Word Study
Greek-English
New Testament

WORD STUDY GREEK-ENGLISH NEW TESTAMENT

A literal, interlinear word study of the *Greek New Testament*
United Bible Societies' Third Corrected Edition
with
New Revised Standard Version, New Testament
and Word Study Concordance

Editor: Paul R. McReynolds

Editors of the *Greek New Testament,* United Bible Societies' Third Corrected
Edition (which has the same text as *Novum Testamentum Graece,* 26th edition):
Kurt Aland, Matthew Black, Carlo M. Martini, Bruce M. Metzger, and Allen
Wikgren in cooperation with the Institute for New Testament Textual Research,
Münster/Westphalia; under the direction of Kurt Aland and Barbara Aland
    Chairperson of the Standard Bible Committee that produced the New Revised
Standard Version: Bruce M. Metzger

Tyndale House Publishers, Inc., Wheaton, Illinois

Library of Congress Cataloging-in-Publication Data

Bible. N.T. Greek. 1999.
 Word study Greek-English New Testament : a literal, interlinear word study of the Greek New Testament United Bible Societies' third corrected edition with New Revised Standard Version, New Testament, and word study concordance / editor, Paul R. McReynolds.
  p. cm.
  ISBN 0-8423-8290-9 (alk. paper)
  1. Bible. N.T.—Interlinear translations, English. I. McReynolds, Paul R., date.
II. Bible. N.T. English. New Revised Standard. 1999. III. Title.
BS1965.5. 1999
225.4'8—dc21   98-56040

Printed in the United States of America

09 08 07 06 05 04 03
9   8   7   6   5   4   3   2

CONTENTS

PREFACE

THIS VOLUME grew out of my teaching at Pacific Christian College. Because of the importance of knowing the correct definition of words, I started teaching a Greek tools class for students who were not taking Greek but were very interested in the biblical text. At the time I started this in the 1970s, most references works were to the King James Version. We utilized the *Word Study Concordance*. While very valuable, it was outdated in terms of the Greek text underlying it and the concordance. The *Word Study New Testament* did not reference many Greek words and was a KJV text. So I started doing my own very literal interlinear Greek-English text. With an interlinear text and an up-to-date Greek-English concordance, students without a thorough knowledge of Greek can utilize the best of the Greek-English reference works to the New Testament.

I owe a debt of thanks to many of my students, who helped refine the interlinear translation. Also, many thanks to those who helped in the typing and editing of the concordance, including Graham Gourley, Karen McReynolds, and my wife, Madeline. As both translator and typesetter of the Greek-English interlinear, I have done my utmost to ensure accuracy. In the interest of making it as accurate as possible, I would appreciate input on corrections from any reader.

A debt beyond thanks goes to Bruce Morrill, who not only gave me good advice and encouragement for the interlinear but also set up the concordance so that it could be edited by computer. This saved thousands of hours and ensured much greater accuracy. He also devised computer programs to detect errors in Strong's numbers, in the Greek text, and in translation.

It is my firm hope and expectation that this volume will enable many students to become more independent learners of the biblical text with greater accuracy and understanding of the meaning of words. All this comes with the expectation that the increased knowledge will help them understand the New Testament text and utilize its life-giving principles in their own lives and continue to teach those principles to others.

Grace and Peace.

INTRODUCTION

THERE ARE five major components to this book: (1) the Greek text of the New Testament, which is the third edition of the United Bible Societies' *Greek New Testament* (1993); (2) numbers above the Greek words with references to the concordance; (3) an interlinear English word-for-word gloss or translation; (4) a side-column version, which is the New Revised Standard Version; and (5) a concordance based on the NRSV. The second, third, and fifth components require further explanation, given below:

Numbers in the Greek Text

The numbers above each Greek word are from *An Exhaustive Concordance of the Bible* by James Strong. Because several words in the Greek text used by Strong are not in the UBS[3] edition, there are several numbers missing. There are also several Greek words that were not in the Greek text used by Strong but are in the UBS[3] edition. These new words have an a, b, or c after the immediately preceding Strong's number. For some unknown reason, Strong skipped numbers 3203 through 3302, so these numbers are also missing. Another major exception concerned the forms of the definite article. Because there are 24 forms, I have identified each form by case, number, and gender by creating new numbers as follows:

01 = NSM	02 = GSM	03 = DSM	04 = ASM
05 = NSF	06 = GSF	07 = DSF	08 = ASF
09 = NSN	010 = GSN	011 = DSN	012 = ASN
013 = NPM	014 = GPM	015 = DPM	016 = APM
017 = NPF	018 = GPF	019 = DPF	020 = APF
021 = NPN	022 = GPN	023 = DPN	024 = APN

The first letter is the case: N = Nominative, G = Genitive, D = Dative, A = Accusative. The second letter is the number: S = Singular, P = Plural. The third letter is the gender: M = Masculine, F = Feminine, N = Neuter.

English Interlinear Translation

*   The lexical meaning—as opposed to the contextual meaning—is used so that learners can know the basic meaning of the word and can judge for themselves what contextual meanings to add. For example, the Greek word *apostolos* is translated as "apostle" by most translators, but there are instances where the word simply means a special envoy or delegate and not one of the 12 Apostles. So all the usages of that Greek word are translated by the English word *delegate*.
*   When possible (and even though some awkward phrases occur), related words in Greek are translated into related words in English. For example, the word series that includes the Greek word *dikaios* I have translated as "right." So *dikaiosune* is "rightness" and *dikaioo* is "I make right."
*   Jargon, archaic, and exclusively religious terms are translated into more currently used common words. This is done so that the learner can determine by context whether a word is used generically or technically. For example, *ekklesia* is normally translated "church" by most translators. But the word occurs in Acts meaning "assembly" (7:38) and "unlawful assembly" (16:32, 39). And because it is jargon, many not familiar with ecclesiastical vocabulary will not understand this as a reference to a group of people rather than a building. *Metanoia* is another example. Although it is commonly translated as "repentance," I have translated it as a "change of mind." I am aware of the dangers of etymological fallacy, but I want learners to be aware of the root meaning so that they can add the appropriate connotations according to the context.
*   Generally, the same English word is translated by the same Greek word, whether the word is a verb or noun. This is to show their relatedness.
*   The interlinear English is an *extremely* literal translation and is not meant to be read like English sentences.
*   Every Greek word is translated by the grammatical equivalent in English— that is, a Greek participle is translated by an English participle, and an

imperfect tense is translated by the English tense form that indicates
continuing action in past time.

♦ Genitive absolutes and articular infinitives are translated literally. These
generally do not make sense in English, so learners should check the
translation in the margin for an accurate, readable translation.

♦ Plural neuters in the nominative case in Greek take singular verbs. In these
cases, I have translated the verbs to agree with the plural subjects.

♦ All proper names are transliterated, though on occasion common English
forms are used.

♦ Aramaic words are transliterated, since they were transliterated in
the Greek.

♦ Monetary and measurement terms are transliterated, unless the equivalent
is commonly accepted.

♦ To differentiate between singular and plural *you,* I have underlined the
singular *you.*

Concordance

This is a Greek-English concordance utilizing as a reference source the
"Computer-Konkordanz zum Novum Testamentum Graece" of the Nestle-
Aland, 26th edition, and *Greek New Testament,* 3rd edition. This concordance
was published by Walter De Gruyter (Berlin, 1980). It should be noted that
several verbs end in *-mai* according to this concordance, while those same verbs
end in *omega* according to Arndt and Gingrich. Thus, some of the Greek words
in this concordance are not in strict alphabetical order. Rather, the order is
according to the Strong's number.

The word in **bold** in each citation is the English word or phrase that is
translated from the Greek word. The New Revised Standard Version is utilized
for the English citations in this concordance, since it is the marginal text for the
interlinear. This has caused some difficulty in choosing which English word to
make bold. For example, the Greek word *amphoteroi* means "both," but the
closest English word I could find in the NRSV in Acts 19:16 was "them"; and in
Acts 23:8, "all." Finding equivalents was especially difficult for some particles
and conjunctions. Some terms had several related translations; for example,
sperma means "seed" as in a literal seed, but it is also translated as "children,"
"descendants," "posterity," and "offspring."

The following is an excerpt from the concordance, explaining the various
numbers:

1248   ᴳᴼ34 ᴬᴳ184 ᴸᴺ59 ᴮ3:544 ᴷ2:87 ᴿ1249
διακονια, service

Lk	10:40	distracted by her many **tasks;**
Ac	1:17	his share in this **ministry.**
	1:25	the place in this **ministry**
	6: 1	daily **distribution** of food.
	6: 4	prayer and to **serving** the word
	11:29	according to their **ability,**
	12:25	after completing their **mission**
	20:24	**ministry** that I received
	21:19	through his **ministry.**
Ro	11:13	I glorify my **ministry**
	12: 7	**ministry,** in ministering;

The boldfaced number is James Strong's number in *The Exhaustive Concordance of the Bible.*

A number with a superscript *GO* before it is the number of occurrences in the Greek text.

A number with a superscript *AG* before it is the page in Arndt and Gingrich's *A Greek-English Lexicon of the Greek New Testament and Other Early Christian Literature.*

A number with a superscript *LN* before it is the page in Louw and Nida's *A Greek-English Lexicon of the New Testament Based on Semantic Domains.*

A number with a superscript *B* before it is the page in C. Brown's *New International Dictionary of New Testament Theology.*

A number with a superscript *K* before it is the page in Kittel's *Theological Dictionary of the New Testament.*

A number with a superscript *R* before it is another Strong's number referring to a related word. When there are two Strong's numbers here, it is a reference to a compound word.

The second line has the Greek word and a very literal English translation, which is generally used in the interlinear text.

Thus, to do a thorough word study of *diakonia,* one could say that it occurs 34 times in the New Testament and then study the context of those 34 times and deduce a meaning. A shortcut would be to look the word up in Arndt and Gingrich on page 184. One could find something about the semantic domains of the word by reading Louw and Nida (p. 59), Brown (vol. 3, p. 544) and Kittel (vol. 2, p. 87). One could also study related words to help formulate a thorough definition.

There are several Strong's numbers that do not have any citations because their inclusion would be too exhaustive. Thus, I have left out the definite article, several prepositions, particles, and conjunctions. If one wants to do a detailed study of those words, the Aland complete concordance lists these in the back of the computer concordance, but without contexts.

INTRODUCTION TO THE NEW REVISED STANDARD VERSION, NEW TESTAMENT

To the Reader

This preface is addressed to you by the Committee of translators, who wish to explain, as briefly as possible, the origin and character of our work. The publication of our revision is yet another step in the long, continual process of making the Bible available in the form of the English language that is most widely current in our day. To summarize in a single sentence: the New Revised Standard Version of the Bible is an authorized revision of the Revised Standard Version, published in 1952, which was a revision of the American Standard Version, published in 1901, which, in turn, embodied earlier revisions of the King James Version, published in 1611.

The need for issuing a revision of the Revised Standard Version of the Bible arises from three circumstances: (a) the acquisition of still older biblical manuscripts, (b) further investigation of linguistic features of the text, and (c) changes in preferred English usage. Consequently, in 1974 the Policies Committee of the Revised Standard Version, which is a standing committee of the National Council of the Churches of Christ in the U.S.A., authorized the preparation of a revision of the entire RSV Bible.

For the New Testament the Committee has based its work on the most recent edition of the *Greek New Testament,* prepared by an interconfessional and international committee and published by the United Bible Societies (1966; 3rd ed. corrected, 1983; information concerning changes to be introduced into the critical apparatus of the forthcoming 4th edition was available to the Committee). As in that edition, double brackets are used to enclose a few passages that are generally regarded to be later additions to the text, but which we have retained because of their evident antiquity and their importance in the textual tradition. Only in very rare instances have we replaced the text or the punctuation of the Bible Societies' edition by an alternative that seemed to us to be superior. Here and there in the footnotes the phrase "Other ancient authorities read" identifies alternative readings preserved by Greek manuscripts and early versions. Alternative renderings of the text are indicated by the word "Or."

As for the style of English adopted for the present revision, among the mandates given to the Committee in 1980 by the Division of Education and Ministry of the National Council of Churches of Christ (which now holds the copyright of the RSV Bible) was the directive to continue in the tradition of the King James Bible, but to introduce such changes as are warranted on the basis of accuracy, clarity, euphony, and current English usage. Within the constraints set by the original texts and by the mandates of the Division, the Committee has followed the maxim "As literal as possible, as free as necessary." As a consequence, the New Revised Standard Version (NRSV) remains essentially a literal translation. Paraphrastic renderings have been adopted only sparingly, and then chiefly to compensate for a deficiency in the English language—the lack of a common-gender third person singular pronoun.

During the almost half a century since the publication of the RSV, many in the churches have become sensitive to the danger of linguistic sexism arising from the inherent bias of the English language toward the masculine gender, a bias that in the case of the Bible has often restricted or obscured the meaning of the original text. The mandates from the Division specified that, in references to men and women, masculine oriented language should be eliminated as far as this can be done without altering passages that reflect the historical situation of ancient patriarchal culture. As can be appreciated, more than once the Committee found that the several mandates stood in tension and even in conflict. The various concerns had to be balanced case by case in order to provide a faithful and acceptable rendering without using contrived English. In the vast majority of cases, however, inclusiveness has been attained by introducing plural forms when this does not distort the meaning of the passage. Of course, in narrative and in parable no attempt was made to generalize the sex of individual persons.

It will be seen that in prayers addressed to God the archaic second person singular pronouns *(thee, thou, thine)* and verb forms *(art, hast, hadst)* are no longer used. Although some readers may regret this change, it should be pointed out that in the original languages neither the Old Testament nor the New makes any linguistic distinction between addressing a human being and addressing the Deity. Furthermore, in the tradition of the King James Bible one will not expect to find the use of capital letters for pronouns that refer to the Deity— such capitalization is an unnecessary innovation that has only recently been introduced into a few English translations of the Bible. Finally, we have left to the discretion of the licensed publishers such matters as section headings, cross-references, and clues to the pronunciation of proper names.

This new version seeks to preserve all that is best in the English Bible as it has been known and used through the years. It is intended for use in public reading and congregational worship, as well as in private study, instruction, and meditation. We have resisted the temptation to introduce terms and phrases that merely reflect current moods, and have tried to put the message of the Scriptures in simple, enduring words and expressions that are worthy to stand in the great tradition of the King James Bible and its predecessors. It is the hope and prayer of the translators that this version may continue to hold a large place in congregation life and to speak to all readers, young and old alike, helping them to understand and believe and respond to its message.

For the Committee,
Bruce M. Metzger

MATTHEW

CHAPTER 1

An account of the genealogy*a* of Jesus the Messiah,*b* the son of David, the son of Abraham.

2 Abraham was the father of Isaac, and Isaac the father of Jacob, and Jacob the father of Judah and his brothers, 3and Judah the father of Perez and Zerah by Tamar, and Perez the father of Hezron, and Hezron the father of Aram, 4and Aram the father of Aminadab, and Aminadab the father of Nahshon, and Nahshon the father of Salmon, 5and Salmon the father of Boaz by Rahab, and Boaz the father of Obed by Ruth, and Obed the father of Jesse, 6and Jesse the father of King David.

And David was the father of Solomon by the wife of Uriah, 7and Solomon the father of Rehoboam, and Rehoboam the father of Abijah, and Abijah the father of Asaph,*c* 8and Asaph*c* the father of Jehoshaphat, and Jehoshaphat the father of Joram, and Joram the father of Uzziah, 9and Uzziah the father of Jotham, and Jotham the father of Ahaz, and Ahaz the father of Hezekiah, 10and Hezekiah the father of Manasseh, and Manasseh the father of Amos,*d* and Amos*d* the father of Josiah, 11and Josiah the father of Jechoniah

a Or *birth*

b Or *Jesus Christ*

c Other ancient authorities read *Asa*

d Other ancient authorities read *Amon*

1:1
976 Βίβλος — Book
1078 γενέσεως — of origin
2424 Ἰησοῦ — of Jesus
5547 Χριστοῦ — Christ
5207 υἱοῦ — son
1160a Δαυὶδ — David
5207 υἱοῦ — son

11 Ἀβραάμ. — Abraham.
2 11 Ἀβραὰμ — Abraham
1080 ἐγέννησεν — gave birth
04 τὸν — the
2464 Ἰσαάκ, — Isaac,
2464 Ἰσαὰκ — Isaac
1161 δὲ — but

1080 ἐγέννησεν — gave birth
04 τὸν — the
2384 Ἰακώβ, — Jacob,
2384 Ἰακὼβ — Jacob
1161 δὲ — but
1080 ἐγέννησεν — gave birth
04 τὸν — the

2455 Ἰούδαν — Judas
2532 καὶ — and
016 τοὺς — the
80 ἀδελφοὺς — brothers
846 αὐτοῦ, — of him,
3 2455 Ἰούδας — Judas
1161 δὲ — but

1080 ἐγέννησεν — gave birth
04 τὸν — the
5329 Φάρες — Phares
2532 καὶ — and
04 τὸν — the
2196 Ζάρα — Zara
1537 ἐκ — out of
06 τῆς — the
2283 Θαμάρ, — Thamar,

5329 Φάρες — Phares
1161 δὲ — but
1080 ἐγέννησεν — gave birth
04 τὸν — the
2074 Ἐσρώμ, — Esrom,
2074 Ἐσρὼμ — Esrom
1161 δὲ — but

1080 ἐγέννησεν — gave birth
04 τὸν — the
689 Ἀράμ, — Aram,
4 689 Ἀρὰμ — Aram
1161 δὲ — but
1080 ἐγέννησεν — gave birth
04 τὸν — the

284 Ἀμιναδάβ, — Aminadab,
284 Ἀμιναδὰβ — Aminadab
1161 δὲ — but
1080 ἐγέννησεν — gave birth
04 τὸν — the
3476 Ναασσών, — Naasson,

3476 Ναασσὼν — Naasson
1161 δὲ — but
1080 ἐγέννησεν — gave birth
04 τὸν — the
4533 Σαλμών, — Salmon,
5 4533 Σαλμὼν — Salmon
1161 δὲ — but

1080 ἐγέννησεν — gave birth
04 τὸν — the
994a Βόες — Boes
1537 ἐκ — out of
06 τῆς — the
4477 Ῥαχάβ, — Rachab,
994a Βόες — Boes
1161 δὲ — but

1080 ἐγέννησεν — gave birth
04 τὸν — the
2492a Ἰωβὴδ — Jobed
1537 ἐκ — out of
06 τῆς — the
4503 Ῥούθ, — Ruth,
2492a Ἰωβὴδ — Jobed
1161 δὲ — but

1080 ἐγέννησεν — gave birth
04 τὸν — the
2421 Ἰεσσαί, — Jesse,
6 2421 Ἰεσσαὶ — Jesse,
1161 δὲ — but
1080 ἐγέννησεν — gave birth
04 τὸν — the

1160a Δαυὶδ — David
04 τὸν — the
935 βασιλέα. — king.
1160a Δαυὶδ — David
1161 δὲ — but
1080 ἐγέννησεν — gave birth
04 τὸν — the
4672 Σολομῶνα — Solomon

1537 ἐκ — out of
06 τῆς — the
02 τοῦ — of the
3774 Οὐρίου, — Ourios,
7 4672 Σολομὼν — Solomon
1161 δὲ — but
1080 ἐγέννησεν — gave birth

04 τὸν — the
4497 Ῥοβοάμ, — Roboam,
4497 Ῥοβοὰμ — Roboam
1161 δὲ — but
1080 ἐγέννησεν — gave birth
04 τὸν — the
7 Ἀβιά, — Abia,
7 Ἀβιὰ — Abia

1161 δὲ — but
1080 ἐγέννησεν — gave birth
04 τὸν — the
760 Ἀσάφ, — Asaph,
8 760 Ἀσὰφ — Asaph
1161 δὲ — but
1080 ἐγέννησεν — gave birth

04 τὸν — the
2498 Ἰωσαφάτ, — Josaphat,
2498 Ἰωσαφὰτ — Josaphat
1161 δὲ — but
1080 ἐγέννησεν — gave birth
04 τὸν — the
2496 Ἰωράμ, — Joram,

2496 Ἰωρὰμ — Joram
1161 δὲ — but
1080 ἐγέννησεν — gave birth
04 τὸν — the
3604 Ὀζίαν, — Ozias,
9 3604 Ὀζίας — Ozias
1161 δὲ — but

1080 ἐγέννησεν — gave birth
04 τὸν — the
2488 Ἰωαθάμ, — Joatham,
2488 Ἰωαθὰμ — Joatham
1161 δὲ — but
1080 ἐγέννησεν — gave birth
04 τὸν — the

881 Ἀχάζ, — Achaz,
881 Ἀχὰζ — Achaz
1161 δὲ — but
1080 ἐγέννησεν — gave birth
04 τὸν — the
1478 Ἐζεκίαν, — Ezekias,

10 1478 Ἐζεκίας — Ezekias
1161 δὲ — but
1080 ἐγέννησεν — gave birth
04 τὸν — the
3128 Μανασσῆ, — Manasses,
3128 Μανασσῆς — Manasses

1161 δὲ — but
1080 ἐγέννησεν — gave birth
04 τὸν — the
301 Ἀμώς, — Amos,
301 Ἀμὼς — Amos
1161 δὲ — but
1080 ἐγέννησεν — gave birth
04 τὸν — the

2502 Ἰωσίαν, — Josias,
11 2502 Ἰωσίας — Josias
1161 δὲ — but
1080 ἐγέννησεν — gave birth
04 τὸν — the
2423 Ἰεχονίαν — Jechonias

```
2532  016   80            846      1909  06  3350
καὶ   τοὺς  ἀδελφοὺς αὐτοῦ  ἐπὶ  τῆς  μετοικεσίας
and   the   brothers  of him at   the  change of home
897            3326  3350   08  3350            897
Βαβυλῶνος.  12  Μετὰ  δὲ   τὴν μετοικεσίαν     Βαβυλῶνος
Babylon.        After but  the change of home  Babylon
 2423        1080         04   4528       4528      1161
Ἰεχονίας    ἐγέννησεν τὸν Σαλαθιήλ,  Σαλαθιὴλ,  δὲ
Jechonias   gave birth the Salathiel, Salathiel, but
1080         04   2216        2216      1161 1080
ἐγέννησεν τὸν Ζοροβαβέλ,  13  Ζοροβαβὲλ δὲ   ἐγέννησεν
gave birth the Zorobabel,      Zorobabel but gave birth
04  10          10     1161 1080        04    1662
τὸν Ἀβιούδ, Ἀβιοὺδ δὲ   ἐγέννησεν τὸν Ἐλιακίμ,
the Abioud, Abioud but  gave birth the Eliakim,
1662       1161 1080        04    107        107  1161
Ἐλιακὶμ δὲ   ἐγέννησεν τὸν Ἀζώρ,  14  Ἀζὼρ δὲ
Eliakim but  gave birth the Azor,     Azor but
1080         04   4524       4524   1161 1080        04
ἐγέννησεν τὸν Σαδώκ, Σαδὼκ δὲ   ἐγέννησεν τὸν
gave birth the Sadok, Sadok but  gave birth the
885       885    1161 1080        04    1664         1664
Ἀχίμ, Ἀχὶμ δὲ   ἐγέννησεν τὸν Ἐλιούδ,  15  Ἐλιοὺδ
Achim, Achim but gave birth the Elioud,     Elioud
1161 1080        04    1648       1648   1161 1080
δὲ   ἐγέννησεν τὸν Ἐλεάζαρ, Ἐλεάζαρ δὲ   ἐγέννησεν
but  gave birth the Eleazar,  Eleazar but gave birth
04  3157       3157    1161 1080        04    2384
τὸν Ματθάν, Ματθὰν δὲ   ἐγέννησεν τὸν Ἰακώβ,
the Matthan, Matthan but gave birth the Jacob,
     2384       1161 1080        04    2501    04  435
16  Ἰακὼβ δὲ   ἐγέννησεν τὸν Ἰωσὴφ τὸν ἄνδρα
     Jacob but gave birth the Joseph the man
3137     1537   3739 1080        2424    01
Μαρίας,  ἐξ  ἧς   ἐγεννήθη Ἰησοῦς ὁ
of Maria, out of whom was born Jesus the
3004            5547        3956  3767 017
λεγόμενος     χριστός.  17  Πᾶσαι οὖν αἱ
one being called Christ.     All   then the
1074        575   11      2193     1160a 1074
γενεαὶ     ἀπὸ Ἀβραὰμ ἕως  Δαυὶδ γενεαὶ
generations from Abraham until David generations
1180             2532 575  1160a 2193  06  3350
δεκατέσσαρες, καὶ ἀπὸ Δαυὶδ ἕως  τῆς  μετοικεσίας
fourteen,     and  from David until the change of home
897            1074        1180         2532 575  06
Βαβυλῶνος γενεαὶ     δεκατέσσαρες, καὶ ἀπὸ τῆς
Babylon    generations fourteen,     and from the
3350          897        2193  02   5547      1074
μετοικεσίας Βαβυλῶνος ἕως  τοῦ Χριστοῦ γενεαὶ
change of home Babylon  until the Christ    generations
1180             02   1161 2424   5547      05
δεκατέσσαρες.  18  Τοῦ δὲ  Ἰησοῦ Χριστοῦ ἡ
fourteen.          Of the but Jesus Christ the
1078      3779   1510 3423               06  3384
γένεσις οὕτως ἦν.  μνηστευθείσης      τῆς μητρὸς
origin  thusly was. Having been engaged the mother
846     3137  03      2501     4250   2228
αὐτοῦ Μαρίας τῷ    Ἰωσήφ,  πρὶν ἢ
of him Maria to the Joseph,  before or
4905               846     2147       1722 1064
συνελθεῖν       αὐτοὺς εὑρέθη    ἐν  γαστρὶ
to come together them   she was found in  womb
2192    1537   4151        40       2501      1161 01
ἔχουσα ἐκ  πνεύματος ἁγίου.  19  Ἰωσὴφ δὲ  ὁ
having out of spirit    holy.      Joseph but the
435     846    1342      1510 2532 3361 2309     846
ἀνὴρ αὐτῆς, δίκαιος ὢν  καὶ μὴ  θέλων  αὐτὴν
man  of her, right   being and not wanting her
```

and his brothers, at the time of the deportation to Babylon. 12 And after the deportation to Babylon: Jechoniah was the father of Salathiel, and Salathiel the father of Zerubbabel, 13 and Zerubbabel the father of Abiud, and Abiud the father of Eliakim, and Eliakim the father of Azor, 14 and Azor the father of Zadok, and Zadok the father of Achim, and Achim the father of Eliud, 15 and Eliud the father of Eleazar, and Eleazar the father of Matthan, and Matthan the father of Jacob, 16 and Jacob the father of Joseph the husband of Mary, of whom Jesus was born, who is called the Messiah.[a]

17 So all the generations from Abraham to David are fourteen generations; and from David to the deportation to Babylon, fourteen generations; and from the deportation to Babylon to the Messiah,[a] fourteen generations.

18 Now the birth of Jesus the Messiah[b] took place in this way. When his mother Mary had been engaged to Joseph, but before they lived together, she was found to be with child from the Holy Spirit. 19 Her husband Joseph, being a righteous man and unwilling

a Or the Christ
b Or Jesus Christ

to expose her to public disgrace, planned to dismiss her quietly. 20But just when he had resolved to do this, an angel of the Lord appeared to him in a dream and said, "Joseph, son of David, do not be afraid to take Mary as your wife, for the child conceived in her is from the Holy Spirit. 21She will bear a son, and you are to name him Jesus, for he will save his people from their sins." 22All this took place to fulfill what had been spoken by the Lord through the prophet: 23"Look, the virgin shall conceive and bear a son, and they shall name him Emmanuel," which means, "God is with us." 24When Joseph awoke from sleep, he did as the angel of the Lord commanded him; he took her as his wife, 25but had no marital relations with her until she had borne a son;a and he named him Jesus.

CHAPTER 2

In the time of King Herod, after Jesus was born in Bethlehem of Judea, wise menb from the East came to Jerusalem, 2asking, "Where is the

a Other ancient authorities read her firstborn son
b Or astrologers; Gk magi

1165	1014	2977	630
δειγματίσαι,	ἐβουλήθη	λάθρα	ἀπολῦσαι
to expose publicly,	planned	privately	to loose off

846	20	3778	1161	846	1760		2400
αὐτήν.		ταῦτα	δὲ	αὐτοῦ	ἐνθυμηθέντος		ἰδοὺ
her.		These	but	of him	having reflected		look

32	2962	2596	3677	5316	846	3004
ἄγγελος	κυρίου	κατ'	ὄναρ	ἐφάνη	αὐτῷ	λέγων·
messenger	of Master	by	dream	shone	to him	saying,

2501	5207	1160a	3361	5399	3880
Ἰωσὴφ	υἱὸς	Δαυίδ,	μὴ	φοβηθῇς	παραλαβεῖν
Joseph	son	David,	not	you might fear	to take along

3137	08	1135	1473	09	1063	1722	846	1080
Μαρίαν	τὴν	γυναῖκά	σου·	τὸ	γὰρ	ἐν	αὐτῇ	γεννηθὲν
Maria	the	woman	of you;	the	for	in	her	having been born

1537	4151	1510	40	21	5088
ἐκ	πνεύματός	ἐστιν	ἁγίου.		τέξεται
out of	spirit	is	holy.		She will give birth

1161	5207	2532	2564	012	3686	846	2424
δὲ	υἱόν, καὶ	καλέσεις		τὸ	ὄνομα	αὐτοῦ	Ἰησοῦν·
but	son, and	you will call		the	name	of him	Jesus;

846	1063	4982	04	2992	846	575	018	266
αὐτὸς	γὰρ	σώσει	τὸν	λαὸν	αὐτοῦ	ἀπὸ	τῶν	ἁμαρτιῶν
himself	for	will deliver	the	people	of him	from	the	sins

846	22	3778	1161	3650	1096	2443	4137	09
αὐτῶν.		τοῦτο	δὲ	ὅλον	γέγονεν	ἵνα	πληρωθῇ	τὸ
them.		This	but	whole	has become	that	might be	the fulfilled

3004	5259	2962	1223	02	4396
ῥηθὲν	ὑπὸ	κυρίου	διὰ	τοῦ	προφήτου
word having been spoken	by	Master	through	the	spokesman

3004	23	2400	05	3933	1722	1064	2192
λέγοντος·		ἰδοὺ	ἡ	παρθένος	ἐν	γαστρὶ	ἕξει
saying,		Look	the	virgin	in	womb	will have

2532	5088	5207	2532	2564	012
καὶ	τέξεται	υἱόν, καὶ	καλέσουσιν		τὸ
and	will give birth	son, and	they will call		the

3686	846	1694	3739	1510	3177
ὄνομα	αὐτοῦ	Ἐμμανουήλ,	ὃ	ἐστιν	μεθερμηνευόμενον
name	of him	Emmanuel,	which	is	being translated

3326	1473	01	2316	24	1453	1161	01	2501
μεθ'	ἡμῶν	ὁ	θεός.		ἐγερθεὶς	δὲ	ὁ	Ἰωσὴφ
with	us	the	God.		Having been raised	but	the	Joseph

575	02	5258	4160	5613	4367	846	01
ἀπὸ	τοῦ	ὕπνου	ἐποίησεν	ὡς	προσέταξεν	αὐτῷ	ὁ
from	the	sleep	did	as	commanded	to him	the

32	2962	2532	3880	08	1135
ἄγγελος	κυρίου	καὶ	παρέλαβεν	τὴν	γυναῖκα
messenger	of Master	and	he took along	the	woman

846	25	2532	3756	1097	846	2193	3739
αὐτοῦ,		καὶ	οὐκ	ἐγίνωσκεν	αὐτὴν	ἕως	οὗ
of him,		and	not	he knew	her	until	which

5088	5207	2532	2564	012	3686	846
ἔτεκεν	υἱόν·	καὶ	ἐκάλεσεν	τὸ	ὄνομα	αὐτοῦ
she gave birth	son;	and	he called	the	name	of him

2424	2:1	02	1161	2424	1080	1722
Ἰησοῦν.		Τοῦ	δὲ	Ἰησοῦ	γεννηθέντος	ἐν
Jesus.		Of the	but	Jesus	having been born	in

965	06	2449	1722	2250	2264	02
Βηθλέεμ	τῆς	Ἰουδαίας	ἐν	ἡμέραις	Ἡρῴδου	τοῦ
Bethlehem	of the	Judea	in	days	of Herod	the

935	2400	3097	575	395	3854
βασιλέως,	ἰδοὺ	μάγοι	ἀπὸ	ἀνατολῶν	παρεγένοντο
king,	look	magicians	from	east	arrived

1519	2414	2	3004	4226	1510	01
εἰς	Ἱεροσόλυμα		λέγοντες·	ποῦ	ἐστιν	ὁ
in	Jerusalem		saying,	where	is	the one

```
5088         935        014      2453       3708      1063
τεχθεὶς  βασιλεὺς τῶν  Ἰουδαίων;  εἴδομεν γὰρ
having been king       of the Judeans?   We saw  for
given birth
846     04    792    1722 07   395      2532 2064
αὐτοῦ  τὸν ἀστέρα ἐν  τῇ ἀνατολῇ καὶ  ἤλθομεν
of him  the star  in  the east   and  we came
4352          846    3  191         1161 01   935
προσκυνῆσαι αὐτῷ.     ἀκούσας   δὲ  ὁ  βασιλεὺς
to worship  him.      Having heard but  the  king
2264    5015           2532 3956   2414        3326 846
Ἡρῴδης ἐταράχθη     καὶ  πᾶσα Ἱεροσόλυμα μετ' αὐτοῦ,
Herod  was troubled and  all   Jerusalem   with him,
4  2532 4863              3956  016  749
καὶ συναγαγὼν        πάντας τοὺς ἀρχιερεῖς
and bringing together   all   the  ruler priests
2532 1122          02      2992     4441           3844
καὶ γραμματεῖς τοῦ  λαοῦ ἐπυνθάνετο    παρ'
and writers       of the people he was inquiring from
846   4226  01    5547    1080          5 013       1161
αὐτῶν ποῦ ὁ  χριστὸς γεννᾶται.       οἱ      δὲ
them where the Christ  is being born.  The ones but
3004  846        1722 965       06     2449     3779
εἶπαν αὐτῷ·  ἐν Βηθλέεμ τῆς  Ἰουδαίας· οὕτως
said  to him; in  Bethlehem of the Judea;  thusly
1063 1125              1223     02   4396       6  2532
γὰρ γέγραπται      διὰ   τοῦ προφήτου·    καὶ
for  it has been written through the spokesman;  and
1473 965        1093  2455       3760       1646
συ  Βηθλέεμ,  γῆ  Ἰούδα, οὐδαμῶς  ἐλαχίστη
you Bethlehem, land of Judas, not at all least
1510   1722 015  2232        2455    1537 1473 1063
εἶ   ἐν  τοῖς ἡγεμόσιν Ἰούδα· ἐκ  σοῦ γὰρ
you are in  the leaders  Judas; from you  for
1831           2233        3748  4165         04
ἐξελεύσεται  ἡγούμενος, ὅστις ποιμανεῖ    τὸν
will come out leader,    who   will shepherd the
2992  1473  04   2474     7 5119   2264    2977
λαόν  μου  τὸν Ἰσραήλ.    Τότε Ἡρῴδης λάθρᾳ
people of me the  Israel.   Then  Herod   privately
2564        016 3097    198
καλέσας   τοὺς μάγους  ἠκρίβωσεν
having called the magicians determined accurately
3844 846   04   5550    02      5316        792
παρ' αὐτῶν τὸν χρόνον τοῦ  φαινομένου ἀστέρος,
from them  the time   of the shining    of star,
8  2532 3992        846      1519 965          3004
καὶ πέμψας     αὐτοὺς εἰς Βηθλέεμ    εἶπεν·
and having sent them   to  Bethlehem  he said,
4198           1833        3748    4012     010
πορευθέντες ἐξετάσατε ἀκριβῶς  περὶ  τοῦ
having traveled inquire  accurately about the
3813          1875 1161 2147          518
παιδίου·   ἐπὰν δὲ  εὕρητε,    ἀπαγγείλατέ
small child; when but  you might find,  tell
1473 3704    2504     2064        4352       846
μοι,  ὅπως κἀγὼ ἐλθὼν     προσκυνήσω  αὐτῷ.
to me, so that also I having come might worship him.
9  013       1161 191       02 935          4198
οἱ      δὲ  ἀκούσαντες τοῦ βασιλέως ἐπορεύθησαν
The ones but having heard the king       traveled
2532 2400 01  792      3739 3708     1722 07   395
καὶ ἰδοὺ ὁ  ἀστήρ, ὃν  εἶδον ἐν  τῇ ἀνατολῇ,
and look the star, which they saw in  the east,
4254        846     2193  2064      2476      1883
προῆγεν αὐτούς, ἕως ἐλθὼν   ἐστάθη ἐπάνω
led before them,  until having come it stood upon
3757 151009 3813       10  3708      1161 04
οὗ  ἦν τὸ παιδίον.      ἰδόντες   δὲ  τὸν
where was the small child.  Having seen but  the
```

child who has been born king of the Jews? For we observed his star at its rising,[a] and have come to pay him homage." [3]When King Herod heard this, he was frightened, and all Jerusalem with him; [4]and calling together all the chief priests and scribes of the people, he inquired of them where the Messiah[b] was to be born. [5]They told him, "In Bethlehem of Judea; for so it has been written by the prophet:

[6] 'And you, Bethlehem,
   in the land of Judah,
are by no means least
   among the rulers of
   Judah;
for from you shall come
   a ruler
who is to shepherd[c] my
   people Israel.'"

[7] Then Herod secretly called for the wise men[d] and learned from them the exact time when the star had appeared. [8]Then he sent them to Bethlehem, saying, "Go and search diligently for the child; and when you have found him, bring me word so that I may also go and pay him homage." [9]When they had heard the king, they set out; and there, ahead of them, went the star that they had seen at its rising,[a] until it stopped over the place where the child was. [10]When they saw that

a Or in the East
b Or the Christ
c Or rule
d Or astrologers; Gk magi

the star had stopped,[a] they were overwhelmed with joy. [11]On entering the house, they saw the child with Mary his mother; and they knelt down and paid him homage. Then, opening their treasure chests, they offered him gifts of gold, frankincense, and myrrh. [12]And having been warned in a dream not to return to Herod, they left for their own country by another road.

[13]Now after they had left, an angel of the Lord appeared to Joseph in a dream and said, "Get up, take the child and his mother, and flee to Egypt, and remain there until I tell you; for Herod is about to search for the child, to destroy him." [14]Then Joseph[b] got up, took the child and his mother by night, and went to Egypt, [15]and remained there until the death of Herod. This was to fulfill what had been spoken by the Lord through the prophet, "Out of Egypt I have called my son."

[16]When Herod saw that he had been tricked by the wise men,[c] he was infuriated, and he sent and killed all the children

[a] Gk *saw the star*
[b] Gk *he*
[c] Or *astrologers*; Gk *magi*

	792	5463		5479	3173	4970	**11**	2532
	ἀστέρα	ἐχάρησαν		χαρὰν	μεγάλῃ	σφόδρα.		καὶ
	star	they rejoiced		joy	great	exceeding.		And

2064   1519 08   3614   3708   012 3813
ἐλθόντες   εἰς τὴν οἰκίαν εἶδον   τὸ παιδίον
having come into the house they saw the small child

3326 3137   06   3384   846   2532 4098
μετὰ Μαρίας τῆς μητρὸς αὐτοῦ, καὶ πεσόντες
with Maria the mother of him, and having fallen

4352   846 2532 455   016 2344
προσεκύνησαν αὐτῷ καὶ ἀνοίξαντες τοὺς θησαυροὺς
they worshiped him and having opened the treasures

846   4374   846   1435   5557 2532
αὐτῶν προσήνεγκαν αὐτῷ δῶρα, χρυσὸν καὶ
of them they offered to him gifts, gold and

3030   2532 4666   **12** 2532 5537
λίβανον   καὶ σμύρναν.   καὶ χρηματισθέντες
frankincense and myrrh. And having been warned

2596 3677 3361 344   4314   2264   1223
κατ' ὄναρ μὴ ἀνακάμψαι πρὸς Ἡρῴδην, δι'
by dream not to bend again toward Herod, through

243   3598 402   1519 08 5561   846
ἄλλης ὁδοῦ ἀνεχώρησαν εἰς τὴν χώραν αὐτῶν.
other way they departed into the country of them.

13 402   1161 846   2400 32
Ἀναχωρησάντων δὲ αὐτῶν ἰδοὺ ἄγγελος
Having departed but of them look messenger

2962   5316   2596 3677 03   2501   3004
κυρίου φαίνεται κατ' ὄναρ τῷ Ἰωσὴφ λέγων·
of Master shines by dream to the Joseph saying,

1453   3880   012 3813   2532 08
ἐγερθεὶς   παράλαβε τὸ παιδίον καὶ τὴν
having been raised take along the small child and the

3384   846   2532 5343 1519 125   2532 1510 1563
μητέρα αὐτοῦ καὶ φεῦγε εἰς Αἴγυπτον καὶ ἴσθι ἐκεῖ
mother of him and flee into Egypt and be there

2193 302 3004   1473   3195   1063   2264
ἕως ἂν εἴπω   σοι·   μέλλει γὰρ Ἡρῴδης
until - I might say to you; is about for Herod

2212   012 3813   010   622   846   01
ζητεῖν τὸ παιδίον τοῦ ἀπολέσαι αὐτό. **14** ὁ
to seek the small child of the to destroy him. The one

1161 1453   3880   012 3813
δὲ   ἐγερθεὶς   παρέλαβεν τὸ παιδίον
but having been raised took along the small child

2532 08 3384   846   3571   2532 402   1519
καὶ τὴν μητέρα αὐτοῦ νυκτὸς καὶ ἀνεχώρησεν εἰς
and the mother of him of night and he departed into

125   2532 1510   1563   2193 06 5054
Αἴγυπτον, **15** καὶ ἦν ἐκεῖ ἕως τῆς τελευτῆς
Egypt, and he was there until the end

2264   2443 4137   09 3004   5259 2962
Ἡρῴδου· ἵνα πληρωθῇ τὸ ῥηθὲν   ὑπὸ κυρίου
of Herod; that might be the thing having by Master
fulfilled been spoken

1223   02 4396   3004   1537   125
διὰ   τοῦ προφήτου λέγοντος· ἐξ Αἰγύπτου
through the spokesman saying, out of Egypt

2564   04 5207 1473   5119 2264   3708
ἐκάλεσα τὸν υἱόν μου. **16** Τότε Ἡρῴδης ἰδὼν
I called the son of me. Then Herod having seen

3754 1702   5259 014 3097   2373   3029
ὅτι ἐνεπαίχθη ὑπὸ τῶν μάγων ἐθυμώθη λίαν,
that he was mocked by the magicians was angry very,

2532 649   337   3956   016 3816   016
καὶ ἀποστείλας ἀνεῖλεν πάντας τοὺς παῖδας   τοὺς
and having he killed all the boy servants the
delegated

1722 965   2532 1722 3956 023   3725   846
ἐν Βηθλέεμ   καὶ ἐν πᾶσι τοῖς ὁρίοις   αὐτῆς
in Bethlehem and in all the territories of it

575 1332   2532 2737   2596 04 5550   3739
ἀπὸ διετοῦς καὶ κατωτέρω,   κατὰ τὸν χρόνον ὃν
from two years and down under, by   the time   which

198   3844 014 3097   17 5119 4137   09
ἠκρίβωσεν   παρὰ τῶν μάγων.   τότε ἐπληρώθη τὸ
he determined from the magicians. Then was   the
accurately   fulfilled

3004   1223   2408   02 4396   3004
ῥηθὲν   διὰ   Ἰερεμίου τοῦ προφήτου λέγοντος·
word having through Jeremiah the spokesman saying,
been spoken

18 5456   1722 4471 191   2805   2532 3602
 φωνὴ ἐν   Ῥαμὰ ἠκούσθη, κλαυθμὸς καὶ ὀδυρμὸς
sound in   Rama was heard, crying   and lamenting

4183   4478   2799   024 5043   846   2532 3756
πολύς·   Ῥαχὴλ κλαίουσα τὰ τέκνα αὐτῆς, καὶ οὐκ
much: Rachel crying the children of her, and not

2309   3870   3754   3756 1510
ἤθελεν   παρακληθῆναι,   ὅτι   οὐκ εἰσίν.
she wanted to be encouraged, because not they are.

19 5053   1161 02   2264   2400 32
Τελευτήσαντος δὲ   τοῦ Ἡρῴδου ἰδοῦ ἄγγελος
Having died   but the Herod look messenger

2962   5316   2596 3677 03   2501 1722 125
κυρίου φαίνεται κατ᾽ ὄναρ τῷ   Ἰωσὴφ ἐν Αἰγύπτῳ
of Master shines by dream to the Joseph in Egypt

20 3004   1453   3880   012 3813   2532 08
λέγων· ἐγερθεὶς παράλαβε τὸ παιδίον καὶ τὴν
saying, having been take along the small and the
        raised   child

3384   846   2532 4198   1519 1093 2474
μητέρα αὐτοῦ καὶ πορεύου εἰς γῆν Ἰσραήλ·
mother of him and travel   to land Israel;

2348   1063 013   2212   08 5590 010
τεθνήκασιν γὰρ οἱ   ζητοῦντες τὴν ψυχὴν τοῦ
have died   for the ones seeking the soul of the

3813   21 01 1161 1453   3880
παιδίου.   ὁ δὲ ἐγερθεὶς   παρέλαβεν
small child. The but having been raised took along

012 3813   2532 08 3384   846   2532 1525
τὸ παιδίον   καὶ τὴν μητέρα αὐτοῦ καὶ εἰσῆλθεν
the small child and the mother of him and went into

1519 1093 2474   22 191   1161 3754 745
εἰς γῆν Ἰσραήλ.   Ἀκούσας   δὲ ὅτι   Ἀρχέλαος
into land Israel.   Having heard but that Archelaos

936   06   2449   473   02   3962   846
βασιλεύει τῆς Ἰουδαίας ἀντὶ τοῦ πατρὸς αὐτοῦ
is king   of the Judea instead of the father of him

2264   5399   1563   565   5537   1161 2596
Ἡρῴδου ἐφοβήθη ἐκει ἀπελθεῖν· χρηματισθεὶς δὲ κατ᾽
Herod he was there to go off; having been but by
       afraid   warned

3677   402   1519 024 3313 06   1056
ὄναρ ἀνεχώρησεν εἰς τὰ μέρη τῆς Γαλιλαίας,
dream he departed to the parts of the Galilee,

23 2532 2064   2730   1519 4172 3004
καὶ ἐλθὼν   κατῴκησεν εἰς πόλιν λεγομένην
and having come he resided in city being called

3478a   3704   4137   09 3004   1223
Ναζαρέτ· ὅπως πληρωθῇ τὸ ῥηθὲν   διὰ
Nazaret; so that might be the word having through
         fulfilled   been spoken

014 4396   3754 3480   2564   3:1 1722
τῶν προφητῶν ὅτι Ναζωραῖος κληθήσεται.   Ἐν
the spokesmen that Nazorean he will be called. In

in and around Bethlehem who were two years old or under, according to the time that he had learned from the wise men.[a] [17]Then was fulfilled what had been spoken through the prophet Jeremiah: [18] "A voice was heard in Ramah,
    wailing and loud lamentation,
Rachel weeping for her children;
    she refused to be consoled, because they are no more."
19 When Herod died, an angel of the Lord suddenly appeared in a dream to Joseph in Egypt and said, [20] "Get up, take the child and his mother, and go to the land of Israel, for those who were seeking the child's life are dead." [21]Then Joseph[b] got up, took the child and his mother, and went to the land of Israel. [22]But when he heard that Archelaus was ruling over Judea in place of his father Herod, he was afraid to go there. And after being warned in a dream, he went away to the district of Galilee. [23]There he made his home in a town called Nazareth, so that what had been spoken through the prophets might be fulfilled, "He will be called a Nazorean."

CHAPTER 3

In those days John the Baptist

[a] Or astrologers; Gk magi
[b] Gk he

appeared in the wilderness
of Judea, proclaiming,
2"Repent, for the king-
dom of heaven has come
near."*a* 3This is the one of
whom the prophet Isaiah
spoke when he said,
  "The voice of one crying
    out in the wilderness:
  'Prepare the way of the
    Lord,
    make his paths straight.'"
4Now John wore clothing
of camel's hair with a
leather belt around his
waist, and his food was
locusts and wild honey.
5Then the people of
Jerusalem and all Judea
were going out to him,
and all the region along
the Jordan, 6and they
were baptized by him in the
river Jordan, confessing
their sins.
  7 But when he saw many
Pharisees and Sadducees
coming for baptism, he said
to them, "You brood of
vipers! Who warned you
to flee from the wrath to
come? 8Bear fruit worthy
of repentance. 9Do not
presume to say to your-
selves, 'We have Abraham
as our ancestor'; for I tell
you, God is able from these
stones to raise up

a Or *is at hand*

```
        1161  019   2250         1565      3854            2491      01
        δὲ    ταῖς  ἡμέραις  ἐκείναις  παραγίνεται  Ἰωάννης  ὁ
        but   the   days      those     arrives        John      the
        910          2784             1722 07  2048   06      2449
        βαπτιστὴς  κηρύσσων     ἐν    τῇ   ἐρήμῳ  τῆς  Ἰουδαίας
        Immerser   announcing   in    the  desert  of the  Judea
        2532   3004      3340            1448          1063 05
    2  [καὶ] λέγων·  μετανοεῖτε·  ἤγγικεν  γὰρ  ἡ
        and    saying, change mind, has neared  for  the
        932         014     3772            3778  1063 1510  01
        βασιλεία  τῶν  οὐρανῶν.  3 οὗτος γάρ ἐστιν ὁ
        kingdom  of the heavens.  This  for  is    the
        3004       1223     2268       02  4396         3004
        ῥηθεὶς  διὰ  Ἡσαΐου  τοῦ προφήτου  λέγοντος·
        word having  through  Isaiah the spokesman saying,
        been spoken
        5456    994          1722 07  2048    2090           08
        φωνὴ  βοῶντος      ἐν   τῇ  ἐρήμῳ·  ἑτοιμάσατε τὴν
        voice  crying aloud  in   the  desert,  prepare        the
        3598 2962       2117a    4160     020  5147       846
        ὁδὸν κυρίου,  εὐθείας  ποιεῖτε  τὰς τρίβους  αὐτοῦ.
        way of Master,  straight make    the  paths    of him.
        846      1161 01  2491     2192 012  1742      846
    4  αὐτὸς  δὲ   ὁ  Ἰωάννης εἶχεν τὸ ἔνδυμα  αὐτοῦ
        Himself but  the  John    had   the clothes  of him
        575   2359     2574      2532 2223  1193          4012   08
        ἀπὸ  τριχῶν καμήλου  καὶ  ζώνην δερματίνην περὶ  τὴν
        from  hairs  of camel  and  belt  of skin       around the
        3751  846       05 1161 5160   1510 846      200       2532
        ὀσφὺν αὐτοῦ, ἡ  δὲ τροφὴ ἦν  αὐτοῦ ἀκρίδες καὶ
        hip    of him,  the but food  was  of him  locusts and
        3192 66      5119 1607           4314    846
        μέλι ἄγριον. 5 Τότε ἐξεπορεύετο  πρὸς  αὐτὸν
        honey wild.    Then traveled out   toward him
        2414          2532 3956 05  2449      2532 3956 05
        Ἱεροσόλυμα καὶ πᾶσα ἡ Ἰουδαία καὶ πᾶσα ἡ
        Jerusalem  and all  the  Judea  and  all  the
        4066        02    2446       6 2532 907
        περίχωρος  τοῦ Ἰορδάνου,  καὶ ἐβαπτίζοντο
        country around the  Jordan,     and they were immersed
        1722 03  2446   4215  5259 846  1843            020
        ἐν   τῷ Ἰορδάνῃ ποταμῷ ὑπ' αὐτοῦ ἐξομολογούμενοι τὰς
        in   the Jordan river  by  him  confessing out  the
        266        846      7 3708        1161 4183      014
        ἁμαρτίας αὐτῶν.  Ἰδὼν       δὲ πολλοὺς τῶν
        sins      of them.  Having seen but many    of the
        5330        2532 4523        2064       1909 012 908
        Φαρισαίων καὶ Σαδδουκαίων ἐρχομένους ἐπὶ τὸ βάπτισμα
        Pharisees and Sadducees    coming      at  the immersion
        846    3004    846       1081        2191
        αὐτοῦ εἶπεν αὐτοῖς· γεννήματα ἐχιδνῶν,
        of him he said to them, generations of poison snakes,
        5101 5263      1473 5343    575  06   3195
        τίς ὑπέδειξεν ὑμῖν φυγεῖν ἀπὸ τῆς μελλούσης
        who exampled  you to flee from the  being about to be
        3709       4160      3767 2590  514    06      3341
        ὀργῆς;  8 ποιήσατε οὖν καρπὸν ἄξιον τῆς  μετανοίας
        anger?     Make     then fruit  worthy of the change of
                                                              mind
        2532 3361 1380              3004     1722 1438
    9  καὶ μὴ δόξητε          λέγειν ἐν ἑαυτοῖς·
        and not you might think to say in  yourselves,
        3962       2192    04  11     3004 1063 1473   3754
        πατέρα ἔχομεν τὸν Ἀβραάμ. λέγω γὰρ ὑμῖν ὅτι
        Father we have the Abraham,  I say for to you that
        1410   01  2316 1537   014  3037   3778    1453
        δύναται ὁ θεὸς ἐκ τῶν λίθων τούτων ἐγεῖραι
        is able the God out of the stones  these  to raise
```

```
5043        03    11              2235 1161  05 513    4314 08
τέκνα    τῷ   Ἀβραάμ. 10 ἤδη   δὲ  ἡ  ἀξίνη πρὸς τὴν
children to the Abraham.   Already but the axe   to   the
4491   022      1186      2749           3956 3767 1186
ῥίζαν τῶν    δένδρων κεῖται·       πᾶν  οὖν  δένδρον
root  of the trees    is being laid; all  then tree
3361 4160    2590    2570 1581            2532 1519
μὴ   ποιοῦν καρπὸν καλὸν ἐκκόπτεται   καὶ  εἰς
not  making fruit  good  is being cut off and into
4442 906                1473 3303   1473 907       1722
πῦρ  βάλλεται.   11  Ἐγὼ  μὲν  ὑμᾶς βαπτίζω ἐν
fire is being thrown.   I    indeed you   immerse in
5204  1519 3341            01     1161 3694   1473
ὕδατι εἰς  μετάνοιαν,   ὁ    δὲ  ὀπίσω μου
water to   change of mind, the one but  after me
2064      2478        1473   1510 3739    3756
ἐρχόμενος ἰσχυρότερός μού ἐστιν, οὗ    οὐκ
coming    stronger    of me is,  of whom not
1510 2425  024 5266       941      846     1473
εἰμὶ ἱκανὸς τὰ ὑποδήματα βαστάσαι· αὐτὸς  ὑμᾶς
I am enough the sandals  to bear;  himself you
907          1722 4151    40   2532 4442  12 3739
βαπτίσει  ἐν  πνεύματι ἁγίῳ καὶ  πυρί·    οὗ
will immerse in  spirit   holy and  fire;   of whom
09 4425         1722 07 5495   846   2532
τὸ πτύον      ἐν τῇ χειρὶ αὐτοῦ καὶ
the winnowing shovel in  the hand of him and
1245          08 257      846   2532 4863
διακαθαριεῖ τὴν ἅλωνα  αὐτοῦ καὶ  συνάξει
he will clean the threshing of  and  he will bring
thoroughly      floor     him       together
04  4621 846    1519 08 596       012 1161 892
τὸν σῖτον αὐτοῦ εἰς τὴν ἀποθήκην, τὸ δὲ ἄχυρον
the wheat of him into the storehouse, the but chaff
2618        4442   762       13 5119
κατακαύσει πυρὶ ἀσβέστῳ.       Τότε
he will burn down in fire unextinguishable.  Then
3854        01 2424    575  06 1056     1909 04
παραγίνεται ὁ Ἰησοῦς ἀπὸ τῆς Γαλιλαίας ἐπὶ τὸν
arrives     the Jesus from the Galilee   at  the
2446     4314  04 2491     010  907
Ἰορδάνην πρὸς τὸν Ἰωάννην τοῦ βαπτισθῆναι
Jordan   toward the John  of the to be immersed
5259 846      01 1161 2491    1254       846
ὑπ' αὐτοῦ. 14 ὁ  δὲ  Ἰωάννης διεκώλυεν  αὐτὸν
by  him.    The but John    was preventing him
3004  1473 5532    2192 5259 1473 907         2532
λέγων· ἐγὼ χρείαν ἔχω ὑπὸ σοῦ βαπτισθῆναι,  καὶ
saying, I   need  have by  you to be immersed, and
1473 2064 4314   1473 15 611         1161 01
σὺ  ἔρχῃ πρός  με;    ἀποκριθεὶς   δὲ  ὁ
you come toward me?    Having answered but the
2424    3004 4314  846    863  737   3779     1063
Ἰησοῦς εἶπεν πρὸς αὐτόν· ἄφες ἄρτι, οὕτως   γὰρ
Jesus  said toward him;  allow now, thusly for
4241   1510 1473 4137    3956 1343         5119
πρέπον ἐστὶν ἡμῖν πληρῶσαι πᾶσαν δικαιοσύνην. τότε
fitting it is to us to fulfill all  rightness.  Then
863     846    16 907          1161 01
ἀφίησιν αὐτόν.   βαπτισθεὶς    δὲ  ὁ
he allowed him.   Having been immersed but the
2424    2117   305   575  010 5204     2532 2400
Ἰησοῦς εὐθὺς ἀνέβη ἀπὸ τοῦ ὕδατος· καὶ  ἰδοὺ
Jesus immediately went up from the water; and look
455       846    013 3772     2532 3708   012 4151
ἠνεῴχθησαν [αὐτῷ] οἱ οὐρανοί, καὶ εἶδεν [τὸ] πνεῦμα
were opened to him the heavens, and he saw the spirit
02    2316 2597      5616 4058     2532 2064
[τοῦ] θεοῦ καταβαῖνον ὡσεὶ περιστερὰν [καὶ] ἐρχόμενον
of the God going down as   dove         and  coming
```

children to Abraham. [10]Even now the ax is lying at the root of the trees; every tree therefore that does not bear good fruit is cut down and thrown into the fire.

[11]"I baptize you with[a] water for repentance, but one who is more powerful than I is coming after him; I am not worthy to carry his sandals. He will baptize you with[a] the Holy Spirit and fire. [12]His winnowing fork is in his hand, and he will clear his threshing floor and will gather his wheat into the granary; but the chaff he will burn with unquenchable fire."

[13] Then Jesus came from Galilee to John at the Jordan, to be baptized by him. [14]John would have prevented him, saying, "I need to be baptized by you, and do you come to me?" [15]But Jesus answered him, "Let it be so now; for it is proper for us in this way to fulfill all righteousness." Then he consented. [16]And when Jesus had been baptized, just as he came up from the water, suddenly the heavens were opened to him and he saw the Spirit of God descending like a dove and alighting

[a] Or in

on him. [17]And a voice from heaven said, "This is my Son, the Beloved,[a] with whom I am well pleased."

CHAPTER 4

Then Jesus was led up by the Spirit into the wilderness to be tempted by the devil. [2]He fasted forty days and forty nights, and afterwards he was famished. [3]The tempter came and said to him, "If you are the Son of God, command these stones to become loaves of bread." [4]But he answered, "It is written,

'One does not live by
    bread alone,
but by every word that
    comes from the mouth
    of God.'"

[5]Then the devil took him to the holy city and placed him on the pinnacle of the temple, [6]saying to him, "If you are the Son of God, throw yourself down; for it is written,

'He will command his
    angels concerning you,'
and 'On their hands
    they will bear you up,
so that you will not dash
    your foot against a
    stone.'"

[7]Jesus said to him, "Again it is written, 'Do not put the Lord your God to the test.'"

[8]Again, the devil took him to a very high mountain and showed him all the kingdoms of the world and their splendor;

a Or my beloved Son

1909	846		2532	2400	5456	1537	014	3772
ἐπ'	αὐτόν·	**17**	καὶ	ἰδοὺ	φωνὴ	ἐκ	τῶν	οὐρανῶν
on	him;		and	look	sound	out of	the	heavens

3004	3778	1510	01	5207	1473	01	27		1722
λέγουσα·	οὗτός	ἐστιν	ὁ	υἱός	μου	ὁ	ἀγαπητός,		ἐν
saying;	this	is	the	son	of me	the	loved one,		in

3739	2106		5119	01	2424	321
ᾧ	εὐδόκησα.	**4:1**	Τότε	ὁ	Ἰησοῦς	ἀνήχθη
whom	I thought well.		Then	the	Jesus	was led up

1519	08	2048	5259	010	4151	3985		5259
εἰς	τὴν	ἔρημον	ὑπὸ	τοῦ	πνεύματος	πειρασθῆναι		ὑπὸ
into	the	desert	by	the	spirit	to be pressured by		by

02	1228		2532	3522		2250	5062
τοῦ	διαβόλου.	**2**	καὶ	νηστεύσας		ἡμέρας	τεσσεράκοντα
the	slanderer.		And	having fasted		days	forty

2532	3571	5062		5306	3983		2532
καὶ	νύκτας	τεσσεράκοντα,		ὕστερον	ἐπείνασεν.	**3**	καὶ
and	nights	forty,		later	he hungered.		And

4334	01	3985		3004	846	1487
προσελθὼν	ὁ	πειράζων		εἶπεν	αὐτῷ·	εἰ
having come to	the one	pressuring		said	to him,	if

5207	1510	02		2316	3004	2443	013	3037	3778
υἱὸς	εἶ	τοῦ		θεοῦ,	εἰπὲ	ἵνα	οἱ	λίθοι	οὗτοι
son	you are	of the		God,	say	that	the	stones	these

740	1096		01	1161	611		3004
ἄρτοι	γένωνται.	**4**	ὁ	δὲ	ἀποκριθεὶς		εἶπεν·
breads	might become.		The one	but	having answered		said,

1125	3756	1909	740	3441	2198	01	444
γέγραπται·	οὐκ	ἐπ'	ἄρτῳ	μόνῳ	ζήσεται	ὁ	ἄνθρωπος,
it has been	not	on	bread	alone	will live	the	man,
written;							

235	1909	3956	4487	1607		1223	4750
ἀλλ'	ἐπὶ	παντὶ	ῥήματι	ἐκπορευομένῳ		διὰ	στόματος
but	on	all	word	traveling out		through	mouth

2316	5	5119	3880		846	01	1228	1519	08
θεοῦ.	**5**	Τότε	παραλαμβάνει		αὐτὸν	ὁ	διάβολος	εἰς	τὴν
of God.		Then	takes along		him	the	slanderer	to	the

40	4172	2532	2476		846	1909	012	4419
ἁγίαν	πόλιν	καὶ	ἔστησεν		αὐτὸν	ἐπὶ	τὸ	πτερύγιον
holy	city	and	he stood		him	on	the	wing

010	2411	6	2532	3004	846		1487	5207	1510
τοῦ	ἱεροῦ	**6**	καὶ	λέγει	αὐτῷ·		εἰ	υἱὸς	εἶ
of the	temple		and	he says	to him,		if	son	you are

02	2316	906	4572	2736	1125
τοῦ	θεοῦ,	βάλε	σεαυτὸν	κάτω·	γέγραπται
of the	God,	throw	yourself	down;	it has been written

1063	3754	015	32		846	1781	4012
γὰρ	ὅτι	τοῖς	ἀγγέλοις		αὐτοῦ	ἐντελεῖται	περὶ
for	that	to the	messengers		of him	he will command	about

1473	2532	1909	5495	142		1473	3379
σοῦ	καὶ	ἐπὶ	χειρῶν	ἀροῦσίν		σε,	μήποτε
you	and	on	hands	they will lift up		you,	then not

4350		4314	3037	04	4228	1473	7	5346
προσκόψῃς		πρὸς	λίθον	τὸν	πόδα	σου.	**7**	ἔφη
you might stumble		toward	stone	the	foot	of you.		Said

846	01	2424	3825	1125	3756	1598
αὐτῷ	ὁ	Ἰησοῦς·	πάλιν	γέγραπται·	οὐκ	ἐκπειράσεις
to him	the	Jesus,	again	it has been	not	you will
				written;		pressure out

2962	04	2316	1473	8	3825	3880	846	01
κύριον	τὸν	θεόν	σου.	**8**	Πάλιν	παραλαμβάνει	αὐτὸν	ὁ
Master	the	God	of you.		Again	takes along	him	the

1228	1519	3735	5308	3029	2532	1166	846
διάβολος	εἰς	ὄρος	ὑψηλὸν	λίαν	καὶ	δείκνυσιν	αὐτῷ
slanderer	to	hill	high	very	and	he shows	to him

3956	020	932	02	2889	2532	08	1391
πάσας	τὰς	βασιλείας	τοῦ	κόσμου	καὶ	τὴν	δοξαν
all	the	kingdoms	of the	world	and	the	splendor

```
846         9  2532 3004       846      3778 1473    3956
αὐτῶν         καὶ εἶπεν    αὐτῷ·   ταῦτά σοι   πάντα
of them      and  he said to him,  these to you all
1325            1437 4098             4352
δώσω,        ἐὰν πεσὼν        προσκυνήσῃς
I will give,  if   having fallen you might worship
1473      5119 3004    846   01  2424    5217   4567
μοι.  10  τότε λέγει αὐτῷ  ὁ  Ἰησοῦς·  ὕπαγε, σατανᾶ·
me.        Then says to him the Jesus,  go off, adversary,
1125            1063 2962   04  2316 1473   4352
γέγραπται    γαρ· κύριον τὸν θεόν σου  προσκυνήσεις
it has been  for; Master the God  of you you will
written                                  worship
2532 846 3441  3000             5119 863        846
καὶ αὐτῷ μόνῳ λατρεύσεις.  11 Τότε ἀφίησιν   αὐτὸν
and him alone you will serve. Then leaves off him
01  1228         2532 2400 32      4334      2532
ὁ  διάβολος,  καὶ ἰδοὺ ἄγγελοι προσῆλθον καὶ
the slanderer, and look messengers came to  and
1247     846    12 191        1161 3754  2491
διηκόνουν αὐτῷ.  Ἀκούσας  δὲ   ὅτι  Ἰωάννης
they were him.  Having heard but that John
serving
3860          402           1519 08  1056        13 2532
παρεδόθη   ἀνεχώρησεν εἰς τὴν Γαλιλαίαν.   καὶ
was given over he departed into the Galilee.  And
2641          08 3477a 2064       2730
καταλιπὼν  τὴν Ναζαρὰ ἐλθὼν  κατῴκησεν
having left behind the Nazara having come he resided
1519 2746a    08 3864       1722 3725
εἰς Καφαρναοὺμ τὴν παραθαλασσίαν ἐν ὁρίοις
in  Capernaum the along the sea in  territories
2194     2532 3508          14 2443 4137
Ζαβουλὼν καὶ Νεφθαλίμ·   ἵνα πληρωθῇ
Zabulon  and Nephthalim;  that might be fulfilled
09  3004      1223      2268  02 4396      3004
τὸ ῥηθὲν    διὰ     Ἠσαΐου τοῦ προφήτου λέγοντος·
the word     through Isaiah the spokesman saying,
been spoken
15 1093     2194     2532 1093 3508        3598 2281
γῆ      Ζαβουλὼν καὶ γῆ   Νεφθαλίμ,  ὁδὸν θαλάσσης,
land    Zabulon  and land Nephthalim, way  of sea,
4008   02  2446      1056   022    1484    16 01
πέραν τοῦ Ἰορδάνου, Γαλιλαία τῶν ἐθνῶν,  ὁ
across the Jordan,   Galilee of the nations, the
2992 01  2521        1722 4655  5457 3708 3173
λαὸς ὁ καθήμενος ἐν σκότει φῶς εἶδεν μέγα,
people the one sitting in dark light saw great,
2532 015   2521         1722 5561    2532 4639
καὶ τοῖς καθημένοις ἐν χώρᾳ  καὶ σκιᾷ
and to the ones sitting in country and shadow
2288    5457 393      846   17 575  5119 757
θανάτου φῶς ἀνέτειλεν αὐτοῖς.  Ἀπὸ τότε ἤρξατο
of death light arose  to them.  From then began
01  2424  2784     2532 3004    3340
ὁ Ἰησοῦς κηρύσσειν καὶ λέγειν· μετανοεῖτε·
the Jesus to announce and to say, change mind;
1448      1063 05  932       014    3772
ἤγγικεν  γὰρ ἡ βασιλεία τῶν  οὐρανῶν.
has neared for the kingdom of the heavens.
18 4043      1161 3844  08 2281     06
Περιπατῶν δὲ  παρὰ τὴν θάλασσαν τῆς
  Walking around but along the sea    of the
1056      3708  1417 80       4613  04
Γαλιλαίας εἶδεν δύο ἀδελφούς, Σίμωνα τὸν
Galilee he saw two brothers, Simon the one
3004         4074  2532 406    04  80     846
λεγόμενον Πέτρον καὶ Ἀνδρέαν τὸν ἀδελφὸν αὐτοῦ,
being called Peter and Andrew the brother of him,
```

9and he said to him, "All these I will give you, if you will fall down and worship me." 10Jesus said to him, "Away with you, Satan! for it is written,

'Worship the Lord your God,
and serve only him.'"

11Then the devil left him, and suddenly angels came and waited on him.

12 Now when Jesus[a] heard that John had been arrested, he withdrew to Galilee. 13He left Nazareth and made his home in Capernaum by the sea, in the territory of Zebulun and Naphtali, 14so that what had been spoken through the prophet Isaiah might be fulfilled:

15 "Land of Zebulun, land of Naphtali,
on the road by the sea,
across the Jordan,
Galilee of the Gentiles—
16 the people who sat in darkness
have seen a great light,
and for those who sat in the region and shadow of death
light has dawned."

17From that time Jesus began to proclaim, "Repent, for the kingdom of heaven has come near."[b]

18 As he walked by the Sea of Galilee, he saw two brothers, Simon, who is called Peter, and Andrew his brother,

a Gk he
b Or is at hand

casting a net into the sea—for they were fishermen. ¹⁹And he said to them, "Follow me, and I will make you fish for people." ²⁰Immediately they left their nets and followed him. ²¹As he went from there, he saw two other brothers, James son of Zebedee and his brother John, in the boat with their father Zebedee, mending their nets, and he called them. ²²Immediately they left the boat and their father, and followed him.

23 Jesus[a] went throughout Galilee, teaching in their synagogues and proclaiming the good news [b] of the kingdom and curing every disease and every sickness among the people. ²⁴So his fame spread throughout all Syria, and they brought to him all the sick, those who were afflicted with various diseases and pains, demoniacs, epileptics, and paralytics, and he cured them. ²⁵And great crowds followed him from Galilee, the Decapolis, Jerusalem, Judea, and from beyond the Jordan.

CHAPTER 5

When Jesus[c] saw the crowds, he went up

[a] Gk *He*
[b] Gk *gospel*
[c] Gk *he*

906	293		1519	08	2281		1510
βάλλοντας	ἀμφίβληστρον		εἰς	τὴν	θάλασσαν·		ἦσαν
throwing	throwing net		into	the	sea;		they were

1063 231 — 19 — 2532 3004 846 — 1205 3694 1473
γὰρ ἁλιεῖς. **19** καὶ λέγει αὐτοῖς· δεῦτε ὀπίσω μου,
for fishermen. And he says to them, come after me,

2532 4160 1473 231 444 — 20 — 013
καὶ ποιήσω ὑμᾶς ἁλιεῖς ἀνθρώπων. **20** οἱ
and I will make you fishermen of men. The ones

1161 2112 863 024 1350 190
δὲ εὐθέως ἀφέντες τὰ δίκτυα ἠκολούθησαν
but immediately having left the nets followed

846 — 21 — 2532 4260 1564 3708
αὐτῷ. **21** καὶ προβὰς ἐκεῖθεν εἶδεν
him. And having gone before from there he saw

243 1417 80 2385 04 02 2199
ἄλλους δύο ἀδελφούς, Ἰάκωβον τὸν τοῦ Ζεβεδαίου
others two brothers, Jacob the of the Zebedee

2532 2491 04 80 846 1722 011 4143 3326
καὶ Ἰωάννην τὸν ἀδελφὸν αὐτοῦ, ἐν τῷ πλοίῳ μετὰ
and John the brother of him, in the boat with

2199 02 3962 846 2675 024
Ζεβεδαίου τοῦ πατρὸς αὐτῶν καταρτίζοντας τὰ
Zebedee the father of them putting in order the

1350 846 2532 2564 846 — 22 — 013 1161
δίκτυα αὐτῶν, καὶ ἐκάλεσεν αὐτούς. **22** οἱ δὲ
nets of them; and he called them. The ones but

2112 863 012 4143 2532 04 3962
εὐθέως ἀφέντες τὸ πλοῖον καὶ τὸν πατέρα
immediately having left the boat and the father

846 190 846 — 23 — 2532 4013 1722
αὐτῶν ἠκολούθησαν αὐτῷ. **23** Καὶ περιῆγεν ἐν
of them followed him. And he led around in

3650 07 1056 1321 1722 019 4864
ὅλῃ τῇ Γαλιλαίᾳ διδάσκων ἐν ταῖς συναγωγαῖς
whole the Galilee, teaching in the synagogues

846 2532 2784 012 2098 06
αὐτῶν καὶ κηρύσσων τὸ εὐαγγέλιον τῆς
of them and announcing the good message of the

932 2532 2323 3956 3554 2532 3956
βασιλείας καὶ θεραπεύων πᾶσαν νόσον καὶ πᾶσαν
kingdom and healing all illness and all

3119 1722 03 2992 — 24 — 2532 565 05 189
μαλακίαν ἐν τῷ λαῷ. **24** Καὶ ἀπῆλθεν ἡ ἀκοὴ
sickness in the people. And went off the hearing

846 1519 3650 08 4947 2532 4374
αὐτοῦ εἰς ὅλην τὴν Συρίαν· καὶ προσήνεγκαν
of him into whole the Syria; and they brought toward

846 3956 016 2560 2192 4164 3554
αὐτῷ πάντας τοὺς κακῶς ἔχοντας ποικίλαις νόσοις
him all the ones badly having various illnesses

2532 931 4912 2532 1139 2532
καὶ βασάνοις συνεχομένους [καὶ] δαιμονιζομένους καὶ
and torments ones being and ones being and
held together demonized

4583 2532 3885 2532
σεληνιαζομένους καὶ παραλυτικούς, καὶ
ones being moonstruck and ones paralyzed, and

2323 846 — 25 — 2532 190 846 3793
ἐθεράπευσεν αὐτούς. **25** καὶ ἠκολούθησαν αὐτῷ ὄχλοι
he healed them. And followed him crowds

4183 575 06 1056 2532 1179 2532
πολλοὶ ἀπὸ τῆς Γαλιλαίας καὶ Δεκαπόλεως καὶ
many from the Galilee and Decapolis and

2414 2532 2449 2532 4008 02 2446
Ἱεροσολύμων καὶ Ἰουδαίας καὶ πέραν τοῦ Ἰορδάνου.
Jerusalem and Judea and across the Jordan.

5:1 3708 1161 016 3793 305 1519 012
Ἰδὼν δὲ τοὺς ὄχλους ἀνέβη εἰς τὸ
Having seen but the crowds he went up into the

```
3735   2532 2523        846    4334      846   013
ὄρος, καὶ καθίσαντος αὐτοῦ προσῆλθαν αὐτῷ οἱ
hill;  and  having sat  of him came toward  him  the
3101      846    2   2532 455           012  4750  846
μαθηταὶ αὐτοῦ·   καὶ ἀνοίξας      τὸ στόμα αὐτοῦ
learners of him;  and having opened the mouth of him
1321    846    3004    3  3107    013  4434   011
ἐδίδασκεν αὐτοὺς λέγων·  Μακάριοι οἱ πτωχοὶ τῷ
he taught them    saying,  Fortunate the poor  in the
4151    3754   846    1510 05  932    014
πνεύματι, ὅτι αὐτῶν ἐστιν ἡ βασιλεία τῶν
spirit,   because of them is  the kingdom of the
3772     4  3107    013 3996       3754
οὐρανῶν.    μακάριοι οἱ πενθοῦντες,  ὅτι
heavens.    Fortunate the ones mourning, because
846    3870             5  3107    013 4239
αὐτοὶ παρακληθήσονται.    μακάριοι οἱ πραεῖς,
themselves will be encouraged. Fortunate the gentle,
3754  846    2816           08  1093
ὅτι αὐτοὶ κληρονομήσουσιν τὴν γῆν.
because themselves will inherit  the land.
6  3107    013 3983        2532 1372    08
μακάριοι οἱ πεινῶντες   καὶ διψῶντες τὴν
Fortunate the ones hungering and thirsting the
1343        3754  846    5526
δικαιοσύνην, ὅτι αὐτοὶ χορτασθήσονται.
rightness,   because themselves they will be satisfied.
7  3107    013 1655    3754  846
μακάριοι οἱ ἐλεήμονες, ὅτι αὐτοὶ
Fortunate the merciful,  because themselves
1653          8  3107    013 2513   07
ἐλεηθήσονται.    μακάριοι οἱ καθαροὶ τῇ
will be shown mercy.  Fortunate the clean  in the
2588   3754  846    04  2316 3708      9  3107
καρδίᾳ, ὅτι αὐτοὶ τὸν θεὸν ὄψονται.  μακάριοι
heart, because themselves the God will see. Fortunate
013 1518        3754  846          5207 2316
οἱ εἰρηνοποιοί, ὅτι αὐτοὶ     υἱοὶ θεοῦ
the peacemakers, because themselves sons of God
2564          10  3107    013 1377       1752
κληθήσονται.     μακάριοι οἱ δεδιωγμένοι ἕνεκεν
will be called.  Fortunate the ones having on account
been pursued
1343       3754   846    1510 05  932     014
δικαιοσύνης, ὅτι αὐτῶν ἐστιν ἡ βασιλεία τῶν
of rightness, because of them is  the kingdom of the
3772    11  3107    1510    3752 3679
οὐρανῶν.    μακάριοί ἐστε ὅταν ὀνειδίσωσιν
heavens.    Fortunate you are when they might revile
1473 2532 1377       2532 3004      3956 4190
ὑμᾶς καὶ διώξωσιν  καὶ εἴπωσιν πᾶν πονηρὸν
you  and might pursue and might say all evil
2596   1473 5574       1752      1473  12  5463   2532
καθ' ὑμῶν [ψευδόμενοι] ἕνεκεν ἐμοῦ.  χαίρετε καὶ
against you lying      on account of me. Rejoice and
21         3754  01  3408   1473  4183 1722 015
ἀγαλλιᾶσθε, ὅτι ὁ μισθὸς ὑμῶν πολὺς ἐν τοῖς
be glad,   because the wage of you much in the
3772     3779  1063 1377      016  4396      016
οὐρανοῖς· οὕτως γὰρ ἐδίωξαν τοὺς προφήτας τοὺς
heavens; thusly for they pursued the spokesmen the
4253   1473  13  1473 1510 09  217  06      1093 1437
πρὸ ὑμῶν.     Ὑμεῖς ἐστε τὸ ἅλας τῆς γῆς· ἐὰν
before you.   You   are the salt of the land; if
1161 09  217  3471     1722 5101 233           1519
δὲ τὸ ἅλας μωρανθῇ, ἐν τίνι ἁλισθήσεται; εἰς
but the salt might be in what will it be  To
foolish,              salted?
```

the mountain; and after he sat down, his disciples came to him. [2]Then he began to speak, and taught them, saying:

3 "Blessed are the poor in spirit, for theirs is the kingdom of heaven.

4 "Blessed are those who mourn, for they will be comforted.

5 "Blessed are the meek, for they will inherit the earth.

6 "Blessed are those who hunger and thirst for righteousness, for they will be filled.

7 "Blessed are the merciful, for they will receive mercy.

8 "Blessed are the pure in heart, for they will see God.

9 "Blessed are the peacemakers, for they will be called children of God.

10 "Blessed are those who are persecuted for righteousness' sake, for theirs is the kingdom of heaven.

11 "Blessed are you when people revile you and persecute you and utter all kinds of evil against you falsely[a] on my account. [12]Rejoice and be glad, for your reward is great in heaven, for in the same way they persecuted the prophets who were before you.

13 "You are the salt of the earth; but if salt has lost its taste, how can its saltiness be restored?

[a] Other ancient authorities lack *falsely*

It is no longer good for anything, but is thrown out and trampled under foot. 14 "You are the light of the world. A city built on a hill cannot be hid. ¹⁵No one after lighting a lamp puts it under the bushel basket, but on the lampstand, and it gives light to all in the house. ¹⁶In the same way, let your light shine before others, so that they may see your good works and give glory to your Father in heaven.

17 "Do not think that I have come to abolish the law or the prophets; I have come not to abolish but to fulfill. ¹⁸For truly I tell you, until heaven and earth pass away, not one letter,ᵃ not one stroke of a letter, will pass from the law until all is accomplished. ¹⁹Therefore, whoever breaksᵇ one of the least of these commandments, and teaches others to do the same, will be called least in the kingdom of heaven; but whoever does them and teaches them will be called great in the kingdom of heaven. ²⁰For I tell you, unless your righteousness exceeds that of the scribes and Pharisees,

ᵃ Gk one iota
ᵇ Or annuls

3762	2480	2089	1487	3361	906		1854
οὐδὲν	ἰσχύει	ἔτι	εἰ	μὴ	βληθὲν		ἔξω
nothing	it is still strong		except		having been thrown		outside

2662		5259	014	444		**14**	1473	1510	09
καταπατεῖσθαι	ὑπὸ	τῶν	ἀνθρώπων.				Ὑμεῖς	ἐστε	τὸ
to be walked by the men.							You	are	the
over

5457	02	2889	3756	1410	4172	2928
φῶς	τοῦ	κόσμου.	οὐ	δύναται	πόλις	κρυβῆναι
light	of the world.		Not	is able	city	to be hidden

1883	3735	2749	**15**	3761	2545	3088	2532
ἐπάνω	ὄρους	κειμένη·		οὐδὲ	καίουσιν	λύχνον	καὶ
upon	hill	lying;		but not	they burn	lamp	and

5087	846	5259	04	3426	235	1909	08
τιθέασιν	αὐτὸν	ὑπὸ	τὸν	μόδιον	ἀλλ’	ἐπὶ	τὴν
they set it	under	the measuring scoop		but	on	the

3087	2532	2989	3956	015	1722	07
λυχνίαν,	καὶ	λάμπει	πᾶσιν	τοῖς	ἐν	τῇ
lampstand,	and	it shines	to all	the ones	in	the

3614	**16**	3779	2989	09	5457	1473	1715
οἰκίᾳ.		οὕτως	λαμψάτω	τὸ	φῶς	ὑμῶν	ἔμπροσθεν
house.		Thusly	let shine	the	light	of you	in front

014	444	3704	3708		1473	024	2570
τῶν	ἀνθρώπων,	ὅπως	ἴδωσιν		ὑμῶν	τὰ	καλὰ
of the men,		so that	they might see		of you	the	good

2041	2532	1392		04	3962	1473	04
ἔργα	καὶ	δοξάσωσιν		τὸν	πατέρα	ὑμῶν	τὸν
works	and	might give splendor		the	father	of you	the

1722	015	3772	**17**	3361	3543		3754	2064
ἐν	τοῖς	οὐρανοῖς.		Μὴ	νομίσητε		ὅτι	ἦλθον
in	the	heavens.		Not you might think		that	I came

2647		04	3551	2228	016	4396		3756	2064
καταλῦσαι	τὸν	νόμον	ἢ	τοὺς	προφήτας·		οὐκ	ἦλθον
to unloose	the law		or	the	spokesmen;		not	I came

2647		235	4137		**18**	281	1063	3004	1473
καταλῦσαι	ἀλλὰ	πληρῶσαι.				ἀμὴν	γὰρ	λέγω	ὑμῖν·
to unloose	but	to fulfill.				Amen	for	I say	to you,

2193	302	3928		01	3772	2532	05	1093
ἕως	ἂν	παρέλθῃ		ὁ	οὐρανὸς	καὶ	ἡ	γῆ,
until	-	might go along		the	heaven	and	the	land,

2503	1520	2228	1520	2762	3756	3361	3928
ἰῶτα	ἓν	ἢ	μία	κεραία	οὐ	μὴ	παρέλθῃ
iota	one	or	one	point	not	not	might go along

575	02	3551	2193	302	3956	1096		**19**	3739
ἀπὸ	τοῦ	νόμου,	ἕως	ἂν	πάντα	γένηται.			ὃς
from	the	law,	until	-	all	might become.			Who

1437	3767	3089		1520	018	1785	3778	018
ἐὰν	οὖν	λύσῃ		μίαν	τῶν	ἐντολῶν	τούτων	τῶν
if	then	might loose		one	of the	commands	these	the

1646	2532	1321	3779	016	444
ἐλαχίστων	καὶ	διδάξῃ	οὕτως	τοὺς	ἀνθρώπους,
least	and	might teach	thusly	the	men,

1646	2564	1722	07	932	014
ἐλάχιστος	κληθήσεται	ἐν	τῇ	βασιλείᾳ	τῶν
least	will be called	in	the	kingdom	of the

3772	3739	1161	302	4160	2532	1321	3778
οὐρανῶν·	ὃς	δ’	ἂν	ποιήσῃ	καὶ	διδάξῃ,	οὗτος
heavens;	who	but	-	might do	and	teach,	this one

3173	2564	1722	07	932	014	3772
μέγας	κληθήσεται	ἐν	τῇ	βασιλείᾳ	τῶν	οὐρανῶν.
great	will be called	in	the	kingdom	of the heavens.	

20	3004	1063	1473	3754	1437	3361	4052		1473
	Λέγω	γὰρ	ὑμῖν	ὅτι	ἐὰν	μὴ	περισσεύσῃ		ὑμῶν
	I say	for	to you	that	if	not	might exceed		of you

05	1343	4183	014	1122	2532	5330
ἡ	δικαιοσύνη	πλεῖον	τῶν	γραμματέων	καὶ	Φαρισαίων,
the	rightness	more	of the	writers	and	Pharisees,

3756	3361	1525		1519	08	932		014		3772

οὐ μὴ εἰσέλθητε εἰς τὴν βασιλείαν τῶν   οὐρανῶν.
not not you might into the kingdom   of the heavens.
go into

21 'Ηκούσατε ὅτι ἐρρέθη τοῖς ἀρχαίοις· οὐ
(191) (3754 3004) (015 744) (3756)
You heard that it was said to the ancients, not

φονεύσεις· ὃς δ᾽ ἂν φονεύσῃ· ἔνοχος
(5407) (3739 1161 302) (5407) (1777)
you will murder; who but - might murder; guilty

ἔσται τῇ κρίσει. **22** ἐγὼ δὲ λέγω ὑμῖν ὅτι
(1510 07 2920) (1473 1161 3004 1473 3754)
he will be to the judgment. I but say you that

πᾶς ὁ ὀργιζόμενος τῷ ἀδελφῷ αὐτοῦ ἔνοχος
(3956 01 3710) (03) (80) (846) (1777)
all the one being angry to the brother of him guilty

ἔσται τῇ κρίσει· ὃς δ᾽ ἂν εἴπῃ τῷ
(1510 07 2920) (3739 1161 302 3004) (03)
will be to the judgment; who but - might say to the

ἀδελφῷ αὐτοῦ· ῥακά, ἔνοχος ἔσται τῷ συνεδρίῳ·
(80) (846) (4469) (1777) (1510) (011) (4892)
brother of him, raca, guilty will be to the council;

ὃς δ᾽ ἂν εἴπῃ· μωρέ, ἔνοχος ἔσται εἰς τὴν
(3739 1161 302 3004) (3474) (1777) (1510) (1519 08)
who but - might say, fool, guilty will be to the

γέενναν τοῦ πυρός. **23** ἐὰν οὖν προσφέρῃς τὸ
(1067) (010) (4442) (1437 3767 4374) (012)
gehenna of the fire. If then you might offer the

δῶρόν σου ἐπὶ τὸ θυσιαστήριον κἀκεῖ
(1435) (1473) (1909 012 2379) (2546)
gift of you on the place of sacrifice and there

μνησθῇς ὅτι ὁ ἀδελφός σου ἔχει τι
(3403) (3754 01 80) (1473) (2192 5100)
you might remember that the brother of you has some

κατὰ σοῦ, **24** ἄφες ἐκεῖ τὸ δῶρόν σου
(2596) (1473) (863) (1563 012 1435 1473)
against you, leave off there the gift of you

ἔμπροσθεν τοῦ θυσιαστηρίου καὶ ὕπαγε πρῶτον
(1715) (010) (2379) (2532 5217 4413)
in front of the place of sacrifice and go off first

διαλλάγηθι τῷ ἀδελφῷ σου, καὶ τότε
(1259) (03) (80) (1473) (2532 5119)
be reconciled to the brother of you, and then

ἐλθὼν πρόσφερε τὸ δῶρόν σου. **25** ἴσθι
(2064) (4374) (012 1435 1473) (1510)
having come offer the gift of you. Be

εὐνοῶν τῷ ἀντιδίκῳ σου ταχύ, ἕως ὅτου εἶ μετ᾽
(2132) (03 476) (1473 5036) (2193) (3755 1510 3326)
well to opponent of you quickly, until when you with
minded the are

αὐτοῦ ἐν τῇ ὁδῷ, μήποτέ σε παραδῷ ὁ ἀντίδικος
(846) (1722 07) (3598 3379) (1473 3860) (01 476)
him in the way, not you might give the opponent
then over

τῷ κριτῇ καὶ ὁ κριτὴς τῷ ὑπηρέτῃ καὶ εἰς
(03) (2923) (2532 01 2923) (03) (5257) (2532 1519)
to the judge and the judge to the assistant and into

φυλακὴν βληθήσῃ· **26** ἀμὴν λέγω σοι, οὐ
(5438) (906) (281 3004 1473) (3756)
guard you might be thrown; amen I say to you, not

μὴ ἐξέλθῃς ἐκεῖθεν, ἕως ἂν ἀποδῷς τὸν ἔσχατον
(3361 1831) (1564) (2193 302 591) (04 2078)
not you might from until - you might the last
come out there, give off

κοδράντην. **27** 'Ηκούσατε ὅτι ἐρρέθη· οὐ
(2835) (191) (3754 3004) (3756)
codrantes. You heard that it was said, not

---

you will never enter the
kingdom of heaven.

21 "You have heard
that it was said to those of
ancient times, 'You shall
not murder'; and 'whoever
murders shall be liable to
judgment.' [22]But I say to
you that if you are angry
with a brother or sister,[a]
you will be liable to judgment; and if you insult[b] a
brother or sister,[c] you will
be liable to the council; and
if you say, 'You fool,' you
will be liable to the hell[d]
of fire. [23]So when you are
offering your gift at the
altar, if you remember that
your brother or sister[e] has
something against you,
[24]leave your gift there
before the altar and go;
first be reconciled to your
brother or sister,[e] and then
come and offer your gift.
[25]Come to terms quickly
with your accuser while you
are on the way to court[f]
with him, or your accuser
may hand you over to the
judge, and the judge to the
guard, and you will be
thrown into prison. [26]Truly
I tell you, you will never get
out until you have paid the
last penny.

27 "You have heard that
it was said,

---

[a] Gk a brother; other ancient
authorities add without cause
[b] Gk say Raca to (an obscure term
of abuse)
[c] Gk a brother
[d] Gk Gehenna
[e] Gk your brother
[f] Gk lacks to court

'You shall not commit adultery.' 28But I say to you that everyone who looks at a woman with lust has already committed adultery with her in his heart. 29If your right eye causes you to sin, tear it out and throw it away; it is better for you to lose one of your members than for your whole body to be thrown into hell.*a* 30And if your right hand causes you to sin, cut it off and throw it away; it is better for you to lose one of your members than for your whole body to go into hell.*a*

31 "It was also said, 'Whoever divorces his wife, let him give her a certificate of divorce.' 32But I say to you that anyone who divorces his wife, except on the ground of unchastity, causes her to commit adultery; and whoever marries a divorced woman commits adultery.

33 "Again, you have heard that it was said to those of ancient times, 'You shall not swear falsely, but carry out the vows you have made to the Lord.' 34But I say to you, Do not swear at all, either by heaven, for it is the throne of God, 35or by the earth, for it is his footstool, or

a Gk *Gehenna*

```
3431                          1473  1161  3004  1473    3754 3956 01
μοιχεύσεις.        28    ἐγὼ  δὲ   λέγω  ὑμῖν   ὅτι  πᾶς  ὁ
you will commit          I   but   say   to you that all  the
adultery.                                                     one
991        1135    4314    012 1937        846      2235
βλέπων   γυναῖκα προς   τὸ ἐπιθυμῆσαι αὐτὴν ἤδη
looking  woman   toward the to desire   her    already
3431              846  1722 07  2588    846
ἐμοίχευσεν     αὐτὴν ἐν  τῇ καρδίᾳ αὐτοῦ.
committed adultery her  in  the  heart of him.
    1487 1161 01   3788       1473  01  1188     4624
29  εἰ   δὲ  ὁ ὀφθαλμός σου  ὁ  δεξιὸς σκανδαλίζει
    If   but the eye    of you the right offends
1473 1807      846  2532 906   575  1473 4851       1063
σε,  ἔξελε   αὐτὸν καὶ βάλε ἀπὸ σοῦ· συμφέρει γάρ
you, lift out it   and throw from you; advantage for
1473 2443 622                1520 022   3196     1473
σοι ἵνα ἀπόληται         ἐν  τῶν  μελῶν σου
you that might be destroyed one of the members of you
2532 3361 3650 09  4983 1473 906           1519
καὶ μὴ ὅλον τὸ σῶμά σου βληθῇ          εἰς
and not whole the body of you might be thrown into
1067        2532 1487 05  1188  1473  5495 4624
γέενναν. 30 καὶ εἰ  ἡ  δεξιά σου  χεὶρ σκανδαλίζει
gehenna.    And if  the right of you hand offends
1473 1581      846  2532 906   575  1473 4851      1063
σε,  ἔκκοψον αὐτὴν καὶ βάλε ἀπὸ σοῦ· συμφέρει γάρ
you, cut off it    and throw from you; advantage for
1473 2443 622                1520 022   3196
σοι ἵνα ἀπόληται         ἐν  τῶν  μελῶν
you that might be destroyed one of the members
1473     2532 3361 3650 09  4983 1473  1519 1067
σου  καὶ μὴ ὅλον τὸ σῶμά σου  εἰς γέενναν
of you and not whole the body of you into gehenna
565           3004      1161 3739 302
ἀπέλθῃ.   31 Ἐρρέθη  δέ· ὃς ἂν
might go off.  It was said but, who  -
630           08   1135    846      1325    846
ἀπολύσῃ    τὴν γυναῖκα αὐτοῦ, δότω   αὐτῇ
might loose off the woman  of him, let give to her
647           1473 1161 3004 1473    3754 3956 01
ἀποστάσιον. 32 ἐγὼ δὲ  λέγω ὑμῖν   ὅτι  πᾶς  ὁ
stand off.     I  but  say   to you that all  the one
630       08   1135    846    3924    3056
ἀπολύων   τὴν γυναῖκα αὐτοῦ παρεκτὸς λόγου
loosing off the woman  of him except   word
4202       4160 846  3431       2532 3739 1437
πορνείας ποιεῖ αὐτὴν μοιχευθῆναι, καὶ ὃς  ἐὰν
of sexual makes her  to commit    and who if
immorality            adultery,
630            1060   3429        3825 191        3754
ἀπολελυμένην γαμήσῃ, μοιχᾶται. 33 Πάλιν ἠκούσατε ὅτι
having been   might  commits     Again you heard that
loosed off    marry, adultery.
3004   015    744         3756 1964        591
ἐρρέθη τοῖς ἀρχαίοις· οὐκ ἐπιορκήσεις, ἀποδώσεις
it was to the ancients; not you will     you will
said                          perjure,     give off
1161 03   2962    016   3727  1473    1473 1161 3004
δὲ  τῷ  κυρίῳ τοὺς ὅρκους σου. 34 ἐγὼ δὲ  λέγω
but to the Master the oaths of you.  I  but  say
1473 3361 3660       3383   1722 03  3772
ὑμῖν μὴ ὀμόσαι    ὅλως·  μήτε  ἐν τῷ οὐρανῷ,
to you not to take oath wholly; and not in the heaven,
3754    2362   1510 02     2316  3383      1722 07
ὅτι   θρόνος ἐστὶν τοῦ  θεοῦ, 35 μήτε  ἐν  τῇ
because throne it is of the God,    and not in the
1093 3754     5286      1510 014 4228 846      3383
γῇ,  ὅτι   ὑποπόδιόν ἐστιν τῶν ποδῶν αὐτοῦ, μήτε
land, because footstool it is the feet of him, and not
```

1519	2414		3754	4172	1510	02	3173

εἰς   Ἰεροσόλυμα,   ὅτι   πόλις   ἐστὶν τοῦ   μεγάλου
in   Jerusalem,   because city   it is of the great

935		**36**	3383	1722 07	2776	1473	3660

βασιλέως,   μήτε ἐν   τῇ κεφαλῇ σου   ὀμόσῃς,
King,   and in   the head   of you you might take
             not   oath,

3754	3756	1410		1520	2359	3022	4160	2228

ὅτι   οὐ   δύνασαι   μίαν τρίχα λευκὴν ποιῆσαι ἢ
because not   you are able   one hair white   to make or

3189		**37**	1510	1161 01	3056	1473	3483	3483	3756a

μέλαιναν.   ἔστω δὲ ὁ   λόγος ὑμῶν ναὶ ναί,   οὐ
black.   Let be but the word   of you yes yes,   no

3756a 09	1161	4053	3778	1537	02	4190

οὔ·   τὸ δὲ   περισσὸν τούτων ἐκ   τοῦ πονηροῦ
no;   the but   excess   of these out of the evil

1510		**38**	191	3754	3004	3788	473

ἐστιν.   Ἠκούσατε ὅτι ἐρρέθη·   ὀφθαλμὸν ἀντὶ
is.   You heard that it was said, eye   instead

3788	2532	3599	473	3599		**39**	1473	1161	3004

ὀφθαλμοῦ καὶ ὀδόντα ἀντὶ   ὀδόντος.   ἐγὼ δὲ λέγω
of eye   and tooth instead of tooth.   I   but say

1473	3361	436		011	4190	235	3748

ὑμῖν μὴ   ἀντιστῆναι   τῷ πονηρῷ· ἀλλ᾽ ὅστις
to you not   to stand against the evil;   but whoever

1473	4474	1519 08	1188	4600	1473	4762

σε   ῥαπίζει εἰς   τὴν δεξιὰν σιαγόνα [σου],   στρέψον
you   slaps   in   the right cheek   of you,   turn

846	2532	08	243		**40**	2532 03	2309	1473

αὐτῷ   καὶ τὴν ἄλλην·   καὶ τῷ   θέλοντί σοι
to him also the other;   and   to the one wanting you

2919		2532 04	5509	1473	2983	863

κριθῆναι   καὶ τὸν χιτῶνά σου   λαβεῖν, ἄφες
to be judged and   the shirt   of you to take,   send off

846	2532	012	2440		**41**	2532 3748	1473	29

αὐτῷ   καὶ τὸ ἱμάτιον·   καὶ ὅστις σε   ἀγγαρεύσει
to him also the clothes;   and whoever you will
                                           conscript

3400	1520 5217	3326 846	1417		**42**	03	154

μίλιον ἕν,   ὕπαγε μετ᾽ αὐτοῦ δύο.   τῷ   αἰτοῦντί
mile   one,   go off with him   two.   To the one asking

1473	1325	2532 04	2309		575	1473	1155

σε   δός, καὶ τὸν θέλοντα   ἀπὸ σοῦ δανίσασθαι
you   give, and the one wanting from you to borrow

3361	654		**43**	191	3754	3004

μὴ   ἀποστραφῇς.   Ἠκούσατε ὅτι ἐρρέθη·
not   you might turn off.   You heard that it was said,

25		04	4139	1473	2532	3404

ἀγαπήσεις   τὸν πλησίον σου   καὶ μισήσεις
you will love the neighbor of you and   you will hate

04	2190		1473		**44**	1473	1161	3004	1473	25

τὸν ἐχθρόν   σου.   ἐγὼ δὲ λέγω ὑμῖν·   ἀγαπᾶτε
the hostile one of you.   I   but say to you,   love

016	2190		1473	2532 4336		5228	014

τοὺς ἐχθροὺς   ὑμῶν καὶ προσεύχεσθε ὑπὲρ τῶν
the hostile ones of you and   pray   for the

1377	1473		**45**	3704	1096	5207 02	3962

διωκόντων ὑμᾶς,   ὅπως γένησθε   υἱοὶ τοῦ   πατρὸς
ones   you,   so that you might sons of the father
pursuing   become

1473	02	1722 3772	3754	04	2246	846

ὑμῶν τοῦ   ἐν οὐρανοῖς, ὅτι   τὸν ἥλιον αὐτοῦ
of you the one in   heavens, because the sun   of him

393	1909 4190	2532 18	2532 1026

ἀνατέλλει ἐπὶ πονηροὺς καὶ   ἀγαθοὺς καὶ βρέχει
he arises on   evil ones and   good ones and rains

1909 1342	2532 94		**46**	1437 1063

ἐπὶ δικαίους καὶ ἀδίκους.   ἐὰν γὰρ
on   right ones and unright ones.   If   for

by Jerusalem, for it is the city of the great King. [36]And do not swear by your head, for you cannot make one hair white or black. [37]Let your word be 'Yes, Yes' or 'No, No'; anything more than this comes from the evil one.[a]

38 "You have heard that it was said, 'An eye for an eye and a tooth for a tooth.' [39]But I say to you, Do not resist an evildoer. But if anyone strikes you on the right cheek, turn the other also; [40]and if anyone wants to sue you and take your coat, give your cloak as well; [41]and if anyone forces you to go one mile, go also the second mile. [42]Give to everyone who begs from you, and do not refuse anyone who wants to borrow from you.

43 "You have heard that it was said, 'You shall love your neighbor and hate your enemy.' [44]But I say to you, Love your enemies and pray for those who persecute you, [45]so that you may be children of your Father in heaven; for he makes his sun rise on the evil and on the good, and sends rain on the righteous and on the unrighteous. [46]For if you love

[a] Or evil

those who love you, what reward do you have? Do not even the tax collectors do the same? [47]And if you greet only your brothers and sisters,[a] what more are you doing than others? Do not even the Gentiles do the same? [48]Be perfect, therefore, as your heavenly Father is perfect.

CHAPTER 6

"Beware of practicing your piety before others in order to be seen by them; for then you have no reward from your Father in heaven.

2 "So whenever you give alms, do not sound a trumpet before you, as the hypocrites do in the synagogues and in the streets, so that they may be praised by others. Truly I tell you, they have received their reward. [3]But when you give alms, do not let your left hand know what your right hand is doing, [4]so that your alms may be done in secret; and your Father who sees in secret will reward you.[b]

5 "And whenever you pray, do not be like the hypocrites; for they love to stand and pray in the synagogues and at the street corners, so that

[a] Gk your brothers
[b] Other ancient authorities add openly

```
       25                    016   25              1473    5101  3408
ἀγαπήσητε           τοὺς ἀγαπῶντας       ὑμᾶς, τίνα μισθὸν
you might love the      ones loving you,     what   wage
2192          3780  2532  013 5057      012  846  4160
ἔχετε;   οὐχὶ καὶ οἱ τελῶναι τὸ αὐτὸ ποιοῦσιν;
have you? Not also the tax men the same do?
    2532 1437 782              016   80           1473
47 καὶ ἐὰν ἀσπάσησθε       τοὺς ἀδελφοὺς ὑμῶν
    And if  you might greet the  brothers  of you
3441     5101 4053          4160        3780 2532 013 1482      012
μόνον, τί περισσὸν ποιεῖτε; οὐχὶ καὶ οἱ ἐθνικοὶ τὸ
alone, what excess  you do?  Not and the nations the
846   4160              1510      3767 1473  5046        5613 01
αὐτὸ ποιοῦσιν;  48 ἔσεσθε οὖν ὑμεῖς τέλειοι ὡς ὁ
same do?           Will be then you   complete  as the
3962     1473    01    3770        5046      1510     4337
πατὴρ ὑμῶν ὁ οὐράνιος τέλειός ἐστιν. 6:1 Προσέχετε
father of you the heavenly complete is.        Hold to
1161 08   1343           1473    3361 4160    1715
[δὲ] τὴν δικαιοσύνην ὑμῶν μὴ ποιεῖν ἔμπροσθεν
but the rightness   of you not to do  in front of
014 444        4314 012 2300           846        1487 1161
τῶν ἀνθρώπων πρὸς τὸ θεαθῆναι   αὐτοῖς· εἰ δὲ
the men         to  the to be watched them;  if but
3361 1065    3408    3756 2192   3844 03  3962
μή γε,     μισθὸν οὐκ ἔχετε παρὰ τῷ πατρὶ
not indeed, wage   not have you from the father
1473  03 1722 015   3772          2   3752 3767 4160
ὑμῶν τῷ ἐν τοῖς οὐρανοῖς.     Ὅταν οὖν ποιῆς
of you the in the heavens.       When then you might do
1654              3361 4537            1715         1473
ἐλεημοσύνην, μὴ σαλπίσῃς    ἔμπροσθέν σου,
mercifulness, not you might trumpet in front of you,
5618    013 5273        4160      1722 019 4864
ὥσπερ οἱ ὑποκριταὶ ποιοῦσιν ἐν ταῖς συναγωγαῖς
as indeed the hypocrites do      in the synagogues
2532 1722 019  4505     3704     1392              5259 014
καὶ ἐν ταῖς ῥύμαις, ὅπως δοξασθῶσιν ὑπὸ των
and in the lanes, so that they might be by the
                                          given splendor
444         281    3004  1473    568            04   3408
ἀνθρώπων· ἀμὴν λέγω ὑμῖν, ἀπέχουσιν τὸν μισθὸν
men;      amen I say to you, they have back the wage
846        3    1473  1161 4160       1654         3361
αὐτῶν.  σοῦ δὲ ποιοῦντος ἐλεημοσύνην μὴ
of them. Of you but doing     mercifulness not
1097         05 710      1473      5101 4160   05 1188
γνώτω    ἡ ἀριστερά σου τί ποιεῖ ἡ δεξιά
let be known the left   of you what does the right
1473    4  3704      1510      1473     05 1654        1722
σου, ὅπως ᾖ      σου ἡ ἐλεημοσύνη ἐν
of you, so that might be of you the mercifulness in
011 2927      2532 01  3962    1473   01  991        1722
τῷ κρυπτῷ· καὶ ὁ πατήρ σου ὁ βλέπων ἐν
the hidden; and the father of you the one seeing in
011 2927    591        1473     5   2532 3752 4336
τῷ κρυπτῷ ἀποδώσει σοι.    Καὶ ὅταν προσεύχησθε,
the hidden will give to you.   And when you might
            off                              pray,
3756 1510        5613 013 5273      3754      5368
οὐκ ἔσεσθε    ὡς οἱ ὑποκριταί, ὅτι φιλοῦσιν
not you will be as the hypocrites, because they love
1722 019  4864        2532 1722 019 1137    018
ἐν ταῖς συναγωγαῖς καὶ ἐν ταῖς γωνίαις τῶν
in the synagogues and in the corners of the
4113      2476         4336       3704
πλατειῶν ἑστῶτες προσεύχεσθαι, ὅπως
wide places having stood to pray,    so that
```

```
5316                015      444        281   3004   1473
φανῶσιν          τοῖς  ἀνθρώποις· ἀμὴν λέγω ὑμῖν,
they might shine  to the men;      amen I say to you,
568         04   3408    846      6  1473 1161 3752  4336
ἀπέχουσιν τὸν μισθὸν αὐτῶν.    σὺ  δὲ  ὅταν προσεύχῃ,
they have the wage  of them. You  but  when you might
back                                             pray,
1525     1519 012 5009          1473    2532 2808
εἴσελθε εἰς τὸ ταμεῖόν σου   καὶ κλείσας
go in    in  the storeroom of you and  having closed
08   2374  1473  4336      03   3962   1473   03
τὴν θύραν σου πρόσευξαι τῷ πατρί σου τῷ
the  door  of you pray   to the father of you the one
1722 011 2927     2532 01  3962   1473   01  991
ἐν  τῷ κρυπτῷ· καὶ ὁ πατήρ σου  ὁ βλέπων
in  the hidden; and  the father of you the one seeing
1722 011 2927    591       1473     7  4336
ἐν  τῷ κρυπτῷ ἀποδώσει   σοι.    Προσευχόμενοι
in  the hidden will give off to you.  Praying
1161 3361 945            5618  013 1482       1380
δὲ  μὴ βατταλογήσητε ὥσπερ οἱ ἐθνικοί, δοκοῦσιν
but not you might     as     the nations, they think
     babble              indeed
1063 3754 1722 07 4180       846      1522
γὰρ ὅτι ἐν  τῇ πολυλογίᾳ αὐτῶν εἰσακουσθήσονται.
for that in  the much word of them they will be
                                      heard thoroughly.
  8 3361 3767 3666            846       3609a 1063 01
   μὴ  οὖν ὁμοιωθῆτε       αὐτοῖς· οἶδεν γὰρ ὁ
   Not then you might be like to them; knows for  the
3962   1473  3739     5532   2192    4253  010 1473
πατὴρ ὑμῶν ὧν       χρείαν ἔχετε πρὸ τοῦ ὑμᾶς
father of you of what need  you have before the you
154      846      9  3779      3767 4336        1473  3962
αἰτῆσαι αὐτόν.    Οὕτως οὖν προσεύχεσθε ὑμεῖς· Πάτερ
to ask   him.     Thusly then pray        you;   Father
1473  01      1722 015  3772      37          09  3686
ἡμῶν ὁ     ἐν  τοῖς οὐρανοῖς· ἁγιασθήτω  τὸ ὄνομά
of us the one in  the heavens;  let be holy the name
1473 10 2064     05  932       1473   1096     09
σου· ἐλθέτω ἡ βασιλεία σου· γενηθήτω τὸ
of you; let come the kingdom of you; let become the
2307    1473   5613 1722 3772   2532 1909 1093   04
θέλημά σου,   ὡς ἐν  οὐρανῷ καὶ ἐπὶ γῆς· 11 τὸν
want   of you, as  in  heaven also on earth;    the
740    1473   04  1967        1325 1473  4594    12 2532
ἄρτον ἡμῶν τὸν ἐπιούσιον δὸς ἡμῖν σήμερον·    καὶ
bread of us the sustaining give to us today;     and
863    1473   024 3783       1473    5613 2532 1473
ἄφες ἡμῖν τὰ ὀφειλήματα ἡμῶν, ὡς καὶ ἡμεῖς
send off to us the debts  of us,  as  also we
863       015  3781       1473   13 2532 3361
ἀφήκαμεν τοῖς ὀφειλέταις ἡμῶν·    καὶ μὴ
have sent off the debtors of us;    and not
1533         1473 1519 3986       235   4506   1473 575
εἰσενέγκῃς ἡμᾶς εἰς πειρασμόν, ἀλλὰ ῥῦσαι ἡμᾶς ἀπὸ
you might    us  into pressure,  but  rescue us  from
bring into
010  4190      14  1437 1063 863        015     444
τοῦ πονηροῦ.   Ἐὰν γὰρ ἀφῆτε    τοῖς ἀνθρώποις
the evil.        If  for  you might  to the men
                         send off
024 3900        846      863        2532 1473    01
τὰ παραπτώματα αὐτῶν, ἀφήσει    καὶ ὑμῖν ὁ
the trespasses of them, will send off also to you the
3962   1473   01  3770       15 1437 1161 3361 863
πατὴρ ὑμῶν ὁ οὐράνιος·     ἐὰν δὲ  μὴ ἀφῆτε
father of you the heavenly;   if  but  not you might
                                           send off
```

they may be seen by others. Truly I tell you, they have received their reward. [6]But whenever you pray, go into your room and shut the door and pray to your Father who is in secret; and your Father who sees in secret will reward you.[a]

7 "When you are praying, do not heap up empty phrases as the Gentiles do; for they think that they will be heard because of their many words. [8]Do not be like them, for your Father knows what you need before you ask him.

9 "Pray then in this way:
Our Father in heaven,
    hallowed be your name.
[10] Your kingdom come.
    Your will be done,
        on earth as it is in
        heaven.
[11] Give us this day our
    daily bread.[b]
[12] And forgive us our debts,
    as we also have
        forgiven our debtors.
[13] And do not bring us to
    the time of trial,[c]
    but rescue us from the
    evil one.[d]
[14]For if you forgive others their trespasses, your heavenly Father will also forgive you; [15]but if you do not forgive

[a] Other ancient authorities add *openly*
[b] Or *our bread for tomorrow*
[c] Or *us into temptation*
[d] Or *from evil*. Other ancient authorities add, in some form, *For the kingdom and the power and the glory are yours forever. Amen.*

others, neither will your
Father forgive your
trespasses.

16 "And whenever you
fast, do not look dismal,
like the hypocrites, for they
disfigure their faces so as to
show others that they are
fasting. Truly I tell you,
they have received their
reward. 17But when you
fast, put oil on your head
and wash your face, 18so
that your fasting may be
seen not by others but by
your Father who is in
secret; and your Father
who sees in secret will
reward you.[a]

19 "Do not store up
for yourselves treasures
on earth, where moth
and rust[b] consume and
where thieves break in and
steal; 20but store up for
yourselves treasures in
heaven, where neither moth
nor rust[b] consumes and
where thieves do not break
in and steal. 21For where
your treasure is, there your
heart will be also.

22 "The eye is the lamp
of the body. So, if your eye
is healthy, your whole body
will be full of light; 23but if
your eye is unhealthy, your
whole body will be full of
darkness. If then the light

[a] Other ancient authorities add
openly
[b] Gk eating

015	444		3761	01	3962	1473	863		024
τοῖς	ἀνθρώποις,	οὐδὲ	ὁ	πατὴρ	ὑμῶν	ἀφήσει		τὰ
to the men,		but	the	father	of	will send		the
		not			you	off		

3900		1473	**16**	3752	1161	3522		3361
παραπτώματα	ὑμῶν.		"Οταν	δὲ	νηστεύητε,		μὴ
trespasses	of you.		When	but	you might fast,		not

1096		5613	013	5273		4659		853
γίνεσθε	ὡς	οἱ	ὑποκριταὶ	σκυθρωποί,		ἀφανίζουσιν
become	as	the	hypocrites	sad faced,		they cause to
						disappear

1063	024	4383		846		3704		5316
γὰρ	τὰ	πρόσωπα	αὐτῶν		ὅπως		φανῶσιν
for	the	faces	of them		so that		they might shine

015	444		3522		281	3004	1473
τοῖς	ἀνθρώποις	νηστεύοντες·		ἀμὴν	λέγω	ὑμῖν,
to the men		fasting;		amen	I say	to you,

568		04	3408	846		**17**	1473	1161	3522
ἀπέχουσιν		τὸν	μισθὸν	αὐτῶν.			σὺ	δὲ	νηστεύων
they have back		the	wage	of them.			You	but	fasting

218	1473	08	2776		2532	012	4383		1473
ἄλειψαί	σου	τὴν	κεφαλὴν	καὶ	τὸ	πρόσωπόν		σου
smear	of you	the	head		and	the	face		of you

3538		3704	**18**	3361	5316		015		444
νίψαι,		ὅπως		μὴ	φανῇς		τοῖς		ἀνθρώποις
wash,		so that		not	you might shine		to the men

3522		235	03		3962	1473	03	1722	011	2930a
νηστεύων	ἀλλὰ	τῷ		πατρί	σου	τῷ	ἐν	τῷ	κρυφαίῳ·
fasting	but	to the		father	of you	the	in	the	hiding;

2532	01	3962	1473		01	991		1722	011	2930a
καὶ	ὁ	πατήρ	σου		ὁ	βλέπων	ἐν	τῷ	κρυφαίῳ
and	the	father	of you		the	one seeing	in	the	hiding

591		1473	**19**	3361	2343		1473	2344
ἀποδώσει		σοι.		Μὴ	θησαυρίζετε		ὑμῖν	θησαυροὺς
will give off	to you.		Not	treasure		to you	treasures

1909	06	1093	3699	4597	2532	1035		853
ἐπὶ	τῆς	γῆς,	ὅπου	σὴς	καὶ	βρῶσις	ἀφανίζει
on	the	land,	where	moth	and	eating	causes to
							disappear

2532	3699	2812		1358		2532	2813
καὶ	ὅπου	κλέπται	διορύσσουσιν	καὶ		κλέπτουσιν·
and	where	thieves	dig through		and	thieve;

20	2343		1161	1473	2344		1722	3772
	θησαυρίζετε	δὲ		ὑμῖν	θησαυροὺς	ἐν	οὐρανῷ,
	treasure	but		to you	treasures	in	heaven,

3699	3777		4597	3777	1035	853		2532
ὅπου	οὔτε	σὴς	οὔτε	βρῶσις	ἀφανίζει		καὶ
where	neither	moth	nor	eating	causes to disappear	and

3699	2812	3756	1358		3761	2813		**21**	3699
ὅπου	κλέπται	οὐ	διορύσσουσιν	οὐδὲ	κλέπτουσιν·			ὅπου
where	thieves	not	dig through	nor	thieve;			where

1063	1510	01	2344	1473	1563	1510	2532
γὰρ	ἐστιν	ὁ	θησαυρός	σου,	ἐκεῖ	ἔσται	καὶ
for	is	the	treasure of	you,	there	will be	also

05	2588	1473	**22**	01	3088	010		4983	1510
ἡ	καρδία	σου.		Ὁ	λύχνος	τοῦ		σώματός	ἐστιν
the	heart	of you.		The	lamp	of the		body	is

01	3788		1437	3767	1510		01	3788	1473
ὁ	ὀφθαλμός.	ἐὰν	οὖν	ᾖ		ὁ	ὀφθαλμός	σου
the	eye.		If	then	might be		the	eye	of you

573		3650	09	4983	1473	5460		1510		**23**	1437
ἁπλοῦς,	ὅλον	τὸ	σῶμά	σου	φωτεινὸν		ἔσται·			ἐὰν
open,	whole	the	body	of you	lightened	will be;			if

1161	01	3788		1473	4190	1510		3650	09
δὲ	ὁ	ὀφθαλμός	σου	πονηρὸς	ᾖ,		ὅλον	τὸ
but	the	eye	of you	evil	might be,	whole	the

4983	1473	4652		1510		1487	3767	09	5457	09
σῶμά	σου	σκοτεινὸν	ἔσται.	εἰ		οὖν	τὸ	φῶς	τὸ
body of	you	darkened	will be.	If		then	the	light	the

1722	1473	4655	1510	09	4655	4214	**24**	3762
ἐν	σοὶ	σκότος	ἐστίν,	τὸ	σκότος	πόσον.		Οὐδεὶς
in	you	dark	is,	the	dark	how much.		No one

1410	1417	2962	1398	2228	1063	04	1520
δύναται	δυσὶ	κυρίοις	δουλεύειν·	ἢ	γὰρ	τὸν	ἕνα
is able	to two	masters	to slave;	either	for	the	one

3404	2532	04	2087	25	2228	1520	472
μισήσει	καὶ	τὸν	ἕτερον	ἀγαπήσει,	ἢ	ἑνὸς	ἀνθέξεται
he will hate	and	the other	he will love,	or	one	he will hold on

2532	02	2087	2706	3756	1410	2316
καὶ	τοῦ	ἑτέρου	καταφρονήσει.	οὐ	δύνασθε	θεῷ
and	the other		he will think down.	Not	you are able	to God

1398	2532	3126	**25**	1223	3778	3004	1473
δουλεύειν	καὶ	μαμωνᾷ.		Διὰ	τοῦτο	λέγω	ὑμῖν·
to slave	and	to mamon.		Through	this	I say	to you;

3361	3309	07	5590	1473	5101	2068	2228
μὴ	μεριμνᾶτε	τῇ	ψυχῇ	ὑμῶν	τί	φάγητε	[ἢ
not	be anxious	in the	soul	of you	what	you might eat	or

5101	4095	3366	011	4983	1473	5101
τί	πίητε],	μηδὲ	τῷ	σώματι	ὑμῶν	τί
what	you might drink,	but not	the	body	of you	what

1746	3780	05	5590	4183	1510	06
ἐνδύσησθε.	οὐχὶ	ἡ	ψυχὴ	πλεῖόν	ἐστιν	τῆς
you might put on.	Not	the	soul	more	is	the

5160	2532	09	4983	010	1742	26	1689	1519
τροφῆς	καὶ	τὸ	σῶμα	τοῦ	ἐνδύματος;		ἐμβλέψατε	εἰς
food	and	the	body	the	clothes?		Look in	into

024	4071	02	3772	3754	3756	4687	3761
τὰ	πετεινὰ	τοῦ	οὐρανοῦ	ὅτι	οὐ	σπείρουσιν	οὐδὲ
the birds		of the	heaven	that	not	they sow	but not

2325	3761	4863	1519	596	2532	01
θερίζουσιν	οὐδὲ	συνάγουσιν	εἰς	ἀποθήκας,	καὶ	ὁ
they harvest	but not	they bring together	into	storehouses,	and	the

3962	1473	01	3770	5142	846	3756	1473
πατὴρ	ὑμῶν	ὁ	οὐράνιος	τρέφει	αὐτά·	οὐχ	ὑμεῖς
father	of you	the	heavenly	feeds	them;	not	you

3123	1308	846	27	5101	1161	1537	1473
μᾶλλον	διαφέρετε	αὐτῶν;		τίς	δὲ	ἐξ	ὑμῶν
more	differ	of them?		Who	but	from	you

3309	1410	4369	1909	08	2244
μεριμνῶν	δύναται	προσθεῖναι	ἐπὶ	τὴν	ἡλικίαν
being anxious	is able	to set toward	on	the	stature

846	4083	1520	28	2532	4012	1742	5101
αὐτοῦ	πῆχυν	ἕνα;		καὶ	περὶ	ἐνδύματος	τί
of him	cubit	one?		And	concerning	clothes	why

3309	2648	024	2918	02	68	4459
μεριμνᾶτε;	καταμάθετε	τὰ	κρίνα	τοῦ	ἀγροῦ	πῶς
are you anxious?	Learn thoroughly	the	lilies	of the	field	how

837	3756	2872	3761	3514	29	3004
αὐξάνουσιν·	οὐ	κοπιῶσιν	οὐδὲ	νήθουσιν·		λέγω
they grow;	not	they labor	but not	they spin;		I say

1161	1473	3754	3761	4672	1722	3956	07	1391
δὲ	ὑμῖν	ὅτι	οὐδὲ	Σολομὼν	ἐν	πάσῃ	τῇ	δόξῃ
but	to you	that	but not	Solomon	in	all	the	splendor

846	4016	5613	1520	3778	30	1487	1161	04
αὐτοῦ	περιεβάλετο	ὡς	ἓν	τούτων.		εἰ	δὲ	τὸν
of him	threw around	as	one	of these.		If	but	the

5528	02	68	4594	1510	2532	839	1519
χόρτον	τοῦ	ἀγροῦ	σήμερον	ὄντα	καὶ	αὔριον	εἰς
grass	of the	field	today	being	and	tomorrow	into

2823	906	01	2316	3779	294	3756
κλίβανον	βαλλόμενον	ὁ	θεὸς	οὕτως	ἀμφιέννυσιν,	οὐ
furnace	being thrown	the	God	thusly	dresses,	not

in you is darkness, how great is the darkness!

24 "No one can serve two masters; for a slave will either hate the one and love the other, or be devoted to the one and despise the other. You cannot serve God and wealth.[a]

25 "Therefore I tell you, do not worry about your life, what you will eat or what you will drink,[b] or about your body, what you will wear. Is not life more than food, and the body more than clothing? 26Look at the birds of the air; they neither sow nor reap nor gather into barns, and yet your heavenly Father feeds them. Are you not of more value than they? 27And can any of you by worrying add a single hour to your span of life?[c] 28And why do you worry about clothing? Consider the lilies of the field, how they grow; they neither toil nor spin, 29yet I tell you, even Solomon in all his glory was not clothed like one of these. 30But if God so clothes the grass of the field, which is alive today and tomorrow is thrown into the oven,

[a] Gk mammon
[b] Other ancient authorities lack or what you will drink
[c] Or add one cubit to your height

will he not much more
clothe you—you of little
faith? ³¹Therefore do not
worry, saying, 'What will
we eat?' or 'What will we
drink?' or 'What will we
wear?' ³²For it is the
Gentiles who strive for all
these things; and indeed
your heavenly Father knows
that you need all these
things. ³³But strive first for
the kingdom of God[a] and
his[b] righteousness, and all
these things will be given to
you as well.

34 "So do not worry
about tomorrow, for
tomorrow will bring
worries of its own. Today's
trouble is enough for
today.

CHAPTER 7

"Do not judge, so that you
may not be judged. ²For
with the judgment you
make you will be judged,
and the measure you give
will be the measure you get.
³Why do you see the speck
in your neighbor's[c] eye,
but do not notice the log in
your own eye? ⁴Or how can
you say to your neighbor,[d]
'Let me take the speck out
of your eye,' while the log
is in your own eye? ⁵You
hypocrite, first take the log
out of your own eye, and
then you will see clearly to
take the speck out

---

a Other ancient authorities lack
  of God
b Or its
c Gk brother's
d Gk brother

4183	3123	1473	3640		**31**	3361	3767
πολλῷ	μᾶλλον	ὑμᾶς,	ὀλιγόπιστοι;			μὴ	οὖν
much	more	you,	little trusting ones?			Not	then

	3309			3004		5101	2068		2228
	μεριμνήσητε			λέγοντες·		τί	φάγωμεν;		ἤ·
	you might be anxious			saying,		what	might we eat,		or;

5101	4095		2228	5101	4016		**32**	3956
τί	πίωμεν;		ἤ·	τί	περιβαλώμεθα;			πάντα
what	might we drink?		or,	what	might we throw around ourselves?			All

1063	3778	021	1484		1934		3609a	1063	01
γὰρ	ταῦτα	τὰ	ἔθνη		ἐπιζητοῦσιν·		οἶδεν	γὰρ	ὁ
for	these	the	nations		seek after;		knows	for	the

3962	1473	01	3770		3754	5535		3778
πατὴρ	ὑμῶν	ὁ	οὐράνιος	ὅτι	χρῄζετε	τούτων
father	of you	the	heavenly	that	you need	these

537		**33**	2212		1161	4413	08	932		02
ἁπάντων.			ζητεῖτε	δὲ	πρῶτον	τὴν	βασιλείαν	[τοῦ
all.			Seek	but	first	the	kingdom	of the

2316	2532	08	1343		846		2532	3778	3956
θεοῦ]	καὶ	τὴν	δικαιοσύνην	αὐτοῦ,	καὶ	ταῦτα	πάντα
God	and	the	rightness	of him,	and	these	all

4369		1473		**34**	3361	3767	3309			1519	08
προστεθήσεται	ὑμῖν.			μὴ	οὖν	μεριμνήσητε	εἰς	τὴν
will be set toward	you.			Not	then	you might be anxious	into	the

839		05	1063	839		3309			1438
αὔριον,	ἡ	γὰρ	αὔριον	μεριμνήσει	ἑαυτῆς·
tomorrow,	the	for	tomorrow	will be anxious	of itself;

713		07		2250	05	2549		846		**7:1**	3361
ἀρκετὸν	τῇ	ἡμέρᾳ	ἡ	κακία	αὐτῆς.			Μὴ
sufficient	to the	day	the	badness	of it.			Not

2919	2443	3361	2919			1722	3739	1063	2917
κρίνετε,	ἵνα	μὴ	κριθῆτε·	**2**	ἐν	ᾧ	γὰρ	κρίματι
judge,	that	not	you might be judged;		in	what	for	judgment

2919			2919			2532	1722	3739	3358
κρίνετε	κριθήσεσθε,	καὶ	ἐν	ᾧ	μέτρῳ
you judge	you will be judged,	and	in	what	measure

3354		3354		1473		**3**	5101	1161	991		012
μετρεῖτε	μετρηθήσεται	ὑμῖν.		τί	δὲ	βλέπεις	τὸ
you measure	it will be measured	to you.		Why	but	do you see	the

2595		012	1722	03		3788		02		80		1473
κάρφος	τὸ	ἐν	τῷ	ὀφθαλμῷ	τοῦ	ἀδελφοῦ	σου,
splinter	the	in	the	eye	of the	brother	of you,

08	1161	1722	03		4674	3788		1385	3756	2657
τὴν	δὲ	ἐν	τῷ	σῷ	ὀφθαλμῷ	δοκὸν	οὐ	κατανοεῖς;
the	but	in	the	your	eye	log	not	you think carefully?

4	2228	4459	3004			03	80			1473	863
	ἢ	πῶς	ἐρεῖς	τῷ	ἀδελφῷ	σου·	ἄφες
	Or	how	will you say	to the	brother	of you;	allow

1544		012	2595		1537	02	3788		1473	2532
ἐκβάλω	τὸ	κάρφος	ἐκ	τοῦ	ὀφθαλμοῦ	σου,	καὶ
I might throw out	the	splinter	from	the	eye	of you,	and

2400	05	1385	1722	03		3788		1473		**5**	5273
ἰδοὺ	ἡ	δοκὸς	ἐν	τῷ	ὀφθαλμῷ	σοῦ;	ὑποκριτά,
look	the	log	in	the	eye	of you?	Hypocrite,

1544		4413	1537	02		3788		1473	08	1385
ἔκβαλε	πρῶτον	ἐκ	τοῦ	ὀφθαλμοῦ	σοῦ	τὴν	δοκόν,
throw out	first	from	the	eye	of you	the	log,

2532	5119	1227		1544		012	2595		1537	02
καὶ	τότε	διαβλέψεις	ἐκβαλεῖν	τὸ	κάρφος	ἐκ	τοῦ·
and	then	you will see clearly	to throw out	the	splinter	from	the

```
3788        02      80           1473    6  3361  1325        012 40
ὀφθαλμοῦ τοῦ   ἀδελφοῦ σου.        Μὴ  δῶτε       τὸ ἅγιον
eye       of the brother  of you.     Not you might the holy
                                          give

015     2965  3366    906        016  3135       1473
τοῖς κυσὶν μηδὲ βάλητε      τοὺς μαργαρίτας ὑμῶν
to the dogs  but not you might the  pearls     of you
                     throw

1715      014 5519   3379   2662            846
ἔμπροσθεν τῶν χοίρων, μήποτε καταπατήσουσιν αὐτοὺς
in front  of  pigs,  then   they will walk  them
          the        not     over

1722 015  4228  846    2532 4762          4486
ἐν   τοῖς ποσὶν αὐτῶν καὶ στραφέντες     ῥήξωσιν
in   the  feet  of them and having turned they will rip

1473   7 154   2532 1325              1473  2212   2532
ὑμᾶς.    Αἰτεῖτε καὶ δοθήσεται       ὑμῖν, ζητεῖτε καὶ
you.     Ask     and it will be given to you, seek    and

2147      2925   2532 455              1473   8  3956 1063
εὑρήσετε, κρούετε καὶ ἀνοιγήσεται ὑμῖν·     πᾶς  γὰρ
you will  knock  and it will be to you;    all  for
find,                  opened

01   154     2983     2532 01    2212   2147
ὁ    αἰτῶν λαμβάνει καὶ ὁ    ζητῶν εὑρίσκει
the one asking receives and the one seeking finds

2532 03  2925     455              9  2228 5101
καὶ τῷ  κρούοντι ἀνοιγήσεται.       ἢ   τίς
and to the one knocking it will be opened. Or  what

1510 1537 1473 444        3739 154    01   5207 846
ἐστιν ἐξ ὑμῶν ἄνθρωπος, ὃν  αἰτήσει ὁ   υἱὸς αὐτοῦ
is    out of you man,    whom will ask the son  of him

740     3361 3037  1929        846   10 2228 2532
ἄρτον, μὴ  λίθον ἐπιδώσει      αὐτῷ;    ἢ   καὶ
bread, not stone he will give on him?    Or  also

2486  154      3361 3789 1929        846
ἰχθὺν αἰτήσει, μὴ  ὄφιν ἐπιδώσει     αὐτῷ;
fish  he will ask, not snake he will give on him?

   1487 3767 1473  4190      1510  3609a 1390   18
11 εἰ  οὖν ὑμεῖς πονηροὶ ὄντες οἴδατε δόματα ἀγαθὰ
   If  then you  evil ones being know  gifts  good

1325   023  5043   1473    4214      3123   01
διδόναι τοῖς τέκνοις ὑμῶν, πόσῳ    μᾶλλον ὁ
to give to the children of you, how much more  the

3962    1473  01   1722 015   3772        18
πατὴρ ὑμῶν ὁ    ἐν τοῖς οὐρανοῖς δώσει     ἀγαθὰ
father of you the one in the  heavens  will give good

015   154      846    12 3956 3767 3745      1437
τοῖς αἰτοῦσιν αὐτόν.   Πάντα οὖν ὅσα      ἐὰν
to the ones asking him.  All  then as much as  if

2309      2443 4160   1473   013 444
θέλητε    ἵνα ποιῶσιν ὑμῖν οἱ ἄνθρωποι,
you might want that might do to you the men,

3779   2532 1473  4160   3778 1063 1510  01
οὕτως καὶ ὑμεῖς ποιεῖτε αὐτοῖς· οὗτος γάρ ἐστιν ὁ
thusly also you  do     to them; this  for is    the

3551 2532 013 4396      13 1525        1223  06  4728
νόμος καὶ οἱ προφῆται.     Εἰσέλθατε διὰ τῆς στενῆς
law   and the spokesmen.    Go in  through the narrow

4439 3754  4113     05  4439 2532 2149
πύλης· ὅτι πλατεῖα ἡ πύλη καὶ εὐρύχωρος
gate; because wide place the gate and broadspaced

05  3598 05  520         1519 08  684       2532
ἡ  ὁδὸς ἡ ἀπάγουσα     εἰς τὴν ἀπώλειαν καὶ
the way the one leading off into the destruction and

4183   1510 013 1525      1223  846   14 5101
πολλοί εἰσιν οἱ εἰσερχόμενοι δι'   αὐτῆς·    τί
many   are  the ones going in through it;    how

4728  05 4439 2532 2346         05 3598
στενὴ ἡ πύλη καὶ τεθλιμμένη    ἡ ὁδὸς
narrow the gate and having been afflicted the way
```

6 "Do not give what is holy to dogs; and do not throw your pearls before swine, or they will trample them under foot and turn and maul you.

7 "Ask, and it will be given you; search, and you will find; knock, and the door will be opened for you. [8]For everyone who asks receives, and everyone who searches finds, and for everyone who knocks, the door will be opened. [9]Is there anyone among you who, if your child asks for bread, will give a stone? [10]Or if the child asks for a fish, will give a snake? [11]If you then, who are evil, know how to give good gifts to your children, how much more will your Father in heaven give good things to those who ask him!

12 "In everything do to others as you would have them do to you; for this is the law and the prophets.

13 "Enter through the narrow gate; for the gate is wide and the road is easy[b] that leads to destruction, and there are many who take it. [14]For the gate is narrow and the road is hard

of your neighbor's[a] eye.

a Gk brother's
b Other ancient authorities read
  for the road is wide and easy

that leads to life, and there are few who find it.

15 "Beware of false prophets, who come to you in sheep's clothing but inwardly are ravenous wolves. 16You will know them by their fruits. Are grapes gathered from thorns, or figs from thistles? 17In the same way, every good tree bears good fruit, but the bad tree bears bad fruit. 18A good tree cannot bear bad fruit, nor can a bad tree bear good fruit. 19Every tree that does not bear good fruit is cut down and thrown into the fire. 20Thus you will know them by their fruits.

21 "Not everyone who says to me, 'Lord, Lord,' will enter the kingdom of heaven, but only the one who does the will of my Father in heaven. 22On that day many will say to me, 'Lord, Lord, did we not prophesy in your name, and cast out demons in your name, and do many deeds of power in your name?' 23Then I will declare to them, 'I never knew you; go away from me, you evildoers.'

24 "Everyone then who hears

```
05        520           1519 08  2222 2532 3641      1510
ἢ     ἀπάγουσα   εἰς  τὴν ζωὴν καὶ ὀλίγοι εἰσὶν
the one leading off into the life and  few    are
013  2147           846      15  4337        575  014
οἱ εὑρίσκοντες   αὐτήν.      Προσέχετε ἀπὸ τῶν
the ones finding  it.       Hold to   from the
5578              3748    2064      4314   1473 1722
ψευδοπροφητῶν, οἵτινες ἔρχονται πρὸς ὑμᾶς ἐν
false spokesmen, who    come     toward you  in
1742        4263       2081          1161 1510     3074
ἐνδύμασιν προβάτων, ἔσωθεν    δέ  εἰσιν λύκοι
clothes  of sheep, from inside but they are wolves
727          16  575  014 2590      846       1921
ἅρπαγες.       ἀπὸ τῶν καρπῶν αὐτῶν ἐπιγνώσεσθε
plunderers. From the fruit  of them you will perceive
846       3385 4816        575 173       4718
αὐτούς. μήτι συλλέγουσιν ἀπὸ ἀκανθῶν σταφυλὰς
them.   Not they collect from thorns clusters of ripe
                                                  grapes
2228 575   5146        4810  17 3779   3956 1186     18
ἢ  ἀπὸ τριβόλων σῦκα;    οὕτως πᾶν δένδρον ἀγαθὸν
or  from thistles figs?   Thusly all  tree    good
2590      2570     4160  09 1161 4550   1186      2590
καρποὺς καλοὺς ποιεῖ, τὸ δὲ  σαπρὸν δένδρον καρποὺς
fruit   good   makes, the but rotten tree   fruit
4190       4160    18 3756 1410     1186    18    2590
πονηροὺς ποιεῖ.     οὐ δύναται δένδρον ἀγαθὸν καρποὺς
evil    makes.     Not is able tree    good   fruit
4190      4160    3761  1186     4550    2590    2570
πονηροὺς ποιεῖν οὐδὲ  δένδρον σαπρὸν καρποὺς καλοὺς
evil    to do but not tree    rotten fruit   good
4160      19 3956 1186    3361 4160   2590   2570
ποιεῖν.     πᾶν δένδρον μὴ  ποιοῦν καρπὸν καλὸν
to make.    All tree    not making fruit  good
1581        2532 1519 4442 906     20 686  1065
ἐκκόπτεται καὶ  εἰς πῦρ βάλλεται.   ἄρα γε
is cut off and into fire is thrown. Then indeed
575  014 2590      846      1921              846
ἀπὸ τῶν καρπῶν αὐτῶν ἐπιγνώσεσθε     αὐτούς.
from the fruit  of them you will perceive them.
        3756 3956 01 3004        1473 2962   2962
21  Οὐ πᾶς ὁ λέγων    μοι· κύριε κύριε,
    Not · all the one saying to me, Master, Master,
1525           1519 08  932        014  3772      235
εἰσελεύσεται εἰς τὴν βασιλείαν τῶν οὐρανῶν, ἀλλ'
will go into into the kingdom   of the heavens, but
01  4160     012 2307    02 3962    1473  02     1722
ὁ  ποιῶν   τὸ θέλημα τοῦ πατρός μου τοῦ  ἐν
the one doing the want  the father of me the one in
015 3772       22 4183   3004     1473 1722 1565
τοῖς οὐρανοῖς.     πολλοὶ ἐροῦσίν μοι ἐν ἐκείνῃ
the heavens.       Many   will say to me in  that
07  2250     2962   2962     3756 011       4674 3686
τῇ ἡμέρᾳ· κύριε κύριε,  οὐ  τῷ  σῷ ὀνόματι
the day,   Master Master, not in the your name
4395             2532 011       4674 3686    1140
ἐπροφητεύσαμεν, καὶ  τῷ  σῷ ὀνόματι δαιμόνια
we spoke before, and in the your name  demons
1544          2532 011    4674 3686   1411     4183
ἐξεβάλομεν, καὶ  τῷ  σῷ ὀνόματι δυνάμεις πολλὰς
we threw out, and in the your name powers   many
4160        23 2532 5119 3670             846     3754
ἐποιήσαμεν;   καὶ τότε ὁμολογήσω   αὐτοῖς ὅτι
we did?       And then I will confess to them that
3763       1097  1473 672          575  1473 013
οὐδέποτε ἔγνων ὑμᾶς· ἀποχωρεῖτε ἀπ' ἐμοῦ οἱ
but not ever I knew you; make room off from me   the
2038          08 458       24 3956 3767 3748   191
ἐργαζόμενοι τὴν ἀνομίαν.   Πᾶς οὖν ὅστις ἀκούει
ones working the lawlessness. All then who    hears
```

```
1473   016   3056    3778    2532 4160   846
μου   τοὺς λόγους τούτους καὶ ποιεῖ αὐτούς,
of me  the   words  these   and  does  them,
3666              435     5429        3748  3618
ὁμοιωθήσεται    ἀνδρὶ  φρονίμῳ,     ὅστις ᾠκοδόμησεν
will be likened to man  thoughtful, who   built
846    08  3614   1909 08  4073        2532 2597
αὐτοῦ τὴν οἰκίαν ἐπὶ τὴν πέτραν·  25  καὶ κατέβη
of him the house on  the  rock;        and went down
05  1028  2532 2064  013  4215    2532 4154    013
ἡ  βροχὴ καὶ ἦλθον οἱ ποταμοὶ καὶ ἔπνευσαν οἱ
the rain  and came  the rivers  and blew      the
417   2532 4363      07  3614  1565     2532 3756
ἄνεμοι καὶ προσέπεσαν τῇ οἰκίᾳ ἐκείνῃ, καὶ οὐκ
winds  and fell to    the house that,   and  not
4098     2311          1063 1909 08  4073       2532
ἔπεσεν, τεθεμελίωτο γὰρ ἐπὶ τὴν πέτραν.  26 καὶ
it fell, it had been for on  the rock.       And
         founded
3956 01 191           1473  016  3056    3778    2532
πᾶς ὁ ἀκούων      μου  τοὺς λόγους τούτους καὶ
all the one hearing of me the   words  these    and
3361 4160  846  3666            435   3474  3748
μὴ  ποιῶν αὐτοὺς ὁμοιωθήσεται  ἀνδρὶ μωρῷ, ὅστις
not doing them   will be likened to man  fool,  who
3618       846   08 3614   1909 08  285      2532
ᾠκοδόμησεν αὐτοῦ τὴν οἰκίαν ἐπὶ τὴν ἄμμον· 27 καὶ
built      of him the house on  the  sand;     and
2597    05  1028  2532 2064  013  4215     2532
κατέβη ἡ  βροχὴ καὶ ἦλθον οἱ ποταμοὶ καὶ
went down the rain  and came  the rivers  and
4154    013 417   2532 4350       07  3614
ἔπνευσαν οἱ ἄνεμοι καὶ προσέκοψαν τῇ   οἰκίᾳ
blew     the winds  and stumbled   to the house
1565    2532 4098     2532 1510 05  4431    846  3173
ἐκείνῃ, καὶ ἔπεσεν καὶ ἦν  ἡ πτῶσις αὐτῆς μεγάλη.
that,    and it fell and was the  fall  of it  great.
28 2532 1096   3753 5055   01  2424  016
   Καὶ ἐγένετο ὅτε ἐτέλεσεν ὁ Ἰησοῦς τοὺς
   And  it became when completed the Jesus  the
3056    3778    1605           013 3793  1909 07
λόγους τούτους, ἐξεπλήσσοντο οἱ ὄχλοι ἐπὶ τῇ
words  these,   were astonished the crowds at  the
1322     846   29 1510   1063 1321       846   5613
διδαχῇ αὐτοῦ·   ἦν   γὰρ διδάσκων αὐτοὺς ὡς
teaching of him;  he was+ for +teaching them  as
1849     2192  2532 3756 5613 013 1122       846
ἐξουσίαν ἔχων καὶ οὐχ ὡς οἱ γραμματεῖς αὐτῶν.
authority having and not as the writers  of them.
8:1 2597       1161 846  575 010 3735
    Καταβάντος δὲ αὐτοῦ ἀπὸ τοῦ ὄρους
    Having gone down but  of him from the hill
190         846  3793  4183     2  2532 2400 3015
ἠκολούθησαν αὐτῷ ὄχλοι πολλοί.   καὶ ἰδοὺ λεπρὸς
followed     him  crowds many.     And look  leper
4334         4352       846  3004   2962  1437
προσελθὼν   προσεκύνει αὐτῷ λέγων· κύριε, ἐὰν
having come to was worshiping him saying, Master, if
2309   1410      1473 2511      3   2532
θέλῃς δύνασαί με καθαρίσαι.     καὶ
you might want you are able me to clean.    And
1614      08 5495   681      846  3004
ἐκτείνας  τὴν χεῖρα ἥψατο  αὐτοῦ λέγων·
having stretched out the hand he touched him  saying;
2309   2511      2532 2112    2511        846
θέλω, καθαρίσθητι· καὶ εὐθέως ἐκαθαρίσθη αὐτοῦ
I want, be clean;  and immediately was cleaned of him
05  3014   4 2532 3004 846  01  2424   3708 3367
ἡ  λέπρα.   καὶ λέγει αὐτῷ ὁ Ἰησοῦς· ὅρα μηδενὶ
the leprosy. And says to him the Jesus, see to no one
```

these words of mine and acts on them will be like a wise man who built his house on rock. [25]The rain fell, the floods came, and the winds blew and beat on that house, but it did not fall, because it had been founded on rock. [26]And everyone who hears these words of mine and does not act on them will be like a foolish man who built his house on sand. [27]The rain fell, and the floods came, and the winds blew and beat against that house, and it fell—and great was its fall!"

28 Now when Jesus had finished saying these things, the crowds were astounded at his teaching, [29]for he taught them as one having authority, and not as their scribes.

CHAPTER 8

When Jesus[a] had come down from the mountain, great crowds followed him; [2]and there was a leper[b] who came to him and knelt before him, saying, "Lord, if you choose, you can make me clean." [3]He stretched out his hand and touched him, saying, "I do choose. Be made clean!" Immediately his leprosy[b] was cleansed. [4]Then Jesus said to him, "See that you say nothing to anyone;

---

[a] Gk he

[b] The terms leper and leprosy can refer to several diseases

but go, show yourself to the priest, and offer the gift that Moses commanded, as a testimony to them."

5 When he entered Capernaum, a centurion came to him, appealing to him 6 and saying, "Lord, my servant is lying at home paralyzed, in terrible distress." 7 And he said to him, "I will come and cure him." 8 The centurion answered, "Lord, I am not worthy to have you come under my roof; but only speak the word, and my servant will be healed. 9 For I also am a man under authority, with soldiers under me; and I say to one, 'Go,' and he goes, and to another, 'Come,' and he comes, and to my slave, 'Do this,' and the slave does it." 10 When Jesus heard him, he was amazed and said to those who followed him, "Truly I tell you, in no one[a] in Israel have I found such faith. 11 I tell you, many will come from east and west and will eat with Abraham and Isaac and Jacob in the kingdom of .heaven, 12 while the heirs of the kingdom will be thrown into the

[a] Other ancient authorities read *Truly I tell you, not even*

3004		235	5217	4572	1166	03	2409
εἴπῃς,		ἀλλὰ	ὕπαγε	σεαυτὸν	δεῖξον	τῷ	ἱερεῖ
you might say,		but	go off	yourself	show	to the	priest

2532	4374	012	1435	3739	4367		3475
καὶ	προσένεγκον	τὸ	δῶρον	ὃ		προσέταξεν	Μωϋσῆς,
and	offer	the	gift	which		commanded	Moses,

1519	3142	846	5	1525		1161	846
εἰς	μαρτύριον	αὐτοῖς.		Εἰσελθόντος		δὲ	αὐτοῦ
for	testimony	to them.		Having gone into		but	of him

1519	2746a	4334		846	1543
εἰς	Καφαρναοὺμ	προσῆλθεν		αὐτῷ	ἑκατόνταρχος
into	Capernaum	came toward		him	ruler of hundred

3870	846	6	2532	3004	2962	01	3816
παρακαλῶν	αὐτὸν		καὶ	λέγων·	κύριε,	ὁ	παῖς
encouraging	him		and	saying,	Master,	the	boy servant

1473	906		1722	07	3614	3885
μου	βέβληται		ἐν	τῇ	οἰκίᾳ	παραλυτικός,
of me	has been thrown		in	the	house	paralyzed one,

1171	928	7	2532	3004	846	1473
δεινῶς	βασανιζόμενος.		καὶ	λέγει	αὐτῷ·	ἐγὼ
terribly	being tormented.		And	he says	to him,	I

2064	2323	846	8	2532	611		01
ἐλθὼν	θεραπεύσω	αὐτόν.		καὶ	ἀποκριθεὶς		ὁ
having come	will heal	him.		And having answered		the

1543	5346	2962	3756	1510	2425	2443	1473
ἑκατόνταρχος	ἔφη·	κύριε,	οὐκ	εἰμὶ	ἱκανὸς	ἵνα	μου
ruler of hundred	said·	Master,	not	I am	enough	that	of me

5259	08	4721	1525		235	3441	3004
ὑπὸ	τὴν	στέγην	εἰσέλθῃς,		ἀλλὰ	μόνον	εἰπὲ
under	the	roof	you might come into,		but	alone	say

3056	2532	2390		01	3816	1473	9	2532
λόγῳ,	καὶ	ἰαθήσεται		ὁ	παῖς	μου.		καὶ
word,	and	will be cured		the	boy servant	of me.		And

1063	1473	444		1510	5259	1849	2192	5259
γὰρ	ἐγὼ	ἄνθρωπός		εἰμι	ὑπὸ	ἐξουσίαν,	ἔχων	ὑπ'
for	I	man		am	under	authority,	having	under

1683	4757		2532	3004	3778		4198
ἐμαυτὸν	στρατιώτας,		καὶ	λέγω	τούτῳ·		πορεύθητι,
myself	soldiers,		and	I say	to this one;		travel,

2532	4198		2532	243		2064	2532	2064
καὶ	πορεύεται,		καὶ	ἄλλῳ·		ἔρχου,	καὶ	ἔρχεται,
and	he travels,		and	to other;		come,	and	he comes,

2532	03	1401	1473	4160	3778	2532	4160
καὶ	τῷ	δούλῳ	μου·	ποίησον	τοῦτο,	καὶ	ποιεῖ.
and	to the	slave	of me,	do	this,	and	he does.

10	191	1161	01	2424	2296		2532	3004
	ἀκούσας	δὲ	ὁ	Ἰησοῦς	ἐθαύμασεν		καὶ	εἶπεν
	Having heard	but	the	Jesus	marveled		and	said

015	190		281	3004	1473	3844	3762
τοῖς	ἀκολουθοῦσιν·		ἀμὴν	λέγω	ὑμῖν,	παρ'	οὐδενὶ
to the	ones following;		amen	I say	to you,	from	no one

5118	4102	1722	03	2474	2147	11	3004	1161
τοσαύτην	πίστιν	ἐν	τῷ	Ἰσραὴλ	εὗρον.		λέγω	δὲ
such kind	trust	in	the	Israel	I found.		I say	but

1473	3754	4183	575	395		2532	1424	2240
ὑμῖν	ὅτι	πολλοὶ	ἀπὸ	ἀνατολῶν		καὶ	δυσμῶν	ἥξουσιν
to you	that	many	from	east		and	west	will come

2532	347			3326	11		2532	2464
καὶ	ἀνακλιθήσονται			μετὰ	Ἀβραὰμ		καὶ	Ἰσαὰκ
and	they will be reclined			with	Abraham		and	Isaac

2532	2384	1722	07	932		014	3772	12	013
καὶ	Ἰακὼβ	ἐν	τῇ	βασιλείᾳ		τῶν	οὐρανῶν,		οἱ
and	Jacob	in	the	kingdom		of the	heavens,		the

1161	5207	06	932		1544		1519	012
δὲ	υἱοὶ	τῆς	βασιλείας		ἐκβληθήσονται		εἰς	τὸ
but	sons	of the	kingdom		will be thrown		into	the

4655	012	1857		1563	1510	01	2805	2532
σκότος	τὸ	ἐξώτερον·	ἐκεῖ	ἔσται	ὁ	κλαυθμὸς	καὶ	
dark	the	outermost;	there	will be	the	crying	and	

01	1030	014	3599		2532	3004	01	2424
ὁ	βρυγμὸς	τῶν	ὀδόντων.	**13**	καὶ	εἶπεν	ὁ	Ἰησοῦς
the	grinding	of the	teeth.		And	said	the	Jesus

03	1543		5217	5613	4100
τῷ	ἑκατοντάρχῃ·	ὕπαγε,	ὡς	ἐπίστευσας
to the	hundred ruler;	go off,	as	you trusted

1096	1473	2532	2390	01	3816	846	1722	07
γενηθήτω	σοι.	καὶ	ἰάθη	ὁ	παῖς	[αὐτοῦ]	ἐν	τῇ
let become to <u>you</u>.		And was	the boy		of him		in	the cured servant

5610	1565		2532	2064		01	2424	1519	08
ὥρᾳ	ἐκείνῃ.	**14**	Καὶ	ἐλθὼν	ὁ	Ἰησοῦς	εἰς	τὴν
hour	that.		And	having come	the	Jesus	into	the

3614	4074	3708	08	3994		846
οἰκίαν	Πέτρου	εἶδεν	τὴν	πενθερὰν	αὐτοῦ
house	of Peter	saw	the	mother-in-law	of him

906		2532	4445		2532	681
βεβλημένην	καὶ	πυρέσσουσαν·	**15**	καὶ	ἥψατο
having been thrown	and	burning;		and	he touched

06	5495	846	2532	863	846	01	4446
τῆς	χειρὸς	αὐτῆς,	καὶ	ἀφῆκεν	αὐτὴν	ὁ	πυρετός,
the	hand	of her,	and	left off	her		the fever,

2532	1453	2532	1247	846
καὶ	ἠγέρθη	καὶ	διηκόνει	αὐτῷ.
and	she was raised	and	she was serving	him.

16	3798	1161	1096	4374	846
	Ὀψίας	δὲ	γενομένης	προσήνεγκαν	αὐτῷ
	Evening	but	having become	they brought	to him

1139	4183	2532	1544	024	4151
δαιμονιζομένους	πολλούς·	καὶ	ἐξέβαλεν	τὰ	πνεύματα
being demonized	many;	and	he threw out	the	spirits

3056	2532	3956	016	2560	2192	2323
λόγῳ	καὶ	πάντας	τοὺς	κακῶς	ἔχοντας	ἐθεράπευσεν,
in word	and	all	the ones	badly	having	he healed,

17	3704	4137	09	3004	1223	2268
	ὅπως	πληρωθῇ	τὸ	ῥηθὲν	διὰ	Ἠσαΐου
	so that	was fulfilled	the	word having been spoken	through	Isaiah

02	4396	3004	846	020	769	1473
τοῦ	προφήτου	λέγοντος·	αὐτὸς	τὰς	ἀσθενείας	ἡμῶν
the	spokesman	saying,	himself	the	weaknesses	of us

2983	2532	020	3554	941		3708
ἔλαβεν	καὶ	τὰς	νόσους	ἐβάστασεν.	**18**	Ἰδὼν
he received	and	the	illnesses	he bore.		Having seen

1161	01	2424	3793	4012	846	2753	565
δὲ	ὁ	Ἰησοῦς	ὄχλον	περὶ	αὐτὸν	ἐκέλευσεν	ἀπελθεῖν
but	the	Jesus	crowd	around	him	commanded	to go off

1519	012	4008		2532	4334	1520	1122
εἰς	τὸ	πέραν.	**19**	καὶ	προσελθὼν	εἰς	γραμματεὺς
into	the	across.		And	having gone	to one	writer

3004	846	1320	190	1473	3699	1437
εἶπεν	αὐτῷ·	διδάσκαλε,	ἀκολουθήσω	σοι	ὅπου	ἐὰν
said	to him;	teacher,	I will follow	<u>you</u>	where	if

565		2532	3004	846	01	2424	017
ἀπέρχῃ.	**20**	καὶ	λέγει	αὐτῷ	ὁ	Ἰησοῦς·	αἱ
<u>you</u> might go off.		And	says	to him	the	Jesus;	the

258	5454	2192	2532	021	4071	02	3772
ἀλώπεκες	φωλεοὺς	ἔχουσιν	καὶ	τὰ	πετεινὰ	τοῦ	οὐρανοῦ
foxes	holes	have	and	the	birds	of the	heaven

2682	01	1161	5207	02	444	3756	2192
κατασκηνώσεις,	ὁ	δὲ	υἱὸς	τοῦ	ἀνθρώπου	οὐκ	ἔχει
set up tents,	the	but	son	of the	man	not	has

4226	08	2776	2827		2087	1161	014	3101
ποῦ	τὴν	κεφαλὴν	κλίνῃ.	**21**	ἕτερος	δὲ	τῶν	μαθητῶν
where	the	head	he might bow.		Other	but	the	learners

outer darkness, where there will be weeping and gnashing of teeth." [13]And to the centurion Jesus said, "Go; let it be done for you according to your faith." And the servant was healed in that hour.

[14]When Jesus entered Peter's house, he saw his mother-in-law lying in bed with a fever; [15]he touched her hand, and the fever left her, and she got up and began to serve him. [16]That evening they brought to him many who were possessed with demons; and he cast out the spirits with a word, and cured all who were sick. [17]This was to fulfill what had been spoken through the prophet Isaiah, "He took our infirmities and bore our diseases."

[18]Now when Jesus saw great crowds around him, he gave orders to go over to the other side. [19]A scribe then approached and said, "Teacher, I will follow you wherever you go." [20]And Jesus said to him, "Foxes have holes, and birds of the air have nests; but the Son of Man has nowhere to lay his head." [21]Another of his disciples

said to him, "Lord, first let me go and bury my father." ²²But Jesus said to him, "Follow me, and let the dead bury their own dead."

23 And when he got into the boat, his disciples followed him. ²⁴A windstorm arose on the sea, so great that the boat was being swamped by the waves; but he was asleep. ²⁵And they went and woke him up, saying, "Lord, save us! We are perishing!" ²⁶And he said to them, "Why are you afraid, you of little faith?" Then he got up and rebuked the winds and the sea; and there was a dead calm. ²⁷They were amazed, saying, "What sort of man is this, that even the winds and the sea obey him?"

28 When he came to the other side, to the country of the Gadarenes,ᵃ two demoniacs coming out of the tombs met him. They were so fierce that no one could pass that way. ²⁹Suddenly they shouted, "What have you to do with us, Son of God? Have you come here to torment us before the time?" ³⁰Now a large herd of swine was feeding at some distance from them.

ᵃ Other ancient authorities read *Gergesenes;* others, *Gerasenes*

846	3004	846	2962	2010		1473 4413
[αὐτοῦ]	εἶπεν	αὐτῷ·	κυρίε,	ἐπιτρεψόν μοι		πρῶτον
of him	said	to him;	Master,	allow me		first

565	2532 2290	04	3962	1473	**22**	01 1161
ἀπελθεῖν καὶ	θάψαι	τὸν	πατέρα μου.			ὁ δὲ
to go off and	to bury	the	father of me.			The but

2424	3004	846	190	1473 2532 863	016
Ἰησοῦς	λέγει	αὐτῷ·	ἀκολούθει	μοι καὶ ἄφες	τοὺς
Jesus	says	to him,	follow	me and send off	the

3498	2290	016 1438	3498	**23**	2532
νεκροὺς	θάψαι	τοὺς ἑαυτῶν	νεκρούς.		Καὶ
dead	to bury	the of themselves	dead.		And

1684	846	1519 012 4143	190	846
ἐμβάντι	αὐτῷ εἰς	τὸ πλοῖον	ἠκολούθησαν	αὐτῷ
having gone in	him into	the boat	followed	him

013 3101	846	**24**	2532 2400 4578	3173	1096
οἱ μαθηταὶ	αὐτοῦ.		καὶ ἰδοὺ σεισμὸς	μέγας	ἐγένετο
the learners of him.			And look shake	great	became

1722 07 2281	5620	012 4143	2572
ἐν τῇ θαλάσσῃ,	ὥστε	τὸ πλοῖον	καλύπτεσθαι
in the sea,	so that	the boat	to be covered

5259 022 2949	846	1161 2518	**25**	2532
ὑπὸ τῶν κυμάτων,	αὐτὸς	δὲ ἐκάθευδεν.		καὶ
by the waves,	himself	but slept.		And

4334	1453	846	3004	2962
προσελθόντες	ἤγειραν	αὐτὸν	λέγοντες·	κύριε,
having gone to	they raised	him	saying,	Master,

4982	622	**26**	2532 3004	846
σῶσον,	ἀπολλύμεθα.		καὶ λέγει	αὐτοῖς·
deliver,	we are being destroyed.		And he says	to them;

5101 1169	1510	3640	5119
τί δειλοί	ἐστε,	ὀλιγόπιστοι;	τότε
why cowards	are you,	little trustful ones?	Then

1453	2008	015 417	2532 07
ἐγερθεὶς	ἐπετίμησεν	τοῖς ἀνέμοις καὶ	τῇ
having been raised	he admonished	the winds and	the

2281	2532 1096	1055	3173	**27**	013 1161
θαλάσσῃ,	καὶ ἐγένετο	γαλήνη	μεγάλη.		οἱ δὲ
sea,	and became	calm	great.		The but

444	2296	3004	4217	1510 3778
ἄνθρωποι	ἐθαύμασαν	λέγοντες·	ποταπός	ἐστιν οὗτος
men	marveled	saying,	what sort is	this

3754 2532 013 417	2532 05	2281	846	5219
ὅτι καὶ οἱ ἄνεμοι	καὶ ἡ	θάλασσα	αὐτῷ	ὑπακούουσιν;
that even the winds	and the	sea	him	obey?

28	2532 2064	846	1519 012 4008	1519
	Καὶ ἐλθόντος	αὐτοῦ	εἰς τὸ πέραν	εἰς
	And having gone	him	into the across	into

08 5561	014	1046	5221	846 1417
τὴν χώραν	τῶν	Γαδαρηνῶν	ὑπήντησαν	αὐτῷ δύο
the country	of the	Gadarenes	met	him two

1139	1537	022 3419	1831
δαιμονιζόμενοι	ἐκ	τῶν μνημείων	ἐξερχόμενοι,
being demonized	out of	the graves	coming out,

5467	3029	5620 3361	2480	5100 3928
χαλεποὶ	λίαν,	ὥστε μὴ	ἰσχύειν	τινὰ παρελθεῖν
difficult	very,	so not that	to be strong	some to go along

1223	06 3598 1565	**29**	2532 2400 2896
διὰ	τῆς ὁδοῦ ἐκείνης.		καὶ ἰδοὺ ἔκραξαν
through	the way that.		And look they shouted

3004	5101 1473 2532 1473	5207 02	2316
λέγοντες· τί	ἡμῖν καὶ σοί,	υἱὲ τοῦ	θεοῦ;
saying; what	to us and to you,	son of the	God?

2064	5602 4253	2540 928	1473
ἦλθες	ὧδε πρὸ	καιροῦ βασανίσαι	ἡμᾶς;
Have you come	here before	season to torment	us?

30	1510 1161 3112	575	846 34	5519	4183
	ἦν δὲ μακρὰν	ἀπ'	αὐτῶν ἀγέλη	χοίρων	πολλῶν
	Was+ but far	from	them herd	of pigs	many

1006   31   013 1161 1142   3870   846
βοσκομένη.   οἱ   δὲ   δαίμονες παρεκάλουν   αὐτὸν
+grazing.   The but demons   were encouraging   him

3004   1487 1544   1473 649   1473
λέγοντες·   εἰ   ἐκβάλλεις   ἡμᾶς, ἀπόστειλον ἡμᾶς
saying,   if   you throw out   us,   delegate   us

1519 08 34   014   5519   32 2532 3004   846
εἰς τὴν ἀγέλην τῶν   χοίρων.   καὶ εἶπεν   αὐτοῖς·
into the herd of the pigs.   And he said to them;

5217   013 1161 1831   565   1519
ὑπάγετε. οἱ   δὲ   ἐξελθόντες   ἀπῆλθον   εἰς
go off.   The but   ones having gone out went off   into

016 5519   2532 2400 3729   3956 05 34   2596 02
τοὺς χοίρους·   καὶ ἰδοὺ ὥρμησεν πᾶσα ἡ ἀγέλη κατὰ τοῦ
the pigs;   and look rushed all the herd down the

2911   1519 08 2281   2532 599   1722 023
κρημνοῦ   εἰς τὴν θάλασσαν καὶ ἀπέθανον ἐν   τοῖς
steep slope into the sea   and died   in   the

5204   33   013 1161 1006   5343   2532
ὕδασιν.   οἱ   δὲ   βόσκοντες ἔφυγον, καὶ
waters.   The but   ones grazing fled, and

565   1519 08 4172 518   3956 2532
ἀπελθόντες   εἰς τὴν πόλιν ἀπήγγειλαν πάντα καὶ
having gone off into the city they told   all   and

024 014   1139   34 2532 2400 3956 05
τὰ τῶν   δαιμονιζομένων.   καὶ ἰδοὺ πᾶσα ἡ
the of the ones being demonized.   And look all   the

4172 1831   1519 5222   03   2424 2532 3708
πόλις ἐξῆλθεν εἰς ὑπάντησιν τῷ Ἰησοῦ καὶ ἰδόντες
city went out to meeting   the Jesus and having seen

846 3870   3704   3327   575
αὐτὸν παρεκάλεσαν   ὅπως   μεταβῇ   ἀπὸ
him   were encouraging so that he might go across from

022 3725   846   9:1 2532 1684   1519
τῶν ὁρίων   αὐτῶν.   Καὶ ἐμβὰς   εἰς
the territories of them.   And having gone in into

4143 1276   2532 2064   1519 08 2398
πλοῖον διεπέρασεν   καὶ ἦλθεν εἰς τὴν ἰδίαν
boat   he crossed over and he came into the own

4172   2   2532 2400 4374   846   3885
πόλιν.   καὶ ἰδοὺ προσέφερον αὐτῷ παραλυτικὸν
city.   And look they offered to him paralyzed one

1909 2825   906   2532 3708   01   2424
ἐπὶ κλίνης βεβλημένον. καὶ ἰδὼν   ὁ Ἰησοῦς
on   bed   being thrown. And having seen the Jesus

08   4102   846   3004 03   3885
τὴν πίστιν αὐτῶν   εἶπεν τῷ   παραλυτικῷ·
the trust of them said to the paralyzed one;

2293   5043   863   1473   017
θάρσει,   τέκνον, ἀφίενταί   σου   αἱ
take courage, child, are being sent off of you the

266   3   2532 2400 5100   014   1122   3004
ἁμαρτίαι.   καὶ ἰδού τινες τῶν   γραμματέων εἶπαν
sins.   And look some of the writers   said

1722 1438   3778   987   2532 3708
ἐν ἑαυτοῖς·   οὗτος   βλασφημεῖ. καὶ ἰδὼν
in themselves, this one insults.   And having seen

01   2424   020 1761   846   3004   2444
ὁ Ἰησοῦς τὰς ἐνθυμήσεις αὐτῶν εἶπεν· ἱνατί
the Jesus the reflections of them said; why

1760   4190   1722 019 2588   1473 5 5101
ἐνθυμεῖσθε   πονηρὰ ἐν ταῖς καρδίαις ὑμῶν;   τί
do you reflect evil   in the hearts   of you? What

1063 1510 2123   3004   863
γάρ ἐστιν εὐκοπώτερον, εἰπεῖν· ἀφίενταί
for is   easier labor, to say; are being sent off

1473 017 266   3778   3004   1453 2532
σου   αἱ ἁμαρτίαι, ἢ   εἰπεῖν· ἔγειρε καὶ
of you the sins,   or   to say; rise   and

31The demons begged him, "If you cast us out, send us into the herd of swine." 32And he said to them, "Go!" So they came out and entered the swine; and suddenly, the whole herd rushed down the steep bank into the sea and perished in the water. 33The swineherds ran off, and on going into the town, they told the whole story about what had happened to the demoniacs. 34Then the whole town came out to meet Jesus; and when they saw him, they begged him to leave their neighborhood. 9:1And after getting into a boat he crossed the sea and came to his own town.

2 And just then some people were carrying a paralyzed man lying on a bed. When Jesus saw their faith, he said to the paralytic, "Take heart, son; your sins are forgiven." 3Then some of the scribes said to themselves, "This man is blaspheming." 4But Jesus, perceiving their thoughts, said, "Why do you think evil in your hearts? 5For which is easier, to say, 'Your sins are forgiven,' or to say, 'Stand up and walk'?

6But so that you may know that the Son of Man has authority on earth to forgive sins"—he then said to the paralytic—"Stand up, take your bed and go to your home." 7And he stood up and went to his home. 8When the crowds saw it, they were filled with awe, and they glorified God, who had given such authority to human beings.

9 As Jesus was walking along, he saw a man called Matthew sitting at the tax booth; and he said to him, "Follow me." And he got up and followed him.

10 And as he sat at dinner[a] in the house, many tax collectors and sinners came and were sitting[b] with him and his disciples. 11When the Pharisees saw this, they said to his disciples, "Why does your teacher eat with tax collectors and sinners?" 12But when he heard this, he said, "Those who are well have no need of a physician, but those who are sick. 13Go and learn what this means, 'I desire mercy, not sacrifice.' For I have come to call not the righteous but sinners."

14 Then the disciples of John came to him, saying, "Why do we and the Pharisees

a Gk reclined
b Gk were reclining

4043		2443 1161 3609a		3754 1849

περιπάτει; 6 ἵνα δὲ εἰδῆτε ὅτι ἐξουσίαν
walk around? That but you might know that authority

2192 01 5207 02 444 1909 06 1093 863
ἔχει ὁ υἱὸς τοῦ ἀνθρώπου ἐπὶ τῆς γῆς ἀφιέναι
has the son of the man on the earth to send off

266 5119 3004 03 3885 1453
ἁμαρτίας – τότε λέγει τῷ παραλυτικῷ· ἐγερθεὶς
sins then he says to the paralyzed, being raised

142 1473 08 2825 2532 5217 1519 04 3624
ἆρόν σου τὴν κλίνην καὶ ὕπαγε εἰς τὸν οἶκόν
lift up of you the bed and go off into the house

1473 7 2532 1453 565 1519 04
σου. καὶ ἐγερθεὶς ἀπῆλθεν εἰς τὸν
of you. And having been raised he went off into the

3624 846 8 3708 1161 013 3793 5399
οἶκον αὐτοῦ. ἰδόντες δὲ οἱ ὄχλοι ἐφοβήθησαν
house of him. Having seen but the crowds were afraid

2532 1392 04 2316 04 1325
καὶ ἐδόξασαν τὸν θεὸν τὸν δόντα
and they gave splendor the God the one having given

1849 5108 015 444 2532 3855
ἐξουσίαν τοιαύτην τοῖς ἀνθρώποις. 9 Καὶ παράγων
authority such to the men. And leading along

01 2424 1564 3708 444 2521 1909
ὁ Ἰησοῦς ἐκεῖθεν εἶδεν ἄνθρωπον καθήμενον ἐπὶ
the Jesus from there saw man sitting on

012 5058 3102a 3004 2532 3004
τὸ τελώνιον, Μαθθαῖον λεγόμενον, καὶ λέγει
the tax table, Matthew being called, and he says

846 190 1473 2532 450 190
αὐτῷ· ἀκολούθει μοι. καὶ ἀναστὰς ἠκολούθησεν
to him, follow me. And having stood up he followed

846 10 2532 1096 846 345 1722 07
αὐτῷ. καὶ ἐγένετο αὐτοῦ ἀνακειμένου ἐν τῇ
him. And it became of him reclining in the

3614 2532 2400 4183 5057 2532 268
οἰκίᾳ, καὶ ἰδοὺ πολλοὶ τελῶναι καὶ ἁμαρτωλοὶ
house, and look many tax men and sinners

2064 4873 03 2424 2532 015 3101
ἐλθόντες συνανέκειντο τῷ Ἰησοῦ καὶ τοῖς μαθηταῖς
having were reclining to Jesus and the learners
come together the

846 11 2532 3708 013 5330 3004
αὐτοῦ. καὶ ἰδόντες οἱ Φαρισαῖοι ἔλεγον
of him. And having seen the Pharisees were saying

015 3101 846 1223 5101 3326 014 5057
τοῖς μαθηταῖς αὐτοῦ· διὰ τί μετὰ τῶν τελωνῶν
to the learners of him, through what with the tax men

2532 268 2068 01 1320 1473 12 01 1161
καὶ ἁμαρτωλῶν ἐσθίει ὁ διδάσκαλος ὑμῶν; ὁ δὲ
and sinners eats the teacher of you? The but

191 3004 3756 5532 2192 013
ἀκούσας εἶπεν· οὐ χρείαν ἔχουσιν οἱ
one having heard said, not need have the ones

2480 2395 235 013 2560 2192
ἰσχύοντες ἰατροῦ ἀλλ᾽ οἱ κακῶς ἔχοντες.
being strong physician but the ones badly having.

13 4198 1161 3129 5101 1510 1656 2309
πορευθέντες δὲ μάθετε τί ἐστιν· ἔλεος θέλω
Traveling but learn what is; mercy I want

2532 3756 2378 3756 1063 2064 2564 1342
καὶ οὐ θυσίαν· οὐ γὰρ ἦλθον καλέσαι δικαίους
and not sacrifice, not for I came to call right ones

235 268 14 5119 4334 846 013 3101
ἀλλὰ ἁμαρτωλούς. Τότε προσέρχονται αὐτῷ οἱ μαθηταὶ
but sinners. Then go toward him the learners

2491 3004 1223 5101 1473 2532 013 5330
Ἰωάννου λέγοντες· διὰ τί ἡμεῖς καὶ οἱ Φαρισαῖοι
of John saying, because what we and the Pharisees

3522	4183	013	1161	3101	1473	3756
νηστεύομεν	[πολλά],	οἱ	δὲ	μαθηταί	σου	οὐ
fast	many,	the	but	learners	of you	not

3522		2532	3004	846	01	2424	3361
νηστεύουσιν;	**15**	καὶ	εἶπεν	αὐτοῖς	ὁ	Ἰησοῦς·	μὴ
fast?		And	said	to them	the	Jesus,	not

1410	013	5207	02	3567	3996	1909
δύνανται	οἱ	υἱοὶ	τοῦ	νυμφῶνος	πενθεῖν	ἐφ᾽
are able	the	sons	of the	bridal chamber	to mourn	on

3745	3326	846	1510	01	3566	2064
ὅσον	μετ᾽	αὐτῶν	ἐστιν	ὁ	νυμφίος;	ἐλεύσονται
as much as	with	them	is	the	bridegroom?	Will go

1161	2250	3752	522	575	846	01
δὲ	ἡμέραι	ὅταν	ἀπαρθῇ	ἀπ᾽	αὐτῶν	ὁ
but	days	when	might be lifted up	from	them	the

3566	2532	5119	3522		3762	1161
νυμφίος,	καὶ	τότε	νηστεύσουσιν.	**16**	οὐδεὶς	δὲ
bridegroom,	and	then	they will fast.		No one	but

1911	1915	4470	46	1909	2440	3820
ἐπιβάλλει	ἐπίβλημα	ῥάκους	ἀγνάφου	ἐπὶ	ἱματίῳ	παλαιῷ·
throws on	patch	cloth	unshrunk	on	clothes	old;

142	1063	012	4138	846	575	010	2440	2532
αἴρει	γὰρ	τὸ	πλήρωμα	αὐτοῦ	ἀπὸ	τοῦ	ἱματίου	καὶ
lifts up	for	the	fullness	of it	from	the	clothes	and

5501	4978	1096		3761	906	3631
χεῖρον	σχίσμα	γίνεται.	**17**	οὐδὲ	βάλλουσιν	οἶνον
worse	split	becomes.		But not	they throw	wine

3501	1519	779	3820	1487	1161	3361	1065
νέον	εἰς	ἀσκοὺς	παλαιούς·	εἰ	δὲ	μή	γε,
new	into	wineskins	old;	if	but	not	indeed,

4486	013	779	2532	01	3631	1632
ῥήγνυνται	οἱ	ἀσκοὶ	καὶ	ὁ	οἶνος	ἐκχεῖται
are ripped	the	wineskins	and	the	wine	is poured out

2532	013	779	622	235	906
καὶ	οἱ	ἀσκοὶ	ἀπόλλυνται·	ἀλλὰ	βάλλουσιν
and	the	wineskins	are destroyed;	but	they throw

3631	3501	1519	779	2537	2532	297
οἶνον	νέον	εἰς	ἀσκοὺς	καινούς,	καὶ	ἀμφότεροι
wine	new	into	wineskins	new,	and	both

4933		3778	846	2980	846
συντηροῦνται.	**18**	Ταῦτα	αὐτοῦ	λαλοῦντος	αὐτοῖς,
are kept together.		These	of him	speaking	to them,

2400	758	1520	2064	4352	846	3004
ἰδοὺ	ἄρχων	εἷς	ἐλθὼν	προσεκύνει	αὐτῷ	λέγων
look	ruler	one	having come	was worshiping	him	saying,

3754	05	2364	1473	737	5053	235
ὅτι	ἡ	θυγάτηρ	μου	ἄρτι	ἐτελεύτησεν·	ἀλλὰ
(")	the	daughter	of me	now	died;	but

2064	2007	08	5495	1473	1909	846	2532
ἐλθὼν	ἐπίθες	τὴν	χεῖρά	σου	ἐπ᾽	αὐτήν,	καὶ
having come	set on	the	hand	of you	on	her,	and

2198		2532	1453	01	2424
ζήσεται.	**19**	καὶ	ἐγερθεὶς	ὁ	Ἰησοῦς
she will live.		And	having raised	the	Jesus

190	846	2532	013	3101	846		2532	2400
ἠκολούθησεν	αὐτῷ	καὶ	οἱ	μαθηταὶ	αὐτοῦ.	**20**	Καὶ	ἰδοὺ
followed	him	and	the	learners	of him.		And	look

1135	131	1427	2094	4334
γυνὴ	αἱμορροοῦσα	δώδεκα	ἔτη	προσελθοῦσα
woman	hemorrhaging	twelve	years	having gone toward

3693	681	010	2899	010	2440
ὄπισθεν	ἥψατο	τοῦ	κρασπέδου	τοῦ	ἱματίου
from behind	touched	the	edge	of	the clothes

846		3004		1063	1722	1438	1437	3441
αὐτοῦ·	**21**	ἔλεγεν		γὰρ	ἐν	ἑαυτῇ·	ἐὰν	μόνον
of him;		she was saying		for	in	herself,	if	alone

681	010	2440	846	4982		01	1161
ἅψωμαι	τοῦ	ἱματίου	αὐτοῦ	σωθήσομαι.	**22**	ὁ	δὲ
I might touch	the	clothes	of him	I will be delivered.		The	but

fast often,[a] but your disciples do not fast?"

[15]And Jesus said to them, "The wedding guests cannot mourn as long as the bridegroom is with them, can they? The days will come when the bridegroom is taken away from them, and then they will fast.

[16]No one sews a piece of unshrunk cloth on an old cloak, for the patch pulls away from the cloak, and a worse tear is made. [17]Neither is new wine put into old wineskins; otherwise, the skins burst, and the wine is spilled, and the skins are destroyed; but new wine is put into fresh wineskins, and so both are preserved."

18 While he was saying these things to them, suddenly a leader of the synagogue[b] came in and knelt before him, saying, "My daughter has just died; but come and lay your hand on her, and she will live." [19]And Jesus got up and followed him, with his disciples. [20]Then suddenly a woman who had been suffering from hemorrhages for twelve years came up behind him and touched the fringe of his cloak, [21]for she said to herself, "If I only touch his cloak, I will be made well." [22]Jesus turned, and seeing her

[a] Other ancient authorities lack *often*

[b] Gk lacks *of the synagogue*

he said, "Take heart, daughter; your faith has made you well." And instantly the woman was made well. ²³When Jesus came to the leader's house and saw the flute players and the crowd making a commotion, ²⁴he said, "Go away; for the girl is not dead but sleeping." And they laughed at him. ²⁵But when the crowd had been put outside, he went in and took her by the hand, and the girl got up. ²⁶And the report of this spread throughout that district.

27 As Jesus went on from there, two blind men followed him, crying loudly, "Have mercy on us, Son of David!" ²⁸When he entered the house, the blind men came to him; and Jesus said to them, "Do you believe that I am able to do this?" They said to him, "Yes, Lord." ²⁹Then he touched their eyes and said, "According to your faith let it be done to you." ³⁰And their eyes were opened. Then Jesus sternly ordered them, "See that no one knows of this." ³¹But they went away and spread the news about him throughout that district. 32 After they had gone away,

2424	4762	2532	3708	846	3004
Ἰησοῦς στραφεὶς		καὶ	ἰδὼν	αὐτὴν	εἶπεν·
Jesus having turned		and	having seen	her	said,

2293 θάρσει, 2364 θύγατερ· 05 ἡ 4102 πίστις 1473 σου 4982 σέσωκέν
take courage, daughter; the trust of you has delivered

1473 σε. 2532 καὶ 4982 ἐσώθη 05 ἡ 1135 γυνὴ 575 ἀπὸ 06 τῆς 5610 ὥρας 1565 ἐκείνης.
you. And was delivered the woman from the hour that.

23 2532 καὶ 2064 ἐλθὼν 01 ὁ 2424 Ἰησοῦς 1519 εἰς 08 τὴν 3614 οἰκίαν 02 τοῦ
And having come the Jesus into the house of the

758 ἄρχοντος 2532 καὶ 3708 ἰδὼν 016 τοὺς 834 αὐλητὰς 2532 καὶ 04 τὸν 3793 ὄχλον
ruler and having seen the flutists and the crowd

2350 θορυβούμενον **24** 3004 ἔλεγεν· 402 ἀναχωρεῖτε, 3756 οὐ 1063 γὰρ
uproaring was saying, depart, not for

599 ἀπέθανεν 09 τὸ 2877 κοράσιον 235 ἀλλὰ 2518 καθεύδει. 2532 καὶ
died the young girl but she sleeps. And

2606 κατεγέλων 846 αὐτοῦ. **25** 3753 ὅτε 1161 δὲ 1544 ἐξεβλήθη
they were laughing at him. When but was thrown out

01 ὁ 3793 ὄχλος 1525 εἰσελθὼν 2902 ἐκράτησεν 06 τῆς 5495 χειρὸς 846 αὐτῆς,
the crowd having gone in he held the hand of her,

2532 καὶ 1453 ἠγέρθη 09 τὸ 2877 κοράσιον. **26** 2532 καὶ 1831 ἐξῆλθεν 05 ἡ 5345 φήμη
and raised the young girl. And went out the report

3778 αὕτη 1519 εἰς 3650 ὅλην 08 τὴν 1093 γῆν 1565 ἐκείνην. **27** 2532 Καὶ 3855 παράγοντι
this into whole the land that. And leading along

1564 ἐκεῖθεν 03 τῷ 2424 Ἰησοῦ 190 ἠκολούθησαν 846 [αὐτῷ] 1417 δύο 5185 τυφλοὶ
from there to the Jesus followed him two blind

2896 κράζοντες 2532 καὶ 3004 λέγοντες· 1653 ἐλέησον 1473 ἡμᾶς, 5207 υἱὸς
shouting and saying, have mercy us, son

1160a Δαυίδ. **28** 2064 ἐλθόντι 1161 δὲ 1519 εἰς 08 τὴν 3614 οἰκίαν 4334 προσῆλθον
of David. Having gone but into the house went toward

846 αὐτῷ 013 οἱ 5185 τυφλοί, 2532 καὶ 3004 λέγει 846 αὐτοῖς 01 ὁ 2424 Ἰησοῦς·
him the blind, and says to them the Jesus;

4100 πιστεύετε 3754 ὅτι 1410 δύναμαι 3778 τοῦτο 4160 ποιῆσαι; 3004 λέγουσιν
do you trust that I am able this to do? They say

846 αὐτῷ· 3483 ναὶ 2962 κύριε. **29** 5119 τότε 681 ἥψατο 014 τῶν 3788 ὀφθαλμῶν
to him; yes Master. Then he touched the eyes

846 αὐτῶν 3004 λέγων· 2596 κατὰ 08 τὴν 4102 πίστιν 1473 ὑμῶν 1096 γενηθήτω
of them saying; by the trust of you let it become

1473 ὑμῖν. **30** 2532 καὶ 455 ἠνεῴχθησαν 846 αὐτῶν 013 οἱ 3788 ὀφθαλμοί. 2532 καὶ
to you. And were opened of them the eyes. And

1690 ἐνεβριμήθη 846 αὐτοῖς 01 ὁ 2424 Ἰησοῦς 3004 λέγων· 3708 ὁρᾶτε 3367 μηδεὶς
was indignant to them the Jesus saying; see no one

1097 γινωσκέτω. **31** 013 οἱ 1161 δὲ 1831 ἐξελθόντες
let know. The ones but having gone out

1310 διεφήμισαν 846 αὐτὸν 1722 ἐν 3650 ὅλῃ 07 τῇ 1093 γῇ 1565 ἐκείνῃ.
spoke thoroughly him in whole the land that.

32 846 Αὐτῶν 1161 δὲ 1831 ἐξερχομένων 2400 ἰδοὺ 4374 προσήνεγκαν
Of them but coming out look they brought toward

846	444	2974	1139		2532
αὐτῷ	ἄνθρωπον	κωφὸν	δαιμονιζόμενον.	**33**	καὶ
him	man	deaf	being demonized.		And

1544		010	1140	2980	01	2974
ἐκβληθέντος		τοῦ	δαιμονίου	ἐλάλησεν	ὁ	κωφός.
having thrown out		the	demon	spoke	the	deaf.

2532	2296	013	3793	3004	3763
καὶ	ἐθαύμασαν	οἱ	ὄχλοι	λέγοντες·	οὐδέποτε
And	marveled	the	crowds	saying;	but not ever

5316	3779	1722 03	2474		013 1161	5330
ἐφάνη	οὕτως	ἐν τῷ	Ἰσραήλ.	**34**	οἱ δὲ	Φαρισαῖοι
shined	thusly	in the	Israel.		The but	Pharisees

3004	1722 03	758	022	1140
ἔλεγον·	ἐν τῷ	ἄρχοντι	τῶν	δαιμονίων
were saying;	in the	ruler	of the	demons

1544		024	1140		2532	4013
ἐκβάλλει		τὰ	δαιμόνια.	**35**	Καὶ	περιῆγεν
he throws out		the	demons.		And	was leading around

01	2424	020	4172	3956	2532 020	2968	1321
ὁ	Ἰησοῦς	τὰς	πόλεις	πάσας	καὶ τὰς	κώμας	διδάσκων
the	Jesus	the	cities	all	and the	villages	teaching

1722 019	4864	846	2532 2784	012
ἐν ταῖς	συναγωγαῖς	αὐτῶν	καὶ κηρύσσων	τὸ
in the	synagogues	of them	and announcing	the

2098	06	932	2532 2323	3956
εὐαγγέλιον	τῆς	βασιλείας	καὶ θεραπεύων	πᾶσαν
good message	of the	kingdom	and healing	all

3554	2532 3956	3119		3708	1161 016
νόσον	καὶ πᾶσαν	μαλακίαν.	**36**	Ἰδὼν	δὲ τοὺς
illness	and all	sickness.		Having seen	but the

3793	4697	4012	846	3754
ὄχλους	ἐσπλαγχνίσθη	περὶ	αὐτῶν,	ὅτι
crowds	he had affection	concerning	them,	because

1510	4660	2532 4496	5616
ἦσαν	ἐσκυλμένοι	καὶ ἐρριμμένοι	ὡσεὶ
they were+	+being annoyed	and +being flung	as

4263	3361 2192	4166		5119 3004	015
πρόβατα	μὴ ἔχοντα	ποιμένα.	**37**	τότε λέγει	τοῖς
sheep	not having	shepherd.		Then he says	to the

3101	846	03	3303	2326	4183	013 1161
μαθηταῖς	αὐτοῦ·	ὁ	μὲν	θερισμὸς	πολύς,	οἱ δὲ
learners	of him,	the	indeed	harvest	much,	the but

2040	3641		1189	3767 02	2962	02
ἐργάται	ὀλίγοι·	**38**	δεήθητε	οὖν τοῦ	κυρίου	τοῦ
workers	few;		beg	then the	Master	of the

2326	3704	1544		2040	1519 04
θερισμοῦ	ὅπως	ἐκβάλῃ		ἐργάτας	εἰς τὸν
harvest	so that	he might throw out		workers	into the

2326	846		2532 4341	016 1427
θερισμὸν	αὐτοῦ.	**10:1**	Καὶ προσκαλεσάμενος	τοὺς δώδεκα
harvest	of him.		And having called	the twelve

3101	846	1325	846	1849	4151
μαθητὰς	αὐτοῦ	ἔδωκεν	αὐτοῖς	ἐξουσίαν	πνευμάτων
learners	of him	he gave	to them	authority	spirits

169	5620	1544	846	2532 2323
ἀκαθάρτων	ὥστε	ἐκβάλλειν	αὐτὰ	καὶ θεραπεύειν
unclean	so that	to throw out	them	and to heal

3956	3554	2532 3956	3119		014	1161
πᾶσαν	νόσον	καὶ πᾶσαν	μαλακίαν.	**2**	Τῶν	δὲ
all	illness	and all	sickness.		Of the	but

1427	652	021 3686	1510	3778	4413	4613
δώδεκα	ἀποστόλων	τὰ ὀνόματά	ἐστιν	ταῦτα·	πρῶτος	Σίμων
twelve	delegates	the names	are	these;	first	Simon

01	3004	4074	2532	406	01	80
ὁ	λεγόμενος	Πέτρος	καὶ	Ἀνδρέας	ὁ	ἀδελφὸς
the	one being called	Peter	and	Andrew	the	brother

846	2532 2385	01 02	2199	2532 2491
αὐτοῦ,	καὶ Ἰάκωβος	ὁ τοῦ	Ζεβεδαίου	καὶ Ἰωάννης
of him,	and Jacob	the of the	Zebedee	and John

a demoniac who was mute was brought to him. [33]And when the demon had been cast out, the one who had been mute spoke; and the crowds were amazed and said, "Never has anything like this been seen in Israel." [34]But the Pharisees said, "By the ruler of the demons he casts out the demons."[a]

35 Then Jesus went about all the cities and villages, teaching in their synagogues, and proclaiming the good news of the kingdom, and curing every disease and every sickness. [36]When he saw the crowds, he had compassion for them, because they were harassed and helpless, like sheep without a shepherd. [37]Then he said to his disciples, "The harvest is plentiful, but the laborers are few; [38]therefore ask the Lord of the harvest to send out laborers into his harvest."

CHAPTER 10

Then Jesus[b] summoned his twelve disciples and gave them authority over unclean spirits, to cast them out, and to cure every disease and every sickness. [2]These are the names of the twelve apostles: first, Simon, also known as Peter, and his brother Andrew; James son of Zebedee, and his brother John;

---

[a] Other ancient authorities lack this verse
[b] Gk he

3Philip and Bartholomew; Thomas and Matthew the tax collector; James son of Alphaeus, and Thaddaeus;[a] 4Simon the Cananaean, and Judas Iscariot, the one who betrayed him.

5 These twelve Jesus sent out with the following instructions: "Go nowhere among the Gentiles, and enter no town of the Samaritans, 6but go rather to the lost sheep of the house of Israel. 7As you go, proclaim the good news, 'The kingdom of heaven has come near.'[b] 8Cure the sick, raise the dead, cleanse the lepers,[c] cast out demons. You received without payment; give without payment. 9Take no gold, or silver, or copper in your belts, 10no bag for your journey, or two tunics, or sandals, or a staff; for laborers deserve their food. 11Whatever town or village you enter, find out who in it is worthy, and stay there until you leave. 12As you enter the house, greet it. 13If the house is worthy, let your peace come upon it; but if it is not worthy, let your peace return to you.

[a] Other ancient authorities read *Lebbaeus*, or *Lebbaeus called Thaddaeus*

[b] Or *is at hand*

[c] The terms *leper* and *leprosy* can refer to several diseases

01   80   846   3   5376   2532 918   2381
ὁ   ἀδελφὸς αὐτοῦ,   3 Φίλιππος καὶ Βαρθολομαῖος, Θωμᾶς
the   brother of him,   Philip   and Bartholomew, Thomas
2532 3102a   01   5057   2385   01 02   256
καὶ Ματθαῖος ὁ τελώνης,   Ἰάκωβος ὁ τοῦ Ἁλφαίου
and   Matthew the tax man, Jacob   the of the Alpheus
2532 2280   4 4613   01 2581   2532   2455
καὶ Θαδδαῖος, 4 Σίμων ὁ Καναναῖος καὶ Ἰούδας
and   Thaddeus,   Simon the Cananean and Judas
01   2469   01   2532 3860   846
ὁ Ἰσκαριώτης ὁ   καὶ παραδοὺς   αὐτόν.
the Iscariot   the one also having given over him.
    3778   016   1427 649   01 2424
5   Τούτους τοὺς δώδεκα ἀπέστειλεν ὁ Ἰησοῦς
    These   the twelve delegated the Jesus
3853   846   3004   1519 3598 1484
παραγγείλας   αὐτοῖς λέγων· εἰς ὁδὸν ἐθνῶν
having commanded them   saying, into way of nations
3361 565   2532 1519 4172 4541   3361
μὴ ἀπέλθητε καὶ εἰς πόλιν Σαμαριτῶν μὴ
not go off   and into city Samaritans not
1525   4198   1161 3123 4314   024
εἰσέλθητε·   6 πορεύεσθε δὲ μᾶλλον πρὸς τὰ
you might go into;   travel   but more   toward the
4263   024 622   3624   2474
πρόβατα τὰ ἀπολωλότα   οἴκου   Ἰσραήλ.
sheep   the having destroyed of house Israel.
  4198   1161 2784   3004   3754 1448
7 πορευόμενοι δὲ κηρύσσετε λέγοντες ὅτι ἤγγικεν
  Traveling   but announce saying, (") has neared
05 932   014   3772   770
ἡ βασιλεία τῶν οὐρανῶν. 8 ἀσθενοῦντας
the kingdom of the heavens. Ones being weak
2323   3498   1453   3015   2511
θεραπεύετε, νεκροὺς ἐγείρετε, λεπροὺς καθαρίζετε,
heal,   dead   raise,   lepers   clean,
1140   1544   1432   2983   1432   1325
δαιμόνια ἐκβάλλετε· δωρεὰν ἐλάβετε,   δωρεὰν δότε.
demons   throw out; as a   you received, as a   give
                        gift   gift
  3361 2932   5557   3366   696   3366   5475
9 Μὴ κτήσησθε χρυσὸν μηδὲ ἄργυρον μηδὲ χαλκὸν
  Not acquire gold   but not silver but not copper
1519 020 2223   1473   3361 4082   1519 3598 3366
εἰς τὰς ζώνας ὑμῶν, 10 μὴ πήραν εἰς ὁδὸν μηδὲ
into the belts of you,   not bag   into way but not
1417 5509   3366   5266   3366   4464   514
δύο χιτῶνας μηδὲ ὑποδήματα μηδὲ ῥάβδον· ἄξιος
two shirts   but not sandals   but not rod;   worthy
1063 01 2040   06   5160   846   1519 3739 1161
γὰρ ὁ ἐργάτης τῆς τροφῆς αὐτοῦ. 11 εἰς ἣν δ᾽
for   the worker of the food   of him.   Into which but
302 4172   2228 2968   1525   1833   5101
ἂν πόλιν ἢ κώμην εἰσέλθητε,   ἐξετάσατε τίς
- city   or village you might go in, inquire   who
1722 846 514   1510 2546   3306   2193 302
ἐν αὐτῇ ἄξιός ἐστιν· κἀκεῖ   μείνατε ἕως ἂν
in   it worthy is;   and there stay   until -
1831   1525   1161 1519 08 3614
ἐξέλθητε.   12 εἰσερχόμενοι δὲ εἰς τὴν οἰκίαν
you might go out. Going into but into the house
782   846   2532 1437 3303   1510   05
ἀσπάσασθε αὐτήν· 13 καὶ ἐὰν μὲν ᾖ   ἡ
greet   it;   and if indeed might be the
3614 514   2064   05   1515   1473   1909 846   1437
οἰκία ἀξία, ἐλθάτω ἡ εἰρήνη ὑμῶν ἐπ᾽ αὐτήν, ἐὰν
house worthy, let go the peace of you on it,   if
1161 3361 1510   514   05 1515 1473   4314 1473
δὲ μὴ ᾖ   ἀξία, ἡ εἰρήνη ὑμῶν πρὸς ὑμᾶς
but not might be worthy, the peace of you to   you

```
1994              2532  3739  302   3361  1209              1473
ἐπιστραφήτω.  14  καὶ   ὃς    ἂν    μὴ    δέξηται          ὑμᾶς
let return.       And   who   -     not   might welcome   you
3366      191        016   3056   1473       1831
μηδὲ      ἀκούσῃ     τοὺς  λόγους ὑμῶν,      ἐξερχόμενοι
but not   might hear the   words  of you,   going out
1854   06    3614     2228 06    4172    1565       1621
ἔξω    τῆς   οἰκίας ἢ   τῆς   πόλεως ἐκείνης ἐκτινάξατε
outside the  house  or  the   city   that    swing out
04     2868         014    4228   1473       281    3004
τὸν    κονιορτὸν    τῶν    ποδῶν  ὑμῶν.  15  ἀμὴν  λέγω
the    blowing dust of the feet   of you.    Amen  I say
1473     414         1510         1093    4670       2532
ὑμῖν,    ἀνεκτότερον ἔσται        γῇ      Σοδόμων   καὶ
to you,  more endurable it will be in land of Sodom and
1116         1722 2250   2920         2228 07   4172
Γομόρρων ἐν   ἡμέρᾳ κρίσεως    ἢ    τῇ   πόλει
Gomorrah in   day   of judgment or   in the city
1565     16   2400 1473  649        1473  5613  4263      1722
ἐκείνη.       Ἰδοὺ ἐγὼ  ἀποστέλλω ὑμᾶς  ὡς   πρόβατα  ἐν
that.         Look I    delegate  you    as   sheep    in
3319    3074     1096   3767 5429       5613 013  3789
μέσῳ    λύκων·  γίνεσθε οὖν  φρόνιμοι  ὡς  οἱ   ὄφεις
middle  wolves; become  then thoughtful as the  snakes
2532 185          5613 017  4058            4337        1161
καὶ  ἀκέραιοι ὡς  αἱ   περιστεραί.  17  Προσέχετε δὲ
and  innocent as  the  doves.          Hold to    but
575  014  444       3860                  1063 1473 1519
ἀπὸ  τῶν  ἀνθρώπων· παραδώσουσιν        γὰρ  ὑμᾶς εἰς
from the  men;       they will give over for  you   into
4892       2532 1722 019  4864     846
συνέδρια καὶ  ἐν   ταῖς συναγωγαῖς αὐτῶν
councils and  in   the  synagogues of them
3146            1473     18  2532 1909 2232        1161
μαστιγώσουσιν  ὑμᾶς·      καὶ  ἐπὶ  ἡγεμόνας δὲ
they will scourge you;        and  on   leaders  but
2532 935      71               1752           1473 1519
καὶ  βασιλεῖς ἀχθήσεσθε       ἕνεκεν        ἐμοῦ εἰς
also kings    you will be led on account of me   in
3142       846       2532 023    1484          3752 1161
μαρτύριον αὐτοῖς καὶ  τοῖς   ἔθνεσιν.  19  ὅταν  δὲ
testimony to them and  to the nations.     When  but
3860          1473 3361 3309      4459 2228 5101 2980
παραδῶσιν ὑμᾶς, μὴ   μεριμνήσητε πῶς ἢ    τί   λαλήσητε·
they give over you,  not be anxious how or what you might
give over                                          say;
1325           1063 1473  1722 1565  07   5610 5101
δοθήσεται     γὰρ  ὑμῖν  ἐν   ἐκείνῃ τῇ  ὥρᾳ  τί
it will be given for  to you in   that   the hour what
2980       20   3756 1063 1473  1510 013  2980
λαλήσητε·      οὐ   γὰρ  ὑμεῖς ἐστε οἱ  λαλοῦντες
you might say; not  for  you   are  the ones speaking
235  09   4151    02    3962    1473   09  2980
ἀλλὰ τὸ  πνεῦμα τοῦ   πατρὸς ὑμῶν  τὸ  λαλοῦν
but  the spirit of the father of you the one speaking
1722 1473  21   3860             1161 80     80     1519
ἐν   ὑμῖν.      Παραδώσει       δὲ  ἀδελφὸς ἀδελφὸν εἰς
in   you.       Will give over  but brother  brother into
2288       2532 3962   5043     2532 1881
θάνατον καὶ  πατὴρ τέκνον, καὶ  ἐπαναστήσονται
death   and  father child,  and  will stand up against
5043     1909 1118    2532 2289            846
τέκνα   ἐπὶ  γονεῖς καὶ  θανατώσουσιν     αὐτούς.
children on  parents and  they will put to death them.
22  2532 1510        3404         5259 3956      1223
    καὶ  ἔσεσθε       μισούμενοι  ὑπὸ  πάντων διὰ
    And  you will be+ +being hated by   all    because of
```

14 If anyone will not welcome you or listen to your words, shake off the dust from your feet as you leave that house or town. 15 Truly I tell you, it will be more tolerable for the land of Sodom and Gomorrah on the day of judgment than for that town.

16 "See, I am sending you out like sheep into the midst of wolves; so be wise as serpents and innocent as doves. 17 Beware of them, for they will hand you over to councils and flog you in their synagogues; 18 and you will be dragged before governors and kings because of me, as a testimony to them and the Gentiles. 19 When they hand you over, do not worry about how you are to speak or what you are to say; for what you are to say will be given to you at that time; 20 for it is not you who speak, but the Spirit of your Father speaking through you. 21 Brother will betray brother to death, and a father his child, and children will rise against parents and have them put to death; 22 and you will be hated by all because of

my name. But the one who endures to the end will be saved. ²³When they persecute you in one town, flee to the next; for truly I tell you, you will not have gone through all the towns of Israel before the Son of Man comes.

24 "A disciple is not above the teacher, nor a slave above the master; ²⁵it is enough for the disciple to be like the teacher, and the slave like the master. If they have called the master of the house Beelzebul, how much more will they malign those of his household!

26 "So have no fear of them; for nothing is covered up that will not be uncovered, and nothing secret that will not become known. ²⁷What I say to you in the dark, tell in the light; and what you hear whispered, proclaim from the housetops. ²⁸Do not fear those who kill the body but cannot kill the soul; rather fear him who can destroy both soul and body in hell.ᵃ ²⁹Are not two sparrows sold for a penny? Yet not one of them will fall to the ground apart from your Father. ³⁰And even the hairs of your head

ᵃ Gk Gehenna

012	3686	1473	01	1161	5278	1519	5056	3778
τὸ	ὄνομά	μου·	ὁ	δὲ	ὑπομείνας	εἰς	τέλος	οὗτος
the	name	of me;	the	but	having	to	completion	this
			one		endured			

4982		3752	1161	1377		1473
σωθήσεται.	**23**	῞Οταν	δὲ	διώκωσιν		ὑμᾶς
will be delivered.		When but		they might pursue		you

1722	07	4172	3778	5343	1519	08	2087	281	1063
ἐν	τῇ	πόλει	ταύτῃ,	φεύγετε	εἰς	τὴν	ἑτέραν·	ἀμὴν	γὰρ
in	the	city	this,	flee	into	the	other;	amen	for

3004	1473	3756	3361	5055	020	4172	02
λέγω	ὑμῖν,	οὐ	μὴ	τελέσητε	τὰς	πόλεις	τοῦ
I say	to you,	not	not	you might	the	cities	of the
				complete			

2474	2193	302	2064	01	5207	02	444
Ἰσραὴλ	ἕως	ἂν	ἔλθῃ	ὁ	υἱὸς	τοῦ	ἀνθρώπου.
Israel	until	-	might come	the	son	of	the man.

3756	1510	3101	5228	04	1320	3761
24 Οὐκ	ἔστιν	μαθητὴς	ὑπὲρ	τὸν	διδάσκαλον	οὐδὲ
Not	is	learner	above	the	teacher	but not

1401	5228	04	2962	846		713	03
δοῦλος	ὑπὲρ	τὸν	κύριον	αὐτοῦ.	**25**	ἀρκετὸν	τῷ
slave	above	the	Master	of him.		Sufficient	to the

3101	2443	1096		5613	01	1320
μαθητῇ	ἵνα	γένηται		ὡς	ὁ	διδάσκαλος
learner	that	he might become		as	the	teacher

846	2532	01	1401	5613	01	2962	846	1487	04
αὐτοῦ	καὶ	ὁ	δοῦλος	ὡς	ὁ	κύριος	αὐτοῦ.	εἰ	τὸν
of him	and	the	slave	as	the	Master	of him.	If	the

3617		954		1941		4214
οἰκοδεσπότην		Βεελζεβοὺλ		ἐπεκάλεσαν,		πόσῳ
house supervisor		Beelzeboul		they called on,		how much

3123	016	3615		846		3361	3767	5399
μᾶλλον	τοὺς	οἰκιακοὺς		αὐτοῦ.	**26**	Μὴ	οὖν	φοβηθῆτε
more	the	households		of him.		Not	then	you might
								be afraid

846		3762		1063	1510	2572		3739
αὐτούς·	οὐδὲν	γάρ	ἐστιν	κεκαλυμμενόν				ὃ
them;	nothing	for	is+	+having been covered which				

3756	601		2532	2927	3739	3756
οὐκ	ἀποκαλυφθήσεται	καὶ	κρυπτὸν	ὃ	οὐ	
not	will be uncovered	and	hidden	which	not	

1097		3739	3004	1473	1722	07	4653
γνωσθήσεται.	**27**	ὃ	λέγω	ὑμῖν	ἐν	τῇ	σκοτίᾳ
will be known.		What	I say	to you	in	the	dark

3004	1722	011	5457	2532	3739	1519	012	3775	191
εἴπατε	ἐν	τῷ	φωτί,	καὶ	ὃ	εἰς	τὸ	οὖς	ἀκούετε
say	in	the	light,	and	what	into	the	ear	you hear

2784		1909	022	1430		2532	3361	5399	575
κηρύξατε	ἐπὶ	τῶν	δωμάτων.	**28**	καὶ	μὴ	φοβεῖσθε	ἀπὸ	
announce	on	the	roofs.		And	not	fear	from	

014	615		012	4983	08	1161	5590	3361
τῶν	ἀποκτεννόντων	τὸ	σῶμα,	τὴν	δὲ	ψυχὴν	μὴ	
the ones	killing	the	body,	the	but	soul	not	

1410	615		5399		1161	3123	04
δυναμένων	ἀποκτεῖναι·	φοβεῖσθε	δὲ	μᾶλλον	τὸν		
being able	to kill;	fear	but	more	the one		

1410		2532	5590	2532	4983	622	1722	1067
δυνάμενον	καὶ	ψυχὴν	καὶ	σῶμα	ἀπολέσαι	ἐν	γεέννῃ.	
being able	both	soul	and	body	to destroy	in	gehenna.	

3780	1417	4765		787		4453	2532	1520	1537
29 οὐχὶ	δύο	στρουθία	ἀσσαρίου	πωλεῖται;	καὶ	ἓν	ἐξ		
Not	two	sparrows	assarion	is sold?	And	one	out		

846	3756	4098		1909	08	1093	427	02
αὐτῶν	οὐ	πεσεῖται	ἐπὶ	τὴν	γῆν	ἄνευ	τοῦ	
of them	not	will fall	on	the	land	without	the	

3962	1473		1473	1161	2532	017	2359	06
πατρὸς	ὑμῶν.	**30**	ὑμῶν	δὲ	καὶ	αἱ	τρίχες	τῆς
father	of you.		Of you	but	also	the	hairs	of the

2776	3956	705		1510	**31**	3361
κεφαλῆς	πᾶσαι	ἠριθμημέναι		εἰσίν.		μὴ
head	all	+having been numbered are+.				Not

3767	5399	4183	4765	1308	1473
οὖν	φοβεῖσθε·	πολλῶν στρουθίων	διαφέρετε	ὑμεῖς.
then fear;	of many sparrows	differ	you.

32
3956	3767	3748	3670		1722	1473	1715
Πᾶς	οὖν	ὅστις	ὁμολογήσει	ἐν	ἐμοὶ	ἔμπροσθεν
All	then	who	might confess	in	me	in front

014	444	3670	2504	1722	846	1715
τῶν	ἀνθρώπων,	ὁμολογήσω	κἀγὼ	ἐν	αὐτῷ	ἔμπροσθεν
of the men,	will confess I also	in	him	in front

02	3962	1473	02	1722	015	3772
τοῦ	πατρός	μου	τοῦ	ἐν	[τοῖς]	οὐρανοῖς·
of the father of me the one in	the	heavens;

33
3748	1161	302	720		1473	1715	014
ὅστις	δ᾽	ἂν	ἀρνήσηταί	με	ἔμπροσθεν	τῶν
who	but	-	might deny me	in front	of the

444	720	2504	846	1715	02
ἀνθρώπων,	ἀρνήσομαι	κἀγὼ	αὐτὸν	ἔμπροσθεν	τοῦ
men,	will deny I also him	in front	of the

3962	1473	02	1722	015	3772	**34**	3361
πατρός	μου	τοῦ	ἐν	[τοῖς]	οὐρανοῖς.		Μὴ
father of me the one in	the	heavens.		Not

3543		3754	2064	906	1515	1909	08
νομίσητε	ὅτι	ἦλθον	βαλεῖν	εἰρήνην	ἐπὶ	τὴν
you might think that I came to throw peace	on	the

1093	3756	2064	906	1515	235	3162
γῆν·	οὐκ	ἦλθον	βαλεῖν	εἰρήνην	ἀλλὰ	μάχαιραν.
land;	not	I came to throw peace	but	sword.

35
2064	1063	1369		444	2596	02
ἦλθον	γὰρ	διχάσαι	ἄνθρωπον	κατὰ	τοῦ
I came for	to split apart man	against	the

3962	846	2532	2264	2596	06	3384	846
πατρὸς	αὐτοῦ	καὶ	θυγατέρα	κατὰ	τῆς	μητρὸς	αὐτῆς
father of him and	daughter against	the mother of her

2532	3565	2596	06	3994	846	**36**	2532
καὶ	νύμφην	κατὰ	τῆς	πενθερᾶς	αὐτῆς,		καὶ
and	bride	against	the mother-in-law of her,		and

2190	02	444	013	3615	846
ἐχθροὶ	τοῦ	ἀνθρώπου οἱ	οἰκιακοὶ	αὐτοῦ.
hostile ones of the man	the households of him.

37
01	5368	3962	2228	3384	5228	1473	3756
΄Ο	φιλῶν	πατέρα	ἢ	μητέρα	ὑπὲρ	ἐμὲ	οὐκ
The one loving father or	mother above me	not

1510	1473	514	2532	01	5368	5207	2228
ἔστιν	μου	ἄξιος,	καὶ	ὁ	φιλῶν	υἱὸν	ἢ
is	of me worthy, and	the one loving son	or

2364	5228	1473	3756	1510	1473	514	**38**	2532
θυγατέρα	ὑπὲρ	ἐμὲ	οὐκ	ἔστιν	μου	ἄξιος·		καὶ
daughter above me	not	is	of me worthy;		And

3739	3756	2983	04	4716	846	2532	190
ὃς	οὐ	λαμβάνει	τὸν	σταυρὸν	αὐτοῦ	καὶ	ἀκολουθεῖ
who	not	receives	the cross	of him and	follows

3694	1473	3756	1510	1473	514	**39**	01	2147
ὀπίσω	μου,	οὐκ	ἔστιν	μου	ἄξιος.		ὁ	εὑρὼν
after me,	not	is	of me worthy.		The one finding

08	5590	846	622	846	2532	01	622
τὴν	ψυχὴν	αὐτοῦ	ἀπολέσει	αὐτήν,	καὶ	ὁ	ἀπολέσας
the soul	of him destroys it,	and	the one having destroyed

08	5590	846	1752	1473	2147	846
τὴν	ψυχὴν	αὐτοῦ	ἕνεκεν	ἐμοῦ	εὑρήσει	αὐτήν.
the soul	of him on account of me will find it.

40
01	1209		1473	1473	1209		2532	01	1473
΄Ο	δεχόμενος	ὑμᾶς	ἐμὲ	δέχεται,	καὶ	ὁ	ἐμὲ
The one welcoming you	me	welcomes, and the me

are all counted. [31]So do not be afraid; you are of more value than many sparrows.

32 "Everyone therefore who acknowledges me before others, I also will acknowledge before my Father in heaven; [33]but whoever denies me before others, I also will deny before my Father in heaven.

34 "Do not think that I have come to bring peace to the earth; I have not come to bring peace, but a sword. [35]For I have come to set a man against his father, and a daughter against her mother, and a daughter-in-law against her mother-in-law; [36]and one's foes will be members of one's own household.

[37]Whoever loves father or mother more than me is not worthy of me; and whoever loves son or daughter more than me is not worthy of me; [38]and whoever does not take up the cross and follow me is not worthy of me. [39]Those who find their life will lose it, and those who lose their life for my sake will find it.

40 "Whoever welcomes you welcomes me,

and whoever welcomes me welcomes the one who sent me. [41]Whoever welcomes a prophet in the name of a prophet will receive a prophet's reward; and whoever welcomes a righteous person in the name of a righteous person will receive the reward of the righteous; [42]and whoever gives even a cup of cold water to one of these little ones in the name of a disciple—truly I tell you, none of these will lose their reward."

CHAPTER 11

Now when Jesus had finished instructing his twelve disciples, he went on from there to teach and proclaim his message in their cities.

2 When John heard in prison what the Messiah[a] was doing, he sent word by his[b] disciples [3]and said to him, "Are you the one who is to come, or are we to wait for another?" [4]Jesus answered them, "Go and tell John what you hear and see: [5]the blind receive their sight, the lame walk, the lepers[c] are cleansed, the deaf hear, the dead are raised, and the poor have good news brought to them. [6]And blessed is anyone who takes no offense at me."

7 As they went away, Jesus began to speak to the crowds about John: "What did you go out into the wilderness

---

a Or the Christ
b Other ancient authorities read two of his
c The terms leper and leprosy can refer to several diseases

1209	1209	04	649		1473	**41**	01
δεχόμενος	δέχεται	τὸν	ἀποστείλαντά		με.		ὁ
one welcoming	welcomes	the	one having		me.		The one delegated

1209		4396	1519	3686	4396		3408
δεχόμενος		προφήτην	εἰς	ὄνομα	προφήτου		μισθὸν
welcoming		spokesman	in	name	of spokesman		wage

4396		2983	2532	01	1209		1342	1519
προφήτου		λήμψεται,	καὶ	ὁ	δεχόμενος		δίκαιον	εἰς
of spokesman		he will receive,	and	the one	welcoming		right	in

3686	1342	3408	1342	2983		**42**	2532
ὄνομα	δικαίου	μισθὸν	δικαίου	λήμψεται.			καὶ
name	of right	wage	of right	will receive.			And

3739	302	4222	1520	014	3398	3778	4221
ὃς	ἂν	ποτίσῃ	ἕνα	τῶν	μικρῶν	τούτων	ποτήριον
who	-	might give drink	one	of the	small	of these	cup

5593	3441	1519	3686	3101		281	3004	1473
ψυχροῦ	μόνον	εἰς	ὄνομα	μαθητοῦ,		ἀμὴν	λέγω	ὑμῖν,
cold	alone	in	name	of learner,		amen	I say	to you,

3756	3361	622		04	3408	846		**11:1**	2532
οὐ	μὴ	ἀπολέσῃ		τὸν	μισθὸν	αὐτοῦ.			Καὶ
not	not	he might destroy		the	wage	of him.			And

1096	3753	5055	01	2424	1299		015
ἐγένετο	ὅτε	ἐτέλεσεν	ὁ	Ἰησοῦς	διατάσσων		τοῖς
it became	when	completed	the	Jesus	directing		the

1427	3101	846	3327		1564		010
δώδεκα	μαθηταῖς	αὐτοῦ,	μετέβη		ἐκεῖθεν		τοῦ
twelve	learners	of him,	he went across		from there		the

1321	2532	2784	1722	019	4172	846
διδάσκειν	καὶ	κηρύσσειν	ἐν	ταῖς	πόλεσιν	αὐτῶν.
to teach	and	to announce	in	the	cities	of them.

2	01	1161	2491	191		1722	011	1201		024
	Ὁ	δὲ	Ἰωάννης	ἀκούσας		ἐν	τῷ	δεσμωτηρίῳ		τὰ
	The	but	John	having heard		in	the	chain place		the

2041	02	5547	3992		1223		014	3101
ἔργα	τοῦ	Χριστοῦ	πέμψας		διὰ		τῶν	μαθητῶν
works	of the	Christ	having sent		through		the	learners

846	**3**	3004	846	1473	1510	01	2064		2228
αὐτοῦ		εἶπεν	αὐτῷ·	σὺ	εἶ	ὁ	ἐρχόμενος		ἢ
of him		he said	to him;	you	are	the	one coming		or

2087	4328			**4**	2532	611		01
ἕτερον	προσδοκῶμεν;				καὶ	ἀποκριθεὶς		ὁ
other	do we wait expectantly?				And	having answered		the

2424	3004	846		4198		518		2491
Ἰησοῦς	εἶπεν	αὐτοῖς·		πορευθέντες		ἀπαγγείλατε		Ἰωάννῃ
Jesus	said	to them;		having traveled		tell		John

3739	191	2532	991		**5**	5185	308		2532
ἃ	ἀκούετε	καὶ	βλέπετε·			τυφλοὶ	ἀναβλέπουσιν		καὶ
what	you hear	and	you see;			blind	see again		and

5560	4043		3015	2511		2532	2974
χωλοὶ	περιπατοῦσιν,		λεπροὶ	καθαρίζονται		καὶ	κωφοὶ
lame	walk around,		lepers	are cleaned		and	deaf

191		2532	3498	1453		2532	4434
ἀκούουσιν,		καὶ	νεκροὶ	ἐγείρονται		καὶ	πτωχοὶ
hear,		and	dead	are raised		and	poor

2097				**6**	2532	3107		1510	3739
εὐαγγελίζονται·					καὶ	μακάριός		ἐστιν	ὃς
are being told good message;					and	fortunate		is	who

1437	3361	4624		1722	1473		**7**	3778	1161
ἐὰν	μὴ	σκανδαλισθῇ		ἐν	ἐμοί.			Τούτων	δὲ
if	not	might be offended		in	me.			Of these	but

4198		757	01	2424	3004		015	3793
πορευομένων		ἤρξατο	ὁ	Ἰησοῦς	λέγειν		τοῖς	ὄχλοις
traveling		began	the	Jesus	to speak		to the	crowds

4012	2491	5101	1831		1519	08	2048
περὶ	Ἰωάννου·	τί	ἐξήλθατε		εἰς	τὴν	ἔρημον
concerning	John;	what	came you out		into	the	desert

```
2300          2563      5259  417    4531                  235
θεάσασθαι;  κάλαμον ὑπὸ ἀνέμου σαλευόμενον;  8 ἀλλὰ
to watch?    Reed     by    wind   being shaken?   But
5101  1831            3708    444         1722 3120
τί    ἐξήλθατε       ἰδεῖν;  ἄνθρωπον ἐν μαλακοῖς
what  came you out to see?  Man        in  soft
294                      2400 013     024 3120    5409
ἠμφιεσμένον;            ἰδοὺ οἱ      τὰ μαλακὰ φοροῦντες
having been dressed?    Look the ones the soft   wearing
1722 015   3624     014    935      1510    9 235  5101
ἐν   τοῖς οἴκοις τῶν βασιλέων εἰσίν.   ἀλλὰ τί
in   the  houses of the kings  are.      But what
1831            3708    4396        3483 3004  1473  2532
ἐξήλθατε       ἰδεῖν;  προφήτην; ναί λέγω ὑμῖν, καὶ
came you out to see?  Spokesman? Yes I say to you, and
4055            4396        1510  4012
περισσότερον προφήτου. 10 οὗτός ἐστιν περὶ
more excessive spokesman.  This one is   concerning
3739 1125                 2400 1473 649       04
οὗ   γέγραπται·          ἰδοὺ ἐγὼ ἀποστέλλω τὸν
whom it has been written; look I    delegate   the
32        1473 4253  4383        1473      3739
ἄγγελόν μου  πρὸ προσώπου σου,  ὃς
messenger of me before face    of you,  who
2680          3598 1473  1715       1473  11  281
κατασκευάσει τὴν ὁδόν σου ἔμπροσθέν σου.    ᾿Αμὴν
will prepare the way of you in front of you.    Amen
3004 1473   3756 1453            1722 1084
λέγω ὑμῖν· οὐκ ἐγήγερται      ἐν γεννητοῖς
I say to you, not has been raised in born ones
1135    3173   2491     02  910         01       1161
γυναικῶν μείζων ᾿Ιωάννου τοῦ βαπτιστοῦ· ὁ      δὲ
of women greater of John the Immerser;  the one but
3398        1722 07 932      014 3772    3173
μικρότερος ἐν  τῇ βασιλείᾳ τῶν οὐρανῶν μείζων
smaller    in  the kingdom of the heavens greater
846   1510   12 575 1161 018 2250    2491     02
αὐτοῦ ἐστιν.   ἀπὸ δὲ τῶν ἡμερῶν ᾿Ιωάννου τοῦ
of him is.     From but the days  of John the
910        2193 737 05 932      014    3772
βαπτιστοῦ ἕως ἄρτι ἡ βασιλεία τῶν οὐρανῶν
immerser until now the kingdom of the heavens
971         2532 973      726       846
βιάζεται    καὶ βιασταὶ ἁρπάζουσιν αὐτήν.
is being forced and violent ones seize    it.
13 3956  1063 013 4396     2532 01 3551    2193
   πάντες γὰρ οἱ προφῆται καὶ ὁ νόμος ἕως
   All    for the spokesmen and the law  until
2491    4395          14 2532 1487 2309
᾿Ιωάννου ἐπροφήτευσαν·  καὶ εἰ  θέλετε
John    spoke before;    and if  you want
1209        846   1510   2243 01     3195
δέξασθαι,  αὐτός ἐστιν ᾿Ηλίας ὁ μέλλων
to welcome, himself is  Elijah the one being about
2064       15 01  2192      3775 191      16 5101
ἔρχεσθαι.    ὁ ἔχων      ὦτα ἀκουέτω.    Τίνι
to come.     The one having ears let hear.  To what
1161 3666        08  1074     3778    3664 1510
δὲ   ὁμοιώσω     τὴν γενεὰν ταύτην; ὁμοία ἐστὶν
but  will I liken the generation this? Like it is
3813           2521          1722 019 58        3739
παιδίοις      καθημένοις ἐν  ταῖς ἀγοραῖς ἃ
to small children sitting  in  the  markets  who
4377           023   2087      17 3004
προσφωνοῦντα τοῖς ἑτέροις   λέγουσιν·
sounding to   to the others   they say;
832                1473  2532 3756 3738            2354
ηὐλήσαμεν         ὑμῖν καὶ οὐκ ὠρχήσασθε, ἐθρηνήσαμεν
we played flute to you and not you danced;  we lamented
```

to look at? A reed shaken by the wind? [8]What then did you go out to see? Someone[a] dressed in soft robes? Look, those who wear soft robes are in royal palaces. [9]What then did you go out to see? A prophet?[b] Yes, I tell you, and more than a prophet. [10]This is the one about whom it is written,

'See, I am sending my
    messenger ahead of you,
who will prepare your
    way before you.'

[11]Truly I tell you, among those born of women no one has arisen greater than John the Baptist; yet the least in the kingdom of heaven is greater than he. [12]From the days of John the Baptist until now the kingdom of heaven has suffered violence,[c] and the violent take it by force. [13]For all the prophets and the law prophesied until John came; [14]and if you are willing to accept it, he is Elijah who is to come. [15]Let anyone with ears[d] listen!

16 "But to what will I compare this generation? It is like children sitting in the marketplaces and calling to one another,

[17]'We played the flute for you, and you did not dance;
we wailed, and you did not mourn.'

[a] Or Why then did you go out? To see someone

[b] Other ancient authorities read Why then did you go out? To see a prophet?

[c] Or has been coming violently

[d] Other ancient authorities add to hear

18For John came neither eating nor drinking, and they say, 'He has a demon'; 19the Son of Man came eating and drinking, and they say, 'Look, a glutton and a drunkard, a friend of tax collectors and sinners!' Yet wisdom is vindicated by her deeds."*a*

20 Then he began to reproach the cities in which most of his deeds of power had been done, because they did not repent. 21"Woe to you, Chorazin! Woe to you, Bethsaida! For if the deeds of power done in you had been done in Tyre and Sidon, they would have repented long ago in sackcloth and ashes. 22But I tell you, on the day of judgment it will be more tolerable for Tyre and Sidon than for you. 23And you, Capernaum, will you be exalted to heaven?

No, you will be brought down to Hades.

For if the deeds of power done in you had been done in Sodom, it would have remained until this day. 24But I tell you that on the day of judgment it will be more tolerable for the land of Sodom than for you."

25 At that time Jesus said, "I thank*b* you, Father, Lord of heaven and earth, because you have hidden these things from the wise and the intelligent

a Other ancient authorities read *children*

b Or *praise*

2532 3756 2875	**18**	2064	1063	2491	3383

καὶ   οὐκ   ἐκόψασθε.   **18**   ἦλθεν   γὰρ   ᾽Ιωάννης   μήτε
and   not   you mourned.   Came   for   John   and not

2068   3383   4095   2532 3004   1140
ἐσθίων μήτε   πίνων,   καὶ   λέγουσιν·   δαιμόνιον
eating and not   drinking,   and   they say;   demon

2192   **19** 2064   01   5207 02   444   2068   2532
ἔχει.   **19** ἦλθεν ὁ   υἱὸς τοῦ   ἀνθρώπου ἐσθίων καὶ
he has.   Came   the son   of the man   eating and

4095   2532 3004   2400 444   5314   2532
πίνων,   καὶ   λέγουσιν·   ἰδοὺ ἄνθρωπος φάγος καὶ
drinking,   and   they say;   look man   eater and

3630   5057   5384   2532 268   2532 1344
οἰνοπότης, τελωνῶν φίλος καὶ ἁμαρτωλῶν. καὶ ἐδικαιώθη
wine   of tax   friend and of sinners. And was made
drinker,   men   right

05   4678   575   022 2041   846   **20** 5119 757
ἡ   σοφία   ἀπὸ   τῶν ἔργων αὐτῆς.   **20** Τότε ἤρξατο
the wisdom from the works of it.   Then he began

3679   020 4172   1722 3739   1096   017 4183
ὀνειδίζειν τὰς πόλεις ἐν   αἷς   ἐγένοντο αἱ πλεῖσται
to revile   the cities in   which became   the most

1411   846   3754   3756 3340   **21** 3759
δυνάμεις αὐτοῦ, ὅτι   οὐ   μετενόησαν·   **21** οὐαί
powers   of him, because not   they changed mind;   woe

1473   5523   3759 1473   966   3754   1487
σοι,   Χοραζίν,   οὐαί σοι,   Βηθσαϊδά·   ὅτι   εἰ
to you, Chorazin,   woe to you,   Bethsaida; because if

1722 5184 2532 4605   1096   017 1411   017
ἐν   Τύρῳ καὶ   Σιδῶνι ἐγένοντο αἱ δυνάμεις αἱ
in   Tyre and Sidon   became   the powers   the

1096   1722 1473   3819   302 1722 4526
γενομέναι   ἐν   ὑμῖν, πάλαι   ἂν ἐν   σάκκῳ
ones having become in   you,   of old   - in   sackcloth

2532 4700 3340   **22** 4133   3004   1473
καὶ   σποδῷ μετενόησαν.   **22** πλὴν   λέγω   ὑμῖν,
and   ash   they changed mind.   Except I say to you,

5184   2532 4605   414   1510   1722 2250
Τύρῳ   καὶ   Σιδῶνι ἀνεκτότερον   ἔσται   ἐν ἡμέρᾳ
in Tyre   and   Sidon   more endurable   it will be in day

2920   2228 1473   **23** 2532 1473 2746a   3361
κρίσεως   ἢ   ὑμῖν.   **23** καὶ   σύ,   Καφαρναούμ, μὴ
of judgment or   to you. And   you   Capernaum,   not

2193 3772 5312   2193 86
ἕως   οὐρανοῦ ὑψωθήσῃ;   ἕως   ἅδου
until heaven will you be elevated?   Until hades

2597   3754   1487 1722 4670   1096
καταβήσῃ·   ὅτι   εἰ   ἐν   Σοδόμοις ἐγενήθησαν
you will go down; because if   in   Sodom   became

017 1411   017 1096   1722 1473 3306
αἱ   δυνάμεις αἱ   γενόμεναι   ἐν   σοί, ἔμεινεν
the powers   the ones having become in   you, it stayed

302 3360 06 4594   **24** 4133   3004 1473   3754
ἂν   μέχρι τῆς σήμερον.   **24** πλὴν   λέγω ὑμῖν ὅτι
-   until the today.   Except I say to you that

1093 4670   414   1510   1722 2250
γῇ   Σοδόμων ἀνεκτότερον   ἔσται   ἐν ἡμέρᾳ
land of Sodom more endurable it will be in   day

2920   2228 1473   **25** 1722 1565   03 2540
κρίσεως   ἢ   σοί.   **25** ᾽Εν   ἐκείνῳ τῷ καιρῷ
of judgment or   to you. In   that   the season

611   01 2424   3004 1843
ἀποκριθεὶς   ὁ   ᾽Ιησοῦς εἶπεν· ἐξομολογοῦμαί
having answered the Jesus   said; I confess out

1473   3962   2962   02   3772   2532 06 1093
σοι,   πάτερ, κύριε τοῦ   οὐρανοῦ καὶ τῆς γῆς,
to you, father, Master of the heaven   and   the land,

3754   2928   3778   575   4680 2532 4908
ὅτι   ἔκρυψας ταῦτα ἀπὸ σοφῶν καὶ συνετῶν
because you hid these from wise   and   understanding

```
2532 601              846   3516        26  3483 01  3962
καὶ  ἀπεκάλυψας  αὐτὰ νηπίοις·          ναὶ  ὁ  πατήρ,
and  you uncovered them to infants;      yes  the father,
3754      3779    2107          1096      1715      1473
ὅτι   οὕτως  εὐδοκία     ἐγένετο  ἔμπροσθέν σου.
because thusly good thought it became in front of you.
    3956  1473  3860              5259 02  3962    1473
27  Πάντα μοι  παρεδόθη      ὑπὸ  τοῦ πατρός μου,
    All  to me was given over by    the father of me,
2532 3762  1921        04   5207 1487 3361 01  3962
καὶ  οὐδεὶς ἐπιγινώσκει τὸν υἱὸν εἰ  μὴ  ὁ  πατήρ,
and  no one perceives    the son except  the father,
3761   04  3962    5100 1921          1487 3361 01  5207
οὐδὲ  τὸν πατέρα τις  ἐπιγινώσκει εἰ  μὴ  ὁ  υἱὸς
but not the father any perceives    except  the son
2532 3739   1437 1014      01  5207 601
καὶ  ᾧ     ἐὰν βούληται ὁ  υἱὸς ἀποκαλύψαι.
and  to whom if might plan the son to uncover.
    1205  4314  1473 3956  013    2872      2532
28  Δεῦτε πρός  με  πάντες οἱ     κοπιῶντες καὶ
    Come toward me  all   the ones laboring and
5412              2504  373        1473
πεφορτισμένοι,   κἀγὼ ἀναπαύσω  ὑμᾶς.
ones having been packed, and I will give rest you.
    142     04  2218  1473 1909 1473 2532 3129   575
29  ἄρατε  τὸν ζυγόν μου  ἐφ' ὑμᾶς καὶ  μάθετε ἀπ'
    Lift up the yoke of me on   you and  learn from
1473 3754    4239    1510 2532 5011    07    2588
ἐμοῦ, ὅτι   πραΰς  εἰμι καὶ ταπεινὸς τῇ   καρδίᾳ,
me,   because gentle I am and humble in the heart,
2532 2147        372          019      5590    1473
καὶ  εὑρήσετε  ἀνάπαυσιν ταῖς  ψυχαῖς ὑμῶν·
and  you will find rest   to the souls of you.
    01  1063 2218  1473 5543      2532 09  5413      1473
30  ὁ   γὰρ ζυγός μου  χρηστὸς καὶ  τὸ  φορτίον μου
    The for  yoke of me kind    and  the pack   of me
1645    1510    12:1  1722 1565   03   2540     4198
ἐλαφρόν ἐστιν.       Ἐν  ἐκείνῳ τῷ  καιρῷ  ἐπορεύθη
light   is.          In  that  the season traveled
01  2424  023     4521      1223    022 4702
ὁ  Ἰησοῦς τοῖς  σάββασιν διὰ  τῶν σπορίμων·
the Jesus in the sabbaths through the sown fields;
013  1161 3101      846    3983      2532 757
οἱ  δὲ  μαθηταὶ αὐτοῦ ἐπείνασαν καὶ  ἤρξαντο
the but learners of him hungered and  began
5089    4719        2532 2068      2  013 1161
τίλλειν στάχυας   καὶ  ἐσθίειν.     οἱ  δὲ
to pick stalks of grain and to eat.  The but
5330      3708          3004  846      2400 013 3101
Φαρισαῖοι ἰδόντες    εἶπαν αὐτῷ·  ἰδοὺ οἱ  μαθηταί
Pharisees having seen said to him; look the learners
1473 4160      3739 3756 1832          4160    1722
σου  ποιοῦσιν ὃ   οὐκ ἔξεστιν     ποιεῖν ἐν
of you do     what not it is possible to do in
4521      3    01  1161 3004  846      3756 314      5101
σαββάτῳ.      ὁ   δὲ εἶπεν αὐτοῖς·  οὐκ ἀνέγνωτε τί
sabbath.      The one but said to them; not you read what
4160      1160a 3753 3983          2532 013        3326
ἐποίησεν Δαυὶδ ὅτε ἐπείνασεν  καὶ  οἱ        μετ'
did      David when he hungered and  the ones with
846      4  4459 1525        1519 04  3624 02      2316
αὐτοῦ,     πῶς  εἰσῆλθεν  εἰς  τὸν οἶκον τοῦ  θεοῦ
him,       how  he went in into the house of the God
2532 016  740   06      4286          3739 3756
καὶ  τοὺς ἄρτους τῆς   προθέσεως ἔφαγον,  ὃ   οὐκ
and  the breads of the purpose    they ate, what not
1832   1510  846    2068    3761 015    3326 846
ἐξὸν   ἦν   αὐτῷ φαγεῖν οὐδὲ τοῖς  μετ' αὐτοῦ
being it was to him to eat but  to the with him
possible                      not  ones
```

and have revealed them to infants; [26]yes, Father, for such was your gracious will.[a] [27]All things have been handed over to me by my Father; and no one knows the Son except the Father, and no one knows the Father except the Son and anyone to whom the Son chooses to reveal him.

[28]"Come to me, all you that are weary and are carrying heavy burdens, and I will give you rest. [29]Take my yoke upon you, and learn from me; for I am gentle and humble in heart, and you will find rest for your souls. [30]For my yoke is easy, and my burden is light."

CHAPTER 12

At that time Jesus went through the grainfields on the sabbath; his disciples were hungry, and they began to pluck heads of grain to eat. [2]When the Pharisees saw it, they said to him, "Look, your disciples are doing what is not lawful to do on the sabbath." [3]He said to them, "Have you not read what David did when he and his companions were hungry? [4]He entered the house of God and ate the bread of the Presence, which it was not lawful for him or his companions to eat,

---

[a] Or for so it was well-pleasing in your sight

but only for the priests. 5Or have you not read in the law that on the sabbath the priests in the temple break the sabbath and yet are guiltless? 6I tell you, something greater than the temple is here. 7But if you had known what this means, 'I desire mercy and not sacrifice,' you would not have condemned the guiltless. 8For the Son of Man is lord of the sabbath."

9 He left that place and entered their synagogue; 10a man was there with a withered hand, and they asked him, "Is it lawful to cure on the sabbath?" so that they might accuse him. 11He said to them, "Suppose one of you has only one sheep and it falls into a pit on the sabbath; will you not lay hold of it and lift it out? 12How much more valuable is a human being than a sheep! So it is lawful to do good on the sabbath." 13Then he said to the man, "Stretch out your hand." He stretched it out, and it was restored, as sound as the other. 14But the Pharisees went out and conspired against him, how to destroy him.

15 When Jesus became aware of this, he departed.

1487	3361	015	2409	3441	5	2228	3756	314
εἰ	μὴ	τοῖς	ἱερεῦσιν	μόνοις;		ἢ	οὐκ	ἀνέγνωτε

except to the priests alone? Or not you read

1722 03　3551 3754 023　4521　013 2409　1722 011
ἐν τῷ νόμῳ ὅτι τοῖς σάββασιν οἱ ἱερεῖς ἐν τῷ
in the law that in the sabbaths the priests in the

2411　012 4521　953　2532 338
ἱερῷ τὸ σάββατον βεβηλοῦσιν καὶ ἀναίτιοί
temple the sabbath they desecrate and blameless

1510　3004 1161 1473　3754 010　2411　3173
εἰσιν; 6 λέγω δὲ ὑμῖν ὅτι τοῦ ἱεροῦ μεῖζόν
they are? I say but to you that of the temple greater

1510 5602 7 1487 1161 1097　5101 1510　1656
ἐστιν ὧδε. εἰ δὲ ἐγνώκειτε τί ἐστιν· ἔλεος
is here. If but you had known what it is; mercy

2309　2532 3756 2378　3756 302 2613　016
θέλω καὶ οὐ θυσίαν, οὐκ ἂν κατεδικάσατε τοὺς
I want and not sacrifice, not - you condemned the

338　2962 1063 1510 010　4521　01 5207
ἀναιτίους. 8 κύριος γάρ ἐστιν τοῦ σαββάτου ὁ υἱὸς
blameless. Master for is of the sabbath the son

02　444　9 2532 3327　1564
τοῦ ἀνθρώπου. Καὶ μεταβὰς ἐκεῖθεν
of the man. And having gone across from there

2064　1519 08 4864　846　10 2532 2400 444
ἦλθεν εἰς τὴν συναγωγὴν αὐτῶν· καὶ ἰδοὺ ἄνθρωπος
he went into the synagogue of them; and look man

5495 2192 3584　2532 1905　846
χεῖρα ἔχων ξηράν. καὶ ἐπηρώτησαν αὐτὸν
hand having dried out. And they asked on him

3004　1487 1832　023　4521
λέγοντες· εἰ ἔξεστιν τοῖς σάββασιν
saying· if it is possible in the sabbaths

2323　2443 2723　846　11 01
θεραπεῦσαι; ἵνα κατηγορήσωσιν αὐτοῦ. ὁ
to heal? that they might accuse him. The one

1161 3004 846　5101 1510　1537 1473 444
δὲ εἶπεν αὐτοῖς· τίς ἔσται ἐξ ὑμῶν ἄνθρωπος
but said to them; what will be from you man

3739 2192　4263　1520 2532 1437 1706
ὃς ἕξει πρόβατον ἓν καὶ ἐὰν ἐμπέσῃ
who will have sheep one and if might fall in

3778 023　4521　1519 999　3780 2902
τοῦτο τοῖς σάββασιν εἰς βόθυνον, οὐχὶ κρατήσει
this in the sabbaths into ditch, not he will hold

846 2532 1453　12 4214　3767 1308　444
αὐτὸ καὶ ἐγερεῖ; πόσῳ οὖν διαφέρει ἄνθρωπος
it and raise? How much then differs man

4263　5620　1832　023　4521
προβάτου. ὥστε ἔξεστιν τοῖς σάββασιν
of sheep. So that it is possible in the sabbaths

2573 4160　13 5119 3004　03 444　1614
καλῶς ποιεῖν. τότε λέγει τῷ ἀνθρώπῳ· ἔκτεινόν
well to do. Then he says to the man, stretch out

1473 08 5495　2532 1614　2532
σου τὴν χεῖρα. καὶ ἐξέτεινεν καὶ
of you the hand. And he stretched out and

600　5199　5613 05 243
ἀπεκατεστάθη ὑγιὴς ὡς ἡ ἄλλη.
it was restored healthy as the other.

14 1831　1161 013 5330　4824
ἐξελθόντες δὲ οἱ Φαρισαῖοι συμβούλιον
Having gone out but the Pharisees council

2983 2596 846 3704　846 622
ἔλαβον κατ᾿ αὐτοῦ ὅπως αὐτὸν ἀπολέσωσιν.
took against him so that him they might destroy.

15 01 1161 2424 1097　402　1564
Ὁ δὲ Ἰησοῦς γνοὺς ἀνεχώρησεν ἐκεῖθεν.
The but Jesus having known departed from there.

2532 190   846   3793   4183   2532 2323
καὶ ἠκολούθησαν αὐτῷ [ὄχλοι] πολλοί, καὶ ἐθεράπευσεν
And followed   him   crowds   many,   and he healed

846   3956   16 2532 2008   846   2443 3361
αὐτοὺς πάντας   καὶ ἐπετίμησεν   αὐτοῖς ἵνα μὴ
them   all   and he admonished them   that not

5318   846   4160   17 2443 4137
φανερὸν αὐτὸν ποιήσωσιν,   ἵνα πληρωθῇ
evident him   they might make,   that might be fulfilled

09   3004   1223   2268   02 4396   3004
τὸ ῥηθὲν   διὰ   Ἠσαΐου τοῦ προφήτου λέγοντος·
the word having through Isaiah the spokesman saying,
    been spoken

18 2400 01 3816   1473 3739 140   01
    ἰδοὺ ὁ παῖς   μου ὃν ἡρέτισα, ὁ
    look the boy servant of me whom I chose, the

27   1473 1519 3739 2106   05   5590 1473 5087
ἀγαπητός μου εἰς ὃν εὐδόκησεν ἡ ψυχή μου· θήσω
loved   of to whom thought the soul of I will
one   me   well   me; set

012 4151   1473 1909 846   2532 2920   023
τὸ πνεῦμά μου ἐπ' αὐτόν, καὶ κρίσιν   τοῖς
the spirit of me on him,   and judgment to the

1484   518   19 3756 2051   3761   2905
ἔθνεσιν ἀπαγγελεῖ.   οὐκ ἐρίσει οὐδὲ κραυγάσει,
nations he will tell. Not he will but not he will
                             strive   shout,

3761   191   5100 1722 019 4113   08 5456
οὐδὲ ἀκούσει   τις ἐν ταῖς πλατείαις τὴν φωνὴν
but not will hear any in the wide places the sound

846   20 2563   4937   3756 2608
αὐτοῦ.   κάλαμον συντετριμμένον οὐ κατεάξει
of him.   Reed   having been broken not he will break

2532 3043 5188   3756 4570   2193 302 1544
καὶ λίνον τυφόμενον οὐ σβέσει, ἕως ἂν ἐκβάλῃ
and linen being   not he will until - he might
           smoked   quench,   throw out

1519 3534   08   2920   21 2532 011   3686
εἰς νῖκος τὴν κρίσιν.   καὶ τῷ   ὀνόματι
to conquest the judgment.   And in the name

846   1484   1679   22 5119 4374
αὐτοῦ ἔθνη ἐλπιοῦσιν.   Τότε προσηνέχθη
of him nations will hope.   Then was brought toward

846   1139   5185   2532 2974   2532
αὐτῷ δαιμονιζόμενος   τυφλὸς καὶ κωφός, καὶ
him one being demonized blind   and deaf;   and

2323   846   5620   04 2974   2980   2532
ἐθεράπευσεν αὐτόν, ὥστε τὸν κωφὸν λαλεῖν καὶ
he healed   him,   so that the deaf to speak and

991   23 2532 1839   3956   013 3793   2532
βλέπειν.   καὶ ἐξίσταντο πάντες οἱ ὄχλοι καὶ
to see.   And were amazed all   the crowds and

3004   3385 3778   1510 01 5207 1160a
ἔλεγον·   μήτι οὗτός ἐστιν ὁ υἱὸς Δαυίδ;
were saying; not this is   the son of David?

24 013 1161 5330   191   3004 3778   3756
    οἱ δὲ Φαρισαῖοι ἀκούσαντες εἶπον· οὗτος   οὐκ
    The but Pharisees having heard said, this one not

1544   024 1140   1487 3361 1722 03 954
ἐκβάλλει τὰ δαιμόνια εἰ μὴ ἐν τῷ Βεελζεβοὺλ
throws out the demons except in the Beelzeboul

758   022 1140   25 3609a   1161 020
ἄρχοντι τῶν δαιμονίων.   εἰδὼς   δὲ τὰς
ruler   of the demons.   Having known but the

1761   846   3004 846   3956 932
ἐνθυμήσεις αὐτῶν εἶπεν αὐτοῖς· πᾶσα βασιλεία
reflections of them he said to them; all   kingdom

3307   2596   1438   2049   2532
μερισθεῖσα καθ' ἑαυτῆς ἐρημοῦται καὶ
having been divided against itself is desolated and

Many crowds[a] followed him, and he cured all of them, [16]and he ordered them not to make him known. [17]This was to fulfill what had been spoken through the prophet Isaiah:
[18] "Here is my servant,
    whom I have chosen,
    my beloved, with whom
    my soul is well
    pleased.
    I will put my Spirit upon
    him,
    and he will proclaim
    justice to the Gentiles.
[19] He will not wrangle or
    cry aloud,
    nor will anyone hear his
    voice in the streets.
[20] He will not break a
    bruised reed
    or quench a smoldering
    wick
    until he brings justice
    to victory.
[21]   And in his name the
    Gentiles will hope."
   22 Then they brought to him a demoniac who was blind and mute; and he cured him, so that the one who had been mute could speak and see. [23]All the crowds were amazed and said, "Can this be the Son of David?" [24]But when the Pharisees heard it, they said, "It is only by Beelzebul, the ruler of the demons, that this fellow casts out the demons." [25]He knew what they were thinking and said to them, "Every kingdom divided against itself is laid waste, and

a Other ancient authorities lack crowds

no city or house divided against itself will stand. 26If Satan casts out Satan, he is divided against himself; how then will his kingdom stand? 27If I cast out demons by Beelzebul, by whom do your own exorcists*a* cast them out? Therefore they will be your judges. 28But if it is by the Spirit of God that I cast out demons, then the kingdom of God has come to you. 29Or how can one enter a strong man's house and plunder his property, without first tying up the strong man? Then indeed the house can be plundered. 30Whoever is not with me is against me, and whoever does not gather with me scatters. 31Therefore I tell you, people will be forgiven for every sin and blasphemy, but blasphemy against the Spirit will not be forgiven. 32Whoever speaks a word against the Son of Man will be forgiven, but whoever speaks against the Holy Spirit will not be forgiven, either in this age or in the age to come.

33 "Either make the tree good, and its fruit good; or

a Gk sons

3956	4172	2228	3614	3307		2596	1438
πᾶσα	πόλις	ἢ	οἰκία	μερισθεῖσα		καθ'	ἑαυτῆς
all	city	or	house	having been divided		against	itself

3756　2476　　　　　2532　1487　01　　4567　　04
οὐ　σταθήσεται.　**26** καὶ　εἰ　ὁ　σατανᾶς　τὸν
not　will stand.　And if　the　adversary　the

4567　　　1544　　　1909　1438　　3307　　　4459
σατανᾶν　ἐκβάλλει,　ἐφ'　ἑαυτὸν　ἐμερίσθη·　πῶς
adversary　throws out,　on　himself　he was divided;　how

3767　2476　　　05　932　　846　　**27** 2532　1487　1473
οὖν　σταθήσεται　ἡ　βασιλεία　αὐτοῦ;　καὶ　εἰ　ἐγὼ
then　will stand　the kingdom　of him?　And　if　I

1722　954　　　1544　024　1140　013　5207　1473
ἐν　Βεελζεβοὺλ　ἐκβάλλω　τὰ　δαιμόνια,　οἱ　υἱοὶ　ὑμῶν
in　Beelzeboul　throw out　the demons,　the　sons　of you

1722　5101　1544　　　1223　　3778　846
ἐν　τίνι　ἐκβάλλουσιν;　διὰ　τοῦτο　αὐτοὶ
in　what　they throw out?　Through　this　themselves

2923　1510　　1473　**28** 1487　1161　1722　4151　2316
κριταὶ　ἔσονται　ὑμῶν.　εἰ　δὲ　ἐν　πνεύματι　θεοῦ
judges　will be　of you.　If　but　in　spirit　of God

1473　1544　　024　1140　686　5348　1909　1473
ἐγὼ　ἐκβάλλω　τὰ　δαιμόνια,　ἄρα　ἔφθασεν　ἐφ'　ὑμᾶς
I　throw out　the demons,　then　arrived　on　you

05　932　　02　2316　**29** 2228　4459　1410　5100
ἡ　βασιλεία　τοῦ　θεοῦ.　Ἢ　πῶς　δύναταί　τις
the kingdom　of the　God.　Or　how　is able　anyone

1525　　1519　08　3614　02　2478　2532　024
εἰσελθεῖν　εἰς　τὴν　οἰκίαν　τοῦ　ἰσχυροῦ　καὶ　τὰ
to come in　into　the　house　of the　strong　and　the

4632　846　726　　1437　3361　4413　1210
σκεύη　αὐτοῦ　ἁρπάσαι,　ἐὰν　μὴ　πρῶτον　δήσῃ
pots　of him to seize,　except　first　he might bind

04　2478　2532　5119　08　3614　846　1283
τὸν　ἰσχυρόν;　καὶ　τότε　τὴν　οἰκίαν　αὐτοῦ　διαρπάσει.
the strong?　And　then　the house　of him　he will seize
　　　　　　　　　　　　　　　　　thoroughly

30 01　3361　1510　3326　1473　2596　1473　1510　2532
ὁ　μὴ　ὢν　μετ'　ἐμοῦ κατ'　ἐμοῦ ἐστιν, καὶ
The one not being with me　against me　is,　and

01　3361　4863　3326　1473　4650　1223　3778
ὁ　μὴ　συνάγων　μετ'　ἐμοῦ σκορπίζει.　**31** Διὰ　τοῦτο
the not bringing with me　scatters.　Through this
one　together

3004　1473　3956　266　2532　988　863
λέγω　ὑμῖν,　πᾶσα　ἁμαρτία καὶ βλασφημία ἀφεθήσεται
I say to you,　all　sin　and insult will be sent off

015　444　05　1161　010　4151　988
τοῖς　ἀνθρώποις,　ἡ　δὲ　τοῦ　πνεύματος βλασφημία
to the men,　the but　of the spirit　insult

3756　863　2532　3739　1437　3004　3056　2596
οὐκ　ἀφεθήσεται.　**32** καὶ　ὃς　ἐὰν　εἴπῃ　λόγον κατὰ
not will be sent　And who if　he　word against
off.　might say

02　5207　02　444　863　846　3739　1161
τοῦ　υἱοῦ　τοῦ　ἀνθρώπου, ἀφεθήσεται αὐτῷ· ὃς δ'
the son　of the man,　it will be to him; who but
sent off

302　3004　2596　010　4151　010　40　3756
ἂν　εἴπῃ　κατὰ　τοῦ πνεύματος τοῦ ἁγίου, οὐκ
- might say against the spirit　the holy,　not

863　846　3777　1722　3778　03　165
ἀφεθήσεται　αὐτῷ　οὔτε　ἐν　τούτῳ τῷ αἰῶνι
it will be sent off to him and not in　this the age

3777　1722　03　3195　**33** 2228　4160
οὔτε　ἐν　τῷ　μέλλοντι.　Ἢ　ποιήσατε
and not in　the one being about to be.　Or　make

012　1186　2570　2532　04　2590　846　2570　2228
τὸ　δένδρον καλὸν καὶ τὸν καρπὸν αὐτοῦ καλόν, ἢ
the tree　good　and the fruit　of it good,　or

```
4160        012  1186    4550    2532 04  2590    846
ποιήσατε τὸ   δένδρον σαπρὸν καὶ  τὸν καρπὸν αὐτοῦ
make      the  tree    rotten and the fruit   of it
4550    1537    1063 02  2590    09 1186    1097
σαπρόν·  ἐκ    γὰρ τοῦ καρποῦ τὸ δένδρον γινώσκεται.
rotten;  out of for the fruit the tree   is known.
   1081          2191            4459 1410          18
34 γεννήματα    ἐχιδνῶν,        πῶς δύνασθε      ἀγαθὰ
   Generations of poison snakes, how are you able good
2980     4190      1510    1537  1063 010 4051
λαλεῖν  πονηροὶ ὄντες; ἐκ   γὰρ τοῦ περισσεύματος
to speak evil    being? Out of for the excess
06       2588      09  4750  2980      01 18      444
τῆς    καρδίας τὸ στόμα λαλεῖ. 35 ὁ  ἀγαθὸς ἄνθρωπος
of the heart  the mouth speaks.   The good   man
1537 02        18   2344      1544        18    2532 01
ἐκ   τοῦ    ἀγαθοῦ θησαυροῦ ἐκβάλλει   ἀγαθά, καὶ ὁ
out  of the good   treasure throws out good,  and  the
4190      444       1537 02  4190    2344        1544
πονηρὸς ἄνθρωπος ἐκ   τοῦ πονηροῦ θησαυροῦ ἐκβάλλει
evil     man      from the evil    treasure throws out
4190     36 3004  1161 1473  3754 3956 4487  692
πονηρά.    λέγω δὲ  ὑμῖν ὅτι πᾶν ῥῆμα ἀργὸν
evil.      I say but to you that all word  idle
3739    2980       013 444      591                  4012
ὃ     λαλήσουσιν οἱ ἄνθρωποι ἀποδώσουσιν         περὶ
which will speak the men       they will give back about
846   3056  1722 2250   2920        37 1537  1063 014
αὐτοῦ λόγον ἐν ἡμέρᾳ κρίσεως·     ἐκ   γὰρ τῶν
it    word in day of judgment;      out of for the
3056   1473 1344          2532 1537  014 3056   1473
λόγων σου  δικαιωθήσῃ, καὶ ἐκ   τῶν λόγων σου
words of  you will be  and out of the words of you
      you made right,
2613                      38 5119 611         846  5100
καταδικασθήσῃ.            Τότε ἀπεκρίθησαν αὐτῷ τινες
you will be condemned.     Then answered      him some
014       1122       2532 5330    3004     1320
τῶν    γραμματέων καὶ Φαρισαίων λέγοντες· διδάσκαλε,
of the writers     and Pharisees saying,    teacher,
2309    575  1473 4592   3708   39 01      1161
θέλομεν ἀπὸ σοῦ σημεῖον ἰδεῖν.   ὁ      δὲ
we want from you sign    to see.  The one but
611            3004 846       1074       4190     2532
ἀποκριθεὶς   εἶπεν αὐτοῖς· γενεὰ    πονηρὰ καὶ
having answered said to them, generation evil   and
3428       4592      1934        2532 4592       3756
μοιχαλὶς σημεῖον ἐπιζητεῖ, καὶ σημεῖον οὐ
adulterous sign    seeks after, and sign    not
1325         846  1487 3361 09 4592       2495 02
δοθήσεται αὐτῇ εἰ μὴ  τὸ σημεῖον Ἰωνᾶ τοῦ
will be given to it except the sign    Jonah the
4396       40 5618     1063 1510 2495 1722 07 2836
προφήτου.   ὥσπερ  γὰρ ἦν Ἰωνᾶς ἐν τῇ κοιλίᾳ
spokesman.  As indeed for was Jonah in the stomach
010    2785      5140   2250   2532 5140  3571
τοῦ  κήτους   τρεῖς ἡμέρας καὶ τρεῖς νύκτας,
of the sea creature three days  and three nights,
3779   1510   01 5207 02  444      1722 07 2588
οὕτως ἔσται ὁ υἱὸς τοῦ ἀνθρώπου ἐν τῇ καρδίᾳ
thusly will be the son of the man      in the heart
06    1093 5140  2250   2532 5140 3571   41 435
τῆς  γῆς τρεῖς ἡμέρας καὶ τρεῖς νύκτας.  ἄνδρες
of the earth three days  and three nights.  Men
3536      450            1722 07 2920       3326 06
Νινευῖται ἀναστήσονται ἐν  τῇ κρίσει  μετὰ τῆς
Ninevites will stand up in  the judgment with the
1074      3778      2532 2632              846      3754
γενεᾶς   ταύτης καὶ κατακρινοῦσιν αὐτήν, ὅτι
generation this  and will condemn    it,     because
```

make the tree bad, and its fruit bad; for the tree is known by its fruit. [34]You brood of vipers! How can you speak good things, when you are evil? For out of the abundance of the heart the mouth speaks. [35]The good person brings good things out of a good treasure, and the evil person brings evil things out of an evil treasure. [36]I tell you, on the day of judgment you will have to give an account for every careless word you utter; [37]for by your words you will be justified, and by your words you will be condemned."

[38]Then some of the scribes and Pharisees said to him, "Teacher, we wish to see a sign from you." [39]But he answered them, "An evil and adulterous generation asks for a sign, but no sign will be given to it except the sign of the prophet Jonah. [40]For just as Jonah was three days and three nights in the belly of the sea monster, so for three days and three nights the Son of Man will be in the heart of the earth. [41]The people of Nineveh will rise up at the judgment with this generation and condemn it, because

they repented at the
proclamation of Jonah, and
see, something greater than
Jonah is here! 42The queen
of the South will rise up at
the judgment with this
generation and condemn it,
because she came from the
ends of the earth to listen
to the wisdom of Solomon,
and see, something greater
than Solomon is here!

43 "When the unclean
spirit has gone out of a
person, it wanders through
waterless regions looking
for a resting place, but it
finds none. 44Then it says,
'I will return to my house
from which I came.' When
it comes, it finds it empty,
swept, and put in order.
45Then it goes and brings
along seven other spirits
more evil than itself, and
they enter and live there;
and the last state of that
person is worse than the
first. So will it be also with
this evil generation."

46 While he was still
speaking to the crowds, his
mother and his brothers
were standing outside,
wanting to speak to him.
47Someone told him,
"Look, your mother and
your brothers are standing
outside, wanting to speak
to you."*a* 48But to the one
who had told him this,
Jesus*b* replied, "Who is
my mother, and who

a Other ancient authorities lack
verse 47
b Gk he

```
3340           1519 012 2782              2495    2532
μετενόησαν     εἰς  τὸ  κήρυγμα          Ἰωνᾶ,  καὶ
they changed mind in   the announcement Jonah,  and
2400 4183      2495 5602        938      3558
ἰδοὺ πλεῖον  Ἰωνᾶ ὧδε.   42  βασίλισσα νότου
look more     Jonah here.     Queen    of south
1453                1722 07 2920      3326 06 1074
ἐγερθήσεται  ἐν   τῇ  κρίσει   μετὰ τῆς γενεᾶς
will be raised in  the judgment with the generation
3778    2532 2632           846    3754    2064        1537
ταύτης καὶ κατακρινεῖ αὐτήν, ὅτι  ἦλθεν  ἐκ
this    and  will condemn  it;    because she came from
022 4009      06    1093 191      08 4678     4672
τῶν περάτων τῆς  γῆς  ἀκοῦσαι τὴν σοφίαν Σολομῶνος,
the limits of the earth to hear the wisdom of Solomon,
2532 2400 4183      4672          5602      3752 1161 09
καὶ  ἰδοὺ πλεῖον Σολομῶνος ὧδε.   43  Ὅταν δὲ  τὸ
and  look more  of Solomon here.    When but the
169         4151       1831     575 02  444        1330
ἀκάθαρτον πνεῦμα ἐξέλθῃ ἀπὸ τοῦ ἀνθρώπου, διέρχεται
unclean    spirit  might from the man,       he goes
                    go out                      through
1223      504       5117      2212      372         2532 3756
δι᾽     ἀνύδρων  τόπων  ζητοῦν ἀνάπαυσιν καὶ  οὐχ
through waterless places seeking rest      and  not
2147        44 5119 3004       1519 04 3624 1473
εὑρίσκει.     τότε λέγει·   εἰς  τὸν οἶκόν μου
he finds.     Then he says,  to  the house of me
1994          3606       1831          2532 2064
ἐπιστρέψω  ὅθεν    ἐξῆλθον·   καὶ  ἐλθὸν
I will return from where I went out; and  having come
2147      4980         4563        2532
εὑρίσκει σχολάζοντα σεσαρωμένον  καὶ
he finds unoccupied having been swept and
2885           45 5119 4198      2532
κεκοσμημένον.     τότε πορεύεται καὶ
having been adorned.  Then he travels and
3880          3326 1438   2033  2087   4151
παραλαμβάνει μεθ᾽ ἑαυτοῦ ἑπτὰ ἕτερα πνεύματα
he takes along with himself seven other spirits
4190         1438     2532 1525            2730
πονηρότερα ἑαυτοῦ  καὶ εἰσελθόντα κατοικεῖ
more evil of himself, and having gone in he resides
1563    2532 1096  021 2078  02  444      1565
ἐκεῖ·  καὶ γίνεται τὰ ἔσχατα τοῦ ἀνθρώπου ἐκείνου
there; and becomes the last of the man  that
5501     022    4413     3779   1510        2532 07
χείρονα τῶν  πρώτων. οὕτως ἔσται  καὶ  τῇ
worse   of the first. Thusly it will be also in the
1074    3778 07 4190      2089 846    2980
γενεᾷ ταύτῃ τῇ πονηρᾷ. 46  Ἔτι αὐτοῦ λαλοῦντος
generation this the evil.   Still of him speaking
015   3793   2400 05  3384   2532 013 80      846
τοῖς ὄχλοις ἰδοὺ ἡ μήτηρ καὶ οἱ ἀδελφοὶ αὐτοῦ
to the crowds look the mother and the brothers of him
2476       1854   2212  846   2980       47 3004
εἱστήκεισαν ἔξω ζητοῦντες αὐτῷ λαλῆσαι.  [εἶπεν
had stood outside seeking  to him to speak.  Said
1161 5100 846    2400 05 3384  1473     2532 013
δέ  τις αὐτῷ·  ἰδοὺ ἡ μήτηρ σου  καὶ οἱ
but some to him, look the mother of you and the
80       1473 1854   2476      2212       1473
ἀδελφοί σου ἔξω ἑστήκασιν ζητοῦντές σοι
brothers of you outside have stood seeking  to you
2980      48 01    1161 611            3004 03
λαλῆσαι.]    ὁ   δὲ ἀποκριθεὶς εἶπεν τῷ
to speak.   The one but having answered said to the
3004      846     5101 1510  05 3384  1473 2532 5101
λέγοντι αὐτῷ· τίς ἐστιν ἡ μήτηρ μου καὶ τίνες
one saying to him; who is  the mother of me and who
```

```
1510   013  80              1473    49  2532 1614
εἰσὶν  οἱ   ἀδελφοί μου;        καὶ ἐκτείνας
are    the  brothers of me?        And having stretched out
08     5495   846      1909 016   3101     846       3004
τὴν    χεῖρα αὐτοῦ  ἐπὶ τοὺς μαθητὰς αὐτοῦ εἶπεν·
the    hand  of him on  the  learners of him  he said,
2400  05   3384   1473 2532 013 80      1473  50  3748
ἰδοὺ ἡ    μήτηρ μου καὶ οἱ ἀδελφοί μου.     ὅστις
look the  mother of me and the brothers of me.    Whoever
1063  302 4160      012 2307   02      3962    1473  02
γὰρ ἂν ποιήσῃ τὸ θέλημα τοῦ πατρός μου τοῦ
for  -  might do the want of the father of me of the
1722 3772    846       1473 80    2532 79     2532
ἐν  οὐρανοῖς αὐτός μου ἀδελφός καὶ ἀδελφὴ καὶ
in  heavens  himself of me brother and sister and
3384  1510      1722 07   2250  1565   1831
μήτηρ ἐστίν. 13:1 Ἐν τῇ ἡμέρᾳ ἐκείνῃ ἐξελθὼν
mother is.       In the day that having gone
                                                    out
01   2424   06       3614  2521   3844 08    2281
ὁ  Ἰησοῦς τῆς  οἰκίας ἐκάθητο παρὰ τὴν θάλασσαν·
the Jesus of the house sat      along the sea;
   2532 4863                4314 846   3793    4183
2  καὶ  συνήχθησαν       πρὸς αὐτὸν ὄχλοι πολλοί,
   and  were brought together to   him   crowds many,
5620    846    1519 4143   1684            2521      2532
ὥστε  αὐτὸν εἰς πλοῖον ἐμβάντα       καθῆσθαι, καὶ
so that him  into boat  having gone in to sit,    and
3956  01   3793 1909 04   123      2476      3 2532
πᾶς ὁ  ὄχλος ἐπὶ τὸν αἰγιαλὸν εἱστήκει.   Καὶ
all the crowd on the shore      had stood.   And
2980      846     4183 1722 3850         3004
ἐλάλησεν αὐτοῖς πολλὰ ἐν  παραβολαῖς λέγων·
he spoke to them much  in  parallel stories saying;
2400 1831     01      4687    010   4687      4 2532
ἰδοὺ ἐξῆλθεν ὁ   σπείρων τοῦ σπείρειν.   καὶ
look went out the one sowing of the to sow.    And
1722 011 4687    846   3739 3303   4098    3844  08
ἐν  τῷ σπείρειν αὐτὸν ἃ  μὲν  ἔπεσεν παρὰ τὴν
in  the to sow  him   what indeed fell  along the
3598  2532 2064    021 4071   2719      846
ὁδόν, καὶ ἐλθόντα τὰ πετεινὰ κατέφαγεν αὐτά.
way,  and having come the birds ate up    them.
  243      1161  4098   1909 024 4075    3699 3756 2192
5 ἄλλα  δὲ  ἔπεσεν ἐπὶ τὰ πετρώδη ὅπου οὐκ εἶχεν
  Others but fell  on  the rocky    where not it had
1093  4183    2532 2112      1816         1223
γῆν  πολλήν, καὶ εὐθέως ἐξανέτειλεν διὰ
earth much,  and immediately it sprang up out through
012 3361 2192    899  1093      6 2246   1161
τὸ μὴ ἔχειν βάθος γῆς·     ἡλίου δὲ
the not to have depth of land; of sun but
393            2739           2532 1223    012 3361
ἀνατείλαντος ἐκαυματίσθη καὶ διὰ  τὸ μὴ
having arisen it was burned and through the not
2192  4491    3583         7 243     1161 4098
ἔχειν ῥίζαν ἐξηράνθη.    ἄλλα δὲ  ἔπεσεν
to have root it was dried out.  Others but fell
1909 020 173      2532 305     017 173      2532
ἐπὶ τὰς ἀκάνθας, καὶ ἀνέβησαν αἱ ἄκανθαι καὶ
on  the thorns,  and went up   the thorns and
4155   846    8 243     1161 4098   1909 08   1093  08
ἔπνιξαν αὐτά.   ἄλλα δὲ  ἔπεσεν ἐπὶ τὴν γῆν τὴν
choked them.   Others but fell  on  the earth the
2570 2532 1325    2590   3739 3303   1540
καλὴν καὶ ἐδίδου καρπόν, ὃ μὲν ἑκατόν,
good  and was giving fruit, what indeed hundred,
3739 1161 1835    3739 1161 5144     9 01
ὃ  δὲ  ἑξήκοντα, ὃ  δὲ  τριάκοντα.   ὁ
what but sixty,    what but thirty.     The one
```

are my brothers?" [49]And pointing to his disciples, he said, "Here are my mother and my brothers! [50]For whoever does the will of my Father in heaven is my brother and sister and mother."

CHAPTER 13

That same day Jesus went out of the house and sat beside the sea. [2]Such great crowds gathered around him that he got into a boat and sat there, while the whole crowd stood on the beach. [3]And he told them many things in parables, saying: "Listen! A sower went out to sow. [4]And as he sowed, some seeds fell on the path, and the birds came and ate them up. [5]Other seeds fell on rocky ground, where they did not have much soil, and they sprang up quickly, since they had no depth of soil. [6]But when the sun rose, they were scorched; and since they had no root, they withered away. [7]Other seeds fell among thorns, and the thorns grew up and choked them. [8]Other seeds fell on good soil and brought forth grain, some a hundred-fold, some sixty, some thirty. [9]Let anyone with ears[a] listen!"

[a] Other ancient authorities add
to hear

10 Then the disciples came and asked him, "Why do you speak to them in parables?" [11]He answered, "To you it has been given to know the secrets[a] of the kingdom of heaven, but to them it has not been given. [12]For to those who have, more will be given, and they will have an abundance; but from those who have nothing, even what they have will be taken away. [13]The reason I speak to them in parables is that 'seeing they do not perceive, and hearing they do not listen, nor do they understand.' [14]With them indeed is fulfilled the prophecy of Isaiah that says:

'You will indeed listen,
  but never understand,
and you will indeed look, but never perceive.
[15]For this people's heart
  has grown dull,
and their ears are hard
  of hearing,
and they have shut
  their eyes;
so that they might not
  look with their eyes,
and listen with their ears,
and understand with their heart and turn—
and I would heal them.'

[16]But blessed are your eyes, for they see, and your ears, for they hear. [17]Truly I tell you, many prophets and righteous people longed to see what

a Or mysteries

2192	3775	191		2532	4334		013
ἔχων	ὦτα	ἀκουέτω.	10	Καὶ	προσελθόντες		οἱ
having	ears	let hear.		And	having gone to the		

3101		3004	846	1223		5101	1722	3850
μαθηταὶ		εἶπαν	αὐτῷ·	διὰ		τί	ἐν	παραβολαῖς
learners		said	to him;	through		what	in	parallel stories

2980		846		01		1161	611
λαλεῖς		αὐτοῖς;	11	ὁ		δὲ	ἀποκριθεὶς
do you speak		to them?		The one		but	having answered

3004	846		3754	1473		1325		1097	024
εἶπεν	αὐτοῖς·		ὅτι	ὑμῖν		δέδοται		γνῶναι	τὰ
said	to them,		(") to	you		has been given		to know	the

3466		06	932		014	3772		1565	1161
μυστήρια		τῆς	βασιλείας		τῶν	οὐρανῶν,		ἐκείνοις	δὲ
mysteries		of the	kingdom		of the	heavens,		to those	but

3756	1325			3748		1063	2192	1325		846
οὐ	δέδοται.	12		ὅστις		γὰρ	ἔχει,	δοθήσεται		αὐτῷ
not	it has been given.			Whoever		for	has,	it will be given		to him

2532	4052			3748		1161	3756	2192	2532
καὶ	περισσευθήσεται·			ὅστις		δὲ	οὐκ	ἔχει,	καὶ
and	it will be exceeded;			whoever		but	not	has,	also

3739	2192	142		575	846		1223
ὃ	ἔχει	ἀρθήσεται		ἀπ᾽	αὐτοῦ.	13	διὰ
what he has		will be lifted up		from	him.		Through

3778	1722	3850		846		2980	3754
τοῦτο	ἐν	παραβολαῖς		αὐτοῖς		λαλῶ,	ὅτι
this	in	parallel stories		to them		I speak,	because

991		3756	991		2532	191		3756	191
βλέποντες		οὐ	βλέπουσιν		καὶ	ἀκούοντες		οὐκ	ἀκούουσιν
seeing		not	they see		and	hearing		not	they hear

3761		4920		2532	378		846	05
οὐδὲ		συνίουσιν,	14	καὶ	ἀναπληροῦται		αὐτοῖς	ἡ
but not		they understand,		and	is filled up		to them	the

4394		2268	05		3004	189
προφητεία		Ἡσαΐου	ἡ		λέγουσα·	ἀκοῇ
speaking before		Isaiah	the one		saying;	hearing

191		2532	3756	3361	4920		2532	991
ἀκούσετε		καὶ	οὐ	μὴ	συνῆτε,		καὶ	βλέποντες
you will hear		and	not	not	you might understand,		and	seeing

991		2532	3756	3361	3708		3975		1063	05
βλέψετε		καὶ	οὐ	μὴ	ἴδητε.	15	ἐπαχύνθη		γὰρ	ἡ
you will see		and	not	not	you might see.		Was thickened		for	the

2588		02	2992	3778		2532	023		3775	917
καρδία		τοῦ	λαοῦ	τούτου,		καὶ	τοῖς		ὠσὶν	βαρέως
heart		of the	people	this,		and	in the		ears	heavily

191		2532	016	3788		846	2576
ἤκουσαν		καὶ	τοὺς	ὀφθαλμοὺς		αὐτῶν	ἐκάμμυσαν,
they heard		and	the	eyes		of them	they shut,

3379		3708		015	3788		2532	023
μήποτε		ἴδωσιν		τοῖς	ὀφθαλμοῖς		καὶ	τοῖς
not then		they might see		in the	eyes		and	in the

3775	191		2532	07		2588	4920		2532
ὠσὶν	ἀκούσωσιν		καὶ	τῇ		καρδίᾳ	συνῶσιν		καὶ
ears	they might hear		and	in the		heart	they might understand		and

1994		2532	2390		846		1473
ἐπιστρέψωσιν		καὶ	ἰάσομαι		αὐτούς.	16	ὑμῶν
they might return		and	I will cure		them.		Of you

1161	3107		013	3788		3754	991		2532	021	3775
δὲ	μακάριοι		οἱ	ὀφθαλμοὶ		ὅτι	βλέπουσιν		καὶ	τὰ	ὦτα
but	fortunate		the	eyes		that	they see		and	the	ears

1473		3754	191		281	1063	3004	1473		3754
ὑμῶν		ὅτι	ἀκούουσιν.	17	ἀμὴν	γὰρ	λέγω	ὑμῖν		ὅτι
of you		that	they hear.		Amen	for	I say	to you		that

4183	4396		2532	1342		1937		3708	3739
πολλοὶ	προφῆται		καὶ	δίκαιοι		ἐπεθύμησαν		ἰδεῖν	ἃ
many	spokesmen		and	right ones		desired		to see	what

991   2532 3756 3708   2532 191   3739 191
βλέπετε καὶ οὐκ εἶδαν,   καὶ ἀκοῦσαι ἃ   ἀκούετε
you see and not they saw, and to hear what you hear

2532 3756 191   1473 3767 191   08
καὶ οὐκ ἤκουσαν. **18** Ὑμεῖς οὖν ἀκούσατε τὴν
and not they heard.   You   then hear   the

3850   02   4687   3956   191
παραβολὴν   τοῦ σπείραντος. **19** παντὸς ἀκούοντος
parallel story of the one sowing.   All   hearing

04   3056 06   932   2532 3361 4920
τὸν λόγον τῆς βασιλείας καὶ μὴ συνιέντος
the word of the kingdom   and not understanding

2064   01 4190   2532 726   012 4687
ἔρχεται ὁ πονηρὸς καὶ ἁρπάζει τὸ ἐσπαρμένον
comes   the evil   and seizes   the having been sown

1722 07 2588   846   3778 1510 01   3844   08
ἐν   τῇ καρδίᾳ αὐτοῦ, οὗτός ἐστιν ὁ   παρὰ τὴν
in   the heart of him, this is   the one along the

3598 4687   01 1161 1909 024 4075   4687
ὁδὸν σπαρείς. **20** ὁ δὲ ἐπὶ τὰ πετρώδη σπαρείς,
way having   The but on   the rocky   having been
been sown.   one   sown,

3778 1510 01   04 3056 191   2532 2117
οὗτός ἐστιν ὁ   τὸν λόγον ἀκούων καὶ εὐθὺς
this is   the one the word hearing and immediately

3326 5479 2983   846   3756 2192 1161 4491
μετὰ χαρᾶς λαμβάνων αὐτόν, **21** οὐκ ἔχει δὲ ῥίζαν
with joy receiving it,   not it has but root

1722 1438 235 4340   1510 1096   1161
ἐν   ἑαυτῷ ἀλλὰ πρόσκαιρός ἐστιν, γενομένης δὲ
in   itself but to season it is, having become but

2347   2228 1375   1223 04 3056 2117
θλίψεως ἢ διωγμοῦ   διὰ τὸν λόγον εὐθὺς
affliction or persecution through the word immediately

4624   01   1161 1519 020 173
σκανδαλίζεται. **22** ὁ δὲ εἰς τὰς ἀκάνθας
it is offended.   The one but into the thorns

4687   3778 1510 01   04 3056 191
σπαρείς,   οὗτός ἐστιν ὁ   τὸν λόγον ἀκούων,
having been sown, this is   the one the word hearing,

2532 05 3308   02   165   2532 05 539
καὶ ἡ μέριμνα τοῦ αἰῶνος καὶ ἡ ἀπάτη
and the anxiety of the age   and the deception

02   4149   4846   04 3056 2532 175
τοῦ πλούτου συμπνίγει τὸν λόγον καὶ ἄκαρπος
of the rich   choke together the word and fruitless

1096   01   1161 1909 08 2570 1093
γίνεται. **23** ὁ δὲ ἐπὶ τὴν καλὴν γῆν
it becomes.   The one but on   the good land

4687   3778 1510 01   04 3056 191
σπαρείς,   οὗτός ἐστιν ὁ   τὸν λόγον ἀκούων
having been sown, this is   the one the word hearing

2532 4920   3739 1211   2592   2532 4160
καὶ συνιείς, ὃς δὴ καρποφορεῖ καὶ ποιεῖ
and understanding, who indeed bears fruit and makes

3739 3303 1540   3739 1161 1835   3739 1161
ὃ   μὲν ἑκατόν, ὃ δὲ ἑξήκοντα, ὃ δὲ
what indeed hundred, what but sixty,   what but

5144   243   3850   3908
τριάκοντα. **24** Ἄλλην παραβολὴν παρέθηκεν
thirty.   Other parallel story he set along

846   3004   3666   05 932   014 3772
αὐτοῖς λέγων· ὡμοιώθη ἡ βασιλεία τῶν οὐρανῶν
to them saying, was likened the kingdom of the heavens

444   4687   2570 4690   1722 03 68   846
ἀνθρώπῳ σπείραντι καλὸν σπέρμα ἐν τῷ ἀγρῷ αὐτοῦ.
to man   having sown good seed in the field of him.

25 1722 1161 011 2518   016 444   2064 846
ἐν   δὲ τῷ καθεύδειν τοὺς ἀνθρώπους ἦλθεν αὐτοῦ
In   but the to sleep   the men   came of him

---

you see, but did not see it,
and to hear what you hear,
but did not hear it.

18 "Hear then the
parable of the sower.
19When anyone hears the
word of the kingdom and
does not understand it, the
evil one comes and snatches
away what is sown in the
heart; this is what was sown
on the path. 20As for what
was sown on rocky ground,
this is the one who hears
the word and immediately
receives it with joy; 21yet
such a person has no root,
but endures only for a
while, and when trouble
or persecution arises on
account of the word, that
person immediately falls
away.a 22As for what was
sown among thorns, this
is the one who hears the
word, but the cares of the
world and the lure of
wealth choke the word,
and it yields nothing.
23But as for what was sown
on good soil, this is the one
who hears the word and
understands it, who indeed
bears fruit and yields, in
one case a hundredfold,
in another sixty, and in
another thirty."

24 He put before them
another parable: "The
kingdom of heaven may be
compared to someone who
sowed good seed in his
field; 25but while everybody
was asleep, an enemy came

a Gk *stumbles*

and sowed weeds among the wheat, and then went away. 26So when the plants came up and bore grain, then the weeds appeared as well. 27And the slaves of the householder came and said to him, 'Master, did you not sow good seed in your field? Where, then, did these weeds come from?' 28He answered, 'An enemy has done this.' The slaves said to him, 'Then do you want us to go and gather them?' 29But he replied, 'No; for in gathering the weeds you would uproot the wheat along with them. 30Let both of them grow together until the harvest; and at harvest time I will tell the reapers, Collect the weeds first and bind them in bundles to be burned, but gather the wheat into my barn.'"

31 He put before them another parable: "The kingdom of heaven is like a mustard seed that someone took and sowed in his field; 32it is the smallest of all the seeds, but when it has grown it is the greatest of shrubs and becomes a tree, so that the birds of the

01	2190		2532 1986a		2215	303 3319
ὁ	ἐχθρὸς	καὶ	ἐπέσπειρεν	ζιζάνια	ἀνὰ	μέσον
the	hostile one	and	sowed on	weeds	up	middle

02	4621	2532	565		**26**	3753 1161	985		01
τοῦ	σίτου	καὶ	ἀπῆλθεν.			ὅτε δὲ	ἐβλάστησεν		ὁ
of the	wheat	and	went off.			When but	sprouted		the

5528	2532	2590	4160		5119 5316	2532 021
χόρτος	καὶ	καρπὸν	ἐποίησεν,	τότε	ἐφάνη καὶ	τὰ
grass	and	fruit	it made,	then	shined	also the

2215		4334		1161 013	1401	02
ζιζάνια.	**27**	προσελθόντες	δὲ	οἱ	δοῦλοι	τοῦ
weeds.		Having come to	but	the	slaves	of the

3617		3004 846		2962	3780 2570
οἰκοδεσπότου		εἶπον αὐτῷ·		κύριε,	οὐχὶ καλὸν
house supervisor		said to him;		Master,	not good

4690	4687		1722 03	4674 68		4159		3767
σπέρμα	ἔσπειρας	ἐν	τῷ	σῷ	ἀγρῷ;	πόθεν		οὖν
seed	you sowed	in	the	your	field?	From where		then

2192 2215		01		1161 5346 846		2190
ἔχει ζιζάνια;	**28**	ὁ		δὲ ἔφη	αὐτοῖς·	ἐχθρὸς
has weeds?		The one	but	said	to them;	hostile

444	3778	4160		013 1161	1401	3004
ἄνθρωπος	τοῦτο	ἐποίησεν.	οἱ δὲ		δοῦλοι	λέγουσιν
man	this	did.	The	but	slaves	say

846	2309	3767 565		4816		846
αὐτῷ·	θέλεις	οὖν ἀπελθόντες		συλλέξωμεν		αὐτά;
to him,	do you	then having gone off		we might		these?
	want	off		collect		

29	01		1161 5346	3756a 3379		4816	024
	ὁ		δὲ φησιν·	οὔ, μήποτε		συλλέγοντες	τὰ
	The one	but	says;	no, not then		collecting	the

2215	1610		260		846	04
ζιζάνια	ἐκριζώσητε		ἅμα	αὐτοῖς		τὸν
weeds	you might root out		at same time	them		the

4621	**30**	863	4885		297		2193	02
σῖτον.		ἄφετε	συναυξάνεσθαι		ἀμφότερα	ἕως		τοῦ
wheat.		Allow	to grow together		both	until		the

2326	2532	1722 2540	02		2326	3004
θερισμοῦ,	καὶ	ἐν καιρῷ	τοῦ		θερισμοῦ	ἐρῶ
harvest,	and	in season of	the		harvest	I will say

015	2327		4816		4413	024 2215	2532
τοῖς	θερισταῖς·		συλλέξατε	πρῶτον		τὰ ζιζάνια	καὶ
to the	harvesters,		collect	first		the weeds	and

1210	846	1519 1197		4314 012 2618		846
δήσατε	αὐτὰ	εἰς δέσμας	πρὸς	τὸ	κατακαῦσαι	αὐτά,
bind	them	into bundles	to	the	to burn down	them,

04 1161 4621	4863		1519 08	596
τὸν δὲ σῖτον	συναγάγετε		εἰς τὴν	ἀποθήκην
the but wheat	bring together		into the	storehouse

1473	**31**	243	3850		3908		846
μου.		Ἄλλην	παραβολὴν		παρέθηκεν		αὐτοῖς
of me.		Other	parallel story		he set along		to them

3004	3664	1510	05	932		014	3772
λέγων·	ὁμοία	ἐστὶν	ἡ	βασιλεία	τῶν		οὐρανῶν
saying:	like	is	the	kingdom	of the		heavens

2848	4615		3739	2983		444
κόκκῳ	σινάπεως,		ὃν	λαβὼν		ἄνθρωπος
to grain	of mustard,		which	having taken		man

4687	1722 03	68	846		**32**	3739 3398
ἔσπειρεν ἐν	τῷ	ἀγρῷ	αὐτοῦ·			ὃ μικρότερον
sowed	in	the	field of him;			that smaller

3303	1510	3956	022 4690		3752 1161
μέν	ἐστιν	πάντων	τῶν σπερμάτων,		ὅταν δὲ
indeed	is	of all	the seeds,		when but

837	3173	022	3001		1510 2532
αὐξηθῇ	μεῖζον	τῶν	λαχάνων		ἐστὶν καὶ
might be grown	greater	of the	vegetables		is and

1096	1186	5620	2064	024 4071	02
γίνεται	δένδρον,	ὥστε	ἐλθεῖν	τὰ πετεινὰ	τοῦ
it becomes	tree,	so that	to come	the birds	of the

3772   2532 2681   1722 015 2798   846
οὐρανοῦ καὶ κατασκηνοῦν   ἐν   τοῖς κλάδοις αὐτοῦ.
heaven and to set up tent   in   the branches of it.

33 243   3850   2980   846   3664   1510
    Ἄλλην παραβολὴν   ἐλάλησεν αὐτοῖς· ὁμοία ἐστὶν
    Other parallel story   he spoke to them: like is

05 932   014   3772   2219   3739 2983
ἡ   βασιλεία τῶν   οὐρανῶν   ζύμῃ,   ἣν   λαβοῦσα
the kingdom of the heavens   yeast, which having taken

1135 1470   1519 224   4568   5140 2193 3739
γυνὴ ἐνέκρυψεν   εἰς ἀλεύρου σάτα τρία ἕως οὗ
woman hid in   into flour sata three until which

2220   3650   **34** 3778 3956   2980   01 2424
ἐζυμώθη   ὅλον.   ταῦτα πάντα ἐλάλησεν ὁ Ἰησοῦς
it yeasts whole.   These all spoke   the Jesus

1722 3850   015   3793   2532 5565   3850
ἐν   παραβολαῖς τοῖς ὄχλοις καὶ χωρὶς παραβολῆς
in   parallel   to the crowds and without parallel
     stories   story

3762   2980   846   **35** 3704   4137   09
οὐδὲν ἐλάλει αὐτοῖς,   ὅπως πληρωθῇ τὸ
nothing he was to them;   so that might be the
        speaking   fulfilled

3004   1223   02   4396   3004   455   1722
ῥηθὲν   διὰ   τοῦ προφήτου λέγοντος· ἀνοίξω ἐν
word having through the spokesman saying; I will in
been spoken   open

3850   012 4750 1473 2044   2928
παραβολαῖς τὸ στόμα μου, ἐρεύξομαι κεκρυμμένα
parallel   the mouth of   I will speak having been
stories   me, out loud   hidden

575   2602   2889   **36** 5119 863   016
ἀπὸ καταβολῆς [κόσμου].   Τότε ἀφεὶς   τοὺς
from foundation of world.   Then having sent off the

3793   2064   1519 08   3614   2532 4334   846
ὄχλους ἦλθεν εἰς τὴν οἰκίαν. καὶ προσῆλθον αὐτῷ
crowds he went into the house. And came towards him

013 3101   846   3004   1285   1473 08
οἱ μαθηταὶ αὐτοῦ λέγοντες· διασάφησον ἡμῖν τὴν
the learners of him saying, tell clearly to us the

3850   022   2215   02   68   **37** 01
παραβολὴν τῶν ζιζανίων τοῦ ἀγροῦ.   ὁ
parallel story of the weeds of the field.   The one

1161 611   3004   01   4687   012 2570
δὲ ἀποκριθεὶς εἶπεν· ὁ   σπείρων τὸ καλὸν
but having answered said, the one sowing the good

4690   1510 01 5207 02   444   **38** 01 1161
σπέρμα ἐστὶν ὁ υἱὸς τοῦ ἀνθρώπου,   ὁ δὲ
seed   is   the son of the man;   the but

68   1510 01   2889   09   1161 2570 4690   3778
ἀγρός ἐστιν ὁ κόσμος, τὸ δὲ καλὸν σπέρμα οὗτοί
field is   the world; the but good seed these

1510 013 5207 06   932   021 1161 2215
εἰσιν οἱ υἱοὶ τῆς βασιλείας· τὰ δὲ ζιζάνιά
are   the sons of the kingdom; the but weeds

1510 013 5207 02   4190   **39** 01 1161 2190
εἰσιν οἱ υἱοὶ τοῦ πονηροῦ,   ὁ δὲ ἐχθρὸς
are   the sons of the evil,   the but hostile one

01 4687   846   1510 01 1228   01 1161
ὁ σπείρας αὐτά ἐστιν ὁ διάβολος, ὁ δὲ
the one having sown them is the slanderer; the but

2326   4930   165   1510 013 1161
θερισμὸς συντέλεια αἰῶνός ἐστιν, οἱ δὲ
harvest full completion of age is, the but

2327   32   1510   **40** 5618 3767
θερισταὶ ἄγγελοί εἰσιν.   ὥσπερ οὖν
harvesters messengers are.   As indeed then

4816   021 2215   2532 4442   2618
συλλέγεται τὰ ζιζάνια καὶ πυρὶ [κατα]καίεται,
is collected the weeds and in fire it is burned down,

---

air come and make nests in
its branches."

33 He told them another
parable: "The kingdom of
heaven is like yeast that a
woman took and mixed in
with[a] three measures of
flour until all of it was
leavened."

34 Jesus told the crowds
all these things in parables;
without a parable he told
them nothing. 35 This was to
fulfill what had been spoken
through the prophet:[b]
"I will open my mouth to
speak in parables;
I will proclaim what has
been hidden from the
foundation of the
world."[c]

36 Then he left the
crowds and went into the
house. And his disciples
approached him, saying,
"Explain to us the parable
of the weeds of the field."
37 He answered, "The one
who sows the good seed is
the Son of Man; 38 the field
is the world, and the good
seed are the children of the
kingdom; the weeds are
the children of the evil
one, 39 and the enemy who
sowed them is the devil;
the harvest is the end of the
age, and the reapers are
angels. 40 Just as the weeds
are collected and burned up
with fire,

---

[a] Gk hid in
[b] Other ancient authorities read
    the prophet Isaiah
[c] Other ancient authorities lack
    of the world

so will it be at the end of
the age. ⁴¹The Son of Man
will send his angels, and
they will collect out of his
kingdom all causes of sin
and all evildoers, ⁴²and
they will throw them into
the furnace of fire, where
there will be weeping and
gnashing of teeth. ⁴³Then
the righteous will shine like
the sun in the kingdom of
their Father. Let anyone
with ears*ᵃ* listen!

44 "The kingdom of
heaven is like treasure
hidden in a field, which
someone found and hid;
then in his joy he goes and
sells all that he has and
buys that field.

45 "Again, the kingdom
of heaven is like a merchant
in search of fine pearls; ⁴⁶on
finding one pearl of great
value, he went and sold all
that he had and bought it.

47 "Again, the kingdom
of heaven is like a net that
was thrown into the sea and
caught fish of every kind;
⁴⁸when it was full, they
drew it ashore, sat down,
and put the good into
baskets but threw out the
bad. ⁴⁹So it will be at the
end of the age.

ᵃ Other ancient authorities add
to hear

3779	1510		1722	07	4930		02
οὕτως	ἔσται		ἐν	τῇ	συντελείᾳ		τοῦ
thusly	it will be	in		the	full completion	of the	

165		**41**	649		01	5207 02	444	016
αἰῶνος·			ἀποστελεῖ	ὁ	υἱὸς τοῦ	ἀνθρώπου τοὺς
age;			will delegate	the	son	of the man		the

32		846	2532	4816		1537	06
ἀγγέλους	αὐτοῦ,	καὶ	συλλέξουσιν		ἐκ	τῆς
messengers	of him,	and	they will collect	from	the	

932	846	3956	024 4625		2532 016
βασιλείας	αὐτοῦ	πάντα	τὰ σκάνδαλα	καὶ	τοὺς
kingdom	of him	all	the offenses	and	the ones

4160	08	458		**42**	2532 906		846
ποιοῦντας	τὴν	ἀνομίαν			καὶ βαλοῦσιν		αὐτοὺς
doing	the	lawlessness		and they will throw		them

1519 08	2575	010	4442	1563	1510	01
εἰς	τὴν κάμινον τοῦ	πυρός·	ἐκεῖ	ἔσται	ὁ
into	the furnace of the	fire;	there	will be	the

2805	2532 01	1030	014	3599		**43**	5119 013
κλαυθμὸς	καὶ ὁ	βρυγμὸς	τῶν	ὀδόντων.			τότε οἱ
crying	and the	grinding	of the teeth.			Then the

1342	1584		5613 01	2246	1722 07	932
δίκαιοι	ἐκλάμψουσιν		ὡς ὁ	ἥλιος	ἐν τῇ	βασιλείᾳ
right	will shine out	as	the sun	in the	kingdom

02	3962	846		01	2192	3775 191
τοῦ	πατρὸς	αὐτῶν.	ὁ		ἔχων	ὦτα ἀκουέτω.
of the	father	of them.	The one	having	ears let hear.

44	3664	1510	05	932		014	3772	2344
	Ὁμοία	ἐστὶν	ἡ	βασιλεία	τῶν	οὐρανῶν θησαυρῷ
	Like	is	the	kingdom	of the heavens	to treasure

2928		1722 03	68	3739	2147		444
κεκρυμμένῳ	ἐν	τῷ ἀγρῷ,	ὃν	εὑρὼν		ἄνθρωπος
having been	in	the field,	which	having found	man
hidden					

2928		2532 575	06	5479	846		5217		2532
ἔκρυψεν,	καὶ	ἀπὸ	τῆς χαρᾶς	αὐτοῦ	ὑπάγει		καὶ
hid,	and	from	the joy	of him	he goes off	and

4453	3956	3745		2192	2532 59		04	68
πωλεῖ	πάντα	ὅσα		ἔχει	καὶ	ἀγοράζει	τὸν ἀγρὸν
sells	all	as much as	he has	and	buys	the field

1565		**45**	3825	3664	1510	05	932		014
ἐκεῖνον.			Πάλιν	ὁμοία	ἐστὶν	ἡ	βασιλεία	τῶν
that.			Again	like	is	the	kingdom	of the

3772	444		1713	2212	2570	3135
οὐρανῶν	ἀνθρώπῳ	ἐμπόρῳ	ζητοῦντι	καλοὺς	μαργαρίτας·
heavens	to man	merchant	seeking	good	pearls;

46	2147		1161	1520	4186		3135·
	εὑρὼν		δὲ	ἕνα	πολύτιμον	μαργαρίτην
	having found	but	one	much value	pearl

565		4097		3956	3745		2192
ἀπελθὼν		πέπρακεν		πάντα	ὅσα		εἶχεν
having gone off	he has sold	all	as much as	he had

2532 59		846		**47**	3825	3664	1510	05	932
καὶ	ἠγόρασεν	αὐτόν.			Πάλιν	ὁμοία	ἐστὶν	ἡ	βασιλεία
and	he bought	it.		Again	like	is	the	kingdom

014	3772	4522		906		1519 08
τῶν	οὐρανῶν	σαγήνῃ		βληθείσῃ		εἰς τὴν
of the	heavens	fishing net	having been thrown	into the	

2281		2532 1537	3956	1085	4863
θάλασσαν	καὶ	ἐκ	παντὸς	γένους	συναγαγούσῃ·
sea	and	from	all	kind	having brought together,

48	3739	3753 4137		307		1909 04
	ἦν	ὅτε ἐπληρώθη		ἀναβιβάσαντες		ἐπὶ τὸν
	which	when it was filled	having brought up	on	the

123		2532 2523		4816		024 2570 1519
αἰγιαλὸν	καὶ	καθίσαντες	συνέλεξαν		τὰ καλὰ εἰς
shore	and	having sat	they collected	the good into

32a		024 1161	4550	1854	906		**49**	3779
ἄγγη,		τὰ δὲ	σαπρὰ	ἔξω	ἔβαλον.			οὕτως
containers,	the but	rotten	outside	they threw.			Thusly

```
1510          1722  07   4930              02       165
ἔσται      ἐν   τῇ   συντελείᾳ      τοῦ    αἰῶνος·
it will be in    the  full completion  of the  age;
1831           013 32            2532 873
ἐξελεύσονται οἱ ἄγγελοι    καὶ  ἀφοριοῦσιν
will go out    the messengers and  they will separate
016  4190      1537 3319   014   1342        50  2532
τοὺς πονηροὺς ἐκ  μέσου τῶν δικαίων      καὶ
the  evil      from middle of  the right      and
906       846       1519 08  2575    010        4442  1563
βαλοῦσιν αὐτοὺς εἰς  τὴν κάμινον τοῦ  πυρός· ἐκεῖ
will throw them   into the furnace  of the fire;  there
1510  01   2805      2532 01  1030     014     3599
ἔσται ὁ  κλαυθμὸς καὶ  ὁ  βρυγμὸς τῶν  ὀδόντων.
will be the crying   and the grinding of the teeth.
   4920            3778  3956  3004      846     3483
51 Συνήκατε      ταῦτα πάντα; λέγουσιν αὐτῷ·  ναί.
   You understand these all?  They say  to him,  yes.
   01     1161  3004   846     1223     3778 3956
52 ὁ   δὲ  εἶπεν αὐτοῖς· διὰ    τοῦτο πᾶς
   The one but  said  to them,  through this  all
1122      3100                07    932          014
γραμματεὺς μαθητευθεὶς   τῇ   βασιλείᾳ τῶν
writer      having been learned in the kingdom of the
3772    3664   1510 444    3617                3748
οὐρανῶν ὅμοιός ἐστιν ἀνθρώπῳ οἰκοδεσπότῃ,   ὅστις
heavens like   is  to man house supervisor,  who
1544       1537 02     2344      846      2537  2532
ἐκβάλλει ἐκ  τοῦ  θησαυροῦ αὐτοῦ καινὰ καὶ
throws out out  of  the treasure of him new   and
3820     53 2532 1096      3753 5055       01   2424
παλαιά.    Καὶ ἐγένετο ὅτε ἐτέλεσεν ὁ  Ἰησοῦς
old.       And it became when completed the Jesus
020 3850      3778      3332      1564       54  2532
τὰς παραβολὰς ταύτας, μετῆρεν ἐκεῖθεν.     καὶ
the parallel  these,  he moved from there. And
    stories            across
2064       1519 08  3968    846      1321        846
ἐλθὼν     εἰς  τὴν πατρίδα αὐτοῦ ἐδίδασκεν αὐτοὺς
having come into the fatherland of him he taught them
1722 07  4864      846        5620     1605      846
ἐν  τῇ  συναγωγῇ αὐτῶν,   ὥστε  ἐκπλήσσεσθαι αὐτοὺς
in   the synagogue of them,  so that to astonish them
2532 3004      4159       3778        05   4678   3778 2532
καὶ λέγειν· πόθεν   τούτῳ     ἡ  σοφία αὕτη καὶ
and to say; from where to this one the wisdom this and
017 1411        55  3756 3778  1510  01   02        5045
αἱ  δυνάμεις;   οὐχ οὗτός ἐστιν ὁ  τοῦ  τέκτονος
the powers?     Not this  is   the of the carpenter
5207 3756 05  3384    846      3004      3137a 2532 013
υἱός; οὐχ ἡ  μήτηρ αὐτοῦ λέγεται Μαριὰμ καὶ  οἱ
son? Not the mother of him is called Mariam and  the
80      846    2385       2532  2501   2532 4613   2532
ἀδελφοὶ αὐτοῦ Ἰάκωβος καὶ  Ἰωσὴφ καὶ Σίμων καὶ
brothers of him Jacob   and  Joseph and Simon and
2455      56  2532 017 79      846      3780 3956   4314
Ἰούδας;     καὶ  αἱ  ἀδελφαὶ αὐτοῦ οὐχὶ πᾶσαι πρὸς
Judas?      And the sisters  of him not  all   toward
1473 1510    4159        3767 3778          3778 3956
ἡμᾶς εἰσιν; πόθεν   οὖν τούτῳ        ταῦτα πάντα;
us   are?  From where then to this one these all?
   2532 4624                1722 846    01   1161  2424
57 καὶ ἐσκανδαλίζοντο  ἐν  αὐτῷ. ὁ  δὲ  Ἰησοῦς
   And they were offended in  him. The but  Jesus
3004  846        3756 1510 4396       846      1487 3361
εἶπεν αὐτοῖς· οὐκ ἔστιν προφήτης ἄτιμος  εἰ  μὴ
said  to them, not is   spokesman dishonored except
1722 07  3968      2532 1722 07  3614   846     58  2532
ἐν  τῇ  πατρίδι καὶ ἐν  τῇ  οἰκίᾳ αὐτοῦ.    καὶ
in   the fatherland and in  the house of him.    And
```

The angels will come out and separate the evil from the righteous [50]and throw them into the furnace of fire, where there will be weeping and gnashing of teeth.

[51] "Have you understood all this?" They answered, "Yes." [52]And he said to them, "Therefore every scribe who has been trained for the kingdom of heaven is like the master of a household who brings out of his treasure what is new and what is old." [53]When Jesus had finished these parables, he left that place.

[54] He came to his hometown and began to teach the people[a] in their synagogue, so that they were astounded and said, "Where did this man get this wisdom and these deeds of power? [55]Is not this the carpenter's son? Is not his mother called Mary? And are not his brothers James and Joseph and Simon and Judas? [56]And are not all his sisters with us? Where then did this man get all this?" [57]And they took offense at him. But Jesus said to them, "Prophets are not without honor except in their own country and in their own house." [58]And he did not do many deeds of power there, because of their unbelief.

---

[a] Gk them

CHAPTER 14

At that time Herod the ruler*a* heard reports about Jesus; ²and he said to his servants, "This is John the Baptist; he has been raised from the dead, and for this reason these powers are at work in him." ³For Herod had arrested John, bound him, and put him in prison on account of Herodias, his brother Philip's wife,*b* ⁴because John had been telling him, "It is not lawful for you to have her." ⁵Though Herod*c* wanted to put him to death, he feared the crowd, because they regarded him as a prophet. ⁶But when Herod's birthday came, the daughter of Herodias danced before the company, and she pleased Herod ⁷so much that he promised on oath to grant her whatever she might ask. ⁸Prompted by her mother, she said, "Give me the head of John the Baptist here on a platter." ⁹The king was grieved, yet out of regard for his oaths and for the guests, he commanded it to be given; ¹⁰he sent and had John beheaded in the prison. ¹¹The head was brought

a Gk *tetrarch*
b Other ancient authorities read *his brother's wife*
c Gk *he*

3756	4160		1563	1411		4183	1223		08
οὐκ	ἐποίησεν	ἐκεῖ	δυνάμεις	πολλὰς	διὰ				τὴν
not	he did	there	powers	many	because of the

570		846	14:1	1722	1565	03	2540	191
ἀπιστίαν	αὐτῶν.		᾿Εν	ἐκείνῳ	τῷ	καιρῷ	ἤκουσεν
untrust	of them.		In	that	the	season	heard

2264 01 5076 08 189 2424 2532
῾Ηρῴδης ὁ τετραάρχης τὴν ἀκοὴν ᾿Ιησοῦ, ² καὶ
Herod the ruler of fourth the hearing of Jesus, and

3004 015 3816 846 3778 1510
εἶπεν τοῖς παισὶν αὐτοῦ· οὗτός ἐστιν
he said to the boy servants of him, this is

2491 01 910 846 1453 575 014
᾿Ιωάννης ὁ βαπτιστής· αὐτὸς ἠγέρθη ἀπὸ τῶν
John the immerser; himself was raised from the

3498 2532 1223 3778 017 1411 1754
νεκρῶν καὶ διὰ τοῦτο αἱ δυνάμεις ἐνεργοῦσιν
dead and because of this the powers operate

1722 846 ³ 01 1063 2264 2902 04 2491
ἐν αὐτῷ. ῾Ο γὰρ ῾Ηρῴδης κρατήσας τὸν ᾿Ιωάννην
in him. The for Herod having held the John

1210 846 2532 1722 5438 659 1223
ἔδησεν [αὐτὸν] καὶ ἐν φυλακῇ ἀπέθετο διὰ
bound him and in guard he set off because of

2266 08 1135 5376 02 80 846
῾Ηρῳδιάδα τὴν γυναῖκα Φιλίππου τοῦ ἀδελφοῦ αὐτοῦ·
Herodias the woman of Philipp the brother of him;

4 3004 1063 01 2491 846 3756 1832
ἔλεγεν γὰρ ὁ ᾿Ιωάννης αὐτῷ· οὐκ ἔξεστίν
was saying for the John to him; not it is
possible

1473 2192 846 ⁵ 2532 2309 846 615
σοι ἔχειν αὐτήν. καὶ θέλων αὐτὸν ἀποκτεῖναι
to you to have her. And wanting him to kill

5399 04 3793 3754 5613 4396 846
ἐφοβήθη τὸν ὄχλον, ὅτι ὡς προφήτην αὐτὸν
he feared the crowd, because as spokesman him

2192 ⁶ 1077 1161 1096 02 2264
εἶχον. Γενεσίοις δὲ γενομένοις τοῦ ῾Ηρῴδου
they had. Birthday but having become of the Herod

3738 05 2364 06 2266 1722 011 3319
ὠρχήσατο ἡ θυγάτηρ τῆς ῾Ηρῳδιάδος ἐν τῷ μέσῳ
danced the daughter of the Herodias in the middle

2532 700 03 2264 ⁷ 3606 3326 3727
καὶ ἤρεσεν τῷ ῾Ηρῴδῃ, ὅθεν μεθ᾿ ὅρκου
and she pleased the Herod, from where with oath

3670 846 1325 3739 1437 154
ὡμολόγησεν αὐτῇ δοῦναι ὃ ἐὰν αἰτήσηται.
he confessed to her to give what if she might ask.

8 05 1161 4264 5259 06 3384
ἡ δὲ προβιβασθεῖσα ὑπὸ τῆς μητρὸς
The one but having been led forward by the mother

846 1325 1473 5346 5602 1909 4094
αὐτῆς· δός μοι, φησίν, ὧδε ἐπὶ πίνακι
of her; give to me, she says, here on platter

08 2776 2491 02 910 ⁹ 2532
τὴν κεφαλὴν ᾿Ιωάννου τοῦ βαπτιστοῦ. καὶ
the head of John the immerser. And

3076 01 935 1223 016
λυπηθεὶς ὁ βασιλεὺς διὰ τοὺς
having been grieved the king on account of the

3727 2532 016 4873 2753
ὅρκους καὶ τοὺς συνανακειμένους ἐκέλευσεν
oaths and the ones reclining together he commanded

1325 2532 3992 607 04
δοθῆναι, ¹⁰ καὶ πέμψας ἀπεκεφάλισεν [τὸν]
to be given, and having sent he cut off head the

2491 1722 07 5438 ¹¹ 2532 5342 05
᾿Ιωάννην ἐν τῇ φυλακῇ. καὶ ἠνέχθη ἡ
John in the guard. And was brought the

2776   846   1909 4094   2532 1325   011
κεφαλὴ αὐτοῦ ἐπὶ πίνακι καὶ ἐδόθη   τῷ
head   of him on   platter and it was given to the

2877   2532 5342   07   3384   846
κορασίῳ,   καὶ ἤνεγκεν   τῇ   μητρὶ   αὐτῆς.
young girl, and she brought to the mother of her.

   2532 4334   013 3101   846   142
12 καὶ προσελθόντες οἱ μαθηταὶ αὐτοῦ ἦραν
   And having come to the learners of him lifted up

012 4430   2532 2290   846   2532 2064
τὸ πτῶμα καὶ ἔθαψαν αὐτὸ[ν] καὶ ἐλθόντες
the corpse and buried him   and having come

518   03   2424   191   1161 01   2424
ἀπήγγειλαν τῷ   Ἰησοῦ. 13 Ἀκούσας δὲ   ὁ   Ἰησοῦς
they told to the Jesus. Having heard but the Jesus

402   1564   1722 4143 1519 2048   5117 2596
ἀνεχώρησεν ἐκεῖθεν ἐν πλοίῳ εἰς ἔρημον τόπον κατ'
departed   from there in boat into desert place by

2398   2532 191   013 3793   190   846
ἰδίαν· καὶ ἀκούσαντες οἱ ὄχλοι ἠκολούθησαν αὐτῷ
own;   and having heard the crowds followed him

3979   575   018 4172   2532 1831
πεζῇ   ἀπὸ τῶν πόλεων. 14 Καὶ ἐξελθὼν
on foot from the cities.   And having gone out

3708   4183   3793 2532 4697   1909 846   2532
εἶδεν πολὺν ὄχλον καὶ ἐσπλαγχνίσθη ἐπ' αὐτοῖς καὶ
he saw much crowd and had affection on   them   and

2323   016 732   846   3798   1161
ἐθεράπευσεν τοὺς ἀρρώστους αὐτῶν. 15 Ὀψίας δὲ
he healed   the feeble   of them. Evening but

1096   4334   846 013 3101   3004
γενομένης προσῆλθον αὐτῷ οἱ μαθηταὶ λέγοντες·
having become came toward him the learners saying,

2048   1510 01 5117 2532 05 5610 2235   3928
ἔρημός ἐστιν ὁ τόπος καὶ ἡ ὥρα ἤδη   παρῆλθεν·
desert is   the place and the hour already came along;

630   016 3793   2443 565   1519 020
ἀπόλυσον τοὺς ὄχλους, ἵνα ἀπελθόντες εἰς τὰς
loose off the crowds, that having gone off into the

2968   59   1438   1033   16 01
κώμας ἀγοράσωσιν ἑαυτοῖς βρώματα.   ὁ
villages they might buy to themselves food. The

1161   2424   3004 846   3756 5532   2192
δὲ [Ἰησοῦς] εἶπεν αὐτοῖς· οὐ χρείαν ἔχουσιν
but   Jesus said to them, not need they have

565   1325 846   1473 2068   17 013   1161
ἀπελθεῖν, δότε αὐτοῖς ὑμεῖς φαγεῖν.   οἱ   δὲ
to go off; give to them you   to eat.   The ones but

3004   846   3756 2192   5602 1487 3361 4002
λέγουσιν αὐτῷ· οὐκ ἔχομεν ὧδε εἰ μὴ πέντε
say   to him; not we have here except five

740   2532 1417 2486   18 01   1161 3004   5342
ἄρτους καὶ δύο ἰχθύας.   ὁ   δὲ εἶπεν· φέρετέ
breads and two fish.   The one but said, carry

1473 5602 846   19 2532 2753   016 3793
μοι ὧδε αὐτούς.   καὶ κελεύσας   τοὺς ὄχλους
to me here them.   And having commanded the crowds

347   1909 02 5528   2983   016 4002
ἀνακλιθῆναι ἐπὶ τοῦ χόρτου, λαβὼν   τοὺς πέντε
to be reclined on the grass, having taken the five

740   2532 016 1417 2486   308   1519
ἄρτους καὶ τοὺς δύο ἰχθύας, ἀναβλέψας εἰς
breads and the two fish,   having looked up into

04 3772   2127   2532 2806 1325
τὸν οὐρανὸν εὐλόγησεν καὶ κλάσας ἔδωκεν
the heaven he spoke well and having broken gave

015   3101   016 740   013 1161 3101   015
τοῖς μαθηταῖς τοὺς ἄρτους, οἱ δὲ μαθηταὶ τοῖς
to the learners the breads, the but learners to the

on a platter and given to the girl, who brought it to her mother. [12]His disciples came and took the body and buried it; then they went and told Jesus.

13 Now when Jesus heard this, he withdrew from there in a boat to a deserted place by himself. But when the crowds heard it, they followed him on foot from the towns. [14]When he went ashore, he saw a great crowd; and he had compassion for them and cured their sick. [15]When it was evening, the disciples came to him and said, "This is a deserted place, and the hour is now late; send the crowds away so that they may go into the villages and buy food for themselves." [16]Jesus said to them, "They need not go away; you give them something to eat." [17]They replied, "We have nothing here but five loaves and two fish." [18]And he said, "Bring them here to me." [19]Then he ordered the crowds to sit down on the grass. Taking the five loaves and the two fish, he looked up to heaven, and blessed and broke the loaves, and gave them to the disciples, and the disciples gave them to the crowds.

20And all ate and were
filled; and they took up
what was left over of the
broken pieces, twelve
baskets full. 21And those
who ate were about five
thousand men, besides
women and children.

22 Immediately he made
the disciples get into the
boat and go on ahead to
the other side, while he
dismissed the crowds.
23And after he had
dismissed the crowds, he
went up the mountain by
himself to pray. When
evening came, he was there
alone, 24but by this time the
boat, battered by the waves,
was far from the land,ᵃ for
the wind was against them.
25And early in the morning
he came walking toward
them on the sea. 26But
when the disciples saw
him walking on the sea,
they were terrified, saying,
"It is a ghost!" And they
cried out in fear. 27But
immediately Jesus spoke to
them and said, "Take heart,
it is I; do not be afraid."

28 Peter answered him,
"Lord, if it is you,
command me to come to
you on the water." 29He
said, "Come." So Peter got
out of the boat, started
walking on the water, and
came toward Jesus.

ᵃ Other ancient authorities read
was out on the sea

```
3793        2532 2068    3956    2532 5526              2532
ὄχλοις.  20  καὶ ἔφαγον πάντες καὶ ἐχορτάσθησαν, καὶ
crowds.     And ate    all    and were satisfied, and
142              012 4052       022    2801          1427
ἦραν          τὸ περισσεῦον τῶν κλασμάτων δώδεκα
they lifted up the exceeding of the fragments twelve
2894           4134       21  013        1161 2068
κοφίνους     πλήρεις.     οἱ    δὲ   ἐσθίοντες
wicker baskets full.        The ones but eating
1510 435    5616 4000          5565      1135     2532
ἦσαν ἄνδρες ὡσεὶ πεντακισχίλιοι χωρὶς γυναικῶν καὶ
were men    as   five thousand without women    and
3813          22 2532 2112       315       016
παιδίων.       Καὶ εὐθέως     ἠνάγκασεν τοὺς
small children. And immediately he compelled the
3101     1684      1519 012 4143   2532 4254
μαθητὰς ἐμβῆναι εἰς τὸ πλοῖον καὶ προάγειν
learners to go in into the boat and to lead before
846    1519 012 4008     2193 3739 630
αὐτὸν εἰς τὸ πέραν,   ἕως οὗ ἀπολύσῃ
him   into the across, until which he might loose off
016   3793     23 2532 630          016   3793
τοὺς ὄχλους.    καὶ ἀπολύσας     τοὺς ὄχλους
the  crowds.    And having loosed off the  crowds
305      1519 012 3735 2596 2398 4336
ἀνέβη  εἰς τὸ ὄρος κατ' ἰδίαν προσεύξασθαι.
he went up into the hill by own  to pray.
3798      1161 1096        3441  1510 1563   24 09
ὀψίας  δὲ γενομένης μόνος ἦν ἐκεῖ.        τὸ
Evening but having become alone he was there.   The
1161 4143  2235    4712       4183   575 06 1093
δὲ πλοῖον ἤδη  σταδίους πολλοὺς ἀπὸ τῆς γῆς
but boat already stadia many     from the land
568      928           5259 022 2949   1510 1063
ἀπεῖχεν βασανιζόμενον ὑπὸ τῶν κυμάτων, ἦν γὰρ
held off being tormented by the waves, was for
1727     01  417     25 5067      1161 5438   06
ἐναντίος ὁ ἄνεμος.    τετάρτη δὲ φυλακῇ τῆς
against the wind.       In fourth but guard of the
3571   2064    4314 846   4043        1909 08
νυκτὸς ἦλθεν πρὸς αὐτοὺς περιπατῶν ἐπὶ τὴν
night he came to   them   walking around on  the
2281      26 013 1161 3101    3708      846   1909
θάλασσαν.   οἱ δὲ μαθηταὶ ἰδόντες αὐτὸν ἐπὶ
sea.         The but learners having seen him on
06 2281     4043         5015        3004
τῆς θαλάσσης περιπατοῦντα ἐταράχθησαν λέγοντες
the sea      walking around were troubled saying,
3754 5326     1510    2532 575 02 5401  2896
ὅτι φάντασμά ἐστιν, καὶ ἀπὸ τοῦ φόβου ἔκραξαν.
(") ghost    he is, and from the fear they shouted.
27 2117       1161 2980     01 2424    846   3004
εὐθὺς      δὲ ἐλάλησεν [ὁ Ἰησοῦς] αὐτοῖς λέγων·
Immediately but spoke    the Jesus  to them saying,
2293       1473 1510 3361 5399   28 611
θαρσεῖτε, ἐγώ εἰμι· μὴ φοβεῖσθε.   ἀποκριθεὶς
take courage, I am;  not be feared. Having answered
1161 846  01 4074   3004     2962     1487 1473 1510
δὲ αὐτῷ ὁ Πέτρος εἶπεν· κύριε, εἰ σὺ εἶ,
but to him the Peter said, Master, if you are,
2753    1473 2064   4314 846  1909 024 5204   29 01
κέλευσόν με ἐλθεῖν πρός σε ἐπὶ τὰ ὕδατα.     ὁ
command me to come to  you on the waters. The one
1161 3004   2064 2532 2597          575 010 4143
δὲ εἶπεν· ἐλθέ. καὶ καταβὰς     ἀπὸ τοῦ πλοίου
but said, come. And having gone down from the boat
01 4074    4043          1909 024 5204   2532 2064
[ὁ] Πέτρος περιεπάτησεν ἐπὶ τὰ ὕδατα καὶ ἦλθεν
the Peter  walked around on  the waters and he came
```

| 4314 | 04 | 2424 | **30** | 991 | 1161 | 04 | 417 | 2478 |
πρὸς τὸν Ἰησοῦν. **30** βλέπων δὲ τὸν ἄνεμον [ἰσχυρὸν]
toward the Jesus.   Seeing but the wind   strong

5399   2532 757   2670
ἐφοβήθη,   καὶ ἀρξάμενος καταποντίζεσθαι
he was feared, and having begun to be drowned

2896   3004   2962   4982   1473 **31** 2112
ἔκραξεν λέγων· κύριε, σῶσόν με.   **31** εὐθέως
he shouted saying, Master, deliver me.   Immediately

1161 01 2424   1614   08   5495   1949
δὲ ὁ Ἰησοῦς ἐκτείνας   τὴν χεῖρα ἐπελάβετο
but the Jesus having stretched out the hand took on

846 2532 3004   846   3640   1519 5101
αὐτοῦ καὶ λέγει αὐτῷ· ὀλιγόπιστε,   εἰς τί
him and says to him, little trusting one, into what

1365   2532 305   846   1519 012
ἐδίστασας; **32** καὶ ἀναβάντων   αὐτῶν εἰς τὸ
you doubted? And having gone up them into the

4143   2869   01 417 **33** 013 1161 1722 011
πλοῖον ἐκόπασεν ὁ ἄνεμος. **33** οἱ   δὲ ἐν τῷ
boat ceased the wind.   The ones but in the

4143 4352   846 3004   230   2316   5207
πλοίῳ προσεκύνησαν αὐτῷ λέγοντες· ἀληθῶς θεοῦ υἱὸς
boat worshiped   him saying,   truly of God son

1510   **34** 2532 1276   2064   1909 08
εἶ.   **34** Καὶ διαπεράσαντες ἦλθον ἐπὶ τὴν
you are. And having crossed over they came on the

1093 1519 1082   **35** 2532 1921   846   013
γῆν εἰς Γεννησαρέτ. **35** καὶ ἐπιγνόντες αὐτὸν οἱ
land into Gennesaret.   And having perceived him the

435 02   5117 1565   649   1519 3650 08
ἄνδρες τοῦ τόπου ἐκείνου ἀπέστειλαν εἰς ὅλην τὴν
men of the place that delegated into whole the

4066   1565   2532 4374   846 3956
περίχωρον ἐκείνην καὶ προσήνεγκαν αὐτῷ πάντας
country around that and they brought to him all

016 2560 2192 **36** 2532 3870   846
τοὺς κακῶς ἔχοντας, **36** καὶ παρεκάλουν αὐτὸν
the badly having,   and they were encouraging him

2443 3441 681   010 2899   010 2440
ἵνα μόνον ἄψωνται τοῦ κρασπέδου τοῦ ἱματίου
that alone they might touch the edge of the clothes

846   2532 3745 681 1295   5119
αὐτοῦ· καὶ ὅσοι ἥψαντο διεσώθησαν. **15:1** Τότε
of him; and as many touched were thoroughly Then
as   delivered.

4334   03   2424 575 2414   5330   2532
προσέρχονται τῷ Ἰησοῦ ἀπὸ Ἱεροσολύμων Φαρισαῖοι καὶ
came toward the Jesus from Jerusalem Pharisees and

1122   3004   **2** 1223   5101 013 3101
γραμματεῖς λέγοντες· **2** διὰ   τί οἱ μαθηταί
writers saying,   on account of what the learners

1473   3845   08 3862   014   4245
σου παραβαίνουσιν τὴν παράδοσιν τῶν πρεσβυτέρων;
of you go across the tradition of the older men?

3756 1063 3538   020 5495 846   3752 740
οὐ γὰρ νίπτονται τὰς χεῖρας [αὐτῶν] ὅταν ἄρτον
Not for they wash the hands of them when bread

2068   **3** 01   1161 611   3004
ἐσθίωσιν. **3** ὁ   δὲ ἀποκριθεὶς εἶπεν
they might eat. The one but having answered said

846   1223   5101 2532 1473 3845   08
αὐτοῖς· διὰ   τί καὶ ὑμεῖς παραβαίνετε τὴν
to them, on account of what also you go across the

1785 02   2316 1223 08 3862   1473 **4** 01
ἐντολὴν τοῦ θεοῦ διὰ τὴν παράδοσιν ὑμῶν; **4** ὁ
command of the God through the tradition of you? The

1063 2316 3004   5091 04 3962 2532 08 3384   2532
γὰρ θεὸς εἶπεν· τίμα τὸν πατέρα καὶ τὴν μητέρα, καί,
for God said, value the father and the mother, and,

[30]But when he noticed the strong wind,[a] he became frightened, and beginning to sink, he cried out, "Lord, save me!" [31]Jesus immediately reached out his hand and caught him, saying to him, "You of little faith, why did you doubt?" [32]When they got into the boat, the wind ceased. [33]And those in the boat worshiped him, saying, "Truly you are the Son of God."

34 When they had crossed over, they came to land at Gennesaret. [35]After the people of that place recognized him, they sent word throughout the region and brought all who were sick to him, [36]and begged him that they might touch even the fringe of his cloak; and all who touched it were healed.

CHAPTER 15

Then Pharisees and scribes came to Jesus from Jerusalem and said, [2]"Why do your disciples break the tradition of the elders? For they do not wash their hands before they eat." [3]He answered them, "And why do you break the commandment of God for the sake of your tradition? [4]For God said,[b] 'Honor your father and your mother,' and,

[a] Other ancient authorities read *the wind*

[b] Other ancient authorities read *commanded, saying*

'Whoever speaks evil of father or mother must surely die.' [5]But you say that whoever tells father or mother, 'Whatever support you might have had from me is given to God,'[a] then that person need not honor the father.[b] [6]So, for the sake of your tradition, you make void the word[c] of God. [7]You hypocrites! Isaiah prophesied rightly about you when he said:

[8] 'This people honors me
    with their lips,
    but their hearts are far
    from me;
[9] in vain do they worship
    me,
    teaching human precepts
    as doctrines.'"

10 Then he called the crowd to him and said to them, "Listen and understand: [11]it is not what goes into the mouth that defiles a person, but it is what comes out of the mouth that defiles." [12]Then the disciples approached and said to him, "Do you know that the Pharisees took offense when they heard what you said?" [13]He answered, "Every plant that my heavenly Father has not planted will be uprooted. [14]Let them alone; they are blind guides of the blind.[d] And if one blind person guides another, both will fall into a pit." [15]But Peter said to him, "Explain this parable to us." [16]Then he said,

a Or is an offering
b Other ancient authorities add or the mother
c Other ancient authorities read law; others, commandment
d Other ancient authorities lack of the blind

01	2551	3962	2228	3384	2288
ὁ	κακολογῶν	πατέρα ἢ		μητέρα	θανάτῳ
the	one speaking bad	father or		mother	death

5053   1473 1161 3004   3739 302 3004
τελευτάτω. **5** ὑμεῖς δὲ λέγετε· ὃς ἂν εἴπῃ
let die. You but say, who - might say

03   3962 2228 07 3384   1435 3739 1437 1537
τῷ πατρὶ ἢ τῇ μητρί· δῶρον ὃ ἐὰν ἐξ
to the father or the mother, gift what if out

1473 5623   3756 3361 5091   04 3962
ἐμοῦ ὠφεληθῇς, **6** οὐ μὴ τιμήσει τὸν πατέρα
of me you might have not not he will the father
    benefitted,   value

846   2532 208   04 3056 02   2316 1223
αὐτοῦ· καὶ ἠκυρώσατε τὸν λόγον τοῦ θεοῦ διὰ
of him; and invalidate the word of the God through

08 3862   1473   5273   2573 4395
τὴν παράδοσιν ὑμῶν. **7** ὑποκριταί, καλῶς ἐπροφήτευσεν
the tradition of you. Hypocrites, well spoke before

4012   1473 2268 3004 **8** 01 2992 3778
περὶ ὑμῶν Ἡσαΐας λέγων· ὁ λαὸς οὗτος
concerning you Isaiah saying, the people this

023   5491   1473 5091   05 1161 2588 846
τοῖς χείλεσίν με τιμᾷ, ἡ δὲ καρδία αὐτῶν
in the lips me values, the but heart of them

4206 568   575 1473 **9** 3155   1161 4576
πόρρω ἀπέχει ἀπ᾽ ἐμοῦ· μάτην δὲ σέβονταί
far holds off from me; in futility but they worship

1473 1321   1319   1778   444
με διδάσκοντες διδασκαλίας ἐντάλματα ἀνθρώπων.
me teaching teachings commands of men.

10 2532 4341   04 3793 3004 846
καὶ προσκαλεσάμενος τὸν ὄχλον εἶπεν αὐτοῖς·
And having called toward the crowd he said to them;

191   2532 4920 **11** 3756 09 1525
ἀκούετε καὶ συνίετε· οὐ τὸ εἰσερχόμενον
hear and understand; not the thing going into

1519 012 4750 2840   04 444   235 09
εἰς τὸ στόμα κοινοῖ τὸν ἄνθρωπον, ἀλλὰ τὸ
into the mouth makes common the man, but the

1607   1537 010 4750 3778 2840
ἐκπορευόμενον ἐκ τοῦ στόματος τοῦτο κοινοῖ
thing traveling out from the mouth this makes common

04 444   12 5119 4334   013 3101
τὸν ἄνθρωπον. **12** Τότε προσελθόντες · οἱ μαθηταὶ
the man. Then having come toward the learners

3004 846   3609a 3754 013 5330   191
λέγουσιν αὐτῷ· οἶδας ὅτι οἱ Φαρισαῖοι ἀκούσαντες
say to him, you know that the Pharisees having heard

04 3056 4624   01 1161 611
τὸν λόγον ἐσκανδαλίσθησαν; **13** ὁ δὲ ἀποκριθεὶς
the word were offended? The one but having answered

3004 3956 5451 3739 3756 5452   01 3962
εἶπεν· πᾶσα φυτεία ἣν οὐκ ἐφύτευσεν ὁ πατήρ
said; all plant which not planted the father

1473 01 3770   1610   14 863
μου ὁ οὐράνιος ἐκριζωθήσεται. **14** ἄφετε
of me the heavenly will be rooted out. Send off

846   5185 1510 3595   5185   5185 1161
αὐτούς· τυφλοί εἰσιν ὁδηγοί [τυφλῶν]· τυφλὸς δὲ
them; blind are guides of blind; blind but

5185 1437 3594   297   1519 999
τυφλὸν ἐὰν ὁδηγῇ ἀμφότεροι εἰς βόθυνον
blind if might guide both into ditch

4098   15 611   1161 01 4074 3004
πεσοῦνται. **15** Ἀποκριθεὶς δὲ ὁ Πέτρος εἶπεν
will fall. Having answered but the Peter said

846   5419   1473 08 3850   3778   16 01
αὐτῷ· φράσον ἡμῖν τὴν παραβολὴν [ταύτην]. **16** ὁ
to him, explain to us the parallel story this. The

1161 3004   188   2532 1473 801   1510
δὲ εἶπεν· ἀκμὴν καὶ ὑμεῖς ἀσύνετοί   ἐστε;
but said;   even now also you   not understanding are?

   3756 3539   3754 3956 09 1531
17 οὐ νοεῖτε   ὅτι πᾶν τὸ εἰσπορευόμενον
   Not you give thought that all the traveling into
1519 012 4750 1519 08 2836   5562   2532 1519
εἰς τὸ στόμα εἰς τὴν κοιλίαν χωρεῖ   καὶ εἰς
into the mouth into the stomach makes room and into
856   1544   021 1161 1607
ἀφεδρῶνα ἐκβάλλεται;   18 τὰ δὲ ἐκπορευόμενα
latrine it is thrown out? The but traveling out
1537 010 4750   1537 06 2588   1831
ἐκ τοῦ στόματος ἐκ τῆς καρδίας ἐξέρχεται,
out of the mouth out of the heart comes out,
2548   2840   04 444   1537 1063 06
κἀκεῖνα κοινοῖ   τὸν ἄνθρωπον. 19 ἐκ γὰρ τῆς
and that makes common the man.   Out of for the
2588   1831   1261   4190   5408
καρδίας ἐξέρχονται διαλογισμοὶ πονηροί, φόνοι,
heart come out   reasonings evil,   murders,
3430   4202   2829   5577
μοιχεῖαι, πορνεῖαι, κλοπαί, ψευδομαρτυρίαι,
adulteries, sexual thefts, false testimonies,
         immoralities,
988   3778 1510 021   2840
βλασφημίαι. 20 ταῦτά ἐστιν τὰ   κοινοῦντα
insults.   These are the things making common
04 444   09 1161 449   5495   2068 3756
τὸν ἄνθρωπον, τὸ δὲ ἀνίπτοις χερσὶν φαγεῖν οὐ
the man,   the but unwashed hands to eat not
2840   04 444   2532 1831
κοινοῖ   τὸν ἄνθρωπον. 21 Καὶ ἐξελθὼν
makes common· the man.   And having gone out
1564   01 2424 402   1519 024 3313
ἐκεῖθεν ὁ ᾿Ιησοῦς ἀνεχώρησεν εἰς τὰ μέρη
from there the Jesus departed   into the parts
5184   2532 4605   2532 2400 1135   5478
Τύρου καὶ Σιδῶνος. 22 καὶ ἰδοὺ γυνὴ Χαναναία
of Tyre and Sidon.   And look woman Canaanite
575 022 3725   1565   1831   2896
ἀπὸ τῶν ὁρίων   ἐκείνων ἐξελθοῦσα ἔκραζεν
from the territories those having come out shouted
3004   1653   1473 3962   5207 1160a 05 2364
λέγουσα· ἐλέησόν με, κύριε υἱὸς Δαυίδ· ἡ θυγάτηρ
saying, mercy me, Master, son David· the daughter
1473 2560 1139   01   1161 3756 611
μου κακῶς δαιμονίζεται. 23 ὁ   δὲ οὐκ ἀπεκρίθη
of me badly is demonized.   The one but not answered
846   3056   2532 4334   013 3101   846
αὐτῇ λόγον. καὶ προσελθόντες οἱ μαθηταὶ αὐτοῦ
to her word. And having come to the learners of him
2065   846   3004   630   846   3754
ἠρώτουν αὐτὸν λέγοντες· ἀπόλυσον αὐτήν, ὅτι
were asking him saying, loose off her,   because
2896   3693   1473   01 1161 611
κράζει ὄπισθεν ἡμῶν. 24 ὁ δὲ ἀποκριθεὶς
she shouts from behind us.   The one but having answered
3004 3756 649   1487 3361 1519 024 4263
εἶπεν· οὐκ ἀπεστάλην εἰ μὴ εἰς τὰ πρόβατα
said, not I was delegated except to the sheep
024 622   3624   2474   05
τὰ ἀπολωλότα   οἴκου ᾿Ισραήλ. 25 ἡ
the ones having destroyed of house Israel.   The one
1161 2064   4352   846 3004   2962
δὲ ἐλθοῦσα προσεκύνει αὐτῷ λέγουσα· κύριε,
but having come was worshiping him saying; Master,
997   1473   01   1161 611   3004
βοήθει μοι. 26 ὁ   δὲ ἀποκριθεὶς εἶπεν·
help me.   The one but having answered said,

"Are you also still without understanding? [17]Do you not see that whatever goes into the mouth enters the stomach, and goes out into the sewer? [18]But what comes out of the mouth proceeds from the heart, and this is what defiles. [19]For out of the heart come evil intentions, murder, adultery, fornication, theft, false witness, slander. [20]These are what defile a person, but to eat with unwashed hands does not defile."

[21]Jesus left that place and went away to the district of Tyre and Sidon. [22]Just then a Canaanite woman from that region came out and started shouting, "Have mercy on me, Lord, Son of David; my daughter is tormented by a demon." [23]But he did not answer her at all. And his disciples came and urged him, saying, "Send her away, for she keeps shouting after us." [24]He answered, "I was sent only to the lost sheep of the house of Israel." [25]But she came and knelt before him, saying, "Lord, help me." [26]He answered,

"It is not fair to take the children's food and throw it to the dogs." [27]She said, "Yes, Lord, yet even the dogs eat the crumbs that fall from their masters' table." [28]Then Jesus answered her, "Woman, great is your faith! Let it be done for you as you wish." And her daughter was healed instantly.

29 After Jesus had left that place, he passed along the Sea of Galilee, and he went up the mountain, where he sat down. [30]Great crowds came to him, bringing with them the lame, the maimed, the blind, the mute, and many others. They put them at his feet, and he cured them, [31]so that the crowd was amazed when they saw the mute speaking, the maimed whole, the lame walking, and the blind seeing. And they praised the God of Israel.

32 Then Jesus called his disciples to him and said, "I have compassion for the crowd, because they have been with me now for three days and have nothing to eat; and I do not want to send them away hungry, for they might faint on the way."

3756	1510	2570	2983	04	740	022	5043
οὐκ	ἔστιν	καλὸν	λαβεῖν	τὸν	ἄρτον	τῶν	τέκνων
not	it is	good	to take	the	bread	of the	children

2532	906	023	2952		05		1161	3004
καὶ	βαλεῖν	τοῖς	κυναρίοις.	27	ἡ		δὲ	εἶπεν·
and	to throw	to the	puppies.		The one		but	said;

3483	2962	2532	1063	021	2952	2068	575	022
ναὶ	κύριε,	καὶ	γὰρ	τὰ	κυνάρια	ἐσθίει	ἀπὸ	τῶν
yes	Master,	even	for	the	puppies	eat	from	the

5589	022	4098	575	06	5132	014
ψιχίων	τῶν	πιπτόντων	ἀπὸ	τῆς	τραπέζης	τῶν
small crumbs	of the	ones falling	from	the	table	the

2962	846	5119	611	01	2424
κυρίων	αὐτῶν. 28	τότε	ἀποκριθεὶς	ὁ	Ἰησοῦς
masters	of them.	Then	having answered	the	Jesus

3004	846	5599	1135	3173	1473	05	4102
εἶπεν	αὐτῇ·	ὦ	γύναι,	μεγάλη	σου	ἡ	πίστις·
said	to her;	o	woman,	great	of	you	the trust;

1096	1473	5613	2309	2532	2390	05	2364
γενηθήτω	σοι	ὡς	θέλεις.	καὶ	ἰάθη	ἡ	θυγάτηρ
let become	to you	as	you want.	And	was	the	daughter cured

846	575	06	5610	1565		2532	3327
αὐτῆς	ἀπὸ	τῆς	ὥρας	ἐκείνης.	29	Καὶ	μεταβὰς
of her	from	the	hour	that.		And	having gone across

1564	01	2424	2064	3844	08	2281	06
ἐκεῖθεν	ὁ	Ἰησοῦς	ἦλθεν	παρὰ	τὴν	θάλασσαν	τῆς
from there	the	Jesus	went	along	the	sea	of the

1056	2532	305	1519	012	3735	2521
Γαλιλαίας,	καὶ	ἀναβὰς	εἰς	τὸ	ὄρος	ἐκάθητο
Galilee,	and	having gone up	into	the	hill	he sat

1563		2532	4334	846	3793	4183	2192
ἐκεῖ.	30	καὶ	προσῆλθον	αὐτῷ	ὄχλοι	πολλοὶ	ἔχοντες
there.		And	came toward	him	crowds	many	having

3326	1438	5560	5185	2948	2974
μεθ᾽	ἑαυτῶν	χωλούς,	τυφλούς,	κυλλούς,	κωφούς,
with	themselves	lame,	blind,	crippled,	deaf,

2532	2087	4183	2532	4496	846	3844	016
καὶ	ἑτέρους	πολλοὺς,	καὶ	ἔρριψαν	αὐτοὺς	παρὰ	τοὺς
and	others	many,	and	they flung	them	along	the

4228	846	2532	2323	846		5620	04
πόδας	αὐτοῦ,	καὶ	ἐθεράπευσεν	αὐτούς·	31	ὥστε	τὸν
feet	of him,	and	he healed	them;		so that	the

3793	2296	991	2974	2980	2948
ὄχλον	θαυμάσαι	βλέποντας	κωφοὺς	λαλοῦντας,	κυλλοὺς
crowd	to marvel	seeing	deaf	speaking,	crippled

5199	2532	5560	4043	2532	5185
ὑγιεῖς	καὶ	χωλοὺς	περιπατοῦντας	καὶ	τυφλοὺς
healthy	and	lame	walking around	and	blind

991	2532	1392	04	2316	2474
βλέποντας·	καὶ	ἐδόξασαν	τὸν	θεὸν	Ἰσραήλ.
seeing;	and	they gave splendor	the	God	Israel.

	01	1161	2424	4341	016	3101
32	Ὁ	δὲ	Ἰησοῦς	προσκαλεσάμενος	τοὺς	μαθητὰς
	The	but	Jesus	having called toward	the	learners

846	3004	4697	1909	04	3793	3754
αὐτοῦ	εἶπεν·	σπλαγχνίζομαι	ἐπὶ	τὸν	ὄχλον,	ὅτι
of him	said;	I have affection	on	the	crowd,	because

2235	2250	5140	4357	1473	2532	3756
ἤδη	ἡμέραι	τρεῖς	προσμένουσίν	μοι	καὶ	οὐκ
already	days	three	they stay toward	me	and	not

2192	5101	2068	2532	630	846
ἔχουσιν	τί	φάγωσιν·	καὶ	ἀπολῦσαι	αὐτοὺς
they have	what	they might eat;	and	to loose off	them

3523	3756	2309	3379	1590	1722	07	3598
νήστεις	οὐ	θέλω,	μήποτε	ἐκλυθῶσιν	ἐν	τῇ	ὁδῷ.
fasting	not	I want,	not then	they might in		the	way.
				be loosed out			

33
```
     2532 3004      846      013  3101          4159        1473
33  καὶ λέγουσιν αὐτῷ  οἱ μαθηταί·  πόθεν       ἡμῖν
    And say      to him the learners, from where to us
```
```
    1722 2047    740    5118       5620        5526      3793
ἐν  ἐρημίᾳ ἄρτοι τοσοῦτοι ὥστε  χορτάσαι  ὄχλον
in  desert  breads such kind so that to satisfy crowd
```
```
    5118            2532 3004  846    01  2424     4214
τοσοῦτον;  34 καὶ λέγει αὐτοῖς ὁ  Ἰησοῦς· πόσους
such kind?    And says to them the Jesus,  how many
```
```
 740    2192      013      1161 3004   2033   2532
ἄρτους ἔχετε;  οἱ  δὲ  εἶπαν· ἑπτὰ καὶ
breads have you? The ones but said;  seven and
```
```
3641   2485           2532 3853         03      3793
ὀλίγα ἰχθύδια.  35 καὶ παραγγείλας  τῷ    ὄχλῳ
few    small fish.   And having commanded to the crowd
```
```
377       1909 08 1093    2983     016  2033  740
ἀναπεσεῖν ἐπὶ τὴν γῆν 36 ἔλαβεν τοὺς ἑπτὰ ἄρτους
to recline on the land    he took the seven breads
```
```
2532 016  2486   2532 2168          2806      2532 1325
καὶ τοὺς ἰχθύας καὶ εὐχαριστήσας ἔκλασεν καὶ ἐδίδου
and the fish   and having given    he broke and he was
                   good favor                    giving
```
```
015     3101      013 1161 3101      015      3793
τοῖς μαθηταῖς, οἱ δὲ  μαθηταὶ τοῖς ὄχλοις.
to the learners, the but learners to the crowds.
```
```
    2532 2068    3956   2532 5526              2532
37  καὶ ἔφαγον πάντες καὶ ἐχορτάσθησαν.    καὶ
    And ate    all     and they were satisfied. And
```
```
012 4052      022      2801       142         2033
τὸ περισσεῦον τῶν κλασμάτων ἦραν      ἑπτὰ
the exceeding of the fragments they lifted up seven
```
```
4711       4134       38 013       1161 2068       1510
σπυρίδας πλήρεις.    οἱ  δὲ  ἐσθίοντες ἦσαν
mat baskets full.      The ones but eating       were
```
```
5070             435        5565     1135       2532
τετρακισχίλιοι ἄνδρες χωρὶς γυναικῶν καὶ
four thousand   men    without women     and
```
```
3813           2532 630                016  3793
παιδίων.   39 Καὶ ἀπολύσας      τοὺς ὄχλους
small children.  And having loosed off the crowds
```
```
1684        1519 012 4143     2532 2064   1519 024
ἐνέβη      εἰς τὸ πλοῖον καὶ ἦλθεν εἰς τὰ
he went in into the boat   and he came into the
```
```
3725        3093           2532 4334            013
ὅρια       Μαγαδάν. 16:1 Καὶ προσελθόντες  οἱ
territories of Magadan.     And having come toward the
```
```
5330       2532 4523         3985        1905
Φαρισαῖοι καὶ Σαδδουκαῖοι πειράζοντες ἐπηρώτησαν
Pharisees and Sadducees    pressuring   asked on
```
```
846   4592   1537  02 3772     1925       846
αὐτὸν σημεῖον ἐκ  τοῦ οὐρανοῦ ἐπιδεῖξαι αὐτοῖς.
him   sign   out of the heaven  to show on to them.
```
```
  01        1161 611        3004  846      3798
2 ὁ   δὲ  ἀποκριθεὶς  εἶπεν αὐτοῖς· [ ὀψίας
  The one but having answered said to them; evening
```
```
1096        3004   2105    4449       1063 01
γενομένης λέγετε· εὐδία,  πυρράζει γὰρ ὁ
having become you say; good weather, reddens  for the
```
```
3772      3 2532 4404   4594    5494     4449    1063
οὐρανός.   καὶ πρωΐ·  σήμερον χειμών, πυρράζει γὰρ
heaven;     and morning; today  winter,  reddens  for
```
```
4768         01 3772     012 3303  4383     02
στυγνάζων ὁ οὐρανός. τὸ μὲν πρόσωπον τοῦ
becoming gloomy the heaven.  The indeed face    of the
```
```
3772      1097     1252              024 1161 4592
οὐρανοῦ γινώσκετε διακρίνειν,    τὰ δὲ σημεῖα
heaven you know  to judge thoroughly, the but signs
```
```
014     2540    3756 1410          4 1074     4190
τῶν  καιρῶν οὐ δύνασθε; ]  γενεὰ   πονηρὰ
of the seasons not you are able?   Generation evil
```

---

[33]The disciples said to him, "Where are we to get enough bread in the desert to feed so great a crowd?" [34]Jesus asked them, "How many loaves have you?" They said, "Seven, and a few small fish." [35]Then ordering the crowd to sit down on the ground, [36]he took the seven loaves and the fish; and after giving thanks he broke them and gave them to the disciples, and the disciples gave them to the crowds. [37]And all of them ate and were filled; and they took up the broken pieces left over, seven baskets full. [38]Those who had eaten were four thousand men, besides women and children. [39]After sending away the crowds, he got into the boat and went to the region of Magadan.[a]

CHAPTER 16

The Pharisees and Sadducees came, and to test Jesus[b] they asked him to show them a sign from heaven. [2]He answered them, "When it is evening, you say, 'It will be fair weather, for the sky is red.' [3]And in the morning, 'It will be stormy today, for the sky is red and threatening.' You know how to interpret the appearance of the sky, but you cannot interpret the signs of the times.[c] [4]An evil and adulterous generation

---

[a] Other ancient authorities read Magdala or Magdalan
[b] Gk him
[c] Other ancient authorities lack [2]When it is . . . of the times

asks for a sign, but no sign will be given to it except the sign of Jonah." Then he left them and went away.

5 When the disciples reached the other side, they had forgotten to bring any bread. 6Jesus said to them, "Watch out, and beware of the yeast of the Pharisees and Sadducees." 7They said to one another, "It is because we have brought no bread." 8And becoming aware of it, Jesus said, "You of little faith, why are you talking about having no bread? 9Do you still not perceive? Do you not remember the five loaves for the five thousand, and how many baskets you gathered? 10Or the seven loaves for the four thousand, and how many baskets you gathered? 11How could you fail to perceive that I was not speaking about bread? Beware of the yeast of the Pharisees and Sadducees!" 12Then they understood that he had not told them to beware of the yeast of bread, but of the teaching of the Pharisees and Sadducees.

13 Now when Jesus came into the district of Caesarea Philippi, he asked his disciples, "Who do people say that the Son of Man is?" 14And they said,

---

2532	3428	4592	1934	2532	4592
καὶ	μοιχαλὶς	σημεῖον	ἐπιζητεῖ,	καὶ	σημεῖον
and	adulterous	sign	seeks after,	and	sign

3756 1325   846   1487 3361 09 4592   2495
οὐ   δοθήσεται   αὐτῇ εἰ μὴ   τὸ σημεῖον Ἰωνᾶ.
not will be given to it except the sign   Jonah.

2532 2641   846   565   5 2532
καὶ καταλιπὼν   αὐτοὺς ἀπῆλθεν.   Καὶ
And having left behind them   he went off.   And

2064   013 3101   1519 012 4008   1950
ἐλθόντες   οἱ μαθηταὶ εἰς τὸ πέραν ἐπελάθοντο
having come the learners into the across forgot

740   2983   6 01 1161 2424   3004 846
ἄρτους λαβεῖν.   ὁ δὲ Ἰησοῦς εἶπεν αὐτοῖς·
breads to take. The but Jesus said to them,

3708   2532 4337   575   06 2219 014   5330
ὁρᾶτε καὶ προσέχετε ἀπὸ τῆς ζύμης τῶν Φαρισαίων
see   and hold to from the yeast of the Pharisees

2532 4523   7 013   1161 1260   1722
καὶ Σαδδουκαίων.   οἱ   δὲ   διελογίζοντο ἐν
and Sadducees.   The ones but reasoned   in

1438   3004   3754 740 3756 2983
ἑαυτοῖς   λέγοντες ὅτι ἄρτους οὐκ ἐλάβομεν.
themselves saying, (") breads not we took.

8 1097   1161 01 2424   3004 5101 1260
   γνοὺς   δὲ ὁ Ἰησοῦς εἶπεν· τί διαλογίζεσθε
   Having known but the Jesus said; why you reason

1722 1438   3640   3754   740
ἐν ἑαυτοῖς,   ὀλιγόπιστοι,   ὅτι   ἄρτους
in yourselves, little trusting ones, because breads

3756 2192   9 3768 3539   3761
οὐκ ἔχετε;   οὔπω νοεῖτε,   οὐδὲ
not you have? Not yet you give thought, but not

3421   016 4002 740   014   4000
μνημονεύετε τοὺς πέντε ἄρτους τῶν πεντακισχιλίων
you remember the five breads of the five thousand

2532 4214   2894   2983   10 3761   016 2033
καὶ πόσους κοφίνους ἐλάβετε;   οὐδὲ τοὺς ἑπτὰ
and how much wicker you took? But not the seven
                                baskets

740   014   5070   2532 4214   4711
ἄρτους τῶν τετρακισχιλίων καὶ πόσας σπυρίδας
breads of the four thousand   and how many mat baskets

2983   11 4459 3756 3539   3754 3756
ἐλάβετε;   πῶς οὐ νοεῖτε   ὅτι οὐ
you took? How not you give thought that not

4012   740   3004 1473   4337   1161 575
περὶ   ἄρτων εἶπον ὑμῖν; προσέχετε δὲ ἀπὸ
concerning breads I said to you? Hold to but from

06 2219 014   5330   2532 4523   12 5119
τῆς ζύμης τῶν Φαρισαίων καὶ Σαδδουκαίων.   τότε
the yeast of the Pharisees and Sadducees.   Then

4920   3754 3756 3004   4337   575
συνῆκαν   ὅτι οὐκ εἶπεν προσέχειν ἀπὸ
they understood that not he said to hold to from

06 2219 014   740   235   575 06 1322   014
τῆς ζύμης τῶν ἄρτων ἀλλὰ ἀπὸ τῆς διδαχῆς τῶν
the yeast of the breads but from the teaching of the

5330   2532 4523   13 2064   1161 01
Φαρισαίων καὶ Σαδδουκαίων.   Ἐλθὼν   δὲ ὁ
Pharisees and Sadducees.   Having come but the

2424   1519 024 3313 2542   06   5376
Ἰησοῦς εἰς τὰ μέρη Καισαρείας τῆς Φιλίππου
Jesus into the parts of Caesarea of the Philipp

2065   016 3101   846   3004   5101 3004
ἠρώτα τοὺς μαθητὰς αὐτοῦ λέγων· τίνα λέγουσιν
was asking the learners of him saying· who say

013 444   1510 04 5207 02   444   14 013
οἱ ἄνθρωποι εἶναι τὸν υἱὸν τοῦ ἀνθρώπου;   οἱ
the men   to be the son of the man?   The ones

1161	3004	013		3303	2491	04	910
δὲ	εἶπαν·	οἱ		μὲν	Ἰωάννην	τὸν	βαπτιστήν,
but	said;	the ones		indeed	John	the	immerser,

243	1161	2243		2087	1161	2408	2228	1520
ἄλλοι	δὲ	Ἠλίαν,		ἕτεροι	δὲ	Ἰερεμίαν	ἤ	ἕνα
others	but	Elijah,		others	but	Jeremiah	or	one

014	4396		3004	846		1473	1161	5101
τῶν	προφητῶν.	**15** λέγει	αὐτοῖς·	ὑμεῖς	δὲ	τίνα
of the	spokesmen.	He says	to them,	you	but	who

1473	3004	1510		611		1161	4613
με	λέγετε	εἶναι;	**16** ἀποκριθεὶς	δὲ	Σίμων
me	you say	to be?	Having answered	but	Simon

4074	3004	1473	1510	01	5547	01	5207	02
Πέτρος	εἶπεν·	σὺ	εἶ	ὁ	χριστὸς	ὁ	υἱὸς	τοῦ
Peter	said;	You	are	the	Christ	the	son	of the

2316	02		2198		611		1161	01	2424
θεοῦ	τοῦ		ζῶντος.	**17** ἀποκριθεὶς	δὲ	ὁ	Ἰησοῦς
God	of the		living.	Having answered	but	the	Jesus

3004	846		3107		1510		4613	920
εἶπεν	αὐτῷ·	μακάριος	εἶ,		Σίμων	Βαριωνᾶ,
said	to him;	fortunate	you are,		Simon	Barjonah,

3754	4561	2532	129		3756	601		1473
ὅτι	σὰρξ	καὶ	αἷμα	οὐκ	ἀπεκάλυψέν	σοι
because	flesh	and	blood	not	uncovered	to you

235	01	3962	1473	01		1722	015	3772
ἀλλ'	ὁ	πατήρ	μου	ὁ		ἐν	τοῖς	οὐρανοῖς.
but	the	father	of me	the one in	the	heavens.

	2504	1161	1473	3004	3754	1473	1510	4074	2532
18	κἀγὼ	δέ	σοι	λέγω	ὅτι	σὺ	εἶ	Πέτρος,	καὶ
	Also I	but	to you	say	that	you	are	Peter,	and

1909	3778	07	4073	3618		1473	08	1577
ἐπὶ	ταύτῃ	τῇ	πέτρᾳ	οἰκοδομήσω	μου	τὴν	ἐκκλησίαν,
on	this	the	rock	I will build	of me	the	assembly,

2532	4439	86		3756	2729		846
καὶ	πύλαι	ᾅδου	οὐ	κατισχύσουσιν	αὐτῆς.
and	gates	of hades	not	will be strong	against it.

	1325		1473	020	2807	06	932
19	δώσω	σοι	τὰς	κλεῖδας	τῆς	βασιλείας
	I will give	to you	the	keys		of the kingdom

014	3772	2532	3739	1437	1210		1909	06
τῶν	οὐρανῶν,	καὶ	ὃ	ἐὰν	δήσῃς		ἐπὶ	τῆς
of the heavens,	and	what if	you might bind on	the

1093	1510		1210		1722	015	3772
γῆς	ἔσται	δεδεμένον		ἐν	τοῖς	οὐρανοῖς,
land	will be+	+having been bound	in	the	heavens,

2532	3739	1437	3089		1909	06	1093	1510
καὶ	ὃ	ἐὰν	λύσῃς		ἐπὶ	τῆς	γῆς	ἔσται
and	what if	you might loose on	the land	will be+

3089		1722	015	3772		5119
λελυμένον	ἐν	τοῖς	οὐρανοῖς.	**20** τότε
+having been loosed	in	the	heavens.		Then

1291		015	3101	2443	3367
διεστείλατο	τοῖς	μαθηταῖς	ἵνα	μηδενὶ
he commanded	to the	learners	that	to no one

3004		3754	846	1510	01	5547		575
εἴπωσιν	ὅτι	αὐτός	ἐστιν	ὁ	χριστός.	**21** Ἀπὸ
they might say	that	himself	is	the	Christ.		From

5119	757	01	2424	1166	015	3101	846
τότε	ἤρξατο	ὁ	Ἰησοῦς	δεικνύειν	τοῖς	μαθηταῖς	αὐτοῦ
then	began	the	Jesus	to show	to the	learners	of him

3754	1163		846	1519	2414	565
ὅτι	δεῖ		αὐτὸν	εἰς	Ἱεροσόλυμα	ἀπελθεῖν
that	it is necessary	him	into	Jerusalem	to go off

2532	4183	3958	575	014	4245		2532
καὶ	πολλὰ	παθεῖν	ἀπὸ	τῶν	πρεσβυτέρων	καὶ
and	many	to suffer	from the	older men		and

749		2532	1122		2532	615		2532
ἀρχιερέων	καὶ	γραμματέων	καὶ	ἀποκτανθῆναι	καὶ
ruler priests	and	writers	and	to be killed	and

"Some say John the Baptist, but others Elijah, and still others Jeremiah or one of the prophets." [15]He said to them, "But who do you say that I am?" [16]Simon Peter answered, "You are the Messiah,[a] the Son of the living God." [17]And Jesus answered him, "Blessed are you, Simon son of Jonah! For flesh and blood has not revealed this to you, but my Father in heaven. [18]And I tell you, you are Peter,[b] and on this rock[c] I will build my church, and the gates of Hades will not prevail against it. [19]I will give you the keys of the kingdom of heaven, and whatever you bind on earth will be bound in heaven, and whatever you loose on earth will be loosed in heaven." [20]Then he sternly ordered the disciples not to tell anyone that he was[d] the Messiah.[a]

21 From that time on, Jesus began to show his disciples that he must go to Jerusalem and undergo great suffering at the hands of the elders and chief priests and scribes, and be killed, and

a Or the Christ
b Gk Petros
c Gk petra
d Other ancient authorities add Jesus

on the third day be raised. 22And Peter took him aside and began to rebuke him, saying, "God forbid it, Lord! This must never happen to you." 23But he turned and said to Peter, "Get behind me, Satan! You are a stumbling block to me; for you are setting your mind not on divine things but on human things."

24 Then Jesus told his disciples, "If any want to become my followers, let them deny themselves and take up their cross and follow me. 25For those who want to save their life will lose it, and those who lose their life for my sake will find it. 26For what will it profit them if they gain the whole world but forfeit their life? Or what will they give in return for their life?

27 "For the Son of Man is to come with his angels in the glory of his Father, and then he will repay everyone for what has been done. 28Truly I tell you, there are some standing here who will not taste death before they see the Son of Man coming in his kingdom."

```
07        5154    2250    1453              22  2532  4355
τῇ        τρίτῃ   ἡμέρᾳ   ἐγερθῆναι.      καὶ  προσλαβόμενος
in the    third   day     to be raised.   And  having taken to
846       01      4074    757     2008         846  3004
αὐτὸν ὁ   Πέτρος  ἤρξατο  ἐπιτιμᾶν         αὐτῷ λέγων·
him   the Peter   began   to admonish him       saying,
2436      1473    2962    3756 3361 1510        1473  3778
ἵλεώς     σοι,    κύριε·  οὐ μὴ ἔσται         σοι  τοῦτο.
merciful  to you, Master; not not will be to  you  this.
     01   1161 4762            3004  03        4074    5217
23 ὁ   δὲ   στραφεὶς       εἶπεν τῷ        Πέτρῳ· ὕπαγε
   The one but having turned said  to the   Peter,  go off
3694  1473 4567          4625       1510   1473  3754
ὀπίσω μου, Σατανᾶ·       σκάνδαλον εἶ    ἐμοῦ, ὅτι
after me,  Adversary;    offense    you are of me, because
3756 5426    024    02        2316 235  024
οὐ φρονεῖς   τὰ     τοῦ       θεοῦ ἀλλὰ τὰ
not you think the things of the God but  the things
014    444              24 5119 01  2424    3004  015
τῶν    ἀνθρώπων.      Τότε ὁ   Ἰησοῦς εἶπεν τοῖς
of the men.             Then the Jesus  said  to the
3101     846     1487 5100 2309  3694 1473 2064
μαθηταῖς αὐτοῦ·  εἴ   τις θέλει ὀπίσω μου ἐλθεῖν,
learners of him, if   one wants after me  to come,
533                 1438     2532 142    04   4716
ἀπαρνησάσθω         ἑαυτὸν  καὶ ἀράτω  τὸν σταυρὸν
let one thoroughly  himself and let one the cross
deny                         lift up
846     2532 190             1473    25 3739 1063 1437
αὐτοῦ   καὶ  ἀκολουθείτω     μοι.     ὃς  γὰρ  ἐὰν
of him  and  let one follow me.       Who for  if
2309      08   5590 846   4982       622
θέλῃ      τὴν ψυχὴν αὐτοῦ σῶσαι      ἀπολέσει
might want the soul  of him to deliver he will destroy
846     3739 1161 302 622         08  5590  846
αὐτήν·  ὃς  δ'   ἂν ἀπολέσῃ      τὴν ψυχὴν αὐτοῦ
it;     who but  -  might destroy the soul  of him
1752       1473  2147      846      26 5101 1063
ἕνεκεν     ἐμου  εὑρήσει   αὐτήν.    τί   γὰρ
on account of me will find it.        What for
5623                 444          1437 04 2889    3650
ὠφεληθήσεται         ἄνθρωπος ἐὰν τὸν κόσμον ὅλον
will be benefitted man          if   the world  whole
2770       08  1161 5590 846    2210       2228 5101 1325
κερδήσῃ    τὴν δὲ  ψυχὴν αὐτοῦ ζημιωθῇ; ἢ   τί  δώσει
he might   the but soul  of him he might Or  what will
gain                             lose?           give
444         465       06   5590 846     27 3195
ἄνθρωπος    ἀντάλλαγμα τῆς ψυχῆς αὐτοῦ;    μέλλει
man         exchange   of the soul of him?   Is about
1063 01  5207 02   444        2064       1722 07 1391
γὰρ  ὁ   υἱὸς τοῦ  ἀνθρώπου ἔρχεσθαι ἐν   τῇ δόξῃ
for  the son  of the man     to come   in   the splendor
02    3962    846  3326 014  32        846     2532
τοῦ   πατρὸς αὐτοῦ μετὰ τῶν ἀγγέλων   αὐτοῦ, καὶ
of the father of him with the messengers of him, and
5119 591     1538    2596    08 4234    846
τότε ἀποδώσει ἑκάστῳ κατὰ   τὴν πρᾶξιν αὐτοῦ.
then he will  to each according the practice of him.
     give off        to
   281 3004 1473 3754 1510      5100 014    5602
28 ἀμὴν λέγω ὑμῖν ὅτι εἰσίν   τινες τῶν  ὧδε
   Amen I say to you that there are some of the here
2476     3748    3756 3361 1089      2288       2193  302
ἑστώτων οἵτινες οὐ μὴ  γεύσωνται θανάτου ἕως  ἂν
ones    who      not not will taste death until -
standing
3708       04  5207 02   444        2064
ἴδωσιν     τὸν υἱὸν τοῦ  ἀνθρώπου ἐρχόμενον
they might see the son  of the man  coming
```

```
1722 07    932      846         17:1  2532 3326  2250    1803
ἐν  τῇ βασιλείᾳ αὐτοῦ.           Καὶ  μεθ' ἡμέρας ἓξ
in  the kingdom  of him.        And after days  six
3880            01  2424   04  4074  2532  2385      2532
παραλαμβάνει ὁ 'Ιησοῦς τὸν Πέτρον καὶ 'Ιάκωβον καὶ
takes along the Jesus the Peter and  Jacob     and
2491      04  80   846     2532 399           846
'Ιωάννην τὸν ἀδελφὸν αὐτοῦ καὶ ἀναφέρει    αὐτοὺς
John      the brother of him and  he bears up them
1519 3735 5308    2596 2398    2  2532 3339
εἰς  ὄρος ὑψηλὸν κατ' ἰδίαν.      καὶ μετεμορφώθη
into hill high   by   own.        And he was transformed
1715         846    2532 2989   09   4383       846
ἔμπροσθεν αὐτῶν, καὶ ἔλαμψεν τὸ πρόσωπον αὐτοῦ
in front of them, and  shone  the face     of him
5613 01  2246   021 1161 2440  846    1096    3022
ὡς  ὁ  ἥλιος, τὰ δὲ ἱμάτια αὐτοῦ ἐγένετο λευκὰ
as  the sun,  the but clothes of him became  white
5613 09  5457   3  2532 2400 3708    846    3475
ὡς  τὸ φῶς.      καὶ ἰδοὺ ὤφθη   αὐτοῖς Μωϋσῆς
as  the light. And look was seen to them Moses
2532 2243   4814              3326 846
καὶ 'Ηλίας συλλαλοῦντες    μετ' αὐτοῦ.
and  Elijah speaking together with him.
   611            1161 01  4074  3004  03        2424
4 ἀποκριθεὶς     δὲ  ὁ Πέτρος εἶπεν τῷ     'Ιησοῦ·
  Having answered but the Peter said to the Jesus,
2962     2570   1510 1473 5602 1510   1487 2309
κύριε, καλόν ἐστιν ἡμᾶς ὧδε εἶναι· εἰ θέλεις,
Master, good it is  us  here to be; if you want,
4160      5602 5140  4633     1473   1520 2532
ποιήσω  ὧδε τρεῖς σκηνάς, σοὶ μίαν καὶ
I will make here three tents, to you one and
3475    1520 2532 2243     1520  5 2089 846
Μωϋσεῖ μίαν καὶ 'Ηλίᾳ μίαν.    ἔτι αὐτοῦ
to Moses one and to Elijah one. Still of him
2980        2400 3507  5460    1982        846
λαλοῦντος ἰδοὺ νεφέλη φωτεινὴ ἐπεσκίασεν αὐτούς,
speaking look cloud lighten overshadowed them,
2532 2400 5456 1537 06   3507   3004    3778
καὶ ἰδοὺ φωνὴ ἐκ τῆς νεφέλης λέγουσα· οὗτός
and look sound out of the cloud saying· this
1510 01  5207 1473 01  27         1722 3739
ἐστιν ὁ  υἱός μου ὁ ἀγαπητός, ἐν ᾧ
is  the son of me the loved one, in whom
2106        191     846    6 2532 191         013
εὐδόκησα· ἀκούετε αὐτοῦ. καὶ ἀκούσαντες οἱ
I thought well; hear him. And having heard the
3101     4098   1909 4383   846      2532 5399
μαθηταὶ ἔπεσαν ἐπὶ πρόσωπον αὐτῶν καὶ ἐφοβήθησαν
learners fell on face of them and were afraid
4970    7 2532 4334        01  2424   2532
σφόδρα.   καὶ προσῆλθεν ὁ 'Ιησοῦς καὶ
exceeding. And went toward the Jesus and
681        846    3004    1453     2532 3361 5399
ἁψάμενος αὐτῶν εἶπεν· ἐγέρθητε καὶ μὴ φοβεῖσθε.
having touched them said; be raised and not fear.
  1869            1161 016  3788       846
8 ἐπάραντες      δὲ τοὺς ὀφθαλμοὺς αὐτῶν
  Having lifted up on but the eyes of them
3762   3708   1487 3361 846   2424   3441  9 2532
οὐδένα εἶδον εἰ μὴ αὐτὸν 'Ιησοῦν μόνον. Καὶ
no one they saw except him Jesus alone. And
2597        846    1537 010  3735  1781       846
καταβαινόντων αὐτῶν ἐκ τοῦ ὄρους ἐνετείλατο αὐτοῖς
going down them out of the hill commanded them
01  2424   3004    3367   3004   012 3705
ὁ 'Ιησοῦς λέγων· μηδενὶ εἴπητε τὸ ὅραμα
the Jesus saying, to no one you might say the sight
```

CHAPTER 17

Six days later, Jesus took with him Peter and James and his brother John and led them up a high mountain, by themselves. [2]And he was transfigured before them, and his face shone like the sun, and his clothes became dazzling white. [3]Suddenly there appeared to them Moses and Elijah, talking with him. [4]Then Peter said to Jesus, "Lord, it is good for us to be here; if you wish, I[a] will make three dwellings[b] here, one for you, one for Moses, and one for Elijah." [5]While he was still speaking, suddenly a bright cloud overshadowed them, and from the cloud a voice said, "This is my Son, the Beloved;[c] with him I am well pleased; listen to him!" [6]When the disciples heard this, they fell to the ground and were overcome by fear. [7]But Jesus came and touched them, saying, "Get up and do not be afraid." [8]And when they looked up, they saw no one except Jesus himself alone.

9 As they were coming down the mountain, Jesus ordered them, "Tell no one about the vision

a Other ancient authorities read *we*
b Or *tents*
c Or *my beloved Son*

until after the Son of Man has been raised from the dead." [10]And the disciples asked him, "Why, then, do the scribes say that Elijah must come first?" [11]He replied, "Elijah is indeed coming and will restore all things; [12]but I tell you that Elijah has already come, and they did not recognize him, but they did to him whatever they pleased. So also the Son of Man is about to suffer at their hands." [13]Then the disciples understood that he was speaking to them about John the Baptist.

[14]When they came to the crowd, a man came to him, knelt before him, [15]and said, "Lord, have mercy on my son, for he is an epileptic and he suffers terribly; he often falls into the fire and often into the water. [16]And I brought him to your disciples, but they could not cure him." [17]Jesus answered, "You faithless and perverse generation, how much longer must I be with you? How much longer must I put up with you? Bring him here to me." [18]And Jesus rebuked the demon,[a] and it[b] came out of him, and the boy was cured instantly.

---

[a] Gk it or him
[b] Gk the demon

2193	3739	01	5207	02	444	1537	3498
ἕως	οὗ	ὁ	υἱὸς	τοῦ	ἀνθρώπου	ἐκ	νεκρῶν
until	which	the	son	of the	man	from	dead

1453			2532	1905	846	013	3101
ἐγερθῇ.		**10** Καὶ	ἐπηρώτησαν	αὐτὸν	οἱ	μαθηταὶ
might be raised.		And	asked on	him	the	learners

3004	5101	3767	013	1122	3004	3754
λέγοντες·	τί	οὖν	οἱ	γραμματεῖς	λέγουσιν	ὅτι
saying;	why	then	the	writers	say	that

2243	1163	2064	4413	**11**	01
Ἡλίαν	δεῖ	ἐλθεῖν	πρῶτον;		ὁ
Elijah	it is necessary	to come	first?		The one

1161	611	3004	2243	3303	2064	2532
δὲ	ἀποκριθεὶς	εἶπεν·	Ἡλίας	μὲν	ἔρχεται	καὶ
but	having answered	said,	Elijah	indeed	comes	and

600	3956	**12**	3004	1161	1473	3754	2243
ἀποκαταστήσει	πάντα·		λέγω	δὲ	ὑμῖν	ὅτι	Ἡλίας
will restore	all;		I say	but	to you	that	Elijah

2235	2064	2532	3756	1921	846	235
ἤδη	ἦλθεν,	καὶ	οὐκ	ἐπέγνωσαν	αὐτὸν	ἀλλὰ
already	came,	and	not	they perceived	him	but

4160	1722	846	3745	2309	3779	2532
ἐποίησαν	ἐν	αὐτῷ	ὅσα	ἠθέλησαν·	οὕτως	καὶ
they did	in	him	as much as	they wanted;	thusly	also

01	5207	02	444	3195	3958	5259	846
ὁ	υἱὸς	τοῦ	ἀνθρώπου	μέλλει	πάσχειν	ὑπ᾽	αὐτῶν.
the	son	of the	man	is about	to suffer	by	them.

13	5119	4920	013	3101	3754	4012
	τότε	συνῆκαν	οἱ	μαθηταὶ	ὅτι	περὶ
	Then	understood	the	learners	that	concerning

2491	02	910	3004	846	2532
Ἰωάννου	τοῦ	βαπτιστοῦ	εἶπεν	αὐτοῖς.	**14** Καὶ
John	the	immerser	he said	to them.	And

2064	4314	04	3793	4334	846	444
ἐλθόντων	πρὸς	τὸν	ὄχλον	προσῆλθεν	αὐτῷ	ἄνθρωπος
having gone	toward	the	crowd	went toward	him	man

1120	846	**15**	2532	3004	2962	1653
γονυπετῶν	αὐτὸν		καὶ	λέγων·	κύριε,	ἐλέησόν
falling on knees	him		and	saying;	Master,	mercy

1473	04	5207	3754	4583	2532	2560
μου	τὸν	υἱόν,	ὅτι	σεληνιάζεται	καὶ	κακῶς
of me	the	son,	because	he is moonstruck	and	badly

3958	4178	1063	4098	1519	012	4442
πάσχει·	πολλάκις	γὰρ	πίπτει	εἰς	τὸ	πῦρ
he suffers;	frequently	for	he falls	into	the	fire

2532	4178	1519	012	5204	**16**	2532	4374
καὶ	πολλάκις	εἰς	τὸ	ὕδωρ.		καὶ	προσήνεγκα
and	frequently	into	the	water.		And	I offered

846	015	3101	1473	2532	3756	1410
αὐτὸν	τοῖς	μαθηταῖς	σου,	καὶ	οὐκ	ἠδυνήθησαν
him	to the	learners	of you,	and	not	they were able to

846	2323	**17**	611	1161	01	2424
αὐτὸν	θεραπεῦσαι.		ἀποκριθεὶς	δὲ	ὁ	Ἰησοῦς
him	to heal.		Having answered	but	the	Jesus

3004	5599	1074	571	2532	1294	2193
εἶπεν·	ὦ	γενεὰ	ἄπιστος	καὶ	διεστραμμένη,	ἕως
said,	o	generation	untrustful	and	having been perverted,	until

4219	3326	1473	1510	2193	4219	430
πότε	μεθ᾽	ὑμῶν	ἔσομαι;	ἕως	πότε	ἀνέξομαι
when	with	you	will I be?	Until	when	will I endure

1473	5342	1473	846	5602	**18**	2532	2008	846
ὑμῶν;	φέρετέ	μοι	αὐτὸν	ὧδε.		καὶ	ἐπετίμησεν	αὐτῷ
you?	Carry	to me	him	here.		And	admonished	him

01	2424	2532	1831	575	846	09	1140	2532
ὁ	Ἰησοῦς	καὶ	ἐξῆλθεν	ἀπ᾽	αὐτοῦ	τὸ	δαιμόνιον	καὶ
the	Jesus	and	went out	from	him	the	demon	and

2323	01	3816	575	06	5610	1565
ἐθεραπεύθη	ὁ	παῖς	ἀπὸ	τῆς	ὥρας	ἐκείνης.
was healed	the	boy servant	from	the	hour	that.

19
| 5119 | 4334 | | 013 | 3101 | 03 | 2424 |

Τότε προσελθόντες   οἱ μαθηταὶ τῷ ᾽Ιησοῦ
Then having gone toward the learners to the Jesus

2596 2398 3004   1223   5101 1473 3756 1410
κατ᾽ ἰδίαν εἶπον· διὰ   τί   ἡμεῖς οὐκ ἠδυνήθημεν
by   own said, through what we   not were able

1544   846   **20** 01   1161 3004 846   1223
ἐκβαλεῖν αὐτό;   ὁ   δὲ λέγει αὐτοῖς· διὰ
to throw out it?   The one but says to them, through

08   3639a   1473   281 1063 3004 1473   1437
τὴν ὀλιγοπιστίαν ὑμῶν· ἀμὴν γὰρ λέγω ὑμῖν, ἐὰν
the little trust of you; amen for I say to you, if

2192   4102   5613 2848   4615
ἔχητε   πίστιν ὡς κόκκον σινάπεως,
you might have trust as grain of mustard,

3004   011   3735 3778 3327   1759a
ἐρεῖτε   τῷ   ὄρει τούτῳ· μετάβα ἔνθεν
you will say to the hill this; go across from here

1563 2532 3327   2532 3762
ἐκεῖ, καὶ μεταβήσεται·   καὶ οὐδὲν
there, and it will go across; and nothing

101   1473   4962   1161 846
ἀδυνατήσει ὑμῖν. **22** Συστρεφομένων δὲ αὐτῶν
will be unable to you. Turning together but them

1722 07 3004 846   01 2424   3195
ἐν τῇ Γαλιλαίᾳ εἶπεν αὐτοῖς ὁ ᾽Ιησοῦς· μέλλει
in the Galilee said to them the Jesus, is about

01 5207 02   444   3860   1519 5495
ὁ υἱὸς τοῦ ἀνθρώπου παραδίδοσθαι εἰς χεῖρας
the son of the man to be given over into hands

444   **23** 2532 615   846   2532 07
ἀνθρώπων,   καὶ ἀποκτενοῦσιν αὐτόν, καὶ τῇ
of men,   and they will kill him, and in the

5154 2250 1453   2532 3076
τρίτῃ ἡμέρᾳ ἐγερθήσεται.   καὶ ἐλυπήθησαν
third day he will be raised. And they grieved

4970   **24** 2064   1161 846   1519 2746a
σφόδρα.   ᾽Ελθόντων δὲ αὐτῶν εἰς Καφαρναοὺμ
exceeding. Having come but of them into Capernaum

4334   013   024 1323   2983   03
προσῆλθον οἱ   τὰ δίδραχμα λαμβάνοντες τῷ
went toward the ones the didrachma receiving to the

4074 2532 3004   01 1320   1473 3756 5055
Πέτρῳ καὶ εἶπαν· ὁ διδάσκαλος ὑμῶν οὐ τελεῖ
Peter and said; the teacher of you not completes

024 1323   **25** 3004   3483 2532 2064   1519
[τὰ] δίδραχμα;   λέγει· ναί. καὶ ἐλθόντα εἰς
the didrachma?   He says, yes. And having gone into

08   3614   4399   846 01 2424 3004   5101
τὴν οἰκίαν προέφθασεν αὐτὸν ὁ ᾽Ιησοῦς λέγων· τί
the house anticipated him the Jesus saying, what

1473 1380   846   013 935   06   1093 575
σοι δοκεῖ,   Σίμων; οἱ βασιλεῖς τῆς γῆς ἀπὸ
to you it thinks, Simon? The kings of the land from

5101 2983   5056   2228 2778   575 014 5207
τίνων λαμβάνουσιν τέλη ἢ κῆνσον; ἀπὸ τῶν υἱῶν
whom receive completion or tribute? From the sons

846   2228 575 014 245   3004   1161
αὐτῶν ἢ ἀπὸ τῶν ἀλλοτρίων; **26** εἰπόντος δέ·
of them or from the others?   Having said but;

575 014 245   5346 846   01 2424   686
ἀπὸ τῶν ἀλλοτρίων, ἔφη αὐτῷ ὁ ᾽Ιησοῦς· ἄρα
from the others, said to him the Jesus; then

1065   1658   1510 013 5207 **27** 2443 1161 3361
γε   ἐλεύθεροί εἰσιν οἱ υἱοί.   ἵνα δὲ μὴ
indeed free   are the sons.   That but not

4624   846   4198   1519 2281   906
σκανδαλίσωμεν αὐτούς, πορευθεὶς εἰς θάλασσαν βάλε
we might offend them, having to sea   throw
              traveled

19Then the disciples came to Jesus privately and said, "Why could we not cast it out?" 20He said to them, "Because of your little faith. For truly I tell you, if you have faith the size of a[a] mustard seed, you will say to this mountain, 'Move from here to there,' and it will move; and nothing will be impossible for you."[b]

22 As they were gathering[c] in Galilee, Jesus said to them, "The Son of Man is going to be betrayed into human hands, 23and they will kill him, and on the third day he will be raised." And they were greatly distressed.

24 When they reached Capernaum, the collectors of the temple tax[d] came to Peter and said, "Does your teacher not pay the temple tax?"[d] 25He said, "Yes, he does." And when he came home, Jesus spoke of it first, asking, "What do you think, Simon? From whom do kings of the earth take toll or tribute? From their children or from others?" 26When Peter[e] said, "From others," Jesus said to him, "Then the children are free. 27However, so that we do not give offense to them, go to the sea and cast

[a] Gk faith as a grain of
[b] Other ancient authorities add verse 21, But this kind does not come out except by prayer and fasting
[c] Other ancient authorities read living
[d] Gk didrachma
[e] Gk he

a hook; take the first fish that comes up; and when you open its mouth, you will find a coin;[a] take that and give it to them for you and me."

CHAPTER 18

At that time the disciples came to Jesus and asked, "Who is the greatest in the kingdom of heaven?" [2]He called a child, whom he put among them, [3]and said, "Truly I tell you, unless you change and become like children, you will never enter the kingdom of heaven. [4]Whoever becomes humble like this child is the greatest in the kingdom of heaven. [5]Whoever welcomes one such child in my name welcomes me.

6 "If any of you put a stumbling block before one of these little ones who believe in me, it would be better for you if a great millstone were fastened around your neck and you were drowned in the depth of the sea. [7]Woe to the world because of stumbling blocks! Occasions for stumbling are bound to come, but woe to the one by whom the stumbling block comes!

8 "If your hand or your foot causes you to stumble, cut it off

[a] Gk stater; the stater was worth two didrachmas

44	2532 04	305		4413	2486	142

ἄγκιστρον καὶ τὸν ἀναβάντα πρῶτον ἰχθὺν ἆρον,
hook   and the having gone up first fish lift up,

2532 455   012 4750 846 2147
καὶ ἀνοίξας   τὸ στόμα αὐτοῦ εὑρήσεις
and having opened the mouth of it you will find

4715   1565   2983   1325 846   473
στατῆρα· ἐκεῖνον λαβὼν   δὸς αὐτοῖς ἀντὶ
stater; that   having received give to them in place

1473 2532 1473   1722 1565 07 5610 4334
ἐμοῦ καὶ σοῦ. **18:1** Ἐν ἐκείνῃ τῇ ὥρᾳ προσῆλθον
of me and you.   In that   the hour came toward

013 3101   03   2424 3004   5101 686 3173
οἱ μαθηταὶ τῷ Ἰησοῦ λέγοντες· τίς ἄρα μείζων
the learners to the Jesus saying, who then greater

1510 1722 07 932   014 3772   **2** 2532
ἐστὶν ἐν τῇ βασιλείᾳ τῶν οὐρανῶν;   καὶ
is   in the kingdom of the heavens?   And

4341   3813   2476   846 1722
προσκαλεσάμενος παιδίον ἔστησεν αὐτὸ ἐν
having called toward small child he stood him in

3319 846 2532 3004   281 3004 1473 1437 3361
μέσῳ αὐτῶν **3** καὶ εἶπεν· ἀμὴν λέγω ὑμῖν, ἐὰν μὴ
middle of them and he said; amen I say to you, except

4762   2532 1096 5613 021 3813   3756
στραφῆτε καὶ γένησθε ὡς τὰ παιδία,   οὐ
you might turn and become as the small children, not

3361 1525   1519 08 932   014 3772
μὴ εἰσέλθητε εἰς τὴν βασιλείαν τῶν οὐρανῶν.
not you might go in into the kingdom of the heavens.

4 3748 3767 5013   1438   5613 09 3813
ὅστις οὖν ταπεινώσει ἑαυτὸν ὡς τὸ παιδίον
Who then will humble himself as the small child

3778 3778 1510 01 3173   1722 07 932   014
τοῦτο, οὗτός ἐστιν ὁ μείζων ἐν τῇ βασιλείᾳ τῶν
this, this is the greater in the kingdom of the

3772   **5** 2532 3739 1437 1209   1520
οὐρανῶν. καὶ ὃς ἐὰν δέξηται   ἐν
heavens. And who if he might welcome one

3813   5108   1909 011 3686   1473 1473
παιδίον τοιοῦτο ἐπὶ τῷ ὀνόματί μου, ἐμὲ
small child such on the name of me, me

1209   **6** 3739 1161 302 4624   1520 014
δέχεται. Ὃς δ' ἂν σκανδαλίσῃ ἕνα τῶν
he welcomes. Who but - might offend one of the

3398 3778   014   4100   1519 1473
μικρῶν τούτων τῶν πιστευόντων εἰς ἐμέ,
small of these of the ones trusting in me,

4851   846 2443 2910   3458
συμφέρει αὐτῷ ἵνα κρεμασθῇ μύλος
it is advantageous to him that be hung millstone

3684   4012 04 5137   846   2532
ὀνικὸς περὶ τὸν τράχηλον αὐτοῦ καὶ
of donkey around the neck of him and

2670   1722 011 3989   06   2281
καταποντισθῇ ἐν τῷ πελάγει τῆς θαλάσσης.
he might be drowned in the open of the sea.

7 3759 03   2889 575 022 4625   318   1063
Οὐαὶ τῷ κόσμῳ ἀπὸ τῶν σκανδάλων· ἀνάγκη γὰρ
Woe to the world from the offenses; necessity for

2064   024 4625   4133   3759 03   444   1223
ἐλθεῖν τὰ σκάνδαλα, πλὴν οὐαὶ τῷ ἀνθρώπῳ δι'
to come the offenses, except woe to the man through

3739 09 4625   2064 **8** 1487 1161 05 5495 1473
οὗ τὸ σκάνδαλον ἔρχεται. Εἰ δὲ ἡ χείρ σου
whom the offense comes. If but the hand of you

2228 01 4228 1473 4624   1473 1581 846
ἢ ὁ πούς σου σκανδαλίζει σε, ἔκκοψον αὐτὸν
or the foot of you offends you, cut off it

2532 906   575 1473 2570 1473   1510 1525   1519
καὶ βάλε ἀπὸ σοῦ· καλόν σοί ἐστιν εἰσελθεῖν εἰς
and throw from you; good to you it is to go in into
08 2222 2948   2228 5560 2228 1417 5495 2228 1417
τὴν ζωὴν κυλλὸν ἢ χωλὸν ἢ δύο χεῖρας ἢ δύο
the life crippled or lame or two hands or two
4228 2192   906   1519 012 4442 012 166
πόδας ἔχοντα βληθῆναι   εἰς τὸ πῦρ τὸ αἰώνιον.
feet having to be thrown into the fire the eternal.

9 2532 1487 01 3788   1473 4624   1473
καὶ εἰ ὁ ὀφθαλμός σου σκανδαλίζει σε,
And if the eye of you offends you,
1807   846 2532 906   575 1473 2570 1473   1510
ἔξελε αὐτὸν καὶ βάλε ἀπὸ σοῦ· καλόν σοί ἐστιν
lift out it and throw from you; good to you it is
3442   1519 08 2222 1525   2228 1417
μονόφθαλμον εἰς τὴν ζωὴν εἰσελθεῖν ἢ δύο
alone eye into the life to go into or two
3788   2192   906   1519 08 1067   010
ὀφθαλμοὺς ἔχοντα βληθῆναι εἰς τὴν γέενναν τοῦ
eyes having to be thrown into the gehenna of the
4442   **10** 3708 3361 2706   1520 014
πυρός.   Ὁρᾶτε μὴ καταφρονήσητε ἑνὸς τῶν
fire.   See not you might think down one of the
3398   3778   3004 1063 1473   3754 013 32
μικρῶν τούτων· λέγω γὰρ ὑμῖν ὅτι οἱ ἄγγελοι
small of these; I say for to you that the messengers
846   1722 2772   1223   3956 991   012
αὐτῶν ἐν οὐρανοῖς διὰ παντὸς βλέπουσι τὸ
of them in heavens through all see the
4383   02   3962 1473 02   1722 3772
πρόσωπον τοῦ πατρός μου τοῦ ἐν οὐρανοῖς.
face of the father of me the one in heavens.

12 5101 1473 1380   1437 1096   5100
Τί ὑμῖν δοκεῖ; ἐὰν γένηταί τινι
What to you thinks? If might become to some
444   1540   4263 2532 4105   1520
ἀνθρώπῳ ἑκατὸν πρόβατα καὶ πλανηθῇ ἓν
man hundred sheep and might be deceived one
1537 846   3780 863   024 1752a
ἐξ αὐτῶν, οὐχὶ ἀφήσει τὰ ἐνενήκοντα
from them, not will he leave off the ninety
1767 1909 024 3735 2532 4198   2212 012
ἐννέα ἐπὶ τὰ ὄρη καὶ πορευθεὶς ζητεῖ τὸ
nine on the hills and having traveled seeks the
4105   **13** 2532 1437 1096   2147
πλανώμενον;   καὶ ἐὰν γένηται εὑρεῖν
one being deceived? And if it might become to find
846   281 3004 1473   3754 5463   1909 846
αὐτό, ἀμὴν λέγω ὑμῖν ὅτι χαίρει ἐπ᾽ αὐτῷ
it, amen I say to you that he rejoices on it
3123   2228 1909 023 1752a   1767 023   3361
μᾶλλον ἢ ἐπὶ τοῖς ἐνενήκοντα ἐννέα τοῖς μὴ
more than on the ninety nine the ones not
4105   **14** 3779 3756 1510 2307
πεπλανημένοις.   οὕτως οὐκ ἔστιν θέλημα
having been deceived. Thusly not it is want
1715   02 3962   1473 02   1722 3772   2443
ἔμπροσθεν τοῦ πατρὸς ὑμῶν τοῦ ἐν οὐρανοῖς ἵνα
in front of the father of you the one in heavens that
622   1520 022   3398   3778   **15** 1437
ἀπόληται   ἓν τῶν μικρῶν τούτων.   Ἐὰν
might be destroyed one of the small of these. If
1161 264   1519 1473 01 80   1473   5217
δὲ ἁμαρτήσῃ [εἰς σὲ] ὁ ἀδελφός σου, ὕπαγε
but might sin to you the brother of you, go off
1651 846 3342   1473 2532 846   3441   1437 1473
ἔλεγξον αὐτὸν μεταξὺ σοῦ καὶ αὐτοῦ μόνου. ἐάν σου
rebuke him between you and him alone. If you

and throw it away; it is better for you to enter life maimed or lame than to have two hands or two feet and to be thrown into the eternal fire. [9] And if your eye causes you to stumble, tear it out and throw it away; it is better for you to enter life with one eye than to have two eyes and to be thrown into the hell[a] of fire.

10 "Take care that you do not despise one of these little ones; for, I tell you, in heaven their angels continually see the face of my Father in heaven.[b] [12] What do you think? If a shepherd has a hundred sheep, and one of them has gone astray, does he not leave the ninety-nine on the mountains and go in search of the one that went astray? [13] And if he finds it, truly I tell you, he rejoices over it more than over the ninety-nine that never went astray. [14] So it is not the will of your[c] Father in heaven that one of these little ones should be lost.

15 "If another member of the church[d] sins against you,[e] go and point out the fault when the two of you are alone.

---

[a] Gk Gehenna
[b] Other ancient authorities add verse 11, For the Son of Man came to save the lost
[c] Other ancient authorities read my
[d] Gk If your brother
[e] Other ancient authorities lack against you

If the member listens to you, you have regained that one.[a] [16]But if you are not listened to, take one or two others along with you, so that every word may be confirmed by the evidence of two or three witnesses. [17]If the member refuses to listen to them, tell it to the church; and if the offender refuses to listen even to the church, let such a one be to you as a Gentile and a tax collector. [18]Truly I tell you, whatever you bind on earth will be bound in heaven, and whatever you loose on earth will be loosed in heaven. [19]Again, truly I tell you, if two of you agree on earth about anything you ask, it will be done for you by my Father in heaven. [20]For where two or three are gathered in my name, I am there among them."

21 Then Peter came and said to him, "Lord, if another member of the church[b] sins against me, how often should I forgive? As many as seven times?" [22]Jesus said to him, "Not seven times, but, I tell you, seventy-seven[c] times.

23 "For this reason the kingdom of heaven may be compared to a king who wished to settle accounts with his slaves.

[a] Gk the brother
[b] Gk if my brother
[c] Or seventy times seven

191		2770		04	80	1473	16	1437
ἀκούσῃ,		ἐκέρδησας	τὸν	ἀδελφόν	σου·			ἐὰν
he might hear,		you gained	the	brother	of you;			if

1161	3361	191		3880		3326	1473	2089	1520
δὲ	μὴ	ἀκούσῃ,		παράλαβε		μετὰ	σοῦ	ἔτι	ἕνα
but	not	he might hear,		take along		with	you	still	one

2228	1417	2443	1909	4750		1417	3144		2228	5140
ἢ	δύο,	ἵνα	ἐπὶ	στόματος	δύο		μαρτύρων	ἢ	τριῶν
or	two,	that on		mouth	of two		testifiers	or	three

2476	3956	4487	17	1437	1161	3878		846		3004
σταθῇ	πᾶν	ῥῆμα·		ἐὰν	δὲ	παρακούσῃ	αὐτῶν,		εἰπὲ
stand	might all	word;		if	but	he might	of them,		say
						ignore hearing				

07	1577		1437	1161	2532	06	1577		3878
τῇ	ἐκκλησίᾳ·	ἐὰν	δὲ	καὶ	τῆς	ἐκκλησίας	παρακούσῃ,
to assembly;	if	but	also	the	assembly	he might
the						ignore hearing,			

1510	1473	5618		01	1482	2532	01	5057
ἔστω	σοι	ὥσπερ	ὁ	ἐθνικὸς	καὶ	ὁ	τελώνης.
let be	to you	as indeed	the	nation	and	the	tax man.

18	281	3004	1473	3745	1437	1210		1909	06	1093
	Ἀμὴν	λέγω	ὑμῖν·	ὅσα	ἐὰν	δήσητε		ἐπὶ	τῆς	γῆς
	Amen I say	to you,	as if		you might		on	the	land
					much as	bind				

1510	1210		1722	3772	2532	3745	1437	3089
ἔσται	δεδεμένα	ἐν	οὐρανῷ,	καὶ	ὅσα	ἐὰν	λύσητε
it will	+having	in	heaven, and	as		if	you might
be+	been bound				much as		loose

1909	06	1093	1510		3089	1722	3772	19	3825
ἐπὶ	τῆς	γῆς	ἔσται		λελυμένα	ἐν	οὐρανῷ.		Πάλιν
on	the	land	it will be+		+having	in heaven.			Again
					been loosed				

281	3004	1473	3754	1437	1417	4856		1537
[ἀμὴν]	λέγω	ὑμῖν	ὅτι	ἐὰν	δύο	συμφωνήσωσιν	ἐξ
amen	I say	to you	that	if	two	agree		out of

1473	1909	06	1093	4012	3956	4229		3739	1437
ὑμῶν	ἐπὶ	τῆς	γῆς	περὶ	παντὸς	πράγματος	οὗ		ἐὰν
you	on	the	land	about	all	practice	of which	if

154		1096		846		3844	02	3962
αἰτήσωνται,		γενήσεται		αὐτοῖς	παρὰ	τοῦ	πατρός
they might ask,		it will become	to them	from	the	father

1473	02		1722	3772	20	3757	1063	1510	1417	2228
μου	τοῦ		ἐν	οὐρανοῖς.		οὗ	γάρ	εἰσιν	δύο	ἢ
of me	the one	in heavens.			Where	for	are+	two	or

5140	4863		1519	012	1699	3686	1563
τρεῖς	συνηγμένοι		εἰς	τὸ	ἐμὸν	ὄνομα,	ἐκεῖ
three	+being brought together	in	the	my	name,	there

1510	1722	3319	846	21	5119	4334		01
εἰμι	ἐν	μέσῳ	αὐτῶν.		Τότε	προσελθὼν		ὁ
I am	in	middle	of them.	Then	having gone toward the

4074	3004	846		2962		4212	264	1519
Πέτρος	εἶπεν	αὐτῷ·		κύριε,		ποσάκις	ἁμαρτήσει	εἰς
Peter	said	to him;	Master,	how often	might sin	to

1473	01	80		1473	2532	863		846	2193
ἐμὲ	ὁ	ἀδελφός	μου	καὶ	ἀφήσω		αὐτῷ;	ἕως
me	the	brother	of me and	I might send off	him?	Until

2034		3004	846	01	2424	3756	3004	1473
ἑπτάκις;	22	λέγει	αὐτῷ	ὁ	Ἰησοῦς·	οὐ	λέγω	σοι
seven times?		Says	to him	the	Jesus;	not	I say	to you

2193	2034	235	2193	1441		2033
ἕως	ἑπτάκις	ἀλλὰ	ἕως	ἑβδομηκοντάκις	ἑπτά.
until	seven times	but	until	seventy times	seven.

23	1223	3778	3666	05	932	014
	Διὰ	τοῦτο	ὡμοιώθη	ἡ	βασιλεία	τῶν
	Through this	was likened	the	kingdom	of the

3772	444	935	3739	2309	4868
οὐρανῶν	ἀνθρώπῳ	βασιλεῖ,	ὃς	ἠθέλησεν	συνᾶραι
heavens	to man	king,	who	wanted	to lift up
					together

```
3056    3326  014   1401    846      24  757          1161  846
λόγον  μετὰ  τῶν  δούλων  αὐτοῦ.      ἀρξαμένου   δὲ   αὐτοῦ
word   with   the  slaves  of him.      Having begun  but   him

4868                4374           846   1520  3781
συναίρειν           προσηνέχθη     αὐτῷ  εἷς   ὀφειλέτης
to lift up together was offered    him   one   debtor

3463          5007       25  3361  2192    1161  846
μυρίων       ταλάντων.       μὴ  ἔχοντος  δὲ   αὐτοῦ
of ten thousand talants.       Not  having  but   him

591        2753       846   01   2962    4097      2532
ἀποδοῦναι  ἐκέλευσεν  αὐτὸν ὁ   κύριος  πραθῆναι  καὶ
to give back commanded him   the  master to be sold and

08    1135     2532 024  5043    2532  3956   3745
τὴν  γυναῖκα  καὶ  τὰ  τέκνα  καὶ  πάντα  ὅσα
the  woman   and  the children and  all    as much as

2192   2532 591          26  4098              3767 01
ἔχει,  καὶ  ἀποδοθῆναι.     πεσὼν              οὖν  ὁ
he has, and  to be given off.  Having fallen then the

1401    4352        846   3004    3114
δοῦλος προσεκύνει  αὐτῷ  λέγων·  μακροθύμησον
slave  was worshiping him  saying,  be long-tempered

1909  1473  2532 3956 591        1473
ἐπ’  ἐμοί,  καὶ  πάντα ἀποδώσω  σοι.
on   me,    and  all   I will give back to you.

27  4697                 1161 01  2962    02   1401
    σπλαγχνισθεὶς      δὲ  ὁ  κύριος  τοῦ  δούλου
    Having had affection but  the  master  of the slave

1565    630        846   2532 012  1156   863
ἐκείνου ἀπέλυσεν  αὐτὸν καὶ  τὸ  δάνειον ἀφῆκεν
that   he loosed off him   and  the loan  he sent off

846    28  1831      1161 01  1401   1565    2147
αὐτῷ.      ἐξελθὼν  δὲ  ὁ  δοῦλος ἐκεῖνος εὗρεν
to him.    Having gone out but  the  slave  that   found

1520 014   4889         846   3739 3784   846   1540
ἕνα  τῶν  συνδούλων  αὐτοῦ, ὃς  ὤφειλεν αὐτῷ ἑκατὸν
one  of the co-slaves  of him, who  owed   him  hundred

1220      2532 2902       846   4155     3004
δηνάρια,  καὶ  κρατήσας  αὐτὸν ἔπνιγεν λέγων·
denaria,  and  having held him  he choked saying,

591      1487 5100 3784      29  4098              3767 01
ἀπόδος  εἴ   τι  ὀφείλεις.     πεσὼν              οὖν  ὁ
give back if   some you owe.    Having fallen then the

4889       846   3870        846   3004
σύνδουλος αὐτοῦ παρεκάλει   αὐτὸν λέγων·
co-slave  of him was encouraging him  saying;

3114           1909 1473  2532 591
μακροθύμησον  ἐπ’  ἐμοί,  καὶ  ἀποδώσω
be long-tempered on  me,   and  I will give back

1473   30  01  1161 3756 2309      235  565
σοι.       ὁ  δὲ  οὐκ  ἤθελεν  ἀλλὰ ἀπελθὼν
to you. The one but  not  wanted  but  having gone off

906      846   1519 5438      2193 591
ἔβαλεν  αὐτὸν εἰς  φυλακὴν ἕως  ἀποδῷ
he threw him   into  guard    until he might give off

012 3784       31  3708    3767 013 4889
τὸ  ὀφειλόμενον.    ἰδόντες  οὖν  οἱ  σύνδουλοι
the thing owed.       Having seen then the co-slaves

846   024 1096       3076           4970      2532
αὐτοῦ τὰ  γενόμενα  ἐλυπήθησαν  σφόδρα   καὶ
of him the things becoming were grieved exceeding and

2064      1285          03  2962   1438        3956
ἐλθόντες διεσάφησαν  τῷ  κυρίῳ  ἑαυτῶν     πάντα
having    they clearly the  master of themselves all
gone      told

024 1096       32  5119 4341                846   01
τὰ  γενόμενα.     τότε προσκαλεσάμενος  αὐτὸν ὁ
the things becoming. Then having called to him   the

2962    846   3004  846   1401   4190    3956  08
κύριος αὐτοῦ λέγει αὐτῷ·  δοῦλε πονηρέ, πᾶσαν τὴν
master of him says  to him; slave  evil,    all   the
```

24When he began the
reckoning, one who owed
him ten thousand talents[a]
was brought to him; 25and,
as he could not pay, his
lord ordered him to be
sold, together with his wife
and children and all his
possessions, and payment to
be made. 26So the slave fell
on his knees before him,
saying, 'Have patience
with me, and I will pay you
everything.' 27And out of
pity for him, the lord of
that slave released him and
forgave him the debt. 28But
that same slave, as he went
out, came upon one of his
fellow slaves who owed him
a hundred denarii;[b] and
seizing him by the throat,
he said, 'Pay what you
owe.' 29Then his fellow
slave fell down and pleaded
with him, 'Have patience
with me, and I will pay
you.' 30But he refused; then
he went and threw him into
prison until he would pay
the debt. 31When his fellow
slaves saw what had
happened, they were greatly
distressed, and they went
and reported to their lord
all that had taken place.
32Then his lord summoned
him and said to him, 'You
wicked slave! I forgave
you all

---

[a] A talent was worth more than
fifteen years' wages of a laborer

[b] The denarius was the usual day's
wage for a laborer

that debt because you
pleaded with me. ³³Should
you not have had mercy on
your fellow slave, as I had
mercy on you?' ³⁴And in
anger his lord handed him
over to be tortured until he
would pay his entire debt.
³⁵So my heavenly Father
will also do to every one of
you, if you do not forgive
your brother or sister^a
from your heart."

CHAPTER 19

When Jesus had finished
saying these things, he left
Galilee and went to the
region of Judea beyond
the Jordan. ²Large crowds
followed him, and he cured
them there.

3 Some Pharisees came
to him, and to test him they
asked, "Is it lawful for a
man to divorce his wife for
any cause?" ⁴He answered,
"Have you not read that the
one who made them at the
beginning 'made them male
and female,' ⁵and said, 'For
this reason a man shall
leave his father and mother
and be joined to his wife,
and the two shall become
one flesh"? ⁶So they are no
longer two, but one flesh.
Therefore what God has
joined together, let no one
separate."

^a Gk brother

| 3782 | 1565 | 863 | 1473 | 1893 | 3870 |

ὀφειλὴν ἐκείνην ἀφῆκά σοι, ἐπεὶ παρεκάλεσάς
debt   that   I sent off to you, since you encouraged

| 1473 | **33** | 3756 | 1163 | | 2532 1473 | 1653 |

με· οὐκ ἔδει   καὶ σὲ ἐλεῆσαι
me; not it was necessary also you to have mercy

| 04 | 4889 | 1473 | 5613 2504 | 1473 1653 | **34** | 2532 |

τὸν σύνδουλόν σου, ὡς κἀγὼ σὲ ἠλέησα; καὶ
the co-slave of you, as also I you had mercy? And

| 3710 | 01 | 2962 | 846 | 3860 | 846 | 015 |

ὀργισθεὶς ὁ κύριος αὐτοῦ παρέδωκεν αὐτὸν τοῖς
having become the master of him gave over him to the
angry

| 930 | 2193 | 3739 | 591 | | 3956 | 012 |

βασανισταῖς ἕως οὗ ἀποδῷ   πᾶν τὸ
tormentors until which he might give back all the

| 3784 | **35** | 3779 | 2532 01 | 3962 | 1473 01 |

ὀφειλόμενον. οὕτως καὶ ὁ πατήρ μου ὁ
thing owed. Thusly also the father of me the

| 3770 | 4160 | 1473 | 1437 3361 | 863 |

οὐράνιος ποιήσει ὑμῖν, ἐὰν μὴ ἀφῆτε
heavenly will do to you, except you might send off

| 1538 | 03 80 | 846 | 575 | 018 2588 | 1473 |

ἕκαστος τῷ ἀδελφῷ αὐτοῦ ἀπὸ τῶν καρδιῶν ὑμῶν.
each   the brother of him from the hearts of you.

| **19:1** | 2532 1096 | 3753 5055 | 01 | 2424 | 016 |

Καὶ ἐγένετο ὅτε ἐτέλεσεν ὁ Ἰησοῦς τοὺς
And it became when completed the Jesus the

| 3056 | 3778 | 3332 | | 575 06 | 1056 |

λόγους τούτους, μετῆρεν   ἀπὸ τῆς Γαλιλαίας
words these, he moved across from the Galilee

| 2532 2064 | 1519 | 024 3725 | | 06 | 2449 | 4008 |

καὶ ἦλθεν εἰς τὰ ὅρια   τῆς Ἰουδαίας πέραν
and went into the territories of the Judea across

| 02 | 2446 | **2** | 2532 190 | | 846 | 3793 | 4183 |

τοῦ Ἰορδάνου. καὶ ἠκολούθησαν αὐτῷ ὄχλοι πολλοί,
the Jordan. And followed   him crowds many,

| 2532 2323 | 846 | 1563 | **3** | 2532 4334 | | 846 |

καὶ ἐθεράπευσεν αὐτοὺς ἐκεῖ. Καὶ προσῆλθον αὐτῷ
and he healed them there. And came toward him

| 5330 | 3985 | 846 | 2532 3004 | 1487 |

Φαρισαῖοι πειράζοντες αὐτὸν καὶ λέγοντες· εἰ
Pharisees pressuring him and saying; if

| 1832 | 444 | 630 | 08 | 1135 | 846 |

ἔξεστιν ἀνθρώπῳ ἀπολῦσαι τὴν γυναῖκα αὐτοῦ
it is possible to man to loose off the woman of him

| 2596 3956 | 156 | **4** | 01 | 1161 611 |

κατὰ πᾶσαν αἰτίαν; ὁ δὲ ἀποκριθεὶς
by all cause? The one but having answered

| 3004 | 3756 314 | 3754 01 | 2936 | | 575 |

εἶπεν· οὐκ ἀνέγνωτε ὅτι ὁ κτίσας   ἀπ᾽
said, not you read that the one having created from

| 746 | 730 | 2532 2338 | 4160 | 846 | **5** | 2532 |

ἀρχῆς ἄρσεν καὶ θῆλυ ἐποίησεν αὐτούς; καὶ
beginning male and female he made them? And

| 3004 | 1752 | 3778 | 2641 | | 444 |

εἶπεν· ἕνεκα τούτου καταλείψει   ἄνθρωπος
he said, on account of this shall leave behind man

| 04 | 3962 2532 08 | 3384 2532 2853 | | 07 |

τὸν πατέρα καὶ τὴν μητέρα καὶ κολληθήσεται τῇ
the father and the mother and he will be joined to the

| 1135 | 846 | 2532 1510 | 013 1417 1519 4561 | 1520 |

γυναικὶ αὐτοῦ, καὶ ἔσονται οἱ δύο εἰς σάρκα μίαν.
woman of him, and will be the two into flesh one.

| **6** | 5620 | 3765 | 1510 | 1417 235 | 4561 | 1520 3739 |

ὥστε οὐκέτι εἰσὶν δύο ἀλλὰ σὰρξ μία. ὃ
So that no longer they are two but flesh one. What

| 3767 01 | 2316 4801 | | 444 | 3361 5563 |

οὖν ὁ θεὸς συνέζευξεν ἄνθρωπος μὴ χωριζέτω.
then the God yoked together man   not let separate.

7
```
3004        846      5101 3767 3475   1781        1325
λέγουσιν αὐτῷ·  τί   οὖν Μωϋσῆς ἐνετείλατο δοῦναι
They say to him, why then Moses  commanded  to give
975         647          2532 630          846
βιβλίον ἀποστασίου καὶ ἀπολῦσαι [αὐτήν];
small book of stand off and  to loose off her?
```
8
```
3004     846      3754 3475    4314   08   4641
λέγει   αὐτοῖς ὅτι Μωϋσῆς πρὸς τὴν σκληροκαρδίαν
He says to them, (") Moses toward the hard heart
1473   2010      1473  630       020 1135
ὑμῶν ἐπέτρεψεν ὑμῖν ἀπολῦσαι τὰς γυναῖκας
of you allowed  to you to loose off the women
1473    575  746    1161 3756 1096       3779
ὑμῶν,  ἀπ’ ἀρχῆς δὲ  οὐ  γέγονεν    οὕτως.
of you, from beginning but not it has become thusly.
```
9
```
3004   1161 1473  3754 3739 302 630          08
λέγω  δὲ  ὑμῖν ὅτι ὃς  ἂν ἀπολύσῃ      τὴν
I say but to you that who -  might loose off the
1135     846   3361 1909 4202          2532
γυναῖκα αὐτοῦ μὴ ἐπὶ πορνείᾳ      καὶ
woman of him not on  sexual immorality and
1060      243     3429        3004     846   013
γαμήσῃ  ἄλλην μοιχᾶται.  10 Λέγουσιν αὐτῷ οἱ
might marry other commits adultery. Say to him the
3101      846    1487 3779  1510  05 156  02
μαθηταὶ [αὐτοῦ]· εἰ οὕτως ἐστὶν ἡ αἰτία τοῦ
learners of him; if thusly is  the cause of the
444       3326 06 1135      3756 4851
ἀνθρώπου μετὰ τῆς γυναικός, οὐ συμφέρει
man  with the woman, not it is advantageous
1060      01     1161 3004  846    3756 3956
γαμῆσαι. 11 ὁ   δὲ εἶπεν αὐτοῖς· οὐ πάντες
to marry. The one but said to them; not all
5562      04  3056 3778   235 3739
χωροῦσιν τὸν λόγον [τοῦτον] ἀλλ’ οἷς
make room the word this    but to whom
1325      12 1510      1063 2135    3748
δέδοται.    εἰσὶν  γὰρ εὐνοῦχοι οἵτινες
it has been given. There are for eunuchs who
1537 2836      3384     1080       3779    2532
ἐκ κοιλίας μητρὸς ἐγεννήθησαν οὕτως, καὶ
out of stomach of mother were born  thusly, and
1510     2135      3748   2134        5259 014
εἰσὶν εὐνοῦχοι οἵτινες εὐνουχίσθησαν ὑπὸ τῶν
there are eunuchs who    were made eunuchs by the
444       2532 1510     2135      3748    2134
ἀνθρώπων, καὶ εἰσὶν εὐνοῦχοι οἵτινες εὐνούχισαν
men,    and there are eunuchs who    make eunuchs
1438     1223    08  932           014 3772
ἑαυτοὺς διὰ  τὴν βασιλείαν τῶν οὐρανῶν.
themselves because of the kingdom  of the heavens.
01 1410        5562        5562          5119
ὁ δυνάμενος χωρεῖν χωρείτω. 13 Τότε
The one being able to make room let make room. Then
4374         846    3813        2443 020 5495
προσηνέχθησαν αὐτῷ παιδία    ἵνα τὰς χεῖρας
were offered to him small children that the hands
2007       846    2532 4336        013 1161
ἐπιθῇ     αὐτοῖς καὶ προσεύξηται· οἱ δὲ
he might set on them and might pray; the but
3101      2008        846   14 01 1161 2424  3004
μαθηταὶ ἐπετίμησαν αὐτοῖς. ὁ  δὲ Ἰησοῦς εἶπεν·
learners admonished them. The but Jesus said;
863  024 3813         2532 3361 2967   846  2064
ἄφετε τὰ παιδία    καὶ μὴ κωλύετε αὐτὰ ἐλθεῖν
allow the small children and not hinder them to come
4314  1473 014    1063 5108      1510  05 932
πρός μᾶς, τῶν γὰρ τοιούτων ἐστὶν ἡ βασιλεία
toward me, of the for such  is  the kingdom
```

15And he laid his hands on them and went on his way.

16Then someone came to him and said, "Teacher, what good deed must I do to have eternal life?" 17And he said to him, "Why do you ask me about what is good? There is only one who is good. If you wish to enter into life, keep the commandments." 18He said to him, "Which ones?" And Jesus said, "You shall not murder; You shall not commit adultery; You shall not steal; You shall not bear false witness; 19Honor your father and mother; also, You shall love your neighbor as yourself."

20The young man said to him, "I have kept all these;*a* what do I still lack?"

21Jesus said to him, "If you wish to be perfect, go, sell your possessions, and give the money*b* to the poor, and you will have treasure in heaven; then come, follow me." 22When the young man heard this word, he went away grieving, for he had many possessions.

23Then Jesus said to his disciples, "Truly I tell you, it will be hard for a rich person to enter the kingdom of heaven. 24Again I tell you, it is easier for a camel to go through the eye of a needle

a Other ancient authorities add *from my youth*

b Gk lacks *the money*

```
014      3772          2532 2007              020  5495
τῶν      οὐρανῶν.  15  καὶ  ἐπιθεὶς         τὰς  χεῖρας
of the   heavens.     And  having set on   the  hands

846      4198        1564            2532 2400 1520
αὐτοῖς  ἐπορεύθη  ἐκεῖθεν.   16  Καὶ  ἰδοὺ  εἷς
them     he traveled from there.    And  look one

4334               846   3004      1320           5101 18
προσελθὼν         αὐτῷ  εἶπεν·  διδάσκαλε,  τί  ἀγαθὸν
having come toward him   said,  teacher,   what good

4160       2443 2192        2222 166           17  01
ποιήσω   ἵνα  σχῶ        ζωὴν αἰώνιον;        ὁ
might I do that I might have life eternal?    The one

1161 3004  846      5101 1473 2065      4012  010 18
δὲ  εἶπεν αὐτῷ·  τί  με  ἐρωτᾷς  περὶ  τοῦ ἀγαθοῦ;
but said to him,  why me  you ask about the good?

1520 1510  01  18        1487 1161 2309      1519 08
εἷς  ἐστιν ὁ  ἀγαθός·  εἰ  δὲ  θέλεις  εἰς  τὴν
One is     the good;   if  but  you want into the

2222 1525       5083       020 1785       18  3004  846
ζωὴν εἰσελθεῖν, τήρησον  τὰς ἐντολάς.     λέγει αὐτῷ·
life to go into, keep     the commands. He says to him;

4169        01  1161 2424  3004    012       3756
ποίας;     ὁ  δὲ  Ἰησοῦς εἶπεν·  τὸ      οὐ
what kind? The but  Jesus  said,   the one not

5407               3756 3431                    3756
φονεύσεις,       οὐ  μοιχεύσεις,             οὐ
you will murder, not  you will commit adultery, not

2813      3756 5576                  5091  04  3962
κλέψεις,  οὐ  ψευδομαρτυρήσεις,  19 τίμα τὸν πατέρα
you will not  you will testify      value the father
thieve,      falsely,

2532 08  3384      2532 25          04  4139      1473
καὶ  τὴν μητέρα, καὶ ἀγαπήσεις  τὸν πλησίον σου
and  the mother, and  you will love  the neighbor of you

5613 4572       20 3004  846   01  3495        3956
ὡς  σεαυτόν.     λέγει αὐτῷ  ὁ  νεανίσκος· πάντα
as yourself.     Says to him the young man, all

3778 5442        5101 2089 5302        21 5346 846
ταῦτα ἐφύλαξα·  τί  ἔτι  ὑστερῶ;       ἔφη αὐτῷ
these I guarded; what still do I lack?   Said to him

01  2424    1487 2309      5046      1510  5217
ὁ  Ἰησοῦς· εἰ  θέλεις  τέλειος  εἶναι, ὕπαγε
the Jesus·  if  you want complete to be, go off

4453      1473 024 5225              2532 1325 015
πώλησόν σου  τὰ ὑπάρχοντα      καὶ  δὸς [τοῖς]
sell      of you the possessions and  give to the

4434      2532 2192          2344    1722 3772      2532
πτωχοῖς, καὶ  ἕξεις        θησαυρὸν ἐν οὐρανοῖς, καὶ
poor,     and  you will have treasure in heavens,    and

1204 190        1473 191     22  1161 01  3495
δεῦρο ἀκολούθει μοι.      ἀκούσας  δὲ  ὁ  νεανίσκος
come follow    me.       Having heard but the young man

04  3056 565      3076          1510      1063 2192
τὸν λόγον ἀπῆλθεν λυπούμενος· ἦν  γὰρ ἔχων
the word went off grieving;    he was+ for +having

2933       4183      23 01  1161 2424   3004  015
κτήματα  πολλά.      Ὁ  δὲ  Ἰησοῦς εἶπεν τοῖς
acquisitions many.   The but  Jesus   said   to the

3101       846    281 3004  1473   3754 4145
μαθηταῖς αὐτοῦ· ἀμὴν λέγω ὑμῖν ὅτι πλούσιος
learners of him, amen I say to you that rich one

1423         1525             1519 08 932          014
δυσκόλως   εἰσελεύσεται  εἰς  τὴν βασιλείαν τῶν
with difficulty will go into  into the kingdom    of the

3772       24 3825 1161 3004  1473   2123
οὐρανῶν.     πάλιν δὲ  λέγω ὑμῖν, εὐκοπώτερόν
heavens.     Again but  I say to you, easier labor

1510 2574  1223        5169        4476
ἐστιν κάμηλον διὰ    τρυπήματος ῥαφίδος
it is camel    through opening    of needle
```

```
1330              2228 4145      1525        1519 08  932
διελθεῖν      ἢ  πλούσιον εἰσελθεῖν εἰς  τὴν βασιλείαν
to go through  or rich       to go into  into the kingdom
02      2316    191              1161 013 3101
τοῦ   θεοῦ.  25 ἀκούσαντες   δὲ   οἱ  μαθηταὶ
of the God.    Having heard   but  the learners
1605             4970       3004          5101 686  1410
ἐξεπλήσσοντο σφόδρα λέγοντες· τίς ἄρα δύναται
were astonished exceeding saying,   who then is able
4982            1689          1161 01  2424
σωθῆναι;   26 ἐμβλέψας     δὲ  ὁ  Ἰησοῦς
to be delivered? Having looked in but  the Jesus
3004 846        3844 444      3778   102      1510
εἶπεν αὐτοῖς· παρὰ ἀνθρώποις τοῦτο ἀδύνατόν ἐστιν,
said  to them, along men       this  unable    is,
3844 1161 2316 3956 1415       5119 611
παρὰ δὲ  θεῷ πάντα δυνατά. 27 Τότε ἀποκριθεὶς
along but God  all  power.       Then having answered
01   4074      3004 846       2400 1473 863       3956
ὁ   Πέτρος εἶπεν αὐτῷ· ἰδοὺ ἡμεῖς ἀφήκαμεν πάντα
the Peter  said  to him, look we    sent off    all
2532 190            1473 5101 686 1510       1473      01
καὶ ἠκολουθήσαμέν σοι· τί ἄρα ἔσται ἡμῖν; 28 ὁ
and followed       you; what then will be to us?    The
1161 2424    3004 846        281  3004  1473    3754
δὲ  Ἰησοῦς εἶπεν αὐτοῖς· ἀμὴν λέγω ὑμῖν ὅτι
but Jesus  said  to them, amen I say to you that
1473 013 190              1473 1722 07  3824
ὑμεῖς οἱ ἀκολουθήσαντές μοι ἐν  τῇ παλιγγενεσίᾳ,
you   the ones having     me  in  the born again,
              followed
3752 2523      01  5207 02       444        1909 2362
ὅταν καθίσῃ  ὁ  υἱὸς τοῦ   ἀνθρώπου ἐπὶ θρόνου
when might sit the son  of the man       on  throne
1391       846       2521          2532 1473 1909 1427
δόξης    αὐτοῦ, καθήσεσθε καὶ ὑμεῖς ἐπὶ δώδεκα
of splendor of him, will sit also you  on  twelve
2362     2919    020 1427     5443    02   2474
θρόνους κρίνοντες τὰς δώδεκα φυλὰς τοῦ  Ἰσραήλ.
thrones judging  the twelve tribes of the Israel.
   2532 3956 3748 863              3614       2228 80
29 καὶ πᾶς ὅστις ἀφῆκεν    οἰκίας ἢ    ἀδελφοὺς
   And all  who   have sent off houses or   brothers
2228 79      2228 3962 2228 3384 2228 5043      2228 68
ἢ ἀδελφὰς ἢ πατέρα ἢ μητέρα ἢ   τέκνα   ἢ ἀγροὺς
or sisters or father or mother or children or fields
1752      010      3686       1473    1542
ἕνεκεν   τοῦ   ὀνόματός μου, ἑκατονταπλασίονα
on account of the name     of me, hundred times
2983            2532 2222 166      2816         30 4183
λήμψεται   καὶ ζωὴν αἰώνιον κληρονομήσει.    πολλοὶ
will receive also life eternal will inherit.    Many
1161 1510  4413    2078      2532 2078    4413
δὲ  ἔσονται πρῶτοι ἔσχατοι καὶ ἔσχατοι πρῶτοι.
but will be first  last     and last     first.
      3664 1063 1510  05   932        014    3772
20:1 Ὁμοία γὰρ ἐστιν ἡ βασιλεία τῶν  οὐρανῶν
      Like for is    the kingdom of the heavens
444      3617        3748 1831      260
ἀνθρώπῳ οἰκοδεσπότῃ, ὅστις ἐξῆλθεν ἅμα
to man  house supervisor, who went out at same time
4404      3409          2040    1519 04  290
πρωῒ    μισθώσασθαι  ἐργάτας εἰς  τὸν ἀμπελῶνα
in morning to hire     for wages workers into the vineyard
846     2 4856        1161 3326 014 2040     1537
αὐτοῦ.   συμφωνήσας δὲ  μετὰ τῶν ἐργατῶν ἐκ
of him. Having agreed but with the workers from
1220      08 2250  649      846      1519 04
δηναρίου τὴν ἡμέραν ἀπέστειλεν αὐτοὺς εἰς  τὸν
denarius the day    he delegated them    into the
```

than for someone who is rich to enter the kingdom of God." 25When the disciples heard this, they were greatly astounded and said, "Then who can be saved?" 26But Jesus looked at them and said, "For mortals it is impossible, but for God all things are possible."

27 Then Peter said in reply, "Look, we have left everything and followed you. What then will we have?" 28Jesus said to them, "Truly I tell you, at the renewal of all things, when the Son of Man is seated on the throne of his glory, you who have followed me will also sit on twelve thrones, judging the twelve tribes of Israel. 29And everyone who has left houses or brothers or sisters or father or mother or children or fields, for my name's sake, will receive a hundredfold,[a] and will inherit eternal life. 30But many who are first will be last, and the last will be first.

CHAPTER 20

"For the kingdom of heaven is like a landowner who went out early in the morning to hire laborers for his vineyard. 2After agreeing with the laborers for the usual daily wage,[b] he sent them into his vineyard.

[a] Other ancient authorities read manifold
[b] Gk a denarius

3When he went out about nine o'clock, he saw others standing idle in the marketplace; 4and he said to them, 'You also go into the vineyard, and I will pay you whatever is right.' So they went. 5When he went out again about noon and about three o'clock, he did the same. 6And about five o'clock he went out and found others standing around; and he said to them, 'Why are you standing here idle all day?' 7They said to him, 'Because no one has hired us.' He said to them, 'You also go into the vineyard.' 8When evening came, the owner of the vineyard said to his manager, 'Call the laborers and give them their pay, beginning with the last and then going to the first.' 9When those hired about five o'clock came, each of them received the usual daily wage.[a] 10Now when the first came, they thought they would receive more; but each of them also received the usual daily wage.[a] 11And when they received it, they grumbled against the landowner, 12saying, 'These last worked only one hour, and you have made them equal to us who have borne the burden of the day and the scorching heat.' 13But he replied to one of them,

[a] Gk a denarius

	290	846	3	2532	1831		4012	5154
	ἀμπελῶνα	αὐτοῦ.		καὶ	ἐξελθὼν		περὶ	τρίτην
	vineyard of	him.		And	having gone out		around	third

5610	3708	243	2476		1722	07	58	692
ὥραν	εἶδεν	ἄλλους	ἑστῶτας		ἐν	τῇ	ἀγορᾷ	ἀργούς
hour	he saw	others	having stood		in	the	market	idle

4 2532 1565 3004 5217 2532 1473 1519 04
καὶ ἐκείνοις εἶπεν· ὑπάγετε καὶ ὑμεῖς εἰς τὸν
and to those he said, go off also you into the

290 2532 3739 1437 1510 1342 1325
ἀμπελῶνα, καὶ ὃ ἐὰν ᾖ δίκαιον δώσω
vineyard, and what if it might be right I will give

1473 013 1161 565 3825 1161 1831
ὑμῖν. 5 οἱ δὲ ἀπῆλθον. πάλιν [δὲ] ἐξελθὼν
to you. The but went off. Again but having gone out

4012 1623 2532 1728a 5610 4160 5615 6 4012
περὶ ἕκτην καὶ ἐνάτην ὥραν ἐποίησεν ὡσαύτως. περὶ
around sixth and ninth hour he did likewise. Around

1161 08 1734 1831 2147 243
δὲ τὴν ἑνδεκάτην ἐξελθὼν εὗρεν ἄλλους
but the eleventh having gone out he found others

2476 2532 3004 846 5101 5602 2476 3650
ἑστῶτας καὶ λέγει αὐτοῖς· τί ὧδε ἑστήκατε ὅλην
having and says to them, why here have you whole
stood stood

08 2250 692 7 3004 846 3754 3762
τὴν ἡμέραν ἀργοί; λέγουσιν αὐτῷ· ὅτι οὐδεὶς
the day idle? They say to him; because no one

1473 3409 3004 846 5217 2532
ἡμᾶς ἐμισθώσατο. λέγει αὐτοῖς· ὑπάγετε καὶ
us hired for wages. He says to them, go off also

1473 1519 04 290 8 3798 1161 1096
ὑμεῖς εἰς τὸν ἀμπελῶνα. ὀψίας δὲ γενομένης
you into the vineyard. Evening but having become

3004 01 2962 02 290 03 2012
λέγει ὁ κύριος τοῦ ἀμπελῶνος τῷ ἐπιτρόπῳ
says the master of the vineyard to the governor

846 2564 016 2040 2532 591 846 04
αὐτοῦ· κάλεσον τοὺς ἐργάτας καὶ ἀπόδος αὐτοῖς τὸν
of him; call the workers and give off to them the

3408 757 575 014 2078 2193 014 4413
μισθὸν ἀρξάμενος ἀπὸ τῶν ἐσχάτων ἕως τῶν πρώτων.
wage having begun from the last until the first.

9 2532 2064 013 4012 08 1734 5610
καὶ ἐλθόντες οἱ περὶ τὴν ἑνδεκάτην ὥραν
And having gone the ones around the eleventh hour

2983 303 1220 10 2532 2064 013 4413
ἔλαβον ἀνὰ δηνάριον. καὶ ἐλθόντες οἱ πρῶτοι
received up denarius. And having gone the first

3543 3754 4183 2983 2532 2983 012 303
ἐνόμισαν ὅτι πλεῖον λήμψονται· καὶ ἔλαβον [τὸ] ἀνὰ
thought that more they will and they the up
receive; received

1220 2532 846 11 2983 1161
δηνάριον καὶ αὐτοί. λαβόντες δὲ
denarius also themselves. Having received but

1111 2596 02 3617 12 3004
ἐγόγγυζον κατὰ τοῦ οἰκοδεσπότου λέγοντες·
they grumbled against the house supervisor saying,

3778 013 2078 1520 5610 4160 2532 2470 1473
οὗτοι οἱ ἔσχατοι μίαν ὥραν ἐποίησαν, καὶ ἴσους ἡμῖν
These the last one hour they did, and equal to us

846 4410 015 941 012 342
αὐτοὺς ἐποίησας τοῖς βαστάσασι τὸ βάρος
them you did to the ones having borne the burden

06 2250 2532 04 2742 13 01 1161
τῆς ἡμέρας καὶ τὸν καύσωνα. ὁ δὲ
of the day and the burning heat. The one but

611   1520   846   3004   2083   3756
ἀποκριθεὶς   ἑνὶ   αὐτῶν   εἶπεν·   ἑταῖρε,   οὐκ
having answered to one   of them   said,   comrade,   not

91   1473   3780 1220   4856   1473
ἀδικῶ   σε·   οὐχὶ δηναρίου συνεφώνησάς μοι;
I do unright   you;   not denarius you agreed   to me?

14 142 012 4674 2532 5217   2309   1161 3778   03
    ἆρον τὸ σὸν   καὶ ὕπαγε.   θέλω   δὲ   τούτῳ   τῷ
    Lift up the yours and go off.   I want but to this   the

2078   1325   5613 2532 1473   2228 3756 1832
ἐσχάτῳ   δοῦναι ὡς   καὶ σοί· 15 [ἢ] οὐκ ἔξεστίν
last   to give as   also to you; or   not is it possible

1473   3739 2309   4160   1722 023   1699   2228 01
μοι   ὃ   θέλω   ποιῆσαι   ἐν   τοῖς ἐμοῖς;   ἢ   ὁ
to me   what I want   to do   in   the mine?   Or   the

3788   1473 4190   1510   3754   1473 18   1510
ὀφθαλμός   σου πονηρός   ἐστιν ὅτι   ἐγὼ ἀγαθός εἰμι;
eye   of you evil   is   because I   good   am?

16 3779   1510   013 2078   4413   2532 013 4413
    οὕτως   ἔσονται   οἱ   ἔσχατοι πρῶτοι   καὶ οἱ   πρῶτοι
    Thusly   will be   the last   first   and the first

2078   2532 305   01   2424   1519 2414
ἔσχατοι.   17 Καὶ ἀναβαίνων ὁ   Ἰησοῦς   εἰς Ἱεροσόλυμα
last.   And going up the Jesus   into Jerusalem

3880   016   1427 3101   2596 2398   2532 1722
παρέλαβεν   τοὺς   δώδεκα [μαθητὰς] κατ᾽ ἰδίαν   καὶ ἐν
took along   the   twelve learners   by   own   and in

07   3598 3004   846   18 2400 305   1519
τῇ   ὁδῷ εἶπεν   αὐτοῖς·   ἰδοὺ ἀναβαίνομεν εἰς
the way he said to them;   look we go up   into

2414   2532 01 5207 02   444
Ἱεροσόλυμα,   καὶ ὁ   υἱὸς τοῦ   ἀνθρώπου
Jerusalem,   and the son of the   man

3860   015   749   2532
παραδοθήσεται   τοῖς ἀρχιερεῦσιν καὶ
will be given over to the ruler priests and

1122   2532 2632   846   2288
γραμματεῦσιν,   καὶ κατακρινοῦσιν αὐτὸν   θανάτῳ
writers,   and they will condemn him   to death

19 2532 3860   846   023 1484   1519 012
    καὶ παραδώσουσιν   αὐτὸν τοῖς ἔθνεσιν   εἰς τὸ
    and they will give over him to the nations for the

1702   2532 3146   2532 4717   2532 07
ἐμπαῖξαι   καὶ μαστιγῶσαι καὶ σταυρῶσαι, καὶ τῇ
to mock   and to scourge and to crucify, and in the

5154   2250   1453   20 5119 4334   846
τρίτῃ   ἡμέρᾳ ἐγερθήσεται.   Τότε προσῆλθεν   αὐτῷ
third   day   he will be raised.   Then went toward him

05 3384   014   5207 2199   3326 014 5207 846
ἡ   μήτηρ τῶν   υἱῶν Ζεβεδαίου μετὰ τῶν υἱῶν αὐτῆς
the mother of the sons of Zebedee with the sons of her

4352   2532 154   5100   575 846   21 01
προσκυνοῦσα   καὶ αἰτοῦσά   τι   ἀπ᾽ αὐτοῦ.   ὁ
worshiping   and asking   something from him.   The one

1161 3004 846   5101 2309   3004   846
δὲ   εἶπεν αὐτῇ·   τί   θέλεις;   λέγει   αὐτῷ·
but said to her,   what do you want? She says to him,

3004 2443 2523   3778 013 1417 5207 1473 1520 1537
εἰπὲ ἵνα καθίσωσιν   οὗτοι οἱ δύο   υἱοί μου εἷς ἐκ
say that might sit   these the two   sons of me one from

1188   1473   2532 1520 1537 2101   1473 1722 07
δεξιῶν   σου   καὶ εἷς ἐξ εὐωνύμων σου ἐν   τῇ
right   of you   and one from left   of you in   the

932   1473 22 611   1161 01 2424   3004
βασιλείᾳ σου.   ἀποκριθεὶς   δὲ   ὁ Ἰησοῦς   εἶπεν·
kingdom of you.   Having answered but the Jesus   said,

3756 3609a   5101 154   1410   4095   012
οὐκ οἴδατε   τί   αἰτεῖσθε.   δύνασθε   πιεῖν   τὸ
not you know   what you ask.   Are you able to drink the

'Friend, I am doing you no wrong; did you not agree with me for the usual daily wage?[a] [14]Take what belongs to you and go; I choose to give to this last the same as I give to you. [15]Am I not allowed to do what I choose with what belongs to me? Or are you envious because I am generous?'[b] [16]So the last will be first, and the first will be last."[c]

[17]While Jesus was going up to Jerusalem, he took the twelve disciples aside by themselves, and said to them on the way, [18]"See, we are going up to Jerusalem, and the Son of Man will be handed over to the chief priests and scribes, and they will condemn him to death; [19]then they will hand him over to the Gentiles to be mocked and flogged and crucified; and on the third day he will be raised."

[20]Then the mother of the sons of Zebedee came to him with her sons, and kneeling before him, she asked a favor of him. [21]And he said to her, "What do you want?" She said to him, "Declare that these two sons of mine will sit, one at your right hand and one at your left, in your kingdom." [22]But Jesus answered, "You do not know what you are asking. Are you able to drink the

a Gk a denarius
b Gk is your eye evil because I am good?
c Other ancient authorities add for many are called but few are chosen

cup that I am about to drink?"[a] They said to him, "We are able." [23]He said to them, "You will indeed drink my cup, but to sit at my right hand and at my left, this is not mine to grant, but it is for those for whom it has been prepared by my Father."

[24]When the ten heard it, they were angry with the two brothers. [25]But Jesus called them to him and said, "You know that the rulers of the Gentiles lord it over them, and their great ones are tyrants over them. [26]It will not be so among you; but whoever wishes to be great among you must be your servant, [27]and whoever wishes to be first among you must be your slave; [28]just as the Son of Man came not to be served but to serve, and to give his life a ransom for many."

[29]As they were leaving Jericho, a large crowd followed him. [30]There were two blind men sitting by the roadside. When they heard that Jesus was passing by, they shouted, "Lord,[b] have mercy on us, Son of David!" [31]The crowd sternly ordered them to be quiet; but they shouted even more loudly, "Have mercy on us, Lord, Son of David!" [32]Jesus stood still

[a] Other ancient authorities add or to be baptized with the baptism that I am baptized with?

[b] Other ancient authorities lack Lord

4221	3739	1473	3195	4095	3004	846
ποτήριον	ὃ	ἐγὼ μέλλω	πίνειν;	λέγουσιν αὐτῷ·
cup	which I	am about to drink?	They say to him,

1410   3004   846   012 3303   4221   1473
δυνάμεθα. [23] λέγει   αὐτοῖς·   τὸ μὲν   ποτήριόν μου
we are able. He says to them, the indeed cup   of me

4095   09   1161 2523   1537   1188   1473 2532
πίεσθε,   τὸ δὲ καθίσαι ἐκ δεξιῶν μου   καὶ
you will drink, the but to sit from right of me and

1537 2176   3756 1510   1699   3778   1325   235
ἐξ εὐωνύμων οὐκ ἔστιν ἐμὸν [τοῦτο] δοῦναι, ἀλλ'
from left   not it is mine this   to give, but

3739   2090   5259 02 3962   1473
οἷς   ἡτοίμασται   ὑπὸ τοῦ πατρός μου.
to whom it has been prepared by the father of me.

        2532 191   013 1176 23   4012   014
[24] Καὶ ἀκούσαντες οἱ δέκα ἠγανάκτησαν   περὶ τῶν
     And having heard the ten   were indignant   about the

1417 80   01 1161 2424   4341
δύο ἀδελφῶν. [25] ὁ δὲ Ἰησοῦς προσκαλεσάμενος
two brothers.   The but Jesus having called toward

846   3004   3609a   3754 013 758   022   1484
αὐτοὺς εἶπεν· οἴδατε   ὅτι οἱ ἄρχοντες τῶν   ἐθνῶν
them   said; you know that the rulers of the nations

2634   846   2532 013 3173   2715
κατακυριεύουσιν αὐτῶν καὶ οἱ μεγάλοι κατεξουσιάζουσιν
master over   them and the great   exercise
                                    ones   authority over

846   26 3756 3779   1510   1722 1473 235   3739
αὐτῶν.   οὐχ οὕτως ἔσται   ἐν ὑμῖν, ἀλλ' ὃς
them.   Not thusly will it be in you, but who

1437 2309   1722 1473 3173 1096   1510
ἐὰν θέλῃ   ἐν ὑμῖν μέγας γενέσθαι ἔσται
if might want in you great to become will be

1473 1249   2532 3739 302 2309   1722
ὑμῶν διάκονος, [27] καὶ ὃς ἂν θέλῃ   ἐν
of you servant,   and who - might want in

1473 1510 4413   1510   1473 1401   28 5618 01
ὑμῖν εἶναι πρῶτος ἔσται   ὑμῶν δοῦλος·   ὥσπερ ὁ
you to be first   will be of you slave;   as indeed the

5207 02   444   3756 2064 1247   235
υἱὸς τοῦ ἀνθρώπου οὐκ ἦλθεν διακονηθῆναι ἀλλὰ
son of the man   not came to be served but

1247   2532 1325   08 5590 846   3083
διακονῆσαι καὶ δοῦναι τὴν ψυχὴν αὐτοῦ λύτρον
to serve   and to give the soul of him ransom

473   4183   29 2532 1607   846   575
ἀντὶ πολλῶν.   Καὶ ἐκπορευομένων αὐτῶν ἀπὸ
in place of many. And traveling out them from

2410   190   846   3793 4183   30 2532 2400
Ἰεριχὼ ἠκολούθησαν αὐτῷ ὄχλος πολύς.   καὶ ἰδοὺ
Jericho followed   him crowd much.   And look

1417 5185 2521   3844 08 3598 191   3754
δύο τυφλοὶ καθήμενοι παρὰ τὴν ὁδόν ἀκούσαντες ὅτι
two blind sitting   along the way having heard that

2424   3855   2896   3004   1653   1473
Ἰησοῦς παράγει,   ἔκραξαν λέγοντες· ἐλέησον ἡμᾶς,
Jesus leads along, shouted saying, have mercy us,

2962   5207 1160a 31 01 1161 3793   2008   846
[κύριε,] υἱὸς Δαυίδ.   ὁ δὲ ὄχλος ἐπετίμησεν αὐτοῖς
Master, son of David. The but crowd admonished them

2443 4623   013 1161 3173   2896   3004
ἵνα σιωπήσωσιν· οἱ δὲ μεῖζον ἔκραξαν λέγοντες·
that they might the ones but greater shouted saying,
     be silent;

1653   1473   2962   5207 1160a 32 2532 2476
ἐλέησον ἡμᾶς, κύριε, υἱὸς Δαυίδ.   καὶ στὰς
have mercy us, Master, son David.   And having stood

```
01    2424   5455        846    2532  3004       5101  2309
ὁ  Ἰησοῦς ἐφώνησεν αὐτοὺς καὶ  εἶπεν·   τί   θέλετε
the Jesus   sounded   them   and   said,   what do you want
4160        1473     33  3004       846    2962     2443
ποιήσω     ὑμῖν;       λέγουσιν αὐτῷ·   κύριε,   ἵνα
I might do to you?      They say to him;  Master,  that
455        013  3788       1473   34    4697        1161
ἀνοιγῶσιν οἱ ὀφθαλμοὶ ἡμῶν.     σπλαγχνισθεὶς δὲ
might be the   eyes     of us.   Having had      but
opened                                  affection
01    2424   681     022  3659       846    2532  2112
ὁ  Ἰησοῦς ἥψατο  τῶν ὀμμάτων αὐτῶν, καὶ εὐθέως
the Jesus   touched the eyes  of them, and  immediately
308          2532  190        846  21:1 2532  3753
ἀνέβλεψαν καὶ ἠκολούθησαν αὐτῷ.    Καὶ  ὅτε
they saw again and they followed him.    And  when
1448        1519   2414          2532 2064  1519  967
ἤγγισαν    εἰς Ἱεροσόλυμα καὶ ἦλθον εἰς Βηθφαγὴ
they neared to  Jerusalem  and  went into Bethphage
1519  012 3735 018    1636     5119  2424     649
εἰς  τὸ ὄρος τῶν  ἐλαιῶν, τότε Ἰησοῦς ἀπέστειλεν
to   the hill of the  olives,  then  Jesus  delegated
1417  3101  2  3004   846        4198       1519 08
δύο μαθητὰς  λέγων  αὐτοῖς·  πορεύεσθε εἰς  τὴν
two  learners saying to them,  travel     into  the
2968   08  2713       1473  2532  2112
κώμην τὴν κατέναντι ὑμῶν, καὶ εὐθέως
village the over against you,  and  immediately
2147         3688  1210            2532 4454   3326
εὑρήσετε    ὄνον δεδεμένην    καὶ πῶλον μετ᾽
you will find donkey having been bound and colt  with
846     3089      71     1473  2532 1437 5100
αὐτῆς· λύσαντες ἀγάγετέ μοι.  3 καὶ ἐάν τις
her;    having loosed bring  to me. And  if   some
1473  3004     5100 3004      3754 01 2962    846
ὑμῖν εἴπη    τι,    ἐρεῖτε ὅτι ὁ κύριος αὐτῶν
to you might say some,  say,  (") the Master of them
5532   2192  2117         1161 649           846
χρείαν ἔχει· εὐθὺς   δὲ  ἀποστελεῖ      αὐτούς.
need   has;  immediately but he will delegate them.
4  3778  1161 1096       2443 4137              09
τοῦτο δὲ  γέγονεν ἵνα πληρωθῇ         τὸ
This  but has become that might be fulfilled the
3004        1223    02 4396       3004     5  3004
ῥηθὲν      διὰ   τοῦ προφήτου λέγοντος,  εἴπατε
word having through the spokesman saying,  say to
been spoken
07   2364      4622     2400 01   935        1473  2064
τῇ θυγατρὶ Σιών·  ἰδοὺ ὁ βασιλεύς σου ἔρχεταί
the daughter of Sion; look the  king    of you comes
1473  4239    2532 1910          1909 3688   2532
σοι  πραΰς καὶ ἐπιβεβηκὼς  ἐπὶ ὄνον  καὶ
to you gentle and having gone on on  donkey and
1909 4454  5207 5268         6  4198           1161 013
ἐπὶ πῶλον υἱὸν ὑποζυγίου.   πορευθέντες δὲ  οἱ
on  colt  son of yoke animal. Having traveled but the
3101   2532 4160        2531  4929       846
μαθηταὶ καὶ ποιήσαντες καθὼς συνέταξεν αὐτοῖς
learners and having done just as fully ordered them
01    2424   7  71     08 3688   2532 04  4454 2532
ὁ  Ἰησοῦς ἤγαγον τὴν ὄνον καὶ τὸν πῶλον καὶ
the Jesus   brought the donkey and the  colt  and
2007      1909 846    024 2440      2532 1940       1883
ἐπέθηκαν ἐπ᾽ αὐτῶν τὰ ἱμάτια, καὶ ἐπεκάθισεν ἐπάνω
set on    on  them the clothes, and he sat on   upon
846     8  01 1161 4183       3793 4766      1438
αὐτῶν.   ὁ  δὲ πλεῖστος ὄχλος ἔστρωσαν ἑαυτῶν
them.     The but most   crowd  spread    of themselves
```

and called them, saying,
"What do you want me to
do for you?" [33]They said
to him, "Lord, let our eyes
be opened." [34]Moved with
compassion, Jesus touched
their eyes. Immediately they
regained their sight and
followed him.

CHAPTER 21

When they had come near
Jerusalem and had reached
Bethphage, at the Mount
of Olives, Jesus sent two
disciples, [2]saying to them,
"Go into the village ahead
of you, and immediately
you will find a donkey tied,
and a colt with her; untie
them and bring them to me.
[3]If anyone says anything to
you, just say this, 'The Lord
needs them.' And he will
send them immediately.[a]"
[4]This took place to fulfill
what had been spoken
through the prophet,
saying,
[5]"Tell the daughter of
    Zion,
  Look, your king is
    coming to you,
  humble, and mounted
    on a donkey,
  and on a colt, the foal
    of a donkey."
[6]The disciples went and did
as Jesus had directed them;
[7]they brought the donkey
and the colt, and put their
cloaks on them, and he sat
on them. [8]A very large
crowd[b] spread

[a] Or 'The Lord needs them and will
    send them back immediately.'
[b] Or Most of the crowd

their cloaks on the road, and others cut branches from the trees and spread them on the road. 9The crowds that went ahead of him and that followed were shouting,

"Hosanna to the Son of David!
Blessed is the one who comes in the name of the Lord!
Hosanna in the highest heaven!"

10When he entered Jerusalem, the whole city was in turmoil, asking, "Who is this?" 11The crowds were saying, "This is the prophet Jesus from Nazareth in Galilee."

12 Then Jesus entered the temple*a* and drove out all who were selling and buying in the temple, and he overturned the tables of the money changers and the seats of those who sold doves. 13He said to them, "It is written,

'My house shall be called a house of prayer';
but you are making it a den of robbers."

14 The blind and the lame came to him in the temple, and he cured them. 15But when the chief priests and the scribes saw the amazing things that he did, and heard*b* the children crying out in the temple, "Hosanna to the Son of David," they became angry 16and said to him, "Do you hear what these are saying?" Jesus

a Other ancient authorities add *of God*
b Gk lacks *heard*

024	2440		1722	07	3598	243		1161	2875		2798
τὰ	ἱμάτια	ἐν	τῇ	ὁδῷ,	ἄλλοι	δὲ		ἔκοπτον	κλάδους		
the	clothes	in	the	way,	others	but		cut	branches		

575	022	1186		2532	4766		1722	07	3598	013
ἀπὸ	τῶν	δένδρων	καὶ	ἐστρώννυον	ἐν	τῇ	ὁδῷ.	9	οἱ	
from	the	trees	and	spread	in	the	way.		The	

1161	3793	013	4254		846	2532	013
δὲ	ὄχλοι	οἱ	προάγοντες		αὐτὸν	καὶ	οἱ
but	crowds	the	ones leading		before him	and	the ones

190		2896		3004		5614	03	5207
ἀκολουθοῦντες	ἔκραζον		λέγοντες·	ὡσαννὰ	τῷ	υἱῷ	
following	were shouting	saying,	hosanna	to	the son	

1160a	2127		01	2064	1722
Δαυίδ·	εὐλογημένος	ὁ	ἐρχόμενος	ἐν	
of David;	having been well spoken	the one	coming	in	

3686	2962		5614	1722	023	5310	2532
ὀνόματι	κυρίου·	ὡσαννὰ	ἐν	τοῖς	ὑψίστοις.	10	Καὶ
name	of Master;	hosanna	in	the	highest.		And

1525	846	1519	2414		4579	3956
εἰσελθόντος	αὐτοῦ	εἰς	Ἱεροσόλυμα	ἐσείσθη	πᾶσα	
having gone in	him	into	Jerusalem	was shaken	all	

05	4172	3004		5101	1510	3778	013	1161
ἡ	πόλις	λέγουσα·	τίς	ἐστιν	οὗτος;	11	οἱ	δὲ
the	city	saying·	who	is	this one?		The	but

3793	3004		3778	1510	01	4396	2424
ὄχλοι	ἔλεγον·	οὗτός	ἐστιν	ὁ	προφήτης	Ἰησοῦς	
crowds	were saying,	this	is	the	spokesman	Jesus	

01	575	3478	06	1056		2532	1525
ὁ	ἀπὸ	Ναζαρὲθ	τῆς	Γαλιλαίας.	12	Καὶ	εἰσῆλθεν
the one	from	Nazareth	of	the Galilee.		And	went in

2424	1519	012	2411	2532	1544	3956	016
Ἰησοῦς	εἰς	τὸ	ἱερὸν	καὶ	ἐξέβαλεν	πάντας	τοὺς
Jesus	into	the	temple	and	threw out	all	the ones

4453	2532	59		1722	011	2411	2532	020
πωλοῦντας	καὶ	ἀγοράζοντας	ἐν	τῷ	ἱερῷ,	καὶ	τὰς	
selling	and	buying	in	the	temple,	and	the	

5132	014	2855		2690		2632	020
τραπέζας	τῶν	κολλυβιστῶν	κατέστρεψεν	καὶ	τὰς	
tables	of	the money changers	he turned over	and	the	

2515	014	4453		020	4058	2532
καθέδρας	τῶν	πωλούντων	τὰς	περιστεράς,	13	καὶ
seats	of	the ones selling	the	doves,		and

3004	846		1125		01	3624	1473
λέγει	αὐτοῖς·	γέγραπται·		ὁ	οἶκός	μου	
he says	to them,	it has been written:		the	house	of me	

3624	4335		2564		1473	1161	846	4160
οἶκος	προσευχῆς	κληθήσεται,		ὑμεῖς	δὲ	αὐτὸν	ποιεῖτε	
house	of prayer	will be called,		you	but	it	made	

4693	3027		2532	4334		846	5185
σπήλαιον	λῃστῶν.	14	καὶ	προσῆλθον	αὐτῷ	τυφλοὶ	
cave	of robbers.		And	went toward	him	blind	

2532	5560	1722	011	2411	2532	2323		846
καὶ	χωλοὶ	ἐν	τῷ	ἱερῷ,	καὶ	ἐθεράπευσεν	αὐτούς.	
and	lame	in	the	temple,	and	he healed	them.	

3708		1161	013	749		2532	013	1122
15 ἰδόντες	δὲ	οἱ	ἀρχιερεῖς	καὶ	οἱ	γραμματεῖς		
Having seen	but	the	ruler priests	and	the	writers		

024	2297		3739	4160	2532	016	3816	016
τὰ	θαυμάσια	ἃ	ἐποίησεν	καὶ	τοὺς	παῖδας	τοὺς	
the	marvels	which	he did	and	the	boy servants	the	

2896		1722	011	2411	2532	3004		5614	03
κράζοντας	ἐν	τῷ	ἱερῷ	καὶ	λέγοντας·	ὡσαννὰ	τῷ		
ones shouting	in	the	temple	and	saying,	hosanna	to the		

5207	1160a	23			2532	3004
υἱῷ	Δαυίδ,	ἠγανάκτησαν	16	καὶ	εἶπαν	
son	of David,	they were indignant		and	they said	

846	191		5101	3778	3004	01	1161	2424
αὐτῷ,	ἀκούεις	τί	οὗτοι	λέγουσιν;	ὁ	δὲ	Ἰησοῦς	
to him,	you hear	what	these	say?	The	but	Jesus	

3004	846		3483	3763		314		3754	1537
λέγει	αὐτοῖς·	ναί.	οὐδέποτε		ἀνέγνωτε		ὅτι	ἐκ
says	to them;	yes.	But not ever you read				that	from

4750		3516		2532	2337		2675		
στόματος	νηπίων		καὶ	θηλαζόντων		κατηρτίσω		
mouth	of infants		and ones nursing		you put in order		

136		**17**	2532	2641		846		1831
αἶνον;			καὶ	καταλιπὼν		αὐτοὺς	ἐξῆλθεν
praise?			And	having left behind	them		he went out

1854		06	4172	1519	963		2532	835		1563
ἔξω		τῆς	πόλεως	εἰς	Βηθανίαν	καὶ	ηὐλίσθη	ἐκεῖ.
outside	the city		to		Bethany	and	lodged	there.

18	4404		1161	1877			1519	08	4172
	Πρωῒ		δὲ	ἐπανάγων			εἰς	τὴν	πόλιν
	In morning	but	having led on up			into	the	city

3983		**19**	2532	3708		4808		1520	1909	06
ἐπείνασεν.			καὶ	ἰδὼν		συκῆν	μίαν	ἐπὶ	τῆς
he hungered.		And	having seen	fig tree	one	on	the

3598	2064		1909	846	2532	3762		2147		1722	846
ὁδοῦ	ἦλθεν	ἐπ'	αὐτὴν	καὶ	οὐδὲν	εὗρεν	ἐν	αὐτῇ
way	he went on	it		and	nothing	he found	in	it

1487	3361	5444		3441		2532	3004		846		3371
εἰ	μὴ	φύλλα	μόνον,	καὶ	λέγει	αὐτῇ·	μηκέτι
except	leaves	alone,	and	he says	to it;	no longer

1537	1473	2590	1096			1519	04	165		2532
ἐκ	σοῦ	καρπὸς	γένηται		εἰς	τὸν	αἰῶνα.	καὶ
from	you	fruit	might become	into the age.		And

3583		3916		05	4808		**20**	2532	3708
ἐξηράνθη	παραχρῆμα	ἡ	συκῆ.			Καὶ	ἰδόντες
was dried out	suddenly	the	fig tree.		And	having seen

013	3101		2296		3004		4459	3916
οἱ	μαθηταὶ	ἐθαύμασαν	λέγοντες·	πῶς	παραχρῆμα
the	learners	marveled	saying,	how	suddenly

3583		05	4808		**21**	611		1161	01		2424
ἐξηράνθη	ἡ	συκῆ;			ἀποκριθεὶς	δὲ	ὁ	Ἰησοῦς
was dried out	the	fig tree?		Having answered	but	the	Jesus

3004	846		281	3004	1473		1437	2192
εἶπεν	αὐτοῖς·	ἀμὴν	λέγω	ὑμῖν,	ἐὰν	ἔχητε
said	to them;	amen I say to you,		if	you might have

4102		2532	3361	1252			3756	3441	012
πίστιν	καὶ	μὴ	διακριθῆτε,		οὐ	μόνον	τὸ
trust	and	not	you might doubt,		not	alone	the

06	4808		4160		235	2579		011		3735
τῆς	συκῆς	ποιήσετε,	ἀλλὰ	κἂν	τῷ	ὄρει
of the	fig tree	you will do,	but	if also	to the	hill

3778	3004		142		2532	906		1519
τούτῳ	εἴπητε·	ἄρθητι		καὶ	βλήθητι	εἰς
this	you might say,	be lifted up	and	be thrown	into

08	2281		1096		**22**	2532	3956	3745		302
τὴν	θάλασσαν,	γενήσεται·		καὶ	πάντα	ὅσα	ἂν
the	sea,	it will become;		and	all	as much as	-

154		1722	07	4335		4100
αἰτήσητε	ἐν	τῇ	προσευχῇ	πιστεύοντες
you might ask	in	the	prayer	trusting

2983		**23**	2532	2064		846	1519	012
λήμψεσθε.		Καὶ	ἐλθόντος	αὐτοῦ	εἰς	τὸ
you will receive.		And	having gone	him	into	the

2411	4334		846	1321		013	749
ἱερὸν	προσῆλθον	αὐτῷ	διδάσκοντι	οἱ	ἀρχιερεῖς
temple	went toward	him	teaching	the	ruler priests

2532	013	4245		02		2992	3004		1722
καὶ	οἱ	πρεσβύτεροι	τοῦ	λαοῦ	λέγοντες·	ἐν
and	the	older men	of the	people	saying,	in

4169		1849		3778	4160		2532	5101	1473
ποίᾳ	ἐξουσίᾳ	ταῦτα	ποιεῖς;	καὶ	τίς	σοι
what kind	authority	these	you do?	And	who	to you

1325	08	1849		3778		**24**	611		1161
ἔδωκεν	τὴν	ἐξουσίαν	ταύτην;		ἀποκριθεὶς	δὲ
gave	the	authority	this?		Having answered	but

said to them, "Yes; have you never read,

'Out of the mouths of infants and nursing babies you have prepared praise for yourself'?" [17]He left them, went out of the city to Bethany, and spent the night there.

18 In the morning, when he returned to the city, he was hungry. [19]And seeing a fig tree by the side of the road, he went to it and found nothing at all on it but leaves. Then he said to it, "May no fruit ever come from you again!" And the fig tree withered at once. [20]When the disciples saw it, they were amazed, saying, "How did the fig tree wither at once?" [21]Jesus answered them, "Truly I tell you, if you have faith and do not doubt, not only will you do what has been done to the fig tree, but even if you say to this mountain, 'Be lifted up and thrown into the sea,' it will be done. [22]Whatever you ask for in prayer with faith, you will receive."

23 When he entered the temple, the chief priests and the elders of the people came to him as he was teaching, and said, "By what authority are you doing these things, and who gave you this authority?" [24]Jesus said to them,

"I will also ask you one question; if you tell me the answer, then I will also tell you by what authority I do these things. 25Did the baptism of John come from heaven, or was it of human origin?" And they argued with one another, "If we say, 'From heaven,' he will say to us, 'Why then did you not believe him?' 26But if we say, 'Of human origin,' we are afraid of the crowd; for all regard John as a prophet." 27So they answered Jesus, "We do not know." And he said to them, "Neither will I tell you by what authority I am doing these things.

28 "What do you think? A man had two sons; he went to the first and said, 'Son, go and work in the vineyard today.' 29He answered, 'I will not'; but later he changed his mind and went. 30The father[a] went to the second and said the same; and he answered, 'I go, sir'; but he did not go. 31Which of the two did the will of his father?" They said, "The first." Jesus said to them, "Truly I tell you, the tax collectors and the prostitutes are going into the kingdom of God ahead of you. 32For John came

[a] Gk He

01	2424	3004	846		2065	1473	2504	3056
ὁ	Ἰησοῦς	εἶπεν	αὐτοῖς·		ἐρωτήσω	ὑμᾶς	κἀγὼ	λόγον
the	Jesus	said	to them,		will ask	you	also I	word

1520	3739	1437	3004		1473	2504	1473
ἕνα,	ὃν	ἐὰν	εἴπητέ		μοι	κἀγὼ	ὑμῖν
one,	which	if	you might say		to me	and I	to you

3004		1722 4169		1849		3778	4160	**25**	09
ἐρῶ		ἐν ποίᾳ		ἐξουσίᾳ		ταῦτα	ποιῶ·		τὸ
will say		in what kind		authority		these	I do;		the

908		09	2491	4159		1510		1537	3772
βάπτισμα		τὸ	Ἰωάννου	πόθεν		ἦν;		ἐξ	οὐρανοῦ
immersion		the	of John	from where		was it?		From	heaven

2228	1537	444		013		1161	1260		1722
ἢ	ἐξ	ἀνθρώπων;		οἱ		δὲ	διελογίζοντο		ἐν
or	from	men?		The ones		but	were reasoning		in

1438		3004		1437	3004		1537	3772
ἑαυτοῖς		λέγοντες·		ἐὰν	εἴπωμεν·		ἐξ	οὐρανοῦ,
themselves		saying;		if	we might say,		from	heaven,

3004		1473	1223		5101	3767	3756	4100
ἐρεῖ		ἡμῖν·	διὰ		τί	οὖν	οὐκ	ἐπιστεύσατε
he will say		to us;	through		what	then	not	you trusted

846	**26**	1437	1161	3004		1537	444		5399
αὐτῷ;		ἐὰν	δὲ	εἴπωμεν·		ἐξ	ἀνθρώπων,		φοβούμεθα
him?		If	but	we might say,		from	men,		we fear

04	3793	3956	1063	5613	4396		2192		04
τὸν	ὄχλον,	πάντες	γὰρ	ὡς	προφήτην		ἔχουσιν		τὸν
the	crowd,	all	for	as	spokesman		they hold		the

2491		**27**	2532	611		03	2424	3004
Ἰωάννην.			καὶ	ἀποκριθέντες		τῷ	Ἰησοῦ	εἶπαν·
John.			And	having answered		the	Jesus	they said,

3756	3609a	5346		846		2532	846		3761	1473
οὐκ	οἴδαμεν.	ἔφη		αὐτοῖς		καὶ	αὐτός·		οὐδὲ	ἐγὼ
not	we know.	He said		to them		even	himself,		but not	I

3004	1473	1722 4169		1849		3778	4160	**28**	5101
λέγω	ὑμῖν	ἐν ποίᾳ		ἐξουσίᾳ		ταῦτα	ποιῶ.		Τί
say	to you	in what kind		authority		these	I do.		What

1161	1473	1380		444		2192	5043	1417	2532
δὲ	ὑμῖν	δοκεῖ;		ἄνθρωπος		εἶχεν	τέκνα	δύο.	καὶ
but	to you	it thinks?		Man		had	children	two.	And

4334		011	4413	3004		5043	5217
προσελθὼν		τῷ	πρώτῳ	εἶπεν·		τέκνον,	ὕπαγε
having gone		toward	the first	he said;		child,	go off

4594	2038		1722	03	290		**29**	01		1161
σήμερον	ἐργάζου		ἐν	τῷ	ἀμπελῶνι.			ὁ		δὲ
today	work		in	the	vineyard.			The one		but

611		3004		3756	2309		5306		1161
ἀποκριθεὶς		εἶπεν·		οὐ	θέλω,		ὕστερον		δὲ
having answered		said,		not	I want,		later		but

3338		565		**30**	4334		1161	03		2087
μεταμεληθεὶς		ἀπῆλθεν.			προσελθὼν		δὲ	τῷ		ἑτέρῳ
having been		he went off.			Having gone		but	to the		other
sorry					toward					

3004		5615		01		1161	611		3004
εἶπεν		ὡσαύτως.		ὁ		δὲ	ἀποκριθεὶς		εἶπεν·
he said		likewise.		The one		but	having answered		said,

1473	2962		2532	3756	565		**31**	5101	1537	014	1417
ἐγώ,	κύριε,		καὶ	οὐκ	ἀπῆλθεν.			τίς	ἐκ	τῶν	δύο
I,	master,		and	not	he went off.			Who	from	the	two

4160		012	2307	02		3962	3004		01
ἐποίησεν		τὸ	θέλημα	τοῦ		πατρός;	λέγουσιν·		ὁ
did		the	want	of the		father?	They say,		the

4413	3004	846		01	2424	281	3004	1473
πρῶτος.	λέγει	αὐτοῖς		ὁ	Ἰησοῦς·	ἀμὴν	λέγω	ὑμῖν
first.	Says	to them		the	Jesus,	amen	I say	to you

3754	013	5057		2532	017	4204		4254
ὅτι	οἱ	τελῶναι	καὶ	αἱ	πόρναι			προάγουσιν
that	the	tax men	and	the	prostitutes			will lead before

1473	1519	08	932		02		2316		2064	1063
ὑμᾶς	εἰς	τὴν	βασιλείαν		τοῦ		θεοῦ.	**32**	ἦλθεν	γὰρ
you	into	the	kingdom		of the		God.		Went	for

2491	4314	1473 1722 3598 1343				2532 3756
Ἰωάννης	πρὸς	ὑμᾶς ἐν ὁδῷ δικαιοσύνης,		καὶ		οὐκ
John	toward	you in way of rightness,		and		not

4100		846	013 1161 5057	2532 017 4204
ἐπιστεύσατε αὐτῷ,		οἱ δὲ τελῶναι καὶ αἱ πόρναι
you trusted him,		the but tax men and the prostitutes

4100	846	1473 1161	3708	3761
ἐπίστευσαν αὐτῷ·	ὑμεῖς δὲ	ἰδόντες	οὐδὲ
trust	him; you but	having seen	but not

3338	5306	010 4100	846	243
μετεμελήθητε	ὕστερον τοῦ	πιστεῦσαι	αὐτῷ. 33 Ἄλλην
you were sorry	later of the	to trust	him. Other

3850	191	444	1510 3617
παραβολὴν	ἀκούσατε.	ἄνθρωπος ἦν	οἰκοδεσπότης
parallel story	hear.	Man was	house supervisor

3748 5452	290	2532 5418	846 4060
ὅστις ἐφύτευσεν	ἀμπελῶνα καὶ	φραγμὸν	αὐτῷ περιέθηκεν
who planted	vineyard and	hedge	it set around

2532 3736	1722 846 3025	2532 3618	4444
καὶ ὤρυξεν ἐν	αὐτῷ ληνὸν	καὶ ᾠκοδόμησεν	πύργον
and he dug in	it winepress	and he built	tower

2532 1554	846	1092	2532 589
καὶ ἐξέδετο	αὐτὸν	γεωργοῖς	καὶ ἀπεδήμησεν.
and he gave out	it	to farmers	and journeyed.

34
3753 1161 1448	01 2540	014	2590
ὅτε δὲ ἤγγισεν ὁ	καιρὸς τῶν		καρπῶν,
When but neared the	season of the		fruit,

649	016 1401	846	4314 016 1092
ἀπέστειλεν	τοὺς δούλους	αὐτοῦ	πρὸς τοὺς γεωργοὺς
he delegated	the slaves	of him	toward the farmers

2983	016	2590	846	2532 2983	013
λαβεῖν	τοὺς	καρποὺς	αὐτοῦ. 35	καὶ λαβόντες	οἱ
to take	the	fruit	of him.	And having taken	the

1092	016 1401	846	3739 3303	1194
γεωργοὶ	τοὺς δούλους	αὐτοῦ	ὃν μὲν	ἔδειραν,
farmers	the slaves	of him	whom indeed	they beat,

3739 1161 615	3739 1161 3036
ὃν δὲ ἀπέκτειναν,	ὃν δὲ ἐλιθοβόλησαν.
whom but they killed,	whom but they threw stones.

36
3825 649	243 1401	4183	014
πάλιν ἀπέστειλεν	ἄλλους δούλους	πλείονας	τῶν
Again he delegated	other slaves	more	of the

4413	2532 4160	846	5615	5306	1161
πρώτων,	καὶ ἐποίησαν	αὐτοῖς	ὡσαύτως. 37	ὕστερον	δὲ
first,	and they did	to them	likewise.	Later	but

649	4314 846	04 5207 846	3004
ἀπέστειλεν	πρὸς αὐτοὺς	τὸν υἱὸν αὐτοῦ	λέγων·
he delegated	toward them	the son of him	saying,

1788	04 5207 1473	38 013 1161 1092
ἐντραπήσονται	τὸν υἱόν μου.	οἱ δὲ γεωργοὶ
they will regard	the son of me.	The but farmers

3708	04 5207 3004	1722 1438	3778
ἰδόντες	τὸν υἱὸν εἶπον	ἐν ἑαυτοῖς·	οὗτός
having seen	the son said	in themselves,	this

1510 01 2818	1205 615	846	2532
ἐστιν ὁ κληρονόμος·	δεῦτε ἀποκτείνωμεν	αὐτὸν	καὶ
is the inheritor	come let us kill	him	and

2192	08 2817	846	39 2532 2983	846
σχῶμεν	τὴν κληρονομίαν	αὐτοῦ,	καὶ λαβόντες	αὐτὸν
we might have	the inheritance	of him,	And having	him taken

1544	1854	02 290	2532 615
ἐξέβαλον	ἔξω	τοῦ ἀμπελῶνος	καὶ ἀπέκτειναν.
they threw out	outside	the vineyard	and they killed.

40
3752 3767 2064	01 2962	02	290	5101
ὅταν οὖν ἔλθῃ	ὁ κύριος τοῦ		ἀμπελῶνος,	τί
When then might go	the master of the		vineyard,	what

4160	015 1092	1565	3004
ποιήσει	τοῖς γεωργοῖς	ἐκείνοις; 41	λέγουσιν
will he do	to the farmers	those?	They say

to you in the way of righteousness and you did not believe him, but the tax collectors and the prostitutes believed him; and even after you saw it, you did not change your minds and believe him.

33 "Listen to another parable. There was a landowner who planted a vineyard, put a fence around it, dug a wine press in it, and built a watchtower. Then he leased it to tenants and went to another country. [34]When the harvest time had come, he sent his slaves to the tenants to collect his produce. [35]But the tenants seized his slaves and beat one, killed another, and stoned another. [36]Again he sent other slaves, more than the first; and they treated them in the same way. [37]Finally he sent his son to them, saying, 'They will respect my son.' [38]But when the tenants saw the son, they said to themselves, 'This is the heir; come, let us kill him and get his inheritance.' [39]So they seized him, threw him out of the vineyard, and killed him. [40]Now when the owner of the vineyard comes, what will he do to those tenants?" [41]They said to him,

"He will put those wretches to a miserable death, and lease the vineyard to other tenants who will give him the produce at the harvest time."

42 Jesus said to them, "Have you never read in the scriptures:

'The stone that the builders rejected has become the cornerstone;[a] this was the Lord's doing, and it is amazing in our eyes"?

43 Therefore I tell you, the kingdom of God will be taken away from you and given to a people that produces the fruits of the kingdom.[b] 44 The one who falls on this stone will be broken to pieces; and it will crush anyone on whom it falls."[c]

45 When the chief priests and the Pharisees heard his parables, they realized that he was speaking about them. 46 They wanted to arrest him, but they feared the crowds, because they regarded him as a prophet.

CHAPTER 22

Once more Jesus spoke to them in parables, saying: 2 "The kingdom of heaven may be compared to a king who gave a wedding banquet for his son. 3 He sent his slaves to call those who had been invited to the wedding banquet, but they would not come. 4 Again he sent other

---

a Or keystone

b Gk the fruits of it

c Other ancient authorities lack verse 44

846	2556	2560	622		846	2532	04

αὐτῷ· κακοὺς κακῶς ἀπολέσει αὐτοὺς καὶ τὸν
to him, bad ones badly he will destroy them and the

290   1554   243   1092   3748
ἀμπελῶνα ἐκδώσεται ἄλλοις γεωργοῖς, οἵτινες
vineyard he will give out to other farmers, who

591   846   016   2590   1722 015 2540
ἀποδώσουσιν αὐτῷ τοὺς καρποὺς ἐν τοῖς καιροῖς
will give off to him the fruit in the seasons

846   3004 846   01 2424   3763
αὐτῶν. 42 Λέγει αὐτοῖς ὁ Ἰησοῦς· οὐδέποτε
of them. Says to them the Jesus, but not ever

314   1722 019 1124   3037 3739 593
ἀνέγνωτε ἐν ταῖς γραφαῖς· λίθον ὃν ἀπεδοκίμασαν
you read in the writings; stone which rejected

013 3618   3778 1096   1519 2776 1137
οἱ οἰκοδομοῦντες, οὗτος ἐγενήθη εἰς κεφαλὴν γωνίας·
the ones building, this became into head corner;

3844 2962   1096   3778 2532 1510 2298   1722
παρὰ κυρίου ἐγένετο αὕτη καὶ ἔστιν θαυμαστὴ ἐν
from Master became this and it is marvelous in

3788   1473 1223   3778 3004 1473 3754
ὀφθαλμοῖς ἡμῶν, 43 διὰ τοῦτο λέγω ὑμῖν ὅτι
eyes of us? Through this I say to you that

142   575 1473 05 932   02   2316
ἀρθήσεται ἀφ᾽ ὑμῶν ἡ βασιλεία τοῦ θεοῦ
will be lifted up from you the kingdom of the God

2532 1325   1484   4160   016 2590
καὶ δοθήσεται ἔθνει ποιοῦντι τοὺς καρποὺς
and will be given to nation doing the fruit

846   2532 01 4098   1909 04 3037 3778
αὐτῆς. 44 [καὶ ὁ πεσὼν ἐπὶ τὸν λίθον τοῦτον
of it. And the one falling on the stone this

4917   1909 3739 1161 302 4098   3039
συνθλασθήσεται· ἐφ᾽ ὃν δ᾽ ἂν πέσῃ λικμήσει
will be crushed on whom but - it might it will
thoroughly.   fall   pulverize

846   45 2532 191   013 749   2532
αὐτόν.] 45 Καὶ ἀκούσαντες οἱ ἀρχιερεῖς καὶ
him. And having heard the ruler priests and

013 5330   020 3850   846 1097
οἱ Φαρισαῖοι τὰς παραβολὰς αὐτοῦ ἔγνωσαν
the Pharisees the parallel stories of him knew

3754 4012   846 3004   46 2532 2212   846
ὅτι περὶ αὐτῶν λέγει· 46 καὶ ζητοῦντες αὐτὸν
that concerning them he says, and seeking him

2902   5399   016 3793   1893 1519 4396
κρατῆσαι ἐφοβήθησαν τοὺς ὄχλους, ἐπεὶ εἰς προφήτην
to hold they feared the crowds, since for spokesman

846 2192   2532 611   01 2424
αὐτὸν εἶχον. 22:1 Καὶ ἀποκριθεὶς ὁ Ἰησοῦς
him they had. And having answered the Jesus

3825 3004 1722 3850   846 3004
πάλιν εἶπεν ἐν παραβολαῖς αὐτοῖς λέγων·
again said in parallel stories to them saying,

2 3666   05 932   014   3772   444
ὡμοιώθη ἡ βασιλεία τῶν οὐρανῶν ἀνθρώπῳ
was likened the kingdom of the heavens to man

935   3748 4160 1062   03   5207 846
βασιλεῖ, ὅστις ἐποίησεν γάμους τῷ υἱῷ αὐτοῦ.
king, who made wedding for the son of him.

3 2532 649   016 1401 846 2564
καὶ ἀπέστειλεν τοὺς δούλους αὐτοῦ καλέσαι
And he delegated the slaves of him to call

016   2564   1519 016 1062   2532 3756
τοὺς κεκλημένους εἰς τοὺς γάμους, καὶ οὐκ
the ones having been called to the wedding, and not

2309   2064   4 3825 649   243
ἤθελον ἐλθεῖν. 4 πάλιν ἀπέστειλεν ἄλλους
they wanted to come. Again he delegated other

```
1401        3004        3004      015       2564
δούλους λέγων·  εἴπατε τοῖς    κεκλημένοις·
slaves    saying, speak  to the ones having been called;
2400 012 712          1473 2090              013 5022   1473
ἰδοὺ τὸ ἄριστόν μου ἡτοίμακα,       οἱ ταῦροί μου
look the meal  of me I have prepared, the bulls of me
2532 021 4619        2380      2532 3956  2092    1205  1519
καὶ  τὰ σιτιστὰ τεθυμένα καὶ πάντα ἕτοιμα· δεῦτε εἰς
and  the fattened having  and all  prepared; come to
                   been sacrificed
016  1062      5  013    1161 272              565
τοὺς γάμους.     οἱ   δὲ ἀμελήσαντες       ἀπῆλθον,
the  wedding. The ones but having not cared went off,
3739 3303   1519 04  2398   68      3739 1161 1909 08
ὃς  μὲν   εἰς τὸν ἴδιον ἀγρόν, ὃς  δὲ  ἐπὶ τὴν
who indeed to  the own  field, who but  on  the
1711        846      6  013 1161 3062      2902
ἐμπορίαν αὐτοῦ·     οἱ  δὲ λοιποὶ κρατήσαντες
merchandise of him;  the but remaining having held
016  1401    846    5195     2532 615        7 01
τοὺς δούλους αὐτοῦ ὕβρισαν καὶ ἀπέκτειναν.    ὁ
the  slaves  of him abused  and killed.      The
1161 935      3710       2532 3992         024 4753
δὲ βασιλεὺς ὠργίσθη   καὶ πέμψας      τὰ στρατεύματα
but king      was angry and having sent the armies
846  622       016 5406    1565      2532 08
αὐτοῦ ἀπώλεσεν τοὺς φονεῖς ἐκείνους καὶ τὴν
of him destroyed the murderers those    and the
4172 846     1705a    8 5119 3004   015      1401
πόλιν αὐτῶν ἐνέπρησεν.  τότε λέγει τοῖς    δούλοις
city of them he burned up. Then he says to the slaves
846  01    3303  1062     2092    1510 013     1161
αὐτοῦ· ὁ μὲν   γάμος ἕτοιμός ἐστιν, οἱ    δὲ
of him; the indeed wedding prepared is,  the ones but
2564           3756 1510 514    9 4198        3767
κεκλημένοι    οὐκ ἦσαν ἄξιοι·  πορεύεσθε οὖν
having been called not were worthy; travel    then
1909 020 1327        018    3598 2532 3745       1437
ἐπὶ τὰς διεξόδους τῶν    ὁδῶν καὶ ὅσους     ἐὰν
on  the throughways of the ways and as many as if
2147        2564      1519 016 1062     10 2532
εὕρητε     καλέσατε εἰς τοὺς γάμους.    καὶ
you might find call   to  the wedding.   And
1831        013 1401   1565     1519 020 3598
ἐξελθόντες οἱ δοῦλοι ἐκεῖνοι εἰς τὰς ὁδοὺς
having gone out the slaves those  in  the ways
4863          3956 3739 2147         4190    5037
συνήγαγον πάντας οὓς εὗρον,    πονηρούς τε
they brought together all  whom they found, evil both
2532 18      2532 4092    01 1062     345
καὶ ἀγαθούς· καὶ ἐπλήσθη ὁ γάμος ἀνακειμένων.
and  good;   and was filled the wedding of ones
                                            reclining.
   1525          1161 01  935     2300       016
11 εἰσελθὼν     δὲ  ὁ βασιλεὺς θεάσασθαι τοὺς
   Having gone in but the king   to watch  the
345           3708  1563 444     3756 1746
ἀνακειμένους εἶδεν ἐκεῖ ἄνθρωπον οὐκ ἐνδεδυμένον
ones reclining he saw there man    not having put on
1742     1062    12 2532 3004  846     2083    4459
ἔνδυμα γάμου,    καὶ λέγει αὐτῷ· ἑταῖρε, πῶς
clothes of wedding, and he says to him, comrade, how
1525        5602 3361 2192   1742     1062
εἰσῆλθες ὧδε μὴ ἔχων ἔνδυμα γάμου;
you come into here not having clothes of wedding?
01   1161 5392      13 5119 01 935     3004
ὁ   δὲ ἐφιμώθη.      τότε ὁ βασιλεὺς εἶπεν
The one but was muzzled. Then the king     said
```

slaves, saying, 'Tell those who have been invited: Look, I have prepared my dinner, my oxen and my fat calves have been slaughtered, and everything is ready; come to the wedding banquet.' [5]But they made light of it and went away, one to his farm, another to his business, [6]while the rest seized his slaves, mistreated them, and killed them. [7]The king was enraged. He sent his troops, destroyed those murderers, and burned their city. [8]Then he said to his slaves, 'The wedding is ready, but the invited were not worthy. [9]Go therefore into the main streets, and invite everyone you find to the wedding banquet.' [10]Those slaves went out into the streets and gathered all whom they found, both good and bad; so the wedding hall was filled with guests.

11 "But when the king came in to see the guests, he noticed a man there who was not wearing a wedding robe, [12]and he said to him, 'Friend, how did you get in here without a wedding robe?' And he was speechless. [13]Then the king said

to the attendants, 'Bind him hand and foot, and throw him into the outer darkness, where there will be weeping and gnashing of teeth.' [14]For many are called, but few are chosen."

15 Then the Pharisees went and plotted to entrap him in what he said. [16]So they sent their disciples to him, along with the Herodians, saying, "Teacher, we know that you are sincere, and teach the way of God in accordance with truth, and show deference to no one; for you do not regard people with partiality. [17]Tell us, then, what you think. Is it lawful to pay taxes to the emperor, or not?" [18]But Jesus, aware of their malice, said, "Why are you putting me to the test, you hypocrites? [19]Show me the coin used for the tax." And they brought him a denarius. [20]Then he said to them, "Whose head is this, and whose title?" [21]They answered, "The emperor's." Then he said to them, "Give therefore to the emperor the things that are the emperor's, and to God the things that are God's." [22]When they heard this, they were amazed; and they left him and went away.

23 The same day some Sadducees came to him, saying there is no resurrection;[a] and they asked him a question, saying,

[a] Other ancient authorities read *who say that there is no resurrection*

```
015       1249         1210          846     4228 2532 5495
τοῖς   διακόνοις· δήσαντες      αὐτοῦ πόδας καὶ χεῖρας
to the  servants,  having bound of him  feet  and hands
1544      846     1519 012 4655    012 1857        1563
ἐκβάλετε αὐτὸν εἰς τὸ σκότος τὸ ἐξώτερον· ἐκεῖ
throw out him  into the dark  the outermost; there
1510    01  2805      2532 01  1030     014    3599
ἔσται  ὁ  κλαυθμὸς καὶ ὁ  βρυγμὸς τῶν  ὀδόντων.
will be the crying  and the grinding of the teeth.
```

14
```
4183    1063 1510   2822      3641  1161 1588
πολλοὶ γάρ  εἰσιν κλητοί, ὀλίγοι δὲ  ἐκλεκτοί.
Many    for  are  called, few    but selected.
```

15
```
5119 4198               013 5330       4824
Τότε πορευθέντες       οἱ Φαρισαῖοι συμβούλιον
Then having traveled   the Pharisees  council
2983    3704     846    3802           1722 3056  16 2532
ἔλαβον ὅπως    αὐτὸν παγιδεύσωσιν ἐν λόγῳ.      καὶ
took    so that him   they might trap in  word.     And
649          846    016  3101      846        3326 014
ἀποστέλλουσιν αὐτῷ τοὺς μαθητὰς αὐτῶν μετὰ τῶν
they delegated to him the learners of them with the
2265         3004       1320       3609a    3754 227
Ἡρῳδιανῶν λέγοντες· διδάσκαλε, οἴδαμεν ὅτι ἀληθὴς
Herodians saying,    teacher,   we know that true
1510    2532 08 3598 02       2316 1722 225
εἶ     καὶ τὴν ὁδὸν τοῦ    θεοῦ ἐν ἀληθείᾳ
you    are and the way of the God in  truth
1321       2532 3756 3190a          1473 4012  3762
διδάσκεις καὶ  οὐ  μέλει        σοι περὶ οὐδενός.
you teach and not it is a care to you about no one.
3756 1063 991       1519 4383       444       3004 3767
οὐ   γὰρ βλέπεις εἰς πρόσωπον ἀνθρώπων,  17 εἰπὲ οὖν
Not  for you see in  face      of men,      say then
1473 5101 1473  1380       1832         1325
ἡμῖν τί σοι δοκεῖ·    ἔξεστιν      δοῦναι
to us what to you it thinks; is it possible to give
2778     2541     2228 3756a 18 1097     1161 01  2424
κῆνσον Καίσαρι ἢ οὔ;     γνοὺς δὲ ὁ Ἰησοῦς
tribute to Caesar or no? Having known but the Jesus
08 4189        846      3004     5101 1473 3985
τὴν πονηρίαν αὐτῶν εἶπεν· τί με πειράζετε,
the evil      of them said;  why me you pressure,
5273         19 1925         1473 012 3546      02
ὑποκριταί;    ἐπιδείξατέ μοι τὸ νόμισμα τοῦ
hypocrites?   Show on   to me the coinage of the
2778      013      1161 4374      846    1220
κήνσου. οἱ   δὲ προσήνεγκαν αὐτῷ δηνάριον.
tribute. The ones but offered   to him denarius.
```

20
```
2532 3004      846        5101    05 1504 3778
καὶ λέγει   αὐτοῖς· τίνος ἡ εἰκὼν αὕτη
And he says to them, of whom the image this
2532 05 1923         21 3004       846    2541          5119
καὶ ἡ ἐπιγραφή;      λέγουσιν αὐτῷ· Καίσαρος. τότε
and the written on?  They say to him, of Caesar. Then
3004  846     591     3767 024 2541      2541
λέγει αὐτοῖς· ἀπόδοτε οὖν τὰ Καίσαρος Καίσαρι
he says to them, give off then the of Caesar to Caesar
2532 024 02   2316 03    2316      2532 191
καὶ τὰ τοῦ  θεοῦ τῷ  θεῷ. 22 καὶ ἀκούσαντες
and the of the God to the God.   And having heard
2296         2532 863          846     565
ἐθαύμασαν,  καὶ ἀφέντες     αὐτὸν ἀπῆλθαν.
they marveled, and having sent off him they went off.
```

23
```
1722 1565   07  2250  4334        846   4523
Ἐν ἐκείνῃ τῇ ἡμέρᾳ προσῆλθον αὐτῷ Σαδδουκαῖοι,
In  that  the day  went toward him Sadducees,
3004    3361 1510 386      2532 1905
λέγοντες μὴ εἶναι ἀνάστασιν, καὶ ἐπηρώτησαν
saying  not to be standing up, and they asked on
```

846　24　3004　　1320　　3475　3004　1437 5100
αὐτὸν 24 λέγοντες· διδάσκαλε, Μωϋσῆς εἶπεν· ἐάν τις
him   saying, teacher, Moses   said; if someone

599　　　3361 2192　5043　　1918　　　　01
ἀποθάνῃ μὴ ἔχων τέκνα, ἐπιγαμβρεύσει ὁ
might die not having children, will marry the

80　　　846　08　1135　　846　　2532 450
ἀδελφὸς αὐτοῦ τὴν γυναῖκα αὐτοῦ καὶ ἀναστήσει
brother of him the woman of him and will stand up

4690　03　80　　846　　25　1510　1161 3844 1473
σπέρμα τῷ ἀδελφῷ αὐτοῦ. 25 ἦσαν δὲ παρ᾽ ἡμῖν
seed to the brother of him. There were but from us

2033 80　　2532 01　4413　1060　　5053
ἑπτὰ ἀδελφοί· καὶ ὁ πρῶτος γήμας ἐτελεύτησεν,
seven brothers; and the first having married died,

2532 3361 2192　4690　863　08　1135　846　03
καὶ μὴ ἔχων σπέρμα ἀφῆκεν τὴν γυναῖκα αὐτοῦ τῷ
and not having seed he left the woman of him to the

80　　846　26　3668　2532 01　1208　2532 01
ἀδελφῷ αὐτοῦ· 26 ὁμοίως καὶ ὁ δεύτερος καὶ ὁ
brother of him; likewise also the second and the

5154　2193　014　5306　1161 3956　599
τρίτος ἕως τῶν ἑπτά. 27 ὕστερον δὲ πάντων ἀπέθανεν
third until the seven. Later but of all died

05　1135　28　1722 07　386　　3767 5101　014
ἡ γυνή. 28 ἐν τῇ ἀναστάσει οὖν τίνος τῶν
the woman. In the standing up then of whom of the

2033 1510　1135　3956　1063 2192　846
ἑπτὰ ἔσται γυνή; πάντες γὰρ ἔσχον αὐτήν·
seven will be woman? All for had her;

29　611　　1161 01　2424　3004　846
29 ἀποκριθεὶς δὲ ὁ Ἰησοῦς εἶπεν αὐτοῖς·
having answered but the Jesus said to them;

4105　　3361 3609a　020 1124　3366
πλανᾶσθε μὴ εἰδότες τὰς γραφὰς μηδὲ
you are deceived not having known the writings but not

08　1411　02　2316　30　1722 1063 07　386
τὴν δύναμιν τοῦ θεοῦ· 30 ἐν γὰρ τῇ ἀναστάσει
the power of the God; in for the standing up

3777　1060　3777 1060a　235 5613
οὔτε γαμοῦσιν οὔτε γαμίζονται, ἀλλ᾽ ὡς
neither they marry nor given in marriage, but as

32　1722 03　3772　1510　31　4012 1161 06
ἄγγελοι ἐν τῷ οὐρανῷ εἰσιν. 31 περὶ δὲ τῆς
messengers in the heaven are. About but the

386　　014 3498　3756 314　012 3004
ἀναστάσεως τῶν νεκρῶν οὐκ ἀνέγνωτε τὸ ῥηθὲν
standing up of dead not you read the word having
          been spoken
          the

1473　5259 02　2316 3004　32　1473 1510 01　2316
ὑμῖν ὑπὸ τοῦ θεοῦ λέγοντος· 32 ἐγώ εἰμι ὁ θεὸς
to you by the God saying; I am the God

11　　2532 01　2316 2464　2532 01　2316
Ἀβραὰμ καὶ ὁ θεὸς Ἰσαὰκ καὶ ὁ θεὸς
of Abraham and the God of Isaac and the God

2384　3756 1510　01　2316 3498　235　2198
Ἰακώβ; οὐκ ἔστιν [ὁ] θεὸς νεκρῶν ἀλλὰ ζώντων.
of Jacob? Not he is the God of dead but living.

33　2532 191　013 3793　1605　　1909
33 καὶ ἀκούσαντες οἱ ὄχλοι ἐξεπλήσσοντο ἐπὶ
And having heard the crowds were astonished on

07　1322　846　34　013 1161 5330　191
τῇ διδαχῇ αὐτοῦ. 34 Οἱ δὲ Φαρισαῖοι ἀκούσαντες
the teaching of him. The but Pharisees having heard

3754 5392　016 4523　　4863
ὅτι ἐφίμωσεν τοὺς Σαδδουκαίους συνήχθησαν
that he muzzled the Sadducees were brought together

1909 012 846　35　2532 1905　1520 1537　846
ἐπὶ τὸ αὐτό, 35 καὶ ἐπηρώτησεν εἷς ἐξ αὐτῶν
on the same, and asked on one out of them

24"Teacher, Moses said,
'If a man dies childless,
his brother shall marry
the widow, and raise up
children for his brother.'
25Now there were seven
brothers among us; the first
married, and died childless,
leaving the widow to his
brother. 26The second did
the same, so also the third,
down to the seventh. 27Last
of all, the woman herself
died. 28In the resurrection,
then, whose wife of the
seven will she be? For all
of them had married her."

29 Jesus answered them,
"You are wrong, because
you know neither the
scriptures nor the power
of God. 30For in the
resurrection they neither
marry nor are given in
marriage, but are like
angels[a] in heaven. 31And as
for the resurrection of the
dead, have you not read
what was said to you by
God, 32'I am the God of
Abraham, the God of Isaac,
and the God of Jacob'? He
is God not of the dead, but
of the living." 33And when
the crowd heard it, they
were astounded at his
teaching.

34 When the Pharisees
heard that he had silenced
the Sadducees, they
gathered together, 35and
one of them,

a Other ancient authorities add
of God

a lawyer, asked him a
question to test him.
36"Teacher, which
commandment in the law
is the greatest?" 37He said
to him, " 'You shall love
the Lord your God with all
your heart, and with all
your soul, and with all your
mind.' 38This is the greatest
and first commandment.
39And a second is like it:
'You shall love your
neighbor as yourself.' 40On
these two commandments
hang all the law and the
prophets."

41 Now while the
Pharisees were gathered
together, Jesus asked them
this question: 42"What do
you think of the Messiah?ᵃ
Whose son is he?" They
said to him, "The son of
David." 43He said to them,
"How is it then that David
by the Spiritᵇ calls him
Lord, saying,
44 'The Lord said to my
      Lord,
   "Sit at my right hand,
      until I put your enemies
      under your feet" '?
45If David thus calls him
Lord, how can he be his
son?"46No one was able to
give him an answer, nor
from that day did anyone
dare to ask him any more
questions.

CHAPTER 23

Then Jesus said to the
crowds and to his disciples,
2"The scribes and the
Pharisees sit on Moses' seat;
3therefore, do whatever
they teach you

ᵃ Or Christ
ᵇ Gk in spirit

3544	3985	846	**36**	1320	4169 1785
[νομικὸς]	πειράζων	αὐτόν·		διδάσκαλε,	ποία ἐντολὴ
lawyer	pressuring	him,		teacher,	what command

3173	1722 03 3551	**37**	01	1161 5346 846
μεγάλη	ἐν τῷ νόμῳ;		ὁ	δὲ ἔφη αὐτῷ·
great	in the law?		The one	but said to him,

25   2962   04   2316 1473   1722 3650   07
ἀγαπήσεις   κύριον   τὸν θεόν σου   ἐν   ὅλῃ   τῇ
you will love Master the God of you in   whole the

2588   1473   2532 1722 3650   07   5590 1473   2532
καρδίᾳ σου   καὶ ἐν   ὅλῃ   τῇ   ψυχῇ σου   καὶ
heart of you and in   whole the soul of you and

1722 3650   07   1271   1473   **38** 3778 1510   05
ἐν   ὅλῃ   τῇ   διανοίᾳ   σου·   αὕτη ἐστὶν ἡ
in   whole the intelligence of you;   this is   the

3173   2532 4413   1785   **39** 1208   1161 3664   846
μεγάλη καὶ πρώτη ἐντολή.   δευτέρα δὲ   ὁμοία αὐτῇ·
great and first command.   Second but   like it;

25   04   4139   1473 5613 4572   **40** 1722
ἀγαπήσεις   τὸν πλησίον σου ὡς σεαυτόν.   ἐν
you will love the neighbor of you as yourself.   In

3778   019   1417   1785   3650 01   3551   2910
ταύταις ταῖς δυσὶν ἐντολαῖς ὅλος ὁ   νόμος κρέμαται
these   the two   commands whole the law   hang

2532 013 4396   **41** 4863   1161 014
καὶ οἱ προφῆται.   Συνηγμένων   δὲ τῶν
and the spokesmen. Having brought together but of the

5330   1905   846   01 2424   3004   5101
Φαρισαίων ἐπηρώτησεν αὐτοὺς ὁ Ἰησοῦς **42** λέγων· τί
Pharisees asked on   them   the Jesus   saying, what

1473   1380 4012 02 5547   5101 5207 1510
ὑμῖν   δοκεῖ περὶ τοῦ χριστοῦ; τίνος υἱός ἐστιν;
to you think about the Christ? Whose son is he?

3004   846   02 1160a **43** 3004   846   4459
λέγουσιν αὐτῷ· τοῦ Δαυίδ.   λέγει αὐτοῖς· πῶς
They say to him; the of David. He says to them, how

3767 1160a 1722 4151   2564   046 2962   3004
οὖν Δαυὶδ ἐν πνεύματι καλεῖ αὐτὸν κύριον λέγων·
then David in spirit   calls him   Master saying,

44 3004 2962   03   2962 1473   2521   1537 1188
εἶπεν κύριος τῷ   κυρίῳ μου· κάθου ἐκ   δεξιῶν
said Master to the Master of me; sit   from right

1473   2193 302 5087   016 2190   1473
μου,   ἕως ἂν θῶ   τοὺς ἐχθρούς σου
of me, until — I might set the hostile of you

5270   014 4228   1473   **45** 1487 3767 1160a 2564
ὑποκάτω τῶν ποδῶν σου;   εἰ οὖν Δαυὶδ καλεῖ
underneath the feet of you? If then David calls

846   2962   4459 5207 846   1510   **46** 2532 3762
αὐτὸν κύριον, πῶς υἱὸς αὐτοῦ ἐστιν; καὶ οὐδεὶς
him   Master, how son of him is he? And no one

1410   611   846   3056 3761   5111
ἐδύνατο ἀποκριθῆναι αὐτῷ λόγον οὐδὲ ἐτόλμησέν
was able to answer   to him word but not dared

5100 575   1565   06   2250   1905   846   3765
τις ἀπ' ἐκείνης τῆς ἡμέρας ἐπερωτῆσαι αὐτὸν οὐκέτι.
any from that the day   to ask on   him   no longer.

23:1 5119 01 2424   2980   015   3793   2532
Τότε ὁ   Ἰησοῦς ἐλάλησεν τοῖς ὄχλοις καὶ
Then the Jesus spoke   to the crowds and

015   3101   846   **2** 3004   1909 06   3475
τοῖς μαθηταῖς αὐτοῦ λέγων· ἐπὶ τῆς Μωϋσέως
to the learners of him saying, on the Moses

2515   2523   013 1122   2532 013 5330
καθέδρας ἐκάθισαν οἱ γραμματεῖς καὶ οἱ Φαρισαῖοι.
seat   sat   the writers   and the Pharisees.

3 3956 3767 3745   1437 3004   1473
πάντα οὖν ὅσα   ἐὰν εἴπωσιν   ὑμῖν
·All then as much as if they might say to you

```
4160        2532 5083      2596            1161 024 2041
ποιήσατε καὶ  τηρεῖτε, κατὰ           δὲ   τὰ  ἔργα
do          and  keep,    according to but  the  works
846      3361 4160    3004        1063 2532 3756 4160
αὐτῶν   μὴ  ποιεῖτε· λέγουσιν γὰρ καὶ  οὐ  ποιοῦσιν.
of them  not  do;      they say  for  and  not  they do.
    1195              1161 5413    926    2532 1419              2532
4  δεσμεύουσιν δὲ  φορτία βαρέα [καὶ δυσβάστακτα] καὶ
   They tie up  but  packs  burden  and  doubly heavy  and
2007          1909 016   5606        014    444
ἐπιτιθέασιν ἐπὶ  τοὺς ὤμους   τῶν  ἀνθρώπων,
they set on  on   the  shoulders of the  men,
846      1161 03   1147        846        3756 2309
αὐτοὶ  δὲ  τῷ  δακτύλῳ αὐτῶν  οὐ  θέλουσιν
themselves but the  finger   of them  not  they want
2795        846      3956 1161 024 2041     846      4160
κινῆσαι αὐτά. 5 πάντα δὲ  τὰ  ἔργα  αὐτῶν  ποιοῦσιν
to move them.  All  but  the  works of them  they do
4314 012 2300        015    444        4115
πρὸς τὸ θεαθῆναι  τοῖς ἀνθρώποις· πλατύνουσιν
toward the to be watched by the men;       they widen
1063 024 5440        846      2532 3170        024
γὰρ τὰ φυλακτήρια αὐτῶν  καὶ μεγαλύνουσιν τὰ
for  the guard places of them and  make great  the
2899         5368      1161 08   4411
κράσπεδα, 6 φιλοῦσιν δὲ  τὴν πρωτοκλισίαν
edges,       they love  but  the  first reclining place
1722 023    1173        2532 020  4410           1722 019
ἐν  τοῖς δείπνοις καὶ  τὰς πρωτοκαθεδρίας ἐν  ταῖς
in   the  dinners  and  the  first chairs    in   the
4864        2532 016  783        1722 019  58        2532
συναγωγαῖς 7 καὶ  τοὺς ἀσπασμοὺς ἐν  ταῖς ἀγοραῖς καὶ
synagogues    and  the  greetings  in   the  markets and
2564         5259 014 444        4461      8   1473 1161 3361
καλεῖσθαι ὑπὸ τῶν ἀνθρώπων ῥαββί.    ῾Υμεῖς δὲ  μὴ
to be called by  the  men       rabbi.       You  but  not
2564         4461      1520 1063 1510   1473   01
κληθῆτε  ῥαββί· εἷς γὰρ ἐστιν ὑμῶν  ὁ
might be called rabbi;  one  for  is     of you the
1320          3956    1161 1473 80        1510    9  2532
διδάσκαλος, πάντες δὲ  ὑμεῖς ἀδελφοί ἐστε.   καὶ
teacher,    all    but  you   brothers are.      And
3962   3361 2564        1473    1909 06  1093    1520
πατέρα μὴ  καλέσητε  ὑμῶν ἐπὶ τῆς γῆς,  εἷς
father not  you might call of you on   the  earth,  one
1063 1510  1473  01  3962   01  3770        10  3366
γὰρ ἐστιν ὑμῶν  ὁ  πατὴρ ὁ  οὐράνιος.    μηδὲ
for  is    of you the father the heavenly.    But not
2564       2519        3754    2519        1473
κληθῆτε  καθηγηταί,  ὅτι    καθηγητὴς ὑμῶν
you might lead teachers,  because lead teacher of you
be called
1510   1520 01 5547      01 1161 3173    1473    1510
ἐστιν εἷς ὁ Χριστός. 11 ὁ  δὲ  μείζων ὑμῶν  ἔσται
is     one the Christ.     The but  greater of you will be
1473    1249        12  3748 1161 5312            1438
ὑμῶν  διάκονος.    ὅστις δὲ  ὑψώσει  •  ἑαυτὸν
of you servant.      Who  but  will elevate  himself
5013              2532 3748  5013          1438
ταπεινωθήσεται καὶ  ὅστις ταπεινώσει ἑαυτὸν
will be humbled  and  who   will humble himself
5312            13 3759 1161 1473    1122        2532
ὑψωθήσεται.     Οὐαὶ δὲ  ὑμῖν,  γραμματεῖς καὶ
will be elevated. Woe  but  to you, writers     and
5330        5273        3754    2808       08  932
Φαρισαῖοι ὑποκριταί,  ὅτι    κλείετε  τὴν βασιλείαν
Pharisees hypocrites, because you close the kingdom
014    3772       1715        014 444        1473   1063
τῶν  οὐρανῶν ἔμπροσθεν τῶν ἀνθρώπων· ὑμεῖς γὰρ
of the heavens in front of the men;       you  for
```

and follow it; but do not do as they do, for they do not practice what they teach. [4]They tie up heavy burdens, hard to bear,[a] and lay them on the shoulders of others; but they themselves are unwilling to lift a finger to move them. [5]They do all their deeds to be seen by others; for they make their phylacteries broad and their fringes long. [6]They love to have the place of honor at banquets and the best seats in the synagogues, [7]and to be greeted with respect in the marketplaces, and to have people call them rabbi. [8]But you are not to be called rabbi, for you have one teacher, and you are all students.[b] [9]And call no one your father on earth, for you have one Father—the one in heaven. [10]Nor are you to be called instructors, for you have one instructor, the Messiah.[c] [11]The greatest among you will be your servant. [12]All who exalt themselves will be humbled, and all who humble themselves will be exalted.

13 "But woe to you, scribes and Pharisees, hypocrites! For you lock people out of the kingdom of heaven. For you do not go in yourselves, and when others are going in, you stop them.[d]

a Other ancient authorities lack
  hard to bear
b Gk brothers
c Or the Christ
d Other authorities add here (or
  after verse 12) verse 14, Woe
  to you, scribes and Pharisees,
  hypocrites! For you devour widows'
  houses and for the sake of
  appearance you make long prayers;
  therefore you will receive the greater
  condemnation

15Woe to you, scribes and Pharisees, hypocrites! For you cross sea and land to make a single convert, and you make the new convert twice as much a child of hell *a* as yourselves.

16 "Woe to you, blind guides, who say, 'Whoever swears by the sanctuary is bound by nothing, but whoever swears by the gold of the sanctuary is bound by the oath.' 17You blind fools! For which is greater, the gold or the sanctuary that has made the gold sacred? 18And you say, 'Whoever swears by the altar is bound by nothing, but whoever swears by the gift that is on the altar is bound by the oath.' 19How blind you are! For which is greater, the gift or the altar that makes the gift sacred? 20So whoever swears by the altar, swears by it and by everything on it; 21and whoever swears by the sanctuary, swears by it and by the one who dwells in it; 22and whoever swears by heaven, swears by the throne of God and by the one who is seated upon it.

23 "Woe to you, scribes and Pharisees, hypocrites! For you tithe

a Gk Gehenna

3756	1525		3761		016	1525		863
οὐκ	εἰσέρχεσθε	οὐδὲ		τοὺς	εἰσερχομένους		ἀφίετε
not	you go in	but not		the	ones going in		you allow

1525   3759 1473   1122   2532 5330
εἰσελθεῖν. **15** Οὐαὶ ὑμῖν,   γραμματεῖς καὶ   Φαρισαῖοι
to go in.   Woe to you,   writers   and   Pharisees

5273   3754   4013   08   2281   2532
ὑποκριταί, ὅτι   περιάγετε   τὴν θάλασσαν καὶ
hypocrites, because you lead around   the sea   and

08   3584   4160   1520 4339   2532 3752
τὴν ξηρὰν   ποιῆσαι ἕνα προσήλυτον, καὶ   ὅταν
the dried out to make one convert,   and when

1096   4160   846   5207 1067   1362
γένηται   ποιεῖτε αὐτὸν υἱὸν γεέννης διπλότερον
it might become you make him son of gehenna two more

1473   **16** 3759 1473   3595   5185   013   3004
ὑμῶν.   Οὐαὶ ὑμῖν, ὁδηγοὶ τυφλοὶ οἱ   λέγοντες·
of you.   Woe to you, guides blind the ones saying,

3739 302 3660   1722 03   3485   3762   1510
ὃς ἂν ὀμόσῃ   ἐν τῷ ναῷ,   οὐδέν ἐστιν·
who - might take oath in the temple, nothing it is;

3739 1161 302 3660   1722 03 3557 02.
ὃς δ' ἂν ὀμόσῃ   ἐν τῷ χρυσῷ τοῦ
who but - might take oath in the gold of the

3485   3784   **17** 3474 2532 5185   5101 1063 3173
ναοῦ, ὀφείλει.   μωροὶ καὶ τυφλοί, τίς γὰρ μείζων
temple, owes.   Fools and blind, what for greater

1510   01 5557 2228 01 3485   01 37
ἐστίν, ὁ χρυσὸς ἢ ὁ ναὸς ὁ ἁγιάσας
is,   the gold or the temple the one having made holy

04 5557   **18** 2532 3739 302 3660   1722 011
τὸν χρυσόν;   καί· ὃς ἂν ὀμόσῃ   ἐν τῷ
the gold?   And, who - might take oath in the

2379   3762   1510   3739 1161 302
θυσιαστηρίῳ,   οὐδέν ἐστιν· ὃς δ' ἂν
place of sacrifice, nothing it is; who but -

0660   1722 011 1435 011 1883   846   3784
ὀμόσῃ   ἐν τῷ δώρῳ τῷ ἐπάνω αὐτοῦ, ὀφείλει.
might take oath in the gift the upon of him, owes.

19 5185   5101 1063 3173   09 1435 2228 09
τυφλοί, τί γὰρ μεῖζον, τὸ δῶρον ἢ   τὸ
Blind, what for greater, the gift or   the

2379   09   37   012 1435
θυσιαστήριον   τὸ ἁγιάζον   τὸ δῶρον;
place of sacrifice the one making holy the gift?

20 01 3767 3660   1722 011 2379   3660 1722
ὁ οὖν ὀμόσας   ἐν τῷ θυσιαστηρίῳ ὀμνύει ἐν
The then having taken in the place of   takes in
       one   oath   sacrifice oath

846   2532 1722 3956 023 1883   846   **21** 2532 01
αὐτῷ καὶ ἐν πᾶσι τοῖς ἐπάνω αὐτοῦ· καὶ ὁ
him and in all the upon of him;   and the one

3660   1722 03 3485   3660   1722 846 2532 1722 03
ὀμόσας ἐν τῷ ναῷ   ὀμνύει ἐν αὐτῷ καὶ ἐν τῷ
having in the temple takes in it   and in the
taken oath   oath

2730   846   **22** 2532 01   3660   1722 03
κατοικοῦντι αὐτόν,   καὶ ὁ ὀμόσας   ἐν τῷ
things residing it,   and the one having in the
                                  taken oath

3772   3660   1722 03 2362   02   2316 2532 1722
οὐρανῷ ὀμνύει   ἐν τῷ θρόνῳ τοῦ θεοῦ καὶ ἐν
heaven takes oath in the throne of the God and in

03 2521   1883   846   **23** 3759 1473   1122
τῷ καθημένῳ ἐπάνω αὐτοῦ.   Οὐαὶ ὑμῖν, γραμματεῖς
the one sitting upon it.   Woe to you, writers

2532 5330   5273   3754   586   012
καὶ Φαρισαῖοι ὑποκριταί, ὅτι   ἀποδεκατοῦτε τὸ
and Pharisees hypocrites, because you give tenth the

2238   2532 012 432   2532 012 2951   2532 863
ἡδύοσμον καὶ τὸ ἄνηθον καὶ τὸ κύμινον καὶ ἀφήκατε
mint   and the anise and the cummin and you leave off
024 926   02   3551   08 2920   2532 012
τὰ βαρύτερα   τοῦ   νόμου, τὴν κρίσιν   καὶ τὸ
the more burdens of the law,   the judgment and   the
1656   2532 08 4102   3778   1161 1163
ἔλεος καὶ   τὴν πίστιν· ταῦτα [δὲ] ἔδει
mercy and   the trust;   these but it was necessary
4160   2548   3361 863   3595   5185
ποιῆσαι κἀκεῖνα μὴ ἀφιέναι.   **24** ὁδηγοὶ τυφλοί,
to do   and those not   to leave off.   Guides blind,
013 1368   04   2971   08 1161 2574
οἱ διϋλίζοντες   τὸν κώνωπα, τὴν δὲ κάμηλον
the ones filtering the gnat,   the but camel
2666   3759 1473   1122   2532 5330
καταπίνοντες. **25** Οὐαὶ ὑμῖν, γραμματεῖς καὶ Φαρισαῖοι
swallowing down. Woe to you, writers   and Pharisees
5273   3754   2511   012 1855   010 4221
ὑποκριταί, ὅτι   καθαρίζετε τὸ ἔξωθεν τοῦ ποτηρίου
hypocrites, because you clean the outside of the cup
2532 06   3953   2081   1161 1073   1537
καὶ τῆς   παροψίδος, ἔσωθεν δὲ γέμουσιν   ἐξ
and of the dish,   inside but they are full from
724   2532 192   5330   5185   2511
ἁρπαγῆς καὶ ἀκρασίας. **26** Φαρισαῖε τυφλέ, καθάρισον
seizure and no strength. Pharisee blind, clean
4413   012 1787   010 4221   2443 1096   2532
πρῶτον τὸ ἐντὸς τοῦ ποτηρίου, ἵνα γένηται   καὶ
first   the within the cup,   that might become also
09 1622   846   2513   3759 1473   1510
τὸ ἐκτὸς αὐτοῦ καθαρόν. **27** Οὐαὶ ὑμῖν, γραμματεῖς
the outside of it clean. Woe to you, writers
2532 5330   5273   3754   3945   5028
καὶ Φαρισαῖοι ὑποκριταί, ὅτι   παρομοιάζετε τάφοις
and Pharisees hypocrites, because you are like tombs
2867   3748   1855   3303   5316
κεκονιαμένοις, οἵτινες ἔξωθεν μὲν φαίνονται
whitewashed,   which outside indeed shine
5611   2081   1161 1073   3747   3498
ὡραῖοι, ἔσωθεν δὲ γέμουσιν ὀστέων νεκρῶν
beautiful, inside but they are full of bones of dead
2532 3956 167   3779   2532 1473 1855
καὶ πάσης ἀκαθαρσίας. **28** οὕτως καὶ ὑμεῖς ἔξωθεν
and all   uncleanness. Thusly also you   outside
3303   5316   015   444   1342   2081   1161
μὲν   φαίνεσθε τοῖς ἀνθρώποις δίκαιοι, ἔσωθεν δέ
indeed shine   to the men   right,   inside but
1510   3324   5272   2532 458   3759
ἐστε μεστοὶ ὑποκρίσεως καὶ ἀνομίας. **29** Οὐαὶ
you are full of hypocrisy and lawlessness. Woe
1473   1122   2532 5330   5273   3754
ὑμῖν, γραμματεῖς καὶ Φαρισαῖοι ὑποκριταί, ὅτι
to you, writers   and Pharisees hypocrites, because
3618   016 5028   014   4396   2532 2885
οἰκοδομεῖτε τοὺς τάφους τῶν προφητῶν καὶ κοσμεῖτε
you build   the tombs of the spokesmen and you adorn
024 3419   014   1342   2532 3004   1487 1510
τὰ μνημεῖα τῶν δικαίων, **30** καὶ λέγετε· εἰ ἤμεθα
the graves of the right ones, and you say, if we were
1722 019 2250   014   3962   1473   3756 302 1510
ἐν ταῖς ἡμέραις τῶν πατέρων ἡμῶν, οὐκ ἂν ἤμεθα
in the days   of the fathers of us, not - we were
846   2844   1722 011 129   014   4396
αὐτῶν κοινωνοὶ ἐν τῷ αἵματι τῶν προφητῶν.
of them partners in the blood of the spokesmen.
5620   3140   1438   3754 5207 1510
31 ὥστε μαρτυρεῖτε ἑαυτοῖς   ὅτι υἱοί ἐστε
So that you testify to yourselves that sons you are

mint, dill, and cummin, and have neglected the weightier matters of the law: justice and mercy and faith. It is these you ought to have practiced without neglecting the others. 24You blind guides! You strain out a gnat but swallow a camel!

25 "Woe to you, scribes and Pharisees, hypocrites! For you clean the outside of the cup and of the plate, but inside they are full of greed and self-indulgence. 26You blind Pharisee! First clean the inside of the cup,[a] so that the outside also may become clean.

27 "Woe to you, scribes and Pharisees, hypocrites! For you are like white-washed tombs, which on the outside look beautiful, but inside they are full of the bones of the dead and of all kinds of filth. 28So you also on the outside look righteous to others, but inside you are full of hypocrisy and lawlessness.

29 "Woe to you, scribes and Pharisees, hypocrites! For you build the tombs of the prophets and decorate the graves of the righteous, 30and you say, 'If we had lived in the days of our ancestors, we would not have taken part with them in shedding the blood of the prophets.' 31Thus you testify against yourselves that you are descendants

---

a Other ancient authorities add *and of the plate*

of those who murdered the prophets. ³²Fill up, then, the measure of your ancestors. ³³You snakes, you brood of vipers! How can you escape being sentenced to hell?ᵃ ³⁴Therefore I send you prophets, sages, and scribes, some of whom you will kill and crucify, and some you will flog in your synagogues and pursue from town to town, ³⁵so that upon you may come all the righteous blood shed on earth, from the blood of righteous Abel to the blood of Zechariah son of Barachiah, whom you murdered between the sanctuary and the altar. ³⁶Truly I tell you, all this will come upon this generation.

37 "Jerusalem, Jerusalem, the city that kills the prophets and stones those who are sent to it! How often have I desired to gather your children together as a hen gathers her brood under her wings, and you were not willing! ³⁸See, your house is left to you, desolate.ᵇ ³⁹For I tell you, you will not see me again until you say, 'Blessed is the one who comes in the name of the Lord.' "

ᵃ Gk Gehenna
ᵇ Other ancient authorities lack desolate

014 5407 016 4396 2532
τῶν φονευσάντων τοὺς προφήτας. 32 καὶ
of the ones having murdered the spokesmen. And
1473 4137 012 3358 014 3962 1473
ὑμεῖς πληρώσατε τὸ μέτρον τῶν πατέρων ὑμῶν.
you fulfill the measure of the fathers of you.
3789 1081 2191 4459
33 ὄφεις, γεννήματα ἐχιδνῶν, πῶς
Snakes, generations of poison snakes, how
5343 575 06 2920 06 1067
φύγητε ἀπὸ τῆς κρίσεως τῆς γεέννης;
you might flee from the judgment of the gehenna?
1223 3778 2400 1473 649 4314 1473
34 Διὰ τοῦτο ἰδοὺ ἐγὼ ἀποστέλλω πρὸς ὑμᾶς
Through this look I delegate toward you
4396 2532 4680 2532 1122 1537 846
προφήτας καὶ σοφοὺς καὶ γραμματεῖς· ἐξ αὐτῶν
spokesmen and wise and writers; out of them
615 2532 4717 2532 1537 846
ἀποκτενεῖτε καὶ σταυρώσετε καὶ ἐξ αὐτῶν
you will kill and will crucify and out of them
3146 1722 019 4864 1473 2532
μαστιγώσετε ἐν ταῖς συναγωγαῖς ὑμῶν καὶ
you will scourge in the synagogues of you and
1377 575 4172 1519 4172 3704
διώξετε ἀπὸ πόλεως εἰς πόλιν· 35 ὅπως
you will pursue from city to city; so that
2064 1909 1473 3956 129 1342 1632a
ἔλθῃ ἐφ᾿ ὑμᾶς πᾶν αἷμα δίκαιον ἐκχυννόμενον
might come on you all blood right being poured out
1909 06 1093 575 010 129 6 02 1342
ἐπὶ τῆς γῆς ἀπὸ τοῦ αἵματος Ἄβελ τοῦ δικαίου
on the land from the blood of Abel the right one
2193 010 129 2197 5207 914
ἕως τοῦ αἵματος Ζαχαρίου υἱοῦ Βαραχίου,
until the blood of Zacharias son of Barachiah,
3739 5407 3342 02 3485 2532 010
ὃν ἐφονεύσατε μεταξὺ τοῦ ναοῦ καὶ τοῦ
who was murdered between the temple and the
2379 281 3004 1473 2240
θυσιαστηρίου. 36 ἀμὴν λέγω ὑμῖν, ἥξει
place of sacrifice. Amen I say to you, will come
3778 3956 1909 08 1074 3778 2419
ταῦτα πάντα ἐπὶ τὴν γενεὰν ταύτην. 37 Ἰερουσαλὴμ
these all on the generation this. Jerusalem
2419 05 615 016 4396 2532
Ἰερουσαλήμ, ἡ ἀποκτείνουσα τοὺς προφήτας καὶ
Jerusalem, the one killing the spokesmen and
3036 016 649 4314
λιθοβολοῦσα τοὺς ἀπεσταλμένους πρὸς
throwing stones the ones having been delegated toward
846 4212 2309 1996 024
αὐτήν, ποσάκις ἠθέλησα ἐπισυναγαγεῖν τὰ
her, how often I wanted to bring together the
5043 1473 3739 5158 3733 1996 024
τέκνα σου, ὃν τρόπον ὄρνις ἐπισυνάγει τὰ
children of you, which manner hen brings together the
3556 846 5259 020 4420 2532 3756 2309
νοσσία αὐτῆς ὑπὸ τὰς πτέρυγας, καὶ οὐκ ἠθελήσατε.
young of her by the wings, and not you wanted.
2400 863 1473 01 3624 1473 2048
38 ἰδοὺ ἀφίεται ὑμῖν ὁ οἶκος ὑμῶν ἔρημος.
Look is left off to you the house of you desert.
3004 1063 1473 3756 3361 1473 3708 575
39 λέγω γὰρ ὑμῖν, οὐ μή με ἴδητε ἀπ᾿
I say for to you, not not me you might see from
737 2193 302 3004 2127 01
ἄρτι ἕως ἂν εἴπητε· εὐλογημένος ὁ
now until - you might say, being well-spoken the

2064	1722	3686	2962	**24:1**	2532 1831
ἐρχόμενος	ἐν	ὀνόματι	κυρίου.		Καὶ ἐξελθὼν
one coming	in	name	of Master.		And having come out

01	2424	575	010 2411	4198	2532
ὁ	Ἰησοῦς	ἀπὸ	τοῦ ἱεροῦ	ἐπορεύετο,	καὶ
the	Jesus	from	the temple	he was traveling,	and

4334	013 3101	846	1925	846	020
προσῆλθον	οἱ μαθηταὶ	αὐτοῦ	ἐπιδεῖξαι	αὐτῷ	τὰς
went toward	the learners	of him	to show	on to him	the

3619	010	2411	**2**	01	1161 611
οἰκοδομὰς	τοῦ	ἱεροῦ.		ὁ	δὲ ἀποκριθεὶς
buildings	of the	temple.		The but	one having answered

3004 846	3756 991	3778	3956	281	3004
εἶπεν αὐτοῖς·	οὐ βλέπετε	ταῦτα	πάντα;	ἀμὴν	λέγω
said to them,	not you see	these	all?	Amen	I say

1473	3756 3361	863	5602	3037	1909	3037 3739	3756
ὑμῖν,	οὐ μὴ	ἀφεθῇ	ὧδε	λίθος	ἐπὶ	λίθον ὃς	οὐ
to you,	not not	might here	stone	on	stone which	not be sent off

2647	**3**	2521	1161 846	1909	010 3735
καταλυθήσεται.		Καθημένου	δὲ αὐτοῦ	ἐπὶ	τοῦ ὄρους
will be unloosed.		Sitting	but him	on	the hill

018	433,4	846 013 3101	2596 2398
τῶν	ἐλαιῶν προσῆλθον	αὐτῷ οἱ μαθηταὶ	κατ᾽ ἰδίαν
of the	olives came toward	him the learners	by own

3004	3004 1473	4219 3778	1510	2532 5101 09
λέγοντες·	εἰπὲ ἡμῖν,	πότε ταῦτα	ἔσται	καὶ τί τὸ
saying,	say to us,	when these	will be	and what the

4592	06	4674 3952	2532 4930
σημεῖον	τῆς	σῆς παρουσίας	καὶ συντελείας
sign	of the	your presence	and full completion

02	165	**4**	2532 611	01 2424	3004
τοῦ	αἰῶνος;		Καὶ ἀποκριθεὶς	ὁ Ἰησοῦς	εἶπεν
of the	age?		And having answered	the Jesus	said

846	991	3361 5100	1473 4105
αὐτοῖς·	βλέπετε	μή τις	ὑμᾶς πλανήσῃ·
to them;	see	not someone	you might deceive;

5 4183	1063 2064	1909 011 3686	1473 3004
πολλοὶ	γὰρ ἐλεύσονται	ἐπὶ τῷ ὀνόματί	μου λέγοντες·
many	for will come	on the name	of me saying,

1473 1510 01	5547	2532 4183	4105
ἐγώ εἰμι ὁ	χριστός,	καὶ πολλοὺς	πλανήσουσιν.
I am the	Christ,	and many	they will deceive.

6 3195	1161 191	4171	2532 189
μελλήσετε	δὲ ἀκούειν	πολέμους	καὶ ἀκοὰς
You will be about	but to hear	wars	and hearings

4171	3708 3361 2360	1163	1063
πολέμων·	ὁρᾶτε μὴ θροεῖσθε·	δεῖ	γὰρ
of wars;	see not be disturbed;	it is necessary	for

1096	235	3768	1510 09	5056
γενέσθαι,	ἀλλ᾽	οὔπω	ἐστὶν τὸ	τέλος.
to become,	but	not yet	is the	completion.

7 1453	1063 1484	1909 1484	2532 932
ἐγερθήσεται	γὰρ ἔθνος	ἐπὶ ἔθνος	καὶ βασιλεία
Will be raised	for nation	on nation	and kingdom

1909 932	2532 1510	3042	2532 4578
ἐπὶ βασιλείαν	καὶ ἔσονται	λιμοὶ	καὶ σεισμοὶ
on kingdom	and there will be	famines	and shakes

2596 5117	**8**	3956 1161 3778 746	5604
κατὰ τόπους·		πάντα δὲ ταῦτα ἀρχὴ	ὠδίνων.
by places;		all but these beginning	of birth pains.

9 5119 3860	1473 1519 2347	2532
Τότε παραδώσουσιν	ὑμᾶς εἰς θλῖψιν	καὶ
Then they will give over	you into affliction	and

615	1473 2532 1510	3404
ἀποκτενοῦσιν	ὑμᾶς, καὶ ἔσεσθε	μισούμενοι
they will kill	you, and you will be+	+being hated

5259 3956	022 1484	1223	012 3686 1473
ὑπὸ πάντων	τῶν ἐθνῶν	διὰ	τὸ ὄνομά μου.
by all	the nations	because of	the name of me.

CHAPTER 24

As Jesus came out of the temple and was going away, his disciples came to point out to him the buildings of the temple. [2]Then he asked them, "You see all these, do you not? Truly I tell you, not one stone will be left here upon another; all will be thrown down."

[3] When he was sitting on the Mount of Olives, the disciples came to him privately, saying, "Tell us, when will this be, and what will be the sign of your coming and of the end of the age?" [4]Jesus answered them, "Beware that no one leads you astray. [5]For many will come in my name, saying, 'I am the Messiah!'[a] and they will lead many astray. [6]And you will hear of wars and rumors of wars; see that you are not alarmed; for this must take place, but the end is not yet. [7]For nation will rise against nation, and kingdom against kingdom, and there will be famines[b] and earthquakes in various places: [8]all this is but the beginning of the birth pangs.

[9] "Then they will hand you over to be tortured and will put you to death, and you will be hated by all nations because of my name.

[a] Or the Christ
[b] Other ancient authorities add and pestilences

10Then many will fall away,ᵃ and they will betray one another and hate one another. 11And many false prophets will arise and lead many astray. 12And because of the increase of lawlessness, the love of many will grow cold. 13But the one who endures to the end will be saved. 14And this good newsᵇ of the kingdom will be proclaimed throughout the world, as a testimony to all the nations; and then the end will come.

15 "So when you see the desolating sacrilege standing in the holy place, as was spoken of by the prophet Daniel (let the reader understand), 16then those in Judea must flee to the mountains; 17the one on the housetop must not go down to take what is in the house; 18the one in the field must not turn back to get a coat. 19Woe to those who are pregnant and to those who are nursing infants in those days. 20Pray that your flight may not be in winter or on a sabbath. 21For at that time there will be great suffering, such as has not been from the beginning of the world until now, no, and never will be.

ᵃ Or stumble
ᵇ Or gospel

```
              2532  5119  4624                    4183    2532  240
10    καὶ    τότε  σκανδαλισθήσονται  πολλοὶ  καὶ  ἀλλήλους
      And    then  will be offended    many   and  one another
3860                      2532  3404                240
παραδώσουσιν            καὶ  μισήσουσιν       ἀλλήλους·
they will give over    and  they will hate  one another;
      2532  4183    5578                1453              2532
11    καὶ  πολλοὶ  ψευδοπροφῆται  ἐγερθήσονται    καὶ
      and  many   false spokesmen  will be raised  and
4105                4183          2532  1223        012
πλανήσουσιν       πολλούς· 12  καὶ  διὰ       τὸ
they will deceive  many;       and  through  the
4129              08   458            5594          05
πληθυνθῆναι      τὴν  ἀνομίαν      ψυγήσεται       ἡ
to be multiplied  the  lawlessness  will grow cold  the
26    014   4183          01   1161  5278              1519
ἀγάπη  τῶν  πολλῶν. 13 ὁ  δὲ  ὑπομείνας          εἰς
love   of the many.    The  but  one having endured  to
5056      3778    4982                14  2532
τέλος    οὗτος  σωθήσεται.             καὶ
completion this one will be delivered. And
2784                3778   09  2098          06     932
κηρυχθήσεται        τοῦτο  τὸ  εὐαγγέλιον  τῆς  βασιλείας
will be announced   this   the  good message  of the  kingdom
1722  3650  07  3625              1519  3142        3956  023
ἐν  ὅλῃ  τῇ  οἰκουμένῃ      εἰς  μαρτύριον  πᾶσιν  τοῖς
in   whole the  inhabited world  for  testimony   to all  the
1484        2532  5119  2240      09   5056        15  3752 3767
ἔθνεσιν, καὶ  τότε  ἥξει      τὸ  τέλος.           Ὅταν  οὖν
nations,  and  then  will come  the  completion.     When  then
3708        012  946         06   2050          012
ἴδητε     τὸ  βδέλυγμα  τῆς  ἐρημώσεως  τὸ
you might see  the  abomination  of the  desolation  the
3004                    1223      1158    02   4396
ῥηθὲν                 διὰ     Δανιὴλ  τοῦ  προφήτου
word having been spoken  through  Daniel  the  spokesman
2476        1722  5117    40     01   314
ἑστὸς     ἐν  τόπῳ  ἁγίῳ, ὁ  ἀναγινώσκων
having stood  in  place  holy,  the  one reading
3539              16  5119  013        1722  07  2449
νοείτω,          τότε  οἱ        ἐν  τῇ  Ἰουδαίᾳ
let give thought,  then  the ones  in  the  Judea
5343          1519 024 3735  17  01        1909 010 1430  3361
φευγέτωσαν εἰς  τὰ  ὄρη,    ὁ        ἐπὶ  τοῦ  δώματος  μὴ
let flee      into  the  hills,  the  one on  the  roof      not
2597      142      024 1537 06  3614      846        18  2532
καταβάτω ἆραι   τὰ  ἐκ  τῆς  οἰκίας  αὐτοῦ,      καὶ
let come  to lift  the  from the  house  of him,    and
down      up      things
01  1722 03  68      3361 1994            3694  142
ὁ  ἐν  τῷ  ἀγρῷ  μὴ  ἐπιστρεψάτω ὀπίσω ἆραι
the  in  the  field  not  let return    after  to lift up
012 2440      846      3759 1161 019          1722 1064
τὸ  ἱμάτιον  αὐτοῦ. 19  οὐαὶ δὲ  ταῖς        ἐν  γαστρὶ
the  clothes  of him.    Woe  but  to the ones in  womb
2192        2532 019 2337              1722 1565      019
ἐχούσαις καὶ  ταῖς  θηλαζούσαις    ἐν  ἐκείναις ταῖς
having     and  the  ones giving nursing  in  those      the
2250          20  4336          1161 2443 3361 1096        05
ἡμέραις.      προσεύχεσθε δὲ  ἵνα  μὴ  γένηται      ἡ
days.         Pray          but  that  not  might become the
5437  1473  5494        3366  4521        21  1510
φυγὴ  ὑμῶν  χειμῶνος  μηδὲ  σαββάτῳ.       ἔσται
flight of you of winter  but not  in sabbath.     Will be
1063  5119  2347        3173    3634 3756 1096        575
γὰρ  τότε  θλῖψις    μεγάλη οἵα  οὐ  γέγονεν    ἀπ'
for   then  affliction  great   such not  has become  from
746        2889      2193  010 3568 3761        3756 3361
ἀρχῆς    κόσμου  ἕως  τοῦ  νῦν  οὐδ'        οὐ  μὴ
beginning world   until  the  now  but not not  not
```

```
1096                          2532 1487 3361 2856              017
γένηται.            22   καὶ  εἰ  μὴ  ἐκολοβώθησαν αἱ
it might become.        And except   be shortened  the
2250   1565      3756 302 4982                  3956 4561
ἡμέραι ἐκεῖναι, οὐκ  ἂν ἐσώθη            πᾶσα σάρξ·
days those,     not  -  will be delivered all   flesh;
1223       1161 016  1588         2856                017
διὰ        δὲ  τοὺς ἐκλεκτοὺς κολοβωθήσονται   αἱ
because of but the  select     will be shortened the
2250   1565     5119 1437 5100 1473    3004
ἡμέραι ἐκεῖναι. 23 Τότε ἐάν τις ὑμῖν εἴπη·
days those.     Then if  some to you might say,
2400 5602 01  5547     2228 5602 3361 4100
ἰδοὺ ὧδε ὁ χριστός, ἤ· ὧδε, μὴ πιστεύσητε·
look here the Christ, or; here, not you might trust;
      1453            1063 5580          2532 5578
24  ἐγερθήσονται γὰρ ψευδόχριστοι καὶ ψευδοπροφῆται
    will be raised for false christs and false spokesmen
2532 1325       4592 3173  2532 5059    5620
καὶ δώσουσιν σημεῖα μεγάλα καὶ τέρατα ὥστε
and they will give signs great and marvels so that
4105      1487 1415   2532 016 1588      2400
πλανῆσαι, εἰ δυνατόν, καὶ τοὺς ἐκλεκτούς. 25 ἰδοὺ
to deceive, if power,  even the select.      Look
4302          1473   1437 3767 3004
προείρηκα    ὑμῖν. 26 ἐὰν οὖν εἴπωσιν
I have spoken before to you. If then they might say
1473    2400 1722 07 2048    1510 3361 1831    2400
ὑμῖν· ἰδοὺ ἐν τῇ ἐρήμῳ ἐστίν, μὴ ἐξέλθητε· ἰδοὺ
to you, look in the desert he is, not go out;  look
1722 023 5009        3361 4100          5618
ἐν τοῖς ταμείοις, μὴ πιστεύσητε· 27 ὥσπερ
in the storerooms, not you might trust; as indeed
1063 05 796      1831     575 395      2532
γὰρ ἡ ἀστραπὴ ἐξέρχεται ἀπὸ ἀνατολῶν καὶ
for the lightning comes out from east   and
5316     2193 1424   3779 1510   05 3952
φαίνεται ἕως δυσμῶν, οὕτως ἔσται ἡ παρουσία
shines until west,  thusly will be the presence
02   5207 02  444        3699 1437 1510      09
τοῦ υἱοῦ τοῦ ἀνθρώπου· 28 ὅπου ἐὰν ᾖ    τὸ
of the son of the man;     where if might be the
4430     1563 4863          013 105
πτῶμα, ἐκεῖ συναχθήσονται οἱ ἀετοί.
corpse, there will be brought together the eagles.
    2112              1161 3326 08 2347      018    2250
29  Εὐθέως        δὲ μετὰ τὴν θλῖψιν τῶν ἡμερῶν
    Immediately but after the affliction of the days
1565   01 2246 4654              2532 05 4582
ἐκείνων ὁ ἥλιος σκοτισθήσεται, καὶ ἡ σελήνη
those   the sun will be darkened, and the moon
3756 1325      012 5338 846    2532 013 792
οὐ δώσει    τὸ φέγγος αὐτῆς, καὶ οἱ ἀστέρες
not will give the light of it, and the stars
4098        575 02 3772      2532 017 1411   014
πεσοῦνται ἀπὸ τοῦ οὐρανοῦ, καὶ αἱ δυνάμεις τῶν
will fall from the heaven, and the powers  of the
3772   4531          2532 5119 5316      09
οὐρανῶν σαλευθήσονται. 30 καὶ τότε φανήσεται τὸ
heavens will be shaken. And then will shine the
4592 02     5207 02  444        1722 1772      2532
σημεῖον τοῦ υἱοῦ τοῦ ἀνθρώπου ἐν οὐρανῷ, καὶ
sign of the son of the man  in heaven, and
5119 2875   3956 017 5443 06    1093 2532
τότε κόψονται πᾶσαι αἱ φυλαὶ τῆς γῆς καὶ
then will mourn all the tribes of the land and
3708       04 5207 02  444        2064     1909
ὄψονται    τὸν υἱὸν τοῦ ἀνθρώπου ἐρχόμενον ἐπὶ
they will see the son of the man  coming on
```

22And if those days had not been cut short, no one would be saved; but for the sake of the elect those days will be cut short. 23Then if anyone says to you, 'Look! Here is the Messiah!'[a] or 'There he is!'—do not believe it. 24For false messiahs[b] and false prophets will appear and produce great signs and omens, to lead astray, if possible, even the elect. 25Take note, I have told you beforehand. 26So, if they say to you, 'Look! He is in the wilderness,' do not go out. If they say, 'Look! He is in the inner rooms,' do not believe it. 27For as the lightning comes from the east and flashes as far as the west, so will be the coming of the Son of Man. 28Wherever the corpse is, there the vultures will gather.

29 "Immediately after the suffering of those days
    the sun will be darkened,
    and the moon will not give its light;
    the stars will fall from heaven,
    and the powers of heaven will be shaken.
30Then the sign of the Son of Man will appear

[a] Or the Christ
[b] Or christs

in heaven, and then all the
tribes of the earth will
mourn, and they will see
'the Son of Man coming on
the clouds of heaven' with
power and great glory.
³¹And he will send out his
angels with a loud trumpet
call, and they will gather
his elect from the four
winds, from one end of
heaven to the other.

32 "From the fig tree
learn its lesson: as soon as
its branch becomes tender
and puts forth its leaves,
you know that summer is
near. ³³So also, when you
see all these things, you
know that he*a* is near, at
the very gates. ³⁴Truly I tell
you, this generation will
not pass away until all these
things have taken place.
³⁵Heaven and earth will
pass away, but my words
will not pass away.

36 "But about that day
and hour no one knows,
neither the angels of
heaven, nor the Son,*b* but
only the Father. ³⁷For as
the days of Noah were, so
will be the coming of the
Son of Man. ³⁸For as in
those days before the flood
they were eating and
drinking, marrying and
giving in marriage, until
the day Noah entered the
ark, ³⁹and they knew
nothing until the flood
came and swept them all
away, so

a Or *it*
b Other ancient authorities lack *nor*
the Son

```
018   3507      02        3772      3326  1411        2532  1391
τῶν  νεφελῶν  τοῦ      οὐρανοῦ μετὰ  δυνάμεως  καὶ   δόξης
the  clouds    of the   heaven   with  power      and   splendor
4183          2532  649                    016    32           846
πολλῆς·   ³¹ καὶ  ἀποστελεῖ          τοὺς  ἀγγέλους  αὐτοῦ
much;         and   he will delegate   the   messengers of him
3326  4536          3173        2532  1996
μετὰ  σάλπιγγος  μεγάλης,  καὶ  ἐπισυνάξουσιν
with  trumpet      great,       and  they will bring together on
016   1588       846     1537    014  5064       417      575
τοὺς  ἐκλεκτοὺς  αὐτοῦ  ἐκ     τῶν  τεσσάρων ἀνέμων ἀπ'
the   select       of him  out of   the   four        winds    from
206   3772        2193   022    206    846         575   1161
ἄκρων οὐρανῶν  ἕως  [τῶν] ἄκρων  αὐτῶν.  ³² Ἀπὸ  δὲ
tips   of heavens until  the    tips   of them.    From  but
06   4808      3129   08   3850                 3752  2235
τῆς  συκῆς    μάθετε τὴν  παραβολήν·     ὅταν  ἤδη
the  fig tree  learn   the  parallel story;  when  already
01   2798      846     1096                527       2532  024  5444
ὁ    κλάδος  αὐτῆς  γένηται          ἁπαλὸς  καὶ  τὰ  φύλλα
the  branch  of it   might become   tender    and   the  leaves
1631        1097          3754 1451   09    2330          3779
ἐκφύῃ,     γινώσκετε  ὅτι  ἐγγὺς  τὸ  θέρος·  ³³ οὕτως
sprout out,  know         that  near    the  summer;  thusly
2532 1473      3752 3708        3956   3778   1097
καὶ  ὑμεῖς,  ὅταν  ἴδητε        πάντα ταῦτα, γινώσκετε
also  you,    when  you might see all     these,  know
3754 1451   1510 1909 2374          281   3004   1473    3754
ὅτι  ἐγγύς ἐστιν ἐπὶ θύραις. ³⁴ ἀμὴν  λέγω  ὑμῖν  ὅτι
that  near  it is  at   doors.       Amen  I say   to you  that
3756 3361 3928              05   1074             3778 2193
οὐ   μὴ   παρέλθῃ          ἡ   γενεὰ           αὕτη ἕως
not  not  might come along  the  generation     this  until
302  3956  3778 1096            01   3772        2532 05  1093
ἂν  πάντα ταῦτα γένηται. ³⁵ ὁ  οὐρανὸς  καὶ  ἡ  γῆ
-    all    these might become. The heaven   and  the  land
3928                    013  1161 3056    1473 3756 3361
παρελεύσεται,       οἱ  δὲ  λόγοι μου  οὐ  μὴ
will go along,          the but  words of me not  not
3928                  4012 1161 06  2250        1565      2532
παρέλθωσιν.   ³⁶ Περὶ  δὲ  τῆς ἡμέρας ἐκείνης  καὶ
they might go along.  About but  the  day      that      and
5610  3762  3609a        3761     013 32        014
ὥρας  οὐδεὶς οἶδεν,    οὐδὲ    οἱ  ἄγγελοι  τῶν
hour  no one has known,  but not  the  messengers of the
3772    3761    01  5207  1487 3361 01  3962    3441
οὐρανῶν οὐδὲ  ὁ  υἱός, εἰ  μὴ  ὁ  πατὴρ  μόνος.
heavens but not the  son,  except  the  father  alone.
       5618        1063 017 2250   02    3575     3779   1510
³⁷ Ὥσπερ     γὰρ αἱ ἡμέραι τοῦ Νῶε, οὕτως ἔσται
       As indeed  for the days  of the Noah, thusly  will be
05  3952       02     5207 02  444           5613 1063
ἡ  παρουσία τοῦ  υἱοῦ τοῦ ἀνθρώπου. ³⁸ ὡς γὰρ
the presence of the son of  the  man.        As  for
1510    1722 019  2250    1565       019     4253
ἦσαν   ἐν  ταῖς ἡμέραις [ἐκείναις] ταῖς  πρὸ
they were in  the  days   those      the ones before
02  2627         5176      2532 4095      1060     2532
τοῦ κατακλυσμοῦ τρώγοντες καὶ πίνοντες, γαμοῦντες καὶ
the flood         gnawing   and drinking,  marrying  and
1060a                891   3739  2250     1525     3575
γαμίζοντες,       ἄχρι ἧς  ἡμέρας εἰσῆλθεν Νῶε
giving in marriage, until which day    went into  Noah
1519 08  2787      2532 3756 1097      2193  2064
εἰς  τὴν κιβωτόν, ³⁹ καὶ  οὐκ ἔγνωσαν ἕως  ἦλθεν
into the box,        and   not  they knew  until  came
01  2627         2532 142   537       3779
ὁ  κατακλυσμὸς καὶ ἦρεν ἅπαντας, οὕτως
the flood         and  it lifted up all,     thusly
```

| 1510 | 2532 | 05 | 3952 | 02 | 5207 02 | 444 |

ἔσται [καὶ] ἡ παρουσία τοῦ υἱοῦ τοῦ ἀνθρώπου.
will be also the presence of the son of the man.

40
| 5119 | 1417 | 1510 | 1722 03 | 68 | 1520 | 3880 |

τότε δύο ἔσονται ἐν τῷ ἀγρῷ, εἷς παραλαμβάνεται
Then two will be in the field, one is taken along

| 2532 | 1520 | 863 | 1417 | 229 | 1722 03 |

καὶ εἷς ἀφίεται·   **41** δύο ἀλήθουσαι ἐν τῷ
and one is sent off;   two grinding in the

| 3458 | 1520 | 3880 | 2532 | 1520 | 863 |

μύλῳ, μία παραλαμβάνεται καὶ μία αφίεται.
mill, one is taken along and one is sent off.

42
| 1127 | 3767 | 3754 | 3756 | 3609a | 4169 |

Γρηγορεῖτε οὖν, ὅτι οὐκ οἴδατε ποίᾳ
Keep awake then, because not you know what kind

| 2250 | 01 | 2962 | 1473 | 2064 | 1565 | 1161 | 1097 |

ἡμέρᾳ ὁ κύριος ὑμῶν ἔρχεται. **43** Ἐκεῖνο δὲ γινώσκετε
day the Master of you comes. That but know

| 3754 | 1487 | 3609a | 01 | 3617 | 4169 | 5438 |

ὅτι εἰ ᾔδει ὁ οἰκοδεσπότης ποίᾳ φυλακῇ
that if had known the house supervisor what guard

| 01 | 2812 | 2064 | 1127 | 302 | 2532 | 3756 | 302 |

ὁ κλέπτης ἔρχεται, ἐγρηγόρησεν ἂν καὶ οὐκ ἂν
the thief comes, he kept awake - and not -

| 1439 | 1358 | 08 | 3614 | 846 | 1223 |

εἴασεν διορυχθῆναι τὴν οἰκίαν αὐτοῦ. **44** διὰ
allowed to be dug through the house of him. Through

| 3778 | 2532 | 1473 | 1096 | 2092 | 3754 | 3739 |

τοῦτο καὶ ὑμεῖς γίνεσθε ἕτοιμοι, ὅτι ᾗ
this also you become prepared, because in which

| 3756 | 1380 | 5610 01 | 5207 02 | 444 | 2064 |

οὐ δοκεῖτε ὥρᾳ ὁ υἱὸς τοῦ ἀνθρώπου ἔρχεται.
not you think hour the son of the man comes.

45
| 5101 | 686 | 1510 | 01 | 4103 | 1401 | 2532 | 5429 |

Τίς ἄρα ἐστὶν ὁ πιστὸς δοῦλος καὶ φρόνιμος
Who then is the trustful slave and thoughtful

| 3739 | 2525 | 01 | 2962 | 1909 | 06 | 3609b | 846 |

ὃν κατέστησεν ὁ κύριος ἐπὶ τῆς οἰκετείας αὐτοῦ
whom appointed the master on the household of him

| 010 | 1325 | 846 | 08 | 5160 | 1722 | 2540 |

τοῦ δοῦναι αὐτοῖς τὴν τροφὴν ἐν καιρῷ;
of the to give to them the food in season?

46
| 3107 | 01 | 1401 | 1565 | 3739 | 2064 | 01 |

μακάριος ὁ δοῦλος ἐκεῖνος ὃν ἐλθὼν ὁ
Fortunate the slave that whom having come the

| 2962 | 846 | 2147 | 3779 | 4160 | 281 | 3004 |

κύριος αὐτοῦ εὑρήσει οὕτως ποιοῦντα· **47** ἀμὴν λέγω
master of him will find thusly doing; amen I say

| 1473 | 3754 | 1909 | 3956 | 023 | 5225 | 846 |

ὑμῖν ὅτι ἐπὶ πᾶσιν τοῖς ὑπάρχουσιν αὐτοῦ
to you that on all the possessions of him

| 2525 | 846 | 1437 | 1161 | 3004 | 01 | 2556 |

καταστήσει αὐτόν. **48** ἐὰν δὲ εἴπῃ ὁ κακὸς
he will appoint him. If but might say the bad

| 1401 | 1565 | 1722 07 | 2588 | 846 | 5549 |

δοῦλος ἐκεῖνος ἐν τῇ καρδίᾳ αὐτοῦ· χρονίζει
slave that in the heart of him; spends time

| 1473 | 01 | 2962 | 2532 | 757 | 5180 | 016 |

μου ὁ κύριος, **49** καὶ ἄρξηται τύπτειν τοὺς
of me the master, and he might begin to beat the

| 4889 | 846 | 2068 | 1161 | 2532 | 4095 |

συνδούλους αὐτοῦ, ἐσθίῃ δὲ καὶ πίνῃ
co-slaves of him, he might eat but also he might drink

| 3326 | 014 | 3184 | 2240 | 01 | 2962 |

μετὰ τῶν μεθυόντων, **50** ἥξει ὁ κύριος
with the ones being drunk, will come the master

| 02 | 1401 | 1565 | 1722 | 2250 | 3739 | 3756 |

τοῦ δούλου ἐκείνου ἐν ἡμέρᾳ ᾗ οὐ
of the slave that in day in which not

too will be the coming of the Son of Man. [40]Then two will be in the field; one will be taken and one will be left. [41]Two women will be grinding meal together; one will be taken and one will be left. [42]Keep awake therefore, for you do not know on what day[a] your Lord is coming. [43]But understand this: if the owner of the house had known in what part of the night the thief was coming, he would have stayed awake and would not have let his house be broken into. [44]Therefore you also must be ready, for the Son of Man is coming at an unexpected hour.

[45]"Who then is the faithful and wise slave, whom his master has put in charge of his household, to give the other slaves[b] their allowance of food at the proper time? [46]Blessed is that slave whom his master will find at work when he arrives. [47]Truly I tell you, he will put that one in charge of all his possessions. [48]But if that wicked slave says to himself, 'My master is delayed,' [49]and he begins to beat his fellow slaves, and eats and drinks with drunkards, [50]the master of that slave will come on a day when he does not

[a] Other ancient authorities read *at what hour*

[b] Gk *to give them*

expect him and at an hour that he does not know. [51]He will cut him in pieces[a] and put him with the hypocrites, where there will be weeping and gnashing of teeth.

CHAPTER 25

"Then the kingdom of heaven will be like this. Ten bridesmaids[b] took their lamps and went to meet the bridegroom.[c] [2]Five of them were foolish, and five were wise. [3]When the foolish took their lamps, they took no oil with them; [4]but the wise took flasks of oil with their lamps. [5]As the bridegroom was delayed, all of them became drowsy and slept. [6]But at midnight there was a shout, 'Look! Here is the bridegroom! Come out to meet him.' [7]Then all those bridesmaids[b] got up and trimmed their lamps. [8]The foolish said to the wise, 'Give us some of your oil, for our lamps are going out.' [9]But the wise replied, 'No! there will not be enough for you and for us; you had better go to the dealers and buy some for yourselves.' [10]And while they went to buy it,

[a] Or cut him off
[b] Gk virgins
[c] Other ancient authorities add and the bride

4328		2532	1722	5610	3739		3756
προσδοκᾷ		καὶ	ἐν	ὥρᾳ	ᾗ		οὐ
he awaits	expectantly	and	in	hour	in which		not

1097		2532	1371		846	2532	012
γινώσκει,	51	καὶ	διχοτομήσει		αὐτὸν	καὶ	τὸ
he knows,		and	he will cut in two		him	and	the

3313	846	3326	014	5273		5087	1563
μέρος	αὐτοῦ	μετὰ	τῶν	ὑποκριτῶν		θήσει·	ἐκεῖ
part	of him	with	the	hypocrites		he will set;	there

1510	01	2805	2532	01	1030	014	3599
ἔσται	ὁ	κλαυθμὸς	καὶ	ὁ	βρυγμὸς	τῶν	ὀδόντων.
will be	the	crying	and	the	grinding	of the	teeth.

	5119	3666		05	932	014	3772
25:1	Τότε	ὁμοιωθήσεται		ἡ	βασιλεία	τῶν	οὐρανῶν
	Then will be	likened		the	kingdom	of the	heavens

1176	3933		3748		2983	020	2985
δέκα	παρθένοις,		αἵτινες		λαβοῦσαι	τὰς	λαμπάδας
to ten	virgins,		who		having taken	the	lamps

1438		1831		1519	5222	02	3566
ἑαυτῶν		ἐξῆλθον		εἰς	ὑπάντησιν	τοῦ	νυμφίου.
of themselves		went out		into	meeting	the	bridegroom.

	4002	1161	1537	846	1510	3474	2532	4002
2	πέντε	δὲ	ἐξ	αὐτῶν	ἦσαν	μωραὶ	καὶ	πέντε
	Five	but	out of	them	were	fools	and	five

5429		017	1063	3474	2983	020	2985
φρόνιμοι.	3	αἱ	γὰρ	μωραὶ	λαβοῦσαι	τὰς	λαμπάδας
thoughtful.		The	for	fools	having taken	the	lamps

846	3756	2983		3326	1438	1637		017
αὐτῶν	οὐκ	ἔλαβον		μεθ'	ἑαυτῶν	ἔλαιον.	4	αἱ
of them	not	they took		with	themselves	oil.		The

1161	5429		2983	1637	1722	023	30	3326
δὲ	φρόνιμοι		ἔλαβον	ἔλαιον	ἐν	τοῖς	ἀγγείοις	μετὰ
but	thoughtful		took	oil	in	the	containers	with

018	2985	1438		5549		1161	02
τῶν	λαμπάδων	ἑαυτῶν.	5	χρονίζοντος		δὲ	τοῦ
the	lamps	of themselves.		Spending time		but	the

3566	3573		3956	2532	2518		3319
νυμφίου	ἐνύσταξαν		πᾶσαι	καὶ	ἐκάθευδον.	6	μέσης
bridegroom	dozed		all	and	were sleeping.		In middle

1161	3571	2906	1096		2400	01	3566
δὲ	νυκτὸς	κραυγὴ	γέγονεν·		ἰδοὺ	ὁ	νυμφίος,
but	of night	shout	had become;		look	the	bridegroom,

1831	1519	529		846		5119	1453
ἐξέρχεσθε	εἰς	ἀπάντησιν	[αὐτοῦ].	7		τότε	ἠγέρθησαν
comes out	into	meeting	of him.			Then	were raised

3956	017	3933		1565	2532	2885	020	2985
πᾶσαι	αἱ	παρθένοι		ἐκεῖναι	καὶ	ἐκόσμησαν	τὰς	λαμπάδας
all	the	virgins		those	and	adorned	the	lamps

1438		017	1161	3474	019	5429
ἑαυτῶν.	8	αἱ	δὲ	μωραὶ	ταῖς	φρονίμοις
of themselves.		The	but	fools	to the	thoughtful

3004	1325	1473	1537	017	1637	1473	3754
εἶπαν·	δότε	ἡμῖν	ἐκ	τοῦ	ἐλαίου	ὑμῶν,	ὅτι
said·	give	to us	out	of the	oil	of you,	because

017	2985	1473	4570		611	1161
αἱ	λαμπάδες	ἡμῶν	σβέννυνται.	9	ἀπεκρίθησαν	δὲ
the	lamps	of us	are quenched.		Answered	but

017	5429	3004	3379	3756	3361
αἱ	φρόνιμοι	λέγουσαι·	μήποτε	οὐ	μὴ
the	thoughtful	saying,	not then	not	not

714		1473	2532	1473	4198	3123
ἀρκέσῃ		ἡμῖν	καὶ	ὑμῖν·	πορεύεσθε	μᾶλλον
it might be enough		to us	and	to you;	travel	more

4314	016	4453	2532	59	1438
πρὸς	τοὺς	πωλοῦντας	καὶ	ἀγοράσατε	ἑαυταῖς.
toward	the	ones selling	and	buy	to yourselves.

	565		1161	846	59	2064	01
10	ἀπερχομένων		δὲ	αὐτῶν	ἀγοράσαι	ἦλθεν	ὁ
	Going off		but	them	to buy	came	the

```
3566              2532 017 2092              1525        3326
νυμφίος,     καὶ  αἱ  ἕτοιμοι     εἰσῆλθον  μετ᾽
bridegroom,  and  the ones prepared  went into  with

846      1519 016   1062    2532 2808        05   2374
αὐτοῦ εἰς  τοὺς  γάμους  καὶ  ἐκλείσθη  ἡ   θύρα.
him    into the  wedding and  was closed  the door.

    5306        1161 2064       2532 017 3062          3933
11 Ὕστερον  δὲ  ἔρχονται  καὶ  αἱ  λοιπαὶ  παρθένοι
   Later    but  come     also the remaining virgins

3004         2962    2962     455        1473      01         1161
λέγουσαι· κύριε  κύριε,  ἄνοιξον  ἡμῖν.  12 ὁ         δὲ
saying,   master master, open    to us.    The one but

611           3004     281  3004   1473     3756  3609a
ἀποκριθεὶς  εἶπεν· ἀμὴν λέγω ὑμῖν, οὐκ  οἶδα
having answered said,  amen I say to you, not  I know

1473    13 1127        3767  3754    3756 3609a       08
ὑμᾶς.     γρηγορεῖτε  οὖν,  ὅτι   οὐκ  οἴδατε  τὴν
you.      Keep awake  then, because not  you know the

2250    3761    08   5610      14  5618       1063  444
ἡμέραν οὐδὲ  τὴν  ὥραν.      ″Ωσπερ    γὰρ  ἄνθρωπος
day     but not the  hour.     As indeed for  man

589         2564     016    2398    1401    2532 3860
ἀποδημῶν  ἐκάλεσεν τοὺς  ἰδίους  δούλους καὶ  παρέδωκεν
journeying called   the   own     slaves  and  gave over

846     024 5225       846      15 2532 3739      3303
αὐτοῖς  τὰ  ὑπάρχοντα  αὐτοῦ,    καὶ  ᾧ        μὲν
to them the possessions of him,   and  to whom indeed

1325    4002  5007      3739      1161 1417 3739      1161
ἔδωκεν πέντε τάλαντα,  ᾧ        δὲ   δύο,  ᾧ        δὲ
he gave five  talents,  to whom but  two,  to whom but

1520 1538   2596 08   2398   1411      2532 589
ἕν,  ἑκάστῳ κατὰ τὴν ἰδίαν δύναμιν, καὶ  ἀπεδήμησεν.
one, each   by   the own    power,   and  he journeyed.

2112      16 4198          01    024 4002  5007
εὐθέως      πορευθεὶς      ὁ    τὰ  πέντε  τάλαντα
Immediately having traveled the one the five  talents

2983    2038       1722 846     2532 2770       243
λαβὼν  ἠργάσατο ἐν  αὐτοῖς καὶ  ἐκέρδησεν ἄλλα
having taken worked  in  them   and  gained    other

4002   17 5615     01  024 1417 2770      243  1417
πέντε·    ὡσαύτως ὁ   τὰ  δύο  ἐκέρδησεν ἄλλα δύο.
five;     likewise the one the two gained   other two.

18 01       1161 012 1520 2983       565
   ὁ        δὲ   τὸ  ἓν  λαβὼν     ἀπελθὼν
   The one but the one  having taken having gone off

3736    1093 2532 2928   012 694        02   2962
ὤρυξεν γῆν  καὶ  ἔκρυψεν τὸ ἀργύριον τοῦ  κυρίου
dug     earth and  hid    the silver   of the master

846      19 3326 1161 4183    5550  2064   01  2962
αὐτοῦ.     μετὰ δὲ  πολὺν χρόνον ἔρχεται ὁ  κύριος
of him.    After but much  time   comes    the master

014      1401    1565    2532 4868     3056
τῶν  δούλων ἐκείνων καὶ  συναίρει  λόγον
of the slaves those   and  lifts up together word

3326 846     20 2532 4334         01      024 4002
μετ᾽ αὐτῶν.    καὶ  προσελθὼν     ὁ       τὰ  πέντε
with them.     And  having come to the one the five

5007    2983        4374         243   4002  5007
τάλαντα λαβὼν      προσήνεγκεν ἄλλα πέντε τάλαντα
talants having taken offered      other five  talents

3004    2962    4002  5007    3860
λέγων· κύριε,  πέντε τάλαντά μοι  παρέδωκας·
saying, master, five  talents to me you gave over;

2396 243   4002  5007    2770       21 5346 846     01
ἴδε  ἄλλα πέντε τάλαντα ἐκέρδησα.    ἔφη  αὐτῷ  ὁ
look other five  talents I gained.     Said to him the

2962    846     2095 1401  18 2532 4103      1909
κύριος αὐτοῦ· εὖ,  δοῦλε ἀγαθὲ καὶ  πιστέ,  ἐπὶ
master of him, well, slave good   and  trustful, on
```

the bridegroom came, and those who were ready went with him into the wedding banquet; and the door was shut. [11]Later the other bridesmaids[a] came also, saying, 'Lord, lord, open to us.' [12]But he replied, 'Truly I tell you, I do not know you.' [13]Keep awake therefore, for you know neither the day nor the hour.[b]

14 "For it is as if a man, going on a journey, summoned his slaves and entrusted his property to them; [15]to one he gave five talents,[c] to another two, to another one, to each according to his ability. Then he went away. [16]The one who had received the five talents went off at once and traded with them, and made five more talents. [17]In the same way, the one who had the two talents made two more talents. [18]But the one who had received the one talent went off and dug a hole in the ground and hid his master's money. [19]After a long time the master of those slaves came and settled accounts with them. [20]Then the one who had received the five talents came forward, bringing five more talents, saying, 'Master, you handed over to me five talents; see, I have made five more talents.' [21]His master said to him, 'Well done, good and trustworthy slave;

---

a Gk virgins
b Other ancient authorities add in which the Son of Man is coming
c A talent was worth more than fifteen years' wages of a laborer

you have been trustworthy in a few things, I will put you in charge of many things; enter into the joy of your master.' 22And the one with the two talents also came forward, saying, 'Master, you handed over to me two talents; see, I have made two more talents.' 23His master said to him, 'Well done, good and trustworthy slave; you have been trustworthy in a few things, I will put you in charge of many things; enter into the joy of your master.' 24Then the one who had received the one talent also came forward, saying, 'Master, I knew that you were a harsh man, reaping where you did not sow, and gathering where you did not scatter seed; 25so I was afraid, and I went and hid your talent in the ground. Here you have what is yours.' 26But his master replied, 'You wicked and lazy slave! You knew, did you, that I reap where I did not sow, and gather where I did not scatter? 27Then you ought to have invested my money with the bankers, and on my return I would have received what was my own with interest. 28So take the talent from him, and give it to the one with the ten talents. 29For to all those who have, more will be given, and they will have an abundance; but from those who have nothing,

```
3641      1510          4103          1909  4183      1473
ὀλίγα     ἦς            πιστός,       ἐπὶ   πολλῶν    σε
few       you   were    trustful,     on    many      you
2525                    1525       1519  08   5479  02        2962
καταστήσω·              εἴσελθε    εἰς  τὴν  χαρὰν  τοῦ       κυρίου
I will appoint;         go    into into the  joy    of        the master
1473     22  4334       1161  1252  01    024  1417  5007
σου.         προσελθὼν  [δὲ]  καὶ   ὁ     τὰ   δύο   τάλαντα
of you.      Having come but   also  the one   the  two   talents
3004     2962      1417  5007       1473  3860             2396
εἶπεν·   κύριε,    δύο   τάλαντά    μοι   παρέδωκας·        ἴδε
said,    master,  two    talents   to me you   gave over;  look
243      1417  5007      2770        23  5346  846      01    2962
ἄλλα     δύο   τάλαντα   ἐκέρδησα.       ἔφη   αὐτῷ     ὁ     κύριος
other    two   talants   I gained.       Said to him    the   master
846      2095  1401  18   2532  4103       1909  3641
αὐτοῦ·   εὖ,   δοῦλε ἀγαθὲ καὶ  πιστέ,     ἐπὶ   ὀλίγα
of him,  well, slave good  and  trustful,  on    few
1510     4103          1909  4183      1473 2525
ἦς       πιστός,       ἐπὶ   πολλῶν    σε   καταστήσω·
you were trustful,     on    many      you  I will appoint;
1525       1519  08   5479  02   2962    1473  24  4334
εἴσελθε    εἰς  τὴν  χαρὰν  τοῦ κυρίου  σου.      προσελθὼν
go    into into the  joy    of  master of you.    Having come
                                                  toward
                                  the
1161 2532  01    012  1520 5007      2983
δὲ   καὶ   ὁ     τὸ   ἓν   τάλαντον εἰληφὼς
but  also  the one   the one   talant   having received
3004     2962      1097  1473 3754 4642      1510 444
εἶπεν·   κύριε,    ἔγνων σε   ὅτι  σκληρὸς   εἶ   ἄνθρωπος,
said,    master,  I knew you  that hard      you  are man,
2325          3699  3756 4687      2532 4863
θερίζων       ὅπου  οὐκ  ἔσπειρας  καὶ  συνάγων
harvesting    where not  you sowed and  bringing together
3606 3756 1287           25  2532 5399      565
ὅθεν οὐ   διεσκόρπισας,     καὶ  φοβηθεὶς  ἀπελθὼν
from not  you scattered      and  having    having gone
where     thoroughly,            feared    off
2928     012 5007      1473  1722 07  1093 2396
ἔκρυψα   τὸ  τάλαντόν σου   ἐν   τῇ  γῇ·  ἴδε
I hid    the talant   of you in   the land; look
2192     012 4674      26  611          1161 01  2962
ἔχεις    τὸ  σόν.          ἀποκριθεὶς   δὲ   ὁ   κύριος
you have the yours.        Having answered but  the master
846      3004     846       4190   1401  2532 3636
αὐτοῦ    εἶπεν αὐτῷ·        πονηρὲ δοῦλε καὶ  ὀκνηρέ,
of him   said  to him,      evil   slave and  troublesome,
3609a    3754 2325         3699 3756 4687      2532
ᾔδεις    ὅτι  θερίζω       ὅπου οὐκ  ἔσπειρα  καὶ
you knew that I harvest    where not  I sowed and
4863     3606 3756 1287           27  1163       1473 3767
συνάγω   ὅθεν οὐ   διεσκόρπισα;      ἔδει       σε   οὖν
I brought from not  I scattered       It was    you  then
together where     thoroughly?        necessary
906      024 694      1473 015 5133        2532 2064 1473
βαλεῖν   τὰ  ἀργύριά μου  τοῖς τραπεζίταις, καὶ  ἐλθὼν ἐγὼ
to       the silver  of   to  at tables,    and  having I
throw        me      the ones                     come
2865        302 012 1699 4862 5110     28 142      3767 575
ἐκομισάμην  ἂν  τὸ  ἐμὸν σὺν  τόκῳ.        ἄρατε    οὖν  ἀπ'
obtained    -   the mine with interest.    Lift up  then off
846      012 5007      2532 1325 03   2192         024 1176
αὐτοῦ    τὸ  τάλαντον καὶ  δότε τῷ   ἔχοντι      τὰ  δέκα
him      the talant   and  give to   the one having the ten
5007        29  03   1063 2192      3956 1325
τάλαντα·        τῷ   γὰρ  ἔχοντι   παντὶ δοθήσεται
talants;        to the one for having all   will be given
2532 4052                02        1161 3361 2192
καὶ  περισσευθήσεται,   τοῦ        δὲ   μὴ   ἔχοντος
and  it will be exceeding, of the one but  not  having
```

2532	3739	2192	142		575	846	**30**	2532
καὶ	ὃ	ἔχει	ἀρθήσεται		ἀπ'	αὐτοῦ.		καὶ
also	what	he has	will be lifted		from	him.		And

04	888		1401	1544	1519 012	4655	012
τὸν	ἀχρεῖον		δοῦλον	ἐκβάλετε	εἰς τὸ	σκότος	τὸ
the	unneeded		slave	throw out	into the	dark	the

1857	1563	1510	01	2805	2532 01	1030
ἐξώτερον·	ἐκεῖ	ἔσται	ὁ	κλαυθμὸς	καὶ ὁ	βρυγμὸς
outermost;	there	will be	the	crying	and the	grinding

014	3599		3752 1161	2064		01	5207 02
τῶν	ὀδόντων.	**31**	Ὅταν δὲ	ἔλθη		ὁ	υἱὸς τοῦ
of the teeth.			When but	might come		the	son of the

444		1722 07	1391	846	2532	3956	013
ἀνθρώπου	ἐν	τῇ	δόξη	αὐτοῦ	καὶ	πάντες	οἱ
man	in	the	splendor	of him	and	all	the

32		3326 846	5119 2523		1909 2362
ἄγγελοι	μετ'	αὐτοῦ,	τότε καθίσει		ἐπὶ θρόνου
messengers	with	him,	then he will sit		on throne

1391	846	**32**	2532 4863
δόξης	αὐτοῦ·		καὶ συναχθήσονται
of splendor	of him;		and they will be brought together

1715	846	3956 021	1484	2532 873
ἔμπροσθεν	αὐτοῦ	πάντα τὰ	ἔθνη,	καὶ ἀφορίσει
in front	of him	all the	nations,	and he will separate

846	575	240	5618	01	4166	873
αὐτοὺς ἀπ'		ἀλλήλων,	ὥσπερ	ὁ	ποιμὴν	ἀφορίζει
them from one		another,	as indeed	the	shepherd	separates

024 4263	575	014 2056	**33**	2532 2476	024
τὰ πρόβατα	ἀπὸ	τῶν ἐρίφων,		καὶ στήσει	τὰ
the sheep	from	the goats,		and he will stand	the

3303	4263	1537 1188	846	024 1161	2055
μὲν	πρόβατα	ἐκ δεξιῶν	αὐτοῦ,	τὰ δὲ	ἐρίφια
indeed	sheep	from right	of him,	the but	goats

1537 2176	**34**	5119 3004	01	935	015 1537
ἐξ εὐωνύμων.		τότε ἐρεῖ	ὁ	βασιλεὺς	τοῖς ἐκ
from left.		Then will say	the	king	to the from

1188	846	1205 013	2127	02	3962
δεξιῶν	αὐτοῦ·	δεῦτε οἱ	εὐλογημένοι	τοῦ	πατρός
right	of him,	come the	ones well-spoken	of the	father

1473	2816	08	2090	1473
μου,	κληρονομήσατε	τὴν	ἡτοιμασμένην	ὑμῖν
of me,	inherit	the	having been prepared	to you

932	575	2602	2889	**35**	3983
βασιλείαν	ἀπὸ	καταβολῆς	κόσμου.		ἐπείνασα
kingdom	from	foundation	of world.		I was hungry

1063 2532	1325	1473	2068	1372	2532
γὰρ καὶ	ἐδώκατέ	μοι	φαγεῖν,	ἐδίψησα	καὶ
for and	you gave	to me	to eat,	I was thirsty	and

4222	1473	3581	1510 2532	4863	1473
ἐποτίσατέ	με,	ξένος	ἤμην καὶ	συνηγάγετέ	με,
you gave drink	me,	stranger	I was and	you brought me,	
				together	

36	1131	2532 4016	1473	770	2532
	γυμνὸς	καὶ περιεβάλετέ	με,	ἠσθένησα	καὶ
	naked	and you threw around	me,	I was weak	and

1980	1473 1722	5438 1510	2532 2064	4314
ἐπεσκέψασθέ	με, ἐν	φυλακῇ ἤμην	καὶ ἤλθατε	πρός
you looked on	me, in	guard I was	and you came	toward

1473	**37**	5119 611	846	013 1342
με.		τότε ἀποκριθήσονται	αὐτῷ	οἱ δίκαιοι
me.		Then will answer	to him	the right ones

3004	2962	4219 1473 3708	3983	2532
λέγοντες·	κύριε,	πότε σε εἴδομεν	πεινῶντα	καὶ
saying,	Master,	when you we saw	hungering	and

5142	2228 1372	2532 4222	**38**	4219
ἐθρέψαμεν,	ἢ διψῶντα	καὶ ἐποτίσαμεν;		πότε
we fed,	or thirsting	and we gave drink?		When

even what they have will be taken away. [30]As for this worthless slave, throw him into the outer darkness, where there will be weeping and gnashing of teeth.'

[31] "When the Son of Man comes in his glory, and all the angels with him, then he will sit on the throne of his glory. [32]All the nations will be gathered before him, and he will separate people one from another as a shepherd separates the sheep from the goats, [33]and he will put the sheep at his right hand and the goats at the left. [34]Then the king will say to those at his right hand, 'Come, you that are blessed by my Father, inherit the kingdom prepared for you from the foundation of the world; [35]for I was hungry and you gave me food, I was thirsty and you gave me something to drink, I was a stranger and you welcomed me, [36]I was naked and you gave me clothing, I was sick and you took care of me, I was in prison and you visited me.' [37]Then the righteous will answer him, 'Lord, when was it that we saw you hungry and gave you food, or thirsty and gave you something to drink? [38]And when was it that

we saw you a stranger and welcomed you, or naked and gave you clothing? [39]And when was it that we saw you sick or in prison and visited you?' [40]And the king will answer them, 'Truly I tell you, just as you did it to one of the least of these who are members of my family,[a] you did it to me.' [41]Then he will say to those at his left hand, 'You that are accursed, depart from me into the eternal fire prepared for the devil and his angels; [42]for I was hungry and you gave me no food, I was thirsty and you gave me nothing to drink, [43]I was a stranger and you did not welcome me, naked and you did not give me clothing, sick and in prison and you did not visit me.' [44]Then they also will answer, 'Lord, when was it that we saw you hungry or thirsty or a stranger or naked or sick or in prison, and did not take care of you?' [45]Then he will answer them, 'Truly I tell you, just as you did not do it to one of the least of these, you did not do it to me.' [46]And these will go away into eternal punishment, but the righteous into eternal life."

CHAPTER 26

When Jesus had finished saying all these things,

[a] Gk these my brothers

1161	1473	3708	3581	2532	4863
δέ   σε   εἴδομεν ξένον   καὶ   συνηγάγομεν,
but you we saw stranger and we brought together,

| 2228 | 1131 | 2532 | 4016 | | 4219 | 1161 | 1473 |
ἢ   γυμνὸν καὶ   περιεβάλομεν; **39** πότε δέ   σε
or naked and we threw around? When but you

| 3708 | 770 | | 2228 | 1722 | 5438 | 2532 | 2064 |
εἴδομεν ἀσθενοῦντα ἢ   ἐν   φυλακῇ καὶ   ἤλθομεν
we saw being weak or   in   guard   and we went

| 4314 | 1473 | **40** | 2532 | 611 | | 01 | 935 | 3004 |
πρός   σε;   καὶ   ἀποκριθεὶς   ὁ   βασιλεὺς ἐρεῖ
toward you?   And having answered the king   will say

| 846 | 281 | 3004 | 1473 | 1909 | 3745 | | 4160 |
αὐτοῖς· ἀμὴν λέγω ὑμῖν, ἐφ' ὅσον   ἐποιήσατε
to them, amen I say to you, on   as much as you did

| 1520 | 3778 | 014 | 80 | 1473 | 014 | 1646 | | 1473 |
ἑνὶ   τούτων τῶν ἀδελφῶν μου τῶν ἐλαχίστων, ἐμοὶ
to one of these the brothers of me the least,   to me

| 4160 | | **41** | 5119 | 3004 | | 2532 | 015 | | 1537 |
ἐποιήσατε.   τότε ἐρεῖ   καὶ   τοῖς   ἐξ
you did.   Then he will say also to the ones from

| 2176 | 4198 | 575 | 1473 | 013 | 2672 | | 1519 |
εὐωνύμων· πορεύεσθε ἀπ' ἐμοῦ [οἱ] κατηραμένοι εἰς
left,   travel   from me   the   ones cursed into

| 012 | 4442 | 012 | 166 | | 012 | 2090 |
τὸ   πῦρ τὸ   αἰώνιον τὸ   ἡτοιμασμένον
the fire the eternal the one having been prepared

| 03 | 1228 | | 2532 | 015 | 32 | | 846 |
τῷ   διαβόλῳ καὶ   τοῖς   ἀγγέλοις αὐτοῦ.
to the slanderer and   to the messengers of him.

| **42** | 3983 | | 1063 | 2532 | 3756 | 1325 | | 1473 | 2068 |
ἐπείνασα   γὰρ καὶ   οὐκ   ἐδώκατέ μοι   φαγεῖν,
I was hungry for   and   not   you gave to me to eat,

| 1372 | | 2532 | 3756 | 4222 | | 1473 | | **43** | 3581 |
ἐδίψησα   καὶ   οὐκ   ἐποτίσατέ   με,   ξένος
I was thirsty and   not   you gave drink me,   stranger

| 1510 | 2532 | 3756 | 4863 | | 1473 | 1131 |
ἤμην καὶ   οὐ   συνηγάγετέ   με,   γυμνὸς
I was and   not   you brought together me,   naked

| 2532 | 3756 | 4016 | | 1473 | 772 | | 2532 | 1722 | 5438 |
καὶ   οὐ   περιεβάλετέ   με,   ἀσθενὴς καὶ   ἐν   φυλακῇ
and   not   you threw around me,   weak   and in   guard

| 2532 | 3756 | 1980 | | 1473 | **44** | 5119 | 611 |
καὶ   οὐκ   ἐπεσκέψασθέ   με.   τότε ἀποκριθήσονται
and   not   you looked on me.   Then will answer

| 2532 | 846 | | 3004 | | 2962 | 4219 | 1473 | 3708 |
καὶ   αὐτοὶ   λέγοντες· κύριε, πότε σε   εἴδομεν
and   themselves saying·   Master, when you   we saw

| 3983 | | 2228 | 1372 | | 2228 | 3581 | | 2228 | 1131 | 2228 |
πεινῶντα ἢ   διψῶντα ἢ   ξένον ἢ   γυμνὸν ἢ
hungering or   thirsting or   stranger or   naked or

| 772 | | 2228 | 1722 | 5438 | 2532 | 3756 | 1247 | | 1473 |
ἀσθενῆ ἢ   ἐν   φυλακῇ καὶ   οὐ   διηκονήσαμέν σοι;
weak   or   in   guard   and   not   we served   you?

| **45** | 5119 | 611 | | 846 | 3004 | 281 | 3004 |
τότε ἀποκριθήσεται   αὐτοῖς λέγων· ἀμὴν λέγω
Then he will answer   to them saying·   amen I say

| 1473 | 1909 | 3745 | | 3756 | 4160 | | 1520 | 3778 |
ὑμῖν, ἐφ' ὅσον   οὐκ ἐποιήσατε ἑνὶ   τούτων
to you on   as much as not   you did   to one of these

| 014 | 1646 | | 3761 | 1473 | 4160 | | **46** | 2532 |
τῶν ἐλαχίστων, οὐδὲ ἐμοὶ ἐποιήσατε.   καὶ
the least,   but not to me you did.   And

| 565 | | 3778 | 1519 | 2851 | | 166 | | 013 | 1161 |
ἀπελεύσονται οὗτοι εἰς κόλασιν   αἰώνιον, οἱ   δὲ
will go off   these into punishment eternal,   the but

| 1342 | | 1519 | 2222 | 166 | | **26:1** | 2532 | 1096 | | 3753 |
δίκαιοι   εἰς ζωὴν αἰώνιον.   Καὶ   ἐγένετο ὅτε
right ones into life eternal.   And   it became when

5055   01   2424   3956   016   3056   3778
ἐτέλεσεν ὁ 'Ἰησοῦς πάντας τοὺς λόγους τούτους,
completed the Jesus all   the words these,

3004   015   3101   846   **2** 3609a   3754 3326
εἶπεν τοῖς μαθηταῖς αὐτοῦ· οἴδατε ὅτι μετὰ
he said to the learners of him, you know that after

1417 2250   09 3957   1096   2532 01 5207 02
δύο ἡμέρας τὸ πάσχα γίνεται, καὶ ὁ υἱὸς τοῦ
two days the passover becomes, and the son of the

444   3860   1519 012 4717
ἀνθρώπου παραδίδοται εἰς τὸ σταυρωθῆναι.
man   is given over into the to be crucified.

3 5119 4863   013 749   2532 013
Τότε συνήχθησαν   οἱ ἀρχιερεῖς   καὶ οἱ
Then were brought together the ruler priests and the

4245   02   2992   1519 08 833   02
πρεσβύτεροι τοῦ λαοῦ εἰς τὴν αὐλὴν τοῦ
older men of the people into the courtyard of the

749   02   3004   2533   **4** 2532
ἀρχιερέως τοῦ λεγομένου Καϊάφα   καὶ
ruler priest of the one being called Caiaphas and

4823   2443 04 2424 1388
συνεβουλεύσαντο ἵνα τὸν 'Ἰησοῦν δόλῳ
they planned together that the Jesus in guile

2902   2532 615   **5** 3004
κρατήσωσιν καὶ ἀποκτείνωσιν· ἔλεγον
they might hold and might kill;   they were saying

1161 3361 1722 07 1859   2443 3361 2351
δέ· μὴ ἐν τῇ ἑορτῇ, ἵνα μὴ θόρυβος
but, not in the festival, that not uproar

1096   1722 03 2992 **6** 02   1161 2424
γένηται ἐν τῷ λαῷ. Τοῦ δὲ 'Ἰησοῦ
might become in the people. Of the but Jesus

1096   1722 963   1722 3614 4613   02
γενομένου ἐν Βηθανίᾳ ἐν οἰκίᾳ Σίμωνος τοῦ
having become in Bethany in house of Simon the

3015   4334   846   1135 2192 211
λεπροῦ, **7** προσῆλθεν αὐτῷ γυνὴ ἔχουσα ἀλάβαστρον
leper, came toward him woman having alabaster jar

3464   927   2532 2708   1909
μυρού βαρυτίμου καὶ κατέχεεν ἐπὶ
of perfume of heavy value and she poured down on

06 2776   846   345   3708   1161 013
τῆς κεφαλῆς αὐτοῦ ἀνακειμένου. **8** ἰδόντες δὲ οἱ
the head of him reclining.   Having seen but the

3101   846   3004   1519 5101 05
μαθηταὶ ἠγανάκτησαν λέγοντες· εἰς τί ἡ
learners were indignant saying, into what the

684   3778 **9** 1410   1063 3778 4097
ἀπώλεια αὕτη; ἐδύνατο γὰρ τοῦτο πραθῆναι
destruction this? Was able for this to be sold

4183   2532 1325   4434   **10** 1097   1161
πολλοῦ καὶ δοθῆναι πτωχοῖς. γνοὺς δὲ
much and to be given to poor. Having known but

01 2424 3004 846   5101 2873 3930   07
ὁ 'Ἰησοῦς εἶπεν αὐτοῖς· τί κόπους παρέχετε τῇ
the Jesus said to them, why labors you hold to the

1135   2041 1063 2570 2038   1519 1473
γυναικί; ἔργον γὰρ καλὸν ἠργάσατο εἰς ἐμέ·
woman? Work for good she worked in me;

11 3842   1063 016 4434   2192   3326 1438
πάντοτε γὰρ τοὺς πτωχοὺς ἔχετε μεθ' ἑαυτῶν,
always for the poor   you have with yourselves,

1473 1161 3756 3842   2192 **12** 906   1063
ἐμὲ δὲ οὐ πάντοτε ἔχετε· βαλοῦσα γὰρ
me but not always you have; having thrown for

3778   012 3464   3778 1909 010 4983   1473 4314
αὕτη τὸ μύρον τοῦτο ἐπὶ τοῦ σώματός μου πρὸς
this one the perfume this on the body of me to

he said to his disciples, [2]"You know that after two days the Passover is coming, and the Son of Man will be handed over to be crucified."

[3] Then the chief priests and the elders of the people gathered in the palace of the high priest, who was called Caiaphas, [4]and they conspired to arrest Jesus by stealth and kill him. [5]But they said, "Not during the festival, or there may be a riot among the people."

[6] Now while Jesus was at Bethany in the house of Simon the leper,[a] [7]a woman came to him with an alabaster jar of very costly ointment, and she poured it on his head as he sat at the table. [8]But when the disciples saw it, they were angry and said, "Why this waste? [9]For this ointment could have been sold for a large sum, and the money given to the poor." [10]But Jesus, aware of this, said to them, "Why do you trouble the woman? She has performed a good service for me. [11]For you always have the poor with you, but you will not always have me. [12]By pouring this ointment on my body

---

[a] The terms *leper* and *leprosy* can refer to several diseases

she has prepared me for burial. [13]Truly I tell you, wherever this good news[a] is proclaimed in the whole world, what she has done will be told in remembrance of her."

[14]Then one of the twelve, who was called Judas Iscariot, went to the chief priests [15]and said, "What will you give me if I betray him to you?" They paid him thirty pieces of silver. [16]And from that moment he began to look for an opportunity to betray him.

[17]On the first day of Unleavened Bread the disciples came to Jesus, saying, "Where do you want us to make the preparations for you to eat the Passover?" [18]He said, "Go into the city to a certain man, and say to him, 'The Teacher says, My time is near; I will keep the Passover at your house with my disciples.'" [19]So the disciples did as Jesus had directed them, and they prepared the Passover meal.

[20]When it was evening, he took his place with the twelve;[b] [21]and while they were eating, he said, "Truly I tell you, one of you will betray me." [22]And they became greatly distressed and began to say to him one after another, "Surely not I, Lord?" [23]He answered,

[a] Or gospel
[b] Other ancient authorities add disciples

```
012   1779        1473 4160              281  3004 1473        3699
τὸ  ἐνταφιάσαι  με ἐποίησεν. 13 ἀμὴν λέγω ὑμῖν,    ὅπου
the  to bury   me she did.    Amen I say to you,   where
1437 2784              09 2098          3778 1722 3650
ἐὰν  κηρυχθῇ          τὸ εὐαγγέλιον   τοῦτο ἐν ὅλῳ
if   might be announced the good message this in whole
03   2889    2980              2532 3739 4160
τῷ  κόσμῳ, λαληθήσεται      καὶ  ὃ   ἐποίησεν
the world, it might be spoken and  what did
3778      1519 3422        846   14 5119 4198
αὕτη  εἰς μνημόσυνον αὐτῆς.    Τότε πορευθεὶς
this one to memorial  of her.   Then having traveled
1520 014    1427    01 3004              2455
εἷς τῶν  δώδεκα, ὁ λεγόμενος      ᾽Ιούδας
one of the twelve, the one being called Judas
2469         4314    016 749          15 3004   5101
᾽Ισκαριώτης, πρὸς τοὺς ἀρχιερεῖς   εἶπεν· τί
Iscariot,   toward the ruler priests  said,  what
2309   1473 1325      2504   1473 3860
θέλετέ μοι  δοῦναι, κἀγὼ ὑμῖν παραδώσω
you want to me to give, and I to you will give over
846   013 1161 2476    846  5144      694        16 2532
αὐτόν; οἱ δὲ  ἔστησαν αὐτῷ τριάκοντα ἀργύρια.    καὶ
him?  The but stood to him thirty    silver.     And
575   5119 2212        2120       2443 846
ἀπὸ τότε ἐζήτει      εὐκαιρίαν ἵνα αὐτὸν
from then he was seeking good season that him
3860         17 07  1161 4413 022    106
παραδῷ.      Τῇ  δὲ  πρώτῃ τῶν ἀζύμων
he might give over. In the but first of the unyeasted
4334     013 3101   03 2424 3004      4226
προσῆλθον οἱ μαθηταὶ τῷ ᾽Ιησοῦ λέγοντες· ποῦ
went to   the learners the Jesus saying,   where
2309   2090      1473 2068 012 3957      18 01
θέλεις ἑτοιμάσωμέν σοι  φαγεῖν τὸ πάσχα;   ὁ
you   we might to  to eat the passover? The one
want   prepare  you
1161 3004   5217   1519 08 4172 4314   04 1170
δὲ  εἶπεν· ὑπάγετε εἰς τὴν πόλιν πρὸς τὸν δεῖνα
but said;  go off into the city toward the such man
2532 3004 846    01 1320       3004  01 2540
καὶ εἴπατε αὐτῷ· ὁ διδάσκαλος λέγει· ὁ καιρός
and say  to him, the teacher  says;  the season
1473 1451 1510    4314  1473 4160 012 3957      3326
μου ἐγγύς ἐστιν, πρὸς σὲ ποιῶ τὸ πάσχα    μετὰ
of me near is,   toward you I do the passover with
014 3101    1473  19 2532 4160      013 3101   5613
τῶν μαθητῶν μου.    καὶ ἐποίησαν οἱ μαθηταὶ ὡς
the learners of me. And did     the learners as
4929        846    01 2424 2532 2090      012
συνέταξεν αὐτοῖς ὁ ᾽Ιησοῦς καὶ ἡτοίμασαν τὸ
ordered fully them the Jesus and they prepared the
3957   20 3798  1161 1096      345
πάσχα.   ᾽Οψίας δὲ  γενομένης ἀνέκειτο
passover. Evening but having become he was reclining
3326 014 1427    21 2532 2068      846 3004    281
μετὰ τῶν δώδεκα.    καὶ ἐσθιόντων αὐτῶν εἶπεν· ἀμὴν
with the twelve.   And eating      them he said, amen
3004 1473   3754 1520 1537  1473 3860      1473
λέγω ὑμῖν ὅτι εἷς ἐξ  ὑμῶν παραδώσει με.
I say to you that one out of you will give over me.
22 2532 3076      4970    757     3004
   καὶ λυπούμενοι σφόδρα ἤρξαντο λέγειν
   And being grieved exceeding they began to say
846   1520 1538    3385  1473 1510 2962    23 01
αὐτῷ εἷς ἕκαστος· μήτι ἐγώ εἰμι, κύριε;    ὁ
to him one each;   and not I  am,   Master?  The
```

1161	611	3004	01	1686	3326 1473	08	5495
δὲ	ἀποκριθεὶς εἶπεν·	ὁ	ἐμβάψας	μετ’ ἐμοῦ	τὴν	χεῖρα
but	one having said, answered	the one dipped in	the having	with me	the	hand

1722	011	5165	3778	1473 3860		24	01	3303
ἐν	τῷ	τρυβλίῳ	οὗτός	με παραδώσει.			ὁ	μὲν
in	the	dish	this	me will give over.			The	indeed

5207	02	444		5217	2531	1125		4012	846
υἱὸς	τοῦ	ἀνθρώπου		ὑπάγει	καθὼς	γέγραπται		περὶ	αὐτοῦ,
son the	of	man		goes off	just as	it has been written		about	him,

3759	1161	03	444		1565	1223	3739 01	5207
οὐαὶ	δὲ	τῷ	ἀνθρώπῳ		ἐκείνῳ	δι’	οὗ ὁ	υἱὸς
woe	but	to the man			that	through	whom the	son

02	444	3860		2570	1510	846	1487	3756
τοῦ	ἀνθρώπου	παραδίδοται·		καλὸν	ἦν	αὐτῷ	εἰ	οὐκ
of the man	is given over;		good	it was	him	if	not

1080		01 444		1565		25	611		1161
ἐγεννήθη		ὁ ἄνθρωπος		ἐκεῖνος.			ἀποκριθεὶς		δὲ
was born		the man		that.			Having answered	but

2455	01	3860		846	3004	3385		1473
Ἰούδας	ὁ	παραδιδοὺς		αὐτὸν	εἶπεν·	μήτι		ἐγώ
Judas	the	one giving over		him	said;	and not		I

1510	4461	3004	846		1473 3004	846		26	2068
εἰμι,	ῥαββί;	λέγει	αὐτῷ·		σὺ εἶπας.				Ἐσθιόντων
am,	rabbi?	Says	to him·		you said.				Eating

1161	846		2983	01	2424	740	2532	2127
δὲ	αὐτῶν		λαβὼν	ὁ	Ἰησοῦς	ἄρτον	καὶ	εὐλογήσας
but	of them		having taken	the	Jesus	bread	and	having well spoken

2806	2532	1325		015	3101	3004	2983
ἔκλασεν	καὶ	δοὺς		τοῖς	μαθηταῖς	εἶπεν·	λάβετε
he broke	and	having given		to the	learners	said,	take

2068	3778	1510	09	4983 1473		27	2532	2983
φάγετε,	τοῦτό	ἐστιν	τὸ	σῶμά μου.			καὶ	λαβὼν
eat,	this	is	the	body of me.			And	having taken

4221	2532	2168				1325	846
ποτήριον	καὶ	εὐχαριστήσας				ἔδωκεν	αὐτοῖς
cup	and	having given good favor				he gave	to them

3004	4095	1537 846	3956		28	3778 1063	1510
λέγων·	πίετε	ἐξ αὐτοῦ	πάντες,			τοῦτο γάρ	ἐστιν
saying,	drink	from it	all,			this for	is

09	129	1473	06	1242		09	4012	4183
τὸ	αἷμά	μου	τῆς	διαθήκης		τὸ	περὶ	πολλῶν
the	blood	of me	of the	agreement		the one	about	many

1632a		1519	859		266		29	3004
ἐκχυννόμενον		εἰς	ἄφεσιν		ἁμαρτιῶν.			λέγω
being poured out		into	sending off		of sins.			I say

1161	1473	3756 3361	4095		575	737	1537
δὲ	ὑμῖν,	οὐ μὴ	πίω		ἀπ’	ἄρτι	ἐκ
but	to you,	not not	I might drink		from	now	from

3778	010	1079a	06	288	2193	06	2250
τούτου	τοῦ	γενήματος	τῆς	ἀμπέλου	ἕως	τῆς	ἡμέρας
this	the	produce	of the	vine	until	the	day

1565	3752	846	4095		3326	1473	2537	1722	07
ἐκείνης	ὅταν	αὐτὸ	πίνω		μεθ’	ὑμῶν	καινὸν	ἐν	τῇ
that	when it	I might drink		with	you	new	in	the

932	02	3962	1473	30	2532	5214
βασιλείᾳ	τοῦ	πατρός	μου.		Καὶ	ὑμνήσαντες
kingdom	of the	father	of me.		And	having sung

1831		1519	012	3735 018		1636		31	5119
ἐξῆλθον		εἰς	τὸ	ὄρος τῶν		ἐλαιῶν.			Τότε
they went out		into	the	hill of the		olives.			Then

3004	846	01 2424		3956	1473	4624
λέγει	αὐτοῖς	ὁ Ἰησοῦς·		πάντες	ὑμεῖς	σκανδαλισθήσεσθε
says	to them	the Jesus;		all	you	will be offended

1722	1473	1722	07	3571	3778	1125
ἐν	ἐμοὶ	ἐν	τῇ	νυκτὶ	ταύτῃ,	γέγραπται
in	me	in	the	night	this,	it has been written

"The one who has dipped his hand into the bowl with me will betray me. 24The Son of Man goes as it is written of him, but woe to that one by whom the Son of Man is betrayed! It would have been better for that one not to have been born." 25Judas, who betrayed him, said, "Surely not I, Rabbi?" He replied, "You have said so."

26 While they were eating, Jesus took a loaf of bread, and after blessing it he broke it, gave it to the disciples, and said, "Take, eat; this is my body." 27Then he took a cup, and after giving thanks he gave it to them, saying, "Drink from it, all of you; 28for this is my blood of thea covenant, which is poured out for many for the forgiveness of sins. 29I tell you, I will never again drink of this fruit of the vine until that day when I drink it new with you in my Father's kingdom."

30 When they had sung the hymn, they went out to the Mount of Olives.

31 Then Jesus said to them, "You will all become deserters because of me this night; for it is written,

a Other ancient authorities add new

'I will strike the
shepherd,
and the sheep of the
flock will be
scattered.'
32But after I am raised up,
I will go ahead of you to
Galilee." 33Peter said to
him, "Though all become
deserters because of you,
I will never desert you."
34Jesus said to him, "Truly
I tell you, this very night,
before the cock crows, you
will deny me three times."
35Peter said to him, "Even
though I must die with you,
I will not deny you." And
so said all the disciples.

36 Then Jesus went
with them to a place called
Gethsemane; and he said
to his disciples, "Sit here
while I go over there and
pray." 37He took with him
Peter and the two sons of
Zebedee, and began to be
grieved and agitated.
38Then he said to them,
"I am deeply grieved, even
to death; remain here, and
stay awake with me."
39And going a little farther,
he threw himself on the
ground and prayed, "My
Father, if it is possible, let
this cup pass from me; yet
not what I want but what
you want."

1063	3960		04	4166		2532	1287
γάρ·	πατάξω		τὸν	ποιμένα,		καὶ	διασκορπισθήσονται
for,	I will hit		the	shepherd,		and	will be thoroughly scattered

021	4263	06	4167		32	3326	1161	012
τὰ	πρόβατα	τῆς	ποίμνης.			μετὰ	δὲ	τὸ
the sheep		of the	flock.			After	but	the

1453		1473	4254		1473	1519	08
ἐγερθῆναί		με	προάξω		ὑμᾶς	εἰς	τὴν
to be raised		me	I will lead before		you	into the

1056		611		1161	01	4074	3004
Γαλιλαίαν.	33	ἀποκριθεὶς		δὲ	ὁ	Πέτρος	εἶπεν
Galilee.		Having answered		but	the	Peter	said

846	1487	3956	4624		1722	1473	1473
αὐτῷ·	εἰ	πάντες	σκανδαλισθήσονται		ἐν	σοί,	ἐγὼ
to him;	if	all	will be offended		in	you,	I

3763		4624		34	5346	846	01
οὐδέποτε		σκανδαλισθήσομαι.			ἔφη	αὐτῷ	ὁ
but not ever		will be offended.			Said to him		the

2424	281	3004	1473	3754	1722	3778	07	3571
Ἰησοῦς·	ἀμὴν	λέγω	σοι	ὅτι	ἐν	ταύτῃ	τῇ	νυκτὶ
Jesus,	amen	I say to	you	that	in	this	the	night

4250	220	5455	5151	533
πρὶν	ἀλέκτορα	φωνῆσαι	τρὶς	ἀπαρνήσῃ
before	rooster	to sound	three	you will deny thoroughly

1473	35	3004	846	01	4074		2579	1163		1473	4862
με.		λέγει	αὐτῷ	ὁ	Πέτρος·		κἂν	δέῃ		με	σὺν
me.		Says	to him	the	Peter;		even	it might be		me	with
							if	be necessary			

1473	599	3756	3361	1473	533		3668	2532
σοὶ	ἀποθανεῖν,	οὐ	μή	σε	ἀπαρνήσομαι.		ὁμοίως	καὶ
you	to die,	not	not	you	I will deny		Likewise	and
							thoroughly.	

3956	013	3101	3004		36	5119	2064	3326	846
πάντες	οἱ	μαθηταὶ	εἶπαν.			Τότε	ἔρχεται	μετ'	αὐτῶν
all	the	learners	said.			Then comes		with	them

01	2424	1519	5564		3004		1068
ὁ	Ἰησοῦς	εἰς	χωρίον		λεγόμενον		Γεθσημανὶ
the	Jesus	into	small field		being called		Gethsemane

2532	3004	015	3101		2523	847	2193
καὶ	λέγει	τοῖς	μαθηταῖς·		καθίσατε	αὐτοῦ	ἕως
and	he says	to the	learners;		sit	there	until

3739	565		1563	4336		37	2532
[οὗ]	ἀπελθὼν		ἐκεῖ	προσεύξωμαι.			καὶ
which	having gone off		there	I might pray.			And

3880		04	4074	2532	016	1417	5207
παραλαβὼν		τὸν	Πέτρον	καὶ	τοὺς	δύο	υἱοὺς
having taken along		the	Peter	and	the	two	sons

2199	757	3076	2532	85		38	5119
Ζεβεδαίου	ἤρξατο	λυπεῖσθαι	καὶ	ἀδημονεῖν.			τότε
of Zebedee	he began to be	grieved	and	to be distressed.			Then

3004	846	4036		1510	05	5590	1473
λέγει	αὐτοῖς·	περίλυπός		ἐστιν	ἡ	ψυχή	μου
he says	to them;	greatly grieved		is		the soul	of me

2193	2288	3306	5602	2532	1127	3326	1473
ἕως	θανάτου·	μείνατε	ὧδε	καὶ	γρηγορεῖτε	μετ'	ἐμοῦ.
until	death;	stay	here	and	keep awake	with	me.

39	2532	4281		3398	4098	1909	4383
	καὶ	προελθὼν		μικρὸν	ἔπεσεν	ἐπὶ	πρόσωπον
	And	having gone before		little	he fell	on	face

846	4336	2532	3004	3962	1473	1487
αὐτοῦ	προσευχόμενος	καὶ	λέγων·	πάτερ	μου,	εἰ
of him	praying	and	saying;	father	of me,	if

1415	1510	3928	575	1473	09	4221
δυνατόν	ἐστιν,	παρελθάτω	ἀπ'	ἐμοῦ	τὸ	ποτήριον
power	it is,	let go along	from	me	the	cup

3778	4133	3756	5613	1473	2309	235	5613	1473
τοῦτο·	πλὴν	οὐχ	ὡς	ἐγὼ	θέλω	ἀλλ'	ὡς	σύ.
this;	except	not	as	I	want	but	as	you.

2532	2064		4314	016	3101	2532	2147

40 καὶ ἔρχεται πρὸς τοὺς μαθητὰς καὶ εὑρίσκει
And he comes toward the learners and finds

846	2518		2532	3004	03	4074	3779

αὐτοὺς καθεύδοντας, καὶ λέγει τῷ Πέτρῳ· οὕτως
them sleeping, and says to the Peter, thusly

3756	2480		1520	5610	1127		3326

οὐκ ἰσχύσατε μίαν ὥραν γρηγορῆσαι μετ᾽
not you were strong one hour to keep awake with

1473		1127	2532	4336		2443	3361

ἐμοῦ; **41** γρηγορεῖτε καὶ προσεύχεσθε, ἵνα μὴ
me? Keep awake and pray, that not

1525		1519	3986		09	3303	4151

εἰσέλθητε εἰς πειρασμόν· τὸ μὲν πνεῦμα
you might go into into pressure; the indeed spirit

4289	05	1161	4561	772		3825	1537	1208

πρόθυμον ἡ δὲ σὰρξ ἀσθενής. **42** πάλιν ἐκ δευτέρου
eager the but flesh weak. Again from second

565		4336		3004	3962	1473	1487

ἀπελθὼν προσηύξατο λέγων· πάτερ μου, εἰ
having gone off he prayed saying· father of me, if

3756	1410		3778	3928		1437	3361	846

οὐ δύναται τοῦτο παρελθεῖν ἐὰν μὴ αὐτὸ
not it is able this to go along except it

4095		1096		09	2307	1473		2532

πίω, γενηθήτω τὸ θέλημά σου. **43** καὶ
I might drink, let become the want of you. And

2064		3825	2147		846	2518		1510

ἐλθὼν πάλιν εὗρεν αὐτοὺς καθεύδοντας, ἦσαν
having come again he found them sleeping, were

1063	846		013	3788	916			2532

γὰρ αὐτῶν οἱ ὀφθαλμοὶ βεβαρημένοι. **44** καὶ
for of them the eyes having been burdened. And

863		846	3825	565

ἀφεὶς αὐτοὺς πάλιν ἀπελθὼν
having sent off them again having gone off

4336		1537	5154	04	846	3056	3004

προσηύξατο ἐκ τρίτου τὸν αὐτὸν λόγον εἰπὼν
he prayed from third the same word having said

3825	45	5119	2064		4314	016	3101	2532	3004

πάλιν. **45** τότε ἔρχεται πρὸς τοὺς μαθητὰς καὶ λέγει
again. Then he comes to the learners and says

846		2518		012	3062	2532	373		2400

αὐτοῖς· καθεύδετε [τὸ] λοιπὸν καὶ ἀναπαύεσθε· ἰδοὺ
to them, sleep the remaining and rest; look

1448		05	5610	2532	01	5207	02		444

ἤγγικεν ἡ ὥρα καὶ ὁ υἱὸς τοῦ ἀνθρώπου
has neared the hour and the son of the man

3860		1519	5495	268		1453

παραδίδοται εἰς χεῖρας ἁμαρτωλῶν. **46** ἐγείρεσθε
is given over into hands of sinners. Be raised

71		2400	1448		01	3860		1473

ἄγωμεν· ἰδοὺ ἤγγικεν ὁ παραδιδούς με.
we might lead; look has neared the one giving over me.

2532	2089	846	2980		2400	2455	1520	014

47 Καὶ ἔτι αὐτοῦ λαλοῦντος ἰδοὺ Ἰούδας εἷς τῶν
And still him speaking look Judas one of the

1427	2064	2532	3326	846	3793	4183	3326	3162

δώδεκα ἦλθεν καὶ μετ᾽ αὐτοῦ ὄχλος πολὺς μετὰ μαχαιρῶν
twelve came and with him crowd much with swords

2532	3586	575	014	749		2532	4245		02

καὶ ξύλων ἀπὸ τῶν ἀρχιερέων καὶ πρεσβυτέρων τοῦ
and woods from the ruler priests and older men of the

2992	48	01	1161	3860		846	1325	846

λαοῦ. **48** ὁ δὲ παραδιδοὺς αὐτὸν ἔδωκεν αὐτοῖς
people. The but one giving over him gave to them

4592		3004	3739	302	5368		846	1510

σημεῖον λέγων· ὃν ἂν φιλήσω αὐτός ἐστιν,
sign saying, whom - I might love himself it is,

[40]Then he came to the disciples and found them sleeping; and he said to Peter, "So, could you not stay awake with me one hour? [41]Stay awake and pray that you may not come into the time of trial;[a] the spirit indeed is willing, but the flesh is weak." [42]Again he went away for the second time and prayed, "My Father, if this cannot pass unless I drink it, your will be done." [43]Again he came and found them sleeping, for their eyes were heavy. [44]So leaving them again, he went away and prayed for the third time, saying the same words. [45]Then he came to the disciples and said to them, "Are you still sleeping and taking your rest? See, the hour is at hand, and the Son of Man is betrayed into the hands of sinners. [46]Get up, let us be going. See, my betrayer is at hand."

[47]While he was still speaking, Judas, one of the twelve, arrived; with him was a large crowd with swords and clubs, from the chief priests and the elders of the people. [48]Now the betrayer had given them a sign, saying, "The one I will kiss is the man; arrest him."

---

[a] Or into temptation

49At once he came up to
Jesus and said, "Greetings,
Rabbi!" and kissed him.
50Jesus said to him,
"Friend, do what you are
here to do." Then they
came and laid hands on
Jesus and arrested him.
51Suddenly, one of those
with Jesus put his hand on
his sword, drew it, and
struck the slave of the high
priest, cutting off his ear.
52Then Jesus said to him,
"Put your sword back into
its place; for all who take
the sword will perish by
the sword. 53Do you think
that I cannot appeal to
my Father, and he will at
once send me more than
twelve legions of angels?
54But how then would
the scriptures be fulfilled,
which say it must happen in
this way?" 55At that hour
Jesus said to the crowds,
"Have you come out with
swords and clubs to arrest
me as though I were a
bandit? Day after day I
sat in the temple teaching,
and you did not arrest me.
56But all this has taken
place, so that the scriptures
of the prophets may be
fulfilled." Then all the
disciples deserted him and
fled.
    57Those who had
arrested

```
2902        846      49  2532 2112          4334
κρατήσατε  αὐτόν.  49  καὶ εὐθέως      προσελθὼν
hold        him.        And immediately having come toward

03    2424    3004      5463      4461    2532 2705
τῷ 'Ιησοῦ εἶπεν·   χαῖρε,  ῥαββί, καὶ κατεφίλησεν
the Jesus he said, rejoice, rabbi, and  he kissed

846       01 1161 2424   3004   846      2083  1909 3739
αὐτόν. 50  ὁ  δὲ 'Ιησοῦς εἶπεν αὐτῷ· ἑταῖρε, ἐφ' ὃ
him.       The but Jesus  said to him; comrade, on what

3918              5119 4334          1911       020
πάρει.           τότε προσελθόντες ἐπέβαλον   τὰς
you are present. Then having come to they threw on the

5495     1909 04  2424    2532 2902       846     51 2532
χεῖρας ἐπὶ τὸν 'Ιησοῦν καὶ ἐκράτησαν αὐτόν.  51 Καὶ
hands   on  the  Jesus  and held        him.        And

2400 1520 014 3326  2424   1614    08  5495  645
ἰδοὺ εἷς τῶν μετὰ 'Ιησοῦ ἐκτείνας τὴν χεῖρα ἀπέσπασεν
look one of with  Jesus having    the hand  drew off
          the ones         stretched out

08   3162      846   2532 3960      04  1401   02
τὴν μάχαιραν αὐτοῦ καὶ πατάξας τὸν δοῦλον τοῦ
the sword    of him and having hit the slave of the

749        851         846    012 5621     52  5119
ἀρχιερέως ἀφεῖλεν    αὐτοῦ τὸ ὠτίον.  52 τότε
ruler priest he lifted off of him the ear.     Then

3004  846   01  2424       654       08 3162      1473
λέγει αὐτῷ ὁ 'Ιησοῦς· ἀπόστρεψον τὴν μάχαιράν σου
says  to him the Jesus, turn off   the sword     of you

1519 04  5117   846     3956    1063 013     2983
εἰς τὸν τόπον αὐτῆς· πάντες γὰρ οἱ      λαβόντες
into the place of it;  all    for the ones having taken

3162      1722 3162    622           53 2228
μάχαιραν ἐν μαχαίρῃ ἀπολοῦνται.   53 ἢ
sword     in sword    will destroy themselves.   Or

1380     3754 3756 1410        3870        04
δοκεῖς   ὅτι οὐ δύναμαι   παρακαλέσαι  τὸν
do you think that not I am able to encourage the

3962   1473   2532 3936              1473 737  4183
πατέρα μου, καὶ παραστήσει     μοι  ἄρτι πλείω
father of me, and he will stand along to me now  more

1427  3003   32           54  4459 3767 4137
δώδεκα λεγιῶνας ἀγγέλων;  54 πῶς οὖν πληρωθῶσιν
twelve legions of messengers? How then might be
                                        fulfilled

017 1124      3754 3779   1163  1096       55  1722
αἱ γραφαὶ  ὅτι οὕτως δεῖ γενέσθαι;  55 'Εν
the writings that thusly it is to become?   In
                                  necessary

1565    07  5610 3004  01  2424    015    3793      5613
ἐκείνῃ τῇ ὥρᾳ εἶπεν ὁ 'Ιησοῦς τοῖς ὄχλοις· ὡς
that    the hour said the Jesus to the crowds, as

1909 3027  1831       3326 3162    2532 3586
ἐπὶ λῃστὴν ἐξήλθατε μετὰ μαχαιρῶν καὶ ξύλων
on robber you came out with swords  and woods

4815            1473 2596 2250   1722 011 2411
συλλαβεῖν    με; καθ' ἡμέραν ἐν τῷ ἱερῷ
to take together me? By  day   in  the temple

2516         1321       2532 3756 2902      1473
ἐκαθεζόμην διδάσκων καὶ οὐκ ἐκρατήσατέ με.
I was sitting teaching and not  you held  me.

56 3778  1161 3650  1096      2443 4137
56 τοῦτο δὲ ὅλον γέγονεν ἵνα πληρωθῶσιν
   This but whole has become that might be fulfilled

017 1124    014  4396         5119 013 3101    3956
αἱ γραφαὶ τῶν προφητῶν. Τότε οἱ μαθηταὶ πάντες
the writings of the spokesmen. Then the learners all

863      846   5343     57 013 1161 2902          04
ἀφέντες αὐτὸν ἔφυγον.  57 Οἱ δὲ κρατήσαντες   τὸν
having him   fled.         The but ones having held the
left off
```

```
2424      520       4314      2533        04    749
'Ἰησοῦν ἀπήγαγον πρὸς   Καϊάφαν τὸν ἀρχιερέα,
 Jesus  led off   toward Caiaphas the ruler priest,
3699   013 1122         2532 013 4245           4863
ὅπου οἱ γραμματεῖς καὶ οἱ πρεσβύτεροι συνήχθησαν.
where the writers    and the older men    were brought
                                              together.
```

58
```
   01 1161 4074      190          846  575 3113      2193
 ὁ δὲ Πέτρος ἠκολούθει   αὐτῷ ἀπὸ μακρόθεν ἕως
 The but Peter  was following him off from far  until
06  833       02    749          2532 1525
τῆς αὐλῆς   τοῦ  ἀρχιερέως  καὶ εἰσελθὼν
the courtyard of the ruler priest and having come into
2080   2521          3326 014 5257       3708    012
ἔσω  ἐκάθητο      μετὰ τῶν ὑπηρετῶν  ἰδεῖν τὸ
inside he was sitting with the assistants to see the
5056           013 1161 749           2532 09  4892
τέλος.      59 Οἱ δὲ ἀρχιερεῖς    καὶ τὸ συνέδριον
completion. The but  ruler priests  and the council
3650  2212        5577        2596    02   2424
ὅλον ἐζήτουν  ψευδομαρτυρίαν κατὰ  τοῦ Ἰησοῦ
whole were seeking false testimony against the  Jesus
3704   846   2289                    2532 3756
ὅπως αὐτὸν θανατώσωσιν,        60 καὶ οὐχ
so that him  they might put to death,  and  not
2147        4183    4334             5577a
εὗρον    πολλῶν προσελθόντων  ψευδομαρτύρων.
they found many   having come toward false testifiers.
5306     1161 4334           1417    3004    3778
ὕστερον δὲ  προσελθόντες δύο 61 εἶπαν· οὗτος
Later   but  having come to two    said,  this one
5346  1410     2647         04 3485   02     2316 2532
ἔφη· δύναμαι καταλῦσαι τὸν ναὸν τοῦ  θεοῦ καὶ
said, I am able to unloose the temple of the God   and
1223   5140   2250    3618        2532 450
διὰ  τριῶν ἡμερῶν οἰκοδομῆσαι. 62 καὶ ἀναστὰς
through three  days    to build.   And having stood up
01   749          3004 846     3762    611        5101
ὁ  ἀρχιερεὺς εἶπεν αὐτῷ· οὐδὲν ἀποκρίνῃ τί
the ruler priest said  to him, nothing you answer what
3778  1473  2649             01 1161    2424
οὗτοί σου καταμαρτυροῦσιν; 63 ὁ δὲ Ἰησοῦς
these of you testify against?  The but Jesus
4623          2532 01   749         3004   846
ἐσιώπα.   καὶ ὁ  ἀρχιερεὺς εἶπεν αὐτῷ·
was silent.  And the ruler priest said  to him,
1844              1473 2596 02 2316 02  2198    2443
ἐξορκίζω       σε κατὰ τοῦ θεοῦ τοῦ ζῶντος ἵνα
I put under oath you by  the God  the  living that
1473  3004          1487 1473 1510 01 5547     01  5207
ἡμῖν εἴπῃς      εἰ σὺ εἶ ὁ χριστὸς ὁ υἱὸς
to us you might say if you are the Christ the son
02       2316       3004  846    01   2424  1473 3004
τοῦ  θεοῦ.  64 λέγει αὐτῷ ὁ Ἰησοῦς· σὺ εἶπας.
of the God.    Says to him the Jesus; you said.
4133  3004 1473   575  737  3708        04  5207
πλὴν λέγω ὑμῖν· ἀπ' ἄρτι ὄψεσθε    τὸν υἱὸν
Except I say to you, from now  you will see the son
02    444       2521     1537 1188    06    1411
τοῦ ἀνθρώπου καθήμενον ἐκ δεξιῶν τῆς δυνάμεως
of the man    sitting   from right of the power
2532 2064      1909 018 3507     02    3772       5119
καὶ ἐρχόμενον ἐπὶ τῶν νεφελῶν τοῦ οὐρανοῦ. 65 τότε
and coming    on the clouds of the heaven.   Then
01  749          1284         024 2440    846    3004
ὁ ἀρχιερεὺς διέρρηξεν τὰ ἱμάτια αὐτοῦ λέγων·
the ruler priest tore apart the clothes of him saying;
987           τί   ἔτι   χρείαν ἔχομεν μαρτύρων;
ἐβλασφήμησεν·
he insulted;  what still  need   we have of testifiers?
```

Jesus took him to Caiaphas the high priest, in whose house the scribes and the elders had gathered. [58]But Peter was following him at a distance, as far as the courtyard of the high priest; and going inside, he sat with the guards in order to see how this would end. [59]Now the chief priests and the whole council were looking for false testimony against Jesus so that they might put him to death, [60]but they found none, though many false witnesses came forward. At last two came forward [61]and said, "This fellow said, 'I am able to destroy the temple of God and to build it in three days.'" [62]The high priest stood up and said, "Have you no answer? What is it that they testify against you?" [63]But Jesus was silent. Then the high priest said to him, "I put you under oath before the living God, tell us if you are the Messiah,[a] the Son of God." [64]Jesus said to him, "You have said so. But I tell you,

From now on you will see
   the Son of Man
seated at the right hand
   of Power
and coming on the
   clouds of heaven."

[65]Then the high priest tore his clothes and said, "He has blasphemed! Why do we still need witnesses?

[a] Or Christ

You have now heard his blasphemy. [66]What is your verdict?" They answered, "He deserves death."

[67]Then they spat in his face and struck him; and some slapped him, [68]saying, "Prophesy to us, you Messiah![a] Who is it that struck you?"

[69]Now Peter was sitting outside in the courtyard. A servant-girl came to him and said, "You also were with Jesus the Galilean." [70]But he denied it before all of them, saying, "I do not know what you are talking about." [71]When he went out to the porch, another servant-girl saw him, and she said to the bystanders, "This man was with Jesus of Nazareth."[b] [72]Again he denied it with an oath, "I do not know the man." [73]After a little while the bystanders came up and said to Peter, "Certainly you are also one of them, for your accent betrays you." [74]Then he began to curse, and he swore an oath, "I do not know the man!" At that moment the cock crowed. [75]Then Peter remembered what Jesus had said: "Before the cock crows, you will deny me three times." And he went out and wept bitterly.

CHAPTER 27

When morning came, all the chief priests and the elders

[a] Or Christ
[b] Gk the Nazorean

2396 3568 191 08 988 **66** 5101 1473
ἴδε νῦν ἠκούσατε τὴν βλασφημίαν· τί ὑμῖν
Look now you heard the insult; what to you

1380 013 1161 611 3004 1777
δοκεῖ; οἱ δὲ ἀποκριθέντες εἶπαν· ἔνοχος
it thinks? The but ones having answered said; guilty

2288 1510 **67** 5119 1716 1519 012 4383
θανάτου ἐστίν. Τότε ἐνέπτυσαν εἰς τὸ πρόσωπον
of death he is. Then they spat on into the face

846 2532 2852 846 013 1161
αὐτοῦ καὶ ἐκολάφισαν αὐτόν, οἱ δὲ
of him and knocked about him, the ones but

4474 **68** 3004 4395 1473 5547
ἐράπισαν λέγοντες· προφήτευσον ἡμῖν, χριστέ,
slapped saying, speak before to us, Christ,

5101 1510 01 3817 1473 01 1161 4074
τίς ἐστιν ὁ παίσας σε; **69** Ὁ δὲ Πέτρος
who is the one having struck you? The but Peter

2521 1854 1722 01 3588 2532 4334 846
ἐκάθητο ἔξω ἐν τῇ αὐλῇ· καὶ προσῆλθεν αὐτῷ
sat outside in the courtyard; and went to him

1520 3814 3004 2532 1473 1510 3326 2424
μία παιδίσκη λέγουσα· καὶ σὺ ἦσθα μετὰ Ἰησοῦ
one servant girl saying; and you were with Jesus

02 1057 **70** 01 1161 720 1715 3956
τοῦ Γαλιλαίου. ὁ δὲ ἠρνήσατο ἔμπροσθεν πάντων
the Galilean. The one but denied in front of all

3004 3756 3609a 5101 3004 **71** 1831 1161
λέγων· οὐκ οἶδα τί λέγεις. ἐξελθόντα δὲ
saying; not I know what you say. Having gone out but

1519 04 4440 3708 846 243 2532 3004 015
εἰς τὸν πυλῶνα εἶδεν αὐτὸν ἄλλη καὶ λέγει τοῖς
into the gate saw him other and says to the ones

1563 3778 1510 3326 2424 02 3480 **72** 2532
ἐκεῖ· οὗτος ἦν μετὰ Ἰησοῦ τοῦ Ναζωραίου. καὶ
there; this one was with Jesus the Nazorean. And

3825 720 3326 3727 3754 3756 3609a 04
πάλιν ἠρνήσατο μετὰ ὅρκου ὅτι οὐκ οἶδα τὸν
again he denied with oath, (") not I know the

444 **73** 3326 3398 1161 4334 013
ἄνθρωπον. μετὰ μικρὸν δὲ προσελθόντες οἱ
man. After little but having come to the ones

2476 3004 03 4074 230 2532 1473 1537
ἑστῶτες εἶπον τῷ Πέτρῳ· ἀληθῶς καὶ σὺ ἐξ
having stood said to the Peter; truly also you from

846 1510 2532 1063 05 2981 1473 1212 1473 4160
αὐτῶν εἶ, καὶ γὰρ ἡ λαλιά σου δῆλόν σε ποιεῖ.
them are, even for the speech of you clear you makes.

74 5119 757 2616b 2532 3660
τότε ἤρξατο καταθεματίζειν καὶ ὀμνύειν
Then he began to curse thoroughly and to take oath,

3754 3756 3609a 04 444 2532 2112
ὅτι οὐκ οἶδα τὸν ἄνθρωπον. καὶ εὐθέως
(") not I know the man. And immediately

220 5455 **75** 2532 3403 01 4074 010
ἀλέκτωρ ἐφώνησεν. καὶ ἐμνήσθη ὁ Πέτρος τοῦ
rooster sounded. And remembered the Peter the

4487 2424 3004 3754 4250 220
ῥήματος Ἰησοῦ εἰρηκότος ὅτι πρὶν ἀλέκτορα
word of Jesus having said, (") before rooster

5455 5151 533 1473 2532 1831 1854
φωνῆσαι τρὶς ἀπαρνήσῃ με· καὶ ἐξελθὼν ἔξω
to sound three you will deny me; and having outside
thoroughly gone out

2799 4090 **27:1** 4405 1161 1096 4824
ἔκλαυσεν πικρῶς. Πρωΐας δὲ γενομένης συμβούλιον
he cried bitterly. Morning but having become council

2983 3956 013 749 2532 013 4245
ἔλαβον πάντες οἱ ἀρχιερεῖς καὶ οἱ πρεσβύτεροι
took all the ruler priests and the older men

02　2992　　2596　　02　　2424　5620　　2289
τοῦ λαοῦ　κατὰ　τοῦ Ἰησοῦ ὥστε　θανατῶσαι
the people against the　Jesus so that to put to death

846　　2　2532 1210　　　　　846　　520　　　　2532
αὐτόν·　καὶ δήσαντες　αὐτὸν ἀπήγαγον　καὶ
him;　and　having bound him　they led off and

3860　　　4091　　03　2232　　5119 3708
παρέδωκαν Πιλάτῳ　τῷ ἡγεμόνι.³ Τότε ἰδὼν
gave over to Pilate the leader.　Then having seen

2455　　01　3860　　　　846　3754 2632
Ἰούδας ὁ　παραδιδοὺς　αὐτὸν ὅτι κατεκρίθη,
Judas　the one giving over him that he was condemned,

3338　　　　　4762　　024 5144　　694　　015
μεταμεληθεὶς　ἔστρεψεν τὰ τριάκοντα ἀργύρια τοῖς
having sorrowed he turned the thirty　silver　to the

749　　　2532 4245　　4　3004　264
ἀρχιερεῦσιν καὶ　πρεσβυτέροις　λέγων·　ἥμαρτον
ruler priests and　older men　saying,　I sinned

3860　　　129　121　013　　1161 3004
παραδοὺς　αἷμα ἀθῷον.　οἱ　δὲ　εἶπαν·
having given over blood innocent. The ones but　said;

5101 4314 1473 1473 3708　5　2532 4496　　024
τί　πρὸς ἡμᾶς; σὺ ὄψῃ.　καὶ ῥίψας　τὰ
what to　us? You　will see. And　having flung the

694　　1519 04 3485　402　　2532
ἀργύρια εἰς τὸν ναὸν ἀνεχώρησεν, καὶ
silver　into the temple he departed, and

565　　　519　　　　6　013 1161
ἀπελθὼν　ἀπήγξατο.　Οἱ　δὲ
having gone off he choked off himself.　The but

749　　　2983　024 694　　3004　3756 1832
ἀρχιερεῖς　λαβόντες τὰ ἀργύρια εἶπαν· οὐκ ἔξεστιν
ruler priests having　the silver　said;　not it is
taken　　　　　　　　　　　　　　　　　possible

906　　846　　1519 04　2878a　1893　5092　129
βαλεῖν αὐτὰ εἰς τὸν κορβανᾶν, ἐπεὶ τιμὴ αἵματός
to throw these into the corban,　since value of blood

1510　7　4824　　　1161 2983　　59　　　1537
ἐστιν.　συμβούλιον δὲ λαβόντες　ἠγόρασαν ἐξ
it is.　Council　but having taken they bought out of

846　04　68　02　　2763　　1519 5027　015
αὐτῶν τὸν ἀγρὸν τοῦ　κεραμέως εἰς ταφὴν τοῖς
them　the field of the　potter　for　burial to the

3581　　8　1352　　2564　　01 68　1565　　68
ξένοις.　διὸ　ἐκλήθη　ὁ ἀγρὸς ἐκεῖνος ἀγρὸς
strangers. Therefore was called the field that　field

129　　　2193 06 4594　　9 5119 4137　　09
αἵματος ἕως τῆς σήμερον.　τότε ἐπληρώθη　τὸ
of blood until the today.　Then was fulfilled the

3004　　　1223　2408　02 4396　　3004
ῥηθὲν　διὰ　Ἰερεμίου τοῦ προφήτου λέγοντος·
word having through Jeremiah the spokesman saying,
been spoken

2532 2983　024 5144　　694　　08 5092
καὶ ἔλαβον τὰ τριάκοντα ἀργύρια, τὴν τιμὴν
also they took the thirty　silver,　the value

02　　　5091　　　3739 5091　　575
τοῦ　τετιμημένου　ὃν ἐτιμήσαντο ἀπὸ
of the one having been valued who they valued from

5207 2474　　10 2532 1325　846 1519 04 68
υἱῶν Ἰσραήλ,　καὶ ἔδωκαν αὐτὰ εἰς τὸν ἀγρὸν
sons Israel,　and　they gave them into the field

02　　2763　　2505　　4929　　1473 2962
τοῦ　κεραμέως, καθὰ　συνέταξέν μοι κύριος.
of the potter,　just as fully ordered me　Master.

11　01 1161　2424　2476　1715　02 2232
Ὁ δὲ　Ἰησοῦς ἐστάθη　ἔμπροσθεν τοῦ ἡγεμόνος·
The but　Jesus　was stood in front of the leader;

of the people conferred together against Jesus in order to bring about his death. ²They bound him, led him away, and handed him over to Pilate the governor.

3 When Judas, his betrayer, saw that Jesus[a] was condemned, he repented and brought back the thirty pieces of silver to the chief priests and the elders. ⁴He said, "I have sinned by betraying innocent[b] blood." But they said, "What is that to us? See to it yourself." ⁵Throwing down the pieces of silver in the temple, he departed; and he went and hanged himself. ⁶But the chief priests, taking the pieces of silver, said, "It is not lawful to put them into the treasury, since they are blood money." ⁷After conferring together, they used them to buy the potter's field as a place to bury foreigners. ⁸For this reason that field has been called the Field of Blood to this day. ⁹Then was fulfilled what had been spoken through the prophet Jeremiah,[c] "And they took[d] the thirty pieces of silver, the price of the one on whom a price had been set,[e] on whom some of the people of Israel had set a price, ¹⁰and they gave[f] them for the potter's field, as the Lord commanded me."

11 Now Jesus stood before the governor;

[a] Gk he
[b] Other ancient authorities read righteous
[c] Other ancient authorities read Zechariah or Isaiah
[d] Or I took
[e] Or the price of the precious One
[f] Other ancient authorities read I gave

and the governor asked him, "Are you the King of the Jews?" Jesus said, "You say so." 12But when he was accused by the chief priests and elders, he did not answer. 13Then Pilate said to him, "Do you not hear how many accusations they make against you?" 14But he gave him no answer, not even to a single charge, so that the governor was greatly amazed.

15Now at the festival the governor was accustomed to release a prisoner for the crowd, anyone whom they wanted. 16At that time they had a notorious prisoner, called Jesus*a* Barabbas. 17So after they had gathered, Pilate said to them, "Whom do you want me to release for you, Jesus*a* Barabbas or Jesus who is called the Messiah?"*b* 18For he realized that it was out of jealousy that they had handed him over. 19While he was sitting on the judgment seat, his wife sent word to him, "Have nothing to do with that innocent man, for today I have suffered a great deal because of a dream about him." 20Now the chief priests and the elders persuaded the crowds to ask for Barabbas and to have Jesus killed. 21The governor again said to them,

a Other ancient authorities lack Jesus
b Or the Christ

2532	1905		846	01	2232	3004		1473	1510	01
καὶ ἐπηρώτησεν αὐτὸν ὁ ἡγεμὼν λέγων· σὺ εἶ ὁ
and asked on him the leader saying· you are the

935		014		2453		01	1161	2424	5346	1473
βασιλεὺς τῶν Ἰουδαίων; ὁ δὲ Ἰησοῦς ἔφη· σὺ
king of the Judeans? The but Jesus said; you

3004		2532	1722	011	2723		846	5259	014
λέγεις. 12 καὶ ἐν τῷ κατηγορεῖσθαι αὐτὸν ὑπὸ τῶν
say. And in the to be accused him by the

749	2532	4245		3762	611
ἀρχιερέων καὶ πρεσβυτέρων οὐδὲν ἀπεκρίνατο.
ruler priests and older men nothing he answered.

5119	3004	846	01	4091		3756	191
13 τότε λέγει αὐτῷ ὁ Πιλᾶτος· οὐκ ἀκούεις
Then says to him the Pilate; not you hear

4214	1473	2649				2532	3756
πόσα σου καταμαρτυροῦσιν; 14 καὶ οὐκ
how much you they testify against? And not

611	846	4314	3761	1520	4487	5620
ἀπεκρίθη αὐτῷ πρὸς οὐδὲ ἓν ῥῆμα, ὥστε
he answered to him to but not one word, so that

2296	04	2232	3029	2596	1161	1859
θαυμάζειν τὸν ἡγεμόνα λίαν. 15 Κατὰ δὲ ἑορτὴν
to marvel the leader very. By but festival

1536a	01	2232	630	1520	013	3793	1198	3739
εἰώθει ὁ ἡγεμὼν ἀπολύειν ἕνα τῷ ὄχλῳ δέσμιον ὃν
had the leader to loose one to crowd prisoner whom
custom off the

2309		2192	1161	5119	1198	1978
ἤθελον. 16 εἶχον δὲ τότε δέσμιον ἐπίσημον
they wanted. They had but then prisoner prominent

3004		2424	912		4863	3767
λεγόμενον [Ἰησοῦν] Βαραββᾶν. 17 συνηγμένων οὖν
being called Jesus Barabbas. Having been then brought together

846	3004	846	01	4091	5101	2309
αὐτῶν εἶπεν αὐτοῖς ὁ Πιλᾶτος· τίνα θέλετε
them said to them the Pilate; whom do you want

630	1473	2424	04	912	2228	2424	04
ἀπολύσω ὑμῖν, [Ἰησοῦν τὸν] Βαραββᾶν ἢ Ἰησοῦν τὸν
I might to you, Jesus the Barabbas or Jesus the
loose off

3004		5547		3609a	1063	3754	1223
λεγόμενον χριστόν; 18 ᾔδει γὰρ ὅτι διὰ
one being called Christ? He knew for that through

5355	3860		846	2521	1161	846
φθόνον παρέδωκαν αὐτόν. 19 Καθημένου δὲ αὐτοῦ
envy they gave over him. Sitting but him

1909	010	968	649	4314	846	05	1135
ἐπὶ τοῦ βήματος ἀπέστειλεν πρὸς αὐτὸν ἡ γυνὴ
on the law court delegated to him the woman

846	3004	846	3367	1473	2532	03	1342
αὐτοῦ λέγουσα· μηδὲν σοὶ καὶ τῷ δικαίῳ
of him saying, nothing to you and to the right one

1565	4183	1063	3958	4594	2596	3677
ἐκείνῳ· πολλὰ γὰρ ἔπαθον σήμερον κατ' ὄναρ
that; many for I suffered today by dream

1223	846	013	1161	749	2532	013
δι' αὐτόν. 20 Οἱ δὲ ἀρχιερεῖς καὶ οἱ
through him. The but ruler priests and the

4245	3982	013	3793	2443	154
πρεσβύτεροι ἔπεισαν τοὺς ὄχλους ἵνα αἰτήσωνται
older men persuaded the crowds that they might ask

04	912	04	1161	2424	622
τὸν Βαραββᾶν, τὸν δὲ Ἰησοῦν ἀπολέσωσιν.
the Barabbas, the but Jesus they might destroy.

	611		1161	01	2232	3004	846	5101
21 ἀποκριθεὶς δὲ ὁ ἡγεμὼν εἶπεν αὐτοῖς· τίνα
Having answered but the leader said to them; whom

2309   575   014 1417 630   1473   013
θέλετε   ἀπὸ   τῶν δύο   ἀπολύσω   ὑμῖν;   οἱ
you want from the two   I might loose off to you? The

1161 3004   04   912   3004   846   91 4091
δὲ   εἶπαν· τὸν Βαραββᾶν. 22 λέγει αὐτοῖς ὁ Πιλᾶτος·
but   said;   the Barabbas.   Says to them the Pilate,

5101 3767 4160   2424   04 3004
τί   οὖν   ποιήσω   Ἰησοῦν τὸν λεγόμενον
what then might I do Jesus the one being called

5547   3004   3956 4717   01   1161
χριστόν; λέγουσιν πάντες· σταυρωθήτω. 23 ὁ   δὲ
Christ?   Say   all,   let be crucified. The one but

5346 5101 1063 2556 4160   013   1161 4057
ἔφη· τί   γὰρ κακὸν ἐποίησεν; οἱ   δὲ   περισσῶς
said; what for bad   he did?   The ones but exceedingly

2896   3004   4717   3708   1161 01
ἔκραζον λέγοντες· σταυρωθήτω. 24 Ἰδὼν   δὲ   ὁ
shouted saying;   let be crucified. Having seen but the

4091   3754 3762   5623   235 3123   2351
Πιλᾶτος ὅτι οὐδὲν ὠφελεῖ   ἀλλὰ μᾶλλον θόρυβος
Pilate   that nothing he benefits but more   uproar

1096   2983   5204 633   020 5495
γίνεται, λαβὼν   ὕδωρ ἀπενίψατο   τὰς χεῖρας
becomes, having taken water he washed off the hands

561   02   3793 3004   121   1510 575   010
ἀπέναντι τοῦ ὄχλου λέγων· ἀθῷός   εἰμι ἀπὸ τοῦ
over against the crowd saying, innocent I am from the

129   3778   1473 3708   2532 611
αἵματος τούτου·   ὑμεῖς ὄψεσθε. 25 καὶ ἀποκριθεὶς
blood of this one; you will see.   And having answered

3956 01 2992   3004   09   129 846   1909 1473 2532
πᾶς ὁ   λαὸς εἶπεν· τὸ αἷμα αὐτοῦ ἐφ' ἡμᾶς καὶ
all the people said,   the blood of him on us and

1909 024 5043   1473   5119 630   846
ἐπὶ τὰ τέκνα ἡμῶν. 26 τότε ἀπέλυσεν   αὐτοῖς
on   the children of us.   Then he loosed off to them

04   912   04 1161 2424   5417   3860
τὸν Βαραββᾶν, τὸν δὲ Ἰησοῦν φραγελλώσας παρέδωκεν
the Barabbas,   the but Jesus having   he gave
                                 whipped   over

2443 4717   5119 013 4757   02
ἵνα σταυρωθῇ.   27 Τότε οἱ στρατιῶται τοῦ
that he might be crucified. Then the soldiers of the

2232   3880   04   2424 1519 012 4232
ἡγεμόνος παραλαβόντες   τὸν Ἰησοῦν εἰς τὸ πραιτώριον
leader   having taken along the Jesus to the praetorium

4863   1909 846   3650 08   4686   2532
συνήγαγον ἐπ' αὐτὸν ὅλην τὴν σπεῖραν. 28 καὶ
brought together on him   whole the squadron. And

1562   846   5511   2847   4060
ἐκδύσαντες αὐτὸν χλαμύδα κοκκίνην περιέθηκαν
having put off him robe   scarlet they set around

846   2532 4120   4735   1537 173
αὐτῷ, 29 καὶ πλέξαντες στέφανον ἐξ ἀκανθῶν
to him,   and having braided crown out of thorns

2007   1909 06   2776   846   2532 2563 1722 07
ἐπέθηκαν ἐπὶ τῆς κεφαλῆς αὐτοῦ καὶ κάλαμον ἐν τῇ
they set on on the head   of him and reed   in the

1188   846   2532 1120   1715
δεξιᾷ αὐτοῦ, καὶ γονυπετήσαντες   ἔμπροσθεν
right of him, and having fallen on knees in front of

846   1702   846 3004   5463   935   014
αὐτοῦ ἐνέπαιξαν αὐτῷ λέγοντες· χαῖρε, βασιλεῦ τῶν
him   they mocked him saying,   rejoice, king of the

2453   2532 1716   1519 846   2983
Ἰουδαίων, 30 καὶ ἐμπτύσαντες εἰς αὐτὸν ἔλαβον
Judeans,   and having spit on to him   they took

04   2563   2532 5180   1519 08   2776   846   2532
τὸν κάλαμον καὶ ἔτυπτον εἰς τὴν κεφαλὴν αὐτοῦ. 31 καὶ
the reed   and beat   in the head   of him.   And

"Which of the two do you want me to release for you?" And they said, "Barabbas." [22]Pilate said to them, "Then what should I do with Jesus who is called the Messiah?"[a] All of them said, "Let him be crucified!" [23]Then he asked, "Why, what evil has he done?" But they shouted all the more, "Let him be crucified!"

[24] So when Pilate saw that he could do nothing, but rather that a riot was beginning, he took some water and washed his hands before the crowd, saying, "I am innocent of this man's blood;[b] see to it yourselves." [25]Then the people as a whole answered, "His blood be on us and on our children!" [26]So he released Barabbas for them; and after flogging Jesus, he handed him over to be crucified.

[27] Then the soldiers of the governor took Jesus into the governor's headquarters,[c] and they gathered the whole cohort around him. [28]They stripped him and put a scarlet robe on him, [29]and after twisting some thorns into a crown, they put it on his head. They put a reed in his right hand and knelt before him and mocked him, saying, "Hail, King of the Jews!" [30]They spat on him, and took the reed and struck him on the head. [31]After mocking him,

---

[a] Or the Christ
[b] Other ancient authorities read this righteous blood, or this righteous man's blood
[c] Gk the praetorium

they stripped him of the
robe and put his own
clothes on him. Then they
led him away to crucify
him.
32 As they went out,
they came upon a man from
Cyrene named Simon; they
compelled this man to carry
his cross. 33And when they
came to a place called
Golgotha (which means
Place of a Skull), 34they
offered him wine to drink,
mixed with gall; but when
he tasted it, he would not
drink it. 35And when they
had crucified him, they
divided his clothes among
themselves by casting lots;[a]
36then they sat down there
and kept watch over him.
37Over his head they put the
charge against him, which
read, "This is Jesus, the
King of the Jews."
38 Then two bandits
were crucified with him,
one on his right and one on
his left. 39Those who passed
by derided[b] him, shaking
their heads 40and saying,
"You who would destroy
the temple and build it in
three days, save yourself!
If you are the Son of God,
come down from the cross."
41In the same way the chief
priests also, along with
the scribes and elders, were
mocking him, saying, 42"He
saved others; he cannot save
himself.[c] He is the King of
Israel;

a Other ancient authorities add in
  order that what had been spoken
  through the prophet might be
  fulfilled, "They divided my clothes
  among themselves, and for my
  clothing they cast lots."
b Or blasphemed
c Or is he unable to save himself?

```
        3753  1702              846        1562           846       08    5511
        ὅτε  ἐνέπαιξαν      αὐτῷ,  ἐξέδυσαν      αὐτὸν  τὴν  χλαμύδα
        when  they mocked him,     they put off him    the robe
        2532  1746        846   024  2440      846      2532  520
        καὶ  ἐνέδυσαν  αὐτὸν τὰ  ἱμάτια  αὐτοῦ  καὶ  ἀπήγαγον
        and   put on    him   the clothes of him  and  they led off
        846      1519 012  4717           1831           1161
        αὐτὸν εἰς  τὸ  σταυρῶσαι. 32 Ἐξερχόμενοι δὲ
        him    to   the to crucify.     Going from   but
        2147      444        2956       3686     4613       3778
        εὗρον  ἄνθρωπον Κυρηναῖον ὀνόματι Σίμωνα, τοῦτον
        they found  man    Cyrenean  in name  Simon,  this one
        29       2443 142      04      4716       846      33 2532
        ἠγγάρευσαν ἵνα  ἄρῃ     τὸν  σταυρὸν αὐτοῦ.    Καὶ
        they        that he might lift the cross  of him.   And
        conscripted      lift up
        2064         1519 5117  3004          1115        3739
        ἐλθόντες    εἰς  τόπον λεγόμενον  Γολγοθᾶ, ὃ
        having gone into place  being called Golgotha, which
        1510  2898     5117  3004         34 1325       846
        ἐστιν Κρανίου Τόπος λεγόμενος,    ἔδωκαν  αὐτῷ
        is     Skull   Place  being called, they gave to him
        4095       3631   3326  5521  3396           2532
        πιεῖν   οἶνον μετὰ χολῆς μεμιγμένον·     καὶ
        to drink wine  with  gall  having been mixed; and
        1089        3756 2309        4095    35 4717
        γευσάμενος οὐκ ἠθέλησεν πιεῖν.     Σταυρώσαντες
        having tasted not he wanted to drink. Having crucified
        1161 846   1266                    024 2440      846
        δὲ  αὐτὸν διεμερίσαντο       τὰ  ἱμάτια  αὐτοῦ
        but  him   they divided completely the clothes of him
        906      2819      2532 2521      5083        846
        βάλλοντες κλῆρον, 36 καὶ καθήμενοι ἐτήρουν    αὐτὸν
        throwing  lot,       and sitting  they were keeping him
        1563   37 2532 2007      1883   06    2776       846   08
        ἐκεῖ.     Καὶ ἐπέθηκαν ἐπάνω τῆς κεφαλῆς αὐτοῦ τὴν
        there.    And they set on upon  the  head     of him the
        156    046      1125                 3778  1510  2424
        αἰτίαν αὐτοῦ γεγραμμένην·      οὗτός ἐστιν Ἰησοῦς
        cause  of him having been written: this  is    Jesus
        01 935       014     2453          5119 4717        4862
        ὁ βασιλεὺς τῶν  Ἰουδαίων. 38 Τότε σταυροῦνται σὺν
        the king    of the Judeans.   Then they crucify with
        846   1417 3027      1520 1537     1188    2532 1520 1537
        αὐτῷ δύο λῃσταί, εἷς ἐκ    δεξιῶν καὶ εἷς ἐξ
        him  two  robbers,  one out of right  and  one out of
        2176       013   1161 3899          987
        εὐωνύμων. 39 Οἱ δὲ παραπορευόμενοι ἐβλασφήμουν
        left.         The ones but traveling along were insulting
        846      2795       020 2776       846     40 2532 3004      01
        αὐτὸν κινοῦντες τὰς κεφαλὰς αὐτῶν   καὶ λέγοντες· ὁ
        him   moving     the heads    of them and saying·   the
        2647        04    3485     2532 1722 5140   2250
        καταλύων  τὸν ναὸν καὶ ἐν τρισὶν ἡμέραις
        one unloosing the temple and in  three  days
        3618        4982       4572     1487 5207 1510     02
        οἰκοδομῶν, σῶσον σεαυτόν, εἰ υἱὸς εἶ      τοῦ
        building,  deliver yourself, if  son  you are of the
        2316   2532 2597     575  02  4716       41 3668      2532
        θεοῦ, [καὶ] κατάβηθι ἀπὸ τοῦ σταυροῦ.   ὁμοίως καὶ
        God,   and  come down from the cross.    Likewise also
        013 749          1702          3326 014    1122         2532
        οἱ ἀρχιερεῖς ἐμπαίζοντες μετὰ τῶν γραμματέων καὶ
        the ruler priests mocking    with the writers      and
        4245           3004     42 243      4982          1438
        πρεσβυτέρων ἔλεγον·   ἄλλους ἔσωσεν,    ἑαυτὸν
        older men    were saying; others he delivered, himself
        3756 1410    4982        935     2474      1510
        οὐ  δύναται σῶσαι·   βασιλεὺς Ἰσραήλ ἐστιν,
        not he is able to deliver; king    of Israel he is,
```

2597		3568 575 02 4716	2532 4100
καταβάτω		νῦν ἀπὸ τοῦ σταυροῦ	καὶ πιστεύσομεν
let come down		now from the cross	and we will trust

1909 846	**43**	3982	1909 04 2316 4506
ἐπ' αὐτόν.		πέποιθεν	ἐπὶ τὸν θεόν, ῥυσάσθω
on him.		Having persuaded	on the God, let rescue

3568 1487 2309	846	3004 1063 3754 2316 1510
νῦν εἰ θέλει	αὐτόν· εἶπεν	γὰρ ὅτι θεοῦ εἰμι
now if he wants	him; he said	for, (") of God I am

5207	**44**	012 1161 846 2532 013 3027 013
υἱός.		Τὸ δ' αὐτὸ καὶ οἱ λῃσταὶ οἱ
son.		The but same also the robbers the ones

4957	4862 846 3679
συσταυρωθέντες	σὺν αὐτῷ ὠνείδιζον
having been crucified together	with him were reviling

846	**45**	575 1161 1623 5610 4655 1096 1909
αὐτόν.		Ἀπὸ δὲ ἕκτης ὥρας σκότος ἐγένετο ἐπὶ
him.		From the sixth hour dark became on

3956 08 1093 2193	5610 1728a	**46**	4012 1161 08
πᾶσαν τὴν γῆν ἕως	ὥρας ἐνάτης.		περὶ δὲ τὴν
all the land until	hour ninth.		Around but the

1728a 5610 310	01 2424 5456 3173
ἐνάτην ὥραν ἀνεβόησεν	ὁ Ἰησοῦς φωνῇ μεγάλῃ
ninth hour shouted out	the Jesus in voice great

3004 2241 2241 3011a 4518	3778 1510 2316
λέγων· ηλι ηλι λεμα σαβαχθανι;	τοῦτ' ἔστιν· Θεέ
saying, eli eli lema sabachthani?	This is; God

1473 2316 1473	2444 1473 1459	**47**	5100
μου θεέ μου,	ἱνατί με ἐγκατέλιπες;		τινὲς
of me God of me,	why me you left behind?		Some

1161 014	1563 2476	191	3004	3754
δὲ τῶν	ἐκεῖ ἑστηκότων	ἀκούσαντες	ἔλεγον	ὅτι
but of the	there having stood	having heard	were saying,	(")

2243 5455 3778	**48**	2532 2112	5143 1520
Ἡλίαν φωνεῖ οὗτος.		καὶ εὐθέως	δραμὼν εἰς
Elijah sounds this one.		And immediately	having run one

1537 846 2532 2983 4699	4092 5037 3690 2532
ἐξ αὐτῶν καὶ λαβὼν σπόγγον	πλήσας τε ὄξους καὶ
out of also having taken sponge	having filled both of sour and wine

4060 2563 4222 846	**49**	013 1161 3062
περιθεὶς καλάμῳ ἐπότιζεν αὐτόν.		οἱ δὲ λοιποὶ
having set around reed he was giving drink him.		The but remaining

3004 863 3708	1487 2064
ἔλεγον· ἄφες ἴδωμεν	εἰ ἔρχεται
were saying, send off we might see	if comes

2243 4982 846	**50**	01 1161 2424 3825
Ἡλίας σώσων αὐτόν.		ὁ δὲ Ἰησοῦς πάλιν
Elijah delivering him.		The but Jesus again

2896	5456 3173 863	012 4151
κράξας	φωνῇ μεγάλῃ ἀφῆκεν	τὸ πνεῦμα.
having shouted	in voice great sent off	the spirit.

51	2532 2400 09 2665	02	3485 4977
	Καὶ ἰδοὺ τὸ καταπέτασμα	τοῦ	ναοῦ ἐσχίσθη
	And look the veil	of the	temple was split

575 509	2193 2736 1519 1417 2532 05 1093
ἀπ' ἄνωθεν	ἕως κάτω εἰς δύο καὶ ἡ γῆ
from from above	until down into two and the land

4579	2532 017 4073 4977	**52**	2532 021
ἐσείσθη	καὶ αἱ πέτραι ἐσχίσθησαν,		καὶ τὰ
was shaken	and the rocks were split,		and the

3419 455	2532 4183 4983 014
μνημεῖα ἀνεῴχθησαν	καὶ πολλὰ σώματα τῶν
graves were opened	and many bodies of the ones

2837 40	1453	**53**	2532
κεκοιμημένων ἁγίων	ἠγέρθησαν,		καὶ
having slept of holy ones	were raised,		and

let him come down from the cross now, and we will believe in him. [43]He trusts in God; let God deliver him now, if he wants to; for he said, 'I am God's Son.'" [44]The bandits who were crucified with him also taunted him in the same way.

[45]From noon on, darkness came over the whole land[a] until three in the afternoon. [46]And about three o'clock Jesus cried with a loud voice, "Eli, Eli, lema sabachthani?" that is, "My God, my God, why have you forsaken me?" [47]When some of the bystanders heard it, they said, "This man is calling for Elijah." [48]At once one of them ran and got a sponge, filled it with sour wine, put it on a stick, and gave it to him to drink. [49]But the others said, "Wait, let us see whether Elijah will come to save him."[b] [50]Then Jesus cried again with a loud voice and breathed his last.[c] [51]At that moment the curtain of the temple was torn in two, from top to bottom. The earth shook, and the rocks were split. [52]The tombs also were opened, and many bodies of the saints who had fallen asleep were raised. [53]After his resurrection

a Or *earth*

b Other ancient authorities add *And another took a spear and pierced his side, and out came water and blood*

c Or *gave up his spirit*

they came out of the tombs
and entered the holy city
and appeared to many.
[54]Now when the centurion
and those with him, who
were keeping watch over
Jesus, saw the earthquake
and what took place, they
were terrified and said,
"Truly this man was God's
Son!"[a]

[55]Many women were
also there, looking on
from a distance; they had
followed Jesus from Galilee
and had provided for him.
[56]Among them were Mary
Magdalene, and Mary
the mother of James and
Joseph, and the mother of
the sons of Zebedee.

[57]When it was evening,
there came a rich man from
Arimathea, named Joseph,
who was also a disciple of
Jesus. [58]He went to Pilate
and asked for the body of
Jesus; then Pilate ordered
it to be given to him. [59]So
Joseph took the body and
wrapped it in a clean linen
cloth [60]and laid it in his
own new tomb, which he
had hewn in the rock. He
then rolled a great stone
to the door of the tomb
and went away. [61]Mary
Magdalene and the other
Mary were there, sitting
opposite the tomb.

[62]The next day, that is,
after the day of Preparation,

[a] Or a son of God

1831		1537 022 3419		3326	08

ἐξελθόντες   ἐκ   τῶν μνημείων μετὰ τὴν
having come out from the graves   after the

1454   846   1525   1519 08 40   4172
ἔγερσιν   αὐτοῦ εἰσῆλθον   εἰς τὴν ἁγίαν πόλιν
resurrection of him they went in into the holy city

2532 1718   4183   54 01 1161
καὶ ἐνεφανίσθησαν   πολλοῖς. 54 ΄Ο δὲ
and were made visible to many.   The but

1543   2532 013   3326 846   5083
ἑκατόνταρχος   καὶ οἱ   μετ᾽ αὐτοῦ τηροῦντες
ruler of hundred and the ones with him   keeping

04   2424   3708   04   4578   2532 024
τὸν ᾽Ιησοῦν ἰδόντες   τὸν σεισμὸν καὶ τὰ
the Jesus having seen the shake   and the

1096   5399   4970   3004   230
γενόμενα   ἐφοβήθησαν σφόδρα, λέγοντες· ἀληθῶς
having become were afraid exceeding, saying; truly

2316   5207 1510 3778   55 1510 1161 1563 1135
θεοῦ υἱὸς ἦν οὗτος. 55 ῏Ησαν δὲ ἐκεῖ γυναῖκες
of God son was this one. Were but there women

4183   575 3113   2334   3748   190   03
πολλαὶ ἀπὸ μακρόθεν θεωροῦσαι, αἵτινες ἠκολούθησαν τῷ
many   off from far to watch,   who   followed   the

2424   575 06 1056   1247   846   56 1722
᾽Ιησοῦ ἀπὸ τῆς Γαλιλαίας διακονοῦσαι αὐτῷ· 56 ἐν
Jesus from the Galilee   serving   him;   in

3739   1510 3137 05 3094   2532 3137 05 02
αἷς ἦν Μαρία ἡ Μαγδαληνὴ καὶ Μαρία ἡ τοῦ
which was Maria the Magdalene and Maria the of the

2385   2532 2501   3384   2532 05 3384   014
᾽Ιακώβου καὶ ᾽Ιωσὴφ μήτηρ καὶ ἡ μήτηρ τῶν
Jacob   and Joseph mother and the mother of the

5207 2199   57 3798   1161 1096   2064
υἱῶν Ζεβεδαίου. 57 ᾽Οψίας δὲ γενομένης   ἦλθεν
sons of Zebedee.   Evening but having become went

444   4145   575 707   5122   2501 3739
ἄνθρωπος πλούσιος ἀπὸ ᾽Αριμαθαίας, τοὔνομα ᾽Ιωσήφ, ὃς
man   rich   from Arimathea,   the name Joseph, who

2532 846   3100   03   2424   58 3778
καὶ αὐτὸς ἐμαθητεύθη τῷ   ᾽Ιησοῦ· 58 οὗτος
also himself was learned to the Jesus;   this one

4334   03   4091   154   012 4983 02
προσελθὼν   τῷ Πιλάτῳ ἠτήσατο τὸ σῶμα τοῦ
having come to the Pilate asked   the body of the

2424   5119 01 4091   2753   591
᾽Ιησοῦ. τότε ὁ Πιλᾶτος ἐκέλευσεν ἀποδοθῆναι.
Jesus. Then the Pilate commanded to be given off.

59 2532 2983   012 4983 01 2501   1794
59 καὶ λαβὼν   τὸ σῶμα ὁ ᾽Ιωσὴφ ἐνετύλιξεν
And having taken the body the Joseph wrapped

846   1722 4616   2513   60 2532 5087   846   1722 011
αὐτὸ [ἐν] σινδόνι καθαρᾷ 60 καὶ ἔθηκεν αὐτὸ ἐν   τῷ
it   in linen   clean   and set   it   in   the

2537   846   3419   3739 2998   1722 07 4073 2532
καινῷ αὐτοῦ μνημείῳ ὃ   ἐλατόμησεν ἐν τῇ πέτρᾳ καὶ
new   of him grave   which was cut   in the rock   and

4351   3037 3173 07   2374 010   3419
προσκυλίσας λίθον μέγαν τῇ   θύρᾳ τοῦ   μνημείου
having rolled stone great in the door of the grave

565   1510 1161 1563 3137a 05 3094   2532
ἀπῆλθεν. 61 ῏Ην δὲ ἐκεῖ Μαριὰμ ἡ Μαγδαληνὴ καὶ
he went off. Was but there Mariam the Magdalene and

05 243 3137 2521   02 5028   62 07
ἡ ἄλλη Μαρία καθήμεναι ἀπέναντι τοῦ τάφου. 62 Τῇ
the other Maria sitting   over against the tomb. In the

1161 1887   3748 1510 3326 08 3904
δὲ ἐπαύριον, ἥτις ἐστὶν μετὰ τὴν παρασκευήν,
but tomorrow, which is   after the preparation,

4863	013 749	2532 013 5330	4314
συνήχθησαν	οἱ ἀρχιερεῖς καὶ	οἱ Φαρισαῖοι	πρὸς
were brought	the ruler	and the Pharisees	toward
together	priests		

4091	**63**	3004	2962	3403	3754
Πιλᾶτον		λέγοντες·	κύριε,	ἐμνήσθημεν	ὅτι
Pilate		saying,	master,	we remembered	that

1565	01 4108	3004	2089	2198	3326	5140
ἐκεῖνος	ὁ πλάνος	εἶπεν	ἔτι	ζῶν·	μετὰ	τρεῖς
that	the deceiver	said	still	living;	after	three

2250	1453	**64**	2753	3767 805
ἡμέρας	ἐγείρομαι.		κέλευσον	οὖν ἀσφαλισθῆναι
days	I am raised.		Command	then to be made secure

04	5028	2193 06	5154	2250	3379	2064
τὸν	τάφον	ἕως τῆς	τρίτης	ἡμέρας,	μήποτε	ἐλθόντες
the	tomb	until the	third	day,	not then	having come

013 3101	846	2813	846	2532 3004
οἱ μαθηταὶ	αὐτοῦ	κλέψωσιν	αὐτὸν καὶ	εἴπωσιν
the learners	of him	might thieve	him and	might say

03	2992	1453	575	014 3498	2532
τῷ	λαῷ·	ἠγέρθη	ἀπὸ	τῶν νεκρῶν,	καὶ
to the	people;	he was raised	from	the dead,	and

1510	05	2078	4106	5501 06	4413	**65**	5346
ἔσται	ἡ	ἐσχάτη	πλάνη	χείρων τῆς	πρώτης.		ἔφη
will be the		last	deceit	worse the	first.		Said

846	01 4091	2192	2892	5217
αὐτοῖς	ὁ Πιλᾶτος·	ἔχετε	κουστωδίαν·	ὑπάγετε
to them	the Pilate,	you have	custodian;	go off

805	5613 3609a	**66**	013 1161 4198
ἀσφαλίσασθε	ὡς οἴδατε.		οἱ δὲ πορεύθεντες
make secure	as you know.		The but ones having traveled

805	04 5028 4972	04 3037	3326 06
ἠσφαλίσαντο	τὸν τάφον σφραγίσαντες	τὸν λίθον	μετὰ τῆς
made secure	the tomb having sealed	the stone	with the

2892	**28:1**	3796	1161 4521	07
κουστωδίας.		Ὀψὲ	δὲ σαββάτων,	τῇ
custodian.		Evening	but of sabbaths,	in the

2020	1519 1520 4521	2064 3137a	05
ἐπιφωσκούσῃ	εἰς μίαν σαββάτων	ἦλθεν Μαριὰμ	ἡ
dawning on	in one of sabbaths	went Mariam	the

3094	2532 05	243	3137	2334	04 5028
Μαγδαληνὴ	καὶ ἡ	ἄλλη	Μαρία	θεωρῆσαι	τὸν τάφον.
Magdalene	and the	other	Maria	to watch	the tomb.

2	2532 2400 4578	1096	3173	32	·	1063
	καὶ ἰδοὺ σεισμὸς	ἐγένετο	μέγας·	ἄγγελος		γὰρ
	And look shake	became	great;	messenger		for

2962	2597	1537	3772	2532
κυρίου	καταβὰς	ἐξ	οὐρανοῦ	καὶ
of Master	having come down	out of	heaven	and

4334	617	04 3037	2532 2521
προσελθὼν	ἀπεκύλισεν	τὸν λίθον	καὶ ἐκάθητο
having come toward	rolled off	the stone	and sat

1883 846	**3**	1510 1161 05	1489a	846	5613
ἐπάνω αὐτοῦ.		ἦν δὲ ἡ	εἰδέα	αὐτοῦ	ὡς
upon it.		Was but the	appearance	of him	as

796	2532 09	1742	846	3022	5613 5510
ἀστραπὴ	καὶ τὸ	ἔνδυμα	αὐτοῦ	λευκὸν	ὡς χιών.
lightning	and the	clothes	of him	white	as snow.

4	575	1161 02	5401	846	4579	013
	ἀπὸ	δὲ τοῦ	φόβου	αὐτοῦ	ἐσείσθησαν	οἱ
	From	but the	fear	of him	were shaken	the ones

5083	2532 1096	5613 3498	**5**	611
τηροῦντες	καὶ ἐγενήθησαν	ὡς νεκροί.		ἀποκριθεὶς
keeping	and they became	as dead.		Having answered

1161 01	32	3004	019	1135	3361 5399
δὲ	ὁ ἄγγελος	εἶπεν	ταῖς	γυναιξίν·	μὴ φοβεῖσθε
but	the messenger	said	to the	women,	not fear

the chief priests and the Pharisees gathered before Pilate [63]and said, "Sir, we remember what that impostor said while he was still alive, 'After three days I will rise again.' [64]Therefore command the tomb to be made secure until the third day; otherwise his disciples may go and steal him away, and tell the people, 'He has been raised from the dead,' and the last deception would be worse than the first." [65]Pilate said to them, "You have a guard[a] of soldiers; go, make it as secure as you can."[b] [66]So they went with the guard and made the tomb secure by sealing the stone.

CHAPTER 28

After the sabbath, as the first day of the week was dawning, Mary Magdalene and the other Mary went to see the tomb. [2]And suddenly there was a great earthquake; for an angel of the Lord, descending from heaven, came and rolled back the stone and sat on it. [3]His appearance was like lightning, and his clothing white as snow. [4]For fear of him the guards shook and became like dead men. [5]But the angel said to the women, "Do not be afraid;

a Or Take a guard
b Gk you know how

I know that you are looking for Jesus who was crucified. ⁶He is not here; for he has been raised, as he said. Come, see the place where he^a lay. ⁷Then go quickly and tell his disciples, 'He has been raised from the dead,^b and indeed he is going ahead of you to Galilee; there you will see him.' This is my message for you." ⁸So they left the tomb quickly with fear and great joy, and ran to tell his disciples. ⁹Suddenly Jesus met them and said, "Greetings!" And they came to him, took hold of his feet, and worshiped him. ¹⁰Then Jesus said to them, "Do not be afraid; go and tell my brothers to go to Galilee; there they will see me."

11 While they were going, some of the guard went into the city and told the chief priests everything that had happened. ¹²After the priests^c had assembled with the elders, they devised a plan to give a large sum of money to the soldiers, ¹³telling them, "You must say, 'His disciples came by night and stole him away while we were asleep.' ¹⁴If this comes to the governor's ears, we will satisfy him and

^a Other ancient authorities read the Lord
^b Other ancient authorities lack from the dead
^c Gk they

1473	3609a	1063	3754	2424	04	4717
ὑμεῖς,	οἶδα	γὰρ	ὅτι	Ἰησοῦν	τὸν	ἐσταυρωμένον
you,	I know	for	that	Jesus	the	one having been crucified

2212		3756	1510	5602	1453		1063	2531
ζητεῖτε·	**6**	οὐκ	ἔστιν	ὧδε,	ἠγέρθη		γὰρ	καθὼς
you seek;		not	he is here,		he was raised		for	just as

3004	1205	3708	04	5117	3699	2749
εἶπεν·	δεῦτε	ἴδετε	τὸν	τόπον	ὅπου	ἔκειτο.
he said,	come	see	the	place	where	he was lying.

	2532	5036	4198		3004	015	3101
7	καὶ	ταχὺ	πορευθεῖσαι	εἴπατε	τοῖς	μαθηταῖς
	And	quickly	travel	say	to the	learners

846	3754	1453		575	014	3498	2532	2400
αὐτοῦ	ὅτι	ἠγέρθη		ἀπὸ	τῶν	νεκρῶν,	καὶ	ἰδοὺ
of him	that	he was raised		from	the	dead,	and	look

4254		1473	1519	08	1056		1563	846
προάγει		ὑμᾶς	εἰς	τὴν	Γαλιλαίαν,	ἐκεῖ	αὐτὸν
he leads before		you	into	the	Galilee,	there	him

3708		2400	3004	1473		2532	565
ὄψεσθε·		ἰδοὺ	εἶπον	ὑμῖν.	**8**	Καὶ	ἀπελθοῦσαι
you will see;		look	I told	you.		And	having gone off

5036	575	010	3419		3326	5401	2532	5479
ταχὺ	ἀπὸ	τοῦ	μνημείου	μετὰ	φόβου	καὶ	χαρᾶς
quickly	from	the	grave	with	fear	and	joy

3173	5143	518		015	3101	846
μεγάλης	ἔδραμον	ἀπαγγεῖλαι	τοῖς	μαθηταῖς	αὐτοῦ.
great	they ran	to tell	the	learners	of him.

	2532	2400	2424	5221		846	3004	5463
9	καὶ	ἰδοὺ	Ἰησοῦς	ὑπήντησεν	αὐταῖς	λέγων·	χαίρετε.
	And	look	Jesus	met	them	saying,	rejoice.

017	1161	4334			2902	846	016
αἱ	δὲ	προσελθοῦσαι		ἐκράτησαν	αὐτοῦ	τοὺς
The	but	ones having come toward		held	of him	the

4228	2532	4352		846		5119	3004	846	01
πόδας	καὶ	προσεκύνησαν	αὐτῷ.	**10**	τότε	λέγει	αὐταῖς	ὁ
feet	and	worshiped		him.		Then	says	to them	the

2424	3361	5399		5217	518	015
Ἰησοῦς·	μὴ	φοβεῖσθε·	ὑπάγετε	ἀπαγγείλατε	τοῖς
Jesus·	not	fear;	go off	tell	to the

80	1473	2443	565		1519	08
ἀδελφοῖς	μου	ἵνα	ἀπέλθωσιν		εἰς	τὴν
brothers	of me	that	they might go off		into	the

1056		2546		1473	3708		4198
Γαλιλαίαν	κἀκεῖ		με	ὄψονται.	**11**	Πορευομένων
Galilee,	and there		me	they will see.		Having traveled

1161	846	2400	5100	06		2892	2064	1519
δὲ	αὐτῶν	ἰδού	τινες	τῆς		κουστωδίας	ἐλθόντες	εἰς
but	them	look	some	of the		custodian	having gone	into

08	4172	518		015	749		537	024
τὴν	πόλιν	ἀπήγγειλαν	τοῖς	ἀρχιερεῦσιν	ἅπαντα	τὰ
the	city	told	to the	ruler priests	all	the

1096		2532	4863			3326	014
γενόμενα.	**12**	καὶ	συναχθέντες		μετὰ	τῶν
having become.		And	having brought together		with	the

4245		4824		5037	2983		694	2425
πρεσβυτέρων	συμβούλιόν	τε	λαβόντες		ἀργύρια	ἱκανὰ
older men	council	indeed	having taken		silver	enough

1325		015	4757		3004	3004	3754
ἔδωκαν	τοῖς	στρατιώταις	**13**	λέγοντες·	εἴπατε	ὅτι
they gave	to the	soldiers		saying,	say	that

013	3101	846	3571	2064		2813	846
οἱ	μαθηταὶ	αὐτοῦ	νυκτὸς	ἐλθόντες		ἔκλεψαν	αὐτὸν
the	learners	of him	of night	having come		thieved	him

1473	2837		2532	1437	191		3778	1909
ἡμῶν	κοιμωμένων.	**14**	καὶ	ἐὰν	ἀκουσθῇ		τοῦτο	ἐπὶ
of us	sleeping.		And	if	might be heard		this	on

02	2232	1473	3982		846	2532	1473
τοῦ	ἡγεμόνος,	ἡμεῖς	πείσομεν	[αὐτὸν]	καὶ	ὑμᾶς
the	leader,	we	will persuade		him	and	you

275   4160   13   1161 2983   024
ἀμερίμνους ποιήσομεν. **15** οἱ   δὲ λαβόντες   τὰ
unanxious   we will make. The ones but having taken the
694   4160   5613 1321   2532
ἀργύρια ἐποίησαν ὡς   ἐδιδάχθησαν.   καὶ
silver   did   as   they were taught.   And
1310   01   3056 3778 3844   2453
διεφημίσθη   ὁ   λόγος οὗτος παρὰ   Ἰουδαίοις
was spoken thoroughly the word this along   Judeans
3360   06   4594   2250   013 1161 1733
μέχρι τῆς σήμερον [ἡμέρας]. **16** Οἱ δὲ ἕνδεκα
until the today   day.   The but eleven
3101   4198   1519 08 1056   1519 012 3735
μαθηταὶ ἐπορεύθησαν εἰς τὴν Γαλιλαίαν εἰς τὸ ὄρος
learners traveled   into the Galilee to the hill
3757 5021   846   01 2424   2532
οὗ   ἐτάξατο   αὐτοῖς ὁ Ἰησοῦς, **17** καὶ
where set in order to them the Jesus,   and
3708   846   4352   013   1161
ἰδόντες   αὐτὸν προσεκύνησαν, οἱ   δὲ
having seen him   they worshiped, the ones but
1365   18   2532 4334   01 2424   2980
ἐδίστασαν.   καὶ προσελθὼν   ὁ Ἰησοῦς ἐλάλησεν
doubted.   And having come to the Jesus   spoke
846   3004   1325   1473 3956 1849   1722
αὐτοῖς λέγων· ἐδόθη   μοι πᾶσα ἐξουσία ἐν
to them saying, was given to me all authority in
3772   2532 1909 06   1093 19 4198   3767
οὐρανῷ καὶ ἐπὶ [τῆς] γῆς.   πορευθέντες   οὖν
heaven and on the   land.   Having traveled then
3100   3956   024 1484   907   846
μαθητεύσατε πάντα τὰ ἔθνη, βαπτίζοντες αὐτοὺς
make learners all the nations, immersing   them
1519 012 3686 02   3962   2532 02   5207 2532
εἰς τὸ ὄνομα τοῦ πατρὸς καὶ τοῦ υἱοῦ καὶ
into the name of the father and of the son and
010   40   4151   1321   846   5083
τοῦ ἁγίου πνεύματος, **20** διδάσκοντες αὐτοὺς τηρεῖν
of the holy spirit,   teaching   them   to keep
3956 3745   1781   1473 2532 2400 1473
πάντα ὅσα   ἐνετειλάμην ὑμῖν· καὶ ἰδοὺ ἐγὼ
all   as much as I commanded to you; and look I
3326 1473 1510 3956 020 2250   2193 06
μεθ᾽ ὑμῶν εἰμι πάσας τὰς ἡμέρας ἕως   τῆς
with you   am all   the days   until the
4930   02   165
συντελείας   τοῦ αἰῶνος.
full completion of the age.

keep you out of trouble." [15]So they took the money and did as they were directed. And this story is still told among the Jews to this day.

[16]Now the eleven disciples went to Galilee, to the mountain to which Jesus had directed them. [17]When they saw him, they worshiped him; but some doubted. [18]And Jesus came and said to them, "All authority in heaven and on earth has been given to me. [19]Go therefore and make disciples of all nations, baptizing them in the name of the Father and of the Son and of the Holy Spirit, [20]and teaching them to obey everything that I have commanded you. And remember, I am with you always, to the end of the age."[a]

[a] Other ancient authorities add *Amen*

MARK

CHAPTER 1

The beginning of the good news[a] of Jesus Christ, the Son of God.[b]

2 As it is written in the prophet Isaiah,[c]

"See, I am sending my messenger ahead of you,[d]

who will prepare your way;

3 the voice of one crying out in the wilderness:

'Prepare the way of the Lord,

make his paths straight,'"

[4]John the baptizer appeared[e] in the wilderness, proclaiming a baptism of repentance for the forgiveness of sins. [5]And people from the whole Judean countryside and all the people of Jerusalem were going out to him, and were baptized by him in the river Jordan, confessing their sins. [6]Now John was clothed with camel's hair, with a leather belt around his waist, and he ate locusts and wild honey. [7]He proclaimed, "The one who is more powerful than I is coming after me; I am not worthy to stoop down and untie the thong of his sandals. [8]I have baptized you with[f] water; but he will baptize you with[f] the Holy Spirit."

9 In those days Jesus came from Nazareth of Galilee and was baptized by John in the Jordan. [10]And just as he was coming out of the water, he saw the heavens torn apart

[a] Or gospel
[b] Other ancient authorities lack the Son of God
[c] Other ancient authorities read in the prophets
[d] Gk before your face
[e] Other ancient authorities read John was baptizing
[f] Or in

1:1

746	010	2098		2424	5547

Ἀρχὴ   τοῦ   εὐαγγελίου   Ἰησοῦ Χριστοῦ
Beginning of the good message of Jesus Christ

| 5207 2316 | | 2531 | 1125 | | 1722 03 | 2268 | 03 |

[υἱοῦ θεοῦ]. **2** Καθὼς γέγραπται ἐν τῷ Ἡσαΐᾳ τῷ
son of God.   Just as it has been in   the Isaiah the
written

| 4396 | 2400 649 | | 04 32 | | 1473 | 4253 |

προφήτῃ·   ἰδοὺ ἀποστέλλω τὸν ἀγγελόν μου   πρὸ
spokesman,   look I delegate the messenger of me before

| 4383 | 1473 | 3739 2680 | | 08 | 3598 1473 |

προσώπου σου,   ὃς   κατασκευάσει τὴν ὁδόν σου·
face   of you, who will prepare the way of you;

3 | 5456 | 994 | | 1722 07 | 2048 | 2090 | 08 |

φωνὴ βοῶντος   ἐν   τῇ ἐρήμῳ·   ἑτοιμάσατε τὴν
voice crying aloud in   the desert, prepare   the

| 3598 2962 | | 2117a | 4160 | 020 5147 | 846 |

ὁδὸν κυρίου,   εὐθείας ποιεῖτε τὰς τρίβους αὐτοῦ,
way of Master, straight make   the paths   of him,

4 | 1096 | 2491 | 01 907 | | 1722 07 | 2048 | 2532 |

ἐγένετο Ἰωάννης [ὁ] βαπτίζων ἐν   τῇ ἐρήμῳ καὶ
became   John   the immersing in   the desert and

| 2784 | 908 | 3341 | | 1519 859 |

κηρύσσων βάπτισμα μετανοίας   εἰς ἄφεσιν
announcing immersion of mind change for   sending off

| 266 | **5** 2532 1607 | | | 4314 | 846 | 3956 |

ἁμαρτιῶν. **5** καὶ ἐξεπορεύετο   πρὸς αὐτὸν πᾶσα
of sins.   And   was traveling out toward him   all

| 05 | 2453 | 2532 013 | 2415 | | 3956 | 2532 |

ἡ Ἰουδαία χώρα καὶ οἱ   Ἰεροσολυμῖται πάντες, καὶ
the Judean country and the   Jerusalemites all,   and

| 907 | | | 5259 846 | 1722 03 | | 2446 |

ἐβαπτίζοντο   ὑπ' αὐτοῦ ἐν   τῷ Ἰορδάνῃ
they were being immersed by   him   in   the Jordan

| 4215 | 1843 | 020 266 | 846 | **6** 2532 |

ποταμῷ ἐξομολογούμενοι τὰς ἁμαρτίας αὐτῶν. **6** καὶ
river confessing out   the sins   of them. And

| 1510 01 | 2491 | 1746 | 2359 | 2435 | 2532 |

ἦν   ὁ   Ἰωάννης ἐνδεδυμένος τρίχας καμήλου καὶ
was+ the John   +having put on   hairs of camel and

| 2223 | 1193 | 4012 | 08 3751 | 846 | 2532 2068 |

ζώνην δερματίνην περὶ   τὴν ὀσφὺν αὐτοῦ καὶ ἐσθίων
belt of skin   around the hip   of him and +eating

| 200 | 2532 3192 | 66 | **7** 2532 2784 |

ἀκρίδας καὶ μέλι ἄγριον. **7** Καὶ ἐκήρυσσεν
locusts and honey wild.   And he was announcing

| 3004 | 2064 | 01 | 2478 | | 1473 3694 | 1473 3739 |

λέγων·   ἔρχεται ὁ   ἰσχυρότερός μου ὀπίσω μου, οὗ
saying,   comes   the stronger of me after me, of whom

| 3756 1510 2425 | 2955 | | 3089 | 04 2438 |

οὐκ εἰμὶ ἱκανὸς κύψας   λῦσαι   τὸν ἱμάντα
not I am enough having bent down to loose the strap

| 022 | 5266 | 846 | **8** 1473 907 | 1473 5204 |

τῶν   ὑποδημάτων αὐτοῦ. **8** ἐγὼ ἐβάπτισα ὑμᾶς ὕδατι,
of the sandals   of him. I   immersed you in water,

| 846 | 1161 907 | | 1473 1722 4151 | 40 | **9** 2532 |

αὐτὸς δὲ βαπτίσει   ὑμᾶς ἐν πνεύματι ἁγίῳ. **9** Καὶ
himself but will immerse you   in spirit   holy.   And

| 1096 | 1722 1565 | 019 | 2250 | 2064 | 2424 |

ἐγένετο ἐν   ἐκείναις ταῖς ἡμέραις ἦλθεν Ἰησοῦς
it became in   those   the days   came Jesus

| 575 3478a | 06 | 1056 | 2532 907 | 1519 |

ἀπὸ Ναζαρὲτ τῆς   Γαλιλαίας καὶ ἐβαπτίσθη   εἰς
from Nazaret of the Galilee   and was immersed into

| 04 | 2446 | 5259 | 2491 | **10** 2532 2117 |

τὸν Ἰορδάνην ὑπὸ Ἰωάννου. **10** καὶ εὐθὺς
the Jordan   by   John.   And immediately

| 305 | 1537 010 | 5204 | 3708 | 4977 |

ἀναβαίνων ἐκ τοῦ   ὕδατος εἶδεν σχιζομένους
coming up out of the water   he saw being split

```
016    3772        2532  012  4151       5613  4058
τοὺς οὐρανοὺς καὶ τὸ πνεῦμα ὡς περιστερὰν
the  heavens  and  the spirit  as  dove
2597           1519  846    11  2532 5456   1096      1537
καταβαῖνον εἰς αὐτόν·      καὶ φωνὴ ἐγένετο ἐκ
coming down into  him;        and sound became  out of
014  3772      1473 1510  01  5207 1473  01   27        1722
τῶν οὐρανῶν· σὺ  εἶ  ὁ  υἱός μου ὁ ἀγαπητός,  ἐν
the heavens,  you  are the son of me the loved one,  in
1473 2106        12  2532 2117        09    4151    846
σοὶ εὐδόκησα.     Καὶ εὐθὺς    τὸ πνεῦμα αὐτὸν
you I thought well. And immediately the spirit him
1544      1519 08 2048      2532 1510    1722 07
ἐκβάλλει εἰς τὴν ἔρημον. 13 καὶ ἦν  ἐν  τῇ
throws out into the desert.    And he was in  the
2048  5062        2250  3985          5259 02
ἐρήμῳ τεσσεράκοντα ἡμέρας πειραζόμενος ὑπὸ τοῦ
desert forty       days  being pressured by  the
4567      2532 1510  3326 022 2342         2532 013
σατανᾶ,  καὶ ἦν  μετὰ τῶν θηρίων,   καὶ οἱ
adversary, and  he was with the wild animals, and  the
32      1247     846   14  3326 1161 012 3860
ἄγγελοι διηκόνουν αὐτῷ.   Μετὰ δὲ τὸ παραδοθῆναι
messengers were   him.   After but the to be
        serving                   given over
04   2491    2064  01  2424    1519 08  1056
τὸν Ἰωάννην ἦλθεν ὁ Ἰησοῦς εἰς τὴν Γαλιλαίαν
the John   came  the Jesus into the Galilee
2784       012 2098        02      2316  15 2532 3004
κηρύσσων τὸ εὐαγγέλιον τοῦ θεοῦ   καὶ λέγων
announcing the good message of the God  and saying,
3754 4137          01   2540   2532 1448       05
ὅτι πεπλήρωται ὁ καιρὸς καὶ ἤγγικεν ἡ
(") has been filled the season and has neared the
932       02     2316  3340      2532 4100      1722
βασιλεία τοῦ θεοῦ· μετανοεῖτε καὶ πιστεύετε ἐν
kingdom of the God;  change mind and trust    in
011 2098       16 2532 3855       3844 08  2281
τῷ εὐαγγελίῳ.    Καὶ παράγων  παρὰ τὴν θάλασσαν
the good message. And leading along along the sea
06    1056       3708  4613   2532 406      04
τῆς Γαλιλαίας εἶδεν Σίμωνα καὶ Ἀνδρέαν τὸν
of the Galilee he saw Simon and Andrew the
80      4613    292a              1722 07  2281
ἀδελφὸν Σίμωνος ἀμφιβάλλοντας ἐν τῇ θαλάσσῃ·
brother of Simon throwing around(nets) in the sea;
1510   1063 231     17 2532 3004   846      01 2424
ἦσαν γὰρ ἁλιεῖς·    καὶ εἶπεν αὐτοῖς ὁ Ἰησους,
they were for fishermen. And said to them the Jesus,
1205  3694  1473 2532 4160       1473 1096
δεῦτε ὀπίσω μου, καὶ ποιήσω ὑμᾶς γενέσθαι
come after me,  and I will make you to become
231    444      18 2532 2117       863
ἁλιεῖς ἀνθρώπων.    καὶ εὐθὺς     ἀφέντες
fishermen of men.    And immediately having sent off
024 1350   190        846     19 2532 4260
τὰ δίκτυα ἠκολούθησαν αὐτῷ.    Καὶ προβὰς
the nets they followed him.    And having gone before
3641   3708  2385    04 02  2199       2532
ὀλίγον εἶδεν Ἰάκωβον τὸν τοῦ Ζεβεδαίου καὶ
little he saw Jacob  the of the Zebedee  and
2491    04 80   846      2532 846   1722 011
Ἰωάννην τὸν ἀδελφὸν αὐτοῦ καὶ αὐτοὺς ἐν τῷ
John   the brother of him and them  in the
4143  2675        024 1350  20 2532 2117
πλοίῳ καταρτίζοντας τὰ δίκτυα,   καὶ εὐθὺς
boat putting in order the nets,  and immediately
2564    846    2532 863        04   3962
ἐκάλεσεν αὐτούς. καὶ ἀφέντες τὸν πατέρα
he called them.  And having sent off the father
```

and the Spirit descending like a dove on him. [11]And a voice came from heaven, "You are my Son, the Beloved;[a] with you I am well pleased."

12 And the Spirit immediately drove him out into the wilderness. [13]He was in the wilderness forty days, tempted by Satan; and he was with the wild beasts; and the angels waited on him.

14 Now after John was arrested, Jesus came to Galilee, proclaiming the good news[b] of God,[c] [15]and saying, "The time is fulfilled, and the kingdom of God has come near;[d] repent, and believe in the good news."[b]

16 As Jesus passed along the Sea of Galilee, he saw Simon and his brother Andrew casting a net into the sea—for they were fishermen. [17]And Jesus said to them, "Follow me and I will make you fish for people." [18]And immediately they left their nets and followed him. [19]As he went a little farther, he saw James son of Zebedee and his brother John, who were in their boat mending the nets. [20]Immediately he called them; and they left their father

[a] Or my beloved Son
[b] Or gospel
[c] Other ancient authorities read of the kingdom
[d] Or is at hand

Zebedee in the boat with
the hired men, and followed
him.
²¹They went to
Capernaum; and when the
sabbath came, he entered
the synagogue and taught.
²²They were astounded at
his teaching, for he taught
them as one having
authority, and not as the
scribes. ²³Just then there
was in their synagogue a
man with an unclean spirit,
²⁴and he cried out, "What
have you to do with us,
Jesus of Nazareth? Have
you come to destroy us?
I know who you are, the
Holy One of God." ²⁵But
Jesus rebuked him, saying,
"Be silent, and come out of
him!" ²⁶And the unclean
spirit, convulsing him and
crying with a loud voice,
came out of him. ²⁷They
were all amazed, and they
kept on asking one another,
"What is this? A new
teaching—with authority!
He*ᵃ* commands even the
unclean spirits, and they
obey him." ²⁰At once his fame
began to spread throughout
the surrounding region of
Galilee.

29 As soon as they*ᵇ* left
the synagogue, they entered
the house of Simon and
Andrew, with James and
John. ³⁰Now Simon's

ᵃ Or *A new teaching! With
authority he*

ᵇ Other ancient authorities read *he*

846	2199		1722 011	4143	3326 014 3411
αὐτῶν	Ζεβεδαῖον	ἐν	τῷ	πλοίῳ μετὰ	τῶν μισθωτῶν
of them	Zebedee	in	the	boat with	the wage earners

565   3694   846   2532 1531   1519
ἀπῆλθον   ὀπίσω αὐτοῦ. **21** Καὶ εἰσπορεύονται   εἰς
they went off after him.   And they travel into into

2746a   2532 2117   023   4521
Καφαρναούμ· καὶ   εὐθὺς   τοῖς σάββασιν
Capernaum;   and immediately in the sabbaths

1525   1519 08 4864   1321
εἰσελθὼν   εἰς τὴν συναγωγὴν ἐδίδασκεν.
having gone into into the synagogue he was teaching.

   2532 1605   1909 07   1322   846
22 καὶ ἐξεπλήσσοντο   ἐπὶ τῇ διδαχῇ   αὐτοῦ·
      And they were astonished at   the teaching of him;

1510   1063 1321   846   5613 1849   2192   2532
ἦν   γὰρ διδάσκων αὐτοὺς ὡς ἐξουσίαν ἔχων καὶ
he was+ for +teaching them as   authority having and

3756 5613 013 1122   2532 2117   1510 1722
οὐχ ὡς οἱ γραμματεῖς. **23** Καὶ εὐθὺς   ἦν   ἐν
not as the writers.   And immediately was in

07 4864   846   444   1722 4151   169
τῇ συναγωγῇ αὐτῶν ἄνθρωπος ἐν πνεύματι ἀκαθάρτῳ
the synagogue of them man   in spirit   unclean

2532 349   3004   5101 1473   2532 1473
καὶ ἀνέκραξεν **24** λέγων· τί ἡμῖν καὶ σοί,
and he shouted out   saying, what to us and to you,

2424   3479   2064   622   1473 3609a 1473
Ἰησοῦ Ναζαρηνέ; ἦλθες ἀπολέσαι ἡμᾶς; οἶδά σε
Jesus Nazarene? Came you to destroy us? I know you

5101 1510   01 40   02   2316   25 2532 2008
τίς εἶ,   ὁ ἅγιος τοῦ θεοῦ. **25** καὶ ἐπετίμησεν
who you are, the holy of the God.   And admonished

846 01 2424   3004   5392   2532 1831   1537
αὐτῷ ὁ Ἰησοῦς λέγων· φιμώθητι καὶ ἔξελθε ἐξ
him the Jesus saying, be muzzled and come out from

846   26 2532 4682   846   09 4151   09
αὐτοῦ. **26** καὶ σπαράξαν   αὐτὸν τὸ πνεῦμα τὸ
him.   And having convulsed him   the spirit the

169   2532 5455   5456   3173   1831
ἀκάθαρτον καὶ φωνῆσαν   φωνῇ μεγάλη ἐξῆλθεν
unclean   and having sounded sound great he came out

1537 846   2532 2284   537   5620
ἐξ αὐτοῦ. **27** καὶ ἐθαμβήθησαν ἅπαντες ὥστε
out of him.   And were astonished all   so that

4802   4314 1438   3004   5101 1510 3778
συζητεῖν πρὸς ἑαυτοὺς λέγοντας· τί ἐστιν τοῦτο;
to dispute to themselves saying, what is   this?

1322   2537 2596 1849   2532 023   4151
διδαχὴ καινὴ κατ' ἐξουσίαν· καὶ τοῖς   πνεύμασι
Teaching new by   authority; and to the spirits

023   169   2004   2532 5219   846
τοῖς ἀκαθάρτοις ἐπιτάσσει, καὶ ὑπακούουσιν αὐτῷ.
the unclean   he orders, and they obey   him.

   2532 1831   05 189   846   2117
28 καὶ ἐξῆλθεν ἡ ἀκοὴ   αὐτοῦ εὐθὺς
      And went out the hearing of him immediately

3837   1519 3650 08 4066   06
πανταχοῦ εἰς ὅλην τὴν περίχωρον   τῆς
all places into whole the country around of the

1056   2532 2117   1537 06 4864
Γαλιλαίας. **29** Καὶ εὐθὺς   ἐκ τῆς συναγωγῆς
Galilee.   And immediately from the synagogue

1831   2064   1519 08 3614   4613
ἐξελθόντες   ἦλθον εἰς τὴν οἰκίαν Σίμωνος
having come out they went into the house of Simon

2532 406   3326 2385   2532 2491   05 1161
καὶ Ἀνδρέου μετὰ Ἰακώβου καὶ Ἰωάννου. **30** ἡ δὲ
and Andrew with Jacob and John.   The but

```
3994          4613      2621              4445              2532
πενθερὰ      Σίμωνος  κατέκειτο        πυρέσσουσα, καὶ
mother-in-law of Simon was lying down burning,          and
2117          3004      846    4012        846          2532
εὐθὺς        λέγουσιν αὐτῷ  περὶ      αὐτῆς.    31 καὶ
immediately they say to him concerning her.       And
4334          1453      846    2902
προσελθὼν    ἤγειρεν  αὐτὴν κρατήσας
having gone toward he raised her having held
06   5495     2532 863  846    01    4446        2532
τῆς χειρός· καὶ ἀφῆκεν αὐτὴν ὁ πυρετός, καὶ
the hand;  and left  her   the fever,   and
1247          846          3798    1161 1096
διηκόνει    αὐτοῖς. 32 Ὀψίας  δὲ γενομένης,
she was serving them.    Evening but having become
3753 1416 01   2246   5342              4314
ὅτε ἔδυ ὁ ἥλιος, ἔφερον          πρὸς
when set the sun,  they were carrying to
846   3956    016   2560  2192        2532 016
αὐτὸν πάντας τοὺς κακῶς ἔχοντας    καὶ τοὺς
him   all   the  badly ones having and the
1139                    2532 1510 3650  05   4172
δαιμονιζομένους· 33 καὶ ἦν ὅλη ἡ πόλις
ones being demonized; and was+ whole the city
1996                        4314 08   2374       34 2532
ἐπισυνηγμένη              πρὸς τὴν θύραν.      καὶ
+having been brought together to   the door.  And
2323          4183      2560 2192        4164
ἐθεράπευσεν πολλοὺς κακῶς ἔχοντας    ποικίλαις
he healed  many    badly ones having various
3554       2532 1140     4183 1544        2532 3756
νόσοις    καὶ δαιμόνια πολλὰ ἐξέβαλεν καὶ οὐκ
illnesses and demons  many he threw out and not
863         2980      024 1140       3754
ἤφιεν      λαλεῖν   τὰ δαιμόνια, ὅτι
he was allowing to speak the demons, because
3609a        846      35 2532 4404   1773     3029
ἤδεισαν    αὐτόν.    Καὶ πρωῒ ἔννυχα λίαν
they had known him.   And morning in night very
450          1831      2532 565      1519 2048
ἀναστὰς    ἐξῆλθεν  καὶ ἀπῆλθεν εἰς ἔρημον
having stood up he went out and he went off to desert
5117 2546    4336          36 2532 2614
τόπον κἀκεῖ προσηύχετο.    καὶ κατεδίωξεν
place and there he was praying.  And pursued after
846   4613 2532 013      3326 846  37 2532
αὐτὸν Σίμων καὶ οἱ    μετ' αὐτοῦ, καὶ
him   Simon and the ones with him,    and
2147         846    2532 3004    846    3754 3956
εὗρον       αὐτὸν καὶ λέγουσιν αὐτῷ ὅτι πάντες
they found him  and they say to him, (") all
2212        1473 38 2532 3004    846    71
ζητοῦσίν σε.   καὶ λέγει αὐτοῖς· ἄγωμεν
seek     you.   And he says to them, we might lead
237a        1519 020 2192     2969        2443 2532
ἀλλαχοῦ εἰς τὰς ἐχομένας κωμοπόλεις, ἵνα καὶ
elsewhere to the having village cities, that also
1563 2784              1519 3778  1063 1831
ἐκεῖ κηρύξω·        εἰς τοῦτο γὰρ ἐξῆλθον.
there I might announce; into this for I came out.
   2532 2064   2784        1519 020 4864      846
39 Καὶ ἦλθεν κηρύσσων εἰς τὰς συναγωγὰς αὐτῶν
   And he went announcing in the synagogues of them
1519-3650  08  1056     2532 024 1140      1544
εἰς ὅλην τὴν Γαλιλαίαν καὶ τὰ δαιμόνια ἐκβάλλων.
in  whole the Galilee  and the demons  throwing out.
   2532 2064   4314    846    3015  3870      846
40 Καὶ ἔρχεται πρὸς αὐτὸν λεπρὸς παρακαλῶν αὐτὸν
   And comes  toward him  leper  encouraging him
```

mother-in-law was in bed with a fever, and they told him about her at once. [31]He came and took her by the hand and lifted her up. Then the fever left her, and she began to serve them.

[32]That evening, at sundown, they brought to him all who were sick or possessed with demons. [33]And the whole city was gathered around the door. [34]And he cured many who were sick with various diseases, and cast out many demons; and he would not permit the demons to speak, because they knew him.

[35]In the morning, while it was still very dark, he got up and went out to a deserted place, and there he prayed. [36]And Simon and his companions hunted for him. [37]When they found him, they said to him, "Everyone is searching for you." [38]He answered, "Let us go on to the neighboring towns, so that I may proclaim the message there also; for that is what I came out to do." [39]And he went throughout Galilee, proclaiming the message in their synagogues and casting out demons.

[40]A leper[a] came to him begging him,

[a] The terms leper and leprosy can refer to several diseases

and kneeling*a* he said to him, "If you choose, you can make me clean." [41]Moved with pity,*b* Jesus*c* stretched out his hand and touched him, and said to him, "I do choose. Be made clean!" [42]Immediately the leprosy*d* left him, and he was made clean. [43]After sternly warning him he sent him away at once, [44]saying to him, "See that you say nothing to anyone; but go, show yourself to the priest, and offer for your cleansing what Moses commanded, as a testimony to them." [45]But he went out and began to proclaim it freely, and to spread the word, so that Jesus*c* could no longer go into a town openly, but stayed out in the country; and people came to him from every quarter.

CHAPTER 2

When he returned to Capernaum after some days, it was reported that he was at home. [2]So many gathered around that there was no longer room for them, not even in front of the door; and he was speaking the word to them. [3]Then some people*e* came, bringing to him a paralyzed man, carried by four of them. [4]And when they could not bring him to Jesus because of the crowd, they removed the roof above him; and

a Other ancient authorities lack kneeling
b Other ancient authorities read anger
c Gk he
d The terms leper and leprosy can refer to several diseases
e Gk they

2532 1120		2532 3004 846	3754 1437
[καὶ γονυπετῶν]	καὶ	λέγων αὐτῷ	ὅτι ἐὰν
and falling on knees	and	saying to him,	(") if

2309	1410	1473 2511	2532
θέλῃς	δύνασαί	με καθαρίσαι. [41]	καὶ
you might want	you are able	me to clean.	And

4697   1614   08 5495
σπλαγχνισθεὶς   ἐκτείνας   τὴν χεῖρα
having had affection having stretched out the hand

846   681   2532 3004   846   2309
αὐτοῦ ἥψατο   καὶ λέγει αὐτῷ·   θέλω,
of him he touched   and he says to him, I want,

2511   2532 2511   565   575
καθαρίσθητι· [42] καὶ εὐθὺς   ἀπῆλθεν ἀπ᾽
be clean;   and immediately went off from

846   05 3014   2532 2511   43 2532
αὐτοῦ ἡ λέπρα,   καὶ ἐκαθαρίσθη.   καὶ
him the leprosy, and he was cleaned. And

1690   846   2117   1544
ἐμβριμησάμενος   αὐτῷ εὐθὺς   ἐξέβαλεν
having been indignant to him immediately he threw out

846   44 2532 3004   846   3708 3367   3367
αὐτόν   καὶ λέγει αὐτῷ·   ὅρα μηδενὶ   μηδὲν
him   and he says to him, see to no one nothing

3004   235 5217   4572   1166   03   2409
εἴπῃς,   ἀλλὰ ὕπαγε σεαυτὸν δεῖξον τῷ ἱερεῖ
you might say, but go off yourself show to the priest

2532 4374   4012 02 2512   1473   3739
καὶ προσένεγκε περὶ τοῦ καθαρισμοῦ σου   ἃ
and make offering about the cleaning of you what

4367   3475   1519 3142   846   45 01
προσέταξεν Μωϋσῆς, εἰς μαρτύριον αὐτοῖς.   ὁ
commanded Moses, for testimony to them. The one

1161 1831   757   2784   4183 2532
δὲ ἐξελθὼν   ἤρξατο κηρύσσειν   πολλὰ καὶ
but having gone out began to announce many and

1310   04 3056   5620   3371   846
διαφημίζειν   τὸν λόγον, ὥστε μηκέτι   αὐτὸν
to speak thoroughly the word, so that no longer him

1410   5320   1519 4172 1525   235   1854
δύνασθαι φανερῶς εἰς πόλιν εἰσελθεῖν, ἀλλ᾽ ἔξω
to be able openly into city to go into, but outside

1909 2048   5117   1510   2532 2064   4314
ἐπ᾽ ἐρήμοις τόποις ἦν·   καὶ ἤρχοντο   πρὸς
on desert places he was; and they were coming to

846   3840   2:1 2532 1525   3825 1519
αὐτὸν πάντοθεν.   Καὶ εἰσελθὼν   πάλιν εἰς
him from everywhere. And having gone into again into

2746a   1223   2250 191   3754 1722 3624
Καφαρναοὺμ δι᾽   ἡμερῶν ἠκούσθη   ὅτι ἐν οἴκῳ
Capernaum through days it was heard that in house

1510   2 2532 4863   4183 5620
ἐστίν.   καὶ συνήχθησαν   πολλοὶ ὥστε
he is.   And were brought together many so that

3371   5562   3366   024 4314 08 2374 2532 2980
μηκέτι χωρεῖν μηδὲ   τὰ πρὸς τὴν θύραν, καὶ ἐλάλει
no   to make but not the to the door, and he was
longer room   speaking

846   04 3056   3 2532 2064   5342   4314
αὐτοῖς τὸν λόγον.   καὶ ἔρχονται φέροντες πρὸς
to them the word.   And they come carrying toward

846   3885   142   5259 5064
αὐτὸν παραλυτικὸν αἰρόμενον   ὑπὸ τεσσάρων.
him paralyzed one being lifted up by four.

4 2532 3361 1410   4374   846 1223   04
   καὶ μὴ δυνάμενοι προσενέγκαι αὐτῷ διὰ   τὸν
   And not being able to bring to him because of the

3793   648   08 4721   3699 1510   2532
ὄχλον ἀπεστέγασαν τὴν στέγην ὅπου ἦν,   καὶ
crowd they unroofed the roof where he was, and

```
1846            5465          04  2895         3699    01
ἐξορύξαντες    χαλῶσι       τὸν κράβαττον ὅπου   ὁ
having dug out they lower  the mat          where  the
3885            2621              5  2532 3708        01
παραλυτικὸς   κατέκειτο.       καὶ ἰδὼν           ὁ
paralyzed one was lying down.  And  having seen the
2424    08   4102    846        3004  03     3885
Ἰησοῦς  τὴν πίστιν αὐτῶν    λέγει  τῷ     παραλυτικῷ·
Jesus  the trust  of them  says   to the paralyzed one,
5043     863             1473  017 266       6  1510
τέκνον, ἀφίενταί        σου   αἱ ἁμαρτίαι.     ἦσαν
child,  are being sent off of you the sins.    Were+
1161 5100 014   1122      1563  2521       2532
δέ  τινες τῶν  γραμματεων ἐκεῖ καθήμενοι καὶ
but some of the writers  there +sitting  and
1260         1722 019  2588    846       7 5101 3778
διαλογιζόμενοι ἐν  ταῖς καρδίαις αὐτῶν·    τί  οὗτος
+reasoning    in  the  hearts of them,    why this
3779   2980    987       5101 1410    863
οὕτως λαλεῖ;  βλασφημεῖ·  τίς δύναται ἀφιέναι
thusly speaks? He insults; who is able to send off
266     1487 3361 1520 01  2316       8 2532 2117
ἁμαρτίας εἰ  μὴ  εἷς  ὁ  θεός;      καὶ εὐθὺς
sins     except one  the God?      And  immediately
1921        01  2424 011    4151     846    3754
ἐπιγνοὺς      ὁ Ἰησοῦς τῷ    πνεύματι αὐτοῦ ὅτι
having perceived the Jesus in the spirit of him that
3779   1260      1722 1438    3004    846
οὕτως διαλογίζονται ἐν  ἑαυτοῖς λέγει αὐτοῖς·
thusly they reason  in  themselves he says to them,
5101 3778 1260      1722 019 2588     1473
τί  ταῦτα διαλογίζεσθε ἐν  ταῖς καρδίαις ὑμῶν;
why these you reason  in  the  hearts  of you?
   9 5101 1510 2123        3004  03     3885
    τί  ἐστιν εὐκοπώτερον, εἰπεῖν τῷ    παραλυτικῷ·
    What is   easier labor, to say to the paralyzed one;
  863           1473  017 266    2228 3004  1453
Ἀφίενταί       σου   αἱ ἁμαρτίαι, ἢ  εἰπεῖν· ἔγειρε
are sent off of you the sins,    or to say, raise
2532 142     04  2895       1473  2532 4043
καὶ ἄρον    τὸν κράβαττόν σου   καὶ περιπάτει;
and lift up the mat        of you and  walk around?
  10 2443 1161 3609a        3754 1849      2192 01
     ἵνα δὲ  εἰδῆτε        ὅτι ἐξουσίαν ἔχει ὁ
     That but  you might know that authority has the
5207 02   444         863         266      1909 06
υἱὸς τοῦ ἀνθρώπου ἀφιέναι    ἁμαρτίας ἐπὶ τῆς
son of the man      to send off sins    on the
1093   3004  03   3885          11 1473 3004
γῆς  - λέγει τῷ    παραλυτικῷ·    σοὶ λέγω,
earth  he says to the paralyzed one, to you I say,
1453   142   04  2895      1473  2532 5217  1519
ἔγειρε ἄρον τὸν κράβαττόν σου   καὶ ὕπαγε εἰς
raise lift up the mat      of you and  go off into
04  3624 1473   12 2532 1453   2532 2117
τὸν οἶκόν σου.    καὶ ἠγέρθη  καὶ εὐθὺς
the house of you.  And he was raised and immediately
142          04  2895     1831     1715
ἄρας       τὸν κράβαττον ἐξῆλθεν ἔμπροσθεν
having lifted up the mat  he went out in front of
3956   5620  1839      3956 2532 1392
πάντων, ὥστε ἐξίστασθαι πάντας καὶ δοξάζειν
all,  so that to be amazed all  and to give splendor
04  2316 3004    3754 3779   3763      3708
τὸν θεὸν λέγοντας ὅτι οὕτως οὐδέποτε εἴδομεν.
the God saying,  (") thusly but not ever we saw.
  13 2532 1831      3825 3844 08  2281    2532 3956
     Καὶ ἐξῆλθεν    πάλιν παρὰ τὴν θάλασσαν· καὶ πᾶς
     And he went out again along the sea;    and all
```

after having dug through it, they let down the mat on which the paralytic lay. [5]When Jesus saw their faith, he said to the paralytic, "Son, your sins are forgiven." [6]Now some of the scribes were sitting there, questioning in their hearts, [7]"Why does this fellow speak in this way? It is blasphemy! Who can forgive sins but God alone?" [8]At once Jesus perceived in his spirit that they were discussing these questions among themselves; and he said to them, "Why do you raise such questions in your hearts? [9]Which is easier, to say to the paralytic, 'Your sins are forgiven,' or to say, 'Stand up and take your mat and walk'? [10]But so that you may know that the Son of Man has authority on earth to forgive sins"—he said to the paralytic— [11]"I say to you, stand up, take your mat and go to your home." [12]And he stood up, and immediately took the mat and went out before all of them; so that they were all amazed and glorified God, saying, "We have never seen anything like this!"

[13]Jesus[a] went out again beside the sea; the whole

[a] Gk He

crowd gathered around
him, and he taught them.
[14]As he was walking along,
he saw Levi son of Alphaeus
sitting at the tax booth,
and he said to him, "Follow
me." And he got up and
followed him.

15 And as he sat at dinner[a]
in Levi's[b] house, many tax
collectors and sinners were
also sitting[c] with Jesus and
his disciples—for there
were many who followed
him. [16]When the scribes of[d]
the Pharisees saw that he
was eating with sinners and
tax collectors, they said to
his disciples, "Why does he
eat[e] with tax collectors and
sinners?" [17]When Jesus
heard this, he said to them,
"Those who are well have
no need of a physician,
but those who are sick;
I have come to call not the
righteous but sinners."

18 Now John's disciples
and the Pharisees were
fasting; and people[f] came
and said to him, "Why do
John's disciples and the
disciples of the Pharisees
fast, but your disciples do
not fast?" [19]Jesus said to
them, "The wedding guests
cannot fast while the
bridegroom is with them,
can they? As long as they
have the bridegroom with
them, they cannot fast.

[a] Gk *reclined*
[b] Gk *his*
[c] Gk *reclining*
[d] Other ancient authorities read *and*
[e] Other ancient authorities add *and drink*
[f] Gk *they*

01	3793	2064		4314	846		2532	1321
ὁ	ὄχλος	ἤρχετο		πρὸς	αὐτόν,	καὶ		ἐδίδασκεν
the	crowd	was coming	to	him,	and		he was teaching

846 2532 2064   3708 3018 04 02
αὐτούς. **14** Καὶ παράγων   εἶδεν Λευὶν τὸν τὸ τοῦ
them.   And leading along he saw Levi the of the

256   2521   1909 012 5058   2532 3004
Ἀλφαίου καθήμενον ἐπὶ τὸ τελώνιον, καὶ λέγει
Alphaeus sitting   on the tax table, and he says

846   190   1473 2532 450   190
αὐτῷ· ἀκολούθει μοι. καὶ ἀναστὰς   ἠκολούθησεν
to him, follow   me. And having stood up he followed

846 2532 1096   2621   846 1722 07
αὐτῷ. **15** Καὶ γίνεται   κατακεῖσθαι αὐτὸν ἐν τῇ
him.   And it becomes to lie down him in   the

3614 846   2532 4183   5057   2532 268
οἰκίᾳ αὐτοῦ, καὶ πολλοὶ τελῶναι καὶ ἁμαρτωλοὶ
house of him, and many tax men and sinners

4873   03   2424 2532 015   3101
συνανέκειντο   τῷ   Ἰησοῦ καὶ τοῖς μαθηταῖς
were reclining together to the Jesus and the learners

846   1510 1063 4183 2532 190   846 16 2532
αὐτοῦ· ἦσαν γὰρ πολλοὶ καὶ ἠκολούθουν αὐτῷ. καὶ
of him; there for many and they were him.   And
       were   following

013 1122   014 5330   3708   3754 2068
οἱ γραμματεῖς τῶν Φαρισαίων ἰδόντες   ὅτι ἐσθίει
the writers of the Pharisees having seen that he eats

3326 014 268   2532 5057 3004   015
μετὰ τῶν ἁμαρτωλῶν καὶ τελωνῶν ἔλεγον   τοῖς
with the sinners   and taxmen were saying to the

3101 846   3754 3326 014 5057   2532 268
μαθηταῖς αὐτοῦ· ὅτι μετὰ τῶν τελωνῶν καὶ ἁμαρτωλῶν
learners of him, (") with the tax men and sinners

2068   17 2532 191   01 2424 3004 846
ἐσθίει; καὶ ἀκούσας   ὁ Ἰησοῦς λέγει αὐτοῖς
he eats? And having heard the Jesus says to them,

3754 3756 5532 2192   013 2480
[ὅτι] οὐ χρείαν ἔχουσιν οἱ ἰσχύοντες
(") not need   have   the ones being strong

2395   235 013   2560 2192   3756 2064
ἰατροῦ ἀλλ' οἱ   κακῶς ἔχοντες· οὐκ ἦλθον
of physician but the ones badly having; not I came

2564 1342   235 268   18 2532 1510 013
καλέσαι δικαίους ἀλλὰ ἁμαρτωλούς. Καὶ ἦσαν οἱ
to call right ones but sinners.   And were+ the

3101 2491 2532 013 5330   3522   2532
μαθηταὶ Ἰωάννου καὶ οἱ Φαρισαῖοι νηστεύοντες. καὶ
learners of John and the Pharisees +fasting.   And

2064   2532 3004   846   1223   5101 013
ἔρχονται καὶ λέγουσιν αὐτῷ· διὰ   τί οἱ
they come and say   to him, on account of what the

3101 2491   2532 013 3101   014 5330
μαθηταὶ Ἰωάννου καὶ οἱ μαθηταὶ τῶν Φαρισαίων
learners of John and the learners of the Pharisees

3522   013 1161 4674 3101   3756 3522
νηστεύουσιν, οἱ δὲ σοὶ μαθηταὶ οὐ νηστεύουσιν;
fast,   the but to you learners not fast?

19 2532 3004 846 01 2424 3361 1410 013
καὶ εἶπεν αὐτοῖς ὁ Ἰησοῦς· μὴ δύνανται οἱ
And said to them the Jesus, not are able the

5207 02   3567   1722 3739 01 3566
υἱοὶ τοῦ νυμφῶνος   ἐν ᾧ ὁ νυμφίος
sons of the bridal chamber in which the bridegroom

3326 846   1510 3522   3745   5550 2192
μετ' αὐτῶν ἐστιν νηστεύειν; ὅσον   χρόνον ἔχουσιν
with them is   to fast? As much as time   they have

04 3566   3326 846 3756 1410   3522
τὸν νυμφίον μετ' αὐτῶν οὐ δύνανται   νηστεύειν.
the bridegroom with them not they are able to fast.

20
```
  2064        1161 2250   3752 522              575
ἐλεύσονται δὲ ἡμέραι ὅταν ἀπαρθῇ          ἀπ᾽
Will come   but  days  when might be lifted up from
846   01   3566          2532 5119 3522          1722
αὐτῶν ὁ νυμφίος,  καὶ τότε νηστεύσουσιν ἐν
them  the bridegroom, and then they will fast in
1565    07 2250        3762    1915     4470    46
ἐκείνῃ τῇ ἡμέρᾳ.  21 Οὐδεὶς ἐπίβλημα ῥάκους ἀγνάφου
that    the day.     No one patch    cloth  unshrunk
1976     1909 2440    3820       1487 1161 3361 142
ἐπιράπτει ἐπὶ ἱμάτιον παλαιόν· εἰ δὲ μή, αἴρει
sews on   on  clothes old;     if but not, lifts up
012 4138    575  846    09 2537   010   3820
τὸ πλήρωμα ἀπ᾽ αὐτοῦ τὸ καινὸν τοῦ παλαιου
the fullness from itself the new of the old
2532 5501  4978   1096     2532 3762   906
καὶ χεῖρον σχίσμα γίνεται. 22 καὶ οὐδεὶς βάλλει
and worse  split  it becomes. And no one throws
3631 3501 1519 779       3820    1487 1161 3361
οἶνον νέον εἰς ἀσκοὺς παλαιούς· εἰ δὲ μή,
wine  new into wineskins old;    if but not,
4486   01 3631 016 779       2532 01 3631
ῥήξει ὁ οἶνος τοὺς ἀσκοὺς καὶ ὁ οἶνος
will rip the wine the wineskins and the wine
622       2532 013 779       235  3631 3501 1519
ἀπόλλυται καὶ οἱ ἀσκοί· ἀλλὰ οἶνον νέον εἰς
is destroyed and the wineskins; but wine new into
779      2537     23 2532 1096    846  1722 023
ἀσκοὺς καινούς.   Καὶ ἐγένετο αὐτὸν ἐν τοῖς
wineskins new.       And became him in the
4521     3899              1223    022 4702        2532
σάββασιν παραπορεύεσθαι διὰ τῶν σπορίμων, καὶ
sabbaths to travel along through the sown fields, and
013 3101   846    757     3598 4160     5089     016
οἱ μαθηταὶ αὐτοῦ ἤρξαντο ὁδὸν ποιεῖν τίλλοντες τοὺς
the learners of him began way to make picking the
4719        24 2532 013    5330       3004
στάχυας.      καὶ οἱ Φαρισαῖοι ἔλεγον
stalks of grain. And the Pharisees were saying
846    2396 5101 4160    023       4521     3739 3756
αὐτῷ· ἴδε τί ποιοῦσιν τοῖς σάββασιν ὃ οὐκ
to him, look why do they on the sabbaths what not
1832        25 2532 3004   846    3763
ἔξεστιν;     καὶ λέγει αὐτοῖς· οὐδέποτε
it is possible? And he says to them, but not ever
314        5101 4160    1160α 3753 5532   2192    2532
ἀνέγνωτε τί ἐποίησεν Δαυὶδ ὅτε χρείαν ἔσχεν καὶ
you read what did    David when need  he had and
3983       846    2532 013    3326 846       26 4459
ἐπείνασεν αὐτὸς καὶ οἱ μετ᾽ αὐτοῦ,    πῶς
he hungered himself and the ones with him,  how
1525      1519 04 3624 02    2316 1909  8
εἰσῆλθεν εἰς τὸν οἶκον τοῦ θεοῦ ἐπὶ Ἀβιαθὰρ
he went into into the house of the God on Abiathar
749       2532 016 740   06   4286       2068
ἀρχιερέως καὶ τοὺς ἄρτους τῆς προθέσεως ἔφαγεν,
ruler priest and the breads of the purpose he ate,
3739 3756 1832    2068 1487 3361 1016 2409
οὓς οὐκ ἔξεστιν φαγεῖν εἰ μὴ τοὺς ἱερεῖς,
which not it is possible to eat except the priests,
2532 1325  2532 015      4862 846 1510    27 2532
καὶ ἔδωκεν καὶ τοῖς σὺν αὐτῷ οὖσιν;    καὶ
and he gave also to the ones with him being? And
3004     846    09 4521     1223        04
ἔλεγεν αὐτοῖς· τὸ σάββατον διὰ      τὸν
he was saying to them, the sabbath on account of the
444       1096     2532 3756 01 444      1223
ἄνθρωπον ἐγένετο καὶ οὐχ ὁ ἄνθρωπος διὰ
man       became and not the man on account of
```

20The days will come when the bridegroom is taken away from them, and then they will fast on that day.

21 "No one sews a piece of unshrunk cloth on an old cloak; otherwise, the patch pulls away from it, the new from the old, and a worse tear is made. 22And no one puts new wine into old wineskins; otherwise, the wine will burst the skins, and the wine is lost, and so are the skins; but one puts new wine into fresh wineskins."[a]

23 One sabbath he was going through the grain-fields; and as they made their way his disciples began to pluck heads of grain. 24The Pharisees said to him, "Look, why are they doing what is not lawful on the sabbath?" 25And he said to them, "Have you never read what David did when he and his companions were hungry and in need of food? 26He entered the house of God, when Abiathar was high priest, and ate the bread of the Presence, which it is not lawful for any but the priests to eat, and he gave some to his companions." 27Then he said to them, "The sabbath was made for humankind, and not humankind for

---

[a] Other ancient authorities lack *but one puts new wine into fresh wineskins*

the sabbath; 28so the Son
of Man is lord even of the
sabbath."

CHAPTER 3

Again he entered the
synagogue, and a man was
there who had a withered
hand. 2They watched him
to see whether he would
cure him on the sabbath, so
that they might accuse him.
3And he said to the man
who had the withered hand,
"Come forward." 4Then he
said to them, "Is it lawful
to do good or to do harm
on the sabbath, to save life
or to kill?" But they were
silent. 5He looked around
at them with anger; he was
grieved at their hardness of
heart and said to the man,
"Stretch out your hand."
He stretched it out, and his
hand was restored. 6The
Pharisees went out and
immediately conspired with
the Herodians against him,
how to destroy him.

7 Jesus departed with
his disciples to the sea,
and a great multitude
from Galilee followed him;
8hearing all that he was
doing, they came to him in
great numbers from Judea,
Jerusalem, Idumea, beyond
the Jordan, and the region
around Tyre and Sidon.

012 4521		5620	2962	1510	01	5207 02
τὸ σάββατον·	**28** ὥστε	κύριός	ἐστιν	ὁ	υἱὸς τοῦ
the sabbath;	so that	Master	is	the	son of the

444	2532 010	4521		2532 1525
ἀνθρώπου	καὶ τοῦ	σαββάτου.	**3:1**	Καὶ εἰσῆλθεν
man	also of the	sabbath.		And he went into

3825	1519 08	4864	2532	1510 1563	444
πάλιν	εἰς τὴν	συναγωγήν.	καὶ	ἦν ἐκεῖ	ἄνθρωπος
again	into the	synagogue.	And	was there	man

3583	2192	08 5495		2532 3906
ἐξηραμμένην	ἔχων	τὴν χεῖρα.	**2**	καὶ παρετήρουν
having been	having	the hand.		And they were keeping
dried out				watch

846 1487 023	4521	2323	846	2443
αὐτὸν εἰ τοῖς	σάββασιν	θεραπεύσει	αὐτόν,	ἵνα
him if on the	sabbaths	he will heal	him,	that

2723	846		2532 3004	03	444
κατηγορήσωσιν	αὐτοῦ.	**3**	καὶ λέγει	τῷ	ἀνθρώπῳ
they might accuse	him.		And he says	to the	man

03 08 3584	5495 2192	1453 1519 012 3319
τῷ τὴν ξηρὰν	χεῖρα ἔχοντι·	ἔγειρε εἰς τὸ μέσον.
the the dried out hand	having,	raise into the middle.

2532 3004	846	1832	023	4521
4 καὶ λέγει	αὐτοῖς·	ἔξεστιν	τοῖς	σάββασιν
And he says	to them,	is it possible	in the	sabbaths

18	4160	2228 2554	5590 4982	2228
ἀγαθὸν	ποιῆσαι ἢ	κακοποιῆσαι,	ψυχὴν σῶσαι	ἢ
good	to do or	bad to do,	soul to deliver	or

615	013 1161 4623		2532 4017
ἀποκτεῖναι;	οἱ δὲ ἐσιώπων.	**5**	καὶ περιβλεψάμενος
to kill?	The but were silent.		And having himself
	ones		looked around

846	3326 3709	4818	1909 07
αὐτοὺς	μετ᾽ ὀργῆς,	συλλυπούμενος	ἐπὶ τῇ
them	with anger,	being greatly grieved	on the

4457	06	2588	846	3004	03	444
πωρώσει	τῆς	καρδίας	αὐτῶν	λέγει	τῷ	ἀνθρώπῳ·
hardness	of the	heart	of them	he says	to the	man,

1614	08 5495	2532 1614	2532
ἔκτεινον	τὴν χεῖρα.	καὶ ἐξέτεινεν	καὶ
stretch out	the hand.	And he stretched out	and

600	05 5495 846		2532 1831
ἀπεκατεστάθη	ἡ χεὶρ αὐτοῦ.	**6**	καὶ ἐξελθόντες
was restored	the hand of him.		And having gone out

013 5330	2117	3326 014	2265
οἱ Φαρισαῖοι	εὐθὺς	μετὰ τῶν	Ἡρῳδιανῶν
the Pharisees	immediately	with the	Herodians

4824	1325	2596	846	3704	846
συμβούλιον	ἐδίδουν	κατ᾽	αὐτοῦ	ὅπως	αὐτὸν
council	were giving	against	him	so that	him

622		2532 01	2424	3326 014 3101
ἀπολέσωσιν.	**7**	Καὶ ὁ	Ἰησοῦς	μετὰ τῶν μαθητῶν
they might destroy.		And the	Jesus	with the learners

846	402	4314	08 2281	2532 4183
αὐτοῦ	ἀνεχώρησεν	πρὸς	τὴν θάλασσαν,	καὶ πολὺ
of him	departed	toward	the sea,	and much

4128	575 06 1056	190	2532 575
πλῆθος	ἀπὸ τῆς Γαλιλαίας	[ἠκολούθησεν],	καὶ ἀπὸ
quantity	from the Galilee	followed,	and from

06 2449	2532 575	2414	2532 575 06
τῆς Ἰουδαίας	**8** καὶ ἀπὸ	Ἱεροσολύμων	καὶ ἀπὸ τῆς
the Judea	and from	Jerusalem	and from the

2401	2532 4008	02	2446	2532 4012	5184
Ἰδουμαίας	καὶ πέραν	τοῦ	Ἰορδάνου	καὶ περὶ	Τύρον
Idumea	and across	the	Jordan	and around	Tyre

2532 4605	4128	4183 191	3745
καὶ Σιδῶνα	πλῆθος	πολὺ ἀκούοντες	ὅσα
and Sidon	quantity	much hearing	as much as

4160		2064	4314	846	9	2532	3004	015
ἐποίει		ἦλθον	πρὸς	αὐτόν.		καὶ	εἶπεν	τοῖς
he was doing		came	toward	him.		And	he said	to the

3101	846	2443	4142		4342
μαθηταῖς	αὐτοῦ	ἵνα	πλοιάριον		προσκαρτερῇ
learners	of him	that	small boat		might remain constant

846	1223	04	3793	2443	3361
αὐτῷ	διὰ	τὸν	ὄχλον	ἵνα	μὴ
to him	because of	the	crowd	that	not

2346	846	10	4183	1063	2323
θλίβωσιν	αὐτόν.		πολλοὺς	γὰρ	ἐθεράπευσεν,
they might afflict	him;		many	for	he healed,

5620	1968	846	2443	846	681
ὥστε	ἐπιπίπτειν	αὐτῷ	ἵνα	αὐτοῦ	ἅψωνται
so that	to fall on	him	that	him	they might touch

3745	2192	3148	11	2532	021	4151
ὅσοι	εἶχον	μάστιγας.		καὶ	τὰ	πνεύματα
as many as	had	scourges.		And	the	spirits

021	169	3752	846	2334
τὰ	ἀκάθαρτα,	ὅταν	αὐτὸν	ἐθεώρουν,
the unclean,		when	him	they were watching,

4363		846	2532	2896
προσέπιπτον		αὐτῷ	καὶ	ἔκραζον
they were falling toward		him	and	were shouting

3004	3754	1473	1510	01	5207	02	2316	12	2532
λέγοντες	ὅτι	σὺ	εἶ	ὁ	υἱὸς	τοῦ	θεοῦ.		καὶ
saying,	(")	You	are	the	son	of the	God.		And

4183	2008	846	2443	3361	846	5318
πολλὰ	ἐπετίμα	αὐτοῖς	ἵνα	μὴ	αὐτὸν	φανερὸν
many	he was admonishing	them	that	not	him	evident

4160	13	2532	305	1519	012	3735	2532
ποιήσωσιν.		Καὶ	ἀναβαίνει	εἰς	τὸ	ὄρος	καὶ
they might make.		And	he goes up	into	the	hill	and

4341	3739	2309	846	2532
προσκαλεῖται	οὓς	ἤθελεν	αὐτός,	καὶ
he calls toward	whom	he was wanting	himself,	and

565	4314	846	14	2532	4160	1427
ἀπῆλθον	πρὸς	αὐτόν.		καὶ	ἐποίησεν	δώδεκα
they went off	toward	him.		And	he made	twelve

3739	2532	652	3687	2443	1510
[οὓς	καὶ	ἀποστόλους	ὠνόμασεν]	ἵνα	ὦσιν
whom	also	delegates	he named	that	they might be

3326	846	2532	2443	649	846
μετ᾽	αὐτοῦ	καὶ	ἵνα	ἀποστέλλη	αὐτοὺς
with	him	and	that	he might delegate	them

2784	15	2532	2192	1849	1544	024
κηρύσσειν		καὶ	ἔχειν	ἐξουσίαν	ἐκβάλλειν	τὰ
to announce		and	to have	authority	to throw out	the

1140	16	2532	4160	016	1427	2532
δαιμόνια·		[καὶ	ἐποίησεν	τοὺς	δώδεκα,]	καὶ
demons;		and	he made	the	twelve,	and

2007	3686	03	4613	4074	17	2532	2385
ἐπέθηκεν	ὄνομα	τῷ	Σίμωνι	Πέτρον,		καὶ	Ἰάκωβον
he set on	name	to the	Simon	Peter,		and	Jacob

04	02	2199	2532	2491	04	80	02
τὸν	τοῦ	Ζεβεδαίου	καὶ	Ἰωάννην	τὸν	ἀδελφὸν	τοῦ
the	of the	Zebedee	and	John	the	brother	of the

2385	2532	2007	846	3686	993
Ἰακώβου	καὶ	ἐπέθηκεν	αὐτοῖς	ὀνόμα[τα]	βοανηργές,
Jacob	and	he set on	to them	names	Boanerges,

3739	1510	5207	1027	18	2532	406	2532
ὅ	ἐστιν	υἱοὶ	βροντῆς·		καὶ	Ἀνδρέαν	καὶ
which	is	sons	of thunder;		and	Andrew	and

5376	2532	918	2532	3102α	2532	2381
Φίλιππον	καὶ	Βαρθολομαῖον	καὶ	Μαθθαῖον	καὶ	Θωμᾶν
Philip	and	Bartholomew	and	Matthew	and	Thomas

2532	2385	04	02	256	2532	2280	2532
καὶ	Ἰάκωβον	τὸν	τοῦ	Ἁλφαίου	καὶ	Θαδδαῖον	καὶ
and	Jacob	the	of the	Alphaeus	and	Thaddeus	and

[9]He told his disciples to have a boat ready for him because of the crowd, so that they would not crush him; [10]for he had cured many, so that all who had diseases pressed upon him to touch him. [11]Whenever the unclean spirits saw him, they fell down before him and shouted, "You are the Son of God!" [12]But he sternly ordered them not to make him known.

[13]He went up the mountain and called to him those whom he wanted, and they came to him. [14]And he appointed twelve, whom he also named apostles,[a] to be with him, and to be sent out to proclaim the message, [15]and to have authority to cast out demons. [16]So he appointed the twelve:[b] Simon (to whom he gave the name Peter); [17]James son of Zebedee and John the brother of James (to whom he gave the name Boanerges, that is, Sons of Thunder); [18]and Andrew, and Philip, and Bartholomew, and Matthew, and Thomas, and James son of Alphaeus, and Thaddaeus, and

[a] Other ancient authorities lack whom he also named apostles
[b] Other ancient authorities lack So he appointed the twelve

Simon the Cananaean, ¹⁹and Judas Iscariot, who betrayed him.

Then he went home; ²⁰and the crowd came together again, so that they could not even eat. ²¹When his family heard it, they went out to restrain him, for people were saying, "He has gone out of his mind." ²²And the scribes who came down from Jerusalem said, "He has Beelzebul, and by the ruler of the demons he casts out demons." ²³And he called them to him, and spoke to them in parables, "How can Satan cast out Satan? ²⁴If a kingdom is divided against itself, that kingdom cannot stand. ²⁵And if a house is divided against itself, that house will not be able to stand. ²⁶And if Satan has risen up against himself and is divided, he cannot stand, but his end has come. ²⁷But no one can enter a strong man's house and plunder his property without first tying up the strong man; then indeed the house can be plundered.

28 "Truly I tell you, people will be forgiven

4613	04	2581		2532	2455	2465a	3739
Σίμωνα	τὸν	Καναναῖον	19	καὶ	Ἰούδαν	Ἰσκαριώθ,	ὃς
Simon	the	Cananean		and	Judas	Iscariot,	who

2532	3860		846		2532	2064	1519	3624	2532
καὶ	παρέδωκεν		αὐτόν.	20	Καὶ	ἔρχεται	εἰς	οἶκον,	καὶ
also	gave over		him.		And	he comes	into	house,	and

4905	3825	01	3793	5620	3361	1410
συνέρχεται	πάλιν	[ὁ]	ὄχλος,	ὥστε	μὴ	δύνασθαι
goes with	again	the	crowd,	so that	not	to be able

846	3366	740	2068		2532	191
αὐτοὺς	μηδὲ	ἄρτον	φαγεῖν.	21	καὶ	ἀκούσαντες
them	but not	bread	to eat.		And	having heard

013		3844	846	1831	2902	846
οἱ	παρ'		αὐτοῦ	ἐξῆλθον	κρατῆσαι	αὐτόν·
the ones	along		him	went out	to hold	him;

3004		1063	3754	1839
ἔλεγον		γὰρ	ὅτι	ἐξέστη.
they were saying		for	that	he was beside himself.

	2532	013	1122		013		575	2414
22	Καὶ	οἱ	γραμματεῖς	οἱ		ἀπὸ	Ἱεροσολύμων
	And	the	writers		the ones		from	Jerusalem

2597		3004		3754	954		2192
καταβάντες		ἔλεγον		ὅτι	Βεελζεβοὺλ		ἔχει
having come down		were saying		that	Beelzeboul		he has

2532	3754	1722	03	758		022	1140		1544
καὶ	ὅτι	ἐν	τῷ	ἄρχοντι	τῶν	δαιμονίων		ἐκβάλλει
and	that	in	the	ruler		of	demons		he throws out

024	1140		2532	4341			846	1722
τὰ	δαιμόνια.	23	Καὶ	προσκαλεσάμενος		αὐτοὺς	ἐν
the	demons.		And	having called		toward them	in

3850		3004		846		4459	1410
παραβολαῖς		ἔλεγεν		αὐτοῖς·		πῶς	δύναται
parallel stories		he was saying		to them,		how	is able

4567	4567		1544			2532	1437	932
σατανᾶς	σατανᾶν		ἐκβάλλειν;		24	καὶ	ἐὰν	βασιλεία
adversary	adversary		to throw out?			And	if	kingdom

1909	1438	3307		3756	1410		2476	05
ἐφ'	ἑαυτὴν	μερισθῇ,		οὐ	δύναται	σταθῆναι	ἡ
on	itself	might be divided,		not	is able	to stand	the

932	1565		2532	1437	3614	1909	1438
βασιλεία	ἐκείνη·	25	καὶ	ἐὰν	οἰκία	ἐφ'	ἑαυτὴν
kingdom	that;		and	if	house	on	itself

3307		3756	1410		05	3614	1565
μερισθῇ,		οὐ	δυνήσεται		ἡ	οἰκία	ἐκείνη
might be divided,		not	will be able		the	house	that

2476		2532	1487	01	4567	450	1909
σταθῆναι.	26	καὶ	εἰ	ὁ	σατανᾶς	ἀνέστη	ἐφ'
to stand.		And	if	the	adversary	stood up	on

1438	2532	3307		3756	1410		2476
ἑαυτὸν	καὶ	ἐμερίσθη,		οὐ	δύναται	στῆναι
himself	also	he is divided,		not	he is able	to stand

235	5056		2192		235	3756	1410	3762	1519
ἀλλὰ	τέλος		ἔχει.	27	ἀλλ'	οὐ	δύναται	οὐδεὶς	εἰς
but	completion		he has.		But	not	is able	no one	into

08	3614	02	2478	1525		024	4632
τὴν	οἰκίαν	τοῦ	ἰσχυροῦ	εἰσελθὼν		τὰ	σκεύη
the	house	of the	strong	having gone in		the	pots

846	1283		1437	3361	4413	04	2478
αὐτοῦ	διαρπάσαι,		ἐὰν	μὴ	πρῶτον	τὸν	ἰσχυρὸν
of him	to seize thoroughly,		except	first		the	strong

1210		2532	5119	08	3614	846
δήσῃ,		καὶ	τότε	τὴν	οἰκίαν	αὐτοῦ
he might bind,		and	then	the	house	of him

1283		281	3004	1473	3754	3956
διαρπάσει.	28	Ἀμὴν	λέγω	ὑμῖν	ὅτι	πάντα
he will seize thoroughly.		Amen	I say	to you	that	all

863		015	5207	014	444	021
ἀφεθήσεται		τοῖς	υἱοῖς	τῶν	ἀνθρώπων	τὰ
will be sent off		to the	sons	of the	men	the

265   2532 017 988   3745   1437
ἁμαρτήματα καὶ αἱ βλασφημίαι ὅσα   ἐὰν
sins   and the insults   as much as if

987   3739 1161 302 987   1519 012
βλασφημήσωσιν· **29** ὃς δ᾽ ἂν βλασφημήσῃ εἰς τὸ
they might insult; who but - might insult in the

4151   012 40   3756 2192   859   1519 04
πνεῦμα τὸ ἅγιον, οὐκ ἔχει ἄφεσιν   εἰς τὸν
spirit the holy, not he has sending off in the

165   235   1777   1510 166   265
αἰῶνα, ἀλλὰ ἔνοχός ἐστιν αἰωνίου ἁμαρτήματος.
age,   but guilty he is of eternal sin.

       3754 3004   4151   169   2192   **31** 2532
30 ὅτι ἔλεγον·   πνεῦμα ἀκάθαρτον ἔχει.   Καὶ
Because they were saying, spirit unclean he has. And

2064   05 3384   846   2532 013 80   846   2532
ἔρχεται ἡ μήτηρ αὐτοῦ καὶ οἱ ἀδελφοὶ αὐτοῦ καὶ
comes the mother of him and the brothers of him and

1854   4739   649   4314   846   2564
ἔξω   στήκοντες ἀπέστειλαν πρὸς αὐτὸν καλοῦντες
outside standing they delegate toward him calling

846   **32** 2532 2521   4012   846   3793 2532
αὐτόν.   καὶ ἐκάθητο περὶ αὐτὸν ὄχλος, καὶ
him.   And was sitting around him crowd, and

3004   846   2400 05 3384   1473   2532 013
λέγουσιν αὐτῷ· ἰδοὺ ἡ μήτηρ σου καὶ οἱ
they say to him, look the mother of you and the

80   1473   2532 017 79   1473   1854
ἀδελφοί σου [καὶ αἱ ἀδελφαί σου] ἔξω
brothers of you and the sisters of you outside

2212   1473 2532 611   846   3004
ζητοῦσίν σε. **33** καὶ ἀποκριθεὶς αὐτοῖς λέγει·
seek   you. And having answered them he says,

5101 1510 05 3384   1473 2532 013 80   1473
τίς ἐστιν ἡ μήτηρ μου καὶ οἱ ἀδελφοί [μου];
who is the mother of me and the brothers of me?

34 2532 4017   016   4012   846
καὶ περιβλεψάμενος   τοὺς περὶ αὐτον
And having looked around the ones around him

2945   2521   3004   2396 05 3384   1473
κύκλῳ καθημένους λέγει· ἴδε ἡ μήτηρ μου
circle sitting   he says, look the mother of me

2532 013 80   1473   **35** 3739 1063 302 4160   012
καὶ οἱ ἀδελφοί μου.   ὃς [γὰρ] ἂν ποιήσῃ τὸ
and the brothers of me. Who for - might do the

2307 02   2316   3778 80   1473 2532 79   2532
θέλημα τοῦ θεοῦ, οὗτος ἀδελφός μου καὶ ἀδελφὴ καὶ
want of the God, this brother of me and sister and

3384   1510   **4:1** 2532 3825 757   1321   3844
μήτηρ ἐστίν.   Καὶ πάλιν ἤρξατο διδάσκειν παρὰ
mother is.   And again he began to teach along

08   2281   2532 4863   4314 846
τὴν θάλασσαν· καὶ συνάγεται   πρὸς αὐτὸν
the sea;   and was brought together toward him

3793 4183   5620   846   1519 4143   1684
ὄχλος πλεῖστος, ὥστε αὐτὸν εἰς πλοῖον ἐμβάντα
crowd most,   so that him into boat having gone in

2521   1722 07   2532 3956 01 3793 4314
καθῆσθαι ἐν τῇ θαλάσσῃ, καὶ πᾶς ὁ ὄχλος πρὸς
to sit in the sea,   and all the crowd toward

08   2281   1909 06 1093 1510 **2** 2532 1321
τὴν θάλασσαν ἐπὶ τῆς γῆς ἦσαν.   καὶ ἐδίδασκεν
the sea   on the earth was.   And he taught

846   1722 3850   4183 2532 3004   846
αὐτοὺς ἐν παραβολαῖς πολλὰ καὶ ἔλεγεν αὐτοῖς
them in parallel stories many and was saying to them

1722 07 1322   846   **3** 191   2400 1831   01
ἐν τῇ διδαχῇ αὐτοῦ· Ἀκούετε. ἰδοὺ ἐξῆλθεν ὁ
in the teaching of him, hear. Look went out the

for their sins and whatever
blasphemies they utter;
[29]but whoever blasphemes
against the Holy Spirit
can never have forgiveness,
but is guilty of an eternal
sin"— [30]for they had said,
"He has an unclean spirit."

[31] Then his mother
and his brothers came; and
standing outside, they sent
to him and called him. [32]A
crowd was sitting around
him; and they said to him,
"Your mother and your
brothers and sisters[a] are
outside, asking for you."
[33]And he replied, "Who
are my mother and my
brothers?" [34]And looking
at those who sat around
him, he said, "Here are my
mother and my brothers!
[35]Whoever does the will
of God is my brother and
sister and mother."

CHAPTER 4

Again he began to teach
beside the sea. Such a very
large crowd gathered
around him that he got
into a boat on the sea and
sat there, while the whole
crowd was beside the sea
on the land. [2]He began
to teach them many things
in parables, and in his
teaching he said to them:
[3]"Listen! A sower went out
to sow.

a Other ancient authorities lack
and sisters

⁴And as he sowed, some seed fell on the path, and the birds came and ate it up. ⁵Other seed fell on rocky ground, where it did not have much soil, and it sprang up quickly, since it had no depth of soil. ⁶And when the sun rose, it was scorched; and since it had no root, it withered away. ⁷Other seed fell among thorns, and the thorns grew up and choked it, and it yielded no grain. ⁸Other seed fell into good soil and brought forth grain, growing up and increasing and yielding thirty and sixty and a hundredfold." ⁹And he said, "Let anyone with ears to hear listen!"

10 When he was alone, those who were around him along with the twelve asked him about the parables. ¹¹And he said to them, "To you has been given the secret^a of the kingdom of God, but for those outside, everything comes in parables; ¹²in order that

'they may indeed look,
   but not perceive,
and may indeed listen,
   but not understand;
so that they may not
   turn again and be
   forgiven.'"

13 And he said to them,

a Or mystery

```
4687          4687          2532  1096         1722  011  4687
σπείρων      σπεῖραι.  4  καὶ  ἐγένετο  ἐν   τῷ   σπείρειν
one sowing   to sow.     And  it became  in   the  to sow
3739  3303    4098    3844  08   3598   2532  2064   021
ὃ    μὲν    ἔπεσεν  παρὰ  τὴν  ὁδόν,  καὶ  ἦλθεν  τὰ
what  indeed  fell   along  the  way,   and  came  the
4071        2532  2719         846     5  2532  243   4098   1909
πετεινὰ  καὶ  κατέφαγεν  αὐτό.     καὶ  ἄλλο  ἔπεσεν  ἐπὶ
birds     and  ate up       it.        And  other  fell    on
012 4075        3699    3756  2192     1093  4183      2532
τὸ  πετρῶδες  ὅπου  οὐκ  εἶχεν  γῆν  πολλήν,  καὶ
the  rocky      where  not  it had  earth  much,    and
2117         1816          1223      012  3361  2192   899
εὐθὺς      ἐξανέτειλεν  διὰ    τὸ  μὴ   ἔχειν  βάθος
immediately  it sprang            because  the  not  to    depth
           up out                             have
1093      6  2532  3753  393      01   2246   2739
γῆς·         καὶ  ὅτε  ἀνέτειλεν  ὁ   ἥλιος  ἐκαυματίσθη
of earth;    and  when  arose    the  sun    it was burned
2532  1223          012  3361  2192    4491    3583
καὶ  διὰ          τὸ  μὴ   ἔχειν  ῥίζαν  ἐξηράνθη.
and  on account of  the  not  to have  root  it dried out.
  7  2532  243   4098    1519  020  173      2532  305     017
     καὶ  ἄλλο  ἔπεσεν  εἰς  τὰς  ἀκάνθας,  καὶ  ἀνέβησαν  αἱ
     And  other  fell    into  the  thorns,   and  went up   the
173       2532  4846          846      2532  2590  3756
ἄκανθαι  καὶ  συνέπνιξαν  αὐτό,  καὶ  καρπὸν  οὐκ
thorns    and  they choked together it,   and  fruit    not
1325      8  2532  243   4098    1519  08   1093  08   2570
ἔδωκεν.     καὶ  ἄλλα  ἔπεσεν  εἰς  τὴν  γῆν  τὴν  καλὴν
it gave.     And  others  fell    into  the  earth  the  good
2532  1325     2590     305       2532  837
καὶ  ἐδίδου  καρπὸν  ἀναβαίνοντα  καὶ  αὐξανόμενα
and  it was giving  fruit  going up       and  growing
2532  5342        1520  5144          2532  1520  1835
καὶ  ἔφερεν    ἐν   τριάκοντα  καὶ  ἐν   ἑξήκοντα
and  it was bearing  one  thirty      and  one  sixty
2532  1520  1540    9  2532  3004            3739  2192
καὶ  ἐν   ἑκατόν.     καὶ  ἔλεγεν·         ὃς   ἔχει
and  one  hundred.     And  he was saying,  who  has
3775  191      191          2532  3753  1096        2596
ὦτα  ἀκούειν  ἀκουέτω.  10 Καὶ  ὅτε  ἐγένετο  κατὰ
ears  to hear  let hear.     And  when  it became  by
3441    2065       846     013    4012    846     4862  015
μόνας,  ἠρώτων  αὐτὸν  οἱ   περὶ  αὐτὸν  σὺν  τοῖς
alone,  were asking  him  the ones around  him   with the
1427    020 3850          11  2532  3004
δώδεκα  τὰς  παραβολάς.     καὶ  ἔλεγεν
twelve  the  parallel stories.  And he was saying
846        1473  09   3466        1325          06
αὐτοῖς·  ὑμῖν  τὸ  μυστήριον  δέδοται       τῆς
to them,  to you  the  mystery  has been given  of the
932          02         2316   1565        1161  015      1854
βασιλείας  τοῦ      θεοῦ·  ἐκείνοις  δὲ   τοῖς     ἔξω
kingdom   of the God;    to those  but  the ones  outside
1722 3850              021  3956  1096        12  2443
ἐν  παραβολαῖς    τὰ  πάντα  γίνεται,      ἵνα
in  parallel stories  the  all  becomes,          that
991       991            2532  3361  3708
βλέποντες  βλέπωσιν  καὶ  μὴ   ἴδωσιν,
seeing    they might see  and  not  they might see,
2532  191        191              2532  3361
καὶ  ἀκούοντες  ἀκούωσιν  καὶ  μὴ
and  hearing    they might hear  and  not
4920          3379      1994
συνιῶσιν,    μήποτε  ἐπιστρέψωσιν
they might understand,  then not  they might return
2532  863          846      13  2532  3004
καὶ  ἀφεθῇ      αὐτοῖς.     Καὶ  λέγει
and  it might be sent off  to them.  And  he says
```

846   3756 3609a   08   3850   3778   2532
αὐτοῖς· οὐκ οἴδατε τὴν παραβολὴν   ταύτην, καὶ
to them, not you know the parallel story this,   and

4459 3956 020 3850   1097   01
πῶς πάσας τὰς παραβολὰς   γνώσεσθε; **14** ὁ
how   all   the parallel stories will you know? The one

4687   04   3056   4687   3778 1161 1510 013
σπείρων τὸν λόγον σπείρει. **15** οὗτοι δέ εἰσιν οἱ
sowing the word sows.   These but are the ones

3844 08 3598 3699 4687   01 3056 2532 3752
παρὰ τὴν ὁδόν· ὅπου σπείρεται ὁ λόγος καὶ ὅταν·
along the way; where is being sown the word and   when

191   2117   2064   01   4567
ἀκούσωσιν,   εὐθὺς   ἔρχεται ὁ σατανᾶς
they might hear, immediately comes   the adversary

2532 142   04 3056   04   4687
καὶ αἴρει   τὸν λόγον τὸν ἐσπαρμένον
and he lifts up the word the one having been sown

1519 846   2532 3778 1510 013   1909 024
εἰς αὐτούς. **16** καὶ οὗτοί εἰσιν οἱ   ἐπὶ τὰ
in   them.   And these are the ones on   the

4075   4687   3739 3752 191   04
πετρώδη σπειρόμενοι, οἳ ὅταν ἀκούσωσιν τὸν
rocky   being sown, which when they might hear the

3056 2117   3326 5479 2983   846
λόγον εὐθὺς   μετὰ χαρᾶς λαμβάνουσιν αὐτόν,
word immediately with joy they receive it,

    2532 3756 2192   4491 1722 1438   235
17 καὶ οὐκ ἔχουσιν ῥίζαν ἐν ἑαυτοῖς ἀλλὰ
   and not they have root in themselves but

4340   1510   1534 1096   2347
πρόσκαιροί εἰσιν, εἶτα γενομένης θλίψεως
to season   they are, then having become of affliction

2228 1375   1223   04 3056   2117
ἢ   διωγμοῦ διὰ   τὸν λόγον εὐθὺς
or   persecution on account of the word immediately

4624   2532 243   1510 013   1519
σκανδαλίζονται. **18** καὶ ἄλλοι εἰσιν οἱ   εἰς
they are offended.   And others are the ones in

020 173   4687   3778 1510 013   04 3056
τὰς ἀκάνθας σπειρόμενοι· οὗτοί εἰσιν οἱ   τὸν λόγον
the thorns being sown; these are the ones the word

191   2532 017 3308   02   165   2532
ἀκούσαντες, **19** καὶ αἱ μέριμναι τοῦ αἰῶνος καὶ
having heard,   and the anxieties of the age   and

05 539   02   4149   2532 017 4012 024
ἡ ἀπάτη τοῦ πλούτου καὶ αἱ περὶ τὰ
the deception of the rich and the about the

3062 1939   1531   4846
λοιπὰ ἐπιθυμίαι εἰσπορευόμεναι συμπνίγουσιν
remaining desires traveling into they choke together

04 3056 2532 175   1096   20 2532 1565
τὸν λόγον καὶ ἄκαρπος γίνεται. **20** καὶ ἐκεῖνοί
the word and fruitless it becomes. And those

1510 013 1909 08 1093 08 2570 4687
εἰσιν οἱ ἐπὶ τὴν γῆν τὴν καλὴν σπαρέντες,
are   the ones on the earth the good having been sown,

3748   191   04 3056   2532 3858   2532
οἵτινες ἀκούουσιν τὸν λόγον καὶ παραδέχονται καὶ
who   hear   the word and they accept   and

2592   1520 5144   2532 1520 1835   2532
καρποφοροῦσιν ἓν τριάκοντα καὶ ἓν ἑξήκοντα καὶ
they bear fruit one thirty   and one sixty   and

1520 1540   2532 3004   846   3385
ἓν ἑκατόν. **21** Καὶ ἔλεγεν αὐτοῖς· μήτι
one hundred.   And he was saying to them, not

2064   01 3088   2443 5259 04 3426
ἔρχεται ὁ λύχνος ἵνα ὑπὸ τὸν μόδιον
comes   the lamp that under the measuring scoop

"Do you not understand this parable? Then how will you understand all the parables? [14]The sower sows the word. [15]These are the ones on the path where the word is sown: when they hear, Satan immediately comes and takes away the word that is sown in them. [16]And these are the ones sown on rocky ground: when they hear the word, they immediately receive it with joy. [17]But they have no root, and endure only for a while; then, when trouble or persecution arises on account of the word, immediately they fall away.[a] [18]And others are those sown among the thorns: these are the ones who hear the word, [19]but the cares of the world, and the lure of wealth, and the desire for other things come in and choke the word, and it yields nothing. [20]And these are the ones sown on the good soil: they hear the word and accept it and bear fruit, thirty and sixty and a hundredfold."

21 He said to them, "Is a lamp brought in to be put under the bushel basket,

[a] Or *stumble*

or under the bed, and not on the lampstand? [22]For there is nothing hidden, except to be disclosed; nor is anything secret, except to come to light. [23]Let anyone with ears to hear listen!" [24]And he said to them, "Pay attention to what you hear; the measure you give will be the measure you get, and still more will be given you. [25]For to those who have, more will be given; and from those who have nothing, even what they have will be taken away." [26]He also said, "The kingdom of God is as if someone would scatter seed on the ground, [27]and would sleep and rise night and day, and the seed would sprout and grow, he does not know how. [28]The earth produces of itself, first the stalk, then the head, then the full grain in the head. [29]But when the grain is ripe, at once he goes in with his sickle, because the harvest has come." [30]He also said, "With what can we compare the kingdom of God, or what parable will we use for it? [31]It is like a mustard seed, which, when sown upon the ground,

5087		2228	5259	08	2825	3756	2443	1909
τεθῇ		ἢ	ὑπὸ	τὴν	κλίνην;	οὐχ	ἵνα	ἐπὶ
it might be set		or	under	the	bed?	Not	that	on

08 3087	5087		3756	1063	1510	2927
τὴν λυχνίαν	τεθῇ;	**22**	οὐ	γάρ	ἐστιν	κρυπτὸν
the lampstand	it might be set?		Not	for	it is	hidden

1437 3361	2443	5319		3761
ἐὰν μὴ	ἵνα	φανερωθῇ,		οὐδὲ
except	that	it might be demonstrated,		but not

1096	614	235	2443 2064	1519
ἐγένετο	ἀπόκρυφον	ἀλλ᾽	ἵνα ἔλθη	εἰς
it became	hidden off	but	that it might come	into

5318		1487	5100	2192	3775	191	191
φανερόν.	**23**	εἴ	τις	ἔχει	ὦτα	ἀκούειν	ἀκουέτω.
evident.		If	some	has	ears	to hear	let hear.

	2532	3004		846		991	5101	191	1722
24	Καὶ	ἔλεγεν		αὐτοῖς·		βλέπετε	τί	ἀκούετε.	ἐν
	And	he was saying		to them,		see	what	you hear.	In

3739 3358	3354	3354		1473
ᾧ μέτρῳ	μετρεῖτε	μετρηθήσεται		ὑμῖν
what measure	you measure	it will be measured		to you

2532	4369		1473		3739	1063	2192
καὶ	προστεθήσεται		ὑμῖν.	**25**	ὃς	γὰρ	ἔχει,
and	it will be set to		you.		Who	for	has,

1325		846	2532	3739	3756	2192	2532
δοθήσεται		αὐτῷ·	καὶ	ὃς	οὐκ	ἔχει,	καὶ
it will be given		to him;	and	who	not	has,	also

3739 2192	142		575 846		2532
ὃ ἔχει	ἀρθήσεται		ἀπ᾽ αὐτοῦ.	**26**	Καὶ
what he has	will be lifted up		from him.		And

3004		3779	1510	05	932	02	2316
ἔλεγεν·		οὕτως	ἐστὶν	ἡ	βασιλεία	τοῦ	θεοῦ
he was saying·		thusly	is	the	kingdom	of the	God

5613 444		906		04	4703	1909	06 1093
ὡς ἄνθρωπος		βάλη		τὸν	σπόρον	ἐπὶ	τῆς γῆς
as man		might throw		the	seed	on	the earth

	2532	2510		2532	1453		3571
27	καὶ	καθεύδη		καὶ	ἐγείρηται		νύκτα
	and	he might sleep		and	he might be raised		night

2532	2250	2532	01	4703	985		2532
καὶ	ἡμέραν,	καὶ	ὁ	σπόρος	βλαστᾷ		καὶ
and	day,	and	the	seed	might sprout		and

3373		5613	3756	3609a	846		844
μηκύνηται		ὡς	οὐκ	οἶδεν	αὐτός.	**28**	αὐτομάτη
might lengthen		as	not	he knows	himself.		By itself

05	1093	2592		4413	5528	1534
ἡ	γῆ	καρποφορεῖ,		πρῶτον	χόρτον	εἶτα
the	earth	bears fruit,		first	grass	then

4719		1534 4134		4621	1722	03
στάχυν		εἶτα πλήρη[ς]		σῖτον	ἐν	τῷ
stalk of grain		then full		wheat	in	the

4719		3752	1161	3860		01	2590
στάχυϊ.	**29**	ὅταν	δὲ	παραδοῖ		ὁ	καρπός,
stalk of grain.		When	but	might give over		the	fruit,

2117	649		012 1407	3754
εὐθὺς	ἀποστέλλει		τὸ δρέπανον,	ὅτι
immediately	he delegates		the sickle,	because

3936	01 2326		2532 3004		4459
παρέστηκεν	ὁ θερισμός.	**30**	Καὶ ἔλεγεν·		πῶς
stands along	the harvest.		And he was saying,		how

3666		08	932	02	2316	2228	1722
ὁμοιώσωμεν		τὴν	βασιλείαν	τοῦ	θεοῦ	ἢ	ἐν
might we liken		the	kingdom	of the	God	or	in

5101 846	3850		5087		5613 2848
τίνι αὐτὴν	παραβολῇ		θῶμεν;	**31**	ὡς κόκκῳ
what it	parallel story		might we set?		As grain

4615	3739	3752 4687		1909 06 1093
σινάπεως,	ὃς	ὅταν σπαρῇ		ἐπὶ τῆς γῆς,
of mustard,	which	when it might be sown		on the earth,

```
3398          1510    3956    022  4690         022        1909 06
μικρότερον ὂν   πάντων τῶν σπερμάτων τῶν        ἐπὶ τῆς
smaller    being of all the seeds    of the ones on the

1093    32  2532 3752 4687      305            2532 1096
γῆς,       καὶ ὅταν σπαρῇ,  ἀναβαίνει καὶ γίνεται
earth,     and when it might it goes up and  it becomes
                       be sown,

3173      3956  022 3001        2532 4160      2798
μεῖζον    πάντων τῶν λαχάνων  καὶ ποιεῖ κλάδους
greater   of all the vegetables and it makes branches

3173      5620   1410      5259 08 4639     846    024
μεγάλους, ὥστε δύνασθαι ὑπὸ τὴν σκιὰν αὐτοῦ τὰ
great,    so that to be able under the shadow of it the

4071   02     3772      2681        33  2532 5108
πετεινὰ τοῦ  οὐρανοῦ κατασκηνοῦν.     Καὶ τοιαύταις
birds   of the heaven to set up tent. And  in such

3850            4183    2980              846      04
παραβολαῖς    πολλαῖς ἐλάλει          αὐτοῖς τὸν
parallel stories many  he was speaking to them the

3056   2531   1410         191      34  5565    1161
λόγον καθὼς ἠδύναντο   ἀκούειν·      χωρὶς δὲ
word just as they were able to hear;   without but

3850    3756 2980   846        2596 2398  1161 015
παραβολῆς οὐκ ἐλάλει αὐτοῖς, κατ᾽ ἰδίαν δὲ τοῖς
parallel not he was to them, by  own   but to the
story        speaking

2398   3101    1956              3956   35  2532
ἰδίοις μαθηταῖς ἐπέλυεν        πάντα.     Καὶ
own    learners he was loosening on all.   And

3004    846    1722 1565    07 2250  3798
λέγει  αὐτοῖς ἐν  ἐκείνῃ τῇ ἡμέρᾳ ὀψίας
he says to them in  that   the day  evening

1096          1330          1519 012 4008
γενομένης·   διέλθωμεν      εἰς τὸ πέραν.
having become, we might go through in  the across.

36  2532 863       04  3793 3880             846
   καὶ ἀφέντες    τὸν ὄχλον παραλαμβάνουσιν αὐτὸν
   And having sent off the crowd they took along him

5613 1510    1722 011 4143   2532 243   4143  1510 3326
ὡς  ἦν   ἐν  τῷ πλοίῳ, καὶ ἄλλα πλοῖα ἦν μετ᾽
as  he was in  the boat, and other boats were with

846   37  2532 1096    2978   3173  417       2532 021
αὐτοῦ.   καὶ γίνεται λαῖλαψ μεγάλη ἀνέμου καὶ τὰ
him.     And becomes storm great of wind and the

2949   1911           1519 012 4143   5620   2235
κύματα ἐπέβαλλεν     εἰς τὸ πλοῖον, ὥστε ἤδη
waves were throwing on in the boat,  so that already

1072        012 4143   38  2532 846       1510 1722 07
γεμίζεσθαι τὸ πλοῖον.    καὶ αὐτὸς ἦν ἐν  τῇ
to be filled the boat.    And himself was in  the

4403    1909 012 4344        2518        2532 1453
πρύμνῃ ἐπὶ τὸ προσκεφάλαιον καθεύδων. καὶ ἐγείρουσιν
stern  on  the head rest     sleeping. And they raise

846    2532 3004      846      1320      3190a
αὐτὸν καὶ λέγουσιν αὐτῷ·  διδάσκαλε, οὐ μέλει
him   and they say to him, teacher,  not it is a care

1473   3754 622          39  2532 1326
σοι    ὅτι ἀπολλύμεθα;     καὶ διεγερθεὶς
to you that we are being    And having been raised
           destroyed?          thoroughly

2008       03  417     2532 3004   07      2281
ἐπετίμησεν τῷ ἀνέμῳ καὶ εἶπεν τῇ θαλάσσῃ·
he admonished the wind and he said to the sea,

4623   5392       2532 2869    01    417    2532
σιώπα, πεφίμωσο. καὶ ἐκόπασεν ὁ ἄνεμος καὶ
be silent, be muzzled. And ceased the wind and

1096    1055    3173      40  2532 3004   846     5101
ἐγένετο γαλήνη μεγάλη.     καὶ εἶπεν αὐτοῖς· τί
became  calm   great.      And he said to them, why
```

is the smallest of all the seeds on earth; [32]yet when it is sown it grows up and becomes the greatest of all shrubs, and puts forth large branches, so that the birds of the air can make nests in its shade."

[33] With many such parables he spoke the word to them, as they were able to hear it; [34]he did not speak to them except in parables, but he explained everything in private to his disciples.

[35] On that day, when evening had come, he said to them, "Let us go across to the other side." [36]And leaving the crowd behind, they took him with them in the boat, just as he was. Other boats were with him. [37]A great windstorm arose, and the waves beat into the boat, so that the boat was already being swamped. [38]But he was in the stern, asleep on the cushion; and they woke him up and said to him, "Teacher, do you not care that we are perishing?" [39]He woke up and rebuked the wind, and said to the sea, "Peace! Be still!" Then the wind ceased, and there was a dead calm. [40]He said to them, "Why

are you afraid? Have you
still no faith?" ⁴¹And they
were filled with great awe
and said to one another,
"Who then is this, that even
the wind and the sea obey
him?"

CHAPTER 5

They came to the other side
of the sea, to the country of
the Gerasenes.ᵃ ²And when
he had stepped out of the
boat, immediately a man
out of the tombs with an
unclean spirit met him.
³He lived among the tombs;
and no one could restrain
him any more, even with
a chain; ⁴for he had often
been restrained with
shackles and chains, but the
chains he wrenched apart,
and the shackles he broke
in pieces; and no one had
the strength to subdue him.
⁵Night and day among
the tombs and on the
mountains he was always
howling and bruising
himself with stones.
⁶When he saw Jesus from a
distance, he ran and bowed
down before him; ⁷and he
shouted at the top of his
voice, "What have you to
do with me, Jesus, Son of
the Most High God? I
adjure you by God, do not
torment me." ⁸For he had
said to him, "Come out
of the man, you unclean
spirit!" ⁹Then Jesusᵇ asked

ᵃ Other ancient authorities read
Gergesenes; others, *Gadarenes*
ᵇ Gk *he*

1169	1510	3768	2192	4102	**41**	2532
δειλοί	ἐστε;	οὔπω	ἔχετε	πίστιν;		καὶ
cowards	are you?	Not yet	you have	trust?		And

5399	5401	3173	2532	3004		4314
ἐφοβήθησαν	φόβον	μέγαν	καὶ	ἔλεγον		πρὸς
they feared	fear	great	and	they were saying		toward

240	5101	686	3778	1510	3754	2532	01
ἀλλήλους·	τίς	ἄρα	οὗτός	ἐστιν	ὅτι	καὶ	ὁ
one another;	who	then	this	is	that	also	the

417	2532	05	2281	5219	846	**5:1**	2532
ἄνεμος	καὶ	ἡ	θάλασσα	ὑπακούει	αὐτῷ;		Καὶ
wind	and	the	sea	obey	him?		And

2064	1519	012	4008	06	2281	1519	08
ἦλθον	εἰς	τὸ	πέραν	τῆς	θαλάσσης	εἰς	τὴν
they went	into	the	across	of the sea		into	the

5561	014	1086	**2**	2532	1831		846
χώραν	τῶν	Γερασηνῶν.		καὶ	ἐξελθόντος		αὐτοῦ
country	of the	Gerasenes.		And	having gone out		him

1537	010	4143	2117	5221	846	1537	022
ἐκ	τοῦ	πλοίου	εὐθὺς	ὑπήντησεν	αὐτῷ	ἐκ	τῶν
from	the	boat	immediately	met	him	from	the

3419	444	1722	4151	169	**3**	3739	08
μνημείων	ἄνθρωπος	ἐν	πνεύματι	ἀκαθάρτῳ,		ὃς	τὴν
graves	man	in	spirit	unclean,		who	the

2731	2192	1722	023	3418	2532	3761
κατοίκησιν	εἶχεν	ἐν	τοῖς	μνήμασιν,	καὶ	οὐδὲ
residence	had	in	the	graves,	and	but not

254	3765	3762	1410	846	1210	**4**	1223
ἁλύσει	οὐκέτι	οὐδεὶς	ἐδύνατο	αὐτὸν	δῆσαι		διὰ
chain	no longer	no one	was able	him	to bind		because

012	846	4178	3976		2532	254
τὸ	αὐτὸν	πολλάκις	πέδαις		καὶ	ἁλύσεσιν
the	him	frequently	in foot shackles		and	chains

1210	2532	1288		5259	846	020
δεδέσθαι	καὶ	διεσπάσθαι		ὑπ'	αὐτοῦ	τὰς
to be bound	and	to be torn in pieces		by	him	the

254	2532	020	3976	4937	0500
ἁλύσεις	καὶ	τὰς	πέδας	συντετρῖφθαι,	καὶ
chains	and	the	foot shackles	to be broken,	and

3762	2480	846	1150	**5**	2532	1223
οὐδεὶς	ἴσχυεν	αὐτὸν	δαμάσαι·		καὶ	διὰ
no one	was having strength	him	to tame;		and	through

3956	3571	2532	2250	1722	023	3418	2532	1722
παντὸς	νυκτὸς	καὶ	ἡμέρας	ἐν	τοῖς	μνήμασιν	καὶ	ἐν
all	night	and	day	in	the	graves	and	in

023	3735	1510	2896	2532	2629
τοῖς	ὄρεσιν	ἦν	κράζων	καὶ	κατακόπτων
the	hills	he was	shouting	and	cutting in pieces

1438	3037	**6**	2532	3708	04	2424	575
ἑαυτὸν	λίθοις.		καὶ	ἰδὼν		τὸν Ἰησοῦν	ἀπὸ
himself	in stones.		And	having seen		the Jesus	from

3113	5143	2532	4352	846	**7**	2532
μακρόθεν	ἔδραμεν	καὶ	προσεκύνησεν	αὐτῷ		καὶ
from far	he ran	and	he worshiped	him		and

2896	5456	3173	3004	5101	1473	2532
κράξας	φωνῇ	μεγάλῃ	λέγει·	τί	ἐμοὶ	καὶ
having shouted	sound	great	he says;	what	to me	and

1473	2424	5207	02	2316	02	5310	3726
σοί,	Ἰησοῦ	υἱὲ	τοῦ	θεοῦ	τοῦ	ὑψίστου;	ὁρκίζω
to you,	Jesus	son	of the	God	the	highest?	I put under oath

1473	04	2316	3361	1473	928
σε	τὸν	θεόν,	μή	με	βασανίσῃς.
you	the	God,	not	me	you might torment.

8	3004	1063	846	1831	09	4151	09
	ἔλεγεν	γὰρ	αὐτῷ·	ἔξελθε	τὸ	πνεῦμα	τὸ
	He was saying	for	to him;	come out	the	spirit	the

169	1537	02	1831	**9**	2532	1905
ἀκάθαρτον	ἐκ	τοῦ	ἀνθρώπου.		καὶ	ἐπηρώτα
unclean	out of	the	man.		And	he was asking on

846   5101   3686   1473   2532 3004   846   3003
αὐτόν· τί   ὄνομά σοι;   καὶ λέγει αὐτῷ· λεγιὼν
him;   what name to you? And he says to him; legion

3686   1473   3754   4183   1510   **10** 2532
ὄνομά μοι, ὅτι   πολλοί ἐσμεν.   καὶ
name   to me, because many   we are.   And

3870   846   4183   2443 3361   846
παρεκάλει   αὐτὸν πολλὰ ἵνα μὴ   αὐτὰ
he encourages him   much   that not them

649   1854   06   5561   **11** 1510   1161
ἀποστείλῃ   ἔξω   τῆς χώρας.   ἦν   δὲ
he might delegate outside the country.   There was but

1563   4314   011   3735 34   5519   3173   1006
ἐκεῖ πρὸς τῷ ὄρει ἀγέλη χοίρων μεγάλη βοσκομένη·
there toward the hill   herd of pigs great   grazing;

12 2532 3870   846   3004   3992
       καὶ παρεκάλεσαν   αὐτὸν λέγοντες· πέμψον
       and they were encouraging him   saying;   send

1473 1519 016   5519   2443 1519 846
ἡμᾶς εἰς τοὺς χοίρους, ἵνα εἰς αὐτοὺς
us   into the pigs,   that into them

1525   **13** 2532 2010   846   2532
εἰσέλθωμεν.   καὶ ἐπέτρεψεν αὐτοῖς. καὶ
we might go in.   And he allowed them.   And

1831   021 4151   021 169   1525
ἐξελθόντα   τὰ πνεύματα τὰ ἀκάθαρτα εἰσῆλθον
having gone out the spirits   the unclean   went into

1519 016   5519   2532 3729   05 34   2596 02
εἰς τοὺς χοίρους, καὶ ὥρμησεν ἡ ἀγέλη κατὰ τοῦ
into the pigs,   and rushed   the herd   down the

2911   1519 08 2281   5613 1367   2532
κρημνοῦ εἰς τὴν θάλασσαν, ὡς δισχίλιοι, καὶ
steep slope into the   sea,   as   two thousand, and

4155   1722 07 2281   **14** 2532 013
ἐπνίγοντο   ἐν   τῇ θαλάσσῃ.   Καὶ οἱ
they were choking in   the   sea.   And the ones

1006   846   5343   2532 518   1519 08 4172
βόσκοντες αὐτοὺς ἔφυγον καὶ ἀπήγγειλαν εἰς τὴν πόλιν
grazing   them   fled   and told   in   the city

2532 1519 016   68   2532 2064   3708   5101 1510
καὶ εἰς τοὺς ἀγρούς· καὶ ἦλθον   ἰδεῖν τί   ἐστιν
and   in the   fields;   and they went to see what is

09   1096   **15** 2532 2064   4314   04 2424
τὸ γεγονὸς   καὶ ἔρχονται πρὸς τὸν Ἰησοῦν
the having become   and they come toward the   Jesus

2532 2334   04 1139   2521
καὶ θεωροῦσιν τὸν δαιμονιζόμενον καθήμενον
and they watch   the one being demonized sitting

2439   2532 4993   04
ἱματισμένον καὶ σωφρονοῦντα, τὸν
having been clothed and thinking soberly, the

2192   04 3003   2532 5399   **16** 2532
ἐσχηκότα   τὸν λεγιῶνα, καὶ ἐφοβήθησαν.   καὶ
one having had the legion, and they were afraid. And

1334   846   013 3708   4459 1096
διηγήσαντο αὐτοῖς οἱ ἰδόντες   πῶς ἐγένετο
narrated   to them the ones having seen how it became

03   1139   2532 4012   014 5519
τῷ   δαιμονιζομένῳ   καὶ περὶ   τῶν χοίρων.
to the one being demonized and concerning the pigs.

17 2532 757   3870   846   565   575
       καὶ ἤρξαντο   παρακαλεῖν αὐτὸν ἀπελθεῖν ἀπὸ
       And they began to encourage him   to go off from

022 3725   846   2532 1684   846   1519
τῶν ὁρίων   αὐτῶν. **18** Καὶ ἐμβαίνοντος αὐτοῦ εἰς
the territories of them. And going in   him   into

012 4143   3870   846   01 1139   2443 3326
τὸ πλοῖον παρεκάλει αὐτὸν ὁ δαιμονισθεὶς ἵνα μετ'
the boat   was   him   the one having   that with
                    encouraging   been demonized

him, "What is your name?"
He replied, "My name is
Legion; for we are many."
[10]He begged him earnestly
not to send them out of the
country. [11]Now there on
the hillside a great herd of
swine was feeding; [12]and the
unclean spirits[a] begged him,
"Send us into the swine;
let us enter them." [13]So he
gave them permission. And
the unclean spirits came
out and entered the swine;
and the herd, numbering
about two thousand, rushed
down the steep bank into
the sea, and were drowned
in the sea.

14 The swineherds ran
off and told it in the city
and in the country. Then
people came to see what
was that had happened.
[15]They came to Jesus and
saw the demoniac sitting
there, clothed and in his
right mind, the very man
who had had the legion;
and they were afraid.
[16]Those who had seen
what had happened to the
demoniac and to the swine
reported it. [17]Then they
began to beg Jesus[b] to leave
their neighborhood. [18]As
he was getting into the
boat, the man who had been
possessed by demons begged
him that

a Gk *they*
b Gk *him*

he might be with him.
[19]But Jesus[a] refused, and said to him, "Go home to your friends, and tell them how much the Lord has done for you, and what mercy he has shown you."
[20]And he went away and began to proclaim in the Decapolis how much Jesus had done for him; and everyone was amazed.

21 When Jesus had crossed again in the boat[b] to the other side, a great crowd gathered around him; and he was by the sea.
[22]Then one of the leaders of the synagogue named Jairus came and, when he saw him, fell at his feet [23]and begged him repeatedly, "My little daughter is at the point of death. Come and lay your hands on her, so that she may be made well, and live." [24]So he went with him.

And a large crowd followed him and pressed in on him. [25]Now there was a woman who had been suffering from hemorrhages for twelve years. [26]She had endured much under many physicians, and had spent all that she had; and she was no better, but rather grew worse. [27]She had heard about Jesus, and came up behind him in the crowd and touched

[a] Gk he
[b] Other ancient authorities lack in the boat

846	1510		2532	3756	863		846	235
αὐτοῦ	ἦ.	**19** καὶ	οὐκ	ἀφῆκεν		αὐτόν,	ἀλλὰ
him	he might be.	And	not	he allowed		him,	but

3004	846	5217	1519	04	3624	1473	4314
λέγει	αὐτῷ·	ὕπαγε	εἰς	τὸν	οἶκόν	σου	πρὸς
he says	to him;	go off	into	the	house of	you	toward

016	4674	2532	518		846	3745	01
τοὺς	σοὺς	καὶ	ἀπάγγειλον	αὐτοῖς	ὅσα	ὁ
the	your	and	tell		to them	as much as	the

2962	1473	4160	2532 1653		1473
κύριός	σοι	πεποίηκεν	καὶ ἠλέησέν		σε.
Master	to you	has done	and he showed mercy		you.

20	2532	565		2532	757		2784		1722	07
	καὶ	ἀπῆλθεν		καὶ	ἤρξατο		κηρύσσειν		ἐν	τῇ
	And	he went off		and	he began		to announce		in	the

1179	3745		4160	846	01	2424	2532
Δεκαπόλει	ὅσα		ἐποίησεν	αὐτῷ	ὁ	Ἰησοῦς,	καὶ
Decapolis	as much as did			to him	the	Jesus,	and

3956	2296		2532	1276		02
πάντες	ἐθαύμαζον.	**21** Καὶ	διαπεράσαντος		τοῦ
all	were marveling.	And	having crossed over		the

2424	1722	011	4143	3825	1519	012	4008
Ἰησοῦ	[ἐν	τῷ	πλοίῳ]	πάλιν	εἰς	τὸ	πέραν
Jesus	in	the	boat	again	into	the	across

4863		3793	4183	1909	846	2532
συνήχθη		ὄχλος	πολὺς	ἐπ'	αὐτόν,	καὶ
was brought together		crowd	much	on	him,	and

1510	3844	08	2281		2532	2064	1520	014
ἦν	παρὰ	τὴν	θάλασσαν.	**22** Καὶ	ἔρχεται	εἰς	τῶν
he was	along	the	sea.	And	comes	one	of the

752		3686	2383	2532	3708
ἀρχισυναγώγων,		ὀνόματι	Ἰάϊρος,	καὶ	ἰδὼν
synagogue rulers,		in name	Jairus,	and	having seen

846	4098	4314	016	4228	846		2532 3870
αὐτὸν	πίπτει	πρὸς	τοὺς	πόδας	αὐτοῦ	**23** καὶ	παρακαλεῖ
him	he falls	to	the	feet	of him	and	encourages

846	4183	3004	3754	09	2365		1470
αὐτὸν	πολλὰ	λέγων	ὅτι	τὸ	θυγάτριόν		μου
him	many	saying,	(")	the	small daughter		of me

2079	2192	2443	2064		2007		020
ἐσχάτως	ἔχει,	ἵνα	ἐλθὼν		ἐπιθῇς		τὰς
lastly	has,	that	having come		you might set on		the

5495	846	2443	4982	2532	2198		2532
χεῖρας	αὐτῇ	ἵνα	σωθῇ	καὶ	ζήσῃ.	**24**	καὶ
hands	to her	that	she might and be delivered		she might live.		And

565		3326	846	2532 190		846	3793
ἀπῆλθεν		μετ'	αὐτοῦ.	καὶ ἠκολούθει		αὐτῷ	ὄχλος
he went off		with	him.	And was following		him	crowd

4183	2532	4918		846		2532	1135
πολὺς	καὶ	συνέθλιβον		αὐτόν.	**25**	Καὶ	γυνὴ
much	and	were pressing together		him.		And	woman

1510	1722	4511	129		1427	2094		2532	4183
οὖσα	ἐν	ῥύσει	αἵματος		δώδεκα	ἔτη	**26**	καὶ	πολλὰ
being	in	flow	of blood		twelve	years		and	many

3958		5259	4183	2395		2532	1159
παθοῦσα		ὑπὸ	πολλῶν	ἰατρῶν		καὶ	δαπανήσασα
having suffered		by	many	physicians		and	having spent

024	3844	846		3956	2532 3367		5623		235
τὰ	παρ'	αὐτῆς		πάντα	καὶ	μηδὲν		ὠφεληθεῖσα	ἀλλὰ
the	from	herself		all	and	nothing		having been benefitted	but

3123	1519	012	5501	2064		191		4012
μᾶλλον	εἰς	τὸ	χεῖρον	ἐλθοῦσα,	**27**	ἀκούσασα		περὶ
more	in	the	worse	having gone,		having heard		about

02	2424	2064		1722	03	3793	3693	681	010
τοῦ	Ἰησοῦ,	ἐλθοῦσα	ἐν		τῷ	ὄχλῳ	ὄπισθεν	ἥψατο	τοῦ
the	Jesus,	having gone		in	the	crowd	from behind	she touched	the

2440   846   3004   1063 3754 1437 681   2579
ἱματίου αὐτοῦ·   28 ἔλεγεν γὰρ ὅτι ἐὰν ἅψωμαι κἂν
clothes of him;   she was for (")   if   I might even
                         saying,   touch   if

022 2440   846   4982   2532 2117
τῶν ἱματίων αὐτοῦ σωθήσομαι.   29 καὶ εὐθὺς
the clothes him   I will be delivered.   And immediately

3583   05   4077   010   129   846   2532
ἐξηράνθη   ἡ πηγὴ τοῦ αἵματος αὐτῆς καὶ
was dried out the spring of the blood   of her and

1097   011   4983   3754 2390   575
ἔγνω   τῷ σώματι ὅτι ἴαται   ἀπὸ
she knew in the body   that she had been cured from

06   3148   30 2532 2117   01   2424
τῆς μάστιγος.   καὶ εὐθὺς   ὁ Ἰησοῦς
the scourge.   And immediately the Jesus

1921   1722 1438   08   1537 846   1411
ἐπιγνοὺς   ἐν ἑαυτῷ τὴν ἐξ αὐτοῦ δύναμιν
having perceived in   himself the from him   power

1831   1994   1722 03   3793
ἐξελθοῦσαν   ἐπιστραφεὶς ἐν τῷ ὄχλῳ
having gone out   having returned in   the crowd

3004   5101 1473 681   022 2440   31 2532
ἔλεγεν·   τίς μου ἥψατο τῶν ἱματίων;   καὶ
he was saying; who of me touched the clothes?   And

3004   846   013 3101   846   991   04
ἔλεγον αὐτῷ οἱ μαθηταὶ αὐτοῦ· βλέπεις τὸν
were saying to him the learners of him; you see the

3793   4918   1473 2532 3004   5101 1473
ὄχλον συνθλίβοντά σε καὶ λέγεις· τίς μου
crowd pressing together you and you say; who   me

681   32 2532 4017   3708   08
ἥψατο;   καὶ περιεβλέπετο   ἰδεῖν τὴν
touched?   And he was looking around to see the one

3778   4160   05   1161 1135 5399   2532
τοῦτο ποιήσασαν.   33 ἡ δὲ γυνὴ φοβηθεῖσα καὶ
this having done.   The but woman having fear and

5141   3609a   3739 1096   846   2064
τρέμουσα, εἰδυῖα   ὃ γέγονεν αὐτῇ, ἦλθεν
trembling, having known what has become to her, went

2532 4363   846   2532 3004 846   3956 08
καὶ προσέπεσεν αὐτῷ καὶ εἶπεν αὐτῷ πᾶσαν τὴν
and fell toward him   and said to him all   the

225   01   1161 3004 846   2364   05
ἀλήθειαν. 34 ὁ   δὲ εἶπεν αὐτῇ· θυγάτηρ, ἡ
truth.   The one but said to her, daughter, the

4102   1473 4982   1473 5217   1519 1515
πίστις σου σέσωκέν   σε· ὕπαγε εἰς εἰρήνην
trust of you has delivered you; go off in peace

2532 1510 5199   575 06   3148   1473 35 2089
καὶ ἴσθι ὑγιὴς ἀπὸ τῆς μάστιγός σου.   Ἔτι
and be   healthy from the scourge of you. Still

846   2980   2064   575 02   752
αὐτοῦ λαλοῦντος ἔρχονται ἀπὸ τοῦ ἀρχισυναγώγου
him   speaking   they come from the synagogue ruler

3004   3754 05 2364   1473 599   5101 2089
λέγοντες ὅτι ἡ θυγάτηρ σου ἀπέθανεν· τί ἔτι
saying, (") the daughter of you died;   why still

4660   04 1320   36 01   1161   2424
σκύλλεις τὸν διδάσκαλον;   ὁ δὲ   Ἰησοῦς
annoy   the teacher?   The but Jesus

3878   04 3056 2980   3004 03
παρακούσας τὸν λόγον λαλούμενον λέγει τῷ
ignored hearing the word being spoken says to the

752   3361 5399   3441 4100   37 2532
ἀρχισυναγώγῳ· μὴ φοβοῦ, μόνον πίστευε.   καὶ
synagogue ruler, not fear, alone trust.   And

3756 863   3762   3326 846   4870
οὐκ ἀφῆκεν οὐδένα μετ' αὐτοῦ συνακολουθῆσαι
not he allowed no one with him   to follow together

---

his cloak, [28]for she said, "If I but touch his clothes, I will be made well." [29]Immediately her hemorrhage stopped; and she felt in her body that she was healed of her disease. [30]Immediately aware that power had gone forth from him, Jesus turned about in the crowd and said, "Who touched my clothes?" [31]And his disciples said to him, "You see the crowd pressing in on you; how can you say, 'Who touched me?' " [32]He looked all around to see who had done it. [33]But the woman, knowing what had happened to her, came in fear and trembling, fell down before him, and told him the whole truth. [34]He said to her, "Daughter, your faith has made you well; go in peace, and be healed of your disease."

35 While he was still speaking, some people came from the leader's house to say, "Your daughter is dead. Why trouble the teacher any further?" [36]But overhearing[a] what they said, Jesus said to the leader of the synagogue, "Do not fear, only believe." [37]He allowed no one to follow him

---

[a] Or *ignoring;* other ancient authorities read *hearing*

except Peter, James, and
John, the brother of James.
³⁸When they came to the
house of the leader of
the synagogue, he saw
a commotion, people
weeping and wailing
loudly. ³⁹When he had
entered, he said to them,
"Why do you make a
commotion and weep?
The child is not dead but
sleeping." ⁴⁰And they
laughed at him. Then he
put them all outside, and
took the child's father and
mother and those who were
with him, and went in
where the child was. ⁴¹He
took her by the hand and
said to her, "Talitha cum,"
which means, "Little girl,
get up!" ⁴²And immediately
the girl got up and began to
walk about (she was twelve
years of age). At this they
were overcome with
amazement. ⁴³He strictly
ordered them that no one
should know this, and told
them to give her something
to eat.

CHAPTER 6

He left that place and came
to his hometown, and his
disciples followed him. ²On
the sabbath he began to
teach in the synagogue,
and many who heard him
were astounded. They said,
"Where did this man get
all this?

1487	3361	04	4074	2532	2385	2532	2491	04
εἰ	μὴ	τὸν	Πέτρον	καὶ	Ἰάκωβον	καὶ	Ἰωάννην	τὸν
except	the	Peter	and	Jacob	and	John	the

80   2385   2532 2064   1519 04   3624
ἀδελφὸν Ἰακώβου. **38** καὶ ἔρχονται εἰς τὸν οἶκον
brother of Jacob.   And they come into the house

02   752   2532 2334   2351   2532
τοῦ ἀρχισυναγώγου, καὶ θεωρεῖ θόρυβον καὶ
of the synagogue ruler, and he watches uproar and

2799   2532 214   4183   **39** 2532 1525
κλαίοντας καὶ ἀλαλάζοντας πολλά,   καὶ εἰσελθὼν
crying   and wailing   many,   and having gone in

3004   846   5101 2350   2532 2799
λέγει αὐτοῖς· τί θορυβεῖσθε   καὶ κλαίετε;
he says to them; why are you in uproar and cry?

09   3813   3756 599   235   2518
τὸ παιδίον οὐκ ἀπέθανεν ἀλλὰ καθεύδει.
The small child not died   but she sleeps.

40 2532 2606   846   846   1161
καὶ κατεγέλων   αὐτοῦ. αὐτὸς δὲ
And they were laughing at him.   Himself but

1544   3956 3880   04 3962
ἐκβαλὼν   πάντας παραλαμβάνει τὸν πατέρα
having thrown out all   takes along   the father

010   3813   2532 08 3384   2532 016   3326
τοῦ παιδίου   καὶ τὴν μητέρα καὶ τοὺς μετ᾽
of the small child and the mother and the ones with

846 2532 1531   3699 1510 09 3813
αὐτοῦ καὶ εἰσπορεύεται ὅπου ἦν τὸ παιδίον.
him   and he travels into where was the small child.

41 2532 2902   06 5495 010   3813
καὶ κρατήσας τῆς χειρὸς τοῦ παιδίου
And having held the hand of the small child

3004   846   5008   2891 3739 1510
λέγει αὐτῇ· ταλιθα κουμ, ὅ ἐστιν
he says to her; talitha coum, which is+

0177   09 2877   1473 3004
μεθερμηνευόμενον· τὸ κοράσιον, σοὶ λέγω,
+being translated; the young girl, to you I say,

1453   **42** 2532 2117   450   09 2877   2532
ἔγειρε.   καὶ εὐθὺς ἀνέστη τὸ κοράσιον καὶ
rise.   And immediately stood up the young girl and

4043   1510 1063 2094 1427   2532 1839
περιεπάτει·   ἦν γὰρ ἐτῶν δώδεκα. καὶ ἐξέστησαν
she was walking she for years twelve. And they were
around;   was   amazed

2117   1611   3173   **43** 2532 1291
[εὐθὺς] ἐκστάσει μεγάλῃ.   καὶ διεστείλατο
immediately in amazement great. And he commanded

846   4183 2443 3367   1097   3778 2532 3004
αὐτοῖς πολλὰ ἵνα μηδεὶς γνοῖ τοῦτο, καὶ εἶπεν
them many that no one might know this, and he said

1325   846   2068   2532 1831
δοθῆναι αὐτῇ φαγεῖν. **6:1** Καὶ ἐξῆλθεν
to be given to her to eat.   And he went out

1564   2532 2064   1519 08 3968   846
ἐκεῖθεν καὶ ἔρχεται εἰς τὴν πατρίδα αὐτοῦ,
from there and he comes into the fatherland of him,

2532 190   846 013 3101   846   **2** 2532
καὶ ἀκολουθοῦσιν αὐτῷ οἱ μαθηταὶ αὐτοῦ. καὶ
and follow   him the learners of him. And

1096   4521   757   1321   1722 07
γενομένου σαββάτου ἤρξατο διδάσκειν ἐν τῇ
having become sabbath he began to teach in the

4864   2532 4183 191   1605
συναγωγῇ, καὶ πολλοὶ ἀκούοντες ἐξεπλήσσοντο
synagogue, and many hearing   were astonished

3004   4159   3778   3778 2532 5101
λέγοντες· πόθεν τούτῳ ταῦτα, καὶ τίς
saying, from where to this one these, and what

05   4678   05   1325   3778   2532
ἡ σοφία ἡ   δοθεῖσα   τούτῳ,   καὶ
the wisdom the one   having been given to this one, and

017 1411   5108   1223   018 5495   846
αἱ δυνάμεις τοιαῦται διὰ   τῶν χειρῶν αὐτοῦ
the powers such   through the hands of him

1096   3756 3778   1510 01 5045   01
γινόμεναι; ³ οὐχ οὗτός ἐστιν ὁ τέκτων,   ὁ
becoming?   Not this one is   the carpenter, the

5207 06   3137   2532 80   2385   2532
υἱὸς τῆς Μαρίας καὶ ἀδελφὸς Ἰακώβου καὶ
son of the Maria and brother of Jacob and

2500   2532 2455   2532 4613   2532 3756 1510
Ἰωσῆτος καὶ Ἰούδα καὶ Σίμωνος; καὶ οὐκ εἰσὶν
of Josetus and Judas and Simon?   And not are

017 79   846   5602 4314   1473 2532
αἱ ἀδελφαὶ αὐτοῦ ὧδε πρὸς ἡμᾶς; καὶ
the sisters of him here toward us?   And

4624   1722 846   2532 3004
ἐσκανδαλίζοντο   ἐν αὐτῷ. ⁴ καὶ ἔλεγεν
they were being offended in him.   And was saying

846   01 2424   3754 3756 1510 4396   820
αὐτοῖς ὁ Ἰησοῦς ὅτι οὐκ ἔστιν προφήτης ἄτιμος
to them the Jesus, (") not is spokesman dishonored

1487 3361 1722 07 3968   846   2532 1722 015
εἰ μὴ ἐν τῇ πατρίδι αὐτοῦ καὶ ἐν τοῖς
except in the fatherland of him and in the

4773   846   2532 1722 07 3614   846   ⁵ 2532
συγγενεῦσιν αὐτοῦ καὶ ἐν τῇ οἰκίᾳ αὐτοῦ.   καὶ
relatives of him and in the house of him.   And

3756 1410   1563   4160   3762   1411
οὐκ ἐδύνατο ἐκεῖ ποιῆσαι οὐδεμίαν δύναμιν,
not he was able there to do no one thing power,

1487 3361 3641 732   2007   020 5495
εἰ μὴ ὀλίγοις ἀρρώστοις ἐπιθεὶς τὰς χεῖρας
except few feeble ones having set on the hands

2323   ⁶ 2532 2296   1223   08 570
ἐθεράπευσεν. καὶ ἐθαύμαζεν   διὰ τὴν ἀπιστίαν
he healed.   And he was marveling through the untrust

846   2532 4013   020 2968   2945   1321
αὐτῶν. Καὶ περιῆγεν τὰς κώμας κύκλῳ διδάσκων.
of them. And he was   the villages in   teaching.
           leading around   circle

⁷ 2532 4341   016   1427   2532 757   846
 Καὶ προσκαλεῖται τοὺς δώδεκα καὶ ἤρξατο αὐτοὺς
 And he calls toward the twelve and he began them

649   1417 1417 2532 1325   846   1849
ἀποστέλλειν δύο δύο καὶ ἐδίδου αὐτοῖς ἐξουσίαν
to delegate two two and was giving to them authority

022   4151   022   169   ⁸ 2532 3853
τῶν πνευμάτων τῶν ἀκαθάρτων, καὶ παρήγγειλεν
of the spirits of the unclean,   and he commanded

846   2443 3367   142   1519 3598
αὐτοῖς ἵνα μηδὲν αἴρωσιν   εἰς ὁδὸν
them   that nothing they might lift up into way

1487 3361 4464   3441   3361 740   3361 4082 3361 1519
εἰ μὴ ῥάβδον μόνον, μὴ ἄρτον, μὴ πήραν, μὴ εἰς
except rod alone, not bread, not bag, not into

08 2223   5475   ⁹ 235 5265   4547   2532
τὴν ζώνην χαλκόν, ἀλλὰ ὑποδεδεμένους σανδάλια, καὶ
the belt copper, but having tied down sandals, and

3361 1746   1417 5509   10 2532 3004
μὴ ἐνδύσησθε   δύο χιτῶνας. καὶ ἔλεγεν
not you might put on twoshirts.   And he was saying

846   3699 1437 1525   1519 3614   1563
αὐτοῖς· ὅπου ἐὰν εἰσέλθητε εἰς οἰκίαν, ἐκεῖ
to them; where if you might go into into house, there

3306   2193 302 1831   1564   11 2532 3739
μένετε ἕως ἂν ἐξέλθητε ἐκεῖθεν   καὶ ὃς
stay   until - you might go out from there and what

What is this wisdom that has been given to him? What deeds of power are being done by his hands! ³Is not this the carpenter, the son of Mary[a] and brother of James and Joses and Judas and Simon, and are not his sisters here with us?" And they took offense[b] at him. ⁴Then Jesus said to them, "Prophets are not without honor, except in their hometown, and among their own kin, and in their own house." ⁵And he could do no deed of power there, except that he laid his hands on a few sick people and cured them. ⁶And he was amazed at their unbelief.

Then he went about among the villages teaching. ⁷He called the twelve and began to send them out two by two, and gave them authority over the unclean spirits. ⁸He ordered them to take nothing for their journey except a staff; no bread, no bag, no money in their belts; ⁹but to wear sandals and not to put on two tunics. ¹⁰He said to them, "Wherever you enter a house, stay there until you leave the place. ¹¹If any place

a Other ancient authorities read son of the carpenter and of Mary
b Or stumbled

will not welcome you and they refuse to hear you, as you leave, shake off the dust that is on your feet as a testimony against them." [12]So they went out and proclaimed that all should repent. [13]They cast out many demons, and anointed with oil many who were sick and cured them.

[14]King Herod heard of it, for Jesus'[a] name had become known. Some were[b] saying, "John the baptizer has been raised from the dead; and for this reason these powers are at work in him." [15]But others said, "It is Elijah." And others said, "It is a prophet, like one of the prophets of old." [16]But when Herod heard of it, he said, "John, whom I beheaded, has been raised."

[17]For Herod himself had sent men who arrested John, bound him, and put him in prison on account of Herodias, his brother Philip's wife, because Herod[c] had married her. [18]For John had been telling Herod, "It is not lawful for you to have your brother's wife." [19]And Herodias had a grudge against him, and wanted to kill him. But she could not, [20]for Herod feared John, knowing

[a] Gk his
[b] Other ancient authorities read He was
[c] Gk he

```
302  5117 3361 1209          1473 3366     191
ἂν τόπος μὴ δέξηται      ὑμᾶς μηδὲ    ἀκούσωσιν
- place not might welcome you but not they might hear
1473  1607          1564          1621        04 5529a 04
ὑμῶν, ἐκπορευόμενοι ἐκεῖθεν    ἐκτινάξατε τὸν χοῦν τὸν
you,  traveling out from there swing out   the dust the
5270        014 4228  1473   1519 3142        846
ὑποκάτω    τῶν ποδῶν ὑμῶν  εἰς μαρτύριον αὐτοῖς.
underneath the feet  of you into testimony to them.
      2532 1831          2784      2443 3340              2532
12  Καὶ ἐξελθόντες  ἐκήρυξαν  ἵνα μετανῶσιν,  13 καὶ
    And  having gone they      that they might      and
         out          announced        change mind,
1140    4183  1544          2532 218          1637  4183
δαιμόνια πολλὰ ἐξέβαλλον, καὶ ἤλειφον ἐλαίῳ πολλοὺς
demons  many they were   and they were oil  many
             throwing out, smearing
732        2532 2323          2532 191     01
ἀρρώστους καὶ ἐθεράπευον. 14 Καὶ ἤκουσεν ὁ
feeble    and they were healing. And heard   the
935        2264   5318     1063 1096   09  3686
βασιλεὺς Ἡρῴδης, φανερὸν γὰρ ἐγένετο τὸ ὄνομα
king      Herod,  evident for became the name
846     2532 3004          3754  2491    01
αὐτοῦ, καὶ ἔλεγον       ὅτι Ἰωάννης ὁ
of him, and they were saying, (") John   the one
907       1453          1537 3498   2532 1223
βαπτίζων ἐγήγερται    ἐκ νεκρῶν καὶ διὰ
immersing has been raised out of dead and through
3778 1754    017 1411      1722 846       243   1161
τοῦτο ἐνεργοῦσιν αἱ δυνάμεις ἐν αὐτῷ. 15 ἄλλοι δὲ
this  operate   the powers   in him.   Others but
3004        3754 2243   1510  243   1161 3004
ἔλεγον     ὅτι Ἠλίας ἐστίν· ἄλλοι δὲ ἔλεγον
were saying, (") Elijah it is; others but were saying,
3754 4396      5613 1520 014      4396     191
ὅτι προφήτης ὡς εἷς τῶν      προφητῶν. 16 ἀκούσας
(") spokesman as one of the spokesmen. Having heard
1161 01  2264   3004          3739 1473 607
δὲ ὁ Ἡρῴδης ἔλεγεν·        ὃν ἐγὼ ἀπεκεφάλισα
but the Herod was saying, whom I   cut off head
2491      3778    1453      846    1063 01  2264
Ἰωάννην, οὗτος ἠγέρθη. 17 Αὐτὸς γὰρ ὁ Ἡρῴδης
John,    this one was raised. Himself for the Herod
649         2902     04  2491       2532 1210
ἀποστείλας ἐκράτησεν τὸν Ἰωάννην καὶ ἔδησεν
having delegated he held the John  and he bound
846   1722 5438  1223          2266    08  1135
αὐτὸν ἐν φυλακῇ διὰ     Ἡρῳδιάδα τὴν γυναῖκα
him  in  guard because of Herodias the woman
5376      02  80      846     3754  846  1060
Φιλίππου τοῦ ἀδελφοῦ αὐτοῦ, ὅτι  αὐτὴν ἐγάμησεν·
of Philipp the brother of him, because he married;
   3004       1063 01  2491     03     2264 3754 3756
18 ἔλεγεν    γὰρ ὁ Ἰωάννης τῷ Ἡρῴδῃ ὅτι οὐκ
   was saying for the John to the Herod that not
1832    1473   2192    08 1133 846      1473
ἔξεστίν σοι ἔχειν τὴν γυναῖκα τοῦ ἀδελφοῦ σου.
it is  to you to have the woman of brother of you.
possible          the
   05 1161 2266     1758        846 2532 2309
19 ἡ δὲ Ἡρῳδιὰς ἐνεῖχεν   αὐτῷ καὶ ἤθελεν
   The but Herodias was holding him and she was
               in                          wanting
846   615          2532 3756 1410        01  1063
αὐτὸν ἀποκτεῖναι, καὶ οὐκ ἠδύνατο· 20 ὁ γὰρ
him  to be killed, and not she was able; the for
2264   5399     04  2491     3609a        846
Ἡρῴδης ἐφοβεῖτο τὸν Ἰωάννην, εἰδὼς      αὐτὸν
Herod  was fearing the John,  having known him
```

435   1342   2532 40   2532 4933
ἄνδρα δίκαιον καὶ ἅγιον, καὶ συνετήρει
man   right   and holy,   and he was keeping together
846   2532 191   846   4183 639
αὐτόν, καὶ ἀκούσας αὐτοῦ πολλὰ ἠπόρει,
him,   and having heard him many he was doubting,
2532 2234   846   191   2532 1096
καὶ ἡδέως αὐτοῦ ἤκουεν. **21** Καὶ γενομένης
and gladly him   he was hearing. And having become
2250 2121   3753 2264   023 1077   846
ἡμέρας εὐκαίρου ὅτε Ἡρῴδης τοῖς γενεσίοις αὐτοῦ
day   good season when Herod the   birthday   of him
1173   4160   015   3175   846   2532 015
δεῖπνον ἐποίησεν τοῖς μεγιστᾶσιν αὐτοῦ καὶ τοῖς
dinner he made to the great ones of him and to the
5506   2532 015 4413   06   1056
χιλιάρχοις   καὶ τοῖς πρώτοις τῆς Γαλιλαίας,
rulers of thousand and the first ones of the Galilee,
22 2532 1525   06 2364   846   2266
καὶ εἰσελθούσης   τῆς θυγατρὸς αὐτοῦ Ἡρῳδιάδος
and having gone into the daughter of him Herodias
2532 3738   700   03 2264   2532 015
καὶ ὀρχησαμένης ἤρεσεν τῷ Ἡρῴδη καὶ τοῖς
and having danced she pleased the Herod and the ones
4873   3004 01 935   011 2877
συνανακειμένοις. εἶπεν ὁ βασιλεὺς τῷ κορασίῳ·
reclining together. Said the king   the young girl;
154   1473 3739 1437 2309   2532 1325
αἴτησόν με ὃ ἐὰν θέλῃς,   καὶ δώσω
ask   me what if you might want, and I will give
1473 **23** 2532 3660   846   4183 3739 5100
σοι·   καὶ ὤμοσεν   αὐτῇ [πολλὰ] ὅ τι
to you; and he took an oath to her many   what any
1437 1473 154   1325   1473   2193 2255
ἐάν με αἰτήσῃς δώσω σοι ἕως ἡμίσους
if   me you might ask I will give to you until half
06   932   1473 **24** 2532 1831   3004
τῆς βασιλείας μου.   καὶ ἐξελθοῦσα εἶπεν
of the kingdom of me. And having gone out she said
07   3384   846   5101 154   05   1161
τῇ μητρὶ αὐτῆς· τί αἰτήσωμαι; ἡ δὲ
to the mother of her, what might I ask? The one but
3004   08 2776   2491   02 907   **25** 2532
εἶπεν· τὴν κεφαλὴν Ἰωάννου τοῦ βαπτίζοντος. καὶ
said; the head   of John the one immersing. And
1525   2117   3326 4710   4314   04
εἰσελθοῦσα εὐθὺς μετὰ σπουδῆς πρὸς τὸν
having gone into immediately with diligence toward the
935   154   3004   2309   2443 1824
βασιλέα ᾐτήσατο λέγουσα· θέλω ἵνα ἐξαυτῆς
king   she asked saying· I want that at once
1325   1473 1909 4094   08 2776   2491
δῷς   μοι ἐπὶ πίνακι τὴν κεφαλὴν Ἰωάννου
you might give to me on platter the head   of John
02 910   2532 4036   1096   01 935
τοῦ βαπτιστοῦ. **26** καὶ περίλυπος γενόμενος ὁ βασιλεὺς
the immerser. And greatly having the king
                    grieved become
1223   016 3727 2532 016   345   3756
διὰ   τοὺς ὅρκους καὶ τοὺς ἀνακειμένους οὐκ
because of the oaths and the ones reclining not
2309   114   846 **27** 2532 2117
ἠθέλησεν ἀθετῆσαι αὐτήν· καὶ εὐθὺς
wanted to set aside her; and immediately
649   01 935   4688   2004
ἀποστείλας ὁ βασιλεὺς σπεκουλάτορα ἐπέταξεν
having delegated the king executioner ordered
5342   08 2776   846 2532 565
ἐνέγκαι τὴν κεφαλὴν αὐτοῦ. καὶ ἀπελθὼν
to bring the head   of him. And having gone off

that he was a righteous and holy man, and he protected him. When he heard him, he was greatly perplexed;[a] and yet he liked to listen to him. [21]But an opportunity came when Herod on his birthday gave a banquet for his courtiers and officers and for the leaders of Galilee. [22]When his daughter Herodias[b] came in and danced, she pleased Herod and his guests; and the king said to the girl, "Ask me for whatever you wish, and I will give it." [23]And he solemnly swore to her, "Whatever you ask me, I will give you, even half of my kingdom." [24]She went out and said to her mother, "What should I ask for?" She replied, "The head of John the baptizer." [25]Immediately she rushed back to the king and requested, "I want you to give me at once the head of John the Baptist on a platter." [26]The king was deeply grieved; yet out of regard for his oaths and for the guests, he did not want to refuse her. [27]Immediately the king sent a soldier of the guard with orders to bring John's[c] head. He went

[a] Other ancient authorities read he did many things
[b] Other ancient authorities read the daughter of Herodias herself
[c] Gk his

and beheaded him in the prison, 28brought his head on a platter, and gave it to the girl. Then the girl gave it to her mother. 29When his disciples heard about it, they came and took his body, and laid it in a tomb.

30 The apostles gathered around Jesus, and told him all that they had done and taught. 31He said to them, "Come away to a deserted place all by yourselves and rest a while." For many were coming and going, and they had no leisure even to eat. 32And they went away in the boat to a deserted place by themselves. 33Now many saw them going and recognized them, and they hurried there on foot from all the towns and arrived ahead of them. 34As he went ashore, he saw a great crowd; and he had compassion for them, because they were like sheep without a shepherd; and he began to teach them many things. 35When it grew late, his disciples came to him and said, "This is a deserted place, and the hour is now very late; 36send them away so that they may go into the surrounding country and villages

607		846	1722	07	5438	**28**	2532
ἀπεκεφάλισεν		αὐτὸν	ἐν	τῇ	φυλακῇ		καὶ
he cut off		head him	in	the	guard		and

5342		08	2776	846	1909	4094	2532	1325
ἤνεγκεν		τὴν	κεφαλὴν	αὐτοῦ	ἐπὶ	πίνακι	καὶ	ἔδωκεν
he brought		the	head	of him	on	platter	and	he gave

846	011	2877		2532	09	2877	1325
αὐτὴν	τῷ	κορασίῳ,		καὶ	τὸ	κοράσιον	ἔδωκεν
it	to the	young girl,		and	the	young girl	gave

846	07	3384	846	**29**	2532	191		013
αὐτὴν	τῇ	μητρὶ	αὐτῆς.		καὶ	ἀκούσαντες		οἱ
it	to the	mother	of her.		And	having heard		the

3101	846	2064	2532	142	012	4430	846
μαθηταὶ	αὐτοῦ	ἦλθον	καὶ	ἦραν	τὸ	πτῶμα	αὐτοῦ
learners	of him	came	and	lifted	up the	corpse	of him

2532	5087	846	1722	3419	**30**	2532
καὶ	ἔθηκαν	αὐτὸ	ἐν	μνημείῳ.		Καὶ
and	set	it	in	grave.		And

4863		013	652	4314	04	2424
συνάγονται		οἱ	ἀπόστολοι	πρὸς	τὸν	Ἰησοῦν
were brought together		the	delegates	toward	the	Jesus

2532	518	846	3956	3745	4160	2532
καὶ	ἀπήγγειλαν	αὐτῷ	πάντα	ὅσα	ἐποίησαν	καὶ
and	they told	him	all	as much	as they did	and

3745	1321	**31**	2532	3004	846	1205	1473
ὅσα	ἐδίδαξαν.		καὶ	λέγει	αὐτοῖς·	δεῦτε	ὑμεῖς
as much as	they taught.		And	he says	to them;	come	you

846		2596	2398	1519	2048	5117	2532	373
αὐτοὶ		κατ᾿	ἰδίαν	εἰς	ἔρημον	τόπον	καὶ	ἀναπαύσασθε
yourselves		by	own	to	desert	place	and	rest

3641	1510	1063	013	2064		2532	013	5217
ὀλίγον.	ἦσαν	γὰρ	οἱ	ἐρχόμενοι		καὶ	οἱ	ὑπάγοντες
little.	Were	for	the	ones coming		and	the	going off

4183	2532	3761	2068	2119		**32**	2532
πολλοί,	καὶ	οὐδὲ	φαγεῖν	εὐκαίρουν.			Καὶ
many,	and	but not	to eat	they had good season.			And

565		1722	011	4143	1519	2048	5117	2596
ἀπῆλθον		ἐν	τῷ	πλοίῳ	εἰς	ἔρημον	τόπον	κατ᾿
they went off		in	the	boat	into	desert	place	by

2398	**33**	2532	3708	846	5217	2532	1921
ἰδίαν.		καὶ	εἶδον	αὐτοὺς	ὑπάγοντας	καὶ	ἐπέγνωσαν
own.		And	they saw	them	going off	and	perceived

4183	2532	3979	575	3956	018	4172	4936
πολλοὶ	καὶ	πεζῇ	ἀπὸ	πασῶν	τῶν	πόλεων	συνέδραμον
many	and	on foot	from	all	the	cities	they ran together

1563	2532	4281	846	**34**	2532	1831
ἐκεῖ	καὶ	προῆλθον	αὐτούς.		Καὶ	ἐξελθὼν
there	and	came before	them.		And	having gone out

3708	4183	3793	2532	4697	1909	846
εἶδεν	πολὺν	ὄχλον	καὶ	ἐσπλαγχνίσθη	ἐπ᾿	αὐτούς,
he saw	much	crowd	and	had affections	on	them,

3754	1510	5613	4263	3361	2192	4166	2532
ὅτι	ἦσαν	ὡς	πρόβατα	μὴ	ἔχοντα	ποιμένα,	καὶ
because	they were	as	sheep	not	having	shepherd,	and

757	1321	846	4183	**35**	2532	2235	5610
ἤρξατο	διδάσκειν	αὐτοὺς	πολλά.		Καὶ	ἤδη	ὥρας
he began	to teach	them	many.		And	already	hour

4183	1096	4334	846	2235	3101
πολλῆς	γενομένης	προσελθόντες	αὐτῷ	οἱ	μαθηταὶ
much	having become	having come	to him	the	learners

846	3004	3754	2048	1510	01	5117	2532
αὐτοῦ	ἔλεγον	ὅτι	ἔρημός	ἐστιν	ὁ	τόπος	καὶ
of him	were saying,	(")	desert	is	the	place	and

2235	5610	4183	**36**	630	846	2443
ἤδη	ὥρα	πολλή·		ἀπόλυσον	αὐτούς,	ἵνα
already	hour	much;		loose off	them,	that

565	1519	016	2945	68	2532	2968
ἀπελθόντες	εἰς	τοὺς	κύκλῳ	ἀγροὺς	καὶ	κώμας
having gone off	into	the	in circle	fields	and	villages

```
59              1438          5100  2068            01
ἀγοράσωσιν      ἑαυτοῖς       τί    φάγωσιν.     37 ὁ
they might buy  themselves    some  they might eat.   The one
1161  611                    3004  846        1325 846       1473
δὲ    ἀποκριθεὶς      εἶπεν αὐτοῖς·   δότε αὐτοῖς   ὑμεῖς
but   having answered said  to them,  give to them  you
2068      2532 3004    846        565
φαγεῖν. καὶ  λέγουσιν αὐτῷ·      ἀπελθόντες
to eat.   And  they say to him,  having gone off
59              1220         1250          740        2532
ἀγοράσωμεν      δηναρίων    διακοσίων    ἄρτους καὶ
we might buy     denaria     two hundred  bread  and
1325            846         2068              01       1161 3004
δώσομεν         αὐτοῖς    φαγεῖν;    38 ὁ      δὲ  λέγει
we will give     to them   to eat?      The one but  says
846       4214       740      2192       5217      3708       2532
αὐτοῖς·   πόσους    ἄρτους ἔχετε;     ὑπάγετε ἴδετε.  καὶ
to them;   how many  bread  have you?  Go off   see.     And
1097       3004        4002      2532 1417 2486          2532
γνόντες    λέγουσιν· πέντε,   καὶ  δύο  ἰχθύας. 39 καὶ
having known they say;  five,   and  two  fish.       And
2004      846         347          3956      4849
ἐπέταξεν  αὐτοῖς   ἀνακλῖναι  πάντας συμπόσια
he ordered them   to recline all      groups
4849         1909 03  5515  5528          2532 377
συμπόσια  ἐπὶ  τῷ  χλωρῷ χόρτῳ.  40 καὶ  ἀνέπεσαν
by groups  on    the  green grass.      And  they reclined
4237      4237        2596 1540      2532 2596 4004
πρασιαὶ πρασιαὶ  κατὰ ἑκατὸν  καὶ  κατὰ πεντήκοντα.
blocks    by blocks by    hundred  and  by    fifty.
    2532 2983              016  4002  740        2532 016  1417
41 καὶ  λαβὼν          τοὺς πέντε ἄρτους καὶ  τοὺς δύο
    And  having taken   the  five  bread  and  the  two
2486     308                  1519 04  3772       2127
ἰχθύας ἀναβλέψας       εἰς  τὸν οὐρανὸν εὐλόγησεν
fish     having looked up into  the heaven    he spoke well
2532 2622            016  740    2532 1325          015
καὶ  κατέκλασεν    τοὺς ἄρτους καὶ  ἐδίδου         τοῖς
and   he broke off   the  bread  and he was giving to the
3101        846      2443 3908              846
μαθηταῖς  [αὐτοῦ] ἵνα  παρατιθῶσιν      αὐτοῖς,
learners    of him   that  they might set along  them,
2532 016  1417 2486    3307        3956          2532 2068
καὶ  τοὺς δύο  ἰχθύας ἐμέρισεν πᾶσιν.   42 καὶ  ἔφαγον
and   the  two  fish   he divided to all.      And  ate
3956      2532 5526                     2532 142
πάντες καὶ  ἐχορτάσθησαν,       43 καὶ  ἦραν
all        and  they were satisfied;      and  they lifted up
2801       1427      2894               4138          2532 575
κλάσματα δώδεκα κοφίνων        πληρώματα καὶ  ἀπὸ
fragments  twelve  wicker baskets  full          and   from
014 2486      2532 1510 013 2068           016  740
τῶν ἰχθύων.  44 καὶ  ἦσαν οἱ  φαγόντες  [τοὺς ἄρτους]
the fish.      And   were the ones eating   the  bread
4000                 435         2532 2117        315
πεντακισχίλιοι ἄνδρες.  45 Καὶ  εὐθὺς     ἠνάγκασεν
five thousand   men.       And immediately he compelled
016  3101        846      1684       1519 012 4143      2532
τοὺς μαθητὰς αὐτοῦ ἐμβῆναι εἰς  τὸ πλοῖον καὶ
the   learners  of him   to go in  into  the  boat    and
4254          1519 012 4008    4314      966            2193
προάγειν   εἰς  τὸ πέραν πρὸς Βηθσαϊδάν, ἕως
to lead before into  the  across toward Bethsaida,  until
846     630        04  3793      2532 657
αὐτὸς  ἀπολύει  τὸν ὄχλον. 46 καὶ  ἀποταξάμενος
himself  he looses  the  crowd.    And  having said
off                                              good-bye
846     565            1519 012 3735 4336            2532
αὐτοῖς ἀπῆλθεν    εἰς  τὸ ὄρος προσεύξασθαι. 47 καὶ
to them he went off  into  the  hill   to pray.       And
```

and buy something for themselves to eat." [37]But he answered them, "You give them something to eat." They said to him, "Are we to go and buy two hundred denarii[a] worth of bread, and give it to them to eat?" [38]And he said to them, "How many loaves have you? Go and see." When they had found out, they said, "Five, and two fish." [39]Then he ordered them to get all the people to sit down in groups on the green grass. [40]So they sat down in groups of hundreds and of fifties. [41]Taking the five loaves and the two fish, he looked up to heaven, and blessed and broke the loaves, and gave them to his disciples to set before the people; and he divided the two fish among them all. [42]And all ate and were filled; [43]and they took up twelve baskets full of broken pieces and of the fish. [44]Those who had eaten the loaves numbered five thousand men.

[45]Immediately he made his disciples get into the boat and go on ahead to the other side, to Bethsaida, while he dismissed the crowd. [46]After saying farewell to them, he went up on the mountain to pray.

[47]When evening came,

---

[a] The denarius was the usual day's wage for a laborer

the boat was out on the sea, and he was alone on the land. ⁴⁸When he saw that they were straining at the oars against an adverse wind, he came towards them early in the morning, walking on the sea. He intended to pass them by. ⁴⁹But when they saw him walking on the sea, they thought it was a ghost and cried out; ⁵⁰for they all saw him and were terrified. But immediately he spoke to them and said, "Take heart, it is I; do not be afraid." ⁵¹Then he got into the boat with them and the wind ceased. And they were utterly astounded, ⁵²for they did not understand about the loaves, but their hearts were hardened.

53 When they had crossed over, they came to land at Gennesaret and moored the boat. ⁵⁴When they got out of the boat, people at once recognized him, ⁵⁵and rushed about that whole region and began to bring the sick on mats to wherever they heard he was. ⁵⁶And wherever he went, into villages or cities or

3798	1096		1510 09	4143	1722 3319
ὀψίας	γενομένης	ἦν	τὸ	πλοῖον ἐν	μέσῳ
evening	having become	was	the	boat in	middle

06	2281	2532 846	3441 1909 06	1093
τῆς	θαλάσσης, καὶ	αὐτὸς	μόνος ἐπὶ τῆς	γῆς.
of the sea,	and	himself	alone on the	land.

48
2532 3708	846	928	1722 011
καὶ ἰδὼν	αὐτοὺς	βασανιζομένους	ἐν τῷ
And having seen	them	being tormented	in the

1643	1510 1063 01	417	1727 846	4012
ἐλαύνειν,	ἦν γὰρ ὁ	ἄνεμος	ἐναντίος αὐτοῖς,	περὶ
to drive,	was for the	wind	against them,	around

5067	5438 06	3571	2064	4314 846
τετάρτην	φυλακὴν τῆς	νυκτὸς	ἔρχεται	πρὸς αὐτοὺς
fourth	guard of the	night	he comes	toward them

4043	1909 06 2281	2532 2309
περιπατῶν	ἐπὶ τῆς θαλάσσης καὶ	ἤθελεν
walking around	on the sea and	he was wanting

3928	846	**49**	013	1161 3708	846
παρελθεῖν	αὐτούς.		οἱ	δὲ ἰδόντες	αὐτὸν
to come along	them.		The ones	but having seen	him

1909 06 2281	4043	1380	3754 5326
ἐπὶ τῆς θαλάσσης	περιπατοῦντα	ἔδοξαν	ὅτι φάντασμά
on the sea	walking around	thought	that ghost

1510	2532 349	**50**	3956	1063 846	3708
ἐστιν,	καὶ ἀνέκραξαν·		πάντες	γὰρ αὐτὸν	εἶδον
it is,	and they shouted out;		all	for him	saw

2532 5015	01	1161 2117	2980
καὶ ἐταράχθησαν.	ὁ	δὲ εὐθὺς	ἐλάλησεν
and were troubled.	The one	but immediately	spoke

3326 846	2532 3004	846	2293	1473
μετ᾽ αὐτῶν,	καὶ λέγει	αὐτοῖς·	θαρσεῖτε,	ἐγώ
with them,	and he says	to them;	take courage,	I

1510	3361 5399	**51**	2532 305	4314 846
εἰμι·	μὴ φοβεῖσθε.		καὶ ἀνέβη	πρὸς αὐτοὺς
am;	not be afraid.		And he went up	toward them

1519 012 4143	2532 2869	01 417	2532 3029
εἰς τὸ πλοῖον	καὶ ἐκόπασεν	ὁ ἄνεμος,	καὶ λίαν
into the boat	and ceased	the wind,	and very

1537 4053	1722 1438	1839	**52**	3756 1063
[ἐκ περισσοῦ]	ἐν ἑαυτοῖς	ἐξίσταντο·		οὐ γὰρ
out of excess	in themselves	they were amazed;		not for

4920	1909 015 740	235 1510 846	05
συνῆκαν	ἐπὶ τοῖς ἄρτοις,	ἀλλ᾽ ἦν αὐτῶν	ἡ
they understood	on the bread,	but was+ of them	the

2588	4456	**53**	2532 1276
καρδια	πεπωρώμενη.		Καὶ διαπεράσαντες
heart	+having been hardened.		And having crossed over

1909 08 1093 2064	1519 1082	2532
ἐπὶ τὴν γῆν ἦλθον	εἰς Γεννησαρὲτ καὶ	
on the land they came	into Gennesaret and	

4358	**54**	2532 1831	846 1537
προσωρμίσθησαν.		καὶ ἐξελθόντων	αὐτῶν ἐκ
they were anchored.		And having gone out	them out of

010 4143	2117	1921	846	**55**	4063
τοῦ πλοίου	εὐθὺς	ἐπιγνόντες	αὐτὸν		περιέδραμον
of boat the	immediately	having perceived	him		they ran around

3650 08	5561	1565	2532 757	1909 015
ὅλην τὴν	χώραν	ἐκείνην καὶ	ἤρξαντο	ἐπὶ τοῖς
whole the	country	that and	they began	on the

2895	016 2560 2192	4064
κραβάττοις	τοὺς κακῶς ἔχοντας	περιφέρειν
mats	the badly ones having	to carry around

3699 191	3754 1510	**56**	2532 3699 302
ὅπου ἤκουον	ὅτι ἐστίν.		καὶ ὅπου ἂν
where they were hearing	that he is.		And where -

1531	1519 2968	2228 1519 4172 2228
εἰσεπορεύετο	εἰς κώμας	ἢ εἰς πόλεις ἢ
he was traveling	into into villages	or into cities or

1519	68		1722	019	58		5087			016
εἰς	ἀγρούς,	ἐν	ταῖς	ἀγοραῖς	ἐτίθεσαν					τοὺς
into	fields,	in	the	markets	they were setting					the

770		2532	3870			846	2443
ἀσθενοῦντας		καὶ	παρεκάλουν			αὐτὸν	ἵνα
ones being weak	and	they were encouraging	him	that

2579	010	2899		010	2440	846	681		2532
κἂν	τοῦ	κρασπέδου	τοῦ	ἱματίου	αὐτοῦ	ἅψωνται·	καὶ
even	the edge	of	clothes	of him	they might	and
if		the					touch;

3745		302	681		846	4982
ὅσοι		ἂν	ἥψαντο	αὐτοῦ	ἐσῴζοντο.
as many as	-	touched	him	they were being delivered.

7:1

2532	4863				4314	846	013
Καὶ	συνάγονται			πρὸς	αὐτὸν	οἱ
And	were being brought together	to	him	the

5330		2532	5100	014		1122		2064		575
Φαρισαῖοι	καί	τινες	τῶν		γραμματέων	ἐλθόντες		ἀπὸ
Pharisees	and	some	of the writers		having come from

2414			2532	3708		5100	014	3101
Ἰεροσολύμων.	**2**	καὶ	ἰδόντες		τινὰς	τῶν	μαθητῶν
Jerusalem.	And	having seen	some	of the learners

846	3754	2839		5495	5778	1510	449
αὐτοῦ	ὅτι	κοιναῖς	χερσίν,	τοῦτ᾽	ἔστιν	ἀνίπτοις,
of him	that	in common	hands,	this	is	unwashed,

2068		016	740		013	1063	5330		2532	3956
ἐσθίουσιν	τοὺς	ἄρτους	**3**	-	οἱ	γὰρ	Φαρισαῖοι	καὶ	πάντες
they eat	the	bread	the	for	Pharisees	and	all

013	2453		1437	3361	4435		3538			020
οἱ	Ἰουδαῖοι	ἐὰν	μὴ	πυγμῇ		νίψωνται			τὰς
the	Judeans	except	in fist	they might wash	the

5495	3756	2068		2902		08	3862		014
χεῖρας	οὐκ	ἐσθίουσιν,	κρατοῦντες	τὴν	παράδοσιν	τῶν
hands	not	they eat,	holding	the	tradition	of the

4245		2532	575	58		1437	3361
πρεσβυτέρων,	**4**	καὶ	ἀπ᾽	ἀγορᾶς	ἐὰν	μὴ
older men,	and	from market	except

907		3756	2068		2532	243	4183	1510
βαπτίσωνται	οὐκ	ἐσθίουσιν,	καὶ	ἄλλα	πολλά	ἐστιν
they might	not	they eat,	and	others many	there are
immerse themselves

3739	3880		2902	909		4221
ἃ	παρέλαβον	κρατεῖν,	βαπτισμοὺς	ποτηρίων
which	they took along	to hold,	immersions	of cups

2532	3582	2532	5473		2532	2825		2532
καὶ	ξεστῶν	καὶ	χαλκίων	[καὶ	κλινῶν]	**5**	καὶ
and	jugs	and	copper things	[and	beds]	and

1905		846	013	5330		2532	013	1122
ἐπερωτῶσιν	αὐτὸν	οἱ	Φαρισαῖοι	καὶ	οἱ	γραμματεῖς·
ask on	him	the	Pharisees	and	the	writers,

1223		5101	3756	4043		013	3101	1473
διὰ	τί	οὐ	περιπατοῦσιν	οἱ	μαθηταί	σου
through	what	not	walk around	the	learners	of you

2596		08	3862	014	4245		235
κατὰ	τὴν	παράδοσιν	τῶν	πρεσβυτέρων,	ἀλλὰ
according to	the	tradition	of the	older men,	but

2839		5495	2068		04	740		01		1161
κοιναῖς	χερσὶν	ἐσθίουσιν	τὸν	ἄρτον;	**6**	Ὁ	δὲ
in common	hands	they eat	the	bread?	The one	but

3004	846		2573	4395		2268	4012	1473
εἶπεν	αὐτοῖς·	καλῶς	ἐπροφήτευσεν	Ἡσαΐας	περὶ	ὑμῶν
said	to them;	well	spoke before	Isaiah	about	you

014	5273		5613	1125		3754	3778	01	2992
τῶν	ὑποκριτῶν,	ὡς	γέγραπται	[ὅτι]	οὗτος	ὁ	λαὸς
the	hypocrites,	as	it has been	(")	this	the	people
			written,

023	5491		1473	5091	05	1161	2588	846	4206
τοῖς	χείλεσίν	με	τιμᾷ,	ἡ	δὲ	καρδία	αὐτῶν	πόρρω
in the lips	me	value,	the	but	heart	of them	far

---

farms, they laid the sick in the marketplaces, and begged him that they might touch even the fringe of his cloak; and all who touched it were healed.

CHAPTER 7

Now when the Pharisees and some of the scribes who had come from Jerusalem gathered around him, [2]they noticed that some of his disciples were eating with defiled hands, that is, without washing them. [3](For the Pharisees, and all the Jews, do not eat unless they thoroughly wash their hands,[a] thus observing the tradition of the elders; [4]and they do not eat anything from the market unless they wash it;[b] and there are also many other traditions that they observe, the washing of cups, pots, and bronze kettles.[c]) [5]So the Pharisees and the scribes asked him, "Why do your disciples not live[d] according to the tradition of the elders, but eat with defiled hands?" [6]He said to them, "Isaiah prophesied rightly about you hypocrites, as it is written,

'This people honors me
  with their lips,
  but their hearts are far
  from me;

---

[a] Meaning of Gk uncertain
[b] Other ancient authorities read and when they come from the marketplace, they do not eat unless they purify themselves
[c] Other ancient authorities add and beds
[d] Gk walk

7 in vain do they worship
me,
teaching human
precepts as doctrines.'
8You abandon the
commandment of God and
hold to human tradition."
9 Then he said to them,
"You have a fine way of
rejecting the commandment
of God in order to keep
your tradition! 10For Moses
said, 'Honor your father
and your mother'; and,
'Whoever speaks evil of
father or mother must
surely die.' 11But you say
that if anyone tells father or
mother, 'Whatever support
you might have had from
me is Corban' (that is, an
offering to God*)— 12then
you no longer permit doing
anything for a father or
mother, 13thus making void
the word of God through
your tradition that you
have handed on. And you
do many things like this."

14Then he called the
crowd again and said to
them, "Listen to me, all
of you, and understand:
15there is nothing outside a
person that by going in can
defile, but the things that
come out are what defile."*

17 When he had left the
crowd and entered the
house, his disciples asked
him about the parable.
18He said to them, "Then
do you also

a Gk lacks *to God*
b Other ancient authorities add
verse 16, "*Let anyone with ears
to hear listen*"

          568   575   1473   **7** 3155   1161   4576
ἀπέχει   ἀπ'   ἐμοῦ·   μάτην   δὲ   σέβονταί
holds off from me;   in futility but   they worship
          1473 1321   1319   1778   444
με   διδάσκοντες διδασκαλίας ἐντάλματα ἀνθρώπων.
me   teaching   teachings   commands   of men.
       863   08   1785   02   2316 2902   08
8 ἀφέντες   τὴν ἐντολὴν τοῦ   θεοῦ κρατεῖτε τὴν
       Having sent off the command of the God you hold the
3862   014   444   **9** 2532 3004   846
παράδοσιν τῶν   ἀνθρώπων.   καὶ ἔλεγεν   αὐτοῖς·
tradition of the men.   And he was saying to them;
2573 114   08   1785   02   2316 2443 08
καλῶς ἀθετεῖτε   τὴν ἐντολὴν τοῦ   θεοῦ, ἵνα τὴν
well you set aside the command of the God, that the
3862   1473 2476   **10** 3475 1063 3004
παράδοσιν ὑμῶν στήσητε.   Μωϋσῆς γὰρ εἶπεν·
tradition of you you might stand. Moses   for said,
5091 04   3962   1473 2532 08   3384   1473   2532 01
τίμα τὸν πατέρα σου   καὶ τὴν μητέρα σου,   καί ὁ
value the father of you and the mother of you, and the
2551   3962 2228 3384   2288   5053
κακολόγων   πατέρα ἢ μητέρα θανάτῳ   τελευτάτω.
one speaking bad father or mother in death let die.
   1473 1161 3004   1437 3004   444   03   3962
11 ὑμεῖς δὲ λέγετε· ἐὰν εἴπῃ   ἄνθρωπος τῷ πατρὶ
       You   but say;   if might say man   to the father
2228 07   3384   2878   3739 1510 1435   3739 1437
ἢ   τῇ μητρί· κορβᾶν, ὅ   ἐστιν δῶρον, ὃ   ἐὰν
or   the mother; corban, which is   gift, what if
1537 1473 5623   3765   863
ἐξ   ἐμοῦ ὠφεληθῇς,   **12** οὐκέτι   ἀφίετε
out of me you might be benefitted, no longer you allow
846   3762 4160   03   3962 2228 07 3384
αὐτὸν οὐδὲν ποιῆσαι τῷ   πατρὶ ἢ τῇ μητρί,
him nothing to do   to the father or the mother,
   208   04   3056   02   2316 07   3862
13 ἀκυροῦντες   τὸν λόγον τοῦ   θεοῦ τῇ   παραδύει
       invalidating the word of the God in the tradition
1473 3739 3860   2532 3946   5108
ὑμῶν ᾗ   παρεδώκατε·   καὶ παρόμοια τοιαῦτα
of you which you gave over; and similar   such things
4183 4160   2532 4341   3825 04
πολλὰ ποιεῖτε. **14** Καὶ προσκαλεσάμενος   πάλιν τὸν
many you do.   And having called toward again the
3793 3004   846   191   1473 3956
ὄχλον ἔλεγεν   αὐτοῖς· ἀκούσατέ μου   πάντες
crowd he was saying to them, hear   of me all
2532 4920   3762   1510 1855   02   444
καὶ σύνετε. **15** οὐδέν ἐστιν ἔξωθεν   τοῦ ἀνθρώπου
and understand. Nothing is   from outside the man
1531   1519 846   3739 1410   2840
εἰσπορευόμενον εἰς   αὐτὸν ὃ   δύναται κοινῶσαι
traveling into into him which is able to make common
846   235   021   1537 02 444   1607
αὐτόν, ἀλλὰ τὰ   ἐκ   τοῦ ἀνθρώπου ἐκπορευόμενά
him,   but the things from the man   traveling out
1510 021   2840   04 444   **17** 2532
ἐστιν τὰ   κοινοῦντα   τὸν ἄνθρωπον.   Καὶ
are   the things making common the man.   And
3753 1525   1519 3624 575 02 3793
ὅτε εἰσῆλθεν   εἰς οἶκον ἀπὸ τοῦ ὄχλου,
when he went into into house from the crowd,
1905   846   013 3101   846   08
ἐπηρώτων   αὐτὸν οἱ μαθηταὶ αὐτοῦ τὴν
were asking on him   the learners of him the
3850   2532 3004   846   3779   2532 1473
παραβολήν. **18** καὶ λέγει   αὐτοῖς· οὕτως καὶ ὑμεῖς
parallel story. And he says to them; thusly also you

801 / 1510 / 3756 3539 / 3754 3956 09
ἀσύνετοί ἐστε; οὐ νοεῖτε ὅτι πᾶν τὸ
not understanding are you? Not you give that all the
thought

1855 / 1531 / 1519 04 444 / 3756
ἔξωθεν εἰσπορευόμενον εἰς τὸν ἄνθρωπον οὐ
from outside traveling into into the man not

1410 846 2840 / **19** / 3754 3756 1531
δύναται αὐτὸν κοινῶσαι ὅτι οὐκ εἰσπορεύεται
is able him to make common because not it travels in

846 1519 08 2588 235 1519 08 2836 2532 1519
αὐτοῦ εἰς τὴν καρδίαν ἀλλ᾽ εἰς τὴν κοιλίαν, καὶ εἰς
him into the heart but into the stomach, and into

04 856 1607 2511 3956 024
τὸν ἀφεδρῶνα ἐκπορεύεται, καθαρίζων πάντα τὰ
the latrine it travels out, cleaning all the

1033 / **20** / 3004 1161 3754 09 1537 02
βρώματα; ἔλεγεν δὲ ὅτι τὸ ἐκ τοῦ
foods? He was saying but, (") the out of the

444 1607 1565 2840 04
ἀνθρώπου ἐκπορευόμενον, ἐκεῖνο κοινοῖ τὸν
man traveling out, that makes common the

444 / **21** / 2081 1063 1537 06 2588 014
ἄνθρωπον. ἔσωθεν γὰρ ἐκ τῆς καρδίας τῶν
man. From inside for from the heart of the

444 013 1261 013 2556 1607
ἀνθρώπων οἱ διαλογισμοὶ οἱ κακοὶ ἐκπορεύονται,
men the reasonings the bad travel out,

4202 2829 5408 / **22** / 3430
πορνεῖαι, κλοπαί, φόνοι, μοιχεῖαι,
sexual immoralities, thefts, murders, adulteries,

4124 4189 1388 766 3788
πλεονεξίαι, πονηρίαι, δόλος, ἀσέλγεια, οφθαλμὸς
greedinesses, evils, guile, debauchery, eye

4190 988 5243 877
πονηρός, βλασφημία, ὑπερηφανία, ἀφροσύνη·
evil, insult, arrogance, thoughtlessness;

23 / 3956 3778 021 4190 2081 1607 2532
πάντα ταῦτα τὰ πονηρὰ ἔσωθεν ἐκπορεύεται καὶ
all these the evils from inside travel out and

2840 04 444 / **24** / 1564 1161 450 565
κοινοῖ τὸν ἄνθρωπον. Ἐκεῖθεν δὲ ἀναστὰς ἀπῆλθεν
make the man. From but having he went
common there stood up off

1519 024 3725 5184 2532 1525
εἰς τὰ ὅρια Τύρου. Καὶ εἰσελθὼν
into the territories of Tyre. And having gone into

1519 3614 3762 2309 1097 2532 3756
εἰς οἰκίαν οὐδένα ἤθελεν γνῶναι, καὶ οὐκ
into house no one he was wanting to know, and not

1410 2990 / **25** / 235 2117
ἠδυνήθη λαθεῖν· ἀλλ᾽ εὐθὺς
he was able to escape notice; but immediately

191 1135 4012 846 3739 2192 09
ἀκούσασα γυνὴ περὶ αὐτοῦ, ἧς εἶχεν τὸ
having heard woman concerning him, who had the

2365 846 4151 169 2064
θυγάτριον αὐτῆς πνεῦμα ἀκάθαρτον, ἐλθοῦσα
small daughter of her spirit unclean, having come

4363 4314 016 4228 846 / **26** / 05 1161
προσέπεσεν πρὸς τοὺς πόδας αὐτοῦ· ἡ δὲ
she fell toward toward the feet of him; the but

1135 1510 1674 4949 011 1085
γυνὴ ἦν Ἑλληνίς, Συροφοινίκισσα τῷ γένει·
woman was Greek, Syrophoenician in the kind;

2532 2065 846 2443 012 1140
καὶ ἠρώτα αὐτὸν ἵνα τὸ δαιμόνιον
and she was asking him that the demon

fail to understand? Do you not see that whatever goes into a person from outside cannot defile, [19]since it enters, not the heart but the stomach, and goes out into the sewer?" (Thus he declared all foods clean.) [20]And he said, "It is what comes out of a person that defiles. [21]For it is from within, from the human heart, that evil intentions come: fornication, theft, murder, [22]adultery, avarice, wickedness, deceit, licentiousness, envy, slander, pride, folly. [23]All these evil things come from within, and they defile a person."

[24]From there he set out and went away to the region of Tyre.[a] He entered a house and did not want anyone to know he was there. Yet he could not escape notice, [25]but a woman whose little daughter had an unclean spirit immediately heard about him, and she came and bowed down at his feet. [26]Now the woman was a Gentile, of Syrophoenician origin. She begged him

[a] Other ancient authorities add and Sidon

to cast the demon out of her daughter. 27He said to her, "Let the children be fed first, for it is not fair to take the children's food and throw it to the dogs." 28But she answered him, "Sir,*a* even the dogs under the table eat the children's crumbs." 29Then he said to her, "For saying that, you may go—the demon has left your daughter." 30So she went home, found the child lying on the bed, and the demon gone.

31 Then he returned from the region of Tyre, and went by way of Sidon towards the Sea of Galilee, in the region of the Decapolis. 32They brought to him a deaf man who had an impediment in his speech; and they begged him to lay his hand on him. 33He took him aside in private, away from the crowd, and put his fingers into his ears, and he spat and touched his tongue. 34Then looking up to heaven, he sighed and said to him, "Ephphatha," that is, "Be opened." 35And immediately his ears were opened,

a Or *Lord;* other ancient authorities prefix *Yes*

| 1544 | | 1537 | 06 | 2364 | | 846 | 27 | 2532 |
| ἐκβάλη | | ἐκ | τῆς | θυγατρὸς | | αὐτῆς. | | καὶ |

he might throw out   out of the daughter of her.   And

| 3004 | | 846 | 863 | 4413 | 5526 | | 024 |
| ἔλεγεν | | αὐτῇ· | ἄφες | πρῶτον | χορτασθῆναι | | τὰ |

he was saying to her; allow first   to be satisfied the

| 5043 | | 3756 | 1063 | 1510 | 2570 | 2983 | 04 | 740 |
| τέκνα, | | οὐ | γάρ | ἐστιν | καλὸν | λαβεῖν | τὸν | ἄρτον |

children, not for it is good to take the bread

| 022 | 5043 | 2532 | 023 | 2952 | | 906 | 28 | 05 |
| τῶν | τέκνων | καὶ | τοῖς | κυναρίοις | | βαλεῖν. | | ἡ |

of the children and to the puppies   to throw. The one

| 1161 | 611 | 2532 | 3004 | 846 | | 2962 | 2532 | 021 |
| δὲ | ἀπεκρίθη | καὶ | λέγει | αὐτῷ· | | κύριε· | καὶ | τὰ |

but answered and says to him; Master; also the

| 2952 | 5270 | 06 | 5132 | 2068 | | 575 | 022 |
| κυνάρια | ὑποκάτω | τῆς | τραπέζης | ἐσθίουσιν | | ἀπὸ | τῶν |

puppies underneath the table   eat   from the

| 5589 | 022 | 3813 | | 29 | 2532 | 3004 |
| ψιχίων | τῶν | παιδίων. | | | καὶ | εἶπεν |

small crumbs of the small children. And   he said

| 846 | 1223 | 3778 | 04 | 3056 | 5217 | | 1831 |
| αὐτῇ· | διὰ | τοῦτον | τὸν | λόγον | ὕπαγε, | | ἐξελήλυθεν |

to her; through this the word go off, has gone out

| 1537 | 06 | 2364 | 1473 | 09 | 1140 | 30 | 2532 |
| ἐκ | τῆς | θυγατρός | σου | τὸ | δαιμόνιον. | | καὶ |

out of the daughter of you the demon.   And

| 565 | | 1519 | 04 | 3624 | 846 | 2147 | 012 |
| ἀπελθοῦσα | | εἰς | τὸν | οἶκον | αὐτῆς | εὗρεν | τὸ |

having gone off into the house of her she found the

| 3813 | 906 | | 1909 | 08 | 2825 | 2532 | 012 |
| παιδίον | βεβλημένον | | ἐπὶ | τὴν | κλίνην | καὶ | τὸ |

small child having been thrown on the bed   and the

| 1140 | 1831 | 31 | 2532 | 3825 | 1831 |
| δαιμόνιον | ἐξεληλυθός. | | Καὶ | πάλιν | ἐξελθὼν |

demon   having gone out.   And again having gone out

| 1537 | 022 | 3725 | | 5184 | 2064 | 1223 |
| ἐκ | τῶν | ὁρίων | | Τύρου | ἦλθεν | διὰ |

out of the territories of Tyre he went through

| 4605 | 1519 | 08 | 2281 | 06 | | 1056 | 303 | 3319 |
| Σιδῶνος | εἰς | τὴν | θάλασσαν | τῆς | | Γαλιλαίας | ἀνὰ | μέσον |

Sidon into the sea   of the Galilee   up middle

| 022 | 3725 | 1179 | 32 | 2532 | 5342 | | 846 |
| τῶν | ὁρίων | Δεκαπόλεως. | | Καὶ | φέρουσιν | | αὐτῷ |

of the territories of Decapolis. And they carry to him

| 2974 | 2532 | 3424 | | 2532 | 3870 | | 846 |
| κωφὸν | καὶ | μογιλάλον | | καὶ | παρακαλοῦσιν | | αὐτὸν |

deaf and speech difficulty and they encourage him

| 2443 | 2007 | 846 | 08 | 5495 | 33 | 2532 | 618 |
| ἵνα | ἐπιθῇ | αὐτῷ | τὴν | χεῖρα. | | καὶ | ἀπολαβόμενος |

that he might him the hand.   And having taken
set on   back

| 846 | 575 | 02 | 3793 | 2596 | 2398 | 906 | 016 | 1147 |
| αὐτὸν | ἀπὸ | τοῦ | ὄχλου | κατ' | ἰδίαν | ἔβαλεν | τοὺς | δακτύλους |

him from the crowd by own he threw the fingers

| 846 | | 1519 | 024 | 3775 | 846 | 2532 | 4429 | | 681 |
| αὐτοῦ | | εἰς | τὰ | ὦτα | αὐτοῦ | καὶ | πτύσας | | ἥψατο |

of him into the ears of him and having spit he touched

| 06 | 1100 | 846 | 34 | 2532 | 308 | | 1519 |
| τῆς | γλώσσης | αὐτοῦ, | | καὶ | ἀναβλέψας | | εἰς |

the tongue of him,   and having looked up into

| 04 | 3772 | 4727 | | 2532 | 3004 | 846 | 2188 |
| τὸν | οὐρανὸν | ἐστέναξεν | | καὶ | λέγει | αὐτῷ· | Εφφαθα, |

the heaven he groaned and says to him; Ephphatha,

| 3739 | 1510 | 1272 | | 35 | 2532 | 2112 |
| ὅ | ἐστιν | διανοίχθητι. | | | καὶ | [εὐθέως] |

which is, be opened completely. And immediately

| 455 | | 846 | 017 | 189 | | 2532 | 3089 |
| ἠνοίγησαν | | αὐτοῦ | αἱ | ἀκοαί, | | καὶ | ἐλύθη |

were opened of him the hearings, and was loosened

```
01      1199    06        1100      846      2532  2980
ὁ    δεσμὸς  τῆς    γλώσσης  αὐτοῦ  καὶ  ἐλάλει
the  chain   of the  tongue   of him and   he was speaking
3723              2532 1291              846       2443  3367
ὀρθῶς.    36   καὶ  διεστείλατο  αὐτοῖς  ἵνα  μηδενὶ
straightly.    And  he commanded  them   that  to no one
3004      3745   1161 846        1291             846
λέγωσιν·  ὅσον  δὲ   αὐτοῖς  διεστέλλετο,  αὐτοὶ
they might as much but  to them  he was        themselves
say;      as                    commanding,
3123     4055          2784                      2532
μᾶλλον περισσότερον  ἐκήρυσσον.    37   καὶ
more    more excessive they were announcing.   And
5249            1605          3004        2573   3956
ὑπερπερισσῶς  ἐξεπλήσσοντο  λέγοντες·  καλῶς  πάντα
exceedingly   they were      saying;    well   all
beyond        astonished
4160          2532 016   2974    4160     191     2532
πεποίηκεν,   καὶ  τοὺς κωφοὺς ποιεῖ  ἀκούειν καὶ
he has done, even  the  deaf   he makes to hear  and
016     216       2980              1722 1565      019
[τοὺς] ἀλάλους  λαλεῖν.   8:1   Ἐν  ἐκείναις ταῖς
the     speechless to speak.    In  those    the
2250      3825   4183  3793   1510  2532 3361  2192
ἡμέραις πάλιν πολλοῦ ὄχλου ὄντος καὶ  μὴ  ἐχόντων
days     again much  crowd being and  not  having
5100  2068          4341                016
τί   φάγωσιν,   προσκαλεσάμενος    τοὺς
some they might eat, having called toward the
3101      3004   846        2   4697           1909 04
μαθητὰς λέγει  αὐτοῖς·    σπλαγχνίζομαι  ἐπὶ  τὸν
learners he says to them;   I have affection on   the
3793   3754   2235   2250      5140  4357
ὄχλον, ὅτι   ἤδη  ἡμέραι  τρεῖς προσμένουσίν
crowd, because already days  three they stay toward
1473 2532 3756 2192      5100 2068         3    2532
μοι  καὶ  οὐκ ἔχουσιν  τί  φάγωσιν·      καὶ
me   and  not  they have some they might eat; and
1437  630                846     3523   1519 3624
ἐὰν  ἀπολύσω          αὐτοὺς νήστεις εἰς οἶκον
if    I might loose off them   fasting into house
846    1590                  1722  07  3598 2532
αὐτῶν, ἐκλυθήσονται        ἐν   τῇ  ὁδῷ· καί
of them, they will be loosed out in   the  way; and
5100  846      575  3113      2240      4    2532
τινες αὐτῶν ἀπὸ μακρόθεν ἥκασιν.    καὶ
some  of them from from far  they have come.  And
611           846    013 3101     846      3754 4159
ἀπεκρίθησαν αὐτῷ οἱ  μαθηταὶ αὐτοῦ ὅτι  πόθεν
answered      him  the learners of him, (")  from where
3778     1410       5100 5602 5526     740     1909
τούτους δυνήσεταί τις ὧδε χορτάσαι ἄρτων ἐπ᾽
these    will be able some here to satisfy bread  at
2047     5  2532 2065           846    4214    2192
ἐρημίας;   καὶ  ἠρώτα        αὐτούς· πόσους ἔχετε
desert?    And  he was asking them;  how many have you
740     013    1161 3004    2033  6   2532 3853
ἄρτους; οἱ   δὲ  εἶπαν· ἑπτά.   καὶ  παραγγέλλει
bread?  The ones but said; seven.  And  he commands
03  3793   377         1909 06  1093   2532 2983
τῷ ὄχλῳ ἀναπεσεῖν  ἐπὶ τῆς γῆς· καὶ  λαβὼν
the crowd to recline on  the earth; and  having taken
016  2033   740     2168            2806    2532
τοὺς ἑπτὰ ἄρτους εὐχαριστήσας  ἔκλασεν καὶ
the  seven bread  having given good favor he broke and
1325  015     3101    846     2443 3908          2532
ἐδίδου τοῖς μαθηταῖς αὐτοῦ ἵνα  παρατιθῶσιν,  καὶ
he was to the learners of him that they might set and
giving                              along,
```

his tongue was released, and he spoke plainly. [36]Then Jesus[a] ordered them to tell no one; but the more he ordered them, the more zealously they proclaimed it. [37]They were astounded beyond measure, saying, "He has done everything well; he even makes the deaf to hear and the mute to speak."

CHAPTER 8

In those days when there was again a great crowd without anything to eat, he called his disciples and said to them, [2]"I have compassion for the crowd, because they have been with me now for three days and have nothing to eat. [3]If I send them away hungry to their homes, they will faint on the way—and some of them have come from a great distance." [4]His disciples replied, "How can one feed these people with bread here in the desert?" [5]He asked them, "How many loaves do you have?" They said, "Seven." [6]Then he ordered the crowd to sit down on the ground; and he took the seven loaves, and after giving thanks he broke them and gave them to his disciples to distribute;

[a] Gk he

and they distributed them to the crowd. ⁷They had also a few small fish; and after blessing them, he ordered that these too should be distributed. ⁸They ate and were filled; and they took up the broken pieces left over, seven baskets full. ⁹Now there were about four thousand people. And he sent them away. ¹⁰And immediately he got into the boat with his disciples and went to the district of Dalmanutha.[a]

11 The Pharisees came and began to argue with him, asking him for a sign from heaven, to test him. ¹²And he sighed deeply in his spirit and said, "Why does this generation ask for a sign? Truly I tell you, no sign will be given to this generation." ¹³And he left them, and getting into the boat again, he went across to the other side.

14 Now the disciples[b] had forgotten to bring any bread; and they had only one loaf with them in the boat. ¹⁵And he cautioned them, saying, "Watch out— beware of the yeast of the Pharisees and the yeast of Herod."[c] ¹⁶They said to one another, "It is because we have no bread." ¹⁷And becoming aware of it, Jesus said to them, "Why are you talking about having no bread? Do you still not perceive or

[a] Other ancient authorities read *Mageda* or *Magdala*

[b] Gk *they*

[c] Other ancient authorities read *the Herodians*

3908		03	3793	**7**	2532	2192		2485

παρέθηκαν   τῷ   ὄχλῳ.   **7** καὶ   εἶχον   ἰχθύδια
they set along to the crowd.   And   they had   small fish

ὀλίγα· καὶ   εὐλογήσας   αὐτὰ εἶπεν   καὶ   ταῦτα
few;   and   having spoken well   them he said also these

παρατιθέναι.   **8** καὶ   ἔφαγον   καὶ   ἐχορτάσθησαν,
to be set along. And   they ate and   were satisfied,

καὶ   ἦραν   περισσεύματα κλασμάτων ἑπτὰ
and   they lifted up excesses   fragments seven

σπυρίδας.   **9** ἦσαν   δὲ   ὡς   τετρακισχίλιοι.
mat baskets.   There were but   as   four thousand.

καὶ   ἀπέλυσεν   αὐτούς.   **10** Καὶ   εὐθὺς
And   he loosed off them.   And   immediately

ἐμβὰς   εἰς   τὸ   πλοῖον μετὰ τῶν μαθητῶν
having gone in into the boat   with the learners

αὐτοῦ   ἦλθεν   εἰς   τὰ   μέρη   Δαλμανουθά.   **11** Καὶ
of him he went into the parts Dalmanoutha.   And

ἐξῆλθον   οἱ   Φαρισαῖοι καὶ   ἤρξαντο συζητεῖν   αὐτῷ,
went out the Pharisees and   began   to dispute him,

ζητοῦντες παρ' αὐτοῦ σημεῖον ἀπὸ τοῦ οὐρανοῦ,
seeking   from him   sign   from the heaven,

πειράζοντες αὐτόν.   **12** καὶ   ἀναστενάξας   τῷ
pressing   him.   And   having groaned up in the

πνεύματι αὐτοῦ λέγει·   τί   ἡ   γενεὰ   αὕτη
spirit   of him he says; why the generation this

ζητεῖ σημεῖον; ἀμὴν λέγω ὑμῖν,   εἰ δοθήσεται   τῇ
seeks sign?   Amen I say to you, if will be given the

γενεᾷ   ταύτῃ σημεῖον.   **13** καὶ   ἀφεὶς   αὐτοὺς
generation this sign.   And   having sent off them

πάλιν ἐμβὰς   ἀπῆλθεν   εἰς   τὸ   πέραν.
again having gone in he went off into the across.

14 Καὶ   ἐπελάθοντο λαβεῖν ἄρτους καὶ   εἰ μὴ ἕνα
And   they forgot   to take bread and   except one

ἄρτον οὐκ   εἶχον   μεθ' ἑαυτῶν   ἐν   τῷ πλοίῳ.
bread not   they had with themselves in   the boat.

15 καὶ   διεστέλλετο   αὐτοῖς λέγων·   ὁρᾶτε,
And   he was commanding them   saying; see,

βλέπετε ἀπὸ   τῆς ζύμης τῶν   Φαρισαίων καὶ   τῆς
see   from the yeast of the Pharisees and   of the

ζύμης Ἡρῴδου.   **16** καὶ   διελογίζοντο   πρὸς
yeast of Herod.   And   they were reasoning toward

ἀλλήλους   ὅτι   ἄρτους οὐκ   ἔχουσιν.   **17** καὶ
one another that bread   not   they have.   And

γνοὺς   λέγει   αὐτοῖς·   τί   διαλογίζεσθε ὅτι
having known he says to them; why reason you   that

ἄρτους οὐκ   ἔχετε;   οὔπω   νοεῖτε   οὐδὲ
bread   not   you have? Not yet you give thought but not

4920   4456   2192   08   2588
συνίετε;   πεπωρωμένην ἔχετε   τὴν καρδίαν
you understand? Having been have you the heart
               hardened

1473   18 3788   2192   3756 991   2532 3775
ὑμῶν;   ὀφθαλμοὺς ἔχοντες οὐ βλέπετε καὶ ὦτα
of you? Eyes   having not you see and ears

2192   3756 191   2532 3756 3421   19 3753
ἔχοντες οὐκ ἀκούετε; καὶ οὐ μνημονεύετε,   ὅτε
having not you hear? And not you remember, when

016 4002 740   2806   1519 016 4000
τοὺς πέντε ἄρτους ἔκλασα εἰς τοὺς πεντακισχιλίους,
the five bread I broke into the five thousand,

4214   2894   2801   4134
πόσους κοφίνους κλασμάτων πλήρεις
how many wicker baskets of fragments full

142   3004   846   1427   20 3753 016
ἤρατε;   λέγουσιν αὐτῷ· δώδεκα.   ὅτε τοὺς
you lifted up? They say to him; twelve. When the

2033 1519 016 5070   4214   4711
ἑπτὰ εἰς τοὺς τετρακισχίλιους, πόσων σπυρίδων
seven into the four thousand, how many mat baskets

4138   2801   142   2532 3004
πληρώματα κλασμάτων ἤρατε;   καὶ λέγουσιν
full   of fragments you lifted up? And they say

846   2033   21 2532 3004   846   3768
[αὐτῷ], ἑπτά.   καὶ ἔλεγεν   αὐτοῖς· οὔπω
to him, seven.   And he was saying to them; not yet

4920   22 2532 2064   1519 966   2532
συνίετε;   Καὶ ἔρχονται εἰς Βηθσαϊδάν. Καὶ
you understand? And they come into Bethsaida. And

5342   846   5185   2532 3870   846
φέρουσιν αὐτῷ τυφλὸν καὶ παρακαλοῦσιν αὐτὸν
they carry to him blind one and they encourage him

2443 846   681   23 2532 1949   06
ἵνα αὐτοῦ ἅψηται.   καὶ ἐπιλαβόμενος τῆς
that him he might touch. And having taken on the

5495   02   5185   1627   846   1854   06
χειρὸς τοῦ τυφλοῦ ἐξήνεγκεν αὐτὸν ἔξω   τῆς
hand of the blind he brought out him outside the

2968   2532 4429   1519 024 3659 846
κώμης καὶ πτύσας   εἰς τὰ ὄμματα αὐτοῦ,
village and having spit into the eyes of him,

2007   020 5495   846   1905   846   1487 5100
ἐπιθεὶς τὰς χεῖρας αὐτῷ ἐπηρώτα αὐτόν· εἴ τι
having   the hands to him he was him; if some
set on   asking on

991   24 2532 308   3004   991
βλέπεις;   καὶ ἀναβλέψας ἔλεγεν·   βλέπω
you see?   And having looked up he was saying; I see

016 444   3754 5613 1186 3708 4043
τοὺς ἀνθρώπους ὅτι ὡς δένδρα ὁρῶ περιπατοῦντας.
the men   that as trees I see walking around.

25 1534 3825 2007   020 5495 1909 016 3788
   εἶτα πάλιν ἐπέθηκεν τὰς χεῖρας ἐπὶ τοὺς ὀφθαλμοὺς
   Then again he set on the hands on the eyes

846   2532 1227   2532 600   2532
αὐτοῦ, καὶ διέβλεψεν   καὶ ἀπεκατέστη   καὶ
of him, and he saw clearly and he was restored and

1689   5081   537   26 2532 649
ἐνέβλεπεν   τηλαυγῶς ἅπαντα.   καὶ ἀπέστειλεν
he was looking in clearly all.   And he delegated

846   1519 3624 846   3004   1519 08
αὐτὸν εἰς οἶκον αὐτοῦ λέγων· μηδὲ εἰς τὴν
him into house of him saying; but not into the

2968   1525   27 2532 1831   01 2424 2532
κώμην εἰσέλθης.   Καὶ ἐξῆλθεν ὁ Ἰησοῦς καὶ
village you might go in. And went out the Jesus and

---

understand? Are your hearts hardened? 18Do you have eyes, and fail to see? Do you have ears, and fail to hear? And do you not remember? 19When I broke the five loaves for the five thousand, how many baskets full of broken pieces did you collect?" They said to him, "Twelve." 20"And the seven for the four thousand, how many baskets full of broken pieces did you collect?" And they said to him, "Seven." 21Then he said to them, "Do you not yet understand?"

22 They came to Bethsaida. Some people[a] brought a blind man to him and begged him to touch him. 23He took the blind man by the hand and led him out of the village; and when he had put saliva on his eyes and laid his hands on him, he asked him, "Can you see anything?" 24And the man[b] looked up and said, "I can see people, but they look like trees, walking." 25Then Jesus[b] laid his hands on his eyes again; and he looked intently and his sight was restored, and he saw everything clearly. 26Then he sent him away to his home, saying, "Do not even go into the village."[c]

27 Jesus went on with

---

a Gk *They*
b Gk *he*
c Other ancient authorities add *or tell anyone in the village*

his disciples to the villages of Caesarea Philippi; and on the way he asked his disciples, "Who do people say that I am?" [28]And they answered him, "John the Baptist; and others, Elijah; and still others, one of the prophets." [29]He asked them, "But who do you say that I am?" Peter answered him, "You are the Messiah."[a] [30]And he sternly ordered them not to tell anyone about him.

[31] Then he began to teach them that the Son of Man must undergo great suffering, and be rejected by the elders, the chief priests, and the scribes, and be killed, and after three days rise again. [32]He said all this quite openly. And Peter took him aside and began to rebuke him. [33]But turning and looking at his disciples, he rebuked Peter and said, "Get behind me, Satan! For you are setting your mind not on divine things but on human things."

[34] He called the crowd with his disciples, and said to them, "If any want to become my followers, let them deny themselves and take up

a Or the Christ

013	3101		846		1519	020	2968		2542		06
οἱ	μαθηταὶ		αὐτοῦ		εἰς	τὰς	κώμας		Καισαρείας		τῆς
the	learners		of him		into	the	villages		Caesarea		of the

5376		2532	1722	07	3598	1905			016
Φιλίππου·		καὶ	ἐν	τῇ	ὁδῷ	ἐπηρώτα			τοὺς
Philipp;		and	in	the	way	he was asking on			the

3101		846		3004		846		5101	1473	3004		013
μαθητὰς		αὐτοῦ		λέγων		αὐτοῖς·		τίνα	με	λέγουσιν		οἱ
learners		of him		saying		to them;		who	me	say		the

444		1510		013			1161	3004	846		3004
ἄνθρωποι		εἶναι;	**28**	οἱ			δὲ	εἶπαν	αὐτῷ		λέγοντες
men		to be?		The ones			but	said	to him		saying,

3754	2491		04	910			2532	243		2243
[ὅτι]	Ἰωάννην		τὸν	βαπτιστήν,		καὶ	ἄλλοι		Ἠλίαν,
(")	John		the	immerser,			and	others		Elijah,

243		1161	3754	1520	014		4396		2532	846
ἄλλοι		δὲ	ὅτι	εἶς	τῶν		προφητῶν.	**29**	καὶ	αὐτὸς
others		but	that	one	of the		spokesmen.		And	himself

1905			846		1473	1161	5101	1473	3004
ἐπηρώτα			αὐτούς·		ὑμεῖς	δὲ	τίνα	με	λέγετε
he was asking on		them;		you	but	who	me	say you

1510	611		01	4074	3004	846		1473
εἶναι;	ἀποκριθεὶς		ὁ	Πέτρος	λέγει	αὐτῷ·		σὺ
to be?	Having answered		the	Peter	says	to him;		you

1510	01	5547		2532	2008			846		2443
εἶ	ὁ	χριστός.	**30**	καὶ	ἐπετίμησεν			αὐτοῖς		ἵνα
are	the	Christ.		And	he admonished			them		that

3367		3004			4012	846		**31**	2532	757
μηδενὶ		λέγωσιν			περὶ	αὐτοῦ.			Καὶ	ἤρξατο
to no one		they might say			about	him.			And	he began

1321		846		3754	1163			04	5207	02
διδάσκειν		αὐτοὺς		ὅτι	δεῖ			τὸν	υἱὸν	τοῦ
to teach		them		that	it is necessary			the	son	of the

444		4183	3958		2532	593				5259	014
ἀνθρώπου		πολλὰ	παθεῖν		καὶ	ἀποδοκιμασθῆναι			ὑπὸ	τῶν
man		many	to suffer		and	to be rejected			by	the

1245		2532	014	749			2532	014	1122
πρεσβυτέρων		καὶ	τῶν	ἀρχιερέων			καὶ	ιῶν	γραμματέων
older men		and	the	ruler priests			and	the	writers

2532	615		2532	3326	5140		2250		450
καὶ	ἀποκτανθῆναι		καὶ	μετὰ	τρεῖς		ἡμέρας		ἀναστῆναι·
and	to be killed		and	after	three		days		to stand up;

	2532	3954		04	3056	2980			2532
32	καὶ	παρρησίᾳ		τὸν	λόγον	ἐλάλει.			καὶ
	and	in boldness		the	word	he was speaking.			And

4355		01	4074	846		757		2008
προσλαβόμενος		ὁ	Πέτρος	αὐτὸν		ἤρξατο		ἐπιτιμᾶν
having taken to		the	Peter	him		began		to admonish

846		01	1161	1994			2532	3708
αὐτῷ.	**33**	ὁ	δὲ	ἐπιστραφεὶς			καὶ	ἰδὼν
him.		The one	but	having been returned			and	having seen

016	3101		846	2008			4074	2532	3004
τοὺς	μαθητὰς		αὐτοῦ	ἐπετίμησεν			Πέτρῳ	καὶ	λέγει·
the	learners		of him	admonished			Peter	and	he says;

5217		3694	1473	4567			3754		3756	5426
ὕπαγε		ὀπίσω	μου,	σατανᾶ,			ὅτι		οὐ	φρονεῖς
go off		after	me,	adversary,			because		not	you think

024	02		2316	235	024	014		444		2532
τὰ	τοῦ		θεοῦ	ἀλλὰ	τὰ	τῶν		ἀνθρώπων.	**34**	Καὶ
the	of the		God	but	the	of the		men.		And
things					things					

4341		04	3793	4862	015	3101		846
προσκαλεσάμενος		τὸν	ὄχλον	σὺν	τοῖς	μαθηταῖς		αὐτοῦ
having called to		the	crowd	with	the	learners		of him

3004		846		1487	5100	2309	3694	1473	190
εἶπεν		αὐτοῖς·		εἴ	τις	θέλει	ὀπίσω	μου	ἀκολουθεῖν,
he said		to them;		if	some	wants	after	me	to follow,

533			1438	2532	142		04
ἀπαρνησάσθω			ἑαυτὸν	καὶ	ἀράτω		τὸν
let deny thoroughly			himself	and	let lift up		the

```
4716       846        2532 190            1473   35  3739 1063 1437
σταυρὸν αὐτοῦ  καὶ  ἀκολουθείτω μοι.      ὃς  γὰρ  ἐὰν
cross   of him and   let follow me.    Who for  if
2309      08  5590   846      4982          622
θέλῃ      τὴν ψυχὴν αὐτοῦ σῶσαι        ἀπολέσει
might want the soul  of him to deliver  he will destroy
846       3739 1161 302 622          08   5590   846
αὐτήν·  ὃς  δ’  ἂν  ἀπολέσει      τὴν ψυχὴν αὐτοῦ
it;     who but  -  will destroy  the soul  of him
1752      1473  2532 010 2098          4982
ἕνεκεν    ἐμοῦ καὶ τοῦ εὐαγγελίου σώσει
on account of me and  the good message he will deliver
846    36  5101 1063 5623      444         2770       04
αὐτήν.      τί  γὰρ ὠφελεῖ ἄνθρωπον κερδῆσαι τὸν
it.         What for benefits man       to gain  the
2889     3650 2532 2210        08  5590   846     37  5101
κόσμον ὅλον καὶ ζημιωθῆναι τὴν ψυχὴν αὐτοῦ;    τί
world  whole and to be lost the soul  of him?   What
1063 1325       444         465        06        5590
γὰρ δοῖ        ἄνθρωπος ἀντάλλαγμα τῆς     ψυχῆς
for  might give man      exchange   of the soul
846   38  3739 1063 1437 1870              1473 2532
αὐτοῦ;     ὃς  γὰρ ἐὰν ἐπαισχυνθῇ        με  καὶ
of him?  Who for  if  might be ashamed me   and
016  1699  3056    1722 07  1074        3778  07
τοὺς ἐμοὺς λόγους ἐν  τῇ γενεᾷ     ταύτῃ τῇ
the  mine  words  in  the generation this  the
3428          2532 268        2532 01  5207 02       444
μοιχαλίδι καὶ ἁμαρτωλῷ, καὶ  ὁ  υἱὸς τοῦ    ἀνθρώπου
adulterous and sinner,  also the son  of the man
1870               846    3752 2064          1722 07
ἐπαισχυνθήσεται αὐτόν, ὅταν ἔλθῃ       ἐν  τῇ
will be ashamed  him,  when he might come in  the
1391  02  3962     846    3326 014 32          014
δόξῃ  τοῦ πατρὸς αὐτοῦ μετὰ τῶν ἀγγέλων τῶν
splendor of the father of him with the messengers the
40       9:1 2532 3004      846       281  3004
ἁγίων.       Καὶ ἔλεγεν  αὐτοῖς· ἀμὴν λέγω
holy.        And he was saying to them; amen I say
1473    3754 1510      5100 5602 014
ὑμῖν  ὅτι  εἰσίν    τινες ὧδε τῶν
to you that there are some here of the ones
2476          3748       3756 3361 1089        2288
ἑστηκότων  οἵτινες οὐ μὴ  γεύσωνται θανάτου
having stood who    not not might taste  death
2193 302 3708          08  932        02       2316
ἕως  ἂν  ἴδωσιν      τὴν βασιλείαν τοῦ   θεοῦ
until -  they might see the kingdom  of the God
2064          1722 1411       2  2532 3326  2250    1803
ἐληλυθυῖαν ἐν  δυνάμει.     Καὶ  μετὰ  ἡμέρας ἓξ
having come in  power.       And  after  days   six
3880           01  2424     04  4074   2532 04   2385
παραλαμβάνει ὁ  Ἰησοῦς τὸν Πέτρον καὶ  τὸν Ἰάκωβον
takes along  the Jesus  the Peter  and  the Jacob
2532 04  2491       2532 399        846       1519 3735
καὶ  τὸν Ἰωάννην καὶ ἀναφέρει  αὐτοὺς εἰς  ὄρος
and  the John     and he brings up them   into hill
5308    2596 2398    3441      2532 3339
ὑψηλὸν κατ’ ἰδίαν μόνους. καὶ  μετεμορφώθη
high   by   own    alone.  And  he was transformed
1715          846     3  2532 021 2440       846      1096
ἔμπροσθεν αὐτῶν,     καὶ  τὰ ἱμάτια αὐτοῦ ἐγένετο
in front  of them,     and  the clothes of him became
4744         3022   3029 3634     1102        1909 06
στίλβοντα λευκὰ λίαν, οἷα  γναφεὺς ἐπὶ τῆς
glistening white very, such as wool cleaner on  the
1093  3756 1410    3779   3021          4  2532
γῆς  οὐ  δύναται οὕτως λευκᾶναι.     καὶ
earth not is able thusly to whiten.    And
```

their cross and follow me. [35]For those who want to save their life will lose it, and those who lose their life for my sake, and for the sake of the gospel,[a] will save it. [36]For what will it profit them to gain the whole world and forfeit their life? [37]Indeed, what can they give in return for their life? [38]Those who are ashamed of me and of my words[b] in this adulterous and sinful generation, of them the Son of Man will also be ashamed when he comes in the glory of his Father with the holy angels." [9:1]And he said to them, "Truly I tell you, there are some standing here who will not taste death until they see that the kingdom of God has come with[c] power."

2 Six days later, Jesus took with him Peter and James and John, and led them up a high mountain apart, by themselves. And he was transfigured before them, [3]and his clothes became dazzling white, such as no one[d] on earth could bleach them. [4]And there appeared to them

[a] Other ancient authorities read *lose their life for the sake of the gospel*
[b] Other ancient authorities read *and of mine*
[c] Or *in*
[d] Gk *no fuller*

Elijah with Moses, who were talking with Jesus. ⁵Then Peter said to Jesus, "Rabbi, it is good for us to be here; let us make three dwellings,ᵃ one for you, one for Moses, and one for Elijah." ⁶He did not know what to say, for they were terrified. ⁷Then a cloud overshadowed them, and from the cloud there came a voice, "This is my Son, the Beloved;ᵇ listen to him!" ⁸Suddenly when they looked around, they saw no one with them any more, but only Jesus.

9 As they were coming down the mountain, he ordered them to tell no one about what they had seen, until after the Son of Man had risen from the dead. ¹⁰So they kept the matter to themselves, questioning what this rising from the dead could mean. ¹¹Then they asked him, "Why do the scribes say that Elijah must come first?" ¹²He said to them, "Elijah is indeed coming first to restore all things. How then is it written about the Son of Man, that he is to go through many sufferings and be treated with contempt? ¹³But I tell you

ᵃ Or tents
ᵇ Or my beloved Son

3708		846		2243		4862	3475	2532	
ὤφθη		αὐτοῖς		Ἡλίας		σὺν	Μωϋσεῖ	καὶ	
there was seen		to them		Elijah		with	Moses	and	

1510	4814		03	2424		2532	611		01
ἦσαν	συλλαλοῦντες		τῷ	Ἰησοῦ.	5	καὶ	ἀποκριθεὶς		ὁ
they were+	+speaking together		the	to Jesus.		And	having answered		the

4074	3004	03	2424	4461	2570	1510	1473
Πέτρος	λέγει	τῷ	Ἰησοῦ·	ῥαββί,	καλόν	ἐστιν	ἡμᾶς
Peter	says	to the	Jesus;	Rabbi,	good	it is	us

5602	1510	2532	4160		5140	4633	1473
ὧδε	εἶναι,	καὶ	ποιήσωμεν		τρεῖς	σκηνάς,	σοὶ
here	to be,	and	might we make		three	tents,	to you

1520	2532	3475		1520	2532	2243		1520		3756	1063
μίαν	καὶ	Μωϋσεῖ		μίαν	καὶ	Ἡλίᾳ		μίαν.	6	οὐ	γὰρ
one	and	to Moses		one	and	Elijah		one.		Not	for

3609a	5101	611		1630		1063
ᾔδει	τί	ἀποκριθῇ,		ἔκφοβοι		γὰρ
he had known	what	he answered,		very fearful		for

1096		2532	1096	3507	1982		846
ἐγένοντο.	7	καὶ	ἐγένετο	νεφέλη	ἐπισκιάζουσα		αὐτοῖς,
they became.		And	became	cloud	overshadowing		them,

2532	1096	5456	1537	06	3507	3778	1510	01
καὶ	ἐγένετο	φωνὴ	ἐκ	τῆς	νεφέλης·	οὗτός	ἐστιν	ὁ
and	became	sound	from	the	cloud;	this	is	the

5207	1473	01	27		191	846		2532
υἱός	μου	ὁ	ἀγαπητός,		ἀκούετε	αὐτοῦ.	8	καὶ
son	of me	the	loved one,		hear	him.		And

1819	4017		3765	3762	3708	235
ἐξάπινα	περιβλεψάμενοι		οὐκέτι	οὐδένα	εἶδον	ἀλλὰ
suddenly	having looked around themselves		no longer	no one	they saw	but

04	2424	3441	3326	1438		2532	2597
τὸν	Ἰησοῦν	μόνον	μεθ'	ἑαυτῶν.	9	Καὶ	καταβαινόντων
the	Jesus	alone	with	themselves.		And	coming down

846		1537	010	3735	1291		846	2443
αὐτῶν		ἐκ	τοῦ	ὄρους	διεστείλατο		αὐτοῖς	ἵνα
of them		from	the	hill	he commanded		them	that

3367	3739	3708	1334		1487	3361
μηδενὶ	ἃ	εἶδον	διηγήσωνται,		εἰ	μὴ
to no one	what	they saw	they might narrate,		except	

3752	01	5207	02	444	1537	3498
ὅταν	ὁ	υἱὸς	τοῦ	ἀνθρώπου	ἐκ	νεκρῶν
when	the	son	of the	man	from	dead

450		2532	04	3056	2902		4314
ἀναστῇ.	10	καὶ	τὸν	λόγον	ἐκράτησαν		πρὸς
might stand up.		And	the	word	they held		to

1438	4802		5101	1510	09	1537	3498
ἑαυτοὺς	συζητοῦντες		τί	ἐστιν	τὸ	ἐκ	νεκρῶν
themselves	disputing		what	is	the	out	of dead

450		2532	1905		846	3004		3754
ἀναστῆναι.	11	Καὶ	ἐπηρώτων		αὐτὸν	λέγοντες·		ὅτι
to stand up.		And	they were		him	saying,		(")
			asking on					

3004		013	1122		3754	2243	1163
λέγουσιν		οἱ	γραμματεῖς		ὅτι	Ἡλίαν	δεῖ
say		the	writers		that	Elijah	it is necessary

2064	4413		01		1161	5346	846		2243
ἐλθεῖν	πρῶτον;	12	ὁ		δὲ	ἔφη	αὐτοῖς·		Ἡλίας
to come first?			The one		but	said	to them;		Elijah

3303	2064	4413	600		3956	2532
μὲν	ἐλθὼν	πρῶτον	ἀποκαθιστάνει		πάντα·	καὶ
indeed	having come	first	restores		all;	and

4459	1125		1909	04	5207	02	444
πῶς	γέγραπται		ἐπὶ	τὸν	υἱὸν	τοῦ	ἀνθρώπου
how	has it been written		on	the	son	of	the man

2443	4183	3958		2532	1847		235	3004
ἵνα	πολλὰ	πάθῃ		καὶ	ἐξουδενηθῇ;	13	ἀλλὰ	λέγω
that	many	he might suffer		and	he might be set to nothing;		but	I say

```
1473        3754  2532  2243      2064           2532  4160
ὑμῖν        ὅτι   καὶ   Ἠλίας     ἐλήλυθεν,       καὶ   ἐποίησαν
to you      that  even  Elijah    has come,       and   they did

846   3745        2309              2531   1125              1909
αὐτῷ  ὅσα         ἤθελον,           καθὼς  γέγραπται          ἐπ᾽
to him as much as they wanted,     just   it has been        on
                                    as     written

846        2532 2064        4314    016   3101
αὐτόν.  14 Καὶ  ἐλθόντες     πρὸς    τοὺς  μαθητὰς
him.       And  having come  toward  the   learners

3708    3793   4183   4012   846     2532 1122
εἶδον   ὄχλον  πολὺν  περὶ   αὐτοὺς  καὶ  γραμματεῖς
they saw crowd much   around them    and  writers

4802            4314   846         2532 2117              3956
συζητοῦντας     πρὸς   αὐτούς.  15 καὶ  εὐθὺς             πᾶς
having disputed toward them.      And  immediately       all

01   3793  3708        846     1569a
ὁ    ὄχλος ἰδόντες     αὐτὸν   ἐξεθαμβήθησαν
the  crowd having seen him     were greatly astonished

2532 4370            782          846        2532
καὶ  προστρέχοντες   ἠσπάζοντο   αὐτόν.  16 καὶ
and  running toward  they were greeting him.  And

1905          846      5101 4802       4314    846
ἐπηρώτησεν    αὐτούς·  τί   συζητεῖτε  πρὸς    αὐτούς;
he asked on   them;    why  dispute    you     toward them?

   2532 611        846   1520 1537 02   3793      1320
17 καὶ  ἀπεκρίθη   αὐτῷ  εἷς  ἐκ   τοῦ  ὄχλου·    διδάσκαλε,
   And  answered   him   one  from the  crowd;    teacher,

5342    04  5207 1473  4314    1473 2192     4151
ἤνεγκα  τὸν υἱόν μου   πρὸς    σέ,  ἔχοντα   πνεῦμα
I carried the son of   me  toward you,  having spirit

216         2532 3699 1437 846    2638
ἄλαλον·  18 καὶ  ὅπου  ἐὰν  αὐτὸν καταλάβῃ
speechless; and  where if   him   it might take over

4486      846     2532 875       2532 5149      016
ῥήσσει    αὐτόν, καὶ  ἀφρίζει   καὶ  τρίζει    τοὺς
it will rip him,  and  he foams and  he grinds  the

3599     2532 3583           2532 3004     015
ὀδόντας  καὶ  ξηραίνεται·     καὶ  εἶπα     τοῖς
teeth    and  he is dried out; and  I said    to the

3101     1473 2443 846  1544               2532 3756
μαθηταῖς σου  ἵνα  αὐτὸ ἐκβάλωσιν,          καὶ  οὐκ
learners of you that it  they might throw out, and  not

2480            01  1161 611             846
ἴσχυσαν.  19 ὁ   δὲ  ἀποκριθεὶς          αὐτοῖς
they were strong. The one but having answered them

3004  5599 1074   571        2193  4219 4314    1473
λέγει· ὦ γενεὰ   ἄπιστος,   ἕως   πότε πρὸς   ὑμᾶς
says; O generation untrustful, until when toward you

1510     2193 4219 430         1473 5342   846
ἔσομαι;  ἕως  πότε ἀνέξομαι   ὑμῶν; φέρετε αὐτὸν
I will be? Until when will I endure you? Carry  him

4314  1473    2532 5342      846     4314  846
πρός  με.  20 καὶ  ἤνεγκαν   αὐτὸν  πρὸς  αὐτόν.
toward me.    And  they carried him   toward him.

2532 3708      846     09  4151    2117
καὶ  ἰδὼν     αὐτὸν   τὸ  πνεῦμα  εὐθὺς
And  having seen him    the spirit  immediately

4952            846     2532 4098    1909 06  1093
συνεσπάραξεν    αὐτόν, καὶ  πεσὼν   ἐπὶ  τῆς γῆς
convulsed       him,   and  falling  on   the earth

2947        875        2532 1905         04  3962
ἐκυλίετο    ἀφρίζων. 21 καὶ  ἐπηρώτησεν  τὸν πατέρα
he was rolling foaming.  And  he asked on  the father

846     4214   5550    1510   5613 3778 1096
αὐτοῦ· πόσος χρόνος ἐστὶν ὡς   τοῦτο γέγονεν
of him; how much time  is it  as   this  has become

846   01   1161 3004   1537   3812          2532
αὐτῷ; ὁ   δὲ   εἶπεν·  ἐκ     παιδιόθεν· 22 καὶ
him?  The one but said;  out of childhood;    and
```

that Elijah has come, and they did to him whatever they pleased, as it is written about him."

14 When they came to the disciples, they saw a great crowd around them, and some scribes arguing with them. [15]When the whole crowd saw him, they were immediately overcome with awe, and they ran forward to greet him. [16]He asked them, "What are you arguing about with them?" [17]Someone from the crowd answered him, "Teacher, I brought you my son; he has a spirit that makes him unable to speak; [18]and whenever it seizes him, it dashes him down; and he foams and grinds his teeth and becomes rigid; and I asked your disciples to cast it out, but they could not do so." [19]He answered them, "You faithless generation, how much longer must I be among you? How much longer must I put up with you? Bring him to me." [20]And they brought the boy[a] to him. When the spirit saw him, immediately it convulsed the boy,[a] and he fell on the ground and rolled about, foaming at the mouth. [21]Jesus[b] asked the father, "How long has this been happening to him?" And he said, "From childhood. [22]It has often cast him

[a] Gk *him*
[b] Gk *He*

into the fire and into the water, to destroy him; but if you are able to do anything, have pity on us and help us." [23]Jesus said to him, "If you are able!— All things can be done for the one who believes." [24]Immediately the father of the child cried out,[a] "I believe; help my unbelief!" [25]When Jesus saw that a crowd came running together, he rebuked the unclean spirit, saying to it, "You spirit that keeps this boy from speaking and hearing, I command you, come out of him, and never enter him again!" [26]After crying out and convulsing him terribly, it came out, and the boy was like a corpse, so that most of them said, "He is dead." [27]But Jesus took him by the hand and lifted him up, and he was able to stand. [28]When he had entered the house, his disciples asked him privately, "Why could we not cast it out?" [29]He said to them, "This kind can come out only through prayer."[b]

30 They went on from there and passed through Galilee. He did not want anyone to know it; [31]for he was teaching his disciples,

[a] Other ancient authorities add *with tears*
[b] Other ancient authorities add *and fasting*

4178	2532	1519	4442	846	906	2532	1519
πολλάκις	καὶ	εἰς	πῦρ	αὐτὸν	ἔβαλεν	καὶ	εἰς
frequently	also	into	fire	him	he threw	and	into

5204 2443 622　　　　　　846　235 1487 5100
ὕδατα ἵνα ἀπολέσῃ　　αὐτόν· ἀλλ᾽ εἴ τι
waters that he might destroy him; but if some

1410　　　997　　1473 4697　　　　　1909
δύνῃ, βοήθησον ἡμῖν σπλαγχνισθεὶς ἐφ᾽
you are able, help us having had affection on

1473 **23** 01 1161 2424 3004 846 012 1487
ἡμᾶς. ὁ δὲ Ἰησοῦς εἶπεν αὐτῷ· Τὸ εἰ
us. The but Jesus said to him, the if

1410 3956 1415 03 4100
δύνῃ, πάντα δυνατὰ τῷ πιστεύοντι.
you are able, all powers to the one trusting.

24 2117 2896 01 3962 010 3813 3004
εὐθὺς κράξας ὁ πατὴρ τοῦ παιδίου ἔλεγεν·
Immediately having shouted the father of small the child was saying;

4100　　997 1473 07 570 **25** 3708 1161
πιστεύω· βοήθει μου τῇ ἀπιστίᾳ. ἰδὼν δὲ
I trust, help of me the untrust. Having seen but

01 2424 3754 1998 3793 2008
ὁ Ἰησοῦς ὅτι ἐπισυντρέχει ὄχλος, ἐπετίμησεν
the Jesus that runs on together crowd, admonished

011 4151 011 169 3004 846 09 216
τῷ πνεύματι τῷ ἀκαθάρτῳ λέγων αὐτῷ· τὸ ἄλαλον
the spirit the unclean saying to it; the speechless

2532 2974 4151 1473 2004 1473 1831 1537
καὶ κωφὸν πνεῦμα, ἐγὼ ἐπιτάσσω σοι, ἔξελθε ἐξ
and deaf spirit, I order you, come out from

846 2532 3371 1525 1519 846
αὐτοῦ καὶ μηκέτι εἰσέλθῃς εἰς αὐτόν.
him and no longer you might go into into him.

26 2532 2896 2532 4183 4682
καὶ κράξας καὶ πολλὰ σπαράξας
And having shouted and many having convulsed

1831 2532 1096 5616 3498 5620 016
ἐξῆλθεν· καὶ ἐγένετο ὡσεὶ νεκρός, ὥστε τοὺς
it went out; and he became as dead, so that the

4183 3004 3754 599 **27** 01 1161 2424
πολλοὺς λέγειν ὅτι ἀπέθανεν. ὁ δὲ Ἰησοῦς
many to say that he died. The but Jesus

2902 06 5495 846 1453 846 2532
κρατήσας τῆς χειρὸς αὐτοῦ ἤγειρεν αὐτόν, καὶ
having held the hand of him raised him, and

450 **28** 2532 1525 846 1519 3624
ἀνέστη. Καὶ εἰσελθόντος αὐτοῦ εἰς οἶκον
he stood up. And having gone into of him into house

013 3101 846 2596 2398 1905 846
οἱ μαθηταὶ αὐτοῦ κατ᾽ ἰδίαν ἐπηρώτων αὐτόν·
the learners of him by own were asking on him;

3754 1473 3756 1410 1544 846 **29** 2532
ὅτι ἡμεῖς οὐκ ἠδυνήθημεν ἐκβαλεῖν αὐτό; καὶ
(") we not were able to throw out it? And

3004 846 3778 09 1085 1722 3762 1410
εἶπεν αὐτοῖς· τοῦτο τὸ γένος ἐν οὐδενὶ δύναται
he said to them; this the kind in no one is able

1831 1487 3361 1722 4335 **30** 2547
ἐξελθεῖν εἰ μὴ ἐν προσευχῇ. Κἀκεῖθεν
to go out except in prayer. And from there

1831 3899 1223 06
ἐξελθόντες παρεπορεύοντο διὰ τῆς
having gone out they were traveling along through the

1056 2532 3756 2309 2443 5100 1097
Γαλιλαίας, καὶ οὐκ ἤθελεν ἵνα τις γνοῖ·
Galilee, and not he wanted that some might know;

31 1321 1063 016 3101 846 2532
ἐδίδασκεν γὰρ τοὺς μαθητὰς αὐτοῦ καὶ
he was teaching for the learners of him and

3004	846	3754 01	5207 02	444

ἔλεγεν   αὐτοῖς   ὅτι   ὁ   υἱὸς τοῦ   ἀνθρώπου
he was saying to them that the son of the man

3860   1519 5495 444   2532 615
παραδίδοται   εἰς χεῖρας ἀνθρώπων, καὶ ἀποκτενοῦσιν
is given over into hands of men,   and they will kill

846   2532 615   3326 5140 2250
αὐτόν, καὶ ἀποκτανθεὶς   μετὰ τρεῖς ἡμέρας
him, and having been killed after three days

450   32 013   1161 50   012
ἀναστήσεται.   οἱ   δὲ   ἠγνόουν   τὸ
he will stand up. The ones but were unknowing the

4487   2532 5399   846 1905   33 2532
ῥῆμα, καὶ ἐφοβοῦντο   αὐτὸν ἐπερωτῆσαι.   Καὶ
word, and they were fearing him to ask on. And

2064   1519 2746a   2532 1722 07 3614
ἦλθον εἰς Καφαρναούμ. Καὶ ἐν τῇ οἰκίᾳ
they went into Capernaum. And in the house

1096   1905   846   5101 1722 07 3598
γενόμενος ἐπηρώτα αὐτούς· τί ἐν τῇ ὁδῷ
having become he asked on them; what in the way

1260   34 013   1161 4623   4314
διελογίζεσθε;   οἱ   δὲ   ἐσιώπων·   πρὸς
were you reasoning? The ones but were silent; toward

240   1063 1256   1722 07 3598 5101
ἀλλήλους γὰρ διελέχθησαν ἐν τῇ ὁδῷ τίς
one another for they were disputing in the way who

3173   35 2532 2523   5455   016 1427   2532
μείζων.   καὶ καθίσας ἐφώνησεν τοὺς δώδεκα καὶ
greater. And having sat he sounded the twelve and

3004 846   1487 5100 2309 4413   1510   1510
λέγει αὐτοῖς· εἴ τις θέλει πρῶτος εἶναι, ἔσται
says to them; if some wants first to be, he will be

3956 2078   2532 3956   1249   36 2532 2983
πάντων ἔσχατος καὶ πάντων διάκονος.   καὶ λαβὼν
of all last   and of all servant.   And having
                                                 taken

3813   2476   846   1722 3319 846   2532
παιδίον   ἔστησεν αὐτὸ ἐν μέσῳ αὐτῶν καὶ
small child he stood it in middle of them and

1723   846   3004   846   37 3739 302 1520
ἐναγκαλισάμενος αὐτὸ εἶπεν αὐτοῖς·   ὃς ἂν ἓν
having embraced it he said to them; who - one

022 5108   3813   1209   1909 011 3686 1473 1473
τῶν τοιούτων παιδίων δέξηται ἐπὶ τῷ ὀνόματί μου, ἐμὲ
of such ones small   might on the name of me
the   children welcome   me,

1209   2532 3739 302 1473 1209   3756 1473
δέχεται·   καὶ ὃς ἂν ἐμὲ δέχηται,   οὐκ ἐμὲ
he welcomes; and who - me might welcome, not me

1209   235 04 649   1473 38 5346
δέχεται   ἀλλὰ τὸν ἀποστείλαντά με.   Ἔφη
he welcomes but the one having delegated me. Said

846   01 2491   1320   3708   5100 1722 011
αὐτῷ ὁ Ἰωάννης· διδάσκαλε, εἴδομέν τινα ἐν τῷ
to him the John; teacher, we saw someone in the

3686   1473   1544   1140   2532
ὀνόματί σου ἐκβάλλοντα δαιμόνια καὶ
name   of you throwing out demons and

2967   846   3754   3756 190
ἐκωλύομεν   αὐτόν, ὅτι   οὐκ ἠκολούθει
we were hindering him, because not he was following

1473 39 01 1161 2424   3004   3361 2967   846
ἡμῖν.   ὁ δὲ Ἰησοῦς εἶπεν· μὴ κωλύετε   αὐτόν.
us.   The but Jesus   said; not you hinder him.

3762   1063 1510   3739 4160   1411   1909 011
οὐδεὶς γάρ ἐστιν ὃς   ποιήσει δύναμιν ἐπὶ τῷ
No one for there is who will do power on the

---

saying to them, "The Son of Man is to be betrayed into human hands, and they will kill him, and three days after being killed, he will rise again." [32]But they did not understand what he was saying and were afraid to ask him.

[33]Then they came to Capernaum; and when he was in the house he asked them, "What were you arguing about on the way?" [34]But they were silent, for on the way they had argued with one another who was the greatest. [35]He sat down, called the twelve, and said to them, "Whoever wants to be first must be last of all and servant of all." [36]Then he took a little child and put it among them; and taking it in his arms, he said to them, [37]"Whoever welcomes one such child in my name welcomes me, and whoever welcomes me welcomes not me but the one who sent me."

[38]John said to him, "Teacher, we saw someone[a] casting out demons in your name, and we tried to stop him, because he was not following us." [39]But Jesus said, "Do not stop him; for no one who does a deed of power in

[a] Other ancient authorities add who does not follow us

my name will be able soon afterward to speak evil of me. [40]Whoever is not against us is for us. [41]For truly I tell you, whoever gives you a cup of water to drink because you bear the name of Christ will by no means lose the reward.

[42] "If any of you put a stumbling block before one of these little ones who believe in me,[a] it would be better for you if a great millstone were hung around your neck and you were thrown into the sea. [43]If your hand causes you to stumble, cut it off; it is better for you to enter life maimed than to have two hands and to go to hell,[b] to the unquenchable fire.[c] [45]And if your foot causes you to stumble, cut it off; it is better for you to enter life lame than to have two feet and to be thrown into hell.[b] [c] [47]And if your eye causes you to stumble, tear it out; it is better for you to enter the kingdom of God with one eye than to have two eyes and to be thrown into hell,[b] [48]where their worm never dies, and the fire is never quenched.

[a] Other ancient authorities lack in me
[b] Gk Gehenna
[c] Verses 44 and 46 (which are identical with verse 48) are lacking in the best ancient authorities

```
3686      1473  2532 1410                  5036       2551
ὀνόματί    μου   καὶ  δυνήσεται            ταχὺ      κακολογῆσαί
name       of me and  he will be able     quickly   to speak bad
1473   40  3739 1063 3756 1510  2596      1473  5228
με·        ὃς   γὰρ  οὐκ ἔστιν καθ᾽      ἡμῶν, ὑπὲρ
me;        who  for  not  is   against   us,   on behalf
1473  1510       3739 1063 302 4222              1473
ἡμῶν  ἐστιν. 41 Ὃς   γὰρ  ἂν  ποτίσῃ            ὑμᾶς
of us is.       Who  for  -   might give drink you
4221      5204    1722 3686    3754       5547
ποτήριον  ὕδατος  ἐν   ὀνόματι ὅτι       Χριστοῦ
cup       of water in  name    because of Christ
1510    281  3004 1473    3754 3756 3361 622       04
ἐστε,   ἀμὴν λέγω ὑμῖν    ὅτι  οὐ   μὴ  ἀπολέσῃ    τὸν
you are, amen I say to you that not  not he might the
                                                  destroy
3408     846     42 2532 3739 302 4624          1520
μισθὸν   αὐτοῦ.    Καὶ  ὃς   ἂν  σκανδαλίσῃ     ἕνα
wage     of him.   And  who  -   might offend   one
014    3398     3778       014 4100        1519 1473
τῶν    μικρῶν   τούτων     τῶν πιστευόντων [εἰς ἐμέ],
of the little  of these   the ones trusting in  me,
2570   1510  846     3123  1487 4029           3458
καλόν  ἐστιν αὐτῷ    μᾶλλον εἰ  περίκειται     μύλος
good   it is to him  more   if  be set around  millstone
3684    4012  04   5137      846      2532 906
ὀνικὸς  περὶ  τὸν  τράχηλον  αὐτοῦ   καὶ βέβληται
of donkey around the neck   of him  and he has been
                                                thrown
1519 08  2281      43 2532 1437 4624        1473 05
εἰς  τὴν θάλασσαν.   Καὶ  ἐὰν  σκανδαλίζῃ σε   ἡ
into the sea.       And  if   might offend you  the
5495 1473  609        846    2570 1510  1473 2948
χείρ σου,  ἀπόκοψον   αὐτήν· καλόν ἐστίν σε   κυλλὸν
hand of you, cut off  it;   good  it is  you  crippled
1525       1519 08  2222 2228 020 1417 5495      2192
εἰσελθεῖν  εἰς  τὴν ζωὴν ἢ    τὰς δύο  χεῖρας   ἔχοντα
to go into into the life or   the two hands    having
565         1519 08  1067      1519 012 4442 012
ἀπελθεῖν   εἰς  τὴν γέενναν,  εἰς τὸ  πῦρ  τὸ       .
to go off  into the gehenna,  into the fire the
762          2532 1437 01   4228 1473
ἄσβεστον.  45 καὶ  ἐὰν  ὁ    πούς σου
unextinguishable. And  if   the  foot of you
4624          1473 609    846     2570 1510  1473
σκανδαλίζῃ   σε,  ἀπόκοψον αὐτόν· καλόν ἐστίν σε
might offend you, cut off  it;    good  it is  you
1525       1519 08  2222 5560 2228 016 1417 4228
εἰσελθεῖν  εἰς  τὴν ζωὴν χωλὸν ἢ    τοὺς δύο  πόδας
to go into into the life lame  or   the  two  feet
2192    906        1519 08  1067      47 2532 1437 01
ἔχοντα  βληθῆναι  εἰς  τὴν γέενναν.   καὶ  ἐὰν  ὁ
having  to be thrown into the gehenna. And  if   the
3788       1473 4624        1473 1544       846
ὀφθαλμός   σου  σκανδαλίζῃ  σε,  ἔκβαλε     αὐτόν·
eye        of you might offend you, throw out it;
2570   1473 1510  3442        1525       1519 08
καλόν  σέ   ἐστιν μονόφθαλμον εἰσελθεῖν  εἰς  τὴν
good   you  it is alone eye   to go into into the
932        02    2316 2228 1417 3788   2192
βασιλείαν  τοῦ   θεοῦ ἢ    δύο  ὀφθαλμοὺς ἔχοντα
kingdom    of the God or   two  eyes      having
906        1519 08  1067      48 3699 01 4663
βληθῆναι  εἰς  τὴν γέενναν,   ὅπου ὁ  σκώληξ
to be thrown into the gehenna, where the worm
846    3756 5053    2532 09  4442 3756 4570
αὐτῶν  οὐ   τελευτᾷ καὶ τὸ  πῦρ  οὐ   σβέννυται.
of them not dies    and the fire not  is quenched.
```

49 3956 1063 4442   233   **50** 2570 09 217
Πᾶς γὰρ πυρὶ ἁλισθήσεται.   καλὸν τὸ ἅλας·
All   for   in fire will be salted.   Good the salt;

1437 1161 09 217   358   1096   1722 5101
ἐὰν δὲ τὸ ἅλας ἄναλον γένηται,   ἐν τίνι
if   but the salt saltless might become, in what

846 741   2192 1722 1438   217 2532
αὐτὸ ἀρτύσετε;   ἔχετε ἐν ἑαυτοῖς ἅλα καὶ
it   will you season? Have in yourselves salt and

1514   1722 240   2532 1564
εἰρηνεύετε ἐν ἀλλήλοις. **10:1** Καὶ ἐκεῖθεν
be at peace in one another.   And from there

450   2064   1519 024 3725   06
ἀναστὰς   ἔρχεται εἰς τὰ ὅρια   τῆς
having stood up he goes into the territories of the

2449   2532 4008 02   2446   2532
Ἰουδαίας [καὶ] πέραν τοῦ Ἰορδάνου, καὶ
Judea   and   across the Jordan,   and

4848   3825 3793 4314   846   2532 5613
συμπορεύονται πάλιν ὄχλοι πρὸς αὐτόν, καὶ ὡς
travel together again crowds toward him,   and as

1536a   3825 1321   846   **2** 2532
εἰώθει   πάλιν ἐδίδασκεν αὐτούς.   Καὶ
he had custom again he was teaching them.   And

4334   5330   1905   846   1487
προσελθόντες Φαρισαῖοι ἐπηρώτων   αὐτὸν εἰ
having come to Pharisees they were asking on him   if

1832   435   1135   630   3985
ἔξεστιν ἀνδρὶ γυναῖκα ἀπολῦσαι, πειράζοντες
it is possible to man woman to loose off, pressuring

846   **3** 01 1161 611   3004 846   5101
αὐτόν.   ὁ δὲ ἀποκριθεὶς εἶπεν αὐτοῖς· τί
him.   The but having answered said to them; what

1473   1781   3475   **4** 013   1161 3004
ὑμῖν ἐνετείλατο Μωϋσῆς;   οἱ   δὲ εἶπαν·
to you commanded Moses?   The ones but said;

2010   3475   5067   647   1125   2532
ἐπέτρεψεν Μωϋσῆς βιβλίον ἀποστασίου γράψαι καὶ
allowed   Moses small book of stand off to write and

630   **5** 01 1161 2424   3004 846   4314
ἀπολῦσαι.   ὁ δὲ Ἰησοῦς εἶπεν αὐτοῖς· πρὸς
to loose off. The but Jesus said to them; toward

08 4641   1473   1125   1473 08 1785
τὴν σκληροκαρδίαν ὑμῶν ἔγραψεν ὑμῖν τὴν ἐντολὴν
the hard heart   of you he wrote to you the command

3778   **6** 575 1161 746   2937   730 2532
ταύτην.   ἀπὸ δὲ ἀρχῆς κτίσεως ἄρσεν καὶ
this.   From but beginning of creation male and

2338 4160   846   **7** 1752   3778 2641
θῆλυ ἐποίησεν αὐτούς· ἕνεκεν   τούτου καταλείψει
female he made them;   on account this   will leave
                                 of   behind

444   04 3962   846   2532 08 3384   2532
ἄνθρωπος τὸν πατέρα αὐτοῦ καὶ τὴν μητέρα [καὶ
man   the father of him and the mother and

4347   4314   08 1135   846   **8** 2532
προσκολληθήσεται   πρὸς τὴν γυναῖκα αὐτοῦ], καὶ
he will be joined to toward the woman of him,   and

1510   1413 1417 1519 4561 1520   5620   3765
ἔσονται οἱ δύο εἰς σάρκα μίαν· ὥστε οὐκέτι
will be the two into flesh one;   so that no longer

1510   1417 235 1520 4561   **9** 3739 3767 01 2316
εἰσὶν δύο ἀλλὰ μία σάρξ.   ὃ   οὖν ὁ θεὸς
they are two but one flesh.   What then the God

4801   444   3361 5563   **10** 2532 1519
συνέζευξεν ἄνθρωπος μὴ χωριζέτω.   Καὶ εἰς
yoked together man   not let separate. And into

08 3614   3825 013 3101   4012 3778   1905
τὴν οἰκίαν πάλιν οἱ μαθηταὶ περὶ τούτου ἐπηρώτων
the house again the learners about this   were asking

49 "For everyone will be salted with fire.[a] 50Salt is good; but if salt has lost its saltiness, how can you season it?[b] Have salt in yourselves, and be at peace with one another."

CHAPTER 10

He left that place and went to the region of Judea and[c] beyond the Jordan. And crowds again gathered around him; and, as was his custom, he again taught them.

2 Some Pharisees came, and to test him they asked, "Is it lawful for a man to divorce his wife?" 3He answered them, "What did Moses command you?" 4They said, "Moses allowed a man to write a certificate of dismissal and to divorce her." 5But Jesus said to them, "Because of your hardness of heart he wrote this commandment for you. 6But from the beginning of creation, 'God made them male and female.' 7'For this reason a man shall leave his father and mother and be joined to his wife,[d] 8and the two shall become one flesh.' So they are no longer two, but one flesh. 9Therefore what God has joined together, let no one separate."

10 Then in the house the disciples asked him again about this matter.

---

a Other ancient authorities either add or substitute and every sacrifice will be salted with salt
b Or how can you restore its saltiness?
c Other ancient authorities lack and
d Other ancient authorities lack and be joined to his wife

11He said to them, "Who-
ever divorces his wife and
marries another commits
adultery against her; 12and
if she divorces her husband
and marries another, she
commits adultery."

13 People were bringing
little children to him in
order that he might touch
them; and the disciples
spoke sternly to them.
14But when Jesus saw this,
he was indignant and said
to them, "Let the little
children come to me; do not
stop them; for it is to such
as these that the kingdom
of God belongs. 15Truly I
tell you, whoever does not
receive the kingdom of God
as a little child will never
enter it." 16And he took
them up in his arms, laid
his hands on them, and
blessed them.

17 As he was setting out
on a journey, a man ran up
and knelt before him, and
asked him, "Good Teacher,
what must I do to inherit
eternal life?" 18Jesus said to
him, "Why do you call me
good? No one is good but
God alone. 19You know the
commandments: 'You shall
not murder; You shall not
commit adultery; You shall
not steal; You shall not
bear false witness; You shall
not defraud; Honor your
father and mother.'" 20He
said to him, "Teacher,

```
846       11  2532 3004      846     3739 302 630
αὐτόν.    11  καὶ λέγει αὐτοῖς· ὃς ἂν ἀπολύσῃ
him.          And  he says to them; who -  might loose off
08  1135      846     2532 1060   243    3429        1909
τὴν γυναῖκα αὐτοῦ καὶ γαμήσῃ ἄλλην μοιχᾶται ἐπ'
the woman    of him and might  other he commits on
                     marry              adultery
846       12 2532 1437 846      630               04
αὐτήν·   12  καὶ ἐὰν αὐτὴ ἀπολύσασα        τὸν
her;         and  if  herself having loosed off the
435    846     1060      243    3429
ἄνδρα αὐτῆς γαμήσῃ  ἄλλον μοιχᾶται.
man    of her might marry other she commits adultery.
       2532 4374              846    3813         2443
13  Καὶ προσέφερον       αὐτῷ παιδία      ἵνα
     And they were bringing to him small children that
846     681              013 1161 3101       2008
αὐτῶν ἅψηται·          οἱ δὲ μαθηταὶ ἐπετίμησαν
of them he might touch; the but learners admonished
846      14 3708      1161 01  2424   23       2532
αὐτοῖς.  14 ἰδὼν      δὲ ὁ Ἰησοῦς ἠγανάκτησεν καὶ
them.       Having seen but the Jesus was indignant and
3004  846     863    024 3813              2064     4314
εἶπεν αὐτοῖς· ἄφετε τὰ παιδία       ἔρχεσθαι πρός
said  to them; allow the small children to come  to
1473 3361 2967      846   022   1063 5108        1510 05
με,  μὴ κωλύετε αὐτά, τῶν γὰρ τοιούτων ἐστὶν ἡ
me,  not hinder them, of the for such ones is  the
932     02    2316 15  281 3004  1473 3739 302 3361
βασιλεία τοῦ θεοῦ. 15 ἀμὴν λέγω ὑμῖν, ὃς ἂν μὴ
kingdom of the God.   Amen I say to you, who - not
1209   08 932       02 2316 5613 3813     3756 3361
δέξηται τὴν βασιλείαν τοῦ θεοῦ ὡς παιδίον, οὐ μὴ
might    the kingdom  of  God as small  not not
welcome             the            child,
1525          1519 846    16 2532 1723          846
εἰσέλθῃ     εἰς αὐτήν. 16 καὶ ἐναγκαλισάμενος αὐτὰ
might go into into it.    And having embraced them
2720a          5087  020 5495 1909 846   17 2532
κατευλόγει   τιθεὶς τὰς χεῖρας ἐπ' αὐτά. 17 Καὶ
he was completely setting the hands on them.     And
speaking well
1607          846   1519 3598 4370              1520
ἐκπορευομένου αὐτοῦ εἰς ὁδὸν προσδραμὼν      εἰς
traveling out him  into way  having run toward one
2532 1120            846   1905            846
καὶ γονυπετήσας      αὐτὸν ἐπηρώτα      αὐτόν·
and having fallen on knees him  was asking on him;
1320       18   5101 4160    2443 2222 166
διδάσκαλε ἀγαθέ, τί ποιήσω ἵνα ζωὴν αἰώνιον
teacher   good, what might I do that life eternal
2816         18  01 1161 2424  3004 846  5101 1473
κληρονομήσω; 18 ὁ δὲ Ἰησοῦς εἶπεν αὐτῷ· τί με
I might inherit? The but Jesus said to him; why me
3004  18    3762  18  1487 3361 1520 01  2316
λέγεις ἀγαθόν; οὐδεὶς ἀγαθὸς εἰ μὴ εἷς ὁ θεός.
you say good?  No one good    except one the God.
   020 1785     3609a    3361 5407           3361
19 τὰς ἐντολὰς οἶδας· μὴ φονεύσῃς,       μὴ
   The commands you know; not you might murder, not
3431      3361 2813    3361 5576           3361
μοιχεύσῃς, μὴ κλέψῃς, μὴ ψευδομαρτυρήσῃς, μὴ
you might  not you might not you might      not
commit adultery, thieve,    testify falsely,
650              5091  04  3962 1473  2532 08
ἀποστερήσῃς,   τίμα τὸν πατέρα σου καὶ τὴν
you might deprive, value the father of you and the
3384     20 01   1161 5346 846   1320      3778
μητέρα. 20 ὁ   δὲ ἔφη αὐτῷ· διδάσκαλε, ταῦτα
mother.     The one but said to him; teacher,  these
```

3956	5442		1537	3503		1473	**21**	01	1161
πάντα	ἐφυλαξάμην		ἐκ	νεότητός	μου.			ὁ	δὲ
all	I myself guarded		from	newness	of me.		The		but

2424	1689			846	25		846	2532	3004
Ἰησοῦς	ἐμβλέψας			αὐτῷ	ἠγάπησεν		αὐτὸν	καὶ	εἶπεν
Jesus	having looked in			him	loved		him	and	said

846	1520	1473	5302		5217	3745			2192
αὐτῷ·	ἕν	σε	ὑστερεῖ·		ὕπαγε,	ὅσα			ἔχεις
him,	one	you	lack;		go off,	as much as			you have

4453	2532	1325	015		4434	2532	2192
πώλησον	καὶ	δὸς	[τοῖς]		πτωχοῖς,	καὶ	ἕξεις
sell	and	give	to the		poor,	and	you will have.

2344	1722	3772		2532	1204	190		1473	**22**	01
θησαυρὸν	ἐν	οὐρανῷ,		καὶ	δεῦρο	ἀκολούθει		μοι.		ὁ
treasure	in	heaven,		and	come	follow		me.	The	one

1161	4768			1909	03	3056	565
δὲ	στυγνάσας			ἐπὶ	τῷ	λόγῳ	ἀπῆλθεν
but	having become gloomy			on	the	word	went off

3076		1510		1063	2192	2933		4183
λυπούμενος·		ἦν		γὰρ	ἔχων	κτήματα		πολλά.
being grieved;		he was+		for	+having	acquisitions		many.

23	2532	4017			01	2424	3004	015
	Καὶ	περιβλεψάμενος			ὁ	Ἰησοῦς	λέγει	τοῖς
	And	having looked around			the	Jesus	says	to the

3101		846		4459	1423		013	024	5536
μαθηταῖς		αὐτοῦ·		πῶς	δυσκόλως		οἱ	τὰ	χρήματα
learners		of him,		how	difficultly		the	the	wealth

2192	1519	08	932		02		2316	1525
ἔχοντες	εἰς	τὴν	βασιλείαν		τοῦ		θεοῦ	εἰσελεύσονται.
having	into	the	kingdom		of the		God	will go into.

24	013	1161	3101		2284			1909	015	3056
	οἱ	δὲ	μαθηταὶ		ἐθαμβοῦντο			ἐπὶ	τοῖς	λόγοις
	The	but	learners		were astonished			on	the	words

846	01	1161	2424	3825	611			3004
αὐτοῦ.	ὁ	δὲ	Ἰησοῦς	πάλιν	ἀποκριθεὶς			λέγει
of him.	The	but	Jesus	again	having answered			says

846	5043		4459	1422		1510	1519	08
αὐτοῖς·	τέκνα,		πῶς	δύσκολόν		ἐστιν	εἰς	τὴν
to them;	children,		how	difficult		it is	into	the

932	02		2316	1525		**25**	2123		1510
βασιλείαν	τοῦ		θεοῦ	εἰσελθεῖν·			εὐκοπώτερόν		ἐστιν
kingdom	of the		God	to go into;			easier labor		it is

2574	1223	06	5168	06		4476
κάμηλον	διὰ	[τῆς]	τρυμαλιᾶς	[τῆς]		ῥαφίδος
camel	through	the	eye			of the needle

1330		2228	4145		1519	08	932		02
διελθεῖν		ἢ	πλούσιον		εἰς	τὴν	βασιλείαν		τοῦ
to go through		or	rich		into	the	kingdom		of the

2316	1525		**26**	013	1161	4057		1605
θεοῦ	εἰσελθεῖν.			οἱ	δὲ	περισσῶς		ἐξεπλήσσοντο
God	to go into.			The	but	exceedingly		were astonished

3004	4314	1438		2532	5101	1410
λέγοντες	πρὸς	ἑαυτούς·		καὶ	τίς	δύναται
saying	toward	themselves;		and	who	is able

4982		**27**	1689		846	01	2424
σωθῆναι;			ἐμβλέψας		αὐτοῖς	ὁ	Ἰησοῦς
to be delivered?			Having looked in		them	the	Jesus

3004	3844	444		102		235	3756	3844
λέγει·	παρὰ	ἀνθρώποις		ἀδύνατον,		ἀλλ᾽	οὐ	παρὰ
says;	alongside	men		unable,		but	not	alongside

2316	3956	1063	1415	3844		03	2316	**28**	757
θεῷ·	πάντα	γὰρ	δυνατὰ	παρὰ		τῷ	θεῷ.		Ἤρξατο
God;	all	for	power	alongside		the	God.		Began

3004	01	4074	846		2400	1473	863
λέγειν	ὁ	Πέτρος	αὐτῷ·		ἰδοὺ	ἡμεῖς	ἀφήκαμεν
to speak	the	Peter	to him;		look	we	have sent off

3956	2532	190		1473	**29**	5346	01	2424	281
πάντα	καὶ	ἠκολουθήκαμέν		σοι.		ἔφη	ὁ	Ἰησοῦς·	ἀμὴν
all	and	have followed		you.		Said	the	Jesus;	amen

I have kept all these since my youth." [21]Jesus, looking at him, loved him and said, "You lack one thing; go, sell what you own, and give the money[a] to the poor, and you will have treasure in heaven; then come, follow me." [22]When he heard this, he was shocked and went away grieving, for he had many possessions.

[23]Then Jesus looked around and said to his disciples, "How hard it will be for those who have wealth to enter the kingdom of God!" [24]And the disciples were perplexed at these words. But Jesus said to them again, "Children, how hard it is[b] to enter the kingdom of God! [25]It is easier for a camel to go through the eye of a needle than for someone who is rich to enter the kingdom of God." [26]They were greatly astounded and said to one another,[c] "Then who can be saved?" [27]Jesus looked at them and said, "For mortals it is impossible, but not for God; for God all things are possible."

[28]Peter began to say to him, "Look, we have left everything and followed you." [29]Jesus said, "Truly

[a] Gk lacks *the money*
[b] Other ancient authorities add *for those who trust in riches*
[c] Other ancient authorities read *to him*

I tell you, there is no one who has left house or brothers or sisters or mother or father or children or fields, for my sake and for the sake of the good news,ᵃ ³⁰who will not receive a hundred-fold now in this age— houses, brothers and sisters, mothers and children, and fields, with persecutions— and in the age to come eternal life. ³¹But many who are first will be last, and the last will be first."

32 They were on the road, going up to Jeru-salem, and Jesus was walking ahead of them; they were amazed, and those who followed were afraid. He took the twelve aside again and began to tell them what was to happen to him, ³³saying, "See, we are going up to Jerusalem, and the Son of Man will be handed over to the chief priests and the scribes, and they will condemn him to death; then they will hand him over to the Gentiles; ³⁴they will mock him, and spit upon him, and flog him, and kill him; and after three days he will rise again."

35 James and John, the sons of Zebedee,

ᵃ Or gospel

3004	1473		3762	1510	3739	863		3614
λέγω	ὑμῖν,	οὐδείς	ἐστιν		ὃς	ἀφῆκεν		οἰκίαν
I say	to you,	no one	there	is	who	has sent	off	house

2228	80		2228	79		2228	3384	2228	3962	2228
ἢ	ἀδελφοὺς	ἢ	ἀδελφὰς	ἢ		μητέρα	ἤ	πατέρα	ἢ
or	brothers	or	sisters	or		mother	or	father	or

5043	2228	68		1752		1473	2532	1752
τέκνα	ἢ	ἀγροὺς	ἕνεκεν		ἐμοῦ	καὶ	ἕνεκεν
children	or	fields	on account of	me	and	on account of

010	2098		1437	3361	2983		1542
τοῦ	εὐαγγελίου,	³⁰	ἐὰν	μὴ	λάβῃ		ἑκατονταπλασίονα
the	good message,		if	not	he might		hundred times
					receive		

3568	1722	03	2540	3778	3614	2532	80		2532
νῦν	ἐν	τῷ	καιρῷ	τούτῳ	οἰκίας	καὶ	ἀδελφοὺς	καὶ
now	in	the	season	this	houses	and	brothers	and

79		2532	3384		2532	5043		2532	68		3326
ἀδελφὰς	καὶ	μητέρας	καὶ	τέκνα		καὶ	ἀγροὺς	μετὰ
sisters	and	mothers	and	children	and	fields	with

1375		2532	1722	03	165	03	2064		2222
διωγμῶν,	καὶ	ἐν	τῷ	αἰῶνι	τῷ	ἐρχομένῳ	ζωὴν
persecutions,	and	in	the	age	the	coming	life

166		4183	1161	1510		4413		2078
αἰώνιον.	³¹	πολλοὶ	δὲ	ἔσονται	πρῶτοι		ἔσχατοι
eternal.		Many	but	will be	first ones		last ones

2532	013	2078		4413		1510		1161	1722
καὶ	[οἱ]	ἔσχατοι	πρῶτοι.	³²	*Ησαν		δὲ	ἐν
and	the	last ones	first ones.		They were+	but	in

07	3598	305		1519	2414		2532	1510
τῇ	ὁδῷ	ἀναβαίνοντες	εἰς	Ἱεροσόλυμα,	καὶ	ἦν
the	way	+going up	into	Jerusalem,	and	was

4254	846	01	2424	2532	2284		013	1161
προάγων	αὐτοὺς	ὁ	Ἰησοῦς,	καὶ	ἐθαμβοῦντο,	οἱ	δὲ
leading	them	the	Jesus,	and	they were	the	but
before					astonished,	ones

190		5399		2532	3880
ἀκολουθοῦντες	ἐφοβοῦντο.		καὶ	παραλαβὼν
following	were fearing,	And	having taken along

3825	016	1427	757		846		3004	024
πάλιν	τοὺς	δώδεκα	ἤρξατο		αὐτοῖς	λέγειν	τὰ
again	the	twelve	he began	to	them	to say	the things

3195		846	4819		3754	2400
μέλλοντα		αὐτῷ	συμβαίνειν	³³	ὅτι	ἰδοὺ
being about	to be	him	to go with,		(")	look

305		1519	2414		2532	01	5207	02
ἀναβαίνομεν	εἰς	Ἱεροσόλυμα,	καὶ	ὁ	υἱὸς	τοῦ
we go up	into	Jerusalem,	and	the	son	of the

444		3860		015	749		2532
ἀνθρώπου	παραδοθήσεται		τοῖς	ἀρχιερεῦσιν	καὶ
man	will be given over	to the	ruler priests	and

015		1122		2532	2632		846
τοῖς	γραμματεῦσιν,	καὶ	κατακρινοῦσιν		αὐτὸν
to the	writers,	and	they will condemn	him

2288		2532	3860		846	023	1484
θανάτῳ	καὶ	παραδώσουσιν		αὐτὸν	τοῖς	ἔθνεσιν
to death	and	they will give over	him	to the	nations

34	2532	1702		846	2532	1716		846
	καὶ	ἐμπαίξουσιν		αὐτῷ	καὶ	ἐμπτύσουσιν		αὐτῷ
	and	they will mock	him	and	they will spit	on him

2532	3146		846	2532	615		2532
καὶ	μαστιγώσουσιν		αὐτὸν	καὶ	ἀποκτενοῦσιν,		καὶ
and	they will scourge	him	and	they will kill,	and

3326	5140	2250	450		2532	4365
μετὰ	τρεῖς	ἡμέρας	ἀναστήσεται.	³⁵	Καὶ	προσπορεύονται
after	three	days	he will stand up.		And	travel toward

846	2385		2532	2491	013	5207	2199
αὐτῷ	Ἰάκωβος	καὶ	Ἰωάννης	οἱ	υἱοὶ	Ζεβεδαίου
him	Jacob	and	John	the	sons	of Zebedee

```
3004        846      1320              2309      2443 3739 1437
λέγοντες αὐτῷ·   διδάσκαλε, θέλομεν ἵνα  ὃ   ἐὰν
saying   to him;  teacher,  we want that what if
154              1473 4160           1473   36  01        1161
αἰτήσωμέν  σε ποιήσῃς   ἡμῖν.       ὁ        δὲ
we might ask you you might do to us.  The one but
3004  846      5101 2309      1473 4160       1473
εἶπεν αὐτοῖς·  τί θέλετέ [με] ποιησώ  ὑμῖν;
said  to them; what you want me I might do to you?
37  013     1161 3004  846     1325 1473 2443 1520 1473
    οἱ    δὲ  εἶπαν αὐτῷ·  δὸς ἡμῖν ἵνα εἷς σου
   The ones but  said  to him; give us  that one of you
1537    1188     2532 1520 1537   710       2523
ἐκ  δεξιῶν καὶ  εἷς ἐξ  ἀριστερῶν καθίσωμεν
out of right  and  one out of left   we might sit
1722 07 1391        1473 38  01  1161  2424     3004 846
ἐν τῇ δόξῃ   σου.    ὁ   δὲ  Ἰησοῦς εἶπεν αὐτοῖς·
in the splendor of you. The but Jesus  said to them,
3756 3609a    5101 154       1410        4095       012
οὐκ οἴδατε  τί  αἰτεῖσθε.  δύνασθε   πιεῖν   τὸ
not you know what you ask.  Are you able to drink the
4221       3739  1473 4095 2228 012 908       3739    1473
ποτήριον ὃ   ἐγὼ πίνω ἢ  τὸ βάπτισμα ὃ     ἐγὼ
cup       which I   drink or the immersion which I
907        907           39  013    1161 3004 846
βαπτίζομαι βαπτισθῆναι;    οἱ   δὲ εἶπαν αὐτῷ·
am immersed to be immersed? The ones but said to him,
1410      01 1161 2424      3004 846      012 4221
δυνάμεθα.  ὁ  δὲ  Ἰησοῦς εἶπεν αὐτοῖς· τὸ ποτήριον
we are able. The but Jesus  said  to them; the cup
3739 1473 4095 4095             2532 012 908           3739
ὃ    ἐγὼ πίνω πίεσθε      καὶ τὸ βάπτισμα ὃ
which I   drink you will drink and the immersion which
1473 907          907             40  09   1161 2523
ἐγὼ βαπτίζομαι βαπτισθήσεσθε,    τὸ  δὲ καθίσαι
I   am immersed you will be immersed, the but to sit
1537    1188     1473 2228 1537   2176       3756 1510  1699
ἐκ  δεξιῶν μου  ἢ  ἐξ  εὐωνύμων οὐκ ἔστιν ἐμὸν
out of right of me or out of left  not is   mine
1325      235 3739    2090          41 2532 191
δοῦναι,  ἀλλ᾽ οἷς  ἡτοίμασται.    Καὶ  ἀκούσαντες
to give, but  to whom it has been  And  having heard
                         prepared.
013 1176 757      23            4012 2385      2532
οἱ δέκα ἤρξαντο ἀγανακτεῖν  περὶ  Ἰακώβου καὶ
the ten began  to be indignant about Jacob  and
2491       42 2532 4341             846     01
Ἰωάννου.     καὶ προσκαλεσάμενος αὐτοὺς ὁ
John.        And having called toward them  the
2424     3004 846      3609a     3754 013 1380
Ἰησοῦς λέγει αὐτοῖς· οἴδατε ὅτι οἱ δοκοῦντες
Jesus says  to them; you know that the ones thinking
757      022 1484   2634          846    2532 013
ἄρχειν τῶν ἐθνῶν κατακυριεύουσιν αὐτῶν καὶ οἱ
to rule the nations master over  them  and the
3173      846     2715           846    43 3756
μεγάλοι αὐτῶν κατεξουσιάζουσιν αὐτῶν.    οὐχ
great ones of them exercise authority over them. Not
3779    1161 1510 1722 1473 235 3739 302 2309     3173
οὕτως δέ ἐστιν ἐν ὑμῖν, ἀλλ᾽ ὃς ἂν θέλῃ    μέγας
thusly but it is in you,  but who - might want great
1096       1722 1473 1510     1473  1249        44 2532
γενέσθαι ἐν  ὑμῖν ἔσται ὑμῶν διάκονος,    καὶ
to become in you will be of you servant,   and
3739 302 2309       1722 1473 1510 4413    1510
ὃς  ἂν θέλῃ      ἐν ὑμῖν εἶναι πρῶτος ἔσται
who - might want in you to be first will be
3956   1401    45 2532 1063 01  5207 02      444
πάντων δοῦλος·   καὶ γὰρ ὁ υἱὸς τοῦ ἀνθρώπου
of all slave;  even for the son of the man
```

came forward to him and said to him, "Teacher, we want you to do for us whatever we ask of you." [36]And he said to them, "What is it you want me to do for you?" [37]And they said to him, "Grant us to sit, one at your right hand and one at your left, in your glory." [38]But Jesus said to them, "You do not know what you are asking. Are you able to drink the cup that I drink, or be baptized with the baptism that I am baptized with?" [39]They replied, "We are able." Then Jesus said to them, "The cup that I drink you will drink; and with the baptism with which I am baptized, you will be baptized; [40]but to sit at my right hand or at my left is not mine to grant, but it is for those for whom it has been prepared."

[41] When the ten heard this, they began to be angry with James and John. [42]So Jesus called them and said to them, "You know that among the Gentiles those whom they recognize as their rulers lord it over them, and their great ones are tyrants over them. [43]But it is not so among you; but whoever wishes to become great among you must be your servant, [44]and whoever wishes to be first among you must be slave of all. [45]For the Son of Man

came not to be served but to serve, and to give his life a ransom for many."

46 They came to Jericho. As he and his disciples and a large crowd were leaving Jericho, Bartimaeus son of Timaeus, a blind beggar, was sitting by the roadside. [47]When he heard that it was Jesus of Nazareth, he began to shout out and say, "Jesus, Son of David, have mercy on me!" [48]Many sternly ordered him to be quiet, but he cried out even more loudly, "Son of David, have mercy on me!" [49]Jesus stood still and said, "Call him here." And they called the blind man, saying to him, "Take heart; get up, he is calling you." [50]So throwing off his cloak, he sprang up and came to Jesus. [51]Then Jesus said to him, "What do you want me to do for you?" The blind man said to him, "My teacher,[a] let me see again." [52]Jesus said to him, "Go; your faith has made you well." Immediately he regained his sight and followed him on the way.

CHAPTER 11

When they were approaching Jerusalem, at Bethphage and Bethany, near the Mount of Olives, he sent two of his disciples [2]and said to them,

[a] Aramaic Rabbouni

3756	2064	1247	235	1247	2532	1325
οὐκ	ἦλθεν	διακονηθῆναι	ἀλλὰ	διακονῆσαι	καὶ	δοῦναι
not	came	to be served	but	to serve	and	to give

08	5590	846	3083	473	4183	46	2532
τὴν	ψυχὴν	αὐτοῦ	λύτρον	ἀντὶ	πολλῶν.		Καὶ
the	soul	of him	ransom	in place of	many.		And

2064	1519	2410	2532 1607	846
ἔρχονται	εἰς	Ἰεριχώ.	Καὶ ἐκπορευομένου	αὐτοῦ
they come	into	Jericho.	And traveling out	him

575	2410	2532 014	3101	846	2532 3793
ἀπὸ	Ἰεριχὼ	καὶ τῶν	μαθητῶν	αὐτοῦ	καὶ ὄχλου
from	Jericho	and of the	learners	of him	and crowd

2425	01	5207 5090	924	5185	4319a
ἱκανοῦ	ὁ	υἱὸς Τιμαίου	Βαρτιμαῖος,	τυφλὸς	προσαίτης,
enough	the	son of Timeus	Bartimeus,	blind	beggar,

2521	3844	08 3598	47	2532 191	3754
ἐκάθητο	παρὰ	τὴν ὁδόν.		καὶ ἀκούσας	ὅτι
sat	alongside	the way.		And having heard	that

2424	01 3479	1510	757	2896	2532
Ἰησοῦς	ὁ Ναζαρηνός	ἐστιν	ἤρξατο	κράζειν	καὶ
Jesus	the Nazarene	is	he began	to shout	and

3004	5207 1160a	2424	1653	1473	48	2532
λέγειν·	υἱὲ Δαυὶδ	Ἰησοῦ,	ἐλέησόν	με.		καὶ
to say,	son David	Jesus,	show mercy	on me.		And

2008	846	4183	2443 4623	01	1161 4183
ἐπετίμων	αὐτῷ	πολλοὶ	ἵνα σιωπήσῃ·	ὁ	δὲ πολλῷ
were admonishing	him	many	that he might be silent;	the one	but much

3123	2896	5207 1160a	1653	1473
μᾶλλον	ἔκραζεν·	υἱὲ Δαυίδ,	ἐλέησόν	με.
more	was shouting;	son David,	have mercy	on me.

49	2532 2476	01	2424	3004	5455	846
	καὶ στὰς	ὁ	Ἰησοῦς	εἶπεν·	φωνήσατε	αὐτόν.
	And having stood	the	Jesus	said;	sound	him.

2532 5455	04	5185	3004	846
καὶ φωνοῦσιν	τὸν	τυφλὸν	λέγοντες	αὐτῷ·
And they sound	the	blind	saying	to him;

2293	1453	5455	1473	50	01 1161 577	012
θάρσει,	ἔγειρε,	φωνεῖ	σε.		ὁ δὲ ἀποβαλὼν	τὸ
take courage,	rise,	he sounds	you.		The but throwing	the
					one	off

2440	846	375a	2064	4314	04
ἱμάτιον	αὐτοῦ	ἀναπηδήσας	ἦλθεν	πρὸς	τὸν
clothes	of him	having jumped up	went	toward	the

2424	51	2532 611	846	01 2424	3004
Ἰησοῦν.		καὶ ἀποκριθεὶς	αὐτῷ	ὁ Ἰησοῦς	εἶπεν,
Jesus.		And having answered	him	the Jesus	said,

5101 1473	2309	4160	01	1161 5185	3004
τί σοι	θέλεις	ποιήσω;	ὁ	δὲ τυφλὸς	εἶπεν
what to you	you want	I might do?	The	but blind	said

846	4462	2443 308	52	2532 01 2424
αὐτῷ·	ραββουνι,	ἵνα ἀναβλέψω.		καὶ ὁ Ἰησοῦς
him;	Rabboni,	that I might see again.		And the Jesus

3004	846	5217	05 4102	1473	4982
εἶπεν	αὐτῷ·	ὕπαγε,	ἡ πίστις	σου	σέσωκέν
said	to him;	go off,	the trust	of you	has delivered

1473 2532 2117	308	2532 190	8461722
σε. καὶ εὐθὺς	ἀνέβλεψεν	καὶ ἠκολούθει	αὐτῷ ἐν
you. And immediately	he saw	and he was	him in
	again	following	

07 3598	11:1	2532 3753 1448	1519	2414
τῇ ὁδῷ.		Καὶ ὅτε ἐγγίζουσιν	εἰς	Ἱεροσόλυμα
the way.		And when they near	into	Jerusalem

1519 967	2532 963	4314	012 3735 018
εἰς Βηθφαγὴ	καὶ Βηθανίαν	πρὸς	τὸ ὄρος τῶν
into Bethphage	and Bethany	toward	the hill of the

1636	649	1417 014	3101	846	2	2532
ἐλαιῶν,	ἀποστέλλει	δύο τῶν	μαθητῶν	αὐτοῦ		καὶ
olives,	he delegates	two of the	learners	of him		and

```
3004      846        5217     1519 08  2968      08
λέγει     αὐτοῖς·    ὑπάγετε  εἰς τὴν κώμην     τὴν
he says   to them;   go off   into the village  the

2713          1473 2532 2117        1531              1519
κατέναντι     ὑμῶν, καὶ εὐθὺς      εἰσπορευόμενοι εἰς
over against  you,  and immediately traveling into into

846    2147      4454    1210               1909 3739
αὐτὴν  εὑρήσετε πῶλον  δεδεμένον          ἐφ᾽  ὃν
it     you will find colt having been bound on   which

3762    3768   444       2523       3089   846  2532
οὐδεὶς  οὔπω   ἀνθρώπων ἐκάθισεν·  λύσατε αὐτὸν καὶ
no one  not yet of men   sat;       loose  it    and

5342    3 2532 1437 5100 1473  3004        5101 4160
φέρετε.    καὶ ἐάν τις ὑμῖν εἴπῃ·        τί   ποιεῖτε
bring.     And if some to you might say; why  you do

3778   3004  01  2962   846    5532    2192 2532
τοῦτο; εἴπατε· ὁ κύριος αὐτοῦ χρείαν ἔχει, καὶ
this?  Say;   the Master of it need   has,  and

2117   846   649        3825  5602  2532
εὐθὺς  αὐτὸν ἀποστέλλει πάλιν ὧδε. 4 καὶ
immediately it  he delegates again here.  And

565        2532 2147 4454  1210       4314  2374
ἀπῆλθον    καὶ εὗρον πῶλον δεδεμένον πρὸς θύραν
they went off and found colt having    toward door
                            been bound

1854    1909 010 296       2532 3089      846   5  2532
ἔξω     ἐπὶ τοῦ ἀμφόδου καὶ λύουσιν   αὐτόν.    καί
outside on  the street   and they loose it.     And

5100 014       1563 2476     3004    846      5101
τινες τῶν      ἐκεῖ ἑστηκότων ἔλεγον αὐτοῖς· τί
some  of the ones there having were   to them; why
                    stood        saying

4160    3089      04   4454   6 013      1161 3004
ποιεῖτε. λύοντες τὸν πῶλον;    οἱ   δὲ  εἶπαν
do you  loosening the colt?    The ones but said

846    2531   3004  01 2424     2532 863
αὐτοῖς καθὼς εἶπεν ὁ Ἰησοῦς, καὶ ἀφῆκαν
to them just as said the Jesus,  and they sent off

846    7 2532 5342      04  4454   4314  04   2424
αὐτούς.   καὶ φέρουσιν τὸν πῶλον πρὸς τὸν Ἰησοῦν
them.     And they bring the colt  toward the Jesus

2532 1911         846 024 2440   846   2532
καὶ ἐπιβάλλουσιν αὐτῷ τὰ ἱμάτια αὐτῶν, καὶ
and they throw on it   the clothes of them, and

2523    1909 846   8 2532 4183   024 2440   846
ἐκάθισεν ἐπ᾽ αὐτόν.   καὶ πολλοὶ τὰ ἱμάτια αὐτῶν
he sat   on  it.      And many   the clothes of them

4766      1519 08  3598 243    1161 4741a
ἔστρωσαν εἰς τὴν ὁδόν, ἄλλοι δὲ  στιβάδας
spread   in  the way,  others but leafy branches

2875      1537 014 68  9 2532 013    4254      2532
κόψαντες ἐκ τῶν ἀγρῶν.  καὶ οἱ   προάγοντες καὶ
having   out of fields.  And the ones leading and
cut          the                    before

013 190          2896     5614    2127       01
οἱ ἀκολουθοῦντες ἔκραζον· ὡσαννά· εὐλογημένος ὁ
the ones following were    hosanna; being well- the
                  shouting;          spoken

2064       1722 3686     2962    10 2127
ἐρχόμενος ἐν ὀνόματι κυρίου·      εὐλογημένη
one coming in  name    of Master;  being well-spoken

05 2064      932       02  3962     1473 1160a
ἡ ἐρχομένη βασιλεία τοῦ πατρὸς ἡμῶν Δαυίδ·
the coming kingdom  of the father of us David;

5614    1722 023   5310      11 2532 1525     1519
ὡσαννὰ ἐν τοῖς ὑψίστοις.    Καὶ εἰσῆλθεν εἰς
hosanna in the highest.      And he went into into

2414       1519 012 2411   2532 4017
Ἰεροσόλυμα εἰς τὸ ἱερὸν καὶ περιβλεψάμενος
Jerusalem into the temple and having looked around
```

"Go into the village ahead of you, and immediately as you enter it, you will find tied there a colt that has never been ridden; untie it and bring it. [3]If anyone says to you, 'Why are you doing this?' just say this, 'The Lord needs it and will send it back here immediately.'" [4]They went away and found a colt tied near a door, outside in the street. As they were untying it, [5]some of the bystanders said to them, "What are you doing, untying the colt?" [6]They told them what Jesus had said; and they allowed them to take it. [7]Then they brought the colt to Jesus and threw their cloaks on it; and he sat on it. [8]Many people spread their cloaks on the road, and others spread leafy branches that they had cut in the fields. [9]Then those who went ahead and those who followed were shouting,

"Hosanna!
Blessed is the one who comes in the name of the Lord!
[10] Blessed is the coming kingdom of our ancestor David!
Hosanna in the highest heaven!"

[11] Then he entered Jerusalem and went into the temple; and when he had looked around

at everything, as it was
already late, he went out to
Bethany with the twelve.
12 On the following
day, when they came from
Bethany, he was hungry.
13 Seeing in the distance a
fig tree in leaf, he went to
see whether perhaps he
would find anything on it.
When he came to it, he
found nothing but leaves,
for it was not the season
for figs. 14 He said to it,
"May no one ever eat fruit
from you again." And his
disciples heard it.
15 Then they came to
Jerusalem. And he entered
the temple and began to
drive out those who were
selling and those who were
buying in the temple, and
he overturned the tables
of the money changers
and the seats of those who
sold doves; 16 and he would
not allow anyone to carry
anything through the
temple. 17 He was teaching
and saying, "Is it not
written,
  'My house shall be called
  a house of prayer for
  all the nations'?
  But you have made it a
  den of robbers."
18 And when the chief priests
and the scribes heard it,
they kept looking for a way
to kill him; for they were
afraid of him, because the
whole crowd was spell-
bound by his teaching.

3956	3798	2235	1510	06	5610	1831
πάντα,	ὀψίας	ἤδη	οὔσης τῆς		ὥρας,	ἐξῆλθεν
all,	evening	already	being of the		hour,	he went out

1519 963	3326 014	1427	12	2532 07	1887
εἰς Βηθανίαν	μετὰ τῶν	δώδεκα.		Καὶ τῇ	ἐπαύριον
into Bethany	with the	twelve.		And in the	tomorrow

1831	846	575	963	3983
ἐξελθόντων	αὐτῶν	ἀπὸ	Βηθανίας	ἐπείνασεν.
having come out	of them	from	Bethany	he hungered.

13	2532 3708	4808	575	3113	2192
	καὶ ἰδὼν	συκῆν	ἀπὸ	μακρόθεν	ἔχουσαν
	And having seen	fig tree	from	from far	having

5444	2064	1487 686	5100 2147		1722 846	2532
φύλλα	ἦλθεν,	εἰ ἄρα	τι εὑρήσει		ἐν αὐτῇ,	καὶ
leaves	he came,	if then	some he will find		in it,	and

2064	1909 846	3762	2147	1487 3361
ἐλθὼν	ἐπ' αὐτὴν	οὐδὲν	εὗρεν	εἰ μὴ
having come on	it	nothing	he found	except

5444	01	1063 2540	3756 1510	4810	14	2532
φύλλα·	ὁ	γὰρ καιρὸς	οὐκ ἦν	σύκων.		καὶ
leaves;	the	for season	not it was	of figs.		And

611	3004	846	3371	1519 04
ἀποκριθεὶς	εἶπεν	αὐτῇ·	μηκέτι	εἰς τὸν
having answered	he said	to it;	no longer	into the

165	1537 1473 3367	2590	2068	2532 191
αἰῶνα	ἐκ σοῦ μηδεὶς	καρπὸν	φάγοι.	καὶ ἤκουον
age	from you no one	fruit	may eat.	And were hearing

013 3101	846	15	2532 2064	1519	2414
οἱ μαθηταὶ	αὐτοῦ.		Καὶ ἔρχονται	εἰς	Ἱεροσόλυμα.
the learners	him.		And they come	into	Jerusalem.

2532 1525		1519 012 2411	757
Καὶ εἰσελθὼν		εἰς τὸ ἱερὸν	ἤρξατο
And having gone into		into the temple	he began

1544	016	4453	2532 016	59	1722
ἐκβάλλειν	τοὺς	πωλοῦντας	καὶ τοὺς	ἀγοράζοντας	ἐν
to throw out	the	ones selling	and the	ones buying	in

011 1473	2532 020 5132	014	2855
τῷ ἱερῷ,	καὶ τὰς τραπέζας	τῶν	κολλυβιστῶν
the temple,	and the tables	of the	money changers

2532 020 2515	014	4453	020 4058
καὶ τὰς καθέδρας	τῶν	πωλούντων	τὰς περιστερὰς
and the seats	of the	ones selling	the doves

2690	16	2532 3756 863		2443 5100
κατέστρεψεν,		καὶ οὐκ ἤφιεν		ἵνα τις
he turned over,		and not he was allowing		that some

1308	4632	1223	010 2411	17	2532
διενέγκῃ	σκεῦος	διὰ	τοῦ ἱεροῦ.		καὶ
might carry through	pot	through	the temple.		And

1321	2532 3004	846	3756 1125	3754
ἐδίδασκεν	καὶ ἔλεγεν	αὐτοῖς·	οὐ γέγραπται	ὅτι
he was teaching	and saying	to them;	not it has been written	that

01	3624 1473	3624 4335	2564	3956
ὁ	οἶκός μου	οἶκος προσευχῆς	κληθήσεται	πᾶσιν
the	house of me	house of prayer	will be called	to all

023 1484	1473 1161 4160	846 4693
τοῖς ἔθνεσιν;	ὑμεῖς δὲ πεποιήκατε	αὐτὸν σπήλαιον
the nations?	You but have made	it cave

3027	18	2532 191	013 749	2532
λῃστῶν.		Καὶ ἤκουσαν	οἱ ἀρχιερεῖς	καὶ
of robbers.		And were hearing	the ruler priests	and

013 1122	2532 2212	4459 846
οἱ γραμματεῖς	καὶ ἐζήτουν	πῶς αὐτὸν
the writers	and they were seeking	how him

622	5399	1063 846	3956
ἀπολέσωσιν·	ἐφοβοῦντο	γὰρ αὐτόν,	πᾶς
they might destroy;	they were fearing	for him,	all

1063 01	3793 1605	1909 07 1322	846
γὰρ ὁ	ὄχλος ἐξεπλήσσετο	ἐπὶ τῇ διδαχῇ	αὐτοῦ.
for the	crowd was astonished	on the teaching	of him.

19
| 2532 | 3752 | 3796 | 1096 | 1607 | 1854 |
Καὶ ὅταν ὀψὲ ἐγένετο, ἐξεπορεύοντο ἔξω
And when evening became, they traveled out outside

| 06 | 4172 | **20** | 2532 | 3899 | 4404 |
τῆς πόλεως. Καὶ παραπορευόμενοι πρωῒ
the city. And traveling along in morning

| 3708 | 08 | 4808 | 3583 | 1537 |
εἶδον τὴν συκῆν ἐξηραμμένην ἐκ
they saw the fig tree having been dried out from

| 4491 | 2532 | 363 | 01 | 4074 | 3004 |
ῥιζῶν. **21** καὶ ἀναμνησθεὶς ὁ Πέτρος λέγει
roots. And having been reminded the Peter says

| 846 | 4461 | 2396 | 05 | 4808 | 3739 | 2672 |
αὐτῷ· ῥαββί, ἴδε ἡ συκῆ ἣν κατηράσω
to him, Rabbi, look the fig tree which you cursed

| 3583 | **22** | 2532 | 611 | 01 | 2424 |
ἐξήρανται. καὶ ἀποκριθεὶς ὁ Ἰησοῦς
it has been dried out. And having answered the Jesus

| 3004 | 846 | 2192 | 4102 | 2316 | **23** | 281 | 3004 | 1473 |
λέγει αὐτοῖς· ἔχετε πίστιν θεοῦ. ἀμὴν λέγω ὑμῖν
says to them; have trust of God. Amen I say to you

| 3754 | 3739 | 302 | 3004 | 011 | 3735 | 3778 | 142 |
ὅτι ὃς ἂν εἴπῃ τῷ ὄρει τούτῳ· ἄρθητι
that who - might say to the hill this; be lifted up

| 2532 | 906 | 1519 | 08 | 2281 | 2532 | 3361 |
καὶ βλήθητι εἰς τὴν θάλασσαν, καὶ μὴ
and be thrown into the sea, and not

| 1252 | 1722 | 07 | 2588 | 846 | 235 | 4100 |
διακριθῇ ἐν τῇ καρδίᾳ αὐτοῦ ἀλλὰ πιστεύῃ
he might doubt in the heart of him but he might trust

| 3754 | 3739 | 2980 | 1096 | 1510 | 846 |
ὅτι ὃ λαλεῖ γίνεται, ἔσται αὐτῷ.
that what he speaks it becomes, it will be to him.

24
| 1223 | 3778 | 3004 | 1473 | 3956 | 3745 | 4336 |
διὰ τοῦτο λέγω ὑμῖν, πάντα ὅσα προσεύχεσθε
Through this I say to you, all as much as you pray

| 2532 | 154 | 4100 | 3754 | 2983 | 2532 |
καὶ αἰτεῖσθε, πιστεύετε ὅτι ἐλάβετε, καὶ
and you ask, trust that you received, and

| 1510 | 1473 | **25** | 2532 | 3752 | 4739 | 4336 |
ἔσται ὑμῖν. Καὶ ὅταν στήκετε προσευχόμενοι,
it will be to you. And when you stand praying,

| 863 | 1487 | 5100 | 2192 | 2596 | 5100 | 2443 | 2532 |
ἀφίετε εἴ τι ἔχετε κατά τινος, ἵνα καὶ
send off if some you have against some, that also

| 01 | 3962 | 1473 | 01 | 1722 | 015 | 3772 | 863 |
ὁ πατὴρ ὑμῶν ὁ ἐν τοῖς οὐρανοῖς ἀφῇ
the father of you the in the heavens might send off

| 1473 | 024 | 3900 | 1473 | **27** | 2532 | 2064 | 3825 |
ὑμῖν τὰ παραπτώματα ὑμῶν. Καὶ ἔρχονται πάλιν
to you the trespasses of you. And they come again

| 1519 | 2414 | 2532 | 1722 | 011 | 2411 | 4043 |
εἰς Ἱεροσόλυμα. καὶ ἐν τῷ ἱερῷ περιπατοῦντος
into Jerusalem. And in the temple walking around

| 846 | 2064 | 4314 | 846 | 013 | 749 | 2532 | 013 |
αὐτοῦ ἔρχονται πρὸς αὐτὸν οἱ ἀρχιερεῖς καὶ οἱ
him come toward him the ruler priests and the

| 1122 | 2532 | 013 | 4245 | **28** | 2532 | 3004 |
γραμματεῖς καὶ οἱ πρεσβύτεροι καὶ ἔλεγον
writers and the older men and they were saying

| 846 | 1722 | 4169 | 1849 | 3778 | 4160 | 2228 | 5101 | 1473 |
αὐτῷ· ἐν ποίᾳ ἐξουσίᾳ ταῦτα ποιεῖς; ἢ τίς σοι
to him; in what authority these you do? Or who to
                kind   you

| 1325 | 08 | 1849 | 3778 | 2443 | 3778 | 4160 |
ἔδωκεν τὴν ἐξουσίαν ταύτην ἵνα ταῦτα ποιῇς;
gave the authority this that these you might do?

29
| 01 | 1161 | 2424 | 3004 | 846 | 1905 | 1473 |
ὁ δὲ Ἰησοῦς εἶπεν αὐτοῖς· ἐπερωτήσω ὑμᾶς
The but Jesus said to them; I will ask on you

[19] And when evening came, Jesus and his disciples[a] went out of the city.

[20] In the morning as they passed by, they saw the fig tree withered away to its roots. [21] Then Peter remembered and said to him, "Rabbi, look! The fig tree that you cursed has withered." [22] Jesus answered them, "Have[b] faith in God. [23] Truly I tell you, if you say to this mountain, 'Be taken up and thrown into the sea,' and if you do not doubt in your heart, but believe that what you say will come to pass, it will be done for you. [24] So I tell you, whatever you ask for in prayer, believe that you have received[c] it, and it will be yours.

[25] "Whenever you stand praying, forgive, if you have anything against anyone; so that your Father in heaven may also forgive you your trespasses."[d]

[27] Again they came to Jerusalem. As he was walking in the temple, the chief priests, the scribes, and the elders came to him [28] and said, "By what authority are you doing these things? Who gave you this authority to do them?" [29] Jesus said to them, "I will ask you

---

[a] Gk they: other ancient authorities read he

[b] Other ancient authorities read "If you have

[c] Other ancient authorities read are receiving

[d] Other ancient authorities add verse 26, "But if you do not forgive, neither will your Father in heaven forgive your trespasses."

one question; answer me, and I will tell you by what authority I do these things. 30Did the baptism of John come from heaven, or was it of human origin? Answer me." 31They argued with one another, "If we say, 'From heaven,' he will say, 'Why then did you not believe him?' 32But shall we say, 'Of human origin'?"— they were afraid of the crowd, for all regarded John as truly a prophet. 33So they answered Jesus, "We do not know." And Jesus said to them, "Neither will I tell you by what authority I am doing these things."

CHAPTER 12

Then he began to speak to them in parables. "A man planted a vineyard, put a fence around it, dug a pit for the wine press, and built a watchtower; then he leased it to tenants and went to another country. 2When the season came, he sent a slave to the tenants to collect from them his share of the produce of the vineyard. 3But they seized him, and beat him, and sent him away empty-handed. 4And again he sent another slave to them; this one they beat over the head and insulted. 5Then he sent another, and that one they killed. And so it was with many others; some they beat, and others they killed.

1520	3056	2532 611		1473 2532 3004		1473
ἕνα	λόγον,	καὶ ἀποκρίθητέ	μοι	καὶ ἐρῶ		ὑμῖν
one	word,	and you answer	me	and I will	say	to you

1722 4169	1849		3778 4160	**30**	09	908
ἐν ποίᾳ	ἐξουσίᾳ	ταῦτα ποιῶ·			τὸ	βάπτισμα
in what kind authority	these I do;				the	immersion

09	2491	1537 3772		1510 2228	1537 444
τὸ	'Ιωάννου ἐξ	οὐρανοῦ	ἦν	ἢ	ἐξ ἀνθρώπων;
the one	of John out	of heaven	was	or	out of men?

611	1473	2532 1260		4314
ἀποκρίθητέ	μοι. **31**	καὶ διελογίζοντο		πρὸς
You answer	me.	And they were reasoning	toward

1438	3004	1437 3004		1537	3772
ἑαυτοὺς	λέγοντες·	ἐὰν εἴπωμεν·		ἐξ	οὐρανοῦ,
themselves	saying;	if we might say;		out of heaven,

3004	1223	5101	3767 3756 4100		846
ἐρεῖ·	διὰ	τί	[οὖν] οὐκ ἐπιστεύσατε αὐτῷ;
he will say;	through	what	then not you trusted him?

32	235	3004	1537 444		5399
ἀλλὰ εἴπωμεν·		ἐξ ἀνθρώπων;	– ἐφοβοῦντο
But we might say;	out of men?	They were fearing

04	3793	537	1063 2192	04	2491	3689	3754
τὸν ὄχλον·	ἅπαντες	γὰρ εἶχον τὸν 'Ιωάννην	ὄντως	ὅτι
the crowd;	all	for held the John	really	that

4396	1510	**33**	2532 611		03	2424
προφήτης	ἦν.	καὶ ἀποκριθέντες	τῷ	'Ιησοῦ
spokesman	he was.	And having answered	to the	Jesus

3004	3756 3609a	2532 01	2424	3004	846
λέγουσιν· οὐκ οἴδαμεν.	καὶ ὁ 'Ιησοῦς λέγει αὐτοῖς·
they say; not we know.	And the Jesus says to them;

3761	1473 3004 1473	1722 4169	1849	3778
οὐδὲ	ἐγὼ λέγω ὑμῖν	ἐν ποίᾳ	ἐξουσίᾳ	ταῦτα
but not I	say to you	in what kind authority	these

4160	**12:1**	2532 757	846	1722 3850
ποιῶ.		Καὶ ἤρξατο	αὐτοῖς ἐν	παραβολαῖς
I do.		And he began	to them in	parallel stories

2980	290	444	5452	2532 4060
λαλεῖν·	ἀμπελῶνα ἄνθρωπος ἐφύτευσεν	καὶ περιέθηκεν
to speak;	vineyard man planted	and he set around

5418	2532 3736	5276		2532 3618
φραγμὸν	καὶ ὤρυξεν	ὑπολήνιον		καὶ ᾠκοδόμησεν
hedge	and he dug pit under	wine press	and he built

4444	2532 1554	846	1092	2532
πύργον	καὶ ἐξέδετο	αὐτὸν	γεωργοῖς	καὶ
tower	and he gave out	it	to farmers	and

589		**2**	2532 649		4314	016	1092
ἀπεδήμησεν.		καὶ ἀπέστειλεν	πρὸς	τοὺς	γεωργοὺς
he journeyed.		And he delegated	toward	the	farmers

03	2540	1401	2443 3844 014 1092
τῷ	καιρῷ	δοῦλον	ἵνα παρὰ τῶν γεωργῶν
in the	season	slave	that from the farmers

2983		575	014 2590	02	290		**3**	2532
λάβῃ		ἀπὸ	τῶν καρπῶν	τοῦ	ἀμπελῶνος·			καὶ
he might receive	from	the fruit	of the	vineyard;			and

2983		846	1194	2532 649	2756
λαβόντες		αὐτὸν ἔδειραν	καὶ ἀπέστειλαν κενόν.
having received	him they beat	and delegated empty.

4	2532 3825	649		4314 846	243	1401
καὶ πάλιν	ἀπέστειλεν		πρὸς αὐτοὺς	ἄλλον	δοῦλον·
And again	he delegated		toward them	other	slave;

2548	2775		2532 818
κἀκεῖνον	ἐκεφαλίωσαν		καὶ ἠτίμασαν.
and that one	they wounded in head	and dishonored.

5	2532 243	649		2548	615
καὶ ἄλλον	ἀπέστειλεν·		κἀκεῖνον	ἀπέκτειναν,
And other	he delegated;		and that one	they killed,

2532 4183	243	3739 3303	1194	3739 1161
καὶ πολλοὺς	ἄλλους,	οὓς μὲν	δέροντες,	οὓς δὲ
and many	others,	whom indeed	beating,	whom but

615
ἀποκτέννοντες. **6** 2089 1520 2192 5207 27
ἔτι ἕνα εἶχεν υἱὸν ἀγαπητόν·
killing.　Still one he had son loved one;

649　846　2078　4314　846　3004　3754
ἀπέστειλεν αὐτὸν ἔσχατον πρὸς αὐτοὺς λέγων ὅτι
he delegated him last toward them saying, (")

1788　04 5207 1473 **7** 1565　1161 013
ἐντραπήσονται τὸν υἱόν μου. ἐκεῖνοι δὲ οἱ
they will regard the son of me. Those but the

1092　4314 1438　3004 3754 4778 1510 01
γεωργοὶ πρὸς ἑαυτοὺς εἶπαν ὅτι οὗτός ἐστιν ὁ
farmers toward themselves said, (") this is the

2818　1205 615　846　2532 1473
κληρονόμος· δεῦτε ἀποκτείνωμεν αὐτόν, καὶ ἡμῶν
inheritor; come we might kill him, and of us

1510　05 2817 **8** 2532 2983　615
ἔσται ἡ κληρονομία. καὶ λαβόντες ἀπέκτειναν
will be the inheritance. And having taken they killed

846　2532 1544　846 1854　02 290
αὐτὸν καὶ ἐξέβαλον αὐτὸν ἔξω τοῦ ἀμπελῶνος.
him and they threw out him outside the vineyard.

9 5101 3767 4160 01 2962 02　290
τί [οὖν] ποιήσει ὁ κύριος τοῦ ἀμπελῶνος;
What then will do the master of the vineyard?

2064　2532 622　016 1092　2532
ἐλεύσεται καὶ ἀπολέσει τοὺς γεωργοὺς καὶ
He will go and he will destroy the farmers and

1325　04 290 243 **10** 3761　08 1124
δώσει τὸν ἀμπελῶνα ἄλλοις. οὐδὲ τὴν γραφὴν
will give the vineyard to others. But not the writing

3778 314　3037 3739 593　013
ταύτην ἀνέγνωτε· λίθον ὃν ἀπεδοκίμασαν οἱ
this you read; stone which rejected the ones

3618　3778 1096　1519 2776　1137
οἰκοδομοῦντες, οὗτος ἐγενήθη εἰς κεφαλὴν γωνίας·
building,　this became into head of corner;

11 3844 2962　1096　3778 2532 1510 2298　1722
παρὰ κυρίου ἐγένετο αὕτη καὶ ἔστιν θαυμαστὴ ἐν
from Master became this and it is marvelous in

3788　1473 **12** 2532 2212　846
ὀφθαλμοῖς ἡμῶν; Καὶ ἐζήτουν αὐτὸν
eyes of us? And they were seeking him

2902　2532 5399　04 3793　1097
κρατῆσαι, καὶ ἐφοβήθησαν τὸν ὄχλον, ἔγνωσαν
to hold, and they were afraid the crowd, they knew

1063 3754 4314　846　08 3850　3004
γὰρ ὅτι πρὸς αὐτοὺς τὴν παραβολὴν εἶπεν.
for that toward them the parallel story he said.

2532 863　846　565 **13** 2532
καὶ ἀφέντες αὐτὸν ἀπῆλθον. Καὶ
And having sent off him they went off. And

649　4314　846 5100 014　5330
ἀποστέλλουσιν πρὸς αὐτόν τινας τῶν Φαρισαίων
they delegate toward him some of the Pharisees

2532 014　2265　2443 846　64
καὶ τῶν Ἡρῳδιανῶν ἵνα αὐτὸν ἀγρεύσωσιν
and of the Herodians that him they might trap

3056 **14** 2532 2064　3004　846　1320
λόγῳ. καὶ ἐλθόντες λέγουσιν αὐτῷ· διδάσκαλε,
in word. And having come they say to him; teacher,

3609a 3754 227　1510　2532 3756 3190a
οἴδαμεν ὅτι ἀληθὴς εἶ καὶ οὐ μέλει
we know that true you are and not it is a care

1473 4012 3762　3756 1063 991　1519 4383
σοι περὶ οὐδενός· οὐ γὰρ βλέπεις εἰς πρόσωπον
to you about nothing; not for you see into face

444　235 1909 225　08 3598 02　2316
ἀνθρώπων, ἀλλ᾽ ἐπ᾽ ἀληθείας τὴν ὁδὸν τοῦ θεοῦ
of men, but on truth the way of the God

[6]He had still one other, a beloved son. Finally he sent him to them, saying, 'They will respect my son.' [7]But those tenants said to one another, 'This is the heir; come, let us kill him, and the inheritance will be ours.' [8]So they seized him, killed him, and threw him out of the vineyard. [9]What then will the owner of the vineyard do? He will come and destroy the tenants and give the vineyard to others. [10]Have you not read this scripture:

'The stone that the builders rejected has become the cornerstone;[a] [11]this was the Lord's doing, and it is amazing in our eyes'?"

[12]When they realized that he had told this parable against them, they wanted to arrest him, but they feared the crowd. So they left him and went away.

[13]Then they sent to him some Pharisees and some Herodians to trap him in what he said. [14]And they came and said to him, "Teacher, we know that you are sincere, and show deference to no one; for you do not regard people with partiality, but teach the way of God in accordance with truth.

[a] Or keystone

Is it lawful to pay taxes
to the emperor, or not?
¹⁵Should we pay them,
or should we not?" But
knowing their hypocrisy,
he said to them, "Why are
you putting me to the test?
Bring me a denarius and
let me see it." ¹⁶And they
brought one. Then he said
to them, "Whose head is
this, and whose title?"
They answered, "The
emperor's." ¹⁷Jesus said to
them, "Give to the emperor
the things that are the
emperor's, and to God the
things that are God's."
And they were utterly
amazed at him.

18 Some Sadducees, who
say there is no resurrection,
came to him and asked
him a question, saying,
¹⁹"Teacher, Moses wrote
for us that if a man's
brother dies, leaving a wife
but no child, the man^a shall
marry the widow and raise
up children for his brother.
²⁰There were seven
brothers; the first married
and, when he died, left no
children; ²¹and the second
married the widow^b and
died, leaving no children;
and the third likewise;
²²none of the seven left
children. Last of all the
woman herself died. ²³In
the

a Gk his brother
b Gk her

1321	1832			1325	2778	2541
διδάσκεις·	ἔξεστιν			δοῦναι	κῆνσον	Καίσαρι
you teach;	is it possible	to give			tribute	to Caesar

2228 3756a	1325		2228 3361	1325	
ἢ οὔ;	δῶμεν		ἢ μὴ	δῶμεν;	
or no?	Might we give	or	not	might we give?	

15 ὁ   δὲ   εἰδὼς   αὐτῶν   τὴν   ὑπόκρισιν   εἶπεν
(01 1161 3609a   846   08   5272   3004)
The one but having known of them the hypocrisy said

αὐτοῖς·   τί   με   πειράζετε;   φέρετέ   μοι   δηνάριον
(846 5101 1473 3985   5342   1473   1220)
to them; why me you pressure? Bring to me denarius

ἵνα   ἴδω.   **16** οἱ   δὲ   ἤνεγκαν.   καὶ   λέγει
(2443 3708)   (013 1161 5342   2532 3004)
that I might see. The ones but brought. And he says

αὐτοῖς·   τίνος   ἡ   εἰκὼν   αὕτη   καὶ   ἡ   ἐπιγραφή;
(846 5101   05 1504 3778 2532 05   1923)
to them; of whom the image this and the writing on?

οἱ   δὲ   εἶπαν   αὐτῷ·   Καίσαρος.   **17** ὁ   δὲ   Ἰησοῦς
(013 1161 3004 846   2541)   (01 1161 2424)
The ones but said to him; of Caesar. The but Jesus

εἶπεν   αὐτοῖς·   τὰ   Καίσαρος   ἀπόδοτε   Καίσαρι
(3004 846   024   2541   591   2541)
said to them; the things of Caesar give off to Caesar

καὶ   τὰ   τοῦ   θεοῦ   τῷ   θεῷ.   καὶ
(2532 024   02   2316 03   2316 2532)
and the things of the God to the God. And

ἐξεθαύμαζον   ἐπ᾽   αὐτῷ.   **18** Καὶ   ἔρχονται
(1569a   1909 846)   (2532 2064)
they were greatly astonished on him. And come

Σαδδουκαῖοι   πρὸς   αὐτόν,   οἵτινες   λέγουσιν   ἀνάστασιν
(4523   4314   846   3748   3004   386)
Sadducees toward him, who say standing up

μὴ   εἶναι,   καὶ   ἐπηρώτων   αὐτὸν   λέγοντες·
(3361 1510   2532 1905   846 3004)
not to be, and they were asking on him saying;

19 Διδάσκαλε,   Μωϋσῆς   ἔγραψεν   ἡμῖν   ὅτι   ἐὰν   τινος
(1320   3475 1125   1473 3754 1437 5100)
teacher, Moses wrote to us that if some

ἀδελφὸς   ἀποθάνῃ   καὶ   καταλίπῃ   γυναῖκα
(80   599   2532 2641   1135)
brother might die and might leave behind woman

καὶ   μὴ   ἀφῇ   τέκνον,   ἵνα   λάβῃ   ὁ   ἀδελφὸς   αὐτοῦ
(2532 3361 863   5043   2443 2983 01 80   846)
and not he might leave off child, that might the brother of him
                     receive

τὴν   γυναῖκα   καὶ   ἐξαναστήσῃ   σπέρμα   τῷ
(08 1135   2532 1817   4690   03)
the woman and he might stand up out seed to the

ἀδελφῷ   αὐτοῦ.   **20** ἑπτὰ   ἀδελφοὶ   ἦσαν·   καὶ   ὁ
(80 846)   (2033 80   1510   2532 01)
brother of him. Seven brothers there were; and the

πρῶτος   ἔλαβεν   γυναῖκα   καὶ   ἀποθνήσκων   οὐκ
(4413   2983   1135   2532 599   3756)
first received woman and dying not

ἀφῆκεν   σπέρμα·   **21** καὶ   ὁ   δεύτερος   ἔλαβεν   αὐτὴν
(863   4690)   (2532 01 1208   2983   846)
he sent off seed; and the second received her

καὶ   ἀπέθανεν   μὴ   καταλιπὼν   σπέρμα·   καὶ   ὁ   τρίτος
(2532 599   3361 2641   4690   2532 01 5154)
and he died not leaving behind seed; and the third

ὡσαύτως·   **22** καὶ   οἱ   ἑπτὰ   οὐκ   ἀφῆκαν   σπέρμα.
(5615)   (2532 013 2033 3756 863   4690)
likewise; and the seven not they sent off seed.

ἔσχατον   πάντων   καὶ   ἡ   γυνὴ   ἀπέθανεν.   **23** ἐν   τῇ
(2078   3956   2532 05 1135 599)   (1722 07)
Last of all also the woman died. In the

```
386              3752 450        5101  846        1510  1135
ἀναστάσει[, ὅταν ἀναστῶσιν] τίνος αὐτῶν  ἔσται γυνή;
standing    when  they might  of     of them  will  woman?
up,                stand up    whom             she be
013 1063 2033  2192  846     1135          5346 846
οἱ  γὰρ ἑπτὰ ἔσχον αὐτὴν γυναῖκα. 24 ἔφη αὐτοῖς
The for  seven had    her   woman.      Said to them
01   2424    3756 1223      3778  4105      3361  3609a
ὁ  Ἰησοῦς· οὐ  διὰ      τοῦτο πλανᾶσθε μὴ   εἰδότες
the Jesus;  not through this   are you   not   having
                                being deceived      known
020 1124     3366   08   1411     02    2316      3752
τὰς γραφὰς μηδὲ τὴν δύναμιν τοῦ  θεοῦ; 25 ὅταν
the writings but not the power  of the God?     When
1063 1537 3498   450                  3777      1060
γὰρ ἐκ  νεκρῶν ἀναστῶσιν      οὔτε   γαμοῦσιν
for from dead   they might stand up neither they marry
3777 1060a                235    1510    5613
οὔτε γαμίζονται,      ἀλλ’ εἰσὶν  ὡς
nor  they are given marriage, but they are as
32       1722 015    3772        4012  1161  014
ἄγγελοι ἐν  τοῖς οὐρανοῖς. 26 περὶ δὲ  τῶν
messengers in the  heavens.    About but  the
3498   3754 1453         3756 314      1722 07
νεκρῶν ὅτι ἐγείρονται οὐκ ἀνέγνωτε ἐν  τῇ
dead   that they are raised not you read in the
976   3475    1909 02  942    4459 3004 846    01
βίβλῳ Μωϋσέως ἐπὶ τοῦ βάτου πῶς εἶπεν αὐτῷ ὁ
book  of Moses on the thornbush how said to him the
2316 3004    1473 01  2316  11      2532 01  2316
θεὸς λέγων· ἐγὼ ὁ θεὸς Ἀβραὰμ καὶ ὁ  θεὸς
God saying· I   the God Abraham and the God
2464   2532 01  2316 2384     3756 1510  2316 3498
Ἰσαὰκ καὶ ὁ θεὸς Ἰακώβ; 27 οὐκ ἔστιν θεὸς νεκρῶν
Isaac and the God Jacob?    Not  is he God of dead
235   2198    4183 4105      2532 4334
ἀλλὰ ζώντων· πολὺ πλανᾶσθε. 28 Καὶ προσελθὼν
but  of living much you are being  And having come
ones;              deceived.            toward
1520 014   1122      191       846    4802
εἷς τῶν  γραμματέων ἀκούσας  αὐτῶν συζητούντων,
one of the writers  having heard them disputing,
3708    3754 2573 611       846    1905
ἰδὼν  ὅτι καλῶς ἀπεκρίθη αὐτοῖς ἐπηρώτησεν
having seen that well  he answered them he asked on
846    4169     1510 1785    4413 3956
αὐτόν· ποία  ἐστιν ἐντολὴ πρώτη πάντων;
him;   of what kind is command first of all?
       611      01  2424    3754 4413 1510  191
29 ἀπεκρίθη ὁ Ἰησοῦς ὅτι πρώτη ἐστίν· ἄκουε,
   Answered the Jesus, (") first is;  hear,
2474      2962 01  2316 1473 2962  1520 1510
Ἰσραήλ, κύριος ὁ θεὸς ἡμῶν κύριος εἷς ἐστιν,
Israel, Master the God of us Master one  is,
   2532 25          2962   04  2316 1473   1537
30 καὶ ἀγαπήσεις κύριον τὸν θεόν σου   ἐξ
   and you will love Master the God of you from
3650 06  2588   1473    2532 1537 3650  06   5590
ὅλης τῆς καρδίας σου  καὶ  ἐξ ὅλης τῆς ψυχῆς
whole the heart  of you and from whole the soul
1473 2532 1537 3650 06  1271        1473   2532
σου καὶ ἐξ ὅλης τῆς διανοίας  σου   καὶ
of you and from whole the intelligence of you and
1537 3650 06  2479    1473    1208  3778
ἐξ ὅλης τῆς ἰσχύος σου. 31 δευτέρα αὕτη·
from whole the strength of you. Second this;
25          04  4139     1473  5613 4572
ἀγαπήσεις τὸν πλησίον σου  ὡς σεαυτόν.
you will love the neighbor of you as yourself.
```

resurrection[a] whose wife will she be? For the seven had married her."

24 Jesus said to them, "Is not this the reason you are wrong, that you know neither the scriptures nor the power of God? 25For when they rise from the dead, they neither marry nor are given in marriage, but are like angels in heaven. 26And as for the dead being raised, have you not read in the book of Moses, in the story about the bush, how God said to him, 'I am the God of Abraham, the God of Isaac, and the God of Jacob'? 27He is God not of the dead, but of the living; you are quite wrong."

28 One of the scribes came near and heard them disputing with one another, and seeing that he answered them well, he asked him, "Which commandment is the first of all?" 29Jesus answered, "The first is, 'Hear, O Israel: the Lord our God, the Lord is one; 30you shall love the Lord your God with all your heart, and with all your soul, and with all your mind, and with all your strength.' 31The second is this, 'You shall love your neighbor as yourself.'

[a] Other ancient authorities add *when they rise*

There is no other commandment greater than these."
³²Then the scribe said to him, "You are right, Teacher; you have truly said that 'he is one, and besides him there is no other'; ³³and 'to love him with all the heart, and with all the understanding, and with all the strength,' and 'to love one's neighbor as oneself,'—this is much more important than all whole burnt offerings and sacrifices." ³⁴When Jesus saw that he answered wisely, he said to him, "You are not far from the kingdom of God." After that no one dared to ask him any question.

35 While Jesus was teaching in the temple, he said, "How can the scribes say that the Messiah^a is the son of David? ³⁶David himself, by the Holy Spirit, declared,

'The Lord said to my Lord,
"Sit at my right hand, until I put your enemies under your feet."'

³⁷David himself calls him Lord; so how can he be his son?" And the large crowd was listening to him with delight.

38 As he taught, he said, "Beware of the scribes, who like to walk around in long robes, and to be greeted with respect in the marketplaces, ³⁹and to have the best seats in

^a Or the Christ

3173	3778	243	1785	3756 1510	**32**	2532
μείζων	τούτων	ἄλλη	ἐντολὴ	οὐκ ἔστιν.		καὶ
Greater	of these	other	command	not there is.		And

3004 846 01 1122 2573 1320 1909
εἶπεν αὐτῷ ὁ γραμματεύς· καλῶς, διδάσκαλε, ἐπ᾽
said to him the writer; well, teacher, on

225 3004 3754 1520 1510 2532 3756 1510
ἀληθείας εἶπες ὅτι εἷς ἐστιν καὶ οὐκ ἔστιν
truth you spoke that one there is and not there is

243 4133 846 **33** 2532 09 25 846 1537
ἄλλος πλὴν αὐτοῦ· καὶ τὸ ἀγαπᾶν αὐτὸν ἐξ
other except him; and the to love him from

3650 06 2588 2532 1537 3650 06 4907 2532
ὅλης τῆς καρδίας καὶ ἐξ ὅλης τῆς συνέσεως καὶ
whole the heart and from whole the understanding and

1537 3650 06 2479 2532 09 25 04 4139
ἐξ ὅλης τῆς ἰσχύος καὶ τὸ ἀγαπᾶν τὸν πλησίον
from whole the strength and the to love the neighbor

5613 1438 4055 1510 3956 022
ὡς ἑαυτὸν περισσότερόν ἐστιν πάντων τῶν
as himself more excessive it is of all the

3646 2532 2378 **34** 2532 01 2424
ὁλοκαυτωμάτων καὶ θυσιῶν. καὶ ὁ Ἰησοῦς
whole burnt offerings and sacrifices. And the Jesus

3708 846 3754 3562 611 3004
ἰδὼν [αὐτὸν] ὅτι νουνεχῶς ἀπεκρίθη εἶπεν
having seen him that thoughtfully he answered said

846 3756 3112 1510 575 06 932 02
αὐτῷ· οὐ μακρὰν εἶ ἀπὸ τῆς βασιλείας τοῦ
to him; not far you are from the kingdom of the

2316 2532 3762 3765 5111 846 1905
θεοῦ. καὶ οὐδεὶς οὐκέτι ἐτόλμα αὐτὸν ἐπερωτῆσαι.
God. And no one no longer was daring him to ask on.

35 2532 611 01 2424 3004 1321
Καὶ ἀποκριθεὶς ὁ Ἰησοῦς ἔλεγεν διδάσκων
And having answered the Jesus was saying teaching

1722 011 2411 4459 3004 013 1122 3754 01
ἐν τῷ ἱερῷ· πῶς λέγουσιν οἱ γραμματεῖς ὅτι ὁ
in the temple; how do say the writers that the

5547 5207 1160a 1510 846 1160a 3004 1722
χριστὸς υἱὸς Δαυὶδ ἐστιν; **36** αὐτὸς Δαυὶδ εἶπεν ἐν
Christ son David is? Himself David said in

011 4151 011 40 3004 2962 03 2962
τῷ πνεύματι τῷ ἁγίῳ· εἶπεν κύριος τῷ κυρίῳ
the spirit the holy; said Master to the Master

1473 2521 1537 1188 1473 2193 302 5087
μου· κάθου ἐκ δεξιῶν μου, ἕως ἂν θῶ
of me; sit from right of me, until - I might set

016 2190 1473 5270 014 4228 1473
τοὺς ἐχθρούς σου ὑποκάτω τῶν ποδῶν σου.
the hostile ones of you underneath the feet of you.

37 846 1160a 3004 846 2962 2532 4159
αὐτὸς Δαυὶδ λέγει αὐτὸν κύριον, καὶ πόθεν
Himself David says him Master, and from where

846 1510 5207 2532 01 4183 3793 191
αὐτοῦ ἐστιν υἱός; Καὶ [ὁ] πολὺς ὄχλος ἤκουεν
of him is son? And the much crowd was hearing

846 2234 2532 1722 07 1322 846
αὐτοῦ ἡδέως. **38** Καὶ ἐν τῇ διδαχῇ αὐτοῦ
him gladly. And in the teaching of him

3004 991 575 014 1122 014
ἔλεγεν· βλέπετε ἀπὸ τῶν γραμματέων τῶν
he was saying; look from the writers of the

2309 1722 4749 4043 2532
θελόντων ἐν στολαῖς περιπατεῖν καὶ
ones wanting in long robes to walk around and

783 1722 019 58 2532 4410 1722
ἀσπασμοὺς ἐν ταῖς ἀγοραῖς **39** καὶ πρωτοκαθεδρίας ἐν
greetings in the markets and first chairs in

```
019    4864        2532 4411                    1722 023
ταῖς  συναγωγαῖς  καὶ  πρωτοκλισίας          ἐν  τοῖς
the   synagogues   and  first reclining places  in  the
1173          013      2719          020 3614  018
δείπνοις,  40  οἱ    κατεσθίοντες  τὰς οἰκίας τῶν
dinners,       the ones eating up    the houses of the
5503   2532 4392      3117   4336           3778
χηρῶν  καὶ  προφάσει  μακρὰ προσευχόμενοι· οὗτοι
widows and  in pretext far   praying;        these
2983        4055          2917     41  2532 2523
λήμψονται  περισσότερον  κρίμα.     Καὶ  καθίσας
will receive more excessive judgment. And  having sat
2713        010 1049          2334         4459 οἱ
κατέναντι  τοῦ γαζοφυλακίου  ἐθεώρει     πῶς  ὁ
over against the treasury box  he was watching how  the
3793   906    5475     1519 012 1049          2532 4183
ὄχλος βάλλει χαλκὸν εἰς τὸ γαζοφυλάκιον. καὶ  πολλοὶ
crowd throws copper into the treasury box. And  many
4145      906        4183      42  2532 2064
πλούσιοι ἔβαλλον    πολλά·     καὶ  ἐλθοῦσα
rich ones were throwing many;      and  having come
1520 5503  4434  906     3016  1417 3739  1510
μία  χήρα πτωχὴ ἔβαλεν λεπτὰ δύο, ὅ    ἐστιν
one  widow poor  threw  lepta  two, which is
2835        43  2532 4341                 016  3101
κοδράντης.      καὶ  προσκαλεσάμενος    τοὺς μαθητὰς
codrantes.      And  having called toward the  learners
846    3004   846    281   3004  1473 3754 05
αὐτοῦ εἶπεν  αὐτοῖς· ἀμὴν λέγω ὑμῖν ὅτι ἡ
of him he said to them; amen I say to you that the
5503   3778 05 4434  4183   3956   906    014
χήρα  αὕτη ἡ πτωχὴ πλεῖον πάντων ἔβαλεν τῶν
widow this the poor  more  of all  she threw of the
906         1519 012 1049        44  3956  1063
βαλλόντων  εἰς τὸ γαζοφυλάκιον·     πάντες γὰρ
ones throwing into the treasury box;   all    for
1537 010 4052         846    906    3778      1161
ἐκ  τοῦ περισσεύοντος αὐτοῖς ἔβαλον, αὕτη    δὲ
from the more exceeding to them threw,  this one but
1537 06 5304       846   3956  3745     2192
ἐκ  τῆς ὑστερήσεως αὐτῆς πάντα ὅσα    εἶχεν
from the lack      of her all   as much as she had
906        3650 04  979  846        2532 1607
ἔβαλεν    ὅλον τὸν βίον αὐτῆς.  13:1  Καὶ  ἐκπορευομένου
she threw whole the life of her.      And  traveling out
846    1537 010 2411  3004  846   1520 014
αὐτοῦ ἐκ  τοῦ ἱεροῦ λέγει αὐτῷ εἷς  τῶν
of him from the temple says  to him one  of the
3101    846      1320    2396 4217      3037   2532
μαθητῶν αὐτοῦ· διδάσκαλε, ἴδε ποταποὶ λίθοι καὶ
learners of him; teacher,  look what sort stones and
4217     3619      2  2532 01 2424   3004  846
ποταπαὶ οἰκοδομαί.   καὶ  ὁ Ἰησοῦς εἶπεν αὐτῷ·
what sort buildings. And  the Jesus  said  to him;
991     3778   020 3173    3619     3756 3361
βλέπεις ταύτας τὰς μεγάλας οἰκοδομάς; οὐ  μὴ
do you see these  the great  buildings? Not not
863        5602 3037  1909 3037   3739 3756 3361
ἀφεθῇ     ὧδε λίθος ἐπὶ λίθον ὃς  οὐ  μὴ
might be sent off here stone upon stone which not not
2647       3  2532 2521      846    1519 012 3735 018
καταλυθῇ.     Καὶ καθημένου αὐτοῦ εἰς τὸ ὄρος τῶν
might be       And sitting   him   into the hill of the
unloosed.
1636    2713         010 2411  1905       846
ἐλαιῶν κατέναντι    τοῦ ἱεροῦ ἐπηρώτα   αὐτὸν
olives over against  the temple were asking on him
2596 2398  4074   2532 2385   2532 2491  2532
κατ' ἰδίαν Πέτρος καὶ Ἰάκωβος καὶ Ἰωάννης καὶ
by   own   Peter  and Jacob    and John     and
```

the synagogues and places of honor at banquets! [40]They devour widows' houses and for the sake of appearance say long prayers. They will receive the greater condemnation."

41 He sat down opposite the treasury, and watched the crowd putting money into the treasury. Many rich people put in large sums. [42]A poor widow came and put in two small copper coins, which are worth a penny. [43]Then he called his disciples and said to them, "Truly I tell you, this poor widow has put in more than all those who are contributing to the treasury. [44]For all of them have contributed out of their abundance; but she out of her poverty has put in everything she had, all she had to live on."

CHAPTER 13

As he came out of the temple, one of his disciples said to him, "Look, Teacher, what large stones and what large buildings!" [2]Then Jesus asked him, "Do you see these great buildings? Not one stone will be left here upon another; all will be thrown down."

3 When he was sitting on the Mount of Olives opposite the temple, Peter, James, John, and Andrew asked him privately,

4"Tell us, when will this be, and what will be the sign that all these things are about to be accomplished?" 5Then Jesus began to say to them, "Beware that no one leads you astray. 6Many will come in my name and say, 'I am he!'[a] and they will lead many astray. 7When you hear of wars and rumors of wars, do not be alarmed; this must take place, but the end is still to come. 8For nation will rise against nation, and kingdom against kingdom; there will be earthquakes in various places; there will be famines. This is but the beginning of the birth pangs.

9 "As for yourselves, beware; for they will hand you over to councils; and you will be beaten in synagogues; and you will stand before governors and kings because of me, as a testimony to them. 10And the good news[b] must first be proclaimed to all nations. 11When they bring you to trial and hand you over, do not worry beforehand about what you are to say; but say whatever is given you at that time, for it is not you who speak, but the Holy Spirit. 12Brother will betray brother to death, and a father his child, and children will rise against parents

a Gk I am
b Gk gospel

406		3004	1473	4219	3778	1510		2532 5101
Ἀνδρέας·	4	εἶπον	ἡμῖν,	πότε	ταῦτα	ἔσται	καὶ	τί
Andrew;		say	to us,	when	these	will be	and	what

09	4592	3752 3195		3778	4931
τὸ	σημεῖον	ὅταν μέλλη	ταῦτα	συντελεῖσθαι	
the	sign	when are about	these	to be fully completed	

3956		01	1161	2424	757	3004	846
πάντα;	5	ὁ	δὲ	Ἰησοῦς	ἤρξατο	λέγειν	αὐτοῖς·
all?		The	but	Jesus	began	to say	to them;

991	3361 5100	1473 4105			4183	2064
βλέπετε	μή τις	ὑμᾶς πλανήση·		6	πολλοὶ	ἐλεύσονται
see	not some	you might deceive;			many	will come

1909 011	3686	1473	3004	3754 1473 1510	2532
ἐπὶ τῷ	ὀνόματί	μου	λέγοντες	ὅτι ἐγώ εἰμι,	καὶ
on the	name	of me	saying,	(") I am,	and

4183	4105		3752 1161 191
πολλοὺς	πλανήσουσιν.	7	ὅταν δὲ ἀκούσητε
many	they will deceive.		When but you might hear

4171	2532 189	4171	3361 2360
πολέμους	καὶ ἀκοὰς	πολέμων,	μὴ θροεῖσθε·
wars	and hearings	of wars,	not be disturbed;

1163	1096	235	3768	09	5056
δεῖ	γενέσθαι,	ἀλλ᾽	οὔπω	τὸ	τέλος.
it is necessary	to become,	but	not yet	the	completion.

8	1453		1063 1484	1909 1484	2532 932
	ἐγερθήσεται		γὰρ ἔθνος	ἐπ᾽ ἔθνος	καὶ βασιλεία
	Will be raised		for nation	on nation	and kingdom

1909 932		1510	4578	2596 5117
ἐπὶ βασιλείαν,		ἔσονται	σεισμοὶ	κατὰ τόπους,
on kingdom,		there will be	shakes	by places,

1510	3042	746	5604	3778	991
ἔσονται	λιμοί·	ἀρχὴ	ὠδίνων	ταῦτα.	9 Βλέπετε
will be	famines;	beginning	of birth	these.	See
			pains		

1161 1473	1438	3860		1473 1519
δὲ ὑμεῖς	ἑαυτούς·	παραδώσουσιν		ὑμᾶς εἰς
but you	yourselves;	they will give over		you to

4892	2532 1519 4864	1194		2532
συνέδρια	καὶ εἰς συναγωγὰς	δαρήσεσθε		καὶ
councils	and in synagogues	you will be beaten		and

1909 2232	2532 935	2476		1752
ἐπὶ ἡγεμόνων	καὶ βασιλέων	σταθήσεσθε		ἕνεκεν
on leaders	and kings	you will be stood		on account

1473 1519 3142	846		2532 1519 3956	024
ἐμοῦ εἰς μαρτύριον	αὐτοῖς.	10	καὶ εἰς πάντα	τὰ
of me in testimony	to them.		And into all	the

1484	4413	1163	2784	012
ἔθνη	πρῶτον	δεῖ	κηρυχθῆναι	τὸ
nations	first	it is necessary	to be announced	the

2098	2532 3752 71	1473
εὐαγγέλιον.	11 καὶ ὅταν ἄγωσιν	ὑμᾶς
good message.	And when they might lead	you

3860	3361 4305	5101 2980	235
παραδιδόντες,	μὴ προμεριμνᾶτετί	λαλήσητε,	ἀλλ᾽
giving over,	not be anxious	what you might say,	but

3739 1437 1325	1473	1722 1565	07 5610
ὃ ἐὰν δοθῇ	ὑμῖν	ἐν ἐκείνη	τῇ ὥρᾳ
what if might be given	to you	in that	the hour

3778 2980	3756 1063 1510 1473	013	2980
τοῦτο λαλεῖτε·	οὐ γὰρ ἐστε ὑμεῖς	οἱ	λαλοῦντες
this speak;	not for are you	the ones	speaking

235	09 4151	09 40	2532 3860
ἀλλὰ	τὸ πνεῦμα	τὸ ἅγιον.	12 καὶ παραδώσει
but	the spirit	the holy.	And will give over

80	80	1519 2288	2532 3962	5043	2532
ἀδελφὸς	ἀδελφὸν	εἰς θάνατον	καὶ πατὴρ	τέκνον,	καὶ
brother	brother	into death	and father	child,	and

1881	5043	1909 1118	2532
ἐπαναστήσονται	τέκνα	ἐπὶ γονεῖς	καὶ
will stand up against	children	upon parents	and

2289   846   2532 1510
θανατώσουσιν   αὐτούς·   **13** καὶ ἔσεσθε
they will put to death them;   and you will be+

3404   5259 3956   1223   012 3686   1473   01 1161
μισούμενοι   ὑπὸ πάντων διὰ   τὸ ὄνομά μου. ὁ   δὲ
+being hated by   all   through the name of me. The but

5278   1519 5056   3778   4982   3752
ὑπομείνας   εἰς τέλος   οὗτος σωθήσεται. **14** ῞Οταν
one having   into completion this   will be   When
endured   one   delivered.

1161 3708   012 946   06   2050   2476
δὲ ἴδητε τὸ βδέλυγμα   τῆς   ἐρημώσεως   ἑστηκότα
but you   the abomination of the desolation having
    might see   stood

3699   3756 1163 01   314   3539   5119 013 1722
ὅπου οὐ δεῖ, ὁ   ἀναγινώσκων νοείτω,   τότε οἱ   ἐν
where not it the one reading let give then the   in
       is necessary,   thought,   ones

07 2449   5343   1519 024 3735   01   1161 1909
τῇ ᾽Ιουδαίᾳ φευγέτωσαν εἰς τὰ ὄρη, **15** ὁ [δὲ] ἐπὶ
the Judea   let flee   into the hills, the one but on

010 1430   3361 2597   3366 1525   142 5100
τοῦ δώματος μὴ καταβάτω   μηδὲ εἰσελθάτω ἆραί τι
the roof   not let go down but let go   to some
                             not into   lift up

1537 06   3614   846   2532 01   1519 04 68   3361
ἐκ τῆς οἰκίας αὐτοῦ, **16** καὶ ὁ   εἰς τὸν ἀγρὸν μὴ
from the house of him,   and the one in the field not

1994   1519 024 3694 142   012 2440
ἐπιστρεψάτω εἰς τὰ ὀπίσω ἆραι   τὸ ἱμάτιον
let return   to   the after to lift up the clothes

846   17 3759 1161 019   1722 1064   2192   2532
αὐτοῦ.   οὐαὶ δὲ ταῖς ἐν γαστρὶ ἐχούσαις καὶ
of him.   Woe but to the in womb ones having and

019 2337   1722 1565   019 2250
ταῖς θηλαζούσαις   ἐν ἐκείναις ταῖς ἡμέραις.
the ones giving nursing in those   the days.

18 4336   1161 2443 3361 1096   5494
προσεύχεσθε δὲ ἵνα μὴ γένηται   χειμῶνος·
Pray   but that not it might become of winter;

19 1510   1063 017 2250   1565   2347
ἔσονται γὰρ αἱ ἡμέραι ἐκεῖναι θλῖψις
will be for the days those   affliction

3634   3756 1096   5108   875 746
οἵα   οὐ γέγονεν   τοιαύτη ἀπ᾽ ἀρχῆς
of what kind not it has become such from beginning

2937   3739 2936   01 2316 2193 02 3568 2532
κτίσεως   ἣν ἔκτισεν ὁ θεὸς ἕως   τοῦ νῦν καὶ
of creation which created the God until the now and

3756 3361 1096   20   2532 1487 3361 2856
οὐ μὴ γένηται.   καὶ εἰ μὴ ἐκολόβωσεν
not not it might become. And if not shortened

2962   020 2250   3756 302 4982   3956
κύριος τὰς ἡμέρας, οὐκ ἂν ἐσώθη   πᾶσα
Master the days,   not - might be delivered all

4561   235 1223   016 1588   3739 1586
σάρξ· ἀλλὰ διὰ   τοὺς ἐκλεκτοὺς οὓς ἐξελέξατο
flesh; but through the select ones whom he selected

2856   020 2250   21 2532 5119 1437 5100 1473
ἐκολόβωσεν τὰς ἡμέρας.   Καὶ τότε ἐάν τις ὑμῖν
he shortened the days.   And then if some to you

3004   2396 5602 01 5547   2396 1563 3361
εἴπῃ·   ἴδε ὧδε ὁ χριστός, ἴδε ἐκεῖ, μὴ
might say; look here the Christ, look there, not

4100   22 1453   1063 5580   2532
πιστεύετε·   ἐγερθήσονται γὰρ ψευδόχριστοι καὶ
you trust;   will be raised for false christs and

5578   2532 1325   4592 2532
ψευδοπροφῆται καὶ δώσουσιν   σημεῖα καὶ
false spokesmen and they will give signs and

and have them put to death; [13]and you will be hated by all because of my name. But the one who endures to the end will be saved.

14 "But when you see the desolating sacrilege set up where it ought not to be (let the reader understand), then those in Judea must flee to the mountains; [15]the one on the housetop must not go down or enter the house to take anything away; [16]the one in the field must not turn back to get a coat. [17]Woe to those who are pregnant and to those who are nursing infants in those days! [18]Pray that it may not be in winter. [19]For in those days there will be suffering, such as has not been from the beginning of the creation that God created until now, no, and never will be. [20]And if the Lord had not cut short those days, no one would be saved; but for the sake of the elect, whom he chose, he has cut short those days. [21]And if anyone says to you at that time, 'Look! Here is the Messiah!'[a] or 'Look! There he is!'—do not believe it. [22]False messiahs[b] and false prophets will appear and produce signs and

[a] Or the Christ
[b] Or christs

omens, to lead astray, if possible, the elect. 23But be alert; I have already told you everything.

24"But in those days, after that suffering,
the sun will be darkened, and the moon will not give its light,
25 and the stars will be falling from heaven, and the powers in the heavens will be shaken.

26Then they will see 'the Son of Man coming in clouds' with great power and glory. 27Then he will send out the angels, and gather his elect from the four winds, from the ends of the earth to the ends of heaven.

28 "From the fig tree learn its lesson: as soon as its branch becomes tender and puts forth its leaves, you know that summer is near. 29So also, when you see these things taking place, you know that he*a* is near, at the very gates. 30Truly I tell you, this generation will not pass away until all these things have taken place. 31Heaven and earth will pass away, but my words will not pass away.

32 "But about that day or hour no one knows,

a Or *it*

5059	4314	012 635		1487 1415	016
τέρατα	πρὸς	τὸ ἀποπλανᾶν,		εἰ δυνατόν,	τοὺς
marvels	toward	the to deceive off,		if power,	the

5059 4314 012 635

1588		1473 1161 991	4302
ἐκλεκτούς.	**23** ὑμεῖς δὲ	βλέπετε·	προείρηκα
select ones.	You but	see;	I said before

1473	3956		235 1722 1565	019
ὑμῖν	πάντα.	**24**	Ἀλλὰ ἐν ἐκείναις ταῖς	
to you	all.		But in those the	

2250	3326	08	2347	1565	01	2246
ἡμέραις	μετὰ	τὴν	θλῖψιν	ἐκείνην	ὁ	ἥλιος
days	after	the	affliction	that	the	sun

4654		2532 05 4582	3756 1325	012
σκοτισθήσεται,		καὶ ἡ σελήνη	οὐ δώσει	τὸ
will be darkened,		and the moon	not will give	the

5338	846		2532 013 792	1510	1537 02
φέγγος	αὐτῆς,	**25**	καὶ οἱ ἀστέρες	ἔσονται	ἐκ τοῦ
light	of it,		and the stars	will be+	out of the

3772	4098	2532 017 1411	017	1722 015
οὐρανοῦ	πίπτοντες,	καὶ αἱ δυνάμεις αἱ		ἐν τοῖς
heaven	+falling,	and the powers the ones		in the

3772	4531		2532 5119 3708
οὐρανοῖς	σαλευθήσονται.	**26**	καὶ τότε ὄψονται
heavens	will be shaken.		And then they will see

04	5207 02	444	2064	1722 3507	3326
τὸν	υἱὸν τοῦ	ἀνθρώπου	ἐρχόμενον	ἐν νεφέλαις	μετὰ
the	son of the	man	coming	in clouds	with

1411	4183	2532 1391		2532 5119 649	016
δυνάμεως	πολλῆς	καὶ δόξης.	**27**	καὶ τότε ἀποστελεῖ	τοὺς
power	much	and splendor.		And then he will	the delegate

32.		2532 1996	016 1588	846
ἀγγέλους	καὶ	ἐπισυνάξει	τοὺς ἐκλεκτοὺς	[αὐτοῦ]
messengers	and	he will bring together	the select ones	of him

1537	014 5064	417	575 206	1093	2193
ἐκ	τῶν τεσσάρων	ἀνέμων	ἀπ' ἄκρου	γῆς	ἕως
out of	the four	winds	from tip	of earth	until

206	3772		575 1161 06 4808	3129 08
ἄκρου	οὐρανοῦ.	**28**	Ἀπὸ δὲ τῆς συκῆς	μάθετε τὴν
tip	of heaven.		From but the fig tree	learn the

3850		3752 2235	01 2798	846	527
παραβολήν·		ὅταν ἤδη	ὁ κλάδος	αὐτῆς	ἀπαλὸς
parallel story;		when already	the branch	of it	tender

1096	2532 1631		024 5444	1097	3754
γένηται	καὶ ἐκφύῃ		τὰ φύλλα,	γινώσκετε	ὅτι
might become	and might sprout		the leaves,	you know	that out

1451	09	2330	1510		3779	2532 1473	3752
ἐγγὺς	τὸ	θέρος	ἐστίν·	**29**	οὕτως	καὶ ὑμεῖς,	ὅταν
near	the	summer	is;		thusly	also you,	when

3708		3778 1096	1097	3754 1451
ἴδητε		ταῦτα γινόμενα,	γινώσκετε ὅτι	ἐγγύς
you might see		these becoming,	know that	near

1510	1909 2374		281 3004	1473 3754 3756 3361
ἐστιν	ἐπὶ θύραις.	**30**	Ἀμὴν λέγω	ὑμῖν ὅτι οὐ μὴ
it is	on doors.		Amen I say	to you that not not

3928	05	1074	3778 3360	3739 3778
παρέλθῃ	ἡ	γενεὰ	αὕτη μέχρις	οὗ ταῦτα
might go along	the	generation	this until	which these

3956 1096	01 3772	2532 05 1093 3928
πάντα γένηται.	**31** ὁ οὐρανὸς	καὶ ἡ γῆ παρελεύσονται
all might become.	The heaven	and the earth will go along,

013 1161 3056 1473 3756 3361 3928		4012
οἱ δὲ λόγοι μου οὐ μὴ παρελεύσονται.	**32**	Περὶ
the but words of me not not will go along.		About

1161 06 2250	1565	2228 06 5610 3762	3609a
δὲ τῆς ἡμέρας ἐκείνης	ἢ	τῆς ὥρας οὐδεὶς	οἶδεν,
but the day that	or	the hour no one	knows,

```
3761        013  32            1722 3772    3761      01   5207
οὐδὲ   οἱ  ἄγγελοι    ἐν οὐρανῷ οὐδὲ   ὁ   υἱός,
but not the messengers  in heaven but not the  son,
1487 3361  01    3962        991       69             3756
εἰ  μὴ  ὁ  πατήρ.  33 Βλέπετε,  ἀγρυπνεῖτε·  οὐκ
except  the father.    See,     stay awake;  not ·
3609a     1063 4219 01    2540    1510        5613 444
οἴδατε  γὰρ  πότε ὁ  καιρός ἐστιν.  34 ῾Ως  ἄνθρωπος
you know for  when the season is.       As   man
590         863         08  3614    846     2532 1325
ἀπόδημος ἀφεὶς   τὴν οἰκίαν αὐτοῦ καὶ  δοὺς
journey having left  the house  of him and having given
015 1401      846    08  1849       1538    012 2041
τοῖς δούλοις αὐτοῦ τὴν ἐξουσίαν ἑκάστῳ τὸ  ἔργον
the  slaves  of him the authority to each the  work
846    2532 03      2377        1781          2443
αὐτοῦ καὶ  τῷ  θυρωρῷ  ἐνετείλατο  ἵνα
of him and  to the doorkeeper he commanded that
1127             1127        3767 3756 3609a       1063
γρηγορῇ.  35 γρηγορεῖτε οὖν·  οὐκ οἴδατε  γὰρ
he might keep awake.  Keep awake then; not you know for
4219 01   2962     06     3614    2064      2228 3796
πότε ὁ  κύριος τῆς  οἰκίας ἔρχεται,  ἢ  ὀψὲ
when the Master of the house  comes,    or  evening
2228 3317      2228 219              2228 4404     36 3361
ἢ  μεσονύκτιον ἢ  ἀλεκτοροφωνίας ἢ  πρωῒ,    μὴ
or  middle night or rooster sounding or morning, not
2064       1810       2147        1473 2518
ἐλθὼν   ἐξαίφνης εὕρῃ    ὑμᾶς καθεύδοντας.
having come suddenly he might find you  sleeping.
37 3739 1161 1473   3004 3956   3004      1127
   ὃ  δὲ  ὑμῖν λέγω πᾶσιν λέγω,  γρηγορεῖτε.
   What but  to you I say to all I say,  keep awake.
14:1  1510   1161 09  3957       2532 021 106
     ῏Ην  δὲ  τὸ πάσχα  καὶ  τὰ ἄζυμα
     It was but  the passover and  the unyeasted
3326 1417 2250   2532 2212       013 749
μετὰ δύο ἡμέρας. καὶ ἐζήτουν  οἱ  ἀρχιερεῖς
after two days.  And were seeking the ruler priests
2532 013 1122    4459 846    1722 1388   2902
καὶ οἱ γραμματεῖς πῶς αὐτὸν ἐν  δόλῳ κρατήσαντες
and the writers  how  him  in  guile having held
615               3004        1063 3361 1722 07
ἀποκτείνωσιν·  2 ἔλεγον  γάρ· μὴ  ἐν  τῇ
they might kill;  they were saying for; not  in  the
1859       3379       1510      2351    02    2992
ἑορτῇ, μήποτε ἔσται θόρυβος τοῦ λαοῦ.
festival, not then  it will be uproar of the people.
3  2532 1510 846    1722 963      1722 07   3614
   Καὶ ὄντος αὐτοῦ ἐν Βηθανίᾳ ἐν  τῇ οἰκίᾳ
   And being him  in Bethany in  the house
4613     02  3015      2621         846    2064   1135
Σίμωνος τοῦ λεπροῦ, κατακειμένου αὐτοῦ ἦλθεν γυνὴ
of Simon the leper,  lying down    him  came  woman
2192      211         3464     3487     4101
ἔχουσα ἀλάβαστρον μύρου νάρδου πιστικῆς
having alabaster jar of perfume of nard genuine
4185        4937           08  211
πολυτελοῦς, συντρίψασα  τὴν ἀλάβαστρον
much cost,  having broken the alabaster jar
2708       846    06  2776          1510  1161
κατέχεεν αὐτοῦ τῆς κεφαλῆς. 4 ἦσαν δέ
she poured down of him the head.    Were+ but
5100 23             4314   1438       1519 5101 05
τινες ἀγανακτοῦντες πρὸς ἑαυτούς·  εἰς τί  ἡ
some +being indignant toward themselves, in what the
684       3778 010   3464    1096       1410
ἀπώλεια αὕτη τοῦ μύρου γέγονεν;  5 ἠδύνατο
destruction this of the perfume has become?  Was able
```

neither the angels in heaven, nor the Son, but only the Father. [33]Beware, keep alert;[a] for you do not know when the time will come. [34]It is like a man going on a journey, when he leaves home and puts his slaves in charge, each with his work, and commands the doorkeeper to be on the watch. [35]Therefore, keep awake—for you do not know when the master of the house will come, in the evening, or at midnight, or at cockcrow, or at dawn, [36]or else he may find you asleep when he comes suddenly. [37]And what I say to you I say to all: Keep awake."

CHAPTER 14

It was two days before the Passover and the festival of Unleavened Bread. The chief priests and the scribes were looking for a way to arrest Jesus[b] by stealth and kill him; [2]for they said, "Not during the festival, or there may be a riot among the people."

[3] While he was at Bethany in the house of Simon the leper,[c] as he sat at the table, a woman came with an alabaster jar of very costly ointment of nard, and she broke open the jar and poured the ointment on his head. [4]But some were there who said to one another in anger, "Why was the ointment wasted in this way? [5]For this ointment

---

a Other ancient authorities add *and pray*

b Gk *him*

c The terms *leper* and *leprosy* can refer to several diseases

could have been sold for
more than three hundred
denarii,[a] and the money
given to the poor." And
they scolded her. [6]But Jesus
said, "Let her alone; why
do you trouble her? She has
performed a good service
for me. [7]For you always
have the poor with you,
and you can show kindness
to them whenever you wish;
but you will not always
have me. [8]She has done
what she could; she has
anointed my body before-
hand for its burial. [9]Truly
I tell you, wherever the
good news[b] is proclaimed
in the whole world, what
she has done will be told in
remembrance of her."

10 Then Judas Iscariot,
who was one of the twelve,
went to the chief priests
in order to betray him to
them. [11]When they heard it,
they were greatly pleased,
and promised to give him
money. So he began to
look for an opportunity
to betray him.

12 On the first day of
Unleavened Bread, when
the Passover lamb is
sacrificed, his disciples said
to him, "Where do you
want us to go and make the
preparations for you to eat
the Passover?" [13]So he sent
two of his disciples, saying
to them, "Go into the city,
and

a The denarius was the usual day's
  wage for a laborer
b Or gospel

```
1063  3778  09    3464    4097        1883    1220
γὰρ  τοῦτο τὸ  μύρον  πραθῆναι  ἐπάνω δηναρίων
for   this  the  perfume  to be sold  upon  denaria
5145        2532 1325          015       4434     2532
τριακοσίων  καὶ  δοθῆναι  τοῖς  πτωχοῖς·  καὶ
three hundred and  to be given to the poor;    and
1690          846      01  1161  2424    3004    863
ἐνεβριμῶντο  αὐτῇ.  [6] ὁ  δὲ  Ἰησοῦς εἶπεν· ἄφετε
they were being to her. The but  Jesus  said;  leave
indignant                                          off
846    5101 846   2873    3930          2570 2041
αὐτήν· τί  αὐτῇ  κόπους παρέχετε;  καλὸν ἔργον
her;   why  to her  labors you hold to? Good  work
2038        1722 1473  [7] 3842      1063 016  4434
ἠργάσατο ἐν  ἐμοί.   πάντοτε γὰρ  τοὺς πτωχοὺς
she worked in  me.      Always  for  the  poor
2192      3326 1438       2532 3752 2309
ἔχετε  μεθ᾽ ἑαυτῶν  καὶ  ὅταν θέλητε
you have with yourselves and  when you might want
1410         846      2095 4160    1473 1161 3756 3842
δύνασθε  αὐτοῖς εὖ  ποιῆσαι, ἐμὲ δὲ  οὐ πάντοτε
you are able to them well to do,  me  but  not always
2192      [8] 3739 2192    4160        4301
ἔχετε.     ὃ  ἔσχεν ἐποίησεν· προέλαβεν
you have.   What she had she did;  she took beforehand
3462               012 4983 1473 1519 04
μυρίσαι          τὸ σῶμά μου εἰς τὸν
to anoint with perfume the body of me to  the
1780            281  1161 3004 1473   3699 1437
ἐνταφιασμόν.  [9] ἀμὴν δὲ  λέγω ὑμῖν, ὅπου ἐὰν
burial in.    Amen but  I say to you, where if
2784          09   2098          1519 3650 04
κηρυχθῇ    τὸ εὐαγγέλιον εἰς ὅλον τὸν
might be announced the good message into whole the
2889    2532 3739 4160     3778      2980         1519
κόσμον, καὶ ὃ  ἐποίησεν αὕτη  λαληθήσεται  εἰς
world,  also what did    this one will be spoken to
3422         846     [10] 2532 2455     2465a    01 1520
μνημόσυνον αὐτῆς.  Καὶ Ἰούδας Ἰσκαριὼθ ὁ  εἷς
memorial  to her.  And  Judas  Iscarioth the one
014    1427    565     4314   016   749        2443
τῶν  δώδεκα ἀπῆλθεν πρὸς τοὺς ἀρχιερεῖς ἵνα
of the twelve went off toward the  ruler priests that
846   3860            846     [11] 013    1161
αὐτὸν παραδοῖ        αὐτοῖς.   οἱ    δὲ
him   he might give over to them.  The ones but
191          5463       2532 1861          846   694
ἀκούσαντες ἐχάρησαν καὶ ἐπηγγείλαντο αὐτῷ ἀργύριον
having heard rejoiced and  they promised to him silver
1325      2532 2212         4459 846   2122
δοῦναι. καὶ ἐζήτει        πῶς αὐτὸν εὐκαίρως
to give. And he was seeking how  him  good seasonally
3860           [12] 2532 07   4413 2250  022
παραδοῖ.     Καὶ  τῇ  πρώτῃ ἡμέρᾳ τῶν
he might give over.  And  the first day  of the
106     3753 012 3957  2380           3004
ἀζύμων, ὅτε τὸ πάσχα ἔθυον,      λέγουσιν
unyeasted, when the passover they sacrificed, say
846   013 3101    846     4226 2309
αὐτῷ οἱ μαθηταὶ αὐτοῦ· ποῦ θέλεις
to him the learners of him; where you want
565              2090            2443 2068
ἀπελθόντες    ἑτοιμάσωμεν   ἵνα φάγῃς
having gone off we might prepare that you might eat
012 3957      [13] 2532 649          1417 014    3101
τὸ πάσχα;     καὶ ἀποστέλλει δύο τῶν μαθητῶν
the passover? And he delegates two of the learners
846    2532 3004 846      5217      1519 08   4172 2532
αὐτοῦ καὶ λέγει αὐτοῖς· ὑπάγετε εἰς τὴν πόλιν, καὶ
of him and says  to them; go off  into the city,  and
```

528   1473 444   2765   5204   941
ἀπαντήσει ὑμῖν ἄνθρωπος κεράμιον ὕδατος βαστάζων·
will meet you man   ceramic pot of water bearing;

190   846   2532 3699 1437 1525
ἀκολουθήσατε αὐτῷ **14** καὶ ὅπου ἐὰν εἰσέλθῃ
follow   him   and where if he might go in

3004 03   3617   3754 01 1320
εἴπατε τῷ οἰκοδεσπότῃ ὅτι ὁ διδάσκαλος
say   to the house supervisor that the teacher

3004 4226 1510 09 2646   1473 3699 012
λέγει· ποῦ ἐστιν τὸ κατάλυμά μου ὅπου τὸ
says, where is the guestlodge of me where the

3957   3326 014 3101   1473 2068   2532
πάσχα μετὰ τῶν μαθητῶν μου φάγω; **15** καὶ
passover with the learners of me I might eat?   And

846   1473 1166   311a   3173
αὐτὸς ὑμῖν δείξει ἀνάγαιον μέγα
himself to you will show upstairs room great

4766   2092   2532 1563 2090
ἐστρωμένον   ἕτοιμον· καὶ ἐκεῖ ἑτοιμάσατε
having been spread prepared; and there prepare

1473 **16** 2532 1831   013 3101   2532 2064
ἡμῖν.   καὶ ἐξῆλθον οἱ μαθηταὶ καὶ ἦλθον
to us.   And went out the learners and they went

1519 08 4172 2532 2147   2531   3004   846
εἰς τὴν πόλιν καὶ εὗρον καθὼς εἶπεν αὐτοῖς
into the city and they found just as he said to them

2532 2090   012 3957   **17** 2532 3798
καὶ ἡτοίμασαν τὸ πάσχα.   Καὶ ὀψίας
and they prepared the passover. And evening

1096   2064   3326 014 1427   2532
γενομένης ἔρχεται μετὰ τῶν δώδεκα. **18** καὶ
having become he comes with the twelve.   And

345   846   2532 2068   01 2424 3004
ἀνακειμένων αὐτῶν καὶ ἐσθιόντων ὁ Ἰησοῦς εἶπεν·
reclining   them and eating   the Jesus said;

281 3004 1473 3754 1520 1537 1473 3860
ἀμὴν λέγω ὑμῖν ὅτι εἷς ἐξ ὑμῶν παραδώσει
amen I say to you that one out of you will give over

1473 01 2068   3326 1473   757
με ὁ ἐσθίων μετ' ἐμοῦ. **19** ἤρξαντο
me the one eating with me.   They began

3076   2532 3004 846   1520 2596 1520 3385
λυπεῖσθαι   καὶ λέγειν αὐτῷ εἷς κατὰ εἷς· μήτι
to be grieved and to say to him one by   one, not

1473 **20** 01   1161 3004 846   1520 014   1427
ἐγώ;   ὁ δὲ εἶπεν αὐτοῖς· εἷς τῶν   δώδεκα,
I?   The one but said to them; one of the twelve,

01 1686   3326 1473 1519 012 5165   3754
ὁ ἐμβαπτόμενος μετ' ἐμοῦ εἰς τὸ τρύβλιον. **21** ὅτι
the one dipping in with me into the dish.   Because

01 3303 5207 02   444   5217   2531
ὁ μὲν υἱὸς τοῦ ἀνθρώπου ὑπάγει καθὼς
the indeed son of the man   goes off just as

1125   4012   846   3759 1161 03
γέγραπται   περὶ   αὐτοῦ, οὐαὶ δὲ τῷ
it has been written concerning him, woe but to the

444   1565 1223 3739 01 5207 02   444
ἀνθρώπῳ ἐκείνῳ δι' οὗ ὁ υἱὸς τοῦ ἀνθρώπου
man   that through whom the son of the man

3860   2570 014   1487 3756 1080   01
παραδίδοται· καλὸν αὐτῷ εἰ οὐκ ἐγεννήθη ὁ
is given over; good to him if not was born the

444   1565 **22** 2532 2068   846   2983
ἄνθρωπος ἐκεῖνος.   Καὶ ἐσθιόντων αὐτῶν λαβὼν
man   that.   And eating   them having taken

740   2127   2806   2532 1325   846
ἄρτον εὐλογήσας   ἔκλασεν καὶ ἔδωκεν αὐτοῖς
bread having spoken well he broke and he gave to them

a man carrying a jar of water will meet you; follow him, [14]and wherever he enters, say to the owner of the house, 'The Teacher asks, Where is my guest room where I may eat the Passover with my disciples?' [15]He will show you a large room upstairs, furnished and ready. Make preparations for us there." [16]So the disciples set out and went to the city, and found everything as he had told them; and they prepared the Passover meal.

[17]When it was evening, he came with the twelve. [18]And when they had taken their places and were eating, Jesus said, "Truly I tell you, one of you will betray me, one who is eating with me." [19]They began to be distressed and to say to him one after another, "Surely, not I?" [20]He said to them, "It is one of the twelve, one who is dipping bread*a* into the bowl*b* with me. [21]For the Son of Man goes as it is written of him, but woe to that one by whom the Son of Man is betrayed! It would have been better for that one not to have been born."

[22]While they were eating, he took a loaf of bread, and after blessing it he broke it, gave it to them,

a Gk lacks *bread*
b Other ancient authorities read *same bowl*

and said, "Take; this is my body." [23]Then he took a cup, and after giving thanks he gave it to them, and all of them drank from it. [24]He said to them, "This is my blood of the[a] covenant, which is poured out for many. [25]Truly I tell you, I will never again drink of the fruit of the vine until that day when I drink it new in the kingdom of God."

[26]When they had sung the hymn, they went out to the Mount of Olives. [27]And Jesus said to them, "You will all become deserters; for it is written,

'I will strike the shepherd,
and the sheep will be scattered.'

[28]But after I am raised up, I will go before you to Galilee." [29]Peter said to him, "Even though all become deserters, I will not." [30]Jesus said to him, "Truly I tell you, this day, this very night, before the cock crows twice, you will deny me three times." [31]But he said vehemently, "Even though I must die with you, I will not deny you." And all of them said the same.

[32]They went to a place called

[a] Other ancient authorities add *new*

```
2532 3004        2983      3778  1510  09  4983 1473
καὶ  εἶπεν·      λάβετε,  τοῦτό ἐστιν τὸ σῶμά μου.
and he said;     take,     this  is     the body of me.
   2532 2983          4221      2168
23 καὶ  λαβὼν        ποτήριον εὐχαριστήσας
   And  having taken  cup       having given good favor
1325      846       2532 4095  1537 846    3956        2532
ἔδωκεν  αὐτοῖς,  καὶ  ἔπιον ἐξ  αὐτοῦ πάντες.  24 καὶ
he gave  to them, and  drank out of it  all.        And
3004   846        3778  1510  09  129 1473   06
εἶπεν  αὐτοῖς·  τοῦτό ἐστιν τὸ αἷμά μου  τῆς
he said to them; this  is     the blood of me of the
1242     09         1632              5228    4183
διαθήκης τὸ        ἐκχυννόμενον ὑπὲρ πολλῶν.
agreement the one being poured out  on behalf of many.
   281 3004  1473    3754 3765         3756 3361
25 ἀμὴν λέγω ὑμῖν  ὅτι  οὐκέτι       οὐ  μὴ
   Amen I say to you that no longer     not not
4095         1537    010 1079a    06       288        2193
πίω          ἐκ     τοῦ γενήματος τῆς     ἀμπέλου ἕως
I might drink out of the produce   of the vine      until
06 2250  1565          3752 846  4095              2537  1722
τῆς ἡμέρας ἐκείνης ὅταν αὐτὸ πίνω            καινὸν ἐν
the day    that     when it   I might drink new      in
07 932       02     2316   26 2532 5214
τῇ βασιλείᾳ τοῦ    θεοῦ.    Καὶ  ὑμνήσαντες
the kingdom of the God.     And  having sung
1831        1519 012 3735 018      1636      27 2532
ἐξῆλθον    εἰς  τὸ  ὄρος τῶν     ἐλαιῶν.    καὶ
they went out to  the  hill  of the olives.     And
3004 846    01 2424 3754 3956     4624
λέγει αὐτοῖς ὁ  Ἰησοῦς ὅτι πάντες σκανδαλισθήσεσθε,
says  to them the Jesus, (") all    you will be
                                                  offended,
3754      1125          3960        04  4166
ὅτι      γέγραπται·    πατάξω      τὸν ποιμένα,
because it has been written; I will hit the shepherd,
2532 021 4263       1287                        28 235
καὶ  τὰ  πρόβατα διασκορπισθήσονται.         ἀλλὰ
and  the sheep    will be thoroughly scattered.   But
3326 012 1453        1473 4254       1473 1519 08
μετὰ τὸ ἐγερθῆναί  με  προάξω     ὑμᾶς εἰς τὴν
after the to be raised me I will lead you  into the
                                                before
1056          29 01 1161 4074  5346 846      1487 2532
Γαλιλαίαν.      ὁ  δὲ  Πέτρος ἔφη αὐτῷ·  εἰ  καὶ
Galilee.         The but Peter  said to him; if  even
3956 4624             235  3756 1473  30 2532 3004
πάντες σκανδαλισθήσονται, ἀλλ᾽ οὐκ ἐγώ.  καὶ λέγει
all    will be offended, but  not  I.       And says
846 01 2424  281 3004 1473   3754 1473 4594
αὐτῷ ὁ Ἰησοῦς· ἀμὴν λέγω σοι  ὅτι σὺ σήμερον
to him the Jesus; amen I say to you that you today
3778 07 3571   4250 2228 1364 220        5455   5151
ταύτη τῇ νυκτὶ πρὶν ἢ  δὶς ἀλέκτορα φωνῆσαι τρίς
this  the night before or twice rooster  to sound three
1473 533                 31 01      1161 1599a
με   ἀπαρνήσῃ.            ὁ      δὲ  ἐκπερισσῶς
me   you will deny thoroughly. The one but excessively
2980    1437 1163     1473 4880           1473 3756 3361
ἐλάλει· ἐὰν δέῃ      με  συναποθανεῖν σοι, οὐ  μὴ
was     if  it might me  to die         to   not not
saying,     be necessary together      you,
1473 533            5615     1161 2532 3956   3004
σε  ἀπαρνήσομαι. ὡσαύτως δὲ  καὶ  πάντες ἔλεγον.
you I will deny   Likewise but also all    were saying.
     thoroughly.
   2532 2064       1519 5564      3739       09 3686
32 Καὶ  ἔρχονται εἰς χωρίον    οὗ         τὸ ὄνομα
   And  they come into small field of which the name
```

```
1068         2532 3004    015      3101      846        2523
Γεθσημανὶ   καὶ λέγει   τοῖς    μαθηταῖς αὐτοῦ·    καθίσατε
Gethsemane and he says  to the learners of him;    sit
5602 2193   4336              2532 3880         04
ὧδε  ἕως   προσεύξωμαι.  33 καὶ παραλαμβάνει τὸν
here until I might pray.     And  he takes along the
4074     2532 04    2385       2532 04     2491      3326 846
Πέτρον καὶ [τὸν] Ἰάκωβον καὶ [τὸν] Ἰωάννην μετ' αὐτοῦ
Peter  and  the  Jacob    and  the   John    with him
2532 757      1568            2532 85
καὶ  ἤρξατο  ἐκθαμβεῖσθαι  καὶ  ἀδημονεῖν
and  he began to be astonished and to be distressed
                                            greatly
    2532 3004    846        4036             1510  05
 34 καὶ λέγει  αὐτοῖς· περίλυπός     ἐστιν ἡ
    and he says to them; greatly grieved is   the
5590 1473 2193  2288       3306     5602 2532 1127
ψυχή μου ἕως  θανάτου· μείνατε ὧδε καὶ γρηγορεῖτε.
soul of me until death;   stay  here and keep awake.
    2532 4281           3398    4098          1909
 35 καὶ προελθὼν     μικρὸν ἔπιπτεν        ἐπὶ
    And having gone before little he was falling upon
06  1093  2532 4336          2443 1487 1415    1510
τῆς γῆς καὶ προσηύχετο ἵνα  εἰ δυνατόν ἐστιν
the earth and  he was praying that if  power    it is
3928      575  846   05  5610      2532 3004      5     01
παρέλθη ἀπ' αὐτοῦ ἡ ὥρα,  36 καὶ ἔλεγεν· αββα ὁ
might    from him the hour,   and he was  Abba the
go along                         saying,
3962    3956 1415   1473        3911        012 4221
πατήρ, πάντα δυνατά σοι·  παρένεγκε τὸ ποτήριον
father, all  powers to you;  carry along the cup
3778   575 1473  235  3756 5101 1473 2309 235  5101
τοῦτο ἀπ' ἐμοῦ· ἀλλ' οὐ  τί  ἐγὼ θέλω ἀλλὰ τί
this  from me;  but  not what I    want but  what
1473    2532 2064    2532 2147     846    2518
σύ.  37 καὶ ἔρχεται καὶ εὑρίσκει αὐτοὺς καθεύδοντας,
you.    And he comes and he finds them  sleeping,
2532 3004    03      4074   4613     2518       3756
καὶ  λέγει  τῷ    Πέτρῳ· Σίμων, καθεύδεις; οὐκ
and  he says to the Peter; Simon,  you sleep?   Not
2480              1520 5610 1127          1127
ἴσχυσας     μίαν ὥραν γρηγορῆσαι; 38 γρηγορειτε
were you strong one hour  to keep awake?    Keep awake
2532 4336             2443 3361 2064       1519
καὶ  προσεύχεσθε, ἵνα  μὴ  ἔλθητε    εἰς
and  pray,        that not you might go into
3986         09  3303 4151   4289      05  1161 4561
πειρασμόν· τὸ μὲν πνεῦμα πρόθυμον ἡ  δὲ  σὰρξ
pressure;  the indeed spirit  eager    the but  flesh
772          2532 3825 565              4336
ἀσθενής. 39 καὶ πάλιν ἀπελθὼν     προσηύξατο
weak.       And again having gone off he prayed
04  846  3056 3004        2532 3825 2064
τὸν αὐτὸν λόγον εἰπών. 40 καὶ πάλιν ἐλθὼν
the same word having said. And again having come
2147    846   2518        1510  1063 846     013
εὗρεν αὐτοὺς καθεύδοντας, ἦσαν γὰρ αὐτῶν οἱ
he found them  sleeping,   were+ for  of them the
3788       2599a               2532 3756 3609a
ὀφθαλμοὶ καταβαρυνόμενοι,  καὶ οὐκ ἤδεισαν
eyes      +being burdened down, and not they had known
5101 611               846    41 2532 2064   012 5154
τί  ἀποκριθῶσιν   αὐτῷ.   καὶ ἔρχεται τὸ τρίτον
what they might answer to him.  And he comes the third
2532 3004    846    2518      013 3062      2532
καὶ  λέγει  αὐτοῖς· καθεύδετε τὸ λοιπὸν καὶ
and  he says to them; sleep     the remaining and
```

Gethsemane; and he said to his disciples, "Sit here while I pray." [33]He took with him Peter and James and John, and began to be distressed and agitated. [34]And he said to them, "I am deeply grieved, even to death; remain here, and keep awake." [35]And going a little farther, he threw himself on the ground and prayed that, if it were possible, the hour might pass from him. [36]He said, "Abba,[a] Father, for you all things are possible; remove this cup from me; yet, not what I want, but what you want." [37]He came and found them sleeping; and he said to Peter, "Simon, are you asleep? Could you not keep awake one hour? [38]Keep awake and pray that you may not come into the time of trial;[b] the spirit indeed is willing, but the flesh is weak." [39]And again he went away and prayed, saying the same words. [40]And once more he came and found them sleeping, for their eyes were very heavy; and they did not know what to say to him. [41]He came a third time and said to them, "Are you still sleeping and

a Aramaic for *Father*

b Or *into temptation*

taking your rest? Enough!
The hour has come; the Son
of Man is betrayed into the
hands of sinners. ⁴²Get up,
let us be going. See, my
betrayer is at hand."

43 Immediately, while
he was still speaking, Judas,
one of the twelve, arrived;
and with him there was a
crowd with swords and
clubs, from the chief priests,
the scribes, and the elders.
⁴⁴Now the betrayer had
given them a sign, saying,
"The one I will kiss is the
man; arrest him and lead
him away under guard."
⁴⁵So when he came, he went
up to him at once and said,
"Rabbi!" and kissed him.
⁴⁶Then they laid hands on
him and arrested him. ⁴⁷But
one of those who stood near
drew his sword and struck
the slave of the high priest,
cutting off his ear. ⁴⁸Then
Jesus said to them, "Have
you come out with swords
and clubs to arrest me as
though I were a bandit?
⁴⁹Day after day I was with
you in the temple teaching,
and you did not arrest me.
But let the scriptures be
fulfilled." ⁵⁰All of them
deserted him and fled.

51 A certain young man
was following him, wearing
nothing but a linen cloth.

373	568	2064	05	5610	2400
ἀναπαύεσθε·	ἀπέχει·	ἦλθεν ἡ	ὥρα,	ἰδοὺ
rest;	hold off;	came	the hour,	look

3860	01	5207	02	444	1519	020	5495
παραδίδοται	ὁ	υἱὸς	τοῦ	ἀνθρώπου	εἰς	τὰς χεῖρας
is given over	the	son	of	the man	into	the hands

014	268	42	1453	71	2400	01
τῶν	ἁμαρτωλῶν.		ἐγείρεσθε	ἄγωμεν·	ἰδοὺ ὁ
of the sinners.			Be raised	we might lead;	look the

3860	1473	1448	43	2532	2117	2089
παραδιδούς	με	ἤγγικεν.		Καὶ	εὐθὺς	ἔτι
one giving over	me	has neared.	And	immediately	still

846	2980	3854	2455	1520	014	1427
αὐτοῦ λαλοῦντος	παραγίνεται	Ἰούδας	εἷς	τῶν	δώδεκα
him speaking	arrives	Judas	one	of	the twelve

2532	3326	846	3793	3326	3162	2532	3586	3844
καὶ	μετ'	αὐτοῦ	ὄχλος	μετὰ μαχαιρῶν	καὶ	ξύλων	παρὰ
and	with	him	crowd	with swords	and	woods	from

014	749	2532	014	1122	2532	014
τῶν	ἀρχιερέων	καὶ	τῶν	γραμματέων	καὶ	τῶν
the	ruler priests	and	the	writers	and	the

4245	44	1325	1161	01	3860	846
πρεσβυτέρων.		δεδώκει	δὲ	ὁ	παραδιδοὺς	αὐτὸν
older men.		Had given	but	the one giving over	him

4953	846	3004	3739	302	5368	846
σύσσημον	αὐτοῖς	λέγων·	ὃν	ἂν	φιλήσω	αὐτός
signal	to them	saying;	whom	-	I might love	himself

1510	2902	846	2532	520	806	45	2532
ἐστιν,	κρατήσατε	αὐτὸν	καὶ	ἀπάγετε	ἀσφαλῶς.		καὶ
it is,	hold	him	and	lead off	securely.		And

2064	2117	4334	846
ἐλθὼν	εὐθὺς	προσελθὼν	αὐτῷ
having come	immediately	having come toward	him

3004	4461	2532	2705	846	46	013	1161
λέγει·	ῥαββί,	καὶ	κατεφίλησεν	αὐτόν·		οἱ	δὲ
he says;	Rabbi,	and	he kissed	him;		the ones	but

1911	020	5495	846	2532	2902	846	47	1520
ἐπέβαλον	τὰς χεῖρας	αὐτῷ	καὶ	ἐκράτησαν	αὐτόν.		εἷς
threw on	the hands	him	and	they held	him.		One

1161	5100	014	3936	4685
δὲ	[τις]	τῶν	παρεστηκότων	σπασάμενος
but	some	of	the ones having stood along	having drawn

08	3162	3817	04	1401	02	749	2532
τὴν	μάχαιραν	ἔπαισεν	τὸν	δοῦλον	τοῦ	ἀρχιερέως	καὶ
the	sword	struck	the	slave	of	the ruler priest	and

851	846	012	5620a	48	2532	611
ἀφεῖλεν	αὐτοῦ	τὸ	ὠτάριον.		Καὶ	ἀποκριθεὶς
he lifted off	of him	the	ear.		And	having answered

01	2424	3004	846	5613	1909	3027	1831
ὁ	Ἰησοῦς	εἶπεν	αὐτοῖς·	ὡς	ἐπὶ	λῃστὴν	ἐξήλθατε
the	Jesus	said	to them;	as	on	robber	you came out

3326	3162	2532	3586	4815	1473	49	2596
μετὰ	μαχαιρῶν	καὶ	ξύλων	συλλαβεῖν	με;		καθ'
with	swords	and	woods	to take together	me?		By

2250	1510	4314	1473	1722	011	2411	1321	2532
ἡμέραν	ἤμην	πρὸς	ὑμᾶς	ἐν	τῷ	ἱερῷ	διδάσκων	καὶ
day	I was	toward	you	in	the	temple	teaching	and

3756	2902	1473	235	2443	4137	017
οὐκ	ἐκρατήσατέ	με·	ἀλλ'	ἵνα	πληρωθῶσιν	αἱ
not	you held	me;	but	that	might be filled	the

1124	50	2532	863	846	5343	3956
γραφαί.		Καὶ	ἀφέντες	αὐτὸν	ἔφυγον	πάντες.
writings.		And	having left off	him	fled	all.

51	2532	3495	5100	4870	846
	καὶ	νεανίσκος	τις	συνηκολούθει	αὐτῷ
	And	young man	some	was following together	him

4016	4616	1909	1131	2532
περιβεβλημένος	σινδόνα	ἐπὶ	γυμνοῦ,	καὶ
having thrown around himself	linen	upon	naked,	and

```
2902        846      52  01      1161 2641
κρατοῦσιν αὐτόν·         ὁ       δὲ  καταλιπὼν
they hold him;          the one but  having left behind
08  4616   1131    5343       53  2532 520      04
τὴν σινδόνα γυμνὸς ἔφυγεν.        Καὶ  ἀπήγαγον    τὸν
the linen  naked  fled.          And  they led off the
2424    4314   04  749            2532 4905
Ἰησοῦν πρὸς  τὸν ἀρχιερέα,     καὶ  συνέρχονται
Jesus  toward the ruler priest, and  come together
3956   013 749        2532 013 4245       2532 013
πάντες οἱ ἀρχιερεῖς  καὶ οἱ πρεσβύτεροι καὶ οἱ
all    the ruler priests and the older men  and  the
1122         2532 01  4074   575  3113
γραμματεῖς.  54 καὶ ὁ  Πέτρος ἀπὸ μακρόθεν
writers.        And the Peter from from far
190          846     2193  2080  1519 08  833       02
ἠκολούθησεν αὐτῷ ἕως  ἔσω  εἰς τὴν αὐλὴν  τοῦ
followed    him  until inside in the courtyard of the
749        2532 1510    4775           3326 014
ἀρχιερέως  καὶ ἦν  συγκαθήμενος  μετὰ τῶν
ruler priest and he was+ +sitting together with the
5257      2532 2328        4314   012 5457  55  013
ὑπηρετῶν καὶ θερμαινόμενος πρὸς τὸ φῶς.    Οἱ
assistants and +warming    toward the light.  The
1161749       2532 3650  09  4892       2212
δὲ ἀρχιερεῖς  καὶ ὅλον τὸ συνέδριον ἐζήτουν
but ruler priests and whole the council   were seeking
2596    02   2424  3141    1519 012 2289
κατὰ  τοῦ Ἰησοῦ μαρτυρίαν εἰς τὸ θανατῶσαι
against the Jesus testimony to  the to put to death
846     2532 3756 2147     56  4183  1063
αὐτόν, καὶ  οὐχ ηὕρισκον·      πολλοὶ γὰρ
him,   and  not they were finding; many   for
5576              2596   846     2532 2470  017
ἐψευδομαρτύρουν  κατ’  αὐτοῦ, καὶ ἴσαι  αἱ
were testifying falsely against him,   and  equal the
3141        3756 1510  57 2532 5100   450
μαρτυρίαι  οὐκ ἦσαν.    καί  τινες ἀναστάντες
testimonies not  were.   And  some  having stood up
5576              2596   846    3004       3754
ἐψευδομαρτύρουν  κατ’  αὐτοῦ λέγοντες 58 ὅτι
were testifying falsely against him  saying,      (")
1473   191       846   3004      3754 1473 2647
ἡμεῖς ἠκούσαμεν αὐτοῦ λέγοντος ὅτι ἐγὼ καταλύσω
we    heard     him   speaking, (") I   will unloose
04  3485    3778   04  5499        2532 1223    5140
τὸν ναὸν  τοῦτον τὸν χειροποίητον καὶ διὰ  τριῶν
the temple this  the handmade     and through three
2250   243   886        3618       59 2532 3761
ἡμερῶν ἄλλον ἀχειροποίητον οἰκοδομήσω.   καὶ  οὐδὲ
days   other unhandmade     I will build. And  but not
3779   2470 1510 05  3141      846     60 2532
οὕτως ἴση  ἦν  ἡ μαρτυρία αὐτῶν.     καὶ
thusly equal was the testimony of them. And
450        01  749           1519 3319   1905
ἀναστὰς        ὁ ἀρχιερεὺς εἰς μέσον ἐπηρώτησεν
having stood up the ruler priest in middle asked on
04  2424  3004  3756 611     3762     5101 3778
τὸν Ἰησοῦν λέγων· οὐκ ἀποκρίνῃ οὐδὲν τί  οὗτοί
the Jesus  saying; not you answer nothing what these
1473  2649           61 01  1161 4623      2532 3756
σου καταμαρτυροῦσιν;    ὁ  δὲ ἐσιώπα  καὶ οὐκ
of you testify against? The one but was silent and not
611         3762   3825   01  749        1905
ἀπεκρίνατο οὐδέν. πάλιν ὁ ἀρχιερεὺς ἐπηρώτα
answered nothing. Again the ruler priest was asking on
846    2532 3004 846      1473 1510 01  5547   01
αὐτὸν καὶ λέγει αὐτῷ·  σὺ εἶ  ὁ χριστὸς ὁ
him   and says to him; you are the Christ the
```

They caught hold of him, [52]but he left the linen cloth and ran off naked.

53 They took Jesus to the high priest; and all the chief priests, the elders, and the scribes were assembled. [54]Peter had followed him at a distance, right into the courtyard of the high priest; and he was sitting with the guards, warming himself at the fire. [55]Now the chief priests and the whole council were looking for testimony against Jesus to put him to death; but they found none. [56]For many gave false testimony against him, and their testimony did not agree. [57]Some stood up and gave false testimony against him, saying, [58]"We heard him say, 'I will destroy this temple that is made with hands, and in three days I will build another, not made with hands.'" [59]But even on this point their testimony did not agree. [60]Then the high priest stood up before them and asked Jesus, "Have you no answer? What is it that they testify against you?" [61]But he was silent and did not answer. Again the high priest asked him, "Are you the Messiah,[a] the

[a] Or the Christ

Son of the Blessed One?"

62Jesus said, "I am; and 'you will see the Son of Man seated at the right hand of the Power,' and 'coming with the clouds of heaven.'"

63Then the high priest tore his clothes and said, "Why do we still need witnesses? 64You have heard his blasphemy! What is your decision?" All of them condemned him as deserving death. 65Some began to spit on him, to blindfold him, and to strike him, saying to him, "Prophesy!" The guards also took him over and beat him.

66While Peter was below in the courtyard, one of the servant-girls of the high priest came by. 67When she saw Peter warming himself, she stared at him and said, "You also were with Jesus, the man from Nazareth." 68But he denied it, saying, "I do not know or understand what you are talking about." And he went out into the forecourt.*a* Then the cock crowed.*b* 69And the servant-girl, on seeing him, began again to say to the bystanders, "This man is one of them." 70But again he denied it. Then after a little while the bystanders

a Or gateway
b Other ancient authorities lack *Then the cock crowed*

5207	02		2128		**62**	01	1161	2424	3004
υἱὸς	τοῦ		εὐλογητοῦ;			ὁ	δὲ	Ἰησοῦς	εἶπεν·
son	of the	well	spoken one?			The	but	Jesus	said;

1473 1510 2532 3708   04 5207 02   444
ἐγώ εἰμι, καὶ ὄψεσθε   τὸν υἱὸν τοῦ ἀνθρώπου
I am, and you will see the son of the man

1537 1188 2521 06 1411 2532 2064
ἐκ δεξιῶν καθήμενον τῆς δυνάμεως καὶ ἐρχόμενον
from right sitting of the power and coming

3326 018 3507 02 3772   **63** 01 1161
μετὰ τῶν νεφελῶν τοῦ οὐρανοῦ.   ὁ δὲ
with the clouds of the heaven.   The but

749 1284 016 5509 846
ἀρχιερεὺς διαρρήξας τοὺς χιτῶνας αὐτοῦ
ruler priest having torn apart the shirts of him

3004 5101 2089 5532 2192 3144
λέγει· τί ἔτι χρείαν ἔχομεν μαρτύρων;
says; what still need we have of testifiers?

64 191 06 988 5101 1473 5316
ἠκούσατε τῆς βλασφημίας· τί ὑμῖν φαίνεται;
You heard the insult; what to you it shines?

013 1161 3956 2632 846 1777 1510
οἱ δὲ πάντες κατέκριναν αὐτὸν ἔνοχον εἶναι
the ones but all condemned him guilty to be

2288 **65** 2532 757 5100 1716 846 2532
θανάτου. Καὶ ἤρξαντό τινες ἐμπτύειν αὐτῷ καὶ
of death. And began some to spit on him and

4028 846 012 4383 2532 2852
περικαλύπτειν αὐτοῦ τὸ πρόσωπον καὶ κολαφίζειν
to cover around him the face and to knock about

846 2532 3004 846 4395 2532 013
αὐτὸν καὶ λέγειν αὐτῷ· προφήτευσον, καὶ οἱ
him and to say to him; speak before, and the

5257 4475 846 2983 **66** 2532 1510 02
ὑπηρέται ῥαπίσμασιν αὐτὸν ἔλαβον. Καὶ ὄντος τοῦ
assistants in slaps him took. And being the

4074 0736 1722 07 833 2064 1520 018
Πέτρου κάτω ἐν τῇ αὐλῇ ἔρχεται μία τῶν
Peter down in the courtyard comes one of the

3814 02 749 **67** 2532 3708 04
παιδισκῶν τοῦ ἀρχιερέως καὶ ἰδοῦσα τὸν
servant girls of the ruler priest and having seen the

4074 2328 1689 846 3004
Πέτρον θερμαινόμενον ἐμβλέψασα αὐτῷ λέγει·
Peter warming having looked in him she says;

2532 1473 3326 02 3479 1510 02 2424 01
καὶ σὺ μετὰ τοῦ Ναζαρηνοῦ ἦσθα τοῦ Ἰησοῦ. ὁ
also you with the Nazarene were the Jesus. The one

1161 720 3004 3777 3609a 3777 1987
δὲ ἠρνήσατο λέγων· οὔτε οἶδα οὔτε ἐπίσταμαι
but denied saying; neither I know nor I understand

1473 5101 3004 2532 1831 1854 1519 012
σὺ τί λέγεις. καὶ ἐξῆλθεν ἔξω εἰς τὸ
you what say. And he went out outside into the

4259 2532 220 5455 **69** 2532 05
προαύλιον [·καὶ ἀλέκτωρ ἐφώνησεν]. καὶ ἡ
forecourt; and rooster sounded. And the

3814 3708 846 757 3825 3004
παιδίσκη ἰδοῦσα αὐτὸν ἤρξατο πάλιν λέγειν
servant girl having seen him began again to say

015 3936 3754 3778 1537
τοῖς παρεστῶσιν ὅτι οὗτος ἐξ
to the ones having stood along, (") this one from

846 1510 **70** 01 1161 3825 720 2532
αὐτῶν ἐστιν. ὁ δὲ πάλιν ἠρνεῖτο. καὶ
them is. The one but again was denying. And

3326 3398 3825 013 3936
μετὰ μικρὸν πάλιν οἱ παρεστῶτες
after little again the ones having stood along

3004		03	4074	230	1537	846	1510
ἔλεγον		τῷ	Πέτρῳ·	ἀληθῶς	ἐξ	αὐτῶν	εἶ,
were saying		to the	Peter;	truly	from	them	you are,

2532	1063	1057	1510			01	1161	757
καὶ	γὰρ	Γαλιλαῖος	εἶ.	**71**	ὁ	δὲ	ἤρξατο
also	for	Galilean	you are.	The one	but	began

332		2532	3660		3754	3756
ἀναθεματίζειν		καὶ	ὀμνύναι		ὅτι	οὐκ
to swear curse on himself		and	to take oath,		(")	not

3609a	04	444	3778	3739	3004		2532
οἶδα	τὸν	ἄνθρωπον	τοῦτον	ὃν	λέγετε.	**72**	καὶ
I know	the man		this	whom	you say.	And

2117	1537	1208	220	5455	2532
εὐθὺς	ἐκ	δευτέρου	ἀλέκτωρ	ἐφώνησεν.	καὶ
immediately	from	second	rooster	sounded.	And

363	01	4074	012	4487	5613	3004	846	01
ἀνεμνήσθη	ὁ	Πέτρος	τὸ	ῥῆμα	ὡς	εἶπεν	αὐτῷ	ὁ
was reminded	the	Peter	the	word	as	said	to him	the

2424	3754	4250	220	5455	1364	5151	1473
Ἰησοῦς	ὅτι	πρὶν	ἀλέκτορα	φωνῆσαι	δὶς	τρίς	με
Jesus,	(")	before	rooster	to sound	twice	three	me

533	2532	1911	2799		2532
ἀπαρνήσῃ·	καὶ	ἐπιβαλὼν	ἔκλαιεν.	**15:1**	Καὶ
you will deny	and	having thrown	he was		And
thoroughly;		on	crying.

2117	4404	4824	4160	013
εὐθὺς	πρωῒ	συμβούλιον	ποιήσαντες	οἱ
immediately	morning	council	having made	the

749	3326	014	4245	2532	1122
ἀρχιερεῖς	μετὰ	τῶν	πρεσβυτέρων	καὶ	γραμματέων
ruler priests	with	the	older men	and	writers

2532	3650	09	4892	1210	04	2424
καὶ	ὅλον	τὸ	συνέδριον,	δήσαντες	τὸν	Ἰησοῦν
and	whole	the	council,	having bound	the	Jesus

667	2532	3860		2532
ἀπήνεγκαν	καὶ	παρέδωκαν Πιλάτῳ.	**2**	Καὶ
they carried off	and	gave over to Pilate.		And

1905	846	01	4091	1473	1510	01	935
ἐπηρώτησεν	αὐτὸν	ὁ	Πιλᾶτος·	σὺ	εἶ	ὁ	βασιλεὺς
asked on	him	the	Pilate;	you	are	the	king

014	2453	01	1161	611	846
τῶν	Ἰουδαίων;	ὁ	δὲ	ἀποκριθεὶς	αὐτῷ
of the Judeans?	The one	but	having answered	him

3004	1473	3004	2532	2723	846	013
λέγει,	Σὺ	λέγεις.	**3**	καὶ	κατηγόρουν	αὐτοῦ	οἱ
says,	You	say.		And	were accusing	him	the

749	4183		01	1161	4091	3825	1905
ἀρχιερεῖς	πολλά.	**4**	ὁ	δὲ	Πιλᾶτος	πάλιν	ἐπηρώτα
ruler priests	many.		The	but	Pilate	again	asked on

846	3004	3756	611	3762	2396	4214
αὐτὸν	λέγων·	οὐκ	ἀποκρίνῃ	οὐδέν;	ἴδε	πόσα
him	saying,	not	you answer	nothing?	Look	how much

1473	2723		01	1161	2424	3765
σου	κατηγοροῦσιν.	**5**	ὁ	δὲ	Ἰησοῦς	οὐκέτι
of you	they accuse.		The	but	Jesus	no longer

3762	611	5620	2296	04	4091
οὐδὲν	ἀπεκρίθη,	ὥστε	θαυμάζειν	τὸν	Πιλᾶτον.
nothing	answered,	so that	to marvel	the	Pilate.

2596	1161	1859	630	846	1520
6 Κατὰ	δὲ	ἑορτὴν	ἀπέλυεν	αὐτοῖς	ἕνα
According to	but	festival	he loosed off	to them	one

1198	3739	3868		1510	1161
δέσμιον	ὃν	παρῃτοῦντο.	**7**	ἦν	δὲ
prisoner	whom	they were asking for.		There was+	but

01	3004	912	3326	014	4713a
ὁ	λεγόμενος	Βαραββᾶς	μετὰ	τῶν	στασιαστῶν
the one being said		Barabbas	with	the	revolutionaries

1210	3748	1722	07	4714	5408
δεδεμένος	οἵτινες	ἐν	τῇ	στάσει	φόνον
+having been bound	who	in	the	revolution	murder

again said to Peter, "Certainly you are one of them; for you are a Galilean." [71]But he began to curse, and he swore an oath, "I do not know this man you are talking about." [72]At that moment the cock crowed for the second time. Then Peter remembered that Jesus had said to him, "Before the cock crows twice, you will deny me three times." And he broke down and wept.

CHAPTER 15

As soon as it was morning, the chief priests held a consultation with the elders and scribes and the whole council. They bound Jesus, led him away, and handed him over to Pilate. [2]Pilate asked him, "Are you the King of the Jews?" He answered him, "You say so." [3]Then the chief priests accused him of many things. [4]Pilate asked him again, "Have you no answer? See how many charges they bring against you." [5]But Jesus made no further reply, so that Pilate was amazed.

6 Now at the festival he used to release a prisoner for them, anyone for whom they asked. [7]Now a man called Barabbas was in prison with the rebels who had committed murder during the insurrection.

8So the crowd came and began to ask Pilate to do for them according to his custom. 9Then he answered them, "Do you want me to release for you the King of the Jews?" 10For he realized that it was out of jealousy that the chief priests had handed him over. 11But the chief priests stirred up the crowd to have him release Barabbas for them instead. 12Pilate spoke to them again, "Then what do you wish me to do[a] with the man you call[b] the King of the Jews?" 13They shouted back, "Crucify him!" 14Pilate asked them, "Why, what evil has he done?" But they shouted all the more, "Crucify him!" 15So Pilate, wishing to satisfy the crowd, released Barabbas for them; and after flogging Jesus, he handed him over to be crucified.

16 Then the soldiers led him into the courtyard of the palace (that is, the governor's headquarters[c]); and they called together the whole cohort. 17And they clothed him in a purple cloak; and after twisting some thorns into a crown, they put it on him. 18And they began saluting him, "Hail, King of the Jews!" 19They struck his head with a reed, spat upon him, and

---

a Other ancient authorities read
  what should I do
b Other ancient authorities lack
  the man you call
c Gk the praetorium

4160
πεποιήκεισαν. 8 2532 305   καὶ ἀναβὰς   01 ὁ 3793 ὄχλος 757 ἤρξατο
had done.   And having gone up the crowd   began

154   2531   4160   846   9 01 1161 4091
αἰτεῖσθαι καθὼς ἐποίει   αὐτοῖς.   ὁ δὲ Πιλᾶτος
to ask   just as he was doing to them. The but Pilate

611   846   3004   2309   630   1473 04
ἀπεκρίθη αὐτοῖς λέγων· θέλετε   ἀπολύσω ὑμῖν τὸν
answered them   saying; want you I might to you the
                                                 loose off

935   014   2453   10 1097   1063 3754 1223
βασιλέα τῶν   Ἰουδαίων,   ἐγίνωσκεν γὰρ ὅτι διὰ
king   of the Judeans?   He knew   for that through

5355   3860   846   013 749   11 013
φθόνον παραδεδώκεισαν αὐτὸν οἱ ἀρχιερεῖς.   οἱ
envy   had given over him   the ruler priests.   The

1161 749   383   04 3793 2443 3123   04
δὲ ἀρχιερεῖς   ἀνέσεισαν τὸν ὄχλον ἵνα μᾶλλον τὸν
but ruler priests shook up the crowd that more   the

912   630   846   12 01 1161
Βαραββᾶν ἀπολύσῃ   αὐτοῖς.   ὁ δὲ
Barabbas he might loose off to them. The but

4091   3825   611   3004   846   5101
Πιλᾶτος πάλιν ἀποκριθεὶς   ἔλεγεν   αὐτοῖς· τί
Pilate   again having answered was saying to them; what

3767 2309   4160   3739 3004   04 935   014
οὖν [θέλετε] ποιήσω   οὗ λέγετε τὸν βασιλέα τῶν
then you want might I do whom you say the king   of the

2453   13   013   1161 3825 2896   4717
Ἰουδαίων;   οἱ   δὲ πάλιν ἔκραξαν· σταύρωσον
Judeans?   The ones but again shouted; crucify

846   14 01 1161 4091   3004   846   5101 1063
αὐτόν.   ὁ δὲ Πιλᾶτος ἔλεγεν   αὐτοῖς· τί γὰρ
him.   The but Pilate was saying to them; what for

4160   2556   013   1161 4057   2896
ἐποίησεν κακόν; οἱ   δὲ περισσῶς ἔκραξαν·
he did   bad?   The ones but exceedingly they shouted;

4717   846   15 01 1161 4091   1014   03
σταύρωσον αὐτόν.   Ὁ δὲ Πιλᾶτος βουλόμενος τῷ
crucify   him.   The but Pilate planning   the

3793 012 2425   4160   630   846   04
ὄχλῳ τὸ ἱκανὸν ποιῆσαι ἀπέλυσεν αὐτοῖς τὸν
crowd the enough to do loosed off to them the

912   2532 3860   04 2424   5417
Βαραββᾶν, καὶ παρέδωκεν τὸν Ἰησοῦν φραγελλώσας
Barabbas, and he gave over the Jesus having whipped

2443 4717   16   013 1161 4757
ἵνα σταυρωθῇ.   Οἱ δὲ στρατιῶται
that he might be crucified. The but soldiers

520   846   2080   06 833   3739 1510
ἀπήγαγον αὐτὸν ἔσω τῆς αὐλῆς,   ὅ   ἐστιν
lead off him inside the courtyard, which is

4232   2532 4779   3650 08 4686
πραιτώριον, καὶ συγκαλοῦσιν   ὅλην τὴν σπεῖραν.
praetorium, and they call together whole the squadron.

17 2532 1737   846   4209   2532 4060
καὶ ἐνδιδύσκουσιν αὐτὸν πορφύραν καὶ περιτιθέασιν
And they put on   him   purple   and set around

846   4120   174   4735   18 2532
αὐτῷ πλέξαντες   ἀκάνθινον στέφανον·   καὶ
to him having braided thorn   crown;   and

757   782   846   5463   935   014
ἤρξαντο ἀσπάζεσθαι αὐτόν· χαῖρε, βασιλεῦ τῶν
they began to greet   him; rejoice, King of the

2453   19 2532 5180   846   08
Ἰουδαίων·   καὶ ἔτυπτον   αὐτοῦ τὴν
Judeans;   and they were beating of him the

2776   2563   2532 1716   846 2532
κεφαλὴν καλάμῳ καὶ ἐνέπτυον   αὐτῷ καὶ
head   in reed and they were spitting on him and

```
5087     024  1119    4352                      846    20  2532
τιθέντες τὰ  γόνατα  προσεκύνουν               αὐτῷ.      καὶ
setting  the knees   they were worshiping      him.      And
```
```
3753  1702        846    1562        846    08    4209
ὅτε  ἐνέπαιξαν    αὐτῷ,  ἐξέδυσαν    αὐτὸν  τὴν  πορφύραν
when they mocked him,   they put off him    the purple
```
```
2532 1746         846    024  2440    846    2532
καὶ  ἐνέδυσαν     αὐτὸν  τὰ  ἱμάτια   αὐτοῦ. Καί
and they put on  him    the clothes of him. And
```
```
1806         846    2443  4717              846
ἐξάγουσιν    αὐτὸν  ἵνα  σταυρώσωσιν        αὐτόν.
they lead out him    that they might crucify him.
```
```
21  2532 29              3855          5100 4613
    καὶ  ἀγγαρεύουσιν    παράγοντά     τινα Σίμωνα
    And they conscript  leading along some Simon
```
```
2956         2064        575 68    04   3962       223
Κυρηναῖον   ἐρχόμενον   ἀπ' ἀγροῦ, τὸν πατέρα    Ἀλεξάνδρου
Cyrenean     coming      from field, the father of Alexander
```
```
2532 4504     2443  142           04   4716     846
καὶ  Ῥούφου,  ἵνα  ἄρῃ            τὸν σταυρὸν   αὐτοῦ.
and Rufus,    that he might lift up the cross  of him.
```
```
22  2532 5342       846    1909 04   1115       5117    3739
    Καὶ  φέρουσιν   αὐτὸν  ἐπὶ  τὸν Γολγοθᾶν    τόπον  ὃ
    And they carry him    on   the Golgotha    place which
```
```
1510 3177          2898      5117       2532
ἐστιν μεθερμηνευόμενον Κρανίου Τόπος.  23  καὶ
is+   +being translated Of Skull Place.     And
```
```
1325            846    4669
ἐδίδουν         αὐτῷ  ἐσμυρνισμένον
they were giving him   having been spiced with myrrh
```
```
3631   3739   1161  3756 2983         24  2532 4717
οἶνον· ὃς    δὲ  οὐκ  ἔλαβεν.            Καὶ  σταυροῦσιν
wine;  which but  not he received.  And they crucify
```
```
846    2532 1266              024  2440     846
αὐτὸν καὶ  διαμερίζονται      τὰ  ἱμάτια   αὐτοῦ,
him   and they divided completely the clothes of him,
```
```
906          2819  1909 846   5101 5101 142
βάλλοντες   κλῆρον ἐπ'  αὐτὰ τίς  τί  ἄρῃ.
throwing    lot    on   them who what might lift up
```
```
25  1510   1161   5610 5154   2532 4717        846
    ἦν    δὲ    ὥρα  τρίτη  καὶ  ἐσταύρωσαν   αὐτόν.
    It was but  hour third and  they crucified him.
```
```
26  2532 1510 05  1923      06    156      846
    καὶ  ἦν   ἡ  ἐπιγραφὴ   τῆς  αἰτίας   αὐτοῦ
    And was+  the written  on   of the cause of him
```
```
1924               01   935     014    2453
ἐπιγεγραμμένη·     ὁ   βασιλεὺς τῶν    Ἰουδαίων.
+having been written on; the king  of the Judeans.
```
```
27  2532 4862 846   4717        1417 3027     1520 1537
    Καὶ  σὺν  αὐτῷ στραυροῦσιν  δύο  λῃστάς,  ἕνα ἐκ
    And with him they crucify  two  robbers, one from
```
```
1188    2532 1520 1537 2176       846        2532 013
δεξιῶν καὶ  ἕνα ἐξ  εὐωνύμων     αὐτοῦ.  29  Καὶ  οἱ
right  and one from left         of him.     And the
```
```
3899              987            846    2795
παραπορευόμενοι   ἐβλασφήμουν    αὐτὸν κινοῦντες
ones traveling along were insulting him   moving
```
```
020  2776    846   2532 3004     3758 01
τὰς κεφαλὰς αὐτῶν καὶ  λέγοντες· οὐά ὁ
the heads  of them and saying;  ha! the one
```
```
2647      04   3485 2532 3618     1722 5140    2250
καταλύων τὸν ναὸν καὶ οἰκοδομῶν ἐν  τρισὶν ἡμέραις,
unloosing the temple and building in three days,
```
```
30  4982    4572    2597       575  02   4716
    σῶσον  σεαυτὸν καταβὰς     ἀπὸ τοῦ σταυροῦ.
    deliver yourself having come down from the cross.
```
```
31  3668    2532 013 749        1702          4314
    ὁμοίως  καὶ  οἱ ἀρχιερεῖς  ἐμπαίζοντες  πρὸς
    Likewise also the ruler priests mocking       toward
```

knelt down in homage to him. [20]After mocking him, they stripped him of the purple cloak and put his own clothes on him. Then they led him out to crucify him.

21 They compelled a passer-by, who was coming in from the country, to carry his cross; it was Simon of Cyrene, the father of Alexander and Rufus. [22]Then they brought Jesus[a] to the place called Golgotha (which means the place of a skull). [23]And they offered him wine mixed with myrrh; but he did not take it. [24]And they crucified him, and divided his clothes among them, casting lots to decide what each should take.

25 It was nine o'clock in the morning when they crucified him. [26]The inscription of the charge against him read, "The King of the Jews." [27]And with him they crucified two bandits, one on his right and one on his left.[b] [29]Those who passed by derided[c] him, shaking their heads and saying, "Aha! You who would destroy the temple and build it in three days, [30]save yourself, and come down from the cross!" [31]In the same way the chief priests,

[a] Gk him
[b] Other ancient authorities add verse 28, And the scripture was fulfilled that says, "And he was counted among the lawless."
[c] Or blasphemed

along with the scribes, were
also mocking him among
themselves and saying, "He
saved others; he cannot save
himself. ³²Let the Messiah,ᵃ
the King of Israel, come
down from the cross now,
so that we may see and
believe." Those who were
crucified with him also
taunted him.
   33 When it was noon,
darkness came over the
whole landᵇ until three in
the afternoon. ³⁴At three
o'clock Jesus cried out with
a loud voice, "Eloi, Eloi,
lema sabachthani?" which
means, "My God, my God,
why have you forsaken
me?"ᶜ ³⁵When some of the
bystanders heard it, they
said, "Listen, he is calling
for Elijah." ³⁶And someone
ran, filled a sponge with
sour wine, put it on a stick,
and gave it to him to drink,
saying, "Wait, let us see
whether Elijah will come
to take him down." ³⁷Then
Jesus gave a loud cry and
breathed his last. ³⁸And the
curtain of the temple was
torn in two, from top to
bottom. ³⁹Now when the
centurion, who stood
facing him, saw that in this
way heᵈ breathed his last,
he said, "Truly this man
was God's Son!"ᵉ
   40 There were also
women looking on from
a distance; among them
were Mary

ᵃ Or the Christ
ᵇ Or earth
ᶜ Other ancient authorities read
   made me a reproach
ᵈ Other ancient authorities add
   cried out and
ᵉ Or a son of God

```
240            3326 014 1122      3004          243
ἀλλήλους  μετὰ τῶν γραμματέων ἔλεγον·  ἄλλους
one another with the writers   were saying; others
4982              1438  3756  1410        4982      01
ἔσωσεν,      ἑαυτὸν οὐ δύναται  σῶσαι·  32 ὁ
he delivered, himself not he is able to deliver; the
5547    01 935      2474  2597        3568 575 02
χριστὸς ὁ βασιλεὺς Ἰσραὴλ καταβάτω  νῦν ἀπὸ τοῦ
Christ the king   Israel let come down now from the
4716    2443 3708       2532 4100          2532
σταυροῦ, ἵνα ἴδωμεν  καὶ πιστεύσωμεν.  καὶ
cross,  that we might see and we might trust. And
013 4957            4862 846  3679          846
οἱ συνεσταυρωμένοι σὺν αὐτῷ ὠνείδιζον  αὐτόν.
the ones being     with him were reviling him.
   crucified together
   2532 1096         5610 1623 4655   1096   1909
33 Καὶ γενομένης   ὥρας ἕκτης σκότος ἐγένετο ἐφ᾽
   And having become hour sixth dark   became on
3650  08  1093 2193  5610 1728a   2532 07   1728a
ὅλην τὴν γῆν ἕως  ὥρας ἐνάτης. 34 καὶ τῇ ἐνάτῃ
whole the earth until hour ninth.   And the ninth
5610 994       01 2424  5456 3173    1682 1682
ὥρᾳ ἐβόησεν  ὁ Ἰησοῦς φωνῇ μεγάλῃ· ελωι ελωι
hour cried aloud the Jesus sound great;  eloi eloi
2982 4518        3739 1510 3177          01
λεμα σαβαχθανι;  ὅ  ἐστιν μεθερμηνευόμενον· ὁ
lema sabachthani? Which is+ +being translated; the
2316 1473 01  2316 1473  1519 5101 1459
θεός μου ὁ θεός μου, εἰς τί ἐγκατέλιπές
God of me the God of me, into why you left behind
1473    35 2532 5100 014        3936
με;      καί τινες τῶν      παρεστηκότων
me?    And some of the ones having stood along
191          3004        2396 2243   5455
ἀκούσαντες ἔλεγον·  ἴδε Ἠλίαν φωνεῖ.
having heard were saying; look Elijah he sounds.
   5143        1161 5100 2532 1072       4699
36 δραμὼν  δέ τις [καὶ] γεμίσας   σπόγγον
   Having run but some and having filled sponge
3690      4060          2563  4222
ὄξους   περιθεὶς      καλάμῳ ἐπότιζεν
of sour wine having set around reed was giving drink
846  3004   863  3708        1487 2064    2243
αὐτόν λέγων· ἄφετε ἴδωμεν  εἰ ἔρχεται Ἠλίας
him saying; allow we might see if comes  Elijah
2507      846   37 01 1161 2424   863
καθελεῖν αὐτόν.  ὁ δὲ Ἰησοῦς ἀφεὶς
to lift down him.  The but Jesus having sent off
5456 3173   1606      2532 09 2665
φωνὴν μεγάλην ἐξέπνευσεν. 38 Καὶ τὸ καταπέτασμα
sound great breathed out.  And the veil
02   3485  4977      1519 1417 575 509       2193
τοῦ ναοῦ ἐσχίσθη εἰς δύο ἀπ᾽ ἄνωθεν   ἕως
of the temple was split into two from from above until
2736   39 3708      1161 01 2760      01
κάτω.   Ἰδὼν  δὲ ὁ κεντυρίων ὁ
down.  Having seen but the centurion the
3936            1537 1727    846     3754
παρεστηκὼς    ἐξ ἐναντίας αὐτοῦ ὅτι
one having stood along out of against of him that
3779 1606        3004   230    3778 01
οὕτως ἐξέπνευσεν  εἶπεν· ἀληθῶς οὗτος ὁ
thusly he breathed out said, truly this the
444       5207 2316 1510   40 1510 1161 2532 1135
ἄνθρωπος υἱὸς θεοῦ ἦν. Ἦσαν δὲ καὶ γυναῖκες
man      son of God was. Were but also women
575 3113      2334     1722 3739 2532 3137 05
ἀπὸ μακρόθεν θεωροῦσαι, ἐν αἷς καὶ Μαρία ἡ
from from far watching, in whom also Maria the
```

```
3094              2532 3137  05   2385      02      3398    2532
Μαγδαληνὴ καὶ  Μαρία ἡ  ᾽Ιακώβου τοῦ  μικροῦ καὶ
Magdalene and  Maria the of Jacob of the little and
2500              3384  2532 4539          3739 3753 1510
᾽Ιωσῆτος μήτηρ καὶ  Σαλώμη,  41 αἳ  ὅτε  ἦν
of Josetus mother and  Salome,       who when he was
1722 07  1056      190              846   2532
ἐν  τῇ Γαλιλαίᾳ ἠκολούθουν  αὐτῷ καὶ
in  the Galilee were following him  and
1247          846   2532 243     4183     017
διηκόνουν    αὐτῷ, καὶ ἄλλαι πολλαὶ αἱ
they were serving him,  and  others many   the ones
4872          846   1519 2414
συναναβᾶσαι  αὐτῷ εἰς  ῾Ιεροσόλυμα.
having gone up together to him into  Jerusalem.
    2532 2235  3798     1096         1893   1510
 42 Καὶ ἤδη  ὀψίας γενομένης, ἐπεὶ ἦν
    And already evening having become, since it was
3904      3739 1510  4315          2064
παρασκευὴ ὅ  ἐστιν προσάββατον, 43 ἐλθὼν
preparation which is  foresabbath,     having come
2501   01   1   575   707      2158        1010
᾽Ιωσὴφ [ὁ]  ἀπὸ ῾Αριμαθαίας εὐσχήμων βουλευτής,
Joseph the one from Arimathea  proper   planner,
3739 2532 846   1510 4327          08     932
ὃς  καὶ αὐτὸς ἦν  προσδεχόμενος τὴν βασιλείαν
who also himself was+ +awaiting  the kingdom
02     2316  5111       1525       4314 04   4091
τοῦ  θεοῦ, τολμήσας εἰσῆλθεν πρὸς τὸν Πιλᾶτον
of the God, having dared to go into to  the Pilate
2532 154      012 4983 02   2424     01  1161
καὶ ἠτήσατο τὸ σῶμα τοῦ ᾽Ιησοῦ. 44 ὁ  δὲ
and he asked the body of the Jesus.    The but
4091     2296       1487 2235  2348        2532
Πιλᾶτος ἐθαύμασεν εἰ ἤδη τέθνηκεν καὶ
Pilate  marveled  if already he had died and
4341           04   2760    1905         846    1487
προσκαλεσάμενος τὸν κεντυρίωνα ἐπηρώτησεν αὐτὸν εἰ
having called to the centurion  he asked on him   if
3819 599        2532 1097        575  02
πάλαι ἀπέθανεν· 45 καὶ γνοὺς  ἀπὸ τοῦ
of old he died;     and having known from the
2760       1433         012 4430 03   2501      46 2532
κεντυρίωνος ἐδωρήσατο τὸ πτῶμα τῷ  ᾽Ιωσήφ.   καὶ
centurion   he gifted the corpse to the Joseph.    And
59       4616   2507       846  1750        07
ἀγοράσας σινδόνα καθελὼν  αὐτὸν ἐνείλησεν τῇ
having  linen   having lifted him  he wrapped in the
bought          down
4616     2532 5087    846  1722 3419   3739 1510
σινδόνι καὶ ἔθηκεν αὐτὸν ἐν μνημείῳ ὃ  ἦν
linen   and he set him   in grave   which was+
2998              1537 4073    2532 4351        3037
λελατομημένον ἐκ  πέτρας καὶ προσεκύλισεν λίθον
+having been cut out of rock  and rolled       stone
1909 08  2374   010  3419       47 05   1161 3137   05
ἐπὶ τὴν θύραν τοῦ μνημείου.  ἡ  δὲ  Μαρία ἡ
upon the door of the grave.     The but Maria the
3094          2532 3137  05  2500      2334          4226
Μαγδαληνὴ καὶ Μαρία ἡ ᾽Ιωσῆτος ἐθεώρουν ποῦ
Magdalene and Maria the of Josetus were watching where
5087        16:1 2532 2235         010
τέθειται.     Καὶ διαγενομένου τοῦ
he had been set. And having become through the
4521     3137  05  3094          2532 3137  05  02
σαββάτου Μαρία ἡ  Μαγδαληνὴ καὶ Μαρία ἡ [τοῦ]
sabbath Maria the Magdalene and Maria the of the
2385      2532 4539     59        759       2443 2064
᾽Ιακώβου καὶ Σαλώμη ἠγόρασαν ἀρώματα ἵνα ἐλθοῦσαι
Jacob    and Salome bought   spices   that having come
```

Magdalene, and Mary the mother of James the younger and of Joses, and Salome. [41]These used to follow him and provided for him when he was in Galilee; and there were many other women who had come up with him to Jerusalem.

[42]When evening had come, and since it was the day of Preparation, that is, the day before the sabbath, [43]Joseph of Arimathea, a respected member of the council, who was also himself waiting expectantly for the kingdom of God, went boldly to Pilate and asked for the body of Jesus. [44]Then Pilate wondered if he were already dead; and summoning the centurion, he asked him whether he had been dead for some time. [45]When he learned from the centurion that he was dead, he granted the body to Joseph. [46]Then Joseph[a] bought a linen cloth, and taking down the body,[b] wrapped it in the linen cloth, and laid it in a tomb that had been hewn out of the rock. He then rolled a stone against the door of the tomb. [47]Mary Magdalene and Mary the mother of Joses saw where the body[b] was laid.

CHAPTER 16

When the sabbath was over, Mary Magdalene, and Mary the mother of James, and Salome bought spices, so that they might go

[a] Gk *he*
[b] Gk *it*

and anoint him. ²And very early on the first day of the week, when the sun had risen, they went to the tomb. ³They had been saying to one another, "Who will roll away the stone for us from the entrance to the tomb?" ⁴When they looked up, they saw that the stone, which was very large, had already been rolled back. ⁵As they entered the tomb, they saw a young man, dressed in a white robe, sitting on the right side; and they were alarmed. ⁶But he said to them, "Do not be alarmed; you are looking for Jesus of Nazareth, who was crucified. He has been raised; he is not here. Look, there is the place they laid him. ⁷But go, tell his disciples and Peter that he is going ahead of you to Galilee; there you will see him, just as he told you." ⁸So they went out and fled from the tomb, for terror and amazement had seized them; and they said nothing to anyone, for they were afraid.ᵃ

THE SHORTER ENDING OF MARK

[[And all that had been commanded them they told briefly to those around Peter. And afterward Jesus himself sent out through them, from east to west, the sacred and imperishable proclamation of eternal salvation.ᵇ]]

THE LONGER ENDING OF MARK

9[[Now after he rose early on the first day of the week, he appeared first to Mary Magdalene, from whom he had cast out seven demons. ¹⁰She went out

---

```
218                    846      2  2532 3029 4404      07
ἀλείψωσιν       αὐτόν.    καὶ λίαν πρωῒ    τῇ
they might smear him.      And  very morning in the
1520 022     4521   2064        1909 012 3419
μιᾷ  τῶν   σαββάτων ἔρχονται ἐπὶ τὸ μνημεῖον
one of the sabbaths they come on the grave
393              02  2246   3  2532 3004          4314
ἀνατείλαντος τοῦ ἡλίου.   καὶ  ἔλεγον      πρὸς
having arisen the sun.    And they were saying toward
1438        5101 617         1473 04 3037 1537
ἑαυτάς·  τίς ἀποκυλίσει ἡμῖν τὸν λίθον ἐκ
themselves; who will roll off to us the stone from
06  2374 010   3419         2532 308
τῆς θύρας τοῦ  μνημείου;  4 καὶ ἀναβλέψασαι
the door of the grave?     And having looked up
2334        3754 617            01  3037   1510
θεωροῦσιν ὅτι ἀποκεκύλισται ὁ λίθος· ἦν
they watch that has been rolled off the stone; it was
1063 3173 4970    5  2532 1525        ·1519 012
γὰρ μέγας σφόδρα.  Καὶ εἰσελθοῦσαι εἰς τὸ
for great exceeding.  And having gone into into the
3419    3708   3495      2521     1722 023  1188
μνημεῖον εἶδον νεανίσκον καθήμενον ἐν τοῖς δεξιοῖς
grave they saw young man sitting in the right
4016              4749   3022   2532
περιβεβλημένον στολὴν λευκήν, καὶ
having thrown around long robe white, and
1568             6  01   1161 3004
ἐξεθαμβήθησαν.    ὁ  δὲ λέγει
they were greatly astonished. The one but says
846      3361 1568              2424  2212
αὐταῖς· μὴ ἐκθαμβεῖσθε· Ἰησοῦν ζητεῖτε
to them, not be greatly astonished; Jesus you seek
04  3479      04  4717
τὸν Ναζαρηνὸν τὸν ἐσταυρωμένον·
the Nazarene the one having been crucified;
1453          3756 1510 5602  2396 01 5117  3699
ἠγέρθη,     οὐκ ἔστιν ὧδε· ἴδε ὁ τόπος ὅπου
he was raised, not he is here; look the place where
5087      846   7  235 5217  3004  015   3101
ἔθηκαν αὐτόν.   ἀλλὰ ὑπάγετε εἴπατε τοῖς μαθηταῖς
they set him.   But go off say to the learners
846    2532 03       4074  3754 4254        1473
αὐτοῦ καὶ τῷ  Πέτρῳ ὅτι προάγει ὑμᾶς
of him also to the Peter, (") he leads before you
1519 08 1056       1563 846  3708        2531
εἰς τὴν Γαλιλαίαν· ἐκεῖ αὐτὸν ὄψεσθε, καθὼς
into the Galilee;  there him you will see, just as
3004  1473    8  2532 1831          5343   575  010
εἶπεν ὑμῖν.   καὶ ἐξελθοῦσαι ἔφυγον ἀπὸ τοῦ
he said to you. And having gone out they fled from the
3419   2192 1063 846  5156    2532 1611
μνημείου, εἶχεν γὰρ αὐτὰς τρόμος καὶ ἔκστασις·
grave,  had for them trembling and amazement;
2532 3762  3762   3004     5399         1063
καὶ οὐδενὶ οὐδὲν εἶπαν· ἐφοβοῦντο γάρ.
and to no one nothing they said; they were afraid for.

9  450           1161 4404      4413 4521
Ἀναστὰς    δὲ πρωῒ  πρώτη σαββάτου
Having stood up but in morning first of sabbath
5316    4413 3137    07 3094      3844 3739
ἐφάνη πρῶτον Μαρίᾳ τῇ Μαγδαληνῇ, παρ᾽ ἧς
he shone first to Maria the Magdalene, from whom
1544        2033 1140    10  1565    4198
ἐκβεβλήκει ἑπτὰ δαιμόνια.  ἐκείνη πορευθεῖσα
he had thrown seven demons.  That one having
out                                traveled
```

ᵃ Some of the most ancient authorities bring the book to a close at the end of verse 8. One authority concludes the book with the shorter ending; others include the shorter ending and then continue with verses 9-20. In most authorities verses 9-20 follow immediately after verse 8, though in some of these authorities the passage is marked as being doubtful.

ᵇ Other ancient authorities add Amen

518	015	3326	846	1096	3996	2532
ἀπήγγειλεν	τοῖς	μετ'	αὐτοῦ	γενομένοις	πενθοῦσι	καὶ
told	to the	with	him	ones having become	mourning	and

2799		2548	191	3754	2198
κλαίουσιν·	**11** κἀκεῖνοι	ἀκούσαντες	ὅτι	ζῇ	
crying;	and those	having heard	that	he lives	

2532	2300	5259	846	569		3326
καὶ	ἐθεάθη	ὑπ'	αὐτῆς	ἠπίστησαν.	**12**	Μετὰ
and	he was watched	by	her	they trusted not.		After

1161	3778	1417	1537	846	4043	5319
δὲ	ταῦτα	δυσὶν	ἐξ	αὐτῶν	περιπατοῦσιν	ἐφανερώθη
but	these	to two	out of	them	walking around	he was demonstrated

1722	2087	3444	4198	1519	68		2548
ἐν	ἑτέρᾳ	μορφῇ	πορευομένοις	εἰς	ἀγρόν·	**13**	κἀκεῖνοι
in	other	form	traveling	in	field;		and those

565	518	015	3062
ἀπελθόντες	ἀπήγγειλαν	τοῖς	λοιποῖς·
having gone off	told	to the ones	remaining;

3761	1565	4100		5306	1161
οὐδὲ	ἐκείνοις	ἐπίστευσαν.	**14**	Ὕστερον	[δὲ]
but not	to those	they trusted.		Later	but

345	846	015	1733	5319	2532
ἀνακειμένοις	αὐτοῖς	τοῖς	ἔνδεκα	ἐφανερώθη	καὶ
to the ones reclining at meal	to them	to the	eleven	he was demonstrated	and

3679	08	570	846	2532	4641
ὠνείδισεν	τὴν	ἀπιστίαν	αὐτῶν	καὶ	σκληροκαρδίαν
he reviled	the	untrust	of them	and	hard heart

3754	015	2300	846	1453
ὅτι	τοῖς	θεασαμένοις	αὐτὸν	ἐγηγερμένον
that	to the ones	having watched	him	having been raised

3756	4100		2532	3004	846
οὐκ	ἐπίστευσαν.	**15**	καὶ	εἶπεν	αὐτοῖς·
not	they trusted.		And	he said	to them;

4198	1519	04	2889	537	2784	012
πορευθέντες	εἰς	τὸν	κόσμον	ἅπαντα	κηρύξατε	τὸ
having traveled	into	the	world	all	announce	the

2098	3956	07	2937		01	4100
εὐαγγέλιον	πάσῃ	τῇ	κτίσει.	**16** ὁ		πιστεύσας
good message	to all	the	creation.		The one	having trusted

2532	907	4982	01	1161	569
καὶ	βαπτισθεὶς	σωθήσεται,	ὁ	δὲ	ἀπιστήσας
and	having been immersed	will be delivered,	the one	but	having not trusted

2632		4592	1161	015
κατακριθήσεται.	**17**	σημεῖα	δὲ	τοῖς
will be condemned.		Signs	but	to the ones

4100	3778	3877	1722	011
πιστεύσασιν	ταῦτα	παρακολουθήσει·	ἐν	τῷ
having trusted	these	will follow along;	in	the

3686	1473	1140	1544	1100
ὀνόματί	μου	δαιμόνια	ἐκβαλοῦσιν,	γλώσσαις
name	of me	demons	they will throw out,	in tongues

2980	2537		2532	1722	019	5495
λαλήσουσιν	καιναῖς,	**18**	καὶ	ἐν	ταῖς	χερσὶν
they will speak	new things,		and	in	the	hands

3789	142	2579	2286	5100
ὄφεις	ἀροῦσιν	κἂν	θανάσιμόν	τι
snakes	they will lift up	and if	deadly	some

4095	3756	3361	846	984	1909
πίωσιν	οὐ	μὴ	αὐτοὺς	βλάψῃ,	ἐπὶ
might drink	not	not	them	it might hurt,	on

732	5495	2007	2532	2573
ἀρρώστους	χεῖρας	ἐπιθήσουσιν	καὶ	καλῶς
feeble ones	hands	they will set on	and	well

and told those who had been with him, while they were mourning and weeping. [11]But when they heard that he was alive and had been seen by her, they would not believe it.

[12]After this he appeared in another form to two of them, as they were walking into the country. [13]And they went back and told the rest, but they did not believe them.

[14]Later he appeared to the eleven themselves as they were sitting at the table; and he upbraided them for their lack of faith and stubbornness, because they had not believed those who saw him after he had risen.[a] [15]And he said to them, "Go into all the world and proclaim the good news[b] to the whole creation. [16]The one who believes and is baptized will be saved; but the one who does not believe will be condemned. [17]And these signs will accompany those who believe: by using my name they will cast out demons; they will speak in new tongues; [18]they will pick up snakes in their hands,[c] and if they drink any deadly thing, it will not hurt them; they will lay their hands on the sick, and they will recover."

a Other ancient authorities add, in whole or in part, And they excused themselves, saying, "This age of lawlessness and unbelief is under Satan, who does not allow the truth and power of God to prevail over the unclean things of the spirits. Therefore reveal your righteousness now"—thus they spoke to Christ. And Christ replied to them, "The term of years of Satan's power has been fulfilled, but other terrible things draw near. And for those who have sinned I was handed over to death, that they may return to the truth and sin no more, that they may inherit the spiritual and imperishable glory of righteousness that is in heaven."

b Or gospel

c Other ancient authorities lack in their hands

19 So then the Lord Jesus, after he had spoken to them, was taken up into heaven and sat down at the right hand of God. 20 And they went out and proclaimed the good news everywhere, while the Lord worked with them and confirmed the message by the signs that accompanied it.[a]]]

[a] Other ancient authorities add *Amen*

```
2192                    01   3303    3767 2962      2424    3326
ἕξουσιν.        19  'Ο  μὲν   οὖν  κύριος 'Ιησοῦς μετὰ
they will have.    The indeed then Master  Jesus   after
012 2980        846   353                1519 04   3772    2532
τὸ λαλῆσαι    αὐτοῖς ἀνελήμφθη          εἰς  τὸν οὐρανὸν καὶ
the to speak to them  was taken up   to    the heaven    and
2523    1537 1188   02       2316   20 1565        1161
ἐκάθισεν ἐκ  δεξιῶν τοῦ      θεοῦ.     ἐκεῖνοι δὲ
he sat    from right of the God.      Those     but
1831          2784        3837       02       2962
ἐξελθόντες   ἐκήρυξαν πανταχοῦ,  τοῦ      κυρίου
having gone out announced all places, of the Master
4903            2532 04  3056   950        1223
συνεργοῦντος    καὶ τὸν λόγον βεβαιοῦντος διὰ
working together and the word  confirming  through
022 1872             4592
τῶν ἐπακολουθούντων σημείων.
the following on     signs.
```

```
3956 1161 024 3853                              015
Πάντα δὲ  τὰ παρηγγελμένα                       τοῖς
All   but the things having been commanded to the ones
4012       04  4074   4935       1804
περὶ       τὸν Πέτρον συντόμως ἐξήγγειλαν.
concerning the Peter  concisely they announced out.
3326   1161 3778   2532 846      01   2424  575
Μετὰ  δὲ  ταῦτα καὶ  αὐτὸς ὁ 'Ιησοῦς ἀπὸ
After but these also himself the Jesus  from
395         2532 891  1421a   1821           1223
ἀνατολῆς καὶ  ἄχρι δύσεως ἐξαπέστειλεν    δι'
east      and until west   he delegated out through
846    012 2413   2532 862        2782
αὐτῶν τὸ ἱερὸν καὶ  ἄφθαρτον    κήρυγμα
them  the sacred and incorruptible announcement
06    166     4991       281
τῆς   αἰωνίου σωτηρίας.  ἀμήν.
of the eternal deliverance. Amen.
```

LUKE

CHAPTER 1

Since many have
undertaken to set down an
orderly account of the events
that have been fulfilled
among us, [2]just as they were
handed on to us by those
who from the beginning
were eyewitnesses and
servants of the word, [3]I too
decided, after investigating
everything carefully from
the very first,[a] to write an
orderly account for you,
most excellent Theophilus,
[4]so that you may know the
truth concerning the things
about which you have been
instructed.

[5]In the days of King
Herod of Judea, there was
a priest named Zechariah,
who belonged to the
priestly order of Abijah.
His wife was a descendant
of Aaron, and her name
was Elizabeth. [6]Both of
them were righteous before
God, living blamelessly
according to all the
commandments and
regulations of the Lord.
[7]But they had no children,
because Elizabeth was
barren, and both were
getting on in years.

[8]Once when he was
serving as priest before
God and his section was on
duty, [9]he was chosen by lot,
according to the custom of
the priesthood, to enter the
sanctuary of the Lord and
offer incense. [10]Now at the
time of the incense offering,
the whole assembly of the
people was praying outside.

---

[a] Or for a long time

1:1
1895		4183	2021		392
Ἐπειδήπερ		πολλοὶ	ἐπεχείρησαν		ἀνατάξασθαι
Since indeed		many	set hand on		to set up in order

1335	4012	022	4135		1722	1473
διήγησιν	περὶ	τῶν	πεπληροφορημένων		ἐν	ἡμῖν
narrative	about	the	having been fully persuaded		in	us

4229		2531	3860	1473	013	575	746
πραγμάτων,	**2**	καθὼς	παρέδοσαν	ἡμῖν	οἱ	ἀπ'	ἀρχῆς
practices,		just as	gave over	to us	the	from	beginning

845		2532	5257	1096		02
αὐτόπται		καὶ	ὑπηρέται	γενόμενοι		τοῦ
eye witnesses	and	assistants	having become		of the

3056		1380	2504	3877		509
λόγου,	**3**	ἔδοξε	κἀμοὶ	παρηκολουθηκότι		ἄνωθεν
word,		it was also	to me	having followed		from above
		thought		along		

3956	199		2517	1473	1125		2903
πᾶσιν	ἀκριβῶς		καθεξῆς	σοι	γράψαι,		κράτιστε
all	accurately	in order	to you	to write,		most strong

2321		2443	1921	4012	3739	2727	3056
Θεόφιλε,	**4**	ἵνα	ἐπιγνῷς	περὶ	ὧν	κατηχήθης	λόγων
Theophilus,		that	you might perceive	about	which	you were instructed	words

08	803		1096	1722	019	2250	2264
τὴν	ἀσφάλειαν.	**5**	Ἐγένετο	ἐν	ταῖς	ἡμέραις	Ἡρῴδου
the	security.		It became	in	the	days	of Herod

935		06	2449	2409	5100	3686	2197
βασιλέως	τῆς		Ἰουδαίας	ἱερεύς	τις	ὀνόματι	Ζαχαρίας
king	of the		Judea	priest	some	in name	Zacharias

1537	2183		7	2532	1135	846	1537	018
ἐξ	ἐφημερίας	Ἀβιά,		καὶ	γυνὴ	αὐτῷ	ἐκ	τῶν
from	division	Abia,	and	woman	to him	from	the

2364		2		2532	09	3686	846	1665
θυγατέρων	Ἀαρὼν		καὶ	τὸ	ὄνομα	αὐτῆς	Ἐλισάβετ.
daughters	of Aaron	and	the	name	of her	Elisabet.

1510	1161	1342	297		1726		02	2316
6 ἦσαν	δὲ	δίκαιοι	ἀμφότεροι	ἐναντίον		τοῦ	θεοῦ,
Were	but	right	both	in presence		of the	God,

4198		1722	3956	019	1785	2532	1345
πορευόμενοι	ἐν	πάσαις	ταῖς	ἐντολαῖς	καί	δικαιώμασιν
traveling	in	all	the	commands	and	right acts

02	2962	273		2532	3756	1510	846
τοῦ	κυρίου	ἄμεμπτοι.	**7**	καὶ	οὐκ	ἦν	αὐτοῖς
of the	Master	faultless.		And	not	there was	to them

5043	2530		1510	05	1665	4723	2532
τέκνον,	καθότι		ἦν	ἡ	Ἐλισάβετ	στεῖρα,	καὶ
child,	according that	was	the	Elisabet	sterile,	and

297		4260		1722	019	2250	846
ἀμφότεροι	προβεβηκότες		ἐν	ταῖς	ἡμέραις	αὐτῶν
both	+having gone before	in	the	days	of them

1510		1096	1161	1722	011	2407	846
ἦσαν.	**8**	Ἐγένετο	δὲ	ἐν	τῷ	ἱερατεύειν	αὐτὸν
were+.		It became	but	in	the	to serve as priest	him

1722	07	5010	06	2183	846	1725
ἐν	τῇ	τάξει	τῆς	ἐφημερίας	αὐτοῦ	ἔναντι
in	the	rank	of the	division	of him	in presence

02	2316		2596	012	1485	06	2405
τοῦ	θεοῦ,	**9**	κατὰ	τὸ	ἔθος	τῆς	ἱερατείας
of the	God,		by	the	custom	of the	priesthood

2975		010	2370		1525		1519
ἔλαχε		τοῦ	θυμιᾶσαι		εἰσελθὼν		εἰς
he obtained	the	to burn incense		having gone into		into

04	3485	02	2962		2532	3956	09	4128
τὸν	ναὸν	τοῦ	κυρίου,	**10**	καὶ	πᾶν	τὸ	πλῆθος
the	temple	of the	Master,		and	all	the	quantity

1510	02		2992	4336		1854	07	5610
ἦν	τοῦ		λαοῦ	προσευχόμενον		ἔξω	τῇ	ὥρᾳ
were+	of the		people	+praying		outside	in	the hour

```
010        2368            3708      1161  846      32
τοῦ    θυμιάματος.  11  ὤφθη   δὲ   αὐτῷ   ἄγγελος
of the  incense.        Was seen but  to him  messenger
2962      2476    1537  1188     010   2379          010
κυρίου  ἑστὼς  ἐκ  δεξιῶν τοῦ  θυσιαστηρίου τοῦ
of Master having  from  right  of the  place of    of the
         stood                         sacrifice
2368          12  2532 5015          2197       3708
θυμιάματος.      καὶ  ἐταράχθη   Ζαχαρίας ἰδὼν
incense.         And  was troubled Zacharias having seen
2532  5401    1968      1909 846       3004   1161  4314
καὶ  φόβος ἐπέπεσεν ἐπ᾽  αὐτόν.  13  εἶπεν  δὲ   πρὸς
and  fear  fell on   on   him.       Said  but  to
846    01   32        3361  5399      2197        1360
αὐτὸν ὁ  ἄγγελος·  μὴ  φοβοῦ, Ζαχαρία,  διότι
him   the messenger; not  fear,  Zacharias, because
1522           05  1162    1473     2532 05  1135    1473
εἰσηκούσθη ἡ  δέησίς  σου,  καὶ ἡ  γυνή  σου
was heard   the request of you, and  the woman of you
1665        1080             5207 1473 2532 2564
Ἐλισάβετ γεννήσει       υἱόν σοι  καὶ καλέσεις
Elisabet  will give birth son to you and you will call
012 3686    846    2491     14  2532 1510          5479
τὸ ὄνομα αὐτοῦ Ἰωάννην.    καὶ ἔσται        χαρά
the name  of him John.        And he will be  joy
1473    2532 20         2532 4183  1909 07  1078
σοι  καὶ ἀγαλλίασις καὶ πολλοὶ ἐπὶ τῇ γενέσει
to you and gladness   and  many   on  the origin
846    5463       15  1510          1063 3173   1799
αὐτοῦ χαρήσονται.    ἔσται       γὰρ μέγας ἐνώπιον
of him will rejoice. He will be for  great  before
02    2962     2532 3631  2532 4608        3756 3361
[τοῦ] κυρίου, καὶ οἶνον καὶ σίκερα   οὐ  μὴ
the   Master, and  wine  and  intoxicant not  not
4095           2532 4151    40    4092
πίῃ,          καὶ πνεύματος ἁγίου πλησθήσεται
he might drink, and of spirit  holy  he will be    filled
2089 1537 2836     3384      846     16  2532 4183
ἔτι ἐκ κοιλίας μητρὸς αὐτοῦ,    καὶ πολλοὺς
still from stomach of mother of him,  and  many
014   5207 2474  1994        1909 2962   04
τῶν υἱῶν Ἰσραὴλ ἐπιστρέψει ἐπὶ κύριον τὸν
of the sons Israel he will return on  Master the
2316 846         17  2532 846       4281        1799
θεὸν αὐτῶν.     καὶ αὐτὸς προελεύσεται ἐνώπιον
God of them.      And himself will go before before
846    1722 4151     2532 1411    2243       1994
αὐτοῦ ἐν πνευματι καὶ δυνάμει Ἠλίου, ἐπιστρέψαι
him   in  spirit  and power   of Elijah, to return
2588     3962      1909 5043     2532 545       1722
καρδίας πατέρων ἐπὶ τέκνα   καὶ ἀπειθεῖς   ἐν
hearts  of fathers on  children and disobedient in
5428        1342      2090       2962    2992
φρονήσει δικαίων, ἑτοιμάσαι κυρίῳ λαὸν
thoughtfulness of right, to prepare to Master people
2680            18  2532 3004  2197      4314 04
κατεσκευασμένον.   καὶ εἶπεν Ζαχαρίας πρὸς τὸν
having been prepared. And said  Zacharias to  the
32        2596 5101 1097        3778    1473 1063 1510
ἄγγελον· κατὰ τί γνώσομαι τοῦτο; ἐγὼ γάρ εἰμι
messenger; by  what I will know this?  I   for  am
4246      2532 05  1135  1473 4260              1722
πρεσβύτης καὶ ἡ γυνή μου προβεβηκυῖα     ἐν
old man   and  the woman of me having gone before in
019 2250    846     19  2532 611       01
ταῖς ἡμέραις αὐτῆς.   καὶ ἀποκριθεὶς ὁ
the days     of her.    And having answered the
32       3004 846      1473 1510 1043    01
ἄγγελος εἶπεν αὐτῷ· ἐγώ εἰμι Γαβριὴλ ὁ
messenger said  to him; I    am  Gabriel the one
```

[11]Then there appeared to him an angel of the Lord, standing at the right side of the altar of incense. [12]When Zechariah saw him, he was terrified; and fear overwhelmed him. [13]But the angel said to him, "Do not be afraid, Zechariah, for your prayer has been heard. Your wife Elizabeth will bear you a son, and you will name him John. [14]You will have joy and gladness, and many will rejoice at his birth, [15]for he will be great in the sight of the Lord. He must never drink wine or strong drink; even before his birth he will be filled with the Holy Spirit. [16]He will turn many of the people of Israel to the Lord their God. [17]With the spirit and power of Elijah he will go before him, to turn the hearts of parents to their children, and the disobedient to the wisdom of the righteous, to make ready a people prepared for the Lord." [18]Zechariah said to the angel, "How will I know that this is so? For I am an old man, and my wife is getting on in years." [19]The angel replied, "I am Gabriel.

I stand in the presence of God, and I have been sent to speak to you and to bring you this good news. 20But now, because you did not believe my words, which will be fulfilled in their time, you will become mute, unable to speak, until the day these things occur."

21 Meanwhile the people were waiting for Zechariah, and wondered at his delay in the sanctuary. 22When he did come out, he could not speak to them, and they realized that he had seen a vision in the sanctuary. He kept motioning to them and remained unable to speak. 23When his time of service was ended, he went to his home.

24 After those days his wife Elizabeth conceived, and for five months she remained in seclusion. She said, 25"This is what the Lord has done for me when he looked favorably on me and took away the disgrace I have endured among my people."

26 In the sixth month the angel Gabriel was sent by God to a town in Galilee called Nazareth, 27to a virgin engaged to a man whose name was Joseph, of the house

	3936		1799	02 2316 2532
παρεστηκὼς		ἐνώπιον	τοῦ θεοῦ καὶ
having stood		along before	the God and

649		2980	4314 1473 2532
ἀπεστάλην	λαλῆσαι	πρὸς σὲ	καὶ
I was delegated	to speak to	you	and

2097		1473	3778	**20**	2532 2400
εὐαγγελίσασθαί	σοι	ταῦτα·		καὶ ἰδοὺ
to tell good message	to you	these;		and look

1510		4623		2532 3361 1410		2980
ἔσῃ	σιωπῶν		καὶ μὴ δυνάμενος	λαλῆσαι
you will be+	+being silent	and not being able	to speak

891	3739	2250	1096		3778	473	3739
ἄχρι	ἧς	ἡμέρας	γένηται	ταῦτα,	ἀνθ'	ὧν
until	that	day	might become	these,	against	which

3756 4100		015	3056	1473	3748
οὐκ ἐπίστευσας	τοῖς	λόγοις	μου,	οἵτινες
not you trusted	in the	words	of me,	which

4137		1519 04	2540	846		2532 1510 01
πληρωθήσονται	εἰς	τὸν καιρὸν	αὐτῶν.	**21**	Καὶ ἦν ὁ
will be filled	in	the season	of them.		And was the

2992	4328	04 2197	2532 2296	1722 011
λαὸς	προσδοκῶν	τὸν Ζαχαρίαν	καὶ ἐθαύμαζον	ἐν τῷ
people	waiting	the Zacharias	and marveled	in the
	expectantly			

5549	1722 03	3485	846		1831
χρονίζειν	ἐν τῷ	ναῷ	αὐτόν.	**22**	ἐξελθὼν
to spend time	in the	temple	him.		Having gone out

1161 3756 1410	2980	846	2532 1921	3754
δὲ οὐκ ἐδύνατο	λαλῆσαι	αὐτοῖς,	καὶ ἐπέγνωσαν	ὅτι
but not he was	to speak	to them,	and they	that
able			perceived	

3701	3708		1722 03	3485	2532 846	1510
ὀπτασίαν	ἑώρακεν	ἐν	τῷ	ναῷ·	καὶ αὐτὸς	ἦν
vision	he has seen	in	the temple;	and himself	was

1269	846	2532 1265		2974	2532
διανεύων	αὐτοῖς	καὶ διέμενεν	κωφός.	**23**	καὶ
nodding	to them	and he was staying	deaf.		And
thoroughly		through			

1096	5613 4092	017 2250	06	3009
ἐγένετο	ὡς ἐπλήσθησαν	αἱ ἡμέραι	τῆς	λειτουργίας
it became	as were filled	the days	of the	service

846	565	1519 04 3624 846	**24**	3326 1161
αὐτοῦ,	ἀπῆλθεν	εἰς τὸν οἶκον αὐτοῦ.		Μετὰ δὲ
of him,	he went off	into the house of him.		After but

3778	020 2250	4815	1665	05	1135	846
ταύτας	τὰς ἡμέρας	συνέλαβεν	Ἐλισάβετ	ἡ	γυνὴ	αὐτοῦ
these	the days	conceived	Elisabet	the	woman of	him

2532 4032		1438	3376 4002 3004
καὶ περιέκρυβεν	ἑαυτὴν	μῆνας πέντε λέγουσα
and she hid	around herself	months five saying,

25	3754 3779	1473 4160	2962 1722 2250	3739
	ὅτι οὕτως	μοι πεποίηκεν	κύριος ἐν ἡμέραις	αἷς
	(") thusly	to me has done	master in days	in which

2186a	851	3681	1473 1722 444
ἐπεῖδεν	ἀφελεῖν	ὄνειδός μου	ἐν ἀνθρώποις.
he looked on	to lift off	reproach of me	in men.

26	1722 1161 03	3376 01 1623	649	01
	Ἐν δὲ τῷ	μηνὶ τῷ ἕκτῳ	ἀπεστάλη	ὁ
	In but in the	month the sixth	was delegated	the

32	1043	575 02 2316 1519 4172	06
ἄγγελος	Γαβριὴλ	ἀπὸ τοῦ θεοῦ εἰς πόλιν	τῆς
messenger	Gabriel	from the God into city	of the

1056	3739	3686 3478	**27**	4314 3933
Γαλιλαίας	ᾗ	ὄνομα Ναζαρὲθ		πρὸς παρθένον
Galilee	in which	name Nazareth		to virgin

3423	435	3739	3686	2501	1537 3624
ἐμνηστευμένην	ἀνδρὶ	ᾧ	ὄνομα	Ἰωσὴφ	ἐξ οἴκου
having been	to man	of whom	name	Joseph	from house
engaged					

```
1160a 2532 09   3686   06      3933       3137a   28  2532
Δαυὶδ καὶ  τὸ  ὄνομα τῆς    παρθένου Μαριάμ.     καὶ
David and the name  of the virgin    Mariam.      And
1525           4314 846   3004      5463
εἰσελθὼν     πρὸς αὐτὴν εἶπεν·   χαῖρε,
having gone in to  her    he said;  rejoice,
5487                 01   2962    3326  1473  29  05
κεχαριτωμένη,       ὁ   κύριος μετὰ σοῦ.      ἡ
one having been favored, the Master with you.   The one
1161 1909 03    3056 1298           2532 1260
δὲ  ἐπὶ τῷ  λόγῳ διεταράχθη  καὶ  διελογίζετο
but on  the word was troubled and  was reasoning
4217      1510  01  783        3778      2532 3004  01
ποταπὸς  εἴη  ὁ ἀσπασμὸς οὗτος.  30 καὶ  εἶπεν ὁ
what sort may be the greeting this.      And said the
32         846        3361 5399   3137a   2147      1063
ἄγγελος αὐτῇ·  μὴ φοβοῦ, Μαριάμ, εὗρες  γὰρ
messenger to her; not  fear,  Mariam, you found for
5485   3844 03 2316  31 2532 2400 4815              1722
χάριν παρὰ τῷ θεῷ.    καὶ  ἰδοὺ συλλήμψῃ          ἐν
favor from the God.    And  look you will conceive in
1064 2532 5088          5207 2532 2564           012
γαστρὶ καὶ  τέξῃ       υἱὸν καὶ  καλέσεις τὸ
womb  and  will give birth son  and  will call the
3686 846   2424    32 3778   1510    3173  2532
ὄνομα αὐτοῦ Ἰησοῦν.   οὗτος ἔσται  μέγας καὶ
name of him Jesus.      This one will be great and
5207 5310       2564          2532 1325       846
υἱὸς ὑψίστου κληθήσεται καὶ  δώσει    αὐτῷ
son of highest will be called and  will give to him
2962   01 2316 04 2362   1160a 02   3962   846
κύριος ὁ  θεὸς τὸν θρόνον Δαυὶδ τοῦ  πατρὸς αὐτοῦ,
Master the God the throne David of the father of him,
33 2532 936          1909 04 3624    2384  1519
   καὶ βασιλεύσει ἐπὶ τὸν οἶκον Ἰακὼβ εἰς
   and he will be king on  the house Jacob into
016 165    2532 06 932        846      3756 1510
τοὺς αἰῶνας καὶ τῆς βασιλείας αὐτοῦ οὐκ ἔσται
the  ages  and the kingdom  of him not  will be
5056    34 3004 1161 3137a   4314 04  32
τέλος.    εἶπεν δὲ  Μαριὰμ πρὸς τὸν ἄγγελον·
completion. Said but Mariam to  the messenger;
4459 1510   3778   1893   435    3756 1097   35 2532
πῶς ἔσται τοῦτο, ἐπεὶ ἄνδρα οὐ γινωσκω;   καὶ
how will be this, since man  not I know?    And
611           01 32        3004 846       4151
ἀποκριθεὶς ὁ ἄγγελος εἶπεν αὐτῇ· πνεῦμα
having answered the messenger said to her; spirit
40       1904        1909 1473 2532 1411     5310
ἅγιον ἐπελεύσεται ἐπὶ σὲ  καὶ δύναμις ὑψίστου
holy will come on on you and power  of highest
1982       1473 1352      2532 09  1080        40
ἐπισκιάσει σοι· διὸ  καὶ  τὸ γεννώμενον ἅγιον
will over you; therefore also the one being born holy
shadow
2564          5207 2316 36 2532 2400  1665    05
κληθήσεται υἱὸς θεοῦ.  καὶ  ἰδοὺ Ἐλισάβετ ἡ
will be called son of God.  And  look Elisabet the
4773a    1473  2532 846  4815         5207 1722
συγγενίς σου  καὶ  αὐτὴ συνείληφεν υἱὸν ἐν
relative of you also she has conceived son  in
1094  846    2532 3778    3376   1623  1510  846    07
γήρει αὐτῆς καὶ  οὗτος μὴν ἔκτος ἐστὶν αὐτῇ τῇ
old age of her and this month sixth is  to her the
2564         4723      37 3754 3756 101
καλουμένη στείρα·    ὅτι  οὐκ ἀδυνατήσει
one being called sterile; because not will be unable
3844 02  2316 3956 4487  38 3004 1161 3137a  2400
παρὰ τοῦ θεοῦ πᾶν ῥῆμα.   εἶπεν δὲ  Μαριάμ· ἰδοὺ
from the God all word.     Said but Mariam; look
```

of David. The virgin's name was Mary. [28]And he came to her and said, "Greetings, favored one! The Lord is with you."[a] [29]But she was much perplexed by his words and pondered what sort of greeting this might be. [30]The angel said to her, "Do not be afraid, Mary, for you have found favor with God. [31]And now, you will conceive in your womb and bear a son, and you will name him Jesus. [32]He will be great, and will be called the Son of the Most High, and the Lord God will give to him the throne of his ancestor David. [33]He will reign over the house of Jacob forever, and of his kingdom there will be no end." [34]Mary said to the angel, "How can this be, since I am a virgin?"[b] [35]The angel said to her, "The Holy Spirit will come upon you, and the power of the Most High will overshadow you; therefore the child to be born[c] will be holy; he will be called Son of God. [36]And now, your relative Elizabeth in her old age has also conceived a son; and this is the sixth month for her who was said to be barren. [37]For nothing will be impossible with God." [38]Then Mary said, "Here am I,

a Other ancient authorities add *Blessed are you among women*
b Gk *I do not know a man*
c Other ancient authorities add *of you*

the servant of the Lord; let
it be with me according to
your word." Then the angel
departed from her.

39 In those days Mary
set out and went with haste
to a Judean town in the
hill country, 40where she
entered the house of
Zechariah and greeted
Elizabeth. 41When
Elizabeth heard Mary's
greeting, the child leaped in
her womb. And Elizabeth
was filled with the Holy
Spirit 42and exclaimed
with a loud cry, "Blessed
are you among women, and
blessed is the fruit of your
womb. 43And why has this
happened to me, that the
mother of my Lord comes
to me? 44For as soon as I
heard the sound of your
greeting, the child in my
womb leaped for joy. 45And
blessed is she who believed
that there would be[a] a
fulfillment of what was
spoken to her by the Lord."

46 And Mary[b] said,
"My soul magnifies the
Lord,
47 and my spirit rejoices in
God my Savior,
48 for he has looked with
favor on the lowliness
of his servant.
Surely, from now on all
generations will call
me blessed;

[a] Or believed, for there will be
[b] Other ancient authorities read
Elizabeth

```
05   1399   2962          1096           1473  2596  012 4487
ἡ   δούλη κυρίου·  γένοιτό       μοι   κατὰ  τὸ  ῥῆμά
the  slave of Master; may it become to me  by   the word
1473    2532 565      575 846    01 32          450
σου.   καὶ ἀπῆλθεν ἀπ' αὐτῆς ὁ ἄγγελος.  39 Ἀναστᾶσα
of you. And went   from her  the messenger.   Having
             off                                 stood up
1161 3137a 1722 019  2250        3778        4198      1519 08
δὲ  Μαριὰμ ἐν ταῖς ἡμέραις ταύταις ἐπορεύθη εἰς τὴν
but  Mariam in the  days   these   traveled into the
3714          3326 4710      1519 4172   2455   40 2532
ὀρεινὴν    μετὰ σπουδῆς εἰς πόλιν Ἰούδα,   καὶ
hill country with diligence into city Judas,  and
1525      1519 04  3624  2197       2532 782   08
εἰσῆλθεν εἰς τὸν οἶκον Ζαχαρίου καὶ ἠσπάσατο τὴν
went into into the house of Zacharias and greeted  the
1665        2532 1096      5613 191    04 783
Ἐλισάβετ. 41 καὶ ἐγένετο ὡς  ἤκουσεν τὸν ἀσπασμόν
Elisabet.   And  it became as  heard  the greeting
06       3137  05 1665       4640       09  1025  1722
τῆς Μαρίας ἡ Ἐλισάβετ, ἐσκίρτησεν τὸ βρέφος ἐν
of the Maria the Elisabet, skipped   the infant  in
07  2836    846     2532 4092       4151     40   05
τῇ κοιλίᾳ αὐτῆς, καὶ ἐπλήσθη πνεύματος ἁγίου ἡ
the stomach of her, and  was filled of spirit holy the
1665       2532 400         2906     3173 2532
Ἐλισάβετ, 42 καὶ ἀνεφώνησεν κραυγῇ μεγάλῃ καὶ
Elisabet,   and she sounded out in shout great  and
3004    2127               1473 1722 1135     2532
εἶπεν· εὐλογημένη       σὺ ἐν γυναιξὶν καὶ
said;  having been well spoken of you in women  and
2127        01  2590   06   2836    1473  43 2532
εὐλογημένος ὁ καρπὸς τῆς κοιλίας σου.   καὶ
having been the fruit  of the stomach of you. And
well spoken of
4159   1473  3778  2443 2064 05  3384  02  2962 1473
πόθεν μοι τοῦτο ἵνα ἔλθῃ ἡ μήτηρ τοῦ κυρίου μου
from  to me this that might the mother of Master of
where              come       the          me
4314 1473 44 2400 1063 5613 1096  05  5456  02
πρὸς ἐμέ; ἰδοὺ γὰρ ὡς ἐγένετο ἡ φωνὴ τοῦ
to me?    Look for as  became the sound of the
783        1473    1519 024 3775 1473  4640     1722
ἀσπασμοῦ σου εἰς τὰ ὦτά μου, ἐσκίρτησεν ἐν
greeting of you in the ears of me, skipped   in
20     09  1025  1722 07 2836  1473 45 2532
ἀγαλλιάσει τὸ βρέφος ἐν τῇ κοιλίᾳ μου.  καὶ
gladness the infant in  the stomach of me. And
3107    05 4100     3754 1510 5050     023
μακαρία ἡ πιστεύσασα ὅτι ἔσται τελείωσις τοῖς
fortunate the one having that there completion to the
           trusted       will be
2980             846    3844 2962   46 2532
λελαλημένοις   αὐτῇ παρὰ κυρίου.   Καὶ
things having been spoken to her from Master.  And
3004 3137a  3170      05 5590 1473 04 2962
εἶπεν Μαριάμ· Μεγαλύνει ἡ ψυχή μου τὸν κύριον,
said Mariam, makes great the soul of me the Master,
47 2532 21      09  4151    1473 1909 03  2316 03
καὶ ἠγαλλίασεν τὸ πνεῦμά μου ἐπὶ τῷ θεῷ τῷ
and was glad  the spirit of me on  the God  the
4990   1473 48 3754  1914      1909 08  5014
σωτῆρί μου,  ὅτι ἐπέβλεψεν ἐπὶ τὴν ταπείνωσιν
deliverer of me, that he looked on on the humility
06   1399  846    2400 1063 575 010 3568
τῆς δούλης αὐτοῦ. ἰδοὺ γὰρ ἀπὸ τοῦ νῦν
of the slave of him. Look for from the now
```

3106	1473	3956	017	1074		3754	4160
μακαριοῦσίν	με	πᾶσαι	αἱ	γενεαί,	**49**	ὅτι	ἐποίησέν
will call fortunate	me	all	the	generations,		that	made

1473	3173	01	1415		2532	40	09	3686
μοι	μεγάλα	ὁ	δυνατός.		καὶ	ἅγιον	τὸ	ὄνομα
me	great	the	power one.		And	holy	the	name

846		2532	09	1656	846		1519	1074		2532
αὐτοῦ,	**50**	καὶ	τὸ	ἔλεος	αὐτοῦ		εἰς	γενεὰς		καὶ
of him,		and	the	mercy	of him		into	generations		and

1074	015	5399	846		4160
γενεὰς	τοῖς	φοβουμένοις	αὐτόν.	**51**	Ἐποίησεν
generations	to the	ones fearing	him.		He made

2904	1722	1023	846	1287
κράτος	ἐν	βραχίονι	αὐτοῦ,	διεσκόρπισεν
strength	in	arm	of him,	he scattered thoroughly

5244	1271	2588	846
ὑπερηφάνους	διανοίᾳ	καρδίας	αὐτῶν·
arrogant	intelligence	heart	of them;

	2507	1413	575	2362	2532
52	καθεῖλεν	δυνάστας	ἀπὸ	θρόνων	καὶ
	he lifted down	power ones	from	thrones	and

5312	5011		3983	1705
ὕψωσεν	ταπεινούς,	**53**	πεινῶντας	ἐνέπλησεν
elevated	humble ones,		ones hungering	he filled in

18	2532	4147	1821	2756
ἀγαθῶν	καὶ	πλουτοῦντας	ἐξαπέστειλεν	κενούς.
good	and	ones being rich	he delegated out	empty.

	482	2474	3816	846	3403
54	ἀντελάβετο	Ἰσραὴλ	παιδὸς	αὐτοῦ,	μνησθῆναι
	He took part	Israel	boy servant	of him,	to remember

1656		2531	2980	4314	016	3962	1473
ἐλέους,	**55**	καθὼς	ἐλάλησεν	πρὸς	τοὺς	πατέρας	ἡμῶν,
mercy,		just as	he spoke to		the	fathers	of us,

03	11	2532	011	4690	846	1519	04	165
τῷ	Ἀβραὰμ	καὶ	τῷ	σπέρματι	αὐτοῦ	εἰς	τὸν	αιωνα.
to the	Abraham	and	to the	seed	of him	into	the	age.

	3306	1161	3137a	4862	846	5613	3376	5140
56	Ἔμεινεν	δὲ	Μαριὰμ	σὺν	αὐτῇ	ὡς	μῆνας	τρεῖς,
	Stayed	but	Mariam	with	her	as	months	three,

2532	5290		1519	04	3624	846		07	1161
καὶ	ὑπέστρεψεν		εἰς	τὸν	οἶκον	αὐτῆς.	**57**	Τῇ	δὲ
and	she returned		into	the	house	of her.		To the	but

1665	4092	01	5550	010	5088	846
Ἐλισάβετ	ἐπλήσθη	ὁ	χρόνος	τοῦ	τεκεῖν	αὐτὴν
Elisabet	was filled	the	time	of the	to give birth	her

2532	1080	5207		2532	191	013	4040
καὶ	ἐγέννησεν	υἱόν.	**58**	καὶ	ἤκουσαν	οἱ	περίοικοι
and	she gave	son.		And	heard	the	households around

2532	013	4773	846	3754	3170	2962	012
καὶ	οἱ	συγγενεῖς	αὐτῆς	ὅτι	ἐμεγάλυνεν	κύριος	τὸ
and	the	relatives	of her	that	made great	Master	the

1656	846	3326	846	2532	4796	846
ἔλεος	αὐτοῦ	μετ’	αὐτῆς	καὶ	συνέχαιρον	αὐτῇ.
mercy	of him	with	her	and	they rejoiced	her. together

	2532	1096	1722	07	2250	07	3590	2064
59	Καὶ	ἐγένετο	ἐν	τῇ	ἡμέρᾳ	τῇ	ὀγδόῃ	ἦλθον
	And	it became	in	the	day	the	eighth	they came

4059	012	3813		2532	2564	846	1909	011
περιτεμεῖν	τὸ	παιδίον		καὶ	ἐκάλουν	αὐτὸ	ἐπὶ	τῷ
to circumcise	the	small child		and	called	him	on	the

3686	02	3962	846	2197		2532
ὀνόματι	τοῦ	πατρὸς	αὐτοῦ	Ζαχαρίαν.	**60**	καὶ
name	of the	father	of him	Zacharias.		And

611	05	3384	846	3004	3780	235
ἀποκριθεῖσα	ἡ	μήτηρ	αὐτοῦ	εἶπεν·	οὐχί,	ἀλλὰ
having answered	the	mother	of him	said;	not,	but

49 for the Mighty One has
  done great things
  for me,
  and holy is his name.
50 His mercy is for those
  who fear him
  from generation to
  generation.
51 He has shown strength
  with his arm;
  he has scattered the
  proud in the thoughts
  of their hearts.
52 He has brought down the
  powerful from their
  thrones,
  and lifted up the lowly;
53 he has filled the hungry
  with good things,
  and sent the rich away
  empty.
54 He has helped his servant
  Israel,
  in remembrance of his
  mercy,
55 according to the promise
  he made to our
  ancestors,
  to Abraham and to his
  descendants forever."
56 And Mary remained
with her about three
months and then returned
to her home.
57 Now the time came
for Elizabeth to give birth,
and she bore a son. 58Her
neighbors and relatives
heard that the Lord had
shown his great mercy to
her, and they rejoiced with
her.
59 On the eighth day
they came to circumcise the
child, and they were going
to name him Zechariah
after his father. 60But his
mother said, "No;

he is to be called John."
61They said to her, "None
of your relatives has this
name." 62Then they began
motioning to his father
to find out what name
he wanted to give him.
63He asked for a writing
tablet and wrote, "His
name is John." And all
of them were amazed.
64Immediately his mouth
was opened and his tongue
freed, and he began to
speak, praising God.
65Fear came over all their
neighbors, and all these
things were talked about
throughout the entire hill
country of Judea. 66All who
heard them pondered them
and said, "What then will
this child become?" For,
indeed, the hand of the
Lord was with him.

67 Then his father
Zechariah was filled with
the Holy Spirit and spoke
this prophecy:
68 "Blessed be the Lord God
    of Israel,
    for he has looked
    favorably on his
    people and redeemed
    them.
69 He has raised up a mighty
    savior[a] for us
    in the house of his
    servant David,
70 as he spoke through the
    mouth of his holy
    prophets from of old,
71 that we would be saved
    from our enemies and
    from the hand of all
    who hate us.
72 Thus he has shown the
    mercy promised to our
    ancestors,

a Gk a horn of salvation

2564   2491   2532 3004   4314 846   3754
κληθήσεται   Ἰωάννης.   61 καὶ εἰπαν   πρὸς αὐτὴν ὅτι
he will be   John.   And they said to   her,   (")
called

3762   1510   1537 06 4772   1473   3739 2564
οὐδείς ἐστιν ἐκ τῆς συγγενείας σου   ὃς καλεῖται
no one is   from the relatives of you who is called

011 3686   3778   62 1770   1161 03   3962
τῷ ὀνόματι τούτῳ.   ἐνένευον   δὲ   τῷ   πατρὶ
the name   this.   They nodded in but to the father

846   012 5101 302 2309   2564   846
αὐτοῦ τὸ τί   ἂν θέλοι   καλεῖσθαι   αὐτό.
of him the what - he may want to be called him.

63 2532 154   4093   1125   3004
κ αὶ αἰτήσας   πινακίδιον   ἔγραψεν λέγων·
And having asked little tablet he wrote   saying;

2491   1510   3686   846   2532 2296   3956
Ἰωάννης ἐστὶν ὄνομα αὐτοῦ. καὶ ἐθαύμασαν πάντες.
John   is   name of him. And marveled   all.

64 455   1161 09 4750 846   3916   2532 05
ἀνεῴχθη   δὲ   τὸ στόμα αὐτοῦ παραχρῆμα καὶ ἡ
Was opened but   the mouth of him suddenly and the

1100   846   2532 2980   2127   04
γλῶσσα αὐτοῦ, καὶ ἐλάλει   εὐλογῶν   τὸν
tongue of him, and he was speaking speaking well the

2316   2532 1096   1909 3956   5401 016
θεόν. 65 Καὶ ἐγένετο ἐπὶ πάντας φόβος τοὺς
God.   And it became on   all   fear the ones

4039   846   2532 1722 3650 07   3714
περιοικοῦντας αὐτούς, καὶ ἐν ὅλῃ τῇ ὀρεινῇ
living around them,   and in whole the hill country

06   2449   1255   3956 021 4487
τῆς   Ἰουδαίας διελαλεῖτο   πάντα τὰ ῥήματα
of the Judea   was spoken thoroughly all   the words

3778   66 2532 5087   3956   013 191   1722
ταῦτα,   καὶ ἔθεντο πάντες οἱ ἀκούσαντες ἐν
these,   and set   all   the ones having heard in

07   2588   846   3004   3101 686   09   3813
τῇ καρδίᾳ αὐτῶν λέγοντες· τί ἄρα τὸ παιδίον
the heart of them saying;   what then the small child

3778 1510   2532 1063 5495 2962   1510 3326 846
τοῦτο ἔσται; καὶ γὰρ χεὶρ κυρίου ἦν μετ' αὐτοῦ.
this will be? And for hand of Master was with him.

67 2532 2197   01 3962 846   4092   4151
Κ αὶ Ζαχαρίας ὁ πατὴρ αὐτοῦ ἐπλήσθη πνεύματος
And Zacharias the father of him was filled of spirit

40   2532 4395   3004   68 2128   2962
ἁγίου καὶ ἐπροφήτευσεν λέγων· Εὐλογητὸς   κύριος
holy and spoke before saying; well-spoken of Master

01   2316 02   2474   3754 1980   2532 4160
ὁ θεὸς τοῦ Ἰσραήλ, ὅτι ἐπεσκέψατο καὶ ἐποίησεν
the God of the Israel, that he looked on and made

3085   03 2992   846   69 2532 1453   2768
λύτρωσιν τῷ λαῷ αὐτοῦ, καὶ ἤγειρεν κέρας
ransom   the people of him, and he raised horn

4991   1473 1722 3624 1160a 3816
σωτηρίας   ἡμῖν ἐν οἴκῳ Δαυὶδ παιδὸς
of deliverance to us in   house David boy servant

846   70 2531   2980   1223 4750   014 40
αὐτοῦ,   καθὼς ἐλάλησεν διὰ στόματος τῶν ἁγίων
of him,   just as he spoke by mouth of the holy ones

575 165   4396   846   71 4991   1537
ἀπ' αἰῶνος προφητῶν αὐτοῦ,   σωτηρίαν   ἐξ
from age   of spokesmen of him, deliverance from

2190   1473 2532 1537 5495   3956   014 3404
ἐχθρῶν ἡμῶν καὶ ἐκ χειρὸς πάντων τῶν μισούντων
hostile of us and from hand of all the ones hating

1473   72 4160   1656   3326 014 3962   1473 2532
ἡμᾶς,   ποιῆσαι ἔλεος μετὰ τῶν πατέρων ἡμῶν καὶ
us,   to make mercy with the fathers of us and

3403	1242	40	846	**73**	3727	3739
μνησθῆναι	διαθήκης	ἁγίας αὐτοῦ,			ὅρκον	ὃν
to remember	agreement	holy	of him,		oath	which

3660	4314	11	04	3962	1473	010
ὤμοσεν	πρὸς	Ἀβραὰμ	τὸν πατέρα	ἡμῶν,	τοῦ
he took an oath	to	Abraham	the father	of us,	of the

1325	1473	**74**	870	1537 5495	2190
δοῦναι	ἡμῖν		ἀφόβως	ἐκ χειρὸς	ἐχθρῶν
to give	to us		fearlessly	from hand	of hostile

4506		3000	846	**75**	1722 3742
ῥυσθέντας		λατρεύειν	αὐτῷ		ἐν ὁσιότητι
having been rescued		to serve	him		in holiness

2532 1343		1799	846	3956	019	2250
καὶ δικαιοσύνῃ		ἐνώπιον	αὐτοῦ	πάσαις	ταῖς	ἡμέραις
and rightness		before	him	in all	the	days

1473	**76**	2532 1473	1161 3813		4396
ἡμῶν.		Καὶ σὺ	δὲ, παιδίον,		προφήτης
of us.		And you	but, small child,		spokesman

5310	2564	4313	1063 1799	2962
ὑψίστου	κληθήσῃ·	προπορεύσῃ	γὰρ ἐνώπιον	κυρίου
of highest	will be called;	will travel	for before	Master

2090	3598 846	**77**	010	1325	1108
ἑτοιμάσαι	ὁδοὺς αὐτοῦ,		τοῦ	δοῦναι	γνῶσιν
to prepare	ways of him,		of the	to give	knowledge

4991	03	2992	846	1722 859
σωτηρίας	τῷ	λαῷ	αὐτοῦ	ἐν ἀφέσει
of deliverance	to the	people	of him	in sending off

266	846	**78**	1223	4698	1656	2316
ἁμαρτιῶν	αὐτῶν,		διὰ	σπλάγχνα	ἐλέους	θεοῦ
of sins	of them,		through	affections	of mercy	of God

1473	1722 3739	1980		1473	395	1537
ἡμῶν,	ἐν οἷς	ἐπισκέψεται		ἡμᾶς	ἀνατολὴ	ἐξ
of us,	in which	he will look on		us	east	from

5311	**79**	2014	015	1722 4655	2532 4639
ὕψους,		ἐπιφᾶναι	τοῖς	ἐν σκότει	καὶ σκιᾷ
height,		to appear	to the	in dark	and shadow

2288	2521	010	2720	016
θανάτου	καθημένοις,	τοῦ	κατευθῦναι	τοὺς
of death	ones sitting,	of the	to make straight	the

4228	1473	1519 3598	1515	**80**	09	1161 3813
πόδας	ἡμῶν	εἰς ὁδὸν	εἰρήνης.		Τὸ	δὲ παιδίον
feet	of us in	way of	peace.		The	but small child

837	2532 2901		4151	2532 1510
ηὔξανεν	καὶ ἐκραταιοῦτο		πνεύματι,	καὶ ἦν
grew	and was being strengthened		in spirit,	and was

1722 019	2048	2193 2250	323	846
ἐν	ταῖς ἐρήμοις	ἕως ἡμέρας	ἀναδείξεως	αὐτοῦ
in	the deserts	until day	of showing up	of him

4314 04	2474	**2:1**	1096	1161 1722 019	2250
πρὸς τὸν	Ἰσραήλ.		Ἐγένετο	δὲ ἐν ταῖς	ἡμέραις
to the	Israel.		It became	but in the	days

1565	1831	1378	3844 2541	828
ἐκείναις	ἐξῆλθεν	δόγμα	παρὰ Καίσαρος	Αὐγούστου
those	went out	decree	from Caesar	Augustus

583	3956 08	3625	**2**	3778
ἀπογράφεσθαι	πᾶσαν τὴν	οἰκουμένην.		αὕτη
to be enrolled	all the	inhabited world.		This

582	4413	1096	2230	06	4947
ἀπογραφὴ	πρώτη	ἐγένετο	ἡγεμονεύοντος	τῆς	Συρίας
enrollment	first	became	leading	of the	Syria

2958	**3**	2532 4198	3956	583
Κυρηνίου.		καὶ ἐπορεύοντο	πάντες	ἀπογράφεσθαι,
Cyrenius.		And traveled	all	to be enrolled,

1538	1519 08	1438	4172	**4**	305	1161
ἕκαστος	εἰς τὴν	ἑαυτοῦ	πόλιν.		Ἀνέβη	δὲ
each	into the	of himself	city.		Went up	but

2532	2501	575	06	1056	1537 4172	3478
καὶ	Ἰωσὴφ	ἀπὸ	τῆς	Γαλιλαίας	ἐκ πόλεως	Ναζαρὲθ
also	Joseph	from	the	Galilee	from city	Nazareth

and has remembered his
holy covenant,
[73] the oath that he swore to
our ancestor
Abraham,
to grant us [74] that we,
being rescued from the
hands of our enemies,
might serve him without
fear, [75] in holiness
and righteousness
before him all our days.
[76] And you, child, will be
called the prophet of
the Most High;
for you will go before
the Lord to prepare
his ways,
[77] to give knowledge of
salvation to his people
by the forgiveness
of their sins.
[78] By the tender mercy
of our God,
the dawn from on high
will break upon[a] us,
[79] to give light to those who
sit in darkness and in
the shadow of death,
to guide our feet into
the way of peace."
80 The child grew and
became strong in spirit, and
he was in the wilderness
until the day he appeared
publicly to Israel.

CHAPTER 2

In those days a decree
went out from Emperor
Augustus that all the world
should be registered. [2]This
was the first registration
and was taken while
Quirinius was governor of
Syria. [3]All went to their
own towns to be registered.
[4]Joseph also went from the
town of Nazareth in Galilee

---

[a] Other ancient authorities read has
broken upon

to Judea, to the city of
David called Bethlehem,
because he was descended
from the house and family
of David. ⁵He went to be
registered with Mary, to
whom he was engaged and
who was expecting a child.
⁶While they were there, the
time came for her to deliver
her child. ⁷And she gave
birth to her firstborn son
and wrapped him in bands
of cloth, and laid him in a
manger, because there was
no place for them in the
inn.

8 In that region there
were shepherds living in the
fields, keeping watch over
their flock by night. ⁹Then
an angel of the Lord stood
before them, and the glory
of the Lord shone around
them, and they were
terrified. ¹⁰But the angel
said to them, "Do not be
afraid; for see—I am
bringing you good news of
great joy for all the people:
¹¹to you is born this day in
the city of David a Savior,
who is the Messiah,ᵃ the
Lord. ¹²This will be a sign
for you: you will find a
child wrapped in bands
of cloth and lying in a
manger." ¹³And suddenly
there was with the angel a
multitude of the heavenly
host,ᵇ praising God and
saying,

ᵃ Or the Christ
ᵇ Gk army

1519 08	2449	1519 4172	1160a 3748	2564
εἰς τὴν	Ἰουδαίαν	εἰς πόλιν	Δαυὶδ ἥτις	καλεῖται
into the	Judea	into city	David which	is called

965   1223   012 1510 846   1537 3624   2532
Βηθλέεμ,   διὰ   τὸ εἶναι αὐτὸν ἐξ   οἴκου καὶ
Bethlehem, through the to be him   from house and

3965   1160a 5 583   4862 3137a   07
πατριᾶς   Δαυίδ,   ἀπογράψασθαι σὺν Μαριὰμ τῇ
fatherhood David,   to be enrolled with Mariam the

3423   846   1510 1471   6 1096   1161 1722
ἐμνηστευμένη αὐτῷ, οὔσῃ ἐγκύῳ.   Ἐγένετο   δὲ   ἐν
one having   him, being pregnant. It became but in
been engaged

011 1510   846   1563 4092   017 2250   010
τῷ εἶναι αυτοὺς ἐκεῖ ἐπλήσθησαν αἱ ἡμέραι τοῦ
the to be them   there was filled the days of the

5088   846   2532 5088   04 5207
τεκεῖν   αὐτήν, 7 καὶ ἔτεκεν   τὸν υἱὸν
to give birth her,   and she gave birth the son

846   04 4416   2532 4683
αὐτῆς   τὸν πρωτότοκον, καὶ ἐσπαργάνωσεν
of her   the firstborn,   and she wrapped cloth strips

846   2532 347   846   1722 5336   1360
αὐτὸν καὶ ἀνέκλινεν αὐτὸν ἐν   φάτνῃ   διότι
him   and reclined him   in   feed trough because

3756 1510   846   5117 1722 011 2646
οὐκ ἦν   αὐτοῖς τόπος ἐν τῷ καταλύματι.
not there was to them place in the guestlodge.

8 2532 4166   1510 1722 07   5561   07 846
Καὶ ποιμένες ἦσαν ἐν τῇ χώρᾳ   τῇ αὐτῇ
And shepherds were+ in the country the same

63   2532 5442   5438   06
ἀγραυλοῦντες   καὶ φυλάσσοντες φυλακὰς τῆς
+making the field home and +guarding   guards of the

3571   1909 08 4167   846   9 2532 32
νυκτὸς ἐπὶ τὴν ποίμνην αὐτῶν.   καὶ ἄγγελος
night on the flock   of them. And messenger

2962   2186   846   0633 1391   2962
κυρίου   ἐπέστη   αὐτοῖς καὶ δόξα   κυρίου
of Master   stood on to them and splendor of Master

4034   846   2532 5399   5401   3173
περιέλαμψεν αὐτούς, καὶ ἐφοβήθησαν φόβον μέγαν.
shone around them,   and they feared fear great.

10 2532 3004 846   01 32   3361 5399
Καὶ εἶπεν αὐτοῖς ὁ ἄγγελος·   μὴ φοβεῖσθε,
And said to them the messenger; not be afraid,

2400 1063 2097   1473   5479   3173
ἰδοὺ γὰρ εὐαγγελίζομαι ὑμῖν χαρὰν μεγάλην
look for I tell good message to you joy great

3748 1510   3956 03 2992   11 3754 5088
ἥτις ἔσται παντὶ τῷ λαῷ,   ὅτι ἐτέχθη
which will be to all the people, that was given birth

1473   4594   4990   3739 1510 5547   2962
ὑμῖν σήμερον σωτὴρ   ὅς ἐστιν χριστὸς κύριος
to you today deliverer who is   Christ Master

1722 4172 1160a 12 2532 3778 1473 09 4592
ἐν πόλει Δαυίδ.   καὶ τοῦτο ὑμῖν τὸ σημεῖον,
in city David.   And this to you the sign,

2147   1025 4683   2532 2749   1722
εὑρήσετε βρέφος ἐσπαργανωμένον καὶ κείμενον ἐν
you will infant having been wrapped and lying   in
find   in cloth strips

5336   13 2532 1810   1096   4862 03   32
φάτνῃ.   καὶ ἐξαίφνης ἐγένετο σὺν τῷ ἀγγέλῳ
feed trough. And suddenly became with the messenger

4128   4756   3770   134   04 2316 2532
πλῆθος στρατιᾶς οὐρανίου αἰνούντων τὸν θεὸν καὶ
quantity of army heavenly praising the God and

3004   1391   1722 5310   2316   2532 1909
λεγόντων· **14** δόξα   ἐν ὑψίστοις θεῷ   καὶ ἐπὶ
saying;   splendor   in highest   to God and on

1093   1515   1722 444   2107   2532
γῆς   εἰρήνη ἐν ἀνθρώποις εὐδοκίας.   **15** Καὶ
earth peace   in men   of good thought. And

1096   5613 565   575   846   1519 04   3772
ἐγένετο ὡς ἀπῆλθον ἀπ᾽ αὐτῶν εἰς τὸν οὐρανὸν
it became as went off from them into the heaven

013 32   013 4166   2980   4314
οἱ ἄγγελοι, οἱ ποιμένες ἐλάλουν πρὸς
the messengers, the shepherds were saying to

240   1330   1211   2193 965
ἀλλήλους· διέλθωμεν   δὴ   ἕως Βηθλέεμ
one another; let us go through indeed until Bethlehem

2532 3708   012 4487 3778   012   1096
καὶ ἴδωμεν   τὸ ῥῆμα τοῦτο τὸ   γεγονὸς
and let us see the word this the one having become

3739 01 2962   1107   1473   **16** 2532 2064
ὃ   ὁ κύριος ἐγνώρισεν ἡμῖν.   καὶ ἦλθαν
that the Master made known to us.   And they went

4692   2532 429   08   5037 3137a 2532
σπεύσαντες   καὶ ἀνεῦραν   τήν τε Μαριὰμ καὶ
having hurried and they discovered the both Mariam and

04   2501 2532 012 1025   2749   1722 07 5336
τὸν Ἰωσὴφ καὶ τὸ βρέφος κείμενον ἐν τῇ φάτνῃ·
the Joseph and the infant lying   in the feed trough;

17 3708   1161 1107   4012   010 4487
ἰδόντες   δὲ   ἐγνώρισαν   περὶ τοῦ ῥήματος
having seen but they made known about the word

010 2980   846   4012 010 3813
τοῦ λαληθέντος   αὐτοῖς περὶ τοῦ παιδίου
of the one having spoken to them about the small child

3778   **18** 2532 3956   013 191   2296
τούτου.   καὶ πάντες οἱ ἀκούσαντες   ἐθαύμασαν
this.   And all   the ones having heard marveled

4012 022 2980   5259 014 4166   4314 846
περὶ τῶν λαληθέντων   ὑπὸ τῶν ποιμένων πρὸς αὐτούς·
about the things having by the shepherds to   them;
             been spoken

19 05   1161 3137a 3956 4933   024
ἡ   δὲ Μαριὰμ πάντα συνετήρει   τὰ
the but Mariam all   was keeping together the

4487   3778   4820   1722 07 2588   846
ῥήματα ταῦτα συμβάλλουσα   ἐν τῇ καρδίᾳ αὐτῆς.
words these throwing together in the heart of her.

20 2532 5290   013 4166   1392   2532
καὶ ὑπέστρεψαν οἱ ποιμένες δοξάζοντες   καὶ
And returned   the shepherds giving splendor and

134   04   2316 1909 3956 3739 191   2532
αἰνοῦντες τὸν θεὸν ἐπὶ πᾶσιν οἷς ἤκουσαν καὶ
praising the God on all   which they heard and

3708 2531   2980   4314 846   **21** 2532 3753
εἶδον καθὼς ἐλαλήθη   πρὸς αὐτούς.   Καὶ ὅτε
saw   just as it was spoken to them.   And when

4092   2250 3638 010 4059   846
ἐπλήσθησαν ἡμέραι ὀκτὼ τοῦ περιτεμεῖν αὐτὸν
was filled days eight of the to circumcise him

2532 2564   09 3686 846   2424   09
καὶ ἐκλήθη   τὸ ὄνομα αὐτοῦ Ἰησοῦς, τὸ
and was called the name of him Jesus, the one

2564   5259 02 32   4253   010
κληθὲν   ὑπὸ τοῦ ἀγγέλου πρὸ   τοῦ
having been called by the messenger before the

4815   846 1722 07 2836   **22** 2532 3753
συλλημφθῆναι αὐτὸν ἐν τῇ κοιλίᾳ.   Καὶ ὅτε
to be conceived him in the stomach. And when

4092   017 2250 02   2512   846   2596
ἐπλήσθησαν αἱ ἡμέραι τοῦ καθαρισμοῦ αὐτῶν κατὰ
was filled the days of the cleaning of them by

14 "Glory to God in the
   highest heaven,
   and on earth peace
   among those whom
   he favors!"[a]

15 When the angels had
left them and gone into
heaven, the shepherds said
to one another, "Let us go
now to Bethlehem and see
this thing that has taken
place, which the Lord has
made known to us." 16So
they went with haste and
found Mary and Joseph,
and the child lying in the
manger. 17When they saw
this, they made known
what had been told them
about this child; 18and all
who heard it were amazed
at what the shepherds told
them. 19But Mary treasured
all these words and pondered
them in her heart. 20The
shepherds returned, glorifying and praising God for all
they had heard and seen, as
it had been told them.

21 After eight days had
passed, it was time to
circumcise the child; and he
was called Jesus, the name
given by the angel before he
was conceived in the womb.

22 When the time came
for their purification
according to the law of
Moses,

a Other ancient authorities read
peace, goodwill among people

they brought him up to
Jerusalem to present him to
the Lord 23(as it is written
in the law of the Lord,
"Every firstborn male shall
be designated as holy to the
Lord"), 24and they offered
a sacrifice according to
what is stated in the law
of the Lord, "a pair of
turtledoves or two young
pigeons."

25 Now there was a man
in Jerusalem whose name
was Simeon;[a] this man
was righteous and devout,
looking forward to the
consolation of Israel, and
the Holy Spirit rested on
him. 26It had been revealed
to him by the Holy Spirit
that he would not see death
before he had seen the
Lord's Messiah.[b] 27Guided
by the Spirit, Simeon[c] came
into the temple; and when
the parents brought in the
child Jesus, to do for him
what was customary under
the law, 28Simeon[d] took
him in his arms and praised
God, saying,

29 "Master, now you are
    dismissing your
    servant[e] in peace,
    according to your
    word;
30 for my eyes have seen
    your salvation,
31 which you have
    prepared in the
    presence of all
    peoples,
32 a light for revelation
    to the Gentiles
    and for glory to your
    people Israel."

33 And the child's

```
04      3551   3475      321           846      1519   2414
τὸν    νόμον  Μωϋσέως, ἀνήγαγον     αὐτὸν   εἰς   Ἱεροσόλυμα
the    law    Moses,   they led up  him     into  Jerusalem
3936          03     2962         23  2531
παραστῆσαι    τῷ     κυρίῳ,           καθὼς
to stand along to the Master,        just as
1125                   1722 3551 2962        3754 3956
γέγραπται             ἐν   νόμῳ κυρίου     ὅτι  πᾶν
it has been writtten  in   law  of Master that all
730    1272              3388        40    03
ἄρσεν  διανοῖγον       μήτραν     ἅγιον  τῷ
male   opening completely motherhood holy  to the
2962   2564          2532 010 1325      2378      2596
κυρίῳ  κληθήσεται,  24 καὶ  τοῦ δοῦναι  θυσίαν   κατὰ
Master will be called, and  the to give sacrifice by
012 3004              1722 03  3551 2962        2201
τὸ  εἰρημένον        ἐν   τῷ  νόμῳ κυρίου,    ζεῦγος
the having been said in   the law  of Master, yoke
5167         2228 1417 3556a     4058         25 2532 2400
τρυγόνων    ἢ   δύο  νοσσοὺς περιστερῶν.     Καὶ  ἰδοὺ
turtle doves or  two  young  doves.             And  look
444         1510 1722 2419        3739      3686  4826 2532
ἄνθρωπος    ἦν   ἐν  Ἱερουσαλὴμ  ᾧ        ὄνομα Συμεὼν καὶ
man         was  in  Jerusalem   of whom   name  Symeon and
01  444        3778  1342      2532 2126     4327
ὁ   ἄνθρωπος  οὗτος δίκαιος καὶ  εὐλαβὴς  προσδεχόμενος
the man        this  right    and  reverent  awaiting
3874         02      2474       2532 4151     1510 40
παράκλησιν  τοῦ    Ἰσραήλ,   καὶ  πνεῦμα  ἦν   ἅγιον
encouragement of the Israel,   and  spirit   was  holy
1909 846        26 2532 1510 846        5537           5259
ἐπ'  αὐτὸν·       καὶ  ἦν  αὐτῷ      κεχρηματισμένον   ὑπὸ
on   him;         and  was to him     having been warned by
010 4151        010  40   3361 3708   2288       4250 2228
τοῦ πνεύματος  τοῦ  ἁγίου μὴ  ἰδεῖν  θάνατον  πρὶν [ἢ]
the spirit      of the holy  not  to see death    before or
302 3708        04   5547    2962      27 2532 2064 1722
ἂν  ἴδῃ         τὸν χριστὸν κυρίου.     καὶ  ἦλθεν  ἐν
-   he might see the Christ of Master.   And  he went in
011 4151        1519 012 2411    2532 1722 011 1521
τῷ  πνεύματι  εἰς  τὸ  ἱερόν·  καὶ  ἐν  τῷ  εἰσαγαγεῖν
the spirit     into the temple; and  in  the to lead into
016 1118       012 3813       2424   010   4160
τοὺς γονεῖς   τὸ  παιδίον   Ἰησοῦν τοῦ  ποιῆσαι
the  parents  the small child Jesus  of the to do
846    2596 012 1480          02    3551 4012
αὐτοὺς κατὰ τὸ  εἰθισμένον   τοῦ  νόμου περὶ
them   by  the having accustomed the law  about
846    28 2532 846      1209       846    1519 020 43
αὐτοῦ     καὶ  αὐτὸς  ἐδέξατο   αὐτὸ  εἰς  τὰς ἀγκάλας
him       and  himself welcomed  him   into the arms
2532 2127      04   2316 2532 3004      29 3568 630
καὶ  εὐλόγησεν τὸν θεὸν καὶ  εἶπεν·     νῦν  ἀπολύεις
and  spoke well the God  and  said;       now  loose off
04  1401    1473    1203        2596 012 4487 1473
τὸν δοῦλόν σου,    δέσποτα,   κατὰ τὸ  ῥῆμά σου
the slave  of you, Supervisor, by  the  word of you
1722 1515      30 3754 3708  013 3788     1473 012
ἐν  εἰρήνῃ·       ὅτι εἶδον οἱ ὀφθαλμοί μου  τὸ
in  peace;        that saw  the eyes     of me the
4992        1473   31 3739 2090        2596     4383
σωτήριόν   σου,     ὃ  ἡτοίμασας    κατὰ   πρόσωπον
deliverance of you,   whom you prepared before  face
3956   014 2992   32 5457 1519 602       1484
πάντων τῶν λαῶν,    φῶς εἰς  ἀποκάλυψιν ἐθνῶν
of all the peoples,  light to  uncovering of nations
2532 1391   2992    1473   2474      33 2532 1510 01
καὶ  δόξαν λαοῦ    σου   Ἰσραήλ.     καὶ  ἦν   ὁ
and  splendor of people of you Israel.   And  was+ the
```

```
3962      846      2532  05    3384    2296          1909  023
πατὴρ    αὐτοῦ    καὶ   ἡ     μήτηρ   θαυμάζοντες   ἐπὶ   τοῖς
father of him and    the   mother  +marveling     on    the

2980           4012    846        2532 2127        846
λαλουμένοις   περὶ    αὐτοῦ.  34  καὶ εὐλόγησεν   αὐτοὺς
being spoken about   him.        And spoke well  them

4826   2532 3004   4314  3137a   08   3384   846      2400
Συμεὼν καὶ εἶπεν  πρὸς  Μαριὰμ τὴν  μητέρα αὐτοῦ·   ἰδοὺ
Symeon and said   to    Mariam the  mother of him;  look

3778   2749    1519  4431    2532 386          4183
οὗτος  κεῖται  εἰς   πτῶσιν καὶ  ἀνάστασιν    πολλῶν
this one is laid for  fall   and  standing up of many

1722 03  2474   2532 1519 4592      483
ἐν  τῷ  Ἰσραὴλ καὶ  εἰς  σημεῖον   ἀντιλεγόμενον -
in  the Israel and  into sign       being spoken against

   2532 1473 1161 846      08   5590  1330
35 καὶ  σοῦ  [δὲ] αὐτῆς   τὴν  ψυχὴν διελεύσεται
   and  of you but yourself the  soul  will go through

4501        3704   302 601          1537  4183
ρομφαία - ὅπως  ἂν  ἀποκαλυφθῶσιν ἐκ    πολλῶν
sword   - so that -  might be uncovered from  many

2588      1261          2532 1510 451   4398
καρδιῶν  διαλογισμοί. 36 Καὶ  ἦν  Ἄννα προφῆτις,
hearts   reasonings.    And  was Anna spokeswoman,

2364      5323       1537 5443   768   3778
θυγάτηρ  Φανουήλ,   ἐκ   φυλῆς  Ἀσήρ· αὕτη
daughter Phanouel,  from tribe  Aser; this

4260          1722 2250       4183     2198
προβεβηκυῖα   ἐν   ἡμέραις πολλαῖς, ζήσασα
having gone before in  days    many,    having lived

3326 435     2094 2033  575  06   3932        846
μετὰ ἀνδρὸς ἔτη  ἑπτὰ  ἀπὸ τῆς  παρθενίας αὐτῆς
with man     years seven from the  virginity of her

   2532 846    5503 2193  2094  3589        5064
37 καὶ  αὐτὴ  χήρα ἕως  ἐτῶν  ὀγδοήκοντα τεσσάρων,
   and  herself widow until years eighty    four,

3739 3756 868      010  2411     3521        2532
ἣ    οὐκ ἀφίστατο τοῦ  ἱεροῦ   νηστείαις   καὶ
who  not stood off the  temple  in fastings  and

1162        3000       3571 2532 2250      38  2532 846
δεήσεσιν    λατρεύουσα νύκτα καὶ ἡμέραν.     καὶ  αὐτῇ
requests    serving    night and day.         And  same

07 5610 2186     437              03   2316 2532
τῇ ὥρᾳ ἐπιστᾶσα ἀνθωμολογεῖτο τῷ   θεῷ  καὶ
in hour having   she was confessing to the God  and
the    stood on  in response

2980        4012   846    3956   015   4327
ἐλάλει     περὶ   αὐτοῦ πᾶσιν τοῖς  προσδεχομένοις
was speaking about him   to all the  ones awaiting

3085       2419               2532 5613 5055
λύτρωσιν   Ἰερουσαλήμ.  39 Καὶ  ὡς   ἐτέλεσαν
ransom     Jerusalem.      And  as   they completed

3956  024  2596 04  3551  2962     1994         1519
πάντα τὰ  κατὰ τὸν νόμον κυρίου,  ἐπέστρεψαν  εἰς
all   the by  the  law   of Master, they returned to

08  1056       1519 4172  1438         3478      40  09
τὴν Γαλιλαίαν εἰς  πόλιν ἑαυτῶν     Ναζαρέθ.      Τὸ
the Galilee    to   city  of themselves Nazareth.      The

1161 3813      837        2532 2901
δὲ  παιδίον  ηὔξανεν   καὶ  ἐκραταιοῦτο
but small child grew    and  was strengthened

4137        4678      2532 5485   2316   1510 1909 846
πληρούμενον σοφίᾳ,    καὶ  χάρις  θεοῦ  ἦν  ἐπ’ αὐτο.
being filled wisdom,  and  favor  of God was on   him.

   2532 4198        013  1118   846     2596 2094 1519
41 Καὶ  ἐπορεύοντο οἱ  γονεῖς αὐτοῦ κατ’ ἔτος εἰς
   And  traveled    the parents of him by  year in

2419        07   1859      010  3957      42  2532
Ἰερουσαλὴμ τῇ  ἑορτῇ    τοῦ πάσχα.       Καὶ
Jerusalem  in  the festival of  the passover.   And
```

father and mother were amazed at what was being said about him. [34]Then Simeon[a] blessed them and said to his mother Mary, "This child is destined for the falling and the rising of many in Israel, and to be a sign that will be opposed [35]so that the inner thoughts of many will be revealed—and a sword will pierce your own soul too."

[36]There was also a prophet, Anna[b] the daughter of Phanuel, of the tribe of Asher. She was of a great age, having lived with her husband seven years after her marriage, [37]then as a widow to the age of eighty-four. She never left the temple but worshiped there with fasting and prayer night and day. [38]At that moment she came, and began to praise God and to speak about the child[c] to all who were looking for the redemption of Jerusalem.

[39]When they had finished everything required by the law of the Lord, they returned to Galilee, to their own town of Nazareth. [40]The child grew and became strong, filled with wisdom; and the favor of God was upon him.

[41]Now every year his parents went to Jerusalem for the festival of the Passover. [42]And when he was

a Gk Symeon
b Gk Hanna
c Gk him

twelve years old, they went
up as usual for the festival.
43When the festival was
ended and they started to
return, the boy Jesus stayed
behind in Jerusalem, but his
parents did not know it.
44Assuming that he was in
the group of travelers, they
went a day's journey. Then
they started to look for him
among their relatives and
friends. 45When they did
not find him, they returned
to Jerusalem to search for
him. 46After three days they
found him in the temple,
sitting among the teachers,
listening to them and
asking them questions.
47And all who heard him
were amazed at his under-
standing and his answers.
48When his parents*a* saw
him they were astonished;
and his mother said to him,
"Child, why have you
treated us like this? Look,
your father and I have been
searching for you in great
anxiety." 49He said to them,
"Why were you searching
for me? Did you not know
that I must be in my
Father's house?"*b* 50But
they did not understand
what he said to them.
51Then he went down with
them and came to Nazareth,
and was obedient to them.
His mother

a Gk *they*

b Or *be about my Father's interests?*

3753	1096		2094	1427	305		846	2596
ὅτε	ἐγένετο	ἐτῶν	δώδεκα,	ἀναβαινόντων		αὐτῶν	κατὰ
when	he became	years	twelve,	going up		of them	by

012	1485	06	1859		2532	5048	
τὸ	ἔθος	τῆς	ἑορτῆς	43	καὶ	τελειωσάντων	
the	custom	of the	festival		and	having completed	

020	2250	1722	011	5290		846	5278
τὰς	ἡμέρας,	ἐν	τῷ	ὑποστρέφειν	αὐτοὺς	ὑπέμεινεν
the	days,	in	the	to return	them	endured

2424	01	3816		1722	2419		2532	3756
Ἰησοῦς	ὁ	παῖς		ἐν	Ἰερουσαλήμ,	καὶ	οὐκ
Jesus	the	boy servant		in	Jerusalem,	and	not

1097	013	1118	846		3543		1161	846
ἔγνωσαν	οἱ	γονεῖς	αὐτοῦ.	44	νομίσαντες		δὲ	αὐτὸν
knew	the	parents	of him.		Having thought		but	him

1510	1722	07	4923		2064		2250	3598	2532
εἶναι	ἐν	τῇ	συνοδίᾳ	ἦλθον		ἡμέρας	ὁδὸν	καὶ
to be	in	the	co-traveler	they went		day	way	and

327		846	1722	015	4773		2532	015
ἀνεζήτουν		αὐτὸν	ἐν	τοῖς	συγγενεῦσιν	καὶ	τοῖς
were seeking	after him	in	the	relatives	and	the

1110		2532	3361	2147		5290		1519
γνωστοῖς,	45	καὶ	μὴ	εὑρόντες		ὑπέστρεψαν	εἰς
known ones,		and	not	having found		they returned to

2419		327		846		2532	1096
Ἰερουσαλὴμ	ἀναζητοῦντες		αὐτόν.	46	καὶ	ἐγένετο
Jerusalem	having sought		after him.		And	it became

3326	2250	5140	2147		846	1722	011	2411
μετὰ	ἡμέρας	τρεῖς	εὗρον		αὐτὸν	ἐν	τῷ	ἱερῷ
after	days	three	they found him		in	the	temple

2516		1722	3319	014		1320		2532	191
καθεζόμενον	ἐν	μέσῳ	τῶν		διδασκάλων	καὶ	ἀκούοντα
sitting		in middle	of the		teachers	and	hearing

846	2532	1905		846		1839		1161
αὐτῶν	καὶ	ἐπερωτῶντα	αὐτούς·	47	ἐξίσταντο		δὲ
them	and	asking on	them;		were amazed		but

3956	013	191		846	1909	07	4907		2532
πάντες	οἱ	ἀκούοντες		αὐτοῦ	ἐπὶ	τῇ	συνέσει		καὶ
all	the ones	hearing	him	on	the	understanding		and

019	612		846		2532	3708		846
ταῖς	ἀποκρίσεσιν	αὐτοῦ.	48	καὶ	ἰδόντες		αὐτὸν
the	answers	of him.		And	having seen		him

1605		2532	3004	4314	846	05	3384
ἐξεπλάγησαν,		καὶ	εἶπεν	πρὸς	αὐτὸν	ἡ	μήτηρ
they were astonished,	and	said	to	him	the	mother

846	5043	5101	4160		1473	3779		2400	01
αὐτοῦ·	τέκνον,	τί	ἐποίησας	ἡμῖν	οὕτως;	ἰδοὺ	ὁ
of him;	child,	why	did you do	to us	thusly?	Look	the

3962	1473	2504	3600		2212		1473
πατήρ	σου	κἀγὼ	ὀδυνώμενοι		ἐζητοῦμέν	σε.
father	of you	and I	being tormented	we sought	you.

	2532	3004	4314	846		5101	3754	2212
49	καὶ	εἶπεν	πρὸς	αὐτούς·	τί	ὅτι	ἐζητεῖτέ
	And	he said	to	them;	why	because	you sought

1473	3756	3609a		3754	1722	023	02		3962
με;	οὐκ	ᾔδειτε		ὅτι	ἐν	τοῖς	τοῦ		πατρός
me?	Not	had you known	that	in	the	of the	of father

1473	1163		1510	1473		2532	846		3756
μου	δεῖ		εἶναί	με;	50	καὶ	αὐτοὶ		οὐ
of me	it is necessary	to be	me?		And	themselves		not

4920		012	4487	3739	2980		846		2532
συνῆκαν		τὸ	ῥῆμα	ὃ	ἐλάλησεν	αὐτοῖς.	51	καὶ
understood		the	word	that	he spoke	to them.		And

2597		3326	846		2532	2064		1519	3478
κατέβη		μετ᾽	αὐτῶν	καὶ	ἦλθεν	εἰς	Ναζαρὲθ
he went down		with	them	and	he went	into	Nazareth

2532	1510	5293		846		2532	05	3384
καὶ	ἦν	ὑποτασσόμενος	αὐτοῖς.	καὶ	ἡ	μήτηρ
and	was+	+being subject	to them.	And	the	mother

846	1301			3956	024	4487	1722	07
αὐτοῦ	διετήρει			πάντα	τὰ	ῥήματα	ἐν	τῇ
of him	was keeping thoroughly			all	the	words	in	the

treasured all these things in her heart.

2588	846		2532	2424	4298		1722	07
καρδίᾳ	αὐτῆς.	**52**	Καὶ	Ἰησοῦς	προέκοπτεν	[ἐν	τῇ]
heart	of her.		And	Jesus	progressed	in	the

52 And Jesus increased in wisdom and in years,[a] and in divine and human favor.

4678	2532	2244		2532	5485		3844	2316	2532
σοφίᾳ	καὶ	ἡλικίᾳ	καὶ	χάριτι	παρὰ	θεῷ	καὶ
wisdom	and	stature	and	favor	with	God	and

444		1722	2094	1161	4003		06
ἀνθρώποις.	**3:1**	Ἐν	ἔτει	δὲ	πεντεκαιδεκάτῳ	τῆς
men.		In	year	but	five and ten	of the

2231		5086		2541		2230		4194
ἡγεμονίας	Τιβερίου	Καίσαρος,	ἡγεμονεύοντος	Ποντίου
leadership	of Tiberius	Caesar,	leading	Pontius

4091	06		2449		2532	5075
Πιλάτου	τῆς	Ἰουδαίας,	καὶ	τετρααρχοῦντος
Pilate	of the	Judea,	and	one ruling a fourth

06		1056		2264		5376		1161	02	80
τῆς	Γαλιλαίας	Ἡρῴδου,	Φιλίππου	δὲ	τοῦ	ἀδελφοῦ
of the	Galilee	Herod,	Philip	but	the	brother

846	5075			06		2484		2532
αὐτοῦ	τετρααρχοῦντος		τῆς	Ἰτουραίας	καὶ
of him	one ruling a fourth		of the	Iturea	and

5139		5561		2532	3078		06		9
Τραχωνίτιδος	χώρας,	καὶ	Λυσανίου	τῆς	Ἀβιληνῆς
Trachonitis	country,	and	Lysanias	of the	Abilene

5075			1909	749		452	2532
τετρααρχοῦντος,	**2**	ἐπὶ	ἀρχιερέως	Ἄννα	καὶ
one ruling a fourth,		on	ruler priest	Annas	and

2533		1096		4487	2316	1909	2491	04
Καϊάφα,	ἐγένετο	ῥῆμα	θεοῦ	ἐπὶ	Ἰωάννην	τὸν
Caiaphas,	became	word	of God	on	John	the

2197		5207	1722	07	2048		2532	2064		1519
Ζαχαρίου	υἱὸν	ἐν	τῇ	ἐρήμῳ.	**3**	καὶ	ἦλθεν	εἰς
Zacharias	son	in	the	desert.		And	he went	into

3956	08	4066		02		2446		2784
πᾶσαν	[τὴν]	περίχωρον	τοῦ	Ἰορδάνου	κηρύσσων
all	the	country around	the	Jordan	announcing

908		3341		1519	859		266
βάπτισμα	μετανοίας	εἰς	ἄφεσιν	ἁμαρτιῶν,
immersion	of change mind	into	sending off	of sins,

4	5613	1125		1722	976	3056		2268
	ὡς	γέγραπται	ἐν	βίβλῳ	λόγων	Ἡσαΐου
	as	it has been written	in	book	of words	of Isaiah

02	4396		5456	994		1722	07	2048
τοῦ	προφήτου·	φωνὴ	βοῶντος	ἐν	τῇ	ἐρήμῳ·
the	spokesman,	sound	crying aloud	in	the	desert;

2090		08	3598	2962		2117a		4160	020
ἑτοιμάσατε	τὴν	ὁδὸν	κυρίου,	εὐθείας	ποιεῖτε	τὰς
prepare	the	way	of Master,	straight	make	the

5147	846		3956	5327	4137		2532	3956
τρίβους	αὐτοῦ·	**5**	πᾶσα	φάραγξ	πληρωθήσεται	καὶ	πᾶν
paths	of him;		all	ravine	will be filled	and	all

3735	2532	1015		5013			2532	1510	021
ὄρος	καὶ	βουνὸς	ταπεινωθήσεται,	καὶ	ἔσται	τὰ
hill	and	hill	will be humbled,	and	will be	the

4646		1519	2117a	2532	017	5138		1519	3598
σκολιὰ	εἰς	εὐθείαν	καὶ	αἱ	τραχεῖαι	εἰς	ὁδοὺς
crooked	into	straight	and	the	roughs	into	ways

3006		2532	3708		3956	4561	012	4992
λείας·	**6**	καὶ	ὄψεται	πᾶσα	σὰρξ	τὸ	σωτήριον
smooth;		and	will see	all	flesh	the	deliverance

02	2316		3004		3767	015	1607
τοῦ	θεοῦ.	**7**	Ἔλεγεν	οὖν	τοῖς	ἐκπορευομένοις
of the	God.		He was saying	then	to the	traveling out

3793	907		5259	846		1081
ὄχλοις	βαπτισθῆναι	ὑπ'	αὐτοῦ·	γεννήματα
crowds	to be immersed	by	him,	generations

CHAPTER 3

In the fifteenth year of the reign of Emperor Tiberius, when Pontius Pilate was governor of Judea, and Herod was ruler[b] of Galilee, and his brother Philip ruler[b] of the region of Ituraea and Trachonitis, and Lysanias ruler[b] of Abilene, 2during the high priesthood of Annas and Caiaphas, the word of God came to John son of Zechariah in the wilderness. 3He went into all the region around the Jordan, proclaiming a baptism of repentance for the forgiveness of sins, 4as it is written in the book of the words of the prophet Isaiah,

"The voice of one crying out in the wilderness:
'Prepare the way of the Lord,
    make his paths straight.
5 Every valley shall be filled,
    and every mountain and hill shall be made low,
and the crooked shall be made straight,
    and the rough ways made smooth;
6 and all flesh shall see the salvation of God.'"

7 John said to the crowds that came out to be baptized by him,

a Or in stature
b Gk tetrarch

"You brood of vipers! Who warned you to flee from the wrath to come? [8]Bear fruits worthy of repentance. Do not begin to say to yourselves, 'We have Abraham as our ancestor'; for I tell you, God is able from these stones to raise up children to Abraham. [9]Even now the ax is lying at the root of the trees; every tree therefore that does not bear good fruit is cut down and thrown into the fire."

[10]And the crowds asked him, "What then should we do?" [11]In reply he said to them, "Whoever has two coats must share with anyone who has none; and whoever has food must do likewise." [12]Even tax collectors came to be baptized, and they asked him, "Teacher, what should we do?" [13]He said to them, "Collect no more than the amount prescribed for you." [14]Soldiers also asked him, "And we, what should we do?" He said to them, "Do not extort money from anyone by threats or false accusation, and be satisfied with your wages."

[15]As the people were filled with expectation, and all were questioning in their hearts concerning John, whether he might be the Messiah,[a]

[a] Or the Christ

2191		5101	5263		1473	5343		575
ἐχιδνῶν,		τίς	ὑπέδειξεν		ὑμῖν	φυγεῖν		ἀπὸ
of poison snakes,		who	exampled		to you	to flee		from

06	3195		3709		**8**	4160	3767	2590
τῆς	μελλούσης		ὀργῆς;			ποιήσατε	οὖν	καρποὺς
the	being about to be		anger?			Make	then	fruit

514	06		3341		2532	3361	757		3004
ἀξίους	τῆς		μετανοίας		καὶ	μὴ	ἄρξησθε		λέγειν
worthy	of the		mind change		and	not	begin		to say

1722	1438		3962	2192		04	11		3004
ἐν	ἑαυτοῖς·		πατέρα	ἔχομεν		τὸν	Ἀβραάμ·		λέγω
in	yourselves;		father	we have		the	Abraham;		I say

1063	1473		3754	1410		01	2316	1537	014	3037
γὰρ	ὑμῖν		ὅτι	δύναται		ὁ	θεὸς	ἐκ	τῶν	λίθων
for	to you		that	is able		the	God	from	the	stones

3778	1453		5043	03	11		**9**	2235	1161	2532
τούτων	ἐγεῖραι		τέκνα	τῷ	Ἀβραάμ.			ἤδη	δὲ	καὶ
these	to raise		children	the	Abraham.			Already	but	also

05	513		4314	08	4491	022		1186	2749
ἡ	ἀξίνη		πρὸς	τὴν	ῥίζαν	τῶν		δένδρων	κεῖται·
the	axe		to	the	root	of the		trees	is being laid;

3956	3767	1186		3361	4160		2590	2570
πᾶν	οὖν	δένδρον		μὴ	ποιοῦν		καρπὸν	καλὸν
all	then	tree		not	making		fruit	good

1581		2532	1519	4442	906			**10**	2532
ἐκκόπτεται		καὶ	εἰς	πῦρ	βάλλεται.				Καὶ
is being cut off		and	into	fire	is being thrown.				And

1905		846	013	3793	3004		5101	3767
ἐπηρώτων		αὐτὸν	οἱ	ὄχλοι	λέγοντες·		τί	οὖν
were asking on		him	the	crowds	saying,		what	then

4160		**11**	611		1161	3004	846		01
ποιήσωμεν;			ἀποκριθεὶς		δὲ	ἔλεγεν	αὐτοῖς·		ὁ
might we do?			Having answered		but	he was	to them;		the one saying

2192	1417	5509	3330		03		3361	2192
ἔχων	δύο	χιτῶνας	μεταδότω		τῷ		μὴ	ἔχοντι,
having	two	shirts	let share		to the		not	one having,

2532	01	2192		1033		3668		1160		**12**	2064
καὶ	ὁ	ἔχων		βρώματα		ὁμοίως		ποιείτω.			ἦλθον
and	the	one having		foods		likewise		let do.			Came

1161	2532	5057		907		2532	3004	4314	846
δὲ	καὶ	τελῶναι		βαπτισθῆναι		καὶ	εἶπαν	πρὸς	αὐτόν·
but	also	tax men		to be immersed		and	said	to	him;

1320		5101	4160		**13**	01		1161	3004	4314
διδάσκαλε,		τί	ποιήσωμεν;			ὁ		δὲ	εἶπεν	πρὸς
teacher,		what	might we do?			The one		but	said	to

846	3367		4183	3844	012	1299
αὐτούς·	μηδὲν		πλέον	παρὰ	τὸ	διατεταγμένον
them;	nothing		more	from	the	having been directed

1473	4238		**14**	1905			1161	846	2532
ὑμῖν	πράσσετε.			ἐπηρώτων			δὲ	αὐτὸν	καὶ
to you	practice.			Were asking on			but	him	also

4754		3004		5101	4160		2532
στρατευόμενοι		λέγοντες·		τί	ποιήσωμεν		καὶ
ones being soldiers		saying;		what	might do		also

1473	2532	3004		846		3367	1286		3366
ἡμεῖς;	καὶ	εἶπεν		αὐτοῖς·		μηδένα	διασείσητε		μηδὲ
we?	And	he said		to them;		no one	shake down		nor

4811		2532	714		023	3800		1473
συκοφαντήσητε		καὶ	ἀρκεῖσθε		τοῖς	ὀψωνίοις		ὑμῶν.
accuse falsely		and	be enough		to the	salaries		of you.

15	4328		1161	02	2992	2532
	Προσδοκῶντος		δὲ	τοῦ	λαοῦ	καὶ
	Waiting expectantly		but	the	people	and

1260		3956	1722	019	2588		846		4012
διαλογιζομένων		πάντων	ἐν	ταῖς	καρδίαις		αὐτῶν		περὶ
reasoning		all	in	the	hearts		of them		about

02	2491		3379		846		1510		01	5547
τοῦ	Ἰωάννου,		μήποτε		αὐτὸς		εἴη		ὁ	χριστός,
the	John,		not then		himself		might be		the	Christ,

```
      611        3004    3956    01   2491      1473 3303
16  ἀπεκρίνατο λέγων  πᾶσιν  ὁ  Ἰωάννης· ἐγὼ  μὲν
    answered   saying to all the John;    I     indeed
5204      907       1473 2064    1161 01  2478
ὕδατι  βαπτίζω ὑμᾶς· ἔρχεται δὲ  ὁ  ἰσχυρότερός
in water immerse you;  comes   but the stronger
1473   3739      3756 1510 2425    3089     04  2438
μου,   οὗ   οὐκ  εἰμὶ ἱκανὸς λῦσαι   τὸν ἱμάντα
of me, of whom not I am enough to loose the strap
022      5266       846     846    1473 907       1722
τῶν ὑποδημάτων αὐτοῦ· αὐτὸς ὑμᾶς βαπτίσει   ἐν
of the sandals    of him; himself you  will immerse in
4151    40  2532 4442       3739  09   4425
πνεύματι ἁγίῳ καὶ πυρί· 17 οὗ   τὸ πτύον
spirit   holy and fire;   of whom the winnowing shovel
1722 07   5495  846    1244a       08   257        846
ἐν  τῇ  χειρὶ αὐτοῦ διακαθᾶραι τὴν ἅλωνα   αὐτοῦ
in  the hand of  to clean    the threshing of him
            him    thoroughly     floor
2532 4863             04   4621     1519 08  596
καὶ  συναγαγεῖν     τὸν σῖτον εἰς τὴν ἀποθήκην
and  to bring together the wheat to  the storehouse
846     012 1161 892    2618            4442
αὐτοῦ, τὸ δὲ  ἄχυρον κατακαύσει    πυρὶ
of him, the but chaff he will burn down in fire
762           4183  3303  3767 2532 2087
ἀσβέστῳ.   18 Πολλὰ μὲν  οὖν  καὶ  ἕτερα
unextinguishable. Many  indeed then also others
3870      2097                      04  2992
παρακαλῶν εὐηγγελίζετο          τὸν λαόν.
encouraging he was telling good message the people.
      01  1161 2264     01 5076        1651
19  Ὁ  δὲ  Ἡρῴδης ὁ τετραάρχης,  ἐλεγχόμενος
    The but  Herod the ruler of fourth, being rebuked
5259 846    4012 2266      06  1135     02    80
ὑπ᾽ αὐτοῦ περὶ Ἡρῳδιάδος τῆς γυναικὸς τοῦ ἀδελφοῦ
by   him  about Herodias the woman   of the brother
846    2532 4012 3956   3739 4160     4190     01
αὐτοῦ καὶ περὶ πάντων ὧν ἐποίησεν πονηρῶν ὁ
of him and about all   which did    evils   the
2264       4369       2532 3778  1909 3956 2532
Ἡρῴδης, 20 προσέθηκεν καὶ  τοῦτο ἐπὶ πᾶσιν [καὶ]
Herod,    he set to also this  at  all   and
2623        04  2491      1722 5438    1096
κατέκλεισεν τὸν Ἰωάννην ἐν φυλακῇ. 21 Ἐγένετο
closed up   the John    in guard.    It became
1161 1722 011 907          537    04  2992    2532
δὲ  ἐν  τῷ βαπτισθῆναι ἅπαντα τὸν λαὸν  καὶ
but in  the to be immersed all  the people also
2424     907          2532 4336
Ἰησοῦ βαπτισθέντος  καὶ προσευχομένου
of Jesus having been immersed and praying
455          04  3772       22 2532 2597       012
ἀνεῳχθῆναι τὸν οὐρανὸν   καὶ καταβῆναι τὸ
to be opened the heaven   and to come down the
4151    012 40    4984    1491        5613 4058
πνεῦμα τὸ ἅγιον σωματικῷ εἴδει    ὡς περιστερὰν
spirit the holy bodily   visible form as  dove
1909 846   2532 5456    1537 3772    1096      1473
ἐπ᾽ αὐτόν, καὶ φωνὴν ἐξ οὐρανοῦ γενέσθαι· σὺ
on  him,   and sound from heaven to become,  you
1510 01   5207 1473 01  27          1722 1473
εἶ ὁ  υἱός μου ὁ  ἀγαπητός, ἐν  σοὶ
are the son of me the loved one,  in  you
2106         23 2532 846      1510 2424     757
εὐδόκησα.   Καὶ αὐτὸς ἦν Ἰησοῦς ἀρχόμενος
I thought well. And himself was+ Jesus +beginning
5616 2094 5144       1510 5207 5613 3543
ὡσεὶ ἐτῶν τριάκοντα, ὢν  υἱός, ὡς ἐνομίζετο,
as   years thirty,   being son, as  it was thought,
```

16John answered all of them by saying, "I baptize you with water; but one who is more powerful than I is coming; I am not worthy to untie the thong of his sandals. He will baptize you with[a] the Holy Spirit and fire. 17His winnowing fork is in his hand, to clear his threshing floor and to gather the wheat into his granary; but the chaff he will burn with unquenchable fire."

18 So, with many other exhortations, he proclaimed the good news to the people. 19But Herod the ruler,[b] who had been rebuked by him because of Herodias, his brother's wife, and because of all the evil things that Herod had done, 20added to them all by shutting up John in prison.

21 Now when all the people were baptized, and when Jesus also had been baptized and was praying, the heaven was opened, 22and the Holy Spirit descended upon him in bodily form like a dove. And a voice came from heaven, "You are my Son, the Beloved;[c] with you I am well pleased."[d]

23 Jesus was about thirty years old when he began his work. He was the son (as was thought)

a Or in
b Gk tetrarch
c Or my beloved Son
d Other ancient authorities read You are my Son, today I have begotten you

of Joseph son of Heli, ²⁴son
of Matthat, son of Levi,
son of Melchi, son of Jannai,
son of Joseph, ²⁵son of
Mattathias, son of Amos,
son of Nahum, son of Esli,
son of Naggai, ²⁶son of
Maath, son of Mattathias,
son of Semein, son of
Josech, son of Joda, ²⁷son
of Joanan, son of Rhesa,
son of Zerubbabel, son of
Shealtiel,ᵃ son of Neri,
²⁸son of Melchi, son of
Addi, son of Cosam, son of
Elmadam, son of Er, ²⁹son
of Joshua, son of Eliezer,
son of Jorim, son of
Matthat, son of Levi, ³⁰son
of Simeon, son of Judah,
son of Joseph, son of
Jonam, son of Eliakim,
³¹son of Melea, son of
Menna, son of Mattatha,
son of Nathan, son of
David, ³²son of Jesse, son
of Obed, son of Boaz, son
of Sala,ᵇ son of Nahshon,
³³son of Amminadab, son
of Admin, son of Arni,ᶜ
son of Hezron, son of Perez,
son of Judah, ³⁴son of
Jacob, son of Isaac, son of
Abraham, son of Terah, son
of Nahor, ³⁵son of Serug,
son of Reu, son of Peleg,
son of Eber, son of Shelah,
³⁶son of Cainan, son of
Arphaxad, son of Shem, son
of Noah, son of Lamech,
³⁷son of Methuselah, son of
Enoch, son of Jared, son of
Mahalaleel, son of Cainan,
³⁸son of Enos, son of Seth,
son of Adam, son of God.

CHAPTER 4

Jesus, full of the Holy
Spirit, returned from the
Jordan and was led by the

ᵃ Gk Salathiel
ᵇ Other ancient authorities read
  Salmon
ᶜ Other ancient authorities read
  Amminadab, son of Aram; others
  vary widely

2501	02	2242	**24**	02	3102b	02	3017
Ἰωσὴφ	τοῦ	Ἡλὶ		τοῦ	Μαθθὰτ	τοῦ	Λευὶ
Joseph	of the	Eli		of the	Maththat	of the	Levi

02	3197	02	2388	02	2501	**25**	02
τοῦ	Μελχὶ	τοῦ	Ἰανναὶ	τοῦ	Ἰωσὴφ		τοῦ
of the	Melchi	of the	Jannai	of the	Joseph		of the

3161	02	301	02	3486	02	2069	02
Ματταθίου	τοῦ	Ἀμὼς	τοῦ	Ναοὺμ	τοῦ	Ἑσλὶ	τοῦ
Mattathias	of the	Amos	of the	Naum	of the	Hesli	of the

3477	02	02	3092	02	3161	02	4584
Ναγγαὶ	**26**	τοῦ	Μάαθ	τοῦ	Ματταθίου	τοῦ	Σεμεῖν
Naggai		of the	Maath	of the	Mattathias	of the	Semein

02	2501a	02	2492b	**27**	02	2488a	02
τοῦ	Ἰωσὴχ	τοῦ	Ἰωδὰ		τοῦ	Ἰωανὰν	τοῦ
of the	Josech	of the	Joda		of the	Joanan	of the

4488	02	2216		4528	02	3518
Ῥησὰ	τοῦ	Ζοροβαβὲλ	τοῦ	Σαλαθιὴλ	τοῦ	Νηρὶ
Rhesa	of the	Zorobabel	of the	Salathiel	of the	Neri

28	02	3197	02	78	02	2973	02
	τοῦ	Μελχὶ	τοῦ	Ἀδδὶ	τοῦ	Κωσὰμ	τοῦ
	of the	Melchi	of the	Addi	of the	Kosam	of the

1678	02	2262	**29**	02	2424	02	1663
Ἐλμαδὰμ	τοῦ	Ἢρ		τοῦ	Ἰησοῦ	τοῦ	Ἐλιέζερ
Elmadam	of the	Er		of the	Jesus	of the	Eliezer

02	2497	02	3102b	02	3017	**30**	02
τοῦ	Ἰωρὶμ	τοῦ	Μαθθὰτ	τοῦ	Λευὶ		τοῦ
of the	Jorim	of the	Maththat	of the	Levi		of the

4826	02	2455	02	2501	02	2494	02
Συμεὼν	τοῦ	Ἰούδα	τοῦ	Ἰωσὴφ	τοῦ	Ἰωνὰμ	τοῦ
Symeon	of the	Judas	of the	Joseph	of the	Jonam	of the

1662	02	3190	02	3303a	02	3160
Ἐλιακὶμ	**31**	τοῦ	Μελεὰ	τοῦ	Μεννὰ	τοῦ	Ματταθὰ
Eliakim		of the	Melea	of the	Menna	of the	Mattatha

02	3481	02	1160a	**32**	02	2421	02
τοῦ	Ναθὰμ	τοῦ	Δαυὶδ		τοῦ	Ἰεσσαὶ	τοῦ
of the	Natham	of the	David		of the	Jesse	of the

2492a	02	1003	02	4527	02	3476
Ἰωβὴδ	τοῦ	Βόος	τοῦ	Σαλὰ	τοῦ	Ναασσὼν
Jobed	of the	Boos	of the	Sala	of the	Naasson

33	02	284	02	95a	02	720a	02
	τοῦ	Ἀμιναδὰβ	τοῦ	Ἀδμὶν	τοῦ	Ἀρνὶ	τοῦ
	of the	Aminadab	of the	Admin	of the	Arni	of the

2074	02	5329	02	2455	**34**	02	2384	02
Ἐσρὼμ	τοῦ	Φάρες	τοῦ	Ἰούδα		τοῦ	Ἰακὼβ	τοῦ
Esrom	of the	Phares	of the	Judas		of the	Jacob	of the

2464	02	11	02	2291	02	3493
Ἰσαὰκ	τοῦ	Ἀβραὰμ	τοῦ	Θάρα	τοῦ	Ναχὼρ
Isaac	of the	Abraham	of the	Thara	of the	Nachor

35	02	4588a	02	4466	02	5317	02
	τοῦ	Σεροὺχ	τοῦ	Ῥαγαὺ	τοῦ	Φάλεκ	τοῦ
	of the	Seruch	of the	Rhagau	of the	Phalek	of the

1443	02	4527	**36**	02	2536	02	742
Ἔβερ	τοῦ	Σαλὰ		τοῦ	Καϊνὰμ	τοῦ	Ἀρφαξὰδ
Eber	of the	Sala		of the	Kenam	of the	Arphaxad

02	4590	02	3575	02	2984	**37**	02
τοῦ	Σὴμ	τοῦ	Νῶε	τοῦ	Λάμεχ		τοῦ
of the	Sem	of the	Noah	of the	Lamech		of the

3103	02	1800	02	2391	02	3121
Μαθουσαλὰ	τοῦ	Ἐνὼχ	τοῦ	Ἰάρετ	τοῦ	Μαλελεὴλ
Mathusala	of the	Henoch	of the	Jaret	of the	Maleleel

02	2536	**38**	02	1802	02	4589	02	76
τοῦ	Καϊνὰμ		τοῦ	Ἐνὼς	τοῦ	Σὴθ	τοῦ	Ἀδὰμ
of the	Kenam		of the	Enoch	of the	Seth	of the	Adam

02	2316	**4:1**	2424	1161	4134	4151	40
τοῦ	θεοῦ.		Ἰησοῦς	δὲ	πλήρης	πνεύματος	ἁγίου
of the	God.		Jesus	but	full	of spirit	holy

5290	575	02	2446	2532	71	1722	011
ὑπέστρεψεν	ἀπὸ	τοῦ	Ἰορδάνου	καὶ	ἤγετο	ἐν	τῷ
returned	from	the	Jordan	and	was led	in	the

4151   1722 07   2048   **2** 2250   5062
πνεύματι ἐν   τῇ   ἐρήμῳ   ἡμέρας τεσσεράκοντα
spirit in   the desert days   forty

3985   5259 02 1228   2532 3756 2068
πειραζόμενος   ὑπὸ τοῦ διαβόλου. Καὶ οὐκ ἔφαγεν
being pressured by   the slanderer. And   not he ate

3762   1722 019 2250   1565   2532 4931
οὐδὲν   ἐν   ταῖς ἡμέραις ἐκείναις καὶ συντελεσθεισῶν
nothing in   the days   those   and having been
                                            fully completed

846   3983   **3** 3004 1161 846   01 1228
αὐτῶν ἐπείνασεν.   εἶπεν δὲ αὐτῷ ὁ διάβολος·
them he hungered. Said but to him the slanderer;

1487 5207 1510   02   2316   3004 03   3037 3778
εἰ   υἱὸς εἶ   τοῦ   θεοῦ, εἰπὲ τῷ   λίθῳ τούτῳ
if   son you are of the God, say to the stone this

2443 1096   740   **4** 2532 611   4314 846
ἵνα γένηται   ἄρτος.   καὶ ἀπεκρίθη πρὸς αὐτὸν
that it might become bread. And answered to   him

01 2424   1125   3754 3756 1909 740
ὁ Ἰησοῦς· γέγραπται   ὅτι οὐκ ἐπ᾽ ἄρτῳ
the Jesus; it has been written (") not on bread
            written,

3441 2198   01 444   **5** 2532 321   846
μόνῳ ζήσεται ὁ ἄνθρωπος.   Καὶ ἀναγαγὼν   αὐτὸν
alone will live the man.   And leading up him

1166   846   3956   020 932   06
ἔδειξεν αὐτῷ πάσας τὰς βασιλείας τῆς
he showed him all the kingdoms of the

3625   1722 4743   5550   **6** 2532 3004 846
οἰκουμένης   ἐν στιγμῇ χρόνου   καὶ εἶπεν αὐτῷ
inhabited world in point of time and said to him

01 1228   1473 1325   08   1849   3778
ὁ διάβολος· σοὶ δώσω   τὴν ἐξουσίαν ταύτην
the slanderer; to you I will give the authority this

537   2532 08 1391   846   3754   1473
ἅπασαν καὶ τὴν δόξαν   αὐτῶν, ὅτι   ἐμοὶ
all   and the splendor of them, because to me

3860   2532 3739 1437 2309 1325   846   **7** 1473
παραδέδοται καὶ ᾧ ἐὰν θέλω   δίδωμι αὐτήν·   σὺ
it has been and to if I want to give it;   you
given over   whom

3767 1437 4352   1799   1473 1510   1473
οὖν ἐὰν προσκυνήσῃς ἐνώπιον ἐμοῦ, ἔσται σοῦ
then if might worship before me,   will be of you

3956   **8** 2532 611   01   2424   3004 846
πᾶσα.   καὶ ἀποκριθεὶς ὁ Ἰησοῦς εἶπεν αὐτῷ·
all.   And having answered the Jesus said to him;

1125   2962 04 2316 1473   4352   2532
γέγραπται· κύριον τὸν θεόν σου προσκυνήσεις καὶ
it has been Master the God of you you will   and
written;   worship

846 3441 3000   **9** 71   1161 846   1519
αὐτῷ μόνῳ λατρεύσεις.   Ἤγαγεν δὲ αὐτὸν εἰς
him alone will serve.   He led but him   into

2419   2532 2476   1909 012 4419   010
Ἰερουσαλὴμ καὶ ἔστησεν ἐπὶ τὸ πτερύγιον τοῦ
Jerusalem and he stood on the wing   of the

2411 2532 3004 846   1487 5207 1510   02   2316
ἱεροῦ καὶ εἶπεν αὐτῷ· εἰ υἱὸς εἶ   τοῦ   θεοῦ,
temple and said to him; if son you are of the God,

906   4572   1782   2736 **10** 1125   1063
βάλε σεαυτὸν ἐντεῦθεν κάτω·   γέγραπται γὰρ
throw yourself from here down; it has been for,
                                written

3754 015   32   846   1781   4012
ὅτι τοῖς ἀγγέλοις αὐτοῦ ἐντελεῖται περὶ
(") to the messengers of him he will command about

Spirit in the wilderness, [2]where for forty days he was tempted by the devil. He ate nothing at all during those days, and when they were over, he was famished. [3]The devil said to him, "If you are the Son of God, command this stone to become a loaf of bread." [4]Jesus answered, "It is written, 'One does not live by bread alone.'"

[5]Then the devil[a] led him up and showed him in an instant all the kingdoms of the world. [6]And the devil[a] said to him, "To you I will give their glory and all this authority; for it has been given over to me, and I give it to anyone I please. [7]If you, then, will worship me, it will all be yours." [8]Jesus answered him, "It is written,

'Worship the Lord your God,
    and serve only him.'"

[9]Then the devil[a] took him to Jerusalem, and placed him on the pinnacle of the temple, saying to him, "If you are the Son of God, throw yourself down from here, [10]for it is written,

'He will command his angels concerning you,

[a] Gk *he*

to protect you,'
[11]and
'On their hands they will
   bear you up,
   so that you will not
   dash your foot against
   a stone.'"
[12]Jesus answered him, "It is
said, 'Do not put the Lord
your God to the test.'"
[13]When the devil had
finished every test, he
departed from him until
an opportune time.

   [14]Then Jesus, filled
with the power of the
Spirit, returned to Galilee,
and a report about him
spread through all the
surrounding country. [15]He
began to teach in their
synagogues and was praised
by everyone.

   [16]When he came to
Nazareth, where he had
been brought up, he went
to the synagogue on the
sabbath day, as was his
custom. He stood up to
read, [17]and the scroll of
the prophet Isaiah was
given to him. He unrolled
the scroll and found the
place where it was written:
[18]"The Spirit of the Lord
   is upon me,
   because he has anointed
   me
   to bring good news
      to the poor.
   He has sent me to
      proclaim release to the
      captives
   and recovery of sight
      to the blind,
      to let the oppressed
         go free,
[19]to proclaim the year of
   the Lord's favor."

1473 010   1314   1473 **11** 2532 3754 1909 5495
σοῦ τοῦ διαφυλάξαι σε   καὶ ὅτι ἐπὶ χειρῶν
you of the to guard   you   and that on hands
             thoroughly

142   1473 3379   4350   4314 3037 04 4228
ἀροῦσίν σε, μήποτε προσκόψῃς πρὸς λίθον τὸν πόδα
they will you, not you might to stone the foot
lift up   then   stumble

1473 2532 611   3004 846   01   2424
σου. **12** καὶ ἀποκριθεὶς εἶπεν αὐτῷ ὁ ʼΙησοῦς
of you. And having answered said to him the Jesus

3754 3004   3756 1598
ὅτι εἴρηται·   οὐκ ἐκπειράσεις
that it has been said; not you will pressure out

2962   04 2316 1473 13 2532 4931
κύριον τὸν θεόν σου.   Καὶ συντελέσας
Master the God of you. And having completed fully

3956 3986   01   1228   868   575 846
πάντα πειρασμὸν ὁ διάβολος ἀπέστη ἀπʼ αὐτοῦ
all   pressure the slanderer stood off from him

891   2540   14 2532 5290   01   2424 1722 07
ἄχρι καιροῦ.   Καὶ ὑπέστρεψεν ὁ ʼΙησοῦς ἐν τῇ
until season.   And returned the Jesus in the

1411   010   4151   1519 08 1056   2532
δυνάμει τοῦ πνεύματος εἰς τὴν Γαλιλαίαν. καὶ
power of the spirit   into the Galilee.   And

5345 1831   2596 3650 06 4066   4012
φήμη ἐξῆλθεν καθʼ ὅλης τῆς περιχώρου περὶ
report went out to whole the country around about

846   15 2532 846   1321   1722 019 4864
αὐτοῦ.   καὶ αὐτὸς ἐδίδασκεν ἐν ταῖς συναγωγαῖς
him.   And himself was teaching in the synagogues

846   1392   5259 3956   16 2532
αὐτῶν δοξαζόμενος ὑπὸ πάντων.   Καὶ
of them being given splendor by all.   And

2064 1519 3477a   3757 1510   5142
ἦλθεν εἰς Ναζαρά, οὗ ἦν   τεθραμμένος,
he went into Nazara, where he was+ +having been fed,

2532 1525   2596 012 1536a 846   1722 07 2250
καὶ εἰσῆλθεν κατὰ τὸ εἰωθὸς αὐτῷ ἐν τῇ ἡμέρᾳ
and he went in by the custom to him in the day

022   4521   1519 08 4864   2532 450
τῶν σαββάτων εἰς τὴν συναγωγὴν καὶ ἀνέστη
of the sabbaths in the synagogue and he stood up

314   17 2532 1929   846   975
ἀναγνῶναι.   καὶ ἐπεδόθη αὐτῷ βιβλίον
to read.   And was given on to him small book

02   4396   2268   2532 380   012
τοῦ προφήτου ʼΗσαΐου καὶ ἀναπτύξας   τὸ
of the spokesman Isaiah and having unrolled the

975   2147   04 5117 3757 1510   1125
βιβλίον εὗρεν τὸν τόπον οὗ ἦν   γεγραμμένον·
small   he found the place where it was+ +having been
book   written;

     4151   2962   1909 1473 3739   1511a
18 πνεῦμα κυρίου ἐπʼ ἐμὲ οὗ   εἴνεκεν
     spirit of Master on me   of whom on account

5548   1473 2097   4434
ἔχρισέν με εὐαγγελίσασθαι πτωχοῖς,
he anointed me to tell good message to poor,

649   1473 2784   164   859
ἀπέσταλκέν με, κηρύξαι αἰχμαλώτοις ἄφεσιν
he delegated me, to announce to captives sending off

2532 5185   309   649   2352   1722
καὶ τυφλοῖς ἀνάβλεψιν, ἀποστεῖλαι τεθραυσμένους ἐν
and blind seeing   to delegate ones having in
           again,   been crushed

859   19 2784   1763   2962
ἀφέσει,   κηρύξαι ἐνιαυτὸν κυρίου
sending off, to announce year of Master

1184		**20**	2532	4428	012	975		591	

δεκτόν. **20** καὶ πτύξας τὸ βιβλίον ἀποδοὺς
acceptable. And having the small book having given
                    rolled   back

03   5257   2523   2532 3956   013 3788
τῷ ὑπηρέτῃ ἐκάθισεν· καὶ πάντων οἱ ὀφθαλμοὶ
to the assistant he sat;   and of all the eyes

1722 07   4864   1510 816   846   **21** 757
ἐν τῇ συναγωγῇ ἦσαν ἀτενίζοντες αὐτῷ. **21** ἤρξατο
in the synagogue were+ +staring at him. He began

1161 3004   4314 846   3754 4594   4137
δὲ λέγειν πρὸς αὐτοὺς ὅτι σήμερον πεπλήρωται
but to speak to them,   (") today   has been filled

05 1124   3778 1722 023   3775 1473 **22** 2532 3956
ἡ γραφὴ αὕτη ἐν τοῖς ὠσὶν ὑμῶν. **22** Καὶ πάντες
the writing this in the ears of you. And all

3140   846   2532 2296   1909 015
ἐμαρτύρουν αὐτῷ καὶ ἐθαύμαζον ἐπὶ τοῖς
were testifying to him and were marveling on the

3056   06   5485   015   1607   1537 010
λόγοις τῆς χάριτος τοῖς ἐκπορευομένοις ἐκ τοῦ
words of the favor the traveling out from the

4750   846   2532 3004   3780 5207 1510
στόματος αὐτοῦ καὶ ἔλεγον·   οὐχὶ υἱός ἐστιν
mouth of him and were saying; not son is

2501   3778   **23** 2532 3004   4314 846   3843
Ἰωσὴφ οὗτος; **23** καὶ εἶπεν πρὸς αὐτούς· πάντως
Joseph this? And he said to them; altogether

3004   1473 08   3850   3778
ἐρεῖτέ μοι τὴν παραβολὴν ταύτην·
you will say to me the parallel story this;

2395   2323   4572   3745   191
ἰατρέ, θεράπευσον σεαυτόν· ὅσα ἠκούσαμεν
physician, heal   yourself; as many as we heard

1096   1519 08 2746a   4160   2532 5602 1722
γενόμενα εἰς τὴν Καφαρναοὺμ ποίησον καὶ ὧδε ἐν
having become in the Capernaum do   also here in

07 3968   1473 **24** 3004 1161 281   3004 1473
τῇ πατρίδι σου. **24** εἶπεν δέ· ἀμὴν λέγω ὑμῖν
the fatherland of you. He said but; amen I say to you

3754 3762   4396   1184   1510 1722 07 3968
ὅτι οὐδεὶς προφήτης δεκτός ἐστιν ἐν τῇ πατρίδι
that no one spokesman acceptable is in the fatherland

846   **25** 1909 225   1161 3004 1473   4183 5503
αὐτοῦ. **25** ἐπ᾽ ἀληθείας δὲ λέγω ὑμῖν, πολλαὶ χῆραι
of him. On truth   but I say to you, many widows

1510 1722 019   2250   2243   1722 03 2474   3753
ἦσαν ἐν ταῖς ἡμέραις Ἠλίου ἐν τῷ Ἰσραήλ, ὅτε
were in the days   of Elijah in the Israel, when

2808   01   3772   1909 2094 5140 2532 3376   1803
ἐκλείσθη ὁ οὐρανὸς ἐπὶ ἔτη τρία καὶ μῆνας ἕξ,
was closed the heaven on years three and months six,

5613 1096   3042   3173 1909 3956 08 1093 **26** 2532
ὡς ἐγένετο λιμὸς μέγας ἐπὶ πᾶσαν τὴν γῆν, **26** καὶ
as became famine great on all the earth,   and

4314 3762   846   3992   2243 1487 3361 1519
πρὸς οὐδεμίαν αὐτῶν ἐπέμφθη Ἠλίας εἰ μὴ εἰς
to but not one of them was sent Elijah except into

4558   06   4606   4314 1135   5503   **27** 2532
Σάρεπτα τῆς Σιδωνίας πρὸς γυναῖκα χήραν. **27** καὶ
Sarepta of the Sidonia to woman widow. And

4183 3015   1510 1722 03   2474 1909 1666   02
πολλοὶ λεπροὶ ἦσαν ἐν τῷ Ἰσραὴλ ἐπὶ Ἐλισαίου τοῦ
many lepers were in the Israel on Elisha the

4396   2532 3762   846   2511   1487 3361
προφήτου, καὶ οὐδεὶς αὐτῶν ἐκαθαρίσθη. εἰ μὴ
spokesman, and no one of them was cleaned except

3483a 01   4948   **28** 2532 4092   3956   2372 1722
Ναιμὰν ὁ Σύρος. **28** καὶ ἐπλήσθησαν πάντες θυμοῦ ἐν
Naaman the Syrian. And were filled all   fury in

[20]And he rolled up the scroll, gave it back to the attendant, and sat down. The eyes of all in the synagogue were fixed on him. [21]Then he began to say to them, "Today this scripture has been fulfilled in your hearing." [22]All spoke well of him and were amazed at the gracious words that came from his mouth. They said, "Is not this Joseph's son?" [23]He said to them, "Doubtless you will quote to me this proverb, 'Doctor, cure yourself!' And you will say, 'Do here also in your hometown the things that we have heard you did at Capernaum.'" [24]And he said, "Truly I tell you, no prophet is accepted in the prophet's hometown. [25]But the truth is, there were many widows in Israel in the time of Elijah, when the heaven was shut up three years and six months, and there was a severe famine over all the land; [26]yet Elijah was sent to none of them except to a widow at Zarephath in Sidon. [27]There were also many lepers[a] in Israel in the time of the prophet Elisha, and none of them was cleansed except Naaman the Syrian." [28]When they heard this, all in the synagogue were filled with rage.

[a] The terms *leper* and *leprosy* can refer to several diseases

²⁹They got up, drove him out of the town, and led him to the brow of the hill on which their town was built, so that they might hurl him off the cliff. ³⁰But he passed through the midst of them and went on his way.

31 He went down to Capernaum, a city in Galilee, and was teaching them on the sabbath. ³²They were astounded at his teaching, because he spoke with authority. ³³In the synagogue there was a man who had the spirit of an unclean demon, and he cried out with a loud voice, ³⁴"Let us alone! What have you to do with us, Jesus of Nazareth? Have you come to destroy us? I know who you are, the Holy One of God." ³⁵But Jesus rebuked him, saying, "Be silent, and come out of him!" When the demon had thrown him down before them, he came out of him without having done him any harm. ³⁶They were all amazed and kept saying to one another, "What kind of utterance is this? For with authority and power he commands the unclean spirits, and out they come!" ³⁷And a report about him began to reach every place in the region.

07 4864 191 3778 29 2532 450
τῇ συναγωγῇ ἀκούοντες ταῦτα καὶ ἀναστάντες
the synagogue hearing these and having stood up
1544 846 1854 06 4172 2533 71
ἐξέβαλον αὐτὸν ἔξω τῆς πόλεως καὶ ἤγαγον
they threw out him outside the city and they led
846 2193 3790 010 3735 1909 3739 05 4172
αὐτὸν ἕως ὀφρύος τοῦ ὄρους ἐφ' οὗ ἡ πόλις
him until brow of the hill on which the city
3618 846 5620 2630
ᾠκοδόμητο αὐτῶν ὥστε κατακρημνίσαι
had been built of them so that to be hurled down steep
846 846 1161 1330 1223 3319 846
αὐτόν· 30 αὐτὸς δὲ διελθὼν διὰ μέσου αὐτῶν
him; himself but having through middle of them gone through
4198 2532 2718 1519 2746a
ἐπορεύετο. 31 Καὶ κατῆλθεν εἰς Καφαρναοὺμ
he was traveling. And he went down into Capernaum
4172 06 1056 2532 1510 1321 846
πόλιν τῆς Γαλιλαίας. καὶ ἦν διδάσκων αὐτοὺς
city of the Galilee. And he was+ +teaching them
1722 023 4521 2532 1605 1909
ἐν τοῖς σάββασιν· 32 καὶ ἐξεπλήσσοντο ἐπὶ
in the sabbaths; and they were astonished at
07 1322 846 3754 1722 1849 1510 01 3056
τῇ διδαχῇ αὐτοῦ, ὅτι ἐν ἐξουσίᾳ ἦν ὁ λόγος
the teaching of him, because in authority was the word
846 2532 1722 07 4864 1510 444 2192
αὐτοῦ. 33 Καὶ ἐν τῇ συναγωγῇ ἦν ἄνθρωπος ἔχων
of him. And in the synagogue was man having
4151 1140 169 2532 349 5456
πνεῦμα δαιμονίου ἀκαθάρτου καὶ ἀνέκραξεν φωνῇ
spirit of demon unclean and it shouted out in sound
3173 1436 5101 1473 2532 1473 2424
μεγάλῃ· 34 ἔα, τί ἡμῖν καὶ σοί, Ἰησοῦ
great, ah, what to us and to you, Jesus
3479 2064 622 1473 3609a 1473 5101
Ναζαρηνέ; ἦλθες ἀπολέσαι ἡμᾶς; οἶδά σε τίς
Nazarene? Came you to destroy us? I know you who
1510 01 40 02 2316 2532 2008 846 01
εἶ, ὁ ἅγιος τοῦ θεοῦ. 35 καὶ ἐπετίμησεν αὐτῷ ὁ
are, the holy of the God. And admonished him the
2424 2004 5392 2532 1831 575 846
Ἰησοῦς λέγων· φιμώθητι καὶ ἔξελθε ἀπ' αὐτοῦ.
Jesus saying· be muzzled and come out from him.
2532 4496 846 09 1140 1519 012 3319
καὶ ῥίψαν αὐτὸν τὸ δαιμόνιον εἰς τὸ μέσον
And having flung him the demon into the middle
1831 575 846 3367 984 846 2532
ἐξῆλθεν ἀπ' αὐτοῦ μηδὲν βλάψαν αὐτόν. 36 καὶ
went out from him nothing having hurt him. And
1096 2285 1909 3956 2532 4814
ἐγένετο θάμβος ἐπὶ πάντας καὶ συνελάλουν
became astonishment on all and they were talking together
4314 240 3004 5101 01 3056 3778 3754
πρὸς ἀλλήλους λέγοντες· τίς ὁ λόγος οὗτος ὅτι
to one another saying, what the word this that
1722 1849 2532 1411 2004 023 169
ἐν ἐξουσίᾳ καὶ δυνάμει ἐπιτάσσει τοῖς ἀκαθάρτοις
in authority and power he orders the unclean
4151 2532 1831 2532 1607 2279
πνεύμασιν καὶ ἐξέρχονται; 37 καὶ ἐξεπορεύετο ἦχος
spirits and they come out? And traveled out sound
4012 846 1519 3956 5117 06 4066
περὶ αὐτοῦ εἰς πάντα τόπον τῆς περιχώρου.
about him into all place of the country around.

```
        450                    1161 575   06   4864
38  Ἀναστὰς           δὲ    ἀπὸ  τῆς  συναγωγῆς
    Having stood up but     from the  synagogue
1525              1519 08  3614   4613      3994
εἰσῆλθεν          εἰς  τὴν οἰκίαν Σίμωνος.  πενθερὰ
he went into      into the house of Simon.  Mother-in-law
1161 02   4613        1510 4912         3173   2532
δὲ   τοῦ  Σίμωνος  ἦν   συνεχομένη πυρετῷ μεγάλῳ καὶ
but  of   Simon    was+ +being held in fever great  and
     the                     together
2065       846    4012  846      39 2532 2186
ἠρώτησαν  αὐτὸν  περὶ  αὐτῆς.      καὶ ἐπιστὰς
they asked him   about her.        And having stood on
asked
1883    846   2008        03   4446  2532 863
ἐπάνω  αὐτῆς ἐπετίμησεν  τῷ  πυρετῷ καὶ ἀφῆκεν
upon   her   he admonished the fever and it left off
846      3916      1161 450            1247
αὐτήν· παραχρῆμα δὲ   ἀναστᾶσα      διηκόνει
her;   suddenly   but having stood up she was serving
846      40 1416        1161 02  2246  537     3745
αὐτοῖς.    Δύνοντος   δὲ   τοῦ ἡλίου ἅπαντες ὅσοι
them.      Having set  but  the sun  all     as many as
2192  770         3554     4164      71     846
εἶχον ἀσθενοῦντας νόσοις  ποικίλαις ἤγαγον αὐτοὺς
had   being weak  illnesses various  they led them
4314  846   01   1161 1520  1538  846    020
πρὸς αὐτόν· ὁ    δὲ   ἑνὶ  ἑκάστῳ αὐτῶν τὰς
to    him;  the one but to one  each   of them the
5495   2007       2323        846     41 1831
χεῖρας ἐπιτιθεὶς ἐθεράπευεν αὐτούς.    ἐξήρχετο
hands  having set on he healed them.    Were coming out
1161 2532 1140     575   4183    2905       2532
δὲ   καὶ δαιμόνια ἀπὸ πολλῶν κρ[αυγ]άζοντα καὶ
but  also demons  from many  shouting      and
3004    1473 1510 01  5207 02    2316   3754
λέγοντα ὅτι σὺ   εἶ  ὁ   υἱὸς τοῦ θεοῦ. καὶ
saying, (") you  are the son of the God.  And
2008      3756 1439        846  2980      3754
ἐπιτιμῶν  οὐκ εἶα       αὐτὰ λαλεῖν,  ὅτι
admonishing not he was allowing them to speak, because
3609a          04    5547  846   1510      1096
ᾔδεισαν        τὸν χριστὸν αὐτὸν εἶναι. 42 Γενομένης
they had known the Christ  him   to be.  Having become
1161 2250  1831       4198          1519 2048
δὲ   ἡμέρας ἐξελθὼν  ἐπορεύθη      εἰς ἔρημον
but  day   having gone out he traveled into desert
5117    2532 013  3793   1934             846  2532
τόπον· καὶ  οἱ  ὄχλοι ἐπεζήτουν      αὐτὸν καὶ
place; and  the crowds were seeking after him  and
2064  2193 846   2532 2722         846     010 3361
ἦλθον ἕως αὐτοῦ καὶ κατεῖχον      αὐτὸν τοῦ μὴ
came  until him  and  were holding on him  the not
4198        575   846   43 01  1161 3004   4314 846
πορεύεσθαι ἀπ᾽ αὐτῶν.    ὁ   δὲ  εἶπεν πρὸς αὐτοὺς
to travel   from them.   The one but said  to   them
3754 2532 019  2087    4172     2097
ὅτι καὶ  ταῖς ἑτέραις πόλεσιν εὐαγγελίσασθαί
that also to the others cities to tell good message
1473 1163        08  932       02   2316   3754
με   δεῖ       τὴν βασιλείαν τοῦ θεοῦ, ὅτι
me   it is necessary the kingdom of the God, because
1909 3778  649         2532 1510      2784
ἐπὶ τοῦτο ἀπεστάλην. 44 Καὶ ἦν      κηρύσσων
on   this I was delegated. And he was+ +announcing
1519 020 4864     06    2449        5:1 1096
εἰς τὰς συναγωγὰς τῆς Ἰουδαίας.       Ἐγένετο
in   the synagogues of the Judea.        It became
```

38 After leaving the synagogue he entered Simon's house. Now Simon's mother-in-law was suffering from a high fever, and they asked him about her. 39 Then he stood over her and rebuked the fever, and it left her. Immediately she got up and began to serve them.

40 As the sun was setting, all those who had any who were sick with various kinds of diseases brought them to him; and he laid his hands on each of them and cured them. 41 Demons also came out of many, shouting, "You are the Son of God!" But he rebuked them and would not allow them to speak, because they knew that he was the Messiah.[a]

42 At daybreak he departed and went into a deserted place. And the crowds were looking for him; and when they reached him, they wanted to prevent him from leaving them. 43 But he said to them, "I must proclaim the good news of the kingdom of God to the other cities also; for I was sent for this purpose." 44 So he continued proclaiming the message in the synagogues of Judea.[b]

CHAPTER 5

Once while Jesus[c] was standing beside

[a] Or the Christ
[b] Other ancient authorities read Galilee
[c] Gk he

the lake of Gennesaret, and
the crowd was pressing in
on him to hear the word
of God, ²he saw two boats
there at the shore of the
lake; the fishermen had
gone out of them and were
washing their nets. ³He got
into one of the boats, the
one belonging to Simon,
and asked him to put out
a little way from the shore.
Then he sat down and
taught the crowds from
the boat. ⁴When he had
finished speaking, he said
to Simon, "Put out into
the deep water and let down
your nets for a catch."
⁵Simon answered, "Master,
we have worked all night
long but have caught
nothing. Yet if you say so,
I will let down the nets."
⁶When they had done this,
they caught so many fish
that their nets were
beginning to break. ⁷So
they signaled their partners
in the other boat to come
and help them. And they
came and filled both boats,
so that they began to sink.
⁸But when Simon Peter saw
it, he fell down at Jesus'
knees, saying, " Go away
from me, Lord, for I am
a sinful man!" ⁹For he
and all who were with him
were amazed

1161	1722	011	04	3793	1945		846	2532	191
δὲ	ἐν	τῷ	τὸν	ὄχλον	ἐπικεῖσθαι		αὐτῷ	καὶ	ἀκούειν
but	in	the	the	crowd	to be laid on		him	and	to hear

04	3056	02	2316	2532	846		1510	2476		3844
τὸν	λόγον	τοῦ	θεοῦ	καὶ	αὐτὸς		ἦν	ἑστὼς		παρὰ
the	word	of the	God	and	himself		was+	+standing		by

08   3041   1082   **2**   2532 3708   1417 4143
τὴν λίμνην Γεννησαρέτ ² καὶ εἶδεν δύο πλοῖα
the lake Gennesaret   and he saw two boats

2476		3844 08	3041		013 1161	231		575
ἑστῶτα		παρὰ τὴν	λίμνην·		οἱ δὲ	ἁλιεῖς		ἀπ᾽
having stood		by the	lake;		the but	fishermen		from

846	576		4150	024 1350		1684 1161
αὐτῶν	ἀποβάντες		ἔπλυνον	τὰ δίκτυα.	**3**	ἐμβὰς δὲ
of them	having gone		were	the nets.		Having but
	off		washing			gone in

1519 1520 022		4143	3739	1510 4613		2065
εἰς ἓν τῶν		πλοίων,	ὃ	ἦν Σίμωνος,		ἠρώτησεν
into one of the		boats,	which	was of Simon,		he asked

846	575 06	1093 1877			3641	2523
αὐτὸν	ἀπὸ τῆς	γῆς ἐπαναγαγεῖν			ὀλίγον·	καθίσας
him	from the	land to lead on up			little;	having sat

1161 1537 010 4143	1321		016 3793
δὲ ἐκ τοῦ πλοίου	ἐδίδασκεν		τοὺς ὄχλους.
but from the boat	he was teaching		the crowds.

4 5613 1161 3973   2980   3004   4314 04
'Ως δὲ ἐπαύσατο λαλῶν, εἶπεν πρὸς τὸν
As but he stopped speaking, he said to the

4613	1877		1519 012 899	2532 5465	024
Σίμωνα·	ἐπανάγαγε		εἰς τὸ βάθος	καὶ χαλάσατε	τὰ
Simon;	lead on up		into the depth	and lower	the

1350	1473	1519 61	**5**	2532 611		4613
δίκτυα	ὑμῶν	εἰς ἄγραν.		καὶ ἀποκριθεὶς		Σίμων
nets	of you	into catch.		And having answered		Simon

3004 1988		1223	3650 3571
εἶπεν· ἐπιστάτα,		δι᾽	ὅλης νυκτὸς
said; Master teacher,		through	whole night

2872	3762	2983		1909 1161 011 4487
κοπιάσαντες	οὐδὲν	ἐλάβομεν·		ἐπὶ δὲ τῷ ῥήματί
having labored	nothing	we took;		on but the word

1473 5465		024 1350		**6**	2532 3778 4160
σου χαλάσω		τὰ δίκτυα.			καὶ τοῦτο ποιήσαντες
of you I will lower		the nets.			And this having done

4788		4128	2486	4183
συνέκλεισαν		πλῆθος	ἰχθύων	πολύ,
they closed together		quantity	of fish	much,

1284		1161 021 1350	846	**7**	2532
διερρήσσετο		δὲ τὰ δίκτυα	αὐτῶν.		καὶ
were tearing apart		but the nets	of them.		And

2656		015 3353	1722 011 2087 4143
κατένευσαν		τοῖς μετόχοις	ἐν τῷ ἑτέρῳ πλοίῳ
they nodded		toward the sharers	in the other boat

010	2064	4815		846	2532
τοῦ	ἐλθόντας	συλλαβέσθαι		αὐτοῖς·	καὶ
of the	having come	to take together		them;	and

2064	2532 4092	297	024 4143	5620
ἦλθον	καὶ ἔπλησαν	ἀμφότερα	τὰ πλοῖα	ὥστε
they came	and filled	both	the boats	so that

1036	846	**8**	3708		1161 4613	4074
βυθίζεσθαι	αὐτά.		ἰδὼν		δὲ Σίμων	Πέτρος
to be sunk	them.		Having seen		but Simon	Peter

4363	023 1119	2424	3004	1831 575
προσέπεσεν	τοῖς γόνασιν	Ἰησοῦ	λέγων·	ἔξελθε ἀπ᾽
fell to	the knees	of Jesus	saying;	go out from

1473 3754	435 268	1510 2962
ἐμοῦ, ὅτι	ἀνὴρ ἁμαρτωλός	εἰμι, κύριε.
me,	because man sinner	I am, Master.

9 2285   1063 4023   846   2532 3956
θάμβος γὰρ περιέσχεν αὐτὸν καὶ πάντας
Astonishment for encircled him and all

016   4862   846   1909 07   61   014   2486   3739
τοὺς   σὺν   αὐτῷ   ἐπὶ   τῇ   ἄγρᾳ   τῶν   ἰχθύων   ὧν
the ones   with   him   on   the   catch   of the   fish   which

4815   3668   1161 2532 2385   2532
συνέλαβον,   10   ὁμοίως   δὲ   καὶ   ᾽Ιάκωβον καὶ
they took together,   likewise but   also Jacob   and

2491   5207   2199   3739 1510 2844   03
᾽Ιωάννην υἱοὺς Ζεβεδαίου,   οἳ   ἦσαν κοινωνοὶ τῷ
John   sons   of Zebedee, who were partners to the

4613   2532 3004   4314 04   4613   01   2424   3361
Σίμωνι.   καὶ   εἶπεν πρὸς τὸν Σίμωνα ὁ   ᾽Ιησοῦς· μὴ
Simon.   And   said   to   the Simon   the Jesus;   not

5399   575   02   3568   444   1510
φοβοῦ· ἀπὸ   τοῦ   νῦν   ἀνθρώπους ἔσῃ
fear;   from   the   now   men   you will be

2221   2532 2609   024   4143 1909
ζωγρῶν.   11   καὶ   καταγαγόντες   τὰ   πλοῖα ἐπὶ
capturing alive. And   having led down the   boats on

08 1093   863   3956   190   846
τὴν γῆν   ἀφέντες   πάντα ἠκολούθησαν αὐτῷ.
the land   having left off all   they followed him.

     2532 1096   1722 011 1510   846   1722 1520 018
12   Καὶ   ἐγένετο   ἐν   τῷ   εἶναι αὐτὸν ἐν   μιᾷ   τῶν
     And   it became in   the to be him   in   one   of the

4172   2532 2400   435   4134   3014   3708   1161
πόλεων καὶ   ἰδοὺ ἀνὴρ πλήρης λέπρας·   ἰδὼν   δὲ
cities and   look man   full   leprosy; having seen but

04   2424   4098   1909 4383   1189   846   3004
τὸν ᾽Ιησοῦν, πεσὼν ἐπὶ   πρόσωπον ἐδεήθη αὐτοῦ λέγων·
the Jesus,   falling on   face   begged him   saying;

2962   1437 2309   1410   1473 2511
κύριε, ἐὰν   θέλῃς   δύνασαί   με   καθαρίσαι.
Master, if   you might want you are able me to clean.

     2532 1614   08   5495   681   846
13   καὶ   ἐκτείνας   τὴν χεῖρα ἥψατο   αὐτοῦ
     And   having stretched out the hand   he touched him

3004   2511   2532 2112   05   3014
λέγων· θέλω, καθαρίσθητι· καὶ   εὐθέως   ἡ   λέπρα
saying; I want, be clean;   and   immediately the leprosy

565   575   846   2532 846   3853   846
ἀπῆλθεν ἀπ᾽ αὐτοῦ.   14 καὶ   αὐτὸς   παρήγγειλεν αὐτῷ
went off from him.   And   himself commanded   to him

3367   3004   235   565   1166   4572
μηδενὶ   εἰπεῖν, ἀλλὰ ἀπελθὼν   δεῖξον   σεαυτὸν
to no one to say, but   having gone off show   yourself

03   2409   2532 4374   4012   02   2512   1473
τῷ   ἱερεῖ καὶ   προσένεγκε περὶ τοῦ καθαρισμοῦ σου
to the priest and offer   about the cleaning of you

2531   4367   3475   1519 3142   846
καθὼς προσέταξεν Μωϋσῆς, εἰς   μαρτύριον αὐτοῖς.
just as commanded Moses,   for   testimony to them.

     1330   1161 3123   01   3056   4012   846
15   διήρχετο   δὲ   μᾶλλον ὁ   λόγος περὶ αὐτοῦ,
     Was going through but   more   the word   about him,

2532 4908   3793   4183   191   2532
καὶ   συνήρχοντο   ὄχλοι πολλοὶ ἀκούειν καὶ
and   were coming together crowds many   to hear and

2323   575   018 769   846   846   1161
θεραπεύεσθαι ἀπὸ τῶν ἀσθενειῶν αὐτῶν· 16 αὐτὸς   δὲ
to be healed   from the weaknesses of them;   himself   but

1510 5298   1722 019   2048   2532 4336
ἦν   ὑποχωρῶν   ἐν   ταῖς ἐρήμοις καὶ προσευχόμενος.
was+ withdrawing in   the   deserts   and +praying.

     2532 1096   1722 1520 018   2250   2532 846
17   Καὶ   ἐγένετο   ἐν   μιᾷ   τῶν   ἡμερῶν καὶ αὐτὸς
     And   it became in   one   of the days   also himself

1510 1321   2532 1510   2521   5330   2532
ἦν   διδάσκων, καὶ   ἦσαν καθήμενοι Φαρισαῖοι καὶ
was   teaching,   and   were+ sitting   Pharisees   and

---

at the catch of fish that they had taken; [10]and so also were James and John, sons of Zebedee, who were partners with Simon. Then Jesus said to Simon, "Do not be afraid; from now on you will be catching people." [11]When they had brought their boats to shore, they left everything and followed him.

[12]Once, when he was in one of the cities, there was a man covered with leprosy.[a] When he saw Jesus, he bowed with his face to the ground and begged him, "Lord, if you choose, you can make me clean." [13]Then Jesus[b] stretched out his hand, touched him, and said, "I do choose. Be made clean." Immediately the leprosy[a] left him. [14]And he ordered him to tell no one. "Go," he said, "and show yourself to the priest, and, as Moses commanded, make an offering for your cleansing, for a testimony to them." [15]But now more than ever the word about Jesus[c] spread abroad; many crowds would gather to hear him and to be cured of their diseases. [16]But he would withdraw to deserted places and pray.

[17]One day, while he was teaching, Pharisees and

---

[a] The terms leper and leprosy can refer to several diseases
[b] Gk he
[c] Gk him

teachers of the law were sitting near by (they had come from every village of Galilee and Judea and from Jerusalem); and the power of the Lord was with him to heal.[a] [18]Just then some men came, carrying a paralyzed man on a bed. They were trying to bring him in and lay him before Jesus;[b] [19]but finding no way to bring him in because of the crowd, they went up on the roof and let him down with his bed through the tiles into the middle of the crowd[c] in front of Jesus. [20]When he saw their faith, he said, "Friend,[d] your sins are forgiven you." [21]Then the scribes and the Pharisees began to question, "Who is this who is speaking blasphemies? Who can forgive sins but God alone?" [22]When Jesus perceived their questionings, he answered them, "Why do you raise such questions in your hearts? [23]Which is easier, to say, 'Your sins are forgiven you,' or to say, 'Stand up and walk'? [24]But so that you may know that the Son of Man has authority on earth to forgive sins"—

a Other ancient authorities read *was present to heal them*
b Gk *him*
c Gk *into the midst*
d Gk *Man*

3547		3739 1510 2064		1537	3956	2968
νομοδιδάσκαλοι	οἱ	ἦσαν ἐληλυθότες	ἐκ	πάσης	κώμης
law teachers	who	were having come	from	all	village

06	1056	2532	2449	2532	2419	2532
τῆς	Γαλιλαίας καὶ	'Ιουδαίας καὶ	'Ιερουσαλήμ· καὶ
of the	Galilee and	Judea and	Jerusalem; and

1411	2962	1510 1519 012	2390	846	2532
δύναμις κυρίου	ἦν εἰς τὸ ἰᾶσθαι αὐτόν.	18	καὶ
power of Master was	into the to cure him.	And

2400	435	5342	1909 2825	444	3739 1510
ἰδοὺ ἄνδρες	φέροντες ἐπὶ κλίνης	ἄνθρωπον ὃς	ἦν
look men	bringing on bed	man who	was+

3886		2532 2212		846
παραλελυμένος	καὶ ἐζήτουν	αὐτὸν
+having been paralyzed and	they were seeking him

1533	2532 5087	846	1799	846	19	2532
εἰσενεγκεῖν καὶ θεῖναι	[αὐτὸν] ἐνώπιον αὐτοῦ.	19	καὶ
to bring in and to place him	before him.	And

3361 2147	4169 1533	846	1223	04
μὴ εὑρόντες	ποίας εἰσενέγκωσιν	αὐτὸν διὰ	τὸν
not having found	what kind they might bring in	him through the

3793	305	1909 012	1430 1223	014
ὄχλον, ἀναβάντες	ἐπὶ τὸ	δῶμα διὰ	τῶν
crowd, having gone up	on the	roof through the

2766	2524	846	4862 011 2826
κεράμων	καθῆκαν	αὐτὸν σὺν	τῷ κλινιδίῳ
ceramic tiles	they let down	him with	the bed

1519 012 3319	1715	02	2424	20	2532
εἰς τὸ μέσον	ἔμπροσθεν τοῦ	'Ιησοῦ.	20	καὶ
into the middle	in front of the	Jesus.	And

3708	08 4102	846	3004	444
ἰδὼν	τὴν πίστιν	αὐτῶν	εἶπεν·	ἄνθρωπε,
having seen	the trust	of them	he said;	man,

863		1473	017 266	1473	21	2532
ἀφέωνταί	σοι	αἱ ἁμαρτίαι σου.	21	καὶ
had been sent off to *you*	the sins	of *you*.	And

757	1260	013 1122	2532 013 5330
ἤρξαντο διαλογίζεσθαι	οἱ γραμματεῖς καὶ οἱ	Φαρισαῖοι
began to reason	the writers and the	Pharisees

3004	5101 1510 3778	3739 2980	988	5101
λέγοντες· τίς ἐστιν	οὗτος ὃς	λαλεῖ βλασφημίας;	τίς
saying; who is	this who	speaks insults?	Who

1410	266	863	1487 3361 3441	01	2316
δύναται ἁμαρτίας	ἀφεῖναι	εἰ μὴ μόνος	ὁ	θεός;
is able sins	to send off	except alone	the	God?

22	1921	1161 01	2424	016	1261
22	ἐπιγνοὺς	δὲ ὁ	'Ιησοῦς	τοὺς διαλογισμοὺς
	Having perceived	but the	Jesus	the reasonings

846	611	3004	4314 846	5101
αὐτῶν	ἀποκριθεὶς	εἶπεν πρὸς	αὐτούς·	τί
of them	having answered	said to	them;	why

1260	1722 019	2588	1473	23	5101 1510
διαλογίζεσθε ἐν	ταῖς καρδίαις	ὑμῶν;	23	τί ἐστιν
reason you in	the hearts	of you?	What is

2123	3004	863	1473	017
εὐκοπώτερον,	εἰπεῖν·	ἀφέωνταί	σοι	αἱ
easier labor,	to say;	had been sent off to *you*	the

266	1473	2228 3004	1453	2532 4043
ἁμαρτίαι σου,	ἢ	εἰπεῖν· ἔγειρε	καὶ	περιπάτει;
sins	of *you*, or	to say; rise	and	walk around?

24	2443 1161 3609a		3754 01	5207 02	444
24	ἵνα δὲ εἰδῆτε	ὅτι ὁ	υἱὸς τοῦ	ἀνθρώπου
	That but you might know	that the	son of	the man

1849	2192 1909 06	1093	863	266
ἐξουσίαν	ἔχει ἐπὶ τῆς	γῆς	ἀφιέναι	ἁμαρτίας -
authority	has on the	earth	to send off	sins

```
3004        03  3886              1473  3004    1453    2532  142
εἶπεν       τῷ παραλελυμένῳ·     σοὶ  λέγω,   ἔγειρε  καὶ  ἄρας
he said     to one being        to   I say,  rise    and  having
            the paralyzed;      you                       lifted up
012  2826           1473    4198      1519  04  3624   1473
τὸ κλινίδιόν       σου    πορεύου   εἰς  τὸν οἶκόν σου.
the bed            of you travel    into the house of you.
```

   25
```
2532 3916      450      1799      846    142      1909
καὶ παραχρῆμα ἀναστὰς ἐνώπιον αὐτῶν, ἄρας    ἐφ'
And suddenly  having   before   them,  having   on
              stood up                 lifted up
3739 2621        565     1519 04 3624 · 846    1392
ὃ   κατέκειτο, ἀπῆλθεν εἰς  τὸν οἶκον αὐτοῦ δοξάζων
what he was    he went into the house of him giving
lying down, off                                splendor
04  2316   2532 1611      2983   537     2532
τὸν θεόν.
```
   26
```
                 καὶ ἔκστασις ἔλαβεν ἅπαντας καὶ
the God.         And amazement took   all      and
1392               04  2316 2532 4092        5401
ἐδόξαζον          τὸν θεὸν καὶ ἐπλήσθησαν φόβου
they gave splendor the God and were filled of fear
3004    3754 3708  3861       4594        2532 3326
λέγοντες ὅτι εἴδομεν παράδοξα σήμερον.
```
   27
```
                                            Καὶ μετὰ
saying, (") we saw paradoxes today.        And after
3778 1831        2532 2300     5057   3686   3018
ταῦτα ἐξῆλθεν    καὶ ἐθεάσατο τελώνην ὀνόματι Λευὶν
these he went out and watched  tax man in name Levi
2521        1909 012 5058        2532 3004    846
καθήμενον ἐπὶ τὸ τελώνιον, καὶ εἶπεν    αὐτῷ·
sitting    on the tax table, and he said to him;
190       1473
ἀκολούθει μοι.
```
   28
```
                 2532 2641      3956  450
                 καὶ καταλιπὼν πάντα ἀναστὰς
follow   me.     And having left all  having stood
190       846
ἠκολούθει αὐτῷ.
```
   29
```
                     2532 4160    1403   3173
                     Καὶ ἐποίησεν δοχὴν μεγάλην
he was following him. And made    reception great
3018  846      1722 07 3614   846       2532 1510 3793
Λευὶς αὐτῷ   ἐν τῇ οἰκίᾳ αὐτοῦ, καὶ ἦν ὄχλος
Levi to him  in the house of him, and was crowd
4183  5057      2532 243    3739 1510 3326 846
πολὺς τελωνῶν καὶ ἄλλων οἳ ἦσαν μετ' αὐτῶν
much of tax men and others who were+ with them
2621            2532 1111         013 5330      2532
κατακείμενοι.
```
   30
```
                καὶ ἐγόγγυζον  οἱ Φαρισαῖοι καὶ
+lying down.    And were grumbling the Pharisees and
013 1122      846      4314   016 3101    846
οἱ γραμματεῖς αὐτῶν πρὸς τοὺς μαθητὰς αὐτοῦ
the writers   of them toward the learners of him
3004     1223   5101  3326 014 5057   2532 268
λέγοντες· διὰ τί μετὰ τῶν τελωνῶν καὶ ἁμαρτωλῶν
saying;  through what with the tax men and sinners
2068    2532 4095       2532 611         01 2424
ἐσθίετε καὶ πίνετε;
```
   31
```
                     καὶ ἀποκριθεὶς   ὁ Ἰησοῦς
you eat and drink?   And having answered the Jesus
3004  4314 846      3756 5532  2192     013 5198
εἶπεν πρὸς αὐτούς· οὐ χρείαν ἔχουσιν οἱ ὑγιαίνοντες
said to them,     not need  have    the ones being
                                              healthy
2395   235 013 2560  2192        3756 2064
ἰατροῦ ἀλλὰ οἱ κακῶς ἔχοντες·
```
   32
```
                                 οὐκ ἐλήλυθα
of physician but the badly having; not I have come
2564    1342     235  268        1519 3341
καλέσαι δικαίους ἀλλὰ ἁμαρτωλοὺς εἰς μετάνοιαν.
to call right ones but sinners   into change mind.
```
   33
```
013      1161 3004  4314 846     013 3101    2491
Οἱ       δὲ εἶπαν πρὸς αὐτόν· οἱ μαθηταὶ Ἰωαννοῦ
The ones but said to   him;   the learners of John
```

he said to the one who was paralyzed—"I say to you, stand up and take your bed and go to your home." [25]Immediately he stood up before them, took what he had been lying on, and went to his home, glorifying God. [26]Amazement seized all of them, and they glorified God and were filled with awe, saying, "We have seen strange things today."

[27]After this he went out and saw a tax collector named Levi, sitting at the tax booth; and he said to him, "Follow me." [28]And he got up, left everything, and followed him.

[29]Then Levi gave a great banquet for him in his house; and there was a large crowd of tax collectors and others sitting at the table[a] with them. [30]The Pharisees and their scribes were complaining to his disciples, saying, "Why do you eat and drink with tax collectors and sinners?" [31]Jesus answered, "Those who are well have no need of a physician, but those who are sick; [32]I have come to call not the righteous but sinners to repentance."

[33]Then they said to him, "John's disciples, like the disciples of the Pharisees,

[a] Gk reclining

frequently fast and pray, but your disciples eat and drink." [34]Jesus said to them, "You cannot make wedding guests fast while the bride- groom is with them, can you? [35]The days will come when the bridegroom will be taken away from them, and then they will fast in those days." [36] He also told them a parable: "No one tears a piece from a new garment and sews it on an old garment; otherwise the new will be torn, and the piece from the new will not match the old. [37]And no one puts new wine into old wineskins; otherwise the new wine will burst the skins and be spilled, and the skins will be destroyed. [38]But new wine must be put into fresh wineskins. [39]And no one after drinking old wine desires new wine, but says, 'The old is good.' "[a]

CHAPTER 6

One sabbath[b] while Jesus[c] was going through the grainfields, his disciples plucked some heads of grain, rubbed them in their hands, and ate them. [2]But some of the Pharisees

[a] Other ancient authorities read better; others lack verse 39
[b] Other ancient authorities read On the second first sabbath
[c] Gk he

3522	4437	2532	1162	4160	3668
νηστεύουσιν	πυκνὰ	καὶ	δεήσεις	ποιοῦνται	ὁμοίως
fast	frequent	and	requests	they make	likewise

2532	013	014		5330		013	1161	4674
καὶ	οἱ	τῶν		Φαρισαίων,	οἱ		δὲ	σοὶ
and	the	ones of	the	Pharisees,	the ones	but		yours

2068	2532	4095	34	01	1161	2424	3004
ἐσθίουσιν	καὶ	πίνουσιν.		ὁ	δὲ	Ἰησοῦς	εἶπεν
eat	and	drink.		The	but	Jesus	said

4314	846	3361	1410		016	5207	02
πρὸς	αὐτούς·	μὴ	δύνασθε		τοὺς	υἱοὺς	τοῦ
to	them;	not	you are able		the	sons	of the

3567		1722	3739	01	3566		3326	846
νυμφῶνος		ἐν	ᾧ	ὁ	νυμφίος		μετ'	αὐτῶν
bridal chamber		in	which	the	bridegroom		with	them

1510	4160	3522	35	2064	1161	2250	2532
ἐστιν	ποιῆσαι	νηστεῦσαι;		ἐλεύσονται	δὲ	ἡμέραι,	καὶ
is	to make	to fast?		Will go	but	days,	and

3752	522		575	846	01	3566
ὅταν	ἀπαρθῇ		ἀπ'	αὐτῶν	ὁ	νυμφίος,
when	he might lifted up		from	them	the	bridegroom,

5119	3522	1722	1565	019	2250
τότε	νηστεύσουσιν	ἐν	ἐκείναις	ταῖς	ἡμέραις.
then	they will fast	in	those	the	days.

36	3004		1161	2532	3850		4314	846
	Ἔλεγεν		δὲ	καὶ	παραβολὴν		πρὸς	αὐτοὺς
	He was saying		but	also	parallel story		to	them,

3754	3762	1915	575	2440	2537	4977
ὅτι	οὐδεὶς	ἐπίβλημα	ἀπὸ	ἱματίου	καινοῦ	σχίσας
(")	no one	patch	from	clothes	new	having split

1911	1909	2440	3820	1487	1161	3361	1065
ἐπιβάλλει	ἐπὶ	ἱμάτιον	παλαιόν·	εἰ	δὲ	μὴ	γε,
throws on	on	clothes	old;	if	but	not	indeed,

2532	012	2537	4977	2532	011	3820	3756
καὶ	τὸ	καινὸν	σχίσει	καὶ	τῷ	παλαιῷ	οὐ
also	the new		it will split	and	the	old	not

4856	09	1915	09	575	010	2537	37	2532
συμφωνήσει	τὸ	ἐπίβλημα	τὸ	ἀπὸ	τοῦ	καινοῦ.		καὶ
will agree	the	patch	the one	from	the	new.		And

3762	906	3631	3501	1519	779	3820	1487
οὐδεὶς	βάλλει	οἶνον	νέον	εἰς	ἀσκοὺς	παλαιούς·	εἰ
no one	throws	wine	new	into	wineskins	old;	if

1161	3361	1065	4486	01	3631	01	3501	016
δὲ	μὴ	γε,	ῥήξει	ὁ	οἶνος	ὁ	νέος	τοὺς
but	not	indeed,	will rip	the	wine	the	new	the

779	2532	846	1632	2532	013
ἀσκοὺς	καὶ	αὐτὸς	ἐκχυθήσεται	καὶ	οἱ
wineskins	and	itself	will be poured out	and	the

779	622	38	235	3631	3501	1519
ἀσκοὶ	ἀπολοῦνται·		ἀλλὰ	οἶνον	νέον	εἰς
wineskins	will be destroyed;		but	wine	new	into

skins destroyed;

779	2537	992	39	2532	3762	4095
ἀσκοὺς	καινοὺς	βλητέον.		[καὶ]	οὐδεὶς	πιὼν
wineskins	new	one must throw.		And	no one	drinking

3820	2309	3501	3004	1063	01	3820	5543
παλαιὸν	θέλει	νέον·	λέγει	γάρ·	ὁ	παλαιὸς	χρηστός
old	wants	new;	he says	for;	the	old	kind

1510	6:1	1096	1161	1722	4521	1279
ἐστιν.		Ἐγένετο	δὲ	ἐν	σαββάτῳ	διαπορεύεσθαι
it is.		It became	but	in	sabbath	to travel through

846	1223	4702	2532	5089	013
αὐτὸν	διὰ	σπορίμων,	καὶ	ἔτιλλον	οἱ
him	through	sown fields,	and	were picking	the

3101	846	2532	2068	016	4719
μαθηταὶ	αὐτοῦ	καὶ	ἤσθιον	τοὺς	στάχυας
learners	of him	and	were eating	the	stalks of grain

5597	019	5495	2	5100	1161	014	5330
ψώχοντες	ταῖς	χερσίν.		τινὲς	δὲ	τῶν	Φαρισαίων
rubbing	in the	hands.		Some	but	of the	Pharisees

3004	5101	4160		3739	3756	1832			023
εἶπαν·	τί	ποιεῖτε	ὃ		οὐκ	ἔξεστιν			τοῖς
said;	why	do you	what		not	it is possible			in the

4521			2532	611			4314	846		3004	01
σάββασιν;	**3**	καὶ	ἀποκριθεὶς			πρὸς	αὐτοὺς		εἶπεν	ὁ
sabbaths?		And	having answered			to	them		said	the

2424	3761		3778	314		3739	4160		1160a
Ἰησοῦς·	οὐδὲ		τοῦτο	ἀνέγνωτε	ὃ		ἐποίησεν		Δαυὶδ
Jesus;	but not		this	you read	what		did		David

3753	3983		846		2532	013		3326	846
ὅτε	ἐπείνασεν		αὐτὸς	καὶ	οἱ			μετ᾽	αὐτοῦ
when	he hungered		himself	and	the			ones with	him

1510		5613	1525		1519	04	3624	02		2316
[ὄντες],	**4**	[ὡς]	εἰσῆλθεν		εἰς	τὸν	οἶκον	τοῦ		θεοῦ
being,		as	he went	into	into	the	house	of		the God

2532	016	740	06		4286		2983			2068
καὶ	τοὺς	ἄρτους	τῆς		προθέσεως		λαβὼν			ἔφαγεν
and	the	bread	of		the purpose		having taken			he ate

2532	1325	015		3326	846		3739	3756
καὶ	ἔδωκεν	τοῖς		μετ᾽	αὐτοῦ,		οὓς	οὐκ
and	gave	to the ones		with	him,		what	not

1832		2068		1487	3361	3441		016	2409
ἔξεστιν		φαγεῖν	εἰ		μὴ	μόνους		τοὺς	ἱερεῖς;
it is possible		to eat	except			alone		the	priests?

2532	3004		846		2962	1510	010
5 καὶ	ἔλεγεν		αὐτοῖς·		κύριός	ἐστιν	τοῦ
And	he was speaking		to them;		Master	is	of the

4521	01	5207	02		444			1096		1161
σαββάτου	ὁ	υἱὸς	τοῦ		ἀνθρώπου.	**6**		Ἐγένετο		δὲ
sabbath	the	son	of		the man.			It became		but

1722	2087	4521		1525		846		1519	08	4864
ἐν	ἑτέρῳ	σαββάτῳ	εἰσελθεῖν		αὐτὸν	εἰς		τὴν		συναγωγὴν
in	other	sabbath	to go into		him	into		the		synagogue

2532	1321		2532	1510	444		1563	2532	05	5495
καὶ	διδάσκειν.	καὶ		ἦν	ἄνθρωπος	ἐκεῖ		καὶ	ἡ	χεὶρ
and	to teach.	And		was	man	there		and	the	hand

846		05	1188	1510	3584			3906
αὐτοῦ	ἡ		δεξιὰ	ἦν	ξηρά.	**7**		παρετηροῦντο
of him	the		right	was	dried out.			Were keeping watch

1161	846		013	1122		2532	013	5330		1487	1722
δὲ	αὐτὸν	οἱ		γραμματεῖς	καὶ		οἱ	Φαρισαῖοι	εἰ		ἐν
but	him	the		writers	and		the	Pharisees	if		in

011	4521		2323		2443	2147			2723
τῷ	σαββάτῳ	θεραπεύει,		ἵνα	εὕρωσιν				κατηγορεῖν
the	sabbath	he heals,		that	they might find				to accuse

846		846		1161	3609a		016	1261
αὐτοῦ	**8**	αὐτὸς	δὲ		ᾔδει		τοὺς	διαλογισμοὺς
him.		Himself	but		had known		the	reasonings

846		3004		1161	03		435	03	3584
αὐτῶν,		εἶπεν	δὲ		τῷ		ἀνδρὶ	τῷ	ξηρὰν
of them,		he said	but		to		the man	the	dried out

2192	08	5495		1453		2532	2476	1519	012	3319
ἔχοντι	τὴν	χεῖρα·		ἔγειρε	καὶ		στῆθι	εἰς	τὸ	μέσον·
having	the hand;			rise	and		stand	into	the	middle;

2532	450		2476			3004	1161	01	2424
καὶ	ἀναστὰς		ἔστη.	**9**		εἶπεν	δὲ	ὁ	Ἰησοῦς
and	having stood up		he stood.			Said	but	the	Jesus

4314	846		1905		1473	1487	1832		011
πρὸς	αὐτούς·		ἐπερωτῶ		ὑμᾶς	εἰ	ἔξεστιν		τῷ
to	them;		I ask		on you	if	it is possible		in the

4521	15		2228	2554		5590	4982
σαββάτῳ	ἀγαθοποιῆσαι	ἢ		κακοποιῆσαι,		ψυχὴν	σῶσαι
sabbath	to do good	or		to do bad,		soul	to deliver

2228	622			2532	4017			3956
ἢ	ἀπολέσαι;	**10**		καὶ	περιβλεψάμενος			πάντας
or	to destroy?			And	having looked around			all

846		3004	846		1614		08	5495	1473
αὐτοὺς	εἶπεν		αὐτῷ·		ἔκτεινον		τὴν	χεῖρά	σου.
them	he said		to him;		stretch out		the	hand	of you.

said, "Why are you doing what is not lawful[a] on the sabbath?" [3]Jesus answered, "Have you not read what David did when he and his companions were hungry? [4]He entered the house of God and took and ate the bread of the Presence, which it is not lawful for any but the priests to eat, and gave some to his companions?" [5]Then he said to them, "The Son of Man is lord of the sabbath."

[6]On another sabbath he entered the synagogue and taught, and there was a man there whose right hand was withered. [7]The scribes and the Pharisees watched him to see whether he would cure on the sabbath, so that they might find an accusation against him. [8]Even though he knew what they were thinking, he said to the man who had the withered hand, "Come and stand here." He got up and stood there. [9]Then Jesus said to them, "I ask you, is it lawful to do good or to do harm on the sabbath, to save life or to destroy it?" [10]After looking around at all of them, he said to him, "Stretch out your hand."

a Other ancient authorities add to do

He did so, and his hand was restored. ¹¹But they were filled with fury and discussed with one another what they might do to Jesus.

12 Now during those days he went out to the mountain to pray; and he spent the night in prayer to God. ¹³And when day came, he called his disciples and chose twelve of them, whom he also named apostles: ¹⁴Simon, whom he named Peter, and his brother Andrew, and James, and John, and Philip, and Bartholomew, ¹⁵and Matthew, and Thomas, and James son of Alphaeus, and Simon, who was called the Zealot, ¹⁶and Judas son of James, and Judas Iscariot, who became a traitor.

17 He came down with them and stood on a level place, with a great crowd of his disciples and a great multitude of people from all Judea, Jerusalem, and the coast of Tyre and Sidon. ¹⁸They had come to hear him and to be healed of their diseases; and those who were troubled with unclean spirits were cured. ¹⁹And all in the crowd were trying to touch him, for power came out from him

01	1161 4160	2532 600		05	5495 846

ὁ   δὲ ἐποίησεν καὶ ἀπεκατεστάθη ἡ χεὶρ αὐτοῦ.
The one but did   and was restored the hand of him.

11 αὐτοὶ   δὲ ἐπλήσθησαν ἀνοίας καὶ διελάλουν
(846 1161 4092   454   2532 1255)
Themselves but were filled mindless and were speaking
                                              thoroughly

πρὸς ἀλλήλους τί ἂν ποιήσαιεν τῷ   Ἰησοῦ.
(4314 240   5101 302 4160   03   2424)
to   one another what - they may do to the Jesus.

12 Ἐγένετο   δὲ ἐν ταῖς ἡμέραις ταύταις ἐξελθεῖν
(1096   1161 1722 019 2250   3778   1831)
It became but in the days   these   to go out

αὐτὸν εἰς τὸ ὄρος προσεύξασθαι, καὶ ἦν
(846 1519 012 3735 4336   2532 1510)
him   into the hill to pray,   and he was+

διανυκτερεύων   ἐν τῇ προσευχῇ τοῦ
(1273   1722 07 4335   03)
+staying through the night in the prayer of the

θεοῦ. **13** καὶ ὅτε ἐγένετο ἡμέρα, προσεφώνησεν
(2316   2532 3753 1096   2250   4377)
God.   And when it became day, he sounded to

τοὺς μαθητὰς αὐτοῦ, καὶ ἐκλεξάμενος
(016 3101   846   2532 1586)
the learners of him, and having selected for himself

ἀπ᾽ αὐτῶν δώδεκα, οὓς καὶ ἀποστόλους ὠνόμασεν·
(575 846 1427   3739 2532 652   3687)
from them twelve, whom also delegates he named;

14 Σίμωνα ὃν καὶ ὠνόμασεν Πέτρον, καὶ Ἀνδρέαν
(4613 3739 2532 3687   4074   2532 406)
Simon whom also he named Peter,   and Andrew

τὸν ἀδελφὸν αὐτοῦ, καὶ Ἰάκωβον καὶ Ἰωάννην καὶ
(04 80   846   2532 2385   2532 2491   2532)
the brother of him, and Jacob   and John   and

Φίλιππον καὶ Βαρθολομαῖον **15** καὶ Μαθθαῖον καὶ
(5376   2532 918   2532 3102a   2532)
Philip   and Bartholomew   and Matthew   and

Θωμᾶν καὶ Ἰάκωβον Ἀλφαίου καὶ Σίμωνα τὸν
(2381 2532 2385   256   2532 4613   04)
Thomas and Jacob of Alpheus and Simon the one

καλούμενον ζηλωτὴν **16** καὶ Ἰούδαν Ἰακώβου καὶ
(2564   2207   2532 2455 2385   2532)
being called jealous   and Judas of Jacob and

Ἰούδαν Ἰσκαριώθ, ὃς ἐγένετο προδότης. **17** Καὶ
(2455 2465a   3739 1096   4273   2532)
Judas Iscariot, who became traitor.   And

καταβὰς   μετ᾽ αὐτῶν ἔστη ἐπὶ τόπου πεδινοῦ,
(2597   3326 846 2476 1909 5117 3977)
having come down with them he stood on place level,

καὶ ὄχλος πολὺς μαθητῶν   αὐτοῦ, καὶ πλῆθος πολὺ
(2532 3793 4183 3101   846   2532 4128   4183)
and crowd much of learners of him, and quantity much

τοῦ λαοῦ ἀπὸ πάσης τῆς Ἰουδαίας καὶ Ἰερουσαλὴμ
(02 2992 575 3956 06 2449   2532 2419)
of the people from all the Judea   and Jerusalem

καὶ τῆς παραλίου Τύρου καὶ Σιδῶνος, **18** οἳ ἦλθον
(2532 06 3882   5184 2532 4605   3739 2064)
and of the along sea Tyre and Sidon,   who came

ἀκοῦσαι αὐτοῦ καὶ ἰαθῆναι ἀπὸ τῶν νόσων
(191 846 2532 2390   575 018 3554)
to hear him and to be cured from the illnesses

αὐτῶν· καὶ οἱ ἐνοχλούμενοι   ἀπὸ πνευμάτων
(846 2532 013 1776   575 4151)
of them; and the ones being annoyed from spirits

ἀκαθάρτων ἐθεραπεύοντο, **19** καὶ πᾶς ὁ ὄχλος
(169 2323   2532 3956 01 3793)
unclean were being healed, and all the crowd

ἐζήτουν ἅπτεσθαι αὐτοῦ, ὅτι δύναμις παρ᾽
(2212 681   846   3754 1411   3844)
was seeking to touch him, because power from

846	1831		2532	2390		3956	**20**	2532
αὐτοῦ	ἐξήρχετο		καὶ	ἰᾶτο		πάντας.		Καὶ
him	was going out	and		was curing		all.		And

846	1869			016	3788		846	1519
αὐτὸς	ἐπάρας			τοὺς	ὀφθαλμοὺς	αὐτοῦ	εἰς
himself	having lifted up	on	the	eyes		of him	into

016	3101	846	3004		3107		013	4434
τοὺς	μαθητὰς	αὐτοῦ	ἔλεγεν,		Μακάριοι	οἱ	πτωχοί,
the	learners	of him	was saying,		Fortunate	the	poor,

3754	5212	1510	05	932		02		2316
ὅτι	ὑμετέρα	ἐστὶν	ἡ	βασιλεία	τοῦ	θεοῦ.
because	yours	is		the kingdom	of	the God.

21
3107		013 3983			3568 3754
μακάριοι	οἱ	πεινῶντες		νῦν, ὅτι
Fortunate	the ones	hungering		now, because

5526		3107	013	2799		3568
χορτασθήσεσθε.		μακάριος	οἱ	κλαίοντες		νῦν,
you will be satisfied.		Fortunate	the ones	crying		now,

3754	1070	**22**	3107	1510	3752 3404
ὅτι	γελάσετε.		μακάριοί	ἐστε	ὅταν μισήσωσιν
because	you will laugh.		Fortunate	are you	when might hate

1473	013	444		2532	3752	873		1473
ὑμᾶς	οἱ	ἄνθρωποι	καὶ	ὅταν	ἀφορίσωσιν		ὑμᾶς
you	the	men		and	when they might separate		you

2532	3679		2532	1544		012	3686	1473
καὶ	ὀνειδίσωσιν	καὶ	ἐκβάλωσιν		τὸ	ὄνομα	ὑμῶν
and	might revile	and	might throw out		the	name	of you

5613	4190	1752		02	5207 02		444
ὡς	πονηρὸν	ἕνεκα		τοῦ	υἱοῦ τοῦ	ἀνθρώπου·
as	evil	on account of		the	son of	the man;

23
5463	1722	1565	07	2250	2532	4640		2400
χάρητε	ἐν	ἐκείνῃ	τῇ	ἡμέρᾳ	καὶ	σκιρτήσατε,		ἰδοὺ
rejoice	in	that	the	day	and	skip,		look

1063 01	3408		4183	1722	03	3772		2596	024
γὰρ ὁ	μισθὸς	ὑμῶν	πολὺς	ἐν	τῷ	οὐρανῷ·	κατὰ	τὰ
for the	wage	of you	much	in	the	heaven;	by	the

846	1063	4160		015	4396		013	3962
αὐτὰ	γὰρ	ἐποίουν		τοῖς	προφήταις	οἱ	πατέρες
same	for	were doing	to the	spokesmen		the	fathers

846	**24**	4133	3759	1473	015	4145		3754
αὐτῶν.		Πλὴν	οὐαὶ	ὑμῖν	τοῖς	πλουσίοις,	ὅτι
of them.		Except	woe	to you	the	rich ones,		because

568		08	3874		1473	**25**	3759	1473
ἀπέχετε		τὴν	παράκλησιν		ὑμῶν.		οὐαὶ	ὑμῖν,
you hold off	the	encouragement		of you.		Woe	to you,

013	1705		3568	3754	3983		3759	013
οἱ	ἐμπεπλησμένοι	νῦν,	ὅτι		πεινάσετε.	οὐαί,	οἱ
the ones	having filled in		now,	because	you will		Woe,	the
						hunger.		

1070		3568	3754	3996			2532
γελῶντες		νῦν,	ὅτι	πενθήσετε			καὶ
ones laughing		now,	because	you will mourn	and

2799	**26**	3759	3752	1473	2573	3004		3956
κλαύσετε.		οὐαὶ	ὅταν	ὑμᾶς	καλῶς	εἴπωσιν		πάντες
cry.		Woe	when	you	well	might speak		all

013	444		2596	024	846	1063	4160		015
οἱ	ἄνθρωποι·		κατὰ	τὰ	αὐτὰ	γὰρ	ἐποίουν		τοῖς
the	men;	by	the	same	for	were doing	to the

5578		013	3962	846		**27**	235	1473
ψευδοπροφήταις	οἱ	πατέρες	αὐτῶν.			Ἀλλὰ	ὑμῖν
false spokesmen	the	fathers	of them.			But	to you

3004	015	191		25		016	2190
λέγω	τοῖς	ἀκούουσιν·		ἀγαπᾶτε	τοὺς	ἐχθροὺς
I say	to the ones	hearing;		love	the	hostile

1473		2573	4160	015	3404		1473
ὑμῶν,		καλῶς	ποιεῖτε	τοῖς	μισοῦσιν		ὑμᾶς,
of you,		well	do	to the ones	hating		you,

and healed all of them.

20 Then he looked up at his disciples and said: "Blessed are you who are poor, for yours is the kingdom of God. 21 "Blessed are you who are hungry now, for you will be filled. "Blessed are you who weep now, for you will laugh. 22 "Blessed are you when people hate you, and when they exclude you, revile you, and defame you[a] on account of the Son of Man. 23 Rejoice in that day and leap for joy, for surely your reward is great in heaven; for that is what their ancestors did to the prophets. 24 "But woe to you who are rich, for you have received your consolation. 25 "Woe to you who are full now, for you will be hungry. "Woe to you who are laughing now, for you will mourn and weep. 26 "Woe to you when all speak well of you, for that is what their ancestors did to the false prophets. 27 "But I say to you that listen, Love your enemies, do good to those who hate you,

[a] Gk cast out your name as evil

28bless those who curse you, pray for those who abuse you. 29If anyone strikes you on the cheek, offer the other also; and from anyone who takes away your coat do not withhold even your shirt. 30Give to everyone who begs from you; and if anyone takes away your goods, do not ask for them again. 31Do to others as you would have them do to you.

32 "If you love those who love you, what credit is that to you? For even sinners love those who love them. 33If you do good to those who do good to you, what credit is that to you? For even sinners do the same. 34If you lend to those from whom you hope to receive, what credit is that to you? Even sinners lend to sinners, to receive as much again. 35But love your enemies, do good, and lend, expecting nothing in return.a Your reward will be great, and you will be children of the Most High; for he is kind to the ungrateful and the wicked. 36Be merciful, just as your Father is merciful.

37 "Do not judge, and you will not be judged; do not

a Other ancient authorities read *despairing of no one*

```
     2127            016    2672            1473   4336            4012
28  εὐλογεῖτε   τοὺς καταρωμένους ὑμᾶς, προσεύχεσθε περὶ
    speak well  the  ones cursing    you,  pray         about
    014 1908                1473        03    5180            1473
    τῶν ἐπηρεαζόντων     ὑμᾶς. 29  τῷ    τύπτοντί     σε
    the  ones mistreating  you.       To the one beating you
    1909 08  4600       3930      2532  08  243      2532 575
    ἐπὶ  τὴν σιαγόνα πάρεχε καὶ τὴν ἄλλην, καὶ  ἀπὸ
    on   the  cheek    hold to also the other,   and   from
    02  142              1473  012  2440        2532 04  5509
    τοῦ αἴροντός       σου  τὸ  ἱμάτιον καὶ  τὸν χιτῶνα
    the one lifting up of you the clothes  and   the shirt
    3361 2967                3956    154        1473 1325
    μὴ  κωλύσῃς.  30     παντὶ  αἰτοῦντί  σε  δίδου,
    not you might hinder. To all one asking you  give,
    2532 575  02  142            024 4674 3361 523                 2532
    καὶ ἀπὸ τοῦ αἴροντος  τὰ σὰ μὴ  ἀπαίτει.  31 Καὶ
    and  from the lifting up the you not  ask back.   And
    2531        2309      2443 4160        1473       013 444
    καθὼς  θέλετε   ἵνα ποιῶσιν ὑμῖν  οἱ ἄνθρωποι
    just as  you want  that might do to you  the men
    4160       846        3668         2532 1487 25
    ποιεῖτε αὐτοῖς ὁμοίως.  32  καὶ εἰ  ἀγαπᾶτε
    do        to them likewise.  And if   you love
    016  25            1473  4169        1473     5485   1510
    τοὺς ἀγαπῶντας ὑμᾶς, ποία    ὑμῖν  χάρις ἐστίν;
    the  ones loving   you,  what kind to you favor is it?
    2532 1063 013 268            016  25            846
    καὶ γὰρ οἱ ἁμαρτωλοὶ τοὺς ἀγαπῶντας  αὐτοὺς
    Also for  the sinners    the  ones loving     them
    25                2532 1063 1437 15                       016
    ἀγαπῶσιν.  33  καὶ [γὰρ] ἐὰν ἀγαθοποιῆτε   τοὺς
    love.            And for  if   you might do good the
    15                1473  4169        1473     5485   1510
    ἀγαθοποιοῦντας ὑμᾶς, ποία    ὑμῖν  χάρις ἐστίν;
    ones doing good you,  what kind to you favor is it?
    2532 013 268            012 846   4160        2532 1437
    καὶ οἱ ἁμαρτωλοὶ τὸ αὐτὸ ποιοῦσιν.  34  καὶ ἐὰν
    Also the sinners    the same  do.        And if
    1155           3844 3739 1679      2983
    δανίσητε     παρ' ὧν ἐλπίζετε λαβεῖν,
    you might lend from whom you hope to receive,
    4169        1473    5485   1510      2532 268
    ποία    ὑμῖν  χάρις [ἐστίν]; καὶ ἁμαρτωλοὶ
    what kind to you favor is it?  Also sinners
    268          1155        2443 618                         024
    ἁμαρτωλοῖς δανίζουσιν ἵνα ἀπολάβωσιν        τὰ
    to sinners lend          that they might receive back the
    2470     4133  25        016  2190     1473 2532
    ἴσα.  35  πλὴν ἀγαπᾶτε τοὺς ἐχθροὺς ὑμῶν καὶ
    equal.   Except you love  the  hostile of you and
    15              2532 1155        3367     560              2532
    ἀγαθοποιεῖτε καὶ δανίζετε μηδὲν ἀπελπίζοντες· καὶ
    do good        and lend    nothing hoping back;  and
    1510  01  3408    1473   4183    2532 1510          5207
    ἔσται ὁ μισθὸς ὑμῶν πολύς, καὶ ἔσεσθε     υἱοὶ
    will be the wage  of you much,  and  you will be sons
    5310     3754    846        5543    1510 1909 016
    ὑψίστου, ὅτι  αὐτὸς χρηστός ἐστιν ἐπὶ τοὺς
    of highest, because himself kind   is    on   the
    884         2532 4190         1096     3629
    ἀχαρίστους καὶ πονηρούς.  36  Γίνεσθε οἰκτίρμονες
    unfavorable and evil.       Become compassionate
    2531      2532 01  3962    1473  3629          1510
    καθὼς [καὶ] ὁ πατὴρ ὑμῶν οἰκτίρμων   ἐστίν.
    just as also the father of you compassionate is.
    2532 3361 2919      2532 3756 3361        2919      2532 3361
37  Καὶ μὴ  κρίνετε, καὶ οὐ  μὴ  κριθῆτε· καὶ μὴ
    And not judge,   and not not  you might and not
                                        be judged;
```

```
2613              2532 3756 3361 2613
καταδικάζετε, καὶ  οὐ  μὴ  καταδικασθῆτε.
condemn,         and not not  you might be condemned.
630            2532 630                      1325    2532
ἀπολύετε,  καὶ  ἀπολυθήσεσθε·        38 δίδοτε, καὶ
Loose off,    and  you will be loosed off;  give,    and
1325            1473    3358   2570  4085
δοθήσεται   ὑμῖν·  μέτρον καλὸν πεπιεσμένον
it will be given to you; measure good  having been
                                             pressed down
4531               5240                  1325        1519 04  2859
σεσαλευμένον ὑπερεκχυννόμενον δώσουσιν εἰς  τὸν κόλπον
having been      being poured out  will be  into the lap
shaken               excessively       given
1473  3739 1063 3358    3354        488
ὑμῶν· ᾧ  γὰρ μέτρῳ μετρεῖτε ἀντιμετρηθήσεται
of    in  for  measure you measure it will be measured
you;  what                           against
1473   39 3004  1161 2532 3850            846     3385
ὑμῖν.    Εἶπεν δὲ  καὶ  παραβολὴν  αὐτοῖς· μήτι
you.     He said but also parallel story to them; not
1410    5185    5185    3594        3780 297       1519
δύναται τυφλὸς τυφλὸν ὁδηγεῖν; οὐχὶ ἀμφότεροι εἰς
is able blind  blind  to guide? Not both         into
999      1706          40 3756 1510  3101    5228
βόθυνον ἐμπεσοῦνται;    οὐκ ἔστιν μαθητὴς ὑπὲρ
ditch   will they fall in? Not is  learner above
04    1320          2675              1161 3956
τὸν διδάσκαλον· κατηρτισμένος     δὲ  πᾶς
the teacher;    having been put in order but all
1510   5613 01 1320        846    41 5101 1161 991
ἔσται ὡς ὁ  διδάσκαλος αὐτοῦ.   Τί  δὲ  βλέπεις
will be as the teacher    of him.  Why but you see
012 2595    012      1722 03 3788      02   80
τὸ κάρφος τὸ    ἐν  τῷ ὀφθαλμῷ τοῦ ἀδελφοῦ
the splinter the one in the eye     of the brother
1473    08 1161 1385  08      1722 03 2398 3788   3756
σου,   τὴν δὲ δοκὸν τὴν  ἐν  τῷ ἰδίῳ ὀφθαλμῷ οὐ
of you, the but log  the one in the own eye       not
2657        42 4459 1410      3004    03
κατανοεῖς;     πῶς δύνασαι λέγειν τῷ
you think carefully? How are you able to say to the
80    1473  80    863  1544                012
ἀδελφῷ σου· ἀδελφέ, ἄφες ἐκβάλω       τὸ
brother of you; brother, allow I might throw out the
2595     012 1722 03 3788      1473 846      08 1722 03
κάρφος τὸ ἐν  τῷ ὀφθαλμῷ σου, αὐτὸς τὴν ἐν τῷ
splinter the in the eye     of  yourself the in the
      one                               you,
3788      1473  1385   3756 991       5273       1544
ὀφθαλμῷ σου  δοκὸν οὐ  βλέπων; ὑποκριτά, ἔκβαλε
eye      of you log   not seeing? Hypocrite, throw out
4413   08 1385 1537 02 3788      1473 2532 5119
πρῶτον τὴν δοκὸν ἐκ τοῦ ὀφθαλμοῦ σου, καὶ τότε
first  the log  from the eye       of you, and then
1227        012 2595    012     1722 03 3788    02
διαβλέψεις τὸ κάρφος τὸ    ἐν  τῷ ὀφθαλμῷ τοῦ
you will  the splinter the one in the eye     of the
see clearly
80      1473  1544         43 3756 1063 1510  1186
ἀδελφοῦ σου ἐκβαλεῖν.      Οὐ  γὰρ  ἐστιν+ δένδρον
brother of you to throw out. Not for  is+    tree
2570    4160   2590   4550    3761   3825 1186
καλὸν ποιοῦν καρπὸν σαπρόν, οὐδὲ πάλιν δένδρον
good +making fruit  rotten, but  not again tree
4550   4160    2590   2570    44 1538   1063 1186
σαπρὸν ποιοῦν καρπὸν καλόν.   ἕκαστον γὰρ δένδρον
rotten making fruit  good.     Each    for tree
```

condemn, and you will not be condemned. Forgive, and you will be forgiven; [38]give, and it will be given to you. A good measure, pressed down, shaken together, running over, will be put into your lap; for the measure you give will be the measure you get back."

39 He also told them a parable: "Can a blind person guide a blind person? Will not both fall into a pit? [40]A disciple is not above the teacher, but everyone who is fully qualified will be like the teacher. [41]Why do you see the speck in your neighbor's[a] eye, but do not notice the log in your own eye? [42]Or how can you say to your neighbor,[b] 'Friend,[b] let me take out the speck in your eye,' when you yourself do not see the log in your own eye? You hypocrite, first take the log out of your own eye, and then you will see clearly to take the speck out of your neighbor's[a] eye.

43 "No good tree bears bad fruit, nor again does a bad tree bear good fruit; [44]for each tree

a Gk *brother's*
b Gk *brother*

is known by its own fruit. Figs are not gathered from thorns, nor are grapes picked from a bramble bush. [45]The good person out of the good treasure of the heart produces good, and the evil person out of evil treasure produces evil; for it is out of the abundance of the heart that the mouth speaks.

46 "Why do you call me 'Lord, Lord,' and do not do what I tell you? [47]I will show you what someone is like who comes to me, hears my words, and acts on them. [48]That one is like a man building a house, who dug deeply and laid the foundation on rock; when a flood arose, the river burst against that house but could not shake it, because it had been well built.[a] [49]But the one who hears and does not act is like a man who built a house on the ground without a foundation. When the river burst against it, immediately it fell, and great was the ruin of that house."

CHAPTER 7

After Jesus[b] had finished all his sayings in the hearing of the people, he entered Capernaum. [2]A centurion there had a slave

a Other ancient authorities read founded upon the rock
b Gk he

1537	02	2398	2590	1097		3756	1063	1537	173
ἐκ	τοῦ	ἰδίου	καρποῦ	γινώσκεται·		οὐ	γὰρ	ἐξ	ἀκανθῶν
from	the	own	fruit	is known;		not	for	from	thorns

4816		4810	3761	1537	942		4718		5166
συλλέγουσιν	σῦκα	οὐδὲ	ἐκ	βάτου	σταφυλὴν		τρυγῶσιν.
do they collect	figs	but not	from	thorn bush	cluster of ripe grapes		they gather.

45 01 18 / 444 / 1537 02 18 / 2344 06
ὁ ἀγαθὸς ἄνθρωπος ἐκ τοῦ ἀγαθοῦ θησαυροῦ τῆς
The good man from the good treasure of the

2588	4393		012 18		2532	01	4190
καρδίας	προφέρει		τὸ ἀγαθόν,		καὶ	ὁ	πονηρὸς
heart	brings forward		the good,		and		the evil

1537	02	4190	4393		012 4190		1537	1063
ἐκ	τοῦ	πονηροῦ	προφέρει		τὸ πονηρόν·		ἐκ	γὰρ
from	the	evil	brings forward		the evil;		from	for

4051	2588	2980	09	4750	846	**46**	5101
περισσεύματος	καρδίας	λαλεῖ	τὸ	στόμα	αὐτοῦ.		Τί
excess	of heart	speaks	the	mouth	of him.		Why

1161	1473	2564		2962	2962	2532	3756	4160
δέ	με	καλεῖτε·		κύριε	κύριε,	καὶ	οὐ	ποιεῖτε
but	me	you call;		Master	Master,	and	not	you do

3739	3004	**47**	3956	01	2064		4314	1473	2532
ἃ	λέγω;		Πᾶς	ὁ	ἐρχόμενος		πρός	με	καὶ
what	I say?		All		the one coming		to	me	and

191	1473	014	3056	2532	4160	846		5263
ἀκούων	μου	τῶν	λόγων	καὶ	ποιῶν	αὐτούς,		ὑποδείξω
hearing	of me	the	words	and	doing	them,		I example

1473	5101	1510	3664	**48**	3664	1510	444
ὑμῖν	τίνι	ἐστὶν	ὅμοιος·		ὅμοιός	ἐστιν	ἀνθρώπῳ
to you	to what	he is	like;		like	he is	to man

3618		3614	3739 4626		2532 900		2532
οἰκοδομοῦντι	οἰκίαν	ὃς	ἔσκαψεν	καὶ	ἐβάθυνεν	καὶ
building	house	who	dug	and	deepened	and

5087	2310	1909 08	4073	4132	1161
ἔθηκεν	θεμέλιον	ἐπὶ τὴν	πέτραν·	πλημμύρης	δὲ
set	foundation	on the	rock;	flood	but

1096	4366	01	4215	07	3614
γενομένης	προσέρηξεν	ὁ	ποταμὸς	τῇ	οἰκίᾳ
having become	broke toward	the	river		the house

1565	2532 3756	2480	4531	846	1223	012
ἐκείνῃ,	καὶ οὐκ	ἴσχυσεν	σαλεῦσαι	αὐτὴν	διὰ	τὸ
that,	and not	was strong	to shake	it	through	the

2573	3618	846	**49**	01 1161	191
καλῶς	οἰκοδομῆσθαι	αὐτήν.		ὁ δὲ	ἀκούσας
well	to be built	it.		The but	one having heard

2532	3361	4160		3664	1510	444	3618
καὶ	μὴ	ποιήσας		ὅμοιός	ἐστιν	ἀνθρώπῳ	οἰκοδομήσαντι
and	not	having done		like	he is	to man	having built

3614	1909 08	1093	5565	2310		3739
οἰκίαν	ἐπὶ τὴν	γῆν	χωρὶς	θεμελίου,		ᾗ
house	on the	land	without	foundation,		to which

4366	01	4215	2532	2117	4844a	2532
προσέρηξεν	ὁ	ποταμός,	καὶ	εὐθὺς	συνέπεσεν	καὶ
broke toward	the	river,	and	immediately	it fell	and together

1096 ·	09	4485	06	3614	1565	3173
ἐγένετο	τὸ	ῥῆγμα	τῆς	οἰκίας	ἐκείνης	μέγα.
became	the	break up	of the	house	that	great.

7:1 1894 4137 3956 024 4487 846 1519 020
Ἐπειδὴ ἐπλήρωσεν πάντα τὰ ῥήματα αὐτοῦ εἰς τὰς
Since he filled all the words of him in the

189	02	2992	1525	1519	2746a
ἀκοὰς	τοῦ	λαοῦ,	εἰσῆλθεν	εἰς	Καφαρναούμ.
hearings	of the	people,	he went	into into	Capernaum.

2 1543 1161 5100 1401 2560 2192
Ἑκατοντάρχου δέ τινος δοῦλος κακῶς ἔχων
Ruler of hundred but some slave badly having

```
3195        5053         3739 1510 846       1784
ἤμελλεν     τελευτᾶν,    ὃς   ἦν   αὐτῷ      ἔντιμος.
was about   to die,      who  was  to him in honor.
```

```
  191                1161 4012  02   2424 649                  4314
3 ἀκούσας    δὲ  περὶ  τοῦ  Ἰησοῦ ἀπέστειλεν  πρὸς
  Having heard but about the  Jesus he delegated to
  heard
```

```
846    4245          014    2453      2065  846   3704
αὐτὸν πρεσβυτέρους τῶν  Ἰουδαίων ἐρωτῶν αὐτὸν ὅπως
him   older men    of the Judeans  asking him  so that
2064     1295                           04   1401
ἐλθὼν    διασώσῃ                        τὸν δοῦλον
having come he might thoroughly deliver the slave
846      013         1161 3854            4314 04  2424
αὐτοῦ. 4 οἱ    δὲ   παραγενόμενοι πρὸς τὸν Ἰησοῦν
of him.  The ones but arriving       to   the  Jesus
3870          846   4709     3004      3754 514
παρεκάλουν   αὐτὸν σπουδαίως λέγοντες ὅτι ἄξιός
were encouraging him diligently saying, (") worthy
1510 3739 3930      3778   5  25          1063 012 1484
ἐστιν ᾧ   παρέξῃ    τοῦτο·   ἀγαπᾷ      γὰρ τὸ ἔθνος
is    to  you will this;     he loves for the nation
         whom hold to
1473 2532 08  4864      846    3618       1473
ἡμῶν καὶ  τὴν συναγωγὴν αὐτὸς ᾠκοδόμησεν ἡμῖν.
of us and the synagogue himself built      to us.
  01  1161 2424     4198         4862 846      2235
6 ὁ   δὲ  Ἰησοῦς ἐπορεύετο    σὺν αὐτοῖς. ἤδη
  The but Jesus was traveling with them.   Already
1161 846   3756 3112 568       575  06  3614
δὲ  αὐτοῦ οὐ  μακρὰν ἀπέχοντος ἀπὸ τῆς οἰκίας
but of him not far   holding off from the house
3992      5384   01  1543         3004   846
ἔπεμψεν φίλους ὁ  ἑκατοντάρχης λέγων αὐτῷ·
sent    friends the ruler of hundred saying to him;
2962   3361 4660    3756 1063 2425   1510 2443
κύριε, μὴ σκύλλου, οὐ  γὰρ ἱκανός εἰμι ἵνα
Master, not be annoyed, not for enough I am that
5259 08  4721     1473 1525            7 1352
ὑπὸ τὴν στέγην μου εἰσέλθῃς·          διὸ
under the roof of me you might go in;  wherefore
3761   1683     515          4314 1473 2064 235
οὐδὲ ἐμαυτὸν ἠξίωσα       πρὸς σὲ ἐλθεῖν· ἀλλὰ
but not myself I was worthy to you to come; but
3004 3056 2532 2390      01  3816      1473 82532
εἰπὲ λόγῳ, καὶ ἰαθήτω   ὁ  παῖς     μου.  καὶ
say word, and let be cured the boy servant of me. And
1063 1473 444     1510 5259 1849     5021
γὰρ ἐγὼ ἄνθρωπός εἰμι ὑπὸ ἐξουσίαν τασσόμενος
for I  man      am   under authority being set in
                                        set in order
2192 5259 1683     4757          2532 3004 3778
ἔχων ὑπ' ἐμαυτὸν στρατιώτας, καὶ λέγω τούτῳ·
having under myself soldiers,    and I say to this;
4198         2532 4198        2532 243       2064    2532
πορεύθητι, καὶ πορεύεται, καὶ ἄλλῳ·   ἔρχου, καὶ
travel,     and he travels, and to other; come,  and
2064       2532 03  1401    1473 4160    3778   2532
ἔρχεται, καὶ τῷ δούλῳ μου· ποίησον τοῦτο, καὶ
he comes, and to the slave of me; do     this,  and
4160    9  191       1161 3778 01  2424  2296
ποιεῖ.    ἀκούσας δὲ ταῦτα ὁ Ἰησοῦς ἐθαύμασεν
he does.  Having heard but these the Jesus  marveled
846  2532 4762     03  190            846    3793
αὐτὸν καὶ στραφεὶς τῷ  ἀκολουθοῦντι αὐτῷ ὄχλῳ
him   and having turned to the following him crowd
3004    3004 1473 3761 1722 03  2474    5118
εἶπεν· λέγω ὑμῖν, οὐδὲ ἐν τῷ Ἰσραὴλ τοσαύτην
said,  I say to you, but not in the Israel such
```

whom he valued highly, and who was ill and close to death. [3]When he heard about Jesus, he sent some Jewish elders to him, asking him to come and heal his slave. [4]When they came to Jesus, they appealed to him earnestly, saying, "He is worthy of having you do this for him, [5]for he loves our people, and it is he who built our synagogue for us." [6]And Jesus went with them, but when he was not far from the house, the centurion sent friends to say to him, "Lord, do not trouble yourself, for I am not worthy to have you come under my roof; [7]therefore I did not presume to come to you. But only speak the word, and let my servant be healed. [8]For I also am a man set under authority, with soldiers under me; and I say to one, 'Go,' and he goes, and to another, 'Come,' and he comes, and to my slave, 'Do this,' and the slave does it." [9]When Jesus heard this he was amazed at him, and turning to the crowd that followed him, he said, "I tell you, not even in Israel have I found such faith."

10When those who had been sent returned to the house, they found the slave in good health.

11 Soon afterwards[a] he went to a town called Nain, and his disciples and a large crowd went with him. 12As he approached the gate of the town, a man who had died was being carried out. He was his mother's only son, and she was a widow; and with her was a large crowd from the town. 13When the Lord saw her, he had compassion for her and said to her, "Do not weep." 14Then he came forward and touched the bier, and the bearers stood still. And he said, "Young man, I say to you, rise!" 15The dead man sat up and began to speak, and Jesus[b] gave him to his mother. 16Fear seized all of them; and they glorified God, saying, "A great prophet has risen among us!" and "God has looked favorably on his people!" 17This word about him spread throughout Judea and all the surrounding country.

18 The disciples of John reported all these things to him. So John summoned two of his disciples 19and sent them to the Lord to ask, "Are you

a Other ancient authorities read Next day
b Gk he

```
4102      2147         10  2532 5290                    1519 04   3624
πίστιν  εὖρον.          Καὶ  ὑποστρέψαντες  εἰς  τὸν οἶκον
trust   I found.       And  having returned  into the house
013  3992             2147   04  1401      5198              11  2532
οἱ  πεμφθέντες  εὖρον τὸν δοῦλον  ὑγιαίνοντα.       Καὶ
the ones having found the slave   being            And
been sent                         healthy.
1096       1722 03    1836  4198           1519  4172
ἐγένετο  ἐν  τῷ ἑξῆς ἐπορεύθη  εἰς  πόλιν
it became in  the next  he traveled into city
2564              3484  2532  4848                   846    013
καλουμένην  Ναῖν καὶ  συνεπορεύοντο     αὐτῷ  οἱ
being called Nain and  were traveling with him the
3101    846    2532 3793  4183     12  5613 1161  1448
μαθηταὶ  αὐτοῦ καὶ  ὄχλος πολύς.    ὡς  δὲ   ἤγγισεν
learners of him and crowd  much.     As  but he neared
07  4439 06       4172     2532 2400 1580
τῇ  πύλῃ τῆς    πόλεως, καὶ ἰδοὺ ἐξεκομίζετο
the gate of the city,   and look was being carried out
2348           3439        5207 07 3384     846      2532 846
τεθνηκὼς  μονογενὴς υἱὸς τῇ μητρὶ  αὐτοῦ καὶ αὐτὴ
one having only born son  to mother of him and she
died                       the
1510 5503    2532 3793  06       4172    2425    1510 4862
ἦν  χήρα,  καὶ  ὄχλος τῆς    πόλεως ἱκανὸς ἦν  σὺν
was widow, and  crowd of the  city   enough was with
846     13  2532 3708      846     01 2962     4697
αὐτῇ.    καὶ  ἰδὼν       αὐτὴν ὁ κύριος ἐσπλαγχνίσθη
him.      And having seen her the Master had affection
1909 846   2532 3004  846      3361 2799        14  2532
ἐπ᾽ αὐτῇ καὶ εἶπεν αὐτῇ·  μὴ  κλαῖε.        καὶ
on  her and said  to her; not cry.           And
4334            681           06  4673    013          1161
προσελθὼν  ἥψατο      τῆς σοροῦ, οἱ       δὲ
having come to he touched the casket, the ones but
941            2476       2532 3004     3495       1473
βαστάζοντες ἔστησαν, καὶ  εἶπεν·  νεανίσκε,  σοὶ
bearing     stood,    and he said, young man, to you,
3004   1453        15  2532  339         01 3498     2532
λέγω,  ἐγέρθητι.     καὶ  ἀνεκάθισεν ὁ νεκρὸς καὶ
I say, be raised.    And sat up        the dead  and
757      2980      2532 1325    846    07  3384    846
ἤρξατο λαλεῖν,  καὶ  ἔδωκεν αὐτὸν τῇ  μητρὶ  αὐτοῦ.
began  to speak, and he gave him to the mother of him.
    2983     1161 5401    3956    2532 1392    04  2316
16  ἔλαβεν δὲ  φόβος πάντας καὶ  ἐδόξαζον τὸν θεὸν
    Took    but fear  all    and  they were the God
                                   giving splendor
3004       3754 4396      3173    1453        1722 1473 2532
λέγοντες ὅτι προφήτης μέγας ἠγέρθη    ἐν  ἡμῖν καὶ
saying    that spokesman great was raised in us  and
3754 1980         01 2316 04  2992     846     17  2532
ὅτι ἐπεσκέψατο ὁ θεὸς τὸν λαὸν αὐτοῦ.      καὶ
that looked on  the God the people of him.      And
1831     01  3056   3778  1722 3650  07  2449     4012
ἐξῆλθεν ὁ  λόγος οὗτος ἐν  ὅλῃ  τῇ Ἰουδαίᾳ περὶ
went out the word this  in  whole the Judea about
846    2532 3956 07  4066            18  2532 518
αὐτοῦ καὶ  πάσῃ τῇ περιχώρῳ.       Καὶ  ἀπήγγειλαν
him   and  all the country around. And  told
2491     013 3101     846    4012 3956    3778    2532
Ἰωάννῃ οἱ  μαθηταὶ αὐτοῦ περὶ πάντων τούτων. καὶ
to John the learners of him about all    these.   And
4341               1417 5100  014      3101     846    01
προσκαλεσάμενος δύο  τινὰς τῶν   μαθητῶν αὐτοῦ ὁ
having called to two some  of the learners of him the
2491     19  3992     4314 04  2962    3004   1473 1510
Ἰωάννης    ἔπεμψεν πρὸς τὸν κύριον λέγων· σὺ  εἶ
John        sent    to   the Master saying, you are
```

01	2064	2228	243	4328		20	3854	

ὁ ἐρχόμενος ἢ ἄλλον προσδοκῶμεν; **20** παραγενόμενοι
the one coming or other we wait   Having arrived
                          expectantly?

1161 4314 846   013 435   3004   2491   01 910
δὲ πρὸς αὐτὸν οἱ ἄνδρες εἶπαν· Ἰωάννης ὁ βαπτιστὴς
but to him   the men said;   John   the immerser

649   1473 4314 1473 3004   1473 1510 01
ἀπέστειλεν ἡμᾶς πρὸς σὲ λέγων·   σὺ εἶ ὁ
delegated us   to you saying;   you are the one

2064   2228 243 4328   1722 1565   07
ἐρχόμενος ἢ ἄλλον προσδοκῶμεν; **21** ἐν ἐκείνῃ τῇ
coming or other we wait expectantly? In that the

5610 2323   4183   575 3554   2532 3148
ὥρᾳ ἐθεράπευσεν πολλοὺς ἀπὸ νόσων καὶ μαστίγων
hour he healed many from illnesses and scourges

2532 4151   4190   2532 5185   4183   5483
καὶ πνευμάτων πονηρῶν καὶ τυφλοῖς πολλοῖς ἐχαρίσατο
and spirits evil   and blind many   he favored

991   **22** 2532 611   3004   846   4198
βλέπειν.   καὶ ἀποκριθεὶς εἶπεν αὐτοῖς· πορευθέντες
to see.   And having   he said to them; having
                answered   traveled

518   2491   3739 3708   2532 191   5185
ἀπαγγείλατε Ἰωάννῃ ἃ εἴδετε καὶ ἠκούσατε· τυφλοὶ
tell   John what you saw and you heard; blind

308   5560 4043   3015   2511
ἀναβλέπουσιν, χωλοὶ περιπατοῦσιν, λεπροὶ καθαρίζονται
see again,   lame walk around,   lepers are cleaned

2532 2974 191   3498 1453   4434
καὶ κωφοὶ ἀκούουσιν, νεκροὶ ἐγείρονται, πτωχοὶ
and deaf hear,   dead are raised,   poor

2097   **23** 2532 3107   1510 3739 1437 3361
εὐαγγελίζονται·   καὶ μακάριός ἐστιν ὃς ἐὰν μὴ
are being told   and fortunate is who if not
told good message;

4624   1722 1473 **24** 565   1161
σκανδαλισθῇ   ἐν ἐμοί.   Ἀπελθόντων   δὲ
might be offended in me.   Having gone off but

014 32   2491   757   3004   4314 016
τῶν ἀγγέλων Ἰωάννου ἤρξατο λέγειν πρὸς τοὺς
of the messengers of John he began to say to the

3793 4012 2491   5101 1831   1519 08 2048
ὄχλους περὶ Ἰωάννου· τί ἐξήλθατε   εἰς τὴν ἔρημον
crowds about John; what you went out into the desert

2300   2563   5259 417   4531   25 235
θεάσασθαι; κάλαμον ὑπὸ ἀνέμου σαλευόμενον;   ἀλλὰ
to watch? Reed   by wind being shaken?   But

5101 1831   3708 444   1722 3120
τί ἐξήλθατε   ἰδεῖν; ἄνθρωπον ἐν μαλακοῖς
what you came out to see? Man   in soft

2440   294   2400 013 1722 2441
ἱματίοις ἠμφιεσμένον; ἰδοὺ οἱ ἐν ἱματισμῷ
clothes having been dressed? Look the in clothing

1741   2532 5172   5225   1722 023
ἐνδόξῳ   καὶ τρυφῇ   ὑπάρχοντες ἐν τοῖς
in-splendor and indulgence existing in the

934   1510 **26** 235 5101 1831   3708
βασιλείοις εἰσίν.   ἀλλὰ τί ἐξήλθατε ἰδεῖν;
kingly places are. But what you came out to see?

4396   3483 3004 1473   2532 4055
προφήτην; ναὶ λέγω ὑμῖν, καὶ περισσότερον
Spokesman? Yes I say to you, and more excessive

4396   **27** 3778 1510 4012 3739 1125
προφήτου.   οὗτός ἐστιν περὶ οὗ γέγραπται·
spokesman. This is about whom it has been written;

2400 649   04 32   1473 4253   4383
ἰδοὺ ἀποστέλλω τὸν ἄγγελόν μου πρὸ προσώπου
look I delegate my messenger of me before face

the one who is to come, or
are we to wait for another?"
[20]When the men had come
to him, they said, "John the
Baptist has sent us to you to
ask, 'Are you the one who is
to come, or are we to wait
for another?' " [21]Jesus[a] had
just then cured many people
of diseases, plagues, and
evil spirits, and had given
sight to many who were
blind. [22]And he answered
them, "Go and tell John
what you have seen and
heard: the blind receive
their sight, the lame walk,
the lepers[b] are cleansed,
the deaf hear, the dead are
raised, the poor have good
news brought to them.
[23]And blessed is anyone
who takes no offense at me."

24 When John's
messengers had gone, Jesus[c]
began to speak to the
crowds about John:[d] "What
did you go out into the
wilderness to look at? A
reed shaken by the wind?
[25]What then did you go
out to see? Someone[e]
dressed in soft robes?
Look, those who put on
fine clothing and live in
luxury are in royal palaces.
[26]What then did you go out
to see? A prophet? Yes, I
tell you, and more than a
prophet. [27]This is the one
about whom it is written,

'See, I am sending my
    messenger ahead
    of you,

[a] Gk He
[b] The terms *leper* and *leprosy* can
    refer to several diseases
[c] Gk he
[d] Gk him
[e] Or *Why then did you go out? To see
    someone*

who will prepare your way before you.'

28I tell you, among those born of women no one is greater than John; yet the least in the kingdom of God is greater than he."

29(And all the people who heard this, including the tax collectors, acknowledged the justice of God,[a] because they had been baptized with John's baptism. 30But by refusing to be baptized by him, the Pharisees and the lawyers rejected God's purpose for themselves.)

31 "To what then will I compare the people of this generation, and what are they like? 32They are like children sitting in the marketplace and calling to one another,

'We played the flute for you, and you did not dance;
we wailed, and you did not weep.'

33For John the Baptist has come eating no bread and drinking no wine, and you say, 'He has a demon'; 34the Son of Man has come eating and drinking, and you say, 'Look, a glutton and a drunkard, a friend of tax collectors and sinners!' 35Nevertheless, wisdom is vindicated by all her children."

36 One of the Pharisees asked Jesus[b] to eat with him, and he went into the Pharisee's house and took his place at the table.

[a] Or praised God
[b] Gk him

1473	3739	2680		08	3598	1473	1715
σου,	ὃς	κατασκευάσει		τὴν	ὁδόν	σου	ἔμπροσθέν
of you,	who	will prepare		the	way	of you	in front of

1473	28	3004	1473	3173	1722	1084	1135
σου.		λέγω	ὑμῖν,	μείζων	ἐν	γεννητοῖς	γυναικῶν
you.		I say	to you,	greater	in	born ones of	women

2491	3762	1510	01	1161	3398	1722	07
Ἰωάννου	οὐδείς	ἐστιν·	ὁ	δὲ	μικρότερος	ἐν	τῇ
John	no one	is;	the	but	smaller	in	the

932	02	2316	3173	846	1510	29	2532	3956
βασιλείᾳ	τοῦ	θεοῦ	μείζων	αὐτοῦ	ἐστιν.		Καὶ	πᾶς
kingdom	of the	God	greater	of him	is.		And	all

01	2992	191	2532	013	5057	1344
ὁ	λαὸς	ἀκούσας	καὶ	οἱ	τελῶναι	ἐδικαίωσαν
the	people	having heard	also	the	tax men	made right

04	2316	907	012	908	2491
τὸν	θεὸν	βαπτισθέντες	τὸ	βάπτισμα	Ἰωάννου·
the	God	having been immersed	the	immersion	of John;

30	013	1161	5330	2532	013	3544	08	1012
	οἱ	δὲ	Φαρισαῖοι	καὶ	οἱ	νομικοὶ	τὴν	βουλὴν
	the	but	Pharisees	and	the	lawyers	the	plan

02	2316	114	1519	1438	3361
τοῦ	θεοῦ	ἠθέτησαν	εἰς	ἑαυτοὺς	μὴ
of the	God	set aside	to	themselves	not

907	5259	846	31	5101	3767	3666	016
βαπτισθέντες	ὑπ᾽	αὐτοῦ.		Τίνι	οὖν	ὁμοιώσω	τοὺς
having been immersed	by	him.		To what	then	will I liken	the

444	06	1074	3778	2532	5101	1510
ἀνθρώπους	τῆς	γενεᾶς	ταύτης	καὶ	τίνι	εἰσὶν
men	of the	generation	this	and	to what	are they

3664	32	3664	1510	3813	023	1722
ὅμοιοι;		ὅμοιοί	εἰσιν	παιδίοις	τοῖς	ἐν
like?		Like	they are to	small children	the	in

58	2521	2532	4377	240	3739	3004
ἀγορᾷ	καθημένοις	καὶ	προσφωνοῦσιν	ἀλλήλοις	ἃ	λέγει·
market	sitting	and	sound to	one another	who	say;

832	1473	2532	3756	3738	2354
ηὐλήσαμεν	ὑμῖν	καὶ	οὐκ	ὠρχήσασθε,	ἐθρηνήσαμεν
we played flute	to you	and	not	you danced,	we lamented

2532	3756	2799	33	2064	1063	2491	01
καὶ	οὐκ	ἐκλαύσατε.		ἐλήλυθεν	γὰρ	Ἰωάννης	ὁ
and	not	you cried.		Has come	for	John	the

910	3361	2068	740	3383	4095	3631	2532
βαπτιστὴς	μὴ	ἐσθίων	ἄρτον	μήτε	πίνων	οἶνον,	καὶ
immerser	not	eating	bread	and not	drinking	wine,	and

3004	1140	2192	34	2064	01	5207	02
λέγετε·	δαιμόνιον	ἔχει.		ἐλήλυθεν	ὁ	υἱὸς	τοῦ
you say;	demon	he has.		Has come	the	son	of the

444	2068	2532	4095	2532	3004	2400
ἀνθρώπου	ἐσθίων	καὶ	πίνων,	καὶ	λέγετε·	ἰδοὺ
man	eating	and	drinking,	and	you say,	look

444	5314	2532	3630	5384	5057	2532
ἄνθρωπος	φάγος	καὶ	οἰνοπότης,	φίλος	τελωνῶν	καὶ
man	eater	and	wine drinker,	friend	of tax men	and

268	35	2532	1344	05	4678	575	3956
ἁμαρτωλῶν.		καὶ	ἐδικαιώθη	ἡ	σοφία	ἀπὸ	πάντων
sinners.		And	was made right	the	wisdom	from	all

022	5043	846	36	2065	1161	5100	846	014
τῶν	τέκνων	αὐτῆς.		Ἠρώτα	δέ	τις	αὐτὸν	τῶν
the	children	of her.		Was asking	but	some	him	of the

5330	2443	2068	3326	846	2532	1525
Φαρισαίων	ἵνα	φάγῃ	μετ᾽	αὐτοῦ,	καὶ	εἰσελθὼν
Pharisees	that	he might eat	with	him,	and	having come into

1519	04	3624	02	5330	2625
εἰς	τὸν	οἶκον	τοῦ	Φαρισαίου	κατεκλίθη.
into	the	house	of the	Pharisee	he reclined.

37
2532	2400	1135	3748	1510	1722	07	4172	268

καὶ   ἰδοὺ γυνὴ ἥτις ἦν   ἐν   τῇ πόλει ἁμαρτωλός,
And   look   woman who   was in   the city   sinner,

2532	1921		3754	2621	1722	07

καὶ   ἐπιγνοῦσα   ὅτι κατάκειται ἐν   τῇ
and   having perceived that he was lying down in the

3614	02	5330	2865	211

οἰκίᾳ τοῦ Φαρισαίου, κομίσασα   ἀλάβαστρον
house of the Pharisee,   having obtained   alabaster jar

3464	**38**	2532	2476	3694	3844	016

μύρου   καὶ   στᾶσα   ὀπίσω παρὰ τοὺς
of perfume   and   having stood after along the

4228	846	2799	023	1144	757	1026

πόδας αὐτοῦ κλαίουσα τοῖς δάκρυσιν ἤρξατο βρέχειν
feet   of him crying   in the tears   she began to rain

016	4228	846	2532	019	2359	06	2776	846

τοὺς πόδας αὐτοῦ καὶ ταῖς θριξὶν τῆς κεφαλῆς αὐτῆς
the   feet   of him and the   hairs   of the head   of her

1591		2532	2705	016	4228	846

ἐξέμασσεν   καὶ κατεφίλει   τοὺς πόδας αὐτοῦ
she was wiping dry and was kissing the   feet   of him

2532	218	011	3464	**39**	3708	1161	01

καὶ   ἤλειφεν   τῷ μύρῳ.   ἰδὼν   δὲ   ὁ
and   was smearing the perfume.   Having seen but the

5330	01	2564	846	3004	1722	1438

Φαρισαῖος ὁ καλέσας   αὐτὸν εἶπεν ἐν   ἑαυτῷ
Pharisee   the one having called him   said   in   himself

3004	3778	1487	1510	4396	1097	302

λέγων· οὗτος εἰ   ἦν   προφήτης, ἐγίνωσκεν   ἂν
saying; this   if   was spokesman, he was knowing -

5101	2532	4217	05	1135	3748	681	846	3754

τίς   καὶ ποταπὴ ἡ γυνὴ ἥτις ἅπτεται αὐτοῦ, ὅτι
who   and what sort the woman who   touched him,   that

268	1510	**40**	2532	611	01	2424

ἁμαρτωλός ἐστιν.   καὶ ἀποκριθεὶς   ὁ Ἰησοῦς
sinner   she is.   And having answered the Jesus

3004	4314	846	4613	2192	1473	5100	3004

εἶπεν πρὸς αὐτόν· Σίμων, ἔχω   σοί   τι   εἰπεῖν.
said   to   him;   Simon, I have to you some to speak.

01	1161	1320	3004	5346	**41**	1417	5533

ὁ   δέ· διδάσκαλε, εἰπέ, φησίν.   δύο χρεοφειλέται
the but; teacher,   say,   he says. Two borrowers

1510	1157	5100	01	1520	3784	1220

ἦσαν δανιστῇ τινι·   ὁ   εἷς ὤφειλεν δηνάρια
were lender   to some; the one was owing denaria

4001	01	1161	2087	4004	**42**	3361	2192

πεντακόσια, ὁ δὲ ἕτερος πεντήκοντα.   μὴ ἐχόντων
five hundred, the but other   fifty.   Not having

846	591	297	5483	5101	3767

αὐτῶν ἀποδοῦναι ἀμφοτέροις ἐχαρίσατο. τίς οὖν
of them to give back both   he favored. Who then

846	4183	25	846	**43**	611

αὐτῶν πλεῖον ἀγαπήσει αὐτόν;   ἀποκριθεὶς
of them more   will love   him?   Having answered

4613	3004	5274	3754	3739	012	4183

Σίμων εἶπεν· ὑπολαμβάνω ὅτι ᾧ   τὸ πλεῖον
Simon said;   I take up   that to whom the more

5483	01	1161	3004	846	3723

ἐχαρίσατο. ὁ   δὲ   εἶπεν αὐτῷ· ὀρθῶς
he favored. The one but said   to him; straightly

2919	**44**	2532	4762	4314	08	1135	03

ἔκρινας.   καὶ στραφεὶς   πρὸς τὴν γυναῖκα τῷ
you judged. And having turned toward the woman   to the

4613	5346	991	3778	08	1135	1525

Σίμωνι ἔφη· βλέπεις ταύτην τὴν γυναῖκα; εἰσῆλθόν
Simon   he said; you see this   the woman?   I came into

1473	1519	08	3614	5204	1473	1909	4228	3756

σου   εἰς τὴν οἰκίαν, ὕδωρ μοι ἐπὶ πόδας οὐκ
of you into the house,   water to me on   feet   not

37 And a woman in the city, who was a sinner, having learned that he was eating in the Pharisee's house, brought an alabaster jar of ointment. 38 She stood behind him at his feet, weeping, and began to bathe his feet with her tears and to dry them with her hair. Then she continued kissing his feet and anointing them with the ointment. 39 Now when the Pharisee who had invited him saw it, he said to himself, "If this man were a prophet, he would have known who and what kind of woman this is who is touching him—that she is a sinner." 40 Jesus spoke up and said to him, "Simon, I have something to say to you." "Teacher," he replied, "speak." 41 "A certain creditor had two debtors; one owed five hundred denarii,[a] and the other fifty. 42 When they could not pay, he canceled the debts for both of them. Now which of them will love him more?" 43 Simon answered, "I suppose the one for whom he canceled the greater debt." And Jesus[b] said to him, "You have judged rightly." 44 Then turning toward the woman, he said to Simon, "Do you see this woman? I entered your house; you gave me no water for my feet,

[a] The denarius was the usual day's wage for a laborer
[b] Gk he

but she has bathed my feet with her tears and dried them with her hair. [45]You gave me no kiss, but from the time I came in she has not stopped kissing my feet. [46]You did not anoint my head with oil, but she has anointed my feet with ointment. [47]Therefore, I tell you, her sins, which were many, have been forgiven; hence she has shown great love. But the one to whom little is forgiven, loves little." [48]Then he said to her, "Your sins are forgiven." [49]But those who were at the table with him began to say among themselves, "Who is this who even forgives sins?" [50]And he said to the woman, "Your faith has saved you; go in peace."

CHAPTER 8

Soon afterwards he went on through cities and villages, proclaiming and bringing the good news of the kingdom of God. The twelve were with him, [2]as well as some women who had been cured of evil spirits and infirmities: Mary, called Magdalene, from whom seven demons had gone out, [3]and Joanna, the wife of Herod's steward Chuza, and Susanna, and many others, who provided for them[a] out of their resources.

[a] Other ancient authorities read him

	1325	3778	1161	023	1144	1026	1473	016
	ἔδωκας·	αὕτη	δὲ	τοῖς	δάκρυσιν	ἔβρεξέν	μου	τοὺς
	you gave;	this	but	in	the tears	rained	of me	the

4228	2532	019	2359	846	1591		5370
πόδας	καὶ	ταῖς	θριξὶν	αὐτῆς	ἐξέμαξεν.	**45**	φίλημά
feet	and	in the hairs	of her	she wiped dry.		Kiss

1473	3756	1325	3778	1161	575	3739	1525	3756
μοι	οὐκ	ἔδωκας·	αὕτη	δὲ	ἀφ'	ἧς	εἰσῆλθον	οὐ
to me	not	you gave;	this	but	from	which	I came in	not

1257	2705	1473	016	4228
διέλιπεν	καταφιλοῦσά	μου	τοὺς	πόδας.
she left	thoroughly kissing	of me	the	feet.

	1637	08	2776	1473	3756	218	3778
46	ἐλαίῳ	τὴν	κεφαλήν	μου	οὐκ	ἤλειψας·	αὕτη
	In oil	the	head	of me	not	you smeared;	this one

1161	3464	218	016	4228	1473	**47**	3739
δὲ	μύρῳ	ἤλειψεν	τοὺς	πόδας	μου.		οὗ
but	in perfume	smeared	the	feet	of me.		Of which

5484	3004	1473	863		017	266
χάριν	λέγω	σοι,	ἀφέωνται		αἱ	ἁμαρτίαι
reason	I say	to you,	have been sent off		the	sins

846	017	4183	3754	25	4183	3739	1161
αὐτῆς	αἱ	πολλαί,	ὅτι	ἠγάπησεν	πολύ·	ᾧ	δὲ
of her	the	many,	because	she loved	much;	to whom	but

3641	863	3641	25	**48**	3004	1161
ὀλίγον	ἀφίεται,	ὀλίγον	ἀγαπᾷ.		εἶπεν	δὲ
little	is sent off,	little	he loves.		He said	but

846	863	1473	017	266	**49**	2532
αὐτῇ·	ἀφέωνταί	σου	αἱ	ἁμαρτίαι.		καὶ
to her;	have been sent off	of you	the	sins.		And

757	013	4873		3004	1722
ἤρξαντο	οἱ	συνανακείμενοι		λέγειν	ἐν
began	the	ones reclining together		to say	in

1438	5101	3778	1510	3739	2532	266
ἑαυτοῖς·	τίς	οὗτός	ἐστιν	ὃς	καὶ	ἁμαρτίας
themselves;	who	this	is	who	also	sins

063	**50**	3004	1161	4314	08	1135	05	4102
ἀφίησιν;		εἶπεν	δὲ	πρὸς	τὴν	γυναῖκα·	ἡ	πίστις
sends off?		He said	but	to	the	woman;	the	trust

1473	4982	1473	4198	1519	1515
σου	σέσωκέν	σε·	πορεύου	εἰς	εἰρήνην.
of you	has delivered	you;	travel	in	peace.

8:1	2532	1096	1722	03	2517	2532	846
	Καὶ	ἐγένετο	ἐν	τῷ	καθεξῆς	καὶ	αὐτὸς
	And	it became in	the	in order	also	himself

1353	2596	4172	2532	2968	2784	2532
διώδευεν	κατὰ	πόλιν	καὶ	κώμην	κηρύσσων	καὶ
was making	by	city	and	village	announcing	and
way through						

2097	08	932	02	2316	2532	013
εὐαγγελιζόμενος	τὴν	βασιλείαν	τοῦ	θεοῦ	καὶ	οἱ
telling good message	the	kingdom	of the	God	and	the

1427	4862	846		2532	1135	5100	3739	1510
δώδεκα	σὺν	αὐτῷ,	**2**	καὶ	γυναῖκές	τινες	αἳ	ἦσαν
twelve	with	him,		and	women	some	who	were+

2323	575	4151	4190	2532
τεθεραπευμέναι	ἀπὸ	πνευμάτων	πονηρῶν	καὶ
+having been healed	from	spirits	evil	and

769	3137	05	2564	3094	575
ἀσθενειῶν,	Μαρία	ἡ	καλουμένη	Μαγδαληνή,	ἀφ'
weaknesses,	Maria	the one	being called	Magdalene,	from

3739	1140	2033	1831	**3**	2532	2489	1135
ἧς	δαιμόνια	ἑπτὰ	ἐξεληλύθει,		καὶ	Ἰωάννα	γυνὴ
whom	demons	seven	had come out,		and	Joanna	woman

5529	2012	2264	2532	4677	2532	2087
Χουζᾶ	ἐπιτρόπου	Ἡρῴδου	καὶ	Σουσάννα	καὶ	ἕτεραι
of Chouza	governor	of Herod	and	Susanna	and	others

4183	3748	1247	846	1537	022	5225
πολλαί,	αἵτινες	διηκόνουν	αὐτοῖς	ἐκ	τῶν	ὑπαρχόντων
many,	who	were serving	them	from	the	possessions

846   4896   1161 3793 4183   2532
αὐταῖς. **4** Συνιόντος   δὲ ὄχλου πολλοῦ καὶ
to them. Having gone together but crowd much   and

014   2596 4172   1975   4314 846
τῶν   κατὰ πόλιν ἐπιπορευομένων   πρὸς αὐτὸν
of the by city   ones traveling on toward him

3004   1223   3850   **5** 1831   01   4687   010
εἶπεν διὰ   παραβολῆς·   ἐξῆλθεν ὁ σπείρων τοῦ
he said through parallel   came out the one   the
                  story;   sowing

4687   04   4703   846   2532 1722 011 4687   846
σπεῖραι τὸν σπόρον αὐτοῦ. καὶ ἐν τῷ σπείρειν αὐτὸν
to sow the seed   of him. And in the to sow   him

3739 3303   4098   3844 08 3598 2532 2662
ὃ μὲν   ἔπεσεν παρὰ τὴν ὁδὸν καὶ κατεπατήθη,
what indeed fell along the way and was walked over,

2532 021 4071   02   3772   2719   846   **6** 2532
καὶ τὰ πετεινὰ τοῦ   οὐρανοῦ κατέφαγεν αὐτό.   καὶ
and the birds of the heaven   ate up   it.   And

2087   2667   1909 08 4073   2532 5453   3583
ἕτερον κατέπεσεν ἐπὶ τὴν πέτραν, καὶ φυὲν   ἐξηράνθη
other fell down on the rock,   and having it was
                                       sprouted dried out

1223   012 3361 2192   2429   **7** 2532 2087   4098
διὰ   τὸ μὴ ἔχειν ἰκμάδα.   καὶ ἕτερον ἔπεσεν
through the not to have moisture. And other fell

1722 3319 018   173   2532 4855
ἐν μέσῳ τῶν ἀκανθῶν, καὶ συμφυεῖσαι
in middle of the thorns, and having sprouted together

017 173   638   846   **8** 2532 2087 4098   1519
αἱ ἄκανθαι ἀπέπνιξαν αὐτό.   καὶ ἕτερον ἔπεσεν εἰς
the thorns choked off it.   And other fell   into

08 1093   08 18   2532 5453   4160   2590
τὴν γῆν τὴν ἀγαθὴν καὶ φυὲν   ἐποίησεν καρπὸν
the earth the good   and having sprouted made   fruit

1542   3778 3004   5455   01
ἑκατονταπλασίονα. ταῦτα λέγων ἐφώνει·   ὁ
hundred times.   These saying he was sounding; the

2192   3775 191   191   1905   1161
ἔχων   ὦτα ἀκούειν ἀκουέτω. **9** Ἐπηρώτων δὲ
having ears to hear let hear. Were asking on but

846   013 3101   846   5101 3778 1510   05
αὐτὸν οἱ μαθηταὶ αὐτοῦ τίς αὕτη εἴη   ἡ
him   the learners of him what this might be the

3850   **10** 01   1161 3004   1473
παραβολή.   ὁ   δὲ εἶπεν· ὑμῖν
parallel story.   The one but said; to you

1325   1097   024 3466   06   932
δέδοται   γνῶναι τὰ μυστήρια τῆς βασιλείας
has been given to know the mysteries of the kingdom

02   2316 015   1161 3062   1722 3850
τοῦ θεοῦ, τοῖς δὲ λοιποῖς ἐν παραβολαῖς,
of the God, to the but remaining in parallel stories,

2443 991   3361 991   2532 191   3361
ἵνα βλέποντες μὴ βλέπωσιν   καὶ ἀκούοντες μὴ
that seeing   not they might see and hearing   not

4920   1510   1161 3778 05 3850
συνιῶσιν.   **11** Ἔστιν δὲ αὕτη ἡ παραβολή·
might understand. Is but this the parallel story;

01 4703   1510   01 3056 02   2316   **12** 013 1161
ὁ σπόρος ἐστὶν ὁ λόγος τοῦ θεοῦ.   οἱ δὲ
the seed   is   the word of the God.   The but

3844 08 3598 1510 013 191   1534
παρὰ τὴν ὁδὸν εἰσιν οἱ ἀκούσαντες,   εἶτα
along the way are the ones having heard, then

2064   01 1228   2532 142   04 3056 575 06
ἔρχεται ὁ διάβολος καὶ αἴρει τὸν λόγον ἀπὸ τῆς
comes the slanderer and lifts up the word from the

---

4 When a great crowd gathered and people from town after town came to him, he said in a parable: 5 "A sower went out to sow his seed; and as he sowed, some fell on the path and was trampled on, and the birds of the air ate it up. 6 Some fell on the rock; and as it grew up, it withered for lack of moisture. 7 Some fell among thorns, and the thorns grew with it and choked it. 8 Some fell into good soil, and when it grew, it produced a hundredfold." As he said this, he called out, "Let anyone with ears to hear listen!"

9 Then his disciples asked him what this parable meant. 10 He said, "To you it has been given to know the secrets[a] of the kingdom of God; but to others I speak[b] in parables, so that
'looking they may not perceive,
and listening they may not understand.'
11 "Now the parable is this: The seed is the word of God. 12 The ones on the path are those who have heard; then the devil comes and takes away the word from

---

[a] Or mysteries
[b] Gk lacks I speak

their hearts, so that they may not believe and be saved. [13]The ones on the rock are those who, when they hear the word, receive it with joy. But these have no root; they believe only for a while and in a time of testing fall away. [14]As for what fell among the thorns, these are the ones who hear; but as they go on their way, they are choked by the cares and riches and pleasures of life, and their fruit does not mature. [15]But as for that in the good soil, these are the ones who, when they hear the word, hold it fast in an honest and good heart, and bear fruit with patient endurance.

16 "No one after lighting a lamp hides it under a jar, or puts it under a bed, but puts it on a lampstand, so that those who enter may see the light. [17]For nothing is hidden that will not be disclosed, nor is anything secret that will not become known and come to light. [18]Then pay attention to how you listen; for to those who have, more will be given; and from those who do not have, even what they seem to have will be taken away."

19 Then his mother and his brothers came to him, but they could not reach him

2588	846		2443 3361	4100
καρδίας	αὐτῶν,	ἵνα	μὴ	πιστεύσαντες
heart	of them,	that	not	ones having trusted

4982		013	1161 1909	06	4073	3739
σωθῶσιν.	[13]	οἱ	δὲ ἐπὶ	τῆς	πέτρας	οἳ
might be delivered.		The ones	but on	the	rock	who

3752 191	3326 5479	1209	04
ὅταν ἀκούσωσιν	μετὰ χαρᾶς	δέχονται	τὸν
when they might hear	with joy	they welcome	the

3056	2532 3778	4491 3756	2192	3739	4314
λόγον,	καὶ οὗτοι	ῥίζαν οὐκ	ἔχουσιν,	οἳ	πρὸς
word,	and these	root not	have,	which	to

2540	4100	2532 1722	2540	3986
καιρὸν	πιστεύουσιν	καὶ ἐν	καιρῷ	πειρασμοῦ
season	they trust	and in	season	of pressure

868		09 1161	1519 020	173	4098
ἀφίστανται.	[14]	τὸ δὲ	εἰς τὰς	ἀκάνθας	πεσόν,
they stand off.		The but	into the	thorns	having fallen,

3778	1510 013 191	2532 5259	3308	2532
οὗτοί	εἰσιν οἱ ἀκούσαντες,	καὶ ὑπὸ	μεριμνῶν	καὶ
these are	the having heard,	and by	anxieties	and

4149	2532 2237	02	979	4198
πλούτου	καὶ ἡδονῶν	τοῦ	βίου	πορευόμενοι
rich	and pleasures	of the	life	traveling

4846	2532 3756	5052
συμπνίγονται	καὶ οὐ	τελεσφοροῦσιν.
choke together	and not	they bring to completion.

	09	1161 1722 07	2570 1093	3778 1510	3748
[15]	τὸ	δὲ ἐν	τῇ καλῇ γῇ,	οὗτοί εἰσιν	οἵτινες
	The	but in	the good earth,	these are	which

1722 2588	2570 2532 18	191	04 3056
ἐν καρδίᾳ	καλῇ καὶ ἀγαθῇ	ἀκούσαντες	τὸν λόγον
in heart	good and good	having heard	the word

2722	2532 2592	1722 5281
κατέχουσιν	καὶ καρποφοροῦσιν	ἐν ὑπομονῇ.
they hold down	and bear fruit	in patience.

	3762	1161 3088	681	2572	846	4632
[16]	Οὐδεὶς	δὲ λύχνον	ἅψας	καλύπτει	αὐτὸν	σκεύει
	No one	but lamp	having lit	covers	it	in pot

2228 5270	2825	5087	235	1909 3087
ἢ ὑποκάτω	κλίνης	τίθησιν,	ἀλλ'	ἐπὶ λυχνίας
or underneath	bed	sets,	but	on lampstand

5087	2443 013 1531	991	012
τίθησιν,	ἵνα οἱ εἰσπορευόμενοι	βλέπωσιν	τὸ
he sets,	that the ones traveling in	might see	the

5457	17	3756 1063 1510	2927	3739 3756 5318
φῶς.		οὐ γάρ ἐστιν	κρυπτὸν	ὃ οὐ φανερὸν
light.		Not for it is	hidden	which not evident

1096	3761	614	3739 3756 3361
γενήσεται	οὐδὲ	ἀπόκρυφον	ὃ οὐ μὴ
will become	but not	hidden off	which not not

1097	2532 1519 5318	2064	18	991
γνωσθῇ	καὶ εἰς φανερὸν	ἔλθῃ.		Βλέπετε
might be known	and in evident	might come.		See

3767 4459 191	3739 302 1063 2192
οὖν πῶς ἀκούετε·	ὃς ἂν γὰρ ἔχῃ,
then how you hear;	who - for might have,

1325	846	2532 3739 302 3361 2192
δοθήσεται	αὐτῷ·	καὶ ὃς ἂν μὴ ἔχῃ,
it shall be given	to him;	and who - not might have,

2532 3739 1380	2192	142	575
καὶ ὃ δοκεῖ	ἔχειν	ἀρθήσεται	ἀπ'
also what he thinks	to have	will be lifted up	from

846	19	3854	1161 4314 846	05 3384	2532
αὐτοῦ.		Παρεγένετο	δὲ πρὸς αὐτὸν	ἡ μήτηρ	καὶ
him.		Arrived	but to him	the mother	and

013 80	846	2532 3756 1410	4940	846
οἱ ἀδελφοὶ	αὐτοῦ	καὶ οὐκ ἠδύναντο	συντυχεῖν	αὐτῷ
the brothers	of him	and not they were	to meet	to
			able	together him

```
1223      04    3793       518              1161  846       05
διὰ       τὸν  ὄχλον.  20  ἀπηγγέλη   δὲ  αὐτῷ·   ἡ
through   the   crowd.      It was told   but  to him;  the
3384    1473  2532 013 80        1473    2476        1854
μήτηρ    σου  καὶ οἱ  ἀδελφοί  σου   ἑστήκασιν  ἔξω
mother  of you and the brothers  of you  stood       outside
3708    2309      1473  21  01  1161  611            3004  4314
ἰδεῖν  θέλοντές σε.      ὁ   δὲ   ἀποκριθεὶς  εἶπεν πρὸς
to see  wanting  you.      The but  having answered said to
846      3384   1473  2532 80         1473  3778  1510
αὐτούς· μήτηρ  μου  καὶ ἀδελφοί  μου  οὗτοί εἰσιν
them,    mother of me and brothers  of me  these are
013 04   3056  02         2316  191          2532  4160
οἱ   τὸν λόγον τοῦ   θεοῦ ἀκούοντες   καὶ  ποιοῦντες.
the  the word  of the God   ones hearing  and  doing.
       1096       1161  1722  1520 018        2250  2532 846
22  Ἐγένετο    δὲ   ἐν   μιᾷ  τῶν   ἡμερῶν καὶ αὐτὸς
    It became  but  in   one  of the days    and himself
1684        1519 4143  2532 013 3101        846   2532
ἐνέβη     εἰς  πλοῖον καὶ οἱ  μαθηταὶ αὐτοῦ καὶ
went in into boat   and  the learners of him and
3004     4314 846       1330            1519 012 4008
εἶπεν    πρὸς αὐτούς· διέλθωμεν       εἰς  τὸ  πέραν
he said to   them;    let us go through to  the  across
06   3041     2532 321           23  4126      1161 846
τῆς λίμνης,  καὶ ἀνήχθησαν.       πλεόντων  δὲ  αὐτῶν
the  lake,   and they were led up. Sailing  but of them
879          2532 2597      2978   417     1519 08
ἀφύπνωσεν.  καὶ κατέβη   λαῖλαψ ἀνέμου εἰς  τὴν
he fell asleep. And  came down storm  of wind in  the
3041    2532 4845         2532 2793
λίμνην καὶ  συνεπληροῦντο  καὶ ἐκινδύνευον.
lake    and  they were filling and were in danger.
             together
24  4334          1161 1326               846
    προσελθόντες δὲ   διήγειραν         αὐτὸν
    Having come to but they raised thoroughly him
3004       1988      1988     622        01
λέγοντες· ἐπιστάτα ἐπιστάτα, ἀπολλύμεθα. ὁ
saying;   Master   Master     we are being The one
          teacher  teacher,    destroyed.
1161 1326        2008      03   417    2532 03  2830
δὲ   διεγερθεὶς ἐπετίμησεν τῷ ἀνέμῳ καὶ τῷ κλύδωνι
but  having been admonished the wind and  the wave
     thoroughly raised
010     5204     2532 3973      2532 1096      1055
τοῦ   ὕδατος·  καὶ ἐπαύσαντο καὶ ἐγένετο   γαλήνη.
of the water;  and  they stopped and it became calm.
25  3004   1161 846       4226  05 4102   1473
    εἶπεν δὲ  αὐτοῖς· ποῦ ἡ πίστις ὑμῶν;
    He said but to them; where the trust of you?
5399        1161 2296      3004        4314
φοβηθέντες δὲ  ἐθαύμασαν λέγοντες πρὸς
Having feared but they marveled saying   to
240        5101 686  3778   1510  3754 2532 015
ἀλλήλους· τίς ἄρα οὗτός ἐστιν ὅτι καὶ τοῖς
one another; who then this  is    that also to the
417      2004       2532 011 5204    2532 5219
ἀνέμοις ἐπιτάσσει καὶ τῷ ὕδατι, καὶ ὑπακούουσιν
winds   he gives   and  the water, and  they obey
846   26 2532 2668           1519 08  5561     014
αὐτῷ;   Καὶ κατέπλευσαν  εἰς τὴν χώραν  τῶν
him?     And  they sailed down into the country of the
1086         3748  1510  495           06  1056
Γερασηνῶν, ἥτις ἐστὶν ἀντιπέρα       τῆς Γαλιλαίας.
Gerasenes,  which is   across against  the Galilee.
27  1831       1161 846       1909 08  1093
    ἐξελθόντι  δὲ   αὐτῷ ἐπὶ τὴν γῆν
    Having gone out but  to him on  the land
```

because of the crowd. [20]And he was told, "Your mother and your brothers are standing outside, wanting to see you." [21]But he said to them, "My mother and my brothers are those who hear the word of God and do it."

[22]One day he got into a boat with his disciples, and he said to them, "Let us go across to the other side of the lake." So they put out, [23]and while they were sailing he fell asleep. A windstorm swept down on the lake, and the boat was filling with water, and they were in danger. [24]They went to him and woke him up, shouting, "Master, Master, we are perishing!" And he woke up and rebuked the wind and the raging waves; they ceased, and there was a calm. [25]He said to them, "Where is your faith?" They were afraid and amazed, and said to one another, "Who then is this, that he commands even the winds and the water, and they obey him?"

[26]Then they arrived at the country of the Gerasenes,[a] which is opposite Galilee. [27]As he stepped out on land,

[a] Other ancient authorities read Gadarenes; others, Gergesenes

a man of the city who had demons met him. For a long time he had worn[a] no clothes, and he did not live in a house but in the tombs. [28]When he saw Jesus, he fell down before him and shouted at the top of his voice, "What have you to do with me, Jesus, Son of the Most High God? I beg you, do not torment me"— [29]for Jesus[b] had commanded the unclean spirit to come out of the man. (For many times it had seized him; he was kept under guard and bound with chains and shackles, but he would break the bonds and be driven by the demon into the wilds.) [30]Jesus then asked him, "What is your name?" He said, "Legion"; for many demons had entered him. [31]They begged him not to order them to go back into the abyss.

32 Now there on the hillside a large herd of ꜱwine was feeding; and the demons[c] begged Jesus[d] to let them enter these. So he gave them permission. [33]Then the demons came out of the man and entered the swine, and the herd rushed down the steep bank into the lake and was drowned.

a Other ancient authorities read a man of the city who had had demons for a long time met him. He wore
b Gk he
c Gk they
d Gk him

5221		435	5100	1537	06	4172	2192	1140
ὑπήντησεν		ἀνήρ	τις	ἐκ	τῆς	πόλεως	ἔχων	δαιμόνια
met		man	some	from	the	city	having	demons

2532	5550	2425		3756	1746		2440	2532	1722
καὶ	χρόνῳ	ἱκανῷ		οὐκ	ἐνεδύσατο		ἱμάτιον	καὶ	ἐν
and	time	enough		not	he puts on		clothes	and	in

3614	3756	3306		235	1722	023	3418
οἰκίᾳ	οὐκ	ἔμενεν		ἀλλ᾽	ἐν	τοῖς	μνήμασιν.
house	not	he was staying		but	in	the	graves.

28
3708		1161	04	2424	349
ἰδὼν		δὲ	τὸν	Ἰησοῦν	ἀνακράξας
Having seen		but	the	Jesus	having shouted out

4363		846	2532	5456		3173	3004	5101
προσέπεσεν		αὐτῷ	καὶ	φωνῇ		μεγάλῃ	εἶπεν·	τί
he fell		to him	and	in sound		great	he said;	what

1473	2532	1473		2424	5207	02		2316	02
ἐμοὶ	καὶ	σοί,		Ἰησοῦ	υἱὲ	τοῦ		θεοῦ	τοῦ
to me	and	to you,		Jesus	son	of the		God	of the

5310		1189		1473	3361	1473	928
ὑψίστου;		δέομαί		σου,	μή	με	βασανίσῃς.
highest?		I beg		you,	not	me	you might torment.

29
3853		1063	011		4151	011	169
παρήγγειλεν		γὰρ	τῷ		πνεύματι	τῷ	ἀκαθάρτῳ
He commanded		for	to the		spirit	the	unclean

1831		575	02	444		4183		1063	5550
ἐξελθεῖν		ἀπὸ	τοῦ	ἀνθρώπου.		πολλοῖς		γὰρ	χρόνοις
to go out		from	the	man.		In many		for	times

4884		846	2532	1195
συνηρπάκει		αὐτὸν	καὶ	ἐδεσμεύετο
it had seized together		him	and	he was tied up

254		2532	3976		5442		2532
ἁλύσεσιν		καὶ	πέδαις		φυλασσόμενος		καὶ
in chains		and	in foot shackles		being guarded		and

1284		024	1199	1643		5259	010
διαρρήσσων		τὰ	δεσμὰ	ἠλαύνετο		ὑπὸ	τοῦ
tearing apart		the	chains	he was being driven		by	the

1140		1519	020	2048	30	1905		1161	846
δαιμονίου		εἰς	τὰς	ἐρήμους	30	ἐπηρώτησεν		δὲ	αὐτὸν
demon		into	the	deserts.		Asked on		but	him

01	2424		5101	1473	3686	1510	01	1161	3004
ὁ	Ἰησοῦς·		τί	σοι	ὄνομά	ἐστιν;	ὁ	δὲ	εἶπεν·
the Jesus;			what	to you	name	is?	The	but	said;

3003		3754		1525		1140		4183	1519	846
λεγιών,		ὅτι		εἰσῆλθεν		δαιμόνια		πολλὰ	εἰς	αὐτόν.
Legion,		because		went in		demons		many	into	him.

31
2532	3870				846	2443	3361
καὶ	παρεκάλουν				αὐτὸν	ἵνα	μὴ
And	they were encouraging				him	that	not

2004		846		1519	08	12		565
ἐπιτάξῃ		αὐτοῖς		εἰς	τὴν	ἄβυσσον		ἀπελθεῖν.
he might order		them		into	the	bottomless		to go off.

32
1510	1161	1563	34		5519	2425	1006		1722
ἦν	δὲ	ἐκεῖ	ἀγέλη		χοίρων	ἱκανῶν	βοσκομένη		ἐν
Was	but	there	herd		of pigs	enough	grazing		in

011	3735	2532	3870			846	2443	2010
τῷ	ὄρει·	καὶ	παρεκάλεσαν			αὐτὸν	ἵνα	ἐπιτρέψῃ
the	hill;	and	they encouraged			him	that	he might allow

846		1519	1565		1525		2532	2010		846
αὐτοῖς		εἰς	ἐκείνους		εἰσελθεῖν·		καὶ	ἐπέτρεψεν		αὐτοῖς.
them		into	those		to go into;		and	he allowed them.

33
1831			1161	021	1140		575	02	444
ἐξελθόντα			δὲ	τὰ	δαιμόνια		ἀπὸ	τοῦ	ἀνθρώπου
Having gone out			but	the	demons		from	the	man

1525		1519	016	5519		2532	3729	05	34
εἰσῆλθον		εἰς	τοὺς	χοίρους,		καὶ	ὥρμησεν	ἡ	ἀγέλη
went into		into	the	pigs,		and	rushed	the	herd

2596	02	2911		1519	08	3041	2532
κατὰ	τοῦ	κρημνοῦ		εἰς	τὴν	λίμνην	καὶ
down	the	steep slope		into	the	lake	and

638		3708	1161	013	1006		012
ἀπεπνίγη.	**34**	Ἰδόντες	δὲ	οἱ	βόσκοντες		τὸ
choked off.		Having seen	but	the	ones grazing		the

1096		5343	2532	518		1519	08	4172
γεγονὸς		ἔφυγον	καὶ	ἀπήγγειλαν		εἰς	τὴν	πόλιν
having become		fled	and	told		in	the	city

2532	1519	016	68		1831		1161	3708	012
καὶ	εἰς	τοὺς	ἀγρούς.	**35**	ἐξῆλθον		δὲ	ἰδεῖν	τὸ
and	in	the	fields.		They went out		but	to see	the

1096		2532	2064	4314	04	2424	2532	2147
γεγονὸς		καὶ	ἦλθον	πρὸς	τὸν	Ἰησοῦν	καὶ	εὗρον
having become		and	went	to	the	Jesus	and	found

2521	04	444		575	3739	021	1140		1831
καθήμενον	τὸν	ἄνθρωπον	ἀφ᾽	οὗ	τὰ	δαιμόνια	ἐξῆλθεν
sitting	the	man		from	whom	the	demons		went out

2439		2532	4993		3844	016
ἱματισμένον		καὶ	σωφρονοῦντα		παρὰ	τοὺς
having been clothed		and	thinking soberly		by	the

4228	02		2424	2532	5399		518		1161
πόδας	τοῦ		Ἰησοῦ,	καὶ	ἐφοβήθησαν.	**36**	ἀπήγγειλαν		δὲ
feet	of the	Jesus,		and	they were afraid.		Told		but

846	013	3708		4459	4982		01
αὐτοῖς	οἱ	ἰδόντες		πῶς	ἐσώθη		ὁ
to them	the	having seen		how	was delivered		the

1139			2532	2065		846	537
δαιμονισθείς.	**37**		καὶ	ἠρώτησεν		αὐτὸν	ἅπαν
one having been demonized.		And	asked		him	all

09	4128	06		4066		014	1086
τὸ	πλῆθος	τῆς		περιχώρου		τῶν	Γερασηνῶν
the	quantity	of the		country around		the	Gerasenes

565		575	846		3754	5401	3173
ἀπελθεῖν	ἀπ᾽	αὐτῶν,	ὅτι		φόβῳ	μεγάλῳ
to go off	from	them,	because		in fear	great

4912		846	1161	1684	1519	4143	5290
συνείχοντο·	αὐτὸς	δὲ	ἐμβὰς	εἰς	πλοῖον	ὑπέστρεψεν.
they were held together;		himself	but	having	into	boat	returned.

38	1189		1161	846	01	435	575	3739	1831
38	ἐδεῖτο		δὲ	αὐτοῦ	ὁ	ἀνὴρ	ἀφ᾽	οὗ	ἐξεληλύθει
Was begging	but	him	the	man	from	whom	had gone out

021	1140		1510	4862	846	630		1161	846
τὰ	δαιμόνια	εἶναι	σὺν	αὐτῷ·	ἀπέλυσεν		δὲ	αὐτὸν
the demons	to be	with	him;		he loosed off		but	him

3004		5290		1519	04	3624	1473	2532	1334
λέγων·	**39**	ὑπόστρεφε	εἰς	τὸν	οἶκόν	σου	καὶ	διηγοῦ
saying;		return	into	the	house	of you	and	narrate

3745		1473	4160	01	2316	2532	565
ὅσα		σοι	ἐποίησεν	ὁ	θεός.	καὶ	ἀπῆλθεν
as much as	to you	did		the	God.	And	he went off

2596	3650	08	4172	2784		3745		4160	846
καθ᾽	ὅλην	τὴν	πόλιν	κηρύσσων		ὅσα		ἐποίησεν	αὐτῷ
by	whole	the	city	announcing		as much as	did	to him

01	2424		1722	1161	011	5290		04	2424
ὁ	Ἰησοῦς.	**40**	Ἐν	δὲ	τῷ	ὑποστρέφειν		τὸν	Ἰησοῦν
the	Jesus.		In	but	the	to return		the	Jesus

588		846	01	3793	1510	1063	3956
ἀπεδέξατο		αὐτὸν	ὁ	ὄχλος·	ἦσαν	γὰρ	πάντες
thoroughly welcomed	him	the	crowd;	were	for	all

4328		846		2532	2400	2064	435
προσδοκῶντες		αὐτόν.	**41**	καὶ	ἰδοὺ	ἦλθεν	ἀνὴρ
waiting expectantly	him.		And	look	came	man

3739	3686	2383	2532	3778	758	06	4864
ᾧ	ὄνομα	Ἰάϊρος	καὶ	οὗτος	ἄρχων	τῆς	συναγωγῆς
of whom	name	Jairus	and	this	ruler	of the	synagogue

5225		2532	4098		3844	016	4228
ὑπῆρχεν,		καὶ	πεσὼν		παρὰ	τοὺς	πόδας
was existing,	and	having fallen		along	the	feet

02	2424	3870		846	1525		1519
[τοῦ]	Ἰησοῦ	παρεκάλει		αὐτὸν	εἰσελθεῖν		εἰς
of the	Jesus	was encouraging	him	to come into		into

34 When the swineherds saw what had happened, they ran off and told it in the city and in the country. [35]Then people came out to see what had happened, and when they came to Jesus, they found the man from whom the demons had gone sitting at the feet of Jesus, clothed and in his right mind. And they were afraid. [36]Those who had seen it told them how the one who had been possessed by demons had been healed. [37]Then all the people of the surrounding country of the Gerasenes[a] asked Jesus[b] to leave him; for they were seized with great fear. So he got into the boat and returned. [38]The man from whom the demons had gone begged that he might be with him; but Jesus[c] sent him away, saying, [39]"Return to your home, and declare how much God has done for you." So he went away, proclaiming throughout the city how much Jesus had done for him.

40 Now when Jesus returned, the crowd welcomed him, for they were all waiting for him. [41]Just then there came a man named Jairus, a leader of the synagogue. He fell at Jesus' feet and begged him to come to his house,

---

[a] Other ancient authorities read Gadarenes; others, Gergesenes
[b] Gk him
[c] Gk he

42for he had an only
daughter, about twelve
years old, who was dying.
    As he went, the crowds
pressed in on him. 43Now
there was a woman who
had been suffering from
hemorrhages for twelve
years; and though she
had spent all she had on
physicians,a no one could
cure her. 44She came up
behind him and touched
the fringe of his clothes,
and immediately her
hemorrhage stopped.
45Then Jesus asked, "Who
touched me?" When all
denied it, Peterb said,
"Master, the crowds
surround you and press in
on you." 46But Jesus said,
"Someone touched me; for
I noticed that power had
gone out from me." 47When
the woman saw that she
could not remain hidden,
she came trembling; and
falling down before him,
she declared in the presence
of all the people why she
had touched him, and how
she had been immediately
healed. 48He said to her,
"Daughter, your faith has
made you well; go in
peace."
    49 While he was still
speaking, someone came
from the leader's house
to say, "Your daughter is
dead; do not trouble the
teacher any longer."
50When Jesus heard this,
he replied, "Do not fear.
Only believe, and

a Other ancient authorities lack and
  though she had spent all she had
  on physicians
b Other ancient authorities add and
  those who were with him

```
04    3624   846        3754      2364        3439        1510
τὸν οἶκον αὐτοῦ, 42 ὅτι     θυγάτηρ μονογενὴς ἦν
the house of him,    because daughter only born was
846        5613 2094   1427    2532 846      599           1722
αὐτῷ  ὡς  ἐτῶν δώδεκα καὶ αὐτὴ  ἀπέθνησκεν. Ἐν
to him as    years twelve and herself was dying.     In
1161   011  5217        846     013 3793    4846
δὲ   τῷ ὑπάγειν    αὐτὸν οἱ ὄχλοι συνέπνιγον
but  the to go off   him   the crowds choked together
846        2532 1135   1510    1722 4511   129       575
αὐτόν.  43 Καὶ  γυνὴ οὖσα ἐν ῥύσει αἵματος ἀπὸ
him.      And woman being in  flow of blood from
2094   1427    3748   2395              4321             3650
ἐτῶν δώδεκα, ἥτις [ἰατροῖς     προσαναλώσασα ὅλον
years twelve, who   in physicians having spent whole
04    979  3756 2480           575 3762       2323
τὸν βίον] οὐκ ἴσχυσεν    ἀπ' οὐδενὸς θεραπευθῆναι,
the life  not she was strong from no one to be healed,
               3693       681        010 2899
44 προσελθοῦσα ὄπισθεν  ἥψατο    τοῦ κρασπέδου
   having come to from behind she touched the edge
010     2440      846     2532 3916           2476   05  4511
τοῦ   ἱματίου αὐτοῦ καὶ παραχρῆμα ἔστη ἡ  ῥύσις
of the clothes of him and suddenly stood the flow
010     129       846     45 2532 3004   01 2424    5101 01
τοῦ  αἵματος αὐτῆς.  καὶ εἶπεν ὁ Ἰησοῦς· τίς ὁ
of the blood  of her.    And said the Jesus; who the
681              1473 720        1161 3956    3004  01
ἁψάμενός      μου; ἀρνουμένων δὲ πάντων εἶπεν ὁ
one having touched me? Denying  but of all said the
4074    1988          013 3793   4912            1473
Πέτρος· ἐπιστάτα,  οἱ ὄχλοι συνέχουσίν σε
Peter;  Master teacher, the crowds hold together you
2532 598               46 01 1161  2424    3004    681
καὶ ἀποθλίβουσιν.    ὁ  δὲ  Ἰησοῦς εἶπεν· ἥψατό
and afflict.          The but Jesus  said;   touched
1473 5100 1473 1063 1097 1411      1831              575
μού  τις, ἐγὼ γὰρ ἔγνων δύναμιν ἐξεληλυθυῖαν ἀπ'
me  who, I  for knew power having gone out from
1473      3708    1161 05   1135    3754 3756 2097
ἐμοῦ.  47 ἰδοῦσα δὲ  ἡ γυνὴ ὅτι οὐκ ἔλαθεν,
me.       Having but the woman that not she escaped
         seen                                  notice,
5141       2064   2532 4363              846    1223
τρέμουσα ἦλθεν καὶ προσπεσοῦσα       αὐτῷ δι'
trembling went and having fallen toward him through
3739  156   681       846   518         1799
ἦν  αἰτίαν ἥψατο  αὐτοῦ ἀπήγγειλεν ἐνώπιον
which cause she touched him she told    before
3956  02  2992   2532 5613 2390        3916
παντὸς τοῦ λαοῦ καὶ ὡς ἰάθη      παραχρῆμα.
all   the people and as she was cured suddenly.
      01  1161 3004  846     2364     05 4102  1473
48  ὁ  δὲ εἶπεν αὐτῇ· θυγάτηρ, ἡ πίστις σου
    The one but said to her; daughter, the trust of you
4982            1473 4198    1519 1515      49 2089
σέσωκέν    σε· πορεύου εἰς εἰρήνην.    Ἔτι
has delivered you; travel  in peace.      Still
846   2980        2064     5100 3844 02  752
αὐτοῦ λαλοῦντος ἔρχεταί τις παρὰ τοῦ ἀρχισυναγώγου
of him speaking  comes  some from the synagogue ruler
3004   3754 2348    05  2364     1473    3371
λέγων ὅτι τέθνηκεν ἡ θυγάτηρ σου· μηκέτι
saying that has died the daughter of you; no longer
4660   04  1320       50 01 1161 2424    191
σκύλλε τὸν διδάσκαλον.  ὁ  δὲ  Ἰησοῦς ἀκούσας
annoy the teacher.       The but Jesus having heard
611      846    3361 5399   3441 4100        2532
ἀπεκρίθη αὐτῷ· μὴ φοβοῦ, μόνον πίστευσον, καὶ
answered to him; not fear, alone trust,       and
```

4982		**51**	2064		1161	1519	08	3614
σωθήσεται.			ἐλθὼν	δὲ		εἰς	τὴν	οἰκίαν
she will be delivered.		Having gone	but		into	the house

3756	863		1525		5100	4862	846	1487	3361
οὐκ	ἀφῆκεν	εἰσελθεῖν		τινα	σὺν	αὐτῷ	εἰ	μὴ
not	he left off	to go into		some	with	him	except

4074	2532	2491		2532	2385		2532	04	3962
Πέτρον	καὶ	Ἰωάννην	καὶ	Ἰάκωβον	καὶ	τὸν	πατέρα
Peter	and	John	and	Jacob	and	the	father

06	3816	2532	08	3384	**52**	2799		1161
τῆς	παιδὸς	καὶ	τὴν	μητέρα.		ἔκλαιον	δὲ
of the	child	and	the	mother.		Were crying	but

3956	2532	2875		846	01	1161	3004
πάντες	καὶ	ἐκόπτοντο	αὐτήν.	ὁ	δὲ	εἶπεν·
all	and	were mourning	her.	The one	but	said;

3361	2799	3756	1063	599		235	2518
μὴ	κλαίετε,	οὐ	γὰρ	ἀπέθανεν	ἀλλὰ	καθεύδει.
not	cry,	not	for	she died	but	sleeps.

53	2532	2606		846	3609a		3754
	καὶ	κατεγέλων	αὐτοῦ	εἰδότες	ὅτι
	And	they were laughing	him	having known	that

599		846	**54**	1161	2902	06	5495
ἀπέθανεν.		αὐτὸς	δὲ	κρατήσας	τῆς	χειρὸς
she died.	Himself	but	having held	the	hand

846	5455	3004	05	3816	1453	**55**	2532
αὐτῆς	ἐφώνησεν	λέγων·	ἡ	παῖς,	ἔγειρε.		καὶ
of her	he sounded	saying;	the	child,	rise.		And

1994	09	4151	846	2532	450	3916
ἐπέστρεψεν	τὸ	πνεῦμα	αὐτῆς	καὶ	ἀνέστη	παραχρῆμα
returned	the	spirit	of her	and	she stood up	suddenly

2532	1299	846	1325	2068	**56**	2532
καὶ	διέταξεν	αὐτῇ	δοθῆναι	φαγεῖν.		καὶ
and	he directed	to her	to be given	to eat.		And

1839	013	1118	846	01	1161	3853
ἐξέστησαν	οἱ	γονεῖς	αὐτῆς·	ὁ	δὲ	παρήγγειλεν
were amazed	the	parents	of her;	the one	but	commanded

846	3367	3004	012	1096	**9:1**	4779
αὐτοῖς	μηδενὶ	εἰπεῖν	τὸ	γεγονός.		Συγκαλεσάμενος
to them	to no one	to say	the	having become.		Having called together

1161	016	1427	1325	846	1411	2532	1849
δὲ	τοὺς	δώδεκα	ἔδωκεν	αὐτοῖς	δύναμιν	καὶ	ἐξουσίαν
but	the	twelve	he gave	to them	power	and	authority

1909	3956	024	1140	2532	3554	2323
ἐπὶ	πάντα	τὰ	δαιμόνια	καὶ	νόσους	θεραπεύειν
on	all	the	demons	and	illnesses	to heal

2	2532	649	846	2784	08	932
	καὶ	ἀπέστειλεν	αὐτοὺς	κηρύσσειν	τὴν	βασιλείαν
	and	he delegated	them	to announce	the	kingdom

02	2316	2532	2390	016	772	**3**	2532
τοῦ	θεοῦ	καὶ	ἰᾶσθαι	[τοὺς	ἀσθενεῖς],		καὶ
of the	God	and	to cure	the	weak ones,		and

3004	4314	846	3367	142	1519	08	3598
εἶπεν	πρὸς	αὐτούς·	μηδὲν	αἴρετε	εἰς	τὴν	ὁδόν,
he said	to	them;	nothing	lift up	into	the	way,

3383	4464	3383	4082	3383	740	3383
μήτε	ῥάβδον	μήτε	πήραν	μήτε	ἄρτον	μήτε
and not	rod	and not	bag	and not	bread	and not

694	3383	303	1417	5509	2192	**4**	2532
ἀργύριον	μήτε	[ἀνὰ]	δύο	χιτῶνας	ἔχειν.		καὶ
silver	and not	up	two	shirts	to have.		And

1519	3739	302	3614	1525		1563	3306
εἰς	ἣν	ἂν	οἰκίαν	εἰσέλθητε,		ἐκεῖ	μένετε
in	which	-	house	you might go in,	there	stay

2532	1564	1831	**5**	2532	3745	302	3361
καὶ	ἐκεῖθεν	ἐξέρχεσθε.		καὶ	ὅσοι	ἂν	μὴ
and	from there	go out.		And	as many as	-	not

1209	1473	1831	575	06	4172	1565
δέχωνται	ὑμᾶς,	ἐξερχόμενοι	ἀπὸ	τῆς	πόλεως	ἐκείνης
might welcome	you,	going out	from	the	city	that

she will be saved." [51]When he came to the house, he did not allow anyone to enter with him, except Peter, John, and James, and the child's father and mother. [52]They were all weeping and wailing for her; but he said, "Do not weep; for she is not dead but sleeping." [53]And they laughed at him, knowing that she was dead. [54]But he took her by the hand and called out, "Child, get up!" [55]Her spirit returned, and she got up at once. Then he directed them to give her something to eat. [56]Her parents were astounded; but he ordered them to tell no one what had happened.

CHAPTER 9

Then Jesus[a] called the twelve together and gave them power and authority over all demons and to cure diseases, [2]and he sent them out to proclaim the kingdom of God and to heal. [3]He said to them, "Take nothing for your journey, no staff, nor bag, nor bread, nor money—not even an extra tunic. [4]Whatever house you enter, stay there, and leave from there. [5]Wherever they do not welcome you, as you are leaving that town

---

[a] Gk he

shake the dust off your feet as a testimony against them." [6]They departed and went through the villages, bringing the good news and curing diseases everywhere.

[7]Now Herod the ruler[a] heard about all that had taken place, and he was perplexed, because it was said by some that John had been raised from the dead, [8]by some that Elijah had appeared, and by others that one of the ancient prophets had arisen. [9]Herod said, "John I beheaded; but who is this about whom I hear such things?" And he tried to see him.

10 On their return the apostles told Jesus[b] all they had done. He took them with him and withdrew privately to a city called Bethsaida. [11]When the crowds found out about it, they followed him; and he welcomed them, and spoke to them about the kingdom of God, and healed those who needed to be cured.

12 The day was drawing to a close, and the twelve came to him and said, "Send the crowd away, so that they may go into the surrounding villages and countryside, to lodge and get

[a] Gk tetrarch
[b] Gk him

04	2868		575	014	4228	1473	660
τὸν	κονιορτὸν		ἀπὸ	τῶν	ποδῶν	ὑμῶν	ἀποτινάσσετε
the	blowing dust		from	the	feet	of you	shake off

1519	3142		1909	846	6	1831	1161
εἰς	μαρτύριον		ἐπ'	αὐτούς.		ἐξερχόμενοι	δέ
for	testimony		on	them.		Going out	but

1330		2596	020	2968	2097		2532
διήρχοντο		κατὰ	τὰς	κώμας	εὐαγγελιζόμενοι		καὶ
they were		by	the	villages	telling good		and
going through					message		

2323		3837		7	191	1161	2264	01
θεραπεύοντες		πανταχοῦ.			Ἤκουσεν	δὲ	Ἡρῴδης	ὁ
healing		all places.			Heard	but	Herod	the

5076		024	1096	3956	2532	1280
τετραάρχης		τὰ	γινόμενα	πάντα	καὶ	διηπόρει
ruler of		the	having become	all	and	he was doubting
fourth						thoroughly

1223		012	3004	5259	5100	3754	2491
διὰ		τὸ	λέγεσθαι	ὑπό	τινων	ὅτι	Ἰωάννης
through		the	to be said	by	some	that	John

1453		1537	3498	8	5259	5100	1161	3754	2243
ἠγέρθη		ἐκ	νεκρῶν,		ὑπό	τινων	δὲ	ὅτι	Ἠλίας
was raised		from	dead,		by	some	but	that	Elijah

5316	243		1161	3754	4396		5100	014	744
ἐφάνη,	ἄλλων		δὲ	ὅτι	προφήτης		τις	τῶν	ἀρχαίων
shone,	others		but	that	spokesman		some	of	the ancients

450		3004	1161	2264	2491	1473
ἀνέστη.	9	εἶπεν	δὲ	Ἡρῴδης·	Ἰωάννην	ἐγὼ
stood up.		Said	but	Herod,	John	I

607		5101	1161	1510	3778	4012	3739	191
ἀπεκεφάλισα·		τίς	δέ	ἐστιν	οὗτος	περὶ	οὗ	ἀκούω
cut off head;		who	but	is	this	about	whom	I hear

5108		2532	2212	3708	846	10	2532
τοιαῦτα;		καὶ	ἐζήτει	ἰδεῖν	αὐτόν.		Καὶ
such things?		And	he was seeking	to see	him.		And

5290		013	652	1334	846
ὑποστρέψαν τες		οἱ	ἀπόστολοι.	διηγήσαντο	αὐτῷ
having returned		the	delegates	narrated	to him

3745	4160		2532	3880	846	5298	2596
ὅσα	ἐποίησαν.		Καὶ	παραλαβὼν	αὐτοὺς	ὑπεχώρησεν	κατ'
as	they did.		And	having	them	he withdrew	by
much as				taken along			

2398	1519	4172	2564		966	11	013	1161
ἰδίαν	εἰς	πόλιν	καλουμένην		Βηθσαϊδά.		οἱ	δὲ
own	into	city	being called		Bethsaida.		The	but

3793	1097	190		846	2532	588
ὄχλοι	γνόντες	ἠκολούθησαν		αὐτῷ·	καὶ	ἀποδεξάμενος
crowds	having	followed		him;	and	having welcomed
	known					thoroughly

846	2980		846	4012	06	932
αὐτοὺς	ἐλάλει		αὐτοῖς	περὶ	τῆς	βασιλείας
them	he was speaking		to them	about	the	kingdom

02	2316	2532	016	5532	2192	2322
τοῦ	θεοῦ,	καὶ	τοὺς	χρείαν	ἔχοντας	θεραπείας
of the	God,	and	the ones	need	having	of healing

2390		05	1161	2250	757	2827
ἰᾶτο.	12	Ἡ	δὲ	ἡμέρα	ἤρξατο	κλίνειν·
he was curing.		The	but	day	began	to bow;
curing.						

4334		1161	013	1427	3004	846	630
προσελθόντες		δὲ	οἱ	δώδεκα	εἶπαν	αὐτῷ·	ἀπόλυσον
having come to		but	the	twelve	said	to him,	loose off

04	3793		2443	4198	1519	020	2945
τὸν	ὄχλον,		ἵνα	πορευθέντες	εἰς	τὰς	κύκλω
the	crowd,		that	having traveled	into	the	circle

2968		2532	68	2647	2532	2147
κώμας		καὶ	ἀγροὺς	καταλύσωσιν	καὶ	εὕρωσιν
villages		and	fields	they might unloose	and	might find

1979		3754	5602 1722 2048	5117 1510

ἐπισιτισμόν, ὅτι   ὧδε ἐν ἐρήμῳ τόπῳ ἐσμέν.
provisions, because here in desert place we are.

13 3004 1161 4314 846   1325 846   1473
εἶπεν δὲ πρὸς αὐτούς· δότε αὐτοῖς ὑμεῖς
He said but to them;   give to them you

2068   013 1161 3004   3756 1510   1473 4183
φαγεῖν. οἱ δὲ εἶπαν· οὐκ εἰσὶν ἡμῖν πλεῖον
to eat. The but said; not there are to us more

2228 740   4002 2532 2486 1417 1487 3385
ἢ ἄρτοι πέντε καὶ ἰχθύες δύο, εἰ μήτι
or bread five and fish two, except

4198   1473 59   1519 3956 04 2992
πορευθέντες ἡμεῖς ἀγοράσωμεν εἰς πάντα τὸν λαὸν
having traveled we might buy for all the people

3778 1033   **14** 1510 1063 5616 435   4000
τοῦτον βρώματα.   ἦσαν γὰρ ὡσεὶ ἄνδρες πεντακισχίλιοι.
this food.   Were for as men five thousand.

3004   1161 4314 016   3101   846   2625
εἶπεν δὲ πρὸς τοὺς μαθητὰς αὐτοῦ· κατακλίνατε
He said but to the learners of him; recline

846   2828   5616 303 4004   2532 4160
αὐτοὺς κλισίας [ὡσεὶ] ἀνὰ πεντήκοντα. **15** καὶ ἐποίησαν
them in groups as up fifty.   And they did

3779   2532 2625   537   **16** 2983
οὕτως καὶ κατέκλιναν ἅπαντας.   λαβὼν
thusly and they reclined all.   Having taken

1161 016   4002 740   2532 016 1417 2486
δὲ τοὺς πέντε ἄρτους καὶ τοὺς δύο ἰχθύας
but the five bread and the two fish

308   1519 04 3772 2127   846
ἀναβλέψας   εἰς τὸν οὐρανὸν εὐλόγησεν αὐτοὺς
having looked up into the heaven he spoke well them

2532 2622   2532 1325   015   3101
καὶ κατέκλασεν καὶ ἐδίδου τοῖς μαθηταῖς
and he broke off and he was giving to the learners

3908   03   3793 **17** 2532 2068   2532
παραθεῖναι τῷ ὄχλῳ.   καὶ ἔφαγον καὶ
to set along to the crowd. And they ate and

5526   3956 2532 142   09 4052
ἐχορτάσθησαν πάντες, καὶ ἤρθη τὸ περισσεῦσαν
were satisfied all, and was lifted up the exceeding

846   2801   2894   1427 **18** 2532 1096
αὐτοῖς κλασμάτων κόφινοι δώδεκα.   Καὶ ἐγένετο
to them fragments wicker twelve. And it became
baskets

1722 011 1510 846   4336   2596 3441
ἐν τῷ εἶναι αὐτὸν προσευχόμενον κατὰ μόνας
in the to be him praying by alone

4895   846 013 3101   2532 1905   846
συνῆσαν αὐτῷ οἱ μαθηταί, καὶ ἐπηρώτησεν αὐτοὺς
were with him the learners, and he asked on them

3004   5101 1473 3004   013 3793 1510   **19** 013
λέγων· τίνα με λέγουσιν οἱ ὄχλοι εἶναι;   οἱ
saying; whom me say the crowds to be? The ones

1161 611   3004   2491   04 910
δὲ ἀποκριθέντες εἶπαν· Ἰωάννην τὸν βαπτιστήν,
but having answered said; John the immerser,

243   1161 2243 243   1161 3754 4396   5100
ἄλλοι δὲ Ἠλίαν, ἄλλοι δὲ ὅτι προφήτης τις
others but Elijah, others but that spokesman some

014 744   450   **20** 3004 1161 846   1473 1161
τῶν ἀρχαίων ἀνέστη.   εἶπεν δὲ αὐτοῖς· ὑμεῖς δὲ
of the ancients stood up. He said but to them; you but

5101 1473 3004   1510   4074 1161 611
τίνα με λέγετε εἶναι; Πέτρος δὲ ἀποκριθεὶς
whom me you say to be? Peter but having answered

provisions; for we are here in a deserted place." [13]But he said to them, "You give them something to eat." They said, "We have no more than five loaves and two fish—unless we are to go and buy food for all these people." [14]For there were about five thousand men. And he said to his disciples, "Make them sit down in groups of about fifty each." [15]They did so and made them all sit down. [16]And taking the five loaves and the two fish, he looked up to heaven, and blessed and broke them, and gave them to the disciples to set before the crowd. [17]And all ate and were filled. What was left over was gathered up, twelve baskets of broken pieces.

[18] Once when Jesus[a] was praying alone, with only the disciples near him, he asked them, "Who do the crowds say that I am?" [19]They answered, "John the Baptist; but others, Elijah; and still others, that one of the ancient prophets has arisen." [20]He said to them, "But who do you say that I am?" Peter answered,

[a] Gk *he*

"The Messiah[a] of God."

21 He sternly ordered and commanded them not to tell anyone, [22]saying, "The Son of Man must undergo great suffering, and be rejected by the elders, chief priests, and scribes, and be killed, and on the third day be raised."

23 Then he said to them all, "If any want to become my followers, let them deny themselves and take up their cross daily and follow me. [24]For those who want to save their life will lose it, and those who lose their life for my sake will save it. [25]What does it profit them if they gain the whole world, but lose or forfeit themselves? [26]Those who are ashamed of me and of my words, of them the Son of Man will be ashamed when he comes in his glory and the glory of the Father and of the holy angels. [27]But truly I tell you, there are some standing here who will not taste death before they see the kingdom of God."

28 Now about eight days after these sayings Jesus[b] took with him Peter and

[a] Or The Christ
[b] Gk he

3004	04	5547	02	2316	**21**	01	1161	2008
εἶπεν·	τὸν	χριστὸν	τοῦ	θεοῦ.		ὁ	δὲ	ἐπιτιμήσας
said;	the	Christ	of the	God.		The	but	having admonished

846	3853		3367	3004	3778	**22**	3004
αὐτοῖς	παρήγγειλεν	μηδενὶ		λέγειν	τοῦτο.		εἰπὼν
to them	commanded		to no one	to say	this.		Having said

3754	1163	04	5207	02	444	4183	3958
ὅτι	δεῖ	τὸν	υἱὸν	τοῦ	ἀνθρώπου	πολλὰ	παθεῖν
that	it is	the son		of the	man	many	to suffer
	necessary						

2532	593		575	014	4245		2532
καὶ	ἀποδοκιμασθῆναι	ἀπὸ		τῶν	πρεσβυτέρων	καὶ
and	to be rejected	from		the older men	and

749		2532	1122		2532	615		2532
ἀρχιερέων	καὶ		γραμματέων	καὶ		ἀποκτανθῆναι	καὶ
ruler priests	and		writers	and		to be killed	and

07	5154	2250	1453		**23**	3004		1161	4314
τῇ	τρίτῃ	ἡμέρᾳ	ἐγερθῆναι.			Ἔλεγεν		δὲ	πρὸς
in the	third	day	to be raised.			He was saying		but	to

3956	1487	5100	2309	3694	1473	2064	720
πάντας·	εἴ	τις	θέλει	ὀπίσω	μου	ἔρχεσθαι,	ἀρνησάσθω
all,	if	some	wants	after	me	to come,	let deny

1438	2532	142	04	4716	846	2596	2250,
ἑαυτὸν	καὶ	ἀράτω	τὸν	σταυρὸν	αὐτοῦ	καθ'	ἡμέραν
himself	and	let lift up	the	cross	of him	by	day

2532	190		1473	**24**	3739	1063	302	2309	08
καὶ	ἀκολουθείτω	μοι.			ὃς	γὰρ	ἂν	θέλῃ	τὴν
and	let follow	me.			Who	for	-	might want	the

5590	846	4982	622	846	3739	1161
ψυχὴν	αὐτοῦ	σῶσαι	ἀπολέσει	αὐτήν·	ὃς	δ'
soul	of him	to deliver	will destroy	it;	who	but

302	622	08	5590	846	1752	1473	3778
ἂν	ἀπολέσῃ	τὴν	ψυχὴν	αὐτοῦ	ἕνεκεν	ἐμοῦ	οὗτος
-	might destroy	the	soul	of him	on account	of me	this

4982	846	**25**	5101	1063	5623	444
σώσει	αὐτήν.		τί	γὰρ	ὠφελεῖται	ἄνθρωπος
will deliver	it.		What	for	is benefitted	man

2770	04	2889	3650	1438	1161	622	2228
κερδήσας	τὸν	κόσμον	ὅλον	ἑαυτὸν	δὲ	ἀπολέσας	ἢ
having gained	the	world	whole	himself	but	having destroyed	or

2210		**26**	3739	1063	302	1870	1473
ζημιωθείς;			ὃς	γὰρ	ἂν	ἐπαισχυνθῇ	με
having been lost?			Who	for	-	might be ashamed	me

2532	016	1699	3056	3778	01	5207	02	444
καὶ	τοὺς	ἐμοὺς	λόγους,	τοῦτον	ὁ	υἱὸς	τοῦ	ἀνθρώπου
and	the	my	words,	this	the	son	of the	man

1870		3752	2064		1722	07	1391
ἐπαισχυνθήσεται,	ὅταν	ἔλθῃ		ἐν	τῇ	δόξῃ
will be ashamed,	when	he might come		in	the	splendor

846	2532	02	3962	2532	014	40	32
αὐτοῦ	καὶ	τοῦ	πατρὸς	καὶ	τῶν	ἁγίων	ἀγγέλων.
of him	and	of the	father	and	of the	holy	messengers.

27	3004	1161	1473	230	1510	5100	014
	λέγω	δὲ	ὑμῖν	ἀληθῶς,	εἰσίν	τινες	τῶν
	I say	but	to you	truly,	are	some	of the ones

847	2476		3739	3756	3361	1089	2288
αὐτοῦ	ἑστηκότων	οἳ		οὐ	μὴ	γεύσωνται	θανάτου
there	having stood	who		not	not	might taste	death

2193	302	3708	08	932	02	2316
ἕως	ἂν	ἴδωσιν	τὴν	βασιλείαν	τοῦ	θεοῦ.
until	-	they might see	the	kingdom	of the	God.

28	1096	1161	3326	016	3056	3778	5616
	Ἐγένετο	δὲ	μετὰ	τοὺς	λόγους	τούτους	ὡσεὶ
	It became	but	after	the	words	these	as

2250	3638	2532	3880	4074	2532
ἡμέραι	ὀκτὼ	[καὶ]	παραλαβὼν	Πέτρον	καὶ
days	eight	and	having taken along	Peter	and

```
 2491        2532   2385     305              1519 012 3735
Ἰωάννην  καὶ   Ἰάκωβον  ἀνέβη       εἰς τὸ ὄρος
John         and    Jacob      he went up  into the hill
4336              29  2532  1096       1722 011  4336
προσεύξασθαι.        καὶ   ἐγένετο   ἐν   τῷ  προσεύχεσθαι
to pray.                And   it became in    the to pray
846      09  1491         010      4383        846   2087    2532
αὐτὸν τὸ εἶδος         τοῦ   προσώπου αὐτοῦ ἕτερον καὶ
him     the visible form  of the   face      of him  other   and
01    2441      846      3022    1823              2532 2400
ὁ  ἱματισμὸς αὐτοῦ λευκὸς ἐξαστράπτων. 30  καὶ ἰδοὺ
the clothing    of him  white  glittering.       And  look
435      1417 4814                846      3748     1510 3475
ἄνδρες δύο συνελάλουν      αὐτῷ, οἵτινες ἦσαν Μωϋσῆς
men      two  were talking with him, who     were  Moses
2532  2243      31  3739 3708              1722 1391
καὶ Ἠλίας,         οἱ  ὀφθέντες      ἐν   δόξῃ
and  Elijah,          who  having been seen in   splendor
3004      08   1841      846      3739    3195
ἔλεγον τὴν ἔξοδον αὐτοῦ, ἣν  ἤμελλεν
were saying the way out of him, which he was about to
4137         1722  2419         32  01   1161  4074   2532 013
πληροῦν ἐν  Ἰερουσαλήμ.     ὁ   δὲ  Πέτρος καὶ οἱ
to fill in     Jerusalem.            The but  Peter     and the
4862  846    1510  916                    5258
σὺν αὐτῷ ἦσαν βεβαρημένοι        ὕπνῳ·
with him  were+  +having been burdened in sleep;
1235               1161 3708  08   1391      846      2532
διαγρηγορήσαντες δὲ  εἶδον τὴν δόξαν   αὐτοῦ καὶ
having awakened  but  they    the splendor of him and
thoroughly                saw
016  1417 435      016      4921                        846
τοὺς δύο ἄνδρας τοὺς  συνεστῶτας           αὐτῷ.
the   two  men     the ones having stood together to him.
33  2532 1096          1722 011  1316
    καὶ  ἐγένετο     ἐν   τῷ  διαχωρίζεσθαι
    And   it became  in    the to separate thoroughly
846      575  846      3004   01   4074    4314 04   2424
αὐτοὺς ἀπ᾽ αὐτοῦ εἶπεν ὁ   Πέτρος πρὸς τὸν Ἰησοῦν·
them     from him  said   the  Peter     to   the   Jesus;
1988            2570   1510  1473 5602 1510   2532
ἐπιστάτα,   καλόν ἐστιν ἡμᾶς ὧδε εἶναι, καὶ
Master teacher, good  it is   us    here  to be,   and
4160           4633      5140    1520 1473   2532 1520
ποιήσωμεν σκηνὰς τρεῖς, μίαν σοὶ  καὶ μίαν
we might make  tents   three,  one  to you and  one
3475       2532 1520 2243          3361 3609a          3739
Μωϋσεῖ καὶ μίαν Ἠλίᾳ,   μὴ  εἰδὼς      ὃ
to Moses and  one  to Elijah, not  having known what
3004      34  3778  1161 846   3004        1096      3507 2532
λέγει.      ταῦτα δὲ  αὐτοῦ λέγοντος ἐγένετο νεφέλη καὶ
he says.   These but  him    saying      became  cloud  and
1982              846      5399            1161 1722 011
ἐπεσκίαζεν   αὐτούς· ἐφοβήθησαν δὲ  ἐν   τῷ
it was overshadowing them;  they feared   but  in    the
1525         846      1519 08  3507          2532 5456
εἰσελθεῖν αὐτοὺς εἰς τὴν νεφέλην. 35 καὶ φωνὴ
to go into  them    into  the  cloud.      And  sound
1096      1537 06  3507          3004        3778  1510  01
ἐγένετο ἐκ  τῆς νεφέλης λέγουσα· οὗτός ἐστιν ὁ
became  from the cloud    saying; this  is    the
5207 1473 01  1586                  846    191
υἱός μου ὁ  ἐκλελεγμένος,     αὐτοῦ ἀκούετε.
son of me the one having been selected, him    hear.
36  2532 1722 011 1096       08  5456    2147       2424
    καὶ ἐν  τῷ  γενέσθαι τὴν φωνὴν εὑρέθη  Ἰησοῦς
    And in   the to become the sound   was  found Jesus
3441      2532 846       4601           2532 3762
μόνος. καὶ αὐτοὶ  ἐσίγησαν  καὶ οὐδενὶ
alone. And themselves were silent and  to no one
```

John and James, and went up on the mountain to pray. ²⁹And while he was praying, the appearance of his face changed, and his clothes became dazzling white. ³⁰Suddenly they saw two men, Moses and Elijah, talking to him. ³¹They appeared in glory and were speaking of his departure, which he was about to accomplish at Jerusalem. ³²Now Peter and his companions were weighed down with sleep; but since they had stayed awake,ᵃ they saw his glory and the two men who stood with him. ³³Just as they were leaving him, Peter said to Jesus, "Master, it is good for us to be here; let us make three dwellings,ᵇ one for you, one for Moses, and one for Elijah"—not knowing what he said. ³⁴While he was saying this, a cloud came and over-shadowed them; and they were terrified as they entered the cloud. ³⁵Then from the cloud came a voice that said, "This is my Son, my Chosen;ᶜ listen to him!" ³⁶When the voice had spoken, Jesus was found alone. And they kept silent and in those days told no one

ᵃ Or but when they were fully awake
ᵇ Or tents
ᶜ Other ancient authorities read my Beloved

any of the things they had
seen.

37 On the next day,
when they had come down
from the mountain, a great
crowd met him. 38 Just then
a man from the crowd
shouted, "Teacher, I beg
you to look at my son; he is
my only child. 39 Suddenly
a spirit seizes him, and all
at once he[a] shrieks. It
convulses him until he
foams at the mouth; it
mauls him and will scarcely
leave him. 40 I begged your
disciples to cast it out, but
they could not." 41 Jesus
answered, "You faithless
and perverse generation,
how much longer must I
be with you and bear with
you? Bring your son here."
42 While he was coming, the
demon dashed him to the
ground in convulsions. But
Jesus rebuked the unclean
spirit, healed the boy, and
gave him back to his father.
43 And all were astounded
at the greatness of God.

While everyone was
amazed at all that he was
doing, he said to his
disciples, 44 "Let these
words sink into your ears:
The Son of Man is going

[a] Or it

518	1722	1565	019	2250	3762	3739
ἀπήγγειλαν	ἐν	ἐκείναις	ταῖς	ἡμέραις	οὐδὲν	ὧν
they told	in	those	the	days	nothing	of what

3708		1096	1161	07	1836	2250
ἑώρακαν.	37	Ἐγένετο	δὲ	τῇ	ἑξῆς	ἡμέρᾳ
they had seen.		It became	but	in	the next	day

2718		846	575	010	3735	4876		846
κατελθόντων		αὐτῶν	ἀπὸ	τοῦ	ὄρους	συνήντησεν		αὐτῷ
having gone down		them	from	the	hill	met		him

3793	4183		2532	2400	435	575	02	3793
ὄχλος	πολύς.	38	καὶ	ἰδοὺ	ἀνὴρ	ἀπὸ	τοῦ	ὄχλου
crowd	much.		And	look	man	from	the	crowd

994		3004	1320		1189	1473	1914
ἐβόησεν		λέγων·	διδάσκαλε,	δέομαί	σου	ἐπιβλέψαι
cried aloud		saying;	teacher,	I beg	you	to look on

1909	04	5207	1473		3754	3439		1473	1510
ἐπὶ	τὸν	υἱόν	μου,	ὅτι		μονογενής	μοί	ἐστιν,
on	the	son	of me,	because		only born	to me	he is,

	2532	2400	4151	2983		846	2532	1810
39	καὶ	ἰδοὺ	πνεῦμα	λαμβάνει	αὐτὸν	καὶ	ἐξαίφνης
	and	look	spirit	takes		him	and	suddenly

2896		2532	4682		846	3326	876	2532	3425
κράζει		καὶ	σπαράσσει	αὐτὸν	μετὰ	ἀφροῦ	καὶ	μόγις
it shouts		and	convulses	him	with	foam	and	hardly

672		575	846	4937		846		2532
ἀποχωρεῖ		ἀπ᾽	αὐτοῦ	συντρῖβον	αὐτόν·		40	καὶ
makes room off		from	him	breaking	him;			and

1189		014	3101		1473	2443	1544
ἐδεήθην		τῶν	μαθητῶν	σου	ἵνα	ἐκβάλωσιν
I begged		the	learners	of you	that	they might throw out

846	2532	3756	1410			611		1161
αὐτό,	καὶ	οὐκ	ἠδυνήθησαν.		41	ἀποκριθεὶς		δὲ
it,	and	not	they were able.			Having answered		but

01	2424	3004	5599	1074		571		2532
ὁ	Ἰησοῦς	εἶπεν·	ὦ	γενεὰ		ἄπιστος		καὶ
the	Jesus	said;	O	generation		untrustful		and

1294			2193	4219	1510		4314	1473
διεστραμμένη,		ἕως	πότε	ἔσομαι		πρὸς	ὑμᾶς
having been perverted,		until	when	I will be		to	you

2532	430		1473	4317	5602	04	5207
καὶ	ἀνέξομαι		ὑμῶν;	προσάγαγε	ὧδε	τὸν	υἱόν
and	I will endure		you?	Lead	to	here	the son

1473		2089	1161	4334		846	4486	846
σου.	42	ἔτι	δὲ	προσερχομένου	αὐτοῦ	ἔρρηξεν	αὐτὸν
of you.		Still	but	coming to		him	ripped	him

09	1140		2532	4952		2008		1161	01
τὸ	δαιμόνιον	καὶ	συνεσπάραξεν·	ἐπετίμησεν	δὲ	ὁ
the	demon		and	convulsed;		admonished		but	the

2424	011	4151	011	169		2532	2390	04
Ἰησοῦς	τῷ	πνεύματι	τῷ	ἀκαθάρτῳ	καὶ	ἰάσατο	τὸν
Jesus	the	spirit	the	unclean		and	he cured	the

3816		2532	591		846	03	3962
παῖδα		καὶ	ἀπέδωκεν	αὐτὸν	τῷ	πατρὶ
boy		servant and	he gave back		him	to the	father

846		1605			1161	3956	1909	07
αὐτοῦ.	43	ἐξεπλήσσοντο		δὲ	πάντες	ἐπὶ	τῇ
of him.		Were being astonished		but	all	on	the

3168		02	2316	3956	1161	2296		1909
μεγαλειότητι	τοῦ	θεοῦ.	Πάντων	δὲ	θαυμαζόντων	ἐπὶ
greatness	of the	God.	All	but	marveling	on

3956	3739	4160		3004	4314	016	3101
πᾶσιν	οἷς	ἐποίει		εἶπεν	πρὸς	τοὺς	μαθητὰς
all	that	he was doing		he said	to	the	learners

846		5087	1473	1519	024	3775	1473	016	3056
αὐτοῦ·	44	θέσθε	ὑμεῖς	εἰς	τὰ	ὦτα	ὑμῶν	τοὺς	λόγους
of him;		set	you	in	the	ears	of you	the	words

3778		01	1063	5207	02		444		3195
τούτους·	ὁ	γὰρ	υἱὸς	τοῦ		ἀνθρώπου	μέλλει
these;	the	for	son	of the		man	is about to

3860   1519 5495   444   45 013   1161
παραδίδοσθαι εἰς χεῖρας ἀνθρώπων.   οἱ   δὲ
be given over into hands of men.   The ones but

50   012 4487 3778   2532 1510 3871
ἠγνόουν   τὸ ῥῆμα τοῦτο καὶ ἦν παρακεκαλυμμένον
were   the word this and it +having been covered
unknowing   was+ along

575   846   2443 3361 143   846   2532
ἀπ᾽ αὐτῶν ἵνα μὴ αἴσθωνται   αὐτό, καὶ
from them   that not they might notice it, and

5399   2065   846   4012 010 4487   3778
ἐφοβοῦντο ἐρωτῆσαι αὐτὸν περὶ τοῦ ῥήματος τούτου.
they feared to ask   him   about the word   this.

46 1525   1161 1261   1722 846   09 5101 302
  Εἰσῆλθεν δὲ διαλογισμὸς ἐν αὐτοῖς, τὸ τίς ἂν
  Went in   but reasoning   in them, the whom -

1510   3173   846   47 01 1161 2424   3609a
εἴη   μείζων αὐτῶν.   ὁ δὲ Ἰησοῦς εἰδὼς
might be greater of them. The but Jesus having known

04   1261   06   2588   846   1949
τὸν διαλογισμὸν τῆς καρδίας αὐτῶν, ἐπιλαβόμενος
the reasoning   of the heart of them, having taken on

3813   2476   846 3844   1438   2532 3004
παιδίον ἔστησεν αὐτὸ παρ᾽ ἑαυτῷ 48 καὶ εἶπεν
small child stood   him along himself   and he said

846   3739 1437 1209   3778 012 3813
αὐτοῖς· ὃς ἐὰν δέξηται   τοῦτο τὸ παιδίον
to them; who if might welcome this the small child

1909 011 3686   1473   1473 1209   2532 3739
ἐπὶ τῷ ὀνόματί μου, ἐμὲ δέχεται·   καὶ ὃς
on   the name   of me, me he welcomes; and who

302 1473 1209   1209   04 649   1473 01
ἂν ἐμὲ δέξηται, δέχεται τὸν ἀποστείλαντά με· ὁ
-   me   might   welcomes the one having   me; the
           welcome,   delegated

1063 3398   1722 3956 1473   5225   3778   1510
γὰρ μικρότερος ἐν πᾶσιν ὑμῖν ὑπάρχων οὗτός ἐστιν
for smaller   in all   to you existing this one is

3173   49 611   1161 2491   3004   1988
μέγας.   Ἀποκριθεὶς δὲ Ἰωάννης εἶπεν· ἐπιστάτα,
great.   Having   but John   said;   Master
              answered   teacher,

3708   5100 1722 011 3686   1473   1544
εἴδομέν τινα ἐν τῷ ὀνόματί σου ἐκβάλλοντα
we saw some in the name   of you throwing out

1140   2532 2967   846   3754   3756
δαιμόνια καὶ ἐκωλύομεν   αὐτόν, ὅτι   οὐκ
demons   and we were hindering him, because not

190   3326 1473   50 3004 1161 4314 846 01
ἀκολουθεῖ μεθ᾽ ἡμῶν.   εἶπεν δὲ πρὸς αὐτὸν ὁ
he follows with us.   Said but to   him   the

2424   3361 2967   3739 1063 3756 1510 2596 1473
Ἰησοῦς· μὴ κωλύετε· ὃς γὰρ οὐκ ἔστιν καθ᾽ ὑμῶν,
Jesus; not hinder; who for not is   against you,

5228   1473   1510   51 1096   1161 1722 011
ὑπὲρ ὑμῶν ἐστιν.   Ἐγένετο δὲ ἐν τῷ
on behalf of you he is.   It became but in the

4845   020 2250   06   354   846
συμπληροῦσθαι   τὰς ἡμέρας τῆς ἀναλήμψεως αὐτοῦ
to be filled together the days of the taken up of him

2532 846   012 4383   4741   010 4198
καὶ αὐτὸς τὸ πρόσωπον ἐστήρισεν   τοῦ πορεύεσθαι
and himself the face   strengthened the to travel

1519 2419   52 2532 649   32   4253
εἰς Ἰερουσαλήμ.   καὶ ἀπέστειλεν ἀγγέλους πρὸ
into Jerusalem.   And he delegated messengers before

4383   846   2532 4198   1525
προσώπου αὐτοῦ. καὶ πορευθέντες   εἰσῆλθον
face   of him. And having traveled they went into

to be betrayed into human hands." [45]But they did not understand this saying; its meaning was concealed from them, so that they could not perceive it. And they were afraid to ask him about this saying.

[46]An argument arose among them as to which one of them was the greatest. [47]But Jesus, aware of their inner thoughts, took a little child and put it by his side, [48]and said to them, "Whoever welcomes this child in my name welcomes me, and whoever welcomes me welcomes the one who sent me; for the least among all of you is the greatest."

[49]John answered, "Master, we saw someone casting out demons in your name, and we tried to stop him, because he does not follow with us." [50]But Jesus said to him, "Do not stop him; for whoever is not against you is for you."

[51]When the days drew near for him to be taken up, he set his face to go to Jerusalem. [52]And he sent messengers ahead of him. On their way they entered

a village of the Samaritans to make ready for him; ⁵³but they did not receive him, because his face was set toward Jerusalem. ⁵⁴When his disciples James and John saw it, they said, "Lord, do you want us to command fire to come down from heaven and consume them?"[a] ⁵⁵But he turned and rebuked them. ⁵⁶Then[b] they went on to another village.

57 As they were going along the road, someone said to him, "I will follow you wherever you go." ⁵⁸And Jesus said to him, "Foxes have holes, and birds of the air have nests; but the Son of Man has nowhere to lay his head." ⁵⁹To another he said, "Follow me." But he said, "Lord, first let me go and bury my father." ⁶⁰But Jesus[c] said to him, "Let the dead bury their own dead; but as for you, go and proclaim the kingdom of God." ⁶¹Another said, "I will follow you, Lord; but let me first say farewell to those at my home." ⁶²Jesus said to him, "No one who puts a hand to the plow and looks back is fit for the kingdom of God."

CHAPTER 10

After this the Lord appointed

a Other ancient authorities add as Elijah did

b Other ancient authorities read rebuked them, and said, "You do not know what spirit you are of, ⁵⁶for the Son of Man has not come to destroy the lives of human beings but to save them." Then

c Gk he

1519	2968	4541	5613 2090	846	**53** 2532
εἰς	κώμην	Σαμαριτῶν	ὡς ἑτοιμάσαι	αὐτῷ·	καὶ
into	village	of Samaritans	as to prepare	him;	and

3756 1209   846   3754 09 4383   846 1510
οὐκ ἐδέξαντο αὐτόν, ὅτι τὸ πρόσωπον αὐτοῦ ἦν
not they welcomed him, because the face of him was

4198   1519 2419   **54** 3708   1161 013
πορευόμενον εἰς Ἰερουσαλήμ. ἰδόντες δὲ οἱ
traveling into Jerusalem. Having seen but the

3101 2385 2532 2491 3004 2962 2309
μαθηταὶ Ἰάκωβος καὶ Ἰωάννης εἶπαν· κύριε, θέλεις
learners Jacob and John said; Master, you want

3004 4442 2597 575 02 3772 2532
εἴπωμεν πῦρ καταβῆναι ἀπὸ τοῦ οὐρανοῦ καὶ
we might say fire to come down from the heaven and

355 846 **55** 4762 1161 2008
ἀναλῶσαι αὐτούς; στραφεὶς δὲ ἐπετίμησεν
to consume them? Having turned but he admonished

846 2532 4198 1519 2087 2968
αὐτοῖς. **56** καὶ ἐπορεύθησαν εἰς ἑτέραν κώμην.
them. And they traveled into other village.

57 2532 4198 846 1722 07 3598 3004 5100
Καὶ πορευομένων αὐτῶν ἐν τῇ ὁδῷ εἶπέν τις
And traveling them in the way said some

4314 846 190 1473 3699 1437 565
πρὸς αὐτόν· ἀκολουθήσω σοι ὅπου ἐὰν ἀπέρχῃ.
to him; I will follow you where if you might go off.

58 2532 3004 846 01 2424 017 258 5454
καὶ εἶπεν αὐτῷ ὁ Ἰησοῦς· αἱ ἀλώπεκες φωλεοὺς
And said to him the Jesus; the foxes holes

2192 2532 021 4071 02 3772 2682
ἔχουσιν καὶ τὰ πετεινὰ τοῦ οὐρανοῦ κατασκηνώσεις,
have and the birds of the heaven set up tents,

01 1161 5207 02 444 3756 2192 4226 08
ὁ δὲ υἱὸς τοῦ ἀνθρώπου οὐκ ἔχει ποῦ τὴν
the but son of the man not has where the

2776 2827 **59** 3004 1161 4314 2087
κεφαλὴν κλίνῃ. Εἶπεν δὲ πρὸς ἕτερον·
head he might bow. He said but to other;

190 1473 01 1161 3004 2962 2010 1473
ἀκολούθει μοι. ὁ δὲ εἶπεν· [κύριε,] ἐπίτρεψόν μοι
follow me. The but said; Master, allow me

565 4413 2290 04 3962 1473
ἀπελθόντι πρῶτον θάψαι τὸν πατέρα μου.
having gone off first to bury the father of me.

60 3004 1161 846 863 016 3498 2290 016
εἶπεν δὲ αὐτῷ· ἄφες τοὺς νεκροὺς θάψαι τοὺς
He said but to him; send off the dead to bury the

1438 3498 1473 1161 565 1229
ἑαυτῶν νεκρούς, σὺ δὲ ἀπελθὼν διάγγελλε
themselves dead, you but having gone off broadcast

08 932 02 2316 **61** 3004 1161 2532 2087
τὴν βασιλείαν τοῦ θεοῦ. Εἶπεν δὲ καὶ ἕτερος·
the kingdom of the God. Said but also other;

190 1473 2962 4413 1161 2010 1473
ἀκολουθήσω σοι, κύριε· πρῶτον δὲ ἐπίτρεψόν μοι
I will follow you, Master; first but allow me

657 015 1519 04 3624 1473 **62** 3004
ἀποτάξασθαι τοῖς εἰς τὸν οἶκόν μου. εἶπεν
to say good-bye to the ones in the house of me. Said

1161 4314 846 01 2424 3762 1911
δὲ [πρὸς αυτὸν] ὁ Ἰησοῦς· οὐδεὶς ἐπιβαλὼν
but to him] the Jesus; no one having thrown on

08 5495 1909 723 2532 991 1519 024 3694
τὴν χεῖρα ἐπ' ἄροτρον καὶ βλέπων εἰς τὰ ὀπίσω
the hand on plow and looking into the after

2111 1510 07 932 02 2316 **10:1** 3326
εὔθετός ἐστιν τῇ βασιλείᾳ τοῦ θεοῦ. Μετὰ
suitable he is to the kingdom of the God. After

1161	3778	322	01	2962	2087	1440
δὲ	ταῦτα	ἀνέδειξεν ὁ		κύριος	ἑτέρους	ἑβδομήκοντα
but	these	showed up the		Master	others	seventy

1417	2532	649	846	303	1417	1417	4253
[δύο]	καὶ	ἀπέστειλεν	αὐτοὺς	ἀνὰ	δύο	[δύο]	πρὸ
two	and	he delegated	them	up	two	two	before

4383	846	1519	3956	4172	2532	5117	3757
προσώπου	αὐτοῦ	εἰς	πᾶσαν	πόλιν	καὶ	τόπον	οὗ
face	of him	into	all	city	and	place	where

3195	846	2064		3004	1161	4314	846
ἤμελλεν	αὐτὸς	ἔρχεσθαι.	2	ἔλεγεν	δὲ	πρὸς	αὐτούς·
he was	himself	to go.		He was saying	but	to	them,
about							

01	3303	2326	4183	013	1161	2040	3641
ὁ	μὲν	θερισμὸς	πολύς,	οἱ	δὲ	ἐργάται	ὀλίγοι·
the	indeed	harvest	much,	the	but	workers	few;

1189	3767	02	2962	02	2326	3704	2040
δεήθητε	οὖν	τοῦ	κυρίου	τοῦ	θερισμοῦ	ὅπως	ἐργάτας
beg	then	the	Master	of the	harvest	so that	workers

1544		1519	04	2326	846		5217
ἐκβάλῃ		εἰς	τὸν	θερισμὸν	αὐτοῦ.	3	ὑπάγετε·
he might throw out		into		the harvest	of him.		Go off,

2400	649	1473	5613	704	1722	3319	3074
ἰδοὺ	ἀποστέλλω	ὑμᾶς	ὡς	ἄρνας	ἐν	μέσῳ	λύκων.
look	I delegate	you	as	sheep	in	middle	of wolves.

	3361	941	905		3361	4082	3361	5266
4	μὴ	βαστάζετε	βαλλάντιον,	μὴ	πήραν,	μὴ	ὑποδήματα,
	Not	bear	purse,		not	bag,	not	sandals,

2532	3367	2596	08	3598	782		1519	3739	1161
καὶ	μηδένα	κατὰ	τὴν	ὁδὸν	ἀσπάσησθε.	5	εἰς	ἣν	δ᾽
and	no one	by	the	way	greet.		Into	which	but

302	1525		3614	4413	3004	1515
ἂν	εἰσέλθητε		οἰκίαν,	πρῶτον	λέγετε·	εἰρήνη
-	you might go into		house,	first	say;	peace

03	3624	3778		2532	1437	1563	1510	5207
τῷ	οἴκῳ	τούτῳ.	6	καὶ	ἐὰν	ἐκεῖ	ᾖ	υἱὸς
to the	house	this.		And	if	there	might be	son

1515	1879		1909	846	05	1515	1473
εἰρήνης,	ἐπαναπαήσεται		ἐπ᾽	αὐτὸν	ἡ	εἰρήνη	ὑμῶν·
of peace,	will rest on		on	him	the	peace	of you;

1487	1161	3361	1065	1909	1473	344
εἰ	δὲ	μή	γε,	ἐφ᾽	ὑμᾶς	ἀνακάμψει.
if	but	not	indeed,	on	you	it will bend again.

	1722	846	1161	07	3614	3306	2068	2532
7	ἐν	αὐτῇ	δὲ	τῇ	οἰκίᾳ	μένετε	ἐσθίοντες	καὶ
	In	same	but	the	house	stay	eating	and

4095	024	3844		846	514	1063	01	2040
πίνοντες	τὰ	παρ᾽		αὐτῶν·	ἄξιος	γὰρ	ὁ	ἐργάτης
drinking	the	alongside		them;	worthy	for	the	worker

02	3408	846		3361	3327		1537	3614
τοῦ	μισθοῦ	αὐτοῦ.		μὴ	μεταβαίνετε	ἐξ		οἰκίας
of the	wage	of him.		Not	go across		from	house

1519	3614		2532	1519	3739	302	4172
εἰς	οἰκίαν.	8	καὶ	εἰς	ἣν	ἂν	πόλιν
to	house.		And	into	which	-	city

1525		2532	1209		1473	2068
εἰσέρχησθε		καὶ	δέχωνται		ὑμᾶς,	ἐσθίετε
you might go into		and	might welcome		you,	eat

024	3908		1473		2532	2323	016	1722
τὰ	παρατιθέμενα		ὑμῖν	9	καὶ	θεραπεύετε	τοὺς	ἐν
the	being set along		you		and	heal	the	in

846	772	2532	3004	846		1448	1909	1473
αὐτῇ	ἀσθενεῖς	καὶ	λέγετε	αὐτοῖς·		ἤγγικεν	ἐφ᾽	ὑμας
it	weak	and	say	to them;		has neared	on	you

05	932	02	2316		1519	3739	1161	302	4172
ἡ	βασιλεία	τοῦ	θεοῦ.	10	εἰς	ἣν	δ᾽	ἂν	πόλιν
the	kingdom	of the	God.		Into	which	but	-	city

seventy[a] others and sent them on ahead of him in pairs to every town and place where he himself intended to go. [2]He said to them, "The harvest is plentiful, but the laborers are few; therefore ask the Lord of the harvest to send out laborers into his harvest. [3]Go on your way. See, I am sending you out like lambs into the midst of wolves. [4]Carry no purse, no bag, no sandals; and greet no one on the road. [5]Whatever house you enter, first say, 'Peace to this house!' [6]And if anyone is there who shares in peace, your peace will rest on that person; but if not, it will return to you. [7]Remain in the same house, eating and drinking whatever they provide, for the laborer deserves to be paid. Do not move about from house to house. [8]Whenever you enter a town and its people welcome you, eat what is set before you; [9]cure the sick who are there, and say to them, 'The kingdom of God has come near to you.'[b] [10]But whenever you enter a town

[a] Other ancient authorities read seventy-two
[b] Or is at hand for you

and they do not welcome you, go out into its streets and say, [11]"Even the dust of your town that clings to our feet, we wipe off in protest against you. Yet know this: the kingdom of God has come near.'[a] [12]I tell you, on that day it will be more tolerable for Sodom than for that town.

[13]"Woe to you, Chorazin! Woe to you, Bethsaida! For if the deeds of power done in you had been done in Tyre and Sidon, they would have repented long ago, sitting in sackcloth and ashes. [14]But at the judgment it will be more tolerable for Tyre and Sidon than for you. [15]And you, Capernaum,

will you be exalted
　to heaven?
No, you will be brought
　down to Hades.

[16]"Whoever listens to you listens to me, and whoever rejects you rejects me, and whoever rejects me rejects the one who sent me."

[17]The seventy[b] returned with joy, saying, "Lord, in your name even the demons submit to us!" [18]He said to them, "I watched Satan fall from heaven like a flash of lightning. [19]See, I have given you authority to tread on snakes and scorpions,

[a] Or is at hand
[b] Other ancient authorities read seventy-two

1525	2532	3361	1209	1473	1831	1519	020
εἰσέλθητε	καὶ	μὴ	δέχωνται	ὑμᾶς,	ἐξελθόντες	εἰς	τὰς
you might	and	not	might	you,	having	into	the
go into			welcome		gone out		

4113	846	3004	04	2532	04	2868	04
πλατείας	αὐτῆς	εἴπατε·	[11]	καὶ	τὸν	κονιορτὸν	τὸν
wide places	of it	say;		and	the	blowing	dust the

2853	1473	1537 06	4172	1473	1519
κολληθέντα	ἡμῖν	ἐκ τῆς	πόλεως	ὑμῶν	εἰς
having been joined	to us	from the	city	of you	into

016	4228	631	1473	4133	3778	1097
τοὺς	πόδας	ἀπομασσόμεθα	ὑμῖν·	πλὴν	τοῦτο	γινώσκετε
the	feet	we wipe off	to you;	except	this	know

3754	1448	05	932	02	2316	3004 1473
ὅτι	ἤγγικεν	ἡ	βασιλεία	τοῦ	θεοῦ. [12]	λέγω ὑμῖν
that	has neared	the	kingdom	of the	God.	I say to you

3754	4670	1722 07	2250	1565	414
ὅτι	Σοδόμοις	ἐν τῇ	ἡμέρᾳ	ἐκείνῃ	ἀνεκτότερον
that	in Sodom	in the	day	that	more endurable

1510	2228 07	4172	1565	3759 1473
ἔσται	ἢ τῇ	πόλει	ἐκείνῃ. [13]	Οὐαί σοι,
it will be	or to the	city	that.	Woe to you,

5523	3759 1473	966	3754	1487 1722 5184
Χοραζίν,	οὐαί σοι,	Βηθσαϊδά·	ὅτι	εἰ ἐν Τύρῳ
Chorazin,	woe to you,	Bethsaida;	because	if in Tyre

2532	4605	1096	017 1411	017 1096
καὶ	Σιδῶνι	ἐγενήθησαν	αἱ δυνάμεις	αἱ γενόμεναι
and	Sidon	had become	the powers	the having become

1722 1473	3819	302 1722 4526	2532 4700
ἐν ὑμῖν,	πάλαι	ἂν ἐν σάκκῳ	καὶ σποδῷ
in you,	of old	- in sackcloth	and ash

2521	3340	4133	5184	2532
καθήμενοι	μετενόησαν. [14]	πλὴν	Τύρῳ	καὶ
sitting	they changed minds.	Except	in Tyre	and

4605	414	1510	1722 07	2920	2228
Σιδῶνι	ἀνεκτότερον	ἔσται	ἐν τῇ	κρίσει	ἢ
Sidon	more endurable	it will be	in the	judgment	or

1473	2532 1473 2746a	3361 3193 3772
ὑμῖν. [15]	καὶ σύ, Καφαρναούμ,	μὴ ἕως οὐρανοῦ
to you.	And you, Capernaum,	not until heaven

5312	2193 02 86	2597	01 191
ὑψωθήσῃ;	ἕως τοῦ ᾅδου	καταβήσῃ. [16]	Ὁ ἀκούων
you will be	Until the hades	you will	The one hearing
elevated?		go down.	

1473	1473 191	2532 01 114	1473 1473
ὑμῶν	ἐμοῦ ἀκούει,	καὶ ὁ ἀθετῶν	ὑμᾶς ἐμὲ
of you	me hears,	and the setting	aside you me

114	01 1161 1473 114	114	04
ἀθετεῖ·	ὁ δὲ ἐμὲ ἀθετῶν	ἀθετεῖ	τὸν
sets aside;	the but me setting	aside sets	aside the

649	1473 [17]	5290	1161 013 1440
ἀποστείλαντά	με.	Ὑπέστρεψαν	δὲ οἱ ἑβδομήκοντα
one having	me.	Returned	but the seventy
delegated			

1417 3326 5479	3004	2962	2532 021 1140
[δύο] μετὰ χαρᾶς	λέγοντες·	κύριε,	καὶ τὰ δαιμόνια
two with joy	saying;	Master,	even the demons

5293	1473 1722 011 3686	1473	3004 1161
ὑποτάσσεται	ἡμῖν ἐν τῷ ὀνόματί	σου. [18]	εἶπεν δὲ
are subject	to us in the name	of you.	He said but

846	2334	04 4567	5613 796
αὐτοῖς·	ἐθεώρουν	τὸν σατανᾶν	ὡς ἀστραπὴν
to them;	I was watching	the adversary	as lightning

1537 02	3772	4098 [19]	2400 1325	1473
ἐκ τοῦ	οὐρανοῦ	πεσόντα.	ἰδοὺ δέδωκα	ὑμῖν
from the	heaven	having fallen.	Look I have given	you

08	1849	010	3961	1883 3789 2532 4651
τὴν	ἐξουσίαν	τοῦ	πατεῖν	ἐπάνω ὄφεων καὶ σκορπίων
the	authority	of the	to walk	upon snakes and scorpions

```
2532 1909  3956   08    1411    02     2190       2532
καὶ  ἐπὶ  πᾶσαν  τὴν  δύναμιν  τοῦ  ἐχθροῦ,   καὶ
and  on   all    the  power   of the hostile,  and
3762      1473  3756  3361 91              4133 1722 3778
οὐδὲν  ὑμᾶς  οὐ   μὴ  ἀδικήσῃ.       20  πλὴν  ἐν  τούτῳ
nothing you   not  not might do unright.  Except  in  this
3361 5463        3754 021 4151          1473      5293
μὴ   χαίρετε ὅτι  τὰ  πνεύματα ὑμῖν  ὑποτάσσεται,
not  rejoice that the spirits   to you are subject,
5463     1161 3754 021 3686       1473 1449
χαίρετε  δὲ   ὅτι  τὰ  ὀνόματα ὑμῶν ἐγγέγραπται
rejoice but  that the names  of you have been written in
1722 015 3772         1722 846  07    5610 21
ἐν  τοῖς οὐρανοῖς. 21 Ἐν  αὐτῇ τῇ  ὥρᾳ ἠγαλλιάσατο
in  the  heavens.     In  same the hour he was glad
1722 011 4151        011 40    2532 3004      1843
[ἐν] τῷ  πνεύματι τῷ  ἁγίῳ καὶ  εἶπεν· ἐξομολογοῦμαι
in   the spirit  the holy and  said;  I confess out
1473      3962     2962    02      3772       2532 06  1093
σοι,    πάτερ,  κύριε  τοῦ   οὐρανοῦ καὶ   τῆς γῆς,
to you,  father, Master of the heaven  and   the earth,
3754     613          3778    575   4680 2532 4908
ὅτι    ἀπέκρυψας  ταῦτα ἀπὸ σοφῶν καὶ συνετῶν
because you hid off these from wise  and understanding
2532 601        846     3516      3483 01  3962
καὶ  ἀπεκάλυψας αὐτὰ νηπίοις·  ναὶ ὁ  πατήρ,
and  you uncovered them to infants; yes the father,
3754 3779  2107       1096     1715        1473
ὅτι  οὕτως εὐδοκία  ἐγένετο ἔμπροσθέν σου.
that thusly good thought it became in front of you.
    3956   1473 3860        5259 02  3962     1473  2532
22  πάντα μοι  παρεδόθη  ὑπὸ τοῦ πατρός μου,  καὶ
    All   to me was given over by the father of me,  and
3762     1097       5101 1510  01   5207 1487 3361 01
οὐδεὶς γινώσκει τίς  ἐστιν ὁ  υἱὸς εἰ  μὴ  ὁ
no one knows    who  is    the son  except  the
3962     2532 5101 1510  01   3962   1487 3361 01  5207
πατήρ,  καὶ  τίς  ἐστιν ὁ  πατὴρ εἰ  μὴ  ὁ  υἱὸς
father, and  who  is    the father except  the son
2532 3739      1437 1014     01  5207 601
καὶ  ᾧ      ἐὰν βούληται ὁ  υἱὸς ἀποκαλύψαι.
and  to whom if  might plan the son  to uncover.
   2532 4762       4314   016    3101       2596 2398
23 Καὶ στραφεὶς  πρὸς τοὺς μαθητὰς κατ᾽ ἰδίαν
   And having turned toward the  learners by   own
3004     3107     013 3788      013 991       3739
εἶπεν·  μακάριοι οἱ  ὀφθαλμοὶ οἱ  βλέποντες ἃ
he said; fortunate the eyes    the ones seeing what
991         3004 1063 1473     3754 4183   4396
βλέπετε. 24 λέγω γὰρ ὑμῖν  ὅτι πολλοὶ προφῆται
you see.    I say for to you that many  spokesmen
2532 935        2309        3708 3739 1473 991      2532
καὶ  βασιλεῖς ἠθέλησαν ἰδεῖν ἃ  ὑμεῖς βλέπετε καὶ
and  kings     wanted     to see what you   see     and
3756 3708      2532 191       3739 191       2532 3756
οὐκ  εἶδαν,  καὶ  ἀκοῦσαι ἃ  ἀκούετε καὶ  οὐκ
not  they saw, and to hear what you hear and  not
191        2532 2400 3544      5100 450
ἤκουσαν. 25 Καὶ  ἰδοὺ νομικός τις  ἀνέστη
they heard.   And  look lawyer  some stood up
1598          846   3004     1320        5101
ἐκπειράζων  αὐτὸν λέγων·  διδάσκαλε, τί
pressuring out him  saying; teacher,    what
4160       2222 166    2816              01 1161 3004
ποιήσας  ζωὴν αἰώνιον κληρονομήσω; 26 ὁ  δὲ εἶπεν
having done life eternal I will inherit?  The but said
4314 846     1722 03  3551 5101 1125             4459
πρὸς αὐτόν· ἐν  τῷ  νόμῳ τί  γέγραπται;        πῶς
to   him;    in  the law  what has been written? How
```

and over all the power of
the enemy; and nothing will
hurt you. [20]Nevertheless,
do not rejoice at this, that
the spirits submit to you,
but rejoice that your names
are written in heaven."

21 At that same hour
Jesus[a] rejoiced in the Holy
Spirit[b] and said, "I thank[c]
you, Father, Lord of
heaven and earth, because
you have hidden these
things from the wise and
the intelligent and have
revealed them to infants;
yes, Father, for such was
your gracious will.[d] [22]All
things have been handed
over to me by my Father;
and no one knows who the
Son is except the Father,
or who the Father is except
the Son and anyone to
whom the Son chooses to
reveal him."

23 Then turning to the
disciples, Jesus[a] said to
them privately, "Blessed
are the eyes that see what
you see! [24]For I tell you
that many prophets and
kings desired to see what
you see, but did not see it,
and to hear what you hear,
but did not hear it."

25 Just then a lawyer
stood up to test Jesus.[e]
"Teacher," he said, "what
must I do to inherit eternal
life?" [26]He said to him,
"What is written in the
law? What

[a] Gk he
[b] Other authorities read in the spirit
[c] Or praise
[d] Or for so it was well-pleasing in
your sight
[e] Gk him

do you read there?" 27He answered, "You shall love the Lord your God with all your heart, and with all your soul, and with all your strength, and with all your mind; and your neighbor as yourself." 28And he said to him, "You have given the right answer; do this, and you will live.

29 But wanting to justify himself, he asked Jesus, "And who is my neighbor?" 30Jesus replied, "A man was going down from Jerusalem to Jericho, and fell into the hands of robbers, who stripped him, beat him, and went away, leaving him half dead. 31Now by chance a priest was going down that road; and when he saw him, he passed by on the other side. 32So likewise a Levite, when he came to the place and saw him, passed by on the other side. 33But a Samaritan while traveling came near him; and when he saw him, he was moved with pity. 34He went to him and bandaged his wounds, having poured oil and wine on them. Then he put him on his own animal, brought him to an inn, and took care of him. 35The next day he took out two denarii,a gave them

---

a The denarius was the usual day's wage for a laborer

314	27	01	1161	611		3004
ἀναγινώσκεις;	27	ὁ	δὲ	ἀποκριθεὶς		εἶπεν·
do you read?		The	but	one having answered		said;

25		2962	04	2316	1473	1537	3650	06
ἀγαπήσεις		κύριον	τὸν	θεόν σου		ἐξ	ὅλης	[τῆς]
you will love		Master	the	God	of you	from	whole	the

2588	1473	2532	1722	3650	07	5590	1473	2532
καρδίας σου		καὶ	ἐν	ὅλῃ	τῇ	ψυχῇ σου		καὶ
heart	of you	and	in	whole	the	soul	of you	and

1722	3650	07	2479		1473	2532	1722	3650	07
ἐν	ὅλῃ	τῇ	ἰσχύϊ		σου	καὶ	ἐν	ὅλῃ	τῇ
in	whole	the	strength		of you	and	in	whole	the

1271		1473	2532	04	4139		1473	5613
διανοίᾳ		σου,	καὶ	τὸν	πλησίον		σου	ὡς
intelligence	of you,	and	the neighbor		of you	as

4572	28	3004	1161	846		3723
σεαυτόν.	28	εἶπεν	δὲ	αὐτῷ·		ὀρθῶς
yourself.		He said	but	to him;		straightly

611		3778	4160	2532	2198		29	01	1161
ἀπεκρίθης·		τοῦτο	ποίει	καὶ	ζήσῃ.		29	ὁ	δὲ
you answered;		this	do	and	you will live.		The	but

2309	1344		1438	3004	4314	04	2424
θέλων	δικαιῶσαι		ἑαυτὸν	εἶπεν	πρὸς	τὸν	Ἰησοῦν·
wanting to make right		himself	said	to	the	Jesus;

2532	5101	1510	1473	4139		30	5274		01
καὶ	τίς	ἐστίν	μου	πλησίον;		30	Ὑπολαβὼν		ὁ
and	who	is	of me	neighbor?		Having taken up		the

2424	3004	444		5100	2597	575	2419
Ἰησοῦς	εἶπεν·	ἀνθρωπός	τις	κατέβαινεν	ἀπὸ	Ἰερουσαλὴμ
Jesus	said;	man	some	went down	from	Jerusalem

1519	2410	2532	3027		4045		3739	2532
εἰς	Ἰεριχὼ	καὶ	λῃσταῖς		περιέπεσεν,		οἳ	καὶ
into	Jericho	and in	robbers		he fell around,		who	also

1562		846	2532	4127	2007		565
ἐκδύσαντες		αὐτὸν	καὶ	πληγὰς	ἐπιθέντες		ἀπῆλθον
having put off		him	and	blows	having set on		went off

060		2253		31	2596	4795		1161	2409
ἀφέντες		ἡμιθανῆ.		31	κατὰ	συγκυρίαν		δὲ	ἱερεύς
having left off		half dead.		By		coincidence		but	priest

5100	2597		1722	07	3598	1565	2532	3708
τις	κατέβαινεν		ἐν	τῇ	ὁδῷ	ἐκείνῃ	καὶ	ἰδὼν
some	went down		in	the	way	that	and	having seen

846	492		32	3668		1161	2532	3019
αὐτὸν	ἀντιπαρῆλθεν·		32	ὁμοίως		δὲ	καὶ	Λευίτης
him	went along opposite;		likewise		but	also	Levite

1096		2596	04	5117	2064		2532
[γενόμενος]		κατὰ	τὸν	τόπον	ἐλθὼν		καὶ
having become	by	the	place	having come	and

3708		492		33	4541		1161	5100
ἰδὼν		ἀντιπαρῆλθεν.		33	Σαμαρίτης		δέ	τις
having seen	went along opposite.		Samaritan		but	some

3593		2064	2596	846		2532	3708		4697
ὁδεύων		ἦλθεν	κατ'	αὐτὸν		καὶ	ἰδὼν		ἐσπλαγχνίσθη,
journeying	came	by	him		and	seen		having had affection,

34	2532	4334		2611		024	5134
34	καὶ	προσελθὼν		κατέδησεν		τὰ	τραύματα
	and	having come toward		he bound	down	the	wounds

846	2022		1637	2532	3631		1913
αὐτοῦ	ἐπιχέων		ἔλαιον	καὶ	οἶνον,		ἐπιβιβάσας
of him	pouring on		oil	and	wine,		having mounted on

1161	846	1909	012	2398	2934	71	846	1519
δὲ	αὐτὸν	ἐπὶ	τὸ	ἴδιον	κτῆνος	ἤγαγεν	αὐτὸν	εἰς
but	him	on	the	own	animal	he led	him	to

3829		2532	1959		846		35	2532	1909	08
πανδοχεῖον		καὶ	ἐπεμελήθη		αὐτοῦ.		35	καὶ	ἐπὶ	τὴν
inn		and	he took care		of him.		And	on	the

839		1544		1325	1417	1220	03
αὔριον		ἐκβαλὼν		ἔδωκεν	δύο	δηνάρια	τῷ
tomorrow	having thrown out		he gave	two	denaria	to the

3830	2532	3004	1959	846	2532 3739
πανδοχεῖ	καὶ	εἶπεν·	ἐπιμελήθητι	αὐτοῦ,	καὶ ὅ
inn person	and	said;	take care	of him,	and what

5100	302	4325		1473 1722	011 1880
τι	ἂν	προσδαπανήσῃς	ἐγὼ	ἐν τῷ	ἐπανέρχεσθαί
some	-	you might spend more	I	in the	to come up on

1473	591		1473	**36** 5101 3778	014 5140
με	ἀποδώσω		σοι.	τίς τούτων	τῶν τριῶν
me	I will give back		to you.	Who of these	the three

4139	1380	1473	1096	02
πλησίον	δοκεῖ	σοι	γεγονέναι	τοῦ
neighbor	thinks	to you	to have become	of the

1706	1519	016	3027	**37** 01 1161 3004 01
ἐμπεσόντος	εἰς	τοὺς	λῃστάς;	ὁ δὲ εἶπεν· ὁ
one having to fallen in	the		robbers?	The but said; the one one

4160	012 1656	3326 846	3004 1161 846 01
ποιήσας	τὸ ἔλεος	μετ᾽ αὐτοῦ.	εἶπεν δὲ αὐτῷ ὁ
having done	the mercy	with him.	Said but to him the

2424	4198	2532 1473 4160	3668	**38** 1722 1161
Ἰησοῦς·	πορεύου καὶ	σὺ	ποίει ὁμοίως.	Ἐν δὲ
Jesus;	travel and	you	do likewise.	In but

011 4198	846	846	1525	1519 2968
τῷ πορεύεσθαι	αὐτοὺς	αὐτὸς	εἰσῆλθεν	εἰς κώμην
the to travel	them	himself	went into	into village

5100 1135	1161 5100	3686	3136 5264	846
τινά· γυνὴ	δέ τις	ὀνόματι	Μάρθα ὑπεδέξατο	αὐτόν.
some; woman	but some	in name	Martha entertained	him.

39 2532 3592	1510 79	2564	3137a 3739
καὶ τῇδε	ἦν ἀδελφὴ	καλουμένη	Μαριάμ, [ἣ]
Also to the	but was sister	being called	Mariam, who

2532 3869	4314 016	4228 02	2962
καὶ παρακαθεσθεῖσα	πρὸς τοὺς	πόδας τοῦ	κυρίου
also having sat along	to the	feet of the	Master

191	04 3056 846	**40** 05 1161 3136
ἤκουεν	τὸν λόγον αὐτοῦ.	ἡ δὲ Μάρθα
was hearing	the word of him.	The but Martha

4049	4012	4183	1248	2186
περιεσπᾶτο	περὶ	πολλὴν	διακονίαν·	ἐπιστᾶσα
was drawn	around	much	service;	having stood on

1161 3004	2962	3756 3190a	1473 3754
δὲ εἶπεν,	κύριε,	οὐ μέλει	σοι ὅτι
but she said,	Master,	not is it a care	to you that

05 79	1473 3441	1473 2641	1247
ἡ ἀδελφή	μου μόνην με	κατέλιπεν	διακονεῖν;
the sister	of me alone me	left behind	to serve?

3004 3767 846	2443 1473	4878
εἰπὲ οὖν αὐτῇ	ἵνα μοι	συναντιλάβηται.
Say then to her	that to me	she might help with.

41 611	1161 3004 846	01 2962	3136
ἀποκριθεὶς	δὲ εἶπεν αὐτῇ	ὁ κύριος·	Μάρθα
Having answered	but said to her	the Master;	Martha

3136	3309	2532 2349a	4012 4183
Μάρθα,	μεριμνᾷς	καὶ θορυβάζῃ	περὶ πολλά,
Martha,	you are anxious	and in uproar	about many,

42 1520 1161 1510	5532	3137a 1063	08 18
ἑνὸς δέ ἐστιν	χρεία·	Μαριὰμ γὰρ	τὴν ἀγαθὴν
one but is	need;	Mariam for	the good

3310	1586	3748 3756 851	846
μερίδα	ἐξελέξατο	ἥτις οὐκ ἀφαιρεθήσεται	αὐτῆς.
part	selected	which not will be lifted off	her.

11:1 2532 1096	1722 011 1510	846 1722 5117 5100
Καὶ ἐγένετο	ἐν τῷ εἶναι	αὐτὸν ἐν τόπῳ τινὶ
And it became	in the to be	him in place some

4336	5613 3973	3004 5100 014
προσευχόμενον,	ὡς ἐπαύσατο,	εἶπέν τις τῶν
praying,	as he stopped,	said some of the

to the innkeeper, and said, 'Take care of him; and when I come back, I will repay you whatever more you spend.' [36]Which of these three, do you think, was a neighbor to the man who fell into the hands of the robbers?" [37]He said, "The one who showed him mercy." Jesus said to him, "Go and do likewise."

[38]Now as they went on their way, he entered a certain village, where a woman named Martha welcomed him into her home. [39]She had a sister named Mary, who sat at the Lord's feet and listened to what he was saying. [40]But Martha was distracted by her many tasks; so she came to him and asked, "Lord, do you not care that my sister has left me to do all the work by myself? Tell her then to help me." [41]But the Lord answered her, "Martha, Martha, you are worried and distracted by many things; [42]there is need of only one thing.[a] Mary has chosen the better part, which will not be taken away from her."

CHAPTER 11

He was praying in a certain place, and after he had finished, one of

[a] Other ancient authorities read few things are necessary, or only one

his disciples said to him,
"Lord, teach us to pray, as
John taught his disciples."
²He said to them, "When
you pray, say:
Father,ᵃ hallowed be
your name.
Your kingdom come.ᵇ
³ Give us each day our
daily bread.ᶜ
⁴ And forgive us our sins,
for we ourselves
forgive everyone
indebted to us.
And do not bring us
to the time of trial."ᵈ

⁵And he said to them,
"Suppose one of you has a
friend, and you go to him
at midnight and say to him,
'Friend, lend me three
loaves of bread; ⁶for a
friend of mine has arrived,
and I have nothing to set
before him.' ⁷And he
answers from within, 'Do
not bother me; the door has
already been locked, and
my children are with me in
bed; I cannot get up and
give you anything.' ⁸I tell
you, even though he will
not get up and give him
anything because he is his
friend, at least because of
his persistence he will get
up and give him whatever
he needs.

9 "So I say to you, Ask,
and it will be given you;
search, and you will find;

ᵃ Other ancient authorities read
   Our Father in heaven
ᵇ A few ancient authorities read
   Your Holy Spirit come upon us
   and cleanse us. Other ancient
   authorities add Your will be done,
   on earth as in heaven
ᶜ Or our bread for tomorrow
ᵈ Or us into temptation. Other
   ancient authorities add but rescue
   us from the evil one (or from evil)

3101	846	4314 846	2962	1321	1473
μαθητῶν	αὐτοῦ	πρὸς αὐτόν·	κύριε,	δίδαξον	ἡμᾶς
learners	of him	to him;	Master,	teach	us

4336	2531 2532	2491	1321	016	3101
προσεύχεσθαι,	καθὼς καὶ	Ἰωάννης	ἐδίδαξεν	τοὺς	μαθητάς
to pray,	just as also	John	taught	the	learners

² | 846 | | 3004 | 1161 | 846 | 3752 4336 |
|------|--|------|------|-----|-----------|
| αὐτοῦ. | | εἶπεν | δὲ | αὐτοῖς· | ὅταν προσεύχησθε |
| of him. | | He said | but | to them; | when you might pray |

3004	3962	37	09	3686 1473	2064
λέγετε·	Πάτερ,	ἁγιασθήτω	τὸ	ὄνομά σου·	ἐλθέτω
say;	Father,	let be holy	the	name of you;	let come

³	05 932	1473	04	740	1473 04	1967
ἡ βασιλεία σου·		τὸν	ἄρτον	ἡμῶν τὸν	ἐπιούσιον
the kingdom of you;		the	bread	of us the	sustaining

⁴	1325	1473 012	2596	2250		2532 863	1473 020
δίδου	ἡμῖν τὸ	καθ᾽	ἡμέραν·		καὶ ἄφες	ἡμῖν τὰς
give	to us the	by	day;		and send off	us the

266	1473	2532	1063 846		863	3956
ἁμαρτίας	ἡμῶν,	καὶ	γὰρ αὐτοὶ		ἀφίομεν	παντὶ
sins	of us,	also	for ourselves		send off	to all

3784	1473	2532	3361	1533		1473 1519
ὀφείλοντι	ἡμῖν·	καὶ	μὴ	εἰσενέγκῃς		ἡμᾶς εἰς
owing	to us;	and	not	you might bring in		us into

⁵	3986		2532 3004	4314 846		5101 1537 1473
πειρασμόν.		Καὶ εἶπεν	πρὸς αὐτούς·		τίς ἐξ ὑμῶν
pressure.		And he said	to them;		who from you

2192 5384	2532 4198	4314 846	3317	2532
ἕξει φίλον	καὶ πορεύσεται	πρὸς αὐτὸν	μεσονυκτίου	καὶ
will friend and	travels	to him	of middle	and
have			night	

3004	846	5384	2797a 1473	5140 740
εἴπῃ	αὐτῷ·	φίλε,	χρῆσόν μοι	τρεῖς ἄρτους,
might say to him;		friend,	lend to me	three bread,

⁶	1894	5384	1473	3854		1537 3598 4314 1473
ἐπειδὴ	φίλος	μου	παρεγένετο		ἐξ ὁδοῦ πρός με
since	friend	of me	arrived		from way to me

2532 3756 2192	3739 3908	846	2548	2081
καὶ οὐκ ἔχω	ὃ παραθήσω	αὐτῷ·	⁷ κἀκεῖνος	ἔσωθεν
and not I have	what I might	to him;	and that	from
	set along			inside

611		3004		3361 1473	2873
ἀποκριθεὶς		εἴπῃ,		μή μοι	κόπους
having answered		he might say,		not to me	labors

3930	2235	05	2374 2808		2532 021
πάρεχε·	ἤδη	ἡ	θύρα κέκλεισται		καὶ τὰ
hold to;	already	the	door has been closed		and the

3813	1473	3326 1473 1519 08	2845	1510
παιδία	μου	μετ᾽ ἐμοῦ εἰς	τὴν κοίτην	εἰσίν·
small children	of me	with me in	the bed	are;

3756 1410	450		1325	1473	3004
οὐ δύναμαι	ἀναστὰς		δοῦναί	σοι.	⁸ λέγω
not I am able	having stood up		to give	to you.	I say

1473	1487 2532 3756 1325		846	450
ὑμῖν,	εἰ καὶ οὐ δώσει		αὐτῷ	ἀναστὰς
to you,	if also not he will give		to him	having
				stood up

1223	012 1510 5384 846	1223	1065	08
διὰ	τὸ εἶναι φίλον αὐτοῦ,	διά	γε	τὴν
through	the to be friend of him,	through	indeed	the

335	846	1453	1325
ἀναίδειαν	αὐτοῦ	ἐγερθεὶς	δώσει
shamelessness	of him	having been raised	he will give

846	3745	5535	⁹ 2504 1473	3004 154
αὐτῷ	ὅσων	χρῄζει.	Κἀγὼ ὑμῖν	λέγω, αἰτεῖτε
to him	as much as	he needs.	And I to you	say, ask

2532	1325	1473	2212	2532 2147
καὶ	δοθήσεται	ὑμῖν,	ζητεῖτε	καὶ εὑρήσετε,
and	it will be given	to you,	seek	and you will find,

```
2925       2532 455                    1473    10  3956 1063 01
κρούετε καὶ  ἀνοιγήσεται         ὑμῖν·      πᾶς γὰρ ὁ
knock   and  it will be opened  to you;    all for  the
154    2983      2532 01  2212      2147    2532 03
αἰτῶν λαμβάνει καὶ ὁ ζητῶν εὑρίσκει καὶ τῷ
asking receives and the seeking finds    and to the
2925      455        5101 1161 1537 1473 04
κρούοντι ἀνοιγ[ήσ]εται. 11  τίνα δὲ ἐξ ὑμῶν τὸν
knocking it will be opened.   Who but from you  the
3962     154       01  5207 2486  2532 473        2486
πατέρα αἰτήσει ὁ υἱὸς ἰχθύν, καὶ ἀντὶ      ἰχθύος
father might ask the son  fish,  and instead of fish
3789 846   1929        12  2228 2532 154
ὄφιν αὐτῷ ἐπιδώσει;      ἢ  καὶ αἰτήσει
snake to him he will give on?  Or  also he might ask
5609 1929     846    4651       13  1487 3767 1473 4190
ᾠόν, ἐπιδώσει αὐτῷ σκορπίον;  εἰ  οὖν ὑμεῖς πονηροὶ
egg, he will to   scorpion?  If  then you  evil
           give on  him
5225        3609a  1390  18  1325     023     5043
ὑπάρχοντες οἴδατε δόματα ἀγαθὰ διδόναι τοῖς τέκνοις
existing   know  gifts good  to give to the children
1473   4214   3123    01  3962  01 1537 3772
ὑμῶν, πόσῳ μᾶλλον ὁ πατὴρ [ὁ] ἐξ οὐρανοῦ
of you, how much more  the father the from heaven
1325    4151    40  015    154      846    14  2532
δώσει πνεῦμα ἅγιον τοῖς αἰτοῦσιν αὐτόν.  Καὶ
will give spirit holy to the asking  him.   And
1510   1544         1140        2532 846 1510 2974
ἦν  ἐκβάλλων      δαιμόνιον [καὶ αὐτὸ ἦν] κωφόν·
he was+ +throwing out demon    and  it  was  deaf;
1096       1161 010 1140      1831           2980    01
ἐγένετο δὲ τοῦ δαιμονίου ἐξελθόντος ἐλάλησεν ὁ
it became but the demon    having gone out spoke the
2974    2532 2296      013 3793   15  5100 1161 1537 846
κωφὸς καὶ ἐθαύμασαν οἱ ὄχλοι.  τινὲς δὲ ἐξ αὐτῶν
deaf and marveled the crowds.   Some but from them
3004    1722 954        03  758      022     1140
εἶπον· ἐν Βεελζεβοὺλ τῷ ἄρχοντι τῶν δαιμονίων
said;  in Beelzeboul the ruler  of the demons
1544       024 1140    16  2087    1161 3985
ἐκβάλλει τὰ δαιμόνια·  ἕτεροι δὲ πειράζοντες
he throws out the demons;  others but pressuring
4592    1537 3772 2212       3844 846    17  846
σημεῖον ἐξ οὐρανοῦ ἐζήτουν παρ' αὐτοῦ.  αὐτὸς
sign    from heaven were seeking from him.  Himself
1161 3609a        846   024 1270          3004
δὲ εἰδὼς      αὐτῶν τὰ διανοήματα εἶπεν
but having known of them the thorough thoughts said
846     3956 932        1909 1438   1266
αὐτοῖς· πᾶσα βασιλεία ἐφ' ἑαυτὴν διαμερισθεῖσα
to them, all kingdom on  itself having been divided
2049      2532 3624  1909 3624 4098   18  1487 1161
ἐρημοῦται καὶ οἶκος ἐπὶ οἶκον πίπτει.  εἰ  δὲ
is desolated and house on  house falls.  If but
2532 01  4567     1909 1438    1266       4459
καὶ ὁ σατανᾶς ἐφ' ἑαυτὸν διεμερίσθη, πῶς
also the adversary on  himself was divided, how
2476         05  932        846    3754     3004
σταθήσεται ἡ βασιλεία αὐτοῦ; ὅτι   λέγετε
will be standing the kingdom of him? Because you say
1722 954         1544          1473 024 1140    19  1487
ἐν Βεελζεβοὺλ ἐκβάλλειν με τὰ δαιμόνια.   εἰ
in Beelzeboul to throw out me the demons.     If
1161 1473 1722 954         1544      024 1140     013
δὲ ἐγὼ ἐν Βεελζεβοὺλ ἐκβάλλω τὰ δαιμόνια, οἱ
but I  in Beelzeboul throw out the demons,  the
5207 1473 1722 5101 1544          1223     3778
υἱοὶ ὑμῶν ἐν τίνι ἐκβάλλουσιν;  διὰ    τοῦτο
sons of you in what do they throw out? Through this
```

knock, and the door will be opened for you. [10]For everyone who asks receives, and everyone who searches finds, and for everyone who knocks, the door will be opened. [11]Is there anyone among you who, if your child asks for[a] a fish, will give a snake instead of a fish? [12]Or if the child asks for an egg, will give a scorpion? [13]If you then, who are evil, know how to give good gifts to your children, how much more will the heavenly Father give the Holy Spirit[b] to those who ask him!"

14 Now he was casting out a demon that was mute; when the demon had gone out, the one who had been mute spoke, and the crowds were amazed. [15]But some of them said, "He casts out demons by Beelzebul, the ruler of the demons." [16]Others, to test him, kept demanding from him a sign from heaven. [17]But he knew what they were thinking and said to them, "Every kingdom divided against itself becomes a desert, and house falls on house. [18]If Satan also is divided against himself, how will his kingdom stand?—for you say that I cast out the demons by Beelzebul. [19]Now if I cast out the demons by Beelzebul, by whom do your exorcists[c] cast them out?

a Other ancient authorities add bread, will give a stone; or if your child asks for
b Other ancient authorities read the Father give the Holy Spirit from heaven
c Gk sons

Therefore they will be your judges. [20]But if it is by the finger of God that I cast out the demons, then the kingdom of God has come to you. [21]When a strong man, fully armed, guards his castle, his property is safe. [22]But when one stronger than he attacks him and overpowers him, he takes away his armor in which he trusted and divides his plunder. [23]Whoever is not with me is against me, and whoever does not gather with me scatters.

[24] "When the unclean spirit has gone out of a person, it wanders through waterless regions looking for a resting place, but not finding any, it says, 'I will return to my house from which I came.' [25]When it comes, it finds it swept and put in order. [26]Then it goes and brings seven other spirits more evil than itself, and they enter and live there; and the last state of that person is worse than the first."

[27] While he was saying this, a woman in the crowd raised her voice and said to him, "Blessed is the womb that

846	1473	2923	1510	**20**	1487	1161	1722
αὐτοὶ	ὑμῶν	κριταὶ	ἔσονται.		εἰ	δὲ	ἐν
themselves	of you	judges	will be.		If	but	in

1147	2316	1473	1544	024	1140	686
δακτύλῳ	θεοῦ	[ἐγὼ]	ἐκβάλλω	τὰ	δαιμόνια,	ἄρα
finger	of God	I	throw out	the	demons,	then

5348	1909	1473	05	932	02	2316	**21**	3752
ἔφθασεν	ἐφ'	ὑμᾶς	ἡ	βασιλεία	τοῦ	θεοῦ.		ὅταν
arrived	on	you	the	kingdom	of	the God.		When

01	2478	2528	5442	08	1438
ὁ	ἰσχυρὸς	καθωπλισμένος	φυλάσσῃ	τὴν	ἑαυτοῦ
the	strong	having armed	might guard	the	of himself
					himself thoroughly

833	1722	1515	1510	021	5225	846
αὐλήν,	ἐν	εἰρήνῃ	ἐστὶν	τὰ	ὑπάρχοντα	αὐτοῦ·
courtyard,	in	peace	are	the	possessions	of him;

22	1875	1161	2478	846	1904
	ἐπὰν	δὲ	ἰσχυρότερος	αὐτοῦ	ἐπελθὼν
	When but		stronger	of him	having come on

3528	846	08	3833	846	142
νικήσῃ	αὐτόν,	τὴν	πανοπλίαν	αὐτοῦ	αἴρει
might conquer	him,	the	all weaponry	of him	he lifts up

1909	3739	3982	2532	024	4661	846
ἐφ'	ᾗ	ἐπεποίθει	καὶ	τὰ	σκῦλα	αὐτοῦ
on	which	he had persuaded	and	the	spoils	of him

1239	01	3361	1510	3326	1473
διαδίδωσιν.	**23** ὁ	μὴ	ὢν	μετ'	ἐμοῦ
he gives thoroughly.	The one	not	being	with	me

2596	1473	1510	2532	01	3361	4863	3326
κατ'	ἐμοῦ	ἐστιν,	καὶ	ὁ	μὴ	συνάγων	μετ'
against	me	is,	and	the one	not	leading with	with

1473	4650	3752	09	169	4151
ἐμοῦ	σκορπίζει.	**24** Ὅταν	τὸ	ἀκάθαρτον	πνεῦμα
me	scatters.	When	the	unclean	spirit

1831	575	02	444	1330	1223
ἐξέλθῃ	ἀπὸ	τοῦ	ἀνθρώπου,	διέρχεται	δι'
might go out	from	the	man,	he goes through	through

504	5117	2212	372	2532	3361	2147
ἀνύδρων	τόπων	ζητοῦν	ἀνάπαυσιν	καὶ	μὴ	εὑρίσκον·
waterless	places	seeking	rest	and	not	finding;

5119	3004	5290	1519	04	3624	1473
[τότε]	λέγει·	ὑποστρέψω	εἰς	τὸν	οἶκόν	μου
then	he says;	I will return	to	the	house	of me

3606	1831	**25**	2532	2064	2147
ὅθεν	ἐξῆλθον·		καὶ	ἐλθὸν	εὑρίσκει
from where	I went out;		and	having come	he finds

4563	2532	2885	**26**	5119
σεσαρωμένον	καὶ	κεκοσμημένον.		τότε
having been swept	and	having been adorned.		Then

4198	2532	3880	2087	4151	4190
πορεύεται	καὶ	παραλαμβάνει	ἕτερα	πνεύματα	πονηρότερα
he travels	and	takes along	other	spirits	more evil

1438	2033	2532	1525	2730	1563
ἑαυτοῦ	ἑπτὰ	καὶ	εἰσελθόντα	κατοικεῖ	ἐκεῖ·
of himself	seven	and	having gone in	resides	there;

2532	1096	021	2078	02	444	1565
καὶ	γίνεται	τὰ	ἔσχατα	τοῦ	ἀνθρώπου	ἐκείνου
and	became	the	last	of	the man	that

5501	022	4413	**27**	1096	1161	1722	011	3004
χείρονα	τῶν	πρώτων.		Ἐγένετο	δὲ	ἐν	τῷ	λέγειν
worse	of	the first.		It became	but	in	the	to say

846	3778	1869	5100	5456	1135	1537
αὐτὸν	ταῦτα	ἐπάρασά	τις	φωνὴν	γυνὴ	ἐκ
him	these	having lifted up on	some	sound	woman	from

02	3793	3004	846	3107	05	2836	05
τοῦ	ὄχλου	εἶπεν	αὐτῷ·	μακαρία	ἡ	κοιλία	ἡ
the	crowd	said	to him;	fortunate	the	stomach	the one

```
941              1473  2532  3149    3739  2337
βαστάσασά        σε    καὶ   μαστοὶ  οὓς   ἐθήλασας.
having borne you  and   breasts which you   nursed.
borne
```

```
    846          1161  3004     3303b         3107      013
28  αὐτὸς   δὲ    εἶπεν·   μενοῦν       μακάριοι   οἱ
    Himself  but   said;    indeed then  fortunate  the ones
191        04    3056   02      2316  2532  5442
ἀκούοντες  τὸν   λόγον  τοῦ     θεοῦ  καὶ   φυλάσσοντες.
hearing    the   word   of the  God   and   guarding.
```

```
    014     1161  3793   1865                 757      3004
29  Τῶν     δὲ    ὄχλων  ἐπαθροιζομένων  ἤρξατο   λέγειν·
    Of the  but   crowds being thronged      he began  to say,
05    1074            3778  1074           4190      1510    4592
ἦ     γενεὰ          αὕτη  γενεὰ          πονηρά  ἐστιν·  σημεῖον
the   generation     this  generation     evil    is;     sign
2212    2532  4592      3756  1325                      846
ζητεῖ,  καὶ   σημεῖον   οὐ    δοθήσεται            αὐτῇ
it seeks, and   sign       not   will be given to  it
1487  3361  09   4592      2495      2531      1063  1096
εἰ    μὴ    τὸ   σημεῖον   Ἰωνᾶ.  30  καθὼς   γὰρ   ἐγένετο
except       the  sign       Jonah.   Just as for   became
2495  015     3536          4592       3779   1510   2532
Ἰωνᾶς τοῖς    Νινευίταις  σημεῖον,  οὕτως  ἔσται  καὶ
Jonah  to the  Ninevites    sign,     thusly  will be  also
01    5207  02    444        07    1074       3778
ὁ     υἱὸς  τοῦ   ἀνθρώπου  τῇ    γενεᾷ      ταύτῃ.
the   son   of    the man    in    the generation  this.
```

```
    938          3558    1453               1722  07
31  βασίλισσα  νότου   ἐγερθήσεται     ἐν    τῇ
    Queen       of south  will be raised in    the
2920      3326  014  435     06      1074       3778   2532
κρίσει    μετὰ  τῶν  ἀνδρῶν  τῆς     γενεᾶς    ταύτης  καὶ
judgment  with  the  men      of the  generation this    and
2632         846      3754   2064       1537  022   4009
κατακρινεῖ  αὐτούς, ὅτι    ἦλθεν      ἐκ    τῶν   περάτων
will condemn  them,   because she came  from  the   limits
0τ    1093  191      08    4678        4672          2532  2400
τῆς   γῆς   ἀκοῦσαι  τὴν   σοφίαν     Σολομῶνος,    καὶ   ἰδοὺ
of the  earth  to hear  the   wisdom      of Solomon,  and   look
4183    4672       5602      32  435      3536       450
πλεῖον  Σολομῶνος  ὧδε.       ἄνδρες   Νινευῖται  ἀναστήσονται
more    of Solomon  here.       Men       Ninevites   will stand up
1722  07  2920   3326  06  1074       3778   2532
ἐν    τῇ   κρίσει  μετὰ  τῆς γενεᾶς    ταύτης καὶ
in    the  judgment with  the generation  this    and
2632            846      3754    3340               1519  012
κατακρινοῦσιν  αὐτήν· ὅτι     μετενόησαν        εἰς   τὸ
will condemn    it;     because  they changed mind in  the
2782       2495    2532  2400  4183    2495    5602
κήρυγμα   Ἰωνᾶ,   καὶ   ἰδοὺ  πλεῖον  Ἰωνᾶ   ὧδε.
announcement of Jonah, and   look   more    Jonah  here.
```

```
    3762    3088    681      1519  2926      5087     3761
33  Οὐδεὶς  λύχνον  ἅψας      εἰς   κρύπτην  τίθησιν [οὐδὲ
    No one   lamp    having lit  in    hidden    sets      but not
5259  04   3426        235   1909  08   3087
ὑπὸ   τὸν  μόδιον]     ἀλλ'  ἐπὶ  τὴν  λυχνίαν,
under  the  measuring scoop  but   on    the  lampstand,
2443  013  1531                012  5457   991
ἵνα   οἱ   εἰσπορευόμενοι    τὸ   φῶς    βλέπωσιν.
that  the  ones traveling into  the  light    might see.
```

```
    01  3088    010    4983      1510  01  3788      1473
34  Ὁ   λύχνος  τοῦ    σώματός  ἐστιν ὁ   ὀφθαλμός  σου.
    The  lamp     of the  body      is     the  eye        of you.
3752  01  3788       1473   573      1510       2532  3650
ὅταν  ὁ   ὀφθαλμός  σου    ἁπλοῦς  ᾖ,         καὶ   ὅλον
When  the  eye         of you  open     might be,    also  whole
09   4983    1473    5460        1510    1875  1161  4190
τὸ   σῶμά   σου     φωτεινόν   ἐστιν·  ἐπὰν   δὲ   πονηρὸς
the  body    of you   lightened   is;      when   but   evil
```

bore you and the breasts that nursed you!" 28But he said, "Blessed rather are those who hear the word of God and obey it!"

29 When the crowds were increasing, he began to say, "This generation is an evil generation; it asks for a sign, but no sign will be given to it except the sign of Jonah. 30For just as Jonah became a sign to the people of Nineveh, so the Son of Man will be to this generation. 31The queen of the South will rise at the judgment with the people of this generation and condemn them, because she came from the ends of the earth to listen to the wisdom of Solomon, and see, something greater than Solomon is here! 32The people of Nineveh will rise up at the judgment with this generation and condemn it, because they repented at the proclamation of Jonah, and see, something greater than Jonah is here!

33 "No one after lighting a lamp puts it in a cellar,[a] but on the lampstand so that those who enter may see the light. 34Your eye is the lamp of your body. If your eye is healthy, your whole body is full of light; but if it is not healthy,

---

[a] Other ancient authorities add or under the bushel basket

your body is full of darkness. 35Therefore consider
whether the light in you is
not darkness. 36If then your
whole body is full of light,
with no part of it in darkness, it will be as full of
light as when a lamp gives
you light with its rays."

37 While he was
speaking, a Pharisee invited
him to dine with him; so he
went in and took his place
at the table. 38The Pharisee
was amazed to see that he
did not first wash before
dinner. 39Then the Lord
said to him, "Now you
Pharisees clean the outside
of the cup and of the dish,
but inside you are full of
greed and wickedness.
40You fools! Did not the
one who made the outside
make the inside also? 41So
give for alms those things
that are within; and see,
everything will be clean
for you.

42 "But woe to you
Pharisees! For you tithe
mint and rue and herbs
of all kinds, and neglect
justice and the love of
God; it is these you ought
to have practiced, without
neglecting the others.
43Woe to you Pharisees!
For you love to have the
seat of honor in the
synagogues and to be
greeted with respect in the
marketplaces. 44Woe to
you! For you are

```
1510           2532 09   4983 1473   4652
ᾖ,           καὶ  τὸ  σῶμά σου  σκοτεινόν.
might be,    also the body of you darkened.

    4648         3767 3361 09  5457  09   1722 1473
35  σκόπει       οὖν  μὴ  τὸ φῶς  τὸ  ἐν  σοὶ
    Look carefully then not the light the in  you
4655     1510        1487 3767 09  4983 1473    3650
σκότος ἐστίν. 36 εἰ  οὖν  τὸ σῶμά σου   ὅλον
dark   is.      If  then the body of you whole
5460          3361 2192  3313  5100 4652        1510
φωτεινόν,  μὴ  ἔχον μέρος τι  σκοτεινόν, ἔσται
lightened, not having part some darkened, it will be
5460     3650 5613 3752 01  3088  07    796
φωτεινὸν ὅλον ὡς ὅταν ὁ  λύχνος τῇ  ἀστραπῇ
lightened whole as when the lamp  in the lightning
5461       1473    37 1722 1161 011 2980     2065
φωτίζῃ   σε.       Ἐν  δὲ  τῷ λαλῆσαι ἐρωτᾷ
might light you.    In  but the to speak asked
846     5330       3704      709       3844  846   1525
αὐτὸν Φαρισαῖος ὅπως   ἀριστήσῃ παρ᾽ αὐτῷ· εἰσελθὼν
him   Pharisee  so that he might along him; having
                         eat a meal         gone in
1161 377           38 01 1161 5330        3708
δὲ  ἀνέπεσεν.      ὁ  δὲ  Φαρισαῖος ἰδὼν
but he reclined.   The but Pharisee   having seen
2296      3754      3756 4413   907        4253
ἐθαύμασεν ὅτι    οὐ  πρῶτον ἐβαπτίσθη  πρὸ
marveled because not first   he was immersed before
010 712        39 3004  1161 01  2962    4314 846    3568
τοῦ ἀρίστου.    εἶπεν δὲ  ὁ  κύριος πρὸς αὐτόν· νῦν
the meal.       Said but the Master to  him;   now
1473 013 5330      012 1855      010      4221        2532
ὑμεῖς οἱ Φαρισαῖοι τὸ ἔξωθεν τοῦ   ποτηρίου καὶ
you   the Pharisees the outside of the cup      and
02 4094    2511      09  1161 2081    1473   1073
τοῦ πίνακος καθαρίζετε, τὸ δὲ  ἔσωθεν ὑμῶν  γέμει
the platter clean,     the but inside of you is full
724       2532 4189       40 978              3756 01
ἁρπαγῆς  καὶ  πονηρίας.   ἄφρονες,       οὐχ ὁ
of seizure and evil.       Unthinking ones, not the
4160          012 1855    2532 012 2081    4160
ποιήσας        τὸ ἔξωθεν καὶ  τὸ ἔσωθεν ἐποίησεν;
one having made the outside also the inside he made?
    4133    024 1751        1325 1654          2532
41  πλὴν  τὰ ἐνόντα        δότε ἐλεημοσύνην, καὶ
    Except the things being in give mercifulness, and
2400 3956   2513    1473    1510     42 235  3759 1473
ἰδοὺ πάντα καθαρὰ ὑμῖν  ἐστιν.   ἀλλὰ οὐαὶ ὑμῖν
look all   clean  to you is.      But  woe to you
015 5330        3754      586              012 2238
τοῖς Φαρισαίοις, ὅτι    ἀποδεκατοῦτε  τὸ ἡδύοσμον
the Pharisees,  because you give tenth the mint
2532 012 4076   2532 3956 3001    2532 3928
καὶ  τὸ πήγανον καὶ  πᾶν λάχανον καὶ παρέρχεσθε
and the rue     and all  vegetable and you go along
08 2920      2532 08  26    02     2316 3778 1161
τὴν κρίσιν  καὶ τὴν ἀγάπην τοῦ θεοῦ· ταῦτα δὲ
the judgment and the love  of the God; these but
1163         4160         2548      3361 3935
ἔδει        ποιῆσαι κἀκεῖνα μὴ  παρεῖναι.
it is necessary to do  and those not  to fall along.
    3759 1473   015 5330        3754   25       08
43  Οὐαὶ ὑμῖν  τοῖς Φαρισαίοις, ὅτι   ἀγαπᾶτε τὴν
    Woe to you the Pharisees,  because you love the
4410           1722 019  4864      2532 016  783
πρωτοκαθεδρίαν ἐν  ταῖς συναγωγαῖς καὶ τοὺς ἀσπασμοὺς
first chair    in  the synagogues and the greetings
1722 019  58        44 3759 1473    3754      1510
ἐν  ταῖς ἀγοραῖς.    Οὐαὶ ὑμῖν,   ὅτι    ἐστὲ
in  the  markets.     Woe to you, because you are
```

```
5613    021  3419        021  82           2532  013  444              013
ὡς      τὰ   μνημεῖα τὰ   ἄδηλα,    καὶ   οἱ   ἄνθρωποι [οἱ]
as      the  graves   the unclear,   and   the  men             the
4043                  1883  3756  3609a              611              1161
περιπατοῦντες ἐπάνω  οὐκ   οἴδασιν.   45  Ἀποκριθεὶς δὲ
ones walking  upon   not   they know.      Having        but
around                                                    answered
5100  014        3544      3004  846        1320              3778
τις   τῶν       νομικῶν λέγει αὐτῷ·   διδάσκαλε, ταῦτα
some of the     lawyers  say  to him;   teacher,       these
3004     2532  1473  5195          01  1161  3004          2532
λέγων   καὶ   ἡμᾶς ὑβρίζεις.  46 ὁ   δὲ   εἶπεν·      καὶ
saying   also  us    you abuse.     The but said;        also
1473   015    3544        3759    3754      5412         016
ὑμῖν  τοῖς  νομικοῖς οὐαί, ὅτι     φορτίζετε τοὺς
to you the  lawyers  woe,   because you pack  the
444          5413    1419              2532  846              1520
ἀνθρώπους φορτία δυσβάστακτα, καὶ  αὐτοὶ         ἑνὶ
men          packs  doubly heavy,  and  yourselves   one
014       1147          1473  3756  4379              023   5413
τῶν      δακτύλων ὑμῶν οὐ   προσψαύετε τοῖς φορτίοις.
of the   fingers   of you  not  you touch to the  packs.
   3759  1473       3754      3618          024  3419      014
47 Οὐαὶ ὑμῖν,    ὅτι      οἰκοδομεῖτε τὰ   μνημεῖα τῶν
   Woe   to you,  because  you build       the  graves   of the
4396         013  1161  3962      1473        615              846
προφητῶν, οἱ   δὲ   πατέρες ὑμῶν  ἀπέκτειναν αὐτούς.
spokesmen,  the  but  fathers  of you  killed          them.
   686      3144          1510       2532  4909
48 ἄρα    μάρτυρές  ἐστε   καὶ  συνευδοκεῖτε
   Then   testifiers  you are  and  you think well together
023       2041     014     3962      1473      3754         846
τοῖς    ἔργοις  τῶν    πατέρων ὑμῶν,  ὅτι       αὐτοὶ
in the  works   of the  fathers  of you,  because  themselves
3303     615              846        1473   1161  3618
μὲν    ἀπέκτειναν αὐτούς, ὑμεῖς δὲ   οἰκοδομεῖτε.
indeed  killed          them,    you    but  build.
   1223      3778    2532  05   4678    02        2316  3004
49 διὰ     τοῦτο καὶ  ἡ   σοφία τοῦ     θεοῦ εἶπεν·
   Through this  also  the  wisdom of the  God  said;
649                  1519  846        4396       2532  652
ἀποστελῶ         εἰς  αὐτοὺς προφήτας καὶ  ἀποστόλους,
I will delegate to   them    spokesmen and  delegates,
2532  1537  846        615              2532  1377          50  2443
καὶ   ἐξ    αὐτῶν ἀποκτενοῦσιν καὶ   διώξουσιν,    ἵνα
and   from  them    they will kill  and   will pursue,       that
1567                  09   129      3956    014  4396          09
ἐκζητηθῇ           τὸ   αἷμα  πάντων τῶν προφητῶν τὸ
might seek out      the  blood  of all  the  spokesmen  the
1632                  575   2602       2889           575
ἐκκεχυμένον       ἀπὸ καταβολῆς κόσμου     ἀπὸ
having been poured out from foundation of world from
06   1074      3778       575  129         6      2193
τῆς γενεᾶς  ταύτης, 51 ἀπὸ αἵματος Ἄβελ ἕως
the  generation this,      from blood    Abel  until
129        2197        02   622                    3342
αἵματος Ζαχαρίου τοῦ ἀπολομένου   μεταξὺ
blood     of Zacharias the having been destroyed between
010  2379             2532  02   3624   3483  3004    1473
τοῦ θυσιαστηρίου  καὶ  τοῦ οἴκου·  ναὶ λέγω  ὑμῖν,
the place of sacrifice and  the  house;  yes  I tell  you,
1567                   575   06   1074      3778        3759
ἐκζητηθήσεται     ἀπὸ τῆς γενεᾶς ταύτης. 52 Οὐαὶ
it will be sought out from the  generation this.      Woe
1473   015    3544        3754  142            08   2807
ὑμῖν  τοῖς  νομικοῖς, ὅτι   ἤρατε        τὴν κλεῖδα
to you the  lawyers,   because you lift up the  key
06   1108        846        3756  1525        2532  016
τῆς γνώσεως· αὐτοὶ  οὐκ   εἰσήλθατε καὶ   τοὺς
of the knowledge; yourselves not  you go in  and   the
```

45 One of the lawyers answered him, "Teacher, when you say these things, you insult us too." 46And he said, "Woe also to you lawyers! For you load people with burdens hard to bear, and you yourselves do not lift a finger to ease them. 47Woe to you! For you build the tombs of the prophets whom your ancestors killed. 48So you are witnesses and approve of the deeds of your ancestors; for they killed them, and you build their tombs. 49Therefore also the Wisdom of God said, 'I will send them prophets and apostles, some of whom they will kill and persecute,' 50so that this generation may be charged with the blood of all the prophets shed since the foundation of the world, 51from the blood of Abel to the blood of Zechariah, who perished between the altar and the sanctuary. Yes, I tell you, it will be charged against this generation. 52Woe to you lawyers! For you have taken away the key of knowledge; you did not enter yourselves, and you

hindered those who were entering."

53 When he went outside, the scribes and the Pharisees began to be very hostile toward him and to cross-examine him about many things, 54lying in wait for him, to catch him in something he might say.

CHAPTER 12

Meanwhile, when the crowd gathered by the thousands, so that they trampled on one another, he began to speak first to his disciples, "Beware of the yeast of the Pharisees, that is, their hypocrisy. 2Nothing is covered up that will not be uncovered, and nothing secret that will not become known. 3Therefore whatever you have said in the dark will be heard in the light, and what you have whispered behind closed doors will be proclaimed from the housetops.

4 "I tell you, my friends, do not fear those who kill the body, and after that can do nothing more. 5But I will warn you whom to fear: fear him who, after he has killed, has authority[a] to cast into hell.[b] Yes, I tell you, fear him! 6Are not five sparrows sold for two pennies? Yet not one of them is forgotten in God's sight. 7But even

---

a Or *power*
b Gk *Gehenna*

1525		2967		**53**	2547	1831		846
εἰσερχομένους		ἐκωλύσατε.			Κἀκεῖθεν	ἐξελθόντος		αὐτοῦ

ones going in   you hindered.   And from having gone him
                                     there   out

757		013	1122			2532	013	5330		1171
ἤρξαντο	οἱ	γραμματεῖς	καὶ		οἱ	Φαρισαῖοι	δεινῶς

began   the writers   and   the Pharisees   terribly

1758		2532	653
ἐνέχειν	καὶ	ἀποστοματίζειν	αὐτὸν	περὶ	πλειόνων,

to hold in and   to speak off   him   about   more,

54 1748   846   2340   5100 1537 010 4750
ἐνεδρεύοντες   αὐτὸν θηρεῦσαί τι   ἐκ   τοῦ στόματος
lying in wait him   to snare some from the mouth

846   **12:1** 1722 3739 1996
αὐτοῦ.   Ἐν   οἷς   ἐπισυναχθεισῶν
of him.   In   which having been brought together

018 3461   02   3793   5620   2662
τῶν μυριάδων   τοῦ   ὄχλου, ὥστε   καταπατεῖν
the ten thousands of the crowd, so that to walk over

240   757   3004   4314 016   3101   846
ἀλλήλους,   ἤρξατο   λέγειν προς τοὺς μαθητὰς αὐτοῦ
one another, he began to speak to the learners of him

4413   4337   1438   575 06 2219   3748
πρῶτον· προσέχετε ἑαυτοῖς ἀπὸ τῆς ζύμης, ἥτις
first;   hold to   yourselves from the yeast, which

1510 5272   014   5330   **2** 3762   1161
ἐστὶν ὑπόκρισις, τῶν Φαρισαίων. Οὐδὲν δὲ
is   hypocrisy, of the Pharisees. Nothing but

4780   1510   3739 3756
συγκεκαλυμμένον   ἐστὶν ὃ οὐκ
+having been covered together is+   that not

601   2532 2927   3739 3756 1097
ἀποκαλυφθήσεται   καὶ κρυπτὸν ὃ οὐ γνωσθήσεται.
will be uncovered and hidden that not will be known.

3 473   3739 3745   1722 07 4653 3004
ἀνθ᾽ ὧν   ὅσα   ἐν τῇ σκοτίᾳ εἴπατε
Against which as much as in the dark   you said

1722 011 5457 191   2532 3739 4314 012
ἐν τῷ φωτὶ ἀκουσθήσεται,   καὶ ὃ   προς τὸ
in the light it will be heard, and what to the

3775 2980   1722 023   5009   2784
οὓς ἐλαλήσατε ἐν τοῖς ταμείοις κηρυχθήσεται
ear you said in the storerooms will be announced

1909 022 1430   3004   1161 1473   015 5384
ἐπὶ τῶν δωμάτων. **4** Λέγω δὲ ὑμῖν τοῖς φίλοις
on the roofs.   I say but to you the friends

1473 3361 5399   575 014 615   012 4983
μου, μὴ φοβηθῆτε ἀπὸ τῶν ἀποκτεινόντων τὸ σῶμα
of me, not be afraid from the ones killing the body

2532 3326 3778 3361 2192   4055   5100
καὶ μετὰ ταῦτα μὴ ἐχόντων περισσότερόν τι
and after these not having more excessive some

4160   5263   1161 1473   5101
ποιῆσαι. **5** ὑποδείξω δὲ ὑμῖν τίνα
to do.   I will example but to you what

5399   5399   04   3326 012 615
φοβηθῆτε· φοβήθητε τὸν   μετὰ τὸ ἀποκτεῖναι
you might fear; fear the one after the to kill

2192   1849   1685   1519 08 1067   3483
ἔχοντα ἐξουσίαν ἐμβαλεῖν εἰς τὴν γέενναν. ναὶ
having authority to throw in into the gehenna.   Yes

3004 1473   3778   5399   **6** 3780 4002 4765
λέγω ὑμῖν, τοῦτον φοβήθητε.   οὐχὶ πέντε στρουθία
I say to you, this fear.   Not five sparrows

4453   787   1417 2532 1520 1537 846 3756
πωλοῦνται ἀσσαρίων δύο; καὶ ἓν ἐξ αὐτῶν οὐκ
are being sold assarions two? And one from them not

1510 1950   1799   02 2316 **7** 235 2532
ἔστιν ἐπιλελησμένον ἐνώπιον τοῦ θεοῦ. ἀλλὰ καὶ
is+ +having been forgotten before the God.   But also

017 2359   06   2776   1473 3956   705   3361
αἱ τρίχες τῆς κεφαλῆς ὑμῶν πᾶσαι ἠρίθμηνται. μὴ
the hairs of   head   of   all   have been   Not
            the   you   numbered.

5399   4183   4765   1308   8 3004   1161
φοβεῖσθε· πολλῶν στρουθίων διαφέρετε.   Λέγω   δὲ
fear;   of many sparrows   you differ.   I say   but

1473   3956 3739 302 3670   1722 1473 1715
ὑμῖν,   πᾶς ὃς ἂν ὁμολογήσῃ   ἐν ἐμοὶ ἔμπροσθεν
to you, all who -   might confess in me   in front

014   444   2532 01 5207 02   444
τῶν ἀνθρώπων, καὶ ὁ υἱὸς τοῦ ἀνθρώπου
of the men,   also the son of the man

3670   1722 846   1715   014 32
ὁμολογήσει ἐν αὐτῷ ἔμπροσθεν τῶν ἀγγέλων
will confess in him   in front of the messengers

02   2316   9 01   1161 720   1473 1799
τοῦ θεοῦ·   ὁ   δὲ ἀρνησάμενός με ἐνώπιον
of the God;   the one but having denied me before

014 444   533   1799   014
τῶν ἀνθρώπων ἀπαρνηθήσεται   ἐνώπιον τῶν
the men   he will thoroughly deny before the

32   02   2316   10 2532 3956 3739 3004   3056
ἀγγέλων   τοῦ θεοῦ.   Καὶ πᾶς ὃς ἐρεῖ λόγον
messengers of the God.   And all who will say word

1519 04 5207 02   444   863
εἰς τὸν υἱὸν τοῦ ἀνθρώπου, ἀφεθήσεται
to   the son of the man,   it will be sent off

846   03   1161 1519 012 40   4151
αὐτῷ· τῷ   δὲ εἰς τὸ ἅγιον πνεῦμα
to him; to the one but to   the holy spirit

987   3756 863   11 3752 1161
βλασφημήσαντι οὐκ ἀφεθήσεται.   Ὅταν δὲ
having insulted not it will be sent off. When but

1533   1473 1909 020 4864   2532 020
εἰσφέρωσιν   ὑμᾶς ἐπὶ τὰς συναγωγὰς καὶ τὰς
they might bear in you on the synagogues and the

746   2532 020 1849   3361 3309
ἀρχὰς καὶ τὰς ἐξουσίας, μὴ μεριμνήσητε
rulers and the authorities, not you might be anxious

4459 2228 5101 626   2228 5101
πῶς ἢ   τί ἀπολογήσησθε   ἢ   τί
how or what you might defend yourself or what

3004   09 1063 40   4151   1321   1473
εἴπητε·   12 τὸ γὰρ ἅγιον πνεῦμα διδάξει ὑμᾶς
you might say; the for holy spirit will teach you

1722 846 07 5610 3739 1163   3004
ἐν αὐτῇ τῇ ὥρᾳ ἃ δεῖ   εἰπεῖν.
in same the hour what it is necessary to say.

13 3004   1161 5100 1537 02 3793 846   1320
    Εἶπεν δέ τις ἐκ τοῦ ὄχλου αὐτῷ· διδάσκαλε,
    Said but some from the crowd to him, teacher,

3004 03   80   1473 3307   3326 1473 08
εἰπὲ τῷ ἀδελφῷ μου μερίσασθαι μετ' ἐμοῦ τὴν
say to the brother of me to divide with me the

2817   01 1161 3004 846   444   5101 1473
κληρονομίαν. 14 ὁ δὲ εἶπεν αὐτῷ· ἄνθρωπε, τίς με
inheritance.   The but said to him, man, who me

2525   2923   2228 3312   1909 1473   15 3004
κατέστησεν κριτὴν ἢ μεριστὴν ἐφ' ὑμᾶς;   εἶπεν
appointed judge or divider on you?   He said

1161 4314 846   3708   2532 5442   575   3956
δὲ πρὸς αὐτούς· ὁρᾶτε καὶ φυλάσσεσθε ἀπὸ πάσης
but to them,   see   and guard   from all

4124   3754   3756 1722 011 4052   5100
πλεονεξίας, ὅτι   οὐκ ἐν τῷ περισσεύειν τινὶ
greediness, because not in the to exceed   in some

05 2222 846   1510 1537 022 5225   846
ἡ ζωὴ αὐτοῦ ἐστιν ἐκ τῶν ὑπαρχόντων αὐτῷ.
the life of him is   from the possessions to him.

the hairs of your head are
all counted. Do not be
afraid; you are of more
value than many sparrows.

8 "And I tell you,
everyone who acknowledges
me before others, the Son of
Man also will acknowledge
before the angels of God;
9but whoever denies me
before others will be denied
before the angels of God.
10And everyone who speaks
a word against the Son
of Man will be forgiven;
but whoever blasphemes
against the Holy Spirit will
not be forgiven. 11When
they bring you before the
synagogues, the rulers,
and the authorities, do not
worry about how[a] you are
to defend yourselves or
what you are to say; 12for
the Holy Spirit will teach
you at that very hour what
you ought to say."

13 Someone in the crowd
said to him, "Teacher, tell
my brother to divide the
family inheritance with
me." 14But he said to him,
"Friend, who set me to be
a judge or arbitrator over
you?" 15And he said to
them, "Take care! Be on
your guard against all
kinds of greed; for one's
life does not consist in the
abundance of possessions."

[a] Other ancient authorities add
or what

¹⁶Then he told them a parable: "The land of a rich man produced abundantly. ¹⁷And he thought to himself, 'What should I do, for I have no place to store my crops?' ¹⁸Then he said, 'I will do this: I will pull down my barns and build larger ones, and there I will store all my grain and my goods. ¹⁹And I will say to my soul, Soul, you have ample goods laid up for many years; relax, eat, drink, be merry.' ²⁰But God said to him, 'You fool! This very night your life is being demanded of you. And the things you have prepared, whose will they be?' ²¹So it is with those who store up treasures for themselves but are not rich toward God."

22 He said to his disciples, "Therefore I tell you, do not worry about your life, what you will eat, or about your body, what you will wear. ²³For life is more than food, and the body more than clothing. ²⁴Consider the ravens: they neither sow nor reap, they have neither storehouse nor barn, and yet God feeds them. Of how much more value are you than the birds! ²⁵And can any of you by worrying

16
| 3004 | 1161 | 3850 | | 4314 | 846 | 3004 |
Εἶπεν δὲ παραβολὴν πρὸς αὐτοὺς λέγων·
He said but parallel story to them saying,

| 444 | 5100 | 4145 | 2164 | 05 | 5561 | **17** | 2532 |
ἀνθρώπου τινὸς πλουσίου εὐφόρησεν ἡ χώρα. καὶ
of man some rich wore well the country. And

| 1260 | 1722 1438 | 3004 | 5101 4160 |
διελογίζετο ἐν ἑαυτῷ λέγων· τί ποιήσω,
he was reasoning in himself saying, what will I do,

| 3754 | 3756 2192 | 4226 4863 | 016 |
ὅτι οὐκ ἔχω ποῦ συνάξω τοὺς
because not I have where I will bring together the

| 2590 1473 | 2532 3004 | **18** | 3778 4160 |
καρποὺς μου; καὶ εἶπεν· τοῦτο ποιήσω,
fruit of me? And he said, this I will do,

| 2507 | 1473 020 596 | 2532 3173 |
καθελῶ μου τὰς ἀποθήκας καὶ μείζονας
I will lift down of me the storehouses and greater

| 3618 | 2532 4863 1563 3956 04 4621 2532 |
οἰκοδομήσω καὶ συνάξω ἐκεῖ πάντα τὸν σῖτον καὶ
I will build and I will there all the wheat and
              bring together

| 024 18 | 1473 | **19** | 2532 3004 | 07 | 5590 1473 |
τὰ ἀγαθά μου καὶ ἐρῶ τῇ ψυχῇ μου,
the goods of me and I will say to the soul of me,

| 5590 2192 | 4183 18 | 2749 | 1519 2094 4183 |
ψυχή, ἔχεις πολλὰ ἀγαθὰ κείμενα εἰς ἔτη πολλά·
soul, you have many goods lying in years many,

| 373 | 2068 4095 2165 | **20** | 3004 1161 846 |
ἀναπαύου, φάγε, πίε, εὐφραίνου. εἶπεν δὲ αὐτῷ
rest, eat, drink, be merry. Said but to him

| 01 2316 878 | 3778 07 3571 08 5590 |
ὁ θεός· ἄφρων, ταύτῃ τῇ νυκτὶ τὴν ψυχήν
the God, unthinking one, in this the night the soul

| 1473 523 | 575 1473 3739 1161 2090 |
σου ἀπαιτοῦσιν ἀπὸ σοῦ· ἃ δὲ ἡτοίμασας,
of you they ask back from you, what but you prepared,

| 5101 | 1510 | **21** | 3779 01 | 2343 |
τίνι ἔσται; οὕτως ὁ θησαυρίζων
to whom will it be? Thusly the one treasuring

| 1438 | 2532 3361 1519 2316 4147 | **22** | 3004 1161 |
ἑαυτῷ καὶ μὴ εἰς θεὸν πλουτῶν. Εἶπεν δὲ
to himself and not to God being rich. He said but

| 4314 016 3101 | 846 | 1223 | 3778 3004 1473 |
πρὸς τοὺς μαθητὰς [αὐτοῦ]· διὰ τοῦτο λέγω ὑμῖν·
to the learners of him, through this I say to you,

| 3361 3309 | 07 | 5590 5101 2068 | 3366 |
μὴ μεριμνᾶτε τῇ ψυχῇ τί φάγητε, μηδὲ
not be anxious in the soul what you might eat, but not

| 011 | 4983 | 5101 1746 | 05 1063 5590 |
τῷ σώματι τί ἐνδύσησθε. ²³ ἡ γὰρ ψυχὴ
in the body what you might put on. The for soul

| 4183 1510 06 | 5160 | 2532 09 4983 010 |
πλεῖόν ἐστιν τῆς τροφῆς καὶ τὸ σῶμα τοῦ
more is of the food and the body of the

| 1742 | **24** | 2657 | 016 2876 | 3754 3756 |
ἐνδύματος. κατανοήσατε τοὺς κόρακας ὅτι οὐ
clothes. Think carefully the ravens that not

| 4687 | 3761 | 2325 | 3739 3756 1510 |
σπείρουσιν οὐδὲ θερίζουσιν, οἷς οὐκ ἔστιν
they sow but not they harvest, whom not there is

| 5009 | 3761 | 596 | 2532 01 2316 5142 |
ταμεῖον οὐδὲ ἀποθήκη, καὶ ὁ θεὸς τρέφει
storeroom but not store house, and the God feeds

| 846 | 4214 | 3123 1473 1308 | 022 |
αὐτούς· πόσῳ μᾶλλον ὑμεῖς διαφέρετε τῶν
them, how much more you differ of the

| 4071 | **25** | 5101 1161 1537 1473 3309 | 1410 |
πετεινῶν. τίς δὲ ἐξ ὑμῶν μεριμνῶν δύναται
birds. Who but from you being anxious is able

1909	08	2244	846	4369	4083	**26**	1487	3767
ἐπὶ	τὴν	ἡλικίαν	αὐτοῦ	προσθεῖναι	πῆχυν;		εἰ	οὖν
on	the	stature	of him	to set to	cubit?		If	then

3761	1646	1410		5101	4012	022	3062
οὐδὲ	ἐλάχιστον	δύνασθε,		τί	περὶ	τῶν	λοιπῶν
but not	least	you are able,		why	about	the	remaining

3309		2657		024	2918	4459
μεριμνᾶτε;	**27**	κατανοήσατε		τὰ	κρίνα	πῶς
are you anxious?		Think carefully		the	lilies	ho

837		3756	2872		3761	3514		3004	1161
αὐξάνει·		οὐ	κοπιᾷ		οὐδὲ	νήθει·		λέγω	δὲ
grows,		not	it labors		but not	it spins;		I say	but

1473	3761	4672		1722	3956	07	1391	846
ὑμῖν,	οὐδὲ	Σολομὼν	ἐν	πάσῃ	τῇ	δόξῃ	αὐτοῦ
to you,	but not	Solomon	in	all	the	splendor	of him

4016		5613	1520	3778		**28**	1487	1161	1722
περιεβάλετο		ὡς	ἓν	τούτων.			εἰ	δὲ	ἐν
was thrown around		as	one	of these.			If	but	in

68	04	5528	1510	4594	2532	839		1519
ἀγρῷ	τὸν	χόρτον	ὄντα	σήμερον	καὶ	αὔριον		εἰς
field	the	grass	being	today	and	tomorrow		into

2823	906		01	2316	3779	293a
κλίβανον	βαλλόμενον		ὁ	θεὸς	οὕτως	ἀμφιέζει,
furnace	being thrown		the	God	thusly	dresses,

4214	3123	1473	3640		**29**	2532	1473
πόσῳ	μᾶλλον	ὑμᾶς,	ὀλιγόπιστοι.			καὶ	ὑμεῖς
how much	more	you,	little trusting ones.			And	you

3361	2212	5101	2068		2532	5101	4095
μὴ	ζητεῖτε	τί	φάγητε		καὶ	τί	πίητε
not	seek	what	you might eat		and	what	you might drink

2532	3361	3349		**30**	3778	1063	3956	021
καὶ	μὴ	μετεωρίζεσθε·			ταῦτα	γὰρ	πάντα	τὰ
and	not	be restless,			these	for	all	the

1484	02	2889	1934		1473	1161	01
ἔθνη	τοῦ	κόσμου	ἐπιζητοῦσιν,		ὑμῶν	δὲ	ὁ
nations	of the	world	seek after,		of you	but	the

3962	3609a		3754	5535	3778	**31**	4133	2212
πατὴρ	οἶδεν		ὅτι	χρῄζετε	τούτων.		πλὴν	ζητεῖτε
father	had known		that	you need	these.		Except	seek

08	932	846	2532	3778	4369		1473
τὴν	βασιλείαν	αὐτοῦ,	καὶ	ταῦτα	προστεθήσεται		ὑμῖν.
the	kingdom	of him,	and	these	will be set to		to you.

32	3361	5399	09	3398	4168		3754	2106
	Μὴ	φοβοῦ,	τὸ	μικρὸν	ποίμνιον,		ὅτι	εὐδόκησεν
	Not	fear,	the	small	flock,		because	thought well

01	3962	1473	1325	1473	08	932
ὁ	πατὴρ	ὑμῶν	δοῦναι	ὑμῖν	τὴν	βασιλείαν.
the	father	of you	to give	to you	the	kingdom.

33	4453	024	5225	1473	2532	1325
	Πωλήσατε	τὰ	ὑπάρχοντα	ὑμῶν	καὶ	δότε
	Sell	the	possessions	of you	and	give

1654	4160	1438		905	3361
ἐλεημοσύνην·	ποιήσατε	ἑαυτοῖς		βαλλάντια	μὴ
mercifulness;	make	to yourselves		purses	not

3822	2344	413		1722	015
παλαιούμενα,	θησαυρὸν	ἀνέκλειπτον	ἐν	τοῖς
being made old,	treasure	unfailable	in	the

3772	3699	2812	3756	1448	3761	4597
οὐρανοῖς,	ὅπου	κλέπτης	οὐκ	ἐγγίζει	οὐδὲ	σὴς
heavens,	where	thief	not	nears	but not	moth

1311		3699	1063	1510	01	2344	1473
διαφθείρει·	**34**	ὅπου	γὰρ	ἐστιν	ὁ	θησαυρὸς	ὑμῶν,
corrupts,		where	for	is	the	treasure	of you,
thoroughly;							

1563	2532	05	2588	1473	1510		1510	1473
ἐκεῖ	καὶ	ἡ	καρδία	ὑμῶν	ἔσται.	**35**	Ἔστωσαν	ὑμῶν
there	also	the	heart	of you	will be.		Let be+	of you

add a single hour to your span of life?[a] [26]If then you are not able to do so small a thing as that, why do you worry about the rest? [27]Consider the lilies, how they grow: they neither toil nor spin;[b] yet I tell you, even Solomon in all his glory was not clothed like one of these. [28]But if God so clothes the grass of the field, which is alive today and tomorrow is thrown into the oven, how much more will he clothe you—you of little faith! [29]And do not keep striving for what you are to eat and what you are to drink, and do not keep worrying. [30]For it is the nations of the world that strive after all these things, and your Father knows that you need them. [31]Instead, strive for his[c] kingdom, and these things will be given to you as well.

[32] "Do not be afraid, little flock, for it is your Father's good pleasure to give you the kingdom. [33]Sell your possessions, and give alms. Make purses for yourselves that do not wear out, an unfailing treasure in heaven, where no thief comes near and no moth destroys. [34]For where your treasure is, there your heart will be also.

[35] "Be dressed for action

_a_ Or add a cubit to your stature

_b_ Other ancient authorities read Consider the lilies; they neither spin nor weave

_c_ Other ancient authorities read God's

and have your lamps lit;
36be like those who are
waiting for their master to
return from the wedding
banquet, so that they may
open the door for him as
soon as he comes and
knocks. 37Blessed are those
slaves whom the master
finds alert when he comes;
truly I tell you, he will
fasten his belt and have
them sit down to eat, and
he will come and serve
them. 38If he comes during
the middle of the night, or
near dawn, and finds them
so, blessed are those slaves.

39 "But know this: if
the owner of the house had
known at what hour the
thief was coming, he[a]
would not have let his
house be broken into.
40You also must be ready,
for the Son of Man is
coming at an unexpected
hour."

41 Peter said, "Lord,
are you telling this parable
for us or for everyone?"
42And the Lord said,
"Who then is the faithful
and prudent manager
whom his master will put
in charge of his slaves, to
give them their allowance
of food at the proper time?
43Blessed is that slave
whom his master

---

a Other ancient authorities add
would have watched and

```
017  3751        4024              2532 013 3088    2545
αἱ  ὀσφύες  περιεζωσμέναι  καὶ  οἱ  λύχνοι  καιόμενοι·
the  hips     +having been    and  the  lamps   burning;
                encircled

    2532  1473  3664      444          4327              04
36  καὶ  ὑμεῖς ὅμοιοι ἀνθρώποις προσδεχομένοις τὸν
    and   you   like    to men      awaiting        the

2962    1438        4219  360                  1537 014
κύριον ἑαυτῶν     πότε ἀναλύσῃ          ἐκ  τῶν
master of themselves when he might depart from the

1062        2443 2064        2532 2925
γάμων,     ἵνα  ἐλθόντος  καὶ  κρούσαντος
marriages, that having gone and  having knocked

2112        455            846     37 3107    013
εὐθέως  ἀνοίξωσιν    αὐτῷ.      μακάριοι οἱ
immediately they might open to him.    Fortunate the

1401  1565      3739 2064        01  2962      2147
δοῦλοι ἐκεῖνοι, οὓς ἐλθὼν    ὁ  κύριος εὑρήσει
slaves those,   who having come the master will find

1127        281  3004  1473  3754 4024
γρηγοροῦντας· ἀμὴν λέγω ὑμῖν ὅτι περιζώσεται
keeping awake; amen I say to you that he will encircle
                                            himself

2532 347      846      2532 3928      1247
καὶ ἀνακλινεῖ αὐτοὺς καὶ παρελθὼν διακονήσει
and will recline them  and having gone he will
                                   along      serve

846    38 2579  1722 07  1208   2579  1722 07
αὐτοῖς.   κἂν ἐν  τῇ δευτέρᾳ κἂν ἐν  τῇ
them.     And if in the second and if in  the

5154  5438  2064          2532 2147    3779
τρίτῃ φυλακῇ ἔλθῃ       καὶ εὕρῃ    οὕτως,
third guard he might come and might find thusly,

3107    1510  1565      3778 1161 1097    3754
μακάριοί εἰσιν ἐκεῖνοι. 39 τοῦτο δὲ  γινώσκετε ὅτι
fortunate are those.    This  but  know        that

1487 3609a      01  3617              4169   5610  01
εἰ  ᾔδει       ὁ  οἰκοδεσπότης     ποίᾳ  ὥρᾳ ὁ
if  had known the house supervisor in what hour the

2812   2064      3756 302 863        1358
κλέπτης ἔρχεται, οὐκ ἂν ἀφῆκεν  διορυχθῆναι
thief  comes,    not  -  he allowed to be dug through

04  3624 846     40 2532 1473 1096    2092
τὸν οἶκον αὐτοῦ.   καὶ ὑμεῖς γίνεσθε ἕτοιμοι,
the house of him.   And you  become  prepared,

3754    3739    5610 3756 1380    01  5207 02
ὅτι    ᾗ      ὥρᾳ οὐ δοκεῖτε ὁ  υἱὸς τοῦ
because in what hour not you think the son of the

444     2064      41 3004 1161 01  4074    2962
ἀνθρώπου ἔρχεται.    Εἶπεν δὲ ὁ  Πέτρος· κύριε,
man       comes.     Said  but the Peter,  Master,

4314 1473 08 3850        3778    3004     2228 2532
πρὸς ἡμᾶς τὴν παραβολὴν ταύτην λέγεις ἢ  καὶ
to   us   the parallel story this you say or  also

4314 3956    42 2532 3004 01 2962   5101 686  1510
πρὸς πάντας;    καὶ εἶπεν ὁ κύριος· τίς ἄρα ἐστὶν
to   all?       And said the Master, who then is

01 4103    3623    01 5429      3739
ὁ πιστὸς οἰκονόμος ὁ φρόνιμος, ὃν
the trustful manager the thoughtful, whom

2525      01 2962  1909 06 2322      846    010
καταστήσει ὁ κύριος ἐπὶ τῆς θεραπείας αὐτοῦ τοῦ
will appoint the master on the service of him of the

1325     1722 2540  012 4620          43 3107   01
διδόναι ἐν καιρῷ [τὸ] σιτομέτριον;     μακάριος ὁ
to give in season the wheat measure?    Fortunate the

1401  1565      3739 2064        01 2962   846
δοῦλος ἐκεῖνος, ὃν ἐλθὼν    ὁ κύριος αὐτοῦ
slave that,     whom having come the master of him
```

2147   4160   3779   44 230   3004   1473   3754
εὑρήσει ποιοῦντα οὕτως.   ἀληθῶς λέγω ὑμῖν ὅτι
will find   doing   thusly.   Truly I say to you that

1909 3956   023   5225   846   2525   846
ἐπὶ πᾶσιν τοῖς ὑπάρχουσιν αὐτοῦ καταστήσει   αὐτόν.
on   all   the possessions of him he will appoint him.

45 1437 1161 3004   01   1401   1565   1722 07
    ἐὰν δὲ εἴπη   ὁ   δοῦλος ἐκεῖνος ἐν τῇ
    If but might say the slave   that   in the

2588   846   5549   01 2962   1473   2064
καρδίᾳ αὐτοῦ· χρονίζει ὁ κύριός μου ἔρχεσθαι,
heart   of him, spends time the master of me to come,

2532 757   5180   016   3816   2532 020   3814
καὶ ἄρξηται τύπτειν τοὺς παῖδας καὶ τὰς παιδίσκας,
and he might to beat the servant and the servant
     begin   boys   girls,

2068   5037 2532 4095   2532 3182
ἐσθίειν τε καὶ πίνειν καὶ μεθύσκεσθαι,
to eat   both and to drink and to be drunk,

46 2240   01 2962   02   1401   1565   1722
    ἥξει   ὁ κύριος τοῦ δούλου ἐκείνου ἐν
    he will come the master of the slave   that   in

2250 3739   3756 4328   2532 1722
ἡμέρᾳ ᾗ   οὐ προσδοκᾷ   καὶ ἐν
day   in which not he waits expectantly and in

5610 3739   3756 1097   2532 1371
ὥρᾳ ᾗ   οὐ γινώσκει, καὶ διχοτομήσει
hour in which not he knows, and he will cut into two

846   2532 012 3313 846   3326 014 571
αὐτὸν καὶ τὸ μέρος αὐτοῦ μετὰ τῶν ἀπίστων
him   and the part of him with the untrustful

5087   47 1565   1161 01 1401   01 1097   012
θήσει.   Ἐκεῖνος δὲ ὁ δοῦλος ὁ γνοὺς τὸ
he will set.   That   but the slave the knowing the

2307 02   2962   846   2532 3361 2090   2228
θέλημα τοῦ κυρίου αὐτοῦ καὶ μὴ ἑτοιμάσας   ἢ
want   of the master of him and not have prepared or

4160   4314 012 2307   846   1194
ποιήσας   πρὸς τὸ θέλημα αὐτοῦ δαρήσεται
having done to   the want   of him he will be beaten

4183   48 01 1161 3361 1097   4160   1161
πολλάς·   ὁ δὲ μὴ γνούς,   ποιήσας   δὲ
many;   the but not having known, having done but

514   4127   1194   3641   3956   1161
ἄξια πληγῶν δαρήσεται   ὀλίγας. παντὶ δὲ
worthy of blows he will be beaten few.   To all but

3739   1325   4183   4183 2212   3844
ᾧ   ἐδόθη   πολύ, πολὺ ζητηθήσεται παρ᾽
to whom was given much, much will be sought from

846   2532 3739   3908   4183   4055
αὐτοῦ, καὶ ᾧ   παρέθεντο πολύ, περισσότερον
him,   and to whom was set along much, more excessive

154   846   49 4442 2064   906   1909 08
αἰτήσουσιν αὐτόν.   Πῦρ ἦλθον βαλεῖν ἐπὶ τὴν
they will ask him.   Fire I came to throw on the

1093   2532 5101 2309 1487 2235   381
γῆν, καὶ τί θέλω εἰ ἤδη ἀνήφθη.
earth, and what I want if already it was ignited.

50 908   1161 2192 907   2532 4459
    βάπτισμα δὲ ἔχω βαπτισθῆναι,   καὶ πῶς
    Immersion but I have to be immersed, and how

4912   2193 3755 5055   51 1380   3754
συνέχομαι ἕως ὅτου τελεσθῇ.   δοκεῖτε ὅτι
I hold   until when it might   You think that
           be completed.

1515   3854   1325   1722 07 1093   3780
εἰρήνην παρεγενόμην δοῦναι ἐν τῇ γῇ; οὐχί,
peace   I arrived   to give in the earth? Not,

---

will find at work when he arrives. [44]Truly I tell you, he will put that one in charge of all his possessions. [45]But if that slave says to himself, 'My master is delayed in coming,' and if he begins to beat the other slaves, men and women, and to eat and drink and get drunk, [46]the master of that slave will come on a day when he does not expect him and at an hour that he does not know, and will cut him in pieces,[a] and put him with the unfaithful. [47]That slave who knew what his master wanted, but did not prepare himself or do what was wanted, will receive a severe beating. [48]But the one who did not know and did what deserved a beating will receive a light beating. From everyone to whom much has been given, much will be required; and from the one to whom much has been entrusted, even more will be demanded.

[49]"I came to bring fire to the earth, and how I wish it were already kindled! [50]I have a baptism with which to be baptized, and what stress I am under until it is completed! [51]Do you think that I have come to bring peace to the earth? No,

a Or cut him off

I tell you, but rather division! 52From now on five in one household will be divided, three against two and two against three; 53they will be divided:

    father against son

    and son against father,

    mother against daughter

    and daughter against mother,

    mother-in-law against her daughter-in-law

    and daughter-in-law against mother-in-law."

54 He also said to the crowds, "When you see a cloud rising in the west, you immediately say, 'It is going to rain'; and so it happens. 55And when you see the south wind blowing, you say, 'There will be scorching heat'; and it happens. 56You hypocrites! You know how to interpret the appearance of earth and sky, but why do you not know how to interpret the present time?

57 "And why do you not judge for yourselves what is right? 58Thus, when you go with your accuser before a magistrate, on the way make an effort to settle the case,[a] or you may be dragged before the judge, and the judge hand you over to the officer, and the officer throw you in prison. 59I tell you, you will never get out until you have paid the very last penny."

CHAPTER 13

At that very time there were some present

[a] Gk settle with him

3004	1473	235	2228	1267		1510	1063	575
λέγω	ὑμῖν,	ἀλλ᾽	ἢ	διαμερισμόν.	**52**	ἔσονται	γὰρ	ἀπὸ
I say to	you,	but	or	thorough division.		There will be	for	from

02	3568	4002	1722	1520	3624	1266
τοῦ	νῦν	πέντε	ἐν	ἑνὶ	οἴκῳ	διαμεμερισμένοι,
the	now	five	in	one	house	having been completely divided,

5140	1909	1417	2532	1417	1909	5140
τρεῖς	ἐπὶ	δυσὶν	καὶ	δύο	ἐπὶ	τρισίν,
three	on	two	and	two	on	three,

53	1266		3962	1909	5207	2532	5207	1909
	διαμερισθήσονται		πατὴρ	ἐπὶ	υἱῷ	καὶ	υἱὸς	ἐπὶ
	they will be completely divided		father	on	son	and	son	on

3962	3384	1909	08	2364	2532	2364	1909
πατρί,	μήτηρ	ἐπὶ	τὴν	θυγατέρα	καὶ	θυγάτηρ	ἐπὶ
father,	mother	on	the	daughter	and	daughter	on

08	3384	3994	1909	08	3565	846
τὴν	μητέρα,	πενθερὰ	ἐπὶ	τὴν	νύμφην	αὐτῆς
the	mother,	mother-in-law	on	the	bride	of her

2532	3565	1909	08	3994		**54**	3004		1161
καὶ	νύμφη	ἐπὶ	τὴν	πενθεράν.			Ἔλεγεν		δὲ
and	bride	on	the	mother-in-law.			He was saying		but

2532	015	3793	3752	3708		08	3507
καὶ	τοῖς	ὄχλοις·	ὅταν	ἴδητε		[τὴν]	νεφέλην
also	to the	crowds,	when	you might see		the	cloud

393	1909	1424	2112	3004	3754
ἀνατέλλουσαν	ἐπὶ	δυσμῶν,	εὐθέως	λέγετε	ὅτι
arising	on	west,	immediately	you say	that

3655	2064	2532	1096	3779		**55**	2532	3752
ὄμβρος	ἔρχεται,	καὶ	γίνεται	οὕτως·			καὶ	ὅταν
rain storm	comes,	and	it becomes	thusly;			and	when

3558	4154	3004	3754	2742	1510	2532
νότον	πνέοντα,	λέγετε	ὅτι	καύσων	ἔσται,	καὶ
south	blowing,	you say	that	burning heat	will be,	and

1096		**56**	5273	012	4383	06	1093	2532
γίνεται.			ὑποκριταί,	τὸ	πρόσωπον	τῆς	γῆς	καὶ
it becomes.			Hypocrites,	the	face	of	the earth	and

02	3772	3609a	1381	04	2540	1161
τοῦ	οὐρανοῦ	οἴδατε	δοκιμάζειν,	τὸν	καιρὸν	δὲ
of	the heaven	you know	to approve,	the	season	but

3778	4459	3756	3609a	1381		**57**	5101	1161	2532
τοῦτον	πῶς	οὐκ	οἴδατε	δοκιμάζειν;			Τί	δὲ	καὶ
this	how	not	you know	to approve?			What	but	also

575	1438	3756	2919	012	1342		**58**	5613	1063
ἀφ᾽	ἑαυτῶν	οὐ	κρίνετε	τὸ	δίκαιον;			ὡς	γὰρ
from	yourselves	not	you judge	the	right?			As	for

5217	3326	02	476	1473	1909	758	1722
ὑπάγεις	μετὰ	τοῦ	ἀντιδίκου	σου	ἐπ᾽	ἄρχοντα,	ἐν
you go off	with	the	opponent	of you	on	ruler,	in

07	3598	1325	2039	525	575	846	3379
τῇ	ὁδῷ	δὸς	ἐργασίαν	ἀπηλλάχθαι	ἀπ᾽	αὐτοῦ,	μήποτε
the way		give	working	to be released	from	him,	not then

2694	1473	4314	04	2923	2532	01
κατασύρῃ	σε	πρὸς	τὸν	κριτήν,	καὶ	ὁ
he might drag down	you	to	the	judge,	and	the

2923	1473	3860	03	4233	2532
κριτής	σε	παραδώσει	τῷ	πράκτορι,	καὶ
judge	you	will give over	to the	court officer,	and

01	4233	1473	906	1519	5438		**59**	3004
ὁ	πράκτωρ	σε	βαλεῖ	εἰς	φυλακήν.			λέγω
the court officer		you	throws	into	guard.			I say

1473	3756	3361	1831	1564	2193
σοι,	οὐ	μὴ	ἐξέλθῃς	ἐκεῖθεν,	ἕως
to you,	not	not	you might go out	from there,	until

2532	012	2078	3016	591		**13:1**	3918	1161
καὶ	τὸ	ἔσχατον	λεπτὸν	ἀποδῷς.			Παρῆσαν	δέ
also	the	last	lepton	you might give off.			Were present	but

5100   1722 846   03   2540   518   846   4012
τινες ἐν   αὐτῷ τῷ καιρῷ ἀπαγγέλλοντες αὐτῷ   περὶ
some   in   same the season telling   to him about
014 1057   3739   012 129   4091   3396   3326
τῶν Γαλιλαίων ὧν   τὸ αἷμα Πιλᾶτος ἔμιξεν μετὰ
the Galileans of whom the blood Pilate   mixed   with
018 2378   846   2   2532 611   3004
τῶν θυσιῶν   αὐτῶν.   καὶ ἀποκριθεὶς   εἶπεν
the sacrifices of them. And having answered he said
846   1380   3754 013 1057   3778   268
αὐτοῖς· δοκεῖτε   ὅτι   οἱ Γαλιλαῖοι οὗτοι ἁμαρτωλοὶ
to them, you think that the Galileans these sinners
3844   3956   016 1057   1096   3754   3778
παρὰ πάντας τοὺς Γαλιλαίους ἐγένοντο, ὅτι   ταῦτα
along all   the Galileans   became,   because these
3958   3780 3004 1473   235   1437 3361
πεπόνθασιν;   3 οὐχί, λέγω ὑμῖν, ἀλλ᾽ ἐὰν μὴ
they have suffered? Not, I say to you, but   except
3340   3956   3668   622   4 2228 1565
μετανοῆτε πάντες ὁμοίως ἀπολεῖσθε.   ἢ ἐκεῖνοι
you might all   likewise you will destroy Or those
change mind   yourselves.
013 1176a   1909 3739 4098   01 4444 1722 03 4611
οἱ δεκαοκτὼ ἐφ᾽ οὓς ἔπεσεν ὁ πύργος ἐν τῷ Σιλωὰμ
the eighteen on whom fell the tower in the Siloam
2532 615   846   1380   3754 846
καὶ ἀπέκτεινεν αὐτούς, δοκεῖτε ὅτι αὐτοὶ
and it killed   them,   you think that themselves
3781   1096   3844 3956   016 444   016
ὀφειλέται ἐγένοντο παρὰ πάντας τοὺς ἀνθρώπους τοὺς
debtors   became   along all   the men   the ones
2730   2419   5 3780 3004 1473   235
κατοικοῦντας Ἰερουσαλήμ; οὐχί, λέγω ὑμῖν, ἀλλ᾽
residing   Jerusalem?   Not, I say to you, but
1437 3361 3340   3956   5615
ἐὰν μὴ μετανοῆτε   πάντες ὡσαύτως
except you might change mind all   likewise
622   3004   1161 3778   08 3850
ἀπολεῖσθε.   6 Ἔλεγεν δὲ ταύτην τὴν παραβολήν·
you will destroy He was but this   the parallel
yourselves.   saying   story;
4808   2192 5100 5452   1722 03 290
συκῆν εἶχέν τις πεφυτευμένην   ἐν τῷ ἀμπελῶνι
fig tree had some having been planted in the vineyard
846   2532 2064   2212   2590 1722 846 2532 3756
αὐτοῦ, καὶ ἦλθεν ζητῶν καρπὸν ἐν αὐτῇ καὶ οὐχ
of him, and he came seeking fruit in it   and not
2147   7 3004   1161 4314 04 289   2400
εὗρεν.   εἶπεν δὲ πρὸς τὸν ἀμπελουργόν·   ἰδοὺ
he found. He said but to   the vineyard worker, look
5140   2094 575 3739 2064   2212   2590 1722 07
τρία ἔτη ἀφ᾽ οὗ ἔρχομαι ζητῶν καρπὸν ἐν τῇ
three years from which I come seeking fruit in the
4808   3778 2532 3756 2147   1581   3767 846
συκῇ   ταύτῃ καὶ οὐχ εὑρίσκω. ἔκκοψον [οὖν] αὐτήν,
fig tree this and not I find.   Cut off then it,
2444   2532 08 1093 2673   01 1161 611
ἱνατί καὶ τὴν γῆν καταργεῖ; 8 ὁ δὲ ἀποκριθεὶς
why   also the earth does it   The but having
                 abolish?   answered
3004   846   2962   863 846 2532 3778 012 2094
λέγει αὐτῷ· κύριε, ἄφες αὐτὴν καὶ τοῦτο τὸ ἔτος,
he says to him, master, allow it also this the year,
2193   3755 4626   4012 846 2532 906 2874   9 2579
ἕως   ὅτου σκάψω περὶ αὐτὴν καὶ βάλω κόπρια, κἂν
until when I might around it and might manure, and
      dig   throw   if
3303   4160   2590 1519 012 3195
μὲν   ποιήσῃ   καρπὸν εἰς τὸ μέλλον·
indeed it might make fruit in the being about to be;

who told him about the
Galileans whose blood
Pilate had mingled with
their sacrifices. [2]He asked
them, "Do you think that
because these Galileans
suffered in this way they
were worse sinners than all
other Galileans? [3]No, I tell
you; but unless you repent,
you will all perish as they
did. [4]Or those eighteen who
were killed when the tower
of Siloam fell on them—do
you think that they were
worse offenders than all the
others living in Jerusalem?
[5]No, I tell you; but unless
you repent, you will all
perish just as they did."

[6]Then he told this
parable: "A man had a fig
tree planted in his vineyard;
and he came looking for
fruit on it and found none.
[7]So he said to the gardener,
'See here! For three years I
have come looking for fruit
on this fig tree, and still I
find none. Cut it down!
Why should it be wasting
the soil?' [8]He replied, 'Sir,
let it alone for one more
year, until I dig around it
and put manure on it. [9]If it
bears fruit next year, well
and good;

but if not, you can cut it
down.'"

10 Now he was teaching
in one of the synagogues
on the sabbath. 11 And
just then there appeared a
woman with a spirit that
had crippled her for
eighteen years. She was
bent over and was quite
unable to stand up straight.
12 When Jesus saw her, he
called her over and said,
"Woman, you are set free
from your ailment."
13 When he laid his hands
on her, immediately she
stood up straight and
began praising God. 14 But
the leader of the synagogue,
indignant because Jesus
had cured on the sabbath,
kept saying to the crowd,
"There are six days on
which work ought to be
done; come on those days
and be cured, and not on
the sabbath day." 15 But
the Lord answered him and
said, "You hypocrites!
Does not each of you on the
sabbath untie his ox or his
donkey from the manger,
and lead it away to give it
water? 16 And ought not
this woman, a daughter
of Abraham whom Satan
bound for eighteen long
years, be set free from this
bondage on the sabbath
day?" 17 When he said this,
all his opponents were put
to shame;

1487	1161	3361	1065	1581		846		10	1510
εἰ	δὲ	μή	γε,	ἐκκόψεις		αὐτήν.			Ἦν
if	but	not	indeed,	you will cut off it.					He was

1161 1321 　　　1722 1520 018 　　4864 　　　1722 023
δὲ διδάσκων ἐν μιᾷ τῶν συναγωγῶν ἐν τοῖς
but teaching in one of the synagogues in the

4521　 11 2532 2400 1135 4151 2192 769
σάββασιν. 11 καὶ ἰδοὺ γυνὴ πνεῦμα ἔχουσα ἀσθενείας
sabbaths. And look woman spirit having weakness

2094 1176a 2532 1510 4794 2532
ἔτη δεκαοκτὼ καὶ ἦν συγκύπτουσα καὶ
years eighteen and she was+ +bending down with and

3361 1410 352 1519 012 3838
μὴ δυναμένη ἀνακύψαι εἰς τὸ παντελές.
not being able to bend up in the all-complete.

12 3708 1161 846 01 2424 4377 2532
ἰδὼν δὲ αὐτὴν ὁ Ἰησοῦς προσεφώνησεν καὶ
Having seen but her the Jesus sounded to and

3004 846 1135 630 06
εἶπεν αὐτῇ· γύναι, ἀπολέλυσαι τῆς
said to her, woman, you have been loosed off of the

769 1473 2532 2007 846 020 5495 2532
ἀσθενείας σου, 13 καὶ ἐπέθηκεν αὐτῇ τὰς χεῖρας· καὶ
weakness of you, and he set on her the hands; and

3916 461 2532 1392
παραχρῆμα ἀνωρθώθη καὶ ἐδόξαζεν
suddenly she was straightened up and she gave splendor

04 2316 611 1161 01 752
τὸν θεόν. 14 ἀποκριθεὶς δὲ ὁ ἀρχισυνάγωγος,
the God. Having answered but the synagogue ruler,

23 3754 011 4521 2323 01
ἀγανακτῶν ὅτι τῷ σαββάτῳ ἐθεράπευσεν ὁ
being indignant that in the sabbath healed the

2424 3004 03 3793 3754 1803 2250
Ἰησοῦς, ἔλεγεν τῷ ὄχλῳ ὅτι ἓξ ἡμέραι
Jesus, was saying to the crowd that six days

1510 1722 3739 1163 2038 1722 846 3767
εἰσὶν ἐν αἷς δεῖ ἐργάζεσθαι· ἐν αὐταῖς οὖν
there in which it is to work; in these then
are necessary

2064 2323 2532 3361 07 2250 010
ἐρχόμενοι θεραπεύεσθε καὶ μὴ τῇ ἡμέρᾳ τοῦ
going heal and not in the day of the

4521 15 611 1161 846 01 2962 2532 3004
σαββάτου. 15 ἀπεκρίθη δὲ αὐτῷ ὁ κύριος καὶ εἶπεν·
sabbath. Answered but him the Master and said,

5273 1538 1473 011 4521 3756
ὑποκριταί, ἕκαστος ὑμῶν τῷ σαββάτῳ οὐ
hypocrites, each of you in the sabbath not

3089 04 1016 846 2228 04 3688 575 06
λύει τὸν βοῦν αὐτοῦ ἢ τὸν ὄνον ἀπὸ τῆς
he looses the ox of him or the donkey from the

5336 2532 520 4222 16 3778 1161
φάτνης καὶ ἀπαγαγὼν ποτίζει; 16 ταύτην δὲ
feed trough and having led off gives drink? This but

2364 11 1510 3739 1210 01 4567 2400
θυγατέρα Ἀβραὰμ οὖσαν, ἣν ἔδησεν ὁ σατανᾶς ἰδοὺ
daughter Abraham being, whom bound the Adversary look

1176 2532 3638 2094 3756 1163 3089 575 02
δέκα καὶ ὀκτὼ ἔτη, οὐκ ἔδει λυθῆναι ἀπὸ τοῦ
ten and eight years, not was it to be loosed from the
necessary

1199 3778 07 2250 010 4521 17 2532 3778
δεσμοῦ τούτου τῇ ἡμέρᾳ τοῦ σαββάτου; 17 καὶ ταῦτα
chain this the day of the sabbath? And these

3004 846 2617 3956 013 480
λέγοντος αὐτοῦ κατῃσχύνοντο πάντες οἱ ἀντικείμενοι
saying him were being all the ones lying
shamed against

846   2532 3956 01   3793   5463   1909 3956   023
αὐτῷ, καὶ πᾶς ὁ ὄχλος ἔχαιρεν ἐπὶ πᾶσιν τοῖς
him, and all the crowd rejoiced at all the

1741   023 1096   5259 846   18 3004
ἐνδόξοις τοῖς γινομένοις ὑπ᾽ αὐτοῦ. Ἔλεγεν
in-splendor the ones becoming by him. He was saying

3767 5101   3664 1510 05 932   02   2316
οὖν· τίνι ὁμοία ἐστὶν ἡ βασιλεία τοῦ θεοῦ
then, in what like is the kingdom of the God

2532 5101   3666   846   19 3664 1510   2848
καὶ τίνι ὁμοιώσω αὐτήν; ὁμοία ἐστὶν κόκκῳ
and to what will I liken it? Like it is grain

4615   3739 2983   444   906   1519
σινάπεως, ὃν λαβὼν ἄνθρωπος ἔβαλεν εἰς
of mustard, that having taken man threw into

2779 1438   2532 837   2532 1096   1519
κῆπον ἑαυτοῦ, καὶ ηὔξησεν καὶ ἐγένετο εἰς
garden of himself, and it grew and it became into

1186   2532 021 4071   02   3772   2681
δένδρον, καὶ τὰ πετεινὰ τοῦ οὐρανοῦ κατεσκήνωσεν
tree, and the birds of the heaven set up a tent

1722 015 2798   846   20 2532 3825 3004   5101
ἐν τοῖς κλάδοις αὐτοῦ. Καὶ πάλιν εἶπεν· τίνι
in the branches of it. And again he said, to what

3666   08 932   02   2316   21 3664 1510
ὁμοιώσω τὴν βασιλείαν τοῦ θεοῦ; ὁμοία ἐστὶν
will I liken the kingdom of the God? Like it is

2219   3739 2983   1135 1470   1519 224
ζύμη, ἣν λαβοῦσα γυνὴ [ἐν]έκρυψεν εἰς ἀλεύρου
yeast, which having taken woman hid in in flour

4568 5140 2193 3739 2220   3650   22 2532
σάτα τρία ἕως οὗ ἐζυμώθη ὅλον. Καὶ
sata three until which was yeasted whole. And

1279   2596 4172   2532 2968   1321   2532
διεπορεύετο κατὰ πόλεις καὶ κώμας διδάσκων καὶ
he was traveling by cities and villages teaching and
through

4197   4160   1519 2414   23 3004   1161 5100
πορείαν ποιούμενος εἰς Ἱεροσόλυμα. Εἶπεν δέ τις
journey making to Jerusalem. Said but some

846   2962   1487 3641   013 4982   01
αὐτῷ· κύριε, εἰ ὀλίγοι οἱ σῳζόμενοι; ὁ
to him, Master, if few the being delivered? The

1161 3004 4314 846   24   75   1525   1223
δὲ εἶπεν πρὸς αὐτούς· ἀγωνίζεσθε εἰσελθεῖν διὰ
but said to them, contest to go into through

06   4728 2374   3754   4183   3004 1473 2212
τῆς στενῆς θύρας, ὅτι πολλοί, λέγω ὑμῖν, ζητήσουσιν
the narrow door, because many, I say to you, will seek

1525   2532 3756 2480   25 575 3739 302
εἰσελθεῖν καὶ οὐκ ἰσχύσουσιν. ἀφ᾽ οὗ ἂν
to go into and not they will be strong. From which -

1453   01   3617   2532 608
ἐγερθῇ ὁ οἰκοδεσπότης καὶ ἀποκλείσῃ
was raised the house supervisor and he might close off

08 2374 2532 757   1854   2476   2532
τὴν θύραν καὶ ἄρξησθε ἔξω ἑστάναι καὶ
the door and you might begin outside to stand and

2925   08 2374 3004   2962   455   1473 2532
κρούειν τὴν θύραν λέγοντες· κύριε, ἄνοιξον ἡμῖν, καὶ
to knock the door saying, Master, open to us, and

611   3004   1473 3756 3609a 1473 4159   1510
ἀποκριθεὶς ἐρεῖ ὑμῖν· οὐκ οἶδα ὑμᾶς πόθεν ἐστέ.
having he will to not I know you from you
answered say you, where are.

26 5119 757   3004   2068   1799 1473 2532
τότε ἄρξεσθε λέγειν· ἐφάγομεν ἐνώπιόν σου καὶ
Then you will begin to say, we ate before you and

---

and the entire crowd was rejoicing at all the wonderful things that he was doing.

18 He said therefore, "What is the kingdom of God like? And to what should I compare it? 19It is like a mustard seed that someone took and sowed in the garden; it grew and became a tree, and the birds of the air made nests in its branches."

20 And again he said, "To what should I compare the kingdom of God? 21It is like yeast that a woman took and mixed in with[a] three measures of flour until all of it was leavened."

22 Jesus[b] went through one town and village after another, teaching as he made his way to Jerusalem. 23Someone asked him, "Lord, will only a few be saved?" He said to them, 24"Strive to enter through the narrow door; for many, I tell you, will try to enter and will not be able. 25When once the owner of the house has got up and shut the door, and you begin to stand outside and to knock at the door, saying, 'Lord, open to us,' then in reply he will say to you, 'I do not know where you come from.' 26Then you will begin to say, 'We ate and

[a] Gk hid in
[b] Gk He

drank with you, and you taught in our streets.' 27But he will say, 'I do not know where you come from; go away from me, all you evildoers!' 28There will be weeping and gnashing of teeth when you see Abraham and Isaac and Jacob and all the prophets in the kingdom of God, and you yourselves thrown out. 29Then people will come from east and west, from north and south, and will eat in the kingdom of God. 30Indeed, some are last who will be first, and some are first who will be last."

31 At that very hour some Pharisees came and said to him, "Get away from here, for Herod wants to kill you." 32He said to them, "Go and tell that fox for me,*a* 'Listen, I am casting out demons and performing cures today and tomorrow, and on the third day I finish my work. 33Yet today, tomorrow, and the next day I must be on my way, because it is impossible for a prophet to be killed outside of Jerusalem.' 34Jerusalem, Jerusalem, the city that kills the prophets and stones those who are sent to

a Gk lacks *for me*

4095	2532	1722	019	4113		1473	1321
ἐπίομεν	καὶ	ἐν	ταῖς	πλατείαις		ἡμῶν	ἐδίδαξας·
we drank	and	in	the	wide places		of us	you taught;

27
2532	3004		3004	1473		3756	3609a	1473	4159
καὶ	ἐρεῖ		λέγων	ὑμῖν·		οὐκ	οἶδα	[ὑμᾶς]	πόθεν
and	he will speak		saying	to you,		not	I know	you	from where

1510	868	575	1473	3956	2040	93
ἐστέ·	ἀπόστητε	ἀπ'	ἐμοῦ	πάντες	ἐργάται	ἀδικίας.
you are;	stand off	from	me	all	workers	of unright.

28
1563	1510	01	2805	2532	01	1030	014
ἐκεῖ	ἔσται	ὁ	κλαυθμὸς	καὶ	ὁ	βρυγμὸς	τῶν
There	will be	the	crying	and	the	grinding	of the

3599	3752	3708	11	2532	2464	2532
ὀδόντων,	ὅταν	ὄψεσθε	Ἀβραὰμ	καὶ	Ἰσαὰκ	καὶ
teeth,	when	you will see	Abraham	and	Isaac	and

2384	2532	3956	016	4396	1722	07	932
Ἰακὼβ	καὶ	πάντας	τοὺς	προφήτας	ἐν	τῇ	βασιλείᾳ
Jacob	and	all	the	spokesmen	in	the	kingdom

02	2316	1473	1161	1544		1854	2532
τοῦ	θεοῦ,	ὑμᾶς	δὲ	ἐκβαλλομένους	ἔξω.		καὶ
of	God,	you	but	having been thrown out	outside.	29	And
the							

2240		575	395	2532	1424	2532	575	1005
ἥξουσιν		ἀπὸ	ἀνατολῶν	καὶ	δυσμῶν	καὶ	ἀπὸ	βορρᾶ
they will come		from	east	and	west	and	from	north

2532	3558	2532	347		1722	07	932	02
καὶ	νότου	καὶ	ἀνακλιθήσονται		ἐν	τῇ	βασιλείᾳ	τοῦ
and	south	and	they will recline		in	the	kingdom	of the

2316		2532	2400	1510	2078	3739	1510	4413
θεοῦ.	30	καὶ	ἰδοὺ	εἰσὶν	ἔσχατοι	οἳ	ἔσονται	πρῶτοι
God.		And	look	are	last	who	will be	first

2532	1510	4413	3739	1510	2078		1722	846
καὶ	εἰσὶν	πρῶτοι	οἳ	ἔσονται	ἔσχατοι.	31	Ἐν	αὐτῇ
and	are	first	who	will be	last.		In	same

07	5610	4334		5100	5330	3004	846
τῇ	ὥρᾳ	προσῆλθάν		τινες	Φαρισαῖοι	λέγοντες	αὐτῷ·
the	hour	came to		some	Pharisees	saying	to him,

1831	2532	4198	1782		3754	2264	2309	1473
ἔξελθε	καὶ	πορεύου	ἐντεῦθεν,		ὅτι	Ἡρῴδης	θέλει	σε
go out	and	travel	from here,		because	Herod	wants	you

615		2532	3004	846		4198
ἀποκτεῖναι.	32	καὶ	εἶπεν	αὐτοῖς·		πορευθέντες
to kill.		And	he said	to them,		having traveled

3004	07	258	3778	2400	1544	1140
εἴπατε	τῇ	ἀλώπεκι	ταύτῃ·	ἰδοὺ	ἐκβάλλω	δαιμόνια
say	to the	fox	this,	look	I throw out	demons

2532	2392	658		4594	2532	839	2532
καὶ	ἰάσεις	ἀποτελῶ		σήμερον	καὶ	αὔριον	καὶ
and	cures	I complete fully		today	and	tomorrow	and

07	5154	5048		4133	1163
τῇ	τρίτῃ	τελειοῦμαι.	33	πλὴν	δεῖ
in the	third	I am completed.		Except	it is necessary

1473	4594	2532	839	2532	07	2192
με	σήμερον	καὶ	αὔριον	καὶ	τῇ	ἐχομένῃ
me	today	and	tomorrow	and	in the	having

4198		3754	3756	1735	4396
πορεύεσθαι,		ὅτι	οὐκ	ἐνδέχεται	προφήτην
to travel,		because	not	it is possible	spokesman

622		1854	2419		2419
ἀπολέσθαι		ἔξω	Ἰερουσαλήμ.	34	Ἰερουσαλὴμ
to be destroyed		outside	Jerusalem.		Jerusalem,

2419	05	615	016	4396	2532
Ἰερουσαλήμ,	ἡ	ἀποκτείνουσα	τοὺς	προφήτας	καὶ
Jerusalem,	the one	killing	the	spokesmen	and

3036	016	649	4314
λιθοβολοῦσα	τοὺς	ἀπεσταλμένους	πρὸς
throwing-stones	the	ones having been delegated	to

846 4212 2309 1996 024
αὐτήν, ποσάκις ἠθέλησα ἐπισυνάξαι τὰ
her, how often I wanted to bring together the

5043 1473 3739 5158 3733 08 1438
τέκνα σου ὃν τρόπον ὄρνις τὴν ἑαυτῆς
children of you what manner hen the of herself

3555 5259 020 4420 2532 3756 2309
νοσσιὰν ὑπὸ τὰς πτέρυγας, καὶ οὐκ ἠθελήσατε.
young one under the wings, and not you wanted.

2400 863 1473 01 3624 1473
35 ἰδοὺ ἀφίεται ὑμῖν ὁ οἶκος ὑμῶν.
Look is being sent off to you the house of you.

3004 1161 1473 3756 3361 3708 1473 2193 2240 3753
λέγω [δὲ] ὑμῖν, οὐ μὴ ἴδητέ με ἕως [ἥξει ὅτε]
I say but to not not you me until will when
you, might see come

3004 2127 01 2064 1722 3686
εἴπητε· εὐλογημένος ὁ ἐρχόμενος ἐν ὀνόματι
you might having been the one coming in name
say, well spoken

2962 2532 1096 1722 011 2064 846 1519
κυρίου. **14:1** Καὶ ἐγένετο ἐν τῷ ἐλθεῖν αὐτὸν εἰς
of Master. And it became in the to go him into

3624 5100 014 758 014 5330 4521
οἶκόν τινος τῶν ἀρχόντων [τῶν] Φαρισαίων σαββάτῳ
house some of the rulers of the Pharisees in sabbath

2068 740 2532 846 1510 3906
φαγεῖν ἄρτον καὶ αὐτοὶ ἦσαν παρατηρούμενοι
to eat bread and themselves were+ +keeping watch

846 2532 2400 444 5100 1510 5203
αὐτόν. **2** Καὶ ἰδοὺ ἄνθρωπός τις ἦν ὑδρωπικὸς
him. And look man some was bitter-water

1715 846 2532 611 01 2424
ἔμπροσθεν αὐτοῦ. **3** καὶ ἀποκριθεὶς ὁ Ἰησοῦς
in front of him. And having answered the Jesus

3004 4314 016 3544 2532 5330 3004
εἶπεν πρὸς τοὺς νομικοὺς καὶ Φαρισαίους λέγων·
spoke to the lawyers and Pharisees saying,

1832 011 4521 2323 2228 3756a 013
ἔξεστιν τῷ σαββάτῳ θεραπεῦσαι ἢ οὔ; **4** οἱ
is it possible to the sabbath to heal or no? The

1161 2270 2532 1949 2390 846 2532
δὲ ἡσύχασαν. καὶ ἐπιλαβόμενος ἰάσατο αὐτὸν καὶ
but were quiet. And having taken on he cured him and

630 2532 4314 846 3004 5101 1473
ἀπέλυσεν. **5** καὶ πρὸς αὐτοὺς εἶπεν· τίνος ὑμῶν
he loosed off. And to them he said, who of you

5207 2228 1016 1519 5421 4098 2532 3756
υἱὸς ἢ βοῦς εἰς φρέαρ πεσεῖται, καὶ οὐκ
son or ox in well will fall, and not

2112 385 846 1722 2250 010
εὐθέως ἀνασπάσει αὐτὸν ἐν ἡμέρᾳ τοῦ
immediately will he draw up him in day of the

4521 2532 3756 2480 470 4314
σαββάτου; **6** καὶ οὐκ ἴσχυσαν ἀνταποκριθῆναι πρὸς
sabbath? And not they were to answer back to
were strong

3778 3004 1161 4314 016 2564 3850
ταῦτα. **7** Ἔλεγεν δὲ πρὸς τοὺς κεκλημένους παραβολήν,
these. He was but to the ones having parallel
saying been called story,

1907 4459 020 4411 1586 3004
ἐπέχων πῶς τὰς πρωτοκλισίας ἐξελέγοντο, λέγων
holding on how the first reclining were saying
places selecting,

4314 846 3752 2564 5259 5100 1519
πρὸς αὐτούς· **8** ὅταν κληθῇς ὑπό τινος εἰς
to them, when you might be called by some to

---

it! How often have I desired to gather your children together as a hen gathers her brood under her wings, and you were not willing! [35]See, your house is left to you. And I tell you, you will not see me until the time comes when[a] you say, 'Blessed is the one who comes in the name of the Lord.'"

CHAPTER 14

On one occasion when Jesus[b] was going to the house of a leader of the Pharisees to eat a meal on the sabbath, they were watching him closely. [2]Just then, in front of him, there was a man who had dropsy. [3]And Jesus asked the lawyers and Pharisees, "Is it lawful to cure people on the sabbath, or not?" [4]But they were silent. So Jesus[b] took him and healed him, and sent him away. [5]Then he said to them, "If one of you has a child[c] or an ox that has fallen into a well, will you not immediately pull it out on a sabbath day?" [6]And they could not reply to this.

7 When he noticed how the guests chose the places of honor, he told them a parable. [8]"When you are invited by someone to

---

[a] Other ancient authorities lack *the time comes when*
[b] Gk *he*
[c] Other ancient authorities read *a donkey*

a wedding banquet, do not sit down at the place of honor, in case someone more distinguished than you has been invited by your host; ⁹and the host who invited both of you may come and say to you, 'Give this person your place,' and then in disgrace you would start to take the lowest place. ¹⁰But when you are invited, go and sit down at the lowest place, so that when your host comes, he may say to you, 'Friend, move up higher'; then you will be honored in the presence of all who sit at the table with you. ¹¹For all who exalt themselves will be humbled, and those who humble themselves will be exalted."

12 He said also to the one who had invited him, "When you give a luncheon or a dinner, do not invite your friends or your brothers or your relatives or rich neighbors, in case they may invite you in return, and you would be repaid. ¹³But when you give a banquet, invite the poor, the crippled, the lame, and the blind. ¹⁴And you will be blessed, because they cannot repay you, for you will be repaid at the

1062	3361	2625	1519 08	4411
γάμους,	μὴ	κατακλιθῇς εἰς	τὴν	πρωτοκλισίαν,
wedding,	not	you might recline	in the	first reclining place,

3379	1784		1473 1510	2564	5259
μήποτε	ἐντιμότερός		σου ᾖ	κεκλημένος	ὑπ'
not then	more in honor of		you might be+	+having been	by
			you	called	

846	9	2532 2064	01	1473 2532 846	2564	3004
αὐτοῦ,		καὶ ἐλθὼν	ὁ	σὲ καὶ αὐτὸν	καλέσας	ἐρεῖ
him,		and having come	the	you and him	having called	will say

1473	1325 3778	5117	2532 5119 757
σοι·	δὸς τούτῳ	τόπον,	καὶ τότε ἄρξῃ
to you,	give to this	place,	and then you will begin

3326 152	04 2078	5117 2722	10	235 3752
μετὰ αἰσχύνης	τὸν ἔσχατον	τόπον κατέχειν.		ἀλλ' ὅταν
with shame	the last	place to hold on.		But when

2564	4198	377	1519 04
κληθῇς,	πορευθεὶς	ἀνάπεσε	εἰς τὸν
you might be called,	having traveled	recline	in the

2078	5117	2443 3752 2064	01	2564
ἔσχατον	τόπον,	ἵνα ὅταν ἔλθῃ	ὁ	κεκληκώς
last	place,	that when might come	the	having called

1473 3004	1473	5384	4320	511
σε ἐρεῖ	σοι·	φίλε,	προσανάβηθι	ἀνώτερον·
you will say	to you;	friend,	go up to	upper;

5119 1510	1473	1391	1799	3956	014
τότε ἔσται	σοι	δόξα	ἐνώπιον	πάντων	τῶν
then will be to	you	splendor	before	all	the ones

4873	1473	11	3754	3956 01	5312 1438
συνανακειμένων	σοι.		ὅτι	πᾶς ὁ	ὑψῶν ἑαυτὸν
reclining together	to you.		Because	all the one	himself elevating

5013	2532 01 5013	1438
ταπεινωθήσεται,	καὶ ὁ ταπεινῶν	ἑαυτὸν
will be humbled,	and the one humbling	himself

5312	12	3004	1161 2532 03
ὑψωθήσεται.		Ἔλεγεν	δὲ καὶ τῷ
will be elevated.		He was saying	but also to the

2564	846	3752 4160	712	2228
κεκληκότι	αὐτόν·	ὅταν ποιῇς	ἄριστον	ἢ
having called	him,	when you might do	meal	or

1173	3361 5455	016 5384	1473	3366	016
δεῖπνον,	μὴ φώνει	τοὺς φίλους	σου	μηδὲ	τοὺς
dinner,	not sound	the friends	of you	but not	the

80	1473	3366	016 4773	1473	3366
ἀδελφούς	σου	μηδὲ	τοὺς συγγενεῖς	σου	μηδὲ
brothers	of you	but not	the relatives	of you	but not

1069	4145	3379	2532 846
γείτονας	πλουσίους,	μήποτε	καὶ αὐτοὶ
neighbors	rich,	not then	also themselves

479	1473 2532 1096	468	1473
ἀντικαλέσωσίν	σε καὶ γένηται	ἀνταπόδομά	σοι.
might call back	you and it might become	given back	to you. again

13	235 3752 1403	4160	2564 4434
	ἀλλ' ὅταν δοχὴν	ποιῇς,	κάλει πτωχούς,
	But when reception	you might do,	call poor,

374 λ	5560	5185	14	2532 3107
ἀναπείρους,	χωλούς,	τυφλούς·		καὶ μακάριος
disabled,	lame,	blind;		and fortunate

1510	3754 3756 2192	467
ἔσῃ,	ὅτι οὐκ ἔχουσιν	ἀνταποδοῦναί
you will be,	that not they have	to give back

1473	467	1063 1473	1722 07
σοι,	ἀνταποδοθήσεται	γάρ σοι	ἐν τῇ
to you,	it will be given back again	for to you	in the

386	014	1342	**15**	191		1161	5100

ἀναστάσει τῶν δικαίων. **15** Ἀκούσας δέ τις
standing up of the right.   Having heard but some

014	4873		3778	3004	846	3107

τῶν συνανακειμένων ταῦτα εἶπεν αὐτῷ· μακάριος
of the ones reclining these said to him, fortunate
   together

3748	2068	740	1722 07	932	02	2316

ὅστις φάγεται ἄρτον ἐν τῇ βασιλείᾳ τοῦ θεοῦ.
who will eat bread in the kingdom of the God.

16	01	1161	3004	846	444	5100	4160

16 Ὁ δὲ εἶπεν αὐτῷ· ἄνθρωπός τις ἐποίει
   The but said to him, man some was making

1173	3173	2532 2564	4183	**17**	2532

δεῖπνον μέγα, καὶ ἐκάλεσεν πολλοὺς **17** καὶ
dinner great, and he called many   and

649	04	1401	846	07	5610 010

ἀπέστειλεν τὸν δοῦλον αὐτοῦ τῇ ὥρᾳ τοῦ
he delegated the slave of him to the hour of the

1173	3004	015	2564	2064

δείπνου εἰπεῖν τοῖς κεκλημένοις· ἔρχεσθε,
dinner to say to the ones having been called; come,

3754	2235	2092	1510	**18**	2532 757

ὅτι ἤδη ἕτοιμά ἐστιν. **18** καὶ ἤρξαντο
because already prepared it is. And they began

575	1520 3956	3868	01	4413	3004 846

ἀπὸ μιᾶς πάντες παραιτεῖσθαι. ὁ πρῶτος εἶπεν αὐτῷ,
from one all to reject. The first said to him,

68	59	2532 2192	318	1831

ἀγρὸν ἠγόρασα καὶ ἔχω ἀνάγκην ἐξελθὼν
field I bought and I have necessity having gone out

3708	846	2065	1473 2192 1473 3868

ἰδεῖν αὐτόν· ἐρωτῶ σε, ἔχε με παρῃτημένον.
to see it; I ask you, have me having rejected.

19	2532 2087	3004	2201	1016	59	4002 2532

19 καὶ ἕτερος εἶπεν, ζεύγη βοῶν ἠγόρασα πέντε καὶ
   And other said, yokes of oxen I bought five and

4198	1381	846	2065	1473 2192 1473

πορεύομαι δοκιμάσαι αὐτά· ἐρωτῶ σε, ἔχε με
I travel to approve them; I ask you, have me

3868	**20**	2532 2087	3004	1135	1060

παρῃτημένον. **20** καὶ ἕτερος εἶπεν, γυναῖκα ἔγημα
having rejected. And other said, woman I married

2532 1223	3778	3756 1410	2064	**21**	2532

καὶ διὰ τοῦτο οὐ δύναμαι ἐλθεῖν. **21** καὶ
and through this not I am able to come. And

3854	01	1401	518	03	2962	846

παραγενόμενος ὁ δοῦλος ἀπήγγειλεν τῷ κυρίῳ αὐτοῦ
having arrived the slave told to the master of him

3778	5119 3710	01	3617	3004

ταῦτα. τότε ὀργισθεὶς ὁ οἰκοδεσπότης εἶπεν
these. Then being angered the house supervisor said

03	1401	846	1831	5030	1519 020

τῷ δούλῳ αὐτοῦ· ἔξελθε ταχέως εἰς τὰς
to the slave of him, go out quickly into the

4113	2532 4505	06	4172	2532 016	4434

πλατείας καὶ ῥύμας τῆς πόλεως καὶ τοὺς πτωχοὺς
wide places and lanes of the city and the poor

2532 374a	2532 5185	2532 5560	1521

καὶ ἀναπείρους καὶ τυφλοὺς καὶ χωλοὺς εἰσάγαγε
and disabled and blind and lame lead in

5602	**22**	2532 3004	01	1401	2962	1096

ὧδε. **22** καὶ εἶπεν ὁ δοῦλος· κύριε, γέγονεν
here. And said the slave, master, it has become

3739 2004	2532 2089	5117 1510	**23**	2532 3004

ὃ ἐπέταξας, καὶ ἔτι τόπος ἐστίν. **23** καὶ εἶπεν
what you ordered, and still place there is. And said

01	2962	4314 04	1401	1831	1519 020	3598

ὁ κύριος πρὸς τὸν δοῦλον· ἔξελθε εἰς τὰς ὁδοὺς
the master to the slave, go out into the ways

resurrection of the righteous."

15 One of the dinner guests, on hearing this, said to him, "Blessed is anyone who will eat bread in the kingdom of God!" [16]Then Jesus[a] said to him, "Someone gave a great dinner and invited many. [17]At the time for the dinner he sent his slave to say to those who had been invited, 'Come; for everything is ready now.' [18]But they all alike began to make excuses. The first said to him, 'I have bought a piece of land, and I must go out and see it; please accept my regrets.' [19]Another said, 'I have bought five yoke of oxen, and I am going to try them out; please accept my regrets.' [20]Another said, 'I have just been married, and therefore I cannot come.' [21]So the slave returned and reported this to his master. Then the owner of the house became angry and said to his slave, 'Go out at once into the streets and lanes of the town and bring in the poor, the crippled, the blind, and the lame.' [22]And the slave said, 'Sir, what you ordered has been done, and there is still room.' [23]Then the master said to the slave, 'Go out into the roads

[a] Gk *he*

and lanes, and compel people to come in, so that my house may be filled. ²⁴For I tell you,ᵃ none of those who were invited will taste my dinner.' "

25 Now large crowds were traveling with him; and he turned and said to them, ²⁶"Whoever comes to me and does not hate father and mother, wife and children, brothers and sisters, yes, and even life itself, cannot be my disciple. ²⁷Whoever does not carry the cross and follow me cannot be my disciple. ²⁸For which of you, intending to build a tower, does not first sit down and estimate the cost, to see whether he has enough to complete it? ²⁹Otherwise, when he has laid a foundation and is not able to finish, all who see it will begin to ridicule him, ³⁰saying, 'This fellow began to build and was not able to finish.' ³¹Or what king, going out to wage war against another king, will not sit down first and consider whether he is able with ten thousand to oppose the one who comes against him with twenty thousand? ³²If he cannot, then,

ᵃ The Greek word for *you* here is plural

2532	5418		2532	315		1525		2443
καὶ	φραγμοὺς	καὶ	ἀνάγκασον	εἰσελθεῖν,		ἵνα
and	hedges	and	compel	to come in,		that

1072		1473	01	3624		3004 1063 1473	3754
γεμισθῇ	μου	ὁ	οἶκος·	²⁴	λέγω γὰρ ὑμῖν	ὅτι
might be full	of me	the	house;		I say for to you	that

3762	014	435	1565	014 2564
οὐδεὶς	τῶν	ἀνδρῶν	ἐκείνων	τῶν κεκλημένων
no one	of the	men	those	the having been called

1089		1473	010 1173		4848
γεύσεταί	μου	τοῦ δείπνου.	²⁵	Συνεπορεύοντο
will taste	of me	the dinner.		Were traveling together

1161 846		3793	4183	2532 4762		3004
δὲ	αὐτῷ	ὄχλοι	πολλοί, καὶ	στραφεὶς		εἶπεν
but	to him	crowds	many, and	having turned		he said

4314 846		1487 5100 2064	4314 1473 2532 3756
πρὸς αὐτούς·	²⁶	εἴ τις ἔρχεται	πρός με καὶ οὐ
to them,		if some comes	to me and not

3404	04	3962	1438		2532 08	3384	2532 08
μισεῖ	τὸν	πατέρα	ἑαυτοῦ	καὶ	τὴν μητέρα καὶ	τὴν
hates	the	father	of himself	and	the mother and	the

1135	2532 024 5043		2532 016	80		2532 020
γυναῖκα	καὶ τὰ τέκνα	καὶ τοὺς	ἀδελφοὺς καὶ	τὰς
woman	and the children	and the	brothers and	the

79	2089	5037	2532 08	5590 1438		3756
ἀδελφὰς	ἔτι	τε	καὶ	τὴν ψυχὴν ἑαυτοῦ,	οὐ
sisters	still	indeed	also	the soul of himself,	not

1410	1510 1473	3101		3748 3756 941
δύναται	εἶναί μου	μαθητής.	²⁷	ὅστις οὐ βαστάζει
is able	to be of me	learner.		Who not bears

04 4716	1438		2532 2064	3694 1473 3756
τὸν σταυρὸν	ἑαυτοῦ	καὶ ἔρχεται	ὀπίσω μου, οὐ
the cross	of himself	and comes	after me, not

1410	1510 1473	3101		5101 1063 1537 1473
δύναται	εἶναί μου	μαθητής.	²⁸	Τίς γὰρ ἐξ ὑμῶν
is able	to be of me	learner.		Who for from you

2309	4444	3618	3780 4413	2523
θέλων	πύργον	οἰκοδομῆσαι	οὐχὶ πρῶτον	καθίσας
wanting	tower	to build	not first	having sat

5585	08	1160	1487 2192	1519 535
ψηφίζει	τὴν	δαπάνην,	εἰ ἔχει	εἰς ἀπαρτισμόν;
calculates	the	cost,	if he has	into well fit?

²⁹	2443 3379		5087	846		2530	2532 3361
	ἵνα μήποτε	θέντος	αὐτοῦ	θεμέλιον	καὶ μὴ
	That then not	having set	of him	foundation	and not

2480	1615	3956	013 2334
ἰσχύοντος	ἐκτελέσαι	πάντες	οἱ θεωροῦντες
being strong	to finish	all	the ones watching

757	846 1702		30	3004	3754 3778	01
ἄρξωνται	αὐτῷ ἐμπαίζειν			λέγοντες ὅτι	οὗτος	ὁ
might begin	him to mock			saying that	this	the

444	757	3618	2532 3756 2480
ἄνθρωπος	ἤρξατο	οἰκοδομεῖν	καὶ οὐκ ἴσχυσεν
man	began	to build	and not he is strong

1615		2228 5101 935		4198		2087
ἐκτελέσαι.	³¹	Ἢ τίς βασιλεὺς	πορευόμενος	ἑτέρῳ
to finish.		Or what king	traveling	to other

935	4820		1519 4171	3780 2523
βασιλεῖ	συμβαλεῖν	εἰς πόλεμον	οὐχὶ καθίσας
king	to throw with	into war	not having sat

4413	1011		1487 1415	1510	1722 1176
πρῶτον	βουλεύσεται	εἰ	δυνατός	ἐστιν ἐν	δέκα
first	he will plan	if	power	he is in	ten

5505	5221	03		3326 1501	5505
χιλιάσιν	ὑπαντῆσαι	τῷ	μετὰ	εἴκοσι	χιλιάδων
thousands	to meet	the	one with	twenty	thousands

2064	1909 846		32	1487 1161 3361 1065		2089
ἐρχομένῳ	ἐπ' αὐτόν;			εἰ δὲ μή γε,		ἔτι
coming	on him?			If but not indeed,		still

846   4206   1510   4242   649   2065   024
αὐτοῦ πόρρω ὄντος πρεσβείαν ἀποστείλας   ἐρωτᾷ   τὰ
him   far   being envoy   having delegated he asks the

4314   1515   3779   3767 3956 1537 1473 3739 3756
πρὸς εἰρήνην. **33** οὕτως οὖν πᾶς ἐξ ὑμῶν ὃς οὐκ
to   peace.   Thusly then all from you who not

657   3956   023   1438   5225   3756
ἀποτάσσεται πᾶσιν τοῖς ἑαυτοῦ   ὑπάρχουσιν   οὐ
says good-bye to all the   of himself   possessions   not

1410   1510   1473   3101   2570   3767 09   217
δύναται εἶναί μου μαθητής. **34** Καλὸν οὖν τὸ ἅλας·
is able to be of me learner.   Good   then the salt;

1437 1161 2532 09   217   3471   1722 5101
ἐὰν δὲ καὶ τὸ ἅλας μωρανθῇ,   ἐν τίνι
if   but also the salt might become foolish, in what

741   3777   1519 1093 3777 1519
ἀρτυθήσεται; **35** οὔτε εἰς γῆν οὔτε εἰς
will it be seasoned?   Neither for earth nor for

2874   2111   1510   1854   906   846   01
κοπρίαν εὔθετόν ἐστιν, ἔξω βάλλουσιν αὐτό. ὁ
manure suitable it is, outside they throw it. The one
                                                  one

2192   3775 191   191   1510   1161 846
ἔχων ὦτα ἀκούειν ἀκουέτω. **15:1** ⁷Ησαν δὲ αὐτῷ
having ears to hear let hear.   Were+ but to him

1448   3956   013 5057   2532 013 268
ἐγγίζοντες πάντες οἱ τελῶναι καὶ οἱ ἁμαρτωλοὶ
+nearing   all   the tax men and the sinners

191   846   2 2532 1234   013
ἀκούειν αὐτοῦ.   καὶ διεγόγγυζον   οἱ
to hear him.   And were grumbling thoroughly the

5037 5330   2532 013 1122   3004   3754
τε Φαρισαῖοι καὶ οἱ γραμματεῖς λέγοντες ὅτι
both Pharisees and the writers   saying,   (")

3778   268   4327   2532 4906   846
οὗτος ἁμαρτωλοὺς προσδέχεται καὶ συνεσθίει αὐτοῖς.
this one sinners   awaits   and eats with them.

3 3004   1161 4314 846   08   3850   3778
Εἶπεν δὲ πρὸς αὐτοὺς τὴν παραβολὴν ταύτην
He said but to   them   the   parallel story this

3004   5101 444   1537 1473 2192   1540   4263
λέγων· **4** τίς ἄνθρωπος ἐξ ὑμῶν ἔχων ἑκατὸν πρόβατα
saying;   what man   from you having hundred sheep

2532 622   1537 846   1520 3756 2641
καὶ ἀπολέσας   ἐξ αὐτῶν ἓν οὐ καταλείπει
and having destroyed from them one not leaves behind

024   1752a   1767 1722 07   2048 2532 4198
τὰ ἐνενήκοντα ἐννέα ἐν τῇ ἐρήμῳ καὶ πορεύεται
the ninety   nine in the desert and travels

1909 012 622   2193   2147
ἐπὶ τὸ ἀπολωλὸς   ἕως εὕρῃ
on   the one having been destroyed until he might find

846   5 2532 2147   2007   1909 016   5606
αὐτό;   καὶ εὑρὼν ἐπιτίθησιν ἐπὶ τοὺς ὤμους
it?   And finding he sets on on   the   shoulders

846   5463   6 2532 2064   1519 04   3624
αὐτοῦ χαίρων   καὶ ἐλθὼν   εἰς τὸν ὅικον
of him rejoicing   and having come into the   house

4779   016   5384   2532 016   1069
συγκαλεῖ   τοὺς φίλους καὶ τοὺς γείτονας
he calls together the   friends and the   neighbors

3004   846   4796   1473 3754 2147   012
λέγων αὐτοῖς· συγχάρητέ μοι, ὅτι εὗρον τὸ
saying to them; rejoice with me, that I found the

4263   1473 012 622   7 3004
πρόβατόν μου τὸ ἀπολωλός.   λέγω
sheep   of me the one having been destroyed. I say

1473 3754 3779   5479 1722 03   3772   1510   1909
ὑμῖν ὅτι οὕτως χαρὰ ἐν τῷ οὐρανῷ ἔσται ἐπὶ
to you that thusly joy in the heaven will be on

---

while the other is still far away, he sends a delegation and asks for the terms of peace. ³³So therefore, none of you can become my disciple if you do not give up all your possessions.

34 "Salt is good; but if salt has lost its taste, how can its saltiness be restored? [a] ³⁵It is fit neither for the soil nor for the manure pile; they throw it away. Let anyone with ears to hear listen!"

CHAPTER 15

Now all the tax collectors and sinners were coming near to listen to him. ²And the Pharisees and the scribes were grumbling and saying, "This fellow welcomes sinners and eats with them."

3 So he told them this parable: ⁴"Which one of you, having a hundred sheep and losing one of them, does not leave the ninety-nine in the wilderness and go after the one that is lost until he finds it? ⁵When he has found it, he lays it on his shoulders and rejoices. ⁶And when he comes home, he calls together his friends and neighbors, saying to them, 'Rejoice with me, for I have found my sheep that was lost.' ⁷Just so, I tell you, there will be more joy in heaven over

---

[a] Or how can it be used for seasoning?

one sinner who repents than over ninety-nine righteous persons who need no repentance.

8 "Or what woman having ten silver coins,[a] if she loses one of them, does not light a lamp, sweep the house, and search carefully until she finds it? [9]When she has found it, she calls together her friends and neighbors, saying, 'Rejoice with me, for I have found the coin that I had lost.' [10]Just so, I tell you, there is joy in the presence of the angels of God over one sinner who repents."

11 Then Jesus[b] said, "There was a man who had two sons. [12]The younger of them said to his father, 'Father, give me the share of the property that will belong to me.' So he divided his property between them. [13]A few days later the younger son gathered all he had and traveled to a distant country, and there he squandered his property in dissolute living. [14]When he had spent everything, a severe famine took place throughout that country, and he began to be in need. [15]So he went and hired himself out to one of the citizens of that country, who sent him to his fields to feed the pigs. [16]He would gladly

a Gk drachmas, each worth about a day's wage for a laborer
b Gk he

1520	268		3340		2228	1909	1752a		1767
ἑνὶ	ἁμαρτωλῷ	μετανοοῦντι		ἢ	ἐπὶ	ἐνενήκοντα	ἐννέα	
one	sinner	changing mind	or	on	ninety	nine	

1342	3748	3756	5532	2192	3341
δικαίοις	οἵτινες	οὐ	χρείαν	ἔχουσιν	μετανοίας.
right	who	not	need	have	of change mind.

8 | 2228 | 5101 | 1135 | 1406 | | 2192 | 1176 | 1437 |
|---|---|---|---|---|---|---|---|
| Ἢ | τίς | γυνὴ | δραχμὰς | ἔχουσα | δέκα | ἐὰν |
| Or | what | woman | drachmas | having | ten | if |

622		1406	1520	3780	681		3088
ἀπολέσῃ		δραχμὴν	μίαν,	οὐχὶ	ἅπτει		λύχνον
she might destroy	drachma	one,	not	she lights	lamp

2532	4563	08	3614	2532	2212	1960	2193
καὶ	σαροῖ	τὴν	οἰκίαν	καὶ	ζητεῖ	ἐπιμελῶς	ἕως
and	sweeps	the	house	and	seeks	carefully	until

3739	2147		9	2532	2147
οὗ	εὕρῃ;			καὶ	εὑροῦσα
which	she might find?		And	having found

4779		020	5384	2532	1069	3004
συγκαλεῖ		τὰς	φίλας	καὶ	γείτονας	λέγουσα·
she calls together	the	friends	and	neighbors	saying;

4796	1473	3754	2147	08	1406	3739
συγχάρητέ	μοι,	ὅτι	εὗρον	τὴν	δραχμὴν	ἣν
rejoice with	me,	that	I found	the	drachma	which

622	10	3779	3004	1473	1096	5479
ἀπώλεσα.		οὕτως,	λέγω	ὑμῖν,	γίνεται	χαρὰ
I destroyed.	Thusly,	I say	to you,	becomes	joy

1799	014	32	02	2316	1909	1520	268
ἐνώπιον	τῶν	ἀγγέλων	τοῦ	θεοῦ	ἐπὶ	ἑνὶ	ἁμαρτωλῷ
before	the	messengers	of the	God	on	one	sinner

3340		3004	1537	1444		5100	2192	1417
μετανοοῦντι.	11	Εἶπεν	δέ·	ἄνθρωπός	τις	εἶχεν	δύο
changing mind.	Said	but;	man	some	had	two

5207	12	2532	3004	01	3501	846	03
υἱούς.		καὶ	εἶπεν	ὁ	νεώτερος	αὐτῶν	τῷ
sons.	And	said	the	newer	of them	to the

3962	3962	1325	1473	012	1911		3313	06
πατρί·	πάτερ,	δός	μοι	τὸ	ἐπιβάλλον	μέρος	τῆς
father;	father,	give	to me	the	throwing on	part	of the

3776	01	1161	1244	846	04	979	13	2532
οὐσίας.	ὁ	δὲ	διεῖλεν	αὐτοῖς	τὸν	βίον.		καὶ
substance.	The	but	divided	to them	the	life.	And

3326	3756	4183	2250	4863		3956
μετ'	οὐ	πολλὰς	ἡμέρας	συναγαγὼν		πάντα
after	not	many	days	having brought together	all

01	3501	5207	589	1519	5561	3117	2532
ὁ	νεώτερος	υἱὸς	ἀπεδήμησεν	εἰς	χώραν	μακρὰν	καὶ
the	newer	son	journeyed	into	country	far	and

1563	1287		08	3776	846
ἐκεῖ	διεσκόρπισεν		τὴν	οὐσίαν	αὐτοῦ
there	he scattered thoroughly	the	substance	of him

2198	811	14	1159		1161	846	3956
ζῶν	ἀσώτως.		δαπανήσαντος	δὲ	αὐτοῦ	πάντα
living	extravagantly.	Having spent	but of	him	all

1096	3042	2478	2596	08	5561	1565	2532
ἐγένετο	λιμὸς	ἰσχυρὰ	κατὰ	τὴν	χώραν	ἐκείνην,	καὶ
became	famine	strong	by	the	country	that,	and

846	757	5302	15	2532	4198
αὐτὸς	ἤρξατο	ὑστερεῖσθαι.		καὶ	πορευθεὶς
himself	began	to be in lack.	And	having traveled

2853	1520	014	4177	06	5561
ἐκολλήθη	ἑνὶ	τῶν	πολιτῶν	τῆς	χώρας
he was joined	to one	of the	citizens	of the	country

1565	2532	3992	846	1519	016	68	846
ἐκείνης,	καὶ	ἔπεμψεν	αὐτὸν	εἰς	τοὺς	ἀγροὺς	αὐτοῦ
that,	and	he sent	him	into	the	fields	of him

1006	1287	16	2532	1937
βόσκειν	χοίρους,		καὶ	ἐπεθύμει
to graze	pigs,	and	he was desiring

```
5526                1537  022  2769      3739  2068
χορτασθῆναι         ἐκ    τῶν κερατίων ὧν    ἤσθιον
to be satisfied    from  the  pods      that were eating
013 5519     2532 3762  1325           846        1519 1438
οἱ  χοῖροι, καὶ  οὐδεὶς ἐδίδου         αὐτῷ.  17  εἰς ἑαυτὸν
the pigs,   and  no one was giving     to him.     In himself
1161 2064          5346     4214      3407          02
δὲ   ἐλθὼν         ἔφη·     πόσοι     μίσθιοι       τοῦ
but  having come he said;  how many wage earners of the
3962  1473  4052         740        1473 1161
πατρός μου περισσεύονται ἄρτων,     ἐγὼ  δὲ
father of me have excess  breads,    I     but
3042    5602 622               450
λιμῷ   ὧδε  ἀπόλλυμαι.   18  ἀναστὰς
in famine here I destroy myself.    Having stood up
4198          4314 04  3962  1473   2532 3004
πορεύσομαι    πρὸς τὸν πατέρα μου  καὶ  ἐρῶ
I will travel to  the  father of me and  I will say
846         3962  264      1519 04  3772    2532 1799
αὐτῷ·      πάτερ, ἥμαρτον εἰς  τὸν οὐρανὸν καὶ  ἐνώπιόν
to him;    father, I sinned to  the heaven  and  before
1473  3765         1510 514    2564         5207 1473
σου, 19  οὐκέτι  εἰμὶ ἄξιος κληθῆναι    υἱός σου·
you,    no longer I am worthy to be called son of you;
4160     1473 5613 1520 014     3407         1473
ποίησόν με  ὡς  ἕνα τῶν  μίσθιων      σου.
make     me  as  one of the wage earners of you.
   2532 450               2064      4314 04  3962
20 καὶ  ἀναστὰς          ἦλθεν     πρὸς τὸν πατέρα
   And  having stood up he went to the  father
1438        2089  1161 846    3112   568        3708
ἑαυτοῦ.    Ἔτι   δὲ   αὐτοῦ μακρὰν ἀπέχοντος εἶδεν
of himself. Still but  of him far    having back  saw
846      01  3962     846     2532 4697       2532
αὐτὸν ὁ  πατὴρ αὐτοῦ καὶ  ἐσπλαγχνίσθη     καὶ
him   the father of him and he had affections and
5143       1968      1909 04  5137      846       2532
δραμὼν     ἐπέπεσεν ἐπὶ  τὸν τράχηλον αὐτοῦ καὶ
having run he fell on on  the  neck      of him and
2705           846       3004   1161 01  5207 846
κατεφίλησεν αὐτόν.  21  εἶπεν δὲ   ὁ  υἱὸς αὐτῷ·
kissed         him.     Said  but  the son  to him;
3962  264        1519 04  3772    2532 1799       1473
πάτερ, ἥμαρτον εἰς  τὸν οὐρανὸν καὶ  ἐνώπιόν σου,
father, I sinned to  the heaven  and  before    you,
3765         1510 514    2564         5207 1473 22 3004
οὐκέτι      εἰμὶ ἄξιος κληθῆναι    υἱός σου.      εἶπεν
no longer   I am worthy to be called son of you. Said
1161 01  3962     4314 016  1401      846        5036
δὲ   ὁ  πατὴρ πρὸς τοὺς δούλους αὐτοῦ, ταχὺ
but  the father to   the  slaves  of him, quickly
1627          4749       08   4413    2532 1746       846
ἐξενέγκατε στολὴν    τὴν πρώτην καὶ  ἐνδύσατε αὐτόν,
bring out  long robe  the first  and  put on     him,
2532 1325 1146      1519 08  5495  846    2532
καὶ  δότε δακτύλιον εἰς  τὴν χεῖρα αὐτοῦ καὶ
and  give ring       in   the hand  of him and
5266       1519 016  4228        23 2532 5342  04   3448
ὑποδήματα εἰς  τοὺς πόδας,       καὶ  φέρετε τὸν μόσχον
sandals    to   the  feet,         and  carry  the calf
04   4618      2380       2532 2068      2165
τὸν σιτευτόν, θύσατε,   καὶ  φαγόντες εὐφρανθῶμεν,
the wheat fed, sacrifice, and  having    let us be
                                     eaten     merry,
   3754      3778  01  5207 1473  3498    1510   2532
24 ὅτι       οὗτος ὁ  υἱός μου  νεκρὸς ἦν    καὶ
   because this   the son of me dead    he was and
```

have filled himself with[a] the pods that the pigs were eating; and no one gave him anything. [17]But when he came to himself he said, 'How many of my father's hired hands have bread enough and to spare, but here I am dying of hunger! [18]I will get up and go to my father, and I will say to him, "Father, I have sinned against heaven and before you; [19]I am no longer worthy to be called your son; treat me like one of your hired hands."' [20]So he set off and went to his father. But while he was still far off, his father saw him and was filled with compassion; he ran and put his arms around him and kissed him. [21]Then the son said to him, 'Father, I have sinned against heaven and before you; I am no longer worthy to be called your son.'[b] [22]But the father said to his slaves, 'Quickly, bring out a robe—the best one—and put it on him; put a ring on his finger and sandals on his feet. [23]And get the fatted calf and kill it, and let us eat and celebrate; [24]for this son of mine was dead and

---

a Other ancient authorities read *filled his stomach with*

b Other ancient authorities add *Treat me like one of your hired servants*

is alive again; he was lost and is found!' And they began to celebrate.

25 "Now his elder son was in the field; and when he came and approached the house, he heard music and dancing. 26He called one of the slaves and asked what was going on. 27He replied, 'Your brother has come, and your father has killed the fatted calf, because he has got him back safe and sound.' 28Then he became angry and refused to go in. His father came out and began to plead with him. 29But he answered his father, 'Listen! For all these years I have been working like a slave for you, and I have never disobeyed your command; yet you have never given me even a young goat so that I might celebrate with my friends. 30But when this son of yours came back, who has devoured your property with prostitutes, you killed the fatted calf for him!' 31Then the father[a] said to him, 'Son, you are always with me, and all that is mine is yours. 32But we had to celebrate and rejoice, because this brother of yours was dead and has come to life; he was lost and has been found.' "

CHAPTER 16

Then Jesus[a] said to the disciples,

[a] Gk he

326		1510	622		2532	2147		2532	757
ἀνέζησεν,		ἦν	ἀπολωλὼς	καὶ		εὑρέθη.		καὶ	ἤρξαντο
he lived		he	+having	and		was found.		And	they began
again,		was+	been destroyed						

2165			1510	1161	01	5207	846		01	4245
εὐφραίνεσθαι.	25	Ἦν	δὲ	ὁ	υἱὸς	αὐτοῦ	ὁ	πρεσβύτερος
to be merry.		Was	but	the	son	of him	the	older

1722	68		2532	5613	2064		1448		07	3614
ἐν	ἀγρῷ·	καὶ	ὡς	ἐρχόμενος	ἤγγισεν		τῇ		οἰκίᾳ,
in	field;	and	as	coming	he neared		to	the house,

191		4858		2532	5525		2532	4341
ἤκουσεν	συμφωνίας	καὶ	χορῶν,	26	καὶ	προσκαλεσάμενος
he heard	music	and	dancings,		and	having called to

1520	014	3816		4441		5101	302	1510
ἕνα	τῶν	παίδων		ἐπυνθάνετο	τί	ἂν	εἴη
one	of the	boy servants	he inquired	what	-	might be

3778		01	1161	3004	846		3754	01	80		1473
ταῦτα.	27	ὁ	δὲ	εἶπεν	αὐτῷ	ὅτι	ὁ	ἀδελφός	σου
these.		The	but	said	to him,	(")	the	brother	of you

2240		2532	2380		01	3962	1473	04	3448
ἥκει,	καὶ	ἔθυσεν	ὁ	πατήρ	σου	τὸν	μόσχον
has come,	and	sacrificed	the	father	of you	the	calf

04	4618		3754		5198		846	618
τὸν	σιτευτόν,	ὅτι	ὑγιαίνοντα	αὐτὸν	ἀπέλαβεν.
the	wheat fed,	because	being healthy	him	he took back.

	3710		1161	2532	3756	2309		1525
28	ὠργίσθη	δὲ	καὶ	οὐκ	ἤθελεν	εἰσελθεῖν,
	He was angry	but	also	not	he wanted	to go in,

01	1161	3962	846	1831		3870
ὁ	δὲ	πατὴρ	αὐτοῦ	ἐξελθὼν	παρεκάλει
the	but	father	of him	having come out	encouraged

846		01	1161	611		3004	03		3962
αὐτόν.	29	ὁ	δὲ	ἀποκριθεὶς	εἶπεν	τῷ	πατρὶ
him.		The	but	having answered	said	to	the father

846		2400	5118	2094	1398		1473	2532
αὐτοῦ·	ἰδοὺ	τοσαῦτα	ἔτη	δουλεύω	σοι	καὶ
of him;	look	so many	years	I slaved	to you	and

3763		1785	1473		3928		2532	1473
οὐδέποτε	ἐντολήν	σου	παρῆλθον,	καὶ	ἐμοὶ
but not ever	command	of you	I went along,	and	to me

3763		1325		2056	2443	3326	014	5384
οὐδέποτε	ἔδωκας	ἔριφον	ἵνα	μετὰ	τῶν	φίλων
but not ever	you gave	goat	that	with	the	friends

1473	2165		3753	1161	01	5207	1473	3778
μου	εὐφρανθῶ·	30	ὅτε	δὲ	ὁ	υἱός	σου	οὗτος
of me	I might merry;		when	but	the	son	of you	this

01	2719		1473	04	979	3326	4204		2064
ὁ	καταφαγών	σου	τὸν	βίον	μετὰ	πορνῶν	ἦλθεν,
the	having	of	the	life	with	prostitutes	came,
	eaten up	you					

2380		846	04	4618		3448		01	1161
ἔθυσας	αὐτῷ	τὸν	σιτευτὸν	μόσχον.	31	ὁ	δὲ
you	sacrificed	to him	the	wheat fed	calf.		The	but

3004	846		5043		1473	3842		3326	1473	1510	2532
εἶπεν	αὐτῷ·	τέκνον,	σὺ	πάντοτε	μετ᾽	ἐμοῦ	εἶ,	καὶ
said	to him;	child,	you	always	with	me	are,	and

3956	021	1699	4674	1510		2165		1161	2532
πάντα	τὰ	ἐμὰ	σά	ἐστιν·	32	εὐφρανθῆναι	δὲ	καὶ
all	the	mine	yours	are;		to be merry	but	also

5463		1163		3754	01	80
χαρῆναι	ἔδει,	ὅτι	ὁ	ἀδελφός
to rejoice	it was necessary,	because	the	brother

1473	3778	3498	1510	2532	2198		2532
σου	οὗτος	νεκρὸς	ἦν	καὶ	ἔζησεν,	καὶ
of you	this	dead	was	and	he lived,	also

622		2532	2147			3004
ἀπολωλὼς	καὶ	εὑρέθη.	16:1	Ἔλεγεν
having been destroyed	and	he was found.		He was saying

```
1161  2532  4314   016    3101        444         5100 1510
δὲ    καὶ   πρὸς  τοὺς  μαθητάς·   ἄνθρωπός  τις   ἦν
but   also  to     the   learners,  man        some was
4145       3739 2192   3623        2532 3778    1225
πλούσιος  ὃς   εἶχεν οἰκονόμον,  καὶ  οὗτος  διεβλήθη
rich       who  had    manager,    and  this    was accused
846      5613 1287                 024  5225
αὐτῷ   ὡς   διασκορπίζων       τὰ  ὑπάρχοντα
to him  as    scattering thoroughly the possessions
846       2532 5455          846    3004   846    5101
αὐτοῦ.  καὶ  φωνήσας      αὐτὸν εἶπεν αὐτῷ·  τί
of him.  And  having sounded him    he said  to him; what
3778  191    4012 1473  591     04  3056   06
τοῦτο ἀκούω περὶ σοῦ; ἀπόδος τὸν λόγον τῆς
this    I hear about you? Give back the word  of the
3622        1473   3756 1063 1410       2089
οἰκονομίας σου,  οὐ  γὰρ δύνῃ      ἔτι
management of you, not for  you are able still
3621         3004   1161 1722 1438    01  3623
οἰκονομεῖν.  εἶπεν δὲ  ἐν  ἑαυτῷ ὁ  οἰκονόμος·
to manage.   Said  but  in  himself the manager,
5101 4160        3754  01  2962   1473   851
τί   ποιήσω,     ὅτι  ὁ  κύριός μου  ἀφαιρεῖται
what will I do, because the master of me lifts off
08   3056      575 1473  4626       3756 2480
τὴν οἰκονομίαν ἀπ᾽ ἐμοῦ; σκάπτειν οὐκ ἰσχύω,
the management from me? To dig    not  I am strong,
1871      153           1097  5101 4160        2443
ἐπαιτεῖν αἰσχύνομαι.  ἔγνων τί   ποιήσω,     ἵνα
to ask on I am ashamed. I know what I might do, that
3752 3179         1537 06  3622        1209      1473
ὅταν μετασταθῶ ἐκ  τῆς οἰκονομίας δέξωνταί με
when I might be from the management they might me
     transferred                    welcome
1519 016  3624   846      2532 4341            1520
εἰς τοὺς οἴκους αὐτῶν. καὶ  προσκαλεσάμενος ἕνα
into the houses of them. And  having called to one
1538   014    5533          02      2962    1438
ἕκαστον τῶν χρεοφειλετῶν τοῦ  κυρίου ἑαυτοῦ
each     of the borrowers    of the master of himself
3004       03   4413    4214    3784    03
ἔλεγεν    τῷ  πρώτῳ· πόσον ὀφείλεις τῷ
he was saying to the first; how much you owe to the
2962  1473   01  1161 3004   1540   943   1637
κυρίῳ μου; ὁ  δὲ  εἶπεν· ἑκατὸν βάτους ἐλαίου.
master of me? The but said; hundred baths of oil.
01 1161 3004  846     1209     1473   024 1121      2532
ὁ  δὲ  εἶπεν αὐτῷ· δέξαι σου  τὰ γράμματα καὶ
The but said  to him; welcome of you the letters and
2523      5030     1125   4004          1899 2087
καθίσας  ταχέως γράψον πεντήκοντα.  ἔπειτα ἑτέρῳ
having sat quickly write fifty.         Then  to other
3004   1473 1161 4214   3784     01  1161 3004
εἶπεν· σὺ δὲ  πόσον ὀφείλεις; ὁ  δὲ  εἶπεν·
he said; you but how much owe? The one but said;
1540   2884    4621   3004   846    1209
ἑκατὸν κόρους σίτου. λέγει αὐτῷ· δέξαι
hundred kors   of wheat. He says to him; welcome
1473  024 1121      2532 1125   3589          2532
σου  τὰ γράμματα καὶ  γράψον ὀγδοήκοντα.  καὶ
of you the letters and  write eighty.         And
1867      01  2962   04  3623       06  93
ἐπήνεσεν ὁ  κύριος τὸν οἰκονόμον τῆς ἀδικίας
praised on the master the manager  of the unright
3754  5430       4160       3754   013 5207 02
ὅτι  φρονίμως ἐποίησεν· ὅτι  οἱ  υἱοὶ τοῦ
because thoughtfully he did; because the sons of the
165    3778   5429         5228 016  5207   010
αἰῶνος τούτου φρονιμώτεροι ὑπὲρ τοὺς υἱοὺς τοῦ
age    this   more thoughtful above the  sons  of the
```

"There was a rich man who had a manager, and charges were brought to him that this man was squandering his property. 2So he summoned him and said to him, 'What is this that I hear about you? Give me an accounting of your management, because you cannot be my manager any longer.' 3Then the manager said to himself, 'What will I do, now that my master is taking the position away from me? I am not strong enough to dig, and I am ashamed to beg. 4I have decided what to do so that, when I am dismissed as manager, people may welcome me into their homes.' 5So, summoning his master's debtors one by one, he asked the first, 'How much do you owe my master?' 6He answered, 'A hundred jugs of olive oil.' He said to him, 'Take your bill, sit down quickly, and make it fifty.' 7Then he asked another, 'And how much do you owe?' He replied, 'A hundred containers of wheat.' He said to him, 'Take your bill and make it eighty.' 8And his master commended the dishonest manager because he had acted shrewdly; for the children of this age are more shrewd in dealing with

their own generation than
are the children of light.
⁹And I tell you, make
friends for yourselves by
means of dishonest wealth*a*
so that when it is gone,
they may welcome you into
the eternal homes.*b*

10 "Whoever is faithful
in a very little is faithful
also in much; and whoever
is dishonest in a very little
is dishonest also in much.
¹¹If then you have not been
faithful with the dishonest
wealth,*a* who will entrust to
you the true riches? ¹²And
if you have not been faithful
with what belongs to
another, who will give you
what is your own? ¹³No
slave can serve two masters;
for a slave will either hate
the one and love the other,
or be devoted to the one
and despise the other. You
cannot serve God and
wealth."*a*

14 The Pharisees, who
were lovers of money, heard
all this, and they ridiculed
him. ¹⁵So he said to them,
"You are those who justify
yourselves in the sight of
others; but God knows
your hearts; for what is
prized by human beings is
an abomination in the sight
of God.

16 "The law and the
prophets were in effect until
John came; since then the
good news of the kingdom
of God is proclaimed, and
everyone tries to enter it by
force.*c*

a Gk *mammon*
b Gk *tents*
c Or *everyone is strongly urged
to enter it*

| 5457 | 1519 08 | 1074 | 08 | 1438 | 1510 |

φωτὸς εἰς τὴν γενεὰν τὴν ἑαυτῶν εἰσιν.
light in the generation the of themselves are.

9 Καὶ ἐγὼ ὑμῖν λέγω, ἑαυτοῖς ποιήσατε
2532 1473 1473 3004 1438 4160
And I to you say, to yourselves make

φίλους ἐκ τοῦ μαμωνᾶ τῆς ἀδικίας, ἵνα ὅταν
5384 1537 02 3126 06 93 2443 3752
friends from the mamon of the unright, that when

ἐκλίπῃ δέξωνται ὑμᾶς εἰς τὰς αἰωνίους σκηνάς.
1587 1209 1473 1519 020 166 4633
it might they might you into the eternal tents.
leave off welcome

10 Ὁ πιστὸς ἐν ἐλαχίστῳ καὶ ἐν πολλῷ πιστός
01 4103 1722 1646 2532 1722 4183 4103
The trustful in least and in much trustful

ἐστιν, καὶ ὁ ἐν ἐλαχίστῳ ἄδικος καὶ ἐν πολλῷ
1510 2532 01 1722 1646 94 2532 1722 4183
is, and the in least unright also in much

ἄδικός ἐστιν. 11 εἰ οὖν ἐν τῷ ἀδίκῳ μαμωνᾷ
94 1510 1487 3767 1722 03 94 3126
unright is. If then in the unright mamon

πιστοὶ οὐκ ἐγένεσθε, τὸ ἀληθινὸν τίς ὑμῖν
4103 3756 1096 012 228 5101 1473
trustful not you became, the true who to you

πιστεύσει; 12 καὶ εἰ ἐν τῷ ἀλλοτρίῳ
4100 2532 1487 1722 011 245
will trust? And if in the belonging to another

πιστοὶ οὐκ ἐγένεσθε, τὸ ὑμέτερον τίς ὑμῖν
4103 3756 1096 012 5212 5101 1473
trustful not you become, the yours who to you

δώσει; 13 Οὐδεὶς οἰκέτης δύναται δυσὶ κυρίοις
1325 3762 3610 1410 1417 2962
will give? No one house servant is able two masters

δουλεύειν· ἢ γὰρ τὸν ἕνα μισήσει καὶ τὸν
1398 2228 1063 04 1520 3404 2532 04
to slave; or for the one he will hate and the

ἕτερον ἀγαπήσει, ἢ ἑνὸς ἀνθέξεται καὶ τοῦ
2087 25 2228 1520 472 2532 02
other he will love, or one he will hold on and the

ἑτέρου καταφρονήσει. οὐ δύνασθε θεῷ
2087 2706 3756 1410 2316
other he will think down on. Not you are able to God

δουλεύειν καὶ μαμωνᾷ. 14 Ἤκουον δὲ ταῦτα πάντα
1398 2532 3126 191 1161 3778 3956
to slave and to mamon. Were hearing but these all

οἱ Φαρισαῖοι φιλάργυροι ὑπάρχοντες καὶ
013 5330 5366 5225 2532
the Pharisees lovers of silver existing and

ἐξεμυκτήριζον αὐτόν. 15 καὶ εἶπεν αὐτοῖς· ὑμεῖς
1592 846 2532 3004 846 1473
were mocking at him. And he said to them; you

ἐστε οἱ δικαιοῦντες ἑαυτοὺς ἐνώπιον τῶν
1510 013 1344 1438 1799 014
are the ones making right yourselves before the

ἀνθρώπων, ὁ δὲ θεὸς γινώσκει τὰς καρδίας ὑμῶν·
444 01 1161 2316 1097 020 2588 1473
men, the but God knows the hearts of you;

ὅτι τὸ ἐν ἀνθρώποις ὑψηλὸν βδέλυγμα ἐνώπιον
3754 09 1722 444 5308 946 1799
because the in men high abomination before

τοῦ θεοῦ. 16 Ὁ νόμος καὶ οἱ προφῆται μέχρι
02 2316 01 3551 2532 013 4396 3360
the God. The law and the spokesmen until

Ἰωάννου· ἀπὸ τότε ἡ βασιλεία τοῦ θεοῦ
2491 575 5119 05 932 02 2316
John; from then the kingdom of the God

εὐαγγελίζεται καὶ πᾶς εἰς αὐτὴν βιάζεται.
2097 2532 3956 1519 846 971
is told good message and all into it force.

17
2123 / εὐκοπώτερον / Easier labor
1161 / δέ / but
1510 / ἐστιν / it is
04 / τὸν / the
3772 / οὐρανὸν / heaven
2532 / καὶ / and
08 / τὴν / the
1093 / γῆν / earth

3928 / παρελθεῖν / to go along
2228 / ἢ / or
02 / τοῦ / the
3551 / νόμου / law
1520 / μίαν / one
2762 / κεραίαν / point
4098 / πεσεῖν. / to fall.

18 3956 / Πᾶς / All

01 / ὁ / the
630 / ἀπολύων / one loosing off
08 / τὴν / the
1135 / γυναῖκα / woman
846 / αὐτοῦ / of him
2532 / καὶ / and
1060 / γαμῶν / marrying

2087 / ἑτέραν / other
3431 / μοιχεύει, / commits adultery,
2532 / καὶ / and
01 / ὁ / the
630 / ἀπολελυμένην / one having loosed off
575 / ἀπὸ / from
435 / ἀνδρὸς / man

1060 / γαμῶν / marrying
3431 / μοιχεύει. / commits adultery.

19 444 / Ἄνθρωπος / Man
1161 / δέ / but
5100 / τις / some
1510 / ἦν / was

4145 / πλούσιος, / rich,
2532 / καὶ / and
1737 / ἐνεδιδύσκετο / he was putting on
4209 / πορφύραν / purple
2532 / καὶ / and
1040 / βύσσον / linen

2165 / εὐφραινόμενος / being merry
2596 / καθ᾽ / by
2250 / ἡμέραν / day
2988 / λαμπρῶς. / brightly.

20 4434 / πτωχὸς / Poor
1161 / δέ / but
5100 / τις / some

3686 / ὀνόματι / in name
2976 / Λάζαρος / Lazarus
906 / ἐβέβλητο / had been thrown
4314 / πρὸς / to
04 / τὸν / the
4440 / πυλῶνα / gate
846 / αὐτοῦ / of him

1669 / εἱλκωμένος / having been full of sores

21 2532 / καὶ / and
1937 / ἐπιθυμῶν / desiring
5526 / χορτασθῆναι / to be satisfied
575 / ἀπὸ / from
022 / τῶν / the

4098 / πιπτόντων / falling
575 / ἀπὸ / from
06 / τῆς / the
5132 / τραπέζης / table
02 / τοῦ / of the
4145 / πλουσίου· / the rich;
235 / ἀλλὰ / but
2532 / καὶ / also

013 / οἱ / the
2965 / κύνες / dogs
2064 / ἐρχόμενοι / coming
1952a / ἐπέλειχον / were licking
024 / τὰ / the
1668 / ἕλκη / sores
846 / αὐτοῦ. / of him.

22 1096 / ἐγένετο / It became
1161 / δὲ / but
599 / ἀποθανεῖν / to die
04 / τὸν / the
4434 / πτωχὸν / poor
2532 / καὶ / and
667 / ἀπενεχθῆναι / to be carried off

846 / αὐτὸν / him
5259 / ὑπὸ / by
014 / τῶν / the
32 / ἀγγέλων / messengers
1519 / εἰς / to
04 / τὸν / the
2859 / κόλπον / lap
11 / Ἀβραάμ· / Abraham;

599 / ἀπέθανεν / died
1161 / δὲ / but
2532 / καὶ / also
01 / ὁ / the
4145 / πλούσιος / rich
2532 / καὶ / and
2290 / ἐτάφη. / was buried.

23 2532 / καὶ / And

1722 / ἐν / in
03 / τῷ / the
86 / ᾅδῃ / hades
1869 / ἐπάρας / having lifted up
016 / τοὺς / the
3788 / ὀφθαλμοὺς / eyes

846 / αὐτοῦ, / of him,
5259 / ὑπάρχων / existing
5225 / ἐν / in
014 / βασάνοις, / torments,
32 / ὁρᾷ / he sees
1519 / ᾿Αβραὰμ / Abraham
... 11 / Ἀβραὰμ /
575 / ἀπὸ / from

3113 / μακρόθεν / from far
2532 / καὶ / and
2976 / Λάζαρον / Lazarus
1722 / ἐν / in
015 / τοῖς / the
2859 / κόλποις / laps
846 / αὐτοῦ. / of him.

24 2532 / καὶ / And
846 / αὐτὸς / himself
5455 / φωνήσας / having sounded
3004 / εἶπεν· / he said;
3962 / πάτερ / father

11 / Ἀβραάμ, / Abraham,
1653 / ἐλέησόν / mercy
1473 / με / me
2532 / καὶ / and
3992 / πέμψον / send
2976 / Λάζαρον / Lazarus
2443 / ἵνα / that

911 / βάψῃ / he might dip
012 / τὸ / the
206 / ἄκρον / tip
02 / τοῦ / of the
1147 / δακτύλου / finger
846 / αὐτοῦ / of him
5204 / ὕδατος / of water

2532 / καὶ / and
2711 / καταψύξῃ / he might cool
08 / τὴν / the
1100 / γλῶσσάν / tongue
1473 / μου, / of me,
3754 / ὅτι / because

3600 / ὀδυνῶμαι / I am tormented
1722 / ἐν / in
07 / τῇ / the
5395 / φλογὶ / flame
3778 / ταύτῃ. / this.

25 3004 / εἶπεν / Said
1161 / δὲ / but

---

[17]But it is easier for heaven and earth to pass away, than for one stroke of a letter in the law to be dropped.

18 "Anyone who divorces his wife and marries another commits adultery, and whoever marries a woman divorced from her husband commits adultery.

19 "There was a rich man who was dressed in purple and fine linen and who feasted sumptuously every day. [20]And at his gate lay a poor man named Lazarus, covered with sores, [21]who longed to satisfy his hunger with what fell from the rich man's table; even the dogs would come and lick his sores. [22]The poor man died and was carried away by the angels to be with Abraham.[a] The rich man also died and was buried. [23]In Hades, where he was being tormented, he looked up and saw Abraham far away with Lazarus by his side.[b] [24]He called out, 'Father Abraham, have mercy on me, and send Lazarus to dip the tip of his finger in water and cool my tongue; for I am in agony in these flames.' [25]But Abraham said,

---

a Gk to Abraham's bosom
b Gk in his bosom

'Child, remember that during your lifetime you received your good things, and Lazarus in like manner evil things; but now he is comforted here, and you are in agony. ²⁶Besides all this, between you and us a great chasm has been fixed, so that those who might want to pass from here to you cannot do so, and no one can cross from there to us.' ²⁷He said, 'Then, father, I beg you to send him to my father's house— ²⁸for I have five brothers—that he may warn them, so that they will not also come into this place of torment.' ²⁹Abraham replied, 'They have Moses and the prophets; they should listen to them.' ³⁰He said, 'No, father Abraham; but if someone goes to them from the dead, they will repent.' ³¹He said to him, 'If they do not listen to Moses and the prophets, neither will they be convinced even if someone rises from the dead.' "

CHAPTER 17

Jesus*a* said to his disciples, "Occasions for stumbling are bound to come, but woe to anyone by whom they come! ²It would be better for you if a millstone were hung around your neck

a Gk He

	5043	3403		3754 618			024 18
Ἀβραάμ·	τέκνον,	μνήσθητι	ὅτι	ἀπέλαβες		τὰ	ἀγαθά
Abraham;	child,	remember	that	you took		from the	goods

1473	1722 07	2222	1473	2532	2976	3668	024
σου	ἐν τῇ	ζωῇ	σου,	καὶ	Λάζαρος	ὁμοίως	τὰ
of you	in the	life	of you,	and	Lazarus	likewise	the

2556	3568	1161	5602	3870		1473	1161
κακά·	νῦν	δὲ	ὧδε	παρακαλεῖται,		σὺ	δὲ
bad;	now	but	here	he is encouraged,		you	but

3600		2532	1722	3956	3778	3342	1473
ὀδυνᾶσαι.	**26**	καὶ	ἐν	πᾶσι	τούτοις	μεταξὺ	ἡμῶν
are in torment.		And	in	all	these	between	us

2532	1473	5490	3173	4741		3704
καὶ	ὑμῶν	χάσμα	μέγα	ἐστήρικται,		ὅπως
and	you	chasm	great	has been strengthened,		so that

013	2309		1224		1759a	4314	1473
οἱ	θέλοντες		διαβῆναι		ἔνθεν	πρὸς	ὑμᾶς
the ones	wanting		to go through		from here	toward	you

3361	1410		3366		1564	4314	1473
μὴ	δύνωνται,		μηδὲ		ἐκεῖθεν	πρὸς	ἡμᾶς
not	they might be able,		but not		from there	toward	us

1276		3004	1161	2065	1473	3767
διαπερῶσιν.	**27**	εἶπεν	δέ·	ἐρωτῶ	σε	οὖν,
they might cross over.		He said	but;	I ask	you	then,

3962	2443	3992		846	1519 04	3624	02
πάτερ,	ἵνα	πέμψῃς		αὐτὸν	εἰς τὸν	οἶκον	τοῦ
father,	that	you might send		him	to the	house	of the

3962	1473		2192	1063	4002	80	3704
πατρός	μου,	**28**	ἔχω	γὰρ	πέντε	ἀδελφούς,	ὅπως
father	of me,		I have	for	five	brothers,	so that

1263		846		2443	3361	2532	846
διαμαρτύρηται		αὐτοῖς,		ἵνα	μὴ	καὶ	αὐτοὶ
he might testify		to them,		that	not	also	themselves
thoroughly							

2064		1519 04	5117	3778	06	931		3004
ἔλθωσιν		εἰς τὸν	τόπον	τοῦτον	τῆς	βασάνου.	**29**	λέγει
might go		into the	place	this	of the	torment.		Says

1161	11		2192	3475	2532	016	4396
δὲ	Ἀβραάμ·		ἔχουσι	Μωϋσέα	καὶ	τοὺς	προφήτας·
but	Abraham;		they have	Moses	and	the	spokesmen;

191		846		01	1161	3004	3780	3962
ἀκουσάτωσαν		αὐτῶν.	**30**	ὁ	δὲ	εἶπεν·	οὐχί,	πάτερ
let hear		them.		The	but	said;	not,	father

11		235	1437	5100	575	3498	4198	4314
Ἀβραάμ,		ἀλλ᾽	ἐάν	τις	ἀπὸ	νεκρῶν	πορευθῇ	πρὸς
Abraham,		but	if	some	from	dead	might travel	to

846	3340			3004	1161	846
αὐτοὺς	μετανοήσουσιν.		**31**	εἶπεν	δὲ	αὐτῷ·
them	they will change mind.			He said	but	to him;

1487	3475	2532	014	4396	3756	191	3761
εἰ	Μωϋσέως	καὶ	τῶν	προφητῶν	οὐκ	ἀκούουσιν,	οὐδ᾽
if	Moses	and	the	spokesmen	not	they hear,	but not

1437	5100	1537	3498	450		3982
ἐάν	τις	ἐκ	νεκρῶν	ἀναστῇ		πεισθήσονται.
if	some	from	dead	might stand		they might be
				up		persuaded.

	3004		1161	4314	016	3101	846
17:1	Εἶπεν		δὲ	πρὸς	τοὺς	μαθητὰς	αὐτοῦ·
	He said		but	to	the	learners	of him;

418		1510	010	024	4625	3361	2064
ἀνένδεκτόν		ἐστιν	τοῦ	τὰ	σκάνδαλα	μὴ	ἐλθεῖν,
unacceptable		it is	of the	the	offenses	not	to come,

4133	3759	1223		3739	2064		3081	846
πλὴν	οὐαὶ	δι᾽		οὗ	ἔρχεται·	**2**	λυσιτελεῖ	αὐτῷ
except	woe	through		whom	it comes;		it is more	to him
								advantageous

1487	3037	3457	4029		4012	04	5137
εἰ	λίθος	μυλικὸς	περίκειται		περὶ	τὸν	τράχηλον
if	stone	of mill	be set around		around	the	neck

846	2532	4496		1519	08	2281	2228
αὐτοῦ	καὶ	ἔρριπται		εἰς	τὴν	θάλασσαν	ἢ
of him	and	he has been flung		into	the	sea	or

2443	4624		014	3398	3778	1520
ἵνα	σκανδαλίσῃ		τῶν	μικρῶν	τούτων	ἕνα.
that	he might offend		of the	small	of these	one.

3
4337	1438		1437	264	01	80	1473
προσέχετε	ἑαυτοῖς.		Ἐὰν	ἁμάρτῃ	ὁ	ἀδελφός	σου
Hold to	themselves.		If	might sin	the	brother	of you

2008	846	2532	1437	3340
ἐπιτίμησον	αὐτῷ,	καὶ	ἐὰν	μετανοήσῃ
admonish	him,	and	if	he might change mind

863	846		2532	1437	2034	06	2250
ἄφες	αὐτῷ.	**4**	καὶ	ἐὰν	ἑπτάκις	τῆς	ἡμέρας
send off	him.		And	if	seven times	of the	day

264	1519	1473	2532	2034	1994
ἁμαρτήσῃ	εἰς	σὲ	καὶ	ἑπτάκις	ἐπιστρέψῃ
he might sin	to	you	and	seven times	he might return

4314	1473	3004	3340	863
πρὸς	σὲ	λέγων·	μετανοῶ,	ἀφήσεις
to	you	saying;	I change mind,	you will send off

846		2532	3004	013	652	03	2962	4369
αὐτῷ.	**5**	Καὶ	εἶπαν	οἱ	ἀπόστολοι	τῷ	κυρίῳ·	πρόσθες
him.		And	said	the	delegates	to the	Master,	set to

1473	4102		3004	1161	01	2962	1487	2192	4102
ἡμῖν	πίστιν.	**6**	εἶπεν	δὲ	ὁ	κύριος·	εἰ	ἔχετε	πίστιν
us	trust.		Said	but	the	Master;	if	you have	trust

5613	2848	4615	3004	302	07
ὡς	κόκκον	σινάπεως,	ἐλέγετε	ἂν	τῇ
as	grain	of mustard,	you were saying	-	to the

4807	3778	1610	2532	5452	1722
συκαμίνῳ [ταύτῃ]·	ἐκριζώθητι	καὶ	φυτεύθητι	ἐν
mulberry this;	be rooted out	and	be planted in

07	2281	2532	5219	302	1473		5101	1161	1537
τῇ	θαλάσσῃ·	καὶ	ὑπήκουσεν	ἂν	ὑμῖν.	**7**	Τίς	δὲ	ἐξ
the	sea;	and	it obeyed	-	you.		Who	but	from

1473	1401	2192	722	2228	4165	3739
ὑμῶν	δοῦλον	ἔχων	ἀροτριῶντα	ἢ	ποιμαίνοντα,	ὃς
you	slave	having	plowing	or	shepherding,	who

1525	1537	02	68	3004	846
εἰσελθόντι	ἐκ	τοῦ	ἀγροῦ	ἐρεῖ	αὐτῷ·
having come in	from	the	field	will say	to him;

2112	3928	377		235	3780
εὐθέως	παρελθὼν	ἀνάπεσε,	**8**	ἀλλ᾽	οὐχὶ
immediately	having come along	recline,		but	not

3004	846	2090	5101	1172	2532
ἐρεῖ	αὐτῷ·	ἑτοίμασον	τί	δειπνήσω	καὶ
will he say	to him;	prepare	what	I might dine	and

4024	1247	1473	2193	2068	2532	4095
περιζωσάμενος	διακόνει	μοι	ἕως	φάγω	καὶ	πίω,
having encircled himself	serve	me	until	I might eat	and	might drink,

2532	3326	3778	2068	2532	4095	1473		3361
καὶ	μετὰ	ταῦτα	φάγεσαι	καὶ	πίεσαι	σύ;	**9**	μὴ
and	after	these	will eat	and	will drink	you?		Not

2192	5485	03	1401	3754	4160	024
ἔχει	χάριν	τῷ	δούλῳ	ὅτι	ἐποίησεν	τὰ
he has	favor	to the	slave	because	he did	the things

1299		3779	2532	1473	3752
διαταχθέντα;	**10**	οὕτως	καὶ	ὑμεῖς,	ὅταν
having been directed?		Thusly	also	you,	when

4160	3956	024	1299	1473
ποιήσητε	πάντα	τὰ	διαταχθέντα	ὑμῖν,
you might do	all	the	having been directed	to you,

3004	3754	1401	888	1510	3739	3784
λέγετε	ὅτι	δοῦλοι	ἀχρεῖοί	ἐσμεν,	ὃ	ὠφείλομεν
say,	(")	slaves	unneeded	we are,	what	we were owing

4160	4160		2532	1096	1722	011	4198
ποιῆσαι	πεποιήκαμεν.	**11**	Καὶ	ἐγένετο	ἐν	τῷ	πορεύεσθαι
to do	we have done.		And	it became	in	the	to travel

and you were thrown into the sea than for you to cause one of these little ones to stumble. [3]Be on your guard! If another disciple[a] sins, you must rebuke the offender, and if there is repentance, you must forgive. [4]And if the same person sins against you seven times a day, and turns back to you seven times and says, 'I repent,' you must forgive."

[5]The apostles said to the Lord, "Increase our faith!" [6]The Lord replied, "If you had faith the size of a[b] mustard seed, you could say to this mulberry tree, 'Be uprooted and planted in the sea,' and it would obey you.

[7]"Who among you would say to your slave who has just come in from plowing or tending sheep in the field, 'Come here at once and take your place at the table'? [8]Would you not rather say to him, 'Prepare supper for me, put on your apron and serve me while I eat and drink; later you may eat and drink'? [9]Do you thank the slave for doing what was commanded? [10]So you also, when you have done all that you were ordered to do, say, 'We are worthless slaves; we have done only what we ought to have done!'"

[11]On the way to

[a] Gk *your brother*
[b] Gk *faith as a grain of*

Jerusalem Jesus[a] was going through the region between Samaria and Galilee. [12]As he entered a village, ten lepers[b] approached him. Keeping their distance, [13]they called out, saying, "Jesus, Master, have mercy on us!" [14]When he saw them, he said to them, "Go and show yourselves to the priests." And as they went, they were made clean. [15]Then one of them, when he saw that he was healed, turned back, praising God with a loud voice. [16]He prostrated himself at Jesus'[c] feet and thanked him. And he was a Samaritan. [17]Then Jesus asked, "Were not ten made clean? But the other nine, where are they? [18]Was none of them found to return and give praise to God except this foreigner?" [19]Then he said to him, "Get up and go on your way; your faith has made you well."

20 Once Jesus[a] was asked by the Pharisees when the kingdom of God was coming, and he answered, "The kingdom of God is not coming with things that can be observed; [21]nor will they say, 'Look, here it is!' or 'There it is!' For, in fact, the kingdom of God is among[d] you."

22 Then he said

[a] Gk he
[b] The terms leper and leprosy can refer to several diseases
[c] Gk his
[d] Or within

1519   2419   2532 846   1330
εἰς   Ἰερουσαλὴμ καὶ   αὐτὸς   διήρχετο
into Jerusalem and   himself was going through
1223   3319   4540   2532 1056   12 2532
διὰ   μέσον   Σαμαρείας καὶ Γαλιλαίας.   Καὶ
through middle Samaria   and Galilee.   And
1525   846   1519 5100 2968   528   846
εἰσερχομένου αὐτοῦ εἰς τινα κώμην ἀπήντησαν [αὐτῷ]
going into   him   into some village met   him
1176 3015   435   3739 2476   4207   13 2532
δέκα λεπροὶ ἄνδρες, οἳ ἔστησαν πόρρωθεν   καὶ
ten lepers men,   who stood   from far   and
846   142   5456 3004   2424
αὐτοὶ ἦραν   φωνὴν λέγοντες· Ἰησοῦ
themselves lifted up sound saying;   Jesus
1988   1653   1473   14 2532 3708
ἐπιστάτα,   ἐλέησον ἡμᾶς.   καὶ ἰδὼν
Master teacher, mercy   us.   And having seen
3004   846   4198   1925   1438
εἶπεν αὐτοῖς· πορευθέντες   ἐπιδείξατε ἑαυτοὺς
he said to them; having traveled show on   yourselves
015   2409   2532 1096   1722 011 5217
τοῖς ἱερεῦσιν. καὶ ἐγένετο ἐν   τῷ ὑπάγειν
to the priests. And it became in   the to go off
846   2511   15 1520 1161 1537 846
αὐτοὺς ἐκαθαρίσθησαν.   εἷς δὲ ἐξ αὐτῶν,
them   they were cleaned. One but from them,
3708   3754 2390   5290   3326 5456
ἰδὼν   ὅτι ἰάθη, ὑπέστρεψεν μετὰ φωνῆς
having seen that he was cured, returned   with sound
3173   1392   04 2316   16 2532 4098   1909
μεγάλης δοξάζων   τὸν θεόν,   καὶ ἔπεσεν ἐπὶ
great   giving splendor the God,   and he fell on
4383   3844   016 4228 846   2168
πρόσωπον παρὰ τοὺς πόδας αὐτοῦ εὐχαριστῶν
face   beside the feet of him giving good favor
046   2532 846   1510 4541   17 611   1161
αὐτῷ· καὶ αὐτὸς ἦν Σαμαρίτης.   ἀποκριθεὶς δὲ
to him; and himself was Samaritan. Having answered but
01 2424   3004   3780 013 1176 2511   013 1161
ὁ Ἰησοῦς εἶπεν· οὐχὶ οἱ δέκα ἐκαθαρίσθησαν; οἱ δὲ
the Jesus said; not the ten were cleaned? The but
1767 4226   18 3756 2147   5290
ἐννέα ποῦ;   οὐχ εὑρέθησαν ὑποστρέψαντες
nine where? Not they were found having returned
1325   1391   03   2316 1487 3361 01 241
δοῦναι δόξαν τῷ θεῷ εἰ μὴ ὁ ἀλλογενὴς
to give splendor to the God except the other race
3778   19 2532 3004   846   450   4198
οὗτος;   καὶ εἶπεν αὐτῷ· ἀναστὰς πορεύου·
this?   And he said to him; having stood up travel;
05 4102 1473 4982   1473 20 1905
ἡ πίστις σου σέσωκέν σε.   Ἐπερωτηθεὶς
the trust of you has delivered you. Having been
                                          asked on
1161 5259 014 5330   4219 2064 05 932
δὲ ὑπὸ τῶν Φαρισαίων πότε ἔρχεται ἡ βασιλεία
but by the Pharisees when comes the kingdom
02   2316 611   846   2532 3004 3756 2064
τοῦ θεοῦ ἀπεκρίθη αὐτοῖς καὶ εἶπεν· οὐκ ἔρχεται
of the God he answered to them and said; not comes
05 932   02   2316 3326 3907   21 3761
ἡ βασιλεία τοῦ θεοῦ μετὰ παρατηρήσεως,   οὐδὲ
the kingdom of the God with watch keeping,   but not
3004   2400 5602 2228 1563   2400 1063 05
ἐροῦσιν·   ἰδοὺ ὧδε ἤ· ἐκεῖ, ἰδοὺ γὰρ ἡ
they will say; look here or; there, look for the
932   02   2316 1787   1473 1510   3004   1161
βασιλεία τοῦ θεοῦ ἐντὸς ὑμῶν ἐστιν. 22 Εἶπεν δὲ
kingdom of the God within you is.   He said but

```
4314  016   3101      2064           2250      3753
πρὸς  τοὺς  μαθητάς·  ἐλεύσονται  ἡμέραι  ὅτε
to    the   learners;  will come    days     when
1937              1520 018    2250      02      5207 02
ἐπιθυμήσετε     μίαν  τῶν    ἡμερῶν  τοῦ   υἱοῦ  τοῦ
you will desire  one   of the  days     of the  son   of the
444          3708 2532 3756 3708          2532 3004
ἀνθρώπου  ἰδεῖν καὶ  οὐκ  ὄψεσθε.   23  καὶ  ερ̣οῦσιν
man        to see and  not you will see.     And they will say
1473     2400  1563    2228  2400 5602   3361
ὑμῖν·  ἰδοὺ ἐκεῖ,  [ἤ·] ἰδοὺ ὧδε·  μὴ
to you;  look there,  or;  look here;   not
565          3366    1377             5618
ἀπέλθητε  μηδὲ  διώξητε.    24  ὥσπερ
you might go off but not you might pursue.   As indeed
1063 05 796        797          1537 06  5259    04
γὰρ ἡ  ἀστραπὴ  ἀστράπτουσα  ἐκ  τῆς  ὑπὸ  τὸν
for the  lightning  flashing       from the under the
3772      1519 08  5259    3772      2989    3779      1510
οὐρανὸν  εἰς  τὴν ὑπ᾽  οὐρανὸν  λάμπει,  οὕτως  ἔσται
heaven   into the under heaven   shines,  thusly will be
01  5207 02   444            1722 07  2250     846
ὁ  υἱὸς τοῦ  ἀνθρώπου [ἐν τῇ  ἡμέρᾳ αὐτοῦ].
the son of the man        in the  day   of him.
     4413   1161 1163       .   846     4183    3958
25  πρῶτον δὲ   δεῖ            αὐτὸν  πολλὰ  παθεῖν
    First   but  it is necessary him    many   to suffer
1532 593           575 06  1074    3778        2532
καὶ  ἀποδοκιμασθῆναι ἀπὸ  τῆς  γενεᾶς ταύτης.  26  καὶ
and  to be rejected    by  the  generation this.    And
2531  1096      1722 019 2250     3575     3779
καθὼς  ἐγένετο  ἐν  ταῖς  ἡμέραις Νῶε,   οὕτως
just as it became in  the   days    of Noah, thusly
1510      2532 1722 019 2250    02      5207 02
ἔσται  καὶ  ἐν  ταῖς  ἡμέραις τοῦ  υἱοῦ τοῦ
it will be·also in  the   days    of the son  of the
444          27  2068                 4095       1060
ἀνθρώπου·      ἤσθιον,           ἔπινον,  ἐγάμουν,
man;            they were eating,  drinking,  marrying,
1060a                 891      3739  2250      1525
ἐγαμίζοντο,        ἄχρι   ἧς  ἡμέρας εἰσῆλθεν
being given in marriage, until which day    went into
3575 1519 08  2787       2532 2064  01  2627          2532
Νῶε  εἰς  τὴν κιβωτὸν καὶ  ἦλθεν ὁ  κατακλυσμὸς καὶ
Noah into the box       and  came  the flood         and
622           3956        3668      2531    1096
ἀπώλεσεν  πάντας.  28  ὁμοίως  καθὼς  ἐγένετο
it destroyed all.       Likewise just as it became
1722 019 2250     3091    2068              4095
ἐν  ταῖς  ἡμέραις Λώτ·  ἤσθιον,          ἔπινον,
in  the   days    of Lot; they were eating,  drinking,
59          4453    5452      3618              3739    1161
ἠγόραζον,  ἐπώλουν, ἐφύτευον, ᾠκοδόμουν·  29  ᾗ   δὲ
buying,    selling,  planting,  building;      in which but
2250  1831     3091 575   4670        1026       4442 2532
ἡμέρᾳ ἐξῆλθεν Λὼτ ἀπὸ  Σοδόμων, ἔβρεξεν  πῦρ  καὶ
day   went out Lot from Sodom,   it rained fire and
2303   575   3772    2532 622       3956        2596
θεῖον  ἀπ᾽ οὐρανοῦ καὶ  ἀπώλεσεν  πάντας.  30  κατὰ
sulphur from heaven  and  it destroyed all.       By
024 846  1510   3739      2250   01  5207 02   444
τὰ  αὐτὰ ἔσται ἦ  ἡμέρᾳ ὁ  υἱὸς τοῦ  ἀνθρώπου
the same will be in which day   the son of the  man
601            31  1722 1565    07  2250 3739 1510
ἀποκαλύπτεται.   ἐν  ἐκείνη τῇ  ἡμέρᾳ ὃς  ἔσται
is uncovered.      In  that   the  day   who will be
1909 010 1430    2532 021 4632   846      1722 07  3614
ἐπὶ  τοῦ δώματος καὶ  τὰ  σκεύη αὐτοῦ ἐν  τῇ  οἰκίᾳ,
on   the roof     and  the pots  of him in  the  house,
```

to the disciples, "The days are coming when you will long to see one of the days of the Son of Man, and you will not see it. [23] They will say to you, 'Look there!' or 'Look here!' Do not go, do not set off in pursuit. [24] For as the lightning flashes and lights up the sky from one side to the other, so will the Son of Man be in his day.[a] [25] But first he must endure much suffering and be rejected by this generation. [26] Just as it was in the days of Noah, so too it will be in the days of the Son of Man. [27] They were eating and drinking, and marrying and being given in marriage, until the day Noah entered the ark, and the flood came and destroyed all of them. [28] Likewise, just as it was in the days of Lot: they were eating and drinking, buying and selling, planting and building, [29] but on the day that Lot left Sodom, it rained fire and sulfur from heaven and destroyed all of them [30]—it will be like that on the day that the Son of Man is revealed. [31] On that day, anyone on the housetop who has belongings in the house

[a] Other ancient authorities lack *in his day*

must not come down to take
them away; and likewise
anyone in the field must not
turn back. ³²Remember
Lot's wife. ³³Those who
try to make their life secure
will lose it, but those who
lose their life will keep it.
³⁴I tell you, on that night
there will be two in one
bed; one will be taken and
the other left. ³⁵There will
be two women grinding
meal together; one will be
taken and the other left."ᵃ
³⁷Then they asked him,
"Where, Lord?" He said
to them, "Where the corpse
is, there the vultures will
gather."

CHAPTER 18

Then Jesusᵇ told them a
parable about their need
to pray always and not to
lose heart. ²He said, "In a
certain city there was a
judge who neither feared
God nor had respect for
people. ³In that city there
was a widow who kept
coming to him and saying,
'Grant me justice against
my opponent.' ⁴For a while
he refused; but later he said
to himself, 'Though I have
no fear of God and no
respect for anyone, ⁵yet
because this widow keeps
bothering me,

ᵃ Other ancient authorities add
verse 36, "Two will be in the field;
one will be taken and the other
left."
ᵇ Gk he

3361	2597	142		846	2532 01		1722	68
μὴ	καταβάτω	ἆραι		αὐτά,	καὶ ὁ		ἐν	ἀγρῷ
not	let go down	to lift up		them,	and the		one in	field

3668		3361	1994		1519 024	3694
ὁμοίως		μὴ	ἐπιστρεψάτω		εἰς τὰ	ὀπίσω.
likewise		not	let return		into the	after.

32 | 3421 | | 06 | 1135 | | 3091 | | 33 | 3739 | 1437 |
| μνημονεύετε | | τῆς | γυναικὸς | | Λώτ. | | | ὃς | ἐὰν |
| Remember | | the | woman | | of Lot. | | | Who | if |

2212		08	5590	846		4046
ζητήσῃ		τὴν	ψυχὴν	αὐτοῦ		περιποιήσασθαι
he might seek		the	soul	of him		to acquire

622		846		3739 1161	302	622
ἀπολέσει		αὐτήν,		ὃς δ'	ἂν	ἀπολέσῃ
will destroy it,		who		but -	might	destroy

2225			846	34	3004	1473		3778		07
ζῳογονήσει			αὐτήν.		λέγω	ὑμῖν,		ταύτῃ		τῇ
will preserve life it.					I say	to you,		in this		the

3571	1510		1417	1909	2825		1520	01	1520
νυκτὶ	ἔσονται		δύο	ἐπὶ	κλίνης	μιᾶς,	ὁ	εἷς
night	will be		two	on	bed		one,	the	one

3880			2532 01		2087	863
παραλημφθήσεται			καὶ ὁ		ἕτερος	ἀφεθήσεται·
will be taken along			and the		other	will be sent off;

35 | 1510 | | 1417 | 229 | | 1909 012 846 | | 05 | 1520 |
| ἔσονται | | δύο | ἀλήθουσαι | | ἐπὶ τὸ αὐτό, | | ἡ | μία |
| there will be+ | | two | +grinding | | on the same, | | the | one |

3880		05	1161	2087	863
παραλημφθήσεται,		ἡ	δὲ	ἑτέρα	ἀφεθήσεται.
will be taken along,		the	but	other	will be sent off.
along,

37 | 2532 611 | | | 3004 | 846 | | 4226 | 2962 |
| καὶ | ἀποκριθέντες | | λέγουσιν | αὐτῷ· | | ποῦ, | κύριε; |
| And | having answered | | they say | to him; | | where | Master? |

01	1161	3004	846		3699 09	4983	1563	2532 013
ὁ	δὲ	εἶπεν	αὐτοῖς·		ὅπου τὸ	σῶμα,	ἐκεῖ	καὶ οἱ
The	but	said	to them;		where the	body,	there	also the

105	1996		18:1		3004		1161
ἀετοὶ	ἐπισυναχθήσονται.				Ἔλεγεν		δὲ
eagles	will be brought together on.				He was saying		but

3850		846	4314 012	1163		3842
παραβολὴν		αὐτοῖς	πρὸς τὸ	δεῖν		πάντοτε
parallel story		to them	to the	it is necessary		always

4336	846		2532 3361	1457a
προσεύχεσθαι	αὐτοὺς	καὶ	μὴ	ἐγκακεῖν,
to pray	them	and	not	to give in to bad,

2 | 3004 | | 2923 5100 1510 | 1722 | 5100 4172 | 04 | 2316 3361 |
| λέγων· | | κριτής τις ἦν | ἔν | τινι πόλει | τὸν | θεὸν μὴ |
| saying; | | judge some was | in | some city | the | God not |

5399		2532 444		3361 1788		5503
φοβούμενος	καὶ	ἄνθρωπον	μὴ	ἐντρεπόμενος	3	χήρα
fearing	and	man	not	regarding.		Widow

1161 1510 1722 07	4172		1565	2532 2064		4314
δὲ ἦν ἐν τῇ	πόλει		ἐκείνῃ	καὶ ἤρχετο		πρὸς
but was in the	city		that	and was coming		to

846	3004	1556		1473 575	02	476
αὐτὸν	λέγουσα·	ἐκδίκησόν		με ἀπὸ	τοῦ	ἀντιδίκου
him	saying;	bring out		right me	from the	opponent

1473	4	2532 3756 2309		1909 5550	3326
μου.		καὶ οὐκ ἤθελεν		ἐπὶ χρόνον.	μετὰ
of me.		And not he was wanting		on time.	After

1161 3778	3004	1722 1438		1487 2532 04	2316
δὲ	ταῦτα	εἶπεν ἐν ἑαυτῷ·		εἰ καὶ	τὸν θεὸν
but	these	he said in himself;		if also	the God

3756 5399		3761	444		1788	5	1223
οὐ	φοβοῦμαι	οὐδὲ	ἄνθρωπον		ἐντρέπομαι,		διά
not	I fear	but not	man		I regard,		because

1065	012 3930		1473 2873	08	5503	3778
γε	τὸ παρέχειν		μοι κόπον	τὴν	χήραν	ταύτην
indeed	the to hold along		to me labor	the	widow	this

```
1556                    846    2443 3361 1519 5056
ἐκδικήσω               αὐτήν, ἵνα μὴ εἰς τέλος
I will bring out right her,   that not in   completion
2064     5299          1473      3004  1161 01  2962
ἐρχομένη ὑπωπιάζῃ      με.  6 ᵗΕιπεν δὲ  ὁ  κύριος·
coming   she might weary me.   Said   but the  Master;
191      5101 01  2923   06   93      3004    7 01
ἀκούσατε τί  ὁ κριτὴς τῆς ἀδικίας λέγει·     ὁ
hear     what the judge of the unright says;     the
1161 2316 3756 3361 4160      08   1557
δὲ  θεὸς οὐ  μὴ ποιήσῃ  τὴν ἐκδίκησιν
but God not not might do the bring out right
014    1588      846    014    994      846
τῶν ἐκλεκτῶν αὐτοῦ τῶν βοώντων αὐτῷ
of the select  of him the ones crying aloud him
2250    2532 3571   2532 3114           1909 846
ἡμέρας καὶ νυκτός, καὶ μακροθυμεῖ ἐπ' αὐτοῖς;
day    and night,  and has long temper on them?
8 3004 1473  3754 4160      08   1557
λέγω ὑμῖν ὅτι ποιήσει τὴν ἐκδίκησιν
I say to you that he will do the bring out right
846    1722 5034      4133  01  5207 02    444
αὐτῶν ἐν τάχει.   πλὴν ὁ υἱὸς τοῦ ἀνθρώπου
of them in quickness. Except the son of the man
2064    687  2147      08   4102   1909 06  1093
ἐλθὼν ἄρα εὑρήσει τὴν πίστιν ἐπὶ τῆς γῆς;
having come then will find the trust  on  the earth?
9 3004   1161 2532 4314 5100 016    3982         1909
Εἶπεν δὲ  καὶ πρός τινας τοὺς πεποιθότας ἐφ'
He said but also to some the ones having on
                                        persuaded
1438    3754 1510    1342      2532 1848
ἑαυτοῖς ὅτι εἰσὶν δίκαιοι καὶ ἐξουθενοῦντας
themselves that they are right and despising
016  3062   08   3850        3778       444
                                  10 ᵗΑνθρωποι
τοὺς λοιποὺς τὴν παραβολὴν ταύτην·   Μεν
the remaining the parallel story this:   Men
1417 305        1519 012 2411   4336        01 1520
δύο ἀνέβησαν εἰς τὸ ἱερὸν προσεύξασθαι, ὁ εἷς
two went up into the temple to pray,      the one
5330       2532 01  2087   5057       01 5330
Φαρισαῖος καὶ ὁ ἕτερος τελώνης. 11 ὁ Φαρισαῖος
Pharisee and the other tax man.   The Pharisee
2476    4314 1438    3778   4336         01
σταθεὶς πρὸς ἑαυτὸν ταῦτα προσηύχετο· ὁ
having stood toward himself these was praying, the
2316   2168           1473  3754 3756 1510
θεός, εὐχαριστῶ       σοι  ὅτι οὐκ εἰμὶ
God, I give good favor to you that not I am
5618     013 3062   014      444        727
ὥσπερ οἱ λοιποὶ τῶν ἀνθρώπων, ἅρπαγες,
as indeed the remaining of the men,      plunderers,
94      3432    2228 2532 5613 3778 01  5057
ἄδικοι, μοιχοί, ἢ καὶ ὡς οὗτος ὁ τελώνης·
unright, adulterers, or even as this the tax man;
12 3522    1364 010   4521      586       3956
νηστεύω δὶς τοῦ σαββάτου, ἀποδεκατῶ πάντα
I fast twice of the sabbath,  give tenth all
3745   2932      13 01 1161 5057     3113
ὅσα κτῶμαι.      ὁ δὲ τελώνης μακρόθεν
as much as I acquire. The but tax man from far
2476    3756 2309      3761  016    3788
ἑστὼς οὐκ ἤθελεν οὐδὲ τοὺς ὀφθαλμοὺς
having stood not he was wanting but not the eyes
1869      1519 04  3772    235  5180        012
ἐπᾶραι  εἰς τὸν οὐρανόν, ἀλλ' ἔτυπτεν τὸ
to lift up on to the heaven, but he was beating the
4738   846  3004    01 2316   2433       1473 03
στῆθος αὐτοῦ λέγων· ὁ θεός, ἱλάσθητί μοι τῷ
chest of him saying; the God, be expiatory to me the
```

I will grant her justice, so that she may not wear me out by continually coming.'"[a] 6 And the Lord said, "Listen to what the unjust judge says. 7 And will not God grant justice to his chosen ones who cry to him day and night? Will he delay long in helping them? 8 I tell you, he will quickly grant justice to them. And yet, when the Son of Man comes, will he find faith on earth?"

9 He also told this parable to some who trusted in themselves that they were righteous and regarded others with contempt: 10 "Two men went up to the temple to pray, one a Pharisee and the other a tax collector. 11 The Pharisee, standing by himself, was praying thus, 'God, I thank you that I am not like other people: thieves, rogues, adulterers, or even like this tax collector. 12 I fast twice a week; I give a tenth of all my income.' 13 But the tax collector, standing far off, would not even look up to heaven, but was beating his breast and saying, 'God, be merciful to me, a sinner!'

---

a Or so that she may not finally come and slap me in the face

14I tell you, this man went down to his home justified rather than the other; for all who exalt themselves will be humbled, but all who humble themselves will be exalted."

15 People were bringing even infants to him that he might touch them; and when the disciples saw it, they sternly ordered them not to do it. 16But Jesus called for them and said, "Let the little children come to me, and do not stop them; for it is to such as these that the kingdom of God belongs. 17Truly I tell you, whoever does not receive the kingdom of God as a little child will never enter it."

18 A certain ruler asked him, "Good Teacher, what must I do to inherit eternal life?" 19Jesus said to him, "Why do you call me good? No one is good but God alone. 20You know the commandments: 'You shall not commit adultery; You shall not murder; You shall not steal; You shall not bear false witness; Honor your father and mother.'" 21He replied, "I have kept all these since my youth." 22When Jesus heard this, he said to him, "There is still one thing lacking. Sell all that you own and

268	14	3004	1473	2597	3778
ἁμαρτωλῷ.		λέγω	ὑμῖν,	κατέβη	οὗτος
sinner.		I say	to you,	went down	this one

1344		1519	04	3624	846	3844
δεδικαιωμένος		εἰς	τὸν	οἶκον	αὐτοῦ	παρ'
having been made right		into	the	house	of him	from

1565	3754	3956 01	5312	1438
ἐκεῖνον·	ὅτι	πᾶς ὁ	ὑψῶν	ἑαυτὸν
that;	because	all the	one elevating	himself

5013	01 1161	5013	1438
ταπεινωθήσεται,	ὁ δὲ	ταπεινῶν	ἑαυτὸν
will be humbled,	the but	one humbling	himself

5312	15	4374	1161	846	2532 024 1025
ὑψωθήσεται.		Προσέφερον	δὲ	αὐτῷ	καὶ τὰ βρέφη
will be elevated.		They were offering	but	to him	also the infants

2443	846	681	3708	1161 013
ἵνα	αὐτῶν	ἅπτηται·	ἰδόντες	δὲ οἱ
that	them	he might touch;	having seen	but the

3101	2008	846	16	01 1161	2424
μαθηταὶ	ἐπετίμων	αὐτοῖς.		ὁ δὲ	Ἰησοῦς
learners	were admonishing	them.		The but	Jesus

4341	846	3004	863	024 3813
προσεκαλέσατο	αὐτὰ	λέγων·	ἄφετε τὰ	παιδία
called to	them	saying,	allow the	small children

2064	4314	1473	2532 3361	2967	846	022	1063
ἔρχεσθαι	πρός	με	καὶ μὴ	κωλύετε	αὐτά,	τῶν	γὰρ
to come	to	me	and not	hinder	them,	of the	for

5108	1510	05	932	02	2316	17	281	3004
τοιούτων	ἐστὶν	ἡ	βασιλεία	τοῦ	θεοῦ.		ἀμὴν	λέγω
such	is	the	kingdom	of the	God.		Amen	I say

1473	3739 302	3361	1209	08	932
ὑμῖν,	ὃς ἂν	μὴ	δέξηται	τὴν	βασιλείαν
to you,	who -	not	might welcome	the	kingdom

02	2316	5613 3813	3756 3361 1525
τοῦ	θεοῦ	ὡς παιδίον,	οὐ μὴ εἰσέλθῃ
of the	God	as small child,	not not he might go into

1519 846	18	2532 1905	5100 846	758
εἰς αὐτήν.		Καὶ ἐπηρώτησέν	τις αὐτὸν	ἄρχων
into it.		And asked on	some him	ruler

3004	1320	18	5101 4160	2222 166
λέγων·	διδάσκαλε	ἀγαθέ,	τί ποιήσας	ζωὴν αἰώνιον
saying;	teacher	good,	what having done	life eternal

2816	19	3004	1161	846	01	2424	5101
κληρονομήσω;		εἶπεν	δὲ	αὐτῷ	ὁ	Ἰησοῦς·	τί
I will inherit?		Said	but	to him	the	Jesus,	why

1473 3004	18	3762	18	1487 3361 1520 01
με λέγεις	ἀγαθόν;	οὐδεὶς	ἀγαθὸς εἰ	μὴ εἷς ὁ
me you say	good?	No one	good except	one the

2316	20	020 1785	3609a 3361 3431	3361
θεός.		τὰς ἐντολὰς	οἶδας· μὴ μοιχεύσῃς,	μὴ
God.		The commands you	not you might commit not	
			know;	adultery,

5407	3361 2813	3361 5576	5091
φονεύσῃς,	μὴ κλέψῃς,	μὴ ψευδομαρτυρήσῃς,	τίμα
you might not murder,	you might not thieve,	you might testify falsely,	value

04	3962	1473	2532 08	3384	21	01	1161	3004
τὸν	πατέρα	σου	καὶ τὴν	μητέρα.		ὁ	δὲ	εἶπεν·
the	father	of you	and the	mother.		The	but	said;

3778	3956	5442	1537 3503	22	191
ταῦτα	πάντα	ἐφύλαξα	ἐκ νεότητος.		ἀκούσας
these	all	I guarded	from newness.		Having heard

1161 01	2424	3004	846	2089	1520 1473
δὲ ὁ	Ἰησοῦς	εἶπεν	αὐτῷ·	ἔτι	ἕν σοι
but the	Jesus	said	to him;	still	one to you

3007	3956	3745	2192	4453	2532
λείπει·	πάντα	ὅσα	ἔχεις	πώλησον	καὶ
it leaves;	all	as much as	you have	sell	and

```
1239              4434         2532 2192              2344
διάδος            πτωχοῖς, καὶ ἕξεις              θησαυρὸν
give thoroughly to poor,   and  you will have  treasure
1722 015   3772        2532        1204   190              1473   23 01
ἐν [τοῖς] οὐρανοῖς, καὶ δεῦρο ἀκολούθει μοι.              ὁ
in   the  heavens,  and  come  follow     me.   The one
1161 191              3778   4036              1096
δὲ  ἀκούσας        ταῦτα περίλυπος        ἐγενήθη·
but  having heard  these greatly grieved  he became;
1510  1063 4145        4970        3708              1161
ἦν   γὰρ πλούσιος σφόδρα.   24 Ἰδὼν              δὲ
he was for  rich       exceeding. Having seen but
846     01  2424       4036              1096              3004
αὐτὸν ὁ Ἰησοῦς [περίλυπον γενόμενον] εἶπεν·
him    the Jesus  greatly grieved having become said,
4459 1423        013        024 5536   2192              1519 08
πῶς δυσκόλως οἱ  τὰ χρήματα ἔχοντες εἰς τὴν
how difficultly the ones the wealth having   into the
932     02  2316 1531              2123
βασιλείαν τοῦ θεοῦ εἰσπορεύονται· 25 εὐκοπώτερον
kingdom of the God travel into;         easier labor
1063 1510 2574   1223        5143a     955a
γάρ ἐστιν κάμηλον διὰ  τρήματος βελόνης
for  it is camel   through opening of needle
1525        2228 4145        1519 08 932        02
εἰσελθεῖν ἢ  πλούσιον εἰς τὴν βασιλείαν τοῦ
to go into or  rich     into the kingdom  of the
2316 1525        3004 1161 013        191
θεοῦ εἰσελθεῖν. 26 εἶπαν δὲ οἱ     ἀκούσαντες·
God to go into.   Said but the ones having heard;
2532 5101 1410   4982              01 1161 3004   021
καὶ τίς δύναται σωθῆναι; 27 ὁ  δὲ εἶπεν· τὰ
and who is able to be delivered? The but said; the
102     3844  444        1415   3844  03  2316 1510
ἀδύνατα παρὰ ἀνθρώποις δυνατὰ παρὰ τῷ θεῷ ἐστιν.
unable along men       power  along the God are.
3004   1161 01  4074        2400 1473   863
28 Εἶπεν δὲ ὁ Πέτρος· ἰδοὺ ἡμεῖς ἀφέντες
   Said but the Peter; look we    having sent off
024 2398 190              1473   01 1161 3004   846
τὰ ἴδια ἠκολουθήσαμέν σοι. 29 ὁ δὲ εἶπεν αὐτοῖς·
the own followed      you.   The but said to them;
281 3004 1473   3754 3762   1510 3739 863
ἀμὴν λέγω ὑμῖν ὅτι οὐδείς ἐστιν ὃς ἀφῆκεν
amen I say to you that no one is    who sent off
3614 2228 1135   2228 80        2228 1118   2228 5043
οἰκίαν ἢ γυναῖκα ἢ ἀδελφοὺς ἢ γονεῖς ἢ τέκνα
house or woman   or brothers or parents or children
1752   06   932     02     2316 3739 3780
ἕνεκεν τῆς βασιλείας τοῦ θεοῦ, 30 ὃς οὐχὶ
on account of the kingdom of the God, who not
3361 618        4179              1722 03 2540
μὴ [ἀπο]λάβῃ πολλαπλασίονα ἐν τῷ καιρῷ
not might take back many times in  the season
3778   2532 1722 03 165   03 2064        2222 166
τούτῳ καὶ ἐν τῷ αἰῶνι τῷ ἐρχομένῳ ζωὴν αἰώνιον.
this   and in  the age the coming   life eternal.
3880              1161 016 1427   3004   4314 846
31 Παραλαβὼν δὲ τοὺς δώδεκα εἶπεν πρὸς αὐτούς·
   Having taken along but the twelve he said to them;
2400 305        1519 2419        2532 5055
ἰδοὺ ἀναβαίνομεν εἰς Ἰερουσαλήμ, καὶ τελεσθήσεται
look we go up    into Jerusalem, and will be completed
3956 021 1125              1223        014 4396
πάντα τὰ γεγραμμένα   διὰ  τῶν προφητῶν
all  the having been written through the spokesmen
03   5207 02  444        3860              1063
τῷ υἱῷ τοῦ ἀνθρώπου· 32 παραδοθήσεται γὰρ
to the son of the man;   he will be given over for
```

distribute the money[a] to the poor, and you will have treasure in heaven; then come, follow me." [23]But when he heard this, he became sad; for he was very rich. [24]Jesus looked at him and said, "How hard it is for those who have wealth to enter the kingdom of God! [25]Indeed, it is easier for a camel to go through the eye of a needle than for someone who is rich to enter the kingdom of God."

[26]Those who heard it said, "Then who can be saved?" [27]He replied, "What is impossible for mortals is possible for God."

[28]Then Peter said, "Look, we have left our homes and followed you." [29]And he said to them, "Truly I tell you, there is no one who has left house or wife or brothers or parents or children, for the sake of the kingdom of God, [30]who will not get back very much more in this age, and in the age to come eternal life."

[31]Then he took the twelve aside and said to them, "See, we are going up to Jerusalem, and everything that is written about the Son of Man by the prophets will be accomplished. [32]For he will be handed over

[a] Gk lacks the money

to the Gentiles; and he will be mocked and insulted and spat upon. ³³After they have flogged him, they will kill him, and on the third day he will rise again." ³⁴But they understood nothing about all these things; in fact, what he said was hidden from them, and they did not grasp what was said.

35 As he approached Jericho, a blind man was sitting by the roadside begging. ³⁶When he heard a crowd going by, he asked what was happening. ³⁷They told him, "Jesus of Nazareth[a] is passing by." ³⁸Then he shouted, "Jesus, Son of David, have mercy on me!" ³⁹Those who were in front sternly ordered him to be quiet; but he shouted even more loudly, "Son of David, have mercy on me!" ⁴⁰Jesus stood still and ordered the man to be brought to him; and when he came near, he asked him, ⁴¹"What do you want me to do for you?" He said, "Lord, let me see again." ⁴²Jesus said to him, "Receive your sight; your faith has saved you." ⁴³Immediately he regained his sight and followed him, glorifying God; and all the people, when they saw it, praised God.

CHAPTER 19

He entered Jericho and

a Gk the Nazorean

```
       023     1484      2532  1702                  2532  5195
τοῖς    ἔθνεσιν  καὶ    ἐμπαιχθήσεται      καὶ   ὑβρισθήσεται
to the  nations  and    he will be mocked  and   abused
       2532  1716               2532  3146
καὶ    ἐμπτυσθήσεται  33  καὶ   μαστιγώσαντες
and    spit on              and   having scourged
       615         846      2532  07       2250    07    5154
ἀποκτενοῦσιν  αὐτόν,  καὶ   τῇ      ἡμέρᾳ  τῇ   τρίτῃ
they will kill  him,    and   in the  day    the  third
       450            2532  846         3762      3778
ἀναστήσεται.  34  καὶ   αὐτοὶ     οὐδὲν  τούτων
he will stand up.  And  themselves  nothing  of these
       4920      2532  1510  09  4487  3778  2928
συνῆκαν  καὶ   ἦν    τὸ   ῥῆμα  τοῦτο  κεκρυμμένον
understood and  was+  the  word  this  +having been hidden
       575   846  2532  3756  1097           024   3004
ἀπ᾽  αὐτῶν  καὶ  οὐκ  ἐγίνωσκον       τὰ   λεγόμενα.
from  them  and  not  they were knowing  the  being said.
            1096       1161  1722  011  1448      846   1519
35  Ἐγένετο    δὲ    ἐν   τῷ   ἐγγίζειν  αὐτὸν  εἰς
    It became  but   in   the  to near   him    into
       2410      5185  5100  2521      3844  08  3598  1871
Ἰεριχὼ  τυφλός  τις  ἐκάθητο  παρὰ  τὴν  ὁδὸν  ἐπαιτῶν.
Jericho  blind  some  sat      along  the  way  asking on.
       191           1161  3793  1279
36  ἀκούσας     δὲ    ὄχλου  διαπορευομένου
    Having heard  but   crowd  traveling through
       4441           5101  1510    3778     37  518        1161
ἐπυνθάνετο  τί    εἴη    τοῦτο.    ἀπήγγειλαν  δὲ
he inquired  what  might  be this.   They told    but
       846  3754  2424    01   3480      3928          38  2532
αὐτῷ  ὅτι  Ἰησοῦς  ὁ   Ναζωραῖος  παρέρχεται.    καὶ
him,  (")  Jesus    the  Nazorean  comes along.   And
       994          3004    2424  5207  1160a  1653    1473
ἐβόησεν     λέγων·  Ἰησοῦ  υἱὲ  Δαυίδ,  ἐλέησόν  με.
he cried aloud saying,  Jesus  son  David,  mercy   me.
       2532  013  1264              2008              846
39  καὶ   οἱ   προάγοντες        ἐπετίμων          αὐτῷ
    And   the  ones leading before  were admonishing  him
       2443  4601           846      1161  4183  3123
ἵνα   σιγήσῃ,        αὐτὸς  δὲ   πολλῷ  μᾶλλον
that he might be silent,  himself  but   much   more
       2896        5207  1160a  1653      1473  40  2476        1161
ἔκραζεν·  υἱὲ  Δαυίδ,  ἐλέησόν  με.    σταθεὶς       δὲ
shouted;  son  David,  mercy   me.      Having stood   but
       01   2424      2753        846  71          4314  846
ὁ   Ἰησοῦς  ἐκέλευσεν  αὐτὸν  ἀχθῆναι    πρὸς  αὐτόν.
the  Jesus  commanded  him   to be led to    him.
       1448         1161  846  1905          846       41  5101
ἐγγίσαντος  δὲ   αὐτοῦ  ἐπηρώτησεν  αὐτόν·    τί
Having neared  but  him   he asked on  him;     what
       1473    2309       4160        01  1161  3004      2962
σοι    θέλεις  ποιήσω;  ὁ   δὲ   εἶπεν·  κύριε,
to you  do you want I might do?  The  but   said;    Master,
       2443  308                 2532  01  2424    3004    846
ἵνα  ἀναβλέψω.   42  καὶ   ὁ   Ἰησοῦς  εἶπεν  αὐτῷ·
that I might see again.  And  the  Jesus   said   to him;
       308          05  4102    1473    4982         1473  2532
ἀνάβλεψον·  ἡ   πίστις  σου   σέσωκέν     σε.   43  καὶ
see again;  the  trust   of you  has delivered  you.     And
       3916      308           2532  190          846
παραχρῆμα  ἀνέβλεψεν  καὶ   ἠκολούθει      αὐτῷ
suddenly   he saw again and   he was following   him
       1392         04   2316  2532  3956  01   2992
δοξάζων     τὸν  θεόν.  καὶ   πᾶς  ὁ   λαὸς
giving splendor  the  God.   And   all  the  people
       3708      1325  136      03    2316      2532
ἰδὼν    ἔδωκεν  αἶνον  τῷ   θεῷ.  19:1  Καὶ
having seen  gave   praise  to the  God.        And
```

```
1525                1330                    08    2410
εἰσελθὼν           διήρχετο                τὴν  Ἰεριχώ.
having gone into   he was going through   the   Jericho.
```

   2532 2400 435 3686   2564   2195   2532
2 Καὶ ἰδοὺ ἀνὴρ ὀνόματι καλούμενος   Ζακχαῖος, καὶ
   And look man in name being called   Zakcheus, and

```
846      1510 754                2532 846         4145
αὐτὸς    ἦν   ἀρχιτελώνης        καὶ αὐτὸς      πλούσιος·
himself was  first tax man       and himself   rich;
```

   2532 2212   3708   04   2424   5101 1510 2532
3 καὶ ἐζήτει   ἰδεῖν τὸν Ἰησοῦν τίς ἐστιν καὶ
   and he was seeking to see the Jesus who he is and

```
3756 1410          575   02  3793   3754    07
οὐκ  ἠδύνατο        ἀπὸ  τοῦ ὄχλου, ὅτι     τῇ
not  he was able   from the crowd, because in the
```

   2244   3398   1510   **4** 2532 4390   1519 012
ἡλικίᾳ   μικρὸς ἦν.   καὶ προδραμὼν   εἰς τὸ
stature small   he was.   And running before into the

```
1715       305       1909 4809           2443 3708
ἔμπροσθεν ἀνέβη     ἐπὶ  συκομορέαν ἵνα  ἴδῃ
in front  he went up on  sycamore     that he might see
```

   846 3754   1565   3195   1330   **5** 2532
αὐτὸν ὅτι   ἐκείνης ἤμελλεν   διέρχεσθαι.   καὶ
him   because that   he was about to go through. And

```
5613 2064    1909 04  5117    308              01
ὡς   ἦλθεν   ἐπὶ  τὸν τόπον, ἀναβλέψας        ὁ
as   he came on   the place, having looked up the
```

   2424   3004   4314 846   2195   4692
Ἰησοῦς εἶπεν πρὸς αὐτόν· Ζακχαῖε, σπεύσας
Jesus said to   him;   Zakcheus, having hurried

```
2597         4594       1063 1722 03  3624   1473 1163 1473
κατάβηθι,   σήμερον γὰρ ἐν   τῷ  οἴκῳ σου δεῖ  με
come down,  today   for in   the house of  it is me
                                                 you  necessary
```

   3306   **6** 2532 4692   2597   2533
μεῖναι.   καὶ σπεύσας   κατέβη   καὶ
to stay.   And having hurried   he went down and

```
5264        846   5463     **7** 2532 3708           3956
ὑπεδέξατο  αὐτὸν χαίρων.     καὶ  ἰδόντες        πάντες
entertained him   rejoicing. And  having seen all
```

   1234   3004   3754 3844 268   435
διεγόγγυζον   λέγοντες ὅτι παρὰ ἁμαρτωλῷ ἀνδρὶ
grumbled thoroughly saying   that with sinner   man

```
1525      2647         **8** 2476    1161 2195      3004
εἰσῆλθεν  καταλῦσαι.      σταθεὶς δὲ  Ζακχαῖος εἶπεν
he went into to lodge. Having stood but Zakcheus said
```

   4314 04 2962   2400 024 2255   1473 022
πρὸς τὸν κύριον· ἰδοὺ τὰ ἡμίσιά μου τῶν
to   the Master; look the half of me of the

```
5225          2962  015   4434     1325      2532 1487
ὑπαρχόντων,  κύριε, τοῖς πτωχοῖς δίδωμι, καὶ  εἴ
possessions, Master, to the poor   I give, and  if
```

   5100 5100 4811   591   5073
τινός τι ἐσυκοφάντησα ἀποδίδωμι τετραπλοῦν.
someone some I accused falsely I give back four times.

   9 3004 1161 4314 846   01   2424   3754 4594   4991
εἶπεν δὲ πρὸς αὐτὸν ὁ Ἰησοῦς ὅτι σήμερον σωτηρία
Said but to   him   the Jesus, (") today deliverance

```
03      3624 3778  1096       2530     2532 846       5207
τῷ      οἴκῳ τούτῳ ἐγένετο, καθότι καὶ  αὐτὸς     υἱὸς
to the house this  became,  because also himself son
```

   11   1510   **10** 2064 1063 01 5207 02   444
Ἀβραάμ ἐστιν·   ἦλθεν γὰρ ὁ υἱὸς τοῦ   ἀνθρώπου
Abraham is;   came for the son of the man

```
2212      2532 4982      012 622
ζητῆσαι καὶ  σῶσαι     τὸ ἀπολωλός.
to seek and  to save   the having been destroyed one.
```

   11 191   1161 846   3778   4369   3004
Ἀκουόντων δὲ αὐτῶν ταῦτα προσθεὶς   εἶπεν
Hearing   but them these having set to he said

---

was passing through it.
[2] A man was there named
Zacchaeus; he was a chief
tax collector and was rich.
[3] He was trying to see who
Jesus was, but on account
of the crowd he could not,
because he was short in
stature. [4] So he ran ahead
and climbed a sycamore
tree to see him, because he
was going to pass that way.
[5] When Jesus came to the
place, he looked up and said
to him, "Zacchaeus, hurry
and come down; for I must
stay at your house today."
[6] So he hurried down and
was happy to welcome
him. [7] All who saw it began
to grumble and said, "He
has gone to be the guest
of one who is a sinner."
[8] Zacchaeus stood there and
said to the Lord, "Look,
half of my possessions, Lord,
I will give to the poor; and
if I have defrauded anyone
of anything, I will pay back
four times as much." [9] Then
Jesus said to him, "Today
salvation has come to this
house, because he too is a
son of Abraham. [10] For the
Son of Man came to seek
out and to save the lost."

[11] As they were listening
to this, he went on to tell

a parable, because he was near Jerusalem, and because they supposed that the kingdom of God was to appear immediately. ¹²So he said, "A nobleman went to a distant country to get royal power for himself and then return. ¹³He summoned ten of his slaves, and gave them ten pounds,ᵃ and said to them, 'Do business with these until I come back.' ¹⁴But the citizens of his country hated him and sent a delegation after him, saying, 'We do not want this man to rule over us.' ¹⁵When he returned, having received royal power, he ordered these slaves, to whom he had given the money, to be summoned so that he might find out what they had gained by trading. ¹⁶The first came forward and said, 'Lord, your pound has made ten more pounds.' ¹⁷He said to him, 'Well done, good slave! Because you have been trustworthy in a very small thing, take charge of ten cities.' ¹⁸Then the second came, saying, 'Lord, your pound has made five pounds.' ¹⁹He said to him, 'And you, rule over five cities.' ²⁰Then the other came, saying, 'Lord, here is your pound. I wrapped it up in a piece of cloth,

ᵃ The mina, rendered here by pound, was about three months' wages for a laborer

3850	1223	012	1451	1510	2419	846
παραβολὴν	διὰ	τὸ	ἐγγὺς	εἶναι	Ἰερουσαλὴμ	αὐτὸν
parallel story	through	the	near	to be	Jerusalem	him

2532	1380	846	3754 3916	3195	05
καὶ	δοκεῖν	αὐτοὺς	ὅτι παραχρῆμα	μέλλει	ἡ
and	to think	them	that suddenly	is about to	the

932	02	2316	398	**12**	3004	3767
βασιλεία	τοῦ	θεοῦ	ἀναφαίνεσθαι.		εἶπεν	οὖν·
kingdom	of the	God	to appear again.		He said	then;

444	5100	2104	4198	1519 5561	3117
ἄνθρωπός	τις	εὐγενὴς	ἐπορεύθη	εἰς χώραν	μακρὰν
man	some	well born	traveled	into country	far

2983	1438	932	2532 5290
λαβεῖν	ἑαυτῷ	βασιλείαν καὶ	ὑποστρέψαι.
to take	to himself	kingdom and	to return.

13	2564	1161	1176 1401	1438	1325
	καλέσας	δὲ	δέκα δούλους	ἑαυτοῦ	ἔδωκεν
	Having called	but	ten slaves	of himself	he gave

846	1176 3414	2532 3004	4314 846
αὐτοῖς	δέκα μνᾶς	καὶ εἶπεν	πρὸς αὐτούς·
to them	ten minas	and said	to them;

4231	1722 3739	2064	**14**	013 1161 4177
πραγματεύσασθε	ἐν ᾧ	ἔρχομαι.		οἱ δὲ πολῖται
practice trade	in which	I go.		The but citizens

846	3404	846	2532 649	4242
αὐτοῦ	ἐμίσουν	αὐτὸν καὶ	ἀπέστειλαν	πρεσβείαν
of him	were hating	him and	delegated	envoy

3694	846	3004	3756 2309	3778	936
ὀπίσω	αὐτοῦ	λέγοντες·	οὐ θέλομεν	τοῦτον	βασιλεῦσαι
after	him	saying,	not we want	this	to be king

1909 1473	**15**	2532 1096	1722 011 1880
ἐφ' ἡμᾶς.		καὶ ἐγένετο	ἐν τῷ ἐπανελθεῖν
on us.		And it became	in the to go up on

846	2983	08 932	2532 3004
αὐτὸν	λαβόντα	τὴν βασιλείαν	καὶ εἶπεν
him	having taken	the kingdom	and he said

5165	846	016 1401	3778	3739
φωνηθῆναι	αὐτῷ	τοὺς δούλους	τούτους	οἷς
to be sounded	to him	the slaves	these	whom

1325	012 694	2443 1097	5101
δεδώκει	τὸ ἀργύριον,	ἵνα γνοῖ	τί
he had given	the silver,	that he might know	what

1281	**16**	3854	1161 01 4413
διεπραγματεύσαντο.		παρεγένετο	δὲ ὁ πρῶτος
they had practiced by trading.		Arrived	but the first

3004	2962	05	3414 1473	1176 4333
λέγων·	κύριε,	ἡ	μνᾶ σου	δέκα προσηργάσατο
saying;	master,	the	mina of you	ten worked to

3414	**17**	2532 3004	846	2095-1065	18	1401
μνᾶς.		καὶ εἶπεν	αὐτῷ·	εὖγε,		ἀγαθὲ δοῦλε,
minas.		And he said	to him,	well indeed,		good slave,

3754	1722 1646	4103	1096	1510 1849
ὅτι	ἐν ἐλαχίστῳ	πιστὸς	ἐγένου,	ἴσθι ἐξουσίαν
because	in least	trustful	you became,	be authority

2192	1883	1176 4172	**18**	2532 2064 01 1208
ἔχων	ἐπάνω	δέκα πόλεων.		καὶ ἦλθεν ὁ δεύτερος
having	upon	ten cities.		And came the second

3004	05	3414 1473	2962	4160	4002 3414
λέγων·	ἡ	μνᾶ σου,	κύριε,	ἐποίησεν	πέντε μνᾶς.
saying;	the	mina of you,	master,	made	five minas.

19	3004	1161 2532 3778	2532 1473 1883 1096	4002
	εἶπεν	δὲ καὶ τούτῳ·	καὶ σὺ ἐπάνω γίνου	πέντε
	He said	but also to this;	and you upon become	five

4172	**20**	2532 01	2087	2064 3004	2962	2400
πόλεων.		καὶ ὁ	ἕτερος	ἦλθεν λέγων·	κύριε,	ἰδοὺ
cities.		And the	other	came saying;	master,	look

05	3414 1473	3739 2192	606	1722 4676
ἡ	μνᾶ σου	ἣν εἶχον	ἀποκειμένην	ἐν σουδαρίῳ·
the	mina of you	which I had	lying off	in handkerchief;

21
```
    5399            1063 1473 3754  444          840        1510
ἐφοβούμην   γάρ σε,  ὅτι ἄνθρωπος αὐστηρὸς εἶ,
I was fearing for you,  that man          severe      you are,
142         3739 3756 5087      2532 2325      3739 3756
αἴρεις      ὃ   οὐκ ἔθηκας καὶ θερίζεις ὃ   οὐκ
you lift up what not  you set and you harvest what not
4687          3004      846    1537 010 4750      1473
ἔσπειρας.  22 λέγει αὐτῷ·  ἐκ  τοῦ στόματός σου
you sowed.     He says to him; from the mouth    of you
2919     1473 4190     1401    3609a        3754 1473
κρινῶ σε, πονηρὲ δοῦλε. ᾔδεις      ὅτι ἐγὼ
I judge you, evil  slave. You had known that I
444        840       1510  142      3739 3756 5087 2532
ἄνθρωπος αὐστηρός εἰμι, αἴρων   ὃ   οὐκ ἔθηκα καὶ
man        severe   am, lifting up what not  I set and
2325        3739 3756 4687       2532 1223   5101 3756
θερίζων ὃ   οὐκ ἔσπειρα; 23 καὶ διὰ   τί  οὐκ
harvesting what not I sowed?     And through what not
1325     1473 012 694       1909 5132         2504
ἔδωκάς μου τὸ ἀργύριον ἐπὶ τράπεζαν; κἀγὼ
you gave me   the silver   on  table?    And I
2064        4862 5110    302 846 4238        2532
ἐλθὼν   σὺν τόκῳ ἂν αὐτὸ ἔπραξα.  24 καὶ
having come with interest - it  I practiced.    And
015 3936        3004   142   575  846   08  3414 2532
τοῖς παρεστῶσιν εἶπεν· ἄρατε ἀπ' αὐτοῦ τὴν μνᾶν καὶ
to  ones having he     lift from him  the mina and
the stood along said;   up
1325 03      020 1176 3414  2192     2532 3004
δότε τῷ     τὰς δέκα μνᾶς ἔχοντι - 25 καὶ εἶπαν
give to the the ten  minas having     and they said
846      2962      2192  1176 3414     3004 1473
αὐτῷ· κύριε, ἔχει δέκα μνᾶς - 26 λέγω ὑμῖν
to him; master, he has ten  minas    I say to you
3754 3956    03  2192       1325               575  1161
ὅτι παντὶ τῷ ἔχοντι     δοθήσεται,      ἀπὸ δὲ
that to all the one having it will be given, from but
02  3361 2192      2532 3739 2192  142
τοῦ μὴ ἔχοντος καὶ ὃ  ἔχει ἀρθήσεται.
the not having even what he has will be lifted up.
   4133    016  2190    1473 3778   016      3361
27 πλὴν τοὺς ἐχθρούς μου τούτους τοὺς   μὴ
   Except the hostile of me these  the  ones not
2309       1473 936    1909 846  71      5602
θελήσαντάς με βασιλεῦσαι ἐπ' αὐτοὺς ἀγάγετε ὧδε
having wanted me  to be king on  them  bring here
2532 2695          846    1715     1473
καὶ κατασφάξατε αὐτοὺς ἔμπροσθέν μου.
and you thoroughly slaughter them  in front of me.
   2532 3004      3778 4198       1715
28 Καὶ εἰπὼν   ταῦτα ἐπορεύετο ἔμπροσθεν
   And having said these he traveled in front of
305        1519 2414      2532 1096         5613
ἀναβαίνων εἰς Ἱεροσόλυμα. 29 Καὶ ἐγένετο ὡς
going up into Jerusalem.    And it became as
1448       1519 967    2532 963       4314 012 3735
ἤγγισεν εἰς Βηθφαγὴ καὶ Βηθανία[ν] πρὸς τὸ ὄρος
he neared into Bethphage and Bethany   to the hill
012 2564       1636       649          1417 014
τὸ καλούμενον Ἐλαιῶν, ἀπέστειλεν δύο τῶν
the being called of Olives, he delegated two  of the
3101    30  3004   5217    1519 08  2713
μαθητῶν   λέγων· ὑπάγετε εἰς τὴν κατέναντι
learners   saying; go off into the over against
2968     1722 3739 1531         2147          4454
κώμην, ἐν ᾗ   εἰσπορευόμενοι εὑρήσετε πῶλον
village, in which traveling into  you will find colt
1210             1909 3739 3762   4455      444
δεδεμένον,   ἐφ' ὃν  οὐδεὶς πώποτε ἀνθρώπων
having been bound, on  which no one ever yet of men
```

²¹for I was afraid of you, because you are a harsh man; you take what you did not deposit, and reap what you did not sow.' ²²He said to him, 'I will judge you by your own words, you wicked slave! You knew, did you, that I was a harsh man, taking what I did not deposit and reaping what I did not sow? ²³Why then did you not put my money into the bank? Then when I returned, I could have collected it with interest.' ²⁴He said to the bystanders, 'Take the pound from him and give it to the one who has ten pounds.' ²⁵(And they said to him, 'Lord, he has ten pounds!') ²⁶'I tell you, to all those who have, more will be given; but from those who have nothing, even what they have will be taken away. ²⁷But as for these enemies of mine who did not want me to be king over them— bring them here and slaughter them in my presence.'"

²⁸After he had said this, he went on ahead, going up to Jerusalem.

²⁹When he had come near Bethphage and Bethany, at the place called the Mount of Olives, he sent two of the disciples, ³⁰saying, "Go into the village ahead of you, and as you enter it you will find tied there a colt that has never been ridden.

Untie it and bring it here.
³¹If anyone asks you, 'Why
are you untying it?' just say
this, 'The Lord needs it.'"
³²So those who were sent
departed and found it as he
had told them. ³³As they
were untying the colt, its
owners asked them, "Why
are you untying the colt?"
³⁴They said, "The Lord
needs it." ³⁵Then they
brought it to Jesus; and
after throwing their cloaks
on the colt, they set Jesus
on it. ³⁶As he rode along,
people kept spreading their
cloaks on the road. ³⁷As
he was now approaching
the path down from the
Mount of Olives, the whole
multitude of the disciples
began to praise God
joyfully with a loud voice for
all the deeds of power that
they had seen, ³⁸saying,
  "Blessed is the king
  who comes in the name
    of the Lord!
  Peace in heaven,
  and glory in the highest
    heaven!"
³⁹Some of the Pharisees
in the crowd said to him,
"Teacher, order your
disciples to stop." ⁴⁰He
answered, "I tell you, if
these were silent, the stones
would shout out."

41 As he came near and
saw the city, he wept over
it, ⁴²saying, "If you, even
you, had only recognized

```
2523            2532  3089            846      71          2532
ἐκάθισεν,   καὶ  λύσαντες       αὐτὸν  ἀγάγετε.   31  καὶ
sat,            and   having loosed it   bring.        And
1437 5100 1473 2065         1223      5101 3089
ἐάν  τις  ὑμᾶς  ἐρωτᾷ·       διὰ  τί  λύετε;
if    some you   might ask;  through what you loose?
3779      3004            3754    01  2962      846      5532
οὕτως  ἐρεῖτε·       ὅτι   ὁ  κύριος αὐτοῦ  χρείαν
Thusly you will say; because the Master of him  need
2192      32   565         1161 013 649            2147
ἔχει.          ἀπελθόντες  δὲ  οἱ  ἀπεσταλμένοι  εὖρον
has.           Having gone but  the ones being      found
                         off         being delegated
2531     3004     846       33  3089    1161 846    04    4454
καθὼς  εἶπεν  αὐτοῖς.       λυόντων δὲ  αὐτῶν τὸν  πῶλον
just as he said to them.    Loosing but  them   the colt
3004   013 2962     846    4314 846    5101 3089       04
εἶπαν οἱ  κύριοι αὐτοῦ πρὸς αὐτούς· τί  λύετε      τὸν
said   the masters of him to  them;  why you loose the
4454       34  013 1161 3004    3754    01  2962    846
πῶλον;         οἱ  δὲ  εἶπαν· ὅτι   ὁ  κύριος αὐτοῦ
colt?          The but  said;  because the Master of him
5532    2192   35  2532 71      846    4314 04   2424
χρείαν ἔχει.       καὶ ἤγαγον  αὐτὸν πρὸς τὸν 'Ιησοῦν
need   has.        And they led him   to  the  Jesus
2532 1977          846    024 2440   1909 04  4454
καὶ  ἐπιρίψαντες  αὐτῶν τὰ  ἱμάτια ἐπὶ τὸν πῶλον
and  having thrown on them the clothes on  the colt
1913       04    2424     36  4198         1161 846
ἐπεβίβασαν  τὸν 'Ιησοῦν.    πορευομένου δὲ  αὐτοῦ
they mounted the Jesus.      Traveling    but  him
5291              024 2440   846    1722 07  3598
ὑπεστρώννυον   τὰ  ἱμάτια αὐτῶν ἐν  τῇ  ὁδῷ.
they were spreading the clothes of them in  the way.
37 1448          1161 846    2235      4314 07  2600
ἐγγίζοντος  δὲ  αὐτοῦ ἤδη     πρὸς τῇ καταβάσει
Nearing      but  him   already to   the going down
010    3735   018   1636     757    537  09  4128
τοῦ  ὄρους τῶν  ἐλαιῶν ἤρξαντο ἅπαν τὸ πλῆθος
of the  hill  of the olives began   all  the quantity
014    3101     5463     134        04  2316 5456
τῶν  μαθητῶν χαίροντες αἰνεῖν    τὸν θεὸν φωνῇ
of the learners rejoicing to praise the God  in sound
3173     4012  3956  3739 3708   1411
μεγάλη περὶ πασῶν ὧν  εἶδον  δυνάμεων,
great   about all   which they saw powers,
38 3004      2127           01 2064        01
λέγοντες· εὐλογημένος   ὁ  ἐρχόμενος,  ὁ
saying,    being well-spoken the one coming, the
935      1722 3686    2962     1722 3772   1515   2532
βασιλεὺς ἐν  ὀνόματι κυρίου·  ἐν οὐρανῷ εἰρήνη καὶ
king    in   name    of Master; in heaven peace  and
1391   1722 5310        39  2532 5100 014   5330
δόξα  ἐν  ὑψίστοις.     καί τινες τῶν  Φαρισαίων
splendor in  highests.   And some of the Pharisees
575  02   3793   3004 4314 846   1320      2008
ἀπὸ τοῦ ὄχλου εἶπαν πρὸς αὐτόν· διδάσκαλε, ἐπιτίμησον
from the crowd said to  him;  teacher,    admonish
015  3101     1473    40  2532 611         3004
τοῖς μαθηταῖς σου.       καὶ ἀποκριθεὶς  εἶπεν·
the learners of you.     And having answered he said;
3004   1473    1437 3778 4623        013 3037
λέγω ὑμῖν, ἐὰν οὗτοι σιωπήσουσιν, οἱ λίθοι
I say to you, if   these will be silent, the stones
2896       41  2532 5613 1448      3708       08
κράξουσιν.     Καὶ ὡς  ἤγγισεν ἰδὼν      τὴν
will shout.    And as  he neared having seen the
4172   2799      1909 846    42  3004   3754 1487 1097
πόλιν ἔκλαυσεν ἐπ' αὐτὴν   λέγων ὅτι  εἰ  ἔγνως
city   he cried on  it       saying, (") if  you knew
```

1722 07   2250   3778   2532 1473 024 4314   1515   3568
ἐν   τῇ ἡμέρᾳ ταύτῃ καὶ σὺ   τὰ πρὸς εἰρήνην· νῦν
in   the day   this even you the toward peace;   now

1161 2928   575 3788   1473   3754
δὲ   ἐκρύβη   ἀπὸ ὀφθαλμῶν σου.   43 ὅτι
but it was hidden from eyes   of you.   Because

2240   2250   1909 1473 2532 3924a   013
ἥξουσιν   ἡμέραι ἐπὶ σὲ   καὶ παρεμβαλοῦσιν οἱ
will come   days   on   you and they will encamp the

2190   1473 5482   1473 2532 4033   1473
ἐχθροί σου χάρακά σοι καὶ περικυκλώσουσίν σε
hostile of   rampart to   and will encircle   you
ones   you   you   around

2532 4912   1473 3840   2532 1474
καὶ συνέξουσίν σε πάντοθεν, 44 καὶ ἐδαφιοῦσίν
and will hold you from   and they will grind
     together   everywhere,   to ground

1473 2532 024 5043   1473   1722 1473 2532 3756
σε   καὶ τὰ τέκνα   σου ἐν σοί, καὶ οὐκ
you and the children of you in   you, and not

863   3037 1909 3037 1722 1473 473
ἀφήσουσιν   λίθον ἐπὶ λίθον ἐν σοί, ἀνθ᾽
they will send off stone on   stone in   you, against

3739 3756 1097   04 2540   06   1984
ὧν   οὐκ ἔγνως   τὸν καιρὸν τῆς ἐπισκοπῆς
which not you knew the season of the oversight

1473   2532 1525   1519 012 2411
σου.   45 Καὶ εἰσελθὼν   εἰς τὸ ἱερὸν
of you.   And having come into into the temple

757   1544   016 4453   3004
ἤρξατο   ἐκβάλλειν   τοὺς πωλοῦντας 46 λέγων
he began to throw out the ones selling   saying

846   1125   2532 1510   01 3624
αὐτοῖς· γέγραπται·   καὶ ἔσται   ὁ   οἶκός
to them; it has been written; and will be the house

1473   3624 4335   1473 1161 846   4160
μου   οἶκος προσευχῆς, ὑμεῖς δὲ αὐτὸν ἐποιήσατε
of me house of prayer, you   but it   made

4693   3027   47 2532 1510   1321   012 2596
σπήλαιον λῃστῶν.   Καὶ ἦν   διδάσκων τὸ καθ᾽
cave   of robbers. And he was+   +teaching the by

2250   1722 011 2411   013 1161 749   2532 013
ἡμέραν ἐν   τῷ ἱερῷ. οἱ δὲ ἀρχιερεῖς   καὶ οἱ
day   in   the temple. The but ruler priests and the

1122   2212   846 622   2532 013
γραμματεῖς ἐζήτουν   αὐτὸν ἀπολέσαι καὶ οἱ
writers   were seeking him   to destroy and the

4413   02   2992   48 2532 3756 2147
πρῶτοι τοῦ λαοῦ,   καὶ οὐχ εὕρισκον
first of the people,   and not they were finding

012 5101 4160   01   2992 1063 537   1582
τὸ τί   ποιήσωσιν, ὁ   λαὸς γὰρ ἅπας ἐξεκρέματο
the what they   the people for all hung on
    might do,

846   191   2532 1096   1722 1520 018
αὐτοῦ ἀκούων. 20:1 Καὶ ἐγένετο   ἐν   μιᾷ τῶν
him   hearing.   And it became in   one of the

2250   1321   846 04 2992   1722 011 2411
ἡμερῶν διδάσκοντος αὐτοῦ τὸν λαὸν· ἐν   τῷ ἱερῷ
days   teaching   him   the people in   the temple

2532 2097   2186   013 749
καὶ εὐαγγελιζομένου   ἐπέστησαν οἱ ἀρχιερεῖς
and telling good message stood on the ruler priests

2532 013 1122   4862 015 4245   2   2532
καὶ οἱ γραμματεῖς σὺν τοῖς πρεσβυτέροις   καὶ
and the writers   with the older men   and

3004   3004   4314 846   3004   1473 1722 4169
εἶπαν   λέγοντες πρὸς αὐτόν· εἰπὸν ἡμῖν ἐν ποίᾳ
they said saying   to   him,   say   to us in what kind

---

on this day the things that
make for peace! But now
they are hidden from your
eyes. [43]Indeed, the days
will come upon you, when
your enemies will set up
ramparts around you and
surround you, and hem you
in on every side. [44]They will
crush you to the ground,
you and your children
within you, and they will not
leave within you one stone
upon another; because
you did not recognize the
time of your visitation from
God."[a]

45 Then he entered the
temple and began to drive
out those who were selling
things there; [46]and he said,
"It is written,

'My house shall be a
house of prayer';
but you have made it a
den of robbers."

47 Every day he was
teaching in the temple.
The chief priests, the
scribes, and the leaders of
the people kept looking
for a way to kill him; [48]but
they did not find anything
they could do, for all the
people were spellbound by
what they heard.

CHAPTER 20

One day, as he was teaching
the people in the temple and
telling the good news, the
chief priests and the scribes
came with the elders [2]and
said to him, "Tell us, by
what

[a] Gk lacks from God

authority are you doing these things? Who is it who gave you this authority?" ³He answered them, "I will also ask you a question, and you tell me: ⁴Did the baptism of John come from heaven, or was it of human origin?" ⁵They discussed it with one another, saying, "If we say, 'From heaven,' he will say, 'Why did you not believe him?' ⁶But if we say, 'Of human origin,' all the people will stone us; for they are convinced that John was a prophet." ⁷So they answered that they did not know where it came from. ⁸Then Jesus said to them, "Neither will I tell you by what authority I am doing these things."

⁹He began to tell the people this parable: "A man planted a vineyard, and leased it to tenants, and went to another country for a long time. ¹⁰When the season came, he sent a slave to the tenants in order that they might give him his share of the produce of the vineyard; but the tenants beat him and sent him away empty-handed. ¹¹Next he sent another slave; that one also they beat and insulted and sent away empty-handed. ¹²And he sent still a third; this one also they wounded and threw out. ¹³Then the owner of the vineyard said,

1849		3778	4160	2228	5101	1510	01	1325
ἐξουσίᾳ		ταῦτα	ποιεῖς,	ἢ	τίς	ἐστιν	ὁ	δούς
authority		these	you do,	or	who	is	the	one giving

1473	08	1849		3778		611		1161
σοι		τὴν ἐξουσίαν		ταύτην;	³	ἀποκριθεὶς		δὲ
to you		the authority		this?		Having answered		but

3004	4314 846	2065	1473 2504	3056	2532
εἶπεν	πρὸς αὐτούς·	ἐρωτήσω	ὑμᾶς κἀγὼ	λόγον,	καὶ
he said to	them;	will ask	you also I	word,	and

3004	1473	09	908		2491	1537	3772
εἶπατέ μοι·		⁴ τὸ	βάπτισμα		᾿Ιωάννου	ἐξ	οὐρανοῦ
say	to me;	the	immersion		of John	from	heaven

1510	2228	1537	444		013	1161	4817
ἦν	ἢ	ἐξ	ἀνθρώπων;	⁵ οἱ	δὲ	συνελογίσαντο
was it	or	from	men?	The	but	reasoned together

4314 1438		3004	3754 1437 3004		1537
πρὸς ἑαυτοὺς		λέγοντες ὅτι	ἐὰν εἴπωμεν·		ἐξ
to themselves		saying, (")	if we might say;		from

3772	3004		1223	5101 3756 4100
οὐρανοῦ,	ἐρεῖ·	διὰ	τί	οὐκ ἐπιστεύσατε
heaven,	he will say;	through	what	not you trusted

846		1437 1161 3004		1537 444	01
αὐτῷ;	⁶ ἐὰν	δὲ	εἴπωμεν·	ἐξ ἀνθρώπων,	ὁ
in him?	If	but	we might say;	from men,	the

2992	537	2642	1473	3982	1063	1510
λαὸς	ἅπας	καταλιθάσει	ἡμᾶς,	πεπεισμένος	γάρ	ἐστιν
people	all	will stone	us,	+having been	for	they
		thoroughly		persuaded		are+

2491	4396	1510	2532 611	3361
᾿Ιωάννην	προφήτην	εἶναι.	⁷ καὶ ἀπεκρίθησαν	μὴ
John	spokesman	to be.	And they answered,	not

3609a	4159		2532 01	2424	3004 846
εἰδέναι	πόθεν.	⁸ καὶ ὁ		᾿Ιησοῦς	εἶπεν αὐτοῖς·
to know	from where.	And the		Jesus	said to them;

3761	1473 3004 1473	1722 4169	1849
οὐδὲ	ἐγὼ λέγω ὑμῖν	ἐν ποίᾳ	ἐξουσίᾳ
but not I	say to you	in what kind	authority

3778 4160	757	1161 4314 04 2992	3004
ταῦτα ποιῶ.	⁹ ῎Ηρξατο	δὲ πρὸς τὸν λαὸν	λέγειν
these I do.	He began	but to the people	to say

08	3850	3778	444	5100 5452
τὴν	παραβολὴν	ταύτην·	ἄνθρωπός [τις]	ἐφύτευσεν
the	parallel story	this;	man some	planted

290	2532 1554	846	1092	2532
ἀμπελῶνα καὶ	ἐξέδετο	αὐτὸν	γεωργοῖς	καὶ
vineyard and	gave out	it	to farmers	and

589	5550	2425	10	2532 2540
ἀπεδήμησεν	χρόνους	ἱκανούς.		καὶ καιρῷ
journeyed	times	enough.	And	in season

649	4314 016	1092	1401	2443 575	02
ἀπέστειλεν	πρὸς τοὺς	γεωργοὺς	δοῦλον	ἵνα ἀπὸ	τοῦ
he delegated	to the	farmers	slave	that from	the

2590	02	290	1325	846	013 1161
καρποῦ	τοῦ	ἀμπελῶνος	δώσουσιν	αὐτῷ.	οἱ δὲ
fruit	of the	vineyard	they will give	to him;	the but

1092	1821	846	1194	2756	11	2532
γεωργοὶ	ἐξαπέστειλαν	αὐτὸν	δείραντες	κενόν.		καὶ
farmers	delegated	out him	having beaten	empty.	And	

4369	2087	3992	1401	013	1161 2548
προσέθετο	ἕτερον	πέμψαι	δοῦλον·	οἱ	δὲ κἀκεῖνον
he set	to other	to send	slave;	the ones	but also that

1194	2532 818	1821	2756
δείραντες	καὶ ἀτιμάσαντες	ἐξαπέστειλαν	κενόν.
having beaten	and dishonored	they delegated	out empty.

12	2532 4369	5154	3992	013 1161 2532 3778
	καὶ προσέθετο	τρίτον	πέμψαι·	οἱ δὲ καὶ τοῦτον
And	he set	to third	to send;	the but also this

5135	1544		3004 1161 01 2962
τραυματίσαντες	ἐξέβαλον.	¹³	εἶπεν δὲ ὁ κύριος
having wounded	they threw out.	Said	but the master

```
02        290         5101  4160          3992           04   5207
τοῦ     ἀμπελῶνος·  τί    ποιήσω;      πέμψω          τὸν  υἱόν
of the vineyard;   what might I do?  I will send the son
1473   04  27              2481    3778    1788
μου   τὸν ἀγαπητόν·  ἴσως  τοῦτον ἐντραπήσονται.
of me the loved;    likely this   they will regard.
    3708        1161  846    013    1092      1260              4314
14  ἰδόντες   δὲ  αὐτὸν οἱ  γεωργοὶ διελογίζοντο   πρὸς
    Having seen but him  the farmers were reasoning to
240            3004        3778  1510  01   2818
ἀλλήλους   λέγοντες·  οὗτός ἐστιν ὁ  κληρονόμος·
one another saying;    this  is    the inheritor;
615            846      2443 1473  1096       05          .
ἀποκτείνωμεν αὐτόν, ἵνα  ἡμῶν γένηται     ἡ
let us kill  him,    that of us  might become the
2817              15  2532 1544                846   1854     02
κληρονομία.       καὶ  ἐκβαλόντες       αὐτὸν ἔξω     τοῦ
inheritance.     And  having thrown out him  outside the
290           615           5101 3767 4160     846         01
ἀμπελῶνος ἀπέκτειναν.  τί   οὖν ποιήσει αὐτοῖς ὁ
vineyard  they killed. What then will do to them the
2962   02    290             2064        2532 622
κύριος τοῦ ἀμπελῶνος; 16 ἐλεύσεται καὶ ἀπολέσει
master of the vineyard?   He will come and will destroy
016   1092      3778      2532 1325      04   290
τοὺς γεωργοὺς τούτους καὶ  δώσει     τὸν ἀμπελῶνα
the  farmers these   and  will give the vineyard
243        191          1161 3004    3361 1096       17  01
ἄλλοις.   ἀκούσαντες δὲ  εἶπαν·  μὴ  γένοιτο.      ὁ
to others. Having   but they   not  may it    The
           heard         said;          become.
1161  1689              846       3004     5101 3767 1510 09
δὲ  ἐμβλέψας         αὐτοῖς εἶπεν· τί   οὖν ἐστιν τὸ
but having looked in to them said; what then is   the
1125            3778    3037   3739  593              013
γεγραμμένον    τοῦτο· λίθον ὃν   ἀπεδοκίμασαν οἱ
having been written this;  stone which rejected    the
3618           3778   1096     1519 2776      1137
οἰκοδομοῦντες, οὗτος ἐγενήθη εἰς  κεφαλὴν γωνίας;
ones building, this  became  into head    of corner?
    3956 01  4098          1909 1565    04   3037
18  πᾶς ὁ  πεσὼν        ἐπ᾽ ἐκεῖνον τὸν λίθον
    All the one falling on  that    the stone
4917              1909 3739  1161 302 4098
συνθλασθήσεται· ἐφ᾽ ὃν   δ᾽  ἂν  πέσῃ,
will be crushed on  which but -  might fall,
thoroughly;
3039            846      19 2532 2212          013
λικμήσει       αὐτόν.    Καὶ ἐζήτησαν      οἱ
it will pulverize him.   And were seeking the
1122         2532 013 749          1911        1909
γραμματεῖς καὶ  οἱ ἀρχιερεῖς    ἐπιβαλεῖν ἐπ᾽
writers     and the ruler priests to throw on on
846    020 5495   1722 846  07  5610  2532 5399
αὐτὸν τὰς χεῖρας ἐν  αὐτῇ τῇ ὥρᾳ,  καὶ  ἐφοβήθησαν
him   the hands  in  same the hour, and they feared
04  2992    1097        1063 3754 4314 846      3004
τὸν λαόν,  ἔγνωσαν   γὰρ ὅτι  πρὸς αὐτοὺς εἶπεν
the people, they knew for  that to   them   he said
08  3850        3778     20 2532 3906
τὴν παραβολὴν ταύτην.   Καὶ  παρατηρήσαντες
the parallel story this.  And having kept watch
649           1455        5271           1438
ἀπέστειλαν  ἐγκαθέτους ὑποκρινομένους ἑαυτοὺς
they delegated spies    pretending      themselves
1342     1510   2443 1949          846   3056
δικαίους εἶναι, ἵνα  ἐπιλάβωνται    αὐτοῦ λόγου,
right    to be, that they might take on him   word,
```

'What shall I do? I will send my beloved son; perhaps they will respect him.' [14]But when the tenants saw him, they discussed it among themselves and said, 'This is the heir; let us kill him so that the inheritance may be ours.' [15]So they threw him out of the vineyard and killed him. What will the owner of the vineyard do to them? [16]He will come and destroy those tenants and give the vineyard to others." When they heard this, they said, "Heaven forbid!" [17]But he looked at them and said, "What then does this text mean:

'The stone that the
    builders rejected
  has become the
    cornerstone'?[a]

[18]Everyone who falls on that stone will be broken to pieces; and it will crush anyone on whom it falls."

[19]When the scribes and chief priests realized that he had told this parable against them, they wanted to lay hands on him at that very hour, but they feared the people.

[20]So they watched him and sent spies who pretended to be honest, in order to trap him by what he said,

[a] Or keystone

so as to hand him over
to the jurisdiction and
authority of the governor.
²¹So they asked him,
"Teacher, we know that
you are right in what you
say and teach, and you
show deference to no one,
but teach the way of God in
accordance with truth. ²²Is
it lawful for us to pay taxes
to the emperor, or not?"
²³But he perceived their
craftiness and said to them,
²⁴"Show me a denarius.
Whose head and whose title
does it bear?" They said,
"The emperor's." ²⁵He said
to them, "Then give to the
emperor the things that are
the emperor's, and to God
the things that are God's."
²⁶And they were not able in
the presence of the people
to trap him by what he said;
and being amazed by his
answer, they became silent.

27 Some Sadducees,
those who say there is no
resurrection, came to him
²⁸and asked him a question,
"Teacher, Moses wrote for
us that if a man's brother
dies, leaving a wife but no
children, the man*a* shall
marry the widow and raise
up children for his brother.
²⁹Now there were seven
brothers; the first married,
and died childless; ³⁰then
the second ³¹and the third

a Gk his brother

5620	3860	846	07	746	2532	07
ὥστε	παραδοῦναι	αὐτὸν	τῇ	ἀρχῇ	καὶ	τῇ
so that	to give over	him	to the	rule	and	the

1849	02	2232		2532	1905	846
ἐξουσίᾳ	τοῦ	ἡγεμόνος.	**21**	καὶ	ἐπηρώτησαν	αὐτὸν
authority	of the	leader.		And	they asked	on him

3004	1320		3609a		3754	3723
λέγοντες·	διδάσκαλε,	οἴδαμεν			ὅτι	ὀρθῶς
saying;	teacher,		we have known		that	straightly

3004	2532	1321		2532	3756	2983	4383
λέγεις	καὶ	διδάσκεις	καὶ		οὐ	λαμβάνεις	πρόσωπον,
you say	and	teach		and	not	receive	face,

235	1909	225	08	3598	02	2316	1321
ἀλλ᾽	ἐπ᾽	ἀληθείας	τὴν	ὁδὸν	τοῦ	θεοῦ	διδάσκεις·
but	on	truth	the	way	of the	God	you teach;

	1832		1473	2541		5411	1325	2228	3756a
22	ἔξεστιν		ἡμᾶς	Καίσαρι		φόρον	δοῦναι	ἢ	οὔ;
	Is it possible		us	to Caesar		tax	to give	or	no?

	2657		1161	846	08	3834		3004
23	κατανοήσας		δὲ	αὐτῶν	τὴν	πανουργίαν	εἶπεν	
	Having thought		but	of them	the	trickery	he said	
	carefully							

4314	846		1166	1473	1220		5101	2192
πρὸς	αὐτούς·	**24**	δείξατέ	μοι	δηνάριον·		τίνος	ἔχει
to	them;		show	to me	denarius;		of whom	has it

1504	2532	1923		013		1161	3004	2541
εἰκόνα	καὶ	ἐπιγραφήν;		οἱ		δὲ	εἶπαν·	Καίσαρος.
image	and	written on?		The ones		but	said;	of Caesar.

	01	1161	3004	4314	846		5106		591	024
25	ὁ	δὲ	εἶπεν	πρὸς	αὐτούς·		τοίνυν		ἀπόδοτε	τὰ
	The	but	said	to	them;		accordingly		give off	the

2541		2541		2532	024	02		2316	03		2316
Καίσαρος		Καίσαρι		καὶ	τὰ	τοῦ		θεοῦ	τῷ		θεῷ.
of Caesar		to Caesar		and	the	of the		God	to the		God.

	2532	3756	2480			1949		846	4487
26	καὶ	οὐκ	ἴσχυσαν			ἐπιλαβέσθαι		αὐτοῦ	ῥήματος
	And	not	they were strong			to take on		of him	word

1726		02		2992		2532	2296		1909
ἐναντίον		τοῦ		λαοῦ		καὶ	θαυμάσαντες		ἐπὶ
in presence of		the		people		and	having marveled		on

07	612		846	4601				4334
τῇ	ἀποκρίσει		αὐτοῦ	ἐσίγησαν.		**27**		Προσελθόντες
the	answer		of him	they were silent.				Having come to

1161	5100	014		4523		013	483
δέ	τινες	τῶν		Σαδδουκαίων,		οἱ	[ἀντι]λέγοντες
but	some	of the		Sadducees,		the ones	speaking against

386		3361	1510		1905		846		3004
ἀνάστασιν		μὴ	εἶναι,		ἐπηρώτησαν		αὐτὸν	**28**	λέγοντες·
standing up		not	to be,		asked		on him		saying;

1320		3475	1125		1473	1437	5100	80
διδάσκαλε,		Μωϋσῆς	ἔγραψεν		ἡμῖν,	ἐάν	τινος	ἀδελφὸς
teacher,		Moses	wrote		to us,	if	some	brother

599		2192	1135		2532	3778	815		1510
ἀποθάνῃ		ἔχων	γυναῖκα,		καὶ	οὗτος	ἄτεκνος		ᾖ,
might die		having	woman,		and	this	childless		might be,

2443	2983		01	80		846	08	1135		2532
ἵνα	λάβῃ		ὁ	ἀδελφὸς	αὐτοῦ		τὴν	γυναῖκα		καὶ
that	might take		the	brother	of him		the	woman		and

1817		4690	03	80		846		2033	3767
ἐξαναστήσῃ		σπέρμα	τῷ	ἀδελφῷ		αὐτοῦ.	**29**	ἑπτὰ	οὖν
might stand		seed	to	brother		of him.		Seven	then
up out				the					

80		1510	2532	01		4413	2983		1135
ἀδελφοὶ		ἦσαν·	καὶ	ὁ		πρῶτος	λαβὼν		γυναῖκα
brothers		were;	and	the		first	having taken		woman

599		815		2532	01	1208		2532	01
ἀπέθανεν		ἄτεκνος·	**30**	καὶ	ὁ	δεύτερος	**31**	καὶ	ὁ
died		childless;		and	the	second		and	the

5154	2983	846	5615	1161	2532	013	2033
τρίτος	ἔλαβεν	αὐτήν,	ὡσαύτως	δὲ	καὶ	οἱ	ἑπτὰ
third	took	her,	likewise	but	also	the	seven

3756	2641		5043		2532	599	**32**	5306
οὐ	κατέλιπον	τέκνα		καὶ	ἀπέθανον.			ὕστερον
not	left behind	children		and	died.			Later

2532	05	1135	599	**33**	05	1135	3767	1722	07
καὶ	ἡ	γυνὴ	ἀπέθανεν.		ἡ	γυνὴ	οὖν	ἐν	τῇ
also	the	woman	died.		The woman	then	in	the

386		5101	846	1096	1135	013	1063
ἀναστάσει	τίνος	αὐτῶν	γίνεται	γυνή;	οἱ	γὰρ
standing up	who	of them	becomes	woman?	The	for

2033	2192	846	1135	**34**	2532	3004	846	01
ἑπτὰ	ἔσχον	αὐτὴν	γυναῖκα.		καὶ	εἶπεν	αὐτοῖς	ὁ
seven	had	her	woman.		And	said	to them	the

2424	013	5207	02	165	3778	1060	2532
Ἰησοῦς·	οἱ	υἱοὶ	τοῦ	αἰῶνος	τούτου	γαμοῦσιν	καὶ
Jesus;	the	sons	of the	age	this	marry	and

1061	**35**	013	1161	2661	02	165
γαμίσκονται,		οἱ	δὲ	καταξιωθέντες	τοῦ	αἰῶνος
are given in marriage,		the	but	ones having been worthy	of the	age

1565	5177	2532	06	386	06	1537
ἐκείνου	τυχεῖν	καὶ	τῆς	ἀναστάσεως	τῆς	ἐκ
that	to obtain	also	the	standing up	the	from

3498	3777	1060	3777	1060a
νεκρῶν	οὔτε	γαμοῦσιν	οὔτε	γαμίζονται·
dead	neither	marry	nor	are given in marriage;

36	3761	1063	599	2089·	1410
	οὐδὲ	γὰρ	ἀποθανεῖν	ἔτι	δύνανται,
	but not	for	to die	still	they are able,

2465		1063	1510	2532	5207	1510
ἰσάγγελοι		γάρ	εἰσιν	καὶ	υἱοί	εἰσιν
equal messengers		for	they are	and	sons	they are

2316	06	386	5207	1510	**37**	3754
Θεοῦ	τῆς	ἀναστάσεως	υἱοὶ	ὄντες.		ὅτι
of God	of the	standing up	sons	being.		Because

1161	1453	013	3498	2532	3475	3377	1909
δὲ	ἐγείρονται	οἱ	νεκροί,	καὶ	Μωϋσῆς	ἐμήνυσεν	ἐπὶ
but	are raised	the	dead,	and	Moses	reported	on

06	942	5613	3004	2962	04	2316	11
τῆς	βάτου,	ὡς	λέγει	κύριον	τὸν	θεὸν	Ἀβραὰμ
the	thornbush,	as	he says	Master	the	God	Abraham

2532	2316	2464	2532	2316	2384	**38**	2316	1161	3756
καὶ	θεὸν	Ἰσαὰκ	καὶ	θεὸν	Ἰακώβ.		θεὸς	δὲ	οὐκ
and	God	Isaac	and	God	Jacob.		God	but	not

1510	3498	235	2198	3956	1063	846	2198
ἔστιν	νεκρῶν	ἀλλὰ	ζώντων,	πάντες	γὰρ	αὐτῷ	ζῶσιν.
he is	of dead	but	of living,	all	for	to him	live.

39	611		1161	5100	014	1122	3004
	Ἀποκριθέντες	δέ	τινες	τῶν	γραμματέων	εἶπαν·
	Having answered	but	some	of the	writers	said;

1320	2573	3004	**40**	3765	1063
διδάσκαλε,	καλῶς	εἶπας.		οὐκέτι	γὰρ
teacher,	well	you said.		No longer	for

5111		1905	846	3762	**41**	3004	1161
ἐτόλμων		ἐπερωτᾶν	αὐτὸν	οὐδέν.		Εἶπεν	δὲ
they were daring		to ask	on him	nothing.		He said	but

4314	846	4459	3004	04	5547	1510	1160a
πρὸς	αὐτούς·	πῶς	λέγουσιν	∙ τὸν	χριστὸν	εἶναι	Δαυὶδ
to	them;	how	do they say	the	Christ	to be	David

5207	**42**	846	1063	1160a	3004	1722	976	5568
υἱόν;		αὐτὸς	γὰρ	Δαυὶδ	λέγει	ἐν	βίβλῳ	ψαλμῶν·
son?		Himself	for	David	says	in	book	of Psalms;

3004	2962	03	2962	1473	2521	1537	1188
εἶπεν	κύριος	τῷ	κυρίῳ	μου·	κάθου	ἐκ	δεξιῶν
said	Master	to the	Master	of me;	sit	from	right

1473	**43**	2193	302	5087	016	2190	1473
μου,		ἕως	ἂν	θῶ	τοὺς	ἐχθρούς	σου
me,		until	-	I might set	the	hostile ones	of you

married her, and so in the same way all seven died childless. [32]Finally the woman also died. [33]In the resurrection, therefore, whose wife will the woman be? For the seven had married her."

[34]Jesus said to them, "Those who belong to this age marry and are given in marriage; [35]but those who are considered worthy of a place in that age and in the resurrection from the dead neither marry nor are given in marriage. [36]Indeed they cannot die anymore, because they are like angels and are children of God, being children of the resurrection. [37]And the fact that the dead are raised Moses himself showed, in the story about the bush, where he speaks of the Lord as the God of Abraham, the God of Isaac, and the God of Jacob. [38]Now he is God not of the dead, but of the living; for to him all of them are alive."

[39]Then some of the scribes answered, "Teacher, you have spoken well." [40]For they no longer dared to ask him another question.

[41]Then he said to them, "How can they say that the Messiah[a] is David's son? [42]For David himself says in the book of Psalms,

'The Lord said to my Lord,

[43]"Sit at my right hand, until I make your enemies your footstool."'

---

[a] Or the Christ

44David thus calls him Lord; so how can he be his son?"

45 In the hearing of all the people he said to the[a] disciples, 46"Beware of the scribes, who like to walk around in long robes, and love to be greeted with respect in the marketplaces, and to have the best seats in the synagogues and places of honor at banquets. 47They devour widows' houses and for the sake of appearance say long prayers. They will receive the greater condemnation."

CHAPTER 21

He looked up and saw rich people putting their gifts into the treasury; 2he also saw a poor widow put in two small copper coins. 3He said, "Truly I tell you, this poor widow has put in more than all of them; 4for all of them have contributed out of their abundance, but she out of her poverty has put in all she had to live on."

5 When some were speaking about the temple, how it was adorned with beautiful stones and gifts dedicated to God, he said, 6"As for these things that you see, the days will come when not one stone will be left upon another; all will be thrown down."

7 They asked him, "Teacher, when

[a] Other ancient authorities read his

| 5286 | 014 | 4228 | 1473 | 44 | 1160a | 3767 | 2962 | 846 |
ὑποπόδιον τῶν ποδῶν σου. 44 Δαυὶδ οὖν κύριον αὐτὸν
footstool of the feet of you. David then Master him

| 2564 | 2532 | 4459 | 846 | 5207 | 1510 | 45 | 191 | 1161 |
καλεῖ, καὶ πῶς αὐτοῦ υἱός ἐστιν; 45 Ἀκούοντος δὲ
calls, and how of him son is he? Hearing but

| 3956 | 02 | 2992 | 3004 | 015 | 3101 | 846 |
παντὸς τοῦ λαοῦ εἶπεν τοῖς μαθηταῖς [αὐτοῦ]·
all of the people he said to the learners of him;

46 | 4337 | 575 | 014 | 1122 | 014 | 2309 |
προσέχετε ἀπὸ τῶν γραμματέων τῶν θελόντων
hold to from the writers of the ones wanting

| 4043 | 1722 | 4749 | 2532 | 5368 | 783 |
περιπατεῖν ἐν στολαῖς καὶ φιλούντων ἀσπασμοὺς
to walk around in long robes and loving greetings

| 1722 | 019 | 58 | 2532 | 4410 | 1722 | 019 |
ἐν ταῖς ἀγοραῖς καὶ πρωτοκαθεδρίας ἐν ταῖς
in the markets and first chairs in the

| 4864 | 2532 | 4411 | 1722 | 023 |
συναγωγαῖς καὶ πρωτοκλισίας ἐν τοῖς
synagogues and first reclining places in the

| 1173 | 3739 | 2719 | 020 | 3614 | 018 |
δείπνοις, 47 οἳ κατεσθίουσιν τὰς οἰκίας τῶν
dinners, who eat up the houses of the

| 5503 | 2532 | 4392 | 3117 | 4336 | 3778 |
χηρῶν καὶ προφάσει μακρὰ προσεύχονται· οὗτοι
widows and in pretext far they pray; these

| 2983 | 4055 | 2917 | 21:1 | 308 |
λήμψονται περισσότερον κρίμα. 21:1 Ἀναβλέψας
will take more excessive judgment. Having looked up

| 1161 | 3708 | 016 | 906 | 1519 | 012 | 1049 |
δὲ εἶδεν τοὺς βάλλοντας εἰς τὸ γαζοφυλάκιον
but he saw the ones throwing into the treasury box

| 024 | 1435 | 846 | 4145 | 2 | 3708 | 1161 | 5100 | 5503 |
τὰ δῶρα αὐτῶν πλουσίους. 2 εἶδεν δέ τινα χήραν
the gifts of them rich. He saw but some widow

| 3998 | 906 | 1563 | 3016 | 1417 | 3 | 2532 | 3004 |
πενιχρὰν βάλλουσαν ἐκεῖ λεπτὰ δύο, 3 καὶ εἶπεν·
very poor throwing there lepta two, and he said;

| 230 | 3004 | 1473 | 3754 | 05 | 5503 | 3778 | 05 | 4434 |
ἀληθῶς λέγω ὑμῖν ὅτι ἡ χήρα αὕτη ἡ πτωχὴ
truly I say to you that the widow this the poor

| 4183 | 3956 | 906 | 4 | 3956 | 1063 | 3778 | 1537 | 010 |
πλεῖον πάντων ἔβαλεν· 4 πάντες γὰρ οὗτοι ἐκ τοῦ
more of all she threw; all for these from the

| 4052 | 846 | 906 | 1519 | 024 | 1435 | 3778 |
περισσεύοντος αὐτοῖς ἔβαλον εἰς τὰ δῶρα, αὕτη
exceeding to them threw into the gifts, this one

| 1161 | 1537 | 010 | 5303 | 846 | 3956 | 04 | 979 | 3739 |
δὲ ἐκ τοῦ ὑστερήματος αὐτῆς πάντα τὸν βίον ὃν
but from the lack of her all the life which

| 2192 | 906 | 5 | 2532 | 5100 | 3004 | 4012 | 010 |
εἶχεν ἔβαλεν. 5 Καί τινων λεγόντων περὶ τοῦ
she had she threw. And some saying about the

| 2411 | 3754 | 3037 | 2570 | 2532 | 334 |
ἱεροῦ ὅτι λίθοις καλοῖς καὶ ἀναθήμασιν
temple that in stones good and dedications

| 2885 | 3004 | 6 | 3778 | 3739 | 2334 |
κεκόσμηται εἶπεν· 6 ταῦτα ἃ θεωρεῖτε
it has been adorned he said; these that you watch

| 2064 | 2250 | 1722 | 3739 | 3756 | 863 |
ἐλεύσονται ἡμέραι ἐν αἷς οὐκ ἀφεθήσεται
will come days in which not it will be sent off

| 3037 | 1909 | 3037 | 3739 | 3756 | 2647 |
λίθος ἐπὶ λίθῳ ὃς οὐ καταλυθήσεται.
stone on stone which not it will be unloosed.

7 | 1905 | 1161 | 846 | 3004 | 1320 | 4219 |
Ἐπηρώτησαν δὲ αὐτὸν λέγοντες· διδάσκαλε, πότε
They asked on but him saying, teacher, when

3767	3778	1510		2532	5101	09	4592		3752
οὖν	ταῦτα	ἔσται	καὶ	τί	τὸ	σημεῖον	ὅταν
then	these	will be and	what	the	sign	when

3195		3778	1096		8	01	1161	3004		991
μέλλῃ	ταῦτα	γίνεσθαι;	ὁ	δὲ	εἶπεν·	βλέπετε
it is about these to become?	The	but	said,	look

3361	4105			4183	1063	2064
μὴ	πλανηθῆτε·	πολλοὶ γὰρ	ἐλεύσονται
not	you might be deceived;	many	for	will come

1909	011	3686	1473	3004		1473	1510	2532	01
ἐπὶ	τῷ	ὀνόματί	μου	λέγοντες·	ἐγώ	εἰμι,	καί·	ὁ
on	the	name	of me	saying,	I	am,	and;	the

2540	1448		3361	4198		3694	846
καιρὸς	ἤγγικεν.	μὴ	πορευθῆτε	ὀπίσω	αὐτῶν.
season has neared.	Not	you might travel	after them.

9	3752	1161	191		4171	2532	181
	ὅταν	δὲ	ἀκούσητε	πολέμους	καὶ	ἀκαταστασίας,
When but	you might hear	wars	and unstablenesses,

3361	4422		1163	1063	3778	1096		4413
μὴ	πτοηθῆτε·	δεῖ	γὰρ	ταῦτα	γενέσθαι	πρῶτον,
not	you might be terrified;	it is	for	these	to become	first,
		necessary

235	3756	2112		09	5056		10	5119	3004
ἀλλ᾽	οὐκ	εὐθέως	τὸ	τέλος.		Τότε	ἔλεγεν
but	not	immediately	the	completion.	Then	he was saying

846		1453		1484	1909	1484	2532	932
αὐτοῖς·	ἐγερθήσεται	ἔθνος	ἐπ᾽	ἔθνος	καὶ	βασιλεία
to them;	will be raised	nation	on	nation	and	kingdom

1909	932		11	4578		5037	3173		2532	2596
ἐπὶ	βασιλείαν,		σεισμοί	τε	μεγάλοι	καὶ	κατὰ
on	kingdom,		shakes	and	great	and	against

5117	3042		2532	3061		1510		5400		5037	2532
τόπους	λιμοὶ	καὶ	λοιμοὶ	ἔσονται,	φόβητρά	τε	καὶ
places	famines	and	plagues	will be,	fearful	both	and

575	3772	4592	3173	1510		12	4253	1161	3778
ἀπ᾽	οὐρανοῦ	σημεῖα	μεγάλα	ἔσται.		Πρὸ	δὲ	τούτων
from heaven	signs	great	will be.	Before	but	these

3956	1911			1909	1473	020	5495	846
πάντων	ἐπιβαλοῦσιν	ἐφ᾽	ὑμᾶς	τὰς	χεῖρας	αὐτῶν
all	they will throw on	on	you	the	hands	of them

2532	1377		3860		1519	020	4864
καὶ	διώξουσιν,	παραδιδόντες	εἰς	τὰς	συναγωγὰς
and	they will pursue,	giving over	into	the	synagogues

2532	5438	520		1909	935		2532	2232
καὶ	φυλακάς,	ἀπαγομένους	ἐπὶ	βασιλεῖς	καὶ	ἡγεμόνας
and	guards,	being led off	on	kings	and	leaders

1752		010	3686	1473	13	576
ἕνεκεν	τοῦ	ὀνόματός	μου·		ἀποβήσεται
on account of	the	name	of me;	it will go off

1473	1519	3142		14	5087	3767	1722	019	2588
ὑμῖν	εἰς	μαρτύριον.		θέτε	οὖν	ἐν	ταῖς	καρδίαις
to you	into testimony.	Set	then	in	the	hearts

1473	3361	4304		626		15	1473
ὑμῶν	μὴ	προμελετᾶν	ἀπολογηθῆναι·		ἐγὼ
of you	not	to take care before	to defend;	I

1063	1325		1473	4750	2532	4678	3739		3756
γὰρ	δώσω	ὑμῖν	στόμα	καὶ	σοφίαν	ᾗ	οὐ
for	will give	to you	mouth	and	wisdom	in which	not

1410		436		2228	483		537		013
δυνήσονται	ἀντιστῆναι	ἢ	ἀντειπεῖν	ἅπαντες	οἱ
will be able	to stand against	or	to speak against	all	the ones

480		1473	16	3860		1161	2532
ἀντικείμενοι	ὑμῖν.		παραδοθήσεσθε	δὲ	καὶ
lying against you.		You will be given over	but	and

5259	1118		2532	80		2532	4773		2532	5384
ὑπὸ	γονέων	καὶ	ἀδελφῶν	καὶ	συγγενῶν	καὶ	φίλων,
by	parents	and	brothers	and	relatives	and	friends,

will this be, and what will be the sign that this is about to take place?" [8]And he said, "Beware that you are not led astray; for many will come in my name and say, 'I am he!'[a] and, 'The time is near!'[b] Do not go after them.

[9] "When you hear of wars and insurrections, do not be terrified; for these things must take place first, but the end will not follow immediately." [10]Then he said to them, "Nation will rise against nation, and kingdom against kingdom; [11]there will be great earthquakes, and in various places famines and plagues; and there will be dreadful portents and great signs from heaven.

[12] "But before all this occurs, they will arrest you and persecute you; they will hand you over to synagogues and prisons, and you will be brought before kings and governors because of my name. [13]This will give you an opportunity to testify. [14]So make up your minds not to prepare your defense in advance; [15]for I will give you words[c] and a wisdom that none of your opponents will be able to withstand or contradict. [16]You will be betrayed even by parents and brothers, by relatives and friends;

a Gk I am
b Or at hand
c Gk a mouth

and they will put some of
you to death. ¹⁷You will be
hated by all because of my
name. ¹⁸But not a hair of
your head will perish. ¹⁹By
your endurance you will
gain your souls.

20 "When you see
Jerusalem surrounded by
armies, then know that its
desolation has come near.ᵃ
²¹Then those in Judea must
flee to the mountains, and
those inside the city must
leave it, and those out in
the country must not enter
it; ²²for these are days of
vengeance, as a fulfillment
of all that is written. ²³Woe
to those who are pregnant
and to those who are
nursing infants in those
days! For there will be
great distress on the earth
and wrath against this
people; ²⁴they will fall by
the edge of the sword and
be taken away as captives
among all nations; and
Jerusalem will be trampled
on by the Gentiles, until
the times of the Gentiles
are fulfilled.

25 "There will be signs
in the sun, the moon, and
the stars, and on the earth
distress among nations
confused by the roaring
of the sea and the waves.
²⁶People will faint from
fear and foreboding of
what is coming upon the
world, for the

ᵃ Or is at hand

2532	2289			1537	1473	**17**	2532
καὶ	θανατώσουσιν			ἐξ	ὑμῶν,		καὶ
and	they will put to death			from	you,		and

1510   3404   5259 3956 1223   012
ἔσεσθε   μισούμενοι   ὑπὸ πάντων διὰ   τὸ
you will be+   +being hated by all   because of the

3686 1473   **18** 2532 2359 1537 06 2776   1473   3756
ὄνομά μου.   καὶ θρὶξ ἐκ τῆς κεφαλῆς ὑμῶν οὐ
name of me.   And hair from the head   of you not

3361 622   **19** 1722 07   5281   1473
μὴ ἀπόληται.   ἐν   τῇ ὑπομονῇ ὑμῶν
not might be destroyed. In the patience of you

2932   020 5590 1473   **20** 3752 1161 3708
κτήσασθε τὰς ψυχὰς ὑμῶν.   Ὅταν δὲ ἴδητε
acquire   the souls of you.   When but you might see

2944   5259 4760   2419   5119
κύκλουμενην   ὑπὸ στρατοπέδων Ἰερουσαλήμ, τότε
being encircled by soldier camps Jerusalem,   then

1097 3754 1448   05   2050   846   **21** 5119
γνῶτε ὅτι ἤγγικεν ἡ   ἐρήμωσις αὐτῆς.   τότε
know that has neared the desolation of it.   Then

013   1722 07 2449   5343   1519 024 3735 2532
οἱ   ἐν τῇ Ἰουδαίᾳ φευγέτωσαν εἰς τὰ ὄρη καὶ
the ones in the Judea   let flee   into the hills and

013   1722 3319 846 1633   2532
οἱ   ἐν μέσῳ αὐτῆς ἐκχωρείτωσαν   καὶ
the ones in middle of it let make room out and

013   1722 019 5561   3361 1525   1519
οἱ   ἐν ταῖς χώραις μὴ εἰσερχέσθωσαν εἰς
the ones in the countries not let go into   into

846   **22** 3754   2250   1557   3778 1510
αὐτήν,   ὅτι   ἡμέραι ἐκδικήσεως   αὐταί εἰσιν
it,   because days of bring out right these are

010   4092   3956 024 1125
τοῦ   πλησθῆναι   πάντα τὰ γεγραμμένα.
of the to be filled all   the having been written.

23 3759 019   1722 1064   2192   2532 019
ουαὶ ταῖς   ἐν γαστρὶ ἐχούσαις καὶ ταῖς
Woe to the ones   in womb   having   and the ones

2337   1722 1565   019 2250   1510   1063
θηλαζούσαις ἐν ἐκείναις ταῖς ἡμέραις· ἔσται γὰρ
giving nursing in those   the days;   will be for

318   3173   1909 06 1093   2532 3709 03
ἀνάγκη μεγάλη ἐπὶ τῆς γῆς καὶ ὀργὴ τῷ
necessity great on the earth and anger to the

2992 3778   **24** 2532 4098   4750   3162
λαῷ τούτῳ,   καὶ πεσοῦνται   στόματι μαχαίρης
people this,   and they will fall in mouth of sword

2532 163   1519 024 1484   3956 2532
καὶ αἰχμαλωτισθήσονται εἰς τὰ ἔθνη   πάντα, καὶ
and they will be captured in the nations all,   and

2419   1510 3961   5259 1484   891
Ἰερουσαλὴμ ἔσται πατουμένη   ὑπὸ ἐθνῶν, ἄχρι
Jerusalem will be+ +being walked by nations, until

3739 4137   2540   1484   **25** 2532 1510   4592
οὗ πληρωθῶσιν καιροὶ ἐθνῶν.   Καὶ ἔσονται σημεῖα
which they might seasons of nations. And will be signs
                          fill

1722 2246 2532 4582   2532 798   2532 1909 06 1093
ἐν ἡλίῳ καὶ σελήνῃ καὶ ἄστροις, καὶ ἐπὶ τῆς γῆς
in sun and moon   and stars,   and on the earth

4928   1484   1722 640   2279 2281   2532 4535
συνοχὴ ἐθνῶν   ἐν ἀπορίᾳ ἤχους θαλάσσης καὶ σάλου,
anguish of nations in doubt sound of sea   and shaking,

26 674   444   575 5401 2532 4329
ἀποψυχόντων ἀνθρώπων ἀπὸ φόβου καὶ προσδοκίας
fainting   of men   from fear and expectation

022   1904   07   3625   017 1063
τῶν ἐπερχομένων τῇ οἰκουμένῃ,   αἱ γὰρ
of the coming on in the inhabited world, the for

```
1411        014      3772      4531              27  2532 5119
δυνάμεις τῶν    οὐρανῶν σαλευθήσονται.        καὶ  τότε
powers   of the heavens will be shaken.    And  then
3708        04   5207 02      444         2064        1722
ὄψονται       τὸν υἱὸν τοῦ   ἀνθρώπου ἐρχόμενον ἐν
they will see the son of the man        coming    in
3507     3326 1411    2532 1391      4183      28  757
νεφέλῃ μετὰ δυνάμεως καὶ δόξης     πολλῆς.       ἀρχομένων
cloud  with power    and splendor much.        Beginning
1161 3778   1096     352       2532 1869          020
δὲ  τούτων γίνεσθαι ἀνακύψατε καὶ ἐπάρατε      τὰς
but these  to become bend up  and lift up on the
2776     1473    1360        1448      05 629
κεφαλὰς ὑμῶν, διότι      ἐγγίζει ἡ  ἀπολύτρωσις
heads   of you, because that nears   the redemption
1473   29  2532 3004    3850           846      3708
ὑμῶν.      Καὶ εἶπεν  παραβολὴν    αὐτοῖς· ἴδετε
of you.    And he said parallel story to them; see
08  4808     2532 3956  024 1186        30 3752
τὴν συκῆν   καὶ πάντα τὰ δένδρα·         ὅταν
the fig tree and all   the trees;         when
4261                   2235      991        575
προβάλωσιν             ἤδη,    βλέποντες ἀφ'
they might thrown before already, seeing   from
1438        1097      3754 2235   1451  09  2330
ἑαυτῶν     γινώσκετε ὅτι ἤδη    ἐγγὺς τὸ θέρος
themselves know      that already near  the summer
1510  31  3779    2532 1473    3752 3708           3778
ἐστίν·    οὕτως καὶ ὑμεῖς, ὅταν ἴδητε         ταῦτα
is;       thusly also you,  when you might see these
1096       1097      3754 1451    1510  05  932
γινόμενα, γινώσκετε ὅτι ἐγγύς ἐστιν ἡ  βασιλεία
becoming, know      that near   is   the kingdom
02       2316   32  281    3004  1473    3754 3756 3361
τοῦ    θεοῦ.      ἀμὴν λέγω ὑμῖν ὅτι οὐ  μὴ
of the God.       Amen I say to you that not  not
3928         05  1074      3778 2193  302 3956
παρέλθῃ      ἡ  γενεὰ    αὕτη ἕως ἂν πάντα
might go along the generation this until -   all
1096       01  3772    2532 05  1093    3928
γένηται.  33  ὁ  οὐρανὸς καὶ ἡ  γῆ     παρελεύσονται,
might become. The heaven and the earth will go along,
013 1161 3056   1473  3756 3361 3928
οἱ  δὲ  λόγοι μου  οὐ  μὴ  παρελεύσονται.
the but words of me not  not will go along.
34  4337         1161 1438     3379      916
    Προσέχετε δὲ  ἑαυτοῖς  μήποτε βαρηθῶσιν
    Hold to   but yourselves not then might be burdened
1473   017 2588      1722 2897         2532 3178
ὑμῶν αἱ καρδίαι ἐν  κραιπάλῃ      καὶ μέθῃ
of you the hearts in  dissipation  and drunkenness
2532 3308       982       2532 2186           1909 1473
καὶ μερίμναις βιωτικαῖς καὶ ἐπιστῇ          ἐφ' ὑμᾶς
and anxieties of life   and might stand on on  you
160        05  2250   1565      35  5613 3803
αἰφνίδιος ἡ  ἡμέρα ἐκείνη      ὡς  παγίς·
sudden    the day   that        as  trap;
1898a                1063 1909 3956   016  2521
ἐπεισελεύσεται      γὰρ ἐπὶ πάντας τοὺς καθημένους
it will come on into for  on  all    the ones sitting
1909 4383   3956  06  1093  36 69           1161 1722
ἐπὶ πρόσωπον πάσης τῆς γῆς.   ἀγρυπνεῖτε δὲ  ἐν
on  face    of all the earth. Stay awake but  in
3956   2540   1189     2443 2729
παντὶ καιρῷ δεόμενοι ἵνα κατισχύσητε
in all season begging that you might be strong against
1628       3778  3956  024 3195      1096
ἐκφυγεῖν   ταῦτα πάντα τὰ μέλλοντα γίνεσθαι
to flee out these all   the being about to become
```

powers of the heavens will be shaken. [27]Then they will see 'the Son of Man coming in a cloud' with power and great glory. [28]Now when these things begin to take place, stand up and raise your heads, because your redemption is drawing near."

29 Then he told them a parable: "Look at the fig tree and all the trees; [30]as soon as they sprout leaves you can see for yourselves and know that summer is already near. [31]So also, when you see these things taking place, you know that the kingdom of God is near. [32]Truly I tell you, this generation will not pass away until all things have taken place. [33]Heaven and earth will pass away, but my words will not pass away.

34 "Be on guard so that your hearts are not weighed down with dissipation and drunkenness and the worries of this life, and that day does not catch you unexpectedly, [35]like a trap. For it will come upon all who live on the face of the whole earth. [36]Be alert at all times, praying that you may have the strength to escape all these things that will take place,

and to stand before the Son of Man."

37 Every day he was teaching in the temple, and at night he would go out and spend the night on the Mount of Olives, as it was called. 38And all the people would get up early in the morning to listen to him in the temple.

CHAPTER 22

Now the festival of Unleavened Bread, which is called the Passover, was near. 2The chief priests and the scribes were looking for a way to put Jesus[a] to death, for they were afraid of the people.

3 Then Satan entered into Judas called Iscariot, who was one of the twelve; 4he went away and conferred with the chief priests and officers of the temple police about how he might betray him to them. 5They were greatly pleased and agreed to give him money. 6So he consented and began to look for an opportunity to betray him to them when no crowd was present.

7 Then came the day of Unleavened Bread, on which the Passover lamb had to be sacrificed. 8So Jesus[b] sent Peter and John, saying, "Go and prepare the Passover meal for us that we may eat it." 9They asked him, "Where do you want us to make preparations for it?"
10"Listen," he said to them,

a Gk him
b Gk he

| 2532 | 2476 | 1715 | 02 5207 02 | 444 |

καὶ σταθῆναι ἔμπροσθεν τοῦ υἱοῦ τοῦ ἀνθρώπου.
and to stand in front of the son of the man.

37 Ἦν δὲ τὰς ἡμέρας ἐν τῷ ἱερῷ διδάσκων,
He was+ but the days in the temple +teaching,

τὰς δὲ νύκτας ἐξερχόμενος ηὐλίζετο εἰς τὸ ὄρος
the but nights going out he was lodging in the hill

τὸ καλούμενον Ἐλαιῶν· 38 καὶ πᾶς ὁ λαὸς
the being called of Olives; and all the people

ὤρθριζεν πρὸς αὐτὸν ἐν τῷ ἱερῷ ἀκούειν
were coming in to him in the temple to hear
early morning

αὐτοῦ. 22:1 Ἤγγιζεν δὲ ἡ ἑορτὴ τῶν
him. Was nearing but the festival of the

ἀζύμων ἡ λεγομένη πάσχα. 2 καὶ ἐζήτουν οἱ
unyeasted the one being passover. And were seeking the
yeasted called

ἀρχιερεῖς καὶ οἱ γραμματεῖς τὸ πῶς
ruler priests and the writers the how

ἀνέλωσιν αὐτόν, ἐφοβοῦντο γὰρ τὸν λαόν. 3 Εἰσῆλθεν
they might him, they were for the people. Went into
kill fearing

δὲ σατανᾶς εἰς Ἰούδαν τὸν καλούμενον
but adversary into Judas the one being called

Ἰσκαριώτην, ὄντα ἐκ τοῦ ἀριθμοῦ τῶν δώδεκα·
Iscariot, being from the number of the twelve;

4 καὶ ἀπελθὼν συνελάλησεν τοῖς ἀρχιερεῦσιν
and having gone off he spoke with the ruler priests

καὶ στρατηγοῖς τὸ πῶς αὐτοῖς παραδῷ
and captains the how to them he might give over

αὐτόν. 5 καὶ ἐχάρησαν καὶ συνέθεντο αὐτῷ
him. And they rejoiced and set together to him

ἀργύριον δοῦναι. 6 καὶ ἐξωμολόγησεν, καὶ
silver to give. And he confessed out, and

ἐζήτει εὐκαιρίαν τοῦ παραδοῦναι αὐτὸν
he was seeking good season the to give over him

ἄτερ ὄχλου αὐτοῖς. 7 Ἦλθεν δὲ ἡ ἡμέρα τῶν
without crowd to them. Came but the day of the

ἀζύμων, [ἐν] ᾗ ἔδει θυέσθαι τὸ πάσχα·
unyeasted, in which it was to be the passover;
necessary sacrificed

8 καὶ ἀπέστειλεν Πέτρον καὶ Ἰωάννην εἰπών·
and he delegated Peter and John having said;

πορευθέντες ἑτοιμάσατε ἡμῖν τὸ πάσχα ἵνα
having traveled prepare to us the passover that

φάγωμεν. 9 οἱ δὲ εἶπαν αὐτῷ· ποῦ θέλεις
we might eat. The but said to him; where you want

ἑτοιμάσωμεν; 10 ὁ δὲ εἶπεν αὐτοῖς· ἰδοὺ
we might prepare? The but said to them; look

```
1525                    1473 1519 08   4172   4876            1473
εἰσελθόντων    ὑμῶν εἰς τὴν πόλιν συναντήσει ὑμῖν
having gone into you    into the city   will meet    you
444           2765       5204   941        190
ἄνθρωπος κεράμιον ὕδατος βαστάζων· ἀκολουθήσατε
man           ceramic pot of water bearing;   follow
846    1519 08  3614    1519 3739 1531                    2532
αὐτῷ εἰς τὴν οἰκίαν εἰς ἣν   εἰσπορεύεται,  11 καὶ
him   into the house into which he travels into, and
3004        03        3617         06   3614   3004   1473
ἐρεῖτε τῷ     οἰκοδεσπότῃ τῆς οἰκίας· λέγει σοι
you will to the house         of house;  says  to you
say             supervisor   the
01   1320          4226  1510   09  2646         3699  012
ὁ  διδάσκαλος· ποῦ ἐστιν τὸ κατάλυμα ὅπου τὸ
the teacher;      where is  the guestlodge where the
3957     3326 014 3101      1473   2068          2548
πάσχα μετὰ τῶν μαθητῶν μου φάγω;  12 κἀκεῖνος
passover with the learners of me I might eat? And that
1473 1166   311a          3173 4766        1563
ὑμῖν δείξει ἀνάγαιον μέγα ἐστρωμένον· ἐκεῖ
to   will  upstairs  great having been there
you  show  room            spead;
2090            565                1161 2147          2531
ἑτοιμάσατε.  13 ἀπελθόντες   δὲ εὗρον        καθὼς
prepare.         Having gone off but they found just as
3004        846       2532 2090          012 3957
εἰρήκει    αὐτοῖς καὶ ἡτοίμασαν τὸ πάσχα.
he had said to them and they prepared the passover.
    2532 3753 1096    05   5610  377          2532 013
14 Καὶ ὅτε ἐγένετο ἡ ὥρα,  ἀνέπεσεν καὶ οἱ
   And when became the hour, he reclined and the
652          4862 846      2532 3004        4314 846
ἀπόστολοι σὺν αὐτῷ.  15 καὶ εἶπεν    πρὸς αὐτούς·
delegates with him.       And he said  to    them;
1939       1937       3778 012 3957        2068     3326
ἐπιθυμίᾳ ἐπεθύμησα τοῦτο τὸ πάσχα  φαγεῖν μεθ᾽
in desire I desired  this  the passover to eat  with
1473 4253   010 1473 3958      1063 1473   3754
ὑμῶν πρὸ τοῦ με παθεῖν·  16 λέγω γὰρ ὑμῖν ὅτι
you before the me to suffer;   I say for to you that
3756 3361 2068        846 2193  3755
οὐ μὴ φάγω   αὐτὸ ἕως ὅτου
not not I might eat it  until when
4137            1722 07  932       02       2316  17 2532
πληρωθῇ     ἐν τῇ βασιλείᾳ τοῦ θεοῦ.   17 καὶ
it might filled in the kingdom of the God.  And
1209      4221     2168          3004      2983   3778
δεξάμενος ποτήριον εὐχαριστήσας εἶπεν· λάβετε τοῦτο
having    cup      having given he said; take  this
welcomed          good favor
2532 1266              1519 1438        18  3004
καὶ διαμερίσατε     εἰς ἑαυτούς·    18 λέγω
and divide completely to yourselves;    I say
1063 1473   3754 3756 3361 4095        575   010 3568
γὰρ ὑμῖν, [ὅτι] οὐ μὴ πίω       ἀπὸ τοῦ νῦν
for to you, that not not I might drink from the now
575   010 1079a  06    288       2193 3739 05
ἀπὸ τοῦ γενήματος τῆς ἀμπέλου ἕως οὗ  ἡ
from the produce  of the vine until which the
932       02    2316 2064        2532 2983
βασιλεία τοῦ θεοῦ ἔλθῃ.  19 καὶ λαβὼν
kingdom of the God might come. And having taken
740    2168            2806    2532 1325
ἄρτον εὐχαριστήσας    ἔκλασεν καὶ ἔδωκεν
bread having given good favor he broke and gave
846     3004     3778 1510  09  4983 1473  09
αὐτοῖς λέγων· τοῦτό ἐστιν τὸ σῶμά μου τὸ
to them saying, this  is    the body of me the
```

"when you have entered the city, a man carrying a jar of water will meet you; follow him into the house he enters [11]and say to the owner of the house, 'The teacher asks you, "Where is the guest room, where I may eat the Passover with my disciples?"' [12]He will show you a large room upstairs, already furnished. Make preparations for us there." [13]So they went and found everything as he had told them; and they prepared the Passover meal.

[14]When the hour came, he took his place at the table, and the apostles with him. [15]He said to them, "I have eagerly desired to eat this Passover with you before I suffer; [16]for I tell you, I will not eat it[a] until it is fulfilled in the kingdom of God." [17]Then he took a cup, and after giving thanks he said, "Take this and divide it among yourselves; [18]for I tell you that from now on I will not drink of the fruit of the vine until the kingdom of God comes." [19]Then he took a loaf of bread, and when he had given thanks, he broke it and gave it to them, saying, "This is my body,

---

[a] Other ancient authorities read *never eat it again*

which is given for you. Do
this in remembrance of
me." [20]And he did the same
with the cup after supper,
saying, "This cup that is
poured out for you is the
new covenant in my blood.[a]
[21]But see, the one who
betrays me is with me, and
his hand is on the table.
[22]For the Son of Man is
going as it has been determined, but woe to that one
by whom he is betrayed!"
[23]Then they began to ask
one another which one of
them it could be who would
do this.

    24 A dispute also arose
among them as to which
one of them was to be
regarded as the greatest.
[25]But he said to them,
"The kings of the Gentiles
lord it over them; and those
in authority over them are
called benefactors. [26]But
not so with you; rather the
greatest among you must
become like the youngest,
and the leader like one
who serves. [27]For who is
greater, the one who is at
the table or the one who
serves? Is it not the one at
the table? But I am among
you as one who serves.

    28 "You are those who
have stood by me in my
trials; [29]and I confer on
you, just as

a Other ancient authorities lack, in
whole or in part, verses 19b-20
(which is given . . . in my blood)

	5228	1473	1325		3778	4160		1519 08
	ὑπὲρ	ὑμῶν	διδόμενον·		τοῦτο	ποιεῖτε	εἰς	τὴν
	on behalf	of you	being given;		this	do		into the

1699 364   2532 012 4221   5615   3326
ἐμὴν ἀνάμνησιν.   **20** καὶ τὸ ποτήριον ὡσαύτως μετὰ
my remembrance.   And the cup   likewise   after

012 1172   3004   3778 09 4221   05 2537
τὸ δειπνῆσαι, λέγων· τοῦτο τὸ ποτήριον ἡ καινὴ
the to dine, saying; this the cup   the new

1242   1722 011 129   1473 09 5228   1473
διαθήκη ἐν τῷ αἵματί μου τὸ ὑπὲρ   ὑμῶν
agreement in the blood of me the on behalf of you

1632   4133   2400 05 5495 02
ἐκχυννόμενον. **21** Πλὴν ἰδοὺ ἡ χεὶρ τοῦ
being poured out. Except look the hand of the one

3860   1473 3326 1473 1909 06 5132   **22** 3754
παραδιδόντος με μετ᾽ ἐμοῦ ἐπὶ τῆς τραπέζης.   ὅτι
giving over me with me at the table.   Because

01 5207 3303 02   444   2596 012
ὁ υἱὸς μὲν τοῦ ἀνθρώπου κατὰ τὸ
the son indeed of the man   by the

3724   4198   4133   3759 03
ὡρισμένον   πορεύεται, πλὴν οὐαὶ τῷ
having been designated travels,   except woe to the

444   1565   1223   3739 3860   **23** 2532
ἀνθρώπῳ ἐκείνῳ δι᾽   οὗ παραδίδοται.   καὶ
man   that through whom he is given over. And

846   757   4802   4314 1438   012 5101
αὐτοὶ ἤρξαντο συζητεῖν πρὸς ἑαυτοὺς τὸ τίς
themselves began to dispute to themselves the who

686 1510   1537 846 01 3778 3195
ἄρα εἴη ἐξ αὐτῶν ὁ τοῦτο μέλλων
then might be from them the this being about to

4238   1096   1161 2532 5379   1722
πράσσειν. **24** Ἐγένετο δὲ καὶ φιλονεικία ἐν
to practice. It became but also friend's quarrel in

846   09 5101 846   1380   1510 3173   **25** 01
αὐτοῖς, τὸ τίς αὐτῶν δοκεῖ εἶναι μείζων.   ὁ
to them, the who of them thinks to be greater. The one

1161 3004 846   013 935   022   1484
δὲ εἶπεν αὐτοῖς· οἱ βασιλεῖς τῶν ἐθνῶν
but said to them; the kings   of the nations

2961   846   2532 013 1850
κυριεύουσιν αὐτῶν καὶ οἱ ἐξουσιάζοντες
act as master of them and the ones having authority

846   2110   2564   **26** 1473 1161 3756
αὐτῶν εὐεργέται καλοῦνται.   ὑμεῖς δὲ οὐχ
of them good workers are called. You but not

3779   235 01 3173   1722 1473 1096   5613 01
οὕτως, ἀλλ᾽ ὁ μείζων ἐν ὑμῖν γινέσθω ὡς ὁ
thusly, but the greater in you let become as the

3501   2532 01 2233   5613 01   1247
νεώτερος καὶ ὁ ἡγούμενος ὡς ὁ   διακονῶν.
newer and the leader   as the one serving.

    27 5101 1063 3173   01 345   2228 01
    τίς γὰρ μείζων, ὁ ἀνακείμενος ἢ ὁ
    Who for greater, the one reclining or the one

1247   3780 01 345   1473 1161 1722 3319
διακονῶν; οὐχὶ ὁ ἀνακείμενος; ἐγὼ δὲ ἐν μέσῳ
serving? Not the one reclining? I but in middle

1473   1510 5613 01 1247   1473 1161 1510
ὑμῶν εἰμι ὡς ὁ διακονῶν.   **28** Ὑμεῖς δέ ἐστε
of you am as the one serving. You but are

013   1265   3326 1473 1722 015
οἱ   διαμεμενηκότες   μετ᾽ ἐμοῦ ἐν τοῖς
the ones having stayed through with me in the
ones through

3986   1473   **29** 2504   1303   1473   2531
πειρασμοῖς μου·   κἀγὼ διατίθεμαι ὑμῖν καθὼς
pressures of me;   and I agree   to you just as

1303	1473	01	3962	1473	932	**30**	2443
διέθετό	μοι	ὁ	πατήρ	μου	βασιλείαν,		ἵνα
agreed	to me	the	father	of me	kingdom,		that

2068		2532	4095		1909	06	5132
ἔσθητε		καὶ	πίνητε		ἐπὶ	τῆς	τραπέζης
you might eat		and	you might drink		on	the	table

1473	1722	07	932		1473	2532	2521		1909
μου	ἐν	τῇ	βασιλείᾳ	μου,	καὶ	καθήσεσθε		ἐπὶ
of me	in	the	kingdom	of me,	and	you will sit		on

2362	020	1427	5443	2919	02	2474
θρόνων	τὰς	δώδεκα	φυλὰς	κρίνοντες	τοῦ	Ἰσραήλ.
thrones	the	twelve	tribes	judging	the	Israel.

31
4613	4613	2400	01	4567	1809	1473
Σίμων	Σίμων,	ἰδοὺ	ὁ	σατανᾶς	ἐξητήσατο	ὑμᾶς
Simon	Simon,	look	the	adversary	asked out	you

010	4617	5613	04	4621	**32**	1473	1161	1189
τοῦ	σινιάσαι	ὡς	τὸν	σῖτον·		ἐγὼ	δὲ	ἐδεήθην
of the	to sift	as	the	wheat;		I	but	begged

4012	1473	2443	3361	1587		05	4102	1473
περὶ	σοῦ	ἵνα	μὴ	ἐκλίπῃ		ἡ	πίστις	σου·
about	you	that	not	might leave off		the	trust	of you;

2532	1473	4218	1994	4741	016
καὶ	σύ	ποτε	ἐπιστρέψας	στήρισον	τοὺς
and	you	then	having returned	strengthen	the

80	1473	**33**	01	1161	3004	846	2962
ἀδελφούς	σου.		ὁ	δὲ	εἶπεν	αὐτῷ·	κύριε,
brothers	of you.		The	but	said	to him;	Master,

3326	1473	2092	1510	2532	1519	5438	2532	1519
μετὰ	σοῦ	ἕτοιμός	εἰμι	καὶ	εἰς	φυλακὴν	καὶ	εἰς
with	you	prepared	I am	and	into	guard	and	into

2288	4198	**34**	01	1161	3004	3004	1473
θάνατον	πορεύεσθαι.		ὁ	δὲ	εἶπεν·	λέγω	σοι,
death	to travel.		The	but	said;	I say	to you,

4074	3756	5455	4594	220	2193	5151
Πέτρε,	οὐ	φωνήσει	σήμερον	ἀλέκτωρ	ἕως	τρίς
Peter,	not	will sound	today	rooster	until	three

1473	533	3609a		**35**	2532
με	ἀπαρνήσῃ	εἰδέναι.			Καὶ
me	you might thoroughly deny	to have known.			And

3004	846	3753	649	1473	817	905
εἶπεν	αὐτοῖς·	ὅτε	ἀπέστειλα	ὑμᾶς	ἄτερ	βαλλαντίου
he said to them;		when	I delegated	you	without	purse

2532	4082	2532	5266	3361	5100	5302
καὶ	πήρας	καὶ	ὑποδημάτων,	μή	τινος	ὑστερήσατε;
and	bag	and	sandals,	not	of some	you lacked?

013	1161	3004	3762	**36**	3004	1161	846	235
οἱ	δὲ	εἶπαν·	οὐθενός.		εἶπεν	δὲ	αὐτοῖς·	ἀλλὰ
The	but	said;	of nothing.		He said	but	to them;	but

3568	01	2192	905	142	3668	2532
νῦν	ὁ	ἔχων	βαλλάντιον	ἀράτω,	ὁμοίως	καὶ
now	the	having	purse	let lift up,	likewise	also

4082	2532	01	3361	2192	4453	012	2440	846
πήραν,	καὶ	ὁ	μὴ	ἔχων	πωλησάτω	τὸ	ἱμάτιον	αὐτοῦ
bag,	and	the	not	having	let sell	the	clothes	of him

2532	59	3162	**37**	3004	1063	1473	3754
καὶ	ἀγορασάτω	μάχαιραν.		λέγω	γὰρ	ὑμῖν	ὅτι
and	let buy	sword.		I say	for	to you	that

3778	012	1125	1163	5055	1722	1473
τοῦτοτὸ	γεγραμμένον	δεῖ		τελεσθῆναι	ἐν	ἐμοί,
this	the having been	it is		to be completed	in	me,
	written	necessary				

012	2532	3326	459	3049	2532	1063	09
τό·	καὶ	μετὰ	ἀνόμων	ἐλογίσθη·	καὶ	γὰρ	τὸ
the;	also	with	lawless	he was reasoned;	and	for	the

4012	1473	5056	2192	**38**	013	1161	3004	2962
περὶ	ἐμοῦ	τέλος	ἔχει.		οἱ	δὲ	εἶπαν·	κύριε,
about me		completion	has.		The	but	said;	Master,

2400	3162	5602	1417	01	1161	3004	846	2425
ἰδοὺ	μάχαιραι	ὧδε	δύο.	ὁ	δὲ	εἶπεν	αὐτοῖς·	ἱκανόν
look	swords	here	two.	The	but	said	to them;	enough

my Father has conferred on me, a kingdom, [30]so that you may eat and drink at my table in my kingdom, and you will sit on thrones judging the twelve tribes of Israel.

[31] "Simon, Simon, listen! Satan has demanded[a] to sift all of you like wheat, [32]but I have prayed for you that your own faith may not fail; and you, when once you have turned back, strengthen your brothers." [33]And he said to him, "Lord, I am ready to go with you to prison and to death!" [34]Jesus[b] said, "I tell you, Peter, the cock will not crow this day, until you have denied three times that you know me."

[35] He said to them, "When I sent you out without a purse, bag, or sandals, did you lack anything?" They said, "No, not a thing." [36]He said to them, "But now, the one who has a purse must take it, and likewise a bag. And the one who has no sword must sell his cloak and buy one. [37]For I tell you, this scripture must be fulfilled in me, 'And he was counted among the lawless'; and indeed what is written about me is being fulfilled." [38]They said, "Lord, look, here are two swords." He replied, "It is enough."

a Or has obtained permission
b Gk He

39 He came out and went, as was his custom, to the Mount of Olives; and the disciples followed him. 40When he reached the place, he said to them, "Pray that you may not come into the time of trial."*a*
41Then he withdrew from them about a stone's throw, knelt down, and prayed, 42"Father, if you are willing, remove this cup from me; yet, not my will but yours be done." [[43Then an angel from heaven appeared to him and gave him strength. 44In his anguish he prayed more earnestly, and his sweat became like great drops of blood falling down on the ground.]]*b* 45When he got up from prayer, he came to the disciples and found them sleeping because of grief, 46and he said to them, "Why are you sleeping? Get up and pray that you may not come into the time of trial."*a*

47 While he was still speaking, suddenly a crowd came, and the one called Judas, one of the twelve, was leading them. He approached Jesus to kiss him; 48but Jesus said to him, "Judas, is it with a kiss that you are betraying the Son of Man?" 49When those who were around him saw what was coming, they asked, "Lord, should we strike with the sword?"

a Or into temptation
b Other ancient authorities lack
    verses 43 and 44

1510		2532 1831		4198	2596 012
ἐστιν.	**39** Καὶ	ἐξελθὼν		ἐπορεύθη	κατὰ τὸ
it is.	And	having gone	out	he traveled by	the

1485   1519 012 3735 018   1636   190   1161
ἔθος   εἰς τὸ ὄρος τῶν   ἐλαιῶν, ἠκολούθησαν δὲ
custom to   the hill of the olives, followed   but

846   2532 013 3101   1096   1161 1909 02
αὐτῷ καὶ οἱ μαθηταί.   **40** γενόμενος   δὲ ἐπὶ τοῦ
him   also the learners.   Having become but   on   the

5117   3004   846   4336   3361 1525
τόπου εἶπεν αὐτοῖς· προσεύχεσθε μὴ   εἰσελθεῖν
place he said to them; pray   not   to go into

1519 3986   2532 846   645   575
εἰς πειρασμόν. **41** καὶ αὐτὸς ἀπεσπάσθη   ἀπ᾽
into pressure.   And himself was drawn off from

846   5616 3037   1000 2532 5087   024 1119
αὐτῶν ὡσεὶ λίθου βολὴν καὶ θεὶς   τὰ γόνατα
them as of stone throw and having set the knees

4336   3004   3962 1487 1014   3911
προσηύχετο **42** λέγων· πάτερ, εἰ βούλει παρένεγκε
he was praying saying; father, if you plan carry along

3778 012 4221   575 1473 4133   3361 09 2307
τοῦτο τὸ ποτήριον ἀπ᾽ ἐμοῦ· πλὴν μὴ τὸ θέλημά
this the cup   from me; except not the want

1473 235 09 4674 1096   3708   1161
μου ἀλλὰ τὸ σὸν γινέσθω. **43** [[ὤφθη   δὲ
of me but the your let become.   Was seen but

846   32   575 3772 1765   846
αὐτῷ ἄγγελος ἀπ᾽ οὐρανοῦ ἐνισχύων   αὐτόν.
to him messenger from heaven strengthening in him.

44 2532 1096   1722 74   1619
καὶ γενόμενος   ἐν ἀγωνίᾳ ἐκτενέστερον
And having become in agony more intensely

4336   2532 1096   01 2402 846   5616
προσηύχετο·   καὶ ἐγένετο ὁ ἱδρὼς αὐτοῦ ὡσεὶ
he was praying; and became the sweat of him as

2361   129   2597   1909 08 1093   2532
θρόμβοι αἵματος καταβαίνοντος ἐπὶ τὴν γῆν.]] **45** καὶ
clots of blood going down   on the earth.   And

450   575 06 4335   2064   4314 016
ἀναστὰς   ἀπὸ τῆς προσευχῆς ἐλθὼν   πρὸς τοὺς
having stood up from the prayer having gone to the

3101   2147   2837   846   575 06 3077
μαθητὰς εὗρεν κοιμωμένους αὐτοὺς ἀπὸ τῆς λύπης,
learners he found being asleep them   from the grief,

46 2532 3004   846   5101 2518   450
καὶ εἶπεν αὐτοῖς· τί καθεύδετε; ἀναστάντες
and he said to them; why you sleep? Having stood up

4336   2443 3361 1525   1519 3986
προσεύχεσθε, ἵνα μὴ εἰσέλθητε   εἰς πειρασμόν.
pray,   that not you might go into into pressure.

47 2089 846 2980   2400 3793 2532 01
Ἔτι αὐτοῦ λαλοῦντος ἰδοὺ ὄχλος, καὶ ὁ
Still him speaking   look crowd, and the one

3004   2455 1520 014   1427 4281
λεγόμενος Ἰούδας εἰς τῶν   δώδεκα προήρχετο
being said Judas one of the twelve was coming before

846   2532 1448   03   2424 5368   846
αὐτοὺς καὶ ἤγγισεν τῷ   Ἰησοῦ φιλῆσαι αὐτόν.
them and he neared to the Jesus to love him.

48 2424 1161 3004 846   2455 5370   04 5207
Ἰησοῦς δὲ   εἶπεν αὐτῷ· Ἰούδα, φιλήματι τὸν υἱὸν
Jesus but said to him; Judas, in kiss the son

02 444   3860   3708   1161 013
τοῦ ἀνθρώπου παραδίδως; **49** ἰδόντες   δὲ οἱ
of the man   are you giving over? Having seen but the

4012 846   012 1510   3004 2962 1487 3960
περὶ αὐτὸν τὸ ἐσόμενον εἶπαν· κύριε, εἰ πατάξομεν
about him the being   said, Master, if we will hit

```
1722  3162        50  2532  3960       1520  5100  1537  846
ἐν    μαχαίρῃ;        καὶ  ἐπάταξεν   εἷς   τις   ἐξ    αὐτῶν
in    sword?          And  hit        one   some  from  them
02    749              04    1401     2532  851          012
τοῦ   ἀρχιερέως        τὸν  δοῦλον    καὶ   ἀφεῖλεν      τὸ
of the ruler priest    the  slave     and   lifted       off the
3775  846   012  1188          611                1161  01  2424
οὖς   αὐτοῦ τὸ   δεξιόν.   51  ἀποκριθεὶς          δὲ    ὁ   Ἰησοῦς
ear   of him the right.       Having answered     but   the Jesus
3004  1439  2193  3778      2532  681               010  5621
εἶπεν· ἐᾶτε ἕως   τούτου·  καὶ   ἀψάμενος          τοῦ  ὠτίου
said;  allow until this;    and   having touched     the  ear
2390  846    52  3004  1161  2424      4314  016
ἰάσατο αὐτόν.     Εἶπεν δὲ  Ἰησοῦς   πρὸς τοὺς
he cured him.     Said  but Jesus     to    the ones
3854          1909 846  749              2532 4755
παραγενομένους ἐπ’ αὐτὸν ἀρχιερεῖς     καὶ  στρατηγοὺς
having arrived on  him   ruler priests and  captains
010   2411  2532 4245            5613 1909 3027
τοῦ   ἱεροῦ καὶ  πρεσβυτέρους· ὡς   ἐπὶ  λῃστὴν
of the temple and older men,     as   on   robber
1831        3326 3162       2532 3586       53  2596 2250
ἐξήλθατε    μετὰ μαχαιρῶν καὶ  ξύλων;        καθ’ ἡμέραν
you came out with swords   and  woods?         By   day
1510   1473 3326 1473  1722 011  2411     3756
ὄντος  μου  μεθ’ ὑμῶν ἐν   τῷ  ἱερῷ     οὐκ
being of me with you   in   the  temple    not
1614          020  5495   1909 1473  235   3778 1510
ἐξετείνατε    τὰς  χεῖρας ἐπ’  ἐμέ, ἀλλ’ αὐτη ἐστὶν
you stretched out the hands on  me,  but   this is
1473  05   5610 2532 05   1849      010  4655
ὑμῶν  ἡ   ὥρα καὶ  ἡ   ἐξουσία  τοῦ  σκότους.
of you the hour and  the authority of the dark.
   4815           1161 846  71        2532 1521
54 Συλλαβόντες     δὲ  αὐτὸν ἤγαγον  καὶ  εἰσήγαγον
   Having taken together but him they led  and  led into
1519 08   3614  02   749           01   1161 4074
εἰς  τὴν οἰκίαν τοῦ  ἀρχιερέως·    ὁ    δὲ  Πέτρος
into the house of the ruler priest; the  but  Peter
190        3113          55  4014a         1161 4442
ἠκολούθει  μακρόθεν.        περιαψάντων    δὲ  πῦρ
was following from far.      Having lit around but fire
1722 3162  06   833        2532 4776
ἐν   μέσῳ  τῆς αὐλῆς     καὶ  συγκαθισάντων
in   middle of the courtyard and  having sat together
2521     01  4074    3319 846      56 3708        1161
ἐκάθητο  ὁ   Πέτρος μέσος αὐτῶν.    ἰδοῦσα        δὲ
sat      the Peter   middle of them.  Having seen  but
846    3814           5100 2521     4314 012 5457   2532
αὐτὸν  παιδίσκη       τις  κάθημενον πρὸς τὸ  φῶς    καὶ
him    servant girl   some sitting    to   the light  and
816          846   3004    2532 3778  4862 846   1510
ἀτενίσασα    αὐτῷ  εἶπεν· καὶ  οὗτος σὺν  αὐτῷ ἦν.
having stared him   said;   and  this  with him   was.
   01  1161 720        3004    3756 3609a 846    1135
57 ὁ   δὲ  ἠρνήσατο  λέγων·  οὐκ  οἶδα  αὐτόν, γύναι.
   The but denied     saying;  not  I know him,   woman.
   2532 3326 1024     2087  3708      846   5346
58 καὶ  μετὰ βραχὺ  ἕτερος ἰδὼν     αὐτὸν ἔφη·
   And  after little other  having seen him   said;
2532 1473 1537 846    1510 01  1161 4074  5346
καὶ  σὺ  ἐξ   αὐτῶν εἶ.  ὁ   δὲ  Πέτρος ἔφη·
also you from them   are. The but Peter   said;
444       3756 1510   59 2532 1339            5616 5610
ἄνθρωπε,  οὐκ εἰμί.     καὶ  διαστάσης      ὡσεὶ ὥρας
man,      not I am.       And  having stood through as hour
1520 243    5100 1340       3004    1909 225       2532
μιᾶς ἄλλος τις  διϊσχυρίζετο λέγων· ἐπ’ ἀληθείας καὶ
one  other some was insisting saying; on  truth     also
```

[50]Then one of them struck the slave of the high priest and cut off his right ear. [51]But Jesus said, "No more of this!" And he touched his ear and healed him. [52]Then Jesus said to the chief priests, the officers of the temple police, and the elders who had come for him, "Have you come out with swords and clubs as if I were a bandit? [53]When I was with you day after day in the temple, you did not lay hands on me. But this is your hour, and the power of darkness!"

[54]Then they seized him and led him away, bringing him into the high priest's house. But Peter was following at a distance. [55]When they had kindled a fire in the middle of the courtyard and sat down together, Peter sat among them. [56]Then a servant-girl, seeing him in the firelight, stared at him and said, "This man also was with him." [57]But he denied it, saying, "Woman, I do not know him." [58]A little later someone else, on seeing him, said, "You also are one of them." But Peter said, "Man, I am not!" [59]Then about an hour later still another kept insisting, "Surely

this man also was with him;
for he is a Galilean." 60But
Peter said, "Man, I do not
know what you are talking
about!" At that moment,
while he was still speaking,
the cock crowed. 61The
Lord turned and looked
at Peter. Then Peter
remembered the word of
the Lord, how he had said
to him, "Before the cock
crows today, you will deny
me three times." 62And he
went out and wept bitterly.

63 Now the men who
were holding Jesus began
to mock him and beat him;
64they also blindfolded
him and kept asking him,
"Prophesy! Who is it that
struck you?" 65They kept
heaping many other insults
on him.

66 When day came,
the assembly of the elders
of the people, both chief
priests and scribes,
gathered together, and
they brought him to their
council. 67They said, "If
you are the Messiah,ᵃ tell
us." He replied, "If I tell
you, you will not believe;
68and if I question you, you
will not answer. 69But from
now on the Son of Man will
be seated at the right hand
of the power of God." 70All
of them asked, "Are you,
then, the Son of God?" He
said to them, "You say that
I am." 71Then they said,

ᵃ Or the Christ

```
3778    3326   846        1510  2532  1063  1057         1510
οὗτος   μετ'   αὐτοῦ   ἦν,   καὶ  γὰρ  Γαλιλαῖός  ἐστιν.
this    with   him     was,  also  for  Galilean    he is.

        3004  1161 01  4074       444          3756 3609α  3739
60      εἶπεν δὲ   ὁ  Πέτρος· ἄνθρωπε,  οὐκ  οἶδα     ὃ
        Said  but  the Peter;   man,     not  I know what

3004       2532 3916         2089 2980        846   5455
λέγεις.  καὶ  παραχρῆμα ἔτι  λαλοῦντος αὐτοῦ ἐφώνησεν
you say.  And  suddenly  still speaking   him  sounded

220           2532 4762      01  2962   1689       03
ἀλέκτωρ.  61  καὶ στραφεὶς  ὁ  κύριος ἐνέβλεψεν τῷ
rooster.      And having turned the Master looked in the

4074   2532 5279       01  4074   010      4487     02
Πέτρῳ, καὶ ὑπεμνήσθη  ὁ  Πέτρος τοῦ  ῥήματος τοῦ
Peter, and  was reminded the Peter  of the word of the

2962   5613 3004      846   3754 4250      220      5455
κυρίου ὡς  εἶπεν   αὐτῷ  ὅτι  πρὶν ἀλέκτορα φωνῆσαι
Master as  he said to him,  (")  before rooster to sound

4594       533                    1473 5151       2532
σήμερον ἀπαρνήσῃ                με   τρίς.  62  καὶ
today    you will deny thoroughly me   three.    And

1831       1854    2799     4090       2532 013
ἐξελθὼν  ἔξω    ἔκλαυσεν πικρῶς. 63  Καὶ  οἱ
having gone out  outside he cried bitterly. And  the

435    013 4912         846   1702       846
ἄνδρες οἱ  συνέχοντες  αὐτὸν ἐνέπαιζον αὐτῷ
men    the ones holding with him   were mocking with

1194        2532 4028           846   1905
δέροντες, 64  καὶ  περικαλύψαντες αὐτὸν ἐπηρώτων
beating,    and  having covered   him  they were
                    around              asking on

3004        4395        5101 1510  01 3817
λέγοντες· προφήτευσον, τίς  ἐστιν ὁ  παίσας
saying;    speak before,  who  is   the one having struck

1473    2532 2087    4183 987                 3004      1519
σε;  65  καὶ ἕτερα  πολλὰ βλασφημοῦντες ἔλεγον  εἰς
you?     And others many  insulting      were saying to

846      66 2532 5613 1096       2250     4863
αὐτόν.     Καὶ ὡς  ἐγένετο ἡμέρα, συνήχθη‖
him.       And as  it became day,  were led together

09  4244          02   2992    749        5037
τὸ  πρεσβυτέριον τοῦ  λαοῦ,  ἀρχιερεῖς τε
the older men group of the people, ruler priests both

2532 1122         2532 520        846  1519 012
καὶ γραμματεῖς, καὶ ἀπήγαγον  αὐτὸν εἰς  τὸ
and  writers,    and they led off him   into the

4892        846   67 3004       1487 1473 1510 01
συνέδριον αὐτῶν   λέγοντες· εἰ  σὺ  εἶ  ὁ
council    of them  saying,  if  you  are the

5547      3004  1473     3004  1161 846       1437 1473
χριστός, εἰπὸν ἡμῖν. εἶπεν δὲ  αὐτοῖς· ἐὰν ὑμῖν
Christ,   say   to us. He said but to them; if   to you

3004      3756 3361 4100              1437 1161
εἴπω,    οὐ  μὴ  πιστεύσητε·  68  ἐὰν δὲ
I might say, not not  you might trust;   if   but

2065       3756 3361 611           69  575  010 3568
ἐρωτήσω,  οὐ  μὴ  ἀποκριθῆτε.    ἀπὸ τοῦ νῦν
I might ask, not not  you might answer.  From the now

1161 1510  01  5207 02      444        2521     1537
δὲ  ἔσται ὁ  υἱὸς τοῦ  ἀνθρώπου καθήμενος ἐκ
but  will be the son of the man     sitting    from

1188    06  1411       02  2316      70 3004  1161
δεξιῶν τῆς δυνάμεως τοῦ θεοῦ.      εἶπαν δὲ
right of the power    of the God.    Said but

3956    1473 3767 1510 01 5207 02  2316   01 1161
πάντες· σὺ  οὖν εἶ  ὁ  υἱὸς τοῦ θεοῦ; ὁ  δὲ
all;     you  then are the son of the God? the but

4314 846     5346  1473 3004    3754 1473 1510  71 013
πρὸς αὐτοὺς ἔφη· ὑμεῖς λέγετε ὅτι  ἐγώ εἰμι.    οἱ
to   them    said; you  say    that  I    am.   The ones
```

```
1161  3004      5101  2089    2192      3141            5532
δὲ   εἶπαν·   τί   ἔτι   ἔχομεν   μαρτυρίας   χρείαν;
but  said;    why  still we have of testimony   need?
846           1063 191      575   010 4750        846
αὐτοὶ   γὰρ   ἠκούσαμεν ἀπὸ τοῦ στόματος αὐτοῦ.
Ourselves for  we heard   from the mouth      of him.
```

"What further testimony do we need? We have heard it ourselves from his own lips!"

```
        2532  450             537   09  4128    846    71
23:1  Καὶ  ἀναστὰν      ἅπαν τὸ πλῆθος αὐτῶν ἤγαγον
      And  having stood up all the quantity of them led
846     1909 04  4091       2    757       1161 2723
αὐτὸν ἐπὶ τὸν Πιλᾶτον.  ῞Ηρξαντο  δὲ   κατηγορεῖν
him    on  the Pilate.      They began but   to accuse
846    3004       3778    2147    1294       012 1484
αὐτοῦ λέγοντες· τοῦτον εὕραμεν διαστρέφοντα τὸ ἔθνος
him    saying;   this   we found perverting   the nation
1473   2532 2967    5411    2541      1325      2532
ἡμῶν  καὶ κωλύοντα φόρους Καίσαρι διδόναι καὶ
of us  and hindering taxes  to Caesar to give and
3004    1438    5547    935     1510    3  01  1161
λέγοντα ἑαυτὸν χριστὸν βασιλέα εἶναι.  ὁ  δὲ
saying  himself Christ  king   to be.  The but
4091    2065      846   3004   1473 1510 01  935
Πιλᾶτος ἠρώτησεν αὐτὸν λέγων· σὺ  εἶ  ὁ βασιλεὺς
Pilate   asked    him   saying; you  are the king
014   2453       01  1161 611        846   5346 1473
τῶν Ἰουδαίων; ὁ  δὲ  ἀποκριθεὶς αὐτῷ ἔφη· σὺ
the  Judeans?  The but having  to him said; you
the                      answered
3004    01 1161 4091    3004   4314 016  749
λέγεις.  ὁ  δὲ Πιλᾶτος εἶπεν πρὸς τοὺς ἀρχιερεῖς
say.     The but Pilate said  to   the ruler priests
2532 016  3793    3762    2147    159  1722 03 444
καὶ  τοὺς ὄχλους· οὐδὲν εὑρίσκω αἴτιον ἐν τῷ ανθρώπῳ
and  the  crowds, nothing I find cause  in the man
3778   5  013 1161 2001         3004      3754
τούτῳ·   οἱ  δὲ ἐπίσχυον      λέγοντες ὅτι
this.     The but were stronger on saying  that
383            04   2992  1321    2596 3650  06
ἀνασείει      τὸν λαὸν διδάσκων καθ᾽ ὅλης τῆς
he shakes up the people teaching by   whole the
2449        2532 757     575   06  1056      2193
Ἰουδαίας, καὶ  ἀρξάμενος ἀπὸ τῆς Γαλιλαίας ἕως
Judea,     and  beginning from the Galilee    until
5602      6  4091    1161 191       1905      1487 01
ὧδε.      Πιλᾶτος δὲ ἀκούσας ἐπηρώτησεν εἰ  ὁ
here.      Pilate but having heard asked on  if  the
444       1057      1510    7 2532 1921         3754
ἄνθρωπος Γαλιλαῖός ἐστιν,  καὶ ἐπιγνοὺς    ὅτι
man       Galilean  is,    and having perceived that
1537 06  1849      2264    1510  375      846   4314
ἐκ  τῆς ἐξουσίας Ἡρῴδου ἐστὶν ἀνέπεμψεν αὐτὸν πρὸς
from the authority of Herod he is he sent up him  to
2264   1510 2532 846 1722  2414       1722 3778
Ἡρῴδην, ὄντα καὶ αὐτὸν ἐν Ἱεροσολύμοις ἐν ταύταις
Herod,  being also him in  Jerusalem    in these
019  2250        01 1161 2264    3708       04
ταῖς ἡμέραις.  8 ῾Ο  δὲ Ἡρῴδης ἰδὼν       τὸν
the   days.      The but Herod having seen the
2424    5463     3029   1510    1063 1537 2425      5550
Ἰησοῦν ἐχάρη   λίαν, ἦν   γὰρ ἐξ ἱκανῶν χρόνων
Jesus   rejoiced very, he was+ for  from enough times
2309   3708   846   1223 012  191      4012 846  2532
θέλων  ἰδεῖν αὐτὸν διὰ τὸ ἀκούειν περὶ αὐτοῦ καὶ
+wanting to see him through the to hear about him  and
1679     5100  4592    3708   5259 846   1096
ἤλπιζέν  τι   σημεῖον ἰδεῖν ὑπ᾽ αὐτοῦ γινόμενον.
was hoping some sign   to see by   him   becoming.
9  1905            1161  846 1722 3056    2425      846
   ἐπηρώτα       δὲ αὐτὸν ἐν λόγοις ἱκανοῖς, αὐτὸς
   He was asking on but him in words  enough,   himself
```

CHAPTER 23

Then the assembly rose as a body and brought Jesus[a] before Pilate. [2]They began to accuse him, saying, "We found this man perverting our nation, forbidding us to pay taxes to the emperor, and saying that he himself is the Messiah, a king."[b] [3]Then Pilate asked him, "Are you the king of the Jews?" He answered, "You say so." [4]Then Pilate said to the chief priests and the crowds, "I find no basis for an accusation against this man." [5]But they were insistent and said, "He stirs up the people by teaching throughout all Judea, from Galilee where he began even to this place."

[6] When Pilate heard this, he asked whether the man was a Galilean. [7]And when he learned that he was under Herod's jurisdiction, he sent him off to Herod, who was himself in Jerusalem at that time. [8]When Herod saw Jesus, he was very glad, for he had been wanting to see him for a long time, because he had heard about him and was hoping to see him perform some sign. [9]He questioned him at some length, but Jesus[c]

a Gk him
b Or is an anointed king
c Gk he

gave him no answer. [10]The chief priests and the scribes stood by, vehemently accusing him. [11]Even Herod with his soldiers treated him with contempt and mocked him; then he put an elegant robe on him, and sent him back to Pilate. [12]That same day Herod and Pilate became friends with each other; before this they had been enemies.

13 Pilate then called together the chief priests, the leaders, and the people, [14]and said to them, "You brought me this man as one who was perverting the people; and here I have examined him in your presence and have not found this man guilty of any of your charges against him. [15]Neither has Herod, for he sent him back to us. Indeed, he has done nothing to deserve death. [16]I will therefore have him flogged and release him."[a]

18 Then they all shouted out together, "Away with this fellow! Release Barabbas for us!" [19](This was a man who had been put in prison for an insurrection that had taken place in the city, and for murder.) [20]Pilate, wanting to release

---

[a] Here, or after verse 19, other ancient authorities add verse 17, *Now he was obliged to release someone for them at the festival*

```
1161  3762        611            846     10  2476        1161  013
δὲ    οὐδὲν    ἀπεκρίνατο    αὐτῷ.        εἱστήκεισαν  δὲ    οἱ
but   nothing  answered       to him.      Had stood     but   the
749                2532 013 1122          2159
ἀρχιερεῖς        καὶ  οἱ  γραμματεῖς    εὐτόνως
ruler priests    and  the  writers        intensely well
2723              846      11  1848                1161  846
κατηγοροῦντες  αὐτοῦ.       ἐξουθενήσας      δὲ    αὐτὸν
accusing         him.          Having despised   but   him
2532 01  2264    4862 023 4753              846      2532
[καὶ] ὁ  Ἡρῴδης σὺν  τοῖς στρατεύμασιν  αὐτοῦ καὶ
and   the Herod   with the  armies          of him and
1702        4016            2066        2986    375     846
ἐμπαίξας  περιβαλὼν    ἐσθῆτα    λαμπρὰν ἀνέπεμψεν αὐτὸν
having       having thrown  clothes    bright   sent up    him
mocked      around
03     4091       12  1096        1161  5384    01  5037
τῷ    Πιλάτῳ.     ἐγένοντο     δὲ   φίλοι   ὅ  τε
to the Pilate.       They became  but   friends  the both
2264    2532 01  4091      1722 846  07   2250  3326
Ἡρῴδης καὶ ὁ  Πιλᾶτος ἐν   αὐτῇ τῇ  ἡμέρᾳ μετ᾿
Herod   and the Pilate    in   same the  day    with
240          4391          1063 1722 2189       1510  4314
ἀλλήλων·   προϋπῆρχον  γὰρ ἐν   ἔχθρᾳ   ὄντες πρὸς
one another; they were     for  in   hostility being  to
                                        existing before
846       13  4091       1161  4779                016
αὐτούς.      Πιλᾶτος δὲ   συγκαλεσάμενος        τοὺς
them.        Pilate   but   having called together  the
749             2532 016 758       2532 04  2992    14  3004
ἀρχιερεῖς    καὶ τοὺς ἄρχοντας καὶ τὸν λαὸν       εἶπεν
ruler priests and the  rulers    and the people      said
4314 846       4374        1473  04  444      3778 5613
πρὸς αὐτούς· προσηνέγκατέ μοι  τὸν ἄνθρωπον τοῦτον ὡς
to    them;   bring toward to me the man       this   as
654               04  2992   2532 2400 1473 1799    1473
ἀποστρέφοντα τὸν λαόν,  καὶ ἰδοὺ ἐγὼ ἐνώπιον ὑμῶν
turning off     the people,  and look  T    before   you
350          3762       2147   1722 03  444          3778
ἀνακρίνας  οὐθὲν   εὗρον ἐν   τῷ ἀνθρώπῳ τούτῳ
having examined nothing found in   the man          this
159      3739 2723           2596       846    15  235  3761
αἴτιον ὧν   κατηγορεῖτε κατ᾿    αὐτοῦ.     ἀλλ᾿ οὐδὲ
cause  what you accuse     against him.      But  but not
2264    375         1063 846   4314 1473 2532 2400
Ἡρῴδης, ἀνέπεμψεν γὰρ αὐτὸν πρὸς ἡμᾶς, καὶ ἰδοὺ
Herod,   he sent up   for  him    to   us,   and look
3762   514    2288      1510   4238
οὐδὲν ἄξιον θανάτου ἐστὶν πεπραγμένον
nothing worthy of death it is+  +having been practiced
846    16  3811               3767 846   630
αὐτῷ·     παιδεύσας          οὖν αὐτὸν ἀπολύσω.
in him;   having instructed   then him   I will loose off.
            as a child
18  349                1161 3826        3004      142
    Ἀνέκραγον       δὲ   παμπληθεὶ λέγοντες· αἶρε
    They shouted out  but  all quantity saying;  lift up
3778     630        1161 1473 04  912         19  3748
τοῦτον, ἀπόλυσον δὲ   ἡμῖν τὸν Βαραββᾶν·     ὅστις
this,    loose off but  to us the Barabbas;       who
1510 1223    4714         5100 1096          1722 07
ἦν   διὰ    στάσιν     τινὰ γενομένην     ἐν   τῇ
was  through revolution some having become  in   the
4172   2532 5408   906         1722 07 5438     20  3825 1161
πόλει καὶ φόνον βληθεὶς ἐν  τῇ  φυλακῇ.      πάλιν δὲ
city   and murder having  in   the guard.         Again but
              been thrown
01  4091       4377           846    2309     630
ὁ  Πιλᾶτος προσεφώνησεν αὐτοῖς θέλων ἀπολῦσαι
the Pilate    sounded to      to them wanting to loose off
```

```
04    2424        013  1161  2019              3004
τὸν  Ἰησοῦν.  21  οἱ   δὲ   ἐπεφώνουν        λέγοντες·
the  Jesus.     The but   were sounding on saying;
4717  4717     846        01   1161  5154   3004   4314
σταύρου σταύρου αὐτόν.  22 ὁ   δὲ   τρίτον εἶπεν πρὸς
crucify crucify him.      The but  third  said  to
846    5101 1063 2556 4160      3778  3762     159
αὐτούς· τί  γὰρ κακὸν ἐποίησεν οὗτος; οὐδὲν  αἴτιον
them;   what for bad   did      this? Nothing cause
2288     2147   1722 846    3811
θανάτου εὗρον  ἐν  αὐτῷ· παιδεύσας
of death I found in  him; having instructed as a child
3767 846   630          23 013  1161  1945
οὖν  αὐτὸν ἀπολύσω.      οἱ   δὲ   ἐπέκειντο
then him   I will loose off. The but  were lying on
5456     3173     154         846    4717
φωναῖς  μεγάλαις αἰτούμενοι αὐτὸν σταυρωθῆναι,
in sounds great   asking     him   to be crucified,
2532 2729           017  5456    846   24 2532
καὶ  κατίσχυον     αἱ   φωναὶ  αὐτῶν.   Καὶ
and  were strong against the sounds of them.  And
4091    1948      1096      012 155    846
Πιλᾶτος ἐπέκρινεν γενέσθαι τὸ  αἴτημα αὐτῶν·
Pilate  judged on to become the asking of them;
   630           1161 04   1223   4714      2532
25 ἀπέλυσεν      δὲ   τὸν διὰ   στάσιν    καὶ
   he loosed off but  the through revolution and
5408    906             1519 5438    3739
φόνον  βεβλημένον      εἰς  φυλακὴν ὃν
murder having been thrown in  guard   who
154         04  1161 2424    3860        011
ᾐτοῦντο,    τὸν δὲ   Ἰησοῦν παρέδωκεν τῷ
they were asking, the but  Jesus  he gave over to the
2307     846    26 2532 5613 520        846
θελήματι αὐτῶν.   Καὶ  ὡς  ἀπήγαγον  αὐτόν,
want     of them. And  as  they led off him,
1949         4613    5100 2956    2064      575
ἐπιλαβόμενοι Σίμωνά τινα Κυρηναῖον ἐρχόμενον ἀπ’
having taken on Simon some Cyrenean coming  from
68   2007     846 04  4716   5342     3693
ἀγροῦ ἐπέθηκαν αὐτῷ τὸν σταυρὸν φέρειν ὄπισθεν
field they set on him the cross  to carry from behind
02   2424    27 190          1161 846  4183 4128
τοῦ Ἰησοῦ.     Ἠκολούθει    δὲ   αὐτῷ πολὺ πλῆθος
the  Jesus.     Was following but  him  much quantity
02   2992   2532 1135    3739 2875         2532
τοῦ λαοῦ  καὶ  γυναικῶν αἱ  ἐκόπτοντο  καὶ
of the people and women   who were mourning and
2354     846   28 4762      1161 4314 846     01
ἐθρήνουν αὐτόν.  στραφεὶς  δὲ   πρὸς αὐτὰς [ὁ]
lamenting him.   Having turned but  to   them  the
2424    3004    2364      2419       3361 2799  1909
Ἰησοῦς εἶπεν· θυγατέρες Ἰερουσαλήμ, μὴ  κλαίετε ἐπ’
Jesus  said;  daughters Jerusalem,  not cry     on
1473 4133  1909 1438   2799      2532 1909 024
ἐμέ· πλὴν ἐφ’ ἑαυτὰς κλαίετε καὶ  ἐπὶ τὰ
me;  except on yourselves cry  and  on  the
5043   1473   29 3754   2400 2064     2250  1722
τέκνα  ὑμῶν,    ὅτι    ἰδοὺ ἔρχονται ἡμέραι ἐν
children of you, because look come   days   in
3739 3004      3107      017 4723    2532 017 2836
αἷς  ἐροῦσιν·  μακάριαι αἱ  στεῖραι καὶ  αἱ  κοιλίαι
which they will fortunate the sterile and  the stomachs
     say,                            ones
3739 3756 1080    2532 3149   3739 3756 5142
αἳ   οὐκ ἐγέννησαν καὶ μαστοὶ οἳ   οὐκ ἔθρεψαν.
which not gave birth and breasts which not they fed.
   5119 757          3004   023     3735     4098
30 τοτέ ἄρξονται    λέγειν τοῖς  ὄρεσιν· πέσετε
   Then they will begin to say to the hills;  fall
```

Jesus, addressed them again; [21]but they kept shouting, "Crucify, crucify him!" [22]A third time he said to them, "Why, what evil has he done? I have found in him no ground for the sentence of death; I will therefore have him flogged and then release him." [23]But they kept demanding with loud shouts that he should be crucified; and their voices prevailed. [24]So Pilate gave his verdict that their demand should be granted. [25]He released the man they asked for, the one who had been put in prison for insurrection and murder, and he handed Jesus over as they wished.

26 As they led him away, they seized a man, Simon of Cyrene, who was coming from the country, and they laid the cross on him, and made him carry it behind Jesus. [27]A great number of the people followed him, and among them were women who were beating their breasts and wailing for him. [28]But Jesus turned to them and said, "Daughters of Jerusalem, do not weep for me, but weep for yourselves and for your children. [29]For the days are surely coming when they will say, 'Blessed are the barren, and the wombs that never bore, and the breasts that never nursed.' [30]Then they will begin to say to the mountains, 'Fall

on us'; and to the hills, 'Cover us.' [31]For if they do this when the wood is green, what will happen when it is dry?"

[32]Two others also, who were criminals, were led away to be put to death with him. [33]When they came to the place that is called The Skull, there they crucified Jesus[a] there with the criminals, one on his right and one on his left. [[[34]Then Jesus said, "Father, forgive them; for they do not know what they are doing."]][b] And they cast lots to divide his clothing. [35]And the people stood by, watching; but the leaders scoffed at him, saying, "He saved others; let him save himself if he is the Messiah[c] of God, his chosen one!" [36]The soldiers also mocked him, coming up and offering him sour wine, [37]and saying, "If you are the King of the Jews, save yourself!" [38]There was also an inscription over him,[d] "This is the King of the Jews."

[39]One of the criminals who were hanged there kept deriding[e] him and saying, "Are you not the Messiah?[c] Save yourself and us!" [40]But the other rebuked him, saying, "Do you not fear God, since you are under the same

[a] Gk him

[b] Other ancient authorities lack the sentence *Then Jesus . . . what they are doing*

[c] Or *the Christ*

[d] Other ancient authorities add *written in Greek and Latin and Hebrew* (that is, *Aramaic*)

[e] Or *blaspheming*

1909	1473	2532	015	1015	2572	1473
ἐφ᾽	ἡμᾶς,	καὶ	τοῖς	βουνοῖς·	καλύψατε	ἡμᾶς·
on	us,	and	to	the hills;	cover	us;

31
3754	1487	1722	011	5200	3586	3778	4160
ὅτι	εἰ	ἐν	τῷ	ὑγρῷ	ξύλῳ	ταῦτα	ποιοῦσιν,
because	if	in	the	moist	wood	these	they do,

1722	011	3584	5101	1096		71	1161	2532
ἐν	τῷ	ξηρῷ	τί	γένηται;	**32**	Ἤγοντο	δὲ	καὶ
in	the	dried	what	might become?		They were but		also
						leading		

2087	2557		1417	4862	846	337
ἕτεροι	κακοῦργοι		δύο	σὺν	αὐτῷ	ἀναιρεθῆναι.
others	workers of bad		two	with	him	to be killed.

33
2532	3753	2064	1909	04	5117	04	2564
Καὶ	ὅτε	ἦλθον	ἐπὶ	τὸν	τόπον	τὸν	καλούμενον
And	when	they came	on		the place		the being called

2898	1563	4717		846	2532	016
Κρανίον,	ἐκεῖ	ἐσταύρωσαν		αὐτὸν	καὶ	τοὺς
Skull,	there	they crucified		him	and	the

2557		3739	3303	1537	1188	3739	1161	1537
κακούργους,		ὃν	μὲν	ἐκ	δεξιῶν	ὃν	δὲ	ἐξ
workers of bad,		who	indeed	from	right	who	but	from

710		01	1161	2424	3004		3962
ἀριστερῶν.	**34**	[[ὁ	δὲ	Ἰησοῦς	ἔλεγεν·		πάτερ,
left.		The	but	Jesus	was saying,		father,

863		846		3756	1063	3609a	5101	4160
ἄφες		αὐτοῖς,		οὐ	γὰρ	οἴδασιν	τί	ποιοῦσιν.]]
send off		to them,		not	for	they know	what	they do.

1266		1161	024	2440	846	906
διαμεριζόμενοι		δὲ	τὰ	ἱμάτια	αὐτοῦ	ἔβαλον
Dividing completely		but	the	clothes	of him	they threw

2819		2532	2476	01	2992	2334
κλήρους.	**35**	Καὶ	εἱστήκει	ὁ	λαὸς	θεωρῶν.
lots.		And	had stood	the	people	watching.

1592		1161	2532	013	758	3004	243
ἐξεμυκτήριζον		δὲ	καὶ	οἱ	ἄρχοντες	λέγοντες·	ἄλλους
Were mocking at		but	also	the	rulers	saying,	others

4982		4982	1438	1487	3778	1510
ἔσωσεν,		σωσάτω	ἑαυτόν,	εἰ	οὗτός	ἐστιν
he delivered,		let deliver	himself,	if	this	is

01	5547	02	2316	01	1588		1702
ὁ	χριστὸς	τοῦ	θεοῦ	ὁ	ἐκλεκτός.	**36**	ἐνέπαιξαν
the	Christ	of the	God	the	select.		Mocked

1161	846	2532	013	4757		4334	3690
δὲ	αὐτῷ	καὶ	οἱ	στρατιῶται		προσερχόμενοι,	ὄξος
but	him	and	the	soldiers		coming to,	sour wine

4374		846	**37**	2532	3004		1487	1473	1510	01
προσφέροντες		αὐτῷ		καὶ	λέγοντες·		εἰ	σὺ	εἶ	ὁ
bringing to		him		and	saying;		if	you	are	the

935		014		2453		4982	4572		1510
βασιλεὺς		τῶν		Ἰουδαίων,		σῶσον	σεαυτόν.	**38**	ἦν
king		of the		Judeans,		deliver	yourself.		There was

1161	2532	1923		1909	846	01	935	014
δὲ	καὶ	ἐπιγραφὴ		ἐπ᾽	αὐτῷ·	ὁ	βασιλεὺς	τῶν
but	also	writing on		on	him;	the	king	of the

2453		3778		**39**	1520	1161	014	2910
Ἰουδαίων		οὗτος.			Εἷς	δὲ	τῶν	κρεμασθέντων
Judeans		this.			One	but	of the	having been hanged

2557		987		846	3004		3780	1473
κακούργων		ἐβλασφήμει		αὐτὸν	λέγων·		οὐχὶ	σὺ
workers of bad		was insulting		him	saying;		not	you

1510	01	5547		4982	4572	2532	1473
εἶ	ὁ	χριστός;		σῶσον	σεαυτὸν	καὶ	ἡμᾶς.
are	the	Christ?		Deliver	yourself	and	us.

40
611		1161	01	2087	2008		846
ἀποκριθεὶς		δὲ	ὁ	ἕτερος	ἐπιτιμῶν		αὐτῷ
Having answered		but	the	other	admonishing		him

5346	3761		5399	1473	04	2316	3754	1722	011	846
ἔφη·	οὐδὲ		φοβῇ	σὺ	τὸν	θεόν,	ὅτι	ἐν	τῷ	αὐτῷ
said,	but not		fear	you	the	God,	because	in	the	same

```
2917        1510      41  2532  1473    3303      1346        514
κρίματι   εἶ;           καὶ  ἡμεῖς  μὲν    δικαίως,  ἄξια
judgment  you  are?  And  we    indeed  rightly,   worthy

1063  3739     4238          618           3778   1161
γὰρ   ὧν      ἐπράξαμεν   ἀπολαμβάνομεν·  οὗτος  δὲ
for   of what  we practiced  we take from;    this   but

3762    824       4238      42  2532  3004
οὐδὲν   ἄτοπον   ἔπραξεν.      καὶ   ἔλεγεν·
nothing out of place he practiced.  And  he was saying;

2424    3403       1473  3752  2064          1519  08
'Ιησοῦ, μνήσθητί μου   ὅταν  ἔλθῃς       εἰς  τὴν
Jesus,  remember  me    when  you might come into the

932          1473  43  2532  3004     846     281  1473
βασιλείαν σου.      καὶ  εἶπεν   αὐτῷ·  ἀμήν σοι
kingdom    of you.  And he said to him;  amen to you

3004   4594      3326 1473 1510       1722 03    3857
λέγω,  σήμερον μετ' ἐμοῦ ἔσῃ      ἐν τῷ  παραδείσῳ.
I say, today     with me  will be in the paradise.

44 2532 1510  2235      5616 5610 1623    2532 4655
   Καὶ ἦν    ἤδη      ὡσεὶ ὥρα ἕκτη καὶ σκότος
   And it was already as   hour sixth and  dark

1096    1909 3650 08   1093   2193    5610 1728a    45 02
ἐγένετο ἐφ' ὅλην τὴν γῆν   ἕως   ὥρας ἐνάτης      τοῦ
became  on  whole the earth until  hour  ninth         the

2246    1587          4977      1161 09   2665
ἡλίου ἐκλιπόντος,   ἐσχίσθη  δὲ   τὸ  καταπέτασμα
sun   having left off,  was split but  the  veil

02    3485  3319   46 2532 5455        5456
τοῦ  ναοῦ  μέσον.     καὶ  φωνήσας   φωνῇ
of the temple middle.  And  having sounded in sound

3173  01  2424    3004    3962     1519 5495    1473
μεγάλη ὁ 'Ιησοῦς εἶπεν· πάτερ, εἰς χεῖράς σου
great  the Jesus  said;  father, into hands  of you

3908         012 4151    1473   3778  1161 3004
παρατίθεμαι τὸ πνεῦμά μου.  τοῦτο δὲ  εἰπὼν
I set along the spirit of me.  This  but  having said

1606         47 3708     1161 01   1543
ἐξέπνευσεν.    'Ιδὼν   δὲ  ὁ  ἑκατοντάρχης
he breathed out. Having seen but  the ruler of hundred

012 1096      1392        04  2316 3004
τὸ γενόμενον  ἐδόξαζεν     τὸν θεὸν λέγων·
the having become he gave splendor the God saying;

3689  01  444       3778  1342     1510  48 2532 3956
ὄντως ὁ ἄνθρωπος οὗτος δίκαιος ἦν.    καὶ πάντες
really the man      this   right    was.   And  all

013 4836          3793    1909 08  2335      3778
οἱ συμπαραγενόμενοι ὄχλοι ἐπὶ τὴν θεωρίαν ταύτην,
the having become    crowds on  the thing   this,
   along with                              watched

2334          024 1096     5180       024 4738
θεωρήσαντες  τὰ γενόμενα,  τύπτοντες τὰ στήθη
having watched the having become, beating  the chests

5290        49 2476        1161 3956    013
ὑπέστρεφον.    Εἱστήκεισαν δὲ  πάντες οἱ
they were returning. Had stood   but  all     the

1110      846  575  3113     2532 1135   017
γνωστοὶ  αὐτῷ ἀπὸ μακρόθεν καὶ γυναῖκες αἱ
ones knowing him from from far and women     the ones

4870           846 575 06  1056      3708  3778
συνακολουθοῦσαι αὐτῷ ἀπὸ τῆς Γαλιλαίας ὁρῶσαι ταῦτα.
following  with  him from the Galilee    seeing these.

50 2532 2400 435 3686        2501       1010        5225
   Καὶ ἰδοὺ ἀνὴρ ὀνόματι  'Ιωσὴφ  βουλευτὴς ὑπάρχων
   And look man  in name   Joseph  planner    existing

2532 435 18    2532 1342    51 3778 3756 1510
[καὶ] ἀνὴρ ἀγαθὸς καὶ δίκαιος    - οὗτος οὐκ ἦν
and  man  good   and right        this   not  was
```

sentence of condemnation? [41]And we indeed have been condemned justly, for we are getting what we deserve for our deeds, but this man has done nothing wrong." [42]Then he said, "Jesus, remember me when you come into[a] your kingdom." [43]He replied, "Truly I tell you, today you will be with me in Paradise."

[44]It was now about noon, and darkness came over the whole land[b] until three in the afternoon, [45]while the sun's light failed;[c] and the curtain of the temple was torn in two. [46]Then Jesus, crying with a loud voice, said, "Father, into your hands I commend my spirit." Having said this, he breathed his last. [47]When the centurion saw what had taken place, he praised God and said, "Certainly this man was innocent."[d] [48]And when all the crowds who had gathered there for this spectacle saw what had taken place, they returned home, beating their breasts. [49]But all his acquaintances, including the women who had followed him from Galilee, stood at a distance, watching these things.

[50]Now there was a good and righteous man named Joseph, who, though a member of the council, [51]had not agreed

a Other ancient authorities read in
b Or earth
c Or the sun was eclipsed. Other ancient authorities read the sun was darkened
d Or righteous

to their plan and action. He came from the Jewish town of Arimathea, and he was waiting expectantly for the kingdom of God. ⁵²This man went to Pilate and asked for the body of Jesus. ⁵³Then he took it down, wrapped it in a linen cloth, and laid it in a rock-hewn tomb where no one had ever been laid. ⁵⁴It was the day of Preparation, and the sabbath was beginning.ᵃ ⁵⁵The women who had come with him from Galilee followed, and they saw the tomb and how his body was laid. ⁵⁶Then they returned, and prepared spices and ointments.

On the sabbath they rested according to the commandment.

CHAPTER 24

But on the first day of the week, at early dawn, they came to the tomb, taking the spices that they had prepared. ²They found the stone rolled away from the tomb, ³but when they went in, they did not find the body.ᵇ ⁴While they were perplexed about this, suddenly two men in dazzling clothes stood beside them. ⁵The womenᶜ were terrified and bowed their faces to the ground, but the menᵈ said to them, "Why do you look for the living among the dead? He is not here, but has risen.ᵉ

ᵃ Gk was dawning
ᵇ Other ancient authorities add
　of the Lord Jesus
ᶜ Gk They
ᵈ Gk but they
ᵉ Other ancient authorities lack
　He is not here, but has risen

```
4784a                   07   1012  2532  07   4234      846
συγκατατεθειμένος τῇ   βουλῇ  καὶ   τῇ   πράξει   αὐτῶν -
having been set       the   plan   and  the  practice of them
together against
575   707            4172   014    2453      3739 4327
ἀπὸ ʽΑριμαθαίας πόλεως τῶν  ʼΙουδαίων, ὃς προσεδέχετο
from Arimathea  city   of the Judeans, who was awaiting
08  932     02       2316      3778 4334          03
τὴν βασιλείαν τοῦ   θεοῦ, 52 οὗτος προσελθὼν    τῷ
the kingdom   of the God,     this  having gone to the
4091   154    012 4983 02       2424   53 2532
Πιλάτῳ ᾐτήσατο τὸ σῶμα τοῦ   ʼΙησοῦ    καὶ
Pilate asked   the body of the Jesus      and
2507               1794       846  4616      2532
καθελὼν           ἐνετύλιξεν αὐτὸ σινδόνι  καὶ
having lifted down he wrapped it   in linen and
5087   846   1722 3418    2991         3757  3756 1510
ἔθηκεν αὐτὸν ἐν  μνήματι λαξευτῷ     οὗ   οὐκ  ἦν
he set him   in  grave   in cut stone where not  was+
3762   3768  2749        2532 2250 1510 3904
οὐδεὶς οὔπω  κείμενος. 54 καὶ  ἡμέρα ἦν  παρασκευῆς
no one not yet +lying.     And day   was preparation
2532 4521    2020         2628
καὶ  σάββατον ἐπέφωσκεν. 55 Κατακολουθήσασαι
and  sabbath  was dawning on. Having followed after
1161 017  1135    3748   1510 4905        1537
δὲ   αἱ  γυναῖκες, αἵτινες ἦσαν συνεληλυθυῖαι ἐκ
but  the women,   who    were having come with from
06   1056    846   2300       012 3419     2532
τῆς Γαλιλαίας αὐτῷ, ἐθεάσαντο τὸ μνημεῖον καὶ
the Galilee   to him, they watched the grave  and
5613 5087  09  4983 846  5290           1161
ὡς  ἐτέθη τὸ  σῶμα αὐτοῦ, 56 ὑποστρέψασαι δὲ
as  was set the body of him,   having returned but
2090      759      2532 3464    2532 012 3303
ἡτοίμασαν ἀρώματα καὶ  μύρα.   καὶ  τὸ μὲν
they prepared spices and  perfumes. And  the indeed
4521     2270     3696 08  1785       24:1  07
σάββατον ἡσύχασαν κατὰ τὴν ἐντολήν.      Τῇ
sabbath  they were quiet by  the  command.    In the
1161 1520 022  4521      3722    901    1909 012 3418
δὲ   μιᾷ  τῶν σαββάτων ὄρθρου βαθέως ἐπὶ τὸ μνῆμα
but  one  of the sabbaths of dawn deep   on  the grave
2064  5342      3739 2090     759
ἦλθον φέρουσαι ἃ   ἡτοίμασαν ἀρώματα.
they came carrying what they prepared spices.
    2147    1161 04  3037  617
2  εὗρον   δὲ   τὸν λίθον ἀποκεκυλισμένον
   They found but  the stone having been rolled off
575  010 3419       1525      1161 3756 2147
ἀπὸ τοῦ μνημείου, 3 εἰσελθοῦσαι δὲ  οὐχ εὗρον
from the grave,     having gone in but not they found
012 4983 02      2962     2424    2532 1096      1722
τὸ σῶμα τοῦ   κυρίου ʼΙησοῦ. 4 καὶ ἐγένετο    ἐν
the body of the Master Jesus.    And it became   in
011 639       846   4012   3778   2532 2400 435
τῷ ἀπορεῖσθαι αὐτὰς περὶ τούτου καὶ  ἰδοὺ ἄνδρες
the to doubt  them   about this  and  look men
1417 2186     846   1722 2066    797
δύο ἐπέστησαν αὐταῖς ἐν  ἐσθῆτι ἀστραπτούσῃ.
two stood     them   in  clothes flashing.
   1719   1161 1096       846   2532 2827     024
5  ἐμφόβων δὲ  γενομένων αὐτῶν καὶ  κλινουσῶν τὰ
   In fear but having become them and  bowing    the
4383    1519 08  1093 3004      4314 846   5101
πρόσωπα εἰς τὴν γῆν  εἶπαν    πρὸς αὐτάς· τί
faces   into the earth they said to  them;  why
2212    04  2198   3326 014 3498     3756 1510
ζητεῖτε τὸν ζῶντα μετὰ τῶν νεκρῶν· 6 οὐκ ἔστιν
seek you the living with the dead;    not he is
```

5602   235   1453   3403   5613 2980   1473
ὧδε,   ἀλλὰ   ἠγέρθη.   μνήσθητε ὡς   ἐλάλησεν ὑμῖν
here,   but   he was raised.   Remember as   he spoke to you

2089   1510   1722 07   1056   7 3004   04   5207 02
ἔτι   ὢν   ἐν   τῇ   Γαλιλαίᾳ   λέγων   τὸν υἱὸν τοῦ
still being in   the Galilee   saying the son   of the

444   3754 1163   3860   1519
ἀνθρώπου ὅτι δεῖ   παραδοθῆναι   εἰς
man   that it is necessary to be given over   into

5495   444   268   2532 4717   2532
χεῖρας ἀνθρώπων ἁμαρτωλῶν καὶ σταυρωθῆναι   καὶ
hands of men   sinners   and to be crucified and

07   5154   2250 450   8 2532 3403
τῇ   τρίτῃ ἡμέρᾳ ἀναστῆναι.   καὶ ἐμνήσθησαν
in the third day   to stand up. And they remembered

022 4487   846   2532 5290   575   010
τῶν ῥημάτων αὐτοῦ. 9 Καὶ ὑποστρέψασαι   ἀπὸ τοῦ
the words   of him. And having returned from the

3419   518   3778   3956 015   1733 2532 3956
μνημείου ἀπήγγειλαν ταῦτα πάντα τοῖς ἕνδεκα καὶ πᾶσιν
grave   they told these all   to the eleven and all

015 3062   10 1510   1161 05   3094   3137
τοῖς λοιποῖς.   ἦσαν   δὲ ἡ   Μαγδαληνὴ Μαρία
the remaining.   There were but the Magdalene Maria

2532 2489   2532 3137 05   2385   2532 017 3062
καὶ Ἰωάννα καὶ Μαρία ἡ   Ἰακώβου καὶ αἱ λοιπαὶ
and Joanna and Maria the of Jacob   and the remaining

4862 846   3004   4314 016 652
σὺν αὐταῖς. ἔλεγον   πρὸς τοὺς ἀποστόλους
with them. They were saying to   the delegates

3778   11 2532 5316   1799   846   5616 3026
ταῦτα,   καὶ ἐφάνησαν ἐνώπιον αὐτῶν ὡσεὶ λῆρος
these,   and were shone before them as   nonsense

021 4487   3778   2532 569   846
τὰ ῥήματα ταῦτα, καὶ ἠπίστουν   αὐταῖς.
the words these, and they were untrusting them.

01 1161 4074   450   5143   1909 012
12 Ὁ δὲ Πέτρος ἀναστὰς   ἔδραμεν ἐπὶ τὸ
   The but Peter having stood up ran   on   the

3419   2532 3879   991   024 3608 3441   2532
μνημεῖον καὶ παρακύψας βλέπει τὰ ὀθόνια μόνα,   καὶ
grave   and having   he sees the linen alone, and
             stooped down   strips

565   4314 1438   2296   012 1096
ἀπῆλθεν πρὸς ἑαυτὸν θαυμάζων τὸ γεγονός.
he went off to himself marveling the having become.

     2532 2400 1417 1537 846   1722 846   07   2250 1510
13 Καὶ ἰδοὺ δύο ἐξ αὐτῶν ἐν αὐτῇ τῇ ἡμέρᾳ ἦσαν
   And look two from them in   same the day   were

4198   1519 2968 568   4712   1835
πορευόμενοι εἰς κώμην ἀπέχουσαν σταδίους ἑξήκοντα
traveling   into village holding off stadia   sixty

575   2419   3739   3686 1695   14 2532
ἀπὸ Ἰερουσαλήμ, ᾗ   ὄνομα Ἐμμαοῦς,   καὶ
from Jerusalem, in which name Emmaus,   and

846   3656   4314 240   4012
αὐτοὶ ὡμίλουν   πρὸς ἀλλήλους περὶ
themselves were conversing to   one another about

3956   4819   3778   15 2532
πάντων τῶν συμβεβηκότων   τούτων.   καὶ
all   the ones having gone together these.   And

1096   1722 011 3656   846   2532 4802
ἐγένετο ἐν τῷ ὁμιλεῖν   αὐτοὺς καὶ συζητεῖν
it became in the to converse them and to dispute

2532 846   2424   1448   4848
καὶ αὐτὸς Ἰησοῦς ἐγγίσας   συνεπορεύετο
and himself Jesus having neared was traveling with

846   16 013 1161 3788   846   2902
αὐτοῖς,   οἱ δὲ ὀφθαλμοὶ αὐτῶν ἐκρατοῦντο
them,   the but eyes   of them were being held

[6]Remember how he told
you, while he was still in
Galilee, [7]that the Son of
Man must be handed over
to sinners, and be crucified,
and on the third day rise
again." [8]Then they
remembered his words,
[9]and returning from the
tomb, they told all this to
the eleven and to all the
rest. [10]Now it was Mary
Magdalene, Joanna, Mary
the mother of James, and
the other women with
them who told this to the
apostles. [11]But these words
seemed to them an idle tale,
and they did not believe
them. [12]But Peter got up
and ran to the tomb;
stooping and looking in,
he saw the linen cloths by
themselves; then he went
home, amazed at what had
happened.[a]

[13]Now on that same day
two of them were going to a
village called Emmaus, about
seven miles[b] from Jerusalem,
[14]and talking with each
other about all these things
that had happened. [15]While
they were talking and
discussing, Jesus himself
came near and went with
them, [16]but their eyes were
kept

[a] Other ancient authorities lack
verse 12

[b] Gk sixty stadia; other ancient
authorities read a hundred sixty
stadia

from recognizing him.
[17]And he said to them,
"What are you discussing
with each other while you
walk along?" They stood
still, looking sad.[a] [18]Then
one of them, whose name
was Cleopas, answered him,
"Are you the only stranger
in Jerusalem who does not
know the things that have
taken place there in these
days?" [19]He asked them,
"What things?" They
replied, "The things about
Jesus of Nazareth,[b] who
was a prophet mighty in
deed and word before God
and all the people, [20]and
how our chief priests and
leaders handed him over to
be condemned to death and
crucified him. [21]But we had
hoped that he was the one
to redeem Israel.[c] Yes, and
besides all this, it is now the
third day since these things
took place. [22]Moreover,
some women of our group
astounded us. They were
at the tomb early this
morning, [23]and when they
did not find his body there,
they came back and told us
that they had indeed seen
a vision of angels who said
that he was alive. [24]Some
of those who were with us
went to the tomb and found
it just as the women had
said; but they did not see
him."

a Other ancient authorities read
walk along, looking sad?"
b Other ancient authorities read
Jesus the Nazorean
c Or to set Israel free

```
010  3361  1921          846    17  3004     1161  4314
τοῦ  μὴ    ἐπιγνῶναι     αὐτόν.      εἶπεν    δὲ    πρὸς
the  not   to perceive   him.        He said  but   to

846     5101  013   3056  3778  3739  474
αὐτούς· τίνες οἱ    λόγοι οὗτοι οὓς   ἀντιβάλλετε
them;   what  the   words these which you throw against

4314  240       4043              2532  2476
πρὸς  ἀλλήλους  περιπατοῦντες;    καὶ   ἐστάθησαν
to    one another walking around?  And   they stood

4659          611          1161  1520  3686
σκυθρωποί. 18 ἀποκριθεὶς  δὲ    εἷς   ὀνόματι
sad faced.    Having answered but  one   in name

2810     3004   4314 846    1473 3441  3939
Κλεοπᾶς  εἶπεν  πρὸς αὐτόν· σὺ   μόνος παροικεῖς
Cleopas  said   to   him;   you  alone live transiently

2419         2532 3756 1097   024 1096           1722
Ἰερουσαλὴμ  καὶ  οὐκ  ἔγνως  τὰ  γενόμενα       ἐν
Jerusalem   and  not  you knew the having become  in

846 1722 019  2250      3778     19 2532 3004
αὐτῇ ἐν  ταῖς ἡμέραις  ταύταις;    καὶ  εἶπεν
it  in  the  days      these?       And  he said

846      4169     013 1161 3004   846    024 4012
αὐτοῖς·  ποῖα;    οἱ  δὲ  εἶπαν  αὐτῷ· τὰ  περὶ
to them; what kind? The but said   to him; the about

2424   02   3479        3739 1096    435   4396
Ἰησοῦ  τοῦ Ναζαρηνοῦ,  ὃς   ἐγένετο ἀνὴρ προφήτης
Jesus  the Nazarene,   who  became  man  spokesman

1415     1722 2041  2532 3056 1726       02   2316
δυνατὸς ἐν   ἔργῳ καὶ  λόγῳ ἐναντίον    τοῦ  θεοῦ
power   in   work and  word in presence of the God

2532 3956    02    2992   20 3704  5037  3860
καὶ  παντὸς τοῦ   λαοῦ,     ὅπως  τε    παρέδωκαν
and  all     the   people,    so that indeed gave over

846   013 749           2532 013 758       1473 1519
αὐτὸν οἱ  ἀρχιερεῖς     καὶ  οἱ  ἄρχοντες  ἡμῶν εἰς
him    the ruler priests and  the rulers    of us in

2917  2288      2532 4717        846     21 1473
κρίμα θανάτου  καὶ  ἐσταύρωσαν  αὐτόν.     ἡμεῖς
judgment of death and  they crucified him.   We

1161 1679      3754 846       1510 01 3195
δὲ   ἠλπίζομεν ὅτι  αὐτός     ἐστιν ὁ μέλλων
but  were hoping that himself  is    the one being about

3084       04   2474     235  1065  2532 4862 3956
λυτροῦσθαι τὸν Ἰσραήλ· ἀλλά γε    καὶ  σὺν  πᾶσιν
to redeem  the Israel; but  indeed also with all

3778      5154    3778    2250     71   575  3739  3778
τούτοις  τρίτην  ταύτην ἡμέραν  ἄγει ἀφ’  οὗ    ταῦτα
these    third   this   day     it leads from which these

1096        22 235  2532 1135    5100 1537 1473
ἐγένετο.       ἀλλὰ καὶ  γυναῖκές τινες ἐξ ἡμῶν
became.        But  also women    some  from us

1839       1473  1096        3720        1909 012
ἐξέστησαν ἡμᾶς, γενόμεναι  ὀρθριναὶ   ἐπὶ  τὸ
amazed     us,   having become in dawn  on   the

3419        23 2532 3361 2147     012 4983 846
μνημεῖον,      καὶ  μὴ   εὑροῦσαι τὸ  σῶμα αὐτοῦ
grave,         and  not  having found the body of him

2064   3004       2532 3701    32
ἦλθον  λέγουσαι  καὶ  ὀπτασίαν ἀγγέλων
they came saying  also vision   of messengers

3708        3739 3004    846   2198   24 2532 565
ἑωρακέναι,  οἳ   λέγουσιν αὐτὸν ζῆν.     καὶ  ἀπῆλθόν
to have seen, who say     him   to live.  And went off

5100 014  4862 1473 1909 012 3419     2532 2147
τινες τῶν σὺν  ἡμῖν ἐπὶ  τὸ  μνημεῖον καὶ  εὗρον
some  of the with us   on   the grave    and  found

3779  2531   2532 017 1135     3004  846   1161 3756
οὕτως καθὼς καὶ  αἱ  γυναῖκες εἶπον, αὐτὸν δὲ  οὐκ
thusly just as also the women  said,  him    but not
```

3708   25   2532   846   3004   4314   846   5599   453
εἶδον. 25 καὶ   αὐτὸς   εἶπεν πρὸς αὐτούς· ὦ ἀνόητοι
they saw. And himself said to them; O unmindful

2532 1021   07   2588   010   4100   1909 3956
καὶ βραδεῖς τῇ καρδίᾳ τοῦ πιστεύειν ἐπὶ πᾶσιν
and slow in the heart of the to trust on all

3739 2980   013 4396   26   3780 3778   1163
οἷς ἐλάλησαν οἱ προφῆται· 26 οὐχὶ ταῦτα ἔδει
that spoke the spokesmen; not these it was
                                              necessary

3958   04   5547   2532 1525   1519 08   1391
παθεῖν τὸν χριστὸν καὶ εἰσελθεῖν εἰς τὴν δόξαν
to suffer the Christ and to go into into the splendor

846   27   2532 757   575   3475   2532   3956
αὐτοῦ; 27 καὶ ἀρξάμενος ἀπὸ Μωϋσέως καὶ ἀπὸ πάντων
of him? And beginning from Moses and from all

014 4396   1329   846   1722
τῶν προφητῶν διερμήνευσεν   αὐτοῖς ἐν
the spokesmen he translated completely to them in

3956   019   1124   024   4012   1438   28   2532
πάσαις ταῖς γραφαῖς τὰ   περὶ ἑαυτοῦ. 28 Καὶ
all the writings the things about himself. And

1448   1519 08   2968   3757   4198   2532   846
ἤγγισαν εἰς τὴν κώμην οὗ ᾽ επορεύοντο, καὶ αὐτὸς
they into the village where they were and himself
neared   traveling,

4364   4206   4198   29   2532
προσεποιήσατο πορρώτερον πορεύεσθαι. 29 καὶ
made toward further to travel. And

3849   846   3004   3306 3326 1473
παρεβιάσαντο αὐτὸν λέγοντες· μεῖνον μεθ᾽ ἡμῶν,
they pressed along him saying; stay with us,

3754   4314   2073   1510 2532 2827   2235   05
ὅτι πρὸς ἑσπέραν ἐστὶν καὶ κέκλικεν ἤδη ἡ
because toward evening it is and has bowed already the

2250   2532 1525   010 3306   4862 846   30   2532
ἡμέρα. καὶ εἰσῆλθεν τοῦ μεῖναι σὺν αὐτοῖς. 30 καὶ
day. And he went into the to stay with them. And

1096   1722 011 2625   846   3326 846
ἐγένετο ἐν τῷ κατακλιθῆναι αὐτὸν μετ᾽ αὐτῶν
it became in the to recline him with them

2983   04   740   2127   2532 2806   1929
λαβὼν τὸν ἄρτον εὐλόγησεν καὶ κλασάς ἐπεδίδου
having the bread he spoke and having he was
taken   well   broken giving on

846   31   846   1161 1272   013
αὐτοῖς, 31 αὐτῶν δὲ διηνοίχθησαν   οἱ
to them, of them but were opened completely the

3788   2532 1921   846   2532 846
ὀφθαλμοὶ καὶ ἐπέγνωσαν αὐτόν· καὶ αὐτὸς
eyes and they perceived him; and himself

855   1096   575   846   32   2532 3004
ἄφαντος ἐγένετο ἀπ᾽ αὐτῶν. 32 καὶ εἶπαν
disappeared became from them. And they said

4314   240   3780 08   2588   1473   2545   1510
πρὸς ἀλλήλους· οὐχὶ ἡ καρδία ἡμῶν καιομένη ἦν
to one another, not the heart of us +burning was+

1722 1473   5613 2980   1473   1722 07   3598
[ἐν ἡμῖν] ὡς ἐλάλει   ἡμῖν ἐν τῇ ὁδῷ,
in us] as he was speaking to us in the way,

5613 1272   1473   020 1124   33   2532
ὡς διήνοιγεν ἡμῖν τὰς γραφάς; 33 Καὶ
as he completely opened to us the writings? And

450   846   07   5610 5290   1519
ἀναστάντες αὐτῇ τῇ ὥρᾳ ὑπέστρεψαν εἰς
having stood up same the hour they returned to

2419   2532 2147   119a   016   1733
Ἰερουσαλὴμ καὶ εὗρον ἠθροισμένους   τοὺς ἕνδεκα
Jerusalem and found having been gathered the eleven

25Then he said to them, "Oh, how foolish you are, and how slow of heart to believe all that the prophets have declared! 26Was it not necessary that the Messiah[a] should suffer these things and then enter into his glory?" 27Then beginning with Moses and all the prophets, he interpreted to them the things about himself in all the scriptures.

28 As they came near the village to which they were going, he walked ahead as if he were going on. 29But they urged him strongly, saying, "Stay with us, because it is almost evening and the day is now nearly over." So he went in to stay with them. 30When he was at the table with them, he took bread, blessed and broke it, and gave it to them. 31Then their eyes were opened, and they recognized him; and he vanished from their sight. 32They said to each other, "Were not our hearts burning within us[b] while he was talking to us on the road, while he was opening the scriptures to us?" 33That same hour they got up and returned to Jerusalem; and they found the eleven and their companions gathered together.

a. Or the Christ
b Other ancient authorities lack within us

34They were saying, "The Lord has risen indeed, and he has appeared to Simon!" 35Then they told what had happened on the road, and how he had been made known to them in the breaking of the bread.

36 While they were talking about this, Jesus himself stood among them and said to them, "Peace be with you."[a] 37They were startled and terrified, and thought that they were seeing a ghost. 38He said to them, "Why are you frightened, and why do doubts arise in your hearts? 39Look at my hands and my feet; see that it is I myself. Touch me and see; for a ghost does not have flesh and bones as you see that I have." 40And when he had said this, he showed them his hands and his feet.[b] 41While in their joy they were disbelieving and still wondering, he said to them, "Have you anything here to eat?" 42They gave him a piece of broiled fish, 43and he took it and ate in their presence.

44 Then he said to them, "These are my words that I spoke to you while I was still with you—that everything written about me in the law of Moses, the prophets, and the psalms must be fulfilled."

a Other ancient authorities lack and said to them, "Peace be with you."

b Other ancient authorities lack verse 40

2532 016 4862 846
καὶ τοὺς σὺν αὐτοῖς,
and the with them,

34 3004 3754 3689
λέγοντας ὅτι ὄντως
saying that really

1453 01 2962 2532 3708 4613
ἠγέρθη ὁ κύριος καὶ ὤφθη Σίμωνι.
was raised the Master and he was seen in Simon.

35 2532
καὶ
And

846 1834 024 1722 07 3598 2532 5613
αὐτοὶ ἐξηγοῦντο τὰ ἐν τῇ ὁδῷ καὶ ὡς
themselves were explaining the in the way and as

1097 846 1722 07 2800 02 740
ἐγνώσθη αὐτοῖς ἐν τῇ κλάσει τοῦ ἄρτου.
he was known to them in the breaking of the bread.

36 3778 1161 846 2980 846 2476 1722 3319
Ταῦτα δὲ αὐτῶν λαλούντων αὐτὸς ἔστη ἐν μέσῳ
These but them speaking himself stood in middle

846 2532 3004 846 1515 1473
αὐτῶν καὶ λέγει αὐτοῖς· εἰρήνη ὑμῖν.
of them and says to them; peace to you.

37 4422 1161 2532 1719 1096 1380
πτοηθέντες δὲ καὶ ἔμφοβοι γενόμενοι ἐδόκουν
Having been but also in fear having they were
terrified become thinking

4151 2334 **38** 2532 3004 846 5101
πνεῦμα θεωρεῖν. καὶ εἶπεν αὐτοῖς· τί
spirit to watch. And he said to them; why

5015 1510 2532 1223 5101
τεταραγμένοι ἐστὲ καὶ διὰ τί
+having been troubled you are+ and through what

1261 305 1722 07 2588 1473
διαλογισμοὶ ἀναβαίνουσιν ἐν τῇ καρδίᾳ ὑμῶν;
reasonings go up in the heart of you?

39 3708 020 5495 1473 2532 016 4228 1473 3754
ἴδετε τὰς χεῖράς μου καὶ τοὺς πόδας μου ὅτι
See the hands of me and the feet of me that

1473 1510 846 5584 1473 2532 3708 3754
ἐγώ εἰμι αὐτός· ψηλαφήσατέ με καὶ ἴδετε, ὅτι
I am myself; touch me and see, that

4151 4561 2532 3747 3756 2192 2531 1473
πνεῦμα σάρκα καὶ ὀστέα οὐκ ἔχει καθὼς ἐμὲ
spirit flesh and bones not has just as me

2334 2192 **40** 2532 3778 3004 1166
θεωρεῖτε ἔχοντα. καὶ τοῦτο εἰπὼν ἔδειξεν
you watch having. And this having said he showed

846 020 5495 2532 016 4228 **41** 2089 1161
αὐτοῖς τὰς χεῖρας καὶ τοὺς πόδας. ἔτι δὲ
to them the hands and the feet. Still but

569 846 575 06 5479 2532 2296
ἀπιστούντων αὐτῶν ἀπὸ τῆς χαρᾶς καὶ θαυμαζόντων
untrusting them from the joy and marveling

3004 846 2192 5100 1034 1759
εἶπεν αὐτοῖς· ἔχετέ τι βρώσιμον ἐνθάδε;
he said to them; have you some edible in this place?

42 013 1161 1929 846 2486 3702 3313
οἱ δὲ ἐπέδωκαν αὐτῷ ἰχθύος ὀπτοῦ μέρος·
The but gave on to him fish grilled part;

43 2532 2983 1799 846 2068 **44** 3004
καὶ λαβὼν ἐνώπιον αὐτῶν ἔφαγεν. Εἶπεν
and having taken before them he ate. He said

1161 4314 846 3778 013 3056 1473 3739 2980
δὲ πρὸς αὐτούς· οὗτοι οἱ λόγοι μου οὓς ἐλάλησα
but toward them; these the words of me that I spoke

4314 1473 2089 1510 4862 1473 3754 1163
πρὸς ὑμᾶς ἔτι ὢν σὺν ὑμῖν, ὅτι δεῖ
to you still being with you, because it is necessary

4137 3956 024 1125 1722 03
πληρωθῆναι πάντα τὰ γεγραμμένα ἐν τῷ
to be filled all the having been written in the

3551 3475 2532 015 4396 2532 5568 4012
νόμῳ Μωϋσέως καὶ τοῖς προφήταις καὶ ψαλμοῖς περὶ
law of Moses and the spokesmen and psalms about

```
1473        5119  1272                    846        04    3563
ἐμοῦ.  45  τότε  διήνοιξεν              αὐτῶν    τὸν  νοῦν
me.        Then  he completely opened  of them   the  mind
010  4920             020  1124       46  2532  3004     846
τοῦ  συνιέναι        τὰς  γραφάς·        καὶ  εἶπεν    αὐτοῖς
the  to understand  the  writings;      and  he said  to them,
3754 3779   1125                  3958     04    5547
ὅτι  οὕτως  γέγραπται           παθεῖν   τὸν  χριστὸν
(")  thusly it has been written to suffer the  Christ
2532 450         1537 3498   07   5154  2250      47  2532
καὶ  ἀναστῆναι  ἐκ  νεκρῶν  τῇ  τρίτῃ  ἡμέρᾳ,       καὶ
and  to stand up from dead  in the third  day,       and
2784            1909 011 3686     846  3341        1519
κηρυχθῆναι     ἐπὶ  τῷ  ὀνόματι  αὐτοῦ μετάνοιαν  εἰς
to be announced on  the name     of him change mind into
859        266        1519 3956  024 1484     757
ἄφεσιν    ἁμαρτιῶν  εἰς  πάντα τὰ  ἔθνη.    ἀρξάμενοι
sending off of sins  into  all   the nations. Beginning
575   2419            48  1473  3144      3778     2532
ἀπὸ  Ἰερουσαλὴμ        ὑμεῖς μάρτυρες  τούτων.  49  καὶ
from  Jerusalem           you   testifiers of these.  And
2400   1473 649         08   1860      02      3962
[ἰδοὺ]  ἐγὼ ἀποστέλλω  τὴν  ἐπαγγελίαν τοῦ  πατρός
look    I   delegate    the  promise     of the father
1473  1909 1473 1473  1161 2523      1722 07    4172  2193
μου   ἐφ'  ὑμᾶς· ὑμεῖς δὲ  καθίσατε  ἐν  τῇ  πόλει ἕως
of me on  you;  you   but sit         in the city  until
3739 1746           1537 5311   1411      50  1806
οὗ  ἐνδύσησθε       ἐξ  ὕψους  δύναμιν.      Ἐξήγαγεν
which you might put on from height power.    He led out
1161 846      1854        2193 4314  963          2532
δὲ  αὐτοὺς [ἔξω]      ἕως  πρὸς Βηθανίαν,  καὶ
but  them    outside   until toward Bethany,    and
1869            020 5495     846    2127
ἐπάρας         τὰς  χεῖρας  αὐτοῦ  εὐλόγησεν
having lifted up on the hands of him he spoke well
846        51  2532 1096     1722 011 2127           846
αὐτοὺς.       καὶ  ἐγένετο  ἐν  τῷ  εὐλογεῖν       αὐτὸν
them.          And  it became in  the to speak well   him
846        1339       575  846   2532 399         1519 04
αὐτοὺς  διέστη      ἀπ'  αὐτῶν καὶ  ανεφερετο   εἰς  τὸν
them    he stood    from them  and  was being    into the
       through     from them and  carried up
3772       52  2532 846           4352               846
οὐρανόν.      Καὶ  αὐτοὶ       προσκυνήσαντες  αὐτὸν
heaven.        And  themselves having worshiped him
5290          1519 2419        3326 5479 3173    53  2532
ὑπέστρεψαν  εἰς  Ἰερουσαλὴμ μετὰ χαρᾶς μεγάλης    καὶ
returned      into Jerusalem    with joy   great       and
1510     1223      3956    1722 011 2411
ἦσαν   διὰ       παντὸς  ἐν  τῷ  ἱερῷ
they were+ through all      in  the temple
2127             04   2316
εὐλογοῦντες    τὸν  θεόν.
+speaking well the God.
```

[45] Then he opened their minds to understand the scriptures, [46] and he said to them, "Thus it is written, that the Messiah[a] is to suffer and to rise from the dead on the third day, [47] and that repentance and forgiveness of sins is to be proclaimed in his name to all nations beginning from Jerusalem. [48] You are witnesses[b] of these things. [49] And see, I am sending upon you what my Father promised; so stay here in the city until you have been clothed with power from on high."

[50] Then he led them out as far as Bethany, and, lifting up his hands, he blessed them. [51] While he was blessing them, he withdrew from them and was carried up into heaven.[c] [52] And they worshiped him, and[d] returned to Jerusalem with great joy; [53] and they were continually in the temple blessing God. [e]

a Or the Christ
b Or nations. Beginning from Jerusalem [48] you are witnesses
c Other ancient authorities lack and was carried up into heaven
d Other ancient authorities lack worshiped him, and
e Other ancient authorities add Amen

JOHN

CHAPTER 1

In the beginning was the Word, and the Word was with God, and the Word was God. [2]He was in the beginning with God. [3]All things came into being through him, and without him not one thing came into being. What has come into being [4]in him was life, [a] and the life was the light of all people. [5]The light shines in the darkness, and the darkness did not overcome it.

6 There was a man sent from God, whose name was John. [7]He came as a witness to testify to the light, so that all might believe through him. [8]He himself was not the light, but he came to testify to the light. [9]The true light, which enlightens everyone, was coming into the world.[b]

10 He was in the world, and the world came into being through him; yet the world did not know him. [11]He came to what was his own,[c] and his own people did not accept him. [12]But to all who received him, who believed in his name, he gave power to become children of God, [13]who were born, not of blood or of the will of the flesh or of the will of man, but of God.

14 And the Word became flesh and lived among

[a] Or [3]through him. And without him not one thing came into being that has come into being. [4]In him was life

[b] Or He was the true light that enlightens everyone coming into the world

[c] Or to his own home

1:1
1722 746   1510 01 3056 2532 01   3056   1510
Ἐν ἀρχῇ   ἦν ὁ λόγος, καὶ ὁ λόγος ἦν
In beginning was the word, and the word was

4314 04   2316 2532 2316 1510 01   3056   **2** 3778 1510
πρὸς τὸν θεόν, καὶ θεὸς ἦν ὁ λόγος.   οὗτος ἦν
toward the God, and God was the word.   This was

1722 746   4314 04 2316   **3** 3956 1223   846
ἐν ἀρχῇ   πρὸς τὸν θεόν.   πάντα δι᾽   αὐτοῦ
in beginning toward the God.   All through him

1096   2532 5565   846   1096   3761   1520
ἐγένετο, καὶ χωρὶς αὐτοῦ ἐγένετο οὐδὲ ἕν.
became, and without him became but not one thing.

3739 1096   **4** 1722 846   2222 1510 2532 05   2222
ὃ γεγόνεν   ἐν αυτῷ ζωὴ ἦν, καὶ ἡ ζωὴ
That had become in him life was, and the life

1510 09 5457 014   444   **5** 2532 09 5457 1722
ἦν τὸ φῶς τῶν ἀνθρώπων·   καὶ τὸ φῶς ἐν
was the light of the men;   and the light in

07   4653   5316 2532 05 4653   846   3756 2638
τῇ σκοτίᾳ φαίνει, καὶ ἡ σκοτία αὐτὸ οὐ κατέλαβεν.
the dark shines, and the dark it not overtook.

6 1096   444   649   3844 2316
Ἐγένετο ἄνθρωπος, ἀπεσταλμένος   παρὰ θεοῦ,
Became man,   having been delegated from God,

3686 846   2491   **7** 3778   2064 1519 3141
ὄνομα αὐτῷ Ἰωάννης· οὗτος ἦλθεν εἰς μαρτυρίαν
name to him John;   this one came for testimony

2443 3140   4012   010 5457   2443
ἵνα μαρτυρήσῃ   περὶ τοῦ φωτός, ἵνα
that he might testify concerning the light, that

3956   4100   1223   846   **8** 3756 1510 1565
πάντες πιστεύσωσιν δι᾽   αὐτοῦ.   οὐκ ἦν ἐκεῖνος
all might trust through him.   Not was that one

09 5457   235 2443 3140   4012   010
τὸ φῶς, ἀλλ᾽ ἵνα μαρτυρήσῃ   περὶ τοῦ
the light, but that he might testify concerning the

5457   **9** 1510 09 5457 09 228   3739 5461
φωτός.   Ἦν τὸ φῶς τὸ ἀληθινόν, ὃ φωτίζει
light. He was the light the true, who lightens

3956 444   2064   1519 04 2889   **10** 1722 03
πάντα ἄνθρωπον, ἐρχόμενον εἰς τὸν κόσμον.   ἐν τῷ
all man,   coming into the world.   In the

2889 1510   2532 01 2889   1223   846   1096
κόσμῳ ἦν,   καὶ ὁ κόσμος δι᾽   αὐτοῦ ἐγένετο,
world he was, and the world through him became,

2532 01 2889   846   3756 1097   **11** 1519 024 2398
καὶ ὁ κόσμος αὐτὸν οὐκ ἔγνω.   εἰς τὰ ἴδια
and the world him not knew.   To the own

2064   2532 013 2398   846   3756 3880
ἦλθεν, καὶ οἱ ἴδιοι αὐτὸν οὐ παρέλαβον.
he came, and the own him not took along.

12 3745   1161 2983   846   1325   846
ὅσοι   δὲ ἔλαβον αὐτόν, ἔδωκεν αὐτοῖς
As many as but took him,   he gave to them

1849   5043   2316 1096   015
ἐξουσίαν τέκνα θεοῦ γενέσθαι, τοῖς
authority children of God to become, to the

4100   1519 012 3686   846   **13** 3739 3756 1537
πιστεύουσιν εἰς τὸ ὄνομα αὐτοῦ,   οἳ οὐκ ἐξ
ones trusting into the name of him,   who not out of

129   3761   1537 2307   4561   3761   1537
αἱμάτων οὐδὲ ἐκ θελήματος σαρκὸς οὐδὲ ἐκ
bloods but not out of want of flesh but not out of

2307   435 235 1537   2316 1080
θελήματος ἀνδρὸς ἀλλ᾽ ἐκ θεοῦ ἐγεννήθησαν.
want of man but out of God they were born.

14 2532 01 3056   4561 1096   2532 4637   1722
Καὶ ὁ λόγος σὰρξ ἐγένετο καὶ ἐσκήνωσεν ἐν
And the word flesh became and he tented in

```
1473    2532  2300           08   1391      846      1391      5613
ἡμῖν,  καὶ  ἐθεασάμεθα τὴν δόξαν   αὐτοῦ,  δόξαν   ὡς
us,    and  we watched  the splendor of him, splendor as
3439         3844 3962      4134    5485        2532  225
μονογενοῦς παρὰ πατρός, πλήρης χάριτος  καὶ  ἀληθείας.
only born  from father, full   of favor and  truth.
       2491      3140       4012      846    2532 2896
15  Ἰωάννης μαρτυρεῖ περὶ      αὐτοῦ καὶ  κέκραγεν
    John    testifies concerning him   and  has shouted
3004    3778   1510 3739 3004    01       3694  1473
λέγων· οὗτος ἦν  ὃν  εἶπον· ὁ       ὀπίσω μου
saying, this was whom I said; the one after me
2064        1715        1473 1096        3754    4413
ἐρχόμενος ἔμπροσθέν μου γέγονεν,  ὅτι    πρῶτός
coming     in front  of me has become, because first
1473 1510  16 3754     1537  010 4138          846    1473
μου  ἦν.      ὅτι    ἐκ   τοῦ πληρώματος αὐτοῦ ἡμεῖς
of me he was. Because out  of the fullness  of him we
3956    2983     2532 5485  473          5485    17 3754
πάντες ἐλάβομεν καὶ χάριν ἀντὶ    χάριτος·      ὅτι
all     received and favor in place of favor;    because
01 3551   1223   3475       1325    05  5485    2532 05
ὁ  νόμος διὰ  Μωϋσέως ἐδόθη,   ἡ  χάρις καὶ  ἡ
the law  through Moses   was given, the favor and the
225       1223    2424    5547    1096      18 2316 3762
ἀλήθεια διὰ  Ἰησοῦ Χριστοῦ ἐγένετο.    Θεὸν οὐδεὶς
truth    through Jesus Christ  became.      God  no one
3708     4455     3439       2316 01  1510       1519
ἑώρακεν πώποτε·  μονογενὴς θεὸς ὁ  ὢν        εἰς
has seen ever yet; only born God the one being in
04  2859    02   3962    1565      1834        19 2532
τὸν κόλπον τοῦ πατρὸς ἐκεῖνος ἐξηγήσατο.     Καὶ
the lap     of the father that one explained.     And
3778 1510  05 3141     02   2491      3753  649
αὕτη ἐστὶν ἡ μαρτυρία τοῦ  Ἰωάννου, ὅτε  ἀπέστειλαν
this is    the testimony of the John,  when delegated
4314  846      013 2453      1537   2414      2409
[πρὸς αὐτὸν] οἱ Ἰουδαῖοι ἐξ   Ἱεροσολύμων ἱερεῖς
toward him   the Judeans out of Jerusalem  priests
2532 3019     2443 2065           846    1473 5101 1510
καὶ Λευίτας ἵνα ἐρωτήσωσιν αὐτόν· τί   εἶ;
and  Levites that they might ask him;  you who are?
   2532 3670           2532 3756 720         2532
20 καὶ  ὡμολόγησεν καὶ  οὐκ  ἠρνήσατο, καὶ
   And  he confessed and  not   he denied, and
3670          3754 1473 3756 1510 01  5547       21 2532
ὡμολόγησεν ὅτι  ἐγὼ οὐκ  εἰμὶ ὁ  χριστός.      καὶ
he confessed, (") I   not   am  the Christ.       And
2065       846      5101 3767 1473 2243     1510 2532
ἠρώτησαν αὐτόν· τί   οὖν;  σὺ  Ἠλίας εἶ;  καὶ
they asked him;  who then? You Elijah are? And
3004    3756 1510  01  4396        1510 1473 2532
λέγει·  οὐκ  εἰμί. ὁ   προφήτης εἶ  σύ;  καὶ
he says; not  I am. The spokesman are you? And
611        3756a  22 3004    3767 846     5101
ἀπεκρίθη·  οὔ.      εἶπαν οὖν  αὐτῷ· τίς
he answered; no.     They said then to him; who
1510 2443 612         1325   015 3992        1473
εἶ;  ἵνα ἀπόκρισιν δῶμεν τοῖς πέμψασιν ἡμᾶς·
are that answer    we might to ones having us;
you? give                  the   sent
5101 3004    4012   4572      23 5346     1473 5456
τί   λέγεις περὶ σεαυτοῦ;    ἔφη·     ἐγὼ φωνὴ
what you say about yourself? He said; I   sound
994         1722 07  2048     2116        08   3598
βοῶντος    ἐν  τῇ ἐρήμῳ· εὐθύνατε τὴν ὁδὸν
crying aloud in  the desert; straighten the way
2962     2531   3004    2036   4396          24 2532
κυρίου,  καθὼς εἶπεν Ἠσαΐας ὁ προφήτης.      Καὶ
of Master, just as said Isaiah the spokesman.   And
```

us, and we have seen his glory, the glory as of a father's only son,[a] full of grace and truth. [15](John testified to him and cried out, "This was he of whom I said, 'He who comes after me ranks ahead of me because he was before me.' ") [16]From his fullness we have all received, grace upon grace. [17]The law indeed was given through Moses; grace and truth came through Jesus Christ. [18]No one has ever seen God. It is God the only Son,[b] who is close to the Father's heart,[c] who has made him known.

[19]This is the testimony given by John when the Jews sent priests and Levites from Jerusalem to ask him, "Who are you?" [20]He confessed and did not deny it, but confessed, "I am not the Messiah."[d] [21]And they asked him, "What then? Are you Elijah?" He said, "I am not." "Are you the prophet?" He answered, "No." [22]Then they said to him, "Who are you? Let us have an answer for those who sent us. What do you say about yourself?" [23]He said,

"I am the voice of one crying out in the wilderness, 'Make straight the way of the Lord,' "

as the prophet Isaiah said. [24]Now they had been sent

---

[a] Or the Father's only Son
[b] Other ancient authorities read It is an only Son, God, or It is the only Son
[c] Gk bosom
[d] Or the Christ

from the Pharisees. ²⁵They asked him, "Why then are you baptizing if you are neither the Messiah,^a nor Elijah, nor the prophet?" ²⁶John answered them, "I baptize with water. Among you stands one whom you do not know, ²⁷the one who is coming after me; I am not worthy to untie the thong of his sandal." ²⁸This took place in Bethany across the Jordan where John was baptizing.

29 The next day he saw Jesus coming toward him and declared, "Here is the Lamb of God who takes away the sin of the world! ³⁰This is he of whom I said, 'After me comes a man who ranks ahead of me because he was before me.' ³¹I myself did not know him; but I came baptizing with water for this reason, that he might be revealed to Israel." ³²And John testified, "I saw the Spirit descending from heaven like a dove, and it remained on him. ³³I myself did not know him, but the one who sent me to baptize with water said to me, 'He on whom you see the Spirit

a Or the Christ

649		1510 1537	014 5330
ἀπεσταλμένοι		ἦσαν ἐκ	τῶν Φαρισαίων.
ones having delegated		were out of	the Pharisees.

25 καὶ ἠρώτησαν αὐτὸν καὶ εἶπαν αὐτῷ· τί
And they asked him and they said to him; why
(2532 2065 / 846 / 2532 3004 / 846 / 5101)

οὖν βαπτίζεις εἰ σὺ οὐκ εἶ ὁ χριστὸς οὐδὲ
then you immerse if you not are the Christ but not
(3767 907 / 1487 1473 / 3756 1510 01 / 5547 / 3761)

Ἠλίας οὐδὲ ὁ προφήτης; **26** ἀπεκρίθη αὐτοῖς ὁ
Elijah but not the spokesman? Answered them the
(2243 3761 / 01 4396 / 611 / 846 / 01)

Ἰωάννης λέγων· ἐγὼ βαπτίζω ἐν ὕδατι· μέσος ὑμῶν
John saying; I immerse in water; middle of you
(2491 3004 / 1473 907 / 1722 5204 / 3319 1473)

ἕστηκεν ὃν ὑμεῖς οὐκ οἴδατε, **27** ὁ ὀπίσω μου
he has stood whom you not know, the after me
(2476 / 3739 1473 3756 3609a / 01 3694 1473)

ἐρχόμενος, οὗ οὐκ εἰμὶ [ἐγὼ] ἄξιος ἵνα
one coming, of whom not I am I worthy that
(2064 / 3739 / 3756 1510 1473 514 / 2443)

λύσω αὐτοῦ τὸν ἱμάντα τοῦ ὑποδήματος.
I might loose of him the strap of the sandal.
(3089 / 846 / 04 2438 / 010 5266)

28 ταῦτα ἐν Βηθανίᾳ ἐγένετο πέραν τοῦ Ἰορδάνου,
These in Bethany became across the Jordan,
(3778 1722 963 1096 4008 02 2446)

ὅπου ἦν ὁ Ἰωάννης βαπτίζων. **29** Τῇ ἐπαύριον
where was+ the John +immersing. In the tomorrow
(3699 1510 01 2491 907 07 1887)

βλέπει τὸν Ἰησοῦν ἐρχόμενον πρὸς αὐτὸν καὶ
he sees the Jesus coming toward him and
(991 04 2424 2064 4314 846 2532)

λέγει· ἴδε ὁ ἀμνὸς τοῦ θεοῦ ὁ αἴρων
he says; look the lamb of the God the one lifting up
(3004 2396 01 286 02 2316 01 142)

τὴν ἁμαρτίαν τοῦ κόσμου. **30** οὗτός ἐστιν ὑπὲρ
the sin of the world. This is on behalf
(00 266 02 2889 3778 1510 5228)

οὗ ἐγὼ εἶπον· ὀπίσω μου ἔρχεται ἀνὴρ ὃς
of whom I said; after me comes man who
(3739 1473 1473 3694 1473 2064 435 3739)

ἔμπροσθέν μου γέγονεν, ὅτι πρῶτός μου
in front of me has become, because first of me
(1715 1473 1096 3754 4413 1473)

ἦν. **31** κἀγὼ οὐκ ᾔδειν αὐτόν, ἀλλ᾽ ἵνα
he was. And I not I had known him, but that
(1510 2504 3756 3609a 846 235 2443)

φανερωθῇ τῷ Ἰσραὴλ διὰ τοῦτο
he might be demonstrated to the Israel through this
(5319 03 2474 1223 3778)

ἦλθον ἐγὼ ἐν ὕδατι βαπτίζων. **32** Καὶ ἐμαρτύρησεν
came I in water immersing. And testified
(2064 1473 1722 5204 907 2532 3140)

Ἰωάννης λέγων ὅτι τεθέαμαι τὸ πνεῦμα
John saying, (") I have watched the spirit
(2491 3004 3754 2300 012 4151)

καταβαῖνον ὡς περιστερὰν ἐξ οὐρανοῦ καὶ ἔμεινεν
coming down as dove from heaven and it stayed
(2597 5613 4058 1537 3772 2532 3306)

ἐπ᾽ αὐτόν. **33** κἀγὼ οὐκ ᾔδειν αὐτόν, ἀλλ᾽ ὁ
on him. And I not had known him, but the one
(1909 846 2504 3756 3609a 846 235 01)

πέμψας με βαπτίζειν ἐν ὕδατι ἐκεῖνός μοι
having sent me to immerse in water that one to me
(3992 1473 907 1722 5204 1565 1473)

εἶπεν· ἐφ᾽ ὃν ἂν ἴδῃς τὸ πνεῦμα
said; on whom - you might see the spirit
(3004 1909 3739 302 3708 012 4151)

2597   2532 3306   1909 846   3778 1510
καταβαῖνον καὶ μένον ἐπ’ αὐτόν, οὗτός ἐστιν
coming down and staying on him,   this   is
01 907   1722 4151   40   2504 3708
ὁ βαπτίζων   ἐν πνεύματι ἁγίῳ. **34** κἀγὼ ἑώρακα
the one immersing in spirit holy.   And I have seen
2532 3140   3754 3778 1510 01 5207 02
καὶ μεμαρτύρηκα   ὅτι οὗτός ἐστιν ὁ υἱὸς τοῦ
and I have testified that this is   the son of the
2316   07 1887   3825 2476   01 2491   2532
θεοῦ. **35** Τῇ ἐπαύριον πάλιν εἱστήκει ὁ Ἰωάννης καὶ
God.   In the tomorrow again had stood the John   and
1537   014 3101   846   1417   2532 1689
ἐκ τῶν μαθητῶν αὐτοῦ δύο **36** καὶ ἐμβλέψας
out of the learners of him two   and having looked in
03 2424 4043   3004   2396 01 286   02
τῷ Ἰησοῦ περιπατοῦντι λέγει· ἴδε ὁ ἀμνὸς τοῦ
the Jesus walking around he says; look the lamb of the
2316   37 2532 191   013 1417 3101   846   2980
θεοῦ. **37** καὶ ἤκουσαν οἱ δύο μαθηταὶ αὐτοῦ λαλοῦντος
God.   And heard the two learners of him speaking
2532 190   03 2424   4762   1161 01
καὶ ἠκολούθησαν τῷ Ἰησοῦ. **38** στραφεὶς δὲ ὁ
and they followed the Jesus. Having turned but the
2424 2532 2300   846   190   3004
Ἰησοῦς καὶ θεασάμενος αὐτοὺς ἀκολουθοῦντας λέγει
Jesus and having watched them   following   says
846   5101 2212   013   1161 3004 846
αὐτοῖς· τί ζητεῖτε; οἱ   δὲ εἶπαν αὐτῷ·
to them; what you seek? The ones but said to him;
4461 3739 3004   3177
ῥαββί, ὃ λέγεται   μεθερμηνευόμενον
Rabbi, which is being called being translated
1320   4226 3306   3004 846   2064
διδάσκαλε, ποῦ μένεις; **39** λέγει αὐτοῖς· ἔρχεσθε
teacher,   where stay you? He says to them; come
2532 3708   2064   3767 2532 3708 4226 3306
καὶ ὄψεσθε. ἦλθαν οὖν καὶ εἶδαν ποῦ μένει
and see.   They went then and saw where he stays
2532 3844   846 3005   08 2250 1565
καὶ παρ’ αὐτῷ ἔμειναν τὴν ἡμέραν ἐκείνην·
and alongside him they stayed the day   that;
5610 1510 5613 1182   1510 406   01 80
ὥρα ἦν ὡς δεκάτη. **40** Ἦν Ἀνδρέας ὁ ἀδελφὸς
hour was as tenth.   Was Andrew the brother
4613   4074   1520 1537   014 1417 014
Σίμωνος Πέτρου εἷς ἐκ   τῶν δύο τῶν
of Simon Peter one out of the two of the ones
191   3844 2491   2532 190   846
ἀκουσάντων παρὰ Ἰωάννου καὶ ἀκολουθησάντων αὐτῷ·
having heard from John   and having followed him;
  2147   3778   4413   04 80   04 2398
41 εὑρίσκει οὗτος πρῶτον τὸν ἀδελφὸν τὸν ἴδιον
finds   this one first the brother the own
4613   2532 3004 846   2147   04 3323
Σίμωνα καὶ λέγει αὐτῷ· εὑρήκαμεν τὸν Μεσσίαν,
Simon and says to him; we have found the Messiah,
3739 1510 3177   5547   71 846
ὃ ἐστιν μεθερμηνευόμενον χριστός. **42** ἤγαγεν αὐτὸν
which is+ +being translated, Christ. He led him
4314   04 2424   1689   846 01 2424
πρὸς τὸν Ἰησοῦν. ἐμβλέψας αὐτῷ ὁ Ἰησοῦς
toward the Jesus. Having looked in him the Jesus
3004   1473 1510 4613   01 5207 2491   1473
εἶπεν· σὺ εἶ Σίμων ὁ υἱὸς Ἰωάννου, σὺ
said; you are Simon the son of John, you
2564   2786   3739 2059   4074
κληθήσῃ Κηφᾶς, ὃ ἑρμηνεύεται Πέτρος.
will be called Cephas, which is interpreted, Peter.

descend and remain is the one who baptizes with the Holy Spirit.' [34]And I myself have seen and have testified that this is the Son of God."[a]

35 The next day John again was standing with two of his disciples, [36]and as he watched Jesus walk by, he exclaimed, "Look, here is the Lamb of God!" [37]The two disciples heard him say this, and they followed Jesus. [38]When Jesus turned and saw them following, he said to them, "What are you looking for?" They said to him, "Rabbi" (which translated means Teacher), "where are you staying?" [39]He said to them, "Come and see." They came and saw where he was staying, and they remained with him that day. It was about four o'clock in the afternoon. [40]One of the two who heard John speak and followed him was Andrew, Simon Peter's brother. [41]He first found his brother Simon and said to him, "We have found the Messiah" (which is translated Anointed[b]). [42]He brought Simon[c] to Jesus, who looked at him and said, "You are Simon son of John. You are to be called Cephas" (which is translated Peter[d]).

[a] Other ancient authorities read is God's chosen one
[b] Or Christ
[c] Gk him
[d] From the word for rock in Aramaic (kepha) and Greek (petra), respectively

43 The next day Jesus decided to go to Galilee. He found Philip and said to him, "Follow me." 44Now Philip was from Bethsaida, the city of Andrew and Peter. 45Philip found Nathanael and said to him, "We have found him about whom Moses in the law and also the prophets wrote, Jesus son of Joseph from Nazareth." 46Nathanael said to him, "Can anything good come out of Nazareth?" Philip said to him, "Come and see." 47When Jesus saw Nathanael coming toward him, he said of him, "Here is truly an Israelite in whom there is no deceit!" 48Nathanael asked him, "Where did you get to know me?" Jesus answered, "I saw you under the fig tree before Philip called you." 49Nathanael replied, "Rabbi, you are the Son of God! You are the King of Israel!" 50Jesus answered, "Do you believe because I told you that I saw you under the fig tree? You will see greater things than these." 51And he said to him, "Very truly, I tell you,[a] you will see heaven opened and the angels of God ascending and descending upon the Son of Man."

---

[a] Both instances of the Greek word for *you* in this verse are plural

---

43
07	1887	2309	1831	1519	08
Τῇ	ἐπαύριον	ἠθέλησεν	ἐξελθεῖν	εἰς	τὴν
In the	tomorrow	he wanted	to go out	into	the

1056	2532	2147	5376	2532	3004	846
Γαλιλαίαν	καὶ	εὑρίσκει	Φίλιππον.	καὶ	λέγει	αὐτῷ
Galilee	and	he finds	Philip,	and	says	to him

01	2424	190	1473	**44**	1510	1161	01	5376
ὁ	Ἰησοῦς·	ἀκολούθει	μοι.		ἦν	δὲ	ὁ	Φίλιππος
the	Jesus;	follow	me.		Was	but	the	Philip

575	966	1537	06	4172	406	2532
ἀπὸ	Βηθσαϊδά,	ἐκ	τῆς	πόλεως	Ἀνδρέου	καὶ
from	Bethsaida,	out of	the	city	of Andrew	and

4074	**45**	2147	5376	04	3482	2532	3004
Πέτρου.		εὑρίσκει	Φίλιππος	τὸν	Ναθαναὴλ	καὶ	λέγει
Peter.		Finds	Philip	the	Nathanael	and	says

846	3739	1125	3475	1722	03	3551	2532	013
αὐτῷ·	ὃν	ἔγραψεν	Μωϋσῆς	ἐν	τῷ	νόμῳ	καὶ	οἱ
to him;	whom	wrote	Moses	in	the	law	and	the

4396	2147		2424	5207	02		2501	04
προφῆται	εὑρήκαμεν,		Ἰησοῦν	υἱὸν	τοῦ		Ἰωσὴφ	τὸν
spokesmen	we have found,		Jesus	son	of the		Joseph	the

575	3478a		2532	3004	846	3482	1537
ἀπὸ	Ναζαρέτ.	**46**	καὶ	εἶπεν	αὐτῷ	Ναθαναήλ·	ἐκ
from	Nazaret.		And	said	to him	Nathanael;	out of

3478a	1410	5100	18	1510	3004	846	01
Ναζαρὲτ	δύναταί	τι	ἀγαθὸν	εἶναι;	λέγει	αὐτῷ	ὁ
Nazaret	is able	what	good	to be?	Says	to him	the

5376	2064	2532	2396	**47**	3708	01	2424	04
Φίλιππος·	ἔρχου	καὶ	ἴδε.		εἶδεν	ὁ	Ἰησοῦς	τὸν
Philip;	come	and	look.		Saw	the	Jesus	the

3482	2064	4314	846	2532	3004	4012
Ναθαναὴλ	ἐρχόμενον	πρὸς	αὐτὸν	καὶ	λέγει	περὶ
Nathanael	coming	toward	him	and	he says	about

846	2396	230	2475	1722	3739	1388	3756
αὐτοῦ·	ἴδε	ἀληθῶς	Ἰσραηλίτης	ἐν	ᾧ	δόλος	οὐκ
him;	look	truly	Israelite	in	whom	guile	not

1510	**48**	3004	846	3482	4159	1473
ἔστιν.		λέγει	αὐτῷ	Ναθαναήλ·	πόθεν	με
there is.		Says	to him	Nathanael;	from where	me

1097	611	2424	2532	3004	846	4253
γινώσκεις;	ἀπεκρίθη	Ἰησοῦς	καὶ	εἶπεν	αὐτῷ·	πρὸ
you know?	Answered	Jesus	and	said	to him;	before

010	1473	5376	5455	1510	5259	08	4808
τοῦ	σε	Φίλιππον	φωνῆσαι	ὄντα	ὑπὸ	τὴν	συκῆν
the	you	Philip	to sound	being	under	the	fig tree

3708	1473	**49**	611	846	3482	4461	1473
εἶδόν	σε.		ἀπεκρίθη	αὐτῷ	Ναθαναήλ·	ῥαββί,	σὺ
I saw	you.		Answered	him	Nathanael,	Rabbi,	you

1510	01	5207	02	2316	1473	935	1510	02
εἶ	ὁ	υἱὸς	τοῦ	θεοῦ,	σὺ	βασιλεὺς	εἶ	τοῦ
are	the	son	of the	God,	you	king	are	of the

2474	**50**	611	2424	2532	3004	846	3754
Ἰσραήλ.		ἀπεκρίθη	Ἰησοῦς	καὶ	εἶπεν	αὐτῷ·	ὅτι
Israel.		Answered	Jesus	and	said to him;		because

3004	1473	3754	3708	1473	5270	06	4808
εἶπόν	σοι	ὅτι	εἶδόν	σε	ὑποκάτω	τῆς	συκῆς,
I said	to you	that	I saw	you	underneath	the	fig tree,

4100	3173	3778	3708			2532	3004
πιστεύεις;	μείζω	τούτων	ὄψῃ.		**51**	καὶ	λέγει
you trust?	Greater	of these	you will see.			And	he says

846	281	281	3004	1473	3708	04
αὐτῷ·	ἀμὴν	ἀμὴν	λέγω	ὑμῖν,	ὄψεσθε	τὸν
to him;	amen	amen	I say	to you,	you will see	the

3772	455		2532	016	32	02
οὐρανὸν	ἀνεῳγότα		καὶ	τοὺς	ἀγγέλους	τοῦ
heaven	having opened		and	the	messengers	of the

2316	305		2532	2597	1909	04	5207
θεοῦ	ἀναβαίνοντας		καὶ	καταβαίνοντας	ἐπὶ	τὸν	υἱὸν
God	going up		and	going down	upon	the	son

```
02       444          2:1  2532 07        2250  07    5154
τοῦ     ἀνθρώπου.          Καὶ  τῇ     ἡμέρᾳ  τῇ   τρίτῃ
of the man.               And  in the day    the  third
1062     1096       1722 2580 06       1056          2532 1510
γάμος   ἐγένετο ἐν  Κανὰ τῆς  Γαλιλαίας, καὶ  ἦν
marriage became  in  Cana of the Galilee,   and  was
05   3384    02      2424   1563  2  2564        1161 2532
ἡ   μήτηρ  τοῦ   Ἰησοῦ ἐκεῖ·    ἐκλήθη   δὲ   καὶ
the mother of the Jesus there;   was called but  also
01   2424    2532 013 3101    846      1519 04  1062
ὁ   Ἰησοῦς καὶ  οἱ  μαθηταὶ αὐτοῦ εἰς  τὸν γάμον.
the Jesus  and  the learners of him to    the marriage.
   2532 5302                  3631 3004   05   3384
 3 καὶ  ὑστερήσαντος        οἴνου λέγει ἡ   μήτηρ
   And  having been in lack wine  says  the mother
02   2424    4314   846     3631 3756 2192       4  2532
τοῦ Ἰησοῦ πρὸς  αὐτόν· οἶνον οὐκ ἔχουσιν.     [καὶ]
of the Jesus toward him;  wine  not  they have.    And
3004 846    01  2424    5101 1473 2532 1473      1135
λέγει αὐτῇ ὁ  Ἰησοῦς· τί  ἐμοὶ καὶ  σοί,    γύναι;
says  to her the Jesus; what to me and to you,    woman?
3768 2240     05  5610 1473  5  3004 05  3384
οὔπω ἥκει    ἡ  ὥρα  μου.    λέγει ἡ  μήτηρ
Not yet is come the hour of me.  Says  the mother
846    015    1249        3739  5100 302 3004
αὐτοῦ τοῖς διακόνοις· ὅ    τι   ἂν λέγῃ
of him to the servants;   what some -  he might say
1473 4160       6  1510 1161 1563 3035    5201
ὑμῖν ποιήσατε.   ἦσαν δὲ  ἐκεῖ λίθιναι ὑδρίαι
to you do.        Were+ but there of stone waterpots
1803 2596 04 2512       014       2453     2749
ἓξ   κατὰ τὸν καθαρισμὸν τῶν   Ἰουδαίων κείμεναι,
six  by   the cleaning    of the Judeans +lying,
5562         303 3355      1417 2228 5140   7  3004
χωροῦσαι    ἀνὰ μετρητὰς δύο ἢ    τρεῖς.    λέγει
making room up  measures  two or    three.     Says
846    01  2424    1072      020 5201    5204
αὐτοῖς ὁ  Ἰησοῦς· γεμίσατε τὰς ὑδρίας ὕδατος.
to them the Jesus; fill      the waterpots of water.
2532 1072     846   2193 507  8  2532 3004
καὶ  ἐγέμισαν αὐτὰς ἕως ἄνω.   καὶ  λέγει
And  they filled them until up.  And  he says
846     501          3568 2532 5342  03    755
αὐτοῖς· ἀντλήσατε νῦν καὶ  φέρετε τῷ  ἀρχιτρικλίνῳ·
to them; draw out  now and  carry  to the first banquet
                                                 steward;
013     1161 5342      9  5613 1161 1089      01
οἱ     δὲ   ἤνεγκαν.    ὡς   δὲ   ἐγεύσατο ὁ
the ones but  carried.   As   but  tasted    the
755                     012  5204 3631  1096
ἀρχιτρίκλινος          τὸ  ὕδωρ οἶνον γεγενημένον
first banquet steward   the water wine  having become
2532 3756 3609a        4159     1510 013 1161
καὶ  οὐκ ᾔδει         πόθεν   ἐστίν, οἱ  δὲ
and  not  he had known from where it is,   the but
1249     3609a     013 501          012 5204
διάκονοι ᾔδεισαν οἱ  ἠντληκότες  τὸ  ὕδωρ,
servants had known the having drawn out the water,
5455    04  3566      01  755                 2532
φωνεῖ  τὸν νυμφίον ὁ  ἀρχιτρίκλινος  10 καὶ
sounds  the bridegroom the first banquet steward  and
3004 846     3956 444    4413 04  2570 3631
λέγει αὐτῷ· πᾶς ἄνθρωπος πρῶτον τὸν καλὸν οἶνον
says  to him; all  man      first  the good  wine
5087      2532 3752 3182           04  1640      1473
τίθησιν καὶ  ὅταν μεθυσθῶσιν     τὸν ἐλάσσω· σὺ
places  and  when they might be drunk the lesser; you
5083        04  2570 3631  2193 737     11 3778
τετήρηκας τὸν καλὸν οἶνον ἕως ἄρτι.     Ταύτην
have kept  the good  wine  until now.    This
```

CHAPTER 2

On the third day there
was a wedding in Cana of
Galilee, and the mother of
Jesus was there. [2]Jesus and
his disciples had also been
invited to the wedding.
[3]When the wine gave out,
the mother of Jesus said to
him, "They have no wine."
[4]And Jesus said to her,
"Woman, what concern is
that to you and to me? My
hour has not yet come."
[5]His mother said to the
servants, "Do whatever he
tells you." [6]Now standing
there were six stone water
jars for the Jewish rites of
purification, each holding
twenty or thirty gallons.
[7]Jesus said to them, "Fill
the jars with water." And
they filled them up to the
brim. [8]He said to them,
"Now draw some out,
and take it to the chief
steward." So they took it.
[9]When the steward tasted
the water that had become
wine, and did not know
where it came from (though
the servants who had
drawn the water knew),
the steward called the
bridegroom [10]and said to
him, "Everyone serves the
good wine first, and then
the inferior wine after the
guests have become drunk.
But you have kept the good
wine until now." [11]Jesus
did this,

the first of his signs, in Cana of Galilee, and revealed his glory; and his disciples believed in him.

12 After this he went down to Capernaum with his mother, his brothers, and his disciples; and they remained there a few days.

13 The Passover of the Jews was near, and Jesus went up to Jerusalem. 14In the temple he found people selling cattle, sheep, and doves, and the money changers seated at their tables. 15Making a whip of cords, he drove all of them out of the temple, both the sheep and the cattle. He also poured out the coins of the money changers and overturned their tables. 16He told those who were selling the doves, "Take these things out of here! Stop making my Father's house a marketplace!" 17His disciples remembered that it was written, "Zeal for your house will consume me." 18The Jews then said to him, "What sign can you show us for doing this?" 19Jesus answered them, "Destroy this temple, and in three days

4160	746	022	4592	01	2424	1722	2580
ἐποίησεν	ἀρχὴν	τῶν	σημείων	ὁ	Ἰησοῦς	ἐν	Κανὰ
did	beginning	of the	signs		the Jesus	in	Cana

06	1056		2532	5319		08	1391
τῆς	Γαλιλαίας	καὶ	ἐφανέρωσεν			τὴν	δόξαν
of the	Galilee	and	he demonstrated			the	splendor

846		2532	4100		1519	846	013	3101	846
αὐτοῦ,	καὶ	ἐπίστευσαν	εἰς	αὐτὸν	οἱ	μαθηταὶ	αὐτοῦ.
of him,	and	trusted		in	him	the	learners of him.

12 3326 3778 2597 1519 2746a 846 2532
Μετὰ τοῦτο κατέβη εἰς Καφαρναοὺμ αὐτὸς καὶ
After this went down into Capernaum himself and

05 3384 846 2532 013 80 846 2532 013
ἡ μήτηρ αὐτοῦ καὶ οἱ ἀδελφοὶ αὐτοῦ καὶ οἱ
the mother of him and the brothers of him and the

3101 846 2532 1563 3306 3756 4183
μαθηταὶ αὐτοῦ καὶ ἐκεῖ ἔμειναν οὐ πολλὰς
learners of him and there they stayed not many

2250 **13** 2532 1451 1510 09 3957 014
ἡμέρας. Καὶ ἐγγὺς ἦν τὸ πάσχα τῶν
days. And near was the passover of the

2453 2532 305 1519 2414 01 2424
Ἰουδαίων, καὶ ἀνέβη εἰς Ἱεροσόλυμα ὁ Ἰησοῦς.
Judeans, and went up into Jerusalem the Jesus.

14 2532 2147 1722 011 2411 016 4453
Καὶ εὗρεν ἐν τῷ ἱερῷ τοὺς πωλοῦντας
And he found in the temple the ones selling

1016 2532 4263 2532 4058 2532 016
βόας καὶ πρόβατα καὶ περιστερὰς καὶ τοὺς
oxen and sheep and doves and the

2773 2521 **15** 2532 4160 5416
κερματιστὰς καθημένους, καὶ ποιήσας φράγελλιον
money changers sitting, And having made whip

1537 4979 3956 1544 1537 010
ἐκ σχοινίων πάντας ἐξέβαλεν ἐκ τοῦ
out of small cords all he threw out out of the

2411 024 5037 4263 2532 016 1016 2532 014
ἱεροῦ τά τε πρόβατα καὶ τοὺς βόας, καὶ τῶν
temple the both sheep and the oxen, and of the

2855 1632 012 2772 2532 020 5132
κολλυβιστῶν ἐξέχεεν τὸ κέρμα καὶ τὰς τραπέζας
money changers he poured out the money and the tables

396 2532 015 020 4058 4453
ἀνέτρεψεν, **16** καὶ τοῖς τὰς περιστερὰς πωλοῦσιν
he turned up, and to the ones the doves selling

3004 142 3778 1782 3361 4160 04
εἶπεν· ἄρατε ταῦτα ἐντεῦθεν, μὴ ποιεῖτε τὸν
he said; lift up these from here, not make the

3624 02 3962 1473 3624 1712
οἶκον τοῦ πατρός μου οἶκον ἐμπορίου.
house of the father of me house of merchandise.

17 3403 013 3101 846 3754 1125
ἐμνήσθησαν οἱ μαθηταὶ αὐτοῦ ὅτι γεγραμμένον
Remembered the learners of him that +having been written,

1510 01 2205 02 3624 1473 2719
ἐστίν· ὁ ζῆλος τοῦ οἴκου σου καταφάγεταί
it is+; the jealousy of the house of you will eat up

1473 **18** 611 3767 013 2453 2532 3004
με. Ἀπεκρίθησαν οὖν οἱ Ἰουδαῖοι καὶ εἶπαν
me. Answered then the Judeans and said

846 5101 4592 1166 1473 3754 3778
αὐτῷ· τί σημεῖον δεικνύεις ἡμῖν ὅτι ταῦτα
to him; what sign you show to us, that these

4160 **19** 611 2424 2532 3004 846
ποιεῖς; ἀπεκρίθη Ἰησοῦς καὶ εἶπεν αὐτοῖς·
you do? Answered Jesus and said to them;

3089 04 3485 3778 2532 1722 5140 2250
λύσατε τὸν ναὸν τοῦτον καὶ ἐν τρισὶν ἡμέραις
loose the temple this and in three days

1453	846	**20**	3004	3767	013	2453

ἐγερῶ   αὐτόν.   **20** εἶπαν οὖν οἱ Ἰουδαῖοι·
I will raise it.   Said then the Judeans;

5062   2532 1803 2094   3618   01   3485
τεσσεράκοντα καὶ ἓξ   ἔτεσιν οἰκοδομήθη ὁ ναὸς
forty   and six years   was built the temple

3778   2532 1473 1722 5140   2250   1453   846
οὗτος, καὶ σὺ ἐν τρισὶν ἡμέραις ἐγερεῖς αὐτόν;
this, and you in three days   will raise it?

21 1565   1161 3004   4012 02 3485   010
ἐκεῖνος δὲ ἔλεγεν   περὶ τοῦ ναοῦ τοῦ
    That one but was speaking about the temple of the

4983   846   **22** 3753 ουν ἠγέρθη 1453   1537
σώματος αὐτοῦ. **22** ὅτε οὖν ἠγέρθη   ἐκ
body   of him.   When then he was raised out of

3498   3403   013 3101   846   3754 3778
νεκρῶν, ἐμνήσθησαν οἱ μαθηταὶ αὐτοῦ ὅτι τοῦτο
dead, remembered the learners of him that this

3004   2532 4100   07 1124   2532 03
ἔλεγεν,   καὶ ἐπίστευσαν τῇ γραφῇ καὶ τῷ
he was saying, and they trusted the writing and the

3056 3739 3004 01 2424   **23** 5613 1161 1510 1722
λόγῳ ὃν εἶπεν ὁ Ἰησοῦς. **23** Ὡς δὲ ἦν ἐν
word which said the Jesus.   As but he was in

023   2414   1722 011 3957   1722 07   1859
τοῖς Ἱεροσολύμοις ἐν τῷ πάσχα ἐν τῇ ἑορτῇ,
the Jerusalem   in the passover in the festival,

4183   4100   1519 012 3686 846   2334
πολλοὶ ἐπίστευσαν εἰς τὸ ὄνομα αὐτοῦ θεωροῦντες
many   trusted   in the name of him watching

846 024 4592   3739 4160   **24** 846   1161
αὐτοῦ τὰ σημεῖα ἃ ἐποίει· **24** αὐτὸς δὲ
of him the signs which he was doing; himself but

2424   3756 4100   846   846   1223
Ἰησοῦς οὐκ ἐπίστευεν αὐτὸν αὐτοῖς διὰ
Jesus not was trusting himself to them on account

012 846 1097   3956   **25** 2532 3754   3756 5532
τὸ αὐτὸν γινώσκειν πάντας **25** καὶ ὅτι οὐ χρείαν
the him to know all   and because not need

2192 2443 5100 3140   4012   02 444
εἶχεν ἵνα τις μαρτυρήσῃ περὶ   τοῦ ἀνθρώπου·
he had that some might testify concerning the man;

846   1063 1097   5101 1510 1722 03 444
αὐτὸς γὰρ ἐγίνωσκεν τί ἦν ἐν τῷ ἀνθρώπῳ.
himself for was knowing what was in the man.

3:1 1510 1161 444   1537 014 5330   3530
3:1 Ἦν δὲ ἄνθρωπος ἐκ τῶν Φαρισαίων, Νικόδημος
     Was but man   from the Pharisees, Nicodemus

3686 846 758 014   2453   **2** 3778   2064
ὄνομα αὐτῷ, ἄρχων τῶν Ἰουδαίων· **2** οὗτος ἦλθεν
name to him, ruler of the Judeans;   this one came

4314 846 3571   2532 3004 846 4461
πρὸς αὐτὸν νυκτὸς καὶ εἶπεν αὐτῷ· ῥαββί,
toward him of night and said to him; Rabbi,

3609a 3754 575 2316 2064   1320
οἴδαμεν ὅτι ἀπὸ θεοῦ ἐλήλυθας διδάσκαλος·
we know that from God you have come teacher;

3762 1063 1410 3778 024 4592 4160 3739 1473
οὐδεὶς γὰρ δύναται ταῦτα τὰ σημεῖα ποιεῖν ἃ σὺ
no one for is able these the signs to do which you

4160 1437 3361 1510 01 2316 3326 846
ποιεῖς, ἐὰν μὴ ᾖ ὁ θεὸς μετ' αὐτοῦ.
do,   except might be the God with him.

3 611   2424   2532 3004 846   281 281 3004
3 ἀπεκρίθη Ἰησοῦς καὶ εἶπεν αὐτῷ· ἀμὴν ἀμὴν λέγω
   Answered Jesus and said to him, amen amen I say

1473 1437 3361 5100 1080   509   3756
σοι, ἐὰν μὴ τις γεννηθῇ ἄνωθεν, οὐ
to you, except some might be born from above, not

I will raise it up." [20]The
Jews then said, "This
temple has been under
construction for forty-six
years, and will you raise it
up in three days?" [21]But he
was speaking of the temple
of his body. [22]After he was
raised from the dead, his
disciples remembered that
he had said this; and they
believed the scripture and
the word that Jesus had
spoken.

[23]When he was in
Jerusalem during the Passover festival, many believed
in his name because they
saw the signs that he was
doing. [24]But Jesus on his
part would not entrust
himself to them, because
he knew all people [25]and
needed no one to testify
about anyone; for he himself
knew what was in everyone.

CHAPTER 3

Now there was a Pharisee
named Nicodemus, a leader
of the Jews. [2]He came to
Jesus[a] by night and said to
him, "Rabbi, we know that
you are a teacher who has
come from God; for no one
can do these signs that you
do apart from the presence
of God." [3]Jesus answered
him, "Very truly, I tell you,
no one can see the kingdom
of God without being born
from above."[b]

[a] Gk him
[b] Or born anew

⁴Nicodemus said to him, "How can anyone be born after having grown old? Can one enter a second time into the mother's womb and be born?" ⁵Jesus answered, "Very truly, I tell you, no one can enter the kingdom of God without being born of water and Spirit. ⁶What is born of the flesh is flesh, and what is born of the Spirit is spirit.ᵃ ⁷Do not be astonished that I said to you, 'Youᵇ must be born from above.'ᶜ ⁸The windᵃ blows where it chooses, and you hear the sound of it, but you do not know where it comes from or where it goes. So it is with everyone who is born of the Spirit." ⁹Nicodemus said to him, "How can these things be?" ¹⁰Jesus answered him, "Are you a teacher of Israel, and yet you do not understand these things?

11 "Very truly, I tell you, we speak of what we know and testify to what we have seen; yet youᵈ do not receive our testimony. ¹²If I have told you about earthly things and you do not believe, how can you

ᵃ The same Greek word means both wind and spirit
ᵇ The Greek word for you here is plural
ᶜ Or anew
ᵈ The Greek word for you here and in verse 12 is plural

1410	3708	08	932		02	2316	3004
δύναται	ἰδεῖν	τὴν	βασιλείαν	τοῦ	θεοῦ.	**4**	λέγει
he is able	to see	the	kingdom	of the	God.		Says

4314	846	01	3530		4459	1410	444
πρὸς	αὐτὸν	[ὁ]	Νικόδημος·	πῶς	δύναται	ἄνθρωπος	
toward	him	the	Nicodemus;	how	is able	man	

1080	1088	1510	3361	1410		1519	08
γεννηθῆναι	γέρων	ὤν;	μὴ	δύναται		εἰς	τὴν
to be born	old	man being?	Not	he is able		into	the

2836	06	3384	846	1208	1525		2532
κοιλίαν	τῆς	μητρὸς	αὐτοῦ	δεύτερον	εἰσελθεῖν		καὶ
stomach	of the	mother	of him	second	to go into		and

1080		611	2424	281	281	3004	
γεννηθῆναι;	**5**	ἀπεκρίθη	Ἰησοῦς·	ἀμὴν	ἀμὴν	λέγω	
to be born?		Answered	Jesus,	amen	amen	I say	

1473	1437	3361	5100	1080		1537	5204	2532
σοι,	ἐὰν	μὴ	τις	γεννηθῇ		ἐξ	ὕδατος	καὶ
to you,	except		some	might be born		from	water	and

4151		3756	1410		1525		1519	08
πνεύματος,		οὐ	δύναται		εἰσελθεῖν		εἰς	τὴν
spirit,		not	one is able		to go into		into	the

932		02	2316	09	1080			1537
βασιλείαν	τοῦ		θεοῦ.	**6**	τὸ	γεγεννημένον		ἐκ
kingdom	of the		God.		The	one having been born		from

06	4561	4561	1510	2532	09	1080	
τῆς	σαρκὸς	σάρξ	ἐστιν,	καὶ	τὸ	γεγεννημένον	
the	flesh	flesh is,		and	the	one having been born	

1537	010	4151	4151	1510		3361	2296
ἐκ	τοῦ	πνεύματος	πνεῦμά	ἐστιν.	**7**	μὴ	θαυμάσῃς
from	of the	spirit	spirit	he is.		Not	marvel

3754	3004	1473	1510		1473	1080	
ὅτι	εἶπόν	σοι·	δεῖ		ὑμᾶς	γεννηθῆναι	
that	I said	to you,	it is necessary		you	to be born	

509		09	4151	3699	2309	4154	2532	08
ἄνωθεν.	**8**	τὸ	πνεῦμα	ὅπου	θέλει	πνεῖ	καὶ	τὴν
from above.		The	spirit	where	it wants	blows	and	the

5456	846	191	235	3756	3609a		4159
φωνὴν	αὐτοῦ	ἀκούεις,	ἀλλ'	οὐκ	οἶδας		πόθεν
sound	of it	you hear,	but	not	you know		from where

2064	2532	4226	5217		3779	1510	3956	01
ἔρχεται	καὶ	ποῦ	ὑπάγει·		οὕτως	ἐστὶν	πᾶς	ὁ
it comes	and	where	it goes off;		thusly	is	all	the

1080			1537	010	4151		611
γεγεννημένος			ἐκ	τοῦ	πνεύματος.	**9**	ἀπεκρίθη
one having been born			from	the	spirit.		Answered

3530		2532	3004	846		4459	1410	3778
Νικόδημος	καὶ		εἶπεν	αὐτῷ·		πῶς	δύναται	ταῦτα
Nicodemus	and		said	to him;		how	are able	these

1096		611	2424	2532	3004	846		1473
γενέσθαι;	**10**	ἀπεκρίθη	Ἰησοῦς	καὶ	εἶπεν	αὐτῷ·		σὺ
to become?		Answered	Jesus	and	said	to him,		You

1510	01	1320		02	2474	2532	3778	3756
εἶ	ὁ	διδάσκαλος	τοῦ		Ἰσραὴλ	καὶ	ταῦτα	οὐ
are	the	teacher	of the		Israel	and	these	not

1097		281	281	3004	1473	3754	3739
γινώσκεις;	**11**	ἀμὴν	ἀμὴν	λέγω	σοι	ὅτι	ὃ
you know?		Amen	amen	I say	to you	that	what

3609a		2980		2532	3739	3708	
οἴδαμεν		λαλοῦμεν	καὶ	ὃ		ἑωράκαμεν	
we have known		we speak	and	what		we have seen	

3140		2532	08	3141		1473	3756	2983
μαρτυροῦμεν,		καὶ	τὴν	μαρτυρίαν	ἡμῶν	οὐ	λαμβάνετε.	
we testify,		and	the	testimony	of us	not	you receive.	

	1487	024	1919		3004	1473	2532	3756
12	εἰ	τὰ	ἐπίγεια		εἶπον	ὑμῖν	καὶ	οὐ
	If	the	on earth things		I said	to you	and	not

4100		4459	1437	3004		1473	024	
πιστεύετε,	πῶς	ἐὰν	εἴπω		ὑμῖν	τὰ		
you trust,	how	if	I might say		to you	the		

2032		4100		**13**	2532	3762
ἐπουράνια		πιστεύσετε;			καὶ	οὐδεὶς
on heaven things		will you trust?		And	no one

305		1519	04	3772	1487	3361	01	1537	02
ἀναβέβηκεν	εἰς	τὸν	οὐρανὸν	εἰ	μὴ	ὁ	ἐκ	τοῦ
has gone up	into	the	heaven	except	the	out of	the

3772	2597		01	5207	02	444
οὐρανοῦ	καταβάς,		ὁ	υἱὸς	τοῦ	ἀνθρώπου.
heaven	one having gone down,	the	son	of the man.

14 | 2532 | 2531 | 3475 | 5312 | 04 | 3789 | 1722 | 07 |
|---|---|---|---|---|---|---|---|
| Καὶ | καθὼς | Μωϋσῆς | ὕψωσεν | τὸν | ὄφιν | ἐν | τῇ |
| And | just as | Moses | elevated | the | snake | in | the |

2048	3779	5312		1163		04	5207
ἐρήμῳ,	οὕτως	ὑψωθῆναι		δεῖ		τὸν	υἱὸν
desert,	thusly	to be elevated	it is necessary	the	son

02	444	**15**	2443	3956	01	4100		1722	846
τοῦ	ἀνθρώπου,		ἵνα	πᾶς	ὁ	πιστεύων		ἐν	αὐτῷ
of the man,		that	all	the	one trusting	in	him

2192		2222	166	**16**	3779	1063	25		01
ἔχῃ		ζωὴν	αἰώνιον.		οὕτως	γὰρ	ἠγάπησεν		ὁ
might have	life eternal.	Thusly	for	loved	the

2316	04	2889	5620	04	5207	04	3439
θεὸς	τὸν	κόσμον,	ὥστε	τὸν	υἱὸν	τὸν	μονογενῆ
God	the	world,	so that	the	son	the	only born

1325	2443	3956	01	4100		1519	846	3361
ἔδωκεν,	ἵνα	πᾶς	ὁ	πιστεύων		εἰς	αὐτὸν	μὴ
he gave,	that	all	the	one trusting	into	him	not

622		235	2192		2222	166
ἀπόληται		ἀλλ᾽	ἔχῃ		ζωὴν	αἰώνιον.
might be destroyed	but	might have	life eternal.

17 | 3756 | 1063 | 649 | | 01 | 2316 | 04 | 5207 | 1519 | 04 |
|---|---|---|---|---|---|---|---|---|---|
| οὐ | γὰρ | ἀπέστειλεν | ὁ | θεὸς | τὸν | υἱὸν | εἰς | τὸν |
| Not | for | delegated | the | God | the | son | into | the |

2889	2443	2919		04	2889	235	2443
κόσμον	ἵνα	κρινῇ		τὸν	κόσμον,	ἀλλ᾽	ἵνα
world	that	he might judge	the	world,	but	that

4982		01	2889	1223	846	**18**	01
σωθῇ		ὁ	κόσμος	δι᾽	αὐτοῦ.		ὁ
might be delivered	the	world	through	him.	The one

4100		1519	846	3756	2919		01	1161	3361
πιστεύων	εἰς	αὐτὸν	οὐ	κρίνεται·		ὁ	δὲ	μὴ
trusting	into	him	not	is judged;	the	one but	not

4100	2235	2919	3754	3361	4100		1519
πιστεύων	ἤδη	κέκριται,	ὅτι	μὴ	πεπίστευκεν	εἰς
trusting	already	has been	because	not	he has	in
		judged,			trusted

012	3686	02	3439		5207	02	2316	**19**	3778
τὸ	ὄνομα	τοῦ	μονογενοῦς	υἱοῦ	τοῦ	θεοῦ.		αὕτη
the	name	of the	only born	son	of the	God.	This

1161	1510	05	2920	3754	09	5457	2064	1519
δέ	ἐστιν	ἡ	κρίσις	ὅτι	τὸ	φῶς	ἐλήλυθεν	εἰς
but	is	the	judgment	that	the	light	has come	into

04	2889	2532	25	013	444	3123	012	4655
τὸν	κόσμον	καὶ	ἠγάπησαν	οἱ	ἄνθρωποι	μᾶλλον	τὸ	σκότος
the	world	and	loved	the	men	more	the	dark

2228	012	5457	1510	1063	846	4190	021	2041
ἢ	τὸ	φῶς·	ἦν	γὰρ	αὐτῶν	πονηρὰ	τὰ	ἔργα.
or	the	light;	were	for	of them	evil	the	works.

20	3956	1063	01	5337	4238	3404	012	5457
πᾶς	γὰρ	ὁ	φαῦλα	πράσσων	μισεῖ	τὸ	φῶς
All	for	the	one foul	practicing	hates	the	light

2532	3756	2064	4314	012	5457	2443	3361
καὶ	οὐκ	ἔρχεται	πρὸς	τὸ	φῶς,	ἵνα	μὴ
and	not	comes	to	the	light,	that	not

1651		021	2041	846	**21**	01	1161	4160
ἐλεγχθῇ		τὰ	ἔργα	αὐτοῦ·		ὁ	δὲ	ποιῶν
might be rebuked	the	works	of him;	the one but	doing

08	225	2064	4314	012	5457	2443
τὴν	ἀλήθειαν	ἔρχεται	πρὸς	τὸ	φῶς,	ἵνα
the	truth	comes	to	the	light,	that

believe if I tell you about heavenly things? [13]No one has ascended into heaven except the one who descended from heaven, the Son of Man.[a] [14]And just as Moses lifted up the serpent in the wilderness, so must the Son of Man be lifted up, [15]that whoever believes in him may have eternal life.[b]

[16] "For God so loved the world that he gave his only Son, so that everyone who believes in him may not perish but may have eternal life.

[17] "Indeed, God did not send the Son into the world to condemn the world, but in order that the world might be saved through him. [18]Those who believe in him are not condemned; but those who do not believe are condemned already, because they have not believed in the name of the only Son of God. [19]And this is the judgment, that the light has come into the world, and people loved darkness rather than light because their deeds were evil. [20]For all who do evil hate the light and do not come to the light, so that their deeds may not be exposed. [21]But those who do what is true come to the light, so that

a Other ancient authorities add *who is in heaven*

b Some interpreters hold that the quotation concludes with verse 15

it may be clearly seen that their deeds have been done in God."[a]

22 After this Jesus and his disciples went into the Judean countryside, and he spent some time there with them and baptized. [23]John also was baptizing at Aenon near Salim because water was abundant there; and people kept coming and were being baptized [24]—John, of course, had not yet been thrown into prison.

25 Now a discussion about purification arose between John's disciples and a Jew.[b] [26]They came to John and said to him, "Rabbi, the one who was with you across the Jordan, to whom you testified, here he is baptizing, and all are going to him." [27]John answered, "No one can receive anything except what has been given from heaven. [28]You yourselves are my witnesses that I said, 'I am not the Messiah,[c] but I have been sent ahead of him.' [29]He who has the bride is the bridegroom. The friend of the bridegroom, who stands and hears him, rejoices greatly at the bridegroom's voice. For this reason my joy has been fulfilled.

---

[a] Some interpreters hold that the quotation concludes with verse 15

[b] Other ancient authorities read the Jews

[c] Or the Christ

5319		846	021	2041	3754	1722	2316
φανερωθῇ　　　　　　αὐτοῦ τὰ ἔργα ὅτι ἐν θεῷ
might be demonstrated of him the works that in　God

1510　2038　　　　　　3326　3778　2064　01
ἐστιν εἰργασμένα.　**22** Μετὰ ταῦτα ἦλθεν ὁ
it is+ +having been worked. After these went　the

2424　2532　013　3101　　846　1519 08　2449
Ἰησοῦς καὶ οἱ μαθηταὶ αὐτοῦ εἰς τὴν Ἰουδαίαν
Jesus　and the learners of him into the　Judea

1093　2532　1563　1304　　3326 846　2532
γῆν καὶ ἐκεῖ διέτριβεν μετ' αὐτῶν καὶ
land, and there he continued with them　and

907　　　　　1510 1161 2532 01 2491　907
ἐβάπτιζεν.　**23** Ἦν δὲ καὶ ὁ Ἰωάννης βαπτίζων
he was immersing. Was+ but also the John　+immersing

1722 137　1451　010 4530　3754　5204　4183　1510
ἐν Αἰνὼν ἐγγὺς τοῦ Σαλείμ, ὅτι ὕδατα πολλὰ ἦν
in Aenon near the Saleim, because waters much were

1563　2532 3854　2532 907　　3768　1063
ἐκεῖ, καὶ παρεγίνοντο καὶ ἐβαπτίζοντο· **24** οὔπω γὰρ
there, and they were and they were　not yet for
　　　　　　arriving　being immersed;

1510　906　　1519 08 5438　01 2491
ἦν βεβλημένος εἰς τὴν φυλακὴν ὁ Ἰωάννης.
was+ +having been thrown into the guard　the John.

25 1096　3767 2214　1537　014 3101
Ἐγένετο οὖν ζήτησις ἐκ τῶν μαθητῶν
Became then speculation out of the learners

2491　3326 2453　4012　2512　**26** 2532
Ἰωάννου μετὰ Ἰουδαίου περὶ καθαρισμοῦ.　καὶ
of John with Judean concerning cleaning.　And

2064　4314　04　2491　2532 3004　846
ἦλθον πρὸς τὸν Ἰωάννην καὶ εἶπαν αὐτῷ·
they came toward the John　and they said to him;

4461　3739 1510 3326 1473 4008　02　2446　3739
ῥαββί, ὃς ἦν μετὰ σοῦ πέραν τοῦ Ἰορδάνου, ᾧ
rabbi, who was with you across the Jordan, to whom

1473 3140　2396 3778　907　2532 3956
σὺ μεμαρτύρηκας, ἴδε οὗτος βαπτίζει καὶ πάντες
you have testified, look this one immerses and all

2064　4314　846　**27** 611　2491　2532 3004
ἔρχονται πρὸς αὐτόν.　ἀπεκρίθη Ἰωάννης καὶ εἶπεν·
come　toward him.　Answered John　and said;

3756 1410　444　2983　3761　1520 1437 3361
οὐ δύναται ἄνθρωπος λαμβάνειν οὐδὲ ἓν ἐὰν μὴ
not is able man　to receive but not one except

1510　1325　846　1537 02
ᾖ δεδομένον αὐτῷ ἐκ τοῦ
it might be+ +having been given to him from the

3772　**28** 846　1473 1473 3140　3754
οὐρανοῦ.　αὐτοὶ ὑμεῖς μοι μαρτυρεῖτε ὅτι
heaven.　Yourselves you to me testify　that

3004　3754 3756 1510 1473 3756 5547　235　3754
εἶπον [ὅτι] οὐκ εἰμὶ ἐγὼ ὁ Χριστός, ἀλλ' ὅτι
I said, (") not am I the Christ, but that

649　1510 1715　1565
ἀπεσταλμένος εἰμὶ ἔμπροσθεν ἐκείνου.
one having been delegated I am in front of that one.

29 01　2192　08 3565　3566　1510　01
ὁ ἔχων τὴν νύμφην νυμφίος ἐστίν· ὁ
The one having the bride bridegroom is;　the

1161 5384　02　3566　01 2476　2532
δὲ φίλος τοῦ νυμφίου ὁ ἑστηκὼς καὶ
but friend of the bridegroom the one having stood and

191　846 5479　5463　1223　08 5456　02
ἀκούων αὐτοῦ χαρᾷ χαίρει διὰ τὴν φωνὴν τοῦ
hearing him in joy rejoices because the sound of the

3566　3778 3767 05 5479 05 1699 4137
νυμφίου. αὕτη οὖν ἡ χαρὰ ἡ ἐμὴ πεπλήρωται.
bridegroom. This then the joy the my has been filled.

30 ¹⁵⁶⁵ ¹¹⁶³   ⁸³⁷   ¹⁴⁷³ ¹¹⁶¹
ἐκεῖνον δεῖ   αὐξάνειν, ἐμὲ δὲ
That one it is necessary to grow,   me   but
¹⁶⁴²   .01   ⁵⁰⁹   ²⁰⁶⁴   ¹⁸⁸³
ἐλαττοῦσθαι. 31 ʽΟ   ἄνωθεν ἐρχόμενος ἐπάνω
to be lessened. The one from above coming   upon
³⁹⁵⁶ ¹⁵¹⁰   ⁰¹   ¹⁵¹⁰ ¹⁵³⁷ ⁰⁶ ¹⁰⁹³ ¹⁵³⁷ ⁰⁶ ¹⁰⁹³
πάντων ἐστίν· ὁ ὢν ἐκ τῆς γῆς ἐκ τῆς γῆς
all   is; the one being from the earth from the earth
¹⁵¹⁰ ²⁵³² ¹⁵³⁷ ⁰⁶ ¹⁰⁹³ ²⁹⁸⁰   ⁰¹   ¹⁵³⁷ ⁰²
ἐστιν καὶ ἐκ τῆς γῆς λαλεῖ. ὁ   ἐκ τοῦ
is   and from the earth he speaks. The one from the
³⁷⁷²   ²⁰⁶⁴   ¹⁸⁸³ ³⁹⁵⁶ ¹⁵¹⁰   ³⁷³⁹
οὐρανοῦ ἐρχόμενος [ἐπάνω πάντων ἐστίν·] 32 ὁ
heaven coming   upon all   is;   what
³⁷⁰⁸   ²⁵³² ¹⁹¹   ³⁷⁷⁸ ³¹⁴⁰   ²⁵³² ⁰⁸
ἑώρακεν και ἤκουσεν τοῦτο μαρτυρεῖ, καὶ τὴν
he has seen and heard this he testifies, and the
³¹⁴¹   ⁸⁴⁶   ³⁷⁶² ²⁹⁸³   ⁰¹
μαρτυρίαν αὐτοῦ οὐδεὶς λαμβάνει. 33 ὁ
testimony of him no one receives.   The one
²⁹⁸³   ⁸⁴⁶   ⁰⁸ ³¹⁴¹   ⁴⁹⁷²
λαβὼν   αὐτοῦ τὴν μαρτυρίαν ἐσφράγισεν
having received of him the testimony sealed
³⁷⁵⁴   ⁰¹ ²³¹⁶ ²²⁷   ¹⁵¹⁰   ³⁷³⁹ ¹⁰⁶³ ⁶⁴⁹
ὅτι   ὁ θεὸς ἀληθής ἐστιν. 34 ὃν γὰρ ἀπέστειλεν
because the God true   is.   Whom for delegated
⁰¹   ²³¹⁶ ⁰²⁴ ⁴⁴⁸⁷   ⁰²   ²³¹⁶ ²⁹⁸⁰   ³⁷⁵⁶ ¹⁰⁶³
ὁ θεὸς τὰ ῥήματα τοῦ θεοῦ λαλεῖ,   οὐ γὰρ
the God the words of the God he speaks, not for
¹⁵³⁷   ³³⁵⁸   ¹³²⁵   ⁰¹² ⁴¹⁵¹   ⁰¹ ³⁹⁶²
ἐκ   μέτρου δίδωσιν τὸ πνεῦμα. 35 ὁ πατὴρ
out of measure he gives the spirit. The father
²⁵   ⁰⁴ ⁵²⁰⁷ ²⁵³² ³⁹⁵⁶ ¹³²⁵   ¹⁷²² ⁰⁷ ⁵⁴⁹⁵
ἀγαπᾷ τὸν υἱὸν καὶ πάντα δέδωκεν ἐν τῇ χειρὶ
loves the son and all he has given in the hand
⁸⁴⁶   ⁰¹ ⁴¹⁰⁰   ¹⁵¹⁹ ⁰⁴ ⁵²⁰⁷ ²¹⁹² ²²²²
αὐτοῦ. 36 ὁ πιστεύων εἰς τὸν υἱὸν ἔχει ζωὴν
of him. The one trusting into the son has life
¹⁶⁶   ⁰¹ ¹¹⁶¹ ⁵⁴⁴   ⁰³ ⁵²⁰⁷ ³⁷⁵⁶ ³⁷⁰⁸
αἰώνιον· ὁ δὲ ἀπειθῶν τῷ υἱῷ οὐκ ὄψεται
eternal; the but one disobeying the son not will see
²²²² ²³⁵ ⁰⁵ ³⁷⁰⁹ ⁰²   ²³¹⁶ ³³⁰⁶ ¹⁹⁰⁹ ⁸⁴⁶
ζωήν, ἀλλ᾽ ἡ ὀργὴ τοῦ θεοῦ μένει ἐπ᾽ αὐτόν.
life, but the anger of the God stays on him.
4:1 ⁵⁶¹³ ³⁷⁶⁷ ¹⁰⁹⁷ ⁰¹ ²⁴²⁴ ³⁷⁵⁴ ¹⁹¹   ⁰¹³
ʽΩς   οὖν ἔγνω ὁ Ἰησοῦς ὅτι ἤκουσαν οἱ
As then knew the Jesus that heard the
⁵³³⁰   ³⁷⁵⁴ ²⁴²⁴ ⁴¹⁸³   ³¹⁰¹   ⁴¹⁶⁰ ²⁵³²
Φαρισαῖοι ὅτι Ἰησοῦς πλείονας μαθητὰς ποιεῖ καὶ
Pharisees that Jesus more   learners makes and
⁹⁰⁷   ²²²⁸ ²⁴⁹¹   ²⁵⁴⁴   ²⁴²⁴
βαπτίζει ἢ Ἰωάννης 2 - καίτοιγε   Ἰησοῦς
immerses or John   even though indeed Jesus
⁸⁴⁶   ³⁷⁵⁶ ⁹⁰⁷   ²³⁵ ⁰¹³ ³¹⁰¹   ⁸⁴⁶
αὐτὸς οὐκ ἐβάπτιζεν ἀλλ᾽ οἱ μαθηταὶ αὐτοῦ -
himself not was immersing but the learners of him
3 ⁸⁶³   ⁰⁸ ²⁴⁴⁹   ²⁵³² ⁵⁶⁵   ³⁸²⁵
ἀφῆκεν τὴν Ἰουδαίαν καὶ ἀπῆλθεν πάλιν
he left off the Judea   and he went off again
¹⁵¹⁹ ⁰⁸ ¹⁰⁵⁶   ⁴   ¹¹⁶³ ⁸⁴⁶
εἰς τὴν Γαλιλαίαν. Ἔδει   δὲ αὐτὸν
into the Galilee.   It was necessary but him
¹³³⁰   ¹²²³   ⁰⁶ ⁴⁵⁴⁰   ⁵ ²⁰⁶⁴   ³⁷⁶⁷
διέρχεσθαι διὰ τῆς Σαμαρείας. ἔρχεται οὖν
to go through through the Samaria. He comes then
¹⁵¹⁹ ⁴¹⁷² ⁰⁶   ⁴⁵⁴⁰   ³⁰⁰⁴   ⁴⁹⁶⁵ ⁴¹³⁹
εἰς πόλιν τῆς Σαμαρείας λεγομένην Συχὰρ πλησίον
into city of the Samaria being said Sychar neighbor

³⁰He must increase, but I must decrease."[a]

31 The one who comes from above is above all; the one who is of the earth belongs to the earth and speaks about earthly things. The one who comes from heaven is above all. ³²He testifies to what he has seen and heard, yet no one accepts his testimony. ³³Whoever has accepted his testimony has certified[b] this, that God is true. ³⁴He whom God has sent speaks the words of God, for he gives the Spirit without measure. ³⁵The Father loves the Son and has placed all things in his hands. ³⁶Whoever believes in the Son has eternal life; whoever disobeys the Son will not see life, but must endure God's wrath.

CHAPTER 4

Now when Jesus[c] learned that the Pharisees had heard, "Jesus is making and baptizing more disciples than John" [2] —although it was not Jesus himself but his disciples who baptized— ³he left Judea and started back to Galilee. ⁴But he had to go through Samaria. ⁵So he came to a Samaritan city called Sychar, near

---

[a] Some interpreters hold that the quotation continues through verse 36

[b] Gk set a seal to

[c] Other ancient authorities read the Lord

the plot of ground that Jacob had given to his son Joseph. [6]Jacob's well was there, and Jesus, tired out by his journey, was sitting by the well. It was about noon.

[7]A Samaritan woman came to draw water, and Jesus said to her, "Give me a drink." [8](His disciples had gone to the city to buy food.) [9]The Samaritan woman said to him, "How is it that you, a Jew, ask a drink of me, a woman of Samaria?" (Jews do not share things in common with Samaritans.)[a] [10]Jesus answered her, "If you knew the gift of God, and who it is that is saying to you, 'Give me a drink,' you would have asked him, and he would have given you living water." [11]The woman said to him, "Sir, you have no bucket, and the well is deep. Where do you get that living water? [12]Are you greater than our ancestor Jacob, who gave us the well, and with his sons and his flocks drank from it?" [13]Jesus said to her, "Everyone who drinks of this water will be thirsty again, [14]but those who drink of the water

---

[a] Other ancient authorities lack this sentence

```
010  5564           3739   1325        2384    03       2501     03
τοῦ χωρίου      ὃ    ἔδωκεν  Ἰακὼβ [τῷ]  Ἰωσὴφ τῷ
the small field which gave    Jacob to the Joseph the
5207 846      6 1510 1161 1563  4077   02      2384    01
υἱῷ αὐτοῦ·    ἦν  δὲ  ἐκεῖ πηγὴ τοῦ   Ἰακώβ. ὁ
son of him;   was but there spring of the Jacob. The
3767 2424  2872           1537  06  3597
οὖν Ἰησοῦς κεκοπιακὼς    ἐκ    τῆς ὁδοιπορίας
then Jesus having labored out of the walking travel
2516         3779     1909 07 4077    5610 1510 5613
ἐκαθέζετο   οὕτως  ἐπὶ τῇ πηγῇ· ὥρα ἦν ὡς
he was sitting thusly on  the spring; hour was as
1623  7 2064     1135  1537   06 4540        501
ἕκτη.   ἔρχεται γυνὴ ἐκ  τῆς Σαμαρείας ἀντλῆσαι
sixth.  Comes   woman out of the Samaria   to draw out
5204   3004  846    01 2424    1325 1473 4095
ὕδωρ.  λέγει αὐτῇ ὁ Ἰησοῦς· δός μοι πεῖν·    8
water. Says to her the Jesus; give to me to drink;
013 1063 3101       846    565            1519 08  4172
οἱ γὰρ μαθηταὶ αὐτοῦ ἀπεληλύθεισαν εἰς τὴν πόλιν
the for learners of him had gone off  into the city
2443 5160     59              3004 3767 846     05
ἵνα τροφὰς ἀγοράσωσιν.   9 λέγει οὖν αὐτῷ ἡ
that foods they might buy.   Says then to him the
1135   05 4542        4459 1473 2453     1510  3844
γυνὴ ἡ Σαμαρῖτις· πῶς σὺ Ἰουδαῖος ὢν   παρ'
woman the Samaritan; how you Judean   being from
1473 4095      154     1135       4541       1510    3756
ἐμοῦ πεῖν   αἰτεῖς γυναικὸς Σαμαρίτιδος οὔσης; οὐ
me   to drink you ask of woman Samaritan  being? Not
1063 4798             2453      4541
γὰρ συγχρῶνται    Ἰουδαῖοι Σαμαρίταις.
for  make use of together Judeans Samaritans.
    611      2424  2532 3004   846   1487 3609a
10 ἀπεκρίθη Ἰησοῦς καὶ εἶπεν αὐτῇ· εἰ ᾔδεις
   Answered Jesus and said to her; if you had known
08  1431   02       2316 2532 5101 1510  01   3004
τὴν δωρεὰν τοῦ  Θεοῦ καὶ τίς ἐστιν ὁ  λέγων
the gift   of the God and who is  the one saying
1473  1325 1473  4095      1473 302 154  846    2532
σοι·  δός μοι πεῖν,   σὺ ἂν ᾔτησας αὐτὸν καὶ
to you; give to me to drink, you - asked  him  and
1325   302 1473   5204 2198  3004 846   05
ἔδωκεν ἄν σοι ὕδωρ ζῶν. 11 λέγει αὐτῷ [ἡ
he gave - to you water living. Says to him the
1135   2962      3777    502        2192   2532 09 5421
γυνή·] κύριε, οὔτε ἄντλημα ἔχεις καὶ τὸ φρέαρ
woman, Master, neither bucket you have and the well
1510 901    4159    3767 2192    012 5204  012
ἐστὶν βαθύ· πόθεν οὖν ἔχεις  τὸ ὕδωρ τὸ
is    deep; from where then you have the water the
2198  12 3361 1473   1510 02  3962     1473
ζῶν;    μὴ σὺ μείζων εἶ τοῦ πατρὸς ἡμῶν
living?  Not you greater are of the father of us
2384  3739 1325   1473  012 5421  2532 846       1537
Ἰακώβ, ὃς ἔδωκεν ἡμῖν τὸ φρέαρ καὶ αὐτὸς ἐξ
Jacob, who gave  to us the well and himself from
846   4095    2532 013 5207 846    2532 021 2353
αὐτοῦ ἔπιεν καὶ οἱ υἱοὶ αὐτοῦ καὶ τὰ θρέμματα
it   drank and the sons of him and the livestock
846    13 611      2424  2532 3004  846    3956 01
αὐτοῦ;   ἀπεκρίθη Ἰησοῦς καὶ εἶπεν αὐτῇ· πᾶς ὁ
of him? Answered Jesus and said to her; all the
4095       1537 010 5204 3778   1372
πίνων    ἐκ  τοῦ ὕδατος τούτου διψήσει
one drinking out of the water this will thirst
3825    14 3739 1161 302 4095    1537 010 5204
πάλιν·    ὃς δ'  ἂν πίῃ  ἐκ τοῦ ὕδατος
again;    who but -  might drink from the water
```

3739	1473	1325		846		3756	3361	1372
οὗ	ἐγὼ	δώσω		αὐτῷ,	οὐ	μὴ		διψήσει
which	I	will	give	to him,	not	not		he will thirst

1519 04 165   235 09 5204 3739 1325   846
εἰς τὸν αἰῶνα, ἀλλὰ τὸ ὕδωρ ὃ δώσω αὐτῷ
into the age, but the water which I will give to him

1096   1722 846 4077   5204   242   1519
γενήσεται ἐν αὐτῷ πηγὴ ὕδατος ἀλλομένου εἰς
will become in him spring of water leaping into

2222 166   3004 4314 846 05 1135 2962
ζωὴν αἰώνιον. 15 λέγει πρὸς αὐτὸν ἡ γυνή· κύριε,
life eternal. Says toward him the woman; Master,

1325 1473 3778 012 5204 2443 3361 1372
δός μοι τοῦτο τὸ ὕδωρ, ἵνα μὴ διψῶ
give to me this the water, that not I might thirst

3366 1330   1759 501   16 3004 846 5217
μηδὲ διέρχωμαι ἐνθάδε ἀντλεῖν. 16 λέγει αὐτῇ· ὕπαγε
but not I come through to this place to draw He says to her; go off

5455 04 435 1473 2532 2064 1759
φώνησον τὸν ἄνδρα σου καὶ ἐλθὲ ἐνθάδε.
sound the man of you and come to this place.

17 611   05 1135 2532 3004 846   3756 2192
ἀπεκρίθη ἡ γυνὴ καὶ εἶπεν αὐτῷ· οὐκ ἔχω
Answered the woman and said to him; not I have

435 3004 846 01 2424 2573 3004   3754
ἄνδρα. λέγει αὐτῇ ὁ Ἰησοῦς· καλῶς εἶπας ὅτι
man. Says to her the Jesus; well you said, (")

435 3756 2192 18 4002 1063 435 2192 2532
ἄνδρα οὐκ ἔχω· 18 πέντε γὰρ ἄνδρας ἔσχες καὶ
man not I have; five for men you had, and

3568 3739 2192   3756 1510 1473 435 3778 227
νῦν ὃν ἔχεις οὐκ ἔστιν σου ἀνήρ· τοῦτο ἀληθὲς
now whom you have not he is of you man; this true

3004   19 3004 846 05 1135 2962 2334
εἴρηκας. 19 λέγει αὐτῷ ἡ γυνή· κύριε, θεωρῶ
you have said. Says to him the woman; Master, I watch

3754 4396   1510 1473 20 013 3962 1473 1722 011
ὅτι προφήτης εἶ σύ. 20 οἱ πατέρες ἡμῶν ἐν τῷ
that spokesman are you. The fathers of us in the

3735 3778 4352   2532 1473 3004 3754 1722
ὄρει τούτῳ προσεκύνησαν· καὶ ὑμεῖς λέγετε ὅτι ἐν
hill this worshiped; and you say that in

2414   1510 01 5117 3699 4352
Ἰεροσολύμοις ἐστὶν ὁ τόπος ὅπου προσκυνεῖν
Jerusalem is the place where to worship

1163   21 3004 846 01 2424 4100 1473
δεῖ. 21 λέγει αὐτῇ ὁ Ἰησοῦς· πίστευέ μοι,
it is necessary. Says to her the Jesus; trust me,

1135 2532 2064 5610 3753 3777 1722 011 3735
γύναι, ὅτι ἔρχεται ὥρα ὅτε οὔτε ἐν τῷ ὄρει
woman, because comes hour when neither in the hill

3778 3777 1722 2414   4352   03
τούτῳ οὔτε ἐν Ἰεροσολύμοις προσκυνήσετε τῷ
this nor in Jerusalem you will worship the

3962 1473 4352 3739 3756 3609a 1473
πατρί. 22 ὑμεῖς προσκυνεῖτε ὃ οὐκ οἴδατε· ἡμεῖς
father. You worship what not you know; we

4352   3739 3609a 3754 05 4991
προσκυνοῦμεν ὃ οἴδαμεν, ὅτι ἡ σωτηρία
worship what we know, because the deliverance

1537 014 2453 1510 23 235 2064 5610 2532
ἐκ τῶν Ἰουδαίων ἐστίν. 23 ἀλλὰ ἔρχεται ὥρα καὶ
from the Judeans is. But comes hour and

3568 1510 3753 013 228 4353
νῦν ἐστιν, ὅτε οἱ ἀληθινοὶ προσκυνηταὶ
now it is, when the true worshipers

4352   03 3962 1722 4151 2532 225
προσκυνήσουσιν τῷ πατρὶ ἐν πνεύματι καὶ ἀληθείᾳ·
will worship the father in spirit and truth;

that I will give them will never be thirsty. The water that I will give will become in them a spring of water gushing up to eternal life." [15]The woman said to him, "Sir, give me this water, so that I may never be thirsty or have to keep coming here to draw water."

[16]Jesus said to her, "Go, call your husband, and come back." [17]The woman answered him, "I have no husband." Jesus said to her, "You are right in saying, 'I have no husband'; [18]for you have had five husbands, and the one you have now is not your husband. What you have said is true!" [19]The woman said to him, "Sir, I see that you are a prophet. [20]Our ancestors worshiped on this mountain, but you[a] say that the place where people must worship is in Jerusalem." [21]Jesus said to her, "Woman, believe me, the hour is coming when you will worship the Father neither on this mountain nor in Jerusalem. [22]You worship what you do not know; we worship what we know, for salvation is from the Jews. [23]But the hour is coming, and is now here, when the true worshipers will worship the Father in spirit and truth,

a The Greek word for you here and in verses 21 and 22 is plural

for the Father seeks such as these to worship him. [24]God is spirit, and those who worship him must worship in spirit and truth." [25]The woman said to him, "I know that Messiah is coming" (who is called Christ). "When he comes, he will proclaim all things to us." [26]Jesus said to her, "I am he,[a] the one who is speaking to you."

27 Just then his disciples came. They were astonished that he was speaking with a woman, but no one said, "What do you want?" or, "Why are you speaking with her?" [28]Then the woman left her water jar and went back to the city. She said to the people, [29]"Come and see a man who told me everything I have ever done! He cannot be the Messiah,[b] can he?" [30]They left the city and were on their way to him.

31 Meanwhile the disciples were urging him, "Rabbi, eat something." [32]But he said to them, "I have food to eat that you do not know about." [33]So the disciples said to one another, "Surely no one has brought him something to eat?" [34]Jesus said to them, "My food is to do the will of him who sent me and to complete his work. [35]Do you not

a Gk I am
b Or the Christ

2532	1063	01	3962	5108		2212	016
καὶ	γὰρ	ὁ	πατὴρ	τοιούτους		ζητεῖ	τοὺς
also	for	the	father	such ones		seeks	the ones

4352		846		4151		01	2316	2532	016
προσκυνοῦντας		αὐτόν.	**24**	πνεῦμα		ὁ	θεός,	καὶ	τοὺς
worshiping		him.		Spirit		the	God,	and	the ones

4352		846	1722	4151	2532	225
προσκυνοῦντας		αὐτὸν	ἐν	πνεύματι	καὶ	ἀληθείᾳ
worshiping		him	in	spirit	and	in truth

1163		4352		3004	846	05	1135
δεῖ		προσκυνεῖν.	**25**	λέγει	αὐτῷ	ἡ	γυνή·
it is necessary		to worship.		Says	to him	the	woman;

3609a	3754	3323	2064	01	3004	5547
οἶδα	ὅτι	Μεσσίας	ἔρχεται	ὁ	λεγόμενος	χριστός·
I know	that	Messiah	comes	the one	being said	Christ;

3752	2064	1565	312	1473	537
ὅταν	ἔλθῃ	ἐκεῖνος,	ἀναγγελεῖ	ἡμῖν	ἅπαντα.
when	might come	that one,	he will declare	to us	all.

	3004	846	01	2424	1473	1510	01	2980
26	λέγει	αὐτῇ	ὁ	Ἰησοῦς·	ἐγώ	εἰμι,	ὁ	λαλῶν
	Says	to her	the	Jesus;	I	am,	the	one speaking

1473		2532	1909	3778	2064	013	3101	846	2532
σοι.	**27**	Καὶ	ἐπὶ	τούτῳ	ἦλθαν	οἱ	μαθηταὶ	αὐτοῦ	καὶ
to you.		And	on	this	came	the	learners	of him	and

2296		3754	3326	1135	2980
ἐθαύμαζον		ὅτι	μετὰ	γυναικὸς	ἐλάλει·
they were marveling		that	with	woman	he was speaking;

3762	3305	3004	5101	2212	2228	5101	2980
οὐδεὶς	μέντοι	εἶπεν·	τί	ζητεῖς	ἢ	τί	λαλεῖς
no one	however	said;	what	you seek,	or	why	you speak

3326	846		863	3767	08	5201	846	05
μετ᾽	αὐτῆς;	**28**	ἀφῆκεν	οὖν	τὴν	ὑδρίαν	αὐτῆς	ἡ
with	her?		Left off	then	the	waterpot	of her	the

1135	2532	565	1519	08	4172	2532	3004
γυνὴ	καὶ	ἀπῆλθεν	εἰς	τὴν	πόλιν	καὶ	λέγει
woman	and	went off	into	the	city	and	she says

015	444		1205	3708	444	3739	3004
τοῖς	ἀνθρώποις·	**29**	δεῦτε	ἴδετε	ἄνθρωπον	ὃς	εἶπέν
to the	men;		come	see	man	who	said

1473	3956	3745	4160	3385	3778	1510	01
μοι	πάντα	ὅσα	ἐποίησα,	μήτι	οὗτός	ἐστιν	ὁ
to me	all	as much as	I did,	not	this one	is	the

5547		1831	1537	06	4172	2532
χριστός;	**30**	ἐξῆλθον	ἐκ	τῆς	πόλεως	καὶ
Christ?		They went out	from	the	city	and

2064	4314	846		1722	011	3342
ἤρχοντο	πρὸς	αὐτόν.	**31**	Ἐν	τῷ	μεταξὺ
they were going	toward	him.		In	the	between

2065	846	013	3101	3004	4461	2068
ἠρώτων	αὐτὸν	οἱ	μαθηταὶ	λέγοντες·	ῥαββί,	φάγε.
were asking	him	the	learners	saying;	Rabbi,	eat.

	01	1161	3004	846	1473	1035	2192	2068
32	ὁ	δὲ	εἶπεν	αὐτοῖς·	ἐγὼ	βρῶσιν	ἔχω	φαγεῖν
	The one	but	said	to them,	I	food	have	to eat

3739	1473	3756	3609a		3004	3767	013
ἣν	ὑμεῖς	οὐκ	οἴδατε.	**33**	ἔλεγον	οὖν	οἱ
which	you	not	know.		Were saying	then	the

3101	4314	240	3361	5100	5342	846
μαθηταὶ	πρὸς	ἀλλήλους·	μή	τις	ἤνεγκεν	αὐτῷ
learners	toward	one another;	not	some	brought	to him

2068		3004	846	01	2424	1699	1033	1510
φαγεῖν;	**34**	λέγει	αὐτοῖς	ὁ	Ἰησοῦς·	ἐμὸν	βρῶμά	ἐστιν
to eat?		Says	to them	the	Jesus;	my	food	it is

2443	4160	012	2307	02	3992	1473
ἵνα	ποιήσω	τὸ	θέλημα	τοῦ	πέμψαντός	με
that	I might do	the	want	of	the one having sent	me

2532	5048	846	012	2041		3756	1473
καὶ	τελειώσω	αὐτοῦ	τὸ	ἔργον.	**35**	οὐχ	ὑμεῖς
and	I might complete	of him	the	work.		Not	you

```
3004   3754 2089   5072          1510   2532 01   2326
```
λέγετε ὅτι ἔτι τετράμηνός ἐστιν καὶ ὁ θερισμὸς
say,   (") still four months it is and the harvest
```
2064      2400 3004   1473     1869          016   3788
```
ἔρχεται; ἰδοὺ λέγω ὑμῖν, ἐπάρατε τοὺς ὀφθαλμοὺς
comes? Look I say to you, lift up on the eyes
```
1473    2532 2300      020 5561        3754 3022
```
ὑμῶν καὶ θεάσασθε τὰς χώρας ὅτι λευκάι
of you and watch the countries that white
```
1510     4314    2326       2235       01   2325
```
εἰσιν πρὸς θερισμόν. ἤδη **36** ὁ θερίζων
they are toward harvest. Already the one harvesting
```
3408    2983     2532 4863          2590   1519 2222
```
μισθὸν λαμβάνει καὶ συνάγει   καρπὸν εἰς ζωὴν
wage receives and he brings together fruit into life
```
166      2443 01  4687        3674 5463           2532
```
αἰώνιον, ἵνα ὁ σπείρων ὁμοῦ χαίρῃ   καὶ
eternal, that the one sowing same might rejoice and
```
01   2325            1722 1063 3778  01  3056  1510
```
ὁ θερίζων.   **37** ἐν γὰρ τούτῳ ὁ λόγος ἐστὶν
the one harvesting. In for this the word is
```
228       3754 243    1510   01       4687    2532 243
```
ἀληθινὸς ὅτι ἄλλος ἐστὶν ὁ   σπείρων καὶ ἄλλος
true,   (") other is the one sowing and other
```
01   2325        1473 649        1473 2325
```
ὁ θερίζων.   **38** ἐγὼ ἀπέστειλα ὑμᾶς θερίζειν
the one harvesting. I delegated you to harvest
```
3739 3756 1473  2872         243   2872          2532
```
ὃ οὐχ ὑμεῖς κεκοπιάκατε· ἄλλοι κεκοπιάκασιν καὶ
what not you have labored; others have labored and
```
1473  1519  04  2873   846     1525         1537
```
ὑμεῖς εἰς τὸν κόπον αὐτῶν εἰσεληλύθατε. **39** Ἐκ
you into the labor of them went into. Out of
```
1161  06  4172    1565    4183    4100      1519 846
```
δὲ τῆς πόλεως ἐκείνης πολλοὶ ἐπίστευσαν εἰς αὐτὸν
but the city that many trusted in him
```
014      4541        1223   04  3056  06      1135
```
τῶν Σαμαριτῶν διὰ τὸν λόγον τῆς γυναικὸς
of the Samaritans through the word of the woman
```
3140         3754 3004    1473 3956  3739 4160
```
μαρτυρούσης ὅτι εἶπέν μοι πάντα ἃ ἐποίησα.
testifying, (") he said to me all which I did.
```
   5613 3767 2064  4314    846    013 4541
```
40 ὡς οὖν ἦλθον πρὸς αὐτὸν οἱ Σαμαρῖται,
As then came toward him the Samaritans,
```
2065        846    3306    3844       846        2532
```
ἠρώτων   αὐτὸν μεῖναι παρ᾿   αὐτοῖς· καὶ
they were asking him to stay alongside them; and
```
3306     1563  1417 2250       2532 4183   4183
```
ἔμεινεν ἐκεῖ δύο ἡμέρας. **41** καὶ πολλῷ πλείους
he stayed there two days.   And much more
```
4100      1223   04  3056 846          07        5037
```
ἐπίστευσαν διὰ τὸν λόγον αὐτοῦ, **42** τῇ τε
trusted through the word of him,   to the and
```
1135       3004          3754 3765       1223     08
```
γυναικὶ ἔλεγον   ὅτι οὐκέτι διὰ   τὴν
woman they were saying, (") no longer through the
```
4674 2981    4100      846      1063 191        2532
```
σὴν λαλιὰν πιστεύομεν, αὐτοὶ γὰρ ἀκηκόαμεν καὶ
your speech we trust, ourselves for have heard and
```
3609a 3754 3778   1510  230    01 4990      02
```
οἴδαμεν ὅτι οὗτός ἐστιν ἀληθῶς ὁ σωτὴρ τοῦ
we know that this one is truly the deliverer of the
```
2889      3326  1161 020 1417 2250       1831
```
κόσμου. **43** Μετὰ δὲ τὰς δύο ἡμέρας ἐξῆλθεν
world.   After but the two days he went out
```
1564       1519 08 1056           846     1063 2424
```
ἐκεῖθεν εἰς τὴν Γαλιλαίαν· **44** αὐτὸς γὰρ Ἰησοῦς
from there into the Galilee; himself for Jesus

say, 'Four months more,
then comes the harvest'?
But I tell you, look around
you, and see how the fields
are ripe for harvesting.
[36]The reaper is already
receiving[a] wages and is
gathering fruit for eternal
life, so that sower and
reaper may rejoice together.
[37]For here the saying holds
true, 'One sows and another
reaps.' [38]I sent you to reap
that for which you did not
labor. Others have labored,
and you have entered into
their labor."

39 Many Samaritans
from that city believed in
him because of the woman's
testimony, "He told me
everything I have ever done."
[40]So when the Samaritans
came to him, they asked
him to stay with them; and
he stayed there two days.
[41]And many more believed
because of his word. [42]They
said to the woman, "It is
no longer because of what
you said that we believe, for
we have heard for ourselves,
and we know that this is
truly the Savior of the
world."

43 When the two days
were over, he went from
that place to Galilee [44](for
Jesus himself

_a_ Or [35]. . . the fields are already ripe
for harvesting. [36]The reaper is
receiving

had testified that a prophet has no honor in the prophet's own country). ⁴⁵When he came to Galilee, the Galileans welcomed him, since they had seen all that he had done in Jerusalem at the festival; for they too had gone to the festival.

46 Then he came again to Cana in Galilee where he had changed the water into wine. Now there was a royal official whose son lay ill in Capernaum. ⁴⁷When he heard that Jesus had come from Judea to Galilee, he went and begged him to come down and heal his son, for he was at the point of death. ⁴⁸Then Jesus said to him, "Unless you^a see signs and wonders you will not believe." ⁴⁹The official said to him, "Sir, come down before my little boy dies." ⁵⁰Jesus said to him, "Go; your son will live." The man believed the word that Jesus spoke to him and started on his way. ⁵¹As he was going down, his slaves met him and told him that his child was alive. ⁵²So he asked them the hour when he began to recover, and they said to him, "Yesterday at one in the afternoon the fever left him."

a Both instances of the Greek word for *you* in this verse are plural

3140	3754 4396	1722 07	2398 3968
ἐμαρτύρησεν	ὅτι προφήτης	ἐν τῇ	ἰδίᾳ πατρίδι
testified	that spokesman	in the	own fatherland

5092	3756 2192		3753 3767	2064	1519 08
τιμὴν	οὐκ ἔχει.	**45**	ὅτε οὖν	ἦλθεν	εἰς τὴν
value	not has.		When then	he came	into the

1056   1209   846   013 1057   3956
Γαλιλαίαν, ἐδέξαντο αὐτὸν οἱ Γαλιλαῖοι πάντα
Galilee,   welcomed him the Galileans, all

3708   3745   4160   1722 2414   1722
ἑωρακότες ὅσα   ἐποίησεν ἐν ˊΙεροσολύμοις ἐν
having seen as much as he did in Jerusalem   in

07   1859   2532 846   1063 2064   1519 08
τῇ ἑορτῇ,   καὶ αὐτοὶ   γὰρ ἦλθον εἰς τὴν
the festival, and themselves for went into the

1859   **46** 2064   3767 3825   1519 08 2580 06
ἑορτήν.   ˋΗλθεν   οὖν πάλιν εἰς τὴν Κανὰ τῆς
festival.   He went   then again into the Cana of the

1056   3699 4160   012 5204   3631   2532 1510
Γαλιλαίας, ὅπου ἐποίησεν τὸ ὕδωρ οἶνον. Καὶ ἦν
Galilee,   where he made the water wine. And was

5100 937   3739   01 5207 770   1722 2746a
τις βασιλικὸς οὗ   ὁ   υἱὸς ἠσθένει ἐν Καφαρναούμ.
some kingly of whom the son was weak in Capernaum.

47 3778   191   3754 2424   2240   1537 06
οὗτος ἀκούσας   ὅτι ˊΙησοῦς ἥκει   ἐκ   τῆς
This one having heard that Jesus is come out of the

2449   1519 08 1056   565   4314   846
ˊΙουδαίας εἰς τὴν Γαλιλαίαν ἀπῆλθεν πρὸς αὐτὸν
Judea   into the Galilee went off toward him

2532 2065 2443 2597   2532 2390   846   04
καὶ ἠρώτα ἵνα καταβῇ καὶ ἰάσηται αὐτοῦ τὸν
and he was that he might and he might of him the
     asking   come down   cure

5207 3195   1063 599   **48** 3004 3767
υἱόν, ἤμελλεν γὰρ ἀποθνήσκειν.   εἶπεν οὖν
son, he was about to for to die.   Said then

01 2424   4314   846   1407 3361 4592   2532 5059
ὁ ˊΙησοῦς πρὸς αὐτόν· ἐὰν μὴ σημεῖα καὶ τέρατα
the Jesus toward him, except signs and marvels

3708   3756 3361 4100   **49** 3004 4314
ἴδητε,   οὐ μὴ πιστεύσητε.   λέγει πρὸς
you might see, not not you might trust. Says toward

846   01 937   2962   2597   4250
αὐτὸν ὁ βασιλικός· κύριε, κατάβηθι πρὶν
him the kingly one; Master, come down before

599   012 3813   1473   **50** 3004 846   01
ἀποθανεῖν τὸ παιδίον   μου.   λέγει αὐτῷ ὁ
to die   the small child of me. Says to him the

2424   4198   01 5207 1473   2198   4100
ˊΙησοῦς· πορεύου, ὁ υἱός σου   ζῇ.   ἐπίστευσεν
Jesus,   travel, the son of you lives. Trusted

01 444   03   3056 3739 3004 846   01 2424
ὁ ἄνθρωπος τῷ   λόγῳ ὃν εἶπεν αὐτῷ ὁ ˊΙησοῦς
the man   in the word which said to him the Jesus

2532 4198   **51** 2235   1161 846   2597
καὶ ἐπορεύετο.   ἤδη   δὲ αὐτοῦ καταβαίνοντος
and he traveled.   Already but of him going down

013 1401   846   5221   846   3004   3754 01
οἱ δοῦλοι αὐτοῦ ὑπήντησαν αὐτῷ λέγοντες ὅτι ὁ
the slaves of him met   him saying   that the

3816   846   2198 **52** 4441   3767 08 5610
παῖς   αὐτοῦ ζῇ.   ἐπύθετο   οὖν τὴν ὥραν
boy servant of him lives. He inquired then the hour

3844 846 1722 3739 2866   2192   3004   3767
παρ᾿ αὐτῶν ἐν ᾗ   κομψότερον ἔσχεν· εἶπαν   οὖν
from them in which more fine he had; they said then

846   3754 2188a   5610 1442   863   846 01
αὐτῷ   ὅτι ἐχθὲς   ὥραν ἑβδόμην ἀφῆκεν αὐτὸν ὁ
to him, (") yesterday hour seventh left off him   the

```
4446        1097 3767 01   3962    3754 1722 1565    07
πυρετός.  53  ἔγνω οὖν ὁ  πατὴρ  ὅτι [ἐν] ἐκείνῃ τῇ
fever.       Knew then the father that  in  that   the
5610 1722 3739   3004   846      01   2424     01  5207
ὥρα  ἐν  ᾗ    εἶπεν αὐτῷ  ὁ  Ἰησοῦς·  ὁ  υἱός
hour in  which said  to him the Jesus,  the son
1473    2198   2532 4100          846      2532 05  3614
σου   ζῇ,  καὶ ἐπίστευσεν αὐτὸς  καὶ  ἡ  οἰκία
of you lives and he trusted   himself and the house
846   3650   3778  1161 3825  1208      4592
αὐτοῦ ὅλη. 54 Τοῦτο [δὲ] πάλιν δεύτερον σημεῖον
of him whole.  This  but again  second   sign
4160      01  2424   2064       1537  06   2449
ἐποίησεν ὁ  Ἰησοῦς ἐλθὼν  ἐκ   τῆς Ἰουδαίας
did       the Jesus having come out of the Judea
1519 08 1056          3326  3778  1510      1859
εἰς τὴν Γαλιλαίαν. 5:1 Μετὰ ταῦτα ἦν      ἑορτὴ
into the Galilee.      After these there was festival
014     2453      2532 305    2424   1519 2414
τῶν  Ἰουδαίων καὶ ἀνέβη Ἰησοῦς εἰς Ἱεροσόλυμα.
of the Judeans and went up Jesus into Jerusalem.
   1510       1161 1722 023    2414      1909 07
2 Ἔστιν   δὲ  ἐν  τοῖς Ἱεροσολύμοις ἐπὶ τῇ
  There is but in  the  Jerusalem     on  the
4262       2861       05   1951
προβατικῇ κολυμβήθρα ἡ  ἐπιλεγομένη
sheep place pool      the one being called on
1447     964α      4002 4745   2192   3 1722
Ἑβραϊστὶ Βηθζαθὰ πέντε στοὰς ἔχουσα.  ἐν
in Hebrew Bethzatha five colonnades having.  In
3778    2621        4128    014
ταύταις κατέκειτο πλῆθος τῶν
these    were lying down quantity of the ones
770        5185    5560    3584   5 1510 1161 5100
ἀσθενούντων, τυφλῶν, χωλῶν, ξηρῶν.  ἦν  δέ   τις
being weak, blind,   lame,  dried out. Was but some
444       1563  5144     2532 3638 2094  2192  1722
ἄνθρωπος ἐκεῖ τριάκοντα [καὶ] ὀκτὼ ἔτη ἔχων  ἐν
man       there thirty    and  eight years having in
07  769     846    6 3778   3708      01  2424
τῇ ἀσθενείᾳ αὐτοῦ·  τοῦτον ἰδὼν     ὁ  Ἰησοῦς
the weakness of him;  this one having seen the Jesus
2621        2532 1097      3754 4183  2235  5550
κατακείμενον καὶ γνοὺς  ὅτι πολὺν ἤδη χρόνον
lying down    and having known that much already time
2192  3004   846    2309    5199    1096
ἔχει, λέγει αὐτῷ· θέλεις ὑγιὴς γενέσθαι;
he has, he says to him; want you healthy to become?
  611       846     01  770       2962   444
7 ἀπεκρίθη αὐτῷ ὁ ἀσθενῶν· κύριε, ἄνθρωπον
  Answered to him the one being weak, Master, man
3756 2192  2443 3752 5015        09  5204
οὐκ ἔχω  ἵνα ὅταν ταραχθῇ    τὸ ὕδωρ
not I have that when might be troubled the water
906      3004    1473 1519 08 2861     1722 3739
βάλῃ    με  εἰς τὴν κολυμβήθραν· ἐν  ᾧ
he might throw me into the pool;      in  which
1161 2064   1473 243    4253   1473 2597
δὲ ἔρχομαι ἐγώ, ἄλλος πρὸ ἐμοῦ καταβαίνει.
but come   I,   other before me  goes down.
  3004 846   01  2424   1453 142    04  2895
8 λέγει αὐτῷ ὁ Ἰησοῦς· ἔγειρε ἄρον τὸν κράβαττόν
  Says to him the Jesus; rise   lift up the mat
1473  2532 4043    9 2532 2112     1096
σου  καὶ περιπάτει.  καὶ εὐθέως  ἐγένετο
of you and walk around. And immediately became
5199  01  444      2532 142    04  2895
ὑγιὴς ὁ ἄνθρωπος καὶ ἦρεν   τὸν κράβαττον
healthy the man    and lifted up the mat
```

53The father realized that this was the hour when Jesus had said to him, "Your son will live." So he himself believed, along with his whole household. 54Now this was the second sign that Jesus did after coming from Judea to Galilee.

CHAPTER 5

After this there was a festival of the Jews, and Jesus went up to Jerusalem.

2 Now in Jerusalem by the Sheep Gate there is a pool, called in Hebrew[a] Beth-zatha,[b] which has five porticoes. 3In these lay many invalids—blind, lame, and paralyzed.[c] 5One man was there who had been ill for thirty-eight years. 6When Jesus saw him lying there and knew that he had been there a long time, he said to him, "Do you want to be made well?" 7The sick man answered him, "Sir, I have no one to put me into the pool when the water is stirred up; and while I am making my way, someone else steps down ahead of me." 8Jesus said to him, "Stand up, take your mat and walk." 9At once the man was made well, and he took up his mat

---

a That is, *Aramaic*
b Other ancient authorities read *Bethesda*, others *Bethsaida*
c Other ancient authorities add, wholly or in part, *waiting for the stirring of the water;* [*for an angel of the Lord went down at certain seasons into the pool, and stirred up the water; whoever stepped in first after the stirring of the water was made well from whatever disease that person had.*]

and began to walk.
Now that day was a
sabbath. ¹⁰So the Jews said
to the man who had been
cured, "It is the sabbath;
it is not lawful for you to
carry your mat." ¹¹But he
answered them, "The man
who made me well said to
me, 'Take up your mat and
walk.' " ¹²They asked him,
"Who is the man who said
to you, 'Take it up and
walk'?" ¹³Now the man
who had been healed did
not know who it was, for
Jesus had disappeared in ͣ
the crowd that was there.
¹⁴Later Jesus found him in
the temple and said to him,
"See, you have been made
well! Do not sin any more,
so that nothing worse
happens to you." ¹⁵The
man went away and told
the Jews that it was Jesus
who had made him well.
¹⁶Therefore the Jews started
persecuting Jesus, because
he was doing such things
on the sabbath. ¹⁷But Jesus
answered them, "My Father
is still working, and I also
am working." ¹⁸For this
reason the Jews were
seeking all the more to kill
him, because he was not
only breaking the sabbath,
but was also calling God
his own Father, thereby
making himself equal to
God.

ͣ Or *had left because of*

846	2532 4043		1510	1161 4521
αὐτοῦ	καὶ περιεπάτει.		Ἦν	δὲ σάββατον
of him	and he was walking around.		It was	but sabbath

1722 1565   07   2250   **10** 3004   3767 013   2453
ἐν ἐκείνῃ τῇ ἡμέρᾳ.   ἔλεγον   οὖν οἱ Ἰουδαῖοι
in that   the day.   Were saying then the Judeans

03   2323   4521   1510 2532 3756
τῷ   τεθεραπευμένῳ·   σάββατόν ἐστιν, καὶ οὐκ
to the one having been healed, sabbath it is, and not

1832   1473   142   04 2895   1473
ἔξεστίν   σοι   ἆραι   τὸν κράβαττόν σου.
it is possible to you to lift up the mat   of you.

11 01 1161 611   846   01 4160   1473 5199
ὁ δὲ ἀπεκρίθη αὐτοῖς· ὁ ποιήσας μέ ὑγιῆ
The but answered to them; the having me healthy
one   one made

1565   1473 3004   142   04 2895   1473 2532
ἐκεῖνός μοι εἶπεν· ἆρον τὸν κράβαττόν σου καὶ
that one to me said; lift up the mat   of you and

4043   **12** 2065   846   5101 1510 01 444
περιπάτει. ἠρώτησαν αὐτόν· τίς ἐστιν ὁ ἄνθρωπος
walk around. They asked him; who is the man

01 3004   1473   142 2532 4043   **13** 01
ὁ εἰπών   σοι·   ἆρον καὶ περιπάτει;   ὁ
the one saying to you; lift up and walk around? The

1161 2390   3756 3609a 5101 1510 01 1063 2424
δὲ ἰαθεὶς   οὐκ ᾔδει τίς ἐστιν, ὁ γὰρ Ἰησοῦς
but one having not had who he is, the for Jesus
been cured   known

1593   3793 1510 1722 03 5117 **14** 3326 3778
ἐξένευσεν ὄχλου ὄντος ἐν τῷ τόπῳ. μετὰ ταῦτα
withdrew crowd being in the place. After these

2147   846 01 2424   1722 011 2411 2532 3004
εὑρίσκει αὐτὸν ὁ Ἰησοῦς ἐν τῷ ἱερῷ καὶ εἶπεν
finds   him the Jesus in the temple and he said

846   2396 5199   1096   3371   264
αὐτῷ· ἴδε ὑγιὴς γέγονας,   μηκέτι ἁμάρτανε,
to him; look healthy you have become, no longer sin,

2443 3361 5501   1473   5100 1096   **15** 565
ἵνα μὴ χεῖρόν σοί τι γένηται.   ἀπῆλθεν
that not worse to you some might become. Went off

01 444   2532 312   015   2453   3754
ὁ ἄνθρωπος καὶ ἀνήγγειλεν τοῖς Ἰουδαίοις ὅτι
the man   and declared to the Judeans that

2424 1510 01 4160   846 5199 **16** 2532
Ἰησοῦς ἐστιν ὁ ποιήσας   αὐτὸν ὑγιῆ.   καὶ
Jesus is the one having made him healthy. And

1223   3778 1377 013 2453   04 2424   3754
διὰ   τοῦτο ἐδίωκον οἱ Ἰουδαῖοι τὸν Ἰησοῦν, ὅτι
through this pursued the Judeans the Jesus, because

3778   4160   1722 4521   **17** 01 1161
ταῦτα   ἐποίει   ἐν σαββάτῳ.   Ὁ δὲ
these things he was doing in sabbath. The but

2424   611   846   01 3962 1473 2193
[Ἰησοῦς] ἀπεκρίνατο αὐτοῖς· ὁ πατήρ μου ἕως
Jesus answered to them; the father of me until

737 2038   2504 2038   **18** 1223   3778 3767
ἄρτι ἐργάζεται κἀγὼ ἐργάζομαι· διὰ τοῦτο οὖν
now works and I work;   through this then

3123 2212   846 013 2453   615
μᾶλλον ἐζήτουν αὐτὸν οἱ Ἰουδαῖοι ἀποκτεῖναι,
more were seeking him the Judeans to kill,

3754   3756 3441 3089 012 4521   235 2532
ὅτι   οὐ μόνον ἔλυεν τὸ σάββατον, ἀλλὰ καὶ
because not alone he was the sabbath, but also
loosing

3962 2398   04 2316 2470 1438
πατέρα ἴδιον ἔλεγεν τὸν θεὸν ἴσον ἑαυτὸν
father own he was saying the God equal himself

```
4160      03        2316  19  611              3767 01   2424
ποιῶν    τῷ        θεῷ.       Ἀπεκρίνατο οὖν   ὁ   Ἰησοῦς
making to the God.         Answered    then  the Jesus
2532 3004            846        281  281  3004  1473
καὶ ἔλεγεν          αὐτοῖς· ἀμὴν ἀμὴν λέγω ὑμῖν,
and he was saying to them; amen amen I say to you,
3756 1410   01   5207 4160   575   1438    3762
οὐ  δύναται ὁ  υἱὸς ποιεῖν ἀφ᾽ ἑαυτοῦ οὐδὲν
not is able the son to do from himself nothing
1437 3361 5100 991       04  3962    4160       3739
ἐὰν μή   τι  βλέπῃ      τὸν πατέρα ποιοῦντα· ἃ
except  what he might see the father doing;  what
1063 302 1565    4160    3778  2532 01  5207 3668
γὰρ ἂν ἐκεῖνος ποιῇ,   ταῦτα καὶ ὁ  υἱὸς ὁμοίως
for  -  that one might do, these also the son likewise
4160  20  01  1063 3962   5368  04  5207 2532 3956
ποιεῖ.    ὁ  γὰρ πατὴρ φιλεῖ τὸν υἱὸν καὶ πάντα
does.     The for father loves the son and all
1166     846    3739 846    4160    2532 3173
δείκνυσιν αὐτῷ ἃ  αὐτὸς ποιεῖ, καὶ μείζονα
shows    to him what himself does,  and greater
3778      1166       846    2041  2443 1473
τούτων δείξει      αὐτῷ ἔργα, ἵνα ὑμεῖς
of these he will show to him works, that you
2296         21  5618       1063 01  3962    1453      016
θαυμάζητε.     ὥσπερ     γὰρ ὁ  πατὴρ ἐγείρει τοὺς
might marvel.  As indeed for the father raises  the
3498    2532 2227         3779   2532 01  5207 3739
νεκροὺς καὶ ζῳοποιεῖ,  οὕτως καὶ ὁ  υἱὸς οὓς
dead    and makes alive, thusly also the son whom
2309     2227             3761    1063 01  3962   2919
θέλει   ζῳοποιεῖ.  22  οὐδὲ   γὰρ ὁ  πατὴρ κρίνει
he wants makes alive.   But not for  the father judges
3762    235   08   2920     3956  1325       03
οὐδένα, ἀλλὰ τὴν κρίσιν πᾶσαν δέδωκεν     τῷ
nothing, but the judgment all  he has given to the
5207  23  2443 3956   5091       04  5207 2531
υἱῷ,      ἵνα πάντες τιμῶσι  τὸν υἱὸν καθὼς
son,      that all  might value the son just as
5091       04  3962   01   3361 5091      04
τιμῶσι    τὸν πατέρα. ὁ   μὴ  τιμῶν    τὸν
they might value the father. The one not valuing the
5207 3756 5091     04  3962    04  3992
υἱὸν οὐ  τιμᾷ    τὸν πατέρα τὸν πέμψαντα
son  not he values the father, the one having sent
846    24  281  281  3004 1473  3754 01      04
αὐτόν.    Ἀμὴν ἀμὴν λέγω ὑμῖν ὅτι ὁ       τὸν
him.      Amen amen I say to you that the one the
3056   1473  191      2532 4100 01          03
λόγον μου ἀκούων καὶ πιστεύων τῷ
word  of me hearing and trusting in the one
3992        1473 2192 2222 166       2532 1519 2920
πέμψαντί  με  ἔχει ζωὴν αἰώνιον καὶ εἰς κρίσιν
having sent me  has life eternal and into judgment
3756 2064    235  3327              1537    013
οὐκ ἔρχεται, ἀλλὰ μεταβέβηκεν    ἐκ    τοῦ
not he comes, but he has gone across out of the
2288     1519 08  2222    281  281  3004 1473
θανάτου εἰς τὴν ζωήν. 25  ἀμὴν ἀμὴν λέγω ὑμῖν
death   into the life.    Amen amen I say to you
3754 2064    5610 2532 3568 1510  3753 013 3498
ὅτι ἔρχεται ὥρα καὶ νῦν ἐστιν ὅτε οἱ νεκροὶ
that comes  hour and now it is when the dead
191        06  5456  02       5207 02    2316 2532 013
ἀκούσουσιν τῆς φωνῆς τοῦ  υἱοῦ τοῦ  θεοῦ καὶ οἱ
will hear the sound of the son of the God and the
191        2198      26  5618      1063 01  3962
ἀκούσαντες ζήσουσιν.   ὥσπερ  γὰρ ὁ  πατὴρ
ones having heard will live. As indeed for the father
```

19 Jesus said to them, "Very truly, I tell you, the Son can do nothing on his own, but only what he sees the Father doing; for whatever the Father[a] does, the Son does likewise. [20]The Father loves the Son and shows him all that he himself is doing; and he will show him greater works than these, so that you will be astonished. [21]Indeed, just as the Father raises the dead and gives them life, so also the Son gives life to whomever he wishes. [22]The Father judges no one but has given all judgment to the Son, [23]so that all may honor the Son just as they honor the Father. Anyone who does not honor the Son does not honor the Father who sent him. [24]Very truly, I tell you, anyone who hears my word and believes him who sent me has eternal life, and does not come under judgment, but has passed from death to life.

25 "Very truly, I tell you, the hour is coming, and is now here, when the dead will hear the voice of the Son of God, and those who hear will live. [26]For just as the Father

---

[a] Gk that one

has life in himself, so he has granted the Son also to have life in himself; ²⁷and he has given him authority to execute judgment, because he is the Son of Man. ²⁸Do not be astonished at this; for the hour is coming when all who are in their graves will hear his voice ²⁹and will come out—those who have done good, to the resurrection of life, and those who have done evil, to the resurrection of condemnation.

30 "I can do nothing on my own. As I hear, I judge; and my judgment is just, because I seek to do not my own will but the will of him who sent me.

31 "If I testify about myself, my testimony is not true. ³²There is another who testifies on my behalf, and I know that his testimony to me is true. ³³You sent messengers to John, and he testified to the truth. ³⁴Not that I accept such human testimony, but I say these things so that you may be saved. ³⁵He was a burning and shining lamp, and you were willing to rejoice for a while in his light. ³⁶But I have a testimony greater than John's. The

2192	2222	1722	1438	3779	2532 03	5207 1325
ἔχει	ζωὴν	ἐν	ἑαυτῷ,	οὕτως	καὶ τῷ	υἱῷ ἔδωκεν
has	life	in	himself,	thusly	also to the	son he gave

2222	2192	1722	1438	27	2532 1849	1325
ζωὴν	ἔχειν	ἐν	ἑαυτῷ.		καὶ ἐξουσίαν	ἔδωκεν
life	to have	in	himself.		And authority	he gave

846	2920	4160	3754	5207 444	1510
αὐτῷ	κρίσιν	ποιεῖν,	ὅτι	υἱὸς ἀνθρώπου	ἐστίν.
to him	judgment	to make,	because	son of man	he is.

28	3361 2296	3778	3754	2064	5610 1722
	μὴ θαυμάζετε	τοῦτο,	ὅτι	ἔρχεται	ὥρα ἐν
	Not marvel	this,	because	comes	hour in

3739 3956	013	1722 023	3419	191
ᾗ πάντες	οἱ	ἐν τοῖς	μνημείοις	ἀκούσουσιν
which all	the ones	in the	graves	will hear

06 5456 846	29	2532 1607	013	024
τῆς φωνῆς αὐτοῦ		καὶ ἐκπορεύσονται	οἱ	τὰ
the sound of him		and will travel out	the ones	the

18	4160	1519 386	2222	013
ἀγαθὰ	ποιήσαντες	εἰς ἀνάστασιν	ζωῆς,	οἱ
good	having done	into standing up	of life,	the ones

1161 024 5337	4238	1519 386
δὲ τὰ φαῦλα	πράξαντες	εἰς ἀνάστασιν
but the foul	having practiced	into standing up

2920	30	3756 1410	1473 4160	575 1683
κρίσεως.		Οὐ δύναμαι	ἐγὼ ποιεῖν	ἀπ' ἐμαυτοῦ
of judgment.		Not am able	I to do	from myself

3762	2531	191	2919	2532 05 2920	05
οὐδέν·	καθὼς	ἀκούω	κρίνω,	καὶ ἡ κρίσις	ἡ
nothing;	just as	I hear	I judge,	and the judgment	the

1699 1342	1510	3754	3756 2212	012 2307	012
ἐμὴ δικαία	ἐστίν,	ὅτι	οὐ ζητῶ	τὸ θέλημα	τὸ
mine right	it is,	because	not I seek	the want	the

1699 235	012 2307	02	3992	1473
ἐμὸν ἀλλὰ	τὸ θέλημα	τοῦ	πέμψαντός	με.
mine but	the want	of	the one having sent	me.

31	1437 1473	3140	4012	1683	05 3141
	Ἐὰν ἐγὼ	μαρτυρῶ	περὶ	ἐμαυτοῦ,	ἡ μαρτυρία
	If I	testify	about	myself,	the testimony

1473 3756	1510 227	32	243 1510	01
μου οὐκ	ἔστιν ἀληθής·		ἄλλος ἐστὶν	ὁ
of me not	is true;		other there is	the one

3140	4012 1473	2532	3609a 3754 227	1510
μαρτυρῶν	περὶ ἐμοῦ,	καὶ	οἶδα ὅτι ἀληθής	ἐστιν
testifying	about me,	and	I know that true	is

05 3141	3739 3140	4012 1473	33	1473
ἡ μαρτυρία	ἣν μαρτυρεῖ	περὶ ἐμοῦ.		ὑμεῖς
the testimony	which he testifies	about me.		You

649	4314 2491	2532 3140
ἀπεστάλκατε	πρὸς Ἰωάννην,	καὶ μεμαρτύρηκεν
have delegated	toward John,	and he has testified

07	225	34	1473 1161 3756 3844 444	08
τῇ	ἀληθείᾳ·		ἐγὼ δὲ οὐ παρὰ ἀνθρώπου	τὴν
to the truth;			I but not from man	the

3141	2983	235 3778 3004 2443 1473
μαρτυρίαν	λαμβάνω,	ἀλλὰ ταῦτα λέγω ἵνα ὑμεῖς
testimony	receive,	but these I say that you

4982	35	1565	1510 01 3088	01
σωθῆτε.		ἐκεῖνος	ἦν ὁ λύχνος	ὁ
might be delivered.		That one	was the lamp	the one

2545	2532 5316	1473 1161 2309
καιόμενος	καὶ φαίνων,	ὑμεῖς δὲ ἠθελήσατε
burning	and shining,	you but wanted

21	4314	5610 1722 011 5457 846	36	1473
ἀγαλλιαθῆναι	πρὸς	ὥραν ἐν τῷ φωτὶ αὐτοῦ.		Ἐγὼ
to be glad	toward	hour in the light of him.		I

1161 2192 08	3141	3173	02 2491	021
δὲ ἔχω	τὴν μαρτυρίαν	μείζω	τοῦ Ἰωάννου·	τὰ
but have	the testimony	greater	of the John;	the

1063	2041	3739	1325		1473	01	3962	2443
γὰρ	ἔργα	ἃ	δέδωκέν		μοι	ὁ	πατὴρ	ἵνα
for	works	which	has given		to me	the	father	that

5048		846	846	021	2041	3739	4160
τελειώσω		αὐτά,	αὐτὰ	τὰ	ἔργα	ἃ	ποιῶ
I might complete		them,	these	the	works	which	I do

3140		4012	1473	3754	01	3962	1473	649
μαρτυρεῖ		περὶ	ἐμοῦ	ὅτι	ὁ	πατήρ	με	ἀπέσταλκεν.
testify		about	me	that	the	father	me	has delegated.

37

2532	01	3992		1473	3962	1565	3140
καὶ	ὁ	πέμψας		με	πατὴρ	ἐκεῖνος	μεμαρτύρηκεν
And	the	having sent		me	father	that	has testified

4012	1473	3777	5456	846	4455	191
περὶ	ἐμοῦ.	οὔτε	φωνὴν	αὐτοῦ	πώποτε	ἀκηκόατε
about	me.	Neither	sound	of him	ever yet	you have heard

3777	1491		846	3708	**38**	2532	04	3056
οὔτε	εἶδος		αὐτοῦ	ἑωράκατε,		καὶ	τὸν	λόγον
nor	visible form		of him	you have seen,		and	the	word

846	3756	2192	1722	1473	3306	3754	3739
αὐτοῦ	οὐκ	ἔχετε	ἐν	ὑμῖν	μένοντα,	ὅτι	ὃν
of him	not	you have	in	you	staying,	because	whom

649	1565	3778		1473	3756	4100
ἀπέστειλεν	ἐκεῖνος,	τούτῳ		ὑμεῖς	οὐ	πιστεύετε.
delegated	that one,	in this one		you	not	trust.

39

2037a	020	1124		3754	1473	1380	1722
ἐραυνᾶτε	τὰς	γραφάς,		ὅτι	ὑμεῖς	δοκεῖτε	ἐν
You search	the	writings,		because	you	think	in

846	2222	166	2192		2532	1565	1510	017
αὐταῖς	ζωὴν	αἰώνιον	ἔχειν·		καὶ	ἐκεῖναί	εἰσιν	αἱ
them	life	eternal	to have;		and	those	are	the ones

3140		4012	1473	**40**	2532 3756	2309	2064
μαρτυροῦσαι		περὶ	ἐμοῦ·		καὶ οὐ	θέλετε	ἐλθεῖν
testifying		about	me;		And not	you want	to come

4314	1473	2443	2222	2192	**41**	1391	3844
πρός	με	ἵνα	ζωὴν	ἔχητε.		Δόξαν	παρὰ
toward	me	that	life	you might have.		Splendor	from

444		3756	2983	**42**	235	1097		1473 3754
ἀνθρώπων		οὐ	λαμβάνω,		ἀλλὰ	ἔγνωκα		ὑμᾶς ὅτι
men		not	I receive,		but	I have known		you that

08	26	02		2316	3756	2192	1722	1438
τὴν	ἀγάπην	τοῦ		θεοῦ	οὐκ	ἔχετε	ἐν	ἑαυτοῖς.
the	love	of the		God	not	you have in		yourselves.

43

1473	2064		1722	011	3686	02		3962	1473
ἐγὼ	ἐλήλυθα		ἐν	τῷ	ὀνόματι	τοῦ		πατρός	μου,
I	have come		in	the	name	of the		father	of me,

2532 3756	2983		1473	1437	243	2064		1722 011
καὶ οὐ	λαμβάνετέ		με·	ἐὰν	ἄλλος	ἔλθη		ἐν τῷ
and not	you receive		me;	if	other	might come		in the

3686	011	2398	1565	2983			4459
ὀνόματι	τῷ	ἰδίῳ,	ἐκεῖνον	λήμψεσθε.	**44**		πῶς
name	the	own,	that one	you will receive.			How

1410		1473	4100		1391	3844	240
δύνασθε		ὑμεῖς	πιστεῦσαι		δόξαν	παρὰ	ἀλλήλων
are able		you	to trust		splendor	from	one another

2983		2532	08	1391	08	3844 02	3441	2316
λαμβάνοντες		καὶ	τὴν	δόξαν	τὴν	παρὰ τοῦ	μόνου	θεοῦ
receiving		and	the	splendor	the	from the	alone	God

3756 2212		**45**	3361 1380		3754 1473	2723
οὐ ζητεῖτε;			Μὴ δοκεῖτε		ὅτι ἐγὼ	κατηγορήσω
not you seek?			Not you think		that I	will accuse

1473	4314	04	3962	1510	01	2723		1473
ὑμῶν	πρὸς	τὸν	πατέρα·	ἔστιν	ὁ	κατηγορῶν		ὑμῶν
you	toward	the	father;	is	the	one accusing		you

3475		1519 3739	1473	1679		1487 1063
Μωϋσῆς,		εἰς ὃν	ὑμεῖς	ἠλπίκατε.	**46**	εἰ γὰρ
Moses,		in whom	you	have hoped.		If for

4100		3475	4100		302
ἐπιστεύετε		Μωϋσεῖ,	ἐπιστεύετε		ἂν
you were trusting		in Moses,	you were trusting		-

---

works that the Father has given me to complete, the very works that I am doing, testify on my behalf that the Father has sent me. [37]And the Father who sent me has himself testified on my behalf. You have never heard his voice or seen his form, [38]and you do not have his word abiding in you, because you do not believe him whom he has sent.

[39]"You search the scriptures because you think that in them you have eternal life; and it is they that testify on my behalf. [40]Yet you refuse to come to me to have life. [41]I do not accept glory from human beings. [42]But I know that you do not have the love of God in[a] you. [43]I have come in my Father's name, and you do not accept me; if another comes in his own name, you will accept him. [44]How can you believe when you accept glory from one another and do not seek the glory that comes from the one who alone is God? [45]Do not think that I will accuse you before the Father; your accuser is Moses, on whom you have set your hope. [46]If you believed Moses, you would believe

[a] Or among

me, for he wrote about me. ⁴⁷But if you do not believe what he wrote, how will you believe what I say?"

CHAPTER 6

After this Jesus went to the other side of the Sea of Galilee, also called the Sea of Tiberias.[a] ²A large crowd kept following him, because they saw the signs that he was doing for the sick. ³Jesus went up the mountain and sat down there with his disciples. ⁴Now the Passover, the festival of the Jews, was near. ⁵When he looked up and saw a large crowd coming toward him, Jesus said to Philip, "Where are we to buy bread for these people to eat?" ⁶He said this to test him, for he himself knew what he was going to do. ⁷Philip answered him, "Six months' wages[b] would not buy enough bread for each of them to get a little." ⁸One of his disciples, Andrew, Simon Peter's brother, said to him, ⁹"There is a boy here who has five barley loaves and two fish. But what are they among so many people?" ¹⁰Jesus said, "Make the people sit down." Now there was a great deal of grass in the place; so they[c] sat down,

---

a Gk of Galilee of Tiberias
b Gk Two hundred denarii; the denarius was the usual day's wage for a laborer
c Gk the men

1473	4012		1063	1473	1565		1125	**47**	1487
ἐμοί·	περὶ		γὰρ	ἐμοῦ	ἐκεῖνος		ἔγραψεν.		εἰ
in me;	concerning	for		me	that one		wrote.		If

1161	023		1565		1121		3756	4100		4459
δὲ	τοῖς		ἐκείνου		γράμμασιν		οὐ	πιστεύετε,		πῶς
but	in the	of that one		letters		not	you trust,		how

023	1699	4487	4100		**6:1**	3326	3778
τοῖς	ἐμοῖς	ῥήμασιν	πιστεύσετε;			Μετὰ	ταῦτα
in the	mine	words	will you trust?			After	these

565	01	2424	4008	06	2281		06	1056
ἀπῆλθεν	ὁ	Ἰησοῦς	πέραν	τῆς	θαλάσσης		τῆς	Γαλιλαίας
went off	the	Jesus	across	the	sea		of the	Galilee

06	5085		**2**	190		1161	846	3793	4183
τῆς	Τιβεριάδος.			ἠκολούθει	δὲ	αὐτῷ	ὄχλος	πολύς,
of the	Tiberias.		Followed		but	him	crowd	much,

3754	2334		024	4592	3739	4160
ὅτι	ἐθεώρουν		τὰ	σημεῖα	ἃ	ἐποίει
because	they were watching		the	signs	that	he was doing

1909	014	770		**3**	424		1161	1519	012	3735
ἐπὶ	τῶν	ἀσθενούντων.			ἀνῆλθεν	δὲ	εἰς	τὸ	ὄρος
on	the	weak ones.		Went up		but	into	the	hill

2424	2532	1563	2521		3326	014	3101		846
Ἰησοῦς	καὶ	ἐκεῖ	ἐκάθητο	μετὰ	τῶν	μαθητῶν	αὐτοῦ
Jesus	and	there	he sat	with	the	learners	of him

4	1510	1161	1451	09	3957		05	1859		014
	ἦν	δὲ	ἐγγὺς	τὸ	πάσχα,		ἡ	ἑορτὴ		τῶν
	Was	but	near	the	Passover,		the	festival		of the

2453		**5**	1869		3767	016	3788		01
Ἰουδαίων.			Ἐπάρας		οὖν	τοὺς	ὀφθαλμοὺς		ὁ
Judeans.		Having lifted up		on then	the	eyes		the

2424	2532	2300		3754	4183	3793	2064
Ἰησοῦς	καὶ	θεασάμενος		ὅτι	πολὺς	ὄχλος	ἔρχεται
Jesus	and	having watched		that	much	crowd	comes

4314	846	3004	4314	5376		4159
πρὸς	αὐτὸν	λέγει	πρὸς	Φίλιππον·		πόθεν
toward	him	says	toward	Philip;		from where

59	740	2443	2068		3778		**6**	3778	1161
ἀγοράσωμεν	ἄρτους	ἵνα	φάγωσιν		οὗτοι;			τοῦτο	δὲ
might we buy	bread	that	might eat	these?		This		but

3004		3985		846	846		1063	3609a	5101
ἔλεγεν		πειράζων		αὐτόν·	αὐτὸς		γὰρ	ᾔδει	τί
he was saying		pressuring	him;	himself		for	knew	what

3195		4160		**7**	611	846		01	5376
ἔμελλεν		ποιεῖν.			ἀπεκρίθη	αὐτῷ		[ὁ]	Φίλιππος·
he was about to do.			Answered	to him		the	Philip,

1250		1220		740	3756	714		846
διακοσίων		δηναρίων		ἄρτοι	οὐκ	ἀρκοῦσιν		αὐτοῖς
two hundred		denari		bread	not	are enough		to them

2443	1538		1024	5100	2983		**8**	3004	846
ἵνα	ἕκαστος		βραχύ	[τι]	λάβῃ.			λέγει	αὐτῷ
that	each		little	some	might receive.		Says	to him

1520	1537		014	3101		846		406	01	80
εἷς	ἐκ		τῶν	μαθητῶν		αὐτοῦ,		Ἀνδρέας	ὁ	ἀδελφὸς
one	out of		the	learners		of him,		Andrew	the	brother

4613		4074		**9**	1510		3808		5602	3739	2192
Σίμωνος		Πέτρου·			ἔστιν		παιδάριον		ὧδε	ὃς	ἔχει
of Simon		Peter;		there is		small child		here	who	has

4002	740		2916		2532	1417	3795		235	3778
πέντε	ἄρτους		κριθίνους		καὶ	δύο	ὀψάρια·		ἀλλὰ	ταῦτα
five	bread		barley		and two		small fish;		but	these

5101	1510		1519	5118		**10**	3004	01	2424
τί	ἐστιν		εἰς	τοσούτους;			εἶπεν	ὁ	Ἰησοῦς·
what	are they		into	such ones?		Said		the	Jesus·

4160	016	444		377		1510		1161
ποιήσατε	τοὺς	ἀνθρώπους		ἀναπεσεῖν.		ἦν		δὲ
make	the	men		to recline.		There was		but

5528	4183	1722	03	5117		377		3767	013	435
χόρτος	πολὺς	ἐν	τῷ	τόπῳ.		ἀνέπεσαν		οὖν	οἱ	ἄνδρες
grass	much	in	the	place.		Reclined		then	the	men

04	706	5613	4000		2983	3767
τὸν	ἀριθμὸν ὡς	πεντακισχίλιοι.	**11**	ἔλαβεν	οὖν
the	number as	five thousand.		Received	then

016	740	01	2424	2532	2168		1239
τοὺς	ἄρτους	ὁ	Ἰησοῦς	καὶ	εὐχαριστήσας	διέδωκεν
the	breads	the	Jesus	and	having given	he gave
						good favor	thoroughly

015	345		3668	2532	1537	022
τοῖς	ἀνακειμένοις	ὁμοίως	καὶ	ἐκ	τῶν
to the	ones reclining	likewise	also	out of	the

3795	3745	2309		5613	1161
ὀψαρίων	ὅσον	ἤθελον.	**12**	ὡς	δὲ
small fish	as much as	they were wanting.		As	but

1705		3004	015	3101	846
ἐνεπλήσθησαν,		λέγει	τοῖς	μαθηταῖς	αὐτοῦ·
they were filled in,		he says	to the	learners	of him;

4863		024	4052		2801		2443	3361
συναγάγετε		τὰ	περισσεύσαντα	κλάσματα,		ἵνα	μή
bring together		the	exceeding	fragments,		that	not

5100	622		4863		3767	2532	1072
τι	ἀπόληται.	**13**	συνήγαγον	οὖν	καὶ	ἐγέμισαν
some	might be		They brought	then,	and	they filled
	destroyed.		together			

1427	2894		2801		1537	014	4002
δώδεκα	κοφίνους	κλασμάτων		ἐκ		τῶν	πέντε
twelve	wicker baskets	of fragments		out of		the	five

740	014	2916		3739	4052		015
ἄρτων	τῶν	κριθίνων	ἃ		ἐπερίσσευσαν	τοῖς
bread	of the	barley	which		they exceeded	to the ones

977		013	3767	444		3708		3739
βεβρωκόσιν.	**14**	Οἱ	οὖν	ἄνθρωποι	ἰδόντες		ὃ
having eaten.		The	then	men		having seen	what

4160		4592		3004		3754	3778	1510	230
ἐποίησεν	σημεῖον	ἔλεγον		ὅτι	οὗτός	ἐστιν	ἀληθῶς
he did	sign	were saying,		(")	this	is	truly

01	4396		01	2064		1519	04	2889
ὁ	προφήτης	ὁ	ἐρχόμενος	εἰς		τὸν	κόσμον.
the	spokesman	the	one coming	into		the	world.

	2424	3767	1097		3754	3195
15	Ἰησοῦς	οὖν	γνοὺς		ὅτι	μέλλουσιν
	Jesus	then	having known		that	they were about to

2064	2532	726		846		2443	4160
ἔρχεσθαι	καὶ	ἁρπάζειν	αὐτὸν		ἵνα	ποιήσωσιν
to come	and	to seize	him		that	they might make

935	402		3825	1519	012	3735	846
βασιλέα,	ἀνεχώρησεν	πάλιν	εἰς	τὸ	ὄρος	αὐτὸς
king,	departed	again	to	the	hill	himself

3441		5613	1161	3798		1096	2597	013
μόνος.	**16**	Ὡς	δὲ	ὀψία		ἐγένετο	κατέβησαν	οἱ
alone.		As	but	evening		became	went down	the

3101	846	1909	08	2281		2532	1684
μαθηταὶ	αὐτοῦ	ἐπὶ	τὴν	θάλασσαν	**17**	καὶ	ἐμβάντες
learners	of him	on	the	sea		and	having gone in

1519	4143	2064		4008	06	2281		1519
εἰς	πλοῖον	ἤρχοντο		πέραν	τῆς	θαλάσσης	εἰς
into	boat	they were going		across	the	sea	into

2746a		2532	4653	2235		1096		2532	3768
Καφαρναούμ.	καὶ	σκοτία	ἤδη		ἐγεγόνει		καὶ	οὔπω
Capernaum.	And	dark	already		had become		and	not yet

2064		4314	846	01	2424		05	5037	2281
ἐληλύθει	πρὸς	αὐτοὺς	ὁ	Ἰησοῦς,	**18**	ἥ	τε	θάλασσα
had come	toward	them	the	Jesus,		the	and	sea

417	3173	4154	1326
ἀνέμου	μεγάλου	πνέοντος	διεγείρετο.
wind	great	blowing	was thoroughly raised.

	1643		3767	5613	4712		1501	4002	2228
19	ἐληλακότες	οὖν	ὡς	σταδίους	εἴκοσι	πέντε	ἢ
	Having driven	then	as	stadia	twenty	five	or

about five thousand in all. [11]Then Jesus took the loaves, and when he had given thanks, he distributed them to those who were seated; so also the fish, as much as they wanted. [12]When they were satisfied, he told his disciples, "Gather up the fragments left over, so that nothing may be lost." [13]So they gathered them up, and from the fragments of the five barley loaves, left by those who had eaten, they filled twelve baskets. [14]When the people saw the sign that he had done, they began to say, "This is indeed the prophet who is to come into the world."

[15]When Jesus realized that they were about to come and take him by force to make him king, he withdrew again to the mountain by himself.

[16]When evening came, his disciples went down to the sea, [17]got into a boat, and started across the sea to Capernaum. It was now dark, and Jesus had not yet come to them. [18]The sea became rough because a strong wind was blowing. [19]When they had rowed about three or four miles,[a] they saw Jesus walking on

_a_ Gk about twenty-five or thirty stadia

the sea and coming near the boat, and they were terrified. 20But he said to them, "It is I;[a] do not be afraid." 21Then they wanted to take him into the boat, and immediately the boat reached the land toward which they were going.

22 The next day the crowd that had stayed on the other side of the sea saw that there had been only one boat there. They also saw that Jesus had not got into the boat with his disciples, but that his disciples had gone away alone. 23Then some boats from Tiberias came near the place where they had eaten the bread after the Lord had given thanks.[b] 24So when the crowd saw that neither Jesus nor his disciples were there, they themselves got into the boats and went to Capernaum looking for Jesus.

25 When they found him on the other side of the sea, they said to him, "Rabbi, when did you come here?" 26Jesus answered them, "Very truly, I tell you, you are looking for me, not because you saw signs, but because you ate your fill of the loaves. 27Do not work for the food that perishes, but for the food that endures for eternal life, which the Son

a Gk I am
b Other ancient authorities lack after the Lord had given thanks

---

5144	2334	04	2424	4043		1909
τριάκοντα	θεωροῦσιν	τὸν	Ἰησοῦν	περιπατοῦντα		ἐπὶ
thirty	they watch	the	Jesus	walking around		on

06	2281	2532	1451	010	4143	1096		2532
τῆς	θαλάσσης	καὶ	ἐγγὺς	τοῦ	πλοίου	γινόμενον,		καὶ
the	sea	and	near	the	boat	becoming,		and

5399		01		1161	3004	846		1473	1510
ἐφοβήθησαν.	**20** ὁ		δὲ	λέγει	αὐτοῖς·		ἐγώ	εἰμι·
they feared.	The one		but	says	to them;		I	am;

3361	5399		2309			3767	2983	846
μὴ	φοβεῖσθε.	**21** ἤθελον				οὖν	λαβεῖν	αὐτὸν
not	fear.	They were wanting				then	to take	him

1519	012	4143		2532	2112		1096	09	4143
εἰς	τὸ	πλοῖον,	καὶ		εὐθέως		ἐγένετο	τὸ	πλοῖον
into	the	boat,	and		immediately		became	the	boat

1909	06	1093	1519	3739	5217			07
ἐπὶ	τῆς	γῆς	εἰς	ἣν	ὑπῆγον.		**22**	Τῇ
on	the	land	into	which	they were going off.			In the

1887	01	3793	01	2476		4008	06
ἐπαύριον	ὁ	ὄχλος	ὁ	ἑστηκὼς		πέραν	τῆς
tomorrow	the	crowd	the one	having stood		across	the

2281		3708	3754	4142		243	3756	1510
θαλάσσης		εἶδον	ὅτι	πλοιάριον		ἄλλο	οὐκ	ἦν
sea		saw	that	small boat		other	not	there was

1563	1487	3361	1520	2532	3754	3756	4897		015
ἐκεῖ	εἰ	μὴ	ἓν	καὶ	ὅτι	οὐ	συνεισῆλθεν		τοῖς
there	except		one,	and	that	not	went into with		the

3101		846	01	2424	1519	012	4143	235	3441
μαθηταῖς	αὐτοῦ	ὁ	Ἰησοῦς	εἰς	τὸ	πλοῖον	ἀλλὰ	μόνοι
learners of	him	the	Jesus	into	the	boat	but	alone

013	3101		846	565		243	2064
οἱ	μαθηταὶ		αὐτοῦ	ἀπῆλθον·	**23**	ἄλλα	ἦλθεν
the	learners		of him	went off;		other	came

4142		1537	5085		1451	02	5117	3699
πλοιά[ρια]	ἐκ		Τιβεριάδος	ἐγγὺς	τοῦ	τόπου	ὅπου
small boats	out of		Tiberias	near	the	place	where

2068	04	740	2168		02	2962
ἔφαγον	τὸν	ἄρτον	εὐχαριστήραντος		τοῦ	κυρίου.
they ate	the	bread	having given good favor		the	Master.

3753	3767	3708	01	3793	3754	2424	3756	1510
24 ὅτε	οὖν	εἶδεν	ὁ	ὄχλος	ὅτι	Ἰησοῦς	οὐκ	ἔστιν
When	then	saw	the	crowd	that	Jesus	not	is

1563	3761	013	3101		846	1684		846
ἐκεῖ	οὐδὲ	οἱ	μαθηταὶ		αὐτοῦ,	ἐνέβησαν		αὐτοὶ
there	but not	the	learners		of him,	went in		themselves

1519	024	4142		2532	2064		1519	2746a
εἰς	τὰ	πλοιάρια		καὶ	ἦλθον		εἰς	Καφαρναοὺμ
to	the	small boats		and	they went		into	Capernaum

2212		04	2424		2532	2147		846
ζητοῦντες		τὸν	Ἰησοῦν.	**25**	καὶ	εὑρόντες		αὐτὸν
seeking		the	Jesus.		And	having found		him

4008	06	2281		3004	846		4461	4219	5602
πέραν	τῆς	θαλάσσης	εἶπον		αὐτῷ·		ῥαββί,	πότε	ὧδε
across	the	sea	they said		to him;		Rabbi,	when	here

1096		611	846	01	2424	2532
γέγονας;	**26**	Ἀπεκρίθη	αὐτοῖς	ὁ	Ἰησοῦς	καὶ
you have become?		Answered	to them	the	Jesus	and
become?						

3004	281	281	3004	1473	2212		1473	3756
εἶπεν·	ἀμὴν	ἀμὴν	λέγω	ὑμῖν,	ζητεῖτέ		με	οὐχ
he said;	amen	amen	I say	to you,	you seek		me	not

3754	3708	4592	235	3754	2068	1537
ὅτι	εἴδετε	σημεῖα,	ἀλλ᾽	ὅτι	ἐφάγετε	ἐκ
because	you saw	signs,	but	because	you ate	out of

014	740	2532	5526		2038		3361	08
τῶν	ἄρτων	καὶ	ἐχορτάσθητε.	**27**	ἐργάζεσθε		μὴ	τὴν
the	bread	and	you were satisfied.		Work		not	the

1035	08	622		235	08	1035	08
βρῶσιν	τὴν	ἀπολλυμένην		ἀλλὰ	τὴν	βρῶσιν	τὴν
food	the one	being destroyed		but	the	food	the one

```
3306        1519 2222 166        3739  01  5207 02
μένουσαν εἰς ζωὴν αἰώνιον, ἣν  ὁ  υἱὸς τοῦ
staying   into life eternal,  which the son  of the
444         1473   1325        3778    1063 01   3962
ἀνθρώπου ὑμῖν  δώσει·   τοῦτον γὰρ ὁ  πατὴρ
man       to you will give; this   for  the father
4972        01  2316    3004    3767 4314    846       5101
ἐσφράγισεν ὁ  θεός. 28 εἶπον οὖν πρὸς αὐτόν· τί
sealed     the God.   They said then toward him;   what
4160         2443 2038            024 2041  02        2316
ποιῶμεν   ἵνα ἐργαζώμεθα  τὰ ἔργα   τοῦ θεοῦ;
might we do that we might work the works of the God?
    611       01  2424  2532 3004  846         3778   1510
29 ἀπεκρίθη [ὁ] Ἰησοῦς καὶ εἶπεν αὐτοῖς· τοῦτό ἐστιν
   Answered the  Jesus and said to them; this   is
09  2041   02  2316   2443 4100            1519 3739
τὸ ἔργον τοῦ θεοῦ, ἵνα πιστεύητε  εἰς ὃν
the work of the God, that you might trust into whom
649         1565        3004   3767 846       5101 3767
ἀπέστειλεν ἐκεῖνος. 30 Εἶπον οὖν αὐτῷ· τί  οὖν
delegated that one.     They said then to him; what then
4160   1473 4592       2443 3708      2532 4100
ποιεῖς σὺ σημεῖον, ἵνα ἴδωμεν καὶ πιστεύσωμέν
do    you sign,    that we might and we might
                                see         trust
1473 5101 2038           013 3962    1473  012 3131
σοι; τί ἐργάζῃ; 31 οἱ πατέρες ἡμῶν τὸ μάννα
you? What work you?   The fathers of us the manna
2068    1722 07  2048      2531     1510   1125
ἔφαγον ἐν τῇ ἐρήμῳ, καθώς ἐστιν γεγραμμένον·
ate    in  the desert, just as it is+ +having been
                                      written;
740    1537  02  3772    1325   846      2068
ἄρτον ἐκ  τοῦ οὐρανοῦ ἔδωκεν αὐτοῖς φαγεῖν.
bread out of the heaven  he gave to them to eat.
   3004 3767 846    01  2424  281  281  3004
32 εἶπεν οὖν αὐτοῖς ὁ Ἰησοῦς· ἀμὴν ἀμὴν λέγω
   Said then to them the Jesus; amen amen I say
1473    3756 3475  1325         1473 04  740  1537
ὑμῖν,  οὐ Μωϋσῆς δέδωκεν ὑμῖν τὸν ἄρτον ἐκ
to you, not Moses has given to you the bread out of
02  3772    235  01 3962   1473 1325    1473   04
τοῦ οὐρανοῦ, ἀλλ᾽ ὁ πατήρ μου δίδωσιν ὑμῖν τὸν
the heaven, but the father of me gives   to you the
740    1537 02  3772    04 228          01 1063 740
ἄρτον ἐκ  τοῦ οὐρανοῦ τὸν ἀληθινόν· 33 ὁ γὰρ ἄρτος
bread from the heaven  the true;       the for bread
02      2316 1510 01 2597          1537  02
τοῦ θεοῦ ἐστιν ὁ καταβαίνων ἐκ τοῦ
of the God is   the one coming down out of the
3772    2532 2222 1325 03     2889   34 3004
οὐρανοῦ καὶ ζωὴν διδοὺς τῷ κόσμῳ. εἶπον
heaven and life giving to the world.   They said
3767 4314  846    2962   3842     1325 1473 04
οὖν πρὸς αὐτόν· κύριε, πάντοτε δὸς ἡμῖν τὸν
then toward him; Master, always give to us the
740   3778       35 3004 846   01 2424    1473 1510
ἄρτον τοῦτον.    εἶπεν αὐτοῖς ὁ Ἰησοῦς· ἐγὼ εἰμι
bread this.       Said to them the Jesus; I    am
01 740    06  2222  01 2064      4314  1473 3756
ὁ ἄρτος τῆς ζωῆς· ὁ ἐρχόμενος πρὸς ἐμὲ οὐ
the bread of the life; the one coming toward me  not
3361 3983          2532 01 4100         1519 1473 3756
μὴ πεινάσῃ,  καὶ ὁ πιστεύων εἰς ἐμὲ οὐ
not might hunger, and the one trusting in me  not
3361 1372        4455        235 3004  1473
μὴ διψήσει πώποτε. 36 Ἀλλ᾽ εἶπον ὑμῖν
not he might thirst ever yet.   But  I said to you
```

of Man will give you. For it is on him that God the Father has set his seal." [28]Then they said to him, "What must we do to perform the works of God?" [29]Jesus answered them, "This is the work of God, that you believe in him whom he has sent." [30]So they said to him, "What sign are you going to give us then, so that we may see it and believe you? What work are you performing? [31]Our ancestors ate the manna in the wilderness; as it is written, 'He gave them bread from heaven to eat.' [32]Then Jesus said to them, "Very truly, I tell you, it was not Moses who gave you the bread from heaven, but it is my Father who gives you the true bread from heaven. [33]For the bread of God is that which[a] comes down from heaven and gives life to the world." [34]They said to him, "Sir, give us this bread always."

[35]Jesus said to them, "I am the bread of life. Whoever comes to me will never be hungry, and whoever believes in me will never be thirsty. [36]But I said to you

[a] Or he who

that you have seen me and yet do not believe. ³⁷Everything that the Father gives me will come to me, and anyone who comes to me I will never drive away; ³⁸for I have come down from heaven, not to do my own will, but the will of him who sent me. ³⁹And this is the will of him who sent me, that I should lose nothing of all that he has given me, but raise it up on the last day. ⁴⁰This is indeed the will of my Father, that all who see the Son and believe in him may have eternal life; and I will raise them up on the last day."

41 Then the Jews began to complain about him because he said, "I am the bread that came down from heaven." ⁴²They were saying, "Is not this Jesus, the son of Joseph, whose father and mother we know? How can he now say, 'I have come down from heaven'?" ⁴³Jesus answered them, "Do not complain among yourselves. ⁴⁴No one can come to me unless drawn by the Father who sent me; and I will raise that person up on the last day. ⁴⁵It is written

3754	2532	3708		1473	2532	3756	4100
ὅτι	καὶ	ἑωράκατέ	[με]	κἀὶ	οὐ		πιστεύετε.
that	also	you have seen	me	and	not		you trust.

37
3956	3739	1325		1473	01	3962	4314	1473
πᾶν	ὃ	δίδωσίν	μοι	ὁ		πατὴρ	πρὸς	ἐμὲ
All	that	gives	to me	the		father	toward	me

2240		2532	04	2064	4314	1473	3756	3361
ἥξει,		καὶ	τὸν	ἐρχόμενον	πρὸς	ἐμὲ	οὐ	μὴ
will come,		and	the	one coming	to	me	not	not

1544		1854		3754	2597		575
ἐκβάλω		ἔξω,	**38** ὅτι		καταβέβηκα		ἀπὸ
I might throw		outside,	because		I have come down		from

02	3772		3756	2443	4160	012	2307	012	1699
τοῦ	οὐρανοῦ		οὐχ	ἵνα	ποιῶ		τὸ	θέλημα τὸ	ἐμὸν
the	heaven		not	that	I might do		the	want the	mine

235	012	2307	02	3992	1473	**39**	3778
ἀλλὰ	τὸ	θέλημα	τοῦ	πέμψαντός	με.		τοῦτο
but	the	want	of the	one having sent	me.		This

1161	1510	09	2307	02	3992	1473	2443
δέ	ἐστιν	τὸ	θέλημα	τοῦ	πέμψαντός	με,	ἵνα
but	is	the	want	of the	one having sent	me,	that

3956	3739	1325		1473	3361	622	1537
πᾶν	ὃ	δέδωκέν	μοι	μὴ	ἀπολέσω		ἐξ
all	whom	he has given	to me	not	I might destroy		from

846	235	450		846	1722	07	2078
αὐτοῦ,	ἀλλὰ	ἀναστήσω		αὐτὸ	[ἐν]	τῇ	ἐσχάτῃ
it,	but	I might make stand up		it	in	the	last

2250	**40**	3778	1063	1510	09	2307	02	3962
ἡμέρᾳ.		τοῦτο	γάρ	ἐστιν	τὸ	θέλημα	τοῦ	πατρός
day.		This	for	is	the	want	of the	father

1473	2443	3956	01	2334	04	5207	2532
μου,	ἵνα	πᾶς	ὁ	θεωρῶν	τὸν	υἱὸν	καὶ
of me,	that	all	the	one watching	the	son	and

4100	1519	846	2192	2222	166	2532
πιστεύων	εἰς	αὐτὸν	ἔχῃ	ζωὴν	αἰώνιον,	καὶ
trusting	into	him	might have	life	eternal,	and

450	846	1473	1722	07	2078	2250
ἀναστήσω	αὐτὸν	ἐγὼ	[ἐν]	τῇ	ἐσχάτῃ	ἡμέρᾳ.
will make stand up	him	I	in	the	last	day.

41
1111		3767	013	2453	4012	846	3754
Ἐγόγγυζον		οὖν	οἱ	Ἰουδαῖοι	περὶ	αὐτοῦ	ὅτι
Were grumbling		then	the	Judeans	about	him	because

3004	1473	1510	01	740	01	2597	1537
εἶπεν·	ἐγώ	εἰμι	ὁ	ἄρτος	ὁ	καταβὰς	ἐκ
he said·	I	am	the	bread	the	one coming down	from

02	3772	**42**	2532	3004	3756	3778	1510
τοῦ	οὐρανοῦ,		καὶ	ἔλεγον·	οὐχ	οὗτός	ἐστιν
the	heaven,		and	they were saying;	not	this	is

2424	01	5207	2501	3739	1473	3609a	01
Ἰησοῦς	ὁ	υἱὸς	Ἰωσήφ,	οὗ	ἡμεῖς	οἴδαμεν	τὸν
Jesus	the	son	Joseph,	of whom	we	know	the

3962	2532	08	3384	4459	3568	3004	3754	1537
πατέρα	καὶ	τὴν	μητέρα;	πῶς	νῦν	λέγει	ὅτι	ἐκ
father	and	the	mother?	How	now	he says,	(")	out of

02	3772	2597	**43**	611	2424	2532
τοῦ	οὐρανοῦ	καταβέβηκα;		ἀπεκρίθη	Ἰησοῦς	καὶ
the	heaven	I have come down?		Answered	Jesus	and

3004	846	3361	1111	3326	240
εἶπεν	αὐτοῖς·	μὴ	γογγύζετε	μετ'	ἀλλήλων.
said	to them·	not	grumble	with	one another.

44
3762	1410	2064	4314	1473	1437	3361	01
οὐδεὶς	δύναται	ἐλθεῖν	πρός	με	ἐὰν	μὴ	ὁ
No one	is able	to come	toward	me	except		the

3962	01	3992	1473	1670	846	2504
πατὴρ	ὁ	πέμψας	με	ἑλκύσῃ	αὐτόν,	κἀγὼ
father	the	one having sent	me	might haul	him,	and I

450	846	1722	07	2078	2250	**45**	1510
ἀναστήσω	αὐτὸν	ἐν	τῇ	ἐσχάτῃ	ἡμέρᾳ.		ἔστιν
will make stand up	him	in	the	last	day.		It is+

1125		1722 015	4396	2532 1510
γεγραμμένον		ἐν τοῖς	προφήταις·	καὶ ἔσονται
+having been written		in the	spokesmen;	and will be

3956 1318   2316   3956 01 191   3844
πάντες διδακτοὶ θεοῦ·   πᾶς ὁ ἀκούσας   παρὰ
all taught of God; all the one having heard from

02   3962   2532 3129   2064   4314 1473
τοῦ πατρὸς καὶ μαθὼν   ἔρχεται πρὸς ἐμέ.
the father and having learned comes toward me.

46 3756 3754 04   3962   3708   5100 1487 3361 01
οὐχ ὅτι τὸν πατέρα ἑώρακέν τις εἰ μὴ ὁ
Not that the father has seen some except the

1510   3844 02 2316 3778   3708   04 3962
ὦν παρὰ τοῦ θεοῦ, οὗτος ἑώρακεν τὸν πατέρα.
one being from the God, this one has seen the father.

47 281 281 3004 1473   01 4100   2192 2222
ἀμὴν ἀμὴν λέγω ὑμῖν, ὁ πιστεύων ἔχει ζωὴν
Amen amen I say to you, the one trusting has life

166   **48** 1473 1510 01   740 06   2222   **49** 013
αἰώνιον. Ἐγώ εἰμι ὁ ἄρτος τῆς ζωῆς. οἱ
eternal. I am the bread of the life. The

3962 1473 2068 1722 07 2048 012 3131 2532
πατέρες ὑμῶν ἔφαγον ἐν τῇ ἐρήμῳ τὸ μάννα καὶ
fathers of you ate in the desert the manna and

599   **50** 3778 1510 01 740 01 1537 02
ἀπέθανον· οὗτός ἐστιν ὁ ἄρτος ὁ ἐκ τοῦ
they died; this is the bread the from the

3772 2597   2443 5100 1537 846   2068
οὐρανοῦ καταβαίνων, ἵνα τις ἐξ αὐτοῦ φάγῃ
heaven one coming down, that some from it might eat

2532 3361 599   **51** 1473 1510 01 740 01 2198
καὶ μὴ ἀποθάνῃ. ἐγώ εἰμι ὁ ἄρτος ὁ ζῶν
and not he might die. I am the bread the living

01   1537 02 3772 2597   1437 5100
ὁ ἐκ τοῦ οὐρανοῦ καταβάς ἐάν τις
the one from the heaven having come down if some

2068   1537 3778 02 740 2198   1519 04
φάγῃ ἐκ τούτου τοῦ ἄρτου ζήσει εἰς τὸν
might eat from this the bread will live into the

165   2532 01 740 1161 3739 1473 1325   05
αἰῶνα, καὶ ὁ ἄρτος δὲ ὃν ἐγὼ δώσω ἡ
age; also the bread but which I will give the

4561 1473 1510 5228   06   02 2889 2222
σάρξ μού ἐστιν ὑπὲρ τῆς τοῦ κόσμου ζωῆς.
flesh of me is on behalf of the of the world life.

52 3164   3767 4314 240   013 2453
Ἐμάχοντο οὖν πρὸς ἀλλήλους οἱ Ἰουδαῖοι
Were battling then toward one another the Judeans

3004   4459 1410 3778 1473 1325 08
λέγοντες· πῶς δύναται οὗτος ἡμῖν δοῦναι τὴν
saying; how is able this one to us to give the

4561 846 2068   **53** 3004 3767 846 01 2424
σάρκα [αὐτοῦ] φαγεῖν; εἶπεν οὖν αὐτοῖς ὁ Ἰησοῦς·
flesh of him to eat? Said then to them the Jesus;

281 281 3004 1473 1437 3361 2068 08
ἀμὴν ἀμὴν λέγω ὑμῖν, ἐὰν μὴ φάγητε τὴν
amen amen I say to you, except you might eat the

4561 02 5207 02 444 2532 4095
σάρκα τοῦ υἱοῦ τοῦ ἀνθρώπου καὶ πίητε .
flesh of the son of the man and you might drink

846 012 129 3756 2192 2222 1722 1438
αὐτοῦ τὸ αἷμα, οὐκ ἔχετε ζωὴν ἐν ἑαυτοῖς.
of him the blood, not you have life in yourselves.

54 01 5176 1473 08 4561 2532 4095 1473
ὁ τρώγων μου τὴν σάρκα καὶ πίνων μου
The one gnawing of me the flesh and drinking of me

012 129 2192 2222 166 2504 450
τὸ αἷμα ἔχει ζωὴν αἰώνιον, κἀγὼ ἀναστήσω
the blood has life eternal, and I will make stand up

in the prophets, 'And they shall all be taught by God.' Everyone who has heard and learned from the Father comes to me. [46]Not that anyone has seen the Father except the one who is from God; he has seen the Father. [47]Very truly, I tell you, whoever believes has eternal life. [48]I am the bread of life. [49]Your ancestors ate the manna in the wilderness, and they died. [50]This is the bread that comes down from heaven, so that one may eat of it and not die. [51]I am the living bread that came down from heaven. Whoever eats of this bread will live forever; and the bread that I will give for the life of the world is my flesh."

[52]The Jews then disputed among themselves, saying, "How can this man give us his flesh to eat?" [53]So Jesus said to them, "Very truly, I tell you, unless you eat the flesh of the Son of Man and drink his blood, you have no life in you. [54]Those who eat my flesh and drink my blood have eternal life, and I will raise them up

on the last day; ⁵⁵for my flesh is true food and my blood is true drink. ⁵⁶Those who eat my flesh and drink my blood abide in me, and I in them. ⁵⁷Just as the living Father sent me, and I live because of the Father, so whoever eats me will live because of me. ⁵⁸This is the bread that came down from heaven, not like that which your ancestors ate, and they died. But the one who eats this bread will live forever." ⁵⁹He said these things while he was teaching in the synagogue at Capernaum.

60 When many of his disciples heard it, they said, "This teaching is difficult; who can accept it?" ⁶¹But Jesus, being aware that his disciples were complaining about it, said to them, "Does this offend you? ⁶²Then what if you were to see the Son of Man ascending to where he was before? ⁶³It is the spirit that gives life; the flesh is useless. The words that I have spoken to you are spirit and life. ⁶⁴But among you there are some who do not believe." For Jesus knew from the first who were the ones that did not

```
846      07      2078     2250        05   1063  4561   1473
αὐτὸν  τῇ    ἐσχάτῃ ἡμέρᾳ.  55  ἡ   γὰρ  σάρξ   μου
him    in the last    day.       The for   flesh  of me
227      1510    1035      2532 09   129   1473  227       1510
ἀληθής ἐστιν βρῶσις, καὶ  τὸ  αἷμά μου  ἀληθής ἐστιν
true     is    food,   and  the blood of me true     is
4213          01   5176         1473   08  4561   2532
πόσις.  56  ὁ  τρώγων        μου   τὴν σάρκα καὶ
drink.      The one gnawing   of me the flesh  and
4095    1473   012  129     1722 1473 3306  2504    1722
πίνων  μου  τὸ  αἷμα   ἐν ἐμοὶ μένει κἀγὼ ἐν
drinking of me the blood in  me   stays and I in
846     57  2531      649          1473 01 2198   3962    2504
αὐτῷ.      καθὼς  ἀπέστειλέν με ὁ ζῶν  πατὴρ κἀγὼ
him.       Just as delegated me the living father and I
2198 1223    04  3962     2532 01  5176        1473
ζῶ   διὰ  τὸν πατέρα, καὶ ὁ  τρώγων      με
live through the father, also the one gnawing me
2548            2198         1223   1473  58  3778  1510
κἀκεῖνος    ζήσει      δι’  ἐμέ.      οὗτός ἐστιν
also that one will live through me.   This  is
01  740   01        1537 3772  2597              3756
ὁ  ἄρτος ὁ       ἐξ  οὐρανοῦ καταβάς,       οὐ
the bread the one from heaven having come down, not
2531      2068    013 3962     2532 599          01
καθὼς  ἔφαγον οἱ πατέρες καὶ ἀπέθανον· ὁ
just as ate     the fathers and died;       the one
5176    3778      04 740    2198          1519 04  165
τρώγων τοῦτον τὸν ἄρτον ζήσει         εἰς τὸν αἰῶνα.
gnawing this    the bread will live into the age.
59  3778   3004       1722 4864      1321      1722
    Ταῦτα εἶπεν     ἐν  συναγωγῇ διδάσκων ἐν
    These he said  in  synagogue teaching in
2746a         4183   3767 191             1537    014
Καφαρναούμ. 60 Πολλοὶ οὖν ἀκούσαντες ἐκ  τῶν
Capernaum.     Many  then having heard out of the
3101    846     3004    4642       1510 01 3056  3778
μαθητῶν αὐτοῦ εἶπαν· σκληρός ἐστιν ὁ λόγος οὗτος·
learners of him said; hard   is   the word this;
5101 1410   846   191              3609a         1161 01
τίς δύναται αὐτοῦ ἀκούειν;  61 εἰδὼς       δὲ  ὁ
who is able of it to hear?    Having known but the
2424    1722  1438      3754 1111         4012  3778    013
Ἰησοῦς ἐν  ἑαυτῷ   ὅτι γογγύζουσιν περὶ τούτου οἱ
Jesus  in  himself that grumble     about this  the
3101     846    3004   846      3778  1473 4624
μαθηταὶ αὐτοῦ εἶπεν αὐτοῖς· τοῦτο ὑμᾶς σκανδαλίζει;
learners of him said to them; this you offends?
62 1437 3767 2334            04  5207 02    444
   ἐὰν οὖν θεωρῆτε      τὸν υἱὸν τοῦ ἀνθρώπου
   If  then you might watch the son of the man
305          3699 1510   012  4387         09   4151
ἀναβαίνοντα ὅπου ἦν   τὸ πρότερον; 63 τὸ πνεῦμά
going up   where he was the former?    The spirit
1510 09          2227        05  4561 3756 5623
ἐστιν τὸ      ζωοποιοῦν, ἡ σὰρξ οὐκ ὠφελεῖ
is   the one making live, the flesh not benefits
3762      021 4487     3739   1473 2980         1473
οὐδέν·  τὰ ῥήματα ἃ    ἐγὼ λελάληκα ὑμῖν
nothing; the words which I   have spoken to you
4151    1510   2532 2222 1510       64 235    1510 1537
πνεῦμά ἐστιν καὶ ζωή ἐστιν.   ἀλλ’ εἰσὶν ἐξ
spirit are   and life are.      But are  out
1473   5100  3739 3756 4100          3609a      1063
ὑμῶν τινες οἱ οὐ πιστεύουσιν. ᾔδει      γὰρ
of you some who not trust.     Had known for
1537 746      01  2424    5101  1510  013      3361
ἐξ  ἀρχῆς   ὁ Ἰησοῦς τίνες εἰσὶν οἱ      μὴ
from beginning the Jesus who are  the ones not
```

4100   2532 5101 1510   01   3860   846
πιστεύοντες καὶ τίς ἐστιν ὁ παραδώσων αὐτόν.
trusting   and who is   the one giving over him.

   2532 3004   1223   3778   3004   1473
65 καὶ ἔλεγεν· διὰ   τοῦτο εἴρηκα   ὑμῖν
   And he said; through this   I have spoken to you

3754 3762   1410   2064   4314   1473 1437 3361
ὅτι οὐδεὶς δύναται ἐλθεῖν πρός με ἐὰν μὴ
that no one is able to come toward me   except

1510   1325   846   1537 02
ἦ   δεδομένον   αὐτῷ ἐκ τοῦ
it might be+ +having been given to him from the

3962   66 1537   3778   4183   1537 014 3101
πατρός.   'Εκ τούτου πολλοὶ [ἐκ] τῶν μαθητῶν
father.   From this   many   from the learners

846   565   1519 024   3694   2532 3765
αὐτοῦ ἀπῆλθον εἰς τὰ   ὀπίσω καὶ οὐκέτι
of him went off to the things after and no longer

3326 846   4043   3004   3767 01
μετ' αὐτοῦ περιεπάτουν.   67 εἶπεν οὖν ὁ
with him   they were walking around. Said then the

 2424   015   1427   3361 2532 1473 2309
'Ιησοῦς τοῖς δώδεκα· μὴ καὶ ὑμεῖς θέλετε
Jesus to the twelve; not also you   want

5217   611   4463   4613 4074   2962
ὑπάγειν; 68 ἀπεκρίθη αὐτῷ Σίμων Πέτρος· κύριε,
to go off?   Answered to him Simon Peter; Master,

4314 5101 565   4487 2222   166
πρὸς τίνα ἀπελευσόμεθα; ῥήματα ζωῆς αἰωνίου
toward whom will we go off? Words of life eternal

2192   69 2532 1473 4100   2532 1097
ἔχεις,   καὶ ἡμεῖς πεπιστεύκαμεν καὶ ἐγνώκαμεν
you have, and we   have trusted   and have known

3754 1473 1510 01   40   02   2316   70 611
ὅτι σὺ εἶ ὁ ἅγιος τοῦ θεοῦ.   ἀπεκρίθη
that you are the holy of the God.   Answered

846   01 2424   3756 1473 1473 016   1427
αὐτοῖς ὁ 'Ιησοῦς· οὐκ ἐγὼ ὑμᾶς τοὺς δώδεκα
to them the Jesus; not I   you the twelve

1586   2532 1537 1473 1520 1228   1510
ἐξελεξάμην; καὶ ἐξ ὑμῶν εἷς διάβολός ἐστιν;
selected? And out of you one slanderer is?

   3004   1161 04 2455   4613   2469
71 ἔλεγεν   δὲ τὸν 'Ιούδαν Σίμωνος 'Ισκαριώτου·
   He was saying but the Judas of Simon Iscariot;

3778   1063 3195   3860   846   1520 1537
οὗτος γὰρ ἔμελλεν παραδιδόναι αὐτόν, εἷς ἐκ
this one for was about to give over him, one out of

014 1427   7:1 2532 3326 3778 4043
τῶν δώδεκα.   Καὶ μετὰ ταῦτα περιεπάτει
the twelve.   And after these was walking around

01 2424   1722 07 1056   3756 1063 2309   1722
ὁ 'Ιησοῦς ἐν τῇ Γαλιλαίᾳ· οὐ γὰρ ἤθελεν ἐν
the Jesus in the Galilee; not for he wanted in

07 2449   4043   3754 2212   846
τῇ 'Ιουδαίᾳ περιπατεῖν, ὅτι ἐζήτουν αὐτὸν
the Judea   to walk around, because were seeking him

013 2453   615   2 1510 1161 1451 05
οἱ 'Ιουδαῖοι ἀποκτεῖναι. Ἦν δὲ ἐγγὺς ἡ
the Judeans to kill.   Was but near the

1859 014   2453   05 4634   3 3004
ἑορτὴ τῶν 'Ιουδαίων ἡ σκηνοπηγία.   εἶπον
festival of the Judeans, the tent pitching.   Said

3767 4314   846   013 80   846   3327
οὖν πρὸς αὐτὸν οἱ ἀδελφοὶ αὐτοῦ· μετάβηθι
then toward him the brothers of him; go across

1782   2532 5217 1519 08 2449   2443 2532
ἐντεῦθεν καὶ ὕπαγε εἰς τὴν 'Ιουδαίαν, ἵνα καὶ
from here and go off into the Judea,   that also

believe, and who was the
one that would betray him.
65And he said, "For this
reason I have told you that
no one can come to me
unless it is granted by the
Father."

66 Because of this many
of his disciples turned back
and no longer went about
with him. 67So Jesus asked
the twelve, "Do you also
wish to go away?" 68Simon
Peter answered him, "Lord,
to whom can we go? You
have the words of eternal
life. 69We have come to
believe and know that you
are the Holy One of God."[a]
70Jesus answered them,
"Did I not choose you, the
twelve? Yet one of you is a
devil." 71He was speaking
of Judas son of Simon
Iscariot,[b] for he, though
one of the twelve, was
going to betray him.

CHAPTER 7

After this Jesus went about
in Galilee. He did not
wish[c] to go about in Judea
because the Jews were
looking for an opportunity
to kill him. 2Now the
Jewish festival of Booths[d]
was near. 3So his brothers
said to him, "Leave here
and go to Judea so that

a Other ancient authorities read the
Christ, the Son of the living God
b Other ancient authorities read
Judas Iscariot son of Simon;
others, Judas son of Simon from
Karyot (Kerioth)
c Other ancient authorities read
was not at liberty
d Or Tabernacles

your disciples also may see the works you are doing; [4]for no one who wants[a] to be widely known acts in secret. If you do these things, show yourself to the world." [5](For not even his brothers believed in him.) [6]Jesus said to them, "My time has not yet come, but your time is always here. [7]The world cannot hate you, but it hates me because I testify against it that its works are evil. [8]Go to the festival yourselves. I am not[b] going to this festival, for my time has not yet fully come." [9]After saying this, he remained in Galilee.

10But after his brothers had gone to the festival, then he also went, not publicly but as it were[c] in secret. [11]The Jews were looking for him at the festival and saying, "Where is he?" [12]And there was considerable complaining about him among the crowds. While some were saying, "He is a good man," others were saying, "No, he is deceiving the crowd." [13]Yet no one would speak openly about him for fear of the Jews.

14 About the middle of the festival

a Other ancient authorities read wants it

b Other ancient authorities add yet

c Other ancient authorities lack as it were

---

013 3101	1473	2334	1473	024 2041 3739
οἱ μαθηταί	σου	θεωρήσουσιν	σοῦ	τὰ ἔργα ἃ
the learners of	you	will watch	of you	the works that

4160   3762   1063 5100 1722 2927   4160   2532
ποιεῖς· **4** οὐδεὶς γάρ τι ἐν κρυπτῷ ποιεῖ καὶ
you do;   no one for some in hiding does and

2212 846   1722 3954   1510   1487 3778   4160
ζητεῖ αὐτὸς ἐν παρρησίᾳ εἶναι. εἰ ταῦτα ποιεῖς,
seeks himself in boldness to be. If these you do,

5319   4572   03   2889   **5** 3761   1063 013
φανέρωσον σεαυτὸν τῷ κόσμῳ. οὐδὲ γὰρ οἱ
demonstrate yourself to the world. But not for the

80   846   4100   1519 846   **6** 3004 3767˙
ἀδελφοὶ αὐτοῦ ἐπίστευον εἰς αὐτόν. λέγει οὖν
brothers of him were trusting into him. Says then

846   01 2424   01 2540   01 1699 3768
αὐτοῖς ὁ Ἰησοῦς· ὁ καιρὸς ὁ ἐμὸς οὔπω
to them the Jesus; the season the mine not yet

3918   01 1161 2540   01 5212   3842   1510
πάρεστιν, ὁ δὲ καιρὸς ὁ ὑμέτερος πάντοτέ ἐστιν
is present, the but season the of you always is

2092   **7** 3756 1410   01 2889   3404   1473 1473
ἕτοιμος. οὐ δύναται ὁ κόσμος μισεῖν ὑμᾶς, ἐμὲ
prepared. Not is able the world to hate you, me

1161 3404   3754   1473 3140   4012   846
δὲ μισεῖ, ὅτι ἐγὼ μαρτυρῶ περὶ αὐτοῦ
but it hates, because I testify concerning it

3754 021 2041 846   4190   1510   **8** 1473 305
ὅτι τὰ ἔργα αὐτοῦ πονηρά ἐστιν. ὑμεῖς ἀνάβητε
that the works of it evil are. You go up

1519 08 1859   1473 3756 305   1519 08 1859
εἰς τὴν ἑορτήν· ἐγὼ οὐκ ἀναβαίνω εἰς τὴν ἑορτὴν
into the festival; I not go up to the festival

3778   3754   01 1699 2540 3768
ταύτην, ὅτι ὁ ἐμὸς καιρὸς οὔπω
this, because the mine season not yet

4137   **9** 3778 1161 3004   846   3306
πεπλήρωται. ταῦτα δὲ εἰπὼν αὐτὸς ἔμεινεν
has been filled. These but saying himself was staying

1722 07 1056   **10** 5613 1161 305   013 80
ἐν τῇ Γαλιλαίᾳ. Ὡς δὲ ἀνέβησαν οἱ ἀδελφοὶ
in the Galilee. As but went up the brothers

846   1519 08 1859   5119 2532 846   305
αὐτοῦ εἰς τὴν ἑορτήν, τότε καὶ αὐτὸς ἀνέβη
of him to the festival, then also himself went up

3756 5320   235   5613 1722 2927   **11** 013 3767
οὐ φανερῶς ἀλλὰ ὡς ἐν κρυπτῷ. Οἱ οὖν
not openly but as in hiding. The then

2453   2212   846   1722 07 1859   2532
Ἰουδαῖοι ἐζήτουν αὐτὸν ἐν τῇ ἑορτῇ καὶ
Judeans were seeking him in the festival and

3004   4226 1510 1565   **12** 2532 1112
ἔλεγον· ποῦ ἐστιν ἐκεῖνος; καὶ γογγυσμὸς
were saying, where is that one? And grumbling

4012 846 1510 4183 1722 015 3793   013   3303
περὶ αὐτοῦ ἦν πολὺς ἐν τοῖς ὄχλοις· οἱ μὲν
about him was much in the crowds; the ones indeed

3004   3754 18   1510   243   1161 3004
ἔλεγον ὅτι ἀγαθός ἐστιν, ἄλλοι δὲ ἔλεγον,
were saying that good he is, others but were saying,

3756a 235 4105   04 3793   **13** 3762 3305
οὔ, ἀλλὰ πλανᾷ τὸν ὄχλον. οὐδεὶς μέντοι
no, but he deceives the crowd. No one indeed

3954   2980   4012 846   1223 04 5401
παρρησίᾳ ἐλάλει περὶ αὐτοῦ διὰ τὸν φόβον
in boldness was speaking about him because the fear

014   2453   **14** 2235   1161 06 1859
τῶν Ἰουδαίων. Ἤδη δὲ τῆς ἑορτῆς
of the Judeans. Already but the festival

3322	305	2424	1519 012	2411	2532
μεσούσης	ἀνέβη	Ἰησοῦς εἰς	τὸ	ἱερὸν	καὶ
being in middle	went up	Jesus	into the	temple	and

1321		2296		3767 013	2453
ἐδίδασκεν.	**15**	ἐθαύμαζον		οὖν οἱ	Ἰουδαῖοι
he was teaching.		Were marveling		then the	Judeans

3004	4459 3778	1121	3609a	3361
λέγοντες·	πῶς οὗτος	γράμματα	οἶδεν	μὴ
saying;	how this	letters	has known	not

3129		611	3767 846	01	2424	2532
μεμαθηκώς;	**16**	ἀπεκρίθη	οὖν αὐτοῖς	ὁ	Ἰησοῦς καὶ·
having learned?		Answered	then to them	the	Jesus	and

3004	05	1699 1322	3756 1510	1699 235	02
εἶπεν·	ἡ	ἐμὴ διδαχὴ	οὐκ ἔστιν	ἐμὴ ἀλλὰ	τοῦ
said;	the	mine teaching	not is	mine but	of the

3992	1473		1437 5100 2309	012
πέμψαντός	με·	**17**	ἐάν τις θέλῃ	τὸ
one having sent me;			if some might want	the

2307 846	4160	1097	4012	06 1322
θέλημα αὐτοῦ	ποιεῖν,	γνώσεται	περὶ	τῆς διδαχῆς
want of him to do,		he will know	about	the teaching

4220	1537	02	2316 1510	2228 1473 575 1683
πότερον ἐκ		τοῦ θεοῦ ἐστιν	ἢ	ἐγὼ ἀπ᾽ ἐμαυτοῦ
whether out of		the God it is	or	I from myself

2980		01	575 1438	2980	08 1391
λαλῶ.	**18**	ὁ	ἀφ᾽ ἑαυτοῦ	λαλῶν	τὴν δόξαν
speak.		The one from himself	speaking	the splendor

08 2398	2212	01	1161 2212	08 1391
τὴν ἰδίαν	ζητεῖ· ὁ		δὲ ζητῶν	τὴν δόξαν
the own	seeks; the one		but seeking	the splendor

02	3992	846	3778	227	1510
τοῦ	πέμψαντος	αὐτὸν,	οὗτος	ἀληθής	ἐστιν
of the one having sent		him,	this one	true	is

2532 93	1722 846	3756 1510		3756 3475
καὶ ἀδικία ἐν	αὐτῷ οὐκ	ἔστιν.	**19**	Οὐ Μωϋσῆς
and unright in	him not	there is.		Not Moses

1325	1473 04	3551	2532 3762	1537 1473 4160
δέδωκεν	ὑμῖν τὸν	νόμον;	καὶ οὐδεὶς ἐξ	ὑμῶν ποιεῖ
has given	you the	law?	And no one from	you does

04 3551	5101 1473 2212	615		611
τὸν νόμον.	τί με ζητεῖτε	ἀποκτεῖναι;	**20**	ἀπεκρίθη
the law.	Why me you seek	to kill?		Answered

01 3793	1140	2192	5101 1473 2212
ὁ ὄχλος·	δαιμόνιον	ἔχεις·	τίς σε ζητεῖ
the crowd;	demon	you have;	who you seeks

615		611	2424 2532 3004 846	1520
ἀποκτεῖναι;	**21**	ἀπεκρίθη	Ἰησοῦς καὶ εἶπεν αὐτοῖς·	ἓν
to kill?		Answered	Jesus and said to them,	one

2041 4160	2532 3956	2296		1223	3778
ἔργον ἐποίησα	καὶ πάντες	θαυμάζετε.	**22**	διὰ	τοῦτο
work I did	and all	marvel.		Through	this

3475 1325	1473	08 4061	3756 3754
Μωϋσῆς δέδωκεν	ὑμῖν	τὴν περιτομήν	- οὐχ ὅτι
Moses has given	to you	the circumcision	not that

1537	02 3475	1510 235	1537	014 3962
ἐκ	τοῦ Μωϋσέως	ἐστιν ἀλλ᾽	ἐκ	τῶν πατέρων -
out of	the Moses	it is but	out of	the fathers

2532 1722 4521	4059	444		1487
καὶ ἐν σαββάτῳ	περιτέμνετε	ἄνθρωπον.	**23**	εἰ
and in sabbath	you circumcise	man.		If

4061	2983	444	1722 4521	2443
περιτομὴν	λαμβάνει	ἄνθρωπος ἐν	σαββάτῳ	ἵνα
circumcision	receives	man in	sabbath	that

3361 3089	01	3551 3475	1473
μὴ λυθῇ	ὁ	νόμος Μωϋσέως,	ἐμοὶ
not might be loosed	the	law of Moses,	to me

5520	3754	3650 444	5199	4160
χολᾶτε	ὅτι	ὅλον ἄνθρωπον	ὑγιῆ	ἐποίησα
you are bitter	because	whole man	healthy	I made

Jesus went up into the temple and began to teach. [15]The Jews were astonished at it, saying, "How does this man have such learning,[a] when he has never been taught?" [16]Then Jesus answered them, "My teaching is not mine but his who sent me. [17]Anyone who resolves to do the will of God will know whether the teaching is from God or whether I am speaking on my own. [18]Those who speak on their own seek their own glory; but the one who seeks the glory of him who sent him is true, and there is nothing false in him.

19 "Did not Moses give you the law? Yet none of you keeps the law. Why are you looking for an opportunity to kill me?" [20]The crowd answered, "You have a demon! Who is trying to kill you?" [21]Jesus answered them, "I performed one work, and all of you are astonished. [22]Moses gave you circumcision (it is, of course, not from Moses, but from the patriarchs), and you circumcise a man on the sabbath. [23]If a man receives circumcision on the sabbath in order that the law of Moses may not be broken, are you angry with me because I healed a man's whole body on the sabbath?

[a] Or *this man know his letters*

24Do not judge by appearances, but judge with right judgment." 25Now some of the people of Jerusalem were saying, "Is not this the man whom they are trying to kill? 26And here he is, speaking openly, but they say nothing to him! Can it be that the authorities really know that this is the Messiah?*a* 27Yet we know where this man is from; but when the Messiah*a* comes, no one will know where he is from." 28Then Jesus cried out as he was teaching in the temple, "You know me, and you know where I am from. I have not come on my own. But the one who sent me is true, and you do not know him. 29I know him, because I am from him, and he sent me." 30Then they tried to arrest him, but no one laid hands on him, because his hour had not yet come. 31Yet many in the crowd believed in him and were saying, "When the Messiah*a* comes, will he do more signs than this man has done?"*b*

32 The Pharisees heard the crowd muttering such things about him, and the chief priests and Pharisees sent temple police to arrest him. 33Jesus then said,

a Or *the Christ*
b Other ancient authorities read *is doing*

1722	4521	**24**	3361	2919	2596		3799	235
ἐν	σαββάτῳ;		μὴ	κρίνετε	κατ'		ὄψιν,	ἀλλὰ
in	sabbath?	Not	judge	according to sight,	but

08   1342   2920   2919   3004   3767
τὴν δικαίαν κρίσιν κρίνετε. **25** Ἔλεγον   οὖν
the right   judgment judge.   Were saying then

5100   1537 014   2415   3756 3778   1510
τινες ἐκ τῶν Ἱεροσολυμιτῶν· οὐχ οὗτός ἐστιν
some from the Jerusalemites; not this one is

3739 2212   615   2532 2396 3954
ὃν ζητοῦσιν ἀποκτεῖναι; **26** καὶ ἴδε παρρησίᾳ
whom they seek to kill?   And look in boldness

2980   2532 3762   846   3004   3379   230
λαλεῖ καὶ οὐδὲν αὐτῷ λέγουσιν. μήποτε ἀληθῶς
he speaks and nothing to him they say. Not then truly

1097   013 758   3754 3778   1510 01 5547
ἔγνωσαν οἱ ἄρχοντες ὅτι οὗτός ἐστιν ὁ χριστός;
knew   the rulers   that this one is the Christ?

27 235 3778   3609a 4159   1510   01 1161
ἀλλὰ τοῦτον οἴδαμεν πόθεν ἐστίν· ὁ δὲ
But this one we know from where he is; the but

5547   3752 2064   3762   1097   4159
χριστὸς ὅταν ἔρχηται   οὐδεὶς γινώσκει πόθεν
Christ when he might come no one knows from where

1510   2896   3767 1722 011 2411   1321   01
ἐστίν. **28** ἔκραξεν οὖν ἐν τῷ ἱερῷ διδάσκων ὁ
he is. Shouted then in the temple teaching the

2424   2532 3004   2504   3609a   2532 3609a
Ἰησοῦς καὶ λέγων· κἀμὲ οἴδατε καὶ οἴδατε
Jesus and saying; both me you know and you know

4159   1510 2532 575 1683   3756 2064
πόθεν εἰμί· καὶ ἀπ' ἐμαυτοῦ οὐκ ἐλήλυθα,
from where I am; and from myself not I have come,

235 1510 228   01 3992   1473 3739 1473
ἀλλ' ἔστιν ἀληθινὸς ὁ πέμψας   με, ὃν ὑμεῖς
but he is true   the one having sent me, whom you

3756 3609a   **29** 1473 3609a 846   3754   3844 846
οὐκ οἴδατε   ἐγὼ οἶδα αὐτόν, ὅτι παρ' αὐτοῦ
not know;   I know him, because by him

1510 2548   1473 649   30 2212
εἰμι κἀκεῖνός   με ἀπέστειλεν. **30** Ἐζήτουν /
I am and that one me delegated.   They were seeking

3767 846   4084   2532 3762   1911   1909 846
οὖν αὐτὸν πιάσαι, καὶ οὐδεὶς ἐπέβαλεν ἐπ' αὐτὸν
then him to capture, and no one threw on on him

08 5495   3754   3768   2064   05   5610 846
τὴν χεῖρα, ὅτι οὔπω ἐληλύθει ἡ ὥρα αὐτοῦ.
the hand, because not yet had come the hour of him.

31 1537 02 3793   1161 4183   4100   1519 846
Ἐκ τοῦ ὄχλου δὲ πολλοὶ ἐπίστευσαν εἰς αὐτὸν
From the crowd but many trusted in him

2532 3004   01 5547   2064
καὶ ἔλεγον·   ὁ χριστὸς ὅταν ἔλθῃ
and they were saying; the Christ when he might come

3361   4183   4592   4160   3739 3778
μὴ πλείονα σημεῖα ποιήσει ὧν οὗτος
not more   signs he will do that this one

4160   **32** 191   013 5330   02 3793
ἐποίησεν; **32** ἤκουσαν οἱ Φαρισαῖοι τοῦ ὄχλου
did?   Heard   the Pharisees the crowd

1111   4012   846   3778   2532 649   013
γογγύζοντος περὶ αὐτοῦ ταῦτα, καὶ ἀπέστειλαν οἱ
grumbling concerning him these, and delegated the

749   2532 013 5330   5257   2443
ἀρχιερεῖς καὶ οἱ Φαρισαῖοι ὑπηρέτας ἵνα
ruler priests and the Pharisees assistants that

4084   846   **33** 3004 3767 01 2424
πιάσωσιν αὐτόν. **33** εἶπεν οὖν ὁ Ἰησοῦς·
they might capture him. Said then the Jesus;

2089	5550	3398	3326	1473	1510	2532	5217
ἔτι	χρόνον	μικρὸν	μεθ᾽	ὑμῶν	εἰμι	καὶ	ὑπάγω
still	time	little	with you	I am	and	I go off

4314	04	3992		1473	**34**	2212		1473
πρὸς	τὸν	πέμψαντά		με.		ζητήσετέ		με
toward	the one	having sent		me.		You will seek		me

2532	3756	2147		1473	2532	3699	1510	1473
καὶ	οὐχ	εὑρήσετέ		με,	καὶ	ὅπου	εἰμὶ	ἐγὼ
and	not	you will find		me,	and	where	am	I

1473	3756	1410		2064	**35**	3004	3767	013	2453
ὑμεῖς	οὐ	δύνασθε		ἐλθεῖν.		εἶπον	οὖν	οἱ	Ἰουδαῖοι
you	not	are able		to come.		Said	then	the	Judeans

4314	1438		4226	3778	3195		4198
πρὸς	ἑαυτούς·		ποῦ	οὗτος	μέλλει		πορεύεσθαι
toward	themselves;		where	this one	is about		to travel

3754	1473	3756	2147		846	3361	1519	08
ὅτι	ἡμεῖς	οὐχ	εὑρήσομεν		αὐτόν;	μὴ	εἰς	τὴν
that	we	not	will find him?			Not	into	the

1290	014	1672		3195		4198
διασπορὰν	τῶν	Ἑλλήνων		μέλλει		πορεύεσθαι
dispersion	of the	Greeks		is he about		to travel

2532	1321	016	1672	**36**	5101	1510	01	3056
καὶ	διδάσκειν	τοὺς	Ἕλληνας;		τίς	ἐστιν	ὁ	λόγος
and	to teach	the	Greeks?		What is		the	word

3778	3739	3004	2212		1473	2532	3756
οὗτος	ὃν	εἶπεν·	ζητήσετέ		με	καὶ	οὐχ
this	which	he said;	you will seek		me	and	not

2147		1473	2532	3699	1510	1473	1473	3756
εὑρήσετέ		με,	καὶ	ὅπου	εἰμὶ	ἐγὼ	ὑμεῖς	οὐ
you will find		me,	and,	where	am	I	you	not

1410		2064	**37**	1722	1161	07	2078	2250	07
δύνασθε		ἐλθεῖν;		Ἐν	δὲ	τῇ	ἐσχάτῃ	ἡμέρᾳ	τῇ
are able		to to come?		In	but	the	last	day	the

3173	06	1859	2476	01	2424	2532
μεγάλῃ	τῆς	ἑορτῆς	εἰστήκει	ὁ	Ἰησοῦς	καὶ
great	of the	festival	had stood	the	Jesus	and

2896	3004	1437	5100	1372		2064	4314
ἔκραξεν	λέγων·	ἐάν	τις	διψᾷ		ἐρχέσθω	πρός
shouted	saying;	if	some	might thirst		let come	toward

1473	2532	4095	**38**	01	4100		1519	1473	2531
με	καὶ	πινέτω.		ὁ	πιστεύων		εἰς	ἐμέ,	καθὼς
me	and	let drink.		The one	trusting in		me,		just as

3004	05	1124	4215	1537	06	2836	846
εἶπεν	ἡ	γραφή,	ποταμοὶ	ἐκ	τῆς	κοιλίας	αὐτοῦ
said	the	writing,	rivers	out of	the	stomach	of him

4482	5204	2198	**39**	3778	1161	3004	4012
ῥεύσουσιν	ὕδατος	ζῶντος.		τοῦτο	δὲ	εἶπεν	περὶ
will flow	of water	living.		This	but	he said	about

010	4151	3739	3195	2983	013
τοῦ	πνεύματος	ὃ	ἔμελλον	λαμβάνειν	οἱ
the	spirit	that	were about	to receive	the ones

4100		1519	846	3768	1063	1510	4151
πιστεύσαντες		εἰς	αὐτόν·	οὔπω	γὰρ	ἦν	πνεῦμα,
having trusted		in	him;	not yet	for	was	spirit,

3754	2424	3764	1392		**40**	1537
ὅτι	Ἰησοῦς	οὐδέπω	ἐδοξάσθη.			Ἐκ
because	Jesus	but not yet	was given splendor.			Out of

02	3793	3767	191	014	3056	3778
τοῦ	ὄχλου	οὖν	ἀκούσαντες	τῶν	λόγων	τούτων
the	crowd	then	having heard	the	words	these

3004		3778	1510	230	01	4396
ἔλεγον·		οὗτός	ἐστιν	ἀληθῶς	ὁ	προφήτης·
they were saying,		this one is		truly	the	spokesman;

41	243	3004		3778	1510	01	5547	013
	ἄλλοι	ἔλεγον·		οὗτός	ἐστιν	ὁ	χριστός,	οἱ
	others	were saying·		this	is	the	Christ,	the ones

1161	3004	3361	1063	1537	06	1056	01
δὲ	ἔλεγον·	μὴ	γὰρ	ἐκ	τῆς	Γαλιλαίας	ὁ
but	were saying;	not	for	from	the	Galilee	the

"I will be with you a little while longer, and then I am going to him who sent me. [34]You will search for me, but you will not find me; and where I am, you cannot come." [35]The Jews said to one another, "Where does this man intend to go that we will not find him? Does he intend to go to the Dispersion among the Greeks and teach the Greeks? [36]What does he mean by saying, 'You will search for me and you will not find me' and 'Where I am, you cannot come'?"

[37]On the last day of the festival, the great day, while Jesus was standing there, he cried out, "Let anyone who is thirsty come to me, [38]and let the one who believes in me drink. As[a] the scripture has said, 'Out of the believer's heart[b] shall flow rivers of living water.'" [39]Now he said this about the Spirit, which believers in him were to receive; for as yet there was no Spirit,[c] because Jesus was not yet glorified.

[40]When they heard these words, some in the crowd said, "This is really the prophet." [41]Others said, "This is the Messiah."[d] But some asked, "Surely the Messiah[d] does not come from Galilee,

---

[a] Or come to me and drink. [38]The one who believes in me, as

[b] Gk out of his belly

[c] Other ancient authorities read for as yet the Spirit (others, Holy Spirit) had not been given

[d] Or the Christ

does he? ⁴²Has not the
scripture said that the
Messiah[a] is descended
from David and comes
from Bethlehem, the village
where David lived?" ⁴³So
there was a division in the
crowd because of him.
⁴⁴Some of them wanted to
arrest him, but no one laid
hands on him.

45 Then the temple
police went back to the
chief priests and Pharisees,
who asked them, "Why did
you not arrest him?" ⁴⁶The
police answered, "Never
has anyone spoken like
this!" ⁴⁷Then the Pharisees
replied, "Surely you have
not been deceived too,
have you? ⁴⁸Has any one
of the authorities or of the
Pharisees believed in him?
⁴⁹But this crowd, which
does not know the law—
they are accursed."
⁵⁰Nicodemus, who had
gone to Jesus[b] before,
and who was one of them,
asked, ⁵¹"Our law does not
judge people without first
giving them a hearing to
find out what they are
doing, does it?" ⁵²They
replied, "Surely you are
not also from Galilee, are
you? Search and you will
see that no prophet is to
arise from Galilee."[c]

[a] Or the Christ

[b] Gk him

[c] The most ancient authorities lack
7.53–8.11; other authorities add
the passage here or after 7.36 or
after 21.25 or after Luke 21.38,
with variations of text; some mark
the passage as doubtful. This
passage is printed at the end of the
Gospel of John.

```
        5547      2064              3756 05   1124      3004  3754 1537
       χριστὸς ἔρχεται;  42  οὐχ  ἡ  γραφὴ  εἶπεν ὅτι   ἐκ
       Christ   comes?       Not the writing said, (")  out of
        010 4690          1160a  2532 575  965        06
       τοῦ σπέρματος Δαυίδ,  καὶ ἀπὸ Βηθλέεμ τῆς
       the seed       David,   and from Bethlehem of the
        2968    3699      1510 1160a 2064      01   5547
       κώμης ὅπου  ἦν  Δαυίδ ἔρχεται ὁ  χριστός;
       village where was  David comes  the Christ?
           4978   3767 1096        1722 03 3793      1223        846
     43  σχίσμα οὖν ἐγένετο ἐν  τῷ ὄχλῳ  δἰ       αὐτόν·
        Split then became  in   the crowd through him.
           5100  1161 2309              1537  846   4084
     44  τινὲς δὲ  ἤθελον      ἐξ  αὐτῶν πιάσαι
        Some  but were wanting out of them  to capture
        846  235  3762   1911      1909 846    020 5495
       αὐτόν, ἀλλ᾽ οὐδεὶς ἐπέβαλεν ἐπ᾽ αὐτὸν τὰς χεῖρας.
       him,   but  no one threw on  on  him  the hands.
           2064   3767 013 5257       4314 016   749
     45  ͂Ηλθον οὖν οἱ ὑπηρέται  πρὸς τοὺς ἀρχιερεῖς
        Came  then the assistants to   the  ruler priests
        2532 5330         2532 3004 846     1565      1223
       καὶ Φαρισαίους, καὶ εἶπον αὐτοῖς ἐκεῖνοι· διὰ
       and Pharisees,   and said to them those;   through
        5101 3756 71       846      611             013
       τί  οὐκ ἠγάγετε  αὐτόν; 46 ἀπεκρίθησαν οἱ
       why not you brought him?   Answered      the
        5257       3763        2980     3779  444
       ὑπηρέται· οὐδέποτε ἐλάλησεν οὕτως ἄνθρωπος.
       assistants; but not ever speak  thusly man.
         611         3767 846   013 5330        3361 2532
     47 ἀπεκρίθησαν οὖν αὐτοῖς οἱ Φαρισαῖοι· μὴ καὶ
        Answered     then to them the Pharisees; not also
        1473 4105          3361 5100 1537   014 758
       ὑμεῖς πεπλάνησθε;  48 μή τις ἐκ  τῶν ἀρχόντων
       you    have been deceived? Not some out of the rulers
        4100         1519 846  2228 1537 014 5330      49  235
       ἐπίστευσεν εἰς αὐτὸν ἢ ἐκ  τῶν Φαρισαίων;    ἀλλὰ
       trusted     in him   or from the Pharisees?       But
        01  3793  3778 01       3361 1097      04   3551
       ὁ  ὄχλος οὗτος ὁ    μὴ γινώσκων τὸν νόμον
       the crowd this  the one not knowing  the law
        1883a     1510      3004  3530        4314 846
       ἐπάρατοί εἰσιν.  50 λέγει Νικόδημος πρὸς αὐτούς,
       cursed ones they are. Says Nicodemus to   them,
        01  2064          4314    846   012 4387      1520
       ὁ  ἐλθὼν        πρὸς αὐτὸν τὸ πρότερον, εἷς
       the one having come toward him  the former,   one
        1510 1537 846     51 3361 01  3551 1473 2919     04
       ὢν  ἐξ αὐτῶν·    μὴ ὁ νόμος ἡμῶν κρίνει τὸν
       being from them;    not the law of us it judges the
        444       1437 3361 191          4413 3844 846 2532
       ἄνθρωπον ἐὰν μὴ ἀκούσῃ  πρῶτον παρ᾽ αὐτοῦ καὶ
       man       except it might hear first from him   and
        1097         5101 4160  52  611         2532 3004
       γνῷ         τί ποιεῖ;   ἀπεκρίθησαν καὶ εἶπαν
       it might know what he does? They answered and said
       might know
        846      3361 2532 1473 1537  06  1056        1510
       αὐτῷ·  μὴ καὶ σὺ ἐκ  τῆς Γαλιλαίας εἶ;
       to him; not also you out of the Galilee   are?
        2037a     2532 2396 3754 1537 06    1056
       ἐραύνησον καὶ ἴδε ὅτι ἐκ τῆς Γαλιλαίας
       Search    and look that out of the Galilee
        4396      3756 1453
       προφήτης οὐκ ἐγείρεται.
       spokesman not  is raised.
```

12
```
3825      3767  846      2980        01  2424    3004
Πάλιν  οὖν  αὐτοῖς  ἐλάλησεν  ὁ  Ἰησοῦς  λέγων,
Again  then  to them  spoke     the Jesus   saying,
1473 1510 09   5457   02      2889    01  190          1473
ἐγώ  εἰμι  τὸ  φῶς  τοῦ  κόσμου·  ὁ  ἀκολουθῶν  ἐμοὶ
I    am    the light of  the world; the one following  me
3756 3361 4043        1722 07  4653    235  2192    012
οὐ  μὴ  περιπατήσῃ  ἐν  τῇ  σκοτίᾳ,  ἀλλ᾽ ἕξει  τὸ
not not might walk  in  the dark,    but  he will the
         around                                    have
5457 06    2222      3004   3767 846      013 5330
φῶς  τῆς  ζωῆς.  13 εἶπον  οὖν  αὐτῷ  οἱ  Φαρισαῖοι·
light of  the life.   Said then to him  the Pharisees;
1473 4012  4572     3140        05 3141     1473  3756
σὺ  περὶ  σεαυτοῦ  μαρτυρεῖς· ἡ  μαρτυρία  σου  οὐκ
you about yourself testify;   the testimony of you not
1510 227        611       2424 2532 3004 846
ἔστιν ἀληθής. 14 ἀπεκρίθη  Ἰησοῦς καὶ εἶπεν αὐτοῖς·
is    true.      Answered  Jesus  and said  to them;
2579 1473 3140    4012 1683     227    1510 05
κἂν  ἐγὼ μαρτυρῶ περὶ ἐμαυτοῦ, ἀληθής ἐστιν ἡ
and if I  testify about myself, true   is    the
3141      1473  3754   3609a  4159       2064  2532
μαρτυρία μου, ὅτι  οἶδα πόθεν  ἦλθον  καὶ
testimony of me, because I know from where I came and
4226 5217     1473 1161 3756 3609a   4159      2064
ποῦ  ὑπάγω· ὑμεῖς δὲ  οὐκ  οἴδατε πόθεν  ἔρχομαι
where I go off; you  but not  know  from where I come
2228 4226 5217    1473  2596 08  4561  2919     1473
ἢ  ποῦ  ὑπάγω. 15 ὑμεῖς κατὰ τὴν σάρκα κρίνετε, ἐγὼ
or where I go off. You by the flesh judge,      I
3756 2919 3762    2532 1437 2919  1161 1473 05
οὐ  κρίνω οὐδένα. 16 καὶ ἐὰν κρίνω δὲ  ἐγώ, ἡ
not judge no one.     Even if  judge but I,  the
2920    05  1699 228     1510    3754     3441 3756
κρίσις ἡ  ἐμὴ  ἀληθινή ἐστιν, ὅτι  μόνος οὐκ
judgment the mine true  is,    because alone not
1510 235   1473 2532 01  3992      1473 3962    2532
εἰμί, ἀλλ᾽ ἐγὼ καὶ ὁ  πέμψας  με πατήρ. 17 καὶ
I am, but I  and the having sent me father.     And
1722 03  3551 1161 03   5212       1125             3754
ἐν  τῷ νόμῳ δὲ  τῷ  ὑμετέρῳ γέγραπται          ὅτι
in  the law but the your     it has been written that
1417 444       05 3141    227     1510       1473 1510
δύο ἀνθρώπων ἡ  μαρτυρία ἀληθής ἐστιν. 18 ἐγώ εἰμι
two men        the testimony true  is.       I    am
01  3140        4012 1683     2532 3140      4012
ὁ  μαρτυρῶν  περὶ ἐμαυτοῦ καὶ μαρτυρεῖ περὶ
the one testifying about myself and testifies about
1473 01    3992     1473 3962    3004
ἐμοῦ ὁ  πέμψας   με πατήρ. 19 ἔλεγον
me    the having sent me father.  They were saying
3767 846    4226 1510 01 3962   1473    611
οὖν  αὐτῷ· ποῦ ἐστιν ὁ πατήρ σου; ἀπεκρίθη
then to him; where is the father of you? Answered
2424    3777   1473 3609a  3777 04  3962    1473
Ἰησοῦς· οὔτε ἐμὲ οἴδατε οὔτε τὸν πατέρα μου·
Jesus; neither me you know nor the father of me;
1487 1473 3609a      2532 04 3962    1473   302
εἰ ἐμὲ ᾔδειτε,     καὶ τὸν πατέρα μου  ἂν
if me you had known, also the father of me -
3609a        3778 024  4487    2980     1722 011
ᾔδειτε. 20 Ταῦτα τὰ ῥήματα ἐλάλησεν ἐν  τῷ
you had known. These the words he spoke in the
1049         1321      1722 011 2411      2532 3762
γαζοφυλακίῳ διδάσκων ἐν  τῷ ἱερῷ·   καὶ οὐδεὶς
treasury box teaching in the temple; and no one
4084     846   3754   3768    2064     05   5610
ἐπίασεν αὐτόν, ὅτι  οὔπω  ἐληλύθει ἡ  ὥρα
captured him,  because not yet has come the hour
```

12 Again Jesus spoke to them, saying, "I am the light of the world. Whoever follows me will never walk in darkness but will have the light of life." [13] Then the Pharisees said to him, "You are testifying on your own behalf; your testimony is not valid." [14] Jesus answered, "Even if I testify on my own behalf, my testimony is valid because I know where I have come from and where I am going, but you do not know where I come from or where I am going. [15] You judge by human standards;[a] I judge no one. [16] Yet even if I do judge, my judgment is valid; for it is not I alone who judge, but I and the Father[b] who sent me. [17] In your law it is written that the testimony of two witnesses is valid. [18] I testify on my own behalf, and the Father who sent me testifies on my behalf." [19] Then they said to him, "Where is your Father?" Jesus answered, "You know neither me nor my Father. If you knew me, you would know my Father also." [20] He spoke these words while he was teaching in the treasury of the temple, but no one arrested him, because his hour had not yet come.

[a] Gk according to the flesh
[b] Other ancient authorities read he

21 Again he said to them, "I am going away, and you will search for me, but you will die in your sin. Where I am going, you cannot come." 22Then the Jews said, "Is he going to kill himself? Is that what he means by saying, 'Where I am going, you cannot come'?" 23He said to them, "You are from below, I am from above; you are of this world, I am not of this world. 24I told you that you would die in your sins, for you will die in your sins unless you believe that I am he."[a] 25They said to him, "Who are you?" Jesus said to them, "Why do I speak to you at all?[b] 26I have much to say about you and much to condemn; but the one who sent me is true, and I declare to the world what I have heard from him." 27They did not understand that he was speaking to them about the Father. 28So Jesus said, "When you have lifted up the Son of Man, then you will realize that I am he,[a] and that I do nothing on my own, but I speak these things as the Father instructed me. 29And the one who sent me is with me;

[a] Gk I am
[b] Or What I have told you from the beginning

---

846   **21** 3004   3767 3825   846   1473 5217   2532
αὐτοῦ.   Εἶπεν οὖν πάλιν αὐτοῖς· ἐγὼ ὑπάγω καὶ
of him.   He said then again to them; I   go off and

2212   1473   2532 1722 07   266   1473
ζητήσετέ   με, καὶ ἐν τῇ ἁμαρτίᾳ ὑμῶν
you will seek me, and in the sin   of you

599   3699 1473 5217   1473   3756 1410
ἀποθανεῖσθε· ὅπου ἐγὼ ὑπάγω ὑμεῖς οὐ δύνασθε
you will die; where I   go off you   not are able

2064   **22** 3004   3767 013 2453   3385
ἐλθεῖν.   ἔλεγον οὖν οἱ Ἰουδαῖοι· μήτι
to go.   Were saying then the Judeans;   not

615   1438   3754   3004   3699 1473
ἀποκτενεῖ ἑαυτόν, ὅτι λέγει· ὅπου ἐγὼ
will he kill himself, because he says; where I

5217   1473 3756 1410   2064   **23** 2532 3004
ὑπάγω ὑμεῖς οὐ δύνασθε ἐλθεῖν;   καὶ ἔλεγεν
go off you   not are able to go?   And he was saying

846   1473   1537 022 2736 1510   1473 1537 022
αὐτοῖς· ὑμεῖς ἐκ τῶν κάτω ἐστέ, ἐγὼ ἐκ τῶν
to them; you   from the down are,   I   from the

507 1510   1473 1537   3778   02 2889   1510   1473
ἄνω εἰμί· ὑμεῖς ἐκ τούτου τοῦ κόσμου ἐστέ, ἐγὼ
up am;   you   out of this the world are,   I

3756 1510 1537   02 2889   3778   **24** 3004   3767
οὐκ εἰμὶ ἐκ τοῦ κόσμου τούτου.   εἶπον οὖν
not am out of the world this.   I said then

1473   3754 599   1722 019   266   1473
ὑμῖν ὅτι ἀποθανεῖσθε ἐν ταῖς ἁμαρτίαις ὑμῶν·
to you that you will die in the sins   of you;

1437 1063 3361 4100   3754 1473 1510
ἐὰν γὰρ μὴ πιστεύσητε ὅτι ἐγώ εἰμι,
if   for not you might trust that I   am,

599   1722 019 266   1473   **25** 3004
ἀποθανεῖσθε ἐν ταῖς ἁμαρτίαις ὑμῶν.   ἔλεγον
you will die in the sins   of you.   They were
                                                       saying

3767 846   1473 5101 1510 3004 846   01 2424
οὖν αὐτῷ· σὺ τίς εἶ; εἶπεν αὐτοῖς ὁ Ἰησοῦς·
then to him; you who are? Said to them the Jesus;

08 746   3739 5100 2532 2980   1473
τὴν ἀρχὴν ὅ τι καὶ λαλῶ ὑμῖν;
the beginning what some also I speak to you?

26 4183   2192 4012 1473 2980   2532
πολλὰ   ἔχω περὶ ὑμῶν λαλεῖν καὶ
Many things I have about you to speak and

2919   235 01 3992   1473   227   1510
κρίνειν, ἀλλ' ὁ πέμψας   με ἀληθής ἐστιν,
to judge, but the one having sent me true   is,

2504   3739 191   3844 846   3778 2980   1519 04
κἀγὼ ἃ ἤκουσα παρ' αὐτοῦ ταῦτα λαλῶ εἰς τὸν
and I what heard from him these speak in   the

2889   **27** 3756 1097   3754 04 3962   846
κόσμον.   οὐκ ἔγνωσαν ὅτι τὸν πατέρα αὐτοῖς
world.   Not they knew that the father to them

3004   **28** 3004   3767 846   01 2424   3752
ἔλεγεν.   εἶπεν οὖν [αὐτοῖς] ὁ Ἰησοῦς· ὅταν
he was speaking. Said then to them the Jesus;   when

5312   04 5207 02   444   5119
ὑψώσητε τὸν υἱὸν τοῦ ἀνθρώπου, τότε
you might elevate the son of the man,   then

1097   3754 1473 1510   2532 575 1683   4160
γνώσεσθε ὅτι ἐγώ εἰμι, καὶ ἀπ' ἐμαυτοῦ ποιῶ
you will know that I   am,   and from myself I do

3762   235 2531   1473 01 3962   3778
οὐδέν, ἀλλὰ καθὼς ἐδίδαξέν με ὁ πατὴρ ταῦτα
nothing, but just as taught   me the father these

2980   **29** 2532 01 3992   1473 3326 1473 1510
λαλῶ.   καὶ ὁ πέμψας   με μετ' ἐμοῦ ἐστιν·
I speak.   And the one having sent me with me   is;

3756 863   1473 3441   3754   1473 024 701
οὐκ ἀφῆκέν   με   μόνον, ὅτι   ἐγὼ τὰ ἀρεστὰ
not   he left off me   alone, because I   the pleasing

846   4160   3842   3778 846   2980   4183
αὐτῷ ποιῶ πάντοτε. **30** Ταῦτα αὐτοῦ λαλοῦντος πολλοὶ
to him I do always.   These of him speaking many

4100   1519 846   3004   3767 01   2424
ἐπίστευσαν εἰς αὐτόν. **31** ἔλεγεν   οὖν ὁ Ἰησοῦς
trusted   into him.   Was saying then the Jesus

4314 016   4100   846   2453   1437
πρὸς τοὺς   πεπιστευκότας αὐτῷ Ἰουδαίους· ἐὰν
toward the ones having trusted in him Judeans;   if

1473 3306   1722 03 3056 03 1699 230
ὑμεῖς μείνητε ἐν τῷ λόγῳ τῷ ἐμῷ, ἀληθῶς
you   might stay in the word the mine, truly

3101   1473 1510   2532 1097   08 225
μαθηταί μού ἐστε **32** καὶ γνώσεσθε τὴν ἀλήθειαν,
learners of me you are and you will know the truth,

2532 05   225   1659   1473 611
καὶ ἡ   ἀλήθεια ἐλευθερώσει ὑμᾶς. **33** ἀπεκρίθησαν
and the truth   will free   you.   They answered

4314 846   4690   11   1510   2532 3762
πρὸς αὐτόν· σπέρμα Ἀβραάμ ἐσμεν καὶ οὐδενὶ
toward him; seed   Abraham we are and to no one

1398   4455   4459 1473 3004   3754
δεδουλεύκαμεν   πώποτε· πῶς σὺ λέγεις ὅτι
have we been slave ever yet; how you say,   (")

1658   1096   611   846   01
ἐλεύθεροι γενήσεσθε; **34** ἀπεκρίθη αὐτοῖς ὁ
free ones you will become? Answered to them the

2424   281 281 3004   1473   3754 3956 01 4160
Ἰησοῦς· ἀμὴν ἀμὴν λέγω ὑμῖν ὅτι πᾶς ὁ ποιῶν
Jesus;   amen amen I say to you that all the one doing

08 266   1401   1510 06   266   01 1161
τὴν ἁμαρτίαν δοῦλός ἐστιν τῆς ἁμαρτίας. **35** ὁ δὲ
the sin   slave   is   of the sin.   The but

1401   3756 3306 1722 07 3614   1519 04 165   01
δοῦλος οὐ μένει ἐν τῇ οἰκίᾳ εἰς τὸν αἰῶνα, ὁ
slave   not stays in the house into the age,   the

5207 3306 1519 04 165   1437 3767 01   5207 1473
υἱὸς μένει εἰς τὸν αἰῶνα. **36** ἐὰν οὖν ὁ υἱὸς ὑμᾶς
son stays into the age.   If then the son you

1659   3689   1658   1510   37 3609a 3754
ἐλευθερώσῃ, ὄντως ἐλεύθεροι ἔσεσθε. **37** Οἶδα ὅτι
might free, really free ones you will be. I know that

4690   11   1510   235   2212   1473 615
σπέρμα Ἀβραάμ ἐστε· ἀλλὰ ζητεῖτέ με ἀποκτεῖναι,
seed   Abraham you are; but you seek me to kill,

3754   01   3004 ὁ 1699 3756 5562   1722 1473
ὅτι   ὁ λόγος ὁ ἐμὸς οὐ χωρεῖ   ἐν ὑμῖν.
because the word the mine not makes room in you.

38 3739 1473 3708   3844 03   3962   2980   2532
ἃ   ἐγὼ ἑώρακα παρὰ τῷ πατρὶ λαλῶ· καὶ
What I   have seen from the father I speak; and

1473 3767 3739 191   3844 03 3962   4160
ὑμεῖς οὖν ἃ ἠκούσατε παρὰ τοῦ πατρὸς ποιεῖτε.
you   then what you heard from the father you do.

39 611   2532 3004 846   01 3962   1473
ἀπεκρίθησαν καὶ εἶπαν αὐτῷ· ὁ πατὴρ ἡμῶν
They answered and said to him, the father of us

11   1510   3004 846   01 2424   1487 5043
Ἀβραάμ ἐστιν. λέγει αὐτοῖς ὁ Ἰησοῦς· εἰ τέκνα
Abraham is.   Says to them the Jesus, if children

02   11   1510   024 2041 02   11
τοῦ Ἀβραάμ ἐστε, τὰ ἔργα τοῦ Ἀβραὰμ
of the Abraham you are, the works of the Abraham

4160   3568 1161 2212   1473 615
ἐποιεῖτε· **40** νῦν δὲ ζητεῖτέ με ἀποκτεῖναι
you were doing; now but you seek me to kill

he has not left me alone, for I always do what is pleasing to him." 30As he was saying these things, many believed in him.

31 Then Jesus said to the Jews who had believed in him, "If you continue in my word, you are truly my disciples; 32and you will know the truth, and the truth will make you free." 33They answered him, "We are descendants of Abraham and have never been slaves to anyone. What do you mean by saying, 'You will be made free'?"

34 Jesus answered them, "Very truly, I tell you, everyone who commits sin is a slave to sin. 35The slave does not have a permanent place in the household; the son has a place there forever. 36So if the Son makes you free, you will be free indeed. 37I know that you are descendants of Abraham; yet you look for an opportunity to kill me, because there is no place in you for my word. 38I declare what I have seen in the Father's presence; as for you, you should do what you have heard from the Father."[a]

39 They answered him, "Abraham is our father." Jesus said to them, "If you were Abraham's children, you would be doing[b] what Abraham did, 40but now you are trying to kill me,

[a] Other ancient authorities read *you do what you have heard from your father*

[b] Other ancient authorities read *If you are Abraham's children, then do*

a man who has told you
the truth that I heard from
God. This is not what
Abraham did. ⁴¹You are
indeed doing what your
father does." They said
to him, "We are not
illegitimate children; we
have one father, God
himself." ⁴²Jesus said to
them, "If God were your
Father, you would love me,
for I came from God and
now I am here. I did not
come on my own, but he
sent me. ⁴³Why do you
not understand what I say?
It is because you cannot
accept my word. ⁴⁴You are
from your father the devil,
and you choose to do your
father's desires. He was
a murderer from the
beginning and does not
stand in the truth, because
there is no truth in him.
When he lies, he speaks
according to his own
nature, for he is a liar and
the father of lies. ⁴⁵But
because I tell the truth,
you do not believe me.
⁴⁶Which of you convicts me
of sin? If I tell the truth,
why do you not believe me?
⁴⁷Whoever is from God
hears the words of God.
The reason you do not hear
them is that you are not
from God."
    48 The Jews answered
him,

```
      444      3739 08   225          1473    2980          3739
Ἄνθρωπον ὃς  τὴν ἀλήθειαν ὑμῖν λελάληκα  ἣν
man      who  the truth   to you has spoken which
  191     3844 02   2316  3778   11         3756 4160
ἤκουσα παρὰ τοῦ θεοῦ· τοῦτο Ἀβραὰμ οὐκ ἐποίησεν.
I heard from the God; this   Abraham  not  did.
       1473    4160      024 2041  02      3962    1473
41 ὑμεῖς ποιεῖτε τὰ ἔργα τοῦ  πατρὸς ὑμῶν.
   You   do      the works of the father of you.
 3004    3767 846      1473 1537 4202
εἶπαν [οὖν] αὐτῷ· ἡμεῖς ἐκ πορνείας
They said then to him; we   from sexual immorality
 3756 1080          1520 3962   2280   04 2316
οὐ γεγεννήμεθα· ἕνα πατέρα ἔχομεν τὸν θεόν.
not have been born; one father we have the God.
       3004    846     01 2424  1487 01 2316 3962  1473
42 εἶπεν αὐτοῖς ὁ Ἰησοῦς· εἰ ὁ θεὸς πατὴρ ὑμῶν
   Said  to them the Jesus,  if the God  father of you
 1510 25              302 1473 1473 1063 1537   02 2316
ἦν ἠγαπᾶτε    ἂν ἐμέ, ἐγὼ γὰρ ἐκ  τοῦ θεοῦ
was you were loving - me,  I   for out of the God
 1831     2532 2240    3761    1063 575 1683
ἐξῆλθον καὶ ἥκω·  οὐδὲ γὰρ ἀπ᾽ ἐμαυτοῦ
came out and I come; but not for from myself
 2064      235 1565     1473 649             43 1223
ἐλήλυθα,  ἀλλ᾽ ἐκεῖνός με ἀπέστειλεν.   δια
I have come, but that one me delegated.  Through
 5101 08  2981    08 1699 3756 1097        3754    3756
τί τὴν λαλιὰν τὴν ἐμὴν οὐ γινώσκετε; ὅτι  οὐ
what the speech the mine not you know? Because not
 1410     191     04 3056 04 1699        1473 1537
δύνασθε ἀκούειν τὸν λόγον τὸν ἐμόν. 44 ὑμεῖς ἐκ
you are able to hear the word the mine.   You  from
 02 3962  02 1228           1510 2532 020 1939    02
τοῦ πατρὸς τοῦ διαβόλου ἐστὲ καὶ τὰς ἐπιθυμίας τοῦ
the father the slanderer are  and  the desires of the
 3962  1473  2309        4160     1565     443
πατρὸς ὑμῶν θέλετε ποιεῖν. ἐκεῖνος ἀνθρωποκτόνος
father of you you want to do. That one man killer
 1510 575 746      2532 1722 07  225        3756
ἦν ἀπ᾽ ἀρχῆς καὶ ἐν τῇ ἀληθείᾳ οὐκ
was from beginning and in the truth   not
 2476           3754    3756 1510    225       1722 846
ἔστηκεν,     ὅτι   οὐκ ἔστιν ἀλήθεια ἐν αὐτῷ.
he was standing, because not there is truth  in him.
 3752 2980         012 5579   1537 022    2398
ὅταν λαλῇ      τὸ ψεῦδος, ἐκ τῶν ἰδίων
When he might speak the lie,  out of the own
 2980      3754    5583     1510 2532 01 3962    846
λαλεῖ,   ὅτι   ψεύστης ἐστὶν καὶ ὁ πατὴρ αὐτοῦ.
he speaks, because liar   he is and the father of it.
    1473 1161 3754  08   225      3004 3756 4100
45 ἐγὼ δὲ ὅτι  τὴν ἀλήθειαν λέγω, οὐ πιστεύετέ
   I  but because the truth   say, not you trust
 1473 46  5101 1537   1473 1651    1473 4012 266
μοι.   τίς ἐξ ὑμῶν ἐλέγχει με περὶ ἁμαρτίας;
in me. Who out of you rebukes me about sin?
 1487 225      3004  1223   5101 1473 3756 4100
εἰ ἀλήθειαν λέγω, διὰ  τί ὑμεῖς οὐ πιστεύετέ
If truth    I say, through what you  not trust
 1473 47 01     1510 1537  02 2316 024 4487   02
μοι;  ὁ   ὢν ἐκ  τοῦ θεοῦ τὰ ῥήματα τοῦ
in me. The one being out of the God the words of the
 2316 191    1223   3778 1473 3756 191        3754
θεοῦ ἀκούει· διὰ  τοῦτο ὑμεῖς οὐκ ἀκούετε, ὅτι
God hears; through this you  not hear,    because
 1537 02 2316 3756  εστε. 48 611         013
ἐκ τοῦ θεοῦ οὐκ ἐστέ.  Ἀπεκρίθησαν οἱ
out of the God not you are. Answered  the
```

```
  2453        2532 3004        846      3756 2573   3004
'Ιουδαῖοι καὶ εἶπαν    αὐτῷ·    οὐ  καλῶς λέγομεν
Judeans   and  they said to him; not  well  say
1473  3754 4541        1510 1473 2532 1140        2192
ἡμεῖς ὅτι  Σαμαρίτης εἶ  σὺ  καὶ δαιμόνιον ἔχεις;
we,   (")  Samaritan are you and demon      you have?
```

49
```
    611              2424   1473  1140    3756 2192    235
ἀπεκρίθη 'Ιησοῦς· ἐγὼ δαιμόνιον οὐκ ἔχω,  ἀλλὰ
Answered Jesus;  I    demon      not have,  but
5091     04   3962   1473   2532 1473 818        1473
τιμῶ     τὸν πατέρα μου,  καὶ ὑμεῖς ἀτιμάζετέ με.
I value the father  of me, and you   dishonor   me.
```

50
```
1473 1161 3756 2212  08  1391      1473    1510
ἐγὼ δὲ   οὐ  ζητῶ τὴν δόξαν   μου·   ἔστιν
I   but  not  seek the splendor of me; there is
01  2212        2532 2919       281  281  3004  1473
ὁ   ζητῶν      καὶ κρίνων. 
the one seeking and judging.
```
51
```
                                  ἀμὴν ἀμὴν λέγω ὑμῖν,
                                  Amen amen I say to you,
1437 5100 04  1699 3056   5083          2288    3756 3361
ἐάν τις  τὸν ἐμὸν λόγον τηρήσῃ,      θάνατον οὐ  μὴ
if   some the mine word  might keep, death    not not
2334           1519 04  165            3004 3767  846
θεωρήσῃ        εἰς τὸν αἰῶνα. 
he might watch into the age.
```
52
```
                                  εἶπον [οὖν] αὐτῷ
                                  Said  then  to him
013 2453        3568 1097        3754 1140
οἱ  'Ιουδαῖοι· νῦν ἐγνώκαμεν ὅτι  δαιμόνιον
the Judeans;   now we have known that demon
2192   11   599        2532 013 4396       2532
ἔχεις.    'Αβραὰμ ἀπέθανεν καὶ οἱ  προφῆται, καὶ
you have.  Abraham  died      and the spokesmen, and
1473 3004   1437 5100 04  3056  1473 5083
σὺ  λέγεις· ἐάν τις  τὸν λόγον μου τηρήσῃ,
you say;    if   some the word  of me might keep,
3756 3361 1089       2288    1519 04  165
οὐ  μὴ  γεύσηται   θανάτου εἰς τὸν αἰῶνα.
not not  he will taste death    into the age.
```
53
```
3361 1473 3173    1510 02   3962    1473   11
μὴ   σὺ  μείζων εἶ  τοῦ πατρὸς ἡμῶν 'Αβραάμ,
Not you greater are of the father  of us Abraham,
3748 599        2532 013 4396      599      5101
ὅστις ἀπέθανεν; καὶ οἱ  προφῆται ἀπέθανον. τίνα
who died?      And the spokesmen died.      Whom
4572     4160     611        2424   1437 1473
σεαυτὸν ποιεῖς;  
yourself do you? 
```
54
```
                 ἀπεκρίθη 'Ιησοῦς· ἐὰν ἐγὼ
                 Answered Jesus;  if   I
1392        1683      05  1391     1473 3762
δοξάσω     ἐμαυτόν, ἡ δόξα   μου οὐδέν
give splendor myself, the splendor of me nothing
1510  1510  01 3962   1473  01  1392
ἐστιν· ἔστιν ὁ  πατήρ μου ὁ  δοξάζων
it is; is the father  of me the one giving splendor
1473 3739 1473 3004    3754 2316 1473 1510      2532
με,   ὃν ὑμεῖς λέγετε ὅτι  θεὸς ἡμῶν ἐστιν, 
me,  whom you say,    (")  God of us he is; 
```
55
```
                                              καὶ
                                              and
3756 1097        846         1473 1161 3609a 846    2579
οὐκ ἐγνώκατε   αὐτόν, ἐγὼ δὲ  οἶδα αὐτόν. κἄν
not you have known him,  I  but know  him. And if
3004        3754 3756 3609a 846    1510     3664
εἴπω       ὅτι  οὐκ οἶδα αὐτόν, ἔσομαι ὅμοιος
I might say that not  I know him,  I will be like
1473 5583    235 3609a 846    2532 04  3056
ὑμῖν ψεύστης· ἀλλὰ οἶδα αὐτὸν καὶ τὸν λόγον
to you liar;   but  I know him   and the word
846   5083   11   01 3962   1473   21
αὐτοῦ τηρῶ. 
of him I keep.  
```
56
```
           'Αβραὰμ ὁ πατὴρ ὑμῶν ἠγαλλιάσατο
           Abraham the father of you was glad
2443 3708        08  2250   08  1699  2532 3708
ἵνα ἴδῃ        τὴν ἡμέραν τὴν ἐμήν, καὶ εἶδεν
that he might see the day    the mine, and he saw
```

"Are we not right in saying that you are a Samaritan and have a demon?" [49]Jesus answered, "I do not have a demon; but I honor my Father, and you dishonor me. [50]Yet I do not seek my own glory; there is one who seeks it and he is the judge. [51]Very truly, I tell you, whoever keeps my word will never see death." [52]The Jews said to him, "Now we know that you have a demon. Abraham died, and so did the prophets; yet you say, 'Whoever keeps my word will never taste death.' [53]Are you greater than our father Abraham, who died? The prophets also died. Who do you claim to be?" [54]Jesus answered, "If I glorify myself, my glory is nothing. It is my Father who glorifies me, he of whom you say, 'He is our God,' [55]though you do not know him. But I know him; if I would say that I do not know him, I would be a liar like you. But I do know him and I keep his word. [56]Your ancestor Abraham rejoiced that he would see my day; he saw it and was glad."

57Then the Jews said to him, "You are not yet fifty years old, and have you seen Abraham?"a 58Jesus said to them, "Very truly, I tell you, before Abraham was, I am." 59So they picked up stones to throw at him, but Jesus hid himself and went out of the temple.

CHAPTER 9

As he walked along, he saw a man blind from birth. 2His disciples asked him, "Rabbi, who sinned, this man or his parents, that he was born blind?" 3Jesus answered, "Neither this man nor his parents sinned; he was born blind so that God's works might be revealed in him. 4Web must work the works of him who sent mec while it is day; night is coming when no one can work. 5As long as I am in the world, I am the light of the world." 6When he had said this, he spat on the ground and made mud with the saliva and spread the mud on the man's eyes, 7saying to him, "Go, wash in the pool of Siloam" (which means Sent). Then he went and washed and came back able to see. 8The neighbors

a Other ancient authorities read has Abraham seen you?
b Other ancient authorities read I
c Other ancient authorities read us

2532	5463	57	3004	3767	013	2453	4314	846
καὶ	ἐχάρη.		εἶπον	οὖν	οἱ	Ἰουδαῖοι	πρὸς	αὐτόν·
and	rejoiced.	Said	then	the		Judeans	toward	him;

4004	2094	3768	2192	2532	11
πεντήκοντα	ἔτη	οὔπω	ἔχεις	καὶ	Ἀβραὰμ
fifty	years	not yet	you have	and	Abraham

3708	3004	846	2424	281	281	3004
ἑώρακας;	58 εἶπεν	αὐτοῖς	Ἰησοῦς·	ἀμὴν	ἀμὴν	λέγω
you have seen?	Said	to them	Jesus;	amen	amen	I say

1473	4250	11	1096	1473	1510
ὑμῖν,	πρὶν	Ἀβραὰμ	γενέσθαι	ἐγὼ	εἰμί.
to you,	before	Abraham	to become	I	am.

59	142		3767	3037	2443	906
	ἦραν		οὖν	λίθους	ἵνα	βάλωσιν
	They lifted up	then		stones	that	they might throw

1909	846	2424	1161	2928	2532	1831
ἐπ᾽	αὐτόν.	Ἰησοῦς	δὲ	ἐκρύβη	καὶ	ἐξῆλθεν
on	him.	Jesus	but	was hidden	and	he went out

1537	010	2411	9:1	2532	3855	3708	444
ἐκ	τοῦ	ἱεροῦ.	Καὶ	παράγων		εἶδεν	ἄνθρωπον
from	the	temple.	And	leading along		he saw	man

5185	1537	1079	2	2532	2065	846	013
τυφλὸν	ἐκ	γενετῆς.		καὶ	ἠρώτησαν	αὐτὸν	οἱ
blind	out of	birth.	And	asked		him	the

3101	846	3004	4461	5101	264
μαθηταὶ	αὐτοῦ	λέγοντες·	ῥαββί,	τίς	ἥμαρτεν,
learners	of him	saying;	Rabbi,	who	sinned,

3778	2228	013	1118	846	2443	5185
οὗτος	ἢ	οἱ	γονεῖς	αὐτοῦ,	ἵνα	τυφλὸς
this one	or	the	parents	of him,	that	blind

1080	3	611	2424	3777	3778
γεννηθῇ;		ἀπεκρίθη	Ἰησοῦς·	οὔτε	οὗτος
he might be born?	Answered	Jesus;	neither	this one

264	3777	013	1118	846	235	2443	5319
ἥμαρτεν	οὔτε	οἱ	γονεῖς	αὐτοῦ,	ἀλλ᾽	ἵνα	φανερωθῇ
sinned	nor	the	parents	of him,	but	that	might be demonstrated

021	2041	02	2316	1722	846	4	1473	1163
τὰ	ἔργα	τοῦ	θεοῦ	ἐν	αὐτῷ.		ἡμᾶς	δεῖ
the	works	of the	God	in	him.	Us	it is necessary

2038	024	2041	02	3992	1473	2193
ἐργάζεσθαι	τὰ	ἔργα	τοῦ	πέμψαντός	με	ἕως
to work	the	works	of the	one having sent	me	until

2250	1510	2064	3571	3753	3762	1410
ἡμέρα	ἐστίν·	ἔρχεται	νὺξ	ὅτε	οὐδεὶς	δύναται
day	it is;	comes	night	when	no one	is able to

2038	5	3752	1722	03	2889	1510	5457
ἐργάζεσθαι.		ὅταν	ἐν	τῷ	κόσμῳ	ὦ,	φῶς
to work.	When	in	the	world	I might be,	light

1510	02	2889	6	3778	3004	4429
εἰμι	τοῦ	κόσμου.		ταῦτα	εἰπὼν	ἔπτυσεν
I am	of the	world.	These	having said	he spit

5476	2532	4160	4081	1537	010	4427	2532
χαμαὶ	καὶ	ἐποίησεν	πηλὸν	ἐκ	τοῦ	πτύσματος	καὶ
on ground	and	he made	clay	out of	the	spit	and

2025	846	04	4081	1909	016	3788
ἐπέχρισεν	αὐτοῦ	τὸν	πηλὸν	ἐπὶ	τοὺς	ὀφθαλμοὺς
he anointed	on him	the	clay	on	the	eyes

7	2532	3004	846	5217	3538	1519	08
	καὶ	εἶπεν	αὐτῷ·	ὕπαγε	νίψαι	εἰς	τὴν
	And	he said	to him;	go off	wash	into	the

2861	02	4611	3739	2059
κολυμβήθραν	τοῦ	Σιλωάμ	(ὃ	ἑρμηνεύεται
pool		of the Siloam	which	is being interpreted

649	565	3767	2532
ἀπεσταλμένος).	ἀπῆλθεν	οὖν	καὶ
one having been delegated.	He went off	then	and

3538	2532	2064	991	8	013	3767	1069
ἐνίψατο	καὶ	ἦλθεν	βλέπων.		Οἱ	οὖν	γείτονες
he washed	and	he came	seeing.	The	then	neighbors

2532 013   2334   846   012 4387   3754
καὶ οἱ   θεωροῦντες αὐτὸν τὸ πρότερον ὅτι
and the ones watching   him   the former   that

4319a   1510   3004   3756 3778   1510   01
προσαίτης ἦν   ἔλεγον·   οὐχ οὗτός   ἐστιν ὁ
beggar   he was they said; not this one   is   the

2521   2532 4319   9 243   3004   3754
καθήμενος καὶ προσαιτῶν;   ἄλλοι ἔλεγον   ὅτι
one sitting and begging?   Others were saying, (")

3778   1510   243   3004   3780 235 3664
οὗτός ἐστιν, ἄλλοι ἔλεγον·   οὐχί, ἀλλὰ ὅμοιος
this one is,   others were saying, not,   but   like

846   1510   1565   3004   3754 1473 1510
αὐτῷ ἐστιν. ἐκεῖνος ἔλεγεν   ὅτι ἐγώ εἰμι.
to him he is. That one was saying, (")   I   am.

10 3004   3767 846   4459 3767   455
ἔλεγον   οὖν αὐτῷ· πῶς [οὖν] ἠνεῴχθησάν
They were saying then to him; how then   were opened

1473   013 3788   11 611   1565   01 444
σου   οἱ ὀφθαλμοί;   ἀπεκρίθη ἐκεῖνος· ὁ ἄνθρωπος
of you the eyes?   Answered that one; the man

01 3004   2424 4081 4160   2532
ὁ λεγόμενος   Ἰησοῦς πηλὸν ἐποίησεν καὶ
the one being called Jesus clay   made   and

2025   1473   016 3788   2532 3004   1473
ἐπέχρισέν   μου   τοὺς ὀφθαλμοὺς καὶ εἶπέν μοι
he anointed on of me the eyes   and he said to me,

3754 5217   1519 04   4611   2532 3538   565
ὅτι ὕπαγε εἰς τὸν Σιλωὰμ καὶ νίψαι· ἀπελθὼν
(")   go off into the Siloam and wash; having gone off

3767 2532 2532   308   12 2532 3004
οὖν καὶ νιψάμενος ἀνέβλεψα.   καὶ εἶπαν
then and having washed I saw again. And they said

846   4226   1510   1565   3004   3756 3609a
αὐτῷ· ποῦ ἐστιν ἐκεῖνος; λέγει·   οὐκ οἶδα.
to him; where is   that one? He says; not I know.

13 „71   846   4314   016 5330   04 4218
Ἄγουσιν   αὐτὸν πρὸς τοὺς Φαρισαίους τόν ποτε
They bring him   toward the Pharisees the once

5185   1510   1161 4521   1722 3739 2250 04
τυφλόν. 14 ἦν δὲ   σάββατον ἐν ᾗ ἡμέρᾳ τὸν
blind.   It was but sabbath in which day   the

4081 4160   01 2424 2532 455   846   016
πηλὸν ἐποίησεν ὁ Ἰησοῦς καὶ ἀνέῳξεν αὐτοῦ τοὺς
clay made   the Jesus and opened of him the

3788   3825 3767 2065   846 2532 013
ὀφθαλμούς. 15 πάλιν οὖν ἠρώτων αὐτὸν καὶ οἱ
eyes.   Again then were asking him   and the

5330   4459 308   01   1161 3004
Φαρισαῖοι πῶς ἀνέβλεψεν. ὁ   δὲ εἶπεν
Pharisees how he saw again. The one but said

846   4081 2007   1473 1909 016   3788
αὐτοῖς· πηλὸν ἐπέθηκέν μου ἐπὶ τοὺς ὀφθαλμοὺς
to them; clay he set on of me on the eyes

2532 3538   2532 991   16 3004   3767
καὶ ἐνιψάμην καὶ βλέπω. ἔλεγον   οὖν
and I washed myself and I see.   Were saying then

1537   014 5330   5100   3756 1510 3778   3844
ἐκ   τῶν Φαρισαίων τινές· οὐκ ἔστιν οὗτος παρὰ
out of the Pharisees some; not is   this one from

2316 01   444   3754   012 4521   3756 5083
θεοῦ ὁ ἄνθρωπος, ὅτι   τὸ σάββατον οὐ τηρεῖ.
God the man,   because the sabbath not he keeps.

243   1161 3004   4459 1410   444   268
ἄλλοι [δὲ] ἔλεγον·   πῶς δύναται ἄνθρωπος ἁμαρτωλὸς
Others but were saying; how is able man   sinner

5108   5922   4160   2532 4978   1510 1722 846
τοιαῦτα σημεῖα ποιεῖν; καὶ σχίσμα ἦν ἐν αὐτοῖς.
such   signs to do? And split was in them.

and those who had seen him before as a beggar began to ask, "Is this not the man who used to sit and beg?" [9]Some were saying, "It is he." Others were saying, "No, but it is someone like him." He kept saying, "I am the man." [10]But they kept asking him, "Then how were your eyes opened?" [11]He answered, "The man called Jesus made mud, spread it on my eyes, and said to me, 'Go to Siloam and wash.' Then I went and washed and received my sight." [12]They said to him, "Where is he?" He said, "I do not know."

[13]They brought to the Pharisees the man who had formerly been blind. [14]Now it was a sabbath day when Jesus made the mud and opened his eyes. [15]Then the Pharisees also began to ask him how he had received his sight. He said to them, "He put mud on my eyes. Then I washed, and now I see." [16]Some of the Pharisees said, "This man is not from God, for he does not observe the sabbath." But others said, "How can a man who is a sinner perform such signs?" And they were divided.

17So they said again to the blind man, "What do you say about him? It was your eyes he opened." He said, "He is a prophet."

18 The Jews did not believe that he had been blind and had received his sight until they called the parents of the man who had received his sight 19and asked them, "Is this your son, who you say was born blind? How then does he now see?" 20His parents answered, "We know that this is our son, and that he was born blind; 21but we do not know how it is that now he sees, nor do we know who opened his eyes. Ask him; he is of age. He will speak for himself."

22His parents said this because they were afraid of the Jews; for the Jews had already agreed that anyone who confessed Jesus[a] to be the Messiah[b] would be put out of the synagogue. 23Therefore his parents said, "He is of age; ask him."

24 So for the second time they called the man who had been blind, and they said to him, "Give glory to God! We know that this man is a sinner." 25He answered,

[a] Gk him
[b] Or the Christ

17
3004   3767 03   5185 3825 5101 1473 3004
λέγουσιν οὖν τῷ   τυφλῷ πάλιν· τί σὺ λέγεις
They say then to the blind again, what you say

4012 846   3754 455   1473 016 3788
περὶ αὐτοῦ, ὅτι ἠνεῳξέν σου τοὺς ὀφθαλμούς;
about him,   because he opened of you the   eyes?

01   1161 3004 3754 4396   1510   **18** 3756
ὁ   δὲ εἶπεν ὅτι προφήτης ἐστίν.   Οὐκ
The one but said, (") spokesman he is.   Not

4100   3767 013 2453   4012   846   3754
ἐπίστευσαν οὖν οἱ Ἰουδαῖοι περὶ   αὐτοῦ ὅτι
trusted   then the Judeans concerning him because

1510 5185 2532 308   2193   ὅτου 5455
ἦν   τυφλὸς καὶ ἀνέβλεψεν ἕως   ὅτου ἐφώνησαν
he was blind and he saw again until when they sounded

016 1118   846   02   308   **19** 2532
τοὺς γονεῖς αὐτοῦ τοῦ ἀναβλέψαντος   καὶ
the parents of him of the one having seen again and

2065   846   3004   3778 1510 01 5207
ἠρώτησαν αὐτοὺς λέγοντες· οὗτός ἐστιν ὁ υἱὸς
they asked them   saying; this is   the son

1473 3739 1473 3004   3754 5185 1080
ὑμῶν, ὃν ὑμεῖς λέγετε ὅτι τυφλὸς ἐγεννήθη;
of you, whom you say   that blind he was born?

4459 3767 991   737   **20** 611   3767 013
πῶς οὖν βλέπει ἄρτι;   ἀπεκρίθησαν οὖν οἱ
How then he sees now?   Answered   then the

1118   846 2532 3004 3609a 3754 3778   1510
γονεῖς αὐτοῦ καὶ εἶπαν· οἴδαμεν ὅτι οὗτός ἐστιν
parents of him and said, we know that this one is

01 5207 1473 2532 3754 5185   1080   4459 1161
ὁ υἱὸς ἡμῶν καὶ ὅτι τυφλὸς ἐγεννήθη· **21** πῶς δὲ
the son of us and that blind he was born; how but

3568 991   3756 3609a   2228 5101 455   846
νῦν βλέπει οὐκ οἴδαμεν, ἢ τίς ἤνοιξεν αὐτοῦ
now he sees not we know, or who opened of him

016 3788   1473 3756 3609a   846   2065
τοὺς ὀφθαλμοὺς ἡμεῖς οὐκ οἴδαμεν· αὐτὸν ἐρωτήσατε,
the eyes   we   not know; him   ask,

2244   2192 846   4012   1438   2980
ἡλικίαν ἔχει, αὐτὸς περὶ   ἑαυτοῦ λαλήσει.
stature he has, himself concerning himself will speak.

22 3778 3004 013 1118   846   3754
ταῦτα εἶπαν οἱ γονεῖς αὐτοῦ ὅτι
These said the parents of him because

5399   016   2453   2235 1063
ἐφοβοῦντο   τοὺς Ἰουδαίους· ἤδη γὰρ
they were fearing the Judeans; already for

4934   013 2453   2443 1437 5100 846
συνετέθειντο   οἱ Ἰουδαῖοι ἵνα ἐάν τις αὐτὸν
had placed together the Judeans that if some him

3670   5547   656   1096
ὁμολογήσῃ χριστόν, ἀποσυνάγωγος γένηται.
might confess Christ, from synagogue he might become.

23 1223   3778 013 1118   846   3004 3754 2244
διὰ   τοῦτο οἱ γονεῖς αὐτοῦ εἶπαν ὅτι ἡλικίαν
Through this the parents of him said, (") stature

2192   846 1905   5455   3767 04
ἔχει,   αὐτὸν ἐπερωτήσατε. **24** Ἐφώνησαν οὖν τὸν
he has, him ask on.   They sounded then the

444   1537 1208   3739 1510 5185 2532 3004
ἄνθρωπον ἐκ δευτέρου ὃς ἦν τυφλὸς καὶ εἶπαν
man   out of second who was blind and they said

846   1325 1391   03   2316 1473 3609a   3754
αὐτῷ· δὸς δόξαν τῷ   θεῷ· ἡμεῖς οἴδαμεν ὅτι
to him; give splendor to the God; we   know   that

3778 01 444   268   1510   **25** 611   3767
οὗτος ὁ ἄνθρωπος ἁμαρτωλός ἐστιν.   ἀπεκρίθη οὖν
this the man   sinner   is.   Answered then

```
1565          1487  268        1510    3756 3609a      1520 3609a
ἐκεῖνος·  εἰ  ἁμαρτωλός ἐστιν οὐκ  οἶδα·   ἓν   οἶδα
that one; if    sinner     he is not  I know; one I know
3754 5185     1510    737   991           3004         3767 846
ὅτι  τυφλὸς ὢν   ἄρτι βλέπω.  26 εἶπον   οὖν  αὐτῷ,
that blind  being now  I see.     They said then to him,
5101 4160           1473       4459 455          1473    016
τί   ἐποίησέν σοι;    πῶς  ἤνοιξέν σου    τοὺς
what did he do to you?  How  he opened of you the
3788              611         846        3004  1473    2235
ὀφθαλμούς; 27 ἀπεκρίθη  αὐτοῖς·  εἶπον ὑμῖν  ἤδη
eyes?         He answered to them; I told to you already
2532 3756 191           5101 3825 2309      191
καὶ  οὐκ ἠκούσατε·  τί  πάλιν θέλετε  ἀκούειν;
and  not  you heard;  why  again you want to hear?
3361 2532 1473  2309    846      3101        1096
μὴ  καὶ  ὑμεῖς θέλετε αὐτοῦ μαθηταὶ  γενέσθαι;
Not  also you   want   of him learners to become?
   2532 3058       846     2532 3004          1473 3101
28 καὶ  ἐλοιδόρησαν αὐτὸν καὶ  εἶπον·   σὺ  μαθητὴς
   And  they abused him   and  they said; you  learner
1510 1565       1473   1161 02     3475    1510
εἶ  ἐκείνου,  ἡμεῖς δὲ  τοῦ  Μωϋσέως ἐσμὲν
are  of that one, we   but  of the Moses  are
3101        1473    3609a    3754 3475     2980       01
μαθηταί· 29 ἡμεῖς οἴδαμεν ὅτι  Μωϋσεῖ  λελάληκεν ὁ
learners.    We   know    that to Moses has spoken the
2316   3778      1161 3756 3609a     4159      1510
θεός, τοῦτον  δὲ  οὐκ οἴδαμεν πόθεν   ἐστίν.
God,  this one but  not  we know from where he is.
   611         01  444       2532 3004     846        1722
30 ἀπεκρίθη ὁ  ἄνθρωπος καὶ  εἶπεν  αὐτοῖς·  ἐν
   Answered the  man      and  he said to them;  in
3778  1063 09  2298        1510     3754 1473 3756 3609a
τούτῳ γὰρ τὸ  θαυμαστόν ἐστιν, ὅτι  ὑμεῖς οὐκ οἴδατε
this  for  the  marvelous it is, that you   not know
4159       1510    2532 455       1473  016  3788
πόθεν   ἐστίν, καὶ  ἤνοιξέν μου  τοὺς ὀφθαλμούς.
from where he is, and  he opened of me the  eyes.
   3609a     3754 268     01  2316 3756 191      235
31 οἴδαμεν ὅτι ἁμαρτωλῶν ὁ  θεὸς οὐκ ἀκούει, ἀλλ᾽
   We know that sinners   the God not  hears,  but
1437 5100 2318        1510      2532 012 2307   846
ἐάν  τις θεοσεβὴς    ᾖ    καὶ τὸ θέλημα αὐτοῦ
if   some God worshiper might be and the want   of him
4160        3778     191      1537  02  165      3756
ποιῇ      τούτου ἀκούει. 32 ἐκ   τοῦ αἰῶνος οὐκ
he might do this one he hears.  Out of the age   not
191          3754 455      5100 3788        5185
ἠκούσθη     ὅτι  ἠνέῳξέν τις ὀφθαλμοὺς τυφλοῦ
it was heard that opened some eyes      of blind one
1080           1487 3361 1510 3778       3844 2316
γεγεννημένου· 33 εἰ  μὴ  ἦν  οὗτος    παρὰ θεοῦ,
having been born; except  was this one from God,
3756 1410        4160     3762         611            2532
οὐκ ἠδύνατο  ποιεῖν οὐδέν. 34 ἀπεκρίθησαν  καὶ
not  he was able to do  nothing.   They answered and
3004  846     1722 266      1473 1080        2532
εἶπαν αὐτῷ·  ἐν  ἁμαρτίαις σὺ  ἐγεννήθης ὅλος  καὶ
said to him; in sin        you  were born whole, and
1473 1321       1473 2532 1544        846      1854
σὺ  διδάσκεις ἡμᾶς; καὶ  ἐξέβαλον  αὐτὸν ἔξω.
you teach      us?   And they threw out him  outside.
   191       2424  3754 1544         846      1854
35 Ἤκουσεν Ἰησοῦς ὅτι  ἐξέβαλον  αὐτὸν ἔξω,
   Heard    Jesus that they threw out him   outside,
2532 2147      846   3004     1473 4100       1519 04
καὶ  εὑρὼν  αὐτὸν εἶπεν·  σὺ  πιστεύεις εἰς τὸν
and  finding him  he said;  you  trust     in  the
```

"I do not know whether he is a sinner. One thing I do know, that though I was blind, now I see." [26] They said to him, "What did he do to you? How did he open your eyes?" [27] He answered them, "I have told you already, and you would not listen. Why do you want to hear it again? Do you also want to become his disciples?" [28] Then they reviled him, saying, "You are his disciple, but we are disciples of Moses. [29] We know that God has spoken to Moses, but as for this man, we do not know where he comes from." [30] The man answered, "Here is an astonishing thing! You do not know where he comes from, and yet he opened my eyes. [31] We know that God does not listen to sinners, but he does listen to one who worships him and obeys his will. [32] Never since the world began has it been heard that anyone opened the eyes of a person born blind. [33] If this man were not from God, he could do nothing." [34] They answered him, "You were born entirely in sins, and are you trying to teach us?" And they drove him out.

[35] Jesus heard that they had driven him out, and when he found him, he said, "Do you believe in the

Son of Man?"*a* 36He answered, "And who is he, sir?*b* Tell me, so that I may believe in him." 37Jesus said to him, "You have seen him, and the one speaking with you is he." 38He said, "Lord,*b* I believe." And he worshiped him. 39Jesus said, "I came into this world for judgment so that those who do not see may see, and those who do see may become blind." 40Some of the Pharisees near him heard this and said to him, "Surely we are not blind, are we?" 41Jesus said to them, "If you were blind, you would not have sin. But now that you say, 'We see,' your sin remains.

CHAPTER 10

"Very truly, I tell you, anyone who does not enter the sheepfold by the gate but climbs in by another way is a thief and a bandit. 2The one who enters by the gate is the shepherd of the sheep. 3The gatekeeper opens the gate for him, and the sheep hear his voice. He calls his own sheep by name and leads them out. 4When he has brought out all his own, he goes ahead of them, and the sheep follow him because they know his voice.

a Other ancient authorities read the Son of God
b Sir and Lord translate the same Greek word

5207 02   444   611   1565   2532 3004
υἱὸν τοῦ ἀνθρώπου; 36 ἀπεκρίθη ἐκεῖνος καὶ εἶπεν,
son of the man?   Answered that one and said,

2532 5101 1510   2962   2443 4100   1519 846
καὶ τίς ἐστιν, κύριε, ἵνα πιστεύσω εἰς αὐτόν;
and who is he, Master, that I might trust in him?

   3004 846   01 2424   2532 3708   846
37 εἶπεν αὐτῷ ὁ Ἰησοῦς· καὶ ἑώρακας αὐτὸν
   Said to him the Jesus; and you have seen him

2532 01 2980   3326 1473 1565   1510   38 01
καὶ ὁ λαλῶν   μετὰ σοῦ ἐκεῖνός ἐστιν.   ὁ
and the one speaking with you that one is. The one

1161 5346 4100   2962   2532 4352   846
δὲ ἔφη· πιστεύω, κύριε· καὶ προσεκύνησεν αὐτῷ.
but said; I trust, Master; and he worshiped him.

   2532 3004 01 2424   1519 2917   1473 1519 04
39 Καὶ εἶπεν ὁ Ἰησοῦς· εἰς κρίμα ἐγὼ εἰς τὸν
   And said the Jesus; into judgment I into the

2889   3778   2064 2443 013 3361 991
κόσμον τοῦτον ἦλθον, ἵνα οἱ μὴ βλέποντες
world this came, that the not ones seeing

991   2532 013 991   5185   1096
βλέπωσιν καὶ οἱ βλέποντες τυφλοὶ γένωνται.
might see and the ones seeing blind they might become.

   191   1537 014 5330   3778 013   3326
40 ἤκουσαν ἐκ τῶν Φαρισαίων ταῦτα οἱ   μετ᾽
   Heard from the Pharisees these the ones with

846   1510 2532 3004   846   3361 2532 1473
αὐτοῦ ὄντες καὶ εἶπον αὐτῷ· μὴ καὶ ἡμεῖς
him being and they said to him; not also we

5185 1510   01 3004 846 01 2424   1487 5185
τυφλοί ἐσμεν; 41 εἶπεν αὐτοῖς ὁ Ἰησοῦς· εἰ τυφλοὶ
blind are?   Said to them the Jesus; if blind

1510   3756 302 2192   266   3568 1161
ἦτε, οὐκ ἂν εἴχετε ἁμαρτίαν· νῦν δὲ
you were, not - you were having sin; now but

3004   3754 991   05 266   1473 3306
λέγετε ὅτι βλέπομεν, ἡ ἁμαρτία ὑμῶν μένει.
you say, (") we see, the sin of you stays.

    281   281 3004 1473   01 3361 1525
10:1 Ἀμὴν ἀμὴν λέγω ὑμῖν, ὁ μὴ εἰσερχόμενος
     Amen amen I say to you, the not one coming in

1223   06 2374 1519 08 833   022   4263
διὰ   τῆς θύρας εἰς τὴν αὐλὴν τῶν προβάτων
through the door into the courtyard of the sheep

235   305   237   1565   2812   1510
ἀλλὰ ἀναβαίνων ἀλλαχόθεν ἐκεῖνος κλέπτης ἐστὶν
but one going up from another that one thief is

2532 3027   2 01   1161 1525   1223   06
καὶ λῃστής·   ὁ   δὲ εἰσερχόμενος διὰ τῆς
and robber; the one but coming into through the

2374 4166   1510 022   4263   3 3778   01
θύρας ποιμήν ἐστιν τῶν προβάτων. τούτῳ ὁ
door shepherd is of the sheep. To this one the

2377   455   2532 021 4263   06 5456 846
θυρωρὸς ἀνοίγει καὶ τὰ πρόβατα τῆς φωνῆς αὐτοῦ
doorkeeper opens and the sheep the sound of him

191   2532 024 2398 4263   5455 2596 3686 2532
ἀκούει καὶ τὰ ἴδια πρόβατα φωνεῖ κατ᾽ ὄνομα καὶ
hear and the own sheep sounds by name and

1806   846   4 3752 024 2398 3956 1544
ἐξάγει αὐτά.   ὅταν τὰ ἴδια πάντα ἐκβάλῃ,
he leads out them. When the own all he might throw out,

1715   846   4198   2532 021 4263   846
ἔμπροσθεν αὐτῶν πορεύεται καὶ τὰ πρόβατα αὐτῷ
in front of them he travels and the sheep him

190   3754   3609a   08 5456 846
ἀκολουθεῖ, ὅτι οἴδασιν τὴν φωνὴν αὐτοῦ·
follow, because they know the sound of him;

```
     245          1161 3756 3361  190                          235
5  ἀλλοτρίῳ   δὲ   οὐ   μὴ   ἀκολουθήσουσιν,   ἀλλὰ
   to other    but  not  not  they will follow,   but
5343              575      846      3754         3756 3609a    014
φεύξονται       ἀπ᾽    αὐτοῦ, ὅτι        οὐκ  οἴδασιν   τῶν
they will flee  from   him,   because  not  they know  the
245           08    5456    6  3778    08    3942        3004
ἀλλοτρίων    τὴν  φωνήν.    Ταύτην  τὴν  παροιμίαν  εἶπεν
of others     the  sound.    This     the  proverb      said
846    01    2424     1565    1161 3756 1097         5101
αὐτοῖς ὁ  Ἰησοῦς,  ἐκεῖνοι δὲ   οὐκ  ἔγνωσαν   τίνα
to them the  Jesus;  those    but  not  they knew    what
1510  3739 2980         846        7  3004 3767 3825
ἦν    ἃ   ἐλάλει       αὐτοῖς.     Εἶπεν οὖν πάλιν
it was that he was speaking to them.     Said    then  again
01   2424    281   281   3004   1473  3754 1473 1510 05
ὁ  Ἰησοῦς·  ἀμὴν  ἀμὴν  λέγω   ὑμῖν  ὅτι  ἐγώ  εἰμι ἡ
the  Jesus;   amen   amen  I say  to you that  I     am    the
2374 022       4263         8  3956  3745      2064       4253
θύρα τῶν    προβάτων.    πάντες ὅσοι    ἦλθον [πρὸ
door of the sheep.         All    as many as came    before
1473 2812     1510  2532 3027     235   3756 191
ἐμοῦ] κλέπται εἰσὶν καὶ ληισταί,  ἀλλ᾽ οὐκ ἤκουσαν
me]    thieves  are   and  robbers;  but   not  heard
846    021  4263      9  1473 1510 05   2374   1223
αὐτῶν τὰ  πρόβατα.    ἐγώ  εἰμι ἡ  θύρα· δι᾽
them    the sheep.        I     am   the door;  through
1473 1437 5100 1525           4982              2532
ἐμοῦ ἐάν  τις  εἰσέλθῃ     σωθήσεται          καὶ
me    if   some might go into he will be delivered and
1525          2532 1831              2532 3542
εἰσελεύσεται καὶ  ἐξελεύσεται     καὶ  νομὴν
he will go into and   he will go out     and  grazing
2147          10  01   2812      3756 2064   1487 3361 2443
εὑρήσει.       ὁ  κλέπτης οὐκ  ἔρχεται εἰ  μὴ  ἵνα
he will find.     The thief   not  comes    except   that
2813      2532 2380     2532 622         1473 2064 2443
κλέψῃ    καὶ  θύσῃ    καὶ  ἀπολέσῃ· ἐγώ  ἦλθον ἵνα
he might   and  he might  and  he might   I     came  that
thieve        sacrifice       destroy;
2222 2192      2532 4053       2192            11  1473
ζωὴν ἔχωσιν  καὶ περισσὸν ἔχωσιν.        Ἐγώ
life they might have and excess    they might have.  I
1510 01   4166     01   2570    01   4166     01   2570
εἰμι ὁ  ποιμὴν ὁ  καλός. ὁ  ποιμὴν ὁ  καλὸς
am    the shepherd the good;  the shepherd the good
08   5590   846      5087   5228     022    4263
τὴν ψυχὴν αὐτοῦ τίθησιν ὑπὲρ  τῶν   προβάτων·
the  soul    of him  places  on behalf of the sheep;
12 01  3411      2532 3756 1510 4166      3739
   ὁ  μισθωτὸς καὶ  οὐκ ὢν  ποιμήν,  οὗ
   the wage earner and   not being shepherd, of whom
3756 1510 021 4263     2398 2334        04  3074
οὐκ  ἔστιν τὰ  πρόβατα ἴδια, θεωρεῖ  τὸν λύκον
not   is    the  sheep    own,  he watches the wolf
2064       2532 863        024 4263      2532 5343
ἐρχόμενον καὶ  ἀφίησιν  τὰ  πρόβατα καὶ  φεύγει –
coming      and  he leaves off the sheep   and  he flees
2532 01  3074   726    846  2532 4650     13 3754
καὶ ὁ  λύκος ἁρπάζει αὐτὰ καὶ σκορπίζει –  ὅτι
and  the wolf  seizes    them and he scatters    because
3411        1510 2532 3756 3190a     846     4012
μισθωτός  ἐστιν καὶ οὐ  μέλει    αὐτῷ  περὶ
wage earner is    and not  it is care to him  about
022   4263    14 1473 1510 01   4166    01   2570 2532
τῶν προβάτων.    Ἐγώ εἰμι ὁ  ποιμὴν ὁ  καλὸς καὶ
the sheep.          I   am   the shepherd the good  and
1097      024 1699 2532 1097       1473 021 1699
γινώσκω τὰ  ἐμὰ καὶ  γινώσκουσί με  τὰ  ἐμά,
I know    the mine  and know        me   the mine,
```

⁵They will not follow a stranger, but they will run from him because they do not know the voice of strangers." ⁶Jesus used this figure of speech with them, but they did not understand what he was saying to them.

7 So again Jesus said to them, "Very truly, I tell you, I am the gate for the sheep. ⁸All who came before me are thieves and bandits; but the sheep did not listen to them. ⁹I am the gate. Whoever enters by me will be saved, and will come in and go out and find pasture. ¹⁰The thief comes only to steal and kill and destroy. I came that they may have life, and have it abundantly.

11 "I am the good shepherd. The good shepherd lays down his life for the sheep. ¹²The hired hand, who is not the shepherd and does not own the sheep, sees the wolf coming and leaves the sheep and runs away—and the wolf snatches them and scatters them. ¹³The hired hand runs away because a hired hand does not care for the sheep. ¹⁴I am the good shepherd. I know my own and my own know me,

¹⁵just as the Father knows me and I know the Father. And I lay down my life for the sheep. ¹⁶I have other sheep that do not belong to this fold. I must bring them also, and they will listen to my voice. So there will be one flock, one shepherd. ¹⁷For this reason the Father loves me, because I lay down my life in order to take it up again. ¹⁸No one takes[a] it from me, but I lay it down of my own accord. I have power to lay it down, and I have power to take it up again. I have received this command from my Father."

19 Again the Jews were divided because of these words. ²⁰Many of them were saying, "He has a demon and is out of his mind. Why listen to him?" ²¹Others were saying, "These are not the words of one who has a demon. Can a demon open the eyes of the blind?"

22 At that time the festival of the Dedication took place in Jerusalem. It was winter, ²³and Jesus was walking in the temple, in the portico of Solomon. ²⁴So the Jews gathered around him and said to him, "How long will you keep us in suspense? If you are the Messiah,[b]

---

[a] Other ancient authorities read *has taken*

[b] Or *the Christ*

2531		1097		1473	01	3962	2504	1097	04

15 καθὼς γινώσκει με ὁ πατὴρ κἀγὼ γινώσκω τὸν
just as knows me the father and I know the

3962　2532 08　5590　1473　5087　5228　　022
πατέρα, καὶ τὴν ψυχήν μου τίθημι ὑπὲρ τῶν
father, and the soul of me I place on behalf of the

4263　　　2532 243　　4263　　2192　3739 3756 1510
προβάτων. **16** καὶ ἄλλα πρόβατα ἔχω ἃ οὐκ ἔστιν
sheep. And other sheep I have that not are

1537 06　833　　3778　2548　1163　　　1473
ἐκ τῆς αὐλῆς ταύτης· κἀκεῖνα δεῖ με
from the courtyard this; and those it is necessary me

71　　2532 06　5456　1473　191　　　　2532
ἀγαγεῖν καὶ τῆς φωνῆς μου ἀκούσουσιν, καὶ
to lead and the sound of me they will hear, and

1096　　　　1520 4167　　1520 4166　　17 1223
γενήσονται μιά ποίμνη, εἷς ποιμήν. **17** Διὰ
they will become one flock, one shepherd. Through

3778　1473 01　3962　25　　3754　　1473 5087　08
τοῦτό με ὁ πατὴρ ἀγαπᾷ ὅτι ἐγὼ τίθημι τὴν
this me the father loves because I place the

5590　1473　2443 3825 2983　　846　　18 3762
ψυχήν μου, ἵνα πάλιν λάβω αὐτήν. **18** οὐδεὶς
soul of me, that again I might take it. No one

142　　846　575　1473　235　1473 5087　846　575
αἴρει αὐτὴν ἀπ' ἐμοῦ, ἀλλ' ἐγὼ τίθημι αὐτὴν ἀπ'
lifts up it from me, but I place it from

1683　1849　2192　5087　846　2532
ἐμαυτοῦ. ἐξουσίαν ἔχω θεῖναι αὐτήν, καὶ
myself. Authority I have to place it, and

1849　2192　3825 2983　846　3778　08
ἐξουσίαν ἔχω πάλιν λαβεῖν αὐτήν· ταύτην τὴν
authority I have again to take it; this the

1785　2983　3844 02　3962　1473　19　4978
ἐντολὴν ἔλαβον παρὰ τοῦ πατρός μου. **19** Σχίσμα
command I received from the father of me. Split

3825　1096　1722 015　2453　1223　016　3056
πάλιν ἐγένετο ἐν τοῖς Ἰουδαίοις διὰ τοὺς λόγους
again became in the Judeans through the words

3778　　20　3004　1161 4183　1537　846
τούτους. **20** ἔλεγον δὲ πολλοὶ ἐξ αὐτῶν·
these. Were saying but many out of them;

1140　2192　2532 3105　5101 846　191
δαιμόνιον ἔχει καὶ μαίνεται· τί αὐτοῦ ἀκούετε;
demon he has and he is crazy; why him hear you?

243　3004　3778　021 4487　3756 1510
21 ἄλλοι ἔλεγον· ταῦτα τὰ ῥήματα οὐκ ἔστιν
Others were saying; these the words not are

1139　　　3361 1140　　1410　5185
δαιμονιζομένου· μὴ δαιμόνιον δύναται τυφλῶν
of one being demonized; not demon is able blind

3788　455　22　1096　5119 021 1456
ὀφθαλμοὺς ἀνοῖξαι; **22** Ἐγένετο τότε τὰ ἐγκαίνια
eyes to open? Became then the festival
of Dedications

1722 023　2414　　5494　1510　23　2532
ἐν τοῖς Ἱεροσολύμοις, χειμὼν ἦν, **23** καὶ
in the Jerusalem, winter it was, and

4043　　01　2424　1722 011 2411　1722 07
περιεπάτει ὁ Ἰησοῦς ἐν τῷ ἱερῷ ἐν τῇ
walked around the Jesus in the temple in the

4745　02　4672　24 2944　3767 846
στοᾷ τοῦ Σολομῶνος. **24** ἐκύκλωσαν οὖν αὐτὸν
colonnade of the Solomon. Encircled then him

013　2453　2532 3004　846　2193 4219
οἱ Ἰουδαῖοι καὶ ἔλεγον αὐτῷ· ἕως πότε
the Judeans and they were saying to him; until when

08　5590 1473 142　1487 1473 1510 01 5547
τὴν ψυχὴν ἡμῶν αἴρεις; εἰ σὺ εἶ ὁ χριστός,
the soul of us you lift up? If you are the Christ,

```
3004 1473      3954            611           846        01   2424
εἰπὲ ἡμῖν  παρρησίᾳ.  25  ἀπεκρίθη αὐτοῖς ὁ  Ἰησοῦς·
say  to us  in boldness.     Answered  to them the  Jesus;
3004    1473    2532 3756 4100          021 2041   3739 1473
εἶπον ὑμῖν  καὶ  οὐ  πιστεύετε· τὰ  ἔργα  ἃ    ἐγὼ
I told to you and  not  you trust;  the works that  I
4160 1722 011 3686      02     3962    1473    3778
ποιῶ ἐν  τῷ  ὀνόματι τοῦ  πατρός μου  ταῦτα
do   in  the  name    of the father of me these
3140    4012 1473      235 3756 4100
μαρτυρεῖ περὶ ἐμοῦ· 26 ἀλλὰ ὑμεῖς οὐ  πιστεύετε,
testify about me;    but   you    not  trust,
3754    3756 1510    1537    022 4263      022 1699
ὅτι   οὐκ ἐστὲ  ἐκ  τῶν προβάτων τῶν ἐμῶν.
because not  you are out of the sheep     the mine.
   021 4263     021 1699 06  5456   1473   191
27 τὰ  πρόβατα τὰ  ἐμὰ τῆς φωνῆς μου  ἀκούουσιν,
   The sheep   the mine the sound of me hear,
2504 1097     846 2532 190        1473    2504
κἀγὼ γινώσκω αὐτὰ καὶ ἀκολουθοῦσίν μοι, 28 κἀγὼ
and I know    them and they follow  me,     and I
1325   846    2222 166      2532 3756 3361 622
δίδωμι αὐτοῖς ζωὴν αἰώνιον καὶ  οὐ  μὴ  ἀπόλωνται
give   to them life eternal and  not  not  they might
                                                be destroyed
1519 04   165    2532 3756 726        5100 846  1537
εἰς  τὸν αἰῶνα καὶ  οὐχ ἁρπάσει τις αὐτὰ ἐκ
into the age    and  not  will seize some them out of
06  5495    1473      01  3962    1473    3739 1325
τῆς χειρός μου. 29 ὁ  πατήρ μου  ὃ    δέδωκέν
the  hand   of me.   The father of me who has given
1473 3956   3173    1510   2532 3762   1410
μοι  πάντων μεῖζόν ἐστιν, καὶ  οὐδεὶς δύναται
to me all    greater he is, and  no one  is able
726      1537  06  5495    02    3962       1473 2532
ἁρπάζειν ἐκ  τῆς χειρὸς τοῦ  πατρός. 30 ἐγὼ καὶ
to seize out of the hand  of the father.    I    and
01  3962    1520 1510    941      3825 3037  013
ὁ  πατήρ ἕν  ἐσμεν. 31 Ἐβάστασαν πάλιν λίθους οἱ
the father one  are.     Bore      again stones the
2453      2443 3034           846         611
Ἰουδαῖοι ἵνα λιθάσωσιν  αὐτόν. 32 ἀπεκρίθη
Judeans  that they might stone him.      Answered
846   01   2424      4183 2041  2570 1166     1473
αὐτοῖς ὁ  Ἰησοῦς· πολλὰ ἔργα καλὰ ἔδειξα ὑμῖν
to them the Jesus;  many  works good I showed to you
1537    02  3962    1223      4169     846   2041
ἐκ   τοῦ πατρός· διὰ  ποῖον αὐτῶν ἔργον
out of the father; through what kind of them work
1473 3034     611        846      013  2453
ἐμὲ λιθάζετε; 33 ἀπεκρίθησαν αὐτῷ  οἱ  Ἰουδαῖοι·
me  you stone?   Answered    to him the Judeans;
4012  2570  2041 3756 3034      1473 235  4012
περὶ καλοῦ ἔργου οὐ  λιθάζομέν σε  ἀλλὰ περὶ
about good work  not  we stone  you but  about
988        2532 3754    1473 444    1510  4160
βλασφημίας, καὶ ὅτι    σὺ  ἄνθρωπος ὢν  ποιεῖς
insult,     and because you man      being make
4572     2316    611       846      01  2424    3756
σεαυτὸν θεόν. 34 ἀπεκρίθη αὐτοῖς [ὁ] Ἰησοῦς· οὐκ
yourself God.    Answered to them the  Jesus;  not
1510   1125                1722 03  3551 1473    3754
ἔστιν γεγραμμένον  ἐν  τῷ  νόμῳ ὑμῶν  ὅτι
it is+ +having been written in  the  law  of you,  (")
1473 3004 2316 1510     1487 1565    3004     2316
ἐγὼ εἶπα· θεοί ἐστε; 35 εἰ  ἐκείνους εἶπεν θεοὺς
I    said, gods are you?  If  those    he said gods
4314 3739 01   3056 02    2316 1096   2532 3756
πρὸς οὓς ὁ  λόγος τοῦ  θεοῦ ἐγένετο, καὶ  οὐ
to    whom the word of the God   became,  and  not
```

tell us plainly." [25]Jesus answered, "I have told you, and you do not believe. The works that I do in my Father's name testify to me; [26]but you do not believe, because you do not belong to my sheep. [27]My sheep hear my voice. I know them, and they follow me. [28]I give them eternal life, and they will never perish. No one will snatch them out of my hand. [29]What my Father has given me is greater than all else, and no one can snatch it out of the Father's hand.[a] [30]The Father and I are one."

[31]The Jews took up stones again to stone him. [32]Jesus replied, "I have shown you many good works from the Father. For which of these are you going to stone me?" [33]The Jews answered, "It is not for a good work that we are going to stone you, but for blasphemy, because you, though only a human being, are making yourself God." [34]Jesus answered, "Is it not written in your law,[b] 'I said, you are gods'? [35]If those to whom the word of God came were called 'gods'—and the

---

[a] Other ancient authorities read *My Father who has given them to me is greater than all, and no one can snatch them out of the Father's hand*

[b] Other ancient authorities read *in the law*

scripture cannot be annulled— 36can you say that the one whom the Father has sanctified and sent into the world is blaspheming because I said, 'I am God's Son'? 37If I am not doing the works of my Father, then do not believe me. 38But if I do them, even though you do not believe me, believe the works, so that you may know and understand*a* that the Father is in me and I am in the Father." 39Then they tried to arrest him again, but he escaped from their hands.

40 He went away again across the Jordan to the place where John had been baptizing earlier, and he remained there. 41Many came to him, and they were saying, "John performed no sign, but everything that John said about this man was true." 42And many believed in him there.

CHAPTER 11

Now a certain man was ill, Lazarus of Bethany, the village of Mary and her sister Martha. 2Mary was the one who anointed the Lord with perfume and wiped his feet with her hair; her brother Lazarus was ill. 3So the sisters sent a message to Jesus,*b* "Lord, he whom you love is ill." 4But when Jesus heard it,

a Other ancient authorities lack *and understand*; others read *and believe*
b Gk *him*

1410	3089		05	1124	**36**	3739	01	3962
δύναται λυθῆναι ἡ γραφή, **36** ὃν ὁ πατὴρ
is able to be loosed the writing, whom the father

| 37 | | 2532 | 649 | | 1519 | 04 | 2889 | 1473 |
ἡγίασεν καὶ ἀπέστειλεν εἰς τὸν κόσμον ὑμεῖς
made holy and he delegated to the world you

| 3004 | 3754 | 987 | | 3754 | | 3004 | 5207 | 02 |
λέγετε ὅτι βλασφημεῖς, ὅτι εἶπον· υἱὸς τοῦ
say, (") you insult, because I said; son of the

| 2316 | 1510 | | 1487 | 3756 | 4160 | 024 | 2041 | 02 | 3962 |
θεοῦ εἰμι, **37** εἰ οὐ ποιῶ τὰ ἔργα τοῦ πατρός
God I am? If not I do the works of the father

| 1473 | 3361 | 4100 | | 1473 | **38** | 1487 | 1161 | 4160 | 2579 |
μου, μὴ πιστεύετέ μοι· **38** εἰ δὲ ποιῶ, κἂν
of me, not you trust in me; if but I do, and if

| 1473 | 3361 | 4100 | | 023 | | 2041 | 4100 |
ἐμοὶ μὴ πιστεύητε, τοῖς ἔργοις πιστεύετε,
to me not you might trust, in the works you trust,

| 2443 | 1097 | | 2532 | 1097 | | 3754 | 1722 | 1473 | 01 | 3962 |
ἵνα γνῶτε καὶ γινώσκητε ὅτι ἐν ἐμοὶ ὁ πατὴρ
that you might and you might that in me the father
know   know(continuously)

| 2504 | 1722 | 03 | 3962 | **39** | 2212 | | 3767 | 846 |
κἀγὼ ἐν τῷ πατρί. **39** Ἐζήτουν [οὖν] αὐτὸν
and I in the father. They were seeking then him

| 3825 | 4084 | | 2532 | 1831 | | 1537 | 06 | 5495 |
πάλιν πιάσαι, καὶ ἐξῆλθεν ἐκ τῆς χειρὸς
again to capture, and he went out out of the hand

| 846 | **40** | 2532 | 565 | | 3825 | 4008 | 02 | 2446 |
αὐτῶν. **40** Καὶ ἀπῆλθεν πάλιν πέραν τοῦ Ἰορδάνου
of them. And he went off again across the Jordan

| 1519 | 04 | 5117 | 3699 | 1510 | 2491 | 012 | 4413 | 907 |
εἰς τὸν τόπον ὅπου ἦν Ἰωάννης τὸ πρῶτον βαπτίζων
into the place where was+ John the first +immersing

| 2532 | 3306 | | 1563 | **41** | 2532 | 4183 | 2064 | 4314 | 846 |
καὶ ἔμεινεν ἐκεῖ. **41** καὶ πολλοὶ ἦλθον πρὸς αὐτὸν
and he stayed there. And many came toward him

| 2532 | 3004 | | 3754 | 2491 | | 3303 | 4592 |
καὶ ἔλεγον ὅτι Ἰωάννης μὲν σημεῖον
and they were saying, (") John indeed sign

| 4160 | 3762 | | 3956 | 1161 | 3745 | | 3004 | 2491 |
ἐποίησεν οὐδέν, πάντα δὲ ὅσα εἶπεν Ἰωάννης
made nothing, all but as much as said John

| 4012 | | 3778 | 227 | 1510 | **42** | 2532 | 4183 | 4100 |
περὶ τούτου ἀληθῆ ἦν. **42** καὶ πολλοὶ ἐπίστευσαν
concerning this true was. And many trusted

| 1519 | 846 | 1563 | **11:1** | 1510 | 1161 | 5100 | 770 |
εἰς αὐτὸν ἐκεῖ. **11:1** Ἦν δέ τις ἀσθενῶν,
in him there. Was+ but some +being weak,

| 2976 | 575 | 963 | | 1537 | 06 | 2968 | 3137 | 2532 |
Λάζαρος ἀπὸ Βηθανίας, ἐκ τῆς κώμης Μαρίας καὶ
Lazarus from Bethany, out of the village Maria and

| 3136 | 06 | 79 | 846 | **2** | 1510 | 1161 | 3137a | 05 |
Μάρθας τῆς ἀδελφῆς αὐτῆς. **2** ἦν δὲ Μαριὰμ ἡ
Martha the sister of her. Was but Mariam the one

| 218 | | 04 | 2962 | 3464 | | 2532 |
ἀλείψασα τὸν κύριον μύρῳ καὶ
having smeared the master in perfume and

| 1591 | | 016 | 4228 | 846 | 019 | 2359 | 846 |
ἐκμάξασα τοὺς πόδας αὐτοῦ ταῖς θριξὶν αὐτῆς,
having wiped dry the feet of him the hairs of her,

| 3739 | | 01 | 80 | 2976 | 770 | **3** | 649 | 3767 |
ἧς ὁ ἀδελφὸς Λάζαρος ἠσθένει. **3** ἀπέστειλαν οὖν
of whom the brother Lazarus was weak. Delegated then

| 017 | 79 | 4314 | 846 | 3004 | | 2962 | 2396 | 3739 |
αἱ ἀδελφαὶ πρὸς αὐτὸν λέγουσαι· κύριε, ἴδε ὃν
the sisters toward him saying; Master, look whom

| 5368 | 770 | | 191 | | 1161 | 01 | 2424 |
φιλεῖς ἀσθενεῖ. **4** ἀκούσας δὲ ὁ Ἰησοῦς
you love is weak. Having heard but the Jesus

3004　　3778　05　769　　　　3756　1510　4314　　2288
εἶπεν·　αὕτη　ἡ　ἀσθένεια　οὐκ　ἔστιν　πρὸς　θάνατον
said;　this　the　weakness　not　it is　toward　death

235　5228　　　06　　　1391　　02　　　2316　2443
ἀλλ᾽　ὑπὲρ　　τῆς　δόξης　τοῦ　θεοῦ,　ἵνα
but　on behalf　of the　splendor　of the　God,　that

1392　　　　　　　01　5207　02　　　2316　1223
δοξασθῇ　　　　ὁ　υἱὸς　τοῦ　　θεοῦ　δι᾽
might be given splendor　the son　of the God　through

846　　　5　25　　1161　01　　2424　　08　3136　　2532
αὐτῆς.　　ἠγάπα　δὲ　ὁ　᾽Ιησοῦς　τὴν Μάρθαν καὶ
it.　Loved but　the Jesus　the Martha and

08　79　　　846　　2532　04　2976　　　6　5613　3767　191
τὴν ἀδελφὴν αὐτῆς καὶ τὸν Λάζαρον.　ὡς οὖν ἤκουσεν
the sister　of her and the Lazarus.　As then he heard

3754　770　　　　5119　3303　3306　　　　1722　3739
ὅτι　ἀσθενεῖ,　τότε μὲν　ἔμεινεν　ἐν　ᾧ
that　he is weak,　then indeed he stayed in　which

1510　5117　1417　2250　　7　1899　　3326　3778　　3004
ἦν　τόπῳ　δύο　ἡμέρας,　ἔπειτα μετὰ　τοῦτο λέγει
he was place two　days;　then　after this　he says

015　3101　　71　　　1519 08　2449　　　3825
τοῖς　μαθηταῖς·　ἄγωμεν　εἰς τὴν ᾽Ιουδαίαν πάλιν.
to the learners;　we might lead to the Judea　again.

8　3004　　　846　013 3101　　　4461　3568 2212
λέγουσιν αὐτῷ οἱ μαθηταί·　ῥαββί,　νῦν ἐζήτουν
Say　to him the learners;　Rabbi,　now were seeking

1473 3034　　013　2453　　　2532 3825　5217
σε　λιθάσαι οἱ　᾽Ιουδαῖοι, καὶ　πάλιν ὑπάγεις
you　to stone the　Judeans,　and　again you go off

1563　　9　611　　2424　　3780 1427　5610　1510
ἐκεῖ;　ἀπεκρίθη ᾽Ιησοῦς· οὐχὶ δώδεκα ὧραί εἰσιν
there? Answered Jesus·　not　twelve hours are there

06　　2250　　1437 5100 4043　　　　　1722 07 2250
τῆς　ἡμέρας; ἐάν τις　περιπατῇ　　ἐν τῇ ἡμέρᾳ,
of the day?　If　some might walk around in the day,

3756 4350　　　3754　012 5457　02　　2889
οὐ　προσκόπτει,　ὅτι　τὸ φῶς τοῦ　κόσμου
not　he stumbles, because the light of the world

3778　991　　10　1437 1161 5100 4043
τούτου βλέπει·　ἐὰν δέ τις　περιπατῇ
this　he sees;　if but　some might walk around

1722 07　3571　4350　　　3754　09　5457　3756
ἐν τῇ νυκτί, προσκόπτει, ὅτι　τὸ φῶς οὐκ
in the night, he stumbles, because the light not

1510 1722 846　11　3778　3004　　2532 3326　3778
ἔστιν ἐν αὐτῷ.　Ταῦτα εἶπεν,　καὶ μετὰ τοῦτο
is　in him.　These he said, and after this

3004　846　2976　　01　5384　1473
λέγει αὐτοῖς· Λάζαρος ὁ φίλος ἡμῶν
he says to them; Lazarus the friend of us

2837　　　　235　4198　　　2443 1852
κεκοίμηται·　ἀλλὰ πορεύομαι ἵνα ἐξυπνίσω
has fallen asleep; but　I travel　that I might awaken

846　12　3004　3767 013 3101　　846　2962　1487
αὐτόν.　εἶπαν οὖν οἱ μαθηταὶ αὐτῷ·　κύριε, εἰ
him.　Said then the learners to him, Master, if

2837　　　　4982　　　13　3004　　1161 01　2424
κεκοίμηται　σωθήσεται.　εἰρήκει　δὲ ὁ ᾽Ιησοῦς
he has fallen he will be　Had spoken but the Jesus
asleep　delivered.

4012　　02　2288　846　　1565　　1161 1380
περὶ　τοῦ θανάτου αὐτοῦ, ἐκεῖνοι δὲ　ἔδοξαν
concerning the death　of him, those　but thought

3754 4012　　06 2838　　02　5258　3004
ὅτι περὶ　τῆς κοιμήσεως τοῦ　ὕπνου λέγει.
that concerning the sleep　of the sleep he says.

14　5119 3767 3004 846　　01　2424　3954
τότε οὖν　εἶπεν αὐτοῖς ὁ ᾽Ιησοῦς παρρησίᾳ·
Then then said　to them the Jesus in boldness,

---

he said, "This illness does not lead to death; rather it is for God's glory, so that the Son of God may be glorified through it." [5]Accordingly, though Jesus loved Martha and her sister and Lazarus, [6]after having heard that Lazarus[a] was ill, he stayed two days longer in the place where he was.

[7]Then after this he said to the disciples, "Let us go to Judea again." [8]The disciples said to him, "Rabbi, the Jews were just now trying to stone you, and are you going there again?" [9]Jesus answered, "Are there not twelve hours of daylight? Those who walk during the day do not stumble, because they see the light of this world. [10]But those who walk at night stumble, because the light is not in them." [11]After saying this, he told them, "Our friend Lazarus has fallen asleep, but I am going there to awaken him." [12]The disciples said to him, "Lord, if he has fallen asleep, he will be all right." [13]Jesus, however, had been speaking about his death, but they thought that he was referring merely to sleep. [14]Then Jesus told them plainly,

[a] Gk he

"Lazarus is dead. [15]For your sake I am glad I was not there, so that you may believe. But let us go to him." [16]Thomas, who was called the Twin,[a] said to his fellow disciples, "Let us also go, that we may die with him."

[17]When Jesus arrived, he found that Lazarus[b] had already been in the tomb four days. [18]Now Bethany was near Jerusalem, some two miles[c] away, [19]and many of the Jews had come to Martha and Mary to console them about their brother. [20]When Martha heard that Jesus was coming, she went and met him, while Mary stayed at home. [21]Martha said to Jesus, "Lord, if you had been here, my brother would not have died. [22]But even now I know that God will give you whatever you ask of him." [23]Jesus said to her, "Your brother will rise again." [24]Martha said to him, "I know that he will rise again in the resurrection on the last day." [25]Jesus said to her, "I am the resurrection and the life.[d] Those who believe in me, even though they die, will live, [26]and everyone who lives and believes in me will never die.

[a] Gk Didymus
[b] Gk he
[c] Gk fifteen stadia
[d] Other ancient authorities lack and the life

2976	599		15	2532	5463	1223		1473	2443
Λάζαρος	ἀπέθανεν,			καὶ	χαίρω	δι᾽		ὑμᾶς	ἵνα
Lazarus	died,			and	I rejoice	through		you	that

4100		3754	3756	1510	1563		235
πιστεύσητε,		ὅτι	οὐκ	ἤμην	ἐκεῖ·		ἀλλὰ
you might trust,		because	not	I was	there;		but

71		4314	846	16	3004	3767	2381		01
ἄγωμεν		πρὸς	αὐτόν.		εἶπεν	οὖν	Θωμᾶς		ὁ
we might lead		toward	him.		Said	then	Thomas		the

3004		1324	015	4827		71
λεγόμενος		Δίδυμος	τοῖς	συμμαθηταῖς·		ἄγωμεν
one being said		Didymus	to the	co-learners;		might lead

2532	1473	2443	599		3326	846		17	2064
καὶ	ἡμεῖς	ἵνα	ἀποθάνωμεν		μετ᾽	αὐτοῦ.			Ἐλθὼν
also we		that	we might die		with	him.			Having gone

3767	01	2424	2147	846	5064		2235	2250
οὖν	ὁ	Ἰησοῦς	εὗρεν	αὐτὸν	τέσσαρας		ἤδη	ἡμέρας
then the		Jesus	found	him	four		already	days

2192		1722	011	3419	18	1510	1161	05	963
ἔχοντα		ἐν	τῷ	μνημείῳ.		ἦν	δὲ	ἡ	Βηθανία
having		in	the	grave.		Was	but	the	Bethany

1451	022	2414		5613	575	4712		1178
ἐγγὺς	τῶν	Ἱεροσολύμων	ὡς		ἀπὸ	σταδίων		δεκαπέντε.
near	the	Jerusalem	as		from	stadia		fifteen.

19	4183	1161	1537	014	2453		2064		4314
	πολλοὶ	δὲ	ἐκ	τῶν	Ἰουδαίων		ἐληλύθεισαν		πρὸς
	Many	but	out of	the	Judeans		had gone		toward

08	3136	2532	3137a	2443	3888		846
τὴν	Μάρθαν	καὶ	Μαριὰμ	ἵνα	παραμυθήσωνται		αὐτὰς
the	Martha	and	Mariam	that	they might comfort		them

4012	02	80	20	05	3767	3136		5613	191
περὶ	τοῦ	ἀδελφοῦ.		ἡ	οὖν	Μάρθα	ὡς		ἤκουσεν
about	the	brother.		The	then	Martha	as		she heard

3754	2424	2064		5221		846	3137a	1161	1722
ὅτι	Ἰησοῦς	ἔρχεται		ὑπήντησεν		αὐτῷ·	Μαριὰμ	δὲ	ἐν
that	Jesus	comes		she met		him;	Mariam	but	in

03	3624	2516		21	3004	3767	05	3136	4314	04
τῷ	οἴκῳ	ἐκαθέζετο.			εἶπεν	οὖν	ἡ	Μάρθα	πρὸς	τὸν
the	house	was sitting.			Said	then	the	Martha	to	the

2424	2962	1487	1510		5602	3756	302	599
Ἰησοῦν·	κύριε,	εἰ	ἦς		ὧδε	οὐκ	ἂν	ἀπέθανεν
Jesus;	Master,	if	you were here		not	-		died

01	80		1473	22	235	2532	3568	3609a	3754
ὁ	ἀδελφός	μου·			[ἀλλὰ]	καὶ	νῦν	οἶδα	ὅτι
the	brother	of me;			but	also now		I know	that

3745		302	154		04	2316	1325		1473
ὅσα		ἂν	αἰτήσῃ		τὸν	θεὸν	δώσει		σοι
as much as		-	you might ask		the	God	will		give to you

01	2316	23		3004	846	01	2424	450
ὁ	θεός.			λέγει	αὐτῇ	ὁ	Ἰησοῦς·	ἀναστήσεται
the	God.			Says	to her	the	Jesus;	will stand up

01	80		1473	24	3004	846	05	3136	3609a
ὁ	ἀδελφός	σου.			λέγει	αὐτῷ	ἡ	Μάρθα·	οἶδα
the	brother of	you.			Says	to him	the	Martha;	I know

3754	450		1722	07	386		1722	07
ὅτι	ἀναστήσεται		ἐν	τῇ	ἀναστάσει		ἐν	τῇ
that	he will stand up		in	the	standing up		in	the

2078	2250	25	3004	846	01	2424	1473	1510
ἐσχάτῃ	ἡμέρᾳ.		εἶπεν	αὐτῇ	ὁ	Ἰησοῦς·	ἐγώ	εἰμι
last	day.		Said	to her	the	Jesus;	I	am

05	386		2532	05	2222	01	4100		1519
ἡ	ἀνάστασις		καὶ	ἡ	ζωή·	ὁ	πιστεύων		εἰς
the	standing up		and	the	life;	the	one trusting		into

1473	2579	599		2198		26	2532	3956	01
ἐμὲ	κἂν	ἀποθάνῃ		ζήσεται,			καὶ	πᾶς	ὁ
me	if also	he might die		he will live,			and	all	the

2198		2532	4100	1519	1473	3756	3361	599		1519
ζῶν		καὶ	πιστεύων	εἰς	ἐμὲ	οὐ	μὴ	ἀποθάνῃ		εἰς
one living		and	trusting in		me	not	not	he might		into die

```
04   165      4100        3778      27  3004      846         3483
τὸν αἰῶνα· πιστεύεις τοῦτο;          λέγει     αὐτῷ·        ναὶ
the age;   you trust this?              She says to him; yes
2962      1473 4100                  3754 1473 1510 01   5547
κύριε,   ἐγὼ πεπίστευκα      ὅτι σὺ   εἶ  ὁ  χριστὸς
Master,  I   have trusted that you  are  the Christ
01   5207 02      2316 01   1519 04   2889   2064
ὁ  υἱὸς τοῦ     θεοῦ ὁ  εἰς  τὸν κόσμον ἐρχόμενος.
the son of the God  the into the world   one coming.
   2532 3778   3004        565          2532
28 Καὶ τοῦτο εἰποῦσα    ἀπῆλθεν      καὶ
   And this having said she went off and
5455        3137a 08 79        846      2977
ἐφώνησεν Μαριὰμ τὴν ἀδελφὴν αὐτῆς λάθρᾳ
she sounded Mariam the sister   of her  privately
3004         01  1320         3918       2532 5455
εἰποῦσα·   ὁ  διδάσκαλος πάρεστιν  καὶ  φωνεῖ
having said; the teacher    is present and  sounds
1473 29 1565        1161 5613 191       1453
σε.     ἐκείνη   δὲ  ὡς  ἤκουσεν ἠγέρθη
you.    That one but as  heard    she was raised
5036      2532 2064         4314    846       30 3768      1161
ταχὺ   καὶ ἤρχετο       πρὸς αὐτόν.    οὔπω    δὲ
quickly and she was going toward him.    Not yet but
2064       01  2424     1519 08 2968      235   1510 2089
ἐληλύθει ὁ  Ἰησοῦς εἰς τὴν κώμην,  ἀλλ' ἦν   ἔτι
had come the Jesus into the village, but he was still
1722 03  5117  3699   5221      846  05  3136      31 013
ἐν τῷ τόπῳ ὅπου ὑπήντησεν αὐτῷ ἡ Μάρθα.     οἱ
in the place where met     him the Martha. The
3767  2453     013 1510    3326 846  1722 07  3614
οὖν  Ἰουδαῖοι οἱ ὄντες   μετ' αὐτῆς ἐν τῇ οἰκίᾳ
then Judeans the ones being with her  in the house
2532 3888          846    3708       08  3137a   3754
καὶ παραμυθούμενοι αὐτήν, ἰδόντες   τὴν Μαριὰμ ὅτι
and comforting    her,  having seen the Mariam that
5030    450        2532 1831       190
ταχέως ἀνέστη     καὶ ἐξῆλθεν,  ἠκολούθησαν
quickly she stood up and she went out, they followed
846  1380        3754 5217      1519 012 3419
αὐτῇ δόξαντες   ὅτι ὑπάγει     εἰς τὸ μνημεῖον
her having thought that she goes off to the grave
2443 2799         1563    32 05     3767 3137a 5613 2064
ἵνα κλαύσῃ      ἐκεῖ.     Ἡ   οὖν Μαριὰμ ὡς ἦλθεν
that she might cry there.   The then Mariam as went
3699 1510 2424    3708      846    4098   846
ὅπου ἦν  Ἰησοῦς ἰδοῦσα   αὐτὸν ἔπεσεν αὐτοῦ
where was Jesus having seen him   she fell of him
4314   016  4228   3004      846   2962      1487 1510
πρὸς τοὺς πόδας λέγουσα αὐτῷ· κύριε,  εἰ  ἧς
toward the feet  saying to him; Master, if  you were
5602 3756 302 1473 599        01  80          33 2424
ὧδε οὐκ ἂν μου ἀπέθανεν ὁ  ἀδελφός.     Ἰησοῦς
here not - of me died     the brother.    Jesus
3767 5613 3708  846   2799       2532 016
οὖν ὡς  εἶδεν αὐτὴν κλαίουσαν καὶ τοὺς
then as saw her    crying      and the ones
4905          846  2453      2799        1690
συνελθόντας αὐτῇ Ἰουδαίους κλαίοντας, ἐνεβριμήσατο
having come to her Judeans  crying,    he was
together                                indignant
011  4151       2532 5015      1438      34 2532
τῷ  πνεύματι καὶ ἐτάραξεν ἑαυτὸν      καὶ
in the spirit  and he troubled himself  and
3004    4226  5087          846   3004       846
εἶπεν· ποῦ τεθείκατε     αὐτόν; λέγουσιν αὐτῷ·
he said; where have you placed him? They say to him;
2962    2064 2532 2396    35 1145     01 2424
κύριε, ἔρχου καὶ ἴδε.      ἐδάκρυσεν ὁ  Ἰησοῦς.
Master, come and look.    Cried     the Jesus.
```

Do you believe this?" [27]She said to him, "Yes, Lord, I believe that you are the Messiah,[a] the Son of God, the one coming into the world."

28 When she had said this, she went back and called her sister Mary, and told her privately, "The Teacher is here and is calling for you." [29]And when she heard it, she got up quickly and went to him. [30]Now Jesus had not yet come to the village, but was still at the place where Martha had met him. [31]The Jews who were with her in the house, consoling her, saw Mary get up quickly and go out. They followed her because they thought that she was going to the tomb to weep there. [32]When Mary came where Jesus was and saw him, she knelt at his feet and said to him, "Lord, if you had been here, my brother would not have died." [33]When Jesus saw her weeping, and the Jews who came with her also weeping, he was greatly disturbed in spirit and deeply moved. [34]He said, "Where have you laid him?" They said to him, "Lord, come and see." [35]Jesus began to weep.

[a] Or the Christ

36So the Jews said, "See how he loved him!" 37But some of them said, "Could not he who opened the eyes of the blind man have kept this man from dying?"

38 Then Jesus, again greatly disturbed, came to the tomb. It was a cave, and a stone was lying against it. 39Jesus said, "Take away the stone." Martha, the sister of the dead man, said to him, "Lord, already there is a stench because he has been dead four days." 40Jesus said to her, "Did I not tell you that if you believed, you would see the glory of God?" 41So they took away the stone. And Jesus looked upward and said, "Father, I thank you for having heard me. 42I knew that you always hear me, but I have said this for the sake of the crowd standing here, so that they may believe that you sent me." 43When he had said this, he cried with a loud voice, "Lazarus, come out!" 44The dead man came out, his hands and feet bound with strips of cloth, and his face wrapped in a cloth. Jesus said to them, "Unbind him, and let him go."

36
3004   3767 013   2453   2396 4459
ἔλεγον οὖν οἱ Ἰουδαῖοι· ἴδε πῶς
Were saying then the Judeans; look how

5368   846   **37** 5100 1161 1537 846   3004
ἐφίλει αὐτόν. τινὲς δὲ ἐξ αὐτῶν εἶπαν·
he was loving him. Some but out of them said;

3756 1410   3778 01   455   016
οὐκ ἐδύνατο οὗτος ὁ ἀνοίξας τοὺς
not was able this the one having opened the

3788   02 5185   4160 2443 2532 3778   3361
ὀφθαλμοὺς τοῦ τυφλοῦ ποιῆσαι ἵνα καὶ οὗτος μὴ
eyes the blind to make that also this one not

599   2424 3767 3825 1690   1722
ἀποθάνῃ; **38** Ἰησοῦς οὖν πάλιν ἐμβριμώμενος ἐν
might die? Jesus then again being indignant in

1438   2064   1519 012 3419   1510 1161 4693
ἑαυτῷ ἔρχεται εἰς τὸ μνημεῖον· ἦν δὲ σπήλαιον
himself comes to the grave; it was but cave

2532 3037 1945   1909 846 **39** 3004 01 2424
καὶ λίθος ἐπέκειτο ἐπ' αὐτῷ. λέγει ὁ Ἰησοῦς·
and stone was lying on on it. Says the Jesus;

142   04 3037 3004 846   05 79   02
ἄρατε τὸν λίθον. λέγει αὐτῷ ἡ ἀδελφὴ τοῦ
lift up the stone. Says to him the sister of the

5053   3136 2962 2235 3605
τετελευτηκότος Μάρθα· κύριε, ἤδη ὄζει,
one having died Martha; Master, already he stinks,

5066   1063 1510 **40** 3004 846 01 2424
τεταρταῖος γάρ ἐστιν. λέγει αὐτῇ ὁ Ἰησοῦς·
of the fourth for it is. Says to her the Jesus;

3756 3004 1473   3754 1437 4100
οὐκ εἶπόν σοι ὅτι ἐὰν πιστεύσῃς
not I told to <u>you</u> that if <u>you</u> might trust

3708   08 1391   02 2316 **41** 142
ὄψῃ τὴν δόξαν τοῦ θεοῦ; ἦραν
<u>you</u> might see the splendor of the God? They lifted up

07-67 04 3037 01 1161 2424 142   016
οὖν τὸν λίθον. ὁ δὲ Ἰησοῦς ἦρεν τοὺς
then the stone. The but Jesus lifted up the

3788   507 2532 3004   3962   2168
ὀφθαλμοὺς ἄνω καὶ εἶπεν· πάτερ, εὐχαριστῶ
eyes up and he said; father, I give good favor

1473   3754 191   1473 **42** 1473 1161 3609a   3754
σοι ὅτι ἤκουσάς μου. ἐγὼ δὲ ἤδειν ὅτι
to you that you heard me. I but have known that

3842   1473 191   235 1223   04 3793 04
πάντοτέ μου ἀκούεις, ἀλλὰ διὰ τὸν ὄχλον τὸν
always me <u>you</u> hear; but through the crowd the

4026   3004 2443 4100
περιεστῶτα εἶπον, ἵνα πιστεύσωσιν
one standing around I said, that they might trust

3754 1473 1473 649   **43** 2532 3778 3004
ὅτι σύ με ἀπέστειλας. καὶ ταῦτα εἰπὼν
that <u>you</u> me delegated. And these having said

5456 3173 2905   2976 1204 1854
φωνῇ μεγάλῃ ἐκραύγασεν· Λάζαρε, δεῦρο ἔξω.
sound great he shouted; Lazarus, come outside.

44 1831 01 2348   1210
ἐξῆλθεν ὁ τεθνηκὼς δεδεμένος
Came out the one having died having been bound

016 4228 2532 020 5495 2750   2532 05 3799
τοὺς πόδας καὶ τὰς χεῖρας κειρίαις καὶ ἡ ὄψις
the feet and the hands in wrappings and the sight

846   4676   4019   3004 846
αὐτοῦ σουδαρίῳ περιεδέδετο. λέγει αὐτοῖς
of him in handkerchief was bound around. Says to them

01 2424   3089   846 2532 863 846 5217
ὁ Ἰησοῦς· λύσατε αὐτὸν καὶ ἄφετε αὐτὸν ὑπάγειν.
the Jesus; loose him and allow him to go off.

45
4183	3767	1537	014	2453	013	2064
Πολλοὶ	οὖν	ἐκ	τῶν	Ἰουδαίων	οἱ	ἐλθόντες
Many	then	from	the	Judeans	the	ones having come

4314	08	3137a	2532	2300		3739	4160
πρὸς	τὴν	Μαριὰμ	καὶ	θεασάμενοι		ἃ	ἐποίησεν
toward	the	Mariam	and	having watched		what	he did

4100		1519	846	**46**	5100	1161	1537	846
ἐπίστευσαν	εἰς	αὐτόν·		τινὲς	δὲ	ἐξ	αὐτῶν
trusted	in	him;		some	but	out of	them

565	4314	016	5330	2532	3004	846
ἀπῆλθον	πρὸς	τοὺς	Φαρισαίους	καὶ	εἶπαν	αὐτοῖς
went off	toward	the	Pharisees	and	said	to them

3739	846	2424		4863		3767	013
ἃ	ἐποίησεν	Ἰησοῦς.	**47**	Συνήγαγον		οὖν	οἱ
what	did	Jesus.		Brought together		then	the

749		2532	013	5330		4892		2532
ἀρχιερεῖς	καὶ	οἱ	Φαρισαῖοι	συνέδριον	καὶ
ruler priests	and	the	Pharisees	council	and

3004		5101	4160	3754		3778	01	444
ἔλεγον·	τί	ποιοῦμεν	ὅτι		οὗτος	ὁ	ἄνθρωπος
they were saying,	what	we do	because		this	the	man

4183	4160	4592	**48**	1437	863		846
πολλὰ	ποιεῖ	σημεῖα;		ἐὰν	ἀφῶμεν		αὐτὸν
many	does	signs?		If	we might allow		him

3779	3956	4100		1519	846	2532	2064
οὕτως,	πάντες	πιστεύσουσιν	εἰς	αὐτόν,	καὶ	ἐλεύσονται
thusly,	all	will trust	in	him,	and	will come

013	4514	2532	142		1473	2532	04	5117
οἱ	Ῥωμαῖοι	καὶ	ἀροῦσιν		ἡμῶν	καὶ	τὸν	τόπον
the	Romans	and	they will lift		up us	and	the	place

2532 012	1484	**49**	1520	1161	5100	1537	846	2533
καὶ	τὸ	ἔθνος.		εἷς	δέ	τις	ἐξ	αὐτῶν	Καϊάφας,
and	the	nation.		One	but	some	from	them	Caiaphas,

749		1510	02	1763	1565	3004
ἀρχιερεὺς	ὢν	τοῦ	ἐνιαυτοῦ	ἐκείνου,	εἶπεν
ruler priest	being	of the	year	that,	he said

846	1473	3756	3609a	3762	**50**	3761	3049
αὐτοῖς·	ὑμεῖς	οὐκ	οἴδατε	οὐδέν,		οὐδὲ	λογίζεσθε
to them;	you	not	know	nothing,		but not	you reason

3754	4851		1473	2443	1520	444
ὅτι	συμφέρει		ὑμῖν	ἵνα	εἷς	ἄνθρωπος
that it	is advantageous		to you	that	one	man

599	5228	02	2992	2532	3361	3650	09
ἀποθάνῃ	ὑπὲρ	τοῦ	λαοῦ	καὶ	μὴ	ὅλον	τὸ
might die	on behalf	of the	people	and	not	whole	the

1484	622	**51**	3778	1161	575	1438	3756	3004
ἔθνος	ἀπόληται.		τοῦτο	δὲ	ἀφ᾽	ἑαυτοῦ	οὐκ	εἶπεν,
nation	might be destroyed.		This	but	from	himself	not	he said,

235	749		1510	02	1763	1565
ἀλλὰ	ἀρχιερεὺς	ὢν	τοῦ	ἐνιαυτοῦ	ἐκείνου
but	ruler priest	being	of the	year	that

4395		3754	3195		2424	599
ἐπροφήτευσεν	ὅτι	ἔμελλεν		Ἰησοῦς	ἀποθνῄσκειν
spoke before	because	was about		Jesus	to die

5228	010	1484	**52**	2532 3756	5228	010
ὑπὲρ	τοῦ	ἔθνους,		καὶ	οὐχ	ὑπὲρ	τοῦ
on behalf	of the	nation,		and	not	on behalf	of the

1484	3441	235	2443	2532	024	5043	02	2316
ἔθνους	μόνον	ἀλλ᾽	ἵνα	καὶ	τὰ	τέκνα	τοῦ	θεοῦ
nation	alone	but	that	also	the	children	of the	God

024	1287		4863	1519	1520
τὰ	διεσκορπισμένα	συναγάγῃ		εἰς	ἕν.
the ones having been scattered		he might bring		into	one.
	together				

53
575	1565	3767	06	2250	1011	2443
ἀπ᾽	ἐκείνης	οὖν	τῆς	ἡμέρας	ἐβουλεύσαντο	ἵνα
From that		then	the	day	they planned	that

45 Many of the Jews therefore, who had come with Mary and had seen what Jesus did, believed in him. 46But some of them went to the Pharisees and told them what he had done. 47So the chief priests and the Pharisees called a meeting of the council, and said, "What are we to do? This man is performing many signs. 48If we let him go on like this, everyone will believe in him, and the Romans will come and destroy both our holy place[a] and our nation." 49But one of them, Caiaphas, who was high priest that year, said to them, "You know nothing at all! 50You do not understand that it is better for you to have one man die for the people than to have the whole nation destroyed." 51He did not say this on his own, but being high priest that year he prophesied that Jesus was about to die for the nation, 52and not for the nation only, but to gather into one the dispersed children of God. 53So from that day on they planned

---

a Or our temple; Greek our place

to put him to death.
54 Jesus therefore no longer walked about openly among the Jews, but went from there to a town called Ephraim in the region near the wilderness; and he remained there with the disciples.
55 Now the Passover of the Jews was near, and many went up from the country to Jerusalem before the Passover to purify themselves. 56 They were looking for Jesus and were asking one another as they stood in the temple, "What do you think? Surely he will not come to the festival, will he?" 57 Now the chief priests and the Pharisees had given orders that anyone who knew where Jesus[a] was should let them know, so that they might arrest him.

CHAPTER 12

Six days before the Passover Jesus came to Bethany, the home of Lazarus, whom he had raised from the dead. 2 There they gave a dinner for him. Martha served, and Lazarus was one of those at the table with him. 3 Mary took a pound of costly perfume made of pure nard, anointed Jesus' feet, and wiped them[b] with her hair. The house was filled with the fragrance of the perfume. 4 But Judas

[a] Gk he
[b] Gk his feet

| 615 | 846 | 54 | 01 | 3767 | 2424 | 3765 |
ἀποκτείνωσιν αὐτόν. Ὁ οὖν Ἰησοῦς οὐκέτι
they might kill him. The then Jesus no longer

3954 4043 1722 015 2453 235
παρρησίᾳ περιεπάτει ἐν τοῖς Ἰουδαίοις, ἀλλὰ
in boldness walked around in the Judeans, but

565 1564 1519 08 5561 1451 06
ἀπῆλθεν ἐκεῖθεν εἰς τὴν χώραν ἐγγὺς τῆς
he went off from there into the country near the

2048 1519 2187 3004 4172 2546
ἐρήμου, εἰς Ἐφραὶμ λεγομένην πόλιν, κἀκεῖ
desert, into Ephraim being said city, and there

3306 3326 014 3101 55 1510 1161 1451 09
ἔμεινεν μετὰ τῶν μαθητῶν. Ἦν δὲ ἐγγὺς τὸ
he stayed with the learners. Was but near the

3957 014 2453 2532 305 4183 1519
πάσχα τῶν Ἰουδαίων, καὶ ἀνέβησαν πολλοὶ εἰς
passover of the Judeans, and went up many into

2414 1537 06 5561 4253 010 3957 2443
Ἱεροσόλυμα ἐκ τῆς χώρας πρὸ τοῦ πάσχα ἵνα
Jerusalem from the country before the passover that

48 1438 56 2212 3767
ἁγνίσωσιν ἑαυτούς. ἐζήτουν οὖν
they might purify themselves. They were seeking then

04 2424 2532 3004 3326 240 1722 011
τὸν Ἰησοῦν καὶ ἔλεγον μετ' ἀλλήλων ἐν τῷ
the Jesus and were saying with one another in the

2411 2476 5101 1380 1473 3754 3756
ἱερῷ ἑστηκότες· τί δοκεῖ ὑμῖν; ὅτι οὐ
temple having stood, what it thinks to you? That not

3361 2064 1519 08 1859 57 1325
μὴ ἔλθῃ εἰς τὴν ἑορτήν; δεδώκεισαν
not he might come to the festival? Had given

1161 013 749 2532 013 5330 1785
δὲ οἱ ἀρχιερεῖς καὶ οἱ Φαρισαῖοι ἐντολὰς
but the ruler priests and the Pharisees commands

2443 1437 5100 1097 4226 1510 3377
ἵνα ἐάν τις γνῷ ποῦ ἐστιν μηνύσῃ,
that if some might know where he is he might report,

3704 4084 846 12:1 01 3767 2424
ὅπως πιάσωσιν αὐτόν. Ὁ οὖν Ἰησοῦς
so that they might capture him. The then Jesus

4253 1803 2250 010 3957 2064 1519 963
πρὸ ἓξ ἡμερῶν τοῦ πάσχα ἦλθεν εἰς Βηθανίαν,
before six days of the passover went to Bethany,

3699 1510 2976 3739 1453 1537 3498 2424
ὅπου ἦν Λάζαρος, ὃν ἤγειρεν ἐκ νεκρῶν Ἰησοῦς.
where was Lazarus, whom raised out of dead Jesus.

2 4160 3767 846 1173 1563 2532 05 3136
ἐποίησαν οὖν αὐτῷ δεῖπνον ἐκεῖ, καὶ ἡ Μάρθα
They made then to him dinner there, and the Martha

1247 01 1161 2976 1520 1510 1537 014
διηκόνει, ὁ δὲ Λάζαρος εἷς ἦν ἐκ τῶν
was serving, the but Lazarus one was out of the ones

345 4862 846 3 05 3767 3137a 2983
ἀνακειμένων σὺν αὐτῷ. Ἡ οὖν Μαριὰμ λαβοῦσα
reclining with him. The then Mariam having taken

3046 3464 3487 4101 4186 218
λίτραν μύρου νάρδου πιστικῆς πολυτίμου ἤλειψεν
litre of perfume of nard genuine much value smeared

016 4228 02 2424 2532 1591 019 2359
τοὺς πόδας τοῦ Ἰησοῦ καὶ ἐξέμαξεν ταῖς θριξὶν
the feet of the Jesus and wiped dry in the hairs

846 016 4228 846 05 1161 3614 4137
αὐτῆς τοὺς πόδας αὐτοῦ· ἡ δὲ οἰκία ἐπληρώθη
of her the feet of him; the but house was filled

1537 06 3744 010 3464 4 3004 1161 2455
ἐκ τῆς ὀσμῆς τοῦ μύρου. λέγει δὲ Ἰούδας
out of the odor of the perfume. Says but Judas

01 2469   1520 1537   014 3101   846   01
ὁ Ἰσκαριώτης εἷς [ἐκ] τῶν μαθητῶν αὐτοῦ, ὁ
the Iscariot   one out of the learners of him, the

3195   846   3860   5 1223   5101 3778
μέλλων   αὐτὸν παραδιδόναι ·   διὰ   τί   τοῦτο
one being about him   to give over;   through what this

09 3464   3756 4097   5145   1220
τὸ μύρον   οὐκ ἐπράθη τριακοσίων   δηναρίων
the perfume not was sold of three hundred denaria

2532 1325   4434   6 3004   1161 3778   3756
καὶ ἐδόθη   πτωχοῖς;   εἶπεν δὲ τοῦτο οὐχ
and was given to poor?   He said but this   not

3754   4012   014 4434   3190a   846   235
ὅτι   περὶ τῶν πτωχῶν ἔμελεν   αὐτῷ, ἀλλ᾽
because about the poor   it was a care to him, but

3754   2812 1510   2532 012 1101   2192
ὅτι   κλέπτης ἦν   καὶ τὸ γλωσσόκομον ἔχων
because thief   he was and the treasure box having

024 906   941   3004   3767 01
τὰ βαλλόμενα   ἐβάσταζεν.   7 εἶπεν οὖν ὁ
the things being thrown he was bearing. Said then the

2424   863   846   2443 1519 08   2250   02
Ἰησοῦς· ἄφες αὐτήν, ἵνα εἰς τὴν ἡμέραν τοῦ
Jesus;   allow her,   that into the day   of the

1780   1473 5083   846   8 016   4434
ἐνταφιασμοῦ μου τηρήσῃ   αὐτό ·   τοὺς πτωχοὺς
burial   of me she might keep it;   the   poor

1063 3842   2192   3326 1438   1473 1161 3756
γὰρ πάντοτε ἔχετε   μεθ᾽ ἑαυτῶν,   ἐμὲ δὲ οὐ
for always you have with yourselves, me but not

3842   2192   9 1097 3767 01 3793   4183 1537 014
πάντοτε ἔχετε.   Ἔγνω οὖν [ὁ] ὄχλος πολὺς ἐκ τῶν
always you have. Knew then the crowd much from the

2453   3754 1563   1510 2532 2064   3756 1223
Ἰουδαίων ὅτι ἐκεῖ ἐστιν καὶ ἦλθον   οὐ διὰ
Judeans that there he is and they came not because

04 2424   3441   235   2443 2532 04   2976
τὸν Ἰησοῦν μόνον, ἀλλ᾽ ἵνα καὶ τὸν Λάζαρον
the Jesus   alone, but   that also the Lazarus

3708   3739 1453   1537   3498
ἴδωσιν   ὃν ἤγειρεν ἐκ νεκρῶν.
they might see whom he raised out of dead.

10 1011   1161 013 749   2443 2532 04
ἐβουλεύσαντο δὲ οἱ ἀρχιερεῖς   ἵνα καὶ τὸν
Planned   but the ruler priests that also the

2976   615   3754   4183 1223   846
Λάζαρον ἀποκτείνωσιν, 11 ὅτι πολλοὶ δι᾽ αὐτὸν
Lazarus they might kill,   because many through him

5217   014   2453   2532 4100   1519 04
ὑπῆγον τῶν Ἰουδαίων καὶ ἐπίστευον   εἰς τὸν
went off the Judeans and they were trusting in the

2424   12 07   1887   01 3793 4183 01
Ἰησοῦν.   Τῇ ἐπαύριον ὁ ὄχλος πολὺς ὁ
Jesus.   In the tomorrow the crowd much the one

2064   1519 08 1859   191   3754 2064
ἐλθὼν   εἰς τὴν ἑορτήν, ἀκούσαντες ὅτι ἔρχεται
having come to the festival, having heard that comes

01 2424   1519 2414   13 2983   024 902
ὁ Ἰησοῦς εἰς Ἱεροσόλυμα   ἔλαβον   τὰ βαΐα
the Jesus into Jerusalem   they took the branches

014   5404   2532 1831   1519 5222   846
τῶν φοινίκων καὶ ἐξῆλθον   εἰς ὑπάντησιν αὐτῷ
of the palms   and they went out into meeting   him

2532 2905   5614   2127
καὶ ἐκραύγαζον· ὡσαννά· εὐλογημένος
and they shouted; hosanna; having been well spoken

01 2064   1722 3686   2962   2532 01 935
ὁ ἐρχόμενος ἐν ὀνόματι κυρίου, [καὶ] ὁ βασιλεὺς
the one coming in name   of Master, and the king

Iscariot, one of his disciples (the one who was about to betray him), said, [5]"Why was this perfume not sold for three hundred denarii[a] and the money given to the poor?" [6](He said this not because he cared about the poor, but because he was a thief; he kept the common purse and used to steal what was put into it.) [7]Jesus said, "Leave her alone. She bought it[b] so that she might keep it for the day of my burial. [8]You always have the poor with you, but you do not always have me."

[9]When the great crowd of the Jews learned that he was there, they came not only because of Jesus but also to see Lazarus, whom he had raised from the dead. [10]So the chief priests planned to put Lazarus to death as well, [11]since it was on account of him that many of the Jews were deserting and were believing in Jesus.

[12]The next day the great crowd that had come to the festival heard that Jesus was coming to Jerusalem. [13]So they took branches of palm trees and went out to meet him, shouting,

"Hosanna!
Blessed is the one who
comes in the name of
the Lord—
the King of Israel!"

a Three hundred denarii would be nearly a year's wages for a laborer
b Gk lacks She bought it

14Jesus found a young donkey and sat on it; as it is written:

15 "Do not be afraid, daughter of Zion.
   Look, your king is coming,
   sitting on a donkey's colt!"

16His disciples did not understand these things at first; but when Jesus was glorified, then they remembered that these things had been written of him and had been done to him. 17So the crowd that had been with him when he called Lazarus out of the tomb and raised him from the dead continued to testify.ᵃ 18It was also because they heard that he had performed this sign that the crowd went to meet him. 19The Pharisees then said to one another, "You see, you can do nothing. Look, the world has gone after him!"

20 Now among those who went up to worship at the festival were some Greeks. 21They came to Philip, who was from Bethsaida in Galilee, and said to him, "Sir, we wish to see Jesus." 22Philip went and told Andrew; then Andrew and Philip went and told Jesus. 23Jesus answered them,

---

ᵃ Other ancient authorities read with him began to testify that he had called . . . from the dead

---

	02	2474		2147		1161	01	2424
	τοῦ	Ἰσραήλ.	**14**	εὑρὼν	δὲ	ὁ	Ἰησοῦς	
	of the	Israel.		Having found	but	the	Jesus	

3678 ... 2523 ... 1909 846 ... 2531 ... 1510
ὀνάριον ἐκάθισεν ἐπ᾽ αὐτό, καθὼς ἐστιν+
small donkey sat on it, just as it is+

1125 ... 3361 5399 2364 ... 4622 2400
γεγραμμένον· **15** μὴ φοβοῦ, θυγάτηρ Σιών· ἰδοὺ
+having been written; not fear, daughter Sion; look

01 935 1473 2064 2521 1909 4454
ὁ βασιλεύς σου ἔρχεται, καθήμενος ἐπὶ πῶλον
the king of you comes, sitting on colt

3688 ... 3778 3756 1097 846 013 3101 012
ὄνου. **16** ταῦτα οὐκ ἔγνωσαν αὐτοῦ οἱ μαθηταὶ τὸ
of donkey. These not knew of him the learners the

4413 235 3753 1392 2424 5119
πρῶτον, ἀλλ᾽ ὅτε ἐδοξάσθη Ἰησοῦς τότε
first, but when was given splendor Jesus then

3403 3754 3778 1510 1909 846
ἐμνήσθησαν ὅτι ταῦτα ἦν ἐπ᾽ αὐτῷ
they remembered that these it was on him

1125 2532 3778 4160 846
γεγραμμένα καὶ ταῦτα ἐποίησαν αὐτῷ.
having been written and these they did to him.

17 3140 3767 01 3793 01 1510 3326 846
ἐμαρτύρει οὖν ὁ ὄχλος ὁ ὢν μετ᾽ αὐτοῦ
Was testifying then the crowd the one being with him

3753 04 2976 5455 1537 010 3419 2532
ὅτε τὸν Λάζαρον ἐφώνησεν ἐκ τοῦ μνημείου καὶ
when the Lazarus he sounded from the grave and

1453 846 1537 3498 **18** 1223 3778 2532
ἤγειρεν αὐτὸν ἐκ νεκρῶν. διὰ τοῦτο [κὰι]
he raised him from dead. Through this also

5221 846 01 3793 3754 191 3778
ὑπήντησεν αὐτῷ ὁ ὄχλος, ὅτι ἤκουσαν τοῦτο
met him the crowd, because they heard this

846 4160 013 4592 **19** 013 3767 5330
αὐτὸν πεποιηκέναι τὸ σημεῖον. οἱ οὖν Φαρισαῖοι
him to be done the sign. The then Pharisees

3004 4314 1438 2334 3754 3756 5623
εἶπαν πρὸς ἑαυτούς· θεωρεῖτε ὅτι οὐκ ὠφελεῖτε
said toward themselves; watch that not you benefit

3762 2396 01 2889 3694 846 565
οὐδέν· ἴδε ὁ κόσμος ὀπίσω αὐτοῦ ἀπῆλθεν.
nothing; look the world after him went off.

20 1510 1161 1672 5100 1537 014
Ἦσαν δὲ Ἕλληνές τινες ἐκ τῶν
There were but Greeks some out of the ones

305 2443 4352 1722 07 1859
ἀναβαινόντων ἵνα προσκυνήσωσιν ἐν τῇ ἑορτῇ·
going up that they might worship in the festival;

21 3778 3767 4334 5376 03 575 966
οὗτοι οὖν προσῆλθον Φιλίππῳ τῷ ἀπὸ Βηθσαϊδὰ
these then came toward Philip the from Bethsaida

06 1056 2532 2065 846 3004
τῆς Γαλιλαίας καὶ ἠρώτων αὐτὸν λέγοντες·
of the Galilee and they were asking him saying;

2962 2309 04 2424 3708 **22** 2064 01
κύριε, θέλομεν τὸν Ἰησοῦν ἰδεῖν. ἔρχεται ὁ
master, we want the Jesus to see. Comes the

5376 2532 3004 03 406 2064 406
Φίλιππος καὶ λέγει τῷ Ἀνδρέᾳ, ἔρχεται Ἀνδρέας
Philip and says to the Andrew; comes Andrew

2532 5376 2532 3004 03 **23** 01 1161
καὶ Φίλιππος καὶ λέγουσιν τῷ Ἰησοῦ. ὁ δὲ
and Philip also say to the Jesus. The but

2424 611 846 3004 2064 05 5610
Ἰησοῦς ἀποκρίνεται αὐτοῖς λέγων· ἐλήλυθεν ἡ ὥρα
Jesus answers to them saying; has come the hour

2443 1392   01   5207 02
ἵνα   δοξασθῇ   ὁ   υἱὸς τοῦ
that might be given splendor   the   son   of the

444   281   281   3004 1473   1437 3361 01
ἀνθρώπου.   **24** ἀμὴν ἀμὴν λέγω ὑμῖν,   ἐὰν   μὴ   ὁ
man.   Amen amen I say to you,   except   the

2848   02   4621   4098   1519 08   1093 599
κόκκος τοῦ   σίτου πεσὼν   εἰς τὴν γῆν   ἀποθάνῃ,
grain of the wheat falling into the earth might die,

846   3441   3306   1437 1161 599   4183
αὐτὸς μόνος μένει· ἐὰν   δὲ   ἀποθάνῃ,   πολὺν
it   alone stays; if   but   it might die, much

2590   5342   01   5368 08   5590 846
καρπὸν φέρει. **25** ὁ   φιλῶν τὴν ψυχὴν αὐτοῦ
fruit it carries. The one loving the soul of him

622   846   2532 01   3404   08   5590 846   1722
ἀπολλύει αὐτήν,   καὶ   ὁ   μισῶν τὴν ψυχὴν αὐτοῦ   ἐν
destroys it,   and   the hating the soul of him   in

03   2889   3778   1519 2222 166   5442   846
τῷ   κόσμῳ τούτῳ εἰς ζωὴν αἰώνιον φυλάξει   αὐτήν.
the world this   into life eternal he will guard it.

        1437 1473   5100 1247   1473 190
26 ἐὰν   ἐμοί   τις   διακονῇ,   ἐμοὶ ἀκολουθείτω,
If   to me some might serve,   to me let him follow,

2532 3699   1510 1473 1563   2532 01   1249   01   1699
καὶ   ὅπου   εἰμὶ ἐγὼ ἐκεῖ καὶ ὁ   διάκονος ὁ   ἐμὸς
and   where am   I   there also the servant   the mine

1510   1437 5100 1473 1247   5091   846
ἔσται·   ἐάν   τις   ἐμοὶ διακονῇ τιμήσει   αὐτὸν
will be;   if   some to me might serve will value him

01   3962   3568 05   5590 1473 5015
ὁ   πατήρ. **27** Νῦν ἡ   ψυχή μου τετάρακται,
the   father.   Now the soul of me has been troubled,

2532 5101 3004   3962   4982   1473 1537   06
καὶ   τί   εἴπω;   πάτερ, σῶσόν   με   ἐκ   τῆς
and   what might I say? Father, deliver me   out of the

5610 3778   235   1223   3778   2064   1519 08 5610
ὥρας ταύτης·   ἀλλὰ διὰ   τοῦτο ἦλθον εἰς τὴν ὥραν
hour this?   But   through this   I came into the hour

3778   3962   1392   1473   012 3686
ταύτην. **28** πάτερ, δόξασόν   σου   τὸ   ὄνομα.
this.   Father, give splendor of you the name.

2064   3767 5456 1537 02   3772   2532
ἦλθεν οὖν   φωνὴ ἐκ   τοῦ   οὐρανοῦ· καὶ
Came   then sound from of the heaven;   and

1392   2532 3825 1392
ἐδόξασα   καὶ   πάλιν δοξάσω.   **29** 01
I gave splendor and   again I will give splendor. ὁ
                                                   The

3767 3793 01   2476   2532 191
οὖν   ὄχλος ὁ   ἑστὼς   καὶ   ἀκούσας
then crowd the one having stood and having heard

3004   1027   1096   243   3004
ἔλεγεν   βροντὴν γεγονέναι,   ἄλλοι ἔλεγον·
was saying thunder to have become, others were saying;

32   846   2980   611   2424   2532
ἄγγελος αὐτῷ λελάληκεν. **30** ἀπεκρίθη Ἰησοῦς καὶ
messenger to him has spoken.   Answered Jesus and

3004   3756 1223   1473 05   5456   3778 1096
εἶπεν· οὐ   δι'   ἐμὲ ἡ   φωνὴ αὕτη γέγονεν
said; not   on account me the sound this has become

235   1223   1473   3568 2920   1510 02
ἀλλὰ δι'   ὑμᾶς. **31** νῦν κρίσις ἐστὶν τοῦ
but   on account you.   Now judgment is   of the

2889   3778   3568 01   758   02 2889   3778
κόσμου τούτου, νῦν ὁ   ἄρχων τοῦ κόσμου τούτου
world this,   now the ruler the world this

1544   1854   2504 1437 5312   1537 06
ἐκβληθήσεται ἔξω·   **32** κἀγὼ ἐὰν ὑψωθῶ ἐκ   τῆς
will be thrown outside; and I if   might be from the
out   elevated

"The hour has come for the Son of Man to be glorified. [24]Very truly, I tell you, unless a grain of wheat falls into the earth and dies, it remains just a single grain; but if it dies, it bears much fruit. [25]Those who love their life lose it, and those who hate their life in this world will keep it for eternal life. [26]Whoever serves me must follow me, and where I am, there will my servant be also. Whoever serves me, the Father will honor.

27 "Now my soul is troubled. And what should I say—'Father, save me from this hour'? No, it is for this reason that I have come to this hour. [28]Father, glorify your name." Then a voice came from heaven, "I have glorified it, and I will glorify it again." [29]The crowd standing there heard it and said that it was thunder. Others said, "An angel has spoken to him." [30]Jesus answered, "This voice has come for your sake, not for mine. [31]Now is the judgment of this world; now the ruler of this world will be driven out. [32]And I, when I am lifted up from the

earth, will draw all people[a] to myself." [33]He said this to indicate the kind of death he was to die. [34]The crowd answered him, "We have heard from the law that the Messiah[b] remains forever. How can you say that the Son of Man must be lifted up? Who is this Son of Man?" [35]Jesus said to them, "The light is with you for a little longer. Walk while you have the light, so that the darkness may not overtake you. If you walk in the darkness, you do not know where you are going. [36]While you have the light, believe in the light, so that you may become children of light."

After Jesus had said this, he departed and hid from them. [37]Although he had performed so many signs in their presence, they did not believe in him. [38]This was to fulfill the word spoken by the prophet Isaiah:

"Lord, who has believed our message, and to whom has the arm of the Lord been revealed?"

[39]And so they could not believe, because Isaiah also said,

[40]"He has blinded their eyes and hardened their heart,

[a] Other ancient authorities read all things
[b] Or the Christ

1093	3956	1670	4314 1683	**33** 3778 1161
γῆς,	πάντας	ἑλκύσω	πρὸς ἐμαυτόν.	τοῦτο δὲ
earth,	all	I will haul	to myself.	This but

3004	4591	4169	2288	3195
ἔλεγεν	σημαίνων	ποίῳ	θανάτῳ	ἤμελλεν
he was saying	signifying	what kind	death	he was about

599		611	3767 846	01	3793	1473
ἀποθνῄσκειν.	**34**	Ἀπεκρίθη	οὖν αὐτῷ	ὁ	ὄχλος·	ἡμεῖς
to die.		Answered	then to him	the	crowd;	we

191	1537	02	3551 3754 01	5547	3306 1519
ἠκούσαμεν ἐκ		τοῦ νόμου ὅτι ὁ		χριστὸς μένει εἰς	
heard	out	of the law	that the	Christ	stays into

04	165	2532 4459 3004	1473 3754 1163
τὸν αἰῶνα,	καὶ	πῶς λέγεις σὺ	ὅτι δεῖ
the age,	and	how say you	that it is necessary

5312	04 5207 02	444	5101 1510
ὑψωθῆναι	τὸν υἱὸν τοῦ	ἀνθρώπου;	τίς ἐστιν
to be elevated	the son of	the man?	Who is

3778	01 5207 02	444	**35** 3004 3767 846
οὗτος ὁ	υἱὸς τοῦ	ἀνθρώπου;	εἶπεν οὖν αὐτοῖς
this the	son of	the man?	Said then to them

01	2424	2089 3398	5550 09 5457	1722 1473
ὁ	Ἰησοῦς·	ἔτι μικρὸν	χρόνον τὸ φῶς	ἐν ὑμῖν
the	Jesus;	still small	time the light	in you

1510	4043	5613 012 5457	2192	2443 3361
ἐστιν.	περιπατεῖτε ὡς	τὸ φῶς	ἔχετε,	ἵνα μὴ
is.	Walk around as	the light	you have,	that not

4653	1473 2638	2532 01 4043	1722 07
σκοτία	ὑμᾶς καταλάβῃ·	καὶ ὁ περιπατῶν	ἐν τῇ
dark	you might overtake;	and the one walking	in the
		around	

4653	3756 3609a 4226 5217	**36** 5613 012 5457
σκοτία	οὐκ οἶδεν ποῦ ὑπάγει.	ὡς τὸ φῶς
dark	not knows where he goes off.	As the light

2192	4100	1519 012 5457	2443 5207 5457
ἔχετε,	πιστεύετε εἰς	τὸ φῶς,	ἵνα υἱοὶ φωτὸς
you have,	trust	in the light,	that sons of light

1096		3778 2980	2424 2532
γένησθε.		ταῦτα ἐλάλησεν	Ἰησοῦς, καὶ
you might become.		These spoke	Jesus, and

565	2928	575 846	**37** 5118	1161
ἀπελθὼν	ἐκρύβη	ἀπ' αὐτῶν.	Τοσαῦτα	δὲ
having gone	he was	from them.	Such things	but
off		hidden		

846	4592 4160	1715	846	3756
αὐτοῦ	σημεῖα πεποιηκότος	ἔμπροσθεν	αὐτῶν	οὐκ
of him	signs having done	in front	of them	not

4100	1519 846	**38** 2443 01	3056
ἐπίστευον	εἰς αὐτόν,	ἵνα ὁ	λόγος
they were trusting	into him,	that the	word

2268	02 4396	4137	3739 3004
Ἡσαΐου	τοῦ προφήτου	πληρωθῇ	ὃν εἶπεν·
of Isaiah	the spokesman	might be filled	that he said;

2962	5101 4100	07	189	1473 2532 01
κύριε,	τίς ἐπίστευσεν	τῇ	ἀκοῇ	ἡμῶν; καὶ ὁ
Master,	who trusted	in the	hearing	of us? And the

1023	2962	5101	601	**39** 1223
βραχίων	κυρίου	τίνι	ἀπεκαλύφθη;	διὰ
arm	of Master	to whom	has been uncovered?	Through

3778	3756 1410	4100	3754	3825
τοῦτο	οὐκ ἠδύναντο	πιστεύειν,	ὅτι	πάλιν
this	not they were able	to trust,	because	again

3004	2268	**40** 5186	846	016
εἶπεν	Ἡσαΐας·	τετύφλωκεν	αὐτῶν	τοὺς
said	Isaiah;	he has blinded	of them	the

3788	2532 4456	846	08 2588	2443 3361
ὀφθαλμοὺς	καὶ ἐπώρωσεν	αὐτῶν	τὴν καρδίαν,	ἵνα μὴ
eyes	and hardened	of them	the heart,	that not

3708	015	3788	2532	3539	07

ἴδωσιν   τοῖς   ὀφθαλμοῖς καὶ   νοήσωσιν   τῇ
they might in the eyes   and   they might in the
see   give thought

2588	2532	4762	2532	2390	846

καρδίᾳ καὶ στραφῶσιν, καὶ ἰάσομαι αὐτούς.
heart   and they might turn, and I will cure them.

41
3778	3004	2268	3754	3708	08	1391

ταῦτα εἶπεν Ἠσαΐας ὅτι   εἶδεν τὴν δόξαν
These said Isaiah because he saw the splendor

846	2532	2980	4012	846	3676	3305

αὐτοῦ, καὶ ἐλάλησεν περὶ αὐτοῦ. **42** ὅμως   μέντοι
of him, and he spoke about him.   Likewise indeed

2532	1537	014	758	4183	4100	1519	846

καὶ ἐκ τῶν ἀρχόντων πολλοὶ ἐπίστευσαν εἰς αὐτόν,
also out of the rulers   many   trusted   in him,

235	1223	016	5330	3756	3670

ἀλλὰ διὰ   τοὺς Φαρισαίους οὐχ ὡμολόγουν
but through the Pharisees   not they were confessing

2443	3361	656	1096

ἵνα μὴ ἀποσυνάγωγοι γένωνται·
that not from synagogue ones they might be become;

43
25	1063	08	1391	014	444	3123

ἠγάπησαν γὰρ τὴν δόξαν τῶν ἀνθρώπων μᾶλλον
they loved for the splendor of the men more

2260	08	1391	02	2316	2424	1161	2896

ἤπερ τὴν δόξαν τοῦ θεοῦ. **44** Ἰησοῦς δὲ ἔκραξεν
than the splendor of the God. Jesus but shouted

2532	3004	01	4100	1519	1473	3756	4100

καὶ εἶπεν· ὁ πιστεύων εἰς ἐμὲ οὐ πιστεύει
and said; the one trusting in me not he trusts

1519	1473	235	1519	04	3992	1473	2532

εἰς ἐμὲ ἀλλὰ εἰς τὸν πέμψαντά με, **45** καὶ
in me but in the one having sent me, and

01	2334	1473	2334	04	3992	1473

ὁ θεωρῶν   ἐμὲ θεωρεῖ τὸν πέμψαντά με.
the one watching me watches the one having sent me.

46
1473	5457	1519	04	2889	2064	2443	3956	01

ἐγὼ φῶς εἰς τὸν κόσμον ἐλήλυθα, ἵνα πᾶς ὁ
I   light into the world have come, that all the

4100	1519	1473	1722	07	4653	3361

πιστεύων εἰς ἐμὲ ἐν τῇ σκοτίᾳ μὴ
one trusting in me in the dark not

3306	2532	1437	5100	1473	191	022

μείνῃ. **47** καὶ ἐάν τίς μου ἀκούσῃ τῶν
he might stay. And if some me might hear the

4487	2532	3361	5442	1473	3756	2919	846

ῥημάτων καὶ μὴ φυλάξῃ,   ἐγὼ οὐ κρίνω αὐτόν·
words and not he might guard, I not judge him;

3756	1063	2064	2443	2919	04	2889	235

οὐ γὰρ ἦλθον ἵνα κρίνω τὸν κόσμον, ἀλλ᾽
not for I came that I might judge the world, but

2443	4982	04	2889	01	114

ἵνα σώσω   τὸν κόσμον. **48** ὁ ἀθετῶν
that I might deliver the world. The one setting aside

1473	2532	3361	2983	024	4487	1473	2192	04

ἐμὲ καὶ μὴ λαμβάνων τὰ ῥήματά μου ἔχει τὸν
me and not receiving the words of me has the

2919	846	01	3056	3739	2980	1565

κρίνοντα αὐτόν· ὁ λόγος ὃν ἐλάλησα ἐκεῖνος
one judging him; the word that I spoke that

2919	846	1722	07	2078	2250	3754	1473

κρινεῖ αὐτὸν ἐν τῇ ἐσχάτῃ ἡμέρᾳ. **49** ὅτι ἐγὼ
judges him in the last day. Because I

1537	1683	3756	2980	235	01	3992

ἐξ ἐμαυτοῦ οὐκ ἐλάλησα, ἀλλ᾽ ὁ πέμψας
out of myself not spoke, but the one having sent

1473	3962	846	1473	1785	1325	5101

με πατὴρ αὐτός μοι ἐντολὴν δέδωκεν τί
me father himself to me command has given what

so that they might not
  look with their eyes,
  and understand with
  their heart and
  turn—
  and I would heal them."
[41]Isaiah said this because *a*
he saw his glory and spoke
about him. [42]Neverthe-
less many, even of the
authorities, believed in
him. But because of the
Pharisees they did not
confess it, for fear that they
would be put out of the
synagogue; [43]for they loved
human glory more than the
glory that comes from God.
  44 Then Jesus cried
aloud: "Whoever believes
in me believes not in me but
in him who sent me. [45]And
whoever sees me sees him
who sent me. [46]I have come
as light into the world, so
that everyone who believes
in me should not remain
in the darkness. [47]I do not
judge anyone who hears
my words and does not
keep them, for I came not
to judge the world, but to
save the world. [48]The one
who rejects me and does
not receive my word has a
judge; on the last day the
word that I have spoken
will serve as judge, [49]for
I have not spoken on my
own, but the Father who
sent me has himself given
me a commandment about

a Other ancient witnesses read *when*

what to say and what to speak. ⁵⁰And I know that his commandment is eternal life. What I speak, therefore, I speak just as the Father has told me."

CHAPTER 13

Now before the festival of the Passover, Jesus knew that his hour had come to depart from this world and go to the Father. Having loved his own who were in the world, he loved them to the end. ²The devil had already put it into the heart of Judas son of Simon Iscariot to betray him. And during supper ³Jesus, knowing that the Father had given all things into his hands, and that he had come from God and was going to God, ⁴got up from the table,ᵃ took off his outer robe, and tied a towel around himself. ⁵Then he poured water into a basin and began to wash the disciples' feet and to wipe them with the towel that was tied around him. ⁶He came to Simon Peter, who said to him, "Lord, are you going to wash my feet?" ⁷Jesus answered, "You do not know now what I am doing, but later you will understand." ⁸Peter said to him, "You will never wash my

ᵃ Gk from supper

```
3004      2532 5101  2980            2532  3609a  3754
εἴπω      καὶ  τί    λαλήσω.   50   καὶ   οἶδα  ὅτι
I might say and  what I might speak.  And   I know that
05   1785    846      2222    166    1510   3739 3767 1473
ἡ    ἐντολὴ  αὐτοῦ   ζωὴ   αἰώνιός  ἐστιν.  ἃ    οὖν  ἐγὼ
the command of him  life  eternal  it is. What then I
2980  2531   3004           1473 01 3962    3779
λαλῶ, κάθως  εἴρηκέν       μοι  ὁ  πατήρ,  οὕτως
speak, just as has spoken to me the father, thusly
2980         4253    1161 06  1859      010  3957
λαλῶ.  13:1 Πρὸ  δὲ   τῆς ἑορτῆς  τοῦ  πάσχα
I speak.    Before but the festival of the passover
3609a        01   2424   3754 2064  846      05  5610
εἰδὼς        ὁ  Ἰησοῦς ὅτι  ἦλθεν αὐτοῦ ἡ  ὥρα
having known the Jesus  that came  of him the hour
2443 3327              1537 02  2889    3778
ἵνα  μεταβῇ            ἐκ  τοῦ  κόσμου τούτου
that he might go across out  of the world  this
4314  04  3962      25      016 2398    016
πρὸς τὸν πατέρα, ἀγαπήσας τοὺς ἰδίους τοὺς
toward the father, having loved the  own   the ones
1722 03  2889    1519 5056         25       846       2  2532
ἐν   τῷ  κόσμῳ εἰς  τέλος       ἠγάπησεν αὐτούς.  καὶ
in   the world into completion he loved  them.   And
1173    1096        02   1228     2235
δείπνου γινομένου, τοῦ  διαβόλου ἤδη
dinner  becoming, of the slanderer already
906          1519 08  2588    2443 3860
βεβληκότος   εἰς  τὴν καρδίαν ἵνα  παραδοῖ
having thrown into the heart   that might give over
846    2455    4613    2469          3  3609a      3754
αὐτὸν Ἰούδας Σίμωνος Ἰσκαριώτου,   εἰδὼς       ὅτι
him    Judas  of Simon Iscariot,     having known that
3956   1325    846  01  3962   1519 020  5495   2532
πάντα ἔδωκεν αὐτῷ ὁ  πατὴρ εἰς  τὰς χεῖρας καὶ
all    gave   to him the father into the hands  and
3754 5/5  3216 1831        2532 4314   04  2316
ὅτι  ἀπὸ θεοῦ ἐξῆλθεν      καὶ πρὸς  τὸν θεὸν
that from God he came out and toward the God
5217     4 1453            1537 010 1173    2532 5087
ὑπάγει,    ἐγείρεται      ἐκ  τοῦ δείπνου καὶ τίθησιν
he goes off, he is raised from the dinner  and places
024 2440    2532 2983             3012   1241
τὰ  ἱμάτια  καὶ  λαβὼν      λέντιον διέζωσεν
the clothes and  having taken towel  he belted
1438       5 1534 906      5204 1519 04  3537       2532
ἑαυτόν·      εἶτα βάλλει  ὕδωρ εἰς  τὸν νιπτῆρα  καὶ
himself;    then he throws water into the wash bowl and
757     3538   016     4228  014    3101      2532
ἤρξατο νίπτειν τοὺς πόδας τῶν   μαθητῶν καὶ
he began to wash the feet  of the learners and
1591       011   3012  3739       1510
ἐκμάσσειν τῷ  λεντίῳ ᾧ         ἦν
to wipe dry in the towel in which he was+
1241            6 2064   3767 4314 4613     4074
διεζωσμένος.      ἔρχεται οὖν  πρὸς Σίμωνα Πέτρον·
+having been belted. He comes then to   Simon  Peter;
3004   846     2962    1473 1473 3538    016   4228
λέγει αὐτῷ· κύριε, σὺ  μου  νίπτεις τοὺς πόδας;
he says to him; Master, you of me wash  the  feet?
7 611          2424   2532 3004 846    3739 1473 4160
  ἀπεκρίθη Ἰησοῦς καὶ  εἶπεν αὐτῷ· ὃ    ἐγὼ ποιῶ
  Answered Jesus  and  said to him; what I   do
1473 3756 3609a 737      1097       1161 3326  3778
σὺ   οὐκ οἶδας ἄρτι,   γνώσῃ      δὲ  μετὰ ταῦτα.
you  not know now,    you will know but after these.
8 3004   846   4074      3756 3361 3538          1473
  λέγει αὐτῷ Πέτρος·  οὐ  μὴ  νίψῃς        μου
  Says to him Peter;  not not you might wash of me
```

```
016    4228   1519 04   165      611        2424      846
τοὺς πόδας εἰς τὸν αἰῶνα. ἀπεκρίθη Ἰησοῦς αὐτῷ·
the  feet   into the  age.  Answered  Jesus   to him;
1437 3361 3538          1473 3756 2192      3313    3326
ἐὰν μὴ νίψω      σε, οὐκ ἔχεις μέρος μετ᾽
except I might wash you, not  you have part  with
1473  9 3004  846    4613   4074   2962    3361 016
ἐμοῦ.   λέγει αὐτῷ Σίμων Πέτρος· κύριε, μὴ τοὺς
me.     Says to him Simon Peter; Master, not the
4228 1473 3441   235   2532 020  5495    2532 08
πόδας μου μόνον ἀλλὰ καὶ τὰς χεῖρας καὶ τὴν
feet of me alone but  also the hands  and the
2776    10 3004  846   01  2424   01  3068
κεφαλήν.   λέγει αὐτῷ ὁ Ἰησοῦς· ὁ λελουμένος
head.      Says to him the Jesus; the one having
                                            been washed
3756 2192 5532   1487 3361 016   4228  3538        235
οὐκ ἔχει χρείαν εἰ μὴ τοὺς πόδας νίψασθαι, ᾽αλλ᾽
not has   need  except the feet  to be washed, but
1510  2513    3650  2532 1473  2513     1510  235 3780
ἔστιν καθαρὸς ὅλος· καὶ ὑμεῖς καθαροί ἐστε, ἀλλ᾽ οὐχὶ
he is clean whole; and you   clean   are,  but  not
3956     11 3609a     1063 04    3860    846
πάντες.    ᾔδει     γὰρ τὸν  παραδιδόντα αὐτόν·
all.      He had known for the one giving over him;
1223   3778   3004  3754 3780 3956  2513    1510
διὰ  τοῦτο εἶπεν ὅτι οὐχὶ πάντες καθαροί ἐστε.
through this he said, (") not  all   clean   you are.
    3753 3767 3538     016  4228 846     2532
12 Ὅτε οὖν ἔνιψεν τοὺς πόδας αὐτῶν [καὶ]
   When then he washed the  feet  of them and
2983   024 2440    846   2532 377       3825
ἔλαβεν τὰ ἱμάτια αὐτοῦ καὶ ἀνέπεσεν πάλιν,
he took the clothes of him and he reclined again,
3004   846     1097     5101 4160      1473
εἶπεν αὐτοῖς· γινώσκετε τί πεποίηκα ὑμῖν;
he said to them; know you what I have done to you?
   1473 5455    1473 01 1320        2532 01 2962
13 ὑμεῖς φωνεῖτέ με ὁ διδάσκαλος καί ὁ κύριος,
   You sound  me the teacher   and the Master,
2532 2573 3004    1510 1063 1487 3767 1473 3538
καὶ καλῶς λέγετε· εἰμὶ γάρ. 14 εἰ οὖν ἐγὼ ἔνιψα
and well you say; I am for.   If then I  washed
1473 016 4228  01 2962  2532 01 1320       2532
ὑμῶν τοὺς πόδας ὁ κύριος καὶ ὁ διδάσκαλος, καὶ
of you the feet the Master and the teacher,  also
1473 3784      240        3538   016  4228
ὑμεῖς ὀφείλετε ἀλλήλων νίπτειν τοὺς πόδας·
you   owe     of one another to wash the feet;
   5262    1063 1325   1473  2443 2531    1473
15 ὑπόδειγμα γὰρ ἔδωκα ὑμῖν ἵνα καθὼς ἐγὼ
   example  for I gave to you that just as I
4160    1473  2532 1473 4160      281 281 3004
ἐποίησα ὑμῖν καὶ ὑμεῖς ποιῆτε. 16 ἀμὴν ἀμὴν λέγω
did    to you also you might do. Amen amen I say
1473  3756 1510 1401   3173   02  2962    846
ὑμῖν, οὐκ ἔστιν δοῦλος μείζων τοῦ κυρίου αὐτοῦ
to you, not is  slave greater of the master of him
3761  652      3173   02  3992       846
οὐδὲ ἀπόστολος μείζων τοῦ πέμψαντος αὐτόν.
but not delegate greater of the one having sent him.
   1487 3778 3609a    3107     1510    1437
17 εἰ ταῦτα οἴδατε, μακάριοί ἐστε ἐὰν
   If these you know, fortunate you are if
4160       846    18 3756 4012 3956  1473  3004
ποιῆτε αὐτά.   Οὐ περὶ πάντων ὑμῶν λέγω·
you might do these. Not about all  of you I say;
1473 3609a 5101 1586      235 2443 05
ἐγὼ οἶδα τίνας ἐξελεξάμην· ἀλλ᾽ ἵνα ἡ
I   know whom I myself selected; but that the
```

feet." Jesus answered, "Unless I wash you, you have no share with me." 9Simon Peter said to him, "Lord, not my feet only but also my hands and my head!" 10Jesus said to him, "One who has bathed does not need to wash, except for the feet,[a] but is entirely clean. And you[b] are clean, though not all of you." 11For he knew who was to betray him; for this reason he said, "Not all of you are clean."

12 After he had washed their feet, had put on his robe, and had returned to the table, he said to them, "Do you know what I have done to you? 13You call me Teacher and Lord—and you are right, for that is what I am. 14So if I, your Lord and Teacher, have washed your feet, you also ought to wash one another's feet. 15For I have set you an example, that you also should do as I have done to you. 16Very truly, I tell you, servants[c] are not greater than their master, nor are messengers greater than the one who sent them. 17If you know these things, you are blessed if you do them. 18I am not speaking of all of you; I know whom I have chosen. But it is

---

a Other ancient authorities lack
  except for the feet
b The Greek word for you here
  is plural
c Gk slaves

to fulfill the scripture, 'The one who ate my bread*a* has lifted his heel against me.' [19]I tell you this now, before it occurs, so that when it does occur, you may believe that I am he.*b* [20]Very truly, I tell you, whoever receives one whom I send receives me; and whoever receives me receives him who sent me."

21 After saying this Jesus was troubled in spirit, and declared, "Very truly, I tell you, one of you will betray me." [22]The disciples looked at one another, uncertain of whom he was speaking. [23]One of his disciples—the one whom Jesus loved—was reclining next to him; [24]Simon Peter therefore motioned to him to ask Jesus of whom he was speaking. [25]So while reclining next to Jesus, he asked him, "Lord, who is it?" [26]Jesus answered, "It is the one to whom I give this piece of bread when I have dipped it in the dish."*c* So when he had dipped the piece of bread, he gave it to Judas son of Simon Iscariot.*d* [27]After he received the piece of bread,*e* Satan entered into him. Jesus said to him,

a Other ancient authorities read *ate bread with me*
b Gk *I am*
c Gk *dipped it*
d Other ancient authorities read *Judas Iscariot son of Simon;* others, *Judas son of Simon from Karyot* (Kerioth)
e Gk *After the piece of bread*

1124	4137		01	5176	1473	04
γραφὴ	πληρωθῇ·		ὁ	τρώγων	μου	τὸν

writing might be filled; the one gnawing of me the

740	1869		1909	1473	08	4418
ἄρτον	ἐπῆρεν		ἐπ᾽	ἐμὲ	τὴν	πτέρναν

bread he lifted up on on on me   the heel

846	**19**	575	737	3004	1473	4253	010	1096
αὐτοῦ.		ἀπ᾽	ἄρτι	λέγω	ὑμῖν	πρὸ	τοῦ	γενέσθαι,

of him.   From now I say to you before the to become,

2443	4100		3752	1096		3754
ἵνα	πιστεύσητε		ὅταν	γένηται		ὅτι

that you might trust when it might become because

1473	1510	**20**	281	281	3004	1473	01
ἐγώ	εἰμι.		ἀμὴν	ἀμὴν	λέγω	ὑμῖν,	ὁ

I am.   Amen amen I say to you, the

	2983		302	5100	3992		1473	2983	01
	λαμβάνων		ἄν	τινα	πέμψω		ἐμὲ	λαμβάνει,	ὁ

one receiving - some I might send me   receives, the

1161	1473	2983		2983	04	3992
δὲ	ἐμὲ	λαμβάνων		λαμβάνει	τὸν	πέμψαντά

but me   one receiving receives the one having sent

1473	**21**	3778	3004		01	2424	5015
με.		Ταῦτα	εἰπὼν		[ὁ]	Ἰησοῦς	ἐταράχθη

me.   These having said the Jesus was troubled

011	4151	2532	3140		2532	3004	281
τῷ	πνεύματι	καὶ	ἐμαρτύρησεν		καὶ	εἶπεν,	ἀμὴν

in the spirit   and he testified and   he said, amen

281	3004	1473	3754	1520	1537	1473	3860
ἀμὴν	λέγω	ὑμῖν	ὅτι	εἷς	ἐξ	ὑμῶν	παραδώσει

amen I say to you that one out of you   will give over

1473	**22**	991		1519	240		013	3101
με.		ἔβλεπον		εἰς	ἀλλήλους		οἱ	μαθηταὶ

me.   Were seeing into one another the learners

639		4012		5101	3004	**23**	1510	345
ἀπορούμενοι		περὶ		τίνος	λέγει.		ἦν	ἀνακείμενος

doubting   concerning whom he says. Was+ +reclining

1520	1537	014	3101		846	1722	03	2836	03
εἷς	ἐκ	τῶν	μαθητῶν		αὐτοῦ	ἐν	τῷ	κόλπῳ	τοῦ

one out of the learners of him in the lap   of the

2424	3739	25		01	2424	**24**	3506	3767	3778
Ἰησοῦ,	ὃν	ἠγάπα		ὁ	Ἰησοῦς.		νεύει	οὖν	τούτῳ

Jesus, whom loved the Jesus.   Nods then to this

4613	4074	4441		5101	302	1510		4012	3739
Σίμων	Πέτρος	πυθέσθαι		τίς	ἂν	εἴη		περὶ	οὗ

Simon Peter to inquire who - it may be about whom

3004	**25**	377		3767	1565	3779	1909
λέγει.		ἀναπεσὼν		οὖν	ἐκεῖνος	οὕτως	ἐπὶ

he says. Having reclined then that one thusly on

012	4738	02		2424	3004	846		2962	5101
τὸ	στῆθος	τοῦ		Ἰησοῦ	λέγει	αὐτῷ·		κύριε,	τίς

the chest of the Jesus says to him; Master, who

1510	**26**	611		01	2424	1565	1510
ἐστιν;		ἀποκρίνεται		[ὁ]	Ἰησοῦς·	ἐκεῖνός	ἐστιν

is it?   Answers   the Jesus; that one is

3739		1473	911	012	5596	2532	1325
ᾧ		ἐγὼ	βάψω	τὸ	ψωμίον	καὶ	δώσω

to whom I   will dip the small bit and I will give

846	911		3767	012	5596	2983
αὐτῷ.	βάψας		οὖν	τὸ	ψωμίον	λαμβάνει

to him. Having dipped then the small bit he takes

2532	1325	2455	4613	2469	**27**	2532
καὶ	δίδωσιν	Ἰούδᾳ	Σίμωνος	Ἰσκαριώτου.		καὶ

and he gives to Judas of Simon Iscariot.   And

3326	012	5596	5119	1525	1519	1565	01
μετὰ	τὸ	ψωμίον	τότε	εἰσῆλθεν	εἰς	ἐκεῖνον	ὁ

after the small bit then went into into that one the

4567	3004	3767	846	01	2424	3739	4160
σατανᾶς.	λέγει	οὖν	αὐτῷ	ὁ	Ἰησοῦς·	ὃ	ποιεῖς

adversary. Says then to him the Jesus; what you do

```
4160      5030            3778   1161  3762      1097  014
ποίησον   τάχιον.    28   τοῦτο  [δὲ]  οὐδεὶς    ἔγνω  τῶν
do        more quickly.   This   but   no one    knew of the

345              4314    5101  3004    846       5100
ἀνακειμένων      πρὸς    τί    εἶπεν   αὐτῷ·  29  τινὲς
ones reclining   toward  what  he said to him;      some

1063 1380        1893    012  1101             2192
γὰρ  ἐδόκουν,     ἐπεὶ    τὸ   γλωσσόκομον      εἶχεν
for  were thinking, since  the  treasure box     had

2455     3754  3004   846    01   2424   59
Ἰούδας,  ὅτι   λέγει  αὐτῷ   [ὁ]  Ἰησοῦς· ἀγόρασον
Judas,   that  says   to him the  Jesus;  buy

3739     5532     2192     1519 08  1859     2228 015
ὧν       χρείαν   ἔχομεν   εἰς  τὴν ἑορτήν,  ἢ    τοῖς
of which need     we have  into the festival, or   to the

4434     2443 5100 1325          2983         3767
πτωχοῖς  ἵνα  τι   δῷ.      30   λαβὼν        οὖν
poor     that some he might give. Having taken then

012 5596       1565      1831    2117         1510
τὸ  ψωμίον     ἐκεῖνος   ἐξῆλθεν εὐθύς.       ἦν
the small bit  that one  went out immediately. It was

1161 3571    31  3753  3767 1831       3004   2424
δὲ   νύξ.         Ὅτε   οὖν  ἐξῆλθεν,   λέγει  Ἰησοῦς·
but  night.   When then he went out, says   Jesus;

3568 1392              01   5207 02   444         2532
νῦν  ἐδοξάσθη          ὁ    υἱὸς τοῦ  ἀνθρώπου καὶ
now  was given splendor the  son  of the man    and

01  2316 1392            1722 846     1487 01
ὁ   θεὸς ἐδοξάσθη        ἐν   αὐτῷ· 32 [εἰ  ὁ
the God  was given splendor in   him;     if  the

2316 1392                1722 846     2532 01  2316
θεὸς ἐδοξάσθη            ἐν   αὐτῷ,]  καὶ  ὁ   θεὸς
God  might be given splendor in   him,   also the God

1392           846   1722 846   2532 2117
δοξάσει        αὐτὸν ἐν   αὐτῷ, καὶ  εὐθὺς
will give splendor him   in   him,  and  immediately

1392           846     33  5040    2089 3398   3326
δοξάσει        αὐτόν.      τεκνία,  ἔτι  μικρὸν μεθ᾽
he will give him.         Little    still little with
splendor                 children,

1473 1510 2212         1473 2532 2531      3004
ὑμῶν εἰμι· ζητήσετέ    με,  καὶ  καθὼς     εἶπον
you  I am; you will seek me,  and  just as    I said

015     2453          3754 3699  1473 5217   1473   3756
τοῖς    Ἰουδαίοις ὅτι  ὅπου ἐγὼ  ὑπάγω ὑμεῖς οὐ
to the  Judeans,  (")  where I    go off you   not

1410      2064     2532 1473 3004  737     1785
δύνασθε   ἐλθεῖν,  καὶ  ὑμῖν λέγω ἄρτι.  34 Ἐντολὴν
are able to go,    and  to you I say now.    Command

2537    1325   1473    2443 25      240
καινὴν  δίδωμι ὑμῖν,   ἵνα  ἀγαπᾶτε ἀλλήλους,
new     I give to you, that you love one another,

2531    25        1473 2443 2532 1473 25       240
καθὼς   ἠγάπησα   ὑμᾶς ἵνα  καὶ  ὑμεῖς ἀγαπᾶτε ἀλλήλους.
just as I loved you that also  you   love one another.

35  1722 3778   1097        3956   3754 1473  3101
    ἐν   τούτῳ  γνώσονται   πάντες ὅτι  ἐμοὶ  μαθηταί
    In   this   will know    all    that in me learners

1510   1437 26     2192        1722 240
ἐστε,  ἐὰν  ἀγάπην ἔχητε      ἐν   ἀλλήλοις.
you are, if  love   you might have in   one another.

36  3004 846    4613      4074     2962  4226
    Λέγει αὐτῷ   Σίμων    Πέτρος· κύριε, ποῦ
    Says  to him Simon Peter; Master, where

5217        611          846    2424    3699
ὑπάγεις;    ἀπεκρίθη [αὐτῷ]  Ἰησοῦς· ὅπου
are you going off? Answered to him Jesus; where

5217   3756 1410    1473    3568 190
ὑπάγω  οὐ   δύνασαί μοι     νῦν  ἀκολουθῆσαι,
I go off not you are able to me now  to follow,
```

"Do quickly what you are going to do." [28]Now no one at the table knew why he said this to him. [29]Some thought that, because Judas had the common purse, Jesus was telling him, "Buy what we need for the festival"; or, that he should give something to the poor. [30]So, after receiving the piece of bread, he immediately went out. And it was night.

31 When he had gone out, Jesus said, "Now the Son of Man has been glorified, and God has been glorified in him. [32]If God has been glorified in him,[a] God will also glorify him in himself and will glorify him at once. [33]Little children, I am with you only a little longer. You will look for me; and as I said to the Jews so now I say to you, 'Where I am going, you cannot come.' [34]I give you a new commandment, that you love one another. Just as I have loved you, you also should love one another. [35]By this everyone will know that you are my disciples, if you have love for one another."

36 Simon Peter said to him, "Lord, where are you going?" Jesus answered, "Where I am going, you cannot follow me now;

_a_ Other ancient authorities lack
If God has been glorified in him

but you will follow afterward." [37]Peter said to him,
"Lord, why can I not
follow you now? I will lay
down my life for you."
[38]Jesus answered, "Will
you lay down your life for
me? Very truly, I tell you,
before the cock crows, you
will have denied me three
times.

CHAPTER 14

"Do not let your hearts be
troubled. Believe[a] in God,
believe also in me. [2]In my
Father's house there are
many dwelling places. If
it were not so, would I
have told you that I go to
prepare a place for you?[b]
[3]And if I go and prepare a
place for you, I will come
again and will take you to
myself, so that where I am,
there you may be also.
[4]And you know the way
to the place where I am
going."[c] [5]Thomas said
to him, "Lord, we do not
know where you are going.
How can we know the
way?" [6]Jesus said to him,
"I am the way, and the
truth, and the life. No one
comes to the Father except
through me. [7]If you know
me, you will know[d] my
Father also. From now on
you do know him and have
seen him."

8 Philip said to him,
"Lord, show us

---

[a] Or You believe
[b] Or If it were not so, I would have
told you; for I go to prepare a place
for you
[c] Other ancient authorities read
Where I am going you know, and
the way you know
[d] Other ancient authorities read
If you had known me, you would
have known

190		1161	5306		3004	846		01
ἀκολουθήσεις		δὲ	ὕστερον.	37	λέγει	αὐτῷ		ὁ
you will follow		but	later.		Says	to him		the

4074	2962	1223		5101	3756	1410		1473
Πέτρος·	κύριε,	διὰ		τί	οὐ	δύναμαί		σοι
Peter;	Master,	through		what	not	I am able		to you

190		737	08	5590	1473	5228		1473
ἀκολουθῆσαι		ἄρτι;	τὴν	ψυχήν	μου	ὑπὲρ		σοῦ
to follow		now?	The	soul	of me	on behalf of		you

5087			611		2424	08	5590	1473
θήσω.		38	ἀποκρίνεται		Ἰησοῦς·	τὴν	ψυχήν	σου
I will place.			Answers		Jesus;	the	soul	of you

place.

5228		1473	5087		281	281	3004
ὑπὲρ		ἐμοῦ	θήσεις;		ἀμὴν	ἀμὴν	λέγω
on behalf of		of me	will you place?		Amen	amen	I say

1473		3756	3361	220		5455		2193	3739
σοι,		οὐ	μὴ	ἀλέκτωρ		φωνήσῃ		ἕως	οὗ
to you,		not	not	rooster		might sound		until	which

720		1473	5151		3361	5015
ἀρνήσῃ		με	τρίς.	14:1	Μὴ	ταρασσέσθω
you will deny		me	three.		Not	let be troubled

1473	05	2588		4100		1519	04	2316	2532	1519
ὑμῶν	ἡ	καρδία·		πιστεύετε		εἰς	τὸν	θεὸν	καὶ	εἰς
of you	the	heart;		trust		in	the	God,	also	in

1473	4100		1722	07	3614	02		3962	1473
ἐμὲ	πιστεύετε.	2	ἐν		τῇ	οἰκίᾳ	τοῦ		πατρός	μου
me	trust.		In		the	house	of the		father	of me

3438		4183	1510		1487	1161	3361	3004
μοναὶ		πολλαί	εἰσιν·		εἰ	δὲ	μή,	εἶπον
rooms to stay		many	there are;		if	but	not,	I told

302	1473	3754	4198		2090		5117	1473
ἂν	ὑμῖν	ὅτι	πορεύομαι		ἑτοιμάσαι		τόπον	ὑμῖν;
-	to you	that	I travel		to prepare		place	to you?

3	2532	1437	4198		2532	2090		5117	1473	3825
	καὶ	ἐὰν	πορευθῶ		καὶ	ἑτοιμάσω		τόπον	ὑμῖν,	πάλιν
	And	if	I might		also	I might		place	to you,	again
			travel			prepare				

2064	2532	3880		1473	4314	1683
ἔρχομαι	καὶ	παραλήμψομαι		ὑμᾶς	πρὸς	ἐμαυτόν,
I come	and	I will take along		you	toward	myself,

2443	3699	1510	1473	2532	1473	1510		4	2532	3699
ἵνα	ὅπου	εἰμὶ	ἐγὼ	καὶ	ὑμεῖς	ἦτε.			καὶ	ὅπου
that	where	am	I	also	you	might be.			And	where

1473	5217	3609a		08	3598		5	3004	846	2381
[ἐγὼ]	ὑπάγω	οἴδατε		τὴν	ὁδόν.			Λέγει	αὐτῷ	Θωμᾶς·
I	go off	you know		the	way.			Says	to him	Thomas;

2962	3756	3609a	4226	5217		4459	1410
κύριε,	οὐκ	οἴδαμεν	ποῦ	ὑπάγεις·		πῶς	δυνάμεθα
Master,	not	we know	where	you go off;		how	are we able

08	3598	3609a		6	3004	846		01	2424	1473
τὴν	ὁδὸν	εἰδέναι;			λέγει	αὐτῷ		[ὁ]	Ἰησοῦς·	ἐγώ
the way	to know?				Says	to him		the	Jesus;	I

1510	05	3598	2532	05	225		2532	05	2222	3762
εἰμι	ἡ	ὁδὸς	καὶ	ἡ	ἀλήθεια		καὶ	ἡ	ζωή·	οὐδεὶς
am	the	way	and	the	truth		and	the	life;	no one

2064	4314	04	3962	1487	3361	1223		1473
ἔρχεται	πρὸς	τὸν	πατέρα	εἰ	μὴ	δι'		ἐμοῦ.
comes	toward	the	father	except		through		me.

7	1487	1097		1473	2532	04	3962	1473	1097
	εἰ	ἐγνώκατέ		με,	καὶ	τὸν	πατέρα	μου	γνώσεσθε.
	If	you had		me,	and	the	father	of me	you will
		known							know.

2532	575	737	1097		846	2532	3708
καὶ	ἀπ'	ἄρτι	γινώσκετε		αὐτὸν	καὶ	ἑωράκατε
And	from	now	you know		him	and	you have seen

846		8	3004	846	5376		2962	1166	1473
αὐτόν.			Λέγει	αὐτῷ	Φίλιππος·		κύριε,	δεῖξον	ἡμῖν
him.			Says	to him	Philip;		Master,	show	to us

```
04   3962     2532  714              1473    9  3004   846
τὸν πατέρα,  καὶ  ἀρκεῖ            ἡμῖν.    λέγει αὐτῷ
the father,  and  it is enough to us.      Says to him
01   2424     5118      5550    3326 1473 1510 2532 3756
ὁ  Ἰησοῦς·  τοσούτῳ χρόνῳ μεθ᾽ ὑμῶν εἰμι καὶ  οὐκ
the Jesus;  in such time   with you  I am  and  not
1097          1473 5376    01   3708              1473
ἔγνωκάς     με, Φίλιππε; ὁ  ἑωρακὼς         ἐμὲ
you have known me, Philip?  The one having seen me
3708       04   3962       4459 1473 3004       1166      1473
ἑώρακεν  τὸν πατέρα·  πῶς σὺ  λέγεις· δεῖξον ἡμῖν
has seen the father;   how you  say;    show   to us
04   3962      10  3756 4100           3754 1473 1722 03
τὸν πατέρα;       οὐ πιστεύεις ὅτι ἐγὼ ἐν  τῷ
the father?      Not you trust  that I    in  the
3962    2532 01   3962     1722 1473 1510    024 4487
πατρὶ καὶ ὁ  πατὴρ ἐν  ἐμοί ἐστιν; τὰ  ῥήματα
father and the father in   me   is?    The words
3739 1473 3004 1473      575  1683      3756 2980
ἃ    ἐγὼ λέγω ὑμῖν ἀπ᾽ ἐμαυτοῦ οὐ  λαλῶ,
which I    say  to you from myself not  I speak,
01   1161 3962    1722 1473 3306       4160  024 2041
ὁ  δὲ  πατὴρ ἐν  ἐμοὶ μένων ποιεῖ τὰ  ἔργα
the but father in   me   staying does the works
846        11  4100          1473 3754 1473 1722 03   3962
αὐτοῦ.       πιστεύετέ μοι  ὅτι ἐγὼ ἐν  τῷ πατρὶ
of him.  Trust       in me that I    in   the father
2532 01   3962      1722 1473 1487 1161 3361 1223   024
καὶ ὁ  πατὴρ ἐν  ἐμοί· εἰ  δὲ  μή, διὰ τὰ
and the father in   me;   if  but  not, through the
2041 846    4100        12  281  281  3004 1473     01
ἔργα αὐτὰ πιστεύετε.    Ἀμὴν ἀμὴν λέγω ὑμῖν, ὁ
works these trust.       Amen amen I say to you, the
4100               1519 1473 024 2041 3739    1473 4160
πιστεύων      εἰς ἐμὲ τὰ ἔργα ἃ    ἐγὼ ποιῶ
one trusting in   me   the works which I    do
2548              4160       2532 3173    3778      4160
κἀκεῖνος     ποιήσει καὶ μείζονα τούτων ποιήσει,
also that one will do and greater of these he will do,
3754      1473 4314 04   3962     4198        13  2532 3739
ὅτι      ἐγὼ πρὸς τὸν πατέρα πορεύομαι·    καὶ ὅ
because I    to   the father travel;         and  what
5100 302 154             1722 011 3686      1473 3778
τι  ἂν αἰτήσητε      ἐν  τῷ ὀνόματί μου τοῦτο
some -  you might ask in   the name    of me this
4160       2443 1392        01   3962    1722 03   5207
ποιήσω, ἵνα δοξασθῇ  ὁ  πατὴρ ἐν  τῷ υἱῷ.
I will    that might be given the father in   the son.
do,           splendor
     14  1437 5100 154             1473 1722 011 3686       1473
        ἐάν τι  αἰτήσητέ       με  ἐν  τῷ ὀνόματί μου
        If  some you might ask me  in   the name      of me
1473 4160       15  1437 25           1473 020 1785
ἐγὼ ποιήσω.      Ἐὰν ἀγαπᾶτέ     με, τὰς ἐντολὰς
I    will do.      If  you might love me, the commands
020 1699 5083            16  2504  2065    04   3962    2532
τὰς ἐμὰς τηρήσετε·      κἀγὼ ἐρωτήσω τὸν πατέρα καὶ
the mine you will keep;  and I will ask the father and
243  3875        1325       1473       2443 3326 1473
ἄλλον παράκλητον δώσει   ὑμῖν, ἵνα μεθ᾽ ὑμῶν
other encourager he will give to you, that with you
1519 04   165  1510           17  012 4151   06   225
εἰς τὸν αἰῶνα ᾖ,           τὸ πνεῦμα τῆς ἀληθείας,
in   the age  he might be,  the spirit of the truth,
3739 01   2889     3756 1410      2983         3754       3756
ὃ  ὁ  κόσμος οὐ  δύναται λαβεῖν, ὅτι      οὐ
which the world not  is able to receive, because not
2334       846  3761   1097         1473 1097
θεωρεῖ  αὐτὸ οὐδὲ γινώσκει· ὑμεῖς γινώσκετε
it watches it   but not it knows,  you    know
```

the Father, and we will be
satisfied." [9]Jesus said to
him, "Have I been with you
all this time, Philip, and
you still do not know me?
Whoever has seen me has
seen the Father. How can
you say, 'Show us the
Father'? [10]Do you not
believe that I am in the
Father and the Father is
in me? The words that I say
to you I do not speak on my
own; but the Father who
dwells in me does his works.
[11]Believe me that I am in
the Father and the Father
is in me; but if you do not,
then believe me because
of the works themselves.
[12]Very truly, I tell you, the
one who believes in me will
also do the works that I do
and, in fact, will do greater
works than these, because
I am going to the Father.
[13]I will do whatever you
ask in my name, so that the
Father may be glorified in
the Son. [14]If in my name
you ask me[a] for anything,
I will do it.

[15] "If you love me, you
will keep[b] my command-
ments. [16]And I will ask the
Father, and he will give you
another Advocate,[c] to be
with you forever. [17]This is
the Spirit of truth, whom
the world cannot receive,
because it neither sees him
nor knows him. You know

[a] Other ancient authorities lack *me*
[b] Other ancient authorities read *me,
keep*
[c] Or *Helper*

him, because he abides with you, and he will be in*a* you.

18 "I will not leave you orphaned; I am coming to you. 19In a little while the world will no longer see me, but you will see me; because I live, you also will live. 20On that day you will know that I am in my Father, and you in me, and I in you. 21They who have my commandments and keep them are those who love me; and those who love me will be loved by my Father, and I will love them and reveal myself to them." 22Judas (not Iscariot) said to him, "Lord, how is it that you will reveal yourself to us, and not to the world?" 23Jesus answered him, "Those who love me will keep my word, and my Father will love them, and we will come to them and make our home with them. 24Whoever does not love me does not keep my words; and the word that you hear is not mine, but is from the Father who sent me.

25 "I have said these things to you while I am still with you. 26But the Advocate,*b* the Holy Spirit, whom the Father will send in my name,

a Or among
b Or Helper

846	3754	3844	1473 3306	2532 1722 1473
αὐτό,	ὅτι	παρ᾽	ὑμῖν μένει	καὶ ἐν ὑμῖν
it,	because	beside	you it stays	and in you

1510   3756 863   1473 3737
ἔσται.   **18**   Οὐκ ἀφήσω   ὑμᾶς ὀρφανούς,
it will be.   Not I will leave off you orphans,

2064   4314   1473   **19** 2089   3398   2532 01   2889
ἔρχομαι πρὸς   ὑμᾶς.   ἔτι   μικρὸν καὶ ὁ κόσμος
I come   toward you.   Still little and the world

1473 3765   2334   1473 1161 2334   1473
με οὐκέτι   θεωρεῖ,   ὑμεῖς δὲ   θεωρεῖτέ με,
me no longer watches, you but watch me,

3754   1473 2198 2532 1473   2198   **20** 1722 1565
ὅτι   ἐγὼ ζῶ καὶ ὑμεῖς ζήσετε.   ἐν ἐκείνῃ
because I live also you will live.   In that

07 2250 1097   1473 3754 1473 1722 03 3962
τῇ ἡμέρᾳ γνώσεσθε ὑμεῖς ὅτι ἐγὼ ἐν τῷ πατρί
the day will know you that I in the father

1473 2532 1473 1722 1473 2504 1722 1473   01
μου καὶ ὑμεῖς ἐν ἐμοὶ κἀγὼ ἐν ὑμῖν. **21** ὁ
of me and you in me and I in you. The one

2192   020 1785   1473 2532 5083   846   1565
ἔχων τὰς ἐντολάς μου καὶ τηρῶν αὐτὰς ἐκεῖνός
having the commands of me and keeping them that one

1510 01 25   1473 01 1161 25   1473
ἐστιν ὁ ἀγαπῶν   με· ὁ δὲ ἀγαπῶν   με
is the one loving me; the but one loving me

25   5259 02 3962   1473   2504 25
ἀγαπηθήσεται ὑπὸ τοῦ πατρός μου, κἀγὼ ἀγαπήσω
will be loved by the father of me, and I will love

846 2532 1718   846   1683   **22** 3004
αὐτὸν καὶ ἐμφανίσω   αὐτῷ ἐμαυτόν.   Λέγει
him and I will be visible to him myself. Says

846   2455   3756 01 2469   2962   2532 5101
αὐτῷ Ἰούδας, οὐχ ὁ Ἰσκαριώτης· κύριε, [καὶ] τί
to him Judas, not the Iscariot; Master, and what

1096   3754 1473 3195   1718
γέγονεν ὅτι ἡμῖν μέλλεις   ἐμφανίζειν
has become that to us you are about to be visible

4572   2532 3780 03   2889   **23** 611   2424
σεαυτὸν καὶ οὐχὶ τῷ κόσμῳ;   ἀπεκρίθη Ἰησοῦς
yourself and not to the world? Answered Jesus

2532 3004   846   1437 5100 25   1473 04 3056
καὶ εἶπεν αὐτῷ· ἐάν τις ἀγαπᾷ   με τὸν λόγον
and he said to him; if some might love me the word

1473 5083   2532 01 3962   1473 25
μου τηρήσει,   καὶ ὁ πατήρ μου ἀγαπήσει
of me he will keep, and the father of me will love

846 2532 4314   846 2064   2532 3438
αὐτὸν καὶ πρὸς αὐτὸν ἐλευσόμεθα καὶ μονὴν
him and toward him we will come and room to stay

3844᾽   846 4160   **24** 01   3361 25   1473
παρ᾽ αὐτῷ ποιησόμεθα.   ὁ μὴ ἀγαπῶν με
alongside him we will make. The one not loving me

016 3056   1473 3756 5083   2532 01 3056 3739
τοὺς λόγους μου οὐ τηρεῖ· καὶ ὁ λόγος ὃν
the words of me not he keeps; and the word that

191   3756 1510 1699 235 02   3992
ἀκούετε οὐκ ἔστιν ἐμὸς ἀλλὰ τοῦ πέμψαντός
you hear not it is mine but of the one having sent

1473 3962   **25** 3778 2980   1473 3844 1473
με πατρός.   Ταῦτα λελάληκα ὑμῖν παρ᾽ ὑμῖν
me father. These I have spoken to you from you

3306   **26** 01 1161 3875   09 4151 09 40
μένων·   ὁ δὲ παράκλητος, τὸ πνεῦμα τὸ ἅγιον,
staying; the but encourager, the spirit the holy,

3739 3992   01 3962   1722 011 3686   1473
ὃ πέμψει   ὁ πατὴρ ἐν τῷ ὀνόματί μου,
whom will send the father in the name of me,

1565   1473 1321   3956 2532 5279   1473
ἐκεῖνος ὑμᾶς διδάξει   πάντα καὶ ὑπομνήσει   ὑμᾶς
that one you will teach all   and he will remind you
3956   3739 3004   1473 1473   1515   863
πάντα ἃ   εἶπον ὑμῖν [ἐγώ]. **27** Εἰρηνην ἀφιημι
all   that said to you I.   Peace   I leave off
1473   1515   08   1699 1325   1473   3756 2531   01
ὑμῖν, εἰρήνην τὴν ἐμὴν δίδωμι ὑμῖν· οὐ καθὼς ὁ
to you, peace the mine I give to you; not just as the
2889   1325   1473 1325   1473   3361 5015
κόσμος δίδωσιν ἐγὼ δίδωμι ὑμῖν. μὴ ταρασσέσθω
world gives   I   give to you. Not let be troubled
1473 05   2588   3366   1168   191
ὑμῶν ἡ καρδία μηδὲ δειλιάτω.   **28** ἠκούσατε
of you the heart but not let be coward.   You heard
3754 1473 3004   1473   5217   2532 2064   4314
ὅτι ἐγὼ εἶπον ὑμῖν· ὑπάγω καὶ ἔρχομαι πρὸς
that I   said to you; I go off and I come toward
1473 1487 25   1473 5463   302 3754
ὑμᾶς. εἰ ἠγαπᾶτέ   με ἐχάρητε   ἂν ὅτι
you. If you were loving me you rejoiced - because
4198   4314 04 3962   3754   01 3962   3173
πορεύομαι πρὸς τὸν πατέρα, ὅτι ὁ πατὴρ μείζων
I travel to the father, because the father greater
1473 1510   2532 3568 3004   1473   4250
μού ἐστιν. **29** καὶ νῦν εἴρηκα ὑμῖν πρὶν
of me is.   And now I have said to you before
1096   2443 3752 1096   4100
γενέσθαι, ἵνα ὅταν γένηται   πιστεύσητε.
to become, that when it might become you might trust.
30 3765   4183 2980   3326 1473 2064   1063
οὐκέτι   πολλὰ λαλήσω   μεθ᾽ ὑμῶν, ἔρχεται γὰρ
No longer many I will speak with you, comes   for
01 02   2889   758   2532 1722 1473 3756 2192
ὁ τοῦ κόσμου ἄρχων· καὶ ἐν ἐμοὶ οὐκ ἔχει
the the of world ruler; and in me not he has
3762   235   2443 1097   01 2889   3754 25
οὐδέν, **31** ἀλλ᾽ ἵνα γνῷ   ὁ κόσμος ὅτι ἀγαπῶ
nothing, but that might know the world that I love
04 3962   2532 2532 2531   1781   01 3962
τὸν πατέρα, καὶ καθὼς ἐνετείλατό μοι ὁ πατήρ,
the father, and just as commanded to me the father,
3779   4160 1453   71   1782
οὕτως ποιῶ. ἐγείρεσθε, ἄγωμεν ἐντεῦθεν.
thusly I do. Be raised, we might lead from here.
15:1 1473 1510 05 288   05 228   2532 01 3962
Ἐγώ εἰμι ἡ ἄμπελος ἡ ἀληθινὴ καὶ ὁ πατήρ
I   am the vine   the true   and the father
1473 01 1092   1510   3956 2814   1722 1473 3361
μου ὁ γεωργός ἐστιν. **2** πᾶν κλῆμα ἐν ἐμοὶ μὴ
of me the farmer is.   All branch in me   not
5342   2590   142   846   2532 3956 012 2590
φέρον καρπὸν αἴρει αὐτό, καὶ πᾶν τὸ καρπὸν
carrying fruit he lifts up it, and all the fruit
5342   2508   846 2443 2590 4183
φέρον καθαίρει αὐτὸ ἵνα καρπὸν πλείονα
one carrying he cleans it that fruit more
5342   2235   1473 2513   1510 1223   04
φέρῃ. **3** ἤδη ὑμεῖς καθαροί ἐστε διὰ τὸν
it might carry. Already you clean   are through the
3056 3739 2980   1473   3306   1722 1473
λόγον ὃν λελάληκα ὑμῖν· **4** μείνατε ἐν ἐμοί,
word that I have spoken to you; stay in me,
2504 1722 1473 2531   09 2814   3756 1410   2590
κἀγὼ ἐν ὑμῖν. καθὼς τὸ κλῆμα οὐ δύναται καρπὸν
and I in you. Just as the branch not is able fruit
5342   575 1438   1437 3361 3306   1722 07
φέρειν ἀφ᾽ ἑαυτοῦ ἐὰν μὴ μένῃ   ἐν τῇ
to carry from itself except it might stay in the

will teach you everything, and remind you of all that I have said to you. [27]Peace I leave with you; my peace I give to you. I do not give to you as the world gives. Do not let your hearts be troubled, and do not let them be afraid. [28]You heard me say to you, 'I am going away, and I am coming to you.' If you loved me, you would rejoice that I am going to the Father, because the Father is greater than I. [29]And now I have told you this before it occurs, so that when it does occur, you may believe. [30]I will no longer talk much with you, for the ruler of this world is coming. He has no power over me; [31]but I do as the Father has commanded me, so that the world may know that I love the Father. Rise, let us be on our way.

CHAPTER 15

"I am the true vine, and my Father is the vinegrower. [2]He removes every branch in me that bears no fruit. Every branch that bears fruit he prunes[a] to make it bear more fruit. [3]You have already been cleansed[a] by the word that I have spoken to you. [4]Abide in me as I abide in you. Just as the branch cannot bear fruit by itself unless it abides in the

[a] The same Greek root refers to pruning and cleansing

vine, neither can you unless you abide in me. ⁵I am the vine, you are the branches. Those who abide in me and I in them bear much fruit, because apart from me you can do nothing. ⁶Whoever does not abide in me is thrown away like a branch and withers; such branches are gathered, thrown into the fire, and burned. ⁷If you abide in me, and my words abide in you, ask for whatever you wish, and it will be done for you. ⁸My Father is glorified by this, that you bear much fruit and become*a* my disciples. ⁹As the Father has loved me, so I have loved you; abide in my love. ¹⁰If you keep my commandments, you will abide in my love, just as I have kept my Father's commandments and abide in his love. ¹¹I have said these things to you so that my joy may be in you, and that your joy may be complete.

12 "This is my commandment, that you love one another as I have loved you. ¹³No one has greater love than this,

a Or *be*

288	3779	3761	1473 1437 3361	1722 1473
ἀμπέλῳ,	οὕτως	οὐδὲ	ὑμεῖς ἐὰν μὴ	ἐν ἐμοὶ
vine,	thusly	but not	you except	in me

3306   5 ¹⁴⁷³ ¹⁵¹⁰ ⁰⁵ ²⁸⁸   ¹⁴⁷³ ⁰²¹
μένητε.   ἐγώ εἰμι ἡ ἄμπελος, ὑμεῖς τὰ
you might stay.   I am the vine,   you the

2814   01   3306   1722 1473 2504 1722 846
κλήματα. ὁ   μένων   ἐν ἐμοὶ κἀγὼ ἐν αὐτῷ
branches. The one staying in me and I in him

3778   5342 2590   4183   3754   5565   1473 3756
οὗτος   φέρει καρπὸν πολύν, ὅτι   χωρὶς ἐμοῦ οὐ
this one bears fruit much, because without me not

1410   4160   3762   6 ¹⁴³⁷ ³³⁶¹ ⁵¹⁰⁰ ³³⁰⁶
δύνασθε   ποιεῖν οὐδέν.   ἐὰν μὴ τις μένῃ
you are able to do nothing. Except one might stay

1722 1473   906   1854   5613 09 2814   2532
ἐν ἐμοί, ἐβλήθη   ἔξω   ὡς τὸ κλῆμα καὶ
in me, he was thrown outside as the branch and

3583   2532 4863   846   2532
ἐξηράνθη   καὶ συνάγουσιν   αὐτὰ καὶ
it was dried out and they bring together these and

1519 012 4442 906   2532 2545   7 ¹⁴³⁷
εἰς τὸ πῦρ βάλλουσιν καὶ καίεται.   ἐὰν
into the fire they throw and it is burned. If

3306   1722 1473 2532 021 4487   1473   1722
μείνητε   ἐν ἐμοὶ καὶ τὰ ῥήματά μου ἐν
you might stay in me and the words of me in

1473 3306   3739 1437 2309   154
ὑμῖν μείνῃ,   ὃ ἐὰν θέλητε   αἰτήσασθε,
you might stay, what if you might want ask,

2532 1096   1473 8 ¹⁷²² ³⁷⁷⁸ ¹³⁹²   01 3962
καὶ γενήσεται ὑμῖν. ἐν τούτῳ ἐδοξάσθη ὁ πατήρ
and it will to you. In this was given the father
      become   splendor

1473   2443 2590   4183 5342   2532 1096
μου, ἵνα καρπὸν πολὺν φέρητε   καὶ γένησθε
of me, that fruit much you might and you might
                            carry   become

1473 3101   9 ²⁵³¹   25   1473 01 3962
ἐμοὶ μαθηταί. Καθὼς   ἠγάπησέν με ὁ πατήρ,
to me learners. Just as loved me the father,

2504 1473 25   3306   1722 07   26   07 1699
κἀγὼ ὑμᾶς ἠγάπησα· μείνατε ἐν τῇ ἀγάπῃ τῇ ἐμῇ.
and I you loved; stay in the love the mine.

    10 ¹⁴³⁷ ⁰²⁰ ¹⁷⁸⁵   ¹⁴⁷³ ⁵⁰⁸³
       ἐὰν τὰς ἐντολάς μου τηρήσητε,
       If the commands of me you might keep,

3306   1722 07 26   1473   2531   1473 020
μενεῖτε   ἐν τῇ ἀγάπῃ μου, καθὼς ἐγὼ τὰς
you will stay in the love of me, just as I the

1785   02   3962   1473 5083   2532 3306
ἐντολὰς τοῦ   πατρός μου τετήρηκα καὶ μένω
commands of the father of me have kept and I stay

846   1722 07 26   11 ³⁷⁷⁸ ²⁹⁸⁰   ¹⁴⁷³
αὐτοῦ ἐν τῇ ἀγάπῃ. Ταῦτα λελάληκα ὑμῖν
of him in the love. These I have spoken to you

2443 05 5479 05 1699 1722 1473 1510   2532 05 5479
ἵνα ἡ χαρὰ ἡ ἐμὴ ἐν ὑμῖν ᾖ   καὶ ἡ χαρὰ
that the joy the mine in you might be and the joy

1473 4137   12 ³⁷⁷⁸ ¹⁵¹⁰ ⁰⁵ ¹⁷⁸⁵   ⁰⁵
ὑμῶν πληρωθῇ.   Αὕτη ἐστὶν ἡ ἐντολὴ ἡ
of you might be filled. This is the command the

1699 2443 25   240   2531   25
ἐμή, ἵνα ἀγαπᾶτε   ἀλλήλους καθὼς ἠγάπησα
mine, that you might love one another just as I loved

1473   13 ³¹⁷³   ³⁷⁷⁸ ²⁶   ³⁷⁶² ²¹⁹² ²⁴⁴³ ⁵¹⁰⁰
ὑμᾶς. μείζονα ταύτης ἀγάπην οὐδεὶς ἔχει, ἵνα τις
you.   Greater this love no one has, that some

```
08     5590   846      5087        5228        014      5384
τὴν   ψυχὴν αὐτοῦ θῇ       ὑπὲρ      τῶν      φίλων
the    soul   of him he might on behalf of the  friends
                                place
846       14  1473  5384        1473   1510  1437  4160
αὐτοῦ.  14   ὑμεῖς φίλοι   μού   ἐστε ἐὰν  ποιῆτε
of him.       You   friends of me are  if   you might do
3739  1473  1781         1473      15  3765        3004   1473
ἃ    ἐγὼ  ἐντέλλομαι ὑμῖν.  15  οὐκέτι    λέγω  ὑμᾶς
what  I    command    to you.    No longer I say  you
1401        3754     01  1401    3756 3609a 5101 4160
δούλους, ὅτι     ὁ  δοῦλος οὐκ  οἶδεν τί  ποιεῖ
slaves,  because  the slave   not  knows what does
846    01  2962      1473 1161 3004         5384
αὐτοῦ ὁ κύριος· ὑμᾶς δὲ εἴρηκα    φίλους,
of him the Master;  you but I have said friends,
3754     3956   3739  191        3844 02  3962    1473
ὅτι    πάντα ἃ   ἤκουσα παρὰ τοῦ πατρός μου
because all    that I heard from the father of me
1107         1473        16 3756 1473 1473 1586
ἐγνώρισα  ὑμῖν.  16  οὐχ ὑμεῖς με ἐξελέξασθε,
I made known to you.  Not  you  me yourself selected,
235   1473 1586          1473 2532 5087        1473
ἀλλ᾽ ἐγὼ ἐξελεξάμην ὑμᾶς καὶ  ἔθηκα     ὑμᾶς
but   I    myself selected you and  I have placed you
2443 1473 5217          2532 2590  5342
ἵνα ὑμεῖς ὑπάγητε   καὶ καρπὸν φέρητε
that you   might go off and fruit  you might carry
2532 01  2590   1473  3306          2443 3739 5100 302
καὶ ὁ καρπὸς ὑμῶν μένῃ,      ἵνα ὅ  τι   ἂν
and the fruit of you might stay, that what some -
154         04  3962     1722 011 3686      1473
αἰτήσητε     τὸν πατέρα ἐν  τῷ ὀνόματί μου
you might ask the father in   the  name   of me
1325         1473     17 3778 1781         1473      2443
δῷ          ὑμῖν.  17 ταῦτα ἐντέλλομαι ὑμῖν,  ἵνα
he might give to you.  These I command  to you, that
25         240          18 1487 01  2889  1473
ἀγαπᾶτε    ἀλλήλους.  18 Εἰ  ὁ  κόσμος ὑμᾶς
you might love one another. If  the world  you
3404  1097      3754 1473 4413    1473     3404
μισεῖ, γινώσκετε ὅτι ἐμὲ πρῶτον ὑμῶν μεμίσηκεν.
hates, know     that me  first   of you it has hated.
   19 1487 1537  02  2889   1510     01  2889    302 012
19  εἰ  ἐκ  τοῦ κόσμου ἦτε,    ὁ  κόσμος ἂν  τὸ
     If  out of the world  you were, the world  -   the
2398  5368      3754    1161 1537 02  2889    3756
ἴδιον ἐφίλει·  ὅτι   δὲ  ᾽εκ τοῦ κόσμου οὐκ
own  was loving; because but from the world not
1510      235 1473 1586        1473 1537  02
ἐστέ,   ἀλλ᾽ ἐγὼ ἐξελεξάμην ὑμᾶς ἐκ  τοῦ
you are, but   I   myself selected you out of the
2889    1223    3778 3404  1473 01  2889
κόσμου, διὰ   τοῦτο μισεῖ ὑμᾶς ὁ  κόσμος.
world,  through this hates you  the world.
   20 3421       02    3056  3739 1473 3004  1473
20  μνημονεύετε τοῦ  λόγου οὗ  ἐγὼ εἶπον ὑμῖν·
     You remember of the word that I   said  to you;
3756 1510  1401     3173  02   2962    846     1487
οὐκ ἔστιν δοῦλος μείζων τοῦ κυρίου αὐτοῦ. εἰ
not  is    slave  greater of the Master of him. If
1473 1377        2532 1473 1377             1487 04
ἐμὲ ἐδίωξαν,   καὶ ὑμᾶς διώξουσιν·     εἰ  τὸν
me   they pursued, also you they will pursue; if  the
3056 1473 5083       2532 04  5212      5083
λόγον μου ἐτήρησαν, καὶ τὸν ὑμέτερον τηρήσουσιν.
word of me they kept, also the yours  they will keep.
   21 235   3778  3956  4160       1519 1473 1223
21  ἀλλὰ ταῦτα πάντα ποιήσουσιν εἰς ὑμᾶς διὰ
     But  these all   they will do into you because of
```

to lay down one's life for one's friends. [14]You are my friends if you do what I command you. [15]I do not call you servants[a] any longer, because the servant[b] does not know what the master is doing; but I have called you friends, because I have made known to you everything that I have heard from my Father. [16]You did not choose me but I chose you. And I appointed you to go and bear fruit, fruit that will last, so that the Father will give you whatever you ask him in my name. [17]I am giving you these commands so that you may love one another.

18 "If the world hates you, be aware that it hated me before it hated you. [19]If you belonged to the world,[c] the world would love you as its own. Because you do not belong to the world, but I have chosen you out of the world— therefore the world hates you. [20]Remember the word that I said to you, 'Servants[d] are not greater than their master.' If they persecuted me, they will persecute you; if they kept my word, they will keep yours also. [21]But they will do all these things to you on account of

a Gk slaves
b Gk slave
c Gk were of the world
d Gk Slaves

my name, because they do
not know him who sent me.
²²If I had not come and
spoken to them, they would
not have sin; but now they
have no excuse for their sin.
²³Whoever hates me hates
my Father also. ²⁴If I had
not done among them the
works that no one else did,
they would not have sin.
But now they have seen
and hated both me and my
Father. ²⁵It was to fulfill
the word that is written in
their law, 'They hated me
without a cause.'

26"When the Advocate[a]
comes, whom I will send to
you from the Father, the
Spirit of truth who comes
from the Father, he will
testify on my behalf. ²⁷You
also are to testify because
you have been with me from
the beginning.

CHAPTER 16

"I have said these things to
you to keep you from
stumbling. ²They will put
you out of the synagogues.
Indeed, an hour is coming
when those who kill you
will think that by doing so
they are offering worship
to God. ³And they will do
this because they have not
known the Father or me.
⁴But I have said these things
to you so that when their
hour comes you may
remember that I told you
about them.

"I did not say these
things to you from

[a] Or Helper

012	3686	1473	3754	3756	3609a	04
τὸ	ὄνομά	μου,	ὅτι	οὐκ	οἴδασιν	τὸν
the	name	of me,	because	not	they know	the

3992		1473	**22**	1487	3361	2064	2532	2980
πέμψαντά		με.		εἰ	μὴ	ἦλθον	καὶ	ἐλάλησα
one having sent		me.		Except		I came	and	I spoke

846	266		3756	2192		3568	1161
αὐτοῖς,	ἁμαρτίαν	οὐκ	εἴχοσαν·		νῦν	δὲ
to them,	sin		not	they were having;		now	but

4392		3756	2192	4012	06	266	846
πρόφασιν	οὐκ	ἔχουσιν	περὶ	τῆς	ἁμαρτίας	αὐτῶν.
pretext	not	they have	about	the	sin	of them.

23	01	1473	3404	2532	04	3962	1473	3404	**24**	1487
	ὁ	ἐμὲ	μισῶν	καὶ	τὸν	πατέρα	μου	μισεῖ.		εἰ
	The one	me	hating	also	the	father	of me	hates.		If

024	2041	3361	4160	1722	846	3739	3762	243
τὰ	ἔργα	μὴ	ἐποίησα	ἐν	αὐτοῖς	ἃ	οὐδεὶς	ἄλλος
the works		not	I did	in	them	which	no one	other

4160	266		3756	2192		3568	1161	2532
ἐποίησεν,	ἁμαρτίαν	οὐκ	εἴχοσαν·		νῦν	δὲ	καὶ
did,	sin		not	they were having;		now	but	also

3708		2532	3404		2532	1473	2532	04
ἑωράκασιν	καὶ	μεμισήκασιν	καὶ	ἐμὲ	καὶ	τὸν
they have seen	and	they have hated	also	me	and	the

3962	1473	**25**	235	2443	4137		01	3056
πατέρα	μου.		ἀλλ᾽	ἵνα	πληρωθῇ		ὁ	λόγος
father	of me.		But	that	might be filled		the	word

01	1722	03	3551	846	1125		3754
ὁ	ἐν	τῷ	νόμῳ	αὐτῶν	γεγραμμένος		ὅτι
the	in	the	law	of them	having been written,		(")

3404	1473	1432	**26**	3752	2064	01
ἐμίσησάν	με	δωρεάν.		Ὅταν	ἔλθη	ὁ
they hated	me	as a gift.		When	might come	the

3875		3739	1473	3992		1473	3844	02	3962
παράκλητος	ὃν	ἐγὼ	πέμψω		ὑμῖν	παρὰ	τοῦ	πατρός,
encourager	whom	I	will send		to you	from	the	father,

09	4151	06		225		3739	3844	02	3962
τὸ	πνεῦμα	τῆς	ἀληθείας	ὃ		παρὰ	τοῦ	πατρὸς
the	spirit	of the	truth	who		from	the	father

1607		1565	3140		4012	1473	**27**	2532
ἐκπορεύεται,	ἐκεῖνος	μαρτυρήσει		περὶ	ἐμοῦ·		καὶ
travels out,	that one	will testify		about	me;		also

1473	1161	3140		3754	575	746		3326	1473
ὑμεῖς	δὲ	μαρτυρεῖτε,	ὅτι	ἀπ᾽	ἀρχῆς		μετ᾽	ἐμοῦ
you	but	testify,		that	from	beginning	with	me

1510		3778		2980		1473	2443
ἐστε.	**16:1**	Ταῦτα		λελάληκα		ὑμῖν	ἵνα
you are.		These things		I have spoken		to you	that

3361	4624		**2**	656		4160
μὴ	σκανδαλισθῆτε.			ἀποσυναγώγους		ποιήσουσιν
not	you might be offended.			From synagogue		they will do

1473	235	2064	5610	2443	3956	01	615
ὑμᾶς·	ἀλλ᾽	ἔρχεται	ὥρα	ἵνα	πᾶς	ὁ	ἀποκτείνας
you;	but	comes	hour	that	all	the	one having killed

1473	1380		2999	4374	03	2316	**3**	2532
ὑμᾶς	δόξῃ		λατρείαν	προσφέρειν	τῷ	θεῷ.		καὶ
you	might think		service	to offer	to the	God.		And

3778	4160		3754	3756	1097		04	3962
ταῦτα	ποιήσουσιν	ὅτι	οὐκ	ἔγνωσαν		τὸν	πατέρα
these	they will do		that	not	they knew		the	father

3761	1473	**4**	235	3778	2980		1473	2443
οὐδὲ	ἐμέ.		ἀλλὰ	ταῦτα	λελάληκα		ὑμῖν	ἵνα
but not	me.		But	these	I have spoken		to you	that

3752	2064		05	5610	846		3421
ὅταν	ἔλθη	ἡ	ὥρα	αὐτῶν		μνημονεύητε
when	might come	the	hour	of them		you might remember

846		3754	1473	3004	1473	3778	1161	1473	1537
αὐτῶν	ὅτι	ἐγὼ	εἶπον	ὑμῖν.	Ταῦτα	δὲ	ὑμῖν	ἐξ
of them		that I		told	you.	These	but	to you	from

746	3756 3004	3754	3326 1473 1510	5 3568
ἀρχῆς	οὐκ εἶπον,	ὅτι	μεθ᾽ ὑμῶν ἤμην.	Νῦν
beginning	not I told,	because	with you I was.	Now

1161 5217	4314 04	3992	1473 2532 3762
δὲ ὑπάγω	πρὸς τὸν	πέμψαντά	με, καὶ οὐδεὶς
but I go off to	the	one having sent me,	and no one

1537	1473 2065	1473 4226	5217	6 235 3754
ἐξ	ὑμῶν ἐρωτᾷ	με· ποῦ	ὑπάγεις;	ἀλλ᾽ ὅτι
out of	you asks	me; where	go off you?	But because

3778 2980	1473 05	3077 4137	1473 08
ταῦτα λελάληκα	ὑμῖν ἡ	λύπη πεπλήρωκεν	ὑμῶν τὴν
these I have	to the grief has	of you the
	spoken you		filled

2588	7 235	1473 08	225	3004 1473
καρδίαν.	ἀλλ᾽ ἐγὼ	τὴν	ἀλήθειαν λέγω ὑμῖν,
heart.	But I	the	truth say to you,

4851	1473 2443 1473 565	1437 1063 3361 565
συμφέρει	ὑμῖν ἵνα ἐγὼ ἀπέλθω.	ἐὰν γὰρ μὴ ἀπέλθω,
it is	to you that I go off.	If for not I might
advantageous		go off,

01 3875	3756 2064	4314 1473	1437 1161
ὁ παράκλητος	οὐκ ἐλεύσεται	πρὸς ὑμᾶς·	ἐὰν δὲ
the encourager	not will come to	you;	if but

4198	3992 846	4314 1473	8 2532 2064	1565
πορευθῶ,	πέμψω αὐτὸν	πρὸς ὑμᾶς.	καὶ ἐλθὼν	ἐκεῖνος
I might	I will him	to you.	And having	that one
travel,	send		come

1651	04 2889	4012 266	2532 4012
ἐλέγξει	τὸν κόσμον	περὶ ἁμαρτίας	καὶ περὶ
will rebuke	the world	about sin	and about

1343	2532 4012 2920	9 4012 266
δικαιοσύνης	καὶ περὶ κρίσεως·	περὶ ἁμαρτίας
rightness	and about judgment;	about sin

3303	3754	3756 4100	1519 1473	10 4012
μέν,	ὅτι	οὐ πιστεύουσιν	εἰς ἐμέ·	περὶ
indeed,	because	not they trust	in me;	about

1343	1161 3754	4314 04 3962	5217
δικαιοσύνης	δέ, ὅτι	πρὸς τὸν πατέρα	ὑπάγω
rightness	but, because	toward the father	I go off

2532 3765	2334	1473	11 4012 1161 2920
καὶ οὐκέτι	θεωρεῖτέ	με·	περὶ δὲ κρίσεως,
and no longer	you watch	me;	about but judgment,

3754	01 758 02	2889 3778	2919
ὅτι	ὁ ἄρχων τοῦ	κόσμου τούτου	κέκριται.
because	the ruler of the	world this	has been judged.

12 2089	4183 2192	1473 3004	235 3756
Ἔτι	πολλὰ ἔχω	ὑμῖν λέγειν,	ἀλλ᾽ οὐ
Still	many I have	to you to say,	but not

1410	941	737	13 3752 1161 2064
δύνασθε	βαστάζειν	ἄρτι·	ὅταν δὲ ἔλθῃ
you are able	to bear	now;	when but might come

1565	09 4151 06	225	3594 1473
ἐκεῖνος,	τὸ πνεῦμα τῆς	ἀληθείας,	ὁδηγήσει ὑμᾶς
that one,	the spirit of the	truth,	he will guide you

1722 07	225	3956 3756	1063 2980	575
ἐν τῇ	ἀληθείᾳ	πάσῃ· οὐ	γὰρ λαλήσει	ἀφ᾽
in the	truth	all; not	for he will speak	from

1438	235 3745 191	2980 2532 024 2064
ἑαυτοῦ,	ἀλλ᾽ ὅσα ἀκούσει	λαλήσει καὶ τὰ ἐρχόμενα
himself,	but as he hears	he will and the things
	much as	speak, coming

312	1473 1565	14 1565 1473 1392	3754
ἀναγγελεῖ ὑμῖν.	ἐκεῖνος ἐμὲ δοξάσει,	ὅτι
he will to you.	That one me will give	because
declare	splendor,

1537	010 1699 2983	2532 312	1473	15 3956
ἐκ	τοῦ ἐμοῦ λήμψεται	καὶ ἀναγγελεῖ ὑμῖν.	πάντα
out of the	me he will	and he will	to you.	All
	receive	declare

the beginning, because I was with you. [5]But now I am going to him who sent me; yet none of you asks me, 'Where are you going?' [6]But because I have said these things to you, sorrow has filled your hearts. [7]Nevertheless I tell you the truth: it is to your advantage that I go away, for if I do not go away, the Advocate[a] will not come to you; but if I go, I will send him to you. [8]And when he comes, he will prove the world wrong about[b] sin and righteousness and judgment: [9]about sin, because they do not believe in me; [10]about righteousness, because I am going to the Father and you will see me no longer; [11]about judgment, because the ruler of this world has been condemned.

12 "I still have many things to say to you, but you cannot bear them now. [13]When the Spirit of truth comes, he will guide you into all the truth; for he will not speak on his own, but will speak whatever he hears, and he will declare to you the things that are to come. [14]He will glorify me, because he will take what is mine and declare it to you. [15]All that the

a Or Helper
b Or convict the world of

Father has is mine. For this reason I said that he will take what is mine and declare it to you.

16 "A little while, and you will no longer see me, and again a little while, and you will see me." 17Then some of his disciples said to one another, "What does he mean by saying to us, 'A little while, and you will no longer see me, and again a little while, and you will see me'; and 'Because I am going to the Father'?" 18They said, "What does he mean by this 'a little while'? We do not know what he is talking about." 19Jesus knew that they wanted to ask him, so he said to them, "Are you discussing among yourselves what I meant when I said, 'A little while, and you will no longer see me, and again a little while, and you will see me'? 20Very truly, I tell you, you will weep and mourn, but the world will rejoice; you will have pain, but your pain will turn into joy. 21When a woman is in labor, she has pain, because her hour has come. But when her child is born, she no longer remembers the anguish because of the joy of having brought a human being into the world. 22So you have pain now; but I will see you again, and your hearts will rejoice,

3745	2192 01	3962	1699 1510	1223	3778
ὅσα   ἔχει ὁ   πατὴρ ἐμά ἐστιν· διὰ   τοῦτο
as much as has the father mine it is; through this

| 3004 | 3754 | 1537 | 010 1699 2983 | | 2532 |
ἔιπον ὅτι   ἐκ   τοῦ ἐμοῦ λαμβάνει   καὶ
I told because out of the me   he receives and

| 312 | 1473 | 16 | 3398 | 2532 3765 | 2334 |
ἀναγγελεῖ   ὑμῖν. 16 Μικρὸν καὶ   οὐκέτι   θεωρεῖτέ
he declares to you. Little and no longer you watch

| 1473 2532 3825 | 3398 | 2532 3708 | | 1473 | 17 | 3004 |
με,   καὶ   πάλιν μικρὸν καὶ ὄψεσθέ   με. 17 εἶπαν
me, and again little and you will see me. They said

| 3767 1537 014 3101 | 846 | 4314 240 | 5101 |
οὖν   ἐκ τῶν μαθητῶν αὐτοῦ πρὸς ἀλλήλους·   τί
then from the learners of him to   one another; what

| 1510 3778 3739 3004 | 1473 | 3398 2532 3756 |
ἐστιν τοῦτο ὃ   λέγει   ἡμῖν· μικρὸν καὶ οὐ
is   this that he says to us; little and not

| 2334 | 1473 2532 3825 | 3398 | 2532 3708 | 1473 |
θεωρεῖτέ με, καὶ   πάλιν μικρὸν καὶ ὄψεσθέ   με;
you watch me, and again little and you will see me?

| 2532 3754 5217 | 4314 04 3962 | 18 | 3004 |
καί·   ὅτι ὑπάγω   πρὸς τὸν πατέρα; 18 ἔλεγον
And; that I go off to   the father? They were saying

| 3767 | 5101 1510 3778 | 3739 3004 | 09 3398 | 3756 |
οὖν· τί   ἐστιν τοῦτο [ὃ   λέγει] τὸ μικρόν; οὐκ
then; what is   this that he says the little? Not

| 3609a | 5101 2980 | 19 | 1097 01 | 2424 | 3754 |
οἴδαμεν τί   λαλεῖ. 19 Ἔγνω [ὁ] Ἰησοῦς ὅτι
we know what he speaks. Knew the Jesus that

| 2309 | 846 | 2065 2532 3004 | 846 |
ἤθελον   αὐτὸν ἐρωτᾶν, καὶ εἶπεν   αὐτοῖς·
they were wanting him to ask, and he said to them;

| 4012 3778 2212 | 3326 240 | 3754 | 3004 |
περὶ τούτου ζητεῖτε μετ' ἀλλήλων ὅτι   εἶπον·
about this you seek with one another because I said;

| 3398 | 2532 3756 2334 | 1473 2532 3825 3398 | 2532 |
μικρὸν καὶ οὐ   θεωρεῖτέ με, καὶ πάλιν μικρὸν καὶ
little and not you watch me, and again little and

| 3708 | 1473 | 20 | 281 281 3004 1473 | 3754 |
ὄψεσθέ   με; 20 ἀμὴν ἀμὴν λέγω ὑμῖν   ὅτι
you will see me? Amen amen I say to you that

| 2799 | 2532 2354 | 1473 | 01 1161 2889 |
κλαύσετε καὶ θρηνήσετε ὑμεῖς, ὁ δὲ κόσμος
will cry and will lament you, the but world

| 5463 | 1473 3076 | 235 05 3077 |
χαρήσεται·   ὑμεῖς λυπηθήσεσθε,   ἀλλ' ἡ λύπη
will rejoice; you will be grieved, but the grief

| 1473 1519 5479 1096 | 05 1135 3752 |
ὑμῶν εἰς χαρὰν γενήσεται. 21 ἡ γυνὴ ὅταν
of you into joy will become. 21 The woman when

| 5088 | 3077 2192 3754 | 2064 05 5610 846 |
τίκτη   λύπην ἔχει, ὅτι   ἦλθεν ἡ ὥρα αὐτῆς·
she might grief has, because came the hour of her;
give birth

| 3752 1161 1080 | 012 3813 |
ὅταν δὲ γεννήση   τὸ παιδίον,
when but she might give birth the small child,

| 3765 | 3421 | 06 2347 | 1223 | 08 |
οὐκέτι   μνημονεύει τῆς θλίψεως διὰ   τὴν
no longer she remembers the affliction because the

| 5479 1080 | 444 | 1519 04 2889 |
χαρὰν ὅτι   ἐγεννήθη ἄνθρωπος εἰς τὸν κόσμον.
joy because was born man   into the world.

| 22 | 2532 1473 | 3767 3568 3303 | 3077 2192 | 3825 |
22 καὶ ὑμεῖς οὖν νῦν μὲν   λύπην ἔχετε·   πάλιν
And you then now indeed grief will have; again

| 1161 3708 | 1473 2532 5463 | 1473 | 05 |
δὲ ὄψομαι   ὑμᾶς, καὶ χαρήσεται ὑμῶν ἡ
but I will see you, and will rejoice of you the

```
2588        2532 08    5479   1473   3762   142        575  1473
καρδία, καὶ τὴν χαρὰν ὑμῶν οὐδεὶς αἴρει     ἀφ' ὑμῶν.
heart,  and the joy   of you no one lifts up from you.
```

```
    2532 1722 1565    07   2250   1473 3756 2065
23 Καὶ ἐν ἐκείνῃ τῇ ἡμέρᾳ ἐμὲ οὐκ ἐρωτήσετε
   And in that   the day  me  not  you will ask
3762      281  281   3004  1473  302 5101  154
οὐδέν. ἀμὴν ἀμὴν λέγω ὑμῖν, ἄν τι αἰτήσητε
nothing. Amen amen I say to you, - what you might ask
04  3962   1722 011 3686    1473 1325        1473
τὸν πατέρα ἐν τῷ ὀνόματί μου δώσει      ὑμῖν.
the father in  the name  of me he will give to you.
```

```
   2193 737  3756  154       3762   1722 011 3686
24 ἕως ἄρτι οὐκ ἠτήσατε οὐδὲν ἐν τῷ ὀνόματί
   Until now not you asked nothing in  the name
1473 154     2532 2983            2443 05   5479
μου· αἰτεῖτε καὶ λήμψεσθε,     ἵνα ἡ  χαρὰ
of me; ask  and  you will receive, that the joy
1473 1510   4137              25  3778      1722
ὑμῶν ᾖ      πεπληρωμένη.     25 Ταῦτα      ἐν
of you might be+ +having been filled. These things in
3942          2980        1473   2064   5610 3753
παροιμίαις λελάληκα ὑμῖν· ἔρχεται ὥρα ὅτε
proverbs   I have spoken to you; comes  hour when
3765    1722 3942      2980       1473      235
οὐκέτι ἐν παροιμίαις λαλήσω     ὑμῖν, ἀλλὰ
no longer in proverbs I will speak to you, but
3954       4012 02  3962  518       1473    1722
παρρησίᾳ περὶ τοῦ πατρὸς ἀπαγγελῶ ὑμῖν. 26 ἐν
in boldness about the father I will tell to you.   In
1565    07   2250  1722 011 3686   1473     154
ἐκείνῃ τῇ ἡμέρᾳ ἐν τῷ ὀνόματί μου αἰτήσεσθε,
that   the day  in  the name  of me you will ask,
2532 3756 3004  1473   3754 1473 2065    04  3962
καὶ οὐ λέγω ὑμῖν ὅτι ἐγὼ ἐρωτήσω τὸν πατέρα
and not I say to you, (") I   will ask the father
4012 1473     846   1063 01  3962   5368  1473
περὶ ὑμῶν· 27 αὐτὸς γὰρ ὁ πατὴρ φιλεῖ ὑμᾶς,
about you;   himself for  the father loves you,
3754   1473 1473 5368        2532 4100         3754 1473
ὅτι ὑμεῖς ἐμὲ πεφιλήκατε καὶ πεπιστεύκατε ὅτι ἐγὼ
because you me  have loved  and have trusted that I
3844  02   2316 1831     1831       3844 02  3962
παρὰ [τοῦ] θεοῦ ἐξῆλθον. 28 ἐξῆλθον παρὰ τοῦ πατρὸς
from  the   God came out.   I came out from the father
2532 2064    1519 04  2889   3825    863
καὶ ἐλήλυθα εἰς τὸν κόσμον· πάλιν ἀφίημι
and I have come into the world;  again I leave off
04  2889   2532 4198        4314 04  3962     29 3004
τὸν κόσμον καὶ πορεύομαι πρὸς τὸν πατέρα.   29 Λέγουσιν
the world  and I travel  to  the father.   Say
013 3101    846     2396 3568 1722 3954     2980
οἱ μαθηταὶ αὐτοῦ· ἴδε νῦν ἐν παρρησίᾳ λαλεῖς
the learners of him; look now in boldness you speak
2532 3942     3762       3004      30 3568 3609α    3754
καὶ παροιμίαν οὐδεμίαν λέγεις. 30 νῦν οἴδαμεν ὅτι
and proverb   but not one you say. Now we know that
3609α 3956   2532 3756 5532   2192      2443 5100 1473
οἶδας πάντα καὶ οὐ χρείαν ἔχεις ἵνα τίς σε
you know all and  not need  you have that some you
2065       1722 3778 4100        3754 575  2316
ἐρωτᾷ·    ἐν τούτῳ πιστεύομεν ὅτι ἀπὸ θεοῦ
might ask; in this  we trust  that from God
1831        611        846    2424    737
ἐξῆλθες. 31 ἀπεκρίθη αὐτοῖς Ἰησοῦς· ἄρτι
you came out.   Answered them   Jesus;  now
4100         32 2400 2064   5610 2532 2064    2443
πιστεύετε; 32 ἰδοὺ ἔρχεται ὥρα καὶ ἐλήλυθεν ἵνα
do you trust?   Look comes  hour and has come that
```

and no one will take your joy from you. [23]On that day you will ask nothing of me.[a] Very truly, I tell you, if you ask anything of the Father in my name, he will give it to you.[b] [24]Until now you have not asked for anything in my name. Ask and you will receive, so that your joy may be complete.

[25]"I have said these things to you in figures of speech. The hour is coming when I will no longer speak to you in figures, but will tell you plainly of the Father. [26]On that day you will ask in my name. I do not say to you that I will ask the Father on your behalf; [27]for the Father himself loves you, because you have loved me and have believed that I came from God.[c] [28]I came from the Father and have come into the world; again, I am leaving the world and am going to the Father."

[29]His disciples said, "Yes, now you are speaking plainly, not in any figure of speech! [30]Now we know that you know all things, and do not need to have anyone question you; by this we believe that you came from God." [31]Jesus answered them, "Do you now believe? [32]The hour is coming, indeed it has come, when

[a] Or will ask me no question
[b] Other ancient authorities read Father, he will give it to you in my name
[c] Other ancient authorities read the Father

you will be scattered, each one to his home, and you will leave me alone. Yet I am not alone because the Father is with me. [33] I have said this to you, so that in me you may have peace. In the world you face persecution. But take courage; I have conquered the world!"

CHAPTER 17

After Jesus had spoken these words, he looked up to heaven and said, "Father, the hour has come; glorify your Son so that the Son may glorify you, [2] since you have given him authority over all people,[a] to give eternal life to all whom you have given him. [3] And this is eternal life, that they may know you, the only true God, and Jesus Christ whom you have sent. [4] I glorified you on earth by finishing the work that you gave me to do. [5] So now, Father, glorify me in your own presence with the glory that I had in your presence before the world existed.

6 "I have made your name known to those whom you gave me from the world. They were yours, and you gave them to me, and they have kept your word. [7] Now they know that everything you have given me is from you;

_a_ Gk _flesh_

```
4650                      1538      1519  024  2398  2504
σκορπισθῆτε               ἕκαστος   εἰς   τὰ   ἴδια  κἀμὲ
you might be scattered each       in    the  own   and me
3441    863               2532 3756 1510 3441   3754    01
μόνον ἀφῆτε·              καὶ  οὐκ  εἰμὶ μόνος, ὅτι    ὁ
alone you leave off;      and  not  I am alone,  because the
3962    3326 1473 1510        3778  2980           1473
πατὴρ μετ' ἐμοῦ ἐστιν.    33  ταῦτα λελάληκα      ὑμῖν
father with me    is.         These I have spoken to you
2443 1722 1473 1515      2192            1722 03  2889
ἵνα  ἐν  ἐμοὶ εἰρήνην    ἔχητε.          ἐν  τῷ  κόσμῳ
that in  me   peace      you might have. In  the world
2347       2192     235  2293           1473
θλῖψιν     ἔχετε·   ἀλλὰ θαρσεῖτε,       ἐγὼ
affliction you have; but take courage,   I
3528       04  2889           3778   2980          2424
νενίκηκα   τὸν κόσμον.  17:1  Ταῦτα ἐλάλησεν      Ἰησοῦς
have conquered the world.     These spoke         Jesus
2532 1869                016  3788       846      1519
καὶ  ἐπάρας              τοὺς ὀφθαλμοὺς αὐτοῦ εἰς
and  having lifted up   on the eyes    of him to
04  3772     3004  3962    2064       05  5610
τὸν οὐρανὸν εἶπεν· πάτερ, ἐλήλυθεν ἡ ὥρα·
the heaven  said;  father, has come the hour;
1392       1473  04  5207 2443 01  5207
δόξασόν    σου  τὸν υἱόν, ἵνα ὁ  υἱὸς
give splendor of you the son,  that the son
1392      1473        2531 2    1325       846
δοξάσῃ    σέ,  καθὼς ἔδωκας     αὐτῷ
might give splendor you,  just as you gave to him
1849       3956 4561    2443 3956 3739 1325
ἐξουσίαν πάσης σαρκός, ἵνα πᾶν ὃ  δέδωκας
authority all  flesh,   that all who you have given
846   1325       846    2222 166     3  3778 1161
αὐτῷ δώσῃ       αὐτοῖς ζωὴν αἰώνιον.  αὕτη δέ
to him he might give to them life eternal. This but
1510 05  166     2222 2443 1097         1473 04
ἐστιν ἡ  αἰώνιος ζωὴ ἵνα γινώσκωσιν   σὲ τὸν
is    the eternal life that they might know you the
3441    228        2316 2532 3739 649          2424
μόνον ἀληθινὸν θεὸν καὶ ὃν ἀπέστειλας      Ἰησοῦν
alone true     God  and whom you delegated Jesus
5547      4  1473 1473 1392       1909 06  1093 012
Χριστόν.    ἐγώ σε   ἐδόξασα     ἐπὶ  τῆς γῆς  τὸ
Christ.     I   you  gave splendor on   the earth the
2041 5048         3739 1325       1473        2443
ἔργον τελειώσας   ὃ   δέδωκάς    μοι        ἵνα
work  having completed that you have given to me that
4160      5  2532 3568 1392       1473 1473 3962
ποιήσω·     καὶ  νῦν δόξασόν     με  σύ, πάτερ,
I might do;  and now give splendor me  you, father,
3844 4572    07   1391      3739 2192 4253    010 04
παρὰ σεαυτῷ τῇ  δόξῃ      ᾗ   εἶχον πρὸ   τοῦ τὸν
from yourself the splendor that I had before the the
2889     1510 3844 1473  6  1473       012
κόσμον εἶναι παρὰ σοί.  Ἐφανέρωσά   σου  τὸ
world  to be from you.   I demonstrated of you the
3686  015   444         3739 1325   1473 1537 02
ὄνομα τοῖς ἀνθρώποις οὓς ἔδωκάς μοι ἐκ  τοῦ
name  to the men       whom you gave me  from the
2889    1473  1510   2504   846    1325     2532
κόσμου. σοὶ ἦσαν  κἀμοὶ αὐτοὺς ἔδωκας και
world.  To you they were and to me them  you gave and
04  3056 1473 5083          7  3568 1097      3754
τὸν λόγον σου τετήρηκαν.   νῦν ἔγνωκαν   ὅτι
the word of you they have kept. Now they know that
3956 3745      1325          1473 3844 1473 1510
πάντα ὅσα     δέδωκάς      μοι παρὰ σοῦ εἰσιν·
all   as much as you have given to me from you are;
```

```
      3754      024  4487    3739 1325       1473   1325
8  ὅτι    τὰ  ῥήματα  ἃ   ἔδωκάς  μοι  δέδωκα
   because the words  that  you gave  to me I have given
   846       2532 846      2983       2532 1097    230
αὐτοῖς,  καὶ αὐτοὶ    ἔλαβον  καὶ ἔγνωσαν ἀληθῶς
to them,  and  themselves received and know    truly
3754 3844 1473 1831         2532 4100          3754 1473
ὅτι  παρὰ σοῦ ἐξῆλθον,   καὶ ἐπίστευσαν ὅτι  σύ
that from  you I came out, and  they trusted that you
1473 649         ,1473 4012  846      2065  3756 4012
με  ἀπέστειλας. 9 Ἐγὼ περὶ αὐτῶν ἐρωτῶ, οὐ περὶ
me  delegated.     I  about them ask,   not about
02  2889     2065  235  4012  3739 1325              1473
τοῦ κόσμου ἐρωτῶ ἀλλὰ περὶ ὧν  δέδωκάς       μοι,
the world  I ask but  about whom you have given me,
3754 1473  1510  10  2532 021 1699 3956 4674  1510
ὅτι  σοί  εἰσιν,    καὶ τὰ ἐμὰ πάντα σά  ἐστιν
that to you they are, and  the mine all  yours are
2532 021 4674  1699  2532 1392
καὶ τὰ σὰ  ἐμά, καὶ δεδόξασμαι
and  the yours mine, and  I have been given splendor
1722 846     11  2532 3765       1510 1722 03  2889  2532
ἐν  αὐτοῖς.   καὶ οὐκέτι    εἰμὶ ἐν  τῷ κόσμῳ, καὶ
in  them.     And no longer I am in  the world, and
846        1722 03  2889  1510  2504  4314 1473
αὐτοὶ   ἐν  τῷ κόσμῳ εἰσίν, κἀγὼ πρὸς σὲ
themselves in  the world are,  and I to   you
2064      3962  40  5083    846    1722 011 3686
ἔρχομαι. πάτερ ἅγιε, τήρησον αὐτοὺς ἐν  τῷ ὀνόματί
come.    Father holy, keep    them  in  the name
1473   3739 1325          1473   2443 1510
σου  ᾧ  δέδωκάς   μοι,  ἵνα  ὦσιν
of you that you have given to me, that they might be
1520 2531    1473  12  3753 1510  3326 846    1473
ἓν  καθὼς ἡμεῖς.    ὅτε ἤμην μετ' αὐτῶν ἐγὼ
one  just as we.      When I was with them  I
5083     846  1722 011 3686    1473  3739
ἐτήρουν αὐτοὺς ἐν τῷ ὀνόματί σου  ᾧ
was keeping them  in the name  of you that
1325       1473  2532 5442     2532 3762   1537
δέδωκάς  μοι, καὶ ἐφύλαξα, καὶ οὐδεὶς ἐξ
you have given to me, and  I guarded, and no one from
846     622            1487 3361 01  5207 06
αὐτῶν ἀπώλετο      εἰ  μὴ ὁ  υἱὸς τῆς
them  destroyed himself except the son  of the
684      2443 05  1124   4137             3568
ἀπωλείας, ἵνα ἡ  γραφὴ πληρωθῇ.    13 νῦν
destruction, that the writing might be filled.  Now
1161 4314 1473 2064     2532 3778 2980   1722 03 2889
δὲ  πρὸς σὲ ἔρχομαι καὶ ταῦτα λαλῶ  ἐν  τῷ κόσμῳ
but  to  you I come and  these I speak in  the world
2443 2192    08  5479  1699 4137         1722
ἵνα ἔχωσιν τὴν χαρὰν τὴν ἐμὴν πεπληρωμένην ἐν
that they might the joy  the mine having been  in
have                             filled
1438      14  1473 1325    846    04  3056  1473 2532
ἑαυτοῖς.   ἐγὼ δέδωκα  αὐτοῖς τὸν λόγον σου καὶ
themselves. I  have given to them the word of you and
01  2889    3404     846    3754  3756 1510   1537
ὁ  κόσμος ἐμίσησεν αὐτούς, ὅτι  οὐκ εἰσὶν ἐκ
the world  hated    them, because not they are out of
02  2889   2531    1473 3756 1510 1537 02  2889
τοῦ κόσμου καθὼς ἐγὼ οὐκ εἰμὶ ἐκ  τοῦ κόσμου.
the world  just as I  not am  from the world.
   3756 2065  2443 142       846    1537 02  2889
15 οὐκ ἐρωτῶ ἵνα ἄρῃς     αὐτοὺς ἐκ  τοῦ κόσμου,
   Not I ask that you lift up them  from the world,
235  2443 5083     846    1537 02  4190
ἀλλ' ἵνα τηρήσῃς  αὐτοὺς ἐκ  τοῦ πονηροῦ.
but  that you might keep them  from the evil.
```

8for the words that you gave to me I have given to them, and they have received them and know in truth that I came from you; and they have believed that you sent me. 9I am asking on their behalf; I am not asking on behalf of the world, but on behalf of those whom you gave me, because they are yours. 10All mine are yours, and yours are mine; and I have been glorified in them. 11And now I am no longer in the world, but they are in the world, and I am coming to you. Holy Father, protect them in your name that you have given me, so that they may be one, as we are one. 12While I was with them, I protected them in your name that[a] you have given me. I guarded them, and not one of them was lost except the one destined to be lost,[b] so that the scripture might be fulfilled. 13But now I am coming to you, and I speak these things in the world so that they may have my joy made complete in themselves.[c] 14I have given them your word, and the world has hated them because they do not belong to the world, just as I do not belong to the world. 15I am not asking you to take them out of the world, but I ask you to protect them from the evil one.[d]

a Other ancient authorities read protected in your name those whom
b Gk except the son of destruction
c Or among themselves
d Or from evil

16They do not belong to the world, just as I do not belong to the world. 17Sanctify them in the truth; your word is truth. 18As you have sent me into the world, so I have sent them into the world. 19And for their sakes I sanctify myself, so that they also may be sanctified in truth.

20 "I ask not only on behalf of these, but also on behalf of those who will believe in me through their word, 21that they may all be one. As you, Father, are in me and I am in you, may they also be in us,[a] so that the world may believe that you have sent me. 22The glory that you have given me I have given them, so that they may be one, as we are one, 23I in them and you in me, that they may become completely one, so that the world may know that you have sent me and have loved them even as you have loved me. 24Father, I desire that those also, whom you have given me, may be with me where I am, to see my glory, which you have given me because you loved me before the foundation of the world.

25 "Righteous Father, the world does not know you, but I

[a] Other ancient authorities read be one in us

```
          1537  02   2889    3756  1510        2531     1473 3756
16        ἐκ   τοῦ  κόσμου  οὐκ  εἰσὶν      καθὼς    ἐγὼ  οὐκ
          From the  world   not  they are  just as   I    not
1510 1537 02   2889            37           846       1722 07
εἰμὶ ἐκ  τοῦ  κόσμου.   17  ἀγίασον    αὐτοὺς   ἐν   τῇ
am   from the  world.      Make holy  them     in   the
225       01   3056  01   4674 225        1510        18  2531
ἀληθείᾳ·  ὁ   λόγος ὁ   σὸς  ἀλήθειά   ἐστιν.          καθὼς
truth;    the  word  the your  truth    is.             Just as
1473 649                1519 04   2889       2504 649
ἐμὲ  ἀπέστειλας        εἰς  τὸν  κόσμον,    κἀγὼ  ἀπέστειλα
me   you delegated    into the  world,     also I delegated
846      1519 04   2889       19  2532 5228          846     1473
αὐτοὺς  εἰς  τὸν  κόσμον·       καὶ  ὑπὲρ        αὐτῶν  ἐγὼ
them    into the  world·          and on behalf of them  I
37·        1683      2443 1510             2532 846
ἀγιάζω    ἐμαυτόν,  ἵνα  ὦσιν           καὶ  αὐτοὶ
make holy myself,   that they might be+ also themselves
37              1722 225           3756 4012
ἡγιασμένοι     ἐν  ἀληθείᾳ.   20  Οὐ  περὶ
+having been made holy in truth.      Not about
3778    1161 2065   3441   235  2532 4012  014
τούτων  δὲ  ἐρωτῶ  μόνον, ἀλλὰ καὶ  περὶ   τῶν
these   but I ask  alone, but  also about  the ones
4100         1223    02  3056  846        1519 1473  21  2443
πιστευόντων  διὰ    τοῦ  λόγου αὐτῶν    εἰς  ἐμέ,        ἵνα
trusting     through the  word  of them  in   me,          that
3956   1520 1510      2531      1473 3962  1722 1473 2504
πάντες ἓν  ὦσιν,     καθὼς    σύ,  πάτερ, ἐν  ἐμοὶ κἀγὼ
all    one might be, just as  you, father in  me   and I
1722 1473 2443 2532 846          1722 1473 1510        2443
ἐν  σοί, ἵνα καὶ  αὐτοὶ        ἐν  ἡμῖν ὦσιν,       ἵνα
in  you, that also themselves  in  us   might be,    that
01  2889    4100         3754 1473 1473 649
ὁ   κόσμος πιστεύῃ      ὅτι  σύ  με  ἀπέστειλας.
the world  might trust  that you me  delegated.
22  2504    08   1391     3739 1325          1473
κἀγὼ τὴν  δόξαν    ἣν  δέδωκάς         μοι
And I the  splendor that you have given me
1325       846       2443 1510          1520 2531
δέδωκα    αὐτοῖς,   ἵνα  ὦσιν          ἓν  καθὼς
I have given to them, that they might be one just as
1473 1520  23 1473 1722 846    2532 1473 1722 1473 2443
ἡμεῖς ἕν·    ἐγὼ ἐν  αὐτοῖς καὶ  σὺ  ἐν  ἐμοί, ἵνα
we    one;   I   in  them  and you in  me,   that
1510       5048                1519 1520 2443
ὦσιν       τετελειωμένοι       εἰς  ἓν,  ἵνα
they might be+ +having been completed into one, that
1097        01   2889    3754 1473 1473 649         2532
γινώσκῃ    ὁ   κόσμος ὅτι  σύ  με  ἀπέστειλας καὶ
might know the world  that you me  delegated  and
25          846       2531      1473  25   24  3962
ἠγάπησας   αὐτοὺς  καθὼς    ἐμὲ  ἠγάπησας.    Πάτερ,
you loved  them    just as  me   loved.        Father,
3739 1325             1473    2309    2443 3699  1510 1473
ὃ    δέδωκάς         μοι,   θέλω    ἵνα  ὅπου  εἰμὶ ἐγὼ
what you have given to me,   I want  that where am   I
2548          1510    3326 1473    2443 2334
κἀκεῖνοι     ὦσιν   μετ' ἐμοῦ,  ἵνα  θεωρῶσιν
also those   might be with me,  that they might watch
08  1391      08   1699  3739 1325            1473  3754
τὴν δόξαν    τὴν  ἐμήν,  ἣν  δέδωκάς         μοι  ὅτι
the splendor the  mine,  which you have given to me that
25         1473  4253   2602        2889       25  3962
ἠγάπησάς   με   πρὸ  καταβολῆς   κόσμου.       πάτερ
you loved  me   before foundation of world.    Father
1342    2532  01  2889    4674 3756 1097       1473 1161
δίκαιε, καὶ  ὁ   κόσμος σε  οὐκ  ἔγνω,       ἐγὼ  δὲ
right,  also the world  you not  was knowing, I   but
```

```
1473 1097              2532 3778  1097      3754 1473 1473
σε  ἔγνων,         καὶ  οὗτοι ἔγνωσαν ὅτι  σύ  με
you  was knowing,  and  these  knew    that you  me
649                2532 1107        846      012 3686
ἀπέστειλας·  26 καὶ  ἐγνώρισα  αὐτοῖς  τὸ  ὄνομά
delegated;      and  I made known to  them the name
1473 2532 1107              2443 05  26      3739
σου  καὶ  γνωρίσω,      ἵνα  ἡ  ἀγάπη ἣν
of you and  I will make known, that the love  which
25      1473 1722 846      1510    2504  1722 846
ἠγάπησάς με  ἐν  αὐτοῖς ᾖ     κἀγὼ ἐν  αὐτοῖς.
you loved me  in  them  might be and I in  them.
        3778 3004            2424  1831      4862 015
18:1 Ταῦτα εἰπὼν      Ἰησοῦς ἐξῆλθεν σὺν  τοῖς
     These having said Jesus  went out with the
3101    846      4008  02  5493        02      2748
μαθηταῖς αὐτοῦ πέραν  τοῦ χειμάρρου τοῦ  Κεδρὼν
learners of him  across the winter flow of the Kedron
3699 1510 2779     1519 3739  1525      846      2532 013
ὅπου ἦν κῆπος, εἰς  ὃν  εἰσῆλθεν αὐτὸς κὰι ὁι
where was garden, into which went into himself and the
3101    846      3609a    1161 2532 2455    01
μαθηταὶ αὐτοῦ. 2 ᾔδει  δὲ  καὶ  Ἰούδας ὁ
learners of him.  Had known but  also  Judas  the one
3860      846      04  5117  3754    4178
παραδιδοὺς αὐτὸν τὸν τόπον, ὅτι     πολλάκις
giving over him  the place, because frequently
4863           2424  1563  3326 014 3101
συνήχθη       Ἰησοῦς ἐκεῖ μετὰ τῶν μαθητῶν
was brought together Jesus there with the learners
846        01 3767 2455  2983      08  4686
αὐτοῦ. 3 ὁ  οὖν  Ἰούδας λαβὼν    τὴν σπεῖραν
of him.  The then  Judas having taken the squadron
2532 1537 014 749              2532 1537 014 5330
καὶ  ἐκ  τῶν ἀρχιερέων  καὶ  ἐκ  τῶν Φαρισαίων
and  from the ruler priests and  from the Pharisees
5257      2064      1563  3326 5322    2532 2985
ὑπηρέτας ἔρχεται ἐκεῖ μετὰ φανῶν  καὶ  λαμπάδων
assistants comes  there with torches and  lamps
2532 3696        4 2424  3767 3609a      3956 024
καὶ  ὅπλων.      Ἰησοῦς οὖν  εἰδὼς     πάντα τὰ
and  weapons.    Jesus  then having known all  the
2064        1909 846  1831    2532 3004    846
ἐρχόμενα    ἐπ’ αὐτὸν ἐξῆλθεν καὶ  λέγει  αὐτοῖς·
things coming on  him  went out and he says to them;
5101 2212        611          846    2424    04
τίνα ζητεῖτε; 5 ἀπεκρίθησαν αὐτῷ· Ἰησοῦν τὸν
whom seek you? They answered to him; Jesus  the
3480      3004      846      1473 1510  2476    1161
Ναζωραῖον. λέγει  αὐτοῖς· ἐγώ  εἰμι. εἱστήκει δὲ
Nazorean.  He says to them; I   am.   Had stood but
2532 2455    01 3860        846      3326 846
καὶ  Ἰούδας ὁ  παραδιδοὺς αὐτὸν μετ’ αὐτῶν.
also  Judas the one giving over him  with them.
   5613 3767 3004      846      1473 1510  565
6  ὡς  οὖν εἶπεν  αὐτοῖς· ἐγώ  εἰμι, ἀπῆλθον
   As  then he said to them; I   am,  they went off
1519 024 3694  2532 4098      5476     7 3825 3767
εἰς  τὰ  ὀπίσω καὶ  ἔπεσαν χαμαί.   πάλιν οὖν
into the  after and  they fell on ground. Again then
1905        846      5101 2212    013      1161 3004
ἐπηρώτησεν αὐτούς· τίνα ζητεῖτε; οἱ     δὲ  εἶπαν·
he asked on them;  whom seek you? The ones but  said,
 2424    04 3480      8 611        2424  3004    1473
Ἰησοῦν τὸν Ναζωραῖον. ἀπεκρίθη Ἰησοῦς εἶπον ὑμῖν
Jesus  the Nazorean.  Answered Jesus; I said to you
3754 1473 1510  1487 3767 1473 2212    863
ὅτι  ἐγὼ εἰμι. εἰ  οὖν  ἐμὲ  ζητεῖτε, ἄφετε
that I  am.   If  then me   you seek, leave off
```

know you; and these know that you have sent me. [26]I made your name known to them, and I will make it known, so that the love with which you have loved me may be in them, and I in them."

CHAPTER 18

After Jesus had spoken these words, he went out with his disciples across the Kidron valley to a place where there was a garden, which he and his disciples entered. [2]Now Judas, who betrayed him, also knew the place, because Jesus often met there with his disciples. [3]So Judas brought a detachment of soldiers together with police from the chief priests and the Pharisees, and they came there with lanterns and torches and weapons. [4]Then Jesus, knowing all that was to happen to him, came forward and asked them, "Whom are you looking for?" [5]They answered, "Jesus of Nazareth."[a] Jesus replied, "I am he."[b] Judas, who betrayed him, was standing with them. [6]When Jesus[c] said to them, "I am he,"[b] they stepped back and fell to the ground. [7]Again he asked them, "Whom are you looking for?" And they said, "Jesus of Nazareth."[a] [8]Jesus answered, "I told you that I am he.[b] So if you are looking for me, let

a Gk the Nazorean
b Gk I am
c Gk he

these men go." ⁹This was to fulfill the word that he had spoken, "I did not lose a single one of those whom you gave me." ¹⁰Then Simon Peter, who had a sword, drew it, struck the high priest's slave, and cut off his right ear. The slave's name was Malchus. ¹¹Jesus said to Peter, "Put your sword back into its sheath. Am I not to drink the cup that the Father has given me?"

12 So the soldiers, their officer, and the Jewish police arrested Jesus and bound him. ¹³First they took him to Annas, who was the father-in-law of Caiaphas, the high priest that year. ¹⁴Caiaphas was the one who had advised the Jews that it was better to have one person die for the people.

15 Simon Peter and another disciple followed Jesus. Since that disciple was known to the high priest, he went with Jesus into the courtyard of the high priest, ¹⁶but Peter was standing outside at the gate. So the other disciple, who was known to the high priest, went out, spoke to the

3778	5217		2443	4137		01	3056	3739
τούτους	ὑπάγειν·	9	ἵνα	πληρωθῇ		ὁ	λόγος	ὃν
these	to go off;		that	might filled		the	word	which

3004		3754	3739	1325		1473	3756
εἶπεν		ὅτι	οὓς	δέδωκάς		μοι	οὐκ
he said,		(")	whom	you have given		to me	not

622		1537	846	3762	10	4613	3767
ἀπώλεσα		ἐξ	αὐτῶν	οὐδένα.		Σίμων	οὖν
I have destroyed		out of	them	no one.		Simon	then

4074	2192	3162	1670	846	2532	3817
Πέτρος	ἔχων	μάχαιραν	εἵλκυσεν	αὐτὴν	καὶ	ἔπαισεν
Peter	having	sword	hauled	it	and	he struck

04	02	749		1401	2532	609		846
τὸν	τοῦ	ἀρχιερέως		δοῦλον	καὶ	ἀπέκοψεν		αὐτοῦ
the	of the	ruler priest		slave	and	he cut off		of him

012	5620a	012	1188	1510	1161	3686	03		1401
τὸ	ὠτάριον	τὸ	δεξιόν·	ἦν	δὲ	ὄνομα	τῷ		δούλῳ
the ear		the	right;	was	but	name	to the		slave

3124		3004	3767	01	2424	03		4074	906
Μάλχος.	11	εἶπεν	οὖν	ὁ	Ἰησοῦς	τῷ		Πέτρῳ·	βάλε
Malchus.		Said	then	the	Jesus	to the		Peter;	throw

08	3162		1519	08	2336	012	4221		3739
τὴν	μάχαιραν		εἰς	τὴν	θήκην·	τὸ	ποτήριον		ὃ
the	sword		into	the	place;	the	cup		that

1325		1473	01	3962	3756	3361	4095
δέδωκέν		μοι	ὁ	πατὴρ	οὐ	μὴ	πίω
has given		to me	the	father	not	not	I might drink

846		05	3767	4686		2532	01	5506
αὐτο;	12	Ἡ	οὖν	σπεῖρα		καὶ	ὁ	χιλίαρχος
it?		The	then	squadron		and	the	thousand ruler

2532	013	5257		014		2453	4815		04
καὶ	οἱ	ὑπηρέται		τῶν		Ἰουδαίων	συνέλαβον		τὸν
and	the	assistants		of the		Judeans	took together		the

2424	2532	1210		846	13	2532	71		4314
Ἰησοῦν	καὶ	ἔδησαν		αὐτὸν		καὶ	ἤγαγον		πρὸς
Jesus	and they bound			him		and	they led		toward

450	4413		1510	1063	3995		02
Ἄνναν	πρῶτον·		ἦν	γὰρ	πενθερὸς		τοῦ
Annas	first;		he was	for	father-in-law		of the

2533		3739	1510	749		02	1763		1565
Καϊάφα,		ὃς	ἦν	ἀρχιερεὺς		τοῦ	ἐνιαυτοῦ		ἐκείνου·
Caiaphas,		who	was	ruler priest		of the	year		that;

14	1510	1161	2533		01	4823
	ἦν	δὲ	Καϊάφας		ὁ	συμβουλεύσας
	was	but	Caiaphas		the	one having planned together

015	2453		3754	4851		1520	444
τοῖς	Ἰουδαίοις		ὅτι	συμφέρει		ἕνα	ἄνθρωπον
the	Judeans		that	it is advantageous		one	man

599		5228	02		2992	15	190		1161
ἀποθανεῖν		ὑπὲρ	τοῦ		λαοῦ.		Ἠκολούθει		δὲ
to die		on behalf of	the		people.		Was following		but

03	2424	4613	4074	2532	243	3101		01	1161
τῷ	Ἰησοῦ	Σίμων	Πέτρος	καὶ	ἄλλος	μαθητής.		ὁ	δὲ
the Jesus		Simon	Peter	and	other	learner.		The	but

3101	1565		1510	1110	03		749		2532
μαθητὴς	ἐκεῖνος		ἦν	γνωστὸς	τῷ		ἀρχιερεῖ		καὶ
learner that			was	known	to the		ruler priest		and

4897		03	2424	1519	08	833		02
συνεισῆλθεν		τῷ	Ἰησοῦ	εἰς	τὴν	αὐλὴν		τοῦ
he went in with		the Jesus		into	the	courtyard		of the

749		16	01	1161	4074	2476		4314	07	2374
ἀρχιερέως,			ὁ	δὲ	Πέτρος	εἱστήκει		πρὸς	τῇ	θύρᾳ
ruler priest,			the	but	Peter	had stood		to	the	door

1854	1831		3767	01	3101		01	243	01
ἔξω.	ἐξῆλθεν		οὖν	ὁ	μαθητὴς		ὁ	ἄλλος	ὁ
outside.	Came out		then	the	learner		the	other	the

1110	02	749		2532	3004	07
γνωστὸς	τοῦ	ἀρχιερέως		καὶ	εἶπεν	τῇ
known	of the	ruler priest		and	he said	to the

2377   2532 1521   04   4074   17 3004 3767
θυρωρῷ   καὶ εἰσήγαγεν τὸν Πέτρον.   λέγει οὖν
doorkeeper and   he led in the   Peter.   Says   then

03   4074   05   3814   05   2377   3361 2532
τῷ   Πέτρῳ ἡ   παιδίσκη   ἡ θυρωρός·   μὴ καὶ
to the Peter the girl servant the doorkeeper; not also

1473 1537 014 3101   1510 02   444   3778
σὺ   ἐκ   τῶν μαθητῶν εἶ   τοῦ ἀνθρώπου τούτου;
you from the learners are of the man   this?

3004 1565   3756 1510   18 2476   1161 013
λέγει ἐκεῖνος· οὐκ εἰμί.   εἰστήκεισαν δὲ   οἱ
Says   that one; not   I am.   Had stood   but the

1401   2532 013 5257   439   4160
δοῦλοι καὶ οἱ ὑπηρέται ἀνθρακιὰν πεποιηκότες,
slaves   and the assistants coal fire   having made,

3754   5592   1510 2532 2328   1510 1161 2532
ὅτι   ψῦχος ἦν, καὶ ἐθερμαίνοντο· ἦν   δὲ   καὶ
because cold   it   and they were   was+ but also
              was,   warming themselves;

01   4074   3326 846   2476   2532 2328
ὁ   Πέτρος μετ᾽ αὐτῶν ἑστὼς   καὶ θερμαινόμενος.
the Peter   with them   +having stood and +warming.

     01   3767 749   2065   04   2424   4012
19 Ὁ   οὖν ἀρχιερεὺς ἠρώτησεν τὸν Ἰησοῦν περὶ
     The then ruler priest asked   the   Jesus   about

014 3101   846   2532 4012 06   1322   846
τῶν μαθητῶν αὐτοῦ καὶ περὶ τῆς διδαχῆς αὐτοῦ.
the   learners of him and about the teaching of him.

     611   846   2424   1473 3954   2980
20 ἀπεκρίθη αὐτῷ Ἰησοῦς· ἐγὼ παρρησίᾳ λελάληκα
     Answered to him Jesus;   I   in boldness have spoken

03   2889   1473 3842   1321   1722 4864   2532
τῷ   κόσμῳ, ἐγὼ πάντοτε ἐδίδαξα ἐν συναγωγῇ καὶ
to the world, I   always   taught   in   synagogue and

1722 011   2411   3699   3956   013   2453
ἐν τῷ ἱερῷ, ὅπου πάντες οἱ Ἰουδαῖοι
in   the temple, where all   the Judeans

4905   2532 1722 2927   2980   3762   21 5101
συνέρχονται, καὶ ἐν κρυπτῷ ἐλάλησα οὐδέν.   τί
come together, and in   hiding I spoke   nothing.   Why

1473 2065   2065   016   191   5101
με   ἐρωτᾷς; ἐρώτησον τοὺς ἀκηκοότας τί
me   you ask? Ask   the   ones having heard what

2980   846   2396 3778   3609α   3739 3004 1473
ἐλάλησα αὐτοῖς· ἴδε οὗτοι οἴδασιν ἃ   εἶπον ἐγώ.
I spoke   to them;   look these   know   what said   I.

     3778 1161 846   3004   1520 3936
22 ταῦτα δὲ   αὐτοῦ εἰπόντος   εἷς παρεστηκὼς
     These but of him having said   one having stood along

014 5257   1325   4475   03   2424   3004
τῶν ὑπηρετῶν ἔδωκεν ῥάπισμα τῷ Ἰησοῦ εἰπών·
the   assistants gave   slap   to the Jesus   having said;

3779   611   03   749   23 611
οὕτως ἀποκρίνῃ τῷ ἀρχιερεῖ;   ἀπεκρίθη
thusly you answer to the ruler priest?   Answered

846   2424   1487 2560 2980   3140   4012
αὐτῷ Ἰησοῦς· εἰ κακῶς ἐλάλησα, μαρτύρησον περὶ
to him Jesus;   if   badly I spoke,   testify   about

010 2556   1487 1161 2573   5101 1473 1194
τοῦ κακοῦ· εἰ   δὲ   καλῶς, τί   με   δέρεις;
the bad;   if   but well,   why me   you beat?

     649   3767 846   01   452   1210
24 ἀπέστειλεν οὖν αὐτὸν ὁ   Ἅννας δεδεμένον
     Delegated   then him   the Annas having been bound

4314   2533   04   749   25 1510 1161 4613
πρὸς Καϊάφαν τὸν ἀρχιερέα.   Ἦν   δὲ   Σίμων
toward Caiaphas the ruler priest.   Was+ but Simon

4074   2476   2532 2328   3004   3767
Πέτρος ἑστὼς   καὶ θερμαινόμενος. εἶπον οὖν
Peter   +having stood and +warming.   They said then

woman who guarded the
gate, and brought Peter in.
[17]The woman said to Peter,
"You are not also one of
this man's disciples, are
you?" He said, "I am not."
[18]Now the slaves and the
police had made a charcoal
fire because it was cold, and
they were standing around
it and warming themselves.
Peter also was standing
with them and warming
himself.

   19 Then the high priest
questioned Jesus about his
disciples and about his
teaching. [20]Jesus answered,
"I have spoken openly to
the world; I have always
taught in synagogues and
in the temple, where all the
Jews come together. I have
said nothing in secret.
[21]Why do you ask me? Ask
those who heard what I
said to them; they know
what I said." [22]When he
had said this, one of the
police standing nearby
struck Jesus on the face,
saying, "Is that how you
answer the high priest?"
[23]Jesus answered, "If I have
spoken wrongly, testify to
the wrong. But if I have
spoken rightly, why do you
strike me?" [24]Then Annas
sent him bound to Caiaphas
the high priest.

   25 Now Simon Peter
was standing and warming
himself. They asked

him, "You are not also one
of his disciples, are you?"
He denied it and said, "I
am not." [26]One of the slaves
of the high priest, a relative
of the man whose ear Peter
had cut off, asked, "Did I
not see you in the garden
with him?" [27]Again Peter
denied it, and at that
moment the cock crowed.

28 Then they took Jesus
from Caiaphas to Pilate's
headquarters.[a] It was early
in the morning. They themselves did not enter the
headquarters,[a] so as to
avoid ritual defilement
and to be able to eat the
Passover. [29]So Pilate went
out to them and said,
"What accusation do you
bring against this man?"
[30]They answered, "If this
man were not a criminal,
we would not have handed
him over to you." [31]Pilate
said to them, "Take him
yourselves and judge him
according to your law."
The Jews replied, "We are
not permitted to put
anyone to death." [32](This
was to fulfill what Jesus
had said when he indicated
the kind of death he was
to die.)

33 Then Pilate entered
the headquarters[a] again,
summoned Jesus, and asked
him, "Are you the King
of the Jews?" [34]Jesus
answered,

[a] Gk the praetorium

|846| |3361|2532|1473|1537|014|3101| |846| |1510|
αὐτῷ· μὴ καὶ σὺ ἐκ τῶν μαθητῶν αὐτοῦ εἶ;
to him; not also you from the learners of him are?

|720| |1565| |2532 3004| |3756 1510| |3004|
ἠρνήσατο ἐκεῖνος καὶ εἶπεν· οὐκ εἰμί. **26** λέγει
Denied   that one and he said; not I am.   Says

|1520 1537 014 1401| |02| |749| |4773|
εἷς ἐκ τῶν δούλων τοῦ   ἀρχιερέως,   συγγενὴς
one from the slaves of the ruler priest, relative

|1510| |3739 609| |4074| |012 5621| |3756 1473 1473|
ὢν οὗ ἀπέκοψεν Πέτρος τὸ ὠτίον· οὐκ ἐγώ σε
being whom cut off Peter the ear; not I you

|3708 1722 03| |2779| |3326 846| |27 3825 3767|
εἶδον ἐν τῷ κήπῳ μετ' αὐτοῦ;   πάλιν οὖν
saw in the garden with him?   Again then

|720| |4074| |2532 2112| |220| |5455|
ἠρνήσατο Πέτρος, καὶ εὐθέως ἀλέκτωρ ἐφώνησεν.
denied   Peter, and immediately rooster sounded.

28 |71| |3767 04| |2424| |575 02 2533| |1519|
Ἄγουσιν οὖν τὸν Ἰησοῦν ἀπὸ τοῦ Καϊάφα εἰς
They lead then the Jesus from the Caiaphas into

|012 4232| |1510| |1161 4404| |2532 846|
τὸ πραιτώριον· ἦν δὲ πρωΐ· καὶ αὐτοὶ
the praetorium; it was but morning; and themselves

|3756 1525| |1519 012 4232| |2443 3361|
οὐκ εἰσῆλθον εἰς τὸ πραιτώριον, ἵνα μὴ
not went into into the praetorium, that not

|3392| |235 2068| |012|
μιανθῶσιν   ἀλλὰ φάγωσιν   τὸ
they might be defiled but they might eat the

|3957| |1831| |3767 01 4091| |1854| |4314|
πάσχα. **29** ἐξῆλθεν οὖν ὁ Πιλᾶτος ἔξω πρὸς
passover. Went out then the Pilate outside toward

|846| |2532 5346| |5101 2724| |5342| |2596|
αὐτοὺς καὶ φησίν· τίνα κατηγορίαν φέρετε κατὰ
them and says; what accusation bear you against

|02 444| |3778| |611| |2532 3004|
τοῦ ἀνθρώπου τούτου; **30** ἀπεκρίθησαν καὶ εἶπαν
the man   this?   They answered and said

|846| |1487 3361 1510 3778| |2556 4160| |3756 302|
αὐτῷ· εἰ μὴ ἦν οὗτος κακὸν ποιῶν, οὐκ ἂν
to him; except was+ this bad +doing, not -

|1473| |3860| |846| |31 3004 3767 846|
σοι   παρεδώκαμεν   αὐτόν. εἶπεν οὖν αὐτοῖς
to you we have given over him. Said then to them

|01 4091| |2983| |846| |1473 2532 2596 04| |3551|
ὁ Πιλᾶτος· λάβετε αὐτὸν ὑμεῖς καὶ κατὰ τὸν νόμον
the Pilate; take him   you, and by the law

|1473| |2919| |846| |3004 846| |013 2453|
ὑμῶν κρίνατε αὐτόν. εἶπον αὐτῷ οἱ Ἰουδαῖοι·
of you judge him. Said to him the Judeans;

|1473 3756 1832| |615| |3762| |32 2443|
ἡμῖν οὐκ ἔξεστιν   ἀποκτεῖναι οὐδένα·   ἵνα
to us not it is possible to kill no one;   that

|01 3056 02| |2424 4137| |3739 3004|
ὁ λόγος τοῦ Ἰησοῦ πληρωθῇ   ὃν εἶπεν
the word of the Jesus might be filled what he said

|4591| |4169| |2288 3195| |599|
σημαίνων ποίῳ θανάτῳ ἤμελλεν ἀποθνῄσκειν.
signifying what kind death he was about to die.

33 |1525| |3767 3825| |1519 012 4232| |01 4091|
Εἰσῆλθεν οὖν πάλιν εἰς τὸ πραιτώριον ὁ Πιλᾶτος
Went into then again into the praetorium the Pilate

|2532 5455| |04| |2424| |2532 3004| |846| |1473|
καὶ ἐφώνησεν τὸν Ἰησοῦν καὶ εἶπεν αὐτῷ· σὺ
and he sounded the Jesus and he said to him; you

|1510 01| |935| |012 2453| |34 611|
εἶ ὁ βασιλεὺς τῶν Ἰουδαίων;   ἀπεκρίθη
are the king of the Judeans?   Answered

```
2424      575    4572         1473  3778   3004      2228  243
Ἰησοῦς·  ἀπὸ  σεαυτοῦ  σὺ  τοῦτο  λέγεις  ἢ    ἄλλοι
Jesus;   from  yourself  you  this  say     or    others
3004  1473     4012         1473        611      01   4091
εἶπόν  σοι   περὶ        ἐμοῦ;  35 ἀπεκρίθη  ὁ    Πιλᾶτος·
said   to you concerning  me?      Answered the  Pilate;
3385  1473  2453         1510  09  1484   09  4674   2532 013
μήτι  ἐγὼ  Ἰουδαῖός  εἰμι;  τὸ  ἔθνος  τὸ  σὸν  καὶ  οἱ
not    I    Judean     am?   The nation the your  and  the
749           3860        1473 1473   5101 4160
ἀρχιερεῖς  παρέδωκάν  σε  ἐμοί·  τί  ἐποίησας;
ruler priests gave over you  to me;  what did you?
    611       2424     05   932      05  1699 3756 1510
36 ἀπεκρίθη  Ἰησοῦς·  ἡ  βασιλεία  ἡ  ἐμὴ  οὐκ  ἔστιν
   Answered  Jesus·    the kingdom  the mine  not  is
1537   02    2889    3778       1487 1537 02    2889    3778
ἐκ    τοῦ  κόσμου  τούτου·  εἰ  ἐκ  τοῦ  κόσμου  τούτου
out of the  world   this;   if  from the  world   this
1510 05   932     05  1699  013  5257        013
ἦν    ἡ  βασιλεία ἡ  ἐμή,  οἱ  ὑπηρέται  οἱ
was  the kingdom  the mine, the assistants the ones
1699  75         302   2443 3361 3860        015
ἐμοὶ  ἠγωνίζοντο  [ἂν] ἵνα  μὴ  παραδοθῶ  τοῖς
to me were contesting -    that not  I might be  to the
                                             given over
2453        3568 1161 05  932      05  1699 3756 1510
Ἰουδαίοις·  νῦν  δὲ  ἡ  βασιλεία ἡ  ἐμὴ  οὐκ  ἔστιν
Judeans;    now  but the kingdom  the mine  not  is
1782         37 3004  3767 846    01   4091        3766
ἐντεῦθεν.      εἶπεν  οὖν  αὐτῷ  ὁ   Πιλᾶτος·  οὐκοῦν
from here.    Said  then to him the Pilate;  not then
935        1510 1473 611       01  2424      1473 3004
βασιλεὺς  εἶ  σύ;  ἀπεκρίθη  ὁ  Ἰησοῦς·  σὺ  λέγεις
king      are you? Answered the Jesus;  you  say
3754 935       1510 1473 1519 3778  1080                2532
ὅτι  βασιλεύς  εἰμι.  ἐγὼ εἰς  τοῦτο γεγέννημαι      καὶ
that king      I am.  I into this have been born and
1519 3778  2064      1519 04   2889     2443
εἰς τοῦτο ἐλήλυθα  εἰς  τὸν κόσμον,  ἵνα
into this I have come into the world,  that
3140        07   225        3956 01   1510
μαρτυρήσω  τῇ  ἀληθεια· πᾶς ὁ   ὢν
I might testify to the truth;  all the one being
1537 06   225       191     1473 06   5456        38 3004
ἐκ  τῆς  ἀληθείας ἀκούει μου  τῆς φωνῆς.      λέγει
from the truth     hears of me  of the sound.    Says
846    01   4091       5101 1510 225        2532 3778
αὐτῷ  ὁ  Πιλᾶτος·  τί  ἐστιν ἀλήθεια;  Καὶ  τοῦτο
to him the Pilate;  what is   truth?    And  this
3004      3825  1831       4314 016   2453
εἰπὼν    πάλιν ἐξῆλθεν  πρὸς τοὺς Ἰουδαίους
having said again he went out to  the  Judeans
2532 3004  846     1473 3762         2147      1722
καὶ  λέγει  αὐτοῖς·  ἐγὼ οὐδεμίαν  εὑρίσκω ἐν
and  he says to them, I   but not one  find  in
846   156       39 1510  1161 4914        1473 2443 1520
αὐτῷ αἰτίαν.      ἔστιν δὲ  συνήθεια ὑμῖν ἵνα ἕνα
him  cause.       It is but custom  to you that one
630        1473 1722 011 3957        1014        3767
ἀπολύσω  ὑμῖν ἐν  τῷ πάσχα·  βούλεσθε οὖν
I will loose off to you in the passover; you plan then
630        1473 04   935      014    2453
ἀπολύσω  ὑμῖν τὸν βασιλέα τῶν Ἰουδαίων;
I will loose off to you the king  of the Judeans?
   2905         3767 3825 3004      3361 3778
40 ἐκραύγασαν  οὖν  πάλιν λέγοντες μὴ  τοῦτον
   They shouted then again saying;  not this one
235 04   912       1510 1161 01   912        3027
ἀλλὰ τὸν Βαραββᾶν. ἦν  δὲ  ὁ  Βαραββᾶς λῃστής.
but  the Barabbas. Was  but the Barabbas robber.
```

"Do you ask this on your own, or did others tell you about me?" [35]Pilate replied, "I am not a Jew, am I? Your own nation and the chief priests have handed you over to me. What have you done?" [36]Jesus answered, "My kingdom is not from this world. If my kingdom were from this world, my followers would be fighting to keep me from being handed over to the Jews. But as it is, my kingdom is not from here." [37]Pilate asked him, "So you are a king?" Jesus answered, "You say that I am a king. For this I was born, and for this I came into the world, to testify to the truth. Everyone who belongs to the truth listens to my voice." [38]Pilate asked him, "What is truth?"

After he had said this, he went out to the Jews again and told them, "I find no case against him. [39]But you have a custom that I release someone for you at the Passover. Do you want me to release for you the King of the Jews?" [40]They shouted in reply, "Not this man, but Barabbas!" Now Barabbas was a bandit.

CHAPTER 19

Then Pilate took Jesus and had him flogged. ²And the soldiers wove a crown of thorns and put it on his head, and they dressed him in a purple robe. ³They kept coming up to him, saying, "Hail, King of the Jews!" and striking him on the face. ⁴Pilate went out again and said to them, "Look, I am bringing him out to you to let you know that I find no case against him." ⁵So Jesus came out, wearing the crown of thorns and the purple robe. Pilate said to them, "Here is the man!" ⁶When the chief priests and the police saw him, they shouted, "Crucify him! Crucify him!" Pilate said to them, "Take him yourselves and crucify him; I find no case against him." ⁷The Jews answered him, "We have a law, and according to that law he ought to die because he has claimed to be the Son of God."

8 Now when Pilate heard this, he was more afraid than ever. ⁹He entered his headquarters*ᵃ* again and asked Jesus, "Where are you from?" But Jesus gave him no answer.

ᵃ Gk the praetorium

19:1
5119 3767 2983   01   4091   04   2424   2532
Τότε οὖν ἔλαβεν ὁ Πιλᾶτος τὸν Ἰησοῦν καὶ
Then then took. the Pilate the Jesus and

3146   **2** 2532 013 4757   4120
ἐμαστίγωσεν. ² καὶ οἱ στρατιῶται πλέξαντες
he scourged.   And the soldiers   having braided

4735   1537   1537   173   2007   846 07 2776
στέφανον ἐξ ἀκανθῶν ἐπέθηκαν αὐτοῦ τῇ κεφαλῇ
crown out of thorns set on of him the head

2532 2440   4210   4016   846 **3** 2532
καὶ ἱμάτιον πορφυροῦν περιέβαλον   αὐτὸν ³ καὶ
and clothes purple   they threw around him   and

2064   4314 846   2532 3004
ἤρχοντο   πρὸς αὐτὸν καὶ ἔλεγον·
they were coming to   him and they were saying;

5463   01 935   014   2453   2532
χαῖρε ὁ βασιλεὺς τῶν Ἰουδαίων· καὶ
rejoice the king   of the Judeans; and

1325   846   4475   2532 1831
ἐδίδοσαν   αὐτῷ ῥαπίσματα. ⁴ Καὶ ἐξῆλθεν
they were giving to him slaps.   And went out

3825 1854   01   4091   2532 3004   846   2396
πάλιν ἔξω   ὁ Πιλᾶτος καὶ λέγει αὐτοῖς· ἴδε
again outside the Pilate and he says to them; look

71   1473 846 1854   2443 1097   3754
ἄγω ὑμῖν αὐτὸν ἔξω,   ἵνα γνῶτε   ὅτι
I lead to you him   outside, that you might know that

3762   156   2147   1722 846   1831   3767
οὐδεμίαν αἰτίαν εὑρίσκω ἐν αὐτῷ. ⁵ ἐξῆλθεν οὖν
but not one cause I find in him. Went out then

01 2424 1854   5409   04 174   4735
ὁ Ἰησοῦς ἔξω,   φορῶν τὸν ἀκάνθινον στέφανον
the Jesus outside, bearing the thorn   crown

2532 012 4210   2440   2532 3004   846   2400
καὶ τὸ πορφυροῦν ἱμάτιον. καὶ λέγει αὐτοῖς· ἰδοὺ
and the purple   clothes. And he says to them; look

01 444   3753 3767 3708 846 013
ὁ ἄνθρωπος. ⁶ Ὅτε οὖν εἶδον αὐτὸν οἱ
the man.   When then saw him the

749   2532 013 5257   2905
ἀρχιερεῖς καὶ οἱ ὑπηρέται ἐκραύγασαν
ruler priests and the assistants they shouted

3004   4717   4717   3004 846   01
λέγοντες· σταύρωσον σταύρωσον. λέγει αὐτοῖς ὁ
saying; crucify   crucify. Says to them the

4091   2983   846   1473 2532 4717   1473
Πιλᾶτος· λάβετε αὐτὸν ὑμεῖς καὶ σταυρώσατε· ἐγὼ
Pilate; take   him   you   and you crucify; I

1063 3756 2147   1722 846 156 **7** 611
γὰρ οὐχ εὑρίσκω ἐν αὐτῷ αἰτίαν. ⁷ ἀπεκρίθησαν
for not find   in him cause.   Answered

846 013 2453   1473 3551 2192   2532 2596 04
αὐτῷ οἱ Ἰουδαῖοι· ἡμεῖς νόμον ἔχομεν καὶ κατὰ τὸν
to him the Judeans; we   law   have and by   the

3551 3784 599   3754   5207 2316 1438
νόμον ὀφείλει ἀποθανεῖν, ὅτι υἱὸν θεοῦ αὐτὸν
law he owes to die,   because son of God himself

4160   **8** 3753 3767 191   01 4091   3778 04
ἐποίησεν. ⁸ Ὅτε οὖν ἤκουσεν ὁ Πιλᾶτος τοῦτον τὸν
he made. When then heard the Pilate this   the

3056 3123 5399   2532 1525   1519
λόγον, μᾶλλον ἐφοβήθη, ⁹ καὶ εἰσῆλθεν εἰς
word, more   he was afraid, and he went into into

012 4232   3825 2532 3004   03   2424
τὸ πραιτώριον πάλιν καὶ λέγει τῷ Ἰησοῦ·
the praetorium again and he says to the Jesus;

4159   1510 1473 01 1161 2424   612   3756
πόθεν   εἶ σύ; ὁ δὲ Ἰησοῦς ἀπόκρισιν οὐκ
from where are you? The but Jesus answer   not

1325	846	**10**	3004	3767	846	01	4091	1473
ἔδωκεν	αὐτῷ.		λέγει	οὖν	αὐτῷ	ὁ	Πιλᾶτος·	ἐμοὶ
gave	to him.		Says	then	to him	the	Pilate;	to me

3756	2980	3756	3609a	3754	1849	2192
οὐ	λαλεῖς;	οὐκ	οἶδας	ὅτι	ἐξουσίαν	ἔχω
not	you speak?	Not	you know	that	authority	I have

630		1473	2532	1849	2192	4717
ἀπολῦσαί	σε	καὶ	ἐξουσίαν	ἔχω	σταυρῶσαί	
to loose off you		and	authority	I have	to crucify	

1473	**11**	611	846	2424	3756	2192	1849
σε;		ἀπεκρίθη [αὐτῷ]	Ἰησοῦς·	οὐκ εἶχες		ἐξουσίαν
you?		Answered to him	Jesus;	not you had		authority

2596	1473	3762	1487	3361	1510
κατ'	ἐμοῦ οὐδεμίαν		εἰ	μὴ	ἦν
against me	but not one		except		it was+

1325		1473	509	1223	3778	01
δεδομένον		σοι	ἄνωθεν·	διὰ	τοῦτο	ὁ
+having been given		to you	from above;	through	this	the

3860	1473	1473	3173	266	2192	**12**	1537
παραδούς	μέ	σοι	μείζονα	ἁμαρτίαν	ἔχει.		ἐκ
one having me	to	greater	sin	has.			Out of
given over		you					

3778	01	4091	2212	630	846
τούτου	ὁ	Πιλᾶτος	ἐζήτει	ἀπολῦσαι	αὐτόν·
this	the	Pilate	was seeking	to loose	off him;

013	1161	2453	2905	3004	1437	3778
οἱ	δὲ	Ἰουδαῖοι	ἐκραύγασαν	λέγοντες·	ἐὰν	τοῦτον
the but		Judeans	shouted	saying;	if	this one

630		3756	1510	5384	02	2541
ἀπολύσῃς,		οὐκ εἶ		φίλος	τοῦ	Καίσαρος·
you might loose off,		not are you		friend	of the	Caesar;

3956	01	935	1438	4160	483
πᾶς	ὁ	βασιλέα	ἑαυτὸν	ποιῶν	ἀντιλέγει
all	the one	king	himself	making	speaks against

03	2541	**13**	01	3767	4091	191	014	3056
τῷ	Καίσαρι.		ὁ	οὖν	Πιλᾶτος	ἀκούσας		τῶν λόγων
the	Caesar.		The	then	Pilate	having heard		the words

3778	71	1854	04	2424	2532	2523	1909
τούτων	ἤγαγεν	ἔξω	τὸν	Ἰησοῦν	καὶ	ἐκάθισεν	ἐπὶ
these	led	outside the		Jesus	and	he sat	on

968	1519	5117	3004	3038
βήματος	εἰς	τόπον	λεγόμενον	Λιθόστρωτον,
law court	in	place	being called	Stone pavement,

1447	1161	1042	**14**	1510	1161	3904
Ἑβραϊστὶ	δὲ	Γαββαθα.		ἦν	δὲ	παρασκευὴ
in Hebrew	but	Gabbatha.		It was	but	preparation

010	3957	5610	1510	5613	1623	2532	3004	015
τοῦ	πάσχα,	ὥρα	ἦν	ὡς	ἕκτη.	καὶ	λέγει	τοῖς
of the	passover,	hour	was	as	sixth.	And	he says	to the

2453	2396	01	935	1473	**15**	2905	3767
Ἰουδαίοις·	ἴδε	ὁ	βασιλεὺς	ὑμῶν.		ἐκραύγασαν	οὖν
Judeans;	look	the	king	of you.		Shouted	then

1565	142	142	4717	846	3004
ἐκεῖνοι·	ἆρον	ἆρον,	σταύρωσον	αὐτόν.	λέγει
those;	lift up	lift up,	crucify	him.	Says

846	01	4091	04	935	1473	4717
αὐτοῖς	ὁ	Πιλᾶτος·	τὸν	βασιλέα	ὑμῶν	σταυρώσω;
to them	the	Pilate;	the	king	of you	shall I crucify?

611	013	749	3756	2192	935
ἀπεκρίθησαν	οἱ	ἀρχιερεῖς·	οὐκ	ἔχομεν	βασιλέα
Answered	the	ruler priests	not	we have	king

1487	3361	2541	**16**	5119	3767	3860	846
εἰ	μὴ	Καίσαρα.		Τότε	οὖν	παρέδωκεν	αὐτὸν
except		Caesar.		Then	then	he gave over	him

846	2443	4717		3880
αὐτοῖς	ἵνα	σταυρωθῇ.		Παρέλαβον
to them	that	he might be crucified.		They took along

3767	04	2424	**17**	2532	941	1438	04	4716
οὖν	τὸν	Ἰησοῦν,		καὶ	βαστάζων	ἑαυτῷ	τὸν	σταυρὸν
then	the	Jesus,		and	bearing	himself	the	cross

[10]Pilate therefore said to him, "Do you refuse to speak to me? Do you not know that I have power to release you, and power to crucify you?" [11]Jesus answered him, "You would have no power over me unless it had been given you from above; therefore the one who handed me over to you is guilty of a greater sin." [12]From then on Pilate tried to release him, but the Jews cried out, "If you release this man, you are no friend of the emperor. Everyone who claims to be a king sets himself against the emperor."

[13] When Pilate heard these words, he brought Jesus outside and sat[a] on the judge's bench at a place called The Stone Pavement, or in Hebrew[b] Gabbatha. [14]Now it was the day of Preparation for the Passover; and it was about noon. He said to the Jews, "Here is your King!" [15]They cried out, "Away with him! Away with him! Crucify him!" Pilate asked them, "Shall I crucify your King?" The chief priests answered, "We have no king but the emperor." [16]Then he handed him over to them to be crucified.

So they took Jesus; [17]and carrying the cross by himself,

a Or *seated him*
b That is, *Aramaic*

he went out to what is called The Place of the Skull, which in Hebrew[a] is called Golgotha. [18]There they crucified him, and with him two others, one on either side, with Jesus between them. [19]Pilate also had an inscription written and put on the cross. It read, "Jesus of Nazareth,[b] the King of the Jews." [20]Many of the Jews read this inscription, because the place where Jesus was crucified was near the city; and it was written in Hebrew,[a] in Latin, and in Greek. [21]Then the chief priests of the Jews said to Pilate, "Do not write, 'The King of the Jews,' but, 'This man said, I am King of the Jews.' " [22]Pilate answered, "What I have written I have written." [23]When the soldiers had crucified Jesus, they took his clothes and divided them into four parts, one for each soldier. They also took his tunic; now the tunic was seamless, woven in one piece from the top. [24]So they said to one another, "Let us not tear it, but cast lots for it to see who will get it." This was to fulfill what the scripture says,
"They divided my clothes among themselves,

---

[a] That is, Aramaic
[b] Gk the Nazorean

1831		1519 04	3004		2898	5117	3739
ἐξῆλθεν	εἰς	τὸν	λεγόμενον	Κρανίου	Τόπον,	ὃ	
he went out	into	the	being said	of Skull	Place,	which	

3004	1447	1115		18	3699	846	
λέγεται	Ἑβραϊστὶ	Γολγοθα,			ὅπου	αὐτὸν	
is said	in Hebrew	Golgotha,			where	him	

4717		2532 3326 846	243		1417	1782
ἐσταύρωσαν,	καὶ	μετ' αὐτοῦ	ἄλλους	δύο	ἐντεῦθεν
they crucified,	and	with him	others	two	from here

2532 1782	3319	1161 04	2424		19	1125
καὶ ἐντεῦθεν,	μέσον	δὲ	τὸν	Ἰησοῦν.		ἔγραψεν
and from here,	middle	but	the	Jesus.		Wrote

1161 2532 5102	01	4091		2532 5087		1909 02
δὲ καὶ τίτλον	ὁ	Πιλᾶτος	καὶ	ἔθηκεν	ἐπὶ	τοῦ
but also notice	the	Pilate	and	he placed	on	the

4716	1510	1161 1125			2424	01
σταυροῦ.	ἦν	δὲ	γεγραμμένον·		Ἰησοῦς	ὁ
cross;	it was+	but	+having been written,		Jesus	the

3480	01 935	014	2453		20	3778	3767
Ναζωραῖος	ὁ βασιλεὺς	τῶν	Ἰουδαίων.			τοῦτον	οὖν
Nazorean	the king	of the	Judeans.			This	then

04 5102	4183	314		014	2453	3754
τὸν τίτλον	πολλοὶ	ἀνέγνωσαν	τῶν		Ἰουδαίων,	ὅτι
the notice	many	read	of the		Judeans,	because

1451	1510	01	5117	06	4172	3699	4717
ἐγγὺς	ἦν	ὁ	τόπος	τῆς	πόλεως	ὅπου	ἐσταυρώθη
near	was	the	place	of the	city	where	was crucified

01	2424	2532 1510	1125		1447
ὁ	Ἰησοῦς·	καὶ ἦν	γεγραμμένον		Ἑβραϊστί,
the	Jesus;	and it was+	+having been		written in Hebrew,

4515	1676		21	3004	3767 03	4091
Ῥωμαϊστί,	Ἑλληνιστί.			ἔλεγον	οὖν	τῷ Πιλάτῳ
in Roman,	in Greek.			Were saying	then	to the Pilate

013 749		014	2453	3361	1125	01
οἱ ἀρχιερεῖς	τῶν		Ἰουδαίων·	μὴ	γράφε·	ὁ
the ruler priests	of the		Judeans;	not	write;	the

933	014	2453	235	3754	1565	3004
βασιλεὺς	τῶν	Ἰουδαίων,	ἀλλ'	ὅτι	ἐκεῖνος	εἶπεν·
king	of the	Judeans,	but,	(")	that one	said;

935	1510 014	2453		611	01	4091
βασιλεύς	εἰμι τῶν	Ἰουδαίων.	22	ἀπεκρίθη	ὁ	Πιλᾶτος·
king	I am of the	Judeans.		Answered	the	Pilate;

3739 1125		1125		23	013 3767
ὃ γέγραφα,		γέγραφα.			Οἱ οὖν
what I have written,		I have written.			The then

4757	3753 4717		04	2424	2983
στρατιῶται,	ὅτε ἐσταύρωσαν		τὸν	Ἰησοῦν,	ἔλαβον
soldiers,	when they crucified		the	Jesus,	took

024 2440	846	2532 4160		5064	3313
τὰ ἱμάτια	αὐτοῦ	καὶ ἐποίησαν		τέσσαρα	μέρη,
the clothes	of him	and they made		four	parts,

1538	4757	3313	2532 04	5509	1510 1161 01
ἑκάστῳ	στρατιώτῃ	μέρος,	καὶ τὸν	χιτῶνα.	ἦν δὲ ὁ
to each	soldier	part,	and the	shirt.	Was but the

5509	689a	1537 022 509		5307
χιτὼν	ἄραφος,	ἐκ τῶν ἄνωθεν		ὑφαντὸς
shirt	without sewing,	from the from above		woven

1223	3650		24	3004	3767 4314	240
δι'	ὅλου.			εἶπαν	οὖν πρὸς	ἀλλήλους·
through	whole.			They said	then toward	one another;

3361 4977		846	235	2975
μὴ σχίσωμεν		αὐτόν,	ἀλλὰ	λάχωμεν
not we might split it,		it,	but	we might obtain by lot

4012	846	5101	1510	2443 05	1124
περὶ	αὐτοῦ	τίνος	ἔσται·	ἵνα ἡ	γραφὴ
about	it	whose	it will be;	that the	writing

4137	05 3004	1266		024 2440
πληρωθῇ	[ἡ λέγουσα],	διεμέρισαντο		τὰ ἱμάτιά
might be	the being said,	they divided		the clothes
filled		completely		

1473   1438   2532 1909 04 2441   1473
μου   ἑαυτοῖς   καὶ ἐπὶ τὸν ἱματισμόν μου
of me in themselves   and on   the clothing   of me
906   2819   013 3303   3767 4757   3778
ἔβαλον   κλῆρον. Οἱ μὲν οὖν στρατιῶται ταῦτα
they threw lot.   The indeed then soldiers   these
4160   25 2476   1161 3844   03   4716
ἐποίησαν.   Εἱστήκεισαν δὲ παρὰ   τῷ σταυρῷ
did.   Had stood   but alongside the cross
02   2424   05 3384   846   2532 05 79·   06
τοῦ ᾽Ιησοῦ ἡ μήτηρ αὐτοῦ καὶ ἡ ἀδελφὴ τῆς
of the Jesus the mother of him and the sister of the
3384   846   3137 05 02   2832   2532 3137 05
μητρὸς αὐτοῦ, Μαρία ἡ τοῦ Κλωπᾶ καὶ Μαρία ἡ
mother of him, Maria the of the Clopas and Maria the
3094   26   2424   3767 3708   08 3384   2532
Μαγδαληνή.   ᾽Ιησοῦς οὖν ἰδὼν   τὴν μητέρα καὶ
Magdalene.   Jesus   then having seen the mother and
04 3101   3936   3739 25   3004
τὸν μαθητὴν παρεστῶτα   ὃν ἠγάπα,   λέγει
the learner having stood along whom he loved, says
07   3384   1135   2396 01 5207 1473 27 1534
τῇ   μητρί· γύναι, ἴδε ὁ υἱός σου.   εἶτα
to the mother; woman, look the son of you. Then
3004   03   3101   2396 05 3384   1473   2532
λέγει τῷ   μαθητῇ· ἴδε ἡ μήτηρ σου.   καὶ
he says to the learner; look the mother of you. And
575 1565   06 5610 2983   01 3101   846 1519 024
ἀπ᾽ ἐκείνης τῆς ὥρας ἔλαβεν ὁ μαθητὴς αὐτὴν εἰς τὰ
from that   the hour took   the learner her into the
2398   28 3326 3778 3609a   01 2424   3754 2235
ἴδια.   Μετὰ τοῦτο εἰδὼς   ὁ ᾽Ιησοῦς ὅτι ἤδη
own.   After these having known the Jesus that already
3956   5055   2443 5048   05 1124   3004
πάντα τετέλεσται, ἵνα τελειωθῇ ἡ γραφή,   λέγει·
all   has been   that might be the writing, he says,
        completed,   completed
1372   29 4632   2749   3690   3324   4699
διψῶ.   σκεῦος ἔκειτο   ὄξους   μεστόν· σπόγγον
I thirst. Pot   was lying sour wine full; sponge
3767 3324   010 3690   5301   4060
οὖν μεστὸν τοῦ ὄξους   ὑσσώπῳ περιθέντες
then full of the sour wine in hyssop having set around
4374   846   011   4750   30 3753 3767
προσήνεγκαν αὐτοῦ τῷ στόματι.   ὅτε οὖν
they brought to of him the mouth.   When then
2983   012 3690 01 2424   3004   5055   2532
ἔλαβεν τὸ ὄξος [ὁ] ᾽Ιησοῦς εἶπεν· τετέλεσται, καὶ
he took the sour the Jesus said; it has been and
         wine   completed,
2827   08   2776   3860   012 4151
κλίνας   τὴν κεφαλὴν παρέδωκεν τὸ πνεῦμα.
having bowed the head he gave over the spirit.
bowed
31 013 3767 2453   1893   3904   1510   2443
    Οἱ οὖν ᾽Ιουδαῖοι, ἐπεὶ παρασκευὴ ἦν,   ἵνα
    The then Judeans, since preparation it was, that
3361 3306   1909 02 4716   021 4983   1722 011
μὴ μείνῃ ἐπὶ τοῦ σταυροῦ τὰ σώματα ἐν τῷ
not might stay on the cross the bodies in the
4521   1510   1063 3173   05 2250   1565   010
σαββάτῳ, ἦν γὰρ μεγάλη ἡ ἡμέρα ἐκείνου τοῦ
sabbath, it was for great the day of that the
4521   2065   04 4091   2443 2608
σαββάτου, ἠρώτησαν τὸν Πιλᾶτον ἵνα κατεαγῶσιν
sabbath, they asked the Pilate that they might break
846   024 4628 2532 142   32 2064
αὐτῶν τὰ σκέλη καὶ ἀρθῶσιν.   ἦλθον
of them the legs and they might be lifted up. Came

and for my clothing
they cast lots."
25And that is what the
soldiers did.

Meanwhile, standing
near the cross of Jesus
were his mother, and his
mother's sister, Mary the
wife of Clopas, and Mary
Magdalene. 26When Jesus
saw his mother and the
disciple whom he loved
standing beside her, he said
to his mother, "Woman,
here is your son." 27Then
he said to the disciple,
"Here is your mother."
And from that hour the
disciple took her into his
own home.

28 After this, when
Jesus knew that all was now
finished, he said (in order
to fulfill the scripture), "I
am thirsty." 29A jar full of
sour wine was standing
there. So they put a sponge
full of the wine on a branch
of hyssop and held it to his
mouth. 30When Jesus had
received the wine, he said,
"It is finished." Then he
bowed his head and gave
up his spirit.

31 Since it was the day
of Preparation, the Jews
did not want the bodies left
on the cross during the
sabbath, especially because
that sabbath was a day of
great solemnity. So they
asked Pilate to have the legs
of the crucified men broken
and the bodies removed.
32Then the soldiers came

and broke the legs of the first and of the other who had been crucified with him. ³³But when they came to Jesus and saw that he was already dead, they did not break his legs. ³⁴Instead, one of the soldiers pierced his side with a spear, and at once blood and water came out. ³⁵(He who saw this has testified so that you also may believe. His testimony is true, and he knows*a* that he tells the truth.) ³⁶These things occurred so that the scripture might be fulfilled, "None of his bones shall be broken." ³⁷And again another passage of scripture says, "They will look on the one whom they have pierced."

38 After these things, Joseph of Arimathea, who was a disciple of Jesus, though a secret one because of his fear of the Jews, asked Pilate to let him take away the body of Jesus. Pilate gave him permission; so he came and removed his body. ³⁹Nicodemus, who had at first come to Jesus by night, also came, bringing a mixture of myrrh and aloes, weighing about a hundred pounds. ⁴⁰They took the body of Jesus and wrapped it with the spices in linen cloths, according to the burial custom of the Jews.

a Or there is one who knows

3767	013	4757		2532 02	3303	4413	2608
οὖν	οἱ	στρατιῶται	καὶ	τοῦ	μὲν	πρώτου	κατέαξαν
then	the	soldiers	and	of the	indeed	first	they broke

024	4628	2532 02	243	02	4957
τὰ	σκέλη	καὶ	τοῦ ἄλλου	τοῦ	συσταυρωθέντος
the	legs	and	the other	of the	one having been crucified together

846 **33** 1909 1161 04 2424 2064 5613
αὐτῷ **33** ἐπὶ δὲ τὸν Ἰησοῦν ἐλθόντες, ὡς
to him; on but the Jesus having come, as

3708 2235 846 2348 3756 2608
εἶδον ἤδη αὐτὸν τεθνηκότα, οὐ κατέαξαν
they saw already him having died, not they broke

846 024 4628 **34** 235 1520 014 4757 3057
αὐτοῦ τὰ σκέλη, **34** ἀλλ' εἷς τῶν στρατιωτῶν λόγχῃ
of him the legs, but one of the soldiers spear

846 08 4125 3572 2532 1831 2117
αὐτοῦ τὴν πλευρὰν ἔνυξεν, καὶ ἐξῆλθεν εὐθὺς
of him the side stabbed, and came out immediately

129 2532 5204 **35** 2532 01 3708
αἷμα καὶ ὕδωρ. **35** καὶ ὁ ἑωρακὼς
blood and water. And the one having seen

3140 2532 228 846 1510 05 3141
μεμαρτύρηκεν, καὶ ἀληθινὴ αὐτοῦ ἐστιν ἡ μαρτυρία,
has testified, and true of him is the testimony,

2532 1565 3609a 3754 227 3004 2443 2532
καὶ ἐκεῖνος οἶδεν ὅτι ἀληθῆ λέγει, ἵνα καὶ
and that one knew that true he says, that also

1473 4100 **36** 1096 1063 3778 2443 05
ὑμεῖς πιστεύ[σ]ητε. **36** ἐγένετο γὰρ ταῦτα ἵνα ἡ
you might trust. Became for these that the

1124 4137 3747 3756 4937
γραφὴ πληρωθῇ· ὀστοῦν οὐ συντριβήσεται
writing might be filled; bone not will be broken

846 **37** 2532 3825 2087 1124 3004 3708
αὐτοῦ. **37** καὶ πάλιν ἑτέρα γραφὴ λέγει· ὄψονται
of him. And again other writing says; they will see

1519 3739 1574 **38** 3326 1161 3778 2065
εἰς ὃν ἐξεκέντησαν. **38** Μετὰ δὲ ταῦτα ἠρώτησεν
into whom they pierced. After but these asked

04 4091 2501 01 575 707 1510 3101
τὸν Πιλᾶτον Ἰωσὴφ [ὁ] ἀπὸ Ἀριμαθαίας, ὢν μαθητὴς
the Pilate Joseph the from Arimathea, being learner

02 2424 2928 1161 1223 04 5401
τοῦ Ἰησοῦ κεκρυμμένος δὲ διὰ τὸν φόβον
of the Jesus having been hidden but through the fear

014 2453 2443 142 012 4983 02
τῶν Ἰουδαίων, ἵνα ἄρῃ τὸ σῶμα τοῦ
of the Judeans, that he might lift up the body of the

2424 2532 2010 01 4091 2064 3767 2532
Ἰησοῦ· καὶ ἐπέτρεψεν ὁ Πιλᾶτος. ἦλθεν οὖν καὶ
Jesus; and allowed the Pilate. He went then and

142 012 4983 846 **39** 2064 1161 2532
ἦρεν τὸ σῶμα αὐτοῦ. **39** ἦλθεν δὲ καὶ
lifted up the body of him. Went but also

3530 01 2064 4314 846 3571 012
Νικόδημος, ὁ ἐλθὼν πρὸς αὐτὸν νυκτὸς τὸ
Nicodemus, the one having come to him of night the

4413 5342 3395 4666 2532 250 5613
πρῶτον, φέρων μίγμα σμύρνης καὶ ἀλόης ὡς
first, bearing mixture of myrrh and of aloes as

3046 1540 **40** 2983 3767 012 4983 02 2424
λίτρας ἑκατόν. **40** ἔλαβον οὖν τὸ σῶμα τοῦ Ἰησοῦ
litres hundred. They took then the body of the Jesus

2532 1210 846 3608 3326 022
καὶ ἔδησαν αὐτὸ ὀθονίοις μετὰ τῶν
and they bound it in linen strips with the

759 2531 1485 1510 015 2453
ἀρωμάτων, καθὼς ἔθος ἐστὶν τοῖς Ἰουδαίοις
spices, just as custom it is to the Judeans

| 1779 | 41 | 1510 | | 1161 | 1722 | 03 | 5117 | 3699 |
ἐνταφιάζειν. **41** ἦν δὲ ἐν τῷ τόπῳ ὅπου
to bury.   There was but in   the place where

4717   2779   2532 1722 03   2779   3419
ἐσταυρώθη   κῆπος, καὶ ἐν τῷ κήπῳ   μνημεῖον
he was crucified garden, and in the garden grave

2537   1722 3739 3764   3762   1510
καινὸν ἐν ᾧ οὐδέπω   οὐδεὶς ἦν
new   in which but not yet no one was+

5087   1563   42 3767 1223   08
τεθειμένος·   **42** ἐκεῖ οὖν διὰ   τὴν
+having been placed;   there then through the

3904   014   2453   3754   1451   1510 09
παρασκευὴν τῶν ᾿Ιουδαίων, ὅτι ἐγγὺς ἦν τὸ
preparation of the Judeans, because near was the

3419   5087   04   2424   **20:1** 07   1161 1520
μνημεῖον, ἔθηκαν τὸν ᾿Ιησοῦν. **20:1** Τῇ δὲ μιᾷ
grave,   they placed the Jesus.   In the but one

022   4521   3137   05 3094   2064   4404
τῶν σαββάτων Μαρία ἡ Μαγδαληνὴ ἔρχεται πρωῒ
of the sabbaths Maria the Magdalene comes in morning

4653   2089   1510 1519 012 3419   2532 991   04
σκοτίας ἔτι οὔσης εἰς τὸ μνημεῖον καὶ βλέπει   τὸν
dark   still being to the grave   and she sees the

3037   142   1537 010 3419
λίθον ἠρμένον   ἐκ τοῦ μνημείου.
stone having been lifted up from the grave.

2 5143   3767 2532 2064   4314 4613   4074   2532
2 τρέχει οὖν καὶ ἔρχεται πρὸς Σίμωνα Πέτρον καὶ
     She runs then and she comes to Simon Peter and

4314   04 243   3101   3739 5368   01 2424
πρὸς τὸν ἄλλον μαθητὴν ὃν ἐφίλει ὁ ᾿Ιησοῦς
toward the other learner whom was loving the Jesus

2532 3004   846   142   04 2962   1537
καὶ λέγει   αὐτοῖς· ἦραν   τὸν κύριον ἐκ
and she says to them; they lifted up the Master from

010 3419   2532 3756 3609a   4226   5087   846
τοῦ μνημείου καὶ οὐκ οἴδαμεν ποῦ ἔθηκαν   αὐτόν.
the grave   and not we know where they placed him.

3 1831   3767 01 4074   2532 01 243   3101
3 ᾿Εξῆλθεν οὖν ὁ Πέτρος καὶ ὁ ἄλλος μαθητὴς
     Went out then the Peter and the other learner

2532 2064   1519 012 3419   4 5143
καὶ ἤρχοντο   εἰς τὸ μνημεῖον. **4** ἔτρεχον
and they were coming to the grave.   Were running

1161 013 1417 3674   2532 01 243   3101   4390
δὲ οἱ δύο ὁμοῦ· καὶ ὁ ἄλλος μαθητὴς προέδραμεν
but the two same; and the other learner ran before

5030   02 4074   2532 2064   4413   1519 012
τάχιον τοῦ Πέτρου καὶ ἦλθεν πρῶτος εἰς τὸ
more quickly the Peter and he went first into the

3419   5 2532 3879   991   2749
μνημεῖον, **5** καὶ παρακύψας   βλέπει κείμενα
grave,   and having stooped down he sees lying

024 3608   3756 3305   1525   6 2064
τὰ ὀθόνια,   οὐ μέντοι εἰσῆλθεν. **6** ἔρχεται
the linen strips, not however he went into. Comes

3767 2532 4613 4074   190   846 2532 1525
οὖν καὶ Σίμων Πέτρος ἀκολουθῶν αὐτῷ καὶ εἰσῆλθεν
then and Simon Peter following him and he went in

1519 012 3419   2532 2334   024 3608
εἰς τὸ μνημεῖον, καὶ θεωρεῖ τὰ ὀθόνια
into the grave,   and he watches the linen strips

2749   7 2532 012 4676   3739 1510 1909 06
κείμενα, **7** καὶ τὸ σουδάριον, ὃ ἦν ἐπὶ τῆς
lying,   and the handkerchief, which was on the

2776   846   3756 3326 022 3608   2749
κεφαλῆς αὐτοῦ, οὐ μετὰ τῶν ὀθονίων κείμενον
head   of him, not with the linen strips lying

[41]Now there was a garden in the place where he was crucified, and in the garden there was a new tomb in which no one had ever been laid. [42]And so, because it was the Jewish day of Preparation, and the tomb was nearby, they laid Jesus there.

CHAPTER 20

Early on the first day of the week, while it was still dark, Mary Magdalene came to the tomb and saw that the stone had been removed from the tomb. [2]So she ran and went to Simon Peter and the other disciple, the one whom Jesus loved, and said to them, "They have taken the Lord out of the tomb, and we do not know where they have laid him." [3]Then Peter and the other disciple set out and went toward the tomb. [4]The two were running together, but the other disciple outran Peter and reached the tomb first. [5]He bent down to look in and saw the linen wrappings lying there, but he did not go in. [6]Then Simon Peter came, following him, and went into the tomb. He saw the linen wrappings lying there, [7]and the cloth that had been on Jesus' head, not lying with the linen wrappings but rolled up in a place by itself. ⁸Then the other disciple, who reached the tomb first, also went in, and he saw and believed; ⁹for as yet they did not understand the scripture, that he must rise from the dead. ¹⁰Then the disciples returned to their homes.

11 But Mary stood weeping outside the tomb. As she wept, she bent over to look*a* into the tomb; ¹²and she saw two angels in white, sitting where the body of Jesus had been lying, one at the head and the other at the feet. ¹³They said to her, "Woman, why are you weeping?" She said to them, "They have taken away my Lord, and I do not know where they have laid him." ¹⁴When she had said this, she turned around and saw Jesus standing there, but she did not know that it was Jesus. ¹⁵Jesus said to her, "Woman, why are you weeping? Whom are you looking for?" Supposing him to be the gardener, she said to him, "Sir, if you have carried him away, tell me where you have laid him, and I will take him away." ¹⁶Jesus said to her, "Mary!" She turned and said to him in Hebrew,*b* "Rabbouni!" (which means Teacher). ¹⁷Jesus said to her,

a Gk lacks *to look*
b That is, *Aramaic*

235	5565	1794		1519	1520	5117

ἀλλὰ χωρὶς ἐντετυλιγμένον εἰς ἕνα τόπον.
but without having been wrapped into one place.

8 5119 3767 1525 2532 01 243 3101 01
τότε οὖν εἰσῆλθεν καὶ ὁ ἄλλος μαθητὴς ὁ
Then then went into also the other learner the one

2064 4413 1519 012 3419 2532 3708 2532
ἐλθὼν πρῶτος εἰς τὸ μνημεῖον καὶ εἶδεν καὶ
having come first to the grave and he saw and

4100 9 3764 1063 3609a 08
ἐπίστευσεν· οὐδέπω γὰρ ᾔδεισαν τὴν
he trusted; but not yet for they had known the

1124 3754 1163 846 1537 3498
γραφὴν ὅτι δεῖ αὐτὸν ἐκ νεκρῶν
writing that it is necessary him out of dead

450 10 565 3767 3825 4314 846 013
ἀναστῆναι. ἀπῆλθον οὖν πάλιν πρὸς αὐτοὺς οἱ
to stand up. Went off then again toward them the

3101 3137 1161 2476 4314 011 3419
μαθηταί. **11** Μαρία δὲ εἱστήκει πρὸς τῷ μνημείῳ
learners. Maria but had stood to the grave

1854 2799 5613 3767 2799 3879 1519
ἔξω κλαίουσα. ὡς οὖν ἔκλαιεν, παρέκυψεν εἰς
outside crying. As then she was she stooped into
                                    crying. down

012 3419 12 2532 2334 1417 32 1722
τὸ μνημεῖον, καὶ θεωρεῖ δύο ἀγγέλους ἐν
the grave, and she watches two messengers in

3022 2516 1520 4314 07 2776 2532 1520
λευκοῖς καθεζομένους, ἕνα πρὸς τῇ κεφαλῇ καὶ ἕνα
white sitting, one toward the head and one

4314 015 4228 3699 2749 09 4983 02
πρὸς τοῖς ποσίν, ὅπου ἔκειτο τὸ σῶμα τοῦ
toward the feet, where was lying the body of the

2424 13 2532 3004 846 1565 1135 5101
Ἰησοῦ. καὶ λέγουσιν αὐτῇ ἐκεῖνοι· γύναι, τί
Jesus. And say to her those; woman, why

2799 3004 846 3754 142 04
κλαίεις; λέγει αὐτοῖς ὅτι ἦραν τὸν
you cry? She says to them, (") they lifted up the

2962 1473 2532 3756 3609a 4226 5087 846
κύριόν μου, καὶ οὐκ οἶδα ποῦ ἔθηκαν αὐτόν.
Master of me, and not I know where they placed him.

14 3778 3004 4762 1519 024 3694 2532
ταῦτα εἰποῦσα ἐστράφη εἰς τὰ ὀπίσω καὶ
These having said she was turned to the after and

2334 04 2424 2476 2532 3756 3609a
θεωρεῖ τὸν Ἰησοῦν ἑστῶτα καὶ οὐκ ᾔδει
she watches the Jesus having stood and not she knew

3754 2424 1510 15 3004 846 2424 1135 5101
ὅτι Ἰησοῦς ἐστιν. λέγει αὐτῇ Ἰησοῦς· γύναι, τί
that Jesus he is. Says to her Jesus; woman, why

2799 5101 2212 1565 1380 3754 01
κλαίεις; τίνα ζητεῖς; ἐκείνη δοκοῦσα ὅτι ὁ
you cry? Whom you seek? That one thinking that the

2780 1510 3004 846 2962 1487 1473
κηπουρός ἐστιν λέγει αὐτῷ· κύριε, εἰ σὺ
garden keeper it is says to him; Master, if you

941 846 3004 1473 4226 5087 846
ἐβάστασας αὐτόν, εἰπέ μοι ποῦ ἔθηκας αὐτόν,
borne him, say to me where you placed him,

2504 846 142 16 3004 846 2424 3137a
κἀγὼ αὐτὸν ἀρῶ. λέγει αὐτῇ Ἰησοῦς· Μαριάμ.
and I him will lift up. Says to her Jesus; Mariam.

4762 1565 3004 846 1447
στραφεῖσα ἐκείνη λέγει αὐτῷ Ἑβραϊστί·
Having been turned that one says to him in Hebrew;

4462 3739 3004 1320 17 3004 846
ῥαββουνι [ὃ λέγεται διδάσκαλε]. λέγει αὐτῇ
Rabboni which is said Teacher. Says to her

```
  2424      3361  1473    681       3768       1063 305
'Ιησοῦς· μή  μου  ἅπτου, οὔπω  γὰρ  ἀναβέβηκα
Jesus;  not  of me touch, not yet for  I have gone up
 4314     04   3962     4198      1161 4314    016 80
πρὸς  τὸν πατέρα· πορεύου δὲ  πρὸς  τοὺς ἀδελφούς
toward the father; travel but  toward the  brothers
1473    2532 3004 846      305        4314   04  3962
μου  καὶ  εἰπὲ αὐτοῖς· ἀναβαίνω πρὸς  τὸν πατέρα
of me and  say to them; I go up  toward the father
1473  2532 3962   1473    2532 2316 1473  2532 2316
μου  καὶ  πατέρα ὑμῶν  καὶ  θεόν μου  καὶ  θεὸν
of me and  father of you and  God of me and  God
1473         2064      3137a  05   3094       31a
ὑμῶν.   18  ἔρχεται Μαριὰμ ἡ  Μαγδαληνὴ ἀγγέλλουσα
of you.   Comes  Mariam the Magdalene giving message
 015       3101        3754 3708    04   2962     2532 3778
τοῖς  μαθηταῖς ὅτι ἑώρακα  τὸν κύριον, καὶ  ταῦτα
to the learners, (") I have seen the Master, and these
3004   846        1510 3767 3798   07    2250  1565
εἶπεν  αὐτῇ.  19  Οὔσης οὖν ὀψίας τῇ  ἡμέρᾳ ἐκείνῃ
he said to her.   Being then evening in the day  that
07  1520 4521      2532 018 2374     2808
τῇ  μίᾳ  σαββάτων καὶ  τῶν θυρῶν κεκλεισμένων
the one  of sabbaths and  the doors having been closed
3699   1510 013 3101      1223      04   5401   014
ὅπου  ἦσαν οἱ  μαθηταὶ διὰ  τὸν φόβον τῶν
where were the  learners through the fear  of the
 2453       2064  01  2424    2532 2476      1519 012
'Ιουδαίων, ἦλθεν ὁ  'Ιησοῦς καὶ  ἔστη  εἰς  τὸ
Judeans,  came the Jesus and  he stood in  the
3319   2532 3004   846      1515  1473     2532 3778
μέσον καὶ  λέγει  αὐτοῖς· εἰρήνη ὑμῖν.  20  καὶ τοῦτο
middle and  he says to them; peace  to you.  And this
3004        1166     020 5495 2532 08  4125
εἰπὼν   ἔδειξεν  τὰς χεῖρας καὶ  τὴν πλευρὰν
having said he showed the hands and  the side
846     5463        3767 013 3101     3708
αὐτοῖς. ἐχάρησαν  οὖν  οἱ  μαθηταὶ ἰδόντες
to them. They rejoiced then the  learners having seen
04  2962        3004 3767 846     01   2424    3825
τὸν κύριον.  21  εἶπεν οὖν  αὐτοῖς [ὁ  'Ιησοῦς] πάλιν·
the Master.   Said then to them the Jesus  again;
1515   1473     2531     649        1473 01  3962
εἰρήνη ὑμῖν·  καθὼς  ἀπέσταλκέν  με  ὁ  πατήρ,
peace  to you; just as has delegated me  the father,
2504  3992  1473    2532 3778  3004        1720
κἀγὼ  πέμπω ὑμᾶς.  22  καὶ  τοῦτο εἰπὼν    ἐνεφύσησεν
also I send you.  And this  having said he blew in
2532 3004  846      2983     4151  40    302 5100
καὶ  λέγει αὐτοῖς· λάβετε πνεῦμα ἅγιον·  23  ἄν  τινων
and  says to them; take  spirit holy;  - of whom
863       020 266        863       846      302 5100
ἀφῆτε  τὰς ἁμαρτίας ἀφέωνται  αὐτοῖς, ἄν  τινων
you might the sins   they have to them,  - of whom
send off              been sent off
2902      2902         2381  1161 1520 1537   014
κρατῆτε κεκράτηνται.  24  Θωμᾶς δὲ  εἷς ἐκ  τῶν
you might they have    Thomas but  one out of the
hold   been held.
1427    01   3004        1324     3756 1510   3326
δώδεκα, ὁ  λεγόμενος Δίδυμος, οὐκ ἦν  μετ'
twelve, the one being said Didymus, not  he was with
846    3753 2064  2424      3004        3767 846
αὐτῶν ὅτε  ἦλθεν 'Ιησοῦς.  25  ἔλεγον  οὖν  αὐτῷ
them when came  Jesus.   Were saying then to him
013 243  3101      3708      04   2962     01  1161
οἱ  ἄλλοι μαθηταί· ἑωράκαμεν τὸν κύριον. ὁ  δὲ
the others learners; we have seen the Master. The but
```

"Do not hold on to me, because I have not yet ascended to the Father. But go to my brothers and say to them, 'I am ascending to my Father and your Father, to my God and your God.'" [18]Mary Magdalene went and announced to the disciples, "I have seen the Lord"; and she told them that he had said these things to her.

[19]When it was evening on that day, the first day of the week, and the doors of the house where the disciples had met were locked for fear of the Jews, Jesus came and stood among them and said, "Peace be with you." [20]After he said this, he showed them his hands and his side. Then the disciples rejoiced when they saw the Lord. [21]Jesus said to them again, "Peace be with you. As the Father has sent me, so I send you." [22]When he had said this, he breathed on them and said to them, "Receive the Holy Spirit. [23]If you forgive the sins of any, they are forgiven them; if you retain the sins of any, they are retained."

[24]But Thomas (who was called the Twin[a]), one of the twelve, was not with them when Jesus came. [25]So the other disciples told him, "We have seen the Lord." But he said

[a] Gk Didymus

to them, "Unless I see the mark of the nails in his hands, and put my finger in the mark of the nails and my hand in his side, I will not believe."

26 A week later his disciples were again in the house, and Thomas was with them. Although the doors were shut, Jesus came and stood among them and said, "Peace be with you." 27Then he said to Thomas, "Put your finger here and see my hands. Reach out your hand and put it in my side. Do not doubt but believe." 28Thomas answered him, "My Lord and my God!" 29Jesus said to him, "Have you believed because you have seen me? Blessed are those who have not seen and yet have come to believe."

30 Now Jesus did many other signs in the presence of his disciples, which are not written in this book. 31But these are written so that you may come to believe*a* that Jesus is the Messiah,*b* the Son of God, and that through believing you may have life in his name.

CHAPTER 21

After these things Jesus showed himself again to

a Other ancient authorities read *may continue to believe*

b Or *the Christ*

3004	846	1437 3361	3708		1722	019	5495
εἶπεν	αὐτοῖς·	ἐὰν μὴ	ἴδω		ἐν	ταῖς	χερσὶν
said	to them;	except	I might see		in	the	hands

846   04   5179   014   2247   2532 906   04
αὐτοῦ τὸν τύπον τῶν   ἥλων καὶ βάλω   τὸν
of him the example of the nails and I might throw the

1147   1473   1519 04   5179   014   2247 2532
δάκτυλόν μου   εἰς τὸν τύπον τῶν   ἥλων καὶ
finger   of me into the example of the nails and

906   1473   08   5495   1519 08 4125   846
βάλω   μου   τὴν χεῖρα εἰς τὴν πλευρὰν αὐτοῦ,
I might throw of me the hand into the side   of him,

3756 3361 4100   2532 3326 2250   3638 3825
οὐ μὴ πιστεύσω. 26 Καὶ μεθ' ἡμέρας ὀκτὼ πάλιν
not not I will trust. And after days eight again

1510 2080 013 3101   846   2532 2381   3326 846
ἦσαν ἔσω   οἱ μαθηταὶ αὐτοῦ καὶ Θωμᾶς μετ' αὐτῶν.
were inside the learners of him and Thomas with them.

2064   01 2424   018   2374   2808
ἔρχεται ὁ Ἰησοῦς τῶν   θυρῶν κεκλεισμένων,
Comes the Jesus of the doors having been closed,

2532 2476   1519 012 3319   2532 3004   1515
καὶ ἔστη   εἰς τὸ μέσον καὶ εἶπεν· εἰρήνη
and he stood in the middle and he said; peace

1473   27 1534 3004   03   2381   5342 04
ὑμῖν.   εἶτα λέγει τῷ   Θωμᾷ· φέρε τὸν
to you. Then he says to the Thomas; carry the

1147   1473   5602 2532 2396 020 5495 1473 2532
δάκτυλόν σου   ὧδε καὶ ἴδε τὰς χεῖράς μου καὶ
finger of you here and look the hands of me and

5342 08 5495 1473   2532 846   1519 08 4125
φέρε τὴν χεῖρά σου καὶ βάλε εἰς τὴν πλευράν
carry the hand of you and throw into the side

1473   2532 3361 1096 571   235 4103
μου, καὶ μὴ γίνου ἄπιστος ἀλλὰ πιστός.
of me, and not become untrustful but trustful.

28 611   2381 2532 3004 846   01 2962   1473
ἀπεκρίθη Θωμᾶς καὶ εἶπεν αὐτῷ· ὁ κύριός μου
Answered Thomas and said to him; the Master of me

2532 01 2316 1473   29 3004 846   01 2424   3754
καὶ ὁ θεός μου.   λέγει αὐτῷ ὁ Ἰησοῦς· ὅτι
and the God of me. Says to him the Jesus; because

3708   1473   4100   3107   013 3361 3708
ἑώρακάς με   πεπίστευκας; μακάριοι οἱ μὴ ἰδόντες
you have me   have you   Fortunate the not having
seen   trusted?   ones   seen

2532 4100   30 4183   3303   3767 2532 243
καὶ πιστεύσαντες. Πολλὰ μὲν   οὖν καὶ ἄλλα
and having trusted. Many indeed then also other

4592   4160   01 2424   1799   014 3101
σημεῖα ἐποίησεν ὁ Ἰησοῦς ἐνώπιον τῶν μαθητῶν
signs did   the Jesus before the learners

846   3739 3756 1510   1125   1722
[αὐτοῦ,] ἃ   οὐκ ἔστιν γεγραμμένα   ἐν
of him, which not they are+ +having been written in

011 975   3778 31 3778 1161 1125
τῷ βιβλίῳ   τούτῳ·   ταῦτα δὲ γέγραπται
the small book this;   these but have been written

2443 4100   3754 2424   1510 01 5547
ἵνα πιστεύ[σ]ητε ὅτι Ἰησοῦς ἐστιν ὁ χριστὸς
that you might trust that Jesus is the Christ

01 5207 02   2316 2532 2443 4100   2222
ὁ υἱὸς τοῦ θεοῦ, καὶ ἵνα πιστεύοντες ζωὴν
the son of the God, and that trusting life

2192   1722 011 3686   846   21:1 3326
ἔχητε   ἐν τῷ ὀνόματι αὐτοῦ.   Μετὰ
you might have in the name of him.   After

3778 5319   1438   3825 01 2424 015
ταῦτα ἐφανέρωσεν ἑαυτὸν πάλιν ὁ Ἰησοῦς τοῖς
these demonstrated himself again the Jesus to the

```
3101          1909 06   2281      06      5085
μαθηταῖς ἐπὶ τῆς θαλάσσης τῆς    Τιβεριάδος·
learners on    the sea        of the Tiberias;
5319              1161 3779        1510 3674 4613   4074
ἐφανέρωσεν       δὲ   οὕτως.  2  ἦσαν ὁμοῦ Σίμων Πέτρος
he demonstrated but  thusly.     Were same Simon Peter
2532 2381     01   3004              1324      2532 3482
καὶ Θωμᾶς ὁ   λεγόμενος       Δίδυμος καὶ Ναθαναὴλ
and  Thomas the one being said Didymus and  Nathanael
01       575  2580 06     1056          2532 013       02
ὁ   ἀπὸ Κανὰ τῆς   Γαλιλαίας καὶ οἱ      τοῦ
the one from Cana of the Galilee   and the ones of the
2199        2532 243      1537 014 3101        846     1417
Ζεβεδαίου καὶ ἄλλοι ἐκ  τῶν μαθητῶν αὐτοῦ δύο.
Zebedee   and others from the  learners of him two.
    3004    846     4613  4074     5217      232
  3 λέγει αὐτοῖς Σίμων Πέτρος· ὑπάγω ἁλιεύειν.
    Says  to them Simon Peter;  I go off to fish.
3004      846    2064        2532 1473 4862 1473
λέγουσιν αὐτῷ· ἐρχόμεθα καὶ ἡμεῖς σὺν σοί.
They say to him; go        also  we    with you.
1831        2532 1684      1519 012 4143        2532 1722
ἐξῆλθον     καὶ ἐνέβησαν εἰς τὸ πλοῖον, καὶ ἐν
They went out and  went in  into the boat,   and  in
1565     07   3571    4084      3762      4405      1161
ἐκείνῃ τῇ  νυκτὶ ἐπίασαν οὐδέν. 4 πρωΐας δὲ
that    the night they captured nothing.  Morning but
2235      1096         2476 2424   1519 04  123
ἤδη      γενομένης     ἔστη Ἰησοῦς εἰς τὸν αἰγιαλόν,
already having become  stood Jesus into the shore,
3756 3305  3609a       013 3101      3754  2424    1510
οὐ μέντοι ᾔδεισαν οἱ μαθηταὶ ὅτι Ἰησοῦς ἐστιν.
not however had known the learners that Jesus  it is.
  3004 3767 846      01   2424      3813           3361
5 λέγει οὖν αὐτοῖς [ὁ] Ἰησοῦς· παιδία,        μὴ
  Says  then to them the Jesus;  small children, not
5100 4371      2192     611          846      3756a
τι  προσφάγιον ἔχετε; ἀπεκρίθησαν αὐτῷ οὔ.
some thing to eat have you? They answered to him no.
  01   1161 3004  846      906      1519 024 1188
6 ὁ    δὲ  εἶπεν αὐτοῖς· βάλετε εἰς τὰ δεξιὰ
  The one but  said  to them; throw  into the right
3313  010    4143  012 1350     2532 2147
μέρη τοῦ    πλοίου τὸ δίκτυον, καὶ εὑρήσετε.
parts of the boat  the net,   and you will find.
906        3767 2532 3765     846  1670
ἔβαλον     οὖν, καὶ οὐκέτι αὐτὸ ἑλκύσαι
They threw then, and  no longer it   to haul
2480       575  010 4128    014     2486
ἴσχυον     ἀπὸ τοῦ πλήθους τῶν ἰχθύων.
they were strong from the quantity of the fish.
  3004 3767 01    3101      1565      5739 25   01   2424
7 λέγει οὖν ὁ   μαθητὴς ἐκεῖνος ὃν ἡγάπα ὁ Ἰησοῦς
  Says  then the learner that   whom loved the Jesus
03       4074 01   2962    1510   4613 3767 4074
τῷ    Πέτρῳ· ὁ  κύριός ἐστιν. Σίμων οὖν Πέτρος
to the Peter; the Master it is. Simon then Peter
191          3754 01  2962    1510  04  1903
ἀκούσας     ὅτι ὁ   κύριός ἐστιν τὸν ἐπενδύτην
having heard that the Master it is  the outer coat
1241         1510  1063 1131     2532 906       1438
διεζώσατο, ἦν  γὰρ γυμνός, καὶ ἔβαλεν ἑαυτὸν
he belted, he was for naked,  and  he threw himself
1519 08  2281       8 013 1161 243      3101      011
εἰς τὴν θάλασσαν,   οἱ δὲ  ἄλλοι μαθηταὶ τῷ
into the sea,        the but other learners in the
4142      2064    3756 1063 1510      3112     575  06
πλοιαρίῳ ἦλθον, οὐ γὰρ ἦσαν     μακρὰν ἀπὸ τῆς
small boat came,  not for they were far     from the
```

the disciples by the Sea of Tiberias; and he showed himself in this way. [2]Gathered there together were Simon Peter, Thomas called the Twin,[a] Nathanael of Cana in Galilee, the sons of Zebedee, and two others of his disciples. [3]Simon Peter said to them, "I am going fishing." They said to him, "We will go with you." They went out and got into the boat, but that night they caught nothing.

[4]Just after daybreak, Jesus stood on the beach; but the disciples did not know that it was Jesus. [5]Jesus said to them, "Children, you have no fish, have you?" They answered him, "No." [6]He said to them, "Cast the net to the right side of the boat, and you will find some." So they cast it, and now they were not able to haul it in because there were so many fish. [7]That disciple whom Jesus loved said to Peter, "It is the Lord!" When Simon Peter heard that it was the Lord, he put on some clothes, for he was naked, and jumped into the sea. [8]But the other disciples came in the boat, dragging the net full of fish, for they were not far from the

[a] Gk Didymus

land, only about a hundred yards[a] off.

9 When they had gone ashore, they saw a charcoal fire there, with fish on it, and bread. [10]Jesus said to them, "Bring some of the fish that you have just caught." [11]So Simon Peter went aboard and hauled the net ashore, full of large fish, a hundred fifty-three of them; and though there were so many, the net was not torn. [12]Jesus said to them, "Come and have breakfast." Now none of the disciples dared to ask him, "Who are you?" because they knew it was the Lord. [13]Jesus came and took the bread and gave it to them, and did the same with the fish. [14]This was now the third time that Jesus appeared to the disciples after he was raised from the dead.

15 When they had finished breakfast, Jesus said to Simon Peter, "Simon son of John, do you love me more than these?" He said to him, "Yes, Lord; you know that I love you." Jesus said to him, "Feed my lambs." [16]A second time he said to him, "Simon son of John, do you love me?" He said to him, "Yes, Lord; you know that I love you." Jesus said to him, "Tend my sheep." [17]He said to him the third time,

[a] Gk two hundred cubits

1093	235	5613	575	4083	1250		4951	012
γῆς ἀλλὰ ὡς ἀπὸ πηχῶν διακοσίων, σύροντες τὸ
land but as from cubits two hundred, dragging the

1350   014   2486   5613 3767 576   1519
δίκτυον τῶν   ἰχθύων. 9 ὡς   οὖν ἀπέβησαν εἰς
net   of the fish.   As then they went off into

08 1093 991   439   2749   2532 3795
τὴν γῆν βλέπουσιν ἀνθρακιὰν κειμένην καὶ ὀψάριον
the land they see coal fire lying and small fish

1945   2532 740   3004 846   01 2424
ἐπικείμενον καὶ ἄρτον. 10 λέγει αὐτοῖς ὁ Ἰησοῦς·
lying on   and bread.   Says to them the Jesus;

5342   575   022 2795   3739 4084   3568
ἐνέγκατε ἀπὸ τῶν ὀψαρίων ὧν ἐπιάσατε νῦν.
bring from the small fish which you captured now.

    305   3767 4613 4074   2532 1670   012
11 ἀνέβη   οὖν Σίμων Πέτρος καὶ εἵλκυσεν τὸ
    Went up then Simon Peter and he hauled the

1350   1519 08 1093 3324 2486   3173   1540
δίκτυον εἰς τὴν γῆν μεστὸν ἰχθύων μεγάλων ἑκατὸν
net   into the land full of fish great hundred

4004   5140   2532 5118   1510 3756 4977
πεντήκοντα τριῶν· καὶ τοσούτων ὄντων οὐκ ἐσχίσθη
fifty   three; and of such being not was split

09 1350   3004 846   01 2424   1205
τὸ δίκτυον. 12 λέγει αὐτοῖς ὁ Ἰησοῦς· δεῦτε
the net.   Says to them the Jesus; come

709   3762 1161 5111   014   3101
ἀριστήσατε. οὐδεὶς δὲ ἐτόλμα τῶν μαθητῶν
eat a meal. No one but was daring of the learners

1833   846   1473 5101 1510 3609a   3754
ἐξετάσαι αὐτόν· σὺ τίς εἶ; εἰδότες ὅτι
to inquire him; you who are? Having known that

01 2962   1510   2064   2424 2532 2983   04
ὁ κύριός ἐστιν. 13 ἔρχεται Ἰησοῦς καὶ λαμβάνει τὸν
the Master it is.   Comes Jesus and he takes the

740   2532 1325   846   2532 012 3795
ἄρτον καὶ δίδωσιν αὐτοῖς, καὶ τὸ ὀψάριον
bread and he gives to them, and the small fish

3668   3778 2235   5154 5319   2424
ὁμοίως. 14 τοῦτο ἤδη τρίτον ἐφανερώθη Ἰησοῦς
likewise.   This already third demonstrated Jesus

015   3101   1453   1537 3498
τοῖς μαθηταῖς ἐγερθεὶς ἐκ νεκρῶν.
to the learners having been raised out of dead.

   3753 3767 709   3004 03   4613   4074
15 Ὅτε οὖν ἠρίστησαν λέγει τῷ Σίμωνι Πέτρῳ
   When then they ate a meal says to the Simon Peter

01 2424   4613 2491   25   1473 4183
ὁ Ἰησοῦς· Σίμων Ἰωάννου, ἀγαπᾷς με πλέον
the Jesus; Simon of John, love you me more

3778   3004   846   3483 2962   1473 3609a
τούτων; λέγει αὐτῷ· ναὶ κύριε, σὺ οἶδας
of these? He says to him; yes Master, you know

3754 5368   1473 3004   846   1006 024 721
ὅτι φιλῶ σε. λέγει αὐτῷ· βόσκε τὰ ἀρνία
that I love you. He says to him; graze the lambs

1473   3004   846   3825 1208   4613
μου. 16 λέγει αὐτῷ πάλιν δεύτερον· Σίμων
of me.   He says to him again second; Simon

2491   25   1473 3004   846   3483 2962
Ἰωάννου, ἀγαπᾷς με; λέγει αὐτῷ, ναὶ κύριε,
of John, love you me? He says to him, yes Master,

1473 3609a 3754 5368   1473 3004   846   4165
σὺ οἶδας ὅτι φιλῶ σε. λέγει αὐτῷ· ποίμαινε
you know that I love you. He says to him; shepherd

024 4263   1473   3004 846   012 5154   4613
τὰ πρόβατά μου. 17 λέγει αὐτῷ τὸ τρίτον· Σίμων
the sheep of me.   He says to him the third; Simon

```
   2491        5368       1473 3076        01   4074   3754
Ἰωάννου, φιλεῖς   με;   ἐλυπήθη   ὁ  Πέτρος ὅτι
of John,  love you me?  Was grieved the Peter because
3004        846      012 2154     5368      1473 2532 3004
εἶπεν   αὐτῷ   τὸ  τρίτον· φιλεῖς  με;  καὶ  λέγει
he said to him the third;  love you me? And  he says
846      2962     3956 1473 3609a  1473 1097        3754
αὐτῷ·  κύριε,  πάντα σὺ οἶδας, σὺ  γινώσκεις ὅτι
to him; Master, all  you know,  you know        that
5368   1473 3004     846      01 2424      1006  024
φιλῶ  σε.  λέγει αὐτῷ  [ὁ Ἰησοῦς]· βόσκε τὰ
I love you. Says  to him the Jesus;   graze the
4263      1473    281    281  3004   1473      3753 1510
πρόβατά μου.  18 ἀμὴν ἀμὴν λέγω σοι,  ὅτε ἦς
sheep    of me.    Amen amen I say to you, when you were
3501        2224      4572       2532 4043       3699
νεώτερος, ἐζώννυες σεαυτὸν καὶ  περιεπάτεις ὅπου
newer,    you were  yourself and  you were     where
          belting                 walking around
2309      3752 1161 1095        1614      020 5495    1473
ἤθελες· ὅταν δὲ  γηράσης, ἐκτενεῖς τὰς χεῖράς σου,
you were when but  you might you will the hands    of
wanting;           grow old, stretch out         you,
2532 243   1473 2224    2532 5342        3699
καὶ ἄλλος σε  ζώσει  καὶ οἴσει       ὅπου
and  other you will belt and  he will bring where
3756 2309      3778 1161 3004        4591
οὐ  θέλεις.  19 τοῦτο δὲ  εἶπεν  σημαίνων
not  you want.   This  but he said signifying
4169      2288     1392        04  2316 2532 3778  3004
ποίῳ   θανάτῳ δοξάσει    τὸν θεόν. καὶ τοῦτο εἰπὼν
in what death  he will give the God. And this     having
kind          splendor                            said
3004   846      190        1473      1994
λέγει αὐτῷ·  ἀκολούθει μοι.  20 Ἐπιστραφεὶς
he says to him; follow    me.      Having been returned
01  4074   991     04  3101     3739 25   01 2424
ὁ  Πέτρος βλέπει τὸν μαθητὴν ὃν  ἠγάπα ὁ Ἰησοῦς
the Peter  sees   the learner whom loved the Jesus
190            3739 2532 377      1722 011 1173    1909
ἀκολουθοῦντα, ὃς  καὶ ἀνέπεσεν ἐν  τῷ δείπνῳ ἐπὶ
following,    who also reclined in  the dinner  on
012 4738      846    2532 3004      2962      5101 1510   01
τὸ στῆθος αὐτοῦ καὶ εἶπεν, Κύριε, τίς ἐστιν ὁ
the chest  of him and said, Master, who  is     the
3860          1473    3778       3767 3708       01
παραδιδούς σε;  21 τοῦτον   οὖν ἰδὼν      ὁ
one giving over you?   This one then having seen the
4074   3004   03       2424     2962      1161 5101
Πέτρος λέγει τῷ    Ἰησοῦ, Κύριε, οὗτος δὲ  τί;
Peter  says  to the Jesus, Master, this one but what?
     3004   846      01  2424      1437 846      2309    3306
22 λέγει αὐτῷ  ὁ Ἰησοῦς, ἐὰν αὐτὸν θέλω  μένειν
   Says  to him the Jesus, if  him   I want to stay
2193 2064    5101 4314 1473 1473 1473 190
ἕως ἔρχομαι, τί  πρὸς σέ; σύ μοι ἀκολούθει.
until I come, what to  you? You me  follow.
     1831     3767 3778  01 3056 1519 016 80
23 ἐξῆλθεν οὖν οὗτος ὁ λόγος εἰς τοὺς ἀδελφοὺς
   Went out then this the  word to  the  brothers
3754 01 3101     1565     3756 599        3756 3004
ὅτι ὁ  μαθητὴς ἐκεῖνος οὐκ ἀποθνήσκει· οὐκ εἶπεν
that the learner that   not  dies;        not said
1161 846      01 2424      3754 3756 599      235   1437
δὲ  αὐτῷ  ὁ Ἰησοῦς ὅτι οὐκ ἀποθνήσκει ἀλλ᾽ ἐὰν
but  to him the Jesus that not  he dies       but,  if
846      2309    3306     2193 2064       5101 4314 1473
αὐτὸν θέλω  μένειν ἕως ἔρχομαι[, τί  πρὸς σέ];
him    I want to stay until I  come,  what to  you?
```

"Simon son of John, do you love me?" Peter felt hurt because he said to him the third time, "Do you love me?" And he said to him, "Lord, you know everything; you know that I love you." Jesus said to him, "Feed my sheep. [18]Very truly, I tell you, when you were younger, you used to fasten your own belt and to go wherever you wished. But when you grow old, you will stretch out your hands, and someone else will fasten a belt around you and take you where you do not wish to go." [19](He said this to indicate the kind of death by which he would glorify God.) After this he said to him, "Follow me."

[20] Peter turned and saw the disciple whom Jesus loved following them; he was the one who had reclined next to Jesus at the supper and had said, "Lord, who is it that is going to betray you?" [21]When Peter saw him, he said to Jesus, "Lord, what about him?" [22]Jesus said to him, "If it is my will that he remain until I come, what is that to you? Follow me!" [23]So the rumor spread in the community[a] that this disciple would not die. Yet Jesus did not say to him that he would not die, but, "If it is my will that he remain until I come, what is that to you?"[b]

[a] Gk *among the brothers*
[b] Other ancient authorities lack *what is that to you*

24 This is the disciple who is testifying to these things and has written them, and we know that his testimony is true. 25But there are also many other things that Jesus did; if every one of them were written down, I suppose that the world itself could not contain the books that would be written.

THIS STORY, TRADITIONALLY PLACED AT THE END OF JOHN 7, IS PRINTED HERE AS FOLLOWS:

[[53Then each of them went home, 8:1while Jesus went to the Mount of Olives. 2Early in the morning he came again to the temple. All the people came to him and he sat down and began to teach them. 3The scribes and the Pharisees brought a woman who had been caught in adultery; and making her stand before all of them, 4they said to him, "Teacher, this woman was caught in the very act of committing adultery. 5Now in the law Moses commanded us to stone such women. Now what do you say?" 6They said this to test him, so that they might have some charge to bring against him. Jesus bent down and wrote with his finger on the ground. 7When they kept on questioning him, he straightened up and said to them, "Let anyone among you who is without sin be the first

3778	1510	01	3101	01	3140		4012
24 οὗτος ἐστιν ὁ μαθητὴς ὁ μαρτυρῶν περὶ
This is the learner the one testifying about

3778	2532	01	1125		3778	2532	3609a
τούτων καὶ ὁ γράψας ταῦτα, καὶ οἴδαμεν
these and the one having written these, and we know

3754	227	846	05	3141	1510	1510	1161
ὅτι ἀληθὴς αὐτοῦ ἡ μαρτυρία ἐστίν. 25 ἔστιν δὲ
that true of him the testimony is. There are but

2532	243	4183	3739	4160	01	2424	3748	1437
καὶ ἄλλα πολλὰ ἃ ἐποίησεν ὁ Ἰησοῦς, ἅτινα ἐὰν
also others many that did the Jesus, which if

1125		2596	1520	3761	846	3633
γραφῆται καθ᾽ ἕν, οὐδ᾽ αὐτὸν οἶμαι
it might be written by one, but not it I expect

04	2889	5562	024	1125	975
τὸν κόσμον χωρῆσαι τὰ γραφόμενα βιβλία.
the world to make room the being written small books.

	2532	4198	1538	1519	04	3624	846
[[53 Καὶ ἐπορεύθησαν ἕκαστος εἰς τὸν οἶκον αὐτοῦ,
And traveled each into the house of him,

	2424	1161	4198	1519	012	3735	018
8:1 Ἰησοῦς δὲ ἐπορεύθη εἰς τὸ Ὄρος τῶν
Jesus but traveled into the Hill of the

1636		3722	1161	3825	3854	1519	012
Ἐλαιῶν. 2 Ὄρθρου δὲ πάλιν παρεγένετο εἰς τὸ
Olives. Of dawn but again he arrived in the

2411	2532	3956	01	2992	2064	4314	846
ἱερὸν καὶ πᾶς ὁ λαὸς ἤρχετο πρὸς αὐτόν,
temple and all the people were coming toward him,

2532	2523	1321	846	71	1161
καὶ καθίσας ἐδίδασκεν αὐτούς. 3 ἄγουσιν δὲ
and having sat he was teaching them. Bring but

013	1122	2532	013	5330	1135	1909	3430
οἱ γραμματεῖς καὶ οἱ Φαρισαῖοι γυναῖκα ἐπὶ μοιχείᾳ
the writers and the Pharisees woman on adultery

2638		2532	2476	846	1722
κατειλημμένην καὶ στήσαντες αὐτὴν ἐν
having been overtaken and having stood her in

3319	3004	846	1320	3778	05	1135
μέσῳ 4 λέγουσιν αὐτῷ, Διδάσκαλε, αὕτη ἡ γυνὴ
middle they say to him, Teacher, this the woman

2638	1909	848a	3431	1722	1161	03
κατείληπται ἐπ᾽ αὐτοφώρῳ μοιχευομένη· 5 ἐν δὲ τῷ
has been on self-act of committing in but the
overtaken adultery;

3551	1473	3475	1781	020	5108	3034
νόμῳ ἡμῖν Μωϋσῆς ἐνετείλατο τὰς τοιαύτας λιθάζειν.
law to us Moses commanded the such ones to stone.

1473	3767	5101	3004	3778	1161	3004
σὺ οὖν τί λέγεις; 6 τοῦτο δὲ ἔλεγον
You then what say? This but they were saying

3985	846	2443	2192	2723
πειράζοντες αὐτόν, ἵνα ἔχωσιν κατηγορεῖν
pressuring him, that they might have to accuse

846	01	1161	2424	2736	2955	03
αὐτοῦ. ὁ δὲ Ἰησοῦς κάτω κύψας τῷ
him. The but Jesus down having bent down in the

1147	2608a	1519	08	1093	5613	1161
δακτύλῳ κατέγραφεν εἰς τὴν γῆν. 7 ὡς δὲ
finger was writing down in the earth. As but

1961	2065	846	352	2532
ἐπέμενον ἐρωτῶντες αὐτόν, ἀνέκυψεν καὶ
they were staying on asking him, he bent up and

3004	846	01	361	1473	4413	1909
εἶπεν αὐτοῖς, Ὁ ἀναμάρτητος ὑμῶν πρῶτος ἐπ᾽
said to them, The unsinful one of you first on

846	906	3037	**8**	2532	3825	2633a

αὐτὴν βαλέτω λίθον. **8** καὶ πάλιν κατακύψας
her   let throw stone.   And again having bent down

1125	1519	08	1093	**9**	013	1161	191

ἔγραφεν εἰς τὴν γῆν. **9** οἱ δὲ ἀκούσαντες
he was writing in the earth. The but ones having
                                           heard

1831	1520	2596	1520	757	575	014

ἐξήρχοντο εἰς καθ' εἰς ἀρξάμενοι ἀπὸ τῶν
were going out one by one having begun from the

4245	2532	2641	3441	2532	05

πρεσβυτέρων καὶ κατελείφθη μόνος καὶ ἡ
older men and he was left behind alone and the

1135	1722	3319	1510	**10**	352	1161	01

γυνὴ ἐν μέσῳ οὖσα. **10** ἀνακύψας δὲ ὁ
woman in middle being. Having bent up but the

2424	3004	846	1135	4226	1510	3762

Ἰησοῦς εἶπεν αὐτῇ, Γύναι, ποῦ εἰσιν; οὐδείς
Jesus said to her, Woman, where are they? No one

1473	2632	**11**	05	1161	3004	3762	2962

σε κατέκρινεν; **11** ἡ δὲ εἶπεν, Οὐδεις, κύριε.
you condemned?   The one but said, no one, Master.

3004	1161	01	2424	3761	1473	1473	2632

εἶπεν δὲ ὁ Ἰησοῦς, Οὐδὲ ἐγώ σε κατακρίνω·
Said but the Jesus, but not I you condemn;

4198	2532	575	010	3568	3371	264

πορεύου, [καὶ] ἀπὸ τοῦ νῦν μηκέτι ἀμάρτανε.]]
travel, and from the now no longer sin.

to throw a stone at her." [8]And once again he bent down and wrote on the ground.[a] [9]When they heard it, they went away, one by one, beginning with the elders; and Jesus was left alone with the woman standing before him. [10]Jesus straightened up and said to her, "Woman, where are they? Has no one condemned you?" [11]She said, "No one, sir."[b] And Jesus said, "Neither do I condemn you. Go your way, and from now on do not sin again."]]

[a] Other ancient authorities add *the sins of each of them*
[b] Or *Lord*

ACTS

CHAPTER 1

In the first book, Theophilus, I wrote about all that Jesus did and taught from the beginning [2]until the day when he was taken up to heaven, after giving instructions through the Holy Spirit to the apostles whom he had chosen. [3]After his suffering he presented himself alive to them by many convincing proofs, appearing to them during forty days and speaking about the kingdom of God. [4]While staying[a] with them, he ordered them not to leave Jerusalem, but to wait there for the promise of the Father. "This," he said, "is what you have heard from me; [5]for John baptized with water, but you will be baptized with[b] the Holy Spirit not many days from now."

6 So when they had come together, they asked him, "Lord, is this the time when you will restore the kingdom to Israel?" [7]He replied, "It is not for you to know the times or periods that the Father has set by his own authority. [8]But you will receive power when the Holy Spirit has come upon you; and you will be my witnesses in Jerusalem, in all Judea and Samaria, and to the ends of the earth." [9]When he had said this, as they were watching,

a Or eating
b Or by

```
         04    3303      4413    3056   4160        4012   3956   5599
1:1   Τὸν  μὲν    πρῶτον  λόγον ἐποιησάμην περὶ  πάντων, ὦ
      The indeed first    word  I made      about  all,    O
2321              3739      757   01  2424   4160      5037 2532
Θεόφιλε,   ὧν    ἤρξατο ὁ  Ἰησοῦς ποιεῖν τε   καὶ
Theophilus, of what began the Jesus  to do   both and
1321          2  891   3739  2250   1781             015
διδάσκειν,   ἄχρι ἧς    ἡμέρας ἐντειλάμενος    τοῖς
to teach,     until which day   having commanded the
652        1223 4151      40   3739 1586
ἀποστόλοις διὰ πνεύματος ἁγίου οὓς ἐξελέξατο
delegates  by  spirit     holy whom he himself selected
353            3739 2532 3936       1438     2198   3326
ἀνελήμφθη.  3  οἷς καὶ  παρέστησεν ἑαυτὸν ζῶντα μετὰ
he was         To  also he stood    himself living after
taken up.      whom     along
012 3958      846   1722 4183    5039                1223
τὸ παθεῖν   αὐτὸν ἐν  πολλοῖς τεκμηρίοις,      δι
the to suffer him   in  many   convincing proofs, by
2250   5062        3700      846    2532 3004
ἡμερῶν τεσσεράκοντα ὀπτανόμενος αὐτοῖς καὶ λέγων
days    forty        being seen   in them and saying
024    4012   06 932       02     2316 1223          2532
τὰ    περὶ τῆς βασιλείας τοῦ θεοῦ·  4  καὶ
the things about the kingdom of the God;      and
4871          3853       846   575
συναλιζόμενος παρήγγειλεν αὐτοῖς ἀπὸ
taking salt together he commanded them  from
2414        3361 5563       235   4037            08
Ἱεροσολύμων μὴ  χωρίζεσθαι ἀλλὰ περιμένειν   τὴν
Jerusalem    not to be separate but to stay around the
1860        02   3962   3739 191      1473 3754
ἐπαγγελίαν τοῦ πατρὸς ἣν ἠκούσατέ μου, 5 ὅτι
promise     of the father which you heard of me, because
2491     3303  907      5204    1473 1161 1722
Ἰωάννης μὲν  ἐβάπτισεν ὕδατι,  ὑμεῖς δὲ  ἐν
John     indeed immersed  in water, you but in
4151     907             40   3756 3326 4183
πνεύματι βαπτισθήσεσθε ἁγίῳ οὐ  μετὰ πολλὰς
spirit    will be immersed in holy not after many
3778    2250     6  013  3303      3767 4905
ταύτας ἡμέρας.   Οἱ μὲν  οὖν συνελθόντες
these  days.    The ones indeed then having come together
2065   846    3004       2962   1487 1722
ἠρώτων αὐτὸν λέγοντες· κύριε, εἰ ἐν
were asking him  saying,   Master, if in
03   5550  3778 600          08 932        03
τῷ  χρόνῳ τούτῳ ἀποκαθιστάνεις τὴν βασιλείαν τῷ
the time this  you restore      the kingdom    to the
2474    7 3004  1161 4314 846    3756 1473 1510
Ἰσραήλ;  εἶπεν δὲ  πρὸς αὐτούς· οὐχ ὑμῶν ἐστιν
Israel?  He said but to   them;   not of you is it
1097    5550    2228 2540  3739 01 3962  5087
γνῶναι χρόνους ἢ   καιροὺς οὓς ὁ πατὴρ ἔθετο
to know times   or  seasons which the father set
1722 07 2398 1849     8  235   2983        1411
ἐν  τῇ ἰδίᾳ ἐξουσίᾳ,   ἀλλὰ λήμψεσθε     δύναμιν
in  the own authority, but  you will receive power
1904       010 40  4151      1909 1473 2532
ἐπελθόντος τοῦ ἁγίου πνεύματος ἐφ᾽ ὑμᾶς καὶ
having come on of the holy spirit  on   you  and
1510   1473 3144    1722 5037 2419        2532
ἔσεσθέ μου μάρτυρες ἔν  τε  Ἱερουσαλὴμ καὶ
you will be of me testifiers in both Jerusalem   and
1722 3956 07 2449   2532 4540     2532 2193 2078
[ἐν] πάσῃ τῇ Ἰουδαίᾳ καὶ Σαμαρείᾳ καὶ ἕως ἐσχάτου
in   all the Judea   and Samaria  and until last
06   1093  9  2532 3778 3004     991     846
τῆς γῆς.   Καὶ ταῦτα εἰπὼν βλεπόντων αὐτῶν
of the earth. And these having said seeing   them
```

```
1869                    2532 3507    5274      846
ἐπήρθη                 καὶ νεφέλη ὑπέλαβεν αὐτὸν
he was lifted up on and cloud    took up   him
575  014 3788    846        2532  5613 816
ἀπὸ τῶν ὀφθαλμῶν αὐτῶν. 10 καὶ ὡς ἀτενιζοντες
from the eyes    of them.   And as   +staring
1510        1519 04  3772    4198         846      2532
ἦσαν       εἰς τὸν οὐρανὸν πορευομένου αὐτοῦ, καὶ
they were+ into the heaven traveling  of him, and
2400 435   1417 3936          846   '1722 2066
ἰδοὺ ἄνδρες δύο παρειστήκεισαν αὐτοῖς ἐν ἐσθήσεσι
look men  two had stood along them  in  clothes
3022     3739 2532 3004   435    1057       5101
λευκαῖς, 11 οἳ καὶ εἶπαν· ἄνδρες Γαλιλαῖοι, τί
white,      who also said; men  Galileans,  why
2476         1689        1519 04 3772     3778
ἑστήκατε  [ἐμ]βλέποντες εἰς τὸν οὐρανόν; οὗτος
have you stood looking in  into the heaven? This
01  2424  01  353           575  1473 1519 04
ὁ 'Ἰησοῦς ὁ ἀναλημφθεὶς   ἀφ' ὑμῶν εἰς τὸν
the Jesus the having been taken up from you  into the
3772     3779  2064      3739 5158 2300
οὐρανὸν οὕτως ἐλεύσεται ὃν τρόπον ἐθεάσασθε
heaven thusly he will come which manner you watched
846  4198      1519 04 3772    12 5119
αὐτὸν πορευόμενον εἰς τὸν οὐρανόν.   Τότε
him  traveling   into the heaven.      Then
5290         1519 2419      575  3735 010
ὑπέστρεψαν  εἰς 'Ἰερουσαλὴμ ἀπὸ ὄρους τοῦ
they returned into Jerusalem from hill of the one
2564       1638      3739 1510 1451  2419
καλουμένου 'Ἐλαιῶνος, ὅ ἐστιν ἐγγὺς 'Ἰερουσαλὴμ
being called of Olive, which is near Jerusalem
4521     2192  3598   13 2532 3753 1525        1519
σαββάτου ἔχον ὁδόν.   καὶ ὅτε εἰσῆλθον,       εἰς
sabbath having way.  And when they went into, in
012 5253     305        3757 1510
τὸ ὑπερῷον ἀνέβησαν   οὗ ἦσαν
the upstairs room they went up where they were
2650         01  5037 4074     2532 2491    2532
καταμένοντες, ὅ τε Πέτρος καὶ 'Ἰωάννης καὶ
staying down, the both Peter and John  and
2385    2532 406]     5376      2532 2381
'Ἰάκωβος καὶ 'Ἀνδρέας, Φίλιππος καὶ Θωμᾶς,
Jacob   and Andrew,   Philip   and Thomas,
918           2532 3102a     2385    256      2532
Βαρθολομαῖος καὶ Μαθθαῖος, 'Ἰάκωβος 'Ἀλφαίου καὶ
Bartholomew and Matthew,  Jacob   of Alpheus and
4613  01  2207       2532 2455    2385      14 3778
Σίμων ὁ ζηλωτὴς    καὶ 'Ἰούδας 'Ἰακώβου.   οὗτοι
Simon the jealous one and Judas of Jacob.   These
3956  1510 4342           3661        07
πάντες ἦσαν προσκαρτεροῦντες ὁμοθυμαδὸν τῇ
all  were+ +remaining constant with one mind in the
4335     4862 1135     2532 3137a 07  3384 02
προσευχῇ σὺν γυναιξὶν καὶ Μαριὰμ τῇ μητρὶ τοῦ
prayer  with women   and Mariam the mother of the
2424  2532 015  80      846  15 2532 1722 019
'Ἰησοῦ καὶ τοῖς ἀδελφοῖς αὐτοῦ.   Καὶ ἐν ταῖς
Jesus and the brothers of him.   And in  the
2250      3778   450          4074   1722 3319
ἡμέραις ταύταις ἀναστὰς     Πέτρος ἐν μέσῳ
days   these  having stood up Peter in middle
014     80      3004    1510 5037 3793 3686    1909
τῶν ἀδελφῶν εἶπεν· ἦν τε ὄχλος ὀνομάτων ἐπὶ
of the brothers said; was indeed crowd of names on
012 846  5616 1540   1501      16 435   80
τὸ αὐτὸ ὡσεὶ ἑκατὸν εἴκοσι·    ἄνδρες ἀδελφοί,
the same as hundred twenty;    men  brothers,
```

he was lifted up, and a cloud took him out of their sight. [10]While he was going and they were gazing up toward heaven, suddenly two men in white robes stood by them. [11]They said, "Men of Galilee, why do you stand looking up toward heaven? This Jesus, who has been taken up from you into heaven, will come in the same way as you saw him go into heaven."

[12]Then they returned to Jerusalem from the mount called Olivet, which is near Jerusalem, a sabbath day's journey away. [13]When they had entered the city, they went to the room upstairs where they were staying, Peter, and John, and James, and Andrew, Philip and Thomas, Bartholomew and Matthew, James son of Alphaeus, and Simon the Zealot, and Judas son of[a] James. [14]All these were constantly devoting themselves to prayer, together with certain women, including Mary the mother of Jesus, as well as his brothers.

[15]In those days Peter stood up among the believers[b] (together the crowd numbered about one hundred twenty persons) and said, [16]"Friends,[c]

[a] Or the brother of
[b] Gk brothers
[c] Gk Men, brothers

the scripture had to be fulfilled, which the Holy Spirit through David foretold concerning Judas, who became a guide for those who arrested Jesus— [17]for he was numbered among us and was allotted his share in this ministry." [18](Now this man acquired a field with the reward of his wickedness; and falling headlong,[a] he burst open in the middle and all his bowels gushed out. [19]This became known to all the residents of Jerusalem, so that the field was called in their language Hakeldama, that is, Field of Blood.) [20]"For it is written in the book of Psalms,

'Let his homestead
    become desolate,
and let there be no one
    to live in it';
and
'Let another take his
    position of overseer.'

[21]So one of the men who have accompanied us during all the time that the Lord Jesus went in and out among us, [22]beginning from the baptism of John until the day when he was taken up from us—one of these must become a witness with us to his resurrection." [23]So they proposed two, Joseph called Barsabbas, who was also known as Justus, and

[a] Or swelling up

1163		4137		08	1124	3739
ἔδει		πληρωθῆναι	τὴν		γραφὴν	ἣν
it was necessary		to be filled	the		writing	which

4302		09	4151	09	40	1223	4750		1160a
προεῖπεν		τὸ	πνεῦμα	τὸ	ἅγιον	διὰ	στόματος		Δαυὶδ
to say before		the	spirit	the	holy	by	mouth		David

4012		2455	02	1096		3595	015
περὶ		Ἰούδα	τοῦ	γενομένου		ὁδηγοῦ	τοῖς
concerning		Judas	the	one having become		guide	to the

4815		2424	**17**	3754	2674
συλλαβοῦσιν		Ἰησοῦν,		ὅτι	κατηριθμημένος
ones having		Jesus,		because	+having been numbered
taken together					

1510	1722	1473	2532	2975		04	2819	06
ἦν	ἐν	ἡμῖν	καὶ	ἔλαχεν		τὸν	κλῆρον	τῆς
he was+	in	us	and	he obtained		the	lot	of the

1248		3778	**18**	3778	3303	3767	2932
διακονίας	ταύτης.			οὗτος	μὲν	οὖν	ἐκτήσατο
service	this.			This one	indeed	then	acquired

5564		1537	3408	06	93		2532	4248
χωρίον		ἐκ	μισθοῦ	τῆς	ἀδικίας		καὶ	πρηνὴς
small field		from	wage	of the	unright		and	head first

1096		2978a		3319	2532	1632
γενόμενος		ἐλάκησεν		μέσος	καὶ	ἐξεχύθη
having become		he burst open		middle	and	were poured out

3956	021	4698		846		2532	1110
πάντα	τὰ	σπλάγχνα		αὐτοῦ·	**19**	καὶ	γνωστὸν
all	the	internal organs		of him;		and	known

1096	3956	015	2730		2419		5620
ἐγένετο	πᾶσι	τοῖς	κατοικοῦσιν		Ἰερουσαλήμ,		ὥστε
it became	to all	the	ones residing		Jerusalem,		so that

2564		012	5564		1565	07	2398
κληθῆναι		τὸ	χωρίον		ἐκεῖνο	τῇ	ἰδίᾳ
to be called		the	small field		that	in the	own

1258		846		184		3778	1510	5564
διαλέκτῳ		αὐτῶν		Ἀκελδαμάχ,		τοῦτ'	ἔστιν	χωρίον
dialect		of them		Aceldamach,		this	is	small field

129		**20**	1125		1063	1722	976	5568
αἵματος.			γέγραπται		γὰρ	ἐν	βίβλῳ	ψαλμῶν·
of blood.			It has been written		for	in	book	of Psalms;

1096	05	1886	846		2048	2532	3361	1510
γενηθήτω	ἡ	ἔπαυλις	αὐτοῦ		ἔρημος	καὶ	μὴ	ἔστω
let become	the	cottage	of him		desert	and	not	let be

01	2730		1722	846	2532	08	1984		846
ὁ	κατοικῶν		ἐν	αὐτῇ,	καί·	τὴν	ἐπισκοπὴν		αὐτοῦ
the	residing		in	it,	and;	the	oversight		of him

2983	2087		**21**	1163		3767	014
λαβέτω	ἕτερος.			δεῖ		οὖν	τῶν
let take	other.			It is necessary		then	of the ones

4905		1473	435	1722	3956	5550	3739
συνελθόντων		ἡμῖν	ἀνδρῶν	ἐν	παντὶ	χρόνῳ	ᾧ
having come with		us	of men	in	all	time	in which

1525		2532	1831		1909	1473	01	2962		2424
εἰσῆλθεν		καὶ	ἐξῆλθεν		ἐφ'	ἡμᾶς	ὁ	κύριος		Ἰησοῦς,
went in		and	went out		on	us	the	Master		Jesus,

22	757		575	010	908		2491	2193
	ἀρξάμενος		ἀπὸ	τοῦ	βαπτίσματος		Ἰωάννου	ἕως
	having begun		from	the	immersion		of John	until

06	2250	3739	353		575	1473	3144
τῆς	ἡμέρας	ἧς	ἀνελήμφθη		ἀφ'	ἡμῶν,	μάρτυρα
the day		which	he was taken up		from	us,	testifier

06	386		846	4862	1473	1096	1520
τῆς	ἀναστάσεως		αὐτοῦ	σὺν	ἡμῖν	γενέσθαι	ἕνα
of the	standing up		of him	with	us	to become	one

3778		**23**	2532	2476		1417	2501	04
τούτων.			Καὶ	ἔστησαν		δύο,	Ἰωσὴφ	τὸν
of these.			And	they stood		two,	Joseph	the one

2564		923		3739	1941		2459	2532
καλούμενον		Βαρσαββᾶν		ὃς	ἐπεκλήθη		Ἰοῦστος,	καὶ
being called		Barsabbas		who	was called on		Justus,	and

```
3102c          2532 4336                    3004           1473 2962
Μαθθίαν.  24  καὶ  προσευξάμενοι  εἶπαν·    σὺ  κύριε
Matthias.     And  having prayed  they said; you Master

2589            3956      322     3739 1586              1537
καρδιογνῶστα πάντων, ἀνάδειξον ὃν  ἐξελέξω           ἐκ
heart knower of all, show up  whom you selected from

3778   014      1417 1520  25  2983        04  5117   06
τούτων τῶν   δύο ἕνα        λαβεῖν  τὸν τόπον τῆς
these  of the two one          to take the place of the

1248          3778 2532 651            575  3739
διακονίας ταύτης καὶ ἀποστολῆς  ἀφ’  ἧς
service    this  and delegateship from which

3845              2455      4198     1519 04  5117   04
παρέβη        Ἰούδας πορευθῆναι εἰς  τὸν τόπον τὸν
went across  Judas  to travel  into the place the

2398    26  2532 1325     2819     846        2532 4098
ἴδιον.      καὶ ἔδωκαν κλήρους αὐτοῖς καὶ ἔπεσεν
own.        And they gave lots  to them and  fell

01  2819    1909  3102c       2532 4785
ὁ  κλῆρος ἐπὶ Μαθθίαν καὶ συγκατεψηφίσθη
the lot    on  Matthias and he was counted together

3326 014 1733    652        2:1  2532 1722 011
μετὰ τῶν ἕνδεκα ἀποστόλων.    Καὶ ἐν   τῷ
with the eleven delegates.      And in   the

4845                  08      2250    06        4005
συμπληροῦσθαι      τὴν ἡμέραν τῆς   πεντηκοστῆς
to be filled together the day  of the fiftieth

1510 3956   3674 1909 012 846  2  2532 1096
ἦσαν πάντες ὁμοῦ ἐπὶ τὸ αὐτό.   καὶ ἐγένετο
were  all    same on  the same.  And it became

869        1537 02 3772     2279 5618         5342
ἄφνω    ἐκ  τοῦ οὐρανοῦ ἦχος ὥσπερ    φερομένης
suddenly from the heaven sound as indeed being carried

4157  972      2532 4137     3650 04  3624 3757
πνοῆς βιαίας καὶ ἐπλήρωσεν ὅλον τὸν οἶκον οὗ
wind  violent and it filled whole the house where

1510      2521      3  2532 3708      846
ἦσαν   καθήμενοι    καὶ ὤφθησαν αὐτοῖς
they were+ +sitting    and were seen to them

1266                   1100       5616 4442 2532
διαμεριζόμεναι        γλῶσσαι ὡσεὶ πυρὸς καὶ
being completely divided tongues as  fire  and

2523      1909 1520 1538     846         2532 4092
ἐκάθισεν ἐφ’ ἕνα ἕκαστον αὐτῶν, 4 καὶ ἐπλήσθησαν
it sat    on  one each   of them, and were filled

3956   4151      40   2532 757      2980       2087
πάντες πνεύματος ἁγίου καὶ ἤρξαντο λαλεῖν  ἑτέραις
all   of spirit holy and they began to speak in other

1100   2531     09  4151    1325       669
γλώσσαις καθὼς τὸ πνεῦμα ἐδίδου ἀποφθέγγεσθαι
tongues just as the spirit was giving to speak off

846     5  1510          1161 1519  2419
αὐτοῖς.    Ἦσαν    δὲ εἰς  ’Ιερουσαλὴμ
to them.  There were+ but in  Jerusalem

2730            2453      435    2126     575 3956
κατοικοῦντες Ἰουδαῖοι, ἄνδρες εὐλαβεῖς ἀπὸ παντὸς
+residing     Judeans,  men   reverent from all

1484   022 5259  04 3772      6  1096          1161
ἔθνους τῶν ὑπὸ τὸν οὐρανόν.   γενομένης      δὲ
nation the under the heaven.    Having become but

06  5456 3778   4905          09  4128     2532
τῆς φωνῆς ταύτης συνῆλθεν τὸ πλῆθος καὶ
the sound this  went together the quantity and

4797        3754   191            1520 1538
συνεχύθη, ὅτι  ἤκουον       εἷς  ἕκαστος
were confused, because they were hearing one each

07  2398 1258     2980       846   7  1839
τῇ  ἰδίᾳ διαλέκτῳ λαλούντων αὐτῶν. ἐξίσταντο
in the own dialect speaking them.    They were
                                       being amazed
```

Matthias. [24]Then they prayed and said, "Lord, you know everyone's heart. Show us which one of these two you have chosen [25]to take the place[a] in this ministry and apostleship from which Judas turned aside to go to his own place." [26]And they cast lots for them, and the lot fell on Matthias; and he was added to the eleven apostles.

CHAPTER 2

When the day of Pentecost had come, they were all together in one place. [2]And suddenly from heaven there came a sound like the rush of a violent wind, and it filled the entire house where they were sitting. [3]Divided tongues, as of fire, appeared among them, and a tongue rested on each of them. [4]All of them were filled with the Holy Spirit and began to speak in other languages, as the Spirit gave them ability.

5 Now there were devout Jews from every nation under heaven living in Jerusalem. [6]And at this sound the crowd gathered and was bewildered, because each one heard them speaking in the native language of each. [7]Amazed and

_a_ Other ancient authorities read
the share

astonished, they asked,
"Are not all these who are
speaking Galileans? 8And
how is it that we hear, each
of us, in our own native
language? 9Parthians,
Medes, Elamites, and
residents of Mesopotamia,
Judea and Cappadocia,
Pontus and Asia, 10Phrygia
and Pamphylia, Egypt
and the parts of Libya
belonging to Cyrene, and
visitors from Rome, both
Jews and proselytes,
11Cretans and Arabs—
in our own languages we
hear them speaking about
God's deeds of power."
12All were amazed and
perplexed, saying to one
another, "What does this
mean?" 13But others
sneered and said, "They
are filled with new wine."

14 But Peter, standing
with the eleven, raised his
voice and addressed them,
"Men of Judea and all who
live in Jerusalem, let this be
known to you, and listen to
what I say. 15Indeed, these
are not drunk, as you
suppose, for it is only nine
o'clock in the morning.
16No, this is what was
spoken through the
prophet Joel:

1161	2532	2296		3004		3756	2400	537
δὲ	καὶ	ἐθαύμαζον		λέγοντες·		οὐχ	ἰδοὺ	ἅπαντες
but	also	were marveling		saying;		not	look	all

3778	1510	013	2980		1057		8	2532	4459
οὗτοί	εἰσιν	οἱ	λαλοῦντες		Γαλιλαῖοι;			καὶ	πῶς
these	are	the ones	speaking		Galileans?			And	how

1473 191 1538 07 2398 1258 1473 1722
ἡμεῖς ἀκούομεν ἕκαστος τῇ ἰδίᾳ διαλέκτῳ ἡμῶν ἐν
we hear each in the own dialect of us in

3739 1080 9 3934 2532 3370 2532 1639
ᾗ ἐγεννήθημεν; Πάρθοι καὶ Μῆδοι καὶ Ἐλαμῖται
which we were born? Parthians and Medes and Elamites

2532 013 2730 08 3318 2449 5037
καὶ οἱ κατοικοῦντες τὴν Μεσοποταμίαν, Ἰουδαίαν τε
and the ones residing the Mesopotamia, Judea both

2532 2587 4195 2532 08 773 10 5435
καὶ Καππαδοκίαν, Πόντον καὶ τὴν Ἀσίαν, Φρυγίαν
and Cappadocian, Pontus and the Asia, Phrygia

5037 2532 3828 125 2532 024 3313 06
τε καὶ Παμφυλίαν, Αἴγυπτον καὶ τὰ μέρη τῆς
both and Pamphylia, Egypt and the parts of the

3033 06 2596 2957 2532 013
Λιβύης τῆς κατὰ Κυρήνην, καὶ οἱ
Libya of the by Cyrene, and the ones

1927 4514 2453 5037 2532
ἐπιδημοῦντες Ῥωμαῖοι, 11 Ἰουδαῖοί τε καὶ
living temporarily Romans, Judeans both and

4339 2912 2532 690 191 2980
προσήλυτοι, Κρῆτες καὶ Ἄραβες, ἀκούομεν λαλούντων
converts, Cretans and Arabians, we hear speaking

846 019 2251 1100 024 3167 02
αὐτῶν ταῖς ἡμετέραις γλώσσαις τὰ μεγαλεῖα τοῦ
them in the our tongues the greatnesses of the

2316 1839 1161 3956 2532 1280
θεοῦ. 12 ἐξίσταντο δὲ πάντες καὶ διηπόρουν,
God. Were amazed but all and they were doubting
thoroughly,

243 4314 343 3004 5101 2309 3778 1510
ἄλλος πρὸς ἄλλον λέγοντες τί θέλει τοῦτο εἶναι;
other to other saying what wants this to be?

13 2087 1161 1315a 3004 3754
ἕτεροι δὲ διαχλευάζοντες ἔλεγον ὅτι
Others but jeering thoroughly were saying, (")

1098 3325 1510 14 2476 1161 01
γλεύκους μεμεστωμένοι εἰσίν. Σταθεὶς δὲ ὁ
sweet wine having been they are+. Having but the
full stood

4074 4862 015 1733 1869 08 5456 846
Πέτρος σὺν τοῖς ἕνδεκα ἐπῆρεν τὴν φωνὴν αὐτοῦ
Peter with the eleven lifted up on the voice of him

2532 669 846 435 2453 2532 013
καὶ ἀπεφθέγξατο αὐτοῖς· ἄνδρες Ἰουδαῖοι καὶ οἱ
and spoke off to them; men Judeans and the

2730 2419 3956 3778 1473 1110
κατοικοῦντες Ἰερουσαλὴμ πάντες, τοῦτο ὑμῖν γνωστὸν
ones residing Jerusalem all, this to you known

1510 2532 1801 024 4487 1473 15 3756 1063
ἔστω καὶ ἐνωτίσασθε τὰ ῥήματά μου. οὐ γὰρ
let be and give ear to the words of me. Not for

5613 1473 5274 3778 3184 1510 1063
ὡς ὑμεῖς ὑπολαμβάνετε οὗτοι μεθύουσιν, ἔστιν γὰρ
as you take up these are drunk, it is for

5610 5154 06 2250 16 235 3778 1510 09
ὥρα τρίτη τῆς ἡμέρας, ἀλλὰ τοῦτό ἐστιν τὸ
hour third of the day, but this is the

3004 1223 02 4396 2493 17 2532
εἰρημένον διὰ τοῦ προφήτου Ἰωήλ· καὶ
thing having through the spokesman Joel; and
been said

1510   1722 019 2078   2250   3004 01 2316
ἔσται   ἐν ταῖς ἐσχάταις ἡμέραις, λέγει ὁ   θεός,
it will be in the last   days,   says the God,
1632   575 010 4151   1473 1909 3956
ἐκχεῶ   ἀπὸ τοῦ πνεύματός μου ἐπὶ πᾶσαν
I will pour out from the spirit   of me on all
4561   2532 4395   013 5207 1473   2532 017
σάρκα, καὶ προφητεύσουσιν οἱ υἱοὶ ὑμῶν καὶ αἱ
flesh, and will speak before the sons of you and the
2364   1473 2532 013 3495   1473   3706
θυγατέρες ὑμῶν καὶ οἱ νεανίσκοι ὑμῶν ὁράσεις
daughters of you and the young men of you sights
3708   2532 013 4245   1473   1798
ὄψονται καὶ οἱ πρεσβύτεροι ὑμῶν ἐνυπνίοις
will see and the older men   of you in dreams
1797   2532 1065   1909 016 1401
ἐνυπνιασθήσονται· 18 καί γε   ἐπὶ τοὺς δούλους
will dream;   and indeed on the men slaves
1473 2532 1909 020 1399   1473 1722 019 2250
μου καὶ ἐπὶ τὰς δούλας   μου ἐν ταῖς ἡμέραις
of me and on the women slaves of me in the days
1565   1632   575 010 4151   1473 2532
ἐκείναις ἐκχεῶ   ἀπὸ τοῦ πνεύματός μου, καὶ
those   I will pour out from the spirit   of me, and
4395   2532 1325   5059   1722
προφητεύσουσιν. 19 καὶ δώσω   τέρατα ἐν
they will speak before. And I will give marvels in
03 3772   507 2532 4592   1909 06 1093 2736
τῷ οὐρανῷ ἄνω καὶ σημεῖα ἐπὶ τῆς γῆς κάτω,
the heaven up and signs on the earth down,
129   2532 4442 2532 822   2586   01 2246
αἷμα καὶ πῦρ καὶ ἀτμίδα καπνοῦ. 20 ὁ   ἥλιος
blood and fire and vapor of smoke. The sun
3344   1519 4655   2532 05 4582   1519
μεταστραφήσεται εἰς σκότος καὶ ἡ σελήνη εἰς
will be turned across into dark and the moon into
129   4250   2064   2250   2962   08 3173   2532
αἷμα, πρὶν ἐλθεῖν ἡμέραν κυρίου τὴν μεγάλην καὶ
blood, before to come day   of Master the great   and
2016   2532 1510   3956 3739 302 1941
ἐπιφανῇ. 21 καὶ ἔσται   πᾶς ὃς ἂν ἐπικαλέσηται
appearance. And it will be all who - might call on
012 3686 2962   4982   435
τὸ ὄνομα κυρίου σωθήσεται. 22 Ἄνδρες
the name of Master will be delivered. Men
2475   191   016   3056   3778   2424 04
Ἰσραηλῖται, ἀκούσατε τοὺς λόγους τούτους· Ἰησοῦν τὸν
Israelites, hear   the words these;   Jesus the
3480   435   584   575 02 2316
Ναζωραῖον, ἄνδρα ἀποδεδειγμένον   ἀπὸ τοῦ θεοῦ
Nazorean, man   having been shown off from the God
1519 1473 1411   2532 5059   2532 4592   3739
εἰς ὑμᾶς δυνάμεσι καὶ τέρασι καὶ σημείοις οἷς
to   you in powers and marvels and signs   in which
4160   1223   846   01 2316 1722 3319   1473
ἐποίησεν δι'   αὐτοῦ ὁ θεὸς ἐν μέσῳ ὑμῶν
did   through him the God in middle of you
2531   846   3609a   3778 07
καθὼς αὐτοὶ   οἴδατε, 23 τοῦτον τῇ
just as yourselves know,   this   in the
3724   1012   2532 4268   02
ὡρισμένῃ   βουλῇ καὶ προγνώσει   τοῦ
having been designated plan and foreknowledge of the
2316 1560   1223 5495   459   4362
θεοῦ ἔκδοτον διὰ χειρὸς ἀνόμων προσπήξαντες
God given out by hand lawless having affixed to
337   3739 01 2316 450   3089
ἀνείλατε, 24 ὃν ὁ   θεὸς ἀνέστησεν λύσας
you killed, whom the God stood up having loosed

17 'In the last days it will be,
    God declares,
    that I will pour out my
    Spirit upon all flesh,
    and your sons and your
       daughters shall
       prophesy,
    and your young men shall
       see visions,
    and your old men shall
       dream dreams.
18 Even upon my slaves,
    both men and women,
    in those days I will pour
    out my Spirit;
    and they shall
       prophesy.
19 And I will show portents
    in the heaven above
    and signs on the earth
       below,
    blood, and fire, and
       smoky mist.
20 The sun shall be turned to
       darkness
    and the moon to blood,
    before the coming of
    the Lord's great and
       glorious day.
21 Then everyone who calls
    on the name of the
    Lord shall be saved.'
22 "You that are
Israelites,[a] listen to what
I have to say: Jesus of
Nazareth,[b] a man attested
to you by God with deeds
of power, wonders, and
signs that God did through
him among you, as you
yourselves know— 23 this
man, handed over to you
according to the definite
plan and foreknowledge of
God, you crucified and
killed by the hands of those
outside the law. 24 But God
raised him up, having freed

a Gk Men, Israelites
b Gk the Nazorean

him from death,[a] because it
was impossible for him to
be held in its power. [25]For
David says concerning him,
'I saw the Lord always
before me,
for he is at my right
hand so that I will
not be shaken;
[26]therefore my heart was
glad, and my tongue
rejoiced;
moreover my flesh will
live in hope.
[27]For you will not abandon
my soul to Hades,
or let your Holy
One experience
corruption.
[28]You have made known
to me the ways of life;
you will make me full
of gladness with your
presence.'
29 "Fellow Israelites,[b] I
may say to you confidently
of our ancestor David that
he both died and was buried,
and his tomb is with us to
this day. [30]Since he was a
prophet, he knew that God
had sworn with an oath to
him that he would put one
of his descendants on his
throne. [31]Foreseeing this,
David[c] spoke of the resurrection of the Messiah,[d]
saying,
'He was not abandoned
to Hades,
nor did his flesh
experience
corruption.'
[32]This Jesus God raised up,
and of that all of us are
witnesses. [33]Being therefore
exalted at[e] the right hand
of God,

[a] Gk the pains of death
[b] Gk Men, brothers
[c] Gk he
[d] Or the Christ
[e] Or by

---

020 5604		02	2288	2530		3756
τὰς ὠδῖνας		τοῦ	θανάτου,	καθότι		οὐκ
the birth pains		of the	death,	according that		not

1510　1415　2902　　　846　5259 846　　1160a
ἦν　δυνατὸν κρατεῖσθαι αὐτὸν ὑπ᾽ αὐτοῦ. [25] Δαυὶδ
it was power　to be held him　by　him.　David

1063 3004　1519 846　4308　　04 2962
γὰρ λέγει εἰς αὐτόν· προορώμην　τὸν κύριον
for says to him;　I was seeing before the Master

1799　1473 1223　3956　3754 1537 1188　1473
ἐνώπιόν μου διὰ　παντός, ὅτι ἐκ δεξιῶν μού
before me through all,　that from right of me

1510　2443 3361 4531　　1223 3778 2165
ἐστιν ἵνα μὴ σαλευθῶ. [26] διὰ τοῦτο ηὐφράνθη
he is that not I might be shaken. By this was merry

05 2588　1473 2532 21　　05　1100 1473
ἡ καρδία μου καὶ ἠγαλλιάσατο ἡ γλῶσσά μου,
the heart of me and was glad the tongue of me,

2089 1161 2532 05 4561　1473 2681　　1909
ἔτι δὲ καὶ ἡ σάρξ μου κατασκηνώσει ἐπ᾽
still but also the flesh of me will set up a tent on

1680　[27] 3754 3756 1459　　08 5590
ἐλπίδι, ὅτι οὐκ ἐγκαταλείψεις τὴν ψυχήν
hope,　that not you will leave behind the soul

1473　3708　86　3761　1325　04 3741
μου εἰς ἅδην οὐδὲ δώσεις　τὸν ὅσιόν
of me in hades but not you will give the holy one

1473　3708　1312　　[28] 1107　1473 3598
σου ἰδεῖν διαφθοράν. ἐγνώρισάς μοι ὁδοὺς
of you to see corruption. You made known to me ways

2222　4137　1473 2167　3326 010
ζωῆς, πληρώσεις με εὐφροσύνης μετὰ τοῦ
of life, you will fill me of merriment with the

4383　1473　435 80　1832
προσώπου σου. [29] Ἄνδρες ἀδελφοί, ἐξὸν
face　of you. Men brothers, being possible

3004　3326 3954　4314 1473 4012 02 3966
εἰπεῖν μετὰ παρρησίας πρὸς ὑμᾶς περὶ τοῦ πατριάρχου
to say with boldness to you about the father ruler

1160a 3754 2532 5053　2532 2290　2532 09
Δαυὶδ ὅτι καὶ ἐτελεύτησεν καὶ ἐτάφη, καὶ τὸ
David that both he died and he was buried, and the

3418　846　1510 1722 1473 891　06 2250 3778
μνῆμα αὐτοῦ ἔστιν ἐν ἡμῖν ἄχρι τῆς ἡμέρας ταύτης.
grave of him is in us until the day this.

[30] 4396　3767 5225　2532 3609a　3754 3727
προφήτης οὖν ὑπάρχων καὶ εἰδὼς　ὅτι ὅρκῳ
Spokesman then existing and having known that oath

3660　846　01 2316 1537 2590　06　3751
ὤμοσεν αὐτῷ ὁ θεὸς ἐκ καρποῦ τῆς ὀσφύος
took an oath to him the God from fruit of the hip

846　2523　1909 04 2362 846
αὐτοῦ καθίσαι ἐπὶ τὸν θρόνον αὐτοῦ,
of him to sit on the throne of him,

[31] 4308　2980　4012 06 386
προϊδὼν ἐλάλησεν περὶ τῆς ἀναστάσεως
having seen before he spoke about the standing up

02　5547　3754 3777　1459　1519
τοῦ Χριστοῦ ὅτι οὔτε ἐγκατελείφθη εἰς
of the Christ that neither he was left behind in

86　3777 05 4561 846 3708 1312　3778
ἅδην οὔτε ἡ σάρξ αὐτοῦ εἶδεν διαφθοράν. [32] τοῦτον
hades nor the flesh of him saw corruption. This

04　2424 450　01 2316 3739　3956 1473
τὸν Ἰησοῦν ἀνέστησεν ὁ θεός, οὗ πάντες ἡμεῖς
the Jesus stood up the God, of whom all we

1510 3144　[33] 07　1188 3767 02　2316
ἐσμεν μάρτυρες· τῇ δεξιᾷ οὖν τοῦ θεοῦ
are testifiers; in the right then of the God

```
5312                      08   5037 1860            010
ὑψωθείς,              τήν τε ἐπαγγελίαν τοῦ
having been elevated, the both promise    of the
4151      010    40    2983           3844 02  3962
πνεύματος τοῦ  ἁγίου λαβὼν          παρὰ τοῦ πατρός,
spirit    of the holy  having taken from the father,
1632        3778  3739 1473  2532 991     2532
ἐξέχεεν     τοῦτο ὃ    ὑμεῖς [καὶ] βλέπετε καὶ
he poured out this which you  both    see    and
191        3756 1063 1160a 305       1519 016
ἀκούετε. 34 οὐ γὰρ Δαυὶδ ἀνέβη    εἰς τοὺς
hear.       Not for David went up into the
3772       3004     1161 846    01    2962    03
οὐρανούς, λέγει   δὲ αὐτός·  εἶπεν [ὁ] κύριος τῷ
heavens,   he says but himself; said the Master to the
2962   1473  2521    1537 1188      1473 35 2193 302
κυρίῳ μου·  κάθου ἐκ δεξιῶν μου,     ἕως ἂν
Master of me, sit   from right of me,  until -
5087        016    2190      1473  5286       014
θῶ        τοὺς ἐχθρούς     σου  ὑποπόδιον τῶν
I might set the hostile ones of you footstool of the
4228  1473  806   3767 1097     3956 3624
ποδῶν σου. 36 ἀσφαλῶς οὖν γινωσκέτω πᾶς οἶκος
feet of you. Securely then let know all house
2474     3754 2532 2962   846   2532 5547      4160
Ἰσραὴλ ὅτι καὶ κύριον αὐτὸν καὶ χριστὸν ἐποίησεν
Israel that both Master him   and Christ made
01   2316 3778  04    2424    3739 1473 4717
ὁ   θεός, τοῦτον τὸν Ἰησοῦν ὃν  ὑμεῖς ἐσταυρώσατε.
the God, this   the Jesus  whom you    crucified.
37 191       1161 2660        08   2588      3004
Ἀκούσαντες δὲ κατενύγησαν τὴν καρδίαν εἶπόν
Having      but they were stabbed the heart   said
heard                    thoroughly
5037 4314 04   4074       2532 2016  3062       652
τε πρὸς τὸν Πέτρον καὶ τοὺς λοιποὺς ἀποστόλους·
and to the Peter  and the remaining delegates;
5101 4160       435     80     38 4074    1161 4314
τί πόιησωμεν, ἄνδρες ἀδελφοί;   Πέτρος δὲ πρὸς
what might we do, men  brothers?  Peter but toward
846    3340          5346     2532 907
αὐτούς· μετανοήσατε, [φησίν,] καὶ βαπτισθήτω
them;  change mind,  says,    and let be immersed
1538    1473  1909 011 3686    2424       1519
ἕκαστος ὑμῶν ἐπὶ τῷ ὀνόματι Ἰησοῦ  Χριστοῦ εἰς
each   of you on the name  of Jesus Christ into
859       018    266       1473 2532 2983
ἄφεσιν  τῶν ἁμαρτιῶν ὑμῶν καὶ λήμψεσθε
sending off of the sins   of you and you will receive
08  1431   010  40     4151       1473 1063 1510
τὴν δωρεὰν τοῦ ἁγίου πνεύματος. 39 ὑμῖν γάρ ἐστιν
the gift   of the holy spirit.     To you for is
05  1860     2532 2532  5043       1473 2532 3956
ἡ ἐπαγγελία καὶ τοῖς τέκνοις ὑμῶν καὶ πᾶσιν
the promise  and to the children of you and to all
015        1519 3112    3745       302 4341
τοῖς   εἰς μακράν, ὅσους  ἂν προσκαλέσηται
the ones in far,    as many as - might call to
2962   01  2316 1473  40 2087    5037 3056    4183
κύριος ὁ θεὸς ἡμῶν.  ἑτέροις τε λόγοις πλείοσιν
Master the God of us.  In other but words  more
1263       2532 3870    846    3004     4982
διεμαρτύρατο καὶ παρεκάλει αὐτοὺς λέγων· σώθητε
he thoroughly and he was     them    saying; deliver
testified     encouraging
575 06 1074    06  4646     3778      41 013
ἀπὸ τῆς γενεᾶς τῆς σκολιᾶς ταύτης.  οἱ
from the generation the crooked this.   The ones
```

and having received from the Father the promise of the Holy Spirit, he has poured out this that you both see and hear. 34For David did not ascend into the heavens, but he himself says,

'The Lord said to my Lord,
    "Sit at my right hand,
35 until I make your
    enemies your
    footstool." '

36Therefore let the entire house of Israel know with certainty that God has made him both Lord and Messiah,[a] this Jesus whom you crucified."

37 Now when they heard this, they were cut to the heart and said to Peter and to the other apostles, "Brothers,[b] what should we do?" 38Peter said to them, "Repent, and be baptized every one of you in the name of Jesus Christ so that your sins may be forgiven; and you will receive the gift of the Holy Spirit. 39For the promise is for you, for your children, and for all who are far away, everyone whom the Lord our God calls to him." 40And he testified with many other arguments and exhorted them, saying, "Save yourselves from this corrupt generation." 41So those who

a Or Christ
b Gk Men, brothers

welcomed his message were baptized, and that day about three thousand persons were added. 42They devoted themselves to the apostles' teaching and fellowship, to the breaking of bread and the prayers.

43 Awe came upon everyone, because many wonders and signs were being done by the apostles. 44All who believed were together and had all things in common; 45they would sell their possessions and goods and distribute the proceeds*a* to all, as any had need. 46Day by day, as they spent much time together in the temple, they broke bread at home*b* and ate their food with glad and generous*c* hearts, 47praising God and having the goodwill of all the people. And day by day the Lord added to their number those who were being saved.

CHAPTER 3

One day Peter and John were going up to the temple at the hour of prayer, at three o'clock in the afternoon. 2And a man lame from birth was being carried in. People would lay him daily at the gate of the temple called the Beautiful Gate

a Gk them

b Or from house to house

c Or sincere

3303	3767	588		04	3056
μὲν	οὖν	ἀποδεξάμενοι		τὸν	λόγον
indeed	then	having welcomed thoroughly		the	word

846 907 2532 4369 1722 07 2250
αὐτοῦ ἐβαπτίσθησαν καὶ προσετέθησαν ἐν τῇ ἡμέρᾳ
of him were immersed and were set to in the day

1565 5590 5616 5153 **42** 1510 1161
ἐκείνῃ ψυχαὶ ὡσεὶ τρισχίλιαι. ᾿Ησαν δὲ
that souls as three thousand. They were+ but

4342 07 1322 014 652 2532
προσκαρτεροῦντες τῇ διδαχῇ τῶν ἀποστόλων καὶ
+remaining constant the teaching of the delegates and

07 2842 07 2800 02 740 2532 019
τῇ κοινωνίᾳ τῇ κλάσει τοῦ ἄρτου καὶ ταῖς
the partnership the breaking of the bread and the

4335 1096 1161 3956 5590 5401
προσευχαῖς. **43** ἐγίνετο δὲ πάσῃ ψυχῇ φόβος,
prayers. Was becoming but in all soul fear,

4183 5037 5059 2532 4592 1223 014 652
πολλά τε τέρατα καὶ σημεῖα διὰ τῶν ἀποστόλων
many both marvels and signs through the delegates

1096 3956 1161 013 4100 1510 1909
ἐγίνετο. **44** πάντες δὲ οἱ πιστεύοντες ἦσαν ἐπὶ
was becoming. All but the ones trusting were on

012 846 2532 2192 537 2839 **45** 2532 024
τὸ αὐτὸ καὶ εἶχον ἅπαντα κοινά καὶ τὰ
the same and had all common and the

2933 2532 020 5223 4097 2532
κτήματα καὶ τὰς ὑπάρξεις ἐπίπρασκον καὶ
acquisitions and the possessions they were selling and

1266 846 3956 2530
διεμέριζον αὐτὰ πᾶσιν καθότι
were dividing completely these to all according that

302 5100 5532 2192 **46** 2596 2250 5037
ἄν τις χρείαν εἶχεν· καθ᾽ ἡμέραν τε
- some need had; by day both

4342 3661 1722 011 2411
προσκαρτεροῦντες ὁμοθυμαδὸν ἐν τῷ ἱερῷ,
remaining constant with one mind in the temple,

2806 5037 2596 3624 740 3335
κλῶντές τε κατ᾽ οἶκον ἄρτον, μετελάμβανον
breaking and by house bread, they were taking with

5160 1722 20 2532 858 2588
τροφῆς ἐν ἀγαλλιάσει καὶ ἀφελότητι καρδίας
food in gladness and simplicity of heart

47 134 04 2316 2532 2192 5485 4314 3650
αἰνοῦντες τὸν θεὸν καὶ ἔχοντες χάριν πρὸς ὅλον
praising the God and having favor toward whole

04 2992 01 1161 2962 4369 016
τὸν λαόν. ὁ δὲ κύριος προσετίθει τοὺς
the people. The but Master set to the ones

4982 2596 2250 1909 012 846 **3:1** 4074
σωζομένους καθ᾽ ἡμέραν ἐπὶ τὸ αὐτό. Πέτρος
being delivered by day on the same. Peter

1161 2532 2491 305 1519 012 2411 1909 08
δὲ καὶ ᾿Ιωάννης ἀνέβαινον εἰς τὸ ἱερὸν ἐπὶ τὴν
but also John went up to the temple on the

5610 06 4335 08 1728a **2** 2532 5100 435
ὥραν τῆς προσευχῆς τὴν ἐνάτην. καί τις ἀνὴρ
hour of the prayer the ninth. And some man

5560 1537 2836 3384 846 5225
χωλὸς ἐκ κοιλίας μητρὸς αὐτοῦ ὑπάρχων
lame from stomach of mother of him existing

941 3739 5087 2596 2250 4314 08 2374
ἐβαστάζετο, ὃν ἐτίθουν καθ᾽ ἡμέραν πρὸς τὴν θύραν
was being whom they were by day to the door
borne, setting

010 2411 08 3004 5611 010
τοῦ ἱεροῦ τὴν λεγομένην ῾Ωραίαν τοῦ
of the temple the one being called Beautiful the

154   1654   3844 014   1531   1519
αἰτεῖν ἐλεημοσύνην παρὰ τῶν   εἰσπορευομένων εἰς
to ask mercifulness from the ones traveling into into

012 2411   3739 3708   4074 2532 2491
τὸ ἱερόν· **3** ὃς ἰδὼν   Πέτρον καὶ ᾽Ιωάννην
the temple; who having seen Peter and John

3195   1524   1519 012 2411   2065
μέλλοντας εἰσιέναι εἰς τὸ ἱερόν, ἠρώτα
being about to go into into the temple, was asking

1654   2983   816   1161 4074   1519
ἐλεημοσύνην λαβεῖν. **4** ἀτενίσας   δὲ Πέτρος εἰς
mercifulness to receive. Having stared but Peter into

846   4862 03 2491   3004   991   1519 1473   01
αὐτὸν σὺν τῷ ᾽Ιωάννῃ εἶπεν· βλέψον εἰς ἡμᾶς, **5** ὁ
him   with the John   said; look to us. The one

1161 1907   846   4328   5100 3844
δὲ ἐπεῖχεν αὐτοῖς προσδοκῶν   τι παρ᾽
but held on to them waiting expectantly some from

846   2983   3004 1161 4074   694   2532
αὐτῶν λαβεῖν. **6** εἶπεν δὲ Πέτρος· ἀργύριον καὶ
them to receive. Said but Peter; silver and

5553   3756 5225   1473   3739 1161 2192   3778
χρυσίον οὐχ ὑπάρχει μοι, ὃ δὲ ἔχω τοῦτό
gold   not exists to me, what but I have this

1473   1325   1722 011 3686   2424   5547   02
σοι δίδωμι· ἐν τῷ ὀνόματι ᾽Ιησοῦ Χριστοῦ τοῦ
to you I give; in the name of Jesus Christ the

3480   1453   2532 4043   2532 4084
Ναζωραίου [ἔγειρε καὶ] περιπάτει. **7** καὶ πιάσας
Nazorean rise and walk around. And having captured

846   06 1188   5495 1453   846   3916   1161
αὐτὸν τῆς δεξιᾶς χειρὸς ἤγειρεν   αὐτόν· παραχρῆμα δὲ
him   the right hand he raised him; suddenly but

4732   017 939   846   2532 021 4974
ἐστερεώθησαν   αἱ βάσεις αὐτοῦ καὶ τὰ σφυδρά,
were solidified the feet of him and the ankles,

     2532 1814   2476   2532 4043   2532
8 καὶ ἐξαλλόμενος ἔστη καὶ περιεπάτει   καὶ
and leaping out he stood and was walking around and

1525   4862 846   1519 012 2411   4043
εἰσῆλθεν σὺν αὐτοῖς εἰς τὸ ἱερὸν περιπατῶν
he went in with them into the temple walking around

2532 242   2532 134   04 2316   2532 3708 3956
καὶ ἀλλόμενος καὶ αἰνῶν τὸν θεόν. **9** καὶ εἶδεν πᾶς
and leaping and praising the God. And saw all

01 2992   846   4043   2532 134   04 2316
ὁ λαὸς αὐτὸν περιπατοῦντα καὶ αἰνοῦντα τὸν θεόν·
the people him walking around and praising the God;

     1921   1161 846   3754 846   1510
10 ἐπεγίνωσκον   δὲ αὐτὸν ὅτι αὐτὸς ἦν
They were perceiving but him that himself was

01   4314 08 1654   2521   1909 07
ὁ πρὸς τὴν ἐλεημοσύνην καθήμενος ἐπὶ τῇ
the one to the mercifulness sitting on the

5611   4439 010   2411 2532 4092
ὡραίᾳ πύλῃ τοῦ ἱεροῦ καὶ ἐπλήσθησαν
beautiful gate of the temple and they were filled

2285   2532 1611   1909 011 4819
θάμβους καὶ ἐκστάσεως ἐπὶ τῷ συμβεβηκότι
astonishment and amazement on the having come with

846   11 2902   1161 846   04 4074   2532 04
αὐτῷ. **11** Κρατοῦντος δὲ αὐτοῦ τὸν Πέτρον καὶ τὸν
him. Holding but him the Peter and the

2491   4936   3956 01 2992   4314 846
᾽Ιωάννην συνέδραμεν πᾶς ὁ λαὸς πρὸς αὐτοὺς
John ran together all the people toward them

1909 07 4745   07   2564   4672
ἐπὶ τῇ στοᾷ τῇ καλουμένῃ Σολομῶντος
on the colonnade in the being called of Solomon

so that he could ask for alms from those entering the temple. ³When he saw Peter and John about to go into the temple, he asked them for alms. ⁴Peter looked intently at him, as did John, and said, "Look at us." ⁵And he fixed his attention on them, expecting to receive something from them. ⁶But Peter said, "I have no silver or gold, but what I have I give you; in the name of Jesus Christ of Nazareth,ᵃ stand up and walk." ⁷And he took him by the right hand and raised him up; and immediately his feet and ankles were made strong. ⁸Jumping up, he stood and began to walk, and he entered the temple with them, walking and leaping and praising God. ⁹All the people saw him walking and praising God, ¹⁰and they recognized him as the one who used to sit and ask for alms at the Beautiful Gate of the temple; and they were filled with wonder and amazement at what had happened to him.

11 While he clung to Peter and John, all the people ran together to them in the portico called Solomon's Portico,

ᵃ Gk the Nazorean

utterly astonished. [12]When Peter saw it, he addressed the people, "You Israelites,[a] why do you wonder at this, or why do you stare at us, as though by our own power or piety we had made him walk? [13]The God of Abraham, the God of Isaac, and the God of Jacob, the God of our ancestors has glorified his servant[b] Jesus, whom you handed over and rejected in the presence of Pilate, though he had decided to release him. [14]But you rejected the Holy and Righteous One and asked to have a murderer given to you, [15]and you killed the Author of life, whom God raised from the dead. To this we are witnesses. [16]And by faith in his name, his name itself has made this man strong, whom you see and know; and the faith that is through Jesus[c] has given him this perfect health in the presence of all of you.

[17]"And now, friends,[d] I know that you acted in ignorance, as did also your rulers. [18]In this way God fulfilled what he had foretold through all the prophets, that his Messiah[e] would suffer. [19]Repent therefore, and turn to God so that your sins may be wiped out,

[a] Gk Men, Israelites
[b] Or child
[c] Gk him
[d] Gk brothers
[e] Or his Christ

1569		**12**	3708		1161 01	4074
ἔκθαμβοι.			ἰδὼν		δὲ ὁ	Πέτρος
greatly astonished.		Having	seen but		the Peter

611   4314 04   2992   435   2475   5101
ἀπεκρίνατο πρὸς τὸν λαόν·   ἄνδρες Ἰσραηλῖται, τί
answered   to   the people, men   Israelites, why

2296   1909 3778   2228 1473   5101 816
θαυμάζετε   ἐπὶ τούτῳ ἢ   ἡμῖν τί   ἀτενίζετε
do you marvel on this or   to us why   do you stare

5613 2398   1411   2228 2150   4160   010
ὡς   ἰδίᾳ   δυνάμει ἢ   εὐσεβείᾳ πεποιηκόσιν τοῦ
as   in own power   or   reverence having done the

4043   846   01   2316   11   2532 01
περιπατεῖν   αὐτόν;   **13** ὁ θεὸς Ἀβραὰμ καὶ [ὁ
to walk around him?   The God Abraham and the

2316   2464   2532 01   2316   2384   01 2316 014
θεὸς] Ἰσαὰκ καὶ [ὁ   θεὸς] Ἰακώβ, ὁ θεὸς τῶν
God   Isaac and the God]   Jacob, the God of the

3962   1473   1392   04 3816   846
πατέρων ἡμῶν, ἐδόξασεν   τὸν παῖδα   αὐτοῦ
fathers of us, gave splendor the boy servant of him

2424   3739 1473   3303   3860   2532 720
Ἰησοῦν ὃν ὑμεῖς μὲν   παρεδώκατε καὶ ἠρνήσασθε
Jesus whom you   indeed gave over   and denied

2596 4383   4091   2919   1565
κατὰ πρόσωπον Πιλάτου,   κρίναντος   εκείνου
by   face   of Pilate, having judged that one

630   **14** 1473 1161 04   40   2532 1342   720
ἀπολύειν·   ὑμεῖς δὲ   τὸν ἅγιον καὶ δίκαιον ἠρνήσασθε
to loose off; you but   the holy and right   denied

2532 154   435   5406   5483   1473   **15** 04
καὶ ἠτήσασθε ἄνδρα φονέα   χαρισθῆναι ὑμῖν,   τὸν
and asked   man murderer to be favored to you,   the

1161 747   06   2222 615   3739 01 2316
δὲ   ἀρχηγὸν τῆς   ζωῆς ἀπεκτείνατε ὃν ὁ θεὸς
but beginner of the life you killed   whom the God

1453   1537 3498   3739   1473 3144   1510
ἤγειρεν ἐκ νεκρῶν, οὗ   ἡμεῖς μάρτυρές ἐσμεν.
raised from dead,   of which we   testifiers are.

16 2532 1909 07   4102   010   3686   846   3778
καὶ ἐπὶ τῇ πίστει τοῦ   ὀνόματος αὐτοῦ τοῦτον
And on the trust of the name   of him this one

3739 2334   2532 3609α   4732   09 3686
ὃν θεωρεῖτε καὶ οἴδατε,   ἐστερέωσεν τὸ ὄνομα
whom you watch and have known, solidified the name

846   2532 05   4102   05 1223   846   1325   846
αὐτοῦ, καὶ ἡ πίστις ἡ δι'   αὐτοῦ ἔδωκεν αὐτῷ
of him, and the trust the through him   gave   to him

08 3647   3778   561   3956   1473
τὴν ὁλοκληρίαν ταύτην ἀπέναντι   πάντων ὑμῶν.
the whole share this   over against all   you.

17 2532 3568 80   3609α 3754 2596 52
Καὶ νῦν, ἀδελφοί, οἶδα ὅτι κατὰ ἄγνοιαν
And now, brothers, I know that by   unknowingness

4238   5618   2532 013 758   1473
ἐπράξατε   ὥσπερ   καὶ οἱ ἄρχοντες ὑμῶν·
you practiced as indeed also the rulers   of you;

18 01 1161 2316   3739 4293   1223
ὁ δὲ θεός, ἃ   προκατήγγειλεν διὰ
the but God, what he proclaimed before through

4750   3956   014 4396   3958   04 5547
στόματος πάντων τῶν προφητῶν παθεῖν τὸν χριστὸν
mouth   of all the spokesmen to suffer the Christ

846   4137   3779   **19** 3340   3767 2532
αὐτοῦ, ἐπλήρωσεν οὕτως.   μετανοήσατε οὖν καὶ
of him, he filled thusly.   Change mind then and

1994   1519 012 1813   1473   020
ἐπιστρέψατε εἰς τὸ ἐξαλειφθῆναι ὑμῶν τὰς
return   into the to be wiped off of you the

266   3704 302 2064   2540   403
ἁμαρτίας, **20** ὅπως ἂν ἔλθωσιν   καιροὶ ἀναψύξεως
sins,   so that - might come seasons of refreshment

575 4383   02   2962 2532 649   04
ἀπὸ προσώπου τοῦ κυρίου καὶ ἀποστείλῃ   τὸν
from face   of the Master and he might delegate the

4400   1473 5547   2424   3739
προκεχειρισμένον   ὑμῖν χριστόν ᾿Ιησοῦν, **21** ὅν
having set hand before you Christ Jesus,   whom

1163   3772   3303   1209   891   5550
δεῖ   οὐρανὸν μὲν δέξασθαι ἄχρι χρόνων
it is necessary heaven indeed to welcome until times

605   3956   3739 2980   01 2316 1223
ἀποκαταστάσεως πάντων ὧν ἐλάλησεν ὁ θεὸς διὰ
of restoration of all which spoke   the God through

4750   014   40   575 165   846   4396
στόματος τῶν   ἁγίων   ἀπ᾽ αἰῶνος αὐτοῦ προφητῶν.
mouth   of the holy ones from age of him spokesmen.

   3475   3303   3004   3754 4396   1473
22 Μωϋσῆς μὲν   εἶπεν ὅτι προφήτην ὑμῖν
   Moses indeed said that spokesman to you

450   2962   01 2316 1473   1537 014 80
ἀναστήσει   κύριος ὁ θεὸς ὑμῶν ἐκ τῶν ἀδελφῶν
will stand up Master the God of you from the brothers

1473   5613 1473 846   191   2596 3956
ὑμῶν ὡς ἐμέ· αὐτοῦ ἀκούσεσθε κατὰ πάντα
of you as me; him you will hear by all

3745   302 2980   4314 1473   **23** 1510   1161
ὅσα   ἂν λαλήσῃ   πρὸς ὑμᾶς.   ἔσται   δὲ
as much as - he might say to you.   Will be but

3956 5590 3748 1437 3361 191   02 4396
πᾶσα ψυχὴ ἥτις ἐὰν μὴ ἀκούσῃ   τοῦ προφήτου
all soul which except he might hear the spokesman

1565   1842   1537 02 2992   **24** 2532 3956
ἐκείνου ἐξολεθρευθήσεται ἐκ τοῦ λαοῦ.   καὶ πάντες
that   will be ruined from the people. And all
        completely

1161 013 4396   575 4545   2532 014 2517
δὲ οἱ προφῆται ἀπὸ Σαμουὴλ καὶ τῶν καθεξῆς
but the spokesmen from Samuel and the in order

3745   2980   2532 2605   020 2250   3778
ὅσοι   ἐλάλησαν καὶ κατήγγειλαν τὰς ἡμέρας ταύτας.
as many as spoke also proclaimed the days these.

   1473 1510 013 5207 014   4396   2532 06
25 ὑμεῖς ἐστε οἱ υἱοὶ τῶν   προφητῶν καὶ τῆς
   You are the sons of the spokesmen and of the

1242   3739 1303   01   2316 4314 016 3962
διαθήκης ἧς διέθετο ὁ   θεὸς πρὸς τοὺς πατέρας
agreement which agreed the God to the fathers

1473   3004   4314 11   2532 1722 011 4690
ὑμῶν λέγων πρὸς ᾿Αβραάμ· καὶ ἐν τῷ σπέρματί
of you saying to Abraham; also in the seed

1473   1757   3956 017 3965
σου ἐν]ευλογηθήσονται   πᾶσαι αἱ πατριαὶ
of you will be well spoken in all the fatherhoods

06   1093   **26** 1473 4413   450   01 2316
τῆς γῆς.   ὑμῖν πρῶτον ἀναστήσας ὁ θεὸς
of the earth. To you first having stood up the God

04 3816   846   649   846   2127
τὸν παῖδα   αὐτοῦ ἀπέστειλεν αὐτὸν εὐλογοῦντα
the boy servant of him delegated him speaking well

1473 1722 011 654   1538   575 018 4189
ὑμᾶς ἐν τῷ ἀποστρέφειν ἕκαστον ἀπὸ τῶν πονηριῶν
you in the to turn off each from the evils

1473   **4:1** 2980   1161 846   4314 04 2992
ὑμῶν.   Λαλούντων δὲ αὐτῶν πρὸς τὸν λαὸν
of you.   Speaking but them toward the people

2186   846   013 2409   2532 01 4755   010
ἐπέστησαν αὐτοῖς οἱ ἱερεῖς καὶ ὁ στρατηγὸς τοῦ
stood on to them the priests and the captain of the

[20] so that times of refreshing may come from the presence of the Lord, and that he may send the Messiah[a] appointed for you, that is, Jesus, [21] who must remain in heaven until the time of universal restoration that God announced long ago through his holy prophets. [22] Moses said, 'The Lord your God will raise up for you from your own people[b] a prophet like me. You must listen to whatever he tells you. [23] And it will be that everyone who does not listen to that prophet will be utterly rooted out of the people.' [24] And all the prophets, as many as have spoken, from Samuel and those after him, also predicted these days. [25] You are the descendants of the prophets and of the covenant that God gave to your ancestors, saying to Abraham, 'And in your descendants all the families of the earth shall be blessed.' [26] When God raised up his servant,[c] he sent him first to you, to bless you by turning each of you from your wicked ways."

CHAPTER 4

While Peter and John[d] were speaking to the people, the priests, the captain of the

---

[a] Or the Christ
[b] Gk brothers
[c] Or child
[d] Gk While they

temple, and the Sadducees came to them, ²much annoyed because they were teaching the people and proclaiming that in Jesus there is the resurrection of the dead. ³So they arrested them and put them in custody until the next day, for it was already evening. ⁴But many of those who heard the word believed; and they numbered about five thousand.

5 The next day their rulers, elders, and scribes assembled in Jerusalem, ⁶with Annas the high priest, Caiaphas, John,ᵃ and Alexander, and all who were of the high-priestly family. ⁷When they had made the prisonersᵇ stand in their midst, they inquired, "By what power or by what name did you do this?" ⁸Then Peter, filled with the Holy Spirit, said to them, "Rulers of the people and elders, ⁹if we are questioned today because of a good deed done to someone who was sick and are asked how this man has been healed, ¹⁰let it be known to all of you, and to all the people of Israel, that this man is standing

ᵃ Other ancient authorities read *Jonathan*
ᵇ Gk *them*

2411	2532	013	4523	**2**	1278	1223
ἱεροῦ	καὶ	οἱ	Σαδδουκαῖοι,		διαπονούμενοι	διὰ
temple	and	the	Sadducees,		being pained	through

012	1321	846	04	2992	2532	2605
τὸ	διδάσκειν	αὐτοὺς	τὸν	λαὸν	καὶ	καταγγέλλειν
the	to teach	them	the	people	and	to proclaim

1722	03	2424	08	386		08	1537	3498	**3**	2532
ἐν	τῷ	Ἰησοῦ	τὴν	ἀνάστασιν	τὴν	ἐκ	νεκρῶν,		καὶ
in	the	Jesus	the	standing up	the	from	dead,		and

1911		846	020	5495	2532	5087	1519
ἐπέβαλον	αὐτοῖς	τὰς	χεῖρας	καὶ	ἔθεντο	εἰς
they threw on	to them	the	hands	and	set	into

5084	1519	08	839		1510	1063	2073
τήρησιν	εἰς	τὴν	αὔριον·	ἦν	γὰρ	ἑσπέρα
keeping place	in	the	tomorrow;	it was	for	evening

2235	**4**	4183	1161	014	191		04	3056
ἤδη.		πολλοὶ	δὲ	τῶν	ἀκουσάντων	τὸν	λόγον
already.		Many	but	of the	ones having heard	the	word

4100		2532	1096	01	706	014	435	5613
ἐπίστευσαν	καὶ	ἐγενήθη	[ὁ]	ἀριθμὸς	τῶν	ἀνδρῶν	[ὡς]
trusted	and	became	the	number	of the	men	as

5505	4002	**5**	1096	1161	1909	08	839
χιλιάδες	πέντε.		Ἐγένετο	δὲ	ἐπὶ	τὴν	αὔριον
thousands	five.		It became	but	on	the	tomorrow

4863		846	016	758		2532	016
συναχθῆναι	αὐτῶν	τοὺς	ἄρχοντας	καὶ	τοὺς
to be led together	of them	the	rulers	and	the

4245		2532	016	1122		1722	2419
πρεσβυτέρους	καὶ	τοὺς	γραμματεῖς	ἐν	Ἰερουσαλήμ,
older men	and	the	writers	in	Jerusalem,

6	2532	452	01	749		2532	2533	2532
	καὶ	Ἄννας	ὁ	ἀρχιερεὺς	καὶ	Καϊάφας	καὶ
	and	Annas	the	ruler priest	and	Caiaphas	and

2491	2532	223		2532	3745		1510	1537
Ἰωάννης	καὶ	Ἀλέξανδρος	καὶ	ὅσοι	ἦσαν	ἐκ
John	and	Alexander	and	as many as	were	from

1085	748		**7**	2532	2476		846
γένους	ἀρχιερατικοῦ,		καὶ	στήσαντες	αὐτοὺς
kind	of ruler priesthood,		and	having stood	them

1722	011	3319	4441		1722	4169	1411
ἐν	τῷ	μέσῳ	ἐπυνθάνοντο·	ἐν	ποίᾳ	δυνάμει
in	the	middle	they inquired;	in	what kind	power

2228	1722	4169		3686	4160	3778	1473
ἢ	ἐν	ποίῳ	ὀνόματι	ἐποιήσατε	τοῦτο	ὑμεῖς;
or	in	what kind	name	did	this	you?

8	5119	4074	4092		4151	40	3004
	Τότε	Πέτρος	πλησθεὶς	πνεύματος	ἁγίου	εἶπεν
	Then	Peter	having been filled	of spirit	holy	said

4314	846	758	02	2992	2532	4245
πρὸς	αὐτούς·	ἄρχοντες	τοῦ	λαοῦ	καὶ	πρεσβύτεροι,
to	them;	rulers	of the	people	and	older men,

9	1487	1473	4594	350		1909	2108
	εἰ	ἡμεῖς	σήμερον	ἀνακρινόμεθα	ἐπὶ	εὐεργεσίᾳ
	if	we	today	are being examined	on	good work

444	772		1722	5101	3778	4982
ἀνθρώπου	ἀσθενοῦς	ἐν	τίνι	οὗτος	σέσωται,
of man	weak	in	what	this one	has been delivered,

10	1110	1510	3956	1473	2532	3956	03	2992
	γνωστὸν	ἔστω	πᾶσιν	ὑμῖν	καὶ	παντὶ	τῷ	λαῷ
	known	let be	to all	you	and	to all	the	people

2474	3754	1722	011	3686		2424	5547	02
Ἰσραὴλ	ὅτι	ἐν	τῷ	ὀνόματι	Ἰησοῦ	Χριστοῦ	τοῦ
Israel	that	in	the	name	of Jesus	Christ	the

3480		3739	1473	4717		3739	01	2316
Ναζωραίου	ὃν	ὑμεῖς	ἐσταυρώσατε,	ὃν	ὁ	θεὸς
Nazorean	whom	you	crucified,	whom	the	God

1453	1537	3498	1722	3778	3778	3936
ἤγειρεν	ἐκ	νεκρῶν,	ἐν	τούτῳ	οὗτος	παρέστηκεν
raised	from	dead,	in	this	this one	has stood along

1799	1473	5199		3778	1510	01	3037	01
ἐνώπιον	ὑμῶν	ὑγιής.	**11**	οὗτός	ἐστιν	ὁ	λίθος,	ὁ
before	you	healthy.		This	is	the	stone,	the one

1848		5259	1473	014	3618		01
ἐξουθενηθεὶς		ὑφ'	ὑμῶν	τῶν	οἰκοδόμων,		ὁ
having been despised		by	you	the	builders,		the one

1096		1519	2776		1137		**12**	2532	3756	1510
γενόμενος		εἰς	κεφαλὴν		γωνίας.			καὶ	οὐκ	ἔστιν
having become		to	head		of corner.			And	not	is

1722	243	3762	05	4991		3761	1063	3686
ἐν	ἄλλῳ	οὐδενὶ	ἡ	σωτηρία,		οὐδὲ	γὰρ	ὄνομά
in	other	no one	the	deliverance,		but not	for	name

1510	2087	5259	04	3772	09	1325		1722
ἐστιν	ἕτερον	ὑπὸ	τὸν	οὐρανὸν	τὸ	δεδομένον		ἐν
is	other	under	the	heaven	the	having been		in
						one given		

444		1722	3739	1163		4982
ἀνθρώποις		ἐν	ᾧ	δεῖ		σωθῆναι
men		in	which	it is necessary		to be delivered

1473	**13**	2334		1161	08	02	4074	3954
ἡμᾶς.		Θεωροῦντες	δὲ	τὴν	τοῦ		Πέτρου	παρρησίαν
us.		Watching	but	the	of the		Peter	boldness

2532	2491	2532	2638		3754	444
καὶ	Ἰωάννου	καὶ	καταλαβόμενοι		ὅτι	ἄνθρωποι
and	John	and	having overtaken		that	men

62		1510	2532	2399		2296
ἀγράμματοί		εἰσιν	καὶ	ἰδιῶται,		ἐθαύμαζον
unlettered		they are	and	unlearned,		they were marveling

1921		5037	846		3754	4862	03	2424
ἐπεγίνωσκόν		τε	αὐτοὺς	ὅτι	σὺν	τῷ	Ἰησοῦ
were perceiving		and	them		that	with	the	Jesus

1510	**14**	04	5037	444		991	4862	846
ἦσαν,		τόν	τε	ἄνθρωπον	βλέποντες	σὺν	αὐτοῖς
they were,		the	and	man		seeing	with	them

2476		04	2323		3762
ἑστῶτα		τὸν	τεθεραπευμένον		οὐδὲν
having stood		the	one having been healed		nothing

2192	483		**15**	2753		1161	846	1854
εἶχον	ἀντειπεῖν.			κελεύσαντες	δὲ	αὐτοὺς	ἔξω
they had	to speak			Having	but	them	outside
	against.			commanded			

010	4892		565		4820
τοῦ	συνεδρίου	ἀπελθεῖν	συνέβαλλον
of the	council	to go off	they were throwing together

4314	240	**16**	3004		5101	4160		015
πρὸς	ἀλλήλους		λέγοντες·	τί	ποιήσωμεν		τοῖς
toward	one another		saying;		what	might we do		to the

444	3778		3754	3303	1063	1110	4592
ἀνθρώποις	τούτοις;		ὅτι	μὲν	γὰρ	γνωστὸν	σημεῖον
men	these?		That	indeed	for	known	sign

1096	1223	846	3956	015	2730
γέγονεν	δι'	αὐτῶν	πᾶσιν	τοῖς	κατοικοῦσιν
has become	through	them	to all	the	ones residing

2419		5318	2532	3756	1410		720
Ἰερουσαλὴμ	φανερὸν	καὶ	οὐ	δυνάμεθα		ἀρνεῖσθαι·
Jerusalem		evident	and	not	we are able		to deny;

17	235	2443	3361	1909	4183	1268		1519
	ἀλλ'	ἵνα	μὴ	ἐπὶ	πλεῖον	διανεμηθῇ		εἰς
	but	that	not	on	more	it might be spread		to

04	2992	546		846	3371	2980
τὸν	λαὸν	ἀπειλησώμεθα		αὐτοῖς	μηκέτι	λαλεῖν
the	people	we might threaten		them	no longer	to speak

1909	011	3686	3778	3367		444	**18**	2532
ἐπὶ	τῷ	ὀνόματι	τούτῳ	μηδενὶ		ἀνθρώπων.		Καὶ
on	the	name	this	to no one		of men.		And

2564		846	3853		012	2527	3361
καλέσαντες		αὐτοὺς	παρήγγειλαν		τὸ	καθόλου	μὴ
having called		them	they commanded		the	by whole	not

before you in good health by the name of Jesus Christ of Nazareth,[a] whom you crucified, whom God raised from the dead. [11]This Jesus[b] is

'the stone that was
  rejected by you, the
   builders;
 it has become the
  cornerstone.'[c]

[12]There is salvation in no one else, for there is no other name under heaven given among mortals by which we must be saved."

[13]Now when they saw the boldness of Peter and John and realized that they were uneducated and ordinary men, they were amazed and recognized them as companions of Jesus. [14]When they saw the man who had been cured standing beside them, they had nothing to say in opposition. [15]So they ordered them to leave the council while they discussed the matter with one another. [16]They said, "What will we do with them? For it is obvious to all who live in Jerusalem that a notable sign has been done through them; we cannot deny it. [17]But to keep it from spreading further among the people, let us warn them to speak no more to anyone in this name." [18]So they called them and ordered them not

a Gk the Nazorean
b Gk This
c Or keystone

to speak or teach at all in
the name of Jesus. ¹⁹But
Peter and John answered
them, "Whether it is right
in God's sight to listen to
you rather than to God,
you must judge; ²⁰for we
cannot keep from speaking
about what we have seen
and heard." ²¹After
threatening them again,
they let them go, finding no
way to punish them because
of the people, for all of
them praised God for what
had happened. ²²For the
man on whom this sign of
healing had been performed
was more than forty years
old.

23 After they were
released, they went to
their friends[a] and reported
what the chief priests and
the elders had said to them.
²⁴When they heard it, they
raised their voices
together to God and said,
"Sovereign Lord, who
made the heaven and the
earth, the sea, and everything in them, ²⁵it is you
who said by the Holy Spirit
through our ancestor
David, your servant:[b]
'Why did the Gentiles
    rage,
  and the peoples imagine
    vain things?
²⁶The kings of the earth
    took their stand,
  and the rulers have
    gathered together
    against the Lord
    and against his
    Messiah.'[c]

a Gk their own
b Or child
c Or his Christ

| 5350 | 3366 | 1321 | 1909 | 011 | 3686 | 02 |

φθέγγεσθαι μηδὲ διδάσκειν ἐπὶ τῷ ὀνόματι τοῦ
to speak   but not to teach   on the name   of the

2424   01 1161 4074   2532 2491   611
Ἰησοῦ. **19** ὁ δὲ Πέτρος καὶ Ἰωάννης ἀποκριθέντες
Jesus.   The but Peter   and   John   having answered

3004   4314   846   1487 1342   1510   1799   02
εἶπον πρὸς αὐτούς· εἰ δίκαιόν ἐστιν ἐνώπιον τοῦ
said toward them,   if right   it is before the

2316 1473   191   3123   2228 02 2316   2919
θεοῦ ὑμῶν ἀκούειν μᾶλλον ἢ   τοῦ θεοῦ, κρίνατε·
God of you to hear more   than the God, you judge;

    3756 1410   1063 1473 3739 3708   2532 191
20 οὐ δυνάμεθα γὰρ ἡμεῖς ἃ εἴδαμεν καὶ ἠκούσαμεν
    not are able for we   what we saw and we heard

3361 2980   013 1161 4324   630
μὴ λαλεῖν. **21** οἱ δὲ προσαπειλησάμενοι ἀπέλυσαν
not to speak.   The but ones having   loosed off
                                threatened thoroughly

846   3367   2147   012 4459 2849
αὐτούς, μηδὲν εὑρίσκοντες τὸ πῶς κολάσωνται
them,   nothing finding   the how they might punish

846   1223 04   2992   3754   3956
αὐτούς, διὰ τὸν λαόν, ὅτι πάντες
them,   because the people, because all

1392   04 2316 1909 011 1096
ἐδόξαζον   τὸν θεὸν ἐπὶ τῷ γεγονότι·
were giving splendor the God on the having become;

    2094 1063 1510 4183   5062   01 444
22 ἐτῶν γὰρ ἦν πλειόνων τεσσεράκοντα ὁ ἄνθρωπος
    years for was more   forty   the man

1909 3739 1096   09   4592   3778 06   2392
ἐφ' ὃν γεγόνει τὸ σημεῖον τοῦτο τῆς ἰάσεως.
on whom had become the sign this of the cure.

    630   1161 2064   4314 016
23 Ἀπολυθέντες   δὲ ἦλθον πρὸς τοὺς
    Having been loosed off but they went to the

2398   2532 518   0745   4314 846   013
ἰδίους καὶ ἀπήγγειλαν ὅσα   πρὸς αὐτοὺς οἱ
own   and told   as much as to them   the

749   2532 013 4245   3004   **24** 013 1161
ἀρχιερεῖς καὶ οἱ πρεσβύτεροι εἶπαν.   οἱ δὲ
ruler priests and the older men said.   The ones but

191   3661   142   5456 4314 04
ἀκούσαντες ὁμοθυμαδὸν ἦραν φωνὴν πρὸς τὸν
having heard with one mind lifted up sound toward the

2316 2532 3004   1203   1473 01 4160
θεὸν καὶ εἶπαν· δέσποτα, σὺ ὁ ποιήσας
God and said; supervisor, you the one having made

04   3772   2532 08 1093 2532 08   2281   2532 3956
τὸν οὐρανὸν καὶ τὴν γῆν καὶ τὴν θάλασσαν καὶ πάντα
the heaven and the earth and the sea   and all

024 1722 846   01 02 3962   1473 1223
τὰ ἐν αὐτοῖς, **25** ὁ τοῦ πατρὸς ἡμῶν διὰ
the in them,   the of the father of us through

4151   40   4750   1160a 3816   1473
πνεύματος ἁγίου στόματος Δαυὶδ παιδός σου
spirit   holy mouth   David boy servant of you

3004   2444 5433   1484   2532 2992
εἰπών·   ἱνατί ἐφρύαξαν ἔθνη καὶ λαοὶ
having said; why rage   nations and peoples

3191   2756   26 3936   013 935   06
ἐμελέτησαν κενά;   παρέστησαν οἱ βασιλεῖς τῆς
take a care empty? Stood along the kings of the

1093 2532 013 758   4863   1909 012
γῆς καὶ οἱ ἄρχοντες συνήχθησαν   ἐπὶ τὸ
earth and the rulers were led together on the

846   2596 02 2962   2532 2596 02   5547   846
αὐτὸ κατὰ τοῦ κυρίου καὶ κατὰ τοῦ χριστοῦ αὐτοῦ.
same by the Master and by the Christ of him.

27
4863
συνήχθησαν
They were led together

1063 1909 225
γὰρ ἐπ᾽ ἀληθείας ἐν τῇ
for on truth in the

4172 3778 1909 04 40   3816   1473   2424
πόλει ταύτῃ ἐπὶ τὸν ἅγιον παῖδά σου Ἰησοῦν
city this on the holy boy servant of you Jesus

3739 5548   2264   5037 2532 4194   4091
ὃν ἔχρισας, Ἡρῴδης τε καὶ Πόντιος Πιλᾶτος
whom you anointed, Herod both and Pontius Pilate

4862 1484   2532 2992   2474   4160   3745
σὺν ἔθνεσιν καὶ λαοῖς Ἰσραήλ, **28** ποιῆσαι ὅσα
with nations and peoples Israel, to make as much as

05 5495 1473 2532 05 1012   1473 4309
ἡ χείρ σου καὶ ἡ βουλή [σου] προώρισεν
the hand of you and the plan of you set bounds before

1096   **29** 2532 024 3568 2962   2186a 1909 020
γενέσθαι. καὶ τὰ νῦν, κύριε, ἔπιδε ἐπὶ τὰς
to become. And the now, Master, look on on the

547   846   2532 1325 015   1401   1473
ἀπειλὰς αὐτῶν καὶ δὸς τοῖς δούλοις σου
threatenings of them and give to the slaves of you

3326 3954   3956 2980   04 3056 1473 **30** 1722
μετὰ παρρησίας πάσης λαλεῖν τὸν λόγον σου, ἐν
with boldness all to speak the word of you, in

011 08 5495 1473 1614   1473 1519 2392
τῷ τὴν χεῖρά [σου] ἐκτείνειν σε εἰς ἴασιν
the the hand of you to stretch out you into cure

2532 4852 2532 5059   1096   1223 010 3686
καὶ σημεῖα καὶ τέρατα γίνεσθαι διὰ τοῦ ὀνόματος
and signs and marvels to become by the name

02 40   3816   1473 2424 **31** 2532
τοῦ ἁγίου παιδός σου Ἰησοῦ. καὶ
of the holy boy servant of you Jesus. And

1189   846 4531   01 5117 1722 3739
δεηθέντων αὐτῶν ἐσαλεύθη ὁ τόπος ἐν ᾧ
having begged them was shaken the place in which

1510 4863   2532 4092   537   010   40
ἦσαν συνηγμένοι, καὶ ἐπλήσθησαν ἅπαντες τοῦ ἁγίου
they +having been and were filled all of the holy
were+ led together,

4151   2532 2980   04 3056 02   2316 3326
πνεύματος καὶ ἐλάλουν τὸν λόγον τοῦ θεοῦ μετὰ
spirit and were speaking the word of the God with

3954   **32** 010 1161 4128 014   4100
παρρησίας. Τοῦ δὲ πλήθους τῶν πιστευσάντων
boldness. The but quantity of the ones trusting

1510 2588   2532 5590 1520 2532 3761   1520 5100
ἦν καρδία καὶ ψυχὴ μία, καὶ οὐδὲ εἷς τι
was in heart and soul one, and but not one some

022   5225   846   3004   2398 1510 235
τῶν ὑπαρχόντων αὐτῷ ἔλεγεν ἴδιον εἶναι ἀλλ᾽
of the possessions to him was saying own to be but

1510 846 537 2839 **33** 2532 1411   3173
ἦν αὐτοῖς ἅπαντα κοινά. καὶ δυνάμει μεγάλη
was to them all common. And in power great

591   012 3142   013 652   06
ἀπεδίδουν τὸ μαρτύριον οἱ ἀπόστολοι τῆς
were giving off the testimony the delegates of the

386   02   2962   2424 5485 5037 3173
ἀναστάσεως τοῦ κυρίου Ἰησοῦ, χάρις τε μεγάλη
standing up of the Master Jesus, favor both great

1510 1909 3956 846   **34** 3761 1063 1729 5100 1510
ἦν ἐπὶ πάντας αὐτούς. οὐδὲ γὰρ ἐνδεής τις ἦν
was on all them. But not for in need some was

1722 846   3745   1063 2935   5564   2228
ἐν αὐτοῖς· ὅσοι γὰρ κτήτορες χωρίων ἢ
in them; as many as for acquisitions small fields or

3614   5225   4453   5342   020
οἰκιῶν ὑπῆρχον, πωλοῦντες ἔφερον τὰς
houses were possessing, selling were bringing the

27For in this city, in fact, both Herod and Pontius Pilate, with the Gentiles and the peoples of Israel, gathered together against your holy servant[a] Jesus, whom you anointed, 28to do whatever your hand and your plan had predestined to take place. 29And now, Lord, look at their threats, and grant to your servants[b] to speak your word with all boldness, 30while you stretch out your hand to heal, and signs and wonders are performed through the name of your holy servant[a] Jesus." 31When they had prayed, the place in which they were gathered together was shaken; and they were all filled with the Holy Spirit and spoke the word of God with boldness.

32 Now the whole group of those who believed were of one heart and soul, and no one claimed private ownership of any possessions, but everything they owned was held in common. 33With great power the apostles gave their testimony to the resurrection of the Lord Jesus, and great grace was upon them all. 34There was not a needy person among them, for as many as owned lands or houses sold them and brought the

a Or child
b Gk slaves

proceeds of what was sold. 35They laid it at the apostles' feet, and it was distributed to each as any had need. 36There was a Levite, a native of Cyprus, Joseph, to whom the apostles gave the name Barnabas (which means "son of encouragement"). 37He sold a field that belonged to him, then brought the money, and laid it at the apostles' feet.

CHAPTER 5

But a man named Ananias, with the consent of his wife Sapphira, sold a piece of property; 2with his wife's knowledge, he kept back some of the proceeds, and brought only a part and laid it at the apostles' feet. 3"Ananias," Peter asked, "why has Satan filled your heart to lie to the Holy Spirit and to keep back part of the proceeds of the land? 4While it remained unsold, did it not remain your own? And after it was sold, were not the proceeds at your disposal? How is it that you have contrived this deed in your heart? You did not lie to us*a* but to God!" 5Now when Ananias heard these words, he fell down and died. And great fear seized all who heard of it.

a Gk to men

5092	022	4097	**35**	2532	5087		3844
τιμὰς	τῶν	πιπρασκομένων		καὶ	ἐτίθουν		παρὰ
values	of the	ones being sold		and	were setting		along

016   4228   014   652   1239
τοὺς πόδας τῶν   ἀποστόλων, διεδίδετο
the feet of the delegates, it was given thoroughly

1161 1538   2530   302 5100 5532   2192
δὲ ἑκάστῳ καθότι   ἄν τις χρείαν εἶχεν.
but to each according that - some need had.

           2501 1161 01   1941   921
36 Ἰωσὴφ δὲ ὁ   ἐπικληθεὶς   Βαρναβᾶς
       Joseph but the one having been called on Barnabas

575 014 652   3739 1510 3177   5207
ἀπὸ τῶν ἀποστόλων, ὅ   ἐστιν μεθερμηνευόμενον υἱὸς
of the delegates, that is+ +being translated son

3874   3019   2953   011 1085
παρακλήσεως,   Λευΐτης,   Κύπριος τῷ γένει,
of encouragement, Levite,   Cypriot the kind,

        5225   846   68   4453   5342   012
37 ὑπάρχοντος αὐτῷ   ἀγροῦ πωλήσας   ἤνεγκεν τὸ
       existing   to him field having sold brought the

5536   2532 5087   4314 016   4228 014   652
χρῆμα καὶ ἔθηκεν πρὸς τοὺς πόδας τῶν   ἀποστόλων.
wealth and set   to   the feet of the delegates.

       435 1161 5100 367   3686   4862 4551   07
5:1 Ἀνὴρ δέ τις Ἀνανίας ὀνόματι σὺν Σαπφίρῃ τῇ
        Man but some Ananias in name with Sapphire the

1135   846   4453   2933   **2** 2532 3557
γυναικὶ αὐτοῦ ἐπώλησεν κτῆμα   καὶ ἐνοσφίσατο
woman of him sold   acquisition   and misappropriated
                                                  for himself

575 06 5092   4923a   2532 06
ἀπὸ τῆς τιμῆς, συνειδυίης   καὶ τῆς
of the value, having known together also the

1135   2532 5342   3313 5100 3844   016
γυναικός, καὶ ἐνέγκας   μέρος τι παρὰ τοὺς
woman,   and having brought part some along the

4228 014   652   5087   **3** 3004 1161 01   4074
πόδας τῶν   ἀποστόλων ἔθηκεν.   εἶπεν δὲ ὁ   Πέτρος·
feet of the delegates he set.   Said but the Peter;

367   1223   5101 4137   01 4567   08
Ἀνανία, διὰ   τί ἐπλήρωσεν ὁ σατανᾶς τὴν
Ananias, because why filled   the adversary the

2588   1473   5574   1473 012 4151   012 40
καρδίαν σου, ψεύσασθαί σε τὸ πνεῦμα τὸ ἅγιον
heart of you, to lie you the spirit the holy

2532 3557   575 06 5092
καὶ νοσφίσασθαι   ἀπὸ τῆς τιμῆς
and to misappropriate for yourself from the value

010   5564   **4** 3780 3306   1473   3306
τοῦ χωρίου;   οὐχὶ μένον σοὶ   ἔμενεν
of the small field? Not staying to you it was staying

2532 4097   1722 07 4674 1849
καὶ πραθὲν   ἐν τῇ σῇ ἐξουσίᾳ
and having been sold in the your authority

5225   5101 3754   5087   1722 07 2588
ὑπῆρχεν;   τί ὅτι   ἔθου ἐν τῇ καρδίᾳ
did it exist? why because you set in the heart

1473 012 4229   3778   3756 5574   444
σου τὸ πρᾶγμα τοῦτο; οὐκ ἐψεύσω ἀνθρώποις
of you the practice this? Not you lied to men

235 03   2316 5 191   1161 01 367   016
ἀλλὰ τῷ θεῷ.   ἀκούων   δὲ ὁ Ἀνανίας τοὺς
but to the God. Having heard but the Ananias the

3056   3778   4098   1634   2532 1096
λόγους τούτους πεσὼν   ἐξέψυξεν, καὶ ἐγένετο
words these   having fallen expired, and became

5401   3173   1909 3956 016   191
φόβος μέγας ἐπὶ πάντας τοὺς   ἀκούοντας.
fear great on all   the ones hearing.

450		1161	013	3501		4958	
6 ἀναστάντες		δὲ	οἱ	νεώτεροι		συνέστειλαν	
Having stood up		but	the	newer ones		sent together	

846	2532	1627		2290		1096	
αὐτὸν	καὶ	ἐξενέγκαντες		ἔθαψαν.	7	Ἐγένετο	
him	and	having carried out		they buried.		It became	

1161	5613	5610	5140	1292		2532	05	1135	846
δὲ	ὡς	ὡρῶν	τριῶν	διάστημα	καὶ	ἡ		γυνὴ	αὐτοῦ
but	as	hours	three	interval	and	the		woman	of him

3361	3609a		012	1096		1525		611
μὴ	εἰδυῖα		τὸ	γεγονὸς		εἰσῆλθεν.	8	ἀπεκρίθη
not having known			the	having become		went in.		Answered

1161	4314	846	4074		3004	1473	1487	5118	012
δὲ	πρὸς	αὐτὴν	Πέτρος·		εἰπέ	μοι,	εἰ	τοσούτου	τὸ
but	to	her	Peter;		say	to me,	if	so much	the

5564	591		05		1161	3004	3483
χωρίον	ἀπέδοσθε;		ἡ		δὲ	εἶπεν·	ναί,
small field	you gave off?		The one		but	said;	yes,

5118		01	1161	4074	4314	846		5101	3754
τοσούτου.	9	ὁ	δὲ	Πέτρος	πρὸς	αὐτήν·		τί	ὅτι
so much.		The	but	Peter	to	her;		why	because

4856		1473	3985		012	4151	2962
συνεφωνήθη		ὑμῖν	πειράσαι		τὸ	πνεῦμα	κυρίου;
it was agreed		to you	to pressure		the	spirit	of Master?

2400	013	4228	014		2290		04	435
ἰδοὺ	οἱ	πόδες	τῶν		θαψάντων		τὸν	ἄνδρα
Look	the	feet	of the ones		having buried		the	man

1473	1909	07	2374	2532	1627		1473
σου	ἐπὶ	τῇ	θύρᾳ	καὶ	ἐξοίσουσίν		σε.
of you	at	the	door	and	they will carry out		you.

10	4098		1161	3916		4314	016	4228	846	2532
	ἔπεσεν		δὲ	παραχρῆμα		πρὸς	τοὺς	πόδας	αὐτοῦ	καὶ
	She fell		but	suddenly		to	the	feet	of him	and

1634		1525		1161	013	3495		2147
ἐξέψυξεν·		εἰσελθόντες		δὲ	οἱ	νεανίσκοι		εὗρον
expired;		having come in		but	the	young men		found

846	3498	2532	1627		2290		4314
αὐτὴν	νεκρὰν	καὶ	ἐξενέγκαντες		ἔθαψαν		πρὸς
her	dead	and	having carried out		they buried		toward

04	435	846		2532	1096		5401	3173	1909	3650
τὸν	ἄνδρα	αὐτῆς,	11	καὶ	ἐγένετο		φόβος	μέγας	ἐφ᾽	ὅλην
the	man	of her,		and	became		fear	great	on	whole

08	1577		2532	1909	3956	016	191		3778
τὴν	ἐκκλησίαν		καὶ	ἐπὶ	πάντας	τοὺς	ἀκούοντας		ταῦτα.
the	assembly		and	on	all	the	ones hearing		these.

12	1223		1161	018	5495	014		652
	Διὰ		δὲ	τῶν	χειρῶν	τῶν		ἀποστόλων
	Through		but	the	hands	of the		delegates

1096		4592	2532	5059		4183	1722	03	2992
ἐγίνετο		σημεῖα	καὶ	τέρατα		πολλὰ	ἐν	τῷ	λαῷ.
were becoming		signs	and	marvels		many	in	the	people.

2532	1510	3661		537		1722	07	4745
καὶ	ἦσαν	ὁμοθυμαδὸν		ἅπαντες		ἐν	τῇ	στοᾷ
And	were	with one mind		all		in	the	colonnade

4672		13	014		1161	3062		3762	5111
Σολομῶντος,			τῶν		δὲ	λοιπῶν		οὐδεὶς	ἐτόλμα
of Solomon,			of the		but	remaining		no one	was daring

2853		846		235	3170		846
κολλᾶσθαι		αὐτοῖς,		ἀλλ᾽	ἐμεγάλυνεν		αὐτοὺς
to be joined		to them,		but	were making great		them

01	2992		14	3123	1161	4369		4100
ὁ	λαός.			μᾶλλον	δὲ	προσετίθεντο		πιστεύοντες
the	people.			More	but	were being set		to ones trusting

03	2962		4128		435		5037	2532	1135
τῷ	κυρίῳ,		πλήθη		ἀνδρῶν		τε	καὶ	γυναικῶν,
the	Master,		quantities		of men		both	and	women,

15	5620		2532	1519	020	4113		1627		016
	ὥστε		καὶ	εἰς	τὰς	πλατείας		ἐκφέρειν		τοὺς
	so that		even	in	the	wide places		to bring out		the

⁶The young men came and wrapped up his body,[a] then carried him out and buried him.

7 After an interval of about three hours his wife came in, not knowing what had happened. ⁸Peter said to her, "Tell me whether you and your husband sold the land for such and such a price." And she said, "Yes, that was the price." ⁹Then Peter said to her, "How is it that you have agreed together to put the Spirit of the Lord to the test? Look, the feet of those who have buried your husband are at the door, and they will carry you out." ¹⁰Immediately she fell down at his feet and died. When the young men came in they found her dead, so they carried her out and buried her beside her husband. ¹¹And great fear seized the whole church and all who heard of these things.

12 Now many signs and wonders were done among the people through the apostles. And they were all together in Solomon's Portico. ¹³None of the rest dared to join them, but the people held them in high esteem. ¹⁴Yet more than ever believers were added to the Lord, great numbers of both men and women, ¹⁵so that they even carried out the sick into the streets,

---

[a] Meaning of Gk uncertain

and laid them on cots and mats, in order that Peter's shadow might fall on some of them as he came by. [16]A great number of people would also gather from the towns around Jerusalem, bringing the sick and those tormented by unclean spirits, and they were all cured.

[17] Then the high priest took action; he and all who were with him (that is, the sect of the Sadducees), being filled with jealousy, [18]arrested the apostles and put them in the public prison. [19]But during the night an angel of the Lord opened the prison doors, brought them out, and said, [20]"Go, stand in the temple and tell the people the whole message about this life." [21]When they heard this, they entered the temple at daybreak and went on with their teaching.

When the high priest and those with him arrived, they called together the council and the whole body of the elders of Israel, and sent to the prison to have them brought. [22]But when the temple police went there, they did not find them in the prison; so they returned and reported, [23]"We found the prison

772	2532	5087	1909	2824a	2532	2895
ἀσθενεῖς	καὶ	τιθέναι	ἐπὶ	κλιναρίων	καὶ	κραβάττων,
weak	and	to set	on	small beds	and	mats,

2443	2064	4074	2579	05	4639	1982	5100
ἵνα	ἐρχομένου	Πέτρου	κᾶν	ἡ	σκιὰ	ἐπισκιάσῃ	τινὶ
that	of coming	Peter	if also	the	shadow	might overshadow	some

846	16	4905		1161	2532	09	4128
αὐτῶν.		συνήρχετο		δὲ	καὶ	τὸ	πλῆθος
of them.		Was coming together		but	also	the	quantity

018	4038	4172	2419	5342	772
τῶν	πέριξ	πόλεων	Ἰερουσαλὴμ	φέροντες	ἀσθενεῖς
of the	around	cities	Jerusalem	bringing	weak ones

2532	3791		5259	4151	169
καὶ	ὀχλουμένους		ὑπὸ	πνευμάτων	ἀκαθάρτων,
and	ones being crowded		by	spirits	unclean,

3748	2323	537	17	450	1161	01
οἵτινες	ἐθεραπεύοντο	ἅπαντες.		Ἀναστὰς	δὲ	ὁ
who	were healing	all.		Having stood up	but	the

749	2532	3956	013	4862	846	05	1510
ἀρχιερεὺς	καὶ	πάντες	οἱ	σὺν	αὐτῷ,	ἡ	οὖσα
ruler priest	and	all	the ones	with	him,	the	being

139	014	4523	4092	2205	18	2532
αἵρεσις	τῶν	Σαδδουκαίων,	ἐπλήσθησαν	ζήλου		καὶ
sect	of the	Sadducees,	were filled	jealousy		and

1911	020	5495	1909	016	652	2532	5087
ἐπέβαλον	τὰς	χεῖρας	ἐπὶ	τοὺς	ἀποστόλους	καὶ	ἔθεντο
threw on	the	hands	on	the	delegates	and	set

846	1722	5084	1219	19	32	1161
αὐτοὺς	ἐν	τηρήσει	δημοσίᾳ.		Ἄγγελος	δὲ
them	in	keeping place	in public.		Messenger	but

2962	1223	3571	455	020	2374	06
κυρίου	διὰ	νυκτὸς	ἀνοίξας	τὰς	θύρας	τῆς
of Master	by	night	having opened	the	doors	of the

5438	1806		5037	846	3004	20	4198
φυλακῆς	ἐξαγαγών	τε	αὐτοὺς	εἶπεν·		πορεύεσθε
guard	having led out	and	them	said;		travel

2532	2476	2980	1722	011	2411	03	2992	3956
καὶ	σταθέντες	λαλεῖτε	ἐν	τῷ	ἱερῷ	τῷ	λαῷ	πάντα
and	having stood	speak	in	the	temple	to	people	all

024	4487	06	2222	3778	21	191	1161
τὰ	ῥήματα	τῆς	ζωῆς	ταύτης.		ἀκούσαντες	δὲ
the	words	of the	life	this.		Having heard	but

1525	5259	04	3722	1519	012	2411	2532
εἰσῆλθον	ὑπὸ	τὸν	ὄρθρον	εἰς	τὸ	ἱερὸν	καὶ
they went in	by	the	dawn	to	the	temple	and

1321	3854	1161	01	749	2532
ἐδίδασκον.	Παραγενόμενος	δὲ	ὁ	ἀρχιερεὺς	καὶ
were teaching.	Having arrived	but	the	ruler priest	and

013	4862	846	4779	012	4892	2532
οἱ	σὺν	αὐτῷ	συνεκάλεσαν	τὸ	συνέδριον	καὶ
the ones	with	him	called together	the	council	and

3956	08	1087	014	5207	2474	2532	649
πᾶσαν	τὴν	γερουσίαν	τῶν	υἱῶν	Ἰσραὴλ	καὶ	ἀπέστειλαν
all	the	older one	of the	sons	Israel	and	delegated

1519	012	1201	71	846	22	013	1161
εἰς	τὸ	δεσμωτήριον	ἀχθῆναι	αὐτούς.		οἱ	δὲ
to	the	chain place	to be led	them.		The	but

3854	5257	3756	2147	846	1722
παραγενόμενοι	ὑπηρέται	οὐχ	εὗρον	αὐτοὺς	ἐν
having arrived	assistants	not	they found	them	in

07	5438	390	1161	518	23	3004
τῇ	φυλακῇ·	ἀναστρέψαντες	δὲ	ἀπήγγειλαν		λέγοντες
the	guard;	having returned	but	they told		saying

3754	012	1201	2147	2808	1722
ὅτι	τὸ	δεσμωτήριον	εὕρομεν	κεκλεισμένον	ἐν
that	the	chain place	we found	having been closed	in

3956	803		2532	016	5441		2476		1909	018
πάσῃ	ἀσφαλείᾳ	καὶ	τοὺς	φύλακας	ἑστῶτας		ἐπὶ		τῶν	
all	security	and	the	guards	having stood		on		the	

2374	455		1161	2080	3762	2147
θυρῶν,	ἀνοίξαντες	δὲ	ἔσω,	οὐδένα	εὕρομεν.
doors,	having opened	but	inside,	nothing	we found.

24

5613	1161	191	016	3056	3778	01	5037
ὡς	δὲ	ἤκουσαν	τοὺς	λόγους	τούτους	ὅ	τε
As	but	heard	the	words	these	the	both

4755	010	2411	2532	013	749
στρατηγὸς	τοῦ	ἱεροῦ	καὶ	οἱ	ἀρχιερεῖς,
captain	of the	temple	and	the	ruler priests,

1280	4012	846	5101	302	1096	3778
διηπόρουν	περὶ	αὐτῶν	τί	ἂν	γένοιτο	τοῦτο.
they were doubting thoroughly	about	them	what	-	may	become this.

25

3854	1161	5100	518	846	3754	2400
παραγενόμενος	δέ	τις	ἀπήγγειλεν	αὐτοῖς	ὅτι	ἰδοὺ
Having arrived	but	some	told	them,	(")	look

013	435	3739	5087	1722	07	5438	1510	1722	011
οἱ	ἄνδρες	οὓς	ἔθεσθε	ἐν	τῇ	φυλακῇ	εἰσὶν	ἐν	τῷ
the	men	whom	you set in	the		guard	are+	in	the

2411	2476	2532	1321	04	2992		5119
ἱερῷ	ἑστῶτες	καὶ	διδάσκοντες	τὸν	λαόν.	**26**	Τότε
temple	+standing	and	+teaching	the	people.		Then

565	01	4755	4862	015	5257
ἀπελθὼν	ὁ	στρατηγὸς	σὺν	τοῖς	ὑπηρέταις
having gone off	the	captain	with	the	assistants

71	846	3756	3326	970	5399
ἦγεν	αὐτοὺς	οὐ	μετὰ	βίας,	ἐφοβοῦντο
was leading	them	not	with	violence,	they were fearing

1063	04	2992	3361	3034		71
γὰρ	τὸν	λαόν,	μὴ	λιθασθῶσιν.	**27**	Ἀγαγόντες
for	the	people,	not	they might be stoned.		Having led

1161	846	2476	1722	011	4892	2532	1905
δὲ	αὐτοὺς	ἔστησαν	ἐν	τῷ	συνεδρίῳ.	καὶ	ἐπηρώτησεν
but	them	they stood	in	the	council.	And	asked on

846	01	749		3004	3756	3852
αὐτοὺς	ὁ	ἀρχιερεὺς	**28**	λέγων·	[οὐ]	παραγγελίᾳ
them	the	ruler priest		saying;	not	command

3853	1473	3361	1321	1909	011	3686
παρηγγείλαμεν	ὑμῖν	μὴ	διδάσκειν	ἐπὶ	τῷ	ὀνόματι
we commanded	you	not	to teach	on	the	name

3778	2532	2400	4137	08	2419	06
τούτῳ,	καὶ	ἰδοὺ	πεπληρώκατε	τὴν	Ἰερουσαλὴμ	τῆς
this,	and	look	you have filled	the	Jerusalem	of the

1322	1473	2532	1014	1863	1909	1473
διδαχῆς	ὑμῶν	καὶ	βούλεσθε	ἐπαγαγεῖν	ἐφ᾽	ἡμᾶς
teaching	of you	and	you plan	to bring on	on	us

012	129	02	444	3778		611
τὸ	αἷμα	τοῦ	ἀνθρώπου	τούτου.	**29**	ἀποκριθεὶς
the	blood	of the	man	this.		Having answered

1161	4074	2532	013	652	3004	3980
δὲ	Πέτρος	καὶ	οἱ	ἀπόστολοι	εἶπαν·	πειθαρχεῖν
but	Peter	and	the	delegates	said;	to obey

1163	2316	3123	2228	444		01
δεῖ	θεῷ	μᾶλλον	ἢ	ἀνθρώποις.	**30**	ὁ
it is necessary	God	more	than	men.		The

2316	014	3962	1473	1453	2424	3739	1473
θεὸς	τῶν	πατέρων	ἡμῶν	ἤγειρεν	Ἰησοῦν	ὃν	ὑμεῖς
God	of the	fathers	of us	raised	Jesus	whom	you

1315	2910	1909	3586		3778
διεχειρίσασθε	κρεμάσαντες	ἐπὶ	ξύλου·	**31**	τοῦτον
handled thoroughly	having hanged	on	wood;		this one

01	2316	747	2532	4990	5312	07	1188
ὁ	θεὸς	ἀρχηγὸν	καὶ	σωτῆρα	ὕψωσεν	τῇ	δεξιᾷ
the	God	beginner	and	deliverer	elevated	to the	right

846	010	1325	3341	03	2474
αὐτοῦ	[τοῦ]	δοῦναι	μετάνοιαν	τῷ	Ἰσραὴλ
of him	of the	to give	change of mind	to the	Israel

securely locked and the guards standing at the doors, but when we opened them, we found no one inside." [24]Now when the captain of the temple and the chief priests heard these words, they were perplexed about them, wondering what might be going on. [25]Then someone arrived and announced, "Look, the men whom you put in prison are standing in the temple and teaching the people!" [26]Then the captain went with the temple police and brought them, but without violence, for they were afraid of being stoned by the people.

[27]When they had brought them, they had them stand before the council. The high priest questioned them, [28]saying, "We gave you strict orders not to teach in this name,[a] yet here you have filled Jerusalem with your teaching and you are determined to bring this man's blood on us." [29]But Peter and the apostles answered, "We must obey God rather than any human authority.[b] [30]The God of our ancestors raised up Jesus, whom you had killed by hanging him on a tree. [31]God exalted him at his right hand as Leader and Savior that he might give repentance to Israel

[a] Other ancient authorities read Did we not give you strict orders not to teach in this name?

[b] Gk than men

and forgiveness of sins.
32And we are witnesses to
these things, and so is the
Holy Spirit whom God has
given to those who obey
him."
   33 When they heard
this, they were enraged and
wanted to kill them. 34But
a Pharisee in the council
named Gamaliel, a teacher
of the law, respected by
all the people, stood up
and ordered the men to
be put outside for a short
time. 35Then he said to
them, "Fellow Israelites,a
consider carefully what
you propose to do to these
men. 36For some time ago
Theudas rose up, claiming
to be somebody, and a
number of men, about
four hundred, joined him;
but he was killed, and all
who followed him were
dispersed and disappeared.
37After him Judas the
Galilean rose up at the
time of the census and
got people to follow him;
he also perished, and all
who followed him were
scattered. 38So in the
present case, I tell you,
keep away from these men
and let them alone; because
if this plan or this undertaking is of human origin,
it will fail;

a Gk Men, Israelites

2532	859		266		**32**	2532	1473	1510
καὶ	ἄφεσιν		ἁμαρτιῶν.			καὶ	ἡμεῖς	ἐσμεν
and	sending off		of sins.			And	we	are

3144		022	4487	3778	2532	09	4151	09
μάρτυρες		τῶν	ῥημάτων	τούτων	καὶ	τὸ	πνεῦμα	τὸ
testifiers		of the	words	these	and	the	spirit	the

40	3739	1325	01	2316	015	3980		846
ἅγιον	ὃ	ἔδωκεν	ὁ	θεὸς	τοῖς	πειθαρχοῦσιν		αὐτῷ.
holy	that	gave	the	God	to the	ones obeying		him.

33	013		1161	191		1282
	Οἱ		δὲ	ἀκούσαντες		διεπρίοντο
	The ones	but		having heard		were being sawn through

2532	1014		337	846		**34**	450
καὶ	ἐβούλοντο		ἀνελεῖν	αὐτούς.			ἀναστὰς
and	were planning		to kill	them.			Having stood up

1161	5100	1722	011	4892		5330		3686
δέ	τις	ἐν	τῷ	συνεδρίῳ		Φαρισαῖος		ὀνόματι
but	some	in	the	council		Pharisee		in name

1059		3547		5093		3956	03	2992
Γαμαλιήλ,		νομοδιδάσκαλος		τίμιος		παντὶ	τῷ	λαῷ,
Gamaliel,		law-teacher		valuable		to all		the people,

2753		1854		1024	016	444		4160
ἐκέλευσεν		ἔξω		βραχὺ	τοὺς	ἀνθρώπους		ποιῆσαι
commanded		outside		little	the	men		to do

35	3004		5037	4314	846		435		2475
	εἶπέν		τε	πρὸς	αὐτούς·		ἄνδρες		Ἰσραηλῖται,
	he said		and	to	them;		men		Israelites,

4337		1438		1909	011	444		3778	5101
προσέχετε		ἑαυτοῖς		ἐπὶ	τοῖς	ἀνθρώποις		τούτοις	τί
hold to		yourselves		on	the	men		these	what

3195		4238		**36**	4253	1063	3778	018
μέλλετε		πράσσειν.			πρὸ	γὰρ	τούτων	τῶν
you are about		to practice.			Before	for	these	of the

2250	450		2333	3004		1510	5100	1438
ἡμερῶν	ἀνέστη		Θευδᾶς	λέγων		εἶναί	τινα	ἑαυτόν,
days	stood up		Theudas	saying		to be	some	himself,

3739	4345a		435	706		5613	5071
ᾧ	προσεκλίθη		ἀνδρῶν	ἀριθμὸς		ὡς	τετρακοσίων·
to whom	were inclined		of men	number		as	four hundred;

3739	337		2532	3956	3745		3982		846
ὃς	ἀνηρέθη,		καὶ	πάντες	ὅσοι		ἐπείθοντο		αὐτῷ
who	were	and	all		as many as	were being		to him
	killed,			as		persuaded

1262		2532	1096		1519	3762		**37**	3326
διελύθησαν		καὶ	ἐγένοντο		εἰς	οὐδέν.			μετὰ
were thoroughly loosed		and	became		into	nothing.			After

3778	450		2455	01	1057		1722	019	2250
τοῦτον	ἀνέστη		Ἰούδας	ὁ	Γαλιλαῖος		ἐν	ταῖς	ἡμέραις
this	stood up		Judas	the	Galilean		in	the	days

06		582		2532	868		2992	3694	846
τῆς		ἀπογραφῆς		καὶ	ἀπέστησεν		λαὸν	ὀπίσω	αὐτοῦ·
of the		enrollment		and	he stood off		people	after	him

2548		622			2532	3956	3745
κἀκεῖνος		ἀπώλετο			καὶ	πάντες	ὅσοι
and that one		destroyed himself			and	all	as many as

3982		846	1287		**38**	2532	024	3568	3004
ἐπείθοντο		αὐτῷ	διεσκορπίσθησαν.			καὶ	τὰ	νῦν	λέγω
were being		him	were thoroughly			And	the	now	I say
persuaded			scattered.

1473		868		575	014	444		3778	2532	863
ὑμῖν,		ἀπόστητε		ἀπὸ	τῶν	ἀνθρώπων		τούτων	καὶ	ἄφετε
to you,		stand off		from	the	men		these	and	send off

846		3754		1437	1510		1537	444		05
αὐτούς·		ὅτι		ἐὰν	ᾖ		ἐξ	ἀνθρώπων		ἡ
them;		because	if		it might be		from	men		the

1012	3778	2228	09	2041	3778		2647
βουλὴ	αὕτη	ἢ	τὸ	ἔργον	τοῦτο,		καταλυθήσεται,
plan	this	or	the	work	this,		it will be unloosed,

39
1487	1161	1537	2316	1510	3756	1410
εἰ	δὲ	ἐκ	θεοῦ ἐστιν,	οὐ	δυνήσεσθε	
if	but	from	God it is,	not	you will be able	

2647	846	3379	2532	2314
καταλῦσαι	αὐτούς,	μήποτε	καὶ	θεομάχοι
to unloose	them,	not then	also	God fighters

2147	3982	1161	846	**40**	2532	4341
εὑρεθῆτε.	ἐπείσθησαν	δὲ	αὐτῷ		καὶ	προσκαλεσάμενοι
you might be found	They persuaded	but	in him		and	having called to

016	652	1194	3853	3361	2980
τοὺς	ἀποστόλους	δείραντες	παρήγγειλαν	μὴ	λαλεῖν
the	delegates	having beat	they commanded	not	to speak

1909	011	3686	02	2424	2532	630
ἐπὶ	τῷ	ὀνόματι	τοῦ	Ἰησοῦ	καὶ	ἀπέλυσαν.
on	the	name	the	Jesus	and	they loosed off.

41
013	3303	3767	4198	5463	575
Οἱ	μὲν	οὖν	ἐπορεύοντο	χαίροντες	ἀπὸ
The ones	indeed	then	were traveling	rejoicing	from

4383	010	4892	3754	2661
προσώπου	τοῦ	συνεδρίου,	ὅτι	κατηξιώθησαν
face	of the	council,	because	they were worthy

5228	010	3686	818	**42**	3956
ὑπὲρ	τοῦ	ὀνόματος	ἀτιμασθῆναι,		πᾶσάν
on behalf	of the	name	to be dishonored,		all

5037	2250	1722	011	2411	2532	2596	3624	3756
τε	ἡμέραν	ἐν	τῷ	ἱερῷ	καὶ	κατ'	οἶκον	οὐκ
and	day	in	the	temple	and	by	house	not

3973	1321	2532	2097
ἐπαύοντο	διδάσκοντες	καὶ	εὐαγγελιζόμενοι
they stopped	teaching	and	telling good message

04	5547	2424	**6:1**	1722	1161	019	2250
τὸν	χριστόν	Ἰησοῦν.		Ἐν	δὲ	ταῖς	ἡμέραις
the	Christ	Jesus.		In	but	the	days

3778	4129	014	3101	1096	1112
ταύταις	πληθυνόντων	τῶν	μαθητῶν	ἐγένετο	γογγυσμὸς
these	multiplying	the	learners	became	grumbling

014	1675	4314	016	1445	3754
τῶν	Ἑλληνιστῶν	πρὸς	τοὺς	Ἑβραίους,	ὅτι
of the	Hellenists	toward	the	Hebrews,	that

3865	1722	07	1248	07
παρεθεωροῦντο	ἐν	τῇ	διακονίᾳ	τῇ
they were being overlooked	in	the	service	the

2522	017	5503	846	**2**	4341	1161
καθημερινῇ	αἱ	χῆραι	αὐτῶν.		προσκαλεσάμενοι	δὲ
daily	the	widows	of them.		Having called to	but

013	1427	012	4128	014	3101	3004	3756
οἱ	δώδεκα	τὸ	πλῆθος	τῶν	μαθητῶν	εἶπαν·	οὐκ
the	twelve	the	quantity	of the	learners	said;	not

701	1510	1473	2641	04	3056	02
ἀρεστόν	ἐστιν	ἡμᾶς	καταλείψαντας	τὸν	λόγον	τοῦ
pleasing	it is	us	having left behind	the	word	of the

2316	1247	5132	**3**	1980	1161	80
θεοῦ	διακονεῖν	τραπέζαις.		ἐπισκέψασθε	δέ,	ἀδελφοί,
God	to serve	tables.		Look on	but,	brothers,

435	1537	1473	3140	2033	4134
ἄνδρας	ἐξ	ὑμῶν	μαρτυρουμένους	ἑπτά,	πλήρεις
men	from	you	being testified	seven,	full

4151	2532	4678	3739	2525	1909	06
πνεύματος	καὶ	σοφίας,	οὓς	καταστήσομεν	ἐπὶ	τῆς
of spirit	and	wisdom,	whom	we will appoint	on	the

5532	3778	**4**	1473	1161	07	4335	2532	07
χρείας	ταύτης,		ἡμεῖς	δὲ	τῇ	προσευχῇ	καὶ	τῇ
need	this,		we	but	in the	prayer	and	the

1248	02	3056	4342	**5**	2532	700
διακονίᾳ	τοῦ	λόγου	προσκαρτερήσομεν.		καὶ	ἤρεσεν
service	of the	word	will remain constant.		And	pleased

01	3056	1799	3956	010	4128	2532
ὁ	λόγος	ἐνώπιον	παντὸς	τοῦ	πλήθους	καὶ
the	word	before	all	of the	quantity	and

[39]but if it is of God, you will not be able to overthrow them—in that case you may even be found fighting against God!"

They were convinced by him, [40]and when they had called in the apostles, they had them flogged. Then they ordered them not to speak in the name of Jesus, and let them go. [41]As they left the council, they rejoiced that they were considered worthy to suffer dishonor for the sake of the name. [42]And every day in the temple and at home[a] they did not cease to teach and proclaim Jesus as the Messiah.[b]

CHAPTER 6

Now during those days, when the disciples were increasing in number, the Hellenists complained against the Hebrews because their widows were being neglected in the daily distribution of food. [2]And the twelve called together the whole community of the disciples and said, "It is not right that we should neglect the word of God in order to wait on tables.[c] [3]Therefore, friends,[d] select from among yourselves seven men of good standing, full of the Spirit and of wisdom, whom we may appoint to this task, [4]while we, for our part, will devote ourselves to prayer and to serving the word." [5]What they said pleased the whole community, and

[a] Or from house to house
[b] Or the Christ
[c] Or keep accounts
[d] Gk brothers

they chose Stephen, a man full of faith and the Holy Spirit, together with Philip, Prochorus, Nicanor, Timon, Parmenas, and Nicolaus, a proselyte of Antioch. 6They had these men stand before the apostles, who prayed and laid their hands on them.

7 The word of God continued to spread; the number of the disciples increased greatly in Jerusalem, and a great many of the priests became obedient to the faith.

8 Stephen, full of grace and power, did great wonders and signs among the people. 9Then some of those who belonged to the synagogue of the Freedmen (as it was called), Cyrenians, Alexandrians, and others of those from Cilicia and Asia, stood up and argued with Stephen. 10But they could not withstand the wisdom and the Spirit[a] with which he spoke. 11Then they secretly instigated some men to say, "We have heard him speak blasphemous words against Moses and God." 12They stirred up the people as well as the elders and the scribes; then they suddenly confronted him, seized him, and brought him before the council. 13They set up false witnesses who said, "This man never stops saying things against this holy place and the law;

[a] Or spirit

1586	4736	435	4134	4102	2532
ἐξελέξαντο	Στέφανον,	ἄνδρα	πλήρης	πίστεως	καὶ
they selected	Stephan,	man	full	of trust	and

4151	40	2532 5376		2532 4402	2532
πνεύματος	ἁγίου,	καὶ Φίλιππον	καὶ	Πρόχορον	καὶ
spirit	holy,	and Philip	and	Prochorus	and

3527	2532 5096	2532 3937	2532 3532
Νικάνορα	καὶ Τίμωνα	καὶ Παρμενᾶν	καὶ Νικόλαον
Nicanor	and Timon	and Parmenas	and Nicolaos

4339	491	6	3739 2476	1799	014
προσήλυτον	Ἀντιοχέα,		οὓς ἔστησαν	ἐνώπιον	τῶν
convert	Antiochean,	who	stood	before	the

652	2532 4336	2007	846	020
ἀποστόλων,	καὶ προσευξάμενοι	ἐπέθηκαν	αὐτοῖς	τὰς
delegates,	and having prayed	they set on	them	the

5495	7	2532 01	3056 02	2316 837	2532
χεῖρας.		Καὶ ὁ	λόγος τοῦ	θεοῦ ηὔξανεν	καὶ
hands.		And the	word of the	God was growing	and

4129	01 706	014	3101	1722
ἐπληθύνετο	ὁ ἀριθμὸς	τῶν	μαθητῶν	ἐν
was multiplying	the number	of the	learners	in

2419	4970	4183	5037 3793	014	2409
Ἰερουσαλὴμ	σφόδρα,	πολύς	τε ὄχλος	τῶν	ἱερέων
Jerusalem	exceeding,	much	and crowd	of the	priests

5219	07 4102	8	4736	1161 4134	5485
ὑπήκουον	τῇ πίστει.		Στέφανος	δὲ πλήρης	χάριτος
were obeying	the trust.		Stephan	but full	of favor

2532 1411	4160	5059	2532 4592	3173 1722
καὶ δυνάμεως	ἐποίει	τέρατα	καὶ σημεῖα	μεγάλα ἐν
and power	was doing	marvels	and signs	great in

03 2992	450	9	1161 5100	014	1537 06
τῷ λαῷ.	ἀνέστησαν	δέ	τινες	τῶν	ἐκ τῆς
the people.	Stood up	but	some	of the ones	from the

4864	06	3004	3032	2532 2956
συναγωγῆς	τῆς	λεγομένης	Λιβερτίνων	καὶ Κυρηναίων
synagogue	of the	being called	Libertines	and Cyreneans

2532 221		2532 014 575	2791	2532 773
καὶ Ἀλεξανδρέων	καὶ	ἰῶν ἀπὸ	Κιλικίας	καὶ Ἀσίας
and Alexandrians	and	the from	Cilicia	and Asia

4802	03 4736	10	2532 3756 2480
συζητοῦντες	τῷ Στεφάνῳ,		καὶ οὐκ ἴσχυον
disputing	the Stephan,		and not they were strong

436	07 4678	2532 011 4151	3739
ἀντιστῆναι	τῇ σοφίᾳ	καὶ τῷ πνεύματι	ᾧ
to stand against	the wisdom	and the spirit	in what

2980	11	5119 5260	435	3004
ἐλάλει.		τότε ὑπέβαλον	ἄνδρας	λέγοντας
he was speaking.		Then they induced	men	saying,

3754 191	846	2980	4487 989	1519
ὅτι ἀκηκόαμεν	αὐτοῦ	λαλοῦντος	ῥήματα βλάσφημα	εἰς
(") we have heard	him	speaking	words insult	to

3475	2532 04 2316	12	4787	5037 04
Μωϋσῆν	καὶ τὸν θεόν.		συνεκίνησάν	τε τὸν
Moses	and the God.		They stirred together	both the

2992	2532 016 4245	2532 016 1122	2532
λαὸν	καὶ τοὺς πρεσβυτέρους	καὶ τοὺς γραμματεῖς	καὶ
people	and the older men	and the writers	and

2186	4884	846 2532 71	1519 012
ἐπιστάντες	συνήρπασαν	αὐτὸν καὶ	ἤγαγον εἰς τὸ
having stood on	they seized together	him and	led into the

4892	13	2476	5037 3144	5571	3004
συνέδριον,		ἔστησάν	τε μάρτυρας	ψευδεῖς	λέγοντας·
council,		stood	and testifiers	false	saying,

01 444	3778 3756 3973	2980	4487	2596
ὁ ἄνθρωπος	οὗτος οὐ παύεται	λαλῶν	ῥήματα	κατὰ
the man	this not stops	saying	words	against

02 5117 02	40	3778	2532 02 3551
τοῦ τόπου τοῦ	ἁγίου	[τούτου]	καὶ τοῦ νόμου·
the place of the	holy	this	and the law;

14 191   1063 846   3004   3754   2424   01
ἀκηκόαμεν   γὰρ   αὐτοῦ λέγοντος ὅτι ᾿Ιησοῦς ὁ
we have heard for   him   saying,   (") Jesus   the
3480   3778   2647   04 5117 3778   2532
Ναζωραῖος οὗτος καταλύσει τὸν τόπον τοῦτον καὶ
Nazorean   this   will unloose the place this   and
236   024   1485   3739 3860   1473 3475
ἀλλάξει   τὰ   ἔθη   ἃ   παρέδωκεν ἡμῖν Μωϋσῆς.
will change the customs that gave over   to us Moses.

15 2532 816   1519 846   3956   013
καὶ   ἀτενίσαντες   εἰς αὐτὸν πάντες οἱ
And   having stared into him   all   the ones
2516   1722 011 4892   3708 012 4383   846
καθεζόμενοι ἐν   τῷ   συνεδρίῳ εἶδον τὸ πρόσωπον αὐτοῦ
sitting   in   the council   saw   the face   of him
5616 4383   32   **7:1** 3004 1161 01   749
ὡσεὶ πρόσωπον ἀγγέλου.   Εἶπεν δὲ ὁ   ἀρχιερεύς,
as   face   of messenger. Said but the ruler priest,
1487 3778 3779   2192   01 1161 5346   435   80
Εἰ ταῦτα οὕτως ἔχει; **2** ὁ δὲ ἔφη, ῎Ανδρες ἀδελφοὶ
If these thusly have?   The but said, Men   brothers
2532 3962   191   01 2316 06   1391
καὶ πατέρες, ἀκούσατε. ῾Ο θεὸς τῆς δόξης
and fathers, hear.   The God of the splendor
3708   03   3962   1473 11   1510 1722 07
ὤφθη   τῷ   πατρὶ ἡμῶν ᾿Αβραὰμ ὄντι ἐν   τῇ
was seen in the father of us Abraham being in the
3318   4250 2228 2730   846   1722 5488
Μεσοποταμίᾳ πρὶν ἢ   κατοικῆσαι αὐτὸν ἐν Χαρρὰν
Mesopotamia before or to reside him   in Charran
3 2532 3004 4314   846   1537 06 1093 1473
καὶ εἶπεν πρὸς αὐτόν· ἔξελθε ἐκ τῆς γῆς σου
and said to   him,   come out from the land of you
2532 1537 06 4772   1473   2532 1204 1519 08
καὶ [ἐκ] τῆς συγγενείας σου, καὶ δεῦρο εἰς τὴν
and from the relative   of you, and come into the
1093 3739 302 1473   1166   **4** 5119 1831   1537 1093
γῆν ἣν   ἄν σοι δείξω.   τότε ἐξελθὼν ἐκ γῆς
land which -   to you I will   Then having from land
show.   come out
5466   2730   1722 5488   2547
Χαλδαίων κατῴκησεν ἐν Χαρράν. κἀκεῖθεν
Chaldeans he resided in Charran. And from there
3326 012 599   04 3962   846   3351
μετὰ τὸ ἀποθανεῖν τὸν πατέρα αὐτοῦ μετῴκισεν
after the to die   the father of him he changed home
846   1519 08 1093 3778   1519 3739 1473 3568
αὐτὸν εἰς τὴν γῆν ταύτην εἰς ἣν   ὑμεῖς νῦν
him   to   the land this   in   which you   now
2730   **5** 2532 3756 1325   846   2817   1722
κατοικεῖτε,   καὶ οὐκ ἔδωκεν αὐτῷ κληρονομίαν ἐν
reside,   and not he gave to him inheritance in
846 3761   968   4228   2532 1861   1325
αὐτῇ οὐδὲ βῆμα ποδὸς καὶ ἐπηγγείλατο δοῦναι
it   but not room foot and he promised to give
846   1519 2697   846   2532 011 4690   846
αὐτῷ εἰς κατάσχεσιν αὐτὴν καὶ τῷ σπέρματι αὐτοῦ
to him into possession it   and the seed   of him
3326 846   3756 1510 846   5043   **6** 2980   1161
μετ᾿ αὐτόν, οὐκ ὄντος αὐτῷ τέκνου.   ἐλάλησεν δὲ
after him, not being to him child.   Spoke   but
3779   01 2316 3754 1510   09 4690   846
οὕτως ὁ θεὸς ὅτι ἔσται τὸ σπέρμα αὐτοῦ
thusly the God that will be the seed   of him
3941   1722 1093 245   2532 1402   846
πάροικον ἐν γῇ ἀλλοτρίᾳ καὶ δουλώσουσιν αὐτὸ
transient in land to another and they will slave it
2532 2559   2094 5071   **7** 2532 012 1484
καὶ κακώσουσιν ἔτη τετρακόσια· καὶ τὸ ἔθνος
and will do bad years four hundred; and the nation

[14]for we have heard him say
that this Jesus of Nazareth[a]
will destroy this place and
will change the customs
that Moses handed on to us."
[15]And all who sat in the
council looked intently at
him, and they saw that his
face was like the face of an
angel.

CHAPTER 7

Then the high priest asked
him, "Are these things so?"
[2]And Stephen replied:
"Brothers[b] and fathers,
listen to me. The God of
glory appeared to our
ancestor Abraham when he
was in Mesopotamia, before
he lived in Haran, [3]and said
to him, 'Leave your country
and your relatives and go
to the land that I will show
you.' [4]Then he left the
country of the Chaldeans
and settled in Haran. After
his father died, God had
him move from there to this
country in which you are
now living. [5]He did not
give him any of it as a
heritage, not even a foot's
length, but promised to
give it to him as his
possession and to his
descendants after him, even
though he had no child.
[6]And God spoke in these
terms, that his descendants
would be resident aliens
in a country belonging to
others, who would enslave
them and mistreat them
during four hundred years.
[7]"But I will judge the
nation

a Gk the Nazorean
b Gk Men, brothers

that they serve,' said God, 'and after that they shall come out and worship me in this place.' 8Then he gave him the covenant of circumcision. And so Abraham*a* became the father of Isaac and circumcised him on the eighth day; and Isaac became the father of Jacob, and Jacob of the twelve patriarchs.

9 "The patriarchs, jealous of Joseph, sold him into Egypt; but God was with him, 10and rescued him from all his afflictions, and enabled him to win favor and to show wisdom when he stood before Pharaoh, king of Egypt, who appointed him ruler over Egypt and over all his household. 11Now there came a famine throughout Egypt and Canaan, and great suffering, and our ancestors could find no food. 12But when Jacob heard that there was grain in Egypt, he sent our ancestors there on their first visit. 13On the second visit Joseph made himself known to his brothers, and Joseph's family became known to Pharaoh. 14Then Joseph sent and invited his father Jacob and all his relatives to come to him, seventy-five in all; 15so Jacob went down to Egypt. He himself died there

a Gk *he*

	3739	1437	1398		2919		1473	01	2316
	ᾧ	ἐὰν	δουλεύσουσιν		κρινῶ		ἐγώ, ὁ		θεὸς
	in which if		they will slave		will judge		I,	the	God

3004	2532	3326	3778	1831		2532
εἶπεν,	καὶ	μετὰ	ταῦτα	ἐξελεύσονται		καὶ
said,	and	after	these	they will come out and		

3000		1473	1722	03	5117	3778	8	2532	1325
λατρεύσουσίν		μοι	ἐν	τῷ	τόπῳ	τούτῳ.		καὶ	ἔδωκεν
will serve		me	in		the	place this.		And	he gave

846	1242		4061		2532	3779	1080
αὐτῷ	διαθήκην		περιτομῆς·		καὶ	οὕτως	ἐγέννησεν
him	agreement		circumcision;		and	thusly	he gave birth

04	2464	2532	4059		846	07	2250	07
τὸν	Ἰσαὰκ	καὶ	περιέτεμεν		αὐτὸν	τῇ	ἡμέρᾳ	τῇ
the	Isaac	and	he circumcised		him	the	day	the

3590	2532	2464	04	2384	2532	2384	016	1427
ὀγδόῃ,	καὶ	Ἰσαὰκ	τὸν	Ἰακώβ,	καὶ	Ἰακὼβ	τοὺς	δώδεκα
eighth,	and	Isaac	the	Jacob,	and	Jacob	the	twelve

3966	9	2532	013	3966		2206		04
πατριάρχας.		Καὶ	οἱ	πατρίαρχαι		ζηλώσαντες		τὸν
father		And	the	father		having been the		
rulers.				rulers		jealous		

2501	591		1519	125		2532	1510	01	2316
Ἰωσὴφ	ἀπέδοντο		εἰς	Αἴγυπτον.		καὶ	ἦν	ὁ	θεὸς
Joseph	gave back		into	Egypt.		And	was	the	God

3326	846	10	2532	1807		846	1537	3956	018
μετ᾽	αὐτοῦ		καὶ	ἐξείλατο		αὐτὸν	ἐκ	πασῶν	τῶν
with	him		and	he lifted out		him	from	all	the

2347	846	2532	1325	846	5485	2532	4678
θλίψεων	αὐτοῦ	καὶ	ἔδωκεν	αὐτῷ	χάριν	καὶ	σοφίαν
afflictions	of him	and	gave	him	favor	and	wisdom

1726	5328	935	125	2532
ἐναντίον	Φαραὼ	βασιλέως	Αἰγύπτου	καὶ
in presence of	Pharaoh	king	of Egypt	and

2525	846	2233	1909	125	2532	1909
κατέστησεν	αὐτὸν	ἡγούμενον	ἐπ᾽	Αἴγυπτον	καὶ	[ἐφ᾽]
appointed	him	one leading	on	Egypt	and	on

3650	04	3624	846	11	2064	1161	3042	1909	3650
ὅλον	τὸν	οἶκον	αὐτοῦ.		ἦλθεν	δὲ	λιμὸς	ἐφ᾽	ὅλην
whole	the	house of him.			Came	but	famine	on	whole

08	125		2532	5477		2532	2347		3173		2532
τὴν	Αἴγυπτον		καὶ	Χανάαν		καὶ	θλῖψις		μεγάλη,		καὶ
the	Egypt		and	Canaan		and	affliction		great,		and

3756	2147		5527		013	3962	1473
οὐχ	ηὕρισκον		χορτάσματα		οἱ	πατέρες	ἡμῶν.
not	were finding		sustenances		the	fathers of us.	

12	191		1161	2384	1510	4618a	1519	125
	ἀκούσας		δὲ	Ἰακὼβ	ὄντα	σιτία	εἰς	Αἴγυπτον
	Having heard		but	Jacob	being	wheat	in	Egypt

1821		016	3962	1473	4413		13	2532	1722
ἐξαπέστειλεν		τοὺς	πατέρας	ἡμῶν	πρῶτον.			καὶ	ἐν
delegated out		the	fathers	of us	first.			And	in

011	1208	319		2501	015	80
τῷ	δευτέρῳ	ἀνεγνωρίσθη		Ἰωσὴφ	τοῖς	ἀδελφοῖς
the	second	was made known		Joseph	to the	brothers

846	2532	5318	1096	03	5328	09	1085
αὐτοῦ	καὶ	φανερὸν	ἐγένετο	τῷ	Φαραὼ	τὸ	γένος
of him	and	evident	it became	to the	Pharaoh	the	kind

02	2501	14	649		1161	2501
[τοῦ]	Ἰωσήφ.		ἀποστείλας		δὲ	Ἰωσὴφ
of the	Joseph.		Having delegated		but	Joseph

3333	2384	04	3962	846	2532	3956	08
μετεκαλέσατο	Ἰακὼβ	τὸν	πατέρα	αὐτοῦ	καὶ	πᾶσαν	τὴν
called for	Jacob	the	father	of him	and	all	the

4772	1722	5590	1440	4002	15	2532
συγγένειαν	ἐν	ψυχαῖς	ἑβδομήκοντα	πέντε.		καὶ
relative	in	souls	seventy	five.		And

2597	2384	1519	125	2532	5053	846
κατέβη	Ἰακὼβ	εἰς	Αἴγυπτον	καὶ	ἐτελεύτησεν	αὐτὸς
went down	Jacob	into	Egypt	and	died	himself

```
2532    013    3962      1473    16   2532    3346
καὶ    οἱ    πατέρες    ἡμῶν,        καὶ    μετετέθησαν
and    the   fathers    of us,       and    they were changed

1519    4966      2532   5087          1722   011   3418       3739
εἰς    Συχέμ   καὶ    ἐτέθησαν    ἐν    τῷ    μνήματι   ᾧ
into   Sychem  and    was set      in    the   grave      in which

5608        11        5092    694        3844    014   5207
ὠνήσατο   Ἀβραὰμ   τιμῆς   ἀργυρίου   παρὰ   τῶν   υἱῶν
paid price  Abraham   value   of silver    beside  the   sons

1697     1722   4966    17    2531      1161   1448     01    5550
Ἐμμὼρ   ἐν    Συχέμ.       Καθὼς    δὲ    ἤγγιζεν   ὁ    χρόνος
Hemmor   in    Sychem.       Just as    but    neared     the   time

06        1860          3739    3670        01     2316   03
τῆς    ἐπαγγελίας    ἧς    ὡμολόγησεν   ὁ    θεὸς   τῷ
of the   promise        which  confessed     the   God    to the

11          837        01    2992   2532   4129              1722
Ἀβραάμ,   ηὔξησεν   ὁ    λαὸς   καὶ   ἐπληθύνθη            ἐν
Abraham,    grew      the   people  and    were multiplied    in

125      18   891    3739   450       935        2087    1909
Αἰγύπτῳ       ἄχρι   οὗ    ἀνέστη   βασιλεὺς   ἕτερος  [ἐπ'
Egypt         until   which  stood up   king        other    on

125        3739   3756  3609a      04     2501         3778
Αἴγυπτον]  ὃς    οὐκ   ᾔδει     τὸν   Ἰωσήφ.   19  οὗτος
Egypt       which  not   had known  the   Joseph.        This one

2686              012   1085   1473    2559     016
κατασοφισάμενος   τὸ    γένος   ἡμῶν   ἐκάκωσεν   τοὺς
having used wisdom  the   kind    of us    did bad     the
to go against

3962         1473    010    4160     024   1025     1570      846
πατέρας    [ἡμῶν]  τοῦ   ποιεῖν   τὰ   βρέφη    ἔκθετα    αὐτῶν
fathers of us        the   to make   the   infants   set out    of them

1519   012   3361   2225              20   1722  3739   2540
εἰς    τὸ   μὴ   ζωογονεῖσθαι.           Ἐν    ᾧ    καιρῷ
into   the   not   to preserve life.        In    which  season

1080        3475    2532   1510   791        03       2316  3739
ἐγεννήθη   Μωϋσῆς   καὶ   ἦν    ἀστεῖος   τῷ    θεῷ·   ὃς
was born    Moses     and   he was  well-formed  to the  God;   who

397          3376     5140    1722  03   3624    02       3962
ἀνετράφη   μῆνας    τρεῖς   ἐν    τῷ   οἴκῳ   τοῦ    πατρός,
was nourished months   three   in    the  house   of the   father,

21   1620                1161   846     337        846     05
     ἐκτεθέντος         δὲ    αὐτοῦ   ἀνείλατο   αὐτὸν   ἡ
      having been set out  but    him     lifted up    him     the

2364       5328       2532   397          846     1438
θυγάτηρ   Φαραὼ   καὶ   ἀνεθρέψατο   αὐτὸν   ἑαυτῇ
daughter   of Pharaoh  and   she nourished   him     to herself

1519   5207    22   2532  3811                3475     1722
εἰς    υἱόν.        καὶ   ἐπαιδεύθη         Μωϋσῆς  [ἐν]
for    son.         And    was instructed     as a child  Moses

3956    4678       124          1510  1161  1415    1722   3056
πάσῃ   σοφίᾳ   Αἰγυπτίων,   ἦν    δὲ   δυνατὸς   ἐν    λόγοις
all     wisdom   of Egyptians,   he was  but   power       in    words

2532    2041    846         23   5613  1161  03              846
καὶ    ἔργοις   αὐτοῦ.          Ὡς    δὲ   ἐπληροῦτο        αὐτῷ
and     works    of him.           As    but   was being filled   to him

5063                5550     305       1909  08   2588
τεσσερακονταετὴς   χρόνος,   ἀνέβη   ἐπὶ   τὴν   καρδίαν
forty years          time,     it come up  on    the    heart

846      1980           016    80       846      016    5207
αὐτοῦ   ἐπισκέψασθαι   τοὺς   ἀδελφοὺς   αὐτοῦ   τοὺς   υἱοὺς
of him    to look on      the    brothers    of him    the    sons

2474       24   2532  3708         5100  91
Ἰσραήλ.        καὶ   ἰδὼν       τινα   ἀδικούμενον
Israel.         And    having seen   some   being done unright

292         2532   4160        1557          03
ἠμύνατο   καὶ   ἐποίησεν   ἐκδίκησιν      τῷ
he defended  and   did         bring out right  to the one

2669             3960       04    124           25   3543
καταπονουμένῳ   πατάξας   τὸν   Αἰγύπτιον.       ἐνόμιζεν
being worn down   having hit  the   Egyptian.         He thought
```

as well as our ancestors, [16]and their bodies[a] were brought back to Shechem and laid in the tomb that Abraham had bought for a sum of silver from the sons of Hamor in Shechem.

[17] "But as the time drew near for the fulfillment of the promise that God had made to Abraham, our people in Egypt increased and multiplied [18]until another king who had not known Joseph ruled over Egypt. [19]He dealt craftily with our race and forced our ancestors to abandon their infants so that they would die. [20]At this time Moses was born, and he was beautiful before God. For three months he was brought up in his father's house; [21]and when he was abandoned, Pharaoh's daughter adopted him and brought him up as her own son. [22]So Moses was instructed in all the wisdom of the Egyptians and was powerful in his words and deeds.

[23] "When he was forty years old, it came into his heart to visit his relatives, the Israelites.[b] [24]When he saw one of them being wronged, he defended the oppressed man and avenged him by striking down the Egyptian. [25]He supposed that

a Gk they
b Gk his brothers, the sons of Israel

his kinsfolk would under-
stand that God through
him was rescuing them, but
they did not understand.
26The next day he came to
some of them as they were
quarreling and tried to
reconcile them, saying,
'Men, you are brothers;
why do you wrong each
other?' 27But the man who
was wronging his neighbor
pushed Moses*a* aside,
saying, 'Who made you a
ruler and a judge over us?
28Do you want to kill me
as you killed the Egyptian
yesterday?' 29When he
heard this, Moses fled and
became a resident alien in
the land of Midian. There
he became the father of two
sons.

30 "Now when forty
years had passed, an angel
appeared to him in the
wilderness of Mount Sinai,
in the flame of a burning
bush. 31When Moses saw it,
he was amazed at the sight;
and as he approached to
look, there came the voice
of the Lord: 32'I am the
God of your ancestors, the
God of Abraham, Isaac,
and Jacob.' Moses began
to tremble and did not dare
to look. 33Then the Lord
said to him, 'Take off the
sandals from your feet, for
the place where you are
standing is holy ground.
34I have surely seen the
mistreatment of my people
who are in Egypt and have
heard

a Gk *him*

1161	4920		016	80		846		3754	01	2316
δὲ	συνιέναι		τοὺς	ἀδελφοὺς	[αὐτοῦ]	ὅτι	ὁ	θεὸς
but	to understand	the	brothers	of him	that	the	God

1223 5495 846 1325 4991 846 013
διὰ χειρὸς αὐτοῦ δίδωσιν σωτηρίαν αὐτοῖς· οἱ
by hand of him gives deliverance to them; the

1161 3756 4920 **26** 07 5037 1897a 2250
δὲ οὐ συνῆκαν. τῇ τε ἐπιούσῃ ἡμέρᾳ
but not they understood. In the but coming-on day

3708 846 3164 2532 4871a 846
ὤφθη αὐτοῖς μαχομένοις καὶ συνήλλασσεν αὐτοὺς
he was to them battling and he was changing them
seen together

1519 1515 3004 435 80 1510 2444
εἰς εἰρήνην εἰπών· ἄνδρες, ἀδελφοί ἐστε· ἱνατί
to peace saying; men, brothers you are; why

91 240 **27** 01 1161 91 04
ἀδικεῖτε ἀλλήλους; ὁ δὲ ἀδικῶν τὸν
do you unright one another? The but doing unright the

4139 683 846 3004 5101 1473 2525
πλησίον ἀπώσατο αὐτὸν εἰπών· τίς σε κατέστησεν
neighbor shoved off him saying; who you appointed

758 2532 1348 1909 1473 **28** 3361 337
ἄρχοντα καὶ δικαστὴν ἐφ' ἡμῶν; μὴ ἀνελεῖν
ruler and one making right on us? Not to kill

1473 1473 2309 3739 5158 337 2188a
με σὺ θέλεις ὃν τρόπον ἀνεῖλες ἐχθὲς
me you want which manner you killed yesterday

04 124 **29** 5343 1161 3475 1722 03 3056
τὸν Αἰγύπτιον; ἔφυγεν δὲ Μωϋσῆς ἐν τῷ λόγῳ
the Egyptian? Fled but Moses in the word

3778 2532 1096 3941 1722 1093 3099 3757
τούτῳ καὶ ἐγένετο πάροικος ἐν γῇ Μαδιάμ, οὗ
this and became transient in land Madiam, where

1080 5207 1417 **30** 2532 4137
ἐγέννησεν υἱοὺς δύο. Καὶ πληρωθέντων
he gave birth sons two. And having been filled

2094 5062 3708 846 1722 07 2048
ἐτῶν τεσσεράκοντα ὤφθη αὐτῷ ἐν τῇ ἐρήμῳ
years forty was seen to him in the desert

010 3735 4614 32 1722 5395 4442
τοῦ ὄρους Σινᾶ ἄγγελος ἐν φλογὶ πυρὸς
of the hill Sinai messenger in flame of fire

942 **31** 01 1161 3475 3708 2296
βάτου. ὁ δὲ Μωϋσῆς ἰδὼν ἐθαύμαζεν
thorn bush. The but Moses having seen was marveling

012 3705 4334 1161 846 2657
τὸ ὅραμα, προσερχομένου δὲ αὐτοῦ κατανοῆσαι
the sight, coming toward but him to think carefully

1096 5456 2962 **32** 1473 01 2316 014 3962
ἐγένετο φωνὴ κυρίου· ἐγὼ ὁ θεὸς τῶν πατέρων
became sound of master; I the God of the fathers

1473 01 2316 11 2532 2464 2532 2384
σου, ὁ θεὸς Ἀβραὰμ καὶ Ἰσαὰκ καὶ Ἰακώβ.
of you, the God Abraham and Isaac and Jacob.

1790 1161 1096 3475 3756 5111
ἔντρομος δὲ γενόμενος Μωϋσῆς οὐκ ἐτόλμα
Trembling but having become Moses not was daring

2657 **33** 3004 1161 846 01 2962 3089
κατανοῆσαι. εἶπεν δὲ αὐτῷ ὁ κύριος· λῦσον
to think carefully. Said but to him the Master; loose

012 5266 01 4228 1473 01 1063 5117 1909
τὸ ὑπόδημα τῶν ποδῶν σου, ὁ γὰρ τόπος ἐφ'
the sandal of the feet of you, the for place on

3739 2476 1093 40 1510 **34** 3708
ᾧ ἕστηκας γῆ ἁγία ἐστίν. ἰδὼν
which you have stood land holy is. Having seen

3708 08 2561 02 2992 1473 02 1722 125
εἶδον τὴν κάκωσιν τοῦ λαοῦ μου τοῦ ἐν Αἰγύπτῳ
I saw the badness of the people of me the in Egypt

2532 02	4726	846	191	2532 2597
καὶ τοῦ	στεναγμοῦ	αὐτῶν	ἤκουσα,	καὶ κατέβην
and the	groaning	of them	I heard,	and I went down

1807 846 2532 3568 1204 649 1473
ἐξελέσθαι αὐτούς· καὶ νῦν δεῦρο ἀποστείλω σε
to lift out them; and now come I might delegate you

1519 125 **35** 3778 04 3475 3739 720
εἰς Αἴγυπτον. Τοῦτον τὸν Μωϋσῆν ὃν ἠρνήσαντο
to Egypt. This the Moses whom they denied

3004 5101 1473 2525 758 2532
εἰπόντες· τίς σε κατέστησεν ἄρχοντα καὶ
having said, who you appointed ruler and

1348 3778 01 2316 2532 758 2532
δικαστήν; τοῦτον ὁ θεὸς [καὶ] ἄρχοντα καὶ
one making right? This the God both ruler and

3086 649 4862 5495 32 02
λυτρωτὴν ἀπέσταλκεν σὺν χειρὶ ἀγγέλου τοῦ
redeemer has delegated with hand of messenger of the

3708 846 1722 07 942 **36** 3778 1806 846
ὀφθέντος αὐτῷ ἐν τῇ βάτῳ. οὗτος ἐξήγαγεν αὐτοὺς
having him in the thorn This led out them
been seen bush. one

4160 5059 2532 4592 1722 1093 125 2532
ποιήσας τέρατα καὶ σημεῖα ἐν γῇ Αἰγύπτῳ καὶ
having done marvels and signs in land Egypt and

1722 2063 2281 2532 1722 07 2048 2094
ἐν ἐρυθρᾷ θαλάσσῃ καὶ ἐν τῇ ἐρήμῳ ἔτη
in Red Sea and in the desert years

5062 **37** 3778 1510 01 3475 01
τεσσεράκοντα. οὗτός ἐστιν ὁ Μωϋσῆς ὁ
forty. This is the Moses the one

3004 015 5207 2474 4396 1473
εἶπας τοῖς υἱοῖς Ἰσραήλ· προφήτην ὑμῖν
having said to the sons Israel; spokesman to you

450 01 2316 1537 014 80 1473 5613
ἀναστήσει ὁ θεὸς ἐκ τῶν ἀδελφῶν ὑμῶν ὡς
will stand up the God from the brothers of you as

1473 **38** 3778 1510 01 1096 1722 07
ἐμέ. οὗτός ἐστιν ὁ γενόμενος ἐν τῇ
me. This one is the one becoming in the

1577 1722 07 2048 3326 02 32 02
ἐκκλησίᾳ ἐν τῇ ἐρήμῳ μετὰ τοῦ ἀγγέλου τοῦ
assembly in the desert with the messenger the one

2980 846 1722 011 3735 4614 2532 014 3962
λαλοῦντος αὐτῷ ἐν τῷ ὄρει Σινᾶ καὶ τῶν πατέρων
speaking to him in the hill Sinai and the fathers

1473 3739 1209 3051 2198 1325 1473
ἡμῶν, ὃς ἐδέξατο λόγια ζῶντα δοῦναι ἡμῖν,
of us, who welcomed sayings living to give to us,

39 3739 3756 2309 5255 1096 013
ᾧ οὐκ ἠθέλησαν ὑπήκοοι γενέσθαι οἱ
to whom not they wanted obedient to become the

3962 1473 235 683 2532 4762 1722
πατέρες ἡμῶν, ἀλλὰ ἀπώσαντο καὶ ἐστράφησαν ἐν
fathers of us, but they shoved off and were turned in

019 2588 846 1519 125 **40** 3004 03
ταῖς καρδίαις αὐτῶν εἰς Αἴγυπτον εἰπόντες τῷ
the hearts of them to Egypt having said to the

2 4160 1473 2316 3739 4313
Ἀαρών· ποίησον ἡμῖν θεοὺς οἳ προπορεύσονται
Aaron; make us gods which will travel before

1473 01 1063 3475 3778 3739 1806 1473 1537
ἡμῶν· ὁ γὰρ Μωϋσῆς οὗτος, ὃς ἐξήγαγεν ἡμᾶς ἐκ
us; the for Moses this, who led out us from

1093 125 3756 3609a 5101 1096 846
γῆς Αἰγύπτου, οὐκ οἴδαμεν τί ἐγένετο αὐτῷ.
land of Egypt, not we know what it became to him.

41 2532 3447 1722 019 2250 1565
καὶ ἐμοσχοποίησαν ἐν ταῖς ἡμέραις ἐκείναις
·And they made a calf in the days those

their groaning, and I have come down to rescue them. Come now, I will send you to Egypt.'

35 "It was this Moses whom they rejected when they said, 'Who made you a ruler and a judge?' and whom God now sent as both ruler and liberator through the angel who appeared to him in the bush. 36 He led them out, having performed wonders and signs in Egypt, at the Red Sea, and in the wilderness for forty years. 37 This is the Moses who said to the Israelites, 'God will raise up a prophet for you from your own people[a] as he raised me up.' 38 He is the one who was in the congregation in the wilderness with the angel who spoke to him at Mount Sinai, and with our ancestors; and he received living oracles to give to us. 39 Our ancestors were unwilling to obey him; instead, they pushed him aside, and in their hearts they turned back to Egypt, 40 saying to Aaron, 'Make gods for us who will lead the way for us; as for this Moses who led us out from the land of Egypt, we do not know what has happened to him.' 41 At that time they made a calf,

a Gk your brothers

offered a sacrifice to the idol, and reveled in the works of their hands. [42] But God turned away from them and handed them over to worship the host of heaven, as it is written in the book of the prophets:

'Did you offer to me slain victims and sacrifices forty years in the wilderness, O house of Israel?
[43] No; you took along the tent of Moloch, and the star of your god Rephan, the images that you made to worship; so I will remove you beyond Babylon.'

[44] "Our ancestors had the tent of testimony in the wilderness, as God[a] directed when he spoke to Moses, ordering him to make it according to the pattern he had seen. [45] Our ancestors in turn brought it in with Joshua when they dispossessed the nations that God drove out before our ancestors. And it was there until the time of David, [46] who found favor with God and asked that he might find a dwelling place for the house of Jacob.[b] [47] But it was Solomon who built a house for him. [48] Yet the Most High does not dwell in houses made with human hands;[c] as the prophet says,
[49] 'Heaven is my throne, and the earth is my footstool.
What kind of house will you build for me, says the Lord,

[a] Gk he
[b] Other ancient authorities read for the God of Jacob
[c] Gk with hands

2532	321	2378	011	1497	2532
καὶ	ἀνήγαγον	θυσίαν	τῷ	εἰδώλῳ	καὶ
and	led up	sacrifice	to the	idol	and

2165		1722	023	2041	018	5495	846
εὐφραίνοντο		ἐν	τοῖς	ἔργοις	τῶν	χειρῶν	αὐτῶν.
were being merry		in	the	works	of the	hands	of them.

42 | 4762 | 1161 | 01 | 2316 | 2532 | 3860 | | 846 |
| ἔστρεψεν | δὲ | ὁ | θεὸς | καὶ | παρέδωκεν | | αὐτοὺς |
| Turned | but | the | God | and | gave over | | them |

3000		07	4756	02	3772	2531
λατρεύειν		τῇ	στρατιᾷ	τοῦ	οὐρανοῦ	καθὼς
to serve		the	army	of the	heaven	just as

1125		1722	976	014	4396	3361
γέγραπται		ἐν	βίβλῳ	τῶν	προφητῶν·	μὴ
it has been written		in	book	of the	spokesmen;	not

4968	2532	2378	4374	1473	2094
σφάγια	καὶ	θυσίας	προσηνέγκατέ	μοι	ἔτη
slaughters	and	sacrifices	you offered	me	years

5062		1722	07	2048	3624	2474		**43**	2532
τεσσεράκοντα		ἐν	τῇ	ἐρήμῳ,	οἶκος	Ἰσραήλ;			καὶ
forty		in	the	desert,	house	Israel?			And

353		08	4633	02	3434	3522	012	798
ἀνελάβετε		τὴν	σκηνὴν	τοῦ	Μόλοχ	καὶ	τὸ	ἄστρον
you took up		the	tent	of the	Moloch	and	the	star

02	2316	1473	4468a	016	5179	3739
τοῦ	θεοῦ	[ὑμῶν]	Ῥαιφάν,	τοὺς	τύπους	οὓς
of the	god	of you	Raiphan,	the	examples	which

4160	4352	846	2532	3351
ἐποιήσατε	προσκυνεῖν	αὐτοῖς,	καὶ	μετοικιῶ
you made	to worship	them,	and	I will change home

1473	1900	897		**44**	05	4633	010	3142
ὑμᾶς	ἐπέκεινα	Βαβυλῶνος.			Ἡ	σκηνὴ	τοῦ	μαρτυρίου
you	beyond	Babylon.			The	tent	of the	testimony

1510	015	3962	1473	1722	07	2048	2531
ἦν	τοῖς	πατράσιν	ἡμῶν	ἐν	τῇ	ἐρήμῳ	καθὼς
was	to the	fathers	of us	in	the	desert	just as

1299	01	2980	00	9475	4160	846
διετάξατο	ὁ	λαλῶν	τῷ	Μωϋσῇ	ποιῆσαι	αὐτὴν
directed	the	one speaking	to the	Moses	to make	it

2596	04	5179	3739	3708		**45**	3739	2532
κατὰ	τὸν	τύπον	ὃν	ἑωράκει.			ἣν	καὶ
according to	the	example	which	he had seen;			which	also

1521	1237		013	3962	1473	3326	2424
εἰσήγαγον	διαδεξάμενοι		οἱ	πατέρες	ἡμῶν	μετὰ	Ἰησοῦ
led into	having welcomed thoroughly		the	fathers	of us	with	Jesus

1722	07	2697	022	1484	3739	1856
ἐν	τῇ	κατασχέσει	τῶν	ἐθνῶν,	ὧν	ἐξῶσεν
in	the	possession	of the	nations,	whom	pushed out

01	2316	575	4383	014	3962	1473	2193	018
ὁ	θεὸς	ἀπὸ	προσώπου	τῶν	πατέρων	ἡμῶν	ἕως	τῶν
the	God	from	face	of the	fathers	of us	until	the

2250	1160a		3739	2147	5485	1799	02	2316
ἡμερῶν	Δαυίδ,	**46**	ὃς	εὗρεν	χάριν	ἐνώπιον	τοῦ	θεοῦ
days	David,		who	found	favor	before	the	God

2532	154	2147	4638	03	3624	2384
καὶ	ᾐτήσατο	εὑρεῖν	σκήνωμα	τῷ	οἴκῳ	Ἰακώβ.
and	he asked	to find	tent	the	house	Jacob.

47 | 4672 | 1161 | 3618 | 846 | 3624 | | 235 | 3756 |
| Σολομὼν | δὲ | οἰκοδόμησεν | αὐτῷ | οἶκον. | **48** | ἀλλ᾽ | οὐχ |
| Solomon | but | built | to him | house. | | But | not |

01	5310	1722	5499	2730	2531	01
ὁ	ὕψιστος	ἐν	χειροποιήτοις	κατοικεῖ,	καθὼς	ὁ
the	highest	in	handmades	resides,	just as	the

4396	3004		49	01	3772	1473	2362	05	1161
προφήτης	λέγει·			ὁ	οὐρανός	μοι	θρόνος,	ἡ	δὲ
spokesman	says,			the	heaven	to me	throne,	the	but

1093	5286	014	4228	1473	4169	3624
γῆ	ὑποπόδιον	τῶν	ποδῶν	μου·	ποῖον	οἶκον
land	footstool	of the	feet	of me;	what kind	house

```
3618              1473  3004   2962   2228 5101  5117  06
οἰκοδομήσετέ     μοι, λέγει κύριος, ἢ τίς  τόπος τῆς
will you build me,  says  Master, or what place of the
2663             1473      3780 05  5495 1473   4160
καταπαύσεώς     μου;  50  οὐχὶ ἡ  χείρ μου   ἐποίησεν
complete stop of me?  Not the  hand of me made
3778  3956        4644                  2532 564
ταῦτα πάντα;  51 Σκληροτράχηλοι   καὶ ἀπερίτμητοι
these all?       Hard-necked ones and uncircumcised
2588         2532 023    3775 1473  104     011   4151
καρδίαις καὶ τοῖς ὠσίν, ὑμεῖς ἀεὶ  τῷ   πνεύματι
in hearts and in the ears, you  always in the spirit
011 40  496              5613 013 3962    1473   2532
τῷ ἁγίῳ ἀντιπίπτετε   ὡς  οἱ πατέρες ὑμῶν  καὶ
the holy you fall against as  the fathers of you also
1473     52 5101  014     4396       3756 1377    013
ὑμεῖς.      τίνα τῶν   προφητῶν οὐκ ἐδίωξαν οἱ
you.       Which of the spokesmen not  pursued the
3962   1473  2532 615        016
πατέρες ὑμῶν; καὶ ἀπέκτειναν τοὺς
fathers of you? And they killed the ones
4293                4012  06  1660     02
προκαταγγείλαντας  περὶ τῆς ἐλεύσεως τοῦ
having proclaimed before about the coming  of the
1342      3739 3568 1473  4273      2532 5406
δικαίου, οὗ  νῦν  ὑμεῖς προδόται καὶ φονεῖς
right,   whom now  you  traitors and murderers
1096        53 3748   2983     04  3551 1519 1296
ἐγένεσθε,     οἵτινες ἐλάβετε τὸν νόμον εἰς διαταγὰς
became,       who  received the law  in  directions
32         2532 3756 5442      54  191      1161
ἀγγέλων   καὶ οὐκ ἐφυλάξατε.    Ἀκούοντες δὲ
of messengers and not you guarded.  Hearing  but
3778  1282                019     2588
ταῦτα διεπρίοντο              ταῖς καρδίαις
these they were being sawn through in the hearts
846      2532 1031      016  3599  1909 846
αὐτῶν  καὶ ἔβρυχον  τοὺς ὀδόντας ἐπ' αὐτόν.
of them and were grinding the teeth  on  him.
   5225        1161 4134   4151      40   816
55 ὑπάρχων  δὲ  πλήρης πνεύματος ἁγίου ἀτενίσας
   Existing but  full   of spirit holy having stared
1519 04  3772   3708 1391    2316   2532 2424
εἰς τὸν οὐρανὸν εἶδεν δόξαν θεοῦ καὶ Ἰησοῦν
into the heaven he saw splendor of God and Jesus
2476       1537 1188   02      2316  56 2532 3004
ἑστῶτα   ἐκ δεξιῶν τοῦ  θεοῦ     καὶ εἶπεν·
having stood from right of the God    and said;
2400 2334   016  3772    1272
ἰδοὺ θεωρῶ τοὺς οὐρανοὺς διηνοιγμένους
look I watch the heavens having been completely opened
2532 04  5207 02    444       1537 1188  2476
καὶ τὸν υἱὸν τοῦ ἀνθρώπου ἐκ δεξιῶν ἑστῶτα
and the son of the man  from right having stood
02  2316   57 2896      1161 5456     3173
τοῦ θεοῦ.    κράξαντες δὲ  φωνῇ   μεγάλῃ
the God.      Having shouted but in sound great
4912         024 3775 846     2532 3729
συνέσχον   τὰ ὦτα αὐτῶν καὶ ὥρμησαν
they held together the ears of them and rushed
3661       1909 846    58 2532 1544
ὁμοθυμαδὸν ἐπ' αὐτὸν    καὶ ἐκβαλόντες
with one mind on  him     and having thrown out
1854   06  4172   3036                2532 013
ἔξω  τῆς πόλεως ἐλιθοβόλουν.       καὶ οἱ
outside the city  they were throwing stones. And the
3144      659     024 2440    846     3844 016
μάρτυρες ἀπέθεντο τὰ ἱμάτια αὐτῶν παρὰ τοὺς
testifiers set off  the clothes of them along the
```

or what is the place of my rest?

[50] Did not my hand make all these things?'

51 "You stiff-necked people, uncircumcised in heart and ears, you are forever opposing the Holy Spirit, just as your ancestors used to do. [52] Which of the prophets did your ancestors not persecute? They killed those who foretold the coming of the Righteous One, and now you have become his betrayers and murderers. [53] You are the ones that received the law as ordained by angels, and yet you have not kept it."

54 When they heard these things, they became enraged and ground their teeth at Stephen.[a] [55] But filled with the Holy Spirit, he gazed into heaven and saw the glory of God and Jesus standing at the right hand of God. [56] "Look," he said, "I see the heavens opened and the Son of Man standing at the right hand of God!" [57] But they covered their ears, and with a loud shout all rushed together against him. [58] Then they dragged him out of the city and began to stone him; and the witnesses laid their coats at the

---

[a] Gk him

feet of a young man named Saul. [59]While they were stoning Stephen, he prayed, "Lord Jesus, receive my spirit." [60]Then he knelt down and cried out in a loud voice, "Lord, do not hold this sin against them." When he had said this, he died.[a] [8:1]And Saul approved of their killing him.

That day a severe persecution began against the church in Jerusalem, and all except the apostles were scattered throughout the countryside of Judea and Samaria. [2]Devout men buried Stephen and made loud lamentation over him. [3]But Saul was ravaging the church by entering house after house; dragging off both men and women, he committed them to prison.

[4]Now those who were scattered went from place to place, proclaiming the word. [5]Philip went down to the city[b] of Samaria and proclaimed the Messiah[c] to them. [6]The crowds with one accord listened eagerly to what was said by Philip, hearing and seeing the signs that he did, [7]for unclean spirits,

[a] Gk fell asleep
[b] Other ancient authorities read a city
[c] Or the Christ

4228   3494   2564   4569   2532
πόδας νεανίου   καλούμενου   Σαύλου,   59 καὶ
feet of young man being called   Saul,   and

3036   04   4736   1941   2532 3004
ἐλιθοβόλουν   τὸν Στέφανον ἐπικαλούμενον καὶ λέγοντα·
they were   the Stephan   one calling   and saying;
throwing stones   on

2962   2424   1209   012 4151   1473   5087
κύριε 'Ιησοῦ, δέξαι τὸ πνεῦμά μου. 60 θεὶς
Master Jesus, welcome the spirit of me.   Having set

1161 024 1119 2896   5456   3173   2962   3361
δὲ τὰ γόνατα ἔκραξεν φωνῇ μεγάλῃ· κύριε, μὴ
but the knees he shouted sound great; Master, not

2476   846   3778 08 266   2532
στήσῃς   αὐτοῖς ταύτην τὴν ἁμαρτίαν. καὶ
you might stand to them this   the sin.   And

3778 3004   2837   8:1 4569 1161 1510
τοῦτο εἰπὼν ἐκοιμήθη.   Σαῦλος δὲ ἦν
this having said he slept. Saul   but was+

4909   07   336   846
συνευδοκῶν   τῇ   ἀναιρέσει αὐτοῦ.
+thinking well together in the killing of him.
well together

1096   1161 1722 1565   07   2250   1375
'Εγένετο   δὲ ἐν ἐκείνῃ τῇ ἡμέρᾳ διωγμὸς
It became but in that   the day   persecution

3173 1909 08 1577   08 1722 2414
μέγας ἐπὶ τὴν ἐκκλησίαν τὴν ἐν 'Ιεροσολύμοις,
great on the assembly the in Jerusalem,

3956   1161 1289   2596 020 5561
πάντες δὲ διεσπάρησαν   κατὰ τὰς χώρας
all   but were sown thoroughly by the countries

06   2449   2532 4540   4133   014 652
τῆς 'Ιουδαίας καὶ Σαμαρείας πλὴν τῶν ἀποστόλων.
of the Judea and Samaria except the delegates.

4792   1161 04 4736   435   2126
2 συνεκόμισαν δὲ τὸν Στέφανον ἄνδρες εὐλαβεῖς
  Obtained together but the Stephan men   reverent

2532 4160   2870   3173 1909 846   4569 1161
καὶ ἐποίησαν κοπετὸν μέγαν ἐπ' αὐτῷ. 3 Σαῦλος δὲ
and made   mourning great on him.   Saul   but

3075   08 1577   2596 016 3624
ἐλυμαίνετο τὴν ἐκκλησίαν κατὰ τοὺς οἴκους
was ravaging the assembly by   the houses

1531   4951 5037 435   2532 1135
εἰσπορευόμενος, σύρων τε ἄνδρας καὶ γυναῖκας
traveling in, dragging both men and women

3860   1519 5438   013   3303   3767
παρεδίδου εἰς φυλακήν. 4 Οἱ μὲν   οὖν
he was giving over into guard. The ones indeed then

1289   1330   2097   04 3056
διασπαρέντες διῆλθον εὐαγγελιζόμενοι τὸν λόγον.
having been sown went telling good   the word.
thoroughly   through message

5376   1161 2718   1519 08   4172
5 Φίλιππος δὲ κατελθὼν εἰς [τὴν] πόλιν
  Philip   but having gone down into the city

06   4540   2784   846   04 5547
τῆς Σαμαρείας ἐκήρυσσεν αὐτοῖς τὸν Χριστόν.
of the Samaria announced to them the Christ.

4337   1161 013 3793   023 3004
6 προσεῖχον δὲ οἱ ὄχλοι τοῖς λεγομένοις
  Were holding to but the crowds to the being said

5259 02 5376   3661   1722 011 191   846
ὑπὸ τοῦ Φιλίππου ὁμοθυμαδὸν ἐν τῷ ἀκούειν αὐτοὺς
by the Philip   with one mind in the to hear them

2532 991   024 4592 3739 4160   4183 1063
καὶ βλέπειν τὰ σημεῖα ἃ ἐποίει.   7 πολλοὶ γὰρ
and to see the signs that he was doing. Many   for

```
014        2192        4151       169        994            5456
τῶν        ἐχόντων     πνεύματα   ἀκάθαρτα   βοῶντα         φωνῇ
of the     ones having spirits    unclean    crying aloud   sound
3173       1831        4183       1161       3886           2532  5560
μεγάλη     ἐξήρχοντο,  πολλοὶ δὲ  παραλελυμένοι καὶ          χωλοὶ
great      were coming many    but having been    also       lame
           out,                 paralyzed
2323              1096       1161   4183    5479  1722  07
ἐθεραπεύθησαν·  8 ἐγένετο δὲ  πολλὴ χαρὰ ἐν   τῇ
were healed;      became  but  much  joy  in   the
4172   1565       435   1161   5100  3686        4613
πόλει ἐκείνη.   9 Ἀνὴρ δέ   τις  ὀνόματι        Σίμων
city   that.      Man  but  some in name         Simon
4391                  1722 07   4172  3096
προϋπῆρχεν           ἐν    τῇ  πόλει μαγεύων
was existing before  in   the  city  +practicing magic
2532  1839      012  1484      06    4540      3004
καὶ  ἐξιστάνων  τὸ  ἔθνος  τῆς  Σαμαρείας,  λέγων
and  +amazing   the nation of the Samaria,   saying
1510   5100 1438     3173      3739      4337
εἶναί  τινα ἑαυτὸν  μέγαν,  10 ᾧ        προσεῖχον
to be some himself  great,     to whom were holding to
3956   575   3398    2193   3173    3004        3778  1510
πάντες ἀπὸ  μικροῦ ἕως  μεγάλου λέγοντες·  οὗτός ἐστιν
all    from small  until great   saying;     this  is
05    1411    02      2316 05   2564            3173
ἡ    δύναμις τοῦ    θεοῦ ἡ  καλουμένη        μεγάλη.
the  power   of the  God  the one being called great.
    4337                     1161 846      1223       012 2425
 11 προσεῖχον               δὲ  αὐτῷ  διὰ       τὸ ἱκανῷ
    They were holding to but to him through the enough
5550  019    3095      1839          846       3753
χρόνῳ ταῖς  μαγείαις ἐξεστακέναι  αὐτούς.  12 ὅτε
time   in the magic   to have amazed them.    When
1161  4100        03    5376     2097
δὲ   ἐπίστευσαν τῷ  Φιλίππῳ εὐαγγελιζομένῳ
but  they trusted the Philip  telling good message
4012  06   932         02    2316 2532 010      3686
περὶ τῆς βασιλείας τοῦ   θεοῦ καὶ  τοῦ  ὀνόματος
about the kingdom  of the God  and  of the name
2424   5547     907         435        5037 2532
Ἰησοῦ Χριστοῦ, ἐβαπτίζοντο ἄνδρες τε   καὶ
Jesus Christ,   were being immersed men both and
1135        01   1161  4613   2532 846    4100
γυναῖκες. 13 ὁ  δὲ  Σίμων καὶ  αὐτὸς ἐπίστευσεν
women.      The but Simon even himself trusted
2532 907            1510        4342
καὶ βαπτισθεὶς    ἦν         προσκαρτερῶν
and having been immersed he was+ +remaining constant
03    5376       2334      5037 4592    2532 1411
τῷ   Φιλίππῳ, θεωρῶν   τε  σημεῖα καὶ  δυνάμεις
to the Philip,  watching both signs and  powers
3173    1096       1839           191       1161
μεγάλας γινομένας ἐξίστατο.  14 Ἀκούσαντες δὲ
great   becoming  he was amazed. Having heard but
013 1722 2414       652         3754 1209
οἱ  ἐν  Ἱεροσολύμοις ἀπόστολοι ὅτι  δέδεκται
the in   Jerusalem    delegates that had welcomed
05  4540       04  3056  02    2316  649        4314
ἡ   Σαμάρεια τὸν λόγον τοῦ  θεοῦ, ἀπέστειλαν πρὸς
the Samaria  the word of the God,  delegated  to
846    4074    2532 2491       3748       2597
αὐτοὺς Πέτρον καὶ Ἰωάννην,  15 οἵτινες καταβάντες
them    Peter  and John,       who    having come down
4336            4012 846   3704     2983
προσηύξαντο περὶ αὐτῶν ὅπως    λάβωσιν
prayed        about them so that they might receive
4151   40       3764       1063 1510    1909  3762
πνεῦμα ἅγιον· 16 οὐδέπω   γὰρ ἦν    ἐπ' οὐδενὶ
spirit holy;    but not yet for it was+ on  no one
```

crying with loud shrieks, came out of many who were possessed; and many others who were paralyzed or lame were cured. [8]So there was great joy in that city.

[9]Now a certain man named Simon had previously practiced magic in the city and amazed the people of Samaria, saying that he was someone great. [10]All of them, from the least to the greatest, listened to him eagerly, saying, "This man is the power of God that is called Great." [11]And they listened eagerly to him because for a long time he had amazed them with his magic. [12]But when they believed Philip, who was proclaiming the good news about the kingdom of God and the name of Jesus Christ, they were baptized, both men and women. [13]Even Simon himself believed. After being baptized, he stayed constantly with Philip and was amazed when he saw the signs and great miracles that took place.

[14]Now when the apostles at Jerusalem heard that Samaria had accepted the word of God, they sent Peter and John to them. [15]The two went down and prayed for them that they might receive the Holy Spirit [16](for as yet the Spirit

had not come[a] upon any of them; they had only been baptized in the name of the Lord Jesus. [17]Then Peter and John[b] laid their hands on them, and they received the Holy Spirit. [18]Now when Simon saw that the Spirit was given through the laying on of the apostles' hands, he offered them money, [19]saying, "Give me also this power so that anyone on whom I lay my hands may receive the Holy Spirit." [20]But Peter said to him, "May your silver perish with you, because you thought you could obtain God's gift with money! [21]You have no part or share in this, for your heart is not right before God. [22]Repent therefore of this wickedness of yours, and pray to the Lord that, if possible, the intent of your heart may be forgiven you. [23]For I see that you are in the gall of bitterness and the chains of wickedness." [24]Simon answered, "Pray for me to the Lord, that nothing of what you[c] have said may happen to me."

[25] Now after Peter and John[d] had testified and spoken the word of the Lord, they returned to

[a] Gk fallen
[b] Gk they
[c] The Greek word for you and the verb pray are plural
[d] Gk after they

846	1968		3441	1161	907		5225
αὐτῶν	ἐπιπεπτωκός,		μόνον	δὲ	βεβαπτισμένοι		ὑπῆρχον
of them	+having fallen on,		alone	but	+having been immersed		they were existing

1519	012	3686	02		2962	2424	17	5119
εἰς	τὸ	ὄνομα	τοῦ		κυρίου	Ἰησοῦ.		τότε
in		the name	of the		Master	Jesus.		Then

2007		020	5495	1909	846		2532
ἐπετίθεσαν		τὰς	χεῖρας	ἐπ᾽	αὐτοὺς		καὶ
they were setting		on the	hands	on	them		and

2983		4151	40	18	3708		1161	01
ἐλάμβανον		πνεῦμα	ἅγιον.		Ἰδὼν		δὲ	ὁ
were receiving		spirit	holy.		Having seen		but	the

4613	3754	1223	06	1936		018	5495	014
Σίμων	ὅτι	διὰ	τῆς	ἐπιθέσεως		τῶν	χειρῶν	τῶν
Simon	that	through	the	setting on		of the hands		of the

652	1325	09	4151	4374		846
ἀποστόλων	δίδοται	τὸ	πνεῦμα,	προσήνεγκεν		αὐτοῖς
delegates	is given	the	spirit,	he offered		to them

5536	19	3004	1325	2504	08	1849
χρήματα		λέγων·	δότε	κἀμοὶ	τὴν	ἐξουσίαν
wealth		saying,	give	also to me	the	authority

3778	2443	3739	1437	2007		020	5495
ταύτην	ἵνα	ᾧ	ἐὰν	ἐπιθῶ		τὰς	χεῖρας
this	that	on whom	if	I might set on		the hands

2983		4151	40	20	4074	1161	3004
λαμβάνῃ		πνεῦμα	ἅγιον.		Πέτρος	δὲ	εἶπεν
he might receive		spirit	holy.		Peter	but	said

4314	846	09	694		1473	4862	1473	1510	1519
πρὸς	αὐτόν·	τὸ	ἀργύριόν		σου	σὺν	σοὶ	εἴη	εἰς
to	him;	the	silver		of you	with	you	may be	for

684		3754	08	1431	02		2316	3543
ἀπώλειαν		ὅτι	τὴν	δωρεὰν	τοῦ		θεοῦ	ἐνόμισας
destruction		that	the	gift	of the		God	you thought

1223		5536	2932	21	3756	1510	1473	3310
διὰ		χρημάτων	κτᾶσθαι·		οὐκ	ἔστιν	σοι	μερὶς
through		wealth	to acquire;		not	it is	to you	part

3761	2819	1722	03	3056	3778	05	1063	2588
οὐδὲ	κλῆρος	ἐν	τῷ	λόγῳ	τούτῳ,	ἡ	γὰρ	καρδία
but not	lot	in	the	word	this,	the	for	heart

1473	3756	1510	2117a	1725		02	2316
σου	οὐκ	ἔστιν	εὐθεῖα	ἔναντι		τοῦ	θεοῦ.
of you	not	it is	straight	in presence		the	God.

22	3340	3767	575	06	2549	1473	3778	2532
	μετανόησον	οὖν	ἀπὸ	τῆς	κακίας	σου	ταύτης	καὶ
	Change mind	then	from	the	badness	of you	this	and

1189	02	2962	1487	686	863		1473
δεήθητι	τοῦ	κυρίου,	εἰ	ἄρα	ἀφεθήσεταί		σοι
beg	the	Master,	if	then	might be sent off		to you

05	1963	06		2588	1473	23	1519	1063	5521
ἡ	ἐπίνοια	on τῆς		καρδίας	σου,		εἰς	γὰρ	χολὴν
the	thought	of the		heart	of you,		into	for	gall

4088		2532	4886	93		3708	1473
πικρίας		καὶ	σύνδεσμον	ἀδικίας		ὁρῶ	σε
of bitterness		and	co-chain	of unright		I see	you

1510	611			1161	01	4613	3004	1189
ὄντα.	24 ἀποκριθεὶς			δὲ	ὁ	Σίμων	εἶπεν·	δεήθητε
being.	Having answered			but	the	Simon	said;	beg

1473	5228		1473	4314	04	2962	3704		3367
ὑμεῖς	ὑπὲρ		ἐμοῦ	πρὸς	τὸν	κύριον	ὅπως		μηδὲν
you	on behalf		of me	to	the	master	so that		nothing

1904		1909	1473	3739	3004		25	013
ἐπέλθῃ		ἐπ᾽	ἐμὲ	ὧν	εἰρήκατε.			Οἱ
might come on		on	me	of what	you have spoken.			The

3303	3767	1263			2532
μὲν	οὖν	διαμαρτυράμενοι			καὶ
indeed	then	ones having testified thoroughly			and

2980	04	3056	02	2962	5290
λαλήσαντες	τὸν	λόγον	τοῦ	κυρίου	ὑπέστρεφον
having spoken	the	word	of the	Master	were returning

```
1519    2414        4183 5037 2968        014      4541
εἰς   Ἱεροσόλυμα, πολλάς τε κώμας  τῶν    Σαμαριτῶν
to    Jerusalem,  many and villages of the Samaritans
2097                 32        1161 2962    2980
εὐηγγελίζοντο.  26 Ἄγγελος δὲ  κυρίου  ἐλάλησεν
were being told     Messenger but of Master spoke
good message.
4314 5376    3004   450      2532 4198    2596
πρὸς Φίλιππον λέγων· ἀνάστηθι καὶ πορεύου κατὰ
to   Philip   saying, stand up and travel  down
3314          1909 08 3598 08 2597        575
μεσημβρίαν ἐπὶ τὴν ὁδὸν τὴν καταβαίνουσαν ἀπὸ
midday      on  the way the one going down from
2419       1519 1048  3778 1510 2048       2532
Ἱερουσαλὴμ εἰς Γάζαν, αὕτη ἐστὶν ἔρημος. 27 καὶ
Jerusalem  into Gaza, this is    desert.   And
450          4198        2532 2400 435   128
ἀναστὰς    ἐπορεύθη.  καὶ ἰδοὺ ἀνὴρ Αἰθίοψ
having stood up he traveled. And look man Ethiopian
2135       1413     2582     938        128
εὐνοῦχος δυνάστης Κανδάκης βασιλίσσης Αἰθιόπων,
eunuch    power one Candace  queen    of Ethiopians,
3739 1510 1909 3956 06 1047      846      3739
ὃς   ἦν  ἐπὶ πάσης τῆς γάζης  αὐτῆς,  ὃς
who  was on  all   the treasure of her, who
2064      4352        1519 2419        28 1510      5037
ἐληλύθει προσκυνήσων εἰς Ἱερουσαλήμ,   ἦν        τε
had come worshiping in  Jerusalem,      he was+   but
5290         2532 2521    1909 010 716      846    2532
ὑποστρέφων καὶ καθήμενος ἐπὶ τοῦ ἅρματος αὐτοῦ καὶ
+returning and +sitting on  the chariot of him and
314         04  4396        2268      3004 1161 09
ἀνεγίνωσκεν τὸν προφήτην Ἠσαΐαν. 29 εἶπεν δὲ  τὸ
was reading the spokesman Isaiah.    Said but the
4151 03       5376      4334        2532 2853       011
πνεῦμα τῷ   Φιλίππῳ· πρόσελθε καὶ κολλήθητι τῷ
spirit to the Philip;  go toward and be joined to the
716   3778   30 4370        1161 01 5376
ἅρματι τούτῳ.   προσδραμὼν δὲ  ὁ  Φίλιππος
chariot this.    Having run toward but the Philip
191   846 314            2268      04 4396
ἤκουσεν αὐτοῦ ἀναγινώσκοντος Ἠσαΐαν τὸν προφήτην
heard  him   reading        Isaiah the spokesman
2532 3004   687 1065    1097      3739 314
καὶ εἶπεν· ἆρά γε  γινώσκεις ἃ  ἀναγινώσκεις;
and said;  then indeed know you what you read?
31 01 1161 3004    4459 1063 302 1410          1437 3361
ὁ  δὲ εἶπεν· πῶς γὰρ ἂν δυναίμην ἐὰν μὴ
The one but said; how for  -  may I be able except
5100 3594      1473 3870         5037 04 5376
τις ὁδηγήσει με; παρεκάλεσέν τε  τὸν Φίλιππον
some will guide me? He encouraged but the Philip
305        2523       4862 846   32 05 1161 4042
ἀναβάντα καθίσαι σὺν αὐτῷ.    ἡ δὲ  περιοχὴ
having gone up to sit with him. The but section
06  1124    3739 314          1510 3778 5613
τῆς γραφῆς ἦν  ἀνεγίνωσκεν ἦν αὕτη· ὡς
of the writing which he read was this; as
4263       1909 4967   71     2532 5613 286
πρόβατον ἐπὶ σφαγὴν ἤχθη καὶ ὡς ἀμνὸς
sheep     on  slaughter was led and as lamb
1726      02   2751            846     880
ἐναντίον τοῦ κείραντος    αὐτὸν ἄφωνος,
in presence of the one having sheared him soundless,
3779 3756 455      012 4750 846      33 1722 07
οὕτως οὐκ ἀνοίγει τὸ στόμα αὐτοῦ.   Ἐν  τῇ
thusly not he opens the mouth of him.    In  the
5014       846   05 2920   846    142
ταπεινώσει [αὐτοῦ] ἡ κρίσις αὐτοῦ ἤρθη·
humility  of him  the judgment of him is lifted up;
```

Jerusalem, proclaiming the good news to many villages of the Samaritans.

26 Then an angel of the Lord said to Philip, "Get up and go toward the south[a] to the road that goes down from Jerusalem to Gaza." (This is a wilderness road.) 27 So he got up and went. Now there was an Ethiopian eunuch, a court official of the Candace, queen of the Ethiopians, in charge of her entire treasury. He had come to Jerusalem to worship 28 and was returning home; seated in his chariot, he was reading the prophet Isaiah. 29 Then the Spirit said to Philip, "Go over to this chariot and join it." 30 So Philip ran up to it and heard him reading the prophet Isaiah. He asked, "Do you understand what you are reading?" 31 He replied, "How can I, unless someone guides me?" And he invited Philip to get in and sit beside him. 32 Now the passage of the scripture that he was reading was this:

"Like a sheep he was led
    to the slaughter,
and like a lamb silent
    before its shearer,
so he does not open
    his mouth.
33 In his humiliation justice
    was denied him.

a Or go at noon

Who can describe his
generation?
For his life is taken
away from the
earth."
³⁴The eunuch asked Philip,
"About whom, may I ask
you, does the prophet say
this, about himself or about
someone else?" ³⁵Then
Philip began to speak, and
starting with this scripture,
he proclaimed to him the
good news about Jesus.
³⁶As they were going along
the road, they came to
some water; and the eunuch
said, "Look, here is water!
What is to prevent me from
being baptized?"ᵃ ³⁸He
commanded the chariot
to stop, and both of them,
Philip and the eunuch,
went down into the water,
and Philipᵇ baptized him.
³⁹When they came up out
of the water, the Spirit of
the Lord snatched Philip
away; the eunuch saw him
no more, and went on his
way rejoicing. ⁴⁰But Philip
found himself at Azotus,
and as he was passing
through the region, he
proclaimed the good news
to all the towns until he
came to Caesarea.

CHAPTER 9

Meanwhile Saul, still
breathing threats and
murder against the disciples
of the Lord, went to the
high priest ²and asked
him for letters to the
synagogues at Damascus,
so that if

ᵃ Other ancient authorities add all
or most of verse 37, And Philip
said, "If you believe with all your
heart, you may." And he replied,
"I believe that Jesus Christ is the
Son of God."
ᵇ Gk he

```
08       1074         846       5101  1334              3754
τὴν    γενεὰν      αὐτοῦ    τίς   διηγήσεται;   ὅτι
the    generation of him    who   will narrate?  Because
142           575  06   1093    05    2222 846
αἴρεται     ἀπὸ  τῆς γῆς   ἡ    ζωὴ αὐτοῦ.
is lifted up  from the earth   the   life of him.
    611              1161 01    2135       03          5376
34 ἀποκριθεὶς     δὲ   ὁ   εὐνοῦχος  τῷ       Φιλίππῳ
   Having answered but  the  eunuch      to the Philip
3004    1189    1473 4012  5101  01  4396        3004
εἶπεν· δέομαί σου, περὶ  τίνος ὁ προφήτης λέγει
said,   I beg you,  about whom  the spokesman says
3778    4012 1438    2228 4012  2087    5100
τοῦτο; περὶ ἑαυτοῦ ἢ   περὶ  ἑτέρου τινός;
this?   About himself or   about  other  some?
    455              1161 01    5376     012 4750  846     2532
35 ἀνοίξας        δὲ   ὁ   Φίλιππος τὸ στόμα αὐτοῦ  καὶ
   Having opened but  the  Philip      the mouth of him and
757        575  06  1124     3778     2097          846
ἀρξάμενος ἀπὸ τῆς γραφῆς ταύτης εὐηγγελίσατο αὐτῷ
having      from the writing this   he told good to him
begun                                             message
04   2424        5613 1161 4198                     2596 08
τὸν Ἰησοῦν. 36 ὡς   δὲ   ἐπορεύοντο            κατὰ τὴν
the Jesus.      As   but  they were traveling   by   the
3598 2064        1909 5100 5204   2532 5346  01 2135
ὁδόν, ἦλθον   ἐπί τι  ὕδωρ,  καί φησιν ὁ εὐνοῦχος·
way,  they came on  some water, and says  the eunuch;
2400 5204   5101 2967    1473 907              38  2532
ἰδοὺ ὕδωρ, τί κωλύει με  βαπτισθῆναι;        καὶ
look water, what hinders me to be immersed? And
2753         2476        012 716   2532 2597
ἐκέλευσεν στῆναι  τὸ  ἅρμα  καὶ κατέβησαν
he commanded to stand the chariot and they went down
297         1519 012 5204     01 5037   5376       2532 01
ἀμφότεροι εἰς τὸ ὕδωρ,  ὅ  τε   Φίλιππος καὶ ὁ
both        into the water, the both Philip    and the
2135         2532 907          846      39 3753 1161
εὐνοῦχος, καὶ  ἐβάπτισεν αὐτόν.    ὅτε δὲ
eunuch,    and  he immersed him.   When but
305          1537 010 5204      4151   2962        726
ἀνέβησαν  ἐκ  τοῦ ὕδατος, πνεῦμα κυρίου  ἥρπασεν
they went up from the water,  spirit of Master seized
04   5376       2532 3756 3708  846      3765       01
τὸν Φίλιππον καὶ οὐκ  εἶδεν αὐτὸν οὐκέτι  ὁ
the Philip      and not  saw  him   no longer the
2135          4198             1063 08  3598 846
εὐνοῦχος, ἐπορεύετο       γὰρ τὴν ὁδὸν αὐτοῦ
eunuch,   he was traveling for  the way of him
5463          40 5376     1161 2147        1519  108      2532
χαίρων.       Φίλιππος δὲ εὑρέθη    εἰς Ἄζωτον· καὶ
rejoicing.    Philip   but was found in  Azotos; and
1330           2097                        020 4172
διερχόμενος εὐηγγελίζετο            τὰς πόλεις
going through he was telling good message the cities
3956 2193  010 2064     846  1519 2542      9:1    01
πάσας ἕως τοῦ ἐλθεῖν αὐτὸν εἰς Καισάρειαν.      Ὁ
all    until the to come him  into Caesarea.  The
1161 4569 2089  1709      547          2532 5408
δὲ  Σαῦλος ἔτι ἐμπνέων ἀπειλῆς     καὶ φόνου
but  Saul   still blowing in threatening and murder
1519 016 3101      02     2962   4334        03
εἰς τοὺς μαθητὰς τοῦ κυρίου, προσελθὼν τῷ
to   the learners of the Master, having come to the
749               154       3844 846   1992        1519
ἀρχιερεῖ   2 ᾐτήσατο παρ᾽ αὐτοῦ ἐπιστολὰς εἰς
ruler priest  he asked from him  letters    to
1154       4314 020 4864       3704    1437 5100
Δαμασκὸν πρὸς τὰς συναγωγάς, ὅπως ἐάν τινας
Damascus to  the synagogues, so that if  some
```

```
2147            06      3598  1510    435      5037 2532
εὕρῃ           τῆς    ὁδοῦ ὄντας, ἄνδρας τε   καὶ
he might find of the way being,  men      both and
1135      1210              71              1519
γυναῖκας, δεδεμένους     ἀγάγῃ        εἰς
women,    having been bound he might lead to
2419             1722 1161 011  4198        1096
Ἰερουσαλήμ.  3  Ἐν  δὲ  τῷ  πορεύεσθαι ἐγένετο
Jerusalem.   In   but  the to travel    it became
846    1448       07   1154      1810      5037 846
αὐτὸν ἐγγίζειν τῇ Δαμασκῷ, ἐξαίφνης τε   αὐτὸν
him   to near  the Damascus,  suddenly but  him
4015            5457  1537 02  3772       2532 4098
περιήστραψεν  φῶς ἐκ  τοῦ οὐρανοῦ  4 καὶ πεσὼν
glittered around light from the heaven    and  falling
1909 08  1093 191    5456    3004    846   4549
ἐπὶ τὴν γῆν ἤκουσεν φωνὴν λέγουσαν αὐτῷ· Σαοὺλ
on   the earth he heard sound saying   to him, Saul
4549   5101 1473 1377      3004    1161 5101
Σαούλ, τί με  διώκεις; 5 εἶπεν δέ· τίς
Saul,  why me  you pursue? He said but, who
1510   2962    01    1161 1473 1510 2424   3739
εἶ,    κύριε; ὁ  δέ· ἐγώ εἰμι Ἰησοῦς ὃν
are you, Master? The one but; I  am   Jesus whom
1473 1377    235  450     2532 1525      1519 08
σὺ διώκεις· 6 ἀλλὰ ἀνάστηθι καὶ εἴσελθε εἰς τὴν
you pursue·  but  stand up and  go into into the
4172  2532 2980             1473    3739 5101 1473
πόλιν καὶ λαληθήσεταί    σοι    ὅ  τί σε
city  and  it will be spoken to you that what you
1163       4160       013 1161 435      013
δεῖ       ποιεῖν. 7 οἱ δὲ ἄνδρες οἱ
it is necessary to do.  The but men  the ones
4922            846  2476        1752b
συνοδεύοντες    αὐτῷ εἱστήκεισαν ἐνεοί,
journeying together him had stood  speechless,
191        3303  06   5456    3367    1161 2334
ἀκούοντες μὲν τῆς φωνῆς μηδένα δὲ  θεωροῦντες.
hearing    indeed the sound no one but watching.
1453        1161 4569    575  06   1093
8 ἠγέρθη    δὲ  Σαῦλος ἀπὸ τῆς γῆς,
  Was raised but  Saul   from the earth,
455            1161 014  3788       846   3762
ἀνεῳγμένων    δὲ  τῶν ὀφθαλμῶν αὐτοῦ οὐδὲν
having been opened but the eyes     of him nothing
991      5496       1161 846  1521       1519
ἔβλεπεν· χειραγωγοῦντες δὲ αὐτὸν εἰσήγαγον εἰς
he saw;  leading by hand  but him   they led into into
1154         2532 1510 2250  5140  3361 991   2532
Δαμασκόν. 9 καὶ ἦν ἡμέρας τρεῖς μὴ βλέπων καὶ
Damascus.   And was days  three  not seeing and
3756 2068 3761  4095     1510 1161 5100 3101
οὐκ ἔφαγεν οὐδὲ ἔπιεν. 10 Ἦν δέ τις μαθητὴς
not he ate but not he drank.  Was but some learner
1722 1154    3686     367     2532 3004 4314 846
ἐν Δαμασκῷ ὀνόματι Ἀνανίας, καὶ εἶπεν πρὸς αὐτὸν
in Damascus in name Ananias, and  said  to  him
1722 3705    01  2962    367    01 1161 3004   2400
ἐν ὁράματι ὁ κύριος· Ἀνανία. ὁ δὲ εἶπεν· ἰδοὺ
in sight    the Master· Ananias. The but said;  look
1473 2962     01 1161 2962   4314 846   450
ἐγώ, κύριε. 11 ὁ δὲ κύριος πρὸς αὐτόν· ἀναστὰς
I,   Master.  The but Master to  him;  having stood
                                          up
4198        1909 08  4505  08  2564           2117a
πορεύθητι ἐπὶ τὴν ῥύμην τὴν καλουμένην    Εὐθεῖαν
travel     on  the lane  the one being called Straight
2532 2212   1722 3614    2455    4569    3686   5018
καὶ ζήτησον ἐν οἰκίᾳ Ἰούδα Σαῦλον ὀνόματι Ταρσέα·
and  seek    in house of Judas Saul  in name Tarsus;
```

he found any who belonged to the Way, men or women, he might bring them bound to Jerusalem. [3]Now as he was going along and approaching Damascus, suddenly a light from heaven flashed around him. [4]He fell to the ground and heard a voice saying to him, "Saul, Saul, why do you persecute me?" [5]He asked, "Who are you, Lord?" The reply came, "I am Jesus, whom you are persecuting. [6]But get up and enter the city, and you will be told what you are to do." [7]The men who were traveling with him stood speechless because they heard the voice but saw no one. [8]Saul got up from the ground, and though his eyes were open, he could see nothing; so they led him by the hand and brought him into Damascus. [9]For three days he was without sight, and neither ate nor drank.

10 Now there was a disciple in Damascus named Ananias. The Lord said to him in a vision, "Ananias." He answered, "Here I am, Lord." [11]The Lord said to him, "Get up and go to the street called Straight, and at the house of Judas look for a man of Tarsus named Saul.

At this moment he is praying, [12]and he has seen in a vision[a] a man named Ananias come in and lay his ands on him so that he might regain his sight." [13]But Ananias answered, "Lord, I have heard from many about this man, how much evil he has done to your saints in Jerusalem; [14]and here he has authority from the chief priests to bind all who invoke your name." [15]But the Lord said to him, "Go, for he is an instrument whom I have chosen to bring my name before Gentiles and kings and before the people of Israel; [16]I myself will show him how much he must suffer for the sake of my name." [17]So Ananias went and entered the house. He laid his hands on Saul[b] and said, "Brother Saul, the Lord Jesus, who appeared to you on your way here, has sent me so that you may regain your sight and be filled with the Holy Spirit." [18]And immediately something like scales fell from his eyes, and his sight was restored. Then he got up and was baptized, [19]and after taking some food, he regained his strength.

For several days he was with the disciples in Damascus,

[a] Other ancient authorities lack *in a vision*
[b] Gk *him*

2400	1063	4336		2532	3708	435	1722	3705
ἰδοὺ	γὰρ	προσεύχεται	**12**	καὶ	εἶδεν	ἄνδρα	[ἐν	ὁράματι]
look for	he prays			and	he saw	man	in	sight

367	3686	1525		2532	2007
Ἀνανίαν	ὀνόματι	εἰσελθόντα		καὶ	ἐπιθέντα
Ananias	in name	having come into		and	having set on

846	020	5495	3704	308		611
αὐτῷ	[τὰς]	χεῖρας	ὅπως	ἀναβλέψῃ.	**13**	ἀπεκρίθη
him	the	hands	so that	he might see again.		Answered

1161	367	2962	191	575	4183	4012	02
δὲ	Ἀνανίας·	κύριε,	ἤκουσα	ἀπὸ	πολλῶν	περὶ	τοῦ
but	Ananias;	Master,	I heard	from	many	about	the

435	3778	3745	2556	015	40	1473
ἀνδρὸς	τούτου	ὅσα	κακὰ	τοῖς	ἁγίοις	σου
man	this	as much as	bad	to the	holy ones of	you

4160	1722	2419		2532	5602	2192	1849
ἐποίησεν	ἐν	Ἰερουσαλήμ·	**14**	καὶ	ὧδε	ἔχει	ἐξουσίαν
he did	in	Jerusalem;		and	here	he has	authority

3844	014	749		1210		3956	016
παρὰ	τῶν	ἀρχιερέων		δῆσαι		πάντας	τοὺς
from	the	ruler priests		to bind		all	the ones

1941		012	3686	1473		3004	1161	4314	846
ἐπικαλουμένους		τὸ	ὄνομά	σου.	**15**	εἶπεν	δὲ	πρὸς	αὐτὸν
calling on		the	name	of you.		Said	but	to	him

01	2962	4198	3754	4632	1589	1510
ὁ	κύριος·	πορεύου,	ὅτι	σκεῦος	ἐκλογῆς	ἐστίν
the	Master;	travel,	because	pot	select	is

1473	3778	010	941	012	3686	1473	1799
μοι	οὗτος	τοῦ	βαστάσαι	τὸ	ὄνομά	μου	ἐνώπιον
to me	this	the	to bear	the	name	of me	before

1484	5037	2532	935	5207	5037	2474		1473
ἐθνῶν	τε	καὶ	βασιλέων	υἱῶν	τε	Ἰσραήλ·	**16**	ἐγὼ
nations	both	and	kings	sons	and	Israel;		I

1063	5263	846	3745	1163	846
γὰρ	ὑποδείξω	αὐτῷ	ὅσα	δεῖ	αὐτὸν
for	will example	to him	as much as	it is necessary	him

5228	010	3686	1473	3958		565
ὑπὲρ	τοῦ	ὀνόματός	μου	παθεῖν.	**17**	Ἀπῆλθεν
on behalf of	the	name	of me	to suffer.		Went off

1161	367	2532	1525	1519	08	3614	2532
δὲ	Ἀνανίας	καὶ	εἰσῆλθεν	εἰς	τὴν	οἰκίαν	καὶ
but	Ananias	and	went in	into	the	house	and

2007	1909	846	020	5495	3004	4549
ἐπιθεὶς	ἐπ'	αὐτὸν	τὰς	χεῖρας	εἶπεν·	Σαοὺλ
having set on	on	him	the	hands	said;	Saul

80	01	2962	649	1473	2424	01
ἀδελφέ,	ὁ	κύριος	ἀπέσταλκέν	με,	Ἰησοῦς	ὁ
brother,	the	Master	has delegated	me,	Jesus	the one

3708	1473	1722	07	3598	3739
ὀφθείς	σοι	ἐν	τῇ	ὁδῷ	ᾗ
having been seen	to you	in	the	way	which

2064	3704	308	2532
ἤρχου,	ὅπως	ἀναβλέψῃς	καὶ
you were coming,	so that	you might see again	and

4092	4151	40		2532	2112
πλησθῇς	πνεύματος	ἁγίου.	**18**	καὶ	εὐθέως
might be filled	of spirit	holy.		And	immediately

634	846	575	014	3788	5613	3013
ἀπέπεσαν	αὐτοῦ	ἀπὸ	τῶν	ὀφθαλμῶν	ὡς	λεπίδες,
they fell off	of him	from	the	eyes	as	flakes,

308	5037	2532	450	907
ἀνέβλεψέν	τε	καὶ	ἀναστὰς	ἐβαπτίσθη
he saw again	both	and	having stood up	was immersed

	2532	2983	5160	1765
19	καὶ	λαβὼν	τροφὴν	ἐνίσχυσεν.
	and	having taken	food	he strengthened in.

1096	1161	3326	014	1722	1154	3101	2250
Ἐγένετο	δὲ	μετὰ	τῶν	ἐν	Δαμασκῷ	μαθητῶν	ἡμέρας
It became	but	with	the	in	Damascus	learners	days

5100	20	2532	2112		1722	019	4864
τινὰς		καὶ	εὐθέως		ἐν	ταῖς	συναγωγαῖς
some		and	immediately		in	the	synagogues

2784		04	2424	3754	3778	1510	01
ἐκήρυσσεν		τὸν	Ἰησοῦν	ὅτι	οὗτός	ἐστιν	ὁ
he was announcing		the	Jesus,	(")	this	is	the

5207	02		2316	21	1839		1161	3956	013
υἱὸς	τοῦ		θεοῦ.		ἐξίσταντο		δὲ	πάντες	οἱ
son	of		the God.		Were amazed		but	all	the ones

191		2532	3004		3756	3778	1510	01
ἀκούοντες		καὶ	ἔλεγον·		οὐχ	οὗτός	ἐστιν	ὁ
hearing		and	were saying;		not	this	is	the one

4199		1519	2419		016	1941
πορθήσας		εἰς	Ἰερουσαλὴμ		τοὺς	ἐπικαλουμένους
having ravaged		in	Jerusalem		the	ones calling on

012	3686	3778		2532	5602	1519	3778	2064		2443
τὸ	ὄνομα	τοῦτο,		καὶ	ὧδε	εἰς	τοῦτο	ἐλήλύθει		ἵνα
the name	this,			and	here	in	this	he has come		that

1210		846	71		1909	016	749
δεδεμένους		αὐτοὺς	ἀγάγη		ἐπὶ	τοὺς	ἀρχιερεῖς;
having bound		them	he might lead		on	the	ruler priests?

22	4569	1161	3123		1743		2532
	Σαῦλος	δὲ	μᾶλλον		ἐνεδυναμοῦτο		καὶ
	Saul	but	more		was being empowered		and

4797		016	2453		016	2730
συνέχυννεν		[τοὺς]	Ἰουδαίους		τοὺς	κατοικοῦντας
was confusing		the	Judeans		the	ones residing

1722	1154	4822		3754	3778	1510	01
ἐν	Δαμασκῷ	συμβιβάζων		ὅτι	οὗτός	ἐστιν	ὁ
in	Damascus	forcing together		that	this	is	the

5547	23	5613	1161	4137		2250	2425
χριστός.		Ὡς	δὲ	ἐπληροῦντο		ἡμέραι	ἱκαναί,
Christ.		As	but	were being filled		days	enough,

4823		013	2453	337	846
συνεβουλεύσαντο		οἱ	Ἰουδαῖοι	ἀνελεῖν	αὐτόν·
planned together		the	Judeans	to kill	him;

24	1097		1161	03		4569	05	1917		846
	ἐγνώσθη		δὲ	τῷ		Σαύλῳ	ἡ	ἐπιβουλὴ		αὐτῶν.
	was known		but	to the		Saul	the	plan		against of them.

3906		1161	2532	020	4439	2250	5037	2532	3571
παρετηροῦντο		δὲ	καὶ	τὰς	πύλας	ἡμέρας	τε	καὶ	νυκτὸς
They were		but	also	the	gates	day		both and	night
keeping watch									

3704		846	337		25	2983		1161	013
ὅπως		αὐτὸν	ἀνέλωσιν·			λαβόντες		δὲ	οἱ
so that		him	they might kill;			having taken		but	the

3101		846	3571	1223		010	5038	2524
μαθηταὶ		αὐτοῦ	νυκτὸς	διὰ		τοῦ	τείχους	καθῆκαν
learners		of him	night	through		the	wall	let down

846	5465		1722	4711		26	3854		1161
αὐτὸν	χαλάσαντες		ἐν	σπυρίδι.			Παραγενόμενος		δὲ
him	having lowered		in	mat basket.			Having arrived		but

1519	2419		3985		2853		015	3101
εἰς	Ἰερουσαλὴμ		ἐπείραζεν		κολλᾶσθαι		τοῖς	μαθηταῖς,
in	Jerusalem		he was		to be		to the	learners,
			pressuring		joined			

2532	3956	5399		846	3361	4100		3754
καὶ	πάντες	ἐφοβοῦντο		αὐτὸν	μὴ	πιστεύοντες		ὅτι
and	all	were fearing		him	not	trusting		that

1510	3101	27	921		1161	1949		846
ἐστὶν	μαθητής.		Βαρναβᾶς		δὲ	ἐπιλαβόμενος		αὐτὸν
he is	learner.		Barnabas		but	having taken on		him

71		4314	016	652		2532	1334		846
ἤγαγεν		πρὸς	τοὺς	ἀποστόλους		καὶ	διηγήσατο		αὐτοῖς
led		toward	the	delegates		and	narrated		to them

4459	1722	07	3598	3708		04	2962	2532	3754	2980
πῶς	ἐν	τῇ	ὁδῷ	εἶδεν		τὸν	κύριον	καὶ	ὅτι	ἐλάλησεν
how	in	the	way	he saw		the	Master	and	that	he spoke

20and immediately he began to proclaim Jesus in the synagogues, saying, "He is the Son of God." 21All who heard him were amazed and said, "Is not this the man who made havoc in Jerusalem among those who invoked this name? And has he not come here for the purpose of bringing them bound before the chief priests?" 22Saul became increasingly more powerful and confounded the Jews who lived in Damascus by proving that Jesus*a* was the Messiah.*b*

23 After some time had passed, the Jews plotted to kill him, 24but their plot became known to Saul. They were watching the gates day and night so that they might kill him; 25but his disciples took him by night and let him down through an opening in the wall,*c* lowering him in a basket.

26 When he had come to Jerusalem, he attempted to join the disciples; and they were all afraid of him, for they did not believe that he was a disciple. 27But Barnabas took him, brought him to the apostles, and described for them how on the road he had seen the Lord, who had spoken

a Gk that this
b Or the Christ
c Gk through the wall

to him, and how in Damascus he had spoken boldly in the name of Jesus. [28] So he went in and out among them in Jerusalem, speaking boldly in the name of the Lord. [29] He spoke and argued with the Hellenists; but they were attempting to kill him. [30] When the believers[a] learned of it, they brought him down to Caesarea and sent him off to Tarsus.

[31] Meanwhile the church throughout Judea, Galilee, and Samaria had peace and was built up. Living in the fear of the Lord and in the comfort of the Holy Spirit, it increased in numbers.

[32] Now as Peter went here and there among all the believers,[b] he came down also to the saints living in Lydda. [33] There he found a man named Aeneas, who had been bedridden for eight years, for he was paralyzed. [34] Peter said to him, "Aeneas, Jesus Christ heals you; get up and make your bed!" And immediately he got up. [35] And all the residents of Lydda and Sharon saw him and turned to the Lord.

[36] Now in Joppa there was a disciple whose name was Tabitha, which in Greek is Dorcas.[c]

[a] Gk brothers
[b] Gk all of them
[c] The name Tabitha in Aramaic and the name Dorcas in Greek mean a gazelle

---

846　　2532　4459　1722　1154　　　3955　　　　　　1722　011
αὐτῷ καὶ πῶς ἐν Δαμασκῷ ἐπαρρησιάσατο ἐν τῷ
to him and how in Damascus he was bold in the

3686　　2424　　　　2532　1510　　3326　846
ὀνόματι τοῦ ᾽Ιησοῦ. 28 καὶ ἦν μετ᾽ αὐτῶν
name of the Jesus. And he was with them

1531　　　　　2532　1607　　　　1519　2419
εἰσπορευόμενος καὶ ἐκπορευόμενος εἰς ᾽Ιερουσαλήμ,
traveling into and traveling out into Jerusalem,

3955　　　　　1722　011　3686　02　　2962
παρρησιαζόμενος ἐν τῷ ὀνόματι τοῦ κυρίου,
being bold in the name of the Master,

　　2980　　　　5037　2532　4802　　4314　016
29 ἐλάλει τε καὶ συνεζήτει πρὸς τοὺς
he was speaking both and disputing toward the

1675　　　　013　1161　2021　　　　　337
῾Ελληνιστάς, οἱ δὲ ἐπεχείρουν ἀνελεῖν
Hellenists, the but were setting hands on to kill

846　　30　1921　　　　1161　013　80　　　　2609
αὐτόν. ἐπιγνόντες δὲ οἱ ἀδελφοὶ κατήγαγον
him. Having perceived but the brothers led down

846　1519　2542　　　2532　1821　　　846　1519
αὐτὸν εἰς Καισάρειαν καὶ ἐξαπέστειλαν αὐτὸν εἰς
him into Caesarea and delegated out him to

5019　　31　05　3303　3767　1577　　2596　3650　06
Ταρσόν. ῾Η μὲν οὖν ἐκκλησία καθ᾽ ὅλης τῆς
Tarsus. The indeed then assembly by whole the

2449　　　2532　1056　　　2532　4540　　2192　1515
᾽Ιουδαίας καὶ Γαλιλαίας καὶ Σαμαρείας εἶχεν εἰρήνην
Judea and Galilee and Samaria had peace

3618　　　　2532　4198　　　03　　5401　02　2962
οἰκοδομουμένη καὶ πορευομένη τῷ φόβῳ τοῦ κυρίου
being built and traveling in the fear of the Master

2532　07　3874　　　　010　40　　4151
καὶ τῇ παρακλήσει τοῦ ἁγίου πνεύματος
and in the encouragement of the holy spirit

4129　　　　32　1096　　　1161　4074　　1330
ἐπληθύνετο. ᾽Εγένετο δὲ Πέτρον διερχόμενον
was multiplied. It became but Peter going through

1223　3956　2718　　　2532　4314　016　40　　016
διὰ πάντων κατελθεῖν καὶ πρὸς τοὺς ἁγίους τοὺς
through all to go down also toward the holy the

2730　　　3069　　33　2147　　1161　1563　444
κατοικοῦντας Λύδδα. εὗρεν δὲ ἐκεῖ ἄνθρωπόν
ones residing Lydda. He found but there man

5100　3686　132　　1537　2094　3638　2621　　1909
τινα ὀνόματι Αἰνέαν ἐξ ἐτῶν ὀκτὼ κατακείμενον ἐπὶ
some in name Aeneas from years eight lying down on

2895　　3739　1510　3886　　　　　34　2532　3004
κραβάττου, ὃς ἦν παραλελυμένος. καὶ εἶπεν
mat who was+ +having been paralyzed. And said

846　01　4074　132　2390　1473　2424　5547
αὐτῷ ὁ Πέτρος· Αἰνέα, ἰαταί σε ᾽Ιησοῦς Χριστός·
to him the Peter; Aeneas, cures you Jesus Christ;

450　　2532　4766　　4572　　2532　2112
ἀνάστηθι καὶ στρῶσον σεαυτῷ. καὶ εὐθέως
stand up and spread yourself. And immediately

450　　35　2532　3708　846　3956　013　2730
ἀνέστη. καὶ εἶδαν αὐτὸν πάντες οἱ κατοικοῦντες
he stood up. And saw him all the ones residing

3069　2532　04　4565　　3748　1994　　1909　04
Λύδδα καὶ τὸν Σαρῶνα, οἵτινες ἐπέστρεψαν ἐπὶ τὸν
Lydda and the Saron, who returned on the

2962　36　1722　2445　1161　5100　1510　3102　3686
κύριον. ᾽Εν ᾽Ιόππῃ δέ τις ἦν μαθήτρια ὀνόματι
Master. In Joppa but some was learner in name

5000　3739　1329　　　3004　1393　3778
Ταβιθά, ἣ διερμηνευομένη λέγεται Δορκάς· αὕτη
Tabitha, which being completely is said Dorcas; this
translated one

```
1510   4134    2041        18      2532 1654           3739
ἦν   πλήρης  ἔργων   ἀγαθῶν καὶ ἐλεημοσυνῶν  ὧν
was    full    of works   good    and mercifulness  which
4160                    1096     161 1722 019   2250      1565
ἐποίει.      37  ἐγένετο  δὲ  ἐν  ταῖς ἡμέραις ἐκείναις
she was doing.    It became but in  the  days   those
770                 846     599              3068              1161
ἀσθενήσασαν   αὐτὴν ἀποθανεῖν· λούσαντες      δὲ
having weakened  her   to die;   having washed  but
5087           846   1722  5253                 1451  1161  1510
ἔθηκαν  [αὐτὴν] ἐν  ὑπερῴῳ.      38  ἐγγὺς δὲ  οὔσης
they set   her   in  upstairs room.  Near  but  being
3069    07   2445    013 3101      191              3754 4074
Λύδδας τῇ Ἰόππῃ οἱ  μαθηταὶ ἀκούσαντες ὅτι Πέτρος
Lydda  the Joppa  the  learners having heard that Peter
1510 1722 846    649          1417 435        4314    846
ἐστὶν ἐν αὐτῇ ἀπέστειλαν δύο ἄνδρας πρὸς  αὐτὸν
is    in   it  delegated  two  men  toward   him
3870              3361 3635               1330
παρακαλοῦντες· μὴ ὀκνήσῃς      διελθεῖν
encouraging;    not  you might delay to come through
2193 1473      450      1161 4074       4905       846   3739
ἕως  ἡμῶν. 39  ἀναστὰς δὲ  Πέτρος συνῆλθεν αὐτοῖς· ὃν
until us.    Having but Peter  went with them;  who
                     stood up
3854                   321      1519 012 5253            2532
παραγενόμενον ἀνήγαγον εἰς τὸ ὑπερῷον        καὶ
having arrived  they led up into the upstairs room  and
3936          846  3956 017 5503     2799       2532
παρέστησαν αὐτῷ πᾶσαι αἱ χῆραι κλαίουσαι καὶ
stood along him  all  the  widows  crying    and
1925              5509     2532 2440    3745
ἐπιδεικνύμεναι χιτῶνας καὶ ἱμάτια ὅσα
showing on      shirts  and  clothes as much as
4160    3326 846    1510 05  1393       1544         1161
ἐποίει μετ᾽ αὐτῶν οὖσα ἡ Δορκάς. 40 ἐκβαλὼν    δὲ
was    with them  being the Dorcas.  Having thrown but
making                                            out
1854       3956  01  4074   2532 5087        024 1119
ἔξω   πάντας ὁ Πέτρος καὶ θεὶς     τὰ γόνατα
outside all   the Peter  and having set the knees
4336         2532 1994          4314 012 4983 3004
προσηύξατο καὶ ἐπιστρέψας    πρὸς τὸ σῶμα εἶπεν·
prayed     and  having returned to  the body said,
5000     450        05  1161 455      016  3788
Ταβιθά, ἀνάστηθι. ἡ δὲ ἤνοιξεν τοὺς ὀφθαλμοὺς
Tabitha, stand up. The but opened the  eyes
846    2532 3708      04 4074    339
αὐτῆς, καὶ ἰδοῦσα  τὸν Πέτρον ἀνεκάθισεν.
of her, and having seen the Peter  she sat up.
   1325          1161 846  5495    450          846
41 δοὺς       δὲ αὐτῇ χεῖρα ἀνέστησεν αὐτήν·
   Having given but  her  hand  he stood up her;
5455          1161 016  40   2532 020 5503
φωνήσας    δὲ τοὺς ἁγίους καὶ τὰς χήρας
having sounded but the holy   and  the widows
3936          846  2198      1110    1161 1096
παρέστησεν αὐτὴν ζῶσαν. 42 γνωστὸν δὲ ἐγένετο
he presented her  living.  Known  but  it became
2596 3650  06   2445    2532 4100       4183    1909 04
καθ᾽ ὅλης τῆς Ἰόππης καὶ ἐπίστευσαν πολλοὶ ἐπὶ τὸν
by  whole the  Joppa  and trusted   many  on  the
2962      1096    1161 2250   2425    3306    1722
κύριον. 43 Ἐγένετο δὲ ἡμέρας ἱκανὰς μεῖναι ἐν
Master.   It became but  days  enough to stay in
2445  3844   5100 4613 1038         435  1161 5100
Ἰόππῃ παρά τινι Σίμωνι βυρσεῖ. 10:1 Ἀνὴρ δὲ τις
Joppa along some Simon  tanner.       Man  but some
```

She was devoted to good works and acts of charity. [37]At that time she became ill and died. When they had washed her, they laid her in a room upstairs. [38]Since Lydda was near Joppa, the disciples, who heard that Peter was there, sent two men to him with the request, "Please come to us without delay." [39]So Peter got up and went with them; and when he arrived, they took him to the room upstairs. All the widows stood beside him, weeping and showing tunics and other clothing that Dorcas had made while she was with them. [40]Peter put all of them outside, and then he knelt down and prayed. He turned to the body and said, "Tabitha, get up." Then she opened her eyes, and seeing Peter, she sat up. [41]He gave her his hand and helped her up. Then calling the saints and widows, he showed her to be alive. [42]This became known throughout Joppa, and many believed in the Lord. [43]Meanwhile he stayed in Joppa for some time with a certain Simon, a tanner.

CHAPTER 10

In Caesarea there was a man named Cornelius,

a centurion of the Italian Cohort, as it was called. ²He was a devout man who feared God with all his household; he gave alms generously to the people and prayed constantly to God. ³One afternoon at about three o'clock he had a vision in which he clearly saw an angel of God coming in and saying to him, "Cornelius." ⁴He stared at him in terror and said, "What is it, Lord?" He answered, "Your prayers and your alms have ascended as a memorial before God. ⁵Now send men to Joppa for a certain Simon who is called Peter; ⁶he is lodging with Simon, a tanner, whose house is by the seaside." ⁷When the angel who spoke to him had left, he called two of his slaves and a devout soldier from the ranks of those who served him, ⁸and after telling them everything, he sent them to Joppa.

9 About noon the next day, as they were on their journey and approaching the city, Peter went up on the roof to pray. ¹⁰He became hungry and wanted something to eat;

1722	2542		3686	2883		1543		1537
ἐν	Καισαρείᾳ	ὀνόματι	Κορνήλιος,	ἑκατοντάρχης	ἐκ
in	Caesarea	in name	Cornelius,	hundred ruler	from

4686	06	2564		2483	**2**	2152
σπείρης	τῆς	καλουμένης	Ἰταλικῆς,	εὐσεβὴς
squadron	of the	one being called	Italian,	reverent

2532	5399	04	2316	4862	3956	03	3624	846
καὶ	φοβούμενος	τὸν	θεὸν	σὺν	παντὶ	τῷ	οἴκῳ	αὐτοῦ,
and	fearing	the	God	with	all	the	house	of him,

4160	1654		4183	03	2992	2532	1189
ποιῶν	ἐλεημοσύνας	πολλὰς	τῷ	λαῷ	καὶ	δεόμενος
doing	mercifulness	many	to the	people	and	begging

02	2316	1223	3956	**3**	3708	1722	3705	5320
τοῦ	θεοῦ	διὰ	παντός,	εἶδεν	ἐν	ὁράματι	φανερῶς
the	God	through	all,	he saw	in	sight	openly

5616	4012	5610	1728a	06	2250	32	02
ὡσεὶ	περὶ	ὥραν	ἐνάτην	τῆς	ἡμέρας	ἄγγελον	τοῦ
as	about	hour	ninth	of the	day	messenger	of the

2316	1525		4314	846	2532	3004		846
θεοῦ	εἰσελθόντα	πρὸς	αὐτὸν	καὶ	εἰπόντα	αὐτῷ·
God	having gone in to	him	and	having said to him;

2883	**4**	01	1161	816		846	2532	1719
Κορνήλιε.	ὁ	δὲ	ἀτενίσας	αὐτῷ	καὶ	ἔμφοβος
Cornelius.	The	but	having stared	to him	and	in fear

1096	3004	5101	1510	2962	3004	1161
γενόμενος	εἶπεν·	τί	ἐστιν,	κύριε;	εἶπεν	δὲ
having become	said;	what is,	Master?	He said	but

846	017	4335		1473	2532	017	1654
αὐτῷ.	αἱ	προσευχαί	σου	καὶ	αἱ	ἐλεημοσύναι
to him;	the	prayers of	_you_	and	the	mercifulness

1473	305	1519	3422		1715	02	2316
σου	ἀνέβησαν	εἰς	μνημόσυνον	ἔμπροσθεν	τοῦ	θεοῦ.
of _you_	went up	to	memorial	in front	of	the God.

2532	3568	3992	435	1519	2445	2532	3343
5 καὶ	νῦν	πέμψον	ἄνδρας	εἰς	Ἰόππην	καὶ	μετάπεμψαι
And	now	send	men	to	Joppa	and to send for

4613	5100	3739	1941		4074	**6**	3778
Σίμωνά	τινα	ὃς	ἐπικαλεῖται	Πέτρος·	οὗτος
Simon	some	who	is called on	Peter;	this one

3579		3844	5100	4613	1038	3739
ξενίζεται	παρά	τινι	Σίμωνι	βυρσεῖ,	ᾧ
is being entertained by	some	Simon	tanner,	to whom

as a stranger

1510	3614	3844	2281	**7**	5613	1161	565	01
ἐστιν	οἰκία	παρὰ	θάλασσαν.	ὡς	δὲ	ἀπῆλθεν	ὁ
is	house	along	sea.	As	but	went off	the

32	01	2980	846	5455		1417
ἄγγελος	ὁ	λαλῶν	αὐτῷ,	φωνήσας	δύο
messenger	the	speaking	to him,	having sounded	two

014	3610		2532	4757	2152	014
τῶν	οἰκετῶν	καὶ	στρατιώτην	εὐσεβῆ	τῶν
of the	house servants	and	soldier	reverent	of the

4342		846	**8**	2532	1834
προσκαρτερούντων	αὐτῷ	καὶ	ἐξηγησάμενος
ones remaining constant	to him	and	having explained

537	846	649	846	1519	08	2445
ἅπαντα	αὐτοῖς	ἀπέστειλεν	αὐτοὺς	εἰς	τὴν	Ἰόππην.
all	to them	delegated	them	to	the	Joppa.

9 07	1161	1887	3596		1565	2532
Τῇ	δὲ	ἐπαύριον,	ὁδοιπορούντων	ἐκείνων	καὶ
In the	but	tomorrow,	walking travels	of those	and

07	4172	1448	305	4074	1909	012	1430
τῇ	πόλει	ἐγγιζόντων,	ἀνέβη	Πέτρος	ἐπὶ	τὸ	δῶμα
in the	city	nearing,	went up	Peter	on	the	roof

4336	4012	5610	1623	**10**	1096	1161
προσεύξασθαι	περὶ	ὥραν	ἕκτην.	ἐγένετο	δὲ
to pray	about	hour	sixth.	It became	but

4361	2532	2309	1089
πρόσπεινος	καὶ	ἤθελεν	γεύσασθαι.
to hunger	and	he was wanting	to taste.

3903   1161 846   1096   1909 846   1611
παρασκευαζόντων   δὲ   αὐτῶν ἐγένετο ἐπ᾽ αὐτὸν ἔκστασις
Preparing   but   them   became   on   him   amazement

    2532 2334   04   3772   455   2532
11 καὶ θεωρεῖ   τὸν οὐρανὸν ἀνεῳγμένον   καὶ
   and   he watches the heaven   having opened and

2597   4632   5100 5613 3607   3173   5064
καταβαῖνον σκεῦός τι   ὡς   ὀθόνην μεγάλην τέσσαρσιν
coming down pot   some as   sheet   great   in four

746   2524   1909 06 1093   12 1722 3739
ἀρχαῖς καθιέμενον   ἐπὶ τῆς γῆς,   ἐν   ᾧ
corners being let down on   the earth,   in   which

5225   3956 021 5074   2532 2062
ὑπῆρχεν πάντα τὰ τετράποδα   καὶ ἑρπετὰ
were existing all   the four-footed   and   reptiles

06   1093 2532 4071   02   3772   2532 1096
τῆς γῆς καὶ πετεινὰ τοῦ οὐρανοῦ. 13 καὶ ἐγένετο
of the earth and birds   of the heaven.   And became

5456   4314 846   450   4074   2380
φωνὴ πρὸς αὐτόν· ἀναστάς,   Πέτρε, θῦσον
sound to   him;   having stood up, Peter, sacrifice

2532 2068   14 01 1161 4074   3004   3365
καὶ φάγε.   ὁ δὲ Πέτρος εἶπεν· μηδαμῶς,
and   eat.   The but Peter   said;   certainly not,

2962   3754   3763   2068   3956 2839   2532
κύριε, ὅτι   οὐδέποτε ἔφαγον πᾶν κοινὸν καὶ
Master, because but not ever I ate   all   common and

169   15 2532 5456   3825 1537 1208   4314
ἀκάθαρτον.   καὶ φωνὴ πάλιν ἐκ δευτέρου πρὸς
unclean.   And sound again from second   to

846   3739 01 2316 2511   1473 3361 2840
αὐτόν· ἃ ὁ θεὸς ἐκαθάρισεν, σὺ μὴ κοίνου.
him;   what the God cleaned,   you not make common.

   3778   1161 1096   1909 5151 2532 2117
16 τοῦτο δὲ   ἐγένετο ἐπὶ τρὶς καὶ εὐθὺς
   This but   became on   three and immediately

353   09 4632   1519 04 3772   17 5613 1161
ἀνελήμφθη τὸ σκεῦος εἰς τὸν οὐρανόν.   Ὡς   δὲ
was taken up the pot   into the heaven.   As   but

1722 1438   1280   01 4074   5101
ἐν ἑαυτῷ διηπόρει   ὁ Πέτρος τί
in himself was doubting thoroughly the Peter what

302 1510   09 3705   3739 3708   2400 013 435
ἂν εἴη   τὸ ὅραμα ὃ   εἶδεν, ἰδοὺ οἱ ἄνδρες
- might be the sight which he saw, look   the men

013 649   5259 02 2883   1331   08
οἱ ἀπεσταλμένοι ὑπὸ τοῦ Κορνηλίου διερωτήσαντες τὴν
the having been by   the Cornelius having asked   the
ones delegated   thoroughly

3614 02   4613   2186   1909 04 4440
οἰκίαν τοῦ Σίμωνος ἐπέστησαν ἐπὶ τὸν πυλῶνα,
house of the Simon   stood on   on   the gate,

   2532 5455   4441   1487 4613
18 καὶ φωνήσαντες ἐπυνθάνοντο   εἰ Σίμων
   and having sounded they were inquiring if   Simon

01 1941   4074   1759   3579
ὁ ἐπικαλούμενος Πέτρος ἐνθάδε ξενίζεται.
the one being   Peter in this is being entertained
called on   place   as a stranger.

   02 1161 4074   1326a   4012 010 3705
19 Τοῦ δὲ Πέτρου διενθυμουμένου περὶ τοῦ ὁράματος
   The but Peter reflecting   about the sight

3004 846 09 4151   2400 435   5140 2212
εἶπεν [αὐτῷ] τὸ πνεῦμα· ἰδοὺ ἄνδρες τρεῖς ζητοῦντές
said to him the spirit; look men   three seeking

1473 20 235 450   2597   2532 4198
σε,   ἀλλὰ ἀναστὰς κατάβηθι καὶ πορεύου
you,   but having stood up go down and travel

and while it was being
prepared, he fell into a
trance. [11]He saw the heaven
opened and something
like a large sheet coming
down, being lowered to the
ground by its four corners.
[12]In it were all kinds of
four-footed creatures and
reptiles and birds of the air.
[13]Then he heard a voice
saying, "Get up, Peter; kill
and eat." [14]But Peter said,
"By no means, Lord; for I
have never eaten anything
that is profane or unclean."
[15]The voice said to him
again, a second time, "What
God has made clean, you
must not call profane."
[16]This happened three times,
and the thing was suddenly
taken up to heaven.

17 Now while Peter
was greatly puzzled about
what to make of the vision
that he had seen, suddenly
the men sent by Cornelius
appeared. They were asking
for Simon's house and
were standing by the gate.
[18]They called out to ask
whether Simon, who was
called Peter, was staying
there. [19]While Peter was
still thinking about the
vision, the Spirit said to
him, "Look, three[a] men are
searching for you. [20]Now
get up, go down, and go

[a] One ancient authority reads two;
others lack the word

with them without hesitation; for I have sent them." ²¹So Peter went down to the men and said, "I am the one you are looking for; what is the reason for your coming?" ²²They answered, "Cornelius, a centurion, an upright and God-fearing man, who is well spoken of by the whole Jewish nation, was directed by a holy angel to send for you to come to his house and to hear what you have to say." ²³So Peter[a] invited them in and gave them lodging.

The next day he got up and went with them, and some of the believers[b] from Joppa accompanied him. ²⁴The following day they came to Caesarea. Cornelius was expecting them and had called together his relatives and close friends. ²⁵On Peter's arrival Cornelius met him, and falling at his feet, worshiped him. ²⁶But Peter made him get up, saying, "Stand up; I am only a mortal." ²⁷And as he talked with him, he went in and found that many had assembled; ²⁸and he said to them, "You yourselves know that it is unlawful for a Jew to associate with or

[a] Gk he
[b] Gk brothers

4862	846	3367	1252	3754	1473
σὺν	αὐτοῖς	μηδὲν	διακρινόμενος	ὅτι	ἐγὼ
with	them	nothing	doubting	because	I

649		846		2597		1161	4074
ἀπέσταλκα		αὐτούς.	**21**	καταβὰς		δὲ	Πέτρος
have delegated		them.		Having gone down		but	Peter

4314	016	435	3004	2400	1473	1510	3739	2212
πρὸς	τοὺς	ἄνδρας	εἶπεν·	ἰδοὺ	ἐγώ	εἰμι	ὃν	ζητεῖτε·
to	the	men	said;	look	I	am	whom	you seek;

5101	05	156	1223	3739	3918		013	1161
τίς	ἡ	αἰτία	δι᾽	ἣν	πάρεστε;	**22**	οἱ	δὲ
what	the	cause	through	which	you are present?		The ones	but

3004	2883		1543		435	1342	2532
εἶπαν·	Κορνήλιος		ἑκατοντάρχης,		ἀνὴρ	δίκαιος	καὶ
said;	Cornelius		hundred ruler,		man	right	and

5399	04	2316	3140			5037	5259	3650
φοβούμενος	τὸν	θεόν,	μαρτυρούμενός			τε	ὑπὸ	ὅλου
fearing	the	God,	being testified			and	by	whole

010	1484	014	2453	5537		5259	32
τοῦ	ἔθνους	τῶν	Ἰουδαίων,	ἐχρηματίσθη		ὑπὸ	ἀγγέλου
the	nation	of the	Judeans,	was warned		by	messenger

40	3343		1473	1519	04	3624	846	2532
ἁγίου	μεταπέμψασθαί		σε	εἰς	τὸν	οἶκον	αὐτοῦ	καὶ
holy	to be sent for		you	to	the	house	of him	and

191	4487	3844	1473		1528		3767
ἀκοῦσαι	ῥήματα	παρὰ	σοῦ.	**23**	εἰσκαλεσάμενος		οὖν
to hear	words	from	you.		Having called in		then

846	3579		07	1161	1887		450
αὐτοὺς	ἐξένισεν.		Τῇ	δὲ	ἐπαύριον		ἀναστὰς
them	he entertained as strangers.		In	but	tomorrow		having stood up
			the				

1831		4862	846	2532	5100	014	80
ἐξῆλθεν		σὺν	αὐτοῖς	καί	τινες	τῶν	ἀδελφῶν
he went out		with	them	and	some	of the	brothers

014	575	2445	4905	846		07	1161
τῶν	ἀπὸ	Ἰόππης	συνῆλθον	αὐτῷ.	**24**	τῇ	δὲ
of the	from	Joppa	went with	him.		In	but
						the	

1887	1525	1519	08	2542		01	1161
ἐπαύριον	εἰσῆλθεν	εἰς	τὴν	Καισάρειαν.		ὁ	δὲ
tomorrow	he went in	into	the	Caesarea.		The	but

2883	1510	4328		846	4779		016
Κορνήλιος	ἦν	προσδοκῶν		αὐτοὺς	συγκαλεσάμενος		τοὺς
Cornelius	was+	+waiting expectantly		them	having called together		the

4773	846	2532	016	316		5384		**25**	5613
συγγενεῖς	αὐτοῦ	καὶ	τοὺς	ἀναγκαίους		φίλους.			Ὡς
relatives	of him	and	the	necessary		friends.			As

1161	1096	010	1525	04	4074	4876
δὲ	ἐγένετο	τοῦ	εἰσελθεῖν	τὸν	Πέτρον,	συναντήσας
but	it became	the	to go into	the	Peter,	having met

846	01	2883	4098	1909	016	4228
αὐτῷ	ὁ	Κορνήλιος	πεσὼν	ἐπὶ	τοὺς	πόδας
him	the	Cornelius	having fallen	on	the	feet

4352		01	1161	4074	1453	846	3004
προσεκύνησεν.	**26**	ὁ	δὲ	Πέτρος	ἤγειρεν	αὐτὸν	λέγων·
worshiped.		The	but	Peter	raised	him	saying;

450	2532	1473	846	444	1510		2532
ἀνάστηθι·	καὶ	ἐγὼ	αὐτὸς	ἄνθρωπός	εἰμι.	**27**	καὶ
stand up;	also	I	myself	man	am.		And

4926	846	1525	2532	2147	4905
συνομιλῶν	αὐτῷ	εἰσῆλθεν	καὶ	εὑρίσκει	συνεληλυθότας
conversing with	him	he went in	and	finds	having come together

4183		5346	5037	4314	846	1473	1987
πολλούς,	**28**	ἔφη	τε	πρὸς	αὐτούς·	ὑμεῖς	ἐπίστασθε
many,		he said	and	to	them;	you	understand

5613	111		1510	435	2453	2853		2228
ὡς	ἀθέμιτόν		ἐστιν	ἀνδρὶ	Ἰουδαίῳ	κολλᾶσθαι		ἢ
as	unlawful		it is	to man	Judean	to be joined		or

4334	246	2504	01	2316 1166
προσέρχεσθαι	ἀλλοφύλῳ·	κἀμοὶ	ὁ	θεὸς ἔδειξεν
to go towards	other tribe;	and to me	the	God showed

3367	2839 2228 169	3004	444	29	1352
μηδένα	κοινὸν ἢ ἀκάθαρτον	λέγειν	ἄνθρωπον·		διὸ
no one	common or unclean	to say	man;		therefore

2532 369	2064	3343
καὶ ἀναντιρρήτως	ἦλθον	μεταπεμφθείς.
and without contradiction	I came	having been sent for.

4441	3767 5101	3056 3343	1473	30	2532
πυνθάνομαι	οὖν τίνι	λόγῳ μετεπέμψασθέ	με;		καὶ
I inquire	then to what	word you sent	for me?		And

01	2883	5346	575 5067	2250	3360	3778
ὁ	Κορνήλιος	ἔφη·	ἀπὸ τετάρτης	ἡμέρας	μέχρι	ταύτης
the	Cornelius	said;	from fourth	day	until	this

06	5610 1510	08	1728a	4336	1722 03	3624
τῆς	ὥρας ἤμην	τὴν	ἐνάτην	προσευχόμενος	ἐν τῷ	οἴκῳ
the	hour I was+	the	ninth	+praying	in the	house

1473	2532 2400 435	2476	1799	1473	1722 2066
μου,	καὶ ἰδοὺ ἀνὴρ	ἔστη	ἐνώπιόν	μου ἐν	ἐσθῆτι
of me,	and look man	stood	before	me in	clothes

2986	31	2532 5346	2883	1522	1473	05
λαμπρᾷ		καὶ φησίν·	Κορνήλιε,	εἰσηκούσθη	σου	ἡ
bright		and says;	Cornelius,	was heard	of you	the

4335	2532 017 1654	1473	3403
προσευχὴ	καὶ αἱ ἐλεημοσύναι	σου	ἐμνήσθησαν
prayer	and the mercifulness	of you	were remembered

1799	02 2316	32	3992	3767 1519	2445	2532
ἐνώπιον	τοῦ θεοῦ.		πέμψον	οὖν εἰς	Ἰόππην	καὶ
before	the God.		Send	then to	Joppa	and

3333	4613	3739 1941	4074	3778
μετακάλεσαι	Σίμωνα	ὃς ἐπικαλεῖται	Πέτρος,	οὗτος
to call for	Simon	who is called on	Peter,	this one

3579	1722 3614	4613	1038	3844
ξενίζεται	ἐν οἰκίᾳ	Σίμωνος	βυρσέως	παρὰ
is being entertained	in house	of Simon	tanner	along
as a stranger				

2281	33	1824	3767 3992	4314 1473 1473 5037
θάλασσαν.		ἐξαυτῆς	οὖν ἔπεμψα	πρὸς σέ, σύ τε
sea.		At once	then I sent	to you, you indeed

2573 4160	3854	3568 3767 3956	1473
καλῶς ἐποίησας	παραγενόμενος.	νῦν οὖν πάντες	ἡμεῖς
well did	having arrived.	Now then all	we

1799	02 2316 3918	191	3956 024
ἐνώπιον	τοῦ θεοῦ πάρεσμεν	ἀκοῦσαι	πάντα τὰ
before	the God are present	to hear	all the things

4367	1473	5259 02	2962
προστεταγμένα	σοι	ὑπὸ	τοῦ κυρίου.
having been commanded	to you	by	the Master.

34	455	1161 4074	012 4750 3004	1909
	Ἀνοίξας	δὲ Πέτρος	τὸ στόμα εἶπεν·	ἐπ᾽
	Having opened	but Peter	the mouth said;	on

225	2638	3754 3756 1510 4381
ἀληθείας	καταλαμβάνομαι	ὅτι οὐκ ἔστιν προσωπολήμπτης
truth	I over take	that not is receiver of face

01 2316	35	235,	1722 3956 1484	01 5399
ὁ θεός,		ἀλλ᾽	ἐν παντὶ ἔθνει	ὁ φοβούμενος
the God,		but	in all nation	the one fearing

846	2532 2038	1343	1184	846
αὐτὸν	καὶ ἐργαζόμενος	δικαιοσύνην	δεκτὸς	αὐτῷ
him	and working	rightness	acceptable	to him

1510	36	04	3056 3739 649	015	5207
ἐστιν.		τὸν	λόγον [ὃν]	ἀπέστειλεν	τοῖς υἱοῖς
is.		The	word which	he delegated	to the sons

2474	2097	1515	1223	2424
Ἰσραὴλ	εὐαγγελιζόμενος	εἰρήνην	διὰ	Ἰησοῦ
Israel	telling good message	peace	through	Jesus

5547	3778 1510 3956	2962	37	1473	3609a
Χριστοῦ,	οὗτός ἐστιν πάντων	κύριος,		ὑμεῖς	οἴδατε
Christ,	this is of all	Master,		you	know

to visit a Gentile; but God has shown me that I should not call anyone profane or unclean. ²⁹So when I was sent for, I came without objection. Now may I ask why you sent for me?"

³⁰Cornelius replied, "Four days ago at this very hour, at three o'clock, I was praying in my house when suddenly a man in dazzling clothes stood before me. ³¹He said, 'Cornelius, your prayer has been heard and your alms have been remembered before God. ³²Send therefore to Joppa and ask for Simon, who is called Peter; he is staying in the home of Simon, a tanner, by the sea.' ³³Therefore I sent for you immediately, and you have been kind enough to come. So now all of us are here in the presence of God to listen to all that the Lord has commanded you to say."

34 Then Peter began to speak to them: "I truly understand that God shows no partiality, ³⁵but in every nation anyone who fears him and does what is right is acceptable to him. ³⁶You know the message he sent to the people of Israel, preaching peace by Jesus Christ—he is Lord of all. ³⁷That message spread

throughout Judea,
beginning in Galilee after
the baptism that John
announced: 38how God
anointed Jesus of Nazareth
with the Holy Spirit and
with power; how he went
about doing good and
healing all who were
oppressed by the devil, for
God was with him. 39We
are witnesses to all that he
did both in Judea and in
Jerusalem. They put him
to death by hanging him
on a tree; 40but God raised
him on the third day and
allowed him to appear,
41not to all the people but
to us who were chosen by
God as witnesses, and who
ate and drank with him
after he rose from the dead.
42He commanded us to
preach to the people and
to testify that he is the one
ordained by God as judge
of the living and the dead.
43All the prophets testify
about him that everyone
who believes in him receives
forgiveness of sins through
his name."

44 While Peter was still
speaking, the Holy Spirit
fell upon

```
012      1096              4487  2596 3650 06    2449
τὸ    γενόμενον        ῥῆμα καθ᾽ ὅλης τῆς  Ἰουδαίας,
the having become   word  by   whole the Judea,
757           575  06  1056        3326  012  908          3739
ἀρξάμενος  ἀπὸ  τῆς Γαλιλαίας μετὰ  τὸ  βάπτισμα  ὃ
beginning from the Galilee    after  the immersion that
2784        2491              2424    04  575 3478        5613
ἐκήρυξεν Ἰωάννης,  38  Ἰησοῦν τὸν ἀπὸ Ναζαρέθ,  ὡς
announced John,         Jesus  the from Nazareth,  as
5548        846   01  2316 4151    40  2532 1411
ἔχρισεν αὐτὸν ὁ  θεὸς πνεύματι ἁγίῳ καὶ  δυνάμει,
anointed him   the God  in spirit holy and  in power,
3739 1330           2109                 2532 2390     3956  016
ὃς  διῆλθεν    εὐεργετῶν  καὶ ἰώμενος πάντας τοὺς
who  came through working well and curing   all     the
2616                          2659 02  1228          3754   01
καταδυναστευομένους ὑπὸ  τοῦ διαβόλου, ὅτι   ὁ
ones exercising        by   the slanderer, because the
power against
2316 1510 3326 846       2532 1473   3144          3956
θεὸς ἦν  μετ᾽ αὐτοῦ.  39  καὶ ἡμεῖς μάρτυρες πάντων
God was with him.       And we  testifiers  of all
3739  4160    1722 5037 07  5561      014        2453  2532
ὧν   ἐποίησεν ἔν τε  τῇ χώρᾳ  τῶν  Ἰουδαίων καὶ
which he did  in both the country of the Judeans   and
1722  2419        3739 2532 337         2910
[ἐν] Ἰερουσαλήμ. ὃν  καὶ ἀνεῖλαν κρεμάσαντες
in   Jerusalem.  Whom also they killed having hanged
1909  3586      3778   01  2316 1453    1722 07 5154
ἐπὶ  ξυλοῦ,  40  τοῦτον ὁ  θεὸς ἤγειρεν [ἐν] τῇ τρίτῃ
on  wood,      this   the God  raised   in  the third
2250  2532 1325   846    1717     1096       41  3756
ἡμέρᾳ καὶ ἔδωκεν αὐτὸν ἐμφανῆ γενέσθαι,    οὐ
day  and gave    him   visible to become,  not
3956  03   2992    235   3144        015
παντὶ τῷ  λαῷ,  ἀλλὰ μάρτυσιν   τοῖς
to all the people but  to testifiers the ones
4401                    5259 02 2316  1473    3748
προκεχειροτονημένοις ὑπὸ  τοῦ θεοῦ, ἡμῖν, οἵτινες
having stretched out by  the God,  to us, who
his hand on before
4906            2532 4844          846     3326  012
συνεφάγομεν καὶ συνεπίομεν    αὐτῷ μετὰ  τὸ
ate together and drank together in him after the
450            846    1537 3498   42  2532 3853
ἀναστῆναι  αὐτὸν ἐκ  νεκρῶν·   καὶ παρήγγειλεν
to stand up him   from dead;    and he commanded
1473 2784        03  2992  2532 1263         3754
ἡμῖν κηρύξαι  τῷ  λαῷ  καὶ διαμαρτύρασθαι ὅτι
to us to announce to people and to testify      that
the                        thoroughly
3778  1510   01  3724                  5259 02
οὗτός ἐστιν ὁ  ὡρισμένος            ὑπὸ  τοῦ
this  is   the one having been designated by   the
2316 2923  2198       2532 3498   43  3778      3956
θεοῦ κριτὴς ζώντων  καὶ νεκρῶν.   τούτῳ πάντες
God judge of living and dead.    To this all
013 4396         3140       859        266
οἱ  προφῆται μαρτυροῦσιν ἄφεσιν    ἁμαρτιῶν
the spokesmen testify     sending off of sins
2983    1223   010 3686      846    3956 02  3956
λαβεῖν διὰ   τοῦ ὀνόματος αὐτοῦ πάντα τὸν
to receive through the name of him all   the one
4100        1519 846     44  2089 2980     02  4074
πιστεύοντα εἰς αὐτόν.    Ἔτι λαλοῦντος τοῦ Πέτρου
trusting   in  him.     Still speaking   the Peter
024 4487  3778  1968     09  4151  09  40   1909
τὰ ῥήματα ταῦτα ἐπέπεσεν τὸ πνεῦμα τὸ ἅγιον ἐπὶ
the words these fell on   the spirit the holy on
```

3956   016   191   04   3056   2532 1839
πάντας τοὺς ἀκούοντας τὸν λόγον.   **45** καὶ ἐξέστησαν
all   the   hearing   the   word.   And   were amazed

013 1537 4061   4103   3745   4905
οἱ ἐκ περιτομῆς πιστοὶ ὅσοι   συνῆλθαν
the from circumcision trustful as many as went with

03   4074   3754   2532 1909 024 1484   05   1431
τῷ Πέτρῳ, ὅτι   καὶ ἐπὶ τὰ ἔθνη ἡ δωρεὰ
the Peter, because also on the nations the gift

010   40   4151   1632   191
τοῦ ἁγίου πνεύματος ἐκκέχυται· **46** ἤκουον
of the holy spirit   was poured out; they were hearing

1063 846   2980   1100   2532 3170   04
γὰρ αὐτῶν λαλούντων γλώσσαις καὶ μεγαλυνόντων τὸν
for them speaking   in tongues and making great the

2316   5119 611   4074   3385 012 5204 1410
θεόν. τότε ἀπεκρίθη Πέτρος· **47** μήτι τὸ ὕδωρ δύναται
God. then answered Peter;   not the water is able

2967   5100 010 3361 907   3778
κωλῦσαί τις τοῦ μὴ βαπτισθῆναι   τούτους,
to hinder some the not to be immersed these,

3748   012 4151   012 40   2983   5613 2532 1473
οἵτινες τὸ πνεῦμα τὸ ἅγιον ἔλαβον ὡς καὶ ἡμεῖς;
who   the spirit the holy received as   also we?

    4367   1161 846   1722 011 3686   2424
48 προσέταξεν δὲ αὐτοὺς ἐν τῷ ὀνόματι Ἰησοῦ
       He commanded but them   in the name   of Jesus

5547   907   5119 2065   846   1961
Χριστοῦ βαπτισθῆναι. τότε ἠρώτησαν αὐτὸν ἐπιμεῖναι
Christ   to be immersed. Then they asked him to stay on

2250   5100   191   1161 013 652   2532
ἡμέρας τινάς. **11:1** Ἤκουσαν δὲ οἱ ἀπόστολοι καὶ
days   some.   Heard   but the delegates and

013 80   013 1510   2596 08   2449   3754
οἱ ἀδελφοὶ οἱ ὄντες   κατὰ τὴν Ἰουδαίαν ὅτι
the brothers the ones being by   the Judea   because

2532 021 1484   1209   04 3056 02   2316
καὶ τὰ ἔθνη ἐδέξαντο τὸν λόγον τοῦ θεοῦ.
also the nations welcomed the word of the God.

   3753 1161 305   4074   1519 2419
2 Ὅτε δὲ ἀνέβη Πέτρος εἰς Ἰερουσαλήμ,
      When but went up Peter to   Jerusalem,

1252   4314 846   013   1537 4061
διεκρίνοντο πρὸς αὐτὸν οἱ   ἐκ περιτομῆς
were doubting to him   the ones from circumcision

   3004   3754 1525   4314 435   203
3 λέγοντες ὅτι εἰσῆλθες πρὸς ἄνδρας ἀκροβυστίαν
      saying, ("") you come in to men   uncircumcision

2192   2532 4906   846   757   1161
ἔχοντας καὶ συνέφαγες αὐτοῖς. **4** Ἀρξάμενος δὲ
having   and you ate with them.   Having begun but

4074   1420   846 2517   3004   1473 1510
Πέτρος ἐξετίθετο αὐτοῖς καθεξῆς λέγων· **5** ἐγὼ ἤμην
Peter set out   to them in order saying,   I   was

1722 4172   2445   4336   2532 3708 1722 1611
ἐν πόλει Ἰόππη προσευχόμενος καὶ εἶδον ἐν ἐκστάσει
in city   Joppa praying   and saw   in amazement

3705   2597   4632   5100 5613 3607   3173
ὅραμα, καταβαῖνον σκεῦός τι ὡς ὀθόνην μεγάλην
sight, coming down pot   some as sheet great

5064   746   1537 02 3772   2532
τέσσαρσιν ἀρχαῖς καθιεμένην ἐκ τοῦ οὐρανοῦ, καὶ
four   corners being let down from the heaven, and

2064   891   1473 1519 3739 816
ἦλθεν ἄχρι ἐμοῦ. **6** εἰς ἣν ἀτενίσας
it came until me.   Into which having stared

2657   2532 3708 024 5074
κατενόουν   καὶ εἶδον τὰ τετράποδα
I was thinking carefully and saw   the four-footed

all who heard the word.
[45]The circumcised believers who had come with Peter were astounded that the gift of the Holy Spirit had been poured out even on the Gentiles, [46]for they heard them speaking in tongues and extolling God. Then Peter said, [47]"Can anyone withhold the water for baptizing these people who have received the Holy Spirit just as we have?" [48]So he ordered them to be baptized in the name of Jesus Christ. Then they invited him to stay for several days.

CHAPTER 11

Now the apostles and the believers[a] who were in Judea heard that the Gentiles had also accepted the word of God. [2]So when Peter went up to Jerusalem, the circumcised believers[b] criticized him, [3]saying, "Why did you go to uncircumcised men and eat with them?" [4]Then Peter began to explain to them, step by step, saying, [5]"I was in the city of Joppa praying, and in a trance I saw a vision. There was something like a large sheet coming down from heaven, being lowered by its four corners; and it came close to me. [6]As I looked at it closely I saw four-footed animals,

a Gk brothers
b Gk lacks believers

beasts of prey, reptiles, and birds of the air. ⁷I also heard a voice saying to me, 'Get up, Peter; kill and eat.' ⁸But I replied, 'By no means, Lord; for nothing profane or unclean has ever entered my mouth.' ⁹But a second time the voice answered from heaven, 'What God has made clean, you must not call profane.' ¹⁰This happened three times; then everything was pulled up again to heaven. ¹¹At that very moment three men, sent to me from Caesarea, arrived at the house where we were. ¹²The Spirit told me to go with them and not to make a distinction between them and us.ᵃ These six brothers also accompanied me, and we entered the man's house. ¹³He told us how he had seen the angel standing in his house and saying, 'Send to Joppa and bring Simon, who is called Peter; ¹⁴he will give you a message by which you and your entire household will be saved.' ¹⁵And as I began to speak, the Holy Spirit fell upon them just as it had upon us at the beginning. ¹⁶And I remembered the word of

ᵃ Or *not to hesitate*

```
06        1093   2532 024 2342          2532 024 2062
τῆς       γῆς    καὶ  τὰ  θηρία        καὶ  τὰ  ἑρπετὰ
of the    earth  and  the wild animals and  the reptiles
2532 024 4071   02        3772          191   1161 2532
καὶ  τὰ  πετεινὰ τοῦ      οὐρανοῦ. ⁷    ἤκουσα δὲ  καὶ
and  the birds  of the    heaven.       I heard but also
5456  3004      1473 450          4074    2380
φωνῆς λεγούσης  μοι· ἀναστάς,     Πέτρε, θῦσον
sound saying    to me; having stood up, Peter, sacrifice
2532 2068   ₈  3004  1161 3365          2962
καὶ  φάγε.  ⁸  εἶπον δέ·  μηδαμῶς,      κύριε,
and  eat.      I said but; certainly not, Master,
3754      2839     2228 169    3763        1525
ὅτι       κοινὸν  ἢ   ἀκάθαρτον οὐδέποτε  εἰσῆλθεν
because   common  or  unclean   but not ever went in
1519 012 4750   1473  ₉ 611      1161 5456 1537  1208
εἰς  τὸ  στόμα  μου.  ⁹ ἀπεκρίθη δὲ  φωνὴ ἐκ   δευτέρου
into the mouth  of me.  Answered but sound from second
1537 02  3772      3739 01  2316 2511        1473 3361
ἐκ   τοῦ οὐρανοῦ· ἃ    ὁ   θεὸς ἐκαθάρισεν, σὺ  μὴ
from the heaven;  what the  God  cleaned,    you not
2840       ₁₀ 3778  1161 1096   1909 5151   2532
κοίνου.    ¹⁰ τοῦτο δὲ  ἐγένετο ἐπὶ τρίς,  καὶ
make common.  This  but became  on  three, and
385        3825  537   1519 04  3772         ₁₁ 2532
ἀνεσπάσθη  πάλιν ἅπαντα εἰς τὸν οὐρανόν. ¹¹ καὶ
was drawn up again all   in  the heaven.      And
2400 1824    5140  435    2186        1909 08 3614
ἰδοὺ ἐξαυτῆς τρεῖς ἄνδρες ἐπέστησαν ἐπὶ τὴν οἰκίαν
look at once three men    stood on  at  the house
1722 3739  1510   649           575
ἐν   ᾗ     ἦμεν,  ἀπεσταλμένοι  ἀπὸ
in   which we were, having been delegated from
2542      4314 1473 ₁₂ 3004  1161 09   4151  1473
Καισαρείας πρός με.  ¹² εἶπεν δὲ  τὸ   πνεῦμά μοι
Caesarea   to  me.     Said  but the  spirit to me
4905       846    3367  1252              2064 1161
συνελθεῖν  αὐτοῖς μηδὲν διακρίναντα.      ἦλθον δὲ
to go with them   nothing judging thoroughly. Came but
4862 1473 2532 013 1803 80      3778 2532 1525
σὺν ἐμοὶ καὶ  οἱ  ἓξ  ἀδελφοὶ οὗτοι καὶ  εἰσήλθομεν
with me   also the six brothers these and  we went in
1519 04  3624 02        435       ₁₃ 1161 1473
εἰς  τὸν οἶκον τοῦ      ἀνδρός. ¹³ ἀπήγγειλεν δὲ  ἡμῖν
into the house of the  man.      He told  but to us
4459 3708  04  32             1722 03 3624 846
πῶς  εἶδεν [τὸν] ἄγγελον      ἐν   τῷ οἴκῳ αὐτοῦ
how  he saw the  messenger in   the house of him
2476       2532 3004        649         1519 2445
σταθέντα   καὶ  εἰπόντα·     ἀπόστειλον εἰς  Ἰόππην
having stood and having said; delegate  to   Joppa
2532 3343    4613 04 1941             4074
καὶ  μετάπεμψαι Σίμωνα τὸν ἐπικαλούμενον Πέτρον,
and  to send for Simon the being called on Peter,
₁₄ 3739 2980    4487     4314 1473 1722 3739
¹⁴ ὃς  λαλήσει  ῥήματα  πρὸς σὲ  ἐν   οἷς
   who will speak words  to  you  in   which
4982       1473 2532 3956 01  3624 1473
σωθήσῃ     σὺ  καὶ  πᾶς  ὁ   οἶκός σου.
will be delivered you and  all  the house of you.
₁₅ 1722 1161 011 757     1473 2980       1968    09
¹⁵ ἐν   δὲ  τῷ  ἄρξασθαί με  λαλεῖν      ἐπέπεσεν τὸ
   In  but the to begin   me  to speak   fell on   the
4151   09  40  1909 846   5618         2532 1909 1473
πνεῦμα τὸ  ἅγιον ἐπ' αὐτοὺς ὥσπερ      καὶ  ἐφ'  ἡμᾶς
spirit the holy  on  them   as indeed also on   us
1722 746    ₁₆ 3403        1161 010 4487    02
ἐν   ἀρχῇ.  ¹⁶ ἐμνήσθην    δὲ  τοῦ ῥήματος τοῦ
in   beginning. I remembered but the word     of the
```

2962 5613 3004   2491   3303   907
κυρίου ὡς ἔλεγεν·   Ἰωάννης μὲν ἐβάπτισεν
Master as he was saying; John indeed immersed

5204   1473 1161 907   1722 4151   40
ὕδατι, ὑμεῖς δὲ βαπτισθήσεσθε ἐν πνεύματι ἁγίῳ.
in water, you but will be immersed in spirit holy.

   1487 3767 08 2470 1431   1325 846   01 2316
17 εἰ οὖν τὴν ἴσην δωρεὰν ἔδωκεν αὐτοῖς ὁ θεὸς
   If then the equal gift gave to them the God

5613 2532 1473 4100   1909 04 2962   2424
ὡς καὶ ἡμῖν πιστεύσασιν ἐπὶ τὸν κύριον Ἰησοῦν
as also to us having trusted on the Master Jesus

5547   1473 5101 1510 1415   2967   04 2316
Χριστόν, ἐγὼ τίς ἤμην δυνατὸς κωλῦσαι τὸν θεόν;
Christ, I why was power to hinder the God?

  191   1161 3778 2270   2532
18 Ἀκούσαντες δὲ ταῦτα ἡσύχασαν καὶ
   Having heard but these they were quiet and

1392   04 2316 3004   686 2532 023
ἐδόξασαν τὸν θεὸν λέγοντες· ἄρα καὶ τοῖς
gave splendor the God saying; then also to the

1484   01 2316 08 3341   1519 2222 1325
ἔθνεσιν ὁ θεὸς τὴν μετάνοιαν εἰς ζωὴν ἔδωκεν.
nations the God the change mind into life gave.

  013 3303 3767 1289   575
19 Οἱ μὲν οὖν διασπαρέντες ἀπὸ
   The indeed then having been thoroughly sown from

06 2347   06   1096   1909 4736
τῆς θλίψεως τῆς γενομένης ἐπὶ Στεφάνῳ
the affliction of the having become on Stephan

1330   2193 5403   2532 2954 2532
διῆλθον ἕως Φοινίκης καὶ Κύπρου καὶ
went through until Phoenicia and Cyprus and

490   3367   2980   04 3056 1487 3361
Ἀντιοχείας μηδενὶ λαλοῦντες τὸν λόγον εἰ μὴ
Antioch to no one speaking the word except

3441   2453   20 1510 1161 5100 1537 846
μόνον Ἰουδαίοις. Ἦσαν δέ τινες ἐξ αὐτῶν
alone Judeans. Were but some from them

435   2953   2532 2956   3748   2064
ἄνδρες Κύπριοι καὶ Κυρηναῖοι, οἵτινες ἐλθόντες
men Cyprians and Cyreneans, who having come

1519 490   2980   2532 4314 016
εἰς Ἀντιόχειαν ἐλάλουν καὶ πρὸς τοὺς
into Antioch were speaking also to the

1675   2097   04 2962   2424
Ἑλληνιστὰς εὐαγγελιζόμενοι τὸν κύριον Ἰησοῦν.
Hellenists telling good message the Master Jesus.

  2532 1510 5495 2962   3326 846   4183 5037
21 καὶ ἦν χεὶρ κυρίου μετ᾽ αὐτῶν, πολύς τε
   And was hand of Master with them, much and

706   01 4100   1994   1909 04 2962
ἀριθμὸς ὁ πιστεύσας ἐπέστρεψεν ἐπὶ τὸν κύριον.
number the having trusted returned on the Master.

  191   1161 01 3056 1519 024 3775 06
22 Ἠκούσθη δὲ ὁ λόγος εἰς τὰ ὦτα τῆς
   Was heard but the word in the ears of the

1577   06 1510   1722 2419   4012 846
ἐκκλησίας τῆς οὔσης ἐν Ἰερουσαλὴμ περὶ αὐτῶν
assembly the one being in Jerusalem about them

2532 1821   921   1330   2193
καὶ ἐξαπέστειλαν Βαρναβᾶν [διελθεῖν] ἕως
and they delegated out Barnabas to go through until

490   23 3739 3854   2532 3708   08
Ἀντιοχείας. ὃς παραγενόμενος καὶ ἰδὼν τὴν
Antioch. Who having arrived and having seen the

5485 08 02   2316 5463   2532 3870
χάριν [τὴν] τοῦ θεοῦ, ἐχάρη καὶ παρεκάλει
favor the of the God, rejoiced and was encouraging

the Lord, how he had said, 'John baptized with water, but you will be baptized with the Holy Spirit.' [17]If then God gave them the same gift that he gave us when we believed in the Lord Jesus Christ, who was I that I could hinder God?" [18]When they heard this, they were silenced. And they praised God, saying, "Then God has given even to the Gentiles the repentance that leads to life."

[19] Now those who were scattered because of the persecution that took place over Stephen traveled as far as Phoenicia, Cyprus, and Antioch, and they spoke the word to no one except Jews. [20]But among them were some men of Cyprus and Cyrene who, on coming to Antioch, spoke to the Hellenists[a] also, proclaiming the Lord Jesus. [21]The hand of the Lord was with them, and a great number became believers and turned to the Lord. [22]News of this came to the ears of the church in Jerusalem, and they sent Barnabas to Antioch. [23]When he came and saw the grace of God, he rejoiced, and he exhorted them

[a] Other ancient authorities read Greeks

all to remain faithful to the Lord with steadfast devotion; [24]for he was a good man, full of the Holy Spirit and of faith. And a great many people were brought to the Lord. [25]Then Barnabas went to Tarsus to look for Saul, [26]and when he had found him, he brought him to Antioch. So it was that for an entire year they met with[a] the church and taught a great many people, and it was in Antioch that the disciples were first called "Christians."

[27]At that time prophets came down from Jerusalem to Antioch. [28]One of them named Agabus stood up and predicted by the Spirit that there would be a severe famine over all the world; and this took place during the reign of Claudius. [29]The disciples determined that according to their ability, each would send relief to the believers[b] living in Judea; [30]this they did, sending it to the elders by Barnabas and Saul.

CHAPTER 12

About that time King Herod laid violent hands upon some who belonged to the church. [2]He had James, the brother of John, killed with the sword. [3]After he saw that it pleased the

[a] Or were guests of
[b] Gk brothers

```
3956    07       4286       06      2588      4357        03
πάντας τῇ      προθέσει τῆς   καρδίας προσμένειν τῷ
all     in the purpose of the heart    to stay to the
2962         3754     1510    435    18      2532 4134
κυρίῳ,  24  ὅτι    ἦν    ἀνὴρ ἀγαθὸς καὶ  πλήρης
Master,    because he was man   good    and  full
4151       40      2532 4102    2532 4369        3793
πνεύματος ἁγίου καὶ  πίστεως. καὶ προσετέθη ὄχλος
of spirit holy   and  trust.   And was set to crowd
2425    03     2962      1831      1161 1519 5019
ἱκανὸς τῷ    κυρίῳ.  25 ἐξῆλθεν δὲ   εἰς Ταρσὸν
enough in the Master.    He went out but  into Tarsus
327        4569       2532 2147        71      1519
ἀναζητῆσαι Σαῦλον, 26 καὶ εὑρὼν    ἤγαγεν εἰς
to seek after Saul,      and having found he led into
490        1096      1161 846    2532 1763     3650
Ἀντιόχειαν. ἐγένετο δὲ   αὐτοῖς καὶ ἐνιαυτὸν ὅλον
Antioch.    He became but to them and year    whole
4863           1722 07   1577      2532 1321     3793
συναχθῆναι    ἐν τῇ ἐκκλησίᾳ καὶ διδάξαι ὄχλον
to be led together in the assembly and to teach crowd
together
2425    5537          5037 4416a  1722 490         016
ἱκανόν, χρηματίσαι τε  πρώτως ἐν  Ἀντιοχείᾳ τοὺς
enough, to warn    and firstly in  Antioch    the
3101     5546         27 1722 3778   1161 019   2250
μαθητὰς Χριστιανούς.    Ἐν ταύταις δὲ   ταῖς ἡμέραις
learners Christians.    In these    but  the  days
2718      575   2414       4396      1519 490
κατῆλθον ἀπὸ Ἱεροσολύμων προφῆται εἰς Ἀντιόχειαν.
went down from Jerusalem  spokesmen into Antioch.
      450       1161 1520 1537 846   3686    13
28 ἀναστὰς    δὲ  εἷς ἐξ αὐτῶν ὀνόματι Ἅγαβος
   Having stood up but one from them in name Agabus
4591      1223   010 4151   3042    3173
ἐσήμανεν διὰ  τοῦ πνεύματος λιμὸν μεγάλην
signified through the spirit  famine great
3195     1510    1909 0660  08   3625        3748 1096
μέλλειν ἔσεσθαι ἐφ' ὅλην τὴν οἰκουμένην, ἥτις ἐγένετο
to be    to be   on whole the inhabited   which became
about                   world,
1909 2804      29 014    1161 3101    2531
ἐπὶ Κλαυδίου.    τῶν  δὲ   μαθητῶν, καθὼς
on  Claudius.    Of the but  learners, just as
2141        5100 3724    1538    846   1519
εὐπορεῖτό τις, ὥρισαν  ἕκαστος αὐτῶν εἰς
was prospering some, designated each   of them into
1248       3992    015    2730        1722 07  2449
διακονίαν πέμψαι τοῖς κατοικοῦσιν ἐν  τῇ Ἰουδαίᾳ
service   to send to the ones residing in  the Judea
80          30 3739 2532 4160   649             4314
ἀδελφοῖς·    ὃ  καὶ ἐποίησαν ἀποστείλαντες πρὸς
brothers;     what also they did having delegated to
016   4245        1223   5495  921      2532 4569
τοὺς πρεσβυτέρους διὰ  χειρὸς Βαρναβᾶ καὶ Σαύλου.
the  older men    through hand Barnabas and Saul.
      2596 1565      1161 04 2540  1911      2264 01
12:1 Κατ' ἐκεῖνον δὲ   τὸν καιρὸν ἐπέβαλεν Ἡρῴδης ὁ
     By   that    but  the season threw on  Herod   the
935       020 5495   2559      5100 014    575 06
βασιλεὺς τὰς χεῖρας κακῶσαί τινας τῶν  ἀπὸ τῆς
king      the hands to do bad some of the from the
1577        2 337     1161 2385   04 80       2491
ἐκκλησίας.  ἀνεῖλεν δὲ  Ἰάκωβον τὸν ἀδελφὸν Ἰωάννου
assembly.    He killed but Jacob   the brother  of John
3162       3 3708    1161 3754 701      1510 015
μαχαίρῃ.    Ἰδὼν    δὲ   ὅτι ἀρεστόν ἐστιν τοῖς
in sword.   Having seen but that pleasing it is  to the
```

2453   4369   4815   2532 4074
'Ιουδαίοις, προσέθετο συλλαβεῖν   καὶ Πέτρον,
Judeans,   he set to   to take together also Peter,

1510 1161 017 2250   022   106   4 3739 2532
- ἦσαν δὲ [αἱ] ἡμέραι τῶν   ἀζύμων –   ὃν καὶ
- were but the days of the unyeasted -   whom also

4084   5087   1519 5438   3860
πιάσας   ἔθετο εἰς φυλακὴν παραδοὺς
having captured he set into guard   having given over

5064   5069   4757   5442   846
τέσσαρσιν τετραδίοις στρατιωτῶν φυλάσσειν αὐτόν,
to four   groups of four soldiers to guard him,

1014   3326 012 3957   321   846 03
βουλόμενος μετὰ τὸ πάσχα ἀναγαγεῖν αὐτὸν τῷ
planning   after the passover to lead up him   to the

2992   5 01 3303   3767 4074   5083   1722 07
λαῷ.   ὁ μὲν οὖν Πέτρος ἐτηρεῖτο   ἐν τῇ
people.   The indeed then Peter was being kept in the

5438   4335   1161 1510 1619   1096   5259 06
φυλακῇ· προσευχὴ δὲ ἦν ἐκτενῶς γινομένη ὑπὸ τῆς
guard;   prayer   but was+ intensely +becoming by the

1577   4314 04 2316 4012 846   6 3753 1161
ἐκκλησίας πρὸς τὸν θεὸν περὶ αὐτοῦ.   Ὅτε δὲ
assembly   to the God about him.   When but

3195   4254   846   01 2264   07   3571
ἤμελλεν προαγαγεῖν αὐτὸν ὁ 'Ηρῴδης, τῇ νυκτὶ
was about to lead before him the Herod, in the night

1565   1510 01 4074   2837   3342   1417
ἐκείνη ἦν ὁ Πέτρος κοιμώμενος μεταξὺ δύο
that   was+ the Peter +sleeping   between two

4757   1210   254   1417 5441   5037
στρατιωτῶν δεδεμένος   ἁλύσεσιν δυσὶν φύλακές τε
soldiers   having been bound in chains two   guards and

4253   06 2374   5083   08 5438   7 2532
πρὸ τῆς θύρας ἐτήρουν   τὴν φυλακήν.   καὶ
before the door they were keeping the guard.   And

2400 32   2962   2186   2532 5457 2989
ἰδοὺ ἄγγελος κυρίου ἐπέστη καὶ φῶς ἔλαμψεν
look messenger of Master stood on and light shone

1722 011 3612   3960   1161 08 4125   02
ἐν τῷ οἰκήματι· πατάξας δὲ τὴν πλευρὰν τοῦ
in the building; having hit but the side   of the

4074   1453   846   3004   450   1722 5034
Πέτρου ἤγειρεν αὐτὸν λέγων· ἀνάστα ἐν τάχει.
Peter   he raised him   saying; stand up in quickness.

2532 1601   846   017 254   1537 018 5495
καὶ ἐξέπεσαν αὐτοῦ αἱ ἁλύσεις ἐκ τῶν χειρῶν.
And fell out of him the chains from the hands.

      3004 1161 01 32   4314 846   2224
8 εἶπεν δὲ ὁ ἄγγελος πρὸς αὐτόν· ζῶσαι
   Said but the messenger to him; belt yourself

2532 5265   024 4547   1473   4160   1161 3779
καὶ ὑπόδησαι τὰ σανδάλιά σου. ἐποίησεν δὲ οὕτως.
and tie down the sandals of you. He did but thusly.

2532 3004   846   4016   012 2440   1473
καὶ λέγει αὐτῷ· περιβαλοῦ τὸ ἱμάτιόν σου
And he says to him; throw around the clothes of you

2532 190   1473   9 2532 1831   190   2532 3756
καὶ ἀκολούθει μοι.   καὶ ἐξελθὼν ἠκολούθει καὶ οὐκ
and follow   me.   And having   he was   and not
                             come out following

3609a   3754 227   1510 09 1096   1223   02
ᾔδει   ὅτι ἀληθές ἐστιν τὸ γινόμενον διὰ   τοῦ
he knew that true is   the becoming through the

32   1380   1161 3705   991
ἀγγέλου· ἐδόκει   δὲ ὅραμα βλέπειν.
messenger; he was thinking but sight to see.

     1330   1161 4413   5438   2532 1208
10 διελθόντες   δὲ πρώτην φυλακὴν καὶ δευτέραν
    Having gone through but first   guard   and second

Jews, he proceeded to arrest Peter also. (This was during the festival of Unleavened Bread.) [4]When he had seized him, he put him in prison and handed him over to four squads of soldiers to guard him, intending to bring him out to the people after the Passover. [5]While Peter was kept in prison, the church prayed fervently to God for him.

[6]The very night before Herod was going to bring him out, Peter, bound with two chains, was sleeping between two soldiers, while guards in front of the door were keeping watch over the prison. [7]Suddenly an angel of the Lord appeared and a light shone in the cell. He tapped Peter on the side and woke him, saying, "Get up quickly." And the chains fell off his wrists. [8]The angel said to him, "Fasten your belt and put on your sandals." He did so. Then he said to him, "Wrap your cloak around you and follow me." [9]Peter[a] went out and followed him; he did not realize that what was happening with the angel's help was real; he thought he was seeing a vision. [10]After they had passed the first and the second guard,

_a Gk He_

they came before the iron gate leading into the city. It opened for them of its own accord, and they went outside and walked along a lane, when suddenly the angel left him. ¹¹Then Peter came to himself and said, "Now I am sure that the Lord has sent his angel and rescued me from the hands of Herod and from all that the Jewish people were expecting."

12 As soon as he realized this, he went to the house of Mary, the mother of John whose other name was Mark, where many had gathered and were praying. ¹³When he knocked at the outer gate, a maid named Rhoda came to answer. ¹⁴On recognizing Peter's voice, she was so overjoyed that, instead of opening the gate, she ran in and announced that Peter was standing at the gate. ¹⁵They said to her, "You are out of your mind!" But she insisted that it was so. They said, "It is his angel." ¹⁶Meanwhile Peter continued knocking; and when they opened the gate, they saw him and were amazed. ¹⁷He motioned to them with his hand to be silent, and described for them how the Lord

	2064	1909	08	4439	08	4603	08	5342	1519
	ἦλθαν	ἐπὶ		τὴν πύλην	τὴν σιδηρᾶν		τὴν φέρουσαν	εἰς
	they came	on		the gate	the iron		the carrying	to

08	4172	3748	844		455	846	2532
τὴν πόλιν,	ἥτις	αὐτομάτη	ἠνοίγη		αὐτοῖς	καὶ
the city,	that	by itself	was opened		to them	and

1831	4281	4505	1520	2532
ἐξελθόντες	προῆλθον	ῥύμην μίαν,	καὶ
having gone out	they came before	lane one,	and

2112	868	01	32	575	846
εὐθέως	ἀπέστη	ὁ	ἄγγελος	ἀπ᾽	αὐτοῦ.
immediately	stood off	the messenger	from him.

	2532	01	4074	1722	1438	1096	3004	3568
11	Καὶ	ὁ	Πέτρος	ἐν	ἑαυτῷ	γενόμενος	εἶπεν·	νῦν
	And	the	Peter	in	himself	having become	said;	now

3609a	230	3754	1821	01	2962	04
οἶδα	ἀληθῶς	ὅτι	ἐξαπέστειλεν	[ὁ]	κύριος	τὸν
I know	truly	that	delegated out	the	Master	the

32	846	2532	1807	1473	1537	5495
ἄγγελον	αὐτοῦ	καὶ	ἐξείλατό	με	ἐκ	χειρὸς
messenger	of him	and	lifted out	me	from	hand

2264	2532	3956	06	4329	02	2992
Ἡρῴδου	καὶ	πάσης	τῆς	προσδοκίας	τοῦ	λαοῦ
of Herod	and	all	the	expectation	of the	people

014	2453		4927a		5037	2064
τῶν	Ἰουδαίων.	**12**	συνιδών		τε	ἦλθεν
of the	Judeans.		Having seen together		and	he went

1909	08	3614	06	3137	06	3384	2491	02
ἐπὶ	τὴν οἰκίαν	τῆς		Μαρίας	τῆς	μητρὸς	Ἰωάννου	τοῦ
on	the house	of the		Maria	the	mother	of John	the

1941	3138	3757	1510	2425
ἐπικαλουμένου	Μάρκου,	οὗ	ἦσαν	ἱκανοὶ
one being called on	Mark,	where	were	enough

4867	2532	4336		2925	1161
συνηθροισμένοι	καὶ	προσευχόμενοι.	**13**	κρούσαντος	δὲ
having been gathered together	and	praying.		Having knocked	but

846	08	2374	03	4440	4334	3814
αὐτοῦ	τὴν	θύραν	τοῦ	πυλῶνος	προσῆλθεν	παιδίσκη
him	the	door	of the	gate	came to	servant girl

5219	3686	4498		2532	1921	08
ὑπακοῦσαι	ὀνόματι	Ῥόδη,	**14**	καὶ	ἐπιγνοῦσα	τὴν
to obey	in name	Rhoda,		and	having perceived	the

5456	02	4074	575	06	5479	3756	455	04
φωνὴν	τοῦ	Πέτρου	ἀπὸ	τῆς	χαρᾶς	οὐκ	ἤνοιξεν	τὸν
sound	of the	Peter	from	the	joy	not	she opened	the

4440	1532		1161	518		2476	04
πυλῶνα,	εἰσδραμοῦσα		δὲ	ἀπήγγειλεν		ἑστάναι	τὸν
gate,	having run in		but	she told		to stand	the

4074	4253	02	4440		013		1161	4314	846
Πέτρον	πρὸ	τοῦ	πυλῶνος.	**15**	οἱ		δὲ	πρὸς	αὐτὴν
Peter	before	the	gate.		The ones		but	to	her

3004	3105		05	1161	1340	3779
εἶπαν·	μαίνῃ.		ἡ	δὲ	διϊσχυρίζετο	οὕτως
said;	you are crazy.		The	but	was insisting	thusly

2192	013	1161	3004	01	32	1510
ἔχειν.	οἱ	δὲ	ἔλεγον·	ὁ	ἄγγελός	ἐστιν
to have.	The	but	was saying;	the	messenger	is

846		01	1161	4074	1961	2925
αὐτοῦ.	**16**	ὁ	δὲ	Πέτρος	ἐπέμενεν	κρούων·
of him.		The	but	Peter	was staying on	knocking;

455	1161	3708	846	2532	1839
ἀνοίξαντες	δὲ	εἶδαν	αὐτὸν	καὶ	ἐξέστησαν.
having opened	but	they saw	him	and	were amazed.

	2678	1161	846	07	5495
17	κατασείσας	δε	αὐτοῖς	τῇ	χειρὶ
	Having motioned	but	to them	in	the hand

4601	1334	846	4459	01	2962	846
σιγᾶν	διηγήσατο	[αὐτοῖς]	πῶς	ὁ	κύριος	αὐτὸν
to be silent	he narrated	to them	how	the	Master	him

```
1806        1537 06   5438        3004    5037 518
ἐξήγαγεν  ἐκ  τῆς φυλακῆς εἶπέν τε· ἀπαγγείλατε
led out   from the guard    said  and; tell

2385       2532 015  80          3778    2532 1831
'Ιακώβῳ καὶ τοῖς ἀδελφοῖς ταῦτα. καὶ ἐξελθὼν
Jacob   and the brothers these.  And  having gone out

4198        1519 2087  5117       18 1096              1161
ἐπορεύθη εἰς ἕτερον τόπον.       Γενομένης        δὲ
he traveled into other  place.     Having become but

2250    1510 5017   3756 3641   1722 015   4757
ἡμέρας ἦν τάραχος οὐκ ὀλίγος ἐν τοῖς στρατιώταις
day     was trouble not  few   in  the  soldiers

5101 686  01   4074      1096    19  2264     1161
τί ἄρα ὁ Πέτρος ἐγένετο.     'Ηρῴδης δὲ
why then the Peter  became.     Herod    but

1934           846    2532 3361 2147  350      016
ἐπιζητήσας αὐτὸν καὶ μὴ εὑρών, ἀνακρίνας τοὺς
having sought him  and  not having having     the
after                            found, examined

5441     2753      520          2532 2718
φύλακας ἐκέλευσεν ἀπαχθῆναι, καὶ κατελθὼν
guards  commanded to be led off, and having gone down

575 06  2449      1519 2542    1304       1510
ἀπὸ τῆς 'Ιουδαίας εἰς Καισάρειαν διέτριβεν. 20 *Ην
from the Judea    into Caesarea  continued.  He was+

1161 2371           5183      2532 4606
δὲ θυμομάχων      Τυρίοις καὶ Σιδωνίοις·
but +furious fighting Tyreneans and Sidonians;

3661          1161 3918          4314 846     2532
ὁμοθυμαδὸν δὲ παρῆσαν       πρὸς αὐτὸν καὶ
with one mind but they were present to   him   and

3982        986      04  1909 02  2846     02
πείσαντες Βλάστον, τὸν ἐπὶ τοῦ κοιτῶνος τοῦ
having persuaded Blastus, the on  the bedroom  of the

935       154      1515      1223    012 5142
βασιλέως, ἠτοῦντο εἰρήνην διὰ τὸ τρέφεσθαι
king,     were asking peace because the to be fed

846  08  5561    575 06 937           21 5002        1161
αὐτῶν τὴν χώραν ἀπὸ τῆς βασιλικῆς.   τακτῇ     δὲ
them   the country from the kingly.    In ordered but

2250  01 2264 1746         2066     937        2532
ἡμέρᾳ ὁ 'Ηρῴδης ἐνδυσάμενος ἐσθῆτα βασιλικὴν [καὶ]
day   the Herod  having put on  clothes kingly    and

2523       1909 010 968      1215            4314
καθίσας ἐπὶ τοῦ βήματος ἐδημηγόρει      πρὸς
having sat on  the law court was making a speech to

846     22 01  1161 1218  2019              2316
αὐτούς,  ὁ  δὲ δῆμος ἐπεφώνει·         θεοῦ
them,      the but public were sounding on; of god

5456    2532 3756 444     23 3916      1161 3960
φωνὴ καὶ οὐκ ἀνθρώπου.  παραχρῆμα δὲ ἐπάταξεν
sound and not  of man.    Suddenly  but  hit

846  32     2962      473    3739 3756 1325    08
αὐτὸν ἄγγελος κυρίου ἀνθ' ὧν οὐκ ἔδωκεν τὴν
him  messenger of Master against which not he gave the

1391    03   2316 2532 1096         4662
δόξαν τῷ θεῷ, καὶ γενόμενος σκωληκόβρωτος
splendor to the God, and having become food for worms

1634     32  01   1161 3056 02   2316 837
ἐξέψυξεν. 24 'Ο δὲ λόγος τοῦ θεοῦ ηὔξανεν
he expired.   The but word of the God was growing

2532 4129        25 921       1161 2532 4569
καὶ ἐπληθύνετο.   Βαρναβᾶς δὲ καὶ Σαῦλος
and multiplying.   Barnabas  but and  Saul

5290        1519 2419       4137       08 1248
ὑπέστρεψαν εἰς 'Ιερουσαλὴμ πληρώσαντες τὴν διακονίαν,
returned   to  Jerusalem   having filled the service,
```

had brought him out of the prison. And he added, "Tell this to James and to the believers."[a] Then he left and went to another place.

18 When morning came, there was no small commotion among the soldiers over what had become of Peter. 19When Herod had searched for him and could not find him, he examined the guards and ordered them to be put to death. Then he went down from Judea to Caesarea and stayed there.

20 Now Herod[b] was angry with the people of Tyre and Sidon. So they came to him in a body; and after winning over Blastus, the king's chamberlain, they asked for a reconciliation, because their country depended on the king's country for food. 21On an appointed day Herod put on his royal robes, took his seat on the platform, and delivered a public address to them. 22The people kept shouting, "The voice of a god, and not of a mortal!" 23And immediately, because he had not given the glory to God, an angel of the Lord struck him down, and he was eaten by worms and died.

24 But the word of God continued to advance and gain adherents. 25Then after completing their mission Barnabas and Saul returned to[c] Jerusalem

a Gk brothers
b Gk he
c Other ancient authorities read from

and brought with them John, whose other name was Mark.

CHAPTER 13

Now in the church at Antioch there were prophets and teachers: Barnabas, Simeon who was called Niger, Lucius of Cyrene, Manaen a member of the court of Herod the ruler,[a] and Saul. [2]While they were worshiping the Lord and fasting, the Holy Spirit said, "Set apart for me Barnabas and Saul for the work to which I have called them." [3]Then after fasting and praying they laid their hands on them and sent them off.

[4]So, being sent out by the Holy Spirit, they went down to Seleucia; and from there they sailed to Cyprus. [5]When they arrived at Salamis, they proclaimed the word of God in the synagogues of the Jews. And they had John also to assist them. [6]When they had gone through the whole island as far as Paphos, they met a certain magician, a Jewish false prophet, named Bar-Jesus. [7]He was with the proconsul, Sergius Paulus, an intelligent man, who summoned Barnabas and Saul and wanted to hear the word of God. [8]But the magician Elymas

[a] Gk tetrarch

	4838		2491	04	1941		3138
	συμπαραλαβόντες	'Ιωάννην	τὸν	ἐπικληθέντα	Μᾶρκον.
	having taken along together	John	the	having been called on	Mark.

13:1
1510 1161	1722	490		2596 08	1510
Ἦσαν δὲ	ἐν	'Αντιοχείᾳ	κατὰ τὴν	οὖσαν
Were but	in	Antioch	by	the being

1577	4396	2532 1320		01	5037 921
ἐκκλησίαν	προφῆται	καὶ διδάσκαλοι	ὅ	τε	Βαρναβας
assembly	spokesmen	and teachers	the	both	Barnabas

2532 4826	01	2564		3526	2532 3066	01
κἀι Συμεὼν	ὁ	καλούμενος	Νίγερ καὶ	Λούκιος	ὁ
and Symeon	the	being called	Niger and	Lucius	the

2956	3127 5037	2264	02	5076
Κυρηναῖος,	Μαναήν τε	'Ηρῴδου	τοῦ τετραάρχου
Cyrenean,	Manaen and	Herod	the ruler of fourth

4939	2532 4569		3008		1161 846
σύντροφος	καὶ Σαῦλος. [2]	Λειτουργούντων	δὲ	αὐτῶν
fed together	and Saul.	Serving	but	them

03	2962	2532 3522		3004	09	4151	09	40
τῷ	κυρίῳ	καὶ νηστευόντων	εἶπεν τὸ	πνεῦμα	τὸ	ἅγιον·
the	Master	and fasting	said the	spirit	the	holy;

873		1211	1473	04	921		2532 4569	1519 012
ἀφορίσατε	δή	μοι	τὸν Βαρναβᾶν	καὶ Σαῦλον	εἰς τὸ
separate	indeed	to me	the Barnabas	and Saul	to the

2041	3739 4341		846		5119 3522
ἔργον	ὅ	προσκέκλημαι	αὐτούς. [3]	τότε	νηστεύσαντες
work	that	I have called	to them.	Then	having fasted

2532 4336		2532 2007		020 5495	846
καὶ	προσευξάμενοι καὶ	ἐπιθέντες	τὰς χεῖρας	αὐτοῖς
and	prayed	and set on	the hands	to them

630		4	846		3303	3767 1599		5259
ἀπέλυσαν.	[4]	Αὐτοὶ	μὲν	οὖν	ἐκπεμφθέντες	ὑπὸ
they loosed loosed off.		Themselves	indeed	then	having been	by sent out

010 40	4151	2718	1519 4581
τοῦ ἁγίου	πνεύματος	κατῆλθον	εἰς Σελεύκειαν,
the holy	spirit	went down	into Seleucia,

1564		5037 636		1519 2954	5	2532
ἐκεῖθέν	τε	ἀπέπλευσαν	εἰς Κύπρον	[5]	καὶ
from there	and	sailed off	to Cyprus		and

1096		1722 4529		2605
γενόμενοι	ἐν	Σαλαμῖνι	κατήγγελλον
having become	in	in Salamis	they were proclaiming

04	3056	02	2316 1722 019	4864	014
τὸν	λόγον τοῦ	θεοῦ ἐν	ταῖς συναγωγαῖς	τῶν
the	word of the	God in	the synagogues	of the

2453		2192		1161 2532	2491	5257
'Ιουδαίων.	εἶχον	δὲ	καὶ	'Ιωάννην	ὑπηρέτην.
Judeans.	They had	but	also	John	assistant.

6	1330		1161 3650	08	3520	891	3974	2147
	Διελθόντες	δὲ	ὅλην	τὴν νῆσον	ἄχρι	Πάφου	εὗρον
	Having gone through	but	whole	the island	until	Paphos	they found

435	5100 3097		5578		2453	3739
ἄνδρα	τινὰ μάγον		ψευδοπροφήτην	'Ιουδαῖον	ᾧ
man	some magician		false spokesman	Judean	to whom

3686	919	7	3739 1510 4862 03	446	4588
ὄνομα	Βαριησοῦ	[7]	ὃς ἦν σὺν	τῷ ἀνθυπάτῳ	Σεργίῳ
name	Barjesus,		who was with	the deputy	Sergius

3972	435	4908		3778	4341
Παύλῳ,	ἀνδρὶ	συνετῷ.		οὗτος	προσκαλεσάμενος
Paul,	man	understanding.		This	having called to

921		2532 4569	1934		191	04	3056
Βαρναβᾶν	καὶ	Σαῦλον	ἐπεζήτησεν	ἀκοῦσαι	τὸν	λόγον
Barnabas	and	Saul	sought after	to hear	the	word

02	2316	8	436		1161 846	1681
τοῦ	θεοῦ.	[8]	ἀνθίστατο		δὲ αὐτοῖς	'Ελύμας
of the	God.		Was standing against		but them	Elymas

01	3097		3779	1063	3177		09	3686
ὁ	μάγος,	οὕτως	γὰρ	μεθερμηνεύεται	τὸ	ὄνομα
the	magician,	thusly	for	is translated	the	name

846	2212	1294		04	446	575	06
αὐτοῦ,	ζητῶν	διαστρέψαι	τὸν	ἀνθύπατον	ἀπὸ	τῆς
of him,	seeking	to pervert	the	deputy	from	the

4102		9	4569	1161	01	2532	3972
πίστεως.		Σαῦλος	δέ,	ὁ	καὶ	Παῦλος,
trust.	Saul	but,	the	also	Paul,

4092		4151	40	816		1519
πλησθεὶς	πνεύματος	ἁγίου	ἀτενίσας	εἰς
having been filled	of spirit	holy	having stared	into

846	3004	10	5599	4134	3956	1388	2532	3956
αὐτὸν	εἶπεν·	ὦ	πλήρης	παντὸς	δόλου	καὶ	πάσης
him	said;	O	full	of all	guile	and	all

4468		5207	1228		2190		3956
ῥᾳδιουργίας,	υἱὲ	διαβόλου,	ἐχθρὲ	πάσης
fraud,	son	of slanderer,	hostile	one of all

1343		3756	3973		1294		020	3598
δικαιοσύνης,	οὐ	παύσῃ	διαστρέφων	τὰς	ὁδοὺς
rightness,	not	you will stop	perverting	the	ways

02	2962	020	2117a		2532	3568	2400	5495
[τοῦ]	κυρίου	τὰς	εὐθείας;	11	καὶ	νῦν	ἰδοὺ	χεὶρ
of the	Master	the	straight?	And	now	look	hand

2962	1909	1473	2532	1510		5185	3361	991
κυρίου	ἐπὶ	σὲ	καὶ	ἔσῃ	τυφλὸς	μὴ	βλέπων
of Master	on	you	and	you will be	blind	not	seeing

04	2246	891	2540	3916		5037	4098	1909	846
τὸν	ἥλιον	ἄχρι	καιροῦ.	παραχρῆμά	τε	ἔπεσεν	ἐπ᾽	αὐτὸν
the sun	until	season.	Suddenly	and	fell	on	him

887		2532	4655	2532	4013		2212
ἀχλὺς	καὶ	σκότος	καὶ	περιάγων	ἐζήτει
mistiness	and	dark	and	leading	he was seeking around

5497		12	5119	3708		01	446		012
χειραγωγούς.		τότε	ἰδὼν	ὁ	ἀνθύπατος	τὸ
hands leading.	Then	having seen	the	deputy	the

1096		4100		1605		1909	07
γεγονὸς	ἐπίστευσεν	ἐκπλησσόμενος	ἐπὶ	τῇ
having become	trusted	being astonished	at	the

1322	02	2962		13	321		1161
διδαχῇ	τοῦ	κυρίου.	Ἀναχθέντες	δὲ
teaching	of the	Master.	Having been led up	but

575	06	3974	013	4012		3972	2064	1519	4011
ἀπὸ	τῆς	Πάφου	οἱ	περὶ	Παῦλον	ἦλθον	εἰς	Πέργην
from	the	Paphos	the	around	Paul	went	into	Perga

06	3828		2491	1161	672
τῆς	Παμφυλίας,	Ἰωάννης	δὲ	ἀποχωρήσας
of the	Pamphylia,	John	but	having made room off

575	846	5290		1519	2414		14	846		1161
ἀπ᾽	αὐτῶν	ὑπέστρεψεν	εἰς	Ἱεροσόλυμα.	Αὐτοὶ	δὲ
from them	returned	to	Jerusalem.	Themselves	but

1330		575	06	4011	3854		1519
διελθόντες	ἀπὸ	τῆς	Πέργης	παρεγένοντο	εἰς
having gone through	from	the	Perga	arrived	in

490		08	4099	2532	1525		1519	08
Ἀντιόχειαν	τὴν	Πισιδίαν,	καὶ	[εἰσ]ελθόντες	εἰς	τὴν
Antioch	the	Pisidia,	and	having gone in	into	the

4864	07	2250	022	4521		2523		15	3326
συναγωγὴν	τῇ	ἡμέρᾳ	τῶν	σαββάτων	ἐκάθισαν.	μετὰ
synagogue	the	day	of the	sabbaths	they sat.	After

1161	08	320		02	3551	2532	014	4396
δὲ	τὴν	ἀνάγνωσιν	τοῦ	νόμου	καὶ	τῶν	προφητῶν
but	the	reading	of the	law	and	the	spokesmen

649		013	752		4314	846		3004
ἀπέστειλαν	οἱ	ἀρχισυνάγωγοι	πρὸς	αὐτοὺς	λέγοντες·
delegated	the	synagogue rulers	to	them	saying;

435	80		1487	5100	1510	1722	1473	3056
ἄνδρες	ἀδελφοί,	εἴ	τίς	ἐστιν	ἐν	ὑμῖν	λόγος
men	brothers,	if	some	is	in	you	word

(for that is the translation of his name) opposed them and tried to turn the proconsul away from the faith. [9]But Saul, also known as Paul, filled with the Holy Spirit, looked intently at him [10]and said, "You son of the devil, you enemy of all righteousness, full of all deceit and villainy, will you not stop making crooked the straight paths of the Lord? [11]And now listen—the hand of the Lord is against you, and you will be blind for a while, unable to see the sun." Immediately mist and darkness came over him, and he went about groping for someone to lead him by the hand. [12]When the proconsul saw what had happened, he believed, for he was astonished at the teaching about the Lord.

[13] Then Paul and his companions set sail from Paphos and came to Perga in Pamphylia. John, however, left them and returned to Jerusalem; [14]but they went on from Perga and came to Antioch in Pisidia. And on the sabbath day they went into the synagogue and sat down. [15]After the reading of the law and the prophets, the officials of the synagogue sent them a message, saying, "Brothers, if you have any word

of exhortation for the people, give it." 16So Paul stood up and with a gesture began to speak: "You Israelites,*a* and others who fear God, listen. 17The God of this people Israel chose our ancestors and made the people great during their stay in the land of Egypt, and with uplifted arm he led them out of it. 18For about forty years he put up with*b* them in the wilderness. 19After he had destroyed seven nations in the land of Canaan, he gave them their land as an inheritance 20for about four hundred fifty years. After that he gave them judges until the time of the prophet Samuel. 21Then they asked for a king; and God gave them Saul son of Kish, a man of the tribe of Benjamin, who reigned for forty years. 22When he had removed him, he made David their king. In his testimony about him he said, 'I have found David, son of Jesse, to be a man after my heart, who will carry out all my wishes.' 23Of this man's posterity God has brought to Israel a Savior, Jesus, as he promised; 24before his coming John had already proclaimed

a Gk Men, Israelites
b Other ancient authorities read cared for

3874		4314 04	2992	3004	
παρακλήσεως		πρὸς τὸν	λαόν,	λέγετε.	
of encouragement		to the	people,	say.	

16 450
Ἀναστὰς
Having stood up
1161 3972   2532 2678
δὲ Παῦλος καὶ κατασείσας
but Paul and having motioned

07   5495   3004   435   2475   2532 013
τῇ   χειρὶ εἶπεν· ἄνδρες Ἰσραηλῖται καὶ οἱ
in the hand said; men Israelites and the ones

5399   04 2316 191   **17** 01 2316 02
φοβούμενοι τὸν θεόν, ἀκούσατε.   ὁ θεὸς τοῦ
fearing the God, hear.   The God of the

2992   3778   2474   1586   016   3962   1473 2532
λαοῦ τούτου Ἰσραὴλ ἐξελέξατο τοὺς πατέρας ἡμῶν καὶ
people this Israel selected the fathers of us and

04 2992   5312   1722 07   3940   1722 1093
τὸν λαὸν ὕψωσεν ἐν τῇ παροικίᾳ ἐν γῇ
the people elevated in the transiency in land

125   2532 3326 1023   5308   1806   846
Αἰγύπτου καὶ μετὰ βραχίονος ὑψηλοῦ ἐξήγαγεν αὐτοὺς
of Egypt and with arm high he led out them

1537 846   2532 5613 5063   5550
ἐξ αὐτῆς, **18** καὶ ὡς τεσσερακονταετῆ χρόνον
from it, and as forty years time

5159   846   1722 07   2048   **19** 2532
ἐτροποφόρησεν αὐτοὺς ἐν τῇ ἐρήμῳ καὶ
he bore with manners them in the desert and

2507   1484   2033 1722 1093 5477
καθελὼν ἔθνη ἑπτὰ ἐν γῇ Χανάαν
having lifted down nations seven in land Canaan

2624   08 1093 846 **20** 5613
κατεκληρονόμησεν τὴν γῆν αὐτῶν ὡς
he gave as an inheritance the land of them as

2094   5071   2532 4004   2532 3326 3778
ἔτεσιν τετρακοσίοις καὶ πεντήκοντα. καὶ μετὰ ταῦτα
years four hundred and fifty. And after these

1325   2923   2193 4545   02 4396
ἔδωκεν κριτὰς ἕως Σαμουήλ [τοῦ] προφήτου.
he gave judges until Samuel the spokesman.

21 2547   154   935
κἀκεῖθεν ᾐτήσαντο βασιλέα
And from there they asked for themselves king

2532 1325   846   01 2316 04 4549 5207 2797 435
καὶ ἔδωκεν αὐτοῖς ὁ θεὸς τὸν Σαοὺλ υἱὸν Κίς, ἄνδρα
and gave to them the God the Saul son Kis, man

1537 5443 958   2094 5062   **22** 2532
ἐκ φυλῆς Βενιαμίν, ἔτη τεσσεράκοντα, καὶ
from tribe Benjamin, years forty, and

3179   846   1453   04 1160a 846
μεταστήσας αὐτὸν ἤγειρεν τὸν Δαυὶδ αὐτοῖς
having transferred him he raised the David to them

1519 935   3739   2532 3004   3140
εἰς βασιλέα ᾧ καὶ εἶπεν μαρτυρήσας·
to king in whom also he said having testified;

2147   1160a 04 02   2421   435   2596 08
εὗρον Δαυὶδ τὸν τοῦ Ἰεσσαί, ἄνδρα κατὰ τὴν
I found David the of the Jesse, man by the

2588   1473   3739 4160   3956   024 3207   1473
καρδίαν μου, ὃς ποιήσει πάντα τὰ θελήματά μου.
heart of me, who will do all the wants of me.

23 3778   01 2316 575   010 4690   2596 1860
τούτου ὁ θεὸς ἀπὸ τοῦ σπέρματος κατ' ἐπαγγελίαν
Of this the God from the seed by promise

71   03 2474   4990   2424   4296
ἤγαγεν τῷ Ἰσραὴλ σωτῆρα Ἰησοῦν, **24** προκηρύξαντος
led the Israel deliverer Jesus, having announced before

2491   4253   4383   06   1529   846
Ἰωάννου πρὸ προσώπου τῆς εἰσόδου αὐτοῦ
of John before face of the entrance of him

908	334:		3956	03	2992	2474

βάπτισμα μετανοίας παντὶ τῷ λαῷ Ἰσραήλ.
immersion change mind to all the people Israel.

	5613	1161	4137		2491	04	1408

25 ὡς δὲ ἐπλήρου Ἰωάννης τὸν δρόμον,
As but was filling John the race,

3004			5101	1473	5282		1510	3756	1510

ἔλεγεν· τί ἐμὲ ὑπονοεῖτε εἶναι; οὐκ εἰμὶ
he was saying; who me you suppose to be? not am

1473	235	2400	2064		3326	1473	3739	3756	1510

ἐγώ· ἀλλ’ ἰδοὺ ἔρχεται μετ’ ἐμὲ οὗ οὐκ εἰμὶ
I; but look he comes after me who not I am

514	012	5266	014	4228	3089			435

ἄξιος τὸ ὑπόδημα τῶν ποδῶν λῦσαι. 26 Ἄνδρες
worthy the sandal of the feet to loose. Men

80		5207	1085	11		2532	013		1722	1473

ἀδελφοί, υἱοὶ γένους Ἀβραὰμ καὶ οἱ ἐν ὑμῖν
brothers, sons of kind Abraham and the ones in you

5399		04	2316	1473	01	3056	06	4991

φοβούμενοι τὸν θεόν, ἡμῖν ὁ λόγος τῆς σωτηρίας
fearing the God, to us the word of the deliverance

3778	1821			013	1063	2730		1722

ταύτης ἐξαπεστάλη. 27 οἱ γὰρ κατοικοῦντες ἐν
this was delegated out. The for residing in

2419		2532	013	758		846		3778

Ἰερουσαλὴμ καὶ οἱ ἄρχοντες αὐτῶν τοῦτον
Jerusalem and the rulers of them this

50		2532	020	5456	014		4396	020

ἀγνοήσαντες καὶ τὰς φωνὰς τῶν προφητῶν τὰς
having unknown and the sounds of the spokesmen the

2596	3956	4521		314		2919

κατὰ πᾶν σάββατον ἀναγινωσκομένας κρίναντες
by all sabbath being read having judged

4137		2532	3367		156	2288

ἐπλήρωσαν, 28 καὶ μηδεμίαν αἰτίαν θανάτου
they filled, and not even one cause of death

2147		154			4091

εὑρόντες ᾐτήσαντο Πιλᾶτον
having found they asked for themselves Pilate

337		846		5613	1161	5055		3956

ἀναιρεθῆναι αὐτόν. 29 ὡς δὲ ἐτέλεσαν πάντα
to be killed him. As but they completed all

024	4012	846		1125		2507

τὰ περὶ αὐτοῦ γεγραμμένα, καθελόντες
the about him having been written, having lifted down
written,

575	010	3586	5087		1519	3419		01	1161	2316

ἀπὸ τοῦ ξύλου ἔθηκαν εἰς μνημεῖον. 30 ὁ δὲ θεὸς
from the wood they set in grave. The but God

1453		846	1537	3498		3739	3708		1909	2250

ἤγειρεν αὐτὸν ἐκ νεκρῶν, 31 ὃς ὤφθη ἐπὶ ἡμέρας
raised him from dead, who was seen on days

4183	015		4872			846

πλείους τοῖς συναναβᾶσιν αὐτῷ
more to the ones having gone up together to him

575	06	1056		1519	2419		3748	3568

ἀπὸ τῆς Γαλιλαίας εἰς Ἰερουσαλήμ, οἵτινες [νῦν]
from the Galilee to Jerusalem, who now

1510	3144		846		4314	04	2992		2532	1473

εἰσιν μάρτυρες αὐτοῦ πρὸς τὸν λαόν. 32 Καὶ ἡμεῖς
are testifiers of him to the people. And we

1473	2097		08	4314	016	3962

ὑμᾶς εὐαγγελιζόμεθα τὴν πρὸς τοὺς πατέρας
you tell good message the to the fathers

1860		1096		3754	3778	01	2316

ἐπαγγελίαν γενομένην, 33 ὅτι ταύτην ὁ θεὸς
promise having become, because this the God

1603		023	5043	846		1473

ἐκπεπλήρωκεν τοῖς τέκνοις [αὐτῶν] ἡμῖν
has filled out to the children of them to us

a baptism of repentance to all the people of Israel. [25]And as John was finishing his work, he said, 'What do you suppose that I am? I am not he. No, but one is coming after me; I am not worthy to untie the thong of the sandals[a] on his feet.'

26 "My brothers, you descendants of Abraham's family, and others who fear God, to us[b] the message of this salvation has been sent. [27]Because the residents of Jerusalem and their leaders did not recognize him or understand the words of the prophets that are read every sabbath, they fulfilled those words by condemning him. [28]Even though they found no cause for a sentence of death, they asked Pilate to have him killed. [29]When they had carried out everything that was written about him, they took him down from the tree and laid him in a tomb. [30]But God raised him from the dead; [31]and for many days he appeared to those who came up with him from Galilee to Jerusalem, and they are now his witnesses to the people. [32]And we bring you the good news that what God promised to our ancestors [33]he has fulfilled for us, their children,

a Gk untie the sandals
b Other ancient authorities read you

by raising Jesus; as also it is written in the second psalm, 'You are my Son; today I have begotten you.' [34]As to his raising him from the dead, no more to return to corruption, he has spoken in this way, 'I will give you the holy promises made to David.' [35]Therefore he has also said in another psalm, 'You will not let your Holy One experience corruption.' [36]For David, after he had served the purpose of God in his own generation, died,[a] was laid beside his ancestors, and experienced corruption; [37]but he whom God raised up experienced no corruption. [38]Let it be known to you therefore, my brothers, that through this man forgiveness of sins is proclaimed to you; [39]by this Jesus[b] everyone who believes is set free from all those sins[c] from which you could not be freed by the law of Moses. [40]Beware, therefore, that what the prophets said does not happen to you: [41]'Look, you scoffers! Be amazed and perish, for in your days I am doing a work, a work that you will never believe, even if someone tells you.'"

42 As Paul and Barnabas[d] were going out, the people urged them to speak about these things again the next sabbath.

---

[a] Gk fell asleep
[b] Gk this
[c] Gk all
[d] Gk they

		2424	5613	2532	1722	03	5568
450							

ἀναστήσας Ἰησοῦν ὡς καὶ ἐν τῷ ψαλμῷ
having stood up Jesus as also in the psalm

1125   03   1208   5207 1473 1510 1473
γέγραπται   τῷ δευτέρῳ· υἱός μου εἶ σύ,
it has been written the second; son of me are you,

1473 4594   1080   1473   **34** 3754   1161
ἐγὼ σήμερον γεγέννηκά   σε.   ὅτι   δὲ
I today have given birth you.   Because but

450   846   1537 3498 3371   3195
ἀνέστησεν αὐτὸν ἐκ νεκρῶν μηκέτι μέλλοντα
he stood up him from dead no longer being about

5290   1519 1312   3779   3004   3754
ὑποστρέφειν εἰς διαφθοράν, οὕτως εἴρηκεν   ὅτι
to return to corruption, thusly he has spoken, (")

1325   1473   024 3741   1160a 024 4103
δώσω   ὑμῖν τὰ ὅσια Δαυὶδ τὰ πιστά.
I will give to you the holies David the trustful.

35 1360   2532 1722 2087 3004   3756 1325
διότι   καὶ ἐν ἑτέρῳ λέγει·   οὐ δώσεις
Through that also in other he says; not you will give

04   3741   1473   3708   1312   1160a 3303
τὸν ὅσιόν σου   ἰδεῖν διαφθοράν. **36** Δαυὶδ μὲν
the holy of you to see corruption.   David indeed

1063 2398 1074   5256   07   02   2316
γὰρ ἰδίᾳ γενεᾷ   ὑπηρετήσας   τῇ   τοῦ θεοῦ
for own generation having assisted in the of the God

1012 2837   2532 4369   4314 016 3962   846
βουλῇ ἐκοιμήθη καὶ προσετέθη πρὸς τοὺς πατέρας αὐτοῦ
plan slept and was set to to the fathers of him

2532 3708   1312   3739 1161 01 2316 1453
καὶ εἶδεν διαφθοράν· **37** ὃν δὲ ὁ θεὸς ἤγειρεν,
and he saw corruption; whom but the God raised,

3756 3708   1312   1110   3767 1510   1473
οὐκ εἶδεν διαφθοράν. **38** γνωστὸν οὖν ἔστω ὑμῖν,
not he saw corruption. Known then let be to you,

435   80   3754 1223   3778   1473 859
ἄνδρες ἀδελφοί, ὅτι διὰ τούτου ὑμῖν ἄφεσις
men brothers, that through this to you sending off

266   2605   2532 575 3956 3739   3756
ἁμαρτιῶν καταγγέλλεται, [καὶ] ἀπὸ πάντων ὧν   οὐκ
of sins is proclaimed, and from all of which not

1410   1722 3551 3475   1344
ἠδυνήθητε   ἐν νόμῳ Μωϋσέως δικαιωθῆναι,
you were able in law of Moses to be made right,

39 1722 3778 3956 01 4100   1344   991
ἐν τούτῳ πᾶς ὁ πιστεύων δικαιοῦται. **40** βλέπετε
in this all the trusting is made right. See

3767 3361 1904   09 3004   1722 015
οὖν μὴ ἐπέλθῃ τὸ εἰρημένον   ἐν τοῖς
then not might go on the having been said in the

4396   **41** 3708 013 2707   2532 2296
προφήταις·   ἴδετε, οἱ καταφρονηταί, καὶ θαυμάσατε
spokesmen; see, the thinking down, and marvel

2532 853   3754   2041 2038   1473 1722 019
καὶ ἀφανίσθητε, ὅτι   ἔργον ἐργάζομαι ἐγὼ ἐν ταῖς
and disappear, because work work I in the

2250   1473   2041   3739 3756 3361 4100
ἡμέραις ὑμῶν, ἔργον ὃ οὐ μὴ πιστεύσητε
days of you, work that not not you might trust

1437 5100 1555   1473   **42** 1826   1161
ἐὰν τις ἐκδιηγῆται   ὑμῖν.   Ἐξιόντων δὲ
if some might narrate out to you. Going out but

846   3870   1519 012 3342   4521
αὐτῶν παρεκάλουν   εἰς τὸ μεταξὺ σάββατον
them they were encouraging in the between sabbath

2980   846   024 4487 3778
λαληθῆναι αὐτοῖς τὰ ῥήματα ταῦτα.
to be spoken to them the words these.

43
3089 / 1161 06 4864 190
λυθείσης δὲ τῆς συναγωγῆς ἠκολούθησαν
Having been loosed but the synagogue followed

4183 014 2453 2532 014 4576 4339
πολλοὶ τῶν Ἰουδαίων καὶ τῶν σεβομένων προσηλύτων
many of the Judeans and the worshiping converts

03 3972 2532 03 921 3748 4354
τῷ Παύλῳ καὶ τῷ Βαρναβᾷ, οἵτινες προσλαλοῦντες
to the Paul and the Barnabas, who speaking to

846 3982 846 4357 07 5485
αὐτοῖς ἔπειθον αὐτοὺς προσμένειν τῇ χάριτι
them were persuading them to stay to in the favor

02 2316 011 1161 2064 4521 4975
τοῦ θεοῦ. **44** Τῷ δὲ ἐρχομένῳ σαββάτῳ σχεδὸν
of the God. In the but coming sabbath almost

3956 05 4172 4863 191 04 3056
πᾶσα ἡ πόλις συνήχθη ἀκοῦσαι τὸν λόγον
all the city was led together to hear the word

02 2962 3708 1161 013 2453 016
τοῦ κυρίου. **45** ἰδόντες δὲ οἱ Ἰουδαῖοι τοὺς
of the Master. Having seen but the Judeans the

3793 4092 2205 2532 483
ὄχλους ἐπλήσθησαν ζήλου καὶ ἀντέλεγον
crowds were filled jealousy and were speaking against

023 5259 3972 2980 987
τοῖς ὑπὸ Παύλου λαλουμένοις βλασφημοῦντες.
the by Paul things being spoken insulting.

46
3955 5037 01 3972 2532 01 921
παρρησιασάμενοί τε ὁ Παῦλος καὶ ὁ Βαρναβᾶς
Having been bold both the Paul and the Barnabas

3004 1473 1510 316 4413 2980 04
εἶπαν· ὑμῖν ἦν ἀναγκαῖον πρῶτον λαληθῆναι τὸν
said; to you it was necessary first to be spoken the

3056 02 2316 1894 683 846 2532 3756
λόγον τοῦ θεοῦ· ἐπειδὴ ἀπωθεῖσθε αὐτὸν καὶ οὐκ
word of the God; since you shove off him and not

514 2919 1438 06 166 2222 2400
ἀξίους κρίνετε ἑαυτοὺς τῆς αἰωνίου ζωῆς, ἰδοὺ
worthy you judge yourselves of the eternal life, look

4762 1519 024 1484 3779 1063
στρεφόμεθα εἰς τὰ ἔθνη. **47** οὕτως γὰρ
we are turning to the nations. Thusly for

1781 1473 01 2962 5087 1473 1519
ἐντέταλται ἡμῖν ὁ κύριος· τέθεικά σε εἰς
has commanded to us the Master; I have set you to

5457 1484 010 1510 1473 1519 4991
φῶς ἐθνῶν τοῦ εἶναί σε εἰς σωτηρίαν
light of nations of the to be you to deliverance

2193 2078 06 1093 191 1161 021 1484
ἕως ἐσχάτου τῆς γῆς. **48** Ἀκούοντα δὲ τὰ ἔθνη
until last of the earth. Hearing but the nations

5463 2532 1392 04 3056 02
ἔχαιρον καὶ ἐδόξαζον τὸν λόγον τοῦ
were rejoicing and giving splendor the word of the

2962 2532 4100 3745 1510 5021
κυρίου καὶ ἐπίστευσαν ὅσοι ἦσαν τεταγμένοι
Master and trusted as many as were having been
set in order

1519 2222 166 1308 1161 01 3056
εἰς ζωὴν αἰώνιον· **49** διεφέρετο δὲ ὁ λόγος
to life eternal; was carried through but the word

02 2962 1223 3650 06 5561 013 1161
τοῦ κυρίου δι᾽ ὅλης τῆς χώρας. **50** οἱ δὲ
of the Master through whole the country. The but

2453 3951 020 4576 1135 020
Ἰουδαῖοι παρώτρυναν τὰς σεβομένας γυναῖκας τὰς
Judeans stirred up the worshiping women the

2158 2532 016 4413 06 4172 2532 1892
εὐσχήμονας καὶ τοὺς πρώτους τῆς πόλεως καὶ ἐπήγειραν
proper and the first of the city and raised up

---

[43]When the meeting of the synagogue broke up, many Jews and devout converts to Judaism followed Paul and Barnabas, who spoke to them and urged them to continue in the grace of God.

[44] The next sabbath almost the whole city gathered to hear the word of the Lord.[a] [45]But when the Jews saw the crowds, they were filled with jealousy; and blaspheming, they contradicted what was spoken by Paul. [46]Then both Paul and Barnabas spoke out boldly, saying, "It was necessary that the word of God should be spoken first to you. Since you reject it and judge yourselves to be unworthy of eternal life, we are now turning to the Gentiles. [47]For so the Lord has commanded us, saying,

'I have set you to be a
light for the Gentiles,
so that you may bring
salvation to the ends
of the earth.'"

[48] When the Gentiles heard this, they were glad and praised the word of the Lord; and as many as had been destined for eternal life became believers. [49]Thus the word of the Lord spread throughout the region. [50]But the Jews incited the devout women of high standing and the leading men of the city, and stirred up

a Other ancient authorities read *God*

persecution against Paul and Barnabas, and drove them out of their region. 51So they shook the dust off their feet in protest against them, and went to Iconium. 52And the disciples were filled with joy and with the Holy Spirit.

CHAPTER 14

The same thing occurred in Iconium, where Paul and Barnabas[a] went into the Jewish synagogue and spoke in such a way that a great number of both Jews and Greeks became believers. 2But the unbelieving Jews stirred up the Gentiles and poisoned their minds against the brothers. 3So they remained for a long time, speaking boldly for the Lord, who testified to the word of his grace by granting signs and wonders to be done through them. 4But the residents of the city were divided; some sided with the Jews, and some with the apostles. 5And when an attempt was made by both Gentiles and Jews, with their rulers, to mistreat them and to stone them, 6the apostles[a] learned of it and fled to Lystra and Derbe, cities of Lycaonia, and to the surrounding country; 7and there they continued proclaiming the good news.

8 In Lystra there was a man sitting

---

a Gk they

1375	1909	04	3972	2532	921		2532
διωγμὸν	ἐπὶ	τὸν	Παῦλον	καὶ	Βαρναβᾶν		καὶ
persecution	on	the	Paul	and	Barnabas		and

1544	846	575	022	3725	846	51	013
ἐξέβαλον	αὐτοὺς	ἀπὸ	τῶν	ὁρίων	αὐτῶν.		οἱ
threw out	them	from	the	territories	of them.		The

1161	1621		04	2868
δὲ	ἐκτιναξάμενοι		τὸν	κονιορτὸν
but	having swung out themselves		the	blowing dust

014	4228	1909	846	2064	1519	2430	52	013
τῶν	ποδῶν	ἐπ'	αὐτοὺς	ἦλθον	εἰς	Ἰκόνιον,		οἱ
of the	feet	on	them	went	into	Iconium,		the

5037	3101	4137		5479	2532	4151
τε	μαθηταὶ	ἐπληροῦντο		χαρᾶς	καὶ	πνεύματος
but	learners	were being filled		joy	and	spirit

40		1096	1161	1722	2430	2596	012
ἁγίου.	14:1	Ἐγένετο	δὲ	ἐν	Ἰκονίῳ	κατὰ	τὸ
holy.		In became	but	in	Iconium	by	the

846	1525	846	1519	08	4864	014
αὐτὸ	εἰσελθεῖν	αὐτοὺς	εἰς	τὴν	συναγωγὴν	τῶν
same	to go into	them	into	the	synagogue	of the

2453	2532	2980	3779	5620	4100
Ἰουδαίων	καὶ	λαλῆσαι	οὕτως	ὥστε	πιστεῦσαι
Judeans	also	to speak	thusly	so that	to trust

2453	5037	2532	1672	4183	4128	2	013	1161
Ἰουδαίων	τε	καὶ	Ἑλλήνων	πολὺ	πλῆθος.		οἱ	δὲ
of Judeans	both	and	Greeks	much	quantity.		The	but

544		2453	1892		2532	2559	020
ἀπειθήσαντες		Ἰουδαῖοι	ἐπήγειραν		καὶ	ἐκάκωσαν	τὰς
having disobeyed		Judeans	raised up		and	did bad	the

5590	022	1484	2596	014	80	3	2425	3303
ψυχὰς	τῶν	ἐθνῶν	κατὰ	τῶν	ἀδελφῶν.		ἱκανὸν	μὲν
souls	of the	nations	by	the	brothers.		Enough	indeed

3767	5550	1304		3955		1909	03
οὖν	χρόνον	διέτριψαν		παρρησιαζόμενοι		ἐπὶ	τῷ
then	time	they continued		being bold		on	the

2962	03	3140		1909	03	3056	06	5485
κυρίῳ	τῷ	μαρτυροῦντι	[ἐπὶ]	τῷ	λόγῳ	τῆς		χάριτος
Master	the	testifying	on	the	word	of the		favor

846	1325	4592	2532	5059	1096	1223
αὐτοῦ,	διδόντι	σημεῖα	καὶ	τέρατα	γίνεσθαι	διὰ
of him,	giving	signs	and	marvels	to become	through

018	5495	846	4	4977	1161	09	4128	06
τῶν	χειρῶν	αὐτῶν.		ἐσχίσθη	δὲ	τὸ	πλῆθος	τῆς
the	hands	of them.		Was split	but	the	quantity	of the

4172	2532	013	3303	1510	4862	015	2453	013
πόλεως,	καὶ	οἱ	μὲν	ἦσαν	σὺν	τοῖς	Ἰουδαίοις,	οἱ
city,	and	the	indeed	were	with	the	Judeans,	the

1161	4862	015	652	5	5613	1161	1096	3730
δὲ	σὺν	τοῖς	ἀποστόλοις.		ὡς	δὲ	ἐγένετο	ὁρμὴ
but	with	the	delegates.		As	but	became	impulse

022	1484	5037	2532	2453		4862	015	758
τῶν	ἐθνῶν	τε	καὶ	Ἰουδαίων		σὺν	τοῖς	ἄρχουσιν
of the	nations	both	and	Judeans		with	the	rulers

846	5195	2532	3036		846	6	4927a
αὐτῶν	ὑβρίσαι	καὶ	λιθοβολῆσαι		αὐτούς,		συνιδόντες
of them	to abuse	and	throw stones		them,		having seen together

2703		1519	020	4172	06	3071	3082
κατέφυγον		εἰς	τὰς	πόλεις	τῆς	Λυκαονίας	Λύστραν
they fled off		into	the	cities	of the	Lycaonia	Lystra

2532	1191	2532	08	4066	7	2546
καὶ	Δέρβην	καὶ	τὴν	περίχωρον,		κἀκεῖ
and	Derbe	and	the	country around,		and there

2097		1510	8	2532	5100	435
εὐαγγελιζόμενοι		ἦσαν.		Καί	τις	ἀνὴρ
+telling good message		they were+.		And	some	man

102	1722	3082	015	4228	2521	5560
ἀδύνατος	ἐν	Λύστροις	τοῖς	ποσὶν	ἐκάθητο,	χωλὸς
unable	in	Lystra	to the	feet	was sitting,	lame

1537	2836	3384	846	3739	3763
ἐκ	κοιλίας μητρὸς	αὐτοῦ	ὃς	οὐδέποτε
from	stomach of mother	of him	who	but not ever

| 4043 | 9 | 3778 | 191 | 02 | 3972 | 2980 |
περιεπάτησεν. **9** οὗτος ἤκουσεν τοῦ Παύλου λαλοῦντος·
walked around. This heard the Paul speaking;

| 3739 | 816 | 846 | 2532 | 3708 | 3754 | 2192 |
ὃς ἀτενίσας αὐτῷ καὶ ἰδὼν ὅτι ἔχει
who having stared him and having seen that he has

| 4102 | 010 | 4982 | 10 | 3004 | 3173 | 5456 |
πίστιν τοῦ σωθῆναι, **10** εἶπεν μεγάλη φωνῇ·
trust of the to be delivered, said in great sound;

| 450 | 1909 | 016 | 4228 | 1473 | 3717 | 2532 | 242 |
ἀνάστηθι ἐπὶ τοὺς πόδας σου ὀρθός. καὶ ἥλατο
stand up on the feet of you straight. And he leaped

| 2532 | 4043 | 11 | 013 | 5037 | 3793 |
καὶ περιεπάτει. **11** οἵ τε ὄχλοι
and he was walking around. The but crowds

| 3708 | 3739 | 4160 | 3972 | 1869 | 08 |
ἰδόντες ὃ ἐποίησεν Παῦλος ἐπῆραν τὴν
having seen what did Paul lifted up on the

| 5456 | 846 | 3072 | 3004 | 013 | 2316 |
φωνὴν αὐτῶν Λυκαονιστὶ λέγοντες· οἱ θεοὶ
sound of them in Lycaonian saying; the gods

| 3666 | 444 | 2597 | 4314 | 1473 |
ὁμοιωθέντες ἀνθρώποις κατέβησαν πρὸς ἡμᾶς,
having been likened to men came down to us,

| 12 | 2564 | 5037 | 04 | 921 | 2203 | 04 | 1161 |
12 ἐκάλουν τε τὸν Βαρναβᾶν Δία, τὸν δὲ
they were calling but the Barnabas Dios, the but

| 3972 | 2060 | 1894 | 846 | 1510 | 01 | 2233 |
Παῦλον Ἑρμῆν, ἐπειδὴ αὐτὸς ἦν ὁ ἡγούμενος
Paul Hermes, since himself was the leading

| 02 | 3056 | 13 | 01 | 5037 | 2409 | 02 | 2203 | 02 | 1510 |
τοῦ λόγου. **13** ὅ τε ἱερεὺς τοῦ Διὸς τοῦ ὄντος
of the word. The but priest of the Dios the being

| 4253 | 06 | 4172 | 5022 | 2532 | 4725 | 1909 | 016 |
πρὸ τῆς πόλεως ταύρους καὶ στέμματα ἐπὶ τοὺς
before the city bulls and garlands on the

| 4440 | 5342 | 4862 | 015 | 3793 | 2309 |
πυλῶνας ἐνέγκας σὺν τοῖς ὄχλοις ἤθελεν
gates having carried with the crowds was wanting

| 2380 | 14 | 191 | 1161 | 013 | 652 | 921 |
θύειν. **14** Ἀκούσαντες δὲ οἱ ἀπόστολοι Βαρναβᾶς
to sacrifice. Having heard but the delegates Barnabas

| 2532 | 3972 | 1284 | 024 | 2440 | 846 |
καὶ Παῦλος διαρρήξαντες τὰ ἱμάτια αὐτῶν
and Paul having torn apart the clothes of them

| 1600a | 1519 | 04 | 3793 | 2896 | 15 | 2532 | 3004 |
ἐξεπήδησαν εἰς τὸν ὄχλον κράζοντες **15** καὶ λέγοντες·
rushed out into the crowd shouting and saying,

| 435 | 5101 | 3778 | 4160 | 2532 | 1473 | 3663 |
ἄνδρες, τί ταῦτα ποιεῖτε; καὶ ἡμεῖς ὁμοιοπαθεῖς
men, why these do you? Also we like-suffering

| 1510 | 1473 | 444 | 2097 | 1473 | 575 |
ἐσμεν ὑμῖν ἄνθρωποι εὐαγγελιζόμενοι ὑμᾶς ἀπὸ
are to you men telling good message you from

| 3778 | 022 | 3152 | 1994 | 1909 | 2316 | 2198 | 3739 |
τούτων τῶν ματαίων ἐπιστρέφειν ἐπὶ θεὸν ζῶντα, ὃς
these the futile to return on God living, who

| 4160 | 04 | 3772 | 2532 | 08 | 1093 | 2532 | 08 | 2281 |
ἐποίησεν τὸν οὐρανὸν καὶ τὴν γῆν καὶ τὴν θάλασσαν
made the heaven and the earth and the sea

| 2532 | 3956 | 024 | 1722 | 846 | 16 | 3739 | 1722 | 019 |
καὶ πάντα τὰ ἐν αὐτοῖς· **16** ὃς ἐν ταῖς
and all the in them; who in the

| 3944 | 1074 | 1439 | 3956 | 024 | 1484 |
παρῳχημέναις γενεαῖς εἴασεν πάντα τὰ ἔθνη
having passed generations allowed all the nations

who could not use his feet and had never walked, for he had been crippled from birth. [9] He listened to Paul as he was speaking. And Paul, looking at him intently and seeing that he had faith to be healed, [10] said in a loud voice, "Stand upright on your feet." And the man[a] sprang up and began to walk. [11] When the crowds saw what Paul had done, they shouted in the Lycaonian language, "The gods have come down to us in human form!" [12] Barnabas they called Zeus, and Paul they called Hermes, because he was the chief speaker. [13] The priest of Zeus, whose temple was just outside the city,[b] brought oxen and garlands to the gates; he and the crowds wanted to offer sacrifice. [14] When the apostles Barnabas and Paul heard of it, they tore their clothes and rushed out into the crowd, shouting, [15] "Friends,[c] why are you doing this? We are mortals just like you, and we bring you good news, that you should turn from these worthless things to the living God, who made the heaven and the earth and the sea and all that is in them. [16] In past generations he allowed all the nations

a Gk *he*
b Or *The priest of Zeus-Outside-the-City*
c Gk *Men*

to follow their own ways; [17]yet he has not left himself without a witness in doing good—giving you rains from heaven and fruitful seasons, and filling you with food and your hearts with joy." [18]Even with these words, they scarcely restrained the crowds from offering sacrifice to them.

19 But Jews came there from Antioch and Iconium and won over the crowds. Then they stoned Paul and dragged him out of the city, supposing that he was dead. [20]But when the disciples surrounded him, he got up and went into the city. The next day he went on with Barnabas to Derbe.

21 After they had proclaimed the good news to that city and had made many disciples, they returned to Lystra, then on to Iconium and Antioch. [22]There they strengthened the souls of the disciples and encouraged them to continue in the faith, saying, "It is through many persecutions that we must enter the kingdom of God." [23]And after they had appointed elders for them in each church, with prayer and fasting they entrusted them to the Lord in whom they had come to believe.

24 Then they passed through Pisidia and came to Pamphylia. [25]When they

4198	019	3598	846	**17**	2543	3756

πορεύεσθαι ταῖς ὁδοῖς αὐτῶν·   καίτοι οὐκ
to travel   in the ways of them;   and indeed not

267   846   863   18a   3771   1473
ἀμάρτυρον αὐτὸν ἀφῆκεν ἀγαθουργῶν, οὐρανόθεν ὑμῖν
without   him   he send working   from   to you
testimony   off   good,   heaven

5205   1325   2532 2540   2593   1705
ὑετοὺς διδοὺς καὶ καιροὺς καρποφόρους, ἐμπιπλῶν
rains giving and seasons fruit bearing, filling in

5160   2532 2167   020 2588   1473   **18** 2532 3778
τροφῆς καὶ εὐφροσύνης τὰς καρδίας ὑμῶν.   καὶ ταῦτα
food   and   merriment   the hearts of you. And these

3004   3433   2664   016 3793
λέγοντες μόλις κατέπαυσαν   τοὺς ὄχλους
saying   scarcely they stopped completely the crowds

010 3361 2380   846   1904 1161 575
τοῦ μὴ θύειν   αὐτοῖς. **19** Ἐπῆλθαν δὲ ἀπὸ
the not to sacrifice to them.   Went on but from

490   2532 2430   2453   2532 3982
Ἀντιοχείας καὶ Ἰκονίου Ἰουδαῖοι καὶ πείσαντες
Antioch   and   Iconium Judeans and having persuaded

016 3793   2532 3034   04 3972
τοὺς ὄχλους καὶ λιθάσαντες τὸν Παῦλον
the crowds and having stoned the Paul

4951   1854   06 4172 3543   846
ἔσυρον   ἔξω τῆς πόλεως νομίζοντες αὐτὸν
they were dragging outside the city thinking him

2348   **20** 2944   1161 014 3101
τεθνηκέναι.   κυκλωσάντων δὲ τῶν μαθητῶν
to be dead.   Having encircled but the learners

846   450   1525   1519 08 4172   2532
αὐτὸν ἀναστὰς   εἰσῆλθεν εἰς τὴν πόλιν. Καὶ
him having stood up he went in into the city. And

07   1887   1831   4862 03 921   1519
τῇ ἐπαύριον ἐξῆλθεν σὺν τῷ Βαρναβᾷ εἰς
in the tomorrow he went out with the Barnabas into

1191   **21** 2097   5037 08 4172
Δέρβην.   εὐαγγελισάμενοί τε τὴν πόλιν
Derbe.   Having told good message both the city

1565   2532 3100   2425   5290
ἐκείνην καὶ μαθητεύσαντες ἱκανοὺς ὑπέστρεψαν
that   and having made learners enough they returned

1519 08 3082   2532 1519 2430   2532 1519 490
εἰς τὴν Λύστραν καὶ εἰς Ἰκόνιον καὶ εἰς Ἀντιόχειαν
to the Lystra and to Iconium and to Antioch

22 1991   020 5590 014   3101
ἐπιστηρίζοντες τὰς ψυχὰς τῶν μαθητῶν,
strengthening on the souls of the learners,

3870   1696   07 4102   2532 3754 1223
παρακαλοῦντες ἐμμένειν τῇ πίστει καὶ ὅτι διὰ
encouraging   to stay in the trust and that through

4183   2347   1163   1473 1525   1519
πολλῶν θλίψεων δεῖ   ἡμᾶς εἰσελθεῖν εἰς
many   afflictions it is necessary us to go into into

08 932   02   2316 **23** 5500
τὴν βασιλείαν τοῦ θεοῦ.   χειροτονήσαντες
the kingdom of the God.   Having hand stretched on

1161 846   2596 1577   4245   4336
δὲ αὐτοῖς κατ' ἐκκλησίαν πρεσβυτέρους, προσευξάμενοι
but them by assembly older men,   having prayed

3326 3521   3908   846 03   2962 1519
μετὰ νηστειῶν παρέθεντο αὐτοὺς τῷ κυρίῳ εἰς
with fastings they set along them to the Master into

3739 4100   2532 1330   08
ὃν πεπιστεύκεισαν. **24** Καὶ διελθόντες   τὴν
whom they had trusted. And having gone through the

4099   2064   1519 08 3828   **25** 2532
Πισιδίαν ἦλθον εἰς τὴν Παμφυλίαν   καὶ
Pisidia they went into the Pamphylia   and

2980		1722	4011	04	3056	2597		1519
λαλήσαντες	ἐν	Πέργῃ	τὸν	λόγον	κατέβησαν		εἰς	
having spoken	in	Perga	the word		they went down		to	

had spoken the word in Perga, they went down to Attalia.

825		2547		636		1519	490
Ἀττάλειαν	26	κἀκεῖθεν	ἀπέπλευσαν	εἰς	Ἀντιόχειαν,
Attalia		and from there	sailed off	to	Antioch,

[26]From there they sailed back to Antioch, where they had been commended to the grace of God for the work[a] that they had completed.

3606		1510	3860		07		5485	02
ὅθεν	ἦσαν	παραδεδομένοι	τῇ		χάριτι	τοῦ
from where	they +having been were+	given over	in the		favor	of the

[27]When they arrived, they called the church together and related all that God had done with them, and how he had opened a door of faith for the Gentiles.

2316	1519	012	2041	3739	4137		3854
θεοῦ	εἰς	τὸ	ἔργον	ὃ	ἐπλήρωσαν.	27	παραγενόμενοι
God	to	the	work	that	they filled.		Having arrived

1161	2532	4863		08	1577
δὲ	καὶ	συναγόντες		τὴν	ἐκκλησίαν
but	also	having led together		the	assembly

[28]And they stayed there with the disciples for some time.

312		3745		4160	01	2316	3326
ἀνήγγελλον		ὅσα	ἐποίησεν	ὁ	θεὸς	μετ'
they were declaring		as much as	did		the God	with

846	2532	3754	455		023	1484	2374	4102
αὐτῶν	καὶ	ὅτι	ἤνοιξεν		τοῖς	ἔθνεσιν	θύραν	πίστεως.
them	and	that	he opened		the	nations	door	of trust.

	1304			1161	5550	3756	3641	4862
28	διέτριβον		δὲ	χρόνον	οὐκ	ὀλίγον	σὺν
	They were continuing	but	time	not	little	with

Then certain individuals came down from Judea and were teaching the brothers, "Unless you are circumcised according to the custom of Moses, you cannot be saved." [2]And after Paul and Barnabas had no small dissension and debate with them, Paul and Barnabas and some of the others were appointed to go up to Jerusalem to discuss this question with the apostles and the elders. [3]So they were sent on their way by the church, and as they passed through both Phoenicia and Samaria, they reported the conversion of the Gentiles, and brought great joy to all the believers.[b] [4]When they came to Jerusalem, they were welcomed by the church and the

015	3101		2532	5100	2718		575
τοῖς	μαθηταῖς.	15:1	Καὶ	τινες	κατελθόντες		ἀπὸ
the	learners.		And	some	having come	down	from

06	2449		1321		016	80		3754
τῆς	Ἰουδαίας	ἐδίδασκον		τοὺς	ἀδελφοὺς	ὅτι
the	Judea	were teaching		the	brothers,	(")

1437	3361	4059			011	1485	011
ἐὰν	μὴ	περιτμηθῆτε			τῷ	ἔθει	τῷ
except		you might be circumcised		in the	custom	the

3475		3756	1410		4982
Μωϋσέως,	οὐ	δύνασθε		σωθῆναι.
Moses,	not	you are	able	to be delivered.

	1096		1161	4714		2532	2214	3756
2	γενομένης		δὲ	στάσεως	καὶ	ζητήσεως	οὐκ
	Having become	but	revolution	and	speculation	not

3641	03	3972	2532	03	921		4314	846
ὀλίγης	τῷ	Παύλῳ	καὶ	τῷ	Βαρναβᾷ	πρὸς	αὐτούς,
little	the	Paul	and	the	Barnabas	toward	them,

5021		305		3972	2532	922	2532
ἔταξαν		ἀναβαίνειν	Παῦλον	καὶ	Βαρναβᾶν	καί
they set in order		to go up	Paul	and	Barnabas	and

5100	243	1537	846	4314	016	652		2532
τινας	ἄλλους	ἐξ	αὐτῶν	πρὸς	τοὺς	ἀποστόλους	καὶ
some	others	from	them	to	the	delegates	and

4245		1519	2419		4012	010	2213
πρεσβυτέρους	εἰς	Ἰερουσαλὴμ	περὶ	τοῦ	ζητήματος
older men	to	Jerusalem	about	the	question

3778		013	3303	3767	4311		5259
τούτου.	3	Οἱ	μὲν	οὖν	προπεμφθέντες		ὑπὸ
this.		The	indeed	then	having been sent before	by

06	1577		1330		08	5037	5403
τῆς	ἐκκλησίας	διήρχοντο		τήν	τε	Φοινίκην
the	assembly	were going through		the	both	Phoenicia

2532	4540		1555		08	1995	022
καὶ	Σαμάρειαν	ἐκδιηγούμενοι	τὴν	ἐπιστροφὴν	τῶν
and	Samaria	narrating out	the	return	of the

1484	2532	4160		5479	3173	3956	015
ἐθνῶν	καὶ	ἐποίουν		χαρὰν	μεγάλην	πᾶσιν	τοῖς
nations	and	were making	joy	great	in	all	the

80		3854		1161	1519	2419
ἀδελφοῖς.	4	παραγενόμενοι	δὲ	εἰς	Ἰερουσαλὴμ
brothers.		Having arrived	but	in	Jerusalem

3858		575	06	1577	2532	014
παρεδέχθησαν		ἀπὸ	τῆς	ἐκκλησίας	καὶ	τῶν
they were accepted	by	the	assembly	and	the

apostles and the elders, and they reported all that God had done with them. [5]But some believers who belonged to the sect of the Pharisees stood up and said, "It is necessary for them to be circumcised and ordered to keep the law of Moses."

[6]The apostles and the elders met together to consider this matter. [7]After there had been much debate, Peter stood up and said to them, "My brothers,[a] you know that in the early days God made a choice among you, that I should be the one through whom the Gentiles would hear the message of the good news and become believers. [8]And God, who knows the human heart, testified to them by giving them the Holy Spirit, just as he did to us; [9]and in cleansing their hearts by faith he has made no distinction between them and us. [10]Now therefore why are you putting God to the test by placing on the neck of the disciples a yoke that neither our ancestors nor we have been able to bear? [11]On the contrary, we believe that we will be saved through the grace of the Lord Jesus, just as they will."

[12]The whole assembly kept silence, and listened to Barnabas and Paul as they told of

[a] Gk Men, brothers

| 652 | 2532 | 014 | 4245 | | 312 | | 5037 |
ἀποστόλων καὶ τῶν πρεσβυτέρων, ἀνήγγειλάν τε
delegates and the older men, they declared and

| 3745 | 01 | 2316 | 4160 | 3326 | 846 | | 1817 |
ὅσα ὁ θεὸς ἐποίησεν μετ᾽ αὐτῶν. [5] Ἐξανέστησαν
as much as the God did with them. Stood up out

| 1161 | 5100 | 014 | 575 | 06 | 139 | 014 | 5330 |
δέ τινες τῶν ἀπὸ τῆς αἱρέσεως τῶν Φαρισαίων
but some of the from the sect of the Pharisees

| 4100 | | 3004 | 3754 | 1163 |
πεπιστευκότες λέγοντες ὅτι δεῖ
ones having trusted saying, (") it is necessary

| 4059 | | 846 | 3853 | | 5037 | 5083 | 04 |
περιτέμνειν αὐτοὺς παραγγέλλειν τε τηρεῖν τὸν
to circumcise them to command both to keep the

| 3551 | 3475 | | 4863 | | 5037 | 013 | 652 |
νόμον Μωϋσέως. [6] Συνήχθησάν τε οἱ ἀπόστολοι
law of Moses. Were led together both the delegates

| 2532 | 013 | 4245 | | 3708 | 4012 | 02 | 3056 | 3778 |
καὶ οἱ πρεσβύτεροι ἰδεῖν περὶ τοῦ λόγου τούτου.
and the older men to see about the word this.

| 4183 | 1161 | 2214 | | 1096 | | 450 |
[7] Πολλῆς δὲ ζητήσεως γενομένης ἀναστὰς
Much but speculation having become having stood up

| 4074 | 3004 | 4314 | 846 | | 435 | 80 | 1473 |
Πέτρος εἶπεν πρὸς αὐτούς· ἄνδρες ἀδελφοί, ὑμεῖς
Peter said to them; men brothers, you

| 1987 | | 3754 | 575 | 2250 | 744 | 1722 | 1473 | 1586 |
ἐπίστασθε ὅτι ἀφ᾽ ἡμερῶν ἀρχαίων ἐν ὑμῖν ἐξελέξατο
understand that from days ancient in you selected

| 01 | 2316 | 1223 | | 010 | 4750 | 1473 | 191 | 024 |
ὁ θεὸς διὰ τοῦ στόματός μου ἀκοῦσαι τὰ
the God through the mouth of me to hear the

| 1484 | 04 | 3056 | 010 | | 2098 | | 2532 | 4100 |
ἔθνη τὸν λόγον τοῦ εὐαγγελίου καὶ πιστεῦσαι.
nations the word of the good message and to trust.

| | 2532 | 01 | 2589 | | 2316 | 3140 | | 846 |
[8] καὶ ὁ καρδιογνώστης θεὸς ἐμαρτύρησεν αὐτοῖς
And the heart knower God testified to them

| 1325 | | 012 | 4151 | 012 | 40 | 2531 | 2532 | 1473 |
δοὺς τὸ πνεῦμα τὸ ἅγιον καθὼς καὶ ἡμῖν
having given the spirit the holy just as also to us

| | 2532 | 3762 | | 1252 | | 3342 | 1473 | 5037 |
[9] καὶ οὐθὲν διέκρινεν μεταξὺ ἡμῶν τε
and nothing he judged thoroughly between us both

| 2532 | 846 | 07 | | 4102 | 2511 | | 020 | 2588 |
καὶ αὐτῶν τῇ πίστει καθαρίσας τὰς καρδίας
and them in the trust having cleaned the hearts

| 846 | | 3568 | 3767 | 5101 | 3985 | | 04 | 2316 |
αὐτῶν. [10] νῦν οὖν τί πειράζετε τὸν θεὸν
of them. Now then why you pressure the God

| 2007 | | 2218 | 1909 | 04 | 5137 | 014 | 3101 | 3739 |
ἐπιθεῖναι ζυγὸν ἐπὶ τὸν τράχηλον τῶν μαθητῶν ὃν
to set on yoke on the neck of the learners that

| 3777 | 013 | 3962 | 1473 | 3777 | 1473 | 2480 |
οὔτε οἱ πατέρες ἡμῶν οὔτε ἡμεῖς ἰσχύσαμεν
neither the fathers of us nor we were strong

| 941 | | 235 | 1223 | 06 | 5485 | 02 | 2962 |
βαστάσαι; [11] ἀλλὰ διὰ τῆς χάριτος τοῦ κυρίου
to bear? But through the favor of the Master

| 2424 | 4100 | | 4982 | | 2596 | 3739 | 5158 |
Ἰησοῦ πιστεύομεν σωθῆναι καθ᾽ ὃν τρόπον
Jesus we trust to be delivered by which manner

| 2548 | | 12 | 4601 | | 1161 | 3956 | 09 | 4128 | 2532 |
κἀκεῖνοι. [12] Ἐσίγησεν δὲ πᾶν τὸ πλῆθος καὶ
also those. Were silent but all the quantity and

| 191 | | 2532 | 3972 | 1834 |
ἤκουον Βαρναβᾶ καὶ Παύλου ἐξηγουμένων
they were hearing Barnabas and Paul explaining

3745   4160   01   2316 4592   2532 5059 1722 023
ὅσα   ἐποίησεν ὁ   θεὸς σημεῖα καὶ τέρατα ἐν τοῖς
as many as did   the God signs and marvels in the

1484   1223   846   13   3326   1161 012 4601
ἔθνεσιν δι᾿   αὐτῶν.   Μετὰ δὲ   τὸ σιγῆσαι
nations through them.   After but the to be silent

846   611   2385   3004   435   80
αὐτοὺς ἀπεκρίθη ᾿Ιάκωβος λέγων· ἄνδρες ἀδελφοί,
them   answered Jacob   saying, men   brothers,

191   1473   14   4826   1834   2531   4413   01
ἀκούσατέ μου.   Συμεὼν ἐξηγήσατο καθὼς πρῶτον ὁ
hear   me.   Symeon explained just as first the

2316 1980   2983   1537 1484   2992   011
θεὸς ἐπεσκέψατο λαβεῖν ἐξ ἐθνῶν λαὸν τῷ
God looked on to take from nations people in the

3686   846   15   2532 3778   4856   013 3056
ὀνόματι αὐτοῦ.   καὶ τούτῳ συμφωνοῦσιν οἱ λόγοι
name   of him.   And to this agree   the words

014   4396   2531   1125   16   3326
τῶν   προφητῶν καθὼς γέγραπται·   μετὰ
of the spokesmen just as it has been written; after

3778 390   2532 456   08 4633
ταῦτα ἀναστρέψω καὶ ἀνοικοδομήσω τὴν σκηνὴν
these I will return and I will build again the tent

1160a   08   4098   2532 024   2679
Δαυὶδ τὴν πεπτωκυῖαν καὶ τὰ   κατεσκαμμένα
of David the having fallen and the things having been
                                           dug down

846   456   2532 461
αὐτῆς ἀνοικοδομήσω   καὶ ἀνορθώσω
of it I will build again and I will straighten up

846   17   3704   302 1567   013 2645
αὐτήν,   ὅπως   ἂν ἐκζητήσωσιν οἱ κατάλοιποι
it,   so that - will seek out the rest behind

014   444   04 2962   2532 3956 021 1484   1909
τῶν   ἀνθρώπων τὸν κύριον καὶ πάντα τὰ ἔθνη ἐφ᾿
of the men   the Master and all   the nations on

3739 1941   09   3686   1473 1909 846
οὓς ἐπικέκληται   τὸ ὄνομά μου ἐπ᾿ αὐτούς,
whom has been called on the name of me on them,

3004 2962   4160 3778   18   1110   575 165
λέγει κύριος ποιῶν ταῦτα   γνωστὰ ἀπ᾿ αἰῶνος.
says Master doing these   known from age.

19 1352   1473 2919 3361 3926   015
    διὸ   ἐγὼ κρίνω μὴ παρενοχλεῖν τοῖς
    Wherefore I   judge not to annoy along the ones

575 022 1484   1994   1909 04 2316 20 235
ἀπὸ τῶν ἐθνῶν ἐπιστρέφουσιν ἐπὶ τὸν θεόν,   ἀλλὰ
from the nations returning   on the God,   but

1989   846   010 568   022 234
ἐπιστεῖλαι αὐτοῖς τοῦ ἀπέχεσθαι τῶν ἀλισγημάτων
to write letter to them the to hold off the pollutions

022   1497   2532 06   4202   2532 010
τῶν   εἰδώλων καὶ τῆς πορνείας   καὶ τοῦ
of the idols   and of the sexual immorality and the

4156   2532 010 129   21   3475   1063 1537
πνικτοῦ καὶ τοῦ αἵματος.   Μωϋσῆς γὰρ ἐκ
choked and the blood.   Moses for from

1074   744   2596 4172 016 2784
γενεῶν   ἀρχαίων κατὰ πόλιν τοὺς κηρύσσοντας
generations ancient by city the ones announcing

846   2192 1722 019 4864   2596 3956 4521
αὐτὸν ἔχει ἐν ταῖς συναγωγαῖς κατὰ πᾶν σάββατον
him   has in the synagogues by all sabbath

314   22   5119 1380   015   652
ἀναγινωσκόμενος.   Τότε ἔδοξε   τοῖς ἀποστόλοις
being read.   Then it thought to the delegates

2532 015 4245   4862 3650 07 1577
καὶ τοῖς πρεσβυτέροις σὺν ὅλῃ τῇ ἐκκλησίᾳ
and the older men   with whole the assembly

---

all the signs and wonders
that God had done through
them among the Gentiles.
[13]After they finished
speaking, James replied,
"My brothers,[a] listen to
me. [14]Simeon has related
how God first looked
favorably on the Gentiles,
to take from among them a
people for his name. [15]This
agrees with the words of the
prophets, as it is written,
[16]'After this I will return,
    and I will rebuild the
    dwelling of David,
    which has fallen;
    from its ruins I will
    rebuild it,
    and I will set it up,
[17]so that all other peoples
    may seek the Lord—
    even all the Gentiles
    over whom my name
    has been called.
    Thus says the Lord,
    who has been
    making these things
[18] known from long
    ago.'[b]
[19]Therefore I have reached
the decision that we should
not trouble those Gentiles
who are turning to God,
[20]but we should write to
them to abstain only from
things polluted by idols
and from fornication and
from whatever has been
strangled[c] and from blood.
[21]For in every city, for
generations past, Moses has
had those who proclaim
him, for he has been read
aloud every sabbath in the
synagogues."

22 Then the apostles and
the elders, with the consent
of the whole church,
decided

---

[a] Gk Men, brothers
[b] Other ancient authorities read
things. [18]Known to God from of old
are all his works.'
[c] Other ancient authorities lack and
from whatever has been strangled

to choose men from among their members[a] and to send them to Antioch with Paul and Barnabas. They sent Judas called Barsabbas, and Silas, leaders among the brothers, 23with the following letter: "The brothers, both the apostles and the elders, to the believers[b] of Gentile origin in Antioch and Syria and Cilicia, greetings. 24Since we have heard that certain persons who have gone out from us, though with no instructions from us, have said things to disturb you and have unsettled your minds,[c] 25we have decided unanimously to choose representatives[d] and send them to you, along with our beloved Barnabas and Paul, 26who have risked their lives for the sake of our Lord Jesus Christ. 27We have therefore sent Judas and Silas, who themselves will tell you the same things by word of mouth. 28For it has seemed good to the Holy Spirit and to us to impose on you no further burden than these essentials: 29that you abstain from what has been sacrificed to idols and from blood and from what is strangled[e] and from fornication. If you keep yourselves from these, you will do well. Farewell."

30 So they were sent off and went down to Antioch. When they gathered

[a] Gk from among them
[b] Gk brothers
[c] Other ancient authorities add saying, 'You must be circumcised and keep the law.'
[d] Gk men
[e] Other ancient authorities lack and from what is strangled

---

1586   435   1537 846   3992
ἐκλεξαμένους   ἄνδρας ἐξ   αὐτῶν πέμψαι
having selected themselves men   from them to send
1519 490   4862 03   3972   2532 921   2455
εἰς 'Αντιόχειαν συν τῷ Παύλῳ καὶ Βαρναβᾷ, 'Ιούδαν
into Antioch   with the Paul   and Barnabas, Judas
04   2564   923   2532 4609   435
τὸν καλούμενον   Βαρσαββᾶν καὶ Σίλαν, ἄνδρας
the one being called Barsabbas and Silas, men
2233   1722 015 80   1125
ἡγουμένους ἐν τοῖς ἀδελφοῖς, 23 γράψαντες
leading   in the brothers,   having written
1223   5495 846   013 652   2532 013
διὰ   χειρὸς αὐτῶν· Οἱ ἀπόστολοι καὶ οἱ
through hand of them; the delegates and the
4245   80   015   2596 08   490   2532
πρεσβύτεροι ἀδελφοὶ τοῖς κατὰ τὴν 'Αντιόχειαν καὶ
older men brothers to the by the Antioch   and
4947   2532 2791   80   015   1537 1484
Συρίαν καὶ Κιλικίαν ἀδελφοῖς τοῖς   ἐξ ἐθνῶν
Syria and Cilicia brothers to the ones from nations
5463   1894 191   3754 5100   1537 1473
χαίρειν.   24 'Επειδὴ ἠκούσαμεν ὅτι τινὲς ἐξ ἡμῶν
to rejoice.   Since we heard that some from us
1831   5015   1473 3056 384
[ἐξελθόντες] ἐτάραξαν ὑμᾶς λόγοις ἀνασκευάζοντες
having gone out troubled you in words unsettling
020 5590 1473   3739 3756 1291   25 1380
τὰς ψυχὰς ὑμῶν οἷς οὐ διεστειλάμεθα,   25 ἔδοξεν
the souls of you which not we commanded,   it thought
1473 1096   3661   1586   435
ἡμῖν γενομένοις ὁμοθυμαδὸν ἐκλεξαμένοις ἄνδρας
to us having   with one mind having selected men
      become   ourselves
3992   4314   1473 4053 015 27   1473 921
πέμψαι πρὸς ὑμᾶς σὺν τοῖς ἀγαπητοῖς ἡμῶν Βαρναβᾷ
to send to   you with the loved ones of us Barnabas
2532 3972   26 444   3860   020 5590
καὶ Παύλῳ, 26 ἀνθρώποις παραδεδωκόσι   τὰς ψυχὰς
and Paul,   men   having given over the souls
846   5228   010 3686   02   2962   1473
αὐτῶν ὑπὲρ   τοῦ ὀνόματος τοῦ κυρίου ἡμῶν
of them on behalf of the name   of the Master of us
2424 5547   27 649   3767 2455 2532 4609
'Ιησοῦ Χριστοῦ. 27 ἀπεστάλκαμεν οὖν 'Ιούδαν καὶ Σιλᾶν
Jesus Christ.   We have delegated then Judas and Silas
2532 846   1223   3056 518   024 846
καὶ αὐτοὺς διὰ   λόγου ἀπαγγέλλοντας τὰ αὐτά.
and them   through word telling   the same.
28 1380   1063 011   4151   011 40   2532 1473
28 ἔδοξεν   γὰρ τῷ   πνεύματι τῷ ἁγίῳ καὶ ἡμῖν
   It thought for to the spirit   the holy and to us
3367   4183 2007   1473 922   4133 3778
μηδὲν πλέον ἐπιτίθεσθαι ὑμῖν βάρος πλὴν τούτων
nothing more to be set on to you burden except these
022 1876   29 568   1494   2532
τῶν ἐπάναγκες, 29 ἀπέχεσθαι εἰδωλοθύτων καὶ
the necessary,   to hold off idol sacrifices and
129   2532 4156   2532 4202   1537 3739
αἵματος καὶ πνικτῶν καὶ πορνείας,   ἐξ ὧν
blood and choked and sexual immorality, from which
1301   1438   2095 4238
διατηροῦντες ἑαυτοὺς εὖ πράξετε.
keeping thoroughly yourselves well you practice.
4517   30 013 3303   3767 630
Ἔρρωσθε. 30 Οἱ μὲν   οὖν ἀπολυθέντες
Be strong.   The indeed then having been loosed off
2718   1519 490   2532 4863
κατῆλθον εἰς 'Αντιόχειαν, καὶ συναγαγόντες
went down into Antioch,   and having led together

012	4128	1929	08	1992	**31**	314
τὸ	πλῆθος	ἐπέδωκαν	τὴν	ἐπιστολήν.		ἀναγνόντες
the	quantity	they gave	on	the letter.		Having read

1161	5463	1909	07	3874	**32**	2455
δὲ	ἐχάρησαν	ἐπὶ	τῇ	παρακλήσει.		’Ιούδας
but	they rejoiced	on	the	encouragement.		Judas

5037	2532	4609	2532	846	4396	1510
τε	καὶ	Σιλᾶς	καὶ	αὐτοὶ	προφῆται	ὄντες
both	and	Silas	and	themselves	spokesmen	being

1223	3056	4183	3870	016	80	2532
διὰ	λόγου	πολλοῦ	παρεκάλεσαν	τοὺς	ἀδελφοὺς	καὶ
through	word	much	encouraged	the	brothers	and

1991		4160	**33**	1161	5550
ἐπεστήριξαν,		ποιήσαντες		δὲ	χρόνον
strengthened		on, having made		but	time

630	3326	1515	575	014	80	4314
ἀπελύθησαν	μετ’	εἰρήνης	ἀπὸ	τῶν	ἀδελφῶν	πρὸς
they were	with	peace	from	the	brothers	to
loosed off						

016	649	846	**35**	3972	1161
τοὺς	ἀποστείλαντας	αὐτούς.		Παῦλος	δὲ
the ones	having delegated	them.		Paul	but

2532	921	1304	1722	490	1321
καὶ	Βαρναβᾶς	διέτριβον	ἐν	’Αντιοχείᾳ	διδάσκοντες
and	Barnabas	were continuing	in	Antioch	teaching

2532	2097	3326	2532	2087	4183	04
καὶ	εὐαγγελιζόμενοι	μετὰ	καὶ	ἑτέρων	πολλῶν	τὸν
and	telling good message	with	also	others	many	the

3056	02	2962	**36**	3326	1161	5100	2250	3004
λόγον	τοῦ	κυρίου.		Μετὰ	δέ	τινας	ἡμέρας	εἶπεν
word	of the	Master.		After	but	some	days	said

4314	921	3972	1994	1211
πρὸς	Βαρναβᾶν	Παῦλος·	ἐπιστρέψαντες	δὴ
to	Barnabas	Paul;	having returned	indeed

1980	016	80	2596	4172	3956	1722
ἐπισκεψώμεθα	τοὺς	ἀδελφοὺς	κατὰ	πόλιν	πᾶσαν	ἐν
we might look on	the	brothers	by	city	all	in

3739	2605	04	3056	02	2962	4459
αἷς	κατηγγείλαμεν	τὸν	λόγον	τοῦ	κυρίου	πῶς
which	we proclaimed	the	word	of the	Master	how

2192	**37**	921	1161	1014
ἔχουσιν.		Βαρναβᾶς	δὲ	ἐβούλετο
they hold.		Barnabas	but	was planning

4838	2532	04	2491	04
συμπαραλαβεῖν	καὶ	τὸν	’Ιωάννην	τὸν
to take along with	also	the	John	the

2564	3138	**38**	3972	1161
καλούμενον	Μᾶρκον·		Παῦλος	δὲ
one being called	Mark;		Paul	but

515	04	868	575	846
ἠξίου,	τὸν	ἀποστάντα	ἀπ’	αὐτῶν
was thinking worthy,	the	having stood off	from	them

575	3828	2532	3361	4905	846
ἀπὸ	Παμφυλίας	καὶ	μὴ	συνελθόντα	αὐτοῖς
from	Pamphylia	and	not	having gone together	them

1519	012	2041	3361	4838	3778
εἰς	τὸ	ἔργον	μὴ	συμπαραλαμβάνειν	τοῦτον.
to	the	work	not	to take along with	this.

39	1096	1161	3948	5620	673
	ἐγένετο	δὲ	παροξυσμὸς	ὥστε	ἀποχωρισθῆναι
	Became	but	stimulation	so that	to be separated off

846	575	240	04	5037	921
αὐτοὺς	ἀπ’	ἀλλήλων,	τόν	τε	Βαρναβᾶν
them	from	one another,	the	and	Barnabas

3880	04	3138	1602	1519	2954
παραλαβόντα	τὸν	Μᾶρκον	ἐκπλεῦσαι	εἰς	Κύπρον,
having taken along	the	Mark	to sail out	to	Cyprus,

40	3972	1161	1951	4609	1831
	Παῦλος	δὲ	ἐπιλεξάμενος	Σιλᾶν	ἐξῆλθεν
	Paul	but	having called on	Silas	went out

the congregation together, they delivered the letter. [31]When its members[a] read it, they rejoiced at the exhortation. [32]Judas and Silas, who were themselves prophets, said much to encourage and strengthen the believers.[b] [33]After they had been there for some time, they were sent off in peace by the believers[b] to those who had sent them.[c] [35]But Paul and Barnabas remained in Antioch, and there, with many others, they taught and proclaimed the word of the Lord.

[36] After some days Paul said to Barnabas, "Come, let us return and visit the believers[b] in every city where we proclaimed the word of the Lord and see how they are doing." [37]Barnabas wanted to take with them John called Mark. [38]But Paul decided not to take with them one who had deserted them in Pamphylia and had not accompanied them in the work. [39]The disagreement became so sharp that they parted company; Barnabas took Mark with him and sailed away to Cyprus, [40]But Paul chose Silas and set out,

a Gk When they
b Gk brothers
c Other ancient authorities add verse 34, But it seemed good to Silas to remain there

the believers[a] commending him to the grace of the Lord. [41]He went through Syria and Cilicia, strengthening the churches.

CHAPTER 16

Paul[b] went on also to Derbe and to Lystra, where there was a disciple named Timothy, the son of a Jewish woman who was a believer; but his father was a Greek. [2]He was well spoken of by the believers[a] in Lystra and Iconium. [3]Paul wanted Timothy to accompany him; and he took him and had him circumcised because of the Jews who were in those places, for they all knew that his father was a Greek. [4]As they went from town to town, they delivered to them for observance the decisions that had been reached by the apostles and elders who were in Jerusalem. [5]So the churches were strengthened in the faith and increased in numbers daily.

6 They went through the region of Phrygia and Galatia, having been forbidden by the Holy Spirit to speak the word in Asia. [7]When they had come opposite Mysia, they attempted to go into Bithynia, but the Spirit of Jesus

[a] Gk brothers
[b] Gk He

3860		07	5485	02		2962	5259
παραδοθεὶς		τῇ	χάριτι	τοῦ		κυρίου	ὑπὸ
having been given over		to the	favor	of the		Master	by
given over							

014 80		1330			1161	08	4947
τῶν ἀδελφῶν.	**41**	διήρχετο			δὲ	τὴν	Συρίαν
the brothers.		He was going through			but	the	Syria

2532 08	2791	1991		020 1577
καὶ	[τὴν] Κιλικίαν ἐπιστηρίζων		τὰς ἐκκλησίας.
and	the Cilicia strengthening on		the assemblies.

	2658	1161 2532 1519 1191	2532 1519 3082
16:1	Κατήντησεν	δὲ [καὶ] εἰς Δέρβην	καὶ εἰς Λύστραν.
	He arrived	but also in Derbe	and in Lystra.

2532 2400 3101	5100 1510 1563	3686	5095
καὶ ἰδοὺ μαθητής	τις ἦν ἐκεῖ	ὀνόματι	Τιμόθεος,
and look learner	some was there	in name	Timothy,

5207 1135	2453	4103	3962 1161 1672
υἱὸς γυναικὸς	Ἰουδαίας	πιστῆς,	πατρὸς δὲ Ἕλληνος,
son of woman	Judean	trustful,	father but Greek,

	3739 3140		5259 014 1722 3082		2532
2	ὃς ἐμαρτυρεῖτο		ὑπὸ τῶν ἐν Λύστροις καὶ	
	who was being testified		by the in Lystra and	

2430	80		3778	2309	01	3972	4862
Ἰκονίῳ	ἀδελφῶν.	**3**	τοῦτον	ἠθέλησεν	ὁ	Παῦλος	σὺν
Iconium	brothers.		This one	wanted	the	Paul	with

846 1831	2532 2983	4059	846
αὐτῷ ἐξελθεῖν,	καὶ λαβὼν	περιέτεμεν	αὐτὸν
him to go out,	and having taken	he circumcised	him

1223	016	2453	016	1510	1722 015 5117
διὰ	τοὺς Ἰουδαίους	τοὺς ὄντας		ἐν τοῖς τόποις
because	the Judeans	the ones being		in the places

1565	3609a	1063 537	3754	1672 01 3962
ἐκείνοις·	ᾔδεισαν	γὰρ ἅπαντες	ὅτι	Ἕλλην ὁ πατὴρ
those;	had known	for all	that	Greek the father

846	5225	5613 1161 1279	020 4172
αὐτοῦ	ὑπῆρχεν.	**4** Ὡς δὲ	διεπορεύοντο τὰς πόλεις,
of him	was	As but	they were the cities,
	existing		traveling through

3860		846	5442	024 1378
παρεδίδοσαν		αὐτοῖς	φυλάσσειν	τὰ δόγματα
they were giving over		to them	to guard	the decrees

024	2919	5259 014 652	2532
τὰ	κεκριμένα	ὑπὸ τῶν ἀποστόλων	καὶ
the ones having been judged		by the delegates	and

4245	014	1722 2414		017 3303
πρεσβυτέρων	τῶν	ἐν Ἱεροσολύμοις.	**5**	Αἱ μὲν
older men	of the	in Jerusalem.		The indeed

3767 1577	4732		07	4102 2532
οὖν ἐκκλησίαι	ἐστερεοῦντο		τῇ	πίστει καὶ
then assemblies	were being solidified		in	the trust and

4052	03 706	2596 2250	**6** 1330
ἐπερίσσευον	τῷ ἀριθμῷ καθ᾽	ἡμέραν.	Διῆλθον
were exceeding	the number by	day.	They went through

1161 08	5435	2532 1054	5561
δὲ	τὴν Φρυγίαν καὶ	Γαλατικὴν	χώραν
but	the Phrygia and	Galatian	country

2967	5259 010 40	4151	2980	04 3056
κωλυθέντες	ὑπὸ τοῦ ἁγίου	πνεύματος	λαλῆσαι	τὸν λόγον
having been	by the holy	spirit	to speak	the word
hindered				

1722 07	773	2064	1161 2596 08 3465
ἐν τῇ Ἀσίᾳ·	**7**	ἐλθόντες	δὲ κατὰ τὴν Μυσίαν
in the Asia;		having gone	but by the Mysia

3985		1519 08	978	4198
ἐπείραζον		εἰς τὴν	Βιθυνίαν	πορευθῆναι,
they were pressing		into the	Bithynia	to travel,

2532 3756 1439	846	09 4151	2424
καὶ οὐκ εἴασεν	αὐτοὺς	τὸ πνεῦμα	Ἰησοῦ·
and not allowed	them	the spirit	of Jesus;

8
```
3928
παρελθόντες         δὲ     τὴν Μυσίαν κατέβησαν
having gone along  but    the Mysia   they went down
```
```
1519 5174              2532 3705   1223    06    3571  03
εἰς  Τρῳάδα.  9  Καὶ  ὅραμα  διὰ  [τῆς] νυκτὸς τῷ
into Troas.     And  sight through the   night  to the
```
```
3972   3708       435  3110        5100 1510 2476
Παύλῳ ὤφθη,     ἀνὴρ Μακεδών    τις  ἦν  ἑστὼς
Paul  was seen, man Macedonian some was+ +standing
```
```
2532 3870          846   2532 3004     1224
καὶ  παρακαλῶν  αὐτὸν καὶ λέγων·  διαβὰς
and  encouraging him  and saying; having gone through
```
```
1519 3109     997    1473        5613 1161 012  3705
εἰς  Μακεδονίαν βοήθησον ἡμῖν. 10 ὡς   δὲ  τὸ  ὅραμα
into Macedonia help    us.       As  but the  sight
```
```
3708   2112      2212          1831      1519 3109
εἶδεν, εὐθέως   ἐζητήσαμεν ἐξελθεῖν εἰς Μακεδονίαν
he saw, immediately we sought to go out into Macedonia
```
```
4822               3754 4341       1473 01   2316
συμβιβάζοντες  ὅτι  προσκέκληται ἡμᾶς ὁ  θεὸς
forcing together that has called to us  the God
```
```
2097                  846       321          1161 575
εὐαγγελίσασθαι   αὐτούς. 11 Ἀναχθέντες δὲ  ἀπὸ
to tell good message them.  Having been led up but from
```
```
5174    2113          1519 4543         07      1161
Τρῳάδος εὐθυδρομήσαμεν εἰς Σαμοθρᾴκην, τῇ    δὲ
Troas   we ran straight to  Samothrace, in the but
```
```
1966     1519 3496   12 2547          1519 5375
ἐπιούσῃ εἰς Νεάνπολιν   κἀκεῖθεν      εἰς Φιλίππους,
next    into Neapolis    and from there into Philippi
```
```
3748   1510 4413      3310    06    3109     4172
ἥτις  ἐστὶν πρώτη[ς] μερίδος τῆς   Μακεδονίας πόλις,
which is   first    part    of the Macedonia city,
```
```
2862       1510   1161 1722 3778 07 4172   1304
κολωνία.  Ἦμεν  δὲ  ἐν  ταύτῃ τῇ πόλει διατρίβοντες
colony.  We were+ but in this the city +continuing
```
```
2250    5100   13 07   5037 2250 022     4521
ἡμέρας τινάς.    τῇ  τε ἡμέρᾳ τῶν   σαββάτων
days   some.   In the but day  of the sabbaths
```
```
1831          1854   06   4439 3844  4215    3757
ἐξήλθομεν   ἔξω   τῆς πύλης παρὰ ποταμὸν οὗ
we went out outside the gate along river   where
```
```
3543          4335        1510    2532 2523
ἐνομίζομεν    προσευχὴν εἶναι, καὶ καθίσαντες
we were thinking prayer  to be, and having sat
```
```
2980       019     4905         1135         14 2532 5100
ἐλαλοῦμεν ταῖς  συνελθούσαις γυναιξίν.     καί  τις
we were   to the having come  women.        And  some
speaking         together
```
```
1135   3686      3070    4211              4172    2363
γυνὴ  ὀνόματι Λυδία, πορφυρόπωλις πόλεως Θυατείρων
woman in name Lydia, purple seller  of city Thyatira
```
```
4576        04  2316  191       3739 01   2962
σεβομένη  τὸν θεόν, ἤκουεν,    ἧς   ὁ  κύριος
worshiping the God, was hearing, whom the master
```
```
1272          08   2588    4337        023
διήνοιξεν    τὴν καρδίαν προσέχειν τοῖς
opened completely the heart  to hold to to the things
```
```
2980         5259 02 3972        15 5613 1161
λαλουμένοις ὑπὸ τοῦ Παύλου.     ὡς   δὲ
being spoken by  the Paul.        As  but
```
```
907          2532 01 3624 846      3870
ἐβαπτίσθη   καὶ  ὁ  οἶκος αὐτῆς, παρεκάλεσεν
she was immersed and the house of her, she encouraged
```
```
3004     1487 2919     1473 4103    03
λέγουσα· εἰ  κεκρίκατέ με  πιστὴν τῷ
saying;  if  you have judged me trustful in the
```
```
2962   1510  1525         1519 04 3624 1473
κυρίῳ  εἶναι, εἰσελθόντες εἰς τὸν οἶκόν μου
Master to be, having come in into the house of me
```

did not allow them; [8]so, passing by Mysia, they went down to Troas. [9]During the night Paul had a vision: there stood a man of Macedonia pleading with him and saying, "Come over to Macedonia and help us." [10]When he had seen the vision, we immediately tried to cross over to Macedonia, being convinced that God had called us to proclaim the good news to them.

[11]We set sail from Troas and took a straight course to Samothrace, the following day to Neapolis, [12]and from there to Philippi, which is a leading city of the district[a] of Macedonia and a Roman colony. We remained in this city for some days. [13]On the sabbath day we went outside the gate by the river, where we supposed there was a place of prayer; and we sat down and spoke to the women who had gathered there. [14]A certain woman named Lydia, a worshiper of God, was listening to us; she was from the city of Thyatira and a dealer in purple cloth. The Lord opened her heart to listen eagerly to what was said by Paul. [15]When she and her household were baptized, she urged us, saying, "If you have judged me to be faithful to the Lord, come and stay at my home."

[a] Other authorities read a city of the first district

And she prevailed upon us.

16 One day, as we were going to the place of prayer, we met a slave-girl who had a spirit of divination and brought her owners a great deal of money by fortune-telling. [17]While she followed Paul and us, she would cry out, "These men are slaves of the Most High God, who proclaim to you*a* a way of salvation." [18]She kept doing this for many days. But Paul, very much annoyed, turned and said to the spirit, "I order you in the name of Jesus Christ to come out of her." And it came out that very hour.

19 But when her owners saw that their hope of making money was gone, they seized Paul and Silas and dragged them into the marketplace before the authorities. [20]When they had brought them before the magistrates, they said, "These men are disturbing our city; they are Jews [21]and are advocating customs that are not lawful for us as Romans to adopt or observe." [22]The crowd joined in attacking them, and the magistrates had them stripped of their clothing and ordered them to be beaten with rods.

a Other ancient authorities read *to us*

```
3306      2532 3849                  1473     16  1096         1161
μένετε· καὶ παρεβιάσατο        ἡμᾶς.     16 Ἐγένετο    δὲ
stay;     and she pressed along us.        It became but
4198         1473 1519 08  4335          3814          5100
πορευομένων ἡμῶν εἰς τὴν προσευχὴν παιδίσκην   τινὰ
traveling   us    to   the prayer    servant girl some
2192       4151   4436     5221       1473   3748 2039
ἔχουσαν πνεῦμα πύθωνα ὑπαντῆσαι ἡμῖν, ἥτις ἐργασίαν
having  spirit python to meet   us,   who work
4183    3930      015   2962    846
πολλὴν παρεῖχεν τοῖς κυρίοις αὐτῆς
much   held along to the masters of her
3132          17 3778   2628            03  3972
μαντευομένη.  17 αὕτη κατακολουθοῦσα τῷ Παύλῳ
telling       This one following after  the Paul
fortunes.
2532 1473 2896          3004     3778 013 444
καὶ ἡμῖν ἔκραζεν    λέγουσα· οὗτοι οἱ ἄνθρωποι
and to us was shouting saying;  these the men
1401   02     2316 02 5310     1510   3748
δοῦλοι τοῦ θεοῦ τοῦ ὑψίστου εἰσίν, οἵτινες
slaves of the God the highest are,   who
2605          1473 3598 4991          18 3778 1161
καταγγέλλουσιν ὑμῖν ὁδὸν σωτηρίας.  18 τοῦτο δὲ
proclaim      to you way of deliverance. This but
4160       1909 4183 2250    1278         1161
ἐποίει    ἐπὶ πολλὰς ἡμέρας. διαπονηθεὶς δὲ
she was doing on many days.  Having pain but
3972 2532 1994         011   4151       3004
Παῦλος καὶ ἐπιστρέψας τῷ πνεύματι εἶπεν·
Paul   and having returned in the spirit said;
3853     1473 1722 3686     2424 5547    1831
παραγγέλλω σοι ἐν ὀνόματι Ἰησοῦ Χριστοῦ ἐξελθεῖν
I command you in name   Jesus Christ  to go out
575  846    2532 1831      846 07 5610
ἀπ' αὐτῆς· καὶ ἐξῆλθεν αὐτῇ τῇ ὥρᾳ.
from her;  and it went out her the hour.
19 3708          1161 013 2962   846   3754 1831
19 Ἰδόντες    δὲ οἱ κύριοι αὐτῆς ὅτι ἐξῆλθεν
Having seen but the masters of her that went out
05 1680 06     2039        846    1949        04
ἡ ἐλπὶς τῆς ἐργασίας αὐτῶν, ἐπιλαβόμενοι τὸν
the hope of the work   of them, having taken on the
3972 2532 4609 1670        1519 08 58   1909
Παῦλον καὶ τὸν Σιλᾶν εἵλκυσαν εἰς τὴν ἀγορὰν ἐπὶ
Paul   and the Silas they haul to the market on
016   758     20 2532 4317        846    015
τοὺς ἄρχοντας 20 καὶ προσαγαγόντες αὐτοὺς τοῖς
the rulers    and having led to them the
4755    3004      3778 013 444
στρατηγοῖς εἶπαν· οὗτοι οἱ ἄνθρωποι
captains they said; these the men
1613        1473 08 4172    2453
ἐκταράσσουσιν ἡμῶν τὴν πόλιν, Ἰουδαῖοι
trouble thoroughly us the city, Judeans
5225       21 2532 2605          1485   3739 3756
ὑπάρχοντες, 21 καὶ καταγγέλλουσιν ἔθη ἃ οὐκ
existing,    and they proclaim customs that not
1832       1473 3858       3761  4160
ἔξεστιν ἡμῖν παραδέχεσθαι οὐδὲ ποιεῖν
it is possible to us to accept but not to do
4514   1510   22 2532 4911        01 3793
Ῥωμαίοις οὖσιν. 22 καὶ συνεπέστη ὁ ὄχλος
Romans being.   And stood on together the crowd
2596 846   2532 013 4755     4048
κατ' αὐτῶν καὶ οἱ στρατηγοὶ περιρήξαντες
by   them and the captains having ripped around
846  024 2440   2753        4463
αὐτῶν τὰ ἱμάτια ἐκέλευον ῥαβδίζειν,
them the clothes were commanding to beat with rods,
```

23
4183	5037	2007		846	4127	906		1519
πολλάς	τε	ἐπιθέντες		αὐτοῖς	πληγὰς	ἔβαλον		εἰς
many	and	having set		them	blows	they threw		into

5438	3853		03	1200		806
φυλακὴν	παραγγείλαντες		τῷ	δεσμοφύλακι		ἀσφαλῶς
guard	having commanded		the	chain guard		securely

5083	846	**24**	3739	3852		5108
τηρεῖν	αὐτούς.		ὃς	παραγγελίαν		τοιαύτην
to keep	them.		Who	command		such

2983		906	846	1519	08	2082
λαβὼν		ἔβαλεν	αὐτοὺς	εἰς	τὴν	ἐσωτέραν
having taken		threw	them	into	the	inner

5438	2532	016	4228	805		846		1519	012
φυλακὴν	καὶ	τοὺς	πόδας	ἠσφαλίσατο		αὐτῶν		εἰς	τὸ
guard	and	the	feet	he secured		of them		in	the

3586	**25**	2596	1161	012	3317		3972		2532	4609
ξύλον.		Κατὰ	δὲ	τὸ	μεσονύκτιον		Παῦλος	καὶ		Σιλᾶς
wood.		By	but	the	middle night		Paul	and		Silas

4336		5214		04	2316	1874
προσευχόμενοι	ὕμνουν			τὸν	θεόν,	ἐπηκροῶντο
praying	were singing			the	God,	were listening

1161	846	013	1198	**26**	869		1161	4578
δὲ	αὐτῶν	οἱ	δέσμιοι.		ἄφνω		δὲ	σεισμὸς
but	of them	the	prisoners.		Suddenly		but	shake

1096	3173	5620	4531		024	2310
ἐγένετο	μέγας	ὥστε	σαλευθῆναι		τὰ	θεμέλια
became	great	so that	to be shaken		the	foundations

010	1201		455		1161	3916		017
τοῦ	δεσμωτηρίου·		ἠνεῴχθησαν		δὲ	παραχρῆμα		αἱ
of the	chain place;		were opened		but	suddenly		the

2374	3956	2532	3956		021	1199	447
θύραι	πᾶσαι	καὶ	πάντων		τὰ	δεσμὰ	ἀνέθη.
doors	all	and	all		the	chains	were left.

27
1853		1161	1096		01	1200		2532
ἔξυπνος		δὲ	γενόμενος		ὁ	δεσμοφύλαξ		καὶ
Awake		but	having become		the	chain guard		and

3708		455		020	2374	06	5438
ἰδὼν		ἀνεῳγμένας		τὰς	θύρας	τῆς	φυλακῆς,
having seen		having been the		the	doors	of the	guard,
		opened					

4685		08	3162		3195		1438
σπασάμενος		[τὴν]	μάχαιραν		ἤμελλεν		ἑαυτὸν
having drawn		the	sword		he was about		himself

337	3543	1628		016	1198
ἀναιρεῖν	νομίζων	ἐκπεφευγέναι		τοὺς	δεσμίους.
to kill	thinking	to have fled out		the	prisoners.

28
5455		1161	3173	5456	01	3972		3004
ἐφώνησεν		δὲ	μεγάλῃ	φωνῇ	[ὁ]	Παῦλος		λέγων·
Sounded		but	great	sound	the	Paul		saying,

3367	4238		4572		2556	537	1063
μηδὲν	πράξῃς		σεαυτῷ		κακόν,	ἅπαντες	γάρ
nothing	you might practice		yourself		bad,	all	for

1510	1759	**29**	154		1161	5457	1530		2532
ἐσμεν	ἐνθάδε.		αἰτήσας		δὲ	φῶτα	εἰσεπήδησεν		καὶ
are	in this		Having		but	lights	he rushed in		and
	place.		asked						

1790	1096		4363	03	3972	2532	03
ἔντρομος	γενόμενος		προσέπεσεν	τῷ	Παύλῳ	καὶ	[τῷ]
trembling	having become		he fell to	the	Paul	and	the

4609	**30**	2532	4254		846	1854	5346
Σιλᾷ		καὶ	προαγαγὼν		αὐτοὺς	ἔξω	ἔφη·
Silas		and	having led	before them		outside	he said;

2962	5101	1473	1163		4160	2443
κύριοι,	τί	με	δεῖ		ποιεῖν	ἵνα
masters,	what	me	it is necessary		to do	that

4982	**31**	013	1161	3004	4100		1909	04	2962
σωθῶ;		οἱ	δὲ	εἶπαν·	πίστευσον		ἐπὶ	τὸν	κύριον
I might be		The	but	said;	trust		on	the	Master
delivered?									

[23]After they had given them a severe flogging, they threw them into prison and ordered the jailer to keep them securely. [24]Following these instructions, he put them in the innermost cell and fastened their feet in the stocks.

25 About midnight Paul and Silas were praying and singing hymns to God, and the prisoners were listening to them. [26]Suddenly there was an earthquake, so violent that the foundations of the prison were shaken; and immediately all the doors were opened and everyone's chains were unfastened. [27]When the jailer woke up and saw the prison doors wide open, he drew his sword and was about to kill himself, since he supposed that the prisoners had escaped. [28]But Paul shouted in a loud voice, "Do not harm yourself, for we are all here." [29]The jailer[a] called for lights, and rushing in, he fell down trembling before Paul and Silas. [30]Then he brought them outside and said, "Sirs, what must I do to be saved?" [31]They answered, "Believe on the Lord

_a Gk He_

Jesus, and you will be saved, you and your household." [32]They spoke the word of the Lord[a] to him and to all who were in his house. [33]At the same hour of the night he took them and washed their wounds; then he and his entire family were baptized without delay. [34]He brought them up into the house and set food before them; and he and his entire household rejoiced that he had become a believer in God.

[35]When morning came, the magistrates sent the police, saying, "Let those men go." [36]And the jailer reported the message to Paul, saying, "The magistrates sent word to let you go; therefore come out now and go in peace." [37]But Paul replied, "They have beaten us in public, uncondemned, men who are Roman citizens, and have thrown us into prison; and now are they going to discharge us in secret? Certainly not! Let them come and take us out themselves." [38]The police reported these words to the magistrates, and they were afraid when they heard that they were Roman citizens; [39]so they came and apologized to them. And they took them out and asked them to leave the city.

[a] Other ancient authorities read *word of God*

2424	2532 4982	1473 2532 01	3624	1473	**32**	2532
Ἰησοῦν	καὶ σωθήσῃ	σὺ καὶ ὁ	οἶκός	σου.		καὶ
Jesus	and will be	you and the	house of	you.		And
		delivered				

2980	846	04	3056	02	2962	4862 3956
ἐλάλησαν	αὐτῷ	τὸν	λόγον	τοῦ	κυρίου	σὺν πᾶσιν
they spoke	to him	the	word	of	the Master	with all

015	1722 07	τῇ οἰκίᾳ αὐτοῦ.	**33**	2532 3880	846
τοῖς	ἐν	τῇ οἰκίᾳ αὐτοῦ.		καὶ παραλαβὼν	αὐτοὺς
the	in	the house of him.		And having taken them	along

1722	1565	07	5610 06	3571	3068	575 018
ἐν	ἐκείνῃ	τῇ	ὥρᾳ τῆς	νυκτὸς	ἔλουσεν	ἀπὸ τῶν
in	that	the	hour of the	night	he washed	from the

4127	2532 907	846	2532 013 846	3956
πληγῶν,	καὶ ἐβαπτίσθη	αὐτὸς	καὶ οἱ αὐτοῦ	πάντες
blows,	and was immersed	himself	and the of him	all

3916	**34**	321	5037 846	1519 04 3624
παραχρῆμα,		ἀναγαγών	τε αὐτοὺς εἰς	τὸν οἶκον
suddenly,		having led up	but them into	the house

3908	5132	2532 21	3832
παρέθηκεν	τράπεζαν	καὶ ἠγαλλιάσατο	πανοικεὶ
he set along	table	and was glad	all house

4100	03	2316	**35**	2250	1161 1096
πεπιστευκὼς	τῷ	θεῷ.		Ἡμέρας	δὲ γενομένης
having trusted	in the	God.		Day	but having become

649	013 4755	016	4465	3004
ἀπέστειλαν	οἱ στρατηγοὶ	τοὺς	ῥαβδούχους	λέγοντες·
delegated	the captains	the	rodbearers	saying,

630	016 444	1565	**36**	518	1161
ἀπόλυσον	τοὺς ἀνθρώπους	ἐκείνους.		ἀπήγγειλεν	δὲ
loose off	the men	those.		Told	but

01	1200	016	3056	3778	4314 04 3972
ὁ	δεσμοφύλαξ	τοὺς	λόγους	[τούτους]	πρὸς τὸν Παῦλον
the	chain guard	the	words	these	to the Paul

3754 649	013 4755	2443
ὅτι ἀπέσταλκαν	οἱ στρατηγοὶ	ἵνα
that have delegated	the captains	that

630	3568 3767 1831	4198
ἀπολυθῆτε·	νῦν οὖν ἐξελθόντες	πορεύεσθε
you might loose off;	now then having gone out	travel

1722 1515	**37**	01	1161 3972	5346 4314 846
ἐν εἰρήνῃ.		ὁ	δὲ Παῦλος	ἔφη πρὸς αὐτούς·
in peace.		The	but Paul	said to them;

1194	1473 1219	178	444
δείραντες	ἡμᾶς δημοσίᾳ	ἀκατακρίτους,	ἀνθρώπους
having beaten	us in public	uncondemned,	men

4514	5225	906	1519 5438	2532
Ῥωμαίους	ὑπάρχοντας,	ἔβαλαν	εἰς φυλακήν,	καὶ
Romans	existing,	they threw	into guard,	and

3568 2977	1473 1544	3756 1063 235
νῦν λάθρα	ἡμᾶς ἐκβάλλουσιν;	οὐ γάρ, ἀλλὰ
now privately	us they throw out?	Not for, but

2064	846	1473 1806	**38**	518
ἐλθόντες	αὐτοὶ	ἡμᾶς ἐξαγαγέτωσαν.		ἀπήγγειλαν
having come	themselves	us let lead out.		Told

1161 015	4755	013 4465	024 4487
δὲ τοῖς	στρατηγοῖς	οἱ ῥαβδοῦχοι	τὰ ῥήματα
but to the	captains	the rodbearers	the words

3778	5399	1161 191	3754 4514
ταῦτα.	ἐφοβήθησαν	δὲ ἀκούσαντες	ὅτι Ῥωμαῖοί
these.	They were afraid	but having heard	that Romans

1510	**39**	2532 2064	3870	846 2532
εἰσιν,		καὶ ἐλθόντες	παρεκάλεσαν	αὐτοὺς καὶ
they are,		and having come	they encouraged	them and

1806	2065	565	575 06
ἐξαγαγόντες	ἠρώτων	ἀπελθεῖν	ἀπὸ τῆς
having led out	they were asking	to go off	from the

```
4172        1831              1161  575   06   5438
πόλεως.  40 ἐξελθόντες    δὲ  ἀπὸ  τῆς  φυλακῆς
city.       Having come out but from the guard
1525         4314  08   3070   2532  3708          3870
εἰσῆλθον   πρὸς τὴν Λυδίαν καὶ ἰδόντες   παρεκάλεσαν
they went in to the Lydia and having seen encouraged
016   80        2532  1831          1353
τοὺς ἀδελφοὺς καὶ ἐξῆλθαν.  17:1 Διοδεύσαντες
the  brothers  and went out.       Having made way through
1161  08    295           2532  08    624       2064        1519
δὲ   τὴν 'Αμφίπολιν καὶ τὴν 'Απολλωνίαν ἦλθον   εἰς
but  the Amphipolis and the Apollonia they came into
2332           3699  1510  4864        014  2453       2   2596
Θεσσαλονίκην ὅπου ἦν συναγωγὴ τῶν 'Ιουδαίων.     κατὰ
Thessalonica where was synagogue of the Judeans.      By
1161  012   1536a  03      3972  1525          4314    846
δὲ   τὸ   εἰωθὸς τῷ   Παύλῳ εἰσῆλθεν  πρὸς αὐτοὺς
but  the  custom to the Paul  he went into to  them
2532  1909  4521        5140   1256        846       575   018
καὶ  ἐπὶ  σάββατα τρία διελέξατο αὐτοῖς ἀπὸ τῶν
and  on   sabbaths three he disputed to them from the
1124       1272              2532  3908            3754
γραφῶν,  3 διανοίγων     καὶ  παρατιθέμενος ὅτι
writings,  opening completely and  setting along that
04   5547       1163              3958      2532  450
τὸν χριστὸν ἔδει         παθεῖν   καὶ  ἀναστῆναι
the Christ  it was necessary to suffer and to stand up
1537  3498    2532  3754  3778  1510   01   5547    01
ἐκ  νεκρῶν καὶ  ὅτι  οὗτός ἐστιν ὁ  χριστὸς [ὁ]
from dead  and  that this  is     the Christ  the
2424    3739  1473  2605        1473   2532  5100  1537
'Ιησοῦς ὃν  ἐγὼ καταγγέλλω ὑμῖν. 4 καί τινες ἐξ
Jesus  whom I   proclaim   to you.  And some from
846    3982            2532  4345               03    3972
αὐτῶν ἐπείσθησαν    καὶ  προσεκληρώθησαν τῷ   Παύλῳ
them  were persuaded and  they threw lots to the Paul
2532  03   4609    014  5037  4576      1672     4128
καὶ  τῷ Σιλᾷ, τῶν τε σεβομένων 'Ελλήνων πλῆθος
and  the Silas, the both worshiping Greeks quantity
4183   1135      5037  018  4413    3756 3641      2206
πολύ, γυναικῶν τε τῶν πρώτων οὐκ ὀλίγαι. 5 Ζηλώσαντες
much, of women and the first not few.       Having been
                                                   jealous
1161  013   2453       2532  4355            014  60
δὲ   οἱ  'Ιουδαῖοι καὶ προσλαβόμενοι τῶν ἀγοραίων
but  the Judeans  and having taken to the marketers
435        5100  4190    2532  3792
ἄνδρας τινὰς πονηροὺς καὶ ὀχλοποιήσαντες
men      some  evil     and having made crowd
2350           08    4172  2532  2186
ἐθορύβουν    τὴν πόλιν καὶ  ἐπιστάντες
they were uproaring the city and  having stood on
07    3614    2394     2212            846
τῇ  οἰκίᾳ 'Ιάσονος ἐζήτουν    αυτοὺς
the house of Jason they were seeking them
4254         1519  04   1218  6  3361  2147          1161
προαγαγεῖν εἰς  τὸν δῆμον·   μὴ  εὑρόντες     δὲ
to lead     into the public; not having found but
846    4951           2394    2532  5100  80
αὐτοὺς ἔσυρον      'Ιάσονα καί  τινας ἀδελφοὺς
them    they were dragging Jason and  some  brothers
1909  016   4173       994         3754  013  08
ἐπὶ  τοὺς πολιτάρχας βοῶντες    ὅτι  οἱ  τὴν
on    the  city rulers crying aloud that the the
3625           387                3778  2532  1759
οἰκουμένην  ἀναστατώσαντες οὗτοι καὶ  ἐνθάδε
inhabited world having upset these and in this place
3918      7  3739  5264              2394    2532  3778
πάρεισιν,   οὓς  ὑποδέδεκται    'Ιάσων· καὶ  οὗτοι
are present, whom has entertained Jason; and  these
```

40After leaving the prison they went to Lydia's home; and when they had seen and encouraged the brothers and sisters[a] there, they departed.

CHAPTER 17

After Paul and Silas[b] had passed through Amphipolis and Apollonia, they came to Thessalonica, where there was a synagogue of the Jews. 2And Paul went in, as was his custom, and on three sabbath days argued with them from the scriptures, 3explaining and proving that it was necessary for the Messiah[c] to suffer and to rise from the dead, and saying, "This is the Messiah,[c] Jesus whom I am proclaiming to you." 4Some of them were persuaded and joined Paul and Silas, as did a great many of the devout Greeks and not a few of the leading women. 5But the Jews became jealous, and with the help of some ruffians in the marketplaces they formed a mob and set the city in an uproar. While they were searching for Paul and Silas to bring them out to the assembly, they attacked Jason's house. 6When they could not find them, they dragged Jason and some believers[a] before the city authorities,[d] shouting, "These people who have been turning the world upside down have come here also, 7and Jason has entertained them as guests. They are

a Gk brothers
b Gk they
c Or the Christ
d Gk politarchs

all acting contrary to the decrees of the emperor, saying that there is another king named Jesus." [8]The people and the city officials were disturbed when they heard this, [9]and after they had taken bail from Jason and the others, they let them go.

10 That very night the believers[a] sent Paul and Silas off to Beroea; and when they arrived, they went to the Jewish synagogue. [11]These Jews were more receptive than those in Thessalonica, for they welcomed the message very eagerly and examined the scriptures every day to see whether these things were so. [12]Many of them therefore believed, including not a few Greek women and men of high standing. [13]But when the Jews of Thessalonica learned that the word of God had been proclaimed by Paul in Beroea as well, they came there too, to stir up and incite the crowds. [14]Then the believers[a] immediately sent Paul away to the coast, but Silas and Timothy remained behind. [15]Those who conducted Paul brought him as far as Athens; and after receiving instructions to have Silas and Timothy join him as soon as possible, they left him.

---

[a] Gk brothers

3956   561   022 1378   2541   4238
πάντες ἀπέναντι   τῶν δογμάτων Καίσαρος πράσσουσι
all   over against the decrees of Caesar practice
935   2087   3004   1510 2424   5015
βασιλέα ἕτερον λέγοντες εἶναι Ἰησοῦν. 8 ἐτάραξαν
king   other saying to be Jesus.   They troubled
1161 04 3793   2532 016 4173   191   3778
δὲ   τὸν ὄχλον καὶ τοὺς πολιτάρχας ἀκούοντας ταῦτα,
but the crowd and the city rulers hearing these,
          012 2425 3844 02   2394   2532
9 καὶ λαβόντες   τὸ ἱκανὸν παρὰ τοῦ Ἰάσονος καὶ
  and having taken the enough from the Jason   and
014 3062   630   846   013 1161 80
τῶν λοιπῶν   ἀπέλυσαν   αὐτούς. 10 Οἱ δὲ ἀδελφοὶ
the remaining they loosed off them. The but brothers
2112   1223   3571   1599   04 5037 3972 2532
εὐθέως   διὰ   νυκτὸς ἐξέπεμψαν τόν τε Παῦλον καὶ
immediately through night sent out the both Paul and
04 4609 1519 960   3748   3854   1519 08
τὸν Σιλᾶν εἰς Βέροιαν, οἵτινες παραγενόμενοι εἰς τὴν
the Silas to   Berea,   who   having arrived in the
4864   014   2453   549   3778 1161
συναγωγὴν τῶν Ἰουδαίων ἀπῄεσαν. 11 οὗτοι δὲ
synagogue of the Judeans were going off. These but
1510 2104   014   1722 2332   3748
ἦσαν εὐγενέστεροι τῶν   ἐν Θεσσαλονίκῃ, οἵτινες
were more well born the ones in Thessalonica, who
1209   04 3056 3326 3956 4288   2596 2250
ἐδέξαντο τὸν λόγον μετὰ πάσης προθυμίας καθ' ἡμέραν
welcomed the word with all eagerness   by day
350   020 1124   1487 2192   3778 3779
ἀνακρίνοντες τὰς γραφὰς εἰ ἔχοι ταῦτα οὕτως.
examining the writings if may have these thusly.
   4183   3303   3767 1537 846   4100   2532 018
12 πολλοὶ μὲν   οὖν ἐξ αὐτῶν ἐπίστευσαν καὶ τῶν
   Many   indeed then from them trusted   and of the
1674   1135   018 2158   2532 435   3756
Ἑλληνίδων γυναικῶν τῶν εὐσχημόνων καὶ ἀνδρῶν οὐκ
Greek   women   the proper   and men   not
3641   5613 1161 1097   013 575 06 2332
ὀλίγοι. 13 Ὡς δὲ ἔγνωσαν οἱ ἀπὸ τῆς Θεσσαλονίκης
few.   As but knew   the from the Thessalonica
2453   3754 2532 1722 07   960   2605   5259
Ἰουδαῖοι ὅτι καὶ ἐν τῇ Βεροίᾳ κατηγγέλη   ὑπὸ
Judeans that also in the Berea was proclaimed by
02 3972   01 3056 02   2316   2064   2546
τοῦ Παύλου ὁ λόγος τοῦ θεοῦ, ἦλθον κἀκεῖ
the Paul   the word of the God, they went and there
4531   2532 5015   016 3793   2112
σαλεύοντες καὶ ταράσσοντες τοὺς ὄχλους. 14 εὐθέως
shaking   and troubling   the crowds. Immediately
1161 5119 04 3972   1821   013 80
δὲ   τότε τὸν Παῦλον ἐξαπέστειλαν οἱ ἀδελφοὶ
but then the Paul   delegated out the brothers
4198   2193   1909 08 2281   5278   5037 01
πορεύεσθαι ἕως ἐπὶ τὴν θάλασσαν, ὑπέμεινάν τε ὅ
to travel until on the sea,   endured   but the
5037 4609 2532 01 5095   1563   013   1161
τε   Σιλᾶς καὶ ὁ Τιμόθεος ἐκεῖ. 15 οἱ   δὲ
both Silas and the Timothy there. The ones but
2525   04 3972   71   2193 116   2532
καθιστάνοντες τὸν Παῦλον ἤγαγον ἕως Ἀθηνῶν, καὶ
appointing   the Paul   led   until Athens, and
2983   1785   4314 04 4609 2532 04 5095
λαβόντες   ἐντολὴν πρὸς τὸν Σιλᾶν καὶ τὸν Τιμόθεον
having taken command to the Silas and the Timothy
2443 5613 5030   2064   4314 846   1826
ἵνα ὡς τάχιστα   ἔλθωσιν πρὸς αὐτὸν ἐξῄεσαν.
that as most quickly they might to him they were
                             come   going out.

16
1722	1161	019	116	1551	846	02
Ἐν	δὲ	ταῖς	Ἀθήναις	ἐκδεχομένου	αὐτοὺς	τοῦ
In	but	the	Athens	waiting for	them	the

3972	3947		09	4151	846	1722	846
Παύλου	παρωξύνετο		τὸ	πνεῦμα	αὐτοῦ	ἐν	αὐτῷ
Paul	was being provoked		the	spirit	of him	in	him

2334	2712	1510	08	4172
θεωροῦντος	κατείδωλον	οὖσαν	τὴν	πόλιν.
watching	full of idols	being		the city.

17
1256		3303	3767	1722	07	4864
διελέγετο		μὲν	οὖν	ἐν	τῇ	συναγωγῇ
He was disputing		indeed	then	in	the	synagogue

015	2453	2532	015		4576	2532	1722	07
τοῖς	Ἰουδαίοις	καὶ	τοῖς		σεβομένοις	καὶ	ἐν	τῇ
the	Judeans	and	the ones		worshiping	also	in	the

58	2596	3956	2250	4314	016	3909
ἀγορᾷ	κατὰ	πᾶσαν	ἡμέραν	πρὸς	τοὺς	παρατυγχάνοντας.
market	by	all	day	to	the	happening along.

18
5100	1161	2532	014	1946		2532	4770
τινὲς	δὲ	καὶ	τῶν	Ἐπικουρείων		καὶ	Στοϊκῶν
Some	but	also	of the	Epicureans		and	Stoics

5386	4820		846	2532	5100
φιλοσόφων	συνέβαλλον		αὐτῷ,	καί	τινες
philosophers	were throwing together		him,	and	some

3004		5101	302	2309	01	4691
ἔλεγον·		τί	ἂν	θέλοι	ὁ	σπερμολόγος
were saying,		what	-	may want	the	seed collector

3778	3004	013	1161	3581	1140
οὗτος	λέγειν;	οἱ	δέ·	ξένων	δαιμονίων
this	to say?	The	but;	of strangers	demons

1380	2604	1510	3754	04	2424	2532
δοκεῖ	καταγγελεὺς	εἶναι,	ὅτι	τὸν	Ἰησοῦν	καὶ
he thinks	proclaimer	to be,	because	the	Jesus	and

08	386	2097		1949	5037
τὴν	ἀνάστασιν	εὐηγγελίζετο.	**19**	ἐπιλαβόμενοί	τε
the	standing up	he was telling		Having taken on	but
		good message.			

846	1909	04	697	3803a	71	3004
αὐτοῦ	ἐπὶ	τὸν	Ἄρειον	πάγον	ἤγαγον	λέγοντες·
him	on	the	Areo-	pagus	they led	saying;

1410	1097	5101	05	2537	3778	05	5259
δυνάμεθα	γνῶναι	τίς	ἡ	καινὴ	αὕτη	ἡ	ὑπὸ
we are able	to know	what	the	new	this	the	by

1473	2980	1322		3579	1063
σοῦ	λαλουμένη	διδαχή;	**20**	ξενίζοντα	γάρ
you being spoken		teaching?		Thinking strange	for

5100	1533	1519	020	189	1473	1014
τινα	εἰσφέρεις	εἰς	τὰς	ἀκοὰς	ἡμῶν·	βουλόμεθα
some	you carry in	into	the	hearings	of us;	we plan

3767	1097	5101	2309	3778	1510	117
οὖν	γνῶναι	τίνα	θέλει	ταῦτα	εἶναι.	**21** Ἀθηναῖοι
then	to know	what	wants	these	to be.	Atheneans

1161	3956	2532	013	1927	3581
δὲ	πάντες	καὶ	οἱ	ἐπιδημοῦντες	ξένοι
but	all	and	the ones	living temporarily	strangers

1519	3762	2087	2119	2228	3004	5100
εἰς	οὐδὲν	ἕτερον	ηὐκαίρουν	ἢ	λέγειν	τι
in	nothing	other	had good season	or	to say	some

2228	191	5100	2537		2476	1161	01
ἢ	ἀκούειν	τι	καινότερον.	**22**	Σταθεὶς	δὲ	[ὁ]
or	to hear	some	newer.		Having stood	but	the

3972	1722	3319	02	697	3803a	5346	435
Παῦλος	ἐν	μέσῳ	τοῦ	Ἀρείου	πάγου	ἔφη·	ἄνδρες
Paul	in	middle	of the	Areo-	pagus	said;	men

117	2596	3956	5613	1174	1473
Ἀθηναῖοι,	κατὰ	πάντα	ὡς	δεισιδαιμονεστέρους	ὑμᾶς
Atheneans,	by	all	as	more demon fearing	you

2334		1330	1063	2532	333	024
θεωρῶ.	**23**	διερχόμενος	γὰρ	καὶ	ἀναθεωρῶν	τὰ
I watch.		Going through	for	also	watching up	the

16 While Paul was waiting for them in Athens, he was deeply distressed to see that the city was full of idols. ¹⁷So he argued in the synagogue with the Jews and the devout persons, and also in the marketplace[a] every day with those who happened to be there. ¹⁸Also some Epicurean and Stoic philosophers debated with him. Some said, "What does this babbler want to say?" Others said, "He seems to be a proclaimer of foreign divinities." (This was because he was telling the good news about Jesus and the resurrection.) ¹⁹So they took him and brought him to the Areopagus and asked him, "May we know what this new teaching is that you are presenting? ²⁰It sounds rather strange to us, so we would like to know what it means." ²¹Now all the Athenians and the foreigners living there would spend their time in nothing but telling or hearing something new.

22 Then Paul stood in front of the Areopagus and said, "Athenians, I see how extremely religious you are in every way. ²³For as I went through the city and looked carefully at the

---

[a] Or civic center; Gk agora

objects of your worship, I found among them an altar with the inscription, 'To an unknown god.' What therefore you worship as unknown, this I proclaim to you. [24]The God who made the world and everything in it, he who is Lord of heaven and earth, does not live in shrines made by human hands, [25]nor is he served by human hands, as though he needed anything, since he himself gives to all mortals life and breath and all things. [26]From one ancestor[a] he made all nations to inhabit the whole earth, and he allotted the times of their existence and the boundaries of the places where they would live, [27]so that they would search for God[b] and perhaps grope for him and find him—though indeed he is not far from each one of us. [28]For 'In him we live and move and have our being'; as even some of your own poets have said,

'For we too are his offspring.'

[29]Since we are God's offspring, we ought not to think that the deity is like gold, or silver, or stone, an image formed by the art and imagination of mortals. [30]While God has overlooked the times of human ignorance, now he commands all people everywhere to repent,

a Gk From one; other ancient authorities read From one blood
b Other ancient authorities read the Lord

4574   1473   2147   2532 1041
σεβάσματα   ὑμῶν   εὗρον   καὶ βωμὸν
objects of worship of you I found also high places
1722 3739   1924   57   2316 3739 3767
ἐν ᾧ   ἐπεγέγραπτο· Ἀγνώστῳ θεῷ. ὃ   οὖν
in which it had been   to unknown God. What then
                        written on;
50   2151   3778 1473 2605   1473
ἀγνοοῦντες εὐσεβεῖτε, τοῦτο ἐγὼ καταγγέλλω ὑμῖν.
unknowing you revere,   this   I   proclaim   to you.
    01 2316 01   4160   04 2889   2532 3956 024
24 ὁ θεὸς ὁ ποιήσας   τὸν κόσμον καὶ πάντα τὰ
   The God the having made the world and all   the
1722 846   3778 3772   2532 1093 5225   2962
ἐν αὐτῷ, οὗτος οὐρανοῦ καὶ γῆς ὑπάρχων κύριος
in it,   this of heaven and earth existing Master
3756 1722 5499   3485   2730
οὐκ ἐν χειροποιήτοις ναοῖς κατοικεῖ
not in handmade   temples resides
    3761   5259 5495 442   2323
25 οὐδὲ   ὑπὸ χειρῶν ἀνθρωπίνων θεραπεύεται
   but not by hands of man-like is he healed
4326   5100   846   1325 3956   2222 2532
προσδεόμενός τινος, αὐτὸς διδοὺς πᾶσι ζωὴν καὶ
begging toward some, himself giving to all life and
4157   2532 3024 3956   4160   5037 1537 1520
πνοὴν καὶ τὰ πάντα· 26 ἐποίησέν τε ἐξ ἑνὸς
wind and the all;   he made both from one
3956 1484   444   2730   1909 3956   4383
πᾶν ἔθνος ἀνθρώπων κατοικεῖν ἐπὶ παντὸς προσώπου
all nation of men to reside on all   face
06   1093 3724   4367
τῆς γῆς, ὁρίσας   προστεταγμένους
of the earth, having designated having been commanded
2540   2532 2532 020 3734   06   2733
καιροὺς καὶ τὰς ὁροθεσίας   τῆς κατοικίας
seasons and the set territories of the residence
846   27 2212   04 2316 1487 686   1065
αὐτῶν   ζητεῖν τὸν θεόν, εἰ ἄρα γε
of them   to seek the God, if then indeed
5584   846   2532 2147   2532 1065   3756
ψηλαφήσειαν αὐτὸν καὶ εὕροιεν, καί γε   οὐ
they may touch him and may find, and indeed not
3112   575 1520 1538   1473 5225   28 1722 846
μακρὰν ἀπὸ ἑνὸς ἑκάστου ἡμῶν ὑπάρχοντα.   ἐν αὐτῷ
far   from one each   of us existing.   In him
1063 2198   2532 2795   2532 1510   5613 2532
γὰρ ζῶμεν καὶ κινούμεθα καὶ ἐσμέν, ὡς καὶ
for we live and are moved and we are, as also
5100 014   2596 1473 4163   3004   02   1063
τινες τῶν καθ᾽ ὑμᾶς ποιητῶν εἰρήκασιν· τοῦ γὰρ
some of the by you doers have said; of the for
2532 1085 1510   29 1085 3767 5225   02   2316
καὶ γένος ἐσμέν.   γένος οὖν ὑπάρχοντες τοῦ θεοῦ
also kind we are.   Kind then existing of the God
3756 3784   3543   5557   2228 696   2228
οὐκ ὀφείλομεν νομίζειν χρυσῷ ἢ ἀργύρῳ ἢ
not we owe   to think to gold or to silver or
3037   5480   5078   2532 1761   444
λίθῳ, χαράγματι τέχνης καὶ ἐνθυμήσεως ἀνθρώπου,
to stone, in mark of craft and reflection of man,
012 3304 1510 3664   016 3303   3767 5550
τὸ θεῖον εἶναι ὅμοιον. 30 τοὺς μὲν οὖν χρόνους
the godly to be like.   The indeed then times
06   52   5246a   01 2316 024 3568
τῆς ἀγνοίας ὑπεριδὼν   ὁ θεός, τὰ νῦν
of the unknowing having overlooked the God, the now
3853   015 444   3956   3837
παραγγέλλει τοῖς ἀνθρώποις πάντας πανταχοῦ
he commands the men   all   all places

```
3340              2530        2476      2250    1722 3739
μετανοεῖν,    31  καθότι    ἔστησεν ἡμέραν ἐν    ἧ
to change mind, just as that  he stood   day    in   which
3195         2919     08    3625              1722
μέλλει     κρίνειν  τὴν  οἰκουμένην      ἐν
he is about to judge  the  inhabited world  in
1343          1722 435    3739      3724            4102
δικαιοσύνῃ,  ἐν  ἀνδρὶ  ᾧ      ὥρισεν,         πίστιν
rightness,   in  man   in whom he designated, trust
3930       3956   450              846  1537 3498
παρασχὼν  πᾶσιν ἀναστήσας  αὐτὸν ἐκ νεκρῶν.
having held to all  having stood up  him  from dead.
     191           1161 386       3498        013 3303
32 Ἀκούσαντες  δὲ  ἀνάστασιν  νεκρῶν  οἱ μὲν
   Having heard but  standing up  of dead  the indeed
5512         013 1161 3004        191              1473 4012
ἐχλεύαζον,  οἱ δὲ  εἶπαν· ἀκουσόμεθά σου  περὶ
were jeering, the but  said;  we will hear you   about
3778     2532 3825       3779   01   3972    1831      1537
τούτου καὶ  πάλιν.   33 οὕτως ὁ  Παῦλος ἐξῆλθεν  ἐκ
this     also again.    Thusly the Paul   went out from
3319    846       5100 1161 435    2853         846
μέσου  αὐτῶν.  34 τινὲς δὲ ἄνδρες κολληθέντες αὐτῷ
middle of them.     Some  but men  having been  to him
                                                 joined
4100          1722 3739 2532 1354       01  698
ἐπίστευσαν, ἐν  οἷς  καὶ Διονύσιος ὁ  Ἀρεοπαγίτης
trusted,    in  whom also Dionysius the Areopagite
2532 1135   3686        1152      2532 2087    4862 846
καὶ  γυνὴ  ὀνόματι Δάμαρις καὶ  ἕτεροι σὺν αὐτοῖς.
and  woman  in name Damaris and  others with them.
      3326 3778  5563                   1537 018  116
18:1 Μετὰ ταῦτα χωρισθεὶς       ἐκ  τῶν Ἀθηνῶν
     After these having been separated from the Athens
2064     1519 2882           2532 2147        5100
ἦλθεν  εἰς Κόρινθον.  2 καὶ  εὑρών       τινα
he went into Corinth.    And  having found some
2453       3686      207      4193      011    1085
Ἰουδαῖον ὀνόματι Ἀκύλαν,  Ποντικὸν τῷ  γένει
Judean    in name Acquila,  Pontian   in the kind
4373         2064         575  06   2482      2532 4252
προσφάτως ἐληλυθότα ἀπὸ τῆς Ἰταλίας καὶ Πρίσκιλλαν
freshly    having come from the Italy   and Priscilla
1135      846      1223      012 1299         2804
γυναῖκα αὐτοῦ,  διὰ     τὸ διατεταχέναι Κλαύδιον
woman   of him, because the to be directed Claudius
5563           3956   016  2453         575  06   4516
χωρίζεσθαι  πάντας τοὺς Ἰουδαίους ἀπὸ τῆς Ῥώμης,
to be separated all   the  Judeans     from the Rome,
4334        846       2532 1223    012 3673       1510
προσῆλθεν αὐτοῖς  3 καὶ  διὰ    τὸ ὁμότεχνον εἶναι
he came     to them   and because the same craft  to be
3306      3844 846       2532 2038
ἔμενεν   παρ’ αὐτοῖς, καὶ ἠργάζετο·
he was staying with them,  and he was working;
1510      1063  4635       07   5078      1256
ἦσαν    γὰρ σκηνοποιοὶ τῇ τέχνῃ. 4 διελέγετο
they were for  tent makers the craft.  He was disputing
1161 1722 07  4864      2596 3956 4521
δὲ  ἐν  τῇ συναγωγῇ κατὰ πᾶν σάββατον
but  in  the synagogue by  all  sabbath
3982        5037     2453        2532 1672       5613
ἔπειθέν    τε    Ἰουδαίους καὶ Ἕλληνας. 5 Ὡς
he was persuading both  Judeans    and  Greeks.   As
1161 2718       575  06   3109      01  5037 4609 2532
δὲ  κατῆλθον ἀπὸ τῆς Μακεδονίας ὅ  τε  Σιλᾶς καὶ
but  came down from the Macedonia  the both Silas and
01  5095       4912                03    3056 01
ὁ  Τιμόθεος, συνείχετο          τῷ   λόγῳ ὁ
the Timothy,  was being held together in the word the
```

31because he has fixed a day on which he will have the world judged in righteousness by a man whom he has appointed, and of this he has given assurance to all by raising him from the dead."

32 When they heard of the resurrection of the dead, some scoffed; but others said, "We will hear you again about this." 33At that point Paul left them. 34But some of them joined him and became believers, including Dionysius the Areopagite and a woman named Damaris, and others with them.

CHAPTER 18

After this Paul[a] left Athens and went to Corinth. 2There he found a Jew named Aquila, a native of Pontus, who had recently come from Italy with his wife Priscilla, because Claudius had ordered all Jews to leave Rome. Paul[b] went to see them, 3and, because he was of the same trade, he stayed with them, and they worked together—by trade they were tentmakers. 4Every sabbath he would argue in the synagogue and would try to convince Jews and Greeks.

5 When Silas and Timothy arrived from Macedonia, Paul was occupied with proclaiming the word,[c]

a Gk *he*
b Gk *He*
c Gk *with the word*

testifying to the Jews that the Messiah*ᵃ* was Jesus. ⁶When they opposed and reviled him, in protest he shook the dust from his clothes*ᵇ* and said to them, "Your blood be on your own heads! I am innocent. From now on I will go to the Gentiles." ⁷Then he left the synagogue*ᶜ* and went to the house of a man named Titius*ᵈ* Justus, a worshiper of God; his house was next door to the synagogue. ⁸Crispus, the official of the synagogue, became a believer in the Lord, together with all his household; and many of the Corinthians who heard Paul became believers and were baptized. ⁹One night the Lord said to Paul in a vision, "Do not be afraid, but speak and do not be silent; ¹⁰for I am with you, and no one will lay a hand on you to harm you, for there are many in this city who are my people." ¹¹He stayed there a year and six months, teaching the word of God among them.

12 But when Gallio was proconsul of Achaia, the Jews made a united attack on Paul and brought him before the tribunal. ¹³They said, "This man is persuading people to worship God in ways that are contrary to the law." ¹⁴Just as Paul was about

ᵃ Or *the Christ*
ᵇ Gk *reviled him, he shook out his clothes*
ᶜ Gk *left there*
ᵈ Other ancient authorities read *Titus*

| 3972 | 1263 | | 015 | 2453 | 1510 |

Παῦλος διαμαρτυρόμενος τοῖς Ἰουδαίοις εἶναι
Paul testifying thoroughly to the Judeans to be

τὸν χριστὸν Ἰησοῦν. ⁶ ἀντιτασσομένων δὲ
the Christ Jesus. Setting in order against but

αὐτῶν καὶ βλασφημούντων ἐκτιναξάμενος τὰ ἱμάτια
them and insulting having swung out the clothes

εἶπεν πρὸς αὐτούς· τὸ αἷμα ὑμῶν ἐπὶ τὴν κεφαλὴν
he said to them, the blood of you on the head

ὑμῶν· καθαρὸς ἐγὼ ἀπὸ τοῦ νῦν εἰς τὰ ἔθνη
of you; clean I from the now to the nations

πορεύσομαι. ⁷ καὶ μεταβὰς ἐκεῖθεν
will travel. And having gone across from there

εἰσῆλθεν εἰς οἰκίαν τινὸς ὀνόματι Τιτίου
he went into into house of some in name Titius

Ἰούστου σεβομένου τὸν θεόν, οὗ ἡ οἰκία ἦν
Justus worshiping the God, of whom the house was+

συνομοροῦσα τῇ συναγωγῇ. ⁸ Κρίσπος δὲ ὁ
+adjoining the synagogue. Crispus but the

ἀρχισυνάγωγος ἐπίστευσεν τῷ κυρίῳ σὺν ὅλῳ
synagogue ruler trusted in the Master with whole

τῷ οἴκῳ αὐτοῦ, καὶ πολλοὶ τῶν Κορινθίων ἀκούοντες
the house of him, and many of the Corinthians hearing

ἐπίστευον καὶ ἐβαπτίζοντο. ⁹ Εἶπεν δὲ ὁ κύριος ἐν
were and were being Said but the Master in
trusting immersed.

νυκτὶ δι’ ὁράματος τῷ Παύλῳ· μὴ φοβοῦ, ἀλλὰ
night through sight to the Paul; not fear, but

λάλει καὶ μὴ σιωπήσῃς, ¹⁰ διότι ἐγώ
speak and not you might be silent, because that I

εἰμι μετὰ σοῦ καὶ οὐδεὶς ἐπιθήσεταί σοι τοῦ
am with you and no one will set on you the

κακῶσαί σε, διότι λαός ἐστί μοι πολὺς
to do bad you, because that people are to me much

ἐν τῇ πόλει ταύτῃ. ¹¹ Ἐκάθισεν δὲ ἐνιαυτὸν καὶ
in the city this. He sat but year and

μῆνας ἓξ διδάσκων ἐν αὐτοῖς τὸν λόγον τοῦ
months six teaching in them the word of the

θεοῦ. ¹² Γαλλίωνος δὲ ἀνθυπάτου ὄντος τῆς Ἀχαΐας
God. Gallio but deputy being of the Achaia

κατεπέστησαν ὁμοθυμαδὸν οἱ Ἰουδαῖοι τῷ Παύλῳ
stood up against with one mind the Judeans the Paul

καὶ ἤγαγον αὐτὸν ἐπὶ τὸ βῆμα ¹³ λέγοντες ὅτι
and led him on the law court saying that

παρὰ τὸν νόμον ἀναπείθει οὗτος τοὺς ἀνθρώπους
from the law persuades again this the men

σέβεσθαι τὸν θεόν. ¹⁴ μέλλοντος δὲ τοῦ Παύλου
to worship the God. Being about but the Paul

```
455        012 4750  3004   01   1058      4314 016
ἀνοίγειν τὸ στόμα εἶπεν ὁ Γαλλίων πρὸς τοὺς
to open  the mouth said  the Gallio  to   the
2453           1487 3303    1510    92    5100 2228
Ἰουδαίους·  εἰ  μὲν  ἦν  ἀδίκημά τι  ἢ
Judeans;   if  indeed it was unright some or
4467        4190       5599  2453       2596 3056  302
ῥᾳδιούργημα πονηρόν, ὦ   Ἰουδαῖοι, κατὰ λόγον ἂν
fraud       evil,   o   Judeans,  by    word  -
430        1473   15 1487 1161 2213      1510 4012
ἀνεσχόμην ὑμῶν,     εἰ  δὲ  ζητήματά ἐστιν περὶ
I endured you,      if  but questions it is about
3056  2532 3686    2532 3551  02  2596 1473
λόγου καὶ ὀνομάτων καὶ νόμου τοῦ καθ᾽ ὑμᾶς,
word  and names    and law   the by  you,
3708      846        2923  1473 3778       3756
ὄψεσθε   αὐτοί·    κριτὴς ἐγὼ τούτων   οὐ
you will see yourselves; judge I    of these not
1014   1510   16 2532 556  846     575  010
βούλομαι εἶναι.   καὶ ἀπήλασεν αὐτοὺς ἀπὸ τοῦ
I plan  to be.   And he drove off them from the
968      1949       1161 3956  4988      04
βήματος.  17 ἐπιλαβόμενοι δὲ πάντες Σωσθένην τὸν
law court.  Having taken on but all  Sosthenes the
752           5180       1715      010
ἀρχισυνάγωγον ἔτυπτον ἔμπροσθεν τοῦ
synagogue ruler were beating in front of the
968      2532 3762  3778   03    1058
βήματος·  καὶ οὐδὲν τούτων τῷ   Γαλλίωνι
law court; and nothing of these to the Gallio
3190a       01  1161 3972 2089 4357
ἔμελεν.  18 Ὁ δὲ Παῦλος ἔτι προσμείνας
was a care. The but Paul still having stayed to
2250   2425  015  80      657
ἡμέρας ἱκανὰς τοῖς ἀδελφοῖς ἀποταξάμενος
days  enough to the brothers having said good-bye
1602        1519 08 4947     2532 4862 846
ἐξέπλει      εἰς τὴν Συρίαν, καὶ σὺν αὐτῷ
was sailing out into the Syria, and with him
4252      2532 207    2751
Πρίσκιλλα καὶ Ἀκύλας, κειράμενος
Priscilla and Acquila, having sheared himself
1722 2747   08  2776     2192    1063 2171
ἐν Κεγχρεαῖς τὴν κεφαλήν, εἶχεν γὰρ εὐχήν.
in Cenchrea the head,   he had for vow.
19 2658         1161 1519 2181     2548
κατήντησαν δὲ εἰς Ἔφεσον, κἀκείνους
They arrived but in  Ephesus, and those
2641       847    846   1161 1525      1519
κατέλιπεν αὐτοῦ, αὐτὸς δὲ εἰσελθὼν     εἰς
he left behind there, himself but having gone in into
08 4864      1256    015    2453      20 2065
τὴν συναγωγὴν διελέξατο τοῖς Ἰουδαίοις.  ἐρωτώντων
the synagogue disputed to the Judeans.  Asking
1161 846 1909 4183    5550   3306  3756 1962
δὲ αὐτῶν ἐπὶ πλείονα χρόνον μεῖναι οὐκ ἐπένευσεν,
but them on more  time to stay not he nodded on,
21 235 657     2532 3004     3825 344      4314
ἀλλὰ ἀποταξάμενος καὶ εἰπών· πάλιν ἀνακάμψω πρὸς
but having said and having said, again I will bend again toward
good-bye
1473 02 2316 2309    321      575 06  2181
ὑμᾶς τοῦ θεοῦ θέλοντος, ἀνήχθη ἀπὸ τῆς Ἐφέσου,
you the God wanting, he was led up from the Ephesus,
22 2532 2718          1519 2542      305
καὶ κατελθὼν      εἰς Καισάρειαν, ἀναβὰς
and having come down into Caesarea, having gone up
2532 782    08  1577     2597      1519
καὶ ἀσπασάμενος τὴν ἐκκλησίαν κατέβη    εἰς
and having greeted the assembly he went down to
```

to speak, Gallio said to the Jews, "If it were a matter of crime or serious villainy, I would be justified in accepting the complaint of you Jews; [15]but since it is a matter of questions about words and names and your own law, see to it yourselves; I do not wish to be a judge of these matters." [16]And he dismissed them from the tribunal. [17]Then all of them[a] seized Sosthenes, the official of the synagogue, and beat him in front of the tribunal. But Gallio paid no attention to any of these things.

18 After staying there for a considerable time, Paul said farewell to the believers[b] and sailed for Syria, accompanied by Priscilla and Aquila. At Cenchreae he had his hair cut, for he was under a vow. [19]When they reached Ephesus, he left them there, but first he himself went into the synagogue and had a discussion with the Jews. [20]When they asked him to stay longer, he declined; [21]but on taking leave of them, he said, "I[c] will return to you, if God wills." Then he set sail from Ephesus.

22 When he had landed at Caesarea, he went up to Jerusalem[d] and greeted the church, and then went down to Antioch.

[a] Other ancient authorities read *all the Greeks*
[b] Gk *brothers*
[c] Other ancient authorities read *I must at all costs keep the approaching festival in Jerusalem, but I*
[d] Gk *went up*

23After spending some time there he departed and went from place to place through the region of Galatia[a] and Phrygia, strengthening all the disciples.

24Now there came to Ephesus a Jew named Apollos, a native of Alexandria. He was an eloquent man, well-versed in the scriptures. 25He had been instructed in the Way of the Lord; and he spoke with burning enthusiasm and taught accurately the things concerning Jesus, though he knew only the baptism of John. 26He began to speak boldly in the synagogue; but when Priscilla and Aquila heard him, they took him aside and explained the Way of God to him more accurately. 27And when he wished to cross over to Achaia, the believers[b] encouraged him and wrote to the disciples to welcome him. On his arrival he greatly helped those who through grace had become believers, 28for he power-fully refuted the Jews in public, showing by the scriptures that the Messiah[c] is Jesus.

CHAPTER 19

While Apollos was in Corinth, Paul passed through the interior regions and came to Ephesus, where he found

a Gk the Galatian region
b Gk brothers
c Or the Christ

| | 490 | **23** | 2532 | 4160 | | 5550 | 5100 |
'Αντιόχειαν. **23** Καὶ ποιήσας χρόνον τινὰ
Antioch.   And having made time   some
| 1831 | | 1330 | | 2517 | 08 | 1054 |
ἐξῆλθεν διερχόμενος καθεξῆς τὴν Γαλατικὴν
he went out going through in order the Galatian
| 5561 | 2532 | 5435 | | 1991 | | 3956 | 016 |
χώραν καὶ Φρυγίαν, ἐπιστηρίζων πάντας τοὺς
country and Phrygian, strengthening on all   the
| 3101 | **24** | 2453 | 1161 | 5100 | 625 | 3686 |
μαθητάς. **24** 'Ιουδαῖος δέ τις 'Απολλῶς ὀνόματι,
learners.   Judean but some Apollos in name,
| 221 | 011 | 1085 | 435 | 3052 | 2658 |
'Αλεξανδρεὺς τῷ γένει, ἀνὴρ λόγιος, κατήντησεν
Alexandrian in the kind, man wordy, arrived
| 1519 | 2181 | 1415 | 1510 | 1722 | 019 | 1124 |
εἰς "Εφεσον, δυνατὸς ὢν ἐν ταῖς γραφαῖς.
in Ephesus, power being in the writings.
| **25** | 3778 | 1510 | 2727 | | 08 | 3598 |
25 οὗτος ἦν κατηχημένος   τὴν ὁδὸν
This one was+ +having been instructed the way
| 02 | 2962 | 2532 | 2204 | 011 | 4151 |
τοῦ κυρίου καὶ ζέων τῷ πνεύματι
of the Master and boiling in the spirit
| 2980 | | 2532 | 1321 | 199 | 024 | 4012 |
ἐλάλει   καὶ ἐδίδασκεν ἀκριβῶς τὰ περὶ
he was speaking and teaching accurately the about
| 02 | 2424 | 1987 | 3441 | 012 | 908 |
τοῦ 'Ιησοῦ, ἐπιστάμενος μόνον τὸ βάπτισμα
the Jesus, understanding alone the immersion
| 2491 | **26** | 3778 | 5037 | 757 | 3955 | | 1722 | 07 |
'Ιωάννου· **26** οὗτός τε ἤρξατο παρρησιάζεσθαι ἐν τῇ
of John; This but began to be bold in the
| 4864 | 191 | 1161 | 846 | 4252 | 2532 | 207 |
συναγωγῇ. ἀκούσαντες δὲ αὐτοῦ Πρίσκιλλα καὶ 'Ακύλας
synagogue. Having heard but him Priscilla and Acquila
| 4355 | 846 | 2532 | 199 | 846 | 1620 |
προσελάβοντο αὐτὸν καὶ ἀκριβέστερον αὐτῷ ἐξέθεντο
took to him and more accurately to him set out
| 08 | 3598 | 02 | 2316 | **27** | 1014 | 1161 | 846 |
τὴν ὁδὸν [τοῦ θεοῦ]. **27** βουλομένου δὲ αὐτοῦ
the way of the God. Planning but him
| 1330 | 1519 | 08 | 882 | 4389 | 013 |
διελθεῖν εἰς τὴν 'Αχαῖαν, προτρεψάμενοι οἱ
to go through into the Achaia, having urged the
| 80 | 1125 | 015 | 3101 | 588 | 846 |
ἀδελφοὶ ἔγραψαν τοῖς μαθηταῖς ἀποδέξασθαι αὐτόν,
brothers they to the learners to welcome him,
wrote   thoroughly
| 3739 | 3854 | 4820 | 4183 | 015 |
ὃς παραγενόμενος συνεβάλετο πολὺ τοῖς
who having arrived threw together much to the ones
| 4100 | 1223 | 06 | 5485 | **28** | 2159 |
πεπιστευκόσιν διὰ τῆς χάριτος· **28** εὐτόνως
having trusted through the favor; intensely well
| 1063 | 015 | 2453 | 1246 | 1219 |
γὰρ τοῖς 'Ιουδαίοις διακατηλέγχετο δημοσίᾳ
for to the Judeans he rebuked thoroughly in public
| 1925 | 1223 | 018 | 1124 | 1510 | 04 | 5547 |
ἐπιδεικνὺς διὰ τῶν γραφῶν εἶναι τὸν χριστὸν
showing on through the writings to be the Christ
| 2424 | **19:1** | 1096 | 1161 | 1722 | 011 | 04 | 625 |
'Ιησοῦν. **19:1** 'Εγένετο δὲ ἐν τῷ τὸν 'Απολλῶ
Jesus.   It became but in the the Apollos
| 1510 | 1722 | 2882 | 3972 | 1330 | 024 |
εἶναι ἐν Κορίνθῳ Παῦλον διελθόντα τὰ
to be in Corinth Paul having gone through the
| 510 | 3313 | 2718 | 1519 | 2181 | 2532 | 2147 |
ἀνωτερικὰ μέρη [κατ]ελθεῖν εἰς "Εφεσον καὶ εὑρεῖν
upper most parts to go down into Ephesus and to find

5100   3101   **2** 3004   5037 4314 846   1487 4151
τινας μαθητὰς   εἶπέν τε   πρὸς αὐτούς· εἰ   πνεῦμα
some   learners   he said but to   them;   if   spirit

40   2983   4100   013 1161 4314
ἅγιον ἐλάβετε   πιστεύσαντες;   οἱ   δὲ   πρὸς
holy   you received having trusted?   The but   to

846   235   3761   1487 4151   40   1510
αὐτόν· ἀλλ᾽ οὐδ᾽   εἰ   πνεῦμα ἅγιον ἔστιν
him;   but   but not if   spirit   holy   there is

191   **3** 3004   5037 1519 5101 3767
ἠκούσαμεν.   εἶπέν τε· εἰς τί   οὖν
we heard.   He said but; into what then

907   013 1161 3004   1519 012 2491
ἐβαπτίσθητε;   οἱ   δὲ   εἶπαν· εἰς τὸ   Ἰωάννου
were you immersed? The but   said;   into the of John

908   **4** 3004   1161 3972   2491   907
βάπτισμα.   εἶπεν δὲ   Παῦλος· Ἰωάννης ἐβάπτισεν
immersion.   Said   but   Paul;   John   immersed

908   3341   03   2992   3004   1519 04
βάπτισμα μετανοίας   τῷ   λαῷ   λέγων εἰς   τὸν
immersion of change mind to the people saying to   the

2064   3326 846   2443 4100   3778 1510
ἐρχόμενον μετ᾽ αὐτὸν ἵνα πιστεύσωσιν,   τοῦτ᾽ ἔστιν
coming   after him   that they might trust, this is

1519 04   2424   **5** 191   1161 907
εἰς   τὸν Ἰησοῦν.   ἀκούσαντες δὲ   ἐβαπτίσθησαν
in   the   Jesus.   Having heard but   they were immersed

1519 012 3686   02   2962   2424   **6** 2532 2007
εἰς   τὸ   ὄνομα τοῦ κυρίου Ἰησοῦ,   καὶ ἐπιθέντος
into the name   of the Master Jesus,   and   having set on

846   02   3972   020   5495   2064 09   4151   09
αὐτοῖς τοῦ Παύλου [τὰς] χεῖρας ἦλθε τὸ   πνεῦμα τὸ
them   the   Paul   the   hands   came the   spirit   the

40   1909 846   2980   5037 1100   2532
ἅγιον ἐπ᾽ αὐτούς, ἐλάλουν   τε   γλώσσαις   καὶ
holy   on   them,   they were speaking but in tongues   and

4395   **7** 1510   1161 013 3956   435
ἐπροφήτευον.   ἦσαν δὲ   οἱ   πάντες ἄνδρες
were speaking before.   Were but   the   all   men

5616 1427   1525   1161 1519 09   4864
ὡσεὶ δώδεκα. **8** Εἰσελθὼν δὲ   εἰς τὴν συναγωγὴν
as   twelve.   Having gone in but   into the synagogue

3955   1909 3376   5140   1256   2532
ἐπαρρησιάζετο   ἐπὶ μῆνας τρεῖς διαλεγόμενος καὶ
he was being bold   on   months three disputing   and

3982   024 4012 06   932   02   2316   **9** 5613
πείθων [τὰ] περὶ τῆς βασιλείας τοῦ θεοῦ.   ὡς
persuading the about the kingdom   of the God.   As

1161 5100   4645   2532 544
δέ   τινες ἐσκληρύνοντο   καὶ ἠπείθουν
but   some   were being hardened and   were disobedient

2551   08   3598 1799   010   4128   868
κακολογοῦντες τὴν ὁδὸν ἐνώπιον τοῦ πλήθους, ἀποστὰς
speaking bad   the way   before   the quantity,   having
                                                             stood off

575   846   873   016   3101   2596 2250
ἀπ᾽ αὐτῶν ἀφώρισεν   τοὺς μαθητὰς καθ᾽ ἡμέραν
from them   he separated the   learners   by   day

1256   1722 07   4981   5181   **10** 3778
διαλεγόμενος ἐν   τῇ   σχολῇ   Τυράννου.   τοῦτο
disputing   in   the lecture hall of Tyrannus.   This

1161 1096   1909 2094 1417 5620   3956   016
δὲ   ἐγένετο ἐπὶ ἔτη   δύο, ὥστε πάντας τοὺς
but   became   on   years two,   so that all   the

2730   08   773   191   04   3056 02
κατοικοῦντας τὴν Ἀσίαν ἀκοῦσαι τὸν λόγον τοῦ
ones residing   the   Asia   to hear   the   word   of the

2962   2453   5037 2532 1672   **11** 1411   5037
κυρίου, Ἰουδαίους τε   καὶ Ἕλληνας.   Δυνάμεις τε
Master, Judeans   both and   Greeks.   Powers   and

some disciples. [2]He said to them, "Did you receive the Holy Spirit when you became believers?" They replied, "No, we have not even heard that there is a Holy Spirit." [3]Then he said, "Into what then were you baptized?" They answered, "Into John's baptism." [4]Paul said, "John baptized with the baptism of repentance, telling the people to believe in the one who was to come after him, that is, in Jesus." [5]On hearing this, they were baptized in the name of the Lord Jesus. [6]When Paul had laid his hands on them, the Holy Spirit came upon them, and they spoke in tongues and prophesied— [7]altogether there were about twelve of them.

8 He entered the synagogue and for three months spoke out boldly, and argued persuasively about the kingdom of God. [9]When some stubbornly refused to believe and spoke evil of the Way before the congregation, he left them, taking the disciples with him, and argued daily in the lecture hall of Tyrannus.[a] [10]This continued for two years, so that all the residents of Asia, both Jews and Greeks, heard the word of the Lord.

11 God did extra-ordinary miracles

[a] Other ancient authorities read *of a certain Tyrannus, from eleven o'clock in the morning to four in the afternoon*

through Paul, [12]so that when the handkerchiefs or aprons that had touched his skin were brought to the sick, their diseases left them, and the evil spirits came out of them. [13]Then some itinerant Jewish exorcists tried to use the name of the Lord Jesus over those who had evil spirits, saying, "I adjure you by the Jesus whom Paul proclaims." [14]Seven sons of a Jewish high priest named Sceva were doing this. [15]But the evil spirit said to them in reply, "Jesus I know, and Paul I know; but who are you?" [16]Then the man with the evil spirit leaped on them, mastered them all, and so overpowered them that they fled out of the house naked and wounded. [17]When this became known to all residents of Ephesus, both Jews and Greeks, everyone was awestruck; and the name of the Lord Jesus was praised. [18]Also many of those who became believers

3756	020	5177		01	2316	4160	1223	018
οὐ	τὰς	τυχούσας		ὁ	θεὸς	ἐποίει	διὰ	τῶν
not	the	having obtained		the	God	did	through	the

5495	3972		5620	2532	1909	016	770
χειρῶν	Παύλου,	**12** ὥστε	καὶ	ἐπὶ	τοὺς	ἀσθενοῦντας
hands	of Paul,	so that	also	on	the	being weak

667		575	02	5559		846
ἀποφέρεσθαι		ἀπὸ	τοῦ	χρωτὸς		αὐτοῦ
to be carried off		from	the	body surface		of him

4676		2228	4612		2532	525		575
σουδάρια	ἢ	σιμικίνθια	καὶ	ἀπαλλάσσεσθαι	ἀπ'
handkerchiefs	or	aprons	and	to be released	from

846	020	3554		024	5037	4151		024	4190
αὐτῶν	τὰς	νόσους,	τά	τε	πνεύματα	τὰ	πονηρὰ
them	the	illnesses,	the	and	spirits	the	evil

1607		2021		1161	5100
ἐκπορεύεσθαι.	**13** Ἐπεχείρησαν		δέ	τινες
to travel out.	Were setting hands on	but	some

2532	014	4022		2453	1845
καὶ	τῶν	περιερχομένων	Ἰουδαίων	ἐξορκιστῶν
also	of the	coming around	Judeans	exorcists

3687	1909	016	2192	024	4151		024	4190
ὀνομάζειν	ἐπὶ	τοὺς	ἔχοντας	τὰ	πνεύματα	τὰ	πονηρὰ
to name	on	the	having	the	spirits	the	evil

012	3686	02		2962	2424	3004
τὸ	ὄνομα	τοῦ	κυρίου	Ἰησοῦ	λέγοντες·
the	name	of the	Master	Jesus	saying·

3726		1473	04	2424	3739	3972	2784
ὁρκίζω	ὑμᾶς	τὸν	Ἰησοῦν	ὃν	Παῦλος	κηρύσσει.
put under oath	you	the	Jesus	whom	Paul	announces.

	1510	1161	5100	4630	2453	749
14	ἦσαν	δέ	τινος	Σκευᾶ	Ἰουδαίου	ἀρχιερέως
	Were+	but	of some	Skeva	Judean	ruler priest

2033	5207	3778	4160		611		1161
ἑπτὰ	υἱοὶ	τοῦτο	ποιοῦντες.	**15** ἀποκριθὲν		δὲ
seven	sons	this	+doing.	Having answered	but

09	4151	09	4190	3004	846	04	3303
τὸ	πνεῦμα	τὸ	πονηρὸν	εἶπεν	αὐτοῖς·	τὸν	[μὲν]
the	spirit	the	evil	said	to them;	the	indeed

2424	1097		2532	04	3972	1987		1473
Ἰησοῦν	γινώσκω	καὶ	τὸν	Παῦλον	ἐπίσταμαι,	ὑμεῖς
Jesus	I know	and	the	Paul	I understand,	you

1161	5101	1510		2532	2177		01	444
δὲ	τίνες	ἐστέ;	**16** καὶ	ἐφαλόμενος		ὁ	ἄνθρωπος
but	who	are?	And	having leaped	on	the	man

1909	846		1722	3739	1510	09	4151	09	4190
ἐπ'	αὐτοὺς	ἐν	ᾧ	ἦν	τὸ	πνεῦμα	τὸ	πονηρόν,
on	them	in	whom	was	the	spirit	the	evil,

2634		297		2480		2596
κατακυριεύσας	ἀμφοτέρων	ἴσχυσεν		κατ'
having mastered over	both	was strong		against

846	5620		1131		2532	5135
αὐτῶν	ὥστε	γυμνοὺς	καὶ	τετραυματισμένους
them	so that	naked	and	having been wounded

1628		1537	02	3624	1565		3778	1161
ἐκφυγεῖν	ἐκ	τοῦ	οἴκου	ἐκείνου.	**17** τοῦτο	δὲ
to flee out	from	the	house	that.	This	but

1096	1110		3956	2453		5037	2532	1672
ἐγένετο	γνωστὸν	πᾶσιν	Ἰουδαίοις	τε	καὶ	Ἕλλησιν
became	known	to all	Judeans	both	and	Greeks

015	2730		08	2181		2532	1968		5401
τοῖς	κατοικοῦσιν	τὴν	Ἔφεσον	καὶ	ἐπέπεσεν	φόβος
the	ones residing	the	Ephesus	and	fell on	fear

1909	3956	846		2532	3170		09	3686	02
ἐπὶ	πάντας	αὐτοὺς	καὶ	ἐμεγαλύνετο	τὸ	ὄνομα	τοῦ
on	all	them	and	was being made great	the	name	of the

2962	2424		4183	5037	014	4100
κυρίου	Ἰησοῦ.	**18** Πολλοί	τε	τῶν	πεπιστευκότων
Master	Jesus.	Many	but	of the	having trusted

2064	1843		2532 312		020
ἤρχοντο	ἐξομολογούμενοι	καὶ	ἀναγγέλλοντες		τὰς
were coming	confessing out	and	declaring		the

4234	846	**19**	2425	1161 014		024
πράξεις	αὐτῶν.		ἱκανοὶ	δὲ τῶν		τὰ
practices	of them.		Enough	but of the ones		the

4021	4238		4851
περίεργα	πραξάντων		συνενέγκαντες
works around	having practiced		having brought together

020 976	2618		1799	3956	2532
τὰς βίβλους	κατέκαιον		ἐνώπιον	πάντων,	καὶ
the books	were burning down		before	all,	and

4860	020		5092	846	2532 2147
συνεψήφισαν		τὰς	τιμὰς	αὐτῶν	καὶ εὗρον
they calculated together		the	values	of them	and found

694	3461		4002	**20**	3779	2596 2904
ἀργυρίου	μυριάδας		πέντε.		Οὕτως	κατὰ κράτος
of silver	ten thousands		five.		Thusly	by strength

02	2962	01	3056	837		2532
τοῦ	κυρίου	ὁ	λόγος	ηὔξανεν		καὶ
of the Master		the	word	was growing		and

2480		**21**	5613	1161	4137		3778
ἴσχυεν.			Ὡς	δὲ	ἐπληρώθη		ταῦτα,
was strengthening.			As	but	were filled		these,

5087	01	3972	1722	011 4151	1330
ἔθετο	ὁ	Παῦλος	ἐν	τῷ πνεύματι	διελθὼν
set	the	Paul	in	the spirit	having gone through

08	3109		2532	882	4198	1519 2414
τὴν Μακεδονίαν	καὶ	'Αχαΐαν	πορεύεσθαι	εἰς	'Ιεροσόλυμα
the Macedonia	and	Achaia	to travel	into	Jerusalem

3004		3754 3326	012 1096		1473 1563
εἰπὼν		ὅτι μετὰ	τὸ γενέσθαι		με ἐκεῖ
having said,	(")	after the	to become		me there

1163 1473 2532	4516	3708	**22**	649	1161 1519
δεῖ με καὶ	'Ρώμην	ἰδεῖν.		ἀποστείλας	δὲ εἰς
it is me also	Rome	to see.		Having	but into
necessary				delegated	

08	3109		1417 014	1247		846	5095
τὴν Μακεδονίαν	δύο	τῶν	διακονούντων		αὐτῷ,	Τιμόθεον
the Macedonia	two	of the ones serving		him,	Timothy

2532 2037		846	1907	5550	1519 08	773
καὶ Ἔραστον,	αὐτὸς	ἐπέσχεν	χρόνον	εἰς	τὴν	'Ασίαν.
and Erastus,	himself	held on	time	in	the	Asia.

23	1096	1161	2596 04	2540	1565	5017
	Ἐγένετο	δὲ	κατὰ τὸν	καιρὸν	ἐκεῖνον	τάραχος
	It became	by	the	season	that	trouble

3756 3641	4012	06	3598	**24**	1216		1063 5100
οὐκ ὀλίγος	περὶ	τῆς	ὁδοῦ.		Δημήτριος		γάρ τις
not few	about	the	way.		Demetrius		for some

3686	695		4160	3485	693
ὀνόματι,	ἀργυροκόπος,		ποιῶν	ναοὺς	ἀργυροῦς
in name,	silver laborer,		making	temples	silver

735	3930		015	5079	3756
'Αρτέμιδος	παρείχετο		τοῖς	τεχνίταις	οὐκ
of Artemis	was holding		along the	craftsmen	not

3641	2039	**25**	3739 4867
ὀλίγην	ἐργασίαν,		οὓς συναθροίσας
few	working,		whom having gathered together

2532 016	4012	024 5108	2040	3004	435
καὶ τοὺς	περὶ	τὰ τοιαῦτα	ἐργάτας	εἶπεν·	ἄνδρες,
and the	about	the such	workers	said;	men,

1987	3754	1537 3778	06	2039	05	2142
ἐπίστασθε	ὅτι	ἐκ ταύτης	τῆς	ἐργασίας	ἡ	εὐπορία
understand	that	from this	the	working	the	prosperity

1473	1510	**26**	2532 2334		2532 191		3754 3756
ἡμῖν	ἐστιν		καὶ θεωρεῖτε	καὶ	ἀκούετε		ὅτι οὐ
to us	is		and watch	and	hear		that not

3441	2181		235	4975	3956	06	773	01
μόνον	Ἐφέσου		ἀλλὰ	σχεδὸν	πάσης	τῆς	'Ασίας	ὁ
alone	of Ephesus		but	almost	all	the	Asia	the

---

their practices. [19]A number of those who practiced magic collected their books and burned them publicly; when the value of these books[a] was calculated, it was found to come to fifty thousand silver coins. [20]So the word of the Lord grew mightily and prevailed.

[21]Now after these things had been accomplished, Paul resolved in the Spirit to go through Macedonia and Achaia, and then to go on to Jerusalem. He said, "After I have gone there, I must also see Rome." [22]So he sent two of his helpers, Timothy and Erastus, to Macedonia, while he himself stayed for some time longer in Asia.

[23]About that time no little disturbance broke out concerning the Way. [24]A man named Demetrius, a silversmith who made silver shrines of Artemis, brought no little business to the artisans. [25]These he gathered together, with the workers of the same trade, and said, "Men, you know that we get our wealth from this business. [26]You also see and hear that not only in Ephesus but in almost the whole of Asia this

---

[a] Gk *them*

Paul has persuaded and drawn away a considerable number of people by saying that gods made with hands are not gods. ²⁷And there is danger not only that this trade of ours may come into disrepute but also that the temple of the great goddess Artemis will be scorned, and she will be deprived of her majesty that brought all Asia and the world to worship her."

28 When they heard this, they were enraged and shouted, "Great is Artemis of the Ephesians!" ²⁹The city was filled with the confusion; and people*ᵃ* rushed together to the theater, dragging with them Gaius and Aristarchus, Macedonians who were Paul's travel companions. ³⁰Paul wished to go into the crowd, but the disciples would not let him; ³¹even some officials of the province of Asia,*ᵇ* who were friendly to him, sent him a message urging him not to venture into the theater. ³²Meanwhile, some were shouting one thing, some another; for the assembly was in confusion, and most of them did not know why they had come together. ³³Some of the crowd gave instructions to Alexander, whom the Jews had pushed forward.

ᵃ Gk *they*
ᵇ Gk *some of the Asiarchs*

3972	3778	3982		3179		2425	3793
Παῦλος	οὗτος	πείσας		μετέστησεν		ἱκανὸν	ὄχλον
Paul	this	having persuaded		transferred		enough	crowd

3004	3754	3756	1510	2316	013	1223	5495
λέγων	ὅτι	οὐκ	εἰσὶν	θεοὶ	οἱ	διὰ	χειρῶν
saying	that	not	they are	gods	the	through	hands

1096		3756	3441	1161	3778	2793		1473
γινόμενοι.	**27**	οὐ	μόνον	δὲ	τοῦτο	κινδυνεύει		ἡμῖν
becoming.		Not	alone	but	this	is in danger		us

012	3313	1519	557		2064	235	2532 012 06
τὸ	μέρος	εἰς	ἀπελεγμὸν		ἐλθεῖν	ἀλλὰ	καὶ τὸ τῆς
the part		into	disrepute		to come	but	also the of the

3173	2299	735		2411	1519 3762
μεγάλης	θεᾶς	᾿Αρτέμιδος		ἱερὸν	εἰς οὐθὲν
great	goddess	Artemis		temple	into nothing

3049		3195		5037	2532
λογισθῆναι,		μέλλειν		τε	καὶ
to be reasoned,		to be about		indeed	also

2507		06	3168?		846	3739	3650
καθαιρεῖσθαι		τῆς	μεγαλειότητος		αὐτῆς	ἣν	ὅλη
to be lifted down		the	greatness		of her	which	whole

05	773	2532	05	3625		4576
ἡ	᾿Ασία	καὶ	ἡ	οἰκουμένη		σέβεται.
the	Asia	and	the	inhabited world		worship.

	191		1161	2532	1096		4134	2372
28	᾿Ακούσαντες		δὲ	καὶ	γενόμενοι		πλήρεις	θυμοῦ
	Having heard		but	and	having become		full	of fury

2896		3004		3173	05	735
ἔκραζον		λέγοντες·		μεγάλη	ἡ	᾿Αρτεμις
they were shouting		saying,		great	the	Artemis

2180		2532	4092		05	4172	06
᾿Εφεσίων.	**29**	καὶ	ἐπλήσθη		ἡ	πόλις	τῆς
of Ephesians.		And	was filled		the	city	of the

4799		3729		5037	3661		1519 012
συγχύσεως,		ὥρμησάν		τε	ὁμοθυμαδὸν		εἰς τὸ
confusion,		they rushed		and	with one mind		into the

0302	4884		1050	2532	708
θέατρον	συναρπάσαντες		Γάϊον	καὶ.	᾿Αρίσταρχον
theater	having seized together		Gaius	and	Aristarchus

3110		4898	3972		3972	1161
Μακεδόνας,		συνεκδήμους	Παύλου.	**30**	Παύλου	δὲ
Macedonians,		companions	of Paul.		Paul	but

1014		1525		1519 04	1218	3756 1439
βουλομένου		εἰσελθεῖν		εἰς τὸν δῆμον		οὐκ εἴων
planning		to go in		into the public		not were allowing

846	013 3101		5100	1161	2532 014	775
αὐτὸν οἱ	μαθηταί.	**31**	τινὲς	δὲ	καὶ τῶν	᾿Ασιαρχῶν,
him the	learners;		some	but	also of the	Asiarchs,

1510	846	5384		3992		4314 846
ὄντες	αὐτῷ	φίλοι,		πέμψαντες		πρὸς αὐτὸν
being	to him	friends,		having sent		to him

3870		3361	1325		1438	1519 012 2302
παρεκάλουν		μὴ	δοῦναι		ἑαυτὸν	εἰς τὸ θέατρον.
were encouraging		not	to give		himself	into the theater.

	243	3303	3767	243	5100 2896		1510 1063
32	ἄλλοι	μὲν	οὖν	ἄλλο	τι ἔκραζον·		ἦν γὰρ
	Others	indeed	then	other	some were shouting;		was for

05	1577		4797		2532 013 4183	3756
ἡ	ἐκκλησία		συγκεχυμένη		καὶ οἱ πλείους	οὐκ
the	assembly		having been confused		and the more	not

3609a		5101	1752		4905
ᾔδεισαν		τίνος	ἕνεκα		συνεληλύθεισαν.
had known		why	on account of		they had come together.

	1537	1161	02	3793	4822		223
33	ἐκ	δὲ	τοῦ	ὄχλου	συνεβίβασαν		᾿Αλέξανδρον,
	From	but	the	crowd	they forced together		Alexander,

4261		846	014	2453		01	1161
προβαλόντων		αὐτὸν	τῶν	᾿Ιουδαίων·		ὁ	δὲ
having thrown before		him	the	Judeans;		the	but

223   2678   08   5495   2309
Ἀλέξανδρος κατασείσας   τὴν χεῖρα ἤθελεν
Alexander   having motioned the hand   was wanting

626   03 1218   **34** 1921   1161 3754
ἀπολογεῖσθαι τῷ δήμῳ.   ἐπιγνόντες   δὲ ὅτι
to defend   to the public. Having perceived but that

2453   1510   5456   1096   1520 1537 3956   5613
Ἰουδαῖός ἐστιν, φωνὴ ἐγένετο μία ἐκ πάντων ὡς
Judean   he is, sound became one from all   as

1909 5610   1417 2896   3173   05 735
ἐπὶ ὥρας δύο κραζόντων· μεγάλη ἡ Ἄρτεμις
on hours two shouting; great the Artemis

2180   **35** 2687   1161 01 1122   04
Ἐφεσίων.   Καταστείλας δὲ ὁ γραμματεὺς τὸν
of Ephesians. Having calmed but the writer   the

3793   5346   435   2180   5101 1063 1510   444
ὄχλον φησίν· ἄνδρες Ἐφέσιοι, τίς γάρ ἐστιν ἀνθρώπων
crowd says, men   Ephesians, who for is   of men

3739 3756 1097   08   2180   4172 3511
ὃς   οὐ γινώσκει τὴν Ἐφεσίων πόλιν νεωκόρον
who not knows   the of Ephesians city temple keeper

1510 06   3173   735   2532 010   1356
οὖσαν τῆς μεγάλης Ἀρτέμιδος καὶ τοῦ διοπετοῦς;
being of the great Artemis   and of the fallen god?

36 368   3767 1510 3778   1163   1510 1473
ἀναντιρρήτων οὖν ὄντων τούτων δέον ἐστὶν ὑμᾶς
Without   then being these being it is you
contradiction   necessary

2687   5225   2532 3367   4312
κατεσταλμένους ὑπάρχειν καὶ μηδὲν προπετὲς
having been calmed to exist and nothing reckless

4238   **37** 71   1063 016 435   3778   3777
πράσσειν.   ἠγάγετε γὰρ τοὺς ἄνδρας τούτους οὔτε
to practice. You led for the men   these   neither

2417   3777 987   08   2316 1473
ἱεροσύλους οὔτε βλασφημοῦντας τὴν θεὸν ἡμῶν.
temple robbers nor insulters   the god of us.

38 1487 3303   3767 1216   2532 013 4862 846
εἰ μὲν οὖν Δημήτριος καὶ οἱ σὺν αὐτῷ
If indeed then Demetrius and the with him

5079   2192   4314 5100 3056   60   71
τεχνῖται ἔχουσι πρός τινα λόγον, ἀγοραῖοι ἄγονται
craftsmen have to   some word, marketers are brought

2532 446   1510   1458   240
καὶ ἀνθύπατοί εἰσιν, ἐγκαλείτωσαν ἀλλήλοις.
and deputies   there are, let call in one another.

39 1487 1161 5100 4006a   1934   1722 07
εἰ δέ τι περαιτέρω ἐπιζητεῖτε, ἐν τῇ
If but some more beyond you seek after, in the

1772   1577   1956   **40** 2532 1063
ἐννόμῳ ἐκκλησίᾳ ἐπιλυθήσεται.   καὶ γὰρ
in law assembly it will be loosed on. And for

2793   1458   4714   4012 06
κινδυνεύομεν ἐγκαλεῖσθαι στάσεως περὶ τῆς
we are in danger to be called in revolution about the

4594   3367   159   5225   4012 3739 3756
σήμερον, μηδενὸς αἰτίου ὑπάρχοντος περὶ οὗ [οὐ]
today,   of no one cause existing   about which not

1410   591   3056 4012 06   4963
δυνησόμεθα ἀποδοῦναι λόγον περὶ τῆς συστροφῆς
we will be able to give off word about the combination

3778   **41** 2532 3778 3004   630   08
ταύτης.   καὶ ταῦτα εἰπὼν ἀπέλυσεν τὴν
this.   And these having said he loosed off the

1577   **20:1** 3326 1161 012 3973   04
ἐκκλησίαν.   Μετὰ δὲ τὸ παύσασθαι τὸν
assembly.   After but the to be stopped the

2351   3343   01 3972 016 3101   2532
θόρυβον μεταπεμψάμενος ὁ Παῦλος τοὺς μαθητὰς καὶ
uproar having sent for the Paul the learners and

And Alexander motioned for silence and tried to make a defense before the people. [34]But when they recognized that he was a Jew, for about two hours all of them shouted in unison, "Great is Artemis of the Ephesians!" [35]But when the town clerk had quieted the crowd, he said, "Citizens of Ephesus, who is there that does not know that the city of the Ephesians is the temple keeper of the great Artemis and of the statue that fell from heaven?[a] [36]Since these things cannot be denied, you ought to be quiet and do nothing rash. [37]You have brought these men here who are neither temple robbers nor blasphemers of our[b] goddess. [38]If therefore Demetrius and the artisans with him have a complaint against anyone, the courts are open, and there are proconsuls; let them bring charges there against one another. [39]If there is anything further[c] you want to know, it must be settled in the regular assembly. [40]For we are in danger of being charged with rioting today, since there is no cause that we can give to justify this commotion." [41]When he had said this, he dismissed the assembly.

CHAPTER 20

After the uproar had ceased, Paul sent for the disciples; and

Meaning of Gk uncertain
[b] Other ancient authorities read your
[c] Other ancient authorities read about other matters

after encouraging them and saying farewell, he left for Macedonia. ²When he had gone through those regions and had given the believers*a* much encouragement, he came to Greece, ³where he stayed for three months. He was about to set sail for Syria when a plot was made against him by the Jews, and so he decided to return through Macedonia. ⁴He was accompanied by Sopater son of Pyrrhus from Beroea, by Aristarchus and Secundus from Thessalonica, by Gaius from Derbe, and by Timothy, as well as by Tychicus and Trophimus from Asia. ⁵They went ahead and were waiting for us in Troas; ⁶but we sailed from Philippi after the days of Unleavened Bread, and in five days we joined them in Troas, where we stayed for seven days.

7 On the first day of the week, when we met to break bread, Paul was holding a discussion with them; since he intended to leave the next day, he continued speaking until midnight. ⁸There were many lamps in the room upstairs where we were meeting. ⁹A young man named Eutychus, who was sitting in the window, began to sink off into a deep sleep

a Gk given them

3870	782	1831
παρακαλέσας,	ἀσπασάμενος	ἐξῆλθεν
having encouraged,	having greeted	he went out

4198   1519 3109   **2** 1330   1161
πορεύεσθαι εἰς Μακεδονίαν. ² διελθὼν   δὲ
to travel into Macedonia.   Having gone through but

024 3313   1565   2532 3870   846   3056
τὰ μέρη ἐκεῖνα καὶ παρακαλέσας αὐτοὺς λόγῳ
the parts those and having encouraged them in word

4183   2064   1519 08   1671   **3** 4160   5037 3376
πολλῷ ἦλθεν εἰς τὴν Ἑλλάδα ³ ποιήσας τε μῆνας
much he went into the Greece having made but months

5140   1096   1917   846 5259 014
τρεῖς· γενομένης ἐπιβουλῆς αὐτῷ ὑπὸ τῶν
three; having become plan against him by the

   2453   3195   321   1519 08 4947
Ἰουδαίων μέλλοντι ἀνάγεσθαι εἰς τὴν Συρίαν,
Judeans being about to be led up into the Syria,

1096   1106   010   5290   1223 3109
ἐγένετο γνώμης τοῦ ὑποστρέφειν διὰ Μακεδονίας.
it became purpose of the to return through Macedonia.

4 4902   1161 846   4986   4449a
⁴ συνείπετο   δὲ αὐτῷ Σώπατρος Πύρρου
There were accompanying but him Sopater of Pyrrus

961   2331   1161   708   2532
Βεροιαῖος, Θεσσαλονικέων δὲ Ἀρίσταρχος καὶ
Berean, of Thessalonians but Aristarchus and

4580   2532 1050   1190   2532 5095   774
Σεκοῦνδος, καὶ Γάϊος Δερβαῖος καὶ Τιμόθεος, Ἀσιανοὶ
Secundus, and Gaius Derbean and Timothy, Asians

1161 5190   2532 5161   **5** 3778   1161 4281
δὲ Τύχικος καὶ Τρόφιμος. ⁵ οὗτοι δὲ προελθόντες
but Tychicus and Trophimus. These but having gone before

3306   1473 1722 5174 **6** 1473 1161 1602
ἔμενον ἡμᾶς ἐν Τρῳάδι, ⁶ ἡμεῖς δὲ ἐξεπλεύσαμεν
were staying us in Troas, we but sailed out

3326   020 2250   022   106   575 5375   2532
μετὰ τὰς ἡμέρας τῶν ἀζύμων ἀπὸ Φιλίππων καὶ
after the days of the unyeasted from Philippi and

2064   4314 846   1519 08 5174   891   2250 4002
ἤλθομεν πρὸς αὐτοὺς εἰς τὴν Τρῳάδα ἄχρι ἡμερῶν πέντε,
came to them in the Troas until days five,

3699   1304   2250   2033   **7** 1722 1161 07
ὅπου διετρίψαμεν ἡμέρας ἑπτά. ⁷ Ἐν δὲ τῇ
where we continued days seven. In but in the

1520 022   4521   4863   1473
μιᾷ τῶν σαββάτων συνηγμένων ἡμῶν
one of the sabbaths having been brought together us

2806   740   01 3972 1256   846
κλάσαι ἄρτον, ὁ Παῦλος διελέγετο αὐτοῖς
to break bread, the Paul was disputing to them

3195   1826   07   1887   3905
μέλλων ἐξιέναι τῇ ἐπαύριον, παρέτεινέν
being to go out in the tomorrow, he was stretching along
about

5037 04   3056 3360   3317   **8** 1510   1161
τε τὸν λόγον μέχρι μεσονυκτίου. ⁸ ἦσαν δὲ
but the word until middle night. There were but

2985   2425   1722 011 5253   3757 1510
λαμπάδες ἱκαναὶ ἐν τῷ ὑπερῴῳ οὗ ἦμεν
lamps enough in the upstairs room where we were+

4863   2516   **9** 1161 5100 3494   3686
συνηγμένοι. ⁹ καθεζόμενος δέ τις νεανίας ὀνόματι
+having been Sitting but some young man in name
brought together.

2161   1909 06 2376   2702   5258
Εὔτυχος ἐπὶ τῆς θυρίδος, καταφερόμενος ὕπνῳ
Eutychus on the window, being brought down in sleep

```
901      1256          02   3972      1909 4183
βαθεῖ  διαλεγομένου τοῦ Παύλου ἐπὶ  πλεῖον,
deep    disputing    the Paul   on   more,
2702                        575  02   5258  4098    575
κατενεχθεὶς                 ἀπὸ τοῦ ὕπνου ἔπεσεν ἀπὸ
having been brought down from the sleep he fell from
010 5152            2736 2532 142            3498
τοῦ τριστέγου       κάτω καὶ ἤρθη           νεκρός.
the third story     down and was lifted up dead.
     2597            1161 01   3972      1968        846  2532
  10 καταβὰς         δὲ   ὁ    Παῦλος ἐπέπεσεν αὐτῷ καὶ
     Having gone down but  the Paul   fell on     him  and
4843            3004    3361 2350          05   1063
συμπεριλαβὼν    εἶπεν· μὴ  θορυβεῖσθε,  ἡ   γὰρ
having embraced said,  not be in uproar, the for
5590 846      1722 846  1510       305             1161
ψυχὴ αὐτοῦ ἐν  αὐτῷ ἐστιν.  11 ἀναβὰς         δὲ
soul of him  in  him  is.       Having gone up but
2532 2806        04  740     2532 1089         1909
καὶ κλάσας       τὸν ἄρτον καὶ γευσάμενος   ἐφ᾽
also having broken the bread and having tasted on
2425   5037 3656         891   827          3779
ἱκανόν τε  ὁμιλήσας     ἄχρι αὐγῆς,     οὕτως
enough te  having conversed until daybreak, thusly
1831         12 71        1161 04   3816        2198    2532
ἐξῆλθεν.       ἤγαγον   δὲ   τὸν παῖδα     ζῶντα και
he went out.   They led  but  the boy servant living and
3870            3756 3357            1473 1161
παρεκλήθησαν    οὐ   μετρίως.    13 Ἡμεῖς δὲ
were encouraged not  measurably.     We    but
4281            1909 012 4143      321         1909
προελθόντες     ἐπὶ  τὸ πλοῖον ἀνήχθημεν   ἐπὶ
having gone before on   the boat  were led up   upon
08   789   1564       3195        353           04
τὴν Ἄσσον ἐκεῖθεν  μέλλοντες  ἀναλαμβάνειν τὸν
the Assos from there being about  to to take up   the
3972      3779    1063 1299                   1510
Παῦλον· οὕτως γὰρ διατεταγμένος        ἦν
Paul;    thusly  for having directed himself was+
3195     846    3978               5613 1161
μέλλων   αὐτὸς πεζεύειν.    14 ὡς    δὲ
+being about himself to go on foot.  As    but
4820          1473 1519 08   789
συνέβαλλεν    ἡμῖν εἰς τὴν Ἄσσον,
he was thrown together to us in  the  Assos,
353           846   2064       1519 3412
ἀναλαβόντες   αὐτὸν ἤλθομεν εἰς Μιτυλήνην,
having taken up him  we went into Mitylene,
   2547        636                07      1966
15 κἀκεῖθεν    ἀποπλεύσαντες   τῇ    ἐπιούσῃ
   and from there having sailed off in the next
2658         481      5508     07    1161 2087
κατηντήσαμεν ἄντικρυς Χίου,  τῇ    δὲ   ἑτέρᾳ
we arrived   opposite Chios, in the but  other
3846          1519 4544     07    1161 2192     2064
παρεβάλομεν   εἰς Σάμον, τῇ    δὲ   ἐχομένῃ ἤλθομεν
we threw along into Samos, in the but  holding  we came
1519 3399        2919       1063 01  3972      3896
εἰς Μίλητον.  16 κεκρίκει   γὰρ ὁ   Παῦλος παραπλεῦσαι
into Miletus.    Had judged for the Paul   to sail along
08   2181     3704    3361 1096          846
τὴν Ἔφεσον, ὅπως μὴ  γένηται        αὐτῷ
the Ephesus, so that not it might become to him
5551           1722 07  773    4692         1063
χρονοτριβῆσαι ἐν  τῇ Ἀσίᾳ· ἔσπευδεν    γὰρ
to continue time in  the Asia; he was hurrying for
1487 1415    1510          846   08    1050     06
εἰ  δυνατὸν εἴη           αὐτῷ τὴν ἡμέραν τῆς
if  power   it might be to him  the day    of the
```

while Paul talked still longer. Overcome by sleep, he fell to the ground three floors below and was picked up dead. [10]But Paul went down, and bending over him took him in his arms, and said, "Do not be alarmed, for his life is in him." [11]Then Paul went upstairs, and after he had broken bread and eaten, he continued to converse with them until dawn; then he left. [12]Meanwhile they had taken the boy away alive and were not a little comforted.

[13] We went ahead to the ship and set sail for Assos, intending to take Paul on board there; for he had made this arrangement, intending to go by land himself. [14]When he met us in Assos, we took him on board and went to Mitylene. [15]We sailed from there, and on the following day we arrived opposite Chios. The next day we touched at Samos, and[a] the day after that we came to Miletus. [16]For Paul had decided to sail past Ephesus, so that he might not have to spend time in Asia; he was eager to be

[a] Other ancient authorities add *after remaining at Trogyllium*

in Jerusalem, if possible, on the day of Pentecost.

17 From Miletus he sent a message to Ephesus, asking the elders of the church to meet him. [18]When they came to him, he said to them:

"You yourselves know how I lived among you the entire time from the first day that I set foot in Asia, [19]serving the Lord with all humility and with tears, enduring the trials that came to me through the plots of the Jews. [20]I did not shrink from doing anything helpful, proclaiming the message to you and teaching you publicly and from house to house, [21]as I testified to both Jews and Greeks about repentance toward God and faith toward our Lord Jesus. [22]And now, as a captive to the Spirit,[a] I am on my way to Jerusalem, not knowing what will happen to me there, [23]except that the Holy Spirit testifies to me in every city that imprisonment and persecutions are waiting for me. [24]But I do not count my life of any value to myself, if only I may finish my course and the ministry that I received from the Lord Jesus, to testify to the good news of God's grace.

25 "And now

[a] Or And now, bound in the spirit

4005	1096	1519	2414	**17**	575	1161
πεντηκοστῆς	γενέσθαι	εἰς	Ἰεροσόλυμα.		Ἀπὸ	δὲ
fiftieth	to become	into	Jerusalem.		From	but

06	3399	3992		1519	2181	3333
τῆς	Μιλήτου	πέμψας		εἰς	Ἔφεσον	μετεκαλέσατο
the	Miletus	having sent		into	Ephesus	he called for

016	4245		06	1577	**18**	5613	1161
τοὺς	πρεσβυτέρους		τῆς	ἐκκλησίας.		ὡς	δὲ
the	older men		of the	assembly.		As	but

3854		4314	846	3004	846	1473
παρεγένοντο		πρὸς	αὐτὸν	εἶπεν	αὐτοῖς·	ὑμεῖς
they arrived to		him		he said	to them,	you

1987	575	4413	2250	575	3739	1910
ἐπίστασθε,	ἀπὸ	πρώτης	ἡμέρας	ἀφ᾽	ἧς	ἐπέβην
understand,	from	first	day	from	which	I went on

1519	08	773	4459	3326	1473	04	3956	5550
εἰς	τὴν	Ἀσίαν,	πῶς	μεθ᾽	ὑμῶν	τὸν	πάντα	χρόνον
into	the	Asia,	how	with	you	the	all	time

1096	**19**	1398	03	2962	3326	3956
ἐγενόμην,		δουλεύων	τῷ	κυρίῳ	μετὰ	πάσης
I became,		slaving	in the	Master	with	all

5012	2532	1144	2532	3986	014
ταπεινοφροσύνης	καὶ	δακρύων	καὶ	πειρασμῶν	τῶν
humblemindedness	and	tears	and	pressures	the ones

4819		1473	1722	019	1917	014
συμβάντων		μοι	ἐν	ταῖς	ἐπιβουλαῖς	τῶν
having come together to me in		the	plans	against	the

2453	**20**	5613	3762	5288	022
Ἰουδαίων,		ὡς	οὐδὲν	ὑπεστειλάμην	τῶν
Judeans,		as	nothing	I withdrew	of the

4851	010	3361	312	1473	2532	1321
συμφερόντων	τοῦ	μὴ	ἀναγγεῖλαι	ὑμῖν	καὶ	διδάξαι
being advantageous	the	not	to declare	to you	and	to teach

1473	1219	2532	2596	3624	**21**	1263
ὑμᾶς	δημοσίᾳ	καὶ	κατ᾽	οἴκους,		διαμαρτυρόμενος
you	in public	and	by	houses,		thoroughly testifying

2453	5037	2532	1672	08	1519	2316	3341
Ἰουδαίοις	τε	καὶ	Ἕλλησιν	τὴν	εἰς	θεὸν	μετάνοιαν
to Judeans	both	and	Greeks	the	in	God	change mind

2532	4102	1519	04	2962	1473	2424	**22**	2532	3568
καὶ	πίστιν	εἰς	τὸν	κύριον	ἡμῶν	Ἰησοῦν.		Καὶ	νῦν
and	trust	in	the	Master	of us	Jesus.		And	now

2400	1210		1473	011	4151	4198
ἰδοὺ	δεδεμένος		ἐγὼ	τῷ	πνεύματι	πορεύομαι
look	having been bound		I	in the	spirit	travel

1519	2419	024	1722	846	4876	1473	3361
εἰς	Ἰερουσαλὴμ	τὰ	ἐν	αὐτῇ	συναντήσοντά	μοι	μὴ
into	Jerusalem	the	in	it	meeting	to me	not

3609a	**23**	4133	3754	09	4151	09	40	2596
εἰδώς,		πλὴν	ὅτι	τὸ	πνεῦμα	τὸ	ἅγιον	κατὰ
having known,		except	that	the	spirit	the	holy	by

4172	1263		1473	3004	3754	1199	2532
πόλιν	διαμαρτύρεταί		μοι	λέγον	ὅτι	δεσμὰ	καὶ
city	testifies thoroughly		to me	saying	that	chains	and

2347	1473	3306	**24**	235	3762	3056
θλίψεις	με	μένουσιν.		ἀλλ᾽	οὐδενὸς	λόγου
afflictions	me	stay.		But	of nothing	word

4160	08	5590	5093	1683	5613	5048
ποιοῦμαι	τὴν	ψυχὴν	τιμίαν	ἐμαυτῷ	ὡς	τελειῶσαι
I make	the	soul	valuable	to myself	as	to complete

04	1408	1473	2532	08	1248	3739	2983	3844
τὸν	δρόμον	μου	καὶ	τὴν	διακονίαν	ἣν	ἔλαβον	παρὰ
the	race	of me	and	the	service	that	I received	from

02	2962	2424	1263		012
τοῦ	κυρίου	Ἰησοῦ,	διαμαρτύρασθαι		τὸ
the	Master	Jesus,	to testify thoroughly		the

2098	06	5485	02	2316	**25**	2532	3568
εὐαγγέλιον	τῆς	χάριτος	τοῦ	θεοῦ.		Καὶ	νῦν
good message	of the	favor	of the	God.		And	now

2400	1473	3609a	3754	3765		3708	012	4383
ἰδοὺ	ἐγὼ	οἶδα	ὅτι	οὐκέτι		ὄψεσθε	τὸ	πρόσωπόν
look	I	know	that	no longer		will see	the	face

1473	1473	3956	1722	2739	1330		2784
μου	ὑμεῖς	πάντες	ἐν	οἷς	διῆλθον		κηρύσσων
of me	you	all	in	which	I went through		announcing

08	932	**26**	1360		3143		1473	1722 07
τὴν	βασιλείαν.		διότι		μαρτύρομαι		ὑμῖν	ἐν τῇ
the	kingdom.		Because that		I testify		to you	in the

4594	2250	3754	2513		1510 575	010 129
σήμερον	ἡμέρᾳ	ὅτι	καθαρός		εἰμι ἀπὸ	τοῦ αἵματος
today	day	because	clean		I am from	the blood

3956	**27**	3756	1063	5288		010 3361	312
πάντων·		οὐ	γὰρ	ὑπεστειλάμην		τοῦ μὴ	ἀναγγεῖλαι
of all;		not	for	I withdrew		the not	to declare

3956	08	1012	02	2316 1473	**28**	4337		1438
πᾶσαν	τὴν	βουλὴν	τοῦ	θεοῦ ὑμῖν.		προσέχετε		ἑαυτοῖς
all	the	plan	of the	God to you.		Hold to		yourselves

2532 3956	011	4168	1722 2739	1473 09	4151	09
καὶ	παντὶ	τῷ	ποιμνίῳ, ἐν	ᾧ ὑμᾶς	τὸ πνεῦμα	τὸ
and	to all	the flock,	in	which you	the spirit	the

40	5087	1985		4165		08 1577	02
ἅγιον	ἔθετο	ἐπισκόπους		ποιμαίνειν		τὴν ἐκκλησίαν	τοῦ
holy	set	overseers		to shepherd		the assembly	of the

2316	3739	4046		1223 010	129		010 2398
θεοῦ,	ἣν	περιεποιήσατο		διὰ τοῦ	αἵματος		τοῦ ἰδίου.
God,	which	he acquired		by the	blood		the own.

29	1473	3609a	3754	1525		3326	08	867
	ἐγὼ	οἶδα	ὅτι	εἰσελεύσονται		μετὰ	τὴν	ἄφιξίν
	I	know	that	will come in		after	the	departure

1473	3074	926	1519 1473	3361 5339		010
μου	λύκοι	βαρεῖς	εἰς ὑμᾶς	μὴ φειδόμενοι		τοῦ
of me	wolves	burden	to you	not sparing		the

4168·	**30**	2532 1537	1473 846		450
ποιμνίου,		καὶ ἐξ	ὑμῶν αὐτῶν		ἀναστήσονται
flock,		and from	you yourselves		will stand up

435	2980	1294		010 645
ἄνδρες	λαλοῦντες	διεστραμμένα		τοῦ ἀποσπᾶν
men	speaking	having been perverted		the to draw off

016	3101	3694 846	**31**	1352	1127
τοὺς	μαθητὰς	ὀπίσω αὐτῶν.		διὸ	γρηγορεῖτε
the	learners	after them.		Wherefore	keep awake,

3421		3754 5148		3571	2532 2250
μνημονεύοντες		ὅτι τριετίαν		νύκτα	καὶ ἡμέραν
having remembered		that three years		night	and day

3756 3973		3326 1144	3560	1520 1538
οὐκ ἐπαυσάμην		μετὰ δακρύων	νουθετῶν	ἕνα ἕκαστον.
not stopped myself		with tears	warning	one each.

32	2532 024	3568 3908		1473 03	2316	2532 03
	Καὶ τὰ	νῦν παρατίθεμαι		ὑμᾶς τῷ	θεῷ	καὶ τῷ
	And the	now I set along		you to the	God	and the

3056 06	5485	846	03	1410
λόγῳ τῆς	χάριτος	αὐτοῦ,	τῷ	δυναμένῳ
word of the	favor	of him,	to the	one being able

3618	2532 1325	08	2817		1722 015
οἰκοδομῆσαι	καὶ δοῦναι	τὴν	κληρονομίαν	ἐν	τοῖς
to build	and to give	the	inheritance	in	the

37		3956	**33**	694		2228 5553
ἡγιασμένοις		πᾶσιν.		ἀργυρίου	ἢ	χρυσίου
having been made holy		to all.		Silver	or	gold

2228 2441		3762	1937	**34**	846
ἢ ἱματισμοῦ		οὐδενὸς	ἐπεθύμησα·		αὐτοὶ
or clothing		of no one	I desired;		yourselves

1097		3754 019	5532	1473	2532 015	1510
γινώσκετε		ὅτι ταῖς	χρείαις	μου	καὶ τοῖς	οὐσιν
know		that the	needs	of me	and the	ones being

3326 1473	5256	017 5495	3778	**35**	3956
μετ᾽ ἐμοῦ	ὑπηρέτησαν	αἱ χεῖρες	αὗται.		πάντα
with me	assisted	the hands	these.		All

I know that none of you, among whom I have gone about proclaiming the kingdom, will ever see my face again. [26]Therefore I declare to you this day that I am not responsible for the blood of any of you, [27]for I did not shrink from declaring to you the whole purpose of God. [28]Keep watch over yourselves and over all the flock, of which the Holy Spirit has made you overseers, to shepherd the church of God[a] that he obtained with the blood of his own Son.[b] [29]I know that after I have gone, savage wolves will come in among you, not sparing the flock. [30]Some even from your own group will come distorting the truth in order to entice the disciples to follow them. [31]Therefore be alert, remembering that for three years I did not cease night or day to warn everyone with tears. [32]And now I commend you to God and to the message of his grace, a message that is able to build you up and to give you the inheritance among all who are sanctified. [33]I coveted no one's silver or gold or clothing. [34]You know for yourselves that I worked with my own hands to support myself and my companions. [35]In all this

I have given you an example that by such work we must support the weak, remembering the words of the Lord Jesus, for he himself said, 'It is more blessed to give than to receive.'"

36 When he had finished speaking, he knelt down with them all and prayed. [37]There was much weeping among them all; they embraced Paul and kissed him, [38]grieving especially because of what he had said, that they would not see him again. Then they brought him to the ship.

CHAPTER 21

When we had parted from them and set sail, we came by a straight course to Cos, and the next day to Rhodes, and from there to Patara.[a] [2]When we found a ship bound for Phoenicia, we went on board and set sail. [3]We came in sight of Cyprus; and leaving it on our left, we sailed to Syria and landed at Tyre, because the ship was to unload its cargo there. [4]We looked up the disciples and stayed there for seven days. Through the Spirit they told Paul not to go on to Jerusalem.

---

[a] Other ancient authorities add and Myra

	5263	1473	3754	3779	2872	1163
	ὑπέδειξα	ὑμῖν	ὅτι	οὕτως	κοπιῶντας	δεῖ
	I exampled	to you	that	thusly	laboring	it is necessary

482   014 770   3421
ἀντιλαμβάνεσθαι τῶν ἀσθενούντων,   μνημονεύειν
take part of   the ones being weak,   to remember

5037   014 3056 02   2962   2424 3754 846
τε   τῶν λόγων τοῦ   κυρίου 'Ιησοῦ ὅτι αὐτὸς
indeed the words of the Master Jesus that himself

3004   3107   1510   3123   1325 2228 2983
εἶπεν· μακάριόν ἐστιν μᾶλλον διδόναι ἢ   λαμβάνειν.
said, fortunate it is more   to give or to receive.

36 2532 3778 3004   5087   024 1119   846
Καὶ ταῦτα εἰπὼν   θεὶς   τὰ γόνατα αὐτοῦ
And these having said having set the knees of him

4862 3956 846   4336   **37** 2425   1161 2805
σὺν πᾶσιν αὐτοῖς προσηύξατο.   ἱκανὸς δὲ   κλαυθμὸς
with all them   he prayed.   Enough but crying

1096   3956   2532 1968   1909 04 5137
ἐγένετο πάντων καὶ ἐπιπεσόντες   ἐπὶ τὸν τράχηλον
became of all and having fallen on on the neck

02   3972   2705   846   **38** 3600
τοῦ Παύλου κατεφίλουν   αὐτόν,   ὀδυνώμενοι
of the Paul they were kissing him,   being tormented

3122   1909 03 3056 3739 3004   3754
μάλιστα ἐπὶ τῷ λόγῳ ᾧ   εἰρήκει,   ὅτι
especially on the word that he had said, that

3765   3195   012 4383   846   2334
οὐκέτι   μέλλουσιν   τὸ πρόσωπον αὐτοῦ θεωρεῖν.
no longer they are about the face   of him to watch.

4311   1161 846   1519 012 4143
προέπεμπον   δὲ αὐτὸν εἰς τὸ πλοῖον.
They were sending before but him   into the boat.

21:1 5613 1161 1096   321   1473
'Ως δὲ ἐγένετο ἀναχθῆναι   ἡμᾶς
As   but it became to be led up us

645   575 846   2113   2064
ἀποσπασθέντας ἀπ' αὐτῶν, εὐθυδρομήσαντες ἤλθομεν
having been   from them, having run straight we went
drawn off

1519 08 2972 07   1161 1836 1519 08   4499
εἰς τὴν Κῶ, τῇ   δὲ ἐξῆς εἰς τὴν 'Ρόδον
into the Kos, in the but next into the Rhode

2547   1519 3959   **2** 2532 2147   4143
κἀκεῖθεν   εἰς Πάταρα,   καὶ εὑρόντες   πλοῖον
and from there into Patara, and having found boat

1276   1519 5403   1910
διαπερῶν εἰς Φοινίκην ἐπιβάντες
crossing over into Phoenicia having gone on

321   **3** 398   1161 08 2954
ἀνήχθημεν.   ἀναφάναντες   δὲ τὴν Κύπρον
we were led up. Having appeared again but the Cyprus

2532 2641   846   2176   4126
καὶ καταλιπόντες αὐτὴν εὐώνυμον ἐπλέομεν
and having left behind it   left   we were sailing

1519 4947   2532 2718   1519 5184   1566 1063
εἰς Συρίαν καὶ κατήλθομεν εἰς Τύρον· ἐκεῖσε γὰρ
into Syria and we went down into Tyre; there for

09 4143   1510 670   04   1117
τὸ πλοῖον ἦν ἀποφορτιζόμενον τὸν γόμον.
the boat was+ +being packed off the cargo.

4 429   1161 016 3101   1961
ἀνευρόντες   δὲ τοὺς μαθητὰς ἐπεμείναμεν
Having discovered but the learners we stayed on

847   2250 2033 3748 03   3972 3004
αὐτοῦ ἡμέρας ἑπτά, οἵτινες τῷ   Παύλῳ ἔλεγον
there days seven, who   to the Paul were saying

1223 010 4151   3361 1910   1519
διὰ τοῦ πνεύματος μὴ ἐπιβαίνειν εἰς
through the spirit not to go on into

2414	5	3753	1161	1096	1473 1822	020

Ἱεροσόλυμα. **5** ὅτε δὲ ἐγένετο ἡμᾶς ἐξαρτίσαι τὰς
Jerusalem. When but it became us to finish the

2250	1831		4198	4311	1473

ἡμέρας, ἐξελθόντες ἐπορευόμεθα προπεμπόντων ἡμᾶς
days, having gone we were sending before us
out traveling

3956	4862	1135	2532	5043	2193	1854	06

πάντων σὺν γυναιξὶ καὶ τέκνοις ἕως ἔξω τῆς
all with women and children until outside the

4172	2532	5087	024	1119	1909	04	123

πόλεως, καὶ θέντες τὰ γόνατα ἐπὶ τὸν αἰγιαλὸν
city, and having set the knees on the shore

4336	6	537a	240	2532

προσευξάμενοι **6** ἀπησπασάμεθα ἀλλήλους καὶ
having prayed we greeted off one another and

305	1519	012	4143	1565	1161	5290	1519

ἀνέβημεν εἰς τὸ πλοῖον, ἐκεῖνοι δὲ ὑπέστρεψαν εἰς
went up into the boat, those but returned to

024	2398	7	1473	1161	04	4144	1274

τὰ ἴδια. **7** Ἡμεῖς δὲ τὸν πλοῦν διανύσαντες
the own. We but the sailing having completed

575	5184	2658	1519	4424	2532

ἀπὸ Τύρου κατηντήσαμεν εἰς Πτολεμαΐδα καὶ
from Tyre arrived into Ptolemais and

782	016	80	3306	2250	1520

ἀσπασάμενοι τοὺς ἀδελφοὺς ἐμείναμεν ἡμέραν μίαν
having greeted the brothers we stayed day one

3844	846	8	07	1161	1887	1831

παρ' αὐτοῖς. **8** τῇ δὲ ἐπαύριον ἐξελθόντες
along them. In the but tomorrow having gone out

2064	1519	2542	2532	1525	1519	04

ἤλθομεν εἰς Καισάρειαν καὶ εἰσελθόντες εἰς τὸν
we came into Caesarea and having gone in into the

3624	5376	02	2099	1510	1537

οἶκον Φιλίππου τοῦ εὐαγγελιστοῦ, ὄντος ἐκ
house of Philip the good message teller, being from

014	2033	3306	3844	846	9	3778	1161

τῶν ἑπτά, ἐμείναμεν παρ' αὐτῷ. **9** τούτῳ δὲ
the seven, we stayed along him. To this one but

1510	2364	5064	3933	4395

ἦσαν θυγατέρες τέσσαρες παρθένοι προφητεύουσαι.
there were daughters four virgins speaking before.

10	1961	1161	2250	4183	2718	5100	575

10 Ἐπιμενόντων δὲ ἡμέρας πλείους κατῆλθέν τις ἀπὸ
Staying on but days more came down some from

06	2449	4396	3686	13	11	2532

τῆς Ἰουδαίας προφήτης ὀνόματι Ἅγαβος, **11** καὶ
the Judea spokesman in name Agabus, and

2064	4314	1473	2532	142	08	2223

ἐλθὼν πρὸς ἡμᾶς καὶ ἄρας τὴν ζώνην
having come to us and having lifted up the belt

02	3972	1210	1438	016	4228	2532	020

τοῦ Παύλου, δήσας ἑαυτοῦ τοὺς πόδας καὶ τὰς
of the Paul, having bound himself the feet and the

5495	3004	3592	3004	09	4151	09	40

χεῖρας εἶπεν· τάδε λέγει τὸ πνεῦμα τὸ ἅγιον·
hands he said; these but says the spirit the holy;

04	435	3739	1510	05	2223	3778	3779	1210

τὸν ἄνδρα οὗ ἐστιν ἡ ζώνη αὕτη, οὕτως δήσουσιν
the man who is the belt this, thusly will bind

1722	2419	013	2453	2532	3860

ἐν Ἰερουσαλὴμ οἱ Ἰουδαῖοι καὶ παραδώσουσιν
in Jerusalem the Judeans and they will give over

1519	5495	1484	12	5613	1161	191	3778

εἰς χεῖρας ἐθνῶν. **12** ὡς δὲ ἠκούσαμεν ταῦτα,
into hands of nations. As but we heard these,

3870	1473	5037	2532	013	1786	010

παρεκαλοῦμεν ἡμεῖς τε καὶ οἱ ἐντόπιοι τοῦ
were encouraging we both and the local ones the

[5]When our days there were ended, we left and proceeded on our journey; and all of them, with wives and children, escorted us outside the city. There we knelt down on the beach and prayed [6]and said farewell to one another. Then we went on board the ship, and they returned home.

7 When we had finished[a] the voyage from Tyre, we arrived at Ptolemais; and we greeted the believers[b] and stayed with them for one day. [8]The next day we left and came to Caesarea; and we went into the house of Philip the evangelist, one of the seven, and stayed with him. [9]He had four unmarried daughters[c] who had the gift of prophecy. [10]While we were staying there for several days, a prophet named Agabus came down from Judea. [11]He came to us and took Paul's belt, bound his own feet and hands with it, and said, "Thus says the Holy Spirit, 'This is the way the Jews in Jerusalem will bind the man who owns this belt and will hand him over to the Gentiles.'" [12]When we heard this, we and the people there

---

[a] Or continued
[b] Gk brothers
[c] Gk four daughters, virgins,

urged him not to go up to Jerusalem. [13]Then Paul answered, "What are you doing, weeping and breaking my heart? For I am ready not only to be bound but even to die in Jerusalem for the name of the Lord Jesus." [14]Since he would not be persuaded, we remained silent except to say, "The Lord's will be done."

[15] After these days we got ready and started to go up to Jerusalem. [16]Some of the disciples from Caesarea also came along and brought us to the house of Mnason of Cyprus, an early disciple, with whom we were to stay.

[17]When we arrived in Jerusalem, the brothers welcomed us warmly. [18]The next day Paul went with us to visit James; and all the elders were present. [19]After greeting them, he related one by one the things that God had done among the Gentiles through his ministry. [20]When they heard it, they praised God. Then they said to him, "You see, brother, how many thousands of believers there are among the Jews, and they are all zealous for the law. [21]They have been told about you

3361	305	846	1519	2419		5119
μὴ	ἀναβαίνειν	αὐτὸν	εἰς	Ἰερουσαλήμ.	**13**	τότε
not	to go up	him	into	Jerusalem.		Then

611 01 3972 5101 4160 2799 2532
ἀπεκρίθη ὁ Παῦλος· τί ποιεῖτε κλαίοντες καὶ
answered the Paul; what you do crying and

4919 1473 08 2588 1473 1063 3756 3441
συνθρύπτοντές μου τὴν καρδίαν; ἐγὼ γὰρ οὐ μόνον
breaking up of me the heart? I for not alone

1210 235 2532 599 1519 2419
δεθῆναι ἀλλὰ καὶ ἀποθανεῖν εἰς Ἰερουσαλὴμ
to be bound but also to die in Jerusalem

2093 2192 5228 010 3686 02 2962
ἑτοίμως ἔχω ὑπὲρ τοῦ ὀνόματος τοῦ κυρίου
readily I have on behalf of the name of the Master

2424	3361	3982	1161	846	2270
Ἰησοῦ.	**14**	μὴ	πειθομένου	δὲ αὐτοῦ	ἡσυχάσαμεν
Jesus.		Not	being persuaded	but him	we were quiet

3004 02 2962 09 2307 1096 3326
εἰπόντες· τοῦ κυρίου τὸ θέλημα γινέσθω. **15** Μετὰ
having said; of the Master the want let become. After

1161 020 2250 3778 1980a 305
δὲ τὰς ἡμέρας ταύτας ἐπισκευασάμενοι ἀνεβαίνομεν
but the days these having prepared we were going up

1519 2414 1161 4905 1161 2532 014
εἰς Ἱεροσόλυμα· **16** συνῆλθον δὲ καὶ τῶν
into Jerusalem; went with but also of the

3101 575 2542 4862 1473 71 3844 3739
μαθητῶν ἀπὸ Καισαρείας σὺν ἡμῖν, ἄγοντες παρ' ᾧ
learners from Caesarea with us, bringing with whom

3579 3416 5100 2953 744 3101
ξενισθῶμεν Μνασῶνί τινι Κυπρίῳ, ἀρχαίῳ μαθητῇ.
we might be Mnason some Cypriot, ancient learner.
entertained as strangers

1096 1161 1473 1519 2414 780
17 Γενομένων δὲ ἡμῶν εἰς Ἱεροσόλυμα ἀσμένως
Having become but of us into Jerusalem gladly

588 1473 013 80 07 1161 1966
ἀπεδέξαντο ἡμᾶς οἱ ἀδελφοί. **18** Τῇ δὲ ἐπιούσῃ
welcomed us the brothers. In the but next
thoroughly

1524 01 3972 4862 1473 4314 2385
εἰσήει ὁ Παῦλος σὺν ἡμῖν πρὸς Ἰάκωβον,
was going into the Paul with us to Jacob,

3956 5037 3854 013 4245 2532
πάντες τε παρεγένοντο οἱ πρεσβύτεροι. **19** καὶ
all but arrived the older men. And

782 846 1834 2596 1520
ἀσπασάμενος αὐτοὺς ἐξηγεῖτο καθ' ἓν
having greeted them he was explaining by one

1538 3739 4160 01 2316 1722 023 1484
ἕκαστον, ὧν ἐποίησεν ὁ θεὸς ἐν τοῖς ἔθνεσιν
each, what did the God in the nations

1223 06 1248 846 013 1161 191
διὰ τῆς διακονίας αὐτοῦ. **20** Οἱ δὲ ἀκούσαντες
through the service of him. The but having heard

1392 04 2316 3004 5037 846 2334
ἐδόξαζον τὸν θεὸν εἰπόν τε αὐτῷ· Θεωρεῖς,
were giving the God said indeed to him; you watch,
splendor

80 4214 3461 1510 1722 015 2453
ἀδελφέ, πόσαι μυριάδες εἰσὶν ἐν τοῖς Ἰουδαίοις
brother, how many ten thousands are in the Judeans

014 4100 2532 3956 2207 02 3551
τῶν πεπιστευκότων καὶ πάντες ζηλωταὶ τοῦ νόμου
of the having trusted and all jealous of the law

5225 2727 1161 4012 1473 3754
ὑπάρχουσιν· **21** κατηχήθησαν δὲ περὶ σοῦ ὅτι
exist; they were instructed but about you that

646   1321   575   3475   016   2596 024 1484
ἀποστασίαν διδάσκεις ἀπὸ Μωϋσέως τοὺς κατὰ τὰ ἔθνη
stand off you teach from Moses the by the nations

3956   2453   3004   3361 4059   846
πάντας ᾿Ιουδαίους λέγων μὴ περιτέμνειν αὐτοὺς
all   Judeans   saying not to circumcise them

024 5043   3366   023 1485   4043   5101
τὰ τέκνα   μηδὲ τοῖς ἔθεσιν περιπατεῖν. 22 τί
the children but not the customs to walk around. What

3767 1510   3843   191   3754 2064
οὖν ἐστιν; πάντως ἀκούσονται ὅτι ἐλήλυθας.
then is? Altogether they will hear that you have come.

   3778 3767 4160   3739 1473   3004   1510
23 τοῦτο οὖν ποίησον ὅ σοι   λέγομεν· εἰσὶν
   This then do   what to you we say;   there are

1473 435   5064   2171 2192   1909 1438
ἡμῖν ἄνδρες τέσσαρες εὐχὴν ἔχοντες ἐφ᾿ ἑαυτῶν.
to us men   four   vow   holding on themselves.

   3778   3880   48   4862 846
24 τούτους παραλαβὼν   ἁγνίσθητι σὺν αὐτοῖς
   These   having taken along be purified with them

2532 1159   1909 846   2443 3587   08
καὶ δαπάνησον ἐπ᾿ αὐτοῖς ἵνα ξυρήσονται τὴν
and spend   on them   that they will shave the

2776   2532 1097   3956 3754 3739
κεφαλήν, καὶ γνώσονται πάντες ὅτι ὧν
head,   and will know all   that of what

2727   4012 1473 3762   1510 235
κατήχηνται   περὶ σοῦ οὐδέν ἐστιν ἀλλὰ
they had been instructed about you nothing is but

4748   2532 846   5442   04 3551   4012
στοιχεῖς καὶ αὐτὸς φυλάσσων τὸν νόμον. 25 περὶ
you walk also yourself guarding the law.   About

1161 022 4100   1484   1473 1989
δὲ τῶν πεπιστευκότων ἐθνῶν ἡμεῖς ἐπεστείλαμεν
but the having trusted nations we   we wrote letter

2919   5442   846 012 5037 1494
κρίναντες φυλάσσεσθαι αὐτοὺς τό τε εἰδωλόθυτον
having judged to guard them   the both idol
                                           sacrifice

2532 129   2532 4156 2532 4202   5119
καὶ αἷμα καὶ πνικτὸν καὶ πορνειάν. 26 Τότε
and blood and choked and sexual immorality. Then

01   3972   3880   016 435   07
ὁ Παῦλος παραλαβὼν   τοὺς ἄνδρας τῇ
the Paul having taken along the men in the

2192   2250   4862 846   48
ἐχομένη ἡμέρᾳ σὺν αὐτοῖς ἁγνισθείς,
holding day   with them having been purified,

1524   1519 012 2411   1229   08
εἰσήει   εἰς τὸ ἱερὸν διαγγέλλων τὴν
he was going into into the temple broadcasting the

1604   018   2250 02   49   2193
ἐκπλήρωσιν τῶν ἡμερῶν τοῦ ἁγνισμοῦ ἕως
filling out of the days of the purification until

3739 4374   5228 1520 1538   846   05
οὗ προσηνέχθη ὑπὲρ ἑνὸς ἑκάστου αὐτῶν ἡ
which was offered for one each   of them the

4376   27 5613 1161 3195   017 2033 2250
προσφορά.   ῾Ως δὲ ἔμελλον αἱ ἑπτὰ ἡμέραι
offering.   As but were about the seven days

4931   013 575 06   773   2453
συντελεῖσθαι, οἱ ἀπὸ τῆς ᾿Ασίας ᾿Ιουδαῖοι
to be fully completed, the from the Asia Judeans

2300   846   1722 011 2411   4797
θεασάμενοι αὐτὸν ἐν τῷ ἱερῷ συνέχεον
having watched him in the temple were confused

3956 04 3793 2532 1911   1909 846   020 5495
πάντα τὸν ὄχλον καὶ ἐπέβαλον ἐπ᾿ αὐτὸν τὰς χεῖρας
all the crowd and threw on on him the hands

that you teach all the Jews
living among the Gentiles
to forsake Moses, and
that you tell them not to
circumcise their children
or observe the customs.
22What then is to be done?
They will certainly hear
that you have come. 23So
do what we tell you. We
have four men who are
under a vow. 24Join these
men, go through the rite of
purification with them, and
pay for the shaving of their
heads. Thus all will know
that there is nothing in
what they have been told
about you, but that you
yourself observe and guard
the law. 25But as for the
Gentiles who have become
believers, we have sent a
letter with our judgment
that they should abstain
from what has been
sacrificed to idols and
from blood and from what
is strangled[a] and from
fornication." 26Then Paul
took the men, and the next
day, having purified himself,
he entered the temple with
them, making public the
completion of the days of
purification when the
sacrifice would be made
for each of them.

27 When the seven days
were almost completed, the
Jews from Asia, who had
seen him in the temple,
stirred up the whole crowd.
They seized him,

_a_ Other ancient authorities lack _and
from what is strangled_

28shouting, "Fellow
Israelites, help! This is
the man who is teaching
everyone everywhere
against our people, our
law, and this place; more
than that, he has actually
brought Greeks into the
temple and has defiled this
holy place." 29For they had
previously seen Trophimus
the Ephesian with him in
the city, and they supposed
that Paul had brought him
into the temple. 30Then all
the city was aroused, and
the people rushed together.
They seized Paul and
dragged him out of the
temple, and immediately
the doors were shut.
31While they were trying
to kill him, word came to
the tribune of the cohort
that all Jerusalem was in
an uproar. 32Immediately
he took soldiers and
centurions and ran down
to them. When they saw the
tribune and the soldiers,
they stopped beating Paul.
33Then the tribune came,
arrested him, and ordered
him to be bound with two
chains; he inquired who he
was and what he had done.
34Some in the crowd
shouted one thing, some
another; and as he could
not learn the facts because
of the

	2896	435	2475	997	3778
28	κράζοντες·	ἄνδρες	᾽Ισραηλῖται,	βοηθεῖτε·	οὗτός
	shouting;	men	Israelites,	help;	this

1510	01	444	01	2596	02	2992	2532	02
ἐστιν	ὁ	ἄνθρωπος	ὁ	κατὰ	τοῦ	λαοῦ	καὶ	τοῦ
is	the	man	the	against	the	people	and	the

3551 2532 02 5117 3778 3956 3835a 1321
νόμου καὶ τοῦ τόπου τούτου πάντας πανταχῇ διδάσκων,
law and the place this all all places teaching,

2089 5037 2532 1672 1521 1519 012 2411
ἔτι τε καὶ ῞Ελληνας εἰσήγαγεν εἰς τὸ ἱερὸν
still but also Greeks he led into into the temple

2532 2840 04 40 5117 3778 **29** 1510
καὶ κεκοίνωκεν τὸν ἅγιον τόπον τοῦτον. **29** ἦσαν
and has made common the holy place this. They were+

1063 4308 5161 04 2180 1722
γὰρ προεωρακότες Τρόφιμον τὸν ᾽Εφέσιον ἐν
for +having seen before Trophimus the Ephesian in

07 4172 4862 846 3739 3543 3754 1519
τῇ πόλει σὺν αὐτῷ, ὃν ἐνόμιζον ὅτι εἰς
the city with him, whom they were thinking that into

012 2411 1521 01 3972 **30** 2795 5037 05
τὸ ἱερὸν εἰσήγαγεν ὁ Παῦλος. **30** ἐκινήθη τε ἡ
the temple led into the Paul. Was moved but the

4172 3650 2532 1096 4890 02
πόλις ὅλη καὶ ἐγένετο συνδρομὴ τοῦ
city whole and became running together of the

2992 2532 1949 02 3972
λαοῦ, καὶ ἐπιλαβόμενοι τοῦ Παύλου
people, and having taken on of the Paul

1670 846 1854 010 2411 2532
εἵλκον αὐτὸν ἔξω τοῦ ἱεροῦ καὶ
they were hauling him outside the temple and

2112 2808 017 2374 **31** 2212 5037
εὐθέως ἐκλείσθησαν αἱ θύραι. **31** Ζητούντων τε
immediately were closed the doors. Seeking but

846 615 305 5334 03 5506
αὐτὸν ἀποκτεῖναι ἀνέβη φάσις τῷ χιλιάρχῳ
him to kill came up news to the thousand ruler

06 4686 3754 3650 4797 2419
τῆς σπείρης ὅτι ὅλη συγχύννεται ᾽Ιερουσαλήμ.
of the squadron, (") whole is confused Jerusalem.

32 3739 1824 3880 4757 2532
32 ὃς ἐξαυτῆς παραλαβὼν στρατιώτας καὶ
Who at once having taken along soldiers and

1543 2701 1909 846 013 1161
ἑκατοντάρχας κατέδραμεν ἐπ᾽ αὐτούς, οἱ δὲ
hundred rulers ran down on them, the ones but

3708 04 5506 2532 016 4757
ἰδόντες τὸν χιλίαρχον καὶ τοὺς στρατιώτας
having seen the thousand ruler and the soldiers

3973 5180 04 3972 **33** 5119 1448
ἐπαύσαντο τύπτοντες τὸν Παῦλον. **33** τότε ἐγγίσας
stopped beating the Paul. Then having neared

01 5506 1949 846 2532 2753
ὁ χιλίαρχος ἐπελάβετο αὐτοῦ καὶ ἐκέλευσεν
the thousand ruler took on him and commanded

1210 254 1417 2532 4441 5101
δεθῆναι ἁλύσεσι δυσί, καὶ ἐπυνθάνετο τίς
to be bound in chains two, and inquired what

1510 2532 5101 1510 4160 **34** 243 1161
εἴη καὶ τί ἐστιν πεποιηκώς. **34** ἄλλοι δὲ
might be and what he is+ +having done. Others but

243 5100 2019 1722 03 3793 3361
ἄλλο τι ἐπεφώνουν ἐν τῷ ὄχλῳ. μὴ
other some were sounding on in the crowd. Not

1410 1161 846 1097 012 804 1223 04
δυναμένου δὲ αὐτοῦ γνῶναι τὸ ἀσφαλὲς διὰ τὸν
being able but him to know the secure because the
                                                                    of

2351   2753   71   846   1519 08   3925
θόρυβον ἐκέλευσεν   ἄγεσθαι αὐτὸν εἰς τὴν παρεμβολήν.
uproar he commanded to be led him   to the barracks.

    3753 1161 1096   1909 016   304   4819
35 ὅτε δὲ ἐγένετο ἐπὶ τοὺς ἀναβαθμούς, συνέβη
   When but he became on the stairs,   it came
                                                 together
941   846   5259 014 4757   1223   08
βαστάζεσθαι αὐτὸν ὑπὸ τῶν στρατιωτῶν διὰ   τὴν
to be borne him   by   the soldiers because of the
970   02   3793   190   1063 09
βίαν τοῦ ὄχλου, 36 ἠκολούθει   γὰρ τὸ
violence of the crowd,   were following for   the
4128   02   2992   2896   142   846
πλῆθος τοῦ λαοῦ κράζοντες· αἶρε αὐτόν.
quantity of the people shouting; lift up him.

    3195   5037 1521   1519 08   3925
37 Μέλλων   τε εἰσάγεσθαι   εἰς τὴν παρεμβολὴν
   Being about but to be led into into the barracks
01 3972   3004   03   5506   1487
ὁ Παῦλος λέγει τῷ   χιλιάρχῳ·   εἰ
the Paul   says to the thousand ruler; if
1832   1473 3004   5100 4314 1473 01   1161
ἔξεστίν   μοι εἰπεῖν τι πρὸς σέ; ὁ δὲ
is it possible to me to say some to you? The but
5346 1676   1097   3756 686   1473 1510 01
ἔφη· Ἑλληνιστὶ γινώσκεις; 38 οὐκ ἄρα σὺ εἶ ὁ
said; Greek   you know?   Not then you are the
124   01 4253 3778   018 2250   387
Αἰγύπτιος ὁ πρὸ τούτων τῶν ἡμερῶν ἀναστατώσας
Egyptian the before these the days having upset
2532 1806   1519 08 2048   016   5070
καὶ ἐξαγαγὼν   εἰς τὴν ἔρημον τοὺς τετρακισχιλίους
and having led out to the desert the four thousand
435   014   4607   3004 1161 01 3972   1473
ἄνδρας τῶν σικαρίων; 39 εἶπεν δὲ ὁ Παῦλος· ἐγὼ
men   of the assassins? Said but the Paul;   I
444   3303 1510 2453   5018 06   2791
ἄνθρωπος μέν εἰμι Ἰουδαῖος, Ταρσεὺς τῆς Κιλικίας,
man   but am Judean,   Tarsus of the Cilicia,
3756 767   4172   4177   1189   1161 1473
οὐκ ἀσήμου   πόλεως πολίτης· δέομαι δέ σου,
not insignificant city citizen; I beg but of you,
2010   1473 2980   4314 04 2992
ἐπίτρεψόν μοι λαλῆσαι πρὸς τὸν λαόν.
allow   me   to speak to the people.

    2010   1161 846 01 3972   2476   1909
40 ἐπιτρέψαντος δὲ αὐτοῦ ὁ Παῦλος ἑστὼς   ἐπὶ
   Having allowed but him the Paul having stood on
014 304   2678   07   5495 03   2992
τῶν ἀναβαθμῶν κατέσεισεν τῇ χειρὶ τῷ λαῷ.
the stairs   motioned   the hand to the people.
4183   1161 4602   1096   4377   07
πολλῆς δὲ σιγῆς γενομένης προσεφώνησεν τῇ
Much   but silence having become he sounded to in the
1446   1258   3004   22:1 435   80   2532
Ἑβραΐδι διαλέκτῳ λέγων·   Ἄνδρες ἀδελφοὶ καὶ
Hebrew dialect saying,   men   brothers and
3962   191   1473 06 4314 1473 3570 627
πατέρες, ἀκούσατέ μου τῆς πρὸς ὑμᾶς νυνὶ ἀπολογίας.
fathers, hear   me   the to   you now defense.

   191   1161 3754 07   1446   1258
2 ἀκούσαντες δὲ ὅτι τῇ Ἑβραΐδι διαλέκτῳ
  Having heard but that in the Hebrew dialect
4377   846   3123   3930
προσεφώνει   αὐτοῖς, μᾶλλον   παρέσχον
he was sounding to them, more along they held along
sounding   along

uproar, he ordered him
to be brought into the
barracks. [35]When Paul[a]
came to the steps, the
violence of the mob was
so great that he had to be
carried by the soldiers.
[36]The crowd that followed
kept shouting, "Away with
him!"

[37]Just as Paul was
about to be brought into
the barracks, he said to
the tribune, "May I say
something to you?" The
tribune[b] replied, "Do you
know Greek? [38]Then you
are not the Egyptian who
recently stirred up a revolt
and led the four thousand
assassins out into the
wilderness?" [39]Paul replied,
"I am a Jew, from Tarsus
in Cilicia, a citizen of an
important city; I beg you,
let me speak to the people."
[40]When he had given him
permission, Paul stood on
the steps and motioned to
the people for silence; and
when there was a great
hush, he addressed them
in the Hebrew[c] language,
saying:

CHAPTER 22

"Brothers and fathers,
listen to the defense that
I now make before you."

2 When they heard
him addressing them in
Hebrew,[c] they became

a Gk he
b Gk He
c That is, Aramaic

even more quiet. Then he said:

3 "I am a Jew, born in Tarsus in Cilicia, but brought up in this city at the feet of Gamaliel, educated strictly according to our ancestral law, being zealous for God, just as all of you are today. ⁴I persecuted this Way up to the point of death by binding both men and women and putting them in prison, ⁵as the high priest and the whole council of elders can testify about me. From them I also received letters to the brothers in Damascus, and I went there in order to bind those who were there and to bring them back to Jerusalem for punishment.

6 "While I was on my way and approaching Damascus, about noon a great light from heaven suddenly shone about me. ⁷I fell to the ground and heard a voice saying to me, 'Saul, Saul, why are you persecuting me?' ⁸I answered, 'Who are you, Lord?' Then he said to me, 'I am Jesus of Nazareth^a whom you are persecuting.' ⁹Now those who were with me saw the light but did not hear the voice of the one who was speaking to me. ¹⁰I asked, 'What am I to do, Lord?' The Lord

· a Gk the Nazorean

	2271	25325346	**3**	1473	1510	435	2453
	ἡσυχίαν.	καὶ φησίν·		ἐγώ	εἰμι	ἀνὴρ	Ἰουδαῖος,
	quiet.	And he says;		I	am	man	Judean,

1080		1722	5019	06	2791
γεγεννημένος	ἐν	Ταρσῷ	τῆς	Κιλικίας,	
having been born	in	Tarsus	of the	Cilicia,	

397		1161	1722	07	4172	3778	3844
ἀνατεθραμμένος	δὲ	ἐν	τῇ	πόλει	ταύτῃ,	παρὰ
having been nourished	but	in	the	city	this,	along

016	4228	1059	3811		2596
τοὺς	πόδας	Γαμαλιὴλ	πεπαιδευμένος		κατὰ
the	feet	Gamaliel	having been as a child		by

195	02	3971	3551	2207	5225
ἀκρίβειαν	τοῦ	πατρῴου	νόμου,	ζηλωτὴς	ὑπάρχων
accuracy	of the	father	law,	jealous	existing

02	2316	2531	3956	1473	1510	4594	**4**	3739
τοῦ	θεοῦ	καθὼς	πάντες	ὑμεῖς	ἐστε	σήμερον·		ὃς
of the	God	just as	all	you	are	today;		who

3778	08	3598	1377		891	2288	1195	2532
ταύτην	τὴν	ὁδὸν	ἐδίωξα		ἄχρι	θανάτου	δεσμεύων	καὶ
this	the	way	I pursued		until	death	tying up	and

3860		1519	5438	435	5037	2532	1135
παραδιδοὺς	εἰς	φυλακὰς	ἄνδρας	τε	καὶ	γυναῖκας,	
giving over	into	guards	men	both	and	women,	

5	5613	2532	01	749		3140		1473	2532	3956
	ὡς	καὶ	ὁ	ἀρχιερεὺς		μαρτυρεῖ		μοι	καὶ	πᾶν
	as	also	the	ruler priest		testifies		to me	and	all

09	4244		3844	3739	2532	1992
τὸ	πρεσβυτέριον,	παρ'	ὧν	καὶ	ἐπιστολὰς	
the	group of older men,	from	whom	also	letters	

1209		4314	016	80	1519	1154
δεξάμενος	πρὸς	τοὺς	ἀδελφοὺς	εἰς	Δαμασκὸν	
having welcomed	to	the	brothers	in	Damascus	

4198		71	2532	016	1566	1510
ἐπορευόμην,	ἄξων	καὶ	τοὺς	ἐκεῖσε	ὄντας	
I was traveling,	leading	also	the	there	being	

1,210		1519	2419		2443	5097
δεδεμένους	εἰς	Ἰερουσαλὴμ	ἵνα	τιμωρηθῶσιν.		
having been bound	to	Jerusalem	that	they might be punished.		

6	1096		1161	1473	4198		2532	1448		07
	Ἐγένετο	δέ	μοι	πορευομένῳ	καὶ	ἐγγίζοντι	τῇ			
	It became	but	to me	traveling	and	nearing	the			

1154		4012	3314		1810	1537	02	3772
Δαμασκῷ	περὶ	μεσημβρίαν	ἐξαίφνης	ἐκ	τοῦ	οὐρανοῦ		
Damascus	around	midday	suddenly	from	the	heaven		

4015		5457	2425	4012	1473	**7**	4098
περιαστράψαι	φῶς	ἱκανὸν	περὶ	ἐμέ,		ἔπεσά	
to glitter around	light	enough	around	me,		I fell	

5037	1519	012	1475	2532	191		5456	3004
τε	εἰς	τὸ	ἔδαφος	καὶ	ἤκουσα	φωνῆς	λεγούσης	
but	to	the	ground	and	I heard	sound	saying	

1473	4549	4549	5101	1473	1377		**8**	1473	1161
μοι·	Σαοὺλ	Σαούλ,	τί	με	διώκεις;			ἐγὼ	δὲ
to me;	Saul	Saul,	why	me	<u>you</u> pursue?			I	but

611		5101	1510	2962	3004	5037	4314	1473
ἀπεκρίθην·	τίς	εἶ,	κύριε;	εἶπέν	τε	πρός με·		
answered;	who	are <u>you</u>,	Master?	He said	but	to me,		

1473	1510	2424	01	3480		3739	1473	1377
ἐγώ	εἰμι	Ἰησοῦς	ὁ	Ναζωραῖος,	ὃν	σὺ	διώκεις.	
I	am	Jesus	the	Nazorean,	whom,	<u>you</u>	pursue.	

9	013	1161	4862	1473	1510	012	3303	5457	2300
	οἱ	δὲ	σὺν	ἐμοὶ	ὄντες	τὸ	μὲν	φῶς	ἐθεάσαντο
	The	but	with	me	being	the	indeed	light	watched

08	1161	5456	3756	191		02	2980		1473
τὴν	δὲ	φωνὴν	οὐκ	ἤκουσαν	τοῦ	λαλοῦντός	μοι.		
the	but	sound	not	they heard	the	speaking	to me.		

10	3004	1161	5101	4160		2962	01	1161	2962
	εἶπον	δέ·	τί	ποιήσω,	κύριε;	ὁ	δὲ	κύριος	
	I said	but;	what	might I do,	Master?	The	but	Master	

3004	4314	1473	450		4198	1519	1154
εἶπεν	πρός	με·	ἀναστὰς		πορεύου	εἰς	Δαμασκὸν
said	to	me;	having stood up		travel	into	Damascus

2546		1473	2980		4012	3956	3739
κἀκεῖ		σοι	λαληθήσεται		περὶ	πάντων	ὧν
and there		to you	will be said		about	all	which

5021		1473	4160	**11**	5613	1161	3756
τέτακταί		σοι	ποιῆσαι.		ὡς	δὲ	οὐκ
has been set in order		to you	to do.		As	but	not

1689		575	06	1391	010		5457
ἐνέβλεπον		ἀπὸ	τῆς	δόξης	τοῦ		φωτὸς
I was looking in		from	the	splendor	of the		light

1565	5496		5259	014			4895
ἐκείνου,	χειραγωγούμενος		ὑπὸ	τῶν			συνόντων
that,	being led by hand		by	the			ones being with

1473	2064	1519	1154	**12**	367	1161	5100	435
μοι	ἦλθον	εἰς	Δαμασκόν.		Ἀνανίας	δέ	τις,	ἀνὴρ
me	I came	into	Damascus.		Ananias	but	some,	man

2126	2596	04	3551	3140		5259	3956
εὐλαβὴς	κατὰ	τὸν	νόμον,	μαρτυρούμενος		ὑπὸ	πάντων
reverent	by	the	law,	being testified		by	all

014	2730		2453		2064	4314	1473	2532
τῶν	κατοικούντων		Ἰουδαίων,	**13**	ἐλθὼν	πρός	με	καὶ
the residing			Judeans,		having come to	me	and

2186		3004	1473	4549	80		308
ἐπιστὰς		εἶπέν	μοι·	Σαοὺλ	ἀδελφέ,		ἀνάβλεψον.
having stood on		he said to me;	Saul	brother,		look up.

2504	846	07	5610	308		1519	846	**14**	01	1161
κἀγὼ	αὐτῇ	τῇ	ὥρᾳ	ἀνέβλεψα		εἰς	αὐτόν.		ὁ	δὲ
And I	same	the	hour	looked up		to	him.		The	but

3004	01	2316	014	3962	1473	4400
εἶπεν·	ὁ	θεὸς	τῶν	πατέρων	ἡμῶν	προεχειρίσατό
said;	the	God	of the	fathers	of us	set hand before

1473	1097	012	2307	846	2532	3708	04	1342
σε	γνῶναι	τὸ	θέλημα	αὐτοῦ	καὶ	ἰδεῖν	τὸν	δίκαιον
you	to know	the	want	of him	and	to see	the	right

2532	191	5456	1537	010	4750	846	**15**	3754
καὶ	ἀκοῦσαι	φωνὴν	ἐκ	τοῦ	στόματος	αὐτοῦ,		ὅτι
and	to hear	sound	from	the	mouth	of him,		that

1510		3144	846	4314	3956	444		3739
ἔσῃ		μάρτυς	αὐτῷ	πρὸς	πάντας	ἀνθρώπους		ὧν
you will be testifier		to him	to	all	men		whom

3708		2532	191	**16**	2532	3568	5101
ἑώρακας		καὶ	ἤκουσας.		καὶ	νῦν	τί
you have seen and			you heard.		And	now	what

3195	450		907	2532	628		020	266
μέλλεις;	ἀναστὰς		βάπτισαι	καὶ	ἀπόλουσαι		τὰς	ἁμαρτίας
are you	Having		immerse	and	wash off		the	sins
about?	stood up yourself				yourself			

1473	1941		012	3686	846	**17**	1096	1161
σου	ἐπικαλεσάμενος		τὸ	ὄνομα	αὐτοῦ.		Ἐγένετο	δέ
of you	calling on		the	name	of him.		It became	but

1473	5290		1519	2419		2532
μοι	ὑποστρέψαντι		εἰς	Ἰερουσαλὴμ		καὶ
to me	having returned		to	Jerusalem		and

4336		1473	1722	011	2411	1096		1473	1722
προσευχομένου	μου	ἐν	τῷ	ἱερῷ	γενέσθαι		με	ἐν
praying		me	in	the	temple	to become		me	in

1611	**18**	2532	3708	846	3004	1473	4692
ἐκστάσει		καὶ	ἰδεῖν	αὐτὸν	λέγοντά	μοι·	σπεῦσον
amazement		and	to see	him	saying	to me;	hurry

2532	1831	1722	5034		1537	2419	1360
καὶ	ἔξελθε	ἐν	τάχει		ἐξ	Ἰερουσαλήμ,	διότι
and	go out	in	quickness		from	Jerusalem,	because.

3756	3858		1473	3141	4012	1473	**19**	2504
οὐ	παραδέξονταί		σου	μαρτυρίαν	περὶ	ἐμοῦ.		κἀγὼ
not	they accept		of you	testimony	about	me.		And I

3004	2962	846	1987	3754	1473	1510
εἶπον·	κύριε,	αὐτοὶ	ἐπίστανται	ὅτι	ἐγὼ	ἤμην
said;	Master,	they	understand	that	I	was+

said to me, 'Get up and go to Damascus; there you will be told everything that has been assigned to you to do.' [11]Since I could not see · because of the brightness of that light, those who were with me took my hand and led me to Damascus.

[12] "A certain Ananias, who was a devout man according to the law and well spoken of by all the Jews living there, [13]came to me; and standing beside me, he said, 'Brother Saul, regain your sight!' In that very hour I regained my sight and saw him. [14]Then he said, 'The God of our ancestors has chosen you to know his will, to see the Righteous One and to hear his own voice; [15]for you will be his witness to all the world of what you have seen and heard. [16]And now why do you delay? Get up, be baptized, and have your sins washed away, calling on his name.'

[17] "After I had returned to Jerusalem and while I was praying in the temple, I fell into a trance [18]and saw Jesus[a] saying to me, 'Hurry and get out of Jerusalem quickly, because they will not accept your testimony about me.' [19]And I said, 'Lord, they themselves know that

[a] Gk him

in every synagogue I imprisoned and beat those who believed in you. [20]And while the blood of your witness Stephen was shed, I myself was standing by, approving and keeping the coats of those who killed him.' [21]Then he said to me, 'Go, for I will send you far away to the Gentiles.'"

[22]Up to this point they listened to him, but then they shouted, "Away with such a fellow from the earth! For he should not be allowed to live." [23]And while they were shouting, throwing off their cloaks, and tossing dust into the air, [24]the tribune directed that he was to be brought into the barracks, and ordered him to be examined by flogging, to find out the reason for this outcry against him. [25]But when they had tied him up with thongs,[a] Paul said to the centurion who was standing by, "Is it legal for you to flog a Roman citizen who is uncondemned?" [26]When the centurion heard that, he went to the tribune and said to him, "What are you about to do? This man is a Roman citizen." [27]The tribune came and asked Paul,[b] "Tell me, are you a Roman citizen?" And he said,

[a] Or up for the lashes
[b] Gk him

5439		2532	1194		2596 020 4864
φυλακίζων		καὶ	δέρων		κατὰ τὰς συναγωγὰς
+setting under guard	and	+beating		by	the synagogues

016 4100		1909 1473	20	2532 3753 1632
τοὺς πιστεύοντας	ἐπὶ σέ,		20	καὶ ὅτε ἐξεχύννετο
the ones trusting	on <u>you</u>,			and when was poured out

09 129 4736	02 3144	1473 2532 846
τὸ αἷμα Στεφάνου	τοῦ μάρτυρός σου,	καὶ αὐτὸς
the blood of Stephan	the testifier of <u>you</u>,	and himself

1510 2186	2532 4909	2532 5442	024 2440
ἤμην ἐφεστὼς καὶ	συνευδοκῶν καὶ	φυλάσσων τὰ ἱμάτια
was+ +having and stood on	thinking and well together	guarding the clothes

014 337	846	21	2532 3004	4314 1473
τῶν ἀναιρούντων αὐτόν.		21	καὶ εἶπεν	πρός με·
of the ones killing him.			And he said	to me;

4198	3754	1473 1519	1484	3112	1821
πορεύου,	ὅτι	ἐγὼ εἰς	ἔθνη	μακρὰν	ἐξαποστελῶ
travel,	because	I to	nations	far	delegate out

1473	22	191	1161 846	891	3778
σε.	22	Ἤκουον	δὲ αὐτοῦ	ἄχρι	τούτου
<u>you</u>.		They were hearing	but him	until	this

02 3056 2532 1869	08 5456 846
τοῦ λόγου καὶ ἐπῆραν	τὴν φωνὴν αὐτῶν
the word and were lifting up	on the sound of them

3004	142	575 06 1093 04	5108	3756
λέγοντες·	αἶρε	ἀπὸ τῆς γῆς	τὸν τοιοῦτον,	οὐ
saying,	lift up	from the earth	the such one,	not

1063 2520	846 2198	23	2905	5037
γὰρ καθῆκεν	αὐτὸν ζῆν.	23	κραυγαζόντων	τε
for it is proper	him to live.		Shouting	but

846 2532 4495	024 2440 2532 2868
αὐτῶν καὶ ῥιπτούντων	τὰ ἱμάτια καὶ κονιορτὸν
them and flinging	the clothes and blowing dust

906 1519 04 109	24	2753 01 5506
βαλλόντων εἰς τὸν ἀέρα,	24	ἐκέλευσεν ὁ χιλίαρχος
throwing in the air,		commanded the thousand ruler

1521 846 1519 08 3925	3004
εἰσάγεσθαι αὐτὸν εἰς τὴν παρεμβολήν,	εἴπας
to be led in him into the barracks,	having said

3148 426	846 2443 1921
μάστιξιν ἀνετάζεσθαι	αὐτὸν ἵνα ἐπιγνῷ
in scourges to be examined	him that he might perceive

1223 3739 156 3779 2019	846
δι᾽ ἣν αἰτίαν οὕτως ἐπεφώνουν	αὐτῷ.
for what cause thusly they were sounding	on to him.

25	5613 1161 4385	846 015 2438
25	ὡς δὲ προέτειναν	αὐτὸν τοῖς ἱμᾶσιν,
	As but they stretched	before him the straps,

3004 4314 04 2476	1543	01 3972
εἶπεν πρὸς τὸν ἑστῶτα	ἑκατόνταρχον	ὁ Παῦλος·
said to the having stood	hundred ruler	the Paul;

1487 444	4514 2532 178	1832
εἰ ἄνθρωπον	Ῥωμαῖον καὶ ἀκατάκριτον	ἔξεστιν
if man	Roman and uncondemned	it is possible

1473 3147	26	191 1161 01 1543
ὑμῖν μαστίζειν;	26	ἀκούσας δὲ ὁ ἑκατοντάρχης
to you to scourge?		Having heard but the hundred ruler

4334 03 5506	518 3004
προσελθὼν τῷ χιλιάρχῳ	ἀπήγγειλεν λέγων·
having gone to the thousand ruler	told saying,

5101 3195	4160 01 1063 444	3778
τί μέλλεις	ποιεῖν; ὁ γὰρ ἄνθρωπος	οὗτος
what are you about to do?	The for man	this

4514 1510	27	4334	1161 01 5506
Ῥωμαῖός ἐστιν.	27	προσελθὼν	δὲ ὁ χιλίαρχος
Roman is.		Having gone to	but the thousand ruler

3004 846	3004 1473 1473 4514	1510 01 1161 5346
εἶπεν αὐτῷ·	λέγε μοι, σὺ Ῥωμαῖος εἶ;	ὁ δὲ ἔφη·
said to him:	say to me, <u>you</u> Roman are?	The but said;

```
3483   28  611              1161 01    5506                    1473 4183
ναί.      ἀπεκρίθη δὲ   ὁ      χιλίαρχος·        ἐγὼ  πολλοῦ
yes.      Answered but the    thousand ruler;    I    much
2774          08  4174         3778    2932        01   1161
κεφαλαίου τὴν πολιτείαν     ταύτην ἐκτησάμην.    ὁ   δὲ
sum       the citizenship   this    acquired.  The but
3972   5346 1473 1161 2532 1080              29  2112
Παῦλος ἔφη·  ἐγὼ δὲ  καὶ  γεγέννημαι.        εὐθέως
Paul   said; I   but  even  have been born.  Immediately
3767 868      575  846    013 3195               846
οὖν ἀπέστησαν ἀπ᾽ αὐτοῦ οἱ μέλλοντες           αὐτὸν
then stood off from him   the ones being about him
426           2532 01  5506            1161 5399
ἀνετάζειν,  καὶ ὁ χιλίαρχος          δὲ  ἐφοβήθη
to examine, and the thousand ruler   but feared
1921         3754  4514        1510   2532 3754 846
ἐπιγνοὺς    ὅτι  Ῥωμαῖός ἐστιν καὶ  ὅτι  αὐτὸν
having perceived that Roman   he is and  that him
1510   1210              30  07  1161 1887
ἦν    δεδεκώς.         Τῇ  δὲ  ἐπαύριον
he was+ +having bound.  In the but tomorrow
1014          1097       012 804       012 5101 2723
βουλόμενος γνῶναι  τὸ ἀσφαλές, τὸ  τί  κατηγορεῖται
planning    to know the secure, the what he is accused
5259 014   2453       3089     846   2532 2753
ὑπὸ  τῶν  Ἰουδαίων, ἔλυσεν  αὐτὸν καὶ ἐκέλευσεν
by   the  Judeans,  he loosed him  and commanded
4905          016   749        2532 3956 012
συνελθεῖν    τοὺς ἀρχιερεῖς   καὶ  πᾶν  τὸ
to come together the ruler priests and  all  the
4892         2532 2609        04   3972    2476
συνέδριον, καὶ  καταγαγὼν   τὸν Παῦλον ἔστησεν
council,    and having led down the Paul   he stood
1519 846    23:1      816         1161 01  3972    011
εἰς  αὐτούς.       Ἀτενίσας   δὲ  ὁ  Παῦλος τῷ
in   them.         Having stared but the Paul   the
4892         3004   435  80        1473 3956
συνεδρίῳ εἶπεν· ἄνδρες ἀδελφοί, ἐγὼ  πάσῃ
council   said,  men    brothers, I    in all
4893          18    4176            03        2316
συνειδήσει ἀγαθῇ πεπολίτευμαι    τῷ      θεῷ
conscience good  have acted as citizen to the God
891   3778    06  2250        2  01 1161 749
ἄχρι ταύτης τῆς ἡμέρας.       ὁ  δὲ ἀρχιερεὺς
until this   the day.        The but ruler priest
367    2004      015   3936                      846
Ἀνανίας ἐπέταξεν τοῖς παρεστῶσιν              αὐτῷ
Ananias ordered  the  ones having stood along him
5180     846   012 4750        3  5119 01  3972   4314 846
τύπτειν αὐτοῦ τὸ στόμα.          τότε ὁ  Παῦλος πρὸς αὐτὸν
to beat him   the mouth.        Then the Paul   to   him
3004    5180     1473 3195      01  2316  5109
εἶπεν· τύπτειν σε   μέλλει   ὁ  θεός, τοῖχε
said;   to beat you is about  the God,  wall
2867         2532 1473 2521 2919      1473 2596 04
κεκονιαμένε· καὶ  σὺ  κάθη κρίνων  με  κατὰ τὸν
white washed; and you sit   judging me   by   the
3551   2532 3891          2753        1473 5180
νόμον καὶ  παρανομῶν    κελεύεις  με  τύπτεσθαι;
law    and  alongside law you command me to be beaten?
4  013 1161 3936              3004   04  749
   οἱ  δὲ  παρεστῶτες      εἶπαν· τὸν ἀρχιερέα
   The but having stood along said;  the ruler priest
02    2316 3058       5  5346 5037 01  3972    3756
τοῦ  θεοῦ λοιδορεῖς;   ἔφη  τε  ὁ  Παῦλος· οὐκ
of the God you abuse?  Said but the Paul;    not
3609a        80         3754 1510  749
ᾔδειν,      ἀδελφοί, ὅτι  ἐστὶν ἀρχιερεύς·
I had known, brothers, that he is ruler priest;
```

"Yes." [28]The tribune answered, "It cost me a large sum of money to get my citizenship." Paul said, "But I was born a citizen." [29]Immediately those who were about to examine him drew back from him; and the tribune also was afraid, for he realized that Paul was a Roman citizen and that he had bound him.

[30]Since he wanted to find out what Paul[a] was being accused of by the Jews, the next day he released him and ordered the chief priests and the entire council to meet. He brought Paul down and had him stand before them.

CHAPTER 23

While Paul was looking intently at the council he said, "Brothers,[b] up to this day I have lived my life with a clear conscience before God." [2]Then the high priest Ananias ordered those standing near him to strike him on the mouth. [3]At this Paul said to him, "God will strike you, you whitewashed wall! Are you sitting there to judge me according to the law, and yet in violation of the law you order me to be struck?" [4]Those standing nearby said, "Do you dare to insult God's high priest?" [5]And Paul said, "I did not realize, brothers, that he was high priest;

---

a Gk he
b Gk Men, brothers

for it is written, 'You shall not speak evil of a leader of your people.'"

6 When Paul noticed that some were Sadducees and others were Pharisees, he called out in the council, "Brothers, I am a Pharisee, a son of Pharisees. I am on trial concerning the hope of the resurrection[a] of the dead." 7When he said this, a dissension began between the Pharisees and the Sadducees, and the assembly was divided. 8(The Sadducees say that there is no resurrection, or angel, or spirit; but the Pharisees acknowledge all three.) 9Then a great clamor arose, and certain scribes of the Pharisees' group stood up and contended, "We find nothing wrong with this man. What if a spirit or an angel has spoken to him?" 10When the dissension became violent, the tribune, fearing that they would tear Paul to pieces, ordered the soldiers to go down, take him by force, and bring him into the barracks.

11 That night the Lord stood near him and said, "Keep up your courage! For just as you have testified for me in Jerusalem, so you must

---

a Gk concerning hope and
  resurrection

```
1125                    1063 3754 758      02      2992
γέγραπται              γὰρ ὅτι ἄρχοντα τοῦ      λαοῦ
it has been written for that ruler of the people
1473  3756 3004              2560    6  1097       1161
σου   οὐκ ἐρεῖς            κακῶς.   Γνοὺς        δὲ
of you not you will speak badly.  Having known but
01   3972    3754 09   1520 3313  1510  4523     09
ὁ   Παῦλος ὅτι τὸ ἓν μέρος ἐστὶν Σαδδουκαίων τὸ
the Paul  that the one part is   Sadducees   the
1161 2087   5330        2896   1722 011 4892
δὲ  ἕτερον Φαρισαίων ἔκραζεν ἐν τῷ συνεδρίῳ·
but other Pharisees shouted in the council;
435      80   1473 5330      1510   5207 5330
ἄνδρες ἀδελφοί, ἐγὼ Φαρισαῖός εἰμι, υἱὸς Φαρισαίων,
men    brothers, I   Pharisee am,  son of Pharisees,
4012  1680    2532 386        3498    1473 2919
περὶ ἐλπίδος καὶ ἀναστάσεως νεκρῶν [ἐγὼ] κρίνομαι.
about hope and standing up of dead I   am judged.
7 3778 1161 846   3004       1096    4714
  τοῦτο δὲ αὐτοῦ εἰπόντος ἐγένετο στάσις
  This but him having said became revolution
014   5330      2532 4523        2532 4977      09
τῶν  Φαρισαίων καὶ Σαδδουκαίων καὶ ἐσχίσθη τὸ
of the Pharisees and Sadducees and was split the
4128  8 4523      3303    1063 3004      3361 1510
πλῆθος. Σαδδουκαῖοι μὲν γὰρ λέγουσιν μὴ εἶναι
quantity. Sadducees indeed for say not to be
386    3383 32        3383 4151    5330      1161
ἀνάστασιν μήτε ἄγγελον μήτε πνεῦμα, Φαρισαῖοι δὲ
standing up nor messenger nor spirit, Pharisees but
3670      024 297        9 1096   1161 2906    3173
ὁμολογοῦσιν τὰ ἀμφότερα.  ἐγένετο δὲ κραυγὴ μεγάλη,
confess the both.  Became but shout great,
2532 450          5100 014    1122       010
καὶ ἀναστάντες τινὲς τῶν γραμματέων τοῦ
and having stood up some of the writers of the
3313  014    5330      1264         3004
μέρους τῶν Φαρισαίων διεμάχοντο   λέγοντες·
part of the Pharisees fought thoroughly saying,
3762  2556 2147       1722 03  444      3778    1487
οὐδὲν κακὸν εὑρίσκομεν ἐν τῷ ἀνθρώπῳ τούτῳ· εἰ
nothing bad we find in the man this; if
1161 4151  2980      846   2228 32       10 4183
δὲ πνεῦμα ἐλάλησεν αὐτῷ ἢ ἄγγελος; Πολλῆς
but spirit spoke to him or messenger? Much
1161 1096       4714      5399    01
δὲ γινομένης στάσεως φοβηθεὶς ὁ
but becoming revolution having feared the
5506        3361 1288                    01  3972
χιλίαρχος μὴ διασπασθῇ          ὁ Παῦλος
thousand ruler not might be torn in pieces the Paul
5259 846    2753      012 4753    2597
ὑπ' αὐτῶν ἐκέλευσεν τὸ στράτευμα καταβὰν
by them commanded the army having gone down
726     846   1537 3319  846   71      5037 1519
ἁρπάσαι αὐτὸν ἐκ μέσου αὐτῶν ἄγειν τε εἰς
to seize him from middle of them to lead and into
08  3925      07   1161 1966     3571
τὴν παρεμβολήν. 11 Τῇ δὲ ἐπιούσῃ νυκτὶ
the barracks.   In the but next night
2186        846 01 2962    3004      2293       5613
ἐπιστὰς αὐτῷ ὁ κύριος εἶπεν· θάρσει·     ὡς
having stood on him the Master said; take courage; as
1063 1263           024 4012   1473 1519
γὰρ διεμαρτύρω      τὰ περὶ ἐμοῦ εἰς
for you testified thoroughly the about me in
2419        3779   1473 1163        2532 1519
Ἰερουσαλήμ, οὕτω σε δεῖ        καὶ εἰς
Jerusalem, thusly you it is necessary also in
```

```
4516      3140              1096              1161  2250
Ῥώμην  μαρτυρῆσαι.  12  Γενομένης  δὲ  ἡμέρας
Rome    to testify.       Having become  but  day

4160          4963          013   2453        332
ποιήσαντες  συστροφὴν  οἱ  Ἰουδαῖοι  ἀνεθεμάτισαν
having made combination the  Judeans    swore a curse

1438      3004      3383   2068   3383  4095        2193
ἑαυτοὺς  λέγοντες  μήτε  φαγεῖν μήτε  πιεῖν      ἔως
themselves saying  neither to eat nor  to drink until

3739   615                  04    3972        1510 1161 4183
οὗ   ἀποκτείνωσιν  τὸν Παῦλον.  13  ἦσαν δὲ  πλείους
which they might kill the Paul.     Were but   more

5062       013  3778     08   4945              4160
τεσσεράκοντα οἱ ταύτην τὴν συνωμοσίαν ποιησάμενοι,
forty      the this  the co-oath      having made,

    3748       4334          015   749               2532 015
14 οἵτινες  προσελθόντες  τοῖς ἀρχιερεῦσιν  καὶ  τοῖς
   who       having come to the ruler priests and   the

4245         3004  331        332
πρεσβυτέροις εἶπαν· ἀναθέματι ἀνεθεματίσαμεν
older men    said,  in curse we swore a curse

1438       3367        2193      615
ἑαυτοὺς μηδενὸς γεύσασθαι ἔως  οὗ   ἀποκτείνωμεν
ourselves no one  to taste  until which we might kill

04  3972          3568 3767 1473  1718        03
τὸν Παῦλον.  15  νῦν  οὖν  ὑμεῖς ἐμφανίσατε τῷ
the Paul.        Now then you  be visible to the

5506         4862 011 4892         3704
χιλιάρχῳ    σὺν  τῷ συνεδρίῳ ὅπως
thousand ruler with the council  so that

2609          846   1519 1473 5613 3195
καταγάγῃ    αὐτὸν εἰς ὑμᾶς ὡς  μέλλοντας
he might lead down him  to  you  as  being about

1231              199          024 4012  846
διαγινώσκειν  ἀκριβέστερον  τὰ  περὶ  αὐτοῦ·
to know thoroughly more accurately the about him;

1473 1161 4253   010 1448      846   2092    1510
ἡμεῖς δὲ  πρὸ  τοῦ ἐγγίσαι αὐτὸν ἕτοιμοί ἐσμεν
we    but before the to near him  prepared we are

010 337    846          1161 01  5207
τοῦ ἀνελεῖν αὐτόν.  16  Ἀκούσας  δὲ  ὁ  υἱὸς
the to kill him.       Having heard but  the son

06    79       3972   08  1747     3854          2532
τῆς  ἀδελφῆς Παύλου τὴν ἐνέδραν, παραγενόμενος καὶ
of the sister  of Paul the ambush,  having arrived and

1525       1519 08   3925        518    03
εἰσελθὼν  εἰς τὴν παρεμβολὴν ἀπήγγειλεν τῷ
having gone in into the barracks  told      the

3972   4341          1161 01   3972     1520 014
Παύλῳ. 17 προσκαλεσάμενος δὲ  ὁ  Παῦλος ἕνα τῶν
Paul.    Having called to but  the Paul  one of the

1543        5346 04  3494    3778   520
ἑκατονταρχῶν ἔφη· τὸν νεανίαν τοῦτον ἀπάγαγε
hundred rulers said; the young man this  lead off

4314 04 5506        2192 1063 518       5100
πρὸς τὸν χιλίαρχον,  ἔχει γὰρ ἀπαγγεῖλαί τι
to   the thousand ruler, he has for to tell  some

846   18 01 3303  3767 3880              846
αὐτῷ.    ὁ  μὲν οὖν παραλαβὼν       αὐτὸν
to him.  The indeed then having taken along him
him.              taken along

71      4314 04 5506       2532 5346     01 1198
ἤγαγεν πρὸς τὸν χιλίαρχον  καὶ  φησίν· ὁ δέσμιος
he led to   the thousand ruler and  says; the prisoner

3972   4341            1473 2065     3778   04
Παῦλος προσκαλεσάμενός με  ἠρώτησεν τοῦτον τὸν
Paul   having called to me  asked     this   the

3495      71        4314 1473 2192 5100 2980
νεανίσκον ἀγαγεῖν πρὸς σὲ  ἔχοντά τι  λαλῆσαί
young man to lead to   you  having some to speak
```

bear witness also in Rome."

12 In the morning the Jews joined in a conspiracy and bound themselves by an oath neither to eat nor drink until they had killed Paul. [13]There were more than forty who joined in this conspiracy. [14]They went to the chief priests and elders and said, "We have strictly bound ourselves by an oath to taste no food until we have killed Paul. [15]Now then, you and the council must notify the tribune to bring him down to you, on the pretext that you want to make a more thorough examination of his case. And we are ready to do away with him before he arrives."

16 Now the son of Paul's sister heard about the ambush; so he went and gained entrance to the barracks and told Paul. [17]Paul called one of the centurions and said, "Take this young man to the tribune, for he has something to report to him." [18]So he took him, brought him to the tribune, and said, "The prisoner Paul called me and asked me to bring this young man to you; he has something to tell you."

19The tribune took him by the hand, drew him aside privately, and asked, "What is it that you have to report to me?" 20He answered, "The Jews have agreed to ask you to bring Paul down to the council tomorrow, as though they were going to inquire more thoroughly into his case. 21But do not be persuaded by them, for more than forty of their men are lying in ambush for him. They have bound themselves by an oath neither to eat nor drink until they kill him. They are ready now and are waiting for your consent." 22So the tribune dismissed the young man, ordering him, "Tell no one that you have informed me of this."

23 Then he summoned two of the centurions and said, "Get ready to leave by nine o'clock tonight for Caesarea with two hundred soldiers, seventy horsemen, and two hundred spearmen. 24Also provide mounts for Paul to ride, and take him safely to Felix the governor." 25He wrote a letter to this effect:

26 "Claudius Lysias to his Excellency

1473		1949		1161 06	5495	846	01
σοι.	**19**	ἐπιλαβόμενος	δὲ	τῆς	χειρὸς	αὐτοῦ	ὁ
to you.		Having taken on	but	the	hand	of him	the

5506 · 2532 402 · 2596 2398
χιλίαρχος καὶ ἀναχωρήσας κατ' ἰδίαν
thousand ruler and having departed by own

4441 · 5101 1510 3739 2192 · 518
ἐπυνθάνετο, τί ἐστιν ὃ ἔχεις ἀπαγγεῖλαί
was inquiring, what it is that you have to tell

1473 **20** 3004 1161 3754 013 2453 4934
μοι; εἶπεν δὲ ὅτι οἱ Ἰουδαῖοι συνέθεντο
me? He said but that the Judeans set together

010 2065 1473 3704 839 04 3972
τοῦ ἐρωτῆσαί σε ὅπως αὔριον τὸν Παῦλον
the to ask you so that tomorrow the Paul

2609 1519 012 4892 5613 3195 5100
καταγάγῃς εἰς τὸ συνέδριον ὡς μέλλον τι
you might to the council as being some
lead down about

199 4441 4012 846 **21** 1473 3767
ἀκριβέστερον πυνθάνεσθαι περὶ αὐτοῦ. σὺ οὖν
more accurately to inquire about him. You then

3361 3982 846 1748 1063 846
μὴ πεισθῇς αὐτοῖς· ἐνεδρεύουσιν γὰρ αὐτὸν
not might persuade them; lie in wait for him

1537 846 435 4183 5062 3748
ἐξ αὐτῶν ἄνδρες πλείους τεσσεράκοντα, οἵτινες
from them men more forty, who

332 1438 3383 2068 3383 4095
ἀνεθεμάτισαν ἑαυτοὺς μήτε φαγεῖν μήτε πιεῖν
swore a curse themselves neither to eat nor to drink

2193 3739 337 846 2532 3568 1510
ἕως οὗ ἀνέλωσιν αὐτόν, καὶ νῦν εἰσιν
until that they might kill him, and now they are

2092 4327 08 575 1473 1860 **22** 01
ἕτοιμοι προσδεχόμενοι τὴν ἀπὸ σοῦ ἐπαγγελίαν. ὁ
prepared awaiting the from you promise. The

3303 3767 5506 630 04 3495
μὲν οὖν χιλίαρχος ἀπέλυσε τὸν νεανίσκον
indeed then thousand ruler loosed off the young man

3853 3367 1583 3754 3778
παραγγείλας μηδενὶ ἐκλαλῆσαι ὅτι ταῦτα
having commanded to no one to speak out that these

1718 4314 1473 **23** 2532 4341
ἐνεφάνισας πρός με. Καὶ προσκαλεσάμενος
you made visible to me. And having called to

1417 5100 014 1543 3004 2090
δύο [τινὰς] τῶν ἑκατονταρχῶν εἶπεν· ἑτοιμάσατε
two some of the hundred rulers he said, prepare

4757 1250 3704 4198
στρατιώτας διακοσίους, ὅπως πορευθῶσιν
soldiers two hundred, so that they might travel

2193 2542 2532 2460 1440 2532
ἕως Καισαρείας, καὶ ἱππεῖς ἑβδομήκοντα καὶ
until Caesarea, and, horsemen seventy and

1187 1250 575 5154 5610 06 3571
δεξιολάβους διακοσίους ἀπὸ τρίτης ὥρας τῆς νυκτός,
spearmen two hundred from third hour of the night,

24 2934 5037 3936 2443 1913 04
κτήνη τε παραστῆσαι ἵνα ἐπιβιβάσαντες τὸν
animals both to stand along that having mounted the

3972 1295 4314 5344 04
Παῦλον διασώσωσι πρὸς Φήλικα τὸν
Paul they might thoroughly deliver to Felix the

2232 **25** 1125 1992 2192 04
ἡγεμόνα, γράψας ἐπιστολὴν ἔχουσαν τὸν
leader, having written letter having the

5179 3778 **26** 2804 3079 03 2903
τύπον τοῦτον· Κλαύδιος Λυσίας τῷ κρατίστῳ
example this; Claudius Lysias to the most strong

2232	5344	5463		04	435	3778
ἡγεμόνι	Φήλικι	χαίρειν.	**27**	Τὸν	ἄνδρα	τοῦτον
leader	Felix	to rejoice.		The	man	this

4815				5259	014	2453	2532
συλλημφθέντα				ὑπὸ	τῶν	Ἰουδαίων	καὶ
having been taken together				by	the	Judeans	and

3195		337		5259	846	2186
μέλλοντα		ἀναιρεῖσθαι	ὑπ᾽	αὐτῶν	ἐπιστὰς
being about		to be killed	by	them	having stood on

4862	011	4753		1807		3129
σὺν	τῷ	στρατεύματι	ἐξειλάμην		μαθὼν
with	the	army	I myself lifted out		having learned

3754	4514	1510		1014		5037	1921	08
ὅτι	Ῥωμαῖός	ἐστιν.	**28**	βουλόμενός	τε	ἐπιγνῶναι	τὴν
that	Roman	he is.		Planning	but	to perceive	the

156	1223	3739	1458		846
αἰτίαν	δι᾽	ἣν	ἐνεκάλουν		αὐτῷ,
cause	through which		they were calling		in him,

2609		1519	012	4892	846		3739	2147
κατήγαγον	εἰς	τὸ	συνέδριον	αὐτῶν	**29**	ὃν	εὗρον
I led down	to	the	council	of them		whom	I found

1458		4012	2213	02	3551	846
ἐγκαλούμενον	περὶ	ζητημάτων	τοῦ	νόμου	αὐτῶν,
being called in	about	questions	of the	law	of them,

3367	1161	514	2288	2228	1199	2192	1462
μηδὲν	δὲ	ἄξιον	θανάτου	ἢ	δεσμῶν	ἔχοντα	ἔγκλημα.
nothing	but	worthy	of death	or	chains	having	charge.

	3377		1161	1473	1917		1519
30	μηνυθείσης		δέ	μοι	ἐπιβουλῆς		εἰς
	Having been reported	but		to me	plan	against	for

04	435	1510	1824	3992	4314	1473
τὸν	ἄνδρα	ἔσεσθαι	ἐξαυτῆς	ἔπεμψα	πρός	σε
the	man	to be	at once	I sent	to	you

3853		2532	015	2725	3004	024	4314
παραγγείλας	καὶ	τοῖς	κατηγόροις	λέγειν	[τὰ]	πρὸς
having commanded	also	the	accusers	to say	the	to

846	1909	1473		013	3303	3767	4757	2596	012
αὐτὸν	ἐπὶ	σοῦ.	**31**	Οἱ	μὲν	οὖν	στρατιῶται	κατὰ	τὸ
him	on	you.		The	indeed	then	soldiers	by	the

1299		846	353	04
διατεταγμένον	αὐτοῖς	ἀναλαβόντες	τὸν
having been directed	to them	having taken up	the

3972	71	1223	3571	1519	08	494
Παῦλον	ἤγαγον	διὰ	νυκτὸς	εἰς	τὴν	Ἀντιπατρίδα,
Paul	they led	through	night	to	the	Antipatras,

	07	1161	1887	1439	016	2460
32	τῇ	δὲ	ἐπαύριον	ἐάσαντες	τοὺς	ἱππεῖς
	in the	but	tomorrow	having allowed	the	horsemen

565	4862	846	5290	1519	08
ἀπέρχεσθαι	σὺν	αὐτῷ	ὑπέστρεψαν	εἰς	τὴν
to go off	with	him	having returned	to	the

3925		3748	1525	1519	08
παρεμβολήν·	**33**	οἵτινες	εἰσελθόντες	εἰς	τὴν
barracks;		who	having gone in	into	the

2542	2532	325	08	1992	03
Καισάρειαν	καὶ	ἀναδόντες	τὴν	ἐπιστολὴν	τῷ
Caesarea	and	having given up	the	letter	to the

2232	3936		2532	04	3972	846
ἡγεμόνι	παρέστησαν	καὶ	τὸν	Παῦλον	αὐτῷ.
leader	they stood along	also	the	Paul	to him.

	314	1161	2532	1905	1537	4169
34	ἀναγνοὺς	δὲ	καὶ	ἐπερωτήσας	ἐκ	ποίας
	Having read	but	also	having asked	on	from what kind

1885	1510	2532	4441	3754	575	2791
ἐπαρχείας	ἐστίν,	καὶ	πυθόμενος	ὅτι	ἀπὸ	Κιλικίας,
province	he is,	and	having	that	from	Cilicia,
				inquired		

	1251		1473	5346	3752	2532	013
35	διακούσομαί		σου,	ἔφη,	ὅταν	καὶ	οἱ
	I will hear thoroughly		you,	he said,	when	also	the

the governor Felix, greetings. [27]This man was seized by the Jews and was about to be killed by them, but when I had learned that he was a Roman citizen, I came with the guard and rescued him. [28]Since I wanted to know the charge for which they accused him, I had him brought to their council. [29]I found that he was accused concerning questions of their law, but was charged with nothing deserving death or imprisonment. [30]When I was informed that there would be a plot against the man, I sent him to you at once, ordering his accusers also to state before you what they have against him.[a] "

[31]So the soldiers, according to their instructions, took Paul and brought him during the night to Antipatris. [32]The next day they let the horsemen go on with him, while they returned to the barracks. [33]When they came to Caesarea and delivered the letter to the governor, they presented Paul also before him. [34]On reading the letter, he asked what province he belonged to, and when he learned that he was from Cilicia, [35]he said, "I will give you a hearing when

---

[a] Other ancient authorities add *Farewell*

your accusers arrive." Then
he ordered that he be kept
under guard in Herod's
headquarters.[a]

CHAPTER 24

Five days later the high
priest Ananias came
down with some elders
and an attorney, a certain
Tertullus, and they
reported their case against
Paul to the governor.
[2] When Paul[b] had been
summoned, Tertullus began
to accuse him, saying:

"Your Excellency,[c]
because of you we have long
enjoyed peace, and reforms
have been made for this
people because of your
foresight. [3] We welcome
this in every way and
everywhere with utmost
gratitude. [4] But, to detain
you no further, I beg you
to hear us briefly with your
customary graciousness.
[5] We have, in fact, found
this man a pestilent fellow,
an agitator among all the
Jews throughout the world,
and a ringleader of the sect
of the Nazarenes.[d] [6] He even
tried to profane the temple,
and so we seized him.[e] [8] By
examining him yourself you
will be able to learn from
him concerning everything
of which we accuse him."

[9] The Jews also joined in
the charge by asserting that
all this was true.

[10] When the governor
motioned to him to speak,
Paul replied:

[a] Gk praetorium
[b] Gk he
[c] Gk lacks Your Excellency
[d] Gk Nazoreans
[e] Other ancient authorities add
   and we would have judged him
   according to our law. [7] But the chief
   captain Lysias came and with great
   violence took him out of our hands,
   [8] commanding his accusers to come
   before you.

2725   1473   3854   2753   1722
κατήγοροί σου   παραγένωνται· κελεύσας   ἐν
accusers of you might arrive; having commanded in

011 4232   02   2264   5442   846
τῷ πραιτωρίῳ τοῦ   Ἡρῴδου φυλάσσεσθαι   αὐτόν.
the praetorium of the Herod to be guarded him.

           3326 1161 4002 2250   2597   01 749
24:1 Μετὰ δὲ πέντε ἡμέρας κατέβη   ὁ ἀρχιερεὺς
      After but five days went down the ruler priest

  367   3326 4245   5100 2532 4489   5061
Ἀνανίας μετὰ πρεσβυτέρων τινῶν καὶ ῥήτορος Τερτύλλου
Ananias with older men   some and speaker Tertullus

5100   3748   1718   03   2232   2596   02
τινός, οἵτινες ἐνεφάνισαν τῷ   ἡγεμόνι κατὰ τοῦ
some, who   made visible to the leader against the

3972   2564   1161 846   757   2723
Παύλου. [2] κληθέντος   δὲ αὐτοῦ ἤρξατο κατηγορεῖν
Paul.   Having been called but him began to accuse

01 5061   3004   4183   1515   5177
ὁ Τέρτυλλος λέγων· πολλῆς εἰρήνης τυγχάνοντες
the Tertullus saying, much   peace   obtaining

1223   1473 2532 1356a   1096   011   1484
διὰ   σοῦ καὶ διορθωμάτων γινομένων τῷ   ἔθνει
through you and corrections becoming in the nation

3778 1223   06   4674 4307   3839   5037 2532
τούτῳ διὰ τῆς σῆς προνοίας, [3] πάντῃ τε καὶ
this through the your provision, in all both and

3837   588   2903   5344
πανταχοῦ ἀποδεχόμεθα,   κράτιστε   Φῆλιξ,
all places we welcome thoroughly, most strong Felix,

3326 3956 2169   2443 1161 3361 1909 4183
μετὰ πάσης εὐχαριστίας. [4] ἵνα δὲ μὴ ἐπὶ πλεῖόν
with all good favor.   That but not on more

1473 1465   3870   191   1473 1473
σε ἐγκόπτω,   παρακαλῶ   ἀκοῦσαί σε ἡμῶν
you I might hinder, I encourage to hear you of us

4935   07   4674 1932   2147   1063
συντόμως τῇ σῇ ἐπιεικείᾳ. [5] εὑρόντες   γὰρ
concisely in the your gentleness. Having found for

04 435   3778   3061 2532 2795   4714
τὸν ἄνδρα τοῦτον λοιμὸν καὶ κινοῦντα στάσεις
the man this   plague and moving revolutions

3956 015   2453   015 2596 08   3625
πᾶσιν τοῖς Ἰουδαίοις τοῖς κατὰ τὴν οἰκουμένην
to all the Judeans the by the inhabited world

4414   5037 06   014 3480
πρωτοστάτην   τε τῆς τῶν Ναζωραίων
first revolutionary and of the of the Nazoreans

139   3739 2532 012 2411   3985
αἱρέσεως, [6] ὃς καὶ τὸ ἱερὸν ἐπείρασεν
sect,   who also the temple pressured

953   3739 2532 2902   3844 3739
βεβηλῶσαι   ὃν καὶ ἐκρατήσαμεν, [8] παρ' οὗ
to desecrate what also we hold,   along which

1410   846   350   4012 3956
δυνήσῃ   αὐτὸς ἀνακρίνας   περὶ πάντων
you will be able yourself having examined about all

3778   1921   3739 1473 2723   846
τούτων ἐπιγνῶναι ὧν ἡμεῖς κατηγοροῦμεν αὐτοῦ.
these to perceive what we accuse   him.

   4901a   1161 2532 013 2453   5335
[9] συνεπέθεντο   δὲ καὶ οἱ Ἰουδαῖοι φάσκοντες
   Placed together but also the Judeans affirming

3778 3779 2192   611   5037 01 3972
ταῦτα οὕτως ἔχειν. [10] Ἀπεκρίθη τε ὁ Παῦλος
these thusly to have. Answered but the Paul

3506   846   02 2232   3004   1537 4183
νεύσαντος αὐτῷ τοῦ ἡγεμόνος λέγειν· ἐκ πολλῶν
having nodded to him the leader to speak; from many

2094 1510 1473 2923 011 1484 3778
ἐτῶν ὄντα σε κριτὴν τῷ ἔθνει τούτῳ
years being you judge to the nation this

1987 2115a 024 4012 1683 626
ἐπιστάμενος εὐθύμως τὰ περὶ ἐμαυτοῦ ἀπολογοῦμαι,
understanding cheerfully the about myself I defend,

11 1410 1473 1921 3754 3756 4183 1510
δυναμένου σου ἐπιγνῶναι ὅτι οὐ πλείους εἰσίν
being able you to perceive that not more are

1473 2250 1427 575 3739 305 4352
μοι ἡμέραι δώδεκα ἀφ᾽ ἧς ἀνέβην προσκυνήσων
to me days twelve from which I went up worshiping

1519 2419 **12** 2532 3777 1722 011 2411
εἰς Ἰερουσαλήμ. καὶ οὔτε ἐν τῷ ἱερῷ
in Jerusalem. And neither in the temple

2147 1473 4314 5100 1256 2228 1987a
εὑρόν με πρός τινα διαλεγόμενον ἢ ἐπίστασιν
they found me to some disputing or attention

4160 3793 3777 1722 019 4864 3777 2596 08
ποιοῦντα ὄχλου οὔτε ἐν ταῖς συναγωγαῖς οὔτε κατὰ τὴν
making crowd nor in the synagogues nor by the

4172 3761 3936 1410 1473
πόλιν, **13** οὐδὲ παραστῆσαι δύνανταί σοι
city, but not to stand along they are able to you

4012 3739 3570 2723 1473 **14** 3670 1161
περὶ ὧν νυνὶ κατηγοροῦσίν μου. ὁμολογῶ δὲ
about which now they accuse me. I confess but

3778 1473 3754 2596 08 3598 3739 3004
τοῦτό σοι ὅτι κατὰ τὴν ὁδὸν ἣν λέγουσιν
this to you that by the way which they say

139 3779 3000 03 3971 2316 4100 3956
αἵρεσιν, οὕτως λατρεύω τῷ πατρῴῳ θεῷ πιστεύων πᾶσι
sect, thusly I serve the father God trusting all

023 2596 04 3551 2532 023 1722 015 4396
τοῖς κατὰ τὸν νόμον καὶ τοῖς ἐν τοῖς προφήταις
the by the law and the in the spokesmen

1125 **15** 1680 2192 1519 04 2316 3739
γεγραμμένοις, ἐλπίδα ἔχων εἰς τὸν θεὸν ἣν
having been written, hope having in the God who

2532 846 3778 4327 386
καὶ αὐτοὶ οὗτοι προσδέχονται, ἀνάστασιν
also themselves these await, standing up

3195 1510 1342 5037 2532 94 **16** 1722
μέλλειν ἔσεσθαι δικαίων τε καὶ ἀδίκων. ἐν
to be about to be of right both and unright. In

3778 2532 846 778 677 4893 2192
τούτῳ καὶ αὐτὸς ἀσκῶ ἀπρόσκοπον συνείδησιν ἔχειν
this also myself I engage blameless conscience to have

4314 04 2316 2532 016 444 1223 3956
πρὸς τὸν θεὸν καὶ τοὺς ἀνθρώπους διὰ παντός.
to the God and the men through all.

17 1223 2094 1161 4183 1654 4160
δι᾽ ἐτῶν δὲ πλειόνων ἐλεημοσύνας ποιήσων
Through years but more mercifulness having made

1519 012 1484 1473 3854 2532 4376
εἰς τὸ ἔθνος μου παρεγενόμην καὶ προσφοράς,
to the nation of me I arrived and offerings,

18 1722 3739 2147 1473 48 1722
ἐν αἷς εὑρόν με ἡγνισμένον ἐν
in which they found me having been purified in

011 2411 3756 3326 3793 3761 3326 2351
τῷ ἱερῷ οὐ μετὰ ὄχλου οὐδὲ μετὰ θορύβου,
the temple not with crowd but not with uproar,

19 5100 1161 575 06 773 2453 3739
τινὲς δὲ ἀπὸ τῆς Ἀσίας Ἰουδαῖοι, οὓς
some but from the Asia Judeans who

1163 1909 1473 3918 2532 2723
ἔδει ἐπὶ σοῦ παρεῖναι καὶ κατηγορεῖν
it was necessary on you to be present and to accuse

"I cheerfully make my defense, knowing that for many years you have been a judge over this nation. [11]As you can find out, it is not more than twelve days since I went up to worship in Jerusalem. [12]They did not find me disputing with anyone in the temple or stirring up a crowd either in the synagogues or throughout the city. [13]Neither can they prove to you the charge that they now bring against me. [14]But this I admit to you, that according to the Way, which they call a sect, I worship the God of our ancestors, believing everything laid down according to the law or written in the prophets. [15]I have a hope in God— a hope that they themselves also accept—that there will be a resurrection of both[a] the righteous and the unrighteous. [16]Therefore I do my best always to have a clear conscience toward God and all people. [17]Now after some years I came to bring alms to my nation and to offer sacrifices. [18]While I was doing this, they found me in the temple, completing the rite of purification, without any crowd or disturbance. [19]But there were some Jews from Asia—they ought to be here before you to make an accusation,

---

[a] Other ancient authorities read of the dead, both of

if they have anything against me. ²⁰Or let these men here tell what crime they had found when I stood before the council, ²¹unless it was this one sentence that I called out while standing before them, 'It is about the resurrection of the dead that I am on trial before you today.'"

22 But Felix, who was rather well informed about the Way, adjourned the hearing with the comment, "When Lysias the tribune comes down, I will decide your case." ²³Then he ordered the centurion to keep him in custody, but to let him have some liberty and not to prevent any of his friends from taking care of his needs.

24 Some days later when Felix came with his wife Drusilla, who was Jewish, he sent for Paul and heard him speak concerning faith in Christ Jesus. ²⁵And as he discussed justice, self-control, and the coming judgment, Felix became frightened and said, "Go away for the present; when I have an opportunity, I will send for you." ²⁶At the same time he hoped that money would be given him by Paul, and for that reason he used to send for him very often and converse with him.

27 After two years had passed, Felix was succeeded by Porcius Festus; and since he wanted to grant the Jews a favor, Felix left Paul in prison.

1487	5100	2192		4314	1473	**20**	2228	846
εἴ	τι	ἔχοιεν		πρὸς	ἐμέ.		ἢ	αὐτοὶ
if	some	they may have		toward	me.		Or	themselves

3778	3004		5101	2147		92		2476
οὗτοι	εἰπάτωσαν		τί	εὗρον		ἀδίκημα		στάντος
these	let say		what	they found		unright		having stood

1473	1909	010	4892		**21**	2228	4012	1520	3778
μου	ἐπὶ	τοῦ	συνεδρίου,			ἢ	περὶ	μιᾶς	ταύτης
me	on	the	council,			or	about	one	this

5456	3739	2896		1722	846		2476		3754
φωνῆς	ἧς	ἐκέκραξα		ἐν	αὐτοῖς		ἑστὼς		ὅτι
sound	which	I shouted		in	them		having stood		that

4012	386		3498	1473	2919		4594	1909
περὶ	ἀναστάσεως		νεκρῶν	ἐγὼ	κρίνομαι		σήμερον	ἐφ'
about	standing up		of dead	I	am judged		today	on

1473		**22**	306		1161	846		01	5344
ὑμῶν.			ἀνεβάλετο		δὲ	αὐτοὺς		ὁ	Φῆλιξ,
you.			He threw up		but	them		the	Felix,

199		3609a		024	4012	06	3598
ἀκριβέστερον		εἰδὼς		τὰ	περὶ	τῆς	ὁδοῦ
more accurately		having known		the	about	the	way

3004	3752	3079	01	5506		2597		1231
εἴπας·	ὅταν	Λυσίας	ὁ	χιλίαρχος		καταβῇ,		διαγνώσομαι
having said;	when	Lysias	the	thousand ruler		might go down,		I will know thoroughly

024	2596	1473		**23**	1299		03	1543
τὰ	καθ'	ὑμᾶς·			διαταξάμενος		τῷ	ἑκατοντάρχῃ
the	by	you;			having directed		the	hundred ruler

5083		846	2192		5037 425		2532	3367
τηρεῖσθαι		αὐτὸν	ἔχειν		τε ἄνεσιν		καὶ	μηδένα
to be kept		him	to have		both relief		and	no one

2967		014	2398	846		5256		846		3326
κωλύειν		τῶν	ἰδίων	αὐτοῦ		ὑπηρετεῖν		αὐτῷ.		**24** Μετὰ
to hinder		the	own	of him		to assist		him.		After

1161	2250	5100	3854		01	5344	4862
δὲ	ἡμέρας	τινὰς	παραγενόμενος		ὁ	Φῆλιξ	σὺν
but	days	some	having arrived		the	Felix	with

1409	07	2398	1135		1510	2453		3343
Δρουσίλλῃ	τῇ	ἰδίᾳ	γυναικὶ		οὔσῃ	Ἰουδαίᾳ		μετεπέμψατο
Drusilla	the	own	woman		being	Judean		sent for

04	3972	2532	191		846	4012	06	1519	5547
τὸν	Παῦλον	καὶ	ἤκουσεν		αὐτοῦ	περὶ	τῆς	εἰς	Χριστὸν
the	Paul	and	heard		him	about	the	in	Christ

2424	4102		**25**	1256		1161	846	4012
Ἰησοῦν	πίστεως.			διαλεγομένου		δὲ	αὐτοῦ	περὶ
Jesus	trust.			Disputing		but	him	about

1343		2532	1466			2532	010	2917		010
δικαιοσύνης		καὶ	ἐγκρατείας			καὶ	τοῦ	κρίματος		τοῦ
rightness		and	inner strength			and	the	judgment		the

3195		1719	1096		01	5344	611		012
μέλλοντος,		ἔμφοβος	γενόμενος		ὁ	Φῆλιξ	ἀπεκρίθη·		τὸ
being about,		in fear	becoming		the	Felix	answered;		the

3568	2192	4198		2540		1161	3335
νῦν	ἔχον	πορεύου,		καιρὸν		δὲ	μεταλαβὼν
now	having	travel,		season		but	having taken with

3333		1473		**26**	260			2532	1679		3754
μετακαλέσομαί		σε,			ἅμα			καὶ	ἐλπίζων		ὅτι
I will call for		you,			at same time			also	hoping		that

5536	1325		846	5259	02	3972
χρήματα	δοθήσεται		αὐτῷ	ὑπὸ	τοῦ	Παύλου·
wealth	might be given		to him	by	the	Paul;

1352		2532	4437		846	3343
διὸ		καὶ	πυκνότερον		αὐτὸν	μεταπεμπόμενος
wherefore		also	more frequent		him	having sent for

3656		846		**27**	1333		1161
ὡμίλει		αὐτῷ.			Διετίας		δὲ
he was conversing		to him.			Two years		but

4137		2983	1240		01	5344	4201
πληρωθείσης		ἔλαβεν	διάδοχον		ὁ	Φῆλιξ	Πόρκιον
having been filled		took	successor		the	Felix	Porcius

5347	2309	5037	5485	2698		015
Φῆστον,	θέλων	τε	χάριτα	καταθέσθαι		τοῖς
Festus,	wanting	but	favor	to set down		to the

2453	01	5344	2641		04	3972
'Ιουδαίοις	ὁ	Φῆλιξ	κατέλιπε		τὸν	Παῦλον
Judeans	the	Felix	left		behind the	Paul

1210	**25:1**	5347	3767	1910		07
δεδεμένον.		Φῆστος	οὖν	ἐπιβὰς		τῇ
having been bound.		Festus	then	having gone	on the

1885	3326	5140	2250	305		1519	2414
ἐπαρχείᾳ	μετὰ	τρεῖς	ἡμέρας	ἀνέβη		εἰς	'Ιεροσόλυμα
province	after	three	days	went up	to		Jerusalem

575	2542	**2**	1718		5037	846	013
ἀπὸ	Καισαρείας,		ἐνεφάνισάν		τε	αὐτῷ	οἱ
from	Caesarea,		made visible		but	to him	the

749		2532	013	4413		014		2453
ἀρχιερεῖς		καὶ	οἱ	πρῶτοι		τῶν		'Ιουδαίων
ruler priests		and	the	first ones		of the		Judeans

2596	02	3972	2532	3870		846	**3**	154
κατὰ		τοῦ Παύλου	καὶ	παρεκάλουν		αὐτὸν		αἰτούμενοι
against		the Paul	and	they were		him		asking
				encouraging				

5485	2596	846	3704	3343		846
χάριν	κατ'	αὐτοῦ	ὅπως	μεταπέμψηται		αὐτὸν
favor	against	him	so that	he might send for		him

1519	2419		1747	4160		337	846	2596
εἰς	'Ιερουσαλήμ,		ἐνέδραν	ποιοῦντες		ἀνελεῖν	αὐτὸν	κατὰ
to	Jerusalem,		ambush	making		to kill	him	by

08	3598	01	1303	3767	5347	611	5083
τὴν	ὁδόν. **4**	ὁ	μὲν	οὖν	Φῆστος	ἀπεκρίθη	τηρεῖσθαι
the way.		The	but	then	Festus	answered	to be kept

04	3972	1519	2542		1438		1161	3195
τὸν	Παῦλον	εἰς	Καισάρειαν,		ἑαυτὸν		δὲ	μέλλειν
the	Paul	in	Caesarea,		himself		but	to be about

1722	5034		1607		**5**	013	3767	1722	1473
ἐν	τάχει		ἐκπορεύεσθαι·			οἱ	οὖν	ἐν	ὑμῖν,
in	quickness		to travel out;			the	then	in	you,

5346	1415	4782			1487	5100
φησίν,	δυνατοὶ	συγκαταβάντες			εἴ	τί
he says,	power ones	having come down		with	if	some

1510	1722	03	435	824		2723		846
ἐστιν	ἐν	τῷ	ἀνδρὶ	ἄτοπον		κατηγορείτωσαν		αὐτοῦ.
is	in	the	man	out of place		let them accuse		him.

6	1304		1161	1722	846	2250	3756	4183
	Διατρίψας		δὲ	ἐν	αὐτοῖς	ἡμέρας	οὐ	πλείους
	Having continued		but	in	them	days	not	more

3638	2228	1176	2597		1519	2542
ὀκτὼ	ἢ	δέκα,	καταβὰς		εἰς	Καισάρειαν,
eight	or	ten,	having gone down		into	Caesarea,

07	1887	2523		1909	010	968
τῇ	ἐπαύριον	καθίσας		ἐπὶ	τοῦ	βήματος
in the	tomorrow	having sat	on		the	law court

2753	04	3972	71		**7**	3854		1161
ἐκέλευσεν	τὸν	Παῦλον	ἀχθῆναι.			παραγενομένου		δὲ
he commanded	the	Paul	to be led.			Having arrived		but

846	4026		846	013		575	2414
αὐτοῦ	περιέστησαν		αὐτὸν	οἱ		ἀπὸ	'Ιεροσολύμων
him	stood around		him	the ones		from	Jerusalem

2597		2453	4183	2532	926	159a
καταβεβηκότες		'Ιουδαῖοι	πολλὰ	καὶ	βαρέα	αἰτιώματα
having come down		Judeans	many	and	burden	causes

2702		3739	3756	2480
καταφέροντες		ἃ	οὐκ	ἴσχυον
having brought		against that	not	they were strong

584		02	3972	626		3754	3777
ἀποδεῖξαι,	**8**	τοῦ	Παύλου	ἀπολογουμένου		ὅτι	οὔτε
to show off,		the	Paul	defending		that	neither

1519	04	3551	014		2453	3777	1519	012	2411
εἰς	τὸν	νόμον	τῶν		'Ιουδαίων	οὔτε	εἰς	τὸ	ἱερὸν
in	the	law	of the		Judeans	nor	in	the	temple

CHAPTER 25

Three days after Festus had arrived in the province, he went up from Caesarea to Jerusalem [2]where the chief priests and the leaders of the Jews gave him a report against Paul. They appealed to him [3]and requested, as a favor to them against Paul,[a] to have him transferred to Jerusalem. They were, in fact, planning an ambush to kill him along the way. [4]Festus replied that Paul was being kept at Caesarea, and that he himself intended to go there shortly. [5]"So," he said, "let those of you who have the authority come down with me, and if there is anything wrong about the man, let them accuse him."

[6]After he had stayed among them not more than eight or ten days, he went down to Caesarea; the next day he took his seat on the tribunal and ordered Paul to be brought. [7]When he arrived, the Jews who had gone down from Jerusalem surrounded him, bringing many serious charges against him, which they could not prove. [8]Paul said in his defense, "I have in no way committed an offense against the law of the Jews, or against the temple,

[a] Gk him

or against the emperor."
⁹But Festus, wishing to do
the Jews a favor, asked
Paul, "Do you wish to go
up to Jerusalem and be
tried there before me on
these charges?" ¹⁰Paul said,
"I am appealing to the
emperor's tribunal; this
is where I should be tried.
I have done no wrong to
the Jews, as you very well
know. ¹¹Now if I am in the
wrong and have committed
something for which I
deserve to die, I am not
trying to escape death; but
if there is nothing to their
charges against me, no one
can turn me over to them.
I appeal to the emperor."
¹²Then Festus, after he had
conferred with his council,
replied, "You have appealed
to the emperor; to the
emperor you will go."

13 After several days had
passed, King Agrippa and
Bernice arrived at Caesarea
to welcome Festus. ¹⁴Since
they were staying there
several days, Festus laid
Paul's case before the king,
saying, "There is a man
here who was left in prison
by Felix. ¹⁵When I was in
Jerusalem, the chief priests
and the elders of the Jews
informed me about him
and asked

3777	1519	2541		5100	264		9	01	5347	1161
οὔτε	εἰς	Καίσαρά		τι	ἥμαρτον.			῾Ο	Φῆστος	δὲ
nor	in	Caesar		some	I sinned.			The	Festus	but

2309	015		2453		5485	2698
θέλων	τοῖς		Ἰουδαίοις		χάριν	καταθέσθαι
wanting	to the		Judeans		favor	to set down

611		03	3972	3004		2309		1519
ἀποκριθεὶς		τῷ	Παύλῳ	εἶπεν·		θέλεις		εἰς
having answered		the	Paul	said;		you want		to

2414		305		1563	4012	3778
Ἱεροσόλυμα		ἀναβὰς		ἐκεῖ	περὶ	τούτων
Jerusalem		having gone up		there	about	these

2919		1909	1473	10	3004	1161	01	3972	1909
κριθῆναι		ἐπ᾽	ἐμοῦ;		εἶπεν	δὲ	ὁ	Παῦλος·	ἐπὶ
to be judged		by	me?		Said	but	the	Paul	on

010	968		2541		2476		1510	3757	1473
τοῦ	βήματος		Καίσαρος		ἑστώς		εἰμι,	οὗ	με
the	law court		of Caesar		having stood		I am,	where	me

1163		2919		2453		3762
δεῖ		κρινεσθαι.		Ἰουδαίους		οὐδὲν
it is necessary		to be judged.		Judeans		nothing

91		5613	2532	1473	2573	1921
ἠδίκησα		ὡς	καὶ	σὺ	κάλλιον	ἐπιγινώσκεις.
I did unright		as	also	you	well	perceive.

11	1487	3303	3767	91		2532	514	2288
	εἰ	μὲν	οὖν	ἀδικῶ		καὶ	ἄξιον	θανάτου
	If	but	then	I do unright		and	worthy	of death

4238			5100	3756	3868		012	599
πέπραχά			τι,	οὐ	παραιτοῦμαι		τὸ	ἀποθανεῖν·
I have practiced			some,	not	I reject		the	to die;

1487	1161	3762		1510		3739		3778	2723
εἰ	δὲ	οὐδέν		ἐστιν		ὧν		οὗτοι	κατηγοροῦσίν
if	but	nothing		there is		of which		these	accuse

1473	3762		1473	1410		846		5483		2541
μου,	οὐδείς		με	δύναται		αὐτοῖς		χαρίσασθαι·		Καίσαρα
me,	no one		me	is able		to them		to favor;		Caesar

1941		12	5119	01	5347		4814
ἐπικαλοῦμαι.			τότε	ὁ	Φῆστος		συλλαλήσας
I call on.			Then	the	Festus		having spoken together

3326	010	4824		611		2541
μετὰ	τοῦ	συμβουλίου		ἀπεκρίθη·		Καίσαρα
with	the	council		answered;		Caesar

1941		1909	2541		4198
ἐπικέκλησαι,		ἐπὶ	Καίσαρα		πορεύσῃ.
you have called on,		on	Caesar		you will travel.

13	2250		1161	1230			5100	67
	῾Ημερῶν		δὲ	διαγενομένων			τινῶν	᾽Αγρίππας
	Days		but	having become through			some	Agrippa

01	935		2532	959		2658		1519	2542
ὁ	βασιλεὺς		καὶ	Βερνίκη		κατήντησαν		εἰς	Καισάρειαν
the	king		and	Bernice		arrived		in	Caesarea

782		04	5347		14	5613	1161	4183	2250
ἀσπασάμενοι		τὸν	Φῆστον.			ὡς	δὲ	πλείους	ἡμέρας
having greeted		the	Festus.			As	but	many	days

1304		1563	01	5347	03		935
διέτριβον		ἐκεῖ,	ὁ	Φῆστος	τῷ		βασιλεῖ
they continued		there,	the	Festus	to the		king

394		024	2596	04	3972	3004		435	5100	1510
ἀνέθετο		τὰ	κατὰ	τὸν	Παῦλον	λέγων·		ἀνήρ	τίς	ἐστιν
set up		the	against	the	Paul	saying;		man	some	is+

2641			5259	5344	1198		15	4012
καταλελειμμένος			ὑπὸ	Φήλικος	δέσμιος,			περὶ
+having been left behind			by	Felix	prisoner,			about

3739	1096		1473	1519	2414		1718
οὗ	γενομένου		μου	εἰς	Ἱεροσόλυμα		ἐνεφάνισαν
whom	having become		me	in	Jerusalem		made visible

013	749		2532	013	4245		014	2453
οἱ	ἀρχιερεῖς		καὶ	οἱ	πρεσβύτεροι		τῶν	Ἰουδαίων
the	ruler priests		and	the	older men		of the	Judeans

154	2596	846	2613a		4314	3739
αἰτούμενοι	κατ'	αὐτοῦ	καταδίκην.	**16**	πρὸς	οὓς
asking	against him		judgment.		To	whom

611	3754 3756	1510	1485	4514	5483
ἀπεκρίθην	ὅτι οὐκ	ἔστιν	ἔθος	'Ρωμαίοις	χαρίζεσθαί
I answered	that not	it is	custom	to Romans	to favor

5100 444	4250	2228 01	2723	2596
τινα ἄνθρωπον	πρὶν	ἢ ὁ	κατηγορούμενος	κατὰ
some man	before	or the	ones accusing	by

4383	2192	016	2725	5117	5037	627
πρόσωπον	ἔχοι	τοὺς	κατηγόρους	τόπον	τε	ἀπολογίας
face	may have	the	accusers	place	and	defense

2983	4012	010	1462		4905
λάβοι	περὶ	τοῦ	ἐγκλήματος.	**17**	συνελθόντων
may take	about	the	charge.		Having come together

3767 846	1759	311	3367
οὖν [αὐτῶν]	ἐνθάδε	ἀναβολὴν	μηδεμίαν
then them	in this place	no delay	but not one

4160	07	1836	2523	1909 010	968
ποιησάμενος	τῇ	ἑξῆς	καθίσας	ἐπὶ τοῦ	βήματος
having made	the next	having sat	on	the	law court

2753	71	04	435		4012	3739
ἐκέλευσα	ἀχθῆναι	τὸν	ἄνδρα·	**18**	περὶ	οὗ
I commanded	to be led	the	man;		about	whom

2476	013 2725	3762	156
σταθέντες	οἱ κατήγοροι	οὐδεμίαν	αἰτίαν
having been standing	the accusers	but not one	cause

5342	3739	1473 5282	4190
ἔφερον	ὧν	ἐγὼ ὑπενόουν	πονηρῶν,
were bringing	of what	I supposed	evils,

	2213	1161 5100 4012	06	2398	1175
19	ζητήματα	δέ τινα περὶ	τῆς	ἰδίας	δεισιδαιμονίας
	questions	but some about	the	own	demon fearing

2192	4314 846	2532 4012	5100	2424	2348
εἶχον	πρὸς αὐτὸν	καὶ περὶ	τινος	'Ιησοῦ	τεθνηκότος
they had	to him	and about	some	Jesus	having died

3739 5335	01 3972	2198	639	1161
ὃν ἔφασκεν	ὁ Παῦλος	ζῆν.	**20** ἀπορούμενος	δὲ
whom was affirming	the Paul	to live.	Doubting	but

1473 08	4012	3778	2214	3004	1487
ἐγὼ τὴν	περὶ	τούτων	ζήτησιν	ἔλεγον	εἰ
I the	about	these	speculation	was saying	if

1014	4198	1519	2414	2546
βούλοιτο	πορεύεσθαι	εἰς	'Ιεροσόλυμα	κἀκεῖ
he may plan	to travel	to	Jerusalem	and there

2919	4012	3778		02	1161	3972
κρίνεσθαι	περὶ	τούτων.	**21**	τοῦ	δὲ	Παύλου
to be judged	about	these.		The	but	Paul

1941	5083	846	1519 08	02
ἐπικαλεσαμένου	τηρηθῆναι	αὐτὸν	εἰς τὴν	τοῦ
having called on	to be kept	him	in the	of the

4575	1233	2753	5083	846	2193
Σεβαστοῦ	διάγνωσιν,	ἐκέλευσα	τηρεῖσθαι	αυτὸν	ἕως
Sebastus	decision,	I commanded	to be kept	him	until

3739 375	846	4314 2541	67
οὗ ἀναπέμψω	αὐτὸν	πρὸς Καίσαρα.	**22** 'Αγρίππας
which I might send up	him	to Caesar.	Agrippa

1161 4314 04	5347	1014	2532 846	02
δὲ πρὸς τὸν Φῆστον·	ἐβουλόμην		καὶ αὐτὸς	τοῦ
but to the Festus;	I was planning		also myself	the

444	191	839	5346	191	846
ἀνθρώπου	ἀκοῦσαι.	αὔριον,	φησίν,	ἀκούσῃ	αὐτοῦ.
man	to hear.	Tomorrow,	he says,	you will hear	him.

	07	3767 1887	2064	02	67	2532
23	Τῇ	οὖν ἐπαύριον	ἐλθόντος	τοῦ	'Αγρίππα	καὶ
	In the	then tomorrow	having come	the	Agrippa	and

06	959	3326 4183	5325	2532	1525
τῆς	Βερνίκης	μετὰ πολλῆς	φαντασίας	καὶ	εἰσελθόντων
the	Bernice	with much	fantasy	and	having come in

for a sentence against him. [16]I told them that it was not the custom of the Romans to hand over anyone before the accused had met the accusers face to face and had been given an opportunity to make a defense against the charge. [17]So when they met here, I lost no time, but on the next day took my seat on the tribunal and ordered the man to be brought. [18]When the accusers stood up, they did not charge him with any of the crimes[a] that I was expecting. [19]Instead they had certain points of disagreement with him about their own religion and about a certain Jesus, who had died, but whom Paul asserted to be alive. [20]Since I was at a loss how to investigate these questions, I asked whether he wished to go to Jerusalem and be tried there on these charges.[b] [21]But when Paul had appealed to be kept in custody for the decision of his Imperial Majesty, I ordered him to be held until I could send him to the emperor."

[22]Agrippa said to Festus, "I would like to hear the man myself." "Tomorrow," he said, "you will hear him."

23 So on the next day Agrippa and Bernice came with great pomp, and they entered

---

[a] Other ancient authorities read *with anything*
[b] Gk *on them*

the audience hall with the military tribunes and the prominent men of the city. Then Festus gave the order and Paul was brought in. 24And Festus said, "King Agrippa and all here present with us, you see this man about whom the whole Jewish community petitioned me, both in Jerusalem and here, shouting that he ought not to live any longer. 25But I found that he had done nothing deserving death; and when he appealed to his Imperial Majesty, I decided to send him. 26But I have nothing definite to write to our sovereign about him. Therefore I have brought him before all of you, and especially before you, King Agrippa, so that, after we have examined him, I may have something to write— 27for it seems to me unreasonable to send a prisoner without indicating the charges against him."

CHAPTER 26

Agrippa said to Paul, "You have permission to speak for yourself." Then Paul stretched out his hand and began to defend himself:

2 "I consider myself fortunate that it is before you, King Agrippa, I am to make my defense today against all the accusations of the Jews, 3because you are especially

```
      1519  012  201              4862 5037 5506
      εἰς  τὸ  ἀκροατήριον  σύν  τε  χιλιάρχοις
      in   the  hearing place  with  both  rulers of thousand
      2532 435        015  2596 1851      06     4172     2532
      καὶ  ἀνδράσιν  τοῖς κατ᾽ ἐξοχὴν    τῆς   πόλεως  καὶ
      and  men        the  by  prominence  of the city   and
      2753             02   5347   71        01  3972
      κελεύσαντος   τοῦ Φήστου ἤχθη      ὁ  Παῦλος.
      having commanded the Festus was brought the Paul.
   2532 5346  01  5347     67        935     2532 3956
24 καί  φησιν ὁ  Φῆστος· Ἀγρίππα βασιλεῦ καὶ  πάντες
      And  says  the Festus;  Agrippa king   and  all
   013       4840         1473 435     2334        3778
   οἱ  συμπαρόντες  ἡμῖν ἄνδρες, θεωρεῖτε τοῦτον
   the ones being present to us  men,   watch    this
   4012 3739 537  09  4128       014    2453        1793
   περὶ οὗ  ἅπαν τὸ πλῆθος τῶν  Ἰουδαίων ἐνέτυχόν
   about what all  the quantity of the Judeans appealed
   1473 1722 5037 2414          2532 1759
   μοι  ἕν  τε  Ἱεροσολύμοις καὶ  ἐνθάδε
   to me in  both  Jerusalem    and  in this place
   994        3361 1163           846    2198
   βοῶντες  μὴ  δεῖν      αὐτὸν ζῆν
   crying aloud not to be necessary him   to live
   3371    25  1473 1161 2638         3367     514    846
   μηκέτι.     ἐγὼ  δὲ  κατελαβόμην μηδὲν ἄξιον αὐτὸν
   no longer. I   but  took over  nothing worthy him
   2288       4238            846    1161 3778
   θανάτου πεπραχέναι,   αὐτοῦ δὲ  τούτου
   of death to have practiced, him   but  this
   1941             04  4575        2919     3992
   ἐπικαλεσαμένου τὸν Σεβαστὸν ἔκρινα πέμπειν.
   having called on the Sebastus I judged to send.
   26 4012 3739 804        5100 1125     03      2962    3756
   περὶ οὗ  ἀσφαλές τι  γράψαι τῷ  κυρίῳ  οὐκ
   About whom secure  some to write to the master not
   2192    1352      4254        846   1909 1473 2532
   ἔχω,   διὸ  προήγαγον αὐτὸν ἐφ᾽ ὑμῶν καὶ
   I have, wherefore I led before him   on  you  and
   3122       1909 1473 935     67       3704    06
   μάλιστα ἐπὶ σοῦ, βασιλεῦ Ἀγρίππα, ὅπως  τῆς
   especially on you,  king   Agrippa, so that the
   351          1096      2192    5100
   ἀνακρίσεως γενομένης σχῶ  τί
   examination having become I might have some
   1125       27 249       1063 1473 1380      3992
   γράψω·     ἄλογον  γάρ μοι δοκεῖ πέμποντα
   I might write; unspeaking for to me it thinks sending
   1198     3361 2532 020 2596      846   156    4591
   δέσμιον μὴ καὶ  τὰς κατ᾽ αὐτοῦ αἰτίας σημᾶναι.
   prisoner not also the against him  causes to signify.
   26:1 67      1161 4314 04  3972      5346    2010
      Ἀγρίππας δὲ  πρὸς τὸν Παῦλον ἔφη· ἐπιτρέπεταί
      Agrippa but to  the  Paul   said; it is allowed
   1473 4012 4572      3004     5119 01 3972
   σοι  περὶ σεαυτοῦ λέγειν. τότε ὁ  Παῦλος
   to you about yourself to speak. Then the Paul
   1614        08  5495 626
   ἐκτείνας    τὴν χεῖρα ἀπελογεῖτο·
   having stretched out the hand was defending himself,
   2 4012 3956  3739 1458       5259 2453
   Περὶ πάντων ὧν  ἐγκαλοῦμαι ὑπὸ Ἰουδαίων,
   about all   which I am called in by  Judeans,
   935    67       2233      1683    3107   1909 1473
   βασιλεῦ Ἀγρίππα, ἥγημαι ἐμαυτὸν μακάριον ἐπὶ σοῦ
   king   Agrippa, I consider myself fortunate on  you
   3195     4594     626          3 3122
   μέλλων  σήμερον ἀπολογεῖσθαι  μάλιστα
   being about today  to defend      especially
```

```
1109              1510  1473 3956   022 2596  2453
γνώστην           ὄντα σε πάντων τῶν κατὰ ᾽Ιουδαίους
knowledgeable being you of all the by      Judeans
1485       5037 2532 2213        1352      1189
ἐθῶν       τε καὶ ζητημάτων, διὸ       δέομαι
customs    both and questions, wherefore I beg
3116           191      1473   4  08 3303    3767
μακροθύμως     ἀκοῦσαί μου.   Τὴν μὲν    οὖν
long-temperedly to hear me.   The indeed then
981        1473 08  1537 3503     08  575
βίωσίν     μου [τὴν] ἐκ νεότητος τὴν ἀπ᾽
type of life of me the from newness the from
746     1096        1722 011 1484  1473 1722
ἀρχῆς   γενομένην  ἐν  τῷ ἔθνει μου ἔν
beginning having become in the nation of me in
5037 2414          3609a     3956  013  2453
τε  ῾Ιεροσολύμοις ἴσασι    πάντες [οἱ] ᾽Ιουδαῖοι
and Jerusalem    had known all    the Judeans
 5 4267            1473 509       1437 2309
  προγινώσκοντές με ἄνωθεν,    ἐὰν θέλωσι
  knowing before me from above, if  they might want
3140       3754 2596 08 196       139    06
μαρτυρεῖν, ὅτι κατὰ τὴν ἀκριβεστάτην αἵρεσιν τῆς
to testify, that by the most accurate sect  of the
2251      2356      2198  5330        6 2532 3568 1909
ἡμετέρας θρησκείας ἔζησα Φαρισαῖος.  καὶ νῦν ἐπ᾽
our      piety   I lived Pharisaos. And now on
1680    06      1519 016 3962   1473 1860
ἐλπίδι τῆς   εἰς τοὺς πατέρας ἡμῶν ἐπαγγελίας
hope   of the in  the  fathers of us promise
1096       5259 02 2316 2476   2919    7 1519
γενομένης ὑπὸ τοῦ θεοῦ ἔστηκα κρινόμενος, εἰς
having become by the God I stand being judged, to
3739 09 1429      1473 1722 1616      3571
ἦν  τὸ δωδεκάφυλον ἡμῶν ἐν ἐκτενείᾳ νύκτα
which the twelve tribe of us perseverance night
2532 2250 3000     1679    2658    4012 3739
καὶ ἡμέραν λατρεῦον ἐλπίζει καταντῆσαι, περὶ ἧς
and day    serving hopes to arrive, about which
1680  1458       5259 2453     935     8 5101
ἐλπίδος ἐγκαλοῦμαι ὑπὸ ᾽Ιουδαίων, βασιλεῦ. τί
hope   I am called in by Judeans, king.  Why
571        2919      3844 1473 1487 01 2316
ἄπιστον   κρίνεται παρ᾽ ὑμῖν εἰ ὁ θεὸς
untrustful is it judged along you if the God
3498   1453     9 1473 3303 3767 1380    1683
νεκροὺς ἐγείρει;  ᾽Εγὼ μὲν οὖν ἔδοξα ἐμαυτῷ
dead   raises?  I  indeed then thought myself
4314 012 3686   2424    02 3480     1163
πρὸς τὸ ὄνομα ᾽Ιησοῦ τοῦ Ναζωραίου δεῖν
to  the name of Jesus the Nazorean to be necessary
4183 1727   4238    10 3739 2532 4160    1722
πολλὰ ἐναντία πρᾶξαι, ὃ καὶ ἐποίησα ἐν
many against to practice, which also I did in
2414          2532 4183  5037 014   40   1473
῾Ιεροσολύμοις, καὶ πολλούς τε τῶν ἁγίων ἐγὼ
Jerusalem,    and many both of the holy I
1722 5438   2623     08 3844 014 749
ἐν φυλακαῖς κατέκλεισα τὴν παρὰ τῶν ἀρχιερέων
in guards I closed up the along the ruler priests
1849     2983      337         5037 846
ἐξουσίαν λαβὼν ἀναιρουμένων τε αὐτῶν
authority having taken being killed and them
2702        5586     11 2532 2596 3956 020
κατήνεγκα ψῆφον.  καὶ κατὰ πάσας τὰς
I brought against pebble. And against all the
4864     4178     5097     846  315
συναγωγὰς πολλάκις τιμωρῶν αὐτοὺς ἠνάγκαζον
synagogues frequently punishing them I was compelling
```

familiar with all the customs and controversies of the Jews; therefore I beg of you to listen to me patiently.

4 "All the Jews know my way of life from my youth, a life spent from the beginning among my own people and in Jerusalem. [5]They have known for a long time, if they are willing to testify, that I have belonged to the strictest sect of our religion and lived as a Pharisee. [6]And now I stand here on trial on account of my hope in the promise made by God to our ancestors, [7]a promise that our twelve tribes hope to attain, as they earnestly worship day and night. It is for this hope, your Excellency,[a] that I am accused by Jews! [8]Why is it thought incredible by any of you that God raises the dead?

9 "Indeed, I myself was convinced that I ought to do many things against the name of Jesus of Nazareth.[b] [10]And that is what I did in Jerusalem; with authority received from the chief priests, I not only locked up many of the saints in prison, but I also cast my vote against them when they were being condemned to death. [11]By punishing them often in all the synagogues I tried to force them

[a] Gk O king
[b] Gk the Nazorean

to blaspheme; and since I was so furiously enraged at them, I pursued them even to foreign cities.

12 "With this in mind, I was traveling to Damascus with the authority and commission of the chief priests, 13when at midday along the road, your Excellency,*a* I saw a light from heaven, brighter than the sun, shining around me and my companions. 14When we had all fallen to the ground, I heard a voice saying to me in the Hebrew*b* language, 'Saul, Saul, why are you persecuting me? It hurts you to kick against the goads.' 15I asked, 'Who are you, Lord?' The Lord answered, 'I am Jesus whom you are persecuting. 16But get up and stand on your feet; for I have appeared to you for this purpose, to appoint you to serve and testify to the things in which you have seen me*c* and to those in which I will appear to you. 17I will rescue you from your people and from the Gentiles—to whom I am sending you 18to open their eyes so that they may turn from darkness to light and from the power of Satan to God, so that they may receive forgiveness of sins and a place among those who are sanctified by faith in me.'

19 "After that, King Agrippa, I was not

a Gk O king
b That is, Aramaic
c Other ancient authorities read *the things that you have seen*

987	4057	5037	1693	846
βλασφημεῖν	περισσῶς	τε	ἐμμαινόμενος	αὐτοῖς
to insult	exceedingly	and	being mad	against them

1377	2193	2532	1519 020	1854	4172	12	1722
ἐδίωκον	ἕως	καὶ	εἰς τὰς	ἔξω	πόλεις.		Ἐν
I pursued	until	even	in the	outside	cities.		In

3739 4198	1519 08	1154	3326 1849
οἷς πορευόμενος	εἰς τὴν	Δαμασκὸν	μετ' ἐξουσίας
which traveling	to the	Damascus	with authority

2532 2011	06	014 749	13	2250	3319
καὶ ἐπιτροπῆς	τῆς	τῶν ἀρχιερέων		ἡμέρας	μέσης
and allowance	of the	the ruler priests		day	middle

2596 08	3598 3708	935	3771	5228 08
κατὰ τὴν ὁδὸν	εἶδον,	βασιλεῦ,	οὐρανόθεν	ὑπὲρ τὴν
by the way	I saw,	king,	from heaven	above the

2987	02	2246	4034	1473 5457
λαμπρότητα	τοῦ	ἡλίου	περιλάμψαν	με φῶς
brightness	of the	sun	having shone around me	light

2532 016	4862 1473 4198	14	3956 5037
καὶ τοὺς	σὺν ἐμοὶ πορευομένους.		πάντων τε
and the ones	with me traveling.		All and

2667	1473	1519 08	1093	191	5456
καταπεσόντων	ἡμῶν	εἰς τὴν	γῆν	ἤκουσα	φωνὴν
having fallen down	of us	to the	earth	I heard	sound

3004	4314 1473	07	1446	1258	4549
λέγουσαν	πρός με	τῇ	Ἑβραΐδι	διαλέκτῳ·	Σαοὺλ
saying	to me	in the	Hebrew	dialect;	Saul

4549	5101 1473 1377	4642	1473	4314
Σαούλ,	τί με διώκεις;	σκληρόν	σοι	πρός
Saul,	why me you pursue?	Hard	to you	toward

2759	2979	15	1473 1161	3004	5101 1510
κέντρα	λακτίζειν.		ἐγὼ δὲ	εἶπα·	τίς εἶ,
stings	to kick.		I but	said;	who are you,

2962	01	1161	2962	3004	1473 1510	2424	3739
κύριε;	ὁ	δὲ	κύριος	εἶπεν·	ἐγὼ εἰμι	Ἰησοῦς	ὃν
Master?	The	but	Master	said;	I am	Jesus	who

1473 1377	16	235	450	2532 2476	1909 016
σὺ διώκεις.		ἀλλὰ	ἀνάστηθι	καὶ στῆθι	ἐπὶ τοὺς
you pursue.		But	stand up	and stand	on the

4228 1473	1519 3778	1063 3708	1473
πόδας σου·	εἰς τοῦτο	γὰρ ὤφθην	σοι,
feet of you;	for this	for I was seen	to you,

4400	1473 5257	2532 3144	3739
προχειρίσασθαί	σε ὑπηρέτην	καὶ μάρτυρα	ὧν
I set hand before	you assistant	and testifier	of what

5037 3708	1473 3739	5037 3708	1473
τε εἶδές [με]	ὧν	τε ὀφθήσομαί	σοι,
both you saw me	of what	and I will make seen	to you,

17	1807	1473 1537 02	2992	2532 1537 022
	ἐξαιρούμενός	σε ἐκ τοῦ	λαοῦ	καὶ ἐκ τῶν
	lifting out	you from the	people	and from the

1484	1519 3739	1473 649	1473	18	455
ἐθνῶν	εἰς οὓς	ἐγὼ ἀποστέλλω	σε		ἀνοῖξαι
nations	for which	I delegate	you		to open

3788	846	010 1994	575	4655	1519
ὀφθαλμοὺς	αὐτῶν,	τοῦ ἐπιστρέψαι	ἀπὸ	σκότους	εἰς
eyes	of them,	the to return	from	dark	into

5457	2532 06	1849	02	4567	1909 04
φῶς	καὶ τῆς	ἐξουσίας	τοῦ	σατανᾶ	ἐπὶ τὸν
light	and the	authority	of the	adversary	on the

2316	010 2983	846	859	266	2532
θεόν,	τοῦ λαβεῖν	αὐτοὺς	ἄφεσιν	ἁμαρτιῶν	καὶ
God,	the to take	them	sending off	of sins	and

2819	1722 015	37	4102	07 1519 1473
κλῆρον ἐν	τοῖς	ἡγιασμένοις	πίστει	τῇ εἰς ἐμέ.
lot in	the	having been made holy	in trust	the in me.

19	3606	935	67	3756 1096
	Ὅθεν,	βασιλεῦ	Ἀγρίππα,	οὐκ ἐγενόμην
	From where,	king	Agrippa,	not I became

545   07   3770   3701   **20** 235   015
ἀπειθὴς   τῇ   οὐρανίῳ   ὀπτασίᾳ   ἀλλὰ τοῖς
disobedient to the heavenly vision   but   to the
1722 1154   4413   5037 2532   2414   3956
ἐν   Δαμασκῷ πρῶτόν τε   καὶ Ἱεροσολύμοις, πᾶσάν
in   Damascus first both and Jerusalem,   all
5037   08   5561   06   2449   2532 023   1484
τε   τὴν   χώραν   τῆς   Ἰουδαίας καὶ   τοῖς   ἔθνεσιν
indeed the   country of the Judea   and   to the nations
518   3340   2532 1994   1909 04
ἀπήγγελλον μετανοεῖν   καὶ ἐπιστρέφειν ἐπὶ τὸν
I was telling to change mind and to return   on   the
2316 514   06   3341   2041   4238
θεόν, ἄξια   τῆς   μετανοίας ἔργα πράσσοντας.
God, worthy of the change mind works practicing.
    1752   3778   1473 2453   4815
21 ἕνεκα   τούτων με   Ἰουδαῖοι συλλαβόμενοι
On account of these me   Judeans   having taken together
1510   1722 011 2411   3987   1315
[ὄντα] ἐν   τῷ ἱερῷ ἐπειρῶντο   διαχειρίσασθαι.
being in   the temple were pressing to handle
                                     thoroughly.
    1947   3767 5177   06   575   02   2316
22 ἐπικουρίας οὖν τυχὼν   τῆς ἀπὸ τοῦ θεοῦ
    Help   then having obtained the from the God
891   06   2250   3778   2476   3143   3398
ἄχρι τῆς ἡμέρας ταύτης ἕστηκα   μαρτυρόμενος μικρῷ
until the day   this I have stood testifying   small
5037 2532 3173   3762   1622   3004   3739 5037 013
τε καὶ μεγάλῳ οὐδὲν ἐκτὸς λέγων ὧν τε οἱ
both and great nothing outside saying what both the
4396   2980   3195   1096   2532 3475
προφῆται ἐλάλησαν μελλόντων γίνεσθαι καὶ Μωϋσῆς,
spokesmen spoke   being about to become and Moses,
    1487 3805   01   5547   1487 4413   1537
23 εἰ παθητὸς ὁ χριστός, εἰ πρῶτος ἐξ
    if suffering the Christ, if first out of
386   3498   5457 3195   2605   03
ἀναστάσεως νεκρῶν φῶς μέλλει καταγγέλλειν τῷ
standing up dead light is about to proclaim   to the
5037 2992 2532 023   1484   3778 1161 846
τε λαῷ καὶ τοῖς ἔθνεσιν. **24** Ταῦτα δὲ αὐτοῦ
both people and to the nations.   These but him
626   01   5347   3173   07 5456 5346
ἀπολογουμένου ὁ Φῆστος μεγάλῃ τῇ φωνῇ φησιν·
defending   the Festus in great the sound says,
3105   3972   021 4183   1473 1121   1519 3130
μαίνῃ, Παῦλε· τὰ πολλά σε γράμματα εἰς μανίαν
crazy, Paul; the many you letters   into craziness
4062   **25** 01 1161 3972   3756 3105   5346
περιτρέπει.   ὁ δὲ Παῦλος· οὐ μαίνομαι,   φησίν,
turns around.   The but Paul; not I am crazy, says,
2903   5347   235 225   2532 4997
κράτιστε Φῆστε, ἀλλὰ ἀληθείας καὶ σωφροσύνης
most strong Festus, but truth   and sobermindedness
4487   669   **26** 1987   1063 4012   3778
ῥήματα ἀποφθέγγομαι.   ἐπίσταται γὰρ περὶ τούτων
words   I speak off.   Understands for about these
01 935   4314 3739 2532 3955   2980
ὁ βασιλεὺς πρὸς ὃν καὶ παρρησιαζόμενος λαλῶ,
the king   to whom also being bold   I speak,
2990   1063 846   5100 3778   3756
λανθάνειν γὰρ αὐτὸν [τι] τούτων   οὐ
to escape notice for him some of these not
3982   3762   3756 1063 1510   1722 1137
πείθομαι οὐθέν· οὐ γάρ ἐστιν ἐν γωνίᾳ
I am persuaded nothing; not for it is+ in corner
4238   3778   **27** 4100   935
πεπραγμένον τοῦτο.   πιστεύεις, βασιλεῦ
+having been practiced this.   You trust, king

disobedient to the heavenly vision, [20]but declared first to those in Damascus, then in Jerusalem and throughout the countryside of Judea, and also to the Gentiles, that they should repent and turn to God and do deeds consistent with repentance. [21]For this reason the Jews seized me in the temple and tried to kill me. [22]To this day I have had help from God, and so I stand here, testifying to both small and great, saying nothing but what the prophets and Moses said would take place: [23]that the Messiah[a] must suffer, and that, by being the first to rise from the dead, he would proclaim light both to our people and to the Gentiles."

24 While he was making this defense, Festus exclaimed, "You are out of your mind, Paul! Too much learning is driving you insane!" [25]But Paul said, "I am not out of my mind, most excellent Festus, but I am speaking the sober truth. [26]Indeed the king knows about these things, and to him I speak freely; for I am certain that none of these things has escaped his notice, for this was not done in a corner. [27]King Agrippa, do you believe

_a_ Or the Christ

the prophets? I know that you believe." [28]Agrippa said to Paul, "Are you so quickly persuading me to become a Christian?"[a] [29]Paul replied, "Whether quickly or not, I pray to God that not only you but also all who are listening to me today might become such as I am—except for these chains."

30 Then the king got up, and with him the governor and Bernice and those who had been seated with them; [31]and as they were leaving, they said to one another, "This man is doing nothing to deserve death or imprisonment." [32]Agrippa said to Festus, "This man could have been set free if he had not appealed to the emperor."

CHAPTER 27

When it was decided that we were to sail for Italy, they transferred Paul and some other prisoners to a centurion of the Augustan Cohort, named Julius. [2]Embarking on a ship of Adramyttium that was about to set sail to the ports along the coast of Asia, we put to sea, accompanied by Aristarchus, a Macedonian from Thessalonica. [3]The next day we put in at Sidon; and Julius treated Paul kindly, and allowed him to go to his friends to be cared for.

a Or Quickly you will persuade me to play the Christian

67		015	4396		3609a	3754	4100	
Ἀγρίππα,		τοῖς	προφήταις;		οἶδα	ὅτι	πιστεύεις.	
Agrippa,		the	spokesmen?		I know	that	you trust.	

28
01	1161	67		4314	04	3972	1722	3641	1473
ὁ	δὲ	Ἀγρίππας		πρὸς	τὸν	Παῦλον·	ἐν	ὀλίγῳ	με
The	but	Agrippa		to	the	Paul;	in	few	me

3982		5546		4160		01	1161	3972
πείθεις		Χριστιανὸν		ποιῆσαι.	29	ὁ	δὲ	Παῦλος·
you persuade		Christian		to do.		The	but	Paul;

2172		302 03	2316	2532 1722	3641	2532	1722
εὐξαίμην		ἂν τῷ	θεῷ	καὶ ἐν	ὀλίγῳ	καὶ	ἐν
I may wish		- the	God	also in	few	also	in

3173	3756	3441	1473	235	2532	3956	016	191
μεγάλῳ	οὐ	μόνον	σὲ	ἀλλὰ καὶ	πάντας	τοὺς	ἀκούοντάς
great	not	alone	you	but also	all	the	hearing

1473	4594		1096		5108		3697		2532 1473
μου	σήμερον		γενέσθαι		τοιούτους		ὁποῖος		καὶ ἐγώ
me	today		to become		such ones		of what sort		also I

1510	3924		014	1199	3778		450		5037 01
εἰμι	παρεκτὸς		τῶν	δεσμῶν	τούτων.	30	Ἀνέστη		τε ὁ
am	except		the	chains	these.		Stood up		both the

935		2532 01	1232	05	5037 959		2532 013
βασιλεὺς		καὶ ὁ	ἡγεμὼν	ἥ	τε Βερνίκη		καὶ οἱ
king		and the	leader	the	both Bernice		and the

4775		846		2532 402
συγκαθήμενοι		αὐτοῖς,	31	καὶ ἀναχωρήσαντες
sitting together		to them,		and having departed

2980		4314 240		3004	3754
ἐλάλουν		πρὸς ἀλλήλους		λέγοντες	ὅτι
they were speaking		to one another		saying	that

3762	2288		2228 1199	514	5100 4238		01
οὐδὲν	θανάτου		ἢ δεσμῶν	ἄξιόν	[τι] πράσσει		ὁ
nothing	of death		or chains	worthy	some practices		the

444	3778		67	1161 03	5347	5346
ἄνθρωπος	οὗτος.	32	Ἀγρίππας	δὲ τῷ	Φήστῳ	ἔφη·
man	this.		Agrippa	but to the	Festus	said;

630		1410	01	444	3778	1487 3361
ἀπολελύσθαι		ἐδύνατο	ὁ	ἄνθρωπος	οὗτος	εἰ μὴ
to be loosed off		was able	the	man	this	except

1941		2541		5613 1161 2919
ἐπεκέκλητο		Καίσαρα.	27:1	Ὡς δὲ ἐκρίθη
he had called on		Caesar.		As but it was judged

010 636		1473 1519	08	2482	3860
τοῦ ἀποπλεῖν		ἡμᾶς εἰς	τὴν	Ἰταλίαν,	παρεδίδουν
the to sail off		us to	the	Italy,	they gave over

04	5037 3972	2532	5100	2087	1202
τόν	τε Παῦλον	καί	τινας	ἑτέρους	δεσμώτας
the	both Paul	and	some	others	prisoners

1543		3686	2457	4686	4575
ἑκατοντάρχη		ὀνόματι	Ἰουλίῳ	σπείρης	Σεβαστῆς.
to hundred ruler		in name	Julius	squadron	of Sebastus.

2
1910		1161	4143	98		3195
ἐπιβάντες		δὲ	πλοίῳ	Ἀδραμυττηνῷ		μέλλοντι
Having gone on		but	boat	Adramyttium		being about

4126	1519	016	2596	08	773	5117	321
πλεῖν	εἰς	τοὺς	κατὰ	τὴν	Ἀσίαν	τόπους	ἀνήχθημεν
to sail	to	the	by	the	Asia	places	we were led up

1510	4862 1473	708		3110	2331
ὄντος	σὺν ἡμῖν	Ἀριστάρχου		Μακεδόνος	Θεσσαλονικέως.
being	with us	Aristarchus		Macedonian	of Thessalonica.

3
07		5037 2087	2609		1519 4605
τῇ		τε ἑτέρᾳ	κατήχθημεν		εἰς Σιδῶνα,
In the		and other	we were led down		into Sidon,

5364		5037 01	2457	03	3972	5530
φιλανθρώπως		τε ὁ	Ἰούλιος	τῷ	Παύλῳ	χρησάμενος
loving men		and the	Julius	to the	Paul	having used

2010		4314 016	5384	4198		1958
ἐπέτρεψεν		πρὸς τοὺς	φίλους	πορευθέντι		ἐπιμελείας
allowed		to the	friends	having traveled		care

5177	**4**	2547	321	5284	08
τυχεῖν.		κἀκεῖθεν	ἀναχθέντες	ὑπεπλεύσαμεν	τὴν
to obtain.		And from there	having been led up	we sailed	under the

2954	1223	012	016	417	1510	1727
Κύπρον	διὰ	τὸ	τοὺς	ἀνέμους	εἶναι	ἐναντίους,
Cyprus	because	the	the	winds	to be	against,

	012	5037	3989	012	2596	08	2791	2532	3828
5	τό	τε	πέλαγος	τὸ	κατὰ	τὴν	Κιλικίαν	καὶ	Παμφυλίαν
	the	and	open	the	by	the	Cilicia	and	Pamphylia

1277	2718	1519	3460	06
διαπλεύσαντες	κατήλθομεν	εἰς	Μύρα	τῆς
having sailed through	we went down	to	Myra	of the

3073	**6**	2546	2147	01	1543
Λυκίας.		Κἀκεῖ	εὑρὼν	ὁ	ἑκατοντάρχης
Lucia.		And there	having found	the	hundred ruler

4143	222	4126	1519	08	2482
πλοῖον	Ἀλεξανδρῖνον	πλέον	εἰς	τὴν	Ἰταλίαν
boat	Alexandrian	sailing	to	the	Italy

1688	1473	1519	846	**7**	1722	2425	1161	2250
ἐνεβίβασεν	ἡμᾶς	εἰς	αὐτό.		ἐν	ἱκαναῖς	δὲ	ἡμέραις
he boarded	us	into	it.		In	enough	but	days

1020	2532	3433	1096	2596	08
βραδυπλοοῦντες	καὶ	μόλις	γενόμενοι	κατὰ	τὴν
sailing slowly	and	scarcely	having become	by	the

2834	3361	4330	1473	02	417
Κνίδον,	μὴ	προσεῶντος	ἡμᾶς	τοῦ	ἀνέμου
Cnidus,	not	allowing	toward us	the	wind

5284	08	2914	2596	4534	**8**	3433
ὑπεπλεύσαμεν	τὴν	Κρήτην	κατὰ	Σαλμώνην,		μόλις
we sailed under	the	Crete	by	Salmone,		scarcely

5037	3881	846	2064	1519	5117	5100
τε	παραλεγόμενοι	αὐτὴν	ἤλθομεν	εἰς	τόπον	τινὰ
and	coasting along	it	we went	into	place	some

2564	2570	3040	3739	1451	4172	1510
καλούμενον	Καλοὺς	λιμένας	ᾧ	ἐγγὺς	πόλις	ἦν
being called	Good	Harbors	to which	near	city	was

2996	**9**	2425	1161	5550	1230	2532
Λασαία.		Ἱκανοῦ	δὲ	χρόνου	διαγενομένου	καὶ
Lasea.		Enough	but	time	having become through	and

1510	2235	2000	02	4144	1223	012	2532
ὄντος	ἤδη	ἐπισφαλοῦς	τοῦ	πλοὸς	διὰ	τὸ	καὶ
being	already	unsecure	the	sailing	through	the	and

08	3521	2235	3928	3867
τὴν	νηστείαν	ἤδη	παρεληλυθέναι	παρῄνει
the	fasting	already	to have come along	was advising

01	3972	**10**	3004	846	435	2334	3754	3326
ὁ	Παῦλος		λέγων	αὐτοῖς·	ἄνδρες,	θεωρῶ	ὅτι	μετὰ
the	Paul		saying	to them;	men,	I watch	that	with

5196	2532	4183	2209	3756	3441	010	5413
ὕβρεως	καὶ	πολλῆς	ζημίας	οὐ	μόνον	τοῦ	φορτίου
abuse	and	much	loss	not	alone	of the	pack

2532	010	4143	235	2532	018	5590	1473
καὶ	τοῦ	πλοίου	ἀλλὰ	καὶ	τῶν	ψυχῶν	ἡμῶν
and	the	boat	but	also	of the	souls	of us

3195	1510	04	4144	**11**	01	1161	1543
μέλλειν	ἔσεσθαι	τὸν	πλοῦν.		ὁ	δὲ	ἑκατοντάρχης
to be about	to be	the	sailing.		The	but	hundred ruler

03	2942	2532	3490	3123	3982
τῷ	κυβερνήτῃ	καὶ	τῷ	ναυκλήρῳ	μᾶλλον	ἐπείθετο
to the helmsman		and	the	owner	more	was being persuaded

2228	023	5259	3972	3004	**12**	428	1161
ἢ	τοῖς	ὑπὸ	Παύλου	λεγομένοις.		ἀνευθέτου	δὲ
than	the	by	Paul	being said.		Unsuitable	but

02	3040	5225	4314	3915	013
τοῦ	λιμένος	ὑπάρχοντος	πρὸς	παραχειμασίαν	οἱ
the	harbor	existing	toward	wintering	along the

[4] Putting out to sea from there, we sailed under the lee of Cyprus, because the winds were against us. [5] After we had sailed across the sea that is off Cilicia and Pamphylia, we came to Myra in Lycia. [6] There the centurion found an Alexandrian ship bound for Italy and put us on board. [7] We sailed slowly for a number of days and arrived with difficulty off Cnidus, and as the wind was against us, we sailed under the lee of Crete off Salmone. [8] Sailing past it with difficulty, we came to a place called Fair Havens, near the city of Lasea.

[9] Since much time had been lost and sailing was now dangerous, because even the Fast had already gone by, Paul advised them, [10] saying, "Sirs, I can see that the voyage will be with danger and much heavy loss, not only of the cargo and the ship, but also of our lives." [11] But the centurion paid more attention to the pilot and to the owner of the ship than to what Paul said. [12] Since the harbor was not suitable for spending the winter,

the majority was in favor of putting to sea from there, on the chance that somehow they could reach Phoenix, where they could spend the winter. It was a harbor of Crete, facing southwest and northwest.

13 When a moderate south wind began to blow, they thought they could achieve their purpose; so they weighed anchor and began to sail past Crete, close to the shore. [14]But soon a violent wind, called the northeaster, rushed down from Crete.[a] [15]Since the ship was caught and could not be turned head-on into the wind, we gave way to it and were driven. [16]By running under the lee of a small island called Cauda[b] we were scarcely able to get the ship's boat under control. [17]After hoisting it up they took measures[c] to undergird the ship; then, fearing that they would run on the Syrtis, they lowered the sea anchor and so were driven. [18]We were being pounded by the storm so violently that on the next day they began to throw the cargo overboard, [19]and on the third day with their own hands they threw the ship's tackle overboard. [20]When neither sun nor stars appeared for many days, and no small tempest raged, all hope of our being saved was at last abandoned.

21 Since they had been without food

---

[a] Gk it
[b] Other ancient authorities read Clauda
[c] Gk helps

4183	5087	1012	321		1564		1487
πλείονες	ἔθεντο	βουλὴν	ἀναχθῆναι		ἐκεῖθεν,		εἴ
more	set	plan	to be led up		from there,		if

4458	1410		2658		1519	5405
πως	δύναιντο		καταντήσαντες		εἰς	Φοίνικα
how	they may be able		having arrived		in	Phoenix

3914		3040	06	2914	991	2596
παραχειμάσαι		λιμένα	τῆς	Κρήτης	βλέποντα	κατὰ
to winter		along harbor	of the	Crete	seeing	by

3047	2532	2596	5566	**13**	5285		1161
λίβα	καὶ	κατὰ	χῶρον.		Ὑποπνεύσαντος		δὲ
southwest	and	by	northwest.		Having blown by		but

3558	1380		06	4286		2902
νότου	δόξαντες		τῆς	προθέσεως		κεκρατηκέναι,
south	having thought		the	purpose		to have held,

142		788	3881			08	2914
ἄραντες		ἆσσον	παρελέγοντο			τὴν	Κρήτην.
having lifted up		close	they coasted along			the	Crete.

14	3326	3756	4183	1161	906	2596		846	417
	μετ'	οὐ	πολὺ	δὲ	ἔβαλεν	κατ'		αὐτῆς	ἄνεμος
	After	not	much	but	threw	against		it	wind

5189	01	2564		2146a
τυφωνικὸς	ὁ	καλούμενος		εὐρακύλων·
tempest	the	being called		northeast;

15	4884			1161	010	4143	2532	3361
	συναρπασθέντος			δὲ	τοῦ	πλοίου	καὶ	μὴ
	having been seized together			but	the	boat	and	not

1410	503		03	417	1929
δυναμένου	ἀντοφθαλμεῖν		τῷ	ἀνέμῳ	ἐπιδόντες
being able	to eye against		the	wind	having given on

5342	**16**	3519	1161	5100	5295		2564
ἐφερόμεθα.		νησίον	δέ	τι	ὑποδραμόντες		καλούμενον
we were being carried.		small island	but	some	having run under		being called

2737a	2480		3433		4031	1096
Καῦδα	ἰσχύσαμεν		μόλις		περικρατεῖς	γενέσθαι
Cauda	we strengthened		scarcely		in control	to become

06	4627	**17**	3739	142		996
τῆς	σκάφης,		ἣν	ἄραντες		βοηθείαις
the	small boat,		which	having lifted up in		helps

5530		5269		012	4143	5399
ἐχρῶντο		ὑποζωννύντες		τὸ	πλοῖον,	φοβούμενοί
they were using		belting under		the	boat,	fearing

5037	3361	1519	08	4950	1601	5465		012
τε	μὴ	εἰς	τὴν	Σύρτιν	ἐκπέσωσιν,	χαλάσαντες		τὸ
and	not	for	the	Syrtis	they might fall out,	having lowered		the

4632	3779	5342		**18**	4971		1161
σκεῦος,	οὕτως	ἐφέροντο.			σφοδρῶς		δὲ
pot,	thusly	they were carried.			Exceedingly		but

5492		1473	07	1836	1546		4160
χειμαζομένων		ἡμῶν	τῇ	ἐξῆς	ἐκβολὴν		ἐποιοῦντο
being tossed		us	the	next	throw out		they were making

19	2532	07		5154	849		08	4631	010
	καὶ	τῇ		τρίτῃ	αὐτόχειρες		τὴν	σκευὴν	τοῦ
	and	in the		third	own hands		the	tackling	of the

4143	4496		**20**	3383	1161	2246	3383	798
πλοίου	ἔρριψαν.			μήτε	δὲ	ἡλίου	μήτε	ἄστρων
boat	they flung.			Neither	but	sun	nor	stars

2014		1909	4183		2250	5494		5037	3756
ἐπιφαινόντων		ἐπὶ	πλείονας		ἡμέρας,	χειμῶνός		τε	οὐκ
appearing		on	more		days,	of winter		and	not

3641	1945		3062		4014	1680	3956
ὀλίγου	ἐπικειμένου,		λοιπὸν		περιῃρεῖτο	ἐλπὶς	πᾶσα
few	lying on,		remaining		was lifted up around	hope	all

010	4982		1473	**21**	4183	5037	776
τοῦ	σῴζεσθαι		ἡμᾶς.		Πολλῆς	τε	ἀσιτίας
the	to be delivered		us.		Much	and	abstinence

5225   5119 2476   01   3972   1722 3319
ὑπαρχούσης τότε σταθεὶς   ὁ Παῦλος ἐν μέσῳ
existing   then having stood the Paul in   middle

846   3004   1163   3303   5599 435
αὐτῶν εἶπεν· ἔδει   μέν,   ὦ ἄνδρες,
of them said; it was necessary indeed, o   men,

3980   1473 3361 321   575   06   2914
πειθαρχήσαντάς μοι μὴ ἀνάγεσθαι   ἀπὸ τῆς Κρήτης
having obeyed   me not to be led up from the Crete

2770   5037 08 5196   3778   2532 08   2209
κερδῆσαί τε τὴν ὕβριν ταύτην καὶ τὴν ζημίαν.
to gain both the abuse this and the loss.

      2532 024 3568 3867   1473 2114
22 καὶ τὰ νῦν παραινῶ ὑμᾶς εὐθυμεῖν·
    And the now I advise you to be cheerful;

580   1063 5590   3762   1510   1537 1473
ἀποβολὴ γὰρ ψυχῆς οὐδεμία ἔσται ἐξ ὑμῶν
throw off for of soul but not one will be from you

4133   010 4143   23 3936   1063 1473 3778 07
πλὴν τοῦ πλοίου.   παρέστη   γάρ μοι ταύτῃ τῇ
except the boat.   Stood along for to me this the

3571 02   2316 3739   1510 1473 3739   2532
νυκτὶ τοῦ θεοῦ, οὗ εἰμι [ἐγώ] ᾧ   καὶ
night of the God, of whom am I   to whom also

3000   32   3004   3361 5399   3972
λατρεύω, ἄγγελος 24 λέγων· μὴ φοβοῦ, Παῦλε,
I serve, messenger   saying; not fear, Paul,

2541   1473 1163   3936   2532
Καίσαρί σε δεῖ   παραστῆναι,   καὶ
to Caesar you it is necessary to stand along, and

2400 5483   1473   01 2316 3956   016 4126
ἰδοὺ κεχάρισταί σοι ὁ θεὸς πάντας τοὺς πλέοντας
look has favored to you the God all   the sailing

3326 1473 25 1352   2114   435   4100   1063
μετὰ σοῦ.   διὸ   εὐθυμεῖτε, ἄνδρες· πιστεύω γὰρ
with you.   Wherefore cheerful, men;   I trust for

03   2316 3754 3779   1510   2596 3739 5158
τῷ θεῷ ὅτι οὕτως ἔσται   καθ' ὃν   τρόπον
the God that thusly it will be by which manner

2980   1473   26 1519 3520 1161 5100
λελάληταί μοι.   εἰς νῆσον δέ τινα
it was spoken to me.   To island but some

1163   1473 1601   27   5613 1161
δεῖ   ἡμᾶς ἐκπεσεῖν.   Ὡς δὲ
it is necessary us   to fall out. As but

5065   3571 1096   1308
τεσσαρεσκαιδεκάτη νὺξ ἐγένετο διαφερομένων
four and ten   night became being carried through

1473 1722 03 99   2596 3319 06   3571
ἡμῶν ἐν τῷ Ἀδρίᾳ, κατὰ μέσον τῆς   νυκτὸς
us in the Adria, by middle of the night

5282   013 3492   4317   5100 846
ὑπενόουν   οἱ ναῦται προσάγειν τινὰ αὐτοῖς
were supposing the sailors to lead to some them

5561   28 2532 1001   2147   3712
χώραν.   καὶ βολίσαντες εὗρον   ὀργυιὰς
country.   And having sounded they found fathoms

1501   1024   1161 1339   2532 3825
εἴκοσι, βραχὺ δὲ διαστήσαντες καὶ πάλιν
twenty, little but having stood through and again

1001   2147   3712   1178
βολίσαντες εὗρον ὀργυιὰς δεκαπέντε·
having sounded they found fathoms fifteen;

   5399   5037 3361 4225 2596 5138   5117
29 φοβούμενοί τε μὴ που κατὰ τραχεῖς τόπους
   fearing   but not where by rough   places

1601   1537 4403   4496   45
ἐκπέσωμεν, ἐκ πρύμνης ῥίψαντες ἀγκύρας
we might fall out, from stern having flung anchors

for a long time, Paul then stood up among them and said, "Men, you should have listened to me and not have set sail from Crete and thereby avoided this damage and loss. ²²I urge you now to keep up your courage, for there will be no loss of life among you, but only of the ship. ²³For last night there stood by me an angel of the God to whom I belong and whom I worship, ²⁴and he said, 'Do not be afraid, Paul; you must stand before the emperor; and indeed, God has granted safety to all those who are sailing with you.' ²⁵So keep up your courage, men, for I have faith in God that it will be exactly as I have been told. ²⁶But we will have to run aground on some island."

27 When the fourteenth night had come, as we were drifting across the sea of Adria, about midnight the sailors suspected that they were nearing land. ²⁸So they took soundings and found twenty fathoms; a little farther on they took soundings again and found fifteen fathoms. ²⁹Fearing that we might run on the rocks, they let down four anchors from the stern

and prayed for day to come. ³⁰But when the sailors tried to escape from the ship and had lowered the boat into the sea, on the pretext of putting out anchors from the bow, ³¹Paul said to the centurion and the soldiers, "Unless these men stay in the ship, you cannot be saved." ³²Then the soldiers cut away the ropes of the boat and set it adrift.

33 Just before daybreak, Paul urged all of them to take some food, saying, "Today is the fourteenth day that you have been in suspense and remaining without food, having eaten nothing. ³⁴Therefore I urge you to take some food, for it will help you survive; for none of you will lose a hair from your heads." ³⁵After he had said this, he took bread; and giving thanks to God in the presence of all, he broke it and began to eat. ³⁶Then all of them were encouraged and took food for themselves. ³⁷(We were in all two hundred seventy-six[a] persons in the ship.) ³⁸After they had satisfied their hunger, they lightened the ship

[a] Other ancient authorities read seventy-six; others, about seventy-six

5064	2172		2250	1096	**30**	014
τέσσαρας	ηὔχοντο		ἡμέραν	γενέσθαι.		Τῶν
four	they were wishing		day	to become.		Of the

1161	3492	2212	5343	1537	010	4143	2532
δὲ	ναυτῶν	ζητούντων	φυγεῖν	ἐκ	τοῦ πλοίου	καὶ
but	sailors	seeking	to flee	from	the boat	and

5465		08	4627		1519	08	2281
χαλασάντων		τὴν	σκάφην		εἰς	τὴν	θάλασσαν
having lowered		the	small boat		into	the	sea

4392		5613	1537	4408	45		3195
προφάσει		ὡς	ἐκ	πρῴρης	ἀγκύρας		μελλόντων
in pretext		as	from	bow	anchors		being about

1614		3004	01	3972	03		1543
ἐκτείνειν,	**31**	εἶπεν	ὁ	Παῦλος	τῷ		ἑκατοντάρχῃ
to stretch out,		said	the	Paul	to the		hundred ruler

2532	015	4757		1437	3361	3778	3306		1722
καὶ	τοῖς	στρατιώταις·		ἐὰν	μὴ	οὗτοι	μείνωσιν		ἐν
and	the	soldiers;		if	not	these	might stay		in

011	4143	1473	4982			3756	1410	**32**	5119
τῷ	πλοίῳ,	ὑμεῖς	σωθῆναι			οὐ	δύνασθε.		τότε
the boat,		you	to be delivered			not	are able.		Then

609		013	4757		024	4979		06
ἀπέκοψαν		οἱ	στρατιῶται		τὰ	σχοινία		τῆς
having cut off		the	soldiers		the	small cords		of the

4627		2532	1439		846	1601	**33**	891
σκάφης		καὶ	εἴασαν		αὐτὴν	ἐκπεσεῖν.		Ἄχρι
small boat		and	allowed		it	to fall out.		Until

1161	3739	2250	3195			1096			3870
δὲ	οὗ	ἡμέρα	ἤμελλεν			γίνεσθαι,			παρεκάλει
but	what	day	it was about to become,						was encouraging

01	3972	537		3335		5160		3004
ὁ	Παῦλος	ἅπαντας		μεταλαβεῖν		τροφῆς		λέγων·
the	Paul	all		to take with		food		saying,

5065		4594	2250		4328
τεσσαρεσκαιδεκάτην		σήμερον	ἡμέραν		προσδοκῶντες
four and ten		today	day		waiting expectantly

777		1300		3367		4355
ἄσιτοι		διατελεῖτε		μηθὲν		προσλαβόμενοι.
abstaining		you continued		nothing		to take to.

34	1352		3870		1473	3335		5160
	διὸ		παρακαλῶ		ὑμᾶς	μεταλαβεῖν		τροφῆς·
	Wherefore		I encourage		you	to take with		food;

3778	1063	4314	06	5212		4991		5225
τοῦτο	γὰρ	πρὸς	τῆς	ὑμετέρας		σωτηρίας		ὑπάρχει,
this	for	to	the	your		deliverance		exists,

3762		1063	1473	2359	575	06		2776
οὐδενὸς		γὰρ	ὑμῶν	θρὶξ	ἀπὸ	τῆς		κεφαλῆς
no one		for	of you	hair	from	the		head

622				**35**	3004		1161	3778	2532
ἀπολεῖται.					εἴπας		δὲ	ταῦτα	καὶ
will be destroyed.					Having said		but	these	and

2983		740	2168			03		2316
λαβὼν		ἄρτον	εὐχαρίστησεν			τῷ		θεῷ
having taken		bread	he gave good favor			to the		God

1799	3956	2532	2806		757		2068
ἐνώπιον	πάντων	καὶ	κλάσας		ἤρξατο		ἐσθίειν.
before	all	and	having broken		he began		to eat.

36	2115		1161	1096		3956		2532	846
	εὔθυμοι		δὲ	γενόμενοι		πάντες		καὶ	αὐτοὶ
	Cheerful		but	having become		all		and	themselves

4355			5160	**37**	1510	1161	017	3956	5590	1722
προσελάβοντο			τροφῆς.		ἤμεθα	δὲ	αἱ	πᾶσαι	ψυχαὶ	ἐν
took to			food.		Were	but	the	all	souls	in

011	4143	1250		1440		1803	**38**	2880
τῷ	πλοίῳ	διακόσιαι		ἑβδομήκοντα		ἕξ.		κορεσθέντες
the boat		two hundred		seventy		six.		Having been made full

1161	5160	2893			012	4143
δὲ	τροφῆς	ἐκούφιζον			τὸ	πλοῖον
but	food	they were lightening			the	boat

```
1544              04    4621   1519  08   2281        39   3753
ἐκβαλλόμενοι  τὸν σῖτον εἰς  τὴν θάλασσαν.         "Οτε
throwing out the wheat into the sea.              When

1161  2250    1096      08   1093 3756 1921
δὲ   ἡμέρα ἐγένετο,  τὴν γῆν  οὐκ ἐπεγίνωσκον,
but  day    became,  the earth not they were perceiving,

2859    1161 5100 2657                          2192
κόλπον  δέ  τινα κατενόουν               ἔχοντα
lap     but  some they were thinking carefully having

123       1519 3739 1011                1487
αἰγιαλὸν εἰς  ὃν   ἐβουλεύοντο          εἰ
shore    to   which they were planning if

1410           1856       012 4143       40  2532
δύναιντο       ἐξῶσαι     τὸ πλοῖον.          καὶ
they may be able to push out the boat.         And

020 45         4014          1439        1519  08  2281
τὰς ἀγκύρας περιελόντες  εἴων      εἰς  τὴν θάλασσαν,
the anchors having lifted they were to    the sea,
            up around     allowing

260           447         020 2202      022     4079
ἅμα        ἀνέντες    τὰς ζευκτηρίας τῶν   πηδαλίων
at same time having left the bands     of the rudders

2532 1869               04  736    07    4154
καὶ ἐπάραντες          τὸν ἀρτέμωνα τῇ  πνεούσῃ
and  having lifted up on the sail   to the blowing

2722            1519 04 123        41  4045
κατεῖχον     εἰς  τὸν αἰγιαλόν.       περιπεσόντες
they held by to   the shore.           Having fallen around

1161  1519 5117    1337       1945a      08   3491
δὲ   εἰς  τόπον διθάλασσον ἐπέκειλαν    τὴν ναῦν
but  into place  two seas   they grounded the ship

2532 05   3303       4408   2043       3306
καὶ ἡ  μὲν     πρῷρα ἐρείσασα   ἔμεινεν
and the indeed bow        having stuck it stayed

761        05   1161 4403   3089       5269 06
ἀσάλευτος, ἡ  δὲ  πρύμνα ἐλύετο   ὑπὸ τῆς
unshakeable, the but stern  was loosed by   the

970     022    2949      42  014 1161 4757        1012
βίας  [τῶν  κυμάτων].       Τῶν δὲ  στρατιωτῶν βουλὴ
violence of the waves.      The but  soldiers    plan

1096    2443 016 1202     615              3361
ἐγένετο ἵνα τοὺς δεσμώτας ἀποκτείνωσιν,   μή
became that the prisoners might be killed, not

5100 1579      1309          43  01  1161
τις ἐκκολυμβήσας διαφύγῃ.        ὁ  δὲ
some having swum out might flee away. The but

1543           1014        1295                04
ἑκατοντάρχης βουλόμενος διασῶσαι              τὸν
hundred ruler  planning  to deliver thoroughly the

3972   2967    846   010 1013      2753
Παῦλον ἐκώλυσεν αὐτοὺς τοῦ βουλήματος, ἐκέλευσέν
Paul    hindered them    the plan,     he commanded

5037 016   1410       2860      641            4413
τε  τοὺς δυναμένους κολυμβᾶν ἀπορίψαντας  πρώτους
and the being able to swim   having flung off first

1909 08  1093   1826     44  2532 016  3062      3739
ἐπὶ τὴν γῆν  ἐξιέναι        καὶ τοὺς λοιποὺς  οὓς
on  the earth to go out      and the remaining who

3303   1909 4548     3739 1161 1909 5100 022     575
μὲν ἐπὶ σανίσιν, οὓς δὲ ἐπί  τινων τῶν    ἀπὸ
indeed on boards, who but on  some of the from

010 4143    2532 3779  1096     3956
τοῦ πλοίου. καὶ οὕτως ἐγένετο πάντας
the boat.  And thusly it became all

1295                        1909 08  1093    28:1  2532
διασωθῆναι                 ἐπὶ τὴν γῆν.          Καὶ
to be delivered thoroughly on  the earth.        And

1295                               5119 1921
διασωθέντες                       τότε ἐπέγνωμεν
having been thoroughly delivered then we perceived
```

39 In the morning they did not recognize the land, but they noticed a bay with a beach, on which they planned to run the ship ashore, if they could. 40So they cast off the anchors and left them in the sea. At the same time they loosened the ropes that tied the steering-oars; then hoisting the foresail to the wind, they made for the beach. 41But striking a reef,[a] they ran the ship aground; the bow stuck and remained immovable, but the stern was being broken up by the force of the waves. 42The soldiers' plan was to kill the prisoners, so that none might swim away and escape; 43but the centurion, wishing to save Paul, kept them from carrying out their plan. He ordered those who could swim to jump overboard first and make for the land, 44and the rest to follow, some on planks and others on pieces of the ship. And so it was that all were brought safely to land.

CHAPTER 28

After we had reached safety, we then learned

[a] Gk place of two seas

that the island was called Malta. ²The natives showed us unusual kindness. Since it had begun to rain and was cold, they kindled a fire and welcomed all of us around it. ³Paul had gathered a bundle of brushwood and was putting it on the fire, when a viper, driven out by the heat, fastened itself on his hand. ⁴When the natives saw the creature hanging from his hand, they said to one another, "This man must be a murderer; though he has escaped from the sea, justice has not allowed him to live." ⁵He, however, shook off the creature into the fire and suffered no harm. ⁶They were expecting him to swell up or drop dead, but after they had waited a long time and saw that nothing unusual had happened to him, they changed their minds and began to say that he was a god.

7 Now in the neighborhood of that place were lands belonging to the leading man of the island, named Publius, who received us and entertained us hospitably for three days. ⁸It so happened that the father

3754	3194	05	3520	2564		013	5037	915
ὅτι	Μελίτη	ἡ	νῆσος	καλεῖται.	2	οἵ	τε	βάρβαροι
that	Melita	the	island	is called.		The	but	barbarians

3930		3756	08	5177		5363		1473
παρεῖχον		οὐ		τὴν τυχοῦσαν		φιλανθρωπίαν		ἡμῖν,
held along		not		the having obtained		love of man		to us,

681		1063	4443	4355		3956	1473	1223
ἅψαντες		γὰρ	πυρὰν	προσελάβοντο		πάντας	ἡμᾶς	διὰ
having lit		for	fire	they took		to all	us	because

04	5205	04	2186		2532	1223	012	5592
τὸν	ὑετὸν	τὸν	ἐφεστῶτα		καὶ	διὰ	τὸ	ψῦχος.
the	rain	the	having stood on		and	because	the	cold.

	4962		1161	02	3972	5434
3	Συστρέψαντος		δὲ		τοῦ Παύλου	φρυγάνων
	Having turned together		but		the Paul	stick bundle

5100	4128		2532	2007		1909	08	4443
τι	πλῆθος		καὶ	ἐπιθέντος		ἐπὶ	τὴν	πυράν,
some	quantity		and	having set on		on	the	fire,

2191	575	06	2329	1831		2510	06	5495
ἔχιδνα	ἀπὸ	τῆς	θέρμης	ἐξελθοῦσα		καθῆψεν	τῆς	χειρὸς
poison	from	the	heat	having		touched	the	hand
snake				come out		onto		

846		5613	1161	3708	013	915		2910
αὐτοῦ.	4	ὡς	δὲ	εἶδον	οἱ	βάρβαροι		κρεμάμενον
of him.		As	but	saw	the	barbarians		hanging

012	2342		1537	06	5495	846		4314
τὸ	θηρίον		ἐκ	τῆς	χειρὸς	αὐτοῦ,		πρὸς
the	wild animal		from	the	hand	of him,		toward

240		3004		3843		5406		1510	01
ἀλλήλους		ἔλεγον·		πάντως		φονεύς		ἐστιν	ὁ
one another		were saying;		altogether		murderer		is	the

444		3778	3739	1295
ἄνθρωπος		οὗτος	ὃν	διασωθέντα
man		this	who	having been thoroughly delivered

1537	06	2281		05	1349	2198	3756	1439		5	01
ἐκ	τῆς	θαλάσσης		ἡ	δίκη	ζῆν	οὐκ	εἴασεν.		5	ὁ
from	the	sea		the	right	to live	not	allowed.			The

3303	3767	660		012	2342		1519
μὲν	οὖν	ἀποτινάξας		τὸ	θηρίον		εἰς
but	then	having shaken off		the	wild animal		into

012	4442	3958		3762	2556		013	1161
τὸ	πῦρ	ἔπαθεν		οὐδὲν	κακόν,	6	οἱ	δὲ
the	fire	he suffered		nothing	bad,		the	but

4328		846	3195		4092a
προσεδόκων		αὐτὸν	μέλλειν		πίμπρασθαι
waiting expectantly		him	to be about		to be swollen

2228	2667		869		3498	1909	4183	1161
ἢ	καταπίπτειν		ἄφνω		νεκρόν.	ἐπὶ	πολὺ	δὲ
or	to fall down		suddenly		dead.	On	much	but

846	4328		2532	2334		3367
αὐτῶν	προσδοκώντων		καὶ	θεωρούντων		μηδὲν
them	waiting expectantly		and	watching		nothing

824		1519	846	1096		3328
ἄτοπον		εἰς	αὐτὸν	γινόμενον		μεταβαλόμενοι
out of place		in	him	becoming		having thrown with

3004		846	1510	2316		1722	1161	023
ἔλεγον		αὐτὸν	εἶναι	θεόν.	7	Ἐν	δὲ	τοῖς
they were saying		him	to be God.			In	but	the

4012	04	5117	1565	5225		5564
περὶ	τὸν	τόπον	ἐκεῖνον	ὑπῆρχεν		χωρία
around	the	place	that	was existing		small fields

03		4413	06	3520	3686	4196		3739
τῷ		πρώτῳ	τῆς	νήσου	ὀνόματι	Ποπλίῳ,		ὃς
to the		first	of the	island	in name	Poplius,		who

324		1473	5140	2250	5390
ἀναδεξάμενος		ἡμᾶς	τρεῖς	ἡμέρας	φιλοφρόνως
having welcomed again		us	three	days	loving-mindedly

3579		1096	1161	04	3962
ἐξένισεν.	8	ἐγένετο	δὲ	τὸν	πατέρα
he entertained as a stranger.		It became	but	the	father

```
02      4196      4446      2532   1420         4912
τοῦ    Ποπλίου  πυρετοῖς  καὶ  δυσεντερίῳ  συνεχόμενον
of the  Poplius   fevers    and  dysentery   holding together
2621                    4314  3739  01   3972    1525              2532
κατακεῖσθαι,  πρὸς  ὃν   ὁ   Παῦλος  εἰσελθὼν          καὶ
to lie down,   to   whom the  Paul    having come in  and
4336               2007           020    5495    846    2390
προσευξάμενος  ἐπιθεὶς     τὰς  χεῖρας  αὐτῷ  ἰάσατο
having prayed   having set on the  hands   to him  cured
846       3778     1161   1096          2532  013  3062
αὐτόν.  ⁹ τούτου  δὲ   γενομένου   καὶ  οἱ  λοιποὶ
him.      This    but  having become and  the remaining
013 1722  07  3520    2192      769         4334
οἱ   ἐν   τῇ  νήσῳ  ἔχοντες  ἀσθενείας  προσήρχοντο
the  in   the island having   weaknesses  were coming to
2532 2323                       3739 2532  4183      5092
καὶ  ἐθεραπεύοντο,   ¹⁰ οἳ   καὶ  πολλαῖς  τιμαῖς
and   they were being healed, who   also  in many   values
5091       1473 2532 321        2007          024  4314
ἐτίμησαν  ἡμᾶς καὶ  ἀναγομένοις  ἐπέθεντο  τὰ  πρὸς
valued     us   and  being led up  they set on the to
020  5532          3326  1161  5140    3376    321
τὰς  χρείας.  ¹¹ Μετὰ  δὲ  τρεῖς  μῆνας  ἀνήχθημεν
the  needs.     After  but  three  months  we were led up
1722 4143      3914               1722  07   3520
ἐν  πλοίῳ  παρακεχειμακότι    ἐν   τῇ  νήσῳ,
in   boat   having wintered along in   the  island,
222              3902        1359          2532
Ἀλεξανδρίνῳ, παρασήμῳ  Διοσκούροις.  ¹² καὶ
Alexandrian,  signed by  Dioscuri.       And
2609              1519 4946       1961
καταχθέντες   εἰς  Συρακούσας  ἐπεμείναμεν
having been led down to  Syracuse    we stayed on
2250   5140        3606         4014
ἡμέρας  τρεῖς,  ¹³ ὅθεν    περιελόντες
days    three,     from where having lifted up around
2658           1519  4484     2532 3326  1520 2250
κατηντήσαμεν  εἰς  Ῥήγιον.  καὶ  μετὰ  μίαν ἡμέραν
we arrived     in   Rhegium.  And  after  one  day
1920            3558  1206       2064       1519
ἐπιγενομένου  νότου δευτεραῖοι  ἤλθομεν  εἰς
having become  on south second     we came to
4223             3757   2147      80
Ποτιόλους,  ¹⁴ οὗ    εὑρόντες  ἀδελφοὺς
Potioli,       where  having found brothers
3870             3844  846    1961
παρεκλήθημεν   παρ' αὐτοῖς  ἐπιμεῖναι
we were encouraged by   them   to stay on
2250    5140      2532 3779    1519 08   4516  2064
ἡμέρας  ἐπτά·  καὶ  οὕτως  εἰς  τὴν  Ῥώμην ἤλθαμεν.
days    seven;  and  thusly  to   the   Rome   we came.
    2547             013 80         191          024  4012
¹⁵ κἀκεῖθεν       οἱ  ἀδελφοὶ  ἀκούσαντες  τὰ  περὶ
   And from there the  brothers  having heard  the about
1473 2064  1519 529       1473   891     675      5410  2532
ἡμῶν ἦλθαν εἰς ἀπάντησιν ἡμῖν ἄχρι Ἀππίου φόρου καὶ
us   came  to   meeting   us   until Appius  Forum and
5140  4999       3739 3708   01  3972     2168
Τριῶν ταβερνῶν, οὓς  ἰδὼν   ὁ  Παῦλος εὐχαριστήσας
Three Taverns,  whom having  the  Paul   having given
                 seen                    good favor
03     2316 2983   2294      3753 1161 1525           1519
τῷ    θεῷ  ἔλαβε θάρσος. ¹⁶ Ὅτε  δὲ  εἰσήλθομεν εἰς
to the God  take  courage.   When but  we went in  into
4516      2010           03      3972    3306   2596 1438
Ῥώμην, ἐπετράπη        τῷ    Παύλῳ  μένειν καθ' ἑαυτὸν
Rome,   it was allowed  to the  Paul   to stay by himself
4862 03  5442        846     4757            1096       1161
σὺν  τῷ  φυλάσσοντι αὐτὸν στρατιώτῃ. ¹⁷ Ἐγένετο   δὲ
with  the  guarding   him   soldier.      It became but
```

of Publius lay sick in bed with fever and dysentery. Paul visited him and cured him by praying and putting his hands on him. ⁹After this happened, the rest of the people on the island who had diseases also came and were cured. ¹⁰They bestowed many honors on us, and when we were about to sail, they put on board all the provisions we needed.

11 Three months later we set sail on a ship that had wintered at the island, an Alexandrian ship with the Twin Brothers as its figurehead. ¹²We put in at Syracuse and stayed there for three days; ¹³then we weighed anchor and came to Rhegium. After one day there a south wind sprang up, and on the second day we came to Puteoli. ¹⁴There we found believers[a] and were invited to stay with them for seven days. And so we came to Rome. ¹⁵The believers[a] from there, when they heard of us, came as far as the Forum of Appius and Three Taverns to meet us. On seeing them, Paul thanked God and took courage.

16 When we came into Rome, Paul was allowed to live by himself, with the soldier who was guarding him.

17 Three days later

---

[a] Gk brothers

he called together the local leaders of the Jews. When they had assembled, he said to them, "Brothers, though I had done nothing against our people or the customs of our ancestors, yet I was arrested in Jerusalem and handed over to the Romans. [18]When they had examined me, the Romans[a] wanted to release me, because there was no reason for the death penalty in my case. [19]But when the Jews objected, I was compelled to appeal to the emperor—even though I had no charge to bring against my nation. [20]For this reason therefore I have asked to see you and speak with you,[b] since it is for the sake of the hope of Israel that I am bound with this chain." [21]They replied, "We have received no letters from Judea about you, and none of the brothers coming here has reported or spoken anything evil about you. [22]But we would like to hear from you what you think, for with regard to this sect we know that everywhere it is spoken against."

23 After they had set a day to meet with him, they came to him at his lodgings in great numbers. From morning until evening he explained the matter to them, testifying to the kingdom of God

a Gk they
b Or I have asked you to see me and speak with me

3326	2250	5140	4779		846	016
μετὰ	ἡμέρας	τρεῖς	συγκαλέσασθαι		αὐτὸν	τοὺς
after	days	three	to be called together		him	the ones

1510 014　2453　4413　4905
ὄντας τῶν Ἰουδαίων πρώτους· συνελθόντων
being of the Judeans first; having come together

1161 846　3004　　4314 846　1473 435
δὲ αὐτῶν ἔλεγεν πρὸς αὐτούς· ἐγώ, ἄνδρες
but them he was saying to them; I, men

80　3762　1727　4160　03　2992
ἀδελφοί, οὐδὲν ἐναντίον ποιήσας τῷ λαῷ
brothers, nothing against having done to the people

2228 023　1485　023 3971　1198　1537
ἢ τοῖς ἔθεσι τοῖς πατρῴοις δέσμιος ἐξ
or to the customs the fathers prisoner from

2414　3860　1519 020 5495　014
Ἱεροσολύμων παρεδόθην εἰς τὰς χεῖρας τῶν
Jerusalem I was given over into the hands of the

4514 3748　350　1473 1014
Ῥωμαίων, [18] οἵτινες ἀνακρίναντές με ἐβούλοντο
Romans, who having examined me were planning

630　1223　012 3367　156　2288
ἀπολῦσαι διὰ τὸ μηδεμίαν αἰτίαν θανάτου
to loose off because the but not one cause of death

5225　1722 1473 [19] 483　1161 014
ὑπάρχειν ἐν ἐμοί. ἀντιλεγόντων δὲ τῶν
to exist in me speaking against but the

2453　315　1941　2541　3756
Ἰουδαίων ἠναγκάσθην ἐπικαλέσασθαι Καίσαρα οὐχ
Judeans I was compelled to call on Caesar not

5613 010 1484　1473 2192　5100 2723　[20] 1223
ὡς τοῦ ἔθνους μου ἔχων τι κατηγορεῖν. διὰ
as the nation of me having some to accuse. Through

3778　3767 08　156　3870　1473 3708　2532
ταύτην οὖν τὴν αἰτίαν παρεκάλεσα ὑμᾶς ἰδεῖν καὶ
this then the cause I encouraged you to see and

4354　1511a　1063 06 1680　02
προσλαλῆσαι, ἕνεκεν γὰρ τῆς ἐλπίδος ιοῦ
to speak to, on account of for the hope of the

2474　08　254　3778　4029　[21] 013 1161 4314
Ἰσραὴλ τὴν ἅλυσιν ταύτην περίκειμαι. οἱ δὲ πρὸς
Israel the chain this is set around. The but to

846　3004　1473 3777　1121　4012 1473
αὐτὸν εἶπαν· ἡμεῖς οὔτε γράμματα περὶ σοῦ
him said; we neither letters about you

1209　575 06　2449　3777 3854　5100
ἐδεξάμεθα ἀπὸ τῆς Ἰουδαίας οὔτε παραγενόμενός τις
welcomed from the Judea nor having arrived some

014　80　518　2228 2980　5100 4012
τῶν ἀδελφῶν ἀπήγγειλεν ἢ ἐλάλησέν τι περὶ
of the brothers told or spoke some about

1473 4190　[22] 515　1161 3844 1473 191
σοῦ πονηρόν. ἀξιοῦμεν δὲ παρὰ σοῦ ἀκοῦσαι
you evil. We think worthy but from you to hear

3739 5426　4012 3303 1063 06 139　3778
ἃ φρονεῖς, περὶ μὲν γὰρ τῆς αἱρέσεως ταύτης
what you think, about indeed for the sect this

1110　1473 1510 3754 3837　483
γνωστὸν ἡμῖν ἐστιν ὅτι πανταχοῦ ἀντιλέγεται.
known to us is that all places it is spoken against.

[23] 5021　1161 846 2250 2064 4314 846
Ταξάμενοι δὲ αὐτῷ ἡμέραν ἦλθον πρὸς αὐτὸν
Having set in order but him day came to him

1519 08 3578　4183　3739　1620
εἰς τὴν ξενίαν πλείονες οἷς ἐξετίθετο
in the stranger's room more to whom he set out

1263　08 932　02　2316
διαμαρτυρόμενος τὴν βασιλείαν τοῦ θεοῦ,
testifying thoroughly the kingdom of the God,

3982		5037	846		4012	02	2424	575	5037	02

πείθων   τε   αὐτοὺς περὶ τοῦ ᾽Ιησοῦ ἀπό τε   τοῦ
persuading and   them   about the Jesus from both the

3551	3475		2532	014	4396		575	4404		2193

νόμου Μωϋσέως καὶ τῶν προφητῶν, ἀπὸ πρωῒ   ἕως
law   of Moses and the spokesmen, from morning until

2073		**24**	2532	013	3303	3982		023

ἑσπέρας. **24** καὶ οἱ μὲν ἐπείθοντο   τοῖς
evening.   And the but were being persuaded in the

3004		013		1161	569		**25**	800

λεγομένοις, οἱ   δὲ ἠπίστουν·   **25** ἀσύμφωνοι
sayings,   the ones but were untrusting;   disagreement

1161	1510	4314	240		630		3004		02

δὲ ὄντες πρὸς ἀλλήλους ἀπελύοντο εἰπόντος   τοῦ
but being to   one another they were having said the
                                     loosed off

3972	4487	1520	3754	2573	09	4151	09	40

Παύλου ῥῆμα ἕν, ὅτι καλῶς τὸ πνεῦμα τὸ ἅγιον
Paul   word one, that well the spirit the holy

2980		1223		2268	02	4396		4314	016

ἐλάλησεν διὰ   ᾽Ησαΐου τοῦ προφήτου πρὸς τοὺς
spoke   through Isaiah the spokesman to   the

3962	1473	**26**	3004		4198	4314	04	2992

πατέρας ὑμῶν **26** λέγων· πορεύθητι πρὸς τὸν λαὸν
fathers of you   saying· travel   to   the people

3778	2532	3004	189		191		2532	3756	3361

τοῦτον καὶ εἰπόν· ἀκοῇ ἀκούσετε   καὶ οὐ μὴ
this   and say; hearing you will hear and not not

4920			2532	991		991		2532

συνῆτε   καὶ βλέποντες βλέψετε   καὶ
you might understand and seeing   you will see and

3756	3361	3708		**27**	3975		1063	05	2588

οὐ μὴ ἴδητε·   **27** ἐπαχύνθη   γὰρ ἡ καρδία
not not you might see;   was thickened for the heart

02	2992	3778	2532	023	3775	917	191	

τοῦ λαοῦ τούτου καὶ τοῖς ὠσὶν βαρέως ἤκουσαν
of the people this also in the ears heavily they heard

2532	016	3788		846		2576		3379

καὶ τοὺς ὀφθαλμοὺς αὐτῶν ἐκάμμυσαν· μήποτε
and the eyes   of them they shut; not then

3708		015	3788		2532	023	3775

ἴδωσιν   τοῖς ὀφθαλμοῖς καὶ τοῖς ὠσὶν
they might see in the eyes   and in the ears

191		2532	07	2588	4920			2532

ἀκούσωσιν καὶ τῇ καρδίᾳ συνῶσιν   καὶ
might hear and in the heart they might understand and

1994		2532	2390		846	**28**	1110	3767

ἐπιστρέψωσιν, καὶ ἰάσομαι   αὐτούς. **28** γνωστὸν οὖν
might return, and I will cure them.   Known   then

1510	1473	3754	023	1484		649		3778

ἔστω ὑμῖν ὅτι τοῖς ἔθνεσιν ἀπεστάλη   τοῦτο
let be to you that in the nations was delegated this

09	4992		02	2316	846		2532

τὸ σωτήριον τοῦ θεοῦ· αὐτοὶ   καὶ
the deliverance of the God; themselves also

191	**30**	1696		1161	1333		3650	1722

ἀκούσονται. **30** ᾽Ενέμεινεν   δὲ διετίαν ὅλην ἐν
will hear.   He stayed in but two years whole in

2398	3410		2532	588		3956	016

ἰδίῳ μισθώματι καὶ ἀπεδέχετο   πάντας τοὺς
own hired place and thoroughly welcomed all   the

1531		4314	846	**31**	2784		08	932

εἰσπορευομένους πρὸς αὐτόν, **31** κηρύσσων τὴν βασιλείαν
traveling into   to   him,   announcing the kingdom

02		2316	2532	1321		024	4012	02	2962	2424

τοῦ θεοῦ καὶ διδάσκων τὰ περὶ τοῦ κυρίου ᾽Ιησοῦ
of the God and teaching the about the Master Jesus

5547		3326	3956	3954		209

Χριστοῦ μετὰ πάσης παρρησίας ἀκωλύτως.
Christ   with all   boldness   unhinderedly.

and trying to convince them about Jesus both from the law of Moses and from the prophets. [24]Some were convinced by what he had said, while others refused to believe. [25]So they disagreed with each other; and as they were leaving, Paul made one further statement: "The Holy Spirit was right in saying to your ancestors through the prophet Isaiah,
[26]'Go to this people and say,
  You will indeed listen,
    but never understand,
  and you will indeed look,
    but never perceive.
[27]For this people's heart has grown dull,
  and their ears are hard of hearing,
  and they have shut their eyes;
  so that they might not look with their eyes,
  and listen with their ears,
  and understand with their heart and turn—
  and I would heal them.'
[28]Let it be known to you then that this salvation of God has been sent to the Gentiles; they will listen."[a]
30 He lived there two whole years at his own expense[b] and welcomed all who came to him, [31]proclaiming the kingdom of God and teaching about the Lord Jesus Christ with all boldness and without hindrance.

[a] Other ancient authorities add verse 29, And when he had said these words, the Jews departed, arguing vigorously among themselves
[b] Or in his own hired dwelling

ROMANS

CHAPTER 1

Paul, a servant[a] of Jesus Christ, called to be an apostle, set apart for the gospel of God, [2]which he promised beforehand through his prophets in the holy scriptures, [3]the gospel concerning his Son, who was descended from David according to the flesh [4]and was declared to be Son of God with power according to the spirit[b] of holiness by resurrection from the dead, Jesus Christ our Lord, [5]through whom we have received grace and apostleship to bring about the obedience of faith among all the Gentiles for the sake of his name, [6]including yourselves who are called to belong to Jesus Christ,

7 To all God's beloved in Rome, who are called to be saints:

Grace to you and peace from God our Father and the Lord Jesus Christ.

8 First, I thank my God through Jesus Christ for all of you, because your faith is proclaimed throughout the world. [9]For God, whom I serve with my spirit by announcing the gospel[c] of his Son, is my witness that without ceasing I remember you always in my prayers, [10]asking that by God's will I may somehow at last succeed in coming to you. [11]For I am longing to see

a Gk *slave*
b Or *Spirit*
c Gk *my spirit in the gospel*

1:1
3972 1401 5547 2424 2822 652
Παῦλος δοῦλος Χριστοῦ Ἰησοῦ, κλητὸς ἀπόστολος
Paul slave of Christ Jesus, called delegate

873 1519 2098 2316 **2** 3739
ἀφωρισμένος εἰς εὐαγγέλιον θεοῦ, ὃ
having been separated into good message of God, who

4279 1223 014 4396 846 1722
προεπηγγείλατο διὰ τῶν προφητῶν αὐτοῦ ἐν
promised before through the spokesmen of him in

1124 40 **3** 4012 02 5207 846 02
γραφαῖς ἁγίαις, περὶ τοῦ υἱοῦ αὐτοῦ τοῦ
writings holy, about the son of him the one

1096 1537 4690 1160a 2596 4561
γενομένου ἐκ σπέρματος Δαυὶδ κατὰ σάρκα,
having become from seed David according to flesh,

4 02 3724 5207 2316 1722 1411 2596
τοῦ ὁρισθέντος υἱοῦ θεοῦ ἐν δυνάμει κατὰ
the one being designated son of God in power by

4151 42 1537 386 3498 2424
πνεῦμα ἁγιωσύνης ἐξ ἀναστάσεως νεκρῶν, Ἰησοῦ
spirit of holiness from standing up of dead, of Jesus

5547 02 2962 1473 **5** 1223 3739 2983
Χριστοῦ τοῦ κυρίου ἡμῶν, δι' οὗ ἐλάβομεν
Christ of the Master of us, through whom we received

5485 2532 651 1519 5218 4102 1722 3956
χάριν καὶ ἀποστολὴν εἰς ὑπακοὴν πίστεως ἐν πᾶσιν
favor and delegateship into obedience of trust in all

023 1484 5228 010 3686 846 **6** 1722
τοῖς ἔθνεσιν ὑπὲρ τοῦ ὀνόματος αὐτοῦ, ἐν
the nations on behalf of the name of him, in

3739 1510 2532 1473 2822 2424 5547 **7** 3956
οἷς ἐστε καὶ ὑμεῖς κλητοὶ Ἰησοῦ Χριστοῦ, πᾶσιν
which are also you called of Jesus Christ, to all

015 1510 1722 4516 27 2316 2822
τοῖς οὖσιν ἐν Ῥώμῃ ἀγαπητοῖς θεοῦ, κλητοῖς
the ones being in Rome loved ones of God, called

40 5485 1470 2532 1515 575 2316 3962 1473
ἁγίοις, χάρις ὑμῖν καὶ εἰρήνη ἀπὸ θεοῦ πατρὸς ἡμῶν
holy, favor to you and peace from God father of us

2532 2962 2424 5547 **8** 4413 3303
καὶ κυρίου Ἰησοῦ Χριστοῦ. Πρῶτον μὲν
and Master Jesus Christ. First indeed

2168 03 2316 1473 1223 2424
εὐχαριστῶ τῷ θεῷ μου διὰ Ἰησοῦ
I give good favor to the God of me through Jesus

5547 4012 3956 1473 3754 05 4102 1473
Χριστοῦ περὶ πάντων ὑμῶν ὅτι ἡ πίστις ὑμῶν
Christ concerning all of you that the trust of you

2605 1722 3650 03 2889 **9** 3144 1063
καταγγέλλεται ἐν ὅλῳ τῷ κόσμῳ. μάρτυς γάρ
is proclaimed in whole the world. Testifier for

1473 1510 01 2316 3739 3000 1722 011 4151
μού ἐστιν ὁ θεός, ᾧ λατρεύω ἐν τῷ πνεύματί
of me is the God, to whom I serve in the spirit

1473 1722 011 2098 02 5207 846 5613
μου ἐν τῷ εὐαγγελίῳ τοῦ υἱοῦ αὐτοῦ, ὡς
of me in the good message of the son of him, as

89 3417 1473 4160 **10** 3842 1909
ἀδιαλείπτως μνείαν ὑμῶν ποιοῦμαι πάντοτε ἐπὶ
unceasingly memory of you I make myself always on

018 4335 1473 1189 1487 4458 2235 4218
τῶν προσευχῶν μου δεόμενος εἴ πως ἤδη ποτὲ
the prayers of me begging if perhaps already once

2137 1722 011 2307 02 2316
εὐοδωθήσομαι ἐν τῷ θελήματι τοῦ θεοῦ
I will travel well in the want of the God

2064 4314 1473 **11** 1971 1063 3708
ἐλθεῖν πρὸς ὑμᾶς. ἐπιποθῶ γὰρ ἰδεῖν
to come toward you. I desire longingly for to see

```
1473     2443  5100  3330           5486        1473
ὑμᾶς,  ἵνα   τι   μεταδῶ      χάρισμα   ὑμῖν
you,   that some I might share favor gift to you
4152           1519  012  4741                    1473   12  3778
πνευματικὸν εἰς  τὸ  στηριχθῆναι       ὑμᾶς,        τοῦτο
spiritual  to   the to be strengthened you,        this
1161  1510   4837                    1722  1473  1223
δέ   ἐστιν συμπαρακληθῆναι      ἐν   ὑμῖν δια
but  is   to be encouraged together in   you through
06   1722  240            4102     1473    5037  2532  1473
τῆς ἐν  ἀλλήλοις   πίστεως ὑμῶν  τε   καὶ  ἐμοῦ.
the in  one another trust  of you both also of me.
       3756 2309   1161  1473  50        80       3754
13  οὐ  θέλω  δὲ  ὑμᾶς ἀγνοεῖν,  ἀδελφοί, ὅτι
    Not I want but  you  to not know, brothers that
4178        4388          2064     4314   1473  2532
πολλάκις προεθέμην  ἐλθεῖν πρὸς  ὑμᾶς, καὶ
frequently I set forward to come toward you,  and
2967        891  02  1204     2443  5100  2590
ἐκωλύθην  ἄχρι τοῦ δεῦρο, ἵνα  τινὰ καρπὸν
I was hindered until the now,  that some fruit
2192      2532 1722 1473 2531     2532 1722 023
σχῶ     καὶ  ἐν  ὑμῖν καθὼς  καὶ  ἐν   τοῖς
I might have also in  you just as also in  the
3062    1484      14  1672      5037 2532 915
λοιποῖς ἔθνεσιν.  14  Ἕλλησίν τε   καὶ  βαρβάροις,
remaining nations.  Greeks both and  barbarians,
4680   5037 2532 453       3781     1510     3779
σοφοῖς τε  καὶ  ἀνοήτοις ὀφειλέτης εἰμί, 15 οὕτως
wise   both and  unmindful debtor    I am,   thusly
09    2596 1473 4289     2532 1473  015      1722  4516
τὸ  κατ᾽ ἐμὲ  πρόθυμον καὶ  ὑμῖν τοῖς ἐν  Ῥώμῃ
the by  me  eager     also to you the ones in  Rome
2097                 16  3756 1063 1870         012
εὐαγγελίσασθαι.  16  Οὐ  γὰρ ἐπαισχύνομαι τὸ
to tell good message.  Not for  I am ashamed the
2098         1411    1063 2316   1510 1519 4991
εὐαγγέλιον, δύναμις γὰρ θεοῦ  ἐστιν εἰς σωτηρίαν
good message, power  for of God it is to  deliverance
3956   03  4100      2453        5037 4413  2532
παντὶ τῷ  πιστεύοντι, Ἰουδαίῳ τε  πρῶτον καὶ
to all the one trusting, to Judean both first  and
1672      17  1343       1063 2316   1722 846
Ἕλληνι.  17 δικαιοσύνη γὰρ θεοῦ  ἐν  αὐτῷ
to Greek. Rightness   for of God in  him
601             1537 4102    1519 4102     2531
ἀποκαλύπτεται ἐκ  πίστεως εἰς πίστιν, καθὼς
is uncovered  from trust   to  trust,  just as
1125           01  1161 1342    1537 4102
γέγραπται·   ὁ  δὲ  δίκαιος ἐκ  πίστεως
it has been written; the but  right  from trust
2198      18  601         1063 3709   2316    575
ζήσεται.  18 Ἀποκαλύπτεται γὰρ ὀργὴ θεοῦ  ἀπ᾽
will live.  Is uncovered  for anger of God from
3772    1909 3956  763       2532 93      444
οὐρανοῦ ἐπὶ πᾶσαν ἀσέβειαν καὶ  ἀδικίαν ἀνθρώπων
heaven on  all   irreverence and  unright of men
014     08   225    1722 93     2722
τῶν   τὴν ἀλήθειαν ἐν  ἀδικίᾳ κατεχόντων,
the ones the truth  in  unright holding down,
19  1360  09  1110    02      2316 5318    1510  1722
19  διότι τὸ γνωστὸν τοῦ  θεοῦ φανερόν ἐστιν ἐν
    therefore the known  of the God evident is  in
846     01  2316 1063 846     5319     20  021  1063
αὐτοῖς· ὁ  θεὸς γὰρ αὐτοῖς ἐφανέρωσεν. 20 τὰ  γὰρ
them;   the God for to them demonstrated.  The for
517     846   575  2937    2889     023
ἀόρατα αὐτοῦ ἀπὸ κτίσεως κόσμου τοῖς
unseen of him from creation of world to the
```

you so that I may share with you some spiritual gift to strengthen you—[12]or rather so that we may be mutually encouraged by each other's faith, both yours and mine. [13]I want you to know, brothers and sisters,[a] that I have often intended to come to you (but thus far have been prevented), in order that I may reap some harvest among you as I have among the rest of the Gentiles. [14]I am a debtor both to Greeks and to barbarians, both to the wise and to the foolish [15]—hence my eagerness to proclaim the gospel to you also who are in Rome.

16 For I am not ashamed of the gospel; it is the power of God for salvation to everyone who has faith, to the Jew first and also to the Greek. [17]For in it the righteousness of God is revealed through faith for faith; as it is written, "The one who is righteous will live by faith."[b]

18 For the wrath of God is revealed from heaven against all ungodliness and wickedness of those who by their wickedness suppress the truth. [19]For what can be known about God is plain to them, because God has shown it to them. [20]Ever since the creation of the world

---

a Gk brothers
b Or The one who is righteous through faith will live

his eternal power and divine nature, invisible though they are, have been understood and seen through the things he has made. So they are without excuse; ²¹for though they knew God, they did not honor him as God or give thanks to him, but they became futile in their thinking, and their senseless minds were darkened. ²²Claiming to be wise, they became fools; ²³and they exchanged the glory of the immortal God for images resembling a mortal human being or birds or four-footed animals or reptiles.

24 Therefore God gave them up in the lusts of their hearts to impurity, to the degrading of their bodies among themselves, ²⁵because they exchanged the truth about God for a lie and worshiped and served the creature rather than the Creator, who is blessed forever! Amen.

26 For this reason God gave them up to degrading passions. Their women exchanged natural intercourse for unnatural, ²⁷and in the same way also the men, giving up natural intercourse with women, were consumed with passion for one another. Men committed shameless acts with men

4161	3539		2529		
ποιήμασιν	νοούμενα		καθορᾶται,		
made-things	being given thought		are seen thoroughly,		

05	5037 126	846	1411	2532 2305	1519 012
ἥ	τε ἀΐδιος	αὐτοῦ	δύναμις	καὶ θειότης,	εἰς τὸ
the	both eternal	of him	power	and deity,	to the

1510 846	379		1360	1097	04
εἶναι αὐτοὺς	ἀναπολογήτους,	21	διότι	γνόντες	τὸν
to be them	without defense,		therefore	knowing	the

2316 3756 5613 2316 1392		2228
θεὸν οὐχ ὡς θεὸν ἐδόξασαν		ἢ
God not as God they gave splendor		or

2168	235	3154	1722 015
ηὐχαρίστησαν,	ἀλλ'	ἐματαιώθησαν	ἐν τοῖς
gave good favor,	but	they were futile	in the

1261	846	2532 4654	05
διαλογισμοῖς	αὐτῶν	καὶ ἐσκοτίσθη	ἡ
reasonings	of them	and was darkened	the

801	846	2588	5335	1510
ἀσύνετος	αὐτῶν	καρδία. 22	φάσκοντες	εἶναι
not understanding	of them	heart.	Affirming	to be

4680	3471		2532 236	08	1391
σοφοὶ	ἐμωράνθησαν	23	καὶ ἤλλαξαν	τὴν	δόξαν
wise	they became foolish		and changed	the	splendor

02	862		2316 1722 3667	1504
τοῦ	ἀφθάρτου		θεοῦ ἐν ὁμοιώματι	εἰκόνος
of the	incorruptible		God in likeness	of image

5349	444	2532 4071	2532 5074	2532
φθαρτοῦ	ἀνθρώπου καὶ	πετεινῶν καὶ	τετραπόδων	καὶ
corruptible	man and	birds and	four-footed	and

2062	1352	3860	846	01	2316 1722
ἑρπετῶν. 24	Διὸ	παρέδωκεν	αὐτοὺς	ὁ	θεὸς ἐν
reptiles.	Therefore	gave over	them	the	God in

019	1939	018	2588	846	1519 167
ταῖς	ἐπιθυμίαις	τῶν	καρδιῶν	αὐτῶν	εἰς ἀκαθαρσίαν
the	desires	of the	hearts	of them	in uncleanness

010	818	024 4983	846	1722 846
τοῦ	ἀτιμάζεσθαι	τὰ σώματα	αὐτῶν	ἐν αὐτοῖς·
of the	to be dishonored	the bodies	of them	in them;

25	3748	3337	08	225	02	2316 1722
	οἵτινες	μετήλλαξαν	τὴν	ἀλήθειαν	τοῦ	θεοῦ ἐν
	who	changed across	the	truth	of the	God in

011 5579	2532 4573	2532 3000	07
τῷ ψεύδει	καὶ ἐσεβάσθησαν	καὶ ἐλάτρευσαν	τῇ
the lie	and revered	and served	the

2937	3844	04 2936	3739 1510 2128
κτίσει	παρὰ	τὸν κτίσαντα,	ὅς ἐστιν εὐλογητὸς
creation	beyond	the one creating,	who is well-spoken

1519 016	165	281	1223	3778 3860
εἰς τοὺς	αἰῶνας,	ἀμήν. 26	Διὰ	τοῦτο παρέδωκεν
in the	ages,	amen.	Through	this gave over

846	01 2316 1519 3806	819	017 5037
αὐτοὺς	ὁ θεὸς εἰς πάθη	ἀτιμίας,	αἵ τε
them	the God into passions	of dishonor,	the indeed

1063 2338	846	3337	08 5446	5540
γὰρ θήλειαι	αὐτῶν	μετήλλαξαν	τὴν φυσικὴν	χρῆσιν
for females	of them	changed across	the natural	use

1519 08 3844	5449	3668	5037 2532 013
εἰς τὴν παρὰ	φύσιν, 27	ὁμοίως	τε καὶ οἱ
to the beyond	nature,	likewise	indeed also the

730	863	08 5446	5540	06
ἄρσενες	ἀφέντες	τὴν φυσικὴν	χρῆσιν	τῆς
males	having sent off	the natural	use	of the

2338	1572	1722 07	3715 846
θηλείας	ἐξεκαύθησαν	ἐν τῇ	ὀρέξει αὐτῶν
female	were burned thoroughly	in the	lust of them

1519 240	730	1722 730	08 808
εἰς ἀλλήλους,	ἄρσενες	ἐν ἄρσεσιν	τὴν ἀσχημοσύνην
to one another,	males	in males	the shamelessness

```
2716                    2532 08   489              3739
κατεργαζόμενοι     καὶ  τὴν ἀντιμισθίαν ἣν
working thoroughly and  the return wage    which
1163           06   4106     846        1722 1438
ἔδει           τῆς  πλάνης  αὐτῶν     ἐν   ἑαυτοῖς
it is necessary of the deceit of them  in   themselves
618                     28 2532 2531    3756 1381            04
ἀπολαμβάνοντες.         Καὶ καθὼς  οὐκ  ἐδοκίμασαν    τὸν
receiving back.         And just as not  they approved the
2316 2192    1722 1922            3860      846   01   2316
θεὸν ἔχειν  ἐν ἐπιγνώσει,  παρέδωκεν αὐτοὺς ὁ  θεὸς
God to have in  perception, gave over them    the God
1519 96        3563   4160   024 3361 2520
εἰς ἀδόκιμον νοῦν, ποιεῖν τὰ μὴ  καθήκοντα,
into unproved mind, to do  the not being proper,
    4137           3956   93       4189
29 πεπληρωμένους  πάσῃ  ἀδικίᾳ  πονηρίᾳ
    having been filled in all unright, in evil,
4124        2549    3324     5355    5408    2054
πλεονεξίᾳ κακίᾳ,  μεστοὺς φθόνου φόνου ἔριδος
greediness, badness, full   of envy, murder, strife,
1388   2550       5588          30 2637
δόλου κακοηθείας, ψιθυριστάς,    καταλάλους,
guile, malice,    whisperers,       speakers against,
2319         5197      5244        213      2182
θεοστυγεῖς, ὑβριστὰς, ὑπερηφάνους, ἀλαζόνας, ἐφευρετὰς
God-haters, abusers, arrogant,     boasters, inventors
2556   1118      545          31 801
κακῶν, γονεῦσιν ἀπειθεῖς,       ἀσυνέτους,
of bad, to parents disobedient,   not understanding,
802         794                  415
ἀσυνθέτους, ἀστόργους,       ἀνελεήμονας·
disloyal,   no family affection, without mercy;
   3748     012 1345        02   2316 1921
32 οἵτινες τὸ δικαίωμα    τοῦ θεοῦ ἐπιγνόντες
   who      the right thing of the God having perceived
3754 013      024 5108      4238      514    2288
ὅτι οἱ    τὰ τοιαῦτα   πράσσοντες ἄξιοι θανάτου
that the ones the such ones practicing worthy of death
1510  3756 3441  846   4160     235  2532
εἰσίν, οὐ μόνον αὐτὰ ποιοῦσιν ἀλλὰ καὶ
are,   not alone these they do  but  also
4909           015 4238           2:1 1352
συνευδοκοῦσιν τοῖς πράσσουσιν.      Διὸ
they think well the  ones practicing.   Therefore
together
379            1510    5599 444     3956 01
ἀναπολόγητος εἶ,    ὦ  ἄνθρωπε πᾶς ὁ
without defense you are, o  man      all  the one
2919      1722 3739 1063 2919      04 2087     4572
κρίνων· ἐν ᾧ  γὰρ κρίνεις τὸν ἕτερον, σεαυτὸν
judging; in what for  you judge the other,  yourself
2632          024 1063 846  4238        01
κατακρίνεις, τὰ γὰρ αὐτὰ πράσσεις ὁ
you condemn, the for same you practice the one
2919      2 3609a   1161 3754 09  2917      02      2316
κρίνων.    οἴδαμεν δὲ  ὅτι τὸ κρίμα   τοῦ   θεοῦ
judging.   We know but that the judgment of the God
1510 2596         225        1909 016      024 5108
ἐστιν κατὰ      ἀλήθειαν ἐπὶ τοὺς   τὰ τοιαῦτα
is    according to truth  on  the ones the such
4238          3 3049   1161 3778    5599 444      01
πράσσοντας.   λογίζῃ δὲ τοῦτο, ὦ  ἄνθρωπε ὁ
practicing.   You reason but this, o  man      the
2919     016  024 5108      4238       2532 4160  846
κρίνων τοὺς τὰ τοιαῦτα   πράσσοντας καὶ ποιῶν αὐτά,
judging the the such ones practicing and  doing same,
3754 1473 1628        012 2917    02      2316
ὅτι σὺ ἐκφεύξῃ     τὸ κρίμα   τοῦ    θεοῦ;
that you will flee out the judgment of the God?
```

and received in their own persons the due penalty for their error.

28 And since they did not see fit to acknowledge God, God gave them up to a debased mind and to things that should not be done. 29They were filled with every kind of wickedness, evil, covetousness, malice. Full of envy, murder, strife, deceit, craftiness, they are gossips, 30slanderers, God-haters,[a] insolent, haughty, boastful, inventors of evil, rebellious toward parents, 31foolish, faithless, heartless, ruthless. 32They know God's decree, that those who practice such things deserve to die— yet they not only do them but even applaud others who practice them.

CHAPTER 2

Therefore you have no excuse, whoever you are, when you judge others; for in passing judgment on another you condemn yourself, because you, the judge, are doing the very same things. 2You say,[b] "We know that God's judgment on those who do such things is in accordance with truth." 3Do you imagine, whoever you are, that when you judge those who do such things and yet do them yourself, you will escape the judgment of God?

a Or God-hated
b Gk lacks You say

4Or do you despise the riches of his kindness and forbearance and patience? Do you not realize that God's kindness is meant to lead you to repentance? 5But by your hard and impenitent heart you are storing up wrath for yourself on the day of wrath, when God's righteous judgment will be revealed. 6For he will repay according to each one's deeds: 7to those who by patiently doing good seek for glory and honor and immortality, he will give eternal life; 8while for those who are self-seeking and who obey not the truth but wickedness, there will be wrath and fury. 9There will be anguish and distress for everyone who does evil, the Jew first and also the Greek, 10but glory and honor and peace for everyone who does good, the Jew first and also the Greek. 11For God shows no partiality.

12 All who have sinned apart from the law will also perish apart from the law, and all who have sinned under the law will be judged by the law. 13For it is not the hearers of the law who are righteous in God's sight, but the doers of the law who will be justified. 14When Gentiles, who do not possess the law, do instinctively

```
      2228 02    4149    06      5544        846      2532
  4   ἢ   τοῦ  πλούτου τῆς  χρηστότητος αὐτοῦ  καὶ
      Or  of the rich  of the kindness    of him and
  06    463       2532 06   3115        2706
  τῆς  ἀνοχῆς   καὶ  τῆς μακροθυμίας καταφρονεῖς,
  of the restraint and  the long temper you think down,
  50         3754 09  5543    02     2316 1519 3341
  ἀγνοῶν  ὅτι  τὸ  χρηστὸν τοῦ  θεοῦ εἰς  μετάνοιάν
  unknowing that the kind  of the God  to   change mind
  1473 71         2596 1161 08   4643       1473  2532
  σε  ἄγει;  5 κατὰ δὲ  τὴν σκληρότητά σου   καὶ
  you leads?  By  but  the hardness   of you and
  279        2588      2343         4572        3709
  ἀμετανόητον καρδίαν θησαυρίζεις σεαυτῷ    ὀργὴν
  unchange mind heart  you treasure to yourself anger
  1722 2250  3709      2532 602           1341
  ἐν  ἡμέρᾳ ὀργῆς  καὶ ἀποκαλύψεως δικαιοκρισίας
  in   day  of anger and uncovering   right judgment
  02    2316   3739 591          1538    2596 024
  τοῦ  θεοῦ 6 ὃς  ἀποδώσει   ἑκάστῳ κατὰ τὰ
  of the God  who will give off to each by   the
  2041 846        015    3303  2596 5281       2041
  ἔργα αὐτοῦ· 7 τοῖς  μὲν  καθ' ὑπομονὴν ἔργου
  works of him;  to the indeed by   patience  of work
  18    1391    2532 5092 2532 861          2212
  ἀγαθοῦ δόξαν καὶ  τιμὴν καὶ ἀφθαρσίαν ζητοῦσιν
  good  splendor and  value and incorruption they seek
  2222 166       015   1161 1537 2052        2532
  ζωὴν αἰώνιον, 8 τοῖς δὲ  ἐξ ἐριθείας    καὶ
  life eternal,  to the but from selfish ambition and
  544    07  225     3982         1161 07
  ἀπειθοῦσι τῇ ἀληθείᾳ πειθομένοις δὲ  τῇ
  disobeying the truth  being persuaded but  to the
  93    3709  2532 2372   2347        2532 4730
  ἀδικίᾳ ὀργὴ καὶ  θυμός. 9 θλῖψις  καὶ στενοχωρία
  unright anger and fury.   Affliction and  anguish
  1909 3956  5590  444    02  2716          012
  ἐπὶ  πᾶσαν ψυχὴν ἀνθρώπου τοῦ κατεργαζομένου  τὸ
  on   all   soul of man    the working thoroughly the
  2556   2453      5037 4413  2532 1672
  κακόν, Ἰουδαίου τε   πρῶτον καὶ Ἕλληνος·
  bad,   of Judean both first  and  Greek;
      1391      1161 2532 5092 2532 1515    3956   03
  10 δόξα   δὲ  καὶ  τιμὴ καὶ εἰρήνη παντὶ τῷ
     splendor but  and  value and peace to all the one
  2038       012 18      2453       5037 4413   2532
  ἐργαζομένῳ τὸ  ἀγαθόν, Ἰουδαίῳ  τε  πρῶτον καὶ
  working   the good,   to Judean both first  and
  1672       11 3756 1063 1510 4382           3844 03
  Ἕλληνι·   οὐ  γάρ  ἐστιν προσωπολημψία παρὰ τῷ
  Greek;     not for  is   receiving face  with the
  2316   12 3745      1063 460     264     460
  θεῷ.    Ὅσοι    γὰρ ἀνόμως ἥμαρτον, ἀνόμως
  God.     As many as for lawlessly sinned, lawlessly
  2532 622                2532 3745      1722 3551
  καὶ ἀπολοῦνται,      καὶ ὅσοι    ἐν  νόμῳ
  also they will be destroyed, and  as many as in  law
  264    1223    3551    2919        3756 1063 013
  ἥμαρτον, διὰ  νόμου κριθήσονται· 13 οὐ  γὰρ οἱ
  sinned, through law  will be judged; not  for the
  202    3551    1342    3844 03  2316 235  013
  ἀκροαταὶ νόμου δίκαιοι παρὰ [τῷ] θεῷ, ἀλλ' οἱ
  hearers  of law right  with the God, but  the
  4163   3551    1344           3752 1063 1484
  ποιηταὶ νόμου δικαιωθήσονται. 14 ὅταν γὰρ ἔθνη
  doers   of law will be made right. When for  nations
  021 3361 3551 2192      5499    024 02       3551
  τὰ  μὴ  νόμον ἔχοντα φύσει   τὰ  τοῦ  νόμου
  the not law  having in nature the of the law
```

```
4160       3778  3551  3361 2192    1438
ποιῶσιν,   οὗτοι νόμον μὴ   ἔχοντες ἑαυτοῖς
might do,  these law   not  having  to themselves
1510  3551       3748          1731        012 2041   02
εἰσιν νόμος·  15 οἵτινες ἐνδείκνυνται τὸ ἔργον τοῦ
are   law;       who   demonstrate the work  of the
3551  1123      1722 019  2588        846
νόμου γραπτὸν ἐν   ταῖς καρδίαις αὐτῶν,
law   written in  the  hearts   of them,
4828              846    06     4893          2532
συμμαρτυρούσης   αὐτῶν τῆς    συνειδήσεως καὶ
testifying together of them of the conscience and
3342   240     014   3053      2723         2228
μεταξὺ ἀλλήλων τῶν  λογισμῶν κατηγορούντων ἢ
between one another of the reasonings accusing  or
2532 626            1722 2250 3753 2919   01   2316
καὶ  ἀπολογουμένων, 16 ἐν   ἡμέρᾳ ὅτε κρίνει ὁ θεὸς
even defending,      in  day   when judges the God
024 2927  014    444        2596 012 2098        1473
τὰ κρυπτὰ τῶν  ἀνθρώπων κατὰ τὸ εὐαγγέλιόν μου
the hidden of the men    by   the good message of me
1223    5547      2424    17 1487 1161 1473 2453
διὰ    Χριστοῦ Ἰησοῦ.      Εἰ  δὲ  σὺ  Ἰουδαῖος
through Christ  Jesus.     If but you Judean
2028          2532 1879     3551 2532 2744     1722
ἐπονομάζῃ   καὶ  ἐπαναπαύῃ νόμῳ καὶ καυχᾶσαι ἐν
name yourself and rest on   law and brag     in
2316 18 2532 1097    012 2307 2532 1381       024
θεῷ     καὶ  γινώσκεις τὸ θέλημα καὶ δοκιμάζεις τὰ
God     and  you know the want and approve  the
1308       2727             1537 02 3551
διαφέροντα κατηχούμενος  ἐκ  τοῦ νόμου,
differing being instructed from the law,
   3982                  5037 4572      3595    1510
19 πέποιθάς          τε  σεαυτὸν ὁδηγὸν εἶναι
   having been persuaded and  yourself guide to be
5185      5457  014   1722 4655   20  3810
τυφλῶν,   φῶς  τῶν  ἐν  σκότει,    παιδευτὴν
of blind, light of the in  dark,     child instructor
878           1320       3516      2192   08
ἀφρόνων,   διδάσκαλον νηπίων,  ἔχοντα τὴν
of unthinking, teacher of infants, having the
3446      06    1108       2532 06 225      1722 03
μόρφωσιν τῆς  γνώσεως καὶ τῆς ἀληθείας ἐν  τῷ
form    of the knowledge and the truth  in  the
3551  21 01 3767 1321     2087    4572      3756
νόμῳ·    ὁ  οὖν διδάσκων ἕτερον σεαυτὸν οὐ
law;     The then teaching other yourself not
1321     01 2784        3361 2813    2813
διδάσκεις; ὁ κηρύσσων μὴ κλέπτειν κλέπτεις;
you teach? The announcing not to thieve do you thieve?
   01 3004        3361 3431    3431        01
22 ὁ λέγων     μὴ μοιχεύειν μοιχεύεις;    ὁ
   The one saying not to commit do you commit The one
                         adultery  adultery?
948              024 1497   2416          23 3739
βδελυσσόμενος τὰ  εἴδωλα ἱεροσυλεῖς;      ὃς
abominating   the idols do you rob temples? Who
1722 3551 2744      1223   06   3847       02
ἐν  νόμῳ καυχᾶσαι, διὰ   τῆς παραβάσεως τοῦ
in  law brags,    through the transgression of the
3551  04  2316 818       09  1063 3686 02
νόμου τὸν θεὸν ἀτιμάζεις· 24 τὸ γὰρ ὄνομα τοῦ
law   the God you dishonor; the for name  of the
2316 1223    1473 987        1722 023  1484
θεοῦ δι᾽   ὑμᾶς βλασφημεῖται ἐν  τοῖς ἔθνεσιν,
God through you is insulted  in  the  nations,
2531     1125          25  4061       3303
καθὼς   γέγραπται.       Περιτομὴ μὲν
just as it has been written. Circumcision indeed
```

what the law requires, these, though not having the law, are a law to themselves. [15]They show that what the law requires is written on their hearts, to which their own conscience also bears witness; and their conflicting thoughts will accuse or perhaps excuse them [16]on the day when, according to my gospel, God, through Jesus Christ, will judge the secret thoughts of all.

[17]But if you call yourself a Jew and rely on the law and boast of your relation to God [18]and know his will and determine what is best because you are instructed in the law, [19]and if you are sure that you are a guide to the blind, a light to those who are in darkness, [20]a corrector of the foolish, a teacher of children, having in the law the embodiment of knowledge and truth, [21]you, then, that teach others, will you not teach yourself? While you preach against stealing, do you steal? [22]You that forbid adultery, do you commit adultery? You that abhor idols, do you rob temples? [23]You that boast in the law, do you dishonor God by breaking the law? [24]For, as it is written, "The name of God is blasphemed among the Gentiles because of you."

[25]Circumcision indeed

is of value if you obey the law; but if you break the law, your circumcision has become uncircumcision. ²⁶So, if those who are uncircumcised keep the requirements of the law, will not their uncircumcision be regarded as circumcision? ²⁷Then those who are physically uncircumcised but keep the law will condemn you that have the written code and circumcision but break the law. ²⁸For a person is not a Jew who is one outwardly, nor is true circumcision something external and physical. ²⁹Rather, a person is a Jew who is one inwardly, and real circumcision is a matter of the heart—it is spiritual and not literal. Such a person receives praise not from others but from God.

CHAPTER 3

Then what advantage has the Jew? Or what is the value of circumcision? ²Much, in every way. For in the first place the Jews*ᵃ* were entrusted with the oracles of God. ³What if some were unfaithful? Will their faithlessness nullify the faithfulness of God? ⁴By no means! Although everyone is a liar, let God be proved true, as it is written,

"So that you may be
    justified in your
    words,
    and prevail in your
    judging."*ᵇ*

⁵But if our injustice serves to confirm the justice of God,

ᵃ Gk *they*
ᵇ Gk *when you are being judged*

1063	5623		1437	3551	4238	1437	1161
γὰρ	ὠφελεῖ	ἐὰν	νόμον	πράσσῃς·		ἐὰν	δὲ
for	benefits	if	law	you might practice;		if	but

3848 3551 1510 05 4061
παραβάτης νόμου ἧς, ἡ περιτομή
transgressor of law you might be, the circumcision

1473 203 1096 **26** 1437 3767 05
σου ἀκροβυστία γέγονεν. ἐὰν οὖν ἡ
of you uncircumcision has become. If then the

203 024 1345 02 3551
ἀκροβυστία τὰ δικαιώματα τοῦ νόμου
uncircumcision the right things of the law

5442 3756 05 203 846 1519
φυλάσσῃ, οὐχ ἡ ἀκροβυστία αὐτοῦ εἰς
might guard, not the uncircumcision of him into

4061 3049 **27** 2532 2919 05
περιτομὴν λογισθήσεται; καὶ κρινεῖ ἡ
circumcision will be reasoned? And will judge the

1537 5449 203 04 3551 5055 1473
ἐκ φύσεως ἀκροβυστία τὸν νόμον τελοῦσα σὲ
from nature uncircumcision the law completing you

04 1223 1121 2532 4061 3848
τὸν διὰ γράμματος καὶ περιτομῆς παραβάτην
the through letter and circumcision transgressor

3551 **28** 3756 1063 01 1722 011 5318 2453
νόμου. οὐ γὰρ ὁ ἐν τῷ φανερῷ Ἰουδαῖός
of law. Not for the in the evident Judean

1510 3761 05 1722 011 5318 1722 4561
ἐστιν οὐδὲ ἡ ἐν τῷ φανερῷ ἐν σαρκὶ
is but not the in the evident in flesh

4061 **29** 235 01 1722 011 2927 2453 2532
περιτομή, ἀλλ' ὁ ἐν τῷ κρυπτῷ Ἰουδαῖος, καὶ
circumcision, but the in the hidden Judean, and

4061 2588 1722 4151 3756 1121 3739
περιτομὴ καρδίας ἐν πνεύματι οὐ γράμματι, οὗ
circumcision of heart in spirit not letter, of whom

01 1868 3756 1537 444 235 1537 02 2316
ὁ ἔπαινος οὐκ ἐξ ἀνθρώπων ἀλλ' ἐκ τοῦ θεοῦ.
the praise on not from men but from the God.

3:1 5101 3767 09 4053 02 2453 2228 5101
Τί οὖν τὸ περισσὸν τοῦ Ἰουδαίου ἢ τίς
What then the excess of the Judean or what

05 5622 06 4061 **2** 4183 2596 3956
ἡ ὠφέλεια τῆς περιτομῆς; πολὺ κατὰ πάντα
the benefit of the circumcision? Much by all

5158 4413 3303 1063 3754 4100
τρόπον. πρῶτον μὲν [γὰρ] ὅτι ἐπιστεύθησαν
manner. First indeed for because they were trusted

024 3051 02 2316 **3** 5101 1063 1487 569
τὰ λόγια τοῦ θεοῦ. τί γάρ; εἰ ἠπίστησάν
the sayings of the God. What for? If were untrusting

5100 3361 05 570 846 08 4102 02 2316
τινες, μὴ ἡ ἀπιστία αὐτῶν τὴν πίστιν τοῦ θεοῦ
some, not the untrust of them the trust of the God

2673 **4** 3361 1096 1096 1161 01
καταργήσει; μὴ γένοιτο· γινέσθω δὲ ὁ
abolishes? Not may it become; let become but the

2316 227 3956 1161 444 5583 2531
θεὸς ἀληθής, πᾶς δὲ ἄνθρωπος ψεύστης, καθὼς
God of truth, all but man liar, just as

1125 3704 302 1344 1722 015 3056
γέγραπται· ὅπως ἂν δικαιωθῇς ἐν τοῖς λόγοις
it has been so that - you might be in the words
written; made right

1473 2532 3528 1722 011 2919 1473
σου καὶ νικήσεις ἐν τῷ κρίνεσθαί σε.
of you and will conquer in the to be judged you.

5 1487 1161 05 93 1473 2316 1343
εἰ δὲ ἡ ἀδικία ἡμῶν θεοῦ δικαιοσύνην
If but the unright of us of God rightness

```
4921            5101 3004              3361 94      01   2316 01
συνίστησιν,  τί    ἐροῦμεν;     μὴ  ἄδικος ὁ   θεὸς ὁ
commends,    what will we say?  Not unright the God  the

2018           08   3709   2596 444      3004  6  3361
ἐπιφέρων    τὴν ὀργήν; κατὰ ἄνθρωπον λέγω.    μὴ
carrying on the anger? By    man        I say.  Not

1096           1893  4459 2919        01   2316 04
γένοιτο·     ἐπεὶ πῶς κρινεῖ     ὁ   θεὸς τὸν
may it become; since how will judge the God  the

2889      7  1487 1161 05  225        02    2316 1722 011
κόσμον;    εἰ  δὲ  ἡ  ἀλήθεια τοῦ  θεοῦ ἐν  τῷ
world?     If  but the truth   of the God in the

1699 5582     4052        1519 08  1391       846
ἐμῷ ψεύσματι ἐπερίσσευσεν εἰς τὴν δόξαν    αὐτοῦ,
me   lie       exceeds     into the splendor of him,

5101 2089  2504  5613 268   2919
τί   ἔτι  κἀγὼ ὡς ἁμαρτωλὸς κρίνομαι;
why still and I as  sinner     am being judged?

8 2532 3361 2531     987          2532 2531     5346
  καὶ μὴ καθὼς βλασφημούμεθα καὶ καθώς φασίν
  And not just as we insulted   and just as say

5100  1473 3004     3754 4160     024 2556  2443
τινες ἡμᾶς λέγειν ὅτι ποιήσωμεν τὰ κακά, ἵνα
some  us   to say that we might do the bad,  that

2064    021 18      3739  09  2917     1738
ἔλθη   τὰ ἀγαθά; ὧν   τὸ κρίμα  ἔνδικόν
might come the good? Of whom the judgment in right

1510    9 5101 3767 4284        3756 3843
ἐστιν.     Τί  οὖν; προεχόμεθα; οὐ πάντως·
is.       What then? Hold we before? Not altogether;

4256          1063 2453     5037 2532 1672
προῃτιασάμεθα γὰρ Ἰουδαίους τε καὶ Ἕλληνας
before we accused for Judeans  both and Greeks

3956  5259 266       1510      10 2531   1125
πάντας ὑφ' ἁμαρτίαν εἶναι,     καθὼς γέγραπται
all   under sin     to be,   just as it has been
                                        written,

3754 3756 1510   1342    3761     1520  11 3756
ὅτι  οὐκ ἔστιν δίκαιος οὐδὲ εἷς,     οὐκ
(")  not there is right but not one,     not

1510   01  4920        3756 1510   01  1567
ἔστιν ὁ  συνίων,     οὐκ ἔστιν ὁ  ἐκζητῶν
is    the understanding, not is    the seeking out

04  2316  12 3956 1578    260
τὸν θεόν.     πάντες ἐξέκλιναν ἅμα
the God.     All    bowed out  at same time

889            3756 1510   01  4160  5544
ἠχρεώθησαν·    οὐκ ἔστιν ὁ  ποιῶν χρηστότητα,
they were unuseful; not is   the doing kindness,

3756 1510    2193 1520   13 5028   455
[οὐκ ἔστιν] ἕως ἑνός.     τάφος ἀνεῳγμένος
not there is until one.    Tomb having been opened

01  2995  846     019  1100       846
ὁ  λάρυγξ αὐτῶν, ταῖς γλώσσαις αὐτῶν
the throat of them, in the tongues of them

1387          2447 785      5259 024 5491
ἐδολιοῦσαν,   ἰὸς ἀσπίδων ὑπὸ τὰ χείλη
they were beguiling, poison of snakes under the lips

846     14 3739  09  4750 685      2532 4088
αὐτῶν·     ὧν   τὸ στόμα ἀρᾶς   καὶ πικρίας
of them;   of whom the mouth of cursing and bitterness

1073       15 3691 013 4228 846     2532      129
γέμει,       ὀξεῖς οἱ πόδες αὐτῶν ἐκχέαι   αἷμα,
is full,     sharp the feet of them to pour out blood,

16 4938       2532 5004      1722 019 3598     846
   σύντριμμα καὶ ταλαιπωρία ἐν  ταῖς ὁδοῖς αὐτῶν,
   ruin      and misery      in  the ways of them,

17 2532 3598 1515    3756 1097    18 3756 1510  5401
   καὶ ὁδὸν εἰρήνης οὐκ ἔγνωσαν.    οὐκ ἔστιν φόβος
   and way of peace not they knew. Not there is fear
```

what should we say? That
God is unjust to inflict
wrath on us? (I speak in a
human way.) [6]By no means!
For then how could God
judge the world? [7]But if
through my falsehood
God's truthfulness abounds
to his glory, why am I still
condemned as a
sinner? [8]And why not say
(as some people slander
us by saying that we say),
"Let us do evil so that
good may come"? Their
condemnation is deserved!
    9 What then? Are we any
better off?[a] No, not at all;
for we have already charged
that all, both Jews and
Greeks, are under the power
of sin, [10]as it is written:
    "There is no one who is
        righteous, not even
        one;
[11] there is no one who has
        understanding,
        there is no one who
        seeks God.
[12] All have turned aside,
        together they have
        become worthless;
        there is no one who
        shows kindness,
        there is not even one."
[13] "Their throats are
        opened graves;
        they use their tongues
        to deceive."
    "The venom of vipers is
        under their lips."
[14] "Their mouths are full
        of cursing and
        bitterness."
[15] "Their feet are swift
        to shed blood;
[16] ruin and misery are
        in their paths,
[17] and the way of peace they
        have not known."
[18] "There is no fear of God
        before their eyes."

_____
[a] Or at any disadvantage?

19 Now we know that whatever the law says, it speaks to those who are under the law, so that every mouth may be silenced, and the whole world may be held accountable to God. 20 For "no human being will be justified in his sight" by deeds prescribed by the law, for through the law comes the knowledge of sin.

21 But now, apart from law, the righteousness of God has been disclosed, and is attested by the law and the prophets, 22 the righteousness of God through faith in Jesus Christ[a] for all who believe. For there is no distinction, 23 since all have sinned and fall short of the glory of God; 24 they are now justified by his grace as a gift, through the redemption that is in Christ Jesus, 25 whom God put forward as a sacrifice of atonement[b] by his blood, effective through faith. He did this to show his righteousness, because in his divine forbearance he had passed over the sins previously committed; 26 it was to prove at the present time that he himself is righteous and that he justifies the one who has faith in Jesus.[c]

27 Then what becomes of boasting? It is excluded. By what law? By that of works? No, but by the law of faith.

a Or through the faith of Jesus Christ
b Or a place of atonement
c Or who has the faith of Jesus

2316	561		014 3788	846	**19**	3609a	1161

θεοῦ ἀπέναντι   τῶν ὀφθαλμῶν αὐτῶν. **19** οἴδαμεν δὲ
of God over against the eyes   of them. We know but

3754 3745   01   3551 3004   015   1722 03   3551
ὅτι ὅσα   ὁ νόμος λέγει τοῖς ἐν   τῷ νόμῳ
that as many as the law says to the in   the law

2980 2443 3956 4750 5420   2532 5267   1096
λαλεῖ, ἵνα πᾶν στόμα φραγῇ καὶ ὑπόδικος γένηται
speaks, that all mouth might and under   might
                     stopped   right   become

3956 01 2889 τῷ   2316 **20** 1360   1537 2041
πᾶς ὁ κόσμος τῷ   θεῷ· **20** διότι ἐξ ἔργων
all the world to the God;   because from works

3551 3756 1344   3956 4561 1799   846
νόμου οὐ δικαιωθήσεται   πᾶσα σὰρξ ἐνώπιον αὐτοῦ,
of law not will be made right all flesh before him,

1223   1063 3551 1922   266   **21** 3570 1161
διὰ γὰρ νόμου ἐπίγνωσις ἁμαρτίας. **21** Νυνὶ δὲ
through for law perception of sin.   Now but

5565 3551 1343   2316   5319
χωρὶς νόμου δικαιοσύνη θεοῦ πεφανέρωται
without law rightness of God has been demonstrated

3140   5259 02 3551 2532 014 4396
μαρτυρουμένη ὑπὸ τοῦ νόμου καὶ τῶν προφητῶν,
having testified by the law and the spokesmen,

22 1343   1161 2316 1223   4102   2424
22 δικαιοσύνη δὲ θεοῦ διὰ   πίστεως Ἰησοῦ
       rightness but of God through trust of Jesus

5547   1519 3956 016 4100   3756 1063
Χριστοῦ εἰς πάντας τοὺς πιστεύοντας. οὐ γὰρ
Christ in   all   the trusting ones. Not for

1510   1293   **23** 3956 1063 264 2532
ἐστιν διαστολή, **23** πάντες γὰρ ἥμαρτον καὶ
there is difference, all for sinned and

5302   06 1391   02 2316   **24** 1344
ὑστεροῦνται τῆς δόξης τοῦ θεοῦ **24** δικαιούμενοι
lack   the splendor of the God   being made right

1432 07   846 5485 1223 06   629
δωρεὰν τῇ αὐτοῦ χάριτι διὰ τῆς ἀπολυτρώσεως
as a gift in the same favor by the redemption

06 1722 5547   2424   **25** 3739 4388   01 2316
τῆς ἐν Χριστῷ Ἰησοῦ· **25** ὃν προέθετο ὁ θεὸς
the in Christ Jesus;   whom set forward the God

2435   1223   06 4102   1722 011 846
ἱλαστήριον διὰ [τῆς] πίστεως ἐν τῷ αὐτοῦ
place of expiation through the trust in the same

129   1519 1732   06   1343   846
αἵματι εἰς ἔνδειξιν τῆς δικαιοσύνης αὐτοῦ
blood in demonstration of the rightness of him

1223 08 3929   022   4266
διὰ τὴν πάρεσιν τῶν προγεγονότων
through the passing over of the having become before

265   **26** 1722 07 463   02 2316 4314
ἁμαρτημάτων **26** ἐν τῇ ἀνοχῇ τοῦ θεοῦ, πρὸς
sins   in   the restraint of the God, to

08 1732   06   1343   846   1722
τὴν ἔνδειξιν τῆς δικαιοσύνης αὐτοῦ ἐν
the demonstration of the rightness of him in

03 3568 2540   1519 012 1510 846 1342   2532
τῷ νῦν καιρῷ, εἰς τὸ εἶναι αὐτὸν δίκαιον καὶ
the now season, in the to be him right and

1344   04 4102   463   2424   **27** 4226 3767
δικαιοῦντα τὸν ἐκ πίστεως Ἰησοῦ. **27** Ποῦ οὖν
making right the from trust of Jesus. Where then

05 2746   1576   1223 4169 3551
ἡ καύχησις; ἐξεκλείσθη.   διὰ ποίου νόμου;
the brag? It was closed out. By what kind law?

022 2041   3780 235 1223 3551 4102
τῶν ἔργων; οὐχί, ἀλλὰ διὰ νόμου πίστεως.
Of the works? not, but through law of trust.

28
3049　　　　1063 1344　　　　　　4102　　　444
λογιζόμεθα γὰρ δικαιοῦσθαι πίστει ἄνθρωπον
We reason for to be made right in trust man

5565　　2041　3551　　　　2228　2453　　　01　2316
χωρὶς ἔργων νόμου. **29** ἢ Ἰουδαίων ὁ θεὸς
without works of law.　Or of Judeans the God

3441　　3780 2532 1484　　　　3483 2532 1484
μόνον; οὐχὶ καὶ ἐθνῶν; ναὶ καὶ ἐθνῶν,
alone? Not also of nations? Yes also of nations,

30
1512　　　　　1520 01　2316 3739 1344
εἴπερ εἷς ὁ θεὸς ὃς δικαιώσει
if indeed one the God who will make right

4061　　　　1537 4102　　2532 203　　　　　1223
περιτομὴν ἐκ πίστεως καὶ ἀκροβυστίαν διὰ
circumcision from trust and uncircumcision through

06 4102　　　3551　3767 2673　　　　1223　　06
τῆς πίστεως. **31** νόμον οὖν καταργοῦμεν διὰ τῆς
the trust.　Law then we abolish through the

4102　　　3361 1096　　　235　3551　2476
πίστεως; μὴ γένοιτο· ἀλλὰ νόμον ἱστάνομεν.
trust? Not may become; but law we cause to stand.

4:1
5101 3767 3004　　　　2147　　　　11　　04
Τί οὖν ἐροῦμεν εὑρηκέναι Ἀβραὰμ τὸν
What then will we say to have found Abraham the

4310a　　1473　2596 4561　　2 1487 1063　11　　　1537
προπάτορα ἡμῶν κατὰ σάρκα; εἰ γὰρ Ἀβραὰμ ἐξ
forefather of us by flesh? If for Abraham from

2041　1344　　　　　2192　2745　　235　3756 4314
ἔργων ἐδικαιώθη, ἔχει καύχημα, ἀλλ᾽ οὐ πρὸς
works was made right, he has brag, but not toward

2316　3 5101 1063 05　1124　　3004　　4100　　1161
θεόν. τί γὰρ ἡ γραφὴ λέγει; ἐπίστευσεν δὲ
God. What for the writing says? Trusted but

11　　03　2316 2532 3049　　　　846　　1519
Ἀβραὰμ τῷ θεῷ καὶ ἐλογίσθη αὐτῷ εἰς
Abraham the God and it was reasoned to him for

1343　　　　4 03　　1161 2038　　01　3408　　3756
δικαιοσύνην. τῷ δὲ ἐργαζομένῳ ὁ μισθὸς οὐ
rightness.　To the but working the wage not

3049　　　2596 5485　235　2596 3783　　5 03　　1161
λογίζεται κατὰ χάριν ἀλλὰ κατὰ ὀφείλημα, τῷ δὲ
is reasoned by favor but by debt; to the but

3361 2038　　　4100　　1161 1909 04 1344
μὴ ἐργαζομένῳ πιστεύοντι δὲ ἐπὶ τὸν δικαιοῦντα
not one working trusting but on the making right

04　765　　　3049　　　05　4102　846　1519
τὸν ἀσεβῆ λογίζεται ἡ πίστις αὐτοῦ εἰς
the irreverent is reasoned the trust of him for

1343　　　6 2509　　　　2532 1160a 3004 04
δικαιοσύνην· καθάπερ καὶ Δαυὶδ λέγει τὸν
rightness;　just as indeed also David says the

3108　　　02　　444　　　3739　01 2316
μακαρισμὸν τοῦ ἀνθρώπου ᾧ ὁ θεὸς
fortuneness of the man to whom the God

3049　　　1343　　　5565　2041　7 3107
λογίζεται δικαιοσύνην χωρὶς ἔργων· μακάριοι
reasons rightness without works; fortunate

3739　863　　017 458　　　　2532 3739
ὧν ἀφέθησαν αἱ ἀνομίαι καὶ ὧν
of whom were sent off the lawlessnesses and of whom

1943　　　017 266　　8 3107　　　435
ἐπεκαλύφθησαν αἱ ἁμαρτίαι· μακάριος ἀνὴρ
were covered over the sins; fortunate man

3739　3756 3361 3049　　2962　266　9 01
οὗ οὐ μὴ λογίσηται κύριος ἁμαρτίαν. Ὁ
of whom not not might reason Master sin.　The

3108　　　3767 3778 1909 08 4061　　2228 2532
μακαρισμὸς οὖν οὗτος ἐπὶ τὴν περιτομὴν ἢ καὶ
fortuneness then this on the circumcision or also

28For we hold that a person is justified by faith apart from works prescribed by the law. 29Or is God the God of Jews only? Is he not the God of Gentiles also? Yes, of Gentiles also, 30since God is one; and he will justify the circumcised on the ground of faith and the uncircumcised through that same faith. 31Do we then overthrow the law by this faith? By no means! On the contrary, we uphold the law.

CHAPTER 4

What then are we to say was gained by[a] Abraham, our ancestor according to the flesh? 2For if Abraham was justified by works, he has something to boast about, but not before God. 3For what does the scripture say? "Abraham believed God, and it was reckoned to him as righteousness." 4Now to one who works, wages are not reckoned as a gift but as something due. 5But to one who without works trusts him who justifies the ungodly, such faith is reckoned as righteousness. 6So also David speaks of the blessedness of those to whom God reckons righteousness apart from works:

7 "Blessed are those whose iniquities are forgiven, and whose sins are covered;
8 blessed is the one against whom the Lord will not reckon sin."

9 Is this blessedness, then, pronounced only on the circumcised, or also

a Other ancient authorities read say about

on the uncircumcised? We say, "Faith was reckoned to Abraham as righteousness." [10]How then was it reckoned to him? Was it before or after he had been circumcised? It was not after, but before he was circumcised. [11]He received the sign of circumcision as a seal of the righteousness that he had by faith while he was still uncircumcised. The purpose was to make him the ancestor of all who believe without being circumcised and who thus have righteousness reckoned to them, [12]and likewise the ancestor of the circumcised who are not only circumcised but who also follow the example of the faith that our ancestor Abraham had before he was circumcised.

13 For the promise that he would inherit the world did not come to Abraham or to his descendants through the law but through the righteousness of faith. [14]If it is the adherents of the law who are to be the heirs, faith is null and the promise is void. [15]For the law brings wrath; but where there is no law, neither is there violation.

16 For this reason it depends on faith, in order that the promise may rest on grace and be guaranteed to all his descendants, not only to the adherents of the law but also to those who share the faith of Abraham (for he is the father

```
1909 08  203              3004      1063 3049
ἐπὶ  τὴν ἀκροβυστίαν;   λέγομεν γάρ· ἐλογίσθη
on   the uncircumcision? We say  for; was reasoned
03      11    05  4102  1519 1343          4459
τῷ  ᾿Αβραὰμ ἡ πίστις εἰς δικαιοσύνην. 10 πῶς
to the Abraham the trust for rightness.     How
3767 3049          1722 4061        1510 2228
οὖν ἐλογίσθη;    ἐν περιτομῇ ὄντι ἢ
then was it reasoned? In circumcision being or
1722 203           3756 1722 4061       235
ἐν  ἀκροβυστίᾳ;  οὐκ ἐν περιτομῇ ἀλλ᾿
in  uncircumcision? Not in circumcision but
1722 203       11  2532 4592    2983
ἐν  ἀκροβυστίᾳ·    καὶ σημεῖον ἔλαβεν
in  uncircumcision; and sign he received
4061          4973    06 1343       06
περιτομῆς  σφραγῖδα τῆς δικαιοσύνης τῆς
of circumcision seal the of the rightness of the
4102   06 1722 07 203          1519 012 1510
πίστεως τῆς ἐν τῇ ἀκροβυστίᾳ,  εἰς τὸ εἶναι
trust the in the uncircumcision, to the to be
846  3962 3956   014 4100    1223
αὐτὸν πατέρα πάντων τῶν πιστευόντων δι᾿
him father of all the trusting through
203           1519 012 3049         2532 846
ἀκροβυστίας, εἰς τὸ λογισθῆναι [καὶ] αὐτοῖς
uncircumcision, in the to be reasoned and to them
08 1343          12 2532 3962  4061    015
[τὴν] δικαιοσύνην,  καὶ πατέρα περιτομῆς τοῖς
the rightness,   and father circumcision the
3756 1537 4061       3441   235 2532 015  4748
οὐκ ἐκ περιτομῆς μόνον ἀλλὰ καὶ τοῖς στοιχοῦσιν
not from circumcision alone but also the walking
023  2487    06  1722 203        4102
τοῖς ἴχνεσιν τῆς ἐν ἀκροβυστίᾳ πίστεως
the footprints of the in uncircumcision of trust
02   3962    1473 11  13 3756 1063 1223    3551
τοῦ πατρὸς ἡμῶν ᾿Αβραάμ.  Οὐ γὰρ διὰ νόμου
of the father of us Abraham. Not for through law
05 1860    03  11      2228 011    4690
ἡ ἐπαγγελία τῷ ᾿Αβραὰμ ἢ τῷ σπέρματι
the promise to the Abraham or to the seed
846   09 2818       846 1510 2889    235
αὐτοῦ, τὸ κληρονόμον αὐτὸν εἶναι κόσμου, ἀλλὰ
of him, the inheritor him to be of world, but
1223 1343      4102   14 1487 1063 013 1537
διὰ δικαιοσύνης πίστεως.  εἰ γὰρ οἱ ἐκ
through rightness of trust. If for the from
3551 2818   2758       05 4102   2532
νόμου κληρονόμοι, κεκένωται ἡ πίστις καὶ
law inheritors, has been emptied the trust and
2673          05 1860    15 01 1063 3551
κατήργηται ἡ ἐπαγγελία·  ὁ γὰρ νόμος
has been abolished the promise; the for law
3709 2716          3757 1161 3756 1510 3551
ὀργὴν κατεργάζεται· οὗ δὲ οὐκ ἔστιν νόμος
anger thoroughly works; where but not is law
3761 3847      16 1223  3778 1537 4102
οὐδὲ παράβασις.  Διὰ τοῦτο ἐκ πίστεως,
but not transgression. Through this from trust,
2443 2596 5485 1519 012 1510 949   08 1860
ἵνα κατὰ χάριν, εἰς τὸ εἶναι βεβαίαν τὴν ἐπαγγελίαν
that by favor, into the to be firm the promise
3956 011 4690    3756 011    1537 02 3551 3441
παντὶ τῷ σπέρματι, οὐ τῷ ἐκ τοῦ νόμου μόνον
to all the seed, not to the from the law alone
235  2532 011   1537 4102    11  3739 1510 3962
ἀλλὰ καὶ τῷ ἐκ πίστεως ᾿Αβραάμ, ὅς ἐστιν πατὴρ
but also to the from trust Abraham, who is father
```

```
3956      1473   17  2531    1125         3754  3962      4183
πάντων  ἡμῶν,       καθὼς  γέγραπται   ὅτι   πατέρα  πολλῶν
of all   us,        just   it has been  (")   father of many
                    as     written,

1484       5087         1473  2713              3739  4100
ἐθνῶν    τέθεικά    σε,  κατέναντι    οὗ   ἐπίστευσεν
nations  I have set you,  over against whom he trusted

2316 02  2227            016   3498     2532 2564        024
θεοῦ τοῦ ζῳοποιοῦντος  τοὺς νεκροὺς καὶ  καλοῦντος  τὰ
God  the making alive   the  dead    and  calling     the

3361 1510  5613 1510      18  3739 3844 1680    1909 1680
μὴ  ὄντα  ὡς  ὄντα.       Ὃς  παρ' ἐλπίδα ἐπ' ἐλπίδι
not being as being.       Who from hope   on  hope

4100          1519 012 1096      846  3962      4183
ἐπίστευσεν  εἰς  τὸ  γενέσθαι αὐτὸν πατέρα  πολλῶν
trusted      in   the to become him  father of many

1484    2596 012 3004           3779  1510      09
ἐθνῶν  κατὰ τὸ  εἰρημένον·    οὕτως ἔσται    τὸ
nations by   the having been said; thusly will be the

4690     1473   19  2532 3361  770            07    4102
σπέρμα  σου,       καὶ  μὴ   ἀσθενήσας    τῇ   πίστει
seed     of you,   and  not  having weakened in the trust

2657          012 1438    4983     3499
κατενόησεν  τὸ ἑαυτοῦ  σῶμα [ἤδη] νενεκρωμένον,
he thought   the of himself body already having been
carefully                                   dead,

1541           4225  5225          2532 08  3500       06
ἑκατονταετής  που  ὑπάρχων,   καὶ  τὴν νέκρωσιν τῆς
hundred years where existing,   and  the deadness of the

3388       4564    20 1519 1161 08  1860      02
μήτρας   Σάρρας·   εἰς  δὲ  τὴν ἐπαγγελίαν τοῦ
motherhood Sarra;   into but  the promise     of the

2316 3756 1252       07   570       235  1743
θεοῦ οὐ  διεκρίθη  τῇ   ἀπιστίᾳ ἀλλ' ἐνεδυναμώθη
God  not he doubted in the untrust but  was empowered

07   4102      1325   1391      03        2316  21 2532
τῇ   πίστει,  δοὺς δόξαν  τῷ     θεῷ      καὶ
in the trust, giving splendor to the God   and

4135                  3754 3739 1861        1415     1510 2532
πληροφορηθεὶς ὅτι  ὃ    ἐπήγγελται δυνατός ἐστιν καὶ
having been        that what he has   power   he is also
fully persuaded    promised

4160      22  1352   2532 3049                 846      1519
ποιῆσαι.     διὸ  [καὶ] ἐλογίσθη          αὐτῷ    εἰς
to do.       Wherefore also it was reasoned to him  for

1343              3756 1223          1161 1223    846
δικαιοσύνην. 23 Οὐκ ἐγράφη       δὲ  δι'      αὐτὸν
rightness.      Not was it written but through him

3441    3754 3049       846    24 235  2532 1223
μόνον ὅτι ἐλογίσθη    αὐτῷ     ἀλλὰ καὶ  δι'
alone that it was reasoned to him  but  also because

1473  3739   3195        3049          015
ἡμᾶς, οἷς  μέλλει    λογίζεσθαι,   τοῖς
of us, to whom it is about to be reasoned, the

4100          1909 04 1453       2424    04  2962
πιστεύουσιν ἐπὶ τὸν ἐγείραντα  Ἰησοῦν τὸν κύριον
trusting      on  the having raised Jesus the Master

1473  1537 3498      25 3739 3860          1223      024
ἡμῶν ἐκ  νεκρῶν,      ὃς  παρεδόθη      διὰ      τὰ
of us from dead,       who was given over through the

3900            1473  2532 1453        1223 08  1347
παραπτώματα ἡμῶν καὶ  ἠγέρθη      διὰ τὴν δικαίωσιν
trespasses   of us and  was raised by  the rightening

1473    5:1 1344             3767 1537 4102
ἡμῶν.      Δικαιωθέντες   οὖν  ἐκ  πίστεως
of us.     Having been made right then from trust

1515       2192      4314  04  2316 1223      02  2962
εἰρήνην ἔχομεν  πρὸς τὸν θεὸν διὰ      τοῦ κυρίου
peace    we have toward the God through the Master
```

of all of us, [17]as it is written, "I have made you the father of many nations")—in the presence of the God in whom he believed, who gives life to the dead and calls into existence the things that do not exist. [18]Hoping against hope, he believed that he would become "the father of many nations," according to what was said, "So numerous shall your descendants be." [19]He did not weaken in faith when he considered his own body, which was already[a] as good as dead (for he was about a hundred years old), or when he considered the barrenness of Sarah's womb. [20]No distrust made him waver concerning the promise of God, but he grew strong in his faith as he gave glory to God, [21]being fully convinced that God was able to do what he had promised. [22]Therefore his faith[b] "was reckoned to him as righteousness." [23]Now the words, "it was reckoned to him," were written not for his sake alone, [24]but for ours also. It will be reckoned to us who believe in him who raised Jesus our Lord from the dead, [25]who was handed over to death for our trespasses and was raised for our justification.

CHAPTER 5

Therefore, since we are justified by faith, we[c] have peace with God through our Lord

---

[a] Other ancient authorities lack *already*

[b] Gk *Therefore it*

[c] Other ancient authorities read *let us*

Jesus Christ, [2]through whom we have obtained access[a] to this grace in which we stand; and we[b] boast in our hope of sharing the glory of God. [3]And not only that, but we[b] also boast in our sufferings, knowing that suffering produces endurance, [4]and endurance produces character, and character produces hope, [5]and hope does not disappoint us, because God's love has been poured into our hearts through the Holy Spirit that has been given to us.

[6]For while we were still weak, at the right time Christ died for the ungodly. [7]Indeed, rarely will anyone die for a righteous person— though perhaps for a good person someone might actually dare to die. [8]But God proves his love for us in that while we still were sinners Christ died for us. [9]Much more surely then, now that we have been justified by his blood, will we be saved through him from the wrath of God.[c] [10]For if while we were enemies, we were reconciled to God through the death of his Son, much more surely, having been reconciled, will we be saved by his life. [11]But more than that, we even boast in God

a Other ancient authorities add
  by faith
b Or *let us*
c Gk *the wrath*

1473	2424	5547	**2** 1223	3739 2532 08	4318	
ἡμῶν	Ἰησοῦ	Χριστοῦ	δι'	οὗ καὶ τὴν	προσαγωγὴν	
of us	Jesus	Christ	through	whom also the	access	

2192   07   4102   1519 08   5485 3778 1722
ἐσχήκαμεν [τῇ   πίστει] εἰς τὴν χάριν ταύτην ἐν
we have had in the   trust   in   the favor this   in

3739 2476   2532 2744   1909 1680   06
ᾗ   ἑστήκαμεν καὶ καυχώμεθα ἐπ' ἐλπίδι τῆς
which we have stood and we brag   on   hope   of the

1391   02   2316   **3** 3756 3441 1161 235 2532
δόξης τοῦ θεοῦ.   οὐ μόνον δέ, ἀλλὰ καὶ
splendor of the God.   Not alone but, but   also

2744   1722 019 2347   3609α   3754 05
καυχώμεθα ἐν ταῖς θλίψεσιν, εἰδότες ὅτι ἡ
we brag   in   the afflictions, knowing that the

2347   5281   2716   **4** 05   1161
θλῖψις ὑπομονὴν κατεργάζεται,   ἡ δὲ
affliction patience works thoroughly,   the but

5281   1382   05   1161 1382   1680   **5** 05
ὑπομονὴ δοκιμήν, ἡ δὲ δοκιμὴ ἐλπίδα.   ἡ
patience approval, the but approval hope.   The

1161 1680 3756 2617   3754   05 26   02
δὲ ἐλπὶς οὐ καταισχύνει, ὅτι ἡ ἀγάπη τοῦ
but hope not is ashamed, because the love of the

2316 1632   1722 019 2588   1473 1223
θεοῦ ἐκκέχυται ἐν ταῖς καρδίαις ἡμῶν διὰ
God is poured out in   the hearts   of us through

4151   40   010 1325   1473   2089
πνεύματος ἁγίου τοῦ δοθέντος ἡμῖν.   **6** Ἔτι
spirit   holy the having been given to us.   Still

1063 5547   1510 1473 772   2089 2596 2540
γὰρ Χριστὸς ὄντων ἡμῶν ἀσθενῶν ἔτι κατὰ καιρὸν
for Christ being of us weak   still by   season

5228   765   599   **7** 3433   1063
ὑπὲρ ἀσεβῶν ἀπέθανεν.   μόλις γὰρ
on behalf of irreverent died.   Scarcely for

5228   1342   5100 599   5228
ὑπὲρ δικαίου τις ἀποθανεῖται· ὑπὲρ
on behalf of right   some will die;   on behalf of

1063 02 18   5029   5100 2532 5111 599
γὰρ τοῦ ἀγαθοῦ τάχα τις καὶ τολμᾷ ἀποθανεῖν·
for the good   perhaps some even dares to die;

8 4921   1161 08 1438   26   1519 1473 01
συνίστησιν δὲ τὴν ἑαυτοῦ ἀγάπην εἰς ἡμᾶς ὁ
commends but the of himself love   to   us   the

2316 3754 2089 268   1510 1473 5547
θεός, ὅτι ἔτι ἁμαρτωλῶν ὄντων ἡμῶν Χριστὸς
God, that still sinners   being of us Christ

5228   1473 599   **9** 4183 3767 3123
ὑπὲρ ἡμῶν ἀπέθανεν.   πολλῷ οὖν μᾶλλον
on behalf of us died.   Much then more

1344   3568 1722 011 129   846
δικαιωθέντες νῦν ἐν τῷ αἵματι αὐτοῦ
having been made right now   in   the blood   of him

4982   1223   846   575 06 3709
σωθησόμεθα δι' αὐτοῦ ἀπὸ τῆς ὀργῆς.
we will be delivered through him   from the anger.

10 1487 1063 2190   1510 2644   03
εἰ γὰρ ἐχθροὶ ὄντες κατηλλάγημεν τῷ
If for hostile being we were reconciled to the

2316 1223   02 2288   02   5207 846   4183
θεῷ διὰ   τοῦ θανάτου τοῦ υἱοῦ αὐτοῦ, πολλῷ
God through the death   of the son of him, much

3123 2644   4982   1722 07 2222 846
μᾶλλον καταλλαγέντες σωθησόμεθα ἐν τῇ ζωῇ αὐτοῦ·
more having been we will be in   the life of him;
reconciled   delivered

11 3756 3441 1161 235 2532 2744   1722 03 2316
οὐ μόνον δέ, ἀλλὰ καὶ καυχώμενοι ἐν τῷ θεῷ
not alone but, but also bragging   in   the God

1223	02	2962	1473	2424	5547	1223	3739
διὰ	τοῦ	κυρίου	ἡμῶν	'Ιησοῦ	Χριστοῦ	δι'	οὗ
through	the	Master	of us	Jesus	Christ	through	whom

3568 08	2643		2983		**12**	1223	3778
νῦν τὴν	καταλλαγὴν		ἐλάβομεν.			Διὰ	τοῦτο
now the	reconciliation		we received.			Through	this

5618	1223	1520 444	05 266	1519 04
ὥσπερ	δι'	ἑνὸς ἀνθρώπου	ἡ ἁμαρτία εἰς	τὸν
as indeed	through	one man	the sin	into the

2889	1525	2532 1223	06 266	01 2288
κόσμον	εἰσῆλθεν καὶ	διὰ	τῆς ἁμαρτίας ὁ	θάνατος,
world	came in and	through	the sin	the death,

2532 3779	1519 3956	444	01 2288
καὶ οὕτως	εἰς πάντας	ἀνθρώπους ὁ	θάνατος
also thusly	into all	men	the death

1330	1909 3739 3956	264	**13**	891	1063
διῆλθεν,	ἐφ' ᾧ πάντες	ἥμαρτον·		ἄχρι	γὰρ
went through,	on whom all	sinned;		until	for

3551	266	1510 1722 2889	266	1161 3756
νόμου	ἁμαρτία	ἦν ἐν κόσμῳ,	ἁμαρτία	δὲ οὐκ
law	sin	was in world,	sin	but not

1677	3361 1510 3551	**14**	235	936	01
ἐλλογεῖται μὴ	ὄντος νόμου,		ἀλλὰ	ἐβασίλευσεν	ὁ
is charged not	being of law,		but	was king	the

2288	575 76	3360 3475	2532 1909 016	3361
θάνατος	ἀπὸ 'Αδὰμ	μέχρι Μωϋσέως	καὶ ἐπὶ τοὺς	μὴ
death	from Adam	until Moses	and on the	not

264	1909 011 3667	06	3847
ἁμαρτήσαντας	ἐπὶ τῷ ὁμοιώματι	τῆς	παραβάσεως
having sinned	on the likeness	of the	transgression

76	3739 1510 5179	02	3195	**15**	235
'Αδὰμ	ὅς ἐστιν τύπος	τοῦ	μέλλοντος.		'Αλλ'
Adam	who is example	of the	being about to be.		But

3756 5613 09	3900		3779	2532 09	5486
οὐχ ὡς	τὸ παράπτωμα,		οὕτως	καὶ τὸ	χάρισμα·
not as	the trespass,		thusly	also the	favor gift;

1487 1063 011	02	1520 3900	013 4183
εἰ γὰρ τῷ	τοῦ	ἑνὸς παραπτώματι	οἱ πολλοὶ
if for to the	of the	one trespass	the many

599	4183 3123	05 5485 02	2316 2532 05
ἀπέθανον,	πολλῷ μᾶλλον	ἡ χάρις τοῦ	θεοῦ καὶ ἡ
died,	much more	the favor of the	God and the

1431	1722 5485	07 02	1520 444	2424
δωρεὰ	ἐν χάριτι	τῇ τοῦ	ἑνὸς ἀνθρώπου	'Ιησοῦ
gift	in favor	the of the	one man	Jesus

5547	1519 016	4183	4052	**16**	2532 3756
Χριστοῦ	εἰς τοὺς	πολλοὺς	ἐπερίσσευσεν.		καὶ οὐχ
Christ	to the	many	exceeded.		And not

5613 1223	1520 264	09 1434	09 3303
ὡς δι'	ἑνὸς ἁμαρτήσαντος	τὸ δώρημα·	τὸ μὲν
as through one	having sinned	the gift;	the indeed

1063 2917	1537 1520 1519 2631	09 1161
γὰρ κρίμα	ἐξ ἑνὸς εἰς κατάκριμα,	τὸ δὲ
for judgment	from one to condemnation,	the but

5486	1537 4183	3900	1519 1345
χάρισμα	ἐκ πολλῶν	παραπτωμάτων	εἰς δικαίωμα.
favor gift	from many	trespasses	into right.

17	1487 1063 011	02	1520 3900	01
	εἰ γὰρ τῷ	τοῦ	ἑνὸς παραπτώματι	ὁ
	If for in the	of the	one trespass	the

2288	936	1223	02 1520	4183 3123
θάνατος	ἐβασίλευσεν	διὰ	τοῦ ἑνός,	πολλῷ μᾶλλον
death	was king	through	the one,	much more

013	08 4050	06	5485	2532 06 1431
οἱ	τὴν περισσείαν	τῆς	χάριτος	καὶ τῆς δωρεᾶς
the ones	the excess	of the	favor	and the gift

06	1343	2983	1722 2222 936
τῆς	δικαιοσύνης	λαμβάνοντες	ἐν ζωῇ βασιλεύσουσιν
of the	rightness	receiving	in life will be king

through our Lord Jesus Christ, through whom we have now received reconciliation.

12 Therefore, just as sin came into the world through one man, and death came through sin, and so death spread to all because all have sinned— [13]sin was indeed in the world before the law, but sin is not reckoned when there is no law. [14]Yet death exercised dominion from Adam to Moses, even over those whose sins were not like the transgression of Adam, who is a type of the one who was to come.

15 But the free gift is not like the trespass. For if the many died through the one man's trespass, much more surely have the grace of God and the free gift in the grace of the one man, Jesus Christ, abounded for the many. [16]And the free gift is not like the effect of the one man's sin. For the judgment following one trespass brought condemnation, but the free gift following many trespasses brings justification. [17]If, because of the one man's trespass, death exercised dominion through that one, much more surely will those who receive the abundance of grace and the free gift of righteousness exercise dominion

in life through the one man, Jesus Christ.

18 Therefore just as one man's trespass led to condemnation for all, so one man's act of righteousness leads to justification and life for all. 19For just as by the one man's disobedience the many were made sinners, so by the one man's obedience the many will be made righteous. 20But law came in, with the result that the trespass multiplied; but where sin increased, grace abounded all the more, 21so that, just as sin exercised dominion in death, so grace might also exercise dominion through justification[a] leading to eternal life through Jesus Christ our Lord.

CHAPTER 6

What then are we to say? Should we continue in sin in order that grace may abound? 2By no means! How can we who died to sin go on living in it? 3Do you not know that all of us who have been baptized into Christ Jesus were baptized into his death? 4Therefore we have been buried with him by baptism into death, so that, just as Christ was raised from the dead by the glory of the Father, so we too

[a] Or righteousness

1223	02	1520	2424	5547	**18**	686 3767
διὰ	τοῦ	ἑνὸς	'Ιησοῦ	Χριστοῦ.		᾿Άρα οὖν
through	the	one	Jesus	Christ.		Then therefore

5613	1223		1520	3900		1519	3956	444
ὡς	δι'		ἑνὸς	παραπτώματος		εἰς	πάντας	ἀνθρώπους
as	through		one	trespass		into	all	men

1519	2631		3779	2532	1223		1520
εἰς	κατάκριμα,		οὕτως	καὶ	δι'		ἑνὸς
to	condemnation,		thusly	also	through		one

1345		1519	3956	444		1519	1347
δικαιώματος	εἰς	πάντας	ἀνθρώπους	εἰς	δικαίωσιν
right act	into	all	men		into	rightening

2222	**19**	5618		1063	1223	06	3876
ζωῆς·		ὥσπερ		γὰρ	διὰ	τῆς	παρακοῆς
of life;		as indeed		for	through	the	disobedience

02	1520	444		268		2525		013
τοῦ	ἑνὸς	ἀνθρώπου	ἁμαρτωλοὶ	κατεστάθησαν		οἱ
of	the one	man		sinners		were appointed		the

4183	3779	2532	1223	06	5218	02	1520
πολλοί,	οὕτως	καὶ	διὰ	τῆς	ὑπακοῆς	τοῦ	ἑνὸς
many,	thusly	and	through	the	obedience	of the	one

1342	2525		013	4183	**20**	3551	1161
δίκαιοι	κατασταθήσονται		οἱ	πολλοί.		νόμος	δὲ
right	will be appointed		the	many.		Law	but

3922		2443	4121		09	3900
παρεισῆλθεν,		ἵνα	πλεονάσῃ		τὸ	παράπτωμα·
came in along,		that	might increase		the	trespass;

3757	1161	4121		09	05	266	5248
οὗ	δὲ	ἐπλεόνασεν	ἡ	ἁμαρτία,	ὑπερεπερίσσευσεν
where	but	increased	the	sin		exceeded beyond

05	5485	**21**	2443	5618		936		05	266
ἡ	χάρις,		ἵνα	ὥσπερ		ἐβασίλευσεν	ἡ	ἁμαρτία
the	favor,		that	as indeed		was king		the	sin

1722	03	2288		3779	2532	05	5485	936
ἐν	τῷ	θανάτῳ,	οὕτως	καὶ	ἡ	χάρις	βασιλεύσῃ
in	the	death,		thusly	also	the	favor	might be king

1223	1343		1519	2222	166		1223		2424
διὰ	δικαιοσύνης	εἰς	ζωὴν	αἰώνιον	διὰ		'Ιησοῦ
through	rightness		into	life	eternal	through		Jesus

5547	02	2962	1473	**6:1**	5101	3767	3004
Χριστοῦ	τοῦ	κυρίου	ἡμῶν.		Τί	οὖν	ἐροῦμεν;
Christ	the	Master	of us.		What	then will	we say?

1961		07		266		2443	05	5485
ἐπιμένωμεν		τῇ		ἁμαρτίᾳ,		ἵνα	ἡ	χάρις
Might we stay on		in the		sin,		that	the	favor

4121		**2**	3361	1096		3748
πλεονάσῃ;			μὴ	γένοιτο.		οἵτινες
might increase?			Not	may it become.		Who

599	07		266		4459	2089	2198		1722
ἀπεθάνομεν	τῇ		ἁμαρτίᾳ,	πῶς	ἔτι	ζήσομεν		ἐν
we died	in the		sin,		how	still	will we live		in

846		**3**	2228	50		3754	3745
αὐτῇ;			ἢ	ἀγνοεῖτε		ὅτι,	ὅσοι
in it?			Or	do you not know		that,	as many as

907		1519	5547	2424		1519	04
ἐβαπτίσθημεν	εἰς	Χριστὸν	'Ιησοῦν,	εἰς	τὸν
we were immersed		into	Christ	Jesus,		into	the

2288	846	907		**4**	4916
θάνατον	αὐτοῦ	ἐβαπτίσθημεν;			συνετάφημεν
death	of him	we were immersed?			We were buried together

3767	846	1223		010	908		1519	04	2288
οὖν	αὐτῷ	διὰ		τοῦ	βαπτίσματος	εἰς	τὸν	θάνατον,
then	to him	through		the	immersion		into	the	death,

2443	5618		1453		5547	1537	3498	1223
ἵνα	ὥσπερ		ἠγέρθη		Χριστὸς	ἐκ	νεκρῶν	διὰ
that	as indeed		was raised		Christ	from	dead	through

06	1391	02		3962	3779	2532	1473	1722
τῆς	δόξης	τοῦ		πατρός,	οὕτως	καὶ	ἡμεῖς	ἐν
the	splendor	of the		father,	thusly	also	we	in

```
2538       2222      4043                    5 1487 1063
καινότητι  ζωῆς      περιπατήσωμεν.            εἰ   γὰρ
newness    of life   might walk around.  If     for

4854       1096            011      3667
σύμφυτοι   γεγόναμεν        τῷ      ὁμοιώματι
planted together  we have become  in the  likeness

02     2288      846     235    2532 06    386
τοῦ    θανάτου  αὐτοῦ,  ἀλλὰ  καὶ  τῆς   ἀναστάσεως
of the death    of him,  but   also of the standing up

1510        6 3778    1097          3754 01  3820    1473
ἐσόμεθα·      τοῦτο  γινώσκοντες ὅτι  ὁ   παλαιὸς ἡμῶν
we will be;   this   knowing     that the old      of us

444        4957            2443 2673       09   4983  06
ἄνθρωπος   συνεσταυρώθη,  ἵνα  καταργηθῇ τὸ  σῶμα  τῆς
man        was crucified  that might be   the body of the
           together,           abolished

266         010 3371       1398        1473 07   266
ἁμαρτίας,  τοῦ μηκέτι    δουλεύειν   ἡμᾶς τῇ  ἁμαρτίᾳ·
sin,        the no longer to be slave  us    to the sin;

7 01  1063 599            1344               575   06
ὁ    γὰρ  ἀποθανὼν     δεδικαίωται        ἀπὸ  τῆς
the for   having died  has been made right from the

266       8 1487 1161 599              4862 5547
ἁμαρτίας.   εἰ   δὲ   ἀπεθάνομεν  σὺν  Χριστῷ,
sin.        If   but  we died     with Christ,

4100        3754 2532 4800                    846
πιστεύομεν ὅτι  καὶ  συζήσομεν              αὐτῷ,
we trust    that also we will live together  to him,

9 3609a   3754 5547   1453             1537 3498
εἰδότες ὅτι  Χριστὸς ἐγερθεὶς         ἐκ  νεκρῶν
knowing that Christ  having been raised from dead

3765      599            2288      846  3765
οὐκέτι   ἀποθνῄσκει,  θάνατος αὐτοῦ οὐκέτι
no longer dies,        death   of him no longer

2961        10 3739 1063 599          07   266
κυριεύει.     ὃ   γὰρ  ἀπέθανεν,  τῇ  ἁμαρτίᾳ
masters.      That for  he died,  to the sin

599       2178          3739 1161 2198       2198
ἀπέθανεν ἐφάπαξ·       ὃ    δὲ   ζῇ,         ζῇ
he died  once for all; that but he lives,  he lives

03      2316      11 3779      2532 1473   3049     1473
τῷ      θεῷ.        οὕτως    καὶ  ὑμεῖς  λογίζεσθε ἑαυτοὺς
to the God.         Thusly   also you   reason    yourselves

1510     3498      3303    07   266       2198      1161
[εἶναι]  νεκροὺς μὲν   τῇ  ἁμαρτίᾳ ζῶντας δὲ
to be    dead    indeed to the sin  living but

03      2316 1722 5547      2424    12 3361 3767
τῷ      θεῷ  ἐν  Χριστῷ  Ἰησοῦ.     Μὴ   οὖν
to the God   in  Christ   Jesus.     Not  then

936      05   266      1722 011 2349        1473  4983
βασιλευέτω ἡ   ἁμαρτία ἐν  τῷ  θνητῷ      ὑμῶν σώματι
let be king the sin     in  the death like of you body

1519 012 5219          019   1939         846    13 3366
εἰς  τὸ  ὑπακούειν  ταῖς ἐπιθυμίαις αὐτοῦ,     μηδὲ
for  the to obey     the  desires    of it,      but not

3936          024 3196  1473   3696     93
παριστάνετε  τὰ  μέλη  ὑμῶν  ὅπλα   ἀδικίας
stand along  the members of you weapons of unright

07  266      235  3936        1438      03
τῇ  ἁμαρτίᾳ, ἀλλὰ παραστήσατε ἑαυτοὺς  τῷ
to the sin,   but  stand along yourselves to the

2316 5616 1537 3498    2198     2532 024 3196    1473
θεῷ  ὡσεὶ ἐκ  νεκρῶν ζῶντας καὶ  τὰ  μέλη   ὑμῶν
God  as   from dead  living and  the members of you

3696     1343           03      2316 14 266       1063 1473
ὅπλα     δικαιοσύνης   τῷ      θεῷ.    ἁμαρτία γὰρ ὑμῶν
weapons of rightness   to the God.     Sin      for of you

3756 2961       3756 1063 1510      5259  3551  235
οὐ   κυριεύσει·  οὐ  γὰρ  ἐστε    ὑπὸ  νόμον ἀλλὰ
not  will master; not for  you are under law   but
```

might walk in newness of life.

5 For if we have been united with him in a death like his, we will certainly be united with him in a resurrection like his. 6 We know that our old self was crucified with him so that the body of sin might be destroyed, and we might no longer be enslaved to sin. 7 For whoever has died is freed from sin. 8 But if we have died with Christ, we believe that we will also live with him. 9 We know that Christ, being raised from the dead, will never die again; death no longer has dominion over him. 10 The death he died, he died to sin, once for all; but the life he lives, he lives to God. 11 So you also must consider yourselves dead to sin and alive to God in Christ Jesus.

12 Therefore, do not let sin exercise dominion in your mortal bodies, to make you obey their passions. 13 No longer present your members to sin as instruments[a] of wickedness, but present yourselves to God as those who have been brought from death to life, and present your members to God as instruments[a] of righteousness. 14 For sin will have no dominion over you, since you are not under law but under grace.

a Or weapons

15 What then? Should we sin because we are not under law but under grace? By no means! 16Do you not know that if you present yourselves to anyone as obedient slaves, you are slaves of the one whom you obey, either of sin, which leads to death, or of obedience, which leads to righteousness? 17But thanks be to God that you, having once been slaves of sin, have become obedient from the heart to the form of teaching to which you were entrusted, 18and that you, having been set free from sin, have become slaves of righteousness. 19I am speaking in human terms because of your natural limitations.[a] For just as you once presented your members as slaves to impurity and to greater and greater iniquity, so now present your members as slaves to righteousness for sanctification.

20 When you were slaves of sin, you were free in regard to righteousness. 21So what advantage did you then get from the things of which you now are ashamed? The end of those things is death. 22But now that you have been freed from sin and enslaved to God, the advantage you get is sanctification. The end is eternal life. 23For the wages of sin is death, but the

[a] Gk the weakness of your flesh

5259	5485	**15** 5101	3767	264	3754	3756
ὑπὸ	χάριν.	Τί	οὖν;	ἁμαρτήσωμεν,	ὅτι	οὐκ
under	favor.	What then?		Might we sin,	because	not

1510   5259   3551   235   5259   5485   3361
ἐσμὲν ὑπὸ   νόμον ἀλλὰ ὑπὸ χάριν; μὴ
we are under law   but   under favor? Not

1096   **16** 3756 3609a   3754 3739
γένοιτο.   οὐκ οἴδατε   ὅτι   ᾧ
may it become. Not you know that to whom

3936   1438   1401   1519.5218
παριστάνετε   ἑαυτοὺς   δούλους εἰς ὑπακοήν,
you stand along yourselves slaves into obedience,

1401   1510   3739   5219   2273   266
δοῦλοί ἐστε   ᾧ   ὑπακούετε, ἤτοι   ἁμαρτίας
slaves you are to whom you obey, whether of sin

1519 2288   2228 5218   1519 1343   **17** 5485
εἰς θάνατον ἢ   ὑπακοῆς εἰς δικαιοσύνην;   χάρις
into death   or obedience into rightness?   Favor

1161 03   2316 3754   1510   1401   06
δὲ   τῷ   θεῷ ὅτι   ἦτε   δοῦλοι τῆς
but to the God because you were slaves of the

266   5219   1161 1537 2588   1519 3739
ἁμαρτίας ὑπηκούσατε δὲ   ἐκ   καρδίας εἰς ὃν
sin   you obeyed but from heart   into what

3860   5179   1322   **18** 1659   1161
παρεδόθητε τύπον διδαχῆς,   ἐλευθερωθέντες δὲ
you were   example of teaching,   having been   but
given over   freed

575 06 266   1402   07   1343
ἀπὸ τῆς ἁμαρτίας ἐδουλώθητε   τῇ   δικαιοσύνῃ.
from the sin   you were slaved to the rightness.

19 442   3004 1223   08 769   06 4561
Ἀνθρώπινον λέγω διὰ   τὴν ἀσθένειαν τῆς σαρκὸς
Manlike   I say through the weakness of the flesh

1473   5618   1063 3936   024 3196
ὑμῶν. ὥσπερ   γὰρ παρεστήσατε   τὰ μέλη
of you. As indeed for you stand along the members

1473   1400   07   167   2532 07   458
ὑμῶν δοῦλα τῇ   ἀκαθαρσίᾳ καὶ τῇ ἀνομίᾳ
of you slaves to the uncleanness and the lawlessness

1519 08   458   3779 3568 3936   024
εἰς τὴν ἀνομίαν,   οὕτως νῦν παραστήσατε τὰ
for the lawlessness,   thusly now stand along the

3196   1473   1400   07   1343   1519 38
μέλη ὑμῶν δοῦλα τῇ   δικαιοσύνῃ εἰς ἁγιασμόν.
members of you slaves to the rightness   into holiness.

20 3753 1063 1401   1510   06   266
ὅτε γὰρ δοῦλοι ἦτε   τῆς ἁμαρτίας,
When for slaves you were of the sin,

1658   1510   07   1343   **21** 5101 3767
ἐλεύθεροι ἦτε   τῇ   δικαιοσύνῃ   τίνα οὖν
free   you were to the rightness.   What then

2590   2192   5119   1909 3739 3568 1870
καρπὸν εἴχετε τότε; ἐφ᾽ οἷς   νῦν ἐπαισχύνεσθε,
fruit   had you then? On which now you are ashamed,

09   1063 5056   1565   2288   **22** 3570 1161
τὸ γὰρ τέλος   ἐκείνων θάνατος.   νυνὶ δὲ
the for completion of those death.   Now but

1659   575 06 266   1402
ἐλευθερωθέντες ἀπὸ τῆς ἁμαρτίας δουλωθέντες
having been freed from the sin   having been slaved

1161 03   2316 2192   04   2590   1473   1519
δὲ   τῷ   θεῷ ἔχετε   τὸν καρπὸν ὑμῶν εἰς
but to the God you have the fruit of you for

38   012 1161 5056   2222 166   **23** 021
ἁγιασμόν, τὸ δὲ τέλος   ζωὴν αἰώνιον.   τὰ
holiness, the but completion life eternal.   The

1063 3800   06 266   2288   09 1161
γὰρ ὀψώνια τῆς ἁμαρτίας θάνατος, τὸ δὲ
for salaries of the sin   death,   the but

```
5486              02       2316 2222  166    1722 5547      2424   03
χάρισμα      τοῦ   θεοῦ ζωὴ αἰώνιος ἐν Χριστῷ ᾽Ιησοῦ τῷ
favor gift of the God life eternal in Christ Jesus the
2962    1473          2228 50                  80
κυρίῳ ἡμῶν.  7:1  ῍Η   ἀγνοεῖτε,        ἀδελφοί,
Master of us.      Or   do you not know, brothers,
1097               1063 3551  2980        3754 01 3551  2961
γινώσκουσιν γὰρ νόμον λαλῶ,   ὅτι ὁ νόμος κυριεύει
knowing         for  law  I speak, that the law masters
02  444        1909 3745              5550   2198      05 1063
τοῦ ἀνθρώπου ἐφ᾽ ὅσον     χρόνον ζῇ;  2 ἡ  γὰρ
the man        on   as much as time  he lives? The for
5220          1135 03      2198    435   1210
ὕπανδρος γυνὴ τῷ   ζῶντι ἀνδρὶ δέδεται
under man woman to the living man    has been bound
3551      1437 1161 599       01  435    2673
νόμῳ·  ἐὰν  δὲ  ἀποθάνῃ ὁ ἀνήρ, κατήργηται
in law; if  but  might die the man, she has been
                                             abolished
575 02 3551   02      435      3  686  3767        2198
ἀπὸ τοῦ νόμου τοῦ  ἀνδρός.   ἄρα οὖν        ζῶντος
by  the law  of the man.     Then therefore living
02  435    3428        5537               1437
τοῦ ἀνδρὸς μοιχαλὶς χρηματίσει     ἐὰν
the man    adulterous she will be warned if
1096          435     2087   1437 1161 599       01
γένηται     ἀνδρὶ ἑτέρῳ· ἐὰν  δὲ  ἀποθάνῃ ὁ
she might become to man other; if  but  might die the
435   1658      1510  575 02 3551    010 3361 1510
ἀνήρ, ἐλευθέρα ἐστὶν ἀπὸ τοῦ νόμου, τοῦ μὴ  εἶναι
man,  free      she is from the law   the not  to be
846    3428      1096         435   2087       4  5620
αὐτὴν μοιχαλίδα γενομένην ἀνδρὶ ἑτέρῳ.  ὥστε,
her    adulterous having become man other.  So that,
80          1473    2532 1473 2289            03
ἀδελφοί μου,  καὶ ὑμεῖς ἐθανατώθητε      τῷ
brothers of me, and  you   were put to death in the
3551 1223    010 4983    02    5547      1519 012
νόμῳ διὰ    τοῦ σώματος τοῦ   Χριστοῦ, εἰς  τὸ
law  through the body   of the Christ,  into the
1096       1473 2087   03       1537 3498
γενέσθαι ὑμᾶς ἑτέρῳ, τῷ   ἐκ νεκρῶν
to become you  to other, to the from dead
1453               2443 2592           03
ἐγερθέντι,      ἵνα καρποφορήσωμεν    τῷ
having been raised, that we might bear fruit to the
2316   5  3753 1063 1510  1722 07  4561      021 3804
θεῷ.     ὅτε  γὰρ ἦμεν  ἐν τῇ σαρκί, τὰ παθήματα
God.     When for  we were in the flesh, the sufferings
018      266     021 1223   02  3551   1754
τῶν   ἁμαρτιῶν τὰ διὰ    τοῦ νόμου ἐνηργεῖτο
of the sins      the through the law  were operating
1722 023    3196      1473   1519 012 2592       03
ἐν  τοῖς μέλεσιν ἡμῶν, εἰς τὸ καρποφορῆσαι τῷ
in  the  members of us, into the to bear fruit to the
2288     6  3570 1161 2673          575 02 3551
θανάτῳ·   νυνὶ δὲ  κατηργήθημεν   ἀπὸ τοῦ νόμου
death;     now  but  we were abolished from the law
599            1722 3739 2722                5620
ἀποθανόντες ἐν ᾧ   κατειχόμεθα,      ὥστε
having died in which we were being held down, so that
1398        1473 1722 2538     4151        2532 3756
δουλεύειν ἡμᾶς ἐν καινότητι πνεύματος καὶ οὐ
to slave  us  in  newness   of spirit and not
3821        1121       7  5101 3767 3004       01
παλαιότητι γράμματος.  Τί  οὖν ἐροῦμεν;  ὁ
oldness    of letter.  What then will we say? The
3551   266     1096       235  08  266
νόμος ἁμαρτία; μὴ  γένοιτο·    ἀλλὰ τὴν ἁμαρτίαν
law  sin?      Not  may it become; but  the sin
```

free gift of God is eternal life in Christ Jesus our Lord.

Do you not know, brothers and sisters[a]—for I am speaking to those who know the law—that the law is binding on a person only during that person's lifetime? [2]Thus a married woman is bound by the law to her husband as long as he lives; but if her husband dies, she is discharged from the law concerning the husband. [3]Accordingly, she will be called an adulteress if she lives with another man while her husband is alive. But if her husband dies, she is free from that law, and if she marries another man, she is not an adulteress.

4 In the same way, my friends,[a] you have died to the law through the body of Christ, so that you may belong to another, to him who has been raised from the dead in order that we may bear fruit for God. [5]While we were living in the flesh, our sinful passions, aroused by the law, were at work in our members to bear fruit for death. [6]But now we are discharged from the law, dead to that which held us captive, so that we are slaves not under the old written code but in the new life of the Spirit.

7 What then should we say? That the law is sin? By no means! Yet, if it had not been for the law, I would not have known sin.

a Gk brothers

I would not have known
what it is to covet if the
law had not said, "You
shall not covet." [8]But sin,
seizing an opportunity
in the commandment,
produced in me all kinds
of covetousness. Apart
from the law sin lies dead.
[9]I was once alive apart
from the law, but when the
commandment came, sin
revived [10]and I died, and
the very commandment
that promised life proved
to be death to me. [11]For
sin, seizing an opportunity
in the commandment,
deceived me and through it
killed me. [12]So the law is
holy, and the commandment
is holy and just and good.

13 Did what is good,
then, bring death to me?
By no means! It was sin,
working death in me
through what is good,
in order that sin might
be shown to be sin, and
through the commandment
might become sinful beyond
measure.

14 For we know that the
law is spiritual; but I am of
the flesh, sold into slavery
under sin.[a] [15]I do not
understand my own actions.
For I do not do what I
want, but I do the very
thing I hate. [16]Now if I do
what I do not want, I agree
that the law

[a] Gk sold under sin

3756	1097	1487 3361	1223		3551	08	5037	1063
οὐκ	ἔγνων	εἰ μὴ	διὰ		νόμου·	τήν	τε	γὰρ
not	I knew	except	through		law;	the	also	for

1939		3756 3609a		1487 3361	01	3551
ἐπιθυμίαν	οὐκ	ᾔδειν		εἰ μὴ	ὁ	νόμος
desire	not	I had known		except	the	law

3004		3756 1937		874		1161
ἔλεγεν·	οὐκ	ἐπιθυμήσεις.	[8]	ἀφορμὴν	δὲ	
was saying;	not	you will desire.		Opportunity	but	

2983		05	266	1223	06	1785
λαβοῦσα		ἡ	ἁμαρτία	διὰ	τῆς	ἐντολῆς
having received		the	sin	through	the	command

2716		1722	1473	3956	1939		5565
κατειργάσατο		ἐν	ἐμοὶ	πᾶσαν	ἐπιθυμίαν·		χωρὶς
worked thoroughly		in	me	all	desire;		without

1063	3551	266		3498	[9]	1473	1161	2198
γὰρ	νόμου	ἁμαρτία		νεκρά.		ἐγὼ	δὲ	ἔζων
for	law	sin		dead.		I	but	was living

5565	3551	4218	2064		1161	06		1785
χωρὶς	νόμου	ποτέ,	ἐλθούσης		δὲ	τῆς		ἐντολῆς
without	law	then,	having come		but	of the		command

05	266	326		[10]	1473	1161	599		2532
ἡ	ἁμαρτία	ἀνέζησεν,			ἐγὼ	δὲ	ἀπέθανον		καὶ
the	sin	lived again,			I	but	died		and

2147		1473	05	1785		05	1519	2222	3778	1519
εὑρέθη		μοι	ἡ	ἐντολὴ		ἡ	εἰς	ζωήν,	αὕτη	εἰς
was found		in me	the	command		the	into	life,	this	into

2288		05	1063	266		874		2983
θάνατον·	[11]	ἡ	γὰρ	ἁμαρτία		ἀφορμὴν		λαβοῦσα
death;		the	for	sin		opportunity		having received

1223		06	1785	1818			1473	2532
διὰ		τῆς	ἐντολῆς	ἐξηπάτησέν			με	καὶ
through		the	command	deceived thoroughly			me	and

1223	846	615		[12]	5620	01	3303	3551
δι'	αὐτῆς	ἀπέκτεινεν.			ὥστε	ὁ	μὲν	νόμος
through	it	it killed.			So that	the	indeed	law

40	2532	05	1785	40	2532	1342	2532	18
ἅγιος	καὶ	ἡ	ἐντολὴ	ἁγία	καὶ	δικαία	καὶ	ἀγαθή.
holy	and	the	command	holy	and	right	and	good.

[13]	09	3767	18		1473	1096	2288	3361
	Τὸ	οὖν	ἀγαθὸν	ἐμοὶ	ἐγένετο	θάνατος;	μὴ
	The	then	good		to me	became	death?	Not

1096		235	05	266		2443	5316
γένοιτο·		ἀλλὰ	ἡ	ἁμαρτία,		ἵνα	φανῇ
may it become;		but	the	sin,		that	it might shine

266		1223		010	18	1473	2716
ἁμαρτία,		διὰ		τοῦ	ἀγαθοῦ	μοι	κατεργαζομένη
sin,		through		the	good	in me	working thoroughly

2288		2443	1096		2596	5236		268
θάνατον,		ἵνα	γένηται		καθ'	ὑπερβολὴν		ἁμαρτωλὸς
death,		that	might become		by	excess		sinner

05	266	1223		06	1785		[14]	3609a	1063	3754
ἡ	ἁμαρτία	διὰ		τῆς	ἐντολῆς.			Οἴδαμεν	γὰρ	ὅτι
the	sin	through		the	command.			We know	for	that

01	3551	4152		1510	1473	1161	4560		1510
ὁ	νόμος	πνευματικός		ἐστιν,	ἐγὼ	δὲ	σάρκινός		εἰμι
the	law	spiritual		is,	I	but	of flesh		am

4097		5259	08	266		[15]	3739	1063
πεπραμένος		ὑπὸ	τὴν	ἁμαρτίαν.			ὃ	γὰρ
having been sold		under	the	sin.			What	for

2716		3756	1097		3756	1063	3739	2309
κατεργάζομαι		οὐ	γινώσκω·		οὐ	γὰρ	ὃ	θέλω
I work thoroughly		not	I know;		not	for	what	I want

3778	4238		235	3739	3404		3778	4160		[16]	1487
τοῦτο	πράσσω,		ἀλλ'	ὃ	μισῶ		τοῦτο	ποιῶ.			εἰ
this	I practice,		but	what	I hate		this	I do.			If

1161	3739	3756	2309	3778	4160	4852		03	3551
δὲ	ὃ	οὐ	θέλω	τοῦτο	ποιῶ,	σύμφημι		τῷ	νόμῳ
but	what	not	I want	this	I do,	I say with		the	law

3754 2570   3570 1161 3765   1473 2716
ὅτι καλός. **17** νυνὶ δὲ οὐκέτι   ἐγὼ κατεργάζομαι
that good.   Now but no longer I   work thoroughly

846 235 05 3611   1722 1473 266   3609a 1063
αὐτὸ ἀλλὰ ἡ οἰκοῦσα ἐν ἐμοὶ ἁμαρτία. **18** Οἶδα γὰρ
it   but   the housing in me   sin.   I know for

3754 3756 3611   1722 1473 3778 1510 1722 07 4561
ὅτι οὐκ οἰκεῖ ἐν ἐμοί, τοῦτ' ἔστιν ἐν τῇ σαρκί
that not houses in me,   this is   in the flesh

1473 18   09 1063 2309   3873   1473   09
μου, ἀγαθόν· τὸ γὰρ θέλειν παράκειταί μοι,   τὸ
of me, good; the for to want lies along to me, the

1161 2716   012 2570 3756a **19** 3756 1063
δὲ κατεργάζεσθαι   τὸ καλὸν οὔ·   οὐ γὰρ
but to work thoroughly the good no;   not for

3739 2309   4160 18   235 3739 3756 2309   2556
ὃ   θέλω ποιῶ ἀγαθόν, ἀλλὰ ὃ   οὐ θέλω   κακὸν
what I want I do good, but what not I want bad

3778 4238   **20** 1487 1161 3739 3756 2309 1473 3778
τοῦτο πράσσω.   εἰ δὲ ὃ   οὐ θέλω [ἐγὼ] τοῦτο
this I practice. If but what not want I this

4160 3765   1473 2716   846 235 05
ποιῶ, οὐκέτι   ἐγὼ κατεργάζομαι αὐτὸ ἀλλὰ ἡ
I do, no longer I   work thoroughly it but the

3611   1722 1473 266   **21** 2147   686 04 3551
οἰκοῦσα ἐν ἐμοὶ ἁμαρτία.   εὑρίσκω ἄρα τὸν νόμον,
housing in me   sin.   I find then the law,

03 2309   1473 4160 012 2570 3754 1473 09
τῷ θέλοντι ἐμοὶ ποιεῖν τὸ καλόν, ὅτι ἐμοὶ τὸ
the wanting in me to do the good, that to me the

2556 3873   **22** 4913   1063 03
κακὸν παράκειται·   συνήδομαι   γὰρ τῷ
bad lies along;   I have pleasure together for in the

3551 02   2316 2596 04 2080   444   991
νόμῳ τοῦ   θεοῦ κατὰ τὸν ἔσω ἄνθρωπον, **23** βλέπω
law of the God by the inside man,   I see

1161 2087 3551 1722 023 3196   1473
δὲ ἕτερον νόμον ἐν τοῖς μέλεσίν μου
but other law   in the members of me

497   03 3551 02   3563 1473 2532
ἀντιστρατευόμενον   τῷ νόμῳ τοῦ   νοός μου καὶ
soldiering against   the law of the mind of me and

163   1473 1722 03 3551 06   266   03
αἰχμαλωτίζοντά   με ἐν τῷ νόμῳ τῆς ἁμαρτίας τῷ
capturing   me in the law of the sin   the

1510 1722 023 3196   1473 **24** 5005   1473
ὄντι ἐν τοῖς μέλεσίν μου.   Ταλαίπωρος ἐγὼ
being in the members of me.   Miserable I

444   5101 1473 4506   1537 010 4983
ἄνθρωπος· τίς με ῥύσεται   ἐκ τοῦ σώματος
man;   who me will rescue from the body

02 2288   3778   **25** 5485 1161 03   2316
τοῦ θανάτου τούτου;   χάρις δὲ τῷ   θεῷ
of the death this?   Favor but to the God

1223 2424 5547   02 2962   1473   686 3767
διὰ Ἰησοῦ Χριστοῦ τοῦ κυρίου ἡμῶν. Ἄρα οὖν
through Jesus Christ the Master of us. Then therefore

846 1473 03   3303 3563 1398   3551   2316
αὐτὸς ἐγὼ τῷ μὲν νοῒ δουλεύω νόμῳ θεοῦ
myself I the indeed mind slave in law of God

07   1161 4561 3551 266   **8:1** 3762   686 3568
τῇ δὲ σαρκὶ νόμῳ ἁμαρτίας.   Οὐδὲν ἄρα νῦν
in the but flesh law of sin.   Nothing then now

2631   015   1722 2424   01 1063
κατάκριμα   τοῖς   ἐν Χριστῷ Ἰησοῦ. **2** ὁ γὰρ
condemnation to the ones in Christ Jesus.   The for

3551 010 4151   06   2222 1722 5547   2424
νόμος τοῦ πνεύματος τῆς ζωῆς ἐν Χριστῷ Ἰησοῦ
law of the spirit of the life in Christ Jesus

---

[17] But in fact it is no longer I that do it, but sin that dwells within me. [18] For I know that nothing good dwells within me, that is, in my flesh. I can will what is right, but I cannot do it. [19] For I do not do the good I want, but the evil I do not want is what I do. [20] Now if I do what I do not want, it is no longer I that do it, but sin that dwells within me.

21 So I find it to be a law that when I want to do what is good, evil lies close at hand. [22] For I delight in the law of God in my inmost self, [23] but I see in my members another law at war with the law of my mind, making me captive to the law of sin that dwells in my members. [24] Wretched man that I am! Who will rescue me from this body of death? [25] Thanks be to God through Jesus Christ our Lord!

So then, with my mind I am a slave to the law of God, but with my flesh I am a slave to the law of sin.

CHAPTER 8

There is therefore now no condemnation for those who are in Christ Jesus. [2] For the law of the Spirit[a] of life in Christ Jesus

[a] Or spirit

has set you[a] free from the law of sin and of death. ³For God has done what the law, weakened by the flesh, could not do: by sending his own Son in the likeness of sinful flesh, and to deal with sin,[b] he condemned sin in the flesh, ⁴so that the just requirement of the law might be fulfilled in us, who walk not according to the flesh but according to the Spirit.[c] ⁵For those who live according to the flesh set their minds on the things of the flesh, but those who live according to the Spirit[c] set their minds on the things of the Spirit.[c] ⁶To set the mind on the flesh is death, but to set the mind on the Spirit[c] is life and peace. ⁷For this reason the mind that is set on the flesh is hostile to God; it does not submit to God's law—indeed it cannot, ⁸and those who are in the flesh cannot please God.

9 But you are not in the flesh; you are in the Spirit,[c] since the Spirit of God dwells in you. Anyone who does not have the Spirit of Christ does not belong to him. ¹⁰But if Christ is in you, though the body is dead because of sin, the Spirit[c] is life because of righteousness. ¹¹If the Spirit of him who raised Jesus from the dead dwells in you, he who raised Christ[d] from the dead

a Here the Greek word *you* is singular number; other ancient authorities read *me* or *us*

b Or *and as a sin offering*

c Or *spirit*

d Other ancient authorities read *the Christ* or *Christ Jesus* or *Jesus Christ*

1659		1473	575	02	3551	06	266	2532
ἠλευθέρωσέν		σε	ἀπὸ	τοῦ	νόμου	τῆς	ἁμαρτίας	καὶ
has freed		you	from	the	law	of the	sin	and

02	2288		012	1063	102	02	3551	1722
τοῦ	θανάτου.	³ Τὸ	γὰρ	ἀδύνατον	τοῦ	νόμου	ἐν
of the	death.	The	for	unable	of the	law	in

3739	770	1223	06	4561	01	2316	04
ᾧ	ἠσθένει	διὰ	τῆς	σαρκός,	ὁ	θεὸς	τὸν
that	it was weak	through	the	flesh,	the	God	the

1438	5207	3992	1722	3667	4561
ἑαυτοῦ	υἱὸν	πέμψας	ἐν	ὁμοιώματι	σαρκὸς
himself	son	having sent	in	likeness	of flesh

266	2532	4012	266	2632	08	266
ἁμαρτίας	καὶ	περὶ	ἁμαρτίας	κατέκρινεν	τὴν	ἁμαρτίαν
sin	and	about	sin	condemned	the	sin

1722	07	4561		2443	09	1345	02	3551
ἐν	τῇ	σαρκί,	⁴ ἵνα	τὸ	δικαίωμα	τοῦ	νόμου
in	the	flesh,	that	the	right	of the	law

4137	1722	1473	015	3361	2596	4561	4043
πληρωθῇ	ἐν	ἡμῖν	τοῖς	μὴ	κατὰ	σάρκα	περιπατοῦσιν
might be	in	us	the	not	by	flesh	walking around
filled

235	2596	4151		013	1063	2596	4561	1510	024
ἀλλὰ	κατὰ	πνεῦμα.	⁵ οἱ	γὰρ	κατὰ	σάρκα	ὄντες	τὰ
but	by	spirit.	The	for	by	flesh	being	the

06	4561	5426		013	1161	2596	4151	024
τῆς	σαρκὸς	φρονοῦσιν,	οἱ	δὲ	κατὰ	πνεῦμα	τὰ
of the	flesh	think,	the	but	by	spirit	the

010	4151		09	1063	5427	06	4561
τοῦ	πνεύματος.	⁶ τὸ	γὰρ	φρόνημα	τῆς	σαρκὸς
of the	spirit.	The	for	thought	of the	flesh

2288	09	1161	5427	010	4151	2222	2532
θάνατος,	τὸ	δὲ	φρόνημα	τοῦ	πνεύματος	ζωὴ	καὶ
death,	the	but	thought	of the	spirit	life	and

1515		1360	09	5427	06	4561	2189
εἰρήνη·	⁷ διότι	τὸ	φρόνημα	τῆς	σαρκὸς	ἔχθρα
peace;	because	the	thought	of the	flesh	hostility

1519	2316	03		1063	3551	02	2316	3756
εἰς	θεόν,	τῷ	γὰρ	νόμῳ	τοῦ	θεοῦ	οὐχ
to	God,	to the	for	law	of the	God	not

5293		3761	1063	1410		013	1161	1722
ὑποτάσσεται,	οὐδὲ	γὰρ	δύναται·	⁸ οἱ	δὲ	ἐν
is subject,	but not	for	it is able;	the	but	in

4561	1510	2316	700	3756	1410		1473	1161
σαρκὶ	ὄντες	θεῷ	ἀρέσαι	οὐ	δύνανται.	⁹ Ὑμεῖς	δὲ
flesh	being	God	to please	not	are able.	You	but

3756	1510	1722	4561	235	1722	4151	1512
οὐκ	ἐστὲ	ἐν	σαρκὶ	ἀλλὰ	ἐν	πνεύματι,	εἴπερ
not	are	in	flesh	but	in	spirit,	if indeed

4151	2316	3611	1722	1473	1487	1161	5100
πνεῦμα	θεοῦ	οἰκεῖ	ἐν	ὑμῖν.	εἰ	δέ	τις
spirit	of God	houses	in	you.	If	but	some

4151	5547	3756	2192	3778	3756	1510	846
πνεῦμα	Χριστοῦ	οὐκ	ἔχει,	οὗτος	οὐκ	ἔστιν	αὐτοῦ.
spirit	of Christ	not	has,	this	not	is	of him.

	1487	1161	5547	1722	1473	09	3303	4983	3498
¹⁰ εἰ	δὲ	Χριστὸς	ἐν	ὑμῖν,	τὸ	μὲν	σῶμα	νεκρὸν
If	but	Christ	in	you,	the	indeed	body	dead

1223	266	09	1161	4151	2222	1223
διὰ	ἁμαρτίαν	τὸ	δὲ	πνεῦμα	ζωὴ	διὰ
through	sin	the	but	spirit	life	through

1343		1487	1161	09	4151	02
δικαιοσύνην.	¹¹ εἰ	δὲ	τὸ	πνεῦμα	τοῦ
rightness.	If	but	the	spirit	of the one

1453	04	2424	1537	3498	3611	1722
ἐγείραντος	τὸν	Ἰησοῦν	ἐκ	νεκρῶν	οἰκεῖ	ἐν
having raised	the	Jesus	from	dead	houses	in

1473	01	1453	5547	1537	3498
ὑμῖν,	ὁ	ἐγείρας	Χριστὸν	ἐκ	νεκρῶν
you,	the one	having raised	Christ	from	dead

2227		2532 024 2349			4983	1473
ζῳοποιήσει		καὶ τὰ θνητὰ			σώματα	ὑμῶν
will make alive		and the death		like	bodies	of you

1223	010 1774		846	4151		1722 1473
διὰ	τοῦ ἐνοικοῦντος		αὐτοῦ	πνεύματος	ἐν	ὑμῖν.
through	the housing	in	of him	spirit	in	you.

12 686 3767   80   3781   1510   3756
"Αρα οὖν,   ἀδελφοί, ὀφειλέται ἐσμὲν οὐ
Then therefore, brothers, debtors   we are not

07	4561 010 2596 4561 2198	**13**	1487 1063
τῇ	σαρκὶ τοῦ κατὰ σάρκα ζῆν,		εἰ γὰρ
to the	flesh the by flesh to live, if		for

2596 4561 2198   3195   599   1487
κατὰ σάρκα ζῆτε,   μέλλετε   ἀποθνήσκειν· εἰ
by flesh you live, you are about to die;   if

1161 4151   020 4234   010   4983
δὲ πνεύματι τὰς πράξεις τοῦ σώματος
but in spirit the practices of the body

2289   2198   **14** 3745   1063
θανατοῦτε,   ζήσεσθε.   ὅσοι   γὰρ
you put to death, you will live. As many as for

4151   2316 71   3778 5207 2316   1510
πνεύματι θεοῦ ἄγονται, οὗτοι υἱοὶ θεοῦ εἰσιν.
in spirit of God are led, these sons of God are.

15 3756 1063 2983   4151 1397   3825 1519
οὐ γὰρ ἐλάβετε   πνεῦμα δουλείας πάλιν εἰς
Not for you received spirit of slavery again to

5401 235 2983   4151 5206   1722
φόβον ἀλλὰ ἐλάβετε   πνεῦμα υἱοθεσίας   ἐν
fear but you received spirit of adoption as son in

3739 2896   5   01 3962   **16** 846   09   4151
ᾧ κράζομεν· αββα ὁ πατήρ.   αὐτὸ τὸ πνεῦμα
which we shout; abba the father.   Itself the spirit

4828   011   4151   1473 3754 1510
συμμαρτυρεῖ   τῷ   πνεύματι ἡμῶν ὅτι ἐσμὲν
testifies together to the spirit   of us that we are

5043   2316   **17** 1487 1161 5043   2532 2818
τέκνα   θεοῦ.   εἰ δὲ τέκνα,   καὶ κληρονόμοι·
children of God. If   but children also inheritors;

2818   3303   2316 4789   1161 5547
κληρονόμοι μὲν   θεοῦ, συγκληρονόμοι δὲ Χριστοῦ,
inheritors indeed God, co-inheritors but of Christ,

1512   4841   2443 2532 4888
εἴπερ συμπάσχομεν ἵνα καὶ συνδοξασθῶμεν.
if indeed we suffer   that also we might be given
together   splendor together.

18 3049   1063 3754 3756 514   021 3804
Λογίζομαι γὰρ ὅτι οὐκ ἄξια τὰ παθήματα
I reason for that not worthy the sufferings

02   3568 2540 4314   08 3195   1391
τοῦ νῦν καιροῦ πρὸς τὴν μέλλουσαν δόξαν
of the now season toward the being about splendor

601   1519 1473   **19** 05 1063 603
ἀποκαλυφθῆναι εἰς ἡμᾶς.   ἡ γὰρ ἀποκαραδοκία
to be uncovered in us.   The for eager expectation

06   2937   08 602   014   5207 02   2316
τῆς κτίσεως τὴν ἀποκάλυψιν τῶν υἱῶν τοῦ θεοῦ
of the creation the uncovering of the sons of the God

553   **20** 07   1063 3153   05 2937
ἀπεκδέχεται.   τῇ γὰρ ματαιότητι ἡ κτίσις
awaits.   In the for futility the creation

5293   3756 1635 235 1223   04
ὑπετάγη,   οὐχ ἑκοῦσα ἀλλὰ διὰ τὸν
was subjected, not willing but through the one

5293   1909 1680   **21** 3754 2532 846   05
ὑποτάξαντα, ᾽εφ ᾽ἐλπίδι ὅτι καὶ αὐτὴ ἡ
having subjected, on hope   that also itself the

2937   1659   575 06 1397 06
κτίσις ἐλευθερωθήσεται ἀπὸ τῆς δουλείας τῆς
creation will be freed from the slavery of the

---

will give life to your mortal bodies also through[a] his Spirit that dwells in you.

12 So then, brothers and sisters,[b] we are debtors, not to the flesh, to live according to the flesh— 13 for if you live according to the flesh, you will die; but if by the Spirit you put to death the deeds of the body, you will live. 14 For all who are led by the Spirit of God are children of God. 15 For you did not receive a spirit of slavery to fall back into fear, but you have received a spirit of adoption. When we cry, "Abba![c] Father!" 16 it is that very Spirit bearing witness[d] with our spirit that we are children of God, 17 and if children, then heirs, heirs of God and joint heirs with Christ—if, in fact, we suffer with him so that we may also be glorified with him.

18 I consider that the sufferings of this present time are not worth comparing with the glory about to be revealed to us. 19 For the creation waits with eager longing for the revealing of the children of God; 20 for the creation was subjected to futility, not of its own will but by the will of the one who subjected it, in hope 21 that the creation itself will be set free from its bondage

---

a Other ancient authorities read *on account of*

b Gk *brothers*

c Aramaic for *Father*

d Or *15a spirit of adoption, by which we cry, "Abba! Father!" 16The Spirit itself bears witness*

to decay and will obtain the freedom of the glory of the children of God. 22We know that the whole creation has been groaning in labor pains until now; 23and not only the creation, but we ourselves, who have the first fruits of the Spirit, groan inwardly while we wait for adoption, the redemption of our bodies. 24For in[a] hope we were saved. Now hope that is seen is not hope. For who hopes[b] for what is seen? 25But if we hope for what we do not see, we wait for it with patience.

26 Likewise the Spirit helps us in our weakness; for we do not know how to pray as we ought, but that very Spirit intercedes[c] with sighs too deep for words. 27And God,[d] who searches the heart, knows what is the mind of the Spirit, because the Spirit[e] intercedes for the saints according to the will of God.[f]

28 We know that all things work together for good[g] for those who love God, who are called according to his purpose. 29For those whom he foreknew he also predestined to be conformed to the image of his Son, in order that he might be the firstborn within a large family.[h] 30And those whom he predestined

a Or by
b Other ancient authorities read awaits
c Other ancient authorities add for us
d Gk the one
e Gk he or it
f Gk according to God
g Other ancient authorities read God makes all things work together for good, or in all things God works for good
h Gk among many brothers

5356	1519 08	1657	06	1391	022
φθορᾶς	εἰς τὴν	ἐλευθερίαν	τῆς	δόξης	τῶν
corruption	into the	freedom	of the	splendor	of the

5043	02	2316	22	3609a	1063	3754	3956	05
τέκνων	τοῦ	θεοῦ.		οἴδαμεν	γὰρ	ὅτι	πᾶσα	ἡ
children	of the	God.		We know	for	that	all	the

2937	4959	2532	4944		891	02	3568
κτίσις	συστενάζει	καὶ	συνωδίνει		ἄχρι	τοῦ	νῦν·
creation	groans together	and	suffers birth pains together		until	the	now;

23
3756	3441	1161	235	2532	846	08
οὐ	μόνον	δέ,	ἀλλὰ	καὶ	αὐτοὶ	τὴν
not	alone	but,	but	also	ourselves	the

536	010	4151	2192	1473	2532
ἀπαρχὴν	τοῦ	πνεύματος	ἔχοντες,	ἡμεῖς	καὶ
from beginning	of the	spirit	having,	we	also

846	1722	1438	4727	5206
αὐτοὶ	ἐν	ἑαυτοῖς	στενάζομεν	υἱοθεσίαν
ourselves	in	ourselves	groan	adoption as son

553	08	629	010	4983	1473
ἀπεκδεχόμενοι,	τὴν	ἀπολύτρωσιν	τοῦ	σώματος	ἡμῶν.
awaiting,	the	redemption	of the	body	of us.

24
07	1063	1680	4982	1680	1161
τῇ	γὰρ	ἐλπίδι	ἐσώθημεν·	ἐλπὶς	δὲ
In the	for	hope	we were delivered;	hope	but

991	3756	1510	1680	3739	1063	991	5101
βλεπομένη	οὐκ	ἔστιν	ἐλπίς·	ὃ	γὰρ	βλέπει	τίς
being seen	not	is	hope;	what	for	he sees	what

1679	25	1487	1161	3739	3756	991	1679
ἐλπίζει;		εἰ	δὲ	ὃ	οὐ	βλέπομεν	ἐλπίζομεν,
he hopes?		If	but	what	not	we see	we hope,

1223	5281	553	26	5615	1161	2532
δι᾽	ὑπομονῆς	ἀπεκδεχόμεθα.		Ὡσαύτως	δὲ	καὶ
through	patience	we await.		Likewise	but	also

09	4151	4878	07	769	1473	012
τὸ	πνεῦμα	συναντιλαμβάνεται	τῇ	ἀσθενείᾳ	ἡμῶν·	τὸ
the	spirit	helps with	the	weakness	of us;	the

1063	5101	4336	2526	1163	3756
γὰρ	τί	προσευξώμεθα	καθὸ	δεῖ	οὐκ
for	what	we might pray	as	it is necessary	not

3609a	235	846	09	4151	5241
οἴδαμεν,	ἀλλὰ	αὐτὸ	τὸ	πνεῦμα	ὑπερεντυγχάνει
we know,	but	itself	the	spirit	urgently appeals

4726	215	27	01	1161	2037a	020
στεναγμοῖς	ἀλαλήτοις·		ὁ	δὲ	ἐραυνῶν	τὰς
in groans	unspeakable;		the	but	one searching	the

2588	3609a	5101	09	5427	010	4151	3754
καρδίας	οἶδεν	τί	τὸ	φρόνημα	τοῦ	πνεύματος,	ὅτι
hearts	knows	what	the	thought	of the	spirit,	that

2596	2316	1793	5228	40	28	3609a
κατὰ	θεὸν	ἐντυγχάνει	ὑπὲρ	ἁγίων.		Οἴδαμεν
by	God	it appeals	on behalf	of holy ones.		We know

1161	3754	015	25	04	2316	3956
δὲ	ὅτι	τοῖς	ἀγαπῶσιν	τὸν	θεὸν	πάντα
but	that	to the	ones loving	the	God	all

4903	1519 18	015	2596	4286
συνεργεῖ	εἰς ἀγαθόν,	τοῖς	κατὰ	πρόθεσιν
works together	to good,	to the	by	purpose

2822	1510	29	3754	3739	4267	2532
κλητοῖς	οὖσιν.		ὅτι	οὓς	προέγνω,	καὶ
called	being.		Because	whom	he knew before	also

4309	4832	06	1504	02
προώρισεν	συμμόρφους	τῆς	εἰκόνος	τοῦ
he set bounds before	conformed	of the	image	of the

5207	846	1519	012	1510	846	4416	1722
υἱοῦ	αὐτοῦ,	εἰς	τὸ	εἶναι	αὐτὸν	πρωτότοκον	ἐν
son	of him,	to	the	to be	him	first born	in

4183	80	30	3739	1161	4309
πολλοῖς	ἀδελφοῖς·		οὓς	δὲ	προώρισεν,
many	brothers;		whom	but	he set bounds before,

3778   2532 2564   2532 3739 2564   3778
τούτους καὶ ἐκάλεσεν· καὶ οὓς ἐκάλεσεν, τούτους
these   also he called; and whom he called, these
2532 1344   3739 1161 1344   3778
καὶ ἐδικαίωσεν· οὓς δὲ ἐδικαίωσεν, τούτους
also he made right; whom but he made right, these
2532 1392   5101 3767 3004   4314
καὶ ἐδόξασεν. **31** Τί οὖν ἐροῦμεν πρὸς
also he gave splendor. What then will we say to
3778   1487 01 2316 5228   1473   5101 2596
ταῦτα; εἰ ὁ θεὸς ὑπὲρ ἡμῶν, τίς καθ᾽
these? If   the God on behalf of us, who against
1473   **32** 3739 1065   02 2398   5207 3756 5339   235
ἡμῶν;   ὅς γε τοῦ ἰδίου υἱοῦ οὐκ ἐφείσατο ἀλλὰ
us?   Who indeed the own son not spared   but
5228   1473 3956   3860   846   4459 3780 2532
ὑπὲρ   ἡμῶν πάντων παρέδωκεν αὐτόν, πῶς οὐχὶ καὶ
on behalf of us all   gave over him,   how not also
4862 846 024 3956 1473 5483   33 5101
σὺν αὐτῷ τὰ πάντα ἡμῖν χαρίσεται;   **33** τίς
with him the all to us will he favor?   Who
1458   2596   1588   2316   2316 01
ἐγκαλέσει   κατὰ   ἐκλεκτῶν θεοῦ; θεὸς ὁ
will call in against select of God? God the one
1344   **34** 5101 01 2632   5547   2424
δικαιῶν·   τίς ὁ κατακρινῶν; Χριστὸς [Ἰησοῦς]
making right; who the condemning? Christ   Jesus
01 599   3123   1161 1453   3739
ὁ ἀποθανών, μᾶλλον δὲ ἐγερθείς,   ὃς
the having died, more   but having been raised, who
2532 1510   1722 1188   02   2316 3739 2532 1793
καί ἐστιν ἐν δεξιᾷ τοῦ θεοῦ, ὃς καὶ ἐντυγχάνει
also is   in right of the God, who also appeals
5228   1473 **35** 5101 1473 5563   575 06
ὑπὲρ   ἡμῶν. τίς ἡμᾶς χωρίσει   ἀπὸ τῆς
on behalf of us. Who us will separate from the
26   02   5547   2347   2228 4730   2228
ἀγάπης τοῦ Χριστοῦ; θλῖψις ἢ στενοχωρία ἢ
love   of the Christ? Affliction or anguish   or
1375   2228 3042 2228 1132   2228 2794   2228
διωγμὸς   ἢ λιμὸς ἢ γυμνότης ἢ κίνδυνος ἢ
persecution or famine or nakedness or danger   or
3162   **36** 2531 1125   3754 1752   1473
μάχαιρα; καθὼς γέγραπται ὅτι ἕνεκεν   σοῦ
sword?   Just it has been (") on account of you
          as written,
2289   3650 08 2250
θανατούμεθα   ὅλην τὴν ἡμέραν,
we are being put to death whole the day,
3049   5613 4263   4967   235 1722
ἐλογίσθημεν ὡς πρόβατα σφαγῆς. **37** ἀλλ᾽ ἐν
we were reasoned as sheep of slaughter. But in
3778   3956 5245   1223   02
τούτοις πᾶσιν ὑπερνικῶμεν   διὰ   τοῦ
these   all   we are conquerors beyond through the one
25   1473 **38** 3982   1063 3754
ἀγαπήσαντος ἡμᾶς. πέπεισμαι   γὰρ ὅτι
having loved us.   I have been persuaded for that
3777   2288   3777 2222 3777 32   3777
οὔτε θάνατος οὔτε ζωὴ οὔτε ἄγγελοι οὔτε
neither death   nor life neither messengers nor
746   3777   1764   3777 3195   3777
ἀρχαὶ οὔτε ἐνεστῶτα οὔτε μέλλοντα   οὔτε
rulers neither present   nor being about to be nor
1411   **39** 3777 5313 3777 899   3777 5100 2937
δυνάμεις οὔτε ὕψωμα οὔτε βάθος οὔτε τις κτίσις
powers   nor height nor depth nor some creation
2087 1410   1473 5563   575 06   26
ἑτέρα δυνήσεται ἡμᾶς χωρίσαι   ἀπὸ τῆς ἀγάπης
other will be able us to separate from the love

he also called; and those whom he called he also justified; and those whom he justified he also glorified.

31 What then are we to say about these things? If God is for us, who is against us? [32]He who did not withhold his own Son, but gave him up for all of us, will he not with him also give us everything else? [33]Who will bring any charge against God's elect? It is God who justifies. [34]Who is to condemn? It is Christ Jesus, who died, yes, who was raised, who is at the right hand of God, who indeed intercedes for us.[a] [35]Who will separate us from the love of Christ? Will hardship, or distress, or persecution, or famine, or nakedness, or peril, or sword? [36]As it is written,

"For your sake we are being killed all day long;
we are accounted as sheep to be slaughtered."

[37]No, in all these things we are more than conquerors through him who loved us. [38]For I am convinced that neither death, nor life, nor angels, nor rulers, nor things present, nor things to come, nor powers, [39]nor height, nor depth, nor anything else in all creation, will be able to separate us from the love

---

[a] Or Is it Christ Jesus . . . for us?

of God in Christ Jesus our Lord.

CHAPTER 9

I am speaking the truth in Christ—I am not lying; my conscience confirms it by the Holy Spirit— [2]I have great sorrow and unceasing anguish in my heart. [3]For I could wish that I myself were accursed and cut off from Christ for the sake of my own people,[a] my kindred according to the flesh. [4]They are Israelites, and to them belong the adoption, the glory, the covenants, the giving of the law, the worship, and the promises; [5]to them belong the patriarchs, and from them, according to the flesh, comes the Messiah,[b] who is over all, God blessed forever.[c] Amen.

6It is not as though the word of God had failed. For not all Israelites truly belong to Israel, [7]and not all of Abraham's children are his true descendants; but "It is through Isaac that descendants shall be named for you." [8]This means that it is not the children of the flesh who are the children of God, but the children of the promise are counted as descendants. [9]For this is what the promise said, "About this time I will return and Sarah shall have a son." [10]Nor is that all; something similar happened to Rebecca when she had conceived children by one husband, our ancestor Isaac.

a Gk my brothers
b Or the Christ
c Or Messiah, who is God over all, blessed forever; or Messiah. May h who is God over all be blessed forever

02   2316 06   1722 5547   2424   03   2962   1473
τοῦ   θεοῦ τῆς ἐν   Χριστῷ Ἰησοῦ τῷ κυρίῳ ἡμῶν.
of the God the in   Christ Jesus the Master of us.

9:1 225   3004 1722 5547   3756 5574
     Ἀλήθειαν λέγω ἐν   Χριστῷ, οὐ ψεύδομαι,
     Truth   I say in   Christ, not I lie,
4828   1473 06   4893   1473
συμμαρτυρούσης   μοι τῆς συνειδήσεώς μου
testifying together to me of the conscience   of me
1722 4151   40   3754 3077   1473 1510 3173
ἐν πνεύματι ἁγίῳ, 2 ὅτι λύπη   μοί   ἐστιν μεγάλη
in spirit   holy,   that grief to me is   great
2532 88   3601 07   2588   1473
καὶ ἀδιάλειπτος ὀδύνη τῇ   καρδίᾳ μου.
and unceasing   pain in the heart of me.

3 2172   1063 331   1510 846   1473 575
  ηὐχόμην   γὰρ ἀνάθεμα εἶναι αὐτὸς ἐγὼ ἀπὸ
  I was wishing for curse to be myself I   from
02 5547   5228   014 80   1473 014
τοῦ Χριστοῦ ὑπὲρ τῶν ἀδελφῶν μου τῶν
the Christ on behalf of the brothers of me the
4773   1473 2596 4561 4 3748   1510 2475
συγγενῶν μου κατὰ σάρκα, οἵτινές εἰσιν Ἰσραηλῖται,
relatives of me by flesh, who   are   Israelites,
3739 05 5206   2532 05 1391   2532 017
ὧν   ἡ υἱοθεσία   καὶ ἡ δόξα   καὶ αἱ
of whom the adoption as son and the splendor and the
1242   2532 05 3548   2532 05 2999   2532
διαθῆκαι καὶ ἡ νομοθεσία καὶ ἡ λατρεία καὶ
agreements and the law giving and the service and
017 1860   5 3739 013 3962   2532 1537 3739
αἱ ἐπαγγελίαι,   ὧν   οἱ πατέρες καὶ ἐξ ὧν
the promises,   of whom the fathers and from whom
01 5547   012 2596 4561 01 1510 1909 3956   2316
ὁ Χριστὸς τὸ κατὰ σάρκα, ὁ ὢν ἐπὶ πάντων θεὸς
the Christ the by flesh, the being on   all   God
2126   1519 016 165   281   6 3756 3634 1161
εὐλογητὸς εἰς τοὺς αἰῶνας, ἀμήν.   Οὐχ οἷον δὲ
well spoken into the ages, amen.   Not such but
3754 1601   01 3056 02   2316 3756 1063
ὅτι ἐκπέπτωκεν ὁ λόγος τοῦ θεοῦ. οὐ γὰρ
that has fallen out the word of the God. Not for
3956 013 1537 2474   3778 2474   7 3761   3754
πάντες οἱ ἐξ Ἰσραὴλ οὗτοι Ἰσραήλ· οὐδ' ὅτι
all   the from Israel these Israel; but not that
1510   4690   11   3956 5043   235   1722
εἰσὶν σπέρμα Ἀβραὰμ πάντες τέκνα, ἀλλ' ἐν
they are seed Abraham all   children, but; in
2464 2564   1473   4690   8 3778 1510
Ἰσαὰκ κληθήσεταί σοι σπέρμα. τοῦτ' ἔστιν,
Isaac will be called to you seed. This is,
3756 021 5043   06   4561 3778 5043   02
οὐ τὰ τέκνα τῆς σαρκὸς ταῦτα τέκνα τοῦ
not the children of the flesh these children of the
2316 235 021 5043   06   1860   3049
θεοῦ ἀλλὰ τὰ τέκνα τῆς ἐπαγγελίας λογίζεται
God but the children of the promise are reasoned
1519 4690   9 1860   1063 01 3056 3778   2596
εἰς σπέρμα. ἐπαγγελίας γὰρ ὁ λόγος οὗτος· κατὰ
to seed.   Of promise for the word this; by
04 2540 3778   2064   2532 1510   07
τὸν καιρὸν τοῦτον ἐλεύσομαι καὶ ἔσται   τῇ
the season this   I will come and there will be to the
4564 5207   3756 3441 1161 235 2532 4479   1537
Σάρρᾳ υἱός. 10 Οὐ μόνον δέ, ἀλλὰ καὶ Ῥεβέκκα ἐξ
Sarra son.   Not alone but, but also Rebecca from
1520 2845   2192   2464 02   3962   1473
ἑνὸς κοίτην ἔχουσα, Ἰσαὰκ τοῦ πατρὸς ἡμῶν·
one bed   having, Isaac of the father of us;

11
3380	1063	1080		3366	4238	5100	18
μήπω	γὰρ	γεννηθέντων	μηδὲ	πραξάντων	τι	ἀγαθὸν
not yet	for	having been born	but	having not practiced	some	good

2228	5337	2443 05	2596	1589	4286	02
ἢ	φαῦλον,	ἵνα ἡ	κατ'	ἐκλογὴν	πρόθεσις	τοῦ
or	foul,	that the	by	select	purpose	of the

2316	3306	**12**	3756	1537	2041	235	1537	02
θεοῦ	μένῃ,		οὐκ	ἐξ	ἔργων	ἀλλ'	ἐκ	τοῦ
God	might stay,		not	from	works	but	from	the one

2564	3004		846	3754	01	3173
καλοῦντος,	ἐρρέθη	αὐτῇ	ὅτι	ὁ	μείζων
calling,	it was said	to her	that	the	greater

1398	03	1640		2531	1125
δουλεύσει	τῷ	ἐλάσσονι,	**13** καθὼς	γέγραπται·
will slave	the	lesser,	just as	it has been written;

04	2384	25	04	1161	2269	3404		5101
τὸν	Ἰακὼβ	ἠγάπησα,	τὸν δὲ	Ἠσαῦ	ἐμίσησα.	**14** Τί
the	Jacob	I loved,	the but	Esau	I hated.		What

3767	3004		3361	93		3844	03	2316	3361
οὖν	ἐροῦμεν;	μὴ	ἀδικία	παρὰ	τῷ	θεῷ;	μὴ
then	will we say?	Not	unright	along	the	God?	Not

1096		03	3475	1063	3004
γένοιτο.	**15** τῷ	Μωϋσεῖ	γὰρ	λέγει·
may it become.	To the	Moses	for	he says;

1653	3739	302	1653		2532	3627
ἐλεήσω	ὃν	ἂν	ἐλεῶ	καὶ	οἰκτιρήσω
I will show mercy	whom	-	I might show mercy	and	I will have compassion

3739	302	3627		686	3767		3756
ὃν	ἂν	οἰκτίρω.	**16** ἄρα	οὖν	οὐ
whom	-	I might have compassion.	Then	therefore	not

02	2309	3761	02	5143	235	02
τοῦ	θέλοντος	οὐδὲ	τοῦ	τρέχοντος	ἀλλὰ	τοῦ
the	wanting	but not	the	running	but	the

1648a		2316	**17** 3004	1063	05	1124	03
ἐλεῶντος	θεοῦ.	λέγει γὰρ ἡ	γραφὴ	τῷ
showing mercy	of God.	Says for the	writing	to the

5328	3754	1519	846	3778	1825		1473	3704
Φαραὼ	ὅτι	εἰς	αὐτὸ	τοῦτο	ἐξήγειρά	σε	ὅπως
Pharaoh,	(")	into	same	this	I raised out	you	so that

1731		1722	1473	08	1411		1473	2532
ἐνδείξωμαι	ἐν	σοὶ	τὴν	δύναμίν	μου	καὶ
I might demonstrate	in	you	the	power	of me	and

3704	1229		012	3686	1473	1722	3956
ὅπως	διαγγελῇ	τὸ	ὄνομά	μου	ἐν	πάσῃ
so that	might be broadcast	the	name	of me	in	all

07	1093	**18** 686	3767		3739	2309		1653
τῇ	γῇ.	ἄρα οὖν	ὃν	θέλει	ἐλεεῖ
the	earth.	Then therefore	whom	he wants	he shows mercy

3739	1161	2309	4645		3004		1473
ὃν	δὲ	θέλει	σκληρύνει.	**19** Ἐρεῖς	μοι
whom	but	he wants	he hardens.	You will say	to me

3767	5101	3767	2089	3201		011	1063
οὖν·	τί	[οὖν]	ἔτι	μέμφεται;	τῷ	γὰρ
then;	why	then	still	he finds fault?	In the	for

1013	846	5101	436		5599	444
βουλήματι	αὐτοῦ	τίς	ἀνθέστηκεν;	**20** ὦ	ἄνθρωπε,
plan	of him	who	has stood against?	O	man,

3304		1473	5101	1510	01	470		03	2316
μενοῦνγε	σὺ	τίς	εἶ	ὁ	ἀνταποκρινόμενος	τῷ	θεῷ;
on the contrary	you	who	are	the	answering back	the	God?

3361	3004		09	4110	03	4111		5101
μὴ	ἐρεῖ	τὸ	πλάσμα	τῷ	πλάσαντι·	τί
Not	will he say	the	molded	to the	having molded;	why

1473	4160	3779	**21** 2228	3756	2192	1849	01
με	ἐποίησας	οὕτως;	ἢ	οὐκ	ἔχει	ἐξουσίαν	ὁ
me	you made	thusly?	Or	not	has	authority	the

[11]Even before they had been born or had done anything good or bad (so that God's purpose of election might continue, [12]not by works but by his call) she was told, "The elder shall serve the younger." [13]As it is written,

"I have loved Jacob,
    but I have hated Esau."

[14]What then are we to say? Is there injustice on God's part? By no means! [15]For he says to Moses,

"I will have mercy on
    whom I have mercy,
and I will have
    compassion on whom
    I have compassion."

[16]So it depends not on human will or exertion, but on God who shows mercy. [17]For the scripture says to Pharaoh, "I have raised you up for the very purpose of showing my power in you, so that my name may be proclaimed in all the earth." [18]So then he has mercy on whomever he chooses, and he hardens the heart of whomever he chooses.

[19]You will say to me then, "Why then does he still find fault? For who can resist his will?" [20]But who indeed are you, a human being, to argue with God? Will what is molded say to the one who molds it, "Why have you made me like this?" [21]Has the potter no right

over the clay, to make out of the same lump one object for special use and another for ordinary use? ²²What if God, desiring to show his wrath and to make known his power, has endured with much patience the objects of wrath that are made for destruction; ²³and what if he has done so in order to make known the riches of his glory for the objects of mercy, which he has prepared beforehand for glory— ²⁴including us whom he has called, not from the Jews only but also from the Gentiles? ²⁵As indeed he says in Hosea,

"Those who were not my people I will call 'my people,'
and her who was not beloved I will call 'beloved.'"

²⁶"And in the very place where it was said to them, 'You are not my people,'
there they shall be called children of the living God."

27 And Isaiah cries out concerning Israel, "Though the number of the children of Israel were like the sand of the sea, only a remnant of them will be saved; ²⁸for the Lord will execute his sentence on the earth quickly and decisively."ᵃ
²⁹And as Isaiah predicted,

"If the Lord of hosts had not left survivorsᵇ to us,
we would have fared like Sodom
and been made like Gomorrah."

30 What then are we to say?

ᵃ Other ancient authorities read *for he will finish his work and cut it short in righteousness, because the Lord will make the sentence shortened on the earth*
ᵇ Or *descendants*; Gk *seed*

2763	02	4081	1537 010	846	5445	4160
κεραμεὺς	τοῦ	πηλοῦ	ἐκ τοῦ	αὐτοῦ	φυράματος	ποιῆσαι
potter	of the	clay	from the	same	mixture	to make

3739 3303	1519 5092	4632	3739 1161	1519 819
ὃ μὲν	εἰς τιμὴν	σκεῦος	ὃ δὲ	εἰς ἀτιμίαν;
what indeed	into value	pot	what but	into dishonor?

22

1487 1161 2309	01	2316	1731	08 3709
εἰ δὲ θέλων	ὁ	θεὸς	ἐνδείξασθαι	τὴν ὀργὴν
If but wanting	the	God	to demonstrate	the anger

2532 1107	012 1415	846	5342	1722
καὶ γνωρίσαι	τὸ δυνατὸν	αὐτοῦ	ἤνεγκεν	ἐν
and to make known	the power	of him	he brought	in

4183	3115	4632 3709	2675	1519
πολλῇ	μακροθυμίᾳ	σκεύη ὀργῆς	κατηρτισμένα	εἰς
much	long temper	pots of anger	having been put in order	into

684		2532 2443 1107	04
ἀπώλειαν,	**23**	καὶ ἵνα γνωρίσῃ	τὸν
destruction,		and that he might make known	the

4149 06	1391	846	1909 4632	1656
πλοῦτον τῆς	δόξης	αὐτοῦ	ἐπὶ σκεύη	ἐλέους
rich of the	splendor	of him	on pots	of mercy

3739 4282	1519 1391		3739 2532
ἃ προητοίμασεν	εἰς δόξαν;	**24**	Οὓς καὶ
whom he prepared before	for splendor?		Whom also

2564	1473 3756 3441	1537 2453	235 2532
ἐκάλεσεν	ἡμᾶς οὐ μόνον	ἐξ Ἰουδαίων	ἀλλὰ καὶ
he called	us not alone	from Judeans	but also

1537 1484	**25**	5613 2532 1722	03	5617 3004
ἐξ ἐθνῶν,		ὡς καὶ ἐν	τῷ	Ὡσὴ λέγει·
from nations,		as also in	the	Hosea he says,

2564	04	3756 2992	1473 3450	2992 3450 2532
καλέσω	τὸν οὐ	λαόν	μου	λαόν μου καὶ
I will call	the not	people	of me	people of me and

08 3756 25		25	**26**	2532 1510	1722
τὴν οὐκ	ἠγαπημένην	ἠγαπημένην·		καὶ ἔσται	ἐν
the not	having been loved	having been loved;		and it will	in be

03 5117 3757 3004	846	3756 2992 1473
τῷ τόπῳ οὗ ἐρρέθη	αὐτοῖς·	οὐ λαός μου
the place where it was said	to them,	not people of me

1473 1563 2564	5207 2316 2198
ὑμεῖς, ἐκεῖ κληθήσονται	υἱοὶ θεοῦ ζῶντος.
you, there they will be called	sons of God living.

27

2268	1161 2896 5228	02	2474	1437
Ἡσαΐας	δὲ κράζει ὑπὲρ	τοῦ	Ἰσραήλ·	ἐὰν
Isaiah	but shouts on behalf	of the	Israel;	if

1510	01 706	014	5207	2474	5613 05
ᾖ	ὁ ἀριθμὸς	τῶν	υἱῶν	Ἰσραὴλ	ὡς ἡ
might be	the number	of the	sons	Israel	as the

285 06	2281	09 5274a	4982
ἄμμος τῆς	θαλάσσης,	τὸ ὑπόλειμμα	σωθήσεται·
sand of the	sea,	the remnant	will be delivered;

28

3056 1063 4931	2532 4932	4160	2962
λόγον γὰρ συντελῶν	καὶ συντέμνων	ποιήσει	κύριος
word for fully completing	and cutting together	will make	Master

1909 06 1093	**29**	2532 2531	4302	2268
ἐπὶ τῆς γῆς.		καὶ καθὼς	προείρηκεν	Ἡσαΐας·
on the earth.		And just as	had said before	Isaiah;

1487 3361 2962	4519	1459	1473 4690
εἰ μὴ κύριος	σαβαὼθ	ἐγκατέλιπεν	ἡμῖν σπέρμα,
except Master	sabaoth	left behind	to us seed,

5613 4670 302 1096	2532 5613 1116	302
ὡς Σόδομα ἂν ἐγενήθημεν	καὶ ὡς Γόμορρα	ἂν
as Sodom - we might become	also as Gomorrah	-

3666	**30**	5101 3767 3004	3754
ὡμοιώθημεν.		Τί οὖν ἐροῦμεν;	ὅτι
we might be likened.		What then will we say?	that

1484	021	3361	1377	1343	2638

ἔθνη τὰ μὴ διώκοντα δικαιοσύνην κατέλαβεν
nations the not pursuing rightness over took

1343   1343   1161 08 1537 4102
δικαιοσύνην, δικαιοσύνην δὲ τὴν ἐκ πίστεως,
rightness, rightness but the from trust,

31 2474 1161 1377   3551   1343   1519
ʼΙσραὴλ δὲ διώκων νόμον δικαιοσύνης εἰς
Israel but pursuing law of rightness into

3551 3756 5348   **32** 1223   5101 3754   3756 1537
νόμον οὐκ ἔφθασεν. διὰ τί; ὅτι οὐκ ἐκ
law not arrived. Because why? Because not from

4102   235 5613 1537 2041 4350   03
πίστεως ἀλλʼ ὡς ἐξ ἔργων· προσέκοψαν τῷ
trust but as from works; they stumbled in the

3037 010   4348   **33** 2531   1125   2400
λίθῳ τοῦ προσκόμματος, καθὼς γέγραπται· ἰδοὺ
stone of the stumbling, just as it has been look
                                        written;

5087 1722 4622 3037 4348   2532 4073
τιθήμι ἐν Σιὼν λίθον προσκόμματος καὶ πέτραν
I set in Sion stone of stumbling and rock

4625   2532 01 4100   1909 846 3756
σκανδάλου, καὶ ὁ πιστεύων ἐπʼ αὐτῷ οὐ
of offense, and the trusting on him not

2617   **10:1** 80   05 3303
καταισχυνθήσεται. ʼΑδελφοί, ἡ μὲν
will be ashamed. Brothers, the indeed

2107   06   1699 2588   2532 05 1162
εὐδοκία τῆς ἐμῆς καρδίας καὶ ἡ δέησις
good thought of the me heart and the request

4314 04 2316 5228   846   1519 4991
πρὸς τὸν θεὸν ὑπὲρ αὐτῶν εἰς σωτηρίαν.
to the God on behalf of them for deliverance.

2 3140   1063 846   3754 2205   2316   2192
μαρτυρῶ γὰρ αὐτοῖς ὅτι ζῆλον θεοῦ ἔχουσιν
I testify for to them that jealousy of God they have

235 3756 2596 1922 **3** 50   1063 08 02
ἀλλʼ οὐ κατʼ ἐπίγνωσιν· ἀγνοοῦντες γὰρ τὴν τοῦ
but not by perception; unknowing for the of the

2316 1343   2532 08 2398 1343   2212
θεοῦ δικαιοσύνην καὶ τὴν ἰδίαν [δικαιοσύνην] ζητοῦντες
God rightness and the own rightness seeking

2476   07   1343   08   2316 3756
στῆσαι, τῇ δικαιοσύνῃ τοῦ θεοῦ οὐχ
to stand, in the rightness of the God not

5293   **4** 5056   1063 3551 5547 1519
ὑπετάγησαν. τέλος γὰρ νόμου Χριστὸς εἰς
they were subject. Completion for of law, Christ to

1343   3956 04 4100   **5** 3475 1063 1125
δικαιοσύνην παντὶ τῷ πιστεύοντι. Μωϋσῆς γὰρ γράφει
rightness to all the trusting. Moses for writes

08 1343   08 1537 02 3551   3754   01
τὴν δικαιοσύνην τὴν ἐκ [τοῦ] νόμου ὅτι ὁ
the rightness the from the law because the one

4160   846 444   2198   1722 846   **6** 05
ποιήσας αὐτὰ ἄνθρωπος ζήσεται ἐν αὐτοῖς. ἡ
having done them man will live in them. The

1161 1537 4102 1343   3779   3004   3361
δὲ ἐκ πίστεως δικαιοσύνη οὕτως λέγει· μὴ
but from trust rightness thusly he says; not

3004   1722 07 2588   1473   5101 305
εἴπῃς ἐν τῇ καρδίᾳ σου· τίς ἀναβήσεται
you might say in the heart of you; who will go up

1519 04 3772   3778 1510 5547   2609
εἰς τὸν οὐρανόν; τοῦτʼ ἔστιν Χριστὸν καταγαγεῖν·
into the heaven; This is Christ to lead down;

7 2228 5101 2597   1519 08 12   3778
ἤ· τίς καταβήσεται εἰς τὴν ἄβυσσον; τοῦτʼ
or; who will go down into the bottomless? This

Gentiles, who did not strive for righteousness, have attained it, that is, righteousness through faith; [31]but Israel, who did strive for the righteousness that is based on the law, did not succeed in fulfilling that law. [32]Why not? Because they did not strive for it on the basis of faith, but as if it were based on works. They have stumbled over the stumbling stone, [33]as it is written,

"See, I am laying in Zion
a stone that will make
people stumble, a
rock that will make
them fall,
and whoever believes in
him[a] will not be put
to shame."

CHAPTER 10

Brothers and sisters,[b] my heart's desire and prayer to God for them is that they may be saved. [2]I can testify that they have a zeal for God, but it is not enlightened. [3]For, being ignorant of the righteousness that comes from God, and seeking to establish their own, they have not submitted to God's righteousness. [4]For Christ is the end of the law so that there may be righteousness for everyone who believes.

5 Moses writes concerning the righteousness that comes from the law, that "the person who does these things will live by them." [6]But the righteousness that comes from faith says, "Do not say in your heart, 'Who will ascend into heaven?'" (that is, to bring Christ down) [7]"or 'Who will descend into the abyss?'"

[a] Or trusts in it
[b] Gk Brothers

(that is, to bring Christ up from the dead). 8But what does it say?

   "The word is near you, on your lips and in your heart"

(that is, the word of faith that we proclaim); 9because*a* if you confess with your lips that Jesus is Lord and believe in your heart that God raised him from the dead, you will be saved. 10For one believes with the heart and so is justified, and one confesses with the mouth and so is saved. 11The scripture says, "No one who believes in him will be put to shame." 12For there is no distinction between Jew and Greek; the same Lord is Lord of all and is generous to all who call on him. 13For, "Everyone who calls on the name of the Lord shall be saved."

   14But how are they to call on one in whom they have not believed? And how are they to believe in one of whom they have never heard? And how are they to hear without someone to proclaim him? 15And how are they to proclaim him unless they are sent? As it is written, "How beautiful are the feet of those who bring good news!" 16But not all have obeyed the good news;*b* for Isaiah says, "Lord, who has believed our message?" 17So faith comes from what is heard,

a Or *namely, that*

b Or *gospel*

1510	5547	1537	3498	321		235	5101
ἔστιν	Χριστὸν	ἐκ	νεκρῶν	ἀναγαγεῖν.	**8**	ἀλλὰ	τί
is	Christ	from	dead	to lead up.		But	who

3004	1451	1473 09	4487	1510	1722	011	4750
λέγει;	ἐγγύς σου	τὸ	ῥῆμά	ἐστιν	ἐν	τῷ	στόματί
says?	Near you	the	word	is	in	the	mouth

1473	2532	1722 07	2588	1473	3778	1510 09
σου	καὶ	ἐν	τῇ καρδίᾳ σου,	τοῦτ᾽	ἔστιν τὸ
of you	and	in	the heart of you,	this	is the

4487 06	4102	3739	2784		3754	1437
ῥῆμα τῆς	πίστεως	ὃ	κηρύσσομεν.	**9**	ὅτι	ἐὰν
word of the trust	that	we announce.		That	if

3670	1722 011	4750	1473	2962	2424
ὁμολογήσῃς	ἐν τῷ στόματί σου		κύριον	Ἰησοῦν
you might confess	in the mouth	of you	Master	Jesus

2532 4100	1722 07	2588	1473	3754 01	2316
καὶ πιστεύσῃς	ἐν	τῇ καρδίᾳ σου	ὅτι	ὁ	θεὸς
and might trust	in	the heart of you	that	the	God

846	1453	1537	3498	4982
αὐτὸν	ἤγειρεν	ἐκ	νεκρῶν,	σωθήσῃ·
him	raised	from	dead,	you will delivered;

10	2588	1063 4100	1519	1343
	καρδίᾳ	γὰρ πιστεύεται	εἰς	δικαιοσύνην,
	in heart	for he trusts	into	rightness,

4750	1161 3670	1519 4991	**11**	3004
στόματι	δὲ ὁμολογεῖται	εἰς σωτηρίαν.		λέγει
in mouth	but he confesses	into deliverance.		Says

1063 05	1124	3956 01	4100	1909 846	3756
γὰρ	ἡ γραφή·	πᾶς	ὁ πιστεύων	ἐπ᾽ αὐτῷ	οὐ
for	the writing,	all	the one trusting	on him	not

2617	**12**	3756 1063 1510	1293
καταισχυνθήσεται.		οὐ γὰρ ἐστιν	διαστολὴ
will be ashamed.		Not for it is	difference

2453	5037 2532	1672	01 1063 846	2962
Ἰουδαίου	τε καὶ	Ἕλληνος,	ὁ γὰρ αὐτὸς	κύριος
Judean	both and	Greek,	the for himself	Master

3956	4147	1519 3956	016	1941
πάντων,	πλουτῶν	εἰς πάντας	τοὺς	ἐπικαλουμένους
of all,	being rich	to all	the	ones calling on

846	**13**	3956 1063 3739	302	1941	012 3686
αὐτόν·		πᾶς γὰρ ὃς	ἂν	ἐπικαλέσηται	τὸ ὄνομα
him;		all for who	-	might call on	the name

2962	4982	**14**	4459 3767 1941	1519
κυρίου	σωθήσεται.		Πῶς οὖν ἐπικαλέσωνται	εἰς
of Master	will be delivered.		How then might they call	in on

3739 3756 4100	4459 1161 4100
ὃν οὐκ ἐπίστευσαν;	πῶς δὲ πιστεύσωσιν
whom not they trusted?	How but might they trust

3739 3756 191	4459 1161 191	5565
οὗ οὐκ ἤκουσαν;	πῶς δὲ ἀκούσωσιν	χωρὶς
whom not they heard?	How but might they hear	without

2784	**15**	4459 1161 2784	1437 3361
κηρύσσοντος;		πῶς δὲ κηρύξωσιν	ἐὰν μὴ
announcing?		How but might they announce	except

649	2531	1125
ἀποσταλῶσιν;	καθὼς	γέγραπται·
they might be delegated?	Just as	it has been written,

5613 5611	013 4228	014	2097
ὡς ὡραῖοι	οἱ πόδες	τῶν	εὐαγγελιζομένων
as beautiful	the feet	of the	telling good message

024 18	**16**	235	3756 3956 5219	011
[τὰ] ἀγαθά.		Ἀλλ᾽	οὐ πάντες ὑπήκουσαν	τῷ
the good.		But	not all obeyed	the

2098	2268 1063 3004	2962	5101 4100
εὐαγγελίῳ.	Ἡσαΐας γὰρ λέγει·	κύριε,	τίς ἐπίστευσεν
good message.	Isaiah for says,	Master,	who trusted

07	189	1473	**17**	686 05	4102	1537 189
τῇ	ἀκοῇ	ἡμῶν;		ἄρα ἡ	πίστις	ἐξ ἀκοῆς,
in the	hearing	of us?		Then the	trust	from hearing,

05   1161 189   1223   4487   5547   18   235
ἡ   δὲ   ἀκοὴ   διὰ   ῥήματος Χριστοῦ.   ἀλλὰ
the but hearing through word   of Christ.   But

3004   3361 3756 191   3304   1519
λέγω, μὴ   οὐκ ἤκουσαν;   μενοῦνγε·   εἰς
I say, not not they heard? On the contrary; into

3956   08   1093   1831   01   5353   846   2532 1519
πᾶσαν τὴν γῆν   ἐξῆλθεν ὁ   φθόγγος αὐτῶν καὶ εἰς
all   the earth went out the sound   of them and into

024 4009   06   3625   021 4487   846
τὰ   πέρατα τῆς   οἰκουμένης   τὰ   ῥήματα αὐτῶν.
the limits of the inhabited world the words of them.

     235   3004   3361   2474   3756 1097   4413   3475
19 ἀλλὰ λέγω, μὴ   Ἰσραὴλ οὐκ ἔγνω; πρῶτος Μωϋσῆς
     But   I say, not   Israel not   knew? First Moses

3004   1473 3863   1473 1909 3756 1484
λέγει· ἐγὼ παραζηλώσω   ὑμᾶς ἐπ' οὐκ ἔθνει,
says;   I   will make jealous you on not nation,

1909 1484   801   3949   1473
ἐπ' ἔθνει ἀσυνέτῳ   παροργιῶ   ὑμᾶς.
on   nation not understanding I will make angry you.

     2268   1161 662   2532 3004   2147   1722
20 Ἡσαΐας δὲ   ἀποτολμᾷ καὶ λέγει· εὑρέθην   [ἐν]
     Isaiah but   dared more and says,   I was found in

015   1473 3361 2212   1717   1096   015   1473
τοῖς ἐμὲ μὴ ζητοῦσιν, ἐμφανὴς ἐγενόμην τοῖς ἐμὲ
the   me   not seeking, visible I became to the me

3361 1905   4314 1161 04   2474   3004
μὴ ἐπερωτῶσιν. 21 πρὸς δὲ τὸν Ἰσραὴλ λέγει·
not asking on.   To but the Israel he says,

3650   08   2250   1600   020 5495   1473   4314
ὅλην τὴν ἡμέραν ἐξεπέτασα τὰς χεῖράς μου πρὸς
whole the day   I stretched out the hands of me to

2992   544   2532 483   3004   3767
λαὸν ἀπειθοῦντα καὶ ἀντιλέγοντα. 11:1 λέγω οὖν,
people disobeying and speaking against.   I say then,

3361 683   01   2316 04 2992   846   3361
μὴ ἀπώσατο ὁ θεὸς τὸν λαὸν αὐτοῦ; μὴ
not shoved off the God the people of him? Not

1096   2532 1063 1473 2475   1510 1537
γένοιτο·   καὶ γὰρ ἐγὼ Ἰσραηλίτης εἰμί, ἐκ
may it become; and for I   Israelite am, from

4690   11   5443 958   2 3756 683
σπέρματος Ἀβραάμ, φυλῆς Βενιαμίν.   οὐκ ἀπώσατο
seed   Abraham, tribe Benjamin.   Not shoved off

01 2316 04 2992   846   3739 4267   2228
ὁ θεὸς τὸν λαὸν αὐτοῦ ὃν προέγνω.   ἢ
the God the people of him whom he knew before. Or

3756 3609a   1722 2243   5101 3004   05   1124
οὐκ οἴδατε ἐν Ἠλίᾳ τί λέγει ἡ γραφή,
not you know in Elijah what says the writing,

5613 1793   03   2316 2596   02   2474
ὡς ἐντυγχάνει τῷ θεῷ κατὰ τοῦ Ἰσραήλ;
as   he appeals to the God against the Israel?

   2962   016 4396   1473 615   024
3 κύριε, τοὺς προφήτας σου ἀπέκτειναν, τὰ
    Master, the spokesmen of you they killed, the

2379   1473 2679   2504   5275   3441
θυσιαστήριά σου κατέσκαψαν, κἀγὼ ὑπελείφθην μόνος
places of   of you they dug   and I was left alone
sacrifices   down,   under

2532 2212   08   5590 1473   4 235   5101 3004   846
καὶ ζητοῦσιν τὴν ψυχήν μου.   ἀλλὰ τί λέγει αὐτῷ
and they seek the soul of me. But what says to him

01 5538   2641   1683
ὁ χρηματισμός; κατέλιπον ἐμαυτῷ
the warning?   I left behind to myself

2035   435   3748 3756 2578   1119 07
ἑπτακισχιλίους ἄνδρας, οἵτινες οὐκ ἔκαμψαν γόνυ τῇ
seven thousand men,   who   not bowed   knee to the

and what is heard comes
through the word of
Christ.[a]

18 But I ask, have they
not heard? Indeed they
have; for

"Their voice has gone out
  to all the earth,
and their words to the
  ends of the world."

19 Again I ask, did Israel not
understand? First Moses
says,

"I will make you jealous
  of those who are not a
  nation;
with a foolish nation I
  will make you angry."

20 Then Isaiah is so bold as
to say,

"I have been found by
  those who did not
  seek me;
I have shown myself to
  those who did not ask
  for me."

21 But of Israel he says, "All
day long I have held out my
hands to a disobedient and
contrary people."

———————————

CHAPTER 11

I ask, then, has God rejected
his people? By no means!
I myself am an Israelite,
a descendant of Abraham,
a member of the tribe of
Benjamin. 2 God has not
rejected his people whom
he foreknew. Do you not
know what the scripture
says of Elijah, how he
pleads with God against
Israel? 3 "Lord, they have
killed your prophets, they
have demolished your
altars; I alone am left, and
they are seeking my life."
4 But what is the divine
reply to him? "I have kept
for myself seven thousand
who have not bowed the
knee to Baal."

a Or about Christ; other ancient
  authorities read of God

5So too at the present time there is a remnant, chosen by grace. 6But if it is by grace, it is no longer on the basis of works, otherwise grace would no longer be grace.[a]

7 What then? Israel failed to obtain what it was seeking. The elect obtained it, but the rest were hardened, 8as it is written,

"God gave them a
  sluggish spirit,
  eyes that would not see
  and ears that would not
    hear,
down to this very day."

9And David says,
"Let their table become a
  snare and a trap,
  a stumbling block and a
  retribution for them;
10let their eyes be darkened
  so that they cannot
    see,
  and keep their backs
  forever bent."

11 So I ask, have they stumbled so as to fall? By no means! But through their stumbling[b] salvation has come to the Gentiles, so as to make Israel[c] jealous. 12Now if their stumbling[b] means riches for the world, and if their defeat means riches for Gentiles, how much more will their full inclusion mean!

13 Now I am speaking to you Gentiles. Inasmuch then as I am an apostle to the Gentiles, I glorify my ministry 14in order to make my own people[d] jealous,

---

[a] Other ancient authorities add *But if it is by works, it is no longer on the basis of grace, otherwise work would no longer be work*

[b] Gk *transgression*

[c] Gk *them*

[d] Gk *my flesh*

896	5	3779	3767	2532	1722	03	3568	2540	3005
Βάαλ.		οὕτως	οὖν	καὶ	ἐν	τῷ	νῦν	καιρῷ	λεῖμμα
Baal.		Thusly	then	also	in	the	now	season	remnant

2596	1589	5485	1096	6	1487	1161	5485
κατ'	ἐκλογὴν	χάριτος	γέγονεν·		εἰ	δὲ	χάριτι,
by	select	of favor	having become;		if	but	in favor,

3765		1537	2041	1893	05	5485	3765
οὐκέτι		ἐξ	ἔργων,	ἐπεὶ	ἡ	χάρις	οὐκέτι
no longer		from	works,	since	the	favor	no longer

1096	5485	7	5101	3767	3739	1934		2474
γίνεται	χάρις.		Τί	οὖν;	ὃ	ἐπιζητεῖ		Ἰσραήλ,
becomes	favor.		What	then?	What	seeks after		Israel,

3778	3756	2013		05	1161	1589	2013		013
τοῦτο	οὐκ	ἐπέτυχεν,		ἡ	δὲ	ἐκλογὴ	ἐπέτυχεν·		οἱ
this	not	it obtained,		the	but	select	obtained;		the

1161	3062	4456		8	2531	1125
δὲ	λοιποὶ	ἐπωρώθησαν,		καθὼς	γέγραπται·
but	remaining	were hardened,		just as it has been written,

1325	846	01	2316	4151	2659		3788
ἔδωκεν	αὐτοῖς	ὁ	θεὸς	πνεῦμα	κατανύξεως,		ὀφθαλμοὺς
gave	to them	the	God	spirit	of stupor,		eyes

010	3361	991		2532	3775	010	3361	191		2193	06
τοῦ	μὴ	βλέπειν		καὶ	ὦτα	τοῦ	μὴ	ἀκούειν,		ἕως	τῆς
the	not	to see		and	ears	the	not	to hear,		until	the

4594	2250		9	2532	1160a	3004	1096		05
σήμερον	ἡμέρας.			καὶ	Δαυὶδ	λέγει·	γενηθήτω		ἡ
today	day.			And	David	says,	let become		the

5132	846	1519	3803		2532	1519	2339	2532	1519
τράπεζα	αὐτῶν	εἰς	παγίδα	καὶ	εἰς	θήραν	καὶ	εἰς
table	of them	into	trap	and	into	net	and	into

4625	2532	1519	468		846
σκάνδαλον	καὶ	εἰς	ἀνταπόδομα		αὐτοῖς,
offense	and	into	thing given back again		to them,

10	4654	013	3788	846	010	3361
	σκοτισθήτωσαν	οἱ	ὀφθαλμοὶ	αὐτῶν	τοῦ	μὴ
	let be darkened	the	eyes	of them	the	not

991	2532	04	3577	016	1223	3956
βλέπειν	καὶ	τὸν	νῶτον	αὐτῶν	διὰ	παντὸς
to see	and	the	back	of them	through	all

4781		11	3004	3767	3361	4417		2443
σύγκαμψον.			Λέγω	οὖν,	μὴ	ἔπταισαν		ἵνα
might bow together.			I say	then,	not	they stumbled		that

4098		3361	1096		235	011
πέσωσιν;		μὴ	γένοιτο·		ἀλλὰ	τῷ
they might fall?		Not	may it become;		but	in the

846	3900	05	4991	023	1484
αὐτῶν	παραπτώματι	ἡ	σωτηρία	τοῖς	ἔθνεσιν
of them	trespass	the	deliverance	to the	nations

1519	012	3863		846	12	1487	1161	09
εἰς	τὸ	παραζηλῶσαι		αὐτούς.		εἰ	δὲ	τὸ
to	the	to make jealous		them.		If	but	the

3900	846	4149	2889		2532	09	2275
παράπτωμα	αὐτῶν	πλοῦτος	κόσμου		καὶ	τὸ	ἥττημα
trespass	of them	rich	of world		and	the	defeat

846	4149	1484		4214	3123	09
αὐτῶν	πλοῦτος	ἐθνῶν,		πόσῳ	μᾶλλον	τὸ
of them	rich	of nations,		how much more		the

4138	846	13	1473	1161	3004	023	1484
πλήρωμα	αὐτῶν.		Ὑμῖν	δὲ	λέγω	τοῖς	ἔθνεσιν·
fullness	of them.		To you	but	I say	to the	nations;

1909	3745	3303	3767	1510	1473	1484
ἐφ'	ὅσον	μὲν	οὖν	εἰμι	ἐγὼ	ἐθνῶν
on	as much as	indeed	then	am	I	of nations

652	08	1248		1473	1392		14	1487
ἀπόστολος,	τὴν	διακονίαν		μου	δοξάζω,			εἰ
delegate,	the	service		of me	I give splendor,			if

4458	3863		1473	08	4561	2532
πως	παραζηλώσω		μου	τὴν	σάρκα	καὶ
perhaps	I will make jealous		of me	the	flesh	and

4982		5100	1537	846	**15**	1487	1063	05
σώσω		τινὰς	ἐξ	αὐτῶν.		εἰ	γὰρ	ἡ
I will deliver		some	from	them.		If	for	the

580		846	2643		2889		5101	05
ἀποβολὴ		αὐτῶν	καταλλαγὴ		κόσμου,		τίς	ἡ
throw off		of them	reconciliation		of world,		what	the

4356		1487	3361	2222	1537	3498	**16**	1487	1161
πρόσλημψις		εἰ	μὴ	ζωὴ	ἐκ	νεκρῶν;		εἰ	δὲ
acceptance		except		life	from	dead?		If	but

05	536		40		2532	09	5445		2532	1487
ἡ	ἀπαρχὴ		ἁγία,		καὶ	τὸ	φύραμα·		καὶ	εἰ
the	from beginning		holy,		and	the	mixture;		and	if

05	4491	40		2532	013	2798	**17**	1487	1161	5100
ἡ	ῥίζα	ἁγία,		καὶ	οἱ	κλάδοι.		Εἰ	δέ	τινες
the	root	holy,		also	the	branches.		If	but	some

014		2798		1575		1473	1161	65
τῶν		κλάδων		ἐξεκλάσθησαν,		σὺ	δὲ	ἀγριέλαιος
of the		branches		were broken off,		you	but	wild olive

1510	1461			1722	846		2532	4791
ὢν	ἐνεκεντρίσθης			ἐν	αὐτοῖς	καὶ		συγκοινωνὸς
being	you were grafted in			in	them	and		co-partner

06	4491	06		4096	06		1636	1096
τῆς	ῥίζης	τῆς		πιότητος	τῆς		ἐλαίας	ἐγένου,
of the	root	of the		fatness	of the		olive	you become,

18	3361	2620		014	2798		1487	1161
	μὴ	κατακαυχῶ		τῶν	κλάδων		εἰ	δὲ
	not	brag	against	the	branches;		if	but

2620		3756	1473	08	4491	941		235
κατακαυχᾶσαι		οὐ	σὺ	τὴν	ῥίζαν	βαστάζεις		ἀλλὰ
you	brag against	not	you	the	root	bear		but

05	4491	1473	**19**	3004		3767	1575
ἡ	ῥίζα	σέ.		ἐρεῖς		οὖν·	ἐξεκλάσθησαν
the	root	you.		You will say		then;	were broken off

2798		2443	1473	1461		**20**	2573	07
κλάδοι		ἵνα	ἐγὼ	ἐγκεντρισθῶ.			καλῶς·	τῇ
branches		that	I	might be grafted in.			Well;	in the

570		1575		1473	1161	07		4102
ἀπιστίᾳ		ἐξεκλάσθησαν,		σὺ	δὲ	τῇ		πίστει
untrust		they were broken off,		you	but	in the		trust

2476		3361	5308	5426	235	5399	**21**	1487	1063
ἕστηκας.		μὴ	ὑψηλὰ	φρόνει	ἀλλὰ	φοβοῦ·		εἰ	γὰρ
have stood.		Not	high	think	but	fear;		if	for

01	2316	014		2596	5449	2798		3756	5339
ὁ	θεὸς	τῶν		κατὰ	φύσιν	κλάδων		οὐκ	ἐφείσατο,
the	God	of the		by	nature	branches		not	spared,

3361	4458		3761		1473	5339	**22**	2396	3767
[μή	πως]		οὐδὲ		σοῦ	φείσεται.		ἴδε	οὖν
not	perhaps		but not		of you	he will spare.		Look	then

5544		2532	663		2316		1909	3303	016
χρηστότητα		καὶ	ἀποτομίαν		θεοῦ·		ἐπὶ	μὲν	τοὺς
kindness		and	severity		of God;		on	indeed	the ones

4098		663		1909	1161	1473	5544
πεσόντας,		ἀποτομία,		ἐπὶ	δὲ	σὲ	χρηστότης
having fallen		severity,		on	but	you	kindness

2316		1437	1961		07		5544
θεοῦ,		ἐὰν	ἐπιμένῃς		τῇ		χρηστότητι,
of God,		if	you might stay on		in the		kindness,

1893	2532	1473	1581		**23**	2548		1161	1437
ἐπεὶ	καὶ	σὺ	ἐκκοπήσῃ.			κἀκεῖνοι		δέ,	ἐὰν
since	also	you	will be cut off.			And those		but,	if

3361	1961		07		570
μὴ	ἐπιμένωσιν		τῇ		ἀπιστίᾳ,
not	they might stay on		in the		untrust,

1461		1415	1063	1510	01	2316	3825
ἐγκεντρισθήσονται·		δυνατὸς	γάρ	ἐστιν	ὁ	θεὸς	πάλιν
they will be grafted in;		power	for	is	the	God	again

1461	846	**24**	1487	1063	1473	1537	06	2596
ἐγκεντρίσαι	αὐτούς.		εἰ	γὰρ	σὺ	ἐκ	τῆς	κατὰ
to graft in	them.		If	for	you	from	the	by

and thus save some of them. [15]For if their rejection is the reconciliation of the world, what will their acceptance be but life from the dead? [16]If the part of the dough offered as first fruits is holy, then the whole batch is holy; and if the root is holy, then the branches also are holy.

[17]But if some of the branches were broken off, and you, a wild olive shoot, were grafted in their place to share the rich root[a] of the olive tree, [18]do not boast over the branches. If you do boast, remember that it is not you that support the root, but the root that supports you. [19]You will say, "Branches were broken off so that I might be grafted in." [20]That is true. They were broken off because of their unbelief, but you stand only through faith. So do not become proud, but stand in awe. [21]For if God did not spare the natural branches, perhaps he will not spare you.[b] [22]Note then the kindness and the severity of God: severity toward those who have fallen, but God's kindness toward you, provided you continue in his kindness; otherwise you also will be cut off. [23]And even those of Israel,[c] if they do not persist in unbelief, will be grafted in, for God has the power to graft them in again. [24]For if you

[a] Other ancient authorities read *the richness*

[b] Other ancient authorities read *neither will he spare you*

[c] Gk lacks *of Israel*

have been cut from what is by nature a wild olive tree and grafted, contrary to nature, into a cultivated olive tree, how much more will these natural branches be grafted back into their own olive tree.

25 So that you may not claim to be wiser than you are, brothers and sisters,[a] I want you to understand this mystery: a hardening has come upon part of Israel, until the full number of the Gentiles has come in. 26 And so all Israel will be saved; as it is written,

"Out of Zion will come the Deliverer;
he will banish ungodliness from Jacob."

27 "And this is my covenant with them,
when I take away their sins."

28 As regards the gospel they are enemies of God[b] for your sake; but as regards election they are beloved, for the sake of their ancestors; 29 for the gifts and the calling of God are irrevocable. 30 Just as you were once disobedient to God but have now received mercy because of their disobedience, 31 so they have now been disobedient in order that, by the mercy shown to you, they too may now[c] receive mercy. 32 For God has imprisoned all in disobedience so that he may be merciful to all.

33 O the depth of the riches and wisdom and knowledge of God! How unsearchable are his judgments

[a] Gk brothers
[b] Gk lacks of God
[c] Other ancient authorities lack now

5449	1581		65		2532	3844	5449
φύσιν	ἐξεκόπης		ἀγριελαίου	καὶ		παρὰ	φύσιν
nature	were cut off		wild olive	and		along	nature

1461			1519	2565			4214
ἐνεκεντρίσθης			εἰς	καλλιέλαιον,			πόσῳ
you were grafted in			into	cultivated olive,			how much

3123	3778	013	2596	5449	1461		07
μᾶλλον	οὗτοι	οἱ	κατὰ	φύσιν	ἐγκεντρισθήσονται		τῇ
more	these	the	by	nature	will be grafted		in the

2398	1636	25	3756	1063	2309	1473	50
ἰδίᾳ	ἐλαίᾳ.	25	Οὐ	γὰρ	θέλω	ὑμᾶς	ἀγνοεῖν,
own	olive.		Not	for	I want	you	to not know,

80		012	3466		3778	2443	3361	1510
ἀδελφοί,		τὸ	μυστήριον		τοῦτο,	ἵνα	μὴ	ἦτε
brothers,		the	mystery		this,	that	not	you might be

3844	1438		5429		3754	4457	575
[παρ']	ἑαυτοῖς		φρόνιμοι,		ὅτι	πώρωσις	ἀπὸ
beside	yourselves		thoughtful,		that	hardness	from

3313	03	2474		1096		891	3739	09	4138
μέρους	τῷ	Ἰσραὴλ		γέγονεν		ἄχρις	οὗ	τὸ	πλήρωμα
part	the	Israel		has become		until	which	the	fullness

022	1484	1525		2532	3779	3956	2474
τῶν	ἐθνῶν	εἰσέλθῃ	26	καὶ	οὕτως	πᾶς	Ἰσραὴλ
of the	nations	might come in		and	thusly	all	Israel

4982		2531	1125
σωθήσεται,		καθὼς	γέγραπται·
will be delivered,		just as	it has been written,

2240		1537	4622	01	4506		654
ἥξει		ἐκ	Σιὼν	ὁ	ῥυόμενος,		ἀποστρέψει
will come		from	Sion	the	one rescuing,		he will turn off

763		575	2384	27	2532	3778	846	05	3844
ἀσεβείας		ἀπὸ	Ἰακώβ.	27	καὶ	αὕτη	αὐτοῖς	ἡ	παρ'
irreverences		from	Jacob.		And	this	to them	the	from

1473	1242		3752	851		020	266
ἐμοῦ	διαθήκη,		ὅταν	ἀφέλωμαι		τὰς	ἁμαρτίας
me	agreement,		when	I might lift off		the	sins

846		28	2596	3303	012	2098		2190
αὐτῶν.		28	κατὰ	μὲν	τὸ	εὐαγγέλιον		ἐχθροὶ
of them.			By	indeed	the	good message		hostile

1223		1473	2596	1161	08	1589	27		1223
δι'		ὑμᾶς,	κατὰ	δὲ	τὴν	ἐκλογὴν	ἀγαπητοὶ		διὰ
through		you,	by	but	the	select	loved ones		through

016	3962		278			1063	021	5486
τοὺς	πατέρας·	29	ἀμεταμέλητα			γὰρ	τὰ	χαρίσματα
the	fathers;		not give care for			for	the	favor gifts

2532	05	2821	02		2316	30	5618		1063	1473
καὶ	ἡ	κλῆσις	τοῦ		θεοῦ.	30	ὥσπερ		γὰρ	ὑμεῖς
and	the	call	of		the God.		As		indeed for	you

4218	544		03	2316	3568	1161	1653
ποτε	ἠπειθήσατε		τῷ	θεῷ,	νῦν	δὲ	ἠλεήθητε
then	disobeyed		the	God,	now	but	you were shown mercy

07	3778	543		31	3779	2532	3778	3568
τῇ	τούτων	ἀπειθείᾳ,		31	οὕτως	καὶ	οὗτοι	νῦν
in the	of these	disobedience,			thusly	also	these	now

544		011	5212	1656	2443	2532	846		3568
ἠπείθησαν		τῷ	ὑμετέρῳ	ἐλέει,	ἵνα	καὶ	αὐτοὶ		[νῦν]
disobeyed		the	your	mercy,	that	even	themselves		now

1653		32	4788		1063	01	2316
ἐλεηθῶσιν.		32	συνέκλεισεν		γὰρ	ὁ	θεὸς
might be shown mercy.			Closed together		for	the	God

016	3956	1519	543		2443	016	3956
τοὺς	πάντας	εἰς	ἀπείθειαν,		ἵνα	τοὺς	πάντας
the	all	into	disobedience,		that	the	all

1653		33	5599	899	4149	2532	4678	2532
ἐλεήσῃ.		33	Ὦ	βάθος	πλούτου	καὶ	σοφίας	καὶ
he might show mercy.			O	depth	of rich	and	wisdom	and

1108		2316	5613	419		021	2917	846
γνώσεως		θεοῦ·	ὡς	ἀνεξεραύνητα		τὰ	κρίματα	αὐτοῦ
knowledge		of God;	as	unsearchable		the	judgments	of him

2532 421   017 3598 846   34 5101 1063 1097
καὶ ἀνεξιχνίαστοι αἱ ὁδοὶ αὐτοῦ.   τίς γὰρ ἔγνω
and untraceable   the ways of him.   Who for knew

3563 2962   2228 5101 4825   846   1096
νοῦν κυρίου; ἢ τίς σύμβουλος αὐτοῦ ἐγένετο;
mind of Master? Or who councilor of him became?

    2228 5101 4272   846   2532 467
35 ἢ τίς προέδωκεν αὐτῷ, καὶ ἀνταποδοθήσεται
    Or who gave before him, and it will be given
                                                back again

846   36 3754   1537 846   2532 1223   846   2532
αὐτῷ;   ὅτι   ἐξ αὐτοῦ καὶ δι᾽   αὐτοῦ καὶ
to him? Because from him and through him and

1519 846   021 3956   846   05 1391   1519 016
εἰς αὐτὸν τὰ πάντα· αὐτῷ ἡ δόξα   εἰς τοὺς
into him the all;   to him the splendor into the

165   281   3870   3767 1473 80
αἰῶνας, ἀμήν. 12:1 Παρακαλῶ οὖν ὑμᾶς, ἀδελφοί,
ages,   amen.   I encourage then you, brothers,

1223   014 3628   02   2316 3936
διὰ   τῶν οἰκτιρμῶν   τοῦ   θεοῦ παραστῆσαι
through the compassions of the God to stand along

024 4983   1473   2378   2198 40   2101
τὰ σώματα ὑμῶν θυσίαν ζῶσαν ἁγίαν εὐάρεστον
the bodies of you sacrifice living holy well-pleasing

03   2316 08 3050   2999   1473   2 2532 3361
τῷ   θεῷ, τὴν λογικὴν λατρείαν ὑμῶν·   καὶ μὴ
to the God, the reasonable service of you; and not

4964   03   165   3778   235
συσχηματίζεσθε   τῷ   αἰῶνι τούτῳ, ἀλλὰ
be fashioned together to the age   this, but

3339   07 342   02   3563   1519 012
μεταμορφοῦσθε τῇ ἀνακαινώσει τοῦ νοὸς εἰς τὸ
be transformed in the renewal of the mind, into the

1381   1473 5101 09   2307   02   2316 09 18
δοκιμάζειν ὑμᾶς τί τὸ θέλημα τοῦ θεοῦ, τὸ ἀγαθὸν
to approve you what the want of the God, the good

2532 2101   2532 5046   3 3004 1063 1223
καὶ εὐάρεστον καὶ τέλειον.   Λέγω γὰρ διὰ
and well-pleasing and complete. I say for through

06 5485   06   1325   1473 3956   03
τῆς χάριτος τῆς δοθείσης   μοι παντὶ τῷ
the favor of the having been given to me to all the

1510 1722 1473 3361 5252   3844 3739
ὄντι ἐν ὑμῖν μὴ ὑπερφρονεῖν παρ᾽ ὃ
being in you not to think beyond along what

1163   5426   235 5426   1519 012
δεῖ   φρονεῖν ἀλλὰ φρονεῖν εἰς τὸ
it is necessary to think but to think into the

4993   1538   5613 01 2316 3307
σωφρονεῖν,   ἑκάστῳ ὡς ὁ θεὸς ἐμέρισεν
to think soberly, to each as the God divided

3358   4102   4 2509   1063 1722 1520 4983
μέτρον πίστεως. καθάπερ   γὰρ ἐν ἑνὶ σώματι
measure of trust. Just as indeed for in one body

4183 3196   2192   021 1161 3196   3956 3756 08
πολλὰ μέλη ἔχομεν, τὰ δὲ μέλη πάντα οὐ τὴν
many members we have, the but members all not the

846   2192 4234   5 3779 013 4183   1520 4983
αὐτὴν ἔχει πρᾶξιν, οὕτως οἱ πολλοὶ ἓν σῶμά
same have practice, thusly the many one body

1510 1722 5547   012 1161 2596 1520 240
ἐσμεν ἐν Χριστῷ, τὸ δὲ καθ᾽ εἷς ἀλλήλων
are in Christ, the but by one one another

3196   6 2192   1161 5486   2596 08   5485   08
μέλη.   ἔχοντες δὲ χαρίσματα κατὰ τὴν χάριν τὴν
members. Having but favor gifts by the favor the

1325   1473 1313   1535
δοθεῖσαν   ἡμῖν διάφορα, εἴτε
having been given to us differing, whether

---

and how inscrutable his ways!
34 "For who has known the mind of the Lord?
Or who has been his counselor?"
35 "Or who has given a gift to him,
to receive a gift in return?"
36For from him and through him and to him are all things. To him be the glory forever. Amen.

CHAPTER 12

I appeal to you therefore, brothers and sisters,[a] by the mercies of God, to present your bodies as a living sacrifice, holy and acceptable to God, which is your spiritual[b] worship. 2Do not be conformed to this world,[c] but be transformed by the renewing of your minds, so that you may discern what is the will of God—what is good and acceptable and perfect.[d]

3 For by the grace given to me I say to everyone among you not to think of yourself more highly than you ought to think, but to think with sober judgment, each according to the measure of faith that God has assigned. 4For as in one body we have many members, and not all the members have the same function, 5so we, who are many, are one body in Christ, and individually we are members one of another. 6We have gifts that differ according to the grace given to us:

a Gk brothers
b Or reasonable
c Gk age
d Or what is the good and acceptable and perfect will of God

prophecy, in proportion to faith; [7]ministry, in ministering; the teacher, in teaching; [8]the exhorter, in exhortation; the giver, in generosity; the leader, in diligence; the compassionate, in cheerfulness.

[9]Let love be genuine: hate what is evil, hold fast to what is good; [10]love one another with mutual affection; outdo one another in showing honor. [11]Do not lag in zeal, be ardent in spirit, serve the Lord.[a] [12]Rejoice in hope, be patient in suffering, persevere in prayer. [13]Contribute to the needs of the saints; extend hospitality to strangers.

[14]Bless those who persecute you; bless and do not curse them. [15]Rejoice with those who rejoice, weep with those who weep. [16]Live in harmony with one another; do not be haughty, but associate with the lowly;[b] do not claim to be wiser than you are. [17]Do not repay anyone evil for evil, but take thought for what is noble in the sight of all. [18]If it is possible, so far as it depends on you,

[a] Other ancient authorities read *serve the opportune time*
[b] Or *give yourselves to humble tasks*

4394	2596	08 356	06
προφητείαν	κατὰ	τὴν ἀναλογίαν	τῆς
speaking before	according to	the proportion	of the

4102	1535	1248	1722 07 1248
πίστεως, [7]	εἴτε	διακονίαν ἐν	τῇ διακονίᾳ,
trust,	whether	service in	the service,

1535	01 1321	1722 07 1319	8 1535
εἴτε	ὁ διδάσκων ἐν	τῇ διδασκαλίᾳ,	[8] εἴτε
whether	the teaching, in	the teaching,	whether

01 3870	1722 07 3874	01
ὁ παρακαλῶν ἐν	τῇ παρακλήσει·	ὁ
the encouraging in	the encouragement;	the one

3330	1722 572	01 4291	1722
μεταδιδοὺς ἐν	ἁπλότητι, ὁ	προϊστάμενος	ἐν
sharing in	openness, the	one standing before	in

4710	01 1648a	1722 2432	9 05
σπουδῇ,	ὁ ἐλεῶν	ἐν ἱλαρότητι.	[9] Ἡ
diligence,	the one showing mercy	in cheerfulness.	The

26 505	655	012 4190
ἀγάπη ἀνυπόκριτος.	ἀποστυγοῦντες τὸ	πονηρόν,
love unhypocritical.	Abhorring the	evil,

2853	011	18	07	5360
κολλώμενοι	τῷ	ἀγαθῷ, [10]	τῇ	φιλαδελφίᾳ
being joined to	the good,		in the	brotherly love

1519 240	5387	07	5092
εἰς ἀλλήλους	φιλόστοργοι,	τῇ	τιμῇ
in one another	lovingly affectionate,	in the	value

240	4285	11	07	4710	3361
ἀλλήλους	προηγούμενοι, [11]		τῇ	σπουδῇ	μὴ
one another	leading before,		in the	diligence	not

3636	011	4151	2204	03	2962
ὀκνηροί,	τῷ	πνεύματι	ζέοντες,	τῷ	κυρίῳ
troublesome,	in the	spirit	boiling,	in the	Master

1398	07	1680	5463	07
δουλεύοντες, [12]	τῇ	ἐλπίδι	χαίροντες,	τῇ
being slave,	in the	hope	rejoicing,	in the

2347	5278	07	4335
θλίψει	ὑπομένοντες,	τῇ	προσευχῇ
affliction	enduring,	in the	prayer

4342	13	019	5532	014	40
προσκαρτεροῦντες, [13]		ταῖς	χρείαις	τῶν	ἁγίων
remaining constant,		in the	needs	of the	holy ones

2841	08	5381	1377
κοινωνοῦντες,	τὴν	φιλοξενίαν	διώκοντες.
being partner,	the	love to strangers	pursuing.

14	2127	016	1377	1473	2127	2532
[14]	εὐλογεῖτε	τοὺς	διώκοντας	[ὑμᾶς],	εὐλογεῖτε	καὶ
	Speak well	the	pursuing	you,	speak well	and

3361 2672	15	5463	3326 5463	2799
μὴ καταρᾶσθε. [15]		χαίρειν	μετὰ χαιρόντων,	κλαίειν
not curse.		To rejoice	with rejoicing,	to cry

3326 2799	16	012 846	1519 240
μετὰ κλαιόντων. [16]		τὸ αὐτὸ	εἰς ἀλλήλους
with crying.		The same	into one another

5426	3361 024	5308	5426	235 015
φρονοῦντες, μὴ	τὰ ὑψηλὰ	φρονοῦντες	ἀλλὰ	τοῖς
thinking, not	the high	thinking	but	to the

5011	4879	3361 1096
ταπεινοῖς	συναπαγόμενοι.	μὴ γίνεσθε
humble	being led off together.	Not become

5429	3844	1438	17	3367	2556 473
φρόνιμοι	παρ᾽	ἑαυτοῖς. [17]		μηδενὶ	κακὸν ἀντὶ
thoughtful	beside	yourselves.		To no one	bad instead

2556 591	4306	2570 1799
κακοῦ ἀποδιδόντες,	προνοούμενοι	καλὰ ἐνώπιον
of bad giving back,	thinking before	good before
		for yourselves

3956 444	18	1487 1415	012 1537 1473	3326
πάντων ἀνθρώπων· [18]		εἰ δυνατὸν	τὸ ἐξ ὑμῶν,	μετὰ
all men;		if power	the out of you,	with

3956   444   1514   3361 1438
πάντων ἀνθρώπων εἰρηνεύοντες· **19** μὴ   ἑαυτοὺς
all   men   being at peace;   not   yourselves

1556   27   235   1325 5117   07
ἐκδικοῦντες,   ἀγαπητοί,   ἀλλὰ δότε τόπον τῇ
bringing out right, loved ones, but   give place to the

3709   1125   1063 1473   1557
ὀργῇ,   γέγραπται   γάρ· ἐμοὶ ἐκδίκησις,
anger,   it has been written for, to me bring out right,

1473 467   3004 2962   235 1437
ἐγὼ ἀνταποδώσω,   λέγει κύριος. **20** ἀλλὰ ἐὰν
I   will give back again, says Master. But if

3983   01   2190   1473   5595   846
πεινᾷ   ὁ   ἐχθρός σου, ψώμιζε   αὐτόν·
might hunger the hostile of you, give small bits him;

1437 1372   4222   846   3778   1063
ἐὰν διψᾷ,   πότιζε   αὐτόν· τοῦτο γὰρ
if   he might thirst give drink him;   this   for

4160   440   4442   4987   1909 08
ποιῶν ἄνθρακας   πυρὸς σωρεύσεις   ἐπὶ   τὴν
doing burning coals of fire you will heap up on   the

2776   846   3361 3528   5259 010 2556
κεφαλὴν αὐτοῦ. **21** μὴ νικῶ   ὑπὸ τοῦ κακοῦ
head.   of him.   Not be conquered by   the bad

235   3528   1722 011 18   012 2556   **13:1** 3956 5590
ἀλλὰ νίκα   ἐν τῷ ἀγαθῷ τὸ κακόν.   Πᾶσα ψυχὴ
but   conquer in   the good   the bad.   All   soul

1849   5242   5293   3756 1063
ἐξουσίαις ὑπερεχούσαις ὑποτασσέσθω.   οὐ   γὰρ
authorities excelling   let be subject. Not   for

1510   1849   1487 3361 5259 2316 017   1161
ἔστιν   ἐξουσία   εἰ μὴ ὑπὸ θεοῦ, αἱ   δὲ
there is authority   except by   God, the ones but

1510 5259 2316 5021   1510
οὖσαι ὑπὸ θεοῦ τεταγμέναι   εἰσίν.
being by God +having been set in order are+.

   5620 01   498   07 1849   07   02
2 ὥστε ὁ   αντιτασσομένος   τῇ ἐξουσίᾳ τῇ τοῦ
So   the one setting himself the authority the of
that   in order against   the

2316 1296   436   013 1161 436
θεοῦ διαταγῇ ἀνθέστηκεν, οἱ δὲ ἀνθεστηκότες
God direction has stood   the but one having stood
                 against,   against

1438   2917   2983   013 1063 758
ἑαυτοῖς   κρίμα   λήμψονται. **3** οἱ γὰρ ἄρχοντες
to themselves judgment will receive. The for rulers

3756 1510 5401 011   18   2041 235 011   2556
οὐκ εἰσὶν φόβος τῷ   ἀγαθῷ ἔργῳ ἀλλὰ τῷ   κακῷ.
not are fear to the   good work but   to the bad.

2309   1161 3361 5399   08   1849   012 18
θέλεις δὲ μὴ φοβεῖσθαι τὴν ἐξουσίαν· τὸ ἀγαθὸν
You want but not to fear   the authority; the good

4160   2532 2192   1868   1537 846
ποίει, καὶ ἕξεις   ἔπαινον   ἐξ αὐτῆς·
do,   and you will have praise on from of it;

   2316 1063 1249   1510 1473   1519 012 18
4 θεοῦ γὰρ διάκονός ἐστιν σοὶ εἰς τὸ ἀγαθόν.
of God for servant he is to you into the good.

1437 1161 012 2556 4160   5399   3756 1063
ἐὰν δὲ τὸ κακὸν ποιῇς,   φοβοῦ· οὐ   γὰρ
If   but the bad you might do, fear;   not   for

1500   08   3162   5409   2316 1063
εἰκῇ   τὴν μάχαιραν φορεῖ·   θεοῦ γὰρ
without cause the sword   he wears; of God for

1249   1510 1558   1519 3709 03
διάκονός ἐστιν ἔκδικος   εἰς ὀργὴν τῷ
servant he is bring out right into anger to the one

---

live peaceably with all.
[19]Beloved, never avenge
yourselves, but leave room
for the wrath of God;[a] for
it is written, "Vengeance
is mine, I will repay, says
the Lord." [20]No, "if your
enemies are hungry, feed
them; if they are thirsty,
give them something to
drink; for by doing this
you will heap burning coals
on their heads." [21]Do not
be overcome by evil, but
overcome evil with good.

CHAPTER 13

Let every person be subject to
the governing authorities;
for there is no authority
except from God, and those
authorities that exist have
been instituted by God.
[2]Therefore whoever resists
authority resists what God
has appointed, and those
who resist will incur judgment. [3]For rulers are not a
terror to good conduct, but
to bad. Do you wish to have
no fear of the authority?
Then do what is good,
and you will receive its
approval; [4]for it is God's
servant for your good. But
if you do what is wrong,
you should be afraid, for
the authority[b] does not
bear the sword in vain! It
is the servant of God to
execute wrath

a Gk *the wrath*
b Gk *it*

on the wrongdoer. [5]Therefore one must be subject, not only because of wrath but also because of conscience. [6]For the same reason you also pay taxes, for the authorities are God's servants, busy with this very thing. [7]Pay to all what is due them—taxes to whom taxes are due, revenue to whom revenue is due, respect to whom respect is due, honor to whom honor is due.

[8] Owe no one anything, except to love one another; for the one who loves another has fulfilled the law. [9]The commandments, "You shall not commit adultery; You shall not murder; You shall not steal; You shall not covet"; and any other commandment, are summed up in this word, "Love your neighbor as yourself." [10]Love does no wrong to a neighbor; therefore, love is the fulfilling of the law.

[11] Besides this, you know what time it is, how it is now the moment for you to wake from sleep. For salvation is nearer to us now than when we became believers; [12]the night is far gone, the day is near. Let us then lay aside the works of darkness and put on the armor of light; [13]let us live honorably as in the day, not in reveling and drunkenness, not in debauchery and

```
012   2556   4238           1352          318
τὸ   κακὸν  πράσσοντι.  5 διὸ        ἀνάγκη
the   bad    practicing.   Therefore necessity
5293                3756 3441  1223     08   3709   235  2532
ὑποτάσσεσθαι,   οὐ  μόνον διὰ   τὴν ὀργὴν ἀλλὰ καὶ
to be subject,    not  alone because the anger but  also
1223    08  4893            1223     3778   1063 2532
διὰ   τὴν συνείδησιν.  6 διὰ   τοῦτο γὰρ καὶ
because the conscience.   Because this  for  also
5411   5055              3011         1063 2316 1510
φόρους τελεῖτε·       λειτουργοὶ γὰρ θεοῦ εἰσιν
taxes  you complete;  servants   for God they are
1519 846  3778  4342                    7  591        3956
εἰς  αὐτὸ τοῦτο προσκαρτεροῦντες.  ἀπόδοτε  πᾶσιν
into same this  remaining constant.  Give back to all
020 3782    03         04  5411  04  5411   03
τὰς ὀφειλάς, τῷ     τὸν φόρον τὸν φόρον, τῷ
the debts,  to the one the tax  the tax,  to the one
012 5056  012 5056    03          04  5401  04  5401
τὸ  τέλος τὸ  τέλος, τῷ     τὸν φόβον τὸν φόβον,
the toll  the toll,  to the one the fear  the fear,
03         08  5092   08  5092    8 3367       3367
τῷ     τὴν τιμὴν τὴν τιμήν.  Μηδενὶ    μηδὲν
to the one the value the value.  To no one nothing
3784     1487 3361 012 240      25    01
ὀφείλετε εἰ  μὴ  τὸ ἀλλήλους ἀγαπᾶν·  ὁ
owe      except the one another to love;  the one
1063 25    04  2087   3551  4137           9  09  1063
γὰρ ἀγαπῶν τὸν ἕτερον νόμον πεπλήρωκεν.  τὸ γὰρ
for  loving the other  law  has filled.   The for
3756 3431                  3756 5407
οὐ  μοιχεύσεις,        οὐ  φονεύσεις,
not you will commit adultery, not you will murder,
3756 2813        3756 1937      2532 1487 5100 2087
οὐ  κλέψεις,  οὐκ ἐπιθυμήσεις, καὶ εἴ τις ἑτέρα
not you will not you will     and if  some other
                 thieve,       desire,
1785     1722 03  3036 0770  246              1722  03
ἐντολή,  ἐν  τῷ λόγῳ τούτῳ ἀνακεφαλαιοῦται [ἐν τῷ]
command, in  the word this is headed up    in  the
25              04  4139     1473 5613 4572        10 05
ἀγαπήσεις    τὸν πλησίον σου ὡς σεαυτόν.     ἡ
you will love the neighbor of you as yourself.   The
26    03       4139        2556 3756 2038        4138
ἀγάπη τῷ     πλησίον κακὸν οὐκ ἐργάζεται· πλήρωμα
love  to the neighbor bad  not works;    fullness
3767 3551     05 26       11 2532 3778 3609a 04
οὖν νόμου ἡ ἀγάπη.    Καὶ τοῦτο εἰδότες τὸν
then of law the love.   And this  knowing the
2540    3754 5610 2235   1473 1537 5258  1453
καιρόν, ὅτι ὥρα ἤδη  ὑμᾶς ἐξ ὕπνου ἐγερθῆναι,
season, that hour already you from sleep to be raised,
3568 1063 1451       1473 05  4991        2228 3753
νῦν γὰρ ἐγγύτερον ἡμῶν ἡ σωτηρία  ἢ  ὅτε
now for nearer   us  the deliverance or when
4100          12 05 3571 4298      05 1161 2250
ἐπιστεύσαμεν.  ἡ νὺξ προέκοψεν, ἡ δὲ ἡμέρα
we trusted.   The night progressed, the but day
1448      659          3767 024 2041   010
ἤγγικεν. ἀποθώμεθα   οὖν τὰ ἔργα τοῦ
has neared. Let us set off then the works of the
4655     1746       1161 024 3696   010      5457
σκότους, ἐνδυσώμεθα [δὲ] τὰ ὅπλα τοῦ φωτός.
dark,    let put on but the weapons of the light.
13 5613 1722 2250  2156    4043            3361
   ὡς ἐν ἡμέρᾳ εὐσχημόνως περιπατήσωμεν,  μὴ
   As in day  properly  let us walk around, not
2970      2532 3178    3361 2845     2532
κώμοις  καὶ μέθαις,   μὴ κοίταις καὶ
in carousings and drunkenness, not in beds and
```

766		3361	2054		2532	2205	**14**	235
ἀσελγείαις,		μὴ	ἔριδι		καὶ	ζήλῳ,		ἀλλὰ
in debaucheries,		not	in strife		and	jealousy;		but

1746		04	2962		2424	5547	2532	06		4561
ἐνδύσασθε	τὸν	κύριον	Ἰησοῦν	Χριστὸν	καὶ	τῆς	σαρκὸς
put on	the	Master	Jesus	Christ	and	of the	flesh

4307		3361	4160		1519	1939		**14:1**	04	1161
πρόνοιαν	μὴ	ποιεῖσθε	εἰς	ἐπιθυμίας.			Τὸν	δὲ
provision	not	do	for	desires.			The	but

770		07		4102	4355		3361	1519
ἀσθενοῦντα	τῇ		πίστει	προσλαμβάνεσθε,		μὴ	εἰς
being weak	in the		trust	take to yourselves,		not	into

1253		1261	**2**	3739	3303	4100
διακρίσεις	διαλογισμῶν.		ὃς	μὲν	πιστεύει
differentiations	of reasonings.		Who	indeed	trusts

2068	3956	01	1161	770		3001		2068
φαγεῖν	πάντα,	ὁ	δὲ	ἀσθενῶν	λάχανα		ἐσθίει.
to eat	all,	the but		being weak	vegetables		eats.

3	01	2068		04		3361	2068		3361
	ὁ	ἐσθίων	τὸν		μὴ	ἐσθίοντα	μὴ
	The one eating		the		one not	eating	not

1848		01	1161	3361	2068		04	2068
ἐξουθενείτω,	ὁ	δὲ	μὴ	ἐσθίων		τὸν	ἐσθίοντα
let despise,	the but		not	one eating		the	one eating

3361	2919		01	2316	1063	846	4355
μὴ	κρινέτω,	ὁ	θεὸς	γὰρ	αὐτὸν	προσελάβετο.
not	let judge,	the	God	for	him	took to himself.

4	1473	5101	1510	01	2919		245
	σὺ	τίς	εἶ	ὁ	κρίνων		ἀλλότριον
	You	who	are	the one	judging		belonging to other

3610		03		2398	2962	4739		2228
οἰκέτην;	τῷ		ἰδίῳ	κυρίῳ	στήκει		ἢ
house servant?	To the		own	master	he stands		or

4098	2476		1161	1414		1063	01	2962
πίπτει·	σταθήσεται	δέ,	δυνατεῖ	γὰρ	ὁ	κύριος
he falls;	he will stand	but,	is power	for	the	Master

2476	846		**5**	3739	3303	1063	2919	2250
στῆσαι	αὐτόν.			Ὃς	μὲν	[γὰρ]	κρίνει	ἡμέραν
to stand	him.			Who	indeed	for	judges	day

3844	2250		3739	1161	2919	3956	2250	1538
παρ᾽	ἡμέραν,	ὃς	δὲ	κρίνει	πᾶσαν	ἡμέραν·	ἕκαστος
along	day,	who	but	judges	all	day;	each

1722	03	2398	3563	4135		**6**	01
ἐν	τῷ	ἰδίῳ	νοῒ	πληροφορείσθω.			ὁ
in	the	own	mind	let be fully persuaded.			The one

5426		08	2250	2962		5426	2532	01
φρονῶν	τὴν	ἡμέραν	κυρίῳ		φρονεῖ·	καὶ	ὁ
thinking	the	day	to Master		thinks;	and	the one

2068	2962		2068	2168			1063
ἐσθίων	κυρίῳ		ἐσθίει,	εὐχαριστεῖ			γὰρ
eating	to Master		eats,	he gives good favor			for

03	2316	2532	01	3361	2068		2962		3756
τῷ	θεῷ·	καὶ	ὁ	μὴ	ἐσθίων		κυρίῳ		οὐκ
to the	God;	and	the	not	one eating		to Master		not

2068		2532	2168		03		2316	3762
ἐσθίει	καὶ	εὐχαριστεῖ		τῷ		θεῷ.	**7**	οὐδεὶς
he eats,	and	he gives good favor		to the		God.		No one

1063	1473	1438		2198	2532	3762	1438
γὰρ	ἡμῶν	ἑαυτῷ		ζῇ	καὶ	οὐδεὶς	ἑαυτῷ
for	of us	to himself		lives,	and	no one	to himself

599		**8**	1437	5037	1063	2198		03
ἀποθνήσκει·			ἐάν	τε	γὰρ	ζῶμεν,		τῷ
dies;			if	indeed	for	we might live,		to the

2962	2198		1437	5037	599		03
κυρίῳ	ζῶμεν,	ἐάν	τε		ἀποθνήσκωμεν,	τῷ
Master	we live,	if	indeed		we might die,	to the

2962	599		1437	5037	3767	2198
κυρίῳ	ἀποθνήσκομεν.	ἐάν	τε	οὖν	ζῶμεν
Master	we die.	If	indeed	then	we might live

licentiousness, not in quarreling and jealousy. [14]Instead, put on the Lord Jesus Christ, and make no provision for the flesh, to gratify its desires.

CHAPTER 14

Welcome those who are weak in faith,[a] but not for the purpose of quarreling over opinions. [2]Some believe in eating anything, while the weak eat only vegetables. [3]Those who eat must not despise those who abstain, and those who abstain must not pass judgment on those who eat; for God has welcomed them. [4]Who are you to pass judgment on servants of another? It is before their own lord that they stand or fall. And they will be upheld, for the Lord[b] is able to make them stand.

[5]Some judge one day to be better than another, while others judge all days to be alike. Let all be fully convinced in their own minds. [6]Those who observe the day, observe it in honor of the Lord. Also those who eat, eat in honor of the Lord, since they give thanks to God; while those who abstain, abstain in honor of the Lord and give thanks to God.

[7]We do not live to ourselves, and we do not die to ourselves. [8]If we live, we live to the Lord, and if we die, we die to the Lord; so then, whether we live

[a] Or conviction
[b] Other ancient authorities read for God

or whether we die, we are the Lord's. ⁹For to this end Christ died and lived again, so that he might be Lord of both the dead and the living.

10 Why do you pass judgment on your brother or sister?ᵃ Or you, why do you despise your brother or sister?ᵃ For we will all stand before the judgment seat of God.ᵇ ¹¹For it is written,

"As I live, says the Lord,
    every knee shall bow
    to me,
and every tongue shall
    give praise toᶜ God."

¹²So then, each of us will be accountable to God.ᵈ

13 Let us therefore no longer pass judgment on one another, but resolve instead never to put a stumbling block or hindrance in the way of another.ᵉ ¹⁴I know and am persuaded in the Lord Jesus that nothing is unclean in itself; but it is unclean for anyone who thinks it unclean. ¹⁵If your brother or sisterᵃ is being injured by what you eat, you are no longer walking in love. Do not let what you eat cause the ruin of one for whom Christ died. ¹⁶So do not let your good be spoken of as evil. ¹⁷For the kingdom of God is not food and drink but righteousness and peace and joy in the Holy Spirit. ¹⁸The one who thus serves Christ is acceptable to God and has human approval.

ᵃ Gk brother
ᵇ Other ancient authorities read of Christ
ᶜ Or confess
ᵈ Other ancient authorities lack to God
ᵉ Gk of a brother

1437	5037		599		02		2962	1510	**9**	1519
ἐάν	τε		ἀποθνήσκωμεν,		τοῦ		κυρίου	ἐσμέν.		εἰς
if	indeed		we might die,		of the		Master	we are.		Into

3778　1063　5547　　599　　　　2532　2198　　2443　2532
τοῦτο γὰρ Χριστὸς ἀπέθανεν καὶ ἔζησεν, ἵνα καὶ
this for Christ died and lived, that both

3498　　2532　2198　　2961　　　　　　　　　**10** 1473 1161
νεκρῶν καὶ ζώντων κυριεύσῃ. Σὺ δὲ
of dead and of living he might be Master. You but

5101 2919　04　80　　　1473　　2228 2532 1473 5101
τί κρίνεις τὸν ἀδελφόν σου; ἢ καὶ σὺ τί
who judge the brother of you? Or also you who

1848　　04　80　　1473　　3956　1063
ἐξουθενεῖς τὸν ἀδελφόν σου; πάντες γὰρ
despise the brother of you? All for

3936　　　　011　　968　　02　　　2316
παραστησόμεθα τῷ βήματι τοῦ θεοῦ,
we will stand along to the law court of the God,

11 1125　　　　　1063 2198 1473 3004　2962
γέγραπται γάρ· ζῶ ἐγώ, λέγει κύριος,
it has been written for, live I, says Master,

3754 1473 2578　　3956 1119 2532 3956 1100
ὅτι ἐμοὶ κάμψει πᾶν γόνυ καὶ πᾶσα γλῶσσα
that to me will bow all knee, and all tongue

1843　　　03　　　2316　**12** 686 3767　1538
ἐξομολογήσεται τῷ θεῷ. ἄρα [οὖν] ἕκαστος
will confess out to the God. Then therefore each

1473 4012 1438　　3056 1325　　03　　　2316
ἡμῶν περὶ ἑαυτοῦ λόγον δώσει [τῷ θεῷ].
of us about himself word will give to the God.

13 3371　　3767 240　　2919　　　　235
Μηκέτι οὖν ἀλλήλους κρίνωμεν· ἀλλὰ
No longer then one another we might judge; but

3778 2919　3123　　012 3361 5087　4348　　03
τοῦτο κρίνατε μᾶλλον, τὸ μὴ τιθέναι πρόσκομμα τῷ
this judge more, the not to set stumbling to the

80　　2228 4625　　　**14** 3609a 2532 3982
ἀδελφῷ ἢ σκάνδαλυν. οἶδα καὶ πέπεισμαι
brother or offense. I know and have been persuaded

1722 2962　2424　3754 3762　　2839　1223　　1438
ἐν κυρίῳ Ἰησοῦ ὅτι οὐδὲν κοινὸν δι' ἑαυτοῦ,
in Master Jesus that nothing common through itself;

1487 3361 03　　3049　　5100 2839　1510　1565
εἰ μὴ τῷ λογιζομένῳ τι κοινὸν εἶναι, ἐκείνῳ
except to the reasoning some common to be, to that

2839　　　**15** 1487 1063 1223　1033　01 80　1473
κοινόν. εἰ γὰρ διὰ βρῶμα ὁ ἀδελφός σου
common. If for through food the brother of you

3076　　3765　　2596 26　　4043　　　3361
λυπεῖται, οὐκέτι κατὰ ἀγάπην περιπατεῖς· μὴ
is grieved, no longer by love you walk around; not

011 1033　　1473　1565　　622　　5228　　3739
τῷ βρώματί σου ἐκεῖνον ἀπόλλυε ὑπὲρ οὗ
the food of you that one destroy on behalf of whom

5547　　599　　**16** 3361 987　　　3767 1473
Χριστὸς ἀπέθανεν. μὴ βλασφημείσθω οὖν ὑμῶν
Christ died. Not let be insulted then of you

09　18　　**17** 3756 1063 1510　05　932　　02　2316
τὸ ἀγαθόν. οὐ γάρ ἐστιν ἡ βασιλεία τοῦ θεοῦ
the good. Not for is the kingdom of the God

1035　2532 4213　235　1343　　2532 1515　2532 5479
βρῶσις καὶ πόσις ἀλλὰ δικαιοσύνη καὶ εἰρήνη καὶ χαρὰ
food and drink, but rightness and peace and joy

1722 4151　　40　　**18** 01　1063 1722 3778　1398
ἐν πνεύματι ἁγίῳ· ὁ γὰρ ἐν τούτῳ δουλεύων
in spirit holy; the for in this slaving

03　　5547　2101　　03　　　2316 2532 1384
τῷ Χριστῷ εὐάρεστος τῷ θεῷ καὶ δόκιμος
in the Christ well-pleasing to the God and proved

015	444	**19**	686	3767	024 06	1515

τοῖς ἀνθρώποις. **19** Ἄρα οὖν τὰ τῆς εἰρήνης
to the men.   Then therefore the of the peace

1377   2532 024 06   3619   06   1519
διώκωμεν καὶ τὰ τῆς οἰκοδομῆς τῆς εἰς
we might pursue and the of the building the into

240   **20** 3361 1752   1033   2647   012
ἀλλήλους. **20** μὴ ἔνεκεν βρώματος κατάλυε τὸ
one another;   not on account of food unloose the

2041 02   2316   3956 3303   2513   235 2556
ἔργον τοῦ θεοῦ. πάντα μὲν καθαρά, ἀλλὰ κακὸν
work of the God. All indeed clean, but bad

03   444   03 1223   4348   2068
τῷ ἀνθρώπῳ τῷ διὰ προσκόμματος ἐσθίοντι.
to the man   the through stumbling one eating.

2570 09 3361 2068 2907 3366   4095   3631
21 καλὸν τὸ μὴ φαγεῖν κρέα μηδὲ πιεῖν οἶνον
Good the not to eat meat but not to drink wine

3366   1722 3739 01 80   1473   4350
μηδὲ ἐν ᾧ ὁ ἀδελφός σου προσκόπτει.
but not in what the brother of you stumbles.

1473 4102   3739 2192 2596 4572   2192 1799
22 σὺ πίστιν [ἣν] ἔχεις κατὰ σεαυτον ἔχε ἐνώπιον
You trust that have by yourself have before

02 2316 3107   01 3361 2919   1438   1722 3739
τοῦ θεοῦ. μακάριος ὁ μὴ κρίνων ἑαυτον ἐν ᾧ
the God. Fortunate the not judging himself in what

1381   01 1161 1252   1437 2068
δοκιμάζει. **23** ὁ δὲ διακρινόμενος ἐὰν φάγῃ
he approves;   the but one doubting if he might eat

2632   3754   3756 1537 4102   3956
κατακέκριται, ὅτι οὐκ ἐκ πίστεως· πᾶν
has been condemned, because not from trust; all

1161 3739 3756 1537 4102   266   1510
δὲ ὃ οὐκ ἐκ πίστεως ἁμαρτία ἐστίν.
but what not from trust sin is.

3784   1161 1473 013 1415   024
15:1 Ὀφείλομεν δὲ ἡμεῖς οἱ δυνατοὶ τὰ
Owe but we the power ones the

771   014   102   941   2532 3361
ἀσθενήματα τῶν ἀδυνάτων βαστάζειν καὶ μὴ
weaknesses of the unable ones to bear and not

1438   700   2 1538   1473 03 4139
ἑαυτοῖς ἀρέσκειν. **2** ἔκαστος ἡμῶν τῷ πλησίον
ourselves to please. Each of us the neighbor

700   1519 012 18   4314 3619   **3** 2532 1063
ἀρεσκέτω εἰς τὸ ἀγαθὸν πρὸς οἰκοδομήν· **3** καὶ γὰρ
let please into the good to building; also for

01 5547 3756 1438   700   235 2531
ὁ Χριστὸς οὐχ ἑαυτῷ ἤρεσεν, ἀλλὰ καθὼς
the Christ not himself he pleased, but just as

1125   013 3680   014
γέγραπται· οἱ ὀνειδισμοὶ τῶν
it has been written, the revilings of the ones

3679   1473 1968   1909 1473   **4** 3745   1063
ὀνειδιζόντων σε ἐπέπεσαν ἐπ’ ἐμέ. **4** ὅσα γὰρ
reviling you fell on on me. As much as for

4270   1519 08   2251   1319
προεγράφη, εἰς τὴν ἡμετέραν διδασκαλίαν
it was written before, for the our teaching

1125   2443 1223   06   5281   2532 1223
ἐγράφη, ἵνα διὰ τῆς ὑπομονῆς καὶ διὰ
it was written, that through the patience and through

06 3874   018   1124   08 1680
τῆς παρακλήσεως τῶν γραφῶν τὴν ἐλπίδα
the encouragement of the writings the hope

2192   **5** 01 1161 2316 06   5281   2532
ἔχωμεν. **5** ὁ δὲ θεὸς τῆς ὑπομονῆς καὶ
we might have. The but God of the patience and

[19]Let us then pursue what makes for peace and for mutual upbuilding. [20]Do not, for the sake of food, destroy the work of God. Everything is indeed clean, but it is wrong for you to make others fall by what you eat; [21]it is good not to eat meat or drink wine or do anything that makes your brother or sister[a] stumble.[b] [22]The faith that you have, have as your own conviction before God. Blessed are those who have no reason to condemn themselves because of what they approve. [23]But those who have doubts are condemned if they eat, because they do not act from faith;[c] for whatever does not proceed from faith[c] is sin.[d]

CHAPTER 15

We who are strong ought to put up with the failings of the weak, and not to please ourselves. [2]Each of us must please our neighbor for the good purpose of building up the neighbor. [3]For Christ did not please himself; but, as it is written, "The insults of those who insult you have fallen on me." [4]For whatever was written in former days was written for our instruction, so that by steadfastness and by the encouragement of the scriptures we might have hope. [5]May the God of steadfastness and

a Gk brother
b Other ancient authorities add or be upset or be weakened
c Or conviction
d Other authorities, some ancient, add here 16.25-27

encouragement grant you to live in harmony with one another, in accordance with Christ Jesus, [6]so that together you may with one voice glorify the God and Father of our Lord Jesus Christ.

7 Welcome one another, therefore, just as Christ has welcomed you, for the glory of God. [8]For I tell you that Christ has become a servant of the circumcised on behalf of the truth of God in order that he might confirm the promises given to the patriarchs, [9]and in order that the Gentiles might glorify God for his mercy. As it is written,

  "Therefore I will
    confess[a] you among
    the Gentiles,
  and sing praises to your
    name";
[10]and again he says,
  "Rejoice, O Gentiles,
    with his people";
[11]and again,
  "Praise the Lord, all you
    Gentiles,
  and let all the peoples
    praise him";
[12]and again Isaiah says,
  "The root of Jesse shall
    come,
  the one who rises to rule
    the Gentiles;
  in him the Gentiles shall
    hope."
[13]May the God of hope fill you with all joy and peace in believing, so that you may abound in hope by the power of the Holy Spirit.

14 I myself feel confident about you, my brothers and sisters,[b] that you yourselves

a Or thank
b Gk brothers

06	3874	1325	1473	012 846	5426
τῆς	παρακλήσεως	δώη	ὑμῖν	τὸ αὐτὸ	φρονεῖν
of the	encouragement	may give	to you	the same	to think

1722 240 2596 5547 2424 2443
ἐν ἀλλήλοις κατὰ Χριστὸν Ἰησοῦν, [6] ἵνα
in one another according to Christ Jesus, that

3661 1722 1520 4750 1392
ὁμοθυμαδὸν ἐν ἑνὶ στόματι δοξάζητε
with one mind in one mouth you might give splendor

04 2316 2532 3962 02 2962 1473 2424 5547
τὸν θεὸν καὶ πατέρα τοῦ κυρίου ἡμῶν Ἰησοῦ Χριστοῦ.
the God and father of the Master of us Jesus Christ.

[7] 1352 4355 240 2531 2532
Διὸ προσλαμβάνεσθε ἀλλήλους, καθὼς καὶ
Wherefore take to yourself one another, just as also

01 5547 4355 1473 1519 1391 02
ὁ Χριστὸς προσελάβετο ὑμᾶς εἰς δόξαν τοῦ
the Christ took to himself you in splendor of the

2316 [8] 3004 1063 5547 1249 1096
θεοῦ. λέγω γὰρ Χριστὸν διάκονον γεγενῆσθαι
God. I say for Christ servant to have become

4061 5228 225 2316 1519 012
περιτομῆς ὑπὲρ ἀληθείας θεοῦ, εἰς τὸ
of circumcision on behalf of truth of God, for the

950 020 1860 014 3962 024 1161
βεβαιῶσαι τὰς ἐπαγγελίας τῶν πατέρων, [9] τὰ δὲ
to confirm the promises of the fathers, the but

1484 5228 1656 1392 04 2316
ἔθνη ὑπὲρ ἐλέους δοξάσαι τὸν θεόν,
nations on behalf of mercy to give splendor the God,

2531 1125 1223 3778
καθὼς γέγραπται· διὰ τοῦτο
just as it has been written, through this

1843 1473 1722 1484 2532 011
ἐξομολογήσομαί σοι ἐν ἔθνεσιν καὶ τῷ
I will confess out to you in nations and in the

3686 1473 5567 [10] 2532 3825 3004
ὀνόματί σου ψαλῶ. καὶ πάλιν λέγει·
name of you I will psalm. And again it says,

2165 1484 3326 02 2992 846 [11] 2532
εὐφράνθητε, ἔθνη, μετὰ τοῦ λαοῦ αὐτοῦ. καὶ
be merry, nations, with the people of him. And

3825 134 3956 021 1484 04 2962 2532
πάλιν· αἰνεῖτε, πάντα τὰ ἔθνη, τὸν κύριον καὶ
again, praise, all the nations, the Master and

1867 846 3956 013 2992 [12] 2532 3825
ἐπαινεσάτωσαν αὐτὸν πάντες οἱ λαοί. καὶ πάλιν
let praise on him all the peoples. And again

2268 3004 1510 05 4491 02 2421 2532 01
Ἡσαΐας λέγει· ἔσται ἡ ῥίζα τοῦ Ἰεσσαὶ καὶ ὁ
Isaiah says, will be the root of the Jesse and the

450 757 1484 1909 846 1484
ἀνιστάμενος ἄρχειν ἐθνῶν, ἐπ' αὐτῷ ἔθνη
standing up to rule nations, on him nations

1679 [13] 01 1161 2316 06 1680 4137
ἐλπιοῦσιν. Ὁ δὲ θεὸς τῆς ἐλπίδος πληρώσαι
will hope. The but God of the hope may fill

1473 3956 5479 2532 1515 1722 011 4100
ὑμᾶς πάσης χαρᾶς καὶ εἰρήνης ἐν τῷ πιστεύειν,
you of all joy and peace in the to trust,

1519 012 4052 1473 1722 07 1680 1722 1411
εἰς τὸ περισσεύειν ὑμᾶς ἐν τῇ ἐλπίδι ἐν δυνάμει
into the to exceed you in the hope in power

4151 40 3982 1161 80
πνεύματος ἁγίου. [14] Πέπεισμαι δέ, ἀδελφοί
of spirit holy. I have been persuaded but, brothers

1473 2532 846 1473 4012 1473 3754 2532 846
μου, καὶ αὐτὸς ἐγὼ περὶ ὑμῶν ὅτι καὶ αὐτοὶ
of me, and myself I about you that also yourselves

```
3324    1510  19              4137                    3956
μεστοί  ἐστε  ἀγαθωσύνης,   πεπληρωμένοι            πάσης
full    are   of goodness,  having been filled of   all
06    1108          1410          2532 240
[τῆς]  γνώσεως,     δυνάμενοι   καὶ  ἀλλήλους
the    knowledge,   being able  also  one another
3560          5112        1161 1125     1473  575
νουθετεῖν.  15  τολμηρότερον  δὲ   ἔγραψα  ὑμῖν  ἀπὸ
to warn.      More daring    but  I wrote to you  from
3313    5613  1878              1473 1223    08   5485  08
μέρους  ὡς   ἐπαναμιμνῄσκων  ὑμᾶς διὰ    τὴν χάριν τὴν
part    as   reminding again  you  through the favor the
1325            1473 5259 02   2316      1519 012
δοθεῖσάν       μοι  ὑπὸ τοῦ θεοῦ  16  εἰς  τὸ
having been given to me by  the God      for  the
1510   1473 3011      5547        2424 1519 024 1484
εἶναί με   λειτουργὸν Χριστοῦ  Ἰησοῦ εἰς τὰ  ἔθνη,
to be me   servant    of Christ Jesus to  the nations,
2418            012 2098        02       2316   2443
ἱερουργοῦντα   τὸ  εὐαγγέλιον  τοῦ      θεοῦ,  ἵνα
serving as priest the good message of the God,  that
1096        05  4376        022    1484
γένηται    ἡ   προσφορὰ    τῶν    ἐθνῶν
might become the offering   of the nations
2144            37              1722 4151    40
εὐπρόσδεκτος,   ἡγιασμένη      ἐν πνεύματι ἁγίῳ.
well accepted,  having been made holy in spirit  holy.
   2192  3767 08  2746        1722 5547    2424  024
17 ἔχω   οὖν [τὴν] καύχησιν ἐν  Χριστῷ  Ἰησοῦ τὰ
   I have then the  brag    in   Christ  Jesus the
4314 04  2316     3756 1063 5111         5100 2980
πρὸς τὸν θεόν·  18  οὐ  γὰρ  τολμήσω  τι  λαλεῖν
to   the God;       not  for  I will dare some to speak
3739      3756 2716             5547    1223    1473
ὧν      οὐ  κατειργάσατο    Χριστὸς δι᾽   ἐμοῦ
of what not  worked thoroughly Christ  through me
1519 5218        1484          3056   2532 2041    19  1722
εἰς ὑπακοὴν     ἐθνῶν,       λόγῳ   καὶ  ἔργῳ,       ἐν
in  obedience of nations,   in word and in work,      in
1411       4592     2532 5059     1722 1411      4151
δυνάμει σημείων καὶ  τεράτων,  ἐν  δυνάμει πνεύματος
power  of signs and  marvels,  in  power  of spirit
2316      5620    1473 575  2419       2532 2945
[θεοῦ].  ὥστε    με   ἀπὸ Ἰερουσαλὴμ καὶ  κύκλῳ
of God.  So that me   from Jerusalem and  in circle
3360    010   2437      4137            012 2098
μέχρι τοῦ  Ἰλλυρικοῦ πεπληρωκέναι  τὸ  εὐαγγέλιον
until the  Illyricum to have filled the good message
02       5547     20  3779     1161 5389
τοῦ    Χριστοῦ,     οὕτως  δὲ   φιλοτιμούμενον
of the Christ,      thusly  but  loving value
2097              3756 3699  3687       5547     2443
εὐαγγελίζεσθαι   οὐχ ὅπου  ὠνομάσθη Χριστός, ἵνα
to tell good message not  where was named Christ, that
3361 1909 245     2310       3618          21  235
μὴ  ἐπ᾽ ἀλλότριον θεμέλιον  οἰκοδομῶ,      ἀλλὰ
not on  of another foundation I might build, but
2531     1125              3739     3756
καθὼς  γέγραπται·        οἷς     οὐκ
just as it has been written; to whom not
312           4012 846  3708        2532 3739
ἀνηγγέλη    περὶ αὐτοῦ ὄψονται,   καὶ  οἳ
it was declared about him they will see, and  whom
3756 191       4920          22 1352      2532
οὐκ ἀκηκόασιν συνήσουσιν.      Διὸ      καὶ
not having heard they will understand. Wherefore also
1465          024 4183   010 2064     4314 1473
ἐνεκοπτόμην  τὰ  πολλὰ τοῦ ἐλθεῖν  πρὸς ὑμᾶς·
I was being hindered the many the to come to  you;
```

are full of goodness, filled with all knowledge, and able to instruct one another. [15]Nevertheless on some points I have written to you rather boldly by way of reminder, because of the grace given me by God [16]to be a minister of Christ Jesus to the Gentiles in the priestly service of the gospel of God, so that the offering of the Gentiles may be acceptable, sanctified by the Holy Spirit. [17]In Christ Jesus, then, I have reason to boast of my work for God. [18]For I will not venture to speak of anything except what Christ has accomplished[a] through me to win obedience from the Gentiles, by word and deed, [19]by the power of signs and wonders, by the power of the Spirit of God,[b] so that from Jerusalem and as far around as Illyricum I have fully proclaimed the good news[c] of Christ. [20]Thus I make it my ambition to proclaim the good news,[c] not where Christ has already been named, so that I do not build on someone else's foundation, [21]but as it is written,

"Those who have never
    been told of him shall
    see,
and those who have
    never heard of him
    shall understand."

[22]This is the reason that I have so often been hindered from coming to you.

---

[a] Gk *speak of those things that Christ has not accomplished*
[b] Other ancient authorities read *of the Spirit* or *of the Holy Spirit*
[c] Or *gospel*

23But now, with no further place for me in these regions, I desire, as I have for many years, to come to you 24when I go to Spain. For I do hope to see you on my journey and to be sent on by you, once I have enjoyed your company for a little while. 25At present, however, I am going to Jerusalem in a ministry to the saints; 26for Macedonia and Achaia have been pleased to share their resources with the poor among the saints at Jerusalem. 27They were pleased to do this, and indeed they owe it to them; for if the Gentiles have come to share in their spiritual blessings, they ought also to be of service to them in material things. 28So, when I have completed this, and have delivered to them what has been collected,a I will set out by way of you to Spain; 29and I know that when I come to you, I will come in the fullness of the blessingb of Christ.

30 I appeal to you, brothers and sisters,c by our Lord Jesus Christ and by the love of the Spirit, to join me in earnest prayer to God on my behalf, 31that I may be rescued from the unbelievers in Judea, and that my ministryd to Jerusalem may be acceptable

a Gk have sealed to them this fruit
b Other ancient authorities add of the gospel
c Gk brothers
d Other ancient authorities read my bringing of a gift

```
      3570 1161 3371          5117   2192    1722 023    2824
23   νυνὶ  δὲ  μηκέτι     τόπον ἔχων   ἐν  τοῖς κλίμασι
      now  but no longer place having in  the   regions
     3778      1974         1161 2192   010 2064     4314 1473
    τούτοις, ἐπιποθίαν δὲ   ἔχων   τοῦ ἐλθεῖν πρὸς ὑμᾶς
    these,   desire   but  having the to come to   you
     575  4183   2094         5613 302 4198          1519 08
    ἀπὸ πολλῶν ἐτῶν, 24 ὡς  ἂν  πορεύωμαι      εἰς  τὴν
    from many   years,  as   -  I might travel into the
     4681      1679    1063 1279                2300      1473
    Σπανίαν· ἐλπίζω γὰρ διαπορευόμενος  θεάσασθαι ὑμᾶς
    Spain;   I hope for  traveling through to watch  you
    2532 5259 1473 4311                 1563   1437 1473
    καὶ  ὑφ' ὑμῶν προπεμφθῆναι        ἐκεῖ ἐὰν ὑμῶν
    and  by  you  to be sent before there if   of you
    4413   575  3313   1705                    3570 1161
    πρῶτον ἀπὸ μέρους ἐμπλησθῶ. 25 Νυνὶ  δὲ
    first  from part  I might be filled in. Now but
    4198        1519  2419       1247      015 40
    πορεύομαι εἰς  Ἰερουσαλὴμ διακονῶν τοῖς ἁγίοις.
    I travel   into Jerusalem serving   the  holy ones.
      2106          1063 3109    2532  882    2842
26  εὐδόκησαν    γὰρ Μακεδονία καὶ  Ἀχαΐα  κοινωνίαν
    Thought well for Macedonia and  Achaia partnership
    5100 4160         1519 016 4434    014   40    014
    τινὰ ποιήσασθαι εἰς τοὺς πτωχοὺς τῶν ἁγίων τῶν
    some to have made for  the  poor  of the holies the
    1722 2419         2106                 1063 2532
    ἐν  Ἰερουσαλήμ. 27 εὐδόκησαν     γὰρ καὶ
    in  Jerusalem.      They thought well for also
    3781      1510   846      1487 1063 023    4152
    ὀφειλέται εἰσὶν αὐτῶν· εἰ γὰρ τοῖς πνευματικοῖς
    debtors   they are of them; if for  in the spiritual
    846   2841       021 1484    3784       2532
    αὐτῶν ἐκοινώνησαν τὰ ἔθνη, ὀφείλουσιν καὶ
    of them were partners the nations, they owe   also
    1722 023  4559      3008         846      3778  3767
    ἐν  τοῖς σαρκικοῖς λειτουργῆσαι αὐτοῖς. 28 τοῦτο οὖν
    in  the  fleshly   to serve     them.      This  then
    2005                     2532 4972          846
    ἐπιτελέσας            καὶ σφραγισάμενος αὐτοῖς
    having thoroughly completed and having sealed to them
    04  2590  3778    565       1223   1473 1519
    τὸν καρπὸν τοῦτον, ἀπελεύσομαι δι'  ὑμῶν εἰς
    the fruit  this,  I will go off through you  into
    4681      29 3609a  1161 3754 2064       4314 1473 1722
    Σπανίαν·    οἶδα  δὲ  ὅτι ἐρχόμενος πρὸς ὑμᾶς ἐν
    Spain;      I know but that coming    to   you  in
    4138      2129      5547    2064
    πληρώματι εὐλογίας Χριστοῦ ἐλεύσομαι.
    fullness  of good word of Christ I will come.
      3870      1161 1473   80       1223     02
30  Παρακαλῶ   δὲ  ὑμᾶς [ , ἀδελφοί,] διὰ   τοῦ
    I encourage but you     brothers,  through the
    2962   1473 2424  5547    2532 1223   06  26    010
    κυρίου ἡμῶν Ἰησοῦ Χριστοῦ καὶ διὰ  τῆς ἀγάπης τοῦ
    Master of us Jesus Christ and through the love of the
    4151      4865              1473 1722 019  4335
    πνεύματος συναγωνίσασθαί μοι  ἐν ταῖς προσευχαῖς
    spirit    to contend together to me in the prayers
    5228   1473 4314 04  2316       2443
    ὑπὲρ ἐμοῦ πρὸς τὸν θεόν, 31 ἵνα
    on behalf of me to  the God,   that
    4506    575  014 544    1722 07   2449      2532
    ῥυσθῶ  ἀπὸ τῶν ἀπειθούντων ἐν τῇ Ἰουδαίᾳ καὶ
    I might be from the disobeying  in the Judea    and
    rescued
    05 1248       1473 05 1519 2419        2144
    ἡ διακονία μου ἡ εἰς Ἰερουσαλὴμ εὐπρόσδεκτος
    the service of me the in Jerusalem   well accepted
```

015	40	1096		2443	1722	5479	2064
τοῖς	ἁγίοις	γένηται,	**32**	ἵνα ἐν		χαρᾷ	ἐλθὼν
to the	holy	might become,		that in		joy	having come

4314 1473 1223   2307   2316 4875
πρὸς ὑμᾶς διὰ   θελήματος θεοῦ συναναπαύσωμαι
to   you through   want   of God I might be rested
                                          up together

1473	**33**	01	1161 2316 06		1515	3326 3956
ὑμῖν.		ʽΟ	δὲ Θεὸς τῆς		εἰρήνης	μετὰ πάντων
to you.		The but	God of the		peace	with all

1473	281	**16:1**	4921	1161 1473	5402	08
ὑμῶν,	ἀμήν.		Συνίστημι δὲ	ὑμῖν	Φοίβην τὴν	
of you,	amen.		I commend but	to you	Phoebe the	

79   1473   1510   2532   1249   06   1577
ἀδελφὴν ἡμῶν, οὖσαν [καὶ] διάκονον τῆς   ἐκκλησίας
sister of us, being also servant of the assembly

06	1722 2747	**2**	2443 846	4327		1722
τῆς ἐν	Κεγχρεαῖς,		ἵνα αὐτὴν	προσδέξησθε		ἐν
the in	Cenchrea,		that her	you might await		in

2962   516   014   40   2532 3936   846
κυρίῳ ἀξίως   τῶν   ἁγίων καὶ παραστῆτε   αὐτῇ
Master worthily of the holies and stand along her

1722 3739 302 1473   5535   4229   2532
ἐν   ᾧ ἂν ὑμῶν   χρῄζῃ   πράγματι· καὶ
in what - of you she might need practice; and

1063 846   4368   4183   1096   2532 1473 846
γὰρ αὐτὴ προστάτις πολλῶν ἐγενήθη καὶ ἐμοῦ αὐτοῦ.
for she helper   of many became and of me myself.

3	782	4251	2532	207	016	4904
	ʼΑσπάσασθε	Πρίσκαν καὶ	ʼΑκύλαν	τοὺς	συνεργούς	
	Greet	Prisca and	Acquila	the	co-workers	

1473 1722 5547   2424   **4** 3748   5228   06
μου ἐν Χριστῷ ʼΙησοῦ, οἵτινες ὑπὲρ   τῆς
of me in Christ Jesus,   who on behalf of the

5590 1473 04 1438   5137   5294
ψυχῆς μου τὸν ἑαυτῶν   τράχηλον ὑπέθηκαν,
soul of me the of themselves neck set under,

3739   3756 1473 3441   2168   235 2532
οἷς   οὐκ ἐγὼ μόνος εὐχαριστῶ   ἀλλὰ καὶ
to whom not I alone give good favor but also

3956 017 1577   022   1484 **5** 2532 08 2596
πᾶσαι αἱ ἐκκλησίαι τῶν   ἐθνῶν, καὶ τὴν κατʼ
all   the assemblies of the nations, and the by

3624 846   1577   782   1866   04
οἶκον αὐτῶν ἐκκλησίαν. ἀσπάσασθε ʼΕπαίνετον τὸν
house of them assembly. Greet   Epainetus the

27   1473   3739 1510 536   06
ἀγαπητόν μου, ὅς ἐστιν ἀπαρχὴ   τῆς
loved one of me, who is from beginning of the

773   1519 5547   **6** 782   3137   3748 4183
ʼΑσίας εἰς Χριστόν. ἀσπάσασθε Μαρία, ἥτις πολλὰ
Asia   into Christ.   Greet   Maria, who many

2872   1519 1473 **7** 782   408   2532
ἐκοπίασεν εἰς ὑμᾶς. ἀσπάσασθε ʼΑνδρόνικον καὶ
labored   for you.   Greet   Andronicus and

2458   016   4773   1473 2532 4869
ʼΙουνιᾶν τοὺς συγγενεῖς μου καὶ συναιχμαλώτους
Junias   the relatives of me and co-captives

1473   3748   1510 1978   1722 015   652
μου, οἵτινές εἰσιν ἐπίσημοι ἐν τοῖς ἀποστόλοις,
of me, who are prominent in the delegates,

3739 2532 4253   1473 1096   1722 5547
οἳ καὶ πρὸ ἐμοῦ γέγοναν   ἐν Χριστῷ.
who also before me have become in Christ.

8	782	291	04 27	1473	1722 2962
	ἀσπάσασθε	ʼΑμπλιᾶτον	τὸν ἀγαπητόν	μου	ἐν κυρίῳ.
	Greet	Ampliatus	the loved	of me	in Master.

9	782	3773	04 4904	1473	1722 5547
	ἀσπάσασθε	Οὐρβανὸν	τὸν συνεργὸν	ἡμῶν ἐν	Χριστῷ
	Greet	Urbanus	the co-worker	of us in	Christ

to the saints, [32]so that by God's will I may come to you with joy and be refreshed in your company. [33]The God of peace be with all of you.[a] Amen.

CHAPTER 16

I commend to you our sister Phoebe, a deacon[b] of the church at Cenchreae, [2]so that you may welcome her in the Lord as is fitting for the saints, and help her in whatever she may require from you, for she has been a benefactor of many and of myself as well.

[3]Greet Prisca and Aquila, who work with me in Christ Jesus, [4]and who risked their necks for my life, to whom not only I give thanks, but also all the churches of the Gentiles. [5]Greet also the church in their house. Greet my beloved Epaenetus, who was the first convert[c] in Asia for Christ. [6]Greet Mary, who has worked very hard among you. [7]Greet Andronicus and Junia,[d] my relatives[e] who were in prison with me; they are prominent among the apostles, and they were in Christ before I was. [8]Greet Ampliatus, my beloved in the Lord. [9]Greet Urbanus, our co-worker in Christ,

---

[a] One ancient authority adds 16.25-27 here

[b] Or minister

[c] Gk first fruits

[d] Or Junias; other ancient authorities read Julia

[e] Or compatriots

and my beloved Stachys. [10]Greet Apelles, who is approved in Christ. Greet those who belong to the family of Aristobulus. [11]Greet my relative[a] Herodion. Greet those in the Lord who belong to the family of Narcissus. [12]Greet those workers in the Lord, Tryphaena and Tryphosa. Greet the beloved Persis, who has worked hard in the Lord. [13]Greet Rufus, chosen in the Lord; and greet his mother—a mother to me also. [14]Greet Asyncritus, Phlegon, Hermes, Patrobas, Hermas, and the brothers and sisters [b] who are with them. [15]Greet Philologus, Julia, Nereus and his sister, and Olympas, and all the saints who are with them. [16]Greet one another with a holy kiss. All the churches of Christ greet you.

17 I urge you, brothers and sisters,[b] to keep an eye on those who cause dissensions and offenses, in opposition to the teaching that you have learned; avoid them. [18]For such people do not serve our Lord Christ, but their own appetites,[c] and by smooth talk and flattery they deceive the hearts of the simple-minded. [19]For while your obedience is known to all, so that I rejoice over you, I want

a Or compatriot
b Gk brothers
c Gk their own belly

2532	4720	04	27	1473	10	782	559
καὶ	Στάχυν	τὸν	ἀγαπητόν	μου.		ἀσπάσασθε	’Απελλῆν
and	Stachus	the	loved	of me.		Greet	Apelles

04 1384　　　1722 5547　　782　　　016 1537 014
τὸν δόκιμον　ἐν　Χριστῷ. ἀσπάσασθε τοὺς ἐκ　τῶν
the proved one in　Christ. Greet　the from the

711　　　　782　　　　2267　　04 4773
’Αριστοβούλου. 11 ἀσπάσασθε ῾Ηρῳδίωνα τὸν συγγενῆ
Aristobulus.　Greet　Herodian the relative

1473　782　　016 1537 014 3488　　016 1510
μου. ἀσπάσασθε τοὺς ἐκ　τῶν Ναρκίσσου τοὺς ὄντας
of me. Greet　the from the Narcissus the being

1722 2962　12　782　　5170　　2532 5173　　020
ἐν κυρίῳ.　ἀσπάσασθε Τρύφαιναν καὶ　Τρυφῶσαν τὰς
in Master. Greet　Truphaena and　Truphosa the

2872　　　1722 2962　782　　4069　08
κοπιώσας　ἐν κυρίῳ. ἀσπάσασθε Περσίδα τὴν
ones laboring in　Master. Greet　Persida the

27　　3748 4183 2872　　1722 2962　13　782
ἀγαπητήν, ἥτις πολλὰ ἐκοπίασεν ἐν κυρίῳ.　ἀσπάσασθε
loved,　who many labored　in Master. Greet

4504　04 1588　1722 2962　2532 08 3384
῾Ροῦφον τὸν ἐκλεκτὸν ἐν　κυρίῳ καὶ　τὴν μητέρα
Rufus the select　in　Master and　the mother

846　2532 1473　14　782　799　　5393
αὐτοῦ καὶ ἐμοῦ.　ἀσπάσασθε ’Ασύγκριτον, Φλέγοντα,
of him and me.　Greet　Asyncriton, Phlegon,

2060　　3969　　2057 2532 016 4862 846
῾Ερμῆν, Πατροβᾶν, ῾Ερμᾶν καὶ　τοὺς σὺν αὐτοῖς
Hermes, Patrobas, Hermas and　the with them

80　　　782　　5378　　2532 2456　　3517
ἀδελφούς. 15 ἀσπάσασθε Φιλόλογον καὶ　’Ιουλίαν, Νηρέα
brothers.　Greet　Philologus and　Julia,　Nerea

2532 08 79　846　　2532 3652　2532 016 4862
καὶ τὴν ἀδελφὴν αὐτοῦ, καὶ ’Ολυμπᾶν καὶ τοὺς σὺν
and the sister of him, and　Olympus and the with

846　3956　40　16　782　240　　1722
αὐτοῖς πάντας ἁγίους.　ἀσπάσασθε ἀλλήλους ἐν
them　all holy ones. Greet　one another in

5370　40　782　　1473 017 1577　3956
φιλήματι ἁγίῳ. ἀσπάζονται ὑμᾶς αἱ ἐκκλησίαι πᾶσαι
kiss　holy. Greet　you the assemblies all

02　5547　　3870　　1161 1473 80
τοῦ　Χριστοῦ. 17 Παρακαλῶ δὲ ὑμᾶς, ἀδελφοί,
of the Christ.　I encourage but you, brothers,

4648　　016　020 1370　　2532 024
σκοπεῖν　τοὺς τὰς διχοστασίας καὶ τὰ
to look carefully the ones the divisions and the

4625　3844 08 1322　3739 1473 3129
σκάνδαλα παρὰ τὴν διδαχὴν ἣν ὑμεῖς ἐμάθετε
offenses along the teaching which you　learned

4160　2532 1578　575 846　18　013 1063
ποιοῦντας, καὶ ἐκκλίνετε ἀπ’ αὐτῶν·　οἱ γὰρ
doing,　and bow out from them;　the for

5108　03　2962 1473 5547　3756 1398
τοιοῦτοι τῷ　κυρίῳ ἡμῶν Χριστῷ οὐ δουλεύουσιν
such ones in the Master of us Christ not are slaves

235 07　1438　2836　2532 1223　06
ἀλλὰ τῇ　ἑαυτῶν κοιλίᾳ, καὶ διὰ　τῆς
but in the themselves stomach, and through the

5542　2532 2129　1818
χρηστολογίας καὶ εὐλογίας ἐξαπατῶσιν
kind word and good word they deceive thoroughly

020 2588　014　172　19　05 1063 1473　5218
τὰς καρδίας τῶν ἀκάκων.　ἡ γὰρ ὑμῶν ὑπακοὴ
the hearts of the unbad.　The for of you obedience

1519 3956　864　1909 1473 3767 5463　　2309
εἰς πάντας ἀφίκετο· ἐφ’ ὑμῖν οὖν χαίρω,　θέλω
to all reached; on you then I rejoice, I want

```
1161  1473  4680      1510    1519  012  18        185            1161
δὲ    ὑμᾶς σοφοὺς εἶναι εἰς  τὸ  ἀγαθόν,  ἀκεραίους  δὲ
but   you  wise   to be in   the  good,   innocent   but
1519  012  2556     01   1161   2316  06        1515
εἰς   τὸ  κακόν.  20 ὁ  δὲ   θεὸς  τῆς    εἰρήνης
to    the bad.       The but  God  of the peace
4937      04    4567      5259  016   4228  1473     1722
συντρίψει  τὸν σατανᾶν  ὑπὸ  τοὺς  πόδας ὑμῶν   ἐν
will break the adversary under the  feet  of you  in
5034      05   5485   02      2962   1473  2424   3326
τάχει.    Ἡ  χάρις τοῦ   κυρίου ἡμῶν Ἰησοῦ μεθ’
quickness. The favor of the Master of us Jesus with
1473      21    782        1473 5095     01   4904     1473
ὑμῶν.     21  Ἀσπάζεται ὑμᾶς Τιμόθεος ὁ  συνεργός  μου
you.          Greets    you  Timothy  the co-worker of me
2532 3066    2532   2394   2532 4989        013 4773
καὶ Λούκιος καὶ  Ἰάσων καὶ Σωσίπατρος οἱ συγγενεῖς
and Lucius also  Jason and Sosipatros the relatives
1473     22   782        1473 1473 5060    01   1125
μου.     22  ἀσπάζομαι ὑμᾶς ἐγὼ Τέρτιος ὁ  γράψας
of me.  Greet     you  I   Tertius the having written
08   1992       1722 2962      23  782         1473 1050  01
τὴν ἐπιστολὴν ἐν κυρίῳ.    23 ἀσπάζεται ὑμᾶς Γάϊος ὁ
the letter    in Master.      Greets    you  Gaius the
3581     1473   2532 3650  06   1577        782
ξένος    μου  καὶ ὅλης τῆς ἐκκλησίας.  ἀσπάζεται
stranger of me and whole the assembly.   Greets
1473  2037    01   3623      06     4172   2532 2890
ὑμᾶς Ἔραστος ὁ  οἰκονόμος τῆς  πόλεως καὶ Κούαρτος
you   Erastus the manager  of the city  and Quartus
01   80       03         1161 1410        1473
ὁ   ἀδελφός. [ 25 Τῷ   δὲ  δυναμένῳ  ὑμᾶς
the brother.     To the but  being able you
4741      2596 012  2098        1473  2532 012
στηρίξαι  κατὰ τὸ εὐαγγέλιόν μου   καὶ  τὸ
to strengthen by the good message of me and  the
2782      2424     5547      2596 602
κήρυγμα   Ἰησοῦ  Χριστοῦ, κατὰ ἀποκάλυψιν
announcement of Jesus Christ,  by    uncovering
3466      5550     166        4601
μυστηρίου χρόνοις αἰωνίοις σεσιγημένου,
of mystery in times eternal  having been silent,
26  5319                 1161 3568 1223     5037
    φανερωθέντος        δὲ  νῦν  διά   τε
    having been demonstrated but now  through also
1124      4397            2596 2003      02
γραφῶν   προφητικῶν    κατ’ ἐπιταγὴν τοῦ
writings of speaking before by  order   of the
166      2316 1519 5218      4102       1519 3956   024
αἰωνίου θεοῦ εἰς ὑπακοὴν πίστεως εἰς πάντα τὰ
eternal God  for obedience of trust for  all  the
1484      1107               27  3441      4680 2316
ἔθνη     γνωρισθέντος,     27 μόνῳ     σοφῷ θεῷ,
nations having been made known, to alone wise God,
1223     2424  5547      3739   05  1391      1519
διὰ     Ἰησοῦ Χριστοῦ,  ᾧ   ἡ  δόξα     εἰς
through Jesus Christ,   to whom the splendor into
016   165    281
τοὺς αἰῶνας, ἀμήν. ]
the  ages,   amen.
```

you to be wise in what is good and guileless in what is evil. [20]The God of peace will shortly crush Satan under your feet. The grace of our Lord Jesus Christ be with you.[a]

[21]Timothy, my co-worker, greets you; so do Lucius and Jason and Sosipater, my relatives.[b]

[22]I Tertius, the writer of this letter, greet you in the Lord.[c]

[23]Gaius, who is host to me and to the whole church, greets you. Erastus, the city treasurer, and our brother Quartus, greet you.[d]

[25]Now to God[e] who is able to strengthen you according to my gospel and the proclamation of Jesus Christ, according to the revelation of the mystery that was kept secret for long ages [26]but is now disclosed, and through the prophetic writings is made known to all the Gentiles, according to the command of the eternal God, to bring about the obedience of faith— [27]to the only wise God, through Jesus Christ, to whom[f] be the glory forever! Amen.[g]

---

[a] Other ancient authorities lack this sentence

[b] Or compatriots

[c] Or I Tertius, writing this letter in the Lord, greet you

[d] Other ancient authorities add verse 24, The grace of our Lord Jesus Christ be with all of you. Amen.

[e] Gk the one

[f] Other ancient authorities lack to whom. The verse then reads, to the only wise God be the glory through Jesus Christ forever. Amen.

[g] Other ancient authorities lack 16.25-27 or include it after 14.23 or 15.33; others put verse 24 after verse 27

1 CORINTHIANS

CHAPTER 1

Paul, called to be an apostle of Christ Jesus by the will of God, and our brother Sosthenes,

2 To the church of God that is in Corinth, to those who are sanctified in Christ Jesus, called to be saints, together with all those who in every place call on the name of our Lord Jesus Christ, both their Lord[a] and ours:

3 Grace to you and peace from God our Father and the Lord Jesus Christ.

4 I give thanks to my[b] God always for you because of the grace of God that has been given you in Christ Jesus, [5]for in every way you have been enriched in him, in speech and knowledge of every kind— just as the testimony of[c] Christ has been strengthened among you— [7]so that you are not lacking in any spiritual gift as you wait for the revealing of our Lord Jesus Christ. [8]He will also strengthen you to the end, so that you may be blameless on the day of our Lord Jesus Christ. [9]God is faithful; by him you were called into the fellowship of his Son, Jesus Christ our Lord.

10 Now I appeal to you, brothers and sisters,[d] by the name of our Lord Jesus Christ, that all of you be in agreement and that there be no divisions among you,

a Gk theirs
b Other ancient authorities lack my
c Or to
d Gk brothers

1:1

3972	2822	652	5547	2424	1223
Παῦλος	κλητὸς	ἀπόστολος	Χριστοῦ	Ἰησοῦ	διὰ
Paul	called	delegate	of Christ	Jesus	through

2307	2316	2532 4988	01 80	**2**	07
θελήματος	θεοῦ	καὶ Σωσθένης	ὁ ἀδελφὸς		τῇ
want	of God	and Sosthenes	the brother		to the

1577	02	2316 07	1510	1722 2882
ἐκκλησίᾳ	τοῦ	θεοῦ τῇ	οὔσῃ	ἐν Κορίνθῳ,
assembly of	the	God the	being	in Corinth,

37	1722 5547	2424	2822	40
ἡγιασμένοις	ἐν Χριστῷ	Ἰησοῦ,	κλητοῖς	ἁγίοις,
having been in	Christ	Jesus,	called	holy ones,
made holy

4862 3956	015	1941	012 3686	02	2962
σὺν πᾶσιν	τοῖς	ἐπικαλουμένοις	τὸ ὄνομα	τοῦ	κυρίου
with all	the	calling on	the name	of the	Master

1473	2424	5547	1722 3956	5117	846	2532
ἡμῶν	Ἰησοῦ	Χριστοῦ	ἐν παντὶ	τόπῳ,	αὐτῶν	καὶ
of us	Jesus	Christ	in all	place,	of them	and

1473	**3**	5485	1473	2532 1515	575 2316 3962	1473
ἡμῶν·		χάρις	ὑμῖν	καὶ εἰρήνη	ἀπὸ θεοῦ πατρὸς	ἡμῶν
us;		favor	to you	and peace	from God father	of us

2532 2962	2424 5547	**4**	2168	03
καὶ κυρίου	Ἰησοῦ Χριστοῦ.		Εὐχαριστῶ	τῷ
and Master	Jesus Christ.		I give good favor	to the

2316 1473	3842	4012	1473 1909 07	5485	02
θεῷ μου	πάντοτε	περὶ	ὑμῶν ἐπὶ	τῇ χάριτι	τοῦ
God of me	always	about	you on	the favor	of the

2316 07	1325	1473	1722 5547	2424
θεοῦ τῇ	δοθείσῃ	ὑμῖν	ἐν Χριστῷ	Ἰησοῦ,
God to the	having given	to you	in Christ	Jesus,

5	3754 1722 3956	4148	1722 846	1722
	ὅτι ἐν παντὶ	ἐπλουτίσθητε	ἐν αὐτῷ,	ἐν
	that in all	you were made rich	in him,	in

3956	3056 2532 3956 1108	**6**	2531	09 3142
παντὶ	λόγῳ καὶ πάσῃ γνώσει,		καθὼς	τὸ μαρτύριον
all	word and all knowledge,		just as	the testimony

02	5547	950	1722 1473	**7**	5620	1473
τοῦ	Χριστοῦ	ἐβεβαιώθη	ἐν ὑμῖν,		ὥστε	ὑμᾶς
of the	Christ	was confirmed	in you,		so that	you

3361 5302	1722 3367	5486	553
μὴ ὑστερεῖσθαι	ἐν μηδενὶ	χαρίσματι	ἀπεκδεχομένους
not to be lacking	in nothing	favor gift	awaiting

08 602	02	2962	1473 2424 5547
τὴν ἀποκάλυψιν	τοῦ	κυρίου	ἡμῶν Ἰησοῦ Χριστοῦ·
the uncovering	of the	Master	of us Jesus Christ;

8	3739 2532 950	1473 2193	5056
	ὃς καὶ βεβαιώσει	ὑμᾶς ἕως	τέλους
	who also will confirm	you until	completion

410	1722 07	2250 02	2962	1473 2424
ἀνεγκλήτους	ἐν τῇ	ἡμέρᾳ τοῦ	κυρίου	ἡμῶν Ἰησοῦ
unreproachable	in the	day of the	Master	of us Jesus

5547	4103	01 2316 1223	3739
[Χριστοῦ].	**9** πιστὸς	ὁ θεός, δι᾽	οὗ
Christ.	Trustful	the God, through	whom

2564	1519 2842	02	5207 846
ἐκλήθητε	εἰς κοινωνίαν	τοῦ	υἱοῦ αὐτοῦ
you were called	into partnership	of the	son of him

2424 5547 02	2962 1473	**10**	3870	1161
Ἰησοῦ Χριστοῦ τοῦ	κυρίου ἡμῶν.		Παρακαλῶ	δὲ
Jesus Christ of the	Master of us.		I encourage	but

1473 80	1223	010 3686	02	2962
ὑμᾶς, ἀδελφοί,	διὰ	τοῦ ὀνόματος	τοῦ	κυρίου
you, brothers,	through	the name	of the	Master

1473 2424 5547	2443 012 846	3004
ἡμῶν Ἰησοῦ Χριστοῦ,	ἵνα τὸ αὐτὸ	λέγητε
of us Jesus Christ,	that the same	you might say

3956	2532 3361 1510	1722 1473 4978
πάντες	καὶ μὴ ᾖ	ἐν ὑμῖν σχίσματα,
all	and not might be	in you splits,

1510	1161 2675		1722 03	
ἦτε	δὲ κατηρτισμένοι		ἐν τῷ	
you might be+	but +having been put in order		in the	

846   3563 2532 1722 07 846   1106   **11** 1213
αὐτῷ νοῒ καὶ ἐν τῇ αὐτῇ γνώμῃ.   ἐδηλώθη
same mind and in the same purpose.   It was made clear

1063 1473 4012 1473 80   1473 5259 014
γάρ μοι περὶ ὑμῶν, ἀδελφοί μου, ὑπὸ τῶν
for to me about you, brothers of me, by of the

5514   3754 2054 1722 1473 1510 **12** 3004 1161
Χλόης ὅτι ἔριδες ἐν ὑμῖν εἰσιν.   λέγω δὲ
of Chloe that strifes in you are.   I say but

3778 3754 1538   1473 3004   1473 3303   1510
τοῦτο ὅτι ἔκαστος ὑμῶν λέγει· ἐγὼ μέν εἰμι
this that each of you says, I indeed am

3972   1473 1161 625   1473 1161 2786   1473
Παύλου, ἐγὼ δὲ Ἀπολλῶ, ἐγὼ δὲ Κηφᾶ, ἐγὼ
of Paul, I but of Apollos, I but of Cephas, I

1161 5547   **13** 3307   01 5547   3361
δὲ Χριστοῦ.   μεμέρισται ὁ Χριστός; μὴ
but of Christ. Has been divided the Christ? Not

3972   4717   5228   1473 2228 1519 012
Παῦλος ἐσταυρώθη ὑπὲρ ὑμῶν, ἢ εἰς τὸ
Paul was crucified on behalf of you, or into the

3686 3972 907   **14** 2168
ὄνομα Παύλου ἐβαπτίσθητε;   εὐχαριστῶ
name of Paul were you immersed? I give good favor

03   2316 3754 3762   1473 907   1487 3361
[τῷ θεῷ] ὅτι οὐδένα ὑμῶν ἐβάπτισα εἰ μὴ
to the God that no one of you I immersed except

2921   2532 1050 **15** 2443 3361 5100 3004   3754
Κρίσπον καὶ Γάϊον, ἵνα μή τις εἴπῃ ὅτι
Crispus and Gaius, that not some might say that

1519 012 1699 3686 907   **16** 907
εἰς τὸ ἐμὸν ὄνομα ἐβαπτίσθητε.   ἐβάπτισα
into the my name you were immersed. I immersed

1161 2532 04 4734   3624 3062   3756 3609a
δὲ καὶ τὸν Στεφανᾶ οἶκον, λοιπὸν οὐκ οἶδα
but also the of Stephan house, remaining not I know

1487 5100 243   907   **17** 3756 1063 649   1473
εἴ τινα ἄλλον ἐβάπτισα.   οὐ γὰρ ἀπέστειλέν με
if some other I immersed. Not for delegated me

5547   907   235 2097   3756 1722
Χριστὸς βαπτίζειν ἀλλὰ εὐαγγελίζεσθαι, οὐκ ἐν
Christ to immerse but to tell good message, not in

4678   3056   2443 3361 2758   01 4716
σοφίᾳ λόγου, ἵνα μὴ κενωθῇ ὁ σταυρὸς
wisdom of word, that not might be emptied the cross

02   5547   **18** 01 3056 1063 01 02   4716
τοῦ Χριστοῦ.   Ὁ λόγος γὰρ ὁ τοῦ σταυροῦ
of the Christ. The word for the of the cross

015   3303 622   3472   1510
τοῖς μὲν ἀπολλυμένοις μωρία ἐστίν,
to the indeed ones being destroyed foolishness is,

015   1161 4982   1473 1411   2316
τοῖς δὲ σῳζομένοις ἡμῖν δύναμις θεοῦ
to the but ones being delivered to us power of God

1510   **19** 1125   1063 622   08
ἐστιν.   γέγραπται γάρ· ἀπολῶ τὴν
it is. It has been written for, I will destroy the

4678 014   4680 2532 08 4907   014
σοφίαν τῶν σοφῶν καὶ τὴν σύνεσιν τῶν
wisdom of the wise and the understanding of the ones

4908   114   **20** 4226 4680   4226
συνετῶν ἀθετήσω.   ποῦ σοφός; ποῦ
understanding I will set aside. Where wise? Where

1122   4226 4804   02 165   3778 3780
γραμματεύς; ποῦ συζητητὴς τοῦ αἰῶνος τούτου; οὐχὶ
writer? Where disputer of the age this? Not

but that you be united in the same mind and the same purpose. [11]For it has been reported to me by Chloe's people that there are quarrels among you, my brothers and sisters.[a] [12]What I mean is that each of you says, "I belong to Paul," or "I belong to Apollos," or "I belong to Cephas," or "I belong to Christ." [13]Has Christ been divided? Was Paul crucified for you? Or were you baptized in the name of Paul? [14]I thank God[b] that I baptized none of you except Crispus and Gaius, [15]so that no one can say that you were baptized in my name. [16](I did baptize also the household of Stephanas; beyond that, I do not know whether I baptized anyone else.) [17]For Christ did not send me to baptize but to proclaim the gospel, and not with eloquent wisdom, so that the cross of Christ might not be emptied of its power.

[18]For the message about the cross is foolishness to those who are perishing, but to us who are being saved it is the power of God. [19]For it is written,

"I will destroy the
    wisdom of the wise,
and the discernment of
    the discerning I will
    thwart."

[20]Where is the one who is wise? Where is the scribe? Where is the debater of this age? Has not

[a] Gk *my brothers*
[b] Other ancient authorities read *I am thankful*

God made foolish the wisdom of the world? ²¹For since, in the wisdom of God, the world did not know God through wisdom, God decided, through the foolishness of our proclamation, to save those who believe. ²²For Jews demand signs and Greeks desire wisdom, ²³but we proclaim Christ crucified, a stumbling block to Jews and foolishness to Gentiles, ²⁴but to those who are the called, both Jews and Greeks, Christ the power of God and the wisdom of God. ²⁵For God's foolishness is wiser than human wisdom, and God's weakness is stronger than human strength.

²⁶Consider your own call, brothers and sisters:^a not many of you were wise by human standards,^b not many were powerful, not many were of noble birth. ²⁷But God chose what is foolish in the world to shame the wise; God chose what is weak in the world to shame the strong; ²⁸God chose what is low and despised in the world, things that are not, to reduce to nothing things that are, ²⁹so that no one^c might boast in the presence of God. ³⁰He is the source of your life in Christ Jesus, who became for us wisdom from God, and righteousness

^a Gk brothers
^b Gk according to the flesh
^c Gk no flesh

```
           3471              01    2316 08  4678    02      2889
        ἐμώρανεν      ὁ   θεὸς  τὴν σοφίαν τοῦ    κόσμου;
        made foolish the God  the wisdom of the world?

           1894    1063 1722 07   4678    02        2316 3756 1097
     21 ἐπειδὴ γὰρ  ἐν   τῇ  σοφίᾳ τοῦ   θεοῦ οὐκ   ἔγνω
        Since  for  in   the wisdom of the God  not  knew
        01 2889     1223      06  4678    04  2316  2106
        ὁ κόσμος διὰ    τῆς σοφίας τὸν θεόν, εὐδόκησεν
        the world through the wisdom the God,  thought well
        01  2316 1223     06  3472          010      2782
        ὁ  θεὸς διὰ    τῆς μωρίας       τοῦ   κηρύγματος
        the God through the foolishness of the announcement
        4982        016  4100             1894  2532 2453
        σῶσαι    τοὺς πιστεύοντας·   22 ἐπειδὴ καὶ  Ἰουδαῖοι
        to deliver the ones trusting;   since  also  Judeans
        4592   154     2532  1672     2212           2453    1473
        σημεῖα αἰτοῦσιν καὶ Ἕλληνες σοφίαν ζητοῦσιν,  23 ἡμεῖς
        signs   ask      and  Greeks  wisdom seek,       we
        1161 2784       5547     4717             2453        3303
        δὲ  κηρύσσομεν Χριστὸν ἐσταυρωμένον, Ἰουδαίοις  μὲν
        but  announce   Christ  having been    to Judeans  even
                                                crucified,
        4625        1484     1161 3472         846    1161
        σκάνδαλον, ἔθνεσιν δὲ  μωρίαν,  24 αὐτοῖς δὲ
        offense,   to nations but  foolishness,  to them but
        015 2822    2453           5037 2532 1672       5547
        τοῖς κλητοῖς, Ἰουδαίοις τε   καὶ  Ἕλλησιν, Χριστὸν
        the called,  Judeans   both and   Greeks,   Christ
        2316   1411     2532 2316    4678         3754 09  3474
        θεοῦ δύναμιν καὶ θεοῦ σοφίαν·  25 ὅτι τὸ μωρὸν
        of God power  and of God wisdom;   that the foolish
        02   2316 4680      014      444       1510  2532 09
        τοῦ θεοῦ σοφώτερον τῶν ἀνθρώπων ἐστὶν καὶ τὸ
        of the God wiser    of the men   is    and the
        772     02    2316 2478       014     444
        ἀσθενὲς τοῦ  θεοῦ ἰσχυρότερον τῶν ἀνθρώπων.
        weak    of the God stronger   of the men.

           991      1063 08 2821   1473 80     3754 3756
     26 Βλέπετε γὰρ τὴν κλῆσιν ὑμῶν, ἀδελφοί, ὅτι οὐ
        See     for the call  of you, brothers, that not
        4183  4680 2596 4561   3756 4183   1415      3756
        πολλοὶ σοφοὶ κατὰ σάρκα, οὐ πολλοὶ δυνατοί, οὐ
        many   wise  by   flesh,  not many  power,   not
        4183  2104      235  024 3474     02      2889
        πολλοὶ εὐγενεῖς·  27 ἀλλὰ τὰ μωρὰ τοῦ   κόσμου
        many   wellborn;    but  the foolish of the world
        1586     01  2316 2443 2617     016 4680
        ἐξελέξατο ὁ  θεός, ἵνα καταισχύνῃ τοὺς σοφούς,
        selected the God, that he might shame the wise,
        2532 024 772   02    2889  1586      01 2316 2443
        καὶ τὰ ἀσθενῆ τοῦ  κόσμου ἐξελέξατο ὁ θεός, ἵνα
        and the weak of the world selected the God, that
        2617        024 2478    28 2532 024 36    02
        καταισχύνῃ τὰ ἰσχυρά,   καὶ τὰ ἀγενῆ τοῦ
        he might shame the strong,  and the unborn of the
        2889   2532 024 1848          1586     01
        κόσμου καὶ τὰ ἐξουθενημένα ἐξελέξατο ὁ
        world  and the having been despised selected the
        2316  024 3361 1510   2443 024 1510  2673
        θεός, τὰ μὴ ὄντα, ἵνα τὰ ὄντα καταργήσῃ,
        God,  the not being, that the being he might abolish,
           3704   3361 2744       3956 4561  1799    02
     29 ὅπως μὴ καυχήσηται πᾶσα σὰρξ ἐνώπιον τοῦ
        so that not might brag all flesh before the
        2316   1537 846   1161 1473   1510 1722 5547
        θεοῦ.  30 ἐξ αὐτοῦ δὲ ὑμεῖς ἐστε ἐν Χριστῷ
        God.     From him but you  are  in  Christ
        2424   3739 1096   4678   1473 575 2316 1343
        Ἰησοῦ, ὃς ἐγενήθη σοφία ἡμῖν ἀπὸ θεοῦ, δικαιοσύνη
        Jesus, who became wisdom to us from God, rightness
```

5037	2532	38	2532	629	**31**	2443	2531
τε	καὶ	ἁγιασμὸς καὶ	ἀπολύτρωσις,		ἵνα	καθὼς
both	and	holiness and	redemption,		that	just as

1125		01	2744		1722	2962
γέγραπται·		ὁ	καυχώμενος	ἐν	κυρίῳ
it has been written,		the	bragging	in	Master

2744	**2:1**	2504	2064		4314	1473	80
καυχάσθω.		Κἀγὼ	ἐλθὼν		πρὸς	ὑμᾶς,	ἀδελφοί,
let brag.		And I	having come	to	you,	brothers,

2064	3756	2596	5247		3056		2228	4678
ἦλθον	οὐ	καθ᾽	ὑπεροχὴν	λόγου	ἢ		σοφίας
came	not	by	excellence	of word	or		wisdom

2605		1473	012	3466		02		2316	**2**	3756
καταγγέλλων	ὑμῖν	τὸ	μυστήριον	τοῦ	θεοῦ.		οὐ
proclaiming	to you	the	mystery	of the	God.		Not

1063	2919		5100	3609a	1722	1473	1487	3361		2424
γὰρ	ἔκρινά	τι	εἰδέναι	ἐν	ὑμῖν	εἰ	μὴ		Ἰησοῦν
for	I judged	some	to know	in	you	except		Jesus

5547	2532	3778	4717			**3**	2504
Χριστὸν	καὶ	τοῦτον	ἐσταυρωμένον.				κἀγὼ
Christ	and	this	one having been crucified.		And I

1722	769		2532	1722	5401	2532	1722	5156		4183
ἐν	ἀσθενείᾳ	καὶ	ἐν	φόβῳ	καὶ	ἐν	τρόμῳ		πολλῷ
in	weakness	and	in	fear	and	in	trembling		much

1096		4314	1473	**4**	2532	01	3056	1473		2532	09
ἐγενόμην	πρὸς	ὑμᾶς,		καὶ	ὁ	λόγος	μου		καὶ	τὸ
became	to	you,		and	the	word	of me		and	the

2782		1473	3756	1722	3981		4678		3056
κήρυγμά	μου	οὐκ	ἐν	πειθοῖ[ς]	σοφίας	[λόγοις]
announcement	of me	not	in	persuasive	wisdom	words

235	1722	585		4151		2532	1411		**5**	2443	05
ἀλλ᾽	ἐν	ἀποδείξει	πνεύματος	καὶ	δυνάμεως,		ἵνα	ἡ
but	in	show off	of spirit	and	power,		that	the

4102	1473		3361	1510		1722	4678		444		235	1722
πίστις	ὑμῶν	μὴ	ᾖ		ἐν	σοφίᾳ	ἀνθρώπων	ἀλλ᾽	ἐν
trust	of you	not	might be	in	wisdom	of men		but	in

1411	2316	**6**	4678	1161	2980	1722	015	5046
δυνάμει	θεοῦ.		Σοφίαν	δὲ	λαλοῦμεν	ἐν	τοῖς	τελείοις,
power	of God.		Wisdom	but	we speak	in	the	complete,

4678	1161	3756	02		165		3778	3761		014
σοφίαν	δὲ	οὐ	τοῦ		αἰῶνος	τούτου	οὐδὲ		τῶν
wisdom	but	not	of the	age	this	but not	of the

758		02	165		3778	014		2673
ἀρχόντων	τοῦ	αἰῶνος	τούτου	τῶν		καταργουμένων·
rulers	of the	age	this	of the being abolished;

7	235	2980		2316	4678	1722	3466		08
	ἀλλὰ	λαλοῦμεν	θεοῦ	σοφίαν	ἐν	μυστηρίῳ	τὴν
	but	we speak	of God	wisdom	in	mystery	the

613		3739	4309		01
ἀποκεκρυμμένην,		ἣν	προώρισεν		ὁ
having been hidden off,		which	set bounds before	the

2316	4253	014	165	1519	1391		1473	**8**	3739
θεὸς	πρὸ	τῶν	αἰώνων	εἰς	δόξαν	ἡμῶν,		ἣν
God	before	the	ages	to	splendor	of us,		which

3762	014		758	02		165		3778	1097
οὐδεὶς	τῶν		ἀρχόντων	τοῦ		αἰῶνος	τούτου	ἔγνωκεν·
no one	of the	rulers	of the	age	this	had known;

1487	1063	1097		3756	302	04	2962		06
εἰ	γὰρ	ἔγνωσαν,	οὐκ	ἂν	τὸν	κύριον	τῆς
if	for	they knew,	not	-	the	Master	of the

1391	4717		**9**	235	2531		1125
δόξης	ἐσταύρωσαν.		ἀλλὰ	καθὼς		γέγραπται·
splendor	they crucified.		But	just as	it has been
							written,

3739	3788		3756	3708	2532	3775	3756	191		2532
ἃ	ὀφθαλμὸς	οὐκ	εἶδεν	καὶ	οὖς	οὐκ	ἤκουσεν	καὶ
what	eye	not	saw	and	ear	not	heard	and

1909	2588	444		3756	305		3739	2090
ἐπὶ	καρδίαν	ἀνθρώπου	οὐκ	ἀνέβη,	ἃ	ἡτοίμασεν
on	heart	of man	not	went up,	what	prepared

and sanctification and redemption, [31]in order that, as it is written, "Let the one who boasts, boast in[a] the Lord."

CHAPTER 2

When I came to you, brothers and sisters,[b] I did not come proclaiming the mystery[c] of God to you in lofty words or wisdom. [2]For I decided to know nothing among you except Jesus Christ, and him crucified. [3]And I came to you in weakness and in fear and in much trembling. [4]My speech and my proclamation were not with plausible words of wisdom,[d] but with a demonstration of the Spirit and of power, [5]so that your faith might rest not on human wisdom but on the power of God.

[6]Yet among the mature we do speak wisdom, though it is not a wisdom of this age or of the rulers of this age, who are doomed to perish. [7]But we speak God's wisdom, secret and hidden, which God decreed before the ages for our glory. [8]None of the rulers of this age understood this; for if they had, they would not have crucified the Lord of glory. [9]But, as it is written,

"What no eye has seen,
    nor ear heard,
    nor the human heart
    conceived,
what God has prepared
    for those who love
    him"—

_a_ Or of
_b_ Gk brothers
_c_ Other ancient authorities read testimony
_d_ Other ancient authorities read the persuasiveness of wisdom

¹⁰these things God has revealed to us through the Spirit; for the Spirit searches everything, even the depths of God. ¹¹For what human being knows what is truly human except the human spirit that is within? So also no one comprehends what is truly God's except the Spirit of God. ¹²Now we have received not the spirit of the world, but the Spirit that is from God, so that we may understand the gifts bestowed on us by God. ¹³And we speak of these things in words not taught by human wisdom but taught by the Spirit, interpreting spiritual things to those who are spiritual.ᵃ

14 Those who are unspiritualᵇ do not receive the gifts of God's Spirit, for they are foolishness to them, and they are unable to understand them because they are spiritually discerned. ¹⁵Those who are spiritual discern all things, and they are themselves subject to no one else's scrutiny.

¹⁶ "For who has known the mind of the Lord so as to instruct him?" But we have the mind of Christ.

CHAPTER 3

And so, brothers and sisters,ᶜ I could not speak to you as spiritual people, but rather as people of the flesh, as infants in Christ. ²I fed you with milk, not solid food, for you were not ready for solid food. Even now you are still not ready,

---

ᵃ Or interpreting spiritual things in spiritual language, or comparing spiritual things with spiritual
ᵇ Or natural
ᶜ Gk brothers

---

01   2316 015   25   846   10 1473   1161
ὁ   θεὸς τοῖς ἀγαπῶσιν αὐτόν.   ἡμῖν δὲ
the God to the ones loving him.   To us but

601   01   2316 1223   010 4151   09 1063
ἀπεκάλυψεν ὁ θεὸς διὰ   τοῦ πνεύματος· τὸ γὰρ
uncovered the God through the spirit;   the for

4151   3956 2037a   2532 024 899   02   2316
πνεῦμα πάντα ἐραυνᾷ, καὶ τὰ βάθη τοῦ θεοῦ.
spirit all searches, even the depths of the God.

11 5101 1063 3609a 444   024 02   444
τίς γὰρ οἶδεν ἀνθρώπων τὰ τοῦ ἀνθρώπου
Who for knew of men   the of the man

1487 3361 09 4151   02   444   09 1722 846
εἰ μὴ τὸ πνεῦμα τοῦ ἀνθρώπου τὸ ἐν αὐτῷ;
except the spirit of the man   the in him?

3779 2532 024 02   2316 3762   1097   1487 3361
οὕτως καὶ τὰ τοῦ θεοῦ οὐδεὶς ἔγνωκεν εἰ μὴ
Thusly also the of the God no one has known except

09 4151 02   2316   12 1473 1161 3756 012 4151
τὸ πνεῦμα τοῦ θεοῦ.   ἡμεῖς δὲ οὐ τὸ πνεῦμα
the spirit of the God. We but not the spirit

02   2889   2983   235 012 4151   012 1537 02
τοῦ κόσμου ἐλάβομεν ἀλλὰ τὸ πνεῦμα τὸ ἐκ τοῦ
of the world received but the spirit the from the

2316 2443 3609a   024 5259 02   2316 5483
θεοῦ, ἵνα εἰδῶμεν τὰ ὑπὸ τοῦ θεοῦ χαρισθέντα
God, that we might the by the God having been
           know   favored

1473 13 3739 2532 2980   3756 1722 1318
ἡμῖν·   ἃ καὶ λαλοῦμεν οὐκ ἐν διδακτοῖς
to us; which also we speak not in taught

442   4678   3056   235 1722 1318
ἀνθρωπίνης σοφίας λόγοις ἀλλ᾽ ἐν διδακτοῖς
of man-like wisdom in words but in taught

4151   4152   4152
πνεύματος, πνευματικοῖς πνευματικὰ
of spirit, spiritual things spiritual things

4793   14 5591   1161 444   3756 1209
συγκρίνοντες.   ψυχικὸς δὲ ἄνθρωπος οὐ δέχεται
judging together. Soul-like but man   not welcomes

024 010   4151   02   2316 3472   1063 846
τὰ τοῦ πνεύματος τοῦ θεοῦ· μωρία   γὰρ αὐτῷ
the of the spirit of the God; foolishness for to him

1510 2532 3756 1410   1097   3754 4153
ἐστιν καὶ οὐ δύναται γνῶναι, ὅτι πνευματικῶς
it is also not he is able to know, that spiritually

350   15 01 1161 4152   350   024
ἀνακρίνεται.   ὁ δὲ πνευματικὸς ἀνακρίνει [τὰ]
it is examined. The but spiritual   examines the

3956 846   1161 5259 3762   350   16 5101
πάντα, αὐτὸς δὲ ὑπ᾽ οὐδενὸς ἀνακρίνεται.   τίς
all, himself but by no one is examined.   Who

1063 1097 3563 2962   3739 4822
γὰρ ἔγνω νοῦν κυρίου, ὃς συμβιβάσει
for knew mind of Master, who will force together

846   1473   1161 3563 5547   2192   2504
αὐτόν; ἡμεῖς δὲ νοῦν Χριστοῦ ἔχομεν. 3:1 Κἀγώ,
him? We but mind of Christ have.   And I,

80   3756 1410   2980   1473   5613
ἀδελφοί, οὐκ ἠδυνήθην λαλῆσαι ὑμῖν ὡς
brothers, not was able to speak to you as

4152   235 5613 4560   5613 3516   1722
πνευματικοῖς ἀλλ᾽ ὡς σαρκίνοις, ὡς νηπίοις ἐν
spiritual but as of flesh, as infants in

5547   2 1051 1473 4222   3756 1033
Χριστῷ.   γάλα ὑμᾶς ἐπότισα, οὐ βρῶμα·
Christ.   Milk you I gave to drink, not food,

3768 1063 1410   235 3761   2089 3568
οὔπω γὰρ ἐδύνασθε. ἀλλ᾽ οὐδὲ ἔτι νῦν
not yet for you were able. But but not still now

```
1410                3  2089   1063  4559        1510         3699   1063
δύνασθε,              ἔτι    γὰρ  σαρκικοί ἐστε.    ὅπου   γὰρ
you are able,  still  for  fleshly  you are.  Where for

1722 1473 2205        2532 2054   3780 4559      1510
ἐν  ὑμῖν ζῆλος  καὶ  ἔρις,  οὐχὶ σαρκικοί ἐστε
in  you  jealousy and strife, not  fleshly  are you

2532 2596         444        4043              4  3752  1063
καὶ  κατὰ     ἄνθρωπον περιπατεῖτε;     ὅταν  γὰρ
and according to man   you walk around?  When for

3004         5100  1473 3303   1510 3972       2087    1161
λέγῃ    τις·  ἐγὼ μέν  εἰμι Παύλου, ἕτερος δέ·
might say some: I   indeed am  of Paul, other but,

1473  625         3756 444      1510       5  5101 3767
ἐγὼ ’Απολλῶ,  οὐκ ἄνθρωποί ἐστε;     Τί  οὖν
I   of Apollos, not men    are you?  Who then

1510    625         5101 1161 1510 3972      1249
ἐστιν ’Απολλῶς; τί   δέ   ἐστιν Παῦλος; διάκονοι
is  Apollos? Who but  is   Paul?  Servants

1223     3739 4100            2532 1538      5613 01  2962
δι’    ὧν  ἐπιστεύσατε, καὶ  ἑκάστῳ ὡς  ὁ  κύριος
through whom you trusted, and  to each as  the Master

1325      1473 5452          625          235  01
ἔδωκεν. 6 ἐγὼ ἐφύτευσα, ’Απολλῶς ἐπότισεν, ἀλλὰ ὁ
gave.   I  planted,  Apollos gave drink, but  the

2316 837       7  5620    3777   01  5452       1510
θεὸς ηὔξανεν·   ὥστε  οὔτε  ὁ  φυτεύων ἐστίν
God  grew;  so that neither the planting is

5100 3777 01  4222           235  01  837      2316
τι  οὔτε ὁ  ποτίζων  ἀλλ’ ὁ  αὐξάνων θεός.
some nor the giving drink but  the growing God.

   01  5452    1161 2532 01  4222           1520 1510
8  ὁ  φυτεύων δὲ  καὶ ὁ  ποτίζων  ἕν  εἰσιν,
   The planting but also the giving drink one  are,

1538   1161 04  2398  3408   2983             2596
ἕκαστος δὲ  τὸν ἴδιον μισθὸν λήμψεται     κατὰ
each   but the own  wage   will receive according to

04  2398  2873    9  2316    1063 1510    4904
τὸν ἴδιον κόπον·  θεοῦ  γὰρ ἐσμεν συνεργοί,
the own  labor;  of God for  we are co-workers,

2316  1091       2316  3619      1510     10  2596 08
θεοῦ γεώργιον, θεοῦ οἰκοδομή ἐστε.     Κατὰ τὴν
of God farm land, of God building you are.  By  the

5485  02        2316 08  1325          1473 5613 4680
χάριν τοῦ     θεοῦ τὴν δοθεῖσάν      μοι  ὡς σοφος
favor of the God the having been given to me as wise

753           2310         5087  243    1161
ἀρχιτέκτων  θεμέλιον  ἔθηκα, ἄλλος δὲ
first craftsman foundation I set, other but

2026          1538      1161 991      4459 2026
ἐποικοδομεῖ. ἕκαστος δὲ  βλεπέτω πῶς  ἐποικοδομεῖ.
builds on.  Each   but let see how  he builds on.

   2310         1063 243    3762   1410     5087  3844
11 θεμέλιον  γὰρ ἄλλον οὐδεὶς δύναται θεῖναι παρὰ
   Foundation for other no one is able to set along

04  2749        3739 1510   2424    5547      12  1487
τὸν κείμενον,  ὅς  ἐστιν ’Ιησοῦς Χριστός.    εἰ
the being laid, who  is    Jesus  Christ.  If

1161 5100 2026        1909 04  2310       5557
δέ  τις  ἐποικοδομεῖ ἐπὶ τὸν θεμέλιον χρυσόν,
but some builds on  on  the foundation gold,

696      3037   5093      3586    5528      2562
ἄργυρον, λίθους τιμίους, ξύλα, χόρτον, καλάμην,
silver,  stones valuable, woods, grass,  straw,

   1538     09  2041  5318      1096       05  1063
13 ἑκάστου τὸ  ἔργον φανερὸν γενήσεται,  ἡ  γὰρ
   of each the work  evident will become, the for

2250  1213      3754  1722 4442 601
ἡμέρα δηλώσει,   ὅτι  ἐν πυρὶ ἀποκαλύπτεται·
day  will make clear, because in fire it is uncovered;
```

[3]for you are still of the flesh. For as long as there is jealousy and quarreling among you, are you not of the flesh, and behaving according to human inclinations? [4]For when one says, "I belong to Paul," and another, "I belong to Apollos," are you not merely human?

[5] What then is Apollos? What is Paul? Servants through whom you came to believe, as the Lord assigned to each. [6]I planted, Apollos watered, but God gave the growth. [7]So neither the one who plants nor the one who waters is anything, but only God who gives the growth. [8]The one who plants and the one who waters have a common purpose, and each will receive wages according to the labor of each. [9]For we are God's servants, working together; you are God's field, God's building.

[10] According to the grace of God given to me, like a skilled master builder I laid a foundation, and someone else is building on it. Each builder must choose with care how to build on it. [11]For no one can lay any foundation other than the one that has been laid; that foundation is Jesus Christ. [12]Now if anyone builds on the foundation with gold, silver, precious stones, wood, hay, straw— [13]the work of each builder will become visible, for the Day will disclose it, because it will be revealed with fire,

and the fire will test what
sort of work each has done.
[14]If what has been built on
the foundation survives,
the builder will receive a
reward. [15]If the work is
burned up, the builder
will suffer loss; the builder
will be saved, but only as
through fire.

16 Do you not know
that you are God's temple
and that God's Spirit
dwells in you?[a] [17]If anyone
destroys God's temple, God
will destroy that person.
For God's temple is holy,
and you are that temple.

18 Do not deceive
yourselves. If you think
that you are wise in this age,
you should become fools so
that you may become wise.
[19]For the wisdom of this
world is foolishness with
God. For it is written,
    "He catches the wise in
       their craftiness,"
[20]and again,
    "The Lord knows the
       thoughts of the wise,
       that they are futile."
[21]So let no one boast about
human leaders. For all
things are yours, [22]whether
Paul or Apollos or Cephas
or the world or life or
death or the present or the
future—all belong to you,
[23]and you belong to Christ,
and Christ belongs to God.

CHAPTER 4

Think of us in this way,
as servants of Christ and
stewards

[a] In verses 16 and 17 the Greek
word for *you* is plural

2532	1538		012	2041	3697		1510	09	4442	846
καὶ	ἑκάστου	τὸ	ἔργον	ὁποῖόν			ἐστιν	τὸ	πῦρ	[αὐτὸ]
and	of each	the	work	what kind			it is	the	fire	it

1381   **14**   1487 5100   09   2041   3306   3739
δοκιμάσει.   **14**   εἴ   τινος   τὸ   ἔργον μενεῖ ὃ
will approve.   If   some   the work   stays that

2026   3408   2983   **15**   1487 5100
ἐποικοδόμησεν, μισθὸν λήμψεται·   **15**   εἴ   τινος
he builds on,   wage   he will receive;   if   some

09   2041   2618   2210   846
τὸ   ἔργον κατακαήσεται,   ζημιωθήσεται,   αὐτὸς
the   work will be burned down,   it will be lost,   himself

1161   4982   3779   1161 5613 1223   4442
δὲ   σωθήσεται,   οὕτως δὲ ὡς   διὰ   πυρός.
but   will be delivered,   thusly but as   through fire.

16   3756 3609a   3754 3485   2316   1510   2532 09
    Οὐκ οἴδατε   ὅτι   ναὸς   θεοῦ   ἐστε   καὶ   τὸ
    Not you know that   temple of God you are and   the

4151   02   2316 3611   1722 1473   **17**   1487 5100 04
πνεῦμα τοῦ   θεοῦ οἰκεῖ ἐν   ὑμῖν;   **17**   εἴ   τις   τὸν
spirit of the God houses in   you?   If   some the

3485   02   2316 5351   5351   3778   01
ναὸν   τοῦ   θεοῦ φθείρει,   φθερεῖ   τοῦτον ὁ
temple of the God corrupts,   will corrupt this   the

2316   01   1063 3485   02   2316 40   1510   3748
θεός· ὁ   γὰρ   ναὸς   τοῦ   θεοῦ ἅγιός ἐστιν, οἵτινές
God; the for   temple of the   God holy   is,   who

1510 1473   **18**   3367   1438   1818
ἐστε ὑμεῖς.   **18**   Μηδεὶς ἑαυτὸν   ἐξαπατάτω·
are you.   No one himself let deceive thoroughly;

1487 5100 1380   4680   1510   1722 1473 1722 03   165
εἴ   τις   δοκεῖ   σοφὸς εἶναι ἐν   ὑμῖν ἐν   τῷ   αἰῶνι
if   some thinks wise   to be in   you   in   the age

3778   3474 1096   2443 1096   4680
τούτῳ, μωρὸς γενέσθω,   ἵνα   γένηται   σοφός.
this,   fool let become,   that he might become wise.

19   05   1063 4678   02   2889   3778   3472
   ἡ   γὰρ σοφία τοῦ   κόσμου τούτου μωρία
   The for   wisdom of the world this   foolishness

3844   03 2316 1510   1125   1063 01
παρὰ   τῷ   θεῷ ἐστιν. γέγραπται   γὰρ· ὁ
beside the God is.   It has been written for, the

1405   016   4680   1722 07 3834   846
δρασσόμενος τοὺς σοφοὺς ἐν   τῇ πανουργίᾳ αὐτῶν·
trapping   the   wise   in   the trickery   of them;

20   2532 3825   2962   1097   016   1261
   καὶ   πάλιν· κύριος γινώσκει τοὺς διαλογισμοὺς
   and   again, Master knows   the   reasonings

014   4680 3754 1510   3152   **21**   5620   3367
τῶν   σοφῶν ὅτι   εἰσὶν   μάταιοι.   **21**   ὥστε   μηδεὶς
of the wise that they are futile.   So that no one

2744   1722 444   3956   1063 1473   1510
καυχάσθω ἐν   ἀνθρώποις· πάντα γὰρ   ὑμῶν   ἐστιν,
let brag in   men;   all   for   of you is,

22   1535   3972   1535   625   1535 2786   1535
   εἴτε   Παῦλος εἴτε Ἀπολλῶς εἴτε Κηφᾶς,   εἴτε
   whether Paul   or   Apollos or Cephas, whether

2889   1535 2222 1535 2288   1535   1764
κόσμος εἴτε ζωὴ   εἴτε θάνατος,   εἴτε   ἐνεστῶτα
world   or   life or   death,   whether being present

1535 3195   3956   1473   1473   1161
εἴτε μέλλοντα·   πάντα ὑμῶν,   **23**   ὑμεῖς δὲ
or   being about to be;   all   of you,   you   but

5547   5547   1161 2316   **4:1**   3779   1473 3049
Χριστοῦ,   Χριστὸς δὲ   θεοῦ.   **4:1**   Οὕτως ἡμᾶς λογιζέσθω
of Christ,   Christ   but of God.   Thusly us   let reason

444   5613 5257   5547   2532 3623
ἄνθρωπος ὡς   ὑπηρέτας Χριστοῦ καὶ   οἰκονόμους
man   as   assistants of Christ and   managers

3466   2316   2 5602 3062   2212   1 722
μυστηρίων   θεοῦ.   ὧδε λοιπὸν   ζητεῖται   ἐν
of mysteries of God. Here remaining it is sought in

015   3623   2443 4103   5100 2147
τοῖς οἰκονόμοις, ἵνα πιστός τις εὑρεθῇ.
the managers,   that trustful some might be found.

  1473   1161 1519 1646   1510   2443 5259 1473
3 ἐμοὶ δὲ   εἰς ἐλάχιστόν ἐστιν, ἵνα ὑφ' ὑμῶν
  To me but in least   it is, that by you

350   2228 5259 442   2250   235
ἀνακριθῶ   ἢ ὑπὸ ἀνθρωπίνης ἡμέρας· ἀλλ'
I might be examined or by of man-like day; but

3761   1683   350   4 3762   1063 1683
οὐδὲ ἐμαυτὸν ἀνακρίνω.   οὐδὲν γὰρ ἐμαυτῷ
but not myself I examine. Nothing for to myself

4923a   235   3756 1722 3778 1344   01 1161
σύνοιδα, ἀλλ' οὐκ ἐν τούτῳ δεδικαίωμαι, ὁ δὲ
I know with, but not in this I have been the but
                                 made right,

350   1473 2962   1510   5 5620   3361 4253
ἀνακρίνων με κύριός ἐστιν.   ὥστε μὴ πρὸ
examining me Master is.   So that not before

2540   5100 2919   2193 302 2064   01 2962
καιροῦ τι κρίνετε ἕως ἂν ἔλθῃ   ὁ κύριος,
season some judge until - might come the Master,

3739 2532 5461   024 2927 010   4655
ὃς καὶ φωτίσει   τὰ κρυπτὰ τοῦ σκότους
who also will enlighten the hidden of the dark

2532 5319   020 1012 018   2588   2532
καὶ φανερώσει   τὰς βουλὰς τῶν καρδιῶν· καὶ
and will demonstrate the plans of the hearts; and

5119 01 1868   1096   1538   575 02 2316
τότε ὁ ἔπαινος γενήσεται ἑκάστῳ ἀπὸ τοῦ θεοῦ.
then the praise on will become to each from the God.

  3778   1161 80   3345   1519 1683   2532
6 Ταῦτα δέ, ἀδελφοί, μετεσχημάτισα εἰς ἐμαυτὸν καὶ
  These but, brothers, I reshaped   into myself and

  625   1223   1473   2443 1722 1473 3129
Ἀπολλῶν δι' ὑμᾶς, ἵνα ἐν ἡμῖν μάθητε
Apollos through you, that in us you might learn

012 3361 5228   3739 1125   2443 3361 1520
τὸ μὴ ὑπὲρ ἃ γέγραπται,   ἵνα μὴ εἷς
the not beyond what has been written, that not one

5228   02   1520 5448   2596   02 2087
ὑπὲρ τοῦ ἑνὸς φυσιοῦσθε κατὰ τοῦ ἑτέρου.
beyond of the one you be puffed up against the other.

  5101 1063 1473 1252   5101 1161 2192
7 τίς γάρ σε διακρίνει;   τί δὲ ἔχεις
  Who for you judges thoroughly? What but you have

3739 3756 2983   1487 1161 2532 2983
ὃ οὐκ ἔλαβες; εἰ δὲ καὶ ἔλαβες,
that not you received? If but also you received,

5101 2744   5613 3361 2983   2235
τί καυχᾶσαι ὡς μὴ λαβών;   8 ἤδη
why you brag as not having received? Already

2880   1510   2235
κεκορεσμένοι   ἐστέ, ἤδη
+having been full made you are+, already

4147   5565   1473 936   2532
ἐπλουτήσατε, χωρὶς ἡμῶν ἐβασιλεύσατε· καὶ
you were rich, without us you were kings; and

3785   1065   936   2443 2532 1473
ὄφελόν γε ἐβασιλεύσατε, ἵνα καὶ ἡμεῖς
I would indeed you were kings, that also we

1473   4821   9 1380   1063 01 2316
ὑμῖν συμβασιλεύσωμεν. δοκῶ γάρ, ὁ θεὸς
to you might be kings together. I think for, the God

1473 016 652   2078   584   5613
ἡμᾶς τοὺς ἀποστόλους ἐσχάτους ἀπέδειξεν ὡς
us   the delegates   last   showed off as

of God's mysteries. [2]Moreover, it is required of stewards that they be found trustworthy. [3]But with me it is a very small thing that I should be judged by you or by any human court. I do not even judge myself. [4]I am not aware of anything against myself, but I am not thereby acquitted. It is the Lord who judges me. [5]Therefore do not pronounce judgment before the time, before the Lord comes, who will bring to light the things now hidden in darkness and will disclose the purposes of the heart. Then each one will receive commendation from God.

6 I have applied all this to Apollos and myself for your benefit, brothers and sisters,[a] so that you may learn through us the meaning of the saying, "Nothing beyond what is written," so that none of you will be puffed up in favor of one against another. [7]For who sees anything different in you?[b] What do you have that you did not receive? And if you received it, why do you boast as if it were not a gift?

8 Already you have all you want! Already you have become rich! Quite apart from us you have become kings! Indeed, I wish that you had become kings, so that we might be kings with you! [9]For I think that God has exhibited us apostles as last of all,

a Gk brothers
b Or Who makes you different from another?

as though sentenced to death, because we have become a spectacle to the world, to angels and to mortals. [10]We are fools for the sake of Christ, but you are wise in Christ. We are weak, but you are strong. You are held in honor, but we in disrepute. [11]To the present hour we are hungry and thirsty, we are poorly clothed and beaten and homeless, [12]and we grow weary from the work of our own hands. When reviled, we bless; when persecuted, we endure; [13]when slandered, we speak kindly. We have become like the rubbish of the world, the dregs of all things, to this very day.

14 I am not writing this to make you ashamed, but to admonish you as my beloved children. [15]For though you might have ten thousand guardians in Christ, you do not have many fathers. Indeed, in Christ Jesus I became your father through the gospel. [16]I appeal to you, then, be imitators of me. [17]For this reason I sent[a] you Timothy, who is my beloved and faithful child in the Lord, to remind you of my ways in Christ Jesus, as I teach them everywhere in every church. [18]But some of you, thinking that I am not coming to you, have become arrogant. [19]But I will come to you soon, if the

[a] Or am sending

1935	3754	2302	1096		03
ἐπιθανατίους,	ὅτι	θέατρον	ἐγενήθημεν		τῷ
death sentence,	that	theater	we might become		to the

2889	2532 32		2532 444	10	1473
κόσμῳ καὶ	ἀγγέλοις		καὶ ἀνθρώποις.		ἡμεῖς
world and	to messengers	and	to men.		We

3474	1223	5547	1473	1161 5429	1722
μωροὶ	διὰ	Χριστόν,	ὑμεῖς δὲ	φρόνιμοι	ἐν
fools	through	Christ,	you but	thoughtful	in

5547	1473 772		1473	1161 2478	1473
Χριστῷ·	ἡμεῖς ἀσθενεῖς,		ὑμεῖς δὲ	ἰσχυροί·	ὑμεῖς
Christ;	we weak,		you but	strong;	you

1741	1473 1161	820	11	891 06 737
ἔνδοξοι,	ἡμεῖς δὲ	ἄτιμοι.		ἄχρι τῆς ἄρτι
in splendor,	we but	dishonored.		Until the now

5610 2532 3983		2532 1372		2532 1130
ὥρας καὶ πεινῶμεν	καὶ	διψῶμεν	καὶ	γυμνιτεύομεν
hour both we hunger	and	we thirst	and	we are naked

2532 2852		2532 790	12	2532
καὶ κολαφιζόμεθα		καὶ ἀστατοῦμεν		καὶ
and are knocked about	and	and we never stand		and

2872	2038	019 2398 5495	3058
κοπιῶμεν	ἐργαζόμενοι	ταῖς ἰδίαις χερσίν·	λοιδορούμενοι
we labor	working	the own hands;	being abused

2127	1377	430
εὐλογοῦμεν,	διωκόμενοι	ἀνεχόμεθα,
we speak well,	being pursued	we endure,

13	1425a	3870	5613 4027	02
	δυσφημούμενοι	παρακαλοῦμεν·	ὡς περικαθάρματα	τοῦ
	being vilified	we encourage;	as filth	of the

2889 1096	3956 4067	2193 737	14	3756
κόσμου ἐγενήθημεν,	πάντων περίψημα	ἕως ἄρτι.		Οὐκ
world we became,	of all scum	until now.		Not

1788	1473 1125	3778 235	5613 5043	1473
ἐντρέπων	ὑμᾶς γράφω	ταῦτα ἀλλ᾽	ὡς τέκνα	μου
regarding	you I write	these but	as children	of me

27	3560	15	1437 1063 3463
ἀγαπητὰ	νουθετῶ[ν].		ἐὰν γὰρ μυρίους
loved	warning.		If for ten thousand

3807	2192	1722 5547	235 3756
παιδαγωγοὺς	ἔχητε	ἐν Χριστῷ	ἀλλ᾽ οὐ
tutors	you might have	in Christ	but not

4183	3962	1722 1063 5547	2424 1223	010
πολλοὺς	πατέρας·	ἐν γὰρ Χριστῷ	Ἰησοῦ διὰ	τοῦ
many	fathers;	in for Christ	Jesus through	the

2098	1473 1473 1080	16	3870	3767
εὐαγγελίου	ἐγὼ ὑμᾶς ἐγέννησα.		Παρακαλῶ	οὖν
good message	I you gave birth.		I encourage	then

1473 3402	1473 1096	17	1223	3778 3992
ὑμᾶς, μιμηταί	μου γίνεσθε.		Διὰ	τοῦτο ἔπεμψα
you, imitators	of me become.		Through	this I sent

1473 5095	3739 1510	1473 5043 27	2532
ὑμῖν Τιμόθεον,	ὅς ἐστίν	μου τέκνον ἀγαπητὸν	καὶ
to you Timothy,	who is	of me child loved	and

4103	1722 2962	3739 1473 363	020 3598
πιστὸν	ἐν κυρίῳ,	ὃς ὑμᾶς ἀναμνήσει	τὰς ὁδούς
trustful	in Master,	who you will remind	the ways

1473 020 1722 5547	2424	2531	3837
μου τὰς ἐν Χριστῷ	[Ἰησοῦ],	καθὼς	πανταχοῦ
of me the in Christ	Jesus,	just as	all places

1722 3956 1577	1321	18	5613 3361 2064
ἐν πάσῃ ἐκκλησίᾳ διδάσκω.			Ὡς μὴ ἐρχομένου
in all assembly I teach.			As not coming

1161 1473 4314	1473 5448	5100
δέ μου πρὸς	ὑμᾶς ἐφυσιώθησάν	τινες·
but of me toward	you were puffed up	some;

19	2064	1161 5030	4314	1473 1437 01
	ἐλεύσομαι	δὲ ταχέως	πρὸς	ὑμᾶς ἐὰν ὁ
	I will come	but quickly	toward	you if the

2962   2309   2532 1097   3756 04   3056
κύριος θελήσῃ,   καὶ γνώσομαι   οὐ τὸν λόγον
Master might want, and I will know not   the word
014   5448   235   08   1411   3756
τῶν   πεφυσιωμένων   ἀλλὰ τὴν δύναμιν· 20 οὐ
of the having been puffed up but the power;   not
1063 1722 3056 05 932   02   2316 235 1722 1411
γὰρ ἐν λόγῳ ἡ βασιλεία τοῦ θεοῦ ἀλλ᾽ ἐν δυνάμει.
for in word the kingdom of the God but in power.
     5101 2309   1722 4464 2064   4314 1473
21   τί θέλετε; ἐν ῥάβδῳ ἔλθω   πρὸς ὑμᾶς
     What you want? In   rod I might come to   you
2228 1722 26   4151   5037 4240   3654
ἢ ἐν ἀγάπῃ πνεύματί τε πραΰτητος; 5:1 "Ολως
or in love in spirit and gentleness?   Wholly
191   1722 1473 4202   2532 5108
ἀκούεται ἐν ὑμῖν πορνεία,   καὶ τοιαύτη
it is heard in you sexual immorality, and such
4202   3748   3761   1722 023   1484
πορνεία   ἥτις οὐδὲ ἐν τοῖς ἔθνεσιν,
sexual immorality which but not in   the nations,
5620   1135   5100 02   3962   2192   2532 1473
ὥστε   γυναῖκά τινα τοῦ πατρὸς ἔχειν. 2 καὶ ὑμεῖς
so that woman some of the father to have. And you
5448   1510   2532 3780 3123
πεφυσιωμένοι   ἐστὲ   καὶ οὐχὶ μᾶλλον
+having been puffed up you are+ and not more
3996   2443 142   1537 3319
ἐπενθήσατε, ἵνα ἀρθῇ   ἐκ μέσου
you mourned, that might be lifted up from middle
1473   01   012 2041 3778 4238   3 1473
ὑμῶν ὁ   τὸ ἔργον τοῦτο πράξας;   3 ἐγὼ
of you the one the work this having practiced? I
3303   1063 548   011   4983   3918
μὲν   γάρ, ἀπὼν   τῷ σώματι παρὼν
indeed for, being absent to the body   being present
1161 011   4151   2235   2919   5613
δὲ τῷ   πνεύματι, ἤδη κέκρικα   ὡς
but in the spirit,   already I have judged as
3918 04 3779   3778 2716   1722 011
παρὼν τὸν οὕτως τοῦτο κατεργασάμενον· 4 ἐν τῷ
being the thusly this one having worked in   the
present   thoroughly;
3686   02   2962   1473   2424 4863   1473 2532
ὀνόματι τοῦ κυρίου [ἡμῶν] ᾽Ιησοῦ συναχθέντων ὑμῶν καὶ
name   of Master of us   Jesus having been you and
       the   led together
010 1699   4151   4862 07 1411   02   2962
τοῦ ἐμοῦ πνεύματος σὺν τῇ δυνάμει τοῦ κυρίου
the of me spirit   with the power of the Master
1473 2424   5 3860   04 5108   03 4567
ἡμῶν ᾽Ιησοῦ, 5 παραδοῦναι τὸν τοιοῦτον τῷ σατανᾷ
of us Jesus,   to give over the such to the adversary
1519 3639   06   4561   2443 09 4151   4982
εἰς ὄλεθρον τῆς σαρκός, ἵνα τὸ πνεῦμα σωθῇ
for ruin of the flesh, that the spirit might be
                                      delivered
1722 07 2250   02   2962   6 3756 2570 09 2745
ἐν τῇ ἡμέρᾳ τοῦ κυρίου. 6 Οὐ καλὸν τὸ καύχημα
in the day of the Master.   Not good the brag
1473   3756 3609a   3754 3398   2219 3650 012
ὑμῶν. οὐκ οἴδατε ὅτι μικρὰ ζύμη ὅλον τὸ
of you. Not you know that little yeast whole the
5445   2220   7 1571   08 3820   2219   2443
φύραμα ζυμοῖ;   7 ἐκκαθάρατε τὴν παλαιὰν ζύμην, ἵνα
mixture yeasts?   Clean out the old   yeast, that
1510   3501 5445   2531   1510   106
ἦτε   νέον φύραμα, καθὼς ἐστε ἄζυμοι·
you might be new mixture, just as you are unyeast;

Lord wills, and I will find out not the talk of these arrogant people but their power. [20]For the kingdom of God depends not on talk but on power. [21]What would you prefer? Am I to come to you with a stick, or with love in a spirit of gentleness?

CHAPTER 5

It is actually reported that there is sexual immorality among you, and of a kind that is not found even among pagans; for a man is living with his father's wife. [2]And you are arrogant! Should you not rather have mourned, so that he who has done this would have been removed from among you?

3 For though absent in body, I am present in spirit; and as if present I have already pronounced judgment [4]in the name of the Lord Jesus on the man who has done such a thing.[a] When you are assembled, and my spirit is present with the power of our Lord Jesus, [5]you are to hand this man over to Satan for the destruction of the flesh, so that his spirit may be saved in the day of the Lord.[b]

6 Your boasting is not a good thing. Do you not know that a little yeast leavens the whole batch of dough? [7]Clean out the old yeast so that you may be a new batch, as you really are unleavened.

[a] Or on the man who has done such a thing in the name of the Lord Jesus
[b] Other ancient authorities add Jesus

For our paschal lamb, Christ, has been sacrificed. [8]Therefore, let us celebrate the festival, not with the old yeast, the yeast of malice and evil, but with the unleavened bread of sincerity and truth.

9 I wrote to you in my letter not to associate with sexually immoral persons— [10]not at all meaning the immoral of this world, or the greedy and robbers, or idolaters, since you would then need to go out of the world. [11]But now I am writing to you not to associate with anyone who bears the name of brother or sister[a] who is sexually immoral or greedy, or is an idolater, reviler, drunkard, or robber. Do not even eat with such a one. [12]For what have I to do with judging those outside? Is it not those who are inside that you are to judge? [13]God will judge those outside. "Drive out the wicked person from among you."

CHAPTER 6

When any of you has a grievance against another, do you dare to take it to court before the unrighteous, instead of taking it before the saints? [2]Do you not know that the saints will judge the world? And if the world is to be judged by you, are you incompetent to try trivial cases? [3]Do you not know that we are to judge angels—to say nothing of ordinary matters? [4]If you have ordinary cases,

[a] Gk brother

2532	1063	09	3957		1473	2380		5547
καὶ	γὰρ	τὸ	πάσχα		ἡμῶν	ἐτύθη		Χριστός.
also	for	the	passover		of us	was sacrificed		Christ.

8	5620		1858			3361 1722	2219	3820
	ὥστε		ἑορτάζωμεν			μὴ ἐν	ζύμῃ	παλαιᾷ
	So that		we might keep festival			not in	yeast	old

3366	1722 2219	2549		2532 4189	235	1722
μηδὲ	ἐν ζύμῃ	κακίας		καὶ πονηρίας	ἀλλ'	ἐν
but not in	yeast	badness		and evil	but	in

106		1505		2532 225	9	1125	1473
ἀζύμοις		εἰλικρινείας		καὶ ἀληθείας.		Ἔγραψα	ὑμῖν
unyeasted		unmixedness		and truth.		I wrote	to you

1722 07	1992		3361 4874		4205
ἐν	τῇ ἐπιστολῇ	μὴ	συναναμίγνυσθαι		πόρνοις,
in	the letter	not	to be mixed up together		in sexually immoral ones,

10	3756 3843		015	4205		02
	οὐ πάντως		τοῖς	πόρνοις		τοῦ
	not altogether		in the	sexually immoral		of the

2889	3778	2228 015	4123		2532 727
κόσμου	τούτου	ἢ τοῖς	πλεονέκταις		καὶ ἅρπαξιν
world	this	or in the	greedy ones		and plunderers

2228 1496		1893 3784	686	1537 02
ἢ εἰδωλολάτραις,		ἐπεὶ ὠφείλετε	ἄρα	ἐκ τοῦ
or idol servers,		since you owe	then	from the

2889	1831		3568 1161	1125	1473	3361
κόσμου	ἐξελθεῖν.	11	νῦν δὲ	ἔγραψα	ὑμῖν	μὴ
world	to go out.		Now but	I wrote	to you	not

4874		1437 5100 80	3687
συναναμίγνυσθαι		ἐάν τις ἀδελφὸς	ὀνομαζόμενος
to be mixed up together		if some brother	being named

1510	4205		2228 4123	2228 1496
ᾖ	πόρνος		ἢ πλεονέκτης	ἢ εἰδωλολάτρης
might be	sexually immoral		or greedy	or idol server

2228 3060	2228 3183	2228 727	03
ἢ λοίδορος	ἢ μέθυσος	ἢ ἅρπαξ,	τῷ
or abuser	or drunkard	or plunderer,	to the

5108	3366	4906	12	5101 1063	1473	016
τοιούτῳ	μηδὲ	συνεσθίειν.		τί γάρ	μοι	τοὺς
such	but not	to eat with.		What for	to me	the

1854	2919	3780 016	2080	1473 2919
ἔξω	κρίνειν;	οὐχὶ τοὺς	ἔσω	ὑμεῖς κρίνετε;
outside	to judge?	Not the	inside	you judge?

13	016	1161 1854	01	2316 2919	1808	04
	τοὺς	δὲ ἔξω	ὁ	θεὸς κρινεῖ.	ἐξάρατε	τὸν
	The	but outside	the	God judges.	Lift up out	the

4190	1537 1473 846	6:1	5111	5100 1473
πονηρὸν	ἐξ ὑμῶν αὐτῶν.		Τολμᾷ	τις ὑμῶν
evil	from you of them.		Dares	some of you

4229	2192	4314 04	2087	2919		1909 014
πρᾶγμα	ἔχων	πρὸς τὸν	ἕτερον	κρίνεσθαι		ἐπὶ τῶν
practice	having	to the	other	to be judged		on the

94	2532 3780	1909 014 40		2228 3756	3609a
ἀδίκων	καὶ οὐχὶ	ἐπὶ τῶν ἁγίων;	2	ἢ οὐκ	οἴδατε
unright	and not	on the holies?		Or not	you know

3754 013 40	04 2889	2919		2532 1487 1722
ὅτι οἱ ἅγιοι	τὸν κόσμον	κρινοῦσιν;		καὶ εἰ ἐν
that the holies	the world	will judge?		And if in

1473 2919	01 2889	370	1510
ὑμῖν κρίνεται	ὁ κόσμος,	ἀνάξιοί	ἐστε
you is judged	the world,	unworthy	are you

2922	1646	3	3756 3609a	3754
κριτηρίων	ἐλαχίστων;		οὐκ οἴδατε	ὅτι
of judge courts	least?		Not you know	that

32	2919	3385	1065
ἀγγέλους	κρινοῦμεν,	μήτι	γε
messengers	we will judge,	not some	indeed

982	4	982		3303	3767
βιωτικά;		βιωτικὰ		μὲν	οὖν
things of this life?		Things of this life		indeed	then

2922   1437 2192   016   1848   1722 07
κριτήρια ἐὰν ἔχητε,   τοὺς ἐξουθενημένους ἐν τῇ
judge   if   you might the   ones having been in   the
courts   have,   despised

1577   3778   2523   5 4314 1791   1473
ἐκκλησίᾳ, τούτους καθίζετε; 5 πρὸς ἐντροπὴν ὑμῖν
assembly, these   you seat?   To   shame   to you

3004   3779   3756 1762   1722 1473 3762   4680
λέγω.   οὕτως   οὐκ ἔνι   ἐν ὑμῖν οὐδεὶς σοφός,
I say.   Thusly   not   there is in   you no one wise,

3739 1410   1252   303 3319
ὃς δυνήσεται διακρῖναι   ἀνὰ μέσον
who will be able to judge thoroughly up   middle

02   80   846   6 235   80   3326 80
τοῦ ἀδελφοῦ αὐτοῦ; 6 ἀλλὰ ἀδελφὸς μετὰ ἀδελφοῦ
of the brother of him?   But   brother with brother

2919   2532 3778 1909 571   7 2235
κρίνεται   καὶ τοῦτο ἐπὶ ἀπίστων; 7 Ἤδη
is judged and this   on   untrustful?   Already

3303   3767 3654   2275   1473   1510   3754 2917
μὲν [οὖν] ὅλως ἥττημα ὑμῖν ἐστιν ὅτι κρίματα
indeed then wholly defeat to you it is that judgments

2192   3326 1438   1223   5101 3780 3123
ἔχετε   μεθ᾽ ἑαυτῶν.   διὰ τί οὐχὶ μᾶλλον
you have with yourselves. Through what not   more

91   1223   5101 3780 3123
ἀδικεῖσθε;   διὰ τί οὐχὶ μᾶλλον
you be done unright? Through what not   more

650   8 235   1473 91   2532 650
ἀποστερεῖσθε; 8 ἀλλὰ ὑμεῖς ἀδικεῖτε καὶ ἀποστερεῖτε,
you be deprived? But   you do unright and you deprive,

2532 3778 80   9 2228 3756 3609a   3754
καὶ τοῦτο ἀδελφούς. 9 Ἢ οὐκ οἴδατε ὅτι
and   this brothers.   Or   not you know that

94   2316   932   3756 2816   3361
ἄδικοι θεοῦ βασιλείαν οὐ κληρονομήσουσιν; μὴ
unright of God kingdom not   they will inherit?   Not

4105   3777   4205   3777 1496
πλανᾶσθε·   οὔτε   πόρνοι   οὔτε εἰδωλολάτραι
be deceived; neither sexually immoral nor idol servers

3777 3432   3777 3120   3777 733
οὔτε μοιχοὶ οὔτε μαλακοὶ οὔτε ἀρσενοκοῖται
nor adulterers nor   soft ones nor male bed partners

      3777 2812   3777 4123   3756 3183   3756
10 οὔτε κλέπται οὔτε πλεονέκται, οὐ μέθυσοι, οὐ
    nor thieves nor greedy ones, not drunkards, not

3060   3756 727   932   2316
λοίδοροι, οὐχ ἄρπαγες βασιλείαν θεοῦ
abusers,   not plunderers kingdom   of God

2816   11 2532 3778 5100 1510   235
κληρονομήσουσιν. 11 καὶ ταῦτά τινες ἦτε·   ἀλλὰ
will inherit.   And these some you were; but

628   235   37   235
ἀπελούσασθε,   ἀλλὰ ἡγιάσθητε,   ἀλλὰ
you were washed off, but you were made holy, but

1344   1722 011 3686   02   2962
ἐδικαιώθητε   ἐν τῷ ὀνόματι τοῦ κυρίου
you were made right in   the name   of the Master

2424 5547   2532 1722 011 4151   02   2316
Ἰησοῦ Χριστοῦ καὶ ἐν τῷ πνεύματι τοῦ θεοῦ
Jesus Christ and in   the spirit   of the God

1473   12 3956 1473 1832   235   3756 3956
ἡμῶν. 12 Πάντα μοι ἔξεστιν ἀλλ᾽ οὐ πάντα
of us.   All to me is possible but not all

4851   3956 1473 1832   235 3756
συμφέρει·   πάντα μοι ἔξεστιν ἀλλ᾽ οὐκ
is advantageous; all to me is possible but not

1473 1850   5259 5100   021 1033
ἐγὼ ἐξουσιασθήσομαι   ὑπό τινος. 13 τὰ βρώματα
I   will be under authority by some.   The foods

then, do you appoint as judges those who have no standing in the church? [5]I say this to your shame. Can it be that there is no one among you wise enough to decide between one believer[a] and another, [6]but a believer[a] goes to court against a believer[a]—and before unbelievers at that?

[7]In fact, to have lawsuits at all with one another is already a defeat for you. Why not rather be wronged? Why not rather be defrauded? [8]But you yourselves wrong and defraud—and believers[b] at that.

[9]Do you not know that wrongdoers will not inherit the kingdom of God? Do not be deceived! Fornicators, idolaters, adulterers, male prostitutes, sodomites, [10]thieves, the greedy, drunkards, revilers, robbers—none of these will inherit the kingdom of God. [11]And this is what some of you used to be. But you were washed, you were sanctified, you were justified in the name of the Lord Jesus Christ and in the Spirit of our God.

[12]"All things are lawful for me," but not all things are beneficial. "All things are lawful for me," but I will not be dominated by anything. [13]"Food is meant

[a] Gk brother
[b] Gk brothers

for the stomach and the stomach for food,"[a] and God will destroy both one and the other. The body is meant not for fornication but for the Lord, and the Lord for the body. [14]And God raised the Lord and will also raise us by his power. [15]Do you not know that your bodies are members of Christ? Should I therefore take the members of Christ and make them members of a prostitute? Never! [16]Do you not know that whoever is united to a prostitute becomes one body with her? For it is said, "The two shall be one flesh." [17]But anyone united to the Lord becomes one spirit with him. [18]Shun fornication! Every sin that a person commits is outside the body; but the fornicator sins against the body itself. [19]Or do you not know that your body is a temple[b] of the Holy Spirit within you, which you have from God, and that you are not your own? [20]For you were bought with a price; therefore glorify God in your body.

CHAPTER 7

Now concerning the matters about which you wrote: "It is well for a man not to touch a woman." [2]But because of cases of sexual immorality, each man should have his own wife and each

[a] The quotation may extend to the word other

[b] Or sanctuary

07	2836	2532	05	2836	023	1033	01
τῇ	κοιλίᾳ	καὶ	ἡ	κοιλία	τοῖς	βρώμασιν,	ὁ
for the	stomach	and	the	stomach	for the	foods,	the

1161	2316	2532	3778	2532	3778	2673	09
δὲ	θεὸς	καὶ	ταύτην	καὶ	ταῦτα	καταργήσει.	τὸ
but	God	both	this	and	these	will abolish.	The

1161	4983	3756	07	4202		235	03
δὲ	σῶμα	οὐ	τῇ	πορνείᾳ		ἀλλὰ	τῷ
but	body	not	for the	sexual immorality	but		for the

2962	2532	01	2962	011	4983	01	1161
κυρίῳ,	καὶ	ὁ	κύριος	τῷ	σώματι·	[14] ὁ	δὲ
Master,	and	the	Master	for the	body;	the	but

2316	2532	04	2962	1453	2532	1473	1825
θεὸς	καὶ	τὸν	κύριον	ἤγειρεν	καὶ	ἡμᾶς	ἐξεγερεῖ
God	both	the	Master	raised	and	us	will raise out

1223	06	1411	846	15	3756	3609a	3754	021
διὰ	τῆς	δυνάμεως	αὐτοῦ.		οὐκ	οἴδατε	ὅτι	τὰ
through	the	power	of him.		Not	you know	that	the

4983	1473	3196	5547	1510	142
σώματα	ὑμῶν	μέλη	Χριστοῦ	ἐστιν;	ἄρας
bodies	of you	members	of Christ	are?	Having lifted up

3767	024	3196	02	5547	4160
οὖν	τὰ	μέλη	τοῦ	Χριστοῦ	ποιήσω
then	the	members	of the	Christ	I might make

4204	3196	3361	1096	16	2228	3756
πόρνης	μέλη;	μὴ	γένοιτο.		[ἢ]	οὐκ
of prostitute	members?	Not	may it become.		Or	not

3609a	3754	01	2853	07	4204
οἴδατε	ὅτι	ὁ	κολλώμενος	τῇ	πόρνῃ
you know	that	the	one being joined	to the	prostitute

1520	4983	1510	1510	1063	5346	013	1417	1519
ἓν	σῶμά	ἐστιν;	ἔσονται	γάρ,	φησίν,	οἱ	δύο	εἰς
one	body	is?	Will be	for,	it says,	the	two	into

4561	1520	17	01	1161	2853	03	2962
σάρκα	μίαν.		ὁ	δὲ	κολλώμενος	τῷ	κυρίῳ
flesh	one.		The one	but	being joined	to the	Master

1520	4151	1510	18	5343	08	4202
ἓν	πνεῦμά	ἐστιν.		Φεύγετε	τὴν	πορνείαν.
one	spirit	is.		Flee	the	sexual immorality.

3956	265	3739	1437	4160	444	1622	010
πᾶν	ἁμάρτημα	ὃ	ἐὰν	ποιήσῃ	ἄνθρωπος	ἐκτὸς	τοῦ
All	sin	that	if	might do	man	outside	the

4983	1510	01	1161	4203
σώματός	ἐστιν·	ὁ	δὲ	πορνεύων
body	is;	the one	but	committing sexual immorality

1519	012	2398	4983	264	19	2228	3756	3609a
εἰς	τὸ	ἴδιον	σῶμα	ἁμαρτάνει.		ἢ	οὐκ	οἴδατε
into	the	own	body	sins.		Or	not	you know

3754	09	4983	1473	3485	010	1722	1473	40
ὅτι	τὸ	σῶμα	ὑμῶν	ναὸς	τοῦ	ἐν	ὑμῖν	ἁγίου
that	the	body	of you	temple	of the	in	you	holy

4151	1510	3739	2192	575	2316	2532	3756
πνεύματός	ἐστιν	οὗ	ἔχετε	ἀπὸ	θεοῦ,	καὶ	οὐκ
spirit	is	which	you have	from	God,	and	not

1510	1438	20	59	1063	5092
ἐστὲ	ἑαυτῶν;		ἠγοράσθητε	γὰρ	τιμῆς·
you are	of yourselves?		You were bought	for	value;

1392	1211	04	2316	1722	011	4983	1473
δοξάσατε	δὴ		τὸν	θεὸν	ἐν	τῷ σώματι	ὑμῶν.
give splendor	indeed		the	God	in	the body	of you.

7:1	4012	1161	3739	1125	2570	444	1135
	Περὶ	δὲ	ὧν	ἐγράψατε,	καλὸν	ἀνθρώπῳ	γυναικὸς
	About	but	what	you wrote,	good	to man	woman

3361	681	2	1223	1161	020	4202
μὴ	ἅπτεσθαι·		διὰ	δὲ	τὰς	πορνείας
not	to touch;		because	but	the	sexual immoralities

1538	08	1438	1135	2192	2532	1538	04
ἕκαστος	τὴν	ἑαυτοῦ	γυναῖκα	ἐχέτω	καὶ	ἑκάστη	τὸν
each	the	of himself	woman	let have	and	each	the

```
2398    435     2192    3  07         1135        01    435    08
ἴδιον   ἄνδρα   ἐχέτω.   3  τῇ         γυναικὶ  ὁ    ἀνὴρ   τὴν
own     man     let have.   To the woman        the   man    the

3782       591              3668        1161  2532  05    1135
ὀφειλὴν   ἀποδιδότω,       ὁμοίως      δὲ   καὶ   ἡ    γυνὴ
debt       let give back,   likewise    but  also  the  woman

03      435      4  05    1135   010      2398    4983     3756
τῷ      ἀνδρί.    4  ἡ    γυνὴ   τοῦ      ἰδίου   σώματος  οὐκ
to the  man.        The  woman  of the    own      body      not

1850          235   01   435     3668    1161  2532  01  435
ἐξουσιάζει    ἀλλὰ  ὁ    ἀνήρ,   ὁμοίως  δὲ   καὶ   ὁ   ἀνὴρ
has authority but   the  man,    likewise but  also  the man

010     2398    4983     3756   1850          235   05   1135
τοῦ     ἰδίου   σώματος  οὐκ    ἐξουσιάζει    ἀλλὰ  ἡ   γυνή.
of the  own      body     not    has authority but   the woman.

     3361  650           240          1487  3385  302  1537
5    μὴ    ἀποστερεῖτε   ἀλλήλους,   εἰ    μήτι  ἂν   ἐκ
     Not   deprive       one another, except  -    out of

4859       4314  2540     2443  4980
συμφώνου   πρὸς  καιρόν,  ἵνα   σχολάσητε
agreement  to    season,  that  you might concentrate

07    4335         2532  3825    1909  012   846   1510
τῇ    προσευχῇ    καὶ   πάλιν   ἐπὶ   τὸ    αὐτὸ  ἦτε,
in the prayer      and   again   on    the   same  you might be,

2443  3361  3985       1473   01   4567       1223
ἵνα   μὴ    πειράζῃ    ὑμᾶς   ὁ    σατανᾶς    διὰ
that  not   might pressure you  the  adversary  through

08    192       1473    6  3778    1161  3004   2596
τὴν   ἀκρασίαν  ὑμῶν.   6  τοῦτο   δὲ   λέγω   κατὰ
the   no strength of you. This     but  I say   by

4774          3756  2596  2003        7  2309     1161  3956
συγγνώμην     οὐ    κατ'  ἐπιταγήν.   7  θέλω     δὲ   πάντας
concession    not   by    order.        I want    but  all

444          1510   5613  2532  1683       235   1538     2398
ἀνθρώπους    εἶναι  ὡς    καὶ   ἐμαυτόν·   ἀλλὰ  ἕκαστος  ἴδιον
men          to be  as    also  myself;    but   each     own

2192  5486      1537  2316  01   3303      3779     01  1161
ἔχει  χάρισμα   ἐκ    θεοῦ, ὁ    μὲν       οὕτως,   ὁ   δὲ
has   favor gift from  God,  the  indeed    thusly,  the but

3779      8  3004  1161  015    22          2532  019      5503
οὕτως.    8  Λέγω  δὲ   τοῖς   ἀγάμοις    καὶ   ταῖς     χήραις,
thusly.      I say but  to the unmarried  and   to the    widows,

2570  846      1437  3306        5613  2504  9  1487
καλὸν αὐτοῖς   ἐὰν   μείνωσιν    ὡς    κἀγώ·  9  εἰ
good  to them  if    they might stay as also I;    if

1161  3756  1467             1060
δὲ    οὐκ   ἐγκρατεύονται,    γαμησάτωσαν,
but   not   they have inner strength, let marry,

2909      1063  1510  1060    2228  4448       10  015
κρεῖττον  γάρ   ἐστιν γαμῆσαι ἢ    πυροῦσθαι.  10  Τοῖς
better    for   it is to marry or   to be on fire.   To the

1161  1060                 3853          3756  1473  235
δὲ    γεγαμηκόσιν          παραγγέλλω,   οὐκ   ἐγὼ  ἀλλὰ
but   ones having married  I command,    not   I    but

01    2962     1135    575   01    3361  5563
ὁ     κύριος,  γυναῖκα ἀπὸ   ἀνδρὸς μὴ   χωρισθῆναι,
the   Master,  woman   from  man    not  to be separated,

11  1437  1161  2532  5563         3306     2228        2228
11  ἐὰν   δὲ   καὶ   χωρισθῇ,     μενέτω   ἄγαμος      ἢ
    if    but  also  she might    let stay unmarried   or

03    435      2644              2532  435    1135
τῷ    ἀνδρὶ   καταλλαγήτω,  -    καὶ   ἄνδρα  γυναῖκα
to the man    let be reconciled,  and   man    woman

3361  863          015    1161  3062      3004  1473  3756
μὴ    ἀφιέναι.   12  Τοῖς   δὲ   λοιποῖς  λέγω  ἐγὼ  οὐχ
not   to send off. To the  but  remaining say   I    not

01    2962      1487  5100  80      1135     2932  571
ὁ     κύριος·  εἴ    τις   ἀδελφὸς γυναῖκα ἔχει  ἄπιστον
the   Master;  if    some  brother woman   has   untrustful
```

woman her own husband. [3]The husband should give to his wife her conjugal rights, and likewise the wife to her husband. [4]For the wife does not have authority over her own body, but the husband does; likewise the husband does not have authority over his own body, but the wife does. [5]Do not deprive one another except perhaps by agreement for a set time, to devote yourselves to prayer, and then come together again, so that Satan may not tempt you because of your lack of self-control. [6]This I say by way of concession, not of command. [7]I wish that all were as I myself am. But each has a particular gift from God, one having one kind and another a different kind.

8 To the unmarried and the widows I say that it is well for them to remain unmarried as I am. [9]But if they are not practicing self-control, they should marry. For it is better to marry than to be aflame with passion.

10 To the married I give this command—not I but the Lord—that the wife should not separate from her husband [11](but if she does separate, let her remain unmarried or else be reconciled to her husband), and that the husband should not divorce his wife.

12 To the rest I say—I and not the Lord—that if any believer[a] has a wife who is an unbeliever,

---

[a] Gk brother

and she consents to live with him, he should not divorce her. [13]And if any woman has a husband who is an unbeliever, and he consents to live with her, she should not divorce him. [14]For the unbelieving husband is made holy through his wife, and the unbelieving wife is made holy through her husband. Otherwise, your children would be unclean, but as it is, they are holy. [15]But if the unbelieving partner separates, let it be so; in such a case the brother or sister is not bound. It is to peace that God has called you.[a] [16]Wife, for all you know, you might save your husband. Husband, for all you know, you might save your wife.

17 However that may be, let each of you lead the life that the Lord has assigned, to which God called you. This is my rule in all the churches. [18]Was anyone at the time of his call already circumcised? Let him not seek to remove the marks of circumcision. Was anyone at the time of his call uncircumcised? Let him not seek circumcision. [19]Circumcision is nothing, and uncircumcision is nothing; but obeying the commandments of God is everything. [20]Let each of you remain in the condition in which you were called.

21 Were you a slave when called? Do not be concerned about it. Even if

a Other ancient authorities read us

2532	3778	4909		3611	3326
καὶ	αὕτη	συνευδοκεῖ		οἰκεῖν	μετ'
and	this one	thinks well together		to house	with

846	3361	863	846	**13**	2532	1135	1487	5100
αὐτοῦ,	μὴ	ἀφιέτω	αὐτήν·		καὶ	γυνὴ	εἴ	τις
him,	not	let send off	her;		and	woman	if	some

2192	435	571	2532	3778	4909
ἔχει	ἄνδρα	ἄπιστον	καὶ	οὗτος	συνευδοκεῖ
has	man	untrustful	and this one		thinks well together

3611	3326	846	3361	863	04	435
οἰκεῖν	μετ'	αὐτῆς,	μὴ	ἀφιέτω	τὸν	ἄνδρα.
to house	with her,		not	let send off	the	man.

14	37		1063	01	435	01	571
	ἡγίασται		γὰρ	ὁ	ἀνὴρ	ὁ	ἄπιστος
	Has been made holy		for	the	man		the untrustful

1722	07	1135	2532	37		05	1135	05
ἐν	τῇ	γυναικὶ	καὶ	ἡγίασται		ἡ	γυνὴ	ἡ
in	the	woman	and	has been made holy		the	woman	the

571		1722	03	80	1893	686	021	5043
ἄπιστος		ἐν	τῷ	ἀδελφῷ·	ἐπεὶ	ἄρα	τὰ	τέκνα
untrustful		in		the brother;	since then		the	children

1473	169		1510	3568	1161	40	1510		**15**	1487
ὑμῶν	ἀκάθαρτά		ἐστιν,	νῦν	δὲ	ἅγιά	ἐστιν.			εἰ
of you	unclean		are,	now	but	holy	are.			If

1161	01	571	5563		5563		3756
δὲ	ὁ	ἄπιστος	χωρίζεται,		χωριζέσθω·		οὐ
but	the	untrustful	separates,		let separate;		not

1402	01	80	2228	05	79	1722	023
δεδούλωται	ὁ	ἀδελφὸς	ἢ	ἡ	ἀδελφὴ	ἐν	τοῖς
has been slaved	the	brother	or	the	sister	in	the

5108	1722	1161	1515	2564		1473	01	2316
τοιούτοις·	ἐν	δὲ	εἰρήνῃ	κέκληκεν		ὑμᾶς	ὁ	θεός.
such;	in	but	peace	has called		you	the	God.

16	5101	1063	3609a		1135	1487	04	435
	τί	γὰρ	οἶδας,		γύναι,	εἰ	τὸν	ἄνδρα
	What	for	you know,		woman,	if	the	man

4903		2228	5101	3609a		435	1487	08
σώσεις;		ἢ	τί	οἶδας,		ἄνερ,	εἰ	τὴν
you will deliver?		Or	what	you know,		man,	if	the

1135	4982		**17**	1487	3361	1538	5613
γυναῖκα	σώσεις;			Εἰ	μὴ	ἑκάστῳ	ὡς
woman	you will deliver?			Except		to each	as

3307	01	2962	1538	5613	2564	01	2316
ἐμέρισεν	ὁ	κύριος,	ἕκαστον	ὡς	κέκληκεν	ὁ	θεός,
divided	the	Master,	each	as	has called	the	God,

3779	4043		2532	3779	1722	019	1577
οὕτως	περιπατείτω.		καὶ	οὕτως	ἐν	ταῖς	ἐκκλησίαις
thusly	let walk around.		And	thusly	in	the	assemblies

3956	1299		**18**	4059		5100	2564
πάσαις	διατάσσομαι.			περιτετμημένος		τις	ἐκλήθη,
all	I direct.			Having been		some	were called,
				circumcised			

3361	1986		1722	4059		2564
μὴ	ἐπισπάσθω·		ἐν	ἀκροβυστίᾳ		κέκληταί
not	let draw over;		in	uncircumcision		has been called

5100	3361	4059		**19**	05	4061
τις,	μὴ	περιτεμνέσθω.			ἡ	περιτομὴ
some,	not	let be circumcised.			The	circumcision

3762	1510	2532	03	4059		3762	1510
οὐδέν	ἐστιν	καὶ	ἡ	ἀκροβυστία		οὐδέν	ἐστιν,
nothing is		and	the	uncircumcision		nothing is,

235	5084	1785	2316		1538	1722	07	2821
ἀλλὰ	τήρησις	ἐντολῶν	θεοῦ.	**20**	ἕκαστος	ἐν	τῇ	κλήσει
but	keep	commands	of God.		Each	in	the	call

3739	2564		1722	3778	3306	**21**	1401
ᾗ	ἐκλήθη,		ἐν	ταύτῃ	μενέτω.		δοῦλος
in which he was called,		in	this	let stay.		Slave

2564		3361	1473	3190a		235	1487
ἐκλήθης,		μή	σοι	μελέτω·		ἀλλ'	εἰ
were you called,		not	to you	let be care;		but	if

2532 1410   1658   1096   3123   5530
καὶ δύνασαι   ἐλεύθερος γενέσθαι, μᾶλλον χρῆσαι.
also you are able free   to become, more   use.

    01 1063 1722 2962   2564   1401
22 ὁ γὰρ ἐν κυρίῳ κληθεὶς   δοῦλος
   The for in Master having been called slave

558   2962   1510   3668   01 1658
ἀπελεύθερος κυρίου   ἐστίν, ὁμοίως ὁ ἐλεύθερος
freed man   of Master he is,   likewise the free

2564   1401   1510   5547   5092
κληθεὶς   δοῦλός ἐστιν Χριστοῦ. 23 τιμῆς
having been called slave is   of Christ.   Value

59   3361 1096   1401   444
ἠγοράσθητε·   μὴ γίνεσθε δοῦλοι ἀνθρώπων.
you were bought; not become   slaves of men.

    1538   1722 3739 2564   80   1722 3778
24 ἕκαστος ἐν ᾧ   ἐκλήθη,   ἀδελφοί, ἐν τούτῳ
   Each   in which he was called, brothers, in this

3306   3844 2316 25 4012   1161 018 3933
μενέτω παρὰ θεῷ. 25 Περὶ   δὲ τῶν παρθένων
let stay beside God. Concerning but the virgins

2003   2962   3756 2192   1106   1161 1325
ἐπιταγὴν κυρίου   οὐκ ἔχω,   γνώμην δὲ δίδωμι
order   of Master not I have, purpose but I give

5613 1653   5259 2962   4103
ὡς ἠλεημένος   ὑπὸ κυρίου πιστὸς
as having been shown mercy by Master trustful

1510   26 3543   3767 3778 2570 5225   1223
εἶναι. 26 Νομίζω οὖν τοῦτο καλὸν ὑπάρχειν διὰ
to be.   I think then this good to exist through

08 1764   318   3754 2570 444   09
τὴν ἐνεστῶσαν ἀνάγκην, ὅτι καλὸν ἀνθρώπῳ τὸ
the being present necessity, that good to man   the

3779 1510   27 1210   1135   3361
οὕτως εἶναι. 27 δέδεσαι   γυναικί, μὴ
thusly to be.   Have you been bound to woman, not

2212 3080   3089   575 1135
ζήτει λύσιν·   λέλυσαι   ἀπὸ γυναικός,
seek loosening; have you been loosed from woman,

3361 2212 1135   28 1437 1161 2532 1060
μὴ ζήτει γυναῖκα. 28 ἐὰν δὲ καὶ γαμήσῃς,
not seek woman.   If but also you might marry,

3756 264   2532 1437 1060   05 3933
οὐχ ἥμαρτες,   καὶ ἐὰν γήμῃ   ἡ παρθένος,
not you sinned, and if might marry the virgin,

3756 264   2347   1161 07   4561 2192
οὐχ ἥμαρτεν·   θλῖψιν   δὲ τῇ σαρκὶ ἕξουσιν
not she sinned; affliction but in the flesh will have

013 5108   1473 1161 1473 5339   3778 1161
οἱ τοιοῦτοι, ἐγὼ δὲ ὑμῶν φείδομαι. 29 Τοῦτο δέ
the such,   I but you spare.   This but

5346 80   01 2540   4958   1510   012
φημι, ἀδελφοί, ὁ καιρὸς συνεσταλμένος ἐστίν· τὸ
I say, brothers, the season +having been   is+;   the
                             sent together

3062   2443 2532 013   2192   1135   5613
λοιπόν, ἵνα καὶ οἱ   ἔχοντες γυναῖκας ὡς
remaining, that also the ones having women   as

3361 2192   1510   30 2532 013 2799   5613 3361
μὴ ἔχοντες ὦσιν 30 καὶ οἱ κλαίοντες ὡς μὴ
not having might be and the crying   as not

2799   2532 013 5463   5613 3361 5463   2532
κλαίοντες καὶ οἱ χαίροντες ὡς μὴ χαίροντες καὶ
crying   and the rejoicing as not rejoicing and

013 59   5613 3361 2722   31 2532 013
οἱ ἀγοράζοντες ὡς μὴ κατέχοντες, 31 καὶ οἱ
the buying   as not holding on,   and the

5530   04 2889   5613 3361 2710
χρώμενοι τὸν κόσμον ὡς μὴ καταχρώμενοι·
using   the world as not using thoroughly;

you can gain your freedom, make use of your present condition now more than ever.[a] 22For whoever was called in the Lord as a slave is a freed person belonging to the Lord, just as whoever was free when called is a slave of Christ. 23You were bought with a price; do not become slaves of human masters. 24In whatever condition you were called, brothers and sisters,[b] there remain with God.

25 Now concerning virgins, I have no command of the Lord, but I give my opinion as one who by the Lord's mercy is trustworthy. 26I think that, in view of the impending[c] crisis, it is well for you to remain as you are. 27Are you bound to a wife? Do not seek to be free. Are you free from a wife? Do not seek a wife. 28But if you marry, you do not sin, and if a virgin marries, she does not sin. Yet those who marry will experience distress in this life,[d] and I would spare you that. 29I mean, brothers and sisters,[b] the appointed time has grown short; from now on, let even those who have wives be as though they had none, 30and those who mourn as though they were not mourning, and those who rejoice as though they were not rejoicing, and those who buy as though they had no possessions, 31and those who deal with the world as though they had no dealings with it.

a Or avail yourself of the opportunity
b Gk brothers
c Or present
d Gk in the flesh

For the present form of this world is passing away.

32 I want you to be free from anxieties. The unmarried man is anxious about the affairs of the Lord, how to please the Lord; [33]but the married man is anxious about the affairs of the world, how to please his wife, [34]and his interests are divided. And the unmarried woman and the virgin are anxious about the affairs of the Lord, so that they may be holy in body and spirit; but the married woman is anxious about the affairs of the world, how to please her husband. [35]I say this for your own benefit, not to put any restraint upon you, but to promote good order and unhindered devotion to the Lord.

36 If anyone thinks that he is not behaving properly toward his fiancée,[a] if his passions are strong, and so it has to be, let him marry as he wishes; it is no sin. Let them marry. [37]But if someone stands firm in his resolve, being under no necessity but having his own desire under control, and has determined in his own mind to keep her as his fiancée,[a] he will do well. [38]So then, he who marries his fiancée[a] does well; and he who refrains from marriage will do better.

39 A wife is bound as long as

[a] Gk virgin

3855		1063 09	4976 02		2889	3778

παράγει　　γὰρ τὸ σχῆμα τοῦ　κόσμου τούτου.
leads along for　the shape of the world　this.

32 Θέλω δὲ ὑμᾶς ἀμερίμνους εἶναι. ὁ ἄγαμος
(2309 1161 1473 275　　　1510 01 22)
I want but you unanxious to be. The unmarried

μεριμνᾷ τὰ τοῦ κυρίου, πῶς ἀρέσῃ τῷ
(3309　024 02　2962　4459 700　03)
is anxious the of the Master, how he might please the

33 κυρίῳ· ὁ δὲ γαμήσας μεριμνᾷ τὰ τοῦ
(2962　01 1161 1060　3309　024 02)
Master; the but having married is anxious the of the

κόσμου, πῶς ἀρέσῃ τῇ γυναικί, **34** καὶ
(2889　4459 700　07 1135　2532)
world, how he might please the woman,　and

μεμέρισται. καὶ ἡ γυνὴ ἡ ἄγαμος καὶ ἡ
(3307　2532 05 1135 05 22　2532 05)
has been divided. And the woman the unmarried and the

παρθένος μεριμνᾷ τὰ τοῦ κυρίου, ἵνα ᾖ
(3933　3309　024 02　2962　2443 1510)
virgin is anxious the of the Master, that she might be

ἁγία καὶ τῷ σώματι καὶ τῷ πνεύματι· ἡ δὲ
(40 2532 011　4983 2532 011　4151　05 1161)
holy both in the body and in the spirit; the but

γαμήσασα μεριμνᾷ τὰ τοῦ κόσμου, πῶς
(1060　3309　024 02　2889　4459)
having married is anxious the of the world, how

ἀρέσῃ τῷ ἀνδρί. **35** τοῦτο δὲ πρὸς τὸ
(700　03 435　3778 1161 4314 012)
she might please the man.　This but to the

ὑμῶν αὐτῶν σύμφορον λέγω, οὐχ ἵνα βρόχον ὑμῖν
(1473 846 4852a　3004 3756 2443 1029　1473)
of you of them advantage I say, not that noose to you

ἐπιβάλω ἀλλὰ πρὸς τὸ εὔσχημον καὶ εὐπάρεδρον
(1911　235 4314 012 2158　2532 2137a)
I might throw on but to the proper and consistent

τῷ κυρίῳ ἀπερισπάστως. **36** Εἰ δέ τις
(03　2962　563　1487 1161 5100)
to the Master undistractedly. If but some

ἀσχημονεῖν ἐπὶ τὴν παρθένον αὐτοῦ νομίζει, ἐὰν
(807　1909 08 3933　846　3543　1437)
to be shameful on the virgin of him thinks, if

ᾖ ὑπέρακμος καὶ οὕτως ὀφείλει γίνεσθαι,
(1510　5230　2532 3779　3784　1096)
she might be beyond peak and thusly it owes to become,

ὃ θέλει ποιείτω, οὐχ ἁμαρτάνει, γαμείτωσαν.
(3739 2309　4160　3756 264　1060)
what he wants let do, not he sins, let marry.

37 ὃς δὲ ἕστηκεν ἐν τῇ καρδίᾳ αὐτοῦ ἑδραῖος
(3739 1161 2476　1722 07 2588 846　1476)
Who but has stood in the heart of him stable

μὴ ἔχων ἀνάγκην, ἐξουσίαν δὲ ἔχει περὶ τοῦ
(3361 2192 318　1849　1161 2192　4012 010)
not having necessity, authority but he has about the

ἰδίου θελήματος καὶ τοῦτο κέκρικεν ἐν τῇ ἰδίᾳ
(2398 2307　2532 3778 2919　1722 07 2398)
own want and this he has judged in the own

καρδίᾳ, τηρεῖν τὴν ἑαυτοῦ παρθένον, καλῶς
(2588　5083　08 1438　3933　2573)
heart, to keep the of himself virgin, well

ποιήσει. **38** ὥστε καὶ ὁ γαμίζων τὴν ἑαυτοῦ
(4160　5620　2532 01 1060a　08 1438)
he will do. So that both the marrying the of himself

παρθένον καλῶς ποιεῖ καὶ ὁ μὴ γαμίζων κρεῖσσον
(3933　2573 4160　2532 01 3361 1060a　2909)
virgin well he does and the not marrying better

ποιήσει. **39** Γυνὴ δέδεται ἐφ᾽ ὅσον χρόνον
(4160　1135 1210　1909 3745　5550)
he will do. Woman has been on as many as time
bound

```
2198          01   435   846      1437 1161 2837
ζῇ          ὁ ἀνὴρ αὐτῆς· ἐὰν δὲ κοιμηθῇ
might live the man  of her; if  but  might fall asleep
01   435   1658      1510    3739      2309
ὁ ἀνήρ, ἐλευθέρα ἐστὶν ᾧ        θέλει
the man,  free      she is to whom she wants
1060          3441  1722 2962        3107
γαμηθῆναι,   μόνον ἐν κυρίῳ.   40 μακαριωτέρα
to be married, alone in Master.    More fortunate
1161 1510  1437 3779   3306          2596 08  1699
δέ   ἐστιν ἐὰν οὕτως μείνῃ,        κατὰ τὴν ἐμὴν
but   it is if  thusly she might stay, by   the my
1106    1380   1161 2504   4151    2316    2192
γνώμην· δοκῶ δὲ κἀγὼ πνεῦμα θεοῦ ἔχειν.
purpose; think but also I spirit of God to have.
    4012 1161 022 1494           3609a   3754 3956
8:1 Περὶ δὲ τῶν εἰδωλοθύτων,    οἴδαμεν ὅτι πάντες
    About but the idol sacrifices, we know that all
1108      2192    05   1108     5448     05  1161
γνῶσιν ἔχομεν. ἡ γνῶσις φυσιοῖ, ἡ  δὲ
knowledge we have. The knowledge puffs up, the but
26      3618        1487 5100 1380    1097      5100
ἀγάπη οἰκοδομεῖ· 2 εἴ τις δοκεῖ ἐγνωκέναι τι,
love builds;      if  some thinks to have known some,
3768    1097      2531   1163        1097      3 1487
οὔπω  ἔγνω   καθὼς δεῖ          γνῶναι· 3 εἰ
not yet he knew just as it is necessary to know;  if
1161 5100 25   04 2316 3778 1097          5259
δέ   τις ἀγαπᾷ τὸν θεόν, οὗτος ἔγνωσται  ὑπ᾽
but  some loves the God, this  has been known by
846      4012 06  1035   3767 022       1494
αὐτοῦ. 4 Περὶ τῆς βρώσεως οὖν τῶν εἰδωλοθύτων,
him.     About the food  then of the idol sacrifices,
3609a    3754 3762    1497   1722 2889 2532 3754 3762
οἴδαμεν ὅτι οὐδὲν εἴδωλον ἐν κόσμῳ καὶ ὅτι οὐδεὶς
we know that nothing idol  in world and that no one
2316 1487 3361 1520  2532 1063 1512      1510
θεὸς εἰ μὴ εἷς. 5 καὶ γὰρ εἴπερ  εἰσὶν
God  except one.  Also for if indeed there are
3004      2316 1535    1722 3772   1535 1909 1093
λεγόμενοι θεοὶ εἴτε ἐν οὐρανῷ εἴτε ἐπὶ γῆς,
being called gods whether in  heaven or  on earth,
5618      1510       2316 4183   2532 2962    4183
ὥσπερ   εἰσὶν θεοὶ πολλοὶ καὶ κύριοι πολλοί,
as indeed there are gods many  and masters many,
6 235   1473  1520 2316 01  3962  1537 3739 021 3956
  ἀλλ᾽ ἡμῖν εἷς θεὸς ὁ πατὴρ ἐξ οὗ  τὰ πάντα
  but  to us one God the father from whom the all
2532 1473  1519 846  2532 1520 2962     2424  5547
καὶ ἡμεῖς εἰς αὐτόν, καὶ εἷς κύριος Ἰησοῦς Χριστὸς
and we into him,   and one Master Jesus Christ
1223    3739 021 3956   2532 1473  1223    846
δι᾽   οὗ τὰ πάντα καὶ ἡμεῖς δι᾽ αὐτοῦ.
through whom the all and we through him.
7 235   3756 1722 3956  05  1108       5100 1161
  Ἀλλ᾽ οὐκ ἐν πᾶσιν ἡ γνῶσις·   τινὲς δὲ
  But  not in all the knowledge; some but
07     4914     2193 737 010  1497     5613
τῇ   συνηθείᾳ ἕως ἄρτι τοῦ εἰδώλου ὡς
in the custom until now of the idol  as
1494        2068      2532 05  4893      846
εἰδωλόθυτον ἐσθίουσιν, καὶ ἡ συνείδησις αὐτῶν
idol sacrifice eat,   and the conscience of them
772    1510  3435        8 1033 1161 1473 3756
ἀσθενὴς οὖσα μολύνεται. 8 βρῶμα δὲ ἡμᾶς οὐ
weak   being is stained. Food but us not
3936        03     2316 3777  1437 3361
παραστήσει τῷ  θεῷ· οὔτε ἐὰν μὴ
will stand along to the God; neither except
```

her husband lives. But if the husband dies,[a] she is free to marry anyone she wishes, only in the Lord. [40]But in my judgment she is more blessed if she remains as she is. And I think that I too have the Spirit of God.

CHAPTER 8

Now concerning food sacrificed to idols: we know that "all of us possess knowledge." Love builds up, but love builds up. [2]Anyone who claims to know something does not yet have the necessary knowledge; [3]but anyone who loves God is known by him.

[4]Hence, as to the eating of food offered to idols, we know that "no idol in the world really exists," and that "there is no God but one." [5]Indeed, even though there may be so-called gods in heaven or on earth—as in fact there are many gods and many lords— [6]yet for us there is one God, the Father, from whom are all things and for whom we exist, and one Lord, Jesus Christ, through whom are all things and through whom we exist.

[7]It is not everyone, however, who has this knowledge. Since some have become so accustomed to idols until now, they still think of the food they eat as food offered to an idol; and their conscience, being weak, is defiled. [8]"Food will not bring us close to God."[b] We are no worse off

[a] Gk falls asleep

[b] The quotation may extend to the end of the verse

if we do not eat, and no better off if we do. ⁹But take care that this liberty of yours does not somehow become a stumbling block to the weak. ¹⁰For if others see you, who possess knowledge, eating in the temple of an idol, might they not, since their conscience is weak, be encouraged to the point of eating food sacrificed to idols? ¹¹So by your knowledge those weak believers for whom Christ died are destroyed.ᵃ ¹²But when you thus sin against members of your family,ᵇ and wound their conscience when it is weak, you sin against Christ. ¹³Therefore, if food is a cause of their falling,ᶜ I will never eat meat, so that I may not cause one of themᵈ to fall.

CHAPTER 9

Am I not free? Am I not an apostle? Have I not seen Jesus our Lord? Are you not my work in the Lord? ²If I am not an apostle to others, at least I am to you; for you are the seal of my apostleship in the Lord. 3 This is my defense to those who would examine me. ⁴Do we not have the right to our food and drink? ⁵Do we not have the right to be accompanied by a believing wife,ᵉ as do the other apostles and the brothers of the Lord and Cephas? ⁶Or is it only Barnabas and I

ᵃ Gk the weak brother . . . is destroyed
ᵇ Gk against the brothers
ᶜ Gk my brother's falling
ᵈ Gk cause my brother
ᵉ Gk a sister as wife

2068	5302	3777	1437	2068
φάγωμεν	ὑστερούμεθα,	οὔτε	ἐὰν	φάγωμεν
we might eat	are we lacking,	neither	if	we might eat

4052		991	1161	3361	4458	05	1849
περισσεύομεν.	⁹	βλέπετε	δὲ	μή	πως	ἡ	ἐξουσία
we exceed.		See	but	not	perhaps	the	authority

1473	3778	4348	1096	015	772
ὑμῶν	αὕτη	πρόσκομμα	γένηται	τοῖς	ἀσθενέσιν.
of you	this	stumbling	might become	to the	weak ones.

	1437	1063	5100	3708	1473	04	2192	1108
10	ἐὰν	γάρ	τις	ἴδῃ	σὲ	τὸν	ἔχοντα	γνῶσιν
	If	for	some	might see	you	the	having	knowledge

1722	1493	2621	3780	05	4893	846
ἐν	εἰδωλείῳ	κατακείμενον,	οὐχὶ	ἡ	συνείδησις	αὐτοῦ
in	idol temple	lying down,	not	the	conscience	of him

772	1510	3618	1519	012	024	1494
ἀσθενοῦς	ὄντος	οἰκοδομηθήσεται	εἰς	τὸ	τὰ	εἰδωλόθυτα
weak	being	will be built	into	the	the	idol sacrifices

2068		622	1063	01	770	1722	07	4674
ἐσθίειν;	11	ἀπόλλυται	γὰρ	ὁ	ἀσθενῶν	ἐν	τῇ	σῇ
to eat?		Is destroyed	for	the	weak	in	the	your

1108	01	80	1223	3739	5547	599
γνώσει,	ὁ	ἀδελφὸς	δι᾽	ὃν	Χριστὸς	ἀπέθανεν.
knowledge,	the	brother	through	whom	Christ	died.

	3779	1161	264	1519	016	80	2532
12	οὕτως	δὲ	ἁμαρτάνοντες	εἰς	τοὺς	ἀδελφοὺς	καὶ
	Thusly	but	sinning	for	the	brothers	and

5180	846	08	4893	770	1519
τύπτοντες	αὐτῶν	τὴν	συνείδησιν	ἀσθενοῦσαν	εἰς
beating	of them	the	conscience	being weak	for

5547	264		1355	1487	1033	4624
Χριστὸν	ἁμαρτάνετε.	13	διόπερ	εἰ	βρῶμα	σκανδαλίζει
Christ	you sin.		Therefore if		food	offends

04	80	1473	3756	3361	2068	2907	1519	04
τὸν	ἀδελφόν	μου,	οὐ	μὴ	φάγω	κρέα	εἰς	τὸν
the	brother	of me,	not	not	I might eat	meat	into	the

165	2443	3361	04	80	1473	4624
αἰῶνα,	ἵνα	μὴ	τὸν	ἀδελφόν	μου	σκανδαλίσω.
age,	that	not	the	brother	of me	I might offend.

9:1	3756	1510	1658	3756	1510	652	3780
	Οὐκ	εἰμὶ	ἐλεύθερος;	οὐκ	εἰμὶ	ἀπόστολος;	οὐχὶ
	Not	am I	free?	Not	am I	delegate?	Not

2424	04	2962	1473	3708	3756	09	2041
᾿Ιησοῦν	τὸν	κύριον	ἡμῶν	ἑώρακα;	οὐ	τὸ	ἔργον
Jesus	the	Master	of us	I have seen?	Not	the	work

1473	1473	1510	1722	2962		1487	243	3756	1510
μου	ὑμεῖς	ἐστε	ἐν	κυρίῳ;	2	εἰ	ἄλλοις	οὐκ	εἰμὶ
of me	you	are	in	Master?		If	to others	not	I am

652	235	1065	1473	1510	05	1063	4973
ἀπόστολος,	ἀλλά	γε	ὑμῖν	εἰμι·	ἡ	γὰρ	σφραγίς
delegate,	but	indeed	to you	I am;	the	for	seal

1473	06	651	1473	1510	1722	2962	05
μου	τῆς	ἀποστολῆς	ὑμεῖς	ἐστε	ἐν	κυρίῳ.	3 ᾿Η
of me	the	delegateship	you	are	in	Master.	The

1699	627	015	1473	350	1510	3778
ἐμὴ	ἀπολογία	τοῖς	ἐμὲ	ἀνακρίνουσίν	ἐστιν	αὕτη.
my	defense	to the	me	examining	is	this.

	3361	3756	2192	1849	2068	2532	4095
4	μὴ	οὐκ	ἔχομεν	ἐξουσίαν	φαγεῖν	καὶ	πεῖν;
	Not	not	we have	authority	to eat	and	drink?

	3361	3756	2192	1849	79	1135
5	μὴ	οὐκ	ἔχομεν	ἐξουσίαν	ἀδελφὴν	γυναῖκα
	Not	not	we have	authority	sister	woman

4013	5613	2532	013	3062	652	2532
περιάγειν	ὡς	καὶ	οἱ	λοιποὶ	ἀπόστολοι	καὶ
to lead around	as	also	the	remaining	delegates	and

013	80	02	2962	2532	2786		2228	3441	1473
οἱ	ἀδελφοὶ	τοῦ	κυρίου	καὶ	Κηφᾶς;	6	ἢ	μόνος	ἐγὼ
the	brothers	of the	Master	and	Cephas?		Or	alone	I

```
2532 921        3756 2192      1849          3361 2038
καὶ  Βαρναβᾶς οὐκ ἔχομεν ἐξουσίαν μὴ   ἐργάζεσθαι;
and  Barnabas  not  we have authority not   to work?
   5101 4754            2398 3800        4218  5101 5452
 7 Τίς  στρατεύεται ἰδίοις ὀψωνίοις ποτέ; τίς φυτεύει
   Who  soldiers     in own  salaries  ever? Who plants
290          2532 04   2590     846     3756 2068      2228 5101
ἀμπελῶνα καὶ  τὸν καρπὸν αὐτοῦ οὐκ ἐσθίει;  ἢ   τίς
vineyard and  the fruit  of it  not  eats?   Or  who
4165       4167       2532 1537 010 1051       06     4167
ποιμαίνει ποίμνην καὶ  ἐκ  τοῦ γάλακτος τῆς  ποίμνης
shepherds flock    and  from the milk    of the flock
3756 2068       3361 2596 444         3778 2980     2228
οὐκ ἐσθίει;  8 Μὴ  κατὰ ἄνθρωπον ταῦτα λαλῶ    ἢ
not eats?      Not  by   man      these I speak  or
2532 01   3551    3778 3756 3004      1722 1063 03
καὶ  ὁ  νόμος ταῦτα οὐ  λέγει;  9 ἐν  γὰρ τῷ
even the law   these not says?    In  for  the
3475     3551 1125                 3756 2777a           1016
Μωϋσέως νόμῳ γέγραπται·          οὐ κημώσεις βοῦν
Moses    law  it has been written, not you muzzle ox
248        3361 014     1016 3190a       03      2316
ἀλοῶντα.  μὴ  τῶν βοῶν μέλει         τῷ    θεῷ
threshing. Not of the oxen is it a care to the God
   2228 1223          1473 3843       3004     1223
10 ἢ    δι᾽        ἡμᾶς πάντως λέγει;  δι᾽
   or  because of us  altogether it says? Because
1473 1063 1125               3754 3784     1909 1680
ἡμᾶς γὰρ ἐγράφη           ὅτι ὀφείλει ἐπ᾽ ἐλπίδι
of us for  it was written that one owes on   hope
01  722      722     2532 01  248      1909 1680
ὁ  ἀροτριῶν ἀροτριᾶν καὶ  ὁ  ἀλοῶν ἐπ᾽ ἐλπίδι
the plowing  to plow  and the threshing on  hope
010      3348          1487 1473  1473    024 4152
τοῦ  μετέχειν.  11 εἰ  ἡμεῖς ὑμῖν τὰ  πνευματικὰ
of the to have with. If  we         to you the spiritual
4687          3173 1487 1473 1473   024 4559
ἐσπείραμεν, μέγα εἰ  ἡμεῖς ὑμῶν τὰ  σαρκικὰ
sowed,      great if  we    of you the fleshly
2325               1487 1473 06       1473 1849
θερίσομεν;  12 Εἰ  ἄλλοι τῆς  ὑμῶν ἐξουσίας
we will harvest? If  others of the of you authority
3348        3756 3123   1473   235  3756 5530
μετέχουσιν, οὐ  μᾶλλον ἡμεῖς; ἀλλ᾽ οὐκ ἐχρησάμεθα
have with,  not  more   we?   But  not  we made use
07  1849        3778    235  3956 4722        2443 3361
τῇ ἐξουσίᾳ   ταύτῃ, ἀλλὰ πάντα στέγομεν, ἵνα μὴ
the authority this,  but  all  we endure,  that not
5100 1464     1325     011    2098
τινα ἐγκοπὴν δῶμεν τῷ  εὐαγγελίῳ
some hindrance we might give to the good message
02   5547        3756 3609a       3754 013        024
τοῦ  Χριστοῦ. 13 Οὐκ οἴδατε ὅτι οἱ      τὰ
of the Christ.   Not  you know that the ones the
2411     2038        024 1537 010 2411      2068
ἱερὰ   ἐργαζόμενοι [τὰ] ἐκ  τοῦ ἱεροῦ ἐσθίουσιν,
temples working    the  from the temple they eat,
013 011      2379       3917a        011 2379
οἱ  τῷ   θυσιαστηρίῳ παρεδρεύοντες τῷ  θυσιαστηρίῳ
the in the sacrifice  sitting beside the sacrifice
ones     place                              place
4829                 3779    2532 01  2962    1299
συμμερίζονται;  14 οὕτως καὶ  ὁ  κύριος διέταξεν
are dividers with?   Thusly also the Master directed
015         012 2098       2605              1537 010
τοῖς    τὸ εὐαγγέλιον καταγγέλλουσιν ἐκ  τοῦ
to the ones the good message proclaiming  from the
2098       2198        1473 1161 3756 5530
εὐαγγελίου ζῆν.  15 Ἐγὼ δὲ  οὐ  κέχρημαι
good message to live. I    but not have used
```

who have no right to refrain from working for a living? [7]Who at any time pays the expenses for doing military service? Who plants a vineyard and does not eat any of its fruit? Or who tends a flock and does not get any of its milk?

[8]Do I say this on human authority? Does not the law also say the same? [9]For it is written in the law of Moses, "You shall not muzzle an ox while it is treading out the grain." Is it for oxen that God is concerned? [10]Or does he not speak entirely for our sake? It was indeed written for our sake, for whoever plows should plow in hope and whoever threshes should thresh in hope of a share in the crop. [11]If we have sown spiritual good among you, is it too much if we reap your material benefits? [12]If others share this rightful claim on you, do not we still more?

Nevertheless, we have not made use of this right, but we endure anything rather than put an obstacle in the way of the gospel of Christ. [13]Do you not know that those who are employed in the temple service get their food from the temple, and those who serve at the altar share in what is sacrificed on the altar? [14]In the same way, the Lord commanded that those who proclaim the gospel should get their living by the gospel.

[15]But I have made no use

of any of these rights, nor am I writing this so that they may be applied in my case. Indeed, I would rather die than that—no one will deprive me of my ground for boasting! 16If I proclaim the gospel, this gives me no ground for boasting, for an obligation is laid on me, and woe to me if I do not proclaim the gospel! 17For if I do this of my own will, I have a reward; but if not of my own will, I am entrusted with a commission. 18What then is my reward? Just this: that in my proclamation I may make the gospel free of charge, so as not to make full use of my rights in the gospel.

19 For though I am free with respect to all, I have made myself a slave to all, so that I might win more of them. 20To the Jews I became as a Jew, in order to win Jews. To those under the law I became as one under the law (though I myself am not under the law) so that I might win those under the law. 21To those outside the law I became as one outside the law (though I am not free from God's law but am under Christ's law) so that I might win those outside the law. 22To the weak I became weak, so that I might win the weak. I have become all things to all people, that I might by all means save some. 23I do it all for the sake of the gospel, so that I may share in its blessings.

```
3762      3778        3756 1125    1161 3778    2443 3779
οὐδενὶ τούτων.  Οὐκ ἔγραψα δὲ ταῦτα, ἵνα οὕτως
nothing of these. Not I wrote but these, that thusly
1096            1722 1473  2570 1063 1473  3123
γένηται       ἐν ἐμοί· καλὸν γάρ μοι μᾶλλον
it might become in me;  good for me  more
599          2228 012 2745       1473 3762   2758
ἀποθανεῖν ἢ -  τὸ καύχημά μου οὐδεὶς κενώσει.
to die   or  the brag    of me no one will empty.
      1437 1063 2097                  3756 1510
16 ἐὰν γὰρ εὐαγγελίζωμαι,            οὐκ ἔστιν
   If for I might tell good message, not it is
1473 2745     318      1063 1473 1945     3759
μοι καύχημα· ἀνάγκη γάρ μοι ἐπίκειται· οὐαὶ
to me brag; necessity for to me lies on; woe
1063 1473 1510  1437 3361 2097
γάρ μοί ἐστιν ἐὰν μὴ εὐαγγελίσωμαι.
for to me it is if  not I might tell good message.
   1487 1063 1635   3778 4238        3408 2192
17 εἰ γὰρ ἑκὼν τοῦτο πράσσω,    μισθὸν ἔχω·
   If for willing this I practice, wage I have;
1487 1161 210     3622        4100
εἰ δὲ ἄκων, οἰκονομίαν πεπίστευμαι·
if but unwilling, management I have been trusted;
   5101 3767 1473  1510 01  3408    2443
18 τίς οὖν μού ἐστιν ὁ μισθός; ἵνα
   What then of me is  the wage? That
2097          77      5087  012 2098            1519
εὐαγγελιζόμενος ἀδάπανον θήσω τὸ εὐαγγέλιον εἰς
telling good     without I might the good message for
message          expense set
012 3361 2710         07  1849      1473 1722 011
τὸ μὴ καταχρήσασθαι τῇ ἐξουσίᾳ μου ἐν τῷ
the not to use thoroughly the authority of me in the
2098        1658    1063 1510 1537 3956  3956
εὐαγγελίῳ. 19 Ἐλεύθερος γὰρ ὢν ἐκ πάντων πᾶσιν
good message, Free   for being from all  in all
1683    1402       2443 016 4183    2770
ἐμαυτὸν ἐδούλωσα, ἵνα τοὺς πλείονας κερδήσω·
myself I slaved, that the more    I might gain;
   2532 1096   015   2453     5613 2453     2443
20 καὶ ἐγενόμην τοῖς Ἰουδαίοις ὡς Ἰουδαῖος, ἵνα
   and I became to the Judeans as Judean,   that
2453      2770      015   5259 3551 5613 5259
Ἰουδαίους κερδήσω· τοῖς ὑπὸ νόμον ὡς ὑπὸ
Judeans I might gain; to the under law  as under
3551  3361 1510 846  5259 3551  2443 016 5259
νόμον, μὴ ὢν αὐτὸς ὑπὸ νόμον, ἵνα τοὺς ὑπὸ
law,  not being self under law,  that the under
3551 2770       015  459      5613 459     3361
νόμον κερδήσω· 21 τοῖς ἀνόμοις ὡς ἄνομος, μὴ
law I might gain; to the lawless as lawless, not
1510 459    2316   235  1772  5547    2443
ὢν ἄνομος θεοῦ ἀλλ' ἔννομος Χριστοῦ, ἵνα
being lawless of God but in law of Christ, that
2770      016  459      1096   015    772
κερδάνω τοὺς ἀνόμους· 22 ἐγενόμην τοῖς ἀσθενέσιν
I might gain the lawless;   I became to the weak
772    2443 016 772      2770      015   3956
ἀσθενής, ἵνα τοὺς ἀσθενεῖς κερδήσω· τοῖς πᾶσιν
weak,  that the weak    I might gain; to the in all
1096    3956  2443 3843   5100 4982    3956
γέγονα πάντα, ἵνα πάντως τινὰς σώσω. 23 πάντα
I have all, that altogether some I might All
become                           deliver.
1161 4160 1223    012 2098         2443 4791
δὲ ποιῶ διὰ τὸ εὐαγγέλιον, ἵνα συγκοινωνὸς
but I do through the good message, that co-partner
```

846   1096   3756 3609a   3754 013 1722
αὐτοῦ γένωμαι.   **24** Οὐκ οἴδατε   ὅτι   οἱ ἐν
of him I might become.   Not you know that the in
4712   5143   3956   3303   5143   1520 1161
σταδίῳ τρέχοντες πάντες μὲν   τρέχουσιν, εἷς δὲ
stadion running   all   indeed run,   one but
2983   012 1017   3779   5143   2443 2638
λαμβάνει τὸ βραβεῖον; οὕτως τρέχετε ἵνα καταλάβητε.
receives the prize?   Thusly run   that you might
                                                      over take.

        3956 1161 01 75   3956   1467
25 πᾶς   δὲ ὁ ἀγωνιζόμενος πάντα ἐγκρατεύεται,
      All   but the one contesting   all   has inner strength,
1565   3303   3767 2443 5349   4735
ἐκεῖνοι μὲν   οὖν ἵνα φθαρτὸν   στέφανον
those   indeed then that corruptible crown
2983   1473 1161 862   26 1473
λάβωσιν,   ἡμεῖς δὲ ἄφθαρτον.   **26** ἐγὼ
they might receive, we   but incorruptible.   I
5106   3779   5143 5613 3756 84   3779
τοίνυν   οὕτως τρέχω ὡς οὐκ ἀδήλως,   οὕτως
accordingly thusly run   as   not unclearly, thusly
4438   5613 3756 109 1194   27 235 5299   1473
πυκτεύω ὡς   οὐκ ἀέρα δέρων·   **27** ἀλλὰ ὑπωπιάζω μου
I box   as   not   air beating;   but   I weary   of me
012 4983 2532 1396   3361 4458   243
τὸ σῶμα καὶ δουλαγωγῶ,   μή πως   ἄλλοις
the body and lead into slavery, not perhaps to others
2784   846   96   1096
κηρύξας   αὐτὸς ἀδόκιμος γένωμαι.
having announced myself unproved I might become.

        3756 2309   1063 1473 50   80   3754
10:1 Οὐ θέλω   γὰρ ὑμᾶς ἀγνοεῖν,   ἀδελφοί, ὅτι
       Not I want for you   to not know, brothers,   that
013 3962   1473 3956   5259 08   3507   1510 2532
οἱ πατέρες ἡμῶν πάντες ὑπὸ τὴν νεφέλην ἦσαν καὶ
the fathers of us all   under the cloud   were and
3956 1223   06   2281   1330   2 2532 3956
πάντες διὰ   τῆς θαλάσσης διῆλθον   **2** καὶ πάντες
all   through the sea   went through   and   all
1519 04 3475   907   1722 07 3507   2532 1722
εἰς τὸν Μωϋσῆν ἐβαπτίσθησαν ἐν τῇ νεφέλῃ καὶ ἐν
into the Moses   were immersed in the cloud   and   in
07   2281   3 2532 3956   012 846 4152   1033
τῇ θαλάσσῃ **3** καὶ πάντες τὸ αὐτὸ πνευματικὸν βρῶμα
the sea   and   all   the same spiritual   food
2068   4 2532 3956   012 846 4152   4095   4188
ἔφαγον **4** καὶ πάντες τὸ αὐτὸ πνευματικὸν ἔπιον πόμα·
ate   and   all   the same spiritual   drank drink;
4095   1063 1537 4152   190   4073
ἔπινον   γὰρ ἐκ πνευματικῆς ἀκολουθούσης πέτρας,
they drank for from spiritual   following   rock,
05   4073 1161 1510 01 5547   5 235 3756 1722
ἡ πέτρα δὲ ἦν ὁ Χριστός.   **5** Ἀλλ᾽ οὐκ ἐν
the rock but was the Christ.   But not   in
015 4183   846   2106   01 2316
τοῖς πλείοσιν αὐτῶν εὐδόκησεν   ὁ θεός,
the more   of them thought well the God,
2693   1063 1722 07 2048   6 3778
κατεστρώθησαν γὰρ ἐν τῇ ἐρήμῳ.   **6** Ταῦτα
they were thrown down for in the desert.   These
1161 5179   1473 1096   1519 012 3361 1510
δὲ τύποι   ἡμῶν ἐγενήθησαν, εἰς τὸ μὴ εἶναι
but examples of us became,   for the not to be
1473 1938   2556   2531   2548   1937
ἡμᾶς ἐπιθυμητὰς κακῶν, καθὼς κἀκεῖνοι ἐπεθύμησαν.
us   desirers   of bad, just as also those desired.
        3366   1496   1096   2531   5100 846
7 μηδὲ   εἰδωλολάτραι γίνεσθε καθώς τινες αὐτῶν,
      But not idol servers   become, just as some of them,

24 Do you not know
that in a race the runners
all compete, but only one
receives the prize? Run in
such a way that you may
win it. [25]Athletes exercise
self-control in all things;
they do it to receive a
perishable wreath, but we
an imperishable one. [26]So
I do not run aimlessly, nor
do I box as though beating
the air; [27]but I punish my
body and enslave it, so that
after proclaiming to others
I myself should not be
disqualified.

CHAPTER 10

I do not want you to be
unaware, brothers and
sisters,[a] that our ancestors
were all under the cloud,
and all passed through the
sea, [2]and all were baptized
into Moses in the cloud and
in the sea, [3]and all ate the
same spiritual food, [4]and
all drank the same spiritual
drink. For they drank from
the spiritual rock that
followed them, and the
rock was Christ. [5]Never-
theless, God was not
pleased with most of them,
and they were struck down
in the wilderness.

6 Now these things
occurred as examples for us,
so that we might not desire
evil as they did. [7]Do not
become idolaters as some
of them did;

---

[a] Gk brothers

as it is written, "The people sat down to eat and drink, and they rose up to play." [8]We must not indulge in sexual immorality as some of them did, and twenty-three thousand fell in a single day. [9]We must not put Christ[a] to the test, as some of them did, and were destroyed by serpents. [10]And do not complain as some of them did, and were destroyed by the destroyer. [11]These things happened to them to serve as an example, and they were written down to instruct us, on whom the ends of the ages have come. [12]So if you think you are standing, watch out that you do not fall. [13]No testing has overtaken you that is not common to everyone. God is faithful, and he will not let you be tested beyond your strength, but with the testing he will also provide the way out so that you may be able to endure it.

[14]Therefore, my dear friends,[b] flee from the worship of idols. [15]I speak as to sensible people; judge for yourselves what I say. [16]The cup of blessing that we bless, is it not a sharing in the blood of Christ? The bread that we break, is it not a sharing in the body of Christ? [17]Because there is one bread, we who are many are one body,

a Other ancient authorities read the Lord
b Gk my beloved

5618	1125		2523	01	2992
ὥσπερ	γέγραπται·		ἐκάθισεν	ὁ	λαὸς
as indeed	it has been written,		sat	the	people

2068	2532	4095	2532	450	3815		3366
φαγεῖν καὶ		πεῖν	καὶ	ἀνέστησαν	παίζειν.	**8**	μηδὲ
to eat and		to drink and		stood up	to play.		But not

4203		2531	5100	846	4203
πορνεύωμεν,		καθώς	τινες	αὐτῶν	ἐπόρνευσαν
we might commit just as some of them committed sexual					
sexual immorality,					immorality

2532	4098	1520	2250	1501	5140	5505
καὶ	ἔπεσαν	μιᾷ	ἡμέρᾳ	εἴκοσι	τρεῖς	χιλιάδες.
and	fell	in one	day	twenty	three	thousands.

	3366	1598		04	5547	2531
9	μηδὲ	ἐκπειράζωμεν		τὸν	Χριστόν,	καθώς
	But not	we might pressure out		the	Christ,	just as

5100	846	3985	2532	5259	014	3789
τινες	αὐτῶν	ἐπείρασαν	καὶ	ὑπὸ	τῶν	ὄφεων
some	of them	pressured	and	by	the	snakes

622		3366	1111	2509
ἀπώλλυντο.	**10**	μηδὲ	γογγύζετε,	καθάπερ
were destroyed.		But not	grumble,	just as indeed

5100	846	1111	2532	622	5259	02
τινὲς	αὐτῶν	ἐγόγγυσαν	καὶ	ἀπώλοντο	ὑπὸ	τοῦ
some	of them	grumbled	and	were destroyed by		the

3644		3778	1161	5178a	4819
ὀλοθρευτοῦ.	**11**	ταῦτα	δὲ	τυπικῶς	συνέβαινεν
destroyer.		These	but	by example	came together

1565	1125		1161	4314	3559	1473
ἐκείνοις,	ἐγράφη		δὲ	πρὸς	νουθεσίαν	ἡμῶν,
to those,	it was written		but	toward	warning	of us,

1519	3739	021	5056	014	165	2658
εἰς	οὓς	τὰ	τέλη	τῶν	αἰώνων	κατήντηκεν.
to	whom	the completion		of the	ages	have arrived.

	5620	01	1380	2476	991	3361
12	Ὥστε	ὁ	δοκῶν	ἑστάναι	βλεπέτω	μὴ
	So that	the	thinking	to stand	let look	not

4098		3986	1473	3756	2983	1487	3361
πέσῃ.	**13**	πειρασμὸς	ὑμᾶς	οὐκ	εἴληφεν	εἰ	μὴ
he might fall.		Pressure	you	not	has taken		except

442	4103	1161	01	2316	3739	3756	1439
ἀνθρώπινος·	πιστὸς	δὲ	ὁ	θεός,	ὃς	οὐκ	ἐάσει
man-like;	trustful	but	the	God,	who	not	will allow

1473	3985		5228	3739	1410	235
ὑμᾶς	πειρασθῆναι		ὑπὲρ	ὃ	δύνασθε	ἀλλὰ
you	to be pressured		above	what	you are able	but

4160	4862	03	3986	2532	08	1545	010
ποιήσει	σὺν	τῷ	πειρασμῷ	καὶ	τὴν	ἔκβασιν	τοῦ
will make	with	the	pressure	also	the	going out	the

1410	5297		1355		27	1473
δύνασθαι	ὑπενεγκεῖν.	**14**	Διόπερ,		ἀγαπητοί	μου,
to be able	to endure.		Therefore,		loved	of me,

5343	575	06	1495		5613	5429
φεύγετε	ἀπὸ	τῆς	εἰδωλολατρίας.	**15**	ὡς	φρονίμοις
flee	from	the	idol service.		As	thoughtful

3004	2919	1473	3739	5346		09	4221	06
λέγω·	κρίνατε	ὑμεῖς	ὅ	φημι.	**16**	Τὸ	ποτήριον	τῆς
I say,	judge	you	what	I say.		The	cup	of the

2129	3739	2127		3780	2842	1510
εὐλογίας	ὃ	εὐλογοῦμεν,		οὐχὶ	κοινωνία	ἐστὶν
good word	which	we speak well,		not	partnership	is it

010	129	02	5547	04	740	3739	2806
τοῦ	αἵματος	τοῦ	Χριστοῦ;	τὸν	ἄρτον	ὃν	κλῶμεν,
of the	blood	of the	Christ?	The	bread	that	we break,

3780	2842	010	4983	02	5547	1510
οὐχὶ	κοινωνία	τοῦ	σώματος	τοῦ	Χριστοῦ	ἐστιν;
not	partnership	of the	body	of the	Christ	is it?

	3754	1520	740	1520	4983	013	4183	1510	013
17	ὅτι	εἷς	ἄρτος,	ἓν	σῶμα	οἱ	πολλοί	ἐσμεν,	οἱ
	Because	one	bread,	one	body	the	many	are,	the

1063 3956 1537 02 1520 740 3348 **18** 991
γὰρ πάντες ἐκ τοῦ ἑνὸς ἄρτου μετέχομεν. βλέπετε
for all from the one bread we hold with. See

04 2474 2596 4561 3756 013 2068 020
τὸν Ἰσραὴλ κατὰ σάρκα· οὐχ οἱ ἐσθίοντες τὰς
the Israel by flesh; not the ones eating the

2378 2844 010 2379 1510
θυσίας κοινωνοὶ τοῦ θυσιαστηρίου εἰσίν;
sacrifices partners of the sacrifice place are they?

19 5101 3767 5346 3754 1494 5100 1510
Τί οὖν φημι; ὅτι εἰδωλόθυτόν τί ἐστιν
What then I say? That idol sacrifice some is

2228 3754 1497 5100 1510 **20** 235 3754 3739
ἢ ὅτι εἴδωλόν τί ἐστιν; ἀλλ᾽ ὅτι ἃ
or that idol some is? But that what

2380 1140 2532 3756 2316 2380 3756
θύουσιν, δαιμονίοις καὶ οὐ θεῷ [θύουσιν]· οὐ
they to demons and not to God they not
sacrifice, sacrifice;

2309 1161 1473 2844 022 1140 1096
θέλω δὲ ὑμᾶς κοινωνοὺς τῶν δαιμονίων γίνεσθαι.
I want but you partners of the demons to become.

21 3756 1410 4221 2962 4095 2532
οὐ δύνασθε ποτήριον κυρίου πίνειν καὶ
Not you are able cup of Master to drink and

4221 1140 3756 1410 5132
ποτήριον δαιμονίων, οὐ δύνασθε τραπέζης
cup of demons, not you are able table

2962 3348 2532 5132 1140
κυρίου μετέχειν καὶ τραπέζης δαιμονίων.
of Master to hold with and table of demons.

22 2228 3863 04 2962 3361 2478
ἢ παραζηλοῦμεν τὸν κύριον; μὴ ἰσχυρότεροι
Or do we make jealous the Master? Not stronger

846 1510 **23** 3956 1832 235 3756 3956
αὐτοῦ ἐσμεν; Πάντα ἔξεστιν ἀλλ᾽ οὐ πάντα
of him we are? All is possible but not all

4851 3956 1832 235 3756 3956
συμφέρει· πάντα ἔξεστιν ἀλλ᾽ οὐ πάντα
advantageous; all is possible but not all

3618 3367 012 1438 2212 235 012
οἰκοδομεῖ. **24** μηδεὶς τὸ ἑαυτοῦ ζητείτω ἀλλὰ τὸ
builds. No one the of himself let seek but the

02 2087 **25** 3956 012 1722 3111 4453
τοῦ ἑτέρου. Πᾶν τὸ ἐν μακέλλῳ πωλούμενον
of the other. All the in meat market being sold

2068 3367 350 1223 08 4893
ἐσθίετε μηδὲν ἀνακρίνοντες διὰ τὴν συνείδησιν·
eat nothing examining because the conscience;

26 02 2962 1063 05 1093 2532 09 4138 846
τοῦ κυρίου γὰρ ἡ γῆ καὶ τὸ πλήρωμα αὐτῆς.
of the Master for the earth and the fullness of it.

27 1487 5100 2564 1473 014 571 2532 2309
εἴ τις καλεῖ ὑμᾶς τῶν ἀπίστων καὶ θέλετε
If some calls you of the untrustful and you want

4198 3956 012 3908 1473 2068
πορεύεσθαι, πᾶν τὸ παρατιθέμενον ὑμῖν ἐσθίετε
to travel, all the being set along to you eat

3367 350 1223 08 4893
μηδὲν ἀνακρίνοντες διὰ τὴν συνείδησιν.
nothing examining because of the conscience.

28 1437 1161 5100 1473 3004 3778 2410a 1510
ἐὰν δέ τις ὑμῖν εἴπῃ· τοῦτο ἱερόθυτόν ἐστιν,
If but some to you might this temple is,
say; sacrifice

3361 2068 1223 1565 04 3377
μὴ ἐσθίετε δι᾽ ἐκεῖνον τὸν μηνύσαντα
not eat because of that the having reported

for we all partake of the one bread. [18]Consider the people of Israel;[a] are not those who eat the sacrifices partners in the altar? [19]What do I imply then? That food sacrificed to idols is anything, or that an idol is anything? [20]No, I imply that what pagans sacrifice, they sacrifice to demons and not to God. I do not want you to be partners with demons. [21]You cannot drink the cup of the Lord and the cup of demons. You cannot partake of the table of the Lord and the table of demons. [22]Or are we provoking the Lord to jealousy? Are we stronger than he?

[23]"All things are lawful," but not all things are beneficial. "All things are lawful," but not all things build up. [24]Do not seek your own advantage, but that of the other. [25]Eat whatever is sold in the meat market without raising any question on the ground of conscience, [26]for "the earth and its fullness are the Lord's." [27]If an unbeliever invites you to a meal and you are disposed to go, eat whatever is set before you without raising any question on the ground of conscience. [28]But if someone says to you, "This has been offered in sacrifice," then do not eat it, out of consideration for the one who informed you,

a Gk Israel according to the flesh

and for the sake of
conscience— 29I mean
the other's conscience,
not your own. For why
should my liberty be subject
to the judgment of someone
else's conscience? 30If I
partake with thankfulness,
why should I be denounced
because of that for which
I give thanks?

31So, whether you eat
or drink, or whatever you
do, do everything for the
glory of God. 32Give no
offense to Jews or to Greeks
or to the church of God,
33just as I try to please
everyone in everything
I do, not seeking my own
advantage, but that of
many, so that they may
be saved. 11:1Be imitators
of me, as I am of Christ.

2 I commend you
because you remember me
in everything and maintain
the traditions just as I
handed them on to you.
3But I want you to
understand— that Christ is
the head of every man, and
the husband*a* is the head
of his wife,*b* and God is the
head of Christ. 4Any man
who prays or prophesies
with something on his head
disgraces his head, 5but
any woman who prays or
prophesies with her head
unveiled disgraces her
head—it is one and the
same thing as having her
head shaved. 6For if a
woman will not veil herself,
then she should cut off her
hair; but if it is disgraceful

a The same Greek word means *man*
or *husband*

b Or *head of the woman*

2532 08	4893	29 4893	1161 3004 3780 08

καὶ τὴν συνείδησιν· συνείδησιν δὲ λέγω οὐχὶ τὴν
and the conscience; conscience but I say not the

1438   235 08 02   2087   2444 1063 05
ἑαυτοῦ ἀλλὰ τὴν τοῦ ἑτέρου. ἱνατί γὰρ ἡ
of yourself but the of the other. Why for the

1657   1473 2919   5259 243   4893
ἐλευθερία μου κρίνεται ὑπὸ ἄλλης συνειδήσεως;
freedom of me is judged by other conscience?

30 1487 1473 5485   3348   5101 987
εἰ ἐγὼ χάριτι μετέχω, τί βλασφημοῦμαι
If I in favor I hold with, why am I insulted

5228   3739 1473 2168   31 1535   3767
ὑπὲρ οὗ ἐγὼ εὐχαριστῶ; Εἴτε οὖν
on behalf of what I give good favor? Whether then

2068   1535 4095 1535 5100 4160   3956   1519
ἐσθίετε εἴτε πίνετε εἴτε τι ποιεῖτε, πάντα εἰς
you eat or drink or some you do, all to

1391   2316 4160   32 677   2532 2453
δόξαν θεοῦ ποιεῖτε. ἀπρόσκοποι καὶ Ἰουδαίοις
splendor of God do. Blameless both to Judeans

1096   2532 1672   2532 07   1577   02   2316
γίνεσθε καὶ Ἕλλησιν καὶ τῇ ἐκκλησίᾳ τοῦ θεοῦ,
become and to Greeks and to the assembly of the God,

33 2531 2504 3956 3956   700   3361 2212   012
καθὼς κἀγὼ πάντα πᾶσιν ἀρέσκω μὴ ζητῶν τὸ
just as also I all to all I please not seeking the

1683   4852a   235 012 014   4183   2443
ἐμαυτοῦ σύμφορον ἀλλὰ τὸ τῶν πολλῶν, ἵνα
of myself advantage but the of the many, that

4982   11:1 3402   1473 1096
σωθῶσιν. μιμηταί μου γίνεσθε
they might be delivered. Imitators of me become

2531   2504 5547   2 1867   1161 1473 3754
καθὼς κἀγὼ Χριστοῦ. Ἐπαινῶ δὲ ὑμᾶς ὅτι
just as also I of Christ. I praise on but you that

3956 1473 3403   2532 2531
πάντα μου μέμνησθε καί, καθὼς
all of me you have remembered and, just as

3860   1473 020 3862   2722   3 2309
παρέδωκα ὑμῖν, τὰς παραδόσεις κατέχετε. Θέλω
I gave over to you the traditions you hold on. I want

1161 1473 3609a   3754 3956 435 05 2776   01
δὲ ὑμᾶς εἰδέναι ὅτι παντὸς ἀνδρὸς ἡ κεφαλὴ ὁ
but you to know that of all man the head the

5547   1510 2776 1161 1135   01 435 2776
Χριστός ἐστιν, κεφαλὴ δὲ γυναικὸς ὁ ἀνήρ, κεφαλὴ
Christ is, head but of woman the man, head

1161 02   5547   01 2316 3956 435 4336
δὲ τοῦ Χριστοῦ ὁ θεός. 4 πᾶς ἀνὴρ προσευχόμενος
but of the Christ the God. All man praying

2228 4395   2596 2776   2192   2617
ἢ προφητεύων κατὰ κεφαλῆς ἔχων καταισχύνει
or speaking before by head having shames

08 2776   846   5 3956 1161 1135   4336   2228
τὴν κεφαλὴν αὐτοῦ. πᾶσα δὲ γυνὴ προσευχομένη ἢ
the head of him. All but woman praying or

4395   177   07 2776   2617
προφητεύουσα ἀκατακαλύπτῳ τῇ κεφαλῇ καταισχύνει
speaking before uncovered over the head shames

08 2776   846   1520 1063 1510 2532 09 846
τὴν κεφαλὴν αὐτῆς· ἓν γάρ ἐστιν καὶ τὸ αὐτὸ
the head of her; one for it is and the same

07 3587   6 1487 1063 3756 2619
τῇ ἐξυρημένη. εἰ γὰρ οὐ κατακαλύπτεται
to the having been If for not is covered over
shaved.

1135   2532 2751   1487 1161 150
γυνή, καὶ κειράσθω· εἰ δὲ αἰσχρὸν
woman, and let shear herself; if but shame

```
1135        09    2751              2228  3587
γυναικὶ   τὸ  κείρασθαι      ἢ    ξυρᾶσθαι,
to woman the to be sheared  or   to be shaved,
2619                         435  3303    1063  3756  3784
κατακαλυπτέσθω.    7  Ἀνὴρ  μὲν   γὰρ   οὐκ  ὀφείλει
let be covered over.  Man  indeed for   not  owes
2619                 08    2776      1504   2532  1391
κατακαλύπτεσθαι   τὴν  κεφαλὴν  εἰκὼν  καὶ  δόξα
to be covered over the  head     image  and  splendor
2316     5225        05   1135  1161 1391     435   1510
θεοῦ  ὑπάρχων·  ἡ  γυνὴ  δὲ   δόξα   ἀνδρός ἐστιν.
of God existing; the woman but  splendor of man is.
8  3756 1063 1510  435  1537 1135      235   1135 1537
   οὐ  γάρ ἐστιν ἀνὴρ ἐκ  γυναικὸς ἀλλὰ γυνὴ ἐξ
   Not for is    man  from woman   but  woman from
435       9  2532 1063 3756 2936     435  1223     08
ἀνδρός·     καὶ γὰρ οὐκ ἐκτίσθη  ἀνὴρ διὰ   τὴν
man;        also for not was created man  through the
1135      235  1135 1223    04 435       10 1223     3778
γυναῖκα ἀλλὰ γυνὴ διὰ   τὸν ἄνδρα.     διὰ    τοῦτο
woman   but  woman through the man.     Through this
3784       05  1135  1849       2192     1909 06  2776
ὀφείλει ἡ  γυνὴ ἐξουσίαν ἔχειν ἐπὶ τῆς κεφαλῆς
owes    the woman authority to have on  the head
1223      016  32            4133    3777      1135
διὰ     τοὺς ἀγγέλους. 11 πλὴν οὔτε  γυνὴ
because of the messengers.  Except neither woman
5565     435   3777 435  5565     1135      1722 2962
χωρὶς ἀνδρὸς οὔτε ἀνὴρ χωρὶς γυναικὸς ἐν  κυρίῳ·
without man   nor  man without woman    in  Master;
12 5618      1063 05  1135  1537 02  435       3779
   ὥσπερ  γὰρ ἡ  γυνὴ ἐκ  τοῦ ἀνδρός, οὕτως
   as indeed for the woman from the man,    thusly
2532 01  435  1223    06  1135       021 1161 3956 1537
καὶ ὁ  ἀνὴρ διὰ  τῆς γυναικός· τὰ  δὲ  πάντα ἐκ
also the man through the woman;   the but  all  from
02  2316      13 1722 1473 846      2919       4241
τοῦ θεοῦ.       Ἐν ὑμῖν αὐτοῖς κρίνατε· πρέπον
the God.        In  you to them you judge; fitting
1510 1135      177            03     2316 4336
ἐστὶν γυναῖκα ἀκατακάλυπτον τῷ   θεῷ προσεύχεσθαι;
it is woman   uncovered      over to the God to pray?
14 3761    05  5449     846     1321     1473 3754 435
   οὐδὲ  ἡ  φύσις αὐτὴ  διδάσκει ὑμᾶς ὅτι ἀνὴρ
   But not the nature itself teaches  you  that man
3303  1437 2863                819      846    1510
μὲν  ἐὰν κομᾷ          ἀτιμία αὐτῷ ἐστιν,
indeed if might have long hair dishonor to him it is,
15 1135 1161 1437 2863              1391     846
   γυνὴ δὲ  ἐὰν κομᾷ           δόξα   αὐτῇ
   woman but if  might have long hair splendor to her
1510  3754   05 2864      473    4018
ἐστιν; ὅτι  ἡ  κόμη ἀντὶ  περιβολαίου
it is? Because the long hair in place of robe
1325       846     16 1487 1161 5100 1380
δέδοται [αὐτῇ].      Εἰ  δέ  τις δοκεῖ
has been given to her.   If  but  some thinks
5380           1510  1473 5108    4914      3756
φιλόνεικος   εἶναι, ἡμεῖς τοιαύτην συνήθειαν οὐκ
friend of quarrels to be, we    such     custom    not
2192  3761    017 1577      02        2316   17 3778
ἔχομεν οὐδὲ αἱ ἐκκλησίαι τοῦ θεοῦ.     Τοῦτο
have   but not the assemblies of the God.  This
1161 3853        3756 1867        3754 3756 1519 012
δὲ  παραγγέλλων οὐκ ἐπαινῶ  ὅτι οὐκ εἰς τὸ
but  commanding not I praise on that not  into the
2909      235  1519 012 2269α 4905
κρεῖσσον ἀλλὰ εἰς τὸ ἧσσον συνέρχεσθε.
better   but  into the worse you come together.
```

for a woman to have her hair cut off or to be shaved, she should wear a veil. [7]For a man ought not to have his head veiled, since he is the image and reflection[a] of God; but woman is the reflection[a] of man. [8]Indeed, man was not made from woman, but woman from man. [9]Neither was man created for the sake of woman, but woman for the sake of man. [10]For this reason a woman ought to have a symbol of[b] authority on her head,[c] because of the angels. [11]Nevertheless, in the Lord woman is not independent of man or man independent of woman. [12]For just as woman came from man, so man comes through woman; but all things come from God. [13]Judge for yourselves: is it proper for a woman to pray to God with her head unveiled? [14]Does not nature itself teach you that if a man wears long hair, it is degrading to him, [15]but if a woman has long hair, it is her glory? For her hair is given to her for a covering. [16]But if anyone is disposed to be contentious—we have no such custom, nor do the churches of God.

17 Now in the following instructions I do not commend you, because when you come together it is not for the better but for the worse.

a Or glory
b Gk lacks a symbol of
c Or have freedom of choice regarding her head

18For, to begin with, when you come together as a church, I hear that there are divisions among you; and to some extent I believe it. 19Indeed, there have to be factions among you, for only so will it become clear who among you are genuine. 20When you come together, it is not really to eat the Lord's supper. 21For when the time comes to eat, each of you goes ahead with your own supper, and one goes hungry and another becomes drunk. 22What! Do you not have homes to eat and drink in? Or do you show contempt for the church of God and humiliate those who have nothing? What should I say to you? Should I commend you? In this matter I do not commend you!

23 For I received from the Lord what I also handed on to you, that the Lord Jesus on the night when he was betrayed took a loaf of bread, 24and when he had given thanks, he broke it and said, "This is my body that is for*a* you. Do this in remembrance of me." 25In the same way he took the cup also, after supper, saying, "This cup is the new covenant in my blood. Do this, as often as you drink it, in remembrance of me." 26For as often as you eat this bread and drink the cup,

a Other ancient authorities read *is broken for*

4413	3303	1063	4905		1473	1722
18 πρῶτον μὲν γὰρ συνερχομένων ὑμῶν ἐν
First indeed for having come together you in

| 1577 | 191 | 4978 | 1722 1473 | 5225 | 2532 | 3313 |
ἐκκλησίᾳ ἀκούω σχίσματα ἐν ὑμῖν ὑπάρχειν καὶ μέρος
assembly I hear splits in you to exist and part

| 5100 4100 | | 1163 | | 1063 2532 | 139 |
τι πιστεύω. **19** δεῖ γὰρ καὶ αἱρέσεις
some I trust. It is necessary for also sects

| 1722 1473 1510 | 2443 2532 | 013 1384 | 5318 |
ἐν ὑμῖν εἶναι, ἵνα [καὶ] οἱ δόκιμοι φανεροὶ
in you to be, that also the proved evident

| 1096 | 1722 1473 | 4905 | 3767 1473 |
γένωνται ἐν ὑμῖν. **20** Συνερχομένων οὖν ὑμῶν
might become in you. Coming together then you

| 1909 012 846 | 3756 1510 | 2960 | 1173 | 2068 |
ἐπὶ τὸ αὐτὸ οὐκ ἔστιν κυριακὸν δεῖπνον φαγεῖν·
on the same not it is Master's dinner to eat;

| 1538 | 1063 012 2398 | 1173 | 4301 | 1722 |
21 ἕκαστος γὰρ τὸ ἴδιον δεῖπνον προλαμβάνει ἐν
each for the own dinner takes before in

| 011 2068 | 2532 2739 3303 | 3983 | 3739 1161 |
τῷ φαγεῖν, καὶ ὃς μὲν πεινᾷ ὃς δὲ
the to eat, and who indeed hungers who but

| 3184 | 3361 1063 3614 | 3756 2192 | 1519 012 |
μεθύει. **22** μὴ γὰρ οἰκίας οὐκ ἔχετε εἰς τὸ
is drunk. Not for houses not you have for the

| 2068 | 2532 4095 | 2228 06 1577 | 02 | 2316 |
ἐσθίειν καὶ πίνειν; ἢ τῆς ἐκκλησίας τοῦ θεοῦ
to eat and to drink? Or the assembly of the God

| 2706 | 2532 2617 | 016 3361 2192 |
καταφρονεῖτε, καὶ καταισχύνετε τοὺς μὴ ἔχοντας;
you think down, and you shame the not having?

| 5101 3004 | 1473 | 1867 | 1473 1722 |
τί εἴπω ὑμῖν; ἐπαινέσω ὑμᾶς; ἐν
What might I say to you? Might I praise on you? In

| 3778 3756 1867 | 1473 1063 3880 | 575 02 |
τούτῳ οὐκ ἐπαινῶ. **23** Ἐγὼ γὰρ παρέλαβον ἀπὸ τοῦ
this not I praise on. I for took along from the

| 2962 | 3739 2532 3860 | 1473 | 3754 01 2962 |
κυρίου, ὃ καὶ παρέδωκα ὑμῖν, ὅτι ὁ κύριος
Master, what also I gave over to you, that the Master

| 2424 1722 07 3571 3739 | 3860 | 2983 |
Ἰησοῦς ἐν τῇ νυκτὶ ᾗ παρεδίδετο ἔλαβεν
Jesus in the night in which he was given over took

| 740 | 2532 2168 | 2806 | 2532 3004 | 3778 |
24 ἄρτον καὶ εὐχαριστήσας ἔκλασεν καὶ εἶπεν· τοῦτό
bread and having given broke and said; this
              good favor

| 1473 1510 09 4983 09 | 5228 | 1473 | 3778 |
μού ἐστιν τὸ σῶμα τὸ ὑπὲρ ὑμῶν· τοῦτο
of me is the body the on behalf of you; this

| 4160 | 1519 08 1699 364 | 5615 | 2532 012 |
ποιεῖτε εἰς τὴν ἐμὴν ἀνάμνησιν. **25** ὡσαύτως καὶ τὸ
do in the my remembrance. Likewise also the

| 4221 | 3326 012 1172 | 3004 | 3778 09 4221 |
ποτήριον μετὰ τὸ δειπνῆσαι λέγων· τοῦτο τὸ ποτήριον
cup after the to dine saying, this the cup

| 05 2537 1242 | 1510 1722 011 1699 129 | 3778 |
ἡ καινὴ διαθήκη ἐστὶν ἐν τῷ ἐμῷ αἵματι· τοῦτο
the new agreement is in the my blood; this

| 4160 | 3740 | 1437 4095 | 1519 08 |
ποιεῖτε, ὁσάκις ἐὰν πίνητε, εἰς τὴν
do, as often as if you might drink, in the

| 1699 364 | 3740 | 1063 1437 2068 |
ἐμὴν ἀνάμνησιν. **26** ὁσάκις γὰρ ἐὰν ἐσθίητε
my remembrance. As often as for if you might eat

| 04 740 | 3778 2532 012 4221 | 4095 | 04 |
τὸν ἄρτον τοῦτον καὶ τὸ ποτήριον πίνητε, τὸν
the bread this and the cup you might drink, the

2288	02	2962	2605	891	3739

θάνατον τοῦ κυρίου καταγγέλλετε ἄχρις οὗ
death of the Master you proclaim until which

2064
ἔλθῃ. **27** Ὥστε ὃς ἂν ἐσθίῃ τὸν ἄρτον
he might come.   So that who - might eat the bread

5620 3739 302 2068 04 740

2228 4095   012 4221   02   2962   371
ἢ πίνῃ τὸ ποτήριον τοῦ κυρίου ἀναξίως,
or might drink the cup of the Master unworthily,

1777   1510   010   4983   2532 010 129   02
ἔνοχος ἔσται τοῦ σώματος καὶ τοῦ αἵματος τοῦ
guilty will be of the body and the blood of the

2962 **28** 1381   1161 444   1438   2532
κυρίου. δοκιμαζέτω δὲ ἄνθρωπος ἑαυτὸν καὶ
Master. Let prove but man himself and

3779   1537 02 740   2068   2532 1537 010 4221
οὕτως ἐκ τοῦ ἄρτου ἐσθιέτω καὶ ἐκ τοῦ ποτηρίου
thusly from the bread let eat and from the cup

4095 **29** 01 1063 2068 2532 4095   2917
πινέτω· ὁ γὰρ ἐσθίων καὶ πίνων κρίμα
let drink; the for eating and drinking judgment

1438   2068   2532 4095   3361 1252
ἑαυτῷ ἐσθίει καὶ πίνει μὴ διακρίνων
to himself eats and drinks not judging thoroughly

012 4983 **30** 1223 3778 1722 1473 4183 772   2532
τὸ σῶμα. διὰ τοῦτο ἐν ὑμῖν πολλοὶ ἀσθενεῖς καὶ
the body. Because this in you many weak and

732   2532 2837   2425 **31** 1487 1161
ἄρρωστοι καὶ κοιμῶνται ἱκανοί. εἰ δὲ
feeble and fall asleep enough. If but

1438   1252   3756 302
ἑαυτοὺς διεκρίνομεν, οὐκ ἂν
ourselves we judged thoroughly, not -

2919 **32** 2919   1161 5259 02
ἐκρινόμεθα· κρινόμενοι δὲ ὑπὸ [τοῦ]
we would be judged; being judged but by the

2962 3811   2443 3361
κυρίου παιδευόμεθα, ἵνα μὴ
Master we are being instructed as a child, that not

4862 03 2889 2632 **33** 5620
σὺν τῷ κόσμῳ κατακριθῶμεν. Ὥστε,
with the world we might be condemned. So that,

80   1473 4905   1519 012 3588
ἀδελφοί μου, συνερχόμενοι εἰς τὸ φαγεῖν
brothers of me, coming together for the to eat

240   1551 **34** 1487 5100 3983   1722
ἀλλήλους ἐκδέχεσθε. εἰ τις πεινᾷ, ἐν
one another wait for. If some hungers, in

3624 2068   2443 3361 1519 2917   4905
οἴκῳ ἐσθιέτω, ἵνα μὴ εἰς κρίμα συνέρχησθε.
house let eat, that not for judgment you might come
                                        together.

024 1161 3062   5613 302 2064   1299
τὰ δὲ λοιπὰ ὡς ἂν ἔλθω διατάξομαι.
The but remaining as - I might come I will direct.

12:1 4012 1161 022 4152   80   3756 2309
Περὶ δὲ τῶν πνευματικῶν, ἀδελφοί, οὐ θέλω
Concerning but the spiritual, brothers, not I want

1473 50 **2** 3609a 3754 3753 1484   1510
ὑμᾶς ἀγνοεῖν. Οἴδατε ὅτι ὅτε ἔθνη ἦτε
you to not know. You know that when nations you were

4314 024 1497 024 880   5613 302 71
πρὸς τὰ εἴδωλα τὰ ἄφωνα ὡς ἂν ἤγεσθε
to the idols the soundless as - you were led

520   1352 **3** 1107   1473 3754
ἀπαγόμενοι. διὸ γνωρίζω ὑμῖν ὅτι
being led off. Therefore I make known to you that

3762 1722 4151   2316 2980   3004 331
οὐδεὶς ἐν πνεύματι θεοῦ λαλῶν λέγει· Ἀνάθεμα
no one in spirit of God speaking says, curse

you proclaim the Lord's death until he comes.

27 Whoever, therefore, eats the bread or drinks the cup of the Lord in an unworthy manner will be answerable for the body and blood of the Lord. 28Examine yourselves, and only then eat of the bread and drink of the cup. 29For all who eat and drink[a] without discerning the body,[b] eat and drink judgment against themselves. 30For this reason many of you are weak and ill, and some have died.[c] 31But if we judged ourselves, we would not be judged. 32But when we are judged by the Lord, we are disciplined[d] so that we may not be condemned along with the world.

33 So then, my brothers and sisters,[e] when you come together to eat, wait for one another. 34If you are hungry, eat at home, so that when you come together, it will not be for your condemnation. About the other things I will give instructions when I come.

CHAPTER 12

Now concerning spiritual gifts,[f] brothers and sisters,[e] I do not want you to be uninformed. 2You know that when you were pagans, you were enticed and led astray to idols that could not speak. 3Therefore I want you to understand that no one speaking by the Spirit of God ever says

---

a Other ancient authorities add
  in an unworthy manner,
b Other ancient authorities read
  the Lord's body
c Gk fallen asleep
d Or When we are judged, we are
  being disciplined by the Lord
e Gk brothers
f Or spiritual persons

"Let Jesus be cursed!" and no one can say "Jesus is Lord" except by the Holy Spirit.

4 Now there are varieties of gifts, but the same Spirit; 5and there are varieties of services, but the same Lord; 6and there are varieties of activities, but it is the same God who activates all of them in everyone. 7To each is given the manifestation of the Spirit for the common good. 8To one is given through the Spirit the utterance of wisdom, and to another the utterance of knowledge according to the same Spirit, 9to another faith by the same Spirit, to another gifts of healing by the one Spirit, 10to another the working of miracles, to another prophecy, to another the discernment of spirits, to another various kinds of tongues, to another the interpretation of tongues. 11All these are activated by one and the same Spirit, who allots to each one individually just as the Spirit chooses.

12 For just as the body is one and has many members, and all the members of the body, though many, are one body, so it is with Christ. 13For in the one Spirit we were all baptized into one body—Jews

| 2424 | 2532 | 3762 | 1410 | 3004 | 2962 | 2424 |
Ἰησοῦς, καὶ οὐδεὶς δύναται εἰπεῖν· Κύριος Ἰησοῦς,
Jesus, and no one is able to say, Master Jesus,

1487 3361 1722 4151 40 ₄ 1243
εἰ μὴ ἐν πνεύματι ἁγίῳ. ⁴ Διαιρέσεις
except in spirit holy. Different selections

1161 5486 1510 09 1161 846 4151
δὲ χαρισμάτων εἰσίν, τὸ δὲ αὐτὸ πνεῦμα·
but of favor gifts there are, the but same spirit.

₅ 2532 1243 1248 1510 2532
καὶ διαιρέσεις διακονιῶν εἰσιν, καὶ
And different selections of services there are, and

01 846 2962 ₆ 2532 1243 1755
ὁ αὐτὸς κύριος· ⁶ καὶ διαιρέσεις ἐνεργημάτων
the same Master, and different of operations selections

1510 01 1161 846 2316 01 1754 024 3956
εἰσίν, ὁ δὲ αὐτὸς Θεὸς ὁ ἐνεργῶν τὰ πάντα
there are, the but same God the operating the all

1722 3956 ₇ 1538 1161 1325 05 5321
ἐν πᾶσιν. ⁷ ἑκάστῳ δὲ δίδοται ἡ φανέρωσις
in all. To each but is given the demonstration

010 4151 4314 012 4851 ₈ 3739 3303 1063
τοῦ πνεύματος πρὸς τὸ συμφέρον ⁸ ᾧ μὲν γὰρ
of the spirit to the advantage to whom indeed for

1223 010 4151 1325 3056 4678
διὰ τοῦ πνεύματος δίδοται λόγος σοφίας,
through the spirit is given word of wisdom,

243 1161 3056 1108 2596 012 846
ἄλλῳ δὲ λόγος γνώσεως κατὰ τὸ αὐτὸ
to other but word of knowledge by the same

4151 ₉ 2087 4102 1722 011 846 4151
πνεῦμα, ⁹ ἑτέρῳ πίστις ἐν τῷ αὐτῷ πνεύματι,
spirit, to other trust in the same spirit,

243 1161 5486 2386 1722 011 1520
ἄλλῳ δὲ χαρίσματα ἰαμάτων ἐν τῷ ἑνὶ
to other but favor gifts of cures in the one

4151 10 243 1161 1755 1411
πνεύματι, ¹⁰ ἄλλῳ δὲ ἐνεργήματα δυνάμεων,
spirit, to other but operations of powers,

243 1161 4394 243 1161
ἄλλῳ [δὲ] προφητεία, ἄλλῳ [δὲ]
to other but speaking before, to other but

1253 4151 2087 1085
διακρίσεις πνευμάτων, ἑτέρῳ γένη
differentiations of spirits, to other kinds

1100 243 1161 2058 1100
γλωσσῶν, ἄλλῳ δὲ ἑρμηνεία γλωσσῶν·
of tongues, to other but interpretation of tongues;

11 3956 1161 3778 1754 09 1520 2532 09 846
¹¹ πάντα δὲ ταῦτα ἐνεργεῖ τὸ ἓν καὶ τὸ αὐτὸ
all but these operate the one and the same

4151 1244 2398 1538 2531 1014
πνεῦμα διαιροῦν ἰδίᾳ ἑκάστῳ καθὼς βούλεται.
spirit dividing own each just as it plans.

12 2509 1063 09 4983 1510 1510 2532
¹² Καθάπερ γὰρ τὸ σῶμα ἕν ἐστιν καὶ
Just as indeed for the body one is and

3196 4183 2192 3956 1161 021 3196 010
μέλη πολλὰ ἔχει, πάντα δὲ τὰ μέλη τοῦ
members many it has, all but the members of the

4983 4183 1510 1520 1510 4983 3779 2532 01
σώματος πολλὰ ὄντα ἕν ἐστιν σῶμα, οὕτως καὶ ὁ
body many being one is body, thusly also the

5547 13 2532 1063 1722 1520 4151 1473 3956
Χριστός. ¹³ καὶ γὰρ ἐν ἑνὶ πνεύματι ἡμεῖς πάντες
Christ; also for in one spirit we all

1519 1520 4983 907 1535 2453
εἰς ἓν σῶμα ἐβαπτίσθημεν, εἴτε Ἰουδαῖοι
into one body were immersed, whether Judeans

1535	1672	1535	1401	1535	1658	2532
εἴτε	Ἕλληνες	εἴτε	δοῦλοι	εἴτε	ἐλεύθεροι,	καὶ
whether	Greeks	whether	slaves	whether	free ones,	and

3956	1520	4151	4222		2532	1063	09
πάντες	ἓν	πνεῦμα	ἐποτίσθημεν.	**14**	Καὶ	γὰρ	τὸ
all	one	spirit	were made to drink.		Also	for	the

4983	3756	1510	1520	3196	235	4183		1437
σῶμα	οὐκ	ἔστιν	ἓν	μέλος	ἀλλὰ	πολλά.	**15**	ἐὰν
body	not	is	one	member	but	many.		If

3004	01	4228	3754	3756	1510	5495	3756	1510
εἴπῃ	ὁ	πούς·	ὅτι	οὐκ	εἰμὶ	χείρ,	οὐκ	εἰμὶ
might say	the	foot;	because	not	I am	hand,	not	I am

1537	010	4983	3756	3844	3778	3756	1510	1537
ἐκ	τοῦ	σώματος,	οὐ	παρὰ	τοῦτο	οὐκ	ἔστιν	ἐκ
from	the	body;	not	along	this	not	it is	from

010	4983		2532	1437	3004	09	3775	3754
τοῦ	σώματος;	**16**	καὶ	ἐὰν	εἴπῃ	τὸ	οὖς·	ὅτι
the	body?		And	if	might say	the	ear;	because

3756	1510	3788		3756	1510	1537	010	4983		3756
οὐκ	εἰμὶ	ὀφθαλμός,		οὐκ	εἰμὶ	ἐκ	τοῦ	σώματος,		οὐ
not	I am	eye,		not	I am	from	the	body,		not

3844	3778	3756	1510	1537	010	4983		1487	3650
παρὰ	τοῦτο	οὐκ	ἔστιν	ἐκ	τοῦ	σώματος;	**17**	εἰ	ὅλον
along	this	not	it is	from	the	body?		If	whole

09	4983	3788		4226	05	189		1487	3650
τὸ	σῶμα	ὀφθαλμός,		ποῦ	ἡ	ἀκοή;		εἰ	ὅλον
the	body	eye,		where	the	hearing?		If	whole

189		4226	05	3750		3570	1161	01	2316
ἀκοή,		ποῦ	ἡ	ὄσφρησις;	**18**	νυνὶ	δὲ	ὁ	θεὸς
hearing,		where	the	smelling?		Now	but	the	God

5087	024	3196		1520	1538	846		1722	011
ἔθετο	τὰ	μέλη,		ἓν	ἕκαστον	αὐτῶν		ἐν	τῷ
set	the	members,		one	each	of them		in	the

4983	2531	2309		1487	1161	1510	021	3956
σώματι	καθὼς	ἠθέλησεν.	**19**	εἰ	δὲ	ἦν	τὰ	πάντα
body	just as	he wanted.		If	but	was	the	all

1520	3196		4226	09	4983		3568	1161	4183	3303
ἓν	μέλος,		ποῦ	τὸ	σῶμα;	**20**	νῦν	δὲ	πολλὰ	μὲν
one	member,		where	the	body?		Now	but	many	indeed

3196		1520	1161	4983		3756	1410		1161	01
μέλη,		ἓν	δὲ	σῶμα.	**21**	οὐ	δύναται	δὲ	ὁ
members,		one	but	body.		Not	is able	but	the

3788	3004	07		5495	5532	1473	3756	2192
ὀφθαλμὸς	εἰπεῖν	τῇ		χειρί·	χρείαν	σου	οὐκ	ἔχω,
eye	to say	to the		hand,	need	of you	not	I have,

2228	3825	05	2776	015	4228	5532	1473	3756
ἢ	πάλιν	ἡ	κεφαλὴ	τοῖς	ποσίν·	χρείαν	ὑμῶν	οὐκ
or	again	the	head	to the	feet,	need	of you	not

2192		235	4183	3123	021	1380	3196	010
ἔχω·	**22**	ἀλλὰ	πολλῷ	μᾶλλον	τὰ	δοκοῦντα	μέλη	τοῦ
I have;		but	much	more	the	thinking	members	of the

4983	772		5225	316		1510	010		2532
σώματος	ἀσθενέστερα	ὑπάρχειν	ἀναγκαῖά	ἐστιν,	**23**	καὶ
body	weaker ones	to exist	necessary	it is,		and

3739	1380	820		1510	010	4983
ἃ	δοκοῦμεν	ἀτιμότερα		εἶναι	τοῦ	σώματος
what	we think	more dishonorable		to be	of the	body

3778	5092	4055	4060	2532	021
τούτοις	τιμὴν	περισσοτέραν	περιτίθεμεν,	καὶ	τὰ
to these	value	more excessive	we set around,	and	the

809	1473	2157	4055	2192
ἀσχήμονα	ἡμῶν	εὐσχημοσύνην	περισσοτέραν	ἔχει.
shameful	of us	appropriateness	more excessive	has,

	021	1161	2158	1473	3756	5532	2192	235
24	τὰ	δὲ	εὐσχήμονα	ἡμῶν	οὐ	χρείαν	ἔχει.	ἀλλὰ
	the	but	proper	of us	not	need	has.	But

01	2316	4786	012	4983	011	5302
ὁ	θεὸς	συνεκέρασεν	τὸ	σῶμα	τῷ	ὑστερουμένῳ
the	God	mixed together	the	body	to the	lacking one

or Greeks, slaves or free—and we were all made to drink of one Spirit.

14 Indeed, the body does not consist of one member but of many. 15 If the foot would say, "Because I am not a hand, I do not belong to the body," that would not make it any less a part of the body. 16 And if the ear would say, "Because I am not an eye, I do not belong to the body," that would not make it any less a part of the body. 17 If the whole body were an eye, where would the hearing be? If the whole body were hearing, where would the sense of smell be? 18 But as it is, God arranged the members in the body, each one of them, as he chose. 19 If all were a single member, where would the body be? 20 As it is, there are many members, yet one body. 21 The eye cannot say to the hand, "I have no need of you," nor again the head to the feet, "I have no need of you." 22 On the contrary, the members of the body that seem to be weaker are indispensable, 23 and those members of the body that we think less honorable we clothe with greater honor, and our less respectable members are treated with greater respect; 24 whereas our more respectable members do not need this. But God has so arranged the body, giving the greater honor to the inferior member,

²⁵that there may be no dissension within the body, but the members may have the same care for one another. ²⁶If one member suffers, all suffer together with it; if one member is honored, all rejoice together with it.

27 Now you are the body of Christ and individually members of it. ²⁸And God has appointed in the church first apostles, second prophets, third teachers; then deeds of power, then gifts of healing, forms of assistance, forms of leadership, various kinds of tongues. ²⁹Are all apostles? Are all prophets? Are all teachers? Do all work miracles? ³⁰Do all possess gifts of healing? Do all speak in tongues? Do all interpret? ³¹But strive for the greater gifts. And I will show you a still more excellent way.

CHAPTER 13

If I speak in the tongues of mortals and of angels, but do not have love, I am a noisy gong or a clanging cymbal. ²And if I have prophetic powers, and understand all mysteries and all knowledge, and if I have all faith,

4055	1325	5092	**25**	2443 3361	1510	4978
περισσοτέραν	δοὺς	τιμήν,		ἵνα μὴ	ᾖ	σχίσμα
more excessive	having	value,		that not	might	split
	given				be	

1722	011	4983	235	012 846	5228	240
ἐν	τῷ	σώματι	ἀλλὰ	τὸ αὐτὸ	ὑπὲρ	ἀλλήλων
in	the	body	but	the same	on behalf of	one another

3309		021 3196	**26**	2532 1535	3958
μεριμνῶσιν		τὰ μέλη.		καὶ εἴτε	πάσχει
might be anxious		the members.		And whether	suffers

1520 3196	4841	3956 021 3196
ἓν μέλος,	συμπάσχει	πάντα τὰ μέλη·
one member,	suffer together	all the members;

1535	1392	1520 3196	4796
εἴτε	δοξάζεται	[ἓν] μέλος,	συγχαίρει
whether	is given splendor	one member,	rejoice together

3956 021 3196	**27**	1473 1161 1510 4983 5547	2532
πάντα τὰ μέλη.		Ὑμεῖς δέ ἐστε σῶμα Χριστοῦ	καὶ
all the members.		You but are body of Christ	and

3196	1537 3313	**28**	2532 3739 3303	5087 01 1830
μέλη	ἐκ μέρους.		Καὶ οὓς μὲν	ἔθετο ὁ θεὸς
members	from part.		And whom indeed	set the God

1722 07	1577	4413	652	1208
ἐν τῇ	ἐκκλησίᾳ	πρῶτον ἀποστόλους,	δεύτερον
in the	assembly	first delegates,	second

4396	5154	1320	1899 1411	1899
προφήτας,	τρίτον	διδασκάλους,	ἔπειτα δυνάμεις,	ἔπειτα
spokesmen,	third	teachers,	then powers,	then

5486	2386	484	2941
χαρίσματα	ἰαμάτων,	ἀντιλήμψεις,	κυβερνήσεις,
favor gifts	of cures,	assistances,	administrations,

1085	1100	**29**	3361 3956	652	3361 3956
γένη	γλωσσῶν.		μὴ πάντες	ἀπόστολοι;	μὴ πάντες
kinds	of tongues.		Not all	delegates?	Not all

4396	3361 3956	1320	3361 3956
προφῆται;	μὴ πάντες	διδάσκαλοι;	μὴ πάντες
spokesmen?	Not all	teachers?	Not all

1411	**30**	3361 3956	5406	2192	2386
δυνάμεις;		μὴ πάντες	χαρίσματα	ἔχουσιν	ἰαμάτων;
powers?		Not all	favor gifts	have	of cures?

3361 3956	1100	2980	3361 3956
μὴ πάντες	γλώσσαις	λαλοῦσιν;	μὴ πάντες
Not all	in tongues	speak?	Not all

1329	**31**	2206	1161 024 5486
διερμηνεύουσιν;		ζηλοῦτε	δὲ τὰ χαρίσματα
translate completely?		Be jealous	but the favor gifts

024 3173	2532 2089	2596 5236	3598 1473
τὰ μείζονα.	Καὶ ἔτι	καθ' ὑπερβολὴν	ὁδὸν ὑμῖν
the greater.	And still	by excess	way to you

1166	**13:1**	1437 019	1100	014	444
δείκνυμι.		Ἐὰν ταῖς	γλώσσαις	τῶν	ἀνθρώπων
I show.		If in the	tongues	of the	men

2980	2532 014	32	26	1161 3361
λαλῶ	καὶ τῶν	ἀγγέλων,	ἀγάπην	δὲ μὴ
I might speak	and of the	messengers,	love	but not

2192	1096	5475 2278	2228
ἔχω,	γέγονα	χαλκὸς ἠχῶν	ἢ
I might have,	I have become	copper resounding	or

2950	214	**2**	2532 1437 2192	4394	2532
κύμβαλον	ἀλαλάζον.		καὶ ἐὰν ἔχω	προφητείαν	καὶ
cymbal	wailing.		And if I might	speaking	and
				have before	

3609a	024 3466	3956 2532 3956 08
εἰδῶ	τὰ μυστήρια	πάντα καὶ πᾶσαν τὴν
I might have known	the mysteries	all and all the

1108	2532 1437 2192	3956 08 4102
γνῶσιν	καὶ ἐὰν ἔχω	πᾶσαν τὴν πίστιν
knowledge	and if I might have	all the trust

```
5620      3735    3179                        26       1161  3361
ὥστε      ὄρη     μεθιστάναι,          ἀγάπην δὲ    μὴ
so that hills to be transferred, love      but   not
2192           3762    1510   3  2579     5595
ἔχω,           οὐθέν  εἰμι.       κἂν     ψωμίσω
I might have, nothing I am.  And if I might dole out
3956   024  5225            1473   2532 1437 3860
πάντα  τὰ  ὑπάρχοντά  μου   καὶ ἐὰν  παραδῶ
all    the possessions of me, and if I might give over
012  4983   1473  2443  2744              26      1161 3361
τὸ  σῶμά  μου  ἵνα  καυχήσωμαι,  ἀγάπην δὲ   μὴ
the body of me that I might brag,  love     but   not
2192          3762   5623           05  26        3114
ἔχω,          οὐδὲν ὠφελοῦμαι.  4  Ἡ  ἀγάπη μακροθυμεῖ,
I might nothing I might be    The love  is long-
have,         benefitted.               tempered,
5541          05  26       3756 2206       05  26        3756
χρηστεύεται ἡ  ἀγάπη, οὐ ζηλοῖ,  [ἡ  ἀγάπη] οὐ
is kind      the love,  not is jealous, the love   not
4068            3756 5448          5  3756
περπερεύεται,    οὐ  φυσιοῦται,      οὐκ
puts itself forward, not is puffed up, not
807          3756 2212    024 1438         3756
ἀσχημονεῖ,   οὐ  ζητεῖ  τὰ ἑαυτῆς,    οὐ
it is shameful, not it seeks the of itself, not
3947         3756 3049     012 2556   6  3756
παροξύνεται, οὐ  λογίζεται τὸ κακόν,    οὐ
it is provoked, not it reasons the bad,    not
5463       1909 07  93        4796        1161
χαίρει     ἐπὶ τῇ ἀδικίᾳ, συγχαίρει   δὲ
it rejoices on the unright, it rejoices together but
07   225      7  3956 4722      3956 4100
τῇ  ἀληθείᾳ·    πάντα στέγει,  πάντα πιστεύει,
in the truth;  all   it endures, all   it trusts,
3956 1679      3956 5278     8  05  26
πάντα ἐλπίζει, πάντα ὑπομένει.   Ἡ  ἀγάπη
all  it hopes, all  it endures. The love
3763        4098     1535    1161 4394
οὐδέποτε  πίπτει· εἴτε  δὲ  προφητεῖαι,
but not ever falls; whether but speaking before,
2673            1535   1100   3973
καταργηθήσονται· εἴτε  γλῶσσαι, παύσονται
they will be   whether tongues, they will stop
abolished               themselves
1535     1108    2673              9  1537 3313
εἴτε    γνῶσις, καταργηθήσεται.    ἐκ  μέρους
whether knowledge, it will be abolished. From part
1063 1097    2532 1537 3313  4395         10  3752
γὰρ γινώσκομεν καὶ ἐκ μέρους προφητεύομεν·  ὅταν
for we know   and from part we speak before; when
1161 2064    09  5046     09  1537 3313
δὲ  ἔλθῃ    τὸ τέλειον, τὸ ἐκ μέρους
but might come the complete, the from part
2673           11 3753 1510  3516    2980
καταργηθήσεται.   ὅτε ἤμην νήπιος, ἐλάλουν
will be abolished. When I was infant, I was speaking
5613 3516  5426     5613 3516   3049     5613
ὡς  νήπιος, ἐφρόνουν ὡς νήπιος, ἐλογιζόμην ὡς
as infant, I was   as infant, I was    as
            thinking            reasoning
3516  3753 1096  435  2673     024        02
νήπιος· ὅτε γέγονα ἀνήρ, κατήργηκα τὰ    τοῦ
infant; when I have man, I have  the things of the
            become        abolished
3516     12  991      1063 737 1223   2072      1722
νηπίου.   βλέπομεν γὰρ ἄρτι δι᾽ ἐσόπτρου ἐν
infant.   We look for now through mirror  in
135           5119 1161 4383      4314 4383       737
αἰνίγματι, τότε δὲ  πρόσωπον πρὸς πρόσωπον· ἄρτι
riddle,    then but face    toward face;    now
```

so as to remove mountains, but do not have love, I am nothing. [3]If I give away all my possessions, and if I hand over my body so that I may boast,[a] but do not have love, I gain nothing.

4 Love is patient; love is kind; love is not envious or boastful or arrogant [5]or rude. It does not insist on its own way; it is not irritable or resentful; [6]it does not rejoice in wrongdoing, but rejoices in the truth. [7]It bears all things, believes all things, hopes all things, endures all things.

8 Love never ends. But as for prophecies, they will come to an end; as for tongues, they will cease; as for knowledge, it will come to an end. [9]For we know only in part, and we prophesy only in part; [10]but when the complete comes, the partial will come to an end. [11]When I was a child, I spoke like a child, I thought like a child, I reasoned like a child; when I became an adult, I put an end to childish ways. [12]For now we see in a mirror, dimly,[b] but then we will see face to face. Now

a Other ancient authorities read *body to be burned*
b Gk *in a riddle*

I know only in part; then I will know fully, even as I have been fully known. [13]And now faith, hope, and love abide, these three; and the greatest of these is love.

CHAPTER 14

Pursue love and strive for the spiritual gifts, and especially that you may prophesy. [2]For those who speak in a tongue do not speak to other people but to God; for nobody understands them, since they are speaking mysteries in the Spirit. [3]On the other hand, those who prophesy speak to other people for their upbuilding and encouragement and consolation. [4]Those who speak in a tongue build up themselves, but those who prophesy build up the church. [5]Now I would like all of you to speak in tongues, but even more to prophesy. One who prophesies is greater than one who speaks in tongues, unless someone interprets, so that the church may be built up.

6 Now, brothers and sisters,[a] if I come to you speaking in tongues, how will I benefit you unless I speak to you in some revelation or knowledge or prophecy or teaching? [7]It is the same way with lifeless instruments that produce sound, such as the flute or the harp. If they do not give distinct notes, how

---

[a] Gk *brothers*

1097	1537	3313		5119	1161	1921		2531
γινώσκω	ἐκ	μέρους,	τότε	δὲ		ἐπιγνώσομαι		καθὼς
I know	from	part,	then	but		I will perceive		just as

2532	1921			3570	1161	3306	4102	1680
καὶ	ἐπεγνώσθην.	**13**	Νυνὶ	δὲ		μένει	πίστις,	ἐλπίς,
also I	was perceived.		Now	but		stays	trust,	hope,

26	021	5140	3778		3173	1161	3778	05
ἀγάπη,	τὰ	τρία	ταῦτα·	μείζων		δὲ	τούτων	ἡ
love,	the	three	these;	greater		but	of these	the

26		1377	08	26		2206		1161 024
ἀγάπη.	**14:1**	Διώκετε	τὴν	ἀγάπην,	ζηλοῦτε		δὲ	τὰ
love.		Pursue	the	love,	be jealous		but	the

4152		3123	1161	2443	4395
πνευματικά,	μᾶλλον	δὲ		ἵνα	προφητεύητε.
spiritual,	more	but		that	you might speak before.

2	01	1063	2980		1100		3756	444		2980
	ὁ	γὰρ	λαλῶν		γλώσσῃ		οὐκ	ἀνθρώποις		λαλεῖ
	The	for	one speaking		in tongue		not	to men		speaks

235	2316		3762	1063	191		4151		1161
ἀλλὰ	θεῷ.		οὐδεὶς	γὰρ	ἀκούει,		πνεύματι		δὲ
but	to God;		no one	for	hears,		in spirit		but

2980		3466		**3**	01	1161	4395
λαλεῖ	μυστήρια·				ὁ	δὲ	προφητεύων
he speaks	in mysteries;				the	but	one speaking before

444		2980	3619		2532	3874		2532
ἀνθρώποις	λαλεῖ		οἰκοδομὴν	καὶ		παράκλησιν		καὶ
to men	speaks		building	and		encouragement		and

3889		**4**	01	2980		1100		1438	3618
παραμυθίαν.			ὁ	λαλῶν		γλώσσῃ		ἑαυτὸν	οἰκοδομεῖ·
comfort.			The	speaking		in tongue		himself	builds;

01	1161	4395			1577		3618
ὁ	δὲ	προφητεύων			ἐκκλησίαν		οἰκοδομεῖ.
the	but	one speaking before			assembly		builds.

5	2309	1161	3956	1473	3980		1100		3123
	θέλω	δὲ	πάντας	ὑμᾶς	λαλεῖν		γλώσσαις,		μᾶλλον
	I want	but	all	you	to speak		in tongues,		more

1161	2443	4395			3173		1161	01
δὲ	ἵνα	προφητεύητε·			μείζων		δὲ	ὁ
but	that	you might speak before;			greater		but	the one

4395		2228	01	2980		1100
προφητεύων		ἢ	ὁ	λαλῶν		γλώσσαις
speaking before		or	the one	speaking		in tongues

1622	1487	3361	1329		2443	05	1577
ἐκτὸς	εἰ	μὴ	διερμηνεύῃ,		ἵνα	ἡ	ἐκκλησία
outside	except		he might translate		that	the	assembly
							completely,

3619		2983		**6**	3568	1161	80		1437
οἰκοδομὴν	λάβῃ.				Νῦν	δέ,	ἀδελφοί,		ἐὰν
building	might receive.				Now	but,	brothers,		if

2064		4314	1473	1100		2980		5101
ἔλθω		πρὸς	ὑμᾶς	γλώσσαις		λαλῶν,		τί
I might come		toward	you	in tongues		speaking,		what

1473	5623		1437	3361	1473		2980		2228
ὑμᾶς	ὠφελήσω		ἐὰν	μὴ	ὑμῖν		λαλήσω		ἢ
you	will I benefit		except		to you		I might speak		or

1722	602		2228	1722	1108		2228	1722
ἐν	ἀποκαλύψει		ἢ	ἐν	γνώσει		ἢ	ἐν
in	uncovering		or	in	knowledge		or	in

4394		2228	1722	1322		**7**	3676		021
προφητείᾳ		ἢ	[ἐν]	διδαχῇ;			ὅμως		τὰ
speaking before		or	in	teaching?			Likewise		the

895		5456	1325		1535	836		1535	2788
ἄψυχα		φωνὴν	διδόντα,		εἴτε		αὐλὸς εἴτε		κιθάρα,
unsouled		sound	giving,		whether		flute whether		harp,

1437	1293		015		5353	3361	1325		4459
ἐὰν	διαστολὴν		τοῖς		φθόγγοις	μὴ	δῷ,		πῶς
if	difference		to the		sounds	not	it might give,		how

```
1097            09    832           2228 09   2789
γνωσθήσεται    τὸ   αὐλούμενον   ἢ   τὸ   κιθαριζόμενον;
will it be     the   being played  or   the   being played on
known                on flute                 harp?

  2532 1063 1437 82      4536      5456   1325              5101
8 καὶ  γὰρ  ἐὰν ἄδηλον σάλπιγξ φωνὴν δῷ,              τίς
  Also for  if  unclear trumpet  sound might give,    who

3903              1519 4171       3779    2532 1473
παρασκευάσεται εἰς  πόλεμον;  9 οὕτως  καὶ  ὑμεῖς
will prepare    for  war?        Thusly also you
themselves

1223      06    1100    1437 3361  2154           3056
διὰ   τῆς γλώσσης ἐὰν μὴ  εὔσημον       λόγον
through the tongue  except  well-defined word

1325         4459 1097               09  2980
δῶτε,     πῶς γνωσθήσεται      τὸ λαλούμενον;
might give,  how  will it be known  the being spoken?

1510          1063 1519 109   2980                5118    1487
ἔσεσθε     γὰρ εἰς ἀέρα λαλοῦντες. 10 τοσαῦτα εἰ
You will be+ for  into air +speaking.     So many if

5177         1085 5456        1510     1722 2889
τύχοι     γένη φωνῶν   εἰσιν  ἐν  κόσμῳ
it may obtain kinds of sounds there are in   world

2532 3762    880          1437 3767 3361 3609a
καὶ οὐδὲν ἄφωνον· 11 ἐὰν οὖν μὴ  εἰδῶ
and nothing soundless;   if   then not  I might know

08  1411    06   5456    1510      03    2980
τὴν δύναμιν τῆς φωνῆς, ἔσομαι τῷ     λαλοῦντι
the power of the sound, I will be to the one speaking

915        2532 01    2980        1722 1473 915
βάρβαρος καὶ ὁ    λαλῶν  ἐν ἐμοὶ βάρβαρος.
barbarian and the one speaking in   me barbarian.

   3779    2532 1473 1893  2207      1510    4151
12 οὕτως  καὶ ὑμεῖς ἐπεὶ ζηλωταί ἐστε  πνευμάτων,
   Thusly also you  since jealous you are of spirits,

4314 08  3619      06    1577      2212    2443
πρὸς τὴν οἰκοδομὴν τῆς  ἐκκλησίας ζητεῖτε ἵνα
to   the building of the assembly seek   that

4052              1352  01  2980          1100
περισσεύητε. 13 Διὸ  ὁ   λαλῶν    γλώσσῃ
you might exceed. Therefore the one speaking in tongue

4336         2443 1329      1437 1063 4336
προσευχέσθω ἵνα διερμηνεύῃ. 14 ἐὰν [γὰρ] προσεύχωμαι
let pray     that he might   If   for  I might pray
             completely translate.

1100        09   4151    1473 4336      01  1161 3563
γλώσσῃ,   τὸ πνεῦμά μου προσεύχεται, ὁ δὲ νοῦς
in tongue, the spirit of me prays,      the but mind

1473 175      1510  15 5101 3767 1510      4336
μου ἄκαρπός ἐστιν. 15 τί  οὖν ἐστιν; προσεύξομαι
of me fruitless is.    What then is it? I will pray

011    4151      4336        1161 2532 03   3563
τῷ   πνεύματι, προσεύξομαι δὲ καὶ τῷ   νοΐ·
in the spirit,  I will pray  but also in the mind;

5567      011    4151       5567         1161 2532
ψαλῶ    τῷ   πνεύματι, ψαλῶ      δὲ καὶ
I will psalm the spirit,  I will psalm but also

03    3563 16 1893  1437 2127
τῷ   νοΐ. 16 ἐπεὶ ἐὰν εὐλογῇς
in the mind. Since if  you might speak well

1722 4151     01  378      04  5117 02
[ἐν] πνεύματι, ὁ ἀναπληρῶν τὸν τόπον τοῦ
in spirit,   the filling up the place of the

2399       4459 3004    012 281  1909 07  4674
ἰδιώτου πῶς ἐρεῖ    τὸ ἀμὴν ἐπὶ τῇ σῇ
unlearned how will he say the amen on the your

2169       1894  5101 3004   3756 3609a  17 1473
εὐχαριστίᾳ; ἐπειδὴ τί λέγεις οὐκ οἶδεν· 17 σὺ
good favor? Since what you say not  he knew;  you
```

will anyone know what is being played? [8] And if the bugle gives an indistinct sound, who will get ready for battle? [9] So with yourselves; if in a tongue you utter speech that is not intelligible, how will anyone know what is being said? For you will be speaking into the air. [10] There are doubtless many different kinds of sounds in the world, and nothing is without sound. [11] If then I do not know the meaning of a sound, I will be a foreigner to the speaker and the speaker a foreigner to me. [12] So with yourselves; since you are eager for spiritual gifts, strive to excel in them for building up the church.

[13] Therefore, one who speaks in a tongue should pray for the power to interpret. [14] For if I pray in a tongue, my spirit prays but my mind is unproductive. [15] What should I do then? I will pray with the spirit, but I will pray with the mind also; I will sing praise with the spirit, but I will sing praise with the mind also. [16] Otherwise, if you say a blessing with the spirit, how can anyone in the position of an outsider say the "Amen" to your thanksgiving, since the outsider does not know what you are saying? [17] For you may give thanks

well enough, but the other person is not built up. ¹⁸I thank God that I speak in tongues more than all of you; ¹⁹nevertheless, in church I would rather speak five words with my mind, in order to instruct others also, than ten thousand words in a tongue.

20 Brothers and sisters,ᵃ do not be children in your thinking; rather, be infants in evil, but in thinking be adults. ²¹In the law it is written,

"By people of strange tongues
and by the lips of foreigners
I will speak to this people;
yet even then they will not listen to me,"

says the Lord. ²²Tongues, then, are a sign not for believers but for unbelievers, while prophecy is not for unbelievers but for believers. ²³If, therefore, the whole church comes together and all speak in tongues, and outsiders or unbelievers enter, will they not say that you are out of your mind? ²⁴But if all prophesy, an unbeliever or outsider who enters is reproved by all and called to account by all. ²⁵After the secrets of the unbeliever's heart are disclosed, that person will bow down before God and worship him,

---

ᵃ Gk brothers

3303	1063	2573	2168		235	01	2087	3756
μὲν	γὰρ	καλῶς	εὐχαριστεῖς		ἀλλ'	ὁ	ἕτερος	οὐκ
indeed	for	well	give good favor		but	the	other	not

3618		2168		03		2316	3956
οἰκοδομεῖται.	¹⁸	Εὐχαριστῶ		τῷ		θεῷ,	πάντων
is built.		I give good favor		to the		God,	of all

1473	3123	1100		2980		235	1722	1577
ὑμῶν	μᾶλλον	γλώσσαις	λαλῶ·		¹⁹	ἀλλὰ	ἐν	ἐκκλησίᾳ
of you more		in tongues	I speak;			but	in	assembly

2309	4002	3056	03		3563	1473	2980		2443
θέλω	πέντε	λόγους	τῷ		νοΐ	μου	λαλῆσαι,		ἵνα
I want	five	words	in the		mind	of me	to speak,		that

2532	243	2727		2228	3463		3056
καὶ	ἄλλους	κατηχήσω,		ἢ	μυρίους		λόγους
also	others	I might instruct,		or	ten thousand		words

1722	1100	80		3361	3813		1096
ἐν	γλώσσῃ.	²⁰	Ἀδελφοί,	μὴ	παιδία		γίνεσθε
in	tongue.		Brothers,	not	small children		become

019	5424		235	07		2549	3515
ταῖς	φρεσὶν		ἀλλὰ	τῇ		κακίᾳ	νηπιάζετε,
in the understandings		but	to the		badness	be infants,

019	1161	5424		5046	1096		1722
ταῖς	δὲ	φρεσὶν		τέλειοι	γίνεσθε.	²¹	ἐν
in the	but in	understandings		complete	become.		In

03	3551	1125		3754	1722	2084
τῷ	νόμῳ	γέγραπται		ὅτι	ἐν	ἑτερογλώσσοις
the	law	it has been written,		(")	in	other tongues

2532	1722	5491	2087		2980	03
καὶ	ἐν	χείλεσιν	ἑτέρων		λαλήσω	τῷ
and	in	lips	of others		I will speak	to the

2992	3778	2532	3761	3779	1522		1473
λαῷ	τούτῳ	καὶ	οὐδ'	οὕτως	εἰσακούσονταί		μου,
people	this	and	but not	thusly	they will hear		me,

3004	2962		5620	017	1100	1519	4592
λέγει	κύριος	²²	ὥστε	αἱ	γλῶσσαι	εἰς	σημεῖόν
says	Master.		So that	the	tongues	into	sign

1510	3756	015	4100		235	015	571
εἰσιν	οὐ	τοῖς	πιστεύουσιν		ἀλλὰ	τοῖς	ἀπίστοις,
are	not	to the	ones trusting		but	to the	untrustful,

05	1161	4394		3756	015	571	235
ἡ	δὲ	προφητεία		οὐ	τοῖς	ἀπίστοις	ἀλλὰ
the	but	speaking before		not	to the	untrustful	but

015	4100		1437	3767	4905
τοῖς	πιστεύουσιν.	²³	Ἐὰν	οὖν	συνέλθῃ
to the	ones trusting.		If	then	might come together

05	1577	3650	1909	012	846	2532	3956
ἡ	ἐκκλησία	ὅλη	ἐπὶ	τὸ	αὐτὸ	καὶ	πάντες
the	assembly	whole	on	the	same	and	all

2980	1100	1525		1161	2399
λαλῶσιν	γλώσσαις,	εἰσέλθωσιν		δὲ	ἰδιῶται
might speak	in tongues,	might come into		but	unlearned

2228	571		3756	3004	3754	3105
ἢ	ἄπιστοι,		οὐκ	ἐροῦσιν	ὅτι	μαίνεσθε;
or	untrustful,		not	will they say,	(")	are you crazy?

1437	1161	3956	4395		1525
²⁴	Ἐὰν	δὲ	πάντες	προφητεύωσιν,	εἰσέλθῃ
	If	but	all	might speak before,	might come in

1161	5100	571		2228	2399		1651
δέ	τις	ἄπιστος	ἢ	ἰδιώτης,		ἐλέγχεται
but	some	untrustful	or	unlearned,		he is rebuked

5259	3956	350		5259	3956		021	2927
ὑπὸ	πάντων,	ἀνακρίνεται		ὑπὸ	πάντων,	²⁵	τὰ	κρυπτὰ
by	all,	he is examined		by	all,		the	hidden

06	2588	846	5318	1096	2532	3779
τῆς	καρδίας	αὐτοῦ	φανερὰ	γίνεται,	καὶ	οὕτως
of the	heart	of him	evident	becomes,	and	thusly

4098	1909	4383	4352		03	2316
πεσὼν	ἐπὶ	πρόσωπον	προσκυνήσει		τῷ	θεῷ
falling	on	face	he will worship		the	God

518   3754 3689   01   2316 1722 1473   1510
ἀπαγγέλλων ὅτι ὄντως ὁ θεὸς ἐν ὑμῖν ἐστιν.
telling,   (") really the God in you   is.

5101 3767 1510   80   3752 4905
26 Τί   οὖν ἐστιν, ἀδελφοί; ὅταν συνέρχησθε,
What then is it, brothers? When you might come
                                            together

1538   5568   2192 1322   2192   602   2192
ἕκαστος ψαλμὸν ἔχει, διδαχὴν ἔχει, ἀποκάλυψιν ἔχει,
each   psalm has, teaching has, uncovering has,

1100   2192 2058   2192   3956   4314
γλῶσσαν ἔχει, ἑρμηνείαν   ἔχει· πάντα πρὸς
tongue   has, interpretation has· all   to

3619   1096   **27** 1535   1100   5100 2980
οἰκοδομὴν γινέσθω.   εἴτε   γλώσσῃ τις λαλεῖ,
building let become.   Whether in tongue some speaks,

2596 1417 2228 012 4183   5140 2532 303 3313   2532
κατὰ δύο ἢ   τὸ πλεῖστον τρεῖς καὶ ἀνὰ μέρος, καὶ
by   two or the most   three and up part, and

1520 1329   **28** 1437 1161 3361
εἷς διερμηνευέτω·   ἐὰν δὲ   μὴ
one let translate completely; if   but not

1510   1328   4601   1722
ἢ   διερμηνευτής,   σιγάτω   ἐν
there might be thorough translator, let be silent in

1577   1438   1161 2980   2532 03   2316
ἐκκλησίᾳ, ἑαυτῷ   δὲ λαλείτω καὶ τῷ   θεῷ.
assembly, to himself but let speak and to the God.

4396   1161 1417 2228 1510   2980   2532 013
29 προφῆται δὲ   δύο ἢ   τρεῖς λαλείτωσαν καὶ οἱ
Spokesmen but   two or three let speak   and the

243   1252   **30** 1437 1161 243
ἄλλοι διακρινέτωσαν·   ἐὰν δὲ ἄλλῳ
others let judge thoroughly; if but to other

601   2521   01 4413   4601
ἀποκαλυφθῇ   καθημένῳ, ὁ πρῶτος σιγάτω.
it be uncovered sitting,   the first let be silent.

1410   1063 2596 1520 3956   4395
31 δύνασθε   γὰρ καθ᾽ ἕνα πάντες προφητεύειν,
You are able for   by one all to speak before,

2443 3956   3129   2532 3956   3870
ἵνα πάντες μανθάνωσιν καὶ πάντες παρακαλῶνται.
that all   might learn and all   might be encouraged.

2532 4151   4396   4396   5293
32 καὶ πνεύματα προφητῶν   προφήταις ὑποτάσσεται,
And spirits of spokesmen to spokesmen are subject,

3756 1063 1510   181   01   2316 235
33 οὐ   γὰρ ἐστιν ἀκαταστασίας ὁ   θεὸς ἀλλὰ
not for is of unstableness the God but

1515   5613 1722 3956   019 1577   014
εἰρήνης. Ὡς ἐν πάσαις ταῖς ἐκκλησίαις τῶν
of peace. As in all   the assemblies of the

40   017 1135   1722 019 1577
ἁγίων **34** αἱ γυναῖκες ἐν ταῖς ἐκκλησίαις
holy ones   the women   in the assemblies

4601   3756 1063 2010   846
σιγάτωσαν·   οὐ   γὰρ ἐπιτρέπεται   αὐταῖς
let be silent, not for it is allowed to them

2980   235 5293   2531   2532 01 3551
λαλεῖν, ἀλλὰ ὑποτασσέσθωσαν, καθὼς καὶ ὁ νόμος
to speak; but let be subject, just as also the law

3004   **35** 1487 1161 5100 3129   2309   1722 3624
λέγει.   εἰ   δὲ   τι μαθεῖν θέλουσιν, ἐν   οἴκῳ
says.   If but some to learn want,   in   house

016   2398 435   1905   150   1063 1510
τοὺς ἰδίους ἄνδρας ἐπερωτάτωσαν· αἰσχρὸν γάρ ἐστιν
the own   men   let ask on,   shame   for it is

1135   2980   1722 1577   **36** 2228 575 1473
γυναικὶ λαλεῖν ἐν ἐκκλησίᾳ.   ἢ   ἀφ᾽ ὑμῶν
to woman to speak in assembly.   Or from you

---

declaring, "God is really among you."

26 What should be done then, my friends?[a] When you come together, each one has a hymn, a lesson, a revelation, a tongue, or an interpretation. Let all things be done for building up. [27]If anyone speaks in a tongue, let there be only two or at most three, and each in turn; and let one interpret. [28]But if there is no one to interpret, let them be silent in church and speak to themselves and to God. [29]Let two or three prophets speak, and let the others weigh what is said. [30]If a revelation is made to someone else sitting nearby, let the first person be silent. [31]For you can all prophesy one by one, so that all may learn and all be encouraged. [32]And the spirits of prophets are subject to the prophets, [33]for God is a God not of disorder but of peace.

(As in all the churches of the saints, [34]women should be silent in the churches. For they are not permitted to speak, but should be subordinate, as the law also says. [35]If there is anything they desire to know, let them ask their husbands at home. For it is shameful for a woman to speak in church.[b] [36]Or did the word of God originate with you?

[a] Gk brothers
[b] Other ancient authorities put verses 34-35 after verse 40

Or are you the only ones it has reached?)

37 Anyone who claims to be a prophet, or to have spiritual powers, must acknowledge that what I am writing to you is a command of the Lord. 38 Anyone who does not recognize this is not to be recognized. 39 So, my friends,[a] be eager to prophesy, and do not forbid speaking in tongues; 40 but all things should be done decently and in order.

CHAPTER 15

Now I would remind you, brothers and sisters,[b] of the good news[c] that I proclaimed to you, which you in turn received, in which also you stand, 2 through which also you are being saved, if you hold firmly to the message that I proclaimed to you—unless you have come to believe in vain.

3 For I handed on to you as of first importance what I in turn had received: that Christ died for our sins in accordance with the scriptures, 4 and that he was buried, and that he was raised on the third day in accordance with the scriptures, 5 and that he appeared to Cephas, then to the twelve. 6 Then he appeared to more than five hundred brothers and sisters[b] at one time, most of whom are still alive, though some have died.[d] 7 Then he appeared to James, then to all the apostles. 8 Last of all, as to

01	3056	02		2316	1831		2228	1519	1473	3441
ὁ	λόγος	τοῦ		θεοῦ	ἐξῆλθεν,		ἢ	εἰς	ὑμᾶς	μόνους
the	word	of the		God	went out,		or	into	you	alone

2658		**37**	1487	5100	1380		4396		1510	2228
κατήντησεν;			Εἴ	τις	δοκεῖ		προφήτης		εἶναι	ἢ
arrived it?			If	some	thinks		spokesman		to be	or

4152		1921		3739	1125		1473	3754
πνευματικός,		ἐπιγινωσκέτω		ἃ	γράφω		ὑμῖν	ὅτι
spiritual,		let perceive		what	I write		to you	that

2962		1510	1785		**38**	1487	1161	5100	50
κυρίου		ἐστὶν	ἐντολή·			εἰ	δέ	τις	ἀγνοεῖ,
of Master		it is	command;			if	but	some	knows not,

50		**39**	5620		80		1473	2206
ἀγνοεῖται.			Ὥστε,		ἀδελφοί	[μου],		ζηλοῦτε
he is unknowing.			So that,		brothers	of me,		be jealous

012 4395			2532	012	2980		3361	2967
τὸ προφητεύειν			καὶ	τὸ	λαλεῖν		μὴ	κωλύετε
the to speak before			and	the	to speak		not	hinder

1100		**40**	3956	1161	2156		2532	2596	5010
γλώσσαις·			πάντα	δὲ	εὐσχημόνως		καὶ	κατὰ	τάξιν
in tongues;			all	but	properly		and	by	rank

1096		**15:1**	1107		1161	1473		80
γινέσθω.			Γνωρίζω		δὲ	ὑμῖν,		ἀδελφοί,
let become.			I make known		but	to you,		brothers,

012	2098		3739	2097			1473
τὸ	εὐαγγέλιον		ὃ	εὐηγγελισάμην			ὑμῖν,
the	good message		which	I told good message			to you,

3739	2532	3880		1722	3739	2532
ὃ	καὶ	παρελάβετε,		ἐν	ᾧ	καὶ
what	also	you took along,		in	which	also

2476		**2**	1223		3739	2532	4982		5101
ἑστήκατε,			δι᾽		οὗ	καὶ	σῴζεσθε,		τίνι
you have stood,			through		which	also	you are being saved		in what
									delivered,

3056	2097			1473	1487	2722
λόγῳ	εὐηγγελισάμην			ὑμῖν	εἰ	κατέχετε,
word	I told good message			to you	if	you hold on,

1622	1487	3361	1500			4100
ἐκτὸς	εἰ	μὴ	εἰκῇ			ἐπιστεύσατε.
outside	except		without cause			you trusted.

3	3860		1063	1473	1722	4413		3739	2532
	παρέδωκα		γὰρ	ὑμῖν	ἐν	πρώτοις,		ὃ	καὶ
	I gave over		for	to you	in	firsts,		what	also

3880		3754	5547	599		5228		018
παρέλαβον,		ὅτι	Χριστὸς	ἀπέθανεν		ὑπὲρ		τῶν
I took along,		that	Christ	died		on behalf of		the

266		1473	2596		020	1124		**4**	2532	3754
ἁμαρτιῶν		ἡμῶν	κατὰ		τὰς	γραφὰς			καὶ	ὅτι
sins		of us	according to		the	writings			and	that

2290		2532	3754	1453				07
ἐτάφη		καὶ	ὅτι	ἐγήγερται				τῇ
he was buried		and	that	he has been raised				in the

2250	07	5154	2596		020	1124		**5**	2532	3754
ἡμέρᾳ	τῇ	τρίτῃ	κατὰ		τὰς	γραφὰς			καὶ	ὅτι
day	the	third	according to		the	writings			and	that

3708		2786		1534	015	1427		**6**	1899
ὤφθη		Κηφᾷ		εἶτα	τοῖς	δώδεκα·			ἔπειτα
he was seen		by Cephas		then	the	twelve;			then

3708		1883	4001		80		2178
ὤφθη		ἐπάνω	πεντακοσίοις		ἀδελφοῖς		ἐφάπαξ,
he was seen		up on	five hundred		brothers		once for all,

1537	3739	013	4183		3306		2193	737		5100	1161
ἐξ	ὧν	οἱ	πλείονες		μένουσιν		ἕως	ἄρτι,		τινὲς	δὲ
from	whom	the	more		stay		until	now,		some	but

2837		**7**	1899	3708			2385		1534	015
ἐκοιμήθησαν·			ἔπειτα	ὤφθη			Ἰακώβῳ		εἶτα	τοῖς
fell asleep;			then	he was seen			by Jacob		then	the

652		3956		**8**	2078	1161	3956	5619
ἀποστόλοις		πᾶσιν·			ἔσχατον	δὲ	πάντων	ὡσπερεὶ
delegates		all;			last	but	of all	as indeed if

011	1626	3708	2504		1473	1063

τῷ   ἐκτρώματι ὤφθη   κἀμοί. **9** Ἐγὼ γάρ
to the premature he was seen also by me.   I   for

εἰμι ὁ   ἐλάχιστος τῶν   ἀποστόλων ὃς   οὐκ εἰμὶ
am the least of the delegates who   not I am

ἱκανὸς καλεῖσθαι ἀπόστολος, διότι   ἐδίωξα
enough to be called delegate, through that I pursued

τὴν ἐκκλησίαν τοῦ   θεοῦ· **10** χάριτι δὲ θεοῦ εἰμι
the assembly of the God;   in favor but of God I am

ὅ εἰμι, καὶ ἡ   χάρις αὐτοῦ ἡ   εἰς ἐμὲ οὐ
what I am, and the favor of him the in   me   not

κενὴ ἐγενήθη, ἀλλὰ περισσότερον αὐτῶν πάντων
empty became, but more excessive of them all

ἐκοπίασα, οὐκ ἐγὼ δὲ ἀλλὰ ἡ χάρις τοῦ   θεοῦ
I labored, not I but but the favor of the God

[ἡ] σὺν ἐμοί. **11** εἴτε   οὖν ἐγὼ εἴτε ἐκεῖνοι,
the with me.   Whether then I or those,

οὕτως κηρύσσομεν καὶ οὕτως ἐπιστεύσατε. **12** Εἰ
thusly we announce and thusly you trusted.   If

δὲ Χριστὸς κηρύσσεται ὅτι ἐκ νεκρῶν
but Christ is announced that from dead

ἐγήγερται,   πῶς λέγουσιν ἐν ὑμῖν τινες ὅτι
he has been raised, how they say in you some that

ἀνάστασις νεκρῶν οὐκ ἔστιν; **13** εἰ δὲ
standing up of dead not there is? If but

ἀνάστασις νεκρῶν οὐκ ἔστιν, οὐδὲ Χριστὸς
standing up of dead not there is, but not Christ

ἐγήγερται· **14** εἰ δὲ Χριστὸς οὐκ ἐγήγερται,
has been raised; if but Christ not has been raised,

κενὸν ἄρα [καὶ] τὸ κήρυγμα ἡμῶν, κενὴ καὶ
empty then also the announcement of us, empty also

ἡ πίστις ὑμῶν· **15** εὑρισκόμεθα δὲ καὶ
the trust of you; we are found but also

ψευδομάρτυρες τοῦ   θεοῦ, ὅτι ἐμαρτυρήσαμεν κατὰ
false testifiers of the God, that we testified by

τοῦ θεοῦ ὅτι ἤγειρεν τὸν Χριστόν, ὃν οὐκ ἤγειρεν
the God that he raised the Christ, whom not he raised

εἴπερ ἄρα νεκροὶ οὐκ ἐγείρονται. **16** εἰ γὰρ
if indeed then dead not are raised. If for

νεκροὶ οὐκ ἐγείρονται, οὐδὲ Χριστὸς ἐγήγερται·
dead not are raised, but not Christ has been raised;

17 εἰ δὲ Χριστὸς οὐκ ἐγήγερται, ματαία ἡ
if but Christ not has been raised, futile the

πίστις ὑμῶν, ἔτι ἐστὲ ἐν ταῖς ἁμαρτίαις ὑμῶν,
trust of you, still you are in the sins of you,

18 ἄρα καὶ οἱ κοιμηθέντες ἐν Χριστῷ
then also the ones having fallen asleep in Christ

one untimely born, he appeared also to me. [9]For I am the least of the apostles, unfit to be called an apostle, because I persecuted the church of God. [10]But by the grace of God I am what I am, and his grace toward me has not been in vain. On the contrary, I worked harder than any of them—though it was not I, but the grace of God that is with me. [11]Whether then it was I or they, so we proclaim and so you have come to believe.

[12]Now if Christ is proclaimed as raised from the dead, how can some of you say there is no resurrection of the dead? [13]If there is no resurrection of the dead, then Christ has not been raised; [14]and if Christ has not been raised, then our proclamation has been in vain and your faith has been in vain. [15]We are even found to be misrepresenting God, because we testified of God that he raised Christ—whom he did not raise if it is true that the dead are not raised. [16]For if the dead are not raised, then Christ has not been raised. [17]If Christ has not been raised, your faith is futile and you are still in your sins. [18]Then those also who have died[a] in Christ have perished.

[a] Gk fallen asleep

¹⁹If for this life only we have hoped in Christ, we are of all people most to be pitied.

20 But in fact Christ has been raised from the dead, the first fruits of those who have died.ᵃ ²¹For since death came through a human being, the resurrection of the dead has also come through a human being; ²²for as all die in Adam, so all will be made alive in Christ. ²³But each in his own order: Christ the first fruits, then at his coming those who belong to Christ. ²⁴Then comes the end,ᵇ when he hands over the kingdom to God the Father, after he has destroyed every ruler and every authority and power. ²⁵For he must reign until he has put all his enemies under his feet. ²⁶The last enemy to be destroyed is death. ²⁷For "Godᶜ has put all things in subjection under his feet." But when it says, "All things are put in subjection," it is plain that this does not include the one who put all things in subjection under him. ²⁸When all things are subjected to him, then the Son himself will also be subjected to the one who put all things in subjection under him, so that God may be all in all.

ᵃ Gk fallen asleep
ᵇ Or Then come the rest
ᶜ Gk he

622		1487	1722 07	2222 3778	1722 5547
ἀπώλοντο.	**19**	εἰ	ἐν τῇ	ζωῇ ταύτῃ ἐν	Χριστῷ
were destroyed.	If	in	the	life this in	Christ

1679	1510	3441	1652
ἠλπικότες	ἐσμὲν	μόνον,	ἐλεεινότεροι
+having hoped	we are+	alone,	more in need of mercy

3956 444	1510		3570 1161 5547
πάντων ἀνθρώπων	ἐσμέν.	**20**	Νυνὶ δὲ Χριστὸς
of all men	we are.		Now but Christ

1453	1537 3498	536	014	2837
ἐγήγερται	ἐκ νεκρῶν	ἀπαρχὴ	τῶν	κεκοιμημένων.
has been	from dead	from	of the ones having	fallen asleep.
raised		beginning		

	1894	1063 1223	444	2288	2532 1223
21	ἐπειδὴ	γὰρ δι'	ἀνθρώπου	θάνατος, καὶ	δι'
	Since	for through	man	death, also	through

444	386	3498		5618	1063 1722
ἀνθρώπου	ἀνάστασις	νεκρῶν.	**22**	ὥσπερ	γὰρ ἐν
man	standing up	of dead.		As indeed	for in

03 76	3956	599		3779	2532 1722 03
τῷ Ἀδὰμ	πάντες	ἀποθνήσκουσιν,	οὕτως	καὶ ἐν	τῷ
the Adam	all	died,	thusly	also in	the

5547	3956	2227		1538	1161 1722
Χριστῷ	πάντες	ζωοποιηθήσονται.	**23**	Ἕκαστος	δὲ ἐν
Christ	all	will be made alive.		Each	but in

011 2398 5001	536		5547	1899	013
τῷ ἰδίῳ τάγματι·	ἀπαρχὴ		Χριστός,	ἔπειτα	οἱ
the own order;	from beginning		Christ,	then	the

02	5547	1722 07	3952	846		1534 09
τοῦ	Χριστοῦ ἐν	τῇ	παρουσίᾳ	αὐτοῦ,	**24**	εἶτα τὸ
of the	Christ in	the	presence	of him,		then the

5056	3752 3860		08 932	03
τέλος,	ὅταν παραδιδῷ		τὴν βασιλείαν	τῷ
completion,	when he might give over		the kingdom	to the

2316 2532 3962	3752 2673	3956 746
θεῷ καὶ πατρί,	ὅταν καταργήσῃ	πᾶσαν ἀρχὴν
God and father,	when he might abolish	all rule

2532 3956 1849	2532 1411		1163
καὶ πᾶσαν ἐξουσίαν	καὶ δύναμιν.	**25**	δεῖ
and all authority	and power.		It is necessary

1063 846 936	891	3739 5087	3956
γὰρ αὐτὸν βασιλεύειν	ἄχρι	οὗ θῇ	πάντας
for him to be king	until	which he might set	all

016 2190	5259 016	4228 846		2078
τοὺς ἐχθροὺς	ὑπὸ τοὺς	πόδας αὐτοῦ.	**26**	ἔσχατος
the hostile	under the	feet of him.		Last

2190	2673	01 2288		3956 1063
ἐχθρὸς	καταργεῖται	ὁ θάνατος·	**27**	πάντα γὰρ
hostile	is abolished	the death;		all for

5293	5259 016	4228 846	3752 1161
ὑπέταξεν	ὑπὸ τοὺς	πόδας αὐτοῦ.	ὅταν δὲ
he subjected	under the	feet of him.	When but

3004	3754 3956 5293		1212 3754
εἴπῃ	ὅτι πάντα ὑποτέτακται,		δῆλον ὅτι
he might say	that all has been subjected,		clear that

1622	02 5293	846	024 3956		3752
ἐκτὸς	τοῦ ὑποτάξαντος	αὐτῷ	τὰ πάντα.	**28**	ὅταν
outside	the having subjected	to him	the all.		When

1161 5293	846	021 3956	5119 2532
δὲ ὑποταγῇ	αὐτῷ	τὰ πάντα,	τότε [καὶ]
but might be subject	to him	the all,	then also

846	01	5207 5293	03	5293	846
αὐτὸς	ὁ	υἱὸς ὑποταγήσεται	τῷ	ὑποτάξαντι	αὐτῷ
himself	the	son will be		to the one having	to him
		subjected		subjected	

024 3956	2443 1510	01	2316 3956 1722
τὰ πάντα,	ἵνα ᾖ	ὁ	θεὸς [τὰ] πάντα ἐν
the all,	that might be	the	God the all in

```
3956              1893    5101   4160           013  907
πᾶσιν.  29  'Επεὶ   τί    ποιήσουσιν οἱ  βαπτιζόμενοι
all.        Since what  will do    the being immersed
5228        014    3498        1487  3654  3498      3756
ὑπὲρ     τῶν    νεκρῶν;  εἰ   ὅλως νεκροὶ οὐκ
on behalf of the  dead?    If   wholly dead  not
1453          5101  2532  907                5228
ἐγείρονται, τί     καὶ   βαπτίζονται      ὑπὲρ
are raised,  why  also  are they immersed on behalf of
846        5101  2532  1473   2793           3956  5610
αὐτῶν;  30  Τί   καὶ   ἡμεῖς κινδυνεύομεν πᾶσαν ὥραν;
them?      Why  also  we     are in danger  all   hour?
    2596  2250   599        3513  08  5212       2746
31  καθ' ἡμέραν ἀποθνῄσκω, νὴ  τὴν ὑμετέραν καύχησιν,
    By   day     I die,     yea  the  your      brag,
80              3739   2192  1722 5547      2424   03  2962
[ἀδελφοί], ἣν   ἔχω   ἐν  Χριστῷ 'Ιησοῦ τῷ  κυρίῳ
brothers, which I have in  Christ  Jesus  the Master
1473      1487 2596  444       2341             1722
ἡμῶν.  32  εἰ  κατὰ ἄνθρωπον ἐθηριομάχησα       ἐν
of us.     If  by   man       I fought wild animals in
2181       5101  1473  09    3786        1487  3498   3756
'Εφέσῳ,  τί     μοι   τὸ   ὄφελος;   εἰ   νεκροὶ οὐκ
Ephesus, what  to me the  advantage? If   dead   not
1453          2068     2532  4095        839     1063
ἐγείρονται, φάγωμεν καὶ  πίωμεν,     αὔριον  γὰρ
are raised, let us eat and let us drink, tomorrow for
599             3361  4105           5351       2239
ἀποθνῄσκομεν.  33  μὴ  πλανᾶσθε·   φθείρουσιν ἤθη
we die.           Not  be deceived;  corrupt     customs
5543    3657      2556        1594     1346   2532 3361
χρηστὰ ὁμιλίαι  κακαί.  34  ἐκνήψατε δικαίως καὶ μὴ
kind   conversations bad.  Be sober rightly and not
264        56        1063 2316   5100   2192
ἁμαρτάνετε, ἀγνωσίαν γὰρ θεοῦ  τινες ἔχουσιν,
sin,       no knowledge for of God some  have,
4314  1791     1473  2980      235   3004        5100 4459
πρὸς ἐντροπὴν ὑμῖν λαλῶ.  35  'Αλλὰ ἐρεῖ     τις·  πῶς
to   shame   to you I speak. But  will say some; how
1453          013 3498  4169        1161 4983       2064
ἐγείρονται οἱ  νεκροί; ποίῳ    δὲ  σώματι   ἔρχονται;
are raised the dead?  What kind but body     come they?
    878            1473 3739 4687       3756 2227
36  ἄφρων,     σὺ  ὃ  σπείρεις, οὐ  ζωοποιεῖται
    Unthinking, you what sow,    not it is made alive
1437 3361 599           2532 3739 4687      3756 012
ἐὰν μὴ ἀποθάνῃ·  37  καὶ ὃ   σπείρεις, οὐ  τὸ
except it might die; and what you sow,   not the
4983 012 1096          4687     235   1131    2848
σῶμα τὸ γενησόμενον  σπείρεις ἀλλὰ γυμνὸν κόκκον
body the going to become you sow but naked  grain
1487 5177        4621    2228 5100  012          3062
εἰ  τύχοι     σίτου   ἢ  τινος τῶν       λοιπῶν·
if  it may obtain of wheat or some of the remaining;
    01 1161 2316 1325      846   4983 2531      2309
38  ὁ  δὲ  θεὸς δίδωσιν αὐτῷ σῶμα καθὼς  ἠθέλησεν,
    the but God gives   to it body just as he wanted,
2532 1538     022      4690        2398 4983   3756 3956
καὶ  ἑκάστῳ τῶν   σπερμάτων ἴδιον σῶμα.  39  Οὐ  πᾶσα
and  to each of the seeds   own   body.    Not all
4561  05  846   4561     235  243    3303      444       243
σὰρξ ἡ  αὐτὴ σὰρξ ἀλλὰ ἄλλη μὲν    ἀνθρώπων, ἄλλη
flesh the same flesh but  other indeed of men,     other
1161 4561  2934       243  1161 4561  4421      243
δὲ  σὰρξ κτηνῶν,  ἄλλη δὲ  σὰρξ πτηνῶν, ἄλλη
but flesh of animals, other but flesh of birds, other
1161 2486      40  2532 4983    2032        2532 4983
δὲ  ἰχθύων.     καὶ  σώματα ἐπουράνια, καὶ  σώματα
but of fish.    And  bodies on heaven,  and  bodies
```

29 Otherwise, what will those people do who receive baptism on behalf of the dead? If the dead are not raised at all, why are people baptized on their behalf?

30 And why are we putting ourselves in danger every hour? 31I die every day! That is as certain, brothers and sisters,[a] as my boasting of you—a boast that I make in Christ Jesus our Lord. 32If with merely human hopes I fought with wild animals at Ephesus, what would I have gained by it? If the dead are not raised,

"Let us eat and drink,
  for tomorrow we die."

33Do not be deceived:
"Bad company ruins
  good morals."

34Come to a sober and right mind, and sin no more; for some people have no knowledge of God. I say this to your shame.

35 But someone will ask, "How are the dead raised? With what kind of body do they come?" 36Fool! What you sow does not come to life unless it dies. 37And as for what you sow, you do not sow the body that is to be, but a bare seed, perhaps of wheat or of some other grain. 38But God gives it a body as he has chosen, and to each kind of seed its own body. 39Not all flesh is alike, but there is one flesh for human beings, another for animals, another for birds, and another for fish. 40There are both heavenly bodies

a Gk brothers

and earthly bodies, but the glory of the heavenly is one thing, and that of the earthly is another. 41There is one glory of the sun, and another glory of the moon, and another glory of the stars; indeed, star differs from star in glory.

42 So it is with the resurrection of the dead. What is sown is perishable, what is raised is imperishable. 43It is sown in dishonor, it is raised in glory. It is sown in weakness, it is raised in power. 44It is sown a physical body, it is raised a spiritual body. If there is a physical body, there is also a spiritual body. 45Thus it is written, "The first man, Adam, became a living being"; the last Adam became a life-giving spirit. 46But it is not the spiritual that is first, but the physical, and then the spiritual. 47The first man was from the earth, a man of dust; the second man is[a] from heaven. 48As was the man of dust, so are those who are of the dust; and as is the man of heaven, so are those who are of heaven. 49Just as we have borne the image of the man of dust, we will[b] also bear the image of the man of heaven.

50 What I am saying, brothers and sisters,[c] is this: flesh and blood cannot inherit the kingdom of God, nor does the perishable inherit the imperishable. 51Listen, I will tell you a mystery!

[a] Other ancient authorities add the Lord
[b] Other ancient authorities read let us
[c] Gk brothers

1919	235	2087	3303	05	022	2032
ἐπίγεια·	ἀλλὰ	ἑτέρα	μὲν	ἡ	τῶν	ἐπουρανίων
on earth;	but	other	indeed	the	of the	ones on heaven

1391	2087	1161	05	022	1919	243
δόξα,	ἑτέρα	δὲ	ἡ	τῶν	ἐπιγείων.	41 ἄλλη
splendor,	other	but	the	of the	ones on earth.	Other

1391	2246	2532 243	1391	4582	2532 243
δόξα	ἡλίου,	καὶ ἄλλη	δόξα	σελήνης,	καὶ ἄλλη
splendor	of sun,	and other	splendor	of moon,	and other

1391	792	792	1063 792	1308	1722
δόξα	ἀστέρων·	ἀστὴρ	γὰρ ἀστέρος	διαφέρει	ἐν
splendor	of stars;	star	for of star	differs	in

1391	42	3779	2532 05	386	014	3498
δόξῃ.		Οὕτως	καὶ ἡ	ἀνάστασις	τῶν	νεκρῶν.
splendor.		Thusly	also the	standing up	of the	dead.

4687	1722 5356		1453	1722 861
σπείρεται	ἐν φθορᾷ,		ἐγείρεται	ἐν ἀφθαρσίᾳ·
it is sown	in corruption,		it is raised	in incorruption;

43	4687	1722 819	1453	1722 1391
	σπείρεται	ἐν ἀτιμίᾳ,	ἐγείρεται	ἐν δόξῃ·
	it is sown	in dishonor,	it is raised	in splendor;

4687	1722 769	1453	1722 1411
σπείρεται	ἐν ἀσθενείᾳ,	ἐγείρεται	ἐν δυνάμει·
it is sown	in weakness,	it is raised	in power;

44	4687	4983 5591	1453	4983
	σπείρεται	σῶμα ψυχικόν,	ἐγείρεται	σῶμα
	it is sown	body soul-like,	it is raised	body

4152	1487 1510	4983 5591	1510
πνευματικόν.	Εἰ ἔστιν	σῶμα ψυχικόν,	ἔστιν
spiritual.	If there is	body soul-like,	there is

2532 4152		45	3779	2532 1125
καὶ πνευματικόν.			οὕτως	καὶ γέγραπται·
also spiritual.			Thusly	also it has been written,

1096	01	4413	444	76	1519 5590	2198
ἐγένετο	ὁ	πρῶτος	ἄνθρωπος	᾿Αδὰμ	εἰς ψυχὴν	ζῶσαν,
became	the	first	man	Adam	into soul	living,

01	2078	76	1519 4151	2227	46	235 3756
ὁ	ἔσχατος	᾿Αδὰμ	εἰς πνεῦμα	ζωοποιοῦν.		ἀλλ᾿ οὐ
the	last	Adam	into spirit	life making.		But not

4413	09 4152	235 09 5591	1899 09
πρῶτον	τὸ πνευματικὸν	ἀλλὰ τὸ ψυχικόν,	ἔπειτα τὸ
first	the spiritual	but the soul-like,	then the

4152	47	01	4413	444	1537 1093	5517
πνευματικόν.		ὁ	πρῶτος	ἄνθρωπος	ἐκ γῆς	χοϊκός,
spiritual.		The	first	man	from earth	dust,

01 1208	444	1537 3772	48	3634 01 5517
ὁ δεύτερος	ἄνθρωπος	ἐξ οὐρανοῦ.		οἷος ὁ χοϊκός,
the second	man	from heaven.		As such the dust,

5108	2532 013 5517	2532 3634	01 2032
τοιοῦτοι	καὶ οἱ χοϊκοί,	καὶ οἷος	ὁ ἐπουράνιος,
such	also the dusts,	and as such	the on heavenly,

5108	2532 013 2032	49	2532 2531
τοιοῦτοι	καὶ οἱ ἐπουράνιοι·		καὶ καθὼς
such	also the on heavenlies;		and just as

5409	08	1504	02	5517	5409	2532
ἐφορέσαμεν	τὴν	εἰκόνα	τοῦ	χοϊκοῦ,	φορέσομεν	καὶ
we wore	the	image	of the	dust,	we will wear	also

08	1504	02	2032	50	3778 1161 5346
τὴν	εἰκόνα	τοῦ	ἐπουρανίου.		Τοῦτο δέ φημι,
the	image	of the	on heavenly.		This but I say,

80	3754 4561	2532 129	932	2316
ἀδελφοί,	ὅτι σὰρξ	καὶ αἷμα	βασιλείαν	θεοῦ
brothers,	that flesh	and blood	kingdom	of God

2816	3756 1410	3761	05 5356	08
κληρονομῆσαι	οὐ δύναται	οὐδὲ	ἡ φθορὰ	τὴν
to inherit	not is able	but not	the corruption	the

861	2816	51	2400 3466	1473
ἀφθαρσίαν	κληρονομεῖ.		ἰδοὺ μυστήριον	ὑμῖν
incorruption	inherits.		Look mystery	to you

```
3004    3956    3756  2837           3956    1161
λέγω·   πάντες  οὐ    κοιμηθησόμεθα,  πάντες  δὲ
I say;  all     not   we will sleep, all     but
236                   1722 823        1722  4493   3788
ἀλλαγησόμεθα,    52   ἐν  ἀτόμῳ,     ἐν   ῥιπῇ  ὀφθαλμοῦ,
we will be changed,   in  instant,   in   blink of eye,
1722 07  2078   4536          4537              1063 2532 013
ἐν   τῇ  ἐσχάτῃ σάλπιγγι·    σαλπίσει          γὰρ  καὶ  οἱ
in   the last   trumpet;     it will trumpet  for  and  the
3498     1453               862              2532 1473
νεκροὶ  ἐγερθήσονται      ἄφθαρτοι         καὶ  ἡμεῖς
dead     will be raised    incorruptible    and  we
236                   1163        1063 012 5349              3778
ἀλλαγησόμεθα.    53  Δεῖ        γὰρ  τὸ  φθαρτὸν           τοῦτο
will be changed. It is  for     the corruptible this
                      necessary
1746             861            2532 012 2349              3778
ἐνδύσασθαι     ἀφθαρσίαν      καὶ  τὸ  θνητὸν            τοῦτο
to put on      incorruption    and  the death-like       this
1746             110               3752 1161 09  5349
ἐνδύσασθαι     ἀθανασίαν.   54  ὅταν δὲ  τὸ  φθαρτὸν
to put on      deathlessness.    When but   the corruptible
3778  1746           861            2532 09  2349
τοῦτο ἐνδύσηται     ἀφθαρσίαν      καὶ  τὸ  θνητὸν
this  will put on    incorruption    and  the death-like
3778  1746           110            5119 1096          01
τοῦτο ἐνδύσηται     ἀθανασίαν,     τότε γενήσεται      ὁ
this  will put on    deathlessness,  then will become   the
3056    01   1125               2666               01   2288       1519
λόγος   ὁ    γεγραμμένος·      κατεπόθη           ὁ    θάνατος   εἰς
word    the  having been        was swallowed      the death      into
             written,            down
3534          55  4226   1473      2288       09  3534      4226
νῖκος.            ποῦ   σου,     θάνατε,   τὸ  νῖκος;   ποῦ
conquest.         Where of you,  death,    the conquest?  Where
1473    2288       09  2759            09  1161 2759       02
σου,    θάνατε,   τὸ  κέντρον;   56  τὸ  δὲ   κέντρον τοῦ
of you, death,    the sting?        The but   sting   of the
2288      05   266          05  1161 1411           06   266
θανάτου  ἡ    ἁμαρτία,   ἡ   δὲ  δύναμις τῆς       ἁμαρτίας
death     the  sin,        the but power    of the    sin
01   3551       57  03    1161 2316 5485     03   1325
ὁ    νόμος·         τῷ   δὲ   θεῷ  χάρις τῷ   διδόντι
the  law;           to the but  God  favor to the one giving
1473    012 3534     1223    02   2962      1473    2424
ἡμῖν   τὸ  νῖκος    διὰ    τοῦ κυρίου ἡμῶν Ἰησοῦ
to us  the  conquest through the Master of us Jesus
5547           58  5620    80     1473 27         1476
Χριστοῦ.          Ὥστε,   ἀδελφοί μου ἀγαπητοί, ἑδραῖοι
Christ.           So that, brothers of me loved,   stable
1096       277               4052              1722 011 2041
γίνεσθε,  ἀμετακίνητοι,   περισσεύοντες ἐν   τῷ  ἔργῳ
become,   unmovable,       exceeding        in  the work
02   2962     3842         3609a    3754 01  2873    1473
τοῦ  κυρίου πάντοτε,   εἰδότες ὅτι  ὁ   κόπος ὑμῶν
of the Master always,   knowing that the labor of you
3756 1510   2756  1722 2962          4012 1161 06
οὐκ  ἔστιν  κενὸς ἐν  κυρίῳ.  16:1 Περὶ δὲ  τῆς
not  is     empty in  Master.      About but  the
3048           06 1519 016  40          5618     1299
λογείας      τῆς εἰς τοὺς ἁγίους   ὥσπερ  διέταξα
collection   the for the  holy ones  as indeed I directed
019   1577          06   1053       3779   2532 1473
ταῖς ἐκκλησίαις τῆς  Γαλατίας,  οὕτως καὶ  ὑμεῖς
the  assemblies  of the Galatia,   thusly also  you
4160           2596 1520 4521       1538     1473   3844
ποιήσατε.  2  κατὰ μίαν σαββάτου ἕκαστος ὑμῶν παρ᾽
do.           By  one  sabbath    each    of you beside
```

We will not all die,[a] but
we will all be changed, [52]in
a moment, in the twinkling
of an eye, at the last
trumpet. For the trumpet
will sound, and the dead
will be raised imperishable,
and we will be changed.
[53]For this perishable body
must put on imperishability,
and this mortal body must
put on immortality. [54]When
this perishable body puts on
imperishability, and
this mortal body puts on
immortality, then the
saying that is written will
be fulfilled:
    "Death has been
        swallowed up in
        victory."
[55] "Where, O death, is your
        victory?
    Where, O death, is your
        sting?"
[56]The sting of death is sin,
and the power of sin is the
law. [57]But thanks be to
God, who gives us the
victory through our Lord
Jesus Christ.
    [58]Therefore, my
beloved,[b] be steadfast,
immovable, always
excelling in the work of
the Lord, because you
know that in the Lord
your labor is not in vain.

CHAPTER 16

Now concerning the
collection for the saints:
you should follow the
directions I gave to the
churches of Galatia. [2]On
the first day of every week,
each of you is to put aside

[a] Gk fall asleep
[b] Gk beloved brothers

and save whatever extra you earn, so that collections need not be taken when I come. ³And when I arrive, I will send any whom you approve with letters to take your gift to Jerusalem. ⁴If it seems advisable that I should go also, they will accompany me.

5 I will visit you after passing through Macedonia—for I intend to pass through Macedonia— ⁶and perhaps I will stay with you or even spend the winter, so that you may send me on my way, wherever I go. ⁷I do not want to see you now just in passing, for I hope to spend some time with you, if the Lord permits. ⁸But I will stay in Ephesus until Pentecost, ⁹for a wide door for effective work has opened to me, and there are many adversaries.

10 If Timothy comes, see that he has nothing to fear among you, for he is doing the work of the Lord just as I am; ¹¹therefore let no one despise him. Send him on his way in peace, so that he may come to me; for I am expecting him with the brothers.

12 Now concerning our brother Apollos, I strongly urged him to visit you with the other

1438	5087	2343		3739 5100 1437
ἑαυτῷ	τιθέτω	θησαυρίζων	ὅ	τι ἐὰν
himself	let set	treasuring	what	some if

2137		2443 3361	3752 2064	5119
εὐοδῶται,		ἵνα μὴ	ὅταν ἔλθω	τότε
he might travel well,		that not	when I might come	then

3048   1096   3752 1161 3854
λογεῖαι   γίνωνται. ³ ὅταν δὲ   παραγένωμαι,
collections might become.   When but   I might arrive,

3739 1437 1381   1223   1992   3778
οὓς ἐὰν δοκιμάσητε,   δι᾽   ἐπιστολῶν τούτους
whom if   you might prove,   through letters   these

3992   667   08 5485   1473   1519
πέμψω   ἀπενεγκεῖν   τὴν χάριν ὑμῶν   εἰς
I will send   to carry off the favor of you   into

2419   4   1437 1161 514   1510   010 2504
Ἰερουσαλήμ·   ἐὰν δὲ ἄξιον ᾖ   τοῦ κἀμὲ
Jerusalem;   if but worthy might be the also me

4198   4862 1473 4198   5   2064
πορεύεσθαι, σὺν ἐμοὶ πορεύσονται.   Ἐλεύσομαι
to travel, with me they will travel.   I will come

1161 4314 1473 3752 3109   1330
δὲ πρὸς ὑμᾶς ὅταν Μακεδονίαν διέλθω·
but to you when Macedonia I might go through;

3109   1063 1330   6   4314 1473 1161
Μακεδονίαν γὰρ διέρχομαι,   πρὸς ὑμᾶς δὲ
Macedonia for I go through,   to you but

5177   3887   2228 2532 3914   2443 1473
τυχὸν   παραμενῶ   ἢ καὶ παραχειμάσω,   ἵνα ὑμεῖς
having   I stay along or also I will winter   that you
obtained   along,

1473 4311   3757   1437 4198   7   3756
με   προπέμψητε   οὗ ἐὰν πορεύωμαι.   οὐ
me might send before where if I might travel.   Not

2309   1063 1473 737   1722 3938   3708   1679   1063
θέλω γὰρ ὑμᾶς ἄρτι ἐν παρόδῳ ἰδεῖν, ἐλπίζω γὰρ
I want for you now in passage to see, I hope for

5550   5100 1961   4314 1473 1437 01   2962
χρόνον τινὰ ἐπιμεῖναι πρὸς ὑμᾶς ἐὰν ὁ κύριος
time some to stay on to you if the Master

2010   8   1961   1161 1722 2181   2193
ἐπιτρέψῃ.   ἐπιμενῶ   δὲ ἐν Ἐφέσῳ ἕως
might allow.   I will stay on but in Ephesus until

06   4005   9   2374 1063 1473 455   3173
τῆς πεντηκοστῆς·   θύρα γάρ μοι ἀνέῳγεν μεγάλη
the fiftieth;   door for to me has opened great

2532 1756   2532 480   4183   10   1437
καὶ ἐνεργής,   καὶ ἀντικείμενοι πολλοί.   Ἐὰν
and operational,   and lying against many.   If

1161 2064   5095   991   2443 870
δὲ ἔλθῃ   Τιμόθεος, βλέπετε, ἵνα ἀφόβως
but might come Timothy,   see,   that fearlessly

1096   4314 1473 012 1063 2041 2962
γένηται   πρὸς ὑμᾶς· τὸ γὰρ ἔργον κυρίου
he might become to   you; the for work of Master

2038   5613 2504   11   3361 5100 3767 846
ἐργάζεται ὡς κἀγώ·   μή τις οὖν αὐτὸν
he works as   also I;   not some then him

1848   4311   1161 846   1722 1515   2443
ἐξουθενήσῃ. προπέμψατε δὲ αὐτὸν ἐν εἰρήνῃ, ἵνα
might despise. Send before but him in peace, that

2064   4314 1473 1551   1063 846   3326 014
ἔλθῃ   πρός με· ἐκδέχομαι γὰρ αὐτὸν μετὰ τῶν
he might come to   me; I wait for for him with the

80   4012 1161 80   02 80   4183
ἀδελφῶν.   12 Περὶ δὲ   Ἀπολλῶ τοῦ ἀδελφοῦ, πολλὰ
brothers.   About but   Apollos the brother, many

3870   846   2443 2064   4314 1473 3326 014
παρεκάλεσα αὐτόν, ἵνα ἔλθῃ   πρὸς ὑμᾶς μετὰ τῶν
I encouraged him,   that he might go to you with the

80	2532	3843		3756	1510	2307	2443
ἀδελφῶν·	καὶ	πάντως		οὐκ	ἦν	θέλημα	ἵνα
brothers;	and	altogether		not	it was	want	that

3568	2064		2064		1161	3752
νῦν	ἔλθῃ·		ἐλεύσεται		δὲ	ὅταν
now	he might come;		he will come		but	when

2119		**13**	1127		4739		1722	07
εὐκαιρήσῃ.			Γρηγορεῖτε,		στήκετε		ἐν	τῇ
it might be good season.			Keep awake,		stand		in	the

4102	407	2901		**14**	3956	1473	1722
πίστει,	ἀνδρίζεσθε,	κραταιοῦσθε.			πάντα	ὑμῶν	ἐν
trust,	be like men,	be strong.			All	of you	in

26	1096		**15**	3870		1161	1473	80
ἀγάπη	γινέσθω.			Παρακαλῶ		δὲ	ὑμᾶς,	ἀδελφοί·
love	let become.			I encourage		but	you,	brothers;

3609a	08	3614	4734		3754	1510	536
οἴδατε	τὴν	οἰκίαν	Στεφανᾶ,		ὅτι	ἐστὶν	ἀπαρχὴ
you know	the	house	Stephan,		that	he is	from beginning

06	882	2532	1519	1248		015	40
τῆς	Ἀχαΐας	καὶ	εἰς	διακονίαν		τοῖς	ἁγίοις
of the	Achaia	and	in	service		to the	holy ones

5021	1438		**16**	2443	2532	1473
ἔταξαν	ἑαυτούς·			ἵνα	καὶ	ὑμεῖς
they set in order	themselves;			that	also	you

5293		015	5108		2532	3956	03
ὑποτάσσησθε		τοῖς	τοιούτοις		καὶ	παντὶ	τῷ
might be subjected		to the	such		and	to all	the

4903		2532	2872		**17**	5463		1161	1909
συνεργοῦντι		καὶ	κόπιωντι.			χαίρω		δὲ	ἐπὶ
working together		and	laboring.			I rejoice		but	on

07	3952	4734		2532	5415		2532	883
τῇ	παρουσίᾳ	Στεφανᾶ		καὶ	Φορτουνάτου		καὶ	Ἀχαϊκοῦ,
the	presence	Stephan		and	Fortunatus		and	Achaicus,

3754	012	5212		5303		3778	378
ὅτι	τὸ	ὑμέτερον		ὑστέρημα		οὗτοι	ἀνεπλήρωσαν·
that	the	your		lack		these	filled up;

18	373		1063	012	1699	4151		2532	012
	ἀνέπαυσαν		γὰρ	τὸ	ἐμὸν	πνεῦμα		καὶ	τὸ
	they gave rest		for	the	my	spirit		and	the

1473	1921		3767	016	5108
ὑμῶν.	ἐπιγινώσκετε		οὖν	τοὺς	τοιούτους.
of you.	Perceive		then	the	such.

19	782		1473	017	1577		06		773
	Ἀσπάζονται		ὑμᾶς	αἱ	ἐκκλησίαι		τῆς		Ἀσίας.
	Greet		you	the	assemblies		of the		Asia.

782		1473	1722	2962		4183	207		2532	4251
ἀσπάζεται		ὑμᾶς	ἐν	κυρίῳ		πολλὰ	Ἀκύλας		καὶ	Πρίσκα
Greet		you	in	Master		many	Acquila		and	Prisca

4862	07	2596	3624	846		1577		**20**	782
σὺν	τῇ	κατ᾽	οἶκον	αὐτῶν		ἐκκλησίᾳ.			ἀσπάζονται
with	the	by	house	of them		assembly.			Greet

1473	013	80		3956	782		240		1722
ὑμᾶς	οἱ	ἀδελφοὶ		πάντες.	Ἀσπάσασθε		ἀλλήλους		ἐν
you	the	brothers		all.	Greet		one another		in

5370	40		**21**	01	783		07		1699	5495
φιλήματι	ἁγίῳ.			Ὁ	ἀσπασμὸς		τῇ		ἐμῇ	χειρὶ
kiss	holy.			The	greeting		in the		my	hand

3972		**22**	1487	5100	3756	5368	04	2962		1510
Παύλου.			εἴ	τις	οὐ	φιλεῖ	τὸν	κύριον,		ἤτω
of Paul.			If	some	not	loves	the	Master,		let be

331		3134	2279a		**23**	05	5485	02	2962
ἀνάθεμα.		μαράνα	θά.			ἡ	χάρις	τοῦ	κυρίου
curse.		Marana	tha.			The	favor	of the	Master

2424	3326	1473		**24**	05	26	1473	3326	3956	1473
Ἰησοῦ	μεθ᾽	ὑμῶν.			ἡ	ἀγάπη	μου	μετὰ	πάντων	ὑμῶν
Jesus	with	you.			The	love	of me	with	all	you

1722	5547	2424
ἐν	Χριστῷ	Ἰησοῦ.
in	Christ	Jesus.

brothers, but he was not at all willing[a] to come now. He will come when he has the opportunity.

13 Keep alert, stand firm in your faith, be courageous, be strong. [14]Let all that you do be done in love.

15 Now, brothers and sisters,[b] you know that members of the household of Stephanas were the first converts in Achaia, and they have devoted themselves to the service of the saints; [16]I urge you to put yourselves at the service of such people, and of everyone who works and toils with them. [17]I rejoice at the coming of Stephanas and Fortunatus and Achaicus, because they have made up for your absence; [18]for they refreshed my spirit as well as yours. So give recognition to such persons.

19 The churches of Asia send greetings. Aquila and Prisca, together with the church in their house, greet you warmly in the Lord. [20]All the brothers and sisters[b] send greetings. Greet one another with a holy kiss.

21 I, Paul, write this greeting with my own hand. [22]Let anyone be accursed who has no love for the Lord. Our Lord, come![c] [23]The grace of the Lord Jesus be with you. [24]My love be with all of you in Christ Jesus.[d]

a Or it was not at all God's will for him
b Gk brothers
c Gk Marana tha. These Aramaic words can also be read Maran atha, meaning Our Lord has come
d Other ancient authorities add Amen

2 CORINTHIANS

CHAPTER 1

Paul, an apostle of Christ Jesus by the will of God, and Timothy our brother, To the church of God that is in Corinth, including all the saints throughout Achaia:

2 Grace to you and peace from God our Father and the Lord Jesus Christ.

3 Blessed be the God and Father of our Lord Jesus Christ, the Father of mercies and the God of all consolation, 4who consoles us in all our affliction, so that we may be able to console those who are in any affliction with the consolation with which we ourselves are consoled by God. 5For just as the sufferings of Christ are abundant for us, so also our consolation is abundant through Christ. 6If we are being afflicted, it is for your consolation and salvation; if we are being consoled, it is for your consolation, which you experience when you patiently endure the same sufferings that we are also suffering. 7Our hope for you is unshaken; for we know that as you share in our sufferings, so also you share in our consolation.

8 We do not want you to be unaware, brothers and sisters,a of the affliction

a Gk brothers

1:1	3972	652	5547	2424	1223	2307
	Παῦλος	ἀπόστολος	Χριστοῦ	Ἰησοῦ	διὰ	θελήματος
	Paul	delegate	of Christ	Jesus	through	want

2316 2532 5095 01 80 07 1577 02
θεοῦ καὶ Τιμόθεος ὁ ἀδελφὸς τῇ ἐκκλησίᾳ τοῦ
of God and Timothy the brother to the assembly of the

2316 07 1510 1722 2882 4862 015 40 3956
θεοῦ τῇ οὔσῃ ἐν Κορίνθῳ σὺν τοῖς ἁγίοις πᾶσιν
God the being in Corinth with the holy ones to all

015 1510 1722 3650 07 882 2 5485 1473 2532
τοῖς οὖσιν ἐν ὅλῃ τῇ Ἀχαΐᾳ, χάρις ὑμῖν καὶ
the being in whole the Achaia, favor to you and

1515 575 2316 3962 1473 2532 2962 2424
εἰρήνη ἀπὸ θεοῦ πατρὸς ἡμῶν καὶ κυρίου Ἰησοῦ
peace from God father of us and Master Jesus

5547 3 2128 01 2316 2532 3962 02
Χριστοῦ. Εὐλογητὸς ὁ θεὸς καὶ πατὴρ τοῦ
Christ. Well-spoken the God and father of the

2962 1473 2424 5547 01 3962 014
κυρίου ἡμῶν Ἰησοῦ Χριστοῦ, ὁ πατὴρ τῶν
Master of us Jesus Christ, the father of the

3628 2532 2316 3956 3874 4 01
οἰκτιρμῶν καὶ θεὸς πάσης παρακλήσεως, ὁ
compassions and God of all encouragement, the one

3870 1473 1909 3956 07 2347 1473 1519
παρακαλῶν ἡμᾶς ἐπὶ πάσῃ τῇ θλίψει ἡμῶν εἰς
encouraging us on all the affliction of us in

012 1410 1473 3870 016 1722 3956
τὸ δύνασθαι ἡμᾶς παρακαλεῖν τοὺς ἐν πάσῃ
the to be able us to encourage the in all

2347 1223 06 3874 3739
θλίψει διὰ τῆς παρακλήσεως ἧς
affliction through the encouragement of which

3870 846 5259 02 2316 5 3754
παρακαλούμεθα αὐτοὶ ὑπὸ τοῦ θεοῦ. ὅτι
we are encouraged ourselves by the God. Because

2531 4050 021 3804 02 5547 1519
καθὼς περισσεύει τὰ παθήματα τοῦ Χριστοῦ εἰς
just as exceeds the sufferings of the Christ in

1473 3779 1223 02 5547 4052 2532 05
ἡμᾶς, οὕτως διὰ τοῦ Χριστοῦ περισσεύει καὶ ἡ
us, thusly through the Christ exceeds also the

3874 1473 6 1535 1161 2346
παράκλησις ἡμῶν. εἴτε δὲ θλιβόμεθα,
encouragement of us. Whether but we are being
afflicted,

5228 06 1473 3874 2532 4991
ὑπὲρ τῆς ὑμῶν παρακλήσεως καὶ σωτηρίας·
on behalf of the of you encouragement and deliverance;

1535 3870 5228 06 1473
εἴτε παρακαλούμεθα, ὑπὲρ τῆς ὑμῶν
or we are being encouraged, on behalf of the of you

3874 06 1754 1722 5281 022
παρακλήσεως τῆς ἐνεργουμένης ἐν ὑπομονῇ τῶν
encouragement of the operation in patience of the

846 3804 3739 2532 1473 3958 7 2532
αὐτῶν παθημάτων ὧν καὶ ἡμεῖς πάσχομεν. καὶ
of them sufferings which also we suffer. And

05 1680 1473 949 5228 1473 3609a
ἡ ἐλπὶς ἡμῶν βεβαία ὑπὲρ ὑμῶν εἰδότες
the hope of us firm on behalf of you having known

3754 5613 2844 1510 022 3804 3779
ὅτι ὡς κοινωνοί ἐστε τῶν παθημάτων, οὕτως
that as partners you are of the sufferings, thusly

2532 06 3874 8 3756 1063 2309 1473
καὶ τῆς παρακλήσεως. Οὐ γὰρ θέλομεν ὑμᾶς
also of the encouragement. Not for we want you

50 80 5228 06 2347
ἀγνοεῖν, ἀδελφοί, ὑπὲρ τῆς θλίψεως
to not know, brothers, on behalf of the affliction

1473	06	1096		1722	07	773		3754	2596
ἡμῶν	τῆς	γενομένης	ἐν	τῇ	Ἀσίᾳ,	ὅτι	καθ᾽
of us	the	having become	in	the	Asia,	that	by

5236		5228	1411	916		5620
ὑπερβολὴν	ὑπὲρ	δύναμιν	ἐβαρήθημεν	ὥστε
excess	beyond	power	we were burdened	so that

1820   1473 2532 010 2198   9 235
ἐξαπορηθῆναι   ἡμᾶς καὶ τοῦ ζῆν·   ἀλλὰ
to be in great doubt us   even the to live; but

846   1722 1438   012 610   02   2288
αὐτοὶ   ἐν ἑαυτοῖς τὸ ἀπόκριμα τοῦ   θανάτου
ourselves in ourselves the sentence of the death

2192   2443 3361 3982   1510
ἐσχήκαμεν, ἵνα μὴ πεποιθότες   ὦμεν
we have had, that not +having persuaded we might be+

1909 1438   235 1909 03 2316 03   1453   016
ἐφ᾽ ἑαυτοῖς   ἀλλ᾽ ἐπὶ τῷ θεῷ τῷ ἐγείροντι τοὺς
on ourselves but on the God the one raising the

3498   10 3739 1537 5082   2288   4506   1473
νεκρούς·   ὃς ἐκ τηλικούτου θανάτου ἐρρύσατο ἡμᾶς
dead,   who from so great death rescued us

2532 4506   1519 3739 1679   3754 2532
καὶ ῥύσεται,   εἰς ὃν ἠλπίκαμεν   [ὅτι] καὶ
and he will rescue, in what we have hoped that also

2089 4506   11 4943   2532 1473 5228
ἔτι ῥύσεται,   συνυπουργούντων καὶ ὑμῶν ὑπὲρ
still will rescue, working together and you on behalf

1473 07 1162   2443 1537 4183   4383   09 1519
ἡμῶν τῇ δεήσει, ἵνα ἐκ πολλῶν προσώπων τὸ εἰς
of us the request, that from many faces   the into

1473 5486   1223   4183 2168   5228
ἡμᾶς χάρισμα διὰ   πολλῶν εὐχαριστηθῇ ὑπὲρ
us favor   through many he might give on behalf
    gift   good favor

1473   12 05 1063 2746   1473 3778 1510   09
ἡμῶν.   Ἡ γὰρ καύχησις ἡμῶν αὕτη ἐστίν, τὸ
of us.   The for brag   of us this is,   the

3142   06   4893   1473 3754 1722 572
μαρτύριον τῆς   συνειδήσεως ἡμῶν, ὅτι ἐν ἁπλότητι
testimony of the conscience of us, that in openness

2532 1505   02   2316   2532 3756 1722 4678
καὶ εἰλικρινείᾳ τοῦ θεοῦ, [καὶ] οὐκ ἐν σοφίᾳ
and unmixedness of the God, and not in wisdom

4559   235 1722 5485   2316   390   1722
σαρκικῇ ἀλλ᾽ ἐν χάριτι θεοῦ, ἀνεστράφημεν ἐν
fleshly but in favor of God, we behaved   in

03 2889   4056   1161 4314   1473
τῷ κόσμῳ, περισσοτέρως δὲ πρὸς ὑμᾶς.
the world, more exceedingly but toward you.

13 3756 1063 243   1125   1473 235 2228 3739
   οὐ γὰρ ἄλλα γράφομεν ὑμῖν ἀλλ᾽ ἢ ἃ
   Not for others we write to you but or what

314   2228 2532 1921   1679   1161 3754
ἀναγινώσκετε ἢ   καὶ ἐπιγινώσκετε· ἐλπίζω δὲ ὅτι
you read   or   even you perceive; I hope but that

2193 5056   1921   14 2531   2532
ἕως τέλους ἐπιγνώσεσθε,   καθὼς καὶ
until completion you will perceive, just as also

1921   1473 575 3313   3754 2745   1473
ἐπέγνωτε ἡμᾶς ἀπὸ μέρους, ὅτι καύχημα ὑμῶν
so you perceived us from part, that brag   of you

1510 2509   2532 1473 1473 1722 07 2250
ἐσμεν καθάπερ   καὶ ὑμεῖς ἡμῶν ἐν τῇ ἡμέρᾳ
we are just as indeed also you of us in the day

02   2962   1473 2424   15 2532 3778   07
τοῦ κυρίου [ἡμῶν] Ἰησοῦ.   Καὶ ταύτῃ τῇ
of the Master of us Jesus. And in this the

4006   1014   4387   4314 1473 2064
πεποιθήσει ἐβουλόμην πρότερον πρὸς ὑμᾶς ἐλθεῖν,
persuasion I was planning former to you to come,

---

we experienced in Asia; for we were so utterly, unbearably crushed that we despaired of life itself. [9]Indeed, we felt that we had received the sentence of death so that we would rely not on ourselves but on God who raises the dead. [10]He who rescued us from so deadly a peril will continue to rescue us; on him we have set our hope that he will rescue us again, [11]as you also join in helping us by your prayers, so that many will give thanks on our[a] behalf for the blessing granted us through the prayers of many.

12 Indeed, this is our boast, the testimony of our conscience: we have behaved in the world with frankness[b] and godly sincerity, not by earthly wisdom but by the grace of God—and all the more toward you. [13]For we write you nothing other than what you can read and also understand; I hope you will understand until the end—[14]as you have already understood us in part—that on the day of the Lord Jesus we are your boast even as you are our boast.

15 Since I was sure of this, I wanted to come to you first,

---

a Other ancient authorities read *your*
b Other ancient authorities read *holiness*

so that you might have a double favor;[a] [16]I wanted to visit you on my way to Macedonia, and to come back to you from Macedonia and have you send me on to Judea. [17]Was I vacillating when I wanted to do this? Do I make my plans according to ordinary human standards,[b] ready to say "Yes, yes" and "No, no" at the same time? [18]As surely as God is faithful, our word to you has not been "Yes and No." [19]For the Son of God, Jesus Christ, whom we proclaimed among you, Silvanus and Timothy and I, was not "Yes and No"; but in him it is always "Yes." [20]For in him every one of God's promises is a "Yes." For this reason it is through him that we say the "Amen," to the glory of God. [21]But it is God who establishes us with you in Christ and has anointed us, [22]by putting his seal on us and giving us his Spirit in our hearts as a first installment.

23 But I call on God as witness against me: it was to spare you that I did not come again to Corinth. [24]I do not mean to imply that we lord it over your faith; rather, we are workers with you for your joy, because you stand firm in the faith. [2:1] So I made up my mind

[a] Other ancient authorities read *pleasure*
[b] Gk *according to the flesh*

2443	1208	5485	2192	**16** 2532 1223	1473
ἵνα	δευτέραν	χάριν	σχῆτε,	καὶ δι'	ὑμῶν
that	second	favor	you might have,	and through	you

1330   1519 3109   2532 3825 575 3109
διελθεῖν   εἰς Μακεδονίαν καὶ πάλιν ἀπὸ Μακεδονίας
to go through into Macedonia and again from Macedonia

2064   4314 1473 2532 5259 1473 4311
ἐλθεῖν πρὸς ὑμᾶς καὶ ὑφ' ὑμῶν προπεμφθῆναι
to go to you and by you to be sent forward

1519 08   2449   **17** 3778 3767 1014   3385
εἰς τὴν Ἰουδαίαν.   τοῦτο οὖν βουλόμενος μήτι
into the Judea.   This then planning neither

686 07   1644   5530   2228 3739 1011
ἄρα τῇ ἐλαφρίᾳ ἐχρησάμην; ἢ ἃ βουλεύομαι
then in the lightness I used? Or what I plan

2596 4561   1011   2443 1510   3844 1473
κατὰ σάρκα βουλεύομαι, ἵνα ᾖ   παρ' ἐμοὶ
by flesh I plan, that it might be beside me

09 3483 3483 3483 2532 09 3756a 3756a **18** 4103   1161
τὸ ναὶ ναὶ καὶ τὸ οὔ οὔ;   πιστὸς δὲ
the yes yes and the no no?   Trustful but

01 2316 3754 01 3056 1473 01 4314 1473 3756 1510
ὁ θεὸς ὅτι ὁ λόγος ἡμῶν ὁ πρὸς ὑμᾶς οὐκ ἔστιν
the God that the word of us the to you not is

3483 2532 3756a **19** 01 02   2316 1063 5207 2424
ναὶ καὶ οὔ.   ὁ τοῦ   θεοῦ γὰρ υἱὸς Ἰησοῦς
yes and no.   The of the God for son Jesus

5547   01 1722 1473 1223   1473 2784   1223
Χριστὸς ὁ ἐν ὑμῖν δι' ἡμῶν κηρυχθείς, δι'
Christ the in you through us having been through announced,

1473 2532 4610   2532 5095   3756 1096   3483
ἐμοῦ καὶ Σιλουανοῦ καὶ Τιμοθέου, οὐκ ἐγένετο ναὶ
me and Silvanus and Timothy, not it became yes

2532 3756a 235 3483 1722 846 1096
καὶ οὔ ἀλλὰ ναὶ ἐν αὐτῷ γέγονεν.
and no but yes in him it has become.

20 3745   1063 1860 2016   1722 846 09
ὅσαι   γὰρ ἐπαγγελίαι θεοῦ, ἐν αὐτῷ τὸ
As many as for promises of God, in him the

3483 1352   2532 1223 846 09 281 03   2316
ναί· διὸ   καὶ δι' αὐτοῦ τὸ ἀμὴν τῷ   θεῷ
yes; therefore also through him the amen to the God

4314 1391   1223   1473 **21** 01 1161 950
πρὸς δόξαν δι' ἡμῶν.   ὁ δὲ βεβαιῶν
to splendor through us.   The but confirming

1473 4862 1473 1519 5547   2532 5548   1473
ἡμᾶς σὺν ὑμῖν εἰς Χριστὸν καὶ χρίσας ἡμᾶς
us with you in Christ and having anointed us

2316 **22** 01 2532 4972   1473 2532 1325
θεός,   ὁ καὶ σφραγισάμενος ἡμᾶς καὶ δοὺς
God,   the also having sealed us and having given

04 728   010 4151   1722 019 2588
τὸν ἀρραβῶνα τοῦ πνεύματος ἐν ταῖς καρδίαις
the earnest of the spirit in the hearts

1473 **23** 1473 1161 3144   04 2316 1941
ἡμῶν.   Ἐγὼ δὲ μάρτυρα τὸν θεὸν ἐπικαλοῦμαι
of us.   I but testifier the God I myself call on

1909 08 1699 5590 3754 5339   1473 3765
ἐπὶ τὴν ἐμὴν ψυχήν, ὅτι φειδόμενος ὑμῶν οὐκέτι
on the my soul, that sparing of you no longer

2064 1519 2882   **24** 3756 3754 2961   1473
ἦλθον εἰς Κόρινθον.   οὐχ ὅτι κυριεύομεν ὑμῶν
I came into Corinth.   Not that we master of you

06 4102 235 4904   1510 06 5479 1473
τῆς πίστεως ἀλλὰ συνεργοί ἐσμεν τῆς χαρᾶς ὑμῶν·
the trust but co-workers we are of the joy of you;

07   1063 4102 2476   **2:1** 2919 1063 1683
τῇ   γὰρ πίστει ἑστήκατε.   Ἔκρινα γὰρ ἐμαυτῷ
in the for trust you have stood.   I judged for myself

3778	012	3361	3825	1722	3077	4314	1473	2064

τοῦτο τὸ μὴ πάλιν ἐν λύπῃ πρὸς ὑμᾶς ἐλθεῖν.
this the not again in grief to you to come.

2
1487 1063 1473 3076   1473 2532 5101 01 2165
εἰ γὰρ ἐγὼ λυπῶ ὑμᾶς, καὶ τίς ὁ εὐφραίνων
If for I grieve you, and who the making merry

1473 1487 3361 01 3076   1537 1473   2532
με εἰ μὴ ὁ λυπούμενος ἐξ ἐμοῦ; **3** καὶ
me except the being grieved from me? And

1125   3778   846   2443 3361 2064   3077
ἔγραψα τοῦτο αὐτό, ἵνα μὴ ἐλθὼν λύπην
I wrote this same, that not having come grief

2192   575 3739 1163   1473
σχῶ ἀφ' ὧν ἔδει με
I might have from whom it was necessary me

5463   3982   1909 3956 1473 3754 05
χαίρειν, πεποιθὼς ἐπὶ πάντας ὑμᾶς ὅτι ἡ
to rejoice, being persuaded on all you that the

1699 5479 3956   1473 1510   1537 1063 4183
ἐμὴ χαρὰ πάντων ὑμῶν ἐστιν. **4** ἐκ γὰρ πολλῆς
my joy of all you is. From for much

2347   2532 4928   2588   1125   1473
θλίψεως καὶ συνοχῆς καρδίας ἔγραψα ὑμῖν
affliction and anguish of heart I wrote to you

1223   4183   1144   3756 2443 3076
διὰ πολλῶν δακρύων, οὐχ ἵνα λυπηθῆτε
through many tears, not that you might be grieved

235 08 26   2443 1097   3739 2192
ἀλλὰ τὴν ἀγάπην ἵνα γνῶτε ἣν ἔχω
but the love that you might know which I have

4056   1519 1473 **5** 1487 1161 5100 3076
περισσοτέρως εἰς ὑμᾶς. Εἰ δέ τις λελύπηκεν,
more exceedingly to you. If but some has grieved,

3756 1473 3076   235 575 3313   2443 3361
οὐκ ἐμὲ λελύπηκεν, ἀλλὰ ἀπὸ μέρους, ἵνα μὴ
not me he has grieved, but from part, that not

1912   3956 1473 **6** 2425 03   5108
ἐπιβαρῶ, πάντας ὑμᾶς. ἱκανὸν τῷ τοιούτῳ
I might burden on, all you. Enough to the such

05 2009   3778 05 5259 014 4183 **7** 5620
ἡ ἐπιτιμία αὕτη ἡ ὑπὸ τῶν πλειόνων, ὥστε
the admonishment this the by the more, so that

5121   3123   1473 5483   2532
τοὐναντίον μᾶλλον ὑμᾶς χαρίσασθαι καὶ
on the contrary more you to be favored and

3870   3361 4458 07   4055   3077
παρακαλέσαι, μή πως τῇ περισσοτέρᾳ λύπῃ
to encourage, not perhaps in the more excessive grief

2666   01 5108   **8** 1352
καταποθῇ ὁ τοιοῦτος. διὸ
might be swallowed the such. Therefore

3870   1473 2964   1519 846   26
παρακαλῶ ὑμᾶς κυρῶσαι εἰς αὐτὸν ἀγάπην·
I encourage you to authenticate to him love;

9 1519 3778 1063 2532 1125   2443 1097
εἰς τοῦτο γὰρ καὶ ἔγραψα, ἵνα γνῶ
for this for also I wrote, that I might know

08 1382   1473   1487 1519 3956 5255   1510
τὴν δοκιμὴν ὑμῶν, εἰ εἰς πάντα ὑπήκοοί ἐστε.
the approval of you, if in all obedient you are.

10 3739   1161 5100 5483   2504   2532 1063 1473
ᾧ δέ τι χαρίζεσθε, κἀγώ· καὶ γὰρ ἐγὼ
To whom but some you favor, also I; also for I

3739 5483   1487 5100 5483   1223
ὃ κεχάρισμαι, εἴ τι κεχάρισμαι, δι'
what have favored, if some I have favored, through

1473 1722 4383   5547   **11** 2443 3361 4122
ὑμᾶς ἐν προσώπῳ Χριστοῦ, ἵνα μὴ πλεονεκτηθῶμεν
you in face of Christ, that not we might be
taken more of

not to make you another painful visit. [2]For if I cause you pain, who is there to make me glad but the one whom I have pained? [3]And I wrote as I did, so that when I came, I might not suffer pain from those who should have made me rejoice; for I am confident about all of you, that my joy would be the joy of all of you. [4]For I wrote you out of much distress and anguish of heart and with many tears, not to cause you pain, but to let you know the abundant love that I have for you.

5 But if anyone has caused pain, he has caused it not to me, but to some extent—not to exaggerate it—to all of you. [6]This punishment by the majority is enough for such a person; [7]so now instead you should forgive and console him, so that he may not be overwhelmed by excessive sorrow. [8]So I urge you to reaffirm your love for him. [9]I wrote for this reason: to test you and to know whether you are obedient in everything. [10]Anyone whom you forgive, I also forgive. What I have forgiven, if I have forgiven anything, has been for your sake in the presence of Christ. [11]And we do this so that

we may not be outwitted by Satan; for we are not ignorant of his designs.

12 When I came to Troas to proclaim the good news of Christ, a door was opened for me in the Lord; [13]but my mind could not rest because I did not find my brother Titus there. So I said farewell to them and went on to Macedonia.

14 But thanks be to God, who in Christ always leads us in triumphal procession, and through us spreads in every place the fragrance that comes from knowing him. [15]For we are the aroma of Christ to God among those who are being saved and among those who are perishing; [16]to the one a fragrance from death to death, to the other a fragrance from life to life. Who is sufficient for these things? [17]For we are not peddlers of God's word like so many;[a] but in Christ we speak as persons of sincerity, as persons sent from God and standing in his presence.

CHAPTER 3

Are we beginning to commend ourselves again? Surely we do not need, as some do, letters of recommendation to you or from you, do we? [2]You yourselves are our letter, written on our[b] hearts, to be known and read by all; [3]and you show that you are a letter of Christ,

[a] Other ancient authorities read like the others
[b] Other ancient authorities read your

5259	02	4567	3756 1063 846	024 3540	
ὑπὸ	τοῦ	σατανᾶ·	οὐ γὰρ αὐτοῦ	τὰ νοήματα	
by	the	adversary;	not for of him	the thoughts	

50
ἀγνοοῦμεν. **12** Ἐλθὼν
we are unknowing.   Having come

2064   1161 1519 08   5174
δὲ   εἰς τὴν Τρωάδα
but   into the Troas

1519 012 2098   02   5547   2532 2374   1473
εἰς τὸ εὐαγγέλιον τοῦ Χριστοῦ καὶ θύρας μοι
for the good message of the Christ and door to me

455   1722 2962   **13** 3756 2192
ἀνεῳγμένης   ἐν κυρίῳ,   οὐκ ἔσχηκα
having been opened in Master,   not I have had

425   011   4151   1473 011 3361 2147   1473 5103
ἄνεσιν τῷ   πνεύματί μου   τῷ μὴ εὑρεῖν με Τίτον
relief to the spirit   of me the not to find me Titus

04 80   1473   235   657   846
τὸν ἀδελφόν μου,   ἀλλὰ ἀποταξάμενος   αὐτοῖς
the brother of me, but having said good-bye to them

1831   1519 3109   03   1161 2316 5485
ἐξῆλθον εἰς Μακεδονίαν. **14** Τῷ δὲ θεῷ χάρις
I went out into Macedonia.   To the but God favor

03   3842   2358   1473 1722 03
τῷ   πάντοτε θριαμβεύοντι   ἡμᾶς ἐν τῷ
to the always one leading in triumph us   in the

5547   2532 08   3744   06   1108   846
Χριστῷ καὶ τὴν ὀσμὴν τῆς γνώσεως αὐτοῦ
Christ and the odor of the knowledge of him

5319   1223   1473 1722 3956 5117   **15** 3754
φανεροῦντι δι'   ἡμῶν ἐν παντὶ τόπῳ·   ὅτι
demonstrating through us in all place;   because

5547   2175   1510 03   2316 1722 015
Χριστοῦ εὐωδία   ἐσμὲν τῷ θεῷ ἐν τοῖς
of Christ good smell we are to the God in   the ones

4982   2532 1722 015   622
σῳζομένοις καὶ ἐν τοῖς ἀπολλυμένοις,
being delivered and in the ones being destroyed,

16 3739   3303   3744 1537 2288   1519 2288
οἷς μὲν   ὀσμὴ ἐκ θανάτου εἰς θάνατον,
to whom indeed odor from death into death,

3739   1161 3744 1537 2222 1519 2222   2532 4314 3778
οἷς δὲ ὀσμὴ ἐκ ζωῆς εἰς ζωήν. καὶ πρὸς ταῦτα
to whom but odor from life into life. And to these

5101 2425   **17** 3756 1063 1510   5613 013 4183
τίς ἱκανός;   οὐ γὰρ ἐσμεν ὡς οἱ πολλοὶ
who enough?   Not for we are as the many

2585   04 3056 02   2316 235 5613 1537
καπηλεύοντες τὸν λόγον τοῦ θεοῦ, ἀλλ' ὡς ἐξ
trading on the word of the God, but as from

1505   235 5613 1537 2316 2713   2316
εἰλικρινείας, ἀλλ' ὡς ἐκ θεοῦ κατέναντι θεοῦ
unmixedness, but as from God over against God

1722 5547   2980   **3:1** 757   3825 1438
ἐν Χριστῷ λαλοῦμεν.   Ἀρχόμεθα πάλιν ἑαυτοὺς
in Christ we speak.   Do we begin again ourselves

4921   2228 3361 5535   5613 5100 4956
συνιστάνειν; ἢ μὴ χρῄζομεν ὥς τινες συστατικῶν
to commend? Or not we need as some commendation

1992   4314 1473 2228 1537 1473   **2** 05 1992
ἐπιστολῶν πρὸς ὑμᾶς ἢ ἐξ ὑμῶν; ἡ ἐπιστολὴ
letters to you or from you? The letter

1473   1473 1510 1449   1722 019 2588   1473
ἡμῶν ὑμεῖς ἐστε, ἐγγεγραμμένη ἐν ταῖς καρδίαις ἡμῶν,
of us you are, having been in the hearts of us,
written in

1097   2532 314   5259 3956   444
γινωσκομένη καὶ ἀναγινωσκομένη ὑπὸ πάντων ἀνθρώπων,
being known and being read by all men,

3 5319   3756 1510 1992   5547
φανερούμενοι ὅτι ἐστὲ ἐπιστολὴ Χριστοῦ
being demonstrated that you are letter of Christ

```
1247                    5259 1473  1449                        3756
διακονηθεῖσα           ὑφ' ἡμῶν, ἐγγεγραμμένη                   οὐ
having been served by  us,   having been written in      not
3189          235  4151        2316      2198   3756 1722 4109
μέλανι       ἀλλὰ πνεύματι    θεοῦ     ζῶντος, οὐκ ἐν πλαξὶν
in black but  in spirit of  God    living,  not   in tablets
3035       235  1722 4109     2588           4560
λιθίναις ἀλλ' ἐν   πλαξὶν καρδίαις σαρκίναις.
of 'stone but  in  tablets of hearts of flesh.

  4006        1161 5108      2192       1223      02  5547
4 Πεποίθησιν δὲ   τοιαύτην ἔχομεν διὰ      τοῦ Χριστοῦ
  Persuasion but  such      we have through the Christ
4314 04  2316  5 3756 3754 575  1438        2425
πρὸς τὸν θεόν. 5 οὐχ ὅτι ἀφ' ἑαυτῶν       ἱκανοί
to   the God.   Not  that from ourselves enough
1510      3049          5100 5613 1537 1438          235   05
ἐσμεν λογίσασθαί τι ὡς  ἐξ   ἑαυτῶν,   ἀλλ' ἡ
we are to reason  some as  from ourselves, but  the
2426        1473  1537 02  2316  6 3739 2532 2427
ἱκανότης ἡμῶν ἐκ   τοῦ θεοῦ, 6 ὃς  καὶ ἱκάνωσεν
enoughness of us from the God,  who also made enough
1473 1249        2537        3756 1121       235
ἡμᾶς διακόνους καινῆς διαθήκης, οὐ γράμματος ἀλλὰ
us   servants  of new agreement, not of letter but
4151          09  1063 1121     615           09  1161 4151
πνεύματος· τὸ γὰρ γράμμα ἀποκτέννει, τὸ δὲ  πνεῦμα
of spirit; the for  letter kills,   the but  spirit
2227        7 1487 1161 05  1248       02      2288
ζωοποιεῖ. 7 Εἰ   δὲ  ἡ  διακονία τοῦ    θανάτου
makes alive. If  but  the service of the death
1722 1121     1795            3037        1096
ἐν   γράμμασιν ἐντετυπωμένη   λίθοις   ἐγενήθη
in   letters    having been engraved in stones became
1722 1391      5620      3361 1410      816       016
ἐν   δόξῃ,   ὥστε   μὴ δύνασθαι ἀτενίσαι τοὺς
in   splendor, so that not  to be able to stare the
5207    2474   1519 012 4383       3475    1223
υἱοὺς 'Ισραὴλ εἰς τὸ πρόσωπον Μωϋσέως διὰ
sons  Israel in  the face      of Moses because of
08 1391     010    4383        846  08
τὴν δόξαν  τοῦ  προσώπου αὐτοῦ τὴν
the splendor of the face    of him the one
2673                8 4459 3780 3123    05  1248       010
καταργουμένην, 8 πῶς οὐχὶ μᾶλλον ἡ  διακονία τοῦ
being abolished, how  not  more    the service of the
4151        1510      1722 1391     9 1487 1063 07
πνεύματος ἔσται ἐν  δόξῃ; 9 εἰ  γὰρ τῇ
spirit    will be in  splendor? If  for  in the
1248       06  2633         1391      4183 3123
διακονίᾳ τῆς  κατακρίσεως δόξα,   πολλῷ μᾶλλον
service  of the condemnation splendor, much  more
4052       05  1248      06  1343        1391
περισσεύει ἡ  διακονία τῆς  δικαιοσύνης δόξῃ.
exceeds   the service of the rightness  in splendor.
    2532 1063 3756 1392      09  1392
10 καὶ γὰρ οὐ  δεδόξασται    τὸ δεδοξασμένον
   Also for not has been given the one having been
                splendor                  given splendor
1722 3778 011 3313   1511a      06        5235
ἐν   τούτῳ τῷ μέρει εἵνεκεν τῆς  ὑπερβαλλούσης
in   this  the part  on account of the exceeding
1391        11 1487 1063 09  2673
δόξης.  11 εἰ   γὰρ τὸ  καταργούμενον
splendor. If   for  the one being abolished
1223      1391     4183  3123    09  3306       1722
διὰ      δόξης,  πολλῷ μᾶλλον τὸ μένον      ἐν
through splendor, in much more  the one staying in
1391       2192    3767 5108     1680    4183   3954
δόξῃ. 12 Ἔχοντες οὖν τοιαύτην ἐλπίδα πολλῇ παρρησίᾳ
splendor. Having then such      hope   in much boldness
```

prepared by us, written not with ink but with the Spirit of the living God, not on tablets of stone but on tablets of human hearts.

4 Such is the confidence that we have through Christ toward God. [5]Not that we are competent of ourselves to claim anything as coming from us; our competence is from God, [6]who has made us competent to be ministers of a new covenant, not of letter but of spirit; for the letter kills, but the Spirit gives life.

7 Now if the ministry of death, chiseled in letters on stone tablets,[a] came in glory so that the people of Israel could not gaze at Moses' face because of the glory of his face, a glory now set aside, [8]how much more will the ministry of the Spirit come in glory? [9]For if there was glory in the ministry of condemnation, much more does the ministry of justification abound in glory! [10]Indeed, what once had glory has lost its glory because of the greater glory; [11]for if what was set aside came through glory, much more has the permanent come in glory!

12 Since, then, we have such a hope, we act with great boldness,

---

[a] Gk on stones

13not like Moses, who put a veil over his face to keep the people of Israel from gazing at the end of the glory thata was being set aside. 14But their minds were hardened. Indeed, to this very day, when they hear the reading of the old covenant, that same veil is still there, since only in Christ is it set aside. 15Indeed, to this very day whenever Moses is read, a veil lies over their minds; 16but when one turns to the Lord, the veil is removed. 17Now the Lord is the Spirit, and where the Spirit of the Lord is, there is freedom. 18And all of us, with unveiled faces, seeing the glory of the Lord as though reflected in a mirror, are being transformed into the same image from one degree of glory to another; for this comes from the Lord, the Spirit.

CHAPTER 4

Therefore, since it is by God's mercy that we are engaged in this ministry, we do not lose heart. 2We have renounced the shameful things that one hides; we refuse to practice cunning or to falsify God's word; but by the open statement of the truth we commend ourselves to the conscience of everyone in the sight of God. 3And even if

a Gk of what

		5530		2532	3756	2509		3475	5087

5530   2532 3756 2509   3475   5087
χρώμεθα   13 καὶ   οὐ καθάπερ   Μωϋσῆς ἐτίθει
we use   and not just as indeed Moses was setting
2571   1909 012 4383   846   4314 012 3361
κάλυμμα ἐπὶ τὸ πρόσωπον αὐτοῦ πρὸς τὸ μὴ
veil   on the face   of him to the not
816   016 5207   2474   1519 012 5056   010
ἀτενίσαι τοὺς υἱοὺς 'Ισραὴλ εἰς τὸ τέλος   τοῦ
to stare the sons Israel to   the completion of the
2673   235 4456   021 3540
καταργουμένου.   14 ἀλλὰ ἐπωρώθη   τὰ νοήματα
one being abolished.   But were hardened the thoughts
846   891 1063 06 4594   2250 09 846 2571
αὐτῶν. ἄχρι γὰρ τῆς σήμερον ἡμέρας τὸ αὐτὸ κάλυμμα
of them. Until for the today day   the same veil
1909 07 320   06   3820   1242   3306
ἐπὶ τῇ ἀναγνώσει τῆς παλαιᾶς διαθήκης μένει,
on   the reading   of the old   agreement stays,
3361 343   3754 1722 5547   2673
μὴ ἀνακαλυπτόμενον ὅτι   ἐν Χριστῷ καταργεῖται·
not being uncovered because in Christ it is abolished;
      235 2193 4594   2259 302 314   3475
15 ἀλλ' ἕως σήμερον ἡνίκα ἂν ἀναγινώσκηται Μωϋσῆς,
    but until today when   - might be read Moses,
2571   1909 08 2588   846   2749   16 2259
κάλυμμα ἐπὶ τὴν καρδίαν αὐτῶν κεῖται·   16 ἡνίκα
veil   on the heart   of them lies;   when
1161 1437 1994   4314 2962
δὲ ἐὰν ἐπιστρέψῃ   πρὸς κύριον,
but if he might return to   Master,
4014   09 2571   01 1161 2962
περιαιρεῖται   τὸ κάλυμμα. 17 ὁ δὲ κύριος
is lifted up around the veil.   The but Master
09   4151   1510   3757 1161 09 4151   2962
τὸ πνεῦμά ἐστιν· οὗ δὲ τὸ πνεῦμα κυρίου,
the spirit is;   where but the spirit of Master,
1657   18 1473 1161 3956   343
ἐλευθερία.   18 ἡμεῖς δὲ πάντες ἀνακεκαλυμμένῳ
freedom.   We   but all   having been uncovered
4383   08 1391   2962   2734
προσώπῳ τὴν δόξαν κυρίου κατοπτριζόμενοι
in face the splendor of Master producing reflection
08 846   1504 3339   575 1391
τὴν αὐτὴν εἰκόνα μεταμορφούμεθα   ἀπὸ δόξης
the same image we are being transformed from splendor
1519 1391   2509   575 2962   4151
εἰς δόξαν καθάπερ   ἀπὸ κυρίου πνεύματος.
into splendor just as indeed from Master spirit.
    1223   3778   2192   08 1248   3778   2531
4:1 Διὰ   τοῦτο, ἔχοντες τὴν διακονίαν ταύτην καθὼς
    Through this, having the service   this   just as
1653   3756 1457a   2   235
ἠλεήθημεν,   οὐκ ἐγκακοῦμεν   2 ἀλλὰ
we were shown mercy, not we give in to bad but
550   024 2927 06   152   3361
ἀπειπάμεθα τὰ κρυπτὰ τῆς αἰσχύνης, μὴ
we renounced the hidden of the shame,   not
4043   1722 3834   3366   1389   04
περιπατοῦντες ἐν πανουργίᾳ μηδὲ δολοῦντες τὸν
walking around in trickery but not beguiling the
3056 02   2316 235 07   5321   06
λόγον τοῦ θεοῦ ἀλλὰ τῇ φανερώσει   τῆς
word of the God but in the demonstration of the
225   4921   1438   4314 3956 4893
ἀληθείας συνιστάνοντες ἑαυτοὺς πρὸς πᾶσαν συνείδησιν
truth   commending   ourselves to   all   conscience
444   1799   02 2316   3 1487 1161 2532 1510
ἀνθρώπων ἐνώπιον τοῦ θεοῦ. 3 εἰ δὲ καὶ ἔστιν
of men   before the God.   If but also is+

2572	09	2098	1473	1722	015
κεκαλυμμένον	τὸ	εὐαγγέλιον	ἡμῶν,	ἐν	τοῖς
+having been covered	the	good message	of us,	in	the

622		1510	2572		
ἀπολλυμένοις		ἐστὶν	κεκαλυμμένον,		
ones being destroyed		it is+	+having been covered,		

4

1722	3739	01	2316	02	165	3778	5186
ἐν	οἷς	ὁ	θεὸς	τοῦ	αἰῶνος	τούτου	ἐτύφλωσεν
in	whom	the	God	of the	age	this	blinded

024	3540	014	571	1519	012	3361	826
τὰ	νοήματα	τῶν	ἀπίστων	εἰς	τὸ	μὴ	αὐγάσαι
the	thoughts	of the	untrustful	in	the	not	to dawn

04	5462	010	2098	06	1391
τὸν	φωτισμὸν	τοῦ	εὐαγγελίου	τῆς	δόξης
the	lightening	of the	good message	of the	splendor

02	5547	3739	1510	1504	02	2316	3756
τοῦ	Χριστοῦ,	ὅς	ἐστιν	εἰκὼν	τοῦ	θεοῦ.	Οὐ
of the	Christ,	who	is	image	of the	God.	Not

5

1063	1438	2784	235	2424	5547
γὰρ	ἑαυτοὺς	κηρύσσομεν	ἀλλὰ	Ἰησοῦν	Χριστὸν
for	ourselves	we announce	but	Jesus	Christ

2962	1438	1161	1401	1473	1223	2424
κύριον,	ἑαυτοὺς	δὲ	δούλους	ὑμῶν	διὰ	Ἰησοῦν.
Master,	ourselves	but	slaves	of you	through	Jesus.

6

3754	01	3754	01	3004	1537	4655
ὅτι	ὁ	θεὸς	ὁ	εἰπών·	ἐκ	σκότους
Because	the	God	the	one having said,	from	dark

5457	2989	3739	2989	1722	019	2588	1473
φῶς	λάμψει,	ὃς	ἔλαμψεν	ἐν	ταῖς	καρδίαις	ἡμῶν
light	will shine,	who	shined	in	the	hearts	of us

4314	5462	06	1108	06	1391
πρὸς	φωτισμὸν	τῆς	γνώσεως	τῆς	δόξης
to	lightening	of the	knowledge	of the	splendor

02	2316	1722	4383	2424	5547	2192
τοῦ	θεοῦ	ἐν	προσώπῳ	[Ἰησοῦ]	Χριστοῦ.	Ἔχομεν
of the	God	in	face	of Jesus	Christ.	We have

7

1161	04	2344	3778	1722	3749	4632
δὲ	τὸν	θησαυρὸν	τοῦτον	ἐν	ὀστρακίνοις	σκεύεσιν,
but	the	treasure	this	in	clay	pots,

2443	05	5236	06	1411	1510	02	2316
ἵνα	ἡ	ὑπερβολὴ	τῆς	δυνάμεως	ᾖ	τοῦ	θεοῦ
that	the	excess	of the	power	might be	of the	God

2532	3361	1537	1473	1722	3956	2346
καὶ	μὴ	ἐξ	ἡμῶν·	ἐν	παντὶ	θλιβόμενοι
and	not	from	us;	in	all	being afflicted

8

235	3756	4729	639	235	3756
ἀλλ᾽	οὐ	στενοχωρούμενοι,	ἀπορούμενοι	ἀλλ᾽	οὐκ
but	not	being anguished,	doubting	but	not

1820	1377	235	3756
ἐξαπορούμενοι,	διωκόμενοι	ἀλλ᾽	οὐκ
doubting greatly,	being pursued	but	not

9

1459	2598	235	3756
ἐγκαταλειπόμενοι,	καταβαλλόμενοι	ἀλλ᾽	οὐκ
being left behind,	being thrown down	but	not

622	3842	08	3500	02	2424
ἀπολλύμενοι,	πάντοτε	τὴν	νέκρωσιν	τοῦ	Ἰησοῦ
being destroyed,	always	the	deadness	of the	Jesus

10

1722	011	4983	4064	2443	2532	05	2222
ἐν	τῷ	σώματι	περιφέροντες,	ἵνα	καὶ	ἡ	ζωὴ
in	the body	bearing around,		that	also	the	life

02	2424	1722	011	4983	1473	5319
τοῦ	Ἰησοῦ	ἐν	τῷ	σώματι	ἡμῶν	φανερωθῇ.
of the	Jesus	in	the body		of us	might be demonstrated.

11

104	1063	1473	013	2198	1519	2288
ἀεὶ	γὰρ	ἡμεῖς	οἱ	ζῶντες	εἰς	θάνατον
Always	for	we	the	living	into	death

3860	1223	2424	2443	2532	05
παραδιδόμεθα	διὰ	Ἰησοῦν,	ἵνα	καὶ	ἡ
are being given over	through	Jesus,	that	also	the

our gospel is veiled, it is veiled to those who are perishing. [4]In their case the god of this world has blinded the minds of the unbelievers, to keep them from seeing the light of the gospel of the glory of Christ, who is the image of God. [5]For we do not proclaim ourselves; we proclaim Jesus Christ as Lord and ourselves as , your slaves for Jesus' sake. [6]For it is the God who said, "Let light shine out of darkness," who has shone in our hearts to give the light of the knowledge of the glory of God in the face of Jesus Christ.

[7]But we have this treasure in clay jars, so that it may be made clear that this extraordinary power belongs to God and does not come from us. [8]We are afflicted in every way, but not crushed; perplexed, but not driven to despair; [9]persecuted, but not forsaken; struck down, but not destroyed; [10]always carrying in the body the death of Jesus, so that the life of Jesus may also be made visible in our bodies. [11]For while we live, we are always being given up to death for Jesus' sake, so that the

life of Jesus may be made visible in our mortal flesh. [12]So death is at work in us, but life in you.

13 But just as we have the same spirit of faith that is in accordance with scripture—"I believed, and so I spoke"—we also believe, and so we speak, [14]because we know that the one who raised the Lord Jesus will raise us also with Jesus, and will bring us with you into his presence. [15]Yes, everything is for your sake, so that grace, as it extends to more and more people, may increase thanksgiving, to the glory of God.

16 So we do not lose heart. Even though our outer nature is wasting away, our inner nature is being renewed day by day. [17]For this slight momentary affliction is preparing us for an eternal weight of glory beyond all measure, [18]because we look not at what can be seen but at what cannot be seen; for what can be seen is temporary, but what cannot be seen is eternal.

CHAPTER 5

For we know that if the earthly tent we live in is destroyed, we have a building from God, a house not made with hands, eternal in the heavens. [2]For in this tent we groan,

---

2222 02		2424	5319				1722 07
ζωὴ	τοῦ	'Ιησοῦ	φανερωθῇ				ἐν τῇ
life of	the	Jesus	might be demonstrated				in the

2349		4561 1473		5620	01	2288	1722 1473
θνητῇ		σαρκὶ ἡμῶν.	[12]	ὥστε	ὁ	θάνατος	ἐν ἡμῖν
death-like		flesh of us.		So that	the	death	in us

1754		05	1161 2222 1722 1473		2192		1161
ἐνεργεῖται,		ἡ δὲ	ζωὴ ἐν ὑμῖν.	[13]	Ἔχοντες		δὲ
operates,		the but	life in you.		Having		but

012 846	4151	06	4102	2596		012
τὸ αὐτὸ	πνεῦμα	τῆς	πίστεως	κατὰ		τὸ
the same	spirit	of the	trust	according		to the thing

1125		4100	1352	2980	2532
γεγραμμένον·		ἐπίστευσα,	διὸ	ἐλάλησα,	καὶ
having been written,		I trusted,	therefore	I spoke,	and

1473 4100		1352	2532 2980		3609a
ἡμεῖς πιστεύομεν,		διὸ	καὶ λαλοῦμεν,	[14]	εἰδότες
we trust,		therefore	also we speak,		having known

3754 01	1453		04	2962	2424	2532
ὅτι ὁ	ἐγείρας		τὸν	κύριον	'Ιησοῦν	καὶ
that the	one having raised		the	Master	Jesus	also

1473 4862	2424	1453	2532 3936		4862
ἡμᾶς σὺν	'Ιησοῦ	ἐγερεῖ	καὶ παραστήσει		σὺν
us with	Jesus	will raise	and will stand along		with

1473	021 1063 3956	1223		1473	2443 05	5485
ὑμῖν.	[15] τὰ γὰρ πάντα	δι'		ὑμᾶς,	ἵνα ἡ	χάρις
you.	The for all	through		you,	that the	favor

4121		1223	014 4183	08	2169
πλεονάσασα		διὰ	τῶν πλειόνων	τὴν	εὐχαριστίαν
having increased		through	the more	the	good favor

4052		1519 08	1391	02	2316	1352
περισσεύσῃ		εἰς τὴν	δόξαν	τοῦ	θεοῦ.	[16] Διὸ
might exceed		into the	splendor	of the	God.	Therefore

3756 1457a		235	1487 2532 01	1854
οὐκ ἐγκακοῦμεν,		ἀλλ'	εἰ καὶ ὁ	ἔξω
not we give in to bad,		but	if also the	outside

1473	444	1311		235	01 2080
ἡμῶν	ἄνθρωπος	διαφθείρεται,		ἀλλ' ὁ	ἔσω
of us	man	is corrupted thoroughly,		but the	inside

1473	341		2250	2532 2250	09	1063
ἡμῶν	ἀνακαινοῦται		ἡμέρᾳ	καὶ ἡμέρᾳ.	[17] τὸ	γὰρ
of us	is being renewed		day	and day.	The	for

3910	1645	06	2347		1473	2596
παραυτίκα	ἐλαφρὸν	τῆς	θλίψεως		ἡμῶν	καθ'
momentary	light	of the	affliction		of us	by

5236	1519 5236		166	922	1391
ὑπερβολὴν	εἰς ὑπερβολὴν		αἰώνιον	βάρος	δόξης
excess	into excess		eternal	burden	of splendor

2716	1473		3361 4648		1473
κατεργάζεται	ἡμῖν,	[18] μὴ	σκοπούντων		ἡμῶν
works thoroughly	to us,	not	looking carefully		of us

024 991		235	024 3361 991		021 1063
τὰ βλεπόμενα		ἀλλὰ	τὰ μὴ βλεπόμενα·		τὰ γὰρ
the being seen		but	the not being seen;		the for

991		4340	021 1161 3361 991
βλεπόμενα		πρόσκαιρα,	τὰ δὲ μὴ βλεπόμενα
being seen		for season,	the but not being seen

166		3609a	1063 3754 1437 05	1919	1473
αἰώνια.	[5:1]	Οἴδαμεν	γὰρ ὅτι ἐὰν ἡ	ἐπίγειος	ἡμῶν
eternal.		We know	for that if	the on earth	of us

3614 010	01	4636	2647		3619
οἰκία τοῦ		σκήνους	καταλυθῇ,		οἰκοδομὴν
house of the		tent	might be unloosed,		building

1537 2316 2192		3614	886	166	1722
ἐκ θεοῦ ἔχομεν,		οἰκίαν	ἀχειροποίητον	αἰώνιον	ἐν
from God we have,		house	unhandmade	eternal	in

015	3772		2532 1063 1722 3778	4727	012
τοῖς	οὐρανοῖς.	[2]	καὶ γὰρ ἐν τούτῳ	στενάζομεν	τὸ
the	heavens.		Even for in this	we groan	the

3613   1473   012 1537 3772   1902
οἰκητήριον ἡμῶν   τὸ   ἐξ   οὐρανοῦ ἐπενδύσασθαι
house place of us   the from heaven to put on oneself

1971   1487 1065   2532 1562
ἐπιποθοῦντες,   **3** εἴ   γε   καὶ ἐκδυσάμενοι
desiring longingly,   if   indeed and having put off

3756 1131   2147   2532 1063 013 1510
οὐ   γυμνοὶ εὑρεθησόμεθα.   **4** καὶ γὰρ οἱ   ὄντες
not naked we will be found.   And for the ones being

1722 011 4636   4727   916   1909 3739
ἐν   τῷ   σκήνει στενάζομεν βαρούμενοι,   ἐφ' ᾧ
in   the tent   we groan   being burdened, on which

3756 2309   1562   235 1902   2443
οὐ   θέλομεν ἐκδύσασθαι ἀλλ' ἐπενδύσασθαι,   ἵνα
not we want to put off but to put on oneself, that

2666   09   2349   5259 06 2222
καταποθῇ   τὸ   θνητὸν   ὑπὸ τῆς ζωῆς.
might be swallowed down the death-like by the life.

     01   1161 2716   1473 1519 846
5 ὁ   δὲ   κατεργασάμενος   ἡμᾶς εἰς αὐτὸ
     The but having thoroughly worked us for same

3778   2316 01   1325   1473 04 728
τοῦτο θεός, ὁ   δοὺς   ἡμῖν τὸν ἀρραβῶνα
this   God, the one having given to us the earnest

010   4151   2292   3767 3842   2532
τοῦ   πνεύματος. **6** θαρροῦντες   οὖν πάντοτε καὶ
of the spirit.   Being confident then always and

3609a   3754 1736   1722 011 4983
εἰδότες   ὅτι ἐνδημοῦντες ἐν τῷ   σώματι
having known that being at home in the body

1553   575 02 2962   1223   4102
ἐκδημοῦμεν   ἀπὸ τοῦ κυρίου· **7** διὰ   πίστεως
we are out of home from the Master; through trust

1063 4043   3756 1223 1491
γὰρ περιπατοῦμεν, οὐ διὰ   εἴδους·
for we walk around, not through visible form;

     2292   1161 2532 2106   3123
8 θαρροῦμεν   δὲ   καὶ εὐδοκοῦμεν   μᾶλλον
     we are confident but also we think well more

1553   1537 010 4983   2532 1736
ἐκδημῆσαι   ἐκ   τοῦ σώματος καὶ ἐνδημῆσαι
to be out of home from the body   and to be at home

4314 04 2962   1352   2532 5389
πρὸς τὸν κύριον. **9** διὸ   καὶ φιλοτιμούμεθα,
toward the Master. Therefore also we love value,

1535 1736   1535 1553
εἴτε ἐνδημοῦντες εἴτε ἐκδημοῦντες,
whether being at home or being out of home,

2101   846 1510   016 1063 3956 1473
εὐάρεστοι   αὐτῷ εἶναι. **10** τοὺς γὰρ πάντας ἡμᾶς
well-pleasing to him to be. The for all   us

5319   1163   1715   010
φανερωθῆναι   δεῖ   ἔμπροσθεν τοῦ
to be demonstrated it is necessary in front of the

968   02   5547   2443 2865   1538
βήματος τοῦ Χριστοῦ, ἵνα κομίσηται   ἕκαστος
law court of the Christ, that might obtain each

024 1223   010 4983   4314 3739 4238
τὰ διὰ   τοῦ σώματος πρὸς ἃ   ἔπραξεν,
the through the body   toward what he practiced,

1535 18   1535 5337   3609a   3767 04
εἴτε ἀγαθὸν εἴτε φαῦλον. **11** Εἰδότες   οὖν τὸν
whether good or foul.   Having known then the

5401 02   2962   444   3982   2316 1161
φόβον τοῦ κυρίου ἀνθρώπους πείθομεν,   θεῷ δὲ
fear of the Master men   we persuade, to God but

5319   1679   1161 2532 1722 019
πεφανερώμεθα·   ἐλπίζω δὲ καὶ ἐν   ταῖς
we have been demonstrated; I hope but also in the

longing to be clothed with our heavenly dwelling— [3]if indeed, when we have taken it off[a] we will not be found naked. [4]For while we are still in this tent, we groan under our burden, because we wish not to be unclothed but to be further clothed, so that what is mortal may be swallowed up by life. [5]He who has prepared us for this very thing is God, who has given us the Spirit as a guarantee.

[6]So we are always confident; even though we know that while we are at home in the body we are away from the Lord— [7]for we walk by faith, not by sight. [8]Yes, we do have confidence, and we would rather be away from the body and at home with the Lord. [9]So whether we are at home or away, we make it our aim to please him. [10]For all of us must appear before the judgment seat of Christ, so that each may receive recompense for what has been done in the body, whether good or evil.

11 Therefore, knowing the fear of the Lord, we try to persuade others; but we ourselves are well known to God, and I hope that

a Other ancient authorities read *put it on*

we are also well known to your consciences. 12We are not commending ourselves to you again, but giving you an opportunity to boast about us, so that you may be able to answer those who boast in outward appearance and not in the heart. 13For if we are beside ourselves, it is for God; if we are in our right mind, it is for you. 14For the love of Christ urges us on, because we are convinced that one has died for all; therefore all have died. 15And he died for all, so that those who live might live no longer for themselves, but for him who died and was raised for them.

16 From now on, therefore, we regard no one from a human point of view;*a* even though we once knew Christ from a human point of view,*a* we know him no longer in that way. 17So if anyone is in Christ, there is a new creation: everything old has passed away; see, everything has become new! 18All this is from God, who reconciled us to himself through Christ, and has given us the ministry of reconciliation; 19that is, in Christ God was reconciling the world to himself,*b* not counting their trespasses against them, and entrusting the message of reconciliation to us. 20So we are ambassadors for Christ, since

a Gk according to the flesh
b Or God was in Christ reconciling the world to himself

4893	1473	5319		12	3756
συνειδήσεσιν	ὑμῶν	πεφανερῶσθαι.			οὐ
consciences	of you	to have been demonstrated.			Not

3825	1438	4921	1473	235	874
πάλιν	ἑαυτοὺς	συνιστάνομεν	ὑμῖν	ἀλλὰ	ἀφορμὴν
again	ourselves	we commend	to you	but	opportunity

1325	1473	2745	5228	1473	2443
διδόντες	ὑμῖν	καυχήματος	ὑπὲρ	ἡμῶν,	ἵνα
giving	to you	to brag	on behalf of	us,	that

2192	4314 016	1722 4383	2744		2532
ἔχητε	πρὸς τοὺς ἐν	προσώπῳ καυχωμένους	καὶ		
you might have	to the in	face bragging	and		

3361 1722 2588		13	1535	1063 1839	
μὴ ἐν καρδίᾳ.			εἴτε	γὰρ ἐξέστημεν,	
not in heart.			Whether	for we are beside ourselves,	

2316	1535 4993		1473	05	1063 26
θεῷ·	εἴτε σωφρονοῦμεν,		ὑμῖν.	14 ἡ	γὰρ ἀγάπη
to God;	or we think soberly,		to you.	The	for love

02	5547	4912	1473 2919		3778
τοῦ	Χριστοῦ	συνέχει	ἡμᾶς, κρίναντας		τοῦτο,
of the Christ	holds together	us,	having judged		this,

3754 1520 5228		3956	599	686 013 3956	
ὅτι εἷς ὑπὲρ		πάντων	ἀπέθανεν,	ἄρα οἱ πάντες	
that one on behalf of		all	died,	then the all	

599	15 2532 5228	3956	599	2443 013
ἀπέθανον·	καὶ ὑπὲρ	πάντων ἀπέθανεν,	ἵνα οἱ	
died;	and on behalf of	all he died,	that the	

2198	3371	1438	2198	235
ζῶντες	μηκέτι	ἑαυτοῖς	ζῶσιν	ἀλλὰ
ones living	no longer	to themselves	might live	but

03	5228	846	599	2532
τῷ	ὑπὲρ	αὐτῶν	ἀποθανόντι	καὶ
to the one	on behalf of	them	dying	and

1453	5620	1473	575 010 3568 3762
ἐγερθέντι.	16 Ὥστε	ἡμεῖς	ἀπὸ τοῦ νῦν οὐδένα
having been raised.	So that	we	from the now not one

3609a	2596 4561	1487 2532 1097	2596 4561
οἴδαμεν κατὰ σάρκα·	εἰ	καὶ ἐγνώκαμεν	κατὰ σάρκα
we know by flesh;	if	even we have known	by flesh

5547	235 3568 3765	1097	17	5620 1487
Χριστόν,	ἀλλὰ νῦν οὐκέτι	γινώσκομεν.		ὥστε εἴ
Christ,	but now no longer	we know.		So that if

5100 1722 5547	2537 2937	021 744
τις ἐν Χριστῷ,	καινὴ κτίσις·	τὰ ἀρχαῖα
some in Christ,	new creation;	the ancients

3928	2400 1096	2537	18	021 1161
παρῆλθεν,	ἰδοὺ γέγονεν	καινά·		τὰ δὲ
went along,	look it has become	new;		the but

3956 1537 02	2316 02 2644		1473
πάντα ἐκ τοῦ	θεοῦ τοῦ καταλλάξαντος		ἡμᾶς
all from the	God the one having reconciled		us

1438	1223	5547 2532 1325	1473 08
ἑαυτῷ	διὰ	Χριστοῦ καὶ δόντος	ἡμῖν τὴν
to himself	through	Christ and having given	to us the

1248	06	2643	19	5613 3754 2316 1510
διακονίαν	τῆς	καταλλαγῆς,		ὡς ὅτι θεὸς ἦν
service	of the	reconciliation,		as that God was+

1722 5547	2889	2644	1438	3361
ἐν Χριστῷ	κόσμον	καταλλάσσων	ἑαυτῷ,	μὴ
in Christ	world	+reconciling	to himself,	not

3049	846	024 3900	846	2532
λογιζόμενος	αὐτοῖς	τὰ παραπτώματα	αὐτῶν	καὶ
reasoning	to them	the trespasses	of them	and

5087	1722 1473 04	3056 06	2643
θέμενος	ἐν ἡμῖν τὸν	λόγον τῆς	καταλλαγῆς.
having set in	us the	word of the	reconciliation.

20	5228	5547	3767 4243	5613 02
	Ὑπὲρ	Χριστοῦ	οὖν πρεσβεύομεν	ὡς τοῦ
	On behalf	of Christ	then we are envoys	as of the

2316 3870   1223   1473   1189   5228
θεοῦ παρακαλοῦντος δι᾽   ἡμῶν· δεόμεθα ὑπὲρ
God encouraging   through us;   we beg on behalf

5547   2644   03   2316   04   3361
Χριστοῦ, καταλλάγητε τῷ   θεῷ. **21** τὸν   μὴ
of Christ, be reconciled to the God.   The one not

1097   266   5228   1473   266
γνόντα   ἁμαρτίαν ὑπὲρ   ἡμῶν ἁμαρτίαν
having known sin   on behalf of us sin

4160   2443 1473 1096   1343   2316
ἐποίησεν, ἵνα ἡμεῖς γενώμεθα   δικαιοσύνη θεοῦ
he made, that we   might become rightness of God

1722 846   4903   1161 2532 3870
ἐν αὐτῷ. **6:1** Συνεργοῦντες   δὲ καὶ παρακαλοῦμεν
in him.   Working together but also we encourage

3361 1519 2756 08 5485 02   2316 1209   1473
μὴ εἰς κενὸν τὴν χάριν τοῦ   θεοῦ δέξασθαι   ὑμᾶς·
not in empty the favor of the God to welcome you;

2 3004   1063 2540   1184   1873   1473 2532
λέγει   γάρ· καιρῷ   δεκτῷ   ἐπήκουσά σου καὶ
he says for, in season acceptable I heard you and

1722 2250 4991   997   1473 2400 3568
ἐν ἡμέρᾳ σωτηρίας   ἐβοήθησά σοι. ἰδοὺ νῦν
in day of deliverance I helped you. Look now

2540   2144   2400 3568 2250 4991
καιρὸς εὐπρόσδεκτος, ἰδοὺ νῦν ἡμέρα σωτηρίας.
season well accepted, look now day of deliverance.

3 3367   1722 3367   1325   4349   2443
Μηδεμίαν ἐν μηδενὶ διδόντες προσκοπήν, ἵνα
But not one in nothing giving stumble, that

3361 3469   05 1248   235 1722 3956
μὴ μωμηθῇ   ἡ διακονία, **4** ἀλλ᾽ ἐν παντὶ
not might be stained the service, but in all

4921   1438   5613 2316 1249   1722 5281
συνίσταντες ἑαυτοὺς ὡς θεοῦ διάκονοι, ἐν ὑπομονῇ
commending ourselves as of God servants, in patience

4183 1722 2347   1722 318   1722 4730
πολλῇ, ἐν θλίψεσιν, ἐν ἀνάγκαις, ἐν στενοχωρίαις,
much, in afflictions, in necessities, in anguish,

5 1722 4127   1722 5438   1722 181   1722
ἐν πληγαῖς, ἐν φυλακαῖς, ἐν ἀκαταστασίαις, ἐν
in blows, in guards, in unstablenesses, in

2873   1722 70   1722 3521   **6** 1722
κόποις, ἐν ἀγρυπνίαις, ἐν νηστείαις, ἐν
labors, in staying awake, in fastings, in

54   1722 1108   1722 3115   1722
ἁγνότητι, ἐν γνώσει, ἐν μακροθυμίᾳ, ἐν
pureness, in knowledge, in long temper, in

5544   1722 4151   40 1722 26   505
χρηστότητι, ἐν πνεύματι ἁγίῳ, ἐν ἀγάπῃ ἀνυποκρίτῳ,
kindness, in spirit holy, in love unhypocritical,

7 1722 3056 225   1722 1411   2316   1223   022
ἐν λόγῳ ἀληθείας, ἐν δυνάμει θεοῦ· διὰ τῶν
in word of truth, in power of God; through the

3696   06   1343   018   1188   2532
ὅπλων τῆς δικαιοσύνης τῶν δεξιῶν καὶ
weapons of the rightness of the right and

710   **8** 1223   1391   2532 819   1223
ἀριστερῶν, διὰ δόξης καὶ ἀτιμίας, διὰ
left,   through splendor and dishonor, through

1426   2532 2162   5613 4108   2532 227
δυσφημίας καὶ εὐφημίας· ὡς πλάνοι καὶ ἀληθεῖς,
bad report and good report; as deceivers and true,

9 5613 50   2532 1921   5613
ὡς ἀγνοούμενοι καὶ ἐπιγινωσκόμενοι, ὡς
as being unknown and being perceived, as

599   2532 2400 2198   5613 3811
ἀποθνήσκοντες καὶ ἰδοὺ ζῶμεν, ὡς παιδευόμενοι
dying   and look we live, as being instructed
                                  as a child

God is making his appeal
through us; we entreat
you on behalf of Christ,
be reconciled to God.
[21]For our sake he made
him to be sin who knew no
sin, so that in him we might
become the righteousness
of God.

CHAPTER 6

As we work together with
him,[a] we urge you also not
to accept the grace of God
in vain. [2]For he says,
    "At an acceptable time
        I have listened to you,
    and on a day of salvation
        I have helped you."
See, now is the acceptable
time; see, now is the day of
salvation! [3]We are putting
no obstacle in anyone's
way, so that no fault may
be found with our ministry,
[4]but as servants of God we
have commended ourselves
in every way: through great
endurance, in afflictions,
hardships, calamities,
[5]beatings, imprisonments,
riots, labors, sleepless
nights, hunger; [6]by purity,
knowledge, patience,
kindness, holiness of spirit,
genuine love, [7]truthful
speech, and the power of
God; with the weapons of
righteousness for the right
hand and for the left; [8]in
honor and dishonor, in ill
repute and good repute.
We are treated as impostors,
and yet are true; [9]as
unknown, and yet are well
known; as dying, and see—
we are alive; as punished,

---

[a] Gk As we work together

and yet not killed; [10]as sorrowful, yet always rejoicing; as poor, yet making many rich; as having nothing, and yet possessing everything.

11 We have spoken frankly to you Corinthians; our heart is wide open to you. [12]There is no restriction in our affections, but only in yours. [13]In return—I speak as to children—open wide your hearts also.

14 Do not be mismatched with unbelievers. For what partnership is there between righteousness and lawlessness? Or what fellowship is there between light and darkness? [15]What agreement does Christ have with Beliar? Or what does a believer share with an unbeliever? [16]What agreement has the temple of God with idols? For we[a] are the temple of the living God; as God said,

"I will live in them and
　walk among them,
and I will be their God,
　and they shall be my
　people.
[17]Therefore come out from
　them,
　and be separate from
　them, says the Lord,
and touch nothing
　unclean;
　then I will welcome
　you,
[18]and I will be your father,
　and you shall be my
　sons and daughters,
says the Lord Almighty."

CHAPTER 7

Since we have these promises, beloved, let us cleanse ourselves from every defilement of body and

---

[a] Other ancient authorities read you

```
2532 3361 2289                    5613 3076              104 1161
καὶ  μὴ  θανατούμενοι,   10  ὡς  λυπούμενοι ἀεὶ  δὲ
and  not  being put to death, as  grieving    always but
5463      5613 4434  4183     1161 4148              5613
χαίροντες, ὡς  πτωχοὶ πολλοὺς δὲ  πλουτίζοντες, ὡς
rejoicing, as  poor   many    but making rich,   as
3367   2192    2532 3956 2722          09  4750
μηδὲν ἔχοντες καὶ πάντα κατέχοντες.  11 Τὸ στόμα
nothing having and  all  holding down. The mouth
1473  455           4314 1473 2881      05  2588
ἡμῶν ἀνέῳγεν πρὸς ὑμᾶς, Κορίνθιοι, ἡ καρδία
of us has opened to  you,  Corinthians, the heart
1473 4115               3756 4729          1722 1473
ἡμῶν πεπλάτυνται·  12 οὐ στενοχωρεῖσθε ἐν ἡμῖν,
of us has been widened;  not be anguished   in  us,
4729             1161 1722 023  4698           1473   08
στενοχωρεῖσθε δὲ  ἐν  τοῖς σπλάγχνοις ὑμῶν· 13 τὴν
be anguished  but in  the  affections  of you;    the
1161 846   489          5613 5043       3004
δὲ  αὐτὴν ἀντιμισθίαν, ὡς  τέκνοις λέγω,
but same   return wage,  as  to children I say,
4115        2532 1473    3361 1096    2086
πλατύνθητε καὶ ὑμεῖς. 14 Μὴ γίνεσθε ἑτεροζυγοῦντες
be widened also you.    Not become being other yoked
571        5101 1063 3352        1343         2532
ἀπίστοις·  τίς γὰρ μετοχὴ δικαιοσύνῃ καὶ
to untrustful; what for commonality in rightness and
458    2228 5101 2842       5457 4314  4655
ἀνομίᾳ,  ἢ  τίς κοινωνία φωτὶ πρὸς σκότος;
lawlessness, or what partnership light toward dark?
15 5101 1161 4857      5547      4314  4955  2228
   τίς δὲ  συμφώνησις Χριστοῦ πρὸς Βελιάρ, ἢ
   What but harmony   of Christ toward Beliar, or
5101 3310 4103     3326 571         5101 1161
τίς μερὶς πιστῷ μετὰ ἀπίστου; 16 τίς δὲ
what part trustful with untrustful?  What but
4784         3485      2316 3326 1497     1473 1063
συγκατάθεσις ναῷ Θεοῦ μετὰ εἰδώλων; ἡμεῖς γὰρ
pact          in temple of God with idols?  We   for
3485  2316  1510 2198    2531    3004 01 2316 3754
ναὸς Θεοῦ ἐσμεν ζῶντος, καθὼς εἶπεν ὁ Θεὸς ὅτι
temple of God are  living, just as said the God that
1774      1722 846   2532 1704
ἐνοικήσω ἐν αὐτοῖς καὶ ἐμπεριπατήσω
I will house in in them and I will walk around in
2532 1510    846     2316 2532 846    1510
καὶ ἔσομαι αὐτῶν θεὸς καὶ αὐτοὶ ἔσονταί
and I will be of them God and themselves will be
1473 2992   17 1352   1831      1537 3319 846
μου λαός.   διὸ ἐξέλθατε ἐκ μέσου αὐτῶν
of me people. Therefore come out from middle of them
2532 873        3004 2962    2532 169      3361
καὶ ἀφορίσθητε, λέγει κύριος, καὶ ἀκαθάρτου μὴ
and be separated, says Master, and unclean    not
681       2504  1523           1473 18 2532 1510
ἅπτεσθε· κἀγὼ εἰσδέξομαι ὑμᾶς  καὶ ἔσομαι
touch;    and I will welcome in you  and I will be
1473 1519 3962   2532 1473 1510    1473 1519 5207
ὑμῖν εἰς πατέρα καὶ ὑμεῖς ἔσεσθέ μοι εἰς υἱοὺς
to you for father and you  will be to me for sons
2532 2364    3004 2962    3841            3778
καὶ θυγατέρας, λέγει κύριος παντοκράτωρ. 7:1 ταύτας
and daughters, says Master all strength.       These
3767 2192   020 1860        27       2511
οὖν ἔχοντες τὰς ἐπαγγελίας, ἀγαπητοί, καθαρίσωμεν
then having the promises,    loved ones, let us clean
1438    575  3956   3436    4561   2532
ἑαυτοὺς ἀπὸ παντὸς μολυσμοῦ σαρκὸς καὶ
ourselves from all  stainness of flesh and
```

4151   2005   42   1722 5401
πνεύματος, ἐπιτελοῦντες   ἁγιωσύνην ἐν   φόβῳ
spirit,   completing thoroughly holiness   in   fear
2316   5562   1473   3762   91   3762
θεοῦ.   **2** Χωρήσατε ἡμᾶς· οὐδένα ἠδικήσαμεν,   οὐδένα
of God.   Make room us;   no one we did unright,   no one
5351   3762   4122   4314
ἐφθείραμεν,   οὐδένα ἐπλεονεκτήσαμεν. **3** πρὸς
we corrupted,   no one we took more.   To
2633   3756 3004   4302   1063 3754 1722
κατάκρισιν   οὐ λέγω· προείρηκα   γὰρ ὅτι ἐν
condemnation   not I say; I said before for   that in
019   2588   1473   1510   1519 012 4880
ταῖς καρδίαις ἡμῶν ἐστε   εἰς τὸ συναποθανεῖν
the hearts   of us you are in   the to die together
2532 4800   4183   1473   3954   4314 1473
καὶ   συζῆν.   **4** πολλή μοι   παρρησία πρὸς ὑμᾶς,
and   to live together.   Much to me boldness to   you,
4183   1473   2746   5228 1473   4137
πολλή μοι   καύχησις ὑπὲρ ὑμῶν· πεπλήρωμαι
much to me brag   over you;   I have been filled
07   3874   5248   07   5479
τῇ   παρακλήσει,   ὑπερπερισσεύομαι   τῇ   χαρᾷ
in the encouragement, I am exceeding beyond in the joy
1909 3956 07   2347   1473   2532 1063 2064
ἐπὶ   πάσῃ τῇ   θλίψει   ἡμῶν. **5** Καὶ   γὰρ ἐλθόντων
on   all   the affliction of us.   Also for   having come
1473   1519 3109   3762   2192   425   05
ἡμῶν εἰς Μακεδονίαν οὐδεμίαν   ἔσχηκεν ἄνεσιν ἡ
of us into Macedonia but not one has had relief the
4561   1473   235   1722 3956 2346
σὰρξ ἡμῶν ἀλλ’ ἐν   παντὶ θλιβόμενοι·
flesh of us but in   all   being afflicted;
1855   3163   2081   5401   235   01
ἔξωθεν   μάχαι,   ἔσωθεν   φόβοι. **6** ἀλλ’ ὁ
from outside battles,   from inside fears.   But   the
3870   016 5011   3870   1473 01
παρακαλῶν   τοὺς ταπεινοὺς παρεκάλεσεν ἡμᾶς ὁ
one encouraging the humble   encouraged us   the
2316 1722 07   3952   5103   3756 3441 1161 1722
θεὸς ἐν   τῇ   παρουσίᾳ Τίτου, **7** οὐ   μόνον δὲ   ἐν
God in   the presence of Titus, not   alone but   in
07   3952   846   235   2532 1722 07   3874
τῇ   παρουσίᾳ αὐτοῦ ἀλλὰ καὶ ἐν   τῇ   παρακλήσει
the presence of him but   also in   the encouragement
3739   3870   1909 1473   312   1473
ᾗ   παρεκλήθη   ἐφ’ ὑμῖν, ἀναγγέλλων ἡμῖν
by which he was encouraged on   you,   declaring   to us
08   1473   1972   04   1473   3602   04
τὴν ὑμῶν ἐπιπόθησιν,   τὸν ὑμῶν ὀδυρμόν,   τὸν
the of you longing desire, the of you lamenting, the
1473   2205   5228 1473 5620   1473 3123   5463
ὑμῶν   ζῆλον   ὑπὲρ ἐμοῦ ὥστε   με μᾶλλον χαρῆναι.
of you jealousy over me   so that me more to rejoice.
   8 3754 1487 2532 3076   1473 1722 07   1992   3756
"Οτι εἰ   καὶ ἐλύπησα ὑμᾶς ἐν   τῇ ἐπιστολῇ, οὐ
That if   also I grieved you in   the letter,   not
3338   1487 2532 3338   991   1063 3754
μεταμέλομαι· εἰ   καὶ μετεμελόμην, βλέπω [γὰρ] ὅτι
I am sorry;   if   even I was sorry, I see   for   that
05   1992   1565 1487 2532 4314   5610 3076
ἡ   ἐπιστολὴ ἐκείνη εἰ   καὶ πρὸς   ὥραν ἐλύπησεν
the letter   that   if   also toward hour it grieved
1473   **9** 3568 5463   3756 3754 3076   235
ὑμᾶς,   νῦν χαίρω,   οὐχ ὅτι ἐλυπήθητε   ἀλλ’
you,   now I rejoice,   not that you were grieved but
3754 3076   1519 3341   3076   1063
ὅτι ἐλυπήθητε εἰς μετάνοιαν·   ἐλυπήθητε γὰρ
that you were into change of mind; you were for
   grieved   grieved

of spirit, making holiness perfect in the fear of God.

2 Make room in your hearts[a] for us; we have wronged no one, we have corrupted no one, we have taken advantage of no one. 3 I do not say this to condemn you, for I said before that you are in our hearts, to die together and to live together. 4 I often boast about you; I have ˋ great pride in you; I am filled with consolation; I am overjoyed in all our affliction.

5 For even when we came into Macedonia, our bodies had no rest, but we were afflicted in every way—disputes without and fears within. 6 But God, who consoles the downcast, consoled us by the arrival of Titus, 7 and not only by his coming, but also by the consolation with which he was consoled about you, as he told us of your longing, your mourning, your zeal for me, so that I rejoiced still more. 8 For even if I made you sorry with my letter, I do not regret it (though I did regret it, for I see that I grieved you with that letter, though only briefly). 9 Now I rejoice, not because you were grieved, but because your grief led to repentance; for you felt

a Gk lacks in your hearts

a godly grief, so that you were not harmed in any way by us. [10]For godly grief produces a repentance that leads to salvation and brings no regret, but worldly grief produces death. [11]For see what earnestness this godly grief has produced in you, what eagerness to clear yourselves, what indignation, what alarm, what longing, what zeal, what punishment! At every point you have proved yourselves guiltless in the matter. [12]So although I wrote to you, it was not on account of the one who did the wrong, nor on account of the one who was wronged, but in order that your zeal for us might be made known to you before God. [13]In this we find comfort.

In addition to our own consolation, we rejoiced still more at the joy of Titus, because his mind has been set at rest by all of you. [14]For if I have been somewhat boastful about you to him, I was not disgraced; but just as everything we said to you was true, so our boasting to Titus has proved true as well. [15]And his heart goes out all the more to you, as he remembers

```
             2596  2316   2443  1722 3367     2210              1537 1473
             κατὰ θεόν,  ἵνα  ἐν  μηδενὶ  ζημιωθῆτε        ἐξ  ἡμῶν.
             by   God,  that in  nothing you might lose from us.
       05  1063 2596 2316 3077      3341                  1519
10     ἡ  γὰρ  κατὰ θεὸν λύπη  μετάνοιαν              εἰς
       The for  by  God grief change of mind into
     4991        278            2038       05   1161 02
     σωτηρίαν   ἀμεταμέλητον  ἐργάζεται· ἡ  δὲ  τοῦ
     deliverance not give care works;   the but  of the
     2889     3077  2288      2716                  2400 1063
     κόσμου λύπη  θάνατον κατεργάζεται.    11  ἰδοὺ γὰρ
     world  grief death  works thoroughly.   Look for
     846  3778   09  2596 2316 3076          4214
     αὐτὸ τοῦτο τὸ κατὰ θεὸν λυπηθῆναι    πόσην
     same this the by  God to be grieved how much
     2716            1473    4710       235  627
     κατειργάσατο   ὑμῖν  σπουδήν,  ἀλλὰ ἀπολογίαν,
     worked thoroughly to you diligence, but defense,
     235  24           235  5401     235  1972
     ἀλλὰ ἀγανάκτησιν, ἀλλὰ φόβον, ἀλλὰ ἐπιπόθησιν,
     but indignation, but fear,  but  longing desire,
     235  2205       235  1557          1722 3956
     ἀλλὰ ζῆλον,    ἀλλὰ ἐκδίκησιν.    ἐν  παντὶ
     but jealousy, but bring out right. In  all
     4921            1438        53     1510 011      4229
     συνεστήσατε ἑαυτοὺς ἁγνοὺς εἶναι τῷ   πράγματι.
     you commend yourselves pure  to be in the practice.
12   686   1487 2532 1125      1473     3756 1752
     ἄρα  εἰ  καὶ ἔγραψα ὑμῖν,  οὐχ ἕνεκεν
     Then if  also I wrote to you, not  on account
     02        91                   3761   1752
     τοῦ  ἀδικήσαντος              οὐδὲ  ἕνεκεν
     of the one having done unright but not on account
     02        91                     235  1752
     τοῦ  ἀδικηθέντος              ἀλλ᾽ ἕνεκεν
     of the one having been done unright but  on account
     010      5319               08  4710        1473     08
     τοῦ  φανερωθῆναι      τὴν σπουδὴν ὑμῶν τὴν
     of the one to be demonstrated the diligence of you the
     5228     1473  4314    1473 1799   02  2316
     ὑπὲρ  ἡμῶν πρὸς ὑμᾶς ἐνώπιον τοῦ θεοῦ.
     on behalf of us toward you before  the God.
13   1223     3778 3870                    1909 1161
     διὰ  τοῦτο παρακεκλήμεθα.        Ἐπὶ  δὲ
     Through this we have been encouraged. On  but
07  3874             1473  4056            3123
    τῇ παρακλήσει ἡμῶν περισσοτέρως    μᾶλλον
    the encouragement of us more exceedingly more
    5463      1909 07  5479 5103      3754 373
    ἐχάρημεν ἐπὶ τῇ χαρᾷ Τίτου,  ὅτι ἀναπέπαυται
    we rejoice on the joy of Titus, that has been rested
    09  4151   846   575  3956   1473        3754 1487 5100
    τὸ πνεῦμα αὐτοῦ ἀπὸ πάντων ὑμῶν· 14 ὅτι εἴ τι
    the spirit of him from all  of you; that if some
    846    5228    1473  2744          3756
    αὐτῷ ὑπὲρ  ὑμῶν κεκαύχημαι,   οὐ
    to him on behalf of you I have bragged, not
    2617         235   5613 3956 1722 225      2980
    κατησχύνθην, ἀλλ᾽ ὡς  πάντα ἐν ἀληθείᾳ ἐλαλήσαμεν
    I have been but as  all  in  truth  we spoke
    ashamed,
    1473    3779    2532 05  2746       1473   05  1909 5103
    ὑμῖν,  οὕτως καὶ ἡ καύχησις ἡμῶν ἡ ἐπὶ Τίτου
    to you, thusly also the brag  of us the on  Titus
    225      1096      2532 021 4698        846
    ἀλήθεια ἐγενήθη. 15 καὶ τὰ σπλάγχνα αὐτοῦ
    truth  became.   And the affections of him
    4056            1519 1473 1510  363
    περισσοτέρως  εἰς ὑμᾶς ἐστιν ἀναμιμνησκομένου
    more exceedingly in  you  are  being reminded
```

08	3956	1473	5218		5613	3326	5401	2532
τὴν	πάντων	ὑμῶν	ὑπακοήν,		ὡς	μετὰ	φόβου	καὶ
the all		of you	obedience,		as	with	fear	and

5156	1209		846		3754	1722
τρόμου	ἐδέξασθε		αὐτόν. **16**	χαίρω	ὅτι	ἐν
trembling	you welcomed		him.	I rejoice	that	in

3956	2292		1722	1473	**8:1**	1107		1161
παντὶ	θαρρῶ		ἐν	ὑμῖν.		Γνωρίζομεν		δὲ
all	I am confident		in	you.		We make known		but

1473	80		08	5485	02		2316	08
ὑμῖν,	ἀδελφοί,		τὴν	χάριν	τοῦ		θεοῦ	τὴν
to you,	brothers,		the	favor	of the		God	the one

1325		1722	1519	1577		06	3109
δεδομένην		ἐν	ταῖς	ἐκκλησίαις		τῆς	Μακεδονίας,
having been given		in the		assemblies		of the	Macedonia,

2
3754	1722	4183	1382		2347		05	4050
ὅτι	ἐν	πολλῇ	δοκιμῇ		θλίψεως		ἡ	περισσεία
that in		much	approval		of affliction		the	excess

06	5479	846		2532	05	2596	899		4432
τῆς	χαρᾶς	αὐτῶν		καὶ	ἡ	κατὰ	βάθους		πτωχεία
of the	joy	of them		and	the	by	depth		poverty

846	4052		1519	012	4149		06	572
αὐτῶν	ἐπερίσσευσεν		εἰς	τὸ	πλοῦτος		τῆς	ἁπλότητος
of them	exceeded		into	the	rich		of the	openness

846		**3**	3754	2596	1411		3140		2532	3844
αὐτῶν·			ὅτι	κατὰ	δύναμιν,		μαρτυρῶ,		καὶ	παρὰ
of them;			that by		power,		I testify,		and	beside

1411	830		**4**	3326	4183	3874
δύναμιν,	αὐθαίρετοι			μετὰ	πολλῆς	παρακλήσεως
power,	by self-choice			with	much	encouragement

1189	1473	08	5485	2532	08	2842		06
δεόμενοι	ἡμῶν	τὴν	χάριν	καὶ	τὴν	κοινωνίαν		τῆς
begging	us	the	favor	and	the	partnership		of the

1248	06	1519	016	40		**5**	2532	3756	2531
διακονίας	τῆς	εἰς	τοὺς	ἁγίους,			καὶ	οὐ	καθὼς
service	the	for	the	holy ones,			and	not	just as

1679	235	1438		1325		4413	03
ἠλπίσαμεν	ἀλλ᾽	ἑαυτοὺς		ἔδωκαν		πρῶτον	τῷ
we hoped	but	themselves		they gave		first	to the

2962	2532	1473	1223		2307		2316		**6**	1519	012
κυρίῳ	καὶ	ἡμῖν	διὰ		θελήματος		θεοῦ			εἰς	τὸ
Master	and	to us	through		want		of God			for	the

3870		1473	5103	2443	2531		4278
παρακαλέσαι		ἡμᾶς	Τίτον,	ἵνα	καθὼς		προενήρξατο
to encourage		us	Titus,	that	just as		he began before

3779	2532	2005				1519	1473
οὕτως	καὶ	ἐπιτελέσῃ				εἰς	ὑμᾶς
thusly	also	he might complete thoroughly				in	you

2532	08	5485	3778		**7**	235	5618		1722	3956
καὶ	τὴν	χάριν	ταύτην.			Ἀλλ᾽	ὥσπερ		ἐν	παντὶ
also	the	favor	this.			But	as indeed		in	all

4052		4102		2532	3056		2532	1108
περισσεύετε,		πίστει		καὶ	λόγῳ		καὶ	γνώσει
you exceed,		in trust		and	in word		and	in knowledge

2532	3956	4710		2532	07		1537	1473	1722	1473
καὶ	πάσῃ	σπουδῇ		καὶ	τῇ		ἐξ	ἡμῶν	ἐν	ὑμῖν
and	in all	diligence		and	in the		from	us	in	you

26		2443	2532	1722	3778	07	5485		4052
ἀγάπη,		ἵνα	καὶ	ἐν	ταύτῃ	τῇ	χάριτι		περισσεύητε.
love,		that	also	in	this	the	favor		you might exceed.

8
3756	2596	2003		3004	235	1223		06	2087
Οὐ	κατ᾽	ἐπιταγὴν		λέγω	ἀλλὰ	διὰ		τῆς	ἑτέρων
Not	by	order		I say	but	through		the of	others

4710		2532	012	06		5212		26		1103
σπουδῆς		καὶ	τὸ	τῆς		ὑμετέρας		ἀγάπης		γνήσιον
diligence		and	the	of the		your		love		legitimate

1381		**9**	1097		1063	08	5485	02		2962
δοκιμάζων·			γινώσκετε		γὰρ	τὴν	χάριν	τοῦ		κυρίου
proving;			you know		for	the	favor	of the		Master

the obedience of all of you, and how you welcomed him with fear and trembling. [16]I rejoice, because I have complete confidence in you.

CHAPTER 8

We want you to know, brothers and sisters,[a] about the grace of God that has been granted to the churches of Macedonia; [2]for during a severe ordeal of affliction, their abundant joy and their extreme poverty have overflowed in a wealth of generosity on their part. [3]For, as I can testify, they voluntarily gave according to their means, and even beyond their means, [4]begging us earnestly for the privilege[b] of sharing in this ministry to the saints— [5]and this, not merely as we expected; they gave themselves first to the Lord and, by the will of God, to us, [6]so that we might urge Titus that, as he had already made a beginning, so he should also complete this generous undertaking[c] among you. [7]Now as you excel in everything—in faith, in speech, in knowledge, in utmost eagerness, and in our love for you[d]—so we want you to excel also in this generous undertaking.[e]

8 I do not say this as a command, but I am testing the genuineness of your love against the earnestness of others. [9]For you know the generous act [e] of our Lord

a Gk brothers
b Gk grace
c Gk this grace
d Other ancient authorities read your love for us
e Gk the grace

Jesus Christ, that though he was rich, yet for your sakes he became poor, so that by his poverty you might become rich. [10]And in this matter I am giving my advice: it is appropriate for you who began last year not only to do something but even to desire to do something— [11]now finish doing it, so that your eagerness may be matched by completing it according to your means. [12]For if the eagerness is there, the gift is acceptable according to what one has—not according to what one does not have. [13]I do not mean that there should be relief for others and pressure on you, but it is a question of a fair balance between [14]your present abundance and their need, so that their abundance may be for your need, in order that there may be a fair balance. [15]As it is written,

"The one who had much did not have too much,
   and the one who had little did not have too little."

16 But thanks be to God who put in the heart of Titus the same eagerness for you that I myself have. [17]For he not only accepted our appeal, but since he is more eager than ever, he is going to you of his own accord. [18]With him we are sending the brother who is famous

1473	2424	5547	3754 1223		1473
ἡμῶν	Ἰησοῦ	Χριστοῦ,	ὅτι δι'		ὑμᾶς
of us	Jesus	Christ,	that because of		you

4433   4145   1510   2443   1473   07
ἐπτώχευσεν πλούσιος ὤν, ἵνα ὑμεῖς τῇ
he became poor rich being, that you in the

1565   4432   4147   **10**   2532 1106   1722
ἐκείνου πτωχείᾳ πλουτήσητε.   καὶ γνώμην ἐν
of that one poverty might be rich. And purpose in

3778 1325   3778   1063 1473   4851   3748
τούτῳ δίδωμι· τοῦτο γὰρ ὑμῖν συμφέρει, οἵτινες
this I give; this for to you is advantageous, who

3756 3441   012 4160   235   2532 012 2309
οὐ μόνον τὸ ποιῆσαι ἀλλὰ καὶ τὸ θέλειν
not alone the to do but also the to want

4278   575   4070   **11**   3570 1161 2532 012
προενήρξασθε ἀπὸ πέρυσι· νυνὶ δὲ καὶ τὸ
you began before from last year; now but also the

4160   2005   3704   2509
ποιῆσαι ἐπιτελέσατε, ὅπως καθάπερ
to do you complete thoroughly, so that just as indeed

05 4288   010   2309   3779   2532 09
ἡ προθυμία τοῦ θέλειν, οὕτως καὶ τὸ
the eagerness of the to want, thusly also the

2005   1537 010 2192   **12**   1487 1063
ἐπιτελέσαι ἐκ τοῦ ἔχειν. εἰ γὰρ
to thoroughly complete from the to have. If for

05 4288   4295   2526   1437 2192
ἡ προθυμία πρόκειται, καθὸ ἐὰν ἔχῃ
the eagerness lies before, by what if he might have

2144   3756 2526   3756 2192   **13**   3756 1063
εὐπρόσδεκτος, οὐ καθὸ οὐκ ἔχει. οὐ γὰρ
well accepted, not by what not he has. Not for

2443 243   425   1473   2347   235 1537
ἵνα ἄλλοις ἄνεσις, ὑμῖν θλῖψις, ἀλλ' ἐξ
that to others relief, to you affliction, but from

2471   **14**   1722 03   3568 2540   09   1473   4051
ἰσότητος· ἐν τῷ νῦν καιρῷ τὸ ὑμῶν περίσσευμα
equality; in the now season the of you excess

1519 012 1565   5303   2443 2532 09 1565
εἰς τὸ ἐκείνων ὑστέρημα, ἵνα καὶ τὸ ἐκείνων
to the of those lack, that also the of those

4051   1096   1519 012 1473   5303
περίσσευμα γένηται εἰς τὸ ὑμῶν ὑστέρημα,
excess might become to the of you lack,

3704   1096   2471   **15**   2531   1125   01
ὅπως γένηται ἰσότης, καθὼς γέγραπται· ὁ
so that it might equality, just as it has been the one
     become   written,

012 4183 3756 4121   2532 01   012 3641
τὸ πολὺ οὐκ ἐπλεόνασεν, καὶ ὁ τὸ ὀλίγον
the much not he increased, and the one the little

3756 1641   5486 1161 03   2316 03
οὐκ ἠλαττόνησεν.   **16**   Χάρις δὲ τῷ θεῷ τῷ
not he lessened. Favor but to the God the one

1325   08 846   4710   5228   1473   1722
δόντι τὴν αὐτὴν σπουδὴν ὑπὲρ ὑμῶν ἐν
having given the same diligence on behalf of you in

07 2588   5103   **17**   3754 08   3303   3874
τῇ καρδίᾳ Τίτου, ὅτι τὴν μὲν παράκλησιν
the heart of Titus, that the indeed encouragement

1209   4705   1161 5225   830
ἐδέξατο, σπουδαιότερος δὲ ὑπάρχων αὐθαίρετος
he welcomed, more diligent but existing by self-choice

1831   4314 1473   **18**   4842   1161 3326
ἐξῆλθεν πρὸς ὑμᾶς. συνεπέμψαμεν δὲ μετ'
he went out to you. We sent together but with

846   04 80   3739   01   1868   1722 011
αὐτοῦ τὸν ἀδελφὸν οὗ ὁ ἔπαινος ἐν τῷ
him the brother of whom the praise on in the

```
2098         1223      3956   018  1577        19  3756
εὐαγγελίῳ    διὰ       πασῶν  τῶν  ἐκκλησιῶν,       οὐ
good message through   all    the  assemblies,       not
3441   1161  235   2532  5500                  5259 018
μόνον  δέ,   ἀλλὰ  καὶ   χειροτονηθεὶς          ὑπὸ  τῶν
alone  but,  but   also  hand stretched on      by   the
1577         4898         1473   4862 07  5485      3778    07
ἐκκλησιῶν    συνέκδημος   ἡμῶν   σὺν  τῇ   χάριτι    ταύτῃ τῇ
assemblies   companion    of us with the  favor     this  the
1247              5259 1473 4314 08   846      02   2962
διακονουμένῃ      ὑφ'  ἡμῶν πρὸς τὴν  [αὐτοῦ]  τοῦ  κυρίου
one being served  by   us   to   the  of him   the  Master
1391   2532 4288      1473  20  4724       3778
δόξαν  καὶ  προθυμίαν ἡμῶν,     στελλόμενοι τοῦτο,
splendor and eagerness of us,    avoiding    this,
3361 5100 1473 3469          1722 07  100            3778
μή   τις  ἡμᾶς μωμήσηται     ἐν   τῇ   ἀδρότητι      ταύτῃ
not  some us   might stain in the  munificence    this
07   1247              5259 1473  21 4306         1063
τῇ   διακονουμένῃ      ὑφ'  ἡμῶν·   προνοοῦμεν    γὰρ
the  one being served  by   us;     we think before for
2570 3756 3441 1799   2962    235   2532 1799
καλὰ οὐ   μόνον ἐνώπιον κυρίου ἀλλὰ καὶ  ἐνώπιον
good not  alone before Master but  also before
444        22 4842           1161 846      04    80
ἀνθρώπων.     συνεπέμψαμεν   δὲ   αὐτοῖς  τὸν  ἀδελφὸν
men.          We sent together but to them the brother
1473  3739 1381            1722 4183   4178
ἡμῶν  ὃν   ἐδοκιμάσαμεν     ἐν   πολλοῖς πολλάκις
of us whom we proved        in   many    frequently
4705       1510   3570 1161 4183 4705
σπουδαῖον  ὄντα,  νυνὶ δὲ   πολὺ σπουδαιότερον
diligent   being, now  but  much more diligent
4006        4183     07   1519 1473  23 1535  5228
πεποιθήσει  πολλῇ    τῇ   εἰς  ὑμᾶς.   εἴτε  ὑπὲρ
persuasion in much   the  to   you.    Whether on behalf
5103    2844       1699 2532 1519  1473 4904      1535
Τίτου,  κοινωνὸς  ἐμὸς καὶ  εἰς  ὑμᾶς συνεργός·  εἴτε
of Titus, partner my   and  to   you  co-worker;  or
80     1473   652    1577             1391
ἀδελφοὶ ἡμῶν, ἀπόστολοι ἐκκλησιῶν,      δόξα
brothers of us, delegates of assemblies, splendor
5547    24 08   3767 1732       06       26
Χριστοῦ.   τὴν  οὖν  ἔνδειξιν  τῆς      ἀγάπης
of Christ. The then demonstration of the love
1473  2532 1473  2746       5228     1473  1519
ὑμῶν  καὶ  ἡμῶν καυχήσεως  ὑπὲρ     ὑμῶν  εἰς
of you and  of us brag      on behalf of you to
846    1731          1519 4383    018 1577
αὐτοὺς ἐνδεικνύμενοι εἰς  πρόσωπον τῶν ἐκκλησιῶν.
them   demonstrating to   face     of the assemblies.
9:1 4012 3303   1063 06   1248      06   1519 016
    Περὶ  μὲν   γὰρ  τῆς  διακονίας τῆς  εἰς  τοὺς
    About indeed for  the  service   the  to   the
40       4053      1473 1510 09   1125     1473
ἁγίους   περισσόν μοί  ἐστιν τὸ   γράφειν ὑμῖν·
holy ones excess   to me it is the  to write to you;
2 3609a 1063 08  4288       1473  3739 5228 1473
  οἶδα  γὰρ  τὴν προθυμίαν ὑμῶν  ἣν   ὑπὲρ ὑμῶν
  I know for  the eagerness of you which over you
2744      3110         3754 882    3903
καυχῶμαι  Μακεδόσιν,   ὅτι  Ἀχαΐα παρεσκεύασται
I brag     to Macedonians, that Achaia has been
                                              prepared
575  4070    2532 09  1473 2205    2042       016
ἀπὸ  πέρυσι, καὶ  τὸ   ὑμῶν ζῆλος  ἠρέθισεν   τοὺς
from last year, and the of you jealousy provoked the
4183       3 3992      1161 016  80    2443 3361 09
πλείονας.    ἔπεμψα    δὲ   τοὺς ἀδελφούς, ἵνα  μὴ   τὸ
more.        I sent but the brothers, that not the
```

among all the churches for his proclaiming the good news;[a] [19]and not only that, but he has also been appointed by the churches to travel with us while we are administering this generous undertaking[b] for the glory of the Lord himself[c] and to show our goodwill. [20]We intend that no one should blame us about this generous gift that we are administering, [21]for we intend to do what is right not only in the Lord's sight but also in the sight of others. [22]And with them we are sending our brother whom we have often tested and found eager in many matters, but who is now more eager than ever because of his great confidence in you. [23]As for Titus, he is my partner and co-worker in your service; as for our brothers, they are messengers[d] of the churches, the glory of Christ. [24]Therefore openly before the churches, show them the proof of your love and of our reason for boasting about you.

CHAPTER 9

Now it is not necessary for me to write you about the ministry to the saints, [2]for I know your eagerness, which is the subject of my boasting about you to the people of Macedonia, saying that Achaia has been ready since last year; and your zeal has stirred up most of them. [3]But I am sending the brothers in order that

[a] Or the gospel
[b] Gk this grace
[c] Other ancient authorities lack himself
[d] Gk apostles

our boasting about you may not prove to have been empty in this case, so that you may be ready, as I said you would be; 4otherwise, if some Macedonians come with me and find that you are not ready, we would be humiliated—to say nothing of you—in this undertaking.*a* 5So I thought it necessary to urge the brothers to go on ahead to you, and arrange in advance for this bountiful gift that you have promised, so that it may be ready as a voluntary gift and not as an extortion.

6 The point is this: the one who sows sparingly will also reap sparingly, and the one who sows bountifully will also reap bountifully. 7Each of you must give as you have made up your mind, not reluctantly or under compulsion, for God loves a cheerful giver. 8And God is able to provide you with every blessing in abundance, so that by always having enough of everything, you may share abundantly in every good work. 9As it is written,

"He scatters abroad, he
    gives to the poor;
his righteousness*b*
    endures forever."

10He who supplies seed to the sower and bread for food will supply and multiply your seed for sowing and increase the harvest

a Other ancient authorities add *of boasting*

b Or *benevolence*

2745	1473	09	5228	1473	2758		1722	011
καύχημα	ἡμῶν	τὸ	ὑπὲρ	ὑμῶν	κενωθῇ		ἐν	τῷ
brag	of us	the	over	you	might be empty		in	the

3313	3778	2443	2531	3004		3903
μέρει	τούτῳ,	ἵνα	καθὼς	ἔλεγον		παρεσκευασμένοι
part	this,	that	just as	I was saying		having prepared

1510	4	3361	4458	1437	2064		4862	1473
ἦτε,		μή	πως	ἐὰν	ἔλθωσιν		σὺν	ἐμοὶ
you might be,		not	perhaps	if	might come		with	me

3110	2532	2147		1473	532
Μακεδόνες	καὶ	εὕρωσιν		ὑμᾶς	ἀπαρασκευάστους
Macedonians	and	might find		you	unprepared

2617		1473	2443	3361	3004		1473	1722
καταισχυνθῶμεν		ἡμεῖς,	ἵνα	μὴ	λέγω		ὑμεῖς,	ἐν
might be shamed		we,	that	not	I might say		you,	in

07	5287	3778	5	316		3767	2233
τῇ	ὑποστάσει	ταύτῃ.		ἀναγκαῖον		οὖν	ἡγησάμην
the	substance	this.		Necessary		then	I considered

3870		016	80		2443	4281
παρακαλέσαι		τοὺς	ἀδελφούς,		ἵνα	προέλθωσιν
to encourage		the	brothers,		that	they might go before

1519	1473	2532	4294		08
εἰς	ὑμᾶς	καὶ	προκαταρτίσωσιν		τὴν
to	you	and	might organize before		the

4279		2129	1473	3778	2092
προεπηγγελμένην		εὐλογίαν	ὑμῶν,	ταύτην	ἑτοίμην
having promised before		good word	of you,	this	prepared

1510	3779	5613	2129		2532	3361	5613	4124
εἶναι	οὕτως	ὡς	εὐλογίαν		καὶ	μὴ	ὡς	πλεονεξίαν.
to be	thusly	as	good word		and	not	as	greediness.

6	3778	1161	01		4687	5340		5340
	Τοῦτο	δέ,	ὁ		σπείρων	φειδομένως		φειδομένως
	This	but,	the		one sowing	sparingly		sparingly

2532	2325		2532	01	4687	1909	2129		1909
καὶ	θερίσει,		καὶ	ὁ	σπείρων	ἐπ'	εὐλογίαις		ἐπ'
also	harvests,		and	the	sowing	on	good words		on

2129		2532	2325	7	1538		2531
εὐλογίαις		καὶ	θερίσει.		ἕκαστος		καθὼς
good words		also	harvests.		Each		just as

4255		07	2588		3361	1537	3077
προῄρηται		τῇ	καρδίᾳ,		μὴ	ἐκ	λύπης
he has chosen before		in the	heart,		not	from	grief

2228	1537	318		2431	1063	1395	25		01	2316
ἢ	ἐξ	ἀνάγκης·		ἱλαρὸν	γὰρ	δότην	ἀγαπᾷ		ὁ	θεός.
or	from	necessity;		cheerful	for	giver	loves		the	God.

8	1414		1161	01	2316	3956	5485	4052		1519
	δυνατεῖ		δὲ	ὁ	θεὸς	πᾶσαν	χάριν	περισσεῦσαι		εἰς
	Is power		but	the	God	all	favor	to exceed		to

1473	2443	1722	3956	3842		3956	841
ὑμᾶς,	ἵνα	ἐν	παντὶ	πάντοτε		πᾶσαν	αὐτάρκειαν
you,	that	in	all	always		all	self-sufficiency

2192	4052		1519	3956	2041	18
ἔχοντες	περισσεύητε		εἰς	πᾶν	ἔργον	ἀγαθόν,
having	you might exceed		in	all	work	good,

9	2531	1125		4650		1325
	καθὼς	γέγραπται·		ἐσκόρπισεν,		ἔδωκεν
	just as	it has been written,		he scattered,		he gave

015	3993	05	1343		846	3306	1519	04
τοῖς	πένησιν,	ἡ	δικαιοσύνη		αὐτοῦ	μένει	εἰς	τὸν
to the	poor,	the	rightness		of him	stays	into	the

165	10	01	1161	2023		4703	03		4687
αἰῶνα.		ὁ	δὲ	ἐπιχορηγῶν		σπόρον	τῷ		σπείροντι
age.		The	but	supplying		seed	to		the one sowing
		one		further					

2532	740	1519	1035	5524		2532	4129
καὶ	ἄρτον	εἰς	βρῶσιν	χορηγήσει		καὶ	πληθυνεῖ
and	bread	for	food	will supply		and	will multiply

04	4703	1473	2532	837		024	1079a	06
τὸν	σπόρον	ὑμῶν	καὶ	αὐξήσει		τὰ	γενήματα	τῆς
the	seed	of you	and	will grow		the	products	of the

```
1343              1473      11  1722  3956   4148              1519
δικαιοσύνης ὑμῶν.      ἐν    παντὶ πλουτιζόμενοι εἰς
rightness   of you.   In   all   making rich    to
3956  572          3748    2716              1223        1473
πᾶσαν ἁπλότητα, ἥτις κατεργάζεται     δι'       ἡμῶν
all   openness, which works thoroughly through   us
2169          03     2316  12 3754   05    1248        06
εὐχαριστίαν τῷ   θεῷ·   ὅτι    ἡ   διακονία τῆς
good favor  to the God;   because the service  of the
3009         3778   3756  3441   1510   4322
λειτουργίας ταύτης οὐ   μόνον ἐστὶν προσαναπληροῦσα
service     this   not  alone  it is+ +filling up to
024 5303     014    40       235   2532 4052
τὰ ὑστερήματα τῶν  ἁγίων,   ἀλλὰ καὶ περισσεύουσα
the lacks    of the holy ones, but  also +exceeding
1223    4183   2169        03    2316  13 1223     06
διὰ    πολλῶν εὐχαριστιῶν τῷ   θεῷ.  διὰ      τῆς
through many   good favors to the God.   Through the
1382    06   1248       3778   1392         04
δοκιμῆς τῆς διακονίας ταύτης δοξάζοντες    τὸν
approval of the service this  giving splendor the
2316 1909 07  5292      06   3671      1473    1519
θεὸν ἐπὶ  τῇ ὑποταγῇ τῆς ὁμολογίας ὑμῶν εἰς
God  on   the subjection of the confession of you for
012 2098     02    5547    2532 572      06
τὸ εὐαγγέλιον τοῦ Χριστοῦ καὶ ἁπλότητι τῆς
the good message of the Christ and openness of the
2842      1519 846   2532 1519 3956      14 2532
κοινωνίας εἰς αὐτοὺς καὶ εἰς πάντας,    καὶ
partnership to them and to all,       and
846   1162  5228      1473 1971
αὐτῶν δεήσει ὑπὲρ  ὑμῶν ἐπιποθούντων
of them request on behalf of you desiring longingly
1473 1223   08  5235         5485   02     2316 1909
ὑμᾶς διὰ    τὴν ὑπερβάλλουσαν χάριν τοῦ  θεοῦ ἐφ'
you  through the exceeding    favor of the God  on
1473  15 5485 03    2316 1909 07 411
ὑμῖν.  Χάρις τῷ   θεῷ ἐπὶ τῇ ἀνεκδιηγήτῳ
you.    Favor to the God on  the inexpressible
846   1431     10:1  846   1473 3972 3870
αὐτοῦ δωρεᾷ.    Αὐτὸς δὲ ἐγὼ Παῦλος παρακαλῶ
of him gift.    Myself but I   Paul   encourage
1473 1223   06  4240       2532 1932        02
ὑμᾶς διὰ    τῆς πραΰτητος καὶ ἐπιεικείας τοῦ
you  through the gentleness and gentleness of the
5547    3739 2596 4383      3303      5011    1722 1473
Χριστοῦ, ὃς κατὰ πρόσωπον μὲν ταπεινὸς ἐν ὑμῖν,
Christ,  who by   face      indeed humble   in you,
548    1161 2292       1519 1473   2 1189
ἀπὼν  δὲ θαρρῶ      εἰς ὑμᾶς·   δέομαι
being absent but I am confident in you;    I beg
1161 012 3361 3918      2292         07
δὲ  τὸ μὴ  παρὼν    θαρρῆσαι      τῇ
but the not being present to be confident in the
4006        3739   3049       5111    1909 5100  016
πεποιθήσει ᾗ   λογίζομαι τολμῆσαι ἐπί τινας τοὺς
persuasion in which I reason to dare  on  some  the
3049         1473 5613 2596 4561 4043
λογιζομένους ἡμᾶς ὡς κατὰ σάρκα περιπατοῦντας.
ones reasoning us  as  by   flesh walking around.
3  1722 4561  1063 4043           3756 2596 4561
   Ἐν  σαρκὶ γὰρ περιπατοῦντες οὐ κατὰ σάρκα
   In  flesh for  walking around not by   flesh
4754          4  021 1063 3696   06    4752
στρατευόμεθα,   τὰ  γὰρ ὅπλα τῆς  στρατείας
we fight as soldier, the for  weapons of the soldiery
1473 3756 4559     235  1415  03    2316 4314
ἡμῶν οὐ   σαρκικὰ ἀλλὰ δυνατὰ τῷ   θεῷ πρὸς
of us not  fleshly but  powers  to the God to
```

of your righteousness.[a] [11]You will be enriched in every way for your great generosity, which will produce thanksgiving to God through us; [12]for the rendering of this ministry not only supplies the needs of the saints but also overflows with many thanksgivings to God. [13]Through the testing of this ministry you glorify God by your obedience to the confession of the gospel of Christ and by the generosity of your sharing with them and with all others, [14]while they long for you and pray for you because of the surpassing grace of God that he has given you. [15]Thanks be to God for his indescribable gift!

CHAPTER 10

I myself, Paul, appeal to you by the meekness and gentleness of Christ—I who am humble when face to face with you, but bold toward you when I am away!— [2]I ask that when I am present I need not show boldness by daring to oppose those who think we are acting according to human standards.[b] [3]Indeed, we live as human beings,[c] but we do not wage war according to human standards;[b] [4]for the weapons of our warfare are not merely human,[d] but they have divine power

---

a Or benevolence
b Gk according to the flesh
c Gk in the flesh
d Gk fleshly

to destroy strongholds. We destroy arguments [5]and every proud obstacle raised up against the knowledge of God, and we take every thought captive to obey Christ. [6]We are ready to punish every disobedience when your obedience is complete.

[7] Look at what is before your eyes. If you are confident that you belong to Christ, remind yourself of this, that just as you belong to Christ, so also do we. [8]Now, even if I boast a little too much of our authority, which the Lord gave for building you up and not for tearing you down, I will not be ashamed of it. [9]I do not want to seem as though I am trying to frighten you with my letters. [10]For they say, "His letters are weighty and strong, but his bodily presence is weak, and his speech contemptible." [11]Let such people understand that what we say by letter when absent, we will also do when present.

[12] We do not dare to classify or compare ourselves with some of those who commend themselves. But when they measure themselves by one another, and compare themselves with one another, they do not show good sense.

2506	3794	3053	2507
καθαίρεσιν	ὀχυρωμάτων,	λογισμοὺς	καθαιροῦντες
lifting down	fortresses,	reasonings	lifting down

	2532	3956	5313	1869		2596	06	1108
5	καὶ	πᾶν	ὕψωμα	ἐπαιρόμενον		κατὰ		τῆς γνώσεως
	and	all	height	lifting up	on	against		the knowledge

02		2316	2532	163		3956	3540		1519	08
τοῦ		θεοῦ,	καὶ	αἰχμαλωτίζοντες		πᾶν	νόημα		εἰς	τὴν
of the		God,	and	capturing		all	thought		to	the

5218	02	5547		2532	1722	2092		2192
ὑπακοὴν	τοῦ	Χριστοῦ,	6	καὶ	ἐν	ἑτοίμῳ		ἔχοντες
obedience	of the	Christ,		and	in	prepared		having

1556		3956	3876		3752
ἐκδικῆσαι		πᾶσαν	παρακοήν,		ὅταν
to bring out right		all	disobedience,		when

4137		1473	05	5218		024	2596
πληρωθῇ		ὑμῶν	ἡ	ὑπακοή.	7	Τὰ	κατὰ
might be filled		of you	the	obedience.		The	by

4383	991	1487	5100	3982		1438	5547
πρόσωπον	βλέπετε.	εἴ	τις	πέποιθεν		ἑαυτῷ	Χριστοῦ
face	you see.	If	some	persuaded		himself	of Christ

1510	3778	3049		3825	1909	1438		3754
εἶναι,	τοῦτο	λογιζέσθω		πάλιν	ἐφ'	ἑαυτοῦ,		ὅτι
to be,	this	let reason		again	on	himself,		that

2531	846	5547		3779	2532	1473	8	1437
καθὼς	αὐτὸς	Χριστοῦ,		οὕτως	καὶ	ἡμεῖς.		ἐάν
just as	himself	of Christ,		thusly	also	we.		If

5037	1063	4055		5100	2744		4012	06
[τε]	γὰρ	περισσότερόν		τι	καυχήσωμαι		περὶ	τῆς
indeed	for	more excessive		some	I might brag		about	the

1849	1473	3739	1325	01	2962	1519	3619
ἐξουσίας	ἡμῶν	ἧς	ἔδωκεν	ὁ	κύριος	εἰς	οἰκοδομὴν
authority	of us	which	gave	the	Master	for	building

2532	3756	1519	2506		1473		3756
καὶ	οὐκ	εἰς	καθαίρεσιν		ὑμῶν,		οὐκ
and	not	for	lifting down		of you,		not

153		2443	3361	1380			5613	302
αἰσχυνθήσομαι.	9	ἵνα	μὴ	δόξω			ὡς	ἂν
I will be ashamed.		That	not	I might think		as		-

1629		1473	1223		018	1992		10	3754
ἐκφοβεῖν		ὑμᾶς	διὰ		τῶν	ἐπιστολῶν·			ὅτι
to make fearful		you	through		the	letters;			that

017	1992		3303		5346		926		2532	2478
αἱ	ἐπιστολαὶ	μέν,		φησίν,		βαρεῖαι	καὶ	ἰσχυραί,
the	letters		indeed,		he says,		burdens	and	strong,

05	1161	3952		010		4983		772		2532	01	3056
ἡ	δὲ	παρουσία	τοῦ		σώματος	ἀσθενὴς	καὶ	ὁ	λόγος
the	but	presence	of the	body		weak		and	the	word

1848		3778	3049		01	5108
ἐξουθενημένος.	11	τοῦτο	λογιζέσθω	ὁ	τοιοῦτος,
having been despised.		This	let reason		the	such,

3754	3634	1510	03		3056	1223		1992
ὅτι	οἷοί	ἐσμεν	τῷ		λόγῳ	δι'		ἐπιστολῶν
that	such	we are	in the	word		through		letters

548		5108		2532	3918		011	2041
ἀπόντες,		τοιοῦτοι	καὶ		παρόντες		τῷ	ἔργῳ.
being absent,		such		also	being present		in the	work.

	3756	1063	5111		1469		2228	4793
12	Οὐ	γὰρ	τολμῶμεν		ἐγκρῖναι		ἢ	συγκρῖναι
	Not	for	we dare		to judge in		or	to judge with

1438		5100	014		1438		4921
ἑαυτούς		τισιν	τῶν		ἑαυτοὺς	συνιστανόντων,
ourselves		to some	of the		themselves	ones commending,

235	846		1722	1438		1438	3354
ἀλλὰ	αὐτοὶ		ἐν	ἑαυτοῖς		ἑαυτοὺς	μετροῦντες
but	themselves	in		themselves	themselves	measuring

2532	4793		1438		1438		3756
καὶ	συγκρίνοντες	ἑαυτοὺς		ἑαυτοῖς			οὐ
and	judging with	themselves		to themselves			not

2 CORINTHIANS 10:13—11:4

4920
συνιᾶσιν. **13** 1473 1161 3756 1519 024 280
ἡμεῖς δὲ οὐκ εἰς τὰ ἄμετρα
they understand. We but not to the unmeasurable

2744 235 2596 012 3358 02 2583 3739
καυχησόμεθα ἀλλὰ κατὰ τὸ μέτρον τοῦ κανόνος οὗ
will brag but by the measure of the rule which

3307 1473 01 2316 3358 2185 891
ἐμέρισεν ἡμῖν ὁ θεὸς μέτρου, ἐφικέσθαι ἄχρι
divided to us the God of measure, to reach until

2532 1473 **14** 3756 1063 5613 3361 2185 1519
καὶ ὑμῶν. οὐ γὰρ ὡς μὴ ἐφικνούμενοι εἰς
also of you. Not for as not reaching to

1473 5239 1438 891 1063 2532
ὑμᾶς ὑπερεκτείνομεν ἑαυτούς, ἄχρι γὰρ καὶ
you we stretched beyond ourselves, until for also

1473 5348 1722 011 2098 02 5547
ὑμῶν ἐφθάσαμεν ἐν τῷ εὐαγγελίῳ τοῦ χριστοῦ,
of you we arrived in the good message of the Christ,

15 3756 1519 024 280 2744 1722 245
οὐκ εἰς τὰ ἄμετρα καυχώμενοι ἐν ἀλλοτρίοις
not for the unmeasurable bragging in to others

2873 1680 1161 2192 837 06 4102
κόποις, ἐλπίδα δὲ ἔχοντες αὐξανομένης τῆς πίστεως
labors, hope but having being grown of the trust

1473 1722 1473 3170 2596 04 2583 1473
ὑμῶν ἐν ὑμῖν μεγαλυνθῆναι κατὰ τὸν κανόνα ἡμῶν
of you in you to be made great by the rule of us

1519 4050 **16** 1519 024 5238 1473
εἰς περισσείαν εἰς τὰ ὑπερέκεινα ὑμῶν
for excess for the things beyond of you

2097 3756 1722 245 2583 1519
εὐαγγελίσασθαι, οὐκ ἐν ἀλλοτρίῳ κανόνι εἰς
to tell good message, not in to other rule for

024 2092 2744 **17** 01 1161 2744
τὰ ἕτοιμα καυχήσασθαι. Ὁ δὲ καυχώμενος
the prepared to brag. The but one bragging

1722 2962 2744 **18** 3756 1063 01 1438
ἐν κυρίῳ καυχάσθω· οὐ γὰρ ὁ ἑαυτὸν
in Master let brag; not for the himself

4921 1565 1510 1384 235 3739 01
συνιστάνων, ἐκεῖνός ἐστιν δόκιμος, ἀλλὰ ὃν ὁ
commending, that is proved, but what the

2962 4921 **11:1** 3785 430 1473
κύριος συνίστησιν. Ὄφελον ἀνείχεσθέ μου
Master commends. Would that you endure of me

3398 5100 877 235 2532 430 1473
μικρόν τι ἀφροσύνης· ἀλλὰ καὶ ἀνέχεσθέ μου.
little some thoughtlessness; but also you endure me.

2 2206 1063 1473 2316 2205 718
ζηλῶ γὰρ ὑμᾶς θεοῦ ζήλῳ, ἡρμοσάμην
I am jealous for you of God jealousy, I harmonized

1063 1473 1520 435 3933 53 3936
γὰρ ὑμᾶς ἑνὶ ἀνδρὶ παρθένον ἁγνὴν παραστῆσαι
for you to one man virgin pure to stand along

03 5547 **3** 5399 1161 3361 4458 5613 01
τῷ Χριστῷ· φοβοῦμαι δὲ μή πως, ὡς ὁ
to the Christ; I fear but not perhaps, as the

3789 1818 2096 1722 07 3834
ὄφις ἐξηπάτησεν Εὔαν ἐν τῇ πανουργίᾳ
snake thoroughly deceived Eve in the trickery

846 5351 021 3540 1473 575
αὐτοῦ, φθαρῇ τὰ νοήματα ὑμῶν ἀπὸ
of him, might be corrupted the thoughts of you from

06 572 2532 06 54 06 1519 04 5503
τῆς ἁπλότητος [καὶ τῆς ἁγνότητος] τῆς εἰς τὸν Χριστόν.
the openness and the pureness the in the Christ.

4 1487 3303 1063 01 2064 243 2424
εἰ μὲν γὰρ ὁ ἐρχόμενος ἄλλον Ἰησοῦν
If indeed for the one coming other Jesus

[13]We, however, will not boast beyond limits, but will keep within the field that God has assigned to us, to reach out even as far as you. [14]For we were not overstepping our limits when we reached you; we were the first to come all the way to you with the good news[a] of Christ. [15]We do not boast beyond limits, that is, in the labors of others; but our hope is that, as your faith increases, our sphere of action among you may be greatly enlarged, [16]so that we may proclaim the good news[a] in lands beyond you, without boasting of work already done in someone else's sphere of action. [17]"Let the one who boasts, boast in the Lord." [18]For it is not those who commend themselves that are approved, but those whom the Lord commends.

CHAPTER 11

I wish you would bear with me in a little foolishness. Do bear with me! [2]I feel a divine jealousy for you, for I promised you in marriage to one husband, to present you as a chaste virgin to Christ. [3]But I am afraid that as the serpent deceived Eve by its cunning, your thoughts will be led astray from a sincere and pure[b] devotion to Christ. [4]For if someone comes and proclaims another Jesus

a Or the gospel
b Other ancient authorities lack and pure

than the one we proclaimed, or if you receive a different spirit from the one you received, or a different gospel from the one you accepted, you submit to it readily enough. [5]I think that I am not in the least inferior to these super-apostles. [6]I may be untrained in speech, but not in knowledge; certainly in every way and in all things we have made this evident to you.

7 Did I commit a sin by humbling myself so that you might be exalted, because I proclaimed God's good news[a] to you free of charge? [8]I robbed other churches by accepting support from them in order to serve you. [9]And when I was with you and was in need, I did not burden anyone, for my needs were supplied by the friends[b] who came from Macedonia. So I refrained and will continue to refrain from burdening you in any way. [10]As the truth of Christ is in me, this boast of mine will not be silenced in the regions of Achaia. [11]And why? Because I do not love you? God knows I do!

12 And what I do I will also continue to do, in order to deny an opportunity to those who want an opportunity to be recognized as our equals in what they boast about. [13]For such boasters are false apostles,

a Gk the gospel of God
b Gk brothers

2784	3739	3756	2784	2228	4151	2087
κηρύσσει	ὃν	οὐκ	ἐκηρύξαμεν,	ἢ	πνεῦμα	ἕτερον
announces	whom	not	we announced,	or	spirit	other

2983	3739	3756	2983		2228	2098
λαμβάνετε	ὃ	οὐκ	ἐλάβετε,		ἢ	εὐαγγέλιον
receive	whom	not	you received,		or	good message

2087	3739	3756	1209	2573	430
ἕτερον	ὃ	οὐκ	ἐδέξασθε,	καλῶς	ἀνέχεσθε.
other	that	not	you welcomed,	well	you endure.

5 | 3049 | 1063 | 3367 | 5302 | 014 |
|------|------|------|------|-----|
| Λογίζομαι | γὰρ | μηδὲν | ὑστερηκέναι | τῶν |
| I reason | for | nothing | to be lacking | of the |

5244a	652	**6**	1487	1161	2532	2399
ὑπερλίαν	ἀποστόλων.		εἰ	δὲ	καὶ	ἰδιώτης
very beyond	delegates.		If	but	also	unlearned

03	3056	235	3756 07	1108	235	1722
τῷ	λόγῳ,	ἀλλ'	οὐ τῇ	γνώσει,	ἀλλ'	ἐν
in the word,		but	not in	the knowledge,	but	in

3956	5319	1722	3956	1519	1473
παντὶ	φανερώσαντες	ἐν	πᾶσιν	εἰς	ὑμᾶς.
all	having demonstrated	in	all	in	you.

7 | 2228 | 266 | 4160 | 1683 | 5013 | 2443 | 1473 |
|------|------|------|------|------|------|------|
| Ἢ | ἁμαρτίαν | ἐποίησα | ἐμαυτὸν | ταπεινῶν | ἵνα | ὑμεῖς |
| Or | sin | I did | myself | humbling | that | you |

5312	3754 1432	012 02	2316
ὑψωθῆτε,	ὅτι δωρεὰν	τὸ τοῦ	θεοῦ
might be elevated,	that as a gift	the of	the God

2098	2097	1473	243
εὐαγγέλιον	εὐηγγελισάμην	ὑμῖν; **8**	ἄλλας
good message	I told good message	to you?	Other

1577	4813	2983	3800	4314 08
ἐκκλησίας	ἐσύλησα	λαβὼν	ὀψώνιον	πρὸς τὴν
assemblies	I robbed	having taken	salary	to the

1473	1248	2532 3918	4314 1473 2532
ὑμῶν	διακονίαν, **9**	καὶ παρὼν	πρὸς ὑμᾶς καὶ
of you	service,	and being present	to you and

5302	3756 2655	3762	012
ὑστερηθεὶς	οὐ κατενάρκησα	οὐθενός·	τὸ
having been in lack	not I burdened	of nothing;	the

1063 5303	1473 4322	013 80
γὰρ ὑστέρημά	μου προσανεπλήρωσαν	οἱ ἀδελφοὶ
for lack	of me filled up to	the brothers

2064	575	3109	2532 1722 3956 4
ἐλθόντες	ἀπὸ	Μακεδονίας,	καὶ ἐν παντὶ ἀβαρῆ
having come	from	Macedonia,	and in all unburden

1683	1473	5083	2532 5083	**10**	1510	225
ἐμαυτὸν	ὑμῖν	ἐτήρησα	καὶ τηρήσω.		ἔστιν	ἀλήθεια
myself	to you	I kept	and I will keep.		It is	truth

5547	1722 1473 3754 05	2746	3778 3756
Χριστοῦ	ἐν ἐμοὶ ὅτι ἡ	καύχησις	αὕτη οὐ
of Christ	in me that the	brag	this not

5420	1519 1473 1722 023	2824	06
φραγήσεται	εἰς ἐμὲ ἐν	τοῖς κλίμασιν	τῆς
will be stopped	to me in	the regions	of the

882	**11**	1223	5101	3754 3756 25	1473	01
Ἀχαΐας.		διὰ	τί;	ὅτι οὐκ	ἀγαπῶ ὑμᾶς;	ὁ
Achaia.		Through	what?	That not	I love you?	The

2316 3609a	**12**	3739 1161 4160	2532 4160	2443
θεὸς οἶδεν.		Ὃ δὲ ποιῶ,	καὶ ποιήσω,	ἵνα
God has known.		What but I do,	and I will do,	that

1581	08 874	014	2309	874
ἐκκόψω	τὴν ἀφορμὴν	τῶν	θελόντων	ἀφορμήν,
I might cut off	the opportunity	of the	ones wanting	opportunity,

2443 1722 3739 2744	2147	2531
ἵνα ἐν ᾧ καυχῶνται	εὑρεθῶσιν	καθὼς
that in what they brag	they might be found	just as

2532 1473	**13**	013 1063 5108	5570
καὶ ἡμεῖς.		οἱ γὰρ τοιοῦτοι	ψευδαπόστολοι,
also we.		The for such	false delegates,

```
2040      1386        3345                    1519 652
ἐργάται  δόλιοι,   μετασχηματιζόμενοι    εἰς ἀποστόλους
workers  beguiling, reshaping themselves into delegates
5547        14  2532 3756 2295      846       1063 01
Χριστοῦ.  14 καὶ οὐ θαῦμα·  αὐτὸς   γὰρ  ὁ
of Christ.     And not marvel; himself for  the
4567        3345                 1519 32         5457
σατανᾶς  μετασχηματίζεται εἰς ἄγγελον  φωτός.
adversary reshapes himself into messenger of light.
        3756 3173   3767 1487 2532  013 1249       846
15      οὐ μέγα  οὖν  εἰ  καὶ  οἱ διάκονοι αὐτοῦ
        Not great then if  also the servants of him
3345                     5613 1249      1343            3739
μετασχηματίζονται ὡς  διάκονοι δικαιοσύνης· ὧν
reshape themselves as servants of rightness; of which
09     5056           1510      2596 024 2041  846      3825
τὸ τέλος      ἔσται  κατὰ τὰ ἔργα αὐτῶν.  16 Πάλιν
the completion will be by  the works of them.    Again
3004      3361 5100 1473 1380          878         1510
λέγω,  μή  τίς  με  δόξῃ       ἄφρονα   εἶναι·
I say, not some me  might think unthinking to be;
1487 1161 3361 1065  2579    5613 878      1209
εἰ  δὲ  μή  γε,  κἂν  ὡς  ἄφρονα  δέξασθέ
if  but not indeed, if also as  unthinking welcome
1473 2443 2504    3398    5100 2744       17  3739 2980
με,  ἵνα κἀγὼ μικρόν τι καυχήσωμαι.  17 ὃ λαλῶ,
me,  that also I little some might brag.  What I say,
3756 2596 2962    2980   235  5613 1722 877
οὐ  κατὰ κύριον λαλῶ ἀλλ᾽ ὡς ἐν ἀφροσύνῃ,
not by  Master I say but  as  in thoughtlessness,
1722 3778  07 5287      06        2746          18  1893
ἐν  ταύτῃ τῇ ὑποστάσει τῆς καυχήσεως.  18 ἐπεὶ
in  this  the substance of the brag.       Since
4183   2744         2596 4561    2504     2744
πολλοὶ καυχῶνται κατὰ σάρκα, κἀγὼ  καυχήσομαι.
many  might brag by  flesh, also I will brag.
       2234   1063 430     014 878        5429
19     ἡδέως γὰρ ἀνέχεσθε τῶν ἀφρόνων φρόνιμοι
       Gladly for  you endure the unthinking thoughtful
1510       20  430     1063 1487 5100    1473
ὄντες·   20 ἀνέχεσθε γὰρ  εἴ  τις  ὑμᾶς
being;      endure  for if  some you
2615              1487 5100 2719       1487 5100
καταδουλοῖ,   εἴ  τις κατεσθίει,  εἴ  τις
enslaves thoroughly, if  some eats up,  if  some
2983         1487 5100 1869      1487 5100 1519 4383
λαμβάνει, εἴ  τις ἐπαίρεται,  εἴ  τις εἰς πρόσωπον
receives, if  some lifts up on, if some into face
1473 1194      21  2596 819    3004   5613 3754 1473
ὑμᾶς δέρει.  21 κατὰ ἀτιμίαν λέγω, ὡς  ὅτι ἡμεῖς
you beats.      By  dishonor I say, as  that we
770            1722 3739 1161 302 5100 5111       1722
ἠσθενήκαμεν. Ἐν  ᾧ   δ᾽  ἄν τις τολμᾷ,  ἐν
have weakened. In what but  -  some might dare, in
877          3004    5111  2504     22  1445
ἀφροσύνῃ  λέγω, τολμῶ κἀγώ.  22 Ἑβραῖοί
thoughtlessness I say, dare also I.   Hebrews
1510      2504  2475    1510      2504
εἰσιν;  κἀγώ. Ἰσραηλῖταί εἰσιν;  κἀγώ.
are they? Also I. Israelites are they? Also I.
4690    11   1510     2504       23  1249
σπέρμα Ἀβραάμ εἰσιν;  κἀγώ.  23 διάκονοι
Seed   Abraham are they? Also I.   Servants
5547     1510    3912          2980
Χριστοῦ εἰσιν;  παραφρονῶν   λαλῶ,
of Christ are they? Being beside thought I speak,
                                thought
5228   1473 1722 2873     4056         1722 5438
ὑπὲρ ἐγώ· ἐν κόποις περισσοτέρως,  ἐν φυλακαῖς
beyond I;  in labors more exceedingly, in guards
```

deceitful workers, disguising themselves as apostles of Christ. [14]And no wonder! Even Satan disguises himself as an angel of light. [15]So it is not strange if his ministers also disguise themselves as ministers of righteousness. Their end will match their deeds.

[16]I repeat, let no one think that I am a fool; but if you do, then accept me as a fool, so that I too may boast a little. [17]What I am saying in regard to this boastful confidence, I am saying not with the Lord's authority, but as a fool; [18]since many boast according to human standards,[a] I will also boast. [19]For you gladly put up with fools, being wise yourselves! [20]For you put up with it when someone makes slaves of you, or preys upon you, or takes advantage of you, or puts on airs, or gives you a slap in the face. [21]To my shame, I must say, we were too weak for that!

But whatever anyone dares to boast of—I am speaking as a fool—I also dare to boast of that. [22]Are they Hebrews? So am I. Are they Israelites? So am I. Are they descendants of Abraham? So am I. [23]Are they ministers of Christ? I am talking like a madman—I am a better one: with far greater labors, far more imprisonments,

_a_ Gk according to the flesh

with countless floggings, and often near death. ²⁴Five times I have received from the Jews the forty lashes minus one. ²⁵Three times I was beaten with rods. Once I received a stoning. Three times I was shipwrecked; for a night and a day I was adrift at sea; ²⁶on frequent journeys, in danger from rivers, danger from bandits, danger from my own people, danger from Gentiles, danger in the city, danger in the wilderness, danger at sea, danger from false brothers and sisters;ᵃ ²⁷in toil and hardship, through many a sleepless night, hungry and thirsty, often without food, cold and naked. ²⁸And, besides other things, I am under daily pressure because of my anxiety for all the churches. ²⁹Who is weak, and I am not weak? Who is made to stumble, and I am not indignant?

30 If I must boast, I will boast of the things that show my weakness. ³¹The God and Father of the Lord Jesus (blessed be he forever!) knows that I do not lie. ³²In Damascus, the governorᵇ under King Aretas guarded the city of Damascus in order toᶜ seize me, ³³but I was let down in a basket through a window in the wall,ᵈ and escaped from his hands.

ᵃ Gk brothers
ᵇ Gk ethnarch
ᶜ Other ancient authorities read and wanted to
ᵈ Gk through the wall

4056		1722	4127	5234		1722
περισσοτέρως,	ἐν	πληγαῖς	ὑπερβαλλόντως,	ἐν
more excessively,	in	blows	exceedingly,	in

2288	4178	**24**	5259	2453	3999
θανάτοις πολλάκις.		Ὑπὸ	Ἰουδαίων πεντάκις
deaths frequently.		By	Judeans five times

5062	3844	1520 2983	**25**	5151
τεσσεράκοντα παρὰ	μίαν ἔλαβον,		τρὶς
forty beside one	I received,		three

4463	530	3034	5151
ἐραβδίσθην,	ἅπαξ ἐλιθάσθην,	τρὶς
I was beaten with rods,	once I was stoned,	three

3489	3574	1722	03	1037
ἐναυάγησα,	νυχθήμερον	ἐν	τῷ	βυθῷ
I was shipwrecked,	night day	in	the	deep

4160	**26**	3597	4178	2794
πεποίηκα·		ὁδοιπορίαις	πολλάκις,	κινδύνοις
I have done;		walking travels	frequently,	in dangers

4215	2794	3027	2794	1537
ποταμῶν,	κινδύνοις ληστῶν,		κινδύνοις ἐκ
of rivers,	in dangers of robbers,		in dangers from

1085	2794	1537 1484	2794	1722 4172
γένους,	κινδύνοις ἐξ	ἐθνῶν,	κινδύνοις ἐν	πόλει,
kind,	in dangers from	nations,	in dangers in	city,

2794	1722	2047	2794	1722 2281
κινδύνοις	ἐν	ἐρημίᾳ,	κινδύνοις ἐν	θαλάσσῃ,
in dangers	in	desert,	in dangers in	sea,

2794	1722	5569	**27**	2873	2532 3449
κινδύνοις	ἐν	ψευδαδέλφοις,		κόπῳ	καὶ μόχθῳ,
in dangers in	false brothers,			in labor	and toil,

1722 70	4178	1722 3042	2532 1373
ἐν ἀγρυπνίαις	πολλάκις,	ἐν λιμῷ	καὶ δίψει,
in staying awake	frequently,	in famine	and thirst,

1722 3521	4178	1722 5592	2532 1132
ἐν νηστείαις	πολλάκις,	ἐν ψύχει	καὶ γυμνότητι·
in fastings	frequently,	in cold	and nakedness;

28	3565	033	3924	05	1987a	1473	05	2596
	χωρὶς	τῶν παρεκτὸς	ἡ	ἐπίστασίς μοι	ἡ	καθ'
	without	the except	the	attention to me	the	by

2250	05	3308	3956	018 1577	**29**	5101
ἡμέραν,	ἡ	μέριμνα	πασῶν	τῶν ἐκκλησιῶν.		τίς
day,	the	anxiety	of all	the assemblies.		Who

770	2532 3756	770	5101	4624	2532
ἀσθενεῖ καὶ	οὐκ	ἀσθενῶ;	τίς	σκανδαλίζεται καὶ
is weak and	not	I am weak?	Who	is offended and

3756 1473	4448	**30**	1487 2744
οὐκ ἐγὼ	πυροῦμαι;		Εἰ καυχᾶσθαι
not I	am set on fire?		If to brag

1163	024 06	769	1473
δεῖ,	τὰ τῆς	ἀσθενείας	μου
it is necessary,	the of the	weakness	of me

2744	**31**	01	2316	2532 3962	02	2962
καυχήσομαι.		ὁ	θεὸς καὶ	πατὴρ	τοῦ	κυρίου
I will brag.		The	God and	father	of the	Master

2424	3609a	01	1510	2128	1519 016
Ἰησοῦ	οἶδεν,	ὁ	ὢν	εὐλογητὸς	εἰς τοὺς
Jesus	has known,	the one	being	well-spoken	into the

165	3754	3756 5574	**32**	1722 1154	01
αἰῶνας,	ὅτι	οὐ ψεύδομαι.		ἐν	Δαμασκῷ ὁ
ages,	because	not I lie.		In	Damascus the

1481	702	02	935	5432	08 4172
ἐθνάρχης	Ἀρέτα	τοῦ	βασιλέως	ἐφρούρει	τὴν πόλιν
Ethnarch	Aretus	the	king	was guarding	the city

1153	4084	1473	**33**	2532 1223	2376
Δαμασκηνῶν	πιάσαι	με,		καὶ διὰ	θυρίδος
of Damascus	to capture	me,		and through	window

1722	4553	5465	1223	010 5038
ἐν	σαργάνῃ	ἐχαλάσθην	διὰ	τοῦ τείχους
in	rope basket	I was lowered	through	the wall

2532 1628   020 5495   846   **12:1** 2744
καὶ ἐξέφυγον τὰς χεῖρας αὐτοῦ.   Καυχᾶσθαι
and I fled out the hands of him.   To brag
1163   3756 4851   3303   2064
δεῖ,   οὐ συμφέρον μέν, ἐλεύσομαι
it is necessary, not advantageous indeed, I will go
1161 1519 3701   2532 602   2962   **2** 3609a
δὲ εἰς ὀπτασίας καὶ ἀποκαλύψεις κυρίου.   οἶδα
but into visions and uncoverings of Master. I know
444   1722 5547   4253   2094 1180   1535
ἄνθρωπον ἐν Χριστῷ πρὸ ἐτῶν δεκατεσσάρων, εἴτε
man in Christ before years fourteen, whether
1722 4983   3756 3609a   1535 1622   010 4983   3756
ἐν σώματι οὐκ οἶδα, εἴτε ἐκτὸς τοῦ σώματος οὐκ
in body not I know, or outside the body not
3609a 01 2316 3609a   726   04
οἶδα, ὁ θεὸς οἶδεν, ἁρπαγέντα τὸν
I know, the God has known, having been seized the
5108   2193 5154   3772   **3** 2532 3609a 04
τοιοῦτον ἕως τρίτου οὐρανοῦ. καὶ οἶδα τὸν
such until third heaven.   And I know the
5108   444   1535   1722 4983   1535 5565
τοιοῦτον ἄνθρωπον, εἴτε ἐν σώματι εἴτε χωρὶς
such man, whether in body or without
010 4983   3756 3609a   01 2316 3609a   **4** 3754
τοῦ σώματος οὐκ οἶδα, ὁ θεὸς οἶδεν, ὅτι
the body not I know, the God has known, because
726   1519 04 3857   2532 191
ἡρπάγη εἰς τὸν παράδεισον καὶ ἤκουσεν
he was seized into the paradise and he heard
731   4487   3739 3756 1832   444
ἄρρητα ῥήματα ἃ οὐκ ἐξὸν ἀνθρώπῳ
unspeakable words which not it is possible to man
2980   **5** 5228   02   5108   2744
λαλῆσαι. ὑπὲρ τοῦ τοιούτου καυχήσομαι,
to speak. On behalf of the such I will brag,
5228   1161 1683   3756 2744   1487 3361
ὑπὲρ δὲ ἐμαυτοῦ οὐ καυχήσομαι εἰ μὴ
on behalf of but myself not I will brag except
1722 019 769   **6** 1437 1063 2309
ἐν ταῖς ἀσθενείαις. Ἐὰν γὰρ θελήσω
in the weaknesses. If for I might want
2744   3756 1510   878   225   1063
καυχήσασθαι, οὐκ ἔσομαι ἄφρων, ἀλήθειαν γὰρ
to brag, not I will be unthinking truth for
3004   5339   1161 3361 5100 1519 1473
ἐρῶ·   φείδομαι δέ, μή τις εἰς ἐμὲ
I will say; I spare but, not some to me
3049   5228   3739 991   1473 2228 191   5100
λογίσηται ὑπὲρ ὃ βλέπει με ἢ ἀκούει [τι]
might reason beyond what he sees me or hears some
1537 1473 **7** 2532 07   5236   018   602
ἐξ ἐμοῦ καὶ τῇ ὑπερβολῇ τῶν ἀποκαλύψεων.
from me and in the excess of the uncoverings.
1352   2443 3361 5229   1325
διό ἵνα μὴ ὑπεραίρωμαι, ἐδόθη
Therefore that not I might be lifted beyond, was given
1473 4647   07   4561   32   4567
μοι σκόλοψ τῇ σαρκί, ἄγγελος σατανᾶ,
to me thorn in the flesh, messenger of adversary,
2443 1473 2852   2443 3361
ἵνα με κολαφίζῃ, ἵνα μὴ
that me he might knock about, that not
5229   **8** 5228   3778 5151
ὑπεραίρωμαι. ὑπὲρ τούτου τρὶς
I might be lifted beyond. On behalf of this three
04 2962   3870   2443 868
τὸν κύριον παρεκάλεσα ἵνα ἀποστῇ
the Master I encouraged that it might be stood off

CHAPTER 12

It is necessary to boast;
nothing is to be gained
by it, but I will go on to
visions and revelations of
the Lord. [2]I know a person
in Christ who fourteen
years ago was caught up to
the third heaven—whether
in the body or out of the
body I do not know; God
knows. [3]And I know that
such a person—whether
in the body or out of the
body I do not know; God
knows— [4]was caught up
into Paradise and heard
things that are not to be
told, that no mortal is
permitted to repeat. [5]On
behalf of such a one I will
boast, but on my own
behalf I will not boast,
except of my weaknesses.
[6]But if I wish to boast, I
will not be a fool, for I will
be speaking the truth. But
I refrain from it, so that
no one may think better of
me than what is seen in me
or heard from me, [7]even
considering the exceptional
character of the revelations.
Therefore, to keep[a] me
from being too elated, a
thorn was given me in the
flesh, a messenger of Satan
to torment me, to keep me
from being too elated.[b]
[8]Three times I appealed to
the Lord about this, that it

[a] Other ancient authorities read
To keep
[b] Other ancient authorities lack
to keep me from being too elated

would leave me, 9but he said to me, "My grace is sufficient for you, for power[a] is made perfect in weakness." So, I will boast all the more gladly of my weaknesses, so that the power of Christ may dwell in me. 10Therefore I am content with weaknesses, insults, hardships, persecutions, and calamities for the sake of Christ; for whenever I am weak, then I am strong.

11 I have been a fool! You forced me to it. Indeed you should have been the ones commending me, for I am not at all inferior to these super-apostles, even though I am nothing. 12The signs of a true apostle were performed among you with utmost patience, signs and wonders and mighty works. 13How have you been worse off than the other churches, except that I myself did not burden you? Forgive me this wrong!

14 Here I am, ready to come to you this third time. And I will not be a burden, because I do not want what is yours but you; for children ought not to lay up for their parents, but parents for their children. 15I will most gladly spend and be spent for you. If I love you more, am I to be loved less?

_____
a Other ancient authorities read
  my power

575   1473   9 2532 3004   1473   714
ἀπ᾽   ἐμοῦ.   9 καὶ εἴρηκέν   μοι· ἀρκεῖ
from   me.   And he has spoken to me; is enough

1473   05   5485   1473   05 1063 1411   1722 769
σοι   ἡ χάρις μου,   ἡ γὰρ δύναμις ἐν   ἀσθενείᾳ
to you the favor of me, the for power   in   weakness

5055   2234   3767 3123 2744   1722
τελεῖται.   Ἥδιστα   οὖν μᾶλλον καυχήσομαι ἐν
is complete. Most gladly then more I will brag in

019 769   1473   2443 1981   1909 1473
ταῖς ἀσθενείαις μου, ἵνα ἐπισκηνώσῃ   ἐπ᾽ ἐμὲ
the weaknesses of me, that might set up tent on me

05 1411   02   5547   10 1352   2106
ἡ δύναμις τοῦ Χριστοῦ. 10 διὸ   εὐδοκῶ
the power of the Christ.   Therefore I think well

1722 769   1722 5196   1722 318   1722
ἐν ἀσθενείαις,   ἐν ὕβρεσιν, ἐν ἀνάγκαις, ἐν
in weaknesses,   in abuses,   in necessities, in

1375   2532 4730   5228   5547
διωγμοῖς καὶ στενοχωρίαις, ὑπὲρ   Χριστοῦ·
persecutions and anguish,   on behalf of Christ;

3752 1063 770   5119 1415   1510   11 1096
ὅταν γὰρ ἀσθενῶ,   τότε δυνατός εἰμι. 11 Γέγονα
when for I am weak, then power I am. I have become

878   1473 1473 315   1473 1063 3784
ἄφρων,   ὑμεῖς με ἠναγκάσατε. ἐγὼ γὰρ ὤφειλον
unthinking, you me compelled.   I   for owe

5259 1473 4921   3762   1063 5302   014
ὑφ᾽ ὑμῶν συνίστασθαι·   οὐδὲν γὰρ ὑστέρησα τῶν
by you to be commended; nothing for I lacked of the

5244a   652   1487 2532 3762   1510 12 021
ὑπερλίαν ἀποστόλων εἰ καὶ οὐδέν εἰμι. 12 τὰ
very beyond delegates if even nothing I am. The

3303   4592   02   652   2716   1722
μὲν   σημεῖα τοῦ ἀποστόλου κατειργάσθη   ἐν
indeed signs of the delegate worked thoroughly in

1473 1722 3956 5281   4592   5037 2532 5059
ὑμῖν ἐν πάσῃ ὑπομονῇ, σημείοις τε καὶ τέρασιν
you in all patience,   in signs both and marvels

2532 1411   13 5101 1063 1510   3739   2074a
καὶ δυνάμεσιν. 13 τί γὰρ ἐστιν ὃ   ἡσσώθητε
and powers.   What for is it which you were
                                      lessened

5228   020 3062   1577   1487 3361 3754 846
ὑπὲρ τὰς λοιπὰς ἐκκλησίας, εἰ μὴ ὅτι αὐτὸς
beyond the remaining assemblies, except that myself

1473 3756 2655   1473 5483   1473 08
ἐγὼ οὐ κατενάρκησα ὑμῶν; χαρίσασθέ μοι τὴν
I   not burdened   you? Give favor to me the

93   3778   14 2400 5154   3778 2093   2192
ἀδικίαν ταύτην.   14 Ἰδοὺ τρίτον τοῦτο ἑτοίμως ἔχω
unright this.   Look third this readily I have

2064   4314 1473 2532 3756 2655   3756 1063
ἐλθεῖν πρὸς ὑμᾶς, καὶ οὐ καταναρκήσω· οὐ γὰρ
to come to you,   and not I will burden; not for

2212   024 1473 235 1473   3756 1063 3784   021
ζητῶ   τὰ ὑμῶν ἀλλὰ ὑμᾶς. οὐ γὰρ ὀφείλει τὰ
I seek the of you but you. Not for owe   the

5043   015   1118   2843   235 013 1118
τέκνα   τοῖς γονεῦσιν θησαυρίζειν ἀλλὰ οἱ γονεῖς
children to the parents to treasure but the parents

023   5043   15 1473 1161 2234   1159
τοῖς τέκνοις. 15 ἐγὼ δὲ ἥδιστα   δαπανήσω
to the children.   I   but most gladly will spend

2532 1550   5228   018   5590 1473
καὶ ἐκδαπανηθήσομαι ὑπὲρ   τῶν   ψυχῶν ὑμῶν.
and will be spent out on behalf of the souls of you.

1487 4056   1473 25   2269a 25
εἰ περισσοτέρως ὑμᾶς ἀγαπῶ[ν], ἧσσον ἀγαπῶμαι;
If more exceedingly you loving, worse am I loved?

16
1510	1161	1473	3756	2599	1473	235
Ἔστω	δέ,	ἐγὼ	οὐ	κατεβάρησα	ὑμᾶς·	ἀλλὰ
Let be	but,	I	not	burdened down	you;	but

5225	3835	1388	1473	2983	**17**	3361
ὑπάρχων	πανοῦργος	δόλῳ	ὑμᾶς	ἔλαβον.		μή
existing	trickster	in guile	you	I received.		Not

5100 3739	649		4314	1473	1223	846
τινα ὧν	ἀπέσταλκα		πρὸς	ὑμᾶς,	δι᾽	αὐτοῦ
some of whom	I have delegated	to		you,	through	him

4122	1473	**18**	3870	5103	2532
ἐπλεονέκτησα	ὑμᾶς;		παρεκάλεσα	Τίτον	καὶ
I took more	you?		I encouraged	Titus	and

4882	04 80	3385	4122	1473
συναπέστειλα	τὸν ἀδελφόν·	μήτι	ἐπλεονέκτησεν	ὑμᾶς
I delegated together	the brother;	not some	took more	you

5103	3756	011	846	4151	4043
Τίτος;	οὐ	τῷ	αὐτῷ	πνεύματι	περιεπατήσαμεν;
Titus?	Not	in the same		spirit	we walked around?

3756	023	846	2487	**19**	3819	1380	3754
οὐ	τοῖς	αὐτοῖς	ἴχνεσιν;		Πάλαι	δοκεῖτε	ὅτι
Not	in the same		footprints?		Of old	you think	that

1473	626	2713	2316	1722	5547
ὑμῖν	ἀπολογούμεθα.	κατέναντι	θεοῦ ἐν		Χριστῷ
to you	we defend.	Over against	God in		Christ

2980	021 1161	3956	27	5228	06
λαλοῦμεν·	τὰ δὲ	πάντα,	ἀγαπητοί,	ὑπὲρ	τῆς
we speak;	the but	all,	loved ones,	on behalf of	the

1473	3619	**20**	5399	1063 3361	4458
ὑμῶν	οἰκοδομῆς.		φοβοῦμαι	γὰρ μή	πως
of you	building.		I fear	for not	perhaps

2064	3756 3634	2309	2147	1473 2504
ἐλθὼν	οὐχ οἵους	θέλω	εὕρω	ὑμᾶς κἀγὼ
having come	not such as	I want	I might find	you and I

2147	1473 3634	3756 2309	3361 4458
εὑρεθῶ	ὑμῖν οἷον	οὐ θελέτε·	μή πως
I might find	you such as not	you want;	not perhaps

2054	2205	2372	2052
ἔρις,	ζῆλος,	θυμοί,	ἐριθεῖαι,
strife,	jealousy,	furies,	selfish ambitions,

2636	5587	5450
καταλαλιαί,	ψιθυρισμοί,	φυσιώσεις,
speeches against,	whisperings,	puffing ups,

181	**21**	3361 3825	2064	1473
ἀκαταστασίαι·		μὴ πάλιν	ἐλθόντος	μου
unstablenesses;		not again	having come	me

5013	1473 01	2316 1473	4314 1473	2532
ταπεινώσῃ	με ὁ	θεός μου	πρὸς ὑμᾶς	καὶ
might humble	me the	God of me	to you	and

3996	4183	014	4258
πενθήσω	πολλοὺς	τῶν	προημαρτηκότων
I might mourn	much	of the ones	having sinned before

2532 3361	3340	1909 07	167	2532
καὶ μὴ	μετανοησάντων	ἐπὶ τῇ	ἀκαθαρσίᾳ	καὶ
and not	having changed mind	on the	uncleanness	and

4202	2532 766	3739	4238
πορνείᾳ	καὶ ἀσελγείᾳ	ἢ	ἔπραξαν.
sexual immorality	and debauchery	which	they practiced.

13:1
5154	3778	2064	4314 1473	1909 4750	1417
Τρίτον	τοῦτο	ἔρχομαι	πρὸς ὑμᾶς·	ἐπὶ στόματος	δύο
Third	this	I come	to you;	on mouth	two

3144	2532 5140	2476	3956 4487
μαρτύρων	καὶ τριῶν	σταθήσεται	πᾶν ῥῆμα.
testifiers	and of three	will stand	all word.

2
4302	2532 4302	5613
προείρηκα	καὶ προλέγω,	ὡς
I have said before	and I say before,	as

3918	012 1208	2532 548	3568
παρὼν	τὸ δεύτερον	καὶ ἀπὼν	νῦν,
being present	the second	and being absent	now,

[16]Let it be assumed that I did not burden you. Nevertheless (you say) since I was crafty, I took you in by deceit. [17]Did I take advantage of you through any of those whom I sent to you? [18]I urged Titus to go, and sent the brother with him. Titus did not take advantage of you, did he? Did we not conduct ourselves with the same spirit? Did we not take the same steps?

[19]Have you been thinking all along that we have been defending ourselves before you? We are speaking in Christ before God. Everything we do, beloved, is for the sake of building you up. [20]For I fear that when I come, I may find you not as I wish, and that you may find me not as you wish; I fear that there may perhaps be quarreling, jealousy, anger, selfishness, slander, gossip, conceit, and disorder. [21]I fear that when I come again, my God may humble me before you, and that I may have to mourn over many who previously sinned and have not repented of the impurity, sexual immorality, and licentiousness that they have practiced.

CHAPTER 13

This is the third time I am coming to you. "Any charge must be sustained by the evidence of two or three witnesses." [2]I warned those who sinned previously and all the others, and I warn them now while absent, as I did when present on my second visit, that if I come again, I will not be lenient— ³since you desire proof that Christ is speaking in me. He is not weak in dealing with you, but is powerful in you. ⁴For he was crucified in weakness, but lives by the power of God. For we are weak in him,ᵃ but in dealing with you we will live with him by the power of God.

5 Examine yourselves to see whether you are living in the faith. Test yourselves. Do you not realize that Jesus Christ is in you?— unless, indeed, you fail to meet the test! ⁶I hope you will find out that we have not failed. ⁷But we pray to God that you may not do anything wrong—not that we may appear to have met the test, but that you may do what is right, though we may seem to have failed. ⁸For we cannot do anything against the truth, but only for the truth. ⁹For we rejoice when we are weak and you are strong. This is what we pray for, that you may become perfect. ¹⁰So I write these things while I am away from you, so that when I come, I may not have to be severe in using the authority that the Lord has given me for building up

ᵃ Other ancient authorities read with him

015	4258		2532 015	3062
τοῖς	προημαρτηκόσιν	καὶ	τοῖς	λοιποῖς
to the ones	having sinned before	and	to the	remaining

3956	3754	1437	2064	1519	012	3825	3756
πᾶσιν,	ὅτι	ἐὰν	ἔλθω	εἰς	τὸ	πάλιν	οὐ
all,	that	if	I might come	to	the	again	not

³ 5339
φείσομαι,   ³ ἐπεὶ δοκιμὴν ζητεῖτε τοῦ ἐν
I will spare,   since approval you seek of the in

1473 2980   5547   3739 1519 1473 3756 770
ἐμοὶ λαλοῦντος Χριστοῦ, ὃς εἰς ὑμᾶς οὐκ ἀσθενεῖ
me one speaking Christ, who in you not is weak

235 1414   1722 1473   **⁴** 2532 1063 4717
ἀλλὰ δυνατεῖ ἐν ὑμῖν.   ⁴ καὶ γὰρ ἐσταυρώθη
but is power in you.   Also for he was crucified

1537 769   235 2198   1537 1411   2316
ἐξ ἀσθενείας, ἀλλὰ ζῇ ἐκ δυνάμεως θεοῦ.
from weakness, but he lives from power of God.

2532 1063 1473 770   1722 846 235 2198
καὶ γὰρ ἡμεῖς ἀσθενοῦμεν ἐν αὐτῷ, ἀλλὰ ζήσομεν
And for we are weak in him, but we will live

4862 846 1537 1411   2316   1519 1473   **⁵** 1438
σὺν αὐτῷ ἐκ δυνάμεως θεοῦ εἰς ὑμᾶς.   ⁵ Ἑαυτοὺς
with him from power of God to you.   Yourselves

3985   1487 1510   1722 07 4102   1438
πειράζετε εἰ ἐστὲ ἐν τῇ πίστει, ἑαυτοὺς
pressure if you are in the trust, yourselves

1381   2228 3756 1921   1438   3754
δοκιμάζετε· ἢ οὐκ ἐπιγινώσκετε ἑαυτοὺς ὅτι
prove; or not do you perceive yourselves that

2424 5547   1722 1473 1487 3385   96
Ἰησοῦς Χριστὸς ἐν ὑμῖν; εἰ μήτι ἀδόκιμοί
Jesus Christ in you? If not some unproved

1510   **⁶** 1679 1161 3754 1097   3754 1473
ἐστε.   ⁶ ἐλπίζω δὲ ὅτι γνώσεσθε ὅτι ἡμεῖς
you are.   I hope but that you will know that we

3756 1510 96   **⁷** 2172   1161 4314 04 2316
οὐκ ἐσμὲν ἀδόκιμοι.   ⁷ εὐχόμεθα δὲ πρὸς τὸν θεὸν
not are unproved.   We wish but to the God

3361 4160   1473 2556 3367   3756 2443 1473
μὴ ποιῆσαι ὑμᾶς κακὸν μηδέν, οὐχ ἵνα ἡμεῖς
not to do you bad nothing, not that we

1384   5316   235 2443 1473 012 2570
δόκιμοι φανῶμεν, ἀλλ' ἵνα ὑμεῖς τὸ καλὸν
proved might shine, but that you the good

4160   1473 1161 5613 96   1510   **⁸** 3756
ποιῆτε, ἡμεῖς δὲ ὡς ἀδόκιμοι ὦμεν.   ⁸ οὐ
you might do, we but as unproved might be.   Not

1063 1410   5100 2596 06 225   235
γὰρ δυνάμεθά τι κατὰ τῆς ἀληθείας ἀλλὰ
for we are able some against the truth but

5228 06 225   **⁹** 5463   1063 3752
ὑπὲρ τῆς ἀληθείας.   ⁹ χαίρομεν γὰρ ὅταν
on behalf of the truth.   We rejoice for when

1473 770   1473 1161 1415   1510
ἡμεῖς ἀσθενῶμεν, ὑμεῖς δὲ δυνατοὶ ἦτε·
we might be weak, you but power might be;

3778 2532 2172   08 1473   2676
τοῦτο καὶ εὐχόμεθα, τὴν ὑμῶν κατάρτισιν.
this also we wish, the of you putting in order.

10 1223   3778 3778 548   1125   2443
Διὰ τοῦτο ταῦτα ἀπὼν γράφω, ἵνα
Through this these being absent I write, that

3918   3361 664   5530   2596 08
παρὼν μὴ ἀποτόμως χρήσωμαι κατὰ τὴν
being present not severely I might use by the

1849   3739 01 2962 1325   1473 1519 3619
ἐξουσίαν ἣν ὁ κύριος ἔδωκέν μοι εἰς οἰκοδομὴν
authority which the Master gave to me for building

2532	3756	1519	2506		3062		80
καὶ	οὐκ	εἰς	καθαίρεσιν.	**11**	Λοιπόν,		ἀδελφοί,
and	not	for	lifting down.		Remaining,		brothers,

5463	2675		3870		012	846
χαίρετε,	καταρτίζεσθε,		παρακαλεῖσθε,		τὸ	αὐτὸ
rejoice,	be put in order,		encourage,		the	same

5426	1514		2532	01	2316	06	26
φρονεῖτε,	εἰρηνεύετε,		καὶ	ὁ	θεὸς	τῆς	ἀγάπης
think,	be at peace,		and	the	God	of the	love

2532	1515	1510	3326	1473		782
καὶ	εἰρήνης	ἔσται	μεθ'	ὑμῶν.	**12**	Ἀσπάσασθε
and	peace	will be	with	you.		Greet

240	1722	40	5370		782		1473	013
ἀλλήλους	ἐν	ἁγίῳ	φιλήματι.		Ἀσπάζονται		ὑμᾶς	οἱ
one another	in	holy	kiss.		Greet		you	the

40	3956		05	5485	02	2962	2424
ἅγιοι	πάντες.	**13**	Ἡ	χάρις	τοῦ	κυρίου	Ἰησοῦ
holy ones	all.		The	favor	of the	Master	Jesus

5547	2532	05	26	02	2316	2532	05
Χριστοῦ	καὶ	ἡ	ἀγάπη	τοῦ	θεοῦ	καὶ	ἡ
Christ	and	the	love	of the	God	and	the

2842	010	40	4151	3326	3956	1473
κοινωνία	τοῦ	ἁγίου	πνεύματος	μετὰ	πάντων	ὑμῶν.
partnership	of the	holy	spirit	with	all	of you.

and not for tearing down.

11 Finally, brothers and sisters,[a] farewell.[b] Put things in order, listen to my appeal,[c] agree with one another, live in peace; and the God of love and peace will be with you. [12]Greet one another with a holy kiss. All the saints greet you.

13 The grace of the Lord Jesus Christ, the love of God, and the communion of[d] the Holy Spirit be with all of you.

[a] Gk brothers
[b] Or rejoice
[c] Or encourage one another
[d] Or and the sharing in

GALATIANS

CHAPTER 1

Paul an apostle—sent neither by human commission nor from human authorities, but through Jesus Christ and God the Father, who raised him from the dead— [2]and all the members of God's family[a] who are with me,

To the churches of Galatia:

3 Grace to you and peace from God our Father and the Lord Jesus Christ, [4]who gave himself for our sins to set us free from the present evil age, according to the will of our God and Father, [5]to whom be the glory forever and ever. Amen.

6 I am astonished that you are so quickly deserting the one who called you in the grace of Christ and are turning to a different gospel— [7]not that there is another gospel, but there are some who are confusing you and want to pervert the gospel of Christ, [8]But even if we or an angel[b] from heaven should proclaim to you a gospel contrary to what we proclaimed to you, let that one be accursed! [9]As we have said before, so now I repeat, if anyone proclaims to you a gospel contrary to what you received, let that one be accursed!

10 Am I now seeking human approval, or God's approval? Or am I trying to please people? If I were still pleasing people, I would not be a servant[c] of Christ.

a Gk all the brothers
b Or a messenger
c Gk slave

1:1
3972 Παῦλος Paul
652 ἀπόστολος delegate
3756 οὐκ not
575 ἀπ' from
444 ἀνθρώπων men
3761 οὐδὲ but not
1223 δι' through

444 ἀνθρώπου man
235 ἀλλὰ but
1223 διὰ through
2424 Ἰησοῦ Jesus
5547 Χριστοῦ Christ
2532 καὶ and
2316 θεοῦ God
3962 πατρὸς father

02 τοῦ of
1453 ἐγείραντος the one having raised
846 αὐτὸν him
1537 ἐκ from
3498 νεκρῶν, dead,
2 2532 καὶ and
013 οἱ the

4862 σὺν with
1473 ἐμοὶ me
3956 πάντες all
80 ἀδελφοὶ brothers
019 ταῖς to the
1577 ἐκκλησίαις assemblies
06 τῆς of the

1053 Γαλατίας, Galatia,
3 5485 χάρις favor
1473 ὑμῖν to you
2532 καὶ and
1515 εἰρήνη peace
575 ἀπὸ from
2316 θεοῦ God
3962 πατρὸς father

1473 ἡμῶν of us
2532 καὶ and
2962 κυρίου Master
2424 Ἰησοῦ Jesus
5547 Χριστοῦ Christ
4 02 τοῦ the
1325 δόντος one having given

1438 ἑαυτὸν himself
5228 ὑπὲρ on behalf
018 τῶν of the
266 ἁμαρτιῶν sins
1473 ἡμῶν, of us,
3704 ὅπως so that

1807 ἐξέληται he might lift out
1473 ἡμᾶς us
1537 ἐκ from
02 τοῦ the
165 αἰῶνος age
02 τοῦ the
1764 ἐνεστῶτος, present

4190 πονηροῦ evil
2596 κατὰ by
012 τὸ the
2307 θέλημα want
02 τοῦ of the
2316 θεοῦ God
2532 καὶ and
3962 πατρὸς father
1473 ἡμῶν, of us,

5 3739 ᾧ to whom
05 ἡ the
1391 δόξα splendor
1519 εἰς into
016 τοὺς the
165 αἰῶνας ages
014 τῶν of the
165 αἰώνων, ages,

281 ἀμήν. amen.
6 2296 Θαυμάζω I marvel
3754 ὅτι that
3779 οὕτως thusly
5030 ταχέως quickly
3346 μετατίθεσθε you change

575 ἀπὸ from
02 τοῦ the
2564 καλέσαντος one having called
1473 ὑμᾶς you
1722 ἐν in
5485 χάριτι favor
5547 [Χριστοῦ] of Christ

1519 εἰς into
2087 ἕτερον other
2098 εὐαγγέλιον, good message,
7 3739 ὃ what
3756 οὐκ not
1510 ἔστιν is
243 ἄλλο, other,

1487 εἰ except
3361 μή
5100 τινές some
1510 εἰσιν are
013 οἱ the ones
5015 ταράσσοντες troubling
1473 ὑμᾶς you
2532 καὶ and

2309 θέλοντες wanting
3344 μεταστρέψαι to turn across
012 τὸ the
2098 εὐαγγέλιον good message
02 τοῦ of the

5547 Χριστοῦ. Christ.
8 235 ἀλλὰ But
2532 καὶ even
1437 ἐὰν if
1473 ἡμεῖς we
2228 ἢ or
32 ἄγγελος messenger
1537 ἐξ from

3772 οὐρανοῦ heaven
2097 εὐαγγελίζηται might tell good message
1473 [ὑμῖν] to you
3844 παρ' from
3739 ὃ what

2097 εὐηγγελισάμεθα good message we ourselves told
1473 ὑμῖν, to you,
331 ἀνάθεμα curse
1510 ἔστω. let be.

9 5613 ὡς As
4302 προειρήκαμεν we have said before
2532 καὶ and
737 ἄρτι now
3825 πάλιν again
3004 λέγω· I say;
1487 εἰ if

5100 τις some
1473 ὑμᾶς you
2097 εὐαγγελίζεται tells good message
3844 παρ' from
3739 ὃ what
3880 παρελάβετε, you took along,
331 ἀνάθεμα curse

1510 ἔστω. let be.
10 737 Ἄρτι Now
1063 γὰρ for
444 ἀνθρώπους men
3982 πείθω I persuade
2228 ἢ or
04 τὸν the

2316 θεόν; God?
2228 ἢ Or
2212 ζητῶ I seek
444 ἀνθρώποις men
700 ἀρέσκειν; to please?
1487 εἰ If
2089 ἔτι still

444 ἀνθρώποις men
700 ἤρεσκον, I was pleasing,
5547 Χριστοῦ of Christ
1401 δοῦλος slave
3756 οὐκ not
302 ἂν -

1510	**11** 1107	1063 1473	80	012
ἤμην.	Γνωρίζω	γὰρ ὑμῖν,	ἀδελφοί,	τὸ
I was.	I make known	for to you,	brothers	the

2098	012 2097			5259
εὐαγγέλιον	τὸ εὐαγγελισθὲν			ὑπ'
good message	the having been told good message			by

1473 3754 3756 1510	2596 444	**12**	3761	1063 1473
ἐμοῦ ὅτι οὐκ ἔστιν κατὰ ἄνθρωπον·			οὐδὲ	γὰρ ἐγὼ
me that not it is by man;			but not	for I

3844 444	3880	846	3777 1321	235
παρὰ ἀνθρώπου	παρέλαβον	αὐτὸ	οὔτε ἐδιδάχθην	ἀλλὰ
from man	took along	it	nor was I taught	but

1223 602	2424	5547	**13**	191 1063
δι' ἀποκαλύψεως	Ἰησοῦ	Χριστοῦ.		Ἠκούσατε γὰρ
through uncovering	of Jesus	Christ.		You heard for

08 1699 391	4218 1722 03	2454		3754 2596
τὴν ἐμὴν ἀναστροφήν	ποτε ἐν τῷ	Ἰουδαϊσμῷ,		ὅτι καθ'
the my behavior	then in the	Judaism,		that by

5236	1377	08	1577	02	2316
ὑπερβολὴν	ἐδίωκον		τὴν ἐκκλησίαν	τοῦ	θεοῦ
excess	I was pursuing		the assembly	of the	God

2532 4199	846	**14**	2532 4298		1722
καὶ ἐπόρθουν	αὐτήν,		καὶ προέκοπτον		ἐν
and was ravaging	her,		and I was progressing		in

03 2454	5228 4183	4915		1722 011
τῷ Ἰουδαϊσμῷ	ὑπὲρ πολλοὺς	συνηλικιώτας		ἐν τῷ
the Judaism	beyond many	contemporaries		in the

1085 1473	4056	2207	5225	014
γένει μου,	περισσοτέρως	ζηλωτὴς	ὑπάρχων	τῶν
kind of me,	more exceedingly	jealous	existing	of the

3967 1473	3862	**15**	3753	1161 2106
πατρικῶν μου	παραδόσεων.		Ὅτε	δὲ εὐδόκησεν
fathers of me	traditions.		When	but thought well

01 2316 01	873		1473 1537 2836
[ὁ θεὸς] ὁ	ἀφορίσας		με ἐκ κοιλίας
the God the	one having separated		me from stomach

3384	1473	2532 2564		1223	06 5485
μητρός	μου	καὶ καλέσας		διὰ	τῆς χάριτος
of mother	of me	and having called		through	the favor

846	**16**	601	04	5207 846	1722 1473	2443
αὐτοῦ		ἀποκαλύψαι	τὸν	υἱὸν αὐτοῦ	ἐν ἐμοί,	ἵνα
of him		to uncover	the	son of him	in me,	that

2097	846	1722 023	1484	2112	3756
εὐαγγελίζωμαι	αὐτὸν	ἐν τοῖς	ἔθνεσιν,	εὐθέως	οὐ
I might tell	him	in the	nations,	immediately	not
good message					

4323	4561	2532 129	**17**	3761	424
προσανεθέμην	σαρκὶ	καὶ αἵματι		οὐδὲ	ἀνῆλθον
I conferred	in flesh	and blood		but not	I went up

1519 2414	4314	016 4253	1473 652
εἰς Ἱεροσόλυμα	πρὸς	τοὺς πρὸ	ἐμοῦ ἀποστόλους,
into Jerusalem	toward	the before me	delegates,

235 565	1519	688	2532 3825	5290
ἀλλὰ ἀπῆλθον	εἰς	Ἀραβίαν	καὶ πάλιν	ὑπέστρεψα
but I went off	into	Arabia	and again	I returned

1519 1154	**18**	1899	3326 2094	5140 424
εἰς Δαμασκόν.		Ἔπειτα	μετὰ ἔτη	τρία ἀνῆλθον
into Damascus.		Then	after years	three I went up

1519 2414	2477	2786	2532 1961
εἰς Ἱεροσόλυμα	ἱστορῆσαι	Κηφᾶν	καὶ ἐπέμεινα
into Jerusalem	to visit with	Cephas	and I stayed on

4314 846	2250	1178	**19**	2087	1161 014
πρὸς αὐτὸν	ἡμέρας	δεκαπέντε,		ἕτερον	δὲ τῶν
toward him	days	fifteen,		other	but of the

652	3756 3708	1487 3361	2385	04 80
ἀποστόλων	οὐκ εἶδον	εἰ μὴ	Ἰάκωβον	τὸν ἀδελφὸν
delegates	not I saw	except	Jacob	the brother

02	2962	**20**	3739 1161 1125	1473	2400 1799
τοῦ	κυρίου.		ἃ δὲ γράφω	ὑμῖν,	ἰδοὺ ἐνώπιον
of the	Master.		What but I write	to you,	look before

11 For I want you to know, brothers and sisters,[a] that the gospel that was proclaimed by me is not of human origin; [12]for I did not receive it from a human source, nor was I taught it, but I received it through a revelation of Jesus Christ.

13 You have heard, no doubt, of my earlier life in Judaism. I was violently persecuting the church of God and was trying to destroy it. [14]I advanced in Judaism beyond many among my people of the same age, for I was far more zealous for the traditions of my ancestors. [15]But when God, who had set me apart before I was born and called me through his grace, was pleased [16]to reveal his Son to me,[b] so that I might proclaim him among the Gentiles, I did not confer with any human being, [17]nor did I go up to Jerusalem to those who were already apostles before me, but I went away at once into Arabia, and afterwards I returned to Damascus.

18 Then after three years I did go up to Jerusalem to visit Cephas and stayed with him fifteen days; [19]but I did not see any other apostle except James the Lord's brother. [20]In what I am writing to you,

a Gk brothers
b Gk in me

before God, I do not lie!
²¹Then I went into the
regions of Syria and Cilicia,
²²and I was still unknown
by sight to the churches of
Judea that are in Christ;
²³they only heard it said,
"The one who formerly
was persecuting us is now
proclaiming the faith he
once tried to destroy."
²⁴And they glorified God
because of me.

CHAPTER 2

Then after fourteen years
I went up again to Jerusalem
with Barnabas, taking
Titus along with me. ²I
went up in response to a
revelation. Then I laid
before them (though only
in a private meeting with
the acknowledged leaders)
the gospel that I proclaim
among the Gentiles, in
order to make sure that I
was not running, or had
not run, in vain. ³But even
Titus, who was with me,
was not compelled to be
circumcised, though he
was a Greek. ⁴But because
of false believers[a] secretly
brought in, who slipped in
to spy on the freedom we
have in Christ Jesus, so that
they might enslave us—
⁵we did not submit to them
even for a moment, so that
the truth of the gospel
might always remain with
you. ⁶And from those
who were supposed to be
acknowledged leaders
(what they actually were
makes no difference to me;

[a] Gk false brothers

02	2316	3754	3756	5574		1899	2064	1519 024

02   2316   3754   3756   5574   **21** 1899   2064   1519 024
τοῦ θεοῦ ὅτι   οὐ   ψεύδομαι.   ῎Επειτα ἦλθον εἰς   τὰ
the God   (")   not   I lie.   Then   I went into the

2824   06   4947   2532 06 2791   1510   1161
κλίματα τῆς   Συρίας καὶ τῆς Κιλικίας· **22** ἤμην   δὲ
regions of the Syria and the Cilicia;   I was+ but

50   011   4383   019   1577   06
ἀγνοούμενος τῷ   προσώπῳ ταῖς ἐκκλησίαις τῆς
+being unknown in the face   to the assemblies of the

2449   019   1722 5547   3441   1161 191
᾿Ιουδαίας ταῖς ἐν   Χριστῷ. **23** μόνον δὲ   ἀκούοντες
Judea   the in   Christ.   Alone but   +hearing

1510 3754 01   1377   1473 4218 3568 2097   08
ἦσαν ὅτι ὁ   διώκων ἡμᾶς ποτε νῦν   εὐαγγελίζεται τὴν
they that the one   us   then now he tells good the
were+   pursuing   message

4102   3739   4218 4199   2532 1392   1722
πίστιν ἥν   ποτε ἐπόρθει, **24** καὶ ἐδόξαζον   ἐν
trust which then he was   and they were giving in
                ravaging,   splendor

1473 04 2316   1899   1223   1180   2094
ἐμοὶ τὸν θεόν. **2:1** ῎Επειτα διὰ   δεκατεσσάρων ἐτῶν
me   the God.   Then through fourteen   years

3825 305   1519 2414   3326 921
πάλιν ἀνέβην   εἰς   ᾿Ιεροσόλυμα μετὰ Βαρναβᾶ
again I went up into Jerusalem with Barnabas

4838   2532 5103   **2** 305   1161 2596
συμπαραλαβὼν   καὶ Τίτον·   ἀνέβην δὲ κατὰ
having taken along with also Titus; I went up but by

602   2532 394   846   012 2098   3739
ἀποκάλυψιν· καὶ ἀνεθέμην αὐτοῖς τὸ εὐαγγέλιον   ὃ
uncovering; and I set up to them the good message that

2784   1722 023 1484   2596 2398 1161 015
κηρύσσω   ἐν τοῖς ἔθνεσιν, κατ᾿ ἰδίαν δὲ τοῖς
I announce in the nations, by   own but to the

1380   3361 4458   1519 2756 5143   2228
δοκοῦσιν,   μή πως   εἰς κενὸν τρέχω   ἢ
ones thinking, not perhaps in empty I might run or

5143   235 3761   5103 01 4862 1472   1672
ἔδραμον. **3** ἀλλ᾿ οὐδὲ Τίτος ὁ σὺν ἐμοί, ῞Ελλην
I ran.   But but not Titus the with me,   Greek

1510 315   4059   **4** 1223   1161
ὤν,   ἠναγκάσθη   περιτμηθῆναι·   διὰ   δὲ
being, was compelled to be circumcised; through but

016 3920   5569   3748
τοὺς παρεισάκτους   ψευδαδέλφους,   οἵτινες
the brought in secretly false brothers, who

3922   2684   08 1657   1473
παρεισῆλθον κατασκοπῆσαι τὴν ἐλευθερίαν ἡμῶν
came in along to look carefully the freedom of us

3739 2192   1722 5547   2424 2443 1473
ἣν ἔχομεν ἐν Χριστῷ ᾿Ιησοῦ, ἵνα ἡμᾶς
that we have in Christ Jesus, that us

2615   **5** 3739   3761   4314
καταδουλώσουσιν,   οἷς   οὐδὲ   πρὸς
they will enslave thoroughly to whom but not to

5610 1502   07   5292   2443 05 225
ὥραν εἴξαμεν τῇ   ὑποταγῇ,   ἵνα ἡ ἀλήθεια
hour we yielded in the subjection, that the truth

010 2098   1265   4314 1473
τοῦ εὐαγγελίου διαμείνῃ   πρὸς ὑμᾶς.
of the good message might stay through to you.

6 575 1161 014 1380   1510 5100 3697   4218
᾿Απὸ δὲ   τῶν δοκούντων εἶναί τι, – ὁποῖοί ποτε
From but the ones   to be some, what kind then
           thinking

1510   3762 1473 1308   4383   01 2316
ἦσαν   οὐδέν μοι διαφέρει· πρόσωπον [ὁ] θεὸς
they were nothing to me it differs; face   the God

```
444        3756 2983              1473    1063  013  1380
ἀνθρώπου   οὐ   λαμβάνει -        ἐμοὶ    γὰρ  οἱ  δοκοῦντες
of man     not  receives         to me   for  the ones thinking
3762       4323                  7 235  5121
οὐδὲν      προσανέθεντο,           ἀλλὰ   τοὐναντίον
nothing    conferred,             but    on the contrary
3708           3754 4100                  012  2098
ἰδόντες        ὅτι  πεπίστευμαι          τὸ   εὐαγγέλιον
having seen    that I have been trusted  the  good message
06   203             2531      4074 06
τῆς  ἀκροβυστίας      καθὼς     Πέτρος τῆς
of the uncircumcision just as  Peter  of the
4061              8 01       1063 1754              4074
περιτομῆς,          ὁ     γὰρ  ἐνεργήσας           Πέτρῳ
circumcision,      the one for  having operated    in Peter
1519 651           06   4061          1754        2532
εἰς  ἀποστολὴν     τῆς  περιτομῆς     ἐνήργησεν  καὶ
to   delegateship the  circumcision  operated   also
1473 1519 024 1484       9 2532 1097           08  5485
ἐμοὶ εἰς  τὰ  ἔθνη,        καὶ  γνόντες         τὴν χάριν
in me to  the nations,     and  having known   the favor
08            1325          1473   2385    2532 2786
τὴν          δοθεῖσάν       μοι,   Ἰάκωβος καὶ  Κηφᾶς
the one having been given to me,  Jacob   and  Cephas
2532 2491        013 1380              4769     1510    1188
καὶ  Ἰωάννης,   οἱ  δοκοῦντες        στῦλοι  εἶναι,  δεξιὰς
and  John,      the ones thinking    pillars to be,  right
1325         1473   2532 921          2842              2443
ἔδωκαν       ἐμοὶ  καὶ  Βαρναβᾷ       κοινωνίας,         ἵνα
they gave to me and  Barnabas of partnership,        that
1473  1519 024 1484        846           1161 1519 08
ἡμεῖς εἰς  τὰ  ἔθνη,        αὐτοὶ       δὲ   εἰς  τὴν
we    to  the nations,     themselves but  to   the
4061           10 3441   014 4434      2443 3421
περιτομήν·        μόνον τῶν πτωχῶν    ἵνα  μνημονεύωμεν,
circumcision; alone the  poor       that we might remember,
3739 2532 4704          846   3778  4160          3753
ὃ    καὶ  ἐσπούδασα     αὐτὸ τοῦτο ποιῆσαι.    11 "Οτε
that also I was diligent same this to do.        When
1161 2064  2786     1519 490         2596 4383        846
δὲ   ἦλθεν Κηφᾶς εἰς  Ἀντιόχειαν, κατὰ πρόσωπον αὐτῷ
but  came  Cephas into Antioch,     by   face     to him
436            3754    2607
ἀντέστην,      ὅτι    κατεγνωσμένος
I stood against because +having known against himself
1510       4253     010 1063 2064    5100  575  2385
ἦν.        12 πρὸ  τοῦ γὰρ ἐλθεῖν τινας ἀπὸ Ἰακώβου
he was+.  Before the for  to come some  from Jacob
3326 022 1484        4906                3753 1161
μετὰ τῶν ἐθνῶν       συνήσθιεν·          ὅτε  δὲ
with the nations he was eating with; when but
2064    5288              2532 873
ἦλθον,  ὑπέστελλεν        καὶ  ἀφώριζεν
they came, he was withdrawing and  was separating
1438    5399       016     1537 4061          13 2532
ἑαυτόν  φοβούμενος τοὺς  ἐκ   περιτομῆς.       καὶ
himself fearing    the  ones from circumcision. And
4942                    846      2532 013
συνυπεκρίθησαν          αὐτῷ  [καὶ] οἱ
they were hypocritical together to him and  the
3062     2453        5620    2532 921
λοιποὶ  Ἰουδαῖοι,   ὥστε    καὶ  Βαρναβᾶς
remaining Judeans,  so that even Barnabas
4879              846    07   5272            14 235
συναπήχθη         αὐτῶν  τῇ   ὑποκρίσει.        ἀλλ'
was led off together of them in the hypocrisy.  But
3753 3708 3754 3756 3716            4314 08
ὅτε  εἶδον ὅτι οὐκ ὀρθοποδοῦσιν    πρὸς τὴν
when I saw that not they walk straight to  the
```

God shows no partiality)—those leaders contributed nothing to me. [7]On the contrary, when they saw that I had been entrusted with the gospel for the uncircumcised, just as Peter had been entrusted with the gospel for the circumcised [8](for he who worked through Peter making him an apostle to the circumcised also worked through me in sending me to the Gentiles), [9]and when James and Cephas and John, who were acknowledged pillars, recognized the grace that had been given to me, they gave to Barnabas and me the right hand of fellowship, agreeing that we should go to the Gentiles and they to the circumcised. [10]They asked only one thing, that we remember the poor, which was actually what I was[a] eager to do.

[11] But when Cephas came to Antioch, I opposed him to his face, because he stood self-condemned; [12]for until certain people came from James, he used to eat with the Gentiles. But after they came, he drew back and kept himself separate for fear of the circumcision faction. [13]And the other Jews joined him in this hypocrisy, so that even Barnabas was led astray by their hypocrisy. [14]But when I saw that they were not acting consistently with the

[a] Or had been

truth of the gospel, I said to Cephas before them all, "If you, though a Jew, live like a Gentile and not like a Jew, how can you compel the Gentiles to live like Jews?"[a]

15 We ourselves are Jews by birth and not Gentile sinners; [16]yet we know that a person is justified[b] not by the works of the law but through faith in Jesus Christ.[c] And we have come to believe in Christ Jesus, so that we might be justified by faith in Christ,[d] and not by doing the works of the law, because no one will be justified by the works of the law. [17]But if, in our effort to be justified in Christ, we ourselves have been found to be sinners, is Christ then a servant of sin? Certainly not! [18]But if I build up again the very things that I once tore down, then I demonstrate that I am a transgressor. [19]For through the law I died to the law, so that I might live to God. I have been crucified with Christ; [20]and it is no longer I who live, but it is Christ who lives in me. And the life I now live in the flesh I live by faith in the Son of God,[e] who loved me and gave himself for me. [21]I do not nullify the grace of God; for if justification[f] comes through the law, then Christ died for nothing.

[a] Some interpreters hold that the quotation extends into the following paragraph

[b] Or *reckoned as righteous;* and so elsewhere

[c] Or *the faith of Jesus Christ*

[d] Or *the faith of Christ*

[e] Or *by the faith of the Son of God*

[f] Or *righteousness*

225	010	2098	3004	03	2786
ἀλήθειαν	τοῦ	εὐαγγελίου,	εἶπον	τῷ	Κηφᾷ
truth	of the	good message,	I said to the	Cephas

1715	3956	1487	1473	2453	5225
ἔμπροσθεν	πάντων·	εἰ	σὺ	Ἰουδαῖος	ὑπάρχων
in front	of all;	if	you	Judean	existing

1483	2532	3780	2452	2198	4459 024 1484
ἐθνικῶς	καὶ	οὐχὶ	Ἰουδαϊκῶς	ζῇς,	πῶς τὰ ἔθνη
nationally	and	not	Judaically	live,	how the nations

315	2450	**15**	1473	5449	2453
ἀναγκάζεις	ἰουδαΐζειν;		Ἡμεῖς	φύσει	Ἰουδαῖοι
you compel	to judaize?		We	in nature	Judeans

2532	3756	1537	1484	268	**16**	3609a	1161
καὶ	οὐκ	ἐξ	ἐθνῶν	ἁμαρτωλοί·		εἰδότες	[δὲ]
and	not	from	nations	sinners;		having known	but

3754	3756	1344	444	1537 2041	3551
ὅτι	οὐ	δικαιοῦται	ἄνθρωπος ἐξ	ἔργων	νόμου
that	not	is made right	man from	works	of law

1437 3361	1223	4102	2424	5547	2532 1473
ἐὰν μὴ	διὰ	πίστεως	Ἰησοῦ	Χριστοῦ,	καὶ ἡμεῖς
except	through	trust	of Jesus	Christ,	and we

1519 5547	2424	4100	2443
εἰς Χριστὸν	Ἰησοῦν	ἐπιστεύσαμεν,	ἵνα
in Christ	Jesus	trusted,	that

1344	1537 4102	5547	2532
δικαιωθῶμεν	ἐκ πίστεως	Χριστοῦ	καὶ
we might be made right	from trust	of Christ	and

3756 1537 2041 3551	3754 1537 2041 3551	3756
οὐκ ἐξ ἔργων νόμου,	ὅτι ἐξ ἔργων νόμου	οὐ
not from works of law,	that from works of law	not

1344	3956 4561	**17**	1487 1161 2212
δικαιωθήσεται	πᾶσα σάρξ.		εἰ δὲ ζητοῦντες
will be made right	all flesh.		If but seeking

1344	1722 3445	2147	2532
δικαιωθῆναι	ἐν Χριστῷ	εὑρέθημεν	καὶ
to-be made right	in Christ	we were found	also

846	268	687 5547	266	1249
αὐτοὶ	ἁμαρτωλοί,	ἆρα Χριστὸς	ἁμαρτίας	διάκονος;
ourselves	sinners,	then Christ	of sin	servant?

3361 1096	**18**	1487 1063 3739 2647	3778
μὴ γένοιτο.		εἰ γὰρ ἃ κατέλυσα	ταῦτα
Not may it become.		If for what I unloosed	these

3825 3618	3848	1683	4921
πάλιν οἰκοδομῶ,	παραβάτην	ἐμαυτὸν	συνιστάνω.
again I build,	transgressor	myself	I commend.

19	1473 1063 1223	3551	3551	599	2443
	ἐγὼ γὰρ διὰ	νόμου	νόμῳ	ἀπέθανον,	ἵνα
	I for through	law	in law	died,	that

2316	2198	5547	4957
θεῷ	ζήσω.	Χριστῷ	συνεσταύρωμαι·
to God	I might live.	In Christ	I have been crucified together;

20	2198 1161 3765	1473 2198	1161 1722 1473
	ζῶ δὲ οὐκέτι	ἐγώ, ζῇ	δὲ ἐν ἐμοὶ
	live but no longer	I, lives	but in me

5547	3739 1161 3568 2198	1722 4561	1722 4102
Χριστός·	ὃ δὲ νῦν ζῶ	ἐν σαρκί,	ἐν πίστει
Christ;	what but now I live	in flesh,	in trust

2198	07 02	5207 02	2316 02
ζῶ	τῇ τοῦ	υἱοῦ τοῦ	θεοῦ τοῦ
I live	the of the	son of the	God the one

25	1473 2532 3860	1438
ἀγαπήσαντός	με καὶ παραδόντος	ἑαυτὸν
having loved	me and having given over	himself

5228	1473	**21**	3756 114	08 5485 02
ὑπὲρ	ἐμοῦ.		Οὐκ ἀθετῶ	τὴν χάριν τοῦ
on behalf	of me.		Not I set aside	the favor of the

2316 1487 1063 1223	3551	1343	686 5547
θεοῦ· εἰ γὰρ διὰ	νόμου	δικαιοσύνη,	ἄρα Χριστὸς
God; if for through	law	rightness,	then Christ

```
1432      599              5599  453           1052
δωρεὰν    ἀπέθανεν.  3:1   Ὦ     ἀνόητοι   Γαλάται,
as a gift died.           O     unmindful Galatians,
5101  1473  940          3739    2596 3788        2424
τίς   ὑμᾶς ἐβάσκανεν, οἷς     κατ᾽ ὀφθαλμοὺς Ἰησοῦς
who   you  bewitched,  to whom by   eyes      Jesus
5547    4270              4717
Χριστὸς προεγράφη          ἐσταυρωμένος;
Christ  was written before having been crucified?
  3778  3441  2309  3129      575   1473  1537 2041
2 τοῦτο μόνον θέλω  μαθεῖν  ἀφ᾽  ὑμῶν· ἐξ  ἔργων
  This  alone I want to learn from you;  from works
3551  012  4151  2983        2228 1537 189
νόμου τὸ  πνεῦμα ἐλάβετε  ἢ    ἐξ  ἀκοῆς
of law the spirit you received or   from hearing
4102     3779  453       1510    1728
πίστεως; 3 οὕτως ἀνόητοί ἐστε,  ἐναρξάμενοι
of trust? Thusly unmindful you are, having begun in
4151      3568 4561     2005
πνεύματι  νῦν σαρκὶ ἐπιτελεῖσθε;
in spirit now in flesh you are thoroughly completing?
  5118      3958      1500       1487 1065
4 τοσαῦτα   ἐπάθετε   εἰκῇ;      εἴ  γε
  Such things you suffered without cause? If  indeed
2532 1500        01     3767 2023
καὶ  εἰκῇ.   5 ὁ      οὖν ἐπιχορηγῶν
also without cause. The one then supplying further
1473     012 4151   2532 1754      1411      1722 1473
ὑμῖν     τὸ  πνεῦμα καὶ  ἐνεργῶν  δυνάμεις ἐν  ὑμῖν,
to you   the spirit and  operating powers  in  you,
1537 2041 3551  2228 1537 189    4102      2531
ἐξ  ἔργων νόμου ἢ   ἐξ  ἀκοῆς πίστεως;  6 Καθὼς
from works of law or  from hearing of trust? Just as
 11     4100        03   2316 2532 3049
Ἀβραὰμ  ἐπίστευσεν τῷ  θεῷ, καὶ  ἐλογίσθη
Abraham trusted     the God, and  it was reasoned
846    1519 1343       1097        686  3754 013
αὐτῷ  εἰς δικαιοσύνην· 7 γινώσκετε ἄρα ὅτι  οἱ
to him for rightness;   you know   then that the ones
1537 4102     3778 5207 1510   11
ἐκ  πίστεως, οὗτοι υἱοί εἰσιν Ἀβραάμ.
from trust,   these sons are  Abraham.
  4308                 1161 05  1124      3754 1537 4102
8 προϊδοῦσα          δὲ ἡ  γραφὴ ὅτι ἐκ  πίστεως
  Having seen before but the writing that from trust
1344    024 1484   01   2316 4283          03
δικαιοῖ τὰ  ἔθνη  ὁ   θεὸς, προευηγγελίσατο τῷ
makes   the nations the God, he told good     to the
right                           message before
 11       3754 1757               1722 1473
Ἀβραὰμ   ὅτι ἐνευλογηθήσονται       ἐν  σοὶ
Abraham that they will be well-spoken in in  you
3956  021 1484    9 5620     013 1537 4102
πάντα τὰ  ἔθνη·     ὥστε  οἱ ἐκ  πίστεως
all   the nations; so that the from trust
2127           4862 03  4103    11       10  3745
εὐλογοῦνται    σὺν τῷ πιστῷ Ἀβραάμ.     Ὅσοι
are well spoken with the trustful Abraham.  As many as
1063 1537 2041 3551   1510  5259  2671    1510
γὰρ ἐξ  ἔργων νόμου εἰσίν, ὑπὸ  κατάραν εἰσίν·
for from works of law are,  under curse   they are;
1125          1063 3754 1944      3956 3739
γέγραπται     γὰρ ὅτι ἐπικατάρατος πᾶς ὃς
it has been written for, (") curse on  all who
3756 1696    3956 023     1125
οὐκ ἐμμένει πᾶσιν τοῖς γεγραμμένοις
not stay in all  the things having been written
1722 011 975      02   3551  010 4160     846
ἐν  τῷ βιβλίῳ    τοῦ  νόμου τοῦ ποιῆσαι αὐτά.
in  the small book of the law  the to do  them.
```

CHAPTER 3

You foolish Galatians! Who has bewitched you? It was before your eyes that Jesus Christ was publicly exhibited as crucified! [2]The only thing I want to learn from you is this: Did you receive the Spirit by doing the works of the law or by believing what you heard? [3]Are you so foolish? Having started with the Spirit, are you now ending with the flesh? [4]Did you experience so much for nothing?—if it really was for nothing. [5]Well then, does God[a] supply you with the Spirit and work miracles among you by your doing the works of the law, or by your believing what you heard?

6 Just as Abraham "believed God, and it was reckoned to him as righteousness," [7]so, you see, those who believe are the descendants of Abraham. [8]And the scripture, foreseeing that God would justify the Gentiles by faith, declared the gospel beforehand to Abraham, saying, "All the Gentiles shall be blessed in you." [9]For this reason, those who believe are blessed with Abraham who believed.

10 For all who rely on the works of the law are under a curse; for it is written, "Cursed is everyone who does not observe and obey all the things written in the book of the law."

_a_ Gk _he_

11Now it is evident that no one is justified before God by the law; for "The one who is righteous will live by faith."[a] 12But the law does not rest on faith; on the contrary, "Whoever does the works of the law[b] will live by them." 13Christ redeemed us from the curse of the law by becoming a curse for us—for it is written, "Cursed is everyone who hangs on a tree"— 14in order that in Christ Jesus the blessing of Abraham might come to the Gentiles, so that we might receive the promise of the Spirit through faith.

15 Brothers and sisters,[c] I give an example from daily life: once a person's will[d] has been ratified, no one adds to it or annuls it. 16Now the promises were made to Abraham and to his offspring;[e] it does not say, "And to offsprings,"[f] as of many; but it says, "And to your offspring,"[e] that is, to one person, who is Christ. 17My point is this: the law, which came four hundred thirty years later, does not annul a covenant previously ratified by God, so as to nullify the promise. 18For if the inheritance comes from the law, it no longer comes from the promise; but God granted it to Abraham through the promise.

19 Why then the law? It was added because of transgressions,

a Or The one who is righteous through faith will live
b Gk does them
c Gk Brothers
d Or covenant (as in verse 17)
e Gk seed
f Gk seeds

11
3754 — ὅτι — That
1161 — δὲ — but
1722 — ἐν — in
3551 — νόμῳ — law
3762 — οὐδεὶς — no one
1344 — δικαιοῦται — is made right
— παρὰ — along
3844 — τῷ — the
03

2316 — θεῷ — God
1212 — δῆλον, — clear,
3754 — ὅτι — because
01 — ὁ — the
1342 — δίκαιος — right
1537 — ἐκ — from
4102 — πίστεως — trust
2198 — ζήσεται· — will live;

12
01 — ὁ — the
1161 — δὲ — but
3551 — νόμος — law
3756 — οὐκ — not
1510 — ἔστιν — is
1537 — ἐκ — from
4102 — πίστεως, — trust,
235 — ἀλλ᾽ — but
01 — ὁ — the one

4160 — ποιήσας — having done
846 — αὐτὰ — them
2198 — ζήσεται — will live
1722 — ἐν — in
846 — αὐτοῖς. — them.
13
5547 — Χριστὸς — Christ
1473 — ἡμᾶς — us

1805 — ἐξηγόρασεν — bought out
1537 — ἐκ — from
06 — τῆς — the
2671 — κατάρας — curse
02 — τοῦ — of the
3551 — νόμου — law
1096 — γενόμενος — having become

5228 — ὑπὲρ — on behalf
1473 — ἡμῶν — of us
2671 — κατάρα, — curse,
3754 — ὅτι — because
1125 — γέγραπται· — it has been written,

1944 — ἐπικατάρατος — curse on
3956 — πᾶς — all
01 — ὁ — the one
2910 — κρεμάμενος — having hung
1909 — ἐπὶ — on
3586 — ξύλου, — wood,

14
2443 — ἵνα — that
1519 — εἰς — in
024 — τὰ — the
1484 — ἔθνη — nations
05 — ἡ — the
2129 — εὐλογία — good word
02 — τοῦ — of the
11 — Ἀβραὰμ — Abraham

1096 — γένηται — might become
1722 — ἐν — in
5547 — Χριστῷ — Christ
2424 — Ἰησοῦ, — Jesus,
2443 — ἵνα — that
08 — τὴν — the
1860 — ἐπαγγελίαν — promise

010 — τοῦ — of the
4151 — πνεύματος — spirit
2983 — λάβωμεν — we might receive
1223 — διὰ — through
06 — τῆς — the
4102 — πίστεως. — trust.

15
80 — Ἀδελφοί, — Brothers,
2596 — κατὰ — by
444 — ἄνθρωπον — man
3004 — λέγω· — I speak;
3676 — ὅμως — likewise
444 — ἀνθρώπου — of man

2964 — κεκυρωμένην — having been authenticated
1242 — διαθήκην — agreement
3762 — οὐδεὶς — no one
114 — ἀθετεῖ — sets aside

2228 — ἢ — or
1928 — ἐπιδιατάσσεται. — adds.
16
03 — τῷ — To the
1161 — δὲ — but
11 — Ἀβραὰμ — Abraham
3004 — ἐρρέθησαν — were said

017 — αἱ — the
1860 — ἐπαγγελίαι — promises
2532 — καὶ — and
011 — τῷ — to the
4690 — σπέρματι — seed
846 — αὐτοῦ. — of him.
3756 — οὐ — Not

3004 — λέγει· — it says;
2532 — καὶ — and
023 — τοῖς — to the
4690 — σπέρμασιν, — seeds,
5613 — ὡς — as
1909 — ἐπὶ — on
4183 — πολλῶν — many
235 — ἀλλ᾽ — but

5613 — ὡς — as
1909 — ἐφ᾽ — on
1520 — ἑνός· — one;
2532 — καὶ — and
011 — τῷ — to the
4690 — σπέρματί — seed
1473 — σου, — of you,
3739 — ὅς — who
1510 — ἐστιν — is

5547 — Χριστός. — Christ.
17
3778 — τοῦτο — This
1161 — δὲ — but
3004 — λέγω· — I say;
1242 — διαθήκην — agreement
4300 — προκεκυρωμένην — having been validated before

5259 — ὑπὸ — by
02 — τοῦ — the
2316 — θεοῦ — God
01 — ὁ — the
3326 — μετὰ — after
5071 — τετρακόσια — four hundred
2532 — καὶ — and
5144 — τριάκοντα — thirty

2094 — ἔτη — years
1096 — γεγονὼς — having become
3551 — νόμος — law
3756 — οὐκ — not
208 — ἀκυροῖ — invalidates
1519 — εἰς — for
012 — τὸ — the

2673 — καταργῆσαι — to abolish
08 — τὴν — the
1860 — ἐπαγγελίαν. — promise.
18
1487 — εἰ — If
1063 — γὰρ — for
1537 — ἐκ — from
3551 — νόμου — law
05 — ἡ — the

2817 — κληρονομία, — inheritance,
3765 — οὐκέτι — no longer
1537 — ἐξ — from
1860 — ἐπαγγελίας· — promise;
03 — τῷ — to the
1161 — δὲ — but

11 — Ἀβραὰμ — Abraham
1223 — δι᾽ — through
1860 — ἐπαγγελίας — promise
5483 — κεχάρισται — has favored
01 — ὁ — the
2316 — θεός. — God.

19
5101 — Τί — What
3767 — οὖν — then
01 — ὁ — the
3551 — νόμος; — law?
018 — τῶν — Of the
3847 — παραβάσεων — transgressions

5484   4369   891   3739   2064
χάριν   προσετέθη,   ἄχρις οὗ ἔλθῃ
on account   it was set forward, until which might come

09   4690   3739 1861   1299   1223
τὸ σπέρμα ᾧ ἐπήγγελται, διαταγεὶς δι᾽
the seed   to it has been having been through
           whom promised,   directed

32   1722 5495 3316   01   1161 3316
ἀγγέλων   ἐν χειρὶ μεσίτου. 20 ὁ δὲ μεσίτης
messengers in hand of mediator. The but mediator

1520 3756 1510   01   1161 2316 1520 1510   01   3767
ἑνὸς οὐκ ἔστιν, ὁ δὲ θεὸς εἷς ἐστιν. 21 ὁ οὖν
one not is,   the but God one is.   The then

3551 2596   018 1860   02   2316   3361
νόμος κατὰ τῶν ἐπαγγελιῶν [τοῦ θεοῦ]; μὴ
law   against the promises   of the God?   Not

1096   1487 1063 1325   3551 01
γένοιτο.   εἰ γὰρ ἐδόθη   νόμος ὁ
may it become. If for had been given law   the

1410   2227   3689   1537 3551 302 1510 05
δυνάμενος ζωοποιῆσαι, ὄντως ἐκ νόμου ἂν ἦν ἡ
being able to make live, really from law - was the

1343   22 235 4788   05 1124   024
δικαιοσύνη. ἀλλὰ συνέκλεισεν ἡ γραφὴ τὰ
rightness.   But closed together the writing the

3956 5259 266   2443 05 1860   1537 4102
πάντα ὑπὸ ἁμαρτίαν, ἵνα ἡ ἐπαγγελία ἐκ πίστεως
all   under sin,   that the promise   from trust

2424   5547   1325   015   4100
Ἰησοῦ Χριστοῦ δοθῇ   τοῖς πιστεύουσιν.
of Jesus Christ might be given to the ones trusting.

23 4253 010 1161 2064   08 4102   5259   3551
   Πρὸ τοῦ δὲ ἐλθεῖν τὴν πίστιν ὑπὸ νόμον
   Before the but to come the trust under law

5432   4788   1519 08
ἐφρουρούμεθα   συγκλειόμενοι   εἰς τὴν
we were being guarded being closed together for the

3195   4102   601   5620   01 3551
μέλλουσαν πίστιν ἀποκαλυφθῆναι, 24 ὥστε ὁ νόμος
being about trust to be uncovered,   so that the law

3807   1473 1096   1519 5547   2443 1537
παιδαγωγὸς ἡμῶν γέγονεν εἰς Χριστόν, ἵνα ἐκ
tutor   of us has become to   Christ, that from

4102   1344   2064   1161 06
πίστεως δικαιωθῶμεν· 25 ἐλθούσης δὲ τῆς
trust   we might be made right; having come but the

4102   3765   5259 3807   1510   3956
πίστεως οὐκέτι   ὑπὸ παιδαγωγόν ἐσμεν. 26 Πάντες
trust   no longer under tutor   we are.   All

1063 5207 2316   1510   1223   06 4102   1722
γὰρ υἱοὶ θεοῦ   ἐστε   διὰ τῆς πίστεως ἐν
for sons of God you are through the trust   in

5547   2424   27 3745   1063 1519 5547
Χριστῷ Ἰησοῦ· ὅσοι   γὰρ εἰς Χριστὸν
Christ Jesus; as many as for into Christ

907   5547   1746   28 3756 1762
ἐβαπτίσθητε, Χριστὸν ἐνεδύσασθε. οὐκ ἔνι
were immersed, Christ put on.   Not there is

2453   3761   1672   3756 1762   1401   3761
Ἰουδαῖος οὐδὲ Ἕλλην, οὐκ ἔνι   δοῦλος οὐδὲ
Judean but not Greek, not there is slave but not

1658   3756 1762   730   2532 2338   3956
ἐλεύθερος, οὐκ ἔνι   ἄρσεν καὶ θῆλυ· πάντες
free,   not there is male and female; all

1063 1473 1520 1510 1722 5547   2424   1487 1161
γὰρ ὑμεῖς εἷς ἐστε ἐν Χριστῷ Ἰησοῦ. 29 εἰ δὲ
for you one are in Christ Jesus.   If but

1473 5547   686 02   11   4690   1510
ὑμεῖς Χριστοῦ, ἄρα τοῦ Ἀβραὰμ σπέρμα ἐστέ,
you   of Christ, then of the Abraham seed   you are,

until the offspring[a] would come to whom the promise had been made; and it was ordained through angels by a mediator. [20]Now a mediator involves more than one party; but God is one.

[21]Is the law then opposed to the promises of God? Certainly not! For if a law had been given that could make alive, then righteousness would indeed come through the law. [22]But the scripture has imprisoned all things under the power of sin, so that what was promised through faith in Jesus Christ[b] might be given to those who believe.

[23]Now before faith came, we were imprisoned and guarded under the law until faith would be revealed. [24]Therefore the law was our disciplinarian until Christ came, so that we might be justified by faith. [25]But now that faith has come, we are no longer subject to a disciplinarian, [26]for in Christ Jesus you are all children of God through faith. [27]As many of you as were baptized into Christ have clothed yourselves with Christ. [28]There is no longer Jew or Greek, there is no longer slave or free, there is no longer male and female; for all of you are one in Christ Jesus. [29]And if you belong to Christ, then you are Abraham's offspring,[a] heirs according to the promise.

[a] Gk seed
[b] Or through the faith of Jesus Christ

CHAPTER 4

My point is this: heirs, as long as they are minors, are no better than slaves, though they are the owners of all the property; [2]but they remain under guardians and trustees until the date set by the father. [3]So with us; while we were minors, we were enslaved to the elemental spirits[a] of the world. [4]But when the fullness of time had come, God sent his Son, born of a woman, born under the law, [5]in order to redeem those who were under the law, so that we might receive adoption as children. [6]And because you are children, God has sent the Spirit of his Son into our[b] hearts, crying, "Abba![c] Father!" [7]So you are no longer a slave but a child, and if a child then also an heir, through God.[d]

[8]Formerly, when you did not know God, you were enslaved to beings that by nature are not gods. [9]Now, however, that you have come to know God, or rather to be known by God, how can you turn back again to the weak and beggarly elemental spirits?[e] How can you want to be enslaved to them again? [10]You are observing special days, and months, and seasons, and years. [11]I am afraid that my work for you may have been wasted.

[12]Friends,[f] I beg you, become as I am,

[a] Or the rudiments
[b] Other ancient authorities read your
[c] Aramaic for Father
[d] Other ancient authorities read an heir of God through Christ
[e] Or beggarly rudiments
[f] Gk Brothers

2596	1860	2818	**4:1**	3004	1161	1909
κατ'	ἐπαγγελίαν	κληρονόμοι.		Λέγω	δέ,	ἐφ'
by	promise	inheritors.		I say	but,	on

3745	5550	01	2818	3516	1510	3762
ὅσον	χρόνον ὁ		κληρονόμος	νήπιός	ἐστιν,	οὐδὲν
as much as	time the		the inheritor	infant	is,	nothing

1308	1401	2962	3956	1510	**2**	235	5259
διαφέρει	δούλου	κύριος	πάντων	ὤν,		ἀλλὰ	ὑπὸ
he differs	of slave	master	of all	being,		but	under

2012	1510	2532	3623	891	06	4287
ἐπιτρόπους	ἐστὶν	καὶ	οἰκονόμους	ἄχρι	τῆς	προθεσμίας
governors	he is	and	managers	until	the	purpose

02	3962	**3**	3779	2532	1473	3753	1510
τοῦ	πατρός.		οὕτως	καὶ	ἡμεῖς,	ὅτε	ἦμεν
of the	father.		Thusly	also	we,	when	we were

3516	5259	024 4747	02	2889	1510
νήπιοι,	ὑπὸ	τὰ στοιχεῖα	τοῦ	κόσμου	ἤμεθα
infants,	under	the elements	of the	world	we were+

1402	**4**	3753	1161	2064	09	4138
δεδουλωμένοι·		ὅτε	δὲ	ἦλθεν	τὸ	πλήρωμα
+having been enslaved;		when	but	came	the	fullness

02	5550	1821	01	2316 04	5207	846
τοῦ	χρόνου,	ἐξαπέστειλεν	ὁ	θεὸς τὸν	υἱὸν	αὐτοῦ,
of the	time,	delegated out	the	God the	son	of him,

1096	1537 1135	1096	5259	3551
γενόμενον	ἐκ γυναικός,	γενόμενον	ὑπὸ	νόμον,
having become	from woman,	having become	under	law,

5	2443 016	5259	3551	1805	2443 08
	ἵνα τοὺς	ὑπὸ	νόμον	ἐξαγοράσῃ,	ἵνα τὴν
	that the ones	under	law	he might buy out,	that the

5206	618	**6**	3754	1161 1510	5207
υἱοθεσίαν	ἀπολάβωμεν.		Ὅτι	δέ ἐστε	υἱοί,
adoption	we might receive back.		Because	but you are	sons,
as son					

1821	01	2316 012	4151	02	5207 846
ἐξαπέστειλεν	ὁ	θεὸς τὸ	πνεῦμα	τοῦ	υἱοῦ αὐτοῦ
delegated out	the	God the	spirit	of the	son of him

1519 020 2588	1473	2896	5	01	3962
εἰς τὰς καρδίας	ἡμῶν	κρᾶζον·	αββα	ὁ	πατήρ.
into the hearts	of us	shouting;	abba	the	father.

7	5620	3765	1510	1401	235	5207	1487
	ὥστε	οὐκέτι	εἶ	δοῦλος	ἀλλὰ	υἱός·	εἰ
	So that	no longer	you are	slave	but	son;	if

1161	5207	2532 2818	1223	2316	**8**	235	5119
δὲ	υἱός,	καὶ κληρονόμος	διὰ	θεοῦ.		Ἀλλὰ	τότε
but	son,	also inheritor	through	God.		But	then

3303	3756 3609a	2316	1398	015
μὲν	οὐκ εἰδότες	θεὸν	ἐδουλεύσατε	τοῖς
indeed	not having known	God	you were enslaved	to the

5449	3361 1510	2316	**9**	3568 1161	1097
φύσει	μὴ οὖσιν	θεοῖς·		νῦν δὲ	γνόντες
in nature	not being	gods;		now but	having known

2316	3123	1161 1097	5259 2316	4459
θεόν,	μᾶλλον	δὲ γνωσθέντες	ὑπὸ θεοῦ,	πῶς
God,	more	but having been known	by God,	how

1994	3825 1909 024 772	2532 4434	4747
ἐπιστρέφετε	πάλιν ἐπὶ τὰ ἀσθενῆ	καὶ πτωχὰ	στοιχεῖα
you returned	again on the weak	and poor	elements

3739	3825	509	1398	2309	**10**	2250
οἷς	πάλιν	ἄνωθεν	δουλεύειν	θέλετε;		ἡμέρας
to which	again	from above	to slave	you want?		Days

3906	2532 3376	2532 2540	2532 1763
παρατηρεῖσθε	καὶ μῆνας	καὶ καιροὺς	καὶ ἐνιαυτούς,
you keep watch	and months	and seasons	and years,

11	5399	1473 3361 4458	1500
	φοβοῦμαι	ὑμᾶς μή πως	εἰκῇ
	I fear	you not perhaps	without cause

2872	1519 1473	1096	5613 1473 3754
κεκοπίακα	εἰς ὑμᾶς.	**12** Γίνεσθε	ὡς ἐγώ, ὅτι
I have labored	in you.	Become	as I, that

```
2504      5613   1473      80          1189     1473    3762    1473
κἀγὼ      ὡς     ὑμεῖς,    ἀδελφοί,    δέομαι   ὑμῶν.   οὐδέν   με
also I     as     you,      brothers,   I beg     you.    Nothing me

91                    3609a      1161   3754   1223            769
ἠδικήσατε·    13      οἴδατε     δὲ     ὅτι    δι᾽            ἀσθένειαν
you did unright;       you know   but    that   through        weakness

06        4561     2097                      1473  012    4387
τῆς       σαρκὸς   εὐηγγελισάμην             ὑμῖν  τὸ     πρότερον,
of the    flesh    I told good message       to you the    former,

        2532  04    3986            1473      1722  07   4561   1473   3756
14      καὶ   τὸν   πειρασμὸν       ὑμῶν      ἐν    τῇ   σαρκί  μου    οὐκ
        and   the   pressure        of you    in    the  flesh  of me  not

1848              3761    1609               235    5613  32
ἐξουθενήσατε     οὐδὲ    ἐξεπτύσατε,         ἀλλὰ  ὡς    ἄγγελον
you despised     but not  you spit out,       but    as    messenger

2316      1209       1473   5613   5547       2424            4226
θεοῦ      ἐδέξασθέ   με,    ὡς     Χριστὸν   Ἰησοῦν.    15   ποῦ
of God    you welcomed me,  as     Christ     Jesus.          Where

3767   01  3108                  1473       3140        1063  1473
οὖν    ὁ   μακαρισμὸς           ὑμῶν;      μαρτυρῶ     γὰρ   ὑμῖν
then   the fortunateness        of you?     I testify    for   to you

3754  1487  1415     016    3788          1473      1846
ὅτι   εἰ    δυνατὸν  τοὺς   ὀφθαλμοὺς     ὑμῶν      ἐξορύξαντες
that  if    power    the    eyes          of you     having dug out

1325      1473   5620           2190      1473   1096
ἐδώκατέ   μοι.   16   ὥστε     ἐχθρὸς    ὑμῶν   γέγονα
you gave  to me.      So that   hostile    of you  I have become

226          1473    17  2206              1473  3756
ἀληθεύων    ὑμῖν;       ζηλοῦσιν          ὑμᾶς  οὐ
telling truth to you?    They are jealous   you    not

2573   235   1576            1473  2309       2443  846
καλῶς, ἀλλὰ ἐκκλεῖσαι       ὑμᾶς θέλουσιν,  ἵνα   αὐτοὺς
well,  but   to close out     you   they want,  that  them

2206                18   2570   1161  2206            1722
ζηλοῦτε·                καλὸν  δὲ    ζηλοῦσθαι        ἐν
you might be jealous;    good   but   to be jealous     in

2570   3842     2532  3361  3441    1722  011  3918
καλῷ  πάντοτε  καὶ   μὴ    μόνον   ἐν    τῷ   παρεῖναί
good  always    and   not   alone   in    the  to be present

1473  4314   1473   19   5043    1473   3739  3825
με    πρὸς   ὑμᾶς.      τέκνα   μου,   οὓς   πάλιν
me    toward you.        Children of me,  whom  again

5605              3360    3739  3445               5547
ὠδίνω             μέχρις  οὗ    μορφωθῇ            Χριστὸς
I have birth pains until    that  might be formed    Christ

1722  1473   20   2309          1161  3918       4314
ἐν    ὑμῖν·        ἤθελον       δὲ    παρεῖναι   πρὸς
in    you;          I would want but   to be present to

1473  737   2532  236      08     5456  1473   3754
ὑμᾶς  ἄρτι  καὶ   ἀλλάξαι  τὴν   φωνήν μου,   ὅτι
you   now   and   to change the   sound of me,  because

639          1722  1473   21   3004    1473   013  5259  3551
ἀπορούμαι   ἐν    ὑμῖν.       Λέγετέ  μοι,   οἱ   ὑπὸ   νόμον
I doubt      in    you.        Say     to me,  the   under law

2309         1510  04   3551   3756  191            1125
θέλοντες    εἶναι, τὸν  νόμον  οὐκ  ἀκούετε;  22  γέγραπται
wanting      to be,  the  law    not  you hear?      It has been
                                                        written

1063  3754  11           1417  5207   2192   1520  1537 06
γὰρ   ὅτι   Ἀβραὰμ       δύο   υἱοὺς  ἔσχεν, ἕνα   ἐκ   τῆς
for,  (")   Abraham       two   sons   had,   one   from the

3814           2532  1520  1537 06   1658          23   235    01
παιδίσκης      καὶ   ἕνα   ἐκ   τῆς  ἐλευθέρας.       ἀλλ᾽  ὁ
servant girl   and   one   from the  free.              But   the

3303   1537 06   3814           2596  4561  1080
μὲν    ἐκ   τῆς  παιδίσκης      κατὰ σάρκα γεγέννηται,
indeed from the  servant girl    by   flesh has been born,

01    1161  1537 06   1658           1223  1860            24   3748
ὁ     δὲ    ἐκ   τῆς  ἐλευθέρας     δι᾽  ἐπαγγελίας.         ἅτινά
the   but   from the  free           by   promise.                Which
```

for I also have become as you are. You have done me no wrong. [13]You know that it was because of a physical infirmity that I first announced the gospel to you; [14]though my condition put you to the test, you did not scorn or despise me, but welcomed me as an angel of God, as Christ Jesus. [15]What has become of the goodwill you felt? For I testify that, had it been possible, you would have torn out your eyes and given them to me. [16]Have I now become your enemy by telling you the truth? [17]They make much of you, but for no good purpose; they want to exclude you, so that you may make much of them. [18]It is good to be made much of for a good purpose at all times, and not only when I am present with you. [19]My little children, for whom I am again in the pain of childbirth until Christ is formed in you, [20]I wish I were present with you now and could change my tone, for I am perplexed about you.

21 Tell me, you who desire to be subject to the law, will you not listen to the law? [22]For it is written that Abraham had two sons, one by a slave woman and the other by a free woman. [23]One, the child of the slave, was born according to the flesh; the other, the child of the free woman, was born through the promise.

24Now this is an allegory: these women are two covenants. One woman, in fact, is Hagar, from Mount Sinai, bearing children for slavery. 25Now Hagar is Mount Sinai in Arabia*a* and corresponds to the present Jerusalem, for she is in slavery with her children. 26But the other woman corresponds to the Jerusalem above; she is free, and she is our mother. 27For it is written,

"Rejoice, you childless one, you who bear no children,
burst into song and shout, you who endure no birth pangs;
for the children of the desolate woman are more numerous
than the children of the one who is married."

28Now you,*b* my friends,*c* are children of the promise, like Isaac. 29But just as at that time the child who was born according to the flesh persecuted the child who was born according to the Spirit, so it is now also. 30But what does the scripture say? "Drive out the slave and her child; for the child of the slave will not share the inheritance with the child of the free woman." 31So then, friends,*c* we are children, not of the slave but of the free woman.

5:1For freedom Christ has set us free. Stand firm, therefore, and do not submit again to a yoke of slavery.

2Listen! I, Paul, am telling you that if you let yourselves be circumcised, Christ will be of no benefit to you. 3Once again I testify to every

---

1510 238   3778 1063 1510 1417
ἐστιν ἀλληγορούμενα· αὗται γάρ εἰσιν δύο
is+ +being allegorized; these for are two

1242 1520 3303 575 3735 4614 1519 1397
διαθῆκαι, μία μὲν ἀπὸ ὄρους Σινᾶ εἰς δουλείαν
agreements, one indeed from hill Sinai into slavery

1080 3748 1510 28   09 1161 28
γεννῶσα, ἥτις ἐστὶν Ἀγάρ. 25 τὸ δὲ Ἀγὰρ
giving birth, who is Hagar. The but Hagar

4614 3735 1510 1722 07 688 4960
Σινᾶ ὄρος ἐστὶν ἐν τῇ Ἀραβίᾳ· συστοιχεῖ
Sinai hill is in the Arabia; it lines up together

1161 07 3568 2419 1398 1063
δὲ τῇ νῦν Ἰερουσαλήμ, δουλεύει γὰρ
but in the now Jerusalem, she is enslaved for

3326 022 5043 846 05 1161 507 2419
μετὰ τῶν τέκνων αὐτῆς. 26 ἡ δὲ ἄνω Ἰερουσαλὴμ
with the children of her. The but up Jerusalem

1658 1510 3748 1510 3384 1473
ἐλευθέρα ἐστίν, ἥτις ἐστὶν μήτηρ ἡμῶν·
free is, who is mother of us;

27 1125 1063 2165 4723 05
γέγραπται γάρ· εὐφράνθητι, στεῖρα ἡ
it has been written for, be merry, sterile the

3756 5088 4486 2532 994 05 3756
οὐ τίκτουσα, ῥῆξον καὶ βόησον, ἡ οὐκ
not giving birth, rip and cry aloud, the one not

5605 3754 4183 021 5043 06
ὠδίνουσα· ὅτι πολλὰ τὰ τέκνα τῆς
having birth pains; because many the children of the

2048 3123 2228 06 2192 04 435 28 1473
ἐρήμου μᾶλλον ἢ τῆς ἐχούσης τὸν ἄνδρα. Ὑμεῖς
desert more or of the having the man. You

1161 80 2596 2464 1860 5043 1510
δέ, ἀδελφοί, κατὰ Ἰσαὰκ ἐπαγγελίας τέκνα ἐστέ.
but, brothers, by Isaac promise children you are.

29 235 5618 5119 01 2596 4561 1080
ἀλλ᾽ ὥσπερ τότε ὁ κατὰ σάρκα γεννηθεὶς
But as indeed then the by flesh having been born

1377 04 2596 4151 3779 2532 3568 30 235 5101
ἐδίωκεν τὸν κατὰ πνεῦμα, οὕτως καὶ νῦν. ἀλλὰ τί
pursued the by spirit, thusly also now. But what

3004 05 1124 1544 08 3814 2532 04
λέγει ἡ γραφή; ἔκβαλε τὴν παιδίσκην καὶ τὸν
says the writing? Throw out the servant girl and the

5207 846 3756 1063 3361 2816 01 5207 06
υἱὸν αὐτῆς· οὐ γὰρ μὴ κληρονομήσει ὁ υἱὸς τῆς
son of her; not for not will inherit the son of the

3814 3326 02 5207 06 1658 31 1352
παιδίσκης μετὰ τοῦ υἱοῦ τῆς ἐλευθέρας. διό,
servant girl with the son of the free. Therefore,

80 3756 1510 3814 5043 235
ἀδελφοί, οὐκ ἐσμὲν παιδίσκης τέκνα ἀλλὰ
brothers, not we are of servant girl children but

06 1658 5:1 07 1657 1473 5547
τῆς ἐλευθέρας. Τῇ ἐλευθερίᾳ ἡμᾶς Χριστὸς
of the free. In the freedom us Christ

1659 4739 3767 2532 3361 3825 2218
ἠλευθέρωσεν· στήκετε οὖν καὶ μὴ πάλιν ζυγῷ
freed; stand then and not again in yoke

1397 1758 2 2396 1473 3972 3004 1473
δουλείας ἐνέχεσθε. Ἴδε ἐγὼ Παῦλος λέγω ὑμῖν
of slavery be held in. Look I Paul say to you

3754 1437 4059 5547 1473
ὅτι ἐὰν περιτέμνησθε, Χριστὸς ὑμᾶς
that if you might be circumcised, Christ you

3762 5623 3 3143 1161 3825 3956
οὐδὲν ὠφελήσει. μαρτύρομαι δὲ πάλιν παντὶ
nothing will benefit. I testify but again to all

---

a Other ancient authorities read For Sinai is a mountain in Arabia

b Other ancient authorities read we

c Gk brothers

```
444        4059                 3754  3781        1510    3650
ἀνθρώπῳ  περιτεμνομένῳ       ὅτι   ὀφειλέτης  ἐστὶν  ὅλον
man       being circumcised     that  debtor      he is  whole
04   3551   4160       4  2673                          575
τὸν  νόμον  ποιῆσαι.      κατηργήθητε               ἀπὸ
the  law    to do.       You have been abolished from
5547       3748    1722  3551  1344            06   5485
Χριστοῦ,  οἵτινες  ἐν    νόμῳ  δικαιοῦσθε,    τῆς  χάριτος
Christ,    who      in    law   are made right, the  favor
1601           5  1473  1063  4151        1537  4102
ἐξεπέσατε.       ἡμεῖς  γὰρ  πνεύματι  ἐκ   πίστεως
you fell out.   We      for   in spirit  from  trust
1680    1343        553             6  1722  1063  5547
ἐλπίδα  δικαιοσύνης  ἀπεκδεχόμεθα.     ἐν   γὰρ  Χριστῷ
hope    of rightness  we await.        In    for   Christ
2424   3777    4061          5100  2480       3777
Ἰησοῦ  οὔτε   περιτομή     τι   ἰσχύει      οὔτε
Jesus  neither circumcision some  is strong   nor
203          235   4102    1223    26      1754
ἀκροβυστία  ἀλλὰ  πίστις  δι᾽    ἀγάπης  ἐνεργουμένη.
uncircumcision  but  trust   through  love     operating.
7  5143                2573      5101  1473  1465       07
   Ἐτρέχετε           καλῶς·  τίς  ὑμᾶς  ἐνέκοψεν [τῇ]
   You were running well;    who  you   hindered   in the
225       3361  3982           8  05   3988       3756  1537
ἀληθείᾳ  μὴ   πείθεσθαι;       ἡ   πεισμονὴ  οὐκ  ἐκ
truth     not  to be persuaded?  The persuasion not from
02    2564          1473   9  3398   2219  3650  012  5445
τοῦ  καλοῦντος   ὑμᾶς.      μικρὰ  ζύμη  ὅλον  τὸ  φύραμα
the one calling you.        Little  yeast  whole  the  mixture
2220         10  1473  3982            1519  1473  1722
ζυμοῖ.           ἐγὼ  πέποιθα          εἰς  ὑμᾶς  ἐν
yeasts.  I       have been persuaded to  you   in
2962     3754  3762    243   5426            01        1161
κυρίῳ  ὅτι  οὐδὲν  ἄλλο  φρονήσετε·    ὁ      δὲ
master that nothing other you will think; the one but
5015          1473  941        012  2917       3748   1437
ταράσσων  ὑμᾶς  βαστάσει  τὸ  κρίμα,    ὅστις  ἐὰν
troubling you   will bear   the  judgment,  who    if
1510       11  1473  1161  80        1487  4061        2089
ᾖ.             Ἐγὼ  δέ,  ἀδελφοί,  εἰ   περιτομὴν  ἔτι
he might be. I   but, brothers, if   circumcision still
2784         5101  2089  1377     686
κηρύσσω,  τί   ἔτι   διώκομαι;  ἄρα
I announce, why  still  am I pursued?  Then
2673               09    4625        02       4716
κατήργηται        τὸ   σκάνδαλον  τοῦ   σταυροῦ.
has been abolished the  offense    of the  cross.
12  3785          2532  609                        013
    Ὄφελον       καὶ   ἀποκόψονται              οἱ
    Would that also  will cut off themselves  the ones
387              1473     13  1473  1063  1909  1657
ἀναστατοῦντες  ὑμᾶς.        Ὑμεῖς  γὰρ  ἐπ᾽  ἐλευθερίᾳ
upsetting       you.         You    for   on    freedom
2564          80          3441  3361  08   1657        1519
ἐκλήθητε,  ἀδελφοί·   μόνον  μὴ   τὴν  ἐλευθερίαν  εἰς
were called, brothers;  alone  not   the  freedom     into
874          07     4561    235  1223    06    26
ἀφορμὴν  τῇ   σαρκί,  ἀλλὰ  διὰ   τῆς  ἀγάπης
opportunity to the  flesh,  but   through  the  love
1398        240            14  01  1063  3956  3551  1722  1520
δουλεύετε  ἀλλήλοις.        ὁ   γὰρ  πᾶς  νόμος  ἐν  ἑνὶ
slave       to one another.  The for  all   law    in   one
3056  4137              1722  03   25            04
λόγῳ  πεπλήρωται,    ἐν   τῷ·  ἀγαπήσεις     τὸν
word  has been filled,  in   the;  you will love   the
4139      1473   5613  4572      15  1487  1161  240
πλησίον  σου   ὡς   σεαυτόν.     εἰ   δὲ   ἀλλήλους
neighbor of you  as   yourself.   If   but   one another
```

man who lets himself be circumcised that he is obliged to obey the entire law. [4]You who want to be justified by the law have cut yourselves off from Christ; you have fallen away from grace. [5]For through the Spirit, by faith, we eagerly wait for the hope of righteousness. [6]For in Christ Jesus neither circumcision nor uncircumcision counts for anything; the only thing that counts is faith working[a] through love.

[7]You were running well; who prevented you from obeying the truth? [8]Such persuasion does not come from the one who calls you. [9]A little yeast leavens the whole batch of dough. [10]I am confident about you in the Lord that you will not think otherwise. But whoever it is that is confusing you will pay the penalty. [11]But my friends,[b] why am I still being persecuted if I am still preaching circumcision? In that case the offense of the cross has been removed. [12]I wish those who unsettle you would castrate themselves!

13 For you were called to freedom, brothers and sisters;[b] only do not use your freedom as an opportunity for self-indulgence,[c] but through love become slaves to one another. [14]For the whole law is summed up in a single commandment, "You shall love your neighbor as yourself." [15]If, however,

a Or made effective
b Gk brothers
c Gk the flesh

you bite and devour one another, take care that you are not consumed by one another.

16 Live by the Spirit, I say, and do not gratify the desires of the flesh. [17]For what the flesh desires is opposed to the Spirit, and what the Spirit desires is opposed to the flesh; for these are opposed to each other, to prevent you from doing what you want. [18]But if you are led by the Spirit, you are not subject to the law. [19]Now the works of the flesh are obvious: fornication, impurity, licentiousness, [20]idolatry, sorcery, enmities, strife, jealousy, anger, quarrels, dissensions, factions, [21]envy,[a] drunkenness, carousing, and things like these. I am warning you, as I warned you before: those who do such things will not inherit the kingdom of God.

22 By contrast, the fruit of the Spirit is love, joy, peace, patience, kindness, generosity, faithfulness, [23]gentleness, and self-control. There is no law against such things. [24]And those who belong to Christ Jesus have crucified the flesh with its passions and desires. [25]If we live by the Spirit, let us also be guided by the Spirit. [26]Let us not become conceited,

[a] Other ancient authorities add *murder*

1143	2532	2719		991	3361	5259	240
δάκνετε	καὶ	κατεσθίετε,		βλέπετε	μὴ	ὑπ'	ἀλλήλων
you bite and		you eat up,		see	not	by	one another

355
ἀναλωθῆτε. **16**
you might be consumed.

3004 1161 4151
Λέγω δέ, πνεύματι
I say but, in spirit

4043 2532 1939 4561 3756 3361
περιπατεῖτε καὶ ἐπιθυμίαν σαρκὸς οὐ μὴ
walk around and desire of flesh not not

5055
τελέσητε. **17**
you might complete.

05 1063 4561 1937 2596
ἡ γὰρ σὰρξ ἐπιθυμεῖ κατὰ
The for flesh desires against

010 4151 09 1161 4151 2596 06 4561
τοῦ πνεύματος, τὸ δὲ πνεῦμα κατὰ τῆς σαρκός,
the spirit, the but spirit against the flesh,

3778 1063 240 480 2443 3361 3739
ταῦτα γὰρ ἀλλήλοις ἀντίκειται, ἵνα μὴ ἃ
these for one another lie against, that not what

1437 2309 3778 4160 1487 1161
ἐὰν θέλητε ταῦτα ποιῆτε. **18** εἰ δὲ
if you might want these you might do. If but

4151 71 3756 1510 5259 3551
πνεύματι ἄγεσθε, οὐκ ἐστὲ ὑπὸ νόμον.
in spirit you are led, not you are under law.

19
5318 1161 1510 021 2041 06 4561 3748
φανερὰ δέ ἐστιν τὰ ἔργα τῆς σαρκός, ἅτινά
Evident but are the works of the flesh, which

1510 4202 167 766
ἐστιν πορνεία, ἀκαθαρσία, ἀσέλγεια,
is sexual immorality, uncleanness, debauchery,

20
1495 5331 2189 2054
εἰδωλολατρία, φαρμακεία, ἔχθραι, ἔρις,
idol service, magic, hostilities, strife,

2205 2372 2052 1370
ζῆλος, θυμοί, ἐριθεῖαι, διχοστασίαι,
jealousy, furies, selfish ambitions, divisions,

139 **21** 5355 3178 2970 2532 021
αἱρέσεις, φθόνοι, μέθαι, κῶμοι καὶ τὰ
sects, envies, drunkenness, carousings and the

3664 3778 3739 4302 1473 2531
ὅμοια τούτοις, ἃ προλέγω ὑμῖν, καθὼς
like these, that I say before to you, just as

4302 3754 013 024 5108 4238
προεῖπον ὅτι οἱ τὰ τοιαῦτα πράσσοντες
I said before that the ones the such practicing

932 2316 3756 2816 **22** 01 1161
βασιλείαν θεοῦ οὐ κληρονομήσουσιν. ὁ δὲ
kingdom of God not will inherit. The but

2590 010 4151 1510 26 5479 1515
καρπὸς τοῦ πνεύματός ἐστιν ἀγάπη χαρὰ εἰρήνη,
fruit of the spirit is love, joy, peace,

3115 5544 19 4102 **23** 4240
μακροθυμία χρηστότης ἀγαθωσύνη, πίστις πραΰτης
long-temper, kindness, goodness, trust, gentleness,

1466 2596 022 5108 3756 1510 3551
ἐγκράτεια· κατὰ τῶν τοιούτων οὐκ ἔστιν νόμος.
inner strength; against the such not there is law.

24
013 1161 02 5547 2424 08 4561
οἱ δὲ τοῦ Χριστοῦ ['Ιησοῦ] τὴν σάρκα
The ones but of the Christ Jesus the flesh

4717 4862 023 3804 2532 019 1939
ἐσταύρωσαν σὺν τοῖς παθήμασιν καὶ ταῖς ἐπιθυμίαις.
crucified with the sufferings and the desires.

25
1487 2198 4151 4151 2532
Εἰ ζῶμεν πνεύματι, πνεύματι καὶ
If we live in spirit, in spirit also

4748 **26** 3361 1096 2755
στοιχῶμεν. μὴ γινώμεθα κενόδοξοι,
we might walk. Not we might become empty splendor,

240   4292   240   5354
ἀλλήλους προκαλούμενοι, ἀλλήλοις φθονοῦντες.
one another provoking,   one another envying.

6:1 ᾿Αδελφοί, ἐὰν καὶ προλημφθῇ ἄνθρωπος
  80   1437 2532 4301   444
Brothers, if also might be taken before man

1722 5100 3900   1473 013 4152
ἐν τινι παραπτώματι, ὑμεῖς οἱ πνευματικοὶ
in some trespass,   you the spiritual ones

2675   04   5108   1722 4151   4240
καταρτίζετε τὸν τοιοῦτον ἐν πνεύματι πραΰτητος,
put in order the such   in spirit of gentleness,

4648   4572   3361 2532 1473 3985
σκοπῶν σεαυτὸν μὴ καὶ σὺ πειρασθῇς.
looking yourself not also you might be pressured.
carefully

2 ᾿Αλλήλων τὰ βάρη βαστάζετε καὶ οὕτως
240   024 922 941   2532 3779
Of one another the burdens bear and thusly

378   04 3551 02   5547
ἀναπληρώσετε τὸν νόμον τοῦ Χριστοῦ. 3 εἰ γὰρ
you will fill up the law of the Christ. If for
                               1487 1063

1380   5100 1510 5100 3367   1510   5422
δοκεῖ τις εἶναί τι μηδὲν ὤν, φρεναπατᾷ
thinks some to be some nothing being, he deceives mind

1438   012 1161 2041 1438   1381
ἑαυτόν. 4 τὸ δὲ ἔργον ἑαυτοῦ δοκιμαζέτω
himself. The but work of himself let approve

1538   2532 5119 1519 1438   3441 012 2745
ἕκαστος, καὶ τότε εἰς ἑαυτὸν μόνον τὸ καύχημα
each, and then in himself alone the brag

2192   2532 3756 1519 04 2087   1538 1063
ἕξει καὶ οὐκ εἰς τὸν ἕτερον· 5 ἕκαστος γὰρ
he will have and not in the other; each for

012 2398 5413 941   2841   1161 01
τὸ ἴδιον φορτίον βαστάσει. 6 Κοινωνείτω δὲ ὁ
the own pack will bear. Let be partner but the

2727   04 3056 03   2727
κατηχούμενος τὸν λόγον τῷ κατηχοῦντι
one being instructed the word to the one instructing

1722 3956 18 7 3361 4105   2316 3756
ἐν πᾶσιν ἀγαθοῖς. Μὴ πλανᾶσθε, θεὸς οὐ
in all good. Not be deceived, God not

3456   3739 1063 1437 4687 444   3778
μυκτηρίζεται. ὃ γὰρ ἐὰν σπείρῃ ἄνθρωπος, τοῦτο
is mocked. What for if might sow man, this

2532 2325   8 3754 01 4687   1519
καὶ θερίσει· ὅτι ὁ σπείρων εἰς
also he will harvest; because the one sowing in

08 4561 1438   1537 06 4561 2325
τὴν σάρκα ἑαυτοῦ ἐκ τῆς σαρκὸς θερίσει
the flesh of himself from the flesh will harvest

5356   01 1161 4687   1519 012 4151 1537
φθοράν, ὁ δὲ σπείρων εἰς τὸ πνεῦμα ἐκ
corruption, the but one sowing in the spirit from

010 4151   2325   2222 166 9 012
τοῦ πνεύματος θερίσει ζωὴν αἰώνιον. τὸ
the spirit will harvest life eternal. The one

1161 2570 4160   3361 1457a   2540
δὲ καλὸν ποιοῦντες μὴ ἐγκακῶμεν, καιρῷ
but good doing not we give in to bad, in season

1063 2398 2325   3361 1590   686
γὰρ ἰδίῳ θερίσομεν μὴ ἐκλυόμενοι. 10 ῎Αρα
for own we will harvest not being loosed out. Then

3767   5613 2540 2192 2038   012 18
οὖν ὡς καιρὸν ἔχομεν, ἐργαζώμεθα τὸ ἀγαθὸν
therefore as season we have, we might work the good

4314 3956 3122   1161 4314 016 3609
πρὸς πάντας, μάλιστα δὲ πρὸς τοὺς οἰκείους
toward all, especially but toward the households

competing against one
another, envying one
another.

CHAPTER 6

My friends,[a] if anyone is
detected in a transgression,
you who have received the
Spirit should restore such a
one in a spirit of gentleness.
Take care that you your-
selves are not tempted.
[2]Bear one another's
burdens, and in this way
you will fulfill[b] the law of
Christ. [3]For if those who
are nothing think they are
something, they deceive
themselves. [4]All must test
their own work; then that
work, rather than their
neighbor's work, will
become a cause for pride.
[5]For all must carry their
own loads.

6 Those who are taught
the word must share in all
good things with their
teacher.

7 Do not be deceived;
God is not mocked, for
you reap whatever you
sow. [8]If you sow to your
own flesh, you will reap
corruption from the flesh;
but if you sow to the Spirit,
you will reap eternal life
from the Spirit. [9]So let us
not grow weary in doing
what is right, for we will
reap at harvest time, if we
do not give up. [10]So then,
whenever we have an
opportunity, let us work
for the good of all, and
especially for those of the
family of faith.

[a] Gk *Brothers*
[b] Other ancient authorities read
in this way fulfill

11 See what large letters I make when I am writing in my own hand! 12It is those who want to make a good showing in the flesh that try to compel you to be circumcised—only that they may not be persecuted for the cross of Christ. 13Even the circumcised do not themselves obey the law, but they want you to be circumcised so that they may boast about your flesh. 14May I never boast of anything except the cross of our Lord Jesus Christ, by which[a] the world has been crucified to me, and I to the world. 15For[b] neither circumcision nor uncircumcision is anything; but a new creation is everything! 16As for those who will follow this rule—peace be upon them, and mercy, and upon the Israel of God.

17 From now on, let no one make trouble for me; for I carry the marks of Jesus branded on my body.

18 May the grace of our Lord Jesus Christ be with your spirit, brothers and sisters.[c] Amen.

[a] Or through whom
[b] Other ancient authorities add in Christ Jesus
[c] Gk brothers

```
06        4102              3708    4080        1473    1121
τῆς      πίστεως.      11  Ἴδετε   πηλίκοις    ὑμῖν    γράμμασιν
of the   trust.          See      how great   to you  letters
1125   07    1699 5495          3745        2309
ἔγραψα τῇ   ἐμῇ χειρί.   12  Ὅσοι        θέλουσιν
I wrote in the my  hand.     As many as  want
2146                    1722 4561   3778  315          1473
εὐπροσωπῆσαι           ἐν   σαρκί, οὗτοι ἀναγκάζουσιν ὑμᾶς
to put on good face    in   flesh, these compel         you
4059            3441   2443 03       4716   02
περιτέμνεσθαι, μόνον ἵνα τῷ      σταυρῷ τοῦ
to be circumcised, alone that in the cross of the
5547   3361  1377                    3761    1063
Χριστοῦ μὴ  διώκωνται.        13  οὐδὲ   γὰρ
Christ  not they might be pursued.   But not for
013   4059               846      3551
οἱ   περιτεμνόμενοι    αὐτοὶ   νόμον
the ones being circumcised themselves law
5442            235   2309   1473 4059
φυλάσσουσιν,   ἀλλὰ θέλουσιν ὑμᾶς περιτέμνεσθαι
they will guard, but  they want you  to be circumcised
2443 1722 07   5212    4561  2744                1473
ἵνα ἐν  τῇ ὑμετέρᾳ σαρκὶ καυχήσωνται.    14  Ἐμοὶ
that in  the your    flesh they might brag.   To me
1161 3361 1096              2744         1487 3361 1722 03
δὲ  μὴ  γένοιτο       καυχᾶσθαι εἰ  μὴ  ἐν   τῷ
but not may it become to brag     except   in   the
4716  02    2962    1473   2424  5547       1223
σταυρῷ τοῦ  κυρίου ἡμῶν Ἰησοῦ Χριστοῦ, δι'
cross  of the Master of us Jesus Christ,    through
3739 1473 2889  4717            2504  2889
οὗ  ἐμοὶ κόσμος ἐσταύρωται     κἀγὼ κόσμῳ.
whom to me world  has been crucified and I to world.
    3777        1063 4061          5100 1510 3777
15  οὔτε       γὰρ περιτομή    τί  ἐστιν οὔτε
    Neither     for circumcision some is   nor
203            235   2537  2937        2532 3745
ἀκροβυστία    ἀλλὰ καινὴ κτίσις.  16  καὶ  ὅσοι
uncircumcision but  new   creation.   And as many as
03        2583   3778  4748        1515  1909 846
τῷ       κανόνι τούτῳ στοιχήσουσιν, εἰρήνη ἐπ' αὐτοὺς
in the    rule   this  will walk,     peace  on  them
2532 1656 2532 1909 04     2474   02         2316    010
καὶ ἔλεος καὶ ἐπὶ  τὸν  Ἰσραὴλ τοῦ  θεοῦ.  17  Τοῦ
and mercy and on   the  Israel of the God.     Of the
3062     2873    1473 3367    3930          1473 1063
λοιποῦ   κόπους μοι μηδεὶς παρεχέτω·   ἐγὼ γὰρ
remaining labors to me no one let hold to;  I    for
024 4742      02    2424  1722 011 4983   1473
τὰ στίγματα τοῦ  Ἰησοῦ ἐν  τῷ σώματί μου
the brands  of the Jesus in  the body  of me
941           05  5485 02    2962   1473 2424
βαστάζω.  18  Ἡ  χάρις τοῦ  κυρίου ἡμῶν Ἰησοῦ
bear.         The favor of the Master of us Jesus
5547    3326 010 4151      1473  80      281
Χριστοῦ μετὰ τοῦ πνεύματος ὑμῶν, ἀδελφοί· ἀμήν.
Christ  with the spirit    of you, brothers; amen.
```

EPHESIANS

CHAPTER 1

Paul, an apostle of Christ Jesus by the will of God, To the saints who are in Ephesus and are faithful[a] in Christ Jesus:

2 Grace to you and peace from God our Father and the Lord Jesus Christ.

3 Blessed be the God and Father of our Lord Jesus Christ, who has blessed us in Christ with every spiritual blessing in the heavenly places, [4]just as he chose us in Christ[b] before the foundation of the world to be holy and blameless before him in love. [5]He destined us for adoption as his children through Jesus Christ, according to the good pleasure of his will, [6]to the praise of his glorious grace that he freely bestowed on us in the Beloved. [7]In him we have redemption through his blood, the forgiveness of our trespasses, according to the riches of his grace [8]that he lavished on us. With all wisdom and insight [9]he has made known to us the mystery of his will, according to his good pleasure that he set forth in Christ, [10]as a plan for the fullness of time, to gather up all things in him,

[a] Other ancient authorities lack *in Ephesus*, reading *saints who are also faithful*
[b] Gk *in him*

```
           3972       652           5547        2424   1223        2307
1:1  Παῦλος ἀπόστολος Χριστοῦ  Ἰησοῦ  διὰ      θελήματος
     Paul    delegate of Christ  Jesus through want
     2316  015     40        015    1510   1722 2181       2532
     θεοῦ τοῖς  ἁγίοις   τοῖς οὖσιν [ἐν  Ἐφέσῳ]  καὶ
     of God to the holy ones  the being  in   Ephesus and
     4103         1722 5547      2424    2  5485   1473   2532
     πιστοῖς   ἐν  Χριστῷ Ἰησοῦ,   χάρις ὑμῖν  καὶ
     trustful ones in  Christ  Jesus,   favor to you and
     1515   575  2316 3962   1473 2532 2962       2424
     εἰρήνη ἀπὸ θεοῦ πατρὸς ἡμῶν καὶ κυρίου Ἰησοῦ
     peace from God father of us and Master  Jesus
     5547    3  2128          01   2316 2532 3962      02
     Χριστοῦ.  Εὐλογητὸς   ὁ  θεὸς καὶ πατὴρ τοῦ
     Christ.   Well-spoken of the God and father of the
     2962   1473  2424   5547      01   2127
     κυρίου ἡμῶν Ἰησοῦ Χριστοῦ, ὁ  εὐλογήσας
     Master of us Jesus Christ,  the one having spoken well
     1473 1722 3956 2129         4152       1722 023
     ἡμᾶς ἐν  πάσῃ εὐλογίᾳ πνευματικῇ ἐν  τοῖς
     us  in  all  good word spiritual in  the
     2032         1722 5547      4  2531    1586
     ἐπουρανίοις ἐν  Χριστῷ,  καθὼς ἐξελέξατο
     heavenlies in  Christ,  just as he selected
     1473 1722 846   4253   2602        2889     1510  1473
     ἡμᾶς ἐν  αὐτῷ πρὸ καταβολῆς κόσμου εἶναι ἡμᾶς
     us  in  him before foundation of world to be us
     40       2532 299        2714       846   1722 26
     ἁγίους καὶ ἀμώμους κατενώπιον αὐτοῦ ἐν  ἀγάπῃ,
     holy ones and blameless down before him  in  love,
        4309                 1473 1519 5206
     5 προορίσας          ἡμᾶς εἰς υἱοθεσίαν
       having set bounds before us  for  adoption as son
     1223    2424  5547   1519 846    2596 08  2107
     διὰ  Ἰησοῦ Χριστοῦ εἰς αὐτόν, κατὰ τὴν εὐδοκίαν
     through Jesus Christ in  him,   by  the good thought
     010  0307      846    6 1519 1868      1391
     τοῦ  θελήματος ἀυτου,  εἰς ἔπαινον δόξης
     of the want   of him,  for praise on of splendor
     06    5485    846    3739    5487        1473 1722 03
     τῆς  χάριτος αὐτοῦ ἧς     ἐχαρίτωσεν ἡμᾶς ἐν  τῷ
     of the favor of him by which he favored us  in  the
     25             1722 3739 2192    08   629
     ἠγαπημένῳ.  7 Ἐν  ᾧ  ἔχομεν τὴν ἀπολύτρωσιν
     having been loved. In whom we have the redemption
     1223   010 129   846    08  859       022
     διὰ  τοῦ αἵματος αὐτοῦ, τὴν ἄφεσιν τῶν
     through the blood of him, the sending off of the
     3900          2596 012 4149  06   5485    846
     παραπτωμάτων, κατὰ τὸ πλοῦτος τῆς χάριτος αὐτοῦ
     trespasses,  by  the rich  of the favor  of him
       3739      4052        1519 1473 1722 3956 4678
     8 ἧς     ἐπερίσσευσεν εἰς ἡμᾶς, ἐν  πάσῃ σοφίᾳ
       by which he exceeded to  us,  in  all  wisdom
     2532 5428       9 1107              1473  012
     καὶ φρονήσει,   γνωρίσας        ἡμῖν τὸ
     and thoughtfulness, having made known to us the
     3466      010  2307      846    2596 08
     μυστήριον τοῦ θελήματος αὐτοῦ, κατὰ τὴν
     mystery   of the want   of him, by  the
     2107      846   3739 4388         1722 846
     εὐδοκίαν αὐτοῦ ἣν  προέθετο     ἐν  αὐτῷ
     good thought of him which he set forward in  him
        1519 3622       010      4138   014    2540
     10 εἰς οἰκονομίαν τοῦ πληρώματος τῶν καιρῶν,
        for management of the fullness of the seasons,
     346                024 3956 1722 03   5547    024
     ἀνακεφαλαιώσασθαι τὰ πάντα ἐν  τῷ Χριστῷ, τὰ
     to be brought to head the all in  the Christ, the
```

1909	015	3772	2532	024	1909	06	1093	1722	846
ἐπὶ	τοῖς	οὐρανοῖς	καὶ	τὰ	ἐπὶ	τῆς	γῆς	ἐν	αὐτῷ.
on	the	heavens	and	the	on	the	earth	in	him.

11
1722	2739	2532	2820		4309		2596
Ἐν	ᾧ	καὶ	ἐκληρώθημεν	προορισθέντες	κατὰ
In	whom	also	we were	having set	by
			appointed	bounds before

4286	02		024	3956	1754		2596	08
πρόθεσιν	τοῦ	τὰ	πάντα	ἐνεργοῦντος	κατὰ	τὴν
purpose	of	the one	the	all	operating	by	the

1012	010	2307	846		1519	012	1510	1473
βουλὴν	τοῦ	θελήματος	αὐτοῦ	**12**	εἰς	τὸ	εἶναι	ἡμᾶς
plan	of the	want	of him		for	the	to be	us

1519	1868	1391	846	016
εἰς	ἔπαινον	δόξης	αὐτοῦ	τοὺς
for	praise on	of splendor	of him	the ones

4276		1722	03	5547		1722	3739
προηλπικότας	ἐν	τῷ	Χριστῷ.	**13**	Ἐν	ᾧ
having hoped before	in	the	Christ.		In	whom

2532	1473	191		04	3056	06		225		012
καὶ	ὑμεῖς	ἀκούσαντες	τὸν	λόγον	τῆς	ἀληθείας,	τὸ
also	you	having heard	the	word	of the	truth,	the

2098		06	4991		1473	1722	3739	2532
εὐαγγέλιον	τῆς	σωτηρίας	ὑμῶν,	ἐν	ᾧ	καὶ
good message	of the	deliverance	of you,	in	whom	also

4100		4972		011	4151	06
πιστεύσαντες	ἐσφραγίσθητε	τῷ	πνεύματι	τῆς
having trusted	you were sealed	in the	spirit	of the

1860		011	40		3739	1510	728	06
ἐπαγγελίας	τῷ	ἁγίῳ,	**14**	ὅ	ἐστιν	ἀρραβὼν	τῆς
promise	the	holy,		which is	earnest	of the

2817		1473	1519	629	06
κληρονομίας	ἡμῶν,	εἰς	ἀπολύτρωσιν	τῆς
inheritance	of us,	for	redemption	of the

4047		1519	1868	06	1391	846
περιποιήσεως,	εἰς	ἔπαινον	τῆς	δόξης	αὐτοῦ.
possession,	for	praise on	of the	splendor	of him.

15
1223	3778	2504	191		08	2596	1473
Διὰ	τοῦτο	κἀγὼ	ἀκούσας	τὴν	καθ᾽	ὑμᾶς
Through	this	also	I having heard	the	by	you

4102	1722	03	2962	2424	2532	08	26	08	1519
πίστιν	ἐν	τῷ	κυρίῳ	Ἰησοῦ	καὶ	τὴν	ἀγάπην	τὴν	εἰς
trust	in	the	Master	Jesus	and	the	love	the	for

3956	016	40		3756	3973	2168
πάντας	τοὺς	ἁγίους	**16**	οὐ	παύομαι	εὐχαριστῶν
all	the	holy ones		not	I stop	giving good favor

5228		1473	3417	4160		1909	018	4335
ὑπὲρ	ὑμῶν	μνείαν	ποιούμενος	ἐπὶ	τῶν	προσευχῶν
on behalf	of you	memory	making	on	the	prayers

1473		2443	01	2316	02		2962	1473	2424
μου,	**17**	ἵνα	ὁ	θεὸς	τοῦ	κυρίου	ἡμῶν	Ἰησοῦ
of me,		that the	God	of the	Master	of us	Jesus

5547	01	3962	06	1391	1325	1473
Χριστοῦ,	ὁ	πατὴρ	τῆς	δόξης,	δῴη	ὑμῖν
Christ,	the	Father	of the	splendor,	might give	to you

4151	4678	2532	602	1722	1922
πνεῦμα	σοφίας	καὶ	ἀποκαλύψεως	ἐν	ἐπιγνώσει
spirit	of wisdom	and	uncovering	in	perception

846		5461		016	3788	06
αὐτοῦ,	**18**	πεφωτισμένους	τοὺς	ὀφθαλμοὺς	τῆς
of him,		having been lightened	the	eyes	of the

2588	1473	1519	012	3609a	1473	5101	1510	05
καρδίας	[ὑμῶν]	εἰς	τὸ	εἰδέναι	ὑμᾶς	τίς	ἐστιν	ἡ
heart	of you	for	the	to know	you	what	is	the

1680	06	2821	846	5101	01	4149	06
ἐλπὶς	τῆς	κλήσεως	αὐτοῦ,	τίς	ὁ	πλοῦτος	τῆς
hope	of the	call	of him,	what	the	rich	of the

1391	06	2817	846	1722	015
δόξης	τῆς	κληρονομίας	αὐτοῦ	ἐν	τοῖς
splendor	of the	inheritance	of him	in	the

things in heaven and things on earth. [11]In Christ we have also obtained an inheritance,[a] having been destined according to the purpose of him who accomplishes all things according to his counsel and will, [12]so that we, who were the first to set our hope on Christ, might live for the praise of his glory. [13]In him you also, when you had heard the word of truth, the gospel of your salvation, and had believed in him, were marked with the seal of the promised Holy Spirit; [14]this[b] is the pledge of our inheritance toward redemption as God's own people, to the praise of his glory.

15 I have heard of your faith in the Lord Jesus and your love[c] toward all the saints, and for this reason [16]I do not cease to give thanks for you as I remember you in my prayers. [17]I pray that the God of our Lord Jesus Christ, the Father of glory, may give you a spirit of wisdom and revelation as you come to know him, [18]so that, with the eyes of your heart enlightened, you may know what is the hope to which he has called you, what are the riches of his glorious inheritance

[a] Or been made a heritage
[b] Other ancient authorities read who
[c] Other ancient authorities lack and your love

among the saints, [19]and
what is the immeasurable
greatness of his power for
us who believe, according
to the working of his great
power. [20]God[a] put this
power to work in Christ
when he raised him from
the dead and seated him
at his right hand in the
heavenly places, [21]far above
all rule and authority and
power and dominion, and
above every name that is
named, not only in this age
but also in the age to come.
[22]And he has put all things
under his feet and has made
him the head over all things
for the church, [23]which is
his body, the fullness of him
who fills all in all.

CHAPTER 2

You were dead through
the trespasses and sins
[2]in which you once lived,
following the course of this
world, following the ruler
of the power of the air, the
spirit that is now at work
among those who are
disobedient. [3]All of us once
lived among them in the
passions of our flesh,
following the desires of
flesh and senses, and we
were by nature children of
wrath, like everyone else.
[4]But God, who is rich in
mercy, out of the great love

[a] Gk He

	40	**19**	2532	5101	09	5235	3174	06
	ἁγίοις,		καὶ	τί	τὸ	ὑπερβάλλον	μέγεθος	τῆς
	holy ones,		and	what	the	exceeding	greatness	of the

1411   846   1519 1473 016   4100   2596 08
δυνάμεως αὐτοῦ εἰς ἡμᾶς τοὺς πιστεύοντας κατὰ τὴν
power   of him in us   the ones trusting   by   the

1753   010   2904   06   2479   846
ἐνέργειαν τοῦ κράτους τῆς ἰσχύος αὐτοῦ,
operation of the strength of the strength of him,

20 3739   1754   1722 03 5547   1453   846
    Ἣν ἐνήργησεν ἐν τῷ Χριστῷ ἐγείρας αὐτὸν
    which operated in the Christ having raised him

1537 3498   2532 2523   1722 1188 846   1722
ἐκ νεκρῶν καὶ καθίσας ἐν δεξιᾷ αὐτοῦ ἐν
from dead and having seated in right of him in

023   2032   **21** 5231   3956 746   2532
τοῖς ἐπουρανίοις ὑπεράνω πάσης ἀρχῆς καὶ
the heavenlies   up above all   rule and

1849   2532 1411   2532 2963   2532 3956
ἐξουσίας καὶ δυνάμεως καὶ κυριότητος καὶ παντὸς
authority and power   and mastership and all

3686   3687   3756 3441 1722 03 165   3778
ὀνόματος ὀνομαζομένου, οὐ μόνον ἐν τῷ αἰῶνι τούτῳ
name   being named,   not alone in the age this

235 2532 1722 03   3195   **22** 2532 3956
ἀλλὰ καὶ ἐν τῷ μέλλοντι·   καὶ πάντα
but also in the one being about to be; and all

5293   5259 016 4228 846 2532 846 1325
ὑπέταξεν ὑπὸ τοὺς πόδας αὐτοῦ καὶ αὐτὸν ἔδωκεν
he subjected under the feet of him and him   he gave

2776   5228   3956 07 1577   **23** 3748 1510 09
κεφαλὴν ὑπὲρ πάντα τῇ ἐκκλησίᾳ, ἥτις ἐστὶν τὸ
head   above all the assembly,   which is   the

4983 846   09   4138   02   024 3956   1722
σῶμα αὐτοῦ, τὸ πλήρωμα τοῦ   τὰ πάντα ἐν
body of him, the fullness of the one the all in

3956 4137   **2:1** 2532 1473 1510 3498   023
πᾶσιν πληρουμένου.   Καὶ ὑμᾶς ὄντας νεκροὺς τοῖς
all filling.   And you being dead   in the

3900   2532 019   266   1473   **2** 1722 3739
παραπτώμασιν καὶ ταῖς ἁμαρτίαις ὑμῶν, ἐν αἷς
trespasses   and in the sins   of you, in which

4218 4043   2596 04 165   02   2889
ποτε περιεπατήσατε κατὰ τὸν αἰῶνα τοῦ κόσμου
then you walked around by the age   of the world

3778   2596 04 758   06   1849   02   109
τούτου, κατὰ τὸν ἄρχοντα τῆς ἐξουσίας τοῦ ἀέρος,
this,   by the ruler of the authority of the air,

010   4151   010   3568 1754   1722 015
τοῦ πνεύματος τοῦ νῦν ἐνεργοῦντος ἐν τοῖς
of the spirit of the now one operating in the

5207 06   543   **3** 1722 3739 2532 1473 3956
υἱοῖς τῆς ἀπειθείας· ἐν οἷς καὶ ἡμεῖς πάντες
sons of the disobedience, in whom also we   all

390   4218 1722 019 1939   06   4561
ἀνεστράφημέν ποτε ἐν ταῖς ἐπιθυμίαις τῆς σαρκὸς
behaved   then in the desires   of the flesh

1473 4160   024 2307   06   4561 2532 018
ἡμῶν ποιοῦντες τὰ θελήματα τῆς σαρκὸς καὶ τῶν
of us doing   the wants of the flesh and the

1271   2532 1510 5043   5449
διανοιῶν, καὶ ἤμεθα τέκνα φύσει
intelligences, and we were children in nature

3709   5613 2532 013 3062   **4** 01 1161 2316 4145
ὀργῆς· ὡς καὶ οἱ λοιποί·   ὁ δὲ θεὸς πλούσιος
of anger as also the remaining; the but God rich

1510 1722 1656   1223   08 4183 26   846
ὢν   ἐν ἐλέει, διὰ τὴν πολλὴν ἀγάπην αὐτοῦ
being in mercy, through the much love   of him

```
3739    25          1473   5  2532 1510  1473 3498      023
ἦν     ἠγάπησεν ἡμᾶς,      καὶ ὄντας ἡμᾶς νεκροὺς τοῖς
which  he loved us,        and being us  dead     in the
```

```
3900         4806                    03      5547
παραπτώμασιν συνεζωοποίησεν          τῷ   Χριστῷ, -
trespasses   he made alive together in the Christ,
```

```
5485     1510 4982         6  2532 4891         2532
χάριτί  ἐστε σεσῳσμένοι -    καὶ συνήγειρεν καὶ
in favor you being delivered and he raised  and
         are                     together
```

```
4776        1722 023  2032        1722 5547       2424
συνεκάθισεν ἐν τοῖς ἐπουρανίοις ἐν Χριστῷ ᾿Ιησοῦ,
sat together in the on heavenlies in Christ  Jesus,
```

```
  2443 1731              1722 015  165       015
7 ἵνα ἐνδείξηται        ἐν τοῖς αἰῶσιν τοῖς
  that he might demonstrate in   the ages  in the
```

```
1904         012    5235          4149    06       5485
ἐπερχομένοις τὸ  ὑπερβάλλον πλοῦτος τῆς χάριτος
ones coming on the exceeding   rich    of the favor
```

```
846       1722 5544       1909 1473 1722 5547     2424
αὐτοῦ  ἐν χρηστότητι ἐφ᾿ ἡμᾶς ἐν Χριστῷ ᾿Ιησοῦ.
of him in kindness     on   us  in  Christ  Jesus.
```

```
  07     1063 5485      1510      4982          1223
8 Τῇ   γὰρ χάριτί ἐστε      σεσῳσμένοι   διὰ
  In the for favor you are being delivered through
```

```
4102      2532 3778  3756 1537 1473 2316   09  1435
πίστεως· καὶ τοῦτο οὐκ ἐξ ὑμῶν, θεοῦ τὸ δῶρον·
trust;    and this not from you, of God the gift;
```

```
  3756 1537 2041   2443 3361 5100 2744      10  846
9 οὐκ ἐξ ἔργων, ἵνα μή τις καυχήσηται.     αὐτοῦ
  not from works, that not any  might brag.   Of him
```

```
1063 1510  4161      2936               1722 5547
γὰρ ἐσμεν ποίημα, κτισθέντες      ἐν Χριστῷ
for we are made-thing, having been created in Christ
```

```
2424 1909 2041   18       3739     4282
᾿Ιησοῦ ἐπὶ ἔργοις ἀγαθοῖς οἷς προητοίμασεν
Jesus on   works  good    in which prepared before
```

```
01    2316  2443 1722 846       4043
ὁ  θεός, ἵνα ἐν αὐτοῖς περιπατήσωμεν.
the God,  that in  them  we might walk around.
```

```
   1352      3421          3754 4218 1473  021 1484   1722
11 Διὸ     μνημονεύετε ὅτι ποτὲ ὑμεῖς τὰ ἔθνη  ἐν
   Therefore remember      that then you  the nations in
```

```
4561   013 3004         203        5259 06
σαρκί, οἱ λεγόμενοι ἀκροβυστία ὑπὸ τῆς
flesh, the ones being said uncircumcision by  the
```

```
3004          4061        1722 4561   5499
λεγομένης περιτομῆς ἐν σαρκὶ χειροποιήτου,
one being said circumcision in flesh handmade,
```

```
   3754 1510   03    2540     1565    5565     5547
12 ὅτι ἦτε     τῷ  καιρῷ ἐκείνῳ χωρὶς Χριστοῦ,
   that you were in the season that  without Christ,
```

```
526             06       4174      02      2474
ἀπηλλοτριωμένοι τῆς πολιτείας τοῦ ᾿Ισραὴλ
having been alienated of the citizenship of the Israel
```

```
2532 3581     018    1242        06       1860
καὶ ξένοι τῶν διαθηκῶν τῆς ἐπαγγελίας,
and strangers of the agreements of the promise,
```

```
1680     3361 2192     2532 112   1722 03  2889    13  3570
ἐλπίδα μὴ ἔχοντες καὶ ἄθεοι ἐν τῷ κόσμῳ.     νυνὶ
hope   not having and godless in the world.    Now
```

```
1161 1722 5547      2424  1473 013       4218 1510
δὲ ἐν Χριστῷ ᾿Ιησοῦ ὑμεῖς οἱ     ποτε ὄντες
but in Christ Jesus you  the ones then being
```

```
3112   1096      1451 1722 011 129    02       5547
μακρὰν ἐγενήθητε ἐγγὺς ἐν τῷ αἵματι τοῦ Χριστοῦ.
far    became    near in the blood of the Christ.
```

```
   846     1063 1510  05  1515    1473   01
14 Αὐτὸς  γὰρ ἐστιν ἡ εἰρήνη ἡμῶν, ὁ
   Himself for  is   the peace of us, the one
```

5even when we were dead through our trespasses, made us alive together with Christ[a]—by grace you have been saved— 6and raised us up with him and seated us with him in the heavenly places in Christ Jesus, 7so that in the ages to come he might show the immeasurable riches of his grace in kindness toward us in Christ Jesus. 8For by grace you have been saved through faith, and this is not your own doing; it is the gift of God— 9not the result of works, so that no one may boast. 10For we are what he has made us, created in Christ Jesus for good works, which God prepared beforehand to be our way of life.

11 So then, remember that at one time you Gentiles by birth,[b] called "the uncircumcision" by those who are called "the circumcision"—a physical circumcision made in the flesh by human hands— 12remember that you were at that time without Christ, being aliens from the commonwealth of Israel, and strangers to the covenants of promise, having no hope and without God in the world. 13But now in Christ Jesus you who once were far off have been brought near by the blood of Christ. 14For he is our peace;

with which he loved us

a Other ancient authorities read in Christ

b Gk in the flesh

in his flesh he has made both groups into one and has broken down the dividing wall, that is, the hostility between us. [15]He has abolished the law with its commandments and ordinances, that he might create in himself one new humanity in place of the two, thus making peace, [16]and might reconcile both groups to God in one body[a] through the cross, thus putting to death that hostility through it.[b] [17]So he came and proclaimed peace to you who were far off and peace to those who were near; [18]for through him both of us have access in one Spirit to the Father. [19]So then you are no longer strangers and aliens, but you are citizens with the saints and also members of the household of God, [20]built upon the foundation of the apostles and prophets, with Christ Jesus himself as the cornerstone.[c] [21]In him the whole structure is joined together and grows into a holy temple in the Lord; [22]in whom you also are built together spiritually[d] into a dwelling place for God.

CHAPTER 3

This is the reason that I Paul am a prisoner for[e] Christ Jesus for the sake of you Gentiles— [2]for surely you have already heard of the commission of God's grace that was given me

[a] Or reconcile both of us in one body for God
[b] Or in him, or in himself
[c] Or keystone
[d] Gk in the Spirit
[e] Or of

4160	024 297	1520 2532 012 3320
ποιήσας	τὰ ἀμφότερα	ἓν καὶ τὸ μεσότοιχον
having made	the both	one and the middle wall

02	5418	3089	08 2189	1722 07
τοῦ	φραγμοῦ λύσας,	τὴν ἔχθραν	ἐν τῇ
of the	hedge having loosed,	the hostility	in the

4561 846 **15** 04 3551 018 1785 1722 1378
σαρκὶ αὐτοῦ, τὸν νόμον τῶν ἐντολῶν ἐν δόγμασιν
flesh of him, the law of the commands in decrees

2673 2443 016 1417 2936 1722
καταργήσας, ἵνα τοὺς δύο κτίσῃ ἐν
having abolished, that the two he might create in

846 1519 1520 2537 444 4160 1515 **16** 2532
αὐτῷ εἰς ἕνα καινὸν ἄνθρωπον ποιῶν εἰρήνην καὶ
him into one new man making peace and

604 016 297 1722 1520 4983 03
ἀποκαταλλάξῃ τοὺς ἀμφοτέρους ἐν ἑνὶ σώματι τῷ
he might reconcile the both in one body to
thoroughly the

2316 1223 02 4716 615 08 2189
θεῷ διὰ τοῦ σταυροῦ, ἀποκτείνας τὴν ἔχθραν
God through the cross, having killed the hostility

1722 846 **17** 2532 2064 2097
ἐν αὐτῷ. καὶ ἐλθὼν εὐηγγελίσατο
in him. And having come he told good message

1515 1473 015 3112 2532 1515 015
εἰρήνην ὑμῖν τοῖς μακρὰν καὶ εἰρήνην τοῖς
peace to you the ones far and peace the ones

1451 **18** 3754 1223 846 2192 08 4318
ἐγγύς· ὅτι δι’ αὐτοῦ ἔχομεν τὴν προσαγωγὴν
near; that through him we have the access

013 297 1722 1520 4151 4314 04 3962
οἱ ἀμφότεροι ἐν ἑνὶ πνεύματι πρὸς τὸν πατέρα.
the both in one spirit toward the Father.

19 686 3767 3765 1510 3581 2532
Ἄρα οὖν οὐκέτι ἐστὲ ξένοι καὶ
Then therefore no longer you are strangers and

3941 235 1510 4847 014 40
πάροικοι ἀλλὰ ἐστὲ συμπολῖται τῶν ἁγίων
transients but you are co-citizens of the holy ones

2532 3609 02 2316 **20** 2026
καὶ οἰκεῖοι τοῦ θεοῦ, ἐποικοδομηθέντες
and households of the God, having been built on

1909 03 2310 014 652 2532 4396
ἐπὶ τῷ θεμελίῳ τῶν ἀποστόλων καὶ προφητῶν,
on the foundation of the delegates and spokesmen,

1510 204 846 5547 2424 **21** 1722 3739
ὄντος ἀκρογωνιαίου αὐτοῦ Χριστοῦ Ἰησοῦ, ἐν ᾧ
being cornerstone of him Christ Jesus, in whom

3956 3619 4883 837 1519 3485
πᾶσα οἰκοδομὴ συναρμολογουμένη αὔξει εἰς ναὸν
all building being joined together grows into temple

40 1722 2962 **22** 1722 3739 2532 1473
ἅγιον ἐν κυρίῳ, ἐν ᾧ καὶ ὑμεῖς
holy in Master, in whom also you

4925 1519 2732 02 2316
συνοικοδομεῖσθε εἰς κατοικητήριον τοῦ θεοῦ
being built together into residence place of the God

1722 4151 **3:1** 3778 5484 1473 3972 01
ἐν πνεύματι. Τούτου χάριν ἐγὼ Παῦλος ὁ
in spirit. Of this reason I Paul the

1198 02 5547 2424 1519 1473 022
δέσμιος τοῦ Χριστοῦ [Ἰησοῦ] ὑπὲρ ὑμῶν τῶν
prisoner of the Christ Jesus on behalf of you the

1484 **2** 1487 1065 191 08 3622 06
ἐθνῶν - εἴ γε ἠκούσατε τὴν οἰκονομίαν τῆς
nations - if indeed you heard the management of the

5485 02 2316 06 1325 1473
χάριτος τοῦ θεοῦ τῆς δοθείσης μοι
favor of the God of the one having been given to me

1519 1473 **3** 3754 2596 602 1107
εἰς ὑμᾶς, [ὅτι] κατὰ ἀποκάλυψιν ἐγνωρίσθη
for you, that by uncovering was made known

1473 09 3466 2531 4270 1722
μοι τὸ μυστήριον, καθὼς προέγραψα ἐν
to me the mystery, just as I wrote before in

3641 **4** 4314 3739 1410 314
ὀλίγῳ, πρὸς ὃ δύνασθε ἀναγινώσκοντες
little, to which you are able reading

3539 08 4907 1473 1722 011
νοῆσαι τὴν σύνεσίν μου ἐν τῷ
to give thought the understanding of me in the

3466 02 5547 **5** 3739 2087 1074
μυστηρίῳ τοῦ Χριστοῦ, ὃ ἑτέραις γενεαῖς
mystery of the Christ, which in other generations

3756 1107 015 5207 014 444 5613
οὐκ ἐγνωρίσθη τοῖς υἱοῖς τῶν ἀνθρώπων ὡς
not it was made known to the sons of the men as

3568 601 015 40 652 846
νῦν ἀπεκαλύφθη τοῖς ἁγίοις ἀποστόλοις αὐτοῦ
now it was uncovered to the holy delegates of him

2532 4396 1722 4151 **6** 1510 024 1484
καὶ προφήταις ἐν πνεύματι, εἶναι τὰ ἔθνη
and spokesmen in spirit, to be the nations

4789 2532 4954 2532 4830 06
συγκληρονόμα καὶ σύσσωμα καὶ συμμέτοχα τῆς
co-inheritors and co-body and co-partakers of the

1860 1722 5547 2424 1223 010 2098
ἐπαγγελίας ἐν Χριστῷ Ἰησοῦ διὰ τοῦ εὐαγγελίου,
promise in Christ Jesus through the good message,

7 3739 1096 1249 2596 08 1431 06
οὗ ἐγενήθην διάκονος κατὰ τὴν δωρεὰν τῆς
of which I became servant by the gift of the

5485 02 2316 06 1325 1473
χάριτος τοῦ θεοῦ τῆς δοθείσης μοι
favor of the God the one having been given to me

2596 08 1753 06 1411 846 **8** 1473 03
κατὰ τὴν ἐνέργειαν τῆς δυνάμεως αὐτοῦ. Ἐμοὶ τῷ
by the operation of the power of him. To me the

1646 3956 40 1325 05 5485
ἐλαχιστοτέρῳ πάντων ἁγίων ἐδόθη ἡ χάρις
least of all holy ones was given the favor

3778 023 1484 2097 012
αὕτη, τοῖς ἔθνεσιν εὐαγγελίσασθαι τὸ
this, to the nations to tell good message the

421 4149 02 5547 **9** 2532 5461
ἀνεξιχνίαστον πλοῦτος τοῦ Χριστοῦ καὶ φωτίσαι
untraceable rich of the Christ and to lighten

3956 5101 05 3622 010 3466 010
[πάντας] τίς ἡ οἰκονομία τοῦ μυστηρίου τοῦ
all what the management of the mystery of the

613 575 014 165 1722 03 2316 03
ἀποκεκρυμμένου ἀπὸ τῶν αἰώνων ἐν τῷ θεῷ τῷ
one having been from the ages in the God the one
hidden off

024 3956 2936 **10** 2443 1107 3568
τὰ πάντα κτίσαντι, ἵνα γνωρισθῇ νῦν
the all having created, that might be made known now

019 746 2532 019 1849 1722 023 2032
ταῖς ἀρχαῖς καὶ ταῖς ἐξουσίαις ἐν τοῖς ἐπουρανίοις
to the rulers and the authorities in the heavenlies

1223 06 1577 05 4182 4678 02
διὰ τῆς ἐκκλησίας ἡ πολυποίκιλος σοφία τοῦ
through the assembly the much-varied wisdom of the

2316 **11** 2596 4286 014 165 3739 4160
θεοῦ, κατὰ πρόθεσιν τῶν αἰώνων ἣν ἐποίησεν
God, by purpose of the ages which he made

1722 03 5547 2424 03 2962 1473 **12** 1722 3739
ἐν τῷ Χριστῷ Ἰησοῦ τῷ κυρίῳ ἡμῶν, ἐν ᾧ
in the Christ Jesus the Master of us, in whom

for you, [3]and how the mystery was made known to me by revelation, as I wrote above in a few words, [4]a reading of which will enable you to perceive my understanding of the mystery of Christ. [5]In former generations this mystery[a] was not made known to humankind, as it has now been revealed to his holy apostles and prophets by the Spirit: [6]that is, the Gentiles have become fellow heirs, members of the same body, and sharers in the promise in Christ Jesus through the gospel.

[7]Of this gospel I have become a servant according to the gift of God's grace that was given me by the working of his power. [8]Although I am the very least of all the saints, this grace was given to me to bring to the Gentiles the news of the boundless riches of Christ, [9]and to make everyone see[b] what is the plan of the mystery hidden for ages in[c] God who created all things; [10]so that through the church the wisdom of God in its rich variety might now be made known to the rulers and authorities in the heavenly places. [11]This was in accordance with the eternal purpose that he has carried out in Christ Jesus our Lord, [12]in whom

[a] Gk it
[b] Other ancient authorities read *to bring to light*
[c] Or *by*

we have access to God in boldness and confidence through faith in him.[a] [13]I pray therefore that you[b] may not lose heart over my sufferings for you; they are your glory.

14 For this reason I bow my knees before the Father,[c] [15]from whom every family[d] in heaven and on earth takes its name. [16]I pray that, according to the riches of his glory, he may grant that you may be strengthened in your inner being with power through his Spirit, [17]and that Christ may dwell in your hearts through faith, as you are being rooted and grounded in love. [18]I pray that you may have the power to comprehend, with all the saints, what is the breadth and length and height and depth, [19]and to know the love of Christ that surpasses knowledge, so that you may be filled with all the fullness of God.

20 Now to him who by the power at work within us is able to accomplish abundantly far more than all we can ask or imagine, [21]to him be glory in the church and in Christ Jesus to all generations, forever and ever. Amen.

CHAPTER 4

I therefore, the prisoner in the Lord,

a Or the faith of him
b Or I
c Other ancient authorities add of our Lord Jesus Christ
d Gk fatherhood

2192	08	3954		2532	4318		1722	4006
ἔχομεν	τὴν	παρρησίαν	καὶ		προσαγωγὴν	ἐν		πεποιθήσει
we have	the	boldness	and		access	in		persuasion

1223	06	4102	846		1352		154	3361
διὰ	τῆς	πίστεως	αὐτοῦ.	[13]	διὸ		αἰτοῦμαι	μὴ
through	the	trust	of him.		Therefore	I ask		not

1457a		1722	019	2347		1473	5228
ἐγκακεῖν		ἐν	ταῖς	θλίψεσίν	μου		ὑπὲρ
to give in to bad		in	the	afflictions	of me		on behalf

1473	3748	1510	1391		1473		3778
ὑμῶν,	ἥτις	ἐστὶν	δόξα		ὑμῶν.	[14]	Τούτου
of you,	which	is	splendor		of you.		Of this

5484	2578	024	1119	1473	4314	04	3962
χάριν	κάμπτω	τὰ	γόνατά	μου	πρὸς	τὸν	πατέρα,
on account	I bow	the	knees	of me	to	the	Father,

1537	3739	3956	3965		1722	3772		2532	1909
[15] ἐξ	οὗ	πᾶσα	πατριὰ		ἐν	οὐρανοῖς	καὶ		ἐπὶ
from whom	all	fatherhood		in	heavens	and		on

1093	3687		2443	1325		1473	2596
γῆς	ὀνομάζεται,	[16]	ἵνα	δῷ		ὑμῖν	κατὰ
earth	is named,		that he might give		to you	by

012	4149	06		1391	846	1411
τὸ	πλοῦτος	τῆς		δόξης	αὐτοῦ	δυνάμει
the	rich	of the		splendor	of him	power

2901		1223	010	4151		846	1519
κραταιωθῆναι		διὰ	τοῦ	πνεύματος	αὐτοῦ		εἰς
to be strengthened		through	the	spirit	of him		into

04	2080	444		2730		04	5547	1223
τὸν	ἔσω	ἄνθρωπον,	[17]	κατοικῆσαι	τὸν	Χριστὸν	διὰ
the	inside	man,		to reside	the	Christ	through

06	4102	1722	019	2588		1473	1722	26
τῆς	πίστεως	ἐν	ταῖς	καρδίαις	ὑμῶν,		ἐν	ἀγάπῃ
the	trust	in	the	hearts	of you,	in		love

4492		2532	2311			2443
ἐρριζωμένοι		καὶ	τεθεμελιωμένοι,		[18]	ἵνα
having been rooted		and	having been founded,			that

1840		2638		4862	3956	015	40
ἐξισχύσητε		καταλαβέσθαι	σὺν	πᾶσιν	τοῖς	ἁγίοις
you might be made	to overtake	with	all	the	holy
thoroughly strong						ones

5101	09	4114	2532	3372	2532	5311	2532	899
τί	τὸ	πλάτος	καὶ	μῆκος	καὶ	ὕψος	καὶ	βάθος,
what	the	width	and	length	and	height	and	depth,

1097	5037	08	5235		06	1108
[19] γνῶναί	τε	τὴν	ὑπερβάλλουσαν	τῆς		γνώσεως
to know	and	the	exceeding		of the	knowledge

26	02	5547	2443	4137		1519
ἀγάπην	τοῦ	Χριστοῦ,	ἵνα	πληρωθῆτε		εἰς
love	of the	Christ,	that	you might be filled		in

3956	012	4138	02		2316		03	1161
πᾶν	τὸ	πλήρωμα	τοῦ		θεοῦ.	[20]	Τῷ	δὲ
all	the	fullness	of the		God.		To the one	but

1410		5228	3956	4160	5238a
δυναμένῳ		ὑπὲρ	πάντα	ποιῆσαι	ὑπερεκπερισσοῦ
being able		beyond	all	to do	excessively beyond

3739	154	2228	3539		2596	08	1411
ὧν	αἰτούμεθα	ἢ	νοοῦμεν		κατὰ	τὴν	δύναμιν
of what we ask		or	we give thought		by	the	power

08	1754		1722	1473		846	05	1391
τὴν	ἐνεργουμένην	ἐν	ἡμῖν,	[21]	αὐτῷ	ἡ	δόξα
the	one operating	in	us,		to him	the	splendor

1722	07	1577	2532	1722	5547	2424	1519	3956
ἐν	τῇ	ἐκκλησίᾳ	καὶ	ἐν	Χριστῷ	Ἰησοῦ	εἰς	πάσας
in	the	assembly	and	in	Christ	Jesus	for	all

020	1074	02	165	014	165	281
τὰς	γενεὰς	τοῦ	αἰῶνος	τῶν	αἰώνων,	ἀμήν.
the	generations	of the	age	of the	ages,	amen.

	3870	3767	1473	1473	01	1198	1722	2962
4:1	Παρακαλῶ	οὖν	ὑμᾶς	ἐγὼ	ὁ	δέσμιος	ἐν	κυρίῳ
	Encourage	then	you	I	the	prisoner	in	Master

516   4043   06   2821   3739
ἀξίως   περιπατῆσαι   τῆς   κλήσεως ἧς
worthily   to walk around   of the   call   of which

2564   2   3326 3956 5012   2532
ἐκλήθητε,   μετὰ πάσης ταπεινοφροσύνης καὶ
you were called,   with all humblemindedness and

4240   3326 3115   430   240
πραΰτητος, μετὰ μακροθυμίας, ἀνεχόμενοι ἀλλήλων
gentleness, with long temper, enduring   one another

1722 26   3 4704   5083   08   1775   010
ἐν ἀγάπῃ,   σπουδάζοντες τηρεῖν τὴν ἑνότητα τοῦ
in love,   being diligent to keep the oneness of the

4151   1722 03 4886   06   1515   1520
πνεύματος ἐν τῷ συνδέσμῳ τῆς εἰρήνης· 4 Ἓν
spirit   in the co-chain of the peace;   one

4983 2532 1520 4151   2531   2532 2564   1722
σῶμα καὶ ἓν πνεῦμα, καθὼς καὶ ἐκλήθητε   ἐν
body and one spirit, just as also you were called in

1520 1680   06   2821   1473   5 1520 2962   1520
μιᾷ ἐλπίδι τῆς   κλήσεως ὑμῶν·   εἷς κύριος, μία
one hope   of the call   of you;   one Master, one

4102   1520 908   6 1520 2316 2532 3962   3956
πίστις, ἓν βάπτισμα,   εἷς θεὸς καὶ πατὴρ πάντων,
trust, one immersion,   one God and father of all,

01   1909 3956   2532 1223   3956   2532 1722 3956
ὁ   ἐπὶ πάντων καὶ διὰ   πάντων καὶ ἐν πᾶσιν.
the one on all   and through all   and in all.

7 1520   1161 1538   1473 1325   05   5485   2596
   Ἑνὶ   δὲ ἑκάστῳ ἡμῶν ἐδόθη   ἡ χάρις κατὰ
   To one but each   of us was given the favor by

012 3358   06   1431   02   5547   8 1352
τὸ μέτρον τῆς δωρεᾶς τοῦ   Χριστοῦ.   διὸ
the measure the gift of the Christ.   Therefore

3004   305   1519 5311   162
λέγει· ἀναβὰς   εἰς ὕψος   ἠχμαλώτευσεν
it says, having gone up into height he led captive

161   1325   1390   015   444   9 09 1161
αἰχμαλωσίαν, ἔδωκεν δόματα τοῖς ἀνθρώποις.   τὸ δὲ
captivity,   he gave gifts to the men.   The but

305   5101 1510   1487 3361 3754 2532 2597
ἀνέβη   τί ἐστιν, εἰ μὴ ὅτι καὶ κατέβη
he went up what is it, except that also he went down

1519 024 2737   3313 06   1093   10 01
εἰς τὰ κατώτερα [μέρη] τῆς   γῆς;   ὁ
into the underneath parts of the earth?   The one

2597   846   1510 2532 01 305
καταβὰς   αὐτός ἐστιν καὶ ὁ ἀναβὰς
having come down himself is   also the having come up

5231   3956   014 3772   2443 4137   024
ὑπεράνω πάντων τῶν οὐρανῶν, ἵνα πληρώσῃ   τὰ
up above all   the heavens, that he might fill the

3956   11 2532 846   1325   016 3303   652
πάντα.   Καὶ αὐτὸς ἔδωκεν τοὺς μὲν ἀποστόλους,
all.   And himself gave   the indeed delegates,

016   1161 4396   016 1161 2099
τοὺς δὲ προφήτας, τοὺς δὲ εὐαγγελιστάς,
the but spokesmen, the but tellers of good message,

016 1161 4166   2532 1320   12 4314   04
τοὺς δὲ ποιμένας καὶ διδασκάλους,   πρὸς τὸν
the but shepherds and teachers,   toward the

2677   014   40   1519 2041 1248
καταρτισμὸν τῶν   ἁγίων εἰς ἔργον διακονίας,
putting in order of the holy ones to work of service,

1519 3619   010   4983   02   5547   13 3360
εἰς οἰκοδομὴν τοῦ   σώματος τοῦ   Χριστοῦ,   μέχρι
to building of the body   of the Christ,   until

2658   013 3956 1519 08 1775   06   4102
καταντήσωμεν οἱ πάντες εἰς τὴν ἑνότητα τῆς πίστεως
might arrive the all   into the oneness of the trust

beg you to lead a life
worthy of the calling to
which you have been called,
[2]with all humility and
gentleness, with patience,
bearing with one another in
love, [3]making every effort
to maintain the unity of the
Spirit in the bond of peace.
[4]There is one body and one
Spirit, just as you were
called to the one hope of
your calling, [5]one Lord,
one faith, one baptism, [6]one
God and Father of all, who
is above all and through all
and in all.

7 But each of us was
given grace according to
the measure of Christ's gift.
[8]Therefore it is said,
    "When he ascended on
      high he made captivity
      itself a captive;
    he gave gifts to his
      people."
[9](When it says, "He
ascended," what does it
mean but that he had also
descended[a] into the lower
parts of the earth? [10]He
who descended is the same
one who ascended far above
all the heavens, so that he
might fill all things.) [11]The
gifts he gave were that some
would be apostles, some
prophets, some evangelists,
some pastors and teachers,
[12]to equip the saints for
the work of ministry, for
building up the body of
Christ, [13]until all of us
come to the unity of the
faith

<hr>

[a] Other ancient authorities add first

and of the knowledge of the Son of God, to maturity, to the measure of the full stature of Christ. 14We must no longer be children, tossed to and fro and blown about by every wind of doctrine, by people's trickery, by their craftiness in deceitful scheming. 15But speaking the truth in love, we must grow up in every way into him who is the head, into Christ, 16from whom the whole body, joined and knit together by every ligament with which it is equipped, as each part is working properly, promotes the body's growth in building itself up in love.

17 Now this I affirm and insist on in the Lord: you must no longer live as the Gentiles live, in the futility of their minds. 18They are darkened in their understanding, alienated from the life of God because of their ignorance and hardness of heart. 19They have lost all sensitivity and have abandoned themselves to licentiousness, greedy to practice every kind of impurity. 20That is not the way you learned Christ! 21For surely you have heard about him and

2532	06	1922		02	5207 02		2316 1519 435
καὶ	τῆς	ἐπιγνώσεως	τοῦ	υἱοῦ	τοῦ	θεοῦ,	εἰς ἄνδρα
and	the	perception	of the	son	of	the God,	to man

5046 1519 3358   2244   010   4138
τέλειον, εἰς μέτρον ἡλικίας τοῦ πληρώματος
complete, into measure of stature of the fullness

02   5547   **14** 2443 3371   1510   3516
τοῦ Χριστοῦ,   ἵνα μηκέτι ὦμεν νήπιοι,
of the Christ,   that no longer we might be infants,

2831   2532 4064   3956   417
κλυδωνιζόμενοι καὶ περιφερόμενοι   παντὶ ἀνέμῳ
being tossed and being carried around in all wind
by waves

06   1319   1722 07 2940   014   444
τῆς διδασκαλίας ἐν τῇ κυβείᾳ τῶν ἀνθρώπων,
of the teaching in the trickery of the men,

1722 3834   4314   08 3180   06   4106
ἐν πανουργίᾳ πρὸς τὴν μεθοδείαν τῆς πλάνης,
in trickery toward the scheming of the deceit,

15 226   1161 1722 26   837   1519
ἀληθεύοντες δὲ ἐν ἀγάπῃ αὐξήσωμεν εἰς
telling truth but in love we might grow into

846   024 3956   3739 1510 05 2776   5547
αὐτὸν τὰ πάντα, ὅς ἐστιν ἡ κεφαλή, Χριστός,
him the all, who is the head, Christ,

16 1537 3739 3956 09 4983 4883   2532
ἐξ οὗ πᾶν τὸ σῶμα συναρμολογούμενον καὶ
from whom all the body being joined together and

4822   1223   3956 860   06
συμβιβαζόμενον   διὰ πάσης ἁφῆς τῆς
being forced together through all ligament of the

2024   2596 1753   1722 3358   1520 1538
ἐπιχορηγίας κατ' ἐνέργειαν ἐν μέτρῳ ἑνὸς ἑκάστου
support by operation in measure of one each

3313 08 838   010   4983   4160   1519
μέρους τὴν αὔξησιν τοῦ σώματος ποιεῖται εἰς
part the growth of the body makes itself into

3619   1438   1722 26   **17** 3778 3767 3004 2532
οἰκοδομὴν ἑαυτοῦ ἐν ἀγάπῃ.   Τοῦτο οὖν λέγω καὶ
building itself in love.   This then I say and

3143   1722 2962   3371   1473 4043
μαρτύρομαι ἐν κυρίῳ, μηκέτι ὑμᾶς περιπατεῖν,
I testify in Master, no longer you to walk around,

2531   2532 021 1484   4043   1722 3153
καθὼς καὶ τὰ ἔθνη περιπατεῖ ἐν ματαιότητι
just as also the nations walk around in futility

02   3563 846   **18** 4656   07
τοῦ νοὸς αὐτῶν,   ἐσκοτωμένοι   τῇ
of the mind of them,   having been darkened in the

1271   1510 526   06   2222
διανοίᾳ ὄντες, ἀπηλλοτριωμένοι   τῆς ζωῆς
intelligence being, having been alienated of the life

02   2316 1223   08 52   08 1510 1722
τοῦ θεοῦ διὰ τὴν ἄγνοιαν τὴν οὖσαν ἐν
of the God through the unknowingness the being in

846   1223   08 4457   06   2588   846
αὐτοῖς, διὰ τὴν πώρωσιν τῆς καρδίας αὐτῶν,
them, through the hardness of the heart of them,

19 3748   524   1438   3860
οἵτινες ἀπηλγηκότες   ἑαυτοὺς παρέδωκαν
who   being calloused themselves they gave over

07   766   1519 2039   167   3956
τῇ ἀσελγείᾳ εἰς ἐργασίαν ἀκαθαρσίας πάσης
to the debauchery into working of uncleanness all

1722 4124   **20** 1473 1161 3756 3779   3129
ἐν πλεονεξίᾳ.   Ὑμεῖς δὲ οὐχ οὕτως ἐμάθετε
in greediness.   You but not thusly learned

04 5547   **21** 1487 1065 846 191   2532 1722
τὸν Χριστόν,   εἴ γε αὐτὸν ἠκούσατε καὶ ἐν
the Christ,   if indeed him you heard and in

846   1321   2531   1510   225   1722 03
αὐτῷ ἐδιδάχθητε,   καθώς   ἐστιν ἀλήθεια ἐν   τῷ
him   you were taught, just as it is truth   in   the

2424   659   1473 2596 08   4387
Ἰησοῦ, **22** ἀποθέσθαι   ὑμᾶς κατὰ τὴν προτέραν
Jesus,   to be set off you by   the former

391   04   3820   444   04   5351
ἀναστροφὴν τὸν παλαιὸν ἄνθρωπον τὸν φθειρόμενον
behavior   the old   man   the being corrupted

2596 020 1939   06   539   **23** 365   1161
κατὰ τὰς ἐπιθυμίας τῆς   ἀπάτης,   ἀνανεοῦσθαι δὲ
by   the desires of the deception,   to renew   but

011   4151   02   3563 1473   **24** 2532 1746
τῷ   πνεύματι τοῦ νοὸς ὑμῶν   καὶ   ἐνδύσασθαι
in the spirit   of the mind of you   and   to put on

04   2537   444   04   2596 2316 2936
τὸν καινὸν ἄνθρωπον τὸν κατὰ θεὸν κτισθέντα
the new   man   the by   God having been created

1722 1343   2532 3742   06   225   **25** 1352
ἐν   δικαιοσύνῃ καὶ ὁσιότητι τῆς ἀληθείας.   Διὸ
in   rightness   and holiness of the truth.   Therefore

659   012 5579   2980   225   1538   3326
ἀποθέμενοι τὸ ψεῦδος λαλεῖτε ἀλήθειαν ἕκαστος μετὰ
setting off the lie   speak   truth   each   with

02   4139   846   3754   1510   240
τοῦ πλησίον αὐτοῦ, ὅτι   ἐσμὲν ἀλλήλων
the neighbor of him, because we are of one another

3196   **26** 3710   2532 3361 264   01   2246
μέλη.   ὀργίζεσθε καὶ μὴ ἁμαρτάνετε· ὁ   ἥλιος
members.   Be angry   and not sin;   the sun

3361 1931   1909 03 3950   1473   3366
μὴ ἐπιδυέτω ἐπὶ [τῷ] παροργισμῷ ὑμῶν, **27** μηδὲ
not let set on   the angry mood of you,   but not

1325   5117 03 1228   **28** 01   2813
δίδοτε τόπον τῷ διαβόλῳ.   ὁ   κλέπτων
give   place to the slanderer. The one thieving

3371   2813   3123   1161 2872   2038
μηκέτι κλεπτέτω, μᾶλλον δὲ κοπιάτω ἐργαζόμενος
no longer let thieve, more but let labor working

019   2398   5495   012 18   2443 2192
ταῖς [ἰδίαις] χερσὶν τὸ ἀγαθόν, ἵνα ἔχῃ
in the own   hands   the good,   that he might have

3330   03   5532   2192   **29** 3956 3056
μεταδιδόναι τῷ   χρείαν ἔχοντι.   πᾶς λόγος
to share   to the one need   having.   All word

4550   1537 010 4750   1473   3361 1607
σαπρὸς ἐκ   τοῦ στόματος ὑμῶν μὴ ἐκπορευέσθω,
rotten out of the mouth   of you not let travel out,

235   1487 5100 18   4314   3619   06   5532
ἀλλὰ εἴ τις ἀγαθὸς πρὸς οἰκοδομὴν τῆς χρείας,
but if   some good   toward building the need,

2443 1325   5485   015   191   **30** 2532
ἵνα δῷ   χάριν τοῖς ἀκούουσιν.   καὶ
that he might give favor to the ones hearing.   And

3361 3076   012 4151   012 40   02   2316 1722
μὴ λυπεῖτε τὸ πνεῦμα τὸ ἅγιον τοῦ θεοῦ, ἐν
not grieve the spirit the holy of the God,   in

3739 4972   1519 2250   629   **31** 3956
ᾧ   ἐσφραγίσθητε εἰς ἡμέραν ἀπολυτρώσεως.   πᾶσα
whom you were sealed for day   of redemption. All

4088   2532 2372 2532 3709 2532 2906   2532
πικρία   καὶ θυμὸς καὶ ὀργὴ καὶ κραυγὴ καὶ
bitterness   and fury   and anger and shout and

988   142   575   1473 4862 3956
βλασφημία ἀρθήτω   ἀφ᾽ ὑμῶν σὺν πάσῃ
insult   let be lifted up from you with all

2549   **32** 1096   1161 1519 240   5543
κακία.   γίνεσθε [δὲ] εἰς ἀλλήλους χρηστοί,
badness.   Become but for one another kind ones,

were taught in him, as truth is in Jesus. [22]You were taught to put away your former way of life, your old self, corrupt and deluded by its lusts, [23]and to be renewed in the spirit of your minds, [24]and to clothe yourselves with the new self, created according to the likeness of God in true righteousness and holiness.

[25]So then, putting away falsehood, let all of us speak the truth to our neighbors, for we are members of one another. [26]Be angry but do not sin; do not let the sun go down on your anger, [27]and do not make room for the devil. [28]Thieves must give up stealing; rather let them labor and work honestly with their own hands, so as to have something to share with the needy. [29]Let no evil talk come out of your mouths, but only what is useful for building up,[a] as there is need, so that your words may give grace to those who hear. [30]And do not grieve the Holy Spirit of God, with which you were marked with a seal for the day of redemption. [31]Put away from you all bitterness and wrath and anger and wrangling and slander, together with all malice, [32]and be kind to one another,

[a] Other ancient authorities read *building up faith*

tenderhearted, forgiving one another, as God in Christ has forgiven you.[a] **5:1**Therefore be imitators of God, as beloved children, [2]and live in love, as Christ loved us[b] and gave himself up for us, a fragrant offering and sacrifice to God.

3 But fornication and impurity of any kind, or greed, must not even be mentioned among you, as is proper among saints. [4]Entirely out of place is obscene, silly, and vulgar talk; but instead, let there be thanksgiving. [5]Be sure of this, that no fornicator or impure person, or one who is greedy (that is, an idolater), has any inheritance in the kingdom of Christ and of God.

6 Let no one deceive you with empty words, for because of these things the wrath of God comes on those who are disobedient. [7]Therefore do not be associated with them. [8]For once you were darkness, but now in the Lord you are light. Live as children of light— [9]for the fruit of the light is found in all that is good and right and true. [10]Try to find out what is pleasing to the Lord. [11]Take no part in the unfruitful works of

[a] Other ancient authorities read *us*
[b] Other ancient authorities read *you*

2155		5483		1438		2531	2532
εὔσπλαγχνοι,		χαριζόμενοι		ἑαυτοῖς,		καθὼς	καὶ
well affectioned,		favoring		yourselves,		just	as also

01	2316	1722	5547	5483		1473		1096	3767
ὁ	θεὸς	ἐν	Χριστῷ	ἐχαρίσατο		ὑμῖν.	**5:1**	Γίνεσθε	οὖν
the God	in Christ	favored		you.				Become	then

3402	02		2316	5613	5043		27		2532
μιμηταὶ	τοῦ		θεοῦ	ὡς	τέκνα		ἀγαπητὰ	**2**	καὶ
imitators of the God	as	children	loved	and

4043		1722	26		2531		2532	01	5547
περιπατεῖτε	ἐν		ἀγάπῃ,		καθὼς		καὶ	ὁ	Χριστὸς
walk around in	love,	just as also the Christ

25		1473	2532	3860		1438		5228	1473
ἠγάπησεν	ἡμᾶς	καὶ	παρέδωκεν	ἑαυτὸν	ὑπὲρ	ἡμῶν
loved	us	and	gave over	himself	on behalf	of us

4376		2532	2378		03		2316	1519	3744
προσφορὰν	καὶ	θυσίαν	τῷ	θεῷ	εἰς	ὀσμὴν
offering	and	sacrifice	to the God	for	odor

2175		3	4202		1161	2532	167
εὐωδίας.	**3**	Πορνεία		δὲ	καὶ	ἀκαθαρσία
of good smell.	Sexual immorality	but	and	uncleanness

3956	2228	4124		3366		3687		1722	1473
πᾶσα	ἢ	πλεονεξία	μηδὲ	ὀνομαζέσθω	ἐν	ὑμῖν,
all	or	greediness	but not	let be named	in	you,

2531		4241		40			2532	151
καθὼς	πρέπει		ἁγίοις,		**4**	καὶ	αἰσχρότης
just as it is fitting	to holy ones,	and	shamefulness

2532	3473		2228	2160		3739	3756
καὶ	μωρολογία	ἢ	εὐτραπελία,		ἃ	οὐκ
and	foolish words	or	coarse joking,	which not

433		235	3123		2169		5	3778	1063
ἀνῆκεν,	ἀλλὰ	μᾶλλον	εὐχαριστία.		**5**	τοῦτο	γὰρ
is proper,	but	more	good favor.		This	for

3609a	1097		3754	3956	4205			2228
ἴστε	γινώσκοντες,	ὅτι	πᾶς	πόρνος		ἢ
you know knowing,	that	all	sexually immoral one	or

169		2228	4123		3739	1510	1496
ἀκάθαρτος	ἢ	πλεονέκτης,	ὅ	ἐστιν	ϝἰδωλολάτρης,
unclean one	or	greedy one,	who	is	idol server,

3756	2192	2817		1722	07	932		02
οὐκ	ἔχει	κληρονομίαν	ἐν	τῇ	βασιλείᾳ	τοῦ
not	he has	inheritance	in	the	kingdom	of the

5547		2532	2316		6	3367		1473	538		2756
Χριστοῦ	καὶ	θεοῦ.	**6**	Μηδεὶς	ὑμᾶς	ἀπατάτω	κενοῖς
Christ	and	God.	No one	you	let deceive	in empty

3056		1223		3778	1063	2064		05	3709	02		2316
λόγοις·	διὰ	ταῦτα	γὰρ	ἔρχεται	ἡ	ὀργὴ	τοῦ	θεοῦ
words;	through	these	for	comes	the	anger	of the	God

1909	016	5207	06		543			3361	3767	1096
ἐπὶ	τοὺς	υἱοὺς	τῆς	ἀπειθείας.		**7**	μὴ	οὖν	γίνεσθε
upon	the	sons	of the	disobedience.	Not	then	become

4830		846		8	1510		1063	4218	4655		3568
συμμέτοχοι	αὐτῶν·		**8**	ἦτε	γὰρ	ποτε	σκότος,	νῦν
co-partakers	of them;	you were	for	then	dark,	now

1161	5457	1722	2962		5613	5043		5457
δὲ	φῶς	ἐν	κυρίῳ·	ὡς	τέκνα	φωτὸς
but	light	in	Master;	as	children	of light

4043		9	01	1063	2590	010		5457	1722	3956
περιπατεῖτε	**9**	ὁ	γὰρ	καρπὸς	τοῦ	φωτὸς	ἐν	πάσῃ
walk around	the	for	fruit	of the	light	in	all

19		2532	1343		2532	225			10	1381
ἀγαθωσύνῃ	καὶ	δικαιοσύνῃ	καὶ	ἀληθείᾳ -		**10**	δοκιμάζοντες
goodness	and	rightness	and	truth -	proving

5101	1510	2101		03		2962		11	2532	3361
τί	ἐστιν	εὐάρεστον	τῷ	κυρίῳ,		**11**	καὶ	μὴ
what is	well-pleasing	to the Master,	and	not

4790		023		2041	023	175		010
συγκοινωνεῖτε	τοῖς	ἔργοις	τοῖς	ἀκάρποις	τοῦ
be co-partner in	the	works	the	fruitless	of the

```
4655        3123      1161   2532  1651         024                    1063
σκότους, μᾶλλον δὲ   καὶ  ἐλέγχετε.  12  τὰ                γὰρ
dark,       more      but    also   rebuke.      The things           for
2931              1096         5259  846   150          1510   2532
κρυφῇ    γινόμενα ὑπ'  αὐτῶν αἰσχρόν ἐστιν καὶ
in hiding becoming by   them    shame    it is   and
3004        13   021   1161  3956    1651              5259  010   5457
λέγειν,   13  τὰ    δὲ   πάντα ἐλεγχόμενα       ὑπὸ τοῦ φωτὸς
to say,         the   but   all      being rebuked by   the   light
5319            14   3956  1063  09    5319
φανεροῦται,  14  πᾶν  γὰρ  τὸ   φανερούμενον
is demonstrated,   all    for   the   being demonstrated
5457    1510    1352       3004       1453     01
φῶς  ἐστιν. διὸ   λέγει·  ἔγειρε, ὁ
light is.  Therefore it says, rise,   the one
2518             2532  450          1537  014  3498        2532
καθεύδων, καὶ  ἀνάστα ἐκ   τῶν νεκρῶν, καὶ
sleeping,   and   stand up from the   dead,       and
2017              1473  01   5547          15  991         3767
ἐπιφαύσει   σοι   ὁ   Χριστός.  15  Βλέπετε οὖν
will shine on you  the Christ.        See          then
199             4459  4043            3361  5613  781      235
ἀκριβῶς   πῶς  περιπατεῖτε, μὴ   ὡς   ἄσοφοι ἀλλ'
accurately how   you walk around, not   as    unwise   but
5613  4680    16  1805                04   2540          3754      017
ὡς   σοφοί, 16  ἐξαγοραζόμενοι τὸν καιρόν, ὅτι      αἱ
as    wise,       buying out        the season,   because  the
2250     4190       1510    17  1223      3778   3361  1096
ἡμέραι πονηραί εἰσιν.  17  διὰ     τοῦτο μὴ  γίνεσθε
days     evil       are.        Through this    not   become
878         235      4920           5101  09   2307      02
ἄφρονες, ἀλλὰ συνίετε      τί   τὸ   θέλημα τοῦ
unthinking, but   understand what the   want     of the
2962     18   2532  3361  3182        3631      1722  3739
κυρίου.  18  καὶ  μὴ   μεθύσκεσθε οἴνῳ, ἐν   ᾧ
Master.       And  not   be drunk     in wine, in  which
1510   810         235     4137      1722  4151
ἐστιν ἀσωτία,  ἀλλὰ πληροῦσθε ἐν  πνεύματι,
is      dissipation, but   be filled in   spirit,
19  2980          1438           1722  5568      2532  5215
19  λαλοῦντες ἑαυτοῖς [ἐν] ψαλμοῖς καὶ ὕμνοις
    speaking    to yourselves in  psalms    and  hymns
2532  5603    4152            103         2532  5567          07
καὶ  ᾠδαῖς πνευματικαῖς, ᾄδοντες καὶ  ψάλλοντες τῇ
and   songs spiritual,         singing  and   psalming  in the
2588     1473   03      2962      20  2168            3842
καρδίᾳ ὑμῶν τῷ   κυρίῳ,  20  εὐχαριστοῦντες πάντοτε
heart    of you to the Master,      giving good favor   always
5228     3956    1722  3686     02      2962     1473  2424
ὑπὲρ  πάντων ἐν  ὀνόματι τοῦ  κυρίου ἡμῶν Ἰησοῦ
on behalf of all  in   name     of the Master   of us    Jesus
5547    03    2316  2532  3962    21  5293
Χριστοῦ τῷ  θεῷ  καὶ  πατρί.  21  Ὑποτασσόμενοι
Christ    to the God   and   Father.    Being subject
240           1722  5401  5547        017  1135
ἀλλήλοις ἐν  φόβῳ Χριστοῦ, 22  αἱ  γυναῖκες
to one another in  fear   of Christ,      the women
015      2398   435         5613  03    2962       23  3754
τοῖς  ἰδίοις ἀνδράσιν ὡς   τῷ  κυρίῳ,  23  ὅτι
to the own   men         as    in the Master,     because
435    1510   2776    06        1135     5613  2532  01   5547
ἀνήρ ἐστιν κεφαλὴ τῆς   γυναικὸς ὡς  καὶ  ὁ  Χριστὸς
man   is     head    of the woman    as   also  the Christ
2776    06    1577          846     4990          010
κεφαλὴ τῆς  ἐκκλησίας, αὐτὸς σωτὴρ     τοῦ
head    of the assembly,   himself deliverer of the
4983          24  235   5613  05   1577        5293         03
σώματος·  24  ἀλλὰ ὡς  ἡ  ἐκκλησία ὑποτάσσεται τῷ
body;           but   as   the assembly   is subject     to the
```

darkness, but instead expose them. [12]For it is shameful even to mention what such people do secretly; [13]but everything exposed by the light becomes visible, [14]for everything that becomes visible is light. Therefore it says,

"Sleeper, awake!
Rise from the dead,
and Christ will shine
on you."

15 Be careful then how you live, not as unwise people but as wise, [16]making the most of the time, because the days are evil. [17]So do not be foolish, but understand what the will of the Lord is. [18]Do not get drunk with wine, for that is debauchery; but be filled with the Spirit, [19]as you sing psalms and hymns and spiritual songs among yourselves, singing and making melody to the Lord in your hearts, [20]giving thanks to God the Father at all times and for everything in the name of our Lord Jesus Christ.

21 Be subject to one another out of reverence for Christ.

22 Wives, be subject to your husbands as you are to the Lord. [23]For the husband is the head of the wife just as Christ is the head of the church, the body of which he is the Savior. [24]Just as the church is subject to

Christ, so also wives ought to be, in everything, to their husbands.

25 Husbands, love your wives, just as Christ loved the church and gave himself up for her, [26]in order to make her holy by cleansing her with the washing of water by the word, [27]so as to present the church to himself in splendor, without a spot or wrinkle or anything of the kind— yes, so that she may be holy and without blemish. [28]In the same way, husbands should love their wives as they do their own bodies. He who loves his wife loves himself. [29]For no one ever hates his own body, but he nourishes and tenderly cares for it, just as Christ does for the church, [30]because we are members of his body.[a] [31]"For this reason a man will leave his father and mother and be joined to his wife, and the two will become one flesh." [32]This is a great mystery, and I am applying it to Christ and the church. [33]Each of you, however, should love his wife as himself, and a wife should respect her husband.

CHAPTER 6

Children, obey your parents

_____

[a] Other ancient authorities add of his flesh and of his bones

5547	3779	2532	017	1135		015	435	1722
Χριστῷ,	οὕτως	καὶ	αἱ	γυναῖκες	τοῖς	ἀνδράσιν		ἐν
Christ,	thusly	also	the	women		to the men		in

3956		013	435	25		020	1135		2531
παντί.	**25**	Οἱ	ἄνδρες,	ἀγαπᾶτε	τὰς	γυναῖκας,		καθὼς
all.		The	men,	love		the women,		just as

2532	01	5547	25		08	1577		2532	1438
καὶ	ὁ	Χριστὸς	ἠγάπησεν	τὴν	ἐκκλησίαν	καὶ		ἑαυτὸν
also	the	Christ	loved	the	assembly	and		himself

3860		5228		846		2443	846
παρέδωκεν	ὑπὲρ		αὐτῆς,	**26**	ἵνα	αὐτὴν
he gave over	on behalf of her,				that	her

37			2511		011	3067
ἁγιάσῃ		καθαρίσας	τῷ	λουτρῷ
he might make holy	having cleaned	in the washing

010	5204	1722	4487		2443	3936
τοῦ	ὕδατος	ἐν	ῥήματι,	**27**	ἵνα	παραστήσῃ
of the water	in	word,		that	might stand along

846	1438		1741	08	1577		3361
αὐτὸς	ἑαυτῷ		ἔνδοξον	τὴν	ἐκκλησίαν,		μὴ
himself	to himself	in splendor	the	assembly,		not

2192	4696	2228	4512	2228	5100	022	5108
ἔχουσαν	σπίλον	ἢ	ῥυτίδα	ἤ	τι	τῶν	τοιούτων,
having	blot	or	wrinkle	or	any	of	the such things,

235	2443	1510		40	2532	299		3779
ἀλλ᾽	ἵνα	ᾖ		ἁγία	καὶ	ἄμωμος.	**28**	οὕτως
but	that	she might be	holy	and	blameless.		Thusly

3784		2532	013	435	25		020	1438
ὀφείλουσιν	[καὶ]	οἱ	ἄνδρες	ἀγαπᾶν	τὰς	ἑαυτῶν
owe	also	the	men	to love	the	of themselves

1135	5613	024	1438		4983	01	25
γυναῖκας	ὡς	τὰ	ἑαυτῶν		σώματα.	ὁ	ἀγαπῶν
women	as	the	of themselves	bodies.	The one loving

08	1438		1135	1438	25		3762	1063
τὴν	ἑαυτοῦ		γυναῖκα	ἑαυτὸν	ἀγαπᾷ·	**29**	Οὐδεὶς	γάρ
the	of himself	woman	himself	loves;		no one	for

4218	08	1438		4561	3404	235	1625
ποτε	τὴν	ἑαυτοῦ		σάρκα	ἐμίσησεν	ἀλλὰ	ἐκτρέφει
then	the	of himself	flesh	hated	but	he nourishes

2532	2282		846	2531		2532	01	5547	08
καὶ	θάλπει	αὐτήν,	καθὼς		καὶ	ὁ	Χριστὸς	τὴν
and	cherishes	it,	just as	also	the	Christ	the

1577		3754	3196	1510	010	4983
ἐκκλησίαν,	**30**	ὅτι	μέλη	ἐσμὲν	τοῦ	σώματος
assembly,		because	members	we are	of the	body

846		473		3778	2641		444
αὐτοῦ.	**31**	ἀντὶ		τούτου	καταλείψει		ἄνθρωπος
of him.		In place of	this	will leave behind	man

04	3962	2532	08	3384	2532	4347
[τὸν]	πατέρα	καὶ	[τὴν]	μητέρα	καὶ	προσκολληθήσεται
the	father	and	the	mother	and	will be joined to

4314	08	1135	846	2532	1510	013	1417	1519
πρὸς	τὴν	γυναῖκα	αὐτοῦ,	καὶ	ἔσονται	οἱ	δύο	εἰς
toward	the	woman	of him,	and	will be	the	two	into

4561	1520	09	3466		3778	3173	1510	1473
σάρκα	μίαν.	**32**	τὸ	μυστήριον	τοῦτο	μέγα	ἐστίν·	ἐγὼ
flesh	one.		The	mystery	this	great	is;	I

1161	3004	1519	5547	2532	1519	08	1577
δὲ	λέγω	εἰς	Χριστὸν	καὶ	εἰς	τὴν	ἐκκλησίαν.
but	say	for	Christ	and	for	the	assembly.

	4133	2532	1473	013		2596	1520	1538	08
33	πλὴν	καὶ	ὑμεῖς	οἱ		καθ᾽	ἕνα,	ἕκαστος	τὴν
	Except	also	you	the ones	by	one,	each	the

1438		1135	3779	25		5613	1438	05
ἑαυτοῦ		γυναῖκα	οὕτως	ἀγαπάτω	ὡς		ἑαυτόν,	ἡ
of himself	woman	thusly	let love	as		himself,	the

1161	1135	2443	5399		04	435		021
δὲ	γυνὴ	ἵνα	φοβῆται		τὸν	ἄνδρα.	**6:1**	Τὰ
but	woman	that	she might fear	the	man.		The

```
5043        5219        015    1118      1473    1722 2962
τέκνα,    ὑπακούετε τοῖς γονεῦσιν ὑμῶν [ἐν   κυρίῳ]·
children, obey        the  parents  of you in   Master;
3778  1063 1510 1342      2  5091  04  3962  1473
τοῦτο γάρ ἐστιν δίκαιον. 2 τίμα τὸν πατέρα σου
this  for  is   right.     Value the father of you
2532 08  3384      3748   1510 1785    4413  1722
καὶ τὴν μητέρα, ἥτις ἐστὶν ἐντολὴ πρώτη ἐν
and the mother, which is   command first in
1860       3 2443 2095 1473  1096      2532 1510
ἐπαγγελίᾳ, 3 ἵνα εὖ σοι   γένηται καὶ ἔσῃ
promise,     that well to you might  and  you will be
                                             become
3118            1909 06 1093   2532 013 3962      3361
μακροχρόνιος ἐπὶ τῆς γῆς. 4 Καὶ οἱ πατέρες, μὴ
long time    on  the earth. And the fathers, not
3949         024 5043      1473  235 1625        846
παροργίζετε τὰ τέκνα  ὑμῶν ἀλλὰ ἐκτρέφετε αὐτὰ
make angry   the children of you but  nourish    them
1722 3809          2532 3559    2962      5 013
ἐν παιδείᾳ      καὶ νουθεσίᾳ κυρίου. 5 Οἱ
in child instruction and warning of Master. The
1401    5219      015      2596   4561 2962      3326
δοῦλοι, ὑπακούετε τοῖς  κατὰ  σάρκα κυρίοις μετὰ
slaves, obey      the ones by  flesh masters with
5401 2532 5156    1722 572    06      2588    1473
φόβου καὶ τρόμου ἐν ἁπλότητι τῆς καρδίας ὑμῶν
fear  and trembling in openness of the heart   of you
5613 03     5547   6 3361 2596 3787        5613
ὡς τῷ    Χριστῷ, 6 μὴ  κατ’ ὀφθαλμοδουλίαν ὡς
as to the Christ,   not by  eye-slavery      as
441        235   5613 1401   5547      4160     012
ἀνθρωπάρεσκοι ἀλλ’ ὡς δοῦλοι Χριστοῦ ποιοῦντες τὸ
men-pleasers but  as slaves of Christ doing     the
2307  02    2316 1537 5590   7 3326 2133
θέλημα τοῦ θεοῦ ἐκ ψυχῆς, 7 μετ’ εὐνοίας
want   of the God from soul,   with good mind
1398        5613 03   2962    2532 3756 444
δουλεύοντες ὡς τῷ κυρίῳ καὶ οὐκ ἀνθρώποις,
slaving     as to the Master and not to men,
   3609a  3754 1538  1437 5100 4160    18
8 εἰδότες ὅτι ἕκαστος ἐάν τι  ποιήσῃ ἀγαθόν,
  knowing that each  if  any might do good,
3778  2865        3844 2962   1535      1401  1535
τοῦτο κομίσεται παρὰ κυρίου εἴτε   δοῦλος εἴτε
this  he will obtain from Master whether slave or
1658       9 2532 013 2962   024 846        4160
ἐλεύθερος. 9 Καὶ οἱ κύριοι, τὰ αὐτὰ     ποιεῖτε
free.        And the masters, the same things do
4314    846      447   08 547          3609a     3754
πρὸς αὐτούς, ἀνιέντες τὴν ἀπειλήν,  εἰδότες ὅτι
toward them,  leaving  the threatening, knowing that
2532 846     2532 1473  01 2962   1510 1722 3772
καὶ αὐτῶν καὶ ὑμῶν ὁ  κύριός ἐστιν ἐν οὐρανοῖς
also of them and of you the Master he is in heavens
2532 4382           3756 1510    3844 846  10 010
καὶ προσωπολημψία οὐκ ἔστιν παρ’ αὐτῷ. 10 Τοῦ
and receiving of faces not there is from him. Of the
3062    1743         1722 2962 2532 1722 011 2904
λοιποῦ, ἐνδυναμοῦσθε ἐν κυρίῳ καὶ ἐν  τῷ κράτει
remaining, be empowered in Master and in  the strength
06  2479   846    11 1746     08 3833
τῆς ἰσχύος αὐτοῦ. 11 ἐνδύσασθε τὴν πανοπλίαν
of the strength of him. Put on   the all weaponry
02   2316 4314 012 1410     1473 2476    4314
τοῦ θεοῦ πρὸς τὸ δύνασθαι ὑμᾶς στῆναι πρὸς
of the God to  the to be able you  to stand toward
020 3180      02   1228        12 3754 3756 1510
τὰς μεθοδείας τοῦ διαβόλου· 12 ὅτι οὐκ ἔστιν
the schemings of the slanderer;   that not  is
```

in the Lord,[a] for this is right. [2]"Honor your father and mother"—this is the first commandment with a promise: [3]"so that it may be well with you and you may live long on the earth."

4 And, fathers, do not provoke your children to anger, but bring them up in the discipline and instruction of the Lord.

5 Slaves, obey your earthly masters with fear and trembling, in singleness of heart, as you obey Christ; [6]not only while being watched, and in order to please them, but as slaves of Christ, doing the will of God from the heart. [7]Render service with enthusiasm, as to the Lord and not to men and women, [8]knowing that whatever good we do, we will receive the same again from the Lord, whether we are slaves or free.

9 And, masters, do the same to them. Stop threatening them, for you know that both of you have the same Master in heaven, and with him there is no partiality.

10 Finally, be strong in the Lord and in the strength of his power. [11]Put on the whole armor of God, so that you may be able to stand against the wiles of the devil. [12]For our[b] struggle is not

[a] Other ancient authorities lack *in the Lord*

[b] Other ancient authorities read *your*

against enemies of blood and flesh, but against the rulers, against the authorities, against the cosmic powers of this present darkness, against the spiritual forces of evil in the heavenly places. ¹³Therefore take up the whole armor of God, so that you may be able to withstand on that evil day, and having done everything, to stand firm. ¹⁴Stand therefore, and fasten the belt of truth around your waist, and put on the breastplate of righteousness. ¹⁵As shoes for your feet put on whatever will make you ready to proclaim the gospel of peace. ¹⁶With all of these,ᵃ take the shield of faith, with which you will be able to quench all the flaming arrows of the evil one. ¹⁷Take the helmet of salvation, and the sword of the Spirit, which is the word of God.

18 Pray in the Spirit at all times in every prayer and supplication. To that end keep alert and always persevere in supplication for all the saints. ¹⁹Pray also for me, so that when I speak, a message may be given to me to make known with boldness the mystery of the gospel,ᵇ ²⁰for which

---

ᵃ Or In all circumstances
ᵇ Other ancient authorities lack of the gospel

1473	05	3823		4314	129	2532	4561	235	4314
ἡμῖν	ἡ	πάλη		πρὸς	αἷμα	καὶ	σάρκα	ἀλλὰ	πρὸς

to us the wrestling toward blood and flesh but toward

020	746		4314	020	1849		4314	016
τὰς	ἀρχάς,		πρὸς	τὰς	ἐξουσίας,		πρὸς	τοὺς

the rulers, toward the authorities, toward the

2888		010	4655	3778	4314	024
κοσμοκράτορας		τοῦ	σκότους	τούτου,	πρὸς	τὰ

world strengths of the dark this, toward the

4152	06	4189	1722	015	2032
πνευματικὰ	τῆς	πονηρίας	ἐν	τοῖς	ἐπουρανίοις.

spiritual of the evil in the on heavenlies.

13
1223	3778	353		08	3833		02
διὰ	τοῦτο	ἀναλάβετε		τὴν	πανοπλίαν		τοῦ

Through this take up the all weaponry of the

2316	2443	1410		436		1722	07
θεοῦ,	ἵνα	δυνηθῆτε		ἀντιστῆναι		ἐν	τῇ

God, that you might be able to stand against in the

2250	07	4190	2532	537	2716
ἡμέρᾳ	τῇ	πονηρᾷ	καὶ	ἅπαντα	κατεργασάμενοι

day the evil and all having worked thoroughly

2476	**14**	2476	3767	4024		08	3751
στῆναι.		στῆτε	οὖν	περιζωσάμενοι		τὴν	ὀσφὺν

to stand. Stand then having encircled the hip

1473	1722	225		2532	1746		04	2382
ὑμῶν	ἐν	ἀληθείᾳ	καὶ	ἐνδυσάμενοι		τὸν	θώρακα

of you in truth and having put on the breastplate

06	1343	**15**	2532	5265		016	4228
τῆς	δικαιοσύνης		καὶ	ὑποδησάμενοι		τοὺς	πόδας

of the rightness and having tied down the feet

1722	2091	010	2098	06	1515
ἐν	ἑτοιμασίᾳ	τοῦ	εὐαγγελίου	τῆς	εἰρήνης,

in preparation of the good message of the peace,

16
1722	3956	353		04	2375	06
ἐν	πᾶσιν	ἀναλαβόντες		τὸν	θυρεὸν	τῆς

in all having taken up the shield of the

4102	1722	3739	1410		3956	024	956
πίστεως,	ἐν	ᾧ	δυνήσευθε		πάντα	τὰ	βέλη

trust, in which you are able all the darts

02	4190	024	4448
τοῦ	πονηροῦ	[τὰ]	πεπυρωμένα

of the evil one the ones having been set on fire

4570	**17**	2532	08	4030		010	4992
σβέσαι·		καὶ	τὴν	περικεφαλαίαν		τοῦ	σωτηρίου

to quench; and the helmet of the deliverance

1209	2532	08	3162	010	4151	3739
δέξασθε	καὶ	τὴν	μάχαιραν	τοῦ	πνεύματος,	ὅ

welcome and the sword of the spirit, which

1510	4487	2316	**18**	1223	3956	4335	2532
ἐστιν	ῥῆμα	θεοῦ.		Διὰ	πάσης	προσευχῆς	καὶ

is word of God. Through all prayer and

1162	4336		1722	3956	2540	1722	4151
δεήσεως	προσευχόμενοι	ἐν	παντὶ	καιρῷ	ἐν	πνεύματι,

request praying in all season in spirit,

2532	1519	846	69		1722	3956	4343
καὶ	εἰς	αὐτὸ	ἀγρυπνοῦντες	ἐν	πάσῃ	προσκαρτερήσει

and into it staying awake in all constancy

2532	1162	4012	3956	014	40	**19**	2532	5228
καὶ	δεήσει	περὶ	πάντων	τῶν	ἁγίων		καὶ	ὑπὲρ

and request about all the holy ones and on behalf

1473	2443	1473	1325		3056	1722	457
ἐμοῦ,	ἵνα	μοι	δοθῇ		λόγος	ἐν	ἀνοίξει

of me, that to me might be given word in opening

010	4750	1473	1722	3954	1107	012
τοῦ	στόματός	μου,	ἐν	παρρησίᾳ	γνωρίσαι	τὸ

of the mouth of me, in boldness to make known the

3466		010	2098	**20**	5228	3739
μυστήριον		τοῦ	εὐαγγελίου,		ὑπὲρ	οὗ

mystery of the good message, on behalf of which

4243	1722	254	2443	1722	846	3955
πρεσβεύω	ἐν	ἁλύσει,	ἵνα	ἐν	αὐτῷ	παρρησιάσωμαι
I am envoy	in	chain,	that	in	him	I might be bold

5613	1163		1473	2980	21	2443	1161
ὡς	δεῖ	με	λαλῆσαι.		"Ἱνα	δὲ
as	it is necessary	me	to speak.		That	but

3609a	2532	1473	024		2596	1473	5101
εἰδῆτε	καὶ	ὑμεῖς	τὰ		κατ'	ἐμέ,	τί
might know	also	you	the things		by	me,	what

4238	3956	1107		1473	5190	01
πράσσω,	πάντα	γνωρίσει		ὑμῖν	Τύχικος	ὁ
I practice,	all	will make known		to you	Tychicus	the

27		2532	1473		1722	2962
ἀγαπητὸς	ἀδελφὸς	καὶ	πιστὸς	διάκονος	ἐν	κυρίῳ,
loved	brother	and	trustful	servant	in	Master,

22	3739	3992	4314	1473	1519	846	3778	2443
	ὃν	ἔπεμψα	πρὸς	ὑμᾶς	εἰς	αὐτὸ	τοῦτο,	ἵνα
	whom	I sent	toward	you	in	same	this,	that

1097		024	4012	1473	2532	3870
γνῶτε		τὰ	περὶ	ἡμῶν	καὶ	παρακαλέσῃ
you might know		the	about	us	and	he might encourage

020	2588	1473	23	1515	015	80		2532	26
τὰς	καρδίας	ὑμῶν.		Εἰρήνη	τοῖς	ἀδελφοῖς	καὶ	ἀγάπη
the hearts	of you.		Peace	to the	brothers	and	love

3326	4102	575	2316	3962	2532	2962	2424
μετὰ	πίστεως	ἀπὸ	θεοῦ	πατρὸς	καὶ	κυρίου	Ἰησοῦ
with trust		from	God	Father	and	Master	Jesus

5547	24	05	5485	3326	3956	014	25	04
Χριστοῦ.		ἡ	χάρις	μετὰ	πάντων	τῶν	ἀγαπώντων	τὸν
Christ.		The	favor	with	all		the ones loving	the

2962	1473	2424	5547	1722	861
κύριον	ἡμῶν	Ἰησοῦν	Χριστὸν	ἐν	ἀφθαρσίᾳ.
Master	of us	Jesus	Christ	in	incorruption.

I am an ambassador in chains. Pray that I may declare it boldly, as I must speak.

21 So that you also may know how I am and what I am doing, Tychicus will tell you everything. He is a dear brother and a faithful minister in the Lord. 22I am sending him to you for this very purpose, to let you know how we are, and to encourage your hearts.

23 Peace be to the whole community,[a] and love with faith, from God the Father and the Lord Jesus Christ. 24Grace be with all who have an undying love for our Lord Jesus Christ.[b]

a Gk to the brothers
b Other ancient authorities add Amen

PHILIPPIANS

CHAPTER 1

Paul and Timothy,
servants[a] of Christ Jesus,
To all the saints in
Christ Jesus who are in
Philippi, with the bishops[b]
and deacons:[c]

2 Grace to you and peace
from God our Father and
the Lord Jesus Christ.

3 I thank my God every
time I remember you,
[4]constantly praying with
joy in every one of my
prayers for all of you,
[5]because of your sharing
in the gospel from the
first day until now. [6]I am
confident of this, that the
one who began a good
work among you will bring
it to completion by the day
of Jesus Christ. [7]It is right
for me to think this way
about all of you, because
you hold me in your heart,[d]
for all of you share in God's
grace[e] with me, both in my
imprisonment and in the
defense and confirmation of
the gospel. [8]For God is my
witness, how I long for all
of you with the compassion
of Christ Jesus. [9]And this
is my prayer, that your
love may overflow more
and more with knowledge
and full insight [10]to help
you to determine what is
best, so that in the day of
Christ you may be pure
and blameless, [11]having
produced

a Gk slaves
b Or overseers
c Or overseers and helpers
d Or because I hold you in my heart
e Gk in grace

1:1
3972   2532 5095   1401   5547   2424   3956
Παῦλος καὶ   Τιμόθεος δοῦλοι Χριστοῦ ᾿Ιησοῦ πᾶσιν
Paul   and Timothy slaves of Christ Jesus to all

015 40   1722 5547   2424   015   1510 1722
τοῖς ἁγίοις   ἐν   Χριστῷ ᾿Ιησοῦ τοῖς   οὖσιν ἐν
the holy ones in   Christ Jesus the ones being in

5375   4862 1985   2532 1249   **2** 5485
Φιλίπποις σὺν ἐπισκόποις καὶ διακόνοις,   χάρις
Philippi   with overseers   and servants,   favor

1473   2532 1515   575   2316 3962   1473   2532 2962
ὑμῖν καὶ εἰρήνη ἀπὸ θεοῦ πατρὸς ἡμῶν καὶ κυρίου
to you and peace from God Father of us and Master

.2424 5547   **3** 2168   03   2316 1473
᾿Ιησοῦ Χριστοῦ.   Εὐχαριστῶ   τῷ   θεῷ μου
Jesus Christ.   I give good favor to the God of me

1909 3956 07 3417   1473 **4** 3842   1722 3956 1162
ἐπὶ πάσῃ τῇ μνείᾳ ὑμῶν πάντοτε ἐν πάσῃ δεήσει
on all   the memory of you always in all   request

1473 5228   3956   1473   3326 5479 08 1162
μου ὑπὲρ   πάντων ὑμῶν,   μετὰ χαρᾶς τὴν δέησιν
of me on behalf of all of you, with joy   the request

4160   **5** 1909 07 2842   1473   1519 012
ποιούμενος,   ἐπὶ τῇ κοινωνίᾳ ὑμῶν εἰς τὸ
making,   on the partnership of you in the

2098   575   06   4413   2250 891   02 3568
εὐαγγέλιον ἀπὸ τῆς πρώτης ἡμέρας ἄχρι τοῦ νῦν,
good message from the first   day   until the now,

6 3982   846   3778   3754 01   1728
πεποιθὼς   αὐτὸ τοῦτο, ὅτι ὁ   ἐναρξάμενος
being persuaded same this, that the one having begun

1722 1473 2041 18   2005   891
ἐν ὑμῖν ἔργον ἀγαθὸν ἐπιτελέσει   ἄχρι
in you work good   will complete thoroughly until

2250   5547   2424   **7** 2531   1510 1342   1473
ἡμέρας Χριστοῦ ᾿Ιησοῦ· Καθώς ἐστιν δίκαιον ἐμοὶ
day   of Christ Jesus.   Just as it is right   to me

3770 5426   5228   3956   1473   1223   012
τοῦτο φρονεῖν ὑπὲρ   πάντων ὑμῶν διὰ   τὸ
this to think on behalf of all of you because the

2192   1473 1722 07 2588   1473 1722 5037 015
ἔχειν   με ἐν τῇ καρδίᾳ ὑμᾶς, ἔν τε   τοῖς
to have me in the heart you, in both the

1199   1473 2532 1722 07 627   2532 951
δεσμοῖς μου καὶ ἐν τῇ ἀπολογίᾳ καὶ βεβαιώσει
chains of me and in the defense and confirmation

010   2098   4791   1473 06   5485
τοῦ εὐαγγελίου συγκοινωνούς μου τῆς χάριτος
of the good message co-partners of me of the favor

3956   1473 1510   **8** 3144   1063 1473 01 2316 5613
πάντας ὑμᾶς ὄντας.   μάρτυς γάρ μου ὁ θεὸς ὡς
all   you being.   Testifier for of me the God as

1971   3956   1473 1722 4698   5547   2424
ἐπιποθῶ πάντας ὑμᾶς ἐν σπλάγχνοις Χριστοῦ ᾿Ιησοῦ.
I desire all   you in affections of Christ Jesus.
longingly

9 2532 3778 4336   2443 05   26   1473   2089
Καὶ τοῦτο προσεύχομαι, ἵνα ἡ ἀγάπη ὑμῶν ἔτι
And this I pray,   that the love of you still

3123   2532 3123   4052   1722 1922   2532
μᾶλλον καὶ μᾶλλον περισσεύῃ ἐν ἐπιγνώσει καὶ
more   and more   might exceed in perception and

3956 144   **10** 1519 012 1381   1473 024
πάσῃ αἰσθήσει   εἰς τὸ δοκιμάζειν ὑμᾶς τὰ
all notice   into the to prove   you the

1308   2443 1510   1506   2532
διαφέροντα,   ἵνα ἦτε   εἰλικρινεῖς καὶ
differing things, that you might be unmixed   and

677   1519 2250   5547   **11** 4137
ἀπρόσκοποι εἰς ἡμέραν Χριστοῦ,   πεπληρωμένοι
blameless in day   of Christ,   having been filled

2590	1343		04	1223	2424	5547	1519
καρπὸν	δικαιοσύνης	τὸν	διὰ	'Ιησοῦ	Χριστοῦ	εἰς
fruit	of rightness	the one	through	Jesus	Christ	into

1391	2532 1868		2316	**12**	1097		1161 1473
δόξαν	καὶ ἔπαινον	θεοῦ.		Γινώσκειν	δὲ	ὑμᾶς
splendor	and praise	on of God.		To know	but	you

1014	80		3754 021	2596 1473	3123	1519
βούλομαι,	ἀδελφοί,	ὅτι τὰ	κατ' ἐμὲ	μᾶλλον εἰς
I plan,	brothers,	that the	by me	more for

4297	010	2098		2064		**13**	5620	016
προκοπὴν	τοῦ	εὐαγγελίου	ἐλήλυθεν,		ὥστε	τοὺς
progress	of the	good message	has come,		so that	the

1199	1473	5318	1722 5547	1096	1722 3650
δεσμούς	μου	φανεροὺς	ἐν Χριστῷ	γενέσθαι	ἐν ὅλῳ
chains	of me	evident	in Christ	to become	in whole

011 4232		2532 015	3062	3956	**14**	2532
τῷ πραιτωρίῳ	καὶ τοῖς	λοιποῖς	πᾶσιν,		καὶ
the praetorium	and to the	remaining	all,		and

016 4183	014	80	1722 2962	3982
τοὺς πλείονας	τῶν	ἀδελφῶν	ἐν κυρίῳ	πεποιθότας
the more	of the	brothers	in Master	being persuaded

015	1199	1473	4056	5111	870
τοῖς	δεσμοῖς	μου	περισσοτέρως	τολμᾶν	ἀφόβως
the	chains	of me	more exceedingly	to dare	fearlessly

04	3056	2980	**15**	5100	3303	2532 1223	5355
τὸν	λόγον	λαλεῖν.		τινὲς	μὲν	καὶ διὰ	φθόνον
the	word	to speak.		Some	indeed	even through	envy

2532 2054	5100	1161 2532 1223	2107	04
καὶ ἔριν,	τινὲς	δὲ καὶ δι'	εὐδοκίαν	τὸν
and strife,	some	but also through	good thought	the

5547	2784	**16**	013	3303	1537 26
Χριστὸν	κηρύσσουσιν·		οἱ	μὲν ἐξ	ἀγάπης,
Christ	announce;		the ones	indeed from	love,

3609a	3754 1519 627		010	2098
εἰδότες	ὅτι εἰς	ἀπολογίαν	τοῦ	εὐαγγελίου
knowing	that for	defense	of the	good message

2749		013	1161 1537 2052		04
κεῖμαι,	**17**	οἱ	δὲ ἐξ	ἐριθείας	τὸν
I am set,		the ones	but from	selfish ambition	the

5547	2605		3756 55	3633
Χριστὸν	καταγγέλλουσιν,	οὐχ	ἁγνῶς,	οἰόμενοι
Christ	proclaim,	not	purely,	expecting

2347	1453	015	1199	1473	**18**	5101 1063
θλῖψιν	ἐγείρειν	τοῖς	δεσμοῖς	μου.		Τί γάρ;
affliction	to raise	in the	chains	of me.		What for?

4133	3754 3956	5158	1535	4392	1535
πλὴν	ὅτι παντὶ	τρόπῳ,	εἴτε	προφάσει	εἴτε
Except	that in all	manner,	whether	in pretext	or

225	5547	2605		2532 1722 3778
ἀληθείᾳ,	Χριστὸς	καταγγέλλεται,	καὶ	ἐν τούτῳ
in truth,	Christ	is proclaimed,	and	in this

5463	235 2532 5463		**19**	3609a	1063 3754
χαίρω.	'Αλλὰ καὶ	χαρήσομαι,		οἶδα	γὰρ ὅτι
I rejoice.	But also	I will rejoice,		I know	for that

3778 1473	576		1519 4991	1223	06
τοῦτό μοι	ἀποβήσεται	εἰς	σωτηρίαν	διὰ	τῆς
this to me	will go off	for	deliverance	through	the

1473	1162	2532 2024		010	4151
ὑμῶν	δεήσεως	καὶ ἐπιχορηγίας	τοῦ	πνεύματος
of you	request	and support		of the	spirit

2424	5547	**20**	2596 08	603		2532
'Ιησοῦ	Χριστοῦ		κατὰ τὴν	ἀποκαραδοκίαν	καὶ
of Jesus	Christ		by the	eager expectation	and

1680	1473	3754	1722 3762	153	235
ἐλπίδα	μου,	ὅτι	ἐν οὐδενὶ	αἰσχυνθήσομαι,	ἀλλ'
hope	of me,	that	in nothing	I will be ashamed,	but

1722 3956 3954		5613 3842	2532 3568
ἐν πάσῃ παρρησίᾳ	ὡς	πάντοτε	καὶ νῦν
in all boldness	as	always	also now

the harvest of righteousness that comes through Jesus Christ for the glory and praise of God.

12 I want you to know, beloved,[a] that what has happened to me has actually helped to spread the gospel, [13]so that it has become known throughout the whole imperial guard[b] and to everyone else that my imprisonment is for Christ; [14]and most of the brothers and sisters,[a] having been made confident in the Lord by my imprisonment, dare to speak the word[c] with greater boldness and without fear.

15 Some proclaim Christ from envy and rivalry, but others from goodwill. [16]These proclaim Christ out of love, knowing that I have been put here for the defense of the gospel; [17]the others proclaim Christ out of selfish ambition, not sincerely but intending to increase my suffering in my imprisonment. [18]What does it matter? Just this, that Christ is proclaimed in every way, whether out of false motives or true; and in that I rejoice.

Yes, and I will continue to rejoice, [19]for I know that through your prayers and the help of the Spirit of Jesus Christ this will turn out for my deliverance. [20]It is my eager expectation and hope that I will not be put to shame in any way, but that by my speaking with all boldness,

---

a Gk brothers
b Gk whole praetorium
c Other ancient authorities read word of God

Christ will be exalted now as always in my body, whether by life or by death. [21]For to me, living is Christ and dying is gain. [22]If I am to live in the flesh, that means fruitful labor for me; and I do not know which I prefer. [23]I am hard pressed between the two: my desire is to depart and be with Christ, for that is far better; [24]but to remain in the flesh is more necessary for you. [25]Since I am convinced of this, I know that I will remain and continue with all of you for your progress and joy in faith, [26]so that I may share abundantly in your boasting in Christ Jesus when I come to you again.

[27]Only, live your life in a manner worthy of the gospel of Christ, so that, whether I come and see you or am absent and hear about you, I will know that you are standing firm in one spirit, striving side by side with one mind for the faith of the gospel, [28]and are in no way intimidated by your opponents. For them this is evidence of their destruction, but of your salvation. And this is God's doing. [29]For he has graciously granted you the privilege not only of believing in Christ, but

3170		5547	1722	011	4983	1473
μεγαλυνθήσεται		Χριστὸς	ἐν	τῷ	σώματί	μου,
will be made great		Christ	in	the	body	of me,

1535	1223	2222	1535	1223	2288	**21**	1473
εἴτε	διὰ	ζωῆς εἴτε	διὰ		θανάτου.		Ἐμοὶ
whether	through	life or	through		death.		To me

1063	09	2198	5547	2532	09	599	2771
γὰρ	τὸ	ζῆν	Χριστὸς	καὶ	τὸ	ἀποθανεῖν	κέρδος.
for	the	to live	Christ	and	the	to die	gain.

22 | 1487 | 1161 | 09 | 2198 | 1722 | 4561 | 3778 | 1473 | 2590 |
| | εἰ | δὲ | τὸ | ζῆν | ἐν | σαρκί, | τοῦτό | μοι | καρπὸς |
| | If | but | the | to live | in | flesh, | this | to me | fruit |

2041	2532	5101	138	3756	1107
ἔργου,	καὶ	τί	αἱρήσομαι	οὐ	γνωρίζω.
of work,	and	what	I will choose	not	I make known.

23 | 4912 | | 1161 | 1537 | 022 | 1417 | 08 | 1939 |
| | συνέχομαι | | δὲ | ἐκ | τῶν | δύο, | τὴν | ἐπιθυμίαν |
| | I am held together | | but | from | the | two, | the | desire |

2192	1519	012	360	2532	4862	5547	1510	4183
ἔχων	εἰς	τὸ	ἀναλῦσαι	καὶ	σὺν	Χριστῷ	εἶναι,	πολλῷ
having	for	the	to depart	and	with	Christ	to be,	much

1063	3123	2909	**24**	09	1161	1961	1722	07
[γὰρ]	μᾶλλον	κρεῖσσον·		τὸ	δὲ	ἐπιμένειν	ἐν	τῇ
for	more	better;		the	but	to stay on	in	the

4561	316	1223	1473	**25**	2532	3778
σαρκὶ	ἀναγκαιότερον	δι᾽	ὑμᾶς.		καὶ	τοῦτο
flesh	more necessary	because of	you.		And	this

3982	3609a	3754	3306	2532	3887	3956	1473
πεποιθὼς	οἶδα	ὅτι	μενῶ	καὶ	παραμενῶ	πᾶσιν	ὑμῖν
being persuaded	I know	that	I will stay	and	I will stay along	to all	you

1519	08	1473	4297	2532	5479	06	4102
εἰς	τὴν	ὑμῶν	προκοπὴν	καὶ	χαρὰν	τῆς	πίστεως,
for	the	of you	progress	and	joy	of the	trust,

26 | 2443 | 09 | 2745 | 1473 | 4052 | 1722 | 5547 |
| | ἵνα | τὸ | καύχημα | ὑμῶν | περισσεύῃ | ἐν | Χριστῷ |
| | that | the | brag | of you | might exceed | in | Christ |

2424	1722	1473	1223	06	1699	3952	3825	4314
Ἰησοῦ	ἐν	ἐμοὶ	διὰ	τῆς	ἐμῆς	παρουσίας	πάλιν	πρὸς
Jesus	in	me	through	the	my	presence	again	toward

1473	**27**	3441	516	010	2098	02
ὑμᾶς.		Μόνον	ἀξίως	τοῦ	εὐαγγελίου	τοῦ
you.		Alone	worthily	of the	good message	of the

5547	4176	2443	1535	2064	2532
Χριστοῦ	πολιτεύεσθε,	ἵνα	εἴτε	ἐλθὼν	καὶ
Christ	act as citizen,	that	whether	having come	and

3708	1473	1535	548	191	024	4012
ἰδὼν	ὑμᾶς εἴτε		ἀπὼν	ἀκούω	τὰ	περὶ
having seen	you whether		being absent	I hear	the	about

1473	3754	4739	1722	1520	4151	1520	5590
ὑμῶν,	ὅτι	στήκετε	ἐν	ἑνὶ	πνεύματι,	μιᾷ	ψυχῇ
you,	that	you stand	in	one	spirit,	in one	soul

4866	07	4102	010	2098
συναθλοῦντες	τῇ	πίστει	τοῦ	εὐαγγελίου
struggling together	in the	trust	of the	good message

28 | 2532 | 3361 | 4426 | 1722 | 3367 | 5259 | 014 |
| | καὶ | μὴ | πτυρόμενοι | ἐν | μηδενὶ | ὑπὸ | τῶν |
| | and | not | being frightened | in | nothing | by | the |

480	3748	1510	846	1732
ἀντικειμένων,	ἥτις	ἐστὶν	αὐτοῖς	ἔνδειξις
ones lying against,	which	is	to them	demonstration

684	1473	1161	4991	2532	3778	575
ἀπωλείας,	ὑμῶν	δὲ	σωτηρίας,	καὶ	τοῦτο	ἀπὸ
of destruction,	of you	but	deliverance,	and	this	from

2316	**29**	3754	1473	5483	09	5228
θεοῦ·		ὅτι	ὑμῖν	ἐχαρίσθη	τὸ	ὑπὲρ
God.		That	to you	it was favored	the	on behalf of

5547	3756	3441	09	1519	846	4100	235	2532
Χριστοῦ,	οὐ	μόνον	τὸ	εἰς	αὐτὸν	πιστεύειν	ἀλλὰ	καὶ
Christ,	not	alone	the	in	him	to trust	but	also

09   5228   846   3958   **30** 04   846   73
τὸ ὑπὲρ   αὐτοῦ πάσχειν,   τὸν αὐτὸν ἀγῶνα
the on behalf of him to suffer,   the same contest

2192   3634   3708   1722 1473 2532 3568 191   1722
ἔχοντες, οἷον εἴδετε ἐν ἐμοὶ καὶ νῦν ἀκούετε ἐν
having,   which you saw in me and now you hear in

1473   **2:1** 1487 5100 3767 3874   1722 5547
ἐμοί.   Εἴ τις οὖν παράκλησις ἐν Χριστῷ,
me.   If some then encouragement in Christ,

1487 5100 3890   26   1487 5100 2842
εἴ τι παραμύθιον ἀγάπης, εἴ τις κοινωνία
if some comfort   of love, if some partnership

4151   1487 5100 4698   2532 3628
πνεύματος, εἴ τις σπλάγχνα καὶ οἰκτιρμοί,
of spirit, if some affections and compassions,

2 4137   1473 08   5479   2443 012 846
πληρώσατέ μου τὴν χαρὰν ἵνα τὸ αὐτὸ
fill   of me the joy that the same

5426   08 846   26   2192
φρονῆτε,   τὴν αὐτὴν ἀγάπην ἔχοντες
you might think, the same love having

4861   012 1520 5426   **3** 3367   2596
σύμψυχοι,   τὸ ἓν φρονοῦντες,   μηδὲν κατ᾽
together in soul the one thinking,   nothing by

2052   3366   2596 2754   235
ἐριθείαν   μηδὲ κατὰ κενοδοξίαν, ἀλλὰ
selfish ambition but not by empty splendor, but

07   5012   240   2233
τῇ ταπεινοφροσύνῃ ἀλλήλους ἡγούμενοι
in the humblemindedness one another considering

5242   1438   **4** 3361 024 1438   1538
ὑπερέχοντας ἑαυτῶν,   μὴ τὰ ἑαυτῶν ἕκαστος
excelling yourselves, not the of yourselves each

4648   235 2532 024 2087   1538
σκοποῦντες ἀλλὰ καὶ τὰ ἑτέρων ἕκαστοι.
looking carefully but also the of others each.

5 3778 5426   1722 1473 3739 2532 1722 5547
Τοῦτο φρονεῖτε ἐν ὑμῖν ὃ καὶ ἐν Χριστῷ
This think in you which also in Christ

2424   3739 1722 3444   2316   5225   3756
Ἰησοῦ, **6** ὃς ἐν μορφῇ θεοῦ ὑπάρχων οὐχ
Jesus, who in form of God existing not

725   2233   012 1510 2470 2316   **7** 235
ἁρπαγμὸν ἡγήσατο τὸ εἶναι ἴσα θεῷ, ἀλλὰ
seizure considered the to be equal to God, but

1438   2758   3444   1401   2983   1722
ἑαυτὸν ἐκένωσεν μορφὴν δούλου λαβών, ἐν
himself he emptied form of slave having taken, in

3667   444   1096   2532 4976   2147
ὁμοιώματι ἀνθρώπων γενόμενος· καὶ σχήματι εὑρεθεὶς
likeness of men becoming; and in shape being found

5613 444   **8** 5013   1438   1096   5255
ὡς ἄνθρωπος ἐταπείνωσεν ἑαυτὸν γενόμενος ὑπήκοος
as man   he humbled himself becoming obedient

3360 2288   2288   1161 4716   **9** 1352   2532
μέχρι θανάτου, θανάτου δὲ σταυροῦ. διὸ καὶ
until death, of death but of cross. Wherefore also

01 2316 846   5251   2532 5483   846
ὁ θεὸς αὐτὸν ὑπερύψωσεν καὶ ἐχαρίσατο αὐτῷ
the God him elevated beyond and he favored to him

012 3686   012 5228 3956 3686   **10** 2443 1722 011
τὸ ὄνομα τὸ ὑπὲρ πᾶν ὄνομα, ἵνα ἐν τῷ
the name the above all name,   that in the

3686   2424   3956 1119 2578   2032   2532
ὀνόματι Ἰησοῦ πᾶν γόνυ κάμψη ἐπουρανίων καὶ
name   of Jesus all knee might bow on heavens and

1919   2532 2709   **11** 2532 3956 1100
ἐπιγείων καὶ καταχθονίων καὶ πᾶσα γλῶσσα
on earths and subterraneans and all tongue

of suffering for him as well—
[30]since you are having the
same struggle that you saw
I had and now hear that I
still have.

CHAPTER 2

If then there is any
encouragement in Christ,
any consolation from
love, any sharing in the
Spirit, any compassion
and sympathy, [2]make my
joy complete: be of the same
mind, having the same love,
being in full accord and of
one mind. [3]Do nothing
from selfish ambition or
conceit, but in humility
regard others as better
than yourselves. [4]Let each
of you look not to your
own interests, but to the
interests of others. [5]Let the
same mind be in you that
was[a] in Christ Jesus,
[6]who, though he was in
    the form of God,
    did not regard equality
       with God
    as something to be
       exploited,
[7] but emptied himself,
    taking the form of a
       slave,
    being born in human
       likeness.
    And being found in
       human form,
[8] he humbled himself
    and became obedient to
       the point of death—
    even death on a cross.

[9]Therefore God also highly
    exalted him
    and gave him the name
    that is above every
       name,
[10]so that at the name
    of Jesus
    every knee should bend,
    in heaven and on earth
       and under the earth,
[11]and every tongue should
    confess

a Or *that you have*

that Jesus Christ is Lord, to the glory of God the Father.

12 Therefore, my beloved, just as you have always obeyed me, not only in my presence, but much more now in my absence, work out your own salvation with fear and trembling; [13]for it is God who is at work in you, enabling you both to will and to work for his good pleasure.

14 Do all things without murmuring and arguing, [15]so that you may be blameless and innocent, children of God without blemish in the midst of a crooked and perverse generation, in which you shine like stars in the world. [16]It is by your holding fast to the word of life that I can boast on the day of Christ that I did not run in vain or labor in vain. [17]But even if I am being poured out as a libation over the sacrifice and the offering of your faith, I am glad and rejoice with all of you— [18]and in the same way you also must be glad and rejoice with me.

19 I hope in the Lord Jesus to send Timothy to you soon, so that I may be cheered by news of you. [20]I have no one like him who will be genuinely concerned for your welfare.

1843		3754	2962	2424	5547	1519
ἐξομολογήσηται		ὅτι	κύριος	Ἰησοῦς	Χριστὸς	εἰς
might confess out, (")		Master	Jesus	Christ		into

1391	2316	3962		5620	27	1473
δόξαν	θεοῦ	πατρός.	12 "Ωστε,	ἀγαπητοί	μου,
splendor of	God	Father.	So that,	loved	of me,

2531	3842	5219		3361	5613	1722	07	3952
καθὼς	πάντοτε	ὑπηκούσατε,	μὴ	ὡς	ἐν	τῇ	παρουσίᾳ
just as	always	you obeyed,	not	as	in	the presence

1473	3441	235	3568	4183	3123	1722	07	666
μου	μόνον	ἀλλὰ	νῦν	πολλῷ	μᾶλλον	ἐν	τῇ	ἀπουσίᾳ
of me	alone	but	now	much	more	in	the absence

1473	3326	5401	2532	5156	08	1438
μου,	μετὰ	φόβου	καὶ	τρόμου	τὴν	ἑαυτῶν
of me,	with	fear	and	trembling	the	of yourselves

4991		2716		13	2316	1063	1510	01
σωτηρίαν	κατεργάζεσθε·		θεὸς	γάρ	ἐστιν	ὁ
deliverance	work thoroughly;	God	for	is	the one

1754	1722	1473	2532	012	2309		2532	012	1754
ἐνεργῶν	ἐν	ὑμῖν	καὶ	τὸ	θέλειν	καὶ	τὸ	ἐνεργεῖν
operating	in	you	both the	to want	and	the	to operate

5228		06	2107		3956	4160	5565
ὑπὲρ	τῆς	εὐδοκίας.	14 Πάντα	ποιεῖτε	χωρὶς
on behalf	of the	good thought.	All	do	without

1112		2532	1261		15	2443	1096
γογγυσμῶν	καὶ	διαλογισμῶν,	ἵνα	γένησθε
grumblings	and	reasonings,	that	you might become

273		2532	185		5043	2316	298
ἄμεμπτοι	καὶ	ἀκέραιοι,	τέκνα	θεοῦ	ἄμωμα
faultless	and	innocent,	children	of God	blameless

3319	1074		4646	2532
μέσον	γενεᾶς	σκολιᾶς	καὶ
middle	of generation	crooked	and

1294		1722	3739	5316		5613
διεστραμμένης,	ἐν	οἷς	φαίνεσθε	ὡς
having been perverted,	in	which	you shine	as

5458	1722	2889	16	3056	2222	1907		1519
φωστῆρες	ἐν	κόσμῳ,	λόγον	ζωῆς	ἐπέχοντες,	εἰς
lights	in	world,	word	of life	holding on,	in

2745	1473	1519	2250	5547		3754	3756	1519
καύχημα	ἐμοὶ	εἰς	ἡμέραν	Χριστοῦ,	ὅτι	οὐκ	εἰς
brag	to me	in	day	of Christ,	that	not	in

2756	5143	3761		1519	2756	2872		235
κενὸν	ἔδραμον	οὐδὲ	εἰς	κενὸν	ἐκοπίασα.	17 Ἀλλὰ
empty	I ran	but not	in	empty	I labored.	But

1487	2532	4689		1909	07	2378		2532
εἰ	καὶ	σπένδομαι	ἐπὶ	τῇ	θυσίᾳ	καὶ
if	also	I am being poured	on	the	sacrifice	and
		out as a libation				

3009		06		4102	1473	5463		2532
λειτουργίᾳ	τῆς	πίστεως	ὑμῶν,	χαίρω	καὶ
service	of the	trust	of you,	I rejoice	and

4796		3956	1473	18	012	1161	846	2532
συγχαίρω	πᾶσιν	ὑμῖν·	τὸ	δὲ	αὐτὸ	καὶ
I rejoice together	in all	you;	the	but	same	also

1473	5463	2532	4796		1473	19	1679
ὑμεῖς	χαίρετε	καὶ	συγχαίρετέ	μοι.	Ἐλπίζω
you	rejoice	and	rejoice together	in me.	I hope

1161	1722	2962	2424	5095	5030	3992
δὲ	ἐν	κυρίῳ	Ἰησοῦ	Τιμόθεον	ταχέως	πέμψαι
but	in	Master	Jesus	Timothy	quickly	to send

1473	2443	2504	2174		1097
ὑμῖν,	ἵνα	κἀγὼ	εὐψυχῶ	γνοὺς
to you,	that	also I	might have good soul	having known

024	4012	1473	20	3762	1063	2192	2473		3748
τὰ	περὶ	ὑμῶν.	οὐδένα	γὰρ	ἔχω	ἰσόψυχον,	ὅστις
the	about	you.	No one	for	I have	equal soul,	who

1104		024	4012	1473	3309		013
γνησίως	τὰ	περὶ	ὑμῶν	μεριμνήσει,	21 οἱ
legitimately	the	about	you	will be anxious,	the

3956   1063 024   1438   2212   3756 024
πάντες γὰρ   τὰ   ἑαυτῶν   ζητοῦσιν, οὐ   τὰ
all   for   the   of themselves   seek,   not   the

.2424   5547   08 1161   1382   846
'Ιησοῦ   Χριστοῦ. 22 τὴν δὲ   δοκιμὴν   αὐτοῦ
of Jesus Christ.   The but   approval   of him

1097   3754 5613 3962   5043   4862 1473
γινώσκετε, ὅτι   ὡς   πατρὶ τέκνον σὺν   ἐμοὶ
you know,   that as   father child   with me

1398   1519 012 2098   3778   3303   3767
ἐδούλευσεν εἰς   τὸ   εὐαγγέλιον. 23 τοῦτον μὲν   οὖν
he slaved   for   the good message. This   indeed then

1679   3992   5613 302 872   024   4012 1473
ἐλπίζω πέμψαι ὡς   ἂν   ἀφίδω   τὰ   περὶ ἐμὲ
I hope to send as   -   I might see off the about me

1824   3982   1161 1722 2962   3754 2532
ἐξαυτῆς, 24 πέποιθα δὲ   ἐν   κυρίῳ ὅτι   καὶ
at once;   I am persuaded but in Master that also

846   5030   2064   316   1161
αὐτὸς   ταχέως ἐλεύσομαι. 25 'Αναγκαῖον   δὲ
myself quickly I will come. Necessary   but

2233   1891   04   80   2532 4904
ἡγησάμην   'Επαφρόδιτον τὸν ἀδελφὸν καὶ συνεργὸν
I considered Epaphroditus the brother and co-worker

2532 4961   1473   1473   1161 652   2532
καὶ   συστρατιώτην   μου,   ὑμῶν   δὲ   ἀπόστολον καὶ
and   co-soldier   of me, of you but delegate and

3011   06   5532   1473   3992   4314   1473
λειτουργὸν τῆς   χρείας μου,   πέμψαι πρὸς   ὑμᾶς,
servant   of the need   of me, to send toward you,

   1894   1971   1510   3956   1473 2532
26 ἐπειδὴ ἐπιποθῶν   ἦν   πάντας ὑμᾶς καὶ
   since   +desiring longingly he was+ all   you and

85   1360 191   3754 770
ἀδημονῶν,   διότι ἠκούσατε ὅτι ἠσθένησεν.
being distressed, that you heard that he was weak.

   2532 1063 770   3897   2288
27 καὶ   γὰρ ἠσθένησεν   παραπλήσιον   θανάτῳ·
   Even for he was weak neighbor along to death;

235 01   2316 1653   846   3756 846   1161
ἀλλὰ ὁ   θεὸς ἠλέησεν   αὐτόν,   οὐκ αὐτὸν δὲ
but the God showed mercy him,   not him   but

3441   235   2532 1473 2443 3361 3077 1909 3077
μόνον   ἀλλὰ καὶ ἐμέ, ἵνα μὴ   λύπην ἐπὶ λύπην
alone   but also me,   that not grief upon grief

2192   4709   3767 3992   846   2443
σχῶ. 28 σπουδαιοτέρως   οὖν ἔπεμψα αὐτόν,   ἵνα
I might have. More diligently then I sent him,   that

3708   846   3825 5463   2504
ἰδόντες   αὐτὸν πάλιν χαρῆτε   κἀγὼ
having seen him   again you might rejoice and I

253   1510   4327   3767 846   1722
ἀλυπότερος ὦ. 29 προσδέχεσθε οὖν αὐτὸν ἐν
ungrief more I might be. Await   then him   in

2962 3326 3956 5479 2532 016 5108   1784
κυρίῳ μετὰ πάσης χαρᾶς καὶ τοὺς τοιούτους ἐντίμους
Master with all joy   and the such ones in honor

2192   30 3754 1223 012 2041 5547   3360
ἔχετε,   ὅτι   διὰ   τὸ ἔργον Χριστοῦ   μέχρι
you hold,   because through the work of Christ until

2288   1448   3851   07   5590   2443
θανάτου ἤγγισεν παραβολευσάμενος τῇ ψυχῇ, ἵνα
death   he neared having risked   the soul, that

378   012 1473   5303   06 4314   1473
ἀναπληρώσῃ τὸ ὑμῶν   ὑστέρημα   τῆς πρός   με
he might fill up the of you lack   the toward me

3009   012 3062   80   1473
λειτουργίας. 3:1 Τὸ λοιπόν, ἀδελφοί μου,
service.   The remaining, brothers of me,

21All of them are seeking their own interests, not those of Jesus Christ. 22But Timothy's[a] worth you know, how like a son with a father he has served with me in the work of the gospel. 23I hope therefore to send him as soon as I see how things go with me; 24and I trust in the Lord that I will also come soon.

25Still, I think it necessary to send to you Epaphroditus—my brother and co-worker and fellow soldier, your messenger[b] and minister to my need; 26for he has been longing for[c] all of you, and has been distressed because you heard that he was ill. 27He was indeed so ill that he nearly died. But God had mercy on him, and not only on him but on me also, so that I would not have one sorrow after another. 28I am the more eager to send him, therefore, in order that you may rejoice at seeing him again, and that I may be less anxious. 29Welcome him then in the Lord with all joy, and honor such people, 30because he came close to death for the work of Christ,[d] risking his life to make up for those services that you could not give me.

CHAPTER 3

Finally, my brothers and sisters,[e]

a Gk his
b Gk apostle
c Other ancient authorities read longing to see
d Other ancient authorities read of the Lord
e Gk my brothers

rejoice*a* in the Lord.

To write the same things to you is not troublesome to me, and for you it is a safeguard.

2 Beware of the dogs, beware of the evil workers, beware of those who mutilate the flesh!*b*
3For it is we who are the circumcision, who worship in the Spirit of God*c* and boast in Christ Jesus and have no confidence in the flesh— 4even though I, too, have reason for confidence in the flesh.

If anyone else has reason to be confident in the flesh, I have more: 5circumcised on the eighth day, a member of the people of Israel, of the tribe of Benjamin, a Hebrew born of Hebrews; as to the law, a Pharisee; 6as to zeal, a persecutor of the church; as to righteousness under the law, blameless.

7 Yet whatever gains I had, these I have come to regard as loss because of Christ. 8More than that, I regard everything as loss because of the surpassing value of knowing Christ Jesus my Lord. For his sake I have suffered the loss of all things, and I regard them as rubbish, in order that I may gain Christ 9and be found in him, not having a righteousness of my own that comes from the law, but one that comes through faith in Christ,*d* the righteousness from God based on faith. 10I want to know Christ*e* and the power of his resurrection and the sharing of his sufferings

a Or *farewell*
b Gk *the mutilation*
c Other ancient authorities read *worship God in spirit*
d Or *through the faith of Christ*
e Gk *him*

5463	1722	2962		024	846	1125	1473	1473
χαίρετε	ἐν	κυρίῳ.		τὰ	αὐτὰ	γράφειν	ὑμῖν	ἐμοὶ
rejoice	in	Master.		The	same	to write	to you	to me

3303	3756	3636		1473	1161	804	2	991
μὲν	οὐκ	ὀκνηρόν,		ὑμῖν	δὲ	ἀσφαλές.		Βλέπετε
indeed	not	troublesome,		to you	but	secure.		Look

016	2965	991	016	2556	2040	991	08
τοὺς	κύνας,	βλέπετε	τοὺς	κακοὺς	ἐργάτας,	βλέπετε	τὴν
the	dogs,	look	the	bad	workers,	look	the

2699	3	1473	1063	1510	05	4061	013
κατατομήν.		ἡμεῖς	γάρ	ἐσμεν	ἡ	περιτομή,	οἱ
cut down.	We	for	are	the	circumcision,	the ones

4151	2316	3000	2532	2744	1722
πνεύματι	θεοῦ	λατρεύοντες	καὶ	καυχώμενοι	ἐν
in spirit	of God	serving	and	bragging	in

5547	2424	2532	3756	1722	4561	3982
Χριστῷ	Ἰησοῦ	καὶ	οὐκ	ἐν	σαρκὶ	πεποιθότες,
Christ	Jesus	and	not	in	flesh	having persuaded,

4	2539	1473	2192	4006	2532	1722	4561
	καίπερ	ἐγὼ	ἔχων	πεποίθησιν	καὶ	ἐν	σαρκί.
	and indeed	I	having	persuasion	and	in	flesh.

1487	5100	1380	243	3982	1722	4561
Εἴ	τις	δοκεῖ	ἄλλος	πεποιθέναι	ἐν	σαρκί,
If	some	thinks	other	to be persuaded	in	flesh,

1473	3123	4061	3637	1537	1085
ἐγὼ	μᾶλλον· 5	περιτομῇ	ὀκταήμερος,	ἐκ	γένους
I	more;	in circumcision	eighth day,	from	kind

2474	5443	958	1445	1537	1445	2596
Ἰσραήλ,	φυλῆς	Βενιαμίν,	Ἑβραῖος	ἐξ	Ἑβραίων,	κατὰ
Israel,	tribe	Benjamin,	Hebrew	from	Hebrews,	by

3551	5330	6	2596	2205	1377	08
νόμον	Φαρισαῖος,		κατὰ	ζῆλος	διώκων	τὴν
law	Pharisee,	by	jealousy	pursuing	the

1577	2596	1343	08	1722	3551	1096
ἐκκλησίαν,	κατὰ	δικαιοσύνην	τὴν	ἐν	νόμῳ	γενόμενος
assembly,	by	rightness	the	in	law	becoming

273	7	235	3748	1510	1473	2771	3778
ἄμεμπτος.		Ἀλλὰ	ἅτινα	ἦν	μοι	κέρδη,	ταῦτα
faultless.	But	what	was	to me	gains,	these

2233	1223	04	5547	2209	235
ἥγημαι	διὰ	τὸν	Χριστὸν	ζημίαν. 8	ἀλλὰ
I have considered	because of	the	Christ	loss.	But

3304	2532	2233	3956	2209	1510
μενοῦνγε	καὶ	ἡγοῦμαι	πάντα	ζημίαν	εἶναι
on the contrary	also	I consider	all	loss	to be

1223	012	5242	06	1108	5547	2424
διὰ	τὸ	ὑπερέχον	τῆς	γνώσεως	Χριστοῦ	Ἰησοῦ
through	the	excelling	of the	knowledge	of Christ	Jesus

02	2962	1473	1223	3739	024	3956	2210
τοῦ	κυρίου	μου,	δι’	ὃν	τὰ	πάντα	ἐζημιώθην,
the	Master	of me,	through	whom	the	all	I lost,

2532	2233	4657	2443	5547	2770
καὶ	ἡγοῦμαι	σκύβαλα,	ἵνα	Χριστὸν	κερδήσω
and	I consider	garbages,	that	Christ	I might gain

9	2532	2147	1722	846	3361	2192	1699	1343
	καὶ	εὑρεθῶ	ἐν	αὐτῷ,	μὴ	ἔχων	ἐμὴν	δικαιοσύνην
	and	be found	in	him,	not	having	my	rightness

08	1537	3551	235	08	1223	4102	5547	08
τὴν	ἐκ	νόμου	ἀλλὰ	τὴν	διὰ	πίστεως	Χριστοῦ,	τὴν
the	from	law	but	the	through	trust	of Christ,	the

1537	2316	1343	1909	07	4102	10	010
ἐκ	θεοῦ	δικαιοσύνην	ἐπὶ	τῇ	πίστει,		τοῦ
from	God	rightness	upon	the	trust,		of the

1097	846	2532	08	1411	06	386
γνῶναι	αὐτὸν	καὶ	τὴν	δύναμιν	τῆς	ἀναστάσεως
to know	him	and	the	power	of the	standing up

846	2532	08	2842	022	3804	846
αὐτοῦ	καὶ	[τὴν]	κοινωνίαν	τῶν	παθημάτων	αὐτοῦ,
of him	and	the	partnership	of the	sufferings	of him,

4832	03	2288	846	11	1487 4458
συμμορφιζόμενος	τῷ	θανάτῳ	αὐτοῦ,		εἴ πως
being conformed	to the	death	of him,		if perhaps

2658	1519 08	1815	08 1537
καταντήσω	εἰς τὴν	ἐξανάστασιν	τὴν ἐκ
I might arrive	in the	standing up out	the from

3498	12	3756 3754 2235	2983	2228 2235
νεκρῶν.		Οὐχ ὅτι ἤδη	ἔλαβον	ἢ ἤδη
dead.		Not that already	I received	or already

5048	1377	1161 1487 2532
τετελείωμαι,	διώκω	δὲ εἰ καὶ
I have been completed,	I pursue	but if also

2638	1909 3739 2532 2638	5259
καταλάβω,	ἐφ᾽ ᾧ καὶ κατελήμφθην	ὑπὸ
I might overtake	on which also I was overtaken	by

5547 2424	13	80	1473 1683	3756 3049
Χριστοῦ Ἰησοῦ.		ἀδελφοί,	ἐγὼ ἐμαυτὸν	οὐ λογίζομαι
Christ Jesus.		Brothers,	I myself	not reason

2638	1520 1161 024	3303 3694
κατειληφέναι·	ἓν δέ, τὰ	μὲν ὀπίσω
to have overtaken;	one but, the	things indeed after

1950	023 1161 1715	1901
ἐπιλανθανόμενος	τοῖς δὲ ἔμπροσθεν	ἐπεκτεινόμενος,
forgetting	the but in front of	stretching forward,

14	2596 4649	1377	1519 012 1017	06	507
	κατὰ σκοπὸν	διώκω	εἰς τὸ βραβεῖον	τῆς	ἄνω
	by goal	I pursue	to the prize	of the	up

2821	02	2316 1722 5547	2424	15	3745
κλήσεως	τοῦ	θεοῦ ἐν Χριστῷ	Ἰησοῦ.		Ὅσοι
call	of the	God in Christ	Jesus.		As many as

3767 5046	3778 5426	2532 1487 5100
οὖν τέλειοι,	τοῦτο φρονῶμεν·	καὶ εἴ τι
then complete,	this we might think;	and if some

2088	5426	2532 3778 01 2316 1473
ἑτέρως	φρονεῖτε,	καὶ τοῦτο ὁ θεὸς ὑμῖν
otherwise	you think,	also this the God to you

601	16	4133	1519 3739 5348	011
ἀποκαλύψει·		πλὴν	εἰς ὃ ἐφθάσαμεν,	τῷ
will uncover;		except	into what we arrived,	in the

846 4748	17	4831	1473 1096	80
αὐτῷ στοιχεῖν.		Συμμιμηταί	μου γίνεσθε,	ἀδελφοί,
same to walk.		Co-imitators	of me become,	brothers,

2532 4648	016 3779 4043	2531
καὶ σκοπεῖτε	τοὺς οὕτω περιπατοῦντας	καθὼς
and look carefully	the thusly walking around	just as

2192	5179	1473	18	4183	1063 4043
ἔχετε	τύπον	ἡμᾶς.		πολλοὶ	γὰρ περιπατοῦσιν
you have	example	us.		Many	for walk around

3739 4178	3004	1473	3568 1161 2532
οὓς πολλάκις	ἔλεγον	ὑμῖν,	νῦν δὲ καὶ
who frequently	I was saying	to you,	now but also

2799 3004	016 2190 02	4716 02
κλαίων λέγω,	τοὺς ἐχθροὺς τοῦ	σταυροῦ τοῦ
crying I say,	the hostile of the	cross of the

5547,	19	3739	09 5056	684
Χριστοῦ,		ὧν	τὸ τέλος	ἀπώλεια,
Christ,		of whom	the completion	destruction,

3739	01 2316 05	2836	2532 05	1391	1722
ὧν	ὁ θεὸς ἡ	κοιλία	καὶ ἡ	δόξα	ἐν
of whom	the God the	stomach	and the	splendor	in

07 152	846	013	024 1919	5426
τῇ αἰσχύνῃ	αὐτῶν,	οἱ	τὰ ἐπίγεια	φρονοῦντες.
the shame	of them,	the ones	the on earth	thinking.

20	1473	1063 09	4175	1722 3772	5225
	ἡμῶν	γὰρ τὸ	πολίτευμα	ἐν οὐρανοῖς	ὑπάρχει,
	Of us	for the	citizenship	in heavens	exists,

1537 3739	2532 4990	553	2962	2424
ἐξ οὗ	καὶ σωτῆρα	ἀπεκδεχόμεθα	κύριον	Ἰησοῦν
from which	also deliverer	we await	Master	Jesus

by becoming like him in his death, [11]if somehow I may attain the resurrection from the dead.

[12]Not that I have already obtained this or have already reached the goal;[a] but I press on to make it my own, because Christ Jesus has made me his own. [13]Beloved,[b] I do not consider that I have made it my own;[c] but this one thing I do: forgetting what lies behind and straining forward to what lies ahead, [14]I press on toward the goal for the prize of the heavenly[d] call of God in Christ Jesus. [15]Let those of us then who are mature be of the same mind; and if you think differently about anything, this too God will reveal to you. [16]Only let us hold fast to what we have attained.

[17]Brothers and sisters,[b] join in imitating me, and observe those who live according to the example you have in us. [18]For many live as enemies of the cross of Christ; I have often told you of them, and now I tell you even with tears. [19]Their end is destruction; their god is the belly; and their glory is in their shame; their minds are set on earthly things. [20]But our citizenship[e] is in heaven, and it is from there that we are expecting a Savior, the Lord Jesus

a Or have already been made perfect
b Gk Brothers
c Other ancient authorities read my own yet
d Gk upward
e Or commonwealth

Christ. ²¹He will transform the body of our humiliationᵃ that it may be conformed to the body of his glory,ᵇ by the power that also enables him to make all things subject to himself. ⁴:¹Therefore, my brothers and sisters,ᶜ whom I love and long for, my joy and crown, stand firm in the Lord in this way, my beloved.

2 I urge Euodia and I urge Syntyche to be of the same mind in the Lord. ³Yes, and I ask you also, my loyal companion,ᵈ help these women, for they have struggled beside me in the work of the gospel, together with Clement and the rest of my co-workers, whose names are in the book of life.

4 Rejoiceᵉ in the Lord always; again I will say, Rejoice.ᵉ ⁵Let your gentleness be known to everyone. The Lord is near. ⁶Do not worry about anything, but in everything by prayer and supplication with thanksgiving let your requests be made known to God. ⁷And the peace of God, which surpasses all understanding, will guard your hearts and your minds in Christ Jesus.

8 Finally, beloved,ᶠ whatever is true, whatever is honorable, whatever is just, whatever is pure, whatever is pleasing, whatever is commendable, if there is any excellence and if

---

ᵃ Or our humble bodies
ᵇ Or his glorious body
ᶜ Gk my brothers
ᵈ Or loyal Syzygus
ᵉ Or Farewell
ᶠ Gk brothers

5547   **21**   3739   3345   012   4983   06
Χριστόν,   ὃς   μετασχηματίσει   τὸ   σῶμα   τῆς
Christ,   who   will reshape   the body of the
5014   1473   4833   011   4983   06
ταπεινώσεως ἡμῶν σύμμορφον τῷ   σώματι τῆς
humility   of us conformed to the body   of the
1391   846   2596 08   1753   010   1410
δόξης   αὐτοῦ κατὰ τὴν ἐνέργειαν τοῦ   δύνασθαι
splendor of him by   the operation of the to be able
846   2532 5293   846   024 3956   **4:1**   5620
αὐτὸν καὶ ὑποτάξαι αὐτῷ τὰ πάντα.   Ὥστε,
him   and   to subject to him the all.   So that,
80   1473   27   2532 1973   5479 2532
ἀδελφοί μου ἀγαπητοὶ καὶ ἐπιπόθητοι, χαρὰ καὶ
brothers of me loved   and desired ones, joy and
4735   1473   3779   4739   1722 2962   27
στέφανός μου, οὕτως στήκετε ἐν κυρίῳ, ἀγαπητοί.
crown   of me, thusly stand   in Master, loved ones.
2   2136   3870   2532 4941   3870   012
Εὐοδίαν παρακαλῶ   καὶ   Συντύχην παρακαλῶ   τὸ
Euodia I encourage and   Syntyche I encourage the
846   5426   1722 2962   **3**   3483 2065 2532 1473
αὐτὸ φρονεῖν ἐν κυρίῳ.   ναὶ ἐρωτῶ καὶ σέ,
same to think in   Master.   Yes I ask also you,
1103   4805   4815   846   3748
γνήσιε   σύζυγε,   συλλαμβάνου αὐταῖς, αἵτινες
legitimate yoke fellow, help together them,   who
1722 011 2098   4866   1473 3326 2532
ἐν   τῷ εὐαγγελίῳ συνήθλησάν   μοι   μετὰ καὶ
in   the good message struggled with me   with also
2815   2532 014 3062   4904   1473
Κλήμεντος καὶ τῶν λοιπῶν   συνεργῶν μου,
Clement   and the remaining co-workers of me,
3739   021 3686   1722 976   2222   **4**   5463   1722
ὧν   τὰ ὀνόματα ἐν βίβλῳ ζωῆς.   Χαίρετε ἐν
of whom, the names   in   book of life.   Rejoice in
2962   3842   3825 3004   5463   **5** 09
κυρίῳ πάντοτε· πάλιν ἐρῶ,   χαίρετε.   τὸ
Master always; again I will say, rejoice.   The
1933   1473   1097   3956   444   01
ἐπιεικὲς ὑμῶν γνωσθήτω πᾶσιν ἀνθρώποις. ὁ
gentle   of you let be known to all men.   The
2962   1451   **6**   3367   3309   235   1722 3956
κύριος ἐγγύς.   μηδὲν   μεριμνᾶτε, ἀλλ' ἐν παντὶ
Master near.   Nothing be anxious, but in   all
07   4335   2532 07   1162   3326 2169   021
τῇ προσευχῇ καὶ τῇ δεήσει μετὰ εὐχαριστίας τὰ
the prayer   and the request with good favor the
155   1473   1107   4314 04   2316
αἰτήματα ὑμῶν γνωριζέσθω   πρὸς τὸν θεόν.
askings of you let be made known to   the God.
7 2532 05   1515   02   2316 05   5242   3956
καὶ ἡ εἰρήνη τοῦ θεοῦ ἡ ὑπερέχουσα πάντα
And the peace of the God the excelling all
3563 5432   020 2588   1473   2532 024 3540
νοῦν φρουρήσει τὰς καρδίας ὑμῶν καὶ τὰ νοήματα
mind will guard the hearts of you and   the thoughts
1473   1722 5547   2424   012 3062   80
ὑμῶν ἐν Χριστῷ Ἰησοῦ. **8** Τὸ λοιπόν,   ἀδελφοί,
of you in   Christ Jesus.   The remaining, brothers,
3745   1510 227   3745   4586   3745
ὅσα   ἐστιν ἀληθῆ, ὅσα   σεμνά, ὅσα
as much as is   true, as much as grave, as much as
1342   3745   53   3745   4375
δίκαια, ὅσα   ἀγνά, ὅσα   προσφιλῆ,
right,   as much as pure, as much as pleasing,
3745   2163   1487 5100 703   2532 1487
ὅσα   εὔφημα,   εἴ τις ἀρετὴ καὶ εἴ
as much as good saying, if   some virtue and if

5100 1868	3778 3049	**9** 3739 2532
τις ἔπαινος,	ταῦτα λογίζεσθε·	ἃ καὶ
some praise,	on these reason;	what also

3129	2532 3880	2532 191	2532 3708
ἐμάθετε	καὶ παρελάβετε καὶ	ἠκούσατε καὶ	εἴδετε
you learned	and took along and	heard and	saw

1722 1473	3778 4238	2532 01	2316 06
ἐν ἐμοί,	ταῦτα πράσσετε·	καὶ ὁ	θεὸς τῆς
in me,	these practice;	and the	God of the

1515	1510	3326 1473	**10** 5463	1161 1722
εἰρήνης	ἔσται	μεθ’ ὑμῶν.	Ἐχάρην	δὲ ἐν
peace	will	be with you.	I rejoiced	but in

2962	3171	3754 2235	4218 330	012
κυρίῳ	μεγάλως	ὅτι ἤδη	ποτὲ ἀνεθάλετε	τὸ
Master	greatly	that already	then you revived	the

5228	1473	5426	1909 3739	2532 5426
ὑπὲρ	ἐμοῦ	φρονεῖν,	ἐφ’ ᾧ	καὶ ἐφρονεῖτε,
on behalf	of me	to think,	on which	also you thought,

170	1161	**11** 3756 3754	2596 5304
ἠκαιρεῖσθε	δέ.	οὐχ ὅτι	καθ’ ὑστέρησιν
you had no season	but.	Not that	by lack

3004	1473 1063 3129	1722	3739 1510
λέγω,	ἐγὼ γὰρ ἔμαθον	ἐν	οἷς εἰμι
I speak,	I for learned	in	what I am

842	1510	**12** 3609a	2532 5013
αὐτάρκης	εἶναι.	οἶδα καὶ	ταπεινοῦσθαι,
self-sufficient	to be.	I know both	to be humbled,

3609a 2532 4052	1722 3956	2532 1722 3956
οἶδα καὶ περισσεύειν·	ἐν παντὶ	καὶ ἐν πᾶσιν
I know also to exceed;	in all	and in all

3453	2532 5526	2532
μεμύημαι,	καὶ χορτάζεσθαι	καὶ
I have learned secret,	both to be satisfied	and

3983	2532 4052	2532 5302	**13** 3956
πεινᾶν	καὶ περισσεύειν	καὶ ὑστερεῖσθαι·	πάντα
to hunger	both to exceed	and to be in lack;	all

2480	1722 03 1743	1473	**14** 4133
ἰσχύω	ἐν τῷ ἐνδυναμοῦντί	με.	πλὴν
I am strong	in the one empowering	me.	Except

2573 4160	4790	1473 07
καλῶς ἐποιήσατε	συγκοινωνήσαντές	μου τῇ
well you did	being co-partners	of me in the

2347	**15** 3609a	1161 2532 1473	5374
θλίψει.	οἴδατε	δὲ καὶ ὑμεῖς,	Φιλιππήσιοι,
affliction.	Know	but also you,	Philippians,

3754 1722 746	010	2098	3753
ὅτι ἐν ἀρχῇ	τοῦ	εὐαγγελίου,	ὅτε
that in beginning	of the	good message,	when

1831	575 3109	3762	1473
ἐξῆλθον	ἀπὸ Μακεδονίας,	οὐδεμία	μοι
I went out	from Macedonia,	but not one	to me

1577	2841	1519 3056	1394	2532
ἐκκλησία	ἐκοινώνησεν	εἰς λόγον	δόσεως	καὶ
assembly	was partner	in word	of giving	and

3024a	1487 3361 1473	3441	**16** 3754	2532 1722
λήμψεως	εἰ μὴ ὑμεῖς	μόνοι,	ὅτι	καὶ ἐν
receiving	except you	alone,	because	also in

2332	2532 530	2532 1364	1519 08	5532
Θεσσαλονίκη	καὶ ἅπαξ	καὶ δὶς	εἰς τὴν	χρείαν
Thessalonica	both once	and twice	in the	need

1473 3992	**17** 3756 3754 1934	012 1390
μοι ἐπέμψατε.	οὐχ ὅτι ἐπιζητῶ	τὸ δόμα,
to me you sent.	Not that I seek after	the gift,

235 1934	04 2590	04 4121	1519
ἀλλὰ ἐπιζητῶ	τὸν καρπὸν	τὸν πλεονάζοντα	εἰς
but I seek after	the fruit	the one increasing	in

3056 1473	**18** 568	1161 3956	2532 4052
λόγον ὑμῶν.	ἀπέχω	δὲ πάντα	καὶ περισσεύω·
word of you.	I have back	but all	and I exceed;

there is anything worthy of praise, think about[a] these things. [9]Keep on doing the things that you have learned and received and heard and seen in me, and the God of peace will be with you.

10 I rejoice[b] in the Lord greatly that now at last you have revived your concern for me; indeed, you were concerned for me, but had no opportunity to show it.[c] [11]Not that I am referring to being in need; for I have learned to be content with whatever I have. [12]I know what it is to have little, and I know what it is to have plenty. In any and all circumstances I have learned the secret of being well-fed and of going hungry, of having plenty and of being in need. [13]I can do all things through him who strengthens me. [14]In any case, it was kind of you to share my distress.

15 You Philippians indeed know that in the early days of the gospel, when I left Macedonia, no church shared with me in the matter of giving and receiving, except you alone. [16]For even when I was in Thessalonica, you sent me help for my needs more than once. [17]Not that I seek the gift, but I seek the profit that accumulates to your account. [18]I have been paid in full and have more than enough;

---

a Gk take account of
b Gk I rejoiced
c Gk lacks to show it

I am fully satisfied, now that I have received from Epaphroditus the gifts you sent, a fragrant offering, a sacrifice acceptable and pleasing to God. [19]And my God will fully satisfy every need of yours according to his riches in glory in Christ Jesus. [20]To our God and Father be glory forever and ever. Amen.

21 Greet every saint in Christ Jesus. The friends[a] who are with me greet you. [22]All the saints greet you, especially those of the emperor's household.

23 The grace of the Lord Jesus Christ be with your spirit.[b]

[a] Gk brothers
[b] Other ancient authorities add Amen

4137	1209	3844	1891
πεπλήρωμαι	δεξάμενος	παρὰ	Ἐπαφροδίτου
I have been filled	having welcomed	from	Epaphroditus

024 3844	1473	3744	2175	2378
τὰ παρ'	ὑμῶν,	ὀσμὴν εὐωδίας,		θυσίαν
the from	you,	odor of good smell,		sacrifice

1184	2101	03	2316	19	01	1161	2316
δεκτήν,	εὐάρεστον	τῷ	θεῷ.		ὁ	δὲ	θεός
acceptable,	well-pleasing	to the	God.		The	but	God

1473	4137	3956	5532	1473	2596	012	4149
μου	πληρώσει	πᾶσαν	χρείαν	ὑμῶν	κατὰ	τὸ	πλοῦτος
of me	will fill	all	need	of you	by	the	rich

846	1722	1391	1722	5547	2424	20	03
αὐτοῦ	ἐν	δόξῃ	ἐν	Χριστῷ	Ἰησοῦ.		τῷ
of him	in	splendor	in	Christ	Jesus.		To the

1161	2316	2532	3962	1473	05	1391	1519	016
δὲ	θεῷ	καὶ	πατρὶ	ἡμῶν	ἡ	δόξα	εἰς	τοὺς
but	God	and	Father	of us	the	splendor	into	the

165	014	165	281	21	782	3956
αἰῶνας	τῶν	αἰώνων,	ἀμήν.		Ἀσπάσασθε	πάντα
ages	of the	ages,	amen.		Greet	all

40	1722	5547	2424	782	1473	013	4862
ἅγιον	ἐν	Χριστῷ	Ἰησοῦ.	ἀσπάζονται	ὑμᾶς	οἱ	σὺν
holy one	in	Christ	Jesus.	Greet	you	the	with

1473	80	22	782	1473	3956	013
ἐμοὶ	ἀδελφοί.		ἀσπάζονται	ὑμᾶς	πάντες	οἱ
me	brothers.		Greet	you	all	the

40	3122	1161	013	1537	06	2541
ἅγιοι,	μάλιστα	δὲ	οἱ	ἐκ	τῆς	Καίσαρος
holy ones,	especially	but	the	from	the	of Caesar

3614	23	05	5485	02	2962	2424	5547
οἰκίας.		Ἡ	χάρις	τοῦ	κυρίου	Ἰησοῦ	Χριστοῦ
house.		The	favor	of the	Master	Jesus	Christ

3326	010	4151	1473
μετὰ	τοῦ	πνεύματος	ὑμῶν.
with	the	spirit	of you.

COLOSSIANS

CHAPTER 1

Paul, an apostle of Christ Jesus by the will of God, and Timothy our brother,

2 To the saints and faithful brothers and sisters[a] in Christ in Colossae:

Grace to you and peace from God our Father.

3 In our prayers for you we always thank God, the Father of our Lord Jesus Christ, [4]for we have heard of your faith in Christ Jesus and of the love that you have for all the saints, [5]because of the hope laid up for you in heaven. You have heard of this hope before in the word of the truth, the gospel [6]that has come to you. Just as it is bearing fruit and growing in the whole world, so it has been bearing fruit among yourselves from the day you heard it and truly comprehended the grace of God. [7]This you learned from Epaphras, our beloved fellow servant.[b] He is a faithful minister of Christ on your[c] behalf, [8]and he has made known to us your love in the Spirit.

9 For this reason, since the day we heard it, we have not ceased praying for you and asking that you may be filled with the knowledge of God's[d] will in all spiritual wisdom and understanding,

---

[a] Gk brothers
[b] Gk slave
[c] Other ancient authorities read our
[d] Gk his

1:1
3972 652 5547 2424 1223 2307
Παῦλος ἀπόστολος Χριστοῦ Ἰησοῦ διὰ θελήματος
Paul delegate of Christ Jesus through want

2316 2532 5095 01 80 015 1722
θεοῦ καὶ Τιμόθεος ὁ ἀδελφὸς **2** τοῖς ἐν
of God and Timothy the brother to the ones in

2857 40 2532 4103 80 1722 5547
Κολοσσαῖς ἁγίοις καὶ πιστοῖς ἀδελφοῖς ἐν Χριστῷ,
Colossae holy and trustful brothers in Christ,

5485 1473 2532 1515 575 2316 3962 1473
χάρις ὑμῖν καὶ εἰρήνη ἀπὸ θεοῦ πατρὸς ἡμῶν.
favor to you and peace from God Father of us.

3
2168 03 2316 3962 02 2962
Εὐχαριστοῦμεν τῷ θεῷ πατρὶ τοῦ κυρίου
We give good favor to the God Father of the Master

1473 2424 5547 3842 4012 1473 4336
ἡμῶν Ἰησοῦ Χριστοῦ πάντοτε περὶ ὑμῶν προσευχόμενοι,
of us Jesus Christ always about you praying,

4
191 08 4102 1473 1722 5547 2424
ἀκούσαντες τὴν πίστιν ὑμῶν ἐν Χριστῷ Ἰησοῦ
having heard the trust of you in Christ Jesus

2532 08 26 3739 2192 1519 3956 016
καὶ τὴν ἀγάπην ἣν ἔχετε εἰς πάντας τοὺς
and the love which you have to all the

40 1223 08 1680 08 606
ἁγίους **5** διὰ τὴν ἐλπίδα τὴν ἀποκειμένην
holy ones through the hope the one being laid off

1473 1722 015 3772 3739 4257
ὑμῖν ἐν τοῖς οὐρανοῖς, ἣν προηκούσατε
to you in the heavens, which you heard before

1722 03 3056 06 225 010 2098 010
ἐν τῷ λόγῳ τῆς ἀληθείας τοῦ εὐαγγελίου **6** τοῦ
in the word the truth of the good message the one

3918 1519 1473 2531 2532 1722 3956 03
παρόντος εἰς ὑμᾶς, καθὼς καὶ ἐν παντὶ τῷ
being present in you, just as also in all the

2889 1510 2592 2532 837 2531
κόσμῳ ἐστιν καρποφορούμενον καὶ αὐξανόμενον καθὼς
world it is+ +bearing fruit and growing just as

2532 1722 1473 575 3739 2250 191 2532
καὶ ἐν ὑμῖν, ἀφ᾽ ἧς ἡμέρας ἠκούσατε καὶ
also in you, from which day you heard and

1921 08 5485 02 2316 1722 225 7 2531
ἐπέγνωτε τὴν χάριν τοῦ θεοῦ ἐν ἀληθείᾳ· καθὼς
perceived the favor of the God in truth; just as

3129 575 1889 02 27 4889 1473
ἐμάθετε ἀπὸ Ἐπαφρᾶ τοῦ ἀγαπητοῦ συνδούλου ἡμῶν,
you learned from Epaphras the loved co-slave of us,

3739 1510 4103 5228 1473 1249 02
ὅς ἐστιν πιστὸς ὑπὲρ ὑμῶν διάκονος τοῦ
who is trustful on behalf of you servant of the

5547 8 01 2532 1213 1473 08
Χριστοῦ, ὁ καὶ δηλώσας ἡμῖν τὴν
Christ, the also one having made clear to us the

1473 26 1722 4151 1223 3778 2532
ὑμῶν ἀγάπην ἐν πνεύματι. **9** Διὰ τοῦτο καὶ
of you love in spirit. Through this also

1473 575 3739 2250 191 3756 3973
ἡμεῖς, ἀφ᾽ ἧς ἡμέρας ἠκούσαμεν, οὐ παυόμεθα
we, from which day we heard, not we stopped

5228 1473 4336 2532 154 2443
ὑπὲρ ὑμῶν προσευχόμενοι καὶ αἰτούμενοι, ἵνα
on behalf of you praying and asking, that

4137 08 1922 010 2307
πληρωθῆτε τὴν ἐπίγνωσιν τοῦ θελήματος
you might be filled the perception of the want

846 1722 3956 4678 2532 4907 4152
αὐτοῦ ἐν πάσῃ σοφίᾳ καὶ συνέσει πνευματικῇ,
of him in all wisdom and understanding spiritual,

10
4043	516	02	2962	1519	3956
περιπατῆσαι	ἀξίως	τοῦ	κυρίου	εἰς	πᾶσαν
to walk around	worthily	of the	Master	in	all

699	1722	3956	2041	18	2592	2532
ἀρεσκείαν,	ἐν	παντὶ	ἔργῳ	ἀγαθῷ	καρποφοροῦντες	καὶ
pleasing,	in	all	work	good	bearing fruit	and

837	07	1922	02	2316	**11**	1722
αὐξανόμενοι	τῇ	ἐπιγνώσει	τοῦ	θεοῦ,		ἐν
growing	in the	perception	of the	God,		in

3956	1411	1412	2596	012	2904	06
πάσῃ	δυνάμει	δυναμούμενοι	κατὰ	τὸ	κράτος	τῆς
all	power	being powered	by	the	strength	of the

1391	846	1519	3956	5281	2532	3115
δόξης	αὐτοῦ	εἰς	πᾶσαν	ὑπομονὴν	καὶ	μακροθυμίαν.
splendor	of him	in	all	patience	and	long temper.

3326	5479	**12**	2168	03	3962	03
Μετὰ	χαρᾶς		εὐχαριστοῦντες	τῷ	πατρὶ	τῷ
With joy			giving good favor	to the	Father	the

2427	1473	1519	08	3310	02	2819	014
ἱκανώσαντι	ὑμᾶς	εἰς	τὴν	μερίδα	τοῦ	κλήρου	τῶν
one having you		in	the	part	of the	lot	of the
made enough							

40	1722	011	5457	**13**	3739	4506	1473	1537
ἁγίων	ἐν	τῷ	φωτί·		ὃς	ἐρρύσατο	ἡμᾶς	ἐκ
holy ones	in	the	light;		who	rescued	us	from

06	1849	010	4655	2532	3179	1519	08
τῆς	ἐξουσίας	τοῦ	σκότους	καὶ	μετέστησεν	εἰς	τὴν
the	authority	of the	dark	and	transferred	into	the

932	02	5207	06	26	846	**14**	1722
βασιλείαν	τοῦ	υἱοῦ	τῆς	ἀγάπης	αὐτοῦ,		ἐν
kingdom	of the	son	of the	love	of him,		in

3739	2192	08	629	08	859	018
ᾧ	ἔχομεν	τὴν	ἀπολύτρωσιν,	τὴν	ἄφεσιν	τῶν
whom	we have	the	redemption,	the	sending off	of the

266	**15**	3739	1510	1504	02	2316	02	517
ἁμαρτιῶν·		ὅς	ἐστιν	εἰκὼν	τοῦ	θεοῦ	τοῦ	ἀοράτου,
sins;		who	is	image	of the	God	the	unseen,

4416	3956	2937	**16**	3754	1722	846
πρωτότοκος	πάσης	κτίσεως,		ὅτι	ἐν	αὐτῷ
firstborn	of all	creation,		because	in	him

2936	021	3956	1722	015	3772	2532	1909
ἐκτίσθη	τὰ	πάντα	ἐν	τοῖς	οὐρανοῖς	καὶ	ἐπὶ
was created	the	all	in	the	heavens	and	on

06	1093	021	3707	2532	021	517	1535	2362
τῆς	γῆς,	τὰ	ὁρατὰ	καὶ	τὰ	ἀόρατα,	εἴτε	θρόνοι
the	earth,	the	seen	and	the	unseen,	whether	thrones

1535	2963	1535	746	1535	1849	021
εἴτε	κυριότητες	εἴτε	ἀρχαὶ	εἴτε	ἐξουσίαι·	τὰ
or	masterships	or	rulers	or	authorities;	the

3956	1223	846	2532	1519	846	2936
πάντα	δι᾽	αὐτοῦ	καὶ	εἰς	αὐτὸν	ἔκτισται·
all	through	him	and	in	him	have been created;

17	2532	846	1510	4253	3956	2532	021	3956	1722
	καὶ	αὐτός	ἐστιν	πρὸ	πάντων	καὶ	τὰ	πάντα	ἐν
	and	himself	is	before	all	and	the	all	in

846	4921	**18**	2532	846	1510	05	2776
αὐτῷ	συνέστηκεν,		καὶ	αὐτός	ἐστιν	ἡ	κεφαλὴ
him	has stood together,		and	himself	is	the	head

010	4983	06	1577	3739	1510	746
τοῦ	σώματος	τῆς	ἐκκλησίας·	ὅς	ἐστιν	ἀρχή,
of the	body	the	assembly;	who	is	ruler,

4416	1537	014	3498	2443	1096	1722	3956
πρωτότοκος	ἐκ	τῶν	νεκρῶν,	ἵνα	γένηται	ἐν	πᾶσιν
firstborn	from	the	dead,	that	might become	in	all

846	4409	**19**	3754	1722	846	2106
αὐτὸς	πρωτεύων,		ὅτι	ἐν	αὐτῷ	εὐδόκησεν
himself being first,			because	in	him	was thought well

3956	012	4138	2730	**20**	2532	1223	846
πᾶν	τὸ	πλήρωμα	κατοικῆσαι		καὶ	δι᾽	αὐτοῦ
all	the	fullness	to reside		and	through	him

[10]so that you may lead lives worthy of the Lord, fully pleasing to him, as you bear fruit in every good work and as you grow in the knowledge of God. [11]May you be made strong with all the strength that comes from his glorious power, and may you be prepared to endure everything with patience, while joyfully [12]giving thanks to the Father, who has enabled[a] you[b] to share in the inheritance of the saints in the light. [13]He has rescued us from the power of darkness and transferred us into the kingdom of his beloved Son, [14]in whom we have redemption, the forgiveness of sins.[c]

15 He is the image of the invisible God, the firstborn of all creation; [16]for in[d] him all things in heaven and on earth were created, things visible and invisible, whether thrones or dominions or rulers or powers—all things have been created through him and for him. [17]He himself is before all things, and in[d] him all things hold together. [18]He is the head of the body, the church; he is the beginning, the firstborn from the dead, so that he might come to have first place in everything. [19]For in him all the fullness of God was pleased to dwell, [20]and through him

a Other ancient authorities read *called*
b Other ancient authorities read *us*
c Other ancient authorities add *through his blood*
d Or *by*

God was pleased to reconcile to himself all things, whether on earth or in heaven, by making peace through the blood of his cross.

21 And you who were once estranged and hostile in mind, doing evil deeds, [22]he has now reconciled[a] in his fleshly body[b] through death, so as to present you holy and blameless and irreproachable before him— [23]provided that you continue securely established and steadfast in the faith, without shifting from the hope promised by the gospel that you heard, which has been proclaimed to every creature under heaven. I, Paul, became a servant of this gospel.

24 I am now rejoicing in my sufferings for your sake, and in my flesh I am completing what is lacking in Christ's afflictions for the sake of his body, that is, the church. [25]I became its servant according to God's commission that was given to me for you, to make the word of God fully known, [26]the mystery that has been hidden throughout the ages and generations but has now

---

[a] Other ancient authorities read *you have now been reconciled*

[b] Gk *in the body of his flesh*

604		024 3956	1519 846
ἀποκαταλλάξαι		τὰ πάντα	εἰς αὐτόν,
to thoroughly reconcile		the all	in him,

1517	1223	010 129	02	4716
εἰρηνοποιήσας	διὰ	τοῦ αἵματος	τοῦ	σταυροῦ
having made peace	through	the blood	of the	cross

846	1223	846	1535	024 1909 06	1093	1535
αὐτοῦ,	[δι᾿	αὐτοῦ]	εἴτε	τὰ ἐπὶ	τῆς γῆς	εἴτε
of him,	through	him	whether	the on	the earth	or

024 1722 015 3772		2532 1473 4218 1510
τὰ ἐν τοῖς οὐρανοῖς.	**21**	Καὶ ὑμᾶς ποτε ὄντας
the in the heavens.		And you then being

526	2532 2190	07	1271
ἀπηλλοτριωμένους	καὶ ἐχθροὺς	τῇ	διανοίᾳ
having been alienated	and hostiles	in the	intelligence

1722 023 2041	023 4190	**22**	3570 1161
ἐν τοῖς ἔργοις	τοῖς πονηροῖς,		νυνὶ δὲ
in the works	the evil,		now but

604	1722 011 4983	06	4561	846
ἀποκατήλλαξεν ἐν	τῷ σώματι τῆς		σαρκὸς	αὐτοῦ
he reconciled in	the body	of the	flesh	of him
thoroughly				

1223	02 2288	3936	1473 40	2532
διὰ	τοῦ θανάτου	παραστῆσαι	ὑμᾶς ἁγίους	καὶ
through	the death	to stand along	you holy	and

299	2532 410	2714	846
ἀμώμους	καὶ ἀνεγκλήτους	κατενώπιον	αὐτοῦ,
blameless	and unreproachable	down before	him,

23 1487 1065	1961	07 4102
εἴ γε	ἐπιμένετε	τῇ πίστει
if indeed	you stay on	the trust

2311	2532 1476	2532 3361
τεθεμελιωμένοι	καὶ ἑδραῖοι	καὶ μὴ
having been founded	and stable	and not

3334	575 06	1680 010	2098
μετακινούμενοι	ἀπὸ τῆς	ἐλπίδος τοῦ	εὐαγγελίου
being moved about	from the	hope of the	good message

3739 191	010 2704	1722
οὗ ἠκούσατε,	τοῦ κηρυχθέντος	ἐν
which you heard,	the one having been announced	in

3956 2937	07 5259 04 3772	3739	1096
πάσῃ κτίσει	τῇ ὑπὸ τὸν οὐρανόν,	οὗ	ἐγενόμην
all creation	the under the heaven,	of which	became

1473 3972 1249	3568 5463	1722 023
ἐγὼ Παῦλος διάκονος.	**24** Νῦν χαίρω	ἐν τοῖς
I Paul servant.	Now I rejoice	in the

3804	5228	1473	2532 466	024
παθήμασιν	ὑπὲρ	ὑμῶν	καὶ ἀνταναπληρῶ	τὰ
sufferings	on behalf of	you	and I fill up	the

5303	018	2347	02	5547 1722 07
ὑστερήματα	τῶν	θλίψεων	τοῦ	Χριστοῦ ἐν τῇ
lacks	of the	afflictions	of the	Christ in the

4561 1473	5228	010	4983	846 3739 1510
σαρκί μου	ὑπὲρ	τοῦ	σώματος	αὐτοῦ, ὅ ἐστιν
flesh of me	on behalf of	the	body	of him, who is

05 1577	**25** 3739	1096	1473 1249	2596
ἡ ἐκκλησία,	ἧς	ἐγενόμην	ἐγὼ διάκονος	κατὰ
the assembly,	of which	became	I servant	by

08 3622	02	2316 08 1325
τὴν οἰκονομίαν	τοῦ	θεοῦ τὴν δοθεῖσάν
the management	of the	God the one having been given

1473 1519 1473 4137	04 3056 02	2316	**26** 012
μοι εἰς ὑμᾶς πληρῶσαι	τὸν λόγον τοῦ	θεοῦ,	τὸ
to me in you to fill	the word of the	God,	the

3466	012 613	575 014
μυστήριον	τὸ ἀποκεκρυμμένον	ἀπὸ τῶν
mystery	the one having been hidden	off from the

165	2532 575 018 1074	3568 1161
αἰώνων	καὶ ἀπὸ τῶν γενεῶν	- νῦν δὲ
ages	and from the generations	now but

5319	015	40	846	27	3739
ἐφανερώθη	τοῖς	ἁγίοις	αὐτοῦ,		οἷς
was demonstrated	to the	holy ones	of him,		to whom

2309	01	2316	1107		5101	09	4149	06
ἠθέλησεν	ὁ	θεὸς	γνωρίσαι		τί	τὸ	πλοῦτος	τῆς
wanted	the	God	to make known		what	the	rich	of the

1391	010	3466		3778	1722	023	1484
δόξης	τοῦ	μυστηρίου	τούτου	ἐν	τοῖς	ἔθνεσιν,
splendor	of the	mystery	this	in	the	nations,

3739	1510	5547		1722	1473	05	1680	06
ὅ	ἐστιν	Χριστὸς	ἐν	ὑμῖν,	ἡ	ἐλπὶς	τῆς
which is		Christ	in	you,	the	hope	of the

1391	28	3739	1473	2605		3560		3956
δόξης·		ὅν	ἡμεῖς	καταγγέλλομεν	νουθετοῦντες	πάντα
splendor;		which	we	proclaim	warning	all.

444		2532	1321		3956	444		1722	3956
ἄνθρωπον	καὶ	διδάσκοντες	πάντα	ἄνθρωπον	ἐν	πάσῃ
man	and	teaching	all	man	in	all

4678	2443	3936		3956	444
σοφίᾳ,	ἵνα	παραστήσωμεν		πάντα	ἄνθρωπον
wisdom,	that	we might stand along		all	man

5046	1722	5547	29	1519	3739	2532	2872
τέλειον	ἐν	Χριστῷ·		εἰς	ὅ	καὶ	κοπιῶ
complete	in	Christ;		in	which	also	I labor

75		2596		08	1753	846	08
ἀγωνιζόμενος	κατὰ		τὴν	ἐνέργειαν	αὐτοῦ	τὴν
contesting	according to		the	operation	of him	the

1754		1722	1473	1722	1411	2:1	2309	1063
ἐνεργουμένην	ἐν	ἐμοὶ	ἐν	δυνάμει.		Θέλω	γὰρ
one operating	in	me	in	power.		I want	for

1473	3609a	2245		73		2192	5228		1473
ὑμᾶς	εἰδέναι	ἡλίκον	ἀγῶνα	ἔχω	ὑπὲρ	ὑμῶν
you	to know	how great	contest	I have	on behalf of	you

2532	014	1722	2993		2532	3745		3756	3708
καὶ	τῶν	ἐν	Λαοδικείᾳ	καὶ	ὅσοι		οὐχ	ἑόρακαν
and	the	in	Laodicea	and	as many as		not	have seen

012	4383		1473	1722	4561	2	2443	3870		017
τὸ	πρόσωπόν	μου	ἐν	σαρκί,		ἵνα	παρακληθῶσιν	αἱ
the	face	of me	in	flesh,		that	they might	the
								be encouraged	

2588	846		4822			1722	26
καρδίαι	αὐτῶν	συμβιβασθέντες			ἐν	ἀγάπῃ
hearts	of them	having been forced together			in	love

2532	1519	3956	4149		06		4136		06
καὶ	εἰς	πᾶν	πλοῦτος	τῆς		πληροφορίας		τῆς
and	in	all	rich	of the		full persuasion		of the

4907		1519	1922		010		3466		02
συνέσεως,	εἰς	ἐπίγνωσιν	τοῦ		μυστηρίου	τοῦ
understanding,	in	perception	of the		mystery	of the

2316	5547	3	1722	3739	1510	3956		013	2344
θεοῦ,	Χριστοῦ,		ἐν	ᾧ	εἰσιν	πάντες	οἱ	θησαυροὶ
God,	Christ,		in	whom	are	all		the	treasures

06		4678	2532	1108		614		4	3778	3004
τῆς	σοφίας	καὶ	γνώσεως	ἀπόκρυφοι.		Τοῦτο	λέγω,
of the	wisdom	and	knowledge	hidden off.		This	I say,

2443	3367		1473	3884		1722
ἵνα	μηδεὶς	ὑμᾶς	παραλογίζηται		ἐν
that	no one	you	might reason beside		in

4086		5	1487	1063	2532	07	4561
πιθανολογίᾳ.		εἰ	γὰρ	καὶ	τῇ	σαρκὶ
persuasive word.		If	for	also	in the	flesh

548		235	011	4151	4862	1473	1510
ἄπειμι,	ἀλλὰ	τῷ		πνεύματι	σὺν	ὑμῖν	εἰμι,
I am absent,	but	in the		spirit	with	you	I am,

5463	2532	991		1473	08	5010	2532	012
χαίρων	καὶ	βλέπων	ὑμῶν		τὴν	τάξιν	καὶ	τὸ
rejoicing	and	seeing	of you		the	rank	and	the

4733	06		1519	5547	4102		1473	6	5613
στερέωμα	τῆς		εἰς	Χριστὸν	πίστεως	ὑμῶν.		ʽΩς
solidity	of the		in	Christ	trust	of you.		As

been revealed to his saints.
[27]To them God chose to make known how great among the Gentiles are the riches of the glory of this mystery, which is Christ in you, the hope of glory. [28]It is he whom we proclaim, warning everyone and teaching everyone in all wisdom, so that we may present everyone mature in Christ. [29]For this I toil and struggle with all the energy that he powerfully inspires within me.

CHAPTER 2

For I want you to know how much I am struggling for you, and for those in Laodicea, and for all who have not seen me face to face. [2]I want their hearts to be encouraged and united in love, so that they may have all the riches of assured understanding and have the knowledge of God's mystery, that is, Christ himself,[a] [3]in whom are hidden all the treasures of wisdom and knowledge. [4]I am saying this so that no one may deceive you with plausible arguments. [5]For though I am absent in body, yet I am with you in spirit, and I rejoice to see your morale and the firmness of your faith in Christ.

[a] Other ancient authorities read *of the mystery of God, both of the Father and of Christ*

6 As you therefore have received Christ Jesus the Lord, continue to live your lives*a* in him, 7rooted and built up in him and established in the faith, just as you were taught, abounding in thanksgiving.

8 See to it that no one takes you captive through philosophy and empty deceit, according to human tradition, according to the elemental spirits of the universe,*b* and not according to Christ. 9For in him the whole fullness of deity dwells bodily, 10and you have come to fullness in him, who is the head of every ruler and authority. 11In him also you were circumcised with a spiritual circumcision,*c* by putting off the body of the flesh in the circumcision of Christ; 12when you were buried with him in baptism, you were also raised with him through faith in the power of God, who raised him from the dead. 13And when you were dead in trespasses and the uncircumcision of your flesh, God*d* made you*e* alive together with him, when he forgave us all our trespasses, 14erasing the record that stood

a Gk *to walk*

b Or *the rudiments of the world*

c Gk *a circumcision made without hands*

d Gk *he*

e Other ancient authorities read *made us;* others, *made*

3767	3880		04	5547	2424	04	2962
οὖν	παρελάβετε		τὸν	Χριστὸν	Ἰησοῦν	τὸν	κύριον,
then	you took along		the	Christ	Jesus	the	Master,

1722	846	4043	7	4492		2532
ἐν	αὐτῷ	περιπατεῖτε,		ἐρριζωμένοι		καὶ
in	him	walk around,		having been rooted		and

2026		1722	846	2532	950		07
ἐποικοδομούμενοι	ἐν	αὐτῷ	καὶ	βεβαιούμενοι		τῇ
being built on	in	him	and	being confirmed		in the

4102	2531	1321		4052	1722
πίστει	καθὼς	ἐδιδάχθητε,		περισσεύοντες	ἐν
trust	just as	you were taught,		exceeding	in

2169	8	991		3361	5100	1473	1510	01
εὐχαριστίᾳ.		Βλέπετε	μή	τις	ὑμᾶς	ἔσται	ὁ
good favor.		See		not	some	you	will be	the one

4812	1223	06	5385		2532	2756	539
συλαγωγῶν	διὰ	τῆς	φιλοσοφίας	καὶ	κενῆς	ἀπάτης
kidnapping	through	the	philosophy	and	empty	deception

2596	08	3862	014	444	2596	024	4747
κατὰ	τὴν	παράδοσιν	τῶν	ἀνθρώπων,	κατὰ	τὰ	στοιχεῖα
by		the tradition	of the	men,	by		the elements

02	2889	2532	3756	2596	5547	9	3754	1722
τοῦ	κόσμου	καὶ	οὐ	κατὰ	Χριστόν·		ὅτι	ἐν
of the	world	and	not	by	Christ;		because	in

846	2730	3956	09	4138	06	2320
αὐτῷ	κατοικεῖ	πᾶν	τὸ	πλήρωμα	τῆς	θεότητος
him	resides	all		the fullness	of the	Godness

4985	10	2532	1510	1722	846	4137
σωματικῶς,		καὶ	ἐστὲ	ἐν	αὐτῷ	πεπληρωμένοι,
bodily,		and	you are+	in	him	+having been filled,

3739	1510	05	2776	3956	746	2532	1849
ὅς	ἐστιν	ἡ	κεφαλὴ	πάσης	ἀρχῆς	καὶ	ἐξουσίας.
who	is	the	head	of all	rule	and	authority.

11	1722	3739	2532	4059		4061
	Ἐν	ᾧ	καὶ	περιετμήθητε		περιτομῇ
	In	whom	and	you were circumcised		in circumcision

886		1722	07	555		010	4983
ἀχειροποιήτῳ	ἐν	τῇ	ἀπεκδύσει		τοῦ	σώματος
unhandmade	in		the putting off		from the	body

06	4561	1722	07	4061	02	5547
τῆς	σαρκός,	ἐν	τῇ	περιτομῇ	τοῦ	Χριστοῦ,
of the	flesh,	in		the circumcision	of the	Christ,

12	4916	846	1722	03	909	1722
	συνταφέντες	αὐτῷ	ἐν	τῷ	βαπτισμῷ,	ἐν
	having been buried together	in him	in		the immersion,	in

3739	2532	4891		1223	06	4102
ᾧ	καὶ	συνηγέρθητε		διὰ	τῆς	πίστεως
which	also	you were raised together		by		the trust

06	1753	02	2316	02	1453
τῆς	ἐνεργείας	τοῦ	θεοῦ	τοῦ	ἐγείραντος
of the	operation	of the	God	the one	having raised

846	1537	3498	13	2532	1473	3498	1510	1722
αὐτὸν	ἐκ	νεκρῶν·		καὶ	ὑμᾶς	νεκροὺς	ὄντας	[ἐν]
him	from	dead;		and	you	dead	being	in

023	3900	2532	07	203	06	4561
τοῖς	παραπτώμασιν	καὶ	τῇ	ἀκροβυστίᾳ	τῆς	σαρκὸς
the	trespasses	and	the	uncircumcision	of the	flesh

1473	4806		1473	4862	846	5483
ὑμῶν,	συνεζωοποίησεν	ὑμᾶς	σὺν	αὐτῷ,	χαρισάμενος
of you,	he made alive	you	with	him,	having favored together with

1473	3956	024	3900	14	1813		012
ἡμῖν	πάντα	τὰ	παραπτώματα.		ἐξαλείψας		τὸ
to us	all	the	trespasses.		Having wiped off		the

2596	1473	5498	023	1378	3739	1510
καθ᾽	ἡμῶν	χειρόγραφον	τοῖς	δόγμασιν	ὃ	ἦν
by	us	hand written		in the decrees	which	was

```
5227              1473   2532 846   142           1537 010
ὑπεναντίον       ἡμῖν, καὶ  αὐτὸ ἦρκεν           ἐκ  τοῦ
over against us,  and  it    he lifted up        from the
3319  4338              846  03       4716
μέσου προσηλώσας       αὐτὸ τῷ       σταυρῷ·
middle having nailed it    to the cross;
   554                     020 746     2532 020 1849
15 ἀπεκδυσάμενος          τὰς ἀρχὰς καὶ  τὰς ἐξουσίας
   having put off from the rulers and  the authorities
1165        1722 3954      2358        846    1722
ἐδειγμάτισεν ἐν  παρρησίᾳ, θριαμβεύσας αὐτοὺς ἐν
he exposed   in  boldness, having led  them   in
publically                  in triumph
846      16 3361 3767 5100 1473 2919    1722 1035
αὐτῷ.      Μὴ  οὖν  τις  ὑμᾶς κρινέτω  ἐν  βρώσει
him.       Not  then some you  let judge in  food
2532 1722 4213 2228 1722 3313   1859      2228 3500a
καὶ ἐν   πόσει ἢ  ἐν  μέρει ἑορτῆς ἢ    νεομηνίας
and in   drink or in   part festival or  new moon
2228 4521        17 3739 1510  4639    022
ἢ   σαββάτων·      ἅ    ἐστιν σκιὰ  τῶν
or  sabbaths,      which is    shadow of the things
3195        09 1161 4983 02   5547       3367
μελλόντων,  τὸ δὲ  σῶμα τοῦ   Χριστοῦ. 18 μηδεὶς
about to be, the but body of the Christ.   No one
1473 2603            2309    1722 5012
ὑμᾶς καταβραβευέτω  θέλων ἐν  ταπεινοφροσύνῃ
you  let decide against wanting in humblemindedness
2532 2356     014   32        3739 3708
καὶ θρησκείᾳ τῶν  ἀγγέλων,  ἃ   ἑόρακεν
and  piety  of the messengers, that he has seen
1687         1500        5448           5259 02
ἐμβατεύων,  εἰκῇ       φυσιούμενος   ὑπὸ τοῦ
penetrating, without cause being puffed up by  the
3563 06     4561  846    19 2532 3756 2902    08
νοὸς τῆς  σαρκὸς αὐτοῦ,    καὶ  οὐ  κρατῶν τὴν
mind of the flesh of him,   and  not holding the
2776     1537 3739 3956 09  4983 1223    018 860
κεφαλήν, ἐξ  οὗ  πᾶν τὸ σῶμα διὰ   τῶν ἁφῶν
head,    from which all the body through the ligaments
2532 4886     2023              2532 4822
καὶ συνδέσμων ἐπιχορηγούμενον καὶ συμβιβαζόμενον
and  co-chains being supplied  and being forced
              further              together
837    08  838    02      2316  20 1487 599       4862
αὔξει τὴν αὔξησιν τοῦ   θεοῦ.   Εἰ  ἀπεθάνετε σὺν
grows the growth  of the God.  If  you died   with
5547   575  022 4747     02    2889     5101 5613
Χριστῷ ἀπὸ τῶν στοιχείων τοῦ   κόσμου, τί ὡς
Christ from the elements  of the world, why as
2198   1722 2889  1379         3361 681     3366
ζῶντες ἐν  κόσμῳ δογματίζεσθε; 21 μὴ ἅψῃ     μηδὲ
living in   world are you being   Not touch but not
              decreed to?
1089   3366  2345     22 3739 1510  3956  1519
γεύσῃ μηδὲ  θίγῃς,      ἅ    ἐστιν πάντα εἰς
taste but not handle,    which is    all  to
5356     07   671         2596 024 1778      2532
φθορὰν  τῇ   ἀποχρήσει, κατὰ τὰ ἐντάλματα καὶ
corruption in the full use, by  the commands and
1319          014    444        23 3748 1510 3056
διδασκαλίας τῶν  ἀνθρώπων,   ἅτινά ἐστιν λόγον
teachings   of the men,      which is    word
3303  2192   4678    1722 1479           2532
μὲν  ἔχοντα σοφίας ἐν  ἐθελοθρησκίᾳ    καὶ
indeed having wisdom in  self-chosen piety and
5012          2532 857     4983        3756 1722
ταπεινοφροσύνῃ [καὶ] ἀφειδίᾳ σώματος, οὐκ ἐν
humblemindedness and  unsparing of body, not  in
```

against us with its legal demands. He set this aside, nailing it to the cross. [15]He disarmed[a] the rulers and authorities and made a public example of them, triumphing over them in it.

[16]Therefore do not let anyone condemn you in matters of food and drink or of observing festivals, new moons, or sabbaths. [17]These are only a shadow of what is to come, but the substance belongs to Christ. [18]Do not let anyone disqualify you, insisting on self-abasement and worship of angels, dwelling[b] on visions,[c] puffed up without cause by a human way of thinking,[d] [19]and not holding fast to the head, from whom the whole body, nourished and held together by its ligaments and sinews, grows with a growth that is from God.

[20]If with Christ you died to the elemental spirits of the universe,[e] why do you live as if you still belonged to the world? Why do you submit to regulations, [21]"Do not handle, Do not taste, Do not touch"? [22]All these regulations refer to things that perish with use; they are simply human commands and teachings. [23]These have indeed an appearance of wisdom in promoting self-imposed piety, humility, and severe treatment of the body,

---

[a] Or divested himself of
[b] Other ancient authorities read not dwelling
[c] Meaning of Gk uncertain
[d] Gk by the mind of his flesh
[e] Or the rudiments of the world

but they are of no value in checking self-indulgence.[a]

CHAPTER 3

So if you have been raised with Christ, seek the things that are above, where Christ is, seated at the right hand of God. [2]Set your minds on things that are above, not on things that are on earth, [3]for you have died, and your life is hidden with Christ in God. [4]When Christ who is your[b] life is revealed, then you also will be revealed with him in glory.

5 Put to death, therefore, whatever in you is earthly: fornication, impurity, passion, evil desire, and greed (which is idolatry). [6]On account of these the wrath of God is coming on those who are disobedient.[c] [7]These are the ways you also once followed, when you were living that life.[d] [8]But now you must get rid of all such things—anger, wrath, malice, slander, and abusive[e] language from your mouth. [9]Do not lie to one another, seeing that you have stripped off the old self with its practices [10]and have clothed yourselves with the new self, which is being renewed in knowledge according to the image of its creator. [11]In that renewal[f] there is no longer Greek and Jew, circumcised and uncircumcised, barbarian, Scythian, slave and free; but

---

[a] Or are of no value, serving only to indulge the flesh
[b] Other authorities read our
[c] Other ancient authorities lack on those who are disobedient (Gk the children of disobedience)
[d] Or living among such people
[e] Or filthy
[f] Gk its creator, [11]where

| 5092 | 5100 | 4314 | 4140 | | 06 | | 4561 | **3:1** | 1487 |
τιμῇ τινι πρὸς πλησμονὴν τῆς σαρκός. Εἰ
value some to filling up of the flesh. If

| 3767 | 4891 | | | 03 | | 5547 | 024 507 |
οὖν συνηγέρθητε τῷ Χριστῷ, τὰ ἄνω
then you were raised together in the Christ, the up

| 2212 | | 3757 | 01 | 5547 | 1510 | 1722 | 1188 | 02 | 2316 |
ζητεῖτε, οὗ ὁ Χριστός ἐστιν ἐν δεξιᾷ τοῦ θεοῦ
seek, where the Christ is in right of the God

| 2521 | | **2** | 024 507 | 5426 | | 3361 | 024 | 1909 | 06 | 1093 |
καθήμενος· τὰ ἄνω φρονεῖτε, μὴ τὰ ἐπὶ τῆς γῆς.
sitting; the up think, not the on the earth.

| 599 | | 1063 | 2532 | 05 | 2222 | 1473 | 2928 |
3 ἀπεθάνετε γὰρ καὶ ἡ ζωὴ ὑμῶν κέκρυπται
You died for and the life of you has been hidden

| 4862 | 03 | 5547 | 1722 | 03 | 2316 | **4** | 3752 | 01 | 5547 |
σὺν τῷ Χριστῷ ἐν τῷ θεῷ. ὅταν ὁ Χριστὸς
with the Christ in the God. When the Christ

| 5319 | | | 05 | 2222 | 1473 | | 5119 | 2532 |
φανερωθῇ, ἡ ζωὴ ὑμῶν, τότε καὶ
might be demonstrated, the life of you, then and

| 1473 | 4862 | 846 | 5319 | | | 1722 | 1391 |
ὑμεῖς σὺν αὐτῷ φανερωθήσεσθε ἐν δόξῃ.
you with him will be demonstrated in splendor.

| **5** | 3499 | | 3767 | 024 | 3196 | | 024 | 1909 | 06 | 1093 |
Νεκρώσατε οὖν τὰ μέλη τὰ ἐπὶ τῆς γῆς,
Deaden then the members the on the earth,

| 4202 | | 167 | | 3806 | | 1939 |
πορνείαν ἀκαθαρσίαν πάθος ἐπιθυμίαν
sexual immorality, uncleanness, passion, desire

| 2556 | 2532 | 08 | 4124 | | 3748 | 1510 | 1495 |
κακήν, καὶ τὴν πλεονεξίαν, ἥτις ἐστὶν εἰδωλολατρία,
bad, and the greediness, which is idol service,

| 1223 | | 3739 | 2064 | 05 | 3709 | 02 | | 2316 | 1909 |
6 δι' ἃ ἔρχεται ἡ ὀργὴ τοῦ θεοῦ [ἐπὶ
through which comes the anger of the God on

| 016 | 5207 | 06 | 543 | | **7** | 1722 | 3739 | 2532 | 1473 |
τοὺς υἱοὺς τῆς ἀπειθείας]. ἐν οἷς καὶ ὑμεῖς
the sons of the disobedience. In which also you

| 4043 | | 4218 | 3753 | 2198 | | 1722 | 3778 |
περιεπατήσατέ ποτε, ὅτε ἐζῆτε ἐν τούτοις·
walked around then, when you lived in these;

| **8** | 3570 | 1161 | 659 | | 2532 | 1473 | 024 | 3956 | 3709 |
νυνὶ δὲ ἀπόθεσθε καὶ ὑμεῖς τὰ πάντα, ὀργήν,
now but set off also you the all, anger,

| 2372 | 2549 | | 988 | | 148 | | 1537 | 010 |
θυμόν, κακίαν, βλασφημίαν, αἰσχρολογίαν ἐκ τοῦ
fury, badness, insult, shameful word from the

| 4750 | 1473 | | **9** | 3361 | 5574 | | 1519 | 240 |
στόματος ὑμῶν· μὴ ψεύδεσθε εἰς ἀλλήλους,
mouth of you; not lie to one another,

| 554 | | 04 | 3820 | | 444 | | 4862 | 019 |
ἀπεκδυσάμενοι τὸν παλαιὸν ἄνθρωπον σὺν ταῖς
having put off from the old man with the

| 4234 | | 846 | **10** | 2532 | 1746 | | 04 | 3501 | 04 |
πράξεσιν αὐτοῦ καὶ ἐνδυσάμενοι τὸν νέον τὸν
practices of him and having put on the new the one

| 341 | | 1519 | 1922 | | 2596 | 1504 | 02 |
ἀνακαινούμενον εἰς ἐπίγνωσιν κατ' εἰκόνα τοῦ
being renewed in perception by image of the one

| 2936 | | 846 | | **11** | 3699 | 3756 | 1762 | | 1672 |
κτίσαντος αὐτόν, ὅπου οὐκ ἔνι Ἕλλην
having created him, where not there is Greek

| 2532 | 2453 | | 4061 | | 2532 | 203 |
καὶ Ἰουδαῖος, περιτομὴ καὶ ἀκροβυστία,
and Judean, circumcision and uncircumcision,

| 915 | | 4658 | | 1401 | | 1658 | | 235 | 021 |
βάρβαρος, Σκύθης, δοῦλος, ἐλεύθερος, ἀλλὰ [τὰ]
barbarian, Scythian, slave, free, but the

3956 2532 1722 3956 5547　12　1746　　3767
πάντα καὶ ἐν πᾶσιν Χριστός. ᾿Ενδύσασθε οὖν,
all and in all Christ. Put on then,

5613 1588　　02　　2316 40 2532 25
ὡς ἐκλεκτοὶ τοῦ θεοῦ ἅγιοι καὶ ἠγαπημένοι,
as select of the God holy and having been loved,

4698　　3628　　　5544　　5012
σπλάγχνα οἰκτιρμοῦ χρηστότητα ταπεινοφροσύνην
affections of compassion, kindness, humblemindedness,

4240　　3115　　13　430　　240　　2532
πραΰτητα μακροθυμίαν, ἀνεχόμενοι ἀλλήλων καὶ
gentleness, long-temper, enduring one another and

5483　　1438　　1437 5100 4314 5100
χαριζόμενοι ἑαυτοῖς ἐάν τις πρός τινα
being favorable to yourselves if some to some

2192　　3437　　2531 2532 01 2962
ἔχῃ μομφήν· καθὼς καὶ ὁ κύριος
might have complaint; just as also the Master

5483　　1473 3779　2532 1473　14 1909 3956 1161
ἐχαρίσατο ὑμῖν, οὕτως καὶ ὑμεῖς· ἐπὶ πᾶσιν δὲ
favored you, thusly also you; on all but

3778　08 26　3739 1510 4886　06
τούτοις τὴν ἀγάπην, ὅ ἐστιν σύνδεσμος τῆς
these the love, which is co-chain of the

5047　　15 2532 05 1515　02　　5547
τελειότητος. καὶ ἡ εἰρήνη τοῦ Χριστοῦ
completeness. And the peace of the Christ

1018　　1722 019 2588　　1473　1519 3739 2532
βραβευέτω ἐν ταῖς καρδίαις ὑμῶν, εἰς ἣν καὶ
let preside in the hearts of you, in which also

2564　　1722 1520 4983　2532 2170
ἐκλήθητε ἐν ἑνὶ σώματι· καὶ εὐχάριστοι
you were called in one body; and well-favored

1096　16 01 3056 02　　5547　1774　　1722
γίνεσθε. ῾Ο λόγος τοῦ Χριστοῦ ἐνοικείτω ἐν
become. The word of the Christ let house in in

1473 4146　1722 3956 4678 1321　　2532
ὑμῖν πλουσίως, ἐν πάσῃ σοφίᾳ διδάσκοντες καὶ
you richly, in all wisdom teaching and

3560　1438　5568　5215 5603
νουθετοῦντες ἑαυτούς, ψαλμοῖς ὕμνοις ᾠδαῖς
warning yourselves, in psalms, hymns, songs

4152　1722 07 5485 103　1722 019 2588
πνευματικαῖς ἐν [τῇ] χάριτι ᾄδοντες ἐν ταῖς καρδίαις
spiritual in the favor singing in the hearts

1473 03　2316 17 2532 3956 3739 5100 1437
ὑμῶν τῷ θεῷ· καὶ πᾶν ὅ τι ἐὰν
of you to the God; and all what some if

4160　1722 3056 2228 1722 2041　3956 1722 3686
ποιῆτε ἐν λόγῳ ἢ ἐν ἔργῳ, πάντα ἐν ὀνόματι
you might do in word or in work, all in name

2962　　2424 2168　03　2316 3962
κυρίου ᾿Ιησοῦ, εὐχαριστοῦντες τῷ θεῷ πατρὶ
of Master Jesus, giving good favor to the God Father

1223 846　017 1135　5293　015
δι᾿ αὐτοῦ. 18 Αἱ γυναῖκες, ὑποτάσσεσθε τοῖς
through him. The women, be subject to the

435　5613 433　1722 2962　19 013 435
ἀνδράσιν ὡς ἀνῆκεν ἐν κυρίῳ. Οἱ ἄνδρες,
men as it was proper in Master. The men,

25　020 1135　2532 3361 4087　4314
ἀγαπᾶτε τὰς γυναῖκας καὶ μὴ πικραίνεσθε πρὸς
love the women and not be bitter toward

846　20 021 5043　5219　015 1118　2596
αὐτάς. Τὰ τέκνα, ὑπακούετε τοῖς γονεῦσιν κατὰ
them. The children, obey the parents by

3956 3778 1063 2101　1510 1722 2962　21 013
πάντα, τοῦτο γὰρ εὐάρεστόν ἐστιν ἐν κυρίῳ. Οἱ
all, this for well-pleasing is in Master. The

Christ is all and in all!

12 As God's chosen ones, holy and beloved, clothe yourselves with compassion, kindness, humility, meekness, and patience. [13]Bear with one another and, if anyone has a complaint against another, forgive each other; just as the Lord[a] has forgiven you, so you also must forgive. [14]Above all, clothe yourselves with love, which binds everything together in perfect harmony. [15]And let the peace of Christ rule in your hearts, to which indeed you were called in the one body. And be thankful. [16]Let the word of Christ[b] dwell in you richly; teach and admonish one another in all wisdom; and with gratitude in your hearts sing psalms, hymns, and spiritual songs to God.[c] [17]And whatever you do, in word or deed, do everything in the name of the Lord Jesus, giving thanks to God the Father through him.

18 Wives, be subject to your husbands, as is fitting in the Lord. [19]Husbands, love your wives and never treat them harshly.

20 Children, obey your parents in everything, for this is your acceptable duty in the Lord.

a Other ancient authorities read just as Christ
b Other ancient authorities read of God, or of the Lord
c Other ancient authorities read to the Lord

21Fathers, do not provoke your children, or they may lose heart. 22Slaves, obey your earthly masters[a] in everything, not only while being watched and in order to please them, but wholeheartedly, fearing the Lord.[a] 23Whatever your task, put yourselves into it, as done for the Lord and not for your masters,[b] 24since you know that from the Lord you will receive the inheritance as your reward; you serve[c] the Lord Christ. 25For the wrongdoer will be paid back for whatever wrong has been done, and there is no partiality. 4:1Masters, treat your slaves justly and fairly, for you know that you also have a Master in heaven.

2 Devote yourselves to prayer, keeping alert in it with thanksgiving. 3At the same time pray for us as well that God will open to us a door for the word, that we may declare the mystery of Christ, for which I am in prison, 4so that I may reveal it clearly, as I should.

5 Conduct yourselves wisely toward outsiders, making the most of the time.[d] 6Let your speech always be gracious, seasoned with salt, so that you may know how you ought to answer everyone.

a In Greek the same word is used for *master* and *Lord*
b Gk *not for men*
c Or *you are slaves of,* or *be slaves of*
d Or *opportunity*

3962	3361	2042		024	5043		1473		2443	3361
πατέρες,	μὴ	ἐρεθίζετε	τὰ	τέκνα	ὑμῶν,		ἵνα	μὴ		
fathers,	not	provoke	the	children	of you,		that	not		

120			**22**	013	1401		5219		2596
ἀθυμῶσιν.				Οἱ	δοῦλοι,	ὑπακούετε	κατὰ		
they might lose wrath.			The slaves,	obey	by				

lose wrath.

3956	015		2596	4561	2962		3361	1722
πάντα	τοῖς	κατὰ	σάρκα	κυρίοις,	μὴ	ἐν		
all	the ones	by	flesh	masters,	not	in		

3787		5613	441		235	1722	572
ὀφθαλμοδουλίᾳ	ὡς	ἀνθρωπάρεσκοι,	ἀλλ᾽	ἐν	ἁπλότητι		
eye slavery	as	men-pleasers,	but	in	openness		

2588	5399	04	2962		**23**	3739	1437
καρδίας	φοβούμενοι	τὸν	κύριον.			ὃ	ἐὰν
of heart	fearing	the	Master.			What	if

4160		1537	5590	2038		5613	03		2962
ποιῆτε,	ἐκ	ψυχῆς	ἐργάζεσθε	ὡς	τῷ		κυρίῳ		
you might do,	from	soul	work	as	to the Master				

2532	3756	444		**24**	3609a	3754	575	2962
καὶ	οὐκ	ἀνθρώποις,			εἰδότες	ὅτι	ἀπὸ	κυρίου
and	not	to men,			knowing	that	from	Master

618			08	469		06
ἀπολήμψεσθε			τὴν	ἀνταπόδοσιν	τῆς	
you will receive			from the	repayment	of the	

2817		03		2962	5547	1398		**25**	01
κληρονομίας.	τῷ		κυρίῳ	Χριστῷ	δουλεύετε·			ὁ
inheritance.	In the		Master	Christ	slave;			the one

1063	91		2865		3739	91		2532
γὰρ	ἀδικῶν	κομίσεται	ὃ	ἠδίκησεν,		καὶ		
for	doing unright	will obtain	what	he did unright,		and		

3756	1510		4382		013	2962		012
οὐκ	ἔστιν	προσωπολημψία.	**4:1**	Οἱ	κύριοι,	τὸ		
not	there is	face receiving.		The masters,	the			

1342		2532	08	2471		015		1401		3930
δίκαιον	καὶ	τὴν	ἰσότητα	τοῖς	δούλοις	παρέχεσθε,				
right	and	the	equality	to the	slaves	hold along,				

3609a	3754	2532	1473	2192	2962	1722	3772
εἰδότες	ὅτι	καὶ	ὑμεῖς	ἔχετε	κύριον	ἐν	οὐρανῷ.
knowing	that	also	you	have	Master	in	heaven.

2	07	4335	4342		1127		1722
	Τῇ	προσευχῇ	προσκαρτερεῖτε,	γρηγοροῦντες	ἐν		
	In the	prayer	remain constant,	keeping awake	in		

846	1722	2169		**3**	4336		260
αὐτῇ	ἐν	εὐχαριστίᾳ,			προσευχόμενοι	ἅμα	
it	in	good favor,			praying	at same time	

2532	4012	1473	2443	01	2316	455		1473
καὶ	περὶ	ἡμῶν,	ἵνα	ὁ	θεὸς	ἀνοίξῃ		ἡμῖν
also	about us,		that	the	God	might open		to us

2374	02		3056	2980		012	3466		02
θύραν	τοῦ	λόγου	λαλῆσαι	τὸ	μυστήριον	τοῦ			
door	of the	word	to speak	the	mystery	of the			

5547		1223	3739	2532	1210			**4**	2443
Χριστοῦ,	δι᾽	ὃ	καὶ	δέδεμαι,				ἵνα
Christ,	through	whom	also	I have been bound,				that

5319		846	5613	1163		1473
φανερώσω	αὐτὸ	ὡς	δεῖ		με
I might demonstrate	it	as	it is necessary		me

2980		**5**	1722	4678	4043		4314	016
λαλῆσαι.			Ἐν	σοφίᾳ	περιπατεῖτε	πρὸς	τοὺς
to speak.			In	wisdom	walk around	to	the ones

1854		04	2540	1805		**6**	01	3056	1473
ἔξω	τὸν	καιρὸν	ἐξαγοραζόμενοι.			ὁ	λόγος	ὑμῶν
outside	the	season	buying out.			The	word	of you

3842	1722	5485	217		741
πάντοτε	ἐν	χάριτι,	ἅλατι	ἠρτυμένος,	
always	in	favor,	in salt	having been seasoned,	

3609a	4459	1163		1473	1520	1538
εἰδέναι	πῶς	δεῖ		ὑμᾶς	ἑνὶ	ἑκάστῳ
to know	how	it is necessary	you	one	each

611   7 024 2596 1473 3956 1107
ἀποκρίνεσθαι.   7 Τὰ κατ' ἐμὲ πάντα γνωρίσει
to answer.   The by me all will make known

1473 5190   01 27   80   2532 4103
ὑμῖν Τύχικος ὁ ἀγαπητὸς ἀδελφὸς καὶ πιστὸς
to you Tychicus the loved brother and trustful

1249   2532 4889   1722 2962   8 3739 3992
διάκονος καὶ σύνδουλος ἐν κυρίῳ,   8 ὃν ἔπεμψα
servant and co-slave in Master,   whom I sent

4314 1473 1519 846   3778   2443 1097   024
πρὸς ὑμᾶς εἰς αὐτὸ τοῦτο, ἵνα γνῶτε   τὰ
to you for it this, that you might know the

4012 1473 2532 3870   020 2588   1473
περὶ ἡμῶν καὶ παρακαλέσῃ τὰς καρδίας ὑμῶν,
about us and he might encourage the hearts of you,

9 4862 3682   03 4103   2532 27   80
9 σὺν Ὀνησίμῳ τῷ πιστῷ καὶ ἀγαπητῷ ἀδελφῷ,
with Onesimus the trustful and loved brother,

3739 1510   1537 1473   3956 1473   1107
ὅς ἐστιν ἐξ ὑμῶν· πάντα ὑμῖν γνωρίσουσιν
who is from you; all to you they will make known

024   5602   10 782   1473 708   01
τὰ   ὧδε.   10 Ἀσπάζεται ὑμᾶς Ἀρίσταρχος ὁ
the things here.   Greets you Aristarchus the

4869   1473 2532 3138   01 431   921
συναιχμάλωτός μου καὶ Μᾶρκος ὁ ἀνεψιὸς Βαρναβᾶ
co-captive of me and Mark the cousin of Barnabas

4012 3739 2983   1785   1437 2064   4314
(περὶ οὗ ἐλάβετε ἐντολάς, ἐὰν ἔλθῃ   πρὸς
about whom you took commands, if he might come to

1473 1209 846   11 2532 2424   01 3004
ὑμᾶς, δέξασθε αὐτόν)   11 καὶ Ἰησοῦς ὁ λεγόμενος
you, welcome him)   and Jesus the being called

2459   013   1510 1537 4061   3778 3441
Ἰοῦστος, οἱ ὄντες ἐκ περιτομῆς, οὗτοι μόνοι
Justus, the ones being from circumcision, these alone

4904   1519 08 932   02   2316 3748
συνεργοὶ εἰς τὴν βασιλείαν τοῦ θεοῦ, οἵτινες
co-workers in the kingdom of the God, who

1096   1473 3931   12 782   1473
ἐγενήθησάν μοι παρηγορία.   12 ἀσπάζεται ὑμᾶς
became to me comfort.   Greets you

1889   01 1537 1473 1401   5547   2424
Ἐπαφρᾶς ὁ ἐξ ὑμῶν, δοῦλος Χριστοῦ [Ἰησοῦ],
Epaphras the from you, slave of Christ Jesus,

3842   75   5228   1473 1722 019
πάντοτε ἀγωνιζόμενος ὑπὲρ ὑμῶν ἐν ταῖς
always contesting on behalf of you in the

4335   2443 2476   5046   2532
προσευχαῖς, ἵνα σταθῆτε τέλειοι καὶ
prayers, that you might stand complete and

4135   1722 3956 2307   02   2316
πεπληροφορημένοι ἐν παντὶ θελήματι τοῦ θεοῦ.
having been in all want of the God.
fully assured

13 3140   1063 846   3754 2192   4183 4192
13 μαρτυρῶ γὰρ αὐτῷ ὅτι ἔχει πολὺν πόνον
I testify for to him that he has much pain

5228   1473   2532 014 1722 2993   2532 014 1722
ὑπὲρ ὑμῶν καὶ τῶν ἐν Λαοδικείᾳ καὶ τῶν ἐν
on behalf of you and the in Laodicea and the in

2404   14 782   1473 3065 01 2395   01
Ἱεραπόλει.   14 ἀσπάζεται ὑμᾶς Λουκᾶς ὁ ἰατρὸς ὁ
Hierapolis.   Greets you Luke the physician the

27   2532 1214   15 782   016 1722 2993
ἀγαπητὸς καὶ Δημᾶς.   15 Ἀσπάσασθε τοὺς ἐν Λαοδικείᾳ
loved and Demas.   Greet the in Laodicea

80   2532 3564   2532 08 2596 3624 846
ἀδελφοὺς καὶ Νύμφαν καὶ τὴν κατ' οἶκον αὐτῆς
brothers and Nymphas and the by house of her

---

7 Tychicus will tell you all the news about me; he is a beloved brother, a faithful minister, and a fellow servant[a] in the Lord. [8]I have sent him to you for this very purpose, so that you may know how we are[b] and that he may encourage your hearts; [9]he is coming with Onesimus, the faithful and beloved brother, who is one of you. They will tell you about everything here.

10 Aristarchus my fellow prisoner greets you, as does Mark the cousin of Barnabas, concerning whom you have received instructions—if he comes to you, welcome him. [11]And Jesus who is called Justus greets you. These are the only ones of the circumcision among my co-workers for the kingdom of God, and they have been a comfort to me. [12]Epaphras, who is one of you, a servant[a] of Christ Jesus, greets you. He is always wrestling in his prayers on your behalf, so that you may stand mature and fully assured in everything that God wills. [13]For I testify for him that he has worked hard for you and for those in Laodicea and in Hierapolis. [14]Luke, the beloved physician, and Demas greet you. [15]Give my greetings to the brothers and sisters[c] in Laodicea, and to Nympha and

---

a Gk slave
b Other authorities read that I may know how you are
c Gk brothers

the church in her house.
¹⁶And when this letter has
been read among you, have
it read also in the church
of the Laodiceans; and see
that you read also the letter
from Laodicea. ¹⁷And say
to Archippus, "See that you
complete the task that you
have received in the Lord."

18 I, Paul, write this
greeting with my own hand.
Remember my chains.
Grace be with you.ᵃ

ᵃ Other ancient authorities add
  Amen

1577   2532 3752 314   3844   1473 05
ἐκκλησίαν. **16** καὶ ὅταν ἀναγνωσθῇ   παρ' ὑμῖν ἡ
assembly.   And when might be read among you the
1992   4160   2443 2532 1722 07   2994
ἐπιστολή, ποιήσατε ἵνα καὶ ἐν τῇ Λαοδικέων
letter,   make   that also in the Laodicea
1577   314   2532 08 1537 2993
ἐκκλησίᾳ ἀναγνωσθῇ,   καὶ τὴν ἐκ Λαοδικείας
assembly it might be read, and the from Laodicea
2443 2532 1473 314   **17** 2532 3004
ἵνα καὶ ὑμεῖς ἀναγνῶτε.   καὶ εἴπατε
that also you   might read.   And say
.751   991   08 1248   3739 3880
Ἀρχίππῳ·   Βλέπε τὴν διακονίαν ἣν παρέλαβες
 to Archippus, see the service   that you took along
1722 2962   2443 846   4137   **18** .01
ἐν κυρίῳ, ἵνα αὐτὴν πληροῖς.   ·Ο
in Master, that it you might fill. The
783   07   1699 5495 3972   3421   1473
ἀσπασμὸς τῇ   ἐμῇ χειρὶ Παύλου. μνημονεύετέ μου
greeting in the my hand Paul.   Remember   of me
014 1199   05 5485 3326 1473
τῶν δεσμῶν. ἡ χάρις μεθ' ὑμῶν.
the chains. The favor with you.

1 THESSALONIANS

CHAPTER 1

Paul, Silvanus, and Timothy,
To the church of the Thessalonians in God the Father and the Lord Jesus Christ:
Grace to you and peace.

2 We always give thanks to God for all of you and mention you in our prayers, constantly [3]remembering before our God and Father your work of faith and labor of love and steadfastness of hope in our Lord Jesus Christ. [4]For we know, brothers and sisters[a] beloved by God, that he has chosen you, [5]because our message of the gospel came to you not in word only, but also in power and in the Holy Spirit and with full conviction; just as you know what kind of persons we proved to be among you for your sake. [6]And you became imitators of us and of the Lord, for in spite of persecution you received the word with joy inspired by the Holy Spirit, [7]so that you became an example to all the believers in Macedonia and in Achaia. [8]For the word of the Lord has sounded forth from you not only in Macedonia and Achaia, but in every place your faith in God has become known, so that we have no need to speak about it. [9]For the people

a Gk brothers

1:1
3972	2532	4610	2532	5095	07	1577
Παῦλος	καὶ	Σιλουανὸς	καὶ	Τιμόθεος	τῇ	ἐκκλησίᾳ
Paul	and	Silvanus	and	Timothy	to the	assembly

2331		1722	2316	3962	2532	2962	2424
Θεσσαλονικέων		ἐν	θεῷ	πατρὶ	καὶ	κυρίῳ	Ἰησοῦ
of Thessalonians		in	God	father	and	Master	Jesus

5547	5485	1473	2532	1515		2168
Χριστῷ,	χάρις	ὑμῖν	καὶ	εἰρήνη.	**2**	Εὐχαριστοῦμεν
Christ,	favor	to you	and	peace.		We give good favor

03	2316	3842	4012	3956	1473	3417
τῷ	θεῷ	πάντοτε	περὶ	πάντων	ὑμῶν	μνείαν
to the God	always	about	all	of you	memory

4160	1909	018	4335	1473	89
ποιούμενοι	ἐπὶ	τῶν	προσευχῶν	ἡμῶν,	ἀδιαλείπτως
making	on	the	prayers	of us,	unceasingly

3
3421	1473	010	2041	06	4102	2532
μνημονεύοντες	ὑμῶν	τοῦ	ἔργου	τῆς	πίστεως	καὶ
remembering	of you	the	work	of the	trust	and

02	2873	06	26	2532	06	5281	06	1680
τοῦ	κόπου	τῆς	ἀγάπης	καὶ	τῆς	ὑπομονῆς	τῆς	ἐλπίδος
the	labor	of the	love	and	the	patience	of the	hope

02	2962	1473	2424	5547	1715	02	2316
τοῦ	κυρίου	ἡμῶν	Ἰησοῦ	Χριστοῦ	ἔμπροσθεν	τοῦ	θεοῦ
of the	Master	of us	Jesus	Christ	in front of	the	God

2532	3962	1473	**4**	3609a		80		25
καὶ	πατρὸς	ἡμῶν,		εἰδότες,		ἀδελφοὶ		ἠγαπημένοι
and	father	of us,		having known,		brothers		having been loved

5259	02	2316	08	1589	1473	**5**	3754	09
ὑπὸ	[τοῦ]	θεοῦ,	τὴν	ἐκλογὴν	ὑμῶν,		ὅτι	τὸ
by	the	God,	the	select	of you,		because	the

2098	1473	3756	1096	1519	1473	1722	3056
εὐαγγέλιον	ἡμῶν	οὐκ	ἐγενήθη	εἰς	ὑμᾶς	ἐν	λόγῳ
good message	of us	not	became	to	you	in	word

3441	235	2532	1722	1411	2532	1722	4151	40
μόνον	ἀλλὰ	καὶ	ἐν	δυνάμει	καὶ	ἐν	πνεύματι	ἁγίῳ
alone	but	also	in	power	and	in	spirit	holy

2532	1722	4136		4183	2531	3609a
καὶ	[ἐν]	πληροφορίᾳ		πολλῇ,	καθὼς	οἴδατε
and	in	full persuasion		much,	just as	you know

3634	1096	1722	1473	1223	1473	**6**	2532
οἷοι	ἐγενήθημεν	[ἐν]	ὑμῖν	δι᾽	ὑμᾶς.		Καὶ
of what sort	we became	in	you	through	you.		And

1473	3402	1473	1096	2532	02	2962
ὑμεῖς	μιμηταὶ	ἡμῶν	ἐγενήθητε	καὶ	τοῦ	κυρίου,
you	imitators	of us	became	and	of the	Master,

1209	04	3056	1722	2347	4183	3326	5479
δεξάμενοι	τὸν	λόγον	ἐν	θλίψει	πολλῇ	μετὰ	χαρᾶς
welcoming	the	word	in	affliction	much	with	joy

4151	40	**7**	5620	1096	1473	5179
πνεύματος	ἁγίου,		ὥστε	γενέσθαι	ὑμᾶς	τύπον
of spirit	holy,		so that	to become	you	example

3956	015	4100	1722	07	3109	2532	1722
πᾶσιν	τοῖς	πιστεύουσιν	ἐν	τῇ	Μακεδονίᾳ	καὶ	ἐν
to all	the	ones trusting	in	the	Macedonia	and	in

07	882	**8**	575	1473	1063	1837	01
τῇ	Ἀχαΐᾳ.		ἀφ᾽	ὑμῶν	γὰρ	ἐξήχηται	ὁ
the	Achaia.		From	you	for	has been sounded out	the

3056	02	2962	3756	3441	1722	07	3109	2532
λόγος	τοῦ	κυρίου	οὐ	μόνον	ἐν	τῇ	Μακεδονίᾳ	καὶ
word	of the	Master	not	alone	in	the	Macedonia	also

1722	07	882	235	1722	3956	5117	05	4102
[ἐν	τῇ]	Ἀχαΐᾳ,	ἀλλ᾽	ἐν	παντὶ	τόπῳ	ἡ	πίστις
in	the	Achaia,	but	in	all	place	the	trust

1473	05	4314	04	2316	1831		5620	3361
ὑμῶν	ἡ	πρὸς	τὸν	θεὸν	ἐξελήλυθεν,		ὥστε	μὴ
of you	the	to	the	God	has gone out,		so that	not

5532	2192	1473	2980	5100	**9**	846	1063
χρείαν	ἔχειν	ἡμᾶς	λαλεῖν	τι.		αὐτοὶ	γὰρ
need	to have	us	to speak	some.		Themselves	for

```
4012    1473   518                3697           1529         2192
περὶ    ἡμῶν   ἀπαγγέλλουσιν      ὁποίαν         εἴσοδον      ἔσχομεν
about   us     they tell         of what sort   entrance     we had
4314   1473    2532  4459  1994            4314  04    2316  575
πρὸς   ὑμᾶς,   καὶ   πῶς   ἐπεστρέψατε      πρὸς  τὸν   θεὸν  ἀπὸ
to     you,   and   how   you returned     to    the   God   from
022  1497      1398              2316     2198    2532  228
τῶν  εἰδώλων   δουλεύειν        θεῷ      ζῶντι   καὶ   ἀληθινῷ
the  idols    to be slave to   God      living  and   true
    2532  362       04   5207 846        1537  014  3772
10  καὶ   ἀναμένειν   τὸν  υἱὸν αὐτοῦ   ἐκ    τῶν  οὐρανῶν,
    and   to stay for  the  son  of him  from  the  heavens,
3739  1453      1537 014   3498      2424     04
ὃν    ἤγειρεν   ἐκ   [τῶν]  νεκρῶν,   Ἰησοῦν   τὸν
whom  he raised from the    dead,     Jesus    the
4506       1473  1537 06   3709   06   2064
ῥυόμενον   ἡμᾶς ἐκ   τῆς   ὀργῆς τῆς  ἐρχομένης.
one rescuing us   from  the   anger the one coming.
      846            1063 3609a      80        08   1529
2:1   Αὐτοὶ         γὰρ  οἴδατε,     ἀδελφοί,  τὴν  εἴσοδον
      Yourselves    for  you know,   brothers, the  entrance
1473  08  4314      1473 3754  3756  2756   1096
ἡμῶν  τὴν πρὸς      ὑμᾶς ὅτι   οὐ    κενὴ    γέγονεν,
of us the  toward   you  that  not   empty   it has become,
    235   4310              2532 5195          2531
2   ἀλλὰ  προπαθόντες       καὶ  ὑβρισθέντες,  καθὼς
    but   having suffered   and  having been   just as
          before                 abused,
3609a         1722 5375      3955              1722 03   2316
οἴδατε,       ἐν   Φιλίπποις ἐπαρρησιασάμεθα ἐν   τῷ   θεῷ
you know,     in   Philippi  we were bold    in   the  God
1473  2980       4314 1473  012  2098         02    2316
ἡμῶν  λαλῆσαι    πρὸς ὑμᾶς  τὸ   εὐαγγέλιον   τοῦ   θεοῦ
of us to speak   to   you   the  good message of the God
1722  4183  73        05   1063 3874         1473   3756
ἐν    πολλῷ ἀγῶνι. 3 ἡ    γὰρ  παράκλησις   ἡμῶν   οὐκ
in    much  contest. The   for  encouragement of us not
1537  4106   3761     1537 167          3761    1722
ἐκ    πλάνης οὐδὲ    ἐξ   ἀκαθαρσίας   οὐδὲ    ἐν
from  deceit but not from uncleanness  but      not in
1388        235  2531     1381                5259 02   2316
δόλῳ,    4  ἀλλὰ καθὼς    δεδοκιμάσμεθα       ὑπὸ  τοῦ  θεοῦ
guile,      but  just as  we have been proved by   the  God
4100        012 2098        3779  2980        3756
πιστευθῆναι τὸ  εὐαγγέλιον, οὕτως λαλοῦμεν,   οὐχ
to be trusted the good message, thusly we speak, not
5613 444         700         235  2316 03   1381
ὡς   ἀνθρώποις  ἀρέσκοντες  ἀλλὰ θεῷ  τῷ   δοκιμάζοντι
as   men        pleasing    but  God  the one proving
020 2588      1473      5  3777   1063 4218 1722 3056
τὰς καρδίας   ἡμῶν.      Οὔτε   γὰρ  ποτε ἐν   λόγῳ
the hearts    of us.       Neither for  then in   word
2850          1096         2531     3609a     3777 1722
κολακείας     ἐγενήθημεν,  καθὼς   οἴδατε,   οὔτε ἐν
of flattery   we became,   just as  you know, nor  in
4392        4124          2316 3144       6 3777 2212
προφάσει    πλεονεξίας,   θεὸς μάρτυς,     οὔτε ζητοῦντες
pretext     of greediness, God testifier,  nor  seeking
1537 444        1391       3777 575   1473 3777 575
ἐξ   ἀνθρώπων   δόξαν      οὔτε ἀφ᾽   ὑμῶν οὔτε ἀπ᾽
from men        splendor   nor  from  you  nor  from
243        7  1410        1722 922    1510   5613 5547
ἄλλων,       δυνάμενοι    ἐν   βάρει  εἶναι ὡς   Χριστοῦ
others,      being able   in   burden to be as   of Christ
652          235  1096       3516    1722 3319   1473
ἀπόστολοι.   ἀλλὰ ἐγενήθημεν νήπιοι  ἐν   μέσῳ   ὑμῶν,
delegates.   But  we became  infants in   middle of you,
5613 1437 5162    2282      204 1438      5043
ὡς   ἐὰν  τροφὸς θάλπῃ     τὰ  ἑαυτῆς    τέκνα,
as   if   feeder cherishes the of herself children,
```

of those regions[a] report about us what kind of welcome we had among you, and how you turned to God from idols, to serve a living and true God, [10]and to wait for his Son from heaven, whom he raised from the dead—Jesus, who rescues us from the wrath that is coming.

CHAPTER 2

You yourselves know, brothers and sisters,[b] that our coming to you was not in vain, [2]but though we had already suffered and been shamefully mistreated at Philippi, as you know, we had courage in our God to declare to you the gospel of God in spite of great opposition. [3]For our appeal does not spring from deceit or impure motives or trickery, [4]but just as we have been approved by God to be entrusted with the message of the gospel, even so we speak, not to please mortals, but to please God who tests our hearts. [5]As you know and as God is our witness, we never came with words of flattery or with a pretext for greed; [6]nor did we seek praise from mortals, whether from you or from others, [7]though we might have made demands as apostles of Christ. But we were gentle[c] among you, like a nurse tenderly caring for her own children.

[a] Gk For they
[b] Gk brothers
[c] Other ancient authorities read infants

8So deeply do we care for you that we are determined to share with you not only the gospel of God but also our own selves, because you have become very dear to us.

9 You remember our labor and toil, brothers and sisters;[a] we worked night and day, so that we might not burden any of you while we proclaimed to you the gospel of God. 10You are witnesses, and God also, how pure, upright, and blameless our conduct was toward you believers. 11As you know, we dealt with each one of you like a father with his children, 12urging and encouraging you and pleading that you lead a life worthy of God, who calls you into his own kingdom and glory.

13 We also constantly give thanks to God for this, that when you received the word of God that you heard from us, you accepted it not as a human word but as what it really is, God's word, which is also at work in you believers. 14For you, brothers and sisters,[a] became imitators of the churches of God in Christ Jesus that are in Judea, for you suffered the same things from your own

[a] Gk brothers

```
      3779        3655a         1473      2106
8   οὕτως   ὁμειρόμενοι ὑμῶν   εὐδοκοῦμεν
    thusly  yearning     of you  we were thinking well
3330          1473        3756 3441   012 2098            02
μεταδοῦναι ὑμῖν    οὐ   μόνον τὸ  εὐαγγέλιον    τοῦ
to share     to you  not   alone the  good message  of the
2316  235    2532 020 1438              5590    1360
θεοῦ ἀλλὰ  καὶ  τὰς ἑαυτῶν     ψυχάς,  διότι
God   but    also the of ourselves  souls,   because
27            1473  1096          3421              1063
ἀγαπητοὶ  ἡμῖν ἐγενήθητε. 9 Μνημονεύετε  γάρ,
loved ones  to us  you became.   Remember       for,
80      04   2873    1473   2532 04  3449        3571  2532
ἀδελφοί,  τὸν κόπον ἡμῶν καὶ  τὸν μόχθον· νυκτὸς καὶ
brothers,  the  labor of us  and  the  toil;   night  and
2250    2038            4314  012 3361 1912              5100
ἡμέρας ἐργαζόμενοι πρὸς τὸ  μὴ  ἐπιβαρῆσαί  τινα
day     working      to    the not  to burden on  some
1473    2784          1519 1473 012 2098             02
ὑμῶν  ἐκηρύξαμεν  εἰς  ὑμᾶς τὸ  εὐαγγέλιον    τοῦ
of you  we announced to     you   the  good message of the
2316    1473 3144           2532 01  2316  5613 3743
θεοῦ. 10 ὑμεῖς μάρτυρες  καὶ  ὁ  θεός, ὡς  ὁσίως
God.      You   testifiers  and the God,  as  holily
2532 1346     2532 274              1473  015    4100
καὶ  δικαίως καὶ  ἀμέμπτως  ὑμῖν  τοῖς πιστεύουσιν
and  rightly  and  faultlessly to you the  ones trusting
1096               2509     3609a        5613 1520 1538
ἐγενήθημεν, 11 καθάπερ οἴδατε,  ὡς  ἕνα ἕκαστον
we became,      just as you know, as   one  each
                                            indeed
1473    5613 3962    5043         1438           3870
ὑμῶν  ὡς  πατὴρ τέκνα  ἑαυτοῦ 12 παρακαλοῦντες
of you  as   father children of himself    encouraging
1473 2532 3888              2532 3140            1519 012
ὑμᾶς καὶ  παραμυθούμενοι καὶ  μαρτυρόμενοι εἰς  τὸ
you  and   comforting         and  testifying     to   the
4043              1473 516       02        2316 02
περιπατεῖν ὑμᾶς ἀξίως   τοῦ    θεοῦ τοῦ
to walk around you  worthily of the God  the one
2564         1473 1519 08 1438          932         2532
καλοῦντος ὑμᾶς εἰς  τὴν ἑαυτοῦ  βασιλείαν καὶ
calling      you  into the  of himself kingdom    and
1391        2532 1223       3778  2532 1473
δόξαν. 13 Καὶ  διὰ   τοῦτο καὶ  ἡμεῖς
splendor.   And through this  also  we
2168              03        2316 89              3754
εὐχαριστοῦμεν  τῷ    θεῷ ἀδιαλείπτως, ὅτι
give good favor to the God  unceasingly,    that
3880                3056  189       3844 1473 02 2316
παραλαβόντες    λόγον ἀκοῆς   παρ' ἡμῶν τοῦ θεοῦ
having taken along word of hearing from  us   the God
1209         3756 3056 444      235   2531       1510
ἐδέξασθε    οὐ  λόγον ἀνθρώπων ἀλλὰ καθώς  ἐστιν
you welcomed not  word  of men   but  just as it is
230       3056 2316    3739 2532 1754        1722 1473
ἀληθῶς λόγον θεοῦ,  ὃς  καὶ  ἐνεργεῖται ἐν  ὑμῖν
truly   word of God, who  also operates    in   you
015  4100            1473  1063 3402        1096
τοῖς πιστεύουσιν. 14 Ὑμεῖς γὰρ μιμηταὶ ἐγενήθητε,
the  ones trusting.   You   for  imitators became,
80     018    1577       02      2316 018
ἀδελφοί, τῶν ἐκκλησιῶν τοῦ θεοῦ τῶν
brothers,  of the assemblies of the God of the ones
1510  1722 07  2449    1722 5547   2424  3754 024
οὐσῶν ἐν τῇ Ἰουδαίᾳ ἐν Χριστῷ Ἰησοῦ, ὅτι  τὰ
being in the Judea   in  Christ  Jesus, that the
846 3958          2532 1473  5259 014 2398
αὐτὰ ἐπάθετε    καὶ  ὑμεῖς ὑπὸ τῶν ἰδίων
same you suffered also  you   by   the own
```

```
4853            2531      2532 846        5259 014   2453
συμφυλετῶν       καθὼς     καὶ  αὐτοὶ      ὑπὸ τῶν  Ἰουδαίων,
co-tribesmen just as also themselves by the   Judeans,
        014           2532 04  2962   615              2424
15 τῶν            καὶ  τὸν κύριον ἀποκτεινάντων  Ἰησοῦν
   of the ones also the Master having killed   Jesus
2532 016  4396        2532 1473 1559              2532
καὶ  τοὺς προφήτας καὶ  ἡμᾶς ἐκδιωξάντων         καὶ
and  the  spokesmen and  us   having persecuted and
2316 3361 700          2532 3956  444      1727
θεῷ  μὴ  ἀρεσκόντων καὶ  πᾶσιν ἀνθρώποις ἐναντίων,
God  not pleasing   and  to all men       against,
   2967     1473 023    1484     2980     2443
16 κωλυόντων ἡμᾶς τοῖς  ἔθνεσιν λαλῆσαι ἵνα
   hindering us   to the nations to speak that
4982                  1519 012 378            846
σωθῶσιν,              εἰς  τὸ ἀναπληρῶσαι αὐτῶν
they might be delivered, for the to fill up  of them
020 266      3842        5348    1161 1909 846    05
τὰς ἁμαρτίας πάντοτε. ἔφθασεν δὲ  ἐπ’ αὐτοὺς ἡ
the sins     always.  Arrived but on  them    the
3709 1519 5056      1473  1161 80
ὀργὴ εἰς  τέλος.  17 Ἡμεῖς δέ, ἀδελφοί,
anger into completion.  We  but, brothers,
642                      575  1473 4314    2540
ἀπορφανισθέντες          ἀφ’ ὑμῶν πρὸς καιρὸν
having been orphaned off from you  toward season
orphaned off
5610   4383      3756 2588       4056
ὥρας,  προσώπῳ οὐ καρδίᾳ,     περισσοτέρως
of hour, in face not in heart, more exceedingly
4704          012 4383    1473   3708    1722 4183
ἐσπουδάσαμεν  τὸ πρόσωπον ὑμῶν ἰδεῖν ἐν πολλῇ
we did diligence the face   of you to see in  much
1939       18  1360   2309       2064    4314 1473
ἐπιθυμίᾳ.      διότι ἠθελήσαμεν ἐλθεῖν πρὸς ὑμᾶς,
desire.        Because we wanted to come to  you,
1473 3303  3972    2532 530  2532 1364   2532 1465
ἐγὼ μὲν   Παῦλος καὶ ἅπαξ καὶ  δίς,   καὶ ἐνέκοψεν
I    indeed Paul  both once and twice, and hindered
1473 01  4567      19 5101 1063 1473  1680   2228 5479
ἡμᾶς ὁ  σατανᾶς.    τίς γὰρ ἡμῶν ἐλπὶς ἢ  χαρὰ
us   the adversary.  Who for of us hope or  joy
2228 4735      2746         2228 3780 2532 1473
ἢ   στέφανος καυχήσεως - ἢ   οὐχὶ καὶ  ὑμεῖς -
or  crown     of brag    or  not  also you
1715       02       2962    1473  2424   1722 07  846
ἔμπροσθεν τοῦ    κυρίου ἡμῶν Ἰησοῦ ἐν τῇ αὐτοῦ
in front  of the Master of us Jesus in the of him
3952       20 1473 1063 1510 05 1391     1473 2532
παρουσίᾳ;     ὑμεῖς γάρ ἐστε ἡ  δόξα  ἡμῶν καὶ
presence?     You   for are the splendor of us and
05 5479    1352  3371      4722
ἡ  χαρά. 3:1 Διὸ  μηκέτι στέγοντες
the joy.     Wherefore no longer enduring
2106          2641              1722 116     3441
εὐδοκήσαμεν  καταλειφθῆναι   ἐν  Ἀθήναις μόνοι
we thought well to be left behind in  Athens  alone
   2532 3992     5095       04  80      1473 2532
 2 καὶ  ἐπέμψαμεν Τιμόθεον, τὸν ἀδελφὸν ἡμῶν καὶ
   and  we sent   Timothy,  the brother of us and
4904       02    2316 1722 011  2098            02
συνεργὸν τοῦ  θεοῦ ἐν  τῷ  εὐαγγελίῳ      τοῦ
co-worker of the God in  the good message of the
5547     1519 012 4741      1473 2532 3870
Χριστοῦ, εἰς  τὸ στηρίξαι  ὑμᾶς καὶ  παρακαλέσαι
Christ,  for the to strengthen you and  to encourage
5228     06   4102     1473  3 012 3367
ὑπὲρ    τῆς πίστεως ὑμῶν    τὸ μηδένα
on behalf of the trust  of you  the no one
```

compatriots as they did from the Jews, [15]who killed both the Lord Jesus and the prophets,[a] and drove us out; they displease God and oppose everyone [16]by hindering us from speaking to the Gentiles so that they may be saved. Thus they have constantly been filling up the measure of their sins; but God's wrath has overtaken them at last.[b]

[17]As for us, brothers and sisters,[c] when, for a short time, we were made orphans by being separated from you—in person, not in heart—we longed with great eagerness to see you face to face. [18]For we wanted to come to you—certainly I, Paul, wanted to again and again—but Satan blocked our way. [19]For what is our hope or joy or crown of boasting before our Lord Jesus at his coming? Is it not you? [20]Yes, you are our glory and joy!

CHAPTER 3

Therefore when we could bear it no longer, we decided to be left alone in Athens; [2]and we sent Timothy, our brother and co-worker for God in proclaiming[d] the gospel of Christ, to strengthen and encourage you for the sake of your faith, [3]so that no one

---

[a] Other ancient authorities read their own prophets
[b] Or completely or forever
[c] Gk brothers
[d] Gk lacks proclaiming

would be shaken by these persecutions. Indeed, you yourselves know that this is what we are destined for. ⁴In fact, when we were with you, we told you beforehand that we were to suffer persecution; so it turned out, as you know. ⁵For this reason, when I could bear it no longer, I sent to find out about your faith; I was afraid that somehow the tempter had tempted you and that our labor had been in vain.

6 But Timothy has just now come to us from you, and has brought us the good news of your faith and love. He has told us also that you always remember us kindly and long to see us— just as we long to see you. ⁷For this reason, brothers and sisters,ᵃ during all our distress and persecution we have been encouraged about you through your faith. ⁸For we now live, if you continue to stand firm in the Lord. ⁹How can we thank God enough for you in return for all the joy that we feel before our God because of you? ¹⁰Night and day we pray most earnestly that we may see you face to face and restore whatever is lacking in your faith.

11 Now may our God and Father himself and our Lord Jesus direct

ᵃ Gk brothers

4525		1722 019	2347		3778	846
σαίνεσθαι	ἐν	ταῖς	θλίψεσιν	ταύταις.	αὐτοὶ	
to be shaken	in	the	afflictions	these.	Yourselves	

1063 3609a   3754 1519 3778   2749   2532 1063
γὰρ οἴδατε ὅτι εἰς τοῦτο κείμεθα· ⁴ καὶ γὰρ
for you know that for this we are set; also for

3753 4314 1473 1510   4302   1473
ὅτε πρὸς ὑμᾶς ἦμεν, προελέγομεν   ὑμῖν
when to you we were, we were speaking before to you

3754 3195   2346   2531   2532
ὅτι μέλλομεν θλίβεσθαι,   καθὼς καὶ
that we are about to be afflicted, just as also

1096   2532 3609a   1223   3778 2504
ἐγένετο καὶ οἴδατε. ⁵ διὰ τοῦτο κἀγὼ
it became and you know. Through this also I

3371   4722   3992   1519 012 1097   08 4102
μηκέτι στέγων ἔπεμψα εἰς τὸ γνῶναι τὴν πίστιν
no longer enduring sent for the to know the trust

1473   3361 4458   3985   1473 01 3985
ὑμῶν, μή πως ἐπείρασεν ὑμᾶς ὁ πειράζων
of you, not perhaps pressured you the one pressuring

2532 1519 2756 1096   01 2873 1473   737
καὶ εἰς κενὸν γένηται ὁ κόπος ἡμῶν. ⁶ Ἄρτι
and into empty might become the labor of us. Now

1161 2064   5095   4314 1473 575 1473 2532
δὲ ἐλθόντος Τιμοθέου πρὸς ἡμᾶς ἀφ' ὑμῶν καὶ
but having come Timothy to us from you and

2097   1473 08 4102 2532 08 26   1473
εὐαγγελισαμένου ἡμῖν τὴν πίστιν καὶ τὴν ἀγάπην ὑμῶν
having told to us the trust and the love of you
good message

2532 3754 2192   3417   1473 18   3842
καὶ ὅτι ἔχετε μνείαν ἡμῶν ἀγαθὴν πάντοτε,
and that you have memory of us good always,

1971   1473 3708 2509   2532 1473
ἐπιποθοῦντες ἡμᾶς ἰδεῖν καθάπερ καὶ ἡμεῖς
desiring longingly us to see just as also we

1473   ⁷ 1223   3778 3870   80
ὑμᾶς, διὰ τοῦτο παρεκλήθημεν, ἀδελφοί,
you, through this we were encouraged, brothers,

1909 1473 1909 3956 07 318   2532 2347   1473
ἐφ' ὑμῖν ἐπὶ πάσῃ τῇ ἀνάγκῃ καὶ θλίψει ἡμῶν
on you on all the necessity and affliction of us

1223   06 1473   4102   ⁸ 3754   3568 2198
διὰ τῆς ὑμῶν πίστεως, ὅτι νῦν ζῶμεν
through the of you trust, because now we live

1437 1473 4739   1722 2962   ⁹ 5101 1063 2169
ἐὰν ὑμεῖς στήκετε ἐν κυρίῳ. τίνα γὰρ εὐχαριστίαν
if you stand in Master. What for good favor

1410   03   2316 467   4012 1473
δυνάμεθα τῷ θεῷ ἀνταποδοῦναι περὶ ὑμῶν
are we able to the God to give back again about you

1909 3956 07 5479 3739   5463   1223   1473
ἐπὶ πάσῃ τῇ χαρᾷ ᾗ χαίρομεν δι' ὑμᾶς
on all the joy in which we rejoice through you

1715   02   2316 1473 ¹⁰ 3571   2532 2250
ἔμπροσθεν τοῦ θεοῦ ἡμῶν, νυκτὸς καὶ ἡμέρας
in front of the God of us, night and day

5238a   1189   1519 012 3708 1473 012
ὑπερεκπερισσοῦ δεόμενοι εἰς τὸ ἰδεῖν ὑμῶν τὸ
excessively beyond begging for the to see of you the

4383   2532 2675   024 5303   06
πρόσωπον καὶ καταρτίσαι τὰ ὑστερήματα τῆς
face and to put in order the lacks of the

4102   1473 ¹¹ 846   1161 01 2316 2532 3962
πίστεως ὑμῶν; Αὐτὸς δὲ ὁ θεὸς καὶ πατὴρ
trust of you? Himself but the God and father

1473 2532 01 2962   1473 2424   2720
ἡμῶν καὶ ὁ κύριος ἡμῶν Ἰησοῦς κατευθύναι
of us and the Master of us Jesus may make straight

08   3598 1473   4314 1473   **12**   1473 1161 01   2962
τὴν ὁδὸν ἡμῶν πρὸς ὑμᾶς·   ὑμᾶς δὲ   ὁ   κύριος
the   way   of us   to   you;   you   but   the Master

4121   2532 4052   07   26   1519
πλεονάσαι   καὶ   περισσεύσαι τῇ   ἀγάπῃ   εἰς
may increase and   may exceed   in the   love   to

240   2532 1519 3956   2509   2532 1473   1519
ἀλλήλους   καὶ   εἰς πάντας καθάπερ καὶ   ἡμεῖς εἰς
one another   and   to   all   just as   also   we   into

1473   **13** 1519 012 4741   1473 020 2588
ὑμᾶς,   εἰς τὸ   στηρίξαι   ὑμῶν τὰς καρδίας
you,   for   the to strengthen   you   the hearts

273   1722 42   1715   02   2316 2532
ἀμέμπτους ἐν   ἁγιωσύνῃ ἔμπροσθεν   τοῦ   θεοῦ καὶ
faultless   in   holiness in front   of the God   and

3962   1473   1722 07   3952   02   2962   1473
πατρὸς ἡμῶν ἐν   τῇ   παρουσίᾳ   τοῦ   κυρίου ἡμῶν
father   of us   in   the presence   of the Master   of us

2424   3326 3956   2532 40   846   281
Ἰησοῦ   μετὰ πάντων τῶν ἁγίων αὐτοῦ,   [ἀμήν].
Jesus   with all   the   holy ones of him,   amen.

4:1 3062   3767 80   2065   1473 2532
        Λοιπὸν οὖν, ἀδελφοί, ἐρωτῶμεν ὑμᾶς καὶ
        Remaining then, brothers,   we ask   you   and

3870   1722 2962   2424   2443 2531
παρακαλοῦμεν ἐν   κυρίῳ Ἰησοῦ, ἵνα   καθὼς
encourage   in   Master   Jesus,   that   just as

3880   3844   1473 012 4459 1163
παρελάβετε παρ᾽   ἡμῶν τὸ   πῶς δεῖ
you took along beside us   the   how it is necessary

1473 4043   2532 700   2316 2531   2532
ὑμᾶς περιπατεῖν καὶ   ἀρέσκειν θεῷ, καθὼς   καὶ
you   to walk around and   to please   God,   just as   also

4043   2443 4052   3123
περιπατεῖτε,   ἵνα   περισσεύητε μᾶλλον.
you walk around, that   you might exceed more.

2 3609a   1063 5101   3852   1325   1473
      οἴδατε   γὰρ τίνας παραγγελίας ἐδώκαμεν ὑμῖν
      You know for   what   commands   we gave   to you

1223   02   2962   2424   3   3778   1063 1510   2307
διὰ   τοῦ κυρίου Ἰησοῦ.   Τοῦτο γάρ ἐστιν θέλημα
through the Master Jesus.   This   for   is   want

02   2316   01   38   1473   568   1473
τοῦ θεοῦ, ὁ   ἁγιασμὸς ὑμῶν,   ἀπέχεσθαι   ὑμᾶς
of the God, the holiness   of you, to hold off   you

575   06   4202   4 3609a   1538   1473
ἀπὸ τῆς πορνείας,   εἰδέναι   ἕκαστον   ὑμῶν
from the sexual immorality, to know   each   of you

012 1438   4632   2932   1722 38   2532
τὸ   ἑαυτοῦ σκεῦος κτᾶσθαι ἐν   ἁγιασμῷ καὶ
the   of himself pot   to acquire   in   holiness   and

5092   5 3361 1722 3806   1939   2509   2532 021
τιμῇ,   μὴ   ἐν   πάθει ἐπιθυμίας καθάπερ καὶ   τὰ
value,   not   in   passion of desire   just as   also the

1484   021 3361 3609a   04   2316   6 012 3361
ἔθνη   τὰ   μὴ   εἰδότα   τὸν θεόν,   τὸ   μὴ
nations the not   having known the God,   the not

5233   2532 4122   1722 011 4229   04
ὑπερβαίνειν   καὶ   πλεονεκτεῖν ἐν   τῷ πράγματι τὸν
to go beyond   and   to take more   in   the practice   the

80   846   1360   1558   2962   4012
ἀδελφὸν   αὐτοῦ, διότι   ἔκδικος   κύριος   περὶ
brother   of him, because bring out right Master about

3956   3778   2531   2532 4302   1473   2532
πάντων τούτων, καθὼς καὶ   προείπαμεν ὑμῖν καὶ
all   these,   just as   also   we said before to you and

1263   7 3756 1063 2564   1473 01   2316
διεμαρτυράμεθα.   οὐ   γὰρ ἐκάλεσεν ἡμᾶς ὁ   θεὸς
we testify   Not   for   called   us   the God
thoroughly.

---

our way to you. [12]And may
the Lord make you increase
and abound in love for one
another and for all, just as
we abound in love for you.
[13]And may he so strengthen
your hearts in holiness that
you may be blameless before
our God and Father at the
coming of our Lord Jesus
with all his saints.

CHAPTER 4

Finally, brothers and
sisters,[a] we ask and urge
you in the Lord Jesus that,
as you learned from us how
you ought to live and to
please God (as, in fact, you
are doing), you should do
so more and more. [2]For you
know what instructions we
gave you through the Lord
Jesus. [3]For this is the will
of God, your sanctification:
that you abstain from
fornication; [4]that each
one of you know how to
control your own body[b]
in holiness and honor, [5]not
with lustful passion, like
the Gentiles who do not
know God; [6]that no one
wrong or exploit a brother
or sister[c] in this matter,
because the Lord is an
avenger in all these things,
just as we have already
told you beforehand and
solemnly warned you. [7]For
God did not call us

---

[a] Gk brothers
[b] Or how to take a wife for himself
[c] Gk brother

to impurity but in holiness.
[8]Therefore whoever rejects
this rejects not human
authority but God, who
also gives his Holy Spirit
to you.

9 Now concerning love
of the brothers and sisters,[a]
you do not need to have
anyone write to you, for
you yourselves have been
taught by God to love one
another; [10]and indeed you
do love all the brothers
and sisters[a] throughout
Macedonia. But we urge
you, beloved,[a] to do so
more and more, [11]to aspire
to live quietly, to mind
your own affairs, and to
work with your hands, as
we directed you, [12]so that
you may behave properly
toward outsiders and be
dependent on no one.

13 But we do not want
you to be uninformed,
brothers and sisters,[a] about
those who have died,[b] so
that you may not grieve
as others do who have no
hope. [14]For since we believe
that Jesus died and rose
again, even so, through
Jesus, God will bring with
him those who have died.[b]
[15]For this we declare to
you by the word of the
Lord, that we who are
alive, who are left until the
coming of the Lord, will
by no means precede those
who have died.[b] [16]For the
Lord himself, with a

[a] Gk brothers
[b] Gk fallen asleep

```
1909   167              235   1722  38          5105              01
ἐπὶ   ἀκαθαρσίᾳ   ἀλλ'  ἐν   ἁγιασμῷ.  8 τοιγαροῦν   ὁ
on    uncleanness but  in   holiness.   Consequently the
114                    3756 444           114        235  04
ἀθετῶν               οὐκ ἄνθρωπον ἀθετεῖ    ἀλλὰ  τὸν
one setting aside not man       sets aside but   the
2316 04    2532 1325          012  4151    846     012
θεὸν  τὸν  [καὶ]  διδόντα    τὸ  πνεῦμα αὐτοῦ  τὸ
God   the  also  having given the spirit of him the
40    1519 1473     4012   1161 06   5360              3756
ἅγιον εἰς  ὑμᾶς.  9 Περὶ  δὲ  τῆς  φιλαδελφίας   οὐ
holy  to   you.   About but the  brotherly love not
5532   2192        1125      1473    846     1063 1473
χρείαν ἔχετε     γράφειν ὑμῖν,  αὐτοὶ   γὰρ  ὑμεῖς
need   you have to write to you, yourselves for   you
2312          1510 1519 012 25       240           10 2532
θεοδίδακτοί ἐστε εἰς τὸ ἀγαπᾶν ἀλλήλους,    καὶ
God taught are for the to love one another, and
1063 4160    846  1519 3956   016  80       016
γὰρ  ποιεῖτε αὐτὸ εἰς πάντας τοὺς ἀδελφοὺς [τοὺς]
for  you do same to  all    the  brothers  the
1722 3650  07 3109         3870       1161 1473
ἐν   ὅλῃ  τῇ Μακεδονίᾳ. Παρακαλοῦμεν δὲ  ὑμᾶς,
in   whole the Macedonia. We encourage but  you,
80       4052        3123      11 2532 5389
ἀδελφοί, περισσεύειν μᾶλλον   καὶ φιλοτιμεῖσθαι
brothers, to exceed  more        and to love value
2270        2532 4238       024 2398 2532 2038
ἡσυχάζειν  καὶ πράσσειν  τὰ ἴδια καὶ ἐργάζεσθαι
to be quiet and to practice the own and to work
019    2398     5495  1473     2531    1473
ταῖς [ἰδίαις] χερσὶν ὑμῶν, καθὼς  ὑμῖν
in the own   hands of you, just as  to you
3853              12 2443 4043          2156        4314
παρηγγείλαμεν,   ἵνα περιπατῆτε    εὐσχημόνως πρὸς
we commanded,    that you might walk properly    to
                                                around
016    1854    2532 3067      5532    2192
τοὺς  ἔξω   καὶ μηδενὸς  χρείαν ἔχητε.
the   outside and of nothing need  you might have.
      3756 2309    1161 1473 50      80        4012
13  Οὐ  θέλομεν δὲ  ὑμᾶς ἀγνοεῖν,  ἀδελφοί, περὶ
    Not  we want but  you to not know, brothers, about
014 2837         2443 3361 3076             2531
τῶν κοιμωμένων, ἵνα μὴ λυπῆσθε         καθὼς
the ones sleeping, that not you might grieve just as
2532 013 3062     013     3361 2192    1680
καὶ οἱ λοιποὶ  οἱ    μὴ ἔχοντες ἐλπίδα.
also the remaining the ones not having hope.
   1487 1063 4100       3754 2424   599        2532
14 εἰ  γὰρ πιστεύομεν ὅτι Ἰησοῦς ἀπέθανεν καὶ
   If  for we trust    that Jesus died      and
450      3779   2532 01 2316 016 2837
ἀνέστη, οὕτως καὶ ὁ θεὸς τοὺς κοιμηθέντας
stood up, thusly also the God the ones having slept
1223  02   2424  71      4862 846    15 3778 1063
διὰ  τοῦ Ἰησοῦ ἄξει  σὺν αὐτῷ.   Τοῦτο γὰρ
through the Jesus will lead with him.  This for
1473  3004    1722 3056 2962     3754 1473 013
ὑμῖν λέγομεν ἐν λόγῳ κυρίου,  ὅτι ἡμεῖς οἱ
to you we say in  word of Master, that we   the
2198   013 4035        1519 08 3952    02
ζῶντες οἱ περιλειπόμενοι εἰς τὴν παρουσίαν τοῦ
living the being left around for the presence of the
2962    3756 3361 5348       016
κυρίου οὐ  μὴ  φθάσωμεν  τοὺς
Master not not we might arrive the ones
2837         16 3754   846   01 2962   1722
κοιμηθέντας·   ὅτι  αὐτὸς ὁ κύριος ἐν
having slept;    because himself the Master in
```

2752   1722 5456   743   2532 1722
κελεύσματι, ἐν   φωνῇ ἀρχαγγέλου   καὶ ἐν
command,   in   sound first messenger and   in
4536   2316   2597   575   3772
σάλπιγγι θεοῦ, καταβήσεται   ἀπ᾿ οὐρανοῦ
trumpet   of God, will come down from heaven
2532 013 3498   1722 5547   450   4413
καὶ οἱ νεκροὶ ἐν Χριστῷ ἀναστήσονται πρῶτον,
and the dead   in Christ will stand up first,
    1899   1473 013 2198   013 4035
17 ἔπειτα ἡμεῖς οἱ ζῶντες οἱ περιλειπόμενοι
   then   we   the living the ones being left around
260   4862 846   726   1722 3507
ἅμα   σὺν αὐτοῖς ἁρπαγησόμεθα ἐν νεφέλαις
at same time with them we will be seized in clouds
1519 529   02   2962   1519 109   2532 3779
εἰς ἀπάντησιν τοῦ κυρίου εἰς ἀέρα· καὶ οὕτως
for meeting of the Master in air; and thusly
3842   4862 2962 1510   5620   3870
πάντοτε σὺν κυρίῳ ἐσόμεθα.   18 Ὥστε   παρακαλεῖτε
always with Master we will be. So that encourage
240   1722 015 3056 3778   4012 1161
ἀλλήλους ἐν τοῖς λόγοις τούτοις. 5:1 Περὶ δὲ
one another in the words these.   About but
014 5550   2532 014 2540   80   3756 5532
τῶν χρόνων καὶ τῶν καιρῶν, ἀδελφοί, οὐ χρείαν
the times   and the seasons, brothers, not need
2192   1473 1125   846   1063
ἔχετε ὑμῖν γράφεσθαι, 2 αὐτοὶ   γὰρ
you have to you to be written, yourselves for
199   3609a   3754 2250 2962   5613 2812
ἀκριβῶς οἴδατε ὅτι ἡμέρα κυρίου ὡς κλέπτης
accurately you know that day of Master as thief
1722 3571 3779   2064   3 3752 3004   1515
ἐν νυκτὶ οὕτως ἔρχεται. ὅταν λέγωσιν·   εἰρήνη
in night thusly comes. When they might say, peace
2532 803   5119 160   846   2186   3639
καὶ ἀσφάλεια, τότε αἰφνίδιος αὐτοῖς ἐφίσταται ὄλεθρος
and security, then sudden   to them stands on ruin
5618   05 5604   07   1722 1064   2192   2532
ὥσπερ ἡ ὠδὶν τῇ ἐν γαστρὶ ἐχούσῃ, καὶ
as indeed the birth pain in the in womb   having, and
3756 3361 1628   4 1473 1161 80
οὐ μὴ ἐκφύγωσιν.   ὑμεῖς δέ, ἀδελφοί,
not not they might flee out. You but, brothers,
3756 1510   1722 4655 2443 05 2250 1473 5613
οὐκ ἐστὲ ἐν σκότει, ἵνα ἡ ἡμέρα ὑμᾶς ὡς
not you are in dark, that the day   you as
2812 2638   3956 1063 1473 5207 5457
κλέπτης καταλάβῃ· 5 πάντες γὰρ ὑμεῖς υἱοὶ φωτός
thief might overtake; all for you sons of light
1510 2532 5207 2250   3756 1510   3571   3761
ἐστε καὶ υἱοὶ ἡμέρας. Οὐκ ἐσμὲν νυκτὸς οὐδὲ
are and sons of day. Not we are of night but not
4655   686 3767   3361 2518   5613 013
σκότους· 6 ἄρα οὖν μὴ καθεύδωμεν ὡς οἱ
of dark; then therefore not we might sleep as the
3062   235 1127   2532 3525   013
λοιποί ἀλλὰ γρηγορῶμεν καὶ νήφωμεν. 7 Οἱ
remaining but we might and we might be The ones
                     keep awake   well-balanced.
1063 2518   3571   2518   2532 013
γὰρ καθεύδοντες νυκτὸς καθεύδουσιν καὶ οἱ
for sleeping by night they sleep and the ones
3182   3571   3184   8 1473 1161 2250
μεθυσκόμενοι νυκτὸς μεθύουσιν· ἡμεῖς δὲ ἡμέρας
being drunk by night are drunk; we but of day
1510 3525   1746
ὄντες νήφωμεν   ἐνδυσάμενοι
being we might be well-balanced having put on

cry of command, with the archangel's call and with the sound of God's trumpet, will descend from heaven, and the dead in Christ will rise first. [17]Then we who are alive, who are left, will be caught up in the clouds together with them to meet the Lord in the air; and so we will be with the Lord forever. [18]Therefore encourage one another with these words.

CHAPTER 5

Now concerning the times and the seasons, brothers and sisters,[a] you do not need to have anything written to you. [2]For you yourselves know very well that the day of the Lord will come like a thief in the night. [3]When they say, "There is peace and security," then sudden destruction will come upon them, as labor pains come upon a pregnant woman, and there will be no escape! [4]But you, beloved,[a] are not in darkness, for that day to surprise you like a thief; [5]for you are all children of light and children of the day; we are not of the night or of darkness. [6]So then let us not fall asleep as others do, but let us keep awake and be sober; [7]for those who sleep sleep at night, and those who are drunk get drunk at night. [8]But since we belong to the day, let us be sober, and put on

a Gk brothers

the breastplate of faith and love, and for a helmet the hope of salvation. ⁹For God has destined us not for wrath but for obtaining salvation through our Lord Jesus Christ, ¹⁰who died for us, so that whether we are awake or asleep we may live with him. ¹¹Therefore encourage one another and build up each other, as indeed you are doing.

12 But we appeal to you, brothers and sisters,ᵃ to respect those who labor among you, and have charge of you in the Lord and admonish you; ¹³esteem them very highly in love because of their work. Be at peace among yourselves. ¹⁴And we urge you, beloved,ᵃ to admonish the idlers, encourage the fainthearted, help the weak, be patient with all of them. ¹⁵See that none of you repays evil for evil, but always seek to do good to one another and to all. ¹⁶Rejoice always, ¹⁷pray without ceasing, ¹⁸give thanks in all circumstances; for this is the will of God in Christ Jesus for you. ¹⁹Do not quench the Spirit. ²⁰Do not despise the words of prophets,ᵇ ²¹but test everything; hold fast to what is good; ²²abstain from every

ᵃ Gk brothers
ᵇ Gk despise prophecies

2382	4102	2532 26		2532 4030	
θώρακα	πίστεως	καὶ	ἀγάπης καὶ	περικεφαλαίαν	
breastplate	of trust	and	of love and	helmet	

1680	4991		⁹ 3754 3756 5087	1473 01	2316
ἐλπίδα	σωτηρίας·		ὅτι οὐκ ἔθετο	ἡμᾶς ὁ	θεὸς
hope	of deliverance;		that not set	us the	God

1519 3709	235	1519 4047		4991
εἰς ὀργὴν	ἀλλὰ	εἰς περιποίησιν		σωτηρίας
for anger	but	for possession		of deliverance

1223	02 2962	1473	2424 5547	10	02
διὰ	τοῦ κυρίου	ἡμῶν	Ἰησοῦ Χριστοῦ		τοῦ
through	the Master	of us	Jesus Christ		the one

599	5228	1473	2443 1535
ἀποθανόντος	ὑπὲρ	ἡμῶν,	ἵνα εἴτε
having died	on behalf	of us,	that whether

1127	1535 2518	260	4862 846	2198
γρηγορῶμεν	εἴτε καθεύδωμεν	ἅμα	σὺν αὐτῷ	ζήσωμεν.
we might or	might be	at same	with him	we might
kedp awale	sleeping	time		live.

11	1352	3870	240	2532 3618
	Διὸ	παρακαλεῖτε	ἀλλήλους	καὶ οἰκοδομεῖτε
	Wherefore	encourage	one another and	build

1520 04	1520 2531	2532 4160		2065	1161
εἰς τὸν ἕνα,	καθὼς	καὶ ποιεῖτε.	12	Ἐρωτῶμεν	δὲ
one the one,	just as	also you do.		We ask	but

1473	80	3609a	016	2872	1722 1473
ὑμᾶς,	ἀδελφοί,	εἰδέναι	τοὺς κοπιῶντας		ἐν ὑμῖν
you,	brothers,	to know	the ones laboring		in you

2532 4291		1473 1722 2962	2532 3560
καὶ προϊσταμένους		ὑμῶν ἐν κυρίῳ	καὶ νουθετοῦντας
and standing before		you in Master	and warning

1473	13	2532 2233	846	5238a
ὑμᾶς		καὶ ἡγεῖσθαι	αὐτοὺς	ὑπερεκπερισσοῦ
you		and to consider	them	more excessively beyond

1722 26	1223	012 2041 846	1514	1722
ἐν ἀγάπη	διὰ	τὸ ἔργον αὐτῶν.	εἰρηνεύετε	ἐν
in love	through	the work of them.	Be at peace	in

1438	14	3870	1161 1473	80
ἑαυτοῖς.		Παρακαλοῦμεν δὲ	ὑμᾶς,	ἀδελφοί,
yourselves.		We encourage but	you,	brothers,

3560	016	813	3888	016
νουθετεῖτε	τοὺς ἀτάκτους,	παραμυθεῖσθε	τοὺς	
warn	the idle,	comfort	the	

3642	472	014 772	3114
ὀλιγοψύχους,	ἀντέχεσθε	τῶν ἀσθενῶν,	μακροθυμεῖτε
little-souled,	hold on	the weak,	be long-tempered

4314 3956	15	3708 3361 5100 2556	473	2556
πρὸς πάντας.		ὁρᾶτε μή τις κακὸν	ἀντὶ	κακοῦ
to all.		See not some bad	in place of	bad

5100 591		235 3842	012 18	1377
τινι ἀποδῷ,		ἀλλὰ πάντοτε	τὸ ἀγαθὸν	διώκετε
some might give off,		but always	the good	pursue

2532 1519 240		2532 1519 3956	16	3842
[καὶ] εἰς ἀλλήλους		καὶ εἰς πάντας.		πάντοτε
both for one another		and for all.		Always

5463	17	89	4336	18	1722 3956
χαίρετε,		ἀδιαλείπτως	προσεύχεσθε,		ἐν παντὶ
rejoice,		unceasingly	pray,		in all

2168		3778 1063 2307	2316	1722 5547
εὐχαριστεῖτε·		τοῦτο γὰρ θέλημα	θεοῦ	ἐν Χριστῷ
give good favor;		this for want	of God	in Christ

2424	1519 1473	19	012 4151	3361 4570
Ἰησοῦ	εἰς ὑμᾶς.		τὸ πνεῦμα	μὴ σβέννυτε,
Jesus	for you.		The spirit	not quench,

20	4394		3361 1848	21	3956 1161
	προφητείας		μὴ ἐξουθενεῖτε,		πάντα δὲ
	speaking before		not despise,		all but

1381	012 2570 2722	22	575 3956
δοκιμάζετε,	τὸ καλὸν κατέχετε,		ἀπὸ παντὸς
prove,	the good hold down,		from all

1491	4190	568	**23**	846	1161	01	2316
εἴδους	πονηροῦ ἀπέχεσθε.			Αὐτὸς	δὲ	ὁ	θεὸς
visible form of evil hold off.				Himself	but	the	God

06	1515	37	1473	3651
τῆς	εἰρήνης ἁγιάσαι		ὑμᾶς ὁλοτελεῖς,	
of the peace	may make holy you		wholly completed,	

2532	3648	1473	09	4151	2532	05	5590
καὶ	ὁλόκληρον	ὑμῶν	τὸ	πνεῦμα	καὶ	ἡ	ψυχὴ
and wholly called of you the spirit and the soul							

2532	09	4983	274	1722	07	3952	02
καὶ	τὸ	σῶμα	ἀμέμπτως	ἐν	τῇ	παρουσίᾳ	τοῦ
and the body faultlessly in the presence of the							

2962	1473	2424	5547	5083	**24**	4103
κυρίου	ἡμῶν	Ἰησοῦ Χριστοῦ	τηρηθείη.			πιστὸς
Master of us Jesus Christ may keep.						Trustful

01	2564	1473	2532	2532	4160	**25**	80
ὁ	καλῶν	ὑμᾶς, ὃς	καὶ	ποιήσει.			Ἀδελφοί,
the one calling you, who also will do.							Brothers,

4336	2532	4012	1473	**26**	782	016
προσεύχεσθε	[καὶ] περὶ		ἡμῶν.		Ἀσπάσασθε	τοὺς
pray also about us.					Greet	the

80	3956	1722	5370	40	**27**	1774a
ἀδελφοὺς	πάντας ἐν	φιλήματι	ἁγίῳ.			Ἐνορκίζω
brothers all in kiss holy.					I put under oath

1473	04	2962	314	08	1992	3956	015
ὑμᾶς	τὸν	κύριον ἀναγνωσθῆναι	τὴν	ἐπιστολὴν	πᾶσιν	τοῖς
you the Master to be read the letter to all the							

80	**28**	05	5485	02	2962	1473	2424
ἀδελφοῖς.		Ἡ	χάρις τοῦ		κυρίου	ἡμῶν	Ἰησοῦ
brothers.		The favor of the Master of us Jesus					

5547	3326	1473
Χριστοῦ	μεθ᾽	ὑμῶν.
Christ with you.		

form of evil.

23 May the God of peace himself sanctify you entirely; and may your spirit and soul and body be kept sound[a] and blameless at the coming of our Lord Jesus Christ. 24 The one who calls you is faithful, and he will do this.

25 Beloved,[b] pray for us.

26 Greet all the brothers and sisters[c] with a holy kiss. 27 I solemnly command you by the Lord that this letter be read to all of them.[d]

28 The grace of our Lord Jesus Christ be with you.[e]

[a] Or complete
[b] Gk Brothers
[c] Gk brothers
[d] Gk to all the brothers
[e] Other ancient authorities add Amen

2 THESSALONIANS

CHAPTER 1

Paul, Silvanus, and Timothy,
To the church of the Thessalonians in God our Father and the Lord Jesus Christ:
2 Grace to you and peace from God our[a] Father and the Lord Jesus Christ.
3 We must always give thanks to God for you, brothers and sisters,[b] as is right, because your faith is growing abundantly, and the love of everyone of you for one another is increasing. 4 Therefore we ourselves boast of you among the churches of God for your steadfastness and faith during all your persecutions and the afflictions that you are enduring.
5 This is evidence of the righteous judgment of God, and is intended to make you worthy of the kingdom of God, for which you are also suffering. 6 For it is indeed just of God to repay with affliction those who afflict you, 7 and to give relief to the afflicted as well as to us, when the Lord Jesus is revealed from heaven with his mighty angels 8 in flaming fire, inflicting vengeance on those who do not know God and on those who do not obey the gospel of our Lord Jesus. 9 These will suffer the punishment

a Other ancient authorities read the
b Gk brothers

1:1
3972　2532　4610　　　2532　5095　　07　　1577
Παῦλος καὶ Σιλουανὸς καὶ Τιμόθεος τῇ ἐκκλησίᾳ
Paul and Silvanus and Timothy to the assembly
2331　　　　　1722 2316 3962　　1473　2532 2962
Θεσσαλονικέων ἐν θεῷ πατρὶ ἡμῶν καὶ κυρίῳ
of Thessalonians in God father of us and Master
2424　5547　　2　5485　1473　　2532 1515　　575　2316
Ἰησοῦ Χριστῷ, **2** χάρις ὑμῖν καὶ εἰρήνη ἀπὸ θεοῦ
Jesus Christ, favor to you and peace from God
3962　　1473　2532 2962　　　2424　5547
πατρὸς [ἡμῶν] καὶ κυρίου Ἰησοῦ Χριστοῦ.
father of us and Master Jesus Christ.

3
2168　　　　　　3784　　03　　2316　3842
Εὐχαριστεῖν ὀφείλομεν τῷ θεῷ πάντοτε
To give good favor we owe to the God always
4012　1473　80　　　　2531　514　1510　　3754
περὶ ὑμῶν, ἀδελφοί, καθὼς ἄξιόν ἐστιν, ὅτι
about you, brothers, just as worthy it is, because
5232　　05　4102　　1473　　2532 4121　　05
ὑπεραυξάνει ἡ πίστις ὑμῶν καὶ πλεονάζει ἡ
grows beyond the trust of you and increases the
26　　1520　1538　　3956　　1473　1519 240
ἀγάπη ἑνὸς ἑκάστου πάντων ὑμῶν εἰς ἀλλήλους,
love of one of each of all of you to one another,
4　5620　　846　　1473 1722 1473 1460a　　1722 019
ὥστε αὐτοὺς ἡμᾶς ἐν ὑμῖν ἐγκαυχᾶσθαι ἐν ταῖς
so that them us in you to brag in in the
1577　　02　　2316 5228　　06　　5281
ἐκκλησίαις τοῦ θεοῦ ὑπὲρ τῆς ὑπομονῆς
assemblies of the God on behalf of the patience
1473　2532 4102　　1722 3956　015　1375
ὑμῶν καὶ πίστεως ἐν πᾶσιν τοῖς διωγμοῖς
of you and trust in all the persecutions
1473　2532 019　　2347　　3739　430
ὑμῶν καὶ ταῖς θλίψεσιν αἷς ἀνέχεσθε,
of you and in the afflictions which you endure,
5　1730　　06　　1342　2920　02　2316 1519
ἔνδειγμα τῆς δικαίας κρίσεως τοῦ θεοῦ εἰς
evidence of the right judgment of the God for
012 2661　　　1473 06　932　02
τὸ καταξιωθῆναι ὑμᾶς τῆς βασιλείας τοῦ
the to have been worthy you of the kingdom of the
2316　5228　　3739　2532 3958　　6　1512
θεοῦ, ὑπὲρ ἧς καὶ πάσχετε, εἴπερ
God, on behalf of which also you suffer, if though
1342　3844 2316 467　　015
δίκαιον παρὰ θεῷ ἀνταποδοῦναι τοῖς
right from God to be given back again to the ones
2346　1473 2347　　7　2532 1473　015
θλίβουσιν ὑμᾶς θλῖψιν καὶ ὑμῖν τοῖς
afflicting you in affliction and to you the
2346　　425　　3326 1473　1722 07　602
θλιβομένοις ἄνεσιν μεθ᾽ ἡμῶν, ἐν τῇ ἀποκαλύψει
being afflicted relief with us, in the uncovering
02　2962　2424 575 3772　3326 32
τοῦ κυρίου Ἰησοῦ ἀπ᾽ οὐρανοῦ μετ᾽ ἀγγέλων
of the Master Jesus from heaven with messengers
1411　846　8　1722 4442 5395　1325
δυνάμεως αὐτοῦ **8** ἐν πυρὶ φλογός, διδόντος
of power of him in fire of flame, giving
1557　　015　　3361 3609a　　2316 2532
ἐκδίκησιν τοῖς μὴ εἰδόσιν θεὸν καὶ
bring out right to the ones not having known God and
015　　3361 5219　　011 2098　02
τοῖς μὴ ὑπακούουσιν τῷ εὐαγγελίῳ τοῦ
to the ones not obeying the good message of the
2962　1473 2424　9　3748　1349 5099　3639
κυρίου ἡμῶν Ἰησοῦ, **9** οἵτινες δίκην τίσουσιν ὄλεθρον
Master of us Jesus, who right will pay ruin

166   575   4383   02   2962   2532 575   06
αἰώνιον ἀπὸ προσώπου τοῦ   κυρίου καὶ ἀπὸ τῆς
eternal from face   of the Master and from the
1391   06   2479   846   3752 2064
δόξης   τῆς ἰσχύος αὐτοῦ, 10 ὅταν ἔλθῃ
splendor of the strength of him,   when he might come
1740   1722 015 40   846   2532
ἐνδοξασθῆναι   ἐν τοῖς ἁγίοις αὐτοῦ καὶ
to be given splendor in in the holy ones of him and
2296   1722 3956 015   4100   3754
θαυμασθῆναι ἐν πᾶσιν τοῖς πιστεύσασιν, ὅτι
to be marveled in all   the ones trusting, because
4100   09   3142   1473 1909 1473 1722 07
ἐπιστεύθη τὸ μαρτύριον ἡμῶν ἐφ' ὑμᾶς, ἐν τῇ
was trusted the testimony of us on you, in the
2250   1565   11 1519 3739 2532 4336   3842
ἡμέρᾳ ἐκείνῃ.   Εἰς ὃ καὶ προσευχόμεθα πάντοτε
day   that.   For that also we pray   always
4012   1473 2443 1473 515   06   2821
περὶ ὑμῶν, ἵνα ὑμᾶς ἀξιώσῃ   τῆς κλήσεως
about you,   that you might make worthy of the call
01   06   1473   2532 4137   3956   2107
ὁ   θεὸς ἡμῶν καὶ πληρώσῃ   πᾶσαν εὐδοκίαν
the God of us and might fill all   good thought
19   2532 2041 4102   1722 1411   12 3704
ἀγαθωσύνης καὶ ἔργον πίστεως ἐν δυνάμει,   ὅπως
of goodness and work of trust in power,   so that
1740   09 3686 02   2962   1473 2424 1722
ἐνδοξασθῇ   τὸ ὄνομα τοῦ κυρίου ἡμῶν Ἰησοῦ ἐν
might be given the name of the Master of us Jesus in
splendor in
1473   2532 1473 1722 846   2596 08 5485 02   2316
ὑμῖν, καὶ ὑμεῖς ἐν αὐτῷ, κατὰ τὴν χάριν τοῦ θεοῦ
you, and you in him, by the favor of the God
1473 2532 2962   2424 5547   2:1 2065
ἡμῶν καὶ κυρίου Ἰησοῦ Χριστοῦ.   Ἐρωτῶμεν
of us and Master Jesus Christ.   We ask
1161 1473 80   5228   06   3952   02
δὲ ὑμᾶς, ἀδελφοί, ὑπὲρ τῆς παρουσίας τοῦ
but you, brothers, on behalf of the presence of the
2962   1473   2424 5547   2532 1473 1997
κυρίου ἡμῶν Ἰησοῦ Χριστοῦ καὶ ἡμῶν ἐπισυναγωγῆς
Master of us Jesus Christ and of us bring together
1909 846   2 1519 012 3361 5030   4531   1473
ἐπ' αὐτὸν   εἰς τὸ μὴ ταχέως σαλευθῆναι ὑμᾶς
on him   for the not quickly to be shaken you
575 02   3563 3366   2360   3383   1223
ἀπὸ τοῦ νοὸς μηδὲ θροεῖσθαι,   μήτε διὰ
from the mind but not to be disturbed neither through
4151   3383 1223   3056   3383 1223   1992   5613
πνεύματος μήτε διὰ   λόγου μήτε δι' ἐπιστολῆς ὡς
spirit   nor through word nor through letter   as
1223   1473 5613 3754 1764   05 2250 02
δι' ἡμῶν, ὡς ὅτι ἐνέστηκεν ἡ ἡμέρα τοῦ
through us, as that was present the day of the
2962   3 3361 5100 1473 1818
κυρίου· Μή τις ὑμᾶς ἐξαπατήσῃ
Master; not some you might thoroughly deceive
2596 3367 5158   3754   1437 3361 2064   05
κατὰ μηδένα τρόπον. ὅτι ἐὰν μὴ ἔλθῃ   ἡ
by no one manner. Because if not might come the
646   4413   2532 601   01 444
ἀποστασία πρῶτον καὶ ἀποκαλυφθῇ ὁ ἄνθρωπος
standing off first and might be uncovered the man
06   458   01 5207 06   684
τῆς ἀνομίας, ὁ υἱὸς τῆς ἀπωλείας,
of the lawlessness, the son of the destruction,
4 01 480   2532 5229
ὁ ἀντικείμενος καὶ ὑπεραιρόμενος
the one lying against and lifting himself beyond

of eternal destruction, separated from the presence of the Lord and from the glory of his might, [10]when he comes to be glorified by his saints and to be marveled at on that day among all who have believed, because our testimony to you was believed. [11]To this end we always pray for you, asking that our God will make you worthy of his call and will fulfill by his power every good resolve and work of faith, [12]so that the name of our Lord Jesus may be glorified in you, and you in him, according to the grace of our God and the Lord Jesus Christ.

CHAPTER 2

As to the coming of our Lord Jesus Christ and our being gathered together to him, we beg you, brothers and sisters,[a] [2]not to be quickly shaken in mind or alarmed, either by spirit or by word or by letter, as though from us, to the effect that the day of the Lord is already here. [3]Let no one deceive you in any way; for that day will not come unless the rebellion comes first and the lawless one[b] is revealed, the one destined for destruction.[c] [4]He opposes and exalts himself above

a Gk brothers
b Gk the man of lawlessness; other ancient authorities read the man of sin
c Gk the son of destruction

every so-called god or object of worship, so that he takes his seat in the temple of God, declaring himself to be God. 5Do you not remember that I told you these things when I was still with you? 6And you know what is now restraining him, so that he may be revealed when his time comes. 7For the mystery of lawlessness is already at work, but only until the one who now restrains it is removed. 8And then the lawless one will be revealed, whom the Lord Jesus*a* will destroy*b* with the breath of his mouth, annihilating him by the manifestation of his coming. 9The coming of the lawless one is apparent in the working of Satan, who uses all power, signs, lying wonders, 10and every kind of wicked deception for those who are perishing, because they refused to love the truth and so be saved. 11For this reason God sends them a powerful delusion, leading them to believe what is false, 12so that all who have not believed the truth but took pleasure in unrighteousness will be condemned.

13But we must always give thanks

a Other ancient authorities lack *Jesus*

b Other ancient authorities read *consume*

1909	3956	3004		2316	2228	4574
ἐπὶ	πάντα	λεγόμενον		θεὸν	ἢ	σέβασμα,
on	all	being said		God	or	object of worship,

1909 3956 3004 2316 2228 4574
ἐπὶ πάντα λεγόμενον θεὸν ἢ σέβασμα,
on all being said God or object of worship,

5620 846 1519 04 3485 02 2316 2523
ὥστε αὐτὸν εἰς τὸν ναὸν τοῦ θεοῦ καθίσαι
so that him in the temple of the God to sit

584 1438 3754 1510 2316 **5** 3756
ἀποδεικνύντα ἑαυτὸν ὅτι ἔστιν θεός. Οὐ
showing off himself that he is God. Not

3421 3754 2089 1510 4314 1473 3778
μνημονεύετε ὅτι ἔτι ὢν πρὸς ὑμᾶς ταῦτα
you remember that still being toward you these

3004 1473 **6** 2532 3568 012 2722
ἔλεγον ὑμῖν; καὶ νῦν τὸ κατέχον
I was saying to you? And now the one holding down

3609a 1519 012 601 846 1722 03
οἴδατε εἰς τὸ ἀποκαλυφθῆναι αὐτὸν ἐν τῷ
you know for the to be uncovered him in the

1438 2540 **7** 09 1063 3466 2235
ἑαυτοῦ καιρῷ. τὸ γὰρ μυστήριον ἤδη
of himself season. The for mystery already

1754 06 458 3441 01
ἐνεργεῖται τῆς ἀνομίας· μόνον ὁ
operates of the lawlessness; alone the one

2722 737 2193 1537 3319 1096
κατέχων ἄρτι ἕως ἐκ μέσου γένηται.
holding down now until from middle he might become.

8 2532 5119 601 01 459 3739 01
καὶ τότε ἀποκαλυφθήσεται ὁ ἄνομος, ὃν ὁ
And then will be uncovered the lawless, whom the

2962 2424 337 011 4151 010
κύριος [Ἰησοῦς] ἀνελεῖ τῷ πνεύματι τοῦ
Master Jesus will kill in the spirit of the

4750 846 2532 2673 07 2015
στόματος αὐτοῦ καὶ καταργήσει τῇ ἐπιφανείᾳ
mouth of him and will abolish in the appearance

06 3952 846 **9** 3739 1510 05 3952
τῆς παρουσίας αὐτοῦ, οὗ ἐστιν ἡ παρουσία
of the presence of him, whose is the presence

2596 1753 02 4567 1722 3956 1411 2532
κατ᾽ ἐνέργειαν τοῦ σατανᾶ ἐν πάσῃ δυνάμει καὶ
by operation of the adversary in all power and

4592 2532 5059 5579 **10** 2532 1722 3956
σημείοις καὶ τέρασιν ψεύδους καὶ ἐν πάσῃ
signs and marvels of lie and in all

539 93 015 622
ἀπάτῃ ἀδικίας τοῖς ἀπολλυμένοις,
deception of unright to the ones being destroyed,

473 3739 08 26 06 225 3756
ἀνθ᾽ ὧν τὴν ἀγάπην τῆς ἀληθείας οὐκ
against which the love of the truth not

1209 1519 012 4982 846 **11** 2532
ἐδέξαντο εἰς τὸ σωθῆναι αὐτούς. καὶ
they welcomed for the to be delivered them. And

1223 3778 3992 846 01 2316 1753
διὰ τοῦτο πέμπει αὐτοῖς ὁ θεὸς ἐνέργειαν
through this sends to them the God operation

4106 1519 012 4100 846 011 5579
πλάνης εἰς τὸ πιστεῦσαι αὐτοὺς τῷ ψεύδει,
of deceit for the to trust them in the lie,

12 2443 2919 3956 013 3361 4100
ἵνα κριθῶσιν πάντες οἱ μὴ πιστεύσαντες
that might be judged all the not ones trusting

07 225 235 2106 07
τῇ ἀληθείᾳ ἀλλὰ εὐδοκήσαντες τῇ
in the truth but having thought well in the

93 1473 1161 3784 2168
ἀδικίᾳ. **13** Ἡμεῖς δὲ ὀφείλομεν εὐχαριστεῖν
unright. We but owe to give good favor

```
03          2316  3842      4012    1473    80
τῷ      θεῷ  πάντοτε  περὶ  ὑμῶν,  ἀδελφοὶ
to the God  always   about  you,   brothers
25                   5259  2962      3754  138      1473  01
ἠγαπημένοι        ὑπὸ  κυρίου,  ὅτι  εἵλατο  ὑμᾶς  ὁ
having been loved by    Master,  that  chose  you   the
2316  536              1519  4991        1722  38
θεὸς  ἀπαρχὴν      εἰς  σωτηρίαν    ἐν  ἁγιασμῷ
God   from beginning  for  deliverance  in   holiness
4151          2532  4102    225          1519  3739  2532
πνεύματος  καὶ  πίστει  ἀληθείας,  14  εἰς  ὃ   [καὶ]
of spirit    and  trust   truth,       for  which also
2564        1473  1223    010  2098          1473  1519
ἐκάλεσεν  ὑμᾶς  διὰ    τοῦ  εὐαγγελίου  ἡμῶν  εἰς
he called  you   through  the  good message  of us  to
4047              1391      02       2962   1473  2424
περιποίησιν  δόξης    τοῦ  κυρίου  ἡμῶν  Ἰησοῦ
possession   of splendor  of the  Master  of us  Jesus
5547        15  686    3767      80           4739    2532
Χριστοῦ.      Ἄρα  οὖν,    ἀδελφοί,  στήκετε  καὶ
Christ.       Then therefore,  brothers,  stand    and
2902      020  3862        3739   1321           1535
κρατεῖτε  τὰς  παραδόσεις  ἃς   ἐδιδάχθητε    εἴτε
hold       the  traditions  which  you were taught  whether
1223      3056  1535  1223    1992       1473    16  846
διὰ      λόγου  εἴτε  δι’    ἐπιστολῆς  ἡμῶν.       Αὐτὸς
through  word   or    through  letter    of us.       Himself
1161  01    2962    1473  2424    5547      2532  01  2316  01
δὲ   ὁ   κύριος  ἡμῶν  Ἰησοῦς  Χριστὸς  καὶ  [ὁ]  θεὸς  ὁ
but   the  Master of us  Jesus   Christ   and  the  God   the
3962    1473  01  25           1473  2532  1325
πατὴρ  ἡμῶν  ὁ  ἀγαπήσας  ἡμᾶς  καὶ  δοὺς
father  of us  the  having loved us   and   having given
3874              166        2532  1680  18      1722  5485
παράκλησιν  αἰωνίαν  καὶ  ἐλπίδα  ἀγαθὴν  ἐν  χάριτι,
encouragement eternal and  hope     good     in   favor,
17  3870                1473    020  2588    2532  4741
    παρακαλέσαι  ὑμῶν  τὰς  καρδίας  καὶ  στηρίξαι
    to encourage of you  the  hearts    and  to strengthen
1722  3956    2041  2532  3056  18       012  3062
ἐν  παντὶ  ἔργῳ καὶ  λόγῳ  ἀγαθῷ.  3:1  Τὸ  λοιπὸν
in   all    work and   word   good.       The  remaining
4336            80          4012  1473  2443  01  3056
προσεύχεσθε,  ἀδελφοί,  περὶ  ἡμῶν,  ἵνα  ὁ  λόγος
pray,          brothers,  about us,    that  the  word
02      2962    5143        2532  1392              2531
τοῦ  κυρίου  τρέχῃ    καὶ  δοξάζηται        καθὼς
of the  Master  might run  and  be given splendor  just as
2532  4314  1473  2      2532  2443  4506          575
καὶ  πρὸς  ὑμᾶς,    καὶ  ἵνα  ῥυσθῶμεν      ἀπὸ
also to   you,      and  that  we might be rescued from
014  824              2532  4190    444        3756  1063
τῶν  ἀτόπων        καὶ  πονηρῶν ἀνθρώπων·  οὐ  γὰρ
the out of place and    of evil  men;          not  for
3956      05  4102      3  4103        1161  1510  01  2962
πάντων  ἡ  πίστις.      Πιστὸς  δέ  ἐστιν  ὁ  κύριος,
of all the  trust.       Trustful  but  is     the  Master,
3739  4741      1473  2532  5442      575    02  4190
ὃς  στηρίξει  ὑμᾶς  καὶ  φυλάξει  ἀπὸ  τοῦ  πονηροῦ.
who  strengthens you  and  guards   from  the  evil.
4  3982              1161  1722  2962      1909  1473
   πεποίθαμεν        δὲ   ἐν  κυρίῳ  ἐφ’  ὑμᾶς,
   We have been persuaded but  in   Master  on   you,
3754  3739  3853            2532    4160      2532  4160
ὅτι  ἃ    παραγγέλλομεν  [καὶ]  ποιεῖτε καὶ  ποιήσετε.
that what we command       both  you do  and  you will do.
5  01    1161  2962    2720              1473  020
   Ὁ   δὲ   κύριος  κατευθύναι      ὑμῶν  τὰς
   The but  Master  may make straight  of you  the
```

to God for you, brothers and sisters[a] beloved by the Lord, because God chose you as the first fruits[b] for salvation through sanctification by the Spirit and through belief in the truth. [14]For this purpose he called you through our proclamation of the good news,[c] so that you may obtain the glory of our Lord Jesus Christ. [15]So then, brothers and sisters,[a] stand firm and hold fast to the traditions that you were taught by us, either by word of mouth or by our letter.

16 Now may our Lord Jesus Christ himself and God our Father, who loved us and through grace gave us eternal comfort and good hope, [17]comfort your hearts and strengthen them in every good work and word.

CHAPTER 3

Finally, brothers and sisters,[a] pray for us, so that the word of the Lord may spread rapidly and be glorified everywhere, just as it is among you, [2]and that we may be rescued from wicked and evil people; for not all have faith. [3]But the Lord is faithful; he will strengthen you and guard you from the evil one.[d] [4]And we have confidence in the Lord concerning you, that you are doing and will go on doing the things that we command. [5]May the Lord direct

---

[a] Gk brothers
[b] Other ancient authorities read from the beginning
[c] Or through our gospel
[d] Or from evil

your hearts to the love of God and to the steadfastness of Christ.

6 Now we command you, beloved,[a] in the name of our Lord Jesus Christ, to keep away from believers who are[b] living in idleness and not according to the tradition that they[c] received from us. 7For you yourselves know how you ought to imitate us; we were not idle when we were with you, 8and we did not eat anyone's bread without paying for it; but with toil and labor we worked night and day, so that we might not burden any of you. 9This was not because we do not have that right, but in order to give you an example to imitate. 10For even when we were with you, we gave you this command: Anyone unwilling to work should not eat. 11For we hear that some of you are living in idleness, mere busybodies, not doing any work. 12Now such persons we command and exhort in the Lord Jesus Christ to do their work quietly and to earn their own living. 13Brothers and sisters,[d] do not be weary in doing what is right.

14 Take note of those who do not obey what we say in this letter; have nothing to do with them, so that

a Gk brothers
b Gk from every brother who is
c Other ancient authorities read you
d Gk Brothers

2588	1519	08	26		02		2316	2532	1519	08
καρδίας	εἰς	τὴν	ἀγάπην	τοῦ		θεοῦ	καὶ	εἰς	τὴν
hearts	in	the	love	of the		God	and	to	the

5281	02		5547		3853			1161	1473
ὑπομονὴν	τοῦ		Χριστοῦ.	6	Παραγγέλλομεν	δὲ		ὑμῖν,
patience	of the		Christ.		We command	but		you,

80		1722	3686		02		2962		1473		2424
ἀδελφοί,	ἐν	ὀνόματι	τοῦ		κυρίου	[ἡμῶν]	Ἰησοῦ
brothers,	in	name	of the		Master	of us	Jesus

5547		4724		1473	575	3956	80		814
Χριστοῦ	στέλλεσθαι	ὑμᾶς	ἀπὸ	παντὸς	ἀδελφοῦ	ἀτάκτως
Christ	to avoid	you	from	all	brother	idly

4043		2532	3361	2596	08	3862		3739
περιπατοῦντος	καὶ	μὴ	κατὰ	τὴν	παράδοσιν	ἣν
walking around	and	not	by	the	tradition	that

3880		3844	1473		846		1063	3609a
παρελάβοσαν	παρ'	ἡμῶν.	7	Αὐτοὶ		γὰρ	οἴδατε
they took along	from us.			Yourselves	for	you know

4459	1163		3401		1473	3754	3756
πῶς	δεῖ		μιμεῖσθαι	ἡμᾶς,	ὅτι	οὐκ
how	it is necessary	to imitate	us,	that	not

812		1722	1473	3761		1432		740
ἠτακτήσαμεν	ἐν	ὑμῖν	8	οὐδὲ	δωρεὰν	ἄρτον
we were idle	in	you		but not	as a gift	bread

2068		3844	5100		235	1722	2873	2532	3449	3571
ἐφάγομεν	παρά	τινος,	ἀλλ'	ἐν	κόπῳ	καὶ	μόχθῳ	νυκτὸς
we ate	from some,	but	in	labor	and	toil	night

2532	2250	2038		4314	012	3361	1912
καὶ	ἡμέρας	ἐργαζόμενοι	πρὸς	τὸ	μὴ	ἐπιβαρῆσαί
and	day	working	to	the	not	to burden on

5100	1473		3756	3754	3756	2192		1849		235
τινα	ὑμῶν·	9	οὐχ	ὅτι	οὐκ	ἔχομεν	ἐξουσίαν,	ἀλλ'
some	of you;		not	that	not	we have	authority,	but

2443	1438		5179	1325	1473		1519	012
ἵνα	ἑαυτοὺς	τύπον	δῶμεν	ὑμῖν	εἰς	τὸ
that	of ourselves	example	we gave	to you	for	the

3401		1473	10	2532	1063	3753	1510		4314	1473
μιμεῖσθαι	ἡμᾶς.	10	καὶ	γὰρ	ὅτε	ἦμεν	πρὸς	ὑμᾶς,
to imitate	us.		Also	for	when	we were	toward	you,

3778	3853		1473	3754	1487	5100	3756	2309
τοῦτο	παρηγγέλλομεν	ὑμῖν,	ὅτι	εἴ	τις	οὐ	θέλει
this	we commanded	you,	that	if	some	not	wants

2038		3366		2068		191		1063	5100
ἐργάζεσθαι	μηδὲ	ἐσθιέτω.	11	Ἀκούομεν	γάρ	τινας
to work	but not	let eat.		We hear	for	some

4043		1722	1473	814		3367		2038
περιπατοῦντας	ἐν	ὑμῖν	ἀτάκτως	μηδὲν	ἐργαζομένους
walking around	in	you	idly	nothing	working

235	4020		015		1161	5108
ἀλλὰ	περιεργαζομένους·	12	τοῖς	δὲ	τοιούτοις
but	working around;		to the	but	such ones

3853		2532	3870		1722	2962	2424
παραγγέλλομεν	καὶ	παρακαλοῦμεν	ἐν	κυρίῳ	Ἰησοῦ
we command	and	we encourage	in	Master	Jesus

5547		2443	3326	2271	2038		04	1438
Χριστῷ,	ἵνα	μετὰ	ἡσυχίας	ἐργαζόμενοι	τὸν	ἑαυτῶν
Christ,	that	with	quiet	working	the	of themselves

740	2068		1473	1161	80		3361
ἄρτον	ἐσθίωσιν.	13	Ὑμεῖς	δέ,	ἀδελφοί,	μὴ
bread	they might eat.		You	but,	brothers,	not

1457a		2569		14	1487	1161	5100	3756
ἐγκακήσητε	καλοποιοῦντες.	14	Εἰ	δέ	τις	οὐχ
give in to bad	doing good.		If	but	some	not

5219	03	3056	1473	1223	06	1992		3778
ὑπακούει	τῷ	λόγῳ	ἡμῶν	διὰ	τῆς	ἐπιστολῆς,	τοῦτον
obeys	the	word	of us	through	the	letter,	this

4593		3361	4874		846		2443
σημειοῦσθε	μὴ	συναναμίγνυσθαι	αὐτῷ,	ἵνα
signify	not	to be mixed up together	to him,	that

1788		**15**	2532	3361	5613	2190	2233
ἐντραπῇ·			καὶ	μὴ	ὡς	ἐχθρὸν	ἡγεῖσθε,
he might be ashamed;			and	not	as	hostile	consider,

235	3560	5613	80	**16**	846	1161	01	2962
ἀλλὰ	νουθετεῖτε	ὡς	ἀδελφόν.		Αὐτὸς	δὲ	ὁ	κύριος
but	warn	as	brother.		Himself	but	the	Master

06	1515	1325	1473	08	1515	1223	3956
τῆς	εἰρήνης	δῴη	ὑμῖν	τὴν	εἰρήνην	διὰ	παντὸς
of the peace		may give	to you	the	peace	through	all

1722	3956	5158	01	2962	3326	3956	1473
ἐν	παντὶ	τρόπῳ.	ὁ	κύριος	μετὰ	πάντων	ὑμῶν.
in	all	manner.	The	Master	with	all	of you.

17	01	783	07	1699	5495	3972	3739	1510
	Ὁ	ἀσπασμὸς	τῇ	ἐμῇ	χειρὶ	Παύλου,	ὅ	ἐστιν
	The	greeting	in the	my	hand	Paul,	which	is

4592	1722	3956	1992	3779	1125	**18**	05	5485
σημεῖον	ἐν	πάσῃ	ἐπιστολῇ·	οὕτως	γράφω.		Ἡ	χάρις
sign	in	all	letter;	thusly	I write.		The	favor

02	2962	1473	2424	5547	3326	3956	1473
τοῦ	κυρίου	ἡμῶν	Ἰησοῦ	Χριστοῦ	μετὰ	πάντων	ὑμῶν.
of the Master	of us	Jesus	Christ	with	all	of you.

they may be ashamed. [15]Do not regard them as enemies, but warn them as believers.[a]

16 Now may the Lord of peace himself give you peace at all times in all ways. The Lord be with all of you.

17 I, Paul, write this greeting with my own hand. This is the mark in every letter of mine; it is the way I write. [18]The grace of our Lord Jesus Christ be with all of you.[b]

[a] Gk *a brother*

[b] Other ancient authorities add *Amen*

1 TIMOTHY

CHAPTER 1

Paul, an apostle of Christ Jesus by the command of God our Savior and of Christ Jesus our hope,

2 To Timothy, my loyal child in the faith:

Grace, mercy, and peace from God the Father and Christ Jesus our Lord.

3 I urge you, as I did when I was on my way to Macedonia, to remain in Ephesus so that you may instruct certain people not to teach any different doctrine, [4]and not to occupy themselves with myths and endless genealogies that promote speculations rather than the divine training[a] that is known by faith. [5]But the aim of such instruction is love that comes from a pure heart, a good conscience, and sincere faith. [6]Some people have deviated from these and turned to meaningless talk, [7]desiring to be teachers of the law, without understanding either what they are saying or the things about which they make assertions.

8 Now we know that the law is good, if one uses it legitimately. [9]This means understanding that the law is laid down not for the innocent but for the lawless and disobedient, for the godless and sinful, for the unholy and profane, for those who kill their father or mother, for murderers, [10]fornicators, sodomites, slave traders, liars, perjurers, and whatever else is contrary to the sound teaching

[a] Or plan

```
            3972      652              5547          2424   2596  2003
1:1   Παῦλος ἀπόστολος Χριστοῦ  Ἰησοῦ κατ' ἐπιταγὴν
      Paul    delegate  of Christ Jesus by   order
2316        4990          1473  2532 5547       2424   06  1680
θεοῦ   σωτῆρος    ἡμῶν καὶ Χριστοῦ Ἰησοῦ τῆς ἐλπίδος
of God deliverer of us and  Christ   Jesus the hope
1473  2  5095          1103         5043    1722 4102      5485
ἡμῶν   Τιμοθέῳ  γνησίῳ    τέκνῳ ἐν  πίστει, χάρις
of us  to Timothy legitimate child in   trust,  favor,
1656     1515     575   2316 3962    2532 5547       2424   02
ἔλεος  εἰρήνη ἀπὸ θεοῦ πατρὸς καὶ Χριστοῦ Ἰησοῦ τοῦ
mercy, peace  from God father and  Christ  Jesus the
2962    1473   3  2531      3870            1473 4357
κυρίου ἡμῶν.   Καθὼς παρεκάλεσά σε  προσμεῖναι
Master of us.  Just as I encouraged you  to stay to
1722   2181     4198           1519 3109         2443
ἐν  Ἐφέσῳ πορευόμενος εἰς Μακεδονίαν, ἵνα
in   Ephesus traveling  into Macedonia,  that
3853               5100 3361 2085            4  3366
παραγγείλῃς    τισὶν μὴ ἑτεροδιδασκαλεῖν   μηδὲ
you might command some not  to teach other     but not
4337          3454     2532 1076       562        3748
προσέχειν μύθοις καὶ γενεαλογίαις ἀπεράντοις, αἵτινες
to hold to myths and genealogies endless,     which
1567a        3930          3123 2228 3622        2316
ἐκζητήσεις παρέχουσιν μᾶλλον ἢ οἰκονομίαν θεοῦ
speculations they hold to more  or  management of God
08 1722 4102    5  09 1161 5056     06        3852
τὴν ἐν πίστει.   τὸ δὲ τέλος  τῆς παραγγελίας
the in   trust.  The but completion of the command
1510  26    1537 2513       2588      2532 4893
ἐστὶν ἀγάπη ἐκ καθαρᾶς καρδίας καὶ συνειδήσεως
is    love  from clean  heart   and conscience
18    2532 4102     505                6  3739      5100
ἀγαθῆς καὶ πίστεως ἀνυποκρίτου,  ὧν     τινες
good   and  trust  unhypocritical, of which some
795                 1604             1519 3150
ἀστοχήσαντες       ἐξετράπησαν εἰς ματαιολογίαν
having missed mark were turned out into futile talk
7  2309     1510 3547           3361 3539
θέλοντες εἶναι νομοδιδάσκαλοι, μὴ νοοῦντες
wanting  to be  law teachers,  not giving thought
3383      3739 3004      3383 4012    5101
μήτε   ἃ   λέγουσιν μήτε περὶ  τίνων
neither what they say nor  about what
1226                     8  3609a   1161 3754 2570   01
διαβεβαιοῦνται.     Οἴδαμεν δὲ  ὅτι καλὸς ὁ
they firmly assert.     We know but that good the
3551    1437 5100 846   3435              5530      9  3609a
νόμος, ἐάν τις αὐτῷ νομίμως χρῆται,     εἰδὼς
law,   if some  it  lawfully might use,  knowing
3778    3754 1342     3551   3756 2749      459
τοῦτο, ὅτι δικαίῳ νόμος οὐ κεῖται, ἀνόμοις
this,  that to right law  not is set, to lawless
1161 2532 506         765           2532 268
δὲ  καὶ ἀνυποτάκτοις, ἀσεβέσι καὶ ἁμαρτωλοῖς,
but and unsubmitting, irreverent and sinners,
462              952      3969a           2532
ἀνοσίοις καὶ βεβήλοις, πατρολῴαις καὶ
unholy   and desecrators, father-killers and
3389           409        10  4205
μητρολῴαις,  ἀνδροφόνοις    πόρνοις
mother-killers, men-murderers, sexually immoral ones,
733               405              5583      1965
ἀρσενοκοίταις ἀνδραποδισταῖς ψεύσταις ἐπιόρκοις,
male bed partners, man-trappers, liars,    perjurers,
2532 1487 5100 2087   07       5198          1319
καὶ εἴ  τι ἕτερον τῇ ὑγιαινούσῃ διδασκαλίᾳ
and if some other in the being healthy teaching
```

```
480              2596 012 2098                06       1391
ἀντίκειται   11  κατὰ τὸ εὐαγγέλιον   τῆς    δόξης
lies against     by   the good message of the splendor
02      3107        2316 3739 4100        1473       5485
τοῦ     μακαρίου   θεοῦ, ὃ    ἐπιστεύθην ἐγώ.   12  Χάριν
of the  fortunate  God,  which was trusted  I.       Favor
2192  03           1743                 1473 5547      2424
ἔχω   τῷ           ἐνδυναμώσαντί        με   Χριστῷ   Ἰησοῦ
I have in the one  having empowered     me   Christ    Jesus
03    2962   1473   3754       4103    1473  2233
τῷ    κυρίῳ  ἡμῶν, ὅτι        πιστόν  με   ἡγήσατο
the   Master of us, because   trustful me   he considered
5087       1519 1248          012 4387     1510
θέμενος    εἰς διακονίαν   13  τὸ πρότερον ὄντα
having set for service          the former  being
989         2532 1376        2532 5197       235
βλάσφημον  καὶ διώκτην     καὶ ὑβριστήν,  ἀλλὰ
insulter    and persecutor  and abuser,     but
1653        3754    50         4160    1722
ἠλεήθην,   ὅτι     ἀγνοῶν    ἐποίησα ἐν
I was shown mercy, because unknowing I did  in
570         5250             1161 05   5485  02
ἀπιστίᾳ·  14  ὑπερεπλεόνασεν δὲ  ἡ  χάρις τοῦ
untrust;     increased beyond  but the favor of the
2962   1473   3326 4102       2532 26     06   1722 5547
κυρίου ἡμῶν μετὰ πίστεως  καὶ ἀγάπης τῆς ἐν Χριστῷ
Master of us with trust     and love     the in  Christ
2424       4103      01   3056  2532 3956  594
Ἰησοῦ.  15  πιστὸς  ὁ   λόγος καὶ πάσης ἀποδοχῆς
Jesus.     Trustful the  word  and of all acceptance
514        3754 5547      2424    2064  1519 04  2889
ἄξιος,    ὅτι Χριστὸς Ἰησοῦς ἦλθεν εἰς  τὸν κόσμον
worthy,   that Christ  Jesus  came  into the world
268          4982       3739    4413   1510 1473
ἁμαρτωλοὺς σῶσαι,      ὧν     πρῶτός εἰμι ἐγώ.
sinners      to deliver, of whom first   am  I.
   235   1223     3778    1653              2443 1722 1473
16 ἀλλὰ διὰ      τοῦτο ἠλεήθην,            ἵνα  ἐν  ἐμοὶ
   But  through this   I was shown mercy  that in   me
4413 1731                5547     2424   08  537
πρώτῳ ἐνδείξηται         Χριστὸς Ἰησοῦς τὴν ἅπασαν
first might demonstrate  Christ  Jesus  the all
3115           4314 5296          014    3195
μακροθυμίαν   πρὸς ὑποτύπωσιν  τῶν    μελλόντων
long temper to  model             of the ones being about
4100        1909 846  1519 2222 166        03      1161
πιστεύειν ἐπ' αὐτῷ εἰς ζωὴν αἰώνιον.  17 Τῷ      δὲ
to trust   on  him  for life eternal.     To the  but
935     014    165       862          517    3441
βασιλεῖ τῶν   αἰώνων,  ἀφθάρτῳ     ἀοράτῳ μόνῳ
king    of the ages,   incorruptible unseen alone
2316 5092 2532 1391       1519 016  165     014  165
θεῷ, τιμὴ καὶ δόξα       εἰς τοὺς αἰῶνας τῶν αἰώνων,
God, value and splendor into the  ages   of the ages,
281         3778   08  3852            3908         1473
ἀμήν.   18 Ταύτην τὴν παραγγελίαν  παρατίθεμαί σοι,
amen.      This   the command      I set along to you,
5043     5095    2596 020 4254                1909 1473
τέκνον Τιμόθεε, κατὰ τὰς προαγούσας          ἐπὶ σὲ
child  Timothy, by   the ones leading before  on  you
4394         2443 4754       1722 846    08   2570
προφητείας, ἵνα στρατεύῃ    ἐν αὐταῖς τὴν καλὴν
speaking,    that you might fight in them  the good
4752          2192  4102     2532 18   4893
στρατείαν 19 ἔχων πίστιν  καὶ ἀγαθὴν συνείδησιν,
soldiery      having trust and good   conscience,
3739   5100 683            4012 08  4102
ἥν    τινες ἀπωσάμενοι    περὶ τὴν πίστιν
which some  having shoved off about the trust
```

[11]that conforms to the glorious gospel of the blessed God, which he entrusted to me.

12 I am grateful to Christ Jesus our Lord, who has strengthened me, because he judged me faithful and appointed me to his service, [13]even though I was formerly a blasphemer, a persecutor, and a man of violence. But I received mercy because I had acted ignorantly in unbelief, [14]and the grace of our Lord overflowed for me with the faith and love that are in Christ Jesus. [15]The saying is sure and worthy of full acceptance, that Christ Jesus came into the world to save sinners—of whom I am the foremost. [16]But for that very reason I received mercy, so that in me, as the foremost, Jesus Christ might display the utmost patience, making me an example to those who would come to believe in him for eternal life. [17]To the King of the ages, immortal, invisible, the only God, be honor and glory forever and ever.[a] Amen.

18 I am giving you these instructions, Timothy, my child, in accordance with the prophecies made earlier about you, so that by following them you may fight the good fight, [19]having faith and a good conscience. By rejecting conscience, certain persons

---

[a] Gk *to the ages of the ages*

have suffered shipwreck in the faith; 20among them are Hymenaeus and Alexander, whom I have turned over to Satan, so that they may learn not to blaspheme.

CHAPTER 2

First of all, then, I urge that supplications, prayers, intercessions, and thanksgivings be made for everyone, 2for kings and all who are in high positions, so that we may lead a quiet and peaceable life in all godliness and dignity. 3This is right and is acceptable in the sight of God our Savior, 4who desires everyone to be saved and to come to the knowledge of the truth. 5For

    there is one God;
    there is also one
       mediator between
       God and humankind,
    Christ Jesus, himself
       human,
6 who gave himself a
    ransom fur all
—this was attested at the right time. 7For this I was appointed a herald and an apostle (I am telling the truth,[a] I am not lying), a teacher of the Gentiles in faith and truth.

8 I desire, then, that in every place the men should pray, lifting up holy hands without anger or argument; 9also that the women should dress themselves modestly and decently in suitable clothing, not with their hair braided, or with gold, pearls, or expensive clothes, 10but with good works, as is proper for women who profess reverence for God.

---

a Other ancient authorities add
    in Christ

| 3489 | | 20 | 3739 | 1510 | 5211 | 2532 | 223 |
ἐναυάγησαν,   ὧν   ἐστιν Ὑμέναιος καὶ   Ἀλέξανδρος,
shipwrecked, of whom is   Hymeneus and   Alexander,

3739 3860   03 4567   2443 3811
οὓς παρέδωκα τῷ σατανᾷ,   ἵνα   παιδευθῶσιν
whom I gave   to adversary, that they might be
              over the   instructed as a child

3361 987   3870   3767 4413   3956
μὴ   βλασφημεῖν. 2:1 Παρακαλῶ οὖν πρῶτον πάντων
not to insult.   I encourage then first of all

4160   1162   4335   1783   2169
ποιεῖσθαι δεήσεις προσευχὰς ἐντεύξεις εὐχαριστίας
to be done requests, prayers, appeals, good favors

5228   3956   444   2 5228   935   2532
ὑπὲρ   πάντων ἀνθρώπων,   ὑπὲρ   βασιλέων καὶ
on behalf of all men,   on behalf of kings and

3956   014 1722 5247   1510   2443 2263   2532
πάντων τῶν ἐν ὑπεροχῇ   ὄντων, ἵνα   ἤρεμον καὶ
of all the in excellence being, that tranquil and

2272   979 1236   1722 3956 2150
ἡσύχιον βίον διάγωμεν   ἐν   πάσῃ εὐσεβείᾳ
quiet   life we might lead through in all   reverence

2532 4587   3 3778   2570 2532 587   1799
καὶ σεμνότητι.   τοῦτο καλὸν καὶ ἀπόδεκτον ἐνώπιον
and gravity.   This good and acceptable before

02 4990   1473 2316   3739 3956 444
τοῦ σωτῆρος ἡμῶν θεοῦ, 4 ὃς πάντας ἀνθρώπους
the deliverer of us God, who all   men

2309 4982   2532 1519 1922   225
θέλει σωθῆναι   καὶ εἰς ἐπίγνωσιν ἀληθείας
wants to be delivered and into perception of truth

2064   5 1520 1063 2316 1520 2532 3316   2316
ἐλθεῖν. εἷς γὰρ θεός, εἷς καὶ μεσίτης θεοῦ
to come. One for God, one and mediator of God

2532 444   444   5547   2424   01
καὶ ἀνθρώπων, ἄνθρωπος Χριστὸς Ἰησοῦς, 6 ὁ
and men,   man   Christ Jesus,   the one

1325   1438   487   5228   3956   09
δοὺς   ἑαυτὸν ἀντίλυτρον ὑπὲρ   πάντων, τὸ
having given himself ransom on behalf of all, the

3142   2540   2398   7 1519 3739 5087   1473
μαρτύριον καιροῖς ἰδίοις. εἰς ὃ   ἐτέθην ἐγὼ
testimony in seasons own. Into that was set I

2783   2532 652   225   3004 3756 5574
κῆρυξ καὶ ἀπόστολος, ἀλήθειαν λέγω οὐ ψεύδομαι,
announcer and delegate, truth   I say not I lie,

1320   1484   1722 4102 2532 225   8 1014
διδάσκαλος ἐθνῶν   ἐν πίστει καὶ ἀληθείᾳ. Βούλομαι
teacher   of nations in trust and truth.   I plan

3767 4336   016   435   1722 3956 5117
οὖν προσεύχεσθαι τοὺς ἄνδρας ἐν   παντὶ τόπῳ
then to pray   the men   in all   place

1869   3741   5495   5565   3709 2532
ἐπαίροντας ὁσίους χεῖρας χωρὶς ὀργῆς καὶ
lifting up on holy hands without anger and

1261   9 5615   2532 1135   1722 2689
διαλογισμοῦ. Ὡσαύτως [καὶ] γυναῖκας ἐν καταστολῇ
reasoning.   Likewise also women   in apparel

2887   3326 127   2532 4997   2885
κοσμίῳ μετὰ αἰδοῦς καὶ σωφροσύνης κοσμεῖν
respectable with modesty and sobermindedness to adorn

1438   3361 1722 4117   2532 5553   2228
ἑαυτάς, μὴ   ἐν πλέγμασιν καὶ χρυσίῳ ἢ
themselves, not in braids   and gold   or

3135   2228 2441   4185   10 235 3739
μαργαρίταις ἢ ἱματισμῷ πολυτελεῖ,   ἀλλ' ὃ
pearls   or clothing much cost,   but what

4241   1135   1861   2317
πρέπει γυναιξὶν ἐπαγγελλομέναις θεοσέβειαν,
is fitting to women ones promising godly reverence,

1223   2041   18   **11**   1135 1722 2271   3129   1722
δι'   ἔργων ἀγαθῶν.   Γυνὴ ἐν ἡσυχίᾳ μανθανέτω ἐν
through works good.   Woman in quiet   let learn in

3956 5292   **12**   1321   1161 1135   3756 2010
πάσῃ ὑποταγῇ·   διδάσκειν δὲ   γυναικὶ οὐκ ἐπιτρέπω
all subjection;   to teach but to woman not I allow

3761   831   435   235   1510 1722 2271
οὐδὲ αὐθεντεῖν ἀνδρός, ἀλλ' εἶναι ἐν ἡσυχίᾳ.
but not to dominate man,   but to be in quiet.

13   76   1063 4413   4111   1534 2096   **14** 2532
Ἀδὰμ γὰρ πρῶτος ἐπλάσθη,   εἶτα Εὔα.   καὶ
Adam for first was molded,   then Eve.   And

76   3756 538   05 1161 1135   1818
Ἀδὰμ οὐκ ἠπατήθη, ἡ δὲ γυνὴ ἐξαπατηθεῖσα
Adam not was   the but woman having been
               deceived,   thoroughly deceived

1722 3847   1096   **15** 4982
ἐν παραβάσει γέγονεν·   σωθήσεται
in transgression has become;   she will be delivered

1161 1223   06 5042   1437 3306   1722
δὲ διὰ τῆς τεκνογονίας, ἐὰν μείνωσιν ἐν
but through the childbearing, if they might stay in

4102 2532 26   2532 38   3326 4997
πίστει καὶ ἀγάπῃ καὶ ἁγιασμῷ μετὰ σωφροσύνης·
trust and love and holiness with sobermindedness;

3:1 4103   01 3056   1487 5100 1984   3713
Πιστὸς ὁ λόγος. Εἴ τις ἐπισκοπῆς ὀρέγεται,
trustful the word. If some oversight strives,

2570 2041 1937   **2** 1163   3767 04
καλοῦ ἔργου ἐπιθυμεῖ.   δεῖ   οὖν τὸν
good work he desires.   It is necessary then the

1985   423   1510   1520 1135   435
ἐπίσκοπον ἀνεπίλημπτον εἶναι, μιᾶς γυναικὸς ἄνδρα,
overseer unimpeachable to be, of one woman man,

3524   4998   2887   5382
νηφάλιον σώφρονα κόσμιον φιλόξενον
temperate, soberminded, respectable, love to stranger,

1317   **3** 3361 3943   3361 4131   235
διδακτικόν, μὴ πάροινον μὴ πλήκτην, ἀλλὰ
able to teach, not with wine, not hitter,   but

1933 269   866   **4** 02   2398
ἐπιεικῆ ἄμαχον ἀφιλάργυρον, τοῦ ἰδίου
gentle, non-fighter, not silver-lover, of the own

3624 2573 4291   5043   2192 1722
οἴκου καλῶς προϊστάμενον, τέκνα ἔχοντα ἐν
house well standing before, children having in

5292   3326 3956 4587   **5** 1487 1161 5100
ὑποταγῇ, μετὰ πάσης σεμνότητος   (εἰ δέ τις
subjection, with all   gravity   if but some

02   2398 3624 4291   3756 3609a   4459
τοῦ ἰδίου οἴκου προστῆναι οὐκ οἶδεν, πῶς
of the own house to stand before not he knows, how

1577   2316 1959   **6** 3361 3504
ἐκκλησίας θεοῦ ἐπιμελήσεται;), μὴ νεόφυτον,
of assembly of God will he take care? Not new plant,

2443 3361 5187   1519 2917   1706   02
ἵνα μὴ τυφωθεὶς εἰς κρίμα ἐμπέσῃ τοῦ
that not having been into judgment he might the
          puffed up   fall in

1228   **7** 1163   1161 2532 3141   2570
διαβόλου.   δεῖ   δὲ καὶ μαρτυρίαν καλὴν
slanderer.   It is necessary but also testimony good

2192   575 014 1855   2443 3361 1519 3680
ἔχειν ἀπὸ τῶν ἔξωθεν, ἵνα μὴ εἰς ὀνειδισμὸν
to have from the outside that not into reviling

1706   2532 3803 02   1228
ἐμπέσῃ καὶ παγίδα τοῦ διαβόλου.
he might fall in and trap of the slanderer.

---

[11]Let a woman[a] learn in silence with full submission. [12]I permit no woman[a] to teach or to have authority over a man;[b] she is to keep silent. [13]For Adam was formed first, then Eve; [14]and Adam was not deceived, but the woman was deceived and became a transgressor. [15]Yet she will be saved through childbearing, provided they continue in faith and love and holiness, with modesty.

CHAPTER 3

The saying is sure:[c] whoever aspires to the office of bishop[d] desires a noble task. [2]Now a bishop[e] must be above reproach, married only once,[f] temperate, sensible, respectable, hospitable, an apt teacher, [3]not a drunkard, not violent but gentle, not quarrelsome, and not a lover of money. [4]He must manage his own household well, keeping his children submissive and respectful in every way— [5]for if someone does not know how to manage his own household, how can he take care of God's church? [6]He must not be a recent convert, or he may be puffed up with conceit and fall into the condemnation of the devil. [7]Moreover, he must be well thought of by outsiders, so that he may not fall into disgrace and the snare of the devil.

[a] Or wife
[b] Or her husband
[c] Some interpreters place these words at the end of the previous paragraph. Other ancient authorities read The saying is commonly accepted
[d] Or overseer
[e] Or an overseer
[f] Gk the husband of one wife

8 Deacons likewise must be serious, not double-tongued, not indulging in much wine, not greedy for money; [9]they must hold fast to the mystery of the faith with a clear conscience. [10]And let them first be tested; then, if they prove themselves blameless, let them serve as deacons. [11]Women[a] likewise must be serious, not slanderers, but temperate, faithful in all things. [12]Let deacons be married only once,[b] and let them manage their children and their households well; [13]for those who serve well as deacons gain a good standing for themselves and great boldness in the faith that is in Christ Jesus.

14 I hope to come to you soon, but I am writing these instructions to you so that, [15]if I am delayed, you may know how one ought to behave in the household of God, which is the church of the living God, the pillar and bulwark of the truth. [16]Without any doubt, the mystery of our religion is great:

He[c] was revealed in flesh,
    vindicated[d] in spirit,[e]
    seen by angels,
    proclaimed among
        Gentiles,
    believed in throughout
        the world,
    taken up in glory.

CHAPTER 4

Now the Spirit expressly says that in later[f] times some will renounce the faith by paying attention to deceitful spirits and

a Or *Their wives*, or *Women deacons*
b Gk *be husbands of one wife*
c Gk *Who*; other ancient authorities read *God*; others, *Which*
d Or *justified*
e Or *by the Spirit*
f Or *the last*

8
1249 Διακόνους / Servants 5615 ὡσαύτως / likewise 4586 σεμνούς, / grave, 3361 μὴ / not 1351 διλόγους, / double worded, 3361 μὴ / not

3631 οἴνῳ / in wine 4183 πολλῷ / much 4337 προσέχοντας, / holding to, 3361 μὴ / not 146 αἰσχροκερδεῖς, / shameful gainer,

9 2192 ἔχοντας / holding 012 τὸ / the 3466 μυστήριον / mystery 06 τῆς / of the 4102 πίστεως / trust 1722 ἐν / in 2513 καθαρᾷ / clean

4893 συνειδήσει. / conscience. **10** 2532 καὶ / And 3778 οὗτοι / these 1161 δὲ / but 1381 δοκιμαζέσθωσαν / let be proved 4413 πρῶτον, / first,

1534 εἶτα / then 1247 διακονείτωσαν / let serve 410 ἀνέγκλητοι / unreproachable 1510 ὄντες. / being. **11** 1135 Γυναῖκας / Women

5615 ὡσαύτως / likewise 4586 σεμνάς, / grave, 3361 μὴ / not 1228 διαβόλους, / slanderers, 3524 νηφαλίους, / temperate, 4103 πιστὰς / trustful

1722 ἐν / in 3956 πᾶσιν. / all. **12** 1249 διάκονοι / Servants 1510 ἔστωσαν / let be 1520 μιᾶς / of one 1135 γυναικὸς / woman

435 ἄνδρες, / men, 5043 τέκνων / of children 2573 καλῶς / well 4291 προϊστάμενοι / standing before 2532 καὶ / and 014 τῶν / of the

2398 ἰδίων / own 3624 οἴκων. / houses. **13** 013 οἱ / The 1063 γὰρ / for 2573 καλῶς / well 1247 διακονήσαντες / ones having served

898 βαθμὸν / step 1438 ἑαυτοῖς / to themselves 2570 καλὸν / good 4046 περιποιοῦνται / acquire 2532 καὶ / and 4183 πολλὴν / much

3954 παρρησίαν / boldness 1722 ἐν / in 4102 πίστει / trust 07 τῇ / the 1722 ἐν / in 5547 Χριστῷ / Christ 2424 Ἰησοῦ. / Jesus. **14** 3778 Ταῦτά / These

1473 σοι / to you 1125 γράφω / I write 1679 ἐλπίζων / hoping 2064 ἐλθεῖν / to come 4314 πρὸς / to 1473 σὲ / you 1722 ἐν / in

5034 τάχει· / quickness; **15** 1437 ἐὰν / if 1161 δὲ / but 1019 βραδύνω, / I might be slow 2443 ἵνα / that

3609a εἰδῇς / you might know 4459 πῶς / how 1163 δεῖ / it is necessary 1722 ἐν / in 3624 οἴκῳ / house 2316 θεοῦ / of God

390 ἀναστρέφεσθαι, / to behave, 3748 ἥτις / which 1510 ἐστὶν / is 1577 ἐκκλησία / assembly 2316 θεοῦ / of God 2198 ζῶντος, / living,

4769 στῦλος / pillar 2532 καὶ / and 1477 ἑδραίωμα / firmness 06 τῆς / of the 225 ἀληθείας. / truth. **16** 2532 καὶ / And

3672 ὁμολογουμένως / confessionally 3173 μέγα / great 1510 ἐστὶν / is 09 τὸ / the 06 τῆς / of the 2150 εὐσεβείας / reverence

3466 μυστήριον· / mystery; 3739 ὃς / who 5319 ἐφανερώθη / was demonstrated 1722 ἐν / in 4561 σαρκί, / flesh,

1344 ἐδικαιώθη / was made right 1722 ἐν / in 4151 πνεύματι, / spirit, 3708 ὤφθη / was seen 32 ἀγγέλοις, / by messengers,

2784 ἐκηρύχθη / was announced 1722 ἐν / in 1484 ἔθνεσιν, / nations, 4100 ἐπιστεύθη / was trusted 1722 ἐν / in 2889 κόσμῳ, / world,

353 ἀνελήμφθη / was taken up 1722 ἐν / in 1391 δόξῃ. / splendor. **4:1** 09 Τὸ / The 1161 δὲ / but 4151 πνεῦμα / spirit 4490 ῥητῶς / expressly

3004 λέγει / says 3754 ὅτι / that 1722 ἐν / in 5306 ὑστέροις / later 2540 καιροῖς / seasons 868 ἀποστήσονταί / will stand off 5100 τινες / some

06 τῆς / of the 4102 πίστεως / trust 4337 προσέχοντες / holding to 4151 πνεύμασιν / spirits 4108 πλάνοις / deceivers 2532 καὶ / and

```
1319              1140          2  1722  5272         5573
διδασκαλίαις δαιμονίων,     ἐν    ὑποκρίσει ψευδολόγων,
in teachings of demons,    in    hypocrisy false words,
2741a                          08   2398  4893
κεκαυστηριασμένων          τὴν ἰδίαν συνείδησιν,
having been seared by fire the own    conscience,
   2967         1060        568            1033        3739 01
3  κωλυόντων γαμεῖν,  ἀπέχεσθαι  βρωμάτων, ἃ    ὁ
   hindering to marry, to hold off foods,    what the
2316 2936     1519 3336      3326 2169        015
θεὸς ἔκτισεν εἰς  μετάλημψιν μετὰ εὐχαριστίας τοῖς
God created for  sharing   with good favor  to the
4103          2532 1921              08   225
πιστοῖς    καὶ  ἐπεγνωκόσι      τὴν ἀλήθειαν.
trustful ones and  ones having perceived the truth.
   3754 3956 2938      2316    2570 2532 3762
4  ὅτι  πᾶν κτίσμα  θεοῦ  καλὸν καὶ  οὐδὲν
   That all  creation of God good  and  nothing
579        3326 2169       2983
ἀπόβλητον  μετὰ εὐχαριστίας λαμβανόμενον·
thrown off with good favor  being received;
   37              1063 1223    3056  2316     2532
5  ἁγιάζεται      γὰρ διὰ  λόγου θεοῦ  καὶ
   it is made holy for  through word of God and
1783          6 3778 5294        015    80        2570
ἐντεύξεως.      Ταῦτα ὑποτιθέμενος τοῖς  ἀδελφοῖς καλὸς
appeal.         These setting under to the brothers good
1510       1249    5547     2424    1789
ἔσῃ        διάκονος Χριστοῦ Ἰησοῦ, ἐντρεφόμενος
you will be servant  of Christ Jesus, being nourished
015      3056  06     4102   2532 06 2570 1319
τοῖς  λόγοις τῆς  πίστεως καὶ τῆς καλῆς διδασκαλίας
in the words of the trust  and the good  teaching
3739 3877                 7 016   1161  952
ἢ   παρηκολούθηκας·       τοὺς δὲ  βεβήλους
that you have followed along; the but  desecration
2532 1126     3454    3868      1128    1161 4572
καὶ γραώδεις μύθους παραιτοῦ. Γύμναζε δὲ  σεαυτὸν
and old women myths reject.   Exercise but yourself
4314  2150      8 05 1063 4984      1129     4314
πρὸς εὐσέβειαν·   ἡ γὰρ σωματικὴ γυμνασία πρὸς
toward reverence; the for bodily  exercise  toward
3641  1510  5624     05 1161 2150       4314    3956
ὀλίγον ἐστὶν ὠφέλιμος, ἡ  δὲ  εὐσέβεια πρὸς  πάντα
few  is  helpful,  the but reverence toward all
5624     1510  1860    2192   2222   06 3568 2532
ὠφέλιμός ἐστιν ἐπαγγελίαν ἔχουσα ζωῆς  τῆς νῦν καὶ
helpful is  promise  having of life the now  and
06 3195       9 4103    01 3056 2532 3956
τῆς μελλούσης.   πιστὸς ὁ  λόγος καὶ πάσης
the being about to be. Trustful the word and  of all
594        514    10 1519 3778  1063 2872    2532
ἀποδοχῆς ἄξιος·    εἰς τοῦτο γὰρ κοπιῶμεν καὶ
acceptance worthy; into this for  we labor and
75       3754 1679       1909 2316 2198    3739
ἀγωνιζόμεθα, ὅτι ἠλπίκαμεν ἐπὶ θεῷ ζῶντι, ὅς
we contest, that we have hoped on God living, who
1510 4990     3956 444       3122    4103
ἐστιν σωτὴρ  πάντων ἀνθρώπων μάλιστα πιστῶν.
is  deliverer of all men especially trustful.
   3853       3778 2532 1321    12 3367  1473  06
11 Παράγγελλε ταῦτα καὶ διδασκε.   Μηδείς σου  τῆς
   Command  these and teach.  No one of you the
3503    2706       235 5179   1096  014
νεότητος καταφρονείτω, ἀλλὰ τύπος γίνου τῶν
newness let think down, but  example become of the
4103      1722 3056  1722 391       1722 26  1722
πιστῶν  ἐν λόγῳ, ἐν ἀναστροφῇ, ἐν ἀγάπῃ, ἐν
trustful ones in word, in behavior, in love, in
```

teachings of demons, [2]through the hypocrisy of liars whose consciences are seared with a hot iron. [3]They forbid marriage and demand abstinence from foods, which God created to be received with thanksgiving by those who believe and know the truth. [4]For everything created by God is good, and nothing is to be rejected, provided it is received with thanksgiving; [5]for it is sanctified by God's word and by prayer.

[6]If you put these instructions before the brothers and sisters,[a] you will be a good servant[b] of Christ Jesus, nourished on the words of the faith and of the sound teaching that you have followed. [7]Have nothing to do with profane myths and old wives' tales. Train yourself in godliness, [8]for, while physical training is of some value, godliness is valuable in every way, holding promise for both the present life and the life to come. [9]The saying is sure and worthy of full acceptance. [10]For to this end we toil and struggle,[c] because we have our hope set on the living God, who is the Savior of all people, especially of those who believe.

[11]These are the things you must insist on and teach. [12]Let no one despise your youth, but set the believers an example in speech and conduct, in love, in

[a] Gk brothers
[b] Or deacon
[c] Other ancient authorities read suffer reproach

faith, in purity. [13]Until I arrive, give attention to the public reading of scripture,[a] to exhorting, to teaching. [14]Do not neglect the gift that is in you, which was given to you through prophecy with the laying on of hands by the council of elders.[b] [15]Put these things into practice, devote yourself to them, so that all may see your progress. [16]Pay close attention to yourself and to your teaching; continue in these things, for in doing this you will save both yourself and your hearers.

CHAPTER 5

Do not speak harshly to an older man,[c] but speak to him as to a father, to younger men as brothers, [2]to older women as mothers, to younger women as sisters—with absolute purity.

[3]Honor widows who are really widows. [4]If a widow has children or grandchildren, they should first learn their religious duty to their own family and make some repayment to their parents; for this is pleasing in God's sight. [5]The real widow, left alone, has set her hope on God and continues in supplications and prayers night and day; [6]but the widow[d] who lives for pleasure is dead even while she lives. [7]Give these commands as well, so that they may be above reproach. [8]And whoever does not provide for relatives, and especially for family members,

a Gk to the reading
b Gk by the presbytery
c Or an elder, or a presbyter
d Gk she

4102	1722	47		2193	2064	4337	07
πίστει,	ἐν	ἀγνείᾳ.	**13** ἕως		ἔρχομαι	προσέχε	τῇ
trust,	in	purity.	Until		I come	hold to	the

320		07	3874		07	1319	
ἀναγνώσει,		τῇ	παρακλήσει,		τῇ	διδασκαλίᾳ.	**14** 3361 μὴ
reading,		the	encouragement,		the	teaching.	Not

272		010 1722 1473 5486			3739	1325
ἀμέλει		τοῦ ἐν σοὶ χαρίσματος,			ὃ	ἐδόθη
not take care		the in you favor gift,			which	was given

1473	1223	4394		3326 1936	018
σοι	διὰ	προφητείας		μετὰ ἐπιθέσεως	τῶν
to you	through	speaking before		with setting on	of the

5495	010	4244		3778	3191	1722
χειρῶν	τοῦ	πρεσβυτερίου.	**15**	ταῦτα	μελέτα,	ἐν
hands	of the	older men group.		These	take care,	in

3778	1510	2443 1473	05	4297	5318
τούτοις	ἴσθι,	ἵνα σου		ἡ προκοπὴ	φανερὰ
these	be,	that of you		the progress	evident

1510	3956		1907	4572	2532 07
ᾖ	πᾶσιν.	**16**	ἔπεχε	σεαυτῷ	καὶ τῇ
might be	to all.		Hold on	to yourself	and to the

1319	1961	846	3778	1063 4160	2532
διδασκαλίᾳ,	ἐπίμενε	αὐτοῖς·	τοῦτο	γὰρ ποιῶν	καὶ
teaching,	stay on	to them;	this	for doing	both

4572	4982		2532 016	191	1473
σεαυτὸν	σώσεις		καὶ τοὺς	ἀκούοντάς	σου.
yourself	you will deliver		and the	ones hearing	you.

	4245		3361 1969		235
5:1	Πρεσβυτέρῳ		μὴ ἐπιπλήξῃς		ἀλλὰ
	To older man		not you might strike at		but

3870	5613 3962	3501	5613 80
παρακάλει	ὡς πατέρα,	νεωτέρους	ὡς ἀδελφούς,
encourage	as father,	newer	as brothers,

	4245	5613 3384	3501	5613 79	1722
2	πρεσβυτέρας	ὡς μητέρας,	νεωτέρας	ὡς ἀδελφὰς	ἐν
	older women	as mothers,	newer	as sisters	in

3956 47		5503	5091 020 3689	5503		1487
πάσῃ ἀγνείᾳ.	**3**	χήρας	τίμα τὰς ὄντως	χήρας.	**4**	εἰ
all purity.		Widows	value the really	widows.		If

1161 5100 5503	5043	2228 1549	2192
δέ τις χήρα	τέκνα	ἢ ἔκγονα	ἔχει,
but some widow	children	or descendants	has,

3129	4413	04 2398	3624 2151	2532
μανθανέτωσαν	πρῶτον	τὸν ἴδιον	οἶκον εὐσεβεῖν	καὶ
let learn	first	the own	house to reverence	and

287	591	015	4269	3778 1063 1510
ἀμοιβὰς	ἀποδιδόναι	τοῖς	προγόνοις·	τοῦτο γάρ ἐστιν
returns	to give back	to the	parents;	this for is

587	1799	02 2316	05	1161 3689	5503
ἀπόδεκτον	ἐνώπιον	τοῦ θεοῦ.	**5** ἡ	δὲ ὄντως	χήρα
acceptable	before	the God.	The	but really	widow

2532 3443	1679	1909 2316 2532
καὶ μεμονωμένη	ἤλπικεν	ἐπὶ θεὸν καὶ
and one having been alone	has hoped	on God and

4357	019 1162	2532 019 4335	3571 2532
προσμένει	ταῖς δεήσεσιν	καὶ ταῖς προσευχαῖς	νυκτὸς καὶ
stays	to the requests	and the prayers	night and

2250	05	1161 4684	2198 2348
ἡμέρας,	**6** ἡ	δὲ σπαταλῶσα	ζῶσα τέθνηκεν.
day,	the	but self-indulgent living	has died.

7	2532 3778 3853	2443 423
	καὶ ταῦτα παράγγελλε,	ἵνα ἀνεπίλημπτοι
	And these command,	that unimpeachable

1510		1487 1161 5100 014	2398 2532
ὦσιν.	**8**	εἰ δέ τις τῶν	ἰδίων καὶ
they might be.		If but some of the	own and

3122	3609	3756 4306	08 4102
μάλιστα	οἰκείων	οὐ προνοεῖ,	τὴν πίστιν
especially	households	not thinks before,	the trust

720   2532 1510 571   5501   **9** 5503
ἤρνηται   καὶ ἔστιν ἀπίστου   χείρων.   Χήρα
he has denied and he is of untrustful worse.   Widow

2639   3361 1640   2094 1835
καταλεγέσθω   μὴ   ἔλαττον ἐτῶν ἑξήκοντα
let be enrolled not lesser years sixty

1096   1520   435   1135   **10** 1722 2041
γεγονυῖα,   ἑνὸς ἀνδρὸς γυνή,   ἐν ἔργοις
having become, of one man woman, in works

2570   3140   1487 5044   1487
καλοῖς μαρτυρουμένη,   εἰ ἐτεκνοτρόφησεν,   εἰ
good being testified, if she nourished children, if

3580   1487 40   4228 3538   1487
ἐξενοδόχησεν,   εἰ ἁγίων πόδας ἔνιψεν,   εἰ
she welcomed strangers, if holy feet she washed, if

2346   1884   1487 3956
θλιβομένοις   ἐπήρκεσεν,   εἰ παντὶ
to ones being afflicted she gave relief, if in all

2041 18 1872   3501   1161 5503
ἔργῳ ἀγαθῷ ἐπηκολούθησεν. **11** νεωτέρας δὲ χήρας
work good she followed on. Newer but widows

3868   3752 1063 2691   02 5547
παραιτοῦ· ὅταν γὰρ καταστρηνιάσωσιν τοῦ Χριστοῦ,
reject; when for might have sexual the Christ,
                    impulses against

1060   2309   **12** 2192   2917   3754 08
γαμεῖν θέλουσιν   ἔχουσαι κρίμα ὅτι τὴν
to marry they want having judgment because the

4413   4102   114   260   1161 2532
πρώτην πίστιν ἠθέτησαν· **13** ἅμα   δὲ καὶ
first trust they set aside; at same time but also

692   3129   4022   020 3614   3756
ἀργαὶ μανθάνουσιν περιερχόμεναι τὰς οἰκίας, οὐ
idle ones they learn going around the houses, not

3441 1161 692   235 2532 5397   2532
μόνον δὲ ἀργαὶ ἀλλὰ καὶ φλύαροι   καὶ
alone but idle ones but also empty gossips and

4021   2980   024 3361 1163
περίεργοι,   λαλοῦσαι τὰ μὴ δέοντα.
workers around, speaking the not being necessary.

14 1014   3767 3501   1060   5041
Βούλομαι οὖν νεωτέρας γαμεῖν, τεκνογονεῖν,
I plan then newer to marry, to bear children,

3616   3367   874   1325
οἰκοδεσποτεῖν, μηδεμίαν ἀφορμὴν διδόναι
to supervise house, but not one opportunity to give

03   480   3059   5484   **15** 2235
τῷ ἀντικειμένῳ λοιδορίας χάριν·   ἤδη
to the lying against abuse on account of; already

1063 5100 1624   3694 02 4567   **16** 1487 5100
γάρ τινες ἐξετράπησαν ὀπίσω τοῦ σατανᾶ. εἴ τις
for some turned out after the adversary. If some

4103   2192 5503 1884   846   2532
πιστὴ ἔχει χήρας, ἐπαρκείτω αὐταῖς καὶ
trustful has widows, let give relief to them and

3361 916   05 1577   2443 019   3689
μὴ βαρείσθω ἡ ἐκκλησία, ἵνα ταῖς ὄντως
not let be burdened the assembly, that to the really

5503 1884   **17** 013 2573
χήραις ἐπαρκέσῃ.   Οἱ καλῶς
widows it might give relief. The well

4291   4245   1362   5092
προεστῶτες   πρεσβύτεροι διπλῆς τιμῆς
having stood before older men of double value

515   3122   013 2872   1722 3056
ἀξιούσθωσαν, μάλιστα οἱ κοπιῶντες ἐν λόγῳ
let be worthy, especially the ones laboring in word

2532 1319   **18** 3004 1063 05 1124   1016
καὶ διδασκαλίᾳ. λέγει γὰρ ἡ γραφή· βοῦν
and teaching. Says for the writing: ox

9 Let a widow be put on
the list if she is not less than
sixty years old and has been
married only once;[a] [10]she
must be well attested for
her good works, as one who
has brought up children,
shown hospitality, washed
the saints' feet, helped the
afflicted, and devoted herself
to doing good in every way.
[11]But refuse to put younger
widows on the list; for
when their sensual desires
alienate them from Christ,
they want to marry, [12]and
so they incur condemnation
for having violated their
first pledge. [13]Besides
that, they learn to be idle,
gadding about from house
to house; and they are not
merely idle, but also gossips
and busybodies, saying
what they should not say.
[14]So I would have younger
widows marry, bear
children, and manage their
households, so as to give
the adversary no occasion
to revile us. [15]For some
have already turned away
to follow Satan. [16]If any
believing woman[b] has
relatives who are really
widows, let her assist
them; let the church not
be burdened, so that it can
assist those who are real
widows.

17 Let the elders who
rule well be considered
worthy of double honor,[c]
especially those who labor
in preaching and teaching;
[18]for the scripture says,

---

[a] Gk the wife of one husband
[b] Other ancient authorities read
believing man or woman; others,
believing man
[c] Or compensation

"You shall not muzzle an ox while it is treading out the grain," and, "The laborer deserves to be paid." [19]Never accept any accusation against an elder except on the evidence of two or three witnesses. [20]As for those who persist in sin, rebuke them in the presence of all, so that the rest also may stand in fear. [21]In the presence of God and of Christ Jesus and of the elect angels, I warn you to keep these instructions without prejudice, doing nothing on the basis of partiality. [22]Do not ordain[a] anyone hastily, and do not participate in the sins of others; keep yourself pure.

23 No longer drink only water, but take a little wine for the sake of your stomach and your frequent ailments.

24 The sins of some people are conspicuous and precede them to judgment, while the sins of others follow them there. [25]So also good works are conspicuous; and even when they are not, they cannot remain hidden.

CHAPTER 6

Let all who are under the yoke of slavery regard their masters as worthy of all honor, so that the name of God and the teaching may not be blasphemed. [2]Those who have believing masters must not be disrespectful to them on the ground that they are members of the church;[b] rather they must serve them all the more, since those who benefit by their service are believers and beloved.[c]

a Gk Do not lay hands on
b Gk are brothers
c Or since they are believers and beloved, who devote themselves to good deeds

---

248	3756	5392		2532	514	01	2040
ἀλοῶντα	οὐ	φιμώσεις,		καί·	ἄξιος	ὁ	ἐργάτης
threshing	not	you will muzzle,		and:	worthy	the	worker

02   3408   846   2596   4245   2724
τοῦ   μισθοῦ   αὐτοῦ. **19** κατὰ   πρεσβυτέρου   κατηγορίαν
of the wage   of him.   Against   older man   accusation

3361 3858   1622   1487 3361 1909 1417 2228 5140
μὴ   παραδέχου,   ἐκτὸς   εἰ   μὴ   ἐπὶ   δύο   ἢ   τριῶν
not   accept,   outside   except   on   two   or   three

3144   016   264   1799   3956   1651
μαρτύρων. **20** Τοὺς   ἁμαρτάνοντας   ἐνώπιον   πάντων   ἔλεγχε,
testifiers.   The   ones sinning   before   all   rebuke,

2443 2532 013 3062   5401   2192   1263
ἵνα   καὶ   οἱ   λοιποὶ   φόβον   ἔχωσιν. **21** Διαμαρτύρομαι
that   also   the   remaining   fear   might   I testify
                                      have.   thoroughly

1799   02   2316 2532 5547   2424   2532 014 1588
ἐνώπιον   τοῦ   θεοῦ   καὶ   Χριστοῦ   Ἰησοῦ   καὶ   τῶν   ἐκλεκτῶν
before   the   God   and   Christ   Jesus   and   the   select

32   2443 3778 5442   5565
ἀγγέλων,   ἵνα   ταῦτα   φυλάξῃς   χωρὶς
messengers,   that   these   you might guard   without

4299   3367   4160 2596 4346   **22** 5495
προκρίματος,   μηδὲν   ποιῶν κατὰ   πρόσκλισιν.   χεῖρας
prejudgment,   nothing doing by   inclination.   Hands

5030   3367   2007   3366   2841   266
ταχέως   μηδενὶ   ἐπιτίθει   μηδὲ   κοινώνει   ἁμαρτίαις
quickly   to no one set on   but   not be partner   in sins

245   4572   53   5083   **23** 3371
ἀλλοτρίαις·   σεαυτὸν   ἀγνὸν   τήρει.   Μηκέτι
of other ones;   yourself   pure   keep.   No longer

5202   235   3631 3641   5530 1223   04
ὑδροπότει,   ἀλλὰ   οἴνῳ ὀλίγῳ   χρῶ   διὰ   τὸν
drink water,   but   wine few   use   because of the

4751   2532 020 4437   1473   769
στόμαχον   καὶ   τὰς   πυκνάς   σου   ἀσθενείας.
stomach   and   the   frequent   of you   weaknesses.

24 5100   444   017 266   1271   1510
Τινῶν   ἀνθρώπων   αἱ   ἁμαρτίαι   πρόδηλοί   εἰσιν
Of some   men   the   sins   clear before   are

4254   1519 2920   5100 1161 2532
προάγουσαι   εἰς   κρίσιν,   τισὶν   δὲ   καὶ
to lead before   into   judgment,   some   but   also

1872   5615   2532 021 2041 021 2570
ἐπακολουθοῦσιν· **25** ὡσαύτως   καὶ   τὰ   ἔργα   τὰ   καλὰ
follow on·   likewise   also the   works the good

4271   2532 021 247   2192   2928
πρόδηλα,   καὶ   τὰ   ἄλλως   ἔχοντα κρυβῆναι
clear before,   and   the   otherwise   having to be hidden

3756 1410   3745   1510 5259 2218 1401
οὐ   δύνανται. **6:1** Ὅσοι   εἰσὶν ὑπὸ ζυγὸν δοῦλοι,
not   are able.   As many as are   by yoke slaves,

016   2398   1203   3956   5092 514
τοὺς   ἰδίους   δεσπότας   πάσης   τιμῆς ἀξίους
the   own   supervisors   of all   value worthy

2233   2443 3361 09   3686 02   2316 2532 05
ἡγείσθωσαν,   ἵνα   μὴ   τὸ   ὄνομα τοῦ   θεοῦ καὶ   ἡ
let consider,   that not   the   name   of the God   and   the

1319   987   013 1161 4103   2192
διδασκαλία   βλασφημῆται. **2** οἱ   δὲ   πιστοὺς   ἔχοντες
teaching   might be insulted.   The but   trustful having

1203   3361 2706   3754   80
δεσπότας   μὴ   καταφρονείτωσαν,   ὅτι   ἀδελφοί
supervisors   not   let think down,   because   brothers

1510   235   3123   1398   3754   4103
εἰσιν,   ἀλλὰ   μᾶλλον   δουλευέτωσαν,   ὅτι   πιστοί
they are,   but   more   let slave,   because   trustful

1510   2532 27   013   06   2108
εἰσιν   καὶ   ἀγαπητοὶ οἱ   τῆς   εὐεργεσίας
they are   and   loved   the ones   of the good work

482   3778   1321   2532 3870
ἀντιλαμβανόμενοι. Ταῦτα δίδασκε καὶ   παρακάλει.
taking part.   These teach   and   encourage.

3 1487 5100 2085   2532 3361 4334
   εἴ   τις ἑτεροδιδασκαλεῖ καὶ μὴ   προσέρχεται
   If   some teaches other   and not comes to
5198   3056   015 02   2962   1473 2424
ὑγιαίνουσιν λόγοις τοῖς τοῦ κυρίου ἡμῶν Ἰησοῦ
being healthy words the of the Master of us Jesus
5547   2532 07   2596 2150   1319
Χριστοῦ καὶ τῇ κατ᾽ εὐσέβειαν διδασκαλίᾳ,
Christ and in the by reverence teaching,

4 5187   3367   1987   235
   τετύφωται,   μηδὲν ἐπιστάμενος, ἀλλὰ
   he has been puffed up, nothing understanding, but
3552   4012 2214   2532 3055   1537
νοσῶν περὶ ζητήσεις καὶ λογομαχίας, ἐξ
ailing about speculations and word fights, from
3739 1096   5355   2054   988   5283
ὧν   γίνεται φθόνος ἔρις βλασφημίαι ὑπόνοιαι
which becomes envy, strife, insults, conjectures,
4190   1274a   1311   444
πονηραί, 5 διαπαρατριβαὶ διεφθαρμένων ἀνθρώπων
evils,   constant   having been corrupted men
            irritations   thoroughly
04 3563 2532 650   06   225
τὸν νοῦν καὶ ἀπεστερημένων τῆς ἀληθείας,
the mind and having been deprived of the truth,
3543   4200   1510 08 2150   6 1510
νομιζόντων πορισμὸν εἶναι τὴν εὐσέβειαν.   Ἔστιν
thinking means of gain be to the reverence. Is
1161 4200   3173 05 2150   3326
δὲ πορισμὸς μέγας ἡ εὐσέβεια μετὰ
but means of gain great the reverence with
841   3762   1063 1533   1519
αὐταρκείας· 7 οὐδὲν γὰρ εἰσηνέγκαμεν εἰς
self sufficient; nothing for we brought into into
04 2889   3754 3761   1627   5100
τὸν κόσμον, ὅτι οὐδὲ ἐξενεγκεῖν τι
the world, that but not to bring out some
1410   8 2192   1161 1305   2532 4629
δυνάμεθα·   ἔχοντες δὲ διατροφὰς καὶ σκεπάσματα,
are we able; having but sustenance and covering,
3778   714   9 013 1161 1014
τούτοις ἀρκεσθησόμεθα. οἱ δὲ βουλόμενοι
in these we will be enough. The but ones planning
4147   1706   1519 3986   2532 3803   2532
πλουτεῖν ἐμπίπτουσιν εἰς πειρασμὸν καὶ παγίδα καὶ
to be rich fall in   into pressure and trap and
1939   4183 453   2532 983   3748
ἐπιθυμίας πολλὰς ἀνοήτους καὶ βλαβεράς, αἵτινες
desires many   unmindful and harmful, which
1036   016 444   1519 3639 2532 684
βυθίζουσιν τοὺς ἀνθρώπους εἰς ὄλεθρον καὶ ἀπώλειαν.
sink   the men   into ruin and destruction.
10 4491 1063 3956 022 2556 1510 05 5365
   ῥίζα γὰρ πάντων τῶν κακῶν ἐστιν ἡ φιλαργυρία,
   Root for all the bad   is   the love of silver,
3739 5100 3713   635   575 06
ἧς τινες ὀρεγόμενοι ἀπεπλανήθησαν ἀπὸ τῆς
which some striving they were deceived off from the
4102   2532 1438   4044   3601
πίστεως καὶ ἑαυτοὺς περιέπειραν ὀδύναις
trust and themselves they pierced around in pains
4183   11 1473 1161 5599 444   2316   3778 5343
πολλαῖς.   Σὺ δὲ, ὦ ἄνθρωπε θεοῦ, ταῦτα φεῦγε·
many.   You but, O man   of God, these flee;
1377   1161 1343   2150   4102   26
δίωκε δὲ δικαιοσύνην εὐσέβειαν πίστιν, ἀγάπην
pursue but rightness, reverence, trust, love,

Teach and urge these duties. [3]Whoever teaches otherwise and does not agree with the sound words of our Lord Jesus Christ and the teaching that is in accordance with godliness, [4]is conceited, understanding nothing, and has a morbid craving for controversy and for disputes about words. From these come envy, dissension, slander, base suspicions, [5]and - wrangling among those who are depraved in mind and bereft of the truth, imagining that godliness is a means of gain.[a] [6]Of course, there is great gain in godliness combined with contentment; [7]for we brought nothing into the world, so that[b] we can take nothing out of it; [8]but if we have food and clothing, we will be content with these. [9]But those who want to be rich fall into temptation and are trapped by many senseless and harmful desires that plunge people into ruin and destruction. [10]For the love of money is a root of all kinds of evil, and in their eagerness to be rich some have wandered away from the faith and pierced themselves with many pains.

11 But as for you, man of God, shun all this; pursue righteousness, godliness, faith, love,

[a] Other ancient authorities add *Withdraw yourself from such people*
[b] Other ancient authorities read *world—it is certain that*

endurance, gentleness.
[12]Fight the good fight of
the faith; take hold of the
eternal life, to which you
were called and for which
you made[a] the good
confession in the presence
of many witnesses. [13]In the
presence of God, who gives
life to all things, and of
Christ Jesus, who in his
testimony before Pontius
Pilate made the good
confession, I charge you
[14]to keep the
commandment without
spot or blame until the
manifestation of our Lord
Jesus Christ, [15]which he
will bring about at the
right time—he who is the
blessed and only Sovereign,
the King of kings and Lord
of lords. [16]who is he alone
who has immortality and
dwells in unapproachable
light, whom no one has
ever seen or can see; to
him be honor and eternal
dominion. Amen.

17 As for those who in
the present age are rich,
command them not to be
haughty, or to set their
hopes on the uncertainty
of riches, but rather on
God who richly provides
us with everything for our
enjoyment. [18]They are to
do good, to be rich in good
works, generous, and ready
to share, [19]thus storing up
for themselves the treasure
of a good foundation for
the future, so that they may
take hold of the life that
really is life.

20 Timothy, guard what
has been entrusted to you.
Avoid the

[a] Gk *confessed*

5281		4238a		**12**	75		04	2570	73

ὑπομονὴν   πραϋπαθίαν.   **12** ἀγωνίζου τὸν καλὸν ἀγῶνα
patience,   gentle passion.   Contest the good contest

06   4102   1949   06   166   2222   1519 3739
τῆς   πίστεως, ἐπιλαβοῦ τῆς αἰωνίου ζωῆς, εἰς ἣν
of the trust,   take on   the eternal life, into which

2564   2532 3670   08   2570 3671   1799
ἐκλήθης   καὶ ὡμολόγησας τὴν καλὴν ὁμολογίαν ἐνώπιον
you were   and having   the good confession before
called   confessed

4183   3144   **13** 3853   1473 1799   02 2316
πολλῶν μαρτύρων.   **13** παραγγέλλω [σοι] ἐνώπιον τοῦ θεοῦ
many   testifiers.   I command you   before   the God

02 2225   024 3956 2532 5547   2424
τοῦ ζωογονοῦντος τὰ πάντα καὶ Χριστοῦ Ἰησοῦ
the one preserving life the all and Christ   Jesus

02 3140   1909 4194   4091   08   2570
τοῦ μαρτυρήσαντος ἐπὶ Ποντίου Πιλάτου τὴν καλὴν
the one having testified on Pontius Pilate   the good

3671   **14** 5083   1473 08 1785   784
ὁμολογίαν,   **14** τηρῆσαί σε τὴν ἐντολὴν ἄσπιλον
confession,   to keep you the command without stain

423   3360 06 2015   02   2962   1473
ἀνεπίλημπτον μέχρι τῆς ἐπιφανείας τοῦ κυρίου ἡμῶν
unimpeachable until the appearance of the Master of us

2424 5547   **15** 3739 2540   2398 1166   01
Ἰησοῦ Χριστοῦ, **15** ἣν   καιροῖς ἰδίοις δείξει ὁ
Jesus Christ,   which in seasons own   to show the

3107   2532 3441   1413   01 935   014
μακάριος καὶ μόνος δυνάστης, ὁ βασιλεὺς τῶν
fortunate and alone power one, the king   of the

936   2532 2962 014 2961
βασιλευόντων καὶ κύριος τῶν κυριευόντων,
ones being king and Master of the ones being master,

16 01 3441   2192   110   5457 3611
16 ὁ μόνος ἔχων ἀθανασίαν,   φῶς οἰκῶν
the alone having deathlessness,   light housing

676   3739 3708 3762   444   3761
ἀπρόσιτον, ὃν εἶδεν οὐδεὶς ἀνθρώπων οὐδὲ
unapproachable, which saw no one of men but not

3708 1410   3739 5092 2532 2904   166
ἰδεῖν δύναται· ᾧ τιμὴ καὶ κράτος αἰώνιον,
to see is able; to whom value and strength eternal,

281   **17** 015   4145   1722 03 3568 165
ἀμήν. **17** Τοῖς πλουσίοις ἐν τῷ νῦν αἰῶνι
amen.   To the rich ones in the now age

3853   3361 5309   3366   1679
παράγγελλε μὴ ὑψηλοφρονεῖν μηδὲ ἠλπικέναι
command   not to think highly but not to have hoped

1909 4149   83   235 1909 2316 03
ἐπὶ πλούτου ἀδηλότητι ἀλλ᾽ ἐπὶ θεῷ τῷ
on rich   unclearness but on God the one

3930   1473 3956 4146   1519 619
παρέχοντι ἡμῖν πάντα πλουσίως εἰς ἀπόλαυσιν,
holding along to us all   richly   for enjoyment,

18 14   4147   1722 2041   2570
18 ἀγαθοεργεῖν, πλουτεῖν ἐν ἔργοις καλοῖς,
to work good, to be rich in works good,

2130   1510   2843   **19** 597
εὐμεταδότους εἶναι, κοινωνικούς, **19** ἀποθησαυρίζοντας
good exchangers to be, partners,   treasuring up

1438   2310   2570 1519 012 3195
ἑαυτοῖς θεμέλιον καλὸν εἰς τὸ μέλλον,
to yourselves foundation good for the about to be,

2443 1949   06   3689 2222 **20** 5599
ἵνα ἐπιλάβωνται τῆς ὄντως ζωῆς. **20** Ὦ
that they might take on the really life.   O

5095   08   3866   5442   1624   020
Τιμόθεε, τὴν παραθήκην φύλαξον ἐκτρεπόμενος τὰς
Timothy, the commitment guard   turning out the

952	2757	2532	477	06
βεβήλους	κενοφωνίας	καὶ	ἀντιθέσεις	τῆς
desecration	empty sounds	and	oppositions	of the

5581	1108	**21**	3739	5100	1861
ψευδωνύμου	γνώσεως,		ἥν	τινες	ἐπαγγελλόμενοι
false named	knowledge,		which	some	promising

4012	08	4102	795		05	5485	3326	1473
περὶ	τὴν	πίστιν	ἠστόχησαν.		ἩΗ	χάρις	μεθ᾽	ὑμῶν.
about	the	trust	miss the mark.		The	favor	with	you.

profane chatter and contradictions of what is falsely called knowledge; [21]by professing it some have missed the mark as regards the faith.

Grace be with you.[a]

[a] The Greek word for *you* here is plural; in other ancient authorities it is singular. Other ancient authorities add *Amen*

2 TIMOTHY

CHAPTER 1

Paul, an apostle of Christ Jesus by the will of God, for the sake of the promise of life that is in Christ Jesus,

2 To Timothy, my beloved child:

Grace, mercy, and peace from God the Father and Christ Jesus our Lord.

3 I am grateful to God—whom I worship with a clear conscience, as my ancestors did—when I remember you constantly in my prayers night and day. 4Recalling your tears, I long to see you so that I may be filled with joy. 5I am reminded of your sincere faith, a faith that lived first in your grandmother Lois and your mother Eunice and now, I am sure, lives in you. 6For this reason I remind you to rekindle the gift of God that is within you through the laying on of my hands; 7for God did not give us a spirit of cowardice, but rather a spirit of power and of love and of self-discipline.

8 Do not be ashamed, then, of the testimony about our Lord or of me his prisoner, but join with me in suffering for the gospel, relying on the power of God, 9who saved us and called us with a holy calling, not according to our works but according to his own purpose and grace.

	3972	652	5547	2424	1223	2307
1:1	Παῦλος	ἀπόστολος	Χριστοῦ	Ἰησοῦ	διὰ	θελήματος
	Paul	delegate	of Christ	Jesus	through	want

2316	2596	1860	2222	06	1722	5547	2424
θεοῦ	κατ᾽	ἐπαγγελίαν	ζωῆς	τῆς	ἐν	Χριστῷ	Ἰησοῦ
of God	by	promise	of life	the	in	Christ	Jesus

	5095	27	5043	5485	1656	1515	575
2	Τιμοθέῳ	ἀγαπητῷ	τέκνῳ,	χάρις	ἔλεος	εἰρήνη	ἀπὸ
	to Timothy	loved	child,	favor,	mercy,	peace	from

2316	3962	2532	5547	2424	02	2962	1473
θεοῦ	πατρὸς	καὶ	Χριστοῦ	Ἰησοῦ	τοῦ	κυρίου	ἡμῶν.
God	father	and	Christ	Jesus	the	Master	of us.

	5485	2192	03	2316	3739	3000	575	4269
3	Χάριν	ἔχω	τῷ	θεῷ,	ᾧ	λατρεύω	ἀπὸ	προγόνων
	Favor	I have	to the	God,	whom	I serve	from	parents

1722	2513	4893	5613	88	2192	08
ἐν	καθαρᾷ	συνειδήσει,	ὡς	ἀδιάλειπτον	ἔχω	τὴν
in	clean	conscience,	as	unceasing	I have	the

4012	1473	3417	1722	019	1162	1473	3571	2532
περὶ	σοῦ	μνείαν	ἐν	ταῖς	δεήσεσίν	μου	νυκτὸς	καὶ
about	you	memory	in	the	requests	of me	night	and

2250		1971	1473	3708	3403	1473	022
ἡμέρας,	**4**	ἐπιποθῶν	σε	ἰδεῖν,	μεμνημένος	σου	τῶν
day,		desiring longingly	you	to see,	having remembered	of you	the

1144	2443	5479	4137		5280
δακρύων,	ἵνα	χαρᾶς	πληρωθῶ,	**5**	ὑπόμνησιν
tears,	that	joy	I might be filled,		reminder

2983	06	1722	1473	505	4102	3748
λαβὼν	τῆς	ἐν	σοὶ	ἀνυποκρίτου	πίστεως,	ἥτις
having taken	the	in	you	unhypocritical	trust,	which

1774	4413	1722	07	3125	1473	3090	2532
ἐνῴκησεν	πρῶτον	ἐν	τῇ	μάμμῃ	σου	Λωΐδι	καὶ
housed	in first	in	the	grandmother	of you	Lois	and

07	3384	1473	2131	3982	1161
τῇ	μητρί	σου	Εὐνίκῃ,	πέπεισμαι	δὲ
in the mother	of you	Eunice,	I have been persuaded	but

3754	2532	1722	1473	223	3739	156	363
ὅτι	καὶ	ἐν	σοί.	**6** Δι᾽	ἣν	αἰτίαν	ἀναμιμνήσκω
that	also	in	you.	Through	which	cause	I remind

1473	329	012	5486	02
σε	ἀναζωπυρεῖν	τὸ	χάρισμα	τοῦ
you	to fire again to life	the	favor gift	of the

2316	3739	1510	1722	1473	1223	06	1936
θεοῦ,	ὅ	ἐστιν	ἐν	σοὶ	διὰ	τῆς	ἐπιθέσεως
God,	which	is	in	you	through	the	setting on

018	5495	1473	3756	1063	1325	1473	01	2316
τῶν	χειρῶν	μου.	**7** οὐ	γὰρ	ἔδωκεν	ἡμῖν	ὁ	θεὸς
of the	hands	of me.	Not	for	gave	to us	the	God

4151	1167	235	1411	2532	26	2532
πνεῦμα	δειλίας	ἀλλὰ	δυνάμεως	καὶ	ἀγάπης	καὶ
spirit	of cowardice	but	of power	and	of love	and

4995		3361	3767	1870	012
σωφρονισμοῦ.	**8**	μὴ	οὖν	ἐπαισχυνθῇς	τὸ
of sober mind.		Not	then	you might be ashamed	the

3142	02	2962	1473	3366	1473	04	1198
μαρτύριον	τοῦ	κυρίου	ἡμῶν	μηδὲ	ἐμὲ	τὸν	δέσμιον
testimony	of the	Master	of us	but not	me	the	prisoner

846	235	4777	011	2098
αὐτοῦ,	ἀλλὰ	συγκακοπάθησον	τῷ	εὐαγγελίῳ
of him,	but	suffer bad together	in the	good message

2596	1411	2316		02	4982	1473
κατὰ	δύναμιν	θεοῦ,	**9**	τοῦ	σώσαντος	ἡμᾶς
by	power	of God,		the one	having delivered	us

2532	2564	2821	40	3756	2596	024	2041
καὶ	καλέσαντος	κλήσει	ἁγίᾳ,	οὐ	κατὰ	τὰ	ἔργα
and	having called	in call	holy,	not	by	the	works

1473	235	2596	2398	4286	2532	5485	08
ἡμῶν	ἀλλὰ	κατὰ	ἰδίαν	πρόθεσιν	καὶ	χάριν,	τὴν
of us	but	by	own	purpose	and	favor,	the one

1325	1473	1722	5547	2424	4253	5550
δοθεῖσαν	ἡμῖν	ἐν	Χριστῷ	᾽Ιησοῦ	πρὸ	χρόνων
having been given	to us	in	Christ	Jesus	before	times

166		5319			1161	3568	1223
αἰωνίων,	**10**	φανερωθεῖσαν			δὲ	νῦν	διὰ
eternal,		having been demonstrated		but	now	through

06	2015	02	4990	1473	5547	2424
τῆς	ἐπιφανείας	τοῦ	σωτῆρος	ἡμῶν	Χριστοῦ	᾽Ιησοῦ,
the	appearance	of the	deliverer	of us	Christ	Jesus,

2673		3303	04	2288	5461
καταργήσαντος		μὲν	τὸν	θάνατον	φωτίσαντος
having abolished		indeed	the	death	having lightened

1161	2222	2532	861		1223	010	2098
δὲ	ζωὴν	καὶ	ἀφθαρσίαν		διὰ	τοῦ	εὐαγγελίου
but	life	and	incorruption	through	the	good message

	1519	3739	5087	1473	2783		2532	652
11	εἰς	ὃ	ἐτέθην	ἐγὼ	κῆρυξ		καὶ	ἀπόστολος
	to	which	was set	I	announcer	and	delegate

2532	1320		1223	3739	156	2532	3778
καὶ	διδάσκαλος,	**12**	δι᾽	ἣν	αἰτίαν	καὶ	ταῦτα
and	teacher,		through	which	cause	also	these

3958	235	3756	1870		3609a	1063	3739
πάσχω·	ἀλλ᾽	οὐκ	ἐπαισχύνομαι,	οἶδα	γὰρ	ᾧ
I suffer;	but	not	I am ashamed,	I know	for	whom

4100		2532	3982		3754	1415
πεπίστευκα		καὶ	πέπεισμαι		ὅτι	δυνατός
I have trusted	and	I have been persuaded	that	power

1510	08	3866	1473	5442	1519	1565	08
ἐστιν	τὴν	παραθήκην	μου	φυλάξαι	εἰς	ἐκείνην	τὴν
is	the	commitment	of me	to guard	for	that	the

2250		5296	2192	5198	3056	3739
ἡμέραν.	**13**	῾Υποτύπωσιν	ἔχε	ὑγιαινόντων	λόγων	ὧν
day.		Model	hold	of being healthy	words	which

3844	1473	191	1722	4102	2532	26	07	1722	5547
παρ᾽	ἐμοῦ	ἤκουσας	ἐν	πίστει	καὶ	ἀγάπῃ	τῇ	ἐν	Χριστῷ
from me	you heard	in	trust	and	love	the	in	Christ

2424		08	2570	3866	5442	1223	4151
᾽Ιησοῦ·	**14**	τὴν	καλὴν	παραθήκην	φύλαξον	διὰ	πνεύματος
Jesus;		the	good	commitment	guard	by	spirit

40	010	1774	1722	1473	3609a	3778
ἁγίου	τοῦ	ἐνοικοῦντος	ἐν	ἡμῖν.	**15** Οἶδας	τοῦτο,
holy	the	one housing in	in	us.	You know	this,

3754	654	1473	3956	013	1722	07	773
ὅτι	ἀπεστράφησάν	με	πάντες	οἱ	ἐν	τῇ	᾽Ασίᾳ,
that	turned off	me	all	the ones	in	the	Asia,

3739	1510	5436	2532	2061		1325
ὧν	ἐστιν	Φύγελος	καὶ	῾Ερμογένης.	**16**	δώη
of whom	is	Phygelus	and	Hermogenes.		May give

1656	01	2962	03	3683	3624	3754
ἔλεος	ὁ	κύριος	τῷ	᾽Ονησιφόρου	οἴκῳ,	ὅτι
mercy	the	Master	to the	Onesiphorus	house,	because

4178	1473	404	2532	08	254	1473
πολλάκις	με	ἀνέψυξεν	καὶ	τὴν	ἅλυσίν	μου
frequently	me	he refreshed	and	the	chain	of me

3756	1870		235	1096	1722	4516
οὐκ	ἐπαισχύνθη,	**17**	ἀλλὰ	γενόμενος	ἐν	῾Ρώμῃ
not	he was ashamed,	but	having become	in	Rome

4709	2212	1473	2532	2147		1325	846
σπουδαίως	ἐζήτησέν	με καὶ	εὗρεν·	**18**	δώη	αὐτῷ
diligently	he sought	me and	found;		may give	to him

01	2962	2147	1656	3844	2962	1722	1565	07
ὁ	κύριος	εὑρεῖν	ἔλεος	παρὰ	κυρίου	ἐν	ἐκείνῃ	τῇ
the	Master	to find	mercy	from	Master	in	that	the

2250	2532	3745	1722	2181	1247	957
ἡμέρᾳ.	καὶ	ὅσα	ἐν	᾽Εφέσῳ	διηκόνησεν,	βέλτιον
day.	And	as many as	in	Ephesus	he served,	better

1473	1097		1473	3767	5043	1473
σὺ	γινώσκεις.	**2:1**	Σὺ	οὖν,	τέκνον	μου,
you know.			You	then,	child	of me,

This grace was given to us in Christ Jesus before the ages began, [10]but it has now been revealed through the appearing of our Savior Christ Jesus, who abolished death and brought life and immortality to light through the gospel. [11]For this gospel I was appointed a herald and an apostle and a teacher,[a] [12]and for this reason I suffer as I do. But I am not ashamed, for I know the one in whom I have put my trust, and I am sure that he is able to guard until that day what I have entrusted to him.[b] [13]Hold to the standard of sound teaching that you have heard from me, in the faith and love that are in Christ Jesus. [14]Guard the good treasure entrusted to you, with the help of the Holy Spirit living in us.

[15]You are aware that all who are in Asia have turned away from me, including Phygelus and Hermogenes. [16]May the Lord grant mercy to the household of Onesiphorus, because he often refreshed me and was not ashamed of my chain; [17]when he arrived in Rome, he eagerly[c] searched for me and found me [18]—may the Lord grant that he will find mercy from the Lord on that day! And you know very well how much service he rendered in Ephesus.

CHAPTER 2

You then, my child,

a Other ancient authorities add of the Gentiles
b Or what has been entrusted to me
c Or promptly

be strong in the grace that is in Christ Jesus; ²and what you have heard from me through many witnesses entrust to faithful people who will be able to teach others as well. ³Share in suffering like a good soldier of Christ Jesus. ⁴No one serving in the army gets entangled in everyday affairs; the soldier's aim is to please the enlisting officer. ⁵And in the case of an athlete, no one is crowned without competing according to the rules. ⁶It is the farmer who does the work who ought to have the first share of the crops. ⁷Think over what I say, for the Lord will give you understanding in all things.

8 Remember Jesus Christ, raised from the dead, a descendant of David—that is my gospel, ⁹for which I suffer hardship, even to the point of being chained like a criminal. But the word of God is not chained. ¹⁰Therefore I endure everything for the sake of the elect, so that they may also obtain the salvation that is in Christ Jesus, with eternal glory. ¹¹The saying is sure:

If we have died with him,
    we will also live with him;
¹²if we endure, we will also
    reign with him;
if we deny him, he will
    also deny us;

1743		1722 07	5485	07	1722 5547	2424
ἐνδυναμοῦ		ἐν τῇ	χάριτι	τῇ	ἐν	Χριστῷ Ἰησοῦ,
be empowered		in the	favor	the	in	Christ Jesus,

2
2532 3739 191   3844 1473 1223   4183
καὶ ἃ ἥκουσας παρ᾽ ἐμοῦ διὰ πολλῶν
and what you heard from me through many
3144   3778 3908   4103   444
μαρτύρων, ταῦτα παράθου πιστοῖς ἀνθρώποις,
testifiers, these set along to trustful men,
3748   2425   1510   2532 2087   1321
οἵτινες ἱκανοὶ ἔσονται καὶ ἑτέρους διδάξαι.
who   enough will be also others to teach.

3
4777   5613 2570 4757   5547
Συγκακοπάθησον ὡς καλὸς στρατιώτης Χριστοῦ
Suffer bad together as good soldier of Christ
2424   3762   4754   1707   019
Ἰησοῦ. ⁴ οὐδεὶς στρατευόμενος ἐμπλέκεται ταῖς
Jesus.   No one soldiering inweaves himself in the
02   979   4230   2443 03 4758
τοῦ βίου πραγματείαις, ἵνα τῷ στρατολογήσαντι
of the life practices, that the one having enlisted
                                           him as a soldier
700   1437 1161 2532 118   5100
ἀρέσῃ. ⁵ ἐὰν δὲ καὶ ἀθλῇ   τις,
he might please. If but also might wrestle some,
3756 4737   1437 3361 3545   118
οὐ στεφανοῦται ἐὰν μὴ νομίμως ἀθλήσῃ.
not he is crowned except lawfully he might wrestle.

6
04 2872   1092 1163   4413 014
τὸν κοπιῶντα γεωργὸν δεῖ   πρῶτον τῶν
The laboring farmer it is necessary first of the
2590 3335   7 3539   3739 3004
καρπῶν μεταλαμβάνειν. νόει   ὃ λέγω·
fruit to take with. Give thought what I say;
1325   1063 1473 01 2962   4907   1722
δώσει γὰρ σοι ὁ κύριος σύνεσιν ἐν
will give for to you the Master understanding in
3956   8 3421   2424   5547   1453
πᾶσιν. Μνημόνευε Ἰησοῦ Χριστὸν ἐγηγερμένον
all.   Remember Jesus Christ having been raised
1537 3498   1537 4690   1160a 2596 012
ἐκ νεκρῶν, ἐκ σπέρματος Δαυίδ, κατὰ τὸ
from dead, from seed David, by the
2098   1473 9 1722 3739 2553   3360
εὐαγγέλιόν μου, ἐν ᾧ κακοπαθῶ μέχρι
good message of me, in whom I suffer bad until
1199   5613 2557   235 01 3056 02   2316 3756
δεσμῶν ὡς κακοῦργος, ἀλλὰ ὁ λόγος τοῦ θεοῦ οὐ
chains as bad worker, but the word of the God not
1210   10 1223   3778 3956 5278   1223
δέδεται·   διὰ τοῦτο πάντα ὑπομένω διὰ
has been bound; through this all I endure because
016 1588   2443 2532 846   4991
τοὺς ἐκλεκτούς, ἵνα καὶ αὐτοὶ σωτηρίας
the select, that also themselves deliverance
5177   06 1722 5547   2424 3326 1391
τύχωσιν τῆς ἐν Χριστῷ Ἰησοῦ μετὰ δόξης
might obtain the in Christ Jesus with splendor
166   11 4103   01 3056   1487 1063
αἰωνίου. πιστὸς ὁ λόγος· εἰ γὰρ
eternal. Trustful the word; if for
4880   2532 4800   12 1487
συναπεθάνομεν, καὶ συζήσομεν·   εἰ
we die together, also we will live together; if
5278   2532 4821   1487
ὑπομένομεν, καὶ συμβασιλεύσομεν·   εἰ
we endure, also we will be kings together; if
720   2548   720   13 1487
ἀρνησόμεθα, κἀκεῖνος ἀρνήσεται ἡμᾶς· εἰ
we will deny, also that one will deny us;   if

569   1565   4103   3306   720
ἀπιστοῦμεν,   ἐκεῖνος   πιστὸς   μένει,   ἀρνήσασθαι
we do not trust,   that one   trustful   stays,   to deny

1063 1438   3756 1410   **14**   3778   5279
γὰρ   ἑαυτὸν   οὐ   δύναται.   Ταῦτα ὑπομίμνησκε
for   himself   not   he is able.   These remind

1263   1799   02   2316 3361
διαμαρτυρόμενος   ἐνώπιον τοῦ θεοῦ μὴ
thoroughly testifying   before   the God   not

3054   1909 3762   5539   1909
λογομαχεῖν,   ἐπ᾽ οὐδὲν   χρήσιμον,   ἐπὶ
to battle with words,   on   nothing useful,   on

2692   014   191   **15**   4704   4572
καταστροφῇ τῶν   ἀκουόντων.   σπούδασον   σεαυτὸν
overturn   of the ones hearing.   Be diligent yourself

1384   3936   03   2316 2040
δόκιμον παραστῆσαι   τῷ   θεῷ, ἐργάτην
proved to stand along to the God,   worker

422   3718   04   3056   06
ἀνεπαίσχυντον, ὀρθοτομοῦντα   τὸν λόγον τῆς
unashamed,   cutting straight   the word   of the

225   **16**   020 1161 952   2757
ἀληθείας.   τὰς δὲ   βεβήλους   κενοφωνίας
truth.   The but   desecration empty sounds

4026   1909 4183   1063 4298
περιΐστασο·   ἐπὶ πλεῖον γὰρ προκόψουσιν
stand around; on   more   for   they progress

763   **17**   2532 01   3056   846   5613 1044
ἀσεβείας   καὶ ὁ   λόγος αὐτῶν ὡς   γάγγραινα
irreverence   and the word   of them as   gangrene

3542   2192   3739   1510   5211   2532
νομὴν   ἕξει.   ὧν   ἐστιν ʿΥμέναιος καὶ
grazing he will have. Of whom is   Hymeneus and

5372   3748   4012 08   225   795
Φίλητος,   **18**   οἵτινες περὶ   τὴν ἀλήθειαν ἠστόχησαν,
Philetus,   who   about the truth   missed the mark,

3004   08   386   2235   1096
λέγοντες [τὴν] ἀνάστασιν   ἤδη   γεγονέναι,
saying   the   standing up   already to have become,

2532 396   08   5100   4102   **19**   01   3305
καὶ   ἀνατρέπουσιν τήν τινων πίστιν.   ὁ   μέντοι
and   they turn up the of some trust.   The however

4731   2310   02   2316 2476   2192   08
στερεὸς θεμέλιος   τοῦ   θεοῦ ἔστηκεν,   ἔχων   τὴν
solid   foundation of the God   has stood, having the

4973   3778   1097 2962   016   1510 846
σφραγῖδα ταύτην· ἔγνω κύριος τοὺς   ὄντας αὐτοῦ,
seal   this: knew Master the ones being of him,

2532 868   575 93   3956 01   3687
καί, ἀποστήτω   ἀπὸ ἀδικίας πᾶς ὁ   ὀνομάζων
and: let stand off from unright all   the one naming

012 3686   2962   **20**   1722 3173   1161 3614   3756
τὸ   ὄνομα κυρίου.   Ἐν   μεγάλῃ δὲ   οἰκίᾳ οὐκ
the   name   of Master.   In   great   but   house not

1510   3441   4632   5552   2532 693   235   2532
ἔστιν   μόνον σκεύη χρυσᾶ καὶ   ἀργυρᾶ ἀλλὰ   καὶ
there are alone pots gold   and   silver but   also

3585   2532 3749   2532 3739   3303   1519   5092
ξύλινα καὶ   ὀστράκινα, καὶ   ἃ   μὲν   εἰς   τιμὴν
wooden and   clay,   and   what indeed into value

3739 1161 1519   819   **21**   1437 3767 5100
ἃ   δὲ   εἰς   ἀτιμίαν·   ἐὰν   οὖν   τις
what but   into   dishonor;   if   then   some

1571   1438   575 3778   1510   4632
ἐκκαθάρῃ   ἑαυτὸν ἀπὸ τούτων, ἔσται   σκεῦος
might clean out himself from these,   he will be pot

1519 5092   37   2173   03
εἰς   τιμήν, ἡγιασμένον,   εὔχρηστον τῷ
into value, having been made holy, good use   to the

---

[13] if we are faithless, he remains faithful— for he cannot deny himself.

14 Remind them of this, and warn them before God[a] that they are to avoid wrangling over words, which does no good but only ruins those who are listening. [15] Do your best to present yourself to God as one approved by him, a worker who has no need to be ashamed, rightly explaining the word of truth. [16] Avoid profane chatter, for it will lead people into more and more impiety, [17] and their talk will spread like gangrene. Among them are Hymenaeus and Philetus, [18] who have swerved from the truth by claiming that the resurrection has already taken place. They are upsetting the faith of some. [19] But God's firm foundation stands, bearing this inscription: "The Lord knows those who are his," and, "Let everyone who calls on the name of the Lord turn away from wickedness."

20 In a large house there are utensils not only of gold and silver but also of wood and clay, some for special use, some for ordinary. [21] All who cleanse themselves of the things I have mentioned[b] will become special utensils, dedicated and useful to the

a Other ancient authorities read *the Lord*
b Gk *of these things*

owner of the house, ready for every good work. [22]Shun youthful passions and pursue righteousness, faith, love, and peace, along with those who call on the Lord from a pure heart. [23]Have nothing to do with stupid and senseless controversies; you know that they breed quarrels. [24]And the Lord's servant[a] must not be quarrelsome but kindly to everyone, an apt teacher, patient, [25]correcting opponents with gentleness. God may perhaps grant that they will repent and come to know the truth, [26]and that they may escape from the snare of the devil, having been held captive by him to do his will.[b]

CHAPTER 3

You must understand this, that in the last days distressing times will come. [2]For people will be lovers of themselves, lovers of money, boasters, arrogant, abusive, disobedient to their parents, ungrateful, unholy, [3]inhuman, implacable, slanderers, profligates, brutes, haters of good, [4]treacherous, reckless, swollen with conceit, lovers of pleasure rather than lovers of God, [5]holding to the outward form of godliness but denying its power. Avoid them!

[a] Gk slave
[b] Or by him, to do his (that is, God's) will

1203	1519	3956	2041	18	2090
δεσπότῃ,	εἰς	πᾶν	ἔργον	ἀγαθὸν	ἡτοιμασμένον.
supervisor,	for all	work	good	having been prepared.	

22 Τὰς δὲ νεωτερικὰς ἐπιθυμίας φεῦγε, δίωκε δὲ
020 1161 3512 1939 5343 1377 1161
The but youthful desires flee, pursue but

δικαιοσύνην πίστιν ἀγάπην εἰρήνην μετὰ τῶν
1343 4102 26 1515 3326 014
rightness, trust, love, peace, with the ones

ἐπικαλουμένων τὸν κύριον ἐκ καθαρᾶς καρδίας. **23** τὰς
1941 04 2962 1537 2513 2588 020
calling on the Master from clean heart. The

δὲ μωρὰς καὶ ἀπαιδεύτους ζητήσεις
1161 3474 2532 521 2214
but foolish and uninstructed as child speculations

παραιτοῦ, εἰδὼς ὅτι γεννῶσιν μάχας·
3868 3609a 3754 1080 3163
reject, having known that they give birth battles;

24 δοῦλον δὲ κυρίου οὐ δεῖ μάχεσθαι
1401 1161 2962 3756 1163 3164
slave but of Master not it is necessary to battle

ἀλλὰ ἤπιον εἶναι πρὸς πάντας, διδακτικόν,
235 2261 1510 4314 3956 1317
but gentle to be toward all, able to teach,

ἀνεξίκακον, **25** ἐν πραΰτητι παιδεύοντα τοὺς
420 1722 4240 3811 016
putting up in gentleness instructing the ones
with bad, as a child

ἀντιδιατιθεμένους, μήποτε δώῃ αὐτοῖς ὁ
475 3379 1325 846 01
setting firmly against, not then may give to them the

θεὸς μετάνοιαν εἰς ἐπίγνωσιν ἀληθείας **26** καὶ
2316 3341 1519 1922 225 2532
God change of mind for perception of truth and

ἀνανήψωσιν ἐκ τῆς τοῦ διαβόλου παγίδος,
366 1537 06 02 1228 3803
they might be well from the of the slanderer trap,
balanced again

ἐζωγρημένοι ὑπ' αὐτοῦ εἰς τὸ ἐκείνου
2221 5259 846 1519 012 1565
having been captured alive by him for the of that

θέλημα. **3:1** Τοῦτο δὲ γίνωσκε, ὅτι ἐν ἐσχάταις
2307 3778 1161 1097 3754 1722 2078
want. This but know, that in last

ἡμέραις ἐνστήσονται καιροὶ χαλεποί· **2** Ἔσονται γὰρ
2250 1764 2540 5467 1510 1063
days will be present seasons difficult; will be for

οἱ ἄνθρωποι φίλαυτοι φιλάργυροι ἀλαζόνες
013 444 5367 5366 213
the men self-lovers, silver-lovers, boasters,

ὑπερήφανοι βλάσφημοι, γονεῦσιν ἀπειθεῖς,
5244 989 1118 545
arrogant, insulters, to parents disobedient,

ἀχάριστοι ἀνόσιοι **3** ἄστοργοι ἄσπονδοι
884 462 794 786
unfavorable, unholy, no family irreconcilable,
affection,

διάβολοι ἀκρατεῖς ἀνήμεροι ἀφιλάγαθοι
1228 193 434 865
slanderers, no strength, untamed, not lovers of good,

4 προδόται προπετεῖς τετυφωμένοι, φιλήδονοι μᾶλλον ἢ
4273 4312 5187 5369 3123 2228
traitors, reckless, having been lovers of more or
puffed up, pleasures

φιλόθεοι, **5** ἔχοντες μόρφωσιν εὐσεβείας τὴν δὲ
5377 2192 3446 2150 08 1161
lovers of God, having form of reverence the but

δύναμιν αὐτῆς ἠρνημένοι· καὶ τούτους ἀποτρέπου.
1411 846 720 2532 3778 665
power of it having denied; and these turn from.

6
1537	3778	1063	1510	013	1744	1519	020

ἐκ   τούτων γάρ εἰσιν οἱ   ἐνδύνοντες εἰς τὰς
From these for are   the ones creeping   into the

3614	2532	163	1133

οἰκίας καὶ αἰχμαλωτίζοντες γυναικάρια
houses and capturing   little women

4987	266	71	1939

σεσωρευμένα   ἁμαρτίαις, ἀγόμενα ἐπιθυμίαις
having been heaped up in sins, being led in desires

4164	7	3842	3129	2532	3368	1519

ποικίλαις, **7** πάντοτε μανθάνοντα καὶ μηδέποτε εἰς
various,   always learning   and but not yet into

1922	225	2064	1410	8	3739	5158

ἐπίγνωσιν ἀληθείας ἐλθεῖν δυνάμενα. **8** ὃν τρόπον
perception of truth to come being able. Which manner

1161	2389	2532	2387	436	3475

δὲ Ἰάννης καὶ Ἰαμβρῆς ἀντέστησαν   Μωϋσεῖ,
but Jannes and Jambres stood against Moses,

3779	2532	3778	436	07	225	444

οὕτως καὶ οὗτοι ἀνθίστανται τῇ ἀληθείᾳ, ἄνθρωποι
thusly also these stand against the truth,   men

2704	04	3563	96	4012	08

κατεφθαρμένοι   τὸν νοῦν, ἀδόκιμοι περὶ τὴν
completely ruining the mind, unproved about the

4102	9	235	3756	4298	1909	4183

πίστιν. **9** ἀλλ' οὐ προκόψουσιν   ἐπὶ πλεῖον·
trust.   But not they will progress on   more;

05	1063	454	846	1552	1510	3956

ἡ γὰρ ἄνοια   αὐτῶν ἔκδηλος ἔσται πᾶσιν,
the for mindless of them very clear will be to all,

5613	2532	05	1565	1096	10	1473	1161

ὡς καὶ ἡ ἐκείνων ἐγένετο. **10** Σὺ δὲ
as also the of those became.   You but

3877	1473	07	1319	07	72	07

παρηκολούθησάς μου τῇ διδασκαλίᾳ, τῇ ἀγωγῇ, τῇ
followed along me in the teaching,   the conduct, the

4286	07	4102	07	3115	07	26	07

προθέσει, τῇ πίστει, τῇ μακροθυμίᾳ, τῇ ἀγάπῃ, τῇ
purpose, the trust, the long temper, the love, the

5281	11	015	1375	023	3804	3634

ὑπομονῇ, **11** τοῖς διωγμοῖς, τοῖς παθήμασιν, οἷά
patience,   in the persecutions, the sufferings, that

1473	1096	1722	490	1722	2430	1722

μοι ἐγένετο ἐν Ἀντιοχείᾳ, ἐν Ἰκονίῳ, ἐν
to me became in Antioch,   in Iconium, in

3082	3634	1375	5297	2532	1537

Λύστροις, οἵους διωγμοὺς ὑπήνεγκα καὶ ἐκ
Lystra,   what persecutions I endured and from

3956	1473	4506	01	2962	12	2532	3956	1161

πάντων με ἐρρύσατο ὁ κύριος. **12** καὶ πάντες δὲ
all   me rescued the Master.   And all   but

013	2309	2153	2198	1722	5547	2424

οἱ θέλοντες   εὐσεβῶς ζῆν ἐν Χριστῷ Ἰησοῦ
the ones wanting reverently to live in Christ Jesus

1377	13	4190	1161	444	2532

διωχθήσονται. **13** πονηροὶ δὲ ἄνθρωποι καὶ
will be pursued. Evil   but men   and

1114	4298	1909	012	5501	4105

γόητες   προκόψουσιν ἐπὶ τὸ χεῖρον πλανῶντες
charlatans will progress on   the worse deceiving

2532	4105	14	1473	1161	3306	1722	3739

καὶ πλανώμενοι. **14** Σὺ δὲ μένε ἐν οἷς
and being deceived.   You but stay in what

3129	2532	4104	3609a	3844

ἔμαθες καὶ ἐπιστώθης,   εἰδὼς   παρὰ
you learned and you were trusted, having known from

5101	3129	15	2532	3754	575	1025	024	2413

τίνων ἔμαθες, **15** καὶ ὅτι ἀπὸ βρέφους [τὰ] ἱερὰ
whom you learned, and that from infant the sacred

---

[6]For among them are those who make their way into households and captivate silly women, overwhelmed by their sins and swayed by all kinds of desires, [7]who are always being instructed and can never arrive at a knowledge of the truth. [8]As Jannes and Jambres opposed Moses, so these people, of corrupt mind and counterfeit faith, also oppose the truth. [9]But they will not make much progress, because, as in the case of those two men,[a] their folly will become plain to everyone.

10 Now you have observed my teaching, my conduct, my aim in life, my faith, my patience, my love, my steadfastness, [11]my persecutions, and my suffering the things that happened to me in Antioch, Iconium, and Lystra. What persecutions I endured! Yet the Lord rescued me from all of them. [12]Indeed, all who want to live a godly life in Christ Jesus will be persecuted. [13]But wicked people and impostors will go from bad to worse, deceiving others and being deceived. [14]But as for you, continue in what you have learned and firmly believed, knowing from whom you learned it, [15]and how from childhood you have known the sacred writings

---

a Gk lacks *two men*

that are able to instruct you for salvation through faith in Christ Jesus. [16]All scripture is inspired by God and is[a] useful for teaching, for reproof, for correction, and for training in righteousness, [17]so that everyone who belongs to God may be proficient, equipped for every good work.

CHAPTER 4

In the presence of God and of Christ Jesus, who is to judge the living and the dead, and in view of his appearing and his kingdom, I solemnly urge you: [2]proclaim the message; be persistent whether the time is favorable or unfavorable; convince, rebuke, and encourage, with the utmost patience in teaching. [3]For the time is coming when people will not put up with sound doctrine, but having itching cars, they will accumulate for themselves teachers to suit their own desires, [4]and will turn away from listening to the truth and wander away to myths. [5]As for you, always be sober, endure suffering, do the work of an evangelist, carry out your ministry fully.

[6]As for me, I am already being poured out as a libation, and the time of my departure has come. [7]I have fought the good fight,

---

[a] Or Every scripture inspired by God is also

1121	3609a	024 1410	1473 4679	1519
γράμματα	οἶδας,	τὰ δυνάμενά	σε σοφίσαι	εἰς
letters	you knew,	the being able	you to make wise to	

4991	1223	4102	06	1722 5547	2424
σωτηρίαν	διὰ	πίστεως	τῆς ἐν	Χριστῷ	Ἰησοῦ.
deliverance	through	trust	the in	Chri'st	Jesus.

16
3956 1124	2315	2532 5624	4314
πᾶσα γραφὴ	θεόπνευστος	καὶ ὠφέλιμος	πρὸς
All writing	God-breathed	and helpful	to

1319	4314 1648b	4314 1882	4314
διδασκαλίαν,	πρὸς ἐλεγμόν,	πρὸς ἐπανόρθωσιν,	πρὸς
teaching,	to rebuking,	to straightening,	to

3809	08	1722 1343	**17** 2443
παιδείαν	τὴν ἐν	δικαιοσύνῃ,	ἵνα
instruction	as a child the in	rightness,	that

739	1510	01 02	2316 444	4314 3956
ἄρτιος	ᾖ	ὁ τοῦ	θεοῦ ἄνθρωπος,	πρὸς πᾶν
fit	might be	the of the	God man,	to all

2041	18	1822	**4:1** 1263	1799
ἔργον	ἀγαθὸν	ἐξηρτισμένος.	Διαμαρτύρομαι	ἐνώπιον
work	good	having been finished.	I testify thoroughly	before

02	2316 2532 5547	2424 02	3195
τοῦ	θεοῦ καὶ Χριστοῦ	Ἰησοῦ τοῦ	μέλλοντος
the	God and Christ	Jesus the	one being about

2919	2198	2532 3498	2532 08	2015
κρίνειν	ζῶντας	καὶ νεκρούς,	καὶ τὴν	ἐπιφάνειαν
to judge	living	and dead,	and the	appearance

846	2532 08	932	846	**2** 2784	04
αὐτοῦ	καὶ τὴν	βασιλείαν	αὐτοῦ·	κήρυξον	τὸν
of him	and the	kingdom	of him:	announce	the

3056	2186	2122	171	1651
λόγον,	ἐπίστηθι	εὐκαίρως	ἀκαίρως,	ἔλεγξον,
word,	stand on good	seasonally	unseasonally,	rebuke,

2008	3870	1722 3956 3115	2532
ἐπιτίμησον,	παρακάλεσον,	ἐν πάσῃ μακροθυμίᾳ	καὶ
admonish,	encourage,	in all long temper	and

1322	**3** 1510	1063 2540	3753 06	5198
διδαχῇ.	Ἔσται	γὰρ καιρὸς	ὅτε τῆς	ὑγιαινούσης
teaching.	Will be	for season	when the	being healthy

1319	3756 430	235	2596 020 2398
διδασκαλίας	οὐκ ἀνέξονται	ἀλλὰ	κατὰ τὰς ἰδίας
teaching	not they will endure	but	by the own

1939	1438	2002	1320
ἐπιθυμίας	ἑαυτοῖς	ἐπισωρεύσουσιν	διδασκάλους
desires	themselves	they will heap on	teachers

2833	08 189	**4** 2532 575	3303 06	225
κνηθόμενοι	τὴν ἀκοὴν	καὶ ἀπὸ	μὲν	τῆς ἀληθείας
being tickled	the hearing	and from	indeed	the truth

08 189	654	1909 1161 016	3454
τὴν ἀκοὴν	ἀποστρέψουσιν,	ἐπὶ δὲ τοὺς	μύθους
the hearing	they will turn off,	on but the	myths

1624	**5** 1473 1161 3525	1722
ἐκτραπήσονται.	Σὺ δὲ νῆφε	ἐν
they will be turned out.	You but be well-balanced	in

3956 2553	2041 4160	2099
πᾶσιν, κακοπάθησον,	ἔργον ποίησον	εὐαγγελιστοῦ,
all, suffer bad,	work do	of good message teller,

08 1248	1473 4135	**6** 1473 1063
τὴν διακονίαν	σου πληροφόρησον.	Ἐγὼ γὰρ
the service	of you fully persuade.	I for

2235	4689	2532 01 2540	06
ἤδη	σπένδομαι,	καὶ ὁ καιρὸς	τῆς
already	am being poured out as a libation,	and the season	of the

359	1473 2186	**7** 04 2570	73
ἀναλύσεώς	μου ἐφέστηκεν.	τὸν καλὸν	ἀγῶνα
release	of me has stood on.	The good	contest

```
75                 04    1408     5055                08
ἠγώνισμαι,         τὸν δρόμον τετέλεκα,              τὴν
I have contested,  the race   I have completed,     the
4102      5083        3062        606           1473   01
πίστιν τετήρηκα·  8  λοιπὸν   ἀπόκειταί       μοι    ὁ
trust  I have kept;  remaining is laid off to me     the
06        1343       4735       3739  591             1473
τῆς  δικαιοσύνης στέφανος,    ὃν   ἀποδώσει         μοι
of the rightness  crown,      which will give off to me
01   2962   1722  1565    07  2250    01   1342    2923
ὁ   κύριος ἐν  ἐκείνῃ τῇ ἡμέρᾳ, ὁ δίκαιος κριτής,
the Master in   that  the day,   the right   judge,
3756 3441   1161 1473   235  2532  3956     015
οὐ  μόνον δὲ  ἐμοὶ ἀλλὰ καὶ πᾶσι  τοῖς
not alone but to me but  also to all the ones
25              08  2015       846        4704
ἠγαπηκόσι   τὴν ἐπιφάνειαν αὐτοῦ.  9  Σπούδασον
having loved the appearance of him.   Be diligent
2064      4314 1473 5030      10  1214  1063 1473  1459
ἐλθεῖν  πρός με  ταχέως·       Δημᾶς γάρ με  ἐγκατέλιπεν
to come to  me  quickly;       Demas for me  left behind
25           04 3568 165   2532 4198        1519
ἀγαπήσας  τὸν νῦν αἰῶνα καὶ ἐπορεύθη εἰς
having loved the now age   and  traveled into
2332          2913      1519 1053      5103  1519
Θεσσαλονίκην, Κρήσκης εἰς Γαλατίαν, Τίτος εἰς
Thessalonica, Cresces into Galatia,  Titus into
1149           3065      1510   3441  3326 1473   3138
Δαλματίαν·  11  Λουκᾶς ἐστιν μόνος μετ᾽ ἐμοῦ. Μᾶρκον
Dalmatia;     Luke   is   alone with me.  Mark
353            71       3326 4572     1510   1063 1473
ἀναλαβὼν   ἄγε  μετὰ σεαυτοῦ, ἔστιν γάρ μοι
having taken up bring with yourself, he is for  to me
2173      1519 1248         5190      1161 649
εὔχρηστος εἰς διακονίαν. 12 Τύχικον δὲ ἀπέστειλα
good use  in   service.     Tychicus but I delegated
1519   2181      04  5314a     3739  620          1722
εἰς  Ἔφεσον.  13  τὸν φαιλόνην ὃν  ἀπέλιπον  ἐν
to   Ephesus.      The coat    which I left off  in
5174    3844 2591    2064       5342    2532 024
Τρῳάδι παρὰ Κάρπῳ ἐρχόμενος φέρε, καὶ  τὰ
Troas  with Carpus coming     bring,  and the
975           3122       020 3200       223
βιβλία    μάλιστα   τὰς μεμβράνας.  14  Ἀλέξανδρος
small books especially the parchments.  Alexander
01   5471        4183           1473    2556 1731
ὁ χαλκεὺς    πολλά       μοι   κακὰ ἐνεδείξατο·
the coppersmith many things to me to me bad  demonstrated;
591          846    01  2962  2596         024  2041
ἀποδώσει  αὐτῷ   ὁ  κύριος κατὰ      τὰ ἔργα
will give off to him the Master according to the works
846           3739 2532 1473 5442         3029 1063
αὐτοῦ·  15  ὃν  καὶ σὺ φυλάσσου, λίαν γὰρ
of him;     whom also you guard,   very for
436          015 2251      3056        1722 07
ἀντέστη  τοῖς ἡμετέροις λόγοις.  16  Ἐν  τῇ
he stood against the our    words.     In  the
4413 1473 627       3762    1473 3854     235
πρώτῃ μου ἀπολογίᾳ οὐδείς μοι παρεγένετο, ἀλλὰ
first of me defense no one to me arrived,   but
3956  1473 1459        3361 846
πάντες με  ἐγκατέλιπον· μὴ αὐτοῖς
all    me  left behind; not to them
3049               01 1161 2962  1473 3936
λογισθείη·   17  ὁ δὲ  κύριός μοι παρέστη
may it be reasoned;  the but Master to me stood along
2532 1743         1473 2443 1223     1473 09
καὶ ἐνεδυνάμωσέν με, ἵνα δι᾽  ἐμοῦ τὸ
and he empowered me, that through me  the
```

I have finished the race, I have kept the faith. [8]From now on there is reserved for me the crown of righteousness, which the Lord, the righteous judge, will give me on that day, and not only to me but also to all who have longed for his appearing.

[9]Do your best to come to me soon, [10]for Demas, in love with this present world, has deserted me and gone to Thessalonica; Crescens has gone to Galatia,[a] Titus to Dalmatia. [11]Only Luke is with me. Get Mark and bring him with you, for he is useful in my ministry. [12]I have sent Tychicus to Ephesus. [13]When you come, bring the cloak that I left with Carpus at Troas, also the books, and above all the parchments. [14]Alexander the coppersmith did me great harm; the Lord will pay him back for his deeds. [15]You also must beware of him, for he strongly opposed our message.

[16] At my first defense no one came to my support, but all deserted me. May it not be counted against them! [17]But the Lord stood by me and gave me strength, so that through me the

---

[a] Other ancient authorities read Gaul

message might be fully proclaimed and all the Gentiles might hear it. So I was rescued from the lion's mouth. [18]The Lord will rescue me from every evil attack and save me for his heavenly kingdom. To him be the glory forever and ever. Amen.

[19]Greet Prisca and Aquila, and the household of Onesiphorus. [20]Erastus remained in Corinth; Trophimus I left ill in Miletus. [21]Do your best to come before winter. Eubulus sends greetings to you, as do Pudens and Linus and Claudia and all the brothers and sisters.[a]

[22]The Lord be with your spirit. Grace be with you.[b]

a Gk all the brothers
b The Greek word for you here is plural. Other ancient authorities add Amen

2782		4135			2532	191	
κήρυγμα		πληροφορηθῇ			καὶ	ἀκούσωσιν	
announcement		might be fully persuasive			and	might hear	

3956	021	1484		2532	4506		1537	4750
πάντα	τὰ	ἔθνη,		καὶ	ἐρρύσθην		ἐκ	στόματος
all	the	nations,		and	I was rescued		from	mouth

3023		4506		1473	01	2962	575	3956
λέοντος.	**18**	ῥύσεταί		με	ὁ	κύριος	ἀπὸ	παντὸς
of lion.		Will rescue		me	the	Master	from	all

2041	4190		2532	4982		1519	08	932
ἔργου	πονηροῦ		καὶ	σώσει		εἰς	τὴν	βασιλείαν
work	evil		and	will deliver		into	the	kingdom

846	08	2032		3739	05	1391		1519	016
αὐτοῦ	τὴν	ἐπουράνιον·		ᾧ	ἡ	δόξα		εἰς	τοὺς
of him	the	on heaven;		to whom	the	splendor		into	the

165	014	165		281			4251	2532
αἰῶνας	τῶν	αἰώνων,		ἀμήν.	**19**	Ἄσπασαι	Πρίσκαν	καὶ
ages	of	the ages,		amen.		Greet	Prisca	and

207	2532	04	3683		3624		2037
Ἀκύλαν	καὶ	τὸν	Ὀνησιφόρου		οἶκον. **20**		Ἔραστος
Acquila	and	the	of Onesiphorus		house.		Erastus

3306	1722	2882		5161		1161	620		1722
ἔμεινεν	ἐν	Κορίνθῳ,		Τρόφιμον		δὲ	ἀπέλιπον		ἐν
stayed	in	Corinth,		Trophimus		but	I left off		in

3399	770		4704		4253	5494
Μιλήτῳ	ἀσθενοῦντα. **21**		Σπούδασον		πρὸ	χειμῶνος
Miletus	being weak.		Be diligent		before	winter

2064		782		1473	2103		2532	4227	2532
ἐλθεῖν.		Ἀσπάζεταί		σε	Εὔβουλος		καὶ	Πούδης	καὶ
to come.		Greets		you	Eubulus		and	Poudes	and

3044	2532	2803		2532	013	80		3956		01
Λίνος	καὶ	Κλαυδία		καὶ	οἱ	ἀδελφοὶ		πάντες.	**22**	Ὁ
Linus	and	Claudia		and	the	brothers		all.		The

2962	3326	010	4151		1473		05	5485	3326	1473
κύριος	μετὰ	τοῦ	πνεύματός		σου.		ἡ	χάρις	μεθ'	ὑμῶν.
Master	with	the	spirit		of you.		The	favor	with	you.

TITUS

CHAPTER 1

Paul, a servant[a] of God and an apostle of Jesus Christ, for the sake of the faith of God's elect and the knowledge of the truth that is in accordance with godliness, [2]in the hope of eternal life that God, who never lies, promised before the ages began— [3]in due time he revealed his word through the proclamation with which I have been entrusted by the command of God our Savior,

4 To Titus, my loyal child in the faith we share: Grace[b] and peace from God the Father and Christ Jesus our Savior.

5 I left you behind in Crete for this reason, so that you should put in order what remained to be done, and should appoint elders in every town, as I directed you: [6]someone who is blameless, married only once,[c] whose children are believers, not accused of debauchery and not rebellious. [7]For a bishop,[d] as God's steward, must be blameless; he must not be arrogant or quick-tempered or addicted to wine or violent or greedy for gain; [8]but he must be hospitable, a lover of goodness, prudent, upright, devout, and self-controlled. [9]He must have a firm grasp of the word that is trustworthy in accordance with the teaching, so that he may be able both to preach with sound doctrine and to refute those who contradict it.

a Gk slave
b Other ancient authorities read Grace, mercy,
c Gk husband of one wife
d Or an overseer

1:1
3972 1401 2316 652 1161 2424
Παῦλος δοῦλος θεοῦ, ἀπόστολος δὲ Ἰησοῦ
Paul slave of God, delegate but of Jesus

5547 2596 4102 1588 2316 2532
Χριστοῦ κατὰ πίστιν ἐκλεκτῶν θεοῦ καὶ
Christ by trust of select ones of God and

1922 225 06 2596 2150 **2** 1909 1680
ἐπίγνωσιν ἀληθείας τῆς κατ᾽ εὐσέβειαν ἐπ᾽ ἐλπίδι
perception of truth the by reverence on hope

2222 166 3739 1861 01 893 2316
ζωῆς αἰωνίου, ἣν ἐπηγγείλατο ὁ ἀψευδὴς θεὸς
of life eternal, which promised the unlying God

4253 5550 166 **3** 5319 1161 2540
πρὸ χρόνων αἰωνίων, ἐφανέρωσεν δὲ καιροῖς
before times eternal, he demonstrated but in seasons

2398 04 3056 846 1722 2782 3739
ἰδίοις τὸν λόγον αὐτοῦ ἐν κηρύγματι, ὃ
own the word of him in announcement, which

4100 1473 2596 2003 02 4990 1473
ἐπιστεύθην ἐγὼ κατ᾽ ἐπιταγὴν τοῦ σωτῆρος ἡμῶν
was trusted I by order of the deliverer of us

2316 **4** 5103 1103 5043 2596 2839 4102
θεοῦ, Τίτῳ γνησίῳ τέκνῳ κατὰ κοινὴν πίστιν,
God, to Titus legitimate child by common trust,

5485 2532 1515 575 2316 3962 2532 5547 2424
χάρις καὶ εἰρήνη ἀπὸ θεοῦ πατρὸς καὶ Χριστοῦ Ἰησοῦ
favor and peace from God father and Christ Jesus

02 4990 1473 **5** 3778 5484 620 1473
τοῦ σωτῆρος ἡμῶν. Τούτου χάριν ἀπέλιπόν σε
the deliverer of us. Of this because I left off you

1722 2914 2443 024 3007 1930
ἐν Κρήτῃ, ἵνα τὰ λείποντα ἐπιδιορθώσῃ
in Crete, that the being left you might set straight

2532 2525 2596 4172 4245 5613 1473
καὶ καταστήσῃς κατὰ πόλιν πρεσβυτέρους, ὡς ἐγώ
and might appoint by city older men, as I

1472 1299 **6** 1487 5100 1510 410
σοι διεταξάμην, εἴ τίς ἐστιν ἀνέγκλητος,
to you directed, if some is unreproachable,

1520 1135 435 5043 2192 4103 3361
μιᾶς γυναικὸς ἀνήρ, τέκνα ἔχων πιστά, μὴ
of one woman man, children having trustful, not

1722 2724 810 2228 506
ἐν κατηγορίᾳ ἀσωτίας ἢ ἀνυπότακτα.
in accusation of dissipation or unsubmitting.

7 1163 1063 04 1985 410
δεῖ γὰρ τὸν ἐπίσκοπον ἀνέγκλητον
It is necessary for the overseer unreproachable

1510 1510 3623 3361 829 3361
εἶναι ὡς θεοῦ οἰκονόμον, μὴ αὐθάδη, μὴ
to be as of God manager, not self-willed, not

3711 3361 3943 3361 4131 3361
ὀργίλον, μὴ πάροινον, μὴ πλήκτην, μὴ
quick-tempered, not with wine, not hitter, not

146 235 5382 5358
αἰσχροκερδῆ, ἀλλὰ φιλόξενον φιλάγαθον
shameful gainer, but lover of stranger, lover of good,

4998 1342 3741 1468 **9** 472
σώφρονα δίκαιον ὅσιον ἐγκρατῆ, ἀντεχόμενον
soberminded, right, holy, inner strength, holding on

02 2596 08 1322 4103 3056 2443 1415
τοῦ κατὰ τὴν διδαχὴν πιστοῦ λόγου, ἵνα δυνατὸς
the by the teaching of trustful word, that power

1510 2532 3870 1722 07 1319 07
ᾖ καὶ παρακαλεῖν ἐν τῇ διδασκαλίᾳ τῇ
he might be also to encourage in the teaching the

5198 2532 016 483 1651
ὑγιαινούσῃ καὶ τοὺς ἀντιλέγοντας ἐλέγχειν.
being healthy and the ones speaking against to rebuke.

```
      1510         1063  4183    2532 506
10  Εἰσὶν        γὰρ  πολλοὶ [καὶ] ἀνυπότακτοι,
    There are     for  many     also unsubmitting ones,
3151          2532 5423                3122        013 1537
ματαιολόγοι   καὶ  φρεναπάται,    μάλιστα    οἱ  ἐκ
futile words  and  mind-deceivers, especially the from
06  4061                3739 1163    1993
τῆς περιτομῆς, 11 οὓς  δεῖ     ἐπιστομίζειν,
the circumcision,  whom it is  to muzzle mouth,
                                            necessary
3748      3650   3624    396                 1321        3739 3361
οἵτινες ὅλους  οἴκους ἀνατρέπουσιν διδάσκοντες ἃ    μὴ
who      whole houses turn up      teaching    what not
1163       150           2771    5484          3004
δεῖ        αἰσχροῦ   κέρδους χάριν.  12 εἶπέν
it is necessary of shameful gain    because.    Said
5100 1537 846   2398   846    4396         2912    104
τις ἐξ  αὐτῶν ἴδιος αὐτῶν προφήτης· Κρῆτες ἀεὶ
some from them  own  of them spokesman, Cretans always
5583      2556 2342         1064      692    13  05
ψεῦσται, κακὰ θηρία,    γαστέρες ἀργαί.     ἡ
liars,   bad  wild animals, gluttons idle.    The
3141        3778 1510 227       1223    3739   156
μαρτυρία αὕτη ἐστὶν ἀληθής. δι᾽   ἣν  αἰτίαν
testimony this is    true.   Through which cause
1651     846    664         2443 5198               1722
ἔλεγχε αὐτοὺς ἀποτόμως, ἵνα ὑγιαίνωσιν      ἐν
rebuke them    severely, that they might be healthy in
07  4102        3361 4337          2451        3454 2532
τῇ πίστει, 14 μὴ προσέχοντες Ἰουδαϊκοῖς μύθοις καὶ
the trust,     not holding to  Judaic    myths   and
1785      444         654            08  225
ἐντολαῖς ἀνθρώπων ἀποστρεφομένων τὴν ἀλήθειαν.
commands of men    being turned off  the truth.
   3956  2513   015      2513          015         1161
15 πάντα καθαρὰ τοῖς  καθαροῖς·  τοῖς     δὲ
   All   clean  to the clean ones; to the ones but
3392              2532 571        3762 2513       235
μεμιαμμένοις     καὶ  ἀπίστοις  οὐδὲν καθαρόν, ἀλλὰ
having been defiled and untrustful nothing clean,  but
3392          846       2532 01  3563 2532 05
μεμίανται     αὐτῶν καὶ  ὁ  νοῦς καὶ  ἡ
have been defiled of them both the mind and  the
4893          16  2316 3670          3609a   023   1161
συνείδησις.     θεὸν ὁμολογοῦσιν εἰδέναι, τοῖς  δὲ
conscience.      God they confess to know,  in the but
2041     720       947          1510 2532 545
ἔργοις ἀρνοῦνται, βδελυκτοὶ ὄντες καὶ ἀπειθεῖς
works  they deny, abominators being and disobedient
2532 4314 3956 2041  18       96         1473 1161
καὶ πρὸς πᾶν ἔργον ἀγαθὸν ἀδόκιμοι. 2:1 Σὺ  δὲ
and to  all work good   unproved.     You  but
2980 3739 4241       07       5198       1319
λάλει ἃ  πρέπει    τῇ   ὑγιαινούσῃ διδασκαλίᾳ.
speak what is fitting in the being healthy teaching.
  4246        3524      1510     4586      4998
2 Πρεσβύτας νηφαλίους εἶναι, σεμνούς, σώφρονας,
  Old men    temperate to be, grave,   soberminded,
5198          07     4102      07   26      07   5281
ὑγιαίνοντας τῇ  πίστει, τῇ ἀγάπῃ, τῇ ὑπομονῇ·
being healthy in the trust, the love,  the patience;
  4247        5615      1722 2688          2412
3 Πρεσβύτιδας ὡσαύτως ἐν καταστήματι ἱεροπρεπεῖς,
  old women   likewise in demeanor   befitting sacred,
3361 1228        3361 3631      4183 1402
μὴ διαβόλους μὴ οἴνῳ πολλῷ δεδουλωμένας,
not slanderers not in wine much, having been slaved,
2567               4  2443 4994              020
καλοδιδασκάλους,   ἵνα σωφρονίζωσιν      τὰς
teachers of good,  that they might urge sober mind the
```

10 There are also many rebellious people, idle talkers and deceivers, especially those of the circumcision; [11] they must be silenced, since they are upsetting whole families by teaching for sordid gain what it is not right to teach. [12] It was one of them, their very own prophet, who said,

"Cretans are always liars, vicious brutes, lazy gluttons."

[13] That testimony is true. For this reason rebuke them sharply, so that they may become sound in the faith, [14] not paying attention to Jewish myths or to commandments of those who reject the truth. [15] To the pure all things are pure, but to the corrupt and unbelieving nothing is pure. Their very minds and consciences are corrupted. [16] They profess to know God, but they deny him by their actions. They are detestable, disobedient, unfit for any good work.

CHAPTER 2

But as for you, teach what is consistent with sound doctrine. [2] Tell the older men to be temperate, serious, prudent, and sound in faith, in love, and in endurance.

3 Likewise, tell the older women to be reverent in behavior, not to be slanderers or slaves to drink; they are to teach what is good, [4] so that they may encourage

the young women to love
their husbands, to love
their children, 5to be
self-controlled, chaste,
good managers of the
household, kind, being
submissive to their
husbands, so that the
word of God may not
be discredited.

6 Likewise, urge the
younger men to be self-
controlled. 7Show yourself
in all respects a model of
good works, and in your
teaching show integrity,
gravity, 8and sound speech
that cannot be censured;
then any opponent will
be put to shame, having
nothing evil to say of us.

9 Tell slaves to be
submissive to their masters
and to give satisfaction in
every respect; they are not
to talk back, 10not to pilfer,
but to show complete and
perfect fidelity, so that in
everything they may be an
ornament to the doctrine
of God our Savior.

11 For the grace of God
has appeared, bringing
salvation to all,a 12training
us to renounce impiety and
worldly passions, and in the
present age to live lives that
are self-controlled, upright,
and godly, 13while we wait
for the blessed hope and
the manifestation of the
glory of our great God
and Savior,b Jesus Christ.
14He it is who gave himself
for us that he might redeem
us from all iniquity and
purify for himself a people
of his own who are zealous

a Or has appeared to all, bringing
salvation
b Or of the great God and our Savior

3501 5362   1510   5388   5 4998
νέας φιλάνδρους εἶναι, φιλοτέκνους   σώφρονας
new men-lovers to be, children-lovers, soberminded,
53   3626   18   5293   015
ἀγνάς οἰκουργοὺς ἀγαθάς, ὑποτασσομένας τοῖς
pure houseworkers good,   being subjected to the
2398   435   2443 3361 01 3056 02   2316
ἰδίοις ἀνδράσιν, ἵνα μὴ ὁ λόγος τοῦ   θεοῦ
own   men,   that not the word of the God
987   016 3501   5615   3870
βλασφημῆται.   6 Τοὺς νεωτέρους ὡσαύτως παρακάλει
might be insulted. The newer   likewise encourage
4993   7 4012 3956   4572   3930
σωφρονεῖν   περὶ πάντα, σεαυτὸν παρεχόμενος
to think soberly about all, yourself holding along
5179   2570   2041 1722 07 1319   862a
τύπον καλῶν ἔργων, ἐν τῇ διδασκαλίᾳ ἀφθορίαν,
example of good works, in the teaching   incorruptible,
4587   8 3056 5199   176   2443
σεμνότητα,   λόγον ὑγιῆ ἀκατάγνωστον,   ἵνα
gravity,   word healthy not known against, that
01   1537 1727   1788   3367   2192
ὁ   ἐξ ἐναντίας ἐντραπῇ   μηδὲν ἔχων
the one from against might be regarded nothing having
3004   4012 1473 5337   9 1401   2398   1203
λέγειν περὶ ἡμῶν φαῦλον.   Δούλους ἰδίοις δεσπόταις
to say about us foul.   Slaves to own supervisors
5293   1722 3956 2101   1510   3361
ὑποτάσσεσθαι ἐν πᾶσιν, εὐαρέστους εἶναι, μὴ
to be subject in all, well-pleasing to be, not
483   10 3361 3557   235   3956
ἀντιλέγοντας,   μὴ νοσφιζομένους, ἀλλὰ πᾶσαν
speaking against, not misappropriating but all
4102 1731   08   18 2443 08 1319   08
πίστιν ἐνδεικνυμένους ἀγαθήν, ἵνα τὴν διδασκαλίαν τὴν
trust demonstrating   good, that the teaching   the
02   4990   1473 2316 2885   1722 3956
τοῦ σωτῆρος ἡμῶν θεοῦ κοσμῶσιν   ἐν πᾶσιν.
of the deliverer of us God they might adorn in all.
11 2014   1063 05 5485 02   2316 4992
  Ἐπεφάνη γὰρ ἡ χάρις τοῦ θεοῦ σωτήριος
  Appeared for the favor of the God deliverance
3956 444   3811   1473 2443
πᾶσιν ἀνθρώποις 12 παιδεύουσα   ἡμᾶς, ἵνα
to all men   instructing as child us, that
720   08   763   2532 020 2886
ἀρνησάμενοι τὴν ἀσέβειαν καὶ τὰς κοσμικὰς
having denied the irreverence and the worldly
1939   4996   2532 1346 2532 2153
ἐπιθυμίας σωφρόνως καὶ δικαίως καὶ εὐσεβῶς
desires, sobermindedly and rightly and reverently
2198   1722 03 3568 165   13 4327
ζήσωμεν ἐν τῷ νῦν αἰῶνι,   προσδεχόμενοι τὴν
we might live in the now age, awaiting   the
3107   1680 2532 2015   06   1391   02
μακαρίαν ἐλπίδα καὶ ἐπιφάνειαν τῆς δόξης   τοῦ
fortunate hope and appearance of the splendor of the
3173   2316 2532 4990   1473 2424 5547
μεγάλου θεοῦ καὶ σωτῆρος ἡμῶν Ἰησοῦ Χριστοῦ,
great   God and deliverer of us Jesus Christ,
14 3739 1325   1438   2228 1473   2443
  ὃς ἔδωκεν ἑαυτὸν ὑπὲρ ἡμῶν, ἵνα
  who gave himself on behalf of us, that
3084   1473 575 3956 458   2532
λυτρώσηται ἡμᾶς ἀπὸ πάσης ἀνομίας καὶ
he might redeem us from all lawlessness and
2511   1438   2992 4041   2207
καθαρίσῃ ἑαυτῷ λαὸν περιούσιον, ζηλωτὴν
might clean to himself people special,   jealous

2570	2041		3778	2980	2532	3870		2532

καλῶν ἔργων. **15** Ταῦτα λάλει καὶ παρακάλει καὶ
of good works. These speak and encourage and

1651	3326	3956	2003		3367	1473

ἔλεγχε μετὰ πάσης ἐπιταγῆς· μηδείς σου
rebuke with all order; no one of you

4065		5279	846	746

περιφρονείτω. **3:1** Ὑπομίμνησκε αὐτοὺς ἀρχαῖς
let think around. Remind them to rulers

1849	5293	3980	4314 3956 2041

ἐξουσίαις ὑποτάσσεσθαι, πειθαρχεῖν, πρὸς πᾶν ἔργον
authorities to be subject, to obey, to all work

18	2092	1510	**2** 3367	987

ἀγαθὸν ἑτοίμους εἶναι, μηδένα βλασφημεῖν,
good prepared to be, no one to insult,

269	1510	1933	3956	1731

ἀμάχους εἶναι, ἐπιεικεῖς, πᾶσαν ἐνδεικνυμένους
non-fighters to be, gentle, all demonstrating

4240	4314 3956	444	**3** 1510 1063 4218

πραΰτητα πρὸς πάντας ἀνθρώπους. Ἦμεν γάρ ποτε
gentleness to all men. Were for then

2532 1473	453	545	4105

καὶ ἡμεῖς ἀνόητοι, ἀπειθεῖς, πλανώμενοι,
also we unmindful, disobedient, being deceived,

1398	1939	2532 2237	4164	1722

δουλεύοντες ἐπιθυμίαις καὶ ἡδοναῖς ποικίλαις, ἐν
slaving in desires and pleasures various, in

2549	2532 5355	1236	4767	3404

κακίᾳ καὶ φθόνῳ διάγοντες, στυγητοί, μισοῦντες
badness and envy leading detestable, hating
through,

240	**4** 3753 1161 05	5544	2532 05

ἀλλήλους. ὅτε δὲ ἡ χρηστότης καὶ ἡ
one another. When but the kindness and the

5363	2014	02	4990	1473	2316

φιλανθρωπία ἐπεφάνη τοῦ σωτῆρος ἡμῶν θεοῦ,
love of man appeared of the deliverer of us God,

5 3756 1537 2041	022 1722 1343	3739	4160

οὐκ ἐξ ἔργων τῶν ἐν δικαιοσύνῃ ἃ ἐποιήσαμεν
not from works the in rightness which did

1473	235	2596	012 846	1656	4982	1473

ἡμεῖς ἀλλὰ κατὰ τὸ αὐτοῦ ἔλεος ἔσωσεν ἡμᾶς
we but by the of him mercy he delivered us

1223	3067	3824	2532 342

διὰ λουτροῦ παλιγγενεσίας καὶ ἀνακαινώσεως
through washing of born again and renewal

4151	40	**6** 3739	1632	1909 1473

πνεύματος ἁγίου, οὗ ἐξέχεεν ἐφ᾽ ἡμᾶς
of spirit holy, which he poured out on us

4146	1223	2424	5547	02	4990	1473

πλουσίως διὰ Ἰησοῦ Χριστοῦ τοῦ σωτῆρος ἡμῶν,
richly through Jesus Christ the deliverer of us,

7 2443 1344	07	1565	5485

ἵνα δικαιωθέντες τῇ ἐκείνου χάριτι
that having been made right in the of that favor

2818	1096	2596 1680	2222	166

κληρονόμοι γενηθῶμεν κατ᾽ ἐλπίδα ζωῆς αἰωνίου.
inheritors we might become by hope of life eternal.

8 4103	01	3056	2532 4012	3778	1014	1473

Πιστὸς ὁ λόγος· καὶ περὶ τούτων βούλομαί σε
Trustful the word; and about these I plan you

1226	2443 5431	2570 2041

διαβεβαιοῦσθαι, ἵνα φροντίζωσιν καλῶν ἔργων
to firmly assert, that they might think good works

4291	013 4100	2316	3778

προΐστασθαι οἱ πεπιστευκότες θεῷ· ταῦτά
to stand before the ones having trusted in God; these

1510	2570 2532	5624	015	444	**9** 3474	1161

ἐστιν καλὰ καὶ ὠφέλιμα τοῖς ἀνθρώποις. μωρὰς δὲ
are good and helpful to the men. Foolish but

---

for good deeds.

15 Declare these things; exhort and reprove with all authority.[a] Let no one look down on you.

CHAPTER 3

Remind them to be subject to rulers and authorities, to be obedient, to be ready for every good work, [2]to speak evil of no one, to avoid quarreling, to be gentle, and to show every courtesy to everyone. [3]For we ourselves were once foolish, disobedient, led astray, slaves to various passions and pleasures, passing our days in malice and envy, despicable, hating one another. [4]But when the goodness and loving kindness of God our Savior appeared, [5]he saved us, not because of any works of righteousness that we had done, but according to his mercy, through the water[b] of rebirth and renewal by the Holy Spirit. [6]This Spirit he poured out on us richly through Jesus Christ our Savior, [7]so that, having been justified by his grace, we might become heirs according to the hope of eternal life. [8]The saying is sure.

I desire that you insist on these things, so that those who have come to believe in God may be careful to devote themselves to good works; these things are excellent and profitable to everyone. [9]But avoid stupid

a Gk commandment
b Gk washing

controversies, genealogies, dissensions, and quarrels about the law, for they are unprofitable and worthless. [10]After a first and second admonition, have nothing more to do with anyone who causes divisions, [11]since you know that such a person is perverted and sinful, being self-condemned.

12 When I send Artemas to you, or Tychicus, do your best to come to me at Nicopolis, for I have decided to spend the winter there. [13]Make every effort to send Zenas the lawyer and Apollos on their way, and see that they lack nothing. [14]And let people learn to devote themselves to good works in order to meet urgent needs, so that they may not be unproductive.

15 All who are with me send greetings to you. Greet those who love us in the faith.

Grace be with all of you.[a]

[a] Other ancient authorities add *Amen*

2214		2532 1076		2532 2054		2532 3163
ζητήσεις		καὶ γενεαλογίας	καὶ	ἔρεις	καὶ	μάχας
speculations	and genealogies	and	strifes	and	battles

3544	4026		1510	1063 512		2532
νομικὰς περιΐστασο·		εἰσὶν	γὰρ ἀνωφελεῖς		καὶ
lawyers stand around;	they are	for	unprofitable	and

3152
μάταιοι.   **10** 141   444   3326 1520 2532 1208
αἱρετικὸν ἄνθρωπον μετὰ μίαν καὶ δευτέραν
futile.   Sectarian man   after one and second

3559   3868   **11** 3609a 3754 1612
νουθεσίαν παραιτοῦ,   εἰδὼς ὅτι ἐξέστραπται
warning   reject,   knowing that has been turned out

01 5108   2532 264   1510 843
ὁ   τοιοῦτος καὶ ἁμαρτάνει ὢν αὐτοκατάκριτος.
the such   and sins   being self-condemned.

12 3752 3992   734   4314 1473 2228 5190
"Οταν πέμψω   'Αρτεμᾶν πρὸς σὲ ἢ   Τύχικον,
When I might send Artemas to   you or   Tychicus,

4704   2064   4314 1473 1519 3533   1563
σπούδασον ἐλθεῖν πρός με εἰς Νικόπολιν, ἐκεῖ
be diligent to come to   me in Nicopolis, there

1063 2919   3914   **13** 2211 04 3544
γὰρ κέκρικα   παραχειμάσαι.   Ζηνᾶν τὸν νομικὸν
for I have judged to winter along. Zenas the lawyer

2532 625   4709   4311   2443 3367
καὶ 'Απολλῶν σπουδαίως πρόπεμψον, ἵνα μηδὲν
and Apollos diligently send before, that nothing

846   3007   **14** 3129   1161 2532 013
αὐτοῖς λείπῃ.   μανθανέτωσαν δὲ καὶ οἱ
to them might leave. Let learn   but also the

2251   2570 2041 4291   1519 020 316
ἡμέτεροι καλῶν ἔργων προΐστασθαι εἰς τὰς ἀναγκαίας
our   good works to stand before for the necessary

5532   2443 3361 1510   175   **15** 782
χρείας, ἵνα μὴ ὦσιν   ἄκαρποι.   'Ασπάζονταί
needs, that not they might be fruitless. Greet

1473 013   3326 1473 3956   782   016
σε οἱ   μετ' ἐμοῦ πάντες. ἄσπασαι τοὺς
you the ones with me all.   Greet the ones

5368   1473 1722 4102   05 5485 3326 3956
φιλοῦντας ἡμᾶς ἐν πίστει. 'Η χάρις μετὰ πάντων
loving us in trust. The favor with all

1473
ὑμῶν.
of you.

PHILEMON

1 Paul, a prisoner of Christ Jesus, and Timothy our brother,[a]

To Philemon our dear friend and co-worker, [2] to Apphia our sister,[b] to Archippus our fellow soldier, and to the church in your house:

3 Grace to you and peace from God our Father and the Lord Jesus Christ.

4 When I remember you[c] in my prayers, I always thank my God [5] because I hear of your love for all the saints and your faith toward the Lord Jesus. [6] I pray that the sharing of your faith may become effective when you perceive all the good that we[d] may do for Christ. [7] I have indeed received much joy and encouragement from your love, because the hearts of the saints have been refreshed through you, my brother.

8 For this reason, though I am bold enough in Christ to command you to do your duty, [9] yet I would rather appeal to you on the basis of love— and I, Paul, do this as an old man, and now also as a prisoner of Christ Jesus.[e] [10] I am appealing to you for my child, Onesimus, whose father I have become during my imprisonment. [11] Formerly he was useless to you, but now he is indeed useful[f] both to you and to me. [12] I am sending him, that is, my own heart, back to you. [13] I wanted to

[a] Gk the brother
[b] Gk the sister
[c] From verse 4 through verse 21, you is singular
[d] Other ancient authorities read you (plural)
[e] Or as an ambassador of Christ Jesus, and now also his prisoner
[f] The name Onesimus means useful or (compare verse 20) beneficial

---

1:1
3972 Παῦλος — Paul
1198 δέσμιος — prisoner
5547 Χριστοῦ — of Christ
2424 Ἰησοῦ — Jesus
2532 καὶ — and
5095 Τιμόθεος — Timothy
01 ὁ — the
80 ἀδελφὸς — brother
5371 Φιλήμονι — to Philemon
03 τῷ — the
27 ἀγαπητῷ — loved
2532 καὶ — and
4904 συνεργῷ — co-worker
1473 ἡμῶν — of us

2
2532 καὶ — and
682 Ἀπφίᾳ — Apphia
07 τῇ — the
79 ἀδελφῇ — sister
2532 καὶ — and
751 Ἀρχίππῳ — Archippus
03 τῷ — the
4961 συστρατιώτῃ — co-soldier
1473 ἡμῶν — of us
2532 καὶ — and
07 τῇ — to the
2596 κατ' — by
3624 οἶκόν — house
1473 σου — of you
1577 ἐκκλησίᾳ, — assembly,

3
5485 χάρις — favor
1473 ὑμῖν — to you
2532 καὶ — and
1515 εἰρήνη — peace
575 ἀπὸ — from
2316 Θεοῦ — God
3962 πατρὸς — father
1473 ἡμῶν — of us
2532 καὶ — and
2962 κυρίου — Master
2424 Ἰησοῦ — Jesus
5547 Χριστοῦ. — Christ.

4
2168 Εὐχαριστῶ — I give good favor
03 τῷ — to the
2316 Θεῷ — God
1473 μου — of me
3842 πάντοτε — always
3417 μνείαν — memory
1473 σου — of you
4160 ποιούμενος — making
1909 ἐπὶ — on
018 τῶν — the
4335 προσευχῶν — prayers
1473 μου, — of me,

5
191 ἀκούων — hearing
1473 σου — of you
08 τὴν — the
26 ἀγάπην — love
2532 καὶ — and
08 τὴν — the
4102 πίστιν, — trust,
3739 ἣν — which
2192 ἔχεις — you have
4314 πρὸς — to
04 τὸν — the
2962 κύριον — Master
2424 Ἰησοῦν — Jesus
2532 καὶ — and
1519 εἰς — to
3956 πάντας — all
016 τοὺς — the
40 ἁγίους, — holy ones,

6
3704 ὅπως — so that
05 ἡ — the
2842 κοινωνία — partnership
06 τῆς — of the
4102 πίστεώς — trust
1473 σου — of you
1756 ἐνεργὴς — operational
1096 γένηται — might become
1722 ἐν — in
1922 ἐπιγνώσει — perception
3956 παντὸς — of all
18 ἀγαθοῦ — good
010 τοῦ — the
1722 ἐν — in
1473 ἡμῖν — us
1519 εἰς — in
5547 Χριστόν. — Christ.

7
5479 χαρὰν — Joy
1063 γὰρ — for
4183 πολλὴν — much
2192 ἔσχον — I had
2532 καὶ — and
3874 παράκλησιν — encouragement
1909 ἐπὶ — on
07 τῇ — the
26 ἀγάπῃ — love
1473 σου, — of you,
3754 ὅτι — that
021 τὰ — the
4698 σπλάγχνα — affections
014 τῶν — of the
40 ἁγίων — holy
373 ἀναπέπαυται — have been rested up
1223 διὰ — by
4675 σοῦ, — you,
80 ἀδελφέ. — brother.

8
1352 Διὸ — Wherefore
4183 πολλὴν — much
1722 ἐν — in
5547 Χριστῷ — Christ
3954 παρρησίαν — boldness
2192 ἔχων — having
2004 ἐπιτάσσειν — to order
1473 σοι — you
012 τὸ — the
433 ἀνῆκον — proper

9
1223 διὰ — through
08 τὴν — the
26 ἀγάπην — love
3123 μᾶλλον — more
3870 παρακαλῶ, — I encourage,
5108 τοιοῦτος — such
1510 ὢν — being
5613 ὡς — as
3972 Παῦλος — Paul
4246 πρεσβύτης — old man
3570 νυνὶ — now
1161 δὲ — but
2532 καὶ — also
1198 δέσμιος — prisoner
5547 Χριστοῦ — of Christ
2424 Ἰησοῦ· — Jesus;

10
3870 παρακαλῶ — I encourage
1473 σε — you
4012 περὶ — about
010 τοῦ — the
1699 ἐμοῦ — of me
5043 τέκνου, — child,
3739 ὃν — whom
1080 ἐγέννησα — I gave birth
1722 ἐν — in
015 τοῖς — the
1199 δεσμοῖς, — chains,
3682 Ὀνήσιμον, — Onesimus,

11
04 τόν — the
4218 ποτέ — then
1473 σοι — to you
890 ἄχρηστον — unuseful
3570 νυνὶ — now
1161 δὲ — but
2532 [καὶ] — both
1473 σοὶ — to you
2532 καὶ — and
1473 ἐμοὶ — to me
2173 εὔχρηστον, — good use,

12
3739 ὃν — whom
375 ἀνέπεμψά — I sent up
1473 σοι, — to you,
846 αὐτόν, — him,
3778 τοῦτ' — this
1510 ἔστιν — is
024 τὰ — the
1699 ἐμὰ — my
4698 σπλάγχνα· — affections;

13
3739 Ὃν — whom
1473 ἐγὼ — I
1014 ἐβουλόμην — planned
4314 πρὸς — to

```
1683        2722              2443 5228        1473 1473
ἐμαυτὸν κατέχειν,        ἵνα ὑπὲρ          σοῦ  μοι
myself   to hold down,   that on behalf of you  me
1247           1722 015   1199   010    2098
διακονῇ       ἐν τοῖς δεσμοῖς τοῦ   εὐαγγελίου,
he might serve in  the  chains  of the good message,
    5565      1161 06  4674 1106   3762    2309
14 χωρὶς δὲ  τῆς σῆς γνώμης οὐδὲν ἠθέλησα
   without but the your purpose nothing I wanted
4160       2443 3361 5613 2596 318        09   18
ποιῆσαι, ἵνα μὴ ὡς κατὰ ἀνάγκην τὸ ἀγαθόν
to do,    that not as  by  necessity the good
1473  1510    235   2596 1595          5029      1063
σου  ᾖ     ἀλλὰ κατὰ ἑκούσιον. 15 Τάχα    γὰρ
of you might be but  by  willingness. Perhaps for
1223      3778  5563            4314 5610 2443 166
διὰ    τοῦτο ἐχωρίσθη      πρὸς ὥραν, ἵνα αἰώνιον
through this  he was separated for  hour, that eternal
846     568                3765      5613 1401   235
αὐτὸν ἀπέχῃς,        16 οὐκέτι   ὡς  δοῦλον ἀλλ᾽
him    you might have back, no longer as  slave  but
5228   1401    80      27        3122       1473
ὑπὲρ δοῦλον, ἀδελφὸν ἀγαπητόν, μάλιστα ἐμοί,
beyond slave, brother loved,    especially to me,
4214 1161 3123  1473    2532 1722 4561   2532 1722
πόσῳ δὲ μᾶλλον σοὶ καὶ ἐν σαρκὶ καὶ ἐν
how but more    to you both in  flesh and in
2962      17 1487 3767 1473 2192  2844        4355
κυρίῳ.      εἰ οὖν με  ἔχεις κοινωνόν, προσλαβοῦ
Master.   If then me you hold partner,   take to
846   5613 1473  18 1487 1161 5100 91          1473
αὐτὸν ὡς ἐμέ.    εἰ δέ τι  ἠδίκησέν    σε
him   as  me.    If but some he did unright you
2228 3784      3778  1473 1676a      1473 3972
ἢ   ὀφείλει, τοῦτο ἐμοὶ ἐλλόγα. 19 ἐγὼ Παῦλος
or  he owes, this  to me charge.    I   Paul
1125    07   1699 5495   1473 661          2443
ἔγραψα τῇ ἐμῇ χειρί, ἐγὼ ἀποτίσω·        ἵνα
wrote  in the my hand, I   will pay damages; that
3361 3004   1473   3754 2532 4572   1473
μὴ λέγω   σοι ὅτι καὶ σεαυτόν μοι
not I might say to you that also yourself to me
4359            20 3483 80    1473 1473 3685
προσοφείλεις.    ναί ἀδελφέ, ἐγώ σου ὀναίμην
you owe to.       Yes brother, I  of you may benefit
1722 2962   373        1473 024 4698      1722
ἐν κυρίῳ· ἀνάπαυσόν μου τὰ σπλάγχνα ἐν
in Master; give rest of me the affections in
5547      21 3982       07   5218    1473
Χριστῷ. Πεποιθὼς     τῇ ὑπακοῇ σου
Christ.   Being persuaded in the obedience of you
1125   1473 3609a     3754 2532 2532 4572 3739 3004
ἔγραψά σοι, εἰδὼς ὅτι καὶ καὶ ὑπὲρ ὃ λέγω
I wrote you, having known that also beyond what I say
4160        22 260       1161 2532 2090    1473
ποιήσεις.    ἅμα      δὲ καὶ ἑτοίμαζέ μοι
you will do.  At same time but also prepare  to me
3578        1679    1063 3754 1223    018
ξενίαν·   ἐλπίζω γὰρ ὅτι διὰ    τῶν
stranger's room; I hope for that through the
4335      1473 5483            1473
προσευχῶν ὑμῶν χαρισθήσομαι ὑμῖν.
prayers  of you I will be favored to you.
   782       1473 1889      01  4869           1473
23 Ἀσπάζεταί σε Ἐπαφρᾶς ὁ συναιχμάλωτός μου
   Greets   you Epaphras the co-captive  of me
1722 5547·  2424     3138     708        1214
ἐν Χριστῷ Ἰησοῦ, 24 Μᾶρκος, Ἀρίσταρχος, Δημᾶς,
in Christ Jesus,   Mark,    Aristarchus, Demas,
```

keep him with me, so that he might be of service to me in your place during my imprisonment for the gospel; [14]but I preferred to do nothing without your consent, in order that your good deed might be voluntary and not something forced. [15]Perhaps this is the reason he was separated from you for a while, so that you might have him back forever, [16]no longer as a slave but more than a slave, a beloved brother—especially to me but how much more to you, both in the flesh and in the Lord.

[17]So if you consider me your partner, welcome him as you would welcome me. [18]If he has wronged you in any way, or owes you anything, charge that to my account. [19]I, Paul, am writing this with my own hand: I will repay it. I say nothing about your owing me even your own self. [20]Yes, brother, let me have this benefit from you in the Lord! Refresh my heart in Christ. [21]Confident of your obedience, I am writing to you, knowing that you will do even more than I say.

[22]One thing more—prepare a guest room for me, for I am hoping through your prayers to be restored to you.

[23]Epaphras, my fellow prisoner in Christ Jesus, sends greetings to you,[a] [24]and so do Mark, Aristarchus, Demas,

[a] Here you is singular

and Luke, my fellow
workers.

25 The grace of the
Lord Jesus Christ be with
your spirit.[a]

3065	013	4904	1473	**25**	05	5485	02
Λουκᾶς,	οἱ	συνεργοί	μου.		Ἡ	χάρις	τοῦ
Luke,	the	co-workers	of me.		The	favor	of the

2962	2424	5547	3326	010	4151	1473
κυρίου	Ἰησοῦ	Χριστοῦ	μετὰ	τοῦ	πνεύματος	ὑμῶν.
Master	Jesus	Christ	with	the	spirit	of you.

[a] Other ancient authorities add
    Amen

HEBREWS

CHAPTER 1

Long ago God spoke to
our ancestors in many
and various ways by the
prophets, [2]but in these last
days he has spoken to us by
a Son,[a] whom he appointed
heir of all things, through
whom he also created the
worlds. [3]He is the reflection
of God's glory and the
exact imprint of God's very
being, and he sustains[b]
all things by his powerful
word. When he had made
purification for sins, he
sat down at the right hand
of the Majesty on high,
[4]having become as much
superior to angels as the
name he has inherited is
more excellent than theirs.
   5 For to which of the
angels did God ever say,
   "You are my Son;
      today I have begotten
      you"?
Or again,
   "I will be his Father,
      and he will be my Son"?
[6]And again, when he brings
the firstborn into the
world, he says,
   "Let all God's angels
      worship him."
[7]Of the angels he says,
   "He makes his angels
      winds,
   and his servants flames
      of fire."
[8]But of the Son he says,
   "Your throne, O God,
      is[c] forever and ever,
   and the righteous
      scepter is the scepter
      of your[d] kingdom.
[9] You have loved
   righteousness and
   hated wickedness;

a Or the Son
b Or bears along
c Or God is your throne
d Other ancient authorities read his

1:1
4181   2532 4187   3819   01   2316
Πολυμερῶς   καὶ πολυτρόπως πάλαι   ὁ   θεὸς
In many parts and many ways of old the God
2980   015   3962   1722 015   4396
λαλήσας   τοῖς   πατράσιν ἐν   τοῖς προφήταις
having spoken to the   fathers   in   the spokesmen
2 1909 2078   018   2250   3778   2980   1473
ἐπ' ἐσχάτου τῶν   ἡμερῶν τούτων ἐλάλησεν ἡμῖν
on last   of the days   these   spoke   to us
1722 5207 3739 5087   2818   3956   1223   3739
ἐν υἱῷ, ὃν ἔθηκεν κληρονόμον πάντων, δι'   οὗ
in son, whom he set inheritor of all, through whom
2532 4160   016 165   3 3739 1510   541
καὶ ἐποίησεν τοὺς αἰῶνας· ὃς ὢν   ἀπαύγασμα
also he made the ages;   who being radiance
06   1391   2532 5481   06   5287
τῆς δόξης   καὶ χαρακτὴρ τῆς ὑποστάσεως
of the splendor and reproduction of the substance
846   5342   5037 024 3956 011   4487   06
αὐτοῦ, φέρων τε   τὰ πάντα τῷ ῥήματι τῆς
of him, bearing indeed the all in the word of the
1411   846   2512   018   266   4160
δυνάμεως αὐτοῦ, καθαρισμὸν τῶν ἁμαρτιῶν ποιησάμενος
power   of him, cleaning of the sins having made
2523   1722 1188 06   3172   1722 5308
ἐκάθισεν ἐν δεξιᾷ τῆς μεγαλωσύνης ἐν ὑψηλοῖς,
he sat   in right of the greatness in heights,
4 5118   2909   1096   014 32
τοσούτῳ κρείττων γενόμενος τῶν ἀγγέλων
by such better having become of the messengers
3745   1313   3844 846   2816
ὅσῳ   διαφορώτερον παρ' αὐτοὺς κεκληρονόμηκεν
as much as more differing from them he has inherited
3686   **5** 5101 1063 3004   4218 014   32
ὄνομα. Τίνι γὰρ εἶπέν ποτε τῶν ἀγγέλων·
name.   To whom for he said ever of the messengers
5207 1473 1510 1473 1473 4594   1080   1473
υἱός μου εἶ σύ, ἐγὼ σήμερον γεγέννηκά   σε;
son of me are you, I today have given birth you?
2532 3825 1473 1510 846 1519 3962   2532 846
καὶ πάλιν· ἐγὼ ἔσομαι αὐτῷ εἰς πατέρα, καὶ αὐτὸς
And again, I will be to him for father, and himself
1510   1473 1519 5207 6 3752 1161 3825
ἔσται   μοι εἰς υἱόν; ὅταν δὲ πάλιν
will be to me for son? When but again
1521   04   4416   1519 08 3625   3004
εἰσαγάγῃ τὸν πρωτότοκον εἰς τὴν οἰκουμένην, λέγει·
he might lead the firstborn into the inhabited   he says,
in   world,
2532 4352   846 3956 32   2316
καὶ προσκυνησάτωσαν αὐτῷ πάντες ἄγγελοι θεοῦ.
and let worship   him all messengers of God.
7 2532 4314 3303 016 32   3004   01
καὶ πρὸς μὲν τοὺς ἀγγέλους λέγει· ὁ
And to indeed the messengers he says, the one
4160   016 32   846 4151   2532 016
ποιῶν τοὺς ἀγγέλους αὐτοῦ πνεύματα καὶ τοὺς
making the messengers of him spirits and the
3011   846 4442   5395 **8** 4314 1161 04
λειτουργοὺς αὐτοῦ πυρὸς φλόγα, πρὸς δὲ τὸν
servants of him of fire flame, to   but the
5207 01 2362   1473 01 2316 1519 04 165   02
υἱόν· ὁ θρόνος σου ὁ θεὸς εἰς τὸν αἰῶνα τοῦ
son, the throne of you the God into the age of the
165   2532 05 4464   06   2118   4464
αἰῶνος, καὶ ἡ ῥάβδος τῆς εὐθύτητος ῥάβδος
age,   and the rod of the straightness rod
06   932   1473 **9** 25   1343   2532
τῆς βασιλείας σου. ἠγάπησας δικαιοσύνην καὶ
of the kingdom of you. You loved rightness and

3404   458   1223   3778   5548   1473
ἐμίσησας ἀνομίαν·   διὰ   τοῦτο ἔχρισέν σε
you hated lawlessness; through this anointed you

01   2316 01   2316 1473   1637   20   3844   016
ὁ   θεὸς ὁ θεός σου   ἔλαιον ἀγαλλιάσεως παρὰ   τοὺς
the God the God of you oil   of gladness along the

3353   1473   2532 1473 2596 746   2962
μετόχους σου. 10 καί· σὺ κατ᾽ ἀρχάς,   κύριε,
sharers of you. And, you by   beginnings, Master,

08   1093 2311   2532 2041 018   5495   1473
τὴν γῆν ἐθεμελίωσας, καὶ ἔργα τῶν   χειρῶν σού
the earth founded,   and works of the hands of you

1510 013   3772   846   622   1473
εἰσιν οἱ οὐρανοί· 11 αὐτοὶ ἀπολοῦνται,   σὺ
are the heavens;   themselves will be destroyed, you

1161 1265   2532 3956   5613 2440
δὲ διαμένεις, καὶ πάντες ὡς ἱμάτιον
but stay through, and all   as clothes

3822   2532 5616 4018   1667
παλαιωθήσονται, 12 καὶ ὡσεὶ περιβόλαιον ἑλίξεις
will become old,   and as robe   you will roll

846   5613 2440   2532 236   1473
αὐτούς, ὡς ἱμάτιον καὶ ἀλλαγήσονται·   σὺ
them,   as clothes and they will be changed; you

1161 01   846   1510 2532 021 2094 1473   3756
δὲ ὁ αὐτὸς εἶ καὶ τὰ ἔτη σου οὐκ
but the same are and the years of you not

1587   4314 5101 1161 014   32
ἐκλείψουσιν. 13 πρὸς τίνα δὲ τῶν   ἀγγέλων
will leave off.   To   whom but of the messengers

3004   4218   2521   1537 1188   1473   2193 302
εἴρηκέν ποτε· κάθου ἐκ δεξιῶν μου, ἕως ἂν
has he said ever, sit from right of me, until -

5087   016   2190   1473   5286   014
θῶ   τοὺς ἐχθρούς σου ὑποπόδιον τῶν
I might set the hostiles of you footstool of the

4228 1473   3780 3956   1510 3010   4151
ποδῶν σου; 14 οὐχὶ πάντες εἰσὶν λειτουργικὰ πνεύματα
feet of you?   Not all   are serving   spirits

1519 1248   649   1223·   016
εἰς διακονίαν ἀποστελλόμενα διὰ   τοὺς
for service being delegated through the ones

3195   2816   4991   1223   3778
μέλλοντας κληρονομεῖν σωτηρίαν; 2:1 Διὰ   τοῦτο
being about to inherit deliverance?   Through this

1163   4056   4337   1473
δεῖ   περισσοτέρως προσέχειν ἡμᾶς
it is necessary more exceedingly to hold to us

023   191   3379   3901
τοῖς ἀκουσθεῖσιν,   μήποτε παραρυῶμεν.
to the having been heard, not then we might drift.

2 1487 1063 01 1223   32   2980
   εἰ γὰρ ὁ δι᾽ ἀγγέλων λαληθεὶς
   If for the through messengers having been spoken

3056   1096   949   2532 3956 3847   2532
λόγος ἐγένετο βέβαιος καὶ πᾶσα παράβασις καὶ
word became firm   also all transgression and

3876   2983   1738   3405   3 4459
παρακοὴ   ἔλαβεν ἔνδικον μισθαποδοσίαν, πῶς
disobedience received in right wage give back,   how

1473 1628   5082   272
ἡμεῖς ἐκφευξόμεθα τηλικαύτης ἀμελήσαντες
we   will flee out so great   having not taken care

4991   3748 746   2983   2980
σωτηρίας, ἥτις ἀρχὴν λαβοῦσα λαλεῖσθαι
of deliverance, which beginning having to be spoken
                                      received

1223   02   2962   5259 014   191   1519
διὰ τοῦ κυρίου ὑπὸ τῶν ἀκουσάντων   εἰς
through the Master by the ones having heard for

therefore God, your God,
  has anointed you
  with the oil of gladness
  beyond your
  companions."
[10]And,
  "In the beginning, Lord,
  you founded the earth,
  and the heavens are the
  work of your hands;
[11] they will perish, but you
  remain;
  they will all wear out
  like clothing;
[12]like a cloak you will roll
  them up,
  and like clothing[a] they
  will be changed.
  But you are the same,
  and your years will
  never end."
[13]But to which of the angels
has he ever said,
  "Sit at my right hand
  until I make your
  enemies a footstool
  for your feet"?
[14]Are not all angels[b]
spirits in the divine service,
sent to serve for the sake of
those who are to inherit
salvation?

CHAPTER 2

Therefore we must pay
greater attention to what
we have heard, so that we
do not drift away from it.
[2]For if the message declared
through angels was valid,
and every transgression or
disobedience received a just
penalty, [3]how can we escape
if we neglect so great a
salvation? It was declared
at first through the Lord,
and it was attested to us by
those who heard him,

---

[a] Other ancient authorities lack like
clothing
[b] Gk all of them

[4]while God added his testimony by signs and wonders and various miracles, and by gifts of the Holy Spirit, distributed according to his will.

[5]Now God[a] did not subject the coming world, about which we are speaking, to angels. [6]But someone has testified somewhere,

"What are human beings
   that you are mindful
   of them,[b]
or mortals, that you
   care for them?[c]
[7]You have made them
   for a little while
   lower[d] than the
   angels;
you have crowned
   them with glory and
   honor,[e]
[8]subjecting all things
   under their feet."

Now in subjecting all things to them, God[a] left nothing outside their control. As it is, we do not yet see everything in subjection to them, [9]but we do see Jesus, who for a little while was made lower[f] than the angels, now crowned with glory and honor because of the suffering of death, so that by the grace of God[g] he might taste death for everyone.

[10]It was fitting that God,[a] for whom and through whom all things exist, in bringing many children to glory, should make the pioneer of their salvation perfect through sufferings. [11]For the one who sanctifies and those who are sanctified all have one Father.[h]

---

[a] Gk he

[b] Gk What is man that you are mindful of him?

[c] Gk or the son of man that you care for him? In the Hebrew of Psalm 8.4-6 both man and son of man refer to all humankind

[d] Or them only a little lower

[e] Other ancient authorities add and set them over the works of your hands

[f] Or who was made a little lower

[g] Other ancient authorities read apart from God

[h] Gk are all of one

1473	950			4901			02	2316
ἡμᾶς	ἐβεβαιώθη,		**4**	συνεπιμαρτυροῦντος			τοῦ	θεοῦ
us	was confirmed,			testifying together			on the	God

4592		5037	2532	5059	2532	4164		1411
σημείοις		τε	καὶ	τέρασιν	καὶ	ποικίλαις		δυνάμεσιν
in signs		both	and	marvels	and	in various		powers

2532	4151		40	3311		2596 08	846
καὶ	πνεύματος		ἁγίου	μερισμοῖς		κατὰ τὴν	αὐτοῦ
and	of spirit		holy	divisions		by the	of him

2308		**5**	3756	1063	32		5293		08
θέλησιν;			Οὐ	γὰρ	ἀγγέλοις		ὑπέταξεν		τὴν
want?			Not	for	to messengers		he subjected		the

3625		08		3195		4012	3739
οἰκουμένην		τὴν		μέλλουσαν,		περὶ	ἧς
inhabited world		the		one being about to be,		about	which

2980		1263		1161	4225	5100
λαλοῦμεν.	**6**	διεμαρτύρατο		δέ	πού	τις
we speak.		Testified thoroughly		but	where	some

3004	5101	1510	444		3754	3403		846
λέγων·	τί	ἐστιν	ἄνθρωπος		ὅτι	μιμνῄσκῃ		αὐτοῦ,
saying·	who	is	man		that	you remember		him,

2228	5207	444		3754	1980		846	**7**	1642
ἢ	υἱὸς	ἀνθρώπου		ὅτι	ἐπισκέπτῃ		αὐτόν;		ἠλάττωσας
or	son	of man		that	you look on him?				Having lessened

846	1024	5100	3844	32		1391		2532
αὐτὸν	βραχύ	τι	παρ'	ἀγγέλους,		δόξῃ		καὶ
him	little	some	by	messengers,		in splendor		and

5092	4737		846	**8**	3956	5293
τιμῇ	ἐστεφάνωσας		αὐτόν,		πάντα	ὑπέταξας
value	you crowned		him,		all	you subjected

5270		014	4228	846		1722	011	1063	5293
ὑποκάτω		τῶν	ποδῶν	αὐτοῦ.		ἐν	τῷ	γὰρ	ὑποτάξαι
underneath		the	feet	of him.		In	the	for	to subject

846	024	3956	3762		863		846
[αὐτῷ]	τὰ	πάντα	οὐδὲν		ἀφῆκεν		αὐτῷ
him	the	all	nothing		he left off		to him

506		3568	1161	3760		2708	846		024	3956
ἀνυπότακτον.		Νῦν	δὲ	οὔπω		ὁρῶμεν	αὐτῷ		τὰ	πάντα
unsubmitting.		Now	but	not yet		we see	to him		the	all

5293		**9**	04	1161	1024		5100	3844
ὑποτεταγμένα·			τὸν	δὲ	βραχύ		τι	παρ'
having been subjected;			the	but	little		some	from

32		1642			991		2424	1223
ἀγγέλους		ἠλαττωμένον			βλέπομεν		Ἰησοῦν	διὰ
messengers		having been lessened			we see		Jesus	by

012	3804		02		2288	1391		2532	5092
τὸ	πάθημα		τοῦ		θανάτου	δόξῃ		καὶ	τιμῇ
the	suffering		of the		death	in splendor		and	value

4737		3704		5485		2316	5228
ἐστεφανωμένον,		ὅπως		χάριτι		θεοῦ	ὑπὲρ
having been crowned,		so that		in favor		of God	on behalf

3956	1089			2288		**10**	4241		1063
παντὸς	γεύσηται			θανάτου.			Ἔπρεπεν		γὰρ
of all	he might taste			death.			It is fitting		for

846	1223		3739	021	3956	2532	1223		3739
αὐτῷ,	δι'		ὃν	τὰ	πάντα	καὶ	δι'		οὗ
to him,	on account of		whom	the	all	and	through		whom

021	3956	4183	5207	1519	1391	71		04
τὰ	πάντα,	πολλοὺς	υἱοὺς	εἰς	δόξαν	ἀγαγόντα		τὸν
the	all,	many	sons	into	splendor	having led		the

747	06		4991		846	1223		3804
ἀρχηγὸν	τῆς		σωτηρίας		αὐτῶν	διὰ		παθημάτων
beginner	of the		deliverance		of them	through		sufferings

5048		01		5037	1063	37		2532	013
τελειῶσαι.	**11**	ὅ		τε	γὰρ	ἁγιάζων		καὶ	οἱ
to complete.		The one		both	for	making holy		and	the

37		1537	1520	3956		1223		3739
ἁγιαζόμενοι		ἐξ	ἑνὸς	πάντες·		δι'		ἣν
ones being made holy		from	one	all;		through		which

```
 156        3756  1870            80           846        2564
αἰτίαν  οὐκ  ἐπαισχύνεται  ἀδελφοὺς  αὐτοὺς  καλεῖν
cause   not   he is ashamed   brothers   them    to call
         3004      518      012  3686   1473    015    80
12 λέγων·  ἀπαγγελῶ  τὸ  ὄνομά σου  τοῖς  ἀδελφοῖς
    saying,  I tell     the  name  of you  to the  brothers
1473  1722  3319    1577        5214         1473      2532
μου,   ἐν   μέσῳ  ἐκκλησίας  ὑμνήσω    σε,   13 καὶ
of me, in  middle of assembly I will sing you,       and
3825   1473  1510      3982                1909  846
πάλιν·  ἐγὼ  ἔσομαι  πεποιθὼς            ἐπ᾽  αὐτῷ,
again, I    will be+ +having been persuaded on   him,
2532  3825   2400 1473 2532  021  3813              3739
καὶ  πάλιν·  ἰδοὺ ἐγὼ καὶ  τὰ  παιδία            ἅ
and  again, look I   and  the small children that
1473  1325     01  0216          1893  3767 021
μοι   ἔδωκεν ὁ  θεός.  14 Ἐπεὶ  οὖν  τὰ
to me gave    the God.     Since then  the
3813              2841              129        2532 4561    2532
παιδία          κεκοινώνηκεν  αἵματος  καὶ σαρκός, καὶ
small children  have partnered of blood and flesh,  and
846     3898           3348             022 846    2443
αὐτὸς  παραπλησίως  μετέσχεν   τῶν αὐτῶν,  ἵνα
himself nearly        has held with the same,   that
1223    02   2288     2673               04      012
διὰ   τοῦ θανάτου  καταργήσῃ         τὸν    τὸ
through the death  he might abolish the one the
2904     2192    02      2288      3778   1510   04
κράτος  ἔχοντα τοῦ    θανάτου, τοῦτ᾽ ἔστιν τὸν
strength having of the death,   this   is    the
1228        2532 525                3778      3745
διάβολον,  15 καὶ  ἀπαλλάξῃ       τούτους, ὅσοι
slanderer,    and he might release these,   as many as
5401   2288      1223   3956   010 2198   1777
φόβῳ  θανάτου  διὰ   παντὸς τοῦ ζῆν  ἔνοχοι
in fear of death through all    the  to live guilty
1510 1397       3756 1063 1222    32
ἦσαν δουλείας.  16 οὐ  γὰρ  δήπου ἀγγέλων
were of slavery.     Not  for   surely of messengers
1949             235   4690       11    1949
ἐπιλαμβάνεται  ἀλλὰ σπέρματος  Ἀβραὰμ ἐπιλαμβάνεται.
he takes on    but  of seed    Abraham takes on.
   3606     3784    2443 3956  015    80
17 ὅθεν  ὤφειλεν κατὰ πάντα τοῖς  ἀδελφοῖς
   From where he owes by   all    to the  brothers
3666            2443 1655   1096              2532
ὁμοιωθῆναι,  ἵνα ἐλεήμων γένηται           καὶ
to be likened, that merciful he might become and
4103      749        024 4314 04  2316 1519 012
πιστὸς  ἀρχιερεὺς  τὰ  πρὸς τὸν θεὸν εἰς  τὸ
trustful ruler priest the to   the  God  for  the
2433           020 2646       02    2992      1722 3739
ἱλάσκεσθαι  τὰς ἁμαρτίας τοῦ  λαοῦ.  18 ἐν   ᾧ
to be expiation the sins    of the people.  In   what
1063 3958     846       3985           1410    015
γὰρ  πέπονθεν αὐτὸς  πειρασθείς, δύναται  τοῖς
for  he has    himself being      he is   to the ones
     suffered           pressured, able
3985             997        3606            80
πειραζομένοις  βοηθῆσαι.  3:1 Ὅθεν,   ἀδελφοὶ
being pressured to help.     From where, brothers
40     2821    2032     3353       2657        04
ἅγιοι, κλήσεως ἐπουρανίου μέτοχοι, κατανοήσατε τὸν
holy,  of call on heaven  sharers, think carefully the
652          2532 2671   06    3671          1473
ἀπόστολον καὶ ἀρχιερέα τῆς  ὁμολογίας  ἡμῶν
delegate   and ruler priest of the confession of us
2424     2  4103    1510  03    4160          846
Ἰησοῦν,    πιστὸν ὄντα τῷ  ποιήσαντι    αὐτὸν
Jesus,     trustful being to the one having made him
```

For this reason Jesus[a] is not ashamed to call them brothers and sisters,[b] [12]saying,

"I will proclaim your
   name to my brothers
   and sisters,[b]
in the midst of the
   congregation I will
   praise you."

[13]And again,

"I will put my trust in
   him."

And again,

"Here am I and the
   children whom God
   has given me."

[14]Since, therefore, the children share flesh and blood, he himself likewise shared the same things, so that through death he might destroy the one who has the power of death, that is, the devil, [15]and free those who all their lives were held in slavery by the fear of death. [16]For it is clear that he did not come to help angels, but the descendants of Abraham. [17]Therefore he had to become like his brothers and sisters[b] in every respect, so that he might be a merciful and faithful high priest in the service of God, to make a sacrifice of atonement for the sins of the people. [18]Because he himself was tested by what he suffered, he is able to help those who are being tested.

CHAPTER 3

Therefore, brothers and sisters,[b] holy partners in a heavenly calling, consider that Jesus, the apostle and high priest of our confession, [2]was faithful to the one who appointed him,

[a] Gk he
[b] Gk brothers

just as Moses also "was faithful in all[a] God's[b] house." [3]Yet Jesus[c] is worthy of more glory than Moses, just as the builder of a house has more honor than the house itself. [4](For every house is built by someone, but the builder of all things is God.) [5]Now Moses was faithful in all God's[b] house as a servant, to testify to the things that would be spoken later. [6]Christ, however, was faithful over God's[b] house as a son, and we are his house if we hold firm[d] the confidence and the pride that belong to hope.

7 Therefore, as the Holy Spirit says,
"Today, if you hear his voice,
[8] do not harden your hearts as in the rebellion,
as on the day of testing in the wilderness,
[9] where your ancestors put me to the test,
though they had seen my works [10]for forty years.
Therefore I was angry with that generation, and I said, 'They always go astray in their hearts,
and they have not known my ways.'
[11] As in my anger I swore, 'They will not enter my rest.' "

[12]Take care, brothers and sisters,[e] that none of you may have an evil, unbelieving heart that turns away from the living God. [13]But exhort one another

[a] Other ancient authorities lack all
[b] Gk his
[c] Gk this one
[d] Other ancient authorities add to the end
[e] Gk brothers

5613	2532	3475	1722	3650	03	3624	846

5613 2532 3475 1722 3650 03 3624 846 **3** 4183
ὡς καὶ Μωϋσῆς ἐν [ὅλῳ] τῷ οἴκῳ αὐτοῦ. πλείονος
as also Moses in whole the house of him. Of more

1063 3778 1391 3844 3475 515 2596
γὰρ οὗτος δόξης παρὰ Μωϋσῆν ἠξίωται, καθ᾽
for this splendor along Moses has been worthy, by

3745 4183 5092 2192 02 3624 01
ὅσον πλείονα τιμὴν ἔχει τοῦ οἴκου ὁ
as much as more value he has of the house the one

2680 846 **4** 3956 1063 3624 2680
κατασκευάσας αὐτόν· πᾶς γὰρ οἶκος κατασκευάζεται
having prepared him; all for house is prepared

5259 5100 01 1161 3956 2680 2316 **5** 2532
ὑπό τινος, ὁ δὲ πάντα κατασκευάσας θεός. καὶ
by some, the but all having prepared God. And

3475 3303 4103 1722 3650 03 3624 846
Μωϋσῆς μὲν πιστὸς ἐν ὅλῳ τῷ οἴκῳ αὐτοῦ
Moses indeed trustful in whole the house of him

5613 2324 1519 3142 022 2980
ὡς θεράπων εἰς μαρτύριον τῶν λαληθησομένων,
as servant for testimony of the being spoken,

6 5547 1161 5613 5207 1909 04 3624 846 3739
Χριστὸς δὲ ὡς υἱὸς ἐπὶ τὸν οἶκον αὐτοῦ· οὗ
Christ but as son on the house of him; whose

3624 1510 1473 1437a 08 3954 2532 012
οἶκός ἐσμεν ἡμεῖς, ἐάν[περ] τὴν παρρησίαν καὶ τὸ
house are we, if indeed the boldness and the

2745 06 1680 2722 **7** 1352
καύχημα τῆς ἐλπίδος κατάσχωμεν. Διό,
brag of the hope we might hold on. Therefore,

2531 3004 09 4151 09 40 4594 1437 06
καθὼς λέγει τὸ πνεῦμα τὸ ἅγιον· σήμερον ἐὰν τῆς
just as says the spirit the holy: today if the

5456 846 191 **8** 3361 4645
φωνῆς αὐτοῦ ἀκούσητε, μὴ σκληρύνητε
sound of him you might hear, not you might harden

020 2588 1473 5613 1722 03 3894 2596 08
τὰς καρδίας ὑμῶν ὡς ἐν τῷ παραπικρασμῷ κατὰ τὴν
the hearts of you as in the embitterment by the

2250 02 3986 1722 07 2048 **9** 3757
ἡμέραν τοῦ πειρασμοῦ ἐν τῇ ἐρήμῳ, οὗ
day of the pressure in the desert, where

3985 013 3962 1473 1722 1381a 2532
ἐπείρασαν οἱ πατέρες ὑμῶν ἐν δοκιμασίᾳ καὶ
pressured the fathers of you in proving and

3708 024 2041 1473 **10** 5062 2094
εἶδον τὰ ἔργα μου τεσσεράκοντα ἔτη·
they saw the works of me forty years;

1352 4360 07 1074 3778
διὸ προσώχθισα τῇ γενεᾷ ταύτῃ
therefore I was vexed toward the generation this

2532 2036 104 4105 07 2588 846
καὶ εἶπον· ἀεὶ πλανῶνται τῇ καρδίᾳ, αὐτοὶ
and said; always they are in the heart, themselves
deceived

1161 3756 1097 020 3598 1473 **11** 5613 3660
δὲ οὐκ ἔγνωσαν τὰς ὁδούς μου, ὡς ὤμοσα
but not they knew the ways of me, as I took

1722 07 3709 1473 1487 1525 1519
ἐν τῇ ὀργῇ μου· εἰ εἰσελεύσονται εἰς
oath in the anger of me: if they will go in into

08 2663 1473 991 80 3379
τὴν κατάπαυσίν μου. **12** Βλέπετε, ἀδελφοί, μήποτε
the complete stop of me. See, brothers, not then

1510 1722 5100 1473 2588 4190 570
ἔσται ἔν τινι ὑμῶν καρδία πονηρὰ ἀπιστίας
there will be in some of you heart evil of untrust

1722 011 868 575 2316 2198 **13** 235
ἐν τῷ ἀποστῆναι ἀπὸ θεοῦ ζῶντος, ἀλλὰ
in the to stand off from God living, but

3870	1438	2596	1538	2250	891
παρακαλεῖτε	ἑαυτοὺς	καθ'	ἑκάστην	ἡμέραν,	ἄχρις
encourage	yourselves	against	each	day,	until

3739	09	4594	2564		2443	3361	4645
οὗ	τὸ	σήμερον	καλεῖται,		ἵνα	μὴ	σκληρυνθῇ
which	the	today	it is called,		that	not	might be hardened

5100	1537	1473	539		06	266		3353
τις	ἐξ	ὑμῶν	ἀπάτῃ		τῆς	ἁμαρτίας	-14	μέτοχοι
some	from	you	in deception		of the	sin -		sharers

1063	02	5547	1096		1437a	08
γὰρ	τοῦ	Χριστοῦ	γεγόναμεν,		ἐάνπερ	τὴν
for	of the	Christ	we have become,		if indeed	the

746	06	5287	3360	5056	949
ἀρχὴν	τῆς	ὑποστάσεως	μέχρι	τέλους	βεβαίαν
beginning	of the	substance	until	completion	firm

2722		1722	011	3004		4594	1437
κατάσχωμεν -	**15**	ἐν	τῷ	λέγεσθαι·	σήμερον	ἐὰν
we might hold down -		in	the	to be said,	today	if

06	5456	846	191		3361	4645	020
τῆς	φωνῆς	αὐτοῦ	ἀκούσητε,		μὴ	σκληρύνητε	τὰς
the	sound	of him	you might hear,		not	harden	the

2588	1473	5613	1722	03	3894		5100
καρδίας	ὑμῶν	ὡς	ἐν	τῷ	παραπικρασμῷ.	**16**	τίνες
hearts	of you	as	in	the	embitterment.		Some

1063	191		3893		235	3756	3956
γὰρ	ἀκούσαντες		παρεπίκραναν;		ἀλλ'	οὐ	πάντες
for	having heard		were embittered?		But	not	all

013	1831		1537	125		1223	3475
οἱ	ἐξελθόντες		ἐξ	Αἰγύπτου	διὰ		Μωϋσέως;
the	having gone	from	from	Egypt	through		Moses?

	5101	1161	4360		5062		2094
17	τίσιν	δὲ	προσώχθισεν		τεσσεράκοντα	ἔτη;
	To whom	but	he was vexed to		forty		years?

3780	015		264		3739	021	2966
οὐχὶ	τοῖς		ἁμαρτήσασιν,		ὧν	τὰ	κῶλα
Not	to the ones		having sinned,		whose	the	corpses

4098	1722	07	2048		5101	1161	3660
ἔπεσεν	ἐν	τῇ	ἐρήμῳ;	**18**	τίσιν	δὲ	ὤμοσεν
fell	in	the	desert?		To whom	but	he took oath

3361	1525		1519	08	2663		846	1487	3361
μὴ	εἰσελεύσεσθαι	εἰς	τὴν	κατάπαυσιν		αὐτοῦ	εἰ	μὴ
not	to go in		to	the	complete stop		of him	except

015	544			2532	991		3754	3756
τοῖς	ἀπειθήσασιν;	**19**	καὶ	βλέπομεν	ὅτι	οὐκ
to the	having disobeyed?		And	we see	that	not

1410		1525		1223	570
ἠδυνήθησαν		εἰσελθεῖν	δι'		ἀπιστίαν.
they were able		to go in	because of		untrust.

	5399		3767	3379	2641
4:1	Φοβηθῶμεν	οὖν,	μήποτε	καταλειπομένης
	Let fear	then,	not then	being left behind

1860		1525		1519	08	2663		846
ἐπαγγελίας	εἰσελθεῖν	εἰς	τὴν	κατάπαυσιν		αὐτοῦ
promise	to go in	into	the	complete stop		of him

1380		5100	1537	1473	5302		2532	1063
δοκῇ		τις	ἐξ	ὑμῶν	ὑστερηκέναι.	**2**	καὶ	γάρ
might think	some	from	you	to have lacked.		Also	for

1510	2097		2509
ἐσμεν	εὐηγγελισμένοι		καθάπερ
we are+	+having told good message		just as indeed

2548		235	3756	5623		01	3056	06
κἀκεῖνοι·	ἀλλ'	οὐκ	ὠφέλησεν		ὁ	λόγος	τῆς
also those;	but	not	benefitted		the	word	of the

189	1565	3361	4786		07
ἀκοῆς	ἐκείνους	μὴ	συγκεκερασμένους		τῇ
hearing	those	not	having been mixed together		in the

4102	015	191		3	1525		1063
πίστει	τοῖς	ἀκούσασιν.		**3**	Εἰσερχόμεθα	γὰρ
trust	to the ones	having heard.			We go in	for

every day, as long as it is called "today," so that none of you may be hardened by the deceitfulness of sin. [14]For we have become partners of Christ, if only we hold our first confidence firm to the end. [15]As it is said,

"Today, if you hear his voice,
do not harden your hearts as in the rebellion."

[16]Now who were they who heard and yet were rebellious? Was it not all those who left Egypt under the leadership of Moses? [17]But with whom was he angry forty years? Was it not those who sinned, whose bodies fell in the wilderness? [18]And to whom did he swear that they would not enter his rest, if not to those who were disobedient? [19]So we see that they were unable to enter because of unbelief.

CHAPTER 4

Therefore, while the promise of entering his rest is still open, let us take care that none of you should seem to have failed to reach it. [2]For indeed the good news came to us just as to them; but the message they heard did not benefit them, because they were not united by faith with those who listened.[a] [3]For we who have believed enter

---

a Other ancient authorities read *it did not meet with faith in those who listened*

that rest, just as God[a] has said,
"As in my anger I swore, 'They shall not enter my rest,'"
though his works were finished at the foundation of the world. [4]For in one place it speaks about the seventh day as follows, "And God rested on the seventh day from all his works." [5]And again in this place it says, "They shall not enter my rest." [6]Since therefore it remains open for some to enter it, and those who formerly received the good news failed to enter because of disobedience, [7]again he sets a certain day—"today"— saying through David much later, in the words already quoted,
"Today, if you hear his voice, do not harden your hearts."
[8]For if Joshua had given them rest, God[a] would not speak later about another day. [9]So then, a sabbath rest still remains for the people of God; [10]for those who enter God's rest also cease from their labors as God did from his. [11]Let us therefore make every effort to enter that rest, so that no one may fall through such disobedience as theirs.

[a] Gk he

1519 08	2663		013 4100
εἰς [τὴν]	κατάπαυσιν	οἱ	πιστεύσαντες,
into the	complete stop	the ones	having trusted,

2531	3004	5613 3660	1722 07 3709
καθὼς	εἴρηκεν·	ὡς ὤμοσα	ἐν τῇ ὀργῇ
just as	he has said:	as I took oath	in the anger

1473	1487 1525	1519 08	2663
μου·	εἰ εἰσελεύσονται	εἰς τὴν	κατάπαυσίν
of me,	if they will go in	into the complete stop

1473	2543	022 2041 575	2602	2889
μου,	καίτοι	τῶν ἔργων ἀπὸ	καταβολῆς	κόσμου
of me,	and indeed	the works from	foundation	of world

1096	3004	1063 4225 4012	06 1442
γενηθέντων.	[4] εἴρηκεν	γάρ που περὶ	τῆς ἑβδόμης
having become.	He has said	for where about	the seventh

3779	2532 2664	01	2316 1722 07 2250
οὕτως·	καὶ κατέπαυσεν	ὁ	θεὸς ἐν τῇ ἡμέρᾳ
thusly;	and completely stopped	the	God in the day

07 1442	575 3956	022 2041 846	[5] 2532 1722
τῇ ἑβδόμῃ	ἀπὸ πάντων	τῶν ἔργων αὐτοῦ,	καὶ ἐν
the seventh	from all	the works of him,	and in

3778 3825	1487 1525	1519 08
τούτῳ πάλιν·	εἰ εἰσελεύσονται	εἰς τὴν
this again;	if they will go in	into the

2663	1473	1893 3767 620	5100
κατάπαυσίν	μου. [6]	ἐπεὶ οὖν ἀπολείπεται	τινὰς
complete stop	of me.	Since then it is left off	some

1525	1519 846	2532 013 4387	2097
εἰσελθεῖν	εἰς αὐτήν,	καὶ οἱ πρότερον	εὐαγγελισθέντες
to go in	into it,	and the former	having been told good news

3756 1525	1223	543	[7] 3825 5100
οὐκ εἰσῆλθον	δι᾽	ἀπείθειαν,	πάλιν τινὰ
not they went in	through	disobedience,	again some

3724	2250	4594	1722 1160a 3004	3326
ὁρίζει	ἡμέραν,	σήμερον,	ἐν Δαυὶδ λέγων	μετὰ
he designates	day,	today,	in David saying	after

5118	5550	2531	4302	4594
τοσοῦτον	χρόνον,	καθὼς	προείρηται·	σήμερον
such	time,	just as	he has said before,	today

1437 06	5456 846	191	3361 4645
ἐὰν τῆς	φωνῆς αὐτοῦ	ἀκούσητε,	μὴ σκληρύνητε
if the	sound of him	you might hear,	not harden

020 2588	1473	1487 1063 846	2424
τὰς καρδίας	ὑμῶν. [8]	εἰ γὰρ αὐτοὺς	Ἰησοῦς
the hearts	of you. If	for them	Jesus

2664	3756 302 4012	243 2980
κατέπαυσεν,	οὐκ ἂν περὶ	ἄλλης ἐλάλει
completely stopped,	not - about	other he was saying

3326 3778 2250	[9] 686 620
μετὰ ταῦτα ἡμέρας.	ἄρα ἀπολείπεται
after these day.	Then it is left off

4520	03	2992 02	2316	[10] 01
σαββατισμὸς	τῷ	λαῷ τοῦ	θεοῦ.	ὁ
sabbath observance	to the	people of the	God.	The

1063 1525	1519 08 2663	846 2532
γὰρ εἰσελθὼν	εἰς τὴν κατάπαυσιν	αὐτοῦ καὶ
for having come in	into the complete stop	of him and

846	2664	575 022 2041 846
αὐτὸς	κατέπαυσεν	ἀπὸ τῶν ἔργων αὐτοῦ
himself	completely stopped	from the works of him

5618	575 022 2398	01 2316	[11] 4704
ὥσπερ	ἀπὸ τῶν ἰδίων	ὁ θεός.	Σπουδάσωμεν
as	indeed from the own	the God.	We might be diligent

3767 1525	1519 1565	08 2663	2443
οὖν εἰσελθεῖν	εἰς ἐκείνην	τὴν κατάπαυσιν,	ἵνα
then to go in	into that	the complete stop,	that

3361 1722 011 846	5100 5262	4098	06
μὴ ἐν τῷ αὐτῷ	τις ὑποδείγματι	πέσῃ	τῆς
not in the same	some in example	might fall	of the

543
ἀπειθείας. **12** Ζῶν γὰρ ὁ λόγος τοῦ θεοῦ καὶ
disobedience. Living for the word of the God and
                2198 1063 01 3056 02 2316 2532

1756   2532 5114   5228 3956 3162
ἐνεργὴς καὶ τομώτερος ὑπὲρ πᾶσαν μάχαιραν
operational and sharper over all sword

1366   2532 1338   891 3311
δίστομον καὶ διϊκνούμενος ἄχρι μερισμοῦ
two-mouthed and piercing through until division

5590   2532 4151   719 5037 2532 3452 2532
ψυχῆς καὶ πνεύματος, ἁρμῶν τε καὶ μυελῶν, καὶ
of soul and spirit, joints both and marrow, and

2924   1761   2532 1771   2588   2532
κριτικὸς ἐνθυμήσεων καὶ ἐννοιῶν καρδίας· **13** καὶ
judge of reflections and insights heart; and

3756 1510 2937 852   1799 846 3956
οὐκ ἔστιν κτίσις ἀφανὴς ἐνώπιον αὐτοῦ, πάντα
not is creation disappeared before him, all

1161 1131 2532 5136   015 3788
δὲ γυμνὰ καὶ τετραχηλισμένα τοῖς ὀφθαλμοῖς
but naked and neck having been in the eyes
                        stuck out

846   4314 3739 1473 01 3056   2192 3767
αὐτοῦ, πρὸς ὃν ἡμῖν ὁ λόγος. **14** Ἔχοντες οὖν
of him, to whom to us the word. Having then

749   3173 1330   016 3772
ἀρχιερέα μέγαν διεληλυθότα τοὺς οὐρανούς,
ruler priest great having gone through the heavens,

2424 04 5207 02   2316 2902   06
Ἰησοῦν τὸν υἱὸν τοῦ θεοῦ, κρατῶμεν τῆς
Jesus the son of the God, we might hold the

3671   15 3756 1063 2192 749   3361
ὁμολογίας. **15** οὐ γὰρ ἔχομεν ἀρχιερέα μὴ
confession. Not for we have ruler priest not

1410 4834   019 769   1473
δυνάμενον συμπαθῆσαι ταῖς ἀσθενείαις ἡμῶν,
being able to suffer with the weaknesses of us,

3985   1161 2596 3956 2596 3665
πεπειρασμένον δὲ κατὰ πάντα καθ' ὁμοιότητα
having been pressured but by all by likeness

5565 266   16 4334   3767 3326
χωρὶς ἁμαρτίας. **16** προσερχώμεθα οὖν μετὰ
without sin. We might come to then with

3954   03   2362 06   5485   2443
παρρησίας τῷ θρόνῳ τῆς χάριτος, ἵνα
boldness to the throne of the favor, that

2983   1656 2532 5485 2147   1519
λάβωμεν ἔλεος καὶ χάριν εὕρωμεν εἰς
we might receive mercy and favor we might find for

2121   996   5:1 3956 1063 749   1537
εὔκαιρον βοήθειαν. **5:1** Πᾶς γὰρ ἀρχιερεὺς ἐξ
good season help. All for ruler priest from

444   2983   5228 444   2525
ἀνθρώπων λαμβανόμενος ὑπὲρ ἀνθρώπων καθίσταται
men being taken on behalf of men is appointed

024 4314 04 2316 2443 4374   1435 5037 2532
τὰ πρὸς τὸν θεόν, ἵνα προσφέρῃ δῶρά τε καὶ
the to the God, that he might offer gifts both and

2378 5228 266   2 3356
θυσίας ὑπὲρ ἁμαρτιῶν, **2** μετριοπαθεῖν
sacrifices on behalf of sins, in measure to suffer

1410 015 50   2532 4105
δυνάμενος τοῖς ἀγνοοῦσιν καὶ πλανωμένοις,
being able to the ones not knowing and being deceived,

1893 2532 846 4029   769 3 2532
ἐπεὶ καὶ αὐτὸς περίκειται ἀσθένειαν **3** καὶ
since also himself is set around weakness and

1223 846 3784   2531 4012 02 2992 3779
δι' αὐτὴν ὀφείλει, καθὼς περὶ τοῦ λαοῦ, οὕτως
because it he owes, just as about the people, thusly
of

12 Indeed, the word of God is living and active, sharper than any two-edged sword, piercing until it divides soul from spirit, joints from marrow; it is able to judge the thoughts and intentions of the heart. [13]And before him no creature is hidden, but all are naked and laid bare to the eyes of the one to whom we must render an account.

14 Since, then, we have a great high priest who has passed through the heavens, Jesus, the Son of God, let us hold fast to our confession. [15]For we do not have a high priest who is unable to sympathize with our weaknesses, but we have one who in every respect has been tested[a] as we are, yet without sin. [16]Let us therefore approach the throne of grace with boldness, so that we may receive mercy and find grace to help in time of need.

CHAPTER 5

Every high priest chosen from among mortals is put in charge of things pertaining to God on their behalf, to offer gifts and sacrifices for sins. [2]He is able to deal gently with the ignorant and wayward, since he himself is subject to weakness; [3]and because of this he must offer sacrifice

---

[a] Or tempted

for his own sins as well
as for those of the people.
⁴And one does not presume
to take this honor, but
takes it only when called
by God, just as Aaron was.

5 So also Christ did not
glorify himself in becoming
a high priest, but was
appointed by the one who
said to him,
   "You are my Son,
   today I have begotten
   you";
⁶as he says also in another
place,
   "You are a priest forever,
   according to the order
   of Melchizedek."

7 In the days of his flesh,
Jesusᵃ offered up prayers
and supplications, with
loud cries and tears, to the
one who was able to save
him from death, and he
was heard because of his
reverent submission.
⁸Although he was a Son, he
learned obedience through
what he suffered; ⁹and
having been made perfect,
he became the source of
eternal salvation for all
who obey him, ¹⁰having
been designated by God a
high priest according to
the order of Melchizedek.

11 About thisᵇ we have
much to say that is hard
to explain, since you have
become dull in under-
standing. ¹²For though by
this time you ought to be
teachers, you need someone
to teach you again the
basic elements of the oracles
of God.

ᵃ Gk he
ᵇ Or him

2532 4012 846 4374 4012 266 **4** 2532
καὶ περὶ αὐτοῦ προσφέρειν περὶ ἁμαρτιῶν. καὶ
also about him to offer concerning sins. And
3756 1438 5100 2983 08 5092 235
οὐχ ἑαυτῷ τις λαμβάνει τὴν τιμὴν ἀλλὰ
not to himself some receives the value but
2564 5259 02 2316 2531a 2532 2
καλούμενος ὑπὸ τοῦ θεοῦ καθώσπερ καὶ Ἀαρών.
being called by the God just as indeed also Aaron.
5 3779 2532 01 5547 3756 1438 1392
Οὕτως καὶ ὁ Χριστὸς οὐχ ἑαυτὸν ἐδόξασεν
Thusly also the Christ not himself he gave splendor
1096 749 235 01 2980 4314
γενηθῆναι ἀρχιερέα ἀλλ᾽ ὁ λαλήσας πρὸς
to become ruler priest but the one having said to
846 5207 1473 1510 1473 1473 4594
αὐτόν· υἱός μου εἶ σύ, ἐγὼ σήμερον
him, son of me are <u>you</u>, I today
1080 1473 **6** 2531 2532 1722 2087
γεγέννηκά σε· καθὼς καὶ ἐν ἑτέρῳ
have given birth <u>you</u>; just as also in other
3004 1473 2409 1519 04 165 2596 08 5010
λέγει· σὺ ἱερεὺς εἰς τὸν αἰῶνα κατὰ τὴν τάξιν
he says, <u>you</u> priest for the age by the rank
3198 **7** 3739 1722 019 2250 06 4561
Μελχισέδεκ, ὃς ἐν ταῖς ἡμέραις τῆς σαρκὸς
Melchisedek, who in the days of the flesh
846 1162 5037 2532 2428 4314 04
αὐτοῦ δεήσεις τε καὶ ἱκετηρίας πρὸς τὸν
of him requests both and petitions to the
1410 4982 846 1537 2288 3326
δυνάμενον σῴζειν αὐτὸν ἐκ θανάτου μετὰ
one being able to deliver him from death with
2906 2478 2532 1144 4374 2532
κραυγῆς ἰσχυρᾶς καὶ δακρύων προσενέγκας καὶ
shout strong and tears having offered and
1522 575 06 2124 **8** 2539 1510
εἰσακουσθεὶς ἀπὸ τῆς εὐλαβείας, καίπερ ὢν
having been heard from the reverence, and indeed being
5207 3129 575 3739 3958 08 5218
υἱός, ἔμαθεν ἀφ᾽ ὧν ἔπαθεν τὴν ὑπακοήν,
son, he learned from what he suffered the obedience,
9 2532 5048 1096 3956 015
καὶ τελειωθεὶς ἐγένετο πᾶσιν τοῖς
and having been completed he became to all the
5219 846 159 4991 166
ὑπακούουσιν αὐτῷ αἴτιος σωτηρίας αἰωνίου,
one obeying him cause of deliverance eternal,
10 4316 5259 02 2316 749
προσαγορευθεὶς ὑπὸ τοῦ θεοῦ ἀρχιερεὺς
having been given title by the God ruler priest
2596 08 5010 3198 **11** 4012 3739 4183 1473
κατὰ τὴν τάξιν Μελχισέδεκ. Περὶ οὗ πολὺς ἡμῖν
by the rank Melchisedek. About whom much to us
01 3056 2532 1421 3004 1893
ὁ λόγος καὶ δυσερμήνευτος λέγειν, ἐπεὶ
the word and difficult interpretation to say, since
3576 1096 019 189 **12** 2532 1063
νωθροὶ γεγόνατε ταῖς ἀκοαῖς. καὶ γὰρ
dull you have become in the hearings. Also for
3784 1510 1320 1223 04 5550 3825
ὀφείλοντες εἶναι διδάσκαλοι διὰ τὸν χρόνον, πάλιν
owing to be teachers through the time, again
5532 2192 010 1321 1473 5101 024 4747
χρείαν ἔχετε τοῦ διδάσκειν ὑμᾶς τινὰ τὰ στοιχεῖα
need you have the to teach you what the elements
06 746 022 3051 02 2316 2532
τῆς ἀρχῆς τῶν λογίων τοῦ θεοῦ καὶ
of the beginning of the sayings of the God and

1096   5532   2192   1051   2532 3756
γεγόνατε   χρείαν ἔχοντες γάλακτος [καὶ] οὐ
you have become need having   milk   and not
4731   5160   13 3956 1063 01   3348   1051
στερεᾶς τροφῆς.   πᾶς γὰρ ὁ μετέχων   γάλακτος
solid   food.   All for the having with milk
552   3056   1343   3516   1063 1510
ἄπειρος   λόγου   δικαιοσύνης, νήπιος γάρ ἐστιν·
inexperienced of word of rightness, infant for he is;
    5046   1161 1510 05 4731   5160   014
14 τελείων   δέ ἐστιν ἡ στερεὰ τροφή, τῶν
   of complete ones but is   the solid   food, the
1223   08   1838   024 145   1128
διὰ   τὴν ἕξιν τὰ αἰσθητήρια γεγυμνασμένα
through the habit the senses   having been exercised
2192   4314 1253   2570   5037 2532 2556
ἐχόντων πρὸς διάκρισιν καλοῦ τε καὶ κακοῦ.
having to differentiation of good both and bad.
    1352   863   04 06   746
6:1 Διὸ   ἀφέντες   τὸν τῆς ἀρχῆς
   Wherefore having sent off the of the beginning
02   5547   3056 1909 08 5047
τοῦ Χριστοῦ λόγον ἐπὶ τὴν τελειότητα
of the Christ word on the completeness
5342   3361   3825 2310   2598
φερώμεθα,   μὴ πάλιν θεμέλιον καταβαλλόμενοι
we might carry, not again foundation throwing down
3341   575   3498   2041   2532 4102   1909 2316
μετανοίας ἀπὸ νεκρῶν ἔργων καὶ πίστεως ἐπὶ θεόν,
change mind from dead works and trust on God,
  909   1322   1936   5037 5495
2 βαπτισμῶν διδαχῆς ἐπιθέσεώς τε χειρῶν,
  of immersions teaching setting on and of hands,
386   5037 3498   2532 2917   166   3 2532
ἀναστάσεώς τε νεκρῶν καὶ κρίματος αἰωνίου.   καὶ
standing up and of dead and judgment eternal.   And
3778   4160   1437a   2010   01 2316
τοῦτο ποιήσομεν, ἐάνπερ ἐπιτρέπῃ ὁ θεός.
this we will do, if indeed might allow the God.
  102   1063 016 530   5461   1089
4 Ἀδύνατον γὰρ τοὺς ἅπαξ φωτισθέντας, γευσαμένους
  Unable   for the once having been   having tasted
                                lightened,
5037 06 1431   06   2032   2532 3353
τε τῆς δωρεᾶς τῆς ἐπουρανίου καὶ μετόχους
both the gift   of the on heaven and sharers
1096   4151   40   5 2532 2570 1089
γενηθέντας πνεύματος ἁγίου καὶ καλὸν γευσαμένους
having become of spirit holy and good having tasted
2316   4487 1411   5037 3195   165
θεοῦ ῥῆμα δυνάμεις τε μέλλοντος   αἰῶνος
of God word in powers and being about to be age
  2532 3895   3825 340   1519
6 καὶ παραπεσόντας, πάλιν ἀνακαινίζειν εἰς
  and having fallen from, again to renew to
3341   388   1438   04 5207
μετάνοιαν, ἀνασταυροῦντας ἑαυτοῖς τὸν υἱὸν
change mind, crucifying again to themselves the son
02   2316 2532 3856   7 1093 1063 05
τοῦ θεοῦ καὶ παραδειγματίζοντας. γῆ γὰρ ἡ
of the God and exposing publicly.   Earth for the
4095   04   1909 846   2064   4178   5205
πιοῦσα τὸν ἐπ' αὐτῆς ἐρχόμενον πολλάκις ὑετὸν
having drunk the on it coming   frequently rain
2532 5088   1008   2111   1565   1223
καὶ τίκτουσα βοτάνην εὔθετον ἐκείνοις δι'
and giving birth vegetation suitable to those through
3739 2532 1090   3335   2129   575
οὓς καὶ γεωργεῖται, μεταλαμβάνει εὐλογίας ἀπὸ
whom also it is farmed, takes with good word from

You need milk, not solid food; [13]for everyone who lives on milk, being still an infant, is unskilled in the word of righteousness. [14]But solid food is for the mature, for those whose faculties have been trained by practice to distinguish good from evil.

CHAPTER 6

Therefore let us go on toward perfection,[a] leaving behind the basic teaching about Christ, and not laying again the foundation: repentance from dead works and faith toward God, [2]instruction about baptisms, laying on of hands, resurrection of the dead, and eternal judgment. [3]And we will do[b] this, if God permits. [4]For it is impossible to restore again to repentance those who have once been enlightened, and have tasted the heavenly gift, and have shared in the Holy Spirit, [5]and have tasted the goodness of the word of God and the powers of the age to come, [6]and then have fallen away, since on their own they are crucifying again the Son of God and are holding him up to contempt. [7]Ground that drinks up the rain falling on it repeatedly, and that produces a crop useful to those for whom it is cultivated, receives a blessing from God.

a Or toward maturity
b Other ancient authorities read let us do

⁸But if it produces thorns and thistles, it is worthless and on the verge of being cursed; its end is to be burned over.

9 Even though we speak in this way, beloved, we are confident of better things in your case, things that belong to salvation. ¹⁰For God is not unjust; he will not overlook your work and the love that you showed for his sake*a* in serving the saints, as you still do. ¹¹And we want each one of you to show the same diligence so as to realize the full assurance of hope to the very end, ¹²so that you may not become sluggish, but imitators of those who through faith and patience inherit the promises.

13 When God made a promise to Abraham, because he had no one greater by whom to swear, he swore by himself, ¹⁴saying, "I will surely bless you and multiply you." ¹⁵And thus Abraham,*b* having patiently endured, obtained the promise. ¹⁶Human beings, of course, swear by someone greater than themselves, and an oath given as confirmation puts an end to all dispute. ¹⁷In the same way, when God desired to show even more clearly to the heirs of the promise the unchangeable character of his purpose, he guaranteed it by an oath,

a Gk *for his name*
b Gk *he*

02 2316		1627	1161 173	2532 5146
τοῦ θεοῦ·	8	ἐκφέρουσα	δὲ ἀκάνθας καὶ	τριβόλους,
the God;		bringing out	but thorns and	thistles,

96   2532 2671   1451   3739 09   5056   1519
ἀδόκιμος καὶ κατάρας ἐγγύς, ἧς τὸ τέλος εἰς
unproved and curse near, which the completion in

2740   3982   1161 4012 1473
καῦσιν. 9 Πεπείσμεθα δὲ περὶ ὑμῶν,
burning. We have been persuaded but about you,

27   024 2909   2532 2192   4991
ἀγαπητοί, τὰ κρείσσονα καὶ ἐχόμενα σωτηρίας,
loved ones, the better and having deliverance,

1487 2532 3779   2980   10   3756 1063 94   01 2316
εἰ καὶ οὕτως λαλοῦμεν. 10 οὐ γὰρ ἄδικος ὁ θεὸς
if also thusly we speak; not for unright the God

1950   010 2041 1473   2532 06 26   3739
ἐπιλαθέσθαι τοῦ ἔργου ὑμῶν καὶ τῆς ἀγάπης ἧς
to forget the work of you and the love which

1731   1519 012 3686 846   1247
ἐνεδείξασθε εἰς τὸ ὄνομα αὐτοῦ, διακονήσαντες
you demonstrated in the name of him, having served

015   40   2532 1247   11   1937
τοῖς ἁγίοις καὶ διακονοῦντες. 11 ἐπιθυμοῦμεν
to the holy ones and serving. We desire

1161 1538   1473   08 846   1731   4710
δὲ ἕκαστον ὑμῶν τὴν αὐτὴν ἐνδείκνυσθαι σπουδὴν
but each of you the same to demonstrate diligence

4314 08 4136   06 1680 891 5056
πρὸς τὴν πληροφορίαν τῆς ἐλπίδος ἄχρι τέλους,
to the full persuasion the hope until completion,

12   2443 3361 3576   1096   3402   1161
ἵνα μὴ νωθροὶ γένησθε, μιμηταὶ δὲ
that not dull you might become, imitators but

014 1223   4102   2532 3115   2816
τῶν διὰ πίστεως καὶ μακροθυμίας κληρονομούντων
the through trust and long temper ones inheriting

020 1860   03   1063 11   1861
τὰς ἐπαγγελίας. 13 Τῷ γὰρ Ἀβραὰμ ἐπαγγειλάμενος
the promises. To the for Abraham having promised

01 2316 1893 2596 3762   2192   3173
ὁ θεός, ἐπεὶ κατ' οὐδενὸς εἶχεν μείζονος
the God, since by no one he had greater

3660   3660   2596 1438   14   3004
ὀμόσαι, ὤμοσεν καθ' ἑαυτοῦ 14 λέγων·
to take oath, he took oath by himself saying,

1487 3375 2127   2127   1473 2532
εἰ μὴν εὐλογῶν εὐλογήσω σε καὶ
if yet speaking well I will speak well you and

4129   4129   1473 15   2532 3779
πληθύνων πληθυνῶ σε· 15 καὶ οὕτως
multiplying I will multiply you; and thusly

3114   2013   06 1860   444
μακροθυμήσας ἐπέτυχεν τῆς ἐπαγγελίας. 16 ἄνθρωποι
having been he obtained the promise. Men
long-tempered

1063 2596 02 3173   3660   2532 3956
γὰρ κατὰ τοῦ μείζονος ὀμνύουσιν, καὶ πάσης
for by the greater take an oath, and all

846 485   4009 1519 951   01 3727
αὐτοῖς ἀντιλογίας πέρας εἰς βεβαίωσιν ὁ ὅρκος·
to them word against limit for confirmation the oath;

17   1722 3739 4055   1014   01 2316
ἐν ᾧ περισσότερον βουλόμενος ὁ θεὸς
in which more excessive planning the God

1925   015 2818   06 1860   012
ἐπιδεῖξαι τοῖς κληρονόμοις τῆς ἐπαγγελίας τὸ
to show on to the inheritors of the promise the

276   06 1012 846   3315   3727
ἀμετάθετον τῆς βουλῆς αὐτοῦ ἐμεσίτευσεν ὅρκῳ,
irrevocable of the plan of him he mediated in oath,

18
2443	1223	1417	4229	276		1722	3739
ἵνα	διὰ	δύο	πραγμάτων	ἀμεταθέτων,	ἐν	οἷς
that	through	two	practices	irrevocable,	in	which

102		5574		04	2316	2478	3874
ἀδύνατον	ψεύσασθαι	[τὸν]	θεόν,	ἰσχυρὰν	παράκλησιν
unable	to lie	the	God,	strong	encouragement

2192		013	2703		2902	06
ἔχωμεν	οἱ	καταφυγόντες	κρατῆσαι	τῆς
might have	the	having fled off	to hold	the

4295		1680		**19**	3739	5613	45		2192
προκειμένης	ἐλπίδος·		ἣν	ὡς	ἄγκυραν	ἔχομεν
lying before	hope,		which	as	anchor	we have

06		5590	804		5037	2532	949		2532	1525
τῆς	ψυχῆς	ἀσφαλῆ	τε	καὶ	βεβαίαν	καὶ	εἰσερχομένην
of the	soul	secure	both	and	firm	and	going in

1519	012	2082		010	2665		**20**	3699
εἰς	τὸ	ἐσώτερον	τοῦ	καταπετάσματος,			ὅπου
into	the	inner	of the	veil,			where

4274		5228		1473	1525		2424	2596	08
πρόδρομος	ὑπὲρ	ἡμῶν	εἰσῆλθεν	Ἰησοῦς,	κατὰ	τὴν
forerunner	on behalf	of us	went in	Jesus,	by	the

5010	3198		749		1096		1519	04
τάξιν	Μελχισέδεκ	ἀρχιερεὺς	γενόμενος	εἰς	τὸν
rank	Melchisedek	ruler priest	having become	into	the

165		3778	1063	01	3198		935
αἰῶνα.	**7:1**	Οὗτος	γὰρ	ὁ	Μελχισέδεκ,	βασιλεὺς
age.		This	for	the	Melchisedek,	king

4532		2409	02		2316	02	5310		01
Σαλήμ,	ἱερεὺς	τοῦ	θεοῦ	τοῦ	ὑψίστου,	ὁ
of Salem,	priest	of the	God	the	highest,	the

4876		11		5290		575	06	2871
συναντήσας	Ἀβραὰμ	ὑποστρέφοντι	ἀπὸ	τῆς	κοπῆς
having met	Abraham	having returned	from	the	slaughter

014	935		2532	2127		846		2	3739		2532
τῶν	βασιλέων	καὶ	εὐλογήσας	αὐτόν,		ᾧ		καὶ
of the	kings	and	having	him,		to whom		also
			spoken-well					

1181		575	3956	3307		11		4413	3303
δεκάτην	ἀπὸ	πάντων	ἐμέρισεν	Ἀβραάμ,	πρῶτον	μὲν
tenth	from	all	divided	Abraham,	first	indeed

2059		935		1343		1899	1161
ἑρμηνευόμενος	βασιλεὺς	δικαιοσύνης	ἔπειτα	δὲ
being interpreted	king	of rightness	then	but

2532	935		4532		3739	1510	935		1515
καὶ	βασιλεὺς	Σαλήμ,	ὅ	ἐστιν	βασιλεὺς	εἰρήνης,
also	king	of Salem,	that is		king	of peace,

3	540		282		35		3383
	ἀπάτωρ	ἀμήτωρ	ἀγενεαλόγητος,	μήτε
	no father,	no mother,	no genealogy,	neither

746		2250	3383	2222		5056		2192
ἀρχὴν	ἡμερῶν	μήτε	ζωῆς	τέλος	ἔχων,
beginning	of days	not	of life	completion	having,

871		1161	03	5207	02	2316	3306		2409
ἀφωμοιωμένος	δὲ	τῷ	υἱῷ	τοῦ	θεοῦ,	μένει	ἱερεὺς
having been	but	to son	of	God,	he stays	priest
made like		the	the				

1519	012	1336		4	2334		1161	4080		3778
εἰς	τὸ	διηνεκές.		Θεωρεῖτε	δὲ	πηλίκος	οὗτος,
into	the	perpetuity.		You watch	but	how great	this,

3739		2532	1181		11		1325	1537	022
ᾧ	[καὶ]	δεκάτην	Ἀβραὰμ	ἔδωκεν	ἐκ	τῶν
to whom	also	tenth	Abraham	gave	from	the

205		01	3966		5	2532	013	3303		1537	014
ἀκροθινίων	ὁ	πατριάρχης.		καὶ	οἱ	μὲν	ἐκ	τῶν
spoils	the	father-ruler.		And	the	indeed	from	the

5207	3017	08	2405		2983		1785	2192
υἱῶν	Λευὶ	τὴν	ἱερατείαν	λαμβάνοντες	ἐντολὴν	ἔχουσιν
sons	Levi	the	priesthood	receiving	command	have to

---

[18]so that through two unchangeable things, in which it is impossible that God would prove false, we who have taken refuge might be strongly encouraged to seize the hope set before us. [19]We have this hope, a sure and steadfast anchor of the soul, a hope that enters the inner shrine behind the curtain, [20]where Jesus, a forerunner on our behalf, has entered, having become a high priest forever according to the order of Melchizedek.

CHAPTER 7

This "King Melchizedek of Salem, priest of the Most High God, met Abraham as he was returning from defeating the kings and blessed him"; [2]and to him Abraham apportioned "one-tenth of everything." His name, in the first place, means "king of righteousness"; next he is also king of Salem, that is, "king of peace." [3]Without father, without mother, without genealogy, having neither beginning of days nor end of life, but resembling the Son of God, he remains a priest forever.

4 See how great he is! Even[a] Abraham the patriarch gave him a tenth of the spoils. [5]And those descendants of Levi who receive the priestly office have a commandment in the law

---

[a] Other ancient authorities lack *Even*

to collect tithes*a* from the people, that is, from their kindred,*b* though these also are descended from Abraham. 6But this man, who does not belong to their ancestry, collected tithes*a* from Abraham and blessed him who had received the promises. 7It is beyond dispute that the inferior is blessed by the superior. 8In the one case, tithes are received by those who are mortal; in the other, by one of whom it is testified that he lives. 9One might even say that Levi himself, who receives tithes, paid tithes through Abraham, 10for he was still in the loins of his ancestor when Melchizedek met him.

11 Now if perfection had been attainable through the levitical priesthood—for the people received the law under this priesthood—what further need would there have been to speak of another priest arising according to the order of Melchizedek, rather than one according to the order of Aaron? 12For when there is a change in the priesthood, there is necessarily a change in the law as well. 13Now the one of whom these things are spoken belonged to another tribe, from which no one has ever served at the altar. 14For it is evident that our Lord was descended from Judah, and in connection with that tribe Moses said nothing about priests.

15 It is even more obvious

a Or *a tenth*
b Gk *brothers*

586		04	2992	2596 04	3551	3778 1510

ἀποδεκατοῦν τὸν λαὸν κατὰ τὸν νόμον, τοῦτ᾽ ἔστιν
take tenth from the people by the law, this is

016 80　846　2539　1831　1537
τοὺς ἀδελφοὺς αὐτῶν, καίπερ ἐξεληλυθότας ἐκ
the brothers of them, and indeed having come out from

06 3751　11　01 1161 3361 1075
τῆς ὀσφύος ᾽Αβραάμ· 6 ὁ δὲ μὴ γενεαλογούμενος
the hip Abraham; the but not having genealogy

1537 846　1183　11　2532 04 2192 020
ἐξ αὐτῶν δεδεκάτωκεν ᾽Αβραὰμ καὶ τὸν ἔχοντα τὰς
from them has taken tenth Abraham and the having the

1860　2127　5565 1161 3956
ἐπαγγελίας εὐλόγηκεν. 7 χωρὶς δὲ πάσης
promises he spoke well. Without but all

485　09 1640　5259 02 2909
ἀντιλογίας τὸ ἔλαττον ὑπὸ τοῦ κρείττονος
word against the lesser by the better

2127　8 2532 5602 3303　1181　599
εὐλογεῖται. καὶ ὧδε μὲν δεκάτας ἀποθνήσκοντες
is spoken well. And here indeed tenths dying

444　2983　1563 1161 3140　3754
ἄνθρωποι λαμβάνουσιν, ἐκεῖ δὲ μαρτυρούμενος ὅτι
men receive, there but testifying that

2198　9 2532 5613 2031 3004　1223　11　2532
ζῇ. καὶ ὡς ἔπος εἰπεῖν, δι᾽ ᾽Αβραὰμ καὶ
he lives. And as so to say, through Abraham and

3017 01　1181　2983　1183　10 2089 1063
Λευὶ ὁ δεκάτας λαμβάνων δεδεκάτωται· ἔτι γὰρ
Levi the tenths receiving has given tenth; still for

1722 07　3751 02　3962 1510　3753 4876
ἐν τῇ ὀσφύϊ τοῦ πατρὸς ἦν ὅτε συνήντησεν
in the hip of the father he was when met

846 3198　11 1487 3303　3767 5050
αὐτῷ Μελχισέδεκ. Εἰ μὲν οὖν τελείωσις
him Melchisedek. If indeed then completion

1223　06 3020　2420　1510 01 2992　1063
διὰ τῆς Λευιτικῆς ἱερωσύνης ἦν, ὁ λαὸς γὰρ
through the Levitical priesthood was, the people for

1909 846　3549　5101 2089 5532 2596 08
ἐπ᾽ αὐτῆς νενομοθέτηται, τίς ἔτι χρεία κατὰ τὴν
on it has been given what still need by the law,

5010 3198　2087 450　2409　2532 3756
τάξιν Μελχισέδεκ ἕτερον ἀνίστασθαι ἱερέα καὶ οὐ
rank Melchisedek other to stand up priest and not

2596 08 5010　2　3004　12 3346
κατὰ τὴν τάξιν ᾽Ααρὼν λέγεσθαι; μετατιθεμένης
by the rank Aaron to be spoken? Being changed

1063 06 2420　1537 318　2532 3551
γὰρ τῆς ἱερωσύνης ἐξ ἀνάγκης καὶ νόμου
for the priesthood from necessity and law

3331　1096　13 1909 3739 1063 3004　3778
μετάθεσις γίνεται. ἐφ᾽ ὃν γὰρ λέγεται ταῦτα,
change becomes. On whom for are said these,

5443 2087　3348　575 3739 3762
φυλῆς ἑτέρας μετέσχηκεν, ἀφ᾽ ἧς οὐδεὶς
tribe other he has with, from which no one

4337　011 2379　14 4271
προσέσχηκεν τῷ θυσιαστηρίῳ· πρόδηλον
held to the place of sacrifce; clear before

1063 3754 1537 2455 393　01 2962 1473
γὰρ ὅτι ἐξ ᾽Ιούδα ἀνατέταλκεν ὁ κύριος ἡμῶν,
for that from Judas has arisen the Master of us,

1519 3739　5443 4012 2409　3762　3475
εἰς ἣν φυλὴν περὶ ἱερέων οὐδὲν Μωϋσῆς
for which tribe about priests nothing Moses

2980　15 2532 4055　2089 2612
ἐλάλησεν. καὶ περισσότερον ἔτι κατάδηλόν
spoke. And more excessive still very clear

1510   1487 2596 08   3665   3198   450
ἐστιν, εἰ κατὰ τὴν ὁμοιότητα Μελχισέδεκ ἀνίσταται
it is, if by   the likeness   Melchisedek he stands up

2409   2087   3739 3756 2596 3551 1785
ἱερεὺς ἕτερος, **16** ὃς οὐ κατὰ νόμον ἐντολῆς
priest other,   who not by law   command

4560   1096   235 2596 1411   2222
σαρκίνης γέγονεν ἀλλὰ κατὰ δύναμιν ζωῆς
of flesh has become but by power   of life

179   3140   1063 3754 1473 2409
ἀκαταλύτου. **17** μαρτυρεῖται γὰρ ὅτι σὺ ἱερεὺς
indestructible. It is testified for that you priest

1519 04 165   2596 08 5010 3198   115
εἰς τὸν αἰῶνα κατὰ τὴν τάξιν Μελχισέδεκ. **18** ἀθέτησις
into the age   by the rank Melchisedek.   Annulment

3303   1063 1096   4254   1785   1223   012
μὲν γὰρ γίνεται προαγούσης ἐντολῆς διὰ τὸ
indeed for becomes leading before command through the

846   772   2532 512   3762 1063
αὐτῆς ἀσθενὲς καὶ ἀνωφελές – **19** οὐδὲν γὰρ
same weakness and unprofitable   nothing for

5048   01 3551 1898   1161 2909
ἐτελείωσεν ὁ νόμος – ἐπεισαγωγὴ δὲ κρείττονος
completed the law   bringing in on but of better

1680   1223   3739 1448   03   2316   2532
ἐλπίδος δι᾽ ἧς ἐγγίζομεν τῷ θεῷ. **20** Καὶ
hope   through which we near to the God.   And

2596 3745   3756 5565 3728   013 3303 1063
καθ᾽ ὅσον οὐ χωρὶς ὁρκωμοσίας· οἱ μὲν γὰρ
by   as much not with oath-taking; the indeed for
as   out   ones

5565   3728   1510 2409   1096   01
χωρὶς ὁρκωμοσίας εἰσὶν ἱερεῖς γεγονότες, **21** ὁ
without oath-taking are+ priests +having become, the

1161 3326 3728   1223   02 3004   4314
δὲ μετὰ ὁρκωμοσίας διὰ   τοῦ λέγοντος πρὸς
but with oath-taking through the one saying to

846   3660   2962   2532 3756 3338
αὐτόν· ὤμοσεν κύριος καὶ οὐ μεταμεληθήσεται·
him,   took an oath Master and not he will be sorry;

1473 2409 1519 04 165   2596 5118   2532
σὺ ἱερεὺς εἰς τὸν αἰῶνα. **22** κατὰ τοσοῦτο [καὶ]
you priest into the age.   By such   also

2909   1242   1096   1450   2424
κρείττονος διαθήκης γέγονεν ἔγγυος Ἰησοῦς.
of better agreement has become bond Jesus.

        2532 013 3303 4183   1510 1096   2409
23 Καὶ οἱ μὲν πλείονές εἰσιν γεγονότες   ἱερεῖς
    And the indeed more   are+ +having become priests

1223   012 2288 2967   3887
διὰ τὸ θανάτῳ κωλύεσθαι παραμένειν·
through the death to be hindered to stay along;

    01 1161 1223   012 3306   846   1519 04 165
24 ὁ δὲ διὰ τὸ μένειν αὐτὸν εἰς τὸν αἰῶνα
   the but through the to stay him into the age

531   2192 08 2420   3606   2532
ἀπαράβατον ἔχει τὴν ἱερωσύνην· **25** ὅθεν   καὶ
untransferable has the priesthood,   from where also

4982   1519 012 3838   1410   016
σῴζειν εἰς τὸ παντελὲς δύναται τοὺς
to deliver into the all complete he is able the

4334   1223   846 03   2316 3842
προσερχομένους δι᾽ αὐτοῦ τῷ θεῷ, πάντοτε
ones coming to through him to the God, always

2198 1519 012 1793   5228   846   5108
ζῶν εἰς τὸ ἐντυγχάνειν ὑπὲρ αὐτῶν. **26** Τοιοῦτος
living for the to appeal on behalf of them. Such

1063 1473 2532 4241   749   3741 172
γὰρ ἡμῖν καὶ ἔπρεπεν ἀρχιερεύς, ὅσιος ἄκακος
for to us also was fitting ruler priest, holy, unbad,

when another priest arises,
resembling Melchizedek,
[16]one who has become a
priest, not through a legal
requirement concerning
physical descent, but
through the power of an
indestructible life. [17]For
it is attested of him,
  "You are a priest forever,
    according to the order
    of Melchizedek."
[18]There is, on the one hand,
the abrogation of an earlier
commandment because it
was weak and ineffectual
[19](for the law made nothing
perfect); there is, on the other
hand, the introduction of a
better hope, through which
we approach God.
  [20]This was confirmed
with an oath; for others
who became priests took
their office without an oath,
[21]but this one became a
priest with an oath, because
of the one who said to him,
  "The Lord has sworn
    and will not change his
    mind,
  'You are a priest
    forever'"—
[22]accordingly Jesus has
also become the guarantee
of a better covenant.
  [23]Furthermore, the
former priests were many
in number, because they
were prevented by death
from continuing in office;
[24]but he holds his priesthood permanently, because
he continues forever.
[25]Consequently he is able
for all time to save[a] those
who approach God through
him, since he always lives to
make intercession for them.
  [26]For it was fitting
that we should have such a
high priest, holy, blameless,

undefiled, separated from sinners, and exalted above the heavens. [27]Unlike the other[a] high priests, he has no need to offer sacrifices day after day, first for his own sins, and then for those of the people; this he did once for all when he offered himself. [28]For the law appoints as high priests those who are subject to weakness, but the word of the oath, which came later than the law, appoints a Son who has been made perfect forever.

CHAPTER 8

Now the main point in what we are saying is this: we have such a high priest, one who is seated at the right hand of the throne of the Majesty in the heavens, [2]a minister in the sanctuary and the true tent[b] that the Lord, and not any mortal, has set up. [3]For every high priest is appointed to offer gifts and sacrifices; hence it is necessary for this priest also to have something to offer. [4]Now if he were on earth, he would not be a priest at all, since there are priests who offer gifts according to the law. [5]They offer worship in a sanctuary that is a sketch and shadow of the heavenly one; for Moses, when he was about to erect the tent,[b] was warned, "See that you make everything according to the pattern

[a] Gk lacks other
[b] Or tabernacle

283	5563			575 014 268	2532

ἀμίαντος, κεχωρισμένος ἀπὸ τῶν ἁμαρτωλῶν καὶ
undefiled, having been separated from the sinners and

5308 014 3772 1096 **27** 3739 3756
ὑψηλότερος τῶν οὐρανῶν γενόμενος, ὃς οὐκ
higher of the heavens having become, who not

2192 2596 2250 318 5618 013
ἔχει καθ᾽ ἡμέραν ἀνάγκην, ὥσπερ οἱ
has by day necessity, as indeed the

749 4387 5228 018 2398 266
ἀρχιερεῖς, πρότερον ὑπὲρ τῶν ἰδίων ἁμαρτιῶν
ruler priests, former on behalf of the own sins

2378 399 1899 018 02 2992 3778
θυσίας ἀναφέρειν ἔπειτα τῶν τοῦ λαοῦ· τοῦτο
sacrifices to carry up then the of the people; this

1063 4160 2178 1438 399
γὰρ ἐποίησεν ἐφάπαξ ἑαυτὸν ἀνενέγκας.
for he did once for all himself having carried up.

28 01 3551 1063 444 3056
ὁ νόμος γὰρ ἀνθρώπους καθίστησιν ἀρχιερεῖς
The law for men appoints ruler priests

2192 769 01 3056 1161 06 3728
ἔχοντας ἀσθένειαν, ὁ λόγος δὲ τῆς ὁρκωμοσίας
having weakness, the word but of the oath-taking

06 3326 04 3551 5207 1519 04 165
τῆς μετὰ τὸν νόμον υἱὸν εἰς τὸν αἰῶνα
the after the law son into the age

5048 **8:1** 2774 1161 1909 023
τετελειωμένον. Κεφάλαιον δὲ ἐπὶ τοῖς
having been completed. Sum but on the

3004 5108 2192 749 3739
λεγομένοις, τοιοῦτον ἔχομεν ἀρχιερέα, ὃς
being said, such we have ruler priest, who

2523 1722 1188 02 2362 06 3172
ἐκάθισεν ἐν δεξιᾷ τοῦ θρόνου τῆς μεγαλωσύνης
sat in right of the throne of the greatness

1722 013 3772 **2** 022 40 3011 2532
ἐν τοῖς οὐρανοῖς, τῶν ἁγίων λειτουργὸς καὶ
in the heavens, of the holies servant and

06 4633 06 228 3739 4078 01 2962
τῆς σκηνῆς τῆς ἀληθινῆς, ἣν ἔπηξεν ὁ κύριος,
of the tent the true, which affixed the Master,

3756 444 **3** 3956 1063 749 1519 012
οὐκ ἄνθρωπος. Πᾶς γὰρ ἀρχιερεὺς εἰς τὸ
not man. All for ruler priest for the

4374 1435 5037 2532 2378 2525
προσφέρειν δῶρά τε καὶ θυσίας καθίσταται·
to offer gifts both and sacrifices is appointed;

3606 316 2192 5100 2532 3778 3739
ὅθεν ἀναγκαῖον ἔχειν τι καὶ τοῦτον ὃ
from where necessary to have some also this what

4374 **4** 1487 3303 3767 1510 1909 1093
προσενέγκῃ. εἰ μὲν οὖν ἦν ἐπὶ γῆς,
he might offer. If indeed then he was on earth,

3761 302 1510 2409 1510 014 4374 2596
οὐδ᾽ ἂν ἦν ἱερεύς, ὄντων τῶν προσφερόντων κατὰ
but not - he was priest, being the offering by

3551 024 1435 **5** 3748 5262 2532 4639
νόμον τὰ δῶρα· οἵτινες ὑποδείγματι καὶ σκιᾷ
law the gifts, who example and shadow

3000 022 2032 2531 5537
λατρεύουσιν τῶν ἐπουρανίων, καθὼς κεχρημάτισται
they serve the on heavenlies, just as was warned

3475 3195 2005 08 4633
Μωϋσῆς μέλλων ἐπιτελεῖν τὴν σκηνήν·
Moses being about to complete thoroughly the tent;

3708 1063 5346 4160 3956 2596 04 5179
ὅρα γὰρ φησιν, ποιήσεις πάντα κατὰ τὸν τύπον
see for he says, you will make all by the example

04	1166		1473	1722	011	3735	**6**	3570	1161
τὸν	δειχθέντα		σοι	ἐν	τῷ	ὄρει·		Νυν[ὶ]	δὲ
the	one having been shown		to you	in	the	hill;		now	but

1313		5177		3009		3745
διαφορωτέρας		τέτυχεν		λειτουργίας,		ὅσῳ
more differing		he has obtained		service,		as much as

2532	2909		1510	1242	3316		3748	1909
καὶ	κρείττονός		ἐστιν	διαθήκης	μεσίτης,		ἥτις	ἐπὶ
also	of better		he is	agreement	mediator,		which	on

2909		1860		3549		7	1487	1063
κρείττοσιν		ἐπαγγελίαις		νενομοθέτηται.			Εἰ	γὰρ
better		promises		has been given law.			If	for

05	4413	1565		1510	273		3756	302	1208
ἡ	πρώτη	ἐκείνη		ἦν	ἄμεμπτος,		οὐκ	ἂν	δευτέρας
the	first	that		was	faultless,		not	-	second

2212		5117	**8**	3201		1063	846		3004
ἐζητεῖτο		τόπος.		μεμφόμενος		γὰρ	αὐτοὺς		λέγει·
was sought		place.		Finding fault		for	them		he says,

2400	2250		2064		3004	2962		2532
ἰδοὺ	ἡμέραι		ἔρχονται,		λέγει	κύριος,		καὶ
look	days		come,		says	Master,		and

4931		1909	04	3624		2474	2532	1909	04	3624
συντελέσω		ἐπὶ	τὸν	οἶκον		Ἰσραὴλ	καὶ	ἐπὶ	τὸν	οἶκον
I will fully complete		on	the	house		Israel	and	on	the	house

2455	1242		2537	**9**	3756	2596	08	1242
Ἰούδα	διαθήκην		καινήν,		οὐ	κατὰ	τὴν	διαθήκην,
Judas	agreement		new,		not	by	the	agreement,

3739	4160		015		3962		846		1722	2250
ἣν	ἐποίησα		τοῖς		πατράσιν		αὐτῶν		ἐν	ἡμέρᾳ
that	I made		to the		fathers		of them		in	day

1949		1473	06	5495	846		1806
ἐπιλαβομένου		μου	τῆς	χειρὸς	αὐτῶν		ἐξαγαγεῖν
having taken on		of me	the	hand	of them		to lead out

846		1537	1093	125		3754	846		3756
αὐτοὺς		ἐκ	γῆς	Αἰγύπτου,		ὅτι	αὐτοὶ		οὐκ
them		from	land	of Egypt,		because	themselves		not

1696		1722	07	1242		1473	2504	272
ἐνέμειναν		ἐν	τῇ	διαθήκῃ		μου,	κἀγὼ	ἠμέλησα
stayed		in	in the	agreement		of me,	and I	gave not care

846		3004	2962	**10**	3754		3778	05	1242
αὐτῶν,		λέγει	κύριος·		ὅτι		αὕτη	ἡ	διαθήκη,
of them,		says	Master;		because		this	the	agreement,

3739	1303		03		3624	2474	3326	020	2250
ἣν	διαθήσομαι		τῷ		οἴκῳ	Ἰσραὴλ	μετὰ	τὰς	ἡμέρας
that	I agreed		to the		house	Israel	after	the	days

1565		3004	2962		1325	3551	1473	1519	08
ἐκείνας,		λέγει	κύριος·		διδοὺς	νόμους	μου	εἰς	τὴν
those,		says	Master:		giving	laws	of me	into	the

1271		846		2532	1909	2588	846
διάνοιαν		αὐτῶν		καὶ	ἐπὶ	καρδίας	αὐτῶν
intelligence		of them		and	on	hearts	of them

1924		846		2532	1510		846		1519
ἐπιγράψω		αὐτούς,		καὶ	ἔσομαι		αὐτοῖς		εἰς
I will write		on them,		and	I will be		to them		for

2316	2532	846		1510		1473	1519	2992
θεόν,	καὶ	αὐτοὶ		ἔσονταί		μοι	εἰς	λαόν·
God,	and	themselves		will be		to me	for	people;

11	2532	3756	3361	1321		1538	04	4177
	καὶ	οὐ	μὴ	διδάξωσιν		ἕκαστος	τὸν	πολίτην
	and	not	not	will teach		each	the	citizen

846		2532	1538	04	80		846	3004	1097
αὐτοῦ		καὶ	ἕκαστος	τὸν	ἀδελφὸν		αὐτοῦ	λέγων·	γνῶθι
of him		and	each	the	brother		of him	saying·	know

04	2962		3754		3956	3609a		1473	575	3398
τὸν	κύριον,		ὅτι		πάντες	εἰδήσουσίν		με	ἀπὸ	μικροῦ
the	Master,		because		all	will know		me	from	little

---

that was shown you on the mountain." [6]But Jesus[a] has now obtained a more excellent ministry, and to that degree he is the mediator of a better covenant, which has been enacted through better promises. [7]For if that first covenant had been faultless, there would have been no need to look for a second one.

[8]God[b] finds fault with them when he says:
"The days are surely coming, says the Lord,
when I will establish a new covenant with the house of Israel and with the house of Judah;
[9] not like the covenant that I made with their ancestors, on the day when I took them by the hand to lead them out of the land of Egypt; for they did not continue in my covenant, and so I had no concern for them, says the Lord.
[10] This is the covenant that I will make with the house of Israel after those days, says the Lord:
I will put my laws in their minds, and write them on their hearts, and I will be their God, and they shall be my people.
[11] And they shall not teach one another or say to each other, 'Know the Lord,' for they shall all know me, from the least of them to the greatest.

a Gk he
b Gk He

12 For I will be merciful toward their iniquities, and I will remember their sins no more." 13 In speaking of "a new covenant," he has made the first one obsolete. And what is obsolete and growing old will soon disappear.

CHAPTER 9

Now even the first covenant had regulations for worship and an earthly sanctuary. 2 For a tent[a] was constructed, the first one, in which were the lampstand, the table, and the bread of the Presence;[b] this is called the Holy Place. 3 Behind the second curtain was a tent[a] called the Holy of Holies. 4 In it stood the golden altar of incense and the ark of the covenant overlaid on all sides with gold, in which there were a golden urn holding the manna, and Aaron's rod that budded, and the tablets of the covenant; 5 above it were the cherubim of glory overshadowing the mercy seat.[c] Of these things we cannot speak now in detail.

6 Such preparations having been made, the priests go continually into the first tent[a] to carry out their ritual duties; 7 but only the high priest goes into the second, and he but once a year, and not without taking the blood that he offers for himself and for the sins committed unintentionally by the people.

a Or tabernacle
b Gk the presentation of the loaves
c Or the place of atonement

```
2193      3173     846        12  3754     2436       1510
ἕως      μεγάλου  αὐτῶν,          ὅτι     ἵλεως     ἔσομαι
until    great    of them,       because merciful  I will be
019       93          846       2532 018 266          846       3756
ταῖς     ἀδικίαις   αὐτῶν      καὶ  τῶν ἁμαρτιῶν    αὐτῶν      οὐ
to the   unrights   of them   and  the  sins        of them   not
3361 3403            2089     13  1722 011  3004      2537
μὴ  μνησθῶ           ἔτι.         ἐν   τῷ  λέγειν    καινὴν
not  I might remember still.      In   the to say    new
3822               08  4413       09  1161 3822
πεπαλαίωκεν        τὴν πρώτην·    τὸ  δὲ   παλαιούμενον
he has made old   the first;     the but  being made old
2532 1095          1451    854          9:1  2192 3303      3767
καὶ  γηράσκον     ἐγγὺς  ἀφανισμοῦ.       Εἶχε μὲν       οὖν
and  growing old  near    disappearance.  Had  indeed    then
2532 05  4413      1345           2999       012 5037    40
[καὶ] ἡ πρώτη    δικαιώματα    λατρείας    τό  τε      ἅγιον
 also  the first  right acts    of service  the indeed  holy
2886          2  4633  1063 2680        05    4413 1722 3739
κοσμικόν.       σκηνὴ γὰρ κατεσκευάσθη ἡ    πρώτη ἐν    ᾗ
worldly.        Tent   for  was prepared  the  first in  which
05  5037 3087          2532 05  5132      2532 05    4286
ἥ  τε   λυχνία       καὶ  ἡ  τράπεζα   καὶ  ἡ    πρόθεσις
the both lampstand   and  the table    and  the  purpose
014      740      3748   3004      40    3  3326  1161 012
τῶν     ἄρτων,  ἥτις    λέγεται  Ἅγια·    μετὰ  δὲ   τὸ
of the  breads, which  is said   holies;   after but  the
1208      2665           4633 05  3004       40
δεύτερον καταπέτασμα  σκηνὴ ἡ λεγομένη   Ἅγια
second   veil          tent   the being said holies
40          4  5552     2192    2369                2532 08
Ἁγίων,        χρυσοῦν ἔχουσα θυμιατήριον      καὶ  τὴν
of holies,    gold    having place of incense  and  the
2787     06    1242          4028
κιβωτὸν τῆς  διαθήκης   περικεκαλυμμένην
box      of the agreement  having been covered around
3840            5553      1722 3739 4713      5552   2192
πάντοθεν       χρυσίῳ,  ἐν  ᾗ   στάμνος χρυσῆ ἔχουσα
from everywhere in gold, in  which jar    gold   having
012 3131   2532 05  4464       2    05  985
τὸ  μάννα καὶ  ἡ  ῥάβδος   Ἀαρὼν ἡ  βλαστήσασα
the manna and  the rod       Aaron the having sprouted
2532 017 4109     06    1242        5  5231      1161
καὶ  αἱ  πλάκες τῆς  διαθήκης,    ὑπεράνω  δὲ
and  the tablets of the agreement,  up above  but
846      5502    1391      2683         012
αὐτῆς Χερουβὶν δόξης    κατασκιάζοντα τὸ
it      cherubim of splendor shadowing over the
2435           4012 3739  3756 1510   3568 3004
ἱλαστήριον.  περὶ  ὧν    οὐκ ἔστιν νῦν λέγειν
place of expiation, about which not  it is now  to say
2596 3313   6  3778    1161 3779    2680
κατὰ μέρος.   Τούτων δὲ  οὕτως κατεσκευασμένων
by    part.    These  but thusly having been prepared
1519 3303   08  4413    4633     1223  3956   1524
εἰς  μὲν     τὴν πρώτην σκηνὴν διὰ  παντὸς εἰσίασιν
for  indeed  the first  tent    through all   go into
013 2409   020 2999       2005            7  1519
οἱ  ἱερεῖς τὰς λατρείας ἐπιτελοῦντες,      εἰς
the priests the services thoroughly completing, into
1161 08  1208      530  02      1763       3441 01
δὲ  τὴν δευτέραν ἅπαξ τοῦ   ἐνιαυτοῦ μόνος ὁ
but  the second  once of the  year      alone the
749          3756 5565    129       3739 4374
ἀρχιερεύς,  οὐ  χωρὶς αἵματος ὃ   προσφέρει
ruler priest, not  without blood  which he offers
5228    1438      2532 022 02    2992  51
ὑπὲρ   ἑαυτοῦ  καὶ  τῶν τοῦ λαοῦ ἀγνοημάτων,
on behalf of himself and the of the people ignorances,
```

8
3778	1213		010	4151		010	40		3380
τοῦτο	δηλοῦντος		τοῦ	πνεύματος		τοῦ	ἁγίου,		μήπω
this	making clear		the	spirit		the	holy,		not yet

5319		08	022	40		3598	2089	06	4413
πεφανερῶσθαι		τὴν	τῶν	ἁγίων		ὁδὸν	ἔτι	τῆς	πρώτης
to have been		the	of the	holies		way	still	of	first
demonstrated									the

4633	2192	4714		**9**	3748	3850		1519
σκηνῆς	ἐχούσης	στάσιν,			ἥτις	παραβολὴ		εἰς
tent	having	standing,			which	parallel story		for

04	2540	04	1764		2596	3739	1435	5037	2532
τὸν	καιρὸν	τὸν	ἐνεστηκότα,		καθ᾽	ἣν	δῶρά	τε	καὶ
the	season	the	present,		by	which	gifts	both	and

2378		4374		3361	1410		2596	4893
θυσίαι		προσφέρονται		μὴ	δυνάμεναι		κατὰ	συνείδησιν
sacrifices		are being		not	being able		by	conscience
		offered						

5048		04	3000		**10**	3441	1909	1033
τελειῶσαι		τὸν	λατρεύοντα,			μόνον	ἐπὶ	βρώμασιν
to complete		the one	serving,			alone	on	food

2532	4188		2532	1313		909		1345
καὶ	πόμασιν		καὶ	διαφόροις		βαπτισμοῖς,		δικαιώματα
and	drinks		and	differing		immersions,		right acts

4561		3360	2540	1357		1945
σαρκὸς		μέχρι	καιροῦ	διορθώσεως		ἐπικείμενα.
of flesh		until	season	of correction		lying on.

11
5547	1161	3854		749		022
Χριστὸς	δὲ	παραγενόμενος		ἀρχιερεὺς		τῶν
Christ	but	having arrived		ruler priest		of the

1096		18	1223		06	3173		2532
γενομένων		ἀγαθῶν	διὰ		τῆς	μείζονος		καὶ
having become		goods	through		the	greater		and

5046		4633	3756	5499		3778	1510
τελειοτέρας		σκηνῆς	οὐ	χειροποιήτου,		τοῦτ᾽	ἔστιν
more complete		tent	not	handmade,		this	is

3756	3778	06	2937		**12**	3761	1223	129
οὐ	ταύτης	τῆς	κτίσεως,			οὐδὲ	δι᾽	αἵματος
not	of this	the	creation,			but not	through	blood

5131		2532	3448	1223		1161	010	2398	129
τράγων		καὶ	μόσχων	διὰ		δὲ	τοῦ	ἰδίου	αἵματος
of goats		and	calves	through		but	the	own	blood

1525		2178		1519	024	40		166
εἰσῆλθεν		ἐφάπαξ		εἰς	τὰ	ἅγια		αἰωνίαν
he went in		once for all		into	the	holies		eternal

3085		2147		**13**	1487	1063	09	129	5131
λύτρωσιν		εὑράμενος.			εἰ	γὰρ	τὸ	αἷμα	τράγων
ransom		having found.			If	for	the	blood	of goats

2532	5022		2532	4700		1151		4472		016
καὶ	ταύρων		καὶ	σποδὸς		δαμάλεως		ῥαντίζουσα		τοὺς
and	bulls		and	ash		of heifer		sprinkling		the ones

2840		37		4314	08	06
κεκοινωμένους		ἁγιάζει		πρὸς	τὴν	τῆς
having been made common		makes holy		toward	the	of the

4561	2514		**14**	4214		3123	09	129	02
σαρκὸς	καθαρότητα,			πόσῳ		μᾶλλον	τὸ	αἷμα	τοῦ
flesh	cleaning,			how much		more	the	blood	of the

5547	3739	1223		4151		166		1438
Χριστοῦ,	ὃς	διὰ		πνεύματος		αἰωνίου		ἑαυτὸν
Christ,	who	through		spirit		eternal		himself

4374		299		03		2316	2511		08
προσήνεγκεν		ἄμωμον		τῷ		θεῷ,	καθαριεῖ		τὴν
offered		blameless		to the		God,	cleans		the

4893		1473	575	3498		2041	1519	012	3000
συνείδησιν		ἡμῶν	ἀπὸ	νεκρῶν		ἔργων	εἰς	τὸ	λατρεύειν
conscience		of us	from	dead		works	to	the	to serve

2316	2198		**15**	2532	1223		3778	1242		2537
θεῷ	ζῶντι.			Καὶ	διὰ		τοῦτο	διαθήκης		καινῆς
God	living.			And	through		this	agreement		new

---

[8]By this the Holy Spirit indicates that the way into the sanctuary has not yet been disclosed as long as the first tent[a] is still standing. [9]This is a symbol[b] of the present time, during which gifts and sacrifices are offered that cannot perfect the conscience of the worshiper, [10]but deal only with food and drink and various baptisms, regulations for the body imposed until the time comes to set things right.

[11] But when Christ came as a high priest of the good things that have come,[c] then through the greater and perfect[d] tent[a] (not made with hands, that is, not of this creation), [12]he entered once for all into the Holy Place, not with the blood of goats and calves, but with his own blood, thus obtaining eternal redemption. [13]For if the blood of goats and bulls, with the sprinkling of the ashes of a heifer, sanctifies those who have been defiled so that their flesh is purified, [14]how much more will the blood of Christ, who through the eternal Spirit[e] offered himself without blemish to God, purify our[f] conscience from dead works to worship the living God!

[15] For this reason he is the mediator of a new covenant,

---

[a] Or tabernacle
[b] Gk parable
[c] Other ancient authorities read good things to come
[d] Gk more perfect
[e] Other ancient authorities read Holy Spirit
[f] Other ancient authorities read your

so that those who are called may receive the promised eternal inheritance, because a death has occurred that redeems them from the transgressions under the first covenant.[a] 16Where a will[a] is involved, the death of the one who made it must be established. 17For a will[a] takes effect only at death, since it is not in force as long as the one who made it is alive. 18Hence not even the first covenant was inaugurated without blood. 19For when every commandment had been told to all the people by Moses in accordance with the law, he took the blood of calves and goats,[b] with water and scarlet wool and hyssop, and sprinkled both the scroll itself and all the people, 20saying, "This is the blood of the covenant that God has ordained for you." 21And in the same way he sprinkled with the blood both the tent[c] and all the vessels used in worship. 22Indeed, under the law almost everything is purified with blood, and without the shedding of blood there is no forgiveness of sins.

23 Thus it was necessary for the sketches of the heavenly things to be purified with these rites, but the heavenly things themselves need better sacrifices than these. 24For Christ did not enter a sanctuary made by human hands, a mere copy of the

a The Greek word used here means both *covenant* and *will*
b Other ancient authorities lack *and goats*
c Or *tabernacle*

3316	1510	3704	2288	1096	1519
μεσίτης	ἐστίν,	ὅπως	θανάτου	γενομένου	εἰς
mediator	he is,	so that	death	having become	for

629	018	1909	07	4413	1242
ἀπολύτρωσιν	τῶν	ἐπὶ	τῇ	πρώτῃ	διαθήκῃ
redemption	of the	on	the	first	agreement

3847	08	1860	2983	013
παραβάσεων	τὴν	ἐπαγγελίαν	λάβωσιν	οἱ
transgressions	the	promise	might receive	the ones

2564	06	166	2817	16	3699
κεκλημένοι	τῆς	αἰωνίου	κληρονομίας.		Ὅπου
having been called	of the	eternal	inheritance.		Where

1063	1242	2288	318	5342	02
γὰρ	διαθήκη,	θάνατον	ἀνάγκη	φέρεσθαι	τοῦ
for	agreement,	death	necessity	to carry	the one

1303	17	1242	1063	1909	3498	949
διαθεμένου·		διαθήκη	γὰρ	ἐπὶ	νεκροῖς	βεβαία,
agreeing;		agreement	for	on	dead	firm,

1893	3379	2480	3753	2198	01	1303
ἐπεὶ	μήποτε	ἰσχύει	ὅτε	ζῇ	ὁ	διαθέμενος.
since	not	then is strong	when	lives	the	having agreed.

18	3606	3761	05	4413	5565	129
	ὅθεν	οὐδὲ	ἡ	πρώτη	χωρὶς	αἵματος
	From where	but not	the	first	without	blood

1457	19	2980	1063	3956
ἐγκεκαίνισται·		λαληθείσης	γὰρ	πάσης
has been made new;		having been spoken	for	of all

1785	2596	04	3551	5259	3475	3956	03	2992
ἐντολῆς	κατὰ	τὸν	νόμον	ὑπὸ	Μωϋσέως	παντὶ	τῷ	λαῷ,
command	by	the	law	by	Moses	in all	the	people,

2983	012	129	014	3448	2532	014	5131
λαβὼν	τὸ	αἷμα	τῶν	μόσχων	[καὶ	τῶν	τράγων]
having taken	the	blood	of the	calves	and	the	goats

3326	5204	2532	2053	2847	2532	5301	846
μετὰ	ὕδατος	καὶ	ἐρίου	κοκκίνου	καὶ	ὑσσώπου	αὐτό
with	water	and	of wool	scarlet	and	hyssop	itself

5037	012	975	2532	3956	04	2992	4472
τε	τὸ	βιβλίον	καὶ	πάντα	τὸν	λαὸν	ἐράντισεν
both	the	small book	and	all	the	people	he sprinkled

20	3004	3778	09	129	06	1242	3739
	λέγων·	τοῦτο	τὸ	αἷμα	τῆς	διαθήκης	ἧς
	saying,	this	the	blood	of the	agreement	which

1781	4314	1473	01	2316	21	2532	08	4633	1161
ἐνετείλατο	πρὸς	ὑμᾶς	ὁ	θεός.		καὶ	τὴν	σκηνὴν	δὲ
commanded	to	you	the	God.		And	the	tent	but

2532	3956	024	4632	06	3009	011	129
καὶ	πάντα	τὰ	σκεύη	τῆς	λειτουργίας	τῷ	αἵματι
also	all	the	pots	of the	service	in the	blood

3668	4472	22	2532	4975	1722	129	3956
ὁμοίως	ἐράντισεν.		καὶ	σχεδὸν	ἐν	αἵματι	πάντα
likewise	he sprinkled.		And	almost	in	blood	all

2511	2596	04	3551	2532	5565	130
καθαρίζεται	κατὰ	τὸν	νόμον	καὶ	χωρὶς	αἱματεκχυσίας
is cleaned	by	the	law	and	without	blood pouring

3756	1096	859	23	318	3767	024
οὐ	γίνεται	ἄφεσις.		Ἀνάγκη	οὖν	τὰ
not	there becomes	sending off.		Necessity	then	the

3303	5262	022	1722	015	3772	3778
μὲν	ὑποδείγματα	τῶν	ἐν	τοῖς	οὐρανοῖς	τούτοις
indeed	examples	the	in	the	heavens	these

2511	846	1161	024	2032
καθαρίζεσθαι,	αὐτὰ	δὲ	τὰ	ἐπουράνια
to be cleaned,	themselves	but	the	on heavenly

2909	2378	3844	3778	24	3756	1063	1519
κρείττοσιν	θυσίαις	παρὰ	ταύτας.		οὐ	γὰρ	εἰς
better	sacrifices	from	these.		Not	for	into

5499	1525	40	5547	499	022
χειροποίητα	εἰσῆλθεν	ἅγια	Χριστός,	ἀντίτυπα	τῶν
handmade	went into	holies	Christ,	antitypes	of the

```
228          235    1519 846     04   3772        3568
ἀληθινῶν, ἀλλ᾽ εἰς αὐτὸν τὸν οὐρανόν, νῦν
true,        but   into itself the heaven,   now
1718              011     4383    02     2316 5228
ἐμφανισθῆναι τῷ    προσώπῳ τοῦ    θεοῦ ὑπὲρ
to be visible  to the face   of the God  on behalf of
1473    25  3761    2443 4178       4374
ἡμῶν·      οὐδ᾽ ἵνα πολλάκις προσφέρῃ
us;        but not that frequently he might offer
1438        5618    01  749           1525       1519 024
ἑαυτόν, ὥσπερ ὁ ἀρχιερεὺς εἰσέρχεται εἰς τὰ
himself, as indeed the ruler priest comes in  into the
40     2596 1763   1722 129    245          26  1893
ἅγια κατ᾽ ἐνιαυτὸν ἐν αἵματι ἀλλοτρίῳ,      ἐπεὶ
holies by  year     in blood  of other,       since
1163         846    4178       3958     575
ἔδει          αὐτὸν πολλάκις παθεῖν ἀπὸ
it was necessary him  frequently to suffer from
2602       2889     3570 1161 530  1909 4930
καταβολῆς κόσμου· νυνὶ δὲ ἅπαξ ἐπὶ συντελείᾳ
foundation of world; now but once at full completion
014    165       1519 115      06    266        1223
τῶν αἰώνων εἰς ἀθέτησιν [τῆς] ἁμαρτίας διὰ
of the ages  into annulment of the sin     through
06  2378      846    5319                27  2532 2596
τῆς θυσίας αὐτοῦ πεφανέρωται.          καὶ καθ᾽
the sacrifice of him has been demonstrated. And by
3745      606        015  444          530  599
ὅσον   ἀπόκειται τοῖς ἀνθρώποις ἅπαξ ἀποθανεῖν,
as much as it lies off the  men         once to die,
3326 1161 3778  2920     28  3779  2532 01  5547
μετὰ δὲ τοῦτο κρίσις,       οὕτως καὶ ὁ Χριστὸς
after but this judgment,     thusly also the Christ
530  4374                 1519 012 4183      399
ἅπαξ προσενεχθεὶς     εἰς τὸ πολλῶν ἀνενεγκεῖν
once having been offered for the of many to bring up
266       1537 1208      5565   266      3708      015
ἁμαρτίας ἐκ δευτέρου χωρὶς ἁμαρτίας ὀφθήσεται τοῖς
sins     from second  with sin        he will   to the
                                                  be seen
846  553                 1519 4991      10:1  4639  1063
αὐτὸν ἀπεκδεχομένοις εἰς σωτηρίαν.     Σκιὰν γὰρ
him  ones awaiting    for deliverance.  Shadow for
2192   01 3551  022    3195         18        3756
ἔχων ὁ νόμος τῶν μελλόντων ἀγαθῶν, οὐκ
having the law of the being about to be goods,  not
846  08 1504   022    4229         2596 1763     019
αὐτὴν τὴν εἰκόνα τῶν πραγμάτων, κατ᾽ ἐνιαυτὸν ταῖς
same  the image of the practices, by   year    in the
846  2378    3739    4374           1519 012
αὐταῖς θυσίαις ἃς προσφέρουσιν εἰς τὸ
same  sacrifices which they offer into the
1336       3763     1410     016   4334
διηνεκὲς οὐδέποτε δύναται τοὺς προσερχομένους
perpetuity but not ever is able the  ones coming to
5048          2  1893  3756 302 3973       4374
τελειῶσαι·     ἐπεὶ οὐκ ἂν ἐπαύσαντο προσφερόμεναι
to complete; since not  -  they stopped being offered
1223     012 3367       2192    2089 4893
διὰ      τὸ μηδεμίαν ἔχειν ἔτι συνείδησιν
because the but not one to have still conscience
266      016  3000        530  2511
ἁμαρτιῶν τοὺς λατρεύοντας ἅπαξ κεκαθαρισμένους;
of sins  the ones serving  once having been cleaned?
3  235  1722 846    364        266      2596 1763
   ἀλλ᾽ ἐν αὐταῖς ἀνάμνησις ἁμαρτιῶν κατ᾽ ἐνιαυτόν·
   But  in them  remembrance of sins  by   year,
4  102        1063 129   5022    2532 5131    851
   ἀδύνατον γὰρ αἷμα ταύρων καὶ τράγων ἀφαιρεῖν
   is unable for blood of bulls and goats to lift off
```

true one, but he entered into heaven itself, now to appear in the presence of God on our behalf. [25]Nor was it to offer himself again and again, as the high priest enters the Holy Place -year after year with blood that is not his own; [26]for then he would have had to suffer again and again since the foundation of the world. But as it is, he has appeared once for all at the end of the age to remove sin by the sacrifice of himself. [27]And just as it is appointed for mortals to die once, and after that the judgment, [28]so Christ, having been offered once to bear the sins of many, will appear a second time, not to deal with sin, but to save those who are eagerly waiting for him.

CHAPTER 10

Since the law has only a shadow of the good things to come and not the true form of these realities, it[a] can never, by the same sacrifices that are continually offered year after year, make perfect those who approach. [2]Otherwise, would they not have ceased being offered, since the worshipers, cleansed once for all, would no longer have any consciousness of sin? [3]But in these sacrifices there is a reminder of sin year after year. [4]For it is impossible for the blood of bulls and goats to take away sins.

a Other ancient authorities read they

5Consequently, when Christ[a] came into the world, he said,
"Sacrifices and offerings you have not desired, but a body you have prepared for me;
6 in burnt offerings and sin offerings you have taken no pleasure.
7 Then I said, 'See, God, I have come to do your will, O God' (in the scroll of the book[b] it is written of me)."
8When he said above, "You have neither desired nor taken pleasure in sacrifices and offerings and burnt offerings and sin offerings" (these are offered according to the law), 9then he added, "See, I have come to do your will." He abolishes the first in order to establish the second. 10And it is by God's will[c] that we have been sanctified through the offering of the body of Jesus Christ once for all.
11 And every priest stands day after day at his service, offering again and again the same sacrifices that can never take away sins. 12But when Christ[d] had offered for all time a single sacrifice for sins, "he sat down at the right hand of God," 13and since then has been waiting "until his enemies would be made a footstool for his feet." 14For by a single offering he has perfected for all time those who are sanctified.
15And the Holy Spirit

[a] Gk he
[b] Meaning of Gk uncertain
[c] Gk by that will
[d] Gk this one

266	5	1352		1525		1519	04	2889
ἁμαρτίας.		Διὸ		εἰσερχόμενος		εἰς	τὸν	κόσμον
sins.		Wherefore		having come		in	into	the world

3004 2378   2532 4376   3756 2309   4983
λέγει· θυσίαν καὶ προσφορὰν οὐκ ἠθέλησας, σῶμα
he says, sacrifice and offering not you wanted, body

1161 2675   1473   6 3646
δὲ κατηρτίσω   μοι·   ὁλοκαυτώματα
but you put in order to me; whole burnt offerings

2532 4012   266   3756 2106   7 5119
καὶ περὶ ἁμαρτίας οὐκ εὐδόκησας.   τότε
and concerning sin   not you thought well. Then

3004 2400 2240 1722 2777   975
εἶπον· ἰδοὺ ἥκω, ἐν κεφαλίδι βιβλίου
I said, look I come, in heading of small book

1125   4012 1473 010 4160 01 2316 012
γέγραπται   περὶ ἐμοῦ, τοῦ ποιῆσαι ὁ θεὸς τὸ
it has been written about me, the to do the God the

2307 1473 511   3004 3754 2378   2532
θέλημά σου. 8 ἀνώτερον λέγων ὅτι θυσίας καὶ
want of you. Upper saying that sacrifices and

4376   2532 3646   2532 4012 266
προσφορὰς καὶ ὁλοκαυτώματα καὶ περὶ ἁμαρτίας
offerings and whole burnt offerings and about sin

3756 2309   3761   2106   3748 2596
οὐκ ἠθέλησας οὐδὲ εὐδόκησας,   αἵτινες κατὰ
not you wanted but not you thought well, which by

3551 4374   9 5119 3004   2400 2240 010
νόμον προσφέρονται, τότε εἴρηκεν· ἰδοὺ ἥκω τοῦ
law they are offered, then he has said, look I come the

4160 012 2307 1473   337   012 4413 2443
ποιῆσαι τὸ θέλημά σου. ἀναιρεῖ τὸ πρῶτον ἵνα
to do the want of you. He kills the first that

012 1208   2476   10 1722 3739 2307
τὸ δεύτερον στήσῃ,   ἐν ᾧ θελήματι
the second might stand, in whose want

37   1510   1223   06 4376
ἡγιασμένοι   ἐσμὲν διὰ τῆς προσφορᾶς
+having been made holy we are+ through the offering

010 4983   2424   5547 2178   11 2532
τοῦ σώματος Ἰησοῦ Χριστοῦ ἐφάπαξ.   Καὶ
of the body of Jesus Christ once for all. And

3956 3303 2409   2476   2596 2250 3008
πᾶς μὲν ἱερεὺς ἕστηκεν καθ' ἡμέραν λειτουργῶν
all indeed priest has stood by day serving

2532 020 846 4178   4374   2378   3748
καὶ τὰς αὐτὰς πολλάκις προσφέρων θυσίας, αἵτινες
and the same frequently offering sacrifices, which

3763   1410   4014   266
οὐδέποτε δύνανται περιελεῖν ἁμαρτίας,
but not ever is able to lift up around sins,

12 3778 1161 1520 5228   266   4374
οὗτος δὲ μίαν ὑπὲρ ἁμαρτιῶν προσενέγκας
this but one on behalf of sins having offered

2378   1519 012 1336   2523   1722 1188
θυσίαν εἰς τὸ διηνεκὲς ἐκάθισεν ἐν δεξιᾷ
sacrifice into the perpetuity he sat in right

02 2316 012 3062   1551   2193
τοῦ θεοῦ, 13 τὸ λοιπὸν ἐκδεχόμενος ἕως
of the God, the remaining waiting for until

5087   013 2190 846   5286   014   4228
τεθῶσιν οἱ ἐχθροὶ αὐτοῦ ὑποπόδιον τῶν ποδῶν
might be set the hostile of him footstool of the feet

846 14 1520 1063 4376   5048   1519
αὐτοῦ. μιᾷ γὰρ προσφορᾷ τετελείωκεν εἰς
of him. In one for offering he has completed into

012 1336   016 37   3140
τὸ διηνεκὲς τοὺς ἁγιαζομένους. 15 Μαρτυρεῖ
the perpetuity the ones being made holy. Testifies

```
1161  1473  2532  09   4151    09   40     3326  1063  012
δὲ    ἡμῖν  καὶ  τὸ  πνεῦμα  τὸ  ἅγιον·  μετὰ  γὰρ   τὸ
but   to us also  the spirit  the holy;  after  for   the
3004                3778 05   1242        3739  1303
εἰρηκέναι·    16   αὕτη ἡ   διαθήκη    ἣν   διαθήσομαι
to have spoken,    this the  agreement  which I will agree
4314  846   3326  020 2250    1565      3004  2962
πρὸς αὐτοὺς μετὰ  τὰς ἡμέρας ἐκείνας,  λέγει κύριος·
to    them  after  the days   those,   says  Master;
1325   3551  1473  1909 2588   846    2532 1909  08
διδοὺς νόμους μου  ἐπὶ καρδίας αὐτῶν καὶ  ἐπὶ  τὴν
giving laws   of me on  hearts  of them and  on   the
1271    846    1924      846     17  2532
διάνοιαν αὐτῶν ἐπιγράψω  αὐτούς,  17  καὶ
intelligence of them I will write on them,    and
018    266    846   2532 018   458
τῶν  ἁμαρτιῶν αὐτῶν καὶ τῶν  ἀνομιῶν
of the sins  of them and of the lawlessnesses
846    3756 3361 3403       2089  18 3699  1161
αὐτῶν οὐ  μὴ  μνησθήσομαι ἔτι.  18 ὅπου  δὲ
of them not not  I will remember still.   Where but
859    3778   3765    4376    4012
ἄφεσις τούτων, οὐκέτι  προσφορὰ περὶ
sending off of these, no longer offering about
266    19  2192   3767  80   3954      1519
ἁμαρτίας. 19  Ἔχοντες οὖν,  ἀδελφοί,  παρρησίαν εἰς
sin.        Having then,  brothers,  boldness into
08  1529   022   40    1722 011  129     2424
τὴν εἴσοδον τῶν  ἁγίων  ἐν  τῷ αἵματι  Ἰησοῦ,
the entrance of the holies in  the blood  of Jesus,
3739  1457      1473    3598 4372     2532 2198
20 ἣν  ἐνεκαίνισεν ἡμῖν  ὁδὸν πρόσφατον καὶ ζῶσαν
   which he made new for us way  fresh     and living
1223  010 2665          3778 1510  06      4561
διὰ  τοῦ καταπετάσματος, τοῦτ' ἔστιν τῆς  σαρκὸς
through the veil,        this  is    of the flesh
846   21  2532 2409   3173 1909  04 3624  02    2316
αὐτοῦ, 21 καὶ ἱερέα  μέγαν ἐπὶ τὸν οἶκον τοῦ  θεοῦ,
of him,   and priest great on  the house of the God,
4334       3326 228     2588     1722
22 προσερχώμεθα    μετὰ ἀληθινῆς καρδίας ἐν
   we might come to with true    heart    in
4136         4102      4472              020
πληροφορίᾳ  πίστεως  ῥεραντισμένοι      τὰς
full persuasion of trust having been sprinkled the
2588   575   4893     4190     2532 3068
καρδίας ἀπὸ συνειδήσεως πονηρᾶς καὶ λελουσμένοι
hearts from conscience  evil    and having been washed
012 4983 5204    2513    23 2722       08
τὸ  σῶμα ὕδατι καθαρῷ· 23 κατέχωμεν    τὴν
the body in water clean;  we might hold on the
3671   06   1680    186     4103     1063 01
ὁμολογίαν τῆς ἐλπίδος ἀκλινῆ  πιστὸς γὰρ ὁ
confession of the hope unleaning trustful for the
1861           2532 2657
ἐπαγγειλάμενος, 24 καὶ κατανοῶμεν
one having promised, and we might think carefully
240      1519 3948     26    2532 2570 2041
ἀλλήλους εἰς παροξυσμὸν ἀγάπης καὶ καλῶν ἔργων,
one another to stimulation of love and  good  works,
25 3361 1459         08   1997      1438
   μὴ  ἐγκαταλείποντες τὴν ἐπισυναγωγὴν ἑαυτῶν,
   not leaving behind  the bringing    of ourselves,
                           together
2531  1485  5100   235  3870        2532
καθὼς ἔθος τισίν, ἀλλὰ παρακαλοῦντες, καὶ
just as custom in some, but encouraging,  and
5118    3123  3745     991    1448     08
τοσούτῳ μᾶλλον ὅσῳ  βλέπετε ἐγγίζουσαν τὴν
to such  more  as much as you see nearing   the
```

also testifies to us, for after saying,

16 "This is the covenant
    that I will make with
    them
    after those days, says
    the Lord:
I will put my laws in their
    hearts,
    and I will write them
    on their minds,"
17 he also adds,
"I will remember[a] their
    sins and their lawless
    deeds no more."
18 Where there is forgiveness
of these, there is no longer
any offering for sin.

19 Therefore, my friends,[b]
since we have confidence
to enter the sanctuary by
the blood of Jesus, 20 by the
new and living way that he
opened for us through the
curtain (that is, through his
flesh), 21 and since we have a
great priest over the house
of God, 22 let us approach
with a true heart in full
assurance of faith, with our
hearts sprinkled clean from
an evil conscience and our
bodies washed with pure
water. 23 Let us hold fast to
the confession of our hope
without wavering, for he who
has promised is faithful.
24 And let us consider how
to provoke one another
to love and good deeds,
25 not neglecting to meet
together, as is the habit
of some, but encouraging
one another, and all the
more as you see the Day
approaching.

---

a Gk on their minds and I will
  remember
b Gk Therefore, brothers

26 For if we willfully persist in sin after having received the knowledge of the truth, there no longer remains a sacrifice for sins, 27but a fearful prospect of judgment, and a fury of fire that will consume the adversaries. 28Anyone who has violated the law of Moses dies without mercy "on the testimony of two or three witnesses." 29How much worse punishment do you think will be deserved by those who have spurned the Son of God, profaned the blood of the covenant by which they were sanctified, and outraged the Spirit of grace? 30For we know the one who said, "Vengeance is mine, I will repay." And again, "The Lord will judge his people." 31It is a fearful thing to fall into the hands of the living God.

32 But recall those earlier days when, after you had been enlightened, you endured a hard struggle with sufferings, 33sometimes being publicly exposed to abuse and persecution, and sometimes being partners with those so treated. 34For you had compassion for those who were in prison, and you cheerfully accepted the plundering of your possessions, knowing

```
2250        1596       1063 264         1473  3326
ἡμέραν.  26  Ἑκουσίως  γὰρ  ἁμαρτανόντων  ἡμῶν  μετὰ
day.        Willingly  for   sinning       of us  after
012 2983     08  1922          06    225
τὸ  λαβεῖν   τὴν ἐπίγνωσιν  τῆς  ἀληθείας,
the to receive the perception of the truth,
3765        4012  266       620              2378
οὐκέτι  περὶ ἁμαρτιῶν  ἀπολείπεται    θυσία,
no longer about sins      there is left off sacrifice,
       5398    1161 5100 1561    2920       2532 4442
27  φοβερὰ  δέ  τις ἐκδοχὴ  κρίσεως  καὶ  πυρὸς
    fearful but some awaiting of judgment and of fire
2205      2068     3195    016 5227
ζῆλος  ἐσθίειν μέλλοντος τοὺς ὑπεναντίους.
jealousy to eat  being about the over against.
   114                5100 3551 3475       5565
28 ἀθετήσας        τις  νόμον Μωϋσέως  χωρὶς
   Having set aside some law of Moses without
3628       1909 1417 2228 5140   3144
οἰκτιρμῶν ἐπὶ δυσὶν ἢ  τρισὶν μάρτυσιν
compassions on two  or three testifiers
599        4214 1380     5501    515
ἀποθνῄσκει· 29 πόσῳ δοκεῖτε χείρονος ἀξιωθήσεται
dies;      in how much you think worse  will be worthy
5098      01  04  5207 02   2316 2662
τιμωρίας  ὁ  τὸν υἱὸν τοῦ  θεοῦ καταπατήσας
punishment the the son of the God having walked over
2532 012 129  06    1242       2839
καὶ  τὸ αἷμα τῆς  διαθήκης κοινὸν
also the blood of the agreement common
2233        1722 3739 37              2532 012
ἡγησάμενος  ἐν  ᾧ  ἡγιάσθη,      καὶ  τὸ
having considered in what he was made holy, and the
4151    06   5485     1796        3609a  1063 04
πνεῦμα τῆς  χάριτος ἐνυβρίσας; 30 οἴδαμεν γὰρ τὸν
spirit of the favor having abused? We know for the
3004       1473 1557        1473
εἰπόντα·   ἐμοὶ ἐκδίκησις,   ἐγὼ
one having said, to me bring out right, I
467       2532 3825 2919     2962
ἀνταποδώσω.  καὶ  πάλιν· κρινεῖ  κύριος
will give back again. And again, will judge Master
04  2992    846       5398   09 1706    1519
τὸν λαὸν  αὐτοῦ. 31 φοβερὸν τὸ ἐμπεσεῖν εἰς
the people of him. Fearful the to fall in into
5495    2316   2198     363        1161 020
χεῖρας θεοῦ ζῶντος. 32 Ἀναμιμνῄσκεσθε δὲ τὰς
hands of God living.   Remind yourselves but the
4387     2250  1722 3739 5461
πρότερον ἡμέρας, ἐν  αἷς  φωτισθέντες
former  days,   in  which having been lightened
4183   119     5278      3804        33 3778
πολλὴν ἄθλησιν ὑπεμείνατε παθημάτων,  τοῦτο
much   wrestling you endured sufferings, this
3303   3680      5037 2532 2347
μὲν   ὀνειδισμοῖς τε  καὶ  θλίψεσιν
indeed revilings both and  afflictions
2301      3778 1161 2844  014    3779
θεατριζόμενοι, τοῦτο δὲ κοινωνοὶ τῶν  οὕτως
being stared at, this  but partners of the thusly
390          1096         2532 1063 015
ἀναστρεφομένων γενηθέντες. 34 καὶ  γὰρ τοῖς
behaving       having become. And for to the
1198     4834        2532 08 724    022
δεσμίοις συνεπαθήσατε καὶ τὴν ἁρπαγὴν τῶν
prisoners you suffered with and the seizure of the
5225      1473  3326 5479 4327     1097
ὑπαρχόντων ὑμῶν μετὰ χαρᾶς προσεδέξασθε γινώσκοντες
possessions of you with joy you awaited knowing
```

2192	1438	2909	5223	2532 3306
ἔχειν	ἑαυτοὺς	κρείττονα	ὕπαρξιν	καὶ μένουσαν.
to have	yourselves	better	possession	and staying.

35 3361 577   3767 08   3954   1473
Μὴ ἀποβάλητε   οὖν τὴν παρρησίαν ὑμῶν,
Not you might throw off then the boldness of you,

3748 2192 3173   3405   **36** 5281   1063
ἥτις ἔχει μεγάλην μισθαποδοσίαν.   ὑπομονῆς γὰρ
which has great wage give back.   Patience for

2192   5532   2443 012 2307   02   2316 4160
ἔχετε χρείαν ἵνα τὸ θέλημα τοῦ θεοῦ ποιήσαντες
you have need that the want of the God having done

2865   08   1860   **37** 2089 1063 3398
κομίσησθε τὴν ἐπαγγελίαν.   ἔτι γὰρ μικρὸν
you might obtain the promise.   Still for little

3745 3745 01   2064   2240   2532 3756
ὅσον ὅσον, ὁ ἐρχόμενος ἥξει καὶ οὐ
so so, the one coming will come and not

5549   **38** 01 1161 1342   1473 1537
χρονίσει·   ὁ δὲ δίκαιός μου ἐκ
he will spend time; the but right of me from

4102   2198   2532 1437 5288   3756
πίστεως ζήσεται, καὶ ἐὰν ὑποστείληται, οὐκ
trust will live, and if he might withdraw, not

2106   05 5590 1473 1722 846   **39** 1473 1161
εὐδοκεῖ ἡ ψυχή μου ἐν αὐτῷ.   ἡμεῖς δὲ
thinks well the soul of me in him.   We but

3756 1510 5289   1519 684   235
οὐκ ἐσμὲν ὑποστολῆς εἰς ἀπώλειαν ἀλλὰ
not are of withdrawal into destruction but

4102   1519 4047   5590   **11:1** 1510 1161
πίστεως εἰς περιποίησιν ψυχῆς.   Ἔστιν δὲ
of trust into possession of soul.   Is but

4102   1679   5287   4229   1650
πίστις ἐλπιζομένων ὑπόστασις, πραγμάτων ἔλεγχος
trust of being hoped substance, practices rebuke

3756 991   **2** 1722 3778 1063 3140   013
οὐ βλεπομένων. ἐν ταύτῃ γὰρ ἐμαρτυρήθησαν οἱ
not of being seen. In this for testified the

4245   **3** 4102   3539
πρεσβύτεροι. Πίστει νοοῦμεν
older men. In trust we give thought

2675   016   165   4487   2316   1519 012
κατηρτίσθαι τοὺς αἰῶνας ῥήματι θεοῦ, εἰς τὸ
to be put in order the ages in word of God, for the

3361 1537 5316   012 991   1096
μὴ ἐκ φαινομένων τὸ βλεπόμενον γεγονέναι.
not from shining the being seen to have become.

4 4102   4183   2378   6   3844 2535
Πίστει πλείονα θυσίαν Ἅβελ παρὰ Κάϊν
In trust more sacrifice Abel from Cain

4374   03   2316 1223   3739 3140
προσήνεγκεν τῷ θεῷ, δι᾽ ἧς ἐμαρτυρήθη
offered to the God, through which he was testified

1510 1342   3140   1909 023 1435 846
εἶναι δίκαιος, μαρτυροῦντος ἐπὶ τοῖς δώροις αὐτοῦ
to be right, testifying on the gifts of him

02   2316 2532 1223   846   599   2089
τοῦ θεοῦ, καὶ δι᾽ αὐτῆς ἀποθανὼν ἔτι
of the God, and through it having died still

2980   **5** 4102   1802 3346   010 3361
λαλεῖ. Πίστει Ἐνὼχ μετετέθη τοῦ μὴ
he speaks. In trust Enoch was changed the not

3708 2288   2532 3756 2147   1360
ἰδεῖν θάνατον, καὶ οὐχ ηὑρίσκετο διότι
to see death, and not he was found because

3346   846   01 2316   4253   1063 06   3331
μετέθηκεν αὐτὸν ὁ θεός. πρὸ γὰρ τῆς μεταθέσεως
changed him the God. Before for the change

---

that you yourselves possessed something better and more lasting. 35 Do not, therefore, abandon that confidence of yours; it brings a great reward. 36 For you need endurance, so that when you have done the will of God, you may receive what was promised. 37 For yet

"in a very little while,
the one who is coming
will come and will
not delay;
38 but my righteous one
will live by faith.
My soul takes no
pleasure in anyone
who shrinks back."

39 But we are not among those who shrink back and so are lost, but among those who have faith and so are saved.

CHAPTER 11

Now faith is the assurance of things hoped for, the conviction of things not seen. 2 Indeed, by faith[a] our ancestors received approval. 3 By faith we understand that the worlds were prepared by the word of God, so that what is seen was made from things that are not visible.[b]

4 By faith Abel offered to God a more acceptable[c] sacrifice than Cain's. Through this he received approval as righteous, God himself giving approval to his gifts; he died, but through his faith[d] he still speaks. 5 By faith Enoch was taken so that he did not experience death; and "he was not found, because God had taken him."

---

[a] Gk by this
[b] Or was not made out of visible things
[c] Gk greater
[d] Gk through it

For it was attested before he was taken away that "he had pleased God." 6And without faith it is impossible to please God, for whoever would approach him must believe that he exists and that he rewards those who seek him. 7By faith Noah, warned by God about events as yet unseen, respected the warning and built an ark to save his household; by this he condemned the world and became an heir to the righteousness that is in accordance with faith.

8 By faith Abraham obeyed when he was called to set out for a place that he was to receive as an inheritance; and he set out, not knowing where he was going. 9By faith he stayed for a time in the land he had been promised, as in a foreign land, living in tents, as did Isaac and Jacob, who were heirs with him of the same promise. 10For he looked forward to the city that has foundations, whose architect and builder is God. 11By faith he received power of procreation, even though he was too old— and Sarah herself was barren—because he considered him faithful who had promised.[a] 12Therefore from one person,

---

a Or By faith Sarah herself, though
barren, received power to conceive,
even when she was too old, because
she considered him faithful who had
promised.

3140	2100	03	2316	6	5565	1161
μεμαρτύρηται	εὐαρεστηκέναι	τῷ	θεῷ·		χωρὶς	δὲ
he has been testified	to be well pleasing	to the	God;		without	but

4102	102	2100	4100	1063
πίστεως	ἀδύνατον	εὐαρεστῆσαι·	πιστεῦσαι	γὰρ
trust	unable	to well please;	to trust	for

1163	04	4334	03	2316	3754
δεῖ		τὸν προσερχόμενον	τῷ	θεῷ	ὅτι
it is necessary		the one coming to	in	the God	that

1510	2532	015	1567	846	3406
ἔστιν	καὶ	τοῖς	ἐκζητοῦσιν	αὐτὸν	μισθαποδότης
he is	and	to the ones	seeking out	him	wage give back

1096	7	4102	5537	3575	4012	022
γίνεται.		Πίστει	χρηματισθεὶς	Νῶε	περὶ	τῶν
he becomes.		In trust	having been warned	Noah	about	the

3369	991	2125	2680	2787
μηδέπω	βλεπομένων,	εὐλαβηθεὶς	κατεσκεύασεν	κιβωτὸν
but not yet	being seen,	having been reverent	prepared	box

1519	4991	02	3624	846	1223	3739
εἰς	σωτηρίαν	τοῦ	οἴκου	αὐτοῦ	δι'	ἧς
for	deliverance	of the	house	of him	through	which

2632	04	2889	2532	06	2596	4102
κατέκρινεν	τὸν	κόσμον,	καὶ	τῆς	κατὰ	πίστιν
he condemned	the	world,	and	the	by	trust

1343	1096	2818	8	4102
δικαιοσύνης	ἐγένετο	κληρονόμος.		Πίστει
rightness	he became	inheritor.		In trust

2564	11	5219	1831	1519	5117
καλούμενος	Ἀβραὰμ	ὑπήκουσεν	ἐξελθεῖν	εἰς	τόπον
being called	Abraham	obeyed	to go out	to	place

3739	3195	2983	1519	2817	2532
ὃν	ἤμελλεν	λαμβάνειν	εἰς	κληρονομίαν,	καὶ
which	he was about	to receive	for	inheritance,	and

1831	3361	1987	4226	2064
ἐξῆλθεν	μὴ	ἐπιστάμενος	ποῦ	ἔρχεται.
he went out	not	understanding	where	he goes.

9	4102	3939	1519	1093	06
	Πίστει	παρῴκησεν	εἰς	γῆν	τῆς
	In trust	he lived transiently	in	land	of the

1860	5613	245	1722	4633
ἐπαγγελίας	ὡς	ἀλλοτρίαν	ἐν	σκηναῖς
promise	as	belonging to other	in	tents

2730	3326	2464	2532	2384	014
κατοικήσας	μετὰ	Ἰσαὰκ	καὶ	Ἰακὼβ	τῶν
having resided	with	Isaac	and	Jacob	the

4789	06	1860	06	846
συγκληρονόμων	τῆς	ἐπαγγελίας	τῆς	αὐτῆς·
co-inheritors	the	of the promise	the	same;

10	1551	1063	08	016	2310
	ἐξεδέχετο	γὰρ	τὴν	τοὺς	θεμελίους
	he was waiting for	for	the	the	foundations

2192	4172	3739	5079	2532	1217	01
ἔχουσαν	πόλιν	ἧς	τεχνίτης	καὶ	δημιουργὸς	ὁ
having	city	whose	craftsman	and	constructor	the

2316	11	4102	2532	846	4564	4723	1411
θεός.		Πίστει	καὶ	αὐτὴ	Σάρρα	στεῖρα	δύναμιν
God.		In trust	also	herself	Sarra	sterile	power

1519	2602	4690	2983	2532	3844	2540
εἰς	καταβολὴν	σπέρματος	ἔλαβεν	καὶ	παρὰ	καιρὸν
for	foundation	of seed	received	and	from	season

2244	1893	4103	2233	04
ἡλικίας,	ἐπεὶ	πιστὸν	ἡγήσατο	τὸν
of stature,	since	trustful	she considered	the one

1861	12	1352	2532	575	1520
ἐπαγγειλάμενον.		διὸ	καὶ	ἀφ'	ἑνὸς
having promised.		Wherefore	also	from	one

```
1080              2532 3778  3499                    2531    021
ἐγεννήθησαν, καὶ  ταῦτα νενεκρωμένου,      καθὼς  τὰ
were born,    and  these having been dead,  just as  the
798   02     3772   011     4128       2532 5613 05
ἄστρα τοῦ   οὐρανοῦ τῷ    πλήθει    καὶ ὡς   ἡ
stars of the heaven  in the quantity and as   the
285   05   3844  012 5491   06  2281        05
ἄμμος ἡ    παρὰ τὸ χεῖλος τῆς θαλάσσης ἡ
sand  the  along the lip   the  sea        the
382            13 2596   4102  599      3778 3956
ἀναρίθμητος.     Κατὰ  πίστιν ἀπέθανον οὗτοι πάντες,
innumerable.  By   trust  died        these all,
3361 2983           020 1860       235  4207
μὴ   λαβόντες      τὰς ἐπαγγελίας ἀλλὰ πόρρωθεν
not  having received the promises  but  from far
846   3708      2532 782            2532
αὐτὰς ἰδόντες   καὶ ἀσπασάμενοι  καὶ
them  having seen and  having greeted and
3670                3754 3581         2532 3927
ὁμολογήσαντες      ὅτι  ξένοι      καὶ  παρεπίδημοί
having confessed   that strangers  and  transients
1510   1909 06 1093      14 013 1063 5108       3004
εἰσιν  ἐπὶ  τῆς γῆς.      οἱ  γὰρ τοιαῦτα λέγοντες
they are on  the earth.  The for such      saying
1718           3754 3968      1934          15 2532 1487
ἐμφανίζουσιν ὅτι  πατρίδα  ἐπιζητοῦσιν.     καὶ εἰ
make visible that fatherland they seek after. And if
3303  1565       3421           575  3739
μὲν  ἐκείνης ἐμνημόνευον      ἀφ’ ἧς
indeed that    they were remembering from which
1543a        2192    302 2540    344
ἐξέβησαν,   εἶχον  ἂν  καιρὸν ἀνακάμψαι·
they came out, they had -   season to bend again;
16 3568 1161 2909        3713      3778 1510
   νῦν  δὲ  κρείττονος ὀρέγονται, τοῦτ’ ἔστιν
   now  but of better they strive, this is
2032          1352    3756 1870          846     01
ἐπουρανίου. διὸ    οὐκ ἐπαισχύνεται αὐτοὺς ὁ
on heavenly. Wherefore not is ashamed them  the
2316 2316 1941           846    2090         1063 846
θεὸς θεὸς ἐπικαλεῖσθαι αὐτῶν· ἡτοίμασεν γὰρ αὐτοῖς
God  God  to be called on them; he prepared for them
4172       17 4102       4374           11   04  2464
πόλιν.       Πίστει  προσενήνοχεν Ἀβραὰμ τὸν Ἰσαὰκ
city.    In trust  has offered    Abraham the  Isaac
3985              2532 04 3439        4374
πειραζόμενος    καὶ τὸν μονογενῆ προσέφερεν,
being pressured and the only born he was offering,
01 020 1860       324                18 4314 3739
ὁ  τὰς ἐπαγγελίας ἀναδεξάμενος,       πρὸς ὃν
the the promises  having welcomed again, to  whom
2980         3754 1722 2464  2564          1473
ἐλαλήθη     ὅτι  ἐν  Ἰσαὰκ κληθήσεταί  σοι
it was spoken that in  Isaac will be called to you
4690      19 3049            3754 2532 1537 3498
σπέρμα,      λογισάμενος    ὅτι  καὶ  ἐκ  νεκρῶν
seed,     having reasoned   that also from dead
1453       1415    01 2316  3606        846   2532 1722
ἐγείρειν δυνατὸς ὁ θεός, ὅθεν       αὐτὸν καὶ ἐν
to raise power   the God, from where him  also in
3850        2865        20 4102     2532 4012
παραβολῇ   ἐκομίσατο.    Πίστει  καὶ περὶ
parallel story he obtained. In trust also concerning
3195        2127      2464  04  2384   2532 04
μελλόντων εὐλόγησεν Ἰσαὰκ τὸν Ἰακὼβ καὶ τὸν
being about spoke well Isaac the  Jacob and the
2269    21 4102      2384   599         1538  014
Ἡσαῦ.     Πίστει  Ἰακὼβ ἀποθνήσκων ἕκαστον τῶν
Esau.   In trust Jacob dying        each     of the
```

and this one as good as dead, descendants were born, "as many as the stars of heaven and as the innumerable grains of sand by the seashore."

13 All of these died in faith without having received the promises, but from a distance they saw and greeted them. They confessed that they were strangers and foreigners on the earth, [14]for people who speak in this way make it clear that they are seeking a homeland. [15]If they had been thinking of the land that they had left behind, they would have had opportunity to return. [16]But as it is, they desire a better country, that is, a heavenly one. Therefore God is not ashamed to be called their God; indeed, he has prepared a city for them.

17 By faith Abraham, when put to the test, offered up Isaac. He who had received the promises was ready to offer up his only son, [18]of whom he had been told, "It is through Isaac that descendants shall be named for you." [19]He considered the fact that God is able even to raise someone from the dead— and figuratively speaking, he did receive him back. [20]By faith Isaac invoked blessings for the future on Jacob and Esau. [21]By faith Jacob, when dying, blessed each of the

sons of Joseph, "bowing in worship over the top of his staff." 22By faith Joseph, at the end of his life, made mention of the exodus of the Israelites and gave instructions about his burial.*a*

23 By faith Moses was hidden by his parents for three months after his birth, because they saw that the child was beautiful; and they were not afraid of the king's edict.*b* 24By faith Moses, when he was grown up, refused to be called a son of Pharaoh's daughter, 25choosing rather to share ill-treatment with the people of God than to enjoy the fleeting pleasures of sin. 26He considered abuse suffered for the Christ*c* to be greater wealth than the treasures of Egypt, for he was looking ahead to the reward. 27By faith he left Egypt, unafraid of the king's anger; for he persevered as though*d* he saw him who is invisible. 28By faith he kept the Passover and the sprinkling of blood, so that the destroyer of the firstborn would not touch the firstborn of Israel.*e*

29 By faith the people passed through the Red Sea as if it were dry land, but when the Egyptians attempted to do so they were drowned. 30By faith the walls of Jericho fell after they had been encircled for seven days.

---

a Gk *his bones*
b Other ancient authorities add *By faith Moses, when he was grown up, killed the Egyptian, because he observed the humiliation of his people* (Gk *brothers*)
c Or *the Messiah*
d Or *because*
e Gk *would not touch them*

5207	2501	2127	2532	4352	1909	012
υἱῶν	Ἰωσὴφ	εὐλόγησεν καὶ	προσεκύνησεν	ἐπὶ	τὸ
sons	Joseph	spoke well and	he worshiped	on	the

206	06	4464	846	4102	2501	5053
ἄκρον	τῆς	ῥάβδου αὐτοῦ.	22 Πίστει	Ἰωσὴφ	τελευτῶν
tip	of	the rod	of him.	In trust Joseph	dying

4012	06	1841	014	5207	2474	3421
περὶ	τῆς	ἐξόδου	τῶν	υἱῶν	Ἰσραὴλ	ἐμνημόνευσεν
about	the	way out	of the	sons	Israel	remembered

2532	4012	022	3747	846	1781	4102
καὶ	περὶ	τῶν	ὀστέων	αὐτοῦ	ἐνετείλατο.	23 Πίστει
and	about	the	bones	of him	he commanded.	In trust

3475	1080	2928	5150	5259
Μωϋσῆς	γεννηθεὶς	ἐκρύβη	τρίμηνον	ὑπὸ
Moses	having been born	was hidden	three months	by

014	3962	846	1360	3708	791	012
τῶν	πατέρων	αὐτοῦ,	διότι	εἶδον	ἀστεῖον	τὸ
the	fathers	of him,	because	they saw	well-formed	the

3813	2532	3756	5399	012	1297	02
παιδίον	καὶ	οὐκ	ἐφοβήθησαν	τὸ	διάταγμα	τοῦ
small child	and	not	they feared	the	directive	of the

935	4102	3475	3173	1096
βασιλέως.	24 Πίστει	Μωϋσῆς	μέγας	γενόμενος
king.	In trust	Moses	great	having become

720	3004	5207	2364	5328
ἠρνήσατο	λέγεσθαι	υἱὸς	θυγατρὸς	Φαραώ,
denied	to be said	son	of daughter	of Pharaoh,

3123	138	4778	03	2992
25 μᾶλλον	ἑλόμενος	συγκακουχεῖσθαι	τῷ	λαῷ
more	having chosen	to have bad	with	the people

02	2316	2228	4340	2192	266	619
τοῦ	θεοῦ	ἢ	πρόσκαιρον	ἔχειν	ἁμαρτίας	ἀπόλαυσιν,
of	the God	or	to season	to have	of sin	enjoyment,

3173	4149	2233	014	125
26 μείζονα	πλοῦτον	ἡγησάμενος	τῶν	Αἰγύπτου
greater	rich	having considered	the of	Egypt

2344	04	3680	02	5547
θησαυρῶν	τὸν	ὀνειδισμὸν	τοῦ	χριστοῦ·
treasures	the	reviling	of the	Christ;

578	1063	1519	08	3405
ἀπέβλεπεν	γὰρ	εἰς	τὴν	μισθαποδοσίαν.
he was looking off	for	to	the	wage give back.

4102	2641	125	3361	5399
27 Πίστει	κατέλιπεν	Αἴγυπτον	μὴ	φοβηθεὶς
In trust	he left behind	Egypt	not	having feared

04	2372	02	935	04	1063	517	5613	3708
τὸν	θυμὸν	τοῦ	βασιλέως·	τὸν	γὰρ	ἀόρατον	ὡς	ὁρῶν
the	fury	of the	king;	the	for	unseen	as	seeing

2594	4102	4160	012	3957	2532
ἐκαρτέρησεν.	28 Πίστει	πεποίηκεν	τὸ	πάσχα	καὶ
he persevered.	In trust	he has made	the	passover	and

08	4378	010	129	2443	3361	01	3645
τὴν	πρόσχυσιν	τοῦ	αἵματος,	ἵνα	μὴ	ὁ	ὀλοθρεύων
the	pouring	of the	blood,	that	not	the	destroying

024	4416	2345	846	4102
τὰ	πρωτότοκα	θίγῃ	αὐτῶν.	29 Πίστει
the firstborn ones		might handle	them.	In trust

1224	08	2063	2281	5613	1223
διέβησαν	τὴν	ἐρυθρὰν	θάλασσαν	ὡς	διὰ
they went	through	the Red	Sea	as	through

3584	1093	3739	3984	2983	013
ξηρᾶς	γῆς,	ἧς	πεῖραν	λαβόντες	οἱ
dried out	earth,	which	trial	having taken	the

124	2666	4102	021	5038
Αἰγύπτιοι	κατεπόθησαν.	30 Πίστει	τὰ	τείχη
Egyptians	were swallowed down.	In trust	the	walls

2410	4098	2944	1909	2033
Ἰεριχὼ	ἔπεσαν	κυκλωθέντα	ἐπὶ	ἑπτὰ
Jericho	fell	having been encircled	on	seven

2250	**31** 4102	4460	05	4204	3756
ἡμέρας.	Πίστει	ʿΡαὰβ	ἡ	πόρνη	οὐ
days.	In trust	Rahab	the	prostitute	not

4881	015	544	1209	016
συναπώλετο	τοῖς	ἀπειθήσασιν	δεξαμένη	τοὺς
was destroyed	the	ones having	having	the
with		disobeyed	welcomed	

2685	3326	1515	**32** 2532	5101	2089
κατασκόπους	μετ᾽	εἰρήνης.	Καὶ	τί	ἔτι
spies	with	peace.	And	what	still

3004	1952	1473	1063	1334
λέγω;	ἐπιλείψει	με	γὰρ	διηγούμενον
might I say?	It will leave on	me	for	narrating

01	5550	4012	1066	913	4546	2422
ὁ	χρόνος	περὶ	Γεδεών,	Βαράκ,	Σαμψών,	᾽Ιεφθάε,
the	time	about	Gideon,	Barak,	Sampson,	Jephtha,

1160a	5037	2532	4545	2532	014	4396	**33** 3739
Δαυὶδ	τε	καὶ	Σαμουὴλ	καὶ	τῶν	προφητῶν,	οἳ
David	both	and	Samuel	and	the	spokesmen,	who

1223	4102	2610	932	2038
διὰ	πίστεως	κατηγωνίσαντο	βασιλείας,	εἰργάσαντο
through	trust	contended over	kingdoms,	worked

1343	2013	1860	5420	4750
δικαιοσύνην,	ἐπέτυχον	ἐπαγγελιῶν,	ἔφραξαν	στόματα
rightness,	obtained	promises,	stopped	mouths

3023	**34** 4570	1411	4442	5343	4750
λεόντων,	ἔσβεσαν	δύναμιν	πυρός,	ἔφυγον	στόματα
of lions,	quenched	power	of fire,	fled	mouths

3162	1412	575	769	1096
μαχαίρης,	ἐδυναμώθησαν	ἀπὸ	ἀσθενείας,	ἐγενήθησαν
of sword,	were powered	from	weakness,	became

2478	1722	4171	3925	2827	245
ἰσχυροὶ	ἐν	πολέμῳ,	παρεμβολὰς	ἔκλιναν	ἀλλοτρίων.
strong	in	war,	barracks	bowed	of others.

35 2983	1135	1537	386	016	3498
Ἔλαβον	γυναῖκες	ἐξ	ἀναστάσεως	τοὺς	νεκροὺς
Received	women	from	standing up	the	dead

846	243	1161	5178	3756
αὐτῶν·	ἄλλοι	δὲ	ἐτυμπανίσθησαν	οὐ
of them;	others	but	were tortured	not

4327	08	629	2443	2909
προσδεξάμενοι	τὴν	ἀπολύτρωσιν,	ἵνα	κρείττονος
having awaited	the	redemption,	that of	better

386	5177	**36** 2087	1161	1701
ἀναστάσεως	τύχωσιν·	ἕτεροι	δὲ	ἐμπαιγμῶν
standing up	they might obtain;	others	but	mockings

2532	3148	3984	2983	2089	1161	1199
καὶ	μαστίγων	πεῖραν	ἔλαβον,	ἔτι	δὲ	δεσμῶν
and	of scourges	trial	received,	still	but	of chains

2532	5438	**37** 3034	4249	1722
καὶ	φυλακῆς·	ἐλιθάσθησαν,	ἐπρίσθησαν,	ἐν
and	guard;	they were stoned,	were sawn,	in

5408	3162	599	4022	1722
φόνῳ	μαχαίρης	ἀπέθανον,	περιῆλθον	ἐν
murder	of sword	died,	they went around	in

3374	1722	122	1192	5302
μηλωταῖς,	ἐν	αἰγείοις	δέρμασιν,	ὑστερούμενοι,
sheepskins,	in	goats	skins,	being in lack,

2346	2558	**38** 3739	3756	1510
θλιβόμενοι,	κακουχούμενοι,	ὧν	οὐκ	ἦν
being afflicted,	being treated badly,	of whom	not	was

514	01	2889	1909	2047	4105	2532
ἄξιος	ὁ	κόσμος,	ἐπὶ	ἐρημίαις	πλανώμενοι	καὶ
worthy	the	world,	on	deserts	being deceived	and

3735	2532	4693	2532	019	3692	06	1093
ὄρεσιν	καὶ	σπηλαίοις	καὶ	ταῖς	ὀπαῖς	τῆς	γῆς.
in hills	and	caves	and	the	holes	of the	earth.

39 2532	3778	3956	3140	1223	06
Καὶ	οὗτοι	πάντες	μαρτυρηθέντες	διὰ	τῆς
And	these	all	having being testified	through	the

[31]By faith Rahab the prostitute did not perish with those who were disobedient,[a] because she had received the spies in peace.

[32]And what more should I say? For time would fail me to tell of Gideon, Barak, Samson, Jephthah, of David and Samuel and the prophets— [33]who through faith conquered kingdoms, administered justice, obtained promises, shut the mouths of lions, [34]quenched raging fire, escaped the edge of the sword, won strength out of weakness, became mighty in war, put foreign armies to flight. [35]Women received their dead by resurrection. Others were tortured, refusing to accept release, in order to obtain a better resurrection. [36]Others suffered mocking and flogging, and even chains and imprisonment. [37]They were stoned to death, they were sawn in two,[b] they were killed by the sword; they went about in skins of sheep and goats, destitute, persecuted, tormented— [38]of whom the world was not worthy. They wandered in deserts and mountains, and in caves and holes in the ground.

[39]Yet all these, though they were commended for their faith,

---

[a] Or unbelieving

[b] Other ancient authorities add they were tempted

did not receive what was promised, [40]since God had provided something better so that they would not, apart from us, be made perfect.

CHAPTER 12

Therefore, since we are surrounded by so great a cloud of witnesses, let us also lay aside every weight and the sin that clings so closely,[a] and let us run with perseverance the race that is set before us, [2]looking to Jesus the pioneer and perfecter of our faith, who for the sake of[b] the joy that was set before him endured the cross, disregarding its shame, and has taken his seat at the right hand of the throne of God.

3 Consider him who endured such hostility against himself from sinners,[c] so that you may not grow weary or lose heart. [4]In your struggle against sin you have not yet resisted to the point of shedding your blood. [5]And you have forgotten the exhortation that addresses you as children—

"My child, do not regard
    lightly the discipline
    of the Lord,
or lose heart when you
    are punished by him;
[6] for the Lord disciplines
    those whom he loves,
    and chastises every child
    whom he accepts."

[7]Endure trials for the sake of discipline. God is treating you as children; for what child is there whom a parent does not discipline?

---

[a] Other ancient authorities read *sin that easily distracts*

[b] Or *who instead of*

[c] Other ancient authorities read *such hostility from sinners against themselves*

4102	3756	2865	08	1860	**40**	02	2316
πίστεως	οὐκ	ἐκομίσαντο	τὴν	ἐπαγγελίαν,		τοῦ	θεοῦ
trust	not	obtained	the	promise,		of the	God

4012	1473	2909	5100	4265		2443	3361
περὶ	ἡμῶν	κρεῖττόν	τι	προβλεψαμένου,		ἵνα	μὴ
about	us	better	some	having seen before,		that	not

5565	1473	5048		**12:1**	5105
χωρὶς	ἡμῶν	τελειωθῶσιν.			Τοιγαροῦν
without	us	they might be complete.			Consequently

2532	1473	5118	2192	4029	1473	3509
καὶ	ἡμεῖς	τοσοῦτον	ἔχοντες	περικείμενον	ἡμῖν	νέφος
also	we	such	having	setting around us		cloud

3144	3591	659	3956	2532	08
μαρτύρων,	ὄγκον	ἀποθέμενοι	πάντα	καὶ	τὴν
of testifiers	weight	having set off	all	and	the

2139	266	1223	5281	5143
εὐπερίστατον	ἁμαρτίαν,	δι᾽	ὑπομονῆς	τρέχωμεν
well-wrapped	sin,	through	patience	we might run

04	4295	1473	73	**2**	872	1519	04
τὸν	προκείμενον	ἡμῖν	ἀγῶνα		ἀφορῶντες	εἰς	τὸν
the	lying before us		contest		seeing off	into	the

06	4102	747	2532	5051	2424	3739
τῆς	πίστεως	ἀρχηγὸν	καὶ	τελειωτὴν	Ἰησοῦν,	ὃς
of the	trust	beginner	and	completer	Jesus,	who

473	06	4295	846	5479	5278
ἀντὶ	τῆς	προκειμένης	αὐτῷ	χαρᾶς	ὑπέμεινεν
in place of	the	lying before	him	joy	endured

4716	152	2706	1722	1188	5037
σταυρὸν	αἰσχύνης	καταφρονήσας	ἐν	δεξιᾷ	τε
cross	shame	having thought down	in	right	and

02	2362	02	2316	2523	**3**	357
τοῦ	θρόνου	τοῦ	θεοῦ	κεκάθικεν.		ἀναλογίσασθε
of the	throne	of the	God	has sat.		Reason up

1063	04	5108	5278	5259	014	268
γὰρ	τὸν	τοιαύτην	ὑπομεμενηκότα	ὑπὸ	τῶν	ἁμαρτωλῶν
for	the	such one	having endured	by	the	sinners

1519	1438	485	2443	3361	2577
εἰς	ἑαυτὸν	ἀντιλογίαν,	ἵνα	μὴ	κάμητε
for	himself	word against,	that	not	you might weary

019	5590	1473	1590	**4**	3768	3360
ταῖς	ψυχαῖς	ὑμῶν	ἐκλυόμενοι.		Οὔπω	μέχρις
the	souls	of you	being loosed out.		Not yet	until

129	478	4314	08	266
αἵματος	ἀντικατέστητε	πρὸς	τὴν	ἁμαρτίαν
blood	you stood up against	to	the	sin

464	**5**	2532	1585	06
ἀνταγωνιζόμενοι.		καὶ	ἐκλέλησθε	τῆς
contesting against.		And	you have forgotten	the

3874	3748	1473	5613	5207	1256
παρακλήσεως,	ἥτις	ὑμῖν	ὡς	υἱοῖς	διαλέγεται·
encouragement,	which	to you	as	sons	he disputes;

5207	1473	3361	3643	3809
υἱέ	μου,	μὴ	ὀλιγώρει	παιδείας
son	of me,	not	think little of	child instruction

2962	3366	1590	5259	846	1651
κυρίου	μηδὲ	ἐκλύου	ὑπ᾽	αὐτοῦ	ἐλεγχόμενος·
of Master	but not	be loosed out	by	him	being rebuked;

6	3739	1063	25	2962	3811	3146	1161
	ὃν	γὰρ	ἀγαπᾷ	κύριος	παιδεύει,	μαστιγοῖ	δὲ
	whom	for	loves	Master	he instructs	scourges	but
					as child,		

3956	5207	3739	3858	**7**	1519	3809
πάντα	υἱὸν	ὃν	παραδέχεται.		εἰς	παιδείαν
all	son	whom	he accepts.		For	child instruction

5278	5613	5207	1473	4374	01	2316
ὑπομένετε,	ὡς	υἱοῖς	ὑμῖν	προσφέρεται	ὁ	θεός.
endure,	as	sons	to you	offers	the	God.

5101	1063	5207	3739	3756	3811	3962
τίς	γὰρ	υἱὸς	ὃν	οὐ	παιδεύει	πατήρ;
What	for	son	whom	not	instructs	as child father?

8 1487 1161 5565 1510 3809 3739
εἰ δὲ χωρὶς ἐστε παιδείας ἧς
If but without you are child instruction of which

3353 1096 3956 686 3541 2532
μέτοχοι γεγόνασιν πάντες, ἄρα νόθοι καὶ
sharers have become all, then illegitimate and

3756 5207 1510 **9** 1534 016 3303 06 4561
οὐχ υἱοί ἐστε. εἶτα τοὺς μὲν τῆς σαρκὸς
not sons you are. Then the indeed of the flesh

1473 3962 2192 3810 2532
ἡμῶν πατέρας εἴχομεν παιδευτὰς καὶ
of us fathers we had child instructors and

1788 3756 4183 1161 3123
ἐνετρεπόμεθα· οὐ πολὺ [δὲ] μᾶλλον
we were regarding; not much but more

5293 03 3962 022 4151 2532
ὑποταγησόμεθα τῷ πατρὶ τῶν πνευμάτων καὶ
we will be subject to the father of the spirits and

2198 **10** 013 3303 1063 4314 3641 2250 2596
ζήσομεν; οἱ μὲν γὰρ πρὸς ὀλίγας ἡμέρας κατὰ
we will live? The indeed for to few days by

012 1380 846 3811 01
τὸ δοκοῦν αὐτοῖς ἐπαίδευον, ὁ
the thinking to them were instructing as a child, the

1161 1909 012 4851 1519 012 3335 06
δὲ ἐπὶ τὸ συμφέρον εἰς τὸ μεταλαβεῖν τῆς
but on the advantage for the to take with the

41 846 **11** 3956 1161 3809 4314
ἁγιότητος αὐτοῦ. πᾶσα δὲ παιδεία πρὸς
holiness of him. All but child instruction to

3303 012 3918 3756 1380 5479 1510
μὲν τὸ παρὸν οὐ δοκεῖ χαρᾶς εἶναι
indeed the being present not he thinks joy to be

235 3077 5306 1161 2590 1516 015
ἀλλὰ λύπης, ὕστερον δὲ καρπὸν εἰρηνικὸν τοῖς
but grief, later but fruit peaceable to the ones

1223 846 1128 591
δι᾽ αὐτῆς γεγυμνασμένοις ἀποδίδωσιν
through it having been exercised it gives back

1343 **12** 1352 020 3935
δικαιοσύνης. Διὸ τὰς παρειμένας
rightness. Wherefore the having fallen along

5495 2532 024 3886 1119 461
χεῖρας καὶ τὰ παραλελυμένα γόνατα ἀνορθώσατε,
hands and the paralyzed knees straighten up,

13 2532 5163 3717 4160 015 4228 1473
καὶ τροχιὰς ὀρθὰς ποιεῖτε τοῖς ποσὶν ὑμῶν,
and tracks straight make for the feet of you,

2443 3361 09 5560 1624
ἵνα μὴ τὸ χωλὸν ἐκτραπῇ,
that not the lame might be turned out,

2390 1161 3123 **14** 1515 1377 3326
ἰαθῇ δὲ μᾶλλον. Εἰρήνην διώκετε μετὰ
he might be cured but more. Peace pursue with

3956 2532 04 38 3739 5565 3762
πάντων καὶ τὸν ἁγιασμόν, οὗ χωρὶς οὐδεὶς
all and the holiness, which without no one

3708 04 2962 **15** 1983 3361 5100
ὄψεται τὸν κύριον, ἐπισκοποῦντες μή τις
will see the Master, overseeing not some

5302 575 06 5485 02 2316 3361 5100
ὑστερῶν ἀπὸ τῆς χάριτος τοῦ θεοῦ, μή τις
being in lack from the favor of the God, not some

4491 4088 507 5453 1776 2532
ῥίζα πικρίας ἄνω φύουσα ἐνοχλῇ καὶ
root of bitterness up sprouting might annoy and

1223 846 3392 4183 **16** 3361 5100 4205
δι᾽ αὐτῆς μιανθῶσιν πολλοί, μή τις πόρνος
through it might be many, not some sexually
defiled immoral

[8]If you do not have that discipline in which all children share, then you are illegitimate and not his children. [9]Moreover, we had human parents to discipline us, and we respected them. Should we not be even more willing to be subject to the Father of spirits and live? [10]For they disciplined us for a short time as seemed best to them, but he disciplines us for our good, in order that we may share his holiness. [11]Now, discipline always seems painful rather than pleasant at the time, but later it yields the peaceful fruit of righteousness to those who have been trained by it.

[12]Therefore lift your drooping hands and strengthen your weak knees, [13]and make straight paths for your feet, so that what is lame may not be put out of joint, but rather be healed.

[14]Pursue peace with everyone, and the holiness without which no one will see the Lord. [15]See to it that no one fails to obtain the grace of God; that no root of bitterness springs up and causes trouble, and through it many become defiled. [16]See to it that no one

becomes like Esau, an immoral and godless person, who sold his birthright for a single meal. [17]You know that later, when he wanted to inherit the blessing, he was rejected, for he found no chance to repent,[a] even though he sought the blessing[b] with tears.

18 You have not come to something[c] that can be touched, a blazing fire, and darkness, and gloom, and a tempest, [19]and the sound of a trumpet, and a voice whose words made the hearers beg that not another word be spoken to them. [20](For they could not endure the order that was given, "If even an animal touches the mountain, it shall be stoned to death." [21]Indeed, so terrifying was the sight that Moses said, "I tremble with fear.") [22]But you have come to Mount Zion and to the city of the living God, the heavenly Jerusalem, and to innumerable angels in festal gathering, [23]and to the assembly[d] of the firstborn who are enrolled in heaven, and to God the judge of all, and to the spirits of the righteous made perfect, [24]and to Jesus, the mediator of a new covenant, and to the sprinkled blood that speaks a better word than the blood of Abel.

25 See that you do not refuse the one who is speaking; for if they did not escape when they refused the one who warned them on earth,

[a] Or no chance to change his father's mind
[b] Gk it
[c] Other ancient authorities read a mountain
[d] Or angels, and to the festal gathering [23]and assembly

2228	952		5613	2269	3739	473		1035

ἢ βέβηλος ὡς 'Ησαῦ, ὃς ἀντὶ βρώσεως
or desecrator as Esau, who in place of food

1520	591		024	4415		1438

μιᾶς ἀπέδετο τὰ πρωτοτόκια ἑαυτοῦ.
one gave off the first child rights of himself.

17 | 3609a | 1063 | 3754 | 2532 | 3347 | | 2309 |

ἴστε γὰρ ὅτι καὶ μετέπειτα θέλων
You know for that even afterward wanting

| 2816 | 08 | 2129 | 593 |

κληρονομῆσαι τὴν εὐλογίαν ἀπεδοκιμάσθη,
to inherit the good word he was rejected,

| 3341 | 1063 | 5117 | 3756 | 2147 | 2539 |

μετανοίας γὰρ τόπον οὐχ εὗρεν καίπερ
change of mind for place not he found even indeed

| 3326 | 1144 | 1567 | 846 | **18** 3756 1063 |

μετὰ δακρύων ἐκζητήσας αὐτήν. **18** Οὐ γὰρ
with tears having sought out it. Not for

| 4334 | 5584 | 2532 2545 |

προσεληλύθατε ψηλαφωμένῳ καὶ κεκαυμένῳ
you have come to being touched and having been burned

| 4442 | 2532 | 1105 | 2532 | 2217 | 2532 | 2366 | **19** 2532 |

πυρὶ καὶ γνόφῳ καὶ ζόφῳ καὶ θυέλλῃ **19** καὶ
in fire and dark and gloom and storm and

| 4536 | 2279 | 2532 5456 | 4487 | 3739 | 013 |

σάλπιγγος ἤχῳ καὶ φωνῇ ῥημάτων, ἧς οἱ
trumpet sound and sound of words, which the

| 191 | 3868 | 3361 4369 | 846 |

ἀκούσαντες παρῃτήσαντο μὴ προστεθῆναι αὐτοῖς
ones having heard rejected not to be set to them

| 3056 | **20** 3756 5342 | 1063 012 |

λόγον, **20** οὐκ ἔφερον γὰρ τὸ
word, not they were carrying for the

| 1291 | 2579 | 2342 | 2345 | 010 |

διαστελλόμενον· κἂν θηρίον θίγῃ τοῦ
being commanded; even if wild animal might handle the

| 3735 | 3036 | | 2532 3779 | 5398 | 1510 |

ὄρους, λιθοβοληθήσεται· **21** καί, οὕτω φοβερὸν ἦν
hill, it will be stoned; and, thusly fearful was

| 09 | 5324 | 3475 | 3004 | 1630 | 1510 |

τὸ φανταζόμενον, Μωϋσῆς εἶπεν· ἔκφοβός εἰμι
the appearing, Moses said, very fearful I am

| 2532 1790 | **22** 235 | 4334 | 4622 3735 |

καὶ ἔντρομος. **22** ἀλλὰ προσεληλύθατε Σιὼν ὄρει
also trembling. But you have come to Sion hill

| 2532 4172 | 2316 | 2198 | 2419 | 2032 |

καὶ πόλει θεοῦ ζῶντος, 'Ιερουσαλὴμ ἐπουρανίῳ,
and city of God living, Jerusalem on heavenly,

| 2532 3461 | 32 | 3831 | **23** 2532 |

καὶ μυριάσιν ἀγγέλων, πανηγύρει **23** καὶ
and ten thousands of messengers, festive group and

| 1577 | 4416 | 583 | 1722 |

ἐκκλησίᾳ πρωτοτόκων ἀπογεγραμμένων ἐν
assembly of firstborn ones having been enrolled in

| 3772 | 2532 2923 | 2316 3956 | 2532 4151 | 1342 |

οὐρανοῖς καὶ κριτῇ θεῷ πάντων καὶ πνεύμασι δικαίων
heavens and judge God of all and spirits of right

| 5048 | **24** 2532 1242 | 3501 3316 |

τετελειωμένων **24** καὶ διαθήκης νέας μεσίτῃ
having been completed and agreement new mediator

| 2424 | 2532 129 | 4473 | 2909 | 2980 | 3844 |

'Ιησοῦ καὶ αἵματι ῥαντισμοῦ κρεῖττον λαλοῦντι παρὰ
Jesus and blood sprinkling better speaking from

| 04 6 | **25** 991 | 3361 3868 | 04 |

τὸν "Αβελ. **25** Βλέπετε μὴ παραιτήσησθε τὸν
the Abel. See not you might reject the one

| 2980 | 1487 1063 1565 | 3756 1628 | 1909 1093 |

λαλοῦντα· εἰ γὰρ ἐκεῖνοι οὐκ ἐξέφυγον ἐπὶ γῆς
speaking; if for those not fled out on earth

```
3868              04   5537              4183 3123   1473
παραιτησάμενοι  τὸν χρηματίζοντα,  πολὺ μᾶλλον ἡμεῖς
having rejected the one warning,   much more   we
013 04  575  3772      654                  3739 05   5456
οἱ  τὸν ἀπ᾽ οὐρανῶν ἀποστρεφόμενοι, 26 οὗ  ἡ  φωνὴ
the the from heavens being turned off, whose the sound
08   1093  4531          5119  3568 1161 1861
τὴν γῆν   ἐσάλευσεν τότε, νῦν δὲ  ἐπήγγελται
the earth shook       then, now but he has promised
3004    2089 530  1473 4579       3756 3441  08
λέγων· ἔτι ἅπαξ ἐγὼ σείσω    οὐ  μόνον τὴν
saying, still once I    will shake not alone  the
1093  235  2532 04  3772     09 1161 2089  530
γῆν ἀλλὰ καὶ τὸν οὐρανόν. 27 τὸ δὲ ἔτι ἅπαξ
earth but  also the heaven.    The but still once
1213      08  022    4531           3331      5613
δηλοῖ [τὴν] τῶν σαλευομένων μετάθεσιν ὡς
makes clear the of the being shaken  change    as
4160               2443 3306     021 3361
πεποιημένων,    ἵνα μείνῃ   τὰ μὴ
having been done, that might stay the not
4531          1352  932     761
σαλευόμενα. 28 Διὸ βασιλείαν ἀσάλευτον
being shaken.  Wherefore kingdom unshakeable
3880                    2192        5485  1223    3739
παραλαμβάνοντες ἔχωμεν χάριν, δι᾽  ἧς
having taken along we might have favor, through which
3000             2102            03   2316 3326
λατρεύωμεν εὐαρέστως τῷ  θεῷ μετὰ
we might serve well-pleasingly to the God with
2124        2532 1189a   2532 1063 01  2316 1473  4442
εὐλαβείας καὶ δέους· 29 καὶ γὰρ ὁ θεὸς ἡμῶν πῦρ
reverence and awe;     even for the God of us fire
2654             05  5360            3306      2  06
καταναλίσκον. 13:1 Ἡ φιλαδελφία μενέτω.  τῆς
all-consuming.    The brotherly love let stay. The
5381          3361 1950         1223      3778
φιλοξενίας μὴ ἐπιλανθάνεσθε, διὰ  ταύτης
love to strangers not forget,   through this
1063 2990        5100 3579
γὰρ ἔλαθόν τινες ξενίσαντες
for escaped notice some having entertained strangers
32            3  3403           014 1198     5613
ἀγγέλους.    μιμνῄσκεσθε τῶν δεσμίων ὡς
messengers.  Remember     the prisoners as
4887                    014 2558
συνδεδεμένοι,     τῶν κακουχουμένων
having been bound with, the ones being treated badly
5613 2532 846        1510 1722 4983   4  5093     01
ὡς  καὶ αὐτοὶ ὄντες ἐν σώματι.   Τίμιος ὁ
as  also yourselves being in body.  Valuable the
1062     1722 3956 2532 05  2845    283
γάμος ἐν πᾶσιν καὶ ἡ κοίτη ἀμίαντος,
marriage in all   and the bed  undefiled,
4205                1063 2532 3432      2919
πόρνους        γὰρ καὶ μοιχοὺς κρινεῖ
sexually immoral ones for and adulterers will judge
01  2316   5  866           01 5158   714
ὁ  θεός.    Ἀφιλάργυρος ὁ τρόπος, ἀρκούμενοι
the God.    Not loving silver the manner, being enough
023    3918        846    1063 3004        3756 3361
τοῖς παροῦσιν. αὐτὸς γὰρ εἴρηκεν·  οὐ μὴ
in the present. Himself for he has said, not not
1473 447        3761       3756 3361 1473
σε  ἀνῶ      οὐδ᾽     οὐ μή σε
you I might leave but not not   not you
1459            5620        2292      1473
ἐγκαταλίπω,   6 ὥστε    θαρροῦντας ἡμᾶς
I might leave behind, so that being confident us
```

how much less will we escape if we reject the one who warns from heaven! [26]At that time his voice shook the earth; but now he has promised, "Yet once more I will shake not only the earth but also the heaven." [27]This phrase, "Yet once more," indicates the removal of what is shaken—that is, created things—so that what cannot be shaken may remain. [28]Therefore, since we are receiving a kingdom that cannot be shaken, let us give thanks, by which we offer to God an acceptable worship with reverence and awe; [29]for indeed our God is a consuming fire.

CHAPTER 13

Let mutual love continue. [2]Do not neglect to show hospitality to strangers, for by doing that some have entertained angels without knowing it. [3]Remember those who are in prison, as though you were in prison with them; those who are being tortured, as though you yourselves were being tortured.[a] [4]Let marriage be held in honor by all, and let the marriage bed be kept undefiled; for God will judge fornicators and adulterers. [5]Keep your lives free from the love of money, and be content with what you have; for he has said, "I will never leave you or forsake you." [6]So we can say with confidence,

a Gk were in the body

"The Lord is my helper;
I will not be afraid.
What can anyone do
to me?"

7 Remember your
leaders, those who spoke
the word of God to you;
consider the outcome of
their way of life, and
imitate their faith. 8Jesus
Christ is the same yesterday
and today and forever. 9Do
not be carried away by all
kinds of strange teachings;
for it is well for the heart
to be strengthened by
grace, not by regulations
about food,*a* which have
not benefited those who
observe them. 10We have an
altar from which those who
officiate in the tent*b* have
no right to eat. 11For the
bodies of those animals
whose blood is brought
into the sanctuary by the
high priest as a sacrifice for
sin are burned outside the
camp. 12Therefore Jesus
also suffered outside the
city gate in order to
sanctify the people by his
own blood. 13Let us then
go to him outside the camp
and bear the abuse he
endured. 14For here we
have no lasting city, but
we are looking for the
city that is to come.
15Through him, then, let us
continually offer a sacrifice
of praise to God, that is,

a Gk *not by foods*
b Or *tabernacle*

3004	2962	1473	998		2532 3756	5399	
λέγειν·	κύριος	ἐμοὶ	βοηθός,	[καὶ]	οὐ	φοβηθήσομαι,
to say,	Master	to me	helper,	and	not	I will fear,

5101 4160   1473   444   3421   014
τί   ποιήσει μοι   ἄνθρωπος;   7 Μνημονεύετε τῶν
what will do to me man?   Remember   the

2233   1473   3748   2980   1473   04 3056
ἡγουμένων ὑμῶν, οἵτινες ἐλάλησαν ὑμῖν τὸν λόγον
leaders   of you, who   spoke   to you the word

02   2316   3739   333   08   1545
τοῦ θεοῦ, ὧν   ἀναθεωροῦντες τὴν ἔκβασιν
of the God, of whom having watched up the going out

06   391   3401   08 4102   8 2424
τῆς ἀναστροφῆς μιμεῖσθε τὴν πίστιν.   'Ιησοῦς
of the behavior imitate the trust.   Jesus

5547   2188a   2532 4594   01 846 2532 1519
Χριστὸς ἐχθὲς   καὶ σήμερον ὁ αὐτὸς καὶ εἰς
Christ yesterday and today the same and into

016   165   9 1322   4164   2532 3581   3361
τοὺς αἰῶνας. Διδαχαῖς ποικίλαις καὶ ξέναις μὴ
the ages.   In teachings various and strangers not

3911   2570   1063 5485   950
παραφέρεσθε·   καλὸν γὰρ χάριτι βεβαιοῦσθαι
be carried along; good for in favor to be confirmed

08   2588   3756 1033   1722 3739   3756
τὴν καρδίαν, οὐ βρώμασιν ἐν   οἷς   οὐκ
the heart,   not foods   in   which not

5623   013 4043   10 2192
ὠφελήθησαν   οἱ περιπατοῦντες.   ἔχομεν
were benefitted the ones walking around.   We have

2379   1537 3739 2068   3756 2192
θυσιαστήριον ἐξ οὗ   φαγεῖν οὐκ ἔχουσιν
place of sacrifice from which to eat not have

1849   013   07   4633 3000
ἐξουσίαν οἱ   τῇ   σκηνῇ λατρεύοντες.
authority the ones in the tent   serving.

11 3739   1063 1533   2226   09 129
   ὧν   γὰρ εἰσφέρεται ζῴων   τὸ αἷμα
   Of what for is carried in of living ones the blood

4012   266   1519 024 40   1223   02
περὶ ἁμαρτίας εἰς τὰ ἅγια διὰ   τοῦ
concerning sin   into the holies through the

749   3778   021 4983   2618
ἀρχιερέως, τούτων τὰ σώματα κατακαίεται
ruler priest, of these the bodies are burned down

1854   06   3925   12 1352   2532 2424   2443
ἔξω   τῆς παρεμβολῆς.   Διὸ καὶ 'Ιησοῦς, ἵνα
outside the barracks.   Wherefore also Jesus, that

37   1223   010 2398 129   04
ἁγιάσῃ   διὰ   τοῦ ἰδίου αἵματος τὸν
he might make holy through the own blood   the

2992   1854   06 4439   3958   13 5106
λαόν, ἔξω τῆς πύλης ἔπαθεν.   τοίνυν
people, outside the gate he suffered.   Accordingly

1831   4314 846 1854   06 3925   04
ἐξερχώμεθα   πρὸς αὐτὸν ἔξω   τῆς παρεμβολῆς τὸν
we might go out to him   outside the barracks   the

3680   846   5342   14 3756 1063 2192
ὀνειδισμὸν αὐτοῦ φέροντες·   οὐ γὰρ ἔχομεν
reviling   of him carrying;   not for we have

5602 3306   4172 235 08 3195
ὧδε μένουσαν πόλιν ἀλλὰ τὴν μέλλουσαν
here staying city but the one being about to be

1934   15 1223 846   3767 399
ἐπιζητοῦμεν. Δι' αὐτοῦ [οὖν] ἀναφέρωμεν
we seek after.   Through him then we might carry up

2378   133   1223   3956 40 2316 3778
θυσίαν αἰνέσεως διὰ   παντὸς τῷ θεῷ, τοῦτ'
sacrifice of praise through all   to the God, this

```
1510    2590    5491      3670            011 3686    846
ἔστιν  καρπὸν χειλέων ὁμολογούντων τῷ ὀνόματι αὐτοῦ.
is      fruit  of lips  confessing   the name    of him.
```

16
```
        06       1161 2140            2532 2842            3361
τῆς     δὲ     εὐποιΐας    καὶ   κοινωνίας       μὴ
Of the but     doing well  and   of partnership not
```
```
1950                 5108           1063 2378          2100
ἐπιλανθάνεσθε· τοιαύταις γὰρ θυσίαις εὐαρεστεῖται
forget;              to such   for sacrifices is well
                                                        pleased
```

17
```
01  2316         3982       015  2233              1473 2532
ὁ   θεός.        Πείθεσθε τοῖς ἡγουμένοις ὑμῶν καὶ
the God.        Persuade the ones leading you   and
```
```
5226          846          1063 69              5228        018
ὑπείκετε, αὐτοὶ     γὰρ ἀγρυπνοῦσιν ὑπὲρ      τῶν
yield,         themselves for stay awake on behalf of the
```
```
5590 1473   5613 3056  591          2443 3326 5479
ψυχῶν ὑμῶν ὡς  λόγον ἀποδώσοντες, ἵνα μετὰ χαρᾶς
souls of you as word giving back, that with joy
```
```
3778    4160             2532 3361 4727          255
τοῦτο ποιῶσιν       καὶ μὴ στενάζοντες· ἀλυσιτελὲς
this   they might do and not groaning;    unprofitable
```

18
```
1063 1473   3778        4336          4012 1473
γὰρ ὑμῖν τοῦτο.     Προσεύχεσθε περὶ ἡμῶν·
for  to you this.     Pray        about us;
```
```
3982              1063 3754 2570 4893              2192
πειθόμεθα       γὰρ ὅτι καλὴν συνείδησιν ἔχομεν,
we are persuaded for that good conscience we have,
```
```
1722 3956   2573 2309     390
ἐν   πᾶσιν καλῶς θέλοντες ἀναστρέφεσθαι.
in   all    well  wanting to behave.
```

19
```
4056                 1161 3870          3778 4160      2443
περισσοτέρως    δὲ παρακαλῶ τοῦτο ποιῆσαι, ἵνα
More exceedingly but I encourage this to do,     that
```
```
5030         600                  1473        01 1161
τάχιον     ἀποκατασταθῶ    ὑμῖν.  20 Ὁ  δὲ
more quickly I might be restored to you.  The but
```
```
2316 06     1515        01  321              1537 3498
θεὸς τῆς   εἰρήνης, ὁ ἀναγαγὼν     ἐκ νεκρῶν
God of the peace,    the one leading up from dead
```
```
04  4166    022        4263      04  3173 1722 129
τὸν ποιμένα τῶν    προβάτων τὸν μέγαν ἐν  αἵματι
the shepherd of the sheep     the great in  blood
```
```
1242          166        04  2962    1473 2424
διαθήκης  αἰωνίου, τὸν κύριον ἡμῶν Ἰησοῦν,
of agreement eternal, the Master of us Jesus,
```

21
```
2675             1473 1722 3956 18      1519 012
καταρτίσαι   ὑμᾶς ἐν παντὶ ἀγαθῷ εἰς τὸ
to put in order you   in  all   good  to  the
```
```
4160       012 2307  846          4160 1722 1473 012
ποιῆσαι τὸ θέλημα αὐτοῦ,    ποιῶν ἐν ἡμῖν τὸ
to do     the want  of him, doing in   us    the
```
```
2101            1799      846 1223            2424 5547
εὐάρεστον   ἐνώπιον αὐτοῦ διὰ          Ἰησοῦ Χριστοῦ,
well-pleasing before  him   through      Jesus Christ,
```
```
3739      05 1391    1519 016 165      014      165
ᾧ        ἡ δόξα   εἰς τοὺς αἰῶνας [τῶν  αἰώνων],
to whom the splendor into the ages    of the ages,
```
```
281     22 3870      1161 1473 80      430
ἀμήν.     Παρακαλῶ δὲ ὑμᾶς, ἀδελφοί, ἀνέχεσθε
amen.     I encourage but you,  brothers, endure
```
```
02 3056 06    3874          2532 1063 1223
τοῦ λόγου τῆς παρακλήσεως, καὶ γὰρ διὰ
the word of the encouragement, and for through
```
```
1024    1989      1473      1097      04 80
βραχέων ἐπέστειλα ὑμῖν. 23 Γινώσκετε τὸν ἀδελφὸν
little  I wrote letter to you.  You know  the brother
```
```
1473 5095  630                 3326 3739 1437
ἡμῶν Τιμόθεον ἀπολελυμένον,  μεθ' οὗ ἐὰν
of us Timothy having been loosed off, with whom if
```

the fruit of lips that confess his name. [16]Do not neglect to do good and to share what you have, for such sacrifices are pleasing to God.

[17]Obey your leaders and submit to them, for they are keeping watch over your souls and will give an account. Let them do this with joy and not with sighing—for that would be harmful to you.

[18]Pray for us; we are sure that we have a clear conscience, desiring to act honorably in all things. [19]I urge you all the more to do this, so that I may be restored to you very soon.

[20]Now may the God of peace, who brought back from the dead our Lord Jesus, the great shepherd of the sheep, by the blood of the eternal covenant, [21]make you complete in everything good so that you may do his will, working among us[a] that which is pleasing in his sight, through Jesus Christ, to whom be the glory forever and ever. Amen.

[22]I appeal to you, brothers and sisters,[b] bear with my word of exhortation, for I have written to you briefly. [23]I want you to know that our brother Timothy has been set free; and if

---

[a] Other ancient authorities read *you*
[b] Gk *brothers*

he comes in time, he will
be with me when I see you.
²⁴Greet all your leaders and
all the saints. Those from
Italy send you greetings.
²⁵Grace be with all of you.ᵃ

ᵃ Other ancient authorities add
  Amen

5030	2064	3708	1473
τάχιον	ἔρχηται	ὄψομαι	ὑμᾶς.
more quickly	he might come	I will	see you.

24
782	3956	016	2233		1473	2532
Ἀσπάσασθε	πάντας	τοὺς	ἡγουμένους		ὑμῶν	καὶ
Greet	all	the	ones leading		you	and

3956	016	40	782	1473	013	575
πάντας	τοὺς	ἁγίους.	Ἀσπάζονται	ὑμᾶς	οἱ	ἀπὸ
all	the	holy ones.	Greet	you	the ones	from

06	2482		05	5485	3326	3956	1473
τῆς	Ἰταλίας.	**25**	Ἡ	χάρις	μετὰ	πάντων	ὑμῶν.
the	Italy.		The	favor	with	all	of you.

JAMES

CHAPTER 1

James, a servant[a] of God and of the Lord Jesus Christ,
To the twelve tribes in the Dispersion:
Greetings.

2 My brothers and sisters,[b] whenever you face trials of any kind, consider it nothing but joy, [3]because you know that the testing of your faith produces endurance; [4]and let endurance have its full effect, so that you may be mature and complete, lacking in nothing.
5 If any of you is lacking in wisdom, ask God, who gives to all generously and ungrudgingly, and it will be given you. [6]But ask in faith, never doubting, for the one who doubts is like a wave of the sea, driven and tossed by the wind; [7,8]for the doubter, being doubleminded and unstable in every way, must not expect to receive anything from the Lord.
9 Let the believer[c] who is lowly boast in being raised up, [10]and the rich in being brought low, because the rich will disappear like a flower in the field. [11]For the sun rises with its scorching heat and withers the field; its flower falls, and its beauty perishes. It is the same way with the rich;

a Gk slave
b Gk brothers
c Gk brother

	2385	2316	2532	2962		2424	5547	1401
1:1	Ἰάκωβος	θεοῦ	καὶ	κυρίου		Ἰησοῦ	Χριστοῦ	δοῦλος
	Jacob	of God	and	Master		Jesus	Christ	slave

019	1427	5443	019		1722 07	1290
ταῖς	δώδεκα	φυλαῖς	ταῖς		ἐν	τῇ	διασπορᾷ
to the	twelve	tribes	the ones		in	the	dispersion

5463		2	3956	5479	2233		80		1473	3752
χαίρειν.		**2**	Πᾶσαν	χαρὰν	ἡγήσασθε,		ἀδελφοί		μου,	ὅταν
to rejoice.			All	joy	consider,		brothers		of me,	when

3986		4045		4164	
πειρασμοῖς		περίπεσητε		ποικίλοις,	
in pressures		you might fall around		various,	

	1097		3754 09	1383		1473	06		4102
3	γινώσκοντες		ὅτι	τὸ	δοκίμιον	ὑμῶν	τῆς		πίστεως
	knowing		that	the proof		of you	of the		trust

2716			5281		**4**	05	1161	5281		2041
κατεργάζεται			ὑπομονήν.		**4**	ἡ	δὲ	ὑπομονὴ		ἔργον
works thoroughly			patience.			The	but	patience		work

5046	2192		2443	1510		5046	2532
τέλειον	ἐχέτω,		ἵνα	ἦτε		τέλειοι	καὶ
complete	let have,		that	you might be		complete	and

3648		1722	3367	3007			1487	1161
ὁλόκληροι		ἐν	μηδενὶ	λειπόμενοι.		**5**	Εἰ	δέ
wholly called		in	nothing	being left.			If	but

5100	1473	3007		4678	154		3844 02	1325
τις	ὑμῶν	λείπεται		σοφίας,	αἰτείτω		παρὰ τοῦ	διδόντος
some	of you	is left		wisdom,	let ask		from the	giving

2316	3956	574		2532	3361	3679		2532
θεοῦ	πᾶσιν	ἁπλῶς		καὶ	μὴ	ὀνειδίζοντος		καὶ
God	to all	openly		and	not	reviling		and

1325		846		154	1161	1722	4102	3367
δοθήσεται		αὐτῷ.	**6**	αἰτείτω	δὲ	ἐν	πίστει	μηδὲν
it will be given to him.				Let ask	but	in	trust	nothing

1252		01	1063	1252		1857a
διακρινόμενος·		ὁ	γὰρ	διακρινόμενος		ἔοικεν
doubting;		the	for	doubting		has resembled

2830	2281		416		2532
κλύδωνι	θαλάσσης		ἀνεμιζομένῳ		καὶ
wave	of sea		being thrown by wind		and

4494		3361	1063	3633		01	444
ῥιπιζομένῳ.	**7**	μὴ	γὰρ	οἰέσθω		ὁ	ἄνθρωπος
being fanned.		Not	for	let expect		the	man

1565	3754	2983		5100	3844 02	2962
ἐκεῖνος	ὅτι	λήμψεταί		τι	παρὰ τοῦ	κυρίου,
that	that	he will receive		some	from the	Master,

	435	1374		182		1722	3956	019	3598
8	ἀνὴρ	δίψυχος,		ἀκατάστατος		ἐν	πάσαις	ταῖς	ὁδοῖς
	man	two souled,		unstable		in	all		the ways

846		2744		1161	01	80		01	5011	1722	011
αὐτοῦ.	**9**	Καυχάσθω		δὲ	ὁ	ἀδελφὸς	ὁ	ταπεινὸς	ἐν	τῷ
of him.		Let brag		but	the	brother	the	humble	in	the

5311	846		10	01	1161	4145		1722 07	5014
ὕψει	αὐτοῦ,		**10**	ὁ	δὲ	πλούσιος		ἐν	τῇ	ταπεινώσει
height of him,				the	but	rich		in	the	humility

846		3754		5613	438		5528	3928
αὐτοῦ,	ὅτι		ὡς		ἄνθος		χόρτου	παρελεύσεται.
of him,	because		as		flower		of grass	it will go along.

	393		1063	01	2246	4862 03	2742		2532
11	ἀνέτειλεν		γὰρ	ὁ	ἥλιος	σὺν τῷ	καύσωνι		καὶ
	Arose		for	the	sun	with the	burning heat		and

3583		04	5528	2532 09	438	846	1601
ἐξήρανεν		τὸν	χόρτον	καὶ τὸ	ἄνθος	αὐτοῦ	ἐξέπεσεν
it dried out		the	grass	and	the flower	of it	fell out

2532 05	2143		010	4383	846
καὶ	ἡ	εὐπρέπεια		τοῦ	προσώπου	αὐτοῦ
and	the	good appearance		of the	face	of it

622		3779	2532 01	4145		1722	019
ἀπώλετο·		οὕτως	καὶ ὁ	πλούσιος		ἐν	ταῖς
was destroyed;		thusly	also the	rich		in	the

```
4197        846       3133                        3107        435
πορείαις αὐτοῦ  μαρανθήσεται.   12  Μακάριος ἀνὴρ
journeys of him  will be wasting away.   Fortunate man
3739 5278        3986              3754    1384        1096
ὃς  ὑπομένει πειρασμόν, ὅτι    δόκιμος γενόμενος
who endures  pressure,  because proved  having become
2983              04   4735      06        2222 3739
λήμψεται          τὸν στέφανον τῆς  ζωῆς ὃν
he will receive the crown  of the life  which
1861       015     25            846      13  3367
ἐπηγγείλατο τοῖς  ἀγαπῶσιν αὐτόν.      Μηδεὶς
he promised to the ones loving him.      No one
3985              3004     3754 575  2316 3985
πειραζόμενος  λεγέτω ὅτι ἀπὸ  θεοῦ πειράζομαι·
being pressured let say, (") from God  I am pressured;
01   1063 2316 551              1510   2556      3985
ὁ  γὰρ θεὸς ἀπείραστός    ἐστιν κακῶν,  πειράζει
the for God  unpressureable is    of bad,  pressures
1161 846        3762     14 1538      1161 3985          5259
δὲ  αὐτὸς οὐδένα.    ἕκαστος δὲ  πειράζεται ὑπὸ
but himself no one.   Each   but is pressured by
06   2398  1939       1828        2532
τῆς ἰδίας ἐπιθυμίας ἐξελκόμενος καὶ
the own  desire    being dragged out and
1185              15 1534 05  1939      4815
δελεαζόμενος·    εἶτα ἡ  ἐπιθυμία συλλαβοῦσα
being ensnared;   then the desire  having conceived
5088      266       05  1161 266        658
τίκτει ἁμαρτίαν, ἡ  δὲ  ἁμαρτία ἀποτελεσθεῖσα
gives  sin,      the but  sin     having been fully
birth                                         completed
616        2288       16 3361 4105       80          1473
ἀποκύει θάνατον.    Μὴ πλανᾶσθε,  ἀδελφοί μου
engenders death.     Not be deceived, brothers of me
27           17 3956 1394    18   2532 3956 1434
ἀγαπητοί.    πᾶσα δόσις ἀγαθὴ καὶ πᾶν δώρημα
loved ones.  All giving good  and all  gift
5046     509       1510   2597        575 02 3962
τέλειον ἄνωθέν ἐστιν καταβαῖνον ἀπὸ τοῦ πατρὸς
complete from above is    coming down from the father
022      5457      3844 3739 3756 1762      3883        2228
τῶν  φώτων, παρ' ᾧ  οὐκ ἔνι    παραλλαγὴ ἢ
of the lights, from whom not there is change    or
5157      644          18 1014        616
τροπῆς ἀποσκίασμα.   βουληθεὶς ἀπεκύησεν
turning overshadow.   Having planned he engendered
1473 3056   225       1519 012 1510  1473 536
ἡμᾶς λόγῳ ἀληθείας εἰς τὸ  εἶναι ἡμᾶς ἀπαρχήν
us    in word of truth  for the to be us  from beginning
5100 022    846       2938        19 3609a 80        1473
τινα τῶν  αὐτοῦ κτισμάτων.    Ἴστε, ἀδελφοί μου
some of the of him creations.   Know, brothers of me
27           1510   1161 3956 444        5036  1519 012
ἀγαπητοί·  ἔστω δὲ  πᾶς ἄνθρωπος ταχὺς εἰς τὸ
loved ones; let be but all  man      quick for the
191        1021     1519 012 2980       1021   1519 3709
ἀκοῦσαι, βραδὺς εἰς τὸ  λαλῆσαι, βραδὺς εἰς ὀργήν·
to hear, slow   for the to speak, slow   into anger;
20 3709 1063 435    1343        2316 3756 2038
ὀργὴ γὰρ ἀνδρὸς δικαιοσύνην θεοῦ οὐκ ἐργάζεται.
anger for of man rightness   of God not works.
21 1352       659        3956 4507       2532
διὸ      ἀποθέμενοι πᾶσαν ῥυπαρίαν καὶ
Wherefore having set off all  dirtiness and
4050        2549     1722 4240       1209   04
περισσείαν κακίας ἐν πραΰτητι, δέξασθε τὸν
excess     badness in gentleness, welcome the
1721      3056  04  1410          4982        020
ἔμφυτον λόγον τὸν δυνάμενον σῶσαι τὰς
implanted word  the one being able to deliver the
```

in the midst of a busy life, they will wither away.

12 Blessed is anyone who endures temptation. Such a one has stood the test and will receive the crown of life that the Lord[a] has promised to those who love him. [13]No one, when tempted, should say, "I am being tempted by God"; for God cannot be tempted by evil and he himself tempts no one. [14]But one is tempted by one's own desire, being lured and enticed by it; [15]then, when that desire has conceived, it gives birth to sin, and that sin, when it is fully grown, gives birth to death. [16]Do not be deceived, my beloved.[b]

17 Every generous act of giving, with every perfect gift, is from above, coming down from the Father of lights, with whom there is no variation or shadow due to change.[c] [18]In fulfillment of his own purpose he gave us birth by the word of truth, so that we would become a kind of first fruits of his creatures.

19 You must understand this, my beloved:[b] let everyone be quick to listen, slow to speak, slow to anger; [20]for your anger does not produce God's righteousness. [21]Therefore rid yourselves of all sordidness and rank growth of wickedness, and welcome with meekness the implanted word that has the power to save your souls.

_a_ Gk _he_; other ancient authorities read _God_

_b_ Gk _my beloved brothers_

_c_ Other ancient authorities read _variation due to a shadow of turning_

22 But be doers of the word, and not merely hearers who deceive themselves. 23 For if any are hearers of the word and not doers, they are like those who look at themselves[a] in a mirror; 24 for they look at themselves and, on going away, immediately forget what they were like. 25 But those who look into the perfect law, the law of liberty, and persevere, being not hearers who forget but doers who act— they will be blessed in their doing.

26 If any think they are religious, and do not bridle their tongues but deceive their hearts, their religion is worthless. 27 Religion that is pure and undefiled before God, the Father, is this: to care for orphans and widows in their distress, and to keep oneself unstained by the world.

CHAPTER 2

My brothers and sisters,[b] do you with your acts of favoritism really believe in our glorious Lord Jesus Christ?[c] 2 For if a person with gold rings and in fine clothes comes into your assembly, and if a poor person in dirty clothes also comes in, 3 and if you take notice of the one wearing the

[a] Gk at the face of his birth
[b] Gk My brothers
[c] Or hold the faith of our glorious Lord Jesus Christ without acts of favoritism

5590 1473
ψυχὰς ὑμῶν. 22 Γίνεσθε δὲ ποιηταὶ λόγου καὶ μὴ
souls of you. Become but doers of word and not
3441 202 3884 1438 3754
μόνον ἀκροαταὶ παραλογιζόμενοι ἑαυτούς. 23 ὅτι
alone hearers reasoning beside yourselves. Because
1487 5100 202 3056 1510 2532 3756 4163
εἴ τις ἀκροατὴς λόγου ἐστὶν καὶ οὐ ποιητής,
if some hearer of word is and not doer,
3778 1857a 435 2657 012
οὗτος ἔοικεν ἀνδρὶ κατανοοῦντι τὸ
this has resembled to man thinking carefully the
4383 06 1078 846 1722 2072
πρόσωπον τῆς γενέσεως αὐτοῦ ἐν ἐσόπτρῳ·
face of the origin of him in mirror;
2657 1063 1438 2532 565
24 κατενόησεν γὰρ ἑαυτὸν καὶ ἀπελήλυθεν
he thought carefully for himself and he has gone off
carefully
2532 2112 1950 3697 1510 01 1161
καὶ εὐθέως ἐπελάθετο ὁποῖος ἦν. 25 ὁ δὲ
and immediately forgot of what kind he was. The but
3879 1519 3551 5046 04 06
παρακύψας εἰς νόμον τέλειον τὸν τῆς
having stooped down into law complete the of the
1657 2532 3887 3756 202
ἐλευθερίας καὶ παραμείνας, οὐκ ἀκροατὴς
freedom and having stayed along, not hearer
1953 1096 235 4163 2041
ἐπιλησμονῆς γενόμενος ἀλλὰ ποιητὴς ἔργου,
of forgetfulness having become but doer of work,
3778 3107 1722 07 4162 846 1510 1487
οὗτος μακάριος ἐν τῇ ποιήσει αὐτοῦ ἔσται. 26 Εἴ
this fortunate in the doing of him will be. If
5100 1380 2357 1510 3361 5468
τις δοκεῖ θρησκὸς εἶναι μὴ χαλιναγωγῶν
some thinks pious to be not setting a bridle
1100 846 235 500 2588 846 3778
γλῶσσαν αὐτοῦ ἀλλὰ ἀπατῶν καρδίαν αὐτοῦ, τούτου
tongue of him but deceiving heart of him, of this
3152 05 2356 2356 2513 2532 283
μάταιος ἡ θρησκεία. 27 θρησκεία καθαρὰ καὶ ἀμίαντος
futile the piety. Piety clean and undefiled
3844 03 2316 2532 3962 3778 1510 1980
παρὰ τῷ θεῷ καὶ πατρὶ αὕτη ἐστίν, ἐπισκέπτεσθαι
beside the God and father this is, to look on
3737 2532 5503 1722 07 2347 846
ὀρφανοὺς καὶ χήρας ἐν τῇ θλίψει αὐτῶν,
orphans and widows in the affliction of them,
784 1438 5083 575 02 2889
ἄσπιλον ἑαυτὸν τηρεῖν ἀπὸ τοῦ κόσμου.
without stain himself to keep from the world.
80 1473 3361 1722 4382 2192
2:1 Ἀδελφοί μου, μὴ ἐν προσωπολημψίαις ἔχετε
Brothers of me, not in receiving faces hold
08 4102 02 2962 1473 2424 5547 06
τὴν πίστιν τοῦ κυρίου ἡμῶν Ἰησοῦ Χριστοῦ τῆς
the trust of the Master of us Jesus Christ of the
1391 1437 1063 1525 1519 4864
δόξης. 2 ἐὰν γὰρ εἰσέλθῃ εἰς συναγωγὴν
splendor. If for might come in into synagogue
1473 435 5554 1722 2066 2986
ὑμῶν ἀνὴρ χρυσοδακτύλιος ἐν ἐσθῆτι λαμπρᾷ,
of you man gold-fingered in clothes bright,
1525 1161 2532 4434 1722 4508 2066
εἰσέλθῃ δὲ καὶ πτωχὸς ἐν ῥυπαρᾷ ἐσθῆτι,
might come in but also poor in dirty clothes,
1914 1161 1909 04 5409 08
3 ἐπιβλέψητε δὲ ἐπὶ τὸν φοροῦντα τὴν
you might look on but on the one wearing the

2066	08	2986	2532	3004	1473	2521	5602

ἐσθῆτα τὴν λαμπρὰν καὶ εἴπητε· σὺ κάθου ὧδε
clothes the bright and might say, you sit here

2573	2532 03	4434	3004	1473	2476	1563

καλῶς, καὶ τῷ πτωχῷ εἴπητε· σὺ στῆθι ἐκεῖ
well, and to the poor you might say, you stand there

2228 2521	5259	012 5286	1473	**4**	3756 1252

ἢ κάθου ὑπὸ τὸ ὑποπόδιόν μου, **4** οὐ διεκρίθητε
or sit under the footstool of me, not you doubt

1722 1438	2532 1096	2923	1261

ἐν ἑαυτοῖς καὶ ἐγένεσθε κριταὶ διαλογισμῶν
in yourselves and become judges of reasonings

4190	**5**	191	80	1473	27	3756

πονηρῶν; **5** Ἀκούσατε, ἀδελφοί μου ἀγαπητοί· οὐχ
evil? Hear, brothers of me loved ones; not

01	2316 1586	016	4434	03	2889 4145

ὁ θεὸς ἐξελέξατο τοὺς πτωχοὺς τῷ κόσμῳ πλουσίους
the God selected the poor in the world rich

1722 4102	2532 2818	06	932	3739

ἐν πίστει καὶ κληρονόμους τῆς βασιλείας ἧς
in trust and inheritors of the kingdom which

1861	015	25	846	1473	1161

ἐπηγγείλατο τοῖς ἀγαπῶσιν αὐτόν; **6** ὑμεῖς δὲ
he promised to the ones loving him? You but

818	04	4434	3756 013 4145

ἠτιμάσατε τὸν πτωχόν. οὐχ οἱ πλούσιοι
dishonored the poor. Not the rich

2616	1473 2532 846	1670

καταδυναστεύουσιν ὑμῶν καὶ αὐτοὶ ἕλκουσιν
exercise power against you and themselves haul

1473 1519 2922	**7**	3756 846	987

ὑμᾶς εἰς κριτήρια; **7** οὐκ αὐτοὶ βλασφημοῦσιν
you into judge courts? Not themselves insult

012 2570	3686 012 1941	1909 1473

τὸ καλὸν ὄνομα τὸ ἐπικληθὲν ἐφ᾿ ὑμᾶς;
the good name the having been called on on you?

8	1487 3305	3551 5055	937	2596 08

8 Εἰ μέντοι νόμον τελεῖτε βασιλικὸν κατὰ τὴν
If indeed law you complete kingly by the

1124	25	04 4139	1473 5613

γραφήν· ἀγαπήσεις τὸν πλησίον σου ὡς
writing· you will love the neighbor of you as

4572	2573 4160	**9**	1487 1161 4380

σεαυτόν, καλῶς ποιεῖτε· **9** εἰ δὲ προσωπολημπτεῖτε,
yourself, well you do; if but you receive faces,

266	2038	1651	5259 02	3551 5613

ἁμαρτίαν ἐργάζεσθε ἐλεγχόμενοι ὑπὸ τοῦ νόμου ὡς
sin you work being rebuked by the law as

3848		3748 1063 3650 04 3551 5083

παραβάται. **10** ὅστις γὰρ ὅλον τὸν νόμον τηρήσῃ
transgressors. **10** Who for whole the law might keep

4417	1161 1722 1520 1096	3956 1777

πταίσῃ δὲ ἐν ἑνί, γέγονεν πάντων ἔνοχος.
might stumble but in one, has become of all guilty.

11	01 1063 3004	3361 3431

11 ὁ γὰρ εἰπών· μὴ μοιχεύσῃς,
The for having said, not you might commit adultery,

3004 2532	3361 5407	1487 1161 3756

εἶπεν καί· μὴ φονεύσῃς· εἰ δὲ οὐ
said also, not you might murder; if but not

3431	5407	1161 1096

μοιχεύεις φονεύεις δέ, γέγονας
you commit adultery you murder but, you have become

3848	3551	**12**	3779 2980	2532 3779

παραβάτης νόμου. **12** Οὕτως λαλεῖτε καὶ οὕτως
transgressor of law. Thusly you speak and thusly

4160	5613 1223	3551 1657	3195

ποιεῖτε ὡς διὰ νόμου ἐλευθερίας μέλλοντες
you do as through law of freedom being about

fine clothes and say, "Have a seat here, please," while to the one who is poor you say, "Stand there," or, "Sit at my feet,"[a] 4have you not made distinctions among yourselves, and become judges with evil thoughts? 5Listen, my beloved brothers and sisters.[b] Has not God chosen the poor in the world to be rich in faith and to be heirs of the kingdom that he has promised to those who love him? 6But you have dishonored the poor. Is it not the rich who oppress you? Is it not they who drag you into court? 7Is it not they who blaspheme the excellent name that was invoked over you?

8 You do well if you really fulfill the royal law according to the scripture, "You shall love your neighbor as yourself." 9But if you show partiality, you commit sin and are convicted by the law as transgressors. 10For whoever keeps the whole law but fails in one point has become accountable for all of it. 11For the one who said, "You shall not commit adultery," also said, "You shall not murder." Now if you do not commit adultery but if you murder, you have become a transgressor of the law. 12So speak and so act as those who are to be judged by the law of liberty.

a Gk Sit under my footstool
b Gk brothers

¹³For judgment will be without mercy to anyone who has shown no mercy; mercy triumphs over judgment.

¹⁴What good is it, my brothers and sisters,^a if you say you have faith but do not have works? Can faith save you? ¹⁵If a brother or sister is naked and lacks daily food, ¹⁶and one of you says to them, "Go in peace; keep warm and eat your fill," and yet you do not supply their bodily needs, what is the good of that? ¹⁷So faith by itself, if it has no works, is dead.

¹⁸But someone will say, "You have faith and I have works." Show me your faith apart from your works, and I by my works will show you my faith. ¹⁹You believe that God is one; you do well. Even the demons believe—and shudder. ²⁰Do you want to be shown, you senseless person, that faith apart from works is barren? ²¹Was not our ancestor Abraham justified by works when he offered his son Isaac on the altar? ²²You see that faith was active along with his works, and faith was brought to completion by the works.

^a Gk brothers

2919   05   1063 2920   415a   03
κρίνεσθαι. **13** ἡ γὰρ κρίσις ἀνέλεος   τῷ
to be judged.   The for judgment without mercy to the
3361 4160   1656 2620   1656
μὴ ποιήσαντι   ἔλεος· κατακαυχᾶται ἔλεος
not one having done mercy; brags against   mercy
2920   5101 09 3786   80   1473   1437
κρίσεως. **14** Τί τὸ ὄφελος, ἀδελφοί μου, ἐὰν
judgment.   What the advantage, brothers of me, if
4102   3004   5100 2192   2041   1161 3361
πίστιν λέγῃ   τις ἔχειν ἔργα δὲ μὴ
trust might say some to have works but not
2192   3361 1410   05   4102   4982   846
ἔχῃ;   μὴ δύναται ἡ πίστις σῶσαι   αὐτόν;
might have? Not is able the trust to deliver him?
     1437 80   2228 79   1131   5225   2532
15 ἐὰν ἀδελφὸς ἢ ἀδελφὴ γυμνοὶ ὑπάρχωσιν καὶ
     If brother or sister naked might exist and
3007   06 2184   5160   3004   1161 5100
λειπόμενοι τῆς ἐφημέρου τροφῆς **16** εἴπῃ   δέ   τις
leaving   the on day   food   might say but   some
846   1537 1473 5217   1722 1515   2328
αὐτοῖς ἐξ ὑμῶν· ὑπάγετε ἐν εἰρήνη, θερμαίνεσθε
to them from you, go off in peace, be warmed
2532 5526   3361 1325   1161 846
καὶ χορτάζεσθε, μὴ δῶτε   δὲ αὐτοῖς
and be satisfied, not you might give but to them
024 2006   010   4983   5101 09 3786
τὰ ἐπιτήδεια τοῦ σώματος, τί τὸ ὄφελος;
the needful of the body, what the advantage?
     3779   2532 05 4102   1437 3361 2192
17 οὕτως καὶ ἡ πίστις, ἐὰν μὴ ἔχῃ
     Thusly also the trust, if not it might have
2041   3498 1510 2596 1438   235 3004
ἔργα, νεκρά ἐστιν καθ' ἑαυτήν. **18** Ἀλλ' ἐρεῖ
works, dead it is by itself.   But will say
6100 1473 4102   2192   2504 2041 2192 1166   1473
τις· σὺ πίστιν ἔχεις, κἀγὼ ἔργα ἔχω· δεῖξόν μοι
some, you trust have, and I works have; show to me
08 4102   1473   5565   022 2041   2504 1473
τὴν πίστιν σου χωρὶς τῶν ἔργων, κἀγώ σοι
the trust of you without the works, and I to you
1166   1537 022 2041 1473   08 4102   19 1473
δείξω   ἐκ τῶν ἔργων μου τὴν πίστιν.   σὺ
will show from the works of me the trust.   You
4100   3754 1520 1510   01   2316   2573 4160
πιστεύεις ὅτι εἷς ἐστιν ὁ θεός, καλῶς ποιεῖς·
trust   that one is the God, well you do;
2532 021 1140   4100   2532 5425
καὶ τὰ δαιμόνια πιστεύουσιν καὶ φρίσσουσιν.
also the demons   trust   and quiver.
     2309   1161 1097   5599 444   2756   3754
20 Θέλεις   δὲ γνῶναι, ὦ ἄνθρωπε κενέ, ὅτι
     Do you want but to know, o man   empty, that
05 4102   5565   022 2041 692 1510   21 11
ἡ πίστις χωρὶς τῶν ἔργων ἀργή ἐστιν;   Ἀβραὰμ
the trust without the works idle is?   Abraham
01 3962   1473 3756 1537 2041 1344
ὁ πατὴρ ἡμῶν οὐκ ἐξ ἔργων ἐδικαιώθη
the father of us not from works was made right
399   2464 04 5207 846   1909 012
ἀνενέγκας Ἰσαὰκ τὸν υἱὸν αὐτοῦ ἐπὶ τὸ
having brought up Isaac the son of him on the
2379   991   3754 05 4102   4903
θυσιαστήριον; **22** βλέπεις ὅτι ἡ πίστις συνήργει
sacrifice place? You see that the trust was working
                                              together
023   2041   846   2532 1537 022 2041 05 4102
τοῖς ἔργοις αὐτοῦ καὶ ἐκ τῶν ἔργων ἡ πίστις
in the works of him and from the works the trust

5048   23   2532 4137   05   1124   05 3004
ἐτελειώθη,   καὶ ἐπληρώθη ἡ γραφὴ ἡ λέγουσα·
was completed, and   was filled the writing the saying:
4100   1161   11   03   2316 2532 3049
ἐπίστευσεν δὲ ᾿Αβραὰμ τῷ θεῷ, καὶ ἐλογίσθη
trusted   but Abraham the God, and it was reasoned
846   1519 1343   2532 5384   2316
αὐτῷ εἰς δικαιοσύνην καὶ φίλος θεοῦ
to him for   rightness   and friend of God
2564   24   3708 3754 1537 2041   1344
ἐκλήθη.   ὁρᾶτε ὅτι ἐξ ἔργων δικαιοῦται
he was called.   See   that from works is made right
444   2532 3756 1537 4102   3441   25   3668
ἄνθρωπος καὶ οὐκ ἐκ πίστεως μόνον.   ὁμοίως
man   and not from trust   alone.   Likewise
1161 2532 4460 05 4204   3756 1537 2041
δὲ καὶ ῾Ραὰβ ἡ πόρνη   οὐκ ἐξ ἔργων
but also Rahab the prostitute not from works
1344   5264   016 32   2532
ἐδικαιώθη   ὑποδεξαμένη   τοὺς ἀγγέλους καὶ
was made right having entertained the messengers and
2087   3598 1544   26   5618   1063 09 4983
ἑτέρᾳ ὁδῷ ἐκβαλοῦσα;   ὥσπερ   γὰρ τὸ σῶμα
other way having thrown out? As indeed for the body
5565   4151   3498 1510   3779   2532 05 4102
χωρὶς πνεύματος νεκρόν ἐστιν, οὕτως καὶ ἡ πίστις
without spirit   dead   is,   thusly also the trust
5565   2041   3498 1510   3:1 3361 4183   1320
χωρὶς ἔργων νεκρά ἐστιν.   Μὴ πολλοὶ διδάσκαλοι
without works dead is.   Not many   teachers
1096   80   1473   3609a   3754 3173
γίνεσθε, ἀδελφοί μου, εἰδότες ὅτι μεῖζον
become, brothers of me, having known that greater
2917   2983   2   4183 1063 4417
κρίμα λημψόμεθα.   πολλὰ γὰρ πταίομεν
judgment we will receive. Many for we stumble
537   1487 5100 1722 3056 3756 4417   3778
ἅπαντες. εἴ τις ἐν λόγῳ οὐ πταίει, οὗτος
all.   If some in word not stumbles, this
5046   435 1415   5468   2532 3650 012
τέλειος ἀνὴρ δυνατὸς χαλιναγωγῆσαι καὶ ὅλον τὸ
complete man power   to set a bridle even whole the
4983   3   1487 1161 014   2462   016 5469   1519 024
σῶμα.   εἰ δὲ τῶν ἵππων τοὺς χαλινοὺς εἰς τὰ
body. If but of the horses the bridles into the
4750   906   1519 012 3982   846   1473
στόματα βάλλομεν εἰς τὸ πείθεσθαι αὐτοὺς ἡμῖν,
mouths we throw for the to persuade them to us,
2532 3650 012 4983 846   3329   4   2400 2532
καὶ ὅλον τὸ σῶμα αὐτῶν μετάγομεν.   ἰδοὺ καὶ
and whole the body of them we lead about. Look also
021 4143 5082   1510   2532 5259 417   4642
τὰ πλοῖα τηλικαῦτα ὄντα καὶ ὑπὸ ἀνέμων σκληρῶν
the boats so great being and by winds hard
1643   3329   5259 1646   4079   3699
ἐλαυνόμενα, μετάγεται ὑπὸ ἐλαχίστου πηδαλίου ὅπου
being driven, is led about by least   rudder where
05 3730   02   2116   1014   5   3779
ἡ ὁρμὴ τοῦ εὐθύνοντος βούλεται,   οὕτως
the impulse of the one straightening plans,   thusly
2532 05 1100   3398   3196   1510 2532 3173   849a
καὶ ἡ γλῶσσα μικρὸν μέλος ἐστὶν καὶ μεγάλα αὐχεῖ.
also the tongue small member is and great boasts.
2400 2245   4442 2245   5208 381   6   2532 05
ἰδοὺ ἡλίκον πῦρ ἡλίκην ὕλην ἀνάπτει·   καὶ ἡ
Look how great fire how great wood it ignites; and the
1100   4442 01 2889 06   93   05   1100
γλῶσσα πῦρ· ὁ κόσμος τῆς ἀδικίας ἡ γλῶσσα
tongue fire; the world of the unright the tongue

[23]Thus the scripture was fulfilled that says, "Abraham believed God, and it was reckoned to him as righteousness," and he was called the friend of God. [24]You see that a person is justified by works and not by faith alone. [25]Likewise, was not Rahab the prostitute also justified by works when she welcomed the messengers and sent them out by another road? [26]For just as the body without the spirit is dead, so faith without works is also dead.

CHAPTER 3

Not many of you should become teachers, my brothers and sisters,[a] for you know that we who teach will be judged with greater strictness. [2]For all of us make many mistakes. Anyone who makes no mistakes in speaking is perfect, able to keep the whole body in check with a bridle. [3]If we put bits into the mouths of horses to make them obey us, we guide their whole bodies. [4]Or look at ships: though they are so large that it takes strong winds to drive them, yet they are guided by a very small rudder wherever the will of the pilot directs. [5]So also the tongue is a small member, yet it boasts of great exploits.

How great a forest is set ablaze by a small fire! [6]And the tongue is a fire. The tongue is placed among our members as a world of iniquity;

[a] Gk brothers

it stains the whole body, sets on fire the cycle of nature,[a] and is itself set on fire by hell.[b] [7]For every species of beast and bird, of reptile and sea creature, can be tamed and has been tamed by the human species, [8]but no one can tame the tongue—a restless evil, full of deadly poison. [9]With it we bless the Lord and Father, and with it we curse those who are made in the likeness of God. [10]From the same mouth come blessing and cursing. My brothers and sisters,[c] this ought not to be so. [11]Does a spring pour forth from the same opening both fresh and brackish water? [12]Can a fig tree, my brothers and sisters,[d] yield olives, or a grapevine figs? No more can salt water yield fresh.

13 Who is wise and understanding among you? Show by your good life that your works are done with gentleness born of wisdom. [14]But if you have bitter envy and selfish ambition in your hearts, do not be boastful and false to the truth. [15]Such wisdom does not come down from above, but is earthly, unspiritual, devilish. [16]For where there is

[a] Or wheel of birth
[b] Gk Gehenna
[c] Gk My brothers
[d] Gk my brothers

2525	1722	023	3196	1473	05	4695
καθίσταται	ἐν	τοῖς	μέλεσιν	ἡμῶν,	ἡ	σπιλοῦσα
is appointed	in	the	members	of us,	the	one spotting

3650	012	4983	2532	5394	04	5164	06	1078
ὅλον	τὸ	σῶμα	καὶ	φλογίζουσα	τὸν	τροχὸν	τῆς	γενέσεως
whole	the	body	and	inflaming	the	cycle	of the	origin

2532	5394		5259	06	1067	7	3956	1063
καὶ	φλογιζομένη	ὑπὸ	τῆς	γεέννης.		πᾶσα	γὰρ
and	being inflamed	by	the	gehenna.		All	for

5449	2342		5037	2532	4071		2062	5037
φύσις	θηρίων	τε	καὶ	πετεινῶν,	ἑρπετῶν	τε
nature	of wild animals	both	and	birds,	reptiles	both

2532	1724	1150		2532	1150	07
καὶ	ἐναλίων	δαμάζεται	καὶ	δεδάμασται	τῇ
and	sea life	is being tamed	and	has been tamed	in the

5449	07	442	8	08	1161	1100	3762
φύσει	τῇ	ἀνθρωπίνῃ,		τὴν	δὲ	γλῶσσαν	οὐδεὶς
nature	in the	man-like,		the	but	tongue	no one

1150	1410	444	182	2556	3324
δαμάσαι	δύναται	ἀνθρώπων,	ἀκατάστατον	κακόν,	μεστὴ
to tame	is able	of men,	unstable	bad,	full

2447	2287	9	1722	846	2127	04
ἰοῦ	θανατηφόρου.		ἐν	αὐτῇ	εὐλογοῦμεν	τὸν
of poison	carrying death.		In	same	we speak well	the

2962	2532	3962	2532	1722	846	2672	016
κύριον	καὶ	πατέρα	καὶ	ἐν	αὐτῇ	καταρώμεθα	τοὺς
Master	and	father	and	in	same	we curse	the

444	016	2596	3669	2316	1096
ἀνθρώπους	τοὺς	καθ᾽	ὁμοίωσιν	θεοῦ	γεγονότας,
men	the	by	likeness	of God	having become,

10	1537	010	846	4750	1831	2129
	ἐκ	τοῦ	αὐτοῦ	στόματος	ἐξέρχεται	εὐλογία
	from	the	same	mouth	comes out	good word

2532	2671	3756	5534	80	1473	3778
καὶ	κατάρα.	οὐ	χρή,	ἀδελφοί	μου,	ταῦτα
and	curse.	Not	it is useful,	brothers	of me,	these

3779	1096	11	3385	05	4077	1537	06	846
οὕτως	γίνεσθαι.		μήτι	ἡ	πηγὴ	ἐκ	τῆς	αὐτῆς
thusly	to become.		What not	the	spring	from	the	same

3692	1032	012	1099	2532	012	4089	12	3361	1410
ὀπῆς	βρύει	τὸ	γλυκὺ	καὶ	τὸ	πικρόν;		μὴ	δύναται,
hole	gushes	the	sweet	and	the	bitter?		Not	is able,

80	1473	4808	1636	4160	2228	288
ἀδελφοί	μου,	συκῆ	ἐλαίας	ποιῆσαι	ἢ	ἄμπελος
brothers	of me,	fig tree	olives	to make	or	vine

4810	3777	252	1099	4160	5204	13	5101
σῦκα;	οὔτε	ἁλυκὸν	γλυκὺ	ποιῆσαι	ὕδωρ.		Τίς
figs?	Neither	salt	sweet	to make	water.		Who

4680	2532	1990	1722	1473	1166	1537
σοφὸς	καὶ	ἐπιστήμων	ἐν	ὑμῖν;	δειξάτω	ἐκ
wise	and	understanding	in	in you?	Let show	from

06	2570	391	024	2041	846	1722	4240
τῆς	καλῆς	ἀναστροφῆς	τὰ	ἔργα	αὐτοῦ	ἐν	πραΰτητι
the	good	behavior	the	works	of him	in	gentleness

4678	14	1487	1161	2205	4089	2192	2532
σοφίας.		εἰ	δὲ	ζῆλον	πικρὸν	ἔχετε	καὶ
of wisdom.		If	but	jealousy	bitter	you have	and

2052	1722	07	2588	1473	3361
ἐριθείαν	ἐν	τῇ	καρδίᾳ	ὑμῶν,	μὴ
selfish ambition	in	the	heart	of you,	not

2620	2532	5574	2596	06	225
κατακαυχᾶσθε	καὶ	ψεύδεσθε	κατὰ	τῆς	ἀληθείας.
brag against	and	lie	against	the	truth.

15	3756	1510	3778	05	4678	509	2718
	οὐκ	ἔστιν	αὕτη	ἡ	σοφία	ἄνωθεν	κατερχομένη
	Not	is	this	the	wisdom	from above	coming down

235	1919	5591	1141	16	3699	1063
ἀλλὰ	ἐπίγειος,	ψυχική,	δαιμονιώδης.		ὅπου	γὰρ
but	on earth,	soul-like,	demonic.		Where	for

```
2205      2532 2052                    1563  181              2532
ζῆλος     καὶ ἐριθεία,                ἐκεῖ ἀκαταστασία καὶ
jealousy and selfish ambition,       there unstableness and
3956 5337     4229        17  05 1161 509              4678  4413
πᾶν φαῦλον πρᾶγμα.           ἡ  δὲ ἄνωθεν     σοφία πρῶτον
all foul   practice.         The but from above wisdom first
3303  53    1510  1899    1516       1933
μὲν  ἀγνή ἐστιν, ἔπειτα εἰρηνική, ἐπιεικής,
indeed pure is,  then    peaceable, gentle,
2138             3324  1656    2532  2590       18
εὐπειθής,      μεστὴ ἐλέους καὶ καρπῶν ἀγαθῶν,
well-persuaded, full  of mercy and fruit   good,
87               505            18  2590   1161
ἀδιάκριτος,    ἀνυπόκριτος.       καρπὸς δὲ
undifferentiating, unhypocritical.  Fruit  but
1343          1722 1515   4687    015    4160
δικαιοσύνης ἐν εἰρήνῃ σπείρεται τοῖς ποιοῦσιν
of rightness in peace is sown    to the ones doing
1515       4:1 4159       4171    2532 4159    3163
εἰρήνην.      Πόθεν πόλεμοι καὶ πόθεν μάχαι
peace.         From where wars  and from where battles
1722 1473   3756 1782       1537 018 2237      1473
ἐν  ὑμῖν; οὐκ ἐντεῦθεν, ἐκ τῶν ἡδονῶν ὑμῶν
in you?  Not from here, from the pleasures of you
018 4754           1722 023  3196    1473 2 1937
τῶν στρατευομένων ἐν τοῖς μέλεσιν ὑμῶν; ἐπιθυμεῖτε
the soldiering   in the   members of you? You desire
2532 3756 2192    5407       2532 2206      2532
καὶ οὐκ ἔχετε,  φονεύετε καὶ ζηλοῦτε καὶ
and not you have, you murder and are jealous and
3756 1410     2013       3164      2532 4170
οὐ δύνασθε ἐπιτυχεῖν, μάχεσθε καὶ πολεμεῖτε,
not you are able to obtain, you battle and you war,
3756 2192   1223   012 3361 154      1473
οὐκ ἔχετε διὰ τὸ μὴ αἰτεῖσθαι ὑμᾶς,
not you have because the not to ask  you,
3 154   2532 3756 2983      1360        2560
αἰτεῖτε καὶ οὐ λαμβάνετε διότι    κακῶς
you ask and not you receive because that badly
154      2443 1722 019 2237      1473
αἰτεῖσθε, ἵνα ἐν ταῖς ἡδοναῖς ὑμῶν
you ask, that in the pleasures of you
1159          4 3428       3756 3609a    3754 05 5373
δαπανήσητε.  μοιχαλίδες, οὐκ οἴδατε ὅτι ἡ φιλία
you might     Adulterous not you know that the love
spend.        ones,
02    2889      2189      02      2316 1510  3739 1437
τοῦ κόσμου ἔχθρα     τοῦ θεοῦ ἐστιν; ὃς ἐὰν
of the world hostility of the God is?   Who if
3767 1014     5384     1510 02    2889    2190
οὖν βουληθῇ φίλος εἶναι τοῦ κόσμου, ἐχθρὸς
then might plan friend to be of the world, hostile
02    2316 2525           5 2228 1380        3754 2761
τοῦ θεοῦ καθίσταται.   ἢ δοκεῖτε ὅτι κενῶς
of the God is appointed. Or think you that emptily
05 1124    3004    4314 5355    1971          09
ἡ γραφὴ λέγει· πρὸς φθόνον ἐπιποθεῖ       τὸ
the writing says: to envy    desires longingly the
4151   3739 2733a       1722 1473   6 3173    1161
πνεῦμα ὃ κατῴκισεν ἐν ἡμῖν, μείζονα δὲ
spirit which he resided in us,   greater but
1325     5485   1352   3004     01 2316
δίδωσιν χάριν; διὸ λέγει· ὁ θεὸς
he gives favor? Wherefore it says, the God
5244         498            5011      1161
ὑπερηφάνοις ἀντιτάσσεται, ταπεινοῖς δὲ
arrogant   sets in order against, humble but
1325     5485  7 5293       3767 03  2316
δίδωσιν χάριν. ὑποτάγητε οὖν τῷ θεῷ,
he gives favor. Be subject then to the God,
```

envy and selfish ambition, there will also be disorder and wickedness of every kind. [17]But the wisdom from above is first pure, then peaceable, gentle, willing to yield, full of mercy and good fruits, without a trace of partiality or hypocrisy. [18]And a harvest of righteousness is sown in peace for[a] those who make peace.

CHAPTER 4

Those conflicts and disputes among you, where do they come from? Do they not come from your cravings that are at war within you? [2]You want something and do not have it; so you commit murder. And you covet[b] something and cannot obtain it; so you engage in disputes and conflicts. You do not have, because you do not ask. [3]You ask and do not receive, because you ask wrongly, in order to spend what you get on your pleasures. [4]Adulterers! Do you not know that friendship with the world is enmity with God? Therefore whoever wishes to be a friend of the world becomes an enemy of God. [5]Or do you suppose that it is for nothing that the scripture says, "God[c] yearns jealously for the spirit that he has made to dwell in us"? [6]But he gives all the more grace; therefore it says,

> "God opposes the proud,
> but gives grace to the humble."

[7]Submit yourselves therefore to God.

---

[a] Or by
[b] Or you murder and you covet
[c] Gk He

Resist the devil, and he will flee from you. [8]Draw near to God, and he will draw near to you. Cleanse your hands, you sinners, and purify your hearts, you double-minded. [9]Lament and mourn and weep. Let your laughter be turned into mourning and your joy into dejection. [10]Humble yourselves before the Lord, and he will exalt you.

11 Do not speak evil against one another, brothers and sisters.[a] Whoever speaks evil against another or judges another, speaks evil against the law and judges the law; but if you judge the law, you are not a doer of the law but a judge. [12]There is one lawgiver and judge who is able to save and to destroy. So who, then, are you to judge your neighbor?

13 Come now, you who say, "Today or tomorrow we will go to such and such a town and spend a year there, doing business and making money." [14]Yet you do not even know what tomorrow will bring. What is your life? For you are a mist that appears for a little while and then vanishes. [15]Instead you ought to say, "If the Lord wishes, we will live and do this or that." [16]As it is, you boast in your arrogance; all such boasting is evil.

[a] Gk brothers

```
436                    1161 03   1228          2532 5343           575
ἀντίστητε      δὲ   τῷ   διαβόλῳ   καὶ φεύξεται      ἀφ᾽
stand against but   the  slanderer and he will flee from
1473        1448     03   2316 2532 1448            1473
ὑμῶν,   8  ἐγγίσατε τῷ θεῷ καὶ  ἐγγιεῖ       ὑμῖν.
you,       near   the God  and   he will near  you.
2511        5495    268       2532 48        2588
καθαρίσατε χεῖρας, ἁμαρτωλοί, καὶ  ἁγνίσατε καρδίας,
Clean      hands,   sinners,   and  purify    hearts,
1374       9 5003          2532 3996     2532 2799
δίψυχοι.    ταλαιπωρήσατε καὶ πενθήσατε καὶ κλαύσατε.
two-souled. Be miserable  and mourn      and cry.
01   1071   1473   1519 3997    3346a           2532
ὁ  γέλως   ὑμῶν  εἰς  πένθος  μετατραπήτω    καὶ
The laughter of you into mourning let turn across and
05  5479  1519 2726        10 5013            1799
ἡ  χαρὰ  εἰς  κατήφειαν.    ταπεινώθητε ἐνώπιον
the joy  into dejection.     Be humble    before
2962   2532 5312          1473   11 3361 2635
κυρίου καὶ ὑψώσει        ὑμᾶς.    Μὴ καταλαλεῖτε
Master and he will elevate you.    Not talk against
240         80    01    2635           80
ἀλλήλων,  ἀδελφοί. ὁ  καταλαλῶν     ἀδελφοῦ
one another, brothers. The one talking against brother
2228 2919   04 80        846      2635           3551
ἢ  κρίνων  τὸν ἀδελφὸν αὐτοῦ καταλαλεῖ     νόμου
or judging the brother  of him talks against law
2532 2919    3551     1487 1161 3551   2919        3756
καὶ κρίνει νόμον· εἰ  δὲ  νόμον κρίνεις,  οὐκ
and judges law;   if  but law   you judge, not
1510    4163      3551     235  2923       12 1520 1510   01
εἶ    ποιητὴς νόμου ἀλλὰ κριτής.    εἷς ἐστιν [ὁ]
you are doer   of law but  judge.     One is    the
3550        2532 2923   01        1410        4982
νομοθέτης καὶ κριτὴς ὁ    δυνάμενος σῶσαι
law-setter and judge  the  one being able to deliver
2532 622         1473 1161 5101 1510 01  2919
καὶ ἀπολέσαι·  οὐ  δὲ  τίς  εἶ  ὁ  κρίνων
and to destroy; you but  why  are the one judging
04  4139        13 33     3568 013      3004       4594
τὸν πλησίον;    Ἄγε νῦν οἱ    λέγοντες· σήμερον
the neighbor?   Come now the ones saying; today
2228 839    4198         1519 3592   08  4172
ἢ  αὔριον πορευσόμεθα εἰς  τήνδε  τὴν πόλιν
or tomorrow we will travel into this such the city
2532 4160        1563  1763      2532 1710
καὶ ποιήσομεν ἐκεῖ ἐνιαυτὸν καὶ ἐμπορευσόμεθα
and will make there year     and we will exploit
2532 2770        14 3748      3756 1987        012
καὶ κερδήσομεν·   οἵτινες οὐκ ἐπίστασθε    τὸ
and will gain;      who    not you understand the
06  839    4169      05  2222 1473    822   1063
τῆς αὔριον ποία    ἡ  ζωὴ ὑμῶν· ἀτμὶς γὰρ
the tomorrow of what kind the life of you; vapor for
1510  05  4314 3641    5316        1899  2532
ἐστε  ἡ  πρὸς ὀλίγον φαινομένη, ἔπειτα καὶ
you are the to  little  shining,    then   also
853             15 473   010      3004     1473 1437 01
ἀφανιζομένη.     ἀντὶ τοῦ  λέγειν ὑμᾶς· ἐὰν ὁ
disappearing.    In place of the to say you;  if   the
2962   2309      2532 2198      2532 4160
κύριος θελήσῃ   καὶ ζήσομεν   καὶ ποιήσομεν
Master might want both we will live and  will do
3778  2228 1565   16 3568 1161 2744       1722 019
τοῦτο ἢ  ἐκεῖνο.   νῦν δὲ  καυχᾶσθε ἐν  ταῖς
this  or that.      Now but you brag  in   the
212           1473   3956 2746       5108    4190
ἀλαζονείαις ὑμῶν·  πᾶσα καύχησις τοιαύτη πονηρά
boasts      of you;  all  brag     such     evil
```

1510	**17**	3609a		3767	2570	4160		2532	3361

ἐστιν. **17** εἰδότι οὖν καλὸν ποιεῖν καὶ μὴ
is. Having known then good to do and not

4160	266	846	1510	**5:1**	33	3568	013

ποιοῦντι, ἁμαρτία αὐτῷ ἐστιν. **5:1** Ἄγε νῦν οἱ
doing,   sin   to him it is.   Come now the

4145	2799	3649	1909	019	5004

πλούσιοι, κλαύσατε ὀλολύζοντες ἐπὶ ταῖς ταλαιπωρίαις
rich,   cry   wailing   on   the   miseries

1473	019	1904	**2**	01	4149	1473

ὑμῶν ταῖς ἐπερχομέναις. **2** ὁ πλοῦτος ὑμῶν
of you the ones coming on. The rich of you

4595	2532	021	2440	1473	4598

σέσηπεν καὶ τὰ ἱμάτια ὑμῶν σητόβρωτα
is rotten and the clothes of you moth-eaten

1096	**3**	01	5557	1473	2532	01	696

γέγονεν, **3** ὁ χρυσὸς ὑμῶν καὶ ὁ ἄργυρος
have become, the gold of you and the silver

2728	2532	01	2447	846	1519	3142

κατίωται καὶ ὁ ἰὸς αὐτῶν εἰς μαρτύριον
is rust-covered and the poison of them for testimony

1473	1510	2532	2068	020	4561	1473	5613

ὑμῖν ἔσται καὶ φάγεται τὰς σάρκας ὑμῶν ὡς
to you will be and it will eat the flesh of you as

4442	2343	1722	2078	2250	**4**	2400	01

πῦρ. ἐθησαυρίσατε ἐν ἐσχάταις ἡμέραις. **4** ἰδοὺ ὁ
fire. You treasured in last days. Look the

3408	014	2040	014	270	020

μισθὸς τῶν ἐργατῶν τῶν ἀμησάντων τὰς
wage of the workers the ones having reaped the

5561	1473	01	650	575

χώρας ὑμῶν ὁ ἀπεστερημένος ἀφ᾽
countries of you the one having been deprived from

1473	2896	2532	017	995	014	2325	1519	024

ὑμῶν κράζει, καὶ αἱ βοαὶ τῶν θερισάντων εἰς τὰ
you shouts, and the loud of the ones having into the
          cries harvested

3775	2962	4519	1525	**5**	5171

ὦτα κυρίου σαβαὼθ εἰσεληλύθασιν. **5** ἐτρυφήσατε
ears of Master Sabaoth have come in. You indulged

1909	06	1093	2532	4684	5142	020

ἐπὶ τῆς γῆς καὶ ἐσπαταλήσατε, ἐθρέψατε τὰς
on the earth and were self-indulgent, you fed the

2588	1473	1722	2250	4967

καρδίας ὑμῶν ἐν ἡμέρᾳ σφαγῆς,
hearts of you in day of slaughter,

6	2613	5407	04	1342	3756

6 κατεδικάσατε, ἐφονεύσατε τὸν δίκαιον, οὐκ
you condemned, you murdered the right, not

498	1473	**7**	3114	3767

ἀντιτάσσεται ὑμῖν. **7** Μακροθυμήσατε οὖν,
he sets in order against you. Be long-tempered then,

80	2193	06	3952	02	2962	2400	01

ἀδελφοί, ἕως τῆς παρουσίας τοῦ κυρίου. ἰδοὺ ὁ
brothers, until the presence of the Master. Look the

1092	1551	04	5093	2590	06	1093

γεωργὸς ἐκδέχεται τὸν τίμιον καρπὸν τῆς γῆς
farmer waits for the valuable fruit of the earth

3114	1909	846	2193	2983

μακροθυμῶν ἐπ᾽ αὐτῷ ἕως λάβῃ
being long-tempered on it until it might receive

4290a	2532	3797	**8**	3114	2532	1473

πρόϊμον καὶ ὄψιμον. **8** μακροθυμήσατε καὶ ὑμεῖς,
early and evening. Be long-tempered also you,

4741	020	2588	1473	3754	05	3952

στηρίξατε τὰς καρδίας ὑμῶν, ὅτι ἡ παρουσία
strengthen the hearts of you, that the presence

02	2962	1448	**9**	3361	4727	80

τοῦ κυρίου ἤγγικεν. **9** μὴ στενάζετε, ἀδελφοί,
of the Master has neared. Not groan, brothers,

---

[17]Anyone, then, who knows the right thing to do and fails to do it, commits sin.

CHAPTER 5

Come now, you rich people, weep and wail for the miseries that are coming to you. [2]Your riches have rotted, and your clothes are moth-eaten. [3]Your gold and silver have rusted, and their rust will be evidence against you, and it will eat your flesh like fire. You have laid up treasure[a] for the last days. [4]Listen! The wages of the laborers who mowed your fields, which you kept back by fraud, cry out, and the cries of the harvesters have reached the ears of the Lord of hosts. [5]You have lived on the earth in luxury and in pleasure; you have fattened your hearts in a day of slaughter. [6]You have condemned and murdered the righteous one, who does not resist you.

[7]Be patient, therefore, beloved,[b] until the coming of the Lord. The farmer waits for the precious crop from the earth, being patient with it until it receives the early and the late rains. [8]You also must be patient. Strengthen your hearts, for the coming of the Lord is near.[c] [9]Beloved,[d] do not grumble

---

a Or *will eat your flesh, since you have stored up fire*

b Gk *brothers*

c Or *is at hand*

d Gk *Brothers*

against one another, so that you may not be judged. See, the Judge is standing at the doors! ¹⁰As an example of suffering and patience, beloved,*a* take the prophets who spoke in the name of the Lord. ¹¹Indeed we call blessed those who showed endurance. You have heard of the endurance of Job, and you have seen the purpose of the Lord, how the Lord is compassionate and merciful.

12 Above all, my beloved,*a* do not swear, either by heaven or by earth or by any other oath, but let your "Yes" be yes and your "No" be no, so that you may not fall under condemnation.

13 Are any among you suffering? They should pray. Are any cheerful? They should sing songs of praise. ¹⁴Are any among you sick? They should call for the elders of the church and have them pray over them, anointing them with oil in the name of the Lord. ¹⁵The prayer of faith will save the sick, and the Lord will raise them up; and anyone who has committed sins will be forgiven. ¹⁶Therefore confess your sins to one another, and pray for one another, so that you may be healed. The prayer of the righteous is powerful and effective. ¹⁷Elijah was a human being

a Gk brothers

2596	240		2443 3361 2919	
κατ'	ἀλλήλων		ἵνα μὴ	κριθῆτε·
against	one another		that not	you might be judged;

2400 01   2923   4253   018 2374 2476   5262
ἰδοὺ ὁ   κριτὴς πρὸ   τῶν θυρῶν ἔστηκεν.   10 ὑπόδειγμα
look the judge before the doors has stood.   Example

2983   80   06   2552   2532 06
λάβετε, ἀδελφοί, τῆς   κακοπαθείας καὶ τῆς
take, brothers, of the bad suffering and of the

3115   016   4396   3739 2980   1722 011
μακροθυμίας τοὺς προφήτας οἳ   ἐλάλησαν ἐν   τῷ
long temper the spokesmen who spoke   in   the

3686   2962   11 2400 3106   016
ὀνόματι κυρίου.   ἰδοὺ μακαρίζομεν   τοὺς
name   of Master.   Look we call fortunate the ones

5278   08 5281   2492 191   2532 012
ὑπομείναντας· τὴν ὑπομονὴν Ἰὼβ ἠκούσατε καὶ τὸ
having endured; the patience Job you heard and the

5056   2962   3708   3754   4184
τέλος   κυρίου εἴδετε, ὅτι   πολύσπλαγχνός
completion of Master you saw, because much-affectioned

1510 01 2962   2532 3629   4253 3956 1161
ἐστιν ὁ κύριος καὶ οἰκτίρμων. 12 Πρὸ πάντων δέ,
is   the Master and compassionate. Before all but,

80   1473   3361 3660   3383   04 3772
ἀδελφοί μου, μὴ ὀμνύετε   μήτε   τὸν οὐρανὸν
brothers of me, not take an oath neither the heaven

3383 08 1093 3383 243   5100 3727 1510   1161
μήτε τὴν γῆν μήτε ἄλλον τινὰ ὅρκον· ἤτω   δὲ
nor the earth nor other some oath; let be but

1473 09 3483 3483 2532 09 3756a 3.756a 2443 3361
ὑμῶν τὸ ναὶ ναὶ καὶ τὸ οὒ   οὔ,   ἵνα μὴ
of you the yes yes and the no   no,   that not

5259 2920   4098   13 2553   5100 1722
ὑπὸ κρίσιν πέσητε.   Κακοπαθεῖ τις ἐν
by judgment you might fall. Suffers bad some in

1473 4336   2114   5100 5567
ὑμῖν, προσευχέσθω· εὐθυμεῖ   τις, ψαλλέτω·
you, let pray;   is cheerful some, let psalm;

14 770   5100 1722 1473 4341   016
ἀσθενεῖ τις ἐν ὑμῖν, προσκαλεσάσθω τοὺς
is weak some in you, let call to   the

4245   06   1577   2532 4336   1909
πρεσβυτέρους τῆς ἐκκλησίας καὶ προσευξάσθωσαν ἐπ'
older men of the assembly and let pray   on

846 218   846   1637   1722 011 3686
αὐτὸν ἀλείψαντες [αὐτὸν] ἐλαίῳ ἐν τῷ ὀνόματι
him having smeared him in oil in   the name

02   2962   15 2532 05 2171 06   4102
τοῦ κυρίου.   καὶ ἡ εὐχὴ τῆς πίστεως
of the Master. And the vow of the trust

4982   04 2577   2532 1453   846 01
σώσει   τὸν κάμνοντα καὶ ἐγερεῖ   αὐτὸν ὁ
will deliver the wearying and will raise him   the

2962   2579 266   1510   4160
κύριος· κἂν ἁμαρτίας ᾖ   πεποιηκώς,
Master; and if sins   there might be+ +having done,

863   846   16 1843   3767
ἀφεθήσεται   αὐτῷ.   ἐξομολογεῖσθε οὖν
it will be sent off to him. Confess out   then

240   020 266   2532 2172   5228
ἀλλήλοις τὰς ἁμαρτίας καὶ εὔχεσθε ὑπὲρ
to one another the sins and wish on behalf of

240   3704 2390   4183 2480
ἀλλήλων ὅπως ἰαθῆτε.   Πολὺ ἰσχύει
one another so that you might be cured. Much is strong

1162   1342   1754   2243   444   1510
δέησις δικαίου ἐνεργουμένη. 17 Ἡλίας ἄνθρωπος ἦν
request of right operating.   Elijah man   was

3663		1473	2532	4335		4336		010
ὁμοιοπαθὴς		ἡμῖν,	καὶ	προσευχῇ		προσηύξατο		τοῦ
like-suffering		to us,	and	in prayer		he prayed		the

3361	1026		2532	3756	1026		1909	06	1093
μὴ	βρέξαι,		καὶ	οὐκ	ἔβρεξεν		ἐπὶ	τῆς	γῆς
not	to rain,		and	not	it rained		on		the earth

1763		5140	2532	3376		1803	**18**	2532	3825
ἐνιαυτοὺς		τρεῖς	καὶ	μῆνας		ἕξ·		καὶ	πάλιν
years		three	and	months		six;		and	again

4336			2532	01	3772	5205	1325	2532	05
προσηύξατο,			καὶ	ὁ	οὐρανὸς	ὑετὸν	ἔδωκεν	καὶ	ἡ
he prayed,			and	the	heaven	rain	gave	and	the

1093	985		04	2590	846	**19**	80		1473
γῆ	ἐβλάστησεν		τὸν	καρπὸν	αὐτῆς.		Ἀδελφοί		μου,
earth	sprouted		the	fruit	of it.		Brothers		of me,

1437	5100	1722	1473	4105		575	06
ἐάν	τις	ἐν	ὑμῖν	πλανηθῇ		ἀπὸ	τῆς
if	some	in	you	might be deceived		from	the

225		2532	1994		5100	846	**20**	1097
ἀληθείας		καὶ	ἐπιστρέψῃ		τις	αὐτόν,		γινωσκέτω
truth		and	might return		some	him,		let know

3754	01		1994		268		1537	4106
ὅτι	ὁ		ἐπιστρέψας		ἁμαρτωλὸν		ἐκ	πλάνης
that	the		one having returned		sinner		from	deceit

3598	846		4982		5590	846	1537	2288
ὁδοῦ	αὐτοῦ		σώσει		ψυχὴν	αὐτοῦ	ἐκ	θανάτου
way	of him		will deliver		soul	of him	from	death

2532	2572		4128	266
καὶ	καλύψει		πλῆθος	ἁμαρτιῶν.
and	will cover		quantity	of sins.

like us, and he prayed fervently that it might not rain, and for three years and six months it did not rain on the earth. [18]Then he prayed again, and the heaven gave rain and the earth yielded its harvest.

19 My brothers and sisters,[a] if anyone among you wanders from the truth and is brought back by another, [20]you should know that whoever brings back a sinner from wandering will save the sinner's[b] soul from death and will cover a multitude of sins.

[a] Gk *My brothers*
[b] Gk *his*

1 PETER

CHAPTER 1

Peter, an apostle of Jesus Christ,
To the exiles of the Dispersion in Pontus, Galatia, Cappadocia, Asia, and Bithynia, 2who have been chosen and destined by God the Father and sanctified by the Spirit to be obedient to Jesus Christ and to be sprinkled with his blood:
May grace and peace be yours in abundance.
3 Blessed be the God and Father of our Lord Jesus Christ! By his great mercy he has given us a new birth into a living hope through the resurrection of Jesus Christ from the dead, 4and into an inheritance that is imperishable, undefiled, and unfading, kept in heaven for you, 5who are being protected by the power of God through faith for a salvation ready to be revealed in the last time. 6In this you rejoice,[a] even if now for a little while you have had to suffer various trials, 7so that the genuineness of your faith—being more precious than gold that, though perishable, is tested by fire—may be found to result in praise and glory and honor when Jesus Christ is revealed. 8Although you have not seen[b] him, you love him; and even though you do not see him now, you believe in him and rejoice with an indescribable and glorious joy, 9for you are receiving the

a Or Rejoice in this
b Other ancient authorities read known

1:1
| 4074 | 652 | | 2424 | 5547 | 1588 |
Πέτρος ἀπόστολος Ἰησοῦ Χριστοῦ ἐκλεκτοῖς
Peter delegate of Jesus Christ to select

3927 1290 4195 1053
παρεπιδήμοις διασπορᾶς Πόντου, Γαλατίας,
transients of dispersion of Pontus, Galatia,

2587 773 2532 978 **2** 2596 4268
Καππαδοκίας, Ἀσίας καὶ Βιθυνίας, κατὰ πρόγνωσιν
Cappadocia, Asia and Bithynia, by foreknowledge

2316 3962 1722 38 4151 1519 5218
θεοῦ πατρὸς ἐν ἁγιασμῷ πνεύματος εἰς ὑπακοὴν
of God father in holiness of spirit for obedience

2532 4473 129 2424 5547 5485
καὶ ῥαντισμὸν αἵματος Ἰησοῦ Χριστοῦ, χάρις
and sprinkling of blood of Jesus Christ, favor

1473 2532 1515 4129 **3** 2128 01
ὑμῖν καὶ εἰρήνη πληθυνθείη. Εὐλογητὸς ὁ
to you and peace may be multiplied. Well-spoken the

2316 2532 3962 02 2962 1473 2424 5547 01
θεὸς καὶ πατὴρ τοῦ κυρίου ἡμῶν Ἰησοῦ Χριστοῦ, ὁ
God and father of the Master of us Jesus Christ, the

2596 012 4183 846 1656 313
κατὰ τὸ πολὺ αὐτοῦ ἔλεος ἀναγεννήσας
by the much of him mercy having given birth again

1473 1519 1680 2198 1223 386 2424
ἡμᾶς εἰς ἐλπίδα ζῶσαν δι' ἀναστάσεως Ἰησοῦ
us into hope living through standing up of Jesus

5547 1537 3498 **4** 1519 2817 862
Χριστοῦ ἐκ νεκρῶν, εἰς κληρονομίαν ἄφθαρτον
Christ from dead, into inheritance incorruptible

2532 283 2532 263 5083 1722
καὶ ἀμίαντον καὶ ἀμάραντον, τετηρημένην ἐν
and undefiled and unfading, having been kept in

3772 1519 1473 **5** 016 1722 1411 2316
οὐρανοῖς εἰς ὑμᾶς τοὺς ἐν δυνάμει θεοῦ
heavens for you the ones in power of God

5432 1223 4102 1519 4991
φρουρουμένους διὰ πίστεως εἰς σωτηρίαν
being guarded through trust into deliverance

2092 601 1722 2540 2078 **6** 1722 3739
ἑτοίμην ἀποκαλυφθῆναι ἐν καιρῷ ἐσχάτῳ. ἐν ᾧ
prepared to be uncovered in season last. In which

21 3641 737 1487 1163 1510
ἀγαλλιᾶσθε, ὀλίγον ἄρτι εἰ δέον [ἐστὶν]
you are glad, little now if being necessary it is

3076 1722 4164 3986 **7** 2443
λυπηθέντες ἐν ποικίλοις πειρασμοῖς, ἵνα
having been grieved in various pressures, that

09 1383 1473 06 4102 4186
τὸ δοκίμιον ὑμῶν τῆς πίστεως πολυτιμότερον
the proof of you of the trust much more valuable

5553 010 622 1223 4442 1161
χρυσίου τοῦ ἀπολλυμένου διὰ πυρὸς δὲ
of gold the being destroyed through fire but

1381 2147 1519 1868 2532
δοκιμαζομένου, εὑρεθῇ εἰς ἔπαινον καὶ
being proved, it might be found for praise on and

1391 2532 5092 1722 602 2424 5547
δόξαν καὶ τιμὴν ἐν ἀποκαλύψει Ἰησοῦ Χριστοῦ·
splendor and value in uncovering of Jesus Christ;

8 3739 3756 3708 25 1519 3739 737 3361
ὃν οὐκ ἰδόντες ἀγαπᾶτε, εἰς ὃν ἄρτι μὴ
whom not having seen you love, to whom now not

3708 4100 1161 21 5479
ὁρῶντες πιστεύοντες δὲ ἀγαλλιᾶσθε χαρᾷ
seeing trusting but you are glad in joy

412 2532 1392 **9** 2865 012
ἀνεκλαλήτῳ καὶ δεδοξασμένῃ κομιζόμενοι τὸ
unspeakable and having been given splendor obtaining the

5056   06   4102   1473   4991   5590
τέλος   τῆς   πίστεως [ὑμῶν] σωτηρίαν   ψυχῶν.
completion of the trust   of you deliverance of souls.

    4012 3739 4991   1567   2532
10 περὶ ἧς   σωτηρίας   ἐξεζήτησαν   καὶ
   About which deliverance they sought out and

1830   4396   013 4012 06   1519 1473 5485
ἐξηραύνησαν προφῆται οἱ περὶ τῆς εἰς ὑμᾶς χάριτος
searched out spokesmen the about the for you   favor

4395   2037a   1519 5101 2228
προφητεύσαντες,   11 ἐραυνῶντες εἰς τίνα ἢ
having spoken before, searching   for what or

4169   2540   1213   09   1722 846   4151
ποῖον   καιρὸν ἐδήλου   τὸ ἐν αὐτοῖς πνεῦμα
what sort season was made clear the in them   spirit

5547   4303   024 1519 5547
Χριστοῦ προμαρτυρόμενον τὰ εἰς Χριστὸν
of Christ testifying before the for Christ

3804   2532 020 3326 3778 1391   3739
παθήματα καὶ τὰς μετὰ ταῦτα δόξας.   12 οἷς
sufferings and the after these splendors. To whom

601   3754 3756 1438   1473   1161
ἀπεκαλύφθη   ὅτι οὐχ ἑαυτοῖς ὑμῖν δὲ
it was uncovered that not themselves to you but

1247   846   3739 3568 312   1473
διηκόνουν   αὐτά, ἃ   νῦν ἀνηγγέλη   ὑμῖν
they were serving them, which now were declared to you

1223   014   2097   1473 1722
διὰ   τῶν εὐαγγελισαμένων   ὑμᾶς [ἐν]
through the ones having told good message you   in

4151   40   649   575 3772   1519
πνεύματι ἁγίῳ ἀποσταλέντι   ἀπ᾽ οὐρανοῦ, εἰς
spirit   holy having been delegated from heaven,   for

3739 1937   32   3879   13 1352
ἃ   ἐπιθυμοῦσιν ἄγγελοι παρακύψαι.   Διὸ
which desire   messengers to stoop down. Wherefore

328   020 3751   06   1271   1473
ἀναζωσάμενοι τὰς ὀσφύας τῆς διανοίας   ὑμῶν
having bound up the hips   of the intelligence of you

3525   5049   1679   1909 08
νήφοντες   τελείως   ἐλπίσατε ἐπὶ τὴν
being well-balanced completely you hope on   the

5342   1473 5485   1722 602   2424
φερομένην ὑμῖν χάριν ἐν ἀποκαλύψει Ἰησοῦ
being carried to you favor in uncovering   of Jesus

5547   14 5613 5043   5218   3361
Χριστοῦ.   ὡς τέκνα ὑπακοῆς μὴ
Christ.   As children obedience not

4964   019 4387   1722 07   52
συσχηματιζόμενοι ταῖς πρότερον ἐν τῇ ἀγνοίᾳ
being fashioned with the former in the unknowing

1473 1939   235 2596 04   2564
ὑμῶν ἐπιθυμίαις 15 ἀλλὰ κατὰ τὸν καλέσαντα
of you desires   but by   the one having called

1473 40   2532 846   40   1722 3956
ὑμᾶς ἅγιον καὶ αὐτοὶ ἅγιοι   ἐν πάσῃ
you holy and themselves holy ones in all

391   1096   16 1360 1125
ἀναστροφῇ γενήθητε,   διότι γέγραπται
behavior   become,   because it has been written,

3754 40   1510   3754 1473 40   1510
[ὅτι] ἅγιοι ἔσεσθε,   ὅτι ἐγὼ ἅγιός [εἰμι].
(")   holy ones you will be, because I   holy am.

   2532 1487 3962   1941   04   678
17 καὶ εἰ πατέρα ἐπικαλεῖσθε τὸν ἀπροσωπολήμπτως
   And if father you call on the not receiving face

2919   2596 012 1538 2041   1722 5401 04 06
κρίνοντα κατὰ τὸ ἑκάστου ἔργον, ἐν φόβῳ τὸν τῆς
judging   by   the of each work, in fear the of the

---

outcome of your faith, the salvation of your souls.

10 Concerning this salvation, the prophets who prophesied of the grace that was to be yours made careful search and inquiry, 11 inquiring about the person or time that the Spirit of Christ within them indicated when it testified in advance to the sufferings destined for Christ and the subsequent glory. 12 It was revealed to them that they were serving not themselves but you, in regard to the things that have now been announced to you through those who brought you good news by the Holy Spirit sent from heaven—things into which angels long to look!

13 Therefore prepare your minds for action;[a] discipline yourselves; set all your hope on the grace that Jesus Christ will bring you when he is revealed. 14 Like obedient children, do not be conformed to the desires that you formerly had in ignorance. 15 Instead, as he who called you is holy, be holy yourselves in all your conduct; 16 for it is written, "You shall be holy, for I am holy."

17 If you invoke as Father the one who judges all people impartially according to their deeds, live in reverent fear

a Gk gird up the loins of your mind

during the time of your exile. ¹⁸You know that you were ransomed from the futile ways inherited from your ancestors, not with perishable things like silver or gold, ¹⁹but with the precious blood of Christ, like that of a lamb without defect or blemish. ²⁰He was destined before the foundation of the world, but was revealed at the end of the ages for your sake. ²¹Through him you have come to trust in God, who raised him from the dead and gave him glory, so that your faith and hope are set on God.

22 Now that you have purified your souls by your obedience to the truth[a] so that you have genuine mutual love, love one another deeply[b] from the heart.[c] ²³You have been born anew, not of perishable but of imperishable seed, through the living and enduring word of God.[d] ²⁴For

"All flesh is like grass
and all its glory like the
flower of grass.
The grass withers,
and the flower falls,
²⁵but the word of the Lord
endures forever."
That word is the good news that was announced to you.

CHAPTER 2

Rid yourselves, therefore, of all malice, and all guile, insincerity, envy, and all slander. ²Like newborn

a Other ancient authorities add *through the Spirit*
b Or *constantly*
c Other ancient authorities read *a pure heart*
d Or *through the word of the living and enduring God*

3940	1473	5550	390		3609a
παροικίας	ὑμῶν	χρόνον	ἀναστράφητε,	**18**	εἰδότες
transiency	of you	time	behave,		having known

3754	3756	5349		694	2228	5553
ὅτι	οὐ	φθαρτοῖς,		ἀργυρίῳ	ἢ	χρυσίῳ,
that	not	in corruptible,		silver	or	gold,

3084		1537	06	3152	1473	391
ἐλυτρώθητε		ἐκ	τῆς	ματαίας	ὑμῶν	ἀναστροφῆς
you were redeemed		from	the	futile	of you	behavior

3970		19	235	5093	129	5613
πατροπαραδότου			ἀλλὰ	τιμίῳ	αἵματι	ὡς
given over by fathers			but	in valuable	blood	as

286	299	2532	784		5547
ἀμνοῦ	ἀμώμου	καὶ	ἀσπίλου		Χριστοῦ,
of lamb	blameless	and	without stain		Christ,

20	4267		3303	4253	2602
	προεγνωσμένου		μὲν	πρὸ	καταβολῆς
	having been known before		indeed	before	foundation

2889	5319		1161	1909	2078
κόσμου	φανερωθέντος		δὲ	ἐπ᾿	ἐσχάτου
of world	having been demonstrated		but	on	last

014	5550	1223	1473	21	016	1223	846
τῶν	χρόνων	δι᾿	ὑμᾶς		τοὺς	δι᾿	αὐτοῦ
of the times	through you				the	through him

4103		1519	2316	04	1453		846
πιστοὺς		εἰς	θεὸν	τὸν	ἐγείραντα		αὐτὸν
trustful ones		to	God	the one	having raised		him

1537	3498	2532	1391	846	1325		5620
ἐκ	νεκρῶν	καὶ	δόξαν	αὐτῷ	δόντα,		ὥστε
from dead		and	splendor	to him,	having given,		so that

08	4102	1473	2532	1680	1510	1519	2316	22	020
τὴν	πίστιν	ὑμῶν	καὶ	ἐλπίδα	εἶναι	εἰς	θεόν.		Τὰς
the trust	of you	and	hope	to be	in		God.		The

5590	1473	48		1722	07	5218	06
ψυχὰς	ὑμῶν	ἡγνικότες		ἐν	τῇ	ὑπακοῇ	τῆς
souls	of you	having purified		in	the	obedience	of the

225	1519	5360	505		1537
ἀληθείας	εἰς	φιλαδελφίαν	ἀνυπόκριτον,		ἐκ
truth	for	brotherly love	unhypocritical,		from

2513	2588	240	25		1619
[καθαρᾶς]	καρδίας	ἀλλήλους	ἀγαπήσατε		ἐκτενῶς
clean	heart	one another	love		intensely

23	313		3756	1537	4701	5349
	ἀναγεγεννημένοι		οὐκ	ἐκ	σπορᾶς	φθαρτῆς
	having been born again		not	from	seed	corruptible

235	862		1223	3056	2198	2316	2532
ἀλλὰ	ἀφθάρτου		διὰ	λόγου	ζῶντος	θεοῦ	καὶ
but	incorruptible		through	word	of living	God	and

3306	24	1360	3956	4561	5613	5528	2532	3956
μένοντος.		διότι	πᾶσα	σὰρξ	ὡς	χόρτος	καὶ	πᾶσα
staying.		Because	all	flesh	as	grass	and	all

1391	846	5613	438	5528	3583	01
δόξα	αὐτῆς	ὡς	ἄνθος	χόρτου·	ἐξηράνθη	ὁ
splendor	of it	as	flower	of grass;	was dried out	the

5528	2532	09	438	1601	25	09	1161	4487
χόρτος	καὶ	τὸ	ἄνθος	ἐξέπεσεν·		τὸ	δὲ	ῥῆμα
grass	and	the	flower	fell out;		the	but	word

2962	3306	1519	04	165	3778	1161	1510	09
κυρίου	μένει	εἰς	τὸν	αἰῶνα.	τοῦτο	δέ	ἐστιν	τὸ
of Master	stays	into	the	age.	This	but	is	the

4487	09	2097		1519	1473	2:1	659	3767
ῥῆμα	τὸ	εὐαγγελισθὲν		εἰς	ὑμᾶς.		Ἀποθέμενοι	οὖν
word	the	having been		for	you.		Having set	then
		told good message					off	

3956	2549	2532	3956	1388	2532	5272		2532
πᾶσαν	κακίαν	καὶ	πάντα	δόλον	καὶ	ὑποκρίσεις		καὶ
all	badness	and	all	guile	and	hypocrisies		and

5355	2532	3956	2636		5613	738
φθόνους	καὶ	πάσας	καταλαλιάς,	**2**	ὡς	ἀρτιγέννητα
envies	and	all	speeches against,		as	just born

1025   012   3050   97   1051 1971
βρέφη   τὸ   λογικὸν   ἄδολον   γάλα ἐπιποθήσατε,
infants the reasonable unguile milk desire longingly,

2443 1722 846   837   1519 4991   3 1487
ἵνα   ἐν   αὐτῷ αὐξηθῆτε   εἰς σωτηρίαν,   εἰ
that in   it   you might grow   into deliverance,   if

1089   3754 5543   01   2962   4 4314   3739
ἐγεύσασθε ὅτι χρηστὸς ὁ   κύριος.   πρὸς ὃν
you taste that kind   the Master.   Toward whom

4334   3037 2198   5259 444   3303
προσερχόμενοι λίθον ζῶντα ὑπὸ ἀνθρώπων μὲν
coming to   stone living by men   indeed

593   3844   1161 2316 1588   1784
ἀποδεδοκιμασμένον παρὰ δὲ θεῷ ἐκλεκτὸν ἔντιμον,
having been rejected along but God select   in honor,

5 2532 846   5613 3037 2198   3618
   καὶ αὐτοὶ   ὡς λίθοι ζῶντες οἰκοδομεῖσθε
   and yourselves   as stones living are being built

3624 4152   1519 2406   40   399
οἶκος πνευματικὸς εἰς ἱεράτευμα ἅγιον ἀνενέγκαι
house spiritual   into priesthood holy to bring up

4152   2378   2144   03   2316
πνευματικὰς θυσίας εὐπροσδέκτους [τῷ] θεῷ
spiritual   sacrifices well-accepted to the God

1223 2424   5547   6 1360   4023   1722
διὰ Ἰησοῦ Χριστοῦ.   διότι περιέχει   ἐν
through Jesus Christ.   Because it encircles in

1124   2400 5087   1722 4622 3037 204
γραφῇ· ἰδοὺ τίθημι ἐν   Σιὼν λίθον ἀκρογωνιαῖον
writing, look I set in   Sion stone cornerstone

1588   1784   2532 01 4100   1909 846   3756
ἐκλεκτὸν ἔντιμον καὶ ὁ   πιστεύων   ἐπ' αὐτῷ οὐ
select   in honor and the one trusting on him   not

3361 2617   7 1473 3767 05 5092 015
μὴ καταισχυνθῇ.   ὑμῖν οὖν ἡ τιμὴ τοῖς
not might be ashamed. To you then the value to the

4100   569   1161 3037 3739 593
πιστεύουσιν,   ἀπιστοῦσιν δὲ λίθος ὃν   ἀπεδοκίμασαν
ones trusting, untrusting but stone which rejected

013 3618   3778 1096   1519 2776   1137
οἱ οἰκοδομοῦντες, οὗτος ἐγενήθη εἰς κεφαλὴν γωνίας
the ones building, this became for head   of corner

8 2532 3037 4348   2532 4073   4625   3739
  καὶ λίθος προσκόμματος   καὶ πέτρα σκανδάλου·   οἳ
  and stone of stumbling   and rock of offense;   who

4350   03   3056   544   1519 3739 2532
προσκόπτουσιν τῷ λόγῳ ἀπειθοῦντες εἰς ὃ   καὶ
stumble   in the word disobeying for which also

5087   9 1473 1161 1085 1588   934
ἐτέθησαν.   ὑμεῖς δὲ γένος ἐκλεκτόν, βασίλειον
they were set. You   but kind select,   kingly

2406   1484   40   2992   1519 4047
ἱεράτευμα, ἔθνος ἅγιον, λαὸς εἰς περιποίησιν,
priesthood, nation holy, people for possession,

3704 020 703   1804   02 1537
ὅπως τὰς ἀρετὰς ἐξαγγείλητε   τοῦ ἐκ
so that the virtues you might announce out the from

4655   1473 2564   1519 012 2298   846
σκότους ὑμᾶς καλέσαντος εἰς τὸ θαυμαστὸν αὐτοῦ
dark   you having called into the marvelous of him

5457   10 3739 4218 3756 2992   3568 1161 2992
φῶς·   οἳ ποτε οὐ λαὸς νῦν δὲ λαὸς
light;   who then not people now but people

2316 013 3756 1653   3568 1161 1653
θεοῦ, οἱ οὐκ ἠλεημένοι νῦν δὲ ἐλεηθέντες.
of God, the not having been now but having been
      ones   shown mercy   shown mercy.

11 27   3870   5613 3941   2532
   Ἀγαπητοί, παρακαλῶ ὡς παροίκους καὶ
   Loved ones, I encourage as transients and

---

infants, long for the pure, spiritual milk, so that by it you may grow into salvation— [3]if indeed you have tasted that the Lord is good.

4 Come to him, a living stone, though rejected by mortals yet chosen and precious in God's sight, and [5]like living stones, let yourselves be built[a] into a spiritual house, to be a holy priesthood, to offer spiritual sacrifices acceptable to God through Jesus Christ. [6]For it stands in scripture:

"See, I am laying in Zion
    a stone,
  a cornerstone chosen
    and precious;
  and whoever believes in
    him[b] will not be put
    to shame."

[7]To you then who believe, he is precious; but for those who do not believe,

"The stone that the
    builders rejected
  has become the very
    head of the corner,"

[8]and

"A stone that makes them
    stumble,
  and a rock that makes
    them fall."

They stumble because they disobey the word, as they were destined to do.

9 But you are a chosen race, a royal priesthood, a holy nation, God's own people,[c] in order that you may proclaim the mighty acts of him who called you out of darkness into his marvelous light.

[10]Once you were not a
    people,
  but now you are God's
    people;
  once you had not received
    mercy,
  but now you have
    received mercy.

11 Beloved, I urge you as aliens and

---

a Or you yourselves are being built
b Or it
c Gk a people for his possession

exiles to abstain from the desires of the flesh that wage war against the soul. [12]Conduct yourselves honorably among the Gentiles, so that, though they malign you as evil-doers, they may see your honorable deeds and glorify God when he comes to judge.[a]

13 For the Lord's sake accept the authority of every human institution,[b] whether of the emperor as supreme, [14]or of governors, as sent by him to punish those who do wrong and to praise those who do right. [15]For it is God's will that by doing right you should silence the ignorance of the foolish. [16]As servants[c] of God, live as free people, yet do not use your freedom as a pretext for evil. [17]Honor everyone. Love the family of believers.[d] Fear God. Honor the emperor.

18Slaves, accept the authority of your masters with all deference, not only those who are kind and gentle but also those who are harsh. [19]For it is a credit to you if, being aware of God, you endure pain while suffering unjustly. [20]If you endure when you are beaten for doing wrong, what credit is that? But if you endure when you do right and suffer for it,

[a] Gk God on the day of visitation
[b] Or every institution ordained for human beings
[c] Gk slaves
[d] Gk Love the brotherhood

3927	568		018	4559
παρεπιδήμους	ἀπέχεσθαι		τῶν	σαρκικῶν
transients	to hold off yourself		of the	fleshly

1939	3748	4754	2596	06	5590
ἐπιθυμιῶν	αἵτινες	στρατεύονται	κατὰ		τῆς ψυχῆς·
desires	which	soldier	against		the soul;

12 08 391   1473 1722 023 1484   2192
τὴν ἀναστροφὴν ὑμῶν ἐν τοῖς ἔθνεσιν ἔχοντες
the behavior of you in the nations having

2570 2443 1722 3739 2635   1473 5613
καλήν, ἵνα ἐν ᾧ καταλαλοῦσιν ὑμῶν ὡς
good, that in what they talk against you as

2555   1537 022 2570 2041 2029
κακοποιῶν ἐκ τῶν καλῶν ἔργων ἐποπτεύοντες
bad doers from the good works observing

1392   04 2316 1722 2250
δοξάσωσιν τὸν θεὸν ἐν ἡμέρᾳ
they might give splendor the God in day

1984   5293   3956   442   2937
ἐπισκοπῆς. **13** Ὑποτάγητε πάσῃ ἀνθρωπίνῃ κτίσει
of oversight. Be subject to all man-like creation

1223 04 2962 1535 935 5613 5242
διὰ τὸν κύριον, εἴτε βασιλεῖ ὡς ὑπερέχοντι,
through the Master, whether to king as excelling,

14 1535 2232 5613 1223 846 3992 1519
εἴτε ἡγεμόσιν ὡς δι᾽ αὐτοῦ πεμπομένοις εἰς
or to leaders as through him being sent for

1557   2555   1868 1161 17
ἐκδίκησιν κακοποιῶν ἔπαινον δὲ ἀγαθοποιῶν·
bring out right of bad doers praise on but doing good;

15 3754 3779 1510 09 2307 02 2316
ὅτι οὕτως ἐστὶν τὸ θέλημα τοῦ θεοῦ
because thusly it is the want of the God

15   5392   08 014 878   444
ἀγαθοποιοῦντας φιμοῦν τὴν τῶν ἀφρόνων ἀνθρώπων
doing good to muzzle the of the unthinking men

56   5613 1658   2532 3361 5613 1942
ἀγνωσίαν, **16** ὡς ἐλεύθεροι καὶ μὴ ὡς ἐπικάλυμμα
no knowledge, as free and not as cover over

2192 06 2549 08 1657   235 5613 2316
ἔχοντες τῆς κακίας τὴν ἐλευθερίαν ἀλλ᾽ ὡς θεοῦ
having of the badness the freedom but as of God

1401 3956 5091 08 81 25
δοῦλοι. **17** πάντας τιμήσατε, τὴν ἀδελφότητα ἀγαπᾶτε,
slaves. All value, the brotherhood love,

04 2316 5399 04 935 5091   **18** 013
τὸν θεὸν φοβεῖσθε, τὸν βασιλέα τιμᾶτε. Οἱ
the God fear, the king value. The

3610   5293   1722 3956 5401 015
οἰκέται ὑποτασσόμενοι ἐν παντὶ φόβῳ τοῖς
house servants being subject in all fear to the

1203   3756 3441 015 18   2532 1933
δεσπόταις, οὐ μόνον τοῖς ἀγαθοῖς καὶ ἐπιεικέσιν
supervisors, not alone to the good and gentle

235 2532 015 4646   **19** 3778 1063 5485 1487
ἀλλὰ καὶ τοῖς σκολιοῖς. τοῦτο γὰρ χάρις εἰ
but also to the crooked. This for favor if

1223 4893 2316 5297 5100 3077
διὰ συνείδησιν θεοῦ ὑποφέρει τις λύπας
through conscience of God endures some griefs

3958 95   **20** 4169   1063 2811 1487
πάσχων ἀδίκως. ποῖον γὰρ κλέος εἰ
of suffering unrightly. What kind for fame if

264 2532 2852   5278   235 1487
ἁμαρτάνοντες καὶ κολαφιζόμενοι ὑπομενεῖτε; ἀλλ᾽ εἰ
sinning and being knocked you will But if
about endure?

15   2532 3958   5278   3778
ἀγαθοποιοῦντες καὶ πάσχοντες ὑπομενεῖτε, τοῦτο
doing good and suffering you will endure, this

5485   3844 2316   1519 3778   1063 2564
χάρις παρὰ θεῷ. **21** εἰς τοῦτο γὰρ ἐκλήθητε,
favor from God.   Into this for you were called,

3754 2532 5547   3958   5228   1473 1473
ὅτι καὶ Χριστὸς ἔπαθεν ὑπὲρ ὑμῶν ὑμῖν
that also Christ suffered on behalf of you to you

5277   5261   2443 1872
ὑπολιμπάνων ὑπογραμμὸν ἵνα ἐπακολουθήσητε
leaving behind pattern   that you might follow on

023   2487   846   3739 266   3756
τοῖς ἴχνεσιν αὐτοῦ, **22** ὃς ἁμαρτίαν οὐκ
in the footprints of him, who sin   not

4160   2147   1388 1722 011 4750
ἐποίησεν οὐδὲ εὑρέθη δόλος ἐν τῷ στόματι
he did but not was found guile in the mouth

846   3739 3058   3756 486
αὐτοῦ, **23** ὃς λοιδορούμενος οὐκ ἀντελοιδόρει,
of him, who being abused not he abused back,

3958   3756 546   3860
πάσχων οὐκ ἠπείλει,   παρεδίδου
suffering not he was threatening, he was giving over

1161 03   2919   1346   3739 020 266
δὲ   τῷ   κρίνοντι δικαίως· **24** ὃς τὰς ἁμαρτίας
but to the one judging rightly; who the sins

1473 846   399   1722 011 4983   846   1909
ἡμῶν αὐτὸς ἀνήνεγκεν ἐν τῷ σώματι αὐτοῦ ἐπὶ
of us himself brought up in the body of him on

012 3586   2443 019   266   581
τὸ ξύλον, ἵνα ταῖς ἁμαρτίαις ἀπογενόμενοι
the wood, that in the sins   having become off

07   1343   2198   3739 03 3468
τῇ   δικαιοσύνῃ ζήσωμεν,   οὗ   τῷ μώλωπι
in the rightness we might live, whose the wound

2390   1510   1063 5613 4263
ἰάθητε. **25** ἦτε γὰρ ὡς πρόβατα
you were cured. You were for as sheep

4105   235 1994   3568 1909 04
πλανώμενοι, ἀλλὰ ἐπεστράφητε νῦν ἐπὶ τὸν
being deceived, but you were returned now on the

4166   2532 1985   018   5590 1473   3668
ποιμένα καὶ ἐπίσκοπον τῶν ψυχῶν ὑμῶν. **3:1** Ὁμοίως
shepherd and overseer of the souls of you. Likewise

017 1135   5293   015   2398   435
[αἱ] γυναῖκες, ὑποτασσόμεναι τοῖς ἰδίοις ἀνδράσιν,
the women, being subject to the own   men,

2443 2532 1487 5100 544   03 3056 1223   06
ἵνα καὶ εἴ τινες ἀπειθοῦσιν τῷ λόγῳ, διὰ   τῆς
that also if some disobey the word, through the

018 1135   391   427   3056
τῶν γυναικῶν ἀναστροφῆς ἄνευ λόγου
of the women behavior   without word

2770   2029   08   1722 5401
κερδηθήσονται, **2** ἐποπτεύσαντες τὴν ἐν φόβῳ
they will be gained, having observed the in fear

53   391   1473   3739 1510 3756 01
ἁγνὴν ἀναστροφὴν ὑμῶν. **3** ὧν ἔστω οὐχ ὁ
pure behavior of you. Of whom let be not the

1855   1708   2359   2532 4025
ἔξωθεν ἐμπλοκῆς τριχῶν καὶ περιθέσεως
from outside braiding of hairs and setting around

5553   2228 1745   2440   2889   4 235 01
χρυσίων ἢ   ἐνδύσεως ἱματίων κόσμος **4** ἀλλ' ὁ
of golds or dressing of clothes adorned but the

2927   06   2588   444   1722 011 862
κρυπτὸς τῆς καρδίας ἄνθρωπος ἐν τῷ ἀφθάρτῳ
hidden of the heart man   in the incorruptible

010   4239   2532 2272   4151   3739 1510
τοῦ πραέως καὶ ἡσυχίου πνεύματος, ὅ ἐστιν
of the gentle and quiet spirit,   which is

you have God's approval.
[21]For to this you have been
called, because Christ also
suffered for you, leaving
you an example, so that you
should follow in his steps.
[22]"He committed no sin,
 and no deceit was found
 in his mouth."
[23]When he was abused,
he did not return abuse;
when he suffered, he did not
threaten; but he entrusted
himself to the one who
judges justly. [24]He himself
bore our sins in his body
on the cross,[a] so that, free
from sins, we might live
for righteousness; by his
wounds[b] you have been
healed. [25]For you were
going astray like sheep, but
now you have returned to
the shepherd and guardian
of your souls.

CHAPTER 3

Wives, in the same way,
accept the authority of your
husbands, so that, even if
some of them do not obey
the word, they may be
won over without a word
by their wives' conduct,
[2]when they see the purity
and reverence of your lives.
[3]Do not adorn yourselves
outwardly by braiding your
hair, and by wearing gold
ornaments or fine clothing;
[4]rather, let your adornment
be the inner self with the
lasting beauty of a gentle
and quiet spirit, which is

---

[a] Or carried up our sins in his body to
 the tree
[b] Gk bruise

very precious in God's
sight. ⁵It was in this way
long ago that the holy
women who hoped in God
used to adorn themselves
by accepting the authority
of their husbands. ⁶Thus
Sarah obeyed Abraham
and called him lord. You
have become her daughters
as long as you do what is
good and never let fears
alarm you.

7 Husbands, in the same
way, show consideration
for your wives in your life
together, paying honor to
the woman as the weaker
sex,ᵃ since they too are also
heirs of the gracious gift of
life—so that nothing may
hinder your prayers.

8 Finally, all of you,
have unity of spirit,
sympathy, love for one
another, a tender heart,
and a humble mind. ⁹Do
not repay evil for evil or
abuse for abuse; but, on
the contrary, repay with a
blessing. It is for this that
you were called—that you
might inherit a blessing.
¹⁰For
    "Those who desire life
    and desire to see good
       days,
    let them keep their
       tongues from evil
    and their lips from
       speaking deceit;
¹¹ let them turn away from
    evil and do good;
    let them seek peace and
       pursue it.
¹² For the eyes of the Lord
    are on the righteous,
    and his ears are open to
       their prayer.
    But the face of the Lord is
       against those who do
       evil."
13 Now who will harm
you if you are eager to do
what is good?

ᵃ Gk vessel

1799	02	2316	4185		3779	1063	4218	2532
ἐνώπιον	τοῦ	θεοῦ	πολυτελές.	**5**	οὕτως	γὰρ	ποτε	καὶ
before	the	God	much cost.		Thusly	for	then	also

017	40	1135	017	1679		1519	2316
αἱ	ἅγιαι	γυναῖκες	αἱ	ἐλπίζουσαι	εἰς	θεὸν
the	holy	women	the	ones hoping	for	God

2885   1438   5293   015   2398
ἐκόσμουν   ἑαυτάς   ὑποτασσόμεναι τοῖς   ἰδίοις
were adorning themselves   being subject to the own

435   **6** 5613 4564 5219   03 11   2962
ἀνδράσιν,   ὡς   Σάρρα ὑπήκουσεν τῷ ᾿Αβραὰμ κύριον
men,   as   Sarra obeyed   the Abraham master

846   2564   3739   1096   5043 15
αὐτὸν καλοῦσα, ἧς   ἐγενήθητε τέκνα ἀγαθοποιοῦσαι
him   calling, of whom you became children doing good

2532 3361 5399   3367   4423   **7** 013 435
καὶ μὴ φοβούμεναι μηδεμίαν   πτόησιν.   Οἱ ἄνδρες
and not fearing   but not one terror.   The men

3668   4924   2596 1108   5613
ὁμοίως,   συνοικοῦντες   κατὰ γνῶσιν   ὡς
likewise,   housing together by   knowledge as

772   4632   011 1134   632   5092
ἀσθενεστέρῳ σκεύει τῷ γυναικείῳ, ἀπονέμοντες τιμὴν
to weaker   pot   the woman,   assigning   value

5613 2532 4789   5485   2222   1519 012 3361
ὡς καὶ συγκληρονόμοις χάριτος ζωῆς   εἰς τὸ μὴ
as also co-inheritors   of favor of life for the not

1465   020 4335   1473 **8** 012 1161 5056
ἐγκόπτεσθαι   τὰς προσευχὰς ὑμῶν. Τὸ δὲ τέλος
to be hindered the prayers   of you. The but completion

3956   3675   4835   5361
πάντες ὁμόφρονες,   συμπαθεῖς,   φιλάδελφοι,
all   same thinking, co-suffering, brother-lovers,

2155   5012a   **9** 3361 591
εὔσπλαγχνοι, ταπεινόφρονες,   μὴ ἀποδιδόντες
well-affectioned, humbleminded,   not giving back

2556 173   2556 2228 3059   473   3059
κακὸν ἀντὶ κακοῦ ἢ λοιδορίαν ἀντὶ λοιδορίας,
bad   in place of bad or abuse in place of abuse,

5121   1161 2127   3754   1519 3778
τοὐναντίον   δὲ εὐλογοῦντες ὅτι   εἰς τοῦτο
on the contrary but speaking well because for this

2564   2443 2129   2816
ἐκλήθητε   ἵνα εὐλογίαν κληρονομήσητε.
you were called that good word you might inherit.

10 01   1063 2309   2222 25   2532 3708 2250
ὁ   γὰρ θέλων ζωὴν ἀγαπᾶν καὶ ἰδεῖν ἡμέρας
The one for wanting life to love and to see days

18   3973   08 1100   575 2556 2532 5491 010
ἀγαθὰς παυσάτω τὴν γλῶσσαν ἀπὸ κακοῦ καὶ χείλη τοῦ
good   let stop the tongue   from bad and lips the

3361 2980   1388   **11** 1578   1161 575 2556
μὴ λαλῆσαι δόλον,   ἐκκλινάτω δὲ ἀπὸ κακοῦ
not to speak guile,   let bow out but from bad

2532 4160   18 2212   1515   2532 1377
καὶ ποιησάτω ἀγαθόν, ζητησάτω εἰρήνην καὶ διωξάτω
and let do   good,   let seek peace   and let pursue

846   **12** 3754   2962   1909 1342   2532
αὐτήν·   ὅτι   ὀφθαλμοὶ κυρίου ἐπὶ δικαίους καὶ
it;   because eyes   of Master on right   and

3775 846   1519 1162   846   4383   1161
ὦτα αὐτοῦ εἰς δέησιν αὐτῶν, πρόσωπον δὲ
ears of him for request of them, face   but

2962   1909 4160   2556   **13** 2532 5101 01
κυρίου ἐπὶ ποιοῦντας κακά.   Καὶ τίς ὁ
of Master on one doing bad.   And who the one

2559   1473 1437 010   18   2207   2310
κακώσων ὑμᾶς ἐὰν τοῦ ἀγαθοῦ ζηλωταὶ
doing bad you if of the good jealous ones

1096 235 1487 2532 3958 1223
γένεσθε; **14** ἀλλ' εἰ καὶ πάσχοιτε διὰ
you become? But if also you may suffer because of

1343 3107 04 1161 5401 846 3361
δικαιοσύνην, μακάριοι. τὸν δὲ φόβον αὐτῶν μὴ
rightness, fortunate. The but fear of them not

5399 3366 5015 2962
φοβηθῆτε μηδὲ ταραχθῆτε, **15** κύριον
you might fear but not you might be troubled, Master

1161 04 5547 37 1722 019 2588 1473
δὲ τὸν Χριστὸν ἁγιάσατε ἐν ταῖς καρδίαις ὑμῶν,
but the Christ make holy in the hearts of you,

2092 104 4314 627 3956 03 154
ἕτοιμοι ἀεὶ πρὸς ἀπολογίαν παντὶ τῷ αἰτοῦντι
prepared always to defense to all the one asking

1473 3056 4012 06 1722 1473 1680 16 235 3326
ὑμᾶς λόγον περὶ τῆς ἐν ὑμῖν ἐλπίδος, **16** ἀλλὰ μετὰ
you word about the in you hope, but with

4240 2532 5401 4893 2192 18 2443
πραΰτητος καὶ φόβου, συνείδησιν ἔχοντες ἀγαθήν, ἵνα
gentleness and fear, conscience having good, that

1722 3739 2635 2617 013
ἐν ᾧ καταλαλεῖσθε καταισχυνθῶσιν οἱ
in what you are talked against might be ashamed the

1908 1473 18 1722 5547
ἐπηρεάζοντες ὑμῶν τὴν ἀγαθὴν ἐν Χριστῷ
ones mistreating you the good in Christ

391 2909 1063 15 1487
ἀναστροφήν. **17** κρεῖττον γὰρ ἀγαθοποιοῦντας, εἰ
behavior. Better for doing good, if

2309 09 2307 02 2316 3958 2228
θέλοι τὸ θέλημα τοῦ θεοῦ, πάσχειν ἢ
might want the want of the God, to suffer or

2554 18 3754 2532 5547 530 4012
κακοποιοῦντας. **18** ὅτι καὶ Χριστὸς ἅπαξ περὶ
doing bad. Because also Christ once concerning

266 3958 1342 5228 94 2443
ἁμαρτιῶν ἔπαθεν, δίκαιος ὑπὲρ ἀδίκων, ἵνα
sins suffered, right on behalf of unright, that

1473 4317 03 2316 2289 3303 4561
ὑμᾶς προσαγάγῃ τῷ θεῷ θανατωθεὶς μὲν σαρκὶ
you he might the God having been indeed in flesh
lead to put to death

2227 1161 4151 19 1722 3739
ζῳοποιηθεὶς δὲ πνεύματι· **19** ἐν ᾧ
having been made alive but in spirit; in which

2532 023 1722 5438 4151 4198
καὶ τοῖς ἐν φυλακῇ πνεύμασιν πορευθεὶς
also to the in guard spirits having traveled

2784 20 544 4218 3753
ἐκήρυξεν, **20** ἀπειθήσασίν ποτε ὅτε
he announced, to ones having disobeyed then when

553 05 02 2316 3115 1722 2250
ἀπεξεδέχετο ἡ τοῦ θεοῦ μακροθυμία ἐν ἡμέραις
awaited the of the God long temper in days

3575 2680 2787 1519 3739 3641
Νῶε κατασκευαζομένης κιβωτοῦ εἰς ἣν ὀλίγοι,
of Noah being prepared box in which few,

3778 1510 3638 5590 1295
τοῦτ' ἔστιν ὀκτὼ ψυχαί, διεσώθησαν
this is eight souls, were thoroughly delivered

1223 5204 21 3739 2532 1473 499 3568
δι' ὕδατος. **21** ὃ καὶ ὑμᾶς ἀντίτυπον νῦν
through water. which also you antitype now

4982 908 3756 4561 595 4509
σῴζει βάπτισμα, οὐ σαρκὸς ἀπόθεσις ῥύπου
delivers immersion, not of flesh setting off of dirt

235 4893 18 1906 1519 2316 1223
ἀλλὰ συνειδήσεως ἀγαθῆς ἐπερώτημα εἰς θεόν, δι'
but of conscience good asking to God, through

[14] But even if you do suffer for doing what is right, you are blessed. Do not fear what they fear,[a] and do not be intimidated, [15] but in your hearts sanctify Christ as Lord. Always be ready to make your defense to anyone who demands from you an accounting for the hope that is in you; [16] yet do it with gentleness and reverence.[b] Keep your conscience clear, so that, when you are maligned, those who abuse you for your good conduct in Christ may be put to shame. [17] For it is better to suffer for doing good, if suffering should be God's will, than to suffer for doing evil. [18] For Christ also suffered[c] for sins once for all, the righteous for the unrighteous, in order to bring you[d] to God. He was put to death in the flesh, but made alive in the spirit, [19] in which also he went and made a proclamation to the spirits in prison, [20] who in former times did not obey, when God waited patiently in the days of Noah, during the building of the ark, in which a few, that is, eight persons, were saved through water. [21] And baptism, which this prefigured, now saves you—not as a removal of dirt from the body, but as an appeal to God for[e] a good conscience, through

a Gk *their fear*
b Or *respect*
c Other ancient authorities read *died*
d Other ancient authorities read *us*
e Or *a pledge to God from*

the resurrection of Jesus Christ, [22]who has gone into heaven and is at the right hand of God, with angels, authorities, and powers made subject to him.

CHAPTER 4

Since therefore Christ suffered in the flesh,[a] arm yourselves also with the same intention (for whoever has suffered in the flesh has finished with sin), [2]so as to live for the rest of your earthly life[b] no longer by human desires but by the will of God. [3]You have already spent enough time in doing what the Gentiles like to do, living in licentiousness, passions, drunkenness, revels, carousing, and lawless idolatry. [4]They are surprised that you no longer join them in the same excesses of dissipation, and so they blaspheme.[c] [5]But they will have to give an accounting to him who stands ready to judge the living and the dead. [6]For this is the reason the gospel was proclaimed even to the dead, so that, though they had been judged in the flesh as everyone is judged, they might live in the spirit as God does.

[7]The end of all things is near;[d] therefore be serious and discipline yourselves for the sake of your prayers. [8]Above all, maintain constant love for one another, for love covers a multitude of sins.

---

a Other ancient authorities add *for us;* others, *for you*
b Gk *rest of the time in the flesh*
c Or *they malign you*
d Or *is at hand*

386	2424	5547	22	3739	1510	1722
ἀναστάσεως	Ἰησοῦ	Χριστοῦ,		ὅς	ἐστιν	ἐν
standing up	of Jesus	Christ,		who	is	in

1188	02	2316	4198		1519	3772
δεξιᾷ	[τοῦ]	θεοῦ	πορευθεὶς		εἰς	οὐρανόν
right	of the	God	having traveled		into	heaven

5293		846	32		2532
ὑποταγέντων		αὐτῷ	ἀγγέλων		καὶ
having been	subjected	to him	messengers		and

1849	2532	1411	4:1	5547	3767
ἐξουσιῶν	καὶ	δυνάμεων.		Χριστοῦ	οὖν
authorities	and	powers.		Of Christ	then

3958		4561	2532	1473	08	846	1771
παθόντος		σαρκὶ	καὶ	ὑμεῖς	τὴν	αὐτὴν	ἔννοιαν
having suffered		in flesh	and	you	the	same	insight

3695	3754	01	3958		4561
ὁπλίσασθε,	ὅτι	ὁ	παθὼν		σαρκὶ
arm yourself,	because	the	one having suffered		in flesh

3973	266	2	1519	012	3371	444
πέπαυται	ἁμαρτίας		εἰς	τὸ	μηκέτι	ἀνθρώπων
has stopped	sin		for	the	no longer	of men

1939	235	2307	2316	04	1954	1722
ἐπιθυμίαις	ἀλλὰ	θελήματι	θεοῦ	τὸν	ἐπίλοιπον	ἐν
desires	but	want	of God	the	remaining	in

4561	980	5550	713		1063	01
σαρκὶ	βιῶσαι	χρόνον.	3 ἀρκετὸς		γὰρ	ὁ
flesh	to live	time.	Sufficient		for	the

3928	5550	012	1013	022	1484
παρεληλυθὼς	χρόνος	τὸ	βούλημα	τῶν	ἐθνῶν
having gone along	time	the	plan	of	the nations

2716	4198	1722	766
κατειργάσθαι	πεπορευμένους	ἐν	ἀσελγείαις,
to work thoroughly	having traveled	in	debaucheries,

1939	3632	2970	4224	2532
ἐπιθυμίαις,	οἰνοφλυγίαις,	κώμοις,	πότοις	καὶ
in desires,	drunkennesses,	carousings,	drinkings,	and

111	1495	4	1722	3739
ἀθεμίτοις	εἰδωλολατρίαις.		ἐν	ᾧ
unlawful	idol services.		In	which

3579	3361	4936	1473	1519	08
ξενίζονται	μὴ	συντρεχόντων	ὑμῶν	εἰς	τὴν
they think strange	not	running with	you	into	the

846	06	810	401	987
αὐτὴν	τῆς	ἀσωτίας	ἀνάχυσιν	βλασφημοῦντες,
same	of the	dissipation	pouring out	insulting,

5	3739	591	3056	03	2093	2192
	οἳ	ἀποδώσουσιν	λόγον	τῷ	ἑτοίμως	ἔχοντι
	who	will give back	word	to the	readily	one having

2919	2198	2532	3498	6	1519	3778	1063	2532
κρῖναι	ζῶντας	καὶ	νεκρούς.		εἰς	τοῦτο	γὰρ	καὶ
to judge	living	and	dead.		Into	this	for	also

3498	2097	2443	2919	3303	2596
νεκροῖς	εὐηγγελίσθη,	ἵνα	κριθῶσι	μὲν	κατὰ
to dead	good message was told,	that	they might be judged	indeed	by

444	4561	2198	1161	2596	2316
ἀνθρώπους	σαρκὶ	ζῶσι	δὲ	κατὰ	θεὸν
men	in flesh	they might live	but	by	God

4151	7	3956	1161	09	5056	1448
πνεύματι.		Πάντων	δὲ	τὸ	τέλος	ἤγγικεν.
in spirit.		Of all	but	the	completion	has neared.

4993	3767	2532	3525	1519	4335
σωφρονήσατε	οὖν	καὶ	νήψατε	εἰς	προσευχάς·
Think soberly	then	and	well-balanced	in	prayers;

8	4253	3956	08	1519	1438	26	1618
	πρὸ	πάντων	τὴν	εἰς	ἑαυτοὺς	ἀγάπην	ἐκτενῆ
	before	all	the	in	yourselves	love	intense

2192	3754	26	2572	4128	266
ἔχοντες,	ὅτι	ἀγάπη	καλύπτει	πλῆθος	ἁμαρτιῶν.
having,	that	love	covers	quantity	of sins.

9
5382	1519	240	427	1112
φιλόξενοι	εἰς	ἀλλήλους	ἄνευ	γογγυσμοῦ,
Stranger lovers	in	one another	without	grumbling,

10
1538	2531	2983	5486	1519	1438
ἕκαστος	καθὼς	ἔλαβεν	χάρισμα	εἰς	ἑαυτοὺς
each	just as	received	favor gift	for	themselves

846	1247	5613	2570	3623	4164
αὐτὸ	διακονοῦντες	ὡς	καλοὶ οἰκονόμοι	ποικίλης
it serving	as	good managers	of various

5485	2316	1487	5100	2980	5613	3051	2316
χάριτος	θεοῦ.	εἴ	τις	λαλεῖ,	ὡς	λόγια	θεοῦ·
favor	of God.	If	some speaks,	as	sayings of God;

11
1487	5100	1247	5613	1537	2479	3739	5524
εἴ	τις	διακονεῖ,	ὡς	ἐξ	ἰσχύος	ἧς	χορηγεῖ
if	some serves,	as	from strength	which	supplies

01	2316	2443	1722	3956	1392	01
ὁ	θεός,	ἵνα	ἐν	πᾶσιν	δοξάζηται	ὁ
the God,	that	in	all	might be given splendor	the

2316	1223	2424	5547	3739	1510	05	1391
θεὸς	διὰ	Ἰησοῦ Χριστοῦ,	ᾧ	ἐστιν	ἡ	δόξα
God	through Jesus Christ,	to whom is	the	splendor

2532	09	2904	1519	016	165	014	165
καὶ	τὸ	κράτος	εἰς	τοὺς	αἰῶνας	τῶν	αἰώνων,
and	the	strength	into	the	ages	of the ages,

281	27	3361	3579	07	1722
ἀμήν.	Ἀγαπητοί,	μὴ	ξενίζεσθε	τῇ	ἐν
amen.	Loved ones,	not	think strange	in the	in

12

1473	4451	4314	3986	1473	1096	5613
ὑμῖν	πυρώσει	πρὸς	πειρασμὸν	ὑμῖν	γινομένῃ	ὡς
you	burning	to	pressure	to you	becoming	as

3581	1473	4819	235	2526
ξένου	ὑμῖν	συμβαίνοντος,	ἀλλὰ	καθὸ
stranger	to you	going with,	but	just as

13

2841	023	02	5547	3804
κοινωνεῖτε	τοῖς	τοῦ	Χριστοῦ	παθήμασιν
you are partner	in the	of the	Christ	sufferings

5463	2443	2532	1722	07	602	06	1391
χαίρετε,	ἵνα	καὶ	ἐν	τῇ	ἀποκαλύψει	τῆς	δόξης
rejoice,	that	also	in	the	uncovering	of the splendor

846	5463	21	1487
αὐτοῦ	χαρῆτε	ἀγαλλιώμενοι.	εἰ
of him	you might rejoice	being glad.	If

14

3679	1722	3686	5547	3107
ὀνειδίζεσθε	ἐν	ὀνόματι	Χριστοῦ,	μακάριοι,
you are reviled	in	name	of Christ,	fortunate,

3754	09	06	1391	2532	09	02	2316
ὅτι	τὸ	τῆς	δόξης	καὶ	τὸ	τοῦ	θεοῦ
because	the	of the splendor	and	the	the	of the God

4151	1909	1473	373	3361	1063	5100	1473
πνεῦμα	ἐφ᾽	ὑμᾶς	ἀναπαύεται.	μὴ	γάρ	τις	ὑμῶν
spirit	on	you	rests.	Not	for	some	of you

15

3958	5613	5406	2228	2812	2228	2555
πασχέτω	ὡς	φονεὺς	ἢ	κλέπτης	ἢ	κακοποιὸς
let suffer	as	murderer	or	thief	or	bad doer

2228	5613	244	1487	1161	5613
ἢ	ὡς	ἀλλοτριεπίσκοπος·	εἰ	δὲ	ὡς
or	as	overseer of others;	if	but	as

16

5546	3361	153	1392
Χριστιανός,	μὴ	αἰσχυνέσθω,	δοξαζέτω
Christian,	not	let be ashamed,	let give splendor

1161	04	2316	1722	011	3686	3778	3754	01
δὲ	τὸν	θεὸν	ἐν	τῷ	ὀνόματι	τούτῳ.	ὅτι	[ὁ]
but	the God	in	the name	this.	Because	the

17

2540	010	757	012	2917	575	02	3624	02
καιρὸς	τοῦ	ἄρξασθαι	τὸ	κρίμα	ἀπὸ	τοῦ	οἴκου	τοῦ
season	the	to begin	the	judgment	from	the	house	of the

2316	1487	1161	4413	575	1473	5101	09	5056
θεοῦ·	εἰ	δὲ	πρῶτον	ἀφ᾽	ἡμῶν,	τί	τὸ	τέλος
God;	if	but	first	from	us,	what	the	completion

[9] Be hospitable to one another without complaining. [10] Like good stewards of the manifold grace of God, serve one another with whatever gift each of you has received. [11] Whoever speaks must do so as one speaking the very words of God; whoever serves must do so with the strength that God supplies, so that God may be glorified in all things through Jesus Christ. To him belong the glory and the power forever and ever. Amen.

[12] Beloved, do not be surprised at the fiery ordeal that is taking place among you to test you, as though something strange were happening to you. [13] But rejoice insofar as you are sharing Christ's sufferings, so that you may also be glad and shout for joy when his glory is revealed. [14] If you are reviled for the name of Christ, you are blessed, because the spirit of glory,[a] which is the Spirit of God, is resting on you.[b] [15] But let none of you suffer as a murderer, a thief, a criminal, or even as a mischief maker. [16] Yet if any of you suffers as a Christian, do not consider it a disgrace, but glorify God because you bear this name. [17] For the time has come for judgment to begin with the household of God; if it begins with us, what will be the end

---

a Other ancient authorities add and of power

b Other ancient authorities add On their part he is blasphemed, but on your part he is glorified

for those who do not obey the gospel of God? [18]And

"If it is hard for the righteous to be saved, what will become of the ungodly and the sinners?"

[19]Therefore, let those suffering in accordance with God's will entrust themselves to a faithful Creator, while continuing to do good.

CHAPTER 5

Now as an elder myself and a witness of the sufferings of Christ, as well as one who shares in the glory to be revealed, I exhort the elders among you [2]to tend the flock of God that is in your charge, exercising the oversight,[a] not under compulsion but willingly, as God would have you do it[b] —not for sordid gain but eagerly. [3]Do not lord it over those in your charge, but be examples to the flock [4]And when the chief shepherd appears, you will win the crown of glory that never fades away. [5]In the same way, you who are younger must accept the authority of the elders.[c] And all of you must clothe yourselves with humility in your dealings with one another, for

"God opposes the proud, but gives grace to the humble."

[6]Humble yourselves therefore under the mighty hand of God, so that he may exalt you in due time. [7]Cast all your anxiety on him, because he cares for you.

[a] Other ancient authorities lack *exercising the oversight*

[b] Other ancient authorities lack *as God would have you do it*

[c] Or *of those who are older*

014	544	011 02	2316 2098
τῶν	ἀπειθούντων τῷ τοῦ		θεοῦ εὐαγγελίῳ;
of the ones	disobeying the of the God		good message?

18 2532 1487 01 1342 3433 4982 01
καὶ εἰ ὁ δίκαιος μόλις σῴζεται, ὁ
And if the right scarcely is delivered, the

765 2532 268 4226 5316
ἀσεβὴς καὶ ἁμαρτωλὸς ποῦ φανεῖται;
irreverent and sinner where will he shine?

19 5620 2532 013 3958 2596 012 2307
ὥστε καὶ οἱ πάσχοντες κατὰ τὸ θέλημα
So that also the ones suffering by the want

02 2316 4103 2939 3908 020 5590
τοῦ θεοῦ πιστῷ κτίστῃ παρατιθέσθωσαν τὰς ψυχὰς
of the God trustful creator let set along the souls

846 1722 16 4245 3767 1722
αὐτῶν ἐν ἀγαθοποιΐᾳ. **5:1** Πρεσβυτέρους οὖν ἐν
of them in good doing. Older men then in

1473 3870 01 4850 2532 3144
ὑμῖν παρακαλῶ ὁ συμπρεσβύτερος καὶ μάρτυς
you encourage the co-older man and testifier

022 02 5547 3804 01 2532 06
τῶν τοῦ Χριστοῦ παθημάτων, ὁ καὶ τῆς
of the of the Christ sufferings, the also of the

3195 601 1391 2844
μελλούσης ἀποκαλύπτεσθαι δόξης κοινωνός·
being about to be uncovered splendor partner;

2 4165 012 1722 1473 4168 02 2316
ποιμάνατε τὸ ἐν ὑμῖν ποίμνιον τοῦ θεοῦ
shepherd the in you flock of the God

1983 3361 317 235 1596 2596
[ἐπισκοποῦντες] μὴ ἀναγκαστῶς ἀλλὰ ἑκουσίως κατὰ
overseeing not by compulsion but willingly by

2316 3366 147 235 4290
θεόν, μηδὲ αἰσχροκερδῶς ἀλλὰ προθύμως,
God, but not by shameful gain but eagerly,

3 3366 5613 2634 014 2819 235
μηδ' ὡς κατακυριεύοντες τῶν κλήρων ἀλλὰ
but not as mastering over the lots but

5179 1096 010 4168 2532
τύποι γινόμενοι τοῦ ποιμνίου· **4** καὶ
examples becoming of the flock; and

5319 02 750 2865 04
φανερωθέντος τοῦ ἀρχιποίμενος κομιεῖσθε τὸν
having been the ruler shepherd you will obtain the
demonstrated

262 06 1391 4735 3668
ἀμαράντινον τῆς δόξης στέφανον. **5** Ὁμοίως,
unfading of the splendor crown. Likewise

3501 5293 4245 3956 1161
νεώτεροι, ὑποτάγητε πρεσβυτέροις· πάντες δὲ
newer ones, be subject to older men; all but

240 08 5012 1463 3754
ἀλλήλοις τὴν ταπεινοφροσύνην ἐγκομβώσασθε, ὅτι
to one another the humblemindedness be clothed, (")

01 2316 5244 498 5011
[ὁ] θεὸς ὑπερηφάνοις ἀντιτάσσεται, ταπεινοῖς
the God arrogant sets in order against, humble

1161 1325 5485 5013 3767 5259 08 2900
δὲ δίδωσιν χάριν. **6** Ταπεινώθητε οὖν ὑπὸ τὴν κραταιὰν
but gives favor. Be humbled then by the strong

5495 02 2316 2443 1473 5312 1722
χεῖρα τοῦ θεοῦ, ἵνα ὑμᾶς ὑψώσῃ ἐν
hand of the God, that you might be elevated in

2540 7 3956 08 3308 1473 1977
καιρῷ, **7** πᾶσαν τὴν μέριμναν ὑμῶν ἐπιρίψαντες
season, all the anxiety of you having thrown on

1909 846 3754 846 3190a 4012 1473
ἐπ' αὐτόν, ὅτι αὐτῷ μέλει περὶ ὑμῶν.
on him, because to him it is a care about you.

8
3525	1127	01	476	1473
Νήψατε,	γρηγορήσατε.	ὁ	ἀντίδικος	ὑμῶν
Be well-balanced,	keep awake.	The	opponent	of you

1228	5613	3023	5612	4043	2212	5101
διάβολος	ὡς	λέων	ὠρυόμενος	περιπατεῖ	ζητῶν	[τινα]
slanderer	as	lion	roaring	walks around	seeking	whom

9
2666		3739	436	4731	07
καταπιεῖν·	ᾧ	ἀντίστητε	στερεοὶ	τῇ
to swallow down;	whom	stand against	solid	in the

4102	3609a	024	846	022	3804	07	1722
πίστει	εἰδότες	τὰ	αὐτὰ	τῶν	παθημάτων	τῇ	ἐν
trust	having known	the	same	the	sufferings	the	in

03	2889	1473	81	2005		01
[τῷ]	κόσμῳ	ὑμῶν	ἀδελφότητι	ἐπιτελεῖσθαι.		Ὁ
the	world	of you	brotherhood	to be thoroughly completed.	**10**	The

1161	2316	3956	5485	01	2564	1473
δὲ	θεὸς	πάσης	χάριτος,	ὁ	καλέσας	ὑμᾶς
but	God	of all	favor,	the	one having called	you

1519	08	166	846	1391	1722	5547	2424
εἰς	τὴν	αἰώνιον	αὐτοῦ	δόξαν	ἐν	Χριστῷ	[Ἰησοῦ],
into	the	eternal	of him	splendor	in	Christ	Jesus,

3641	3958	846	2675
ὀλίγον	παθόντας	αὐτὸς	καταρτίσει,
few	having suffered	himself	will put in order,

4741	4599	2311	846
στηρίξει,	σθενώσει,	θεμελιώσει.	αὐτῷ
will strengthen,	will invigorate,	will found.	**11** To him

09	2904	1519	016	165	281	1223	4610
τὸ	κράτος	εἰς	τοὺς	αἰῶνας,	ἀμήν.	Διὰ	Σιλουανοῦ
the	strength into		the	ages,	amen.	**12** Through	Silvanus

1473	02	4103	80	5613	3049	1223
ὑμῖν	τοῦ	πιστοῦ	ἀδελφοῦ,	ὡς	λογίζομαι,	δι᾽
to you	the	trustful	brother,	as	I reason,	through

3641	1125	3870	2532	1957	3778
ὀλίγων	ἔγραψα	παρακαλῶν	καὶ	ἐπιμαρτυρῶν	ταύτην
few	I wrote	encouraging	and	testifying	on this

1510	227	5485	02	2316	1519	3739	2476
εἶναι	ἀληθῆ	χάριν	τοῦ	θεοῦ	εἰς	ἣν	στῆτε.
to be true	favor	of the	God	into	which	you stand.

13
782	1473	05	1722	897	4899	2532
Ἀσπάζεται	ὑμᾶς	ἡ	ἐν	Βαβυλῶνι	συνεκλεκτὴ	καὶ
Greets	you	the	in	Babylon	co-elect	and

3138	01	5207	1473	782	240	1722
Μᾶρκος	ὁ	υἱός	μου.	ἀσπάσασθε	ἀλλήλους	ἐν
Mark	the	son	of me.	**14** Greet	one another	in

5370	26	1515	1473	3956	015	1722
φιλήματι	ἀγάπης.	Εἰρήνη	ὑμῖν	πᾶσιν	τοῖς	ἐν
kiss	of love.	Peace	to you	all	the ones	in

5547
Χριστῷ.
Christ.

[8]Discipline yourselves, keep alert.[a] Like a roaring lion your adversary the devil prowls around, looking for someone to devour. [9]Resist him, steadfast in your faith, for you know that your brothers and sisters[b] in all the world are undergoing the same kinds of suffering. [10]And after you have suffered for a little while, the God of all grace, who has called you to his eternal glory in Christ, will himself restore, support, strengthen, and establish you. [11]To him be the power forever and ever. Amen.

12 Through Silvanus, whom I consider a faithful brother, I have written this short letter to encourage you and to testify that this is the true grace of God. Stand fast in it. [13]Your sister church[c] in Babylon, chosen together with you, sends you greetings; and so does my son Mark. [14]Greet one another with a kiss of love.

Peace to all of you who are in Christ.[d]

a Or be vigilant
b Gk your brotherhood
c Gk She who is
d Other ancient authorities add Amen

2 PETER

CHAPTER 1

Simeon[a] Peter, a servant[b] and apostle of Jesus Christ, To those who have received a faith as precious as ours through the righteousness of our God and Savior Jesus Christ:[c]

2 May grace and peace be yours in abundance in the knowledge of God and of Jesus our Lord.

3 His divine power has given us everything needed for life and godliness, through the knowledge of him who called us by[d] his own glory and goodness. 4 Thus he has given us, through these things, his precious and very great promises, so that through them you may escape from the corruption that is in the world because of lust, and may become participants of the divine nature. 5 For this very reason, you must make every effort to support your faith with goodness, and goodness with knowledge, 6 and knowledge with self-control, and self-control with endurance, and endurance with godliness, 7 and godliness with mutual[e] affection, and mutual[e] affection with love. 8 For if these things are yours and are increasing among you, they keep you from being ineffective and unfruitful in the knowledge of our Lord Jesus Christ. 9 For anyone who lacks these things is short-sighted and blind,

---

a Other ancient authorities read *Simon*
b Gk *slave*
c Or *of our God and the Savior Jesus Christ*
d Other ancient authorities read *through*
e Gk *brotherly*

1:1

4826 4074 1401 2532 652 2424 5547
Συμεὼν Πέτρος δοῦλος καὶ ἀπόστολος Ἰησοῦ Χριστοῦ
Symeon Peter slave and delegate of Jesus Christ

015 2472 1473 2975 4102 1722
τοῖς ἰσότιμον ἡμῖν λαχοῦσιν πίστιν ἐν
to the ones equal value to us having obtained trust in

1343 02 2316 1473 2532 4990 2424
δικαιοσύνῃ τοῦ θεοῦ ἡμῶν καὶ σωτῆρος Ἰησοῦ
rightness of the God of us and deliverer Jesus

5547 2 5485 1473 2532 1515 4129
Χριστοῦ, χάρις ὑμῖν καὶ εἰρήνη πληθυνθείη
Christ, favor to you and peace may be multiplied

1722 1922 02 2316 2532 2424 02 2962
ἐν ἐπιγνώσει τοῦ. θεοῦ καὶ Ἰησοῦ τοῦ κυρίου
in perception of the God and Jesus the Master

1473 3 5613 3956 1473 06 2304 1411 846 024
ἡμῶν. Ὡς πάντα ἡμῖν τῆς θείας δυνάμεως αὐτοῦ τὰ
of us. As all to us the godly power of him the

4314 2222 2532 2150 1433 1223 06
πρὸς ζωὴν καὶ εὐσέβειαν δεδωρημένης διὰ τῆς
to life and reverence having gifted through the

1922 02 2564 1473 2398 1391
ἐπιγνώσεως τοῦ καλέσαντος ἡμᾶς ἰδίᾳ δόξῃ
perception of the having called us to own splendor

2532 703 1223 3739 024 5093 2532 3173
καὶ ἀρετῇ, 4 δι’ ὧν τὰ τίμια καὶ μέγιστα
and virtue, through whom the valuable and greatest

1473 1862 1433 2443 1223 3778
ἡμῖν ἐπαγγέλματα δεδώρηται, ἵνα διὰ τούτων
to us promises he has gifted, that through these

1096 2304 2844 5449
γένησθε θείας κοινωνοὶ φύσεως
you might become of godly partners nature

668 06 1722 03 2889 1722 1939
ἀποφυγόντες τῆς ἐν τῷ κόσμῳ ἐν ἐπιθυμίᾳ
having fled from the in the world in desire

5356 5 2532 846 3778 1161 4710 3956
φθορᾶς. Καὶ αὐτὸ τοῦτο δὲ σπουδὴν πᾶσαν
of corruption. And same this but diligence all

3923 2023 1722 07
παρεισενέγκαντες ἐπιχορηγήσατε ἐν τῇ
having brought in along you supply further in the

4102 1473 08 703 1722 1161 07 703 08
πίστει ὑμῶν τὴν ἀρετήν, ἐν δὲ τῇ ἀρετῇ τὴν
trust of you the virtue, in but the virtue the

1108 6 1722 1161 07 1108 08 1466
γνῶσιν, ἐν δὲ τῇ γνώσει τὴν ἐγκράτειαν,
knowledge, in but the knowledge the inner strength,

1722 1161 07 1466 08 5281 1722 1161 07
ἐν δὲ τῇ ἐγκρατείᾳ τὴν ὑπομονήν, ἐν δὲ τῇ
in but the inner strength the patience, in but the

5281 08 2150 7 1722 1161 07 2150 08
ὑπομονῇ τὴν εὐσέβειαν, ἐν δὲ τῇ εὐσεβείᾳ τὴν
patience the reverence, in but the reverence the

5360 1722 1161 07 5360 08 26
φιλαδελφίαν, ἐν δὲ τῇ φιλαδελφίᾳ τὴν ἀγάπην.
brotherly love, in but the brotherly love the love.

8 3778 1063 1473 5225 2532 4121 3756
ταῦτα γὰρ ὑμῖν ὑπάρχοντα καὶ πλεονάζοντα οὐκ
These for in you existing and increasing not

692 3761 175 2525 1519 08 02
ἀργοὺς οὐδὲ ἀκάρπους καθίστησιν εἰς τὴν τοῦ
idle but not fruitless he appoints in the of the

2962 1473 2424 5547 1922 9 3739 1063
κυρίου ἡμῶν Ἰησοῦ Χριστοῦ ἐπίγνωσιν· ᾧ γὰρ
Master of us Jesus Christ perception; to whom for

3361 3918 3778 5185 1510 3467
μὴ πάρεστιν ταῦτα, τυφλός ἐστιν μυωπάζων,
not are present these, blind he is being shortsighted

3024	2983	02	2512	018	3819
λήθην	λαβὼν	τοῦ	καθαρισμοῦ	τῶν	πάλαι
forgetfulness	having taken	the	cleaning		of the old

846	266	**10**	1352	3123	80
αὐτοῦ	ἁμαρτιῶν.		διὸ	μᾶλλον,	ἀδελφοί,
of him	sins.		Wherefore	more,	brothers,

4704	949	1473	08	2821	2532	1589
σπουδάσατε	βεβαίαν	ὑμῶν	τὴν	κλῆσιν	καὶ	ἐκλογὴν
be diligent	firm	of you	the	call	and	select

4160	3778	1063	4160	3756	3361
ποιεῖσθαι·	ταῦτα	γὰρ	ποιοῦντες	οὐ	μὴ
to make;	these	for	doing	not	not

4417		4218	**11**	3779	1063	4146
πταίσητέ		ποτε.		οὕτως	γὰρ	πλουσίως
you might stumble		ever.		Thusly	for	richly

2023		1473	05	1529		1519	08
ἐπιχορηγηθήσεται		ὑμῖν	ἡ	εἴσοδος	εἰς	τὴν	
will be supplied		to you	the	entrance	into	the	

166	932	02	2962	1473	2532	4990
αἰώνιον	βασιλείαν	τοῦ	κυρίου	ἡμῶν	καὶ	σωτῆρος
eternal	kingdom	of the	Master	of us	and	deliverer

2424	5547	**12**	1352	3195	104	1473
Ἰησοῦ	Χριστοῦ.		Διὸ	μελλήσω	ἀεὶ	ὑμᾶς
Jesus	Christ.		Wherefore	I will be about	always	you

5279		4012	3778	2539		3609a		2532
ὑπομιμνῄσκειν	περὶ	τούτων	καίπερ		εἰδότας		καὶ	
to remind	about	these	and indeed	having known		and	

4741		1722	07	3918	225
ἐστηριγμένους		ἐν	τῇ	παρούσῃ	ἀληθείᾳ.
having been strengthened		in	the	present	truth.

13	1342	1161	2233	1909	3745	1510	1722
	δίκαιον	δὲ	ἡγοῦμαι,	ἐφ'	ὅσον	εἰμὶ	ἐν
	Right	but	I consider,	on	as much as	I am	in

3778	011	4638	1326	1473	1722
τούτῳ	τῷ	σκηνώματι,	διεγείρειν	ὑμᾶς	ἐν
this	the	tent,	to raise thoroughly	you	in

5280		3609a	3754	5031	1510	05
ὑπομνήσει,	**14**	εἰδὼς	ὅτι	ταχινή	ἐστιν	ἡ
reminder,		having known	that	quick	is	the

595	010	4638	1473	2531	2532	01
ἀπόθεσις	τοῦ	σκηνώματός	μου	καθὼς	καὶ	ὁ
setting off	of the	tent	of me	just as	also	the

2962	1473	2424	5547	1213	1473
κύριος	ἡμῶν	Ἰησοῦς	Χριστὸς	ἐδήλωσέν	μοι,
Master	of us	Jesus	Christ	made clear	to me,

15	4704		1161	2532	1539	2192	1473
	σπουδάσω		δὲ	καὶ	ἑκάστοτε	ἔχειν	ὑμᾶς
	I will be diligent		but	also	always	to have	you

3326	08	1699	1841	08	3778	3420	4160
μετὰ	τὴν	ἐμὴν	ἔξοδον	τὴν	τούτων	μνήμην	ποιεῖσθαι.
after	the	my	way out	the	of these	memory	to make.

16	3756	1063	4679	3454	1811
	Οὐ	γὰρ	σεσοφισμένοις	μύθοις	ἐξακολουθήσαντες
	Not	for	having been made wise	myths	having followed after

1107	1473	08	02	2962	1473	2424
ἐγνωρίσαμεν	ὑμῖν	τὴν	τοῦ	κυρίου	ἡμῶν	Ἰησοῦ
we made known	to you	the	of the	Master	of us	Jesus

5547	1411	2532	3952	235	2030
Χριστοῦ	δύναμιν	καὶ	παρουσίαν	ἀλλ'	ἐπόπται
Christ	power	and	presence	but	eyewitnesses

1096	06	1565	3168
γενηθέντες	τῆς	ἐκείνου	μεγαλειότητος.
having become	of the	of that	greatness.

17	2983		1063	3844	2316	3962	5092	2532
	λαβὼν		γὰρ	παρὰ	θεοῦ	πατρὸς	τιμὴν	καὶ
	Having received		for	from	God	Father	value	and

1391	5456	5342	846	5107
δόξαν	φωνῆς	ἐνεχθείσης	αὐτῷ	τοιᾶσδε
splendor	of sound	having been brought	to him	such

and is forgetful of the cleansing of past sins. [10]Therefore, brothers and sisters,[a] be all the more eager to confirm your call and election, for if you do this, you will never stumble. [11]For in this way, entry into the eternal kingdom of our Lord and Savior Jesus Christ will be richly provided for you.

12 Therefore I intend to keep on reminding you of these things, though you know them already and are established in the truth that has come to you. [13]I think it right, as long as I am in this body,[b] to refresh your memory, [14]since I know that my death[c] will come soon, as indeed our Lord Jesus Christ has made clear to me. [15]And I will make every effort so that after my departure you may be able at any time to recall these things.

16 For we did not follow cleverly devised myths when we made known to you the power and coming of our Lord Jesus Christ, but we had been eyewitnesses of his majesty. [17]For he received honor and glory from God the Father when that voice was conveyed to him

---

a Gk *brothers*
b Gk *tent*
c Gk *the putting off of my tent*

by the Majestic Glory, saying, "This is my Son, my Beloved,[a] with whom I am well pleased." [18]We ourselves heard this voice come from heaven, while we were with him on the holy mountain.

19 So we have the prophetic message more fully confirmed. You will do well to be attentive to this as to a lamp shining in a dark place, until the day dawns and the morning star rises in your hearts. [20]First of all you must understand this, that no prophecy of scripture is a matter of one's own interpretation, [21]because no prophecy ever came by human will, but men and women moved by the Holy Spirit spoke from God.[b]

CHAPTER 2

But false prophets also arose among the people, just as there will be false teachers among you, who will secretly bring in destructive opinions. They will even deny the Master who bought them— bringing swift destruction on themselves. [2]Even so, many will follow their licentious ways, and because of these teachers[c] the way of truth will be maligned. [3]And in their greed they will exploit you with deceptive words. Their condemnation, pronounced against them long ago, has not been idle, and their destruction is not asleep.

[a] Other ancient authorities read *my beloved Son*
[b] Other ancient authorities read *but moved by the Holy Spirit saints of God spoke*
[c] Gk *because of them*

```
5259 06  3169                    1391        01   5207 1473   01
ὑπὸ  τῆς μεγαλοπρεποῦς     δόξης·     ὁ   υἱός μου  ὁ
by   the greatly fitting   splendor; the  son of me the
27       1473    3778    1510  1519 3739 1473 2106
ἀγαπητός μου  οὗτός ἐστιν εἰς  ὃν   ἐγὼ εὐδόκησα,
loved   of me this  is    in   whom I   thought well,
   2532 3778   08   5456   1473  191       1537 3772
18 καὶ ταύτην τὴν φωνὴν ἡμεῖς ἠκούσαμεν ἐξ  οὐρανοῦ
   and this  the  sound we    heard     from heaven
5342                  4862 846  1510  1722  011 40
ἐνεχθεῖσαν        σὺν αὐτῷ ὄντες ἐν   τῷ  ἁγίῳ
having been brought with him being in   the holy
3735    19  2532 2192  949         04  4397
ὄρει.    19 καὶ ἔχομεν βεβαιότερον τὸν προφητικὸν
hill.       And we have more firm  the speaking before
3056   3739      2573   4160   4337        5613 3088
λόγον, ᾧ       καλῶς ποιεῖτε προσέχοντες ὡς  λύχνῳ
word,  of which well  you do  holding to  as  lamp
5316       1722 850         5117    2193 3739 2250
φαίνοντι ἐν αὐχμηρῷ τόπῳ,  ἕως οὗ  ἡμέρα
shining  in dingy   place, until which day
1306        2532 5459          393         1722 019
διαυγάσῃ καὶ φωσφόρος ἀνατείλῃ ἐν   ταῖς
might dawn and light-bearer might arise in   the
2588     1473   20 3778  4413   1097         3754 3956
καρδίαις ὑμῶν,  20 τοῦτο πρῶτον γινώσκοντες ὅτι  πᾶσα
hearts   of you,   this  first  knowing     that all
4394        1124    2398     1955       3756
προφητεία γραφῆς ἰδίας ἐπιλύσεως οὐ
speaking before of writing of own release    not
1096         21 3756 1063 2307     444      5342
γίνεται·     21 οὐ  γὰρ θελήματι ἀνθρώπου ἠνέχθη
becomes;        not for want     of man    was brought
4394        4218  235  5259 4151    40
προφητεία ποτέ, ἀλλὰ ὑπὸ πνεύματος ἁγίου
speaking before then, but  by  spirit    holy
5342         2980      575  2316 444
φερόμενοι ἐλάλησαν ἀπὸ ΘΕΟΥ ἄνθρωποι.
being brought spoke  from God  men.
      1096      1161 2532 5578            1722 03
2:1 Ἐγένοντο  δὲ  καὶ ψευδοπροφῆται ἐν   τῷ
    There became but also false spokesmen  in   the
2992   5613 2532 1722 1473 1510    5572
λαῷ,  ὡς  καὶ  ἐν  ὑμῖν ἔσονται ψευδοδιδάσκαλοι,
people, as also in   you  will be false teachers,
3748      3919              139      684
οἵτινες παρεισάξουσιν  αἱρέσεις ἀπωλείας
who    will bring in along sects of destruction
2532 04 59              846    1203
καὶ τὸν ἀγοράσαντα    αὐτοὺς δεσπότην
and the one having bought them supervisor
720        1863        1438      5031 684
ἀρνούμενοι. ἐπάγοντες ἑαυτοῖς ταχινὴν ἀπώλειαν,
denying.    Bringing on themselves quick destruction,
   2532 4183   1811               846  019
2  καὶ πολλοὶ ἐξακολουθήσουσιν αὐτῶν ταῖς
   and many will follow after them in the
766         1223     3739   05  3598 06    225
ἀσελγείαις δι'    οὓς  ἡ  ὁδὸς τῆς ἀληθείας
debaucheries through which the way of the truth
987            3  2532 1722 4124   4112      3056
βλασφημηθήσεται, 3 καὶ ἐν πλεονεξίᾳ πλαστοῖς λόγοις
will be insulted,  and in greediness molded  words
1473 1710        3739   09  2917     1597
ὑμᾶς ἐμπορεύσονται, οἷς  τὸ  κρίμα  ἔκπαλαι
you  they will exploit, to whom the judgment from old
3756 691   2532 05 684         846   3756 3573
οὐκ ἀργεῖ καὶ ἡ  ἀπώλεια αὐτῶν οὐ  νυστάζει.
not is idle and the destruction of them not doze.
```

4
1487	1063	01	2316	32		264		3756
Εἰ	γὰρ	ὁ	θεὸς	ἀγγέλων		ἁμαρτησάντων		οὐκ
If	for	the God		of messengers		having sinned		not

5339	235	4577	2217	5020
ἐφείσατο	ἀλλὰ	σειραῖς ζόφου		ταρταρώσας
spared	but	to pits of gloom	being sent	to Tartarus

3860		1519	2920	5083	**5**	2532
παρέδωκεν		εἰς	κρίσιν	τηρουμένους,		καὶ
he gave over	into	judgment	being kept,		and

744	2889	3756	5339	235	3590	3575
ἀρχαίου	κόσμου	οὐκ	ἐφείσατο	ἀλλὰ	ὄγδοον	Νῶε
of ancient	world	not	he spared	but	eighth	Noah

1343		2783	5442	2627		2889
δικαιοσύνης	κήρυκα	ἐφύλαξεν	κατακλυσμὸν		κόσμῳ
of rightness	announcer	he guarded	flood		in world

765		1863	**6**	2532	4172	4670
ἀσεβῶν	ἐπάξας,		καὶ	πόλεις	Σοδόμων
irreverent ones	having brought on,		and	cities	Sodom

2532	1116	5077			2692
καὶ	Γομόρρας	τεφρώσας		[καταστροφῇ]
and	Gomorrah	having covered in ashes		in overturn

2632	5262	3195		764
κατέκρινεν	ὑπόδειγμα	μελλόντων		ἀσεβέ[σ]ιν
he condemned	example	being about to be		irreverent

5087	**7**	2532	1342	3091	2669		5259	06
τεθεικώς,		καὶ	δίκαιον	Λὼτ	καταπονούμενον		ὑπὸ	τῆς
having set,		and	right	Lot	being worn down	by	the

014	113		1722	766		391		4506
τῶν	ἀθέσμων		ἐν	ἀσελγείᾳ		ἀναστροφῆς		ἐρρύσατο·
of the	irreverent		in	debauchery		behavior		he rescued;

8
990	1063	2532	189	01	1342	1460
βλέμματι	γὰρ	καὶ	ἀκοῇ	ὁ	δίκαιος	ἐγκατοικῶν
in seeing	for	and	hearing	the	right	dwelling in

1722	846	2250	1537	2250	5590	1342	459
ἐν	αὐτοῖς	ἡμέραν	ἐξ	ἡμέρας	ψυχὴν	δικαίαν	ἀνόμοις
in	them	day	from	day	soul	right	in lawless

2041	928		**9**	3609a	2962	2152	1537
ἔργοις	ἐβασάνιζεν·			οἶδεν	κύριος	εὐσεβεῖς	ἐκ
works	he is tormented;			knows	Master	reverent	from

3986	4506	94		1161	1519	2250
πειρασμοῦ	ῥύεσθαι,	ἀδίκους	δὲ	εἰς	ἡμέραν
pressure	to rescue,	unright	but	in	day

2920	2849		5083	**10**	3122	1161
κρίσεως	κολαζομένους	τηρεῖν,		μάλιστα	δὲ
of judgment	being punished	to keep,		especially	but

016	3694	4561	1722	1939	3394
τοὺς	ὀπίσω	σαρκὸς	ἐν	ἐπιθυμίᾳ	μιασμοῦ
the ones	after	flesh	in	desire	of pollution

4198	2532	2963	2706		5113
πορευομένους	καὶ	κυριότητος	καταφρονοῦντας.		τολμηταὶ
traveling	and	mastership	thinking down.		Bold ones

829	1391	3756	5141	987
αὐθάδεις,	δόξας	οὐ	τρέμουσιν	βλασφημοῦντες,
self-willed,	splendors	not	they tremble	insulting,

11
3699	32	2479		2532	1411	3173
ὅπου	ἄγγελοι	ἰσχύϊ		καὶ	δυνάμει	μείζονες
where	messengers	in strength	and	in power	greater

1510	3756	5342	2596	846	3844	2962
ὄντες	οὐ	φέρουσιν	κατ’	αὐτῶν	παρὰ	κυρίου
being	not	they bring	against	them	from	Master

989	2920	**12**	3778	1161	5613	249
βλάσφημον	κρίσιν.		Οὗτοι	δὲ	ὡς	ἄλογα
insulting	judgment.		These	but	as	unspeaking

2226	1080		5446	1519	259	2532
ζῷα	γεγεννημένα		φυσικὰ	εἰς	ἅλωσιν	καὶ
living ones	having been born	natural	into	capture	and

5356	1722	3739	50		987
φθορὰν	ἐν	οἷς	ἀγνοοῦσιν		βλασφημοῦντες,
corruption	in	which	they not know		insulting,

4 For if God did not spare the angels when they sinned, but cast them into hell[a] and committed them to chains[b] of deepest darkness to be kept until the judgment; [5]and if he did not spare the ancient world, even though he saved Noah, a herald of righteousness, with seven others, when he brought a flood on a world of the ungodly; [6]and if by turning the cities of Sodom and Gomorrah to ashes he condemned them to extinction[c] and made them an example of what is coming to the ungodly;[d] [7]and if he rescued Lot, a righteous man greatly distressed by the licentiousness of the lawless [8](for that righteous man, living among them day after day, was tormented in his righteous soul by their lawless deeds that he saw and heard), [9]then the Lord knows how to rescue the godly from trial, and to keep the unrighteous under punishment until the day of judgment [10]—especially those who indulge their flesh in depraved lust, and who despise authority.

Bold and willful, they are not afraid to slander the glorious ones,[e] [11]whereas angels, though greater in might and power, do not bring against them a slanderous judgment from the Lord.[f] [12]These people, however, are like irrational animals, mere creatures of instinct, born to be caught and killed. They slander what they do not understand,

a Gk *Tartaros*
b Other ancient authorities read *pits*
c Other ancient authorities lack *to extinction*
d Other ancient authorities read *an example to those who were to be ungodly*
e Or *angels*; Gk *glories*
f Other ancient authorities read *before the Lord*; others lack the phrase

and when those creatures are destroyed,[a] they also will be destroyed, [13]suffering[b] the penalty for doing wrong. They count it a pleasure to revel in the daytime. They are blots and blemishes, reveling in their dissipation[c] while they feast with you. [14]They have eyes full of adultery, insatiable for sin. They entice unsteady souls. They have hearts trained in greed. Accursed children! [15]They have left the straight road and have gone astray, following the road of Balaam son of Bosor,[d] who loved the wages of doing wrong, [16]but was rebuked for his own transgression; a speechless donkey spoke with a human voice and restrained the prophet's madness.

[17]These are waterless springs and mists driven by a storm; for them the deepest darkness has been reserved. [18]For they speak bombastic nonsense, and with licentious desires of the flesh they entice people who have just[e] escaped from those who live in error. [19]They promise them freedom, but they themselves are slaves of corruption; for people are slaves to whatever masters them. [20]For if, after they have escaped the defilements of the

[a] Gk in their destruction
[b] Other ancient authorities read receiving
[c] Other ancient authorities read love-feasts
[d] Other ancient authorities read Beor
[e] Other ancient authorities read actually

```
1722 07    5356              846        2532 5351
ἐν   τῇ   φθορᾷ            αὐτῶν     καὶ  φθαρήσονται
in   the  corruption        of them   and  they will be corrupted

    91                3408      93            2237
13  ἀδικούμενοι      μισθὸν   ἀδικίας,     ἡδονὴν
    being done unright wage    of unright,  pleasure

2233         08   1722 2250  5172        4695   2532
ἡγούμενοι    τὴν ἐν  ἡμέρᾳ  τρυφήν,    σπίλοι καὶ
considering  the in  day     indulgence, spots  and

3470     1792          1722 019  539        846
μῶμοι   ἐντρυφῶντες   ἐν  ταῖς ἀπάταις  αὐτῶν
blemishes indulging    in  the  deceptions of them

4910          1473       14 3788       2192    3324
συνευωχούμενοι ὑμῖν,       ὀφθαλμοὺς  ἔχοντες μεστοὺς
feasting with  you,         eyes        having  full

3428       2532 180           266          1185
μοιχαλίδος καὶ  ἀκαταπαύστους ἁμαρτίας,   δελεάζοντες
adulterous and  unable to stop sin,        ensnaring

5590     793          2588        1128
ψυχὰς    ἀστηρίκτους, καρδίαν     γεγυμνασμένην
souls    unstrengthened, heart     having been exercised

4124         2192      2671      5043
πλεονεξίας   ἔχοντες,  κατάρας   τέκνα·
in greediness having,  of curse   children;

    2641           2117a       3598 4105
15  καταλείποντες  εὐθεῖαν     ὁδὸν ἐπλανήθησαν,
    leaving behind straight     way  they were deceived,

1811             07  3598 02    903      02
ἐξακολουθήσαντες τῇ  ὁδῷ  τοῦ  Βαλαὰμ  τοῦ
having followed after the way  of the Balaam of the

1007   3739 3408   93        25          1649   1161
Βοσόρ, ὃς   μισθὸν ἀδικίας   ἠγάπησεν 16 ἔλεγξιν δὲ
Bosor, who  wage   of unright loved      rebuke  but

2192    2398   3892           5268        880     1722
ἔσχεν   ἰδίας  παρανομίας·    ὑποζύγιον  ἄφωνον  ἐν
he had  of own lawlessness;   yoke-animal soundless in

444       5456   5350          2967      08  02
ἀνθρώπου φωνῇ  φθεγξάμενον   ἐκώλυσεν  τὴν τοῦ
of man    sound having spoken hindered  the of the

4396      3913          17 3778    1510 4077     504
προφήτου παραφρονίαν.     οὗτοί  εἰσιν πηγαὶ ἄνυδροι
spokesman beside thought.  These  are   springs waterless

2532 3657a    5259 2978       1643                    3739
καὶ  ὁμίχλαι ὑπὸ λαίλαπος   ἐλαυνόμεναι,            οἷς
and  mists    by  storm       having been driven,     for whom

01   2217   010    4655      5083              18 5246
ὁ    ζόφος  τοῦ    σκότους   τετήρηται.          ὑπέρογκα
the  gloom  of the dark      has been kept.       Overinflated

1063 3153      5350        1185            1722
γὰρ  ματαιότητος φθεγγόμενοι δελεάζουσιν  ἐν
for  in futility  speaking   they ensnare  in

1939         4561    766          016    3643a
ἐπιθυμίαις  σαρκὸς ἀσελγείαις  τοὺς  ὀλίγως
desires     of flesh debaucheries the   scarcely

668           016    1722 4106   390
ἀποφεύγοντας τοὺς  ἐν  πλάνῃ  ἀναστρεφομένους,
fleeing from the ones in  deceit  behaving,

    1657        846    1861           846
19  ἐλευθερίαν αὐτοῖς ἐπαγγελλόμενοι, αὐτοὶ
    freedom     to them promising,      themselves

1401   5225        06   5356       3739   1063 5100
δοῦλοι ὑπάρχοντες τῆς  φθορᾶς·    ᾧ     γὰρ  τις
slaves existing    of the corruption; to whom for  some

2274       3778    1402
ἥττηται,   τούτῳ   δεδούλωται.
has been defeated, to this he has been enslaved.

    1487 1063 668          024 3393     02
20  εἰ   γὰρ  ἀποφυγόντες  τὰ  μιάσματα τοῦ
    If   for  having fled from the pollutions of the
```

2889	1722	1922	02	2962	1473	2532
κόσμου	ἐν	ἐπιγνώσει	τοῦ	κυρίου	[ἡμῶν]	καὶ
world	in	perception	of the	Master	of us	and

4990	2424	5547	3778	1161	3825
σωτῆρος	Ἰησοῦ	Χριστοῦ,	τούτοις	δὲ	πάλιν
deliverer	Jesus	Christ,	to these	but	again

1707	2274	1096	846	021
ἐμπλακέντες	ἡττῶνται,	γέγονεν	αὐτοῖς	τὰ
having been	they have	has become	to them	the
inweaved	been defeated,			

2078	5501	022	4413	**21**	2909	1063	1510
ἔσχατα	χείρονα	τῶν	πρώτων.		κρεῖττον	γὰρ	ἦν
last	worse	of the	first.		Better	for	it was

846	3361	1921	08	3598	06
αὐτοῖς	μὴ	ἐπεγνωκέναι	τὴν	ὁδὸν	τῆς
to them	not	to have perceived	the	way	of the

1343	2228	1921	5290
δικαιοσύνης	ἢ	ἐπιγνοῦσιν	ὑποστρέψαι
rightness	or	having perceived	to have returned

1537	06	3860	846	40	1785
ἐκ	τῆς	παραδοθείσης	αὐτοῖς	ἁγίας	ἐντολῆς.
from	the	having been given over	to them	holy	command.

22	4819	846	09	06	227	3942
	συμβέβηκεν	αὐτοῖς	τὸ	τῆς	ἀληθοῦς	παροιμίας·
	Came with	to them	the	of the	true	proverb,

2965	1994	1909	012	2398	1829	2532
κύων	ἐπιστρέψας	ἐπὶ	τὸ	ἴδιον	ἐξέραμα,	καί·
dog	having returned	on	the	own	vomit,	and,

5300	3068	1519	2946	1004	**3:1**	3778
ὗς	λουσαμένη	εἰς	κυλισμὸν	βορβόρου.		Ταύτην
pig	having washed	into	rolling	filth.		This

2235	27	1208	1473	1125	1992
ἤδη,	ἀγαπητοί,	δευτέραν	ὑμῖν	γράφω	ἐπιστολήν,
already,	loved ones,	second	to you	I write	letter,

1722	3739	1326	1473	1722	5280	08
ἐν	αἷς	διεγείρω	ὑμῶν	ἐν	ὑπομνήσει	τὴν
in	which	I raise thoroughly	to you	in	reminder	the

1506	1271	**2**	3403	022
εἰλικρινῆ	διάνοιαν		μνησθῆναι	τῶν
unmixed	intelligence		to be remembered	of the

4302	4487	5259	014	40	4396
προειρημένων	ῥημάτων	ὑπὸ	τῶν	ἁγίων	προφητῶν
having been said before	words	by	the	holy	spokesmen

2532	06	014	652	1473	1785	02	2962
καὶ	τῆς	τῶν	ἀποστόλων	ὑμῶν	ἐντολῆς	τοῦ	κυρίου
and	the	of the	delegates	of you	command	of the	Master

2532	4990	**3**	3778	4413	1097	3754
καὶ	σωτῆρος,		τοῦτο	πρῶτον	γινώσκοντες	ὅτι
and	deliverer,		this	first	knowing	that

2064	1909	2078	018	2250	1722
ἐλεύσονται	ἐπ᾽	ἐσχάτων	τῶν	ἡμερῶν	[ἐν]
there will come	on	last	of the	days	in

1700a	1703	2596	020	2398	1939	846
ἐμπαιγμονῇ	ἐμπαῖκται	κατὰ	τὰς	ἰδίας	ἐπιθυμίας	αὐτῶν
in mockery	mockers	by	the	own	desires	of them

4198	**4**	2532	3004	4226	1510	05	1860
πορευόμενοι		καὶ	λέγοντες·	ποῦ	ἐστιν	ἡ	ἐπαγγελία
traveling		and	saying,	where	is	the	promise

06	3952	846	575	3739	1063	013	3962
τῆς	παρουσίας	αὐτοῦ;	ἀφ᾽	ἧς	γὰρ	οἱ	πατέρες
of the	presence	of him?	From which		for	the	fathers

2837	3956	3779	1265	575	746
ἐκοιμήθησαν,	πάντα	οὕτως	διαμένει	ἀπ᾽	ἀρχῆς
slept,	all	thusly	stays through	from	beginning

2937	**5**	2990	1063	846	3778	2309
κτίσεως.		Λανθάνει	γὰρ	αὐτοὺς	τοῦτο	θέλοντας
of creation.		Escapes notice	for	them	this	wanting

3754	3772	1510	1597	2532	1093	1537	5204	2532
ὅτι	οὐρανοὶ	ἦσαν	ἔκπαλαι	καὶ	γῆ	ἐξ	ὕδατος	καὶ
that	heavens	were	from old	and	earth	from	water	and

world through the knowledge of our Lord and Savior Jesus Christ, they are again entangled in them and overpowered, the last state has become worse for them than the first. 21For it would have been better for them never to have known the way of righteousness than, after knowing it, to turn back from the holy commandment that was passed on to them. 22It has happened to them according to the true proverb,

"The dog turns back to
  its own vomit,"
and,
"The sow is washed only
  to wallow in the
  mud."

CHAPTER 3

This is now, beloved, the second letter I am writing to you; in them I am trying to arouse your sincere intention by reminding you 2that you should remember the words spoken in the past by the holy prophets, and the commandment of the Lord and Savior spoken through your apostles. 3First of all you must understand this, that in the last days scoffers will come, scoffing and indulging their own lusts 4and saying, "Where is the promise of his coming? For ever since our ancestors died,a all things continue as they were from the beginning of creation!" 5They deliberately ignore this fact, that by the word of God heavens existed long ago and an earth was formed out of water and

---

a Gk our fathers fell asleep

by means of water,
⁶through which the world
of that time was deluged
with water and perished.
⁷But by the same word the
present heavens and earth
have been reserved for fire,
being kept until the day of
judgment and destruction
of the godless.

8 But do not ignore this
one fact, beloved, that with
the Lord one day is like a
thousand years, and a
thousand years are like one
day. ⁹The Lord is not slow
about his promise, as some
think of slowness, but is
patient with you,ᵃ not
wanting any to perish, but
all to come to repentance.
¹⁰But the day of the Lord
will come like a thief, and
then the heavens will pass
away with a loud noise,
and the elements will be
dissolved with fire, and
the earth and everything
that is done on it will be
disclosed.ᵇ

11 Since all these things
are to be dissolved in this
way, what sort of persons
ought you to be in leading
lives of holiness and
godliness, ¹²waitingᶜ for
and hasteningᶜ the coming
of the day of God, because
of which the heavens will
be set ablaze and dissolved,
and the elements will
melt with fire? ¹³But,
in accordance with his
promise, we wait for new
heavens and a new earth,

ᵃ Other ancient authorities read *on
your account*

ᵇ Other ancient authorities read *will
be burned up*

ᶜ Or *earnestly desiring*

1223	5204	4921		03	02	2316
δι᾽	ὕδατος	συνεστῶσα		τῷ	τοῦ	θεοῦ
through	water	have stood together	in	the	of the	God

3056	**6**	1223	3739	01	5119	2889	5204
λόγῳ,		δι᾽	ὧν	ὁ	τότε	κόσμος	ὕδατι
word,		through	which	the	then	world	in water

2626		622		**7**	013	1161	3568
κατακλυσθεὶς		ἀπώλετο·			οἱ	δὲ	νῦν
having been flooded		was destroyed;			the	but	now

3772	2532	05	1093	03	846	3056
οὐρανοὶ	καὶ	ἡ	γῆ	τῷ	αὐτῷ	λόγῳ
heavens	and	the	earth	in	the same	word

2343		1510	4442	5083	1519
τεθησαυρισμένοι		εἰσὶν	πυρὶ	τηρούμενοι	εἰς
+having been treasured		+are	in fire	being kept	for

2250	2920	2532	684	014	765
ἡμέραν	κρίσεως	καὶ	ἀπωλείας	τῶν	ἀσεβῶν
day	of judgment	and	destruction	of the	irreverent

444	**8**	1520	1161	3778	3361	2990
ἀνθρώπων.		Ἓν	δὲ	τοῦτο	μὴ	λανθανέτω
men.		One	but	this	not	let escape notice

1473	27		3754	1520	2250	3844	2962	5613
ὑμᾶς,	ἀγαπητοί,		ὅτι	μία	ἡμέρα	παρὰ	κυρίῳ	ὡς
you,	loved ones,		that	one	day	along	Master	as

5507	2094	2532	5507	2094	5613	2250	1520
χίλια	ἔτη	καὶ	χίλια	ἔτη	ὡς	ἡμέρα	μία.
thousand	years	and	thousand	years	as	day	one.

9	3756	1019	2962	06	1860	5613	5100
	οὐ	βραδύνει	κύριος	τῆς	ἐπαγγελίας,	ὥς	τινες
	Not	is slow	Master	of the	promise,	as	some

1022	2233	235	3114	1519	1473
βραδύτητα	ἡγοῦνται,	ἀλλὰ	μακροθυμεῖ	εἰς	ὑμᾶς,
slowness	consider,	but	is long-tempered	to	you,

3361	1014	5100	622	235	3956	1519
μὴ	βουλόμενός	τινας	ἀπολέσθαι	ἀλλὰ	πάντας	εἰς
not	planning	some	to destroy	but	all	into

3341	5562	**10**	2240	1161	2250
μετάνοιαν	χωρῆσαι.		Ἥξει	δὲ	ἡμέρα
change of mind	to make room.		Will come	but	day

2962	5613	2812	1722	3739	013	3772
κυρίου	ὡς	κλέπτης,	ἐν	ᾗ	οἱ	οὐρανοὶ
of Master	as	thief,	in	which	the	heavens

4500	3928	4747	1161	2741
ῥοιζηδὸν	παρελεύσονται	στοιχεῖα	δὲ	καυσούμενα
cracking sound	will go along	elements	but	being burned

3089	2532	1093	2532	021	1722	846	2041
λυθήσεται	καὶ	γῆ	καὶ	τὰ	ἐν	αὐτῇ	ἔργα
will be loosed	and	earth	and	the	in	it	works

2147	**11**	3778	3779	3956	3089
εὑρεθήσεται.		Τούτων	οὕτως	πάντων	λυομένων
will be found.		These	thusly	all	being loosed

4217	1163	5225	1473	1722	40
ποταποὺς	δεῖ	ὑπάρχειν	[ὑμᾶς]	ἐν	ἁγίαις
what sort	it is necessary	to exist	you	in	holy

391	2532	2150	**12**	4328
ἀναστροφαῖς	καὶ	εὐσεβείαις,		προσδοκῶντας
behaviors	and	reverences,		waiting expectantly

	08	3952	06	02	2316
καὶ	σπεύδοντας	τὴν παρουσίαν	τῆς	τοῦ	θεοῦ
and	having hurried	the presence	of the	of the	God

2250	1223	3739	3772	4448
ἡμέρας	δι᾽	ἣν	οὐρανοὶ	πυρούμενοι
day	through	which	heavens	being on fire

3089	2532	4747	2741	5080
λυθήσονται	καὶ	στοιχεῖα	καυσούμενα	τήκεται.
they will	and	elements	being burned	are melted.
be loosed				

13	2537	1161	3772	2532	1093	2537	2596	012
	καινοὺς	δὲ	οὐρανοὺς	καὶ	γῆν	καινὴν	κατὰ	τὸ
	New	but	heavens	and	earth	new	by	the

1862   846   4328   1722 3739
ἐπάγγελμα αὐτοῦ προσδοκῶμεν,   ἐν   οἷς
promise   of him we wait expectantly,   in   which

1343   2730   1352   27   3778
δικαιοσύνη κατοικεῖ. **14** διό,   ἀγαπητοί,   ταῦτα
rightness   resides.   Wherefore, loved ones,   these

4328   4704   784   2532
προσδοκῶντες   σπουδάσατε ἄσπιλοι   καὶ
waiting expectantly be diligent without stain and

298   846   2147   1722 1515   **15** 2532 08
ἀμώμητοι αὐτῷ εὑρεθῆναι ἐν   εἰρήνῃ   καὶ   τὴν
blameless to him to be found in   peace   and   the

02   2962   1473   3115   4991   2233
τοῦ   κυρίου ἡμῶν μακροθυμίαν σωτηρίαν ἡγεῖσθε,
of the Master of us long temper deliverance consider,

2531   2532 01   27   1473 80   3972   2596 08
καθὼς   καὶ   ὁ   ἀγαπητὸς ἡμῶν ἀδελφὸς Παῦλος κατὰ τὴν
just as also the   loved   of us brother Paul   by   the

1325   846   4678   1125   1473   **16** 5613
δοθεῖσαν   αὐτῷ σοφίαν ἔγραψεν ὑμῖν,   ὡς
having been given to him wisdom wrote   to you,   as

2532 1722 3956   1992   2980   1722 846   4012
καὶ ἐν   πάσαις ἐπιστολαῖς λαλῶν   ἐν   αὐταῖς περὶ
also in   all   letters   speaking in   them   about

3778   1722 3739   1510   1425   5100
τούτων, ἐν   αἷς   ἐστιν δυσνόητά   τινα,
these,   in   which are   hard to understand some,

3739   013 261   2532 793   4761
ἃ   οἱ ἀμαθεῖς καὶ   ἀστήρικτοι   στρεβλοῦσιν
which the unlearned and   unstrengthened twist

5613 2532 020 3062   1124   4314 08   2398
ὡς   καὶ   τὰς λοιπὰς   γραφὰς   πρὸς τὴν ἰδίαν
as   also the remaining writings to   the own

846   684   **17** 1473 3767   27
αὐτῶν   ἀπώλειαν.   Ὑμεῖς οὖν,   ἀγαπητοί,
of them destruction.   You   then, loved ones,

4267   5442   2443 3361 07
προγινώσκοντες φυλάσσεσθε,   ἵνα   μὴ   τῇ
knowing before guard yourselves, that not   in the

014   113   4106   4879   1601
τῶν   ἀθέσμων πλάνῃ συναπαχθέντες   ἐκπέσητε
of the irreverent deceit having been brought you might
                     off together   fall out

02   2398 4740   **18** 837   1161 1722
τοῦ   ἰδίου στηριγμοῦ,   αὐξάνετε δὲ   ἐν
of the own strengthening,   grow   but   in

5485   2532 1108   02   2962   1473   2532
χάριτι καὶ γνώσει   τοῦ   κυρίου ἡμῶν καὶ
favor   and knowledge of the Master of us and

4990   2424 5547   846   05   1391   2532 3568
σωτῆρος Ἰησοῦ Χριστοῦ. αὐτῷ ἡ   δόξα   καὶ   νῦν
deliverer Jesus Christ.   To him the splendor both now

2532 1519 2250   165   281
καὶ   εἰς ἡμέραν αἰῶνος. [ἀμήν.]
and   in   day   of age.   Amen.

where righteousness is at home.

14 Therefore, beloved, while you are waiting for these things, strive to be found by him at peace, without spot or blemish; [15]and regard the patience of our Lord as salvation. So also our beloved brother Paul wrote to you according to the wisdom given him, [16]speaking of this as he does in all his letters. There are some things in them hard to understand, which the ignorant and unstable twist to their own destruction, as they do the other scriptures. [17]You therefore, beloved, since you are forewarned, beware that you are not carried away with the error of the lawless and lose your own stability. [18]But grow in the grace and knowledge of our Lord and Savior Jesus Christ. To him be the glory both now and to the day of eternity. Amen.[a]

[a] Other ancient authorities lack Amen

1 JOHN

CHAPTER 1

We declare to you what was from the beginning, what we have heard, what we have seen with our eyes, what we have looked at and touched with our hands, concerning the word of life— [2]this life was revealed, and we have seen it and testify to it, and declare to you the eternal life that was with the Father and was revealed to us— [3]we declare to you what we have seen and heard so that you also may have fellowship with us; and truly our fellowship is with the Father and with his Son Jesus Christ. [4]We are writing these things so that our[a] joy may be complete.

5 This is the message we have heard from him and proclaim to you, that God is light and in him there is no darkness at all. [6]If we say that we have fellowship with him while we are walking in darkness, we lie and do not do what is true; [7]but if we walk in the light as he himself is in the light, we have fellowship with one another, and the blood of Jesus his Son cleanses us from all sin. [8]If we say that we have no sin, we deceive ourselves, and the truth

[a] Other ancient authorities read *your*

1:1
```
3739 1510 575   746              3739  191                3739
῝Ο   ἦν  ἀπ᾽  ἀρχῆς,      ὃ    ἀκηκόαμεν,           ὃ
What was from beginning, what we have heard,       what
```
```
3708           015    3788        1473   3739 2300
ἑωράκαμεν      τοῖς   ὀφθαλμοῖς   ἡμῶν,  ὃ    ἐθεασάμεθα
we have seen   in the eyes       of us, what we watched
```
```
2532 017 5495   1473  5584          4012 02   3056  06
καὶ  αἱ  χεῖρες ἡμῶν  ἐψηλάφησαν   περὶ τοῦ  λόγου τῆς
and  the hands  of us touched       about the word  of the
```
```
2222     2532 05 2222 5319                    2532
ζωῆς -  2 καὶ  ἡ  ζωὴ ἐφανερώθη,             καὶ
life     and  the life was demonstrated,    and
```
```
3708           2532 3140         2532 518             1473
ἑωράκαμεν      καὶ  μαρτυροῦμεν  καὶ  ἀπαγγέλλομεν ὑμῖν
we have seen   and  we testify   and  we tell      to you
```
```
08   2222 08  166       3748  1510 4314 04  3962    2532
τὴν  ζωὴν τὴν αἰώνιον  ἥτις  ἦν  πρὸς τὸν πατέρα καὶ
the life the eternal  which was to   the father and
```
```
5319             1473    3 3739 3708         2532
ἐφανερώθη       ἡμῖν -    ὃ    ἑωράκαμεν    καὶ
was demonstrated to us      what we have seen also
```
```
191             518        2532 1473       2443 2532
ἀκηκόαμεν,     ἀπαγγέλλομεν καὶ  ὑμῖν,    ἵνα  καὶ
we have heard,  we tell      also to you,  that also
```
```
1473  2842              2192      3326 1473    2532 05
ὑμεῖς κοινωνίαν        ἔχητε     μεθ᾽ ἡμῶν.   καὶ  ἡ
you   partnership      might have with us.    And  the
```
```
2842            1161 05 2251       3326 02   3962    2532 3326
κοινωνία       δὲ   ἡ  ἡμετέρα   μετὰ τοῦ  πατρὸς καὶ  μετὰ
partnership    but  the our       with the father and  with
```
```
02   5207 846   2424       5547       2532 3778  1125
τοῦ  υἱοῦ αὐτοῦ Ἰησοῦ Χριστοῦ. 4 καὶ  ταῦτα γράφομεν
the  son  of him Jesus Christ.   And  these write
```
```
1473  2443 05 5479 1473  1510    4137            5 2532
ἡμεῖς, ἵνα  ἡ  χαρὰ ἡμῶν ᾖ      πεπληρωμένη.     Καὶ
we,    that the joy of us might +having been      And
                                be+  filled.
```
```
1510  3778 05 31        3739 191              575  846
ἔστιν αὕτη ἡ  ἀγγελία  ἣν   ἀκηκόαμεν       ἀπ᾽ αὐτοῦ
is    this the message which we have heard  from him
```
```
2532 312           1473     3754 01  2316 5457  1510
καὶ  ἀναγγέλλομεν ὑμῖν,    ὅτι  ὁ   θεὸς φῶς   ἐστιν
and  we declare    to you,  that the God  light is
```
```
2532 4653   1722 846  3756 1510     3762           6 1437
καὶ  σκοτία ἐν  αὐτῷ οὐκ ἔστιν     οὐδεμία.        Ἐὰν
and  dark   in  him  not there is but not one.      If
```
```
3004          3754 2842         2192     3326 846   2532
εἴπωμεν      ὅτι  κοινωνίαν    ἔχομεν   μετ᾽ αὐτοῦ καὶ
we might say  that partnership  we have  with him   and
```
```
1722 011 4655      4043                 5574         2532
ἐν   τῷ  σκότει περιπατῶμεν,         ψευδόμεθα καὶ
in   the dark   we might walk around,  we lie       and
```
```
3756 4160    08  225          7 1437 1161 1722 011 5457
οὐ   ποιοῦμεν τὴν ἀλήθειαν·   ἐὰν  δὲ  ἐν   τῷ  φωτὶ
not  we do    the truth;      if   but in   the light
```
```
4043               5613 846         1510 1722 011 5457
περιπατῶμεν,      ὡς  αὐτός       ἐστιν ἐν  τῷ  φωτί,
we might walk around as himself   is    in  the light,
```
```
2842          2192    3326 240        2532 09 129
κοινωνίαν    ἔχομεν  μετ᾽ ἀλλήλων  καὶ  τὸ αἷμα
partnership  we have  with one another and the blood
```
```
2424      02   5207 846   2511      1473  575 3956
Ἰησοῦ    τοῦ  υἱοῦ αὐτοῦ καθαρίζει ἡμᾶς ἀπὸ πάσης
of Jesus  the  son  of him cleans    us   from all
```
```
266         8 1437 3004       3754 266        3756
ἁμαρτίας.    ἐὰν  εἴπωμεν    ὅτι  ἁμαρτίαν οὐκ
sin.         If   we might say that sin       not
```
```
2192    1438       4105       2532 05 225        3756
ἔχομεν, ἑαυτοὺς   πλανῶμεν   καὶ  ἡ  ἀλήθεια οὐκ
we have, ourselves we deceive  and  the truth    not
```

```
1510   1722  1473   9  1437 3670                    020  266
ἔστιν  ἐν   ἡμῖν.     ἐὰν ὁμολογῶμεν           τὰς ἁμαρτίας
is     in   us.    If  we might confess        the sins
1473      4103         1510 2532 1342        2443 863      1473
ἡμῶν,  πιστός    ἐστιν καὶ δίκαιος,    ἵνα  ἀφῇ      ἡμῖν
of us, trustful he is  and  right,      that he might to us
                                                     send off
020  266       2532 2511          1473 575  3956  93
τὰς ἁμαρτίας  καὶ καθαρίσῃ   ἡμᾶς ἀπὸ πάσης ἀδικίας.
the sins       and might clean us   from all   unright.
     1437 3004        3754 3756 264              5583
10  ἐὰν εἴπωμεν    ὅτι οὐχ ἡμαρτήκαμεν,     ψεύστην
    If  we might say that not we have sinned,   liar
4160      846    2532 01   3056  846     3756 1510  1722
ποιοῦμεν αὐτὸν καὶ ὁ λόγος αὐτοῦ οὐκ ἔστιν ἐν
we make   him  and the word of him not  is   in
1473    5040          1473    3778 1125    1473    2443
ἡμῖν. 2:1 Τεκνία   μου,   ταῦτα γράφω ὑμῖν ἵνα
us.   Little children of me, these I write to you that
3361 264              2532 1437 5100 264
μὴ ἁμάρτητε.      καὶ ἐάν τις ἁμάρτῃ,
not you might sin.  And if  some might sin,
3875       2192   4314   04  3962    2424     5547
παράκλητον ἔχομεν πρὸς  τὸν πατέρα Ἰησοῦν Χριστὸν
encourager we have toward the father Jesus  Christ
1342       2  2532 846    2434      1510 4012  018
δίκαιον·    καὶ αὐτὸς ἱλασμός ἐστιν περὶ τῶν
right;       and himself expiation is  about the
266      1473   3756 4012  018 2251      1161 3441
ἁμαρτιῶν ἡμῶν,  οὐ περὶ τῶν ἡμετέρων δὲ  μόνον
sins     of us, not about the ours      but  alone
235  2532 4012  3650  02  2889  3  2532 1722 3778
ἀλλὰ καὶ περὶ ὅλου τοῦ κόσμου.  Καὶ ἐν  τούτῳ
but  also about whole the world.  And in  this
1097       3754  1097          846   1437 020 1785
γινώσκομεν ὅτι ἐγνώκαμεν   αὐτόν, ἐὰν τὰς ἐντολὰς
we know      that we have known him,  if  the commands
846   5083         4  01 3004       3754 1097
αὐτοῦ τηρῶμεν.    ὁ λέγων      ὅτι ἔγνωκα
of him we might keep. The one saying, (") I have known
846   2532 020 1785      846  3361 5083        5583
αὐτόν καὶ τὰς ἐντολὰς αὐτοῦ μὴ τηρῶν,   ψεύστης
him   and the commands of him not keeping,  liar
1510 2532 1722 3778  05 225     3756 1510    5  3739
ἐστίν καὶ ἐν τούτῳ ἡ ἀλήθεια οὐκ ἔστιν·    ὃς
he is  and in this the truth   not  is;     who
1161 302 5083       846   04 3056      230   1722 3778
δ’ ἂν τηρῇ      αὐτοῦ τὸν λόγον, ἀληθῶς ἐν τούτῳ
but -  might keep of him the word,  truly  in  this
05 26    02   2316 5048             1722 3778
ἡ ἀγάπη τοῦ θεοῦ τετελείωται,     ἐν  τούτῳ
the love of the God has been completed, in  this
1097       3754 1722 846   1510  6  01 3004        1722
γινώσκομεν ὅτι ἐν αὐτῷ ἐσμεν.  ὁ λέγων        ἐν
we know     that in  him we are. The one saying in
846   3306    3784     2531   1565    4043
αὐτῷ μένειν ὀφείλει καθὼς ἐκεῖνος περιεπάτησεν
him  to stay  owes    just as that one walked around
2532 846    3779    4043    7  27            3756
καὶ αὐτὸς [οὕτως] περιπατεῖν.  Ἀγαπητοί,  οὐκ
also himself thusly to walk around. Loved ones, not
1785     2537    1125    1473   235  1785    3820
ἐντολὴν καινὴν γράφω ὑμῖν ἀλλ’ ἐντολὴν παλαιὰν
command new   I write to you but command old
3739 2192  575   746      05  1785   05   3820
ἣν εἴχετε ἀπ’ ἀρχῆς·   ἡ ἐντολὴ ἡ παλαιά
which you had from beginning; the command the old
1510 01 3056  3739  191       8  3825 1785       2537
ἐστιν ὁ λόγος ὃν ἠκούσατε.  πάλιν ἐντολὴν καινὴν
is    the word which you heard. Again command new
```

is not in us. [9]If we confess our sins, he who is faithful and just will forgive us our sins and cleanse us from all unrighteousness. [10]If we say that we have not sinned, we make him a liar, and his word is not in us.

CHAPTER 2

My little children, I am writing these things to you so that you may not sin. But if anyone does sin, we have an advocate with the Father, Jesus Christ the righteous; [2]and he is the atoning sacrifice for our sins, and not for ours only but also for the sins of the whole world.

3 Now by this we may be sure that we know him, if we obey his commandments. [4]Whoever says, "I have come to know him," but does not obey his commandments, is a liar, and in such a person the truth does not exist; [5]but whoever obeys his word, truly in this person the love of God has reached perfection. By this we may be sure that we are in him: [6]whoever says, "I abide in him," ought to walk just as he walked.

7 Beloved, I am writing you no new commandment, but an old commandment that you have had from the beginning; the old commandment is the word that you have heard. [8]Yet I am writing you a new commandment

that is true in him and in you, because[a] the darkness is passing away and the true light is already shining. [9]Whoever says, "I am in the light," while hating a brother or sister,[b] is still in the darkness. [10]Whoever loves a brother or sister[c] lives in the light, and in such a person[d] there is no cause for stumbling. [11]But whoever hates another believer[e] is in the darkness, walks in the darkness, and does not know the way to go, because the darkness has brought on blindness. [12]I am writing to you, little children,
   because your sins are forgiven on account of his name.
[13]I am writing to you, fathers,
   because you know him who is from the beginning.
I am writing to you, young people,
   because you have conquered the evil one.
[14]I write to you, children, because you know the Father.
I write to you, fathers, because you know him who is from the beginning.
I write to you, young people, because you are strong and the word of God abides in you, and you have overcome the evil one.
[15]Do not love the world or the things in the world. The love of the Father is not in those who love the world; [16]for all that is in the world—the desire

1125	1473	3739	1510	227	1722 846	2532	1722
γράφω	ὑμῖν,	ὅ	ἐστιν	ἀληθὲς	ἐν αὐτῷ	καὶ	ἐν
I write	to you,	that	is	true	in him	and	in

1473	3754	05 ἡ	4653	3855		2532 09	5457 09
ὑμῖν,	ὅτι	ἡ σκοτία		παράγεται		καὶ τὸ	φῶς τὸ
you,	that	the dark		leads along		and the	light the

228 ... 2235 ... 5316 ... 9 01 3004 ... 1722 011
ἀληθινὸν ἤδη φαίνει. [9] Ὁ λέγων ἐν τῷ
true already shines. The one saying in the

5457 1510 2532 04 80 ... 846 3404 1722 07
φωτὶ εἶναι καὶ τὸν ἀδελφὸν αὐτοῦ μισῶν ἐν τῇ
light to be and the brother of him hating in the

4653 1510 2193 737 ... 01 25 ... 04 80
σκοτίᾳ ἐστὶν ἕως ἄρτι. [10] ὁ ἀγαπῶν τὸν ἀδελφὸν
dark he is until now. The one loving the brother

846 1722 011 5457 3306 2532 4625 1722 846
αὐτοῦ ἐν τῷ φωτὶ μένει καὶ σκάνδαλον ἐν αὐτῷ
of him in the light stays and offense in him

3756 1510 ... 01 1161 3404 ... 04 80 846
οὐκ ἔστιν· [11] ὁ δὲ μισῶν τὸν ἀδελφὸν αὐτοῦ
not there is; the but one hating the brother of him

1722 07 4653 1510 2532 1722 07 4653 4043
ἐν τῇ σκοτίᾳ ἐστὶν καὶ ἐν τῇ σκοτίᾳ περιπατεῖ
in the dark he is and in the dark walks around

2532 3756 3609a 4226 5217 3754 05
καὶ οὐκ οἶδεν ποῦ ὑπάγει, ὅτι ἡ
and not he knows where go goes off, because the

4653 5186 016 3788 846 1125
σκοτία ἐτύφλωσεν τοὺς ὀφθαλμοὺς αὐτοῦ. [12] Γράφω
dark blinded the eyes of him. I write

1473 5040 3754 863 1473 017 266
ὑμῖν, τεκνία, ὅτι ἀφέωνται ὑμῖν αἱ ἁμαρτίαι
to you, little children, because have been to you the sins
   sent off

1223 012 3686 846 13 1125 1473 3962
διὰ τὸ ὄνομα αὐτοῦ. [13] γράφω ὑμῖν, πατέρες,
through the name of him, I write to you, fathers,

3754 1097 04 575 746 1125
ὅτι ἐγνώκατε τὸν ἀπ᾽ ἀρχῆς. γράφω
because you have known the one from beginning. I write

1473 3495 3754 3528 04
ὑμῖν, νεανίσκοι, ὅτι νενικήκατε τὸν
to you, young men, because you have conquered the

4190 14 1125 1473 3813 3754
πονηρόν. [14] ἔγραψα ὑμῖν, παιδία, ὅτι
evil. I wrote to you, small children, because

1097 04 3962 1125 1473 3962
ἐγνώκατε τὸν πατέρα. ἔγραψα ὑμῖν, πατέρες,
you have known the father. I wrote to you, fathers,

3754 1097 04 575 746 1125
ὅτι ἐγνώκατε τὸν ἀπ᾽ ἀρχῆς. ἔγραψα
because you have known the one from beginning. I wrote

1473 3495 3754 2478 1510 2532 01
ὑμῖν, νεανίσκοι, ὅτι ἰσχυροί ἐστε καὶ ὁ
to you, young men, because strong you are and the

3056 02 2316 1722 1473 3306 2532
λόγος τοῦ θεοῦ ἐν ὑμῖν μένει καὶ
word of the God in you stays and

3528 04 4190 15 3361 25 04
νενικήκατε τὸν πονηρόν. [15] Μὴ ἀγαπᾶτε τὸν
you have conquered the evil. Not love the

2889 3366 024 1722 03 2889 1437 5100 25
κόσμον μηδὲ τὰ ἐν τῷ κόσμῳ. ἐάν τις ἀγαπᾷ
world but not the in the world. If some might love

04 2889 3756 1510 05 26 02 3962 1722
τὸν κόσμον, οὐκ ἔστιν ἡ ἀγάπη τοῦ πατρὸς ἐν
the world, not is the love of the father in

846 16 3754 3956 09 1722 03 2889 05 1939
αὐτῷ· [16] ὅτι πᾶν τὸ ἐν τῷ κόσμῳ, ἡ ἐπιθυμία
him; because all the in the world, the desire

---

[a] Or that
[b] Gk hating a brother
[c] Gk loves a brother
[d] Or in it
[e] Gk hates a brother

06	4561	2532	05	1939	014	3788	2532
τῆς	σαρκὸς	καὶ	ἡ	ἐπιθυμία	τῶν	ὀφθαλμῶν	καὶ
of the	flesh	and	the	desire	of the	eyes	and

05	212	02	979	3756	1510	1537 02	3962
ἡ	ἀλαζονεία	τοῦ	βίου,	οὐκ	ἔστιν	ἐκ τοῦ	πατρὸς
the	boast	of the	life,	not	it is	from the	father

235	1537 02	2889	1510		**17** 2532 01	2889
ἀλλὰ	ἐκ τοῦ	κόσμου	ἐστίν.		καὶ ὁ	κόσμος
but	from the	world	it is.		And the	world

3855	2532 05	1939	846	01	1161
παράγεται	καὶ ἡ	ἐπιθυμία	αὐτοῦ, ὁ	δὲ
leads along	and the	desire	of it, the	one but

4160	012 2307	02	2316	3306	1519 04	165
ποιῶν	τὸ θέλημα	τοῦ	θεοῦ	μένει	εἰς τὸν	αἰῶνα.
doing	the want	of the	God	stays	into the	age.

18 3813	2078	5610	1510	2532	2531
Παιδία,	ἐσχάτη	ὥρα	ἐστίν,	καὶ	καθὼς
Small children,	last	hour	it is,	and	just as

191	3754	500	2064	2532	3568
ἠκούσατε	ὅτι	ἀντίχριστος	ἔρχεται,	καὶ	νῦν
you heard	that	antichrist	comes,	and	now

500	4183	1096	3606	1097
ἀντίχριστοι	πολλοὶ	γεγόνασιν,	ὅθεν	γινώσκομεν
antichrists	many	have become,	from where	we know

3754 2078	5610 1510		**19** 1537	1473	1831
ὅτι ἐσχάτη	ὥρα ἐστίν.		ἐξ	ἡμῶν	ἐξῆλθαν
that last	hour it is.		From	us	they have gone out

235	3756	1510	1537	1473	1487	1063	1537	1473
ἀλλ'	οὐκ	ἦσαν	ἐξ	ἡμῶν·	εἰ	γὰρ	ἐξ	ἡμῶν
but	not	they were	from	us;	if	for	from	us

1510	3306	302	3326	1473	235	2443
ἦσαν,	μεμενήκεισαν	ἂν	μεθ'	ἡμῶν·	ἀλλ'	ἵνα
they were,	they had stayed	-	with	us;	but	that

5319		3754	3756	1510	3956
φανερωθῶσιν		ὅτι	οὐκ	εἰσὶν	πάντες
they might be demonstrated		that	not	they are	all

1537 1473	**20** 2532	1473	5545	2192	575	02
ἐξ ἡμῶν.	καὶ	ὑμεῖς	χρῖσμα	ἔχετε	ἀπὸ	τοῦ
from us.	And	you	anointing	you have	from	the

40	2532	3609a	3956	**21** 3756	1125	1473	3754
ἁγίου	καὶ	οἴδατε	πάντες.	οὐκ	ἔγραψα	ὑμῖν	ὅτι
holy	and	you know	all.	Not	I wrote	to you	that

3756	3609a	08	225	235	3754 3609a	846	2532
οὐκ	οἴδατε	τὴν	ἀλήθειαν	ἀλλ'	ὅτι οἴδατε	αὐτὴν	καὶ
not	you know	the	truth	but	that you know	it	and

3754	3956	5579	1537 06	225	3756 1510	**22** 5101
ὅτι	πᾶν	ψεῦδος	ἐκ τῆς	ἀληθείας	οὐκ ἔστιν.	Τίς
that	all	lie	from the	truth	not is.	Who

1510	01	5583	1487	3361	01 720		3754 2424
ἐστιν	ὁ	ψεύστης	εἰ	μὴ	ὁ ἀρνούμενος		ὅτι Ἰησοῦς
is	the	liar	except		the one denying		that Jesus

3756 1510	01	5547	3778	1510	01	500
οὐκ ἔστιν	ὁ	Χριστός;	οὗτός	ἐστιν	ὁ	ἀντίχριστος,
not is	the	Christ?	This	is	the	antichrist,

01	720	04	3962	2532 04	5207	**23** 3956 01
ὁ	ἀρνούμενος	τὸν	πατέρα	καὶ τὸν	υἱόν.	πᾶς ὁ
the	one denying	the	father	and the	son.	All the

720	04	5207	3761	04	3962	2192 01
ἀρνούμενος	τὸν	υἱὸν	οὐδὲ	τὸν	πατέρα	ἔχει, ὁ
one denying	the	son	but not	the	father	has, the one

3670	04	5207 2532 04	3962	2192	**24** 1473
ὁμολογῶν	τὸν	υἱὸν καὶ τὸν	πατέρα	ἔχει.	Ὑμεῖς
confessing	the	son also the	father	has.	You

3739 191	575	746	1722 1473	3306	1437
ὃ ἠκούσατε	ἀπ'	ἀρχῆς,	ἐν ὑμῖν	μενέτω.	ἐὰν
what heard	from	beginning,	in you	let stay.	If

1722	1473 3306	3739	575	746	191
ἐν	ὑμῖν μείνῃ	ὃ	ἀπ'	ἀρχῆς	ἠκούσατε,
in	you it might stay	what	from	beginning	you heard,

---

of the flesh, the desire of the eyes, the pride in riches— comes not from the Father but from the world. [17]And the world and its desire[a] are passing away, but those who do the will of God live forever.

[18]Children, it is the last hour! As you have heard that antichrist is coming, so now many antichrists have come. From this we know that it is the last hour. [19]They went out from us, but they did not belong to us; for if they had belonged to us, they would have remained with us. But by going out they made it plain that none of them belongs to us. [20]But you have been anointed by the Holy One, and all of you have knowledge.[b] [21]I write to you, not because you do not know the truth, but because you know it, and you know that no lie comes from the truth. [22]Who is the liar but the one who denies that Jesus is the Christ?[c] This is the antichrist, the one who denies the Father and the Son. [23]No one who denies the Son has the Father; everyone who confesses the Son has the Father also. [24]Let what you heard from the beginning abide in you. If what you heard from the beginning abides in you,

---

a Or *the desire for it*
b Other ancient authorities read *you know all things*
c Or *the Messiah*

then you will abide in the Son and in the Father. ²⁵And this is what he has promised us,ᵃ eternal life.

26 I write these things to you concerning those who would deceive you. ²⁷As for you, the anointing that you received from him abides in you, and so you do not need anyone to teach you. But as his anointing teaches you about all things, and is true and is not a lie, and just as it has taught you, abide in him.ᵇ

28 And now, little children, abide in him, so that when he is revealed we may have confidence and not be put to shame before him at his coming.

29 If you know that he is righteous, you may be sure that everyone who does right has been born of him. ³:¹See what love the Father has given us, that we should be called children of God; and that is what we are. The reason the world does not know us is that it did not know him. ²Beloved, we are God's children now; what we will be has not yet been revealed. What we do know is this: when heᵇ is revealed, we will be like him, for we will see him as he is. ³And all who have this hope in him purify

ᵃ Other ancient authorities read you
ᵇ Or it

```
2532 1473    1722 03    5207 2532 1722 03    3962
καὶ  ὑμεῖς  ἐν  τῷ  υἱῷ  καὶ  ἐν  τῷ  πατρὶ
and  you    in  the son  and  in  the father
3306            2532 3778 1510  05   1860        3739
μενεῖτε.  25  καὶ  αὕτη ἐστὶν ἡ  ἐπαγγελία ἣν
will stay.     And  this is   the  promise   which
846    1861          1473  08  2222 08 166
αὐτὸς ἐπηγγείλατο ἡμῖν, τὴν ζωὴν τὴν αἰώνιον.
himself promised    to us, the life the eternal.
       3778   1125   1473  4012  014 4105          1473
26  Ταῦτα ἔγραψα ὑμῖν περὶ  τῶν πλανώντων    ὑμᾶς.
    These I wrote to you about the ones deceiving you.
    2532 1473  09  5545          3739 2983         575
27  καὶ  ὑμεῖς τὸ  χρῖσμα    ὃ   ἐλάβετε      ἀπ᾽
    And  you   the anointing that you received from
846    3306  1722 1473 2532 3756 5532    2192      2443
αὐτοῦ, μένει ἐν  ὑμῖν καὶ  οὐ χρείαν ἔχετε    ἵνα
him,   stays in  you  and not  need  you have that
5100 1321        1473  235 5613 09 846       5545
τις  διδάσκη   ὑμᾶς, ἀλλ᾽ ὡς  τὸ αὐτοῦ χρῖσμα
some might teach you,  but  as the of him anointing
1321        1473 4012 3956     2532 2227   1510 2532 3756
διδάσκει ὑμᾶς περὶ πάντων καὶ ἀληθές ἐστιν καὶ οὐκ
teaches  you  about all    and true   it is and not
1510 5579      2532 2531   1321        1473 3306
ἔστιν ψεῦδος, καὶ  καθὼς ἐδίδαξεν ὑμᾶς, μένετε
it is lie,    and  just as he taught you, you stay
1722 846       2532 3568 5040                3306 1722
ἐν  αὐτῷ.  28  Καὶ νῦν, τεκνία,        μένετε ἐν
in  him.      And now, little children, stay  in
846   2443 1437 5319                        2192
αὐτῷ, ἵνα ἐὰν φανερωθῇ            σχῶμεν
him,  that if  he might be demonstrated we might have
3954        2532 3361 153                575  846
παρρησίαν καὶ  μὴ  αἰσχυνθῶμεν     ἀπ᾽ αὐτοῦ
boldness   and not we might be ashamed from him
1722 07  3952         846       1437 3609a   3754 1342
ἐν  τῇ παρουσίᾳ αὐτοῦ.  29  ἐὰν  εἰδῆτε ὅτι δίκαιός
in  the presence of him.    If  you know that right
1510 1097       3754 2532 3956 01  4160        08
ἐστιν, γινώσκετε ὅτι καὶ  πᾶς ὁ  ποιῶν    τὴν
he is, you know   that also all  the one doing the
1343             1537 846  1080          3708
δικαιοσύνην ἐξ  αὐτοῦ γεγέννηται.  3:1 Ἴδετε
rightness    from him  has been born.    See
4217      26      1325      1473  01 3962    2443
ποταπὴν ἀγάπην δέδωκεν ἡμῖν ὁ  πατὴρ, ἵνα
what sort love   has given to us the father, that
5043    2316   2564        2532 1510  1223    3778
τέκνα  θεοῦ  κληθῶμεν, καὶ  ἐσμέν. διὰ  τοῦτο
children of God we might   and  we are. Through this
              be called,
01  2889    3756 1097      1473  3754   3756 1097
ὁ  κόσμος οὐ  γινώσκει ἡμᾶς, ὅτι   οὐκ ἔγνω
the world  not knows   us,   because not it knew
846      27       3568 5043      2316    1510    2532
αὐτόν.  2 ἀγαπητοί, νῦν τέκνα   θεοῦ  ἐσμεν, καὶ
him.     Loved ones, now children of God we are, and
3768     5319              5101 1510       3609a
οὔπω  ἐφανερώθη          τί  ἐσόμεθα. οἴδαμεν
not yet has been demonstrated what we will be. We know
3754 1437 5319        3664   846  1510
ὅτι ἐὰν φανερωθῇ,    ὅμοιοι αὐτῷ ἐσόμεθα,
that if  he is demonstrated, like  him  we will be,
3754    3708      846   2531   1510      2532 3956
ὅτι   ὀψόμεθα   αὐτὸν καθὼς ἐστιν.  3 καὶ  πᾶς
because we will see him  just as he is.  And  all
01  2192       08 1680  3778      1909 846 48
ὁ  ἔχων     τὴν ἐλπίδα ταύτην ἐπ᾽ αὐτῷ ἁγνίζει
the one having the hope  this   on  him  purifies
```

```
1438      2531      1565      53      1510      3956 01
ἑαυτὸν,  καθὼς   ἐκεῖνος  ἁγνός ἐστιν.  4 Πᾶς  ὁ
himself,  just as that one  pure  is.    All  the one
4160   08   266        2532 08  458          4160    2532
ποιῶν τὴν ἁμαρτίαν καὶ τὴν ἀνομίαν  ποιεῖ, καὶ
doing the sin       and the lawlessness  does,  and
05   266        1510 05   458              2532  3609a      3754
ἡ  ἁμαρτία ἐστὶν ἡ  ἀνομία.   5 καὶ  οἴδατε    ὅτι
the sin     is    the lawlessness. And you know  that
1565        5319                    2443 020 266
ἐκεῖνος  ἐφανερώθη,        ἵνα τὰς ἁμαρτίας
that one  was demonstrated, that the sins
142                2532 266        1722 846   3756
ἄρῃ,             καὶ ἁμαρτία ἐν  αὐτῷ οὐκ
might be lifted up, and sin       in   him  not
1510        6 3956 01      1722 846  3306       3756
ἔστιν.       πᾶς  ὁ  ἐν  αὐτῷ μένων    οὐχ
there is.  All the one in  him  staying  not
264        3956 01   264         3756 3708      846
ἁμαρτάνει·  πᾶς  ὁ  ἁμαρτάνων ὀυχ ἑώρακεν αὐτὸν
sins;      all the one sinning   not  has seen  him
3761  1097      846        7 5040          3367
οὐδὲ  ἔγνωκεν αὐτόν.    Τεκνία,     μηδεὶς
but not has known him.  Little children, no one
4105        1473  01  4160       08  1343
πλανάτω  ὑμᾶς· ὁ  ποιῶν τὴν δικαιοσύνην
let deceive you;  the one doing the rightness
1342     1510  2531      1565       1342    1510    8  01
δίκαιός ἐστιν, καθὼς  ἐκεῖνος δίκαιός ἐστιν·   ὁ
right   is,   just as that one right   is;     the
4160   08   266        1537 02  1228       1510
ποιῶν τὴν ἁμαρτίαν ἐκ  τοῦ διαβόλου ἐστίν,
one doing the sin   from the slanderer is,
3754   575   746       01   1228         264         1519
ὅτι   ἀπ᾽ ἀρχῆς  ὁ  διάβολος ἁμαρτάνει. εἰς
because from beginning the slanderer sins.    For
3778   5319          01  5207 02      2316   2443
τοῦτο ἐφανερώθη     ὁ  υἱὸς τοῦ  θεοῦ, ἵνα
this  was demonstrated the son of the God,  that
3089         024 2041 02   1228         9 3956 01
λύσῃ        τὰ ἔργα τοῦ  διαβόλου.    Πᾶς ὁ
he might loose the works of the slanderer. All  the
1080                   1537 02  2316  266         3756
γεγεννημένος       ἐκ  τοῦ θεοῦ ἁμαρτίαν οὐ
one having been born from the God  sin          not
4160   3754     4690      846    1722 846  3306       2532
ποιεῖ, ὅτι    σπέρμα αὐτοῦ ἐν  αὐτῷ μένει,  καὶ
does,  because seed   of him in  him  stays,  and
3756 1410      264          3754    1537 02   2316
οὐ  δύναται ἁμαρτάνειν, ὅτι    ἐκ  τοῦ θεοῦ
not he is able to sin,    because from the God
1080           10 1722 3778  5318      1510   021
γεγέννηται.    ἐν  τούτῳ φανερά ἐστιν τὰ
he has been born. In this  evident is    the
5043     02      2316 2532 021 5043      02
τέκνα  τοῦ  θεοῦ καὶ τὰ τέκνα  τοῦ
children of the God  and the children of the
1228        3956 01   3361 4160   1343
διαβόλου· πᾶς  ὁ  μὴ ποιῶν δικαιοσύνην οὐκ
slanderer; all the one not doing rightness  not
1510  1537 02  2316  2532 01       3361 25       04
ἔστιν ἐκ  τοῦ θεοῦ, καὶ ὁ  μὴ ἀγαπῶν τὸν
is   from the God,  and the one not loving the
80        846     11 3754      3778 1510   05 31
ἀδελφὸν αὐτοῦ.  Ὅτι   αὕτη ἐστὶν ἡ  ἀγγελία
brother of him.  Because this is   the message
3739  191       575   746       2443 25
ἣν  ἠκούσατε ἀπ᾽ ἀρχῆς,  ἵνα ἀγαπῶμεν
which you heard from beginning, that we might love
```

4 Everyone who commits sin is guilty of lawlessness; sin is lawlessness. [5] You know that he was revealed to take away sins, and in him there is no sin. [6] No one who abides in him sins; no one who sins has either seen him or known him. [7] Little children, let no one deceive you. Everyone who does what is right is righteous, just as he is righteous. [8] Everyone who commits sin is a child of the devil; for the devil has been sinning from the beginning. The Son of God was revealed for this purpose, to destroy the works of the devil. [9] Those who have been born of God do not sin, because God's seed abides in them;[a] they cannot sin, because they have been born of God. [10] The children of God and the children of the devil are revealed in this way: all who do not do what is right are not from God, nor are those who do not love their brothers and sisters.[b]

11 For this is the message you have heard from the beginning, that we should love one another.

---

[a] Or *because the children of God abide in him*

[b] Gk *his brother*

12We must not be like Cain who was from the evil one and murdered his brother. And why did he murder him? Because his own deeds were evil and his brother's righteous. 13Do not be astonished, brothers and sisters,*a* that the world hates you. 14We know that we have passed from death to life because we love one another. Whoever does not love abides in death. 15All who hate a brother or sister*b* are murderers, and you know that murderers do not have eternal life abiding in them. 16We know love by this, that he laid down his life for us—and we ought to lay down our lives for one another. 17How does God's love abide in anyone who has the world's goods and sees a brother or sister*c* in need and yet refuses help?

18 Little children, let us love, not in word or speech, but in truth and action. 19And by this we will know that we are from the truth and will reassure our hearts before him 20whenever our hearts condemn us; for God is greater

a Gk brothers
b Gk his brother
c Gk brother

240		**12**	3756	2531		2535	1537	02	4190		1510

ἀλλήλους,   οὐ   καθὼς Κάϊν ἐκ   τοῦ πονηροῦ ἦν
one another,   not just as Cain from the evil   was

2532 4969   04 80   846   2532 5484
καὶ ἔσφαξεν   τὸν ἀδελφὸν αὐτοῦ· καὶ χάριν
and he slaughtered the brother of him; and on account

5101   4969   846   3754   021 2041   846
τίνος ἔσφαξεν   αὐτόν; ὅτι   τὰ ἔργα αὐτοῦ
of what slaughtered he him? Because the works of him

4190   1510 021 1161 02   80   846   1342
πονηρὰ   ἦν τὰ δὲ τοῦ   ἀδελφοῦ αὐτοῦ δίκαια.
evil   were the but of the brother of him right.

13 2532 3361 2296   80   1487 3404 1473 01
[Καὶ] μὴ   θαυμάζετε, ἀδελφοί, εἰ   μισεῖ ὑμᾶς ὁ
And   not marvel,   brothers, if   hates you the

2889   **14** 1473 3609a   3754 3327   1537
κόσμος.   ἡμεῖς οἴδαμεν ὅτι μεταβεβήκαμεν   ἐκ
world.   We   know   that we have gone across from

02 2288   1519 08 2222 3754   25   016
τοῦ θανάτου εἰς τὴν ζωήν, ὅτι   ἀγαπῶμεν τοὺς
the death   into the life, because we love   the

80   01   3361 25   3306 1722 03   2288
ἀδελφούς· ὁ   μὴ ἀγαπῶν μένει ἐν   τῷ θανάτῳ.
brothers; the one not loving stays in the death.

15 3956 01 3404   04 80   846   443
πᾶς ὁ μισῶν   τὸν ἀδελφὸν αὐτοῦ ἀνθρωποκτόνος
All the one hating the brother of him man-killer

1510 2532 3609a   3754 3956 443   3756
ἐστίν, καὶ οἴδατε ὅτι πᾶς ἀνθρωποκτόνος οὐκ
is,   and you know that all man-killer   not

2192 2222 166   1722 846 3306   **16** 1722 3778
ἔχει ζωὴν αἰώνιον ἐν   αὐτῷ μένουσαν.   ἐν   τούτῳ
has life eternal in him staying.   In   this

1097   08 26   3754   1565   5228
ἐγνώκαμεν τὴν ἀγάπην, ὅτι   ἐκεῖνος   ὑπὲρ
we have known the love,   because that one on behalf

1473 08 5590 846   5087   2532 1473 3784
ἡμῶν τὴν ψυχὴν αὐτοῦ ἔθηκεν· καὶ ἡμεῖς ὀφείλομεν
of us the soul of him he set; and we   owe

5228   014 80   5090 5087 **17** 3739
ὑπὲρ τῶν ἀδελφῶν τὰς ψυχὰς θεῖναι.   ὃς
on behalf of the brothers the souls to set.   Who

1161 302 2192   04 979 02   2889   2532
δ'   ἂν ἔχῃ   τὸν βίον τοῦ   κόσμου καὶ
but -   might have the life of the world and

2334   04 80   846   5532 2192   2532
θεωρῇ   τὸν ἀδελφὸν αὐτοῦ χρείαν ἔχοντα καὶ
might watch the brother of him need   having and

2808   024 4698   846   575 846   4459 05
κλείσῃ   τὰ σπλάγχνα αὐτοῦ ἀπ' αὐτοῦ, πῶς ἡ
might close the affections of him from him, how the

26   02   2316 3306 1722 846 **18** 5040
ἀγάπη τοῦ   θεοῦ μένει ἐν   αὐτῷ;   Τεκνία,
love of the God stays in him?   Little children,

3361 25   3056 3366   07   1100   235
μὴ   ἀγαπῶμεν λόγῳ μηδὲ τῇ   γλώσσῃ ἀλλὰ
not we might love in word but not in the tongue but

1722 2041 2532 225   2532 1722 3778 1097
ἐν   ἔργῳ καὶ ἀληθείᾳ. **19** [Καὶ] ἐν   τούτῳ γνωσόμεθα
in   work and truth.   And in   this we know

3754 1537 06 225   1510 2532 1715   846
ὅτι ἐκ   τῆς ἀληθείας ἐσμέν, καὶ ἔμπροσθεν αὐτοῦ
that from the truth   we are, and in front of him

3982   08 2588   1473 **20** 3754 1437
πείσομεν   τὴν καρδίαν ἡμῶν,   ὅτι ἐὰν
we will persuade the heart of us,   that if

2607   1473 05 2588 3754   3173
καταγινώσκῃ   ἡμῶν ἡ καρδία, ὅτι μείζων
might know against us the heart, because greater

1510	01	2316	06		2588	1473	2532	1097
ἐστὶν	ὁ	θεὸς	τῆς		καρδίας	ἡμῶν	καὶ	γινώσκει
is	the	God	of the		heart	of us	and	he knows

3956		27		1437	05	2588		1473	3361
πάντα.	**21**	Ἀγαπητοί,		ἐὰν	ἡ	καρδία		[ἡμῶν]	μὴ
all.		Loved ones,		if	the	heart		of us	not

2607		3954		2192		4314	04	2316
καταγινώσκῃ,		παρρησίαν		ἔχομεν		πρὸς	τὸν	θεόν
might know against,		boldness		we have		to	the	God

	2532	3739	1437	154		2983		575	846
22	καὶ	ὃ	ἐὰν	αἰτῶμεν		λαμβάνομεν		ἀπ'	αὐτοῦ,
	and	what	if	we might ask		we receive		from	him,

3754	020	1785		846		5083		2532	024	701
ὅτι	τὰς	ἐντολὰς		αὐτοῦ		τηροῦμεν		καὶ	τὰ	ἀρεστὰ
because	the	commands		of him		we keep		and	the	pleasing

1799	846	4160			2532	3778	1510	05	1785
ἐνώπιον	αὐτοῦ	ποιοῦμεν.	**23**		Καὶ	αὕτη	ἐστὶν	ἡ	ἐντολὴ
before	him	we do.			And	this	is	the	command

846	2443	4100		011		3686		02		5207
αὐτοῦ,	ἵνα	πιστεύσωμεν		τῷ		ὀνόματι		τοῦ		υἱοῦ
of him,	that	we might trust		in the		name		of the		son

846	2424	5547		2532 25				240
αὐτοῦ	Ἰησοῦ	Χριστοῦ		καὶ ἀγαπῶμεν				ἀλλήλους,
of him	Jesus	Christ		and we might love				one another,

2531		1325	1785		1473		2532	01	5083
καθὼς		ἔδωκεν	ἐντολὴν		ἡμῖν.	**24**	καὶ	ὁ	τηρῶν
just as		he gave	command		to us.		And	the	one keeping

020	1785		846		1722 846	3306	2532	846		1722
τὰς	ἐντολὰς		αὐτοῦ		ἐν αὐτῷ	μένει	καὶ	αὐτὸς		ἐν
the commands			of him		in him	stays	and	himself		in

846	2532	1722	3778	1097		3754	3306		1722
αὐτῷ·	καὶ	ἐν	τούτῳ	γινώσκομεν		ὅτι	μένει		ἐν
him;	and	in	this	we know		that	he stays		in

1473	1537	010	4151		3739	1473	1325
ἡμῖν,	ἐκ	τοῦ	πνεύματος		οὗ	ἡμῖν	ἔδωκεν.
us,	from	the	spirit		that	to us	he gave.

	27		3361	3956	4151		4100		235
4:1	Ἀγαπητοί,		μὴ	παντὶ	πνεύματι		πιστεύετε		ἀλλὰ
	Loved ones,		not	all	spirit		trust		but

1381		024	4151		1487	1537	02	2316	1510
δοκιμάζετε	τὰ	πνεύματα	εἰ		ἐκ	τοῦ	θεοῦ	ἐστιν,
prove		the	spirits	if		from	the	God	they are,

3754	4183	5578		1831		1519	04
ὅτι	πολλοὶ	ψευδοπροφῆται		ἐξεληλύθασιν		εἰς	τὸν
because	many	false spokesmen		have gone out		into	the

2889		1722	3778	1097		012	4151	02		2316
κόσμον.	**2**	ἐν	τούτῳ	γινώσκετε		τὸ	πνεῦμα	τοῦ		θεοῦ·
world.		In	this	you know		the	spirit	of the		God;

3956	4151	3739	3670		2424		5547	1722	4561
πᾶν	πνεῦμα	ὃ	ὁμολογεῖ		Ἰησοῦν		Χριστὸν	ἐν	σαρκὶ
all	spirit	that	confesses		Jesus		Christ	in	flesh

2064		1537	02	2316	1510			2532	3956	4151
ἐληλυθότα		ἐκ	τοῦ	θεοῦ	ἐστιν,	**3**		καὶ	πᾶν	πνεῦμα
having come		from	the	God	is,			and	all	spirit

3739	3361	3670		04		2424	1537	02	2316	3756
ὃ	μὴ	ὁμολογεῖ		τὸν	Ἰησοῦν	ἐκ		τοῦ	θεοῦ	οὐκ
that not		confesses		the	Jesus	from		the	God	not

1510	2532	3778	1510	09	02		500		3739
ἔστιν·	καὶ	τοῦτό	ἐστιν	τὸ	τοῦ		ἀντιχρίστου,		ὃ
it is;	and	this	is	the	of the		antichrist,		that

191		3754	2064		2532	3568	1722	03	2889
ἀκηκόατε		ὅτι	ἔρχεται,		καὶ	νῦν	ἐν	τῷ	κόσμῳ
you have heard		that	he comes,		and	now	in	the	world

1510	2235		1473	1537	02	2316	1510
ἐστὶν	ἤδη.	**4**	Ὑμεῖς	ἐκ	τοῦ	θεοῦ	ἐστε,
is	already.		You	from	the	God	are,

5040		2532	3528			846
τεκνία,		καὶ	νενικήκατε			αὐτούς,
little children,		and	you have conquered			them,

than our hearts, and he knows everything. [21]Beloved, if our hearts do not condemn us, we have boldness before God; [22]and we receive from him whatever we ask, because we obey his commandments and do what pleases him.

23 And this is his commandment, that we should believe in the name of his Son Jesus Christ and love one another, just as he has commanded us. [24]All who obey his commandments abide in him, and he abides in them. And by this we know that he abides in us, by the Spirit that he has given us.

CHAPTER 4

Beloved, do not believe every spirit, but test the spirits to see whether they are from God; for many false prophets have gone out into the world. [2]By this you know the Spirit of God: every spirit that confesses that Jesus Christ has come in the flesh is from God, [3]and every spirit that does not confess Jesus[a] is not from God. And this is the spirit of the antichrist, of which you have heard that it is coming; and now it is already in the world. [4]Little children, you are from God, and have conquered them;

---

[a] Other ancient authorities read *does away with Jesus* (Gk *dissolves Jesus*)

for the one who is in you is greater than the one who is in the world. ⁵They are from the world; therefore what they say is from the world, and the world listens to them. ⁶We are from God. Whoever knows God listens to us, and whoever is not from God does not listen to us. From this we know the spirit of truth and the spirit of error.

7 Beloved, let us love one another, because love is from God; everyone who loves is born of God and knows God. ⁸Whoever does not love does not know God, for God is love. ⁹God's love was revealed among us in this way: God sent his only Son into the world so that we might live through him. ¹⁰In this is love, not that we loved God but that he loved us and sent his Son to be the atoning sacrifice for our sins. ¹¹Beloved, since God loved us so much, we also ought to love one another. ¹²No one has ever seen God; if we love one another, God lives in us, and his love is perfected in us.

13 By this we know that

```
3754      3173       1510    01        1722 1473 2228 01
ὅτι       μείζων    ἐστὶν ὁ          ἐν  ὑμῖν ἢ    ὁ
because   greater   is      the one in  you  or   the one
1722 03   2889            846          1537 02  2889     1510
ἐν  τῷ   κόσμῳ.  5  αὐτοὶ    ἐκ  τοῦ κόσμου εἰσίν,
in  the  world.    Themselves from the world  are,
1223      3778   1537 02  2889     2980           2532 01
διὰ      τοῦτο ἐκ  τοῦ κόσμου λαλοῦσιν καὶ  ὁ
through  this  from the world they speak and  the
2889     846      191          1473 1537 02  2316 1510     01
κόσμος αὐτῶν ἀκούει. 6 ἡμεῖς ἐκ  τοῦ θεοῦ ἐσμεν, ὁ
world  them   hears.     We    from the God  are,     the
1097          04 2316 191      1473  3739 3756 1510  1537
γινώσκων    τὸν θεὸν ἀκούει ἡμῶν, ὃς  οὐκ ἔστιν ἐκ
one knowing the God  hears   us,   who not  is     from
02 2316 3756 191      1473   1537 3778    1097       012
τοῦ θεοῦ οὐκ ἀκούει ἡμῶν. ἐκ  τούτου γινώσκομεν τὸ
the God  not  hears  us.    From this  we know       the
4151   06    225          2532 012 4151    06         4106
πνεῦμα τῆς  ἀληθείας καὶ  τὸ  πνεῦμα τῆς  πλάνης.
spirit of the truth    and  the spirit of the deceit.
     27             25                240             3754    05
7 Ἀγαπητοί,    ἀγαπῶμεν    ἀλλήλους,  ὅτι    ἡ
   Loved ones,  we might love one another, because the
26      1537 02 2316 1510   2532 3956 01    25
ἀγάπη ἐκ  τοῦ θεοῦ ἐστιν, καὶ  πᾶς  ὁ   ἀγαπῶν
love   from the God  is,    and  all  the one loving
1537 02  2316 1080           2532 1097      04 2316
ἐκ  τοῦ θεοῦ γεγέννηται καὶ  γινώσκει τὸν θεόν.
from the God  has been born and  knows     the God.
   01      3361 25       3756 1097 04  2316  3754     01
8 ὁ    μὴ  ἀγαπῶν οὐκ ἔγνω τὸν θεόν, ὅτι    ὁ
   The one not  loving not  knew  the God,  because the
2316 26      1510   9 1722 3778  5319              05
θεὸς ἀγάπη ἐστίν. ἐν  τούτῳ ἐφανερώθη     ἡ
God  love   is.     In  this   was demonstrated the
26     02         2316 1722 1473  3754       04 5207 846
ἀγάπη τοῦ    θεοῦ ἐν  ἡμῖν, ὅτι      τὸν υἱὸν αὐτοῦ
love  of the God  in  us,   because the son  of him
04 3439       649           01  2316 1519 04  2889
τὸν μονογενῆ ἀπέσταλκεν ὁ  θεὸς εἰς τὸν κόσμον
the only born has delegated the God  into the world
2443 2198        1223 '       846          1722 3778  1510
ἵνα ζήσωμεν    δι᾽    αὐτοῦ. 10 ἐν  τούτῳ ἐστὶν
that we might live through him.    In  this   is
05  26          3756 3754 1473  25              04 2316 235
ἡ  ἀγάπη, οὐχ ὅτι  ἡμεῖς ἠγαπήκαμεν τὸν θεὸν ἀλλ᾽
the love,  not that we     have loved the God  but
3754 846       25              1473 2532 649         04 5207
ὅτι  αὐτὸς  ἠγάπησεν ἡμᾶς καὶ  ἀπέστειλεν τὸν υἱὸν
that himself loved    us   and  delegated   the son
846     2434       4012 018 266       1473
αὐτοῦ ἱλασμὸν περὶ τῶν ἁμαρτιῶν ἡμῶν.
of him expiation about the sins    of us.
      27         1487 3779 01  2316 25          1473 2532
11 Ἀγαπητοί,  εἰ  οὕτως ὁ  θεὸς ἠγάπησεν ἡμᾶς, καὶ
   Loved ones, if  thusly the God  loved      us,    also
1473 3784      240            25            2316 3762
ἡμεῖς ὀφείλομεν ἀλλήλους ἀγαπᾶν. 12 θεὸν οὐδεὶς
we    owe          one another to love.    God  no one
4455   2300      1437 25           240
πώποτε τεθέαται. · ἐὰν ἀγαπῶμεν ἀλλήλους,
ever yet has watched.  If  we might love one another,
01  2316 1722 1473 3306 2532 05  26       846    1722 1473
ὁ  θεὸς ἐν  ἡμῖν μένει καὶ ἡ  ἀγάπη αὐτοῦ ἐν  ἡμῖν
the God  in  us   stays and the love  of him in  us
5048              1510  13 1722 3778 1097        3754
τετελειωμένη ἐστίν.  Ἐν  τούτῳ γινώσκομεν ὅτι
+having been  is+.     In  this  we know       that
completed
```

```
1722  846   3306      2532 846      1722 1473   3754        1537
ἐν  αὐτῷ μένομεν καὶ αὐτὸς ἐν  ἡμῖν, ὅτι      ἐκ
in   him  we stay  and himself in   us,   because from
010  4151      846    1325         1473        2532 1473
τοῦ πνεύματος αὐτοῦ δέδωκεν      ἡμῖν.  14 καὶ ἡμεῖς
the  spirit   of him he has given to us.    And  we
2300       2532 3140          3754 01 3962   649
τεθεάμεθα καὶ μαρτυροῦμεν ὅτι ὁ πατὴρ ἀπέσταλκεν
have       and we testify  that the father has
watched                                   delegated
04   5207  4990      02   2889         15 3739 1437
τὸν υἱὸν σωτῆρα τοῦ κόσμου.        Ὃς  ἐὰν
the  son  deliverer of the world.     Who if
3670          3754 2424    1510 01 5207 02   2316
ὁμολογήσῃ  ὅτι Ἰησοῦς ἐστιν ὁ  υἱὸς τοῦ θεοῦ,
might confess that Jesus is   the son  of the God,
01  2316 1722 846   3306     2532 846    1722 03  2316
ὁ  θεὸς ἐν  αὐτῷ μένει καὶ αὐτὸς ἐν  τῷ θεῷ.
the God  in   him  stays and himself in  the God.
   2532 1473  1097          2532 4100            08  26
16 καὶ ἡμεῖς ἐγνώκαμεν καὶ πεπιστεύκαμεν τὴν ἀγάπην
    And  we  have known and have trusted    the love
3739 2192 01  2316 1722 1473  01  2316 26    1510
ἣν ἔχει ὁ  θεὸς ἐν  ἡμῖν. Ὁ θεὸς ἀγάπη ἐστίν,
that has the God  in   us.  The God  love  is,
2532 01  3306         1722 07  26      1722 03 2316 3306
καὶ ὁ  μένων       ἐν  τῇ ἀγάπῃ ἐν  τῷ θεῷ μένει
and the one staying in  the love  in  the God stays
2532 01  2316 1722 846   3306        17 1722 3778
καὶ ὁ  θεὸς ἐν  αὐτῷ μένει.        Ἐν τούτῳ
and the God  in   him  stays.      In  this
5048                     05  26    3326 1473 2443 3954
τετελείωται         ἡ  ἀγάπη μεθ᾽ ἡμῶν, ἵνα παρρησίαν
has been completed the love  with  us,   that boldness
2192       1722 07  2250    06    2920        ὅτι
ἔχωμεν   ἐν  τῇ ἡμέρᾳ τῆς κρίσεως, ὅτι
we might have in  the day  of the judgment, that
2531      1565        1510 2532 1473  1510 1722 03   2889
καθὼς ἐκεῖνός ἐστιν καὶ ἡμεῖς ἐσμεν ἐν  τῷ κόσμῳ
just as that one is   also we   are  in  the world
3778         5401 3756 1510 1722 07  26      235  05
τούτῳ.  18 φόβος οὐκ ἔστιν ἐν  τῇ ἀγάπῃ ἀλλ᾽ ἡ
this.      Fear  not  is    in  the love  but  the
5046    26   1854       906      04  5401    3754     01
τελεία ἀγάπη ἔξω    βάλλει τὸν φόβον, ὅτι      ὁ
complete love outside throws the fear, because the
5401   2851       2192 01  1161 5399          3756
φόβος κόλασιν ἔχει, ὁ  δὲ φοβούμενος οὐ
fear   punishment has, the but one fearing not
5048            1722 07  26      19 1473  25
τετελείωται ἐν  τῇ ἀγάπῃ.   ἡμεῖς ἀγαπῶμεν,
has been completed in  the love.    We   love,
3754 846     4413      25      1473 20 1437 5100
ὅτι αὐτὸς πρῶτος ἠγάπησεν ἡμᾶς.   ἐάν τις
because himself first loved      us.   If  some
3004     3754 25   04  2316 2532 04  80        846
εἴπῃ    ὅτι ἀγαπῶ τὸν θεὸν καὶ τὸν ἀδελφὸν αὐτοῦ
might say, (") I love the God and the brother of him
3404       5583       1510 01 1063 3361 25     04
μισῇ,     ψεύστης ἐστίν· ὁ  γὰρ μὴ ἀγαπῶν τὸν
he might hate, liar  he is; the for  not  loving  the
80       846   3739 3708          04  2316 3739 3756
ἀδελφὸν αὐτοῦ ὃν ἑώρακεν,     τὸν θεὸν ὃν οὐχ
brother of him whom he has seen, the God  whom not
3708       3756 1410       25        21 2532 3778    08
ἑώρακεν  οὐ δύναται  ἀγαπᾶν.   καὶ ταύτην τὴν
he has seen not he is able to love.   And  this    the
1785      2192 575  846   2443 01  25        04
ἐντολὴν ἔχομεν ἀπ᾽ αὐτοῦ, ἵνα ὁ  ἀγαπῶν τὸν
command we have from him, that the one loving the
```

we abide in him and he in us, because he has given us of his Spirit. [14]And we have seen and do testify that the Father has sent his Son as the Savior of the world. [15]God abides in those who confess that Jesus is the Son of God, and they abide in God. [16]So we have known and believe the love that God has for us.

God is love, and those who abide in love abide in God, and God abides in them. [17]Love has been perfected among us in this: that we may have boldness on the day of judgment, because as he is, so are we in this world. [18]There is no fear in love, but perfect love casts out fear; for fear has to do with punishment, and whoever fears has not reached perfection in love. [19]We love[a] because he first loved us. [20]Those who say, "I love God," and hate their brothers or sisters,[b] are liars; for those who do not love a brother or sister[c] whom they have seen, cannot love God whom they have not seen. [21]The commandment we have from him is this: those who love

a Other ancient authorities add him; others add God
b Gk brothers
c Gk brother

God must love their brothers and sisters[a] also.

CHAPTER 5

Everyone who believes that Jesus is the Christ[b] has been born of God, and everyone who loves the parent loves the child. [2]By this we know that we love the children of God, when we love God and obey his commandments. [3]For the love of God is this, that we obey his commandments. And his commandments are not burdensome, [4]for whatever is born of God conquers the world. And this is the victory that conquers the world, our faith. [5]Who is it that conquers the world but the one who believes that Jesus is the Son of God?

6 This is the one who came by water and blood, Jesus Christ, not with the water only but with the water and the blood. And the Spirit is the one that testifies, for the Spirit is the truth. [7]There are three that testify:[c] [8]the Spirit and the water and the blood, and these three agree. [9]If we receive human testimony, the testimony of God is greater; for this is the

---

[a] Gk brothers

[b] Or the Messiah

[c] A few other authorities read (with variations) [7]There are three that testify in heaven, the Father, the Word, and the Holy Spirit, and these three are one. [8]And there are three that testify on earth:

```
2316 25              2532 04  80       846      5:1  3956 01
Θεὸν ἀγαπᾷ       καὶ  τὸν ἀδελφὸν αὐτοῦ.      Πᾶς  ὁ
God   might love also the  brother  of him.        All  the
4100           3754  2424   1510 01  5547        1537 02
πιστεύων       ὅτι  Ἰησοῦς ἐστιν ὁ  Χριστός, ἐκ  τοῦ
one trusting that  Jesus  is     the Christ,  from the
2316 1080           2532 3956 01  25            04
θεοῦ γεγέννηται,   καὶ  πᾶς ὁ  ἀγαπῶν         τὸν
God  has been born, and  all  the one loving  the one
1080                25   2532 04        1080
γεννήσαντα          ἀγαπᾷ [καὶ] τὸν  γεγεννημένον
having given birth loves also the one having been born
1537 846      2      1722 3778      1097        3754 25
ἐξ  αὐτοῦ.    ἐν  τούτῳ γινώσκομεν ὅτι  ἀγαπῶμεν
from him.     In  this  we know     that  we love
024 5043      02       2316 3752 04  2316 25
τὰ  τέκνα    τοῦ  θεοῦ, ὅταν τὸν θεὸν ἀγαπῶμεν
the children of the God,  when the God  we might love
2532 020 1785      846      4160         3  3778 1063 1510
καὶ  τὰς ἐντολὰς αὐτοῦ ποιῶμεν.       αὕτη γάρ ἐστιν
and  the commands of him we might do. This for  is
05 26    02       2316 2443 020 1785      846
ἡ  ἀγάπη τοῦ  θεοῦ, ἵνα  τὰς ἐντολὰς αὐτοῦ
the love  of the God,  that the commands of him
5083              2532 017 1785      846      926     3756
τηρῶμεν,        καὶ  αἱ ἐντολαὶ αὐτοῦ βαρεῖαι οὐκ
we might keep, and  the commands of him burdens not
1510      4  3754    3956 09  1080            1537 02
εἰσίν.      ὅτι    πᾶν τὸ  γεγεννημένον  ἐκ  τοῦ
are.       Because all the one having been born from the
2316 3528      04  2889      2532 3778 1510 05  3529
θεοῦ νικᾷ    τὸν κόσμον· καὶ  αὕτη ἐστιν ἡ  νίκη
God  conquers the world;  and  this is    the conquest
05 3528        04  2889     05  4102  1473  5  5101
ἡ  νικήσασα  τὸν κόσμον, ἡ  πίστις ἡμῶν.   Τίς
the one having the world, the trust of us.   Who
    conquered
1161 1510 01 3528        04  2889      1487 3361 01
[δέ] ἐστιν ὁ  νικῶν     τὸν κόσμον εἰ μὴ ὁ
but is    the one conquering the world except  the
4100           3754  2424   1510 01  5207 02      2316
πιστεύων       ὅτι  Ἰησοῦς ἐστιν ὁ  υἱὸς τοῦ  θεοῦ;
one trusting that  Jesus  is     the son  of the God?
6  3778 1510 01  2064       1223   5204  2532
   οὗτός ἐστιν ὁ  ἐλθὼν    δι’  ὕδατος καὶ
   This is    the one having come through water  and
129      2424   5547      3756 1722 011 5204  3441
αἵματος, Ἰησοῦς Χριστός, οὐκ ἐν  τῷ ὕδατι μόνον
blood,   Jesus  Christ,  not in  the water alone
235  1722 011 5204  2532 1722 011 129      2532 09
ἀλλ’ ἐν  τῷ ὕδατι καὶ ἐν  τῷ αἵματι· καὶ  τὸ
but  in  the water and in  the blood;  and  the
4151      1510 09  3140        3754    09  4151
πνεῦμά ἐστιν τὸ  μαρτυροῦν,  ὅτι    τὸ  πνεῦμά
spirit is    the one testifying, because the  spirit
1510 05 225        3754    5140 1510 013
ἐστιν ἡ  ἀλήθεια. 7 ὅτι    τρεῖς εἰσιν οἱ
is    the truth.    Because three are   the ones
3140            8  09  4151   2532 09  5204  2532 09
μαρτυροῦντες,   τὸ  πνεῦμα καὶ  τὸ  ὕδωρ καὶ  τὸ
testifying,      the spirit and  the water and  the
129   2532 013 5140  1519 012 1520 1510    9  1487 08
αἷμα, καὶ  οἱ τρεῖς εἰς  τὸ  ἓν  εἰσιν.    εἰ  τὴν
blood, and  the three into the one are.      If  the
3141           444      2983          05  3141
μαρτυρίαν τῶν ἀνθρώπων λαμβάνομεν, ἡ  μαρτυρία
testimony of the men               we receive, the testimony
02    2316 3173     1510     3754    3778 1510 05
τοῦ  θεοῦ μείζων ἐστίν· ὅτι    αὕτη ἐστὶν ἡ
of the God  greater is;  because this is    the
```

```
3141        02      2316 3754 3140                    4012  02
μαρτυρία    τοῦ     θεοῦ ὅτι μεμαρτύρηκεν     περὶ    τοῦ
testimony   of the  God  that he has testified about  the
5207 846        01  4100              1519 04  5207  02
υἱοῦ αὐτοῦ.  10 ὁ   πιστεύων      εἰς  τὸν  υἱὸν τοῦ
son  of him.    The one trusting in   the son  of the
2316 2192 08    3141           1722 1438        01      3361
θεοῦ ἔχει τὴν μαρτυρίαν ἐν    ἑαυτῷ,   ὁ      μὴ
God  has  the testimony in   himself,  the one not
4100       03   2316 5583   4160          846       3754
πιστεύων τῷ    θεῷ ψεύστην πεποίηκεν αὐτόν, ὅτι
trusting in the God  liar  has made   him,     because
3756 4100          1519 04  3141          3739
οὐ πεπίστευκεν εἰς τὴν μαρτυρίαν ἣν
not he has trusted in  the testimony which
3140            01  2316 4012 02   5207 846        2532
μεμαρτύρηκεν ὁ   θεὸς περὶ τοῦ υἱοῦ αὐτοῦ.  11 Καὶ
has testified the God  about the son  of him.      And
3778 1510   05   3141            3754 2222 166        1325
αὕτη ἐστὶν ἡ   μαρτυρία,   ὅτι ζωὴν αἰώνιον ἔδωκεν
this is      the testimony,  that life eternal  gave
1473 01   2316 2532 3778 05  2222 1722 03   5207
ἡμῖν ὁ   θεός, καὶ αὕτη ἡ   ζωὴ ἐν   τῷ υἱῷ
to us the God,  and this the life in   the son
846  1510       01  2192          04  5207 2192 08
αὐτοῦ ἐστιν.  12 ὁ   ἔχων      τὸν υἱὸν ἔχει τὴν
of him is.       The one having the son  has  the
2222  01      3361 2192  04  5207 02       2316 08  2222
ζωήν· ὁ     μὴ ἔχων τὸν υἱὸν τοῦ    θεοῦ τὴν ζωὴν
life; the one not having the son  of the God  the life
3756 2192     3778 1125    1473   2443 3609a
οὐκ ἔχει.  13 Ταῦτα ἔγραψα ὑμῖν ἵνα εἰδῆτε
not has.      These I wrote to you that you might know
3754 2222 2192       166      015  4100            1519
ὅτι ζωὴν ἔχετε  αἰώνιον, τοῖς πιστεύουσιν εἰς
that life you have eternal, to the ones trusting in
012 3686  02   5207 02   2316       2532 3778 1510
τὸ ὄνομα τοῦ υἱοῦ τοῦ θεοῦ.  14 Καὶ αὕτη ἐστὶν
the name  of the son of the God.     And  this is
05  3954        3739 2192    4314    846     3754 1437 5100
ἡ παρρησία ἣν ἔχομεν πρὸς αὐτόν ὅτι ἐάν τι
the boldness which we have toward him  that if  what
154             2596 012 3307  846        191     1473
αἰτώμεθα   κατὰ τὸ θέλημα αὐτοῦ ἀκούει ἡμῶν.
we might ask by    the want  of him  he hears us.
     2532 1437 3609a   3754 191       1473 3739 1437
15  καὶ ἐὰν οἴδαμεν ὅτι ἀκούει ἡμῶν ὃ  ἐὰν
     And if    we know  that he hears us   what if
154           3609a   3754 2192   024 155       3739
αἰτώμεθα,  οἴδαμεν ὅτι ἔχομεν τὰ αἰτήματα ἃ
we might ask, we know  that we have the askings  which
154         575 846      1437 5100 3708      04
ᾐτήκαμεν ἀπ᾿ αὐτοῦ.  16 Ἐάν τις ἴδῃ    τὸν
we have asked from him.     If  some might see the
80          846    264       266        3361 4314 2288
ἀδελφὸν αὐτοῦ ἁμαρτάνοντα ἁμαρτίαν μὴ πρὸς θάνατον,
brother of him  sinning      sin        not to death,
154       2532 1325       846  2222    015
αἰτήσει καὶ δώσει   αὐτῷ ζωήν, τοῖς
he will ask and he will give to him life, to the ones
264          3361 4314 2288      1510    266      4314
ἁμαρτάνουσιν μὴ πρὸς θάνατον. ἔστιν ἁμαρτία πρὸς
sinning       not to death.  There is sin      to
2288      3756 4012 1565      3004 2443 2065
θάνατον· οὐ περὶ ἐκείνης λέγω ἵνα ἐρωτήσῃ.
death;    not about that   I say that he might ask.
     3956 93    266       1510 2532 1510      266
17  πᾶσα ἀδικία ἁμαρτία ἐστίν, καὶ ἔστιν ἁμαρτία
     All unright sin      is,    and there is sin
```

testimony of God that he has testified to his Son. [10]Those who believe in the Son of God have the testimony in their hearts. Those who do not believe in God[a] have made him a liar by not believing in the testimony that God has given concerning his Son. [11]And this is the testimony: God gave us eternal life, and this life is in his Son. [12]Whoever has the Son has life; whoever does not have the Son of God does not have life.

[13] I write these things to you who believe in the name of the Son of God, so that you may know that you have eternal life.

[14] And this is the boldness we have in him, that if we ask anything according to his will, he hears us. [15]And if we know that he hears us in whatever we ask, we know that we have obtained the requests made of him. [16]If you see your brother or sister[b] committing what is not a mortal sin, you will ask, and God[c] will give life to such a one—to those whose sin is not mortal. There is sin that is mortal; I do not say that you should pray about that. [17]All wrongdoing is sin, but there is sin that is not mortal.

[a] Other ancient authorities read in the Son

[b] Gk your brother

[c] Gk he

18 We know that those who are born of God do not sin, but the one who was born of God protects them, and the evil one does not touch them. [19]We know that we are God's children, and that the whole world lies under the power of the evil one. [20]And we know that the Son of God has come and has given us understanding so that we may know him who is true;[a] and we are in him who is true, in his Son Jesus Christ. He is the true God and eternal life.

21 Little children, keep yourselves from idols.[b]

---

[a] Other ancient authorities read *know the true God*

[b] Other ancient authorities add *Amen*

3756	4314	2288	**18**	3609a	3754	3956	01		
οὐ	πρὸς	θάνατον.		Οἴδαμεν	ὅτι	πᾶς	ὁ		
not	to	death.		We know	that	all	the one		

1080		1537	02	2316	3756	264		235	01
γεγεννημένος		ἐκ	τοῦ	θεοῦ	οὐχ	ἁμαρτάνει,		ἀλλ᾽	ὁ
having been born		from	the	God	not	sins,		but the	

1080		1537	02	2316	5083	846		2532	
γεννηθεὶς		ἐκ	τοῦ	θεοῦ	τηρεῖ	αὐτόν		καὶ	
one having been born		from	the	God	keeps	him		and	

01	4190	3756	681		846	**19**	3609a	3754	1537
ὁ	πονηρὸς	οὐχ	ἅπτεται		αὐτοῦ.		οἴδαμεν	ὅτι	ἐκ
the	evil	not	touches		him.		We know	that	from

02	2316	1510	2532	01	2889	3650	1722	03	4190
τοῦ	θεοῦ	ἐσμεν	καὶ	ὁ	κόσμος	ὅλος	ἐν	τῷ	πονηρῷ
the	God	we are	and	the	world	whole	in	the	evil

2749		**20**	3609a	1161	3754	01	5207	02		2316
κεῖται.			οἴδαμεν	δὲ	ὅτι	ὁ	υἱὸς	τοῦ		θεοῦ
is set.			We know	but	that	the	son	of the		God

2240	2532	1325		1473	1271		2443		
ἥκει	καὶ	δέδωκεν		ἡμῖν	διάνοιαν		ἵνα		
comes	and	has given		to us	intelligence		that		

1097		04	228		2532	1510	1722	03	
γινώσκωμεν		τὸν	ἀληθινόν,		καὶ	ἐσμὲν	ἐν	τῷ	
we might know		the	true,		and	we are	in	the	

228	1722	03	5207	846	2424	5547		3778	
ἀληθινῷ,	ἐν	τῷ	υἱῷ	αὐτοῦ	᾽Ιησοῦ	Χριστῷ.		οὗτός	
true,	in	the	son	of him	Jesus	Christ.		This	

1510	01	228		2316	2532	2222	166		
ἐστιν	ὁ	ἀληθινὸς		θεὸς	καὶ	ζωὴ	αἰώνιος.		
is	the	true		God	and	life	eternal.		

21	5040		5442	1438		575	022
	Τεκνία,		φυλάξατε	ἑαυτὰ		ἀπὸ	τῶν
	Little children,		guard	yourselves		from	the

1497
εἰδώλων.
idols.

2 JOHN

1 The elder to the elect lady and her children, whom I love in the truth, and not only I but also all who know the truth, 2because of the truth that abides in us and will be with us forever:

3 Grace, mercy, and peace will be with us from God the Father and from[a] Jesus Christ, the Father's Son, in truth and love.

4 I was overjoyed to find some of your children walking in the truth, just as we have been commanded by the Father. 5But now, dear lady, I ask you, not as though I were writing you a new commandment, but one we have had from the beginning, let us love one another. 6And this is love, that we walk according to his commandments; this is the commandment just as you have heard it from the beginning—you must walk in it.

7 Many deceivers have gone out into the world, those who do not confess that Jesus Christ has come in the flesh; any such person is the deceiver and the antichrist! 8Be on your guard, so that you do not lose what we[b] have worked for, but may receive a full reward. 9Everyone who does not abide in the teaching of Christ, but goes beyond it, does not have God; whoever

[a] Other ancient authorities add *the Lord*
[b] Other ancient authorities read *you*

1:1
01 ᾽Ο 4245 πρεσβύτερος 1588 ἐκλεκτῇ 2959 κυρίᾳ 2532 καὶ 023 τοῖς
The older man   to select   lady   and   to the

5043 τέκνοις 846 αὐτῆς, 3739 οὓς 1473 ἐγὼ 25 ἀγαπῶ 1722 ἐν 225 ἀληθείᾳ, 2532 καὶ
children   of her,   whom   I   love   in   truth,   and

3756 οὐκ 1473 ἐγὼ 3441 μόνος 235 ἀλλὰ 2532 καὶ 3956 πάντες 013 οἱ 1097 ἐγνωκότες
not   I   alone   but   also   all   the ones having known

08 τὴν 225 ἀλήθειαν, **2** 1223 διὰ 08 τὴν 225 ἀλήθειαν 08 τὴν 3306 μένουσαν 1722 ἐν
the truth,   through   the   truth   the staying   in

1473 ἡμῖν 2532 καὶ 3326 μεθ᾽ 1473 ἡμῶν 1510 ἔσται 1519 εἰς 04 τὸν 165 αἰῶνα. **3** 1510 ἔσται
us   and   with us   it will be   into   the   age.   Will be

3326 μεθ᾽ 1473 ἡμῶν 5485 χάρις 1656 ἔλεος 1515 εἰρήνη 3844 παρὰ 2316 θεοῦ 3962 πατρὸς 2532 καὶ
with us   favor,   mercy,   peace   from   God   Father   and

3844 παρὰ 2424 ᾽Ιησοῦ 5547 Χριστοῦ 02 τοῦ 5207 υἱοῦ 02 τοῦ 3962 πατρὸς 1722 ἐν 225 ἀληθείᾳ
from   Jesus   Christ   the   son   of the   Father   in   truth

2532 καὶ 26 ἀγάπῃ. **4** 5463 ᾽Εχάρην 3029 λίαν 3754 ὅτι 2147 εὕρηκα 1537 ἐκ
and   love.   I rejoiced   very   that   I have found   from

022 τῶν 5043 τέκνων 1473 σου 4043 περιπατοῦντας 1722 ἐν 225 ἀληθείᾳ, 2531 καθὼς
the   children   of you   walking around   in   truth,   just as

1785 ἐντολὴν 2983 ἐλάβομεν 3844 παρὰ 02 τοῦ 3962 πατρός. **5** 2532 καὶ 3568 νῦν 2065 ἐρωτῶ
command   we received   from   the   Father.   And   now   I ask

1473 σε, 2959 κυρία, 3756 οὐχ 5613 ὡς 1785 ἐντολὴν 2537 καινὴν 1125 γράφων 1473 σοι
you,   lady,   not   as   command   new   writing   to you

235 ἀλλὰ 3739 ἣν 2192 εἴχομεν 575 ἀπ᾽ 746 ἀρχῆς, 2443 ἵνα 25 ἀγαπῶμεν
but   what   we had   from   beginning,   that   we might love

240 ἀλλήλους. **6** 2532 καὶ 3778 αἵτη 1510 ἐστὶν 05 ἡ 26 ἀγάπη, 2443 ἵνα
one another.   And   this   is   the   love,   that

4043 περιπατῶμεν 2596 κατὰ 020 τὰς 1785 ἐντολὰς 846 αὐτοῦ· 3778 αὕτη
we might walk around   by   the   commands   of him;   this

05 ἡ 1785 ἐντολή 1510 ἐστιν, 2531 καθὼς 191 ἠκούσατε 575 ἀπ᾽ 746 ἀρχῆς,
the   command   is,   just as   you heard   from   beginning,

2443 ἵνα 1722 ἐν 846 αὐτῇ 4043 περιπατῆτε. **7** 3754 ῞Οτι 4183 πολλοὶ
that   in   it   you might walk around.   Because   many

4108 πλάνοι 1831 ἐξῆλθον 1519 εἰς 04 τὸν 2889 κόσμον, 013 οἱ 3361 μὴ
deceivers   went out   into   the   world,   the ones   not

3670 ὁμολογοῦντες 2424 ᾽Ιησοῦν 5547 Χριστὸν 2064 ἐρχόμενον 1722 ἐν 4561 σαρκί·
confessing   Jesus   Christ   coming   in   flesh;

3778 οὗτός 1510 ἐστιν 01 ὁ 4108 πλάνος 2532 καὶ 01 ὁ 500 ἀντίχριστος.
this   is   the   deceiver   and   the   antichrist.

8 991 βλέπετε 1438 ἑαυτούς, 2443 ἵνα 3361 μὴ 622 ἀπολέσητε 3739 ἃ
See   yourselves,   that not   you might destroy   what

2038 εἰργασάμεθα 235 ἀλλὰ 3408 μισθὸν 4134 πλήρη 618 ἀπολάβητε.
we worked   but   wage   full   you might take back.

9 3956 Πᾶς 01 ὁ 4254 προάγων 2532 καὶ 3361 μὴ 3306 μένων 1722 ἐν
All   the   one leading before   and   not   staying   in

07 τῇ 1322 διδαχῇ 02 τοῦ 5547 Χριστοῦ 2316 θεὸν 3756 οὐκ 2192 ἔχει· 01 ὁ
the   teaching   of the   Christ   God   not   he has;   the one

3306	1722	07	1322	3778	2532	04	3962	2532
μένων	ἐν	τῇ	διδαχῇ,	οὗτος	καὶ	τὸν	πατέρα	καὶ
staying	in	the	teaching,	this	also	the	Father	and

04	5207	2192		1487	5100	2064	4314	1473	2532
τὸν	υἱὸν	ἔχει.	**10**	εἴ	τις	ἔρχεται	πρὸς	ὑμᾶς	καὶ
the	son	has.		If	some	comes	to	you	and

3778	08	1322		3756	5342		3361	2983
ταύτην	τὴν	διδαχὴν	οὐ	φέρει,		μὴ	λαμβάνετε
this	the	teaching	not	he carries,		not	receive

846	1519	3614	2532	5463		846	3361	3004
αὐτὸν	εἰς	οἰκίαν	καὶ	χαίρειν		αὐτῷ	μὴ	λέγετε·
him	into	house	and	to rejoice		to him	not	say;

	01		3004	1063	846		5463	2841
11	ὁ		λέγων	γὰρ	αὐτῷ		χαίρειν	κοινωνεῖ
	the one		saying	for	to him		to rejoice	is partner

023	2041	846	023	4190		4183	2192
τοῖς	ἔργοις	αὐτοῦ	τοῖς	πονηροῖς.	**12**	Πολλὰ	ἔχων
in the	works	of him	the	evil.		Many	˙having

1473	1125	3756	1014	1223	5489	2532
ὑμῖν	γράφειν	οὐκ	ἐβουλήθην	διὰ	χάρτου	καὶ
to you	to write	not	I planned	through	sheet	and

3189	235	1679	1096	4314	1473	2532	4750
μέλανος,	ἀλλὰ	ἐλπίζω	γενέσθαι	πρὸς	ὑμᾶς	καὶ	στόμα
black(ink),	but	I hope	to become	to	you	and	mouth

4314	4750	2980	2443	05	5479	1473
πρὸς	στόμα	λαλῆσαι,	ἵνα	ἡ	χαρὰ	ἡμῶν
to	mouth	to speak,	that	the	joy	of us

4137		1510		782		1473	021
πεπληρωμένη		ᾖ.	**13**	Ἀσπάζεταί		σε	τὰ
+having been filled		might be+.		Greet		you	the

5043	06	79	1473	06	1588
τέκνα	τῆς	ἀδελφῆς	σου	τῆς	ἐκλεκτῆς.
children	of the	sister	of you	the	select.

abides in the teaching has both the Father and the Son. [10]Do not receive into the house or welcome anyone who comes to you and does not bring this teaching; [11]for to welcome is to participate in the evil deeds of such a person.

12 Although I have much to write to you, I would rather not use paper and ink; instead I hope to come to you and talk with you face to face, so that our joy may be complete.

13 The children of your elect sister send you their greetings.[a]

---

[a] Other ancient authorities add *Amen*

3 JOHN

1 The elder to the beloved Gaius, whom I love in truth. 2 Beloved, I pray that all may go well with you and that you may be in good health, just as it is well with your soul. 3 I was overjoyed when some of the friends[a] arrived and testified to your faithfulness to the truth, namely how you walk in the truth. 4 I have no greater joy than this, to hear that my children are walking in the truth.

5 Beloved, you do faithfully whatever you do for the friends,[a] even though they are strangers to you; 6 they have testified to your love before the church. You will do well to send them on in a manner worthy of God; 7 for they began their journey for the sake of Christ,[b] accepting no support from non-believers.[c] 8 Therefore we ought to support such people, so that we may become co-workers with the truth.

9 I have written something to the church; but Diotrephes, who likes to put himself first, does not acknowledge our authority. 10 So if I come, I will call attention to what he is doing in spreading false charges against us. And not content with those charges, he refuses to welcome the friends,[a] and even prevents those who want to do so and expels them from the church.

a Gk brothers
b Gk for the sake of the name
c Gk the Gentiles

1:1
01 4245 1050 03 27 3739 1473
ʽΟ πρεσβύτερος Γαΐῳ τῷ ἀγαπητῷ, ὃν ἐγὼ
The older man to Gaius the loved one, whom I

25 1722 225 27 4012 3956 2172
ἀγαπῶ ἐν ἀληθείᾳ. 2 Ἀγαπητέ, περὶ πάντων εὔχομαί
love in truth. Loved one, about all I wish

1473 2137 2532 5198 2531
σε εὐοδοῦσθαι καὶ ὑγιαίνειν, καθὼς
you to travel well and to be healthy, just as

2137 1473 05 5590 5463 1063 3029
εὐοδοῦταί σου ἡ ψυχή. 3 ἐχάρην γὰρ λίαν
travels well of you the soul. I rejoiced for very

2064 80 2532 3140 1473 07
ἐρχομένων ἀδελφῶν καὶ μαρτυρούντων σου τῇ
coming brothers and testifying of you in the

225 2531 1473 1722 225 4043
ἀληθείᾳ, καθὼς σὺ ἐν ἀληθείᾳ περιπατεῖς.
truth, just as you in truth walk around.

4 3173 3778 3756 2192 5479 2443
μειζοτέραν τούτων οὐκ ἔχω χαράν, ἵνα
Greater of these not I have joy, that

191 024 1699 5043 1722 07 225
ἀκούω τὰ ἐμὰ τέκνα ἐν τῇ ἀληθείᾳ
I might hear the my children in the truth

4043 27 4103 4160 3739 1437
περιπατοῦντα. 5 Ἀγαπητέ, πιστὸν ποιεῖς ὃ ἐὰν
walking around. Loved one, trustful you do what if

2038 1519 016 80 2532 3778 3581
ἐργάσῃ εἰς τοὺς ἀδελφοὺς καὶ τοῦτο ξένους,
you might work in the brothers and this strangers,

6 3739 3140 1473 07 26 1799 1577
οἳ ἐμαρτύρησάν σου τῇ ἀγάπῃ ἐνώπιον ἐκκλησίας,
who testified of you the love before assembly,

3739 2573 4160 4311 516
οὓς καλῶς ποιήσεις προπέμψας ἀξίως
that well you will do having sent before worthily

02 2316 7 5228 1063 010 3686
τοῦ θεοῦ· ὑπὲρ γὰρ τοῦ ὀνόματος
of the God; on behalf of for the name

1831 3367 2983 575 014 1482
ἐξῆλθον μηδὲν λαμβάνοντες ἀπὸ τῶν ἐθνικῶν.
they went out nothing having taken from the nations.

8 1473 3767 3784 5274 016 5108
ἡμεῖς οὖν ὀφείλομεν ὑπολαμβάνειν τοὺς τοιούτους,
We then owe to take up the such ones,

2443 4904 1096 07 225
ἵνα συνεργοὶ γινώμεθα τῇ ἀληθείᾳ.
that co-workers we might become in the truth.

9 1125 5100 07 1577 235 01
Ἔγραψά τι τῇ ἐκκλησίᾳ· ἀλλ' ὁ
I wrote some to the assembly; but the one

5383 846 1361 3756 1926 1473
φιλοπρωτεύων αὐτῶν Διοτρέφης οὐκ ἐπιδέχεται ἡμᾶς.
loving first of them Diotrephes not he welcomes us.

10 1223 3778 1437 2064 5279
διὰ τοῦτο, ἐὰν ἔλθω, ὑπομνήσω
Through this, if I might come, I will remind

846 024 2041 3739 4160 3056 4190
αὐτοῦ τὰ ἔργα ἃ ποιεῖ λόγοις πονηροῖς
him the works that he does in words evil

5396 1473 2532 3361 714 1909
φλυαρῶν ἡμᾶς, καὶ μὴ ἀρκούμενος ἐπὶ
gossiping about us, and not being enough on

3778 3777 846 1926 016 80 2532
τούτοις οὔτε αὐτὸς ἐπιδέχεται τοὺς ἀδελφοὺς καὶ
these neither himself welcomes the brothers and

016 1014 2967 2532 1537 06 1577
τοὺς βουλομένους κωλύει καὶ ἐκ τῆς ἐκκλησίας
the ones planning he hinders and from the assembly

1544		27	3361	3401	012	2556	235

ἐκβάλλει.   **11** Ἀγαπητέ, μὴ   μιμοῦ τὸ κακὸν ἀλλὰ
he throws out.   Loved one, not   imitate the bad   but

012	18	01	15	1537	02	2316	1510

τὸ ἀγαθόν. ὁ ἀγαθοποιῶν   ἐκ τοῦ θεοῦ ἐστιν·
the good.   The one doing good from the God is;

01	2554	3756 3708	04	2316

ὁ κακοποιῶν   οὐχ ἑώρακεν τὸν θεόν.
the one doing bad not   has seen the God.

12 Δημητρίῳ   μεμαρτύρηται   ὑπὸ πάντων καὶ

1216	3140	5259	3956	2532

To Demetrius it has been testified by all   and

5259	846	06	225	2532	1473	1161	3140

ὑπὸ αὐτῆς τῆς ἀληθείας· καὶ ἡμεῖς δὲ μαρτυροῦμεν,
by   itself the truth;   also we   but testify,

2532	3609a	3754 05	3141	1473	227	1510

καὶ οἶδας ὅτι ἡ μαρτυρία ἡμῶν ἀληθής ἐστιν.
and you know that the testimony of us true   is.

13 Πολλὰ εἶχον γράψαι σοι ἀλλ' οὐ θέλω

4183	2192	1125	1473	235	3756 2309

Many I had to write to you but not I want

1223	3189	2532	2563	1473	1125

διὰ   μέλανος καὶ καλάμου σοι   γράφειν·
through black(ink) and reed   to you to write;

14 ἐλπίζω δὲ εὐθέως   σε ἰδεῖν, καὶ στόμα πρὸς

1679	1161	2112	1473	3708	2532 4750	4314

I hope but immediately you to see, and mouth to

4750	2980	1515	1473	782	1473

στόμα λαλήσομεν.   **15** εἰρήνη σοι.   ἀσπάζονταί σε
mouth we will speak.   Peace to you. Greet   you

013 5384	782	016	5384	2596	3686

οἱ φίλοι. ἀσπάζου τοὺς φίλους κατ' ὄνομα.
the friends. Greet the friends by   name.

11 Beloved, do not imitate what is evil but imitate what is good. Whoever does good is from God; whoever does evil has not seen God. [12]Everyone has testified favorably about Demetrius, and so has the truth itself. We also testify for him,[a] and you know that our testimony is true.

13 I have much to write to you, but I would rather not write with pen and ink; [14]instead I hope to see you soon, and we will talk together face to face.

15 Peace to you. The friends send you their greetings. Greet the friends there, each by name.

[a] Gk lacks *for him*

JUDE

1 Jude,[a] a servant[b] of Jesus Christ and brother of James,

To those who are called, who are beloved[c] in[d] God the Father and kept safe for[d] Jesus Christ:

2 May mercy, peace, and love be yours in abundance.

3 Beloved, while eagerly preparing to write to you about the salvation we share, I find it necessary to write and appeal to you to contend for the faith that was once for all entrusted to the saints. 4For certain intruders have stolen in among you, people who long ago were designated for this condemnation as ungodly, who pervert the grace of our God into licentiousness and deny our only Master and Lord, Jesus Christ.[e]

5 Now I desire to remind you, though you are fully informed, that the Lord, who once for all saved[f] a people out of the land of Egypt, afterward destroyed those who did not believe. 6And the angels who did not keep their own position, but left their proper dwelling, he has kept in eternal chains in deepest darkness for the judgment of the great day. 7Likewise, Sodom and Gomorrah and the surrounding cities, which, in the same manner as they, indulged in sexual immorality and pursued unnatural lust,[g] serve

a Gk Judas
b Gk slave
c Other ancient authorities read sanctified
d Or by
e Or the only Master and our Lord Jesus Christ
f Other ancient authorities read though you were once for all fully informed, that Jesus (or Joshua) who saved
g Gk went after other flesh

1:1
2455 Ἰούδας — Judas
2424 Ἰησοῦ — of Jesus
5547 Χριστοῦ — Christ
1401 δοῦλος, — slave,
80 ἀδελφὸς — brother
1161 δὲ — but

2385 Ἰακώβου, — of Jacob,
015 τοῖς — to the ones
1722 ἐν — in
2316 θεῷ — God
3962 πατρὶ — father
25 ἠγαπημένοις — having been loved

2532 καὶ — and
2424 Ἰησοῦ — Jesus
5547 Χριστῷ — Christ
5083 τετηρημένοις — having been kept
2822 κλητοῖς· — called;
2 1656 ἔλεος — mercy

1473 ὑμῖν — to you
2532 καὶ — and
1515 εἰρήνη — peace
2532 καὶ — and
26 ἀγάπη — love
4129 πληθυνθείη. — may be multiplied.

3
27 Ἀγαπητοί, — Loved ones,
3956 πᾶσαν — all
4710 σπουδὴν — diligence
4160 ποιούμενος — making
1125 γράφειν — to write

1473 ὑμῖν — to you
4012 περὶ — about
06 τῆς — the
2839 κοινῆς — common
1473 ἡμῶν — of us
4991 σωτηρίας — deliverance
318 ἀνάγκην — necessity

2192 ἔσχον — I had
1125 γράψαι — to write
1473 ὑμῖν — to you
3870 παρακαλῶν — encouraging
1864 ἐπαγωνίζεσθαι — to contend
07 τῇ — for the

530 ἅπαξ — once
3860 παραδοθείσῃ — having been given over
015 τοῖς — to the
40 ἁγίοις — holy ones
4102 πίστει. — trust.

4
3921 παρεισέδυσαν — Slipped in beside
1063 γάρ — for
5100 τινες — some
444 ἄνθρωποι, — men,
013 οἱ — the
3819 πάλαι — of old

4270 προγεγραμμένοι — having been written before
1519 εἰς — for
3778 τοῦτο — this
012 τὸ — the
2917 κρίμα, — judgment,

765 ἀσεβεῖς, — irreverent,
08 τὴν — the
02 τοῦ — of the
2316 θεοῦ — God
1473 ἡμῶν — of us
5485 χάριτα — favor
3346 μετατιθέντες — changing

1519 εἰς — into
766 ἀσέλγειαν — debauchery
2532 καὶ — and
04 τὸν — the
3441 μόνον — alone
1203 δεσπότην — supervisor
2532 καὶ — and
2962 κύριον — Master

1473 ἡμῶν — of us
2424 Ἰησοῦν — Jesus
5547 Χριστὸν — Christ
720 ἀρνούμενοι. — denying.
5 5279 Ὑπομνῆσαι — To remind
1161 δὲ — but

1473 ὑμᾶς — you
1014 βούλομαι, — I plan,
3609a εἰδότας — having known
[ὑμᾶς] — you
3956 πάντα — all
3754 ὅτι — that
01 [ὁ] — the

2962 κύριος — Master
530 ἅπαξ — once
2992 λαὸν — people
1537 ἐκ — from
1093 γῆς — land
125 Αἰγύπτου — of Egypt
4982 σώσας — having delivered

012 τὸ — the
1208 δεύτερον — second
016 τοὺς — the
3361 μὴ — not
4100 πιστεύσαντας — having trusted
622 ἀπώλεσεν, — he destroyed,

6
32 ἀγγέλους — messengers
5037 τε — even
016 τοὺς — the ones
3361 μὴ — not
5083 τηρήσαντας — having kept
08 τὴν — the

1438 ἑαυτῶν — of themselves
746 ἀρχὴν — beginning
235 ἀλλὰ — but
620 ἀπολιπόντας — having left off
012 τὸ — the

2398 ἴδιον — own
3613 οἰκητήριον — house place
1519 εἰς — for
2920 κρίσιν — judgment
3173 μεγάλης — of great
2250 ἡμέρας — day
1199 δεσμοῖς — chains

126 ἀϊδίοις — eternal
5259 ὑπὸ — by
2217 ζόφον — gloom
5083 τετήρηκεν, — he has kept,
7 5613 ὡς — as
4670 Σόδομα — Sodom
2532 καὶ — and

1116 Γόμορρα — Gomorrah
2532 καὶ — and
017 αἱ — the
4012 περὶ — around
846 αὐτὰς — them
4172 πόλεις — cities
04 τὸν — the
3664 ὅμοιον — like

5158 τρόπον — manner
3778 τούτοις — to these
1608 ἐκπορνεύσασαι — having been completely and sexually
2532 καὶ — and

565 ἀπελθοῦσαι — having gone off
3694 ὀπίσω — after
4561 σαρκὸς — flesh
2087 ἑτέρας, — other,
4295 πρόκεινται — they lie before

1164	4442	166	1349	5254		3668
δεῖγμα	πυρὸς	αἰωνίου	δίκην	ὑπέχουσαι.	**8** ʻΟμοίως
showing	of fire	eternal	right	holding under.		Likewise

3305	2532	3778	1797		4561	3303
μέντοι	καὶ	οὗτοι	ἐνυπνιαζόμενοι		σάρκα	μὲν
indeed	also	these	dreaming ones		flesh	indeed

3392	2963	1161	114		1391
μιαίνουσιν	κυριότητα	δὲ	ἀθετοῦσιν		δόξας
they defile	mastership	but	they set aside		splendors

1161	987		01	1161	3413	01
δὲ	βλασφημοῦσιν.	**9** ʻΟ	δὲ	Μιχαὴλ	ὁ
but	they insult.	The	but	Michael	the

743		3753	03	1228		1252
ἀρχάγγελος,		ὅτε	τῷ	διαβόλῳ		διακρινόμενος
ruler messenger,		when	the	slanderer		doubting

1256		4012	010	3475	4983	3756
διελέγετο		περὶ	τοῦ	Μωϋσέως	σώματος,	οὐκ
he was disputing		about	the	of Moses	body,	not

5111	2920	2018	988	235
ἐτόλμησεν	κρίσιν	ἐπενεγκεῖν	βλασφημίας	ἀλλὰ
he dared	judgment	to carry on	insult	but

3004	2008	1473	2962		3778	1161
εἶπεν·	Ἐπιτιμήσαι	σοι	κύριος.	**10** Οὗτοι	δὲ
he said;	may admonish	you	Master.		These	but

3745	3303	3756	3609a	987
ὅσα	μὲν	οὐκ	οἴδασιν	βλασφημοῦσιν,
as many as	indeed	not	they knew	they insult,

3745	1161	5447	5613	021	249
ὅσα	δὲ	φυσικῶς	ὡς	τὰ	ἄλογα
as many as	but	naturally	as	the	unspeaking

2226	1987	1722	3778	5351
ζῷα	ἐπίστανται,	ἐν	τούτοις	φθείρονται.
living ones	understand,	in	these	they are corrupted.

3759	846	3754	07	3598	02	2535
11 οὐαὶ	αὐτοῖς,	ὅτι	τῇ	ὁδῷ	τοῦ	Κάϊν
Woe	to them,	because	in the	way	of the	Cain

4198	2532	07	4106	02	903	3408
ἐπορεύθησαν	καὶ	τῇ	πλάνῃ	τοῦ	Βαλαὰμ	μισθοῦ
they traveled	and	in the	deceit	of the	Balaam	wage

1632		2532	07	485		02
ἐξεχύθησαν		καὶ	τῇ	ἀντιλογίᾳ		τοῦ
they were poured out		and	in the	word against		the

2879	622		3778	1510	013
Κόρε	ἀπώλοντο.	**12** Οὗτοί	εἰσιν	οἱ
Korah	they destroyed themselves.		These are		the

1722	1019		1473	4694	4910
ἐν	ταῖς	ἀγάπαις	ὑμῶν	σπιλάδες	συνευωχούμενοι
in	the	love(feasts)	of you	spots	feasting with

870	1438	4165	3507	504
ἀφόβως,	ἑαυτοὺς	ποιμαίνοντες,	νεφέλαι	ἄνυδροι
fearlessly,	themselves	shepherding,	clouds	waterless

5259	417	3911		1186	5352
ὑπὸ	ἀνέμων	παραφερόμεναι,		δένδρα	φθινοπωρινὰ
by	winds	being carried along,		trees	late autumn

175	1364	599	1610
ἄκαρπα	δὶς	ἀποθανόντα	ἐκριζωθέντα,
fruitless	twice	having died	having been rooted out,

2949	66	2281	1890	020	1438
13 κύματα	ἄγρια	θαλάσσης	ἐπαφρίζοντα	τὰς	ἑαυτῶν
waves	wild	of sea	foaming up	the	of themselves

152	792	4107	3739	01	2217	010
αἰσχύνας,	ἀστέρες	πλανῆται	οἷς	ὁ	ζόφος	τοῦ
shames,	stars	deceptive	to whom	the	gloom	of the

4655	1519	165	5083		4395
σκότους	εἰς	αἰῶνα	τετήρηται.	**14** Προεφήτευσεν
dark	into	age	has been kept.		He spoke before

1161	2532	3778	1442	575	76	1802	3004
δὲ	καὶ	τούτοις	ἕβδομος	ἀπὸ	Ἀδὰμ	Ἑνὼχ	λέγων·
but	also	to these	seventh	from	Adam	Enoch	saying,

as an example by undergoing a punishment of eternal fire.

8 Yet in the same way these dreamers also defile the flesh, reject authority, and slander the glorious ones.[a] [9]But when the archangel Michael contended with the devil and disputed about the body of Moses, he did not dare to bring a condemnation of slander[b] against him, but said, "The Lord rebuke you!" [10]But these people slander whatever they do not understand, and they are destroyed by those things that, like irrational animals, they know by instinct. [11]Woe to them! For they go the way of Cain, and abandon themselves to Balaam's error for the sake of gain, and perish in Korah's rebellion. [12]These are blemishes[c] on your love-feasts, while they feast with you without fear, feeding themselves.[d] They are waterless clouds carried along by the winds; autumn trees without fruit, twice dead, uprooted; [13]wild waves of the sea, casting up the foam of their own shame; wandering stars, for whom the deepest darkness has been reserved forever.

14 It was also about these that Enoch, in the seventh generation from Adam, prophesied, saying,

[a] Or angels; Gk glories
[b] Or condemnation for blasphemy
[c] Or reefs
[d] Or without fear. They are shepherds who care only for themselves

"See, the Lord is coming*a* with ten thousands of his holy ones, 15to execute judgment on all, and to convict everyone of all the deeds of ungodliness that they have committed in such an ungodly way, and of all the harsh things that ungodly sinners have spoken against him." 16These are grumblers and malcontents; they indulge their own lusts; they are bombastic in speech, flattering people to their own advantage.

17But you, beloved, must remember the predictions of the apostles of our Lord Jesus Christ; 18for they said to you, "In the last time there will be scoffers, indulging their own ungodly lusts." 19It is these worldly people, devoid of the Spirit, who are causing divisions. 20But you, beloved, build yourselves up on your most holy faith; pray in the Holy Spirit; 21keep yourselves in the love of God; look forward to the mercy of our Lord Jesus Christ that leads to*b* eternal life. 22And have mercy on some who are wavering; 23save others by snatching them out of the fire; and have mercy on still others with fear, hating even the tunic defiled by their bodies.*c*

a Gk *came*
b Gk *Christ to*
c Gk *by the flesh*. The Greek text of verses 22-23 is uncertain at several points

2400	2064	2962	1722	40		3461		846
ἰδοὺ	ἦλθεν	κύριος	ἐν	ἁγίαις	μυριάσιν			αὐτοῦ
look	came	Master	in	holy	ten thousands		of	him

15 4160 2920 2596 3956 2532 1651 3956
ποιῆσαι κρίσιν κατὰ πάντων καὶ ἐλέγξαι πᾶσαν
to do judgment against all and to rebuke all

5590 4012 3956 022 2041 763 846
ψυχὴν περὶ πάντων τῶν ἔργων ἀσεβείας αὐτῶν
soul about all of the works of irreverence of them

3739 764 2532 4012 3956 022 4642
ὧν ἠσέβησαν καὶ περὶ πάντων τῶν σκληρῶν
that they do irreverently and about all the hard

3739 2980 2596 846 268 765
ὧν ἐλάλησαν κατ᾽ αὐτοῦ ἁμαρτωλοὶ ἀσεβεῖς.
which spoke against him sinners irreverent.

16 3778 1510 1113 3202 2596 020
Οὗτοί εἰσιν γογγυσταὶ μεμψίμοιροι κατὰ τὰς
These are grumblers, complainers, against the

1939 1438 4198 2532 09 4750
ἐπιθυμίας ἑαυτῶν πορευόμενοι, καὶ τὸ στόμα
desires of themselves traveling, and the mouth

846 2980 5246 2296 4383
αὐτῶν λαλεῖ ὑπέρογκα, θαυμάζοντες πρόσωπα
of them speaks overinflated, marveling faces

5622 5484 **17** 1473 1161 27
ὠφελείας χάριν. Ὑμεῖς δέ, ἀγαπητοί,
benefit on account of. You but, loved ones,

3403 022 4487 022 4302 5259 014
μνήσθητε τῶν ῥημάτων τῶν προειρημένων ὑπὸ τῶν
remember the words the having been spoken by the

652 02 2962 1473 2424 5547 **18** 3754
ἀποστόλων τοῦ κυρίου ἡμῶν Ἰησοῦ Χριστοῦ ὅτι
delegates of the Master of us Jesus Christ that

3004 1473 3754 1909 2078 02 5550
ἔλεγον ὑμῖν ὅτι· ἐπ᾽ ἐσχάτου [τοῦ] χρόνου
they were saying to you, (") on last of the time

1510 1703 2596 020 1438 1939
ἔσονται ἐμπαῖκται κατὰ τὰς ἑαυτῶν ἐπιθυμίας
will be mockers against the of themselves desires

4198 018 763 **19** 3778 1510 013
πορευόμενοι τῶν ἀσεβειῶν. Οὗτοί εἰσιν οἱ
traveling of the irreverences. These are the ones

592 5591 4151 3361 2192
ἀποδιορίζοντες, ψυχικοί, πνεῦμα μὴ ἔχοντες.
dividing off, soul like ones, spirit not having.

20 1473 1161 27 2026 1438
Ὑμεῖς δέ, ἀγαπητοί, ἐποικοδομοῦντες ἑαυτοὺς
You but, loved ones, building on yourselves

07 40 1473 4102 1722 4151 40
τῇ ἁγιωτάτῃ ὑμῶν πίστει, ἐν πνεύματι ἁγίῳ
in the most holy of you trust, in spirit holy

4336 **21** 1438 1722 26 2316 5083
προσευχόμενοι, ἑαυτοὺς ἐν ἀγάπῃ θεοῦ τηρήσατε
praying, yourselves in love of God keep

4327 012 1656 02 2962 1473 2424
προσδεχόμενοι τὸ ἔλεος τοῦ κυρίου ἡμῶν Ἰησοῦ
awaiting the mercy of the Master of us Jesus

5547 1519 2222 166 **22** 2532 3739 3303
Χριστοῦ εἰς ζωὴν αἰώνιον. Καὶ οὓς μὲν
Christ into life eternal. And whom indeed

1648a 1252 **23** 3739 1161 4982
ἐλεᾶτε διακρινομένους, οὓς δὲ σῴζετε
show mercy ones doubting, whom but deliver

1537 4442 726 3739 1161 1648a 1722 5401
ἐκ πυρὸς ἁρπάζοντες, οὓς δὲ ἐλεᾶτε ἐν φόβῳ
from fire seizing, whom but show mercy in fear

3404 2532 04 575 06 4561 4695
μισοῦντες καὶ τὸν ἀπὸ τῆς σαρκὸς ἐσπιλωμένον
hating even the from the flesh having been spotted

```
5509      24  03           1161 1410      5442      1473
χιτῶνα.       Τῷ        δὲ   δυναμένῳ  φυλάξαι  ὑμᾶς
shirt.        To the one but  being able to guard you
679                    2532 2476    2714          06
ἀπταίστους         καὶ  στῆσαι  κατενώπιον  τῆς
without stumbling and   to stand down before the
1391      846    299      1722 20              25  3441
δόξης    αὐτοῦ ἀμώμους  ἐν  ἀγαλλιάσει,      μόνῳ
splendor of him blameless in  gladness,          to alone
2316 4990      1473 1223     2424 5547     02  2962
θεῷ  σωτῆρι  ἡμῶν  διὰ   Ἰησοῦ Χριστοῦ τοῦ κυρίου
God  deliverer of us through Jesus Christ  the Master
1473 1391      3172        2904        2532 1849
ἡμῶν δόξα   μεγαλωσύνη κράτος   καὶ  ἐξουσία
of us splendor, greatness, strength, and  authority
4253    3956    02  165    2532 3568 2532 1519 3956
πρὸ    παντὸς τοῦ αἰῶνος καὶ  νῦν  καὶ  εἰς  πάντας
before all   the age    both now  and  into all
016  165    281
τοὺς αἰῶνας,  ἀμήν.
the  ages,    amen.
```

24 Now to him who is able to keep you from falling, and to make you stand without blemish in the presence of his glory with rejoicing, 25to the only God our Savior, through Jesus Christ our Lord, be glory, majesty, power, and authority, before all time and now and forever. Amen.

REVELATION

CHAPTER 1

The revelation of Jesus Christ, which God gave him to show his servants[a] what must soon take place; he made[b] it known by sending his angel to his servant[c] John, 2who testified to the word of God and to the testimony of Jesus Christ, even to all that he saw.

3 Blessed is the one who reads aloud the words of the prophecy, and blessed are those who hear and who keep what is written in it; for the time is near.

4 John to the seven churches that are in Asia:

Grace to you and peace from him who is and who was and who is to come, and from the seven spirits who are before his throne, 5and from Jesus Christ, the faithful witness, the firstborn of the dead, and the ruler of the kings of the earth.

To him who loves us and freed[d] us from our sins by his blood, 6and made[b] us to be a kingdom, priests serving[e] his God and Father, to him be glory and dominion forever and ever. Amen.

7 Look! He is coming
   with the clouds;
   every eye will see him,
   even those who pierced
       him;
   and on his account all
       the tribes of the earth
       will wail.

[a] Gk slaves
[b] Gk and he made
[c] Gk slave
[d] Other ancient authorities read
    washed
[e] Gk priests to

1:1
602 2424 5547 3739 1325 846 01
Ἀποκάλυψις Ἰησοῦ Χριστοῦ ἦν ἔδωκεν αὐτῷ ὁ
Uncovering of Jesus Christ that gave to him the

2316 1166 015 1401 846 3739 1163
θεὸς δεῖξαι τοῖς δούλοις αὐτοῦ ἃ δεῖ
God to show to the slaves of him what is necessary

1096 1722 5034 2532 4591
γενέσθαι ἐν τάχει, καὶ ἐσήμανεν
to become in quickness, and he signified

649 1223 02 32 846 03
ἀποστείλας διὰ τοῦ ἀγγέλου αὐτοῦ τῷ
having delegated through the messenger of him to the

1401 846 2491 **2** 3739 3140 04 3056
δούλῳ αὐτοῦ Ἰωάννῃ, ὃς ἐμαρτύρησεν τὸν λόγον
slave of him John, who testified the word

02 2316 2532 08 3141 2424 5547
τοῦ θεοῦ καὶ τὴν μαρτυρίαν Ἰησοῦ Χριστοῦ
of the God and the testimony of Jesus Christ

3745 3708 01 314 2532
ὅσα εἶδεν. **3** Μακάριος ὁ ἀναγινώσκων καὶ
as much as he saw. Fortunate the one reading and

013 191 016 3056 06 4394
οἱ ἀκούοντες τοὺς λόγους τῆς προφητείας
the ones hearing the words of the speaking before

2532 5083 024 1722 846 1125 01
καὶ τηροῦντες τὰ ἐν αὐτῇ γεγραμμένα, ὁ
and keeping the in it having been written, the

1063 2540 1451 2491 019 2033 1577
γὰρ καιρὸς ἐγγύς. **4** Ἰωάννης ταῖς ἑπτὰ ἐκκλησίαις
for season near. John to the seven assemblies

019 1722 07 773 5485 1473 2532 1515 575
ταῖς ἐν τῇ Ἀσίᾳ· χάρις ὑμῖν καὶ εἰρήνη ἀπὸ
the ones in the Asia; favor to you and peace from

01 1510 2532 01 1510 2532 01 2064
ὁ ὢν καὶ ὁ ἦν καὶ ὁ ἐρχόμενος
the one being and the one was and the one coming

2532 575 022 2033 4151 3739 1799 02 2362
καὶ ἀπὸ τῶν ἑπτὰ πνευμάτων ἃ ἐνώπιον τοῦ θρόνου
and from the seven spirits who before the throne

846 **5** 2532 575 2424 5547 01 3144 01
αὐτοῦ καὶ ἀπὸ Ἰησοῦ Χριστοῦ, ὁ μάρτυς, ὁ
of him and from Jesus Christ, the testifier, the

4103 01 4416 014 3498 2532 01 758
πιστός, ὁ πρωτότοκος τῶν νεκρῶν καὶ ὁ ἄρχων
trustful, the firstborn of the dead and the ruler

014 935 06 1093 03 25 1473
τῶν βασιλέων τῆς γῆς. Τῷ ἀγαπῶντι ἡμᾶς
of the kings of the earth. To the one loving us

2532 3089 1473 1537 018 266 1473 1722
καὶ λύσαντι ἡμᾶς ἐκ τῶν ἁμαρτιῶν ἡμῶν ἐν
and having loosed us from the sins of us in

011 129 846 **6** 2532 4160 1473 932
τῷ αἵματι αὐτοῦ, καὶ ἐποίησεν ἡμᾶς βασιλείαν,
the blood of him, and he made us kingdom,

2409 03 2316 2532 3962 846 846 05
ἱερεῖς τῷ θεῷ καὶ πατρὶ αὐτοῦ, αὐτῷ ἡ
priests to the God and Father of him, to him the

1391 2532 09 2904 1519 016 165 014
δόξα καὶ τὸ κράτος εἰς τοὺς αἰῶνας [τῶν
splendor and the strength into the ages of the

165 281 **7** 2400 2064 3326 018 3507 2532
αἰώνων]· ἀμήν. Ἰδοὺ ἔρχεται μετὰ τῶν νεφελῶν, καὶ
ages; amen. Look he comes with the clouds, and

3708 846 3956 3788 2532 3748 846
ὄψεται αὐτὸν πᾶς ὀφθαλμὸς καὶ οἵτινες αὐτὸν
will see him all eye and who him

1574 2532 2875 1909 846 3956 017
ἐξεκέντησαν, καὶ κόψονται ἐπʼ αὐτὸν πᾶσαι αἱ
pierced, and will mourn on him all the

5443   06   1093   3483 281   1473 1510 09   255a
φυλαὶ   τῆς   γῆς.   ναί, ἀμήν.   **8** Ἐγώ εἰμι τὸ ἄλφα
tribes of the earth. Yes, amen.   I   am   the alpha

2532 09   5598   3004   2962   01   2316 01   1510
καὶ τὸ ὦ,   λέγει κύριος ὁ θεός, ὁ   ὢν
and the omega, says   Master the God,   the one being

2532 01   1510 2532 01   2064   01   3841
καὶ ὁ   ἦν καὶ ὁ   ἐρχόμενος, ὁ παντοκράτωρ.
and the one was and the one coming,   the all-strength.

     1473   2491   01 80   1473   2532 4791
9 Ἐγὼ Ἰωάννης, ὁ ἀδελφὸς ὑμῶν καὶ συγκοινωνὸς
     I   John,   the brother of you and co-partner

1722 07   2347   2532 932   2532 5281   1722
ἐν τῇ θλίψει   καὶ βασιλείᾳ καὶ ὑπομονῇ ἐν
in the affliction and kingdom and patience in

2424   1096   1722 07   3520   07   2564
Ἰησοῦ, ἐγενόμην ἐν τῇ νήσῳ τῇ καλουμένῃ
Jesus, I became in the island the one being called

3963 1223   04   3056 02   2316 2532 08
Πάτμῳ διὰ   τὸν λόγον τοῦ   θεοῦ καὶ τὴν
Patmos through the word of the God and the

3141   2424   **10** 1096   1722 4151   1722 07
μαρτυρίαν Ἰησοῦ.   ἐγενόμην ἐν πνεύματι ἐν τῇ
testimony of Jesus.   I became in spirit   in the

2960   2250   2532 191   3694 1473 5456   3173
κυριακῇ ἡμέρᾳ καὶ ἤκουσα ὀπίσω μου φωνὴν μεγάλην
Master's day   and I heard after me   sound great

5613 4536   **11** 3004   3739 991   1125   1519
ὡς σάλπιγγος   λεγούσης· ὃ   βλέπεις γράψον εἰς
as trumpet   saying,   what you see write in

975   2532 3992   019   2033   1577   1519
βιβλίον καὶ πέμψον ταῖς ἑπτὰ ἐκκλησίαις, εἰς
small book and send   to the seven assemblies, to

2181   2532 1519 4667   2532 1519 4010   2532 1519
Ἔφεσον καὶ εἰς Σμύρναν καὶ εἰς Πέργαμον καὶ εἰς
Ephesus and to   Smyrna and to   Pergamum and to

2363   2532 1519 4554   2532 1519 5359   2532
Θυάτειρα καὶ εἰς Σάρδεις καὶ εἰς Φιλαδέλφειαν καὶ
Thyatira and to   Sardis and to   Philadelphia and

1519 2993   **12** 2532 1994   991   08   5456
εἰς Λαοδίκειαν.   Καὶ ἐπέστρεψα βλέπειν τὴν φωνὴν
to   Laodicea.   And I returned to see the sound

3748 2980   3326 1473 2532 1994
ἥτις ἐλάλει   μετ' ἐμοῦ, καὶ ἐπιστρέψας
which was speaking with me,   and having returned

3708 2033 3087   5552   **13** 2532 1722 3319
εἶδον ἑπτὰ λυχνίας   χρυσᾶς   καὶ ἐν μέσῳ
I saw seven lampstands gold   and in middle

018   3087   3664   5207 444   1746
τῶν λυχνιῶν   ὅμοιον υἱὸν ἀνθρώπου ἐνδεδυμένον
of the lampstands like   son of man   having put on

4158   2532 4024   4314   015   3149   2223
ποδήρη καὶ περιεζωσμένον πρὸς τοῖς μαστοῖς ζώνην
to feet and having encircled to   the breasts belt

5552   **14** 05   1161 2776   846   2532 017 2359
χρυσᾶν.   ἡ δὲ κεφαλὴ αὐτοῦ καὶ αἱ τρίχες
gold.   The but head   of him and the hairs

3022   5613 2053 3022   5613 5510 2532 013 3788
λευκαὶ ὡς ἔριον λευκόν ὡς χιὼν καὶ οἱ ὀφθαλμοὶ
white   as wool white   as snow and the eyes

846   5613 5395 4442   **15** 2532 013 4228   846
αὐτοῦ ὡς φλὸξ πυρὸς   καὶ οἱ πόδες αὐτοῦ
of him as flame of fire   and the feet of him

3664   5474   5613 1722 2575   4448
ὅμοιοι χαλκολιβάνῳ   ὡς ἐν καμίνῳ πεπυρωμένης
like   polished copper   as in furnace having been
                                              set on fire

2532 05   5456 846   5613 5456 5204   4183
καὶ ἡ φωνὴ αὐτοῦ ὡς φωνὴ ὑδάτων πολλῶν,
and the sound of him as sound of waters many,

So it is to be. Amen.

8 "I am the Alpha and the Omega," says the Lord God, who is and who was and who is to come, the Almighty.

9 I, John, your brother who share with you in Jesus the persecution and the kingdom and the patient endurance, was on the island called Patmos because of the word of God and the testimony of Jesus.[a] [10]I was in the spirit[b] on the Lord's day, and I heard behind me a loud voice like a trumpet [11]saying, "Write in a book what you see and send it to the seven churches, to Ephesus, to Smyrna, to Pergamum, to Thyatira, to Sardis, to Philadelphia, and to Laodicea."

12 Then I turned to see whose voice it was that spoke to me, and on turning I saw seven golden lampstands, [13]and in the midst of the lampstands I saw one like the Son of Man, clothed with a long robe and with a golden sash across his chest. [14]His head and his hair were white as white wool, white as snow; his eyes were like a flame of fire, [15]his feet were like burnished bronze, refined as in a furnace, and his voice was like the sound of many waters.

[a] Or testimony to Jesus
[b] Or in the Spirit

16In his right hand he held seven stars, and from his mouth came a sharp, two-edged sword, and his face was like the sun shining with full force.

17 When I saw him, I fell at his feet as though dead. But he placed his right hand on me, saying, "Do not be afraid; I am the first and the last, 18and the living one. I was dead, and see, I am alive forever and ever; and I have the keys of Death and of Hades. 19Now write what you have seen, what is, and what is to take place after this. 20As for the mystery of the seven stars that you saw in my right hand, and the seven golden lampstands: the seven stars are the angels of the seven churches, and the seven lampstands are the seven churches.

CHAPTER 2

"To the angel of the church in Ephesus write: These are the words of him who holds the seven stars in his right hand, who walks among the seven golden lampstands:

2 "I know your works, your toil and your patient endurance. I know that you cannot tolerate evildoers; you have tested those who claim to be

2532	2192		1722	07	1188	5495	846		792
16 καὶ ἔχων ἐν τῇ δεξιᾷ χειρὶ αὐτοῦ ἀστέρας
and having in the right hand of him stars

2033 2532 1537 010 4750 846 4501
ἑπτὰ καὶ ἐκ τοῦ στόματος αὐτοῦ ῥομφαία
seven and from the mouth of him sword

1366 3691 1607 2532 05 3799 846
δίστομος ὀξεῖα ἐκπορευομένη καὶ ἡ ὄψις αὐτοῦ
two-mouthed sharp traveling out and the sight of him

5613 01 2246 5316 1722 07 1411 846 2532
ὡς ὁ ἥλιος φαίνει ἐν τῇ δυνάμει αὐτοῦ. **17** Καὶ
as the sun shines in the power of him. And

3753 3708 846 4098 4314 016 4228 846 5613
ὅτε εἶδον αὐτόν, ἔπεσα πρὸς τοὺς πόδας αὐτοῦ ὡς
when I saw him, I fell to the feet of him as

3498 2532 5087 08 1188 846 1909 1473 3004
νεκρός, καὶ ἔθηκεν τὴν δεξιὰν αὐτοῦ ἐπ' ἐμὲ λέγων·
dead, and he set the right of him on me saying,

3361 5399 1473 1510 01 4413 2532 01 2078
μὴ φοβοῦ· ἐγώ εἰμι ὁ πρῶτος καὶ ὁ ἔσχατος
not fear; I am the first and the last

2532 01 2198 2532 1096 3498 2532 2400
18 καὶ ὁ ζῶν, καὶ ἐγενόμην νεκρὸς καὶ ἰδοὺ
and the one living, and I became dead and look

2198 1510 1519 016 165 014 165 2532 2192
ζῶν εἰμι εἰς τοὺς αἰῶνας τῶν αἰώνων καὶ ἔχω
living I am into the ages of the ages and I have

020 2807 02 2288 2532 02 86 1125 3767
τὰς κλεῖς τοῦ θανάτου καὶ τοῦ ᾅδου. **19** γράψον οὖν
the keys of the death and the hades. Write then

3739 3708 2532 3739 1510 2532 3739 3195
ἃ εἶδες καὶ ἃ εἰσὶν καὶ ἃ μέλλει
what you saw and what is and what is about

1096 3326 3778 **20** 09 3466 014 2033
γενέσθαι μετὰ ταῦτα. τὸ μυστήριον τῶν ἑπτὰ
to become after these. The mystery of the seven

792 3739 3708 1909 06 1188 1473 2532 020
ἀστέρων οὓς εἶδες ἐπὶ τῆς δεξιᾶς μου καὶ τὰς
stars which you saw on the right of me and the

2033 3087 020 5552 013 2033 792
ἑπτὰ λυχνίας τὰς χρυσᾶς· οἱ ἑπτὰ ἀστέρες
seven lampstands the gold; the seven stars

32 018 2033 1577 1510 2532 017
ἄγγελοι τῶν ἑπτὰ ἐκκλησιῶν εἰσιν καὶ αἱ
messengers of the seven assemblies are and the

3087 017 2033 2033 1577 1510 03
λυχνίαι αἱ ἑπτὰ ἑπτὰ ἐκκλησίαι εἰσίν. **2:1** Τῷ
lampstands the seven seven assemblies are. To the

32 06 1722 2181 1577 1125
ἀγγέλῳ τῆς ἐν Ἐφέσῳ ἐκκλησίας γράψον·
messenger of the in Ephesus assembly write:

3592 3004 01 2902 016 2033 792
Τάδε λέγει ὁ κρατῶν τοὺς ἑπτὰ ἀστέρας
but these says the one holding the seven stars

1722 07 1188 846 01 4043 1722
ἐν τῇ δεξιᾷ αὐτοῦ, ὁ περιπατῶν ἐν
in the right of him, the one walking around in

3319 018 2033 3087 018 5552 3609a
μέσῳ τῶν ἑπτὰ λυχνιῶν τῶν χρυσῶν· **2** οἶδα
middle of the seven lampstands of the gold; I know

024 2041 1473 2532 04 2873 2532 08 5281
τὰ ἔργα σου καὶ τὸν κόπον καὶ τὴν ὑπομονὴν
the works of you and the labor and the patience

1473 2532 3754 3756 1410 941 2556
σου καὶ ὅτι οὐ δύνῃ βαστάσαι κακούς,
of you and that not you are able to bear bad,

2532 3985 016 3004 1438
καὶ ἐπείρασας τοὺς λέγοντας ἑαυτοὺς
and you pressured the ones saying themselves

```
652           2532 3756 1510        2532 2147      846
ἀποστόλους καὶ  οὐκ εἰσὶν  καὶ  εὖρες  αὐτοὺς
delegates  and  not they are and  you found them
5571       3  2532 5281    2192      2532 941
ψευδεῖς,   3  καὶ ὑπομονὴν ἔχεις  καὶ  ἐβάστασας
false,        and patience you have and  you bore
1223    012 3686  1473 2532 3756 2872
διὰ     τὸ ὄνομά μου  καὶ  οὐ  κεκοπίακες.
through the name of me and  not  you have labored.
       235  2192  2596      1473 3754 08  26      1473   08
4  ἀλλὰ ἔχω   κατὰ  σοῦ ὅτι  τὴν ἀγάπην σου  τὴν
4  But  I have against you  that the love  of you the
4413    863        5  3421    3767 4159
πρώτην ἀφῆκες.    5  μνημόνευε οὖν πόθεν
first  you sent off.  Remember  then from where
4098            2532 3340          2532 024 4413  2041
πέπτωκας    καὶ  μετανόησον καὶ  τὰ πρῶτα ἔργα
you have fallen and  change mind and  the first  works
4160    1487 1161 3361 2064    1473    2532 2795
ποίησον· εἰ  δὲ  μή,  ἔρχομαί σοι   καὶ κινήσω
do;     if  but  not, I come  to you and I will move
08 3087      1473 1537 02 5117    846      1437 3361
τὴν λυχνίαν σου  ἐκ  τοῦ τόπου αὐτῆς, ἐὰν  μὴ
the lampstand of you from the place of it, if   not
3340          6  235  3778 2192       3754
μετανοήσῃς.   6  ἀλλὰ τοῦτο ἔχεις,   ὅτι
you might change mind. But  this  you have, that
3404        024 2041 014    3531      3739 2504
μισεῖς  τὰ ἔργα τῶν Νικολαϊτῶν ἃ   κἀγὼ
you hate the works of the Nicolaitans which also I
3404     01 2192      3775 191      5101 09  4151
μισῶ. 7  Ὁ  ἔχων    οὖς ἀκουσάτω τί  τὸ πνεῦμα
hate. 7  The one having ear let hear what the spirit
3004  019 1577        03   3528
λέγει ταῖς ἐκκλησίαις.  Τῷ  νικῶντι
says  to the assemblies. To the one conquering
1325        846    2068    1537 010 3586  06      2222
δώσω      αὐτῷ  φαγεῖν ἐκ  τοῦ ξύλου τῆς  ζωῆς,
I will give to him to eat from the wood  of the life,
3739 1510 1722 03 3857     02     2316    8  2532
ὅ    ἐστιν ἐν  τῷ  παραδείσῳ τοῦ  θεοῦ. 8  Καὶ
that is    in  the paradise  of the God. And
03   32      06   1722 4667    1577      1125
τῷ  ἀγγέλῳ τῆς  ἐν Σμύρνῃ ἐκκλησίας γράψον·
to the messenger of the in  Smyrna assembly  write:
3592    3004  01 4413    2532 01 2078    3739
Τάδε   λέγει ὁ  πρῶτος καὶ  ὁ  ἔσχατος, ὃς
but these says the first  and the last,   who
1096   3498   2532 2198  9  3609a 1473  08
ἐγένετο νεκρὸς καὶ  ἔζησεν 9  οἶδά  σου  τὴν
became dead   and  lived;  I know of you the
2347        2532 08 4432      235  4145    1510
θλῖψιν   καὶ  τὴν πτωχείαν, ἀλλὰ πλούσιος εἶ,
affliction and  the poverty, but  rich     you are,
2532 08 988      1537 014 3004      2453
καὶ  τὴν βλασφημίαν ἐκ  τῶν λεγόντων  Ἰουδαίους
and  the insult    from the ones saying Judeans
1510 1438      2532 3756 1510    235  4864
εἶναι ἑαυτοὺς  καὶ  οὐκ εἰσὶν  ἀλλὰ συναγωγὴ
to be themselves and  not  they are but  synagogue
02   4567    10  3367    5399 3739 3195
τοῦ  σατανᾶ. 10  μηδὲν φοβοῦ ἃ  μέλλεις
of the adversary. Nothing fear  what you are about
3958      2400 3195    906    01 1228      1537
πάσχειν. ἰδοὺ μέλλει βάλλειν ὁ  διάβολος ἐξ
to suffer. Look is about to throw the slanderer from
1473 1519 5438    2443 3985          2532
ὑμῶν εἰς φυλακὴν ἵνα πειρασθῆτε    καὶ
you  into guard  that you might be pressured and
```

apostles but are not, and have found them to be false. [3]I also know that you are enduring patiently and bearing up for the sake of my name, and that you have not grown weary. [4]But I have this against you, that you have abandoned the love you had at first. [5]Remember then from what you have fallen; repent, and do the works you did at first. If not, I will come to you and remove your lampstand from its place, unless you repent. [6]Yet this is to your credit: you hate the works of the Nicolaitans, which I also hate. [7]Let anyone who has an ear listen to what the Spirit is saying to the churches. To everyone who conquers, I will give permission to eat from the tree of life that is in the paradise of God.

[8] "And to the angel of the church in Smyrna write: These are the words of the first and the last, who was dead and came to life:

[9] "I know your affliction and your poverty, even though you are rich. I know the slander on the part of those who say that they are Jews and are not, but are a synagogue of Satan. [10]Do not fear what you are about to suffer. Beware, the devil is about to throw some of you into prison so that you may be tested, and

for ten days you will have affliction. Be faithful until death, and I will give you the crown of life. [11]Let anyone who has an ear listen to what the Spirit is saying to the churches. Whoever conquers will not be harmed by the second death.

12 "And to the angel of the church in Pergamum write: These are the words of him who has the sharp two-edged sword: [13]"I know where you are living, where Satan's throne is. Yet you are holding fast to my name, and you did not deny your faith in me[a] even in the days of Antipas my witness, my faithful one, who was killed among you, where Satan lives. [14]But I have a few things against you: you have some there who hold to the teaching of Balaam, who taught Balak to put a stumbling block before the people of Israel, so that they would eat food sacrificed to idols and practice fornication. [15]So you also have some who hold to the teaching of the Nicolaitans. [16]Repent then. If not, I will come to you soon and make war against them with the sword of my mouth. [17]Let anyone who has an ear listen to what the Spirit is saying to the churches. To everyone who conquers I will give some of the hidden manna,

[a] Or deny my faith

2192	2347	2250	1176	1096	4103
ἕξετε	θλῖψιν	ἡμερῶν	δέκα.	γίνου	πιστὸς
you will have	affliction	days	ten.	Become	trustful

891	2288	2532 1325	1473	04	4735
ἄχρι	θανάτου,	καὶ δώσω	σοι	τὸν	στέφανον
until	death,	and I will give	to you	the	crown

06	2222	**11**	01	2192	3775 191	5101 09
τῆς	ζωῆς.		Ὁ	ἔχων	οὓς ἀκουσάτω	τί τὸ
of the	life.		The one having	ear	let hear	what the

4151	3004	019	1577	01	3528	3756
πνεῦμα	λέγει	ταῖς	ἐκκλησίαις.	Ὁ	νικῶν	οὐ
spirit	says	to the	assemblies.	The one	conquering	not

3361 91		1537 02	2288	02
μὴ ἀδικηθῇ		ἐκ τοῦ	θανάτου	τοῦ
not might be done unright		from the	death	the

1208	**12**	2532 03	32	06	1722 4010
δευτέρου.		Καὶ τῷ	ἀγγέλῳ	τῆς	ἐν Περγάμῳ
second.		And to the	messenger	of the in	Pergamum

1577	1125	3592	3004 01	2192	08
ἐκκλησίας	γράψον·	Τάδε	λέγει ὁ	ἔχων	τὴν
assembly	write:	but these	says the one having		the

4501	08 1366	08	3691	**13**	3609a 4226
ῥομφαίαν	τὴν δίστομον	τὴν	ὀξεῖαν·		οἶδα ποῦ
sword	the two-mouthed	the	sharp;		I know where

2730	3699 01	2362	02	4567	2532
κατοικεῖς,	ὅπου ὁ	θρόνος	τοῦ	σατανᾶ,	καὶ
you reside,	where the	throne	of the	adversary,	and

2902	012 3686	1473 2532	3756 720	08 4102
κρατεῖς	τὸ ὄνομά	μου καὶ	οὐκ ἠρνήσω	τὴν πίστιν
you hold	the name	of me and	not you denied	the trust

1473	2532 1722	019	2250	493	01	3144
μου	καὶ ἐν	ταῖς	ἡμέραις	Ἀντιπᾶς	ὁ	μάρτυς
of me	and in	the	days	Antipas	the	testifier

1473	01 4103	1473	3739 615	3844 1473
μου	ὁ πιστός	μου,	ὃς ἀπεκτάνθη	παρ' ὑμῖν,
of me	the trustful	of me,	who was killed	among you,

3699	01 4567	2730	**14**	235 2192	2596
ὅπου	ὁ σατανᾶς	κατοικεῖ.		ἀλλ' ἔχω	κατὰ
where	the adversary	resides.		But I have	against

1473	3641 3754	2192	1563	2902	08 1322
σοῦ	ὀλίγα ὅτι	ἔχεις	ἐκεῖ	κρατοῦντας	τὴν διδαχὴν
you	few that	you have	there	holding	the teaching

903	3739 1321	03	904	906	4625
Βαλαάμ,	ὃς ἐδίδασκεν	τῷ	Βαλὰκ	βαλεῖν	σκάνδαλον
Balaam,	who taught	to the	Balak	to throw	offense

1799	014 5207	2474	2068	1494	2532
ἐνώπιον	τῶν υἱῶν	Ἰσραὴλ	φαγεῖν	εἰδωλόθυτα	καὶ
before	the sons	Israel	to eat	idol sacrifices	and

4203		15	3779	2192 2532	1473
πορνεῦσαι.			οὕτως	ἔχεις καὶ	σὺ
to commit sexual immorality.			Thusly	have also	you

2902	08 1322	014	3531	3668
κρατοῦντας	τὴν διδαχὴν	[τῶν]	Νικολαϊτῶν	ὁμοίως.
ones holding	the teaching	of the	Nicolaitans	likewise.

16	3340	3767	1487 1161	3361 2064	1473
	μετανόησον	οὖν·	εἰ δὲ	μή, ἔρχομαί	σοι
	Change mind	then;	if but	not, I come	to you

5036	2532 4170	3326 846	1722 07
ταχὺ	καὶ πολεμήσω	μετ' αὐτῶν	ἐν τῇ
quickly	and I will make war	with them	in the

4501	010	4750	1473	**17**	01 2192	3775
ῥομφαίᾳ	τοῦ	στόματός	μου.		Ὁ ἔχων	οὓς
sword	of the	mouth	of me.		The one having	ear

191	5101 09	4151	3004	019	1577
ἀκουσάτω	τί τὸ	πνεῦμα	λέγει	ταῖς	ἐκκλησίαις.
let hear	what the	spirit	says	to the	assemblies.

03	3528	1325	846	010 3131	010
Τῷ	νικῶντι	δώσω	αὐτῷ	τοῦ μάννα	τοῦ
To the one	conquering	I will give	to him	the manna	the

2928	2532 1325	846	5586
κεκρυμμένου	καὶ δώσω	αὐτῷ	ψῆφον
one having been hidden	and I will give	to him	pebble

3022	2532 1909 08	5586	3686 2537	1125
λευκήν,	καὶ ἐπὶ τὴν	ψῆφον	ὄνομα καινὸν	γεγραμμένον
white,	and on the	pebble	name new	having been written

3739	3762	3609a 1487 3361	01	2983		18	2532
ὃ	οὐδεὶς οἶδεν εἰ	μὴ	ὁ	λαμβάνων.		18	Καὶ
which	no one knows except		the one receiving.				And

03	32	06	1722 2363	1577
τῷ	ἀγγέλῳ	τῆς	ἐν Θυατείροις	ἐκκλησίας
to the	messenger	of the	in Thyatira	assembly

1125	3592	3004 01	2316 01
γράψον·	Τάδε	λέγει ὁ υἱὸς τοῦ	θεοῦ, ὁ
write:	but these	says the son of the God,	the one

2192	016	3788	846	5613 5395	4442	2532
ἔχων	τοὺς	ὀφθαλμοὺς	αὐτοῦ	ὡς φλόγα	πυρὸς	καὶ
having	the	eyes	of him	as flame	of fire	and

013 4228	846	3664	5474		19	3609a 1473
οἱ πόδες	αὐτοῦ	ὅμοιοι	χαλκολιβάνῳ·		19	οἶδά σου
the feet	of him	like	polished copper;			I know of you

024 2041	2532 08	26	2532 08	4102	2532 08
τὰ ἔργα	καὶ τὴν	ἀγάπην	καὶ τὴν	πίστιν	καὶ τὴν
the works	and the	love	and the	trust	and the

1248	2532 08	5281	1473	2532 024 2041
διακονίαν	καὶ τὴν	ὑπομονήν	σου,	καὶ τὰ ἔργα
service	and the	patience	of you,	and the works

1473	024 2078	4·183	022	4413		20	235
σου	τὰ ἔσχατα	πλείονα	τῶν	πρώτων.		20	ἀλλὰ
of you	the last	more	of the	first.			But

2192	2596	1473 3754 863	08	1135
ἔχω	κατὰ	σοῦ ὅτι ἀφεῖς	τὴν	γυναῖκα
I have	against	you that you allow	the	woman

2403	05	3004	1438	4398	2532
Ἰεζάβελ,	ἡ	λέγουσα	ἑαυτὴν	προφῆτιν	καὶ
Jezabel,	the	one saying	herself	spokeswoman	and

1321	2532 4105	016 1699 1401
διδάσκει	καὶ πλανᾷ	τοὺς ἐμοὺς δούλους
she teaches	and deceives	the my slaves

4203	2532 2068	1494		21	2532 1325
πορνεῦσαι	καὶ φαγεῖν	εἰδωλόθυτα.		21	καὶ ἔδωκα
to commit sexual morality	and to eat	idol sacrifices.			And I gave

846	5550	2443 3340	2532
αὐτῇ	χρόνον	ἵνα μετανοήσῃ,	καὶ
to her	time	that she might change mind,	and

3756 2309	3340	1537 06
οὐ θέλει	μετανοῆσαι	ἐκ τῆς
not she wants	to change mind	from the

4202	846	22	2400 906	846 1519
πορνείας	αὐτῆς.	22	ἰδοὺ βάλλω	αὐτὴν εἰς
sexual immorality	of her.		Look I throw	her into

2825	2532 016 3431	3326 846 1519
κλίνην	καὶ τοὺς μοιχεύοντας	μετ᾽ αὐτῆς εἰς
bed	and the committing adultery	with her into

2347	3173	1437 3361	3340
θλῖψιν	μεγάλην,	ἐὰν μὴ	μετανοήσωσιν
affliction	great,	if not	they might change mind

1537 022 2041	846	23	2532 024 5043	846
ἐκ τῶν ἔργων	αὐτῆς,	23	καὶ τὰ τέκνα	αὐτῆς
from the works	of her,		and the children	of her

615	1722 2288	2532 1097	3956 017
ἀποκτενῶ	ἐν θανάτῳ.	καὶ γνώσονται	πᾶσαι αἱ
I will kill	in death.	And will know	all the

1577	3754 1473 1510 01	2037a	3510
ἐκκλησίαι	ὅτι ἐγώ εἰμι ὁ	ἐραυνῶν	νεφροὺς
assemblies	that I am the	one searching	kidneys

and I will give a white stone, and on the white stone is written a new name that no one knows except the one who receives it.

18 "And to the angel of the church in Thyatira write: These are the words of the Son of God, who has eyes like a flame of fire, and whose feet are like burnished bronze:

19 "I know your works—your love, faith, service, and patient endurance. I know that your last works are greater than the first. 20 But I have this against you: you tolerate that woman Jezebel, who calls herself a prophet and is teaching and beguiling my servants[a] to practice fornication and to eat food sacrificed to idols. 21 I gave her time to repent, but she refuses to repent of her fornication. 22 Beware, I am throwing her on a bed, and those who commit adultery with her I am throwing into great distress, unless they repent of her doings; 23 and I will strike her children dead. And all the churches will know that I am the one who searches minds and hearts, and I will give to each

---

[a] Gk slaves

of you as your works deserve. [24]But to the rest of you in Thyatira, who do not hold this teaching, who have not learned what some call 'the deep things of Satan,' to you I say, I do not lay on you any other burden; [25]only hold fast to what you have until I come. [26]To everyone who conquers and continues to do my works to the end,

I will give authority over the nations;
[27]to rule[a] them with an
    iron rod,
    as when clay pots are
    shattered—
[28]even as I also received authority from my Father. To the one who conquers I will also give the morning star. [29]Let anyone who has an ear listen to what the Spirit is saying to the churches.

CHAPTER 3

"And to the angel of the church in Sardis write: These are the words of him who has the seven spirits of God and the seven stars:

"I know your works; you have a name of being alive, but you are dead. [2]Wake up, and strengthen what remains and is on the point of death, for I have not found your works perfect in the sight of my God. [3]Remember then what you received and heard; obey it, and repent. If you do not wake up, I will come like a thief,

[a] Or to shepherd

2532	2588		2532	1325		1473	1538	2596	024
καὶ	καρδίας,		καὶ	δώσω		ὑμῖν	ἑκάστῳ	κατὰ	τὰ
and	hearts,		and	I will give		to you	each	by	the

2041 1473 **24** 1473 1161 3004 015 3062
ἔργα ὑμῶν. ὑμῖν δὲ λέγω τοῖς λοιποῖς
works of you. To you but I say the ones remaining

015 1722 2363 3745 3756 2192 08
τοῖς ἐν Θυατείροις, ὅσοι οὐκ ἔχουσιν τὴν
the in Thyatira, as many as not have the

1322 3778 3748 3756 1097 024 901
διδαχὴν ταύτην, οἵτινες οὐκ ἔγνωσαν τὰ βαθέα
teaching this, who not knew the depths

02 4567 5613 3004 3756 906 1909 1473
τοῦ σατανᾶ ὡς λέγουσιν· οὐ βάλλω ἐφ' ὑμᾶς
of the adversary as they say; not I throw on you

243 922 **25** 4133 3739 2192 2902 891
ἄλλο βάρος, πλὴν ὃ ἔχετε κρατήσατε ἄχρι[ς]
other burden, except what you have hold until

3739 302 2240 **26** 2532 01 3528 2532
οὗ ἂν ἥξω. Καὶ ὁ νικῶν καὶ
which - I might come. And the one conquering and

01 5083 891 5056 024 2041 1473
ὁ τηρῶν ἄχρι τέλους τὰ ἔργα μου,
the one keeping until completion the works of me,

1325 846 1849 1909 022 1484 **27** 2532
δώσω αὐτῷ ἐξουσίαν ἐπὶ τῶν ἐθνῶν καὶ
I will give to him authority on the nations and

4165 846 1722 4464 4603 5613 021
ποιμανεῖ αὐτοὺς ἐν ῥάβδῳ σιδηρᾷ ὡς τὰ
he will shepherd them in rod iron as the

4632 021 2764 4133 **28** 5613 2504
σκεύη τὰ κεραμικὰ συντρίβεται, ὡς κἀγὼ
pots the ceramic are broken, as also I

2983 3844 02 3962 1473 2532 1325
εἴληφα παρὰ τοῦ πατρός μου, καὶ δώσω
have received from the Father of me, also I will give

046 04 792 04 4407 **29** 01 2192 3775
αὐτῷ τὸν ἀστέρα τὸν πρωϊνόν. Ὁ ἔχων οὓς
to him the star the morning. The one having ear

191 5101 09 4151 3004 019 1577
ἀκουσάτω τί τὸ πνεῦμα λέγει ταῖς ἐκκλησίαις.
let hear what the spirit says to the assemblies.

3:1 2532 03 32 06 1722 4554 1577
Καὶ τῷ ἀγγέλῳ τῆς ἐν Σάρδεσιν ἐκκλησίας
And to the messenger of the in Sardis assembly

1125 3592 3004 01 2192 024 2033
γράψον· Τάδε λέγει ὁ ἔχων τὰ ἑπτὰ
write: but these says the one having the seven

4151 02 2316 2532 016 2033 792 3609a
πνεύματα τοῦ θεοῦ καὶ τοὺς ἑπτὰ ἀστέρας· οἶδά
spirits of the God and the seven stars; I know

1473 024 2041 3754 3686 2192 3754 2198
σου τὰ ἔργα ὅτι ὄνομα ἔχεις ὅτι ζῇς,
of you the works that name you have that you live,

2532 3498 1510 **2** 1096 1127 2532
καὶ νεκρὸς εἶ. γίνου γρηγορῶν καὶ
and dead you are. Become keeping awake and

4741 024 3062 3739 3195 599
στήρισον τὰ λοιπὰ ἃ ἔμελλον ἀποθανεῖν,
strengthen the remaining that were about to die,

3756 1063 2147 1473 024 2041 4137 1799
οὐ γὰρ εὕρηκά σου τὰ ἔργα πεπληρωμένα ἐνώπιον
not for I have of you the works having been before
found filled

02 2316 1473 **3** 3421 3767 4459 2983
τοῦ θεοῦ μου. μνημόνευε οὖν πῶς εἴληφας
the God of me. Remember then how you have received

2532 191 2532 5083 2532 3340 1437 3767
καὶ ἤκουσας καὶ τήρει καὶ μετανόησον. ἐὰν οὖν
and you heard and keep and change mind. If then

3361 1127   2240   5613 2812
μὴ   γρηγορήσῃς,   ἥξω   ὡς   κλέπτης,
not you might keep awake,   I will come as   thief,

2532 3756 3361 1097   4169   5610
καὶ οὐ   μὴ γνῷς   ποίαν   ὥραν
and not not you might know what kind hour

2240   1909 1473 4 235   2192   3641   3686   1722
ἥξω   ἐπὶ σέ.   ἀλλὰ ἔχεις   ὀλίγα ὀνόματα ἐν
I will come on   you.   But you have few   names   in

4554   3739 3756 3435   024 2440   846   2532
Σάρδεσιν ἃ   οὐκ ἐμόλυναν τὰ ἱμάτια αὐτῶν,   καὶ
Sardis   who not stained   the clothes of them,   and

4043   3326 1473 1722 3022   3754
περιπατήσουσιν   μετ' ἐμοῦ ἐν λευκοῖς,   ὅτι
they will walk around with me   in white,   because

514   1510   5   01 3528   3779
ἄξιοί εἰσιν.   ῾Ο   νικῶν   οὕτως
worthy they are.   The one conquering thusly

4016   1722 2440   3022   2532 3756
περιβαλεῖται   ἐν   ἱματίοις λευκοῖς καὶ οὐ
will be thrown around in   clothes   white   and not

3361 1813   012 3686   846   1537 06 976
μὴ   ἐξαλείψω   τὸ ὄνομα αὐτοῦ ἐκ   τῆς βίβλου
not will I wipe off the name of him from the book

06   2222 2532 3670   012 3686   846
τῆς ζωῆς καὶ ὁμολογήσω   τὸ ὄνομα αὐτοῦ
of the life and I will confess the name of him

1799   02   3962   1473 2532 1799   014 32
ἐνώπιον τοῦ πατρός μου   καὶ ἐνώπιον τῶν ἀγγέλων
before   the Father of me and before   the messengers

846   01 2192   3775 191   5101 09
αὐτοῦ.   6 ῾Ο ἔχων   οὓς ἀκουσάτω τί   τὸ
of him.   The one having ear let hear   what the

4151   3004 019 1577   7 2532 03
πνεῦμα λέγει ταῖς ἐκκλησίαις.   Καὶ τῷ
spirit says to the assemblies.   And to the

32   06   1722 5359   1577   1125
ἀγγέλῳ   τῆς ἐν Φιλαδελφείᾳ ἐκκλησίας γράψον·
messenger of the in Philadelphia assembly write:

3592   3004 01 40   01 228   01 2192
Τάδε   λέγει ὁ ἅγιος, ὁ ἀληθινός, ὁ ἔχων
but these says the holy, the true,   the one having

08 2807 1160a 01 455   2532 3762 2808
τὴν κλεῖν Δαυίδ, ὁ ἀνοίγων   καὶ οὐδεὶς κλείσει
the key   David, the opening   and no one will close

2532 2808   2532 3762 455   8 3609a 1473   024
καὶ κλείων καὶ οὐδεὶς ἀνοίγει·   οἶδά σου   τὰ
and closing and no one opens;   I know of you the

2041   2400 1325   1799   1473 2374 455   3739
ἔργα,   ἰδοὺ δέδωκα ἐνώπιόν σου θύραν ἠνεῳγμένην, ἣν
works, look I have before you door having been   which
             given   opened,

3762   1410   2808   846   3754   3398   2192
οὐδεὶς δύναται κλεῖσαι αὐτήν, ὅτι   μικρὰν ἔχεις
no one is able to close it,   because little you have

1411   2532 5083   1473 04 3056   2532 3756
δύναμιν καὶ ἐτήρησάς μου τὸν λόγον καὶ οὐκ
power   and you kept of me the word and not

720   012 3686   846   9 2400 1325   1537 06
ἠρνήσω τὸ ὄνομά μου.   ἰδοὺ διδῶ   ἐκ   τῆς
you denied the name of me. Look I might give from the

4864   02   4567   014   3004
συναγωγῆς τοῦ σατανᾶ τῶν λεγόντων
synagogue of the adversary of the ones saying

1438   2453   1510 2532 3756 1510   235
ἑαυτοὺς   ᾿Ιουδαίους εἶναι, καὶ οὐκ εἰσὶν   ἀλλὰ
themselves Judeans   to be, and not they are but

5574   2400 4160   846   2443 2240
ψεύδονται. ἰδοὺ ποιήσω   αὐτοὺς ἵνα ἥξουσιν
they lie.   Look I will make them   that they will come

and you will not know at
what hour I will come to
you. [4]Yet you have still
a few persons in Sardis
who have not soiled their
clothes; they will walk with
me, dressed in white, for
they are worthy. [5]If you
conquer, you will be
clothed like them in white
robes, and I will not blot
your name out of the book
of life; I will confess your
name before my Father
and before his angels.
[6]Let anyone who has an
ear listen to what the Spirit
is saying to the churches.

[7] "And to the angel of
the church in Philadelphia
write:

These are the words of
the holy one, the true
one,
who has the key of
David,
who opens and no one
will shut,
who shuts and no one
opens:
[8] "I know your works.
Look, I have set before you
an open door, which no one
is able to shut. I know that
you have but little power,
and yet you have kept my
word and have not denied
my name. [9]I will make those
of the synagogue of Satan
who say that they are Jews
and are not, but are lying—
I will make them come

and bow down before your
feet, and they will learn
that I have loved you.
[19]Because you have kept my
word of patient endurance,
I will keep you from the
hour of trial that is coming
on the whole world to test
the inhabitants of the earth.
[11]I am coming soon; hold
fast to what you have, so
that no one may seize your
crown. [12]If you conquer,
I will make you a pillar in
the temple of my God; you
will never go out of it. I
will write on you the name
of my God, and the name of
the city of my God, the new
Jerusalem that comes down
from my God out of heaven,
and my own new name.
[13]Let anyone who has an
ear listen to what the Spirit
is saying to the churches.

14 "And to the angel
of the church in Laodicea
write: The words of the
Amen, the faithful and true
witness, the origin[a] of
God's creation:

15 "I know your works,
you are neither cold nor
hot. I wish that you were
either cold or hot. [16]So,
because you are lukewarm,
and neither cold nor hot, I
am about to spit you out of
my mouth. [17]For you say,

[a] Or beginning

2532	4352		1799	014	4228	1473	2532
καὶ	προσκυνήσουσιν	ἐνώπιον	τῶν	ποδῶν	σου	καὶ
and	will worship	before	the	feet	of you	and

1097		3754	1473	25		1473		3754
γνῶσιν		ὅτι	ἐγὼ	ἠγάπησά	σε.	**10**	ὅτι
they might know	that	I	loved	you.	Because

5083	04	3056	06	5281	1473	2504	1473
ἐτήρησας	τὸν	λόγον	τῆς	ὑπομονῆς	μου,	κἀγώ	σε
you	kept	the word	of	the patience	of me,	and I	you

5083	1537 06	5610 02	3986	06
τηρήσω	ἐκ	τῆς ὥρας τοῦ	πειρασμοῦ	τῆς
will keep	from	the hour	of the pressure	the one

3195	2064	1909 06	3625	3650
μελλούσης	ἔρχεσθαι	ἐπὶ	τῆς οἰκουμένης	ὅλης
being about	to come	on	the inhabited world	whole

3985	016	2730	1909 06	1093
πειράσαι	τοὺς	κατοικοῦντας	ἐπὶ	τῆς γῆς.
to pressure	the	ones residing	on	the earth.

	2064	5036	2902	3739 2192	2443 3367
11	ἔρχομαι	ταχύ·	κράτει	ὃ ἔχεις,	ἵνα μηδεὶς
	I come	quickly;	hold	what you have,	that no one

2983	04 4735	1473	01	3528
λάβῃ	τὸν στέφανόν	σου.	**12** Ὁ	νικῶν
might take	the crown	of you.	The one conquering

4160	846	4769	1722 03	3485	02	2316
ποιήσω	αὐτὸν	στῦλον	ἐν	τῷ	ναῷ	τοῦ θεοῦ
I will make	him	pillar	in	the temple	of the God

1473	2532 1854	3756 3361	1831	2089 2532
μου	καὶ ἔξω	οὐ μὴ	ἐξέλθῃ	ἔτι καὶ
of me	and outside	not not	might he go out	still and

1125	1909 846	012 3686	02	2316 1473 2532
γράψω	ἐπ' αὐτὸν	τὸ ὄνομα	τοῦ	θεοῦ μου καὶ
I will write	on him	the name	of the God	of me and

012 3686	06	4172	02	2316 1473	06	2537
τὸ ὄνομα τῆς		πόλεως τοῦ		θεοῦ μου,	τῆς καινῆς
the name	of the	city	of the God	of me,	the new

2419	05	2597	1537 02	3772	575
Ἰερουσαλὴμ ἡ	καταβαίνουσα	ἐκ	τοῦ οὐρανοῦ ἀπὸ
Jerusalem	the one coming down	from	the heaven	from

02	2316 1473	2532 012 3686	1473	012 2537		01
τοῦ θεοῦ μου,	καὶ τὸ ὄνομά	μου	τὸ καινόν.	**13** Ὁ
the God of me,	and the name	of me	the new.	The

2192	3775 191	5101 09	4151	3004	019
ἔχων	οὓς ἀκουσάτω	τί	τὸ	πνεῦμα λέγει	ταῖς
one having ear	let hear	what	the	spirit says	to the

1577		2532 03	32	06	1722
ἐκκλησίαις.	**14** Καὶ	τῷ	ἀγγέλῳ	τῆς ἐν
assemblies.	And	to the	messenger	of the in

2993	1577	1125	3592	3004 01	281
Λαοδικείᾳ	ἐκκλησίας	γράψον·	Τάδε	λέγει ὁ	ἀμήν,
Laodicea	assembly	write:	but these	says the	amen,

01	3144	01	4103	2532 228	05	746
ὁ	μάρτυς	ὁ	πιστὸς	καὶ ἀληθινός,	ἡ	ἀρχὴ
the	testifier	the	trustful	and true,	the	beginning

06	2937	02	2316		3609a 1473	024 2041
τῆς	κτίσεως	τοῦ	θεοῦ·	**15**	οἶδά σου	τὰ ἔργα
of the	creation	of the	God;	I know	of you	the works

3754 3777	5593	1510	3777 2200	3785
ὅτι οὔτε	ψυχρὸς	εἶ	οὔτε ζεστός.	ὄφελον
that neither	cold	you are	nor boiling.	I would

5593	1510	2228 2200		3779	3754	5513
ψυχρὸς	ἦς	ἢ ζεστός.	**16**	οὕτως	ὅτι	χλιαρὸς
cold	you were	or boiling.	Thusly	because	lukewarm

1510	2532 3777	2200	3777 5593	3195
εἶ	καὶ οὔτε	ζεστὸς	οὔτε ψυχρός,	μέλλω
you are	and neither	boiling	nor cold,	I am about

1473 1692	1537 010 4750	1473		3754 3004
σε ἐμέσαι	ἐκ τοῦ στόματός	μου.	**17**	ὅτι λέγεις
you to vomit	from the mouth	of me.	Because	you say,

3754 4145   1510 2532 4147   2532 3762
ὅτι πλούσιός εἰμι καὶ πεπλούτηκα   καὶ οὐδὲν
(") rich   I am and   I have been rich and   nothing
5532   2192   2532 3756 3609a   3754 1473 1510 01
χρείαν ἔχω,   καὶ οὐκ οἶδας ὅτι σὺ εἶ ὁ
need   I have, and not you know that you are the
5005   2532 1652   2532 4434   2532 5185   2532
ταλαίπωρος καὶ ἐλεεινὸς καὶ πτωχὸς καὶ τυφλὸς καὶ
miserable and need mercy and poor   and blind and
1131   18 4823   1473 59   3844 1473
γυμνός, 18 συμβουλεύω   σοι ἀγοράσαι παρ᾽ ἐμοῦ
naked,   I plan together you to buy   from me
5553   4448   1537 4442   2443 4147   2532
χρυσίον πεπυρωμένον ἐκ πυρὸς ἵνα πλουτήσῃς, καὶ
gold   having been from fire that you might and
        set on fire   be rich,
2440   3022   2443 4016   2532 3361 5319
ἱμάτια λευκὰ ἵνα περιβάλῃ   καὶ μὴ φανερωθῇ
clothes white that you might be and not might be
                  thrown around   demonstrated
05   152   06   1132   1473   2532 2854
ἡ αἰσχύνη τῆς γυμνότητός σου, καὶ κολλ[ο]ύριον
the shame of the nakedness of you, and eye salve
1472   016 3788   1473   2443 991
ἐγχρῖσαι   τοὺς ὀφθαλμούς σου ἵνα βλέπῃς.
to anoint on the eyes   of you that you might see.
   1473 3745   1437 5368   1651   2532
19 ἐγὼ ὅσους   ἐὰν φιλῶ   ἐλέγχω καὶ
   I   as many as if might love I rebuke and
3811   2204a   3767 2532 3340
παιδεύω·   ζήλευε   οὖν καὶ μετανόησον.
I instruct as child; be jealous then and change mind.
   2400 2476   1909 08 2374   2532 2925
20 Ἰδοὺ ἕστηκα   ἐπὶ τὴν θύραν καὶ κρούω·
   Look I have stood at the door and I knock;
/ 1437 5100 191   06 5456 1473   2532 455
ἐάν τις ἀκούσῃ   τῆς φωνῆς μου καὶ ἀνοίξῃ
if some might hear the sound of me and might open
08   2374   2532 1525   4314 846   2532
τὴν θύραν, [καὶ] εἰσελεύσομαι πρὸς αὐτὸν καὶ
the door,   also I will go in to him and
1172   3326 846   2532 846   3326 1473   21 01
δειπνήσω   μετ᾽ αὐτοῦ καὶ αὐτὸς μετ᾽ ἐμοῦ. 21 ῾Ο
I will dine with him and himself with me. The one
3528   1325   846   2523   3326 1473 1722
νικῶν   δώσω   αὐτῷ καθίσαι μετ᾽ ἐμοῦ ἐν
conquering I will give to him to sit with me   in
03   2362   1473   5613 2504 3528   2532 2523
τῷ θρόνῳ μου,   ὡς κἀγὼ ἐνίκησα καὶ ἐκάθισα
the throne of me, as also I conquered and I sat
3326 02 3962   1473 1722 03 2362   846   22 01
μετὰ τοῦ πατρός μου ἐν τῷ θρόνῳ αὐτοῦ. 22 ῾Ο
with the Father of me in the throne of him. The one
2192   3775 191   5101 09 4151   3004 019
ἔχων   οὖς ἀκουσάτω τί τὸ πνεῦμα λέγει ταῖς
having ear let hear what the spirit says to the
1577   4:1 3326 3778 3708   2532 2400 2374
ἐκκλησίαις. 4:1 Μετὰ ταῦτα εἶδον, καὶ ἰδοὺ θύρα
assemblies.   After these I saw, and look door
455   1722 03 3772   2532 05   5456 05
ἠνεῳγμένη   ἐν τῷ οὐρανῷ, καὶ ἡ φωνὴ ἡ
having been opened in the heaven, and the sound the
4413 3739 191   5613 4536   2980   3326 1473
πρώτη ἦν ἤκουσα ὡς σάλπιγγος λαλούσης μετ᾽ ἐμοῦ
first which I heard as trumpet speaking with me
3004   305   5602 2532 1166   1473   3739
λέγων· ἀνάβα ὧδε, καὶ δείξω   σοι   ἃ
saying: come up here, and I will show to you what

'I am rich, I have prospered,
and I need nothing.' You
do not realize that you are
wretched, pitiable, poor,
blind, and naked. [18]There-
fore I counsel you to buy
from me gold refined by
fire so that you may be rich;
and white robes to clothe
you and to keep the shame
of your nakedness from
being seen; and salve to
anoint your eyes so that
you may see. [19]I reprove
and discipline those whom
I love. Be earnest, therefore,
and repent. [20]Listen! I am
standing at the door,
knocking; if you hear my
voice and open the door, I
will come in to you and eat
with you, and you with me.
[21]To the one who conquers
I will give a place with me
on my throne, just as I
myself conquered and sat
down with my Father on
his throne. [22]Let anyone
who has an ear listen to
what the Spirit is saying
to the churches."

CHAPTER 4

After this I looked, and
there in heaven a door
stood open! And the first
voice, which I had heard
speaking to me like a
trumpet, said, "Come up
here, and I will show you
what

must take place after this."
²At once I was in the spirit,ᵃ
and there in heaven stood
a throne, with one seated
on the throne! ³And the
one seated there looks like
jasper and carnelian, and
around the throne is a
rainbow that looks like
an emerald. ⁴Around the
throne are twenty-four
thrones, and seated on the
thrones are twenty-four
elders, dressed in white
robes, with golden crowns
on their heads. ⁵Coming
from the throne are flashes
of lightning, and rumblings
and peals of thunder, and
in front of the throne burn
seven flaming torches,
which are the seven spirits
of God; ⁶and in front of the
throne there is something
like a sea of glass, like
crystal.

Around the throne, and
on each side of the throne,
are four living creatures,
full of eyes in front and
behind: ⁷the first living
creature like a lion, the
second living creature
like an ox, the third living
creature with a face like a
human face, and the fourth
living creature like a flying
eagle. ⁸And the four living
creatures, each of them
with six wings, are full of
eyes all around and inside.
Day and

ᵃ Or in the Spirit

1163		1096		3326	3778	**2**	2112
δεῖ		γενέσθαι		μετὰ	ταῦτα.		Εὐθέως
is necessary		to become		after	these.		Immediately

1096		1722	4151		2532	2400	2362	2749	1722
ἐγενόμην		ἐν	πνεύματι,		καὶ	ἰδοὺ	θρόνος	ἔκειτο	ἐν
I became		in	spirit,		and	look	throne	was set	in

03	3772	2532	1909	04	2362	2521		**3**	2532	01
τῷ	οὐρανῷ,	καὶ	ἐπὶ	τὸν	θρόνον	καθήμενος,			καὶ	ὁ
the	heaven,	and	on	the	throne	one sitting,			and	the

2521		3664	3706		3037	2393		2532	4554
καθήμενος		ὅμοιος	ὁράσει		λίθῳ	ἰάσπιδι	καὶ		σαρδίῳ,
one sitting		like	in sight		stone	jasper	and		sardis,

2532	2463		2943		02	2362	3664	3706
καὶ	ἶρις		κυκλόθεν		τοῦ	θρόνου	ὅμοιος	ὁράσει
and	rainbow		circled		the	throne	like	in sight

4664		**4**	2532	2943		02	2362	2362	1501
σμαραγδίνῳ.			Καὶ	κυκλόθεν		τοῦ	θρόνου	θρόνους	εἴκοσι
emerald.			And	circled		the	throne	thrones	twenty

5064		2532	1909	016	2362		1501	5064
τέσσαρες,		καὶ	ἐπὶ	τοὺς	θρόνους		εἴκοσι	τέσσαρας
four,		and	on	the	thrones		twenty	four

4245		2521		4016		1722	2440
πρεσβυτέρους		καθημένους		περιβεβλημένους		ἐν	ἱματίοις
older men		sitting		having thrown		in	clothes
				around themselves			

3022		2532	1909	020	2776	846	4735
λευκοῖς		καὶ	ἐπὶ	τὰς	κεφαλὰς	αὐτῶν	στεφάνους
white		and	on	the	heads	of them	crowns

5552		**5**	2532	1537	02	2362	1607		796
χρυσοῦς.			Καὶ	ἐκ	τοῦ	θρόνου	ἐκπορεύονται		ἀστραπαὶ
gold.			And	from	the	throne	travel out		lightnings

2532	5456		2532	1027		2532	2033	2985		4442
καὶ	φωναὶ		καὶ	βρονταί,		καὶ	ἑπτὰ	λαμπάδες		πυρὸς
and	sounds		and	thunders,		and	seven	lamps		of fire

2545		1799		02	2362		3739	1510	021	2033
καιόμεναι		ἐνώπιον		τοῦ	θρόνου,		ἅ	εἰσιν	τὰ	ἑπτὰ
being burned		before		the	throne,		which is		the	seven

4151		02		2316	**6**	2532	1799	02	2362	5613
πνεύματα		τοῦ		θεοῦ,		καὶ	ἐνώπιον	τοῦ	θρόνου	ὡς
spirits		of the		God,		and	before	the	throne	as

2281	5193		3664	2930		2532	1722	3319	02
θάλασσα	ὑαλίνη		ὁμοία	κρυστάλλῳ.		Καὶ	ἐν	μέσῳ	τοῦ
sea	glass		like	crystal.		And in		middle	of the

2362		2532	2945		02	2362	5064	2226
θρόνου		καὶ	κύκλῳ		τοῦ	θρόνου	τέσσαρα	ζῷα
throne		and	in circle		of the	throne	four	living ones

1073		3788		1715		2532	3693		**7**	2532
γέμοντα		ὀφθαλμῶν		ἔμπροσθεν		καὶ	ὄπισθεν.			καὶ
being full		of eyes		in front		and	from behind.			And

09	2226		09	4413	3664	3023		2532	09
τὸ	ζῷον		τὸ	πρῶτον	ὅμοιον	λέοντι		καὶ	τὸ
the	living one		the	first	like	lion		and	the

1208	2226		3664	3448		2532	09	5154
δεύτερον	ζῷον		ὅμοιον	μόσχῳ		καὶ	τὸ	τρίτον
second	living one		like	calf		and	the	third

2226		2192		012	4383		5613	444		2532	09
ζῷον		ἔχων		τὸ	πρόσωπον		ὡς	ἀνθρώπου		καὶ	τὸ
living one		having		the	face		as	man		and	the

5067	2226		3664	105	4072		**8**	2532
τέταρτον	ζῷον		ὅμοιον	ἀετῷ	πετομένῳ.			καὶ
fourth	living one		like	eagle	flying.			And

021	5064	2226		1520	2596	1520	846		2192
τὰ	τέσσαρα	ζῷα,		ἓν	καθ'	ἓν	αὐτῶν		ἔχων
the	four	living ones,		one	by	one	of them		having

303	4420		1803	2943		2532	2081		1073
ἀνὰ	πτέρυγας		ἕξ,	κυκλόθεν		καὶ	ἔσωθεν		γέμουσιν
up	wings		six,	circled		and	inside		they are full

3788		2532	372		3756	2192		2250	2532
ὀφθαλμῶν,		καὶ	ἀνάπαυσιν		οὐκ	ἔχουσιν		ἡμέρας	καὶ
of eyes,		and	rest		not	they have		day	and

3571   3004   40   40   40   2962   01   2316 01
νυκτὸς λέγοντες· ἅγιος ἅγιος ἅγιος κύριος ὁ θεὸς ὁ
night   saying: holy, holy, holy, Master the God the

3841   01   1510 2532 01 1510   2532 01
παντοκράτωρ, ὁ   ἦν καὶ ὁ ὢν   καὶ ὁ
all strength, the one was and the one being and the

2064   9 2532 3752 1325   021 2226
ἐρχόμενος.   Καὶ ὅταν δώσουσιν τὰ ζῷα
one coming.   And when will give the living ones

1391   2532 5092   2532 2169   03
δόξαν καὶ τιμὴν καὶ εὐχαριστίαν τῷ
splendor and value and good favor to the one

2521   1909 03 2362   03   2198   1519 016
καθημένῳ ἐπὶ τῷ θρόνῳ τῷ ζῶντι εἰς τοὺς
sitting on   the throne to the one living into the

165   014 165   10 4098   013 1501   5064
αἰῶνας τῶν αἰώνων,   πεσοῦνται οἱ εἴκοσι τέσσαρες
ages   of the ages,   will fall the twenty four

4245   1799   02 2521   1909 02 2362
πρεσβύτεροι ἐνώπιον τοῦ καθημένου ἐπὶ τοῦ θρόνου
older men before the one sitting on the throne

2532 4352   03   2198   1519 016   165
καὶ προσκυνήσουσιν τῷ ζῶντι εἰς τοὺς αἰῶνας
and will worship the living one into the ages

014 165   2532 906   016   4735   846
τῶν αἰώνων καὶ βαλοῦσιν τοὺς στεφάνους αὐτῶν
of the ages and will throw the crowns of them

1799   02 2362 3004   11 514   1510   01
ἐνώπιον τοῦ θρόνου λέγοντες· ἄξιος εἶ, ὁ
before the throne saying: worthy are you, the

2962   2532 01 2316 1473 2983   08 1391
κύριος καὶ ὁ θεὸς ἡμῶν, λαβεῖν τὴν δόξαν
Master and the God of us, to receive the splendor

2532 08 5092 2532 08 1411   3754 1473 2936
καὶ τὴν τιμὴν καὶ τὴν δύναμιν, ὅτι σὺ ἔκτισας
and the value and the power, because you created

024 3956 2532 1223   012 2307   1473 1510
τὰ πάντα καὶ διὰ τὸ θέλημά σου ἦσαν
the all and through the want of you they were

2532 2537   5:1 2532 3708 1909 08 1188
καὶ ἐκτίσθησαν.   Καὶ εἶδον ἐπὶ τὴν δεξιὰν
also were created.   And I saw on the right

02   2521   1909 02 2362   975
τοῦ καθημένου ἐπὶ τοῦ θρόνου βιβλίον
of the one sitting on the throne small book

1125   2081   2532 3693   2696
γεγραμμένον ἔσωθεν καὶ ὄπισθεν κατεσφραγισμένον
having been inside and from behind having been sealed
written   thoroughly

4973   2033   2 2532 3708 32   2478
σφραγῖσιν ἑπτά.   καὶ εἶδον ἄγγελον ἰσχυρὸν
in seals seven. And I saw messenger strong

2784   1722 5456 3173   5101 514   455   012
κηρύσσοντα ἐν φωνῇ μεγάλῃ· τίς ἄξιος ἀνοῖξαι τὸ
announcing in voice great: who worthy to open the

975   2532 3089   020 4973   846   3 2532
βιβλίον καὶ λῦσαι τὰς σφραγῖδας αὐτοῦ;   καὶ
small book and to loose the seals of it?   And

3762 1410   1722 03 3772   3761   1909 06 1093
οὐδεὶς ἐδύνατο ἐν τῷ οὐρανῷ οὐδὲ ἐπὶ τῆς γῆς
no one was able in the heaven but not on the earth

3761 5270   06 1093 455   012 975
οὐδὲ ὑποκάτω τῆς γῆς ἀνοῖξαι τὸ βιβλίον
but not underneath the earth to open the small book

3777 991   846   4 2532 2799   4183 3754
οὔτε βλέπειν αὐτό. καὶ ἔκλαιον πολύ, ὅτι
nor to see it.   And I was crying much, because

3762 514   2147   455   012 975   3777
οὐδεὶς ἄξιος εὑρέθη ἀνοῖξαι τὸ βιβλίον οὔτε
no one worthy was found to open the small book nor

---

night without ceasing they sing,

"Holy, holy, holy,
   the Lord God the
   Almighty,
who was and is and is to
   come."

[9]And whenever the living creatures give glory and honor and thanks to the one who is seated on the throne, who lives forever and ever, [10]the twenty-four elders fall before the one who is seated on the throne and worship the one who lives forever and ever; they cast their crowns before the throne, singing,

[11]"You are worthy, our
   Lord and God,
   to receive glory and
   honor and power,
for you created all things,
   and by your will they
   existed and were
   created."

CHAPTER 5

Then I saw in the right hand of the one seated on the throne a scroll written on the inside and on the back, sealed[a] with seven seals; [2]and I saw a mighty angel proclaiming with a loud voice, "Who is worthy to open the scroll and break its seals?" [3]And no one in heaven or on earth or under the earth was able to open the scroll or to look into it. [4]And I began to weep bitterly because no one was found worthy to open the scroll or

a Or written on the inside, and sealed on the back

to look into it. ⁵Then one
of the elders said to me,
"Do not weep. See, the
Lion of the tribe of Judah,
the Root of David, has
conquered, so that he can
open the scroll and its seven
seals."

6 Then I saw between the
throne and the four living
creatures and among the
elders a Lamb standing as
if it had been slaughtered,
having seven horns and
seven eyes, which are the
seven spirits of God sent
out into all the earth. ⁷He
went and took the scroll
from the right hand of the
one who was seated on the
throne. ⁸When he had taken
the scroll, the four living
creatures and the twenty-
four elders fell before the
Lamb, each holding a harp
and golden bowls full of
incense, which are the
prayers of the saints. ⁹They
sing a new song:
"You are worthy to take
     the scroll
   and to open its seals,
 for you were slaughtered
   and by your blood you
     ransomed for God
   saints from[a] every tribe
   and language and
     people and nation;
¹⁰ you have made them to be
   a kingdom and priests
     serving[b] our God,
   and they will reign on
     earth."
11 Then I looked, and
I heard the voice of many
angels

[a] Gk ransomed for God from
[b] Gk priests to

991	846	**5**	2532	1520	1537	014	4245		3004

βλέπειν αὐτό. **5** καὶ εἷς ἐκ τῶν πρεσβυτέρων λέγει
to see it.   And one from the older men   says

1473 3361 2799   2400 3528   01 3023 01   1537
μοι· μὴ κλαῖε, ἰδοὺ ἐνίκησεν ὁ λέων ὁ ἐκ
to me, not cry,   look conquered the lion the from

06   5443   2455   05 4491 1160a   455   012
τῆς φυλῆς Ἰούδα, ἡ ῥίζα Δαυίδ, ἀνοῖξαι τὸ
the tribe Judas, the root David, to open the

975   2532 020   2033 4973   846   **6** 2532 3708
βιβλίον καὶ τὰς ἑπτὰ σφραγῖδας αὐτοῦ. **6** Καὶ εἶδον
small book and the seven seals   of it.   And I saw

1722 3319 02   2362   2532 022   5064
ἐν μέσῳ τοῦ θρόνου καὶ τῶν τεσσάρων
in middle of the throne and of the four

2226   2532 1722 3319   014   4245   721
ζώων καὶ ἐν μέσῳ τῶν πρεσβυτέρων ἀρνίον
living ones and in middle of the older men   lamb

2476   5613 4969   2192   2768
ἑστηκὸς ὡς ἐσφαγμένον   ἔχων κέρατα
having stood as having been slaughtered having horns

2033 2532 3788   3739 1510 021 2033
ἑπτὰ καὶ ὀφθαλμοὺς ἑπτὰ οἵ εἰσιν τὰ [ἑπτὰ]
seven and eyes   seven that are the seven

4151   02   2316 649   1519 3956
πνεύματα τοῦ θεοῦ ἀπεσταλμένοι εἰς πᾶσαν
spirits of the God having been delegated into all

08 1093 **7** 2532 2064   2532 2983   1537 06
τὴν γῆν. **7** καὶ ἦλθεν καὶ εἴληφεν ἐκ τῆς
the earth.   And he went and has received from the

1188   02   2521   1909 02 2362   2532 3753
δεξιᾶς τοῦ καθημένου ἐπὶ τοῦ θρόνου. **8** Καὶ ὅτε
right of the one sitting on the throne.   And when

2983   012 975   021 5064   2226   2532
ἔλαβεν τὸ βιβλίον, τὰ τέσσαρα ζῷα καὶ
he took the small book, the four   living ones and

010 1501   5064   4245   4098 1799   010
οἱ εἴκοσι τέσσαρες πρεσβύτεροι ἔπεσαν ἐνώπιον τοῦ
the twenty four   older men   fell before the

721   2192   1538   2532 5357   5552
ἀρνίου ἔχοντες ἕκαστος κιθάραν καὶ φιάλας χρυσᾶς
lamb having each   harp   and bowls gold

1073   2368   3739 1510 017 4335   014
γεμούσας θυμιαμάτων, αἵ εἰσιν αἱ προσευχαὶ τῶν
being full incense,   that are the prayers of the

40   **9** 2532 103   5603 2537 3004
ἁγίων, **9** καὶ ᾄδουσιν ᾠδὴν καινὴν λέγοντες·
holy ones,   and they sing song new   saying,

514   1510   2983   012 975   2532 455   020
ἄξιος εἶ λαβεῖν τὸ βιβλίον καὶ ἀνοῖξαι τὰς
worthy are you to take the small book and to open the

4973   3684 3754   4969   2532
σφραγῖδας αὐτοῦ, ὅτι ἐσφάγης   καὶ
seals   of it, because you were slaughtered and

59   03   2316 1722 011 129   1473 1537 3956
ἠγόρασας τῷ θεῷ ἐν τῷ αἵματί σου ἐκ πάσης
bought to the God in the blood of you from all

5443 2532 1100   2532 2992 2532 1484   2532
φυλῆς καὶ γλώσσης καὶ λαοῦ καὶ ἔθνους **10** καὶ
tribe and tongue and people and nation   and

4160   846   03   2316 1473 932   2532
ἐποίησας αὐτοὺς τῷ θεῷ ἡμῶν βασιλείαν καὶ
you made them to the God of us kingdom and

2409   2532 936   1909 06 1093   **11** 2532
ἱερεῖς, καὶ βασιλεύσουσιν ἐπὶ τῆς γῆς. **11** Καὶ
priests, and they will be kings on the earth.   And

3708 2532 191   5456 32   4183
εἶδον, καὶ ἤκουσα φωνὴν ἀγγέλων πολλῶν
I saw, also I heard voice of messengers many

2945   02   2362   2532 022   2226   2532
κύκλῳ   τοῦ θρόνου καὶ τῶν   ζῴων   καὶ
in circle the throne and of the living ones and

014   4245   2532 1510 01   706   846
τῶν   πρεσβυτέρων, καὶ ἦν   ὁ ἀριθμὸς αὐτῶν
of the older men,   and was the number of them

3461   3461   2532 5505
μυριάδες   μυριάδων   καὶ χιλιάδες
ten thousands of ten thousands and thousands

5505   3004   5456   3173   514   1510
χιλιάδων 12 λέγοντες φωνῇ   μεγάλη· ἄξιόν ἐστιν
of thousands saying   in voice great,   worthy is

09   721   09 4969   2983   08
τὸ ἀρνίον τὸ ἐσφαγμένον   λαβεῖν τὴν
the lamb the one having been slaughtered to take the

1411   2532 4149   2532 4678   2532 2479   2532
δύναμιν καὶ πλοῦτον καὶ σοφίαν καὶ ἰσχὺν   καὶ
power   and rich   and wisdom and strength and

5092 2532 1391   2532 2129   13 2532 3956 2938
τιμὴν καὶ δόξαν καὶ εὐλογίαν.   καὶ πᾶν κτίσμα
value and splendor and good word. And all creation

3739   1722 03   3772   2532 1909 06 1093 2532
ὃ   ἐν τῷ οὐρανῷ καὶ ἐπὶ τῆς γῆς καὶ
which in the heaven and on the earth and

5270   06   1093 2532 1909 06 2281   2532 024
ὑποκάτω τῆς γῆς καὶ ἐπὶ τῆς θαλάσσης καὶ τὰ
underneath the earth and on the sea   and the

1722 846   3956 191   3004   03
ἐν αὐτοῖς πάντα ἤκουσα λέγοντας· τῷ
in them   all I heard saying,   to the one

2521   1909 03 2362   2532 011   721   05
καθημένῳ ἐπὶ τῷ θρόνῳ καὶ τῷ   ἀρνίῳ ἡ
sitting on the throne and to the lamb the

2129   2532 05 5092 2532 05 1391   2532 09
εὐλογία καὶ ἡ τιμὴ καὶ ἡ δόξα καὶ τὸ
good word and the value and the splendor and the

2904   1519 016 165   014   165   14 2532 021
κράτος εἰς τοὺς αἰῶνας τῶν αἰώνων.   καὶ τὰ
strength into the ages of the ages. And the

5064   2226   3004   281   2532 013
τέσσαρα ζῷα ἔλεγον· ἀμήν. καὶ οἱ
four   living ones were saying, amen. And the

4245   4098 2532 4352   6:1 2532 3708
πρεσβύτεροι ἔπεσαν καὶ προσεκύνησαν.   Καὶ εἶδον
older men   fell and worshiped.   And I saw

3753 455   09 721   1520 1537 018 2033   4973
ὅτε ἤνοιξεν τὸ ἀρνίον μίαν ἐκ τῶν ἑπτὰ σφραγίδων,
when opened the lamb one from the seven seals,

2532 191   1520 1537 022 5064   2226
καὶ ἤκουσα ἑνὸς ἐκ τῶν τεσσάρων ζῴων
and I heard one from the four   living ones

3004   5613 5456 1027   2064   2 2532 3708
λέγοντος ὡς φωνὴ βροντῆς· ἔρχου.   καὶ εἶδον,
saying   as sound of thunder, come. And I saw,

2532 2400 2462 3022   2532 01 2521   1909
καὶ ἰδοὺ ἵππος λευκός, καὶ ὁ καθήμενος ἐπ᾿
and look horse white, and the one sitting on

846   2192   5115   2532   846   4735   2532
αὐτὸν ἔχων τόξον καὶ ἐδόθη αὐτῷ στέφανος καὶ
it having bow and was given to him crown   and

1831   3528   2532 2443 3528
ἐξῆλθεν νικῶν   καὶ ἵνα νικήσῃ.
he went out conquering and that he might conquer.

3 2532 3753 455   08   4973   08   1208
   Καὶ ὅτε ἤνοιξεν τὴν σφραγῖδα τὴν δευτέραν,
   And when he opened the seal   the second,

191   010 1208   2226   3004   2064   4 2532
ἤκουσα τοῦ δευτέρου ζῴου λέγοντος· ἔρχου. καὶ
I heard the second living one saying, come.   And

surrounding the throne
and the living creatures and
the elders; they numbered
myriads of myriads and
thousands of thousands,
[12]singing with full voice,
  "Worthy is the Lamb
     that was slaughtered
  to receive power and
     wealth and wisdom
     and might
  and honor and glory and
     blessing!"
[13]Then I heard every
creature in heaven and on
earth and under the earth
and in the sea, and all that
is in them, singing,
  "To the one seated on the
     throne and to the
     Lamb
  be blessing and honor
     and glory and might
     forever and ever!"
[14]And the four living
creatures said, "Amen!"
And the elders fell down
and worshiped.

CHAPTER 6

Then I saw the Lamb open
one of the seven seals, and I
heard one of the four living
creatures call out, as with a
voice of thunder, "Come!"[a]
[2]I looked, and there was a
white horse! Its rider had
a bow; a crown was given
to him, and he came out
conquering and to conquer.
  3 When he opened the
second seal, I heard the
second living creature call
out, "Come!"[a] [4]And out
came[b] another

a Or "Go!"
b Or went

horse, bright red; its rider was permitted to take peace from the earth, so that people would slaughter one another; and he was given a great sword.

5 When he opened the third seal, I heard the third living creature call out, "Come!"[a] I looked, and there was a black horse! Its rider held a pair of scales in his hand, [6]and I heard what seemed to be a voice in the midst of the four living creatures saying, "A quart of wheat for a day's pay,[b] and three quarts of barley for a day's pay,[b] but do not damage the olive oil and the wine!"

7 When he opened the fourth seal, I heard the voice of the fourth living creature call out, "Come!"[a] [8]I looked and there was a pale green horse! Its rider's name was Death, and Hades followed with him; they were given authority over a fourth of the earth, to kill with sword, famine, and pestilence, and by the wild animals of the earth.

9 When he opened the fifth seal, I saw under the altar the souls of those who had been slaughtered for the word of God and for the testimony they had given; [10]they cried out

[a] Or "Go!"
[b] Gk a denarius

1831	243	2462	4450	2532 03	2521
ἐξῆλθεν	ἄλλος	ἵππος	πυρρός,	καὶ τῷ	καθημένῳ
went out	other	horse	red,	and to	the one sitting

1909 846	1325	846	2983	08 1515	1537
ἐπ' αὐτὸν	ἐδόθη	αὐτῷ	λαβεῖν	τὴν εἰρήνην	ἐκ
on it	was given	to him	to take	the peace	from

06	1093	2532	2443 240	4969
τῆς	γῆς	καὶ	ἵνα ἀλλήλους	σφάξουσιν
the	earth	and	that one another	they will slaughter

2532	1325	846	3162	3173	5	2532 3753
καὶ	ἐδόθη	αὐτῷ	μάχαιρα	μεγάλη.		Καὶ ὅτε
and	was given	to him	sword	great.		And when

455	08	4973	08	5154	191	010 5154
ἤνοιξεν	τὴν	σφραγῖδα	τὴν	τρίτην,	ἤκουσα	τοῦ τρίτου
he opened	the	seal		the third,	I heard	the third

2226	3004	2064	2532 3708	2532 2400
ζῴου	λέγοντος·	ἔρχου.	καὶ εἶδον,	καὶ ἰδοὺ
living one	saying,	come.	And I saw,	and look

2462	3189	2532 01	2521	1909 846	2192
ἵππος	μέλας,	καὶ ὁ	καθήμενος	ἐπ' αὐτὸν	ἔχων
horse	black,	and the	one sitting	on it	having

2218	1722 07	5495 846	6	2532 191	5613 5456
ζυγὸν	ἐν τῇ	χειρὶ αὐτοῦ.		καὶ ἤκουσα	ὡς φωνὴν
yoke	in the	hand of him.		And I heard	as voice

1722 3319	022	5064	2226	3004
ἐν μέσῳ	τῶν	τεσσάρων	ζῴων	λέγουσαν·
in middle	of the	four	living ones	saying,

5518	4621	1220	2532 5140	5518
χοῖνιξ	σίτου	δηναρίου	καὶ τρεῖς	χοίνικες
choinix	of wheat	denarius	and three	choinixes

2915	1220	2532 01	1637	2532 04	3631
κριθῶν	δηναρίου,	καὶ τὸ	ἔλαιον	καὶ τὸν	οἶνον
of barley	denarius,	and the	oil	and the	wine

3361 91		7	2532 3753 455	08
μὴ ἀδικήσῃς.			Καὶ ὅτε ἤνοιξεν	τὴν
not you might do unright.			And when he opened	the

4973	08 5067	191	5456 010	5067
σφραγῖδα	τὴν τετάρτην,	ἤκουσα	φωνὴν τοῦ	τετάρτου
seal	the fourth,	I heard	voice of the	fourth

2226	3004	2064	8	2532 2400
ζῴου	λέγοντος·	ἔρχου.		καὶ εἶδον, καὶ ἰδοὺ
living one	saying,	come.		And I saw, and look

2462	5515	2532 01	2521	1883 846	3686
ἵππος	χλωρός,	καὶ ὁ	καθήμενος	ἐπάνω αὐτοῦ	ὄνομα
horse	green,	and the	one sitting	upon it	name

846	01 2288	2532 01 86	190	3326
αὐτῷ	[ὁ] θάνατος,	καὶ ὁ ᾅδης	ἠκολούθει	μετ'
to him	the death,	and the hades	was following	with

846	2532 1325	846	1849	1909 012
αὐτοῦ	καὶ ἐδόθη	αὐτοῖς	ἐξουσία	ἐπὶ τὸ
him	and was given	to them	authority	on the

5067	06	1093 615	1722 4501	2532 1722
τέταρτον	τῆς	γῆς ἀποκτεῖναι	ἐν ῥομφαίᾳ	καὶ ἐν
fourth	of the	earth to kill	in sword	and in

3042	2532 1722 2288	2532 5259 022	2342
λιμῷ	καὶ ἐν θανάτῳ	καὶ ὑπὸ τῶν	θηρίων
famine	and in death	and by the	wild animals

06	1093	9	2532 3753 455	08 3991
τῆς	γῆς.		Καὶ ὅτε ἤνοιξεν	τὴν πέμπτην
of the	earth.		And when he opened	the fifth

4973	3708	5270	010 2379	020
σφραγῖδα,	εἶδον	ὑποκάτω	τοῦ θυσιαστηρίου	τὰς
seal,	I saw	underneath	the sacrifice place	the

5590	014	4969	1223	04 3056 02	2316
ψυχὰς	τῶν	ἐσφαγμένων	διὰ	τὸν λόγον τοῦ	θεοῦ
souls	of the	having been slaughtered	through	the word of	the God
	ones				

2532 1223	08	3141	3739 2192	10	2532
καὶ διὰ	τὴν	μαρτυρίαν	ἣν εἶχον.		καὶ
and through	the	testimony	which they had.		And

2896	5456	3173	3004	2193	4219	01
ἔκραξαν	φωνῇ	μεγάλῃ	λέγοντες·	ἕως	πότε,	ὁ
they shouted	in voice	great	saying,	until	when,	the

1203	01	40	2532	228		3756	2919
δεσπότης	ὁ	ἅγιος	καὶ	ἀληθινός,		οὐ	κρίνεις
supervisor	the	holy	and	true,		not	you judge

2532	1556			012	129	1473	1537	014
καὶ	ἐκδικεῖς			τὸ	αἷμα	ἡμῶν	ἐκ	τῶν
and	you bring out right			the	blood	of us	from	the

2730	1909	06	1093		2532	1325		846
κατοικούντων	ἐπὶ	τῆς	γῆς;	**11**	καὶ	ἐδόθη		αὐτοῖς
ones residing	on	the	earth?		And	was given		to them

1538	4749	3022	2532	3004		846	2443
ἑκάστῳ	στολὴ	λευκὴ	καὶ	ἐρρέθη		αὐτοῖς	ἵνα
each	long robe	white	and	it was said		to them	that

373		2089	5550	3398	2193
ἀναπαύσονται		ἔτι	χρόνον	μικρόν,	ἕως
they will rest		still	time	small,	until

4137		2532	013	4889		846		2532	013
πληρωθῶσιν		καὶ	οἱ	σύνδουλοι	αὐτῶν		καὶ	οἱ
might be filled		both	the	co-slaves	of them		and	the

80	846		013	3195		615
ἀδελφοὶ	αὐτῶν		οἱ	μέλλοντες		ἀποκτέννεσθαι
brothers	of them		the	ones being about		to be killed

5613	2532	846		2532	3708	3753	455		08
ὡς	καὶ	αὐτοί.	**12**	Καὶ	εἶδον	ὅτε	ἤνοιξεν		τὴν
as	also	themselves.		And	I saw	when	he opened		the

4973		08	1623	2532	4578	3173	1096	2532
σφραγῖδα	τὴν	ἕκτην,	καὶ	σεισμὸς	μέγας	ἐγένετο	καὶ
seal		the	sixth,	and	shake	great	became	and

01	2246	1096	3189	5613	4526		5155	2532
ὁ	ἥλιος	ἐγένετο	μέλας	ὡς	σάκκος		τρίχινος	καὶ
the	sun	became	black	as	sackcloth	of hair		and

05	4582	3650	1096	5613	129		2532	013	792
ἡ	σελήνη	ὅλη	ἐγένετο	ὡς	αἷμα	**13**	καὶ	οἱ	ἀστέρες
the	moon	whole	became	as	blood		and	the	stars

02	3772	4098	1519	08	1093	5613	4808
τοῦ	οὐρανοῦ	ἔπεσαν	εἰς	τὴν	γῆν,	ὡς	συκῆ
of the	heaven	fell	into	the	earth,	as	fig tree

906	016	3653		846	5259	417	3173
βάλλει	τοὺς	ὀλύνθους		αὐτῆς	ὑπὸ	ἀνέμου	μεγάλου
throws	the	unripe ones		of it	by	wind	great

4579		2532	01	3772	673		5613
σειομένη,	**14**	καὶ	ὁ	οὐρανὸς	ἀπεχωρίσθη		ὡς
being shaken,		and	the	heaven	was separated off		as

975	1667		2532	3956	3735	2532	3520
βιβλίον	ἑλισσόμενον		καὶ	πᾶν	ὄρος	καὶ	νῆσος
small book	being rolled		and	all	hill	and	island

1537	014	5117	846	2795		2532	013
ἐκ	τῶν	τόπων	αὐτῶν	ἐκινήθησαν.	**15**	Καὶ	οἱ
from	the	places	of them	were moved.		And	the

935	06	1093	2532	013	3175		2532	013
βασιλεῖς	τῆς	γῆς	καὶ	οἱ	μεγιστᾶνες		καὶ	οἱ
kings	of the earth		and	the	great ones		and	the

5506		2532	013	4145		2532	013	2478
χιλίαρχοι		καὶ	οἱ	πλούσιοι	καὶ		οἱ	ἰσχυροὶ
rulers of thousand		and	the	rich		and	the	strong

2532	3956	1401	2532	1658		2928	1438
καὶ	πᾶς	δοῦλος	καὶ	ἐλεύθερος		ἔκρυψαν	ἑαυτοὺς
and	all	slave	and	free		hid	themselves

1519	024	4693	2532	1519	020	4073	022	3735
εἰς	τὰ	σπήλαια	καὶ	εἰς	τὰς	πέτρας	τῶν	ὀρέων
in	the	caves	and	in	the	rocks	of the	hills

	2532	3004		023		3735	2532	019	4073
16	καὶ	λέγουσιν	τοῖς	ὄρεσιν	καὶ	ταῖς		πέτραις·
	and	they say	to the hills		and	to the rocks,		

4098	1909	1473	2532	2928	1473	575	4383
πέσετε	ἐφ᾽	ἡμᾶς	καὶ	κρύψατε	ἡμᾶς	ἀπὸ	προσώπου
fall	on	us	and	hide	us	from	face

with a loud voice, "Sovereign Lord, holy and true, how long will it be before you judge and avenge our blood on the inhabitants of the earth?" [11]They were each given a white robe and told to rest a little longer, until the number would be complete both of their fellow servants[a] and of their brothers and sisters,[b] who were soon to be killed as they themselves had been killed.

[12]When he opened the sixth seal, I looked, and there came a great earthquake; the sun became black as sackcloth, the full moon became like blood, [13]and the stars of the sky fell to the earth as the fig tree drops its winter fruit when shaken by a gale. [14]The sky vanished like a scroll rolling itself up, and every mountain and island was removed from its place. [15]Then the kings of the earth and the magnates and the generals and the rich and the powerful, and everyone, slave and free, hid in the caves and among the rocks of the mountains, [16]calling to the mountains and rocks, "Fall on us and hide us from the face

a Gk slaves
b Gk brothers

of the one seated on the throne and from the wrath of the Lamb; [17]for the great day of their wrath has come, and who is able to stand?"

CHAPTER 7

After this I saw four angels standing at the four corners of the earth, holding back the four winds of the earth so that no wind could blow on earth or sea or against any tree. [2]I saw another angel ascending from the rising of the sun, having the seal of the living God, and he called with a loud voice to the four angels who had been given power to damage earth and sea, [3]saying, "Do not damage the earth or the sea or the trees, until we have marked the servants[a] of our God with a seal on their foreheads."

4 And I heard the number of those who were sealed, one hundred forty-four thousand, sealed out of every tribe of the people of Israel:
[5] From the tribe of Judah
　　twelve thousand
　　sealed,
　　from the tribe of
　　　Reuben twelve
　　　thousand,
　　from the tribe of Gad
　　　twelve thousand,
[6] from the tribe of Asher
　　twelve thousand,
　　from the tribe of
　　　Naphtali twelve
　　　thousand,
　　from the tribe of
　　　Manasseh twelve
　　　thousand,
[7] from the tribe of Simeon
　　twelve thousand,
　　from the tribe of Levi
　　　twelve thousand,

a Gk slaves

```
02              2521           1909 02  2362        2532 575   06
τοῦ       καθημένου   ἐπὶ  τοῦ θρόνου καὶ   ἀπὸ  τῆς
of the one sitting      on   the throne and   from the
3709 010        721              3754 2064  05   2250  05 3173
ὀργῆς τοῦ    ἀρνίου,  17 ὅτι  ἦλθεν ἡ  ἡμέρα ἡ  μεγάλη
anger of the  lamb,      because came  the  day  the great
06    3709 846           2532 5101 1410      2476
τῆς  ὀργῆς αὐτῶν,   καὶ τίς  δύναται σταθῆναι;
of the anger of them,   and who  is able to stand?
       3326  3778 3708  5064        32        2476
7:1 Μετὰ τοῦτο εἶδον τέσσαρας ἀγγέλους ἐστῶτας
    After this  I saw four      messengers having stood
1909 020 5064        1137   06      1093    2902      016
ἐπὶ τὰς τέσσαρας γωνίας τῆς  γῆς,  κρατοῦντας τοὺς
on   the four   corners of the earth, holding     the
5064       417      06   1093  2443 3361 4154
τέσσαρας ἀνέμους τῆς  γῆς ἵνα  μὴ  πνέῃ
four      winds  of the earth that not might blow
417    1909 06  1093  3383      1909 06  2281      3383
ἄνεμος ἐπὶ τῆς γῆς μήτε     ἐπὶ τῆς θαλάσσης μήτε
wind    on  the earth neither on  the sea        nor
1909 3956 1186       2532 3708  243   32
ἐπὶ πᾶν δένδρον. 2 Καὶ εἶδον ἄλλον ἄγγελον
on   all tree.      And I saw other messenger
305          575 395       2246   2192    4973       2316
ἀναβαίνοντα ἀπὸ ἀνατολῆς ἡλίου ἔχοντα σφραγῖδα θεοῦ
coming up    from east   of sun having seal      of God
2198     2532 2896        5456    3173    015   5064
ζῶντος, καὶ ἔκραξεν   φωνῇ  μεγάλῃ τοῖς τέσσαρσιν
living, and he shouted in sound great  to the four
32        3739  1325       846     91
ἀγγέλοις οἷς  ἐδόθη    αὐτοῖς ἀδικῆσαι
messengers to whom were given to them to do unright
08  1093  2532 08  2281          3004    3361 91
τὴν γῆν καὶ τὴν θάλασσαν 3 λέγων· μὴ ἀδικήσητε
the earth and the sea       saying, not do unright
08  1093  3383 08  2281        3383 024  1186     891
τὴν γῆν μήτε τὴν θάλασσαν μήτε τὰ δένδρα, ἄχρι
the earth nor the sea      nor  the trees,  until
4972          016    1401    02      2316 1473 1909 022
σφραγίσωμεν τοὺς δούλους τοῦ  θεοῦ ἡμῶν ἐπὶ τῶν
we might seal the  slaves  of the God of us  on   the
3359      846      2532 191    04  706    014
μετώπων αὐτῶν. 4 Καὶ ἤκουσα τὸν ἀριθμὸν τῶν
foreheads of them.  And I heard the number  of the
4972              1540   5062        5064
ἐσφραγισμένων,  ἑκατὸν τεσσεράκοντα τέσσαρες
ones having been sealed, hundred forty        four
5505       4972            1537 3956 5443   5207
χιλιάδες, ἐσφραγισμένοι  ἐκ πάσης φυλῆς υἱῶν
thousands, having been sealed from all  tribe of sons
2474        5 1537 5443     1427 1427    5505
Ἰσραήλ· 5 ἐκ  φυλῆς Ἰούδα δώδεκα χιλιάδες
Israel:     from tribe Judas twelve thousands
4972             1537 5443     4502   1427    5505
ἐσφραγισμένοι, ἐκ  φυλῆς Ῥουβὴν δώδεκα χιλιάδες,
having been     from tribe Ruben  twelve thousands,
sealed,
1537 5443 1045 1427    5505         6 1537 5443     768
ἐκ  φυλῆς Γὰδ δώδεκα χιλιάδες, 6 ἐκ  φυλῆς Ἀσὴρ
from tribe Gad twelve thousands,  from tribe Aser
1427    5505         1537 5443 3508     1427
δώδεκα χιλιάδες, ἐκ  φυλῆς Νεφθαλὶμ δώδεκα
twelve thousands, from tribe Nephthalim twelve
5505        1537 5443 3128     1427    5505
χιλιάδες, ἐκ  φυλῆς Μανασσῆ δώδεκα χιλιάδες,
thousands, from tribe Manasses twelve thousands,
  1537 5443 4826    1427    5505         1537 5443 3017
7 ἐκ  φυλῆς Συμεὼν δώδεκα χιλιάδες, ἐκ  φυλῆς Λευὶ
  from tribe Symeon twelve thousands, from tribe Levi
```

```
1427      5505           1537  5443    2475a        1427
δώδεκα χιλιάδες,   ἐκ   φυλῆς 'Ισσαχὰρ δώδεκα
twelve thousands,  from tribe  Issachar twelve
5505          1537  5443  2194        1427    5505        1537
χιλιάδες,  8  ἐκ   φυλῆς Ζαβουλὼν δώδεκα χιλιάδες,  ἐκ
thousands,    from tribe  Zabulon  twelve thousands, from
5443     2501    1427    5505        1537  5443   958
φυλῆς 'Ιωσὴφ δώδεκα χιλιάδες,  ἐκ   φυλῆς Βενιαμὶν
tribe  Joseph twelve thousands, from tribe  Benjamin
1427      5505          4972            9  3326    3778
δώδεκα χιλιάδες ἐσφραγισμένοι.     Μετὰ ταῦτα
twelve thousands having been sealed. After these
3708      2532 2400 3793  4183      3739  705         846
εἶδον, καὶ ἰδοὺ ὄχλος πολύς,  ὃν   ἀριθμῆσαι αὐτὸν
I saw,  and  look crowd much,  which to number   it
3762     1410         1537 3956   1484     2532 5443    2532
οὐδεὶς ἐδύνατο,  ἐκ   παντὸς ἔθνους καὶ  φυλῶν καὶ
no one was able, from  all    nation and  tribes and
2992     2532 1100    2476           1799     02  2362
λαῶν  καὶ  γλωσσῶν ἐστῶτες    ἐνώπιον τοῦ θρόνου
peoples and  tongues having stood before the throne
2532 1799   010 721      4016              4749
καὶ ἐνώπιον τοῦ ἀρνίου περιβεβλημένους στολὰς
and  before  the lamb   having thrown   long robes
                                     around themselves
3022     2532 5404    1722 019   5495    846     10  2532
λευκὰς καὶ φοίνικες ἐν  ταῖς χερσὶν αὐτῶν,     καὶ
white  and  palms   in  the hands of them,  and
2896        5456       3173  3004    05  4991
κράζουσιν φωνῇ    μεγάλη λέγοντες· ἡ σωτηρία
they shout in sound great saying,   the deliverance
03       2316 1473  03  2521       1909 03  2362   2532
τῷ      θεῷ  ἡμῶν τῷ καθημένῳ ἐπὶ τῷ θρόνῳ καὶ
to the God  of us the one sitting on  the throne and
011 721       2532 3956   013 32       2476
τῷ ἀρνίῳ.  11 Καὶ πάντες οἱ ἄγγελοι εἱστήκεισαν
the lamb.    And all    the messengers had stood in
2945    02  2362  2532 014 4245      2532 022 5064
κύκλῳ τοῦ θρόνου καὶ τῶν πρεσβυτέρων καὶ τῶν τεσσάρων
circle the throne and the older men    and the four
2226          2532 4098   1799   02  2362    1909 024
ζῴων    καὶ ἔπεσαν ἐνώπιον τοῦ θρόνου ἐπὶ τὰ
living ones and  fell   before the throne on   the
4383     846    2532 4352        03  2316  12  3004
πρόσωπα αὐτῶν  καὶ προσεκύνησαν τῷ θεῷ    λέγοντες·
faces   of them and worshiped   the God     saying,
281    05  2129       2532 05 1391    2532 05 4678
ἀμήν, ἡ  εὐλογία καὶ  ἡ δόξα καὶ  ἡ σοφία
amen, the good word and the splendor and the wisdom
2532 05 2169      2532 05 5092   2532 05 1411
καὶ  ἡ εὐχαριστία καὶ  ἡ τιμὴ καὶ  ἡ δύναμις
and  the good favor and the value and the power
2532 05 2479    03      2316 1473 1519 016  165
καὶ  ἡ ἰσχὺς τῷ    θεῷ ἡμῶν εἰς τοὺς αἰῶνας
and  the strength to the God of us into the ages
014     165    281   13 2532 611      1520 1537 014
τῶν   αἰώνων· ἀμήν.    Καὶ ἀπεκρίθη εἷς ἐκ  τῶν
of the ages;  amen.    And answered one from the
4245          3004   1473 3778  013 4016
πρεσβυτέρων λέγων μοι· οὗτοι οἱ περιβεβλημένοι
older men   saying to these  the ones having thrown
            me,                around themselves
020 4749        020 3022  5101  1510  2532 4159
τὰς στολὰς    τὰς λευκὰς τίνες εἰσὶν καὶ πόθεν
the long robes the white  who  are   and from where
2064        2532 3004   846    2962  1473 1473
ἦλθον; 14 καὶ εἴρηκα αὐτῷ· κύριέ μου,  σὺ
they come? And I said to him, Master of me, you
```

from the tribe of
  Issachar twelve
  thousand,
8 from the tribe of Zebulun
  twelve thousand,
  from the tribe of
  Joseph twelve
  thousand,
  from the tribe of
  Benjamin twelve
  thousand sealed.
  9 After this I looked,
and there was a great
multitude that no one could
count, from every nation,
from all tribes and peoples
and languages, standing
before the throne and
before the Lamb, robed in
white, with palm branches
in their hands. 10They cried
out in a loud voice, saying,
  "Salvation belongs to
  our God who is seated
  on the throne, and to
  the Lamb!"
11And all the angels stood
around the throne and
around the elders and the
four living creatures, and
they fell on their faces
before the throne and
worshiped God, 12singing,
  "Amen! Blessing and
  glory and wisdom
  and thanksgiving and
  honor
  and power and might
  be to our God forever
  and ever! Amen."
  13 Then one of the elders
addressed me, saying,
"Who are these, robed in
white, and where have they
come from?" 14I said to
him, "Sir, you are the one
that knows."

Then he said to me, "These are they who have come out of the great ordeal; they have washed their robes and made them white in the blood of the Lamb.

15 For this reason they are before the throne of God,

and worship him day and night within his temple,

and the one who is seated on the throne will shelter them.

16 They will hunger no more, and thirst no more;

the sun will not strike them,

nor any scorching heat;

17 for the Lamb at the center of the throne will be their shepherd,

and he will guide them to springs of the water of life,

and God will wipe away every tear from their eyes."

CHAPTER 8

When the Lamb opened the seventh seal, there was silence in heaven for about half an hour. 2 And I saw the seven angels who stand before God, and seven trumpets were given to them.

3 Another angel with a golden censer came and stood at the altar; he was given a great quantity of incense to offer with the prayers of all the saints on the golden altar that is before the throne. 4 And the smoke of the incense,

---

3609a	2532	3004	1473	3778	1510	013	2064
οἶδας.	καὶ	εἶπέν	μοι·	οὗτοί	εἰσιν	οἱ	ἐρχόμενοι
know.	And	he said	to me,	these	are	the	ones coming

1537	06	2347		06	3173	2532	4150		020
ἐκ	τῆς	θλίψεως		τῆς	μεγάλης	καὶ	ἔπλυναν		τὰς
from	the	affliction		the	great	and	they washed		the

4749	846	2532	3021	846	1722	011
στολὰς	αὐτῶν	καὶ	ἐλεύκαναν	αὐτὰς	ἐν	τῷ
long robes	of them	and	whitened	them	in	the

129	010	721	**15**	1223		3778	1510
αἵματι	τοῦ	ἀρνίου.		διὰ		τοῦτό	εἰσιν
blood	of the	lamb.		Because of	this		they are

1799	02	2362	02		2316	2532	3000		846
ἐνώπιον	τοῦ	θρόνου	τοῦ		θεοῦ	καὶ	λατρεύουσιν		αὐτῷ
before	the	throne	of the		God	and	they serve		him

2250	2532	3571	1722	03	3485	846		2532	01
ἡμέρας	καὶ	νυκτὸς	ἐν	τῷ	ναῷ	αὐτοῦ,		καὶ	ὁ
day	and	night	in	the	temple	of him,		and	the

2521	1909	02	2362	4637	1909	846
καθήμενος	ἐπὶ	τοῦ	θρόνου	σκηνώσει	ἐπ'	αὐτούς.
one sitting	on	the	throne	will tent	among	them.

16

3756	3983		2089	3761	1372
οὐ	πεινάσουσιν		ἔτι	οὐδὲ	διψήσουσιν
Not	they will hunger		still	but not	they will thirst

2089	3761	3361	4098	1909	846	01	2246
ἔτι	οὐδὲ	μὴ	πέσῃ	ἐπ'	αὐτοὺς	ὁ	ἥλιος
still	but not	not	might fall	on	them	the	sun

3761	3956	2738	**17**	3754	09	721	09	303
οὐδὲ	πᾶν	καῦμα,		ὅτι	τὸ	ἀρνίον	τὸ	ἀνὰ
but not	all	burn,		because	the	lamb	the	up

3319	02	2362	4165	846	2532
μέσον	τοῦ	θρόνου	ποιμανεῖ	αὐτοὺς	καὶ
middle	of the	throne	will shepherd	them	and

3594	846	1909	2222	4077	5204
ὁδηγήσει	αὐτοὺς	ἐπὶ	ζωῆς	πηγὰς	ὑδάτων,
will guide	them	on	of life	springs	of waters,

2532	1813		01	2316	3956	1144	1537	014
καὶ	ἐξαλείψει		ὁ	θεὸς	πᾶν	δάκρυον	ἐκ	τῶν
and	will wipe off		the	God	all	tear	from	the

3788	846		**8:1**	2532	3752	455		08	4973
ὀφθαλμῶν	αὐτῶν.			Καὶ	ὅταν	ἤνοιξεν		τὴν	σφραγῖδα
eyes	of them.			And	when	he opened		the	seal

08	1442	1096	4602	1722	03	3772	5613
τὴν	ἑβδόμην,	ἐγένετο	σιγὴ	ἐν	τῷ	οὐρανῷ	ὡς
the	seventh,	became	silence	in	the	heaven	as

2256		**2**	2532	3708	016	2033	32		3739
ἡμιώριον.			Καὶ	εἶδον	τοὺς	ἑπτὰ	ἀγγέλους		οἳ
half hour.			And	I saw	the	seven	messengers		who

1799	02	2316	2476		2532	1325	846
ἐνώπιον	τοῦ	θεοῦ	ἑστήκασιν,		καὶ	ἐδόθησαν	αὐτοῖς
before	the	God	have stood,		and	were given	to them

2033	4536		**3**	2532	243	32		2064	2532
ἑπτὰ	σάλπιγγες.			Καὶ	ἄλλος	ἄγγελος		ἦλθεν	καὶ
seven	trumpets.			And	other	messenger		came	and

2476	1909	010	2379		2192	3031
ἐστάθη	ἐπὶ	τοῦ	θυσιαστηρίου		ἔχων	λιβανωτὸν
stood	on	the	sacrifice place		having	incense holder

5552	2532	1325	846	2368	4183	2443
χρυσοῦν,	καὶ	ἐδόθη	αὐτῷ	θυμιάματα	πολλά,	ἵνα
gold,	and	was given	to him	incense	much,	that

1325	019	4335	014	40	3956
δώσει	ταῖς	προσευχαῖς	τῶν	ἁγίων	πάντων
he will give	in the	prayers	of the	holy ones	all

1909	012	2379		012	5552	012	1799	02
ἐπὶ	τὸ	θυσιαστήριον		τὸ	χρυσοῦν	τὸ	ἐνώπιον	τοῦ
on	the	sacrifice place		the	gold	the	before	the

2362		**4**	2532	305	01	2586	022	2368
θρόνου.			καὶ	ἀνέβη	ὁ	καπνὸς	τῶν	θυμιαμάτων
throne.			And	came up	the	smoke	of the	incense

019   4335   014   40   1537 5495   02
ταῖς προσευχαῖς τῶν ἁγίων   ἐκ χειρὸς τοῦ
in the prayers   of the holy ones from hand of the

32   1799   02 2316   2532 2983   01
ἀγγέλου ἐνώπιον τοῦ θεοῦ. 5 καὶ εἴληφεν ὁ
messenger before the God.   And has taken the

32   04 3031   2532 1072   846   1537
ἄγγελος τὸν λιβανωτὸν καὶ ἐγέμισεν αὐτὸν ἐκ
messenger the incense holder and he filled it from

010 4442 010   2379   2532 906   1519 08
τοῦ πυρὸς τοῦ θυσιαστηρίου καὶ ἔβαλεν εἰς τὴν
the fire of the sacrifice place and threw into the

1093   1096   1027   2532 5456   2532
γῆν, καὶ ἐγένοντο βρονταὶ καὶ φωναὶ καὶ
earth, and became thunders and sounds and

796   2532 4578   6 2532 013 2033 32
ἀστραπαὶ καὶ σεισμός. Καὶ οἱ ἑπτὰ ἄγγελοι
lightnings and shake. And the seven messengers

013 2192   020 2033   4536   2090   846   2443
οἱ ἔχοντες τὰς ἑπτὰ σάλπιγγας ἡτοίμασαν αὐτοὺς ἵνα
the having the seven trumpets prepared them that

4537   7 2532 01 4413   4537   2532
σαλπίσωσιν.   Καὶ ὁ πρῶτος ἐσάλπισεν· καὶ
they might trumpet. And the first trumpeted; and

1096   5464   2532 4442 3396   1722 129
ἐγένετο χάλαζα καὶ πῦρ μεμιγμένα ἐν αἵματι
became hail   and fire having been mixed in blood

2532 906   1519 08 1093   2532 09 5154   06
καὶ ἐβλήθη εἰς τὴν γῆν, καὶ τὸ τρίτον τῆς
and was thrown into the earth, and the third of the

1093 2618   2532 09 5154   022   1186
γῆς κατεκάη   καὶ τὸ τρίτον τῶν δένδρων
earth was burned down and the third of the trees

2618   2532 3956 5528   5515   2618
κατεκάη   καὶ πᾶς χόρτος χλωρὸς κατεκάη.
was burned down and all grass green was burned down.

8 2532 01 1208   32   4537   2532 5613
  Καὶ ὁ δεύτερος ἄγγελος ἐσάλπισεν· καὶ ὡς
  And the second messenger trumpeted; and as

3735 3173 4442   2545   906   1519 08
ὄρος μέγα πυρὶ καιόμενον ἐβλήθη εἰς τὴν
hill great in fire being burned was thrown into the

2281   2532 1096   09 5154   06   2281
θάλασσαν, καὶ ἐγένετο τὸ τρίτον τῆς θαλάσσης
sea,   and became the third of the sea

129   9 2532 599   09 5154   022   2938   022
αἷμα   καὶ ἀπέθανεν τὸ τρίτον τῶν κτισμάτων τῶν
blood and died   the third of the creations the

1722 07 2281   021 2192   2590 2532 09 5154
ἐν τῇ θαλάσσῃ τὰ ἔχοντα ψυχὰς καὶ τὸ τρίτον
in the sea   the having souls and the third

022 4143   1311   10 2532 01 5154   32
τῶν πλοίων διεφθάρησαν.   Καὶ ὁ τρίτος ἄγγελος
of boats were corrupted And the third messenger
the   thoroughly.

4537   2532 4098   1537 02 3772   792   3173
ἐσάλπισεν· καὶ ἔπεσεν ἐκ τοῦ οὐρανοῦ ἀστὴρ μέγας
trumpeted; and fell   from the heaven star great

2545   5613 2985   2532 4098   1909 012 5154
καιόμενος ὡς λαμπὰς καὶ ἔπεσεν ἐπὶ τὸ τρίτον
burning   as lamp   and it fell on the third

014   4215   2532 1909 020 4077   022   5204
τῶν ποταμῶν καὶ ἐπὶ τὰς πηγὰς τῶν ὑδάτων,
of the rivers and on the springs of the waters,

11 2532 09 3686   02   792   3004   01
   καὶ τὸ ὄνομα τοῦ ἀστέρος λέγεται ὁ
   and the name of the star is called the

894   2532 1096   09 5154   022   5204   1519
Ἄψινθος, καὶ ἐγένετο τὸ τρίτον τῶν ὑδάτων εἰς
Wormwood, and became the third of the waters into

with the prayers of the
saints, rose before God
from the hand of the angel.
[5]Then the angel took the
censer and filled it with
fire from the altar and
threw it on the earth; and
there were peals of thunder,
rumblings, flashes of lightning, and an earthquake.

[6]Now the seven angels
who had the seven trumpets
made ready to blow them.

[7]The first angel blew
his trumpet, and there came
hail and fire, mixed with
blood, and they were hurled
to the earth; and a third of
the earth was burned up,
and a third of the trees were
burned up, and all green
grass was burned up.

[8]The second angel
blew his trumpet, and
something like a great
mountain, burning with
fire, was thrown into the
sea. [9]A third of the sea
became blood, a third of
the living creatures in the
sea died, and a third of the
ships were destroyed.

[10]The third angel
blew his trumpet, and a
great star fell from heaven,
blazing like a torch, and it
fell on a third of the rivers
and on the springs of water.
[11]The name of the star is
Wormwood. A third of the
waters became

wormwood, and many died from the water, because it was made bitter.

12 The fourth angel blew his trumpet, and a third of the sun was struck, and a third of the moon, and a third of the stars, so that a third of their light was darkened; a third of the day was kept from shining, and likewise the night.

13 Then I looked, and I heard an eagle crying with a loud voice as it flew in midheaven, "Woe, woe, woe to the inhabitants of the earth, at the blasts of the other trumpets that the three angels are about to blow!"

CHAPTER 9

And the fifth angel blew his trumpet, and I saw a star that had fallen from heaven to earth, and he was given the key to the shaft of the bottomless pit; ²he opened the shaft of the bottomless pit, and from the shaft rose smoke like the smoke of a great furnace, and the sun and the air were darkened with the smoke from the shaft. ³Then from the smoke came locusts on the earth, and they were given authority like the authority of scorpions of the earth. ⁴They were told not to damage the grass of the earth or any green growth or any

894	2532	4183	014	444	599	1537 022
ἄψινθον	καὶ	πολλοὶ	τῶν	ἀνθρώπων	ἀπέθανον	ἐκ τῶν
wormwood	and	many	of the men		died	from the

5204	3754	4087		2532 01	5067
ὑδάτων	ὅτι	ἐπικράνθησαν.	**12**	Καὶ ὁ	τέταρτος
waters	because	they were made bitter.		And	the fourth

32	4537	2532 4141	09	5154	02
ἄγγελος	ἐσάλπισεν·	καὶ ἐπλήγη	τὸ	τρίτον	τοῦ
messenger	trumpeted;	and was struck	the	third	of the

2246	2532 09	5154	06	4582	2532 09	5154
ἡλίου	καὶ τὸ	τρίτον	τῆς	σελήνης	καὶ τὸ	τρίτον
sun	and the	third	of the	moon	and the	third

014	792	2443 4654		09	5154
τῶν	ἀστέρων,	ἵνα σκοτισθῇ		τὸ	τρίτον
of the stars,		that might be darkened		the	third

846	2532 05	2250 3361 5316		012 5154
αὐτῶν	καὶ ἡ	ἡμέρα μὴ φάνῃ		τὸ τρίτον
of them	and the	day not might shine		the third

846 2532 05	3571	3668		2532 3708	2532 191
αὐτῆς καὶ ἡ	νὺξ	ὁμοίως.	**13**	Καὶ εἶδον,	καὶ ἤκουσα
of it and the	night	likewise.		And I saw,	and I heard

1520 105	4072	1722 3321	3004
ἑνὸς ἀετοῦ	πετομένου	ἐν μεσουρανήματι	λέγοντος
one eagle	flying	in middle heaven	saying

5456	3173	3759 3759 3759 016	2730	1909
φωνῇ	μεγάλῃ·	οὐαὶ οὐαὶ οὐαὶ τοὺς	κατοικοῦντας	ἐπὶ
in sound	great,	woe woe woe the	ones residing	on

06	1093	1537 018 3062	5456	06	4536
τῆς	γῆς	ἐκ τῶν λοιπῶν	φωνῶν	τῆς	σάλπιγγος
the	earth	from the remaining	sounds	of the	trumpet

014	5140 32	014 3195
τῶν	τριῶν ἀγγέλων	τῶν μελλόντων
of the	three messengers	the ones being about

4537		2532 01	3991	32	4537
σαλπίζειν.	**9:1**	Καὶ ὁ	πέμπτος	ἄγγελος	ἐσάλπισεν·
to trumpet.		And the	fifth	messenger	trumpeted;

2532	3708 792	1537 02 3772	4098	1519
καὶ	εἶδον ἀστέρα	ἐκ τοῦ οὐρανοῦ	πεπτωκότα	εἰς
and	I saw star	from the heaven	having fallen	into

08	1093	2532 1325	846	05 2807	010
τὴν	γῆν,	καὶ ἐδόθη	αὐτῷ	ἡ κλεὶς	τοῦ
the	earth,	and was given	to it	the key	of the

5421	06	12		2532 455	012 5421
φρέατος	τῆς	ἀβύσσου·	**2**	καὶ ἤνοιξεν	τὸ φρέαρ
well	of the	bottomless		and he opened	the well

06	12	2532 305	2586	1537 010 5421
τῆς	ἀβύσσου,	καὶ ἀνέβη	καπνὸς	ἐκ τοῦ φρέατος
of the	bottomless,	and went up	smoke	from the well

5613 2586	2575	3173	2532 4656	01
ὡς καπνὸς	καμίνου	μεγάλης,	καὶ ἐσκοτώθη	ὁ
as smoke	of furnace	great,	and was darkened	the

2246 2532 01	109 1537 02	2586	010	5421
ἥλιος καὶ ὁ	ἀὴρ ἐκ	τοῦ καπνοῦ	τοῦ	φρέατος.
sun and the	air from	the smoke	of the	well.

	2532 1537 02	2586	1831	200	1519 08
3	καὶ ἐκ	τοῦ καπνοῦ	ἐξῆλθον	ἀκρίδες	εἰς τὴν
	And from	the smoke	went out	locusts	into the

1093	2532 1325	846	1849	5613 2192
γῆν,	καὶ ἐδόθη	αὐταῖς	ἐξουσία	ὡς ἔχουσιν
earth,	and was given	to them	authority	as have

1849	013 4651	06	1093	2532
ἐξουσίαν	οἱ σκορπίοι	τῆς	γῆς.	**4** καὶ
authority	the scorpions	of the	earth.	And

3004	846	2443 3361 91		04
ἐρρέθη	αὐταῖς	ἵνα μὴ ἀδικήσουσιν		τὸν
it was said	to them	that not they will do unright		the

5528	06	1093	3761	3956 5515	3761	3956
χόρτον	τῆς	γῆς	οὐδὲ	πᾶν χλωρὸν	οὐδὲ	πᾶν
grass	of the	earth	but not	all green	but not	all

1186	1487 3361 016 444	3748	3756 2192
δένδρον,	εἰ μὴ τοὺς ἀνθρώπους οἵτινες	οὐκ	ἔχουσι
tree,	except the men who	not	have

08 4973 02	2316 1909 022 3359	2532
τὴν σφραγῖδα τοῦ	θεοῦ ἐπὶ τῶν μετώπων. 5	καὶ
the seal of the	God on the foreheads. And	

1325	846	2443 3361 615	846
ἐδόθη	αὐτοῖς	ἵνα μὴ ἀποκτείνωσιν	αὐτούς,
it was given	to them	that not they might kill	them,

235 2443 928	3376 4002 2532 01
ἀλλ᾽ ἵνα βασανισθήσονται	μῆνας πέντε, καὶ ὁ
but that they will be tormented	months five, and the

929	846	5613 929	4651	3752
βασανισμὸς	αὐτῶν	ὡς βασανισμὸς	σκορπίου	ὅταν
torment	of them	as torment	of scorpion	when

3817	444	2532 1722 019 2250
παίσῃ	ἄνθρωπον. 6	καὶ ἐν ταῖς ἡμέραις
it might strike	man. And	in the days

1565	2212	013 444	04 2288	2532
ἐκείναις	ζητήσουσιν	οἱ ἄνθρωποι	τὸν θάνατον	καὶ
those	will seek	the men	the death	and

3756 3361 2147	846	2532 1937
οὐ μὴ εὑρήσουσιν	αὐτόν, καὶ	ἐπιθυμήσουσιν
not not they will find	it, and	they will desire

599	2532 5343 01 2288	575 846	7 2532
ἀποθανεῖν	καὶ φεύγει ὁ θάνατος	ἀπ᾽ αὐτῶν.	Καὶ
to die	and flees the death	from them.	And

021 3667	018	200	3664 2462
τὰ ὁμοιώματα	τῶν	ἀκρίδων	ὅμοια ἵπποις
the likenesses	of the	locusts	like horses

2090	1519 4171	2532 1909 020
ἡτοιμασμένοις	εἰς πόλεμον,	καὶ ἐπὶ τὰς
having been prepared	for war,	and on the

2776	846	5613 4735	3664	5557	2532 021
κεφαλὰς	αὐτῶν	ὡς στέφανοι	ὅμοιοι	χρυσῷ,	καὶ τὰ
heads	of them	as crowns	like	gold,	and the

4383	846	5613 4383	444	8 2532 2192
πρόσωπα	αὐτῶν	ὡς πρόσωπα	ἀνθρώπων,	καὶ εἶχον
faces	of them	as faces	of men,	and they had

2359	5613 2359	1135	2532 013 3599	846
τρίχας	ὡς τρίχας	γυναικῶν,	καὶ οἱ ὀδόντες	αὐτῶν
hairs	as hairs	of women,	and the teeth	of them

5613 3023	1510	9 2532 2192	2382	5613
ὡς λεόντων	ἦσαν,	καὶ εἶχον	θώρακας	ὡς
as of lions	were,	and they had	breastplates	as

2382	4603	2532 05 5456 018	4420
θώρακας	σιδηροῦς,	καὶ ἡ φωνὴ τῶν	πτερύγων
breastplates	iron,	and the sound of the	wings

846	5613 5456 716	2462 4183	5143
αὐτῶν	ὡς φωνὴ ἁρμάτων	ἵππων πολλῶν	τρεχόντων
of them	as sound of chariots	horses many	running

1519 4171	10 2532 2192	3769 3664	4651
εἰς πόλεμον,	καὶ ἔχουσιν	οὐρὰς ὁμοίας	σκορπίοις
to war,	And they have	tails like	scorpions

2532 2759	2532 1722 019 3769 846	05
καὶ κέντρα,	καὶ ἐν ταῖς οὐραῖς αὐτῶν	ἡ
and stings,	and in the tails of them	the

1849	846	91	016 444	3376
ἐξουσία	αὐτῶν	ἀδικῆσαι	τοὺς ἀνθρώπους	μῆνας
authority	of them	to do unright	the men	months

4002	11 2192	1909 846	935	04 32
πέντε,	ἔχουσιν	ἐπ᾽ αὐτῶν	βασιλέα	τὸν ἄγγελον
five,	they have on	them	king	the messenger

06	12	3686 846	1447	3
τῆς	ἀβύσσου,	ὄνομα αὐτῷ	Ἑβραϊστὶ	Ἀβαδδών,
of the	bottomless,	name to him	in Hebrew	Abaddon,

2532 1722 07 1673	3686 2192 623	12 05
καὶ ἐν τῇ Ἑλληνικῇ	ὄνομα ἔχει Ἀπολλύων.	Ἡ
and in the Greek	name he has Apollyon.	The

tree, but only those people who do not have the seal of God on their foreheads. [5]They were allowed to torture them for five months, but not to kill them, and their torture was like the torture of a scorpion when it stings someone. [6]And in those days people will seek death but will not find it; they will long to die, but death will flee from them.

[7]In appearance the locusts were like horses equipped for battle. On their heads were what looked like crowns of gold; their faces were like human faces, [8]their hair like women's hair, and their teeth like lions' teeth; [9]they had scales like iron breastplates, and the noise of their wings was like the noise of many chariots with horses rushing into battle. [10]They have tails like scorpions, with stingers, and in their tails is their power to harm people for five months. [11]They have as king over them the angel of the bottomless pit; his name in Hebrew is Abaddon,[a] and in Greek he is called Apollyon.[b]

[12]The first woe has passed.

[a] That is, *Destruction*
[b] That is, *Destroyer*

There are still two woes to come.

13 Then the sixth angel blew his trumpet, and I heard a voice from the four[a] horns of the golden altar before God, 14saying to the sixth angel who had the trumpet, "Release the four angels who are bound at the great river Euphrates." 15So the four angels were released, who had been held ready for the hour, the day, the month, and the year, to kill a third of humankind. 16The number of the troops of cavalry was two hundred million; I heard their number. 17And this was how I saw the horses in my vision: the riders wore breastplates the color of fire and of sapphire[b] and of sulfur; the heads of the horses were like lions' heads, and fire and smoke and sulfur came out of their mouths. 18By these three plagues a third of humankind was killed, by the fire and smoke and sulfur coming out of their mouths. 19For the power of the horses is in their mouths and in their tails;

[a] Other ancient authorities lack *four*
[b] Gk *hyacinth*

3759	05	1520	565		2400	2064		2089	1417	3759
οὐαὶ	ἡ	μία	ἀπῆλθεν·		ἰδοὺ	ἔρχεται		ἔτι	δύο	οὐαὶ
woe	the	one	went off;		look	comes		still	two	woes

3326	3778		2532	01	1623	32		4537
μετὰ	ταῦτα.	**13**	Καὶ	ὁ	ἕκτος	ἄγγελος		ἐσάλπισεν·
after	these.		And	the	sixth	messenger		trumpeted;

2532	191		5456	1520	1537	022	5064		2768
καὶ	ἤκουσα		φωνὴν	μίαν	ἐκ	τῶν	[τεσσάρων]		κεράτων
and	I heard		sound	one	from	the	four		horns

010	2379		010	5552	010	1799	02
τοῦ	θυσιαστηρίου		τοῦ	χρυσοῦ	τοῦ	ἐνώπιον	τοῦ
of the	sacrifice place		the	gold	the	before	the

2316		3004	03	1623	32		01
θεοῦ,	**14**	λέγοντα	τῷ	ἕκτῳ	ἀγγέλῳ,		ὁ
God,		saying	to the	sixth	messenger,		the one

2192	08	4536		3089	016	5064		32
ἔχων	τὴν	σάλπιγγα·		λῦσον	τοὺς	τέσσαρας		ἀγγέλους
having	the	trumpet,		loose	the	four		messengers

016	1210		1909	03	4215	03	3173
τοὺς	δεδεμένους		ἐπὶ	τῷ	ποταμῷ	τῷ	μεγάλῳ
the	ones having been bound		on	the	river	the	great

2166		2532	3089		013	5064		32
Εὐφράτῃ.	**15**	καὶ	ἐλύθησαν		οἱ	τέσσαρες		ἄγγελοι
Euphrates.		And	were loosed		the	four		messengers

013	2090		1519	08	5610	2532	2250
οἱ	ἡτοιμασμένοι		εἰς	τὴν	ὥραν	καὶ	ἡμέραν
the ones	having prepared		for	the	hour	and	day

2532	3376	2532	1763		2443	615		012
καὶ	μῆνα	καὶ	ἐνιαυτόν,		ἵνα	ἀποκτείνωσιν		τὸ
and	month	and	year,		that	they might kill		the

5154	014	444		2532	01	706	022
τρίτον	τῶν	ἀνθρώπων.	**16**	καὶ	ὁ	ἀριθμὸς	τῶν
third	of the	men.		And	the	number	of the

4753		010		2461		1364a
στρατευμάτων		τοῦ		ἱππικοῦ		δισμυριάδες
armies		of the		horseman		two ten thousands

3461		191		04	706		846		17	2532
μυριάδων,		ἤκουσα		τὸν	ἀριθμὸν		αὐτῶν.		**17**	Καὶ
of ten thousand,		I heard		the	number		of them.			And

3779	3708	016	2462		1722	07	3706	2532	016
οὕτως	εἶδον	τοὺς	ἵππους	ἐν	τῇ	ὁράσει	καὶ	τοὺς
thusly	I saw	the	horses	in	the	sight	and	the

2521		1909	846		2192	2382		4447
καθημένους		ἐπ᾽	αὐτῶν,		ἔχοντας	θώρακας		πυρίνους
ones sitting		on	them,		having	breastplates		of fire

2532	5191		2532	2306		2532	017	2776
καὶ	ὑακινθίνους		καὶ	θειώδεις,		καὶ	αἱ	κεφαλαὶ
and	hyacinth		and	sulphurous,		and	the	heads

014	2462		5613	2776	3023		2532	1537	022
τῶν	ἵππων		ὡς	κεφαλαὶ	λεόντων,		καὶ	ἐκ	τῶν
of the	horses		as	heads	of lions,		and	from	the

4750	846		1607		4442	2532	2586		2532
στομάτων	αὐτῶν		ἐκπορεύεται		πῦρ	καὶ	καπνὸς		καὶ
mouths	of them		travels out		fire	and	smoke		and

2303		18	575	018	5140	4127	3778		615
θεῖον.		**18**	ἀπὸ	τῶν	τριῶν	πληγῶν	τούτων		ἀπεκτάνθησαν
sulphur.			From	the	three	blows	these		were killed

09	5154	014		444		1537	010	4442	2532	02
τὸ	τρίτον	τῶν		ἀνθρώπων,		ἐκ	τοῦ	πυρὸς	καὶ	τοῦ
the	third	of the		men,		from	the	fire	and	the

2586		2532	010	2303		010	1607		1537	022
καπνοῦ		καὶ	τοῦ	θείου		τοῦ	ἐκπορευομένου		ἐκ	τῶν
smoke		and	the	sulphur		the	traveling out		from	the

4750	846		19	05	1063	1849		014	2462
στομάτων	αὐτῶν.		**19**	ἡ	γὰρ	ἐξουσία		τῶν	ἵππων
mouths	of them.			The	for	authority		of the	horses

1722	011	4750	846		1510	2532	1722	019	3769
ἐν	τῷ	στόματι	αὐτῶν		ἐστιν	καὶ	ἐν	ταῖς	οὐραῖς
in	the	mouth	of them		is	and	in	the	tails

846   017 1063 3769 846   3664   3789   2192
αὐτῶν, αἱ γὰρ οὐραὶ αὐτῶν ὅμοιαι ὄφεσιν, ἔχουσαι
of them, the for tails of them like   snakes, having
2776   2532 1722 846   91   2532 013
κεφαλὰς καὶ ἐν αὐταῖς ἀδικοῦσιν.   20 Καὶ οἱ
heads   and in them   they do unright.   And the
3062   014   444   3739 3756 615   1722
λοιποὶ τῶν ἀνθρώπων, οἳ οὐκ ἀπεκτάνθησαν ἐν
remaining of the men,   who not were killed in
019 4127   3778   3761   3340   1537
ταῖς πληγαῖς ταύταις, οὐδὲ μετενόησαν   ἐκ
the blows   these,   but not they changed mind from
022 2041 018   5495 846   2443 3361
τῶν ἔργων τῶν χειρῶν αὐτῶν, ἵνα μὴ
the works of the hands of them, that not
4352   024 1140   2532 024 1497   024
προσκυνήσουσιν τὰ δαιμόνια καὶ τὰ εἴδωλα τὰ
they will worship the demons   and the idols   the
5552   2532 024 693   2532 024 5470   2532 024 3035
χρυσᾶ καὶ τὰ ἀργυρᾶ καὶ τὰ χαλκᾶ καὶ τὰ λίθινα
gold   and the silver and the copper and the of stone
2532 024 3585   3739 3777   991   1410
καὶ τὰ ξύλινα, ἃ οὔτε βλέπειν δύνανται
and the wooden, that neither to see they are able
3777 191   3777 4043   21 2532 3756
οὔτε ἀκούειν οὔτε περιπατεῖν,   καὶ οὐ
nor to hear nor to walk around, and not
3340   1537 014 5408   846   3777 1537
μετενόησαν   ἐκ τῶν φόνων αὐτῶν οὔτε ἐκ
they changed mind from the murders of them nor from
022 5331a   846   3777 1537 06 4202
τῶν φαρμάκων αὐτῶν οὔτε ἐκ τῆς πορνείας
the magic   of them nor from the sexual immorality
846   3777 1537 022 2809   846   10:1 2532 3708
αὐτῶν οὔτε ἐκ τῶν κλεμμάτων αὐτῶν.   Καὶ εἶδον
of them nor from the thefts   of them.   And I saw
243 32   2478   2597   1537 02 3772
ἄλλον ἄγγελον ἰσχυρὸν καταβαίνοντα ἐκ τοῦ οὐρανοῦ
other messenger strong coming down from the heaven
4016   3507   2532 05 2463   1909 06
περιβεβλημένον νεφέλην, καὶ ἡ ἶρις ἐπὶ τῆς
having thrown cloud,   and the rainbow on the
around himself
2776   846   2532 09 4383   846   5613 01 2246
κεφαλῆς αὐτοῦ καὶ τὸ πρόσωπον αὐτοῦ ὡς ὁ ἥλιος
head   of him and the face   of him as the sun
2532 013 4228 846   5613 4769   4442   2 2532 2192
καὶ οἱ πόδες αὐτοῦ ὡς στῦλοι πυρός,   καὶ ἔχων
and the feet of him as pillars of fire, and having
1722 07 5495 846   974   455
ἐν τῇ χειρὶ αὐτοῦ βιβλαρίδιον ἠνεωγμένον.
in the hand of him little book having been opened.
2532 5087 04 4228 846   04 1188   1909 06
καὶ ἔθηκεν τὸν πόδα αὐτοῦ τὸν δεξιὸν ἐπὶ τῆς
And he set the foot of him the right on the
2281   04 1161 2176   1909 06 1093   3 2532
θαλάσσης, τὸν δὲ εὐώνυμον ἐπὶ τῆς γῆς,   καὶ
sea,   the but left   on the earth,   and
2896   5456   3173   5618   3023 3455   2532
ἔκραξεν φωνῇ μεγάλῃ ὥσπερ λέων μυκᾶται. καὶ
he shouted in voice great as indeed lion roars. And
3753 2896   2980   017 2033   1027   020
ὅτε ἔκραξεν, ἐλάλησαν αἱ ἑπτὰ βρονταὶ τὰς
when he shouted, spoke the seven thunders the
1438   5456   4 2532 3753 2980   017 2033
ἑαυτῶν φωνάς. καὶ ὅτε ἐλάλησαν αἱ ἑπτὰ
of themselves sounds. And when spoke   the seven
1027   3195   1125   2532 191   5456
βρονταί, ἤμελλον γράφειν, καὶ ἤκουσα φωνὴν
thunders, I was about to write, and I heard voice

their tails are like serpents,
having heads; and with
them they inflict harm.

20 The rest of human-
kind, who were not killed
by these plagues, did not
repent of the works of
their hands or give up
worshiping demons and
idols of gold and silver and
bronze and stone and wood,
which cannot see or hear
or walk. 21 And they did
not repent of their murders
or their sorceries or their
fornication or their thefts.

CHAPTER 10

And I saw another mighty
angel coming down from
heaven, wrapped in a cloud,
with a rainbow over his
head; his face was like the
sun, and his legs like pillars
of fire. 2 He held a little
scroll open in his hand.
Setting his right foot on
the sea and his left foot on
the land, 3 he gave a great
shout, like a lion roaring.
And when he shouted, the
seven thunders sounded.
4 And when the seven
thunders had sounded,
I was about to write, but
I heard a voice

from heaven saying, "Seal
up what the seven thunders
have said, and do not write
it down." ⁵Then the angel
whom I saw standing on the
sea and the land
  raised his right hand
    to heaven
⁶ and swore by him who
    lives forever and ever,
who created heaven and
what is in it, the earth and
what is in it, and the sea
and what is in it: "There
will be no more delay,
⁷but in the days when the
seventh angel is to blow his
trumpet, the mystery of
God will be fulfilled, as he
announced to his servants[a]
the prophets."

8 Then the voice that
I had heard from heaven
spoke to me again, saying,
"Go, take the scroll that
is open in the hand of the
angel who is standing on
the sea and on the land."
⁹So I went to the angel
and told him to give me
the little scroll; and he
said to me, "Take it, and
eat; it will be bitter to your
stomach, but sweet as honey
in your mouth." ¹⁰So I
took the little scroll from
the hand of the angel and
ate it; it was sweet

[a] Gk slaves

```
1537 02   3772      3004          4972        3739 2980      017
ἐκ  τοῦ οὐρανοῦ λέγουσαν· σφράγισον ἃ  ἐλάλησαν αἱ
from the heaven   saying,    seal    what spoke     the
2033 1027      2532 3361  846  1125                   2532
ἑπτὰ βρονταί, καὶ μὴ αὐτὰ γράψῃς.          5 Καὶ
seven thunders, and not them you might write. And
01 32          3739 3708  2476              1909 06
ὁ  ἄγγελος,  ὃν  εἶδον ἑστῶτα        ἐπὶ τῆς
the messenger, who I saw having stood on    the
2281      2532 1909 06 1093   142        08   5495
θαλάσσης καὶ ἐπὶ τῆς γῆς, ἦρεν  τὴν χεῖρα
sea       and on  the earth, lifted up the hand
846    08   1188   1519 04  3772      2532 3660
αὐτοῦ τὴν δεξιὰν εἰς τὸν οὐρανὸν 6 καὶ ὤμοσεν
of him the right into the heaven    and took an oath
1722 03    2198    1519 016  165    014    165      3739
ἐν  τῷ ζῶντι εἰς τοὺς αἰῶνας τῶν αἰώνων, ὃς
in  the living in  the ages   of the ages,  who
2936    04  3772     2532 024 1722 846  2532 08   1093
ἔκτισεν τὸν οὐρανὸν καὶ τὰ ἐν αὐτῷ καὶ τὴν γῆν
created the heaven  and the in it  and the earth
2532 024 1722 846  2532 08   2281      2532 024 1722
καὶ τὰ ἐν αὐτῇ καὶ τὴν θάλασσαν καὶ τὰ ἐν
and the in it  and the sea      and the in
846  3754 5550  3765        1510    235   1722 019
αὐτῇ, ὅτι χρόνος οὐκέτι ἔσται, 7 ἀλλ᾽ ἐν ταῖς
it,  that time no longer will be, but in  the
2250  06   5456 02      1442    32        3752
ἡμέραις τῆς φωνῆς τοῦ ἑβδόμου ἀγγέλου, ὅταν
days   of the sound of the seventh messenger, when
3195          4537       2532 5055         09
μέλλη       σαλπίζειν, καὶ ἐτελέσθη    τὸ
he might be about to trumpet, and  was completed the
3466    06    2316  5613 2097                016
μυστήριον τοῦ θεοῦ, ὡς εὐηγγέλισεν τοὺς
mystery of the God, as  he told good message the
1438      1401   016 4396       8 2532 05   5456
ἑαυτοῦ δούλους τοὺς προφήτας. Καὶ ἡ φωνὴ
of himself slaves the spokesmen. And the voice
3739 191   1537 02  3772     3825 2980      3326
ἣν ἤκουσα ἐκ  τοῦ οὐρανοῦ πάλιν λαλοῦσαν μετ᾽
which I heard from the heaven again speaking with
1473 2532 3004   5217   2983 012 975      012
ἐμοῦ καὶ λέγουσαν· ὕπαγε λάβε τὸ βιβλίον τὸ
me  and saying,   go off take the small book the
455           1722 07  5495 02  32       02  2476
ἠνεῳγμένον ἐν  τῇ χειρὶ τοῦ ἀγγέλου τοῦ ἑστῶτος
having been in the hand of  messenger the having
opened            the             one stood
1909 06   2281       2532 1909 06  1093    9 2532 565
ἐπὶ τῆς θαλάσσης καὶ ἐπὶ τῆς γῆς.   καὶ ἀπῆλθα
on  the sea       and on  the earth. And I went off
4314 04   32       3004    846   1325    1473 012
πρὸς τὸν ἄγγελον λέγων αὐτῷ δοῦναί μοι τὸ
to   the messenger saying to him to give to me the
974          2532 3004    1473   2983 2532 2719
βιβλαρίδιον. καὶ λέγει μοι·  λάβε καὶ κατάφαγε
little book. and  he says to me, take and eat up
846   2532 4087              1473  08  2836
αὐτό, καὶ πικρανεῖ        σου τὴν κοιλίαν,
it,   and it will make bitter of you the stomach,
235  1722 011 4750    1473  1510    1099 5613
ἀλλ᾽ ἐν τῷ στόματί σου ἔσται  γλυκὺ ὡς
but  in the mouth  of you it will be sweet as
3192   2532 2983   012 974         1537 06  5495
μέλι.  10 Καὶ ἔλαβον τὸ βιβλαρίδιον ἐκ τῆς χειρὸς
honey.   And I took the little book from the hand
02   32        2532 2719    846   2532 1510   1722
τοῦ ἀγγέλου καὶ κατέφαγον αὐτό, καὶ ἦν  ἐν
of the messenger and ate up  it,   and it was in
```

011   4750   1473   5613 3192 1099   2532 3753 2068
τῷ   στόματί μου ὡς   μέλι γλυκὺ καὶ ὅτε ἔφαγον
the   mouth   of me as   honey sweet and when I ate
846   4087   05   2836   1473   2532 3004
αὐτό, ἐπικράνθη   ἡ   κοιλία μου. **11** καὶ λέγουσίν
it,   was made bitter the stomach of me.   And they say
1473   1163   1473 3825 4395   1909
μοι· δεῖ   σε   πάλιν προφητεῦσαι   ἐπὶ
to me, it is necessary you again to speak before on
2992   2532 1484   2532 1100   2532 935
λαοῖς καὶ ἔθνεσιν καὶ γλώσσαις καὶ βασιλεῦσιν
peoples and nations and tongues   and kings
4183   2532 1325   1473 2563   3664
πολλοῖς. **11:1** Καὶ ἐδόθη   μοι κάλαμος ὅμοιος
many.   And was given to me reed   like
4464   3004   1453   2532 3354   04 3485   02
ῥάβδῳ, λέγων· ἔγειρε καὶ μέτρησον τὸν ναὸν τοῦ
rod,   saying, rise   and measure the temple of the
2316 2532 012 2379   2532 016 4352
θεοῦ καὶ τὸ θυσιαστήριον καὶ τοὺς προσκυνοῦντας
God and the sacrifice place and the ones worshiping
1722 846   2532 08 833   08 1855   02 3485
ἐν αὐτῷ. **2** καὶ τὴν αὐλὴν τὴν ἔξωθεν τοῦ ναοῦ
in it.   And the courtyard the outside the temple
1544   1855   2532 3361 846   3354
ἔκβαλε ἔξωθεν καὶ μὴ αὐτὴν μετρήσῃς,
throw out outside and not it   you might measure,
3754   1325   023   1484   2532 08 4172 08
ὅτι   ἐδόθη   τοῖς ἔθνεσιν, καὶ τὴν πόλιν τὴν
because it was given to the nations, and the city the
40   3961   3376 5062   2532 1417
ἁγίαν πατήσουσιν μῆνας τεσσεράκοντα [καὶ] δύο.
holy they will walk months forty   and two.
3 2532 1325   015   1417 3144   1473 2532
Καὶ δώσω   τοῖς δυσὶν μάρτυσίν μου καὶ
And I will give to the two testifiers of me and
4395   2250   5505   1250
προφητεύσουσιν ἡμέρας χιλίας διακοσίας
they will speak before days thousands two hundred
1835   4016   4526   **4** 3778 1510 017
ἑξήκοντα περιβεβλημένοι σάκκους. οὗτοί εἰσιν αἱ
sixty   having thrown sackcloths. These are the
            around themselves
1417 1636   2532 017 1417 3087   017 1799   02
δύο ἐλαῖαι καὶ αἱ δύο λυχνίαι αἱ ἐνώπιον τοῦ
two olives and the two lampstands the before the
2962 06   1093 2476   **5** 2532 1487 5100 846
κυρίου τῆς γῆς ἑστῶτες.   καὶ εἴ τις αὐτοὺς
Master of the earth having stood. And if some them
2309 91   4442 1607   1537 010 4750
θέλει ἀδικῆσαι πῦρ ἐκπορεύεται ἐκ τοῦ στόματος
wants to do unright fire travels out from the mouth
846   2532 2719   016 2190   846   2532 1487
αὐτῶν καὶ κατεσθίει τοὺς ἐχθροὺς αὐτῶν· καὶ εἴ
of them and eats up the hostile of them; and if
5100 2309   846   91   3779
τις θελήσῃ αὐτοὺς ἀδικῆσαι, οὕτως
some might want them to do unright, thusly
1163   846 615   **6** 3778 2192
δεῖ   αὐτὸν ἀποκτανθῆναι. οὗτοι ἔχουσιν
it is necessary him to be killed. These have
08 1849   2808   04 3772   2443 3361 5205
τὴν ἐξουσίαν κλεῖσαι τὸν οὐρανόν, ἵνα μὴ ὑετὸς
the authority to close the heaven, that not rain
1026   020 2250 06   4394
βρέχῃ   τὰς ἡμέρας τῆς προφητείας
it might rain the days of the speaking before
846   2532 1849   2192   1909 022 5204
αὐτῶν, καὶ ἐξουσίαν ἔχουσιν ἐπὶ τῶν ὑδάτων
of them, and authority they have on the waters

as honey in my mouth, but when I had eaten it, my stomach was made bitter.

11 Then they said to me, "You must prophesy again about many peoples and nations and languages and kings."

CHAPTER 11

Then I was given a measuring rod like a staff, and I was told, "Come and measure the temple of God and the altar and those who worship there, [2]but do not measure the court outside the temple; leave that out, for it is given over to the nations, and they will trample over the holy city for forty-two months. [3]And I will grant my two witnesses authority to prophesy for one thousand two hundred sixty days, wearing sackcloth."

[4]These are the two olive trees and the two lampstands that stand before the Lord of the earth. [5]And if anyone wants to harm them, fire pours from their mouth and consumes their foes; anyone who wants to harm them must be killed in this manner. [6]They have authority to shut the sky, so that no rain may fall during the days of their prophesying, and they have authority over the waters

REVELATION 11:7—11:12   Page 914

to turn them into blood, and to strike the earth with every kind of plague, as often as they desire.

7 When they have finished their testimony, the beast that comes up from the bottomless pit will make war on them and conquer them and kill them, ⁸and their dead bodies will lie in the street of the great city that is prophetically*a* called Sodom and Egypt, where also their Lord was crucified. ⁹For three and a half days members of the peoples and tribes and languages and nations will gaze at their dead bodies and refuse to let them be placed in a tomb; ¹⁰and the inhabitants of the earth will gloat over them and celebrate and exchange presents, because these two prophets had been a torment to the inhabitants of the earth.

11 But after the three and a half days, the breath*b* of life from God entered them, and they stood on their feet, and those who saw them were terrified. ¹²Then they*c* heard a loud voice from heaven saying to them, "Come up here!" And they went up to heaven in a cloud while their enemies watched them.

a Or *allegorically;* Gk *spiritually*
b Or *the spirit*
c Other ancient authorities read *I*

4762	846	1519	129	2532	3960	08	1093	1722
στρέφειν	αὐτὰ	εἰς	αἷμα	καὶ	πατάξαι	τὴν	γῆν	ἐν
to turn	them	into	blood	and	to hit	the	earth	in

3956 4127	3740		1437 2309		7	2532
πάσῃ πληγῇ	ὁσάκις	ἐὰν	θελήσωσιν.			Καὶ
all blow	as often as	if	they might want.			And

3752 5055		08 3141		846	09
ὅταν τελέσωσιν		τὴν μαρτυρίαν		αὐτῶν,	τὸ
when they might complete		the testimony		of them,	the

2342	09	305		1537 06	12
θηρίον	τὸ	ἀναβαῖνον	ἐκ	τῆς	ἀβύσσου
wild animal	the	one coming up	from	the	bottomless

4160	3326 846	4171	2532 3528		846
ποιήσει	μετ' αὐτῶν	πόλεμον	καὶ νικήσει		αὐτοὺς
will make	with them	war	and will conquer		them

2532 615	846	8	2532 09	4430	846	1909
καὶ ἀποκτενεῖ	αὐτούς.		καὶ τὸ	πτῶμα	αὐτῶν	ἐπὶ
and will kill	them.		And the	corpse	of them	on

06 4113	06	4172 06	3173	3748
τῆς πλατείας	τῆς	πόλεως τῆς	μεγάλης,	ἥτις
the wide place	of the	city the	great,	which

2564	4153	4670	2532 125		3699	2532
καλεῖται	πνευματικῶς	Σόδομα	καὶ Αἴγυπτος,		ὅπου	καὶ
is called	spiritually	Sodom	and Egypt,		where	also

01	2962	846	4717	9	2532 991
ὁ	κύριος	αὐτῶν	ἐσταυρώθη.		καὶ βλέπουσιν
the	Master	of them	was crucified.		And they see

1537 014 2992		2532 5443	2532 1100		2532 1484
ἐκ τῶν λαῶν		καὶ φυλῶν	καὶ γλωσσῶν		καὶ ἐθνῶν
from the peoples		and tribes	and tongues		and nations

012 4430	846	2250	5140 2532	2255	2532 024
τὸ πτῶμα	αὐτῶν	ἡμέρας	τρεῖς καὶ	ἥμισυ	καὶ τὰ
the corpse	of them	days	three and	half	and the

4430	846	3756 863		5087	1519
πτώματα	αὐτῶν	οὐκ ἀφίουσιν		τεθῆναι	εἰς
corpses	of them	not they allowed		to be set	into

3418	10	2532 013 2730		1909 06	1093
μνῆμα.		καὶ οἱ κατοικοῦντες		ἐπὶ τῆς	γῆς
grave.		And the ones residing		on the	earth

5463	1909 846	2532 2165		2532 1435
χαίρουσιν	ἐπ' αὐτοῖς	καὶ εὐφραίνονται		καὶ δῶρα
rejoice	over them	and are merry		and gifts

3992	240		3754	3778	013 1417
πέμψουσιν	ἀλλήλοις,		ὅτι	οὗτοι	οἱ δύο
they will send	to one another,		because	these	the two

4396	928	016 2730		1909 06
προφῆται	ἐβασάνισαν	τοὺς κατοικοῦντας		ἐπὶ τῆς
spokesmen	tormented	the ones residing		on the

1093	11	2532 3326	020 5140	2250	2532 2255	4151
γῆς.		Καὶ μετὰ	τὰς τρεῖς	ἡμέρας	καὶ ἥμισυ	πνεῦμα
earth.		And after	the three	days	and half	spirit

2222	1537 02	2316 1525		1722 846		2532
ζωῆς	ἐκ	τοῦ θεοῦ εἰσῆλθεν		ἐν αὐτοῖς,		καὶ
of life	from	the God went into		in them,		and

2476	1909 016	4228 846		2532 5401	3173
ἔστησαν	ἐπὶ τοὺς	πόδας αὐτῶν,		καὶ φόβος	μέγας
they stood	on the	feet of them,		and fear	great

1968	1909 016	2334		846	12	2532
ἐπέπεσεν	ἐπὶ τοὺς	θεωροῦντας		αὐτούς.		καὶ
fell	on on the	ones watching		them.		And

191	5456 3173	1537 02	3772	3004
ἤκουσαν	φωνῆς μεγάλης	ἐκ τοῦ	οὐρανοῦ	λεγούσης
they heard	voice great	from the	heaven	saying

846	305	5602	2532 305		1519 04
αὐτοῖς·	ἀνάβατε	ὧδε.	καὶ ἀνέβησαν		εἰς τὸν
to them,	come up	here.	And they went up		into the

3772	1722 07	3507	2532 2334		846	013
οὐρανὸν ἐν	τῇ	νεφέλῃ,	καὶ ἐθεώρησαν		αὐτοὺς	οἱ
heaven in	the	cloud,	and watched		them	the

2190	846	13	2532	1722	1565	07	5610	1096

ἐχθροὶ αὐτῶν. **13** Καὶ ἐν ἐκείνῃ τῇ ὥρᾳ ἐγένετο
hostile of them. And in that the hour became

4578	3173	2532 09	1182	06	4172	4098

σεισμὸς μέγας καὶ τὸ δέκατον τῆς πόλεως ἔπεσεν
shake great and the tenth of the city fell

2532 615	1722 03	4578	3686	444

καὶ ἀπεκτάνθησαν ἐν τῷ σεισμῷ ὀνόματα ἀνθρώπων
and were killed in the shake names of men

5505	2033	2532 013 3062	1719	1096

χιλιάδες ἑπτὰ καὶ οἱ λοιποὶ ἔμφοβοι ἐγένοντο
thousands seven and the remaining in fear became

2532 1325	1391	03	2316 02	3772

καὶ ἔδωκαν δόξαν τῷ θεῷ τοῦ οὐρανοῦ.
and they gave splendor to the God of the heaven.

05	3759 05	1208	565	2400 05	3759 05

14 Ἡ οὐαὶ ἡ δευτέρα ἀπῆλθεν· ἰδοὺ ἡ οὐαὶ ἡ
The woe the second went off; look the woe the

5154	2064	5036	15	2532 01	1442	32

τρίτη ἔρχεται ταχύ. **15** Καὶ ὁ ἕβδομος ἄγγελος
third comes quickly. And the seventh messenger

4537	2532 1096	5456	3173	1722 03	3772

ἐσάλπισεν· καὶ ἐγένοντο φωναὶ μεγάλαι ἐν τῷ οὐρανῷ
trumpeted; and became voices great in the heaven

3004	1096	05	932	02	2889	02

λέγοντες· ἐγένετο ἡ βασιλεία τοῦ κόσμου τοῦ
saying, became the kingdom of the world of the

2962	1473	2532 02	5547	846	2532

κυρίου ἡμῶν καὶ τοῦ χριστοῦ αὐτοῦ, καὶ
Master of us and the Christ of him, and

936	1519 016	165	014	165

βασιλεύσει εἰς τοὺς αἰῶνας τῶν αἰώνων.
he will be king into the ages of the ages.

16	2532 013	1501	5064	4245	013 1799

16 Καὶ οἱ εἴκοσι τέσσαρες πρεσβύτεροι [οἱ] ἐνώπιον
And the twenty four older men the before

02	2316 2521	1909 016	2362	846	4098

τοῦ θεοῦ καθήμενοι ἐπὶ τοὺς θρόνους αὐτῶν ἔπεσαν
the God sitting on the thrones of them fell

1909 024 4383	846	2532 4352	03 2316

ἐπὶ τὰ πρόσωπα αὐτῶν καὶ προσεκύνησαν τῷ θεῷ
on the faces of them and worshiped the God

17	3004	2168	1473	2962	01 2316

17 λέγοντες· εὐχαριστοῦμέν σοι, κύριε ὁ θεὸς
saying, we give good favor to you, Master the God

01	3841	01	1510	2532 01	1510

ὁ παντοκράτωρ, ὁ ὢν καὶ ὁ ἦν,
the all-strength, the one being and the one was,

3754	2983	08	1411	1473 08

ὅτι εἴληφας τὴν δύναμίν σου τὴν
because you have received the power of you the

3173	2532 936	18	2532 021	1484

μεγάλην καὶ ἐβασίλευσας. **18** καὶ τὰ ἔθνη
great and you were king. And the nations

3710	2532 2064	05 3709	1473	2532 01

ὠργίσθησαν, καὶ ἦλθεν ἡ ὀργή σου καὶ ὁ
were angry, and went the anger of you and the

2540	014	3498	2919	2532 1325	04

καιρὸς τῶν νεκρῶν κριθῆναι καὶ δοῦναι τὸν
season of the dead to be judged and to give the

3408	015	1401	1473	015	4396	2532 015

μισθὸν τοῖς δούλοις σου τοῖς προφήταις καὶ τοῖς
wage to the slaves of you the spokesmen and the

40	2532 015 5399	012 3686	1473

ἁγίοις καὶ τοῖς φοβουμένοις τὸ ὄνομά σου,
holy ones and the ones fearing the name of you,

016	3398	2532 016	3173	2532

τοὺς μικροὺς καὶ τοὺς μεγάλους, καὶ
the small and the great, and

13At that moment there was a great earthquake, and a tenth of the city fell; seven thousand people were killed in the earthquake, and the rest were terrified and gave glory to the God of heaven.

14 The second woe has passed. The third woe is coming very soon.

15 Then the seventh angel blew his trumpet, and there were loud voices in heaven, saying,
"The kingdom of the world has become the kingdom of our Lord and of his Messiah,[a] and he will reign forever and ever."

16 Then the twenty-four elders who sit on their thrones before God fell on their faces and worshiped God, 17singing,
"We give you thanks, Lord God Almighty, who are and who were, for you have taken your great power and begun to reign.

18 The nations raged, but your wrath has come, and the time for judging the dead, for rewarding your servants,[b] the prophets and saints and all who fear your name, both small and great,

[a] Gk Christ
[b] Gk slaves

and for destroying those who destroy the earth."

19 Then God's temple in heaven was opened, and the ark of his covenant was seen within his temple; and there were flashes of lightning, rumblings, peals of thunder, an earthquake, and heavy hail.

CHAPTER 12

A great portent appeared in heaven: a woman clothed with the sun, with the moon under her feet, and on her head a crown of twelve stars. [2]She was pregnant and was crying out in birth pangs, in the agony of giving birth. [3]Then another portent appeared in heaven: a great red dragon, with seven heads and ten horns, and seven diadems on his heads. [4]His tail swept down a third of the stars of heaven and threw them to the earth. Then the dragon stood before the woman who was about to bear a child, so that he might devour her child as soon as it was born. [5]And she gave birth to a son, a male child, who is to rule[a] all the nations with a rod of iron. But her child was snatched away and taken to God and to his throne; [6]and the woman fled into the wilderness, where she has a place

[a] Or to shepherd

```
1311                          016     1311
διαφθεῖραι            τοὺς διαφθείροντας
to corrupt thoroughly the   ones corrupting thoroughly
08   1093  19  2532  455      01   3485  02   2316 01
τὴν γῆν.  19  Καὶ ἠνοίγη  ὁ  ναὸς  τοῦ  θεοῦ ὁ
the earth.    And  was opened the temple of the God the
1722 03    3772      2532 3708     05  2787     06
ἐν  τῷ  οὐρανῷ καὶ  ὤφθη  ἡ  κιβωτὸς τῆς
in  the heaven and  was seen the box      of the
1242      846      1722 03  3485   846      2532 1096
διαθήκης αὐτοῦ ἐν  τῷ  ναῷ  αὐτοῦ, καὶ ἐγένοντο
agreement of him in  the temple of him, and  became
796       2532 5456    2532 1027     2532 4578    2532
ἀστραπαὶ καὶ  φωναὶ καὶ  βρονταὶ καὶ σεισμὸς καὶ
lightnings and  sounds and  thunders and shake    and
5464     3173       2532 4592     3173  3708    1722 03
χάλαζα μεγάλη.  12:1  Καὶ σημεῖον μέγα ὤφθη  ἐν  τῷ
hail   great.      And  sign     great was seen in  the
3772      1135    4016      04   2246   2532 05  4582
οὐρανῷ, γυνὴ περιβεβλημένη τὸν ἥλιον, καὶ ἡ  σελήνη
heaven,  woman having thrown the sun,   and  the moon
                  around herself
5270       014 4228   846      2532 1909 06  2776
ὑποκάτω τῶν ποδῶν αὐτῆς καὶ  ἐπὶ τῆς κεφαλῆς
underneath the feet  of her and  on  the head
846     4735      792        1427     2532 1722 1064
αὐτῆς στέφανος ἀστέρων δώδεκα, 2 καὶ ἐν  γαστρὶ
of her crown    of stars twelve,    and in  womb
2192    2532 2896     5605            2532
ἔχουσα, καὶ κράζει ὠδίνουσα        καὶ
having, and she shouts having birth pains and
928           5088      3  2532 3708    243
βασανιζομένη τεκεῖν.    καὶ ὤφθη  ἄλλο
being tormented to give birth.  And  was seen other
4592     1722 03  3772     2532 2400 1404   3173  4450
σημεῖον ἐν  τῷ  οὐρανῷ, καὶ ἰδοὺ δράκων μέγας πυρρὸς
sign   in  the heaven, and  look dragon great red
2192   2776      2033   2532 2768    1176 3532 1909 020
ἔχων κεφαλὰς ἑπτὰ καὶ κέρατα δέκα καὶ ἐπὶ τὰς
having heads seven and horns ten and on  the
2776      846     2033   1238        4  2532 05  3769 846
κεφαλὰς αὐτοῦ ἑπτὰ διαδήματα,  καὶ ἡ  οὐρὰ αὐτοῦ
heads   of him seven diadems,    and the tail of him
4951   012 5154   014    792      02      3772     2532
σύρει τὸ τρίτον τῶν ἀστέρων τοῦ  οὐρανοῦ καὶ
drags the third of the stars  of the heaven and
906      846      1519 08 1093    2532 01  1404    2476
ἔβαλεν αὐτοὺς εἰς τὴν γῆν. Καὶ ὁ  δράκων ἔστηκεν
threw  them   into the earth. And  the dragon stood
1799     06  1135     06   3195        5088
ἐνώπιον τῆς γυναικὸς τῆς μελλούσης τεκεῖν,
before  the woman    the being about to give birth,
2443 3752 5088              012 5043   846
ἵνα ὅταν τέκη            τὸ τέκνον αὐτῆς
that when she might give birth the child  of her
2719                 5  2532 5088      5207 730
καταφάγη.          καὶ ἔτεκεν  υἱὸν ἄρσεν,
might be eaten up.    And  she gave birth son male,
3739 3195     4165        3956  024 1484   1722 4464
ὃς  μέλλει ποιμαίνειν πάντα τὰ ἔθνη ἐν ῥάβδῳ
who is about to shepherd all  the nations in  rod
4603    2532 726     09  5043    846      4314 04
σιδηρᾷ. καὶ ἡρπάσθη τὸ τέκνον αὐτῆς πρὸς τὸν
iron.   And  was seized the child  of her to  the
2316  2532 4314 04  2983  846      6  2532 05  1135
θεὸν καὶ πρὸς τὸν θρόνον αὐτοῦ.  καὶ ἡ  γυνὴ
God  and to  the throne of him.  And  the woman
5343    1519 08 2048     3699  2192   1563 5117
ἔφυγεν εἰς τὴν ἔρημον, ὅπου ἔχει ἐκεῖ τόπον
fled   into the desert, where she has there place
```

2090		575	02	2316	2443	1563
ἡτοιμασμένον		ἀπὸ	τοῦ	θεοῦ,	ἵνα	ἐκεῖ
having been prepared		from	the	God,	that	there

5142		846	2250	5505		1250
τρέφωσιν		αὐτὴν	ἡμέρας	χιλίας		διακοσίας
they might feed		her	days	thousands		two hundred

1835		2532	1096	4171	1722 03	3772	01
ἐξήκοντα.	7	Καὶ	ἐγένετο	πόλεμος	ἐν τῷ	οὐρανῷ,	ὁ
sixty.		And	became	war	in the	heaven,	the

3413	2532	013	32		846	010 4170		3326
Μιχαὴλ	καὶ	οἱ	ἄγγελοι		αὐτοῦ	τοῦ πολεμῆσαι		μετὰ
Michael	and	the	messengers		of him	the to war		with

02	1404		2532	01	1404	4170		2532	013
τοῦ	δράκοντος.		καὶ	ὁ	δράκων	ἐπολέμησεν		καὶ	οἱ
the	dragon.		And	the	dragon	made war		and	the

32		846		2532 3756	2480		3761
ἄγγελοι		αὐτοῦ,	8	καὶ οὐκ	ἴσχυσεν		οὐδὲ
messengers		of him,		and not	he is strong		but not

5117	2147		846	2089	1722 03	3772		9	2532
τόπος	εὑρέθη		αὐτῶν	ἔτι	ἐν τῷ	οὐρανῷ.			καὶ
place	was found		of them	still	in the	heaven.			And

906		01	1404	01	3173	01	3789	01
ἐβλήθη		ὁ	δράκων ὁ	μέγας,	ὁ	ὄφις	ὁ
was thrown		the	dragon the	great,	the	snake	the

744		01	2564		1228		2532	01
ἀρχαῖος,		ὁ	καλούμενος		Διάβολος		καὶ	ὁ
ancient,		the	one being called		Slanderer		and	the

4567		01	4105		08	3625
Σατανᾶς,		ὁ	πλανῶν		τὴν	οἰκουμένην
Adversary,		the	one deceiving		the	inhabited world

3650	906		1519 08	1093	2532	013
ὅλην,	ἐβλήθη		εἰς τὴν	γῆν,	καὶ	οἱ
whole,	he was thrown		into the	earth,	and	the

32		846	3326	846	906		10	2532 191
ἄγγελοι		αὐτοῦ	μετ᾽	αὐτοῦ	ἐβλήθησαν.			καὶ ἤκουσα
messengers		of him	with	him	were thrown.			And I heard

5456	3173	1722 03	3772	3004		737	1096
φωνὴν	μεγάλην	ἐν τῷ	οὐρανῷ	λέγουσαν·		ἄρτι	ἐγένετο
voice	great	in the	heaven	saying,		now	became

05	4991		2532 05	1411		2532 05	932
ἡ	σωτηρία		καὶ ἡ	δύναμις		καὶ ἡ	βασιλεία
the	deliverance		and the	power		and the	kingdom

02		2316 1473	2532 05	1849		02	5547
τοῦ		θεοῦ ἡμῶν	καὶ ἡ	ἐξουσία		τοῦ	χριστοῦ
of the		God of us	and the	authority		of the	Christ

846		3754	906		01	2725a	014	80
αὐτοῦ,		ὅτι	ἐβλήθη		ὁ	κατήγωρ	τῶν	ἀδελφῶν
of him,		because	was thrown		the	accuser	of the	brothers

1473	01	2723		846	1799	02	2316 1473
ἡμῶν,	ὁ	κατηγορῶν		αὐτοὺς	ἐνώπιον	τοῦ	θεοῦ ἡμῶν
of us,	the	one accusing		them	before	the	God of us

2250	2532	3571		11	2532 846		3528	846
ἡμέρας	καὶ	νυκτός.			καὶ αὐτοὶ		ἐνίκησαν	αὐτὸν
day	and	night.			And themselves		conquered	him

1223	012	129	010	721	2532 1223	04	3056
διὰ	τὸ	αἷμα	τοῦ	ἀρνίου	καὶ διὰ	τὸν	λόγον
through	the	blood	of the	lamb	and through	the	word

06	3141		846		2532 3756 25		08
τῆς	μαρτυρίας		αὐτῶν		καὶ οὐκ ἠγάπησαν		τὴν
of the	testimony		of them		and not they loved		the

5590	846		891	2288		12	1223	3778
ψυχὴν	αὐτῶν		ἄχρι	θανάτου.			διὰ	τοῦτο
soul	of them		until	death.			Through	this

2165		013 3772		2532 013	1722	846
εὐφραίνεσθε,		[οἱ] οὐρανοὶ		καὶ οἱ	ἐν	αὐτοῖς
be merry,		the heavens		and the	in	them

4637		3759 08	1093	2532 08	2281		3754
σκηνοῦντες.		οὐαὶ τὴν	γῆν	καὶ τὴν	θάλασσαν,		ὅτι
ones tenting.		Woe the	earth	and the	sea,		because

prepared by God, so that
there she can be nourished
for one thousand two
hundred sixty days.

7 And war broke out in
heaven; Michael and his
angels fought against the
dragon. The dragon and
his angels fought back,
[8]but they were defeated,
and there was no longer
any place for them in
heaven. [9]The great dragon
was thrown down, that
ancient serpent, who is
called the Devil and Satan,
the deceiver of the whole
world—he was thrown
down to the earth, and his
angels were thrown down
with him.

10 Then I heard a loud
voice in heaven, proclaiming,
  "Now have come the
    salvation and the
    power
  and the kingdom of our
    God
  and the authority of his
    Messiah,[a]
for the accuser of our
  comrades[b] has been
  thrown down,
  who accuses them day
  and night before our
  God.
[11] But they have conquered
  him by the blood of
  the Lamb
  and by the word of their
  testimony,
for they did not cling
  to life even in the face
  of death.
[12] Rejoice then, you heavens
  and those who dwell in
  them!
  But woe to the earth and
  the sea,

a Gk *Christ*
b Gk *brothers*

for the devil has come
down to you
with great wrath,
because he knows that
his time is short!"
13 So when the dragon
saw that he had been
thrown down to the earth,
he pursued[a] the woman
who had given birth to the
male child. [14]But the
woman was given the two
wings of the great eagle, so
that she could fly from the
serpent into the wilderness,
to her place where she is
nourished for a time, and
times, and half a time.
[15]Then from his mouth the
serpent poured water like a
river after the woman, to
sweep her away with the
flood. [16]But the earth came
to the help of the woman; it
opened its mouth and
swallowed the river that the
dragon had poured from his
mouth. [17]Then the dragon
was angry with the woman,
and went off to make war
on the rest of her children,
those who keep the
commandments of God and
hold the testimony of Jesus.
18 Then the dragon[b]
took his stand on the sand
of the seashore. [13:1]And I
saw a beast rising out of the
sea, having ten horns and
seven heads; and on its
horns were ten diadems,
and on its heads were
blasphemous names. [2]And
the beast that I saw was

[a] Or persecuted
[b] Gk Then he; other ancient
authorities read Then I stood

```
2597        01   1228        4314 1473 2192    2372   3173
κατέβη      ὁ   διάβολος    πρὸς ὑμᾶς ἔχων   θυμὸν μέγαν,
went down   the  slanderer   to   you  having  fury  great,

3609a          3754 3641      2540   2192        2532 3753
εἰδὼς          ὅτι ὀλίγον καιρὸν ἔχει.      13 Καὶ ὅτε
having known   that little season he has.      And when

3708   01   1404     3754 906              1519 08  1093
εἶδεν ὁ  δράκων ὅτι ἐβλήθη        εἰς τὴν γῆν,
saw    the  dragon that he was thrown into the earth,

1377       08   1135      3748 5088        04  730
ἐδίωξεν  τὴν γυναῖκα ἥτις ἔτεκεν    τὸν ἄρσενα.
he pursued the woman    who gave birth the male.

   2532 1325     07        1135   017 1417 4420
14 καὶ ἐδόθησαν τῇ     γυναικὶ αἱ δύο πτέρυγες
   And were given to the woman   the two wings

02      105    02  3173       2443 4072            1519 08
τοῦ   ἀετοῦ τοῦ μεγάλου, ἵνα πέτηται          εἰς τὴν
of the eagle the great,    that she might fly into the

2048     1519 04  5117 846      3699 5142        1563
ἔρημον εἰς τὸν τόπον αὐτῆς, ὅπου τρέφεται ἐκεῖ
desert into the place of her, where she is fed there

2540    2532 2540    2532 2255    2540  575  4383
καιρὸν καὶ καιροὺς καὶ ἥμισυ καιροῦ ἀπὸ προσώπου
season and seasons and half season from face

02    3789      15 2532 906     01  3789  1537 010
τοῦ ὄφεως.      15 καὶ ἔβαλεν ὁ ὄφις ἐκ τοῦ
of the snake.       And threw the snake from the

4750   846    3694  06  1135    5204 5613 4215
στόματος αὐτοῦ ὀπίσω τῆς γυναικὸς ὕδωρ ὡς ποταμόν,
mouth   of him after the woman    water as river,

2443 846    4216             4160        16 2532
ἵνα αὐτὴν ποταμοφόρητον    ποιήσῃ.      16 καὶ
that her carried away by river he might make. And

997        05 1093  07 1135    2532 455    05 1093
ἐβοήθησεν ἡ γῆ τῇ γυναικὶ καὶ ἤνοιξεν ἡ γῆ
helped    the earth the woman and opened the earth

012 4750    846    2532 2666        04 4215       3739
τὸ στόμα αὐτῆς καὶ κατέπιεν    τὸν ποταμὸν ὃν
the mouth of it and swallowed down the river which

906    01  1404    1537 010 4750      846        17 2532
ἔβαλεν ὁ δράκων ἐκ τοῦ στόματος αὐτοῦ.    17 καὶ
threw the dragon from the mouth   of him.     And

3710      01  1404    1909 07 1135    2532 565
ὠργίσθη ὁ δράκων ἐπὶ τῇ γυναικὶ καὶ ἀπῆλθεν
was angry the dragon on the woman and he went off

4160     4171     3326 014 3062    010     4690
ποιῆσαι πόλεμον μετὰ τῶν λοιπῶν τοῦ σπέρματος
to make war     with the remaining of the seed

846    014 5083     020 1785    02       2316 2532
αὐτῆς τῶν τηρούντων τὰς ἐντολὰς τοῦ θεοῦ καὶ
of her the ones keeping the commands of the God and

2192    08 3141      2424     18 2532 2476      1909
ἐχόντων τὴν μαρτυρίαν Ἰησοῦ. 18 Καὶ ἐστάθη   ἐπὶ
having the testimony of Jesus. And he was stood on

08 285     06    2281          2532 3708 1537 06
τὴν ἄμμον τῆς θαλάσσης. 13:1 Καὶ εἶδον ἐκ τῆς
the sand of the sea.        And I saw from the

2281     2342     305         2192  2768  1176
θαλάσσης θηρίον ἀναβαῖνον, ἔχον κέρατα δέκα
sea     wild animal coming up, having horns ten

2532 2776   2033    2532 1909 022 2768   846    1176
καὶ κεφαλὰς ἑπτὰ καὶ ἐπὶ τῶν κεράτων αὐτοῦ δέκα
and heads seven and on the horns of him ten

1238        2532 1909 020 2776    846    3686
διαδήματα καὶ ἐπὶ τὰς κεφαλὰς αὐτοῦ ὀνόμα[τα]
diadems   and on the heads of him names

988        2 2532 09 2342     3739 3708 1510
βλασφημίας. 2 καὶ τὸ θηρίον ὃ εἶδον ἦν
of insult.    And the wild animal that I saw was
```

```
3664      3917        2532 013 4228  846      5613 715   2532
ὅμοιον παρδάλει καὶ  οἱ πόδες αὐτοῦ ὡς  ἄρκου καὶ
like    leopard  and the feet   of him as  bear  and
09  4750   846    5613 4750 3023      2532 1325    846
τὸ στόμα αὐτοῦ ὡς  στόμα λέοντος. καὶ ἔδωκεν αὐτῷ
the mouth of him as  mouth of lion.  And gave   to him
01  1404    08  1411     846    2532 04  2362    846
ὁ  δράκων τὴν δύναμιν αὐτοῦ καὶ τὸν θρόνον αὐτοῦ
the dragon the power   of him and the throne of him
2532 1849       3173        2532 1520 1537 018 2776
καὶ ἐξουσίαν μεγάλην.  3 καὶ μίαν ἐκ  τῶν κεφαλῶν
and authority great.      And one  from the heads
846    5613 4969        1519 2288     2532 05  4127
αὐτοῦ ὡς  ἐσφαγμένην εἰς θάνατον, καὶ ἡ  πληγὴ
of him as  having been  in death,    and the blow
            slaughtered
02      2288     846    2323        2532 2296    3650
τοῦ  θανάτου αὐτοῦ ἐθεραπεύθη. Καὶ ἐθαυμάσθη ὅλη
of the death   of him was healed. And  marveled   whole
05  1093   3694    010 2342     4  2532 4352         03
ἡ  γῆ  ὀπίσω τοῦ θηρίου    καὶ προσεκύνησαν τῷ
the earth after the wild animal and worshiped     the
1404     3754     1325   08  1849       011
δράκοντι, ὅτι    ἔδωκεν τὴν ἐξουσίαν τῷ
dragon,   because he gave the authority to the
2342       2532 4352        011 2342
θηρίῳ,    καὶ προσεκύνησαν τῷ θηρίῳ
wild animal, and they worshiped the wild animal
3004       5101 3664   011     2342       2532 5101
λέγοντες· τίς ὅμοιος τῷ     θηρίῳ    καὶ τίς
saying,    who like   to the wild animal and who
1410      4170       3326 846   5 2532 1325        846
δύναται πολεμῆσαι μετ' αὐτοῦ; Καὶ ἐδόθη    αὐτῷ
is able to war      with him?   And was given to him
4750   2980       3173     2532 988      2532 1325
στόμα λαλοῦν  μεγάλα καὶ βλασφημίας καὶ ἐδόθη
mouth speaking great  and  insults     and was given
846   1849      4160    3376 5062           2532 1417
αὐτῷ ἐξουσία ποιῆσαι μῆνας τεσσεράκοντα [καὶ] δύο.
to him authority to make months forty         and two.
6 2532 455       012 4750  846    1519 988        4314
καὶ ἤνοιξεν τὸ στόμα αὐτοῦ εἰς βλασφημίας πρὸς
  And opened  the mouth of him into insults     to
04  2316 987          012 3686 846      2532 08  4633
τὸν θεὸν βλασφημῆσαι τὸ ὄνομα αὐτοῦ καὶ τὴν σκηνὴν
the God to insult    the name   of him and the tent
846    016  1722 03  3772    4637        7 2532
αὐτοῦ, τοὺς ἐν τῷ οὐρανῷ σκηνοῦντας.  καὶ
of him, the in  the heaven ones tenting. And
1325      846   4160    4171    3326 014 40
ἐδόθη    αὐτῷ ποιῆσαι πόλεμον μετὰ τῶν ἁγίων
it was given to him to make war   with the holy ones
2532 3528      846     2532 1325    846      1849
καὶ νικῆσαι αὐτούς, καὶ ἐδόθη    αὐτῷ ἐξουσία
and to conquer them,  and was given to him authority
1909 3956   5443    2532 2992   2532 1100    2532 1484
ἐπὶ πᾶσαν φυλὴν καὶ λαὸν  καὶ γλῶσσαν καὶ ἔθνος.
over all   tribe and people and tongue   and nation.
8 2532 4352          846   3956  013 2730
καὶ προσκυνήσουσιν αὐτὸν πάντες οἱ  κατοικοῦντες
  And will worship  him    all    the ones residing
1909 06  1093   3739    3756 1125        09  3686
ἐπὶ τῆς γῆς,  οὗ  οὐ  γέγραπται  τὸ ὄνομα
on  the earth, whose not has been written the name
846    1722 011  975   06      2222 010    721
αὐτοῦ ἐν τῷ βιβλίῳ  τῆς  ζωῆς τοῦ ἀρνίου
of him in  the small book of the life of the lamb
```

like a leopard, its feet were like a bear's, and its mouth was like a lion's mouth. And the dragon gave it his power and his throne and great authority. [3]One of its heads seemed to have received a death-blow, but its mortal wound[a] had been healed. In amazement the whole earth followed the beast. [4]They worshiped the dragon, for he had given his authority to the beast, and they worshiped the beast, saying, "Who is like the beast, and who can fight against it?"

5 The beast was given a mouth uttering haughty and blasphemous words, and it was allowed to exercise authority for forty-two months. [6]It opened its mouth to utter blasphemies against God, blaspheming his name and his dwelling, that is, those who dwell in heaven. [7]Also it was allowed to make war on the saints and to conquer them.[b] It was given authority over every tribe and people and language and nation, [8]and all the inhabitants of the earth will worship it, everyone whose name has not been written from the foundation of the world in the book of life of the Lamb that was slaughtered.[c]

[a] Gk the plague of its death
[b] Other ancient authorities lack this sentence
[c] Or written in the book of life of the Lamb that was slaughtered from the foundation of the world

9 Let anyone who has an ear listen:
[10] If you are to be taken captive,
  into captivity you go;
  if you kill with the sword,
  with the sword you must be killed.
Here is a call for the endurance and faith of the saints.

11 Then I saw another beast that rose out of the earth; it had two horns like a lamb and it spoke like a dragon. [12] It exercises all the authority of the first beast on its behalf, and it makes the earth and its inhabitants worship the first beast, whose mortal wound[a] had been healed. [13] It performs great signs, even making fire come down from heaven to earth in the sight of all; [14] and by the signs that it is allowed to perform on behalf of the beast, it deceives the inhabitants of earth, telling them to make an image for the beast that had been wounded by the sword[b] and yet lived; [15] and it was allowed to give breath[c] to the image of the beast so that the image of the beast could even speak and cause those who would not

a Gk whose plague of its death
b Or that had received the plague of the sword
c Or spirit

---

010 4969   575   2602   2889   **9** 1487 5100
τοῦ ἐσφαγμένου   ἀπὸ καταβολῆς κόσμου.   Εἴ τις
the one having been from foundation of world.   If some
slaughtered

2192 3775 191   **10** 1487 5100 1519 161
ἔχει οὖς ἀκουσάτω.   εἴ τις εἰς αἰχμαλωσίαν,
has ear let hear.   If   some into captivity,

1519 161   5217   1487 5100 1722 3162
εἰς αἰχμαλωσίαν ὑπάγει·   εἴ τις ἐν μαχαίρῃ
into captivity he goes off; if some in sword

615   846   1722 3162   615   5602
ἀποκτανθῆναι αὐτὸν ἐν μαχαίρῃ ἀποκτανθῆναι. Ὧδέ
to be killed him in sword to be killed. Here

1510 05 5281   2532 05 4102 014   40
ἐστιν ἡ ὑπομονὴ καὶ ἡ πίστις τῶν ἁγίων.
is the patience and the trust of the holy ones.

11 2532 3708 243   2342   305   1537 06
Καὶ εἶδον ἄλλο θηρίον ἀναβαῖνον ἐκ τῆς
And I saw other wild animal coming up from the

1093   2532 2192   2768   1417 3664   721   2532
γῆς, καὶ εἶχεν κέρατα δύο ὅμοια ἀρνίῳ καὶ
earth, and he had horns two like lamb and

2980   5613 1404   **12** 2532 08 1849
ἐλάλει ὡς δράκων.   καὶ τὴν ἐξουσίαν
he was speaking as dragon.   And the authority

010   4413   2342   3956 4160   1799   846
τοῦ πρώτου θηρίου πᾶσαν ποιεῖ ἐνώπιον αὐτοῦ,
of the first wild animal all he does before him,

2532 4160   08 1093 2532 016 1722 846   2730
καὶ ποιεῖ τὴν γῆν καὶ τοὺς ἐν αὐτῇ κατοικοῦντας
and he makes the earth and the in it ones residing

2443 4352   012 2342   012 4413
ἵνα προσκυνήσουσιν τὸ θηρίον τὸ πρῶτον,
that they will worship the wild animal the first,

3739 2323   05 4127 02   2288   846
οὗ ἐθεραπεύθη ἡ πληγὴ τοῦ θανάτου αὐτοῦ.
whose was healed the blow of the death of him.

13 2532 4160   4592 3173   2443 2532 4442
καὶ ποιεῖ σημεῖα μεγάλα, ἵνα καὶ πῦρ
And he does signs great, that even fire

4160   1537 02 3772   2597   1519 08
ποιῇ ἐκ τοῦ οὐρανοῦ καταβαίνειν εἰς τὴν
he might make from the heaven to come down into the

1093 1799   014 444   2532 4105   016
γῆν ἐνώπιον τῶν ἀνθρώπων, **14** καὶ πλανᾷ τοὺς
earth before the men,   and he deceives the

2730   1909 06 1093 1223   024 4592 3739
κατοικοῦντας ἐπὶ τῆς γῆς διὰ τὰ σημεῖα ἃ
ones residing on the earth through the signs which

1325   846   4160 1799   010 2342
ἐδόθη αὐτῷ ποιῆσαι ἐνώπιον τοῦ θηρίου,
were given to him to do before the wild animal,

3004   015   2730   1909 06 1093 4160
λέγων τοῖς κατοικοῦσιν ἐπὶ τῆς γῆς ποιῆσαι
saying to the ones residing on the earth to make

1504   011   2342   3739 2192 08 4127   06
εἰκόνα τῷ θηρίῳ, ὃς ἔχει τὴν πληγὴν τῆς
image to the wild animal, who has the blow of the

3162   2532 2198   **15** 2532 1325   846
μαχαίρης καὶ ἔζησεν.   Καὶ ἐδόθη αὐτῷ
sword and he lived. And it was given to him

1325   4151 07   1504 010   2342   2443
δοῦναι πνεῦμα τῇ εἰκόνι τοῦ θηρίου, ἵνα
to give spirit to the image of the wild animal, that

2532 2980   05 1504 010   2342   2532
καὶ λαλήσῃ ἡ εἰκὼν τοῦ θηρίου καὶ
also might speak the image of the wild animal and

4160   2443 3745   1437 3361
ποιήσῃ [ἵνα] ὅσοι ἐὰν μὴ
he might make that as many as if not

4352   07   1504   010   2342
προσκυνήσωσιν   τῇ εἰκόνι τοῦ θηρίου
they might worship the image   of the wild animal

615   2532 4160   3956   016   3398
ἀποκτανθῶσιν. **16** καὶ ποιεῖ πάντας, τοὺς μικροὺς
might be killed. And he does all,   the   small

2532 016   3173   2532 016   4145   2532 016
καὶ τοὺς μεγάλους, καὶ τοὺς πλουσίους καὶ τοὺς
and the great,   and the rich   and the

4434   2532 016   1658   2532 016   1401   2443
πτωχούς, καὶ τοὺς ἐλευθέρους καὶ τοὺς δούλους, ἵνα
poor,   and the free   and the slaves,   that

1325   846   5480   1909 06   5495   846
δῶσιν   αὐτοῖς χάραγμα ἐπὶ τῆς χειρὸς αὐτῶν
they might give to them mark   on the hand   of them

06   1188   2228 1909 012 3359   846   **17** 2532 2443
τῆς δεξιᾶς ἢ ἐπὶ τὸ μέτωπον αὐτῶν   καὶ ἵνα
the right   or on the forehead of them   and that

3361 5100 1410   59   2228 4453   1487 3361
μή τις δύνηται   ἀγοράσαι ἢ πωλῆσαι εἰ μὴ
not some might be able to buy   or to sell except

01   2192   012 5480   012 3686 010
ὁ ἔχων   τὸ χάραγμα τὸ ὄνομα τοῦ
the one having the mark   the name of the

2342   2228 04   706   010   3686   846
θηρίου   ἢ τὸν ἀριθμὸν τοῦ ὀνόματος αὐτοῦ.
wild animal or   the number of the name   of him.

18 5602 05 4678   1510   01   2192   3563
    ῟Ωδε ἡ σοφία ἐστίν. ὁ ἔχων   νοῦν
    Here the wisdom is.   The one having mind

5585   04   706   010   2342   706
ψηφισάτω   τὸν ἀριθμὸν τοῦ θηρίου,   ἀριθμὸς
let calculate the number of the wild animal, number

1063 444   1510   2532 01   706   846
γὰρ ἀνθρώπου ἐστίν, καὶ ὁ ἀριθμὸς αὐτοῦ
for of man   it is, and the number of him

1812   1835   1803   **14:1** 2532 3708   2532 2400
ἑξακόσιοι ἑξήκοντα ἕξ.   Καὶ εἶδον, καὶ ἰδοὺ
six hundred sixty   six.   And I saw, and look

09   721   2476   1909 012 3735 4622 2532 3326
τὸ ἀρνίον ἑστὸς   ἐπὶ τὸ ὄρος Σιὼν καὶ μετ'
the lamb having stood on the hill Sion and with

846   1540   5062   5064   5505   2192
αὐτοῦ ἑκατὸν τεσσεράκοντα τέσσαρες χιλιάδες ἔχουσαι
him   hundred forty   four   thousands having

012 3686   846   2532 012 3686   02   3962   846
τὸ ὄνομα αὐτοῦ καὶ τὸ ὄνομα τοῦ   πατρὸς αὐτοῦ
the name of him and the name of the father of him

1125   1909 022 3359   846   **2** 2532
γεγραμμένον   ἐπὶ τῶν μετώπων αὐτῶν.   καὶ
having been written on the foreheads of them. And

191   5456   1537 02 3772   5613 5456   5204
ἤκουσα φωνὴν ἐκ τοῦ οὐρανοῦ ὡς φωνὴν ὑδάτων
I heard sound from the heaven as   sound of waters

4183   2532 5613 5456 1027   3173   2532 05
πολλῶν καὶ ὡς φωνὴ βροντῆς μεγάλης, καὶ ἡ
many   and as sound of thunder great,   and the

5456   3739 191   5613 2790   2789   1722
φωνὴ ἦν ἤκουσα ὡς κιθαρῳδῶν κιθαριζόντων ἐν
sound which I heard as harpists   playing harps in

019   2788   846   **3** 2532 103   5613 2790 2537
ταῖς κιθάραις αὐτῶν.   καὶ ᾄδουσιν [ὡς] ᾠδὴν καινὴν
the harps   of them.   And they sing as   song new

1799   02   2362   2532 1799   022 5064   2226
ἐνώπιον τοῦ θρόνου καὶ ἐνώπιον τῶν τεσσάρων ζῴων
before   the throne and before   the four   living ones

2532 014 4245   2532 3762   1410
καὶ τῶν πρεσβυτέρων, καὶ οὐδεὶς ἐδύνατο
and the older men,   and no one was being able

worship the image of the
beast to be killed. [16]Also it
causes all, both small and
great, both rich and poor,
both free and slave, to be
marked on the right hand
or the forehead, [17]so that
no one can buy or sell who
does not have the mark,
that is, the name of the
beast or the number of its
name. [18]This calls for
wisdom: let anyone with
understanding calculate
the number of the beast,
for it is the number of a
person. Its number is six
hundred sixty-six.[a]

CHAPTER 14

Then I looked, and there
was the Lamb, standing
on Mount Zion! And with
him were one hundred
forty-four thousand who
had his name and his
Father's name written on
their foreheads. [2]And I
heard a voice from heaven
like the sound of many
waters and like the sound
of loud thunder; the voice
I heard was like the sound
of harpists playing on their
harps, [3]and they sing a
new song before the throne
and before the four living
creatures and before the
elders. No one could

[a] Other ancient authorities read *six
hundred sixteen*

learn that song except the one hundred forty-four thousand who have been redeemed from the earth. [4]It is these who have not defiled themselves with women, for they are virgins; these follow the Lamb wherever he goes. They have been redeemed from humankind as first fruits for God and the Lamb, [5]and in their mouth no lie was found; they are blameless.

[6]Then I saw another angel flying in midheaven, with an eternal gospel to proclaim to those who live[a] on the earth—to every nation and tribe and language and people. [7]He said in a loud voice, "Fear God and give him glory, for the hour of his judgment has come; and worship him who made heaven and earth, the sea and the springs of water."

[8]Then another angel, a second, followed, saying, "Fallen, fallen is Babylon the great! She has made all nations drink of the wine of the wrath of her fornication."

[9]Then another angel, a third, followed them, crying with a loud voice, "Those who worship the beast and its image, and receive a mark on their foreheads

[a] Gk sit

3129   08   5603 1487 3361 017 1540   5062
μαθεῖν   τὴν   ᾠδὴν   εἰ   μὴ   αἱ   ἑκατὸν   τεσσεράκοντα
to learn the   song   except the hundred forty
5064   5505   013   59   575
τέσσαρες χιλιάδες, οἱ   ἠγορασμένοι   ἀπὸ
four   thousands, the ones having been bought from
06   1093   4 3778 1510   013   3326 1135   3756
τῆς γῆς.   οὗτοί εἰσιν οἱ   μετὰ γυναικῶν οὐκ
the earth.   These are   the ones with women   not
3435   3933   1063 1510   3778 013
ἐμολύνθησαν, παρθένοι γάρ εἰσιν,   οὗτοι οἱ
were stained, virgins   for they are, these the ones
190   011 721   3699 302 5217
ἀκολουθοῦντες τῷ ἀρνίῳ ὅπου ἂν ὑπάγῃ.
following   the lamb where - he might go off.
3778 59   575   014 444   536
οὗτοι ἠγοράσθησαν ἀπὸ τῶν ἀνθρώπων ἀπαρχὴ
These were bought from the men   from beginning
03   2316 2532 011   721   5 2532 1722 011 4750
τῷ   θεῷ καὶ τῷ   ἀρνίῳ,   καὶ ἐν τῷ στόματι
to the God and to the lamb,   and in the mouth
846   3756 2147   5579   299   1510
αὐτῶν οὐχ εὑρέθη ψεῦδος, ἄμωμοί εἰσιν.
of them not was found lie,   blameless they are,
6 2532 3708 243 32   4072   1722
Καὶ εἶδον ἄλλον ἄγγελον πετόμενον ἐν
and I saw other messenger flying   in
3321   2192   2098   166
μεσουρανήματι, ἔχοντα εὐαγγέλιον αἰώνιον
middle heaven, having good message eternal
2097   1909 016 2521   1909 06
εὐαγγελίσαι   ἐπὶ τοὺς καθημένους ἐπὶ τῆς
to tell good message to the ones sitting on the
1093   2532 1909 3956 1484   2532 5443 2532 1100
γῆς καὶ ἐπὶ πᾶν ἔθνος καὶ φυλὴν καὶ γλῶσσαν
earth and on all nation and tribe and tongue
2532 2992 7 3004 1722 5456 3173   5399   04
καὶ λαόν,   λέγων ἐν φωνῇ μεγάλῃ· φοβήθητε τὸν
and people, saying in voice great, fear   the
2316 2532 1325 846   1391   3754   2064 05 5610
θεὸν καὶ δότε αὐτῷ δόξαν,   ὅτι   ἦλθεν ἡ ὥρα
God and give to him splendor, because came the hour
06   2920   846   2532 4352   03
τῆς   κρίσεως αὐτοῦ, καὶ προσκυνήσατε τῷ
of the judgment of him, and worship   the one
4160   04 3772   2532 08 1093 2532 2281
ποιήσαντι τὸν οὐρανὸν καὶ τὴν γῆν καὶ θάλασσαν
having made the heaven and the earth and sea
2532 4077   5204   2532 243 32   1208
καὶ πηγὰς ὑδάτων. 8 Καὶ ἄλλος ἄγγελος δεύτερος
and springs of waters. And other messenger second
190   3004   4098 4098   897   05 3173
ἠκολούθησεν λέγων· ἔπεσεν ἔπεσεν Βαβυλὼν ἡ μεγάλη
followed   saying, fell   fell   Babylon the great
3739 1537 02 3631 02 2372 06   4202   846
ἣ   ἐκ τοῦ οἴνου τοῦ θυμοῦ τῆς πορνείας αὐτῆς
which from the wine of fury of the sexual of her
                                          the immorality
4222   3956 024 1484 9 2532 243 32
πεπότικεν πάντα τὰ ἔθνη. Καὶ ἄλλος ἄγγελος
have drank all the nations. And other messenger
5154 190   846   3004   1722 5456 3173
τρίτος ἠκολούθησεν αὐτοῖς λέγων ἐν φωνῇ μεγάλῃ·
third followed   them   saying in voice great:
1487 5100 4352   012 2342   2532 08 1504
εἴ τις προσκυνεῖ τὸ θηρίον   καὶ τὴν εἰκόνα
if some worships the wild animal and the image
846   2532 2983   5480   1909 010 3359   846
αὐτοῦ καὶ λαμβάνει χάραγμα ἐπὶ τοῦ μετώπου αὐτοῦ
of him and receives mark   on the forehead of him

```
2228 1909 08   5495  846      10  2532 846        4095
ἢ    ἐπὶ  τὴν χεῖρα αὐτοῦ,      καὶ αὐτὸς  πίεται
or   on  the hand  of him,      also himself will drink
1537 02  3631 02       2372 02      2316 02
ἐκ   τοῦ οἴνου τοῦ   θυμοῦ τοῦ   θεοῦ τοῦ
from the wine of the fury  of the God  the one
2767              194      1722 011 4221    06
κεκερασμένου     ἀκράτου  ἐν  τῷ  ποτηρίῳ τῆς
having been mixed undiluted in  the cup     of the
3709 846   2532 928              1722 4442 2532
ὀργῆς αὐτοῦ καὶ βασανισθήσεται   ἐν  πυρὶ καὶ
anger of him and he will be tormented in fire and
2303  1799    32    40    2532 1799   010
θείῳ  ἐνώπιον ἀγγέλων ἁγίων καὶ ἐνώπιον τοῦ
sulphur before messengers holy and before the
721     11  2532 01  2586    02    929       846
ἀρνίου.     καὶ  ὁ  καπνὸς τοῦ  βασανισμοῦ αὐτῶν
lamb.       And the smoke of the torment   of them
1519 165   165   305        2532 3756 2192
εἰς  αἰῶνας αἰώνων ἀναβαίνει, καὶ  οὐκ  ἔχουσιν
into ages  of ages goes up,  and not they have
372        2250   2532 3571  013 4352       012
ἀνάπαυσιν ἡμέρας καὶ νυκτὸς οἱ προσκυνοῦντες τὸ
rest       day   and night the ones worshiping the
2342      2532 08 1504   846    2532 1487 5100
θηρίον    καὶ τὴν εἰκόνα αὐτοῦ καὶ εἴ   τις
wild animal and the image of him and if some
2983    012 5480   010    3686     846     12  5602
λαμβάνει τὸ χάραγμα τοῦ  ὀνόματος αὐτοῦ.      Ὧδε
receives the mark  of the name   of him.      Here
05 5281    014  40    1510   013 5083
ἡ  ὑπομονὴ τῶν ἁγίων ἐστίν, οἱ τηροῦντες
the patience of the holy ones is,  the ones keeping
020 1785   02   2316 2532 08 4102    2424
τὰς ἐντολὰς τοῦ θεοῦ καὶ τὴν πίστιν Ἰησοῦ.
the commands of the God and the trust of Jesus.
    13  2532 191    5456 1537 02 3772   3004
        Καὶ ἤκουσα φωνῆς ἐκ  τοῦ οὐρανοῦ λεγούσης·
        And I heard voice from the heaven  saying,
1125   3107    013 3498   013 1722 2962
γράψον· μακάριοι οἱ νεκροὶ οἱ ἐν  κυρίῳ
write;  fortunate the dead the in Master
599              575  737    3483 3004  09  4151     2443
ἀποθνήσκοντες ἀπ᾽ ἄρτι. ναί, λέγει τὸ πνεῦμα, ἵνα
ones dying    from now. Yes, says the spirit, that
373           1537 014 2873   846         021 1063
ἀναπαήσονται  ἐκ  τῶν κόπων αὐτῶν, τὰ γὰρ
they will be rested from the labors of them, the for
2041 846   190       3326 846    14  2532 3708
ἔργα αὐτῶν ἀκολουθεῖ μετ᾽ αὐτῶν.    Καὶ εἶδον,
works of them follow  with them.    And I saw,
2532 2400 3507   3022   2532 1909 08  3507
καὶ ἰδοὺ νεφέλη λευκή, καὶ ἐπὶ  τὴν νεφέλην
and look cloud white, and on  the cloud
2521    3664   5207 444      2192   1909 06
καθήμενον ὅμοιον υἱὸν ἀνθρώπου, ἔχων ἐπὶ  τῆς
sitting like son of man,        having on  the
2776   846   4735     5552    2532 1722 07 5495
κεφαλῆς αὐτοῦ στέφανον χρυσοῦν καὶ ἐν  τῇ χειρὶ
head   of him crown   gold    and in the hand
846   1407   3691  15  2532 243  32     1831
αὐτοῦ δρέπανον ὀξύ.   καὶ ἄλλος ἄγγελος ἐξῆλθεν
of him sickle  sharp. And other messenger came out
1537 02 3485  2896   1722 5456  3173   03
ἐκ  τοῦ ναοῦ κράζων ἐν  φωνῇ μεγάλῃ τῷ
from the temple shouting in voice great  to the one
2521    1909 06 3507   3992     012 1407    1473
καθημένῳ ἐπὶ  τῆς νεφέλης· πέμψον τὸ δρέπανόν σου
sitting on  the cloud;   send the sickle of you
```

or on their hands, [10]they will also drink the wine of God's wrath, poured unmixed into the cup of his anger, and they will be tormented with fire and sulfur in the presence of the holy angels and in the presence of the Lamb. [11]And the smoke of their torment goes up forever and ever. There is no rest day or night for those who worship the beast and its image and for anyone who receives the mark of its name."

[12]Here is a call for the endurance of the saints, those who keep the commandments of God and hold fast to the faith of[a] Jesus.

[13]And I heard a voice from heaven saying, "Write this: Blessed are the dead who from now on die in the Lord." "Yes," says the Spirit, "they will rest from their labors, for their deeds follow them."

[14]Then I looked, and there was a white cloud, and seated on the cloud was one like the Son of Man, with a golden crown on his head, and a sharp sickle in his hand! [15]Another angel came out of the temple, calling with a loud voice to the one who sat on the cloud, "Use your sickle

---

[a] Or to their faith in

and reap, for the hour to reap has come, because the harvest of the earth is fully ripe." ¹⁶So the one who sat on the cloud swung his sickle over the earth, and the earth was reaped.

17 Then another angel came out of the temple in heaven, and he too had a sharp sickle. ¹⁸Then another angel came out from the altar, the angel who has authority over fire, and he called with a loud voice to him who had the sharp sickle, "Use your sharp sickle and gather the clusters of the vine of the earth, for its grapes are ripe." ¹⁹So the angel swung his sickle over the earth and gathered the vintage of the earth, and he threw it into the great wine press of the wrath of God. ²⁰And the wine press was trodden outside the city, and blood flowed from the wine press, as high as a horse's bridle, for a distance of about two hundred miles.ᵃ

CHAPTER 15

Then I saw another portent in heaven, great and amazing: seven angels with seven plagues, which are the last, for with them the wrath of God is ended.

2 And I saw what appeared to be a sea of glass

ᵃ Gk one thousand six hundred stadia

```
2532 2325      3754    2064  05  5610 2325
καὶ  θέρισον,  ὅτι  ἦλθεν ἡ  ὥρα θερίσαι,
and  harvest, because came  the hour to harvest,
3754      3583        01    2326      06     1093        16  2532
ὅτι   ἐξηράνθη    ὁ  θερισμὸς τῆς  γῆς.          καὶ
because was dried out the harvest  of the earth.      And
906      01   2521       1909 06  3507      012 1407
ἔβαλεν ὁ  καθήμενος  ἐπὶ  τῆς νεφέλης τὸ  δρέπανον
threw  the one sitting on  the cloud   the sickle
846     1909 08  1093  2532 2325        05  1093
αὐτοῦ ἐπὶ  τὴν γῆν  καὶ ἐθερίσθη    ἡ  γῆ.
of him on   the earth and was harvested the earth.
   2532 243   32          1831      1537 02 3485  02
17 Καὶ ἄλλος ἄγγελος ἐξῆλθεν ἐκ  τοῦ ναοῦ τοῦ
   And other messenger went out from the temple the
1722 03  3772    2192    2532 846      1407      3691
ἐν  τῷ οὐρανῷ ἔχων  καὶ αὐτὸς δρέπανον ὀξύ.
in  the heaven having also himself sickle   sharp.
   2532 243   32       1831      1537 010
18 καὶ ἄλλος ἄγγελος [ἐξῆλθεν] ἐκ  τοῦ
   And other messenger went out from the
2379        01  2192      1849      1909 010
θυσιαστηρίου [ὁ] ἔχων  ἐξουσίαν ἐπὶ τοῦ
sacrifice place the one having authority on  the
4442   2532 5455     5456    3173   03  2192
πυρός, καὶ ἐφώνησεν φωνῇ μεγάλῃ τῷ ἔχοντι
fire,  and  he sounded in voice great  the one having
012 1407      012 3691   3004    3992  1473  012
τὸ  δρέπανον τὸ  ὀξὺ λέγων· πέμψον σου  τὸ
the sickle   the sharp saying, send   of you the
1407      012 3691  2532 5166     016  1009
δρέπανον τὸ  ὀξὺ  καὶ τρύγησον τοὺς βότρυας
sickle   the sharp and gather   the  bunches of grapes
06  288      06   1093  3754    187     017
τῆς ἀμπέλου τῆς  γῆς, ὅτι   ἤκμασαν αἱ
of the vine  of the earth, because ripened the
1719      846       2532 906    01  32          012
σταφυλαὶ αὐτῆς. 19 καὶ ἔβαλεν ὁ  ἄγγελος  τὸ
grape clusters of it.  And  threw  the messenger the
1407      846      1519 08  1093  2532 5166     08
δρέπανον αὐτοῦ εἰς  τὴν γῆν  καὶ ἐτρύγησεν τὴν
sickle   of him into the earth and  he gathered the
288      06   1093  2532 906   1519 08  3025
ἄμπελον τῆς  γῆς  καὶ ἔβαλεν εἰς  τὴν ληνὸν
vine    of the earth and  threw  into the winepress
02   2372 02    2316  04  3173     20  2532 3961
τοῦ θυμοῦ τοῦ θεοῦ τὸν μέγαν.      καὶ ἐπατήθη
of the fury of the God the great.      And  was walked
05   3025    1855          06  4172    2532 1831
ἡ  ληνὸς  ἔξωθεν    τῆς πόλεως καὶ ἐξῆλθεν
the winepress from outside the city   and  went out
129    1537 06  3025          891   014 5469    014
αἷμα ἐκ  τῆς ληνοῦ  ἄχρι τῶν χαλινῶν τῶν
blood from the winepress until the bridles of the
2462   575  4712      5507     1812       15:1  2532
ἵππων ἀπὸ σταδίων χιλίων ἑξακοσίων.      Καὶ
horses from stadia thousands six hundred.      And
3708  243   4592      1722 03  3772    2532
εἶδον ἄλλο σημεῖον ἐν  τῷ οὐρανῷ μέγα καὶ
I saw other sign   in  the heaven great and
2298         32        2033 2192      4127    2033 020
θαυμαστόν, ἀγγέλους ἑπτὰ ἔχοντας πληγὰς ἑπτὰ τὰς
marvelous, messengers seven having blows seven the
2078      3754   1722 846     5055        01  2372
ἐσχάτας, ὅτι   ἐν  αὐταῖς ἐτελέσθη  ὁ  θυμὸς
last,   because in  them  was completed the fury
02   2316     2  2532 3708  5613 2281    5193
τοῦ θεοῦ.     Καὶ εἶδον ὡς  θάλασσαν ὑαλίνην
of the God.    And I saw as  sea      glass
```

3396 4442 2532 016 3528
μεμιγμένην πυρὶ καὶ τοὺς νικῶντας
having been mixed in fire and the ones conquering

1537 010 2342 2532 1537 06 1504 846 2532
ἐκ τοῦ θηρίου καὶ ἐκ τῆς εἰκόνος αὐτοῦ καὶ
from the wild animal and from the image of him and

1537 02 706 010 3686 846 2476
ἐκ τοῦ ἀριθμοῦ τοῦ ὀνόματος αὐτοῦ ἑστῶτας
from the number of the name of him having stood

1909 08 2281 08 5193 2192 2788 02
ἐπὶ τὴν θάλασσαν τὴν ὑαλίνην ἔχοντας κιθάρας τοῦ
on the sea the glass having harps of the

2316 2532 103 08 5603 3475 02 1401
θεοῦ. 3 καὶ ἄδουσιν τὴν ᾠδὴν Μωϋσέως τοῦ δούλου
God. And they sing the song of Moses the slave

02 2316 2532 08 5603 010 721 3004
τοῦ θεοῦ καὶ τὴν ᾠδὴν τοῦ ἀρνίου λέγοντες·
of the God and the song of the lamb saying:

3173 2532 2298 021 2041 1473 2962 01 2316
μεγάλα καὶ θαυμαστὰ τὰ ἔργα σου, κύριε ὁ θεὸς
great and marvelous the works of you, Master the God

01 3841 1342 2532 228 017 3598
ὁ παντοκράτωρ· δίκαιαι καὶ ἀληθιναὶ αἱ ὁδοί
the all-strength; right and true the ways

1473 01 935 022 1484 4 5101 3756 3361
σου, ὁ βασιλεὺς τῶν ἐθνῶν· τίς οὐ μὴ
of you, the king of the nations; who not not

5399 2962 2532 1392 012 3686
φοβηθῇ, κύριε, καὶ δοξάσει τὸ ὄνομά
might fear, Master, and will give splendor the name

1473 3754 3441 3741 3754 3956 021
σου; ὅτι μόνος ὅσιος, ὅτι πάντα τὰ
of you? Because alone holy, because all the

1484 2240 2532 4352 1799 1473
ἔθνη ἥξουσιν καὶ προσκυνήσουσιν ἐνώπιόν σου,
nations will come and will worship before you,

3754 021 1345 1473 5319
ὅτι τὰ δικαιώματά σου ἐφανερώθησαν.
because the rightnesses of you were demonstrated.

5 2532 3326 3778 3708 2532 455 01 3485
Καὶ μετὰ ταῦτα εἶδον, καὶ ἠνοίγη ὁ ναὸς
And after these I saw, and was opened the temple

06 4633 010 3142 1722 03 3772 6 2532
τῆς σκηνῆς τοῦ μαρτυρίου ἐν τῷ οὐρανῷ, καὶ
of the tent of the testimony in the heaven, and

1831 013 2033 32 013 2192 020
ἐξῆλθον οἱ ἑπτὰ ἄγγελοι [οἱ] ἔχοντες τὰς
came out the seven messengers the ones having the

2033 4127 1537 02 3485 1746
ἑπτὰ πληγὰς ἐκ τοῦ ναοῦ ἐνδεδυμένοι
seven blows from the temple having put on themselves

3043 2513 2986 2532 4024 4012 024
λίνον καθαρὸν λαμπρὸν καὶ περιεζωσμένοι περὶ τὰ
linen clean bright and having encircled around the
themselves

4738 2223 5552 7 2532 1520 1537 022 5064
στήθη ζώνας χρυσᾶς. καὶ ἓν ἐκ τῶν τεσσάρων
chests belts gold. And one from the four

2226 1325 015 2033 32 2033 5357
ζῴων ἔδωκεν τοῖς ἑπτὰ ἀγγέλοις ἑπτὰ φιάλας
living ones gave to the seven messengers seven bowls

5552 1073 02 2372 02 2316 02 2198
χρυσᾶς γεμούσας τοῦ θυμοῦ τοῦ θεοῦ τοῦ ζῶντος
gold being full of the fury of the God the living

1519 016 165 014 165 8 2532 1072 01
εἰς τοὺς αἰῶνας τῶν αἰώνων. καὶ ἐγεμίσθη ὁ
into the ages of the ages. And was filled the

3485 2586 1537 06 1391 02 2316 2532
ναὸς καπνοῦ ἐκ τῆς δόξης τοῦ θεοῦ καὶ
temple of smoke from the splendor of the God and

mixed with fire, and those who had conquered the beast and its image and the number of its name, standing beside the sea of glass with harps of God in their hands. [3] And they sing the song of Moses, the servant[a] of God, and the song of the Lamb:

"Great and amazing are
    your deeds,
Lord God the
    Almighty!
Just and true are your
    ways,
King of the nations![b]
[4] Lord, who will not fear
    and glorify your name?
For you alone are holy.
All nations will come
    and worship before you,
for your judgments have
    been revealed."

[5] After this I looked, and the temple of the tent[c] of witness in heaven was opened, [6] and out of the temple came the seven angels with the seven plagues, robed in pure bright linen,[d] with golden sashes across their chests. [7] Then one of the four living creatures gave the seven angels seven golden bowls full of the wrath of God, who lives forever and ever; [8] and the temple was filled with smoke from the glory of God and

[a] Gk slave
[b] Other ancient authorities read the ages
[c] Or tabernacle
[d] Other ancient authorities read stone

from his power, and no one could enter the temple until the seven plagues of the seven angels were ended.

CHAPTER 16

Then I heard a loud voice from the temple telling the seven angels, "Go and pour out on the earth the seven bowls of the wrath of God."

2 So the first angel went and poured his bowl on the earth, and a foul and painful sore came on those who had the mark of the beast and who worshiped its image.

3 The second angel poured his bowl into the sea, and it became like the blood of a corpse, and every living thing in the sea died.

4 The third angel poured his bowl into the rivers and the springs of water, and they became blood. 5 And I heard the angel of the waters say,

"You are just, O Holy
   One, who are and
   were,
for you have judged
   these things;
6 because they shed the
   blood of saints and
   prophets,
you have given them
   blood to drink.
It is what they deserve!"
7 And I heard the altar respond,
"Yes, O Lord God, the
   Almighty,
your judgments are true
   and just!"
8 The fourth angel poured

1537 06	1411	846	2532 3762	1410
ἐκ τῆς	δυνάμεως	αὐτοῦ,	καὶ οὐδεὶς	ἐδύνατο
from the	power	of him,	and no one	was being able

1525	1519 04	3485	891	5055	017
εἰσελθεῖν εἰς	τὸν	ναὸν	ἄχρι	τελεσθῶσιν	αἱ
to go in into	the	temple	until	might be completed	the

2033 4127 014 2033 32 **16:1** 2532 191
ἑπτὰ πληγαὶ τῶν ἑπτὰ ἀγγέλων. Καὶ ἤκουσα
seven blows of the seven messengers. And I heard

3173 5456 1537 02 3485 3004 015 2033
μεγάλης φωνῆς ἐκ τοῦ ναοῦ λεγούσης τοῖς ἑπτὰ
great sound from the temple saying to the seven

32 5217 2532 1632 020 2033 5357
ἀγγέλοις· ὑπάγετε καὶ ἐκχέετε τὰς ἑπτὰ φιάλας
messengers, go off and pour out the seven bowls

02 2372 02 2316 1519 08 1093 **2** 2532 565
τοῦ θυμοῦ τοῦ θεοῦ εἰς τὴν γῆν. Καὶ ἀπῆλθεν
of the fury of the God into the earth. And went off

01 4413 2532 1632 08 5357 846 1519 08
ὁ πρῶτος καὶ ἐξέχεεν τὴν φιάλην αὐτοῦ εἰς τὴν
the first and poured out the bowl of him into the

1093 2532 1096 1668 2556 2532 4190 016
γῆν, καὶ ἐγένετο ἕλκος κακὸν καὶ πονηρὸν ἐπὶ τοὺς
earth, and became sore bad and evil on the

444 016 2192 012 5480 010
ἀνθρώπους τοὺς ἔχοντας τὸ χάραγμα τοῦ
men the ones having the mark of the

2342 2532 016 4352 07 1504
θηρίου καὶ τοὺς προσκυνοῦντας τῇ εἰκόνι
wild animal and the ones worshiping the image

846 **3** 2532 01 1208 1632 08 5357 846
αὐτοῦ. Καὶ ὁ δεύτερος ἐξέχεεν τὴν φιάλην αὐτοῦ
of him. And the second poured out the bowl of him

1519 08 2281 2532 1096 129 5613 3498
εἰς τὴν θάλασσαν, καὶ ἐγένετο αἷμα ὡς νεκροῦ,
into the sea, and it became blood as of dead,

2533 3956 5590 2222 599 021 1722 07 2281
καὶ πᾶσα ψυχὴ ζωῆς ἀπέθανεν τὰ ἐν τῇ θαλάσσῃ.
and all soul of life died the in the sea.

4 2532 01 5154 1632 08 5357 846 1519 016
Καὶ ὁ τρίτος ἐξέχεεν τὴν φιάλην αὐτοῦ εἰς τοὺς
And the third poured out the bowl of him into the

4215 2532 020 4077 022 5204 2532 1096
ποταμοὺς καὶ τὰς πηγὰς τῶν ὑδάτων, καὶ ἐγένετο
rivers and the springs of the waters, and it became

129 **5** 2532 191 02 32 022 5204
αἷμα. Καὶ ἤκουσα τοῦ ἀγγέλου τῶν ὑδάτων
blood. And I heard the messenger of the waters

3004 1342 1510 01 1510 2532 01 1510
λέγοντος· δίκαιος εἶ, ὁ ὢν καὶ ὁ ἦν,
saying, right you are, the one being and the was,

01 3741 3754 3778 2919 **6** 3754 129
ὁ ὅσιος, ὅτι ταῦτα ἔκρινας, ὅτι αἷμα
the holy, because these you judged, because blood

40 2532 4396 1632 2532 129
ἁγίων καὶ προφητῶν ἐξέχεαν καὶ αἷμα
of holy ones and spokesmen they poured out and blood

846 1325 4095 514 1510
αὐτοῖς [δ]έδωκας πιεῖν, ἄξιοί εἰσιν.
to them you have given to drink, worthy are they.

7 2532 191 010 2379 3004 3483
Καὶ ἤκουσα τοῦ θυσιαστηρίου λέγοντος· ναὶ
And I heard the sacrifice place saying, yes

2962 01 2316 01 3841 228 2532 1342
κύριε ὁ θεὸς ὁ παντοκράτωρ, ἀληθιναὶ καὶ δίκαιαι
Master the God the all-strength, true and right

017 2920 1473 **8** 2532 01 5067 1632
αἱ κρίσεις σου. Καὶ ὁ τέταρτος ἐξέχεεν
the judgments of you. And the fourth poured out

08   5357   846   1909 04   2246   2532 1325
τὴν φιάλην αὐτοῦ ἐπὶ τὸν ἥλιον, καὶ ἐδόθη
the bowl   of him on   the sun,   and it was given
846   2739   016   444   1722 4442   9 2532
αὐτῷ καυματίσαι τοὺς ἀνθρώπους ἐν πυρί.   καὶ
to it to burn   the men   in fire.   And
2739   013 444   2738   3173 2532
ἐκαυματίσθησαν οἱ ἄνθρωποι καῦμα μέγα καὶ
were burned   the men   burn great and
987   012 3686 02   2316 02 2192   08
ἐβλασφήμησαν τὸ ὄνομα τοῦ θεοῦ τοῦ ἔχοντος   τὴν
they insulted the name of the God the one having the
1849   1909 020 4127   3778   2532 3756
ἐξουσίαν ἐπὶ τὰς πληγὰς ταύτας καὶ οὐ
authority on the blows these and not
3340   1325   846 1391   10 2532 01
μετενόησαν   δοῦναι αὐτῷ δόξαν.   Καὶ ὁ
they changed mind to give him splendor. And the
3991   1632   08 5357   846   1909 04 2362
πέμπτος ἐξέχεεν τὴν φιάλην αὐτοῦ ἐπὶ τὸν θρόνον
fifth   poured out the bowl of him on the throne
010   2342   2532 1096   05 932   846
τοῦ θηρίου,   καὶ ἐγένετο ἡ βασιλεία αὐτοῦ
of the wild animal, and became+ the kingdom of him
4656   2532 3145   020 1100   846   1537
ἐσκοτωμένη, καὶ ἐμασῶντο τὰς γλώσσας αὐτῶν ἐκ
+having been and they were the tongues of them from
darkened,   chewing
02   4192   11 2532 987   04 2316 02
τοῦ πόνου,   καὶ ἐβλασφήμησαν τὸν θεὸν τοῦ
the pain,   and they insulted the God of the
3772   1537 014 4192 846   2532 1537 022 1668
οὐρανοῦ ἐκ τῶν πόνων αὐτῶν καὶ ἐκ τῶν ἑλκῶν
heaven from the pains of them and from the sores
846   2532 3756 3340   1537 022 2041
αὐτῶν καὶ οὐ μετενόησαν   ἐκ τῶν ἔργων
of them and not they changed mind from the works
846   12 2532 01   1623   1632   08 5357   846
αὐτῶν.   Καὶ ὁ ἕκτος ἐξέχεεν τὴν φιάλην αὐτοῦ
of them. And the sixth poured out the bowl of him
1909 04   4215   04 3173 04   2166   2532
ἐπὶ τὸν ποταμὸν τὸν μέγαν τὸν Εὐφράτην, καὶ
on the river   the great the Euphrates, and
3583   09 5204 846   2443 2090
ἐξηράνθη   τὸ ὕδωρ αὐτοῦ, ἵνα ἑτοιμασθῇ
it dried out the water of it, that might be prepared
05   3598 014   935   014 575   395   2246
ἡ ὁδὸς τῶν βασιλέων τῶν ἀπὸ ἀνατολῆς ἡλίου.
the way of the kings   the from east   of sun.
13 2532 3708 1537 010 4750   02   1404   2532
   Καὶ εἶδον ἐκ τοῦ στόματος τοῦ δράκοντος καὶ
   And I saw from the mouth of the dragon and
1537 010 4750   010   2342   2532 1537 010
ἐκ τοῦ στόματος τοῦ θηρίου   καὶ ἐκ τοῦ
from the mouth   of the wild animal and from the
4750   02   5578   4151   5140
στόματος τοῦ ψευδοπροφήτου πνεύματα τρία
mouth   of the false spokesman spirits three
169   5613 944   14 1510   1063 4151
ἀκάθαρτα ὡς βάτραχοι·   εἰσὶν γὰρ πνεύματα
unclean as frogs;   they are for spirits
1140   4160   4592   3739 1607   1909 016
δαιμονίων ποιοῦντα σημεῖα, ἃ ἐκπορεύεται ἐπὶ τοὺς
of demons doing signs, which travel out on the
935   06   3625   3650
βασιλεῖς τῆς οἰκουμένης ὅλης
kings of the inhabited world whole
4863   846   1519 04 4171   06   2250
συναγαγεῖν αὐτοὺς εἰς τὸν πόλεμον τῆς ἡμέρας
to bring together them to the war   of the day

his bowl on the sun, and
it was allowed to scorch
people with fire; [9]they were
scorched by the fierce heat,
but they cursed the name
of God, who had authority
over these plagues, and they
did not repent and give him
glory.

10 The fifth angel
poured his bowl on the
throne of the beast, and its
kingdom was plunged into
darkness; people gnawed
their tongues in agony,
[11]and cursed the God of
heaven because of their
pains and sores, and they
did not repent of their deeds.

12 The sixth angel
poured his bowl on the
great river Euphrates, and
its water was dried up in
order to prepare the way
for the kings from the east.
[13]And I saw three foul
spirits like frogs coming
from the mouth of the
dragon, from the mouth
of the beast, and from the
mouth of the false prophet.
[14]These are demonic spirits,
performing signs, who go
abroad to the kings of the
whole world, to assemble
them for battle

on the great day of God the Almighty. [15]("See, I am coming like a thief! Blessed is the one who stays awake and is clothed,[a] not going about naked and exposed to shame.") [16]And they assembled them at the place that in Hebrew is called Harmagedon.

[17]The seventh angel poured his bowl into the air, and a loud voice came out of the temple, from the throne, saying, "It is done!" [18]And there came flashes of lightning, rumblings, peals of thunder, and a violent earthquake, such as had not occurred since people were upon the earth, so violent was that earthquake. [19]The great city was split into three parts, and the cities of the nations fell. God remembered great Babylon and gave her the wine-cup of the fury of his wrath. [20]And every island fled away, and no mountains were to be found; [21]and huge hailstones, each weighing about a hundred pounds,[b] dropped from heaven on people, until they cursed God for the plague of the hail, so fearful was that plague.

CHAPTER 17

Then one of the seven angels who had the seven bowls came

[a] Gk and keeps his robes
[b] Gk weighing about a talent

06	3173	02		2316	02	3841		15	2400
τῆς	μεγάλης	τοῦ		θεοῦ	τοῦ	παντοκράτορος.			Ἰδοὺ
the	great	of the		God	the	all-strength.			Look

2064		5613	2812		3107		01	1127
ἔρχομαι		ὡς	κλέπτης.		μακάριος		ὁ	γρηγορῶν
I come		as	thief.		Fortunate		the	one keeping awake

2532	5083		024	2440		846		2443	3361	1131
καὶ	τηρῶν		τὰ	ἱμάτια		αὐτοῦ,		ἵνα	μὴ	γυμνὸς
and	keeping		the	clothes		of him,		that	not	naked

4043		2532	991		08
περιπατῇ		καὶ	βλέπωσιν		τὴν
he might walk around		and	they might see		the

808		846	16	2532	4863		846
ἀσχημοσύνην		αὐτοῦ.		Καὶ	συνήγαγεν		αὐτοὺς
shamelessness		of him.		And	he brought together		them

1519	04	5117	04	2564		1447
εἰς	τὸν	τόπον	τὸν	καλούμενον		Ἑβραϊστὶ
into	the	place	the	one being called		in Hebrew

717		2532	01	1442	1632		08	5357
Ἁρμαγεδών.	17	Καὶ	ὁ	ἕβδομος	ἐξέχεεν		τὴν	φιάλην
Armagedon.		And	the	seventh	poured out		the	bowl

846		1909	04	109	2532	1831		5456	3173	1537
αὐτοῦ		ἐπὶ	τὸν	ἀέρα,	καὶ	ἐξῆλθεν		φωνὴ	μεγάλη	ἐκ
of him		on	the	air,	and	went out		sound	great	from

02	3485	575	02	2362	3004		1096
τοῦ	ναοῦ	ἀπὸ	τοῦ	θρόνου	λέγουσα·		γέγονεν.
the	temple	from	the	throne	saying,		it has become.

18	2532	1096		796		2532	5456	2532
	καὶ	ἐγένοντο		ἀστραπαὶ		καὶ	φωναὶ	καὶ
	And	there became		lightnings		and	sounds	and

1027		2532	4578	1096		3173	3634		3756
βρονταὶ		καὶ	σεισμὸς	ἐγένετο		μέγας,	οἷος		οὐκ
thunders		and	shake	became		great,	of such kind		not

1096		575	3739	444		1096		1909	06	1093
ἐγένετο		ἀφ᾽	οὗ	ἄνθρωπος		ἐγένετο		ἐπὶ	τῆς	γῆς
it became		from	which	man		became		on	the	earth

5082		4578	3779	0173	19	2532	1096	05
τηλικοῦτος		σεισμὸς	οὕτω	μέγας.		καὶ	ἐγένετο	ἡ
so great		shake	thusly	great.		And	became	the

4172	05	3173	1519	5140	3313	2532	017	4172
πόλις	ἡ	μεγάλη	εἰς	τρία	μέρη	καὶ	αἱ	πόλεις
city	the	great	into	three	parts	and	the	cities

022	1484	4098	2532	897	05	3173
τῶν	ἐθνῶν	ἔπεσαν.	καὶ	Βαβυλὼν	ἡ	μεγάλη
of the	nations	fell.	And	Babylon	the	great

3403		1799	02	2316	1325	846
ἐμνήσθη		ἐνώπιον	τοῦ	θεοῦ	δοῦναι	αὐτῇ
was remembered		before	the	God	to give	to her

012	4221	02		3631	02		2372	06		3709
τὸ	ποτήριον	τοῦ		οἴνου	τοῦ		θυμοῦ	τῆς		ὀργῆς
the	cup	of the		wine	of the		fury	of the		anger

846	20	2532	3956	3520		5343	2532	3735	3756
αὐτοῦ.		καὶ	πᾶσα	νῆσος		ἔφυγεν	καὶ	ὄρη	οὐχ
of him.		And	all	island		fled	and	hills	not

2147	21	2532	5464	3173	5613	5006
εὑρέθησαν.		καὶ	χάλαζα	μεγάλη	ὡς	ταλαντιαία
were found.		And	hail	great	as	talant weight

2597		1537	02	3772	1909	016	444
καταβαίνει		ἐκ	τοῦ	οὐρανοῦ	ἐπὶ	τοὺς	ἀνθρώπους,
comes down		from	the	heaven	on	the	men,

2532	987		013	444		04	2316	1537	06
καὶ	ἐβλασφήμησαν		οἱ	ἄνθρωποι		τὸν	θεὸν	ἐκ	τῆς
and	insulted		the	men		the	God	from	the

4127	06	5464		3754		3173	1510	05
πληγῆς	τῆς	χαλάζης,		ὅτι		μεγάλη	ἐστὶν	ἡ
blow	of the	hail,		because		great	is	the

4127	846	4970	17:1	2532	2064	1520	1537	014
πληγὴ	αὐτῆς	σφόδρα.		Καὶ	ἦλθεν	εἷς	ἐκ	τῶν
blow	of her	exceeding.		And	went	one	from	the

2033   32   014 2192   020 2033 5357   2532
ἑπτὰ ἀγγέλων   τῶν ἐχόντων   τὰς ἑπτὰ φιάλας καὶ
seven messengers the ones having the seven bowls and

2980   3326 1473 3004   1204   1166   1473
ἐλάλησεν μετ᾽ ἐμοῦ λέγων· δεῦρο, δείξω   σοι
he spoke with me   saying; come, I will show to you

012   2917   06   4204   06 3173   06
τὸ κρίμα   τῆς   πόρνης   τῆς μεγάλης τῆς
the judgment of the prostitute the great   the one

2521   1909 5204   4183   2 3326 3739
καθημένης ἐπὶ ὑδάτων πολλῶν,   μεθ᾽ ἧς
sitting   on   waters many,   with whom

4203   013 935   06   1093   2532
ἐπόρνευσαν   οἱ βασιλεῖς τῆς   γῆς   καὶ
committed sexual the kings of the earth and
immorality

3184   013   2730   08 1093   1537
ἐμεθύσθησαν οἱ   κατοικοῦντες τὴν γῆν ἐκ
were made drunk the ones residing   the earth from

02 3631 06   4202   846   3 2532
τοῦ οἴνου τῆς   πορνείας   αὐτῆς.   καὶ
the wine of the sexual immorality of her. And

667   1473 1519 2048 1722 4151   2532
ἀπήνεγκέν   με εἰς ἔρημον ἐν πνεύματι. Καὶ
he carried off me into desert in spirit. And

3708 1135   2521   1909 2342   2847
εἶδον γυναῖκα καθημένην ἐπὶ θηρίον   κόκκινον,
I saw woman sitting   on wild animal scarlet,

1073   3686   988   2192   2776   2033
γέμον[τα] ὀνόματα βλασφημίας, ἔχων κεφαλὰς ἑπτὰ
being full names of insult, having heads   seven

2532 2768   1176   2532 05 1135   1510 4016
καὶ κέρατα δέκα. 4 καὶ ἡ γυνὴ ἦν περιβεβλημένη
and horns ten.   And the woman was+ +having thrown
                                       around herself

4210   2532 2847   2532 5558
πορφυροῦν καὶ κόκκινον καὶ κεχρυσωμένη
purple   and scarlet and having made golden

5553   2532 3037 5093   2532 3135   2192
χρυσίῳ καὶ λίθῳ τιμίῳ   καὶ μαργαρίταις, ἔχουσα
in gold and stone valuable and pearls,   having

4221   5552   1722 07 5495 846   1073
ποτήριον χρυσοῦν ἐν τῇ χειρὶ αὐτῆς γέμον
cup   gold   in the hand of her full

946   2532 024 169   06
βδελυγμάτων καὶ τὰ ἀκάθαρτα τῆς
of abominations and the unclean of the

4202   846   5 2532 1909 012 3359
πορνείας   αὐτῆς   καὶ ἐπὶ τὸ μέτωπον
sexual immorality of her and on the forehead

846   3686   1125   3466   897
αὐτῆς ὄνομα γεγραμμένον,   μυστήριον, Βαβυλὼν
of her name having been written, mystery, Babylon

05 3173   05 3384   018   4204   2532 022
ἡ μεγάλη, ἡ μήτηρ τῶν   πορνῶν   καὶ τῶν
the great, the mother of the prostitutes and the

946   06   1093   6 2532 3708 08 1135
βδελυγμάτων τῆς γῆς.   καὶ εἶδον τὴν γυναῖκα
abominations of the earth. And I saw the woman

3184   1537 010 129   014   40   2532 1537
μεθύουσαν ἐκ τοῦ αἵματος τῶν ἁγίων καὶ ἐκ
being drunk from the blood of the holy ones and from

010 129   014   3144   2424   3532 2296
τοῦ αἵματος τῶν μαρτύρων Ἰησοῦ. Καὶ ἐθαύμασα
the blood of the testifiers of Jesus. And I marveled

3708   846   2295   3173 7 2532 3004 1473 01
ἰδὼν   αὐτὴν θαῦμα μέγα.   Καὶ εἶπέν μοι ὁ
having seen her marvel great. And said to me the

and said to me, "Come, I
will show you the judgment
of the great whore who is
seated on many waters,
[2]with whom the kings of
the earth have committed
fornication, and with the
wine of whose fornication
the inhabitants of the earth
have become drunk." [3]So
he carried me away in the
spirit[a] into a wilderness,
and I saw a woman sitting
on a scarlet beast that was
full of blasphemous names,
and it had seven heads and
ten horns. [4]The woman
was clothed in purple and
scarlet, and adorned with
gold and jewels and pearls,
holding in her hand a
golden cup full of abomi-
nations and the impurities
of her fornication; [5]and on
her forehead was written a
name, a mystery: "Babylon
the great, mother of
whores and of earth's
abominations." [6]And I
saw that the woman was
drunk with the blood of
the saints and the blood
of the witnesses to Jesus.

When I saw her, I was
greatly amazed. [7]But the
angel said to me,

a Or in the Spirit

"Why are you so amazed? I will tell you the mystery of the woman, and of the beast with seven heads and ten horns that carries her. 8The beast that you saw was, and is not, and is about to ascend from the bottomless pit and go to destruction. And the inhabitants of the earth, whose names have not been written in the book of life from the foundation of the world, will be amazed when they see the beast, because it was and is not and is to come.

9"This calls for a mind that has wisdom: the seven heads are seven mountains on which the woman is seated; also, they are seven kings, 10of whom five have fallen, one is living, and the other has not yet come; and when he comes, he must remain only a little while. 11As for the beast that was and is not, it is an eighth but it belongs to the seven, and it goes to destruction. 12And the ten horns that you saw are ten kings who have not yet received a kingdom, but they are to receive authority as kings for one hour, together with the beast. 13These are united in yielding their power and authority to the beast;

32	1223	5101	2296	1473 3004
ἄγγελος·	διὰ	τί	ἐθαύμασας;	ἐγὼ ἐρῶ
messenger;	because of	what	you marveled?	I will say

1473	012 3462	06	1135	2532 010
σοι	τὸ μυστήριον τῆς		γυναικὸς καὶ	τοῦ
to you	the mystery of the		woman and	of the

2342	010 941	846	010 2192	020
θηρίου	τοῦ βαστάζοντος	αὐτὴν	τοῦ ἔχοντος	τὰς
wild animal	the one bearing	her	the one having	the

2033 2776	2532 024 1176 2768	09 2342
ἑπτὰ κεφαλὰς	καὶ τὰ δέκα κέρατα.	8 Τὸ θηρίον
seven heads	and the ten horns.	The wild animal

3739 3708	1510	2532 3756 1510	2532 3195
ὃ εἶδες	ἦν	καὶ οὐκ ἔστιν	καὶ μέλλει
which you saw	he was	and not he is	and is about

305	1537 06 12	2532 1519 684
ἀναβαίνειν	ἐκ τῆς ἀβύσσου	καὶ εἰς ἀπώλειαν
to go up	from the bottomless	and into destruction

5217	2532 2296	013 2730
ὑπάγει,	καὶ θαυμασθήσονται	οἱ κατοικοῦντες
he goes off,	and will be marveling	the ones residing

1909 06 1093	3739 3756 1125	09 3686
ἐπὶ τῆς γῆς,	ὧν οὐ γέγραπται	τὸ ὄνομα
on the earth,	whose not has been written	the name

1909 012 975	06	2222 575 2602
ἐπὶ τὸ βιβλίον	τῆς	ζωῆς ἀπὸ καταβολῆς
on the small book	of the	life from foundation

2889	991	012 2342	3754 1510	2532
κόσμου,	βλεπόντων	τὸ θηρίον	ὅτι ἦν	καὶ
of world,	seeing	the wild animal	that he was	and

3756 1510 2532 3918	5602 01 3563 01
οὐκ ἔστιν καὶ παρέσται.	9 ὧδε ὁ νοῦς ὁ
not he is and will be present.	Here the mind the one

2192	4678	017 2033 2776	2033 3735 1510
ἔχων	σοφίαν.	Αἱ ἑπτὰ κεφαλαὶ	ἑπτὰ ὄρη εἰσίν,
having	wisdom.	The seven heads	seven hills are,

3699 05 1105 2631	1909 846	2532 935	2033
ὅπου ἡ γυνὴ κάθηται	ἐπ᾽ αὐτῶν.	καὶ βασιλεῖς	ἑπτά
where the woman sits	on them.	And kings	seven

1510	013 4002 4098	01 1520 1510	01 243
εἰσίν·	10 οἱ πέντε ἔπεσαν,	ὁ εἷς ἔστιν,	ὁ ἄλλος
there are;	the five fell,	the one is,	the other

3768 2064	2532 3752 2064	3641 846
οὔπω ἦλθεν,	καὶ ὅταν ἔλθῃ	ὀλίγον αὐτὸν
not yet came,	and when he might come	little him

1163	3306	2532 09 2342	3739
δεῖ	μεῖναι.	11 καὶ τὸ θηρίον	ὃ
it is necessary	to stay.	And the wild animal	which

1510 2532 3756 1510 2532 846	3590 1510 2532
ἦν καὶ οὐκ ἔστιν καὶ αὐτὸς	ὄγδοός ἐστιν καὶ
was and not is and himself	eighth he is and

1537 014 2033 1510	2532 1519 684
ἐκ τῶν ἑπτά ἐστιν,	καὶ εἰς ἀπώλειαν
from the seven he is,	and into destruction

5217	2532 021 1176 2768 3739 3708 1176
ὑπάγει.	12 Καὶ τὰ δέκα κέρατα ἃ εἶδες δέκα
he goes off.	And the ten horns which you saw ten

935 1510	3748 932	3768 2983
βασιλεῖς εἰσιν,	οἵτινες βασιλείαν	οὔπω ἔλαβον,
kings are,	who kingdom	not yet received,

235 1849	5613 935	1520 5610 2983
ἀλλὰ ἐξουσίαν	ὡς βασιλεῖς	μίαν ὥραν λαμβάνουσιν
but authority	as kings	one hour they receive

3326 010 2342	3778 1520 1106 2192 2532
μετὰ τοῦ θηρίου.	13 οὗτοι μίαν γνώμην ἔχουσιν καὶ
with the wild animal.	These one purpose have and

08 1411 2532 1849	846 011 2342
τὴν δύναμιν καὶ ἐξουσίαν	αὐτῶν τῷ θηρίῳ
the power and authority	of them to the wild animal

1325		3778	3326	010	721	4170		2532
διδόασιν.	**14**	οὗτοι	μετὰ	τοῦ	ἀρνίου	πολεμήσουσιν		καὶ
they give.		These	with	the	lamb	will make war		and

09	721	3528		846	3754	2962
τὸ	ἀρνίον	νικήσει	αὐτούς,	ὅτι	κύριος
the lamb		will conquer	them,	because	Master

2962	1510	2532	935		935		2532	013	3326
κυρίων	ἐστὶν	καὶ	βασιλεὺς	βασιλέων	καὶ	οἱ	μετ'
of masters	he is	and	king		of kings	and	the	with

846	2822	2532	1588		2532	4103		2532	3004
αὐτοῦ	κλητοὶ	καὶ	ἐκλεκτοὶ	καὶ	πιστοί.	**15**	Καὶ	λέγει
him	called	and	select	and	trustful.		And	he says

1473	021	5204	3739	3708		3757	05	4204
μοι·	τὰ	ὕδατα	ἃ	εἶδες	οὗ	ἡ	πόρνη
to me,	the	waters	which	<u>you</u> saw	where	the	prostitute

2521		2992		2532	3793		1510	2532	1484
κάθηται,	λαοὶ	καὶ	ὄχλοι	εἰσὶν	καὶ	ἔθνη
sits,	peoples	and	crowds	are	and	nations

2532	1100		2532	021	1176	2768	3739	3708
καὶ	γλῶσσαι.	**16**	καὶ	τὰ	δέκα	κέρατα	ἃ	εἶδες
and	tongues.		And	the	ten	horns	which	<u>you</u> saw

2532	09	2342		3778	3404		08	4204
καὶ	τὸ	θηρίον	οὗτοι	μισήσουσιν	τὴν	πόρνην
and	the	wild animal	these	will hate	the	prostitute

2532	2049		4160		846	2532	1131		2532	020
καὶ	ἠρημωμένην	ποιήσουσιν	αὐτὴν	καὶ	γυμνὴν	καὶ	τὰς
and	having been	will	her	and	naked	and	the
	desolated	make					

4561	846		2068		2532	846		2618		1722
σάρκας	αὐτῆς	φάγονται	καὶ	αὐτὴν	κατακαύσουσιν	ἐν
flesh	of her	they will	and	her	they will burn	in
		eat			down	

4442		01	1063	2316	1325		1519	020	2588		846
πυρί.	**17**	ὁ	γὰρ	θεὸς	ἔδωκεν	εἰς	τὰς	καρδίας	αὐτῶν
fire.		The	for	God	gave	into	the	hearts	of them

4160		08	1106		846		2532	4160		1520	1106
ποιῆσαι	τὴν	γνώμην	αὐτοῦ	καὶ	ποιῆσαι	μίαν	γνώμην
to do	the	purpose	of him	and	to do	one	purpose

2532	1325		08	932		846	011		2342
καὶ	δοῦναι	τὴν	βασιλείαν	αὐτῶν	τῷ	θηρίῳ
and	to give	the	kingdom	of them	to the	wild animal

891	5055		013	3056	02		2316		**18**	2532
ἄχρι	τελεσθήσονται	οἱ	λόγοι	τοῦ	θεοῦ.		καὶ
until	will be completed	the	words	of the	God.		And

05	1135	3739	3708		1510	05	4172	05	3173	05
ἡ	γυνὴ	ἣν	εἶδες	ἔστιν	ἡ	πόλις	ἡ	μεγάλη	ἡ
the	woman	whom	<u>you</u> saw	is	the	city	the	great	the

2192		932		1909	014	935		06		1093
ἔχουσα	βασιλείαν	ἐπὶ	τῶν	βασιλέων	τῆς	γῆς.
one having	kingdom	on	the	kings	of the	earth.

18:1	3326	3778	3708	243	32		2597
	Μετὰ	ταῦτα	εἶδον	ἄλλον	ἄγγελον	καταβαίνοντα
	After	these	I saw	other	messenger	coming down

1537	02	3772	2192	1849		3173		2532	05
ἐκ	τοῦ	οὐρανοῦ	ἔχοντα	ἐξουσίαν	μεγάλην,	καὶ	ἡ
from	the	heaven	having	authority	great,	and	the

1093	5461		1537	06	1391		846		**2**	2532
γῆ	ἐφωτίσθη	ἐκ	τῆς	δόξης	αὐτοῦ.		καὶ
earth	was lightened	from	the	splendor	of him.		And

2896		1722	2478	5456	3004		4098	4098
ἔκραξεν	ἐν	ἰσχυρᾷ	φωνῇ	λέγων·	ἔπεσεν	ἔπεσεν
he shouted	in	strong	voice	saying,	fell	fell

897		05	3173		2532	1096		2732
Βαβυλὼν	ἡ	μεγάλη,	καὶ	ἐγένετο	κατοικητήριον
Babylon	the	great,	and	she became	residence place

1140		2532	5438	3956	4151		169		2532
δαιμονίων	καὶ	φυλακὴ	παντὸς	πνεύματος	ἀκαθάρτου	καὶ
of demons	and	guard	of all	spirit	unclean	and

[14]they will make war on the Lamb, and the Lamb will conquer them, for he is Lord of lords and King of kings, and those with him are called and chosen and faithful."

15 And he said to me, "The waters that you saw, where the whore is seated, are peoples and multitudes and nations and languages. [16]And the ten horns that you saw, they and the beast will hate the whore; they will make her desolate and naked; they will devour her flesh and burn her up with fire. [17]For God has put it into their hearts to carry out his purpose by agreeing to give their kingdom to the beast, until the words of God will be fulfilled. [18]The woman you saw is the great city that rules over the kings of the earth."

CHAPTER 18

After this I saw another angel coming down from heaven, having great authority; and the earth was made bright with his splendor. [2]He called out with a mighty voice,
"Fallen, fallen is Babylon the great!
It has become a dwelling place of demons,
a haunt of every foul spirit,

a haunt of every foul
   bird,
a haunt of every foul
   and hateful beast.[a]
3 For all the nations have
   drunk[b]
of the wine of the wrath of
   her fornication,
and the kings of the earth
   have committed
   fornication with her,
and the merchants
   of the earth have
   grown rich from the
   power[c] of her
   luxury."
4 Then I heard another
voice from heaven saying,
   "Come out of her, my
   people,
so that you do not take
   part in her sins,
and so that you do not
   share in her plagues;
5 for her sins are heaped
   high as heaven,
and God has remem-
   bered her iniquities.
6 Render to her as she
   herself has rendered,
and repay her double
   for her deeds;
   mix a double draught
   for her in the cup she
   mixed.
7 As she glorified herself
   and lived luxuriously,
so give her a like
   measure of torment
   and grief.
Since in her heart she says,
   'I rule as a queen;
I am no widow,
   and I will never see
   grief,'
8 therefore her plagues will
   come in a single
   day—
   pestilence and mourn-
   ing and famine—
and she will be burned
   with fire;
for mighty is the Lord
   God who judges her."

a Other ancient authorities lack the
   words a haunt of every foul beast
   and attach the words and hateful
   to the previous line so as to read a
   haunt of every foul and hateful bird.
b Other ancient authorities read She
   has made all nations drink
c Or resources

5438	3956	3732	169		2532 5438	3956
φυλακὴ παντὸς ὀρνέου ἀκαθάρτου [καὶ φυλακὴ παντὸς
guard of all bird unclean and guard of all

2342   169   2532 3404   3754
θηρίου ἀκαθάρτου] καὶ μεμισημένου,   **3** ὅτι
wild animal unclean and having been hated, because

1537 02 3631 02   2372 06   4202
ἐκ τοῦ οἴνου τοῦ θυμοῦ τῆς πορνείας
from the wine of the fury of the sexual immorality

846   4095   3956 021 1484   2532 013 935
αὐτῆς πέπωκαν πάντα τὰ ἔθνη   καὶ οἱ βασιλεῖς
of her have drunk all the nations and the kings

06   1093   3326 846   4203   2532
τῆς γῆς μετ᾽ αὐτῆς ἐπόρνευσαν   καὶ
of the earth with her committed sexual immorality and

013 1713   06   1093 1537 06   1411   010
οἱ ἔμποροι τῆς γῆς ἐκ τῆς δυνάμεως τοῦ
the merchants of the earth from the power of the

4764   846   4147   2532 191   243   5456
στρήνους αὐτῆς ἐπλούτησαν. **4** Καὶ ἤκουσα ἄλλην φωνὴν
luxury   of her were rich.   And I heard other voice

1537 02 3772   3004   1831   01 2992   1473
ἐκ τοῦ οὐρανοῦ λέγουσαν· ἐξέλθατε ὁ λαός μου
from the heaven saying, come out the people of me

1537 846   2443 3361 4790   019
ἐξ αὐτῆς ἵνα μὴ συγκοινωνήσητε   ταῖς
from her that not you might be co-partner in the

266   846   2532 1537 018 4127   846   2443
ἁμαρτίαις αὐτῆς, καὶ ἐκ τῶν πληγῶν αὐτῆς ἵνα
sins   of her, and from the blows of her that

3361 2983   3754   2853   846   017
μὴ λάβητε,   **5** ὅτι   ἐκολλήθησαν αὐτῆς αἱ
not you might take, because were joined of her the

266   891 02 3772   2532 3421   01 2316
ἁμαρτίαι ἄχρι τοῦ οὐρανοῦ καὶ ἐμνημόνευσεν ὁ θεὸς
sins   until the heaven and remembered the God

024 92   846   591   846   5613 2532 846
τὰ ἀδικήματα αὐτῆς. **6** ἀπόδοτε αὐτῇ ὡς καὶ αὐτὴ·
the unrights of her. Give off to her as also she

591   2532 1363   024 1362   2596 024 2041
ἀπέδωκεν καὶ διπλώσατε τὰ διπλᾶ κατὰ τὰ ἔργα
gave off and double   the doubles by the works

846   1722 011 4221   3739   2767   2767
αὐτῆς, ἐν τῷ ποτηρίῳ ᾧ   ἐκέρασεν κεράσατε
of her, in the cup   in which she mixed mix

846   1362   3745   1392   846
αὐτῇ διπλοῦν, **7** ὅσα   ἐδόξασεν   αὐτὴν
to her double,   as many as she gave splendor herself

2532 4763   5118   1325 846 3929   2532
καὶ ἐστρηνίασεν, τοσοῦτον δότε αὐτῇ βασανισμὸν καὶ
and luxuriated, such   give to her torment   and

3997   3754   1722 07 2588   846   3004   3754
πένθος. ὅτι ἐν τῇ καρδίᾳ αὐτῆς λέγει ὅτι (")
mourning. Because in the heart of her she says, (")

2521   938   2532 5503   3756 1510 2532 3997
κάθημαι βασίλισσα καὶ χήρα οὐκ εἰμὶ καὶ πένθος
I sit   queen   and widow not I am and mourning

3756 3361 3708   1223   3778 1722 1520 2250
οὐ μὴ ἴδω.   **8** διὰ τοῦτο ἐν μιᾷ ἡμέρᾳ
not not I might see. Through this in one day

2240   017 4127 846   2288   2532 3997
ἥξουσιν αἱ πληγαὶ αὐτῆς, θάνατος καὶ πένθος
will come the blows of her, death and mourning

2532 3042   2532 1722 4442 2618
καὶ λιμός, καὶ ἐν πυρὶ κατακαυθήσεται,
and famine, and in fire she will be burned down,

3754   2478   2962   01 2316 01 2919
ὅτι ἰσχυρὸς κύριος ὁ θεὸς ὁ κρίνας
because strong Master the God the one having judged

846   9 2532 2799   2532 2875   1909 846
αὐτήν.   Καὶ κλαύσουσιν   καὶ κόψονται   ἐπ’ αὐτὴν
her.   And they will cry and will mourn over her
013 935   06   1093   013 3326 846
οἱ βασιλεῖς τῆς   γῆς   οἱ μετ’ αὐτῆς
the kings   of the earth the with her
4203   2532 4763   3752 991
πορνεύσαντες   καὶ στρηνιάσαντες, ὅταν βλέπωσιν
having committed and having   when they might
sexual immorality   luxuriated,   see
04 2586   06   4451   846   10   575   3113
τὸν καπνὸν τῆς   πυρώσεως αὐτῆς,   ἀπὸ μακρόθεν
the smoke of the   burning of her,   from from far
2476   1223   04 5401   02   929
ἑστηκότες   διὰ   τὸν φόβον τοῦ   βασανισμοῦ
having stood through the fear   of the torment
846   3004   3759 3759   05 4172   05 3173
αὐτῆς λέγοντες· οὐαὶ οὐαί, ἡ πόλις ἡ   μεγάλη,
of her saying,   woe woe, the city the great,
897   05 4172   05 2478   3754   1520   5610
Βαβυλὼν ἡ πόλις ἡ ἰσχυρά, ὅτι   μιᾷ   ὥρᾳ
Babylon the city the strong, because in one hour
2064 05 2920   1473   11 2532 013 1713   06
ἦλθεν ἡ κρίσις σου.   Καὶ οἱ ἔμποροι τῆς
came the judgment of you.   And the merchants of the
1093 2799   2532 3996   1909 846   3754   04
γῆς κλαίουσιν καὶ πενθοῦσιν ἐπ’ αὐτήν, ὅτι   τὸν
earth cry   and mourn   on her, because the
1117 846   3762 59   3765   12 1117
γόμον αὐτῶν οὐδεὶς ἀγοράζει οὐκέτι   γόμον
cargo of her no one buys   no longer   cargo
5557   2532 696   2532 3037 5093   2532
χρυσοῦ καὶ ἀργύρου καὶ λίθου τιμίου καὶ
of gold and silver   and stone valuable and
3135   2532 1039   2532 4209   2532 4617a
μαργαριτῶν καὶ βυσσίνου καὶ πορφύρας καὶ σιρικοῦ
pearls   and linen   and purple   and silk
2532 2847   2532 3956 3586   2367   2532 3956 4632
καὶ κοκκίνου, καὶ πᾶν ξύλον θύϊνον καὶ πᾶν σκεῦος
and scarlet, and all wood citron and all pot
1661   2532 3956 4632   1537 3586   5093
ἐλεφάντινον καὶ πᾶν σκεῦος ἐκ ξύλου τιμιωτάτου
ivory   and all pot   from wood most valuable
2532 5475   2532 4604   2532 3139   2532
καὶ χαλκοῦ καὶ σιδήρου καὶ μαρμάρου, 13 καὶ
and copper and iron   and marble,   and
2792   2532 298a   2532 2368   2532 3464
κιννάμωμον καὶ ἄμωμον καὶ θυμιάματα καὶ μύρον
cinnamon   and spice   and incense   and perfume
2532 3030   2532 3631 2532 1637   2532
καὶ λίβανον   καὶ οἶνον καὶ ἔλαιον καὶ
and frankincense and wine and oil   and
4585   2532 4621   2532 2934   2532 4263   2532
σεμίδαλιν καὶ σῖτον καὶ κτήνη   καὶ πρόβατα, καὶ
fine flour and wheat and animals and sheep,   and
2462   2532 4480   2532 4983   2532 5590
ἵππων καὶ ῥεδῶν καὶ σωμάτων, καὶ ψυχὰς
horses and chariots and bodies,   and souls
444   14 2532 05 3703 1473   06 1939
ἀνθρώπων.   καὶ ἡ ὀπώρα σου   τῆς ἐπιθυμίας
of men.   And the fruit of you the desire
06   5590   565   575 1473 2532 3956   021 3045
τῆς   ψυχῆς ἀπῆλθεν ἀπὸ σοῦ, καὶ πάντα τὰ λιπαρὰ
of the soul   went off from you, and all   the sleek
2532 021 2986   622   575 1473 2532 3765
καὶ τὰ λαμπρὰ ἀπώλετο ἀπὸ σοῦ καὶ οὐκέτι
and the bright are destroyed from you and no longer
3756 3361 846 2147   15 013 1713   3778
οὐ μὴ αὐτὰ εὑρήσουσιν.   Οἱ ἔμποροι τούτων
not not them they will find. The merchants of these

9 And the kings of the earth, who committed fornication and lived in luxury with her, will weep and wail over her when they see the smoke of her burning; [10]they will stand far off, in fear of her torment, and say,

"Alas, alas, the great city,
   Babylon, the mighty city!
For in one hour your
   judgment has come."

11 And the merchants of the earth weep and mourn for her, since no one buys their cargo anymore, [12]cargo of gold, silver, jewels and pearls, fine linen, purple, silk and scarlet, all kinds of scented wood, all articles of ivory, all articles of costly wood, bronze, iron, and marble, [13]cinnamon, spice, incense, myrrh, frankincense, wine, olive oil, choice flour and wheat, cattle and sheep, horses and chariots, slaves— and human lives.[a]

[14] "The fruit for which your soul longed
      has gone from you,
   and all your dainties
      and your splendor
   are lost to you,
      never to be found again!"

[15]The merchants of these wares,

[a] Or chariots, and human bodies and souls

who gained wealth from
her, will stand far off,
in fear of her torment,
weeping and mourning
aloud,
16 "Alas, alas, the great
  city,
    clothed in fine linen,
    in purple and scarlet,
    adorned with gold,
      with jewels, and with
      pearls!
17 For in one hour all this
  wealth has been laid
  waste!"
  And all shipmasters and
seafarers, sailors and all
whose trade is on the sea,
stood far off 18and cried
out as they saw the smoke
of her burning,
  "What city was like the
    great city?"
19And they threw dust on
their heads, as they wept
and mourned, crying out,
  "Alas, alas, the great
    city,
    where all who had ships
      at sea
    grew rich by her
      wealth!
    For in one hour she has
      been laid waste."
20 Rejoice over her,
O heaven, you saints and
apostles and prophets! For
God has given judgment
for you against her.
21 Then a mighty angel
took up a stone like a great
millstone and threw it into
the sea, saying,
  "With such violence
    Babylon the great city
      will be thrown down,
      and will be found no
        more;

---

013   4147   575   846   575   3113
οἱ   πλουτήσαντες   ἀπ’ αὐτῆς ἀπὸ μακρόθεν
the ones being rich   from her   from from far
2476   1223   04   5401   02   929   846
στήσονται διὰ   τὸν φόβον τοῦ   βασανισμοῦ αὐτῆς
will stand through   the fear of the torment   of her
2799   2532 3996   3004   3759 3759 05
κλαίοντες καὶ πενθοῦντες 16 λέγοντες· οὐαὶ οὐαί, ἡ
crying   and mourning   saying,   woe woe, the
4172 05   3173   05   4016   1039   2532
πόλις ἡ   μεγάλη, ἡ   περιβεβλημένη βύσσινον καὶ
city the great,   the having thrown linen   and
                               around herself
4210   2532 2847   2532 5558   1722
πορφυροῦν καὶ κόκκινον καὶ κεχρυσωμένη   [ἐν]
purple   and scarlet   and having made golden in
5553   2532 3037 5093   2532 3135   3754
χρυσίῳ καὶ λίθῳ τιμίῳ   καὶ μαργαρίτῃ,   17 ὅτι
gold   and stone valuable and pearl,   because
1520 5610 2049   01 5118   4149   2532
μιᾷ   ὥρᾳ ἠρημώθη   ὁ τοσοῦτος πλοῦτος. Καὶ
in one hour was desolated the such rich.   And
3956 2942   2532 3956 01   1909 5117   4126
πᾶς κυβερνήτης καὶ πᾶς ὁ   ἐπὶ τόπον πλέων
all helmsman   and all the one on place sailing
2532 3492   2532 3745   08 2281   2038
καὶ ναῦται καὶ ὅσοι   τὴν θάλασσαν ἐργάζονται,
and sailors and as many as the sea   work,
575   3113   2476   2532 2896   991
ἀπὸ μακρόθεν ἔστησαν 18 καὶ ἔκραζον   βλέποντες
from from far they stood and were shouting seeing
04   2586   06   4451   846   3004   5101 3664
τὸν καπνὸν τῆς   πυρώσεως αὐτῆς λέγοντες· τίς ὁμοία
the smoke   of the burning of her saying,   what like
07   4172 07 3173   2532 906   5529a 1909
τῇ   πόλει τῇ μεγάλῃ; 19 καὶ ἔβαλον   χοῦν ἐπὶ
to the city the great?   And they threw dust on
020 2776   846   2532 2896   3799   2532
τὰς κεφαλὰς αὐτῶν καὶ ἔκραζον   κλαίοντες καὶ
the heads   of them and were shouting crying   and
3996   3004   3759 3759 05 4172 05   3173
πενθοῦντες λέγοντες· οὐαὶ οὐαί, ἡ   πόλις ἡ   μεγάλη,
mourning   saying,   woe woe, the city the great,
1722 2739 4147   3956 013 2192   024
ἐν ᾗ   ἐπλούτησαν πάντες οἱ ἔχοντες τὰ
in which were rich   all   the ones having the
4143 1722 07 2281   1537 06 5094   846
πλοῖα ἐν τῇ θαλάσσῃ ἐκ τῆς τιμιότητος αὐτῆς,
boats in the sea   from the most valuable of her,
3754   1520 5610 2049   20 2165   1909
ὅτι   μιᾷ ὥρᾳ ἠρημώθη.   Εὐφραίνου ἐπ’
because in one hour it was desolated. Be merry on
846   3772   2532 013 40   2532 013 652   2532
αὐτῇ, οὐρανὲ καὶ οἱ ἅγιοι   καὶ οἱ ἀπόστολοι καὶ
her, heaven and the holy ones and the delegates and
013 4396   3754   2919   01 2316 012 2917
οἱ προφῆται, ὅτι   ἔκρινεν ὁ θεὸς τὸ κρίμα
the spokesmen, because judged the God the judgment
1473 1537 846   21 2532 142   1520 32
ὑμῶν ἐξ αὐτῆς.   Καὶ ἦρεν   εἷς ἄγγελος
of you from her.   And lifted up one messenger
2478   3037 5613 3457a   3173 2532 906   1519 08
ἰσχυρὸς λίθον ὡς μύλινον μέγαν καὶ ἔβαλεν εἰς τὴν
strong   stone as of mill great and threw into the
2281   3004   3779 3731   906   897
θάλασσαν λέγων· οὕτως ὁρμήματι βληθήσεται Βαβυλὼν
sea   saying, thusly in rush will be thrown Babylon
05   3173 4172 2532 3756 3361 2147
ἡ   μεγάλη πόλις καὶ οὐ μὴ εὑρεθῇ
the great   city and not not it might be found

2089	**22**	2532	5456	2790		2532	3451		2532
ἔτι.		καὶ	φωνὴ	κιθαρῳδῶν	καὶ	μουσικῶν	καὶ		
still.		And	sound	of harpists	and	musicians	and		

834		2532	4538		3756	3361	191		1722
αὐλητῶν	καὶ	σαλπιστῶν	οὐ	μὴ	ἀκουσθῇ		ἐν
flutists	and	trumpeters	not	not	might be heard	in

1473	2089		2532	3956	5079		3956		5078	3756	3361
σοὶ	ἔτι,	καὶ	πᾶς	τεχνίτης	πάσης	τέχνης	οὐ	μὴ
you	still,	and	all	craftsman	of all	craft	not	not

2147			1722	1473	2089		2532	5456	3458		3756
εὑρεθῇ		ἐν	σοὶ	ἔτι,	καὶ	φωνὴ	μύλου	οὐ
might be found	in	you	still,	and	sound	of mill	not

3361	191		1722	1473	2089	**23**	2532	5457	3088
μὴ	ἀκουσθῇ	ἐν	σοὶ	ἔτι,		καὶ	φῶς	λύχνου
not	it was heard	in	you	still,		and	light	of lamp

3756	3361	5316		1722	1473	2089		2532	5456
οὐ	μὴ	φάνῃ	ἐν	σοὶ	ἔτι,	καὶ	φωνὴ
not	not	might shine	in	you	still,	and	voice

3566		2532	3565		3756	3361	191		1722
νυμφίου	καὶ	νύμφης	οὐ	μὴ	ἀκουσθῇ		ἐν
of bridegroom	and	bride	not	not	might be heard		in

1473	2089		3754		013	1713		1473		1510	013
σοὶ	ἔτι·	ὅτι	οἱ	ἔμποροί	σου	ἦσαν	οἱ
you	still;	because	the	merchants	of you	were	the

3175		06		1093		3754		1722	07	5331
μεγιστᾶνες	τῆς		γῆς,	ὅτι	ἐν	τῇ	φαρμακείᾳ
great ones	of the earth,		because	in	the		magic

1473	4105		3956	021	1484	**24**	2532	1722	846
σου	ἐπλανήθησαν	πάντα	τὰ	ἔθνη,		καὶ	ἐν	αὐτῇ
of you	were deceived	all		the nations,		and	in	her

129	4396		2532	40		2147		2532	3956
αἷμα	προφητῶν	καὶ	ἁγίων	εὑρέθη	καὶ	πάντων
blood	of spokesmen	and	holy ones	was found	and	of all

014	4969		1909	06	1093	**19:1**	3326	3778
τῶν	ἐσφαγμένων		ἐπὶ	τῆς	γῆς.		Μετὰ	ταῦτα
the ones having been slaughtered		on	the	earth.		After	these

191		5613	5456	3173		3793		4183		1722	03
ἤκουσα	ὡς		φωνὴν	μεγάλην	ὄχλου		πολλοῦ	ἐν	τῷ
I heard	as	sound	great		of crowd	much		in	the

3772		3004		239		05	4991		2532	05
οὐρανῷ	λεγόντων·	ἀλληλουϊά·	ἡ	σωτηρία	καὶ	ἡ
heaven	saying,	hallelujah;	the	deliverance	and	the

1391		2532	05	1411		02		2316	1473	**2**	3754
δόξα	καὶ	ἡ	δύναμις	τοῦ	θεοῦ	ἡμῶν,		ὅτι
splendor	and	the	power	of the	God	of us,		because

228		2532	1342	017	2920		846		3754
ἀληθιναὶ	καὶ	δίκαιαι	αἱ	κρίσεις	αὐτοῦ·	ὅτι
true	and	right	the	judgments	of him;	because

2919		08	4204		08	3173	3748	5351
ἔκρινεν	τὴν	πόρνην	τὴν	μεγάλην	ἥτις	ἔφθειρεν
he judged	the	prostitute	the	great	who	corrupted

08	1093	1722	07	4202		846		2532	1556		012
τὴν	γῆν	ἐν	τῇ	πορνείᾳ	αὐτῆς,	καὶ	ἐξεδίκησεν	τὸ
the earth	in	the	sexual immorality	of her,	and	he brought out right

129	014		1401	846		1537	5495	846	**3**	2532
αἷμα	τῶν	δούλων	αὐτοῦ	ἐκ	χειρὸς	αὐτῆς.		καὶ
blood	of the	slaves	of him	from	hand	of her.		And

1208		3004		239		2532	01	2586
δεύτερον	εἴρηκαν·	ἀλληλουϊά·	καὶ	ὁ	καπνὸς
second	they have said,	hallelujah;	and	the	smoke

846	305		1519	016	165		014		165	**4**	2532
αὐτῆς	ἀναβαίνει	εἰς	τοὺς	αἰῶνας	τῶν	αἰώνων.		καὶ
of her	goes up	into	the	ages	of the	ages.		And

4098	013	4245		013	1501	5064		2532	021
ἔπεσαν	οἱ	πρεσβύτεροι	οἱ	εἴκοσι	τέσσαρες	καὶ	τὰ
fell	the	older men	the	twenty	four	and	the

22 and the sound of harpists
and minstrels and
of flutists and
trumpeters
will be heard in you
no more;
and an artisan of any
trade
will be found in you
no more;
and the sound of the
millstone
will be heard in you
no more;
23 and the light of a lamp
will shine in you no
more;
and the voice of bride-
groom and bride
will be heard in you
no more;
for your merchants were
the magnates of the
earth,
and all nations were
deceived by your
sorcery.
24 And in you[a] was found
the blood of prophets
and of saints,
and of all who have
been slaughtered on
earth."

CHAPTER 19

After this I heard what
seemed to be the loud voice
of a great multitude in
heaven, saying,
"Hallelujah!
Salvation and glory and
power to our God,
2 for his judgments are
true and just;
he has judged the great
whore
who corrupted the
earth with her
fornication,
and he has avenged on
her the blood of his
servants."[b]
3 Once more they said,
"Hallelujah!
The smoke goes up from
her forever and ever."
4 And the twenty-four elders
and the

a Gk her
b Gk slaves

four living creatures fell
down and worshiped God
who is seated on the throne,
saying,
"Amen. Hallelujah!"
5 And from the throne
came a voice saying,
"Praise our God,
all you his servants,[a]
and all who fear him,
small and great."
6Then I heard what seemed
to be the voice of a great
multitude, like the sound
of many waters and like the
sound of mighty thunder-
peals, crying out,
"Hallelujah!
For the Lord our God
the Almighty reigns.
7 Let us rejoice and exult
and give him the glory,
for the marriage of the
Lamb has come,
and his bride has made
herself ready;
8 to her it has been granted
to be clothed
with fine linen, bright
and pure"—
for the fine linen is the
righteous deeds of the
saints.

9 And the angel said[b]
to me, "Write this: Blessed
are those who are invited to
the marriage supper of the
Lamb." And he said to me,
"These are true words of
God." 10Then I fell down at
his feet to worship him, but
he said to me, "You must
not do that! I am a fellow
servant[c] with you and
your comrades[d] who hold
the testimony of Jesus.[e]
Worship God! For the
testimony of Jesus[e] is the
spirit of prophecy."

a Gk *slaves*
b Gk *he said*
c Gk *slave*
d Gk *brothers*
e Or *to Jesus*

5064 2226 2532 4352 03 2316 03
τέσσαρα ζῷα καὶ προσεκύνησαν τῷ θεῷ τῷ
four living ones and they worshiped the God the
2521 1909 03 2362 3004 281 239
καθημένῳ ἐπὶ τῷ θρόνῳ λέγοντες· ἀμὴν ἁλληλουϊά,
one sitting on the throne saying, amen hallelujah,
5 2532 5456 575 02 2362 1831 3004 134
Καὶ φωνὴ ἀπὸ τοῦ θρόνου ἐξῆλθεν λέγουσα· αἰνεῖτε
and voice from the throne came out saying, praise
03 2316 1473 3956 013 1401 846 2532 013
τῷ θεῷ ἡμῶν πάντες οἱ δοῦλοι αὐτοῦ [καὶ] οἱ
the God of us all the slaves of him and the ones
5399 846 013 3398 2532 013 3173 2532
φοβούμενοι αὐτόν, οἱ μικροὶ καὶ οἱ μεγάλοι. 6 Καὶ
fearing him, the small and the great. And
191 5613 5456 3793 4183 2532 5613 5456
ἤκουσα ὡς φωνὴν ὄχλου πολλοῦ καὶ ὡς φωνὴν
I heard as sound of crowd much and as sound
5204 4183 2532 5613 5456 1027 2478
ὑδάτων πολλῶν καὶ ὡς φωνὴν βροντῶν ἰσχυρῶν
of waters many and as sound of thunders strong
3004 239 3754 936 2962 01
λεγόντων· ἁλληλουϊά, ὅτι ἐβασίλευσεν κύριος ὁ
saying, hallelujah, because was king Master the
2316 1473 01 3841 5463 2532
θεὸς [ἡμῶν] ὁ παντοκράτωρ. 7 χαίρωμεν καὶ
God of us the all-strength. We might rejoice and
21 2532 1325 08 1391
ἀγαλλιῶμεν καὶ δώσωμεν τὴν δόξαν
we might be glad and we might give the splendor
846 3754 2064 01 1062 010 721 2532
αὐτῷ, ὅτι ἦλθεν ὁ γάμος τοῦ ἀρνίου καὶ
to him, because came the marriage of the lamb and
05 1135 846 2090 1438 2532 1325
ἡ γυνὴ αὐτοῦ ἡτοίμασεν ἑαυτὴν 8 καὶ ἐδόθη
the woman of him prepared herself and it was given
846 2443 4016 1039
αὐτῇ ἵνα περιβάληται βύσσινον
to her that she might throw around herself linen
2986 2513 09 1063 1039 021 1345
λαμπρὸν καθαρόν· τὸ γὰρ βύσσινον τὰ δικαιώματα
bright clean; the for linen the right acts
014 40 1510 2532 3004 1473 1125
τῶν ἁγίων ἐστίν. 9 Καὶ λέγει μοι· γράψον·
of the holy is. And he says to me, write:
3107 013 1519 012 1173 02 1062
μακάριοι οἱ εἰς τὸ δεῖπνον τοῦ γάμου
fortunate the ones into the dinner of the marriage
010 721 2564 2532 3004 1473
τοῦ ἀρνίου κεκλημένοι. καὶ λέγει μοι·
of the lamb having been called. And he says to me,
3778 013 3056 228 02 2316 1510 2532
οὗτοι οἱ λόγοι ἀληθινοὶ τοῦ θεοῦ εἰσιν. 10 καὶ
these the words true of the God are. And
4098 1715 014 4228 846 4352 846
ἔπεσα ἔμπροσθεν τῶν ποδῶν αὐτοῦ προσκυνῆσαι αὐτῷ.
I fell in front of the feet of him to worship him.
2532 3004 1473 3708 3361 4889 1473 1510
καὶ λέγει μοι· ὅρα μή· σύνδουλός σού εἰμι
And he says to me, see not; co-slave of you I am
2532 014 80 1473 014 2192 08
καὶ τῶν ἀδελφῶν σου τῶν ἐχόντων τὴν
and of the brothers of you the ones having the
3141 2424 03 2316 4352 05 1063
μαρτυρίαν Ἰησοῦ· τῷ θεῷ προσκύνησον. ἡ γὰρ
testimony of Jesus; to the God worship. The for
3141 2424 1510 09 4151 06
μαρτυρία Ἰησοῦ ἐστιν τὸ πνεῦμα τῆς
testimony of Jesus is the spirit of the

4394
προφητείας. **11**
2532 3708 04 3772
Καὶ εἶδον τὸν οὐρανὸν
speaking before. And I saw the heaven

455
ἠνεῳγμένον,
2532 2400 2462 3022 2532 01
καὶ ἰδοὺ ἵππος λευκός καὶ ὁ
having been opened, and look horse white and the one

2521   1909 846   2564   4103   2532
καθήμενος ἐπ' αὐτὸν [καλούμενος] πιστὸς καὶ
sitting   on it   being called trustful and

228   2532 1722 1343   2919   2532 4170
ἀληθινός, καὶ ἐν δικαιοσύνῃ κρίνει καὶ πολεμεῖ.
true,   and in rightness he judges and makes war.

12
013 1161 3788   846   5613 5395 4442   2532
οἱ δὲ ὀφθαλμοὶ αὐτοῦ [ὡς] φλὸξ πυρός, καὶ
The but eyes   of him as flame of fire, and

1909 08 2776   846   1238   4183   2192 3686
ἐπὶ τὴν κεφαλὴν αὐτοῦ διαδήματα πολλά, ἔχων ὄνομα
on the head   of him diadems   many, having name

1125   3739 3762 3609a 1487 3361
γεγραμμένον   ὃ οὐδεὶς οἶδεν εἰ μὴ
having been written that no one knew except

846   **13** 2532 4016   2440   911
αὐτός,   καὶ περιβεβλημένος ἱμάτιον βεβαμμένον
himself, and having thrown clothes having been
              around himself   dipped

129   2532 2564   09 3686   846   01
αἵματι, καὶ κέκληται   τὸ ὄνομα αὐτοῦ ὁ
in blood, and has been called the name of him the

3056 02   2316 **14** 2532 021 4753   021 1722
λόγος τοῦ θεοῦ. Καὶ τὰ στρατεύματα [τὰ] ἐν
word of the God. And the armies   the in

03 3772 190   846 1909 2462 3022
τῷ οὐρανῷ ἠκολούθει αὐτῷ ἐφ' ἵπποις λευκοῖς,
the heaven were following him on horses white,

1746   1039   3022   2513
ἐνδεδυμένοι   βύσσινον λευκὸν καθαρόν.
having put on themselves linen white clean.

15
2532 1537 010 4750   846   1607   4501
καὶ ἐκ τοῦ στόματος αὐτοῦ ἐκπορεύεται ῥομφαία
And from the mouth of him travels out sword

3691   2443 1722 846 3960   024 1484   2532
ὀξεῖα, ἵνα ἐν αὐτῇ πατάξῃ τὰ ἔθνη, καὶ
sharp, that in it he might hit the nations, and

846   4165   846   1722 4464 4603   2532
αὐτὸς ποιμανεῖ   αὐτοὺς ἐν ῥάβδῳ σιδηρᾷ, καὶ
himself will shepherd them in rod iron,   and

846   3961 08 3025   02   3631 02   2372
αὐτὸς πατεῖ τὴν ληνὸν τοῦ οἴνου τοῦ θυμοῦ
himself walks the winepress of the wine of the fury

06   3709 02   2316 02 3841   **16** 2532
τῆς ὀργῆς τοῦ θεοῦ τοῦ παντοκράτορος, καὶ
of the anger of the God the all-strength, and

2192 1909 012 2440   2532 1909 04 3382 846
ἔχει ἐπὶ τὸ ἱμάτιον καὶ ἐπὶ τὸν μηρὸν αὐτοῦ
he has on the clothes and on the thigh of him

3686 1125   935   935   2532
ὄνομα γεγραμμένον·   Βασιλεὺς βασιλέων καὶ
name having been written, King of kings and

2962 2962   **17** 2532 3708 1520 32
κύριος κυρίων.   Καὶ εἶδον ἕνα ἄγγελον
Master of masters. And I saw one messenger

2476   1722 03 2246 2532 2896   1722 5456
ἑστῶτα ἐν τῷ ἡλίῳ καὶ ἔκραξεν [ἐν] φωνῇ
having stood in the sun and he shouted in voice

3173 3004 3956 023 3732   023 4072
μεγάλῃ λέγων πᾶσιν τοῖς ὀρνέοις τοῖς πετομένοις
great saying to all the birds the ones flying

1722 3321   2532 4863   1519 012
ἐν μεσουρανήματι· Δεῦτε συνάχθητε εἰς τὸ
in middle heaven: come bring together into the

11 Then I saw heaven opened, and there was a white horse! Its rider is called Faithful and True, and in righteousness he judges and makes war. [12]His eyes are like a flame of fire, and on his head are many diadems; and he has a name inscribed that no one knows but himself. [13]He is clothed in a robe dipped in[a] blood, and his name is called The Word of God. [14]And the armies of heaven, wearing fine linen, white and pure, were following him on white horses. [15]From his mouth comes a sharp sword with which to strike down the nations, and he will rule[b] them with a rod of iron; he will tread the wine press of the fury of the wrath of God the Almighty. [16]On his robe and on his thigh he has a name inscribed, "King of kings and Lord of lords."

17 Then I saw an angel standing in the sun, and with a loud voice he called to all the birds that fly in midheaven, "Come, gather for the

---

[a] Other ancient authorities read *sprinkled with*

[b] Or *will shepherd*

great supper of God, [18]to eat the flesh of kings, the flesh of captains, the flesh of the mighty, the flesh of horses and their riders—flesh of all, both free and slave, both small and great." [19]Then I saw the beast and the kings of the earth with their armies gathered to make war against the rider on the horse and against his army. [20]And the beast was captured, and with it the false prophet who had performed in its presence the signs by which he deceived those who had received the mark of the beast and those who worshiped its image. These two were thrown alive into the lake of fire that burns with sulfur. [21]And the rest were killed by the sword of the rider on the horse, the sword that came from his mouth; and all the birds were gorged with their flesh.

CHAPTER 20

Then I saw an angel coming down from heaven, holding in his hand the key to the bottomless pit and a great chain. [2]He seized the dragon, that ancient serpent, who is the Devil and Satan,

1173	012	3173	02		2316	**18**	2443	2068
δεῖπνον	τὸ	μέγα	τοῦ		θεοῦ		ἵνα	φάγητε
dinner	the	great	of the		God		that	you might eat

4561	935		2532	4561	5506			2532
σάρκας	βασιλέων	καὶ		σάρκας	χιλιάρχων			καὶ
flesh	of kings	and		flesh	rulers of thousand			and

4561	2478		2532	4561	2462		2532	014
σάρκας	ἰσχυρῶν	καὶ		σάρκας	ἵππων		καὶ	τῶν
flesh	of strong	and		flesh	of horses		and	of the

2521		1909	846	2532	4561	3956	1658
καθημένων		ἐπ'	αὐτῶν	καὶ	σάρκας	πάντων	ἐλευθέρων
ones sitting		on	them	and	flesh	of all	free

5037	2532	1401		2532	3398	2532	3173		2532
τε	καὶ	δούλων	καὶ		μικρῶν	καὶ	μεγάλων.	**19**	Καὶ
both	and	slaves	and		small	and	great.		And

3708	012	2342		2532	016	935	06	1093
εἶδον	τὸ	θηρίον		καὶ	τοὺς	βασιλεῖς	τῆς	γῆς
I saw	the	wild animal		and	the	kings	of the	earth

2532	024	4753		846	4863		4160	04
καὶ	τὰ	στρατεύματα		αὐτῶν	συνηγμένα		ποιῆσαι	τὸν
and	the	armies		of them	having been brought together		to make	the

4171	3326	02	2521		1909	02	2462	2532	3326
πόλεμον	μετὰ	τοῦ	καθημένου		ἐπὶ	τοῦ	ἵππου	καὶ	μετὰ
war	with	the	one sitting		on	the	horse	and	with

010	4753		846		2532	4084		09
τοῦ	στρατεύματος		αὐτοῦ.	**20**	καὶ	ἐπιάσθη		τὸ
the	army		of him.		And	was captured		the

2342		2532	3326	846	01	5578		01
θηρίον		καὶ	μετ'	αὐτοῦ	ὁ	ψευδοπροφήτης		ὁ
wild animal		and	with him		the	false spokesman		the

4160		024	4592	1799		846	1722	3739
ποιήσας		τὰ	σημεῖα	ἐνώπιον		αὐτοῦ,	ἐν	οἷς
one having done		the	signs	before		it,	in	which

4105		016		2983		012	5480
ἐπλάνησεν		τοὺς		λαβόντας		τὸ	χάραγμα
he deceived		the		ones having received		the	mark

010	2342		2532	016	4352		07
τοῦ	θηρίου		καὶ	τοὺς	προσκυνοῦντας		τῇ
of the	wild animal		and	the	ones worshiping		the

1504	846		2198	906		013	1417	1519	08
εἰκόνι	αὐτοῦ·		ζῶντες	ἐβλήθησαν		οἱ	δύο	εἰς	τὴν
image	of him;		living	were thrown		the	two	into	the

3041	010	4442	06	2545		1722	2303
λίμνην	τοῦ	πυρὸς	τῆς	καιομένης		ἐν	θείῳ.
lake	of the	fire	the	one being burned		in	sulphur.

21	2532	013	3062		615		1722	07	4501
	καὶ	οἱ	λοιποὶ		ἀπεκτάνθησαν	ἐν		τῇ	ῥομφαίᾳ
	And	the	remaining		were killed	in		the	sword

02		2521		1909	02	2462	07	1831
τοῦ		καθημένου		ἐπὶ	τοῦ	ἵππου	τῇ	ἐξελθούσῃ
of the		one sitting		on	the	horse	the	having gone out

1537	010	4750		846		2532	3956	021	3732
ἐκ	τοῦ	στόματος		αὐτοῦ,		καὶ	πάντα	τὰ	ὄρνεα
from	the	mouth		of him,		and	all	the	birds

5526		1537	018	4561	846		**20:1**	2532	3708
ἐχορτάσθησαν		ἐκ	τῶν	σαρκῶν	αὐτῶν.			Καὶ	εἶδον
were satisfied		from	the	flesh	of them.			And	I saw

32		2597		1537	02	3772	2192	08
ἄγγελον		καταβαίνοντα	ἐκ		τοῦ	οὐρανοῦ	ἔχοντα	τὴν
messenger		coming down	from		the	heaven	having	the

2807	06	12		2532	254	3173	1909	08
κλεῖν	τῆς	ἀβύσσου		καὶ	ἅλυσιν	μεγάλην	ἐπὶ	τὴν
key	of the	bottomless		and	chain	great	on	the

5495	846	**2**	2532	2902		04	1404	01	3789
χεῖρα	αὐτοῦ.		καὶ	ἐκράτησεν		τὸν	δράκοντα,	ὁ	ὄφις
hand	of him.		And	he held		the	dragon,	the	snake

01	744		3739	1510	1228		2532	01	4567
ὁ	ἀρχαῖος,		ὅς	ἐστιν	Διάβολος		καὶ	ὁ	Σατανᾶς,
the	ancient,		who	is	Slanderer		and	the	Adversary,

2532 1210   846   5507   2094 **3** 2532 906
καὶ ἔδησεν αὐτὸν χίλια   ἔτη   καὶ ἔβαλεν
and he bound him   thousand years   and he threw

846   1519 08   12   2532 2808   2532 4972
αὐτὸν εἰς τὴν ἄβυσσον   καὶ ἔκλεισεν καὶ ἐσφράγισεν
him   into the bottomless and closed   and sealed

1883 846   2443 3361 4105   2089 024
ἐπάνω αὐτοῦ, ἵνα μὴ πλανήσῃ   ἔτι τὰ
upon him,   that not he might deceive still the

1484   891   5055   021 5507   2094   3326
ἔθνη ἄχρι τελεσθῇ   τὰ χίλια   ἔτη. μετὰ
nations until were completed the thousand years. After

3778 1163   3089   846   3398
ταῦτα δεῖ   λυθῆναι   αὐτὸν μικρὸν
these it is necessary to be loosed him   small

5550   **4** 2532 3708 2362   2532 2523   1909 846
χρόνον.   Καὶ εἶδον θρόνους καὶ ἐκάθισαν ἐπ᾿ αὐτοὺς
time.   And I saw thrones and they sat on   them

2532 2917   1325   846   2532 020 5590 '014
καὶ κρίμα ἐδόθη   αὐτοῖς, καὶ τὰς ψυχὰς τῶν
and judgment was given to them, and the souls of the

3990   1223   08 3141   2424   2532
πεπελεκισμένων διὰ   τὴν μαρτυρίαν ᾿Ιησοῦ καὶ
ones having   because the testimony of Jesus and
been beheaded

1223 04   3056 02   2316 2532 3748   3756
διὰ   τὸν λόγον τοῦ   θεοῦ καὶ οἵτινες οὐ
because the word of the God and who   not

4352   012 2342   3761   08 1504   846
προσεκύνησαν τὸ θηρίον   οὐδὲ τὴν εἰκόνα αὐτοῦ
worshiped   the wild animal but not the image of him

2532 3756 2983   012 5480   1909 012 3359
καὶ οὐκ ἔλαβον   τὸ χάραγμα ἐπὶ τὸ μέτωπον
and not they received the mark   on the forehead

2532 1909 08 5495 846   2532 2198   2532
καὶ ἐπὶ τὴν χεῖρα αὐτῶν. καὶ ἔζησαν καὶ
and on the hand of them. And they lived and

936   3326 02 5547   5507   2094 **5** 013
ἐβασίλευσαν μετὰ τοῦ Χριστοῦ χίλια   ἔτη.   οἱ
were kings   with the Christ thousand years. The

3062   014   3498   3756 2198   891
λοιποὶ τῶν νεκρῶν οὐκ ἔζησαν ἄχρι
remaining of the dead not they lived until

5055   021 5507   2094   3778 05
τελεσθῇ   τὰ χίλια   ἔτη. Αὕτη ἡ
were completed the thousand years. This the

386   05 4413   3107   2532 40   01
ἀνάστασις ἡ πρώτη. **6** μακάριος καὶ ἅγιος ὁ
standing up the first.   Fortunate and holy the one

2192 3313 1722 07 386   07 4413   1909 3778
ἔχων μέρος ἐν τῇ ἀναστάσει τῇ πρώτη· ἐπὶ τούτων
having part in the standing up the first; on these

01 1208   2288   3756 2192 1849   235
ὁ δεύτερος θάνατος οὐκ ἔχει ἐξουσίαν, ἀλλ᾿
the second   death   not has authority, but

1510   2409   02   2316 2532 02   5547
ἔσονται ἱερεῖς τοῦ θεοῦ καὶ τοῦ   Χριστοῦ
they will be priests of the God and of the Christ

2532 936   3326 846   024 5507   2094
καὶ βασιλεύσουσιν μετ᾿ αὐτοῦ [τὰ] χίλια   ἔτη.
and they will be king with him   the thousand years.

7 2532 3752 5055   021 5507   2094
Καὶ ὅταν τελεσθῇ   τὰ χίλια   ἔτη,
And when were completed the thousand years,

3089   01 4567   1537 06 5438   846
λυθήσεται ὁ σατανᾶς ἐκ τῆς φυλακῆς αὐτοῦ
will be loosed the adversary from the guard   of him

8 2532 1831   4105   024 1484   024 1722
καὶ ἐξελεύσεται πλανῆσαι τὰ ἔθνη τὰ ἐν
and he will go out to deceive the nations the in

and bound him for a
thousand years, [3]and threw
him into the pit, and locked
and sealed it over him, so
that he would deceive the
nations no more, until the
thousand years were ended.
After that he must be let
out for a little while.

4 Then I saw thrones, and
those seated on them were
given authority to judge. I
also saw the souls of those
who had been beheaded for
their testimony to Jesus[a]
and for the word of God.
They had not worshiped
the beast or its image and
had not received its mark
on their foreheads or their
hands. They came to life
and reigned with Christ a
thousand years. [5](The rest
of the dead did not come
to life until the thousand
years were ended.) This
is the first resurrection.
[6]Blessed and holy are
those who share in the first
resurrection. Over these the
second death has no power,
but they will be priests
of God and of Christ, and
they will reign with him a
thousand years.

7 When the thousand
years are ended, Satan will
be released from his prison
[8]and will come out to
deceive the nations at

---

[a] Or for the testimony of Jesus

the four corners of the earth, Gog and Magog, in order to gather them for battle; they are as numerous as the sands of the sea. 9They marched up over the breadth of the earth and surrounded the camp of the saints and the beloved city. And fire came down from heaven[a] and consumed them. 10And the devil who had deceived them was thrown into the lake of fire and sulfur, where the beast and the false prophet were, and they will be tormented day and night forever and ever.

11 Then I saw a great white throne and the one who sat on it; the earth and the heaven fled from his presence, and no place was found for them. 12And I saw the dead, great and small, standing before the throne, and books were opened. Also another book was opened, the book of life. And the dead were judged according to their works, as recorded in the books. 13And the sea gave up the dead that were in it, Death and Hades gave up the dead that were in them, and all were judged

[a] Other ancient authorities read *from God, out of heaven,* or *out of heaven from God*

```
019    5064      1137     06      1093    04   1136  2532
ταῖς  τέσσαρσιν γωνίαις τῆς    γῆς,   τὸν  Γὼγ  καὶ
the    four      corners  of the  earth,  the  Gog  and
3098     4863              846    1519 04  4171         3739
Μαγώγ, συναγαγεῖν         αὐτοὺς εἰς  τὸν πόλεμον,  ὧν
Magog, to bring together  them   into the  war,       whose
01  706    846      5613 05  285    06        2281
ὁ  ἀριθμὸς αὐτῶν  ὡς  ἡ  ἄμμος τῆς   θαλάσσης.
the number  of them  as  the  sand  of the  sea.
    2532 305         1909 012 4114   06      1093  2532
  9 καὶ  ἀνέβησαν  ἐπὶ  τὸ πλάτος τῆς    γῆς  καὶ
    And  they went up on  the  width  of the  earth and
2942a       08   3925        014    40          2532 08
ἐκύκλευσαν  τὴν παρεμβολὴν τῶν   ἁγίων      καὶ  τὴν
they circled the barracks     of the  holy ones and  the
4172  08  25               2532 2597       4442
πόλιν τὴν ἠγαπημένην,       καὶ  κατέβη    πῦρ
city  the one having been loved, and  went down fire
1537 02  3772     2532 2719      846     10 2532 01
ἐκ  τοῦ οὐρανοῦ καὶ κατέφαγεν αὐτούς.     καὶ  ὁ
from the heaven and ate up      them.       And  the
1228     01  4105         846      906        1519 08
διάβολος ὁ  πλανῶν       αὐτοὺς ἐβλήθη     εἰς  τὴν
slanderer the one deceiving them  was thrown into the
3041  010   4442 2532 2303     3699 2532 09
λίμνην τοῦ  πυρὸς καὶ θείου ὅπου καὶ  τὸ
lake  of the fire  and sulphur where also the
2342      2532 01  5578            2532
θηρίον    καὶ  ὁ  ψευδοπροφήτης, καὶ
wild animal and  the false spokesman, and
928              2250   2532 3571   1519 016
βασανισθήσονται ἡμέρας καὶ νυκτὸς εἰς  τοὺς
they will be tormented day  and  night into the
165   014   165         2532 3708 2362  3173
αἰῶνας τῶν  αἰώνων.   11 Καὶ  εἶδον θρόνον μέγαν
ages  of the ages.       And  I saw throne great
3022   2532 04  2521        1909 846      3739     575
λευκὸν καὶ  τὸν καθίμενον ἐπ’ αὐτόν, οὗ     ἀπὸ
white  and  the one sitting on  it,   of whom from
010 4383        5343     05  1093 2532 01  3772    2532
τοῦ προσώπου ἔφυγεν ἡ  γῆ  καὶ  ὁ  οὐρανὸς καὶ
the face        fled    the earth and the heaven and
5117 3756 2147         846     12 2532 3708 016
τόπος οὐχ εὑρέθη      αὐτοῖς.     καὶ  εἶδον τοὺς
place not  was found to them.     And  I saw the
3498     016  3173        2532 016  3398     2476
νεκρούς, τοὺς μεγάλους καὶ τοὺς μικρούς, ἑστῶτας
dead,    the  great     and the  small,   having stood
1799      02  2362     2532 975     455        2532
ἐνώπιον τοῦ θρόνου. καὶ βιβλία    ἠνοίχθησαν, καὶ
before   the throne. And small books were opened  and
243   975     455        3739 1510 06  2222
ἄλλο βιβλίον ἠνοίχθη,    ὅ  ἐστιν τῆς  ζωῆς,
other small book was opened, which is  of the life,
2532 2919      013 3498  1537 022
καὶ  ἐκρίθησαν οἱ  νεκροὶ ἐκ  τῶν
and  were judged the dead  from the
1125                1722 023 975        2596 024
γεγραμμένων       ἐν  τοῖς βιβλίοις  κατὰ τὰ
having been written in  the  small books by   the
2041 846     13 2532 1325    05 2532 016 3498
ἔργα αὐτῶν.     καὶ  ἔδωκεν ἡ  θάλασσα τοὺς νεκροὺς
works of them.  And  gave   the sea      the dead
016 1722 846   2532 01  2288      2532 01  86    1325
τοὺς ἐν  αὐτῇ καὶ  ὁ  θάνατος καὶ  ὁ  ἅδης ἔδωκαν
the  in  it   and  the death   and  the hades gave
016 3498     016  1722 846   2532 2919
τοὺς νεκροὺς τοὺς ἐν  αὐτοῖς, καὶ  ἐκρίθησαν
the  dead    the  in  them,    and  were judged
```

1538   2596 024 2041   846   **14** 2532 01   2288   2532
ἕκαστος κατὰ τὰ ἔργα αὐτῶν.   καὶ ὁ θάνατος καὶ
each   by   the works of them.   And the death and

01 86   906   1519 08 3041   010   4442
ὁ ᾅδης ἐβλήθησαν εἰς τὴν λίμνην τοῦ πυρός.
the hades were thrown into the lake of the fire.

3778 01 2288   01 1208   1510 05 3041 010
οὗτος ὁ θάνατος ὁ δεύτερός ἐστιν, ἡ λίμνη τοῦ
This the death the second is,   the lake of the

4442   **15** 2532 1487 5100 3756 2147   1722 07 976
πυρός.   καὶ εἴ τις οὐχ εὑρέθη ἐν τῇ βίβλῳ
fire.   And if some not was found in the book

06   2222 1125   906   1519
τῆς ζωῆς γεγραμμένος,   ἐβλήθη   εἰς
of the life having been written, he was thrown into

08 3041   010   4442   **21:1** 2532 3708 3772
τὴν λίμνην τοῦ πυρός.   Καὶ εἶδον οὐρανὸν
the lake of the fire.   And I saw heaven

2537   2532 1093 2537   01 1063 4413   3772   2532
καινὸν καὶ γῆν καινήν. ὁ γὰρ πρῶτος οὐρανὸς καὶ
new   and earth new. The for first heaven and

05 4413 1093 565   2532 05 2281   3756 1510
ἡ πρώτη γῆ ἀπῆλθαν καὶ ἡ θάλασσα οὐκ ἔστιν
the first earth went off and the sea   not is

2089   **2** 2532 08 4172 08 40   2419   2537
ἔτι.   καὶ τὴν πόλιν τὴν ἁγίαν Ἰερουσαλὴμ καινὴν
still.   And the city the holy Jerusalem new

3708 2597   1537 02 3772   575 02 2316
εἶδον καταβαίνουσαν ἐκ τοῦ οὐρανοῦ ἀπὸ τοῦ θεοῦ
I saw coming down   from the heaven from the God

2090   5613 3565   2885   03   435
ἡτοιμασμένην ὡς νύμφην κεκοσμημένην τῷ ἀνδρὶ
having been as bride having been   to the man
prepared   adorned

846   **3** 2532 191   5456   3173 1537 02 2362
αὐτῆς.   καὶ ἤκουσα φωνῆς μεγάλης ἐκ τοῦ θρόνου
of her.   And I heard voice great   from the throne

3004   2400 05 4633 02   2316 3326 014
λεγούσης· ἰδοὺ ἡ σκηνὴ τοῦ θεοῦ μετὰ τῶν
saying,   look the tent of the God with the

444   2532 4637   3326 846   2532
ἀνθρώπων, καὶ σκηνώσει μετ᾽ αὐτῶν, καὶ
men,   and he will tent with them, and

846   2992   846   1510   2532 846   01 2316
αὐτοὶ λαοὶ αὐτοῦ ἔσονται, καὶ αὐτὸς ὁ θεὸς
themselves peoples of him will be, and himself the God

3326 846   1510 846   2316   **4** 2532
μετ᾽ αὐτῶν ἔσται [αὐτῶν θεός],   καὶ
with them will be of them God,   and

1813   3956 1144 1537 014 3788   846
ἐξαλείψει πᾶν δάκρυον ἐκ τῶν ὀφθαλμῶν αὐτῶν,
he will wipe off all tear from the eyes   of them,

2532 01 2288   3756 1510 2089 3777   3997
καὶ ὁ θάνατος οὐκ ἔσται ἔτι οὔτε πένθος
and the death not will be still neither mourning

3777 2906   3777 4192 3756 1510 2089 3774   021
οὔτε κραυγὴ οὔτε πόνος οὐκ ἔσται ἔτι, [ὅτι] τὰ
nor shout   nor pain not will be still, because the

4413 565   **5** 2532 3004 01 2521   1909 03
πρῶτα ἀπῆλθαν. Καὶ εἶπεν ὁ καθήμενος ἐπὶ τῷ
first went off. And said the one sitting on the

2362   2400 2537 4160 3956 2532 3004   1125
θρόνῳ· ἰδοὺ καινὰ ποιῶ πάντα καὶ λέγει· γράψον,
throne, look new I make all and he says, write,

3754   3778 013 3056 4103   2532 228   1510
ὅτι οὗτοι οἱ λόγοι πιστοὶ καὶ ἀληθινοί εἰσιν.
because these the words trustful and true   are.

6 2532 3004 1473 1096   1473 1510 09
καὶ εἶπέν μοι· γέγοναν.   ἐγώ [εἰμι] τὸ
And he said to me, they have become. I am the

---

according to what they
had done. [14]Then Death
and Hades were thrown
into the lake of fire. This is
the second death, the lake
of fire; [15]and anyone whose
name was not found written
in the book of life was
thrown into the lake of fire.

CHAPTER 21

Then I saw a new heaven
and a new earth; for the
first heaven and the first
earth had passed away,
and the sea was no more.
[2]And I saw the holy city,
the new Jerusalem, coming
down out of heaven from
God, prepared as a bride
adorned for her husband.
[3]And I heard a loud voice
from the throne saying,
    "See, the home[a] of God is
        among mortals.
    He will dwell[b] with
        them;
    they will be his peoples,[c]
    and God himself will be
        with them;[d]
[4] he will wipe every tear
        from their eyes.
    Death will be no more;
    mourning and crying and
        pain will be no more,
    for the first things have
        passed away."

    5 And the one who was
seated on the throne said,
"See, I am making all
things new." Also he said,
"Write this, for these words
are trustworthy and true."
[6]Then he said to me, "It is
done! I am the

---

a Gk the tabernacle
b Gk will tabernacle
c Other ancient authorities read
  people
d Other ancient authorities add
  and be their God

Alpha and the Omega, the beginning and the end. To the thirsty I will give water as a gift from the spring of the water of life. 7Those who conquer will inherit these things, and I will be their God and they will be my children. 8But as for the cowardly, the faithless,[a] the polluted, the murderers, the fornicators, the sorcerers, the idolaters, and all liars, their place will be in the lake that burns with fire and sulfur, which is the second death."

9 Then one of the seven angels who had the seven bowls full of the seven last plagues came and said to me, "Come, I will show you the bride, the wife of the Lamb." 10And in the spirit[b] he carried me away to a great, high mountain and showed me the holy city Jerusalem coming down out of heaven from God. 11It has the glory of God and a radiance like a very rare jewel, like jasper, clear as crystal. 12It has a great, high wall with twelve gates, and at the gates twelve angels, and on the gates are inscribed the names of the twelve tribes of the Israelites;

a Or the unbelieving
b Or in the Spirit

255a	2532	09	5598	05	746		2532	09	5056
ἄλφα	καὶ	τὸ	ὦ,	ἡ	ἀρχὴ		καὶ	τὸ	τέλος.
alpha	and	the	omega,	the	beginning		and	the	completion.

1473	03		1372		1325		1537	06	4077
ἐγὼ	τῷ		διψῶντι		δώσω		ἐκ	τῆς	πηγῆς
I	to the		one thirsting		will give		from	the	spring

010	5204	06	2222	1432		01	3528
τοῦ	ὕδατος	τῆς	ζωῆς	δωρεάν.	7	ὁ	νικῶν
of the	water	of the	life	as gift.		The	one conquering

2816		3778	2532	1510		846		2316	2532
κληρονομήσει		ταῦτα	καὶ	ἔσομαι		αὐτῷ		θεὸς	καὶ
will inherit		these	and	I will be		to him		God	and

846		1510		1473	5207	8	015		1161	1169		2532
αὐτὸς		ἔσται		μοι	υἱός.		τοῖς		δὲ	δειλοῖς		καὶ
himself		will be		to me	son.		To the		but	cowards		and

571		2532	948		2532	5406		2532
ἀπίστοις		καὶ	ἐβδελυγμένοις		καὶ	φονεῦσιν		καὶ
untrustful		and	ones abominating		and	murderers		and

4205		2532	5333		2532	1496
πόρνοις		καὶ	φαρμάκοις	καὶ	εἰδωλολάτραις
sexually immoral ones		and	magicians	and	idol-servers

2532	3956	015	5571		09	3313	846		1722	07
καὶ	πᾶσιν	τοῖς	ψευδέσιν		τὸ	μέρος	αὐτῶν		ἐν	τῇ
and	all	the	false ones		the	part	of them		in	the

3041	07	2545		4442	2532	2303		3739
λίμνη	τῇ	καιομένῃ		πυρὶ	καὶ	θείῳ,		ὅ
lake	the	one being burned		in fire	and	sulphur,		which

1510	01	2288	01	1208		2532	2064	1520	1537
ἐστιν	ὁ	θάνατος	ὁ	δεύτερος.	9	Καὶ	ἦλθεν	εἷς	ἐκ
is	the	death	the	second.		And	came	one	from

014	2033	32		014		2192		020	2033
τῶν	ἑπτὰ	ἀγγέλων		τῶν		ἐχόντων		τὰς	ἑπτὰ
the	seven	messengers		of the ones		having		the	seven

5357	018	1073		018		2033	4127		018	2078
φιάλας	τῶν	γεμόντων		τῶν		ἑπτὰ	πληγῶν		τῶν	ἐσχάτων
bowls	the	being full		of the		seven	blows		the	last

2532	2980		3326	1473	3004		1204		1166
καὶ	ἐλάλησεν		μετ’	ἐμοῦ	λέγων·		δεῦρο,		δείξω
and	he spoke		with	me	saying,		come,		I will show

1473	08	3565	08	1135		010		721	10	2532
σοι	τὴν	νύμφην	τὴν	γυναῖκα		τοῦ		ἀρνίου.		καὶ
to you	the	bride	the	woman		of the		lamb.		And

667		1473	1722	4151		1909	3735	3173	2532
ἀπήνεγκέν		με	ἐν	πνεύματι		ἐπὶ	ὄρος	μέγα	καὶ
he carried off		me	in	spirit		on	hill	great	and

5308		2532	1166		1473	08	4172	08	40
ὑψηλόν,		καὶ	ἔδειξέν		μοι	τὴν	πόλιν	τὴν	ἁγίαν
high,		and	he showed		to me	the	city	the	holy

2419		2597		1537	02	3772		575	02
Ἰερουσαλὴμ		καταβαίνουσαν	ἐκ		τοῦ	οὐρανοῦ	ἀπὸ		τοῦ
Jerusalem		coming down		from	the	heaven	from	the

2316	11	2192		08	1391		02		2316	01	5458
θεοῦ		ἔχουσαν		τὴν	δόξαν		τοῦ		θεοῦ,	ὁ	φωστὴρ
God		having		the	splendor		of the		God,	the	light

846	3664	3037	5093		5613	3037	2393
αὐτῆς	ὅμοιος	λίθῳ	τιμιωτάτῳ		ὡς	λίθῳ	ἰάσπιδι
of her	like	stone	most valuable		as	stone	jasper

2929			12	2192	5038	3173	2532
κρυσταλλίζοντι.				ἔχουσα	τεῖχος	μέγα	καὶ
sparkling like crystal.				Having	wall	great	and

5308		2192	4440		1427	2532	1909	015	4440
ὑψηλόν,		ἔχουσα	πυλῶνας		δώδεκα	καὶ	ἐπὶ	τοῖς	πυλῶσιν
high,		having	gates		twelve	and	on	the	gates

32		1427	2532	3686		1924
ἀγγέλους		δώδεκα	καὶ	ὀνόματα		ἐπιγεγραμμένα,
messengers		twelve	and	names		having been written on,

3739	1510		021	3686		018		1427	5443	5207
ἃ	ἐστιν		[τὰ	ὀνόματα]		τῶν		δώδεκα	φυλῶν	υἱῶν
which	are		the	names		of the		twelve	tribes	sons

```
 2474        575    395       4440      5140 2532 575   1005
Ἰσραήλ·  13 ἀπὸ  ἀνατολῆς  πυλῶνες  τρεῖς καὶ ἀπὸ βορρᾶ
Israel;     from east       gates     three and from north

4440     5140  2532 575  3558    4440     5140  2532 575
πυλῶνες  τρεῖς καὶ ἀπὸ  νότου  πυλῶνες  τρεῖς καὶ ἀπὸ
gates    three and from south   gates    three and from

1424    4440     5140       2532 09  5038    06     4172
δυσμῶν πυλῶνες τρεῖς.  14 καὶ  τὸ  τεῖχος τῆς   πόλεως
west    gates   three.     And the  wall   of the city

2192     2310            1427     2532 1909 846     1427
ἔχων  θεμελίους  δώδεκα  καὶ ἐπ᾽ αὐτῶν δώδεκα
having foundations twelve and on  them   twelve

3686     014    1427    652         010    721       2532
ὀνόματα τῶν  δώδεκα ἀποστόλων τοῦ  ἀρνίου.  15 Καὶ
names   of the twelve delegates  of the lamb.      And

01   2980           3326  1473 2192  3358     2563
ὁ  λαλῶν       μετ᾽ ἐμοῦ εἶχεν μέτρον κάλαμον
the one speaking with me   had   measure reed

5552     2443  3354         08  4172   2532 016
χρυσοῦν, ἵνα  μετρήσῃ     τὴν πόλιν καὶ τοὺς
gold,    that he might measure the city and  the

4440    846   2532 012 5038    846      2532 05  4172
πυλῶνας αὐτῆς καὶ  τὸ τεῖχος αὐτῆς.  16 καὶ ἡ  πόλις
gates   of it and the  wall  of it.     And the city

5068       2749    2532 09  3372   846     3745
τετράγωνος κεῖται καὶ  τὸ μῆκος αὐτῆς ὅσον
four-cornered is set and the length of it as much as

2532 09  4114      2532 3354       08  4172   03
[καὶ] τὸ πλάτος. καὶ ἐμέτρησεν τὴν πόλιν τῷ
also the width.  And  he measured the city  in the

2563    1909 4712    1427    5505      09  3372   2532
καλάμῳ ἐπὶ σταδίων δώδεκα χιλιάδων, τὸ μῆκος καὶ
reed    on  stadia  twelve thousands, the length and

09  4114    2532 09  5311   846   2470  1510     2532
τὸ πλάτος καὶ  τὸ ὕψος αὐτῆς ἴσα ἐστίν. 17 καὶ
the width  and the height of it equal is.     And

3354       012 5038   846    1540      5062
ἐμέτρησεν τὸ τεῖχος αὐτῆς ἑκατὸν τεσσεράκοντα
he measured the  wall  of it hundred forty

5064      4083   3358  444       3739  1510
τεσσάρων πηχῶν μέτρον ἀνθρώπου, ὅ  ἐστιν
four     cubits measure of man,   which is

32             2532 05  1746a       010      5038
ἀγγέλου.  18 καὶ  ἡ  ἐνδώμησις τοῦ  τείχους
of messenger.  And the construction of the wall

846   2393   2532 05  4172  5553     2513     3664
αὐτῆς ἴασπις καὶ  ἡ  πόλις χρυσίον καθαρὸν ὅμοιον
of it jasper and the  city  gold    clean    like

5194  2513      013 2310        010     5038      06
ὑάλῳ καθαρῷ.  19 οἱ θεμέλιοι τοῦ  τείχους τῆς
glass clean.      The foundations of the wall   of the

4172   3956  3037    1909      2885               01
πόλεως παντὶ λίθῳ τιμίῳ κεκοσμημένοι·       ὁ
city   in all stone valuable having been adorned; the

2310     01   4413   2393    01  1208     4552
θεμέλιος ὁ  πρῶτος ἴασπις, ὁ δεύτερος σάπφιρος,
foundation the first jasper, the second  sapphire,

01  5154   5472      01  5067    4665         20 01
ὁ  τρίτος χαλκηδών, ὁ τέταρτος σμάραγδος,    ὁ
the third chalcedon, the fourth  emerald,       the

3991    4557     01  1623  4556      01 1442
πέμπτος σαρδόνυξ, ὁ ἕκτος σάρδιον, ὁ ἕβδομος
fifth   sardonyx, the sixth sardis, the seventh

5555       01   3590   969      01  1728a  5116
χρυσόλιθος, ὁ ὄγδοος βήρυλλος, ὁ ἔνατος τοπάζιον,
gold stone, the eighth beryl,   the ninth  topaz,

01 1182    5556       01  1734    5192      01
ὁ δέκατος χρυσόπρασος, ὁ ἑνδέκατος ὑάκινθος, ὁ
the tenth chrysoprase, the eleventh hyacinth, the
```

[13]on the east three gates, on the north three gates, on the south three gates, and on the west three gates. [14]And the wall of the city has twelve foundations, and on them are the twelve names of the twelve apostles of the Lamb.

[15]The angel[a] who talked to me had a measuring rod of gold to measure the city and its gates and walls. [16]The city lies foursquare, its length the same as its width; and he measured the city with his rod, fifteen hundred miles;[b] its length and width and height are equal. [17]He also measured its wall, one hundred forty-four cubits[c] by human measurement, which the angel was using. [18]The wall is built of jasper, while the city is pure gold, clear as glass. [19]The foundations of the wall of the city are adorned with every jewel; the first was jasper, the second sapphire, the third agate, the fourth emerald, [20]the fifth onyx, the sixth carnelian, the seventh chrysolite, the eighth beryl, the ninth topaz, the tenth chrysoprase, the eleventh jacinth, the

a Gk He
b Gk twelve thousand stadia
c That is, almost seventy-five yards

twelfth amethyst. [21]And the twelve gates are twelve pearls, each of the gates is a single pearl, and the street of the city is pure gold, transparent as glass.

[22]I saw no temple in the city, for its temple is the Lord God the Almighty and the Lamb. [23]And the city has no need of sun or moon to shine on it, for the glory of God is its light, and its lamp is the Lamb. [24]The nations will walk by its light, and the kings of the earth will bring their glory into it. [25]Its gates will never be shut by day—and there will be no night there. [26]People will bring into it the glory and the honor of the nations. [27]But nothing unclean will enter it, nor anyone who practices abomination or falsehood, but only those who are written in the Lamb's book of life.

CHAPTER 22

Then the angel[a] showed me the river of the water of life, bright as crystal, flowing from the throne of God and of the Lamb [2]through the middle of the street of the city. On either side of the river is the tree of life[b] with its twelve kinds of fruit, producing its fruit

[a] Gk he
[b] Or the Lamb. [2]In the middle of the street of the city, and on either side of the river, is the tree of life

1428 271 2532 013 1427 4440 1427
δωδέκατος ἀμέθυστος, **21** καὶ οἱ δώδεκα πυλῶνες δώδεκα
twelfth amethyst, and the twelve gates twelve

3135 303 1520 1538 014 4440 1510 1537
μαργαρῖται, ἀνὰ εἷς ἕκαστος τῶν πυλώνων ἦν ἐξ
pearls, up one each of the gates was from

1520 3135 2532 05 4113 06 4172
ἑνὸς μαργαρίτου. καὶ ἡ πλατεῖα τῆς πόλεως
one pearl. And the wide place of the city

5553 2513 5613 5194 1306a 2532 3485
χρυσίον καθαρὸν ὡς ὕαλος διαυγής. **22** Καὶ ναὸν
gold clean as glass transparent. And temple

3756 3708 1722 846 01 1063 2962 01 2316 01
οὐκ εἶδον ἐν αὐτῇ, ὁ γὰρ κύριος ὁ θεὸς ὁ
not I saw in it, the for Master the God the

3841 3485 846 1510 2532 09 721
παντοκράτωρ ναὸς αὐτῆς ἐστιν καὶ τὸ ἀρνίον.
all-strength temple of it is and the lamb.

2532 05 4172 3756 5532 2192 02 2246 3761
23 καὶ ἡ πόλις οὐ χρείαν ἔχει τοῦ ἡλίου οὐδὲ
And the city not need has of the sun but not

06 4582 2443 5316 846 05 1063
τῆς σελήνης ἵνα φαίνωσιν αὐτῇ, ἡ γὰρ
of the moon that they might shine in it, the for

1391 02 2316 5461 846 2532 01 3088
δόξα τοῦ θεοῦ ἐφώτισεν αὐτήν, καὶ ὁ λύχνος
splendor of the God lightened it, and the lamp

846 09 721 2532 4043 021 1484
αὐτῆς τὸ ἀρνίον. **24** καὶ περιπατήσουσιν τὰ ἔθνη
of it the lamb. And will walk around the nations

1223 010 5457 846 2532 013 935 06 1093
διὰ τοῦ φωτὸς αὐτῆς, καὶ οἱ βασιλεῖς τῆς γῆς
through the light of it, and the kings of the earth

5342 08 1391 846 1519 846 2532 013
φέρουσιν τὴν δόξαν αὐτῶν εἰς αὐτήν, **25** καὶ οἱ
carry the splendor of them into it, and the

4440 846 3756 3361 2808 2250 3571
πυλῶνες αὐτῆς οὐ μὴ κλεισθῶσιν ἡμέρας, νὺξ
gates of it not not might be closed day, night

1063 3756 1510 1563 2532 5342 08
γὰρ οὐκ ἔσται ἐκεῖ, **26** καὶ οἴσουσιν τὴν
for not will be there, and they will carry the

1391 2532 08 5092 022 1484 1519 846
δόξαν καὶ τὴν τιμὴν τῶν ἐθνῶν εἰς αὐτήν.
splendor and the value of the nations into it.

2532 3756 3361 1525 1519 846 3956 2839
27 καὶ οὐ μὴ εἰσέλθῃ εἰς αὐτὴν πᾶν κοινὸν
And not not might go in into it all common

2532 01 4160 946 2532 5579 1487 3361
καὶ [ὁ] ποιῶν βδέλυγμα καὶ ψεῦδος εἰ μὴ
and the one doing abomination and lie except

013 1125 1722 011 975 06 2222 010 721
οἱ γεγραμμένοι ἐν τῷ βιβλίῳ τῆς ζωῆς τοῦ ἀρνίου.
the ones having in the small of life of lamb.
been written book the the

2532 1166 1473 4215 5204 2222
22:1 Καὶ ἔδειξέν μοι ποταμὸν ὕδατος ζωῆς
And he showed to me river of water of life

2986 5613 2930 1607 1537 02 2362
λαμπρὸν ὡς κρύσταλλον, ἐκπορευόμενον ἐκ τοῦ θρόνου
bright as crystal, traveling out from the throne

02 2316 2532 010 721 1722 3319 06
τοῦ θεοῦ καὶ τοῦ ἀρνίου. **2** ἐν μέσῳ τῆς
of the God and of the lamb. In middle of the

4113 846 2532 02 4215 1782 2532
πλατείας αὐτῆς καὶ τοῦ ποταμοῦ ἐντεῦθεν καὶ
wide place of it and of the river from here and

1564 3586 2222 4160 2590 1427 2596
ἐκεῖθεν ξύλον ζωῆς ποιοῦν καρποὺς δώδεκα, κατὰ
from there wood of life making fruit twelve, by

3376   1538   591   04   2590   846   2532 021
μῆνα   ἕκαστον   ἀποδιδοῦν   τὸν   καρπὸν   αὐτοῦ, καὶ   τὰ
month   each   giving off   the   fruit   of it, and   the

5444   010   3586 1519 2322   022   1484   **3** 2532
φύλλα   τοῦ   ξύλου εἰς θεραπείαν   τῶν   ἐθνῶν.   καὶ
leaves   of the   wood for service   of the   nations. And

3956   2616a   3756 1510   2089   2532 01   2362   02
πᾶν   κατάθεμα οὐκ ἔσται   ἔτι.   καὶ ὁ   θρόνος   τοῦ
all   curse   not will be still,   and the   throne   of the

2316 2532 010   721   1722 846   1510   2532 013
θεοῦ καὶ τοῦ   ἀρνίου   ἐν αὐτῇ   ἔσται,   καὶ οἱ
God and of the   of the lamb in it   will be, and   the

1401   846   3000   846   **4** 2532 3708
δοῦλοι   αὐτοῦ   λατρεύσουσιν   αὐτῷ   καὶ ὄψονται
slaves   of him   will serve   him   and they will see

012 4383   846   2532 09   3686   846   1909 022
τὸ πρόσωπον   αὐτοῦ,   καὶ τὸ   ὄνομα   αὐτοῦ ἐπὶ τῶν
the face   of him, and   the   name   of him on   the

3359   846   **5** 2532 3571   3756 1510   2089 2532
μετώπων   αὐτῶν.   καὶ νὺξ   οὐκ ἔσται   ἔτι καὶ
foreheads of them. And   night not   will be still and

3756 2192   5532   5457   3088   2532 5457
οὐκ ἔχουσιν   χρείαν   φωτὸς   λύχνου   καὶ φωτὸς
not they have need   of light of lamp and   of light

2246   3754   2962   01   2316 5461   1909
ἡλίου,   ὅτι   κύριος   ὁ   θεὸς φωτίσει   ἐπ᾽
of sun,   because Master   the   God will light on

846   2532 936   1519 016   165   014
αὐτούς,   καὶ βασιλεύσουσιν   εἰς τοὺς   αἰῶνας τῶν
them,   and they will be kings into the   ages of the

165   **6** 2532 3004   1473   3778 013 3056   4103
αἰώνων.   Καὶ εἶπέν   μοι·   οὗτοι οἱ λόγοι   πιστοὶ
ages.   And he said to me, these the words   trustful

2532 228   2532 01   2962   01   2316 022
καὶ ἀληθινοί,   καὶ ὁ   κύριος   ὁ   θεὸς τῶν
and true,   and   the Master   the   God of the

4151   014   4396   649   04   32
πνευμάτων τῶν   προφητῶν   ἀπέστειλεν τὸν ἄγγελον
spirits   of the   spokesmen delegated   the messenger

846   1166   015   1401   846   3739
αὐτοῦ   δεῖξαι   τοῖς   δούλοις   αὐτοῦ   ἃ
of him   to show   to the   slaves   of him   what

1163   1096   1722 5034   **7** 2532 2400
δεῖ   γενέσθαι   ἐν τάχει.   καὶ ἰδοὺ
it is necessary to become in quickness. And   look

2064   5036   3107   01   5083   016 3056
ἔρχομαι   ταχύ.   μακάριος   ὁ   τηρῶν   τοὺς λόγους
I come   quickly. Fortunate   the one keeping the words

06   4394   010   975   3778
τῆς   προφητείας   τοῦ   βιβλίου   τούτου.
of the   speaking before of the   small book this.

8 2504 2491   01   191   2532 1510   3778
Κἀγὼ Ἰωάννης ὁ   ἀκούων   καὶ βλέπων   ταῦτα.
And I John   the one hearing and   seeing   these.

2532 3753 191   2532 991   4098   4352
καὶ ὅτε ἤκουσα   καὶ ἔβλεψα,   ἔπεσα   προσκυνῆσαι
And when I heard   and   saw,   I fell   to worship

1715   014   4228   02   32   02
ἔμπροσθεν τῶν   ποδῶν   τοῦ ἀγγέλου   τοῦ
in front of the   feet   of the messenger of the

1166   1473 3778   **9** 2532 3004   1473   3708
δεικνύοντός μοι ταῦτα.   καὶ λέγει   μοι·   ὅρα
one showing to me these.   And   he says to me,   see

3361 4889   1473   1510 2532 014   80   1473
μή· σύνδουλός σού   εἰμι καὶ τῶν   ἀδελφῶν   σου
not; co-slave of you   I am and   the   brothers of you

014 4396   2532 014 5083   016 3056   010
τῶν προφητῶν   καὶ τῶν τηρούντων   τοὺς λόγους   τοῦ
the spokesmen and   the ones keeping the words   of the

---

each month; and the
leaves of the tree are for
the healing of the nations.
[3]Nothing accursed will be
found there any more. But
the throne of God and of
the Lamb will be in it, and
his servants[a] will worship
him; [4]they will see his face,
and his name will be on
their foreheads. [5]And there
will be no more night; they
need no light of lamp or
sun, for the Lord God will
be their light, and they will
reign forever and ever.

6 And he said to me,
"These words are trust-
worthy and true, for the
Lord, the God of the spirits
of the prophets, has sent his
angel to show his servants[a]
what must soon take
place."

7"See, I am coming
soon! Blessed is the one
who keeps the words of the
prophecy of this book."

8 I, John, am the one
who heard and saw these
things. And when I heard
and saw them, I fell down
to worship at the feet of
the angel who showed
thesm to me; [9]but he said to
me, "You must not do that!
I am a fellow servant[b] with
you and your comrades[c] the
prophets, and with those
who keep the words of

---

[a] Gk slaves
[b] Gk slave
[c] Gk brothers

this book. Worship God!"

10 And he said to me, "Do not seal up the words of the prophecy of this book, for the time is near. [11]Let the evildoer still do evil, and the filthy still be filthy, and the righteous still do right, and the holy still be holy."

12 "See, I am coming soon; my reward is with me, to repay according to everyone's work. [13]I am the Alpha and the Omega, the first and the last, the beginning and the end."

14 Blessed are those who wash their robes,[a] so that they will have the right to the tree of life and may enter the city by the gates. [15]Outside are the dogs and sorcerers and fornicators and murderers and idolaters, and everyone who loves and practices falsehood.

16 "It is I, Jesus, who sent my angel to you with this testimony for the churches. I am the root and the descendant of David, the bright morning star." [17]The Spirit and the bride say, "Come." And let everyone who hears say, "Come." And let everyone who is thirsty come. Let anyone who wishes take the water of life as a gift.

18 I warn everyone

[a] Other ancient authorities read do his commandments

975	3778	03 2316 4352		2532
βιβλίου	τούτου·	τῷ θεῷ προσκύνησον.	**10**	Καὶ
small book	this;	the God worship.		And

3004	1473	3361 4972	016 3056 06
λέγει	μοι·	μὴ σφραγίσῃς	τοὺς λόγους τῆς
he says	to me,	not you might seal	the words of the

4394 010 975 3778 01 2540
προφητείας τοῦ βιβλίου τούτου, ὁ καιρὸς
speaking before of the small book this, the season

1063 1451 1510 01 91 91 2089
γὰρ ἐγγύς ἐστιν. **11** ὁ ἀδικῶν ἀδικησάτω ἔτι
for near is. The one doing let do still
unright unright

2532 01 4508 4506a 2089 2532 01 1342
καὶ ὁ ῥυπαρὸς ῥυπανθήτω ἔτι, καὶ ὁ δίκαιος
and the dirty let be dirty still, and the right

1343 4160 2089 2532 01 40 37
δικαιοσύνην ποιησάτω ἔτι καὶ ὁ ἅγιος ἁγιασθήτω
rightness let do still and the holy let be holy

2089 2400 2064 5036 2532 01 3408 1473
ἔτι. **12** Ἰδοὺ ἔρχομαι ταχύ, καὶ ὁ μισθός μου
still. Look I come quickly, and the wage of me

3326 1473 591 1538 5613 09 2041 1510
μετ' ἐμοῦ ἀποδοῦναι ἑκάστῳ ὡς τὸ ἔργον ἐστὶν
with me to give off to each as the work is

846 1473 09 255a 2532 09 5598 01 4413
αὐτοῦ. **13** ἐγὼ τὸ ἄλφα καὶ τὸ ὦ, ὁ πρῶτος
of him. I the alpha and the omega, the first

2532 01 2078 05 746 2532 09 5056
καὶ ὁ ἔσχατος, ἡ ἀρχὴ καὶ τὸ τέλος.
and the last, the beginning and the completion.

3107 013 4150 020 4749 846
14 Μακάριοι οἱ πλύνοντες τὰς στολὰς αὐτῶν,
Fortunate the ones washing the long robes of them,

2443 1510 05 1849 846 1909 012 3586
ἵνα ἔσται ἡ ἐξουσία αὐτῶν ἐπὶ τὸ ξύλον
that will be the authority of them on the wood

06 2222 2532 015 4440 1525 1519
τῆς ζωῆς καὶ τοῖς πυλῶσιν εἰσέλθωσιν εἰς
of the life and in the gates they might go in into

08 4172 1854 013 2965 2532 013 5333 2532
τὴν πόλιν. **15** ἔξω οἱ κύνες καὶ οἱ φάρμακοι καὶ
the city. Outside the dogs and the magicians and

013 4205 2532 013 5406 2532 013
οἱ πόρνοι καὶ οἱ φονεῖς καὶ οἱ
the sexually immoral ones and the murderers and the

1496 2532 3956 5368 2532 4160 5579
εἰδωλολάτραι καὶ πᾶς φιλῶν καὶ ποιῶν ψεῦδος.
idol-servers and all one loving and doing lie.

1473 2424 3992 04 32 1473 3140
16 Ἐγὼ Ἰησοῦς ἔπεμψα τὸν ἄγγελόν μου μαρτυρῆσαι
I Jesus sent the messenger of me to testify

1473 3778 1909 019 1577 1473 1510 05 4491
ὑμῖν ταῦτα ἐπὶ ταῖς ἐκκλησίαις. ἐγὼ εἰμι ἡ ῥίζα
to you these on the assemblies. I am the root

2532 09 1085 1160a 01 792 01 2986 01
καὶ τὸ γένος Δαυίδ, ὁ ἀστὴρ ὁ λαμπρὸς ὁ
and the kind David, the star the bright the

4407 2532 09 4151 2532 05 3565 3004
πρωϊνός. **17** Καὶ τὸ πνεῦμα καὶ ἡ νύμφη λέγουσιν·
morning. And the spirit and the bride say,

2064 2532 01 191 3004 2064 2532 01
ἔρχου. καὶ ὁ ἀκούων εἰπάτω· ἔρχου. καὶ ὁ
come. And the one hearing let say, come. And the

1372 2064 01 2309 2983
διψῶν ἐρχέσθω, ὁ θέλων λαβέτω
one thirsting let come, the one wanting let receive

5204 2222 1432 3140 1473 3956 03
ὕδωρ ζωῆς δωρεάν. **18** Μαρτυρῶ ἐγὼ παντὶ τῷ
water of life as gift. Testify I to all the one

191　　　016　3056　　06　　4394　　　　　010
ἀκούοντι τοὺς λόγους τῆς προφητείας τοῦ
hearing the words of the speaking before of the

975　　　　3778　　1437 5100 2007　　　　　1909 846
βιβλίου τούτου· ἐάν τις ἐπιθῇ ἐπ' αὐτά,
small book this; if some might set on on them,

2007　　　01　2316 1909 846　020 4127　020
ἐπιθήσει ὁ θεὸς ἐπ' αὐτὸν τὰς πληγὰς τὰς
will set on the God on him the blows the ones

1125　　　　　　1722 011 975　　　3778　19 2532
γεγραμμένας ἐν τῷ βιβλίῳ τούτῳ, καὶ
having been written in the small book this, and

1437 5100 851　　　575　014 3056 010
ἐάν τις ἀφέλῃ ἀπὸ τῶν λόγων τοῦ
if some might lift off from the words of the

975　　06　4394　　　　3778　851
βιβλίου τῆς προφητείας ταύτης, ἀφελεῖ
small book of the speaking before this, will lift off

01　2316 012 3313 846　575　010 3586 06　　2222
ὁ θεὸς τὸ μέρος αὐτοῦ ἀπὸ τοῦ ξύλου τῆς ζωῆς
the God the part of him from the wood of the life

2532 1537 06　4172　06　40　014　1125
καὶ ἐκ τῆς πόλεως τῆς ἁγίας τῶν γεγραμμένων
and from the city the holy of the having been

1722 011· 975　　3778　20 3004 01 3140
ἐν τῷ βιβλίῳ τούτῳ. Λέγει ὁ μαρτυρῶν
in the small book this. Says the one testifying

3778　3483 2064 2064　2064 2962 2424
ταῦτα· ναί, ἔρχομαι ταχύ. Ἀμήν, ἔρχου κύριε Ἰησοῦ.
these, yes, I come quickly. Amen, come Master Jesus.

21 05 5485 02　2962　2424 3326 3956
Ἡ χάρις τοῦ κυρίου Ἰησοῦ μετὰ πάντων.
The favor of the Master Jesus with all.

who hears the words of the prophecy of this book: if anyone adds to them, God will add to that person the plagues described in this book; [19]if anyone takes away from the words of the book of this prophecy, God will take away that person's share in the tree of life and in the holy city, which are described in this book.

20 The one who testifies to these things says, "Surely I am coming soon." Amen. Come, Lord Jesus!

21 The grace of the Lord Jesus be with all the saints. Amen.[a]

[a] Other ancient authorities lack *all;* others lack *the saints;* others lack *Amen*

CONCORDANCE

α

2 GO5 AG1 LN1 K1:3
ααρων, AARON

Lk	1: 5	wife was a descendant of **Aaron**
Ac	7:40	saying to **Aaron,** 'Make gods
He	5: 4	called by God, just as **Aaron**
	7:11	according to the order of **Aaron**
	9: 4	and **Aaron's** rod that budded,

3 GO1 AG1 LN1 K1:4
αβαδδων, ABADDON

Re	9:11	his name in Hebrew is **Abaddon,**

4 GO1 AG1 LN1 R922
αβαρης, UNBURDEN

2C	11: 9	refrain from **burdening** you

5 GO3 AG1 LN1 B1:614 K1:5
αββα, ABBA

Mk	14:36	He said, "**Abba,** Father,
Ro	8:15	When we cry, "**Abba!** Father!"
Ga	4: 6	hearts, crying, "**Abba!** Father!"

6 GO4 AG1 LN1 K1:6
αβελ, ABEL

Mt	23:35	righteous **Abel** to the blood
Lk	11:51	from the blood of **Abel**
He	11: 4	By faith **Abel** offered to God
	12:24	word than the blood of **Abel.**

7 GO3 AG1 LN1
αβια, ABIA

Mt	1: 7	Rehoboam the father of **Abijah,**
	1: 7	and **Abijah** the father of Asaph,
Lk	1: 5	priestly order of **Abijah.**

8 GO1 AG1 LN1
αβιαθαρ, ABIATHAR

Mk	2:26	when **Abiathar** was high priest,

9 GO1 AG1 LN1
αβιληνη, ABILENE

Lk	3: 1	and Lysanias ruler of **Abilene,**

10 GO2 AG1 LN1
αβιουδ, ABIOUD

Mt	1:13	Zerubbabel the father of **Abiud**
	1:13	**Abiud** the father of Eliakim,

11 GO73 AG1 LN1 B1:76 K1:8
αβρααμ, ABRAHAM

Mt	1: 1	David, the son of **Abraham.**
	1: 2	**Abraham** was the father of
	1:17	generations from **Abraham** to
	3: 9	We have **Abraham** as our ancestor
	3: 9	to raise up children to **Abraham**
	8:11	will eat with **Abraham** and Isaac
	22:32	I am the God of **Abraham,**
Mk	12:26	I am the God of **Abraham**
Lk	1:55	**Abraham** and to his descendants
	1:73	swore to our ancestor **Abraham,**
	3: 8	have **Abraham** as our ancestor';
	3: 8	to raise up children to **Abraham**
	3:34	son of Isaac, son of **Abraham,**
	13:16	a daughter of **Abraham** whom
	13:28	when you see **Abraham** and Isaac
	16:22	the angels to be with **Abraham.**
	16:23	saw **Abraham** far away
	16:24	Father **Abraham,** have mercy on
	16:25	But **Abraham** said, 'Child,
	16:29	**Abraham** replied, 'They have
	16:30	He said, 'No, father **Abraham;**
	19: 9	he too is a son of **Abraham.**
	20:37	Lord as the God of **Abraham,**
Jn	8:33	We are descendants of **Abraham**
	8:37	you are descendants of **Abraham;**
	8:39	**Abraham** is our father
	8:39	If you were **Abraham's**
	8:39	you would be doing what **Abraham**
	8:40	This is not what **Abraham** did.
	8:52	**Abraham** died, and so did the
	8:53	greater than our father **Abraham**

	8:56	Your ancestor **Abraham** rejoiced
	8:57	have you seen **Abraham?**
	8:58	before **Abraham** was, I am.
Ac	3:13	The God of **Abraham,**
	3:25	ancestors, saying to **Abraham,**
	7: 2	to our ancestor **Abraham**
	7:16	tomb that **Abraham** had bought
	7:17	God had made to **Abraham,**
	7:32	ancestors, the God of **Abraham,**
	13:26	descendants of **Abraham's** family
Ro	4: 1	to say was gained by **Abraham,**
	4: 2	For if **Abraham** was justified
	4: 3	**Abraham** believed God,
	4: 9	Faith was reckoned to **Abraham**
	4:12	our ancestor **Abraham** had before
	4:13	did not come to **Abraham**
	4:16	who share the faith of **Abraham**
	9: 7	not all of **Abraham's** children
	11: 1	a descendant of **Abraham,**
2C	11:22	Are they descendants of **Abraham**
Ga	3: 6	Just as **Abraham** "believed God,
	3: 7	are the descendants of **Abraham.**
	3: 8	gospel beforehand to **Abraham,**
	3: 9	blessed with **Abraham** who
	3:14	Jesus the blessing of **Abraham**
	3:16	promises were made to **Abraham**
	3:18	God granted it to **Abraham**
	3:29	you are **Abraham's** offspring,
	4:22	**Abraham** had two sons, one by
He	2:16	but the descendants of **Abraham.**
	6:13	God made a promise to **Abraham,**
	7: 1	met **Abraham** as he was returning
	7: 2	and to him **Abraham** apportioned
	7: 4	Even **Abraham** the patriarch gave
	7: 5	descended from **Abraham.**
	7: 6	collected tithes from **Abraham**
	7: 9	paid tithes through **Abraham,**
	11: 8	By faith **Abraham** obeyed
	11:17	By faith **Abraham,** when put to
Ja	2:21	**Abraham** justified by works
	2:23	**Abraham** believed God, and it
1P	3: 6	Thus Sarah obeyed **Abraham**

12   GO9 AG2 LN1   B2:205 K1:9   R1037
αβυσσος, BOTTOMLESS

Lk	8:31	to go back into the **abyss.**
Ro	10: 7	will descend into the **abyss?'**
Re	9: 1	shaft of the **bottomless** pit;
	9: 2	shaft of the **bottomless** pit,

	9:11	angel of the **bottomless** pit;
	11: 7	up from the **bottomless** pit
	17: 8	ascend from the **bottomless** pit
	20: 1	key to the **bottomless** pit
	20: 3	and threw him into the **pit,**

13   GO2 AG2 LN1
αγαβος, AGABUS

Ac	11:28	One of them named **Agabus** stood
	21:10	a prophet named **Agabus** came

14   GO1 AG2 LN1   B2:98 K1:17 R18,2041
αγαθοεργεω, I WORK GOOD

1Ti	6:18	They are to **do good,**

15   GO9 AG2 LN1   B2:98 K1:17 R18,4160
αγαθοποιεω, I DO GOOD

Lk	6: 9	is it lawful to **do good** or to
	6:33	If you **do good** to those who
	6:33	**do good** to you, what credit
	6:35	But love your enemies, **do good,**
1P	2:15	God's will that by **doing right**
	2:20	you endure when you **do right**
	3: 6	long as you **do** what is **good**
	3:17	better to suffer for **doing good**
3J	1:11	Whoever **does good** is from God;

16   GO1 AG2 LN1   B2:98 K1:17 R15
αγαθοποιια, GOOD DOING

1P	4:19	while continuing to **do good.**

17   GO1 AG2 LN1   B2:98 K1:17 R15
αγαθοποιος, DOING GOOD

1P	2:14	to praise those who **do right.**

18   GO102 AG2 LN1   B2:98 K1:10
αγαθος, GOOD

Mt	5:45	on the evil and on the **good,**
	7:11	know how to give **good** gifts to
	7:11	Father in heaven give **good**
	7:17	every **good** tree bears
	7:18	A **good** tree cannot bear bad
	12:34	How can you speak **good** things,
	12:35	The **good** person brings
	12:35	**good** things out of a
	12:35	**good** treasure, and the evil
	19:16	what **good** deed must I do to
	19:17	you ask me about what is **good?**
	19:17	only one who is **good.**
	20:15	envious because I am **generous?**

	22:10	found, both **good** and bad;
	25:21	**good** and trustworthy slave;
	25:23	Well done, **good** and
Mk	3: 4	Is it lawful to do **good** or to
	10:17	**Good** Teacher, what must I do
	10:18	Why do you call me **good?**
	10:18	No one is **good** but God alone.
Lk	1:53	the hungry with **good** things,
	6:45	The **good** person out of the
	6:45	the **good** treasure of the heart
	6:45	the heart produces **good,**
	8: 8	Some fell into **good** soil,
	8:15	in an honest and **good** heart,
	10:42	Mary has chosen the **better** part
	11:13	know how to give **good** gifts to
	12:18	store all my grain and my **goods**
	12:19	you have ample **goods** laid up
	16:25	you received your **good** things,
	18:18	asked him, "**Good** Teacher,
	18:19	Why do you call me **good?**
	18:19	No one is **good** but God alone.
	19:17	Well done, **good** slave!
	23:50	a **good** and righteous man named
Jn	1:46	Can anything **good** come out of
	5:29	those who have done **good,**
	7:12	He is a **good** man,
Ac	9:36	She was devoted to **good** works
	11:24	for he was a **good** man,
	23: 1	a **clear** conscience before God.
Ro	2: 7	who by patiently doing **good**
	2:10	for everyone who does **good,**
	3: 8	do evil so that **good** may come"?
	5: 7	perhaps for a **good** person
	7:12	is holy and just and **good.**
	7:13	Did what is **good,** then, bring
	7:13	in me through what is **good,**
	7:18	I know that nothing **good** dwells
	7:19	For I do not do the **good** I want
	8:28	work together for **good** for
	9:11	had done anything **good** or bad
	10:15	of those who bring **good** news!
	12: 2	will of God—what is **good**
	12: 9	hold fast to what is **good;**
	12:21	but overcome evil with **good.**
	13: 3	not a terror to **good** conduct,
	13: 3	Then do what is **good,** and you
	13: 4	God's servant for your **good.**
	14:16	let your **good** be spoken of as
	15: 2	for the **good** purpose of

	16:19	wise in what is **good** and
2C	5:10	in the body, whether **good** or
	9: 8	abundantly in every **good** work.
Ga	6: 6	must share in all **good** things
	6:10	let us work for the **good** of all
Ep	2:10	in Christ Jesus for **good** works,
	4:28	work **honestly** with their own
	4:29	what is **useful** for building up,
	6: 8	that whatever **good** we do,
Ph	1: 6	who began a **good** work among
		you
Co	1:10	bear fruit in every **good** work
1Th	3: 6	you always remember us **kindly**
	5:15	always seek to do **good** to one
2Th	2:16	eternal comfort and **good** hope,
	2:17	in every **good** work and word.
1Ti	1: 5	a **good** conscience, and sincere
	1:19	faith and a **good** conscience.
	2:10	but with **good** works,
	5:10	devoted herself to doing **good**
2Ti	2:21	ready for every **good** work.
	3:17	equipped for every **good** work.
Ti	1:16	unfit for any **good** work.
	2: 5	**good** managers of the household
	2:10	complete and **perfect** fidelity,
	3: 1	to be ready for every **good** work
Pm	1: 6	when you perceive all the **good**
	1:14	in order that your **good** deed
He	9:11	high priest of the **good** things
	10: 1	shadow of the **good** things to
	13:21	complete in everything **good**
Ja	1:17	Every **generous** act of giving,
	3:17	full of mercy and **good** fruits,
1P	2:18	not only those who are **kind**
	3:10	desire to see **good** days,
	3:11	away from evil and do **good;**
	3:13	are eager to do what is **good?**
	3:16	Keep your conscience **clear,**
	3:16	abuse you for your **good** conduct
	3:21	to God for a **good** conscience,
3J	1:11	but imitate what is **good.**

18a   GO1   AG3   LN1   B2:98   R14
αγαθουργεω, I WORK GOOD
Ac   14:17   without a witness in **doing good**

---

19   GO4   AG3   LN1   B2:98   K1:18   R18
αγαθωσυνη, GOODNESS
Ro   15:14   yourselves are full of **goodness**
Ga   5:22   patience, kindness, **generosity,**

Ep   5: 9   found in all that is **good** and
2Th 1:11   every **good** resolve and work of

---

20 GO5 AG3 LN1 B2:352 K1:19 R21
αγαλλιασις, GLADNESS
Lk   1:14   You will have joy and **gladness,**
     1:44   child in my womb leaped for **joy**
Ac   2:46   with **glad** and generous hearts,
He   1: 9   oil of **gladness** beyond your
Ju   1:24   of his glory with **rejoicing,**

---

21 GO11 AG3 LN1 B2:355 K1:19
αγαλλιαω, I AM GLAD
Mt   5:12   and be **glad,** for your reward
Lk   1:47   and my spirit **rejoices** in God
    10:21   Jesus **rejoiced** in the Holy
Jn   5:35   you were willing to **rejoice**
     8:56   Your ancestor Abraham **rejoiced**
Ac   2:26   therefore my heart was **glad,**
    16:34   **rejoiced** that he had become a
1P   1: 6   In this you **rejoice,**
     1: 8   **rejoice** with an indescribable
     4:13   you may also be **glad** and shout
Re 19: 7   **exult** and give him the glory,

---

22 GO4 AG4 LN1 B3:536 R1062
αγαμος, UNMARRIED
1C   7: 8   To the **unmarried** and the widows
     7:11   let her remain **unmarried** or
     7:32   The **unmarried** man is anxious
     7:34   the **unmarried** woman and the

---

23 GO7 AG4 LN1
αγανακτεω, I AM INDIGNANT
Mt 21:15   David," they became **angry**
    26: 8   they were **angry** and said, "Why
Mk 10:14   Jesus saw this he was **indignant**
    10:41   they began to be **angry** with
    14: 4   said to one another in **anger,**
Lk 13:14   **indignant** because Jesus had

---

24 GO1 AG4 LN1 R23
αγανακτησις, INDIGNATION
2C   7:11   what **indignation,** what alarm,

---

25 GO143 AG4 LN1 B2:538 K1:21
αγαπαω, I LOVE
Mt   5:43   **love** your neighbor and hate
     5:44   **Love** your enemies and pray
     5:46   if you **love** those who love you,

     5:46   if you love those who **love** you,
     6:24   hate the one and **love** the
    19:19   You shall **love** your neighbor as
    22:37   You shall **love** the Lord your
    22:39   You shall **love** your neighbor as
Mk 10:21   Jesus, looking at him **loved** him
    12:30   you shall **love** the Lord your
    12:31   You shall **love** your neighbor as
    12:33   to **love** him with all the heart
    12:33   to **love** one's neighbor as
Lk   6:27   listen, **Love** your enemies,
     6:32   If you **love** those who love you
     6:32   those who **love** you, what credit
     6:32   sinners **love** those who love
     6:32   love those who **love** them.
     6:35   But **love** your enemies,
     7: 5   for he **loves** our people,
     7:42   of them will **love** him more?
     7:47   hence she has shown great **love.**
     7:47   is forgiven, **loves** little.
    10:27   You shall **love** the Lord your
    11:43   For you **love** to have the seat
    16:13   hate the one and **love** the other
Jn   3:16   For God so **loved** the world
     3:19   people **loved** darkness rather
     3:35   The Father **loves** the Son
     8:42   you would **love** me, for I came
    10:17   reason the Father **loves** me,
    11: 5   though Jesus **loved** Martha and
    12:43   for they **loved** human glory
    13: 1   Having **loved** his own who were
    13: 1   he **loved** them to the end.
    13:23   the one whom Jesus **loved**
    13:34   that you **love** one another.
    13:34   Just as I have **loved** you,
    13:34   also should **love** one another.
    14:15   If you **love** me, you will keep
    14:21   keep them are those who **love** me
    14:21   those who **love** me will be loved
    14:21   will be **loved** by my Father,
    14:21   I will **love** them and reveal
    14:23   who **love** me will keep my word,
    14:23   my Father will **love** them,
    14:24   **love** me does not keep my words;
    14:28   If you **loved** me, you would
    14:31   world may know that I **love**
    15: 9   As the Father has **loved** me,
    15: 9   so I have **loved** you; abide
    15:12   commandment, that you **love** one

	15:12	another as I have **loved** you.
	15:17	that you may **love** one another.
	17:23	sent me and have **loved** them
	17:23	even as you have **loved** me.
	17:24	because you **loved** me before
	17:26	which you have **loved** me may be
	19:26	disciple whom he **loved**
	21: 7	disciple whom Jesus **loved** said
	21:15	do you **love** me more than these?
	21:16	of John, do you **love** me?
	21:20	disciple whom Jesus **loved**
Ro	8:28	for those who **love** God, who
	8:37	through him who **loved** us.
	9:13	I have **loved** Jacob, but
	9:25	and her who was not **beloved**
	9:25	I will call '**beloved.**'
	13: 8	except to **love** one another;
	13: 8	who **loves** another has fulfilled
	13: 9	**Love** your neighbor as yourself
1C	2: 9	prepared for those who **love** him
	8: 3	who **loves** God is known by him.
2C	9: 7	for God **loves** a cheerful giver.
	11:11	Because I do not **love** you?
	12:15	If I **love** you more,
	12:15	am I to be **loved** less?
Ga	2:20	who **loved** me and gave himself
	5:14	You shall **love** your neighbor as
Ep	1: 6	bestowed on us in the **Beloved.**
	2: 4	great love with which he **loved**
	5: 2	as Christ **loved** us and gave
	5:25	Husbands, **love** your wives,
	5:25	just as Christ **loved** the church
	5:28	should **love** their wives as they
	5:28	He who **loves** his wife loves
	5:28	loves his wife **loves** himself.
	5:33	should **love** his wife as himself
	6:24	who have an undying **love** for
Co	3:12	chosen ones, holy and **beloved,**
	3:19	Husbands, **love** your wives
1Th	1: 4	sisters **beloved** by God,
	4: 9	by God to **love** one another;
2Th	2:13	sisters **beloved** by the Lord,
	2:16	God our Father, who **loved** us
2Ti	4: 8	have **longed** for his appearing.
	4:10	in **love** with this present world
He	1: 9	You have **loved** righteousness
	12: 6	disciplines those whom he **loves**
Ja	1:12	promised to those who **love** him.
	2: 5	promised to those who **love** him?

	2: 8	You shall **love** your neighbor as
1P	1: 8	not seen him, you **love** him;
	1:22	**love** one another deeply from
	2:17	**Love** the family of believers.
	3:10	For "Those who **desire** life and
2P	2:15	**loved** the wages of doing wrong,
1J	2:10	**loves** a brother or sister lives
	2:15	Do not **love** the world or the
	2:15	in those who **love** the world;
	3:10	those who do not **love** their
	3:11	that we should **love** one another
	3:14	because we **love** one another.
	3:14	does not **love** abides in death.
	3:18	let us **love,** not in word or
	3:23	and **love** one another, just as
	4: 7	let us **love** one another,
	4: 7	who **loves** is born of God and
	4: 8	does not **love** does not know God
	4:10	not that we **loved** God but that
	4:10	he **loved** us and sent his Son
	4:11	since God **loved** us so much,
	4:11	we also ought to **love** one
	4:12	if we **love** one another,
	4:19	We love because he first **loved**
	4:19	love because he first **loved** us.
	4:20	Those who say, "I **love** God,"
	4:20	who do not **love** a brother or
	4:20	cannot **love** God whom they have
	4:21	those who **love** God must love
	4:21	must **love** their brothers and
	5: 1	everyone who **loves** the parent
	5: 1	the parent **loves** the child.
	5: 2	we **love** the children of God,
	5: 2	when we **love** God and obey his
2J	1: 1	I **love** in the truth, and not
	1: 5	let us **love** one another.
3J	1: 1	whom I **love** in truth.
Ju	1: 1	who are **beloved** in God the
	1:12	blemishes on your **love**-feasts,
Re	1: 5	To him who **loves** us and freed
	3: 9	learn that I have **loved** you.
	12:11	for they did not **cling** to life
	20: 9	saints and the **beloved** city.

---

26   GO116   AG5   LN2   B2:538   K1:21   R25
αγαπη, LOVE

Mt	24:12	the **love** of many will grow cold
Lk	11:42	neglect justice and the **love** of
Jn	5:42	not have the **love** of God in you

	13:35	if you have **love** for one
	15: 9	abide in my **love.**
	15:10	you will abide in my **love,**
	15:10	and abide in his **love.**
	15:13	No one has greater **love** than
	17:26	so that the **love** with which you
Ro	5: 5	God's **love** has been poured into
	5: 8	But God proves his **love** for us
	8:35	separate us from the **love** of
	8:39	from the **love** of God in Christ
	12: 9	Let **love** be genuine;
	13:10	**Love** does no wrong to a
	13:10	**love** is the fulfilling of the
	14:15	are no longer walking in **love.**
	15:30	by the **love** of the Spirit,
1C	4:21	with **love** in a spirit of
	8: 1	puffs up, but **love** builds up.
	13: 1	angels, but do not have **love,**
	13: 2	mountains, but do not have **love**
	13: 3	not have **love,** I gain nothing.
	13: 4	**Love** is patient;
	13: 4	**love** is kind;
	13: 4	**love** is not envious or boastful
	13: 8	**Love** never ends.
	13:13	faith, hope, and **love** abide,
	13:13	the greatest of these is **love.**
	14: 1	Pursue **love** and strive for the
	16:14	that you do be done in **love.**
	16:24	My **love** be with all of you in
2C	2: 4	abundant **love** that I have for
	2: 8	to reaffirm your **love** for him.
	5:14	the **love** of Christ urges us on,
	6: 6	of spirit, genuine **love,**
	8: 7	and in our **love** for you
	8: 8	genuineness of your **love**
	8:24	them the proof of your **love**
	13:11	and the God of **love** and peace
	13:13	the **love** of God,
Ga	5: 6	faith working through **love.**
	5:13	through **love** become slaves to
	5:22	fruit of the Spirit is **love,**
Ep	1: 4	blameless before him in **love.**
	1:15	your **love** toward all the saints
	2: 4	great **love** with which he loved
	3:17	rooted and grounded in **love.**
	3:19	and to know the **love** of Christ
	4: 2	with one another in **love,**
	4:15	But speaking the truth in **love,**
	4:16	building itself up in **love.**

	5: 2	live in **love,** as Christ loved
	6:23	**love** with faith, from God the
Ph	1: 9	your **love** may overflow more
	1:16	proclaim Christ out of **love**
	2: 1	any consolation from **love,**
	2: 2	having the same **love,**
Co	1: 4	**love** that you have for all the
	1: 8	your **love** in the Spirit.
	1:13	kingdom of his **beloved** Son,
	2: 2	united in **love,** so that they
	3:14	clothe yourselves with **love,**
1Th	1: 3	work of faith and labor of **love**
	3: 6	news of your faith and **love.**
	3:12	abound in **love** for one another
	5: 8	breastplate of faith and **love,**
	5:13	esteem them very highly in **love**
2Th	1: 3	the **love** of everyone of you for
	2:10	they refused to **love** the truth
	3: 5	direct your hearts to the **love**
1Ti	1: 5	aim of such instruction is **love**
	1:14	**love** that are in Christ Jesus.
	2:15	they continue in faith and **love**
	4:12	conduct, in **love,** in faith, in
	6:11	godliness, faith, **love,**
2Ti	1: 7	spirit of power and of **love**
	1:13	**love** that are in Christ Jesus,
	2:22	faith, **love,** and peace,
	3:10	my patience, my **love,** my
Ti	2: 2	sound in faith, in **love,**
Pm	1: 5	because I hear of your **love**
	1: 7	encouragement from your **love,**
	1: 9	to you on the basis of **love**
He	6:10	overlook your work and the **love**
	10:24	provoke one another to **love**
1P	4: 8	maintain constant **love** for one
	4: 8	**love** covers a multitude of sins
	5:14	one another with a kiss of **love.**
2P	1: 7	and mutual affection with **love.**
1J	2: 5	**love** of God has reached
	2:15	The **love** of the Father is not
	3: 1	See what **love** the Father has
	3:16	We know **love** by this, that he
	3:17	How does God's **love** abide in
	4: 7	because **love** is from God;
	4: 8	for God is **love.**
	4: 9	God's **love** was revealed among
	4:10	In this is **love,** not that we
	4:12	his **love** is perfected in us.
	4:16	believe the **love** that God has

	4:16	God is **love,** and those who
	4:16	and those who abide in **love**
	4:17	**Love** has been perfected
	4:18	There is no fear in **love,** but
	4:18	perfect **love** casts out fear;
	4:18	not reached perfection in **love.**
	5: 3	For the **love** of God is this,
2J	1: 3	Father's Son, in truth and **love**
	1: 6	And this is **love,** that we walk
3J	1: 6	testified to your **love** before
Ju	1: 2	**love** be yours in abundance.
	1:21	keep yourselves in the **love** of
Re	2: 4	you have abandoned the **love**
	2:19	works—your **love,** faith,

27　GO61　AG6　LN2　B2:538　K1:21　R25
αγαπητος, LOVED ONE

Mt	3:17	This is my Son, the **Beloved,**
	12:18	chosen, my **beloved,** with whom
	17: 5	This is my Son, the **Beloved;**
Mk	1:11	You are my Son, the **Beloved;**
	9: 7	the **Beloved;** listen to him!
	12: 6	one other, a **beloved** son.
Lk	3:22	You are my Son, the **Beloved;**
	20:13	I will send my **beloved** son;
Ac	15:25	along with our **beloved** Barnabas
Ro	1: 7	To all God's **beloved** in Rome,
	11:28	election they are **beloved,**
	12:19	**Beloved,** never avenge
	16: 5	Greet my **beloved** Epaenetus,
	16: 8	Greet Ampliatus, my **beloved**
	16: 9	and my **beloved** Stachys.
	16:12	Greet the **beloved** Persis,
1C	4:14	you as my **beloved** children.
	4:17	Timothy, who is my **beloved**
	10:14	my **dear friends,** flee from
	15:58	my **beloved,** be steadfast,
2C	7: 1	**beloved,** let us cleanse
	12:19	Everything we do, **beloved,**
Ep	5: 1	imitators of God, as **beloved**
	6:21	He is a **dear** brother and a
Ph	2:12	Therefore, my **beloved,** just
	4: 1	whom I **love** and long for,
	4: 1	Lord in this way, my **beloved.**
Co	1: 7	Epaphras, our **beloved** fellow
	4: 7	he is a **beloved** brother,
	4: 9	faithful and **beloved** brother,
	4:14	Luke, the **beloved** physician,
1Th	2: 8	you have become **very dear** to us

1Ti	6: 2	are believers and **beloved.**
2Ti	1: 2	To Timothy, my **beloved** child:
Pm	1: 1	To Philemon our **dear friend**
	1:16	more than a slave, a **beloved**
He	6: 9	**beloved,** we are confident of
Ja	1:16	Do not be deceived, my **beloved.**
	1:19	understand this, my **beloved:**
	2: 5	Listen, my **beloved** brothers
1P	2:11	**Beloved,** I urge you as aliens
	4:12	**Beloved,** do not be surprised
2P	1:17	This is my Son, my **Beloved,**
	3: 1	**beloved,** the second letter
	3: 8	**beloved,** that with the Lord
	3:14	**beloved,** while you are waiting
	3:15	**beloved** brother Paul wrote
	3:17	You therefore, **beloved,** since
1J	2: 7	**Beloved,** I am writing you no
	3: 2	**Beloved,** we are God's children
	3:21	**Beloved,** if our hearts do not
	4: 1	**Beloved,** do not believe every
	4: 7	**Beloved,** let us love one
	4:11	**Beloved,** since God loved us so
3J	1: 1	The elder to the **beloved** Gaius,
	1: 2	**Beloved,** I pray that all may go
	1: 5	**Beloved,** you do faithfully
	1:11	**Beloved,** do not imitate what is
Ju	1: 3	**Beloved,** while eagerly
	1:17	But you, **beloved,** must remember
	1:20	**beloved,** build yourselves up

28　GO2　AG6　LN2　B1:80　K1:55
'αγαρ, HAGAR

Ga	4:24	One woman, in fact, is **Hagar,**
	4:25	Now **Hagar** is Mount Sinai in

29　GO3　AG6　LN2
αγγαρευω, I CONSCRIPT

Mt	5:41	if anyone **forces** you to go one
	27:32	they **compelled** this man to
Mk	15:21	They **compelled** a passer-by,

30　GO1　AG6　LN2　R32a
αγγειον, CONTAINER

Mt	25: 4	but the wise took **flasks** of oil

31　GO2　AG7　LN2　B3:44　K1:56　R31a
αγγελια, MESSAGE

1J	1: 5	This is the **message** we have
	3:11	For this is the **message** you

31a ᴳᴼ1 ᴬᴳ7 ᴸᴺ2 ᴮ3:44 ᴷ1:60
αγγελλω, I GIVE MESSAGE
Jn   20:18   **announced** to the disciples,

---

32 ᴳᴼ176 ᴬᴳ7 ᴸᴺ2 ᴮ1:104 ᴷ1:74 ᴿ31a
αγγελος, MESSENGER

Mt	1:20	an **angel** of the Lord appeared
	1:24	he did as the **angel** of the Lord
	2:13	**angel** of the Lord appeared to
	2:19	**angel** of the Lord suddenly
	4: 6	He will command his **angels**
	4:11	suddenly **angels** came and waited
	11:10	See, I am sending my **messenger**
	13:39	and the reapers are **angels.**
	13:41	Son of Man will send his **angels,**
	13:49	The **angels** will come out
	16:27	to come with his **angels**
	18:10	in heaven their **angels**
	22:30	but are like **angels** in heaven.
	24:31	send out his **angels** with a loud
	24:36	knows, neither the **angels** of
	25:31	glory, and all the **angels** with
	25:41	for the devil and his **angels;**
	26:53	than twelve legions of **angels?**
	28: 2	**angel** of the Lord, descending
	28: 5	But the **angel** said to the women
Mk	1: 2	I am sending my **messenger** ahead
	1:13	and the **angels** waited on him.
	8:38	his Father with the holy **angels**
	12:25	but are like **angels** in heaven.
	13:27	he will send out the **angels,**
	13:32	neither the **angels** in heaven,
Lk	1:11	appeared to him an **angel**
	1:13	But the **angel** said to him,
	1:18	Zechariah said to the **angel,**
	1:19	**angel** replied, "I am Gabriel.
	1:26	**angel** Gabriel was sent by God
	1:30	The **angel** said to her, "Do not
	1:34	Mary said to the **angel,** "How
	1:35	**angel** said to her,
	1:38	Then the **angel** departed
	2: 9	**angel** of the Lord stood before
	2:10	But the **angel** said to them,
	2:13	with the **angel** a multitude
	2:15	**angels** had left them and gone
	2:21	the name given by the **angel**
	4:10	He will command his **angels**
	7:24	When John's **messengers** had
	7:27	I am sending my **messenger**

	9:26	Father and of the holy **angels.**
	9:52	And he sent **messengers** ahead
	12: 8	acknowledge before the **angels**
	12: 9	be denied before the **angels**
	15:10	**angels** of God over one sinner
	16:22	carried away by the **angels**
	22:43	**angel** from heaven appeared
	24:23	seen a vision of **angels** who
Jn	1:51	**angels** of God ascending and
	12:29	An **angel** has spoken to him.
	20:12	and she saw two **angels** in white
Ac	5:19	**angel** of the Lord opened the
	6:15	like the face of an **angel.**
	7:30	an **angel** appeared to him in
	7:35	through the **angel** who appeared
	7:38	**angel** who spoke to him at Mount
	7:53	law as ordained by **angels,**
	8:26	Then an **angel** of the Lord said
	10: 3	saw an **angel** of God coming in
	10: 7	When the **angel** who spoke to him
	10:22	was directed by a holy **angel**
	11:13	how he had seen the **angel**
	12: 7	Suddenly an **angel** of the Lord
	12: 8	The **angel** said to him, "Fasten
	12: 9	happening with the **angel's** help
	12:10	when suddenly the **angel** left
	12:11	Lord has sent his **angel**
	12:15	They said, "It is his **angel."**
	12:23	**angel** of the Lord struck him
	23: 8	is no resurrection, or **angel,**
	23: 9	an **angel** has spoken to him?
	27:23	**angel** of the God to whom I
Ro	8:38	nor **angels,** nor rulers, nor
1C	4: 9	to the world, to **angels** and to
	6: 3	we are to judge **angels**
	11:10	her head, because of the **angels**
	13: 1	mortals and of **angels,**
2C	11:14	disguises himself as an **angel**
	12: 7	a **messenger** of Satan to torment
Ga	1: 8	**angel** from heaven should
	3:19	was ordained through **angels** by
	4:14	welcomed me as an **angel** of God,
Co	2:18	and worship of **angels,** dwelling
2Th	1: 7	heaven with his mighty **angels**
1Ti	3:16	seen by **angels,** proclaimed
	5:21	elect **angels,** I warn you
He	1: 4	superior to **angels** as the name
	1: 5	to which of the **angels** did God
	1: 6	Let all God's **angels** worship

	1: 7	Of the **angels** he says,
	1: 7	He makes his **angels** winds,
	1:13	**angels** has he ever said, "Sit
	2: 2	message declared through **angels**
	2: 5	we are speaking, to **angels.**
	2: 7	lower than the **angels;**
	2: 9	made lower than the **angels,**
	2:16	he did not come to help **angels,**
	12:22	innumerable **angels** in festal
	13: 2	have entertained **angels**
Ja	2:25	she welcomed the **messengers**
1P	1:12	things into which **angels** long
	3:22	with **angels,** authorities,
2P	2: 4	God did not spare the **angels**
	2:11	whereas **angels,** though greater
Ju	1: 6	**angels** who did not keep their
Re	1: 1	sending his **angel** to his
	1:20	the seven stars are the **angels**
	2: 1	**angel** of the church in Ephesus
	2: 8	**angel** of the church in Smyrna
	2:12	**angel** of the church in Pergamum
	2:18	**angel** of the church in Thyatira
	3: 1	**angel** of the church in Sardis
	3: 5	my Father and before his **angels**
	3: 7	**angel** of the church in
	3:14	**angel** of the church in Laodicea
	5: 2	I saw a mighty **angel**
	5:11	heard the voice of many **angels**
	7: 1	After this I saw four **angels**
	7: 2	I saw another **angel** ascending
	7: 2	loud voice to the four **angels**
	7:11	And all the **angels** stood around
	8: 2	And I saw the seven **angels** who
	8: 3	Another **angel** with a golden
	8: 4	God from the hand of the **angel**
	8: 5	Then the **angel** took the censer
	8: 6	Now the seven **angels** who had
	8: 8	second **angel** blew his trumpet,
	8:10	third **angel** blew his trumpet,
	8:12	fourth **angel** blew his trumpet,
	8:13	three **angels** are about to blow!
	9: 1	fifth **angel** blew his trumpet,
	9:11	the **angel** of the bottomless pit
	9:13	sixth **angel** blew his trumpet,
	9:14	sixth **angel** who had the trumpet
	9:14	Release the four **angels** who
	9:15	the four **angels** were released,
	10: 1	And I saw another mighty **angel**
	10: 5	**angel** whom I saw standing on

	10: 7	when the seventh **angel** is to
	10: 8	open in the hand of the **angel**
	10: 9	So I went to the **angel**
	10:10	from the hand of the **angel**
	11:15	seventh **angel** blew his trumpet,
	12: 7	Michael and his **angels** fought
	12: 7	dragon and his **angels** fought
	12: 9	his **angels** were thrown down
	14: 6	Then I saw another **angel** flying
	14: 8	Then another **angel,** a second,
	14: 9	Then another **angel,** a third,
	14:10	presence of the holy **angels**
	14:15	**angel** came out of the temple,
	14:17	**angel** came out of the temple
	14:18	**angel** came out from the altar,
	14:19	So the **angel** swung his sickle
	15: 1	seven **angels** with seven plagues
	15: 6	temple came the seven **angels**
	15: 7	gave the seven **angels** seven
	15: 8	plagues of the seven **angels**
	16: 1	temple telling the seven **angels**
	16: 5	**angel** of the waters say,
	17: 1	Then one of the seven **angels**
	17: 7	But the **angel** said to me,
	18: 1	After this I saw another **angel**
	18:21	mighty **angel** took up a stone
	19:17	**angel** standing in the sun,
	20: 1	Then I saw an **angel** coming
	21: 9	seven **angels** who had the seven
	21:12	at the gates twelve **angels,**
	21:17	which the **angel** was using.
	22: 6	has sent his **angel** to show
	22: 8	the **angel** who showed them to me
	22:16	Jesus, who sent my **angel** to you

32a   GO1 AG8 LN2
αγγος, CONTAINER
Mt 13:48   put the good into **baskets**

---

33   GO2 AG8 LN2 R71
αγε, COME
Ja 4:13   **Come now,** you who say, "Today
      5: 1   **Come now,** you rich people, weep

---

34   GO7 AG8 LN2
αγελη, HERD
Mt 8:30   Now a large **herd** of swine was
      8:31   send us into the **herd** of swine.
      8:32   the whole **herd** rushed down
Mk 5:11   great **herd** of swine was feeding

5:13   and the **herd,** numbering about
Lk   8:32   large **herd** of swine was feeding
     8:33   **herd** rushed down the steep bank

---

35 GO1 AG8 LN2 B2:35 K1:665 R1075
αγενεαλογητος, NO GENEALOGY
He   7: 3   **without genealogy,** having

---

36 GO1 AG8 LN2
αγενης, UNBORN
1C   1:28   God chose what is **low** and

---

37 GO28 AG8 LN2 B2:224 K1:111 R40
'αγιαζω, I MAKE HOLY
Mt   6: 9   **hallowed** be your name.
     23:17   that has made the gold **sacred?**
     23:19   that makes the gift **sacred?**
Lk   11: 2   Father, **hallowed** be your name.
Jn   10:36   Father has **sanctified** and sent
     17:17   **Sanctify** them in the truth;
     17:19   their sakes I **sanctify** myself,
     17:19   they also may be **sanctified**
Ac   20:32   among all who are **sanctified.**
     26:18   who are **sanctified** by faith
Ro   15:16   **sanctified** by the Holy Spirit.
1C   1: 2   **sanctified** in Christ Jesus,
     6:11   you were **sanctified,** you were
     7:14   husband is **made holy** through
     7:14   unbelieving wife is **made holy**
Ep   5:26   in order to **make** her **holy** by
1Th   5:23   God of peace himself **sanctify**
1Ti   4: 5   it is **sanctified** by God's word
2Ti   2:21   utensils, **dedicated** and useful
He   2:11   For the one who **sanctifies** and
     2:11   **sanctified** all have one Father
     9:13   **sanctifies** those who have been
     10:10   **sanctified** through the offering
     10:14   those who are **sanctified.**
     10:29   by which they were **sanctified,**
     13:12   **sanctify** the people by his own
1P   3:15   in your hearts **sanctify** Christ
Re   22:11   and the holy still be **holy.**

---

38 GO10 AG9 LN2 B2:224 K1:113 R37
'αγιασμος, HOLINESS
Ro   6:19   righteousness . . . **sanctification**
     6:22   you get is **sanctification.**
1C   1:30   **sanctification** and redemption,
1Th   4: 3   your **sanctification:** that you
     4: 4   your own body in **holiness** and

4: 7   to impurity but in **holiness.**
2Th   2:13   **sanctification** by the Spirit
1Ti   2:15   faith and love and **holiness,**
He   12:14   the **holiness** without which
1P   1: 2   **sanctified** by the Spirit

---

40 GO233 AG9 LN2 B2:223 K1:88
αγιος, HOLY
Mt   1:18   with child from the **Holy** Spirit
     1:20   in her is from the **Holy** Spirit.
     3:11   baptize you with the **Holy**
     4: 5   devil took him to the **holy** city
     7: 6   Do not give what is **holy** to
     12:32   speaks against the **Holy** Spirit
     24:15   sacrilege standing in the **holy**
     27:52   bodies of the **saints** who had
     27:53   entered the **holy** city and
     28:19   the Son and of the **Holy** Spirit,
Mk   1: 8   baptize you with the **Holy**
     1:24   you are, the **Holy** One of God.
     3:29   blasphemes against the **Holy**
     6:20   he was a righteous and **holy** man
     8:38   Father with the **holy** angels.
     12:36   by the **Holy** Spirit, declared,
     13:11   who speak, but the **Holy** Spirit.
Lk   1:15   he will be filled with the **Holy**
     1:35   **Holy** Spirit will come upon you,
     1:35   child to be born will be **holy;**
     1:41   was filled with the **Holy** Spirit
     1:49   and **holy** is his name.
     1:67   was filled with the **Holy** Spirit
     1:70   the mouth of his **holy** prophets
     1:72   remembered his **holy** covenant,
     2:23   designated as **holy** to the Lord
     2:25   the **Holy** Spirit rested on him.
     2:26   to him by the **Holy** Spirit
     3:16   baptize you with the **Holy**
     3:22   and the **Holy** Spirit descended
     4: 1   Jesus, full of the **Holy** Spirit,
     4:34   you are, the **Holy** One of God.
     9:26   Father and of the **holy** angels.
     10:21   rejoiced in the **Holy** Spirit
     11:13   Father give the **Holy** Spirit
     12:10   blasphemes against the **Holy**
     12:12   the **Holy** Spirit will teach you
Jn   1:33   baptizes with the **Holy** Spirit.
     6:69   you are the **Holy** One of God.
     14:26   Advocate, the **Holy** Spirit,
     17:11   **Holy** Father, protect them in

	20:22	Receive the **Holy** Spirit.
Ac	1: 2	instructions through the **Holy**
	1: 5	baptized with the **Holy** Spirit
	1: 8	receive power when the **Holy**
	1:16	**Holy** Spirit through David
	2: 4	filled with the **Holy** Spirit
	2:33	promise of the **Holy** Spirit,
	2:38	the gift of the **Holy** Spirit.
	3:14	rejected the **Holy** and Righteous
	3:21	ago through his **holy** prophets.
	4: 8	Peter, filled with the **Holy**
	4:25	you who said by the **Holy** Spirit
	4:27	against your **holy** servant Jesus
	4:30	name of your **holy** servant Jesus
	4:31	all filled with the **Holy** Spirit
	5: 3	to lie to the **Holy** Spirit
	5:32	**Holy** Spirit whom God has given
	6: 5	full of faith and the **Holy**
	6:13	things against this **holy** place
	7:33	you are standing is **holy** ground
	7:51	opposing the **Holy** Spirit,
	7:55	filled with the **Holy** Spirit,
	8:15	might receive the **Holy** Spirit
	8:17	they received the **Holy** Spirit.
	8:19	may receive the **Holy** Spirit.
	9:13	evil he has done to your **saints**
	9:17	filled with the **Holy** Spirit.
	9:31	comfort of the **Holy** Spirit,
	9:32	to the **saints** living in Lydda.
	9:41	calling the **saints** and widows,
	10:22	was directed by a **holy** angel
	10:38	**Holy** Spirit and with power;
	10:44	**Holy** Spirit fell upon all who
	10:45	gift of the **Holy** Spirit
	10:47	have received the **Holy** Spirit
	11:15	**Holy** Spirit fell upon them
	11:16	baptized with the **Holy** Spirit.
	11:24	good man, full of the **Holy**
	13: 2	fasting, the **Holy** Spirit said,
	13: 4	being sent out by the **Holy**
	13: 9	filled with the **Holy** Spirit,
	13:52	joy and with the **Holy** Spirit.
	15: 8	by giving them the **Holy** Spirit,
	15:28	seemed good to the **Holy** Spirit
	16: 6	forbidden by the **Holy** Spirit
	19: 2	Did you receive the **Holy** Spirit
	19: 2	that there is a **Holy** Spirit.
	19: 6	**Holy** Spirit came upon them,
	20:23	that the **Holy** Spirit testifies

	20:28	**Holy** Spirit has made you
	21:11	Thus says the **Holy** Spirit,
	21:28	has defiled this **holy** place.
	26:10	locked up many of the **saints**
	28:25	The **Holy** Spirit was right
Ro	1: 2	prophets in the **holy** scriptures
	1: 7	who are called to be **saints:**
	5: 5	hearts through the **Holy** Spirit
	7:12	So the law is **holy,**
	7:12	commandment is **holy** and just
	8:27	intercedes for the **saints**
	9: 1	confirms it by the **Holy** Spirit
	11:16	as first fruits is **holy,**
	11:16	if the root is **holy,** then
	12: 1	**holy** and acceptable to God,
	12:13	to the needs of the **saints;**
	14:17	joy in the **Holy** Spirit.
	15:13	by the power of the **Holy** Spirit
	15:16	sanctified by the **Holy** Spirit.
	15:25	in a ministry to the **saints;**
	15:26	among the **saints** at Jerusalem.
	15:31	may be acceptable to the **saints**
	16: 2	is fitting for the **saints,**
	16:15	all the **saints** who are with
	16:16	one another with a **holy** kiss.
1C	1: 2	called to be **saints**
	3:17	God's temple is **holy,** and you
	6: 1	taking it before the **saints?**
	6: 2	**saints** will judge the world?
	6:19	temple of the **Holy** Spirit
	7:14	as it is, they are **holy.**
	7:34	they may be **holy** in body
	12: 3	except by the **Holy** Spirit.
	14:33	all the churches of the **saints,**
	16: 1	collection for the **saints:**
	16:15	to the service of the **saints;**
	16:20	Greet one another with a **holy**
2C	1: 1	including all the **saints**
	6: 6	kindness, **holiness** of spirit,
	8: 4	in this ministry to the **saints**
	9: 1	the ministry to the **saints,**
	9:12	the needs of the **saints** but
	13:12	one another with a **holy** kiss.
	13:12	one another with a **holy** kiss.
	13:13	communion of the **Holy** Spirit
Ep	1: 1	**saints** who are in Ephesus
	1: 4	to be **holy** and blameless
	1:13	of the promised **Holy** Spirit;
	1:15	love toward all the **saints,**

	1:18	inheritance among the **saints,**
	2:19	citizens with the **saints**
	2:21	grows into a **holy** temple
	3: 5	revealed to his **holy** apostles
	3: 8	very least of all the **saints,**
	3:18	comprehend, with all the **saints**
	4:12	equip the **saints** for the work
	4:30	do not grieve the **Holy** Spirit
	5: 3	as is proper among **saints.**
	5:27	she may be **holy** and without
	6:18	supplication for all the **saints**
Ph	1: 1	To all the **saints** in Christ
	4:21	Greet every **saint** in Christ
	4:22	All the **saints** greet you,
Co	1: 2	To the **saints** and faithful
	1: 4	you have for all the **saints,**
	1:12	inheritance of the **saints**
	1:22	to present you **holy** and
	1:26	been revealed to his **saints.**
	3:12	chosen ones, **holy** and beloved,
1Th	1: 5	power and in the **Holy** Spirit
	1: 6	joy inspired by the **Holy** Spirit
	3:13	Lord Jesus with all his **saints.**
	4: 8	gives his **Holy** Spirit to you.
	5:26	sisters with a **holy** kiss.
2Th	1:10	to be glorified by his **saints**
1Ti	5:10	washed the **saints'** feet,
2Ti	1: 9	called us with a **holy** calling,
	1:14	help of the **Holy** Spirit living
Ti	3: 5	renewal by the **Holy** Spirit.
Pm	1: 5	love for all the **saints**
	1: 7	hearts of the **saints**
He	2: 4	by gifts of the **Holy** Spirit,
	3: 1	**holy** partners in a heavenly
	3: 7	as the **Holy** Spirit says, "Today
	6: 4	shared in the **Holy** Spirit,
	6:10	his sake in serving the **saints,**
	8: 2	a minister in the **sanctuary**
	9: 1	and an earthly **sanctuary.**
	9: 2	this is called the **Holy** Place.
	9: 3	tent called the **Holy** of Holies.
	9: 3	tent called the Holy of **Holies.**
	9: 8	the **Holy** Spirit indicates
	9: 8	way into the **sanctuary** has not
	9:12	once for all into the **Holy**
	9:24	not enter a **sanctuary** made
	9:25	priest enters the **Holy** Place
	10:15	**Holy** Spirit also testifies
	10:19	to enter the **sanctuary** by

	13:11	into the **sanctuary** by the high
	13:24	leaders and all the **saints.**
1P	1:12	**Holy** Spirit sent from heaven
	1:15	as he who called you is **holy,**
	1:15	be **holy** yourselves in all
	1:16	You shall be **holy,**
	1:16	for I am **holy.**
	2: 5	to be a **holy** priesthood,
	2: 9	a **holy** nation, God's own
	3: 5	**holy** women who hoped in God
2P	1:18	with him on the **holy** mountain.
	1:21	women moved by the **Holy** Spirit
	2:21	from the **holy** commandment
	3: 2	by the **holy** prophets, and the
	3:11	leading lives of **holiness**
1J	2:20	anointed by the **Holy** One,
Ju	1: 3	all entrusted to the **saints.**
	1:14	ten thousands of his **holy** ones,
	1:20	on your most **holy** faith;
	1:20	pray in the **Holy** Spirit;
Re	3: 7	words of the **holy** one, the true
	4: 8	sing, **"Holy,** holy, holy,
	4: 8	they sing, "Holy, **holy,** holy,
	4: 8	they sing, "Holy, holy, **holy,"**
	5: 8	are the prayers of the **saints.**
	6:10	Sovereign Lord, **holy** and true,
	8: 3	prayers of all the **saints**
	8: 4	with the prayers of the **saints,**
	11: 2	trample over the **holy** city
	11:18	the prophets and **saints**
	13: 7	to make war on the **saints**
	13:10	faith of the **saints.**
	14:10	presence of the **holy** angels
	14:12	endurance of the **saints,**
	16: 6	shed the blood of **saints**
	17: 6	with the blood of the **saints**
	18:20	O heaven, you **saints** and
	18:24	prophets and of **saints,**
	19: 8	righteous deeds of the **saints.**
	20: 6	Blessed and **holy** are those
	20: 9	the camp of the **saints**
	21: 2	And I saw the **holy** city,
	21:10	showed me the **holy** city
	22:11	and the **holy** still be holy.
	22:19	life and in the **holy** city,

---

41 GO1 AG10 LN2 B2:224 K1:114 R40
ἁγιοτης, HOLINESS
He 12:10 that we may share his **holiness.**

42　GO3　AG10　LN2　B2:224　K1:114　R40
'αγιωσυνη, HOLINESS
Ro　1: 4　spirit of **holiness** by
2C　7: 1　making **holiness** perfect
1Th　3:13　your hearts in **holiness**

43　GO1　AG10　LN2　B1:239
αγκαλη, ARM
Lk　2:28　Simeon took him in his **arms**

44　GO1　AG10　LN2
αγκιστρον, HOOK
Mt　17:27　go to the sea and cast a **hook;**

45　GO4　AG10　LN2
αγκυρα, ANCHOR
Ac　27:29　they let down four **anchors** from
　　27:30　putting out **anchors**
　　27:40　they cast off the **anchors**
He　6:19　sure and steadfast **anchor**

46　GO2　AG10　LN2
αγναφος, UNSHRUNK
Mt　9:16　sews a piece of **unshrunk** cloth
Mk　2:21　sews a piece of **unshrunk** cloth

47　GO2　AG10　LN2　B3:100　K1:123　R53
'αγνεια, PURITY
1Ti　4:12　in love, in faith, in **purity.**
　　5: 2　sisters—with absolute **purity**

48　GO7　AG11　LN2　B3:100　K1:123　R53
'αγνιζω, I PURIFY
Jn　11:55　Passover to **purify** themselves.
Ac　21:24　rite of **purification** with them
　　21:26　having **purified** himself,
　　24:18　rite of **purification,** without
Ja　4: 8　**purify** your hearts, you
1P　1:22　you have **purified** your souls
1J　3: 3　hope in him **purify** themselves,

49　GO1　AG11　LN2　B3:100　K1:124　R53
'αγνισμος, PURIFICATION
Ac　21:26　of the days of **purification**

50　GO22　AG11　LN2　B2:406　K1:115　R3539
αγνοεω, I KNOW NOT
Mk　9:32　But they did **not understand**
Lk　9:45　But they did **not understand**
Ac　13:27　or **understand** the words of the

　　17:23　you worship as **unknown,**
Ro　1:13　I want you to **know,**
　　2: 4　Do you **not realize** that God's
　　6: 3　Do you **not know** that all of us
　　7: 1　Do you **not know,** brothers and
　　10: 3　**ignorant** of the righteousness
　　11:25　I want you to **understand** this
1C　10: 1　I do not want you to be **unaware**
　　12: 1　want you to be **uninformed.**
　　14:38　Anyone who does **not recognize**
　　14:38　this is **not** to be **recognized.**
2C　1: 8　do not want you to be **unaware**
　　2:11　we are not **ignorant** of his
　　6: 9　as **unknown,** and yet are well
Ga　1:22　I was still **unknown** by sight
1Th　4:13　want you to be **uninformed,**
1Ti　1:13　I had acted **ignorantly** in
He　5: 2　deal gently with the **ignorant**
2P　2:12　what they do **not understand,**

51　GO1　AG11　LN3　B2:406　K1:115　R50
αγνοημα, IGNORANCES
He　9: 7　sins committed **unintentionally**

52　GO4　AG11　LN3　B2:406　K1:116　R50
αγνοια, UNKNOWINGNESS
Ac　3:17　you acted in **ignorance,** as did
　　17:30　times of human **ignorance,**
Ep　4:18　because of their **ignorance**
1P　1:14　you formerly had in **ignorance.**

53　GO8　AG11　LN3　B3:100　K1:122
'αγνος, PURE
2C　7:11　proved yourselves **guiltless**
　　11: 2　present you as a **chaste** virgin
Ph　4: 8　whatever is **pure,** whatever
1Ti　5:22　keep yourself **pure.**
Ti　2: 5　to be self-controlled, **chaste,**
Ja　3:17　wisdom from above is first **pure**
1P　3: 2　they see the **purity**
1J　3: 3　just as he is **pure.**

54　GO2　AG12　LN3　B3:100　K1:124　R53
'αγνοτης, PURENESS
2C　6: 6　by **purity,** knowledge, patience,
　　11: 3　astray from a sincere and **pure**

55　GO1　AG12　LN3　B3:101　R53
'αγνως, PURELY
Ph　1:17　selfish ambition, not **sincerely**

56 ᴳᴼ2 ᴬᴳ12 ᴸᴺ3 ᴮ2:406 ᴷ1:116 ᴿ1108
αγνωσια, NO KNOWLEDGE
1C 15:34　people have **no knowledge** of God.
1P　2:15　should silence the **ignorance**

---

57 ᴳᴼ1 ᴬᴳ12 ᴸᴺ3 ᴮ2:406 ᴷ1:119 ᴿ1110
αγνωστος, UNKNOWN
Ac 17:23　To an **unknown** god.

---

58 ᴳᴼ11 ᴬᴳ12 ᴸᴺ3 ᴮ1:267
αγορα, MARKET
Mt 11:16　sitting in the **marketplaces**
　　20: 3　idle in the **marketplace;**
　　23: 7　respect in the **marketplaces,**
Mk　6:56　sick in the **marketplaces,**
　　 7: 4　eat anything from the **market**
　　12:38　respect in the **marketplaces,**
Lk　7:32　sitting in the **marketplace**
　　11:43　respect in the **marketplaces.**
　　20:46　respect in the **marketplaces,**
Ac 16:19　**marketplace** before the
　　17:17　also in the **marketplace** every

---

59 ᴳᴼ30 ᴬᴳ12 ᴸᴺ3 ᴮ1:267 ᴷ1:124 ᴿ58
αγοραζω, I BUY
Mt 13:44　he has and **buys** that field.
　　13:46　all that he had and **bought** it.
　　14:15　and **buy** food for themselves.
　　21:12　who were selling and **buying**
　　25: 9　go to the dealers and **buy** some
　　25:10　And while they went to **buy** it,
　　27: 7　to **buy** the potter's field
Mk　6:36　**buy** something for themselves
　　 6:37　Are we to go and **buy**
　　11:15　who were **buying** in the temple,
　　15:46　Joseph **bought** a linen cloth
　　16: 1　Salome **bought** spices,
Lk　9:13　we are to go and **buy** food
　　14:18　I have **bought** a piece of land,
　　14:19　I have **bought** five yoke
　　17:28　drinking, **buying** and selling,
　　22:36　must sell his cloak and **buy** one
Jn　4: 8　had gone to the city to **buy**
　　 6: 5　Where are we to **buy** bread for
　　13:29　**Buy** what we need for the
1C　6:20　you were **bought** with a price
　　 7:23　You were **bought** with a price;
　　 7:30　and those who **buy** as though
2P　2: 1　deny the Master who **bought**
　　　　　them

Re　3:18　I counsel you to **buy** from me
　　 5: 9　by your blood you **ransomed**
　　13:17　no one can **buy** or sell
　　14: 3　who have been **redeemed** from
　　14: 4　They have been **redeemed** from
　　18:11　no one **buys** their cargo anymore

---

60 ᴳᴼ2 ᴬᴳ13 ᴸᴺ3 ᴿ58 ᴮ1:267
αγοραιος, MARKETERS
Ac 17: 5　ruffians in the **marketplaces**
　　19:38　the **courts** are open,

---

61 ᴳᴼ2 ᴬᴳ13 ᴸᴺ3
αγρα, CATCH
Lk　5: 4　let down your nets for a **catch.**
　　 5: 9　amazed at the **catch** of fish

---

62 ᴳᴼ1 ᴬᴳ13 ᴸᴺ3 ᴮ2:456 ᴿ1121
αγραμματος, UNLETTERED
Ac　4:13　they were **uneducated** and

---

63 ᴳᴼ1 ᴬᴳ13 ᴸᴺ3 ᴿ68
αγραυλεω, I MAKE FIELD HOME
Lk　2: 8　shepherds **living** in the fields,

---

64 ᴳᴼ1 ᴬᴳ13 ᴸᴺ3 ᴿ61
αγρευω, I TRAP
Mk 12:13　Herodians to **trap** him in what

---

65 ᴳᴼ2 ᴬᴳ13 ᴸᴺ3 ᴮ2:710 ᴿ66,1636
αγριελαιος, WILD OLIVE
Ro 11:17　you, a **wild olive** shoot,
　　11:24　**wild olive** tree and grafted,

---

66 ᴳᴼ3 ᴬᴳ13 ᴸᴺ3 ᴮ1:520 ᴿ68
αγριος, WILD
Mt　3: 4　food was locusts and **wild** honey
Mk　1: 6　he ate locusts and **wild** honey.
Ju　1:13　**wild** waves of the sea,

---

67 ᴳᴼ11 ᴬᴳ13 ᴸᴺ3
αγριππας, AGRIPPA
Ac 25:13　King **Agrippa** and Bernice
　　25:22　**Agrippa** said to Festus,
　　25:23　So on the next day **Agrippa**
　　25:24　And Festus said, "King **Agrippa,**
　　25:26　before you, King **Agrippa,**
　　26: 1　**Agrippa** said to Paul,
　　26: 2　it is before you, King **Agrippa,**
　　26:19　**Agrippa,** I was not disobedient

	26:27	King **Agrippa,** do you believe
	26:28	**Agrippa** said to Paul, "Are you
	26:32	**Agrippa** said to Festus,

68   GO37   AG13   LN3   K1:520
αγρος, FIELD

Mt	6:28	the lilies of the **field,**
	6:30	grass of the **field,** which is
	13:24	good seed in his **field;**
	13:27	sow good seed in your **field?**
	13:31	sowed in his **field;**
	13:36	of the weeds of the **field.**
	13:38	the **field** is the world,
	13:44	treasure hidden in a **field,**
	13:44	he has and buys that **field.**
	19:29	**fields,** for my name's sake,
	22: 5	one to his **farm,** another
	24:18	the one in the **field** must
	24:40	two will be in the **field;**
	27: 7	to buy the potter's **field**
	27: 8	For this reason that **field**
	27: 8	called the **Field** of Blood
	27:10	them for the potter's **field,**
Mk	5:14	in the city and in the **country.**
	6:36	go into the surrounding **country**
	6:56	**farms,** they laid the sick
	10:29	**fields,** for my sake and for
	10:30	and **fields** with persecutions
	11: 8	they had cut in the **fields.**
	13:16	in the **field** must not turn back
	15:21	was coming in from the **country,**
	16:12	were walking into the **country.**
Lk	8:34	in the city and in the **country.**
	9:12	**countryside,** to lodge and get
	12:28	clothes the grass of the **field,**
	14:18	I have bought a **piece of land,**
	15:15	who sent him to his **fields**
	15:25	elder son was in the **field;**
	17: 7	tending sheep in the **field,**
	17:31	in the **field** must not turn back
	23:26	**country,** and they laid the
Ac	4:37	sold a **field** that belonged

69   GO4   AG14   LN3   B2:137   K2:338   R5258
αγρυπνεω, I STAY AWAKE

Mk	13:33	Beware, **keep alert;** for you
Lk	21:36	**Be alert** at all times,
Ep	6:18	**keep alert** and always persevere
He	13:17	for they are **keeping watch**

70   GO2   AG14   LN3   K2:137   R69
αγρυπνια, STAYING AWAKE

2C	6: 5	riots, labors, **sleepless nights**
	11:27	through many a **sleepless night,**

71   GO67   AG14   LN3   K1:645
αγω, I LEAD, I BRING

Mt	10:18	you will be **dragged** before
	21: 2	untie them and **bring** them to me
	21: 7	they **brought** the donkey
	26:46	Get up, **let us be going.**
Mk	1:38	He answered, **"Let us go** on to
	13:11	When **they bring** you to trial
	14:42	Get up, **let us be going.**
Lk	4: 1	**was led** by the Spirit in the
	4: 9	devil **took** him to Jerusalem,
	4:29	**led** him to the brow of the hill
	4:40	diseases **brought** them to him;
	10:34	**brought** him to an inn,
	18:40	ordered the man to be **brought**
	19:27	**bring** them here and slaughter
	19:30	Untie it and **bring** it here.
	19:35	Then they **brought** it to Jesus;
	22:54	seized him and **led** him away,
	23: 1	**brought** Jesus before Pilate.
	23:32	who were criminals, **were led**
	24:21	it is now the third day
Jn	1:42	He **brought** Simon to Jesus,
	7:45	Why did you not **arrest** him?
	8: 3	Pharisees **brought** a woman
	9:13	They **brought** to the Pharisees
	10:16	I must **bring** them also,
	11: 7	**Let us go** to Judea again.
	11:15	But **let us go** to him.
	11:16	**Let us also go,** that we may
	14:31	Rise, **let us be on** our way.
	18:13	First they **took** him to Annas,
	18:28	they **took** Jesus from Caiaphas
	19: 4	Look, I am **bringing** him out
	19:13	he **brought** Jesus outside
Ac	5:21	the prison to have them **brought**
	5:26	temple police and **brought** them
	5:27	When they had **brought** them,
	6:12	**brought** him before the council.
	8:32	Like a sheep he **was led** to the
	9: 2	he might **bring** them bound to
	9:21	of **bringing** them bound before
	9:27	**brought** him to the apostles,
	11:26	he **brought** him to Antioch.

13:23	man's posterity God has **brought**
17:15	who conducted Paul **brought** him
17:19	they took him and **brought** him
18:12	**brought** him before the tribunal
19:37	You have **brought** these men here
19:38	let them **bring** charges there
20:12	they had **taken** the boy away
21:16	**brought** us to the house of
21:34	he ordered him to be **brought**
22: 5	to **bring** them back to Jerusalem
23:10	**bring** him into the barracks.
23:18	took him, **brought** him to the
23:18	me to **bring** this young man
23:31	**brought** him during the night
25: 6	ordered Paul to be **brought.**
25:17	ordered the man to be **brought.**
25:23	Paul was **brought** in.
Ro 2: 4	is meant to **lead** you to
8:14	who are **led** by the Spirit
1C 12: 2	**led** astray to idols that
Ga 5:18	if you are **led** by the Spirit,
1Th 4:14	God will **bring** with him
2Ti 3: 6	**swayed** by all kinds of desires,
4:11	Get Mark and **bring** him with you
He 2:10	in **bringing** many children to

---

72 GO1 AG14 LN3 B3:935 K1:128
αγωγη, CONDUCT
2Ti 3:10   my teaching, my **conduct,** my aim

---

73 GO6 AG15 LN3 B1:644 K1:135
αγων, CONTEST
Ph 1:30   are having the same **struggle**
Co 2: 1   how much I am **struggling** for
1Th 2: 2   in spite of **great opposition.**
1Ti 6:12   Fight the good **fight** of the
2Ti 4: 7   I have fought the good **fight,**
He 12: 1   **race** that is set before us,

---

74 GO1 AG15 LN3 B1:645 K1:140 R73
αγωνια, AGONY
Lk 22:44   In his **anguish** he prayed more

---

75 GO8 AG15 LN3 B1:644 K1:135 R73
αγωνιζομαι, I CONTEST
Lk 13:24   **Strive** to enter through
Jn 18:36   my followers would be **fighting**
1C 9:25   Athletes **exercise** self-control
Co 1:29   For this I toil and **struggle**
4:12   He is always **wrestling** in his

1Ti 4:10	this end we toil and **struggle,**
6:12	**Fight** the good fight of the
2Ti 4: 7	I have **fought** the good fight,

---

76 GO9 AG15 LN3 B1:84 K1:141
αδαμ, ADAM
Lk 3:38   son of **Adam,** son of God.
Ro 5:14   dominion from **Adam** to Moses,
5:14   the transgression of **Adam,**
1C 15:22   for as all die in **Adam,**
15:45   The first man, **Adam,**
15:45   last **Adam** became a life-giving
1Ti 2:13   For **Adam** was formed first,
2:14   and **Adam** was not deceived,
Ju 1:14   seventh generation from **Adam,**

---

77 GO1 AG15 LN3 R1160
αδαπανος, WITHOUT EXPENSE
1C 9:18   make the gospel **free of charge**

---

78 GO1 AG15 LN4
αδδι, ADDI
Lk 3:28   son of Melchi, son of **Addi,**

---

79 GO26 AG15 LN4 B1:254 K1:144 R80
αδελφη, SISTER
Mt 12:50   brother and **sister** and mother.
13:56   are not all his **sisters** with us
19:29   houses or brothers or **sisters**
Mk 3:32   **sisters** are outside, asking for
3:35   of God is my brother and **sister**
6: 3   his **sisters** here with us?
10:29   house or brothers or **sisters**
10:30   **sisters,** mothers and children,
Lk 10:39   She had a **sister** named Mary,
10:40   do you not care that my **sister**
14:26   **sisters,** yes, and even life
Jn 11: 1   Mary and her **sister** Martha.
11: 3   So the **sisters** sent a message
11: 5   loved Martha and her **sister**
11:28   called her **sister** Mary,
11:39   Martha, the **sister** of the dead
19:25   his mother's **sister,** Mary the
Ac 23:16   son of Paul's **sister** heard
Ro 16: 1   I commend to you our **sister**
16:15   Julia, Nereus and his **sister,**
1C 7:15   brother or **sister** is not bound.
9: 5   accompanied by a **believing wife**
1Ti 5: 2   to younger women as **sisters**
Pm 1: 2   to Apphia our **sister,**

| Ja | 2:15 | If a brother or **sister** is naked |
| 2J | 1:13 | children of your elect **sister** |

80　GO343　AG15　LN4　B1:254　K1:144　R79
αδελφος, BROTHER

Mt	1: 2	Judah and his **brothers,**
	1:11	Jechoniah and his **brothers,**
	4:18	he saw two **brothers,** Simon,
	4:18	and Andrew his **brother,**
	4:21	he saw two other **brothers,**
	4:21	of Zebedee and his **brother** John
	5:22	are angry with a **brother**
	5:22	and if you insult a **brother**
	5:23	you remember that your **brother**
	5:24	be reconciled to your **brother**
	5:47	you greet only your **brothers**
	7: 3	the speck in your **neighbor's**
	7: 4	can you say to your **neighbor,**
	7: 5	speck out of your **neighbor's**
	10: 2	Peter, and his **brother** Andrew;
	10: 2	Zebedee, and his **brother** John;
	10:21	**Brother** will betray brother
	10:21	will betray **brother** to death,
	12:46	his **brothers** were standing
	12:47	**brothers** are standing outside,
	12:48	and who are my **brothers?**
	12:49	are my mother and my **brothers!**
	12:50	in heaven is my **brother** and
	13:55	are not his **brothers** James
	14: 3	his **brother** Philip's wife,
	17: 1	James and his **brother** John
	18:15	another **member of the church**
	18:15	If the **member** listens to you,
	18:21	**member of the church** sins
	18:35	forgive your **brother**
	19:29	has left houses or **brothers**
	20:24	angry with the two **brothers.**
	22:24	his **brother** shall marry the
	22:24	children for his **brother.**
	22:25	Now there were seven **brothers**
	22:25	the widow to his **brother**
	23: 8	and you are all **students.**
	25:40	are **members of my family,**
	28:10	go and tell my **brothers** to go
Mk	1:16	Simon and his **brother** Andrew
	1:19	Zebedee and his **brother** John,
	3:17	John the **brother** of James
	3:31	his mother and his **brothers**
	3:32	Your mother and your **brothers**

	3:33	are my mother and my **brothers?**
	3:34	are my mother and my **brothers!**
	3:35	the will of God is my **brother**
	5:37	John, the **brother** of James.
	6: 3	son of Mary and **brother** of
	6:17	Herodias, his **brother** Philip's
	6:18	you to have your **brother's** wife
	10:29	who has left house or **brothers**
	10:30	in this age—houses, **brothers**
	12:19	if a man's **brother** dies,
	12:19	leaving a wife but no **child,**
	12:19	up children for his **brother.**
	12:20	There were seven **brothers;**
	13:12	**Brother** will betray brother
	13:12	betray **brother** to death,
Lk	3: 1	his **brother** Philip ruler
	3:19	his **brother's** wife, and
	6:14	and his **brother** Andrew,
	6:41	speck in your **neighbor's**
	6:42	you say to your **neighbor,**
	6:42	'Friend, let me take out the
	6:42	out of your **neighbor's** eye.
	8:19	his mother and his **brothers**
	8:20	Your mother and your **brothers**
	8:21	My mother and my **brothers**
	12:13	tell my **brother** to divide
	14:12	your friends or your **brothers**
	14:26	wife and children, **brothers**
	15:27	Your **brother** has come,
	15:32	because this **brother** of
	16:28	for I have five **brothers**
	17: 3	If another **disciple** sins,
	18:29	or wife or **brothers** or
	20:28	if a man's **brother** dies,
	20:28	leaving a wife but no **children**
	20:28	up children for his **brother.**
	20:29	Now there were seven **brothers;**
	21:16	even by parents and **brothers,**
	22:32	strengthen your **brothers.**
Jn	1:40	Andrew, Simon Peter's **brother.**
	1:41	first found his **brother** Simon
	2:12	with his mother, his **brothers,**
	6: 8	Andrew, Simon Peter's **brother,**
	7: 3	So his **brothers** said to him,
	7: 5	not even his **brothers** believed
	7:10	But after his **brothers** had gone
	11: 2	her **brother** Lazarus was ill.
	11:19	them about their **brother.**
	11:21	my **brother** would not have died

	11:23	Your **brother** will rise again.	21:17	**brothers** welcomed us warmly.
	11:32	my **brother** would not have died.	21:20	You see, **brother,** how many
	20:17	But go to my **brothers** and say	22: 1	**Brothers** and fathers,
	21:23	rumor spread in the **community**	22: 5	letters to the **brothers** in
Ac	1:14	as well as his **brothers.**	22:13	**Brother** Saul, regain your
	1:15	stood up among the **believers**	23: 1	**Brothers,** up to this day
	1:16	**Friends,** the scripture had	23: 5	I did not realize, **brothers,**
	2:29	**Fellow Israelites,**	23: 6	**Brothers,** I am a Pharisee,
	2:37	**Brothers,** what should we do?	28:14	There we found **believers**
	3:17	And now, **friends,** I know that	28:15	The **believers** from there,
	3:22	for you from your own **people**	28:17	he said to them, "**Brothers,**
	6: 3	**friends,** select from among	28:21	none of the **brothers** coming
	7: 2	Stephen replied: "**Brothers**	Ro 1:13	I want you to know, **brothers**
	7:13	himself known to his **brothers,**	7: 1	Do you not know, **brothers**
	7:23	heart to visit his **relatives,**	7: 4	In the same way, my **friends,**
	7:25	He supposed that his **kinsfolk**	8:12	So then, **brothers** and
	7:26	Men, you are **brothers;** why do	8:29	firstborn within a **large family**
	7:37	your own **people** as he raised me	9: 3	for the sake of my own **people,**
	9:17	**Brother** Saul, the Lord Jesus,	10: 1	**Brothers** and sisters, my heart
	9:30	When the **believers** learned of	11:25	be wiser than you are, **brothers**
	10:23	the **believers** from Joppa	12: 1	to you therefore, **brothers**
	11: 1	**believers** who were in Judea	14:10	pass judgment on your **brother**
	11:12	six **brothers** also accompanied	14:10	why do you despise your **brother**
	11:29	send relief to the **believers**	14:13	hindrance in the way of **another**
	12: 2	**brother** of John, killed with	14:15	If your **brother** or sister
	12:17	James and to the **believers.**	14:21	**brother** or sister stumble.
	13:15	saying, "**Brothers,** if you have	15:14	about you, my **brothers** and
	13:26	My **brothers,** you descendants	15:30	I appeal to you, **brothers**
	13:38	my **brothers,** that through this	16:14	Hermas, and the **brothers**
	14: 2	minds against the **brothers.**	16:17	I urge you, **brothers** and
	15: 1	were teaching the **brothers,**	16:23	and our **brother** Quartus,
	15: 3	great joy to all the **believers.**	1C 1: 1	and our **brother** Sosthenes,
	15: 7	My **brothers,** you know that in	1:10	I appeal to you, **brothers**
	15:13	My **brothers,** listen to me.	1:11	quarrels among you, my **brothers**
	15:22	leaders among the **brothers,**	1:26	your own call, **brothers**
	15:23	The **brothers,** both the apostles	2: 1	I came to you, **brothers**
	15:23	to the **believers** of Gentile	3: 1	And so, **brothers** and sisters,
	15:32	and strengthen the **believers.**	4: 6	for your benefit, **brothers**
	15:33	in peace by the **believers**	5:11	who bears the name of **brother**
	15:36	visit the **believers** in every	6: 5	to decide between one **believer**
	15:40	**believers** commending him	6: 6	but a **believer** goes to court
	16: 2	by the **believers** in Lystra	6: 6	to court against a **believer**
	16:40	encouraged the **brothers**	6: 8	defraud—and **believers** at
	17: 6	Jason and some **believers**	7:12	if any **believer** has a wife
	17:10	**believers** sent Paul and Silas	7:14	made holy through her **husband.**
	17:14	**believers** immediately sent Paul	7:15	**brother** or sister is not bound.
	18:18	farewell to the **believers**	7:24	you were called, **brothers** and
	18:27	**believers** encouraged him and	7:29	I mean, **brothers** and sisters,
	21: 7	we greeted the **believers**	8:11	weak **believers** for whom Christ

	8:12	against **members of your family,**		3: 1	Finally, my **brothers** and
	8:13	if food is a cause of **their**		3:13	**Beloved,** I do not consider
	8:13	I may not cause **one of them**		3:17	**Brothers** and sisters, join in
	9: 5	**brothers** of the Lord and Cephas		4: 1	Therefore, my **brothers** and
	10: 1	you to be unaware, **brothers**		4: 8	Finally, **beloved,** whatever is
	11:33	So then, my **brothers** and		4:21	The **friends** who are with me
	12: 1	spiritual gifts, **brothers**	Co	1: 1	God, and Timothy our **brother,**
	14: 6	Now, **brothers** and sisters,		1: 2	saints and faithful **brothers**
	14:20	**Brothers** and sisters, do not		4: 7	he is a beloved **brother,**
	14:26	my **friends?** When you come		4: 9	faithful and beloved **brother,**
	14:39	**friends,** be eager to prophesy,		4:15	my greetings to the **brothers**
	15: 1	I would remind you, **brothers**	1Th	1: 4	For we know, **brothers** and
	15: 6	than five hundred **brothers**		2: 1	yourselves know, **brothers**
	15:31	That is as certain, **brothers**		2: 9	our labor and toil, **brothers**
	15:50	What I am saying, **brothers**		2:14	For you, **brothers** and sisters,
	15:58	Therefore, my **beloved,** be		2:17	As for us, **brothers** and sisters
	16:11	expecting him with the **brothers**		3: 2	we sent Timothy, our **brother**
	16:12	concerning our **brother** Apollos,		3: 7	For this reason, **brothers**
	16:12	you with the other **brothers,**		4: 1	Finally, **brothers** and sisters,
	16:15	Now, **brothers** and sisters,		4: 6	wrong or exploit a **brother**
	16:20	All the **brothers** and sisters		4:10	you do love all the **brothers**
2C	1: 1	Timothy our **brother,** To the		4:10	we urge you, **beloved,** to do
	1: 8	you to be unaware, **brothers**		4:13	you to be uninformed, **brothers**
	2:13	I did not find my **brother** Titus		5: 1	times and the seasons, **brothers**
	8: 1	We want you to know, **brothers**		5: 4	**beloved,** are not in darkness,
	8:18	we are sending the **brother** who		5:12	But we appeal to you, **brothers**
	8:22	we are sending our **brother**		5:14	And we urge you, **beloved,** to
	8:23	as for our **brothers,** they are		5:25	**Beloved,** pray for us.
	9: 3	I am sending the **brothers**		5:26	Greet all the **brothers** and
	9: 5	to urge the **brothers** to go on		5:27	letter be read to all of **them.**
	11: 9	**friends** who came from Macedonia	2Th	1: 3	thanks to God for you, **brothers**
	12:18	sent the **brother** with him.		2: 1	we beg you, **brothers** and
	13:11	Finally, **brothers** and sisters,		2:13	to God for you, **brothers**
Ga	1: 2	all the **members of God's family**		2:15	So then, **brothers** and sisters
	1:11	you to know, **brothers** and		3: 1	Finally, **brothers** and sisters,
	1:19	except James the Lord's **brother**		3: 6	Now we command you, **beloved,**
	3:15	**Brothers** and sisters,		3: 6	to keep away from **believers**
	4:12	**Friends,** I beg you, become as I		3:13	**Brothers** and sisters, do not
	4:28	you, my **friends,** are children		3:15	but warn them as **believers.**
	4:31	**friends,** we are children, not	1Ti	4: 6	before the **brothers** and
	5:11	But my **friends,** why am I still		5: 1	to younger men as **brothers,**
	5:13	called to freedom, **brothers**		6: 2	are **members of the church;**
	6: 1	My **friends,** if anyone is	2Ti	4:21	Claudia and all the **brothers**
	6:18	be with your spirit, **brothers**	Pm	1: 1	Timothy our **brother,**
Ep	6:21	He is a dear **brother** and a		1: 7	through you, my **brother.**
	6:23	be to the **whole community,**		1:16	a beloved **brother**—
Ph	1:12	I want you to know, **beloved,**		1:20	Yes, **brother,** let me have this
	1:14	and most of the **brothers**	He	2:11	ashamed to call them **brothers**
	2:25	Epaphroditus—my **brother**		2:12	your name to my **brothers**

	2:17	to become like his **brothers**
	3: 1	Therefore, **brothers** and sisters
	3:12	Take care, **brothers** and sisters
	7: 5	from their **kindred,** though
	8:11	another or say to each **other,**
	10:19	Therefore, my **friends,** since
	13:22	I appeal to you, **brothers**
	13:23	know that our **brother** Timothy
Ja	1: 2	My **brothers** and sisters,
	1: 9	Let the **believer** who is lowly
	1:16	Do not be deceived, my **beloved.**
	1:19	understand this, my **beloved:**
	2: 1	My **brothers** and sisters,
	2: 5	Listen, my beloved **brothers**
	2:14	What good is it, my **brothers**
	2:15	If a **brother** or sister is naked
	3: 1	become teachers, my **brothers**
	3:10	cursing. My **brothers** and
	3:12	Can a fig tree, my **brothers**
	4:11	against one another, **brothers**
	4:11	speaks evil against **another**
	4:11	or judges **another,** speaks evil
	5: 7	Be patient, therefore, **beloved,**
	5: 9	**Beloved,** do not grumble against
	5:10	suffering and patience, **beloved**
	5:12	Above all, my **beloved,** do not
	5:19	My **brothers** and sisters, if
1P	5:12	consider a faithful **brother,**
2P	1:10	Therefore, **brothers** and sisters
	3:15	beloved **brother** Paul wrote
1J	2: 9	while hating a **brother** or
	2:10	Whoever loves a **brother** or
	2:11	whoever hates another **believer**
	3:10	who do not love their **brothers**
	3:12	and murdered his **brother.**
	3:12	his **brother's** righteous.
	3:13	Do not be astonished, **brothers**
	3:14	because we love **one another.**
	3:15	All who hate a **brother** or
	3:16	down our lives for **one another.**
	3:17	sees a **brother** or sister in
	4:20	hate their **brothers** or sisters,
	4:20	who do not love a **brother** or
	4:21	must love their **brothers**
	5:16	If you see your **brother** or
3J	1: 3	some of the **friends** arrived
	1: 5	you do for the **friends,**
	1:10	refuses to welcome the **friends,**
Ju	1: 1	**brother** of James, To those

Re	1: 9	I, John, your **brother** who
	6:11	of their **brothers** and sisters,
	12:10	for the accuser of our **comrades**
	19:10	your **comrades** who hold the
	22: 9	your **comrades** the prophets,

---

81   GO2   AG16   LN4   B1:254   K1:144   R80
αδελφοτης, BROTHERHOOD
1P   2:17   Love the **family of believers.**
   5: 9   that your **brothers and sisters**

---

82   GO2   AG16   LN4   R1212
αδηλος, UNCLEAR
Lk   11:44   you are like **unmarked** graves,
1C   14: 8   bugle gives an **indistinct** sound

---

83   GO1   AG16   LN4   R82
αδηλοτης, UNCLEARNESS
1Ti   6:17   on the **uncertainty** of riches,

---

84   GO1   AG16   LN4   B1:648   R82
αδηλως, UNCLEARLY
1C   9:26   So I do not run **aimlessly,**

---

85   GO3   AG16   LN4
αδημονεω, I AM DISTRESSED
Mt   26:37   to be grieved and **agitated.**
Mk   14:33   to be distressed and **agitated.**
Ph   2:26   has been **distressed** because

---

86   GO10   AG16   LN4   B2:205   K1:146
ᾁδης, HADES
Mt   11:23   be brought down to **Hades.**
     16:18   gates of **Hades** will not prevail
Lk   10:15   will be brought down to **Hades.**
     16:23   In **Hades,** where he was being
Ac   2:27   not abandon my soul to **Hades,**
     2:31   He was not abandoned to
          Hades,
Re   1:18   keys of Death and of **Hades.**
     6: 8   **Hades** followed with him;
     20:13   Death and **Hades** gave up the
     20:14   Death and **Hades** were thrown

---

87   GO1   AG17   LN4   B1:503   K3:950   R1252
αδιακριτος, UNDIFFERENTIATING
Ja   3:17   **without a trace of partiality**

---

88   GO2   AG17   LN4   B3:229   R3007
αδιαλειπτος, UNCEASING

Ro	9: 2	great sorrow and **unceasing**
2Ti	1: 3	when I remember you **constantly**

89　GO4　AG17　LN4　B3:229　R88
αδιαλειπτως, UNCEASINGLY

Ro	1: 9	**without ceasing** I remember you
1Th	1: 2	you in our prayers, **constantly**
	2:13	We also **constantly** give thanks
	5:17	pray **without ceasing**,

91　GO28　AG17　LN4　B3:573　K1:157　R94
αδικεω, I DO UNRIGHT

Mt	20:13	I am doing you no **wrong**;
Lk	10:19	and nothing will **hurt** you.
Ac	7:24	saw one of them being **wronged**,
	7:26	why do you **wrong** each other?
	7:27	was **wronging** his neighbor
	25:10	have done no **wrong** to the Jews,
	25:11	Now if I am in the **wrong**
1C	6: 7	Why not rather be **wronged**?
	6: 8	But you yourselves **wrong**
2C	7:2	we have **wronged** no one,
	7:12	one who **did** the **wrong**,
	7:12	one who was **wronged**,
Ga	4:12	You have done me no **wrong**.
Co	3:25	**wrongdoer** will be paid back
	3:25	whatever **wrong** has been done,
Pm	1:18	If he has **wronged** you in any
2P	2:13	penalty for doing **wrong**.
Re	2:11	conquers will not be **harmed**
	6: 6	but do not **damage** the olive
	7: 2	given power to **damage** earth
	7: 3	Do not **damage** the earth
	9: 4	They were told not to **damage**
	9:10	power to **harm** people for five
	9:19	with them they inflict **harm**.
	11: 5	anyone wants to **harm** them,
	11: 5	to **harm** them must be killed
	22:11	Let the **evildoer** still do evil
	22:11	Let the evildoer still do **evil**

92　GO3　AG17　LN4　B3:573　K1:161　R91
αδικημα, UNRIGHT

Ac	18:14	**crime** or serious villainy,
	24:20	**crime** they had found when I
Re	18: 5	has remembered her **iniquities**.

93　GO25　AG17　LN4　B3:352　K1:153　R94
αδικια, UNRIGHT

Lk	13:27	away from me, all you **evildoers**

	16: 8	commended the **dishonest** manager
	16: 9	by means of **dishonest** wealth
	18: 6	Listen to what the **unjust** judge
Jn	7:18	there is nothing **false** in him.
Ac	1:18	reward of his **wickedness**; and
	8:23	the chains of **wickedness**.
Ro	1:18	ungodliness and **wickedness**
	1:18	by their **wickedness** suppress
	1:29	with every kind of **wickedness**,
	2: 8	the truth but **wickedness**,
	3: 5	But if our **injustice** serves
	6:13	as instruments of **wickedness**,
	9:14	**injustice** on God's part?
1C	13: 6	does not rejoice in **wrongdoing**,
2C	12:13	Forgive me this **wrong**!
2Th	2:10	every kind of wicked **deception**
	2:12	pleasure in **unrighteousness**
2Ti	2:19	Lord turn away from **wickedness**.
He	8:12	toward their **iniquities**,
Ja	3: 6	world of **iniquity**; it stains
2P	2:13	for doing **wrong**. They count it
	2:15	loved the wages of doing **wrong**,
1J	1: 9	us from all **unrighteousness**.
	5:17	All **wrongdoing** is sin,

94　GO12　AG18　LN4　B3:573　K1:149　R1342
αδικος, UNRIGHT

Mt	5:45	and on the **unrighteous**.
Lk	16:10	is **dishonest** in a very little
	16:10	little is **dishonest** also in
	16:11	faithful with the **dishonest**
	18:11	other people: thieves, **rogues**,
Ac	24:15	righteous and the **unrighteous**.
Ro	3: 5	God is **unjust** to inflict wrath
1C	6: 1	court before the **unrighteous**,
	6: 9	**wrongdoers** will not inherit
He	6:10	For God is not **unjust**; he will
1P	3:18	righteous for the **unrighteous**,
2P	2: 9	to keep the **unrighteous** under

95　GO1　AG18　LN4　B3:573　R94
αδικως, UNRIGHTLY

1P	2:19	pain while suffering **unjustly**.

95a　GO1　AG18　LN4
αδμιν, ADMIN

Lk	3:33	son of Amminadab, son of **Admin**,

96　GO8　AG18　LN4　B3:808　K2:255　R1384
αδοκιμος, UNPROVED

Ro   1:28   God gave them up to a **debased**
1C   9:27   should not be **disqualified.**
2C 13: 5   you **fail** to meet the test!
     13: 6   we have not **failed.**
     13: 7   we may seem to have **failed.**
2Ti 3: 8   mind and **counterfeit** faith,
Ti   1:16   disobedient, **unfit** for any good
He   6: 8   it is **worthless** and on the

---

97 GO1 AG18 LN4 R1388
αδολος, UNGUILE
1P   2: 2   long for the **pure,** spiritual

---

98 GO1 AG18 LN4
αδραμυττηνος, ADRAMYTTIUM
Ac 27: 2   ship of **Adramyttium** that was

---

99 GO1 AG18 LN4
αδριας, ADRIA
Ac 27:27   the sea of **Adria,** about

---

100 GO1 AG18 LN4
ʿαδροτης, MUNIFICENCE
2C   8:20   about this **generous gift** that

---

101 GO2 AG19 LN4 K2:284 R102
αδυνατεω, I AM UNABLE
Mt 17:20   and nothing will be **impossible**
Lk   1:37   For nothing will be **impossible**

---

102 GO10 AG19 LN4 B2:601 K2:284 R1415
αδυνατος, UNABLE
Mt 19:26   "For mortals it is **impossible,**
Mk 10:27   "For mortals it is **impossible,**
Lk 18:27   is **impossible** for mortals
Ac 14: 8   man sitting who could **not use**
Ro   8: 3   by the flesh, could **not do**
     15: 1   to put up with the **failings** of
He   6: 4   For it is **impossible** to restore
     6:18   in which it is **impossible** that
     10: 4   it is **impossible** for the blood
     11: 6   without faith it is **impossible**

---

103 GO5 AG19 LN4 B3:672 K1:163
αδω, I SING
Ep   5:19   **singing** and making melody to
Co   3:16   gratitude in your hearts **sing**
Re   5: 9   They **sing** a new song: "You are
     14: 3   **sing** a new song before the
     15: 3   they **sing** the song of Moses

---

104 GO7 AG19 LN4
αει, ALWAYS
Ac   7:51   are **forever** opposing the Holy
2C   4:11   while we live, we are **always**
     6:10   yet **always** rejoicing; as poor,
Ti   1:12   "Cretans are **always** liars,
He   3:10   'They **always** go astray in their
1P   3:15   **Always** be ready to make your
2P   1:12   I intend to **keep on** reminding

---

105 GO5 AG19 LN4
αετος, EAGLE
Mt 24:28   there the **vultures** will gather.
Lk 17:37   there the **vultures** will gather.
Re   4: 7   creature like a flying **eagle.**
     8:13   I looked, and I heard an **eagle**
     12:14   two wings of the great **eagle,**

---

106 GO9 AG19 LN5 B2:461 K2:902 R2219
αζυμος, UNYEASTED
Mt 26:17   first day of **Unleavened**
                 Bread
Mk 14: 1   festival of **Unleavened** Bread.
     14:12   first day of **Unleavened** Bread,
Lk 22: 1   festival of **Unleavened** Bread,
     22: 7   the day of **Unleavened** Bread,
Ac 12: 3   festival of **Unleavened** Bread.
     20: 6   the days of **Unleavened** Bread,
1C   5: 7   as you really are **unleavened.**
     5: 8   but with the **unleavened**
                 bread

---

107 GO2 AG20 LN5
αζωρ, AZOR
Mt   1:13   and Eliakim the father of **Azor,**
     1:14   and **Azor** the father of Zadok,

---

108 GO1 AG20 LN5
αζωτος, AZOTUS
Ac   8:40   Philip found himself at **Azotus,**

---

109 GO7 AG20 LN5 B1:449 K1:165
αηρ, AIR
Ac 22:23   and tossing dust into the **air,**
1C   9:26   box as though beating the **air;**
     14: 9   be we speaking into the **air.**
Ep   2: 2   ruler of the power of the **air,**
1Th 4:17   to meet the Lord in the **air;**
Re   9: 2   and the sun and the **air** were
     16:17   poured his bowl into the **air,**

110 G03 AG20 LN5 B1:430 K3:22 R2288
αθανασια, DEATHLESSNESS
1C 15:53 body must put on **immortality.**
　　15:54 mortal body puts on **immortality**
1Ti 6:16 he alone who has **immortality**

---

111 G02 AG20 LN5 K1:166
αθεμιτος, UNLAWFUL
Ac 10:28 know that it is **unlawful** for
1P 4: 3 revels, carousing, and **lawless**

---

112 G01 AG20 LN5 K3:120 R2316
αθεος, GODLESS
Ep 2:12 having no hope and **without God.**

---

113 G02 AG21 LN5 K1:167
αθεσμος, IRREVERENT
2P 2: 7 licentiousness of the **lawless**
　　3:17 with the error of the **lawless**

---

114 G016 AG21 LN5 B1:74 K8:158
αθετεω, I SET ASIDE
Mk 6:26 he did not want to **refuse** her.
　　7: 9 of **rejecting** the commandment
Lk 7:30 and the lawyers **rejected** God's
　　10:16 whoever **rejects** you rejects me,
　　10:16 whoever rejects you **rejects** me,
　　10:16 and whoever **rejects** me
　　10:16 and whoever rejects me **rejects**
Jn 12:48 The one who **rejects** me
1C 1:19 the discerning I will **thwart.**"
Ga 2:21 I do not **nullify** the grace of
　　3:15 no one adds to it or **annuls** it.
1Th 4: 8 Therefore whoever **rejects** this
　　4: 8 whoever rejects this **rejects**
1Ti 5:12 for having **violated** their first
He 10:28 Anyone who has **violated** the law
Ju 1: 8 also defile the flesh, **reject**

---

115 G02 AG21 LN5 K8:158 R114
αθετησις, ANNULMENT
He 7:18 the **abrogation** of an earlier
　　9:26 at the end of the age to **remove**

---

116 G04 AG21 LN5
αθηναι, ATHENS
Ac 17:15 brought him as far as **Athens**
　　17:16 was waiting for them in **Athens**
　　18: 1 After this Paul left **Athens**
1Th 3: 1 to be left alone in **Athens**

117 G02 AG21 LN5
αθηναιος, ATHENIANS
Ac 17:21 Now all the **Athenians** and the
　　17:22 "**Athenians,** I see how extremely

---

118 G02 AG21 LN5 R1:167
αθλεω, I WRESTLE
2Ti 2: 5 **athlete,** no one is crowned
　　2: 5 And in the case of an **athlete,**

---

119 G01 AG21 LN5 K1:167 R118
αθλησις, WRESTLING
He 10:32 you endured a hard **struggle,**

119a G01 AG21 LN5
αθροιζω, I GATHER
Lk 24:33 companions **gathered together.**

---

120 G01 AG21 LN5
αθυμεω, I LOSE WRATH
Co 3:21 or they may **lose heart.**

---

121 G02 AG21 LN5
αθωος, INNOCENT
Mt 27: 4 by betraying **innocent** blood."
　　27:24 **innocent** of this man's blood;

---

122 G01 AG21 LN5
αιγειος, GOAT
He 11:37 in skins of sheep and **goats,**

---

123 G06 AG21 LN5
αιγιαλος, SHORE
Mt 13: 2 whole crowd stood on the **beach.**
　　13:48 they drew it **ashore,** sat down,
Jn 21: 4 Jesus stood on the **beach;** but
Ac 21: 5 we knelt down on the **beach**
　　27:39 they noticed a bay with a **beach**
　　27:40 they made for the **beach.**

---

124 G05 AG21 LN5 B1:530
αιγυπτιος, EGYPTIAN
Ac 7:22 the wisdom of the **Egyptians**
　　7:24 by striking down the **Egyptian.**
　　7:28 you killed the **Egyptian**
　　21:38 you are not the **Egyptian** who
He 11:29 when the **Egyptians** attempted to

---

125 G025 AG22 LN5 B1:530
αιγυπτος, EGYPT

Mt	2:13	flee to **Egypt,** and remain there
	2:14	by night, and went to **Egypt,**
	2:15	"Out of **Egypt** I have called my
	2:19	in a dream to Joseph in **Egypt**
Ac	2:10	Phrygia and Pamphylia, **Egypt**
	7: 9	sold him into **Egypt;** but God
	7:10	before Pharaoh, king of **Egypt,**
	7:10	before Pharaoh, king of **Egypt,**
	7:11	came a famine throughout **Egypt**
	7:12	that there was grain in **Egypt,**
	7:15	so Jacob went down to **Egypt.**
	7:17	our people in **Egypt** increased
	7:18	known Joseph ruled over **Egypt.**
	7:34	of my people who are in **Egypt**
	7:34	I will send you to **Egypt.**'
	7:36	wonders and signs in **Egypt,**
	7:39	they turned back to **Egypt,**
	7:40	out from the land of **Egypt,**
	13:17	their stay in the land of **Egypt**
He	3:16	not all those who left **Egypt**
	8: 9	them out of the land of **Egypt;**
	11:26	than the treasures of **Egypt,**
	11:27	By faith he left **Egypt,**
Ju	1: 5	people out of the land of **Egypt**
Re	11: 8	called Sodom and **Egypt,** where

---

126   ᴳᴼ2   ᴬᴳ22   ᴸᴺ5   ᴮ3:826   ᴷ1:168
αιδιος, ETERNAL

Ro	1:20	his **eternal** power and divine
Ju	1: 6	he has kept in **eternal** chains

---

127   ᴳᴼ1   ᴬᴳ22   ᴸᴺ5   ᴮ3:561   ᴷ1:169
αιδως, MODESTLY

1Ti	2: 9	should dress themselves **modestly**

---

128   ᴳᴼ2   ᴬᴳ22   ᴸᴺ5
αιθιοψ, ETHIOPIAN

Ac	8:27	there was an **Ethiopian** eunuch
	8:27	Candace queen of the **Ethiopians**

---

129   ᴳᴼ97   ᴬᴳ22   ᴸᴺ5   ᴮ1:220   ᴷ1:172
ʽαιμα, BLOOD

Mt	16:17	**blood** has not revealed
	23:30	shedding the **blood**
	23:35	righteous **blood** shed on earth,
	23:35	**blood** of righteous Abel
	23:35	to the **blood** of Zechariah son
	26:28	is my **blood** of the covenant,
	27: 4	betraying innocent **blood.**"
	27: 6	since they are **blood** money."

	27: 8	called the Field of **Blood**
	27:24	innocent of this man's **blood;**
	27:25	His **blood** be on us and on our
Mk	5:25	suffering from **hemorrhages**
	5:29	her **hemorrhage** stopped;
	14:24	my **blood** of the covenant
Lk	8:43	**hemorrhages** for twelve years;
	8:44	her **hemorrhage** stopped.
	11:50	charged with the **blood**
	11:51	from the **blood** of Abel to
	11:51	Abel to the **blood** of Zechariah,
	13: 1	Galileans whose **blood** Pilate
	22:20	new covenant in my **blood.**
	22:44	great drops of **blood** falling
Jn	1:13	born, not of **blood** or of the
	6:53	Son of Man and drink his **blood,**
	6:54	eat my flesh and drink my **blood**
	6:55	and my **blood** is true drink.
	6:56	my flesh and drink my **blood**
	19:34	once **blood** and water came out.
Ac	1:19	that is, Field of **Blood.**
	2:19	earth below, **blood,** and fire,
	2:20	and the moon to **blood,** before
	5:28	bring this man's **blood** on us."
	15:20	been strangled and from **blood.**
	15:29	to idols and from **blood**
	18: 6	Your **blood** be on your own heads
	20:26	not responsible for the **blood**
	20:28	he obtained with the **blood** of
	21:25	to idols and from **blood**
	22:20	And while the **blood** of your
Ro	3:15	feet are swift to shed **blood;**
	3:25	of atonement by his **blood,**
	5: 9	been justified by his **blood**
1C	10:16	sharing in the **blood** of Christ?
	11:25	the new covenant in my **blood.**
	11:27	the body and **blood** of the Lord.
	15:50	flesh and **blood** cannot inherit.
Ga	1:16	not confer with any **human** being,
Ep	1: 7	redemption through his **blood,**
	2:13	near by the **blood** of Christ.
	6:12	against enemies of **blood**
Co	1:20	making peace through the **blood.**
He	2:14	children share flesh and **blood,**
	9: 7	not without taking the **blood**
	9:12	not with the **blood** of goats
	9:12	Holy Place, not with the **blood**
	9:13	For if the **blood** of goats
	9:14	how much more will the **blood** of

9:18   was inaugurated without **blood.**
9:19   **blood** of calves and goats, with
9:20   the **blood** of the covenant that
9:21   he sprinkled with the **blood**
9:22   without the shedding of **blood**
9:25   with **blood** that is not his own;
10: 4   the **blood** of bulls and goats
10:19   the sanctuary by the **blood** of
10:29   Son of God, profaned the **blood**
11:28   and the sprinkling of **blood,**
12: 4   point of shedding your **blood.**
12:24   word than the **blood** of Abel.
13:11   animals whose **blood** is brought
13:12   the people by his own **blood.**
13:20   **blood** of the eternal covenant,
1P   1: 2   to be sprinkled with his **blood:**
1:19   the precious **blood** of Christ,
1J   1: 7   and the **blood** of Jesus his Son
5: 6   who came by water and **blood,**
5: 6   came by water and **blood,** Jesus
5: 6   with the water and the **blood.**
5: 8   and the water and the **blood,**
Re   1: 5   us from our sins by his **blood,**
5: 9   your **blood** you ransomed for God
6:10   you judge and avenge our **blood**
6:12   the full moon became like **blood,**
7:14   made them white in the **blood** of
8: 7   hail and fire, mixed with **blood,**
8: 8   A third of the sea became **blood**
11: 6   waters to turn them into **blood,**
12:11   conquered him by the **blood** of
14:20   and **blood** flowed from the wine
16: 3   like the **blood** of a corpse,
16: 4   and they became **blood.**
16: 6   because they shed the **blood** of
16: 6   have given them **blood** to drink.
17: 6   the **blood** of the saints and the
17: 6   the **blood** of the witnesses to
18:24   And in you was found the **blood**
19: 2   he has avenged on her the **blood**
19:13   a robe dipped in **blood,**

---

130   GO1   AG23   LN6   B2:853   K1:176   R129,1632
ʿαιματεκχυσια, BLOOD POURING
He   9:22   without the **shedding of blood**

---

131   GO1   AG23   LN6   R129,4482
ʿαιμορροεω, HEMORRHAGING
Mt   9:20   suffering from **hemorrhages** for

132   GO2   AG23   LN6
αινεας, AENEAS
Ac   9:33   he found a man named **Aeneas,**
9:34   Peter said to him, **"Aeneas,**

---

133   GO1   AG23   LN6   B3:816   R136
αινεσις, PRAISE
He   13:15   offer a sacrifice of **praise**

---

134   GO8   AG23   LN6   B2:855   K1:177   R136
αινεω, I PRAISE
Lk   2:13   of the heavenly host, **praising**
2:20   glorifying and **praising** God
19:37   disciples began to **praise** God
Ac   2:47   **praising** God and having the
3: 8   and leaping and **praising** God.
3: 9   walking and **praising** God,
Ro   15:11   and again, **"Praise** the Lord,
Re   19: 5   **"Praise** our God, all you his

---

135   GO1   AG23   LN6   B2:743   K1:178
αινιγμα, RIDDLE
1C   13:12   we see in a mirror, **dimly,** but

---

136   GO2   AG23   LN6   B3:816   K1:177
αινος, PRAISE
Mt   21:16   you have prepared **praise** for
Lk   18:43   when they saw it, **praised** God.

---

137   GO1   AG23   LN6
αινων, AENON
Jn   3:23   baptizing at **Aenon** near Salim

---

138   GO3   AG24   LN6
ʿαιρεω, I CHOOSE
Ph   1:22   I do not know which I **prefer.**
2Th   2:13   God **chose** you as the first
He   11:25   **choosing** rather to share

---

139   GO9   AG23   LN6   B1:533   R138
ʿαιρεσις, SECT
Ac   5:17   the **sect** of the Sadducees,
15: 5   **sect** of the Pharisees stood up
24: 5   the **sect** of the Nazarenes.
24:14   the Way, which they call a **sect**
26: 5   strictest **sect** of our religion
28:22   regard to this **sect** we know
1C   11:19   have to be **factions** among you,
Ga   5:20   quarrels, dissensions, **factions**
2P   2: 1   bring in destructive **opinions.**

140　GO1　AG24　LN6　B1:533　R138
'αιρετιζω, I CHOOSE
Mt　12:18　　whom I **have chosen,** my beloved

141　GO1　AG24　LN6　B1:533
'αιρετικος, SECTARIAN
Ti　3:10　　anyone who causes **divisions,**

142　GO101　AG24　LN6　B1:701　K1:185
αιρω, I LIFT UP
Mt　4: 6　　'On their hands they will **bear**
　　9: 6　　"Stand up, **take** your bed and
　　9:16　　the patch **pulls** away from the
　　11:29　　**Take** my yoke upon you, and
　　13:12　　what they have will be **taken**
　　14:12　　His disciples came and **took**
　　14:20　　they **took** up what was left over
　　15:37　　they **took** up the broken pieces
　　16:24　　deny themselves and **take** up
　　17:27　　**take** the first fish that comes
　　20:14　　**Take** what belongs to you
　　21:21　　'Be **lifted** up and thrown into
　　21:43　　will be **taken** away from you
　　24:17　　go down to **take** what is in the
　　24:18　　not turn back to **get** a coat.
　　24:39　　the flood came and **swept** them
　　25:28　　So **take** the talent from him,
　　25:29　　what they have will be **taken**
　　27:32　　compelled this man to **carry** his
Mk　2: 3　　man, **carried** by four of them.
　　2: 9　　'Stand up and **take** your mat and
　　2:11　　**take** your mat and go to your
　　2:12　　and immediately **took** the mat
　　2:21　　the patch **pulls** away from it,
　　4:15　　comes and **takes** away the word
　　4:25　　what they have will be **taken**
　　6: 8　　He ordered them to **take** nothing
　　6:29　　they came and **took** his body,
　　6:43　　they **took** up twelve baskets
　　8: 8　　they **took** up the broken pieces
　　8:19　　broken pieces did you **collect?"**
　　8:20　　broken pieces did you **collect?"**
　　8:34　　**take** up their cross and follow
　　11:23　　'Be **taken** up and thrown into
　　13:15　　the house to **take** anything
　　13:16　　not turn back to **get** a coat.
　　15:21　　the country, to **carry** his cross
　　15:24　　decide what each should **take.**
　　16:18　　they will **pick** up snakes in
Lk　4:11　　they will **bear** you up, so that

　　5:24　　I say to you, stand up and **take**
　　5:25　　**took** what he had been lying on,
　　6:29　　from anyone who **takes** away your
　　6:30　　if anyone **takes** away your goods,
　　8:12　　the devil comes and **takes** away
　　8:18　　to have will be **taken** away."
　　9: 3　　"**Take** nothing for your journey,
　　9:17　　was **gathered** up, twelve baskets
　　9:23　　**take** up their cross daily and
　　11:22　　he **takes** away his armor
　　11:52　　For you have **taken** away the key
　　17:13　　they **called** out, saying, "Jesus
　　17:31　　must not come down to **take** them
　　19:21　　**take** what you did not deposit,
　　19:22　　**taking** what I did not deposit
　　19:24　　'**Take** the pound from him and
　　19:26　　what they have will be **taken**
　　22:36　　one who has a purse must **take**
　　23:18　　shouted out together, "**Away**
Jn　1:29　　the Lamb of God who **takes** away
　　2:16　　"**Take** these things out of here!
　　5: 8　　"Stand up, **take** your mat and
　　5: 9　　he **took** up his mat and began to
　　5:10　　lawful for you to **carry** your
　　5:11　　**Take** up your mat and walk.
　　5:12　　**Take** it up and walk
　　8:59　　So they **picked** up stones to
　　10:18　　No one **takes** it from me
　　10:24　　"How long will you **keep** us in
　　11:39　　Jesus said, "**Take** away the
　　11:41　　So they **took** away the stone.
　　11:41　　Jesus **looked** upward and said,
　　11:48　　Romans will come and **destroy**
　　15: 2　　He **removes** every branch in me
　　16:22　　no one will **take** your joy from
　　17:15　　not asking you to **take** them
　　19:15　　"**Away** with him! **Away** with him!
　　19:31　　broken and the bodies **removed.**
　　19:38　　**take** away the body of Jesus.
　　19:38　　so he came and **removed** his body
　　20: 1　　the stone had been **removed** from
　　20: 2　　**taken** the Lord out of the tomb,
　　20:13　　"They have **taken** away my Lord,
　　20:15　　and I will **take** him away."
Ac　4:24　　When they heard it, they **raised**
　　8:33　　justice was **denied** him.
　　8:33　　For his life is **taken** away from
　　20: 9　　floors below and was **picked** up
　　21:11　　He came to us and **took** Paul's

	21:36	kept shouting, "**Away** with him!"
	22:22	"**Away** with such a fellow from
	27:13	they **weighed** anchor and began
	27:17	After **hoisting** it up they took
1C	5: 2	would have been **removed** from
	6:15	Should I therefore **take** the
Ep	4:31	**Put** away from you all
1J	3: 5	that he was revealed to **take**
Re	10: 5	on the sea and the land **raised**
	18:21	a mighty angel **took** up a stone

143   GO1   AG24   LN6   B2:390   K1:187
αισθανομαι, I NOTICE
Lk   9:45   so that they could not **perceive**

144   GO1   AG25   LN6   B2:390   K1:187   R143
αισθησις, NOTICE
Ph   1: 9   with knowledge and full **insight**

145   GO1   AG25   LN6   B2:391   K1:187   R143
αισθητηριον, SENSE
He   5:14   for those whose **faculties** have

146   GO2   AG25   LN6   B3:564   R152,2771
αισχροκερδης, SHAMEFUL GAINER
1Ti   3: 8   in much wine, not **greedy** for
Ti   1: 7   wine or violent or **greedy** for

147   GO1   AG25   LN6   R152,2771
αισχροκερδως, BY SHAMEFUL GAIN
1P   5: 2   not for **sordid gain** but eagerly

148   GO1   AG25   LN6   B3:564   R152,3056
αισχρολογια, SHAMEFUL WORD
Co   3: 8   **abusive language** from your mouth.

150   GO4   AG25   LN6   B3:562   K1:189
αισχρος, SHAME
1C   11: 6   but if it is **disgraceful** for a
    14:35   For it is **shameful** for a woman
Ep   5:12   it is **shameful** even to
Ti   1:11   by teaching for **sordid** gain

151   GO1   AG25   LN6   B3:562   K1:189   R150
αισχροτης, SHAMEFULNESS
Ep   5: 4   out of place is **obscene,** silly,

152   GO6   AG25   LN6   B3:562   K1:189   R150
αισχυνη, SHAME
Lk   14: 9   and then in **disgrace** you would

2C	4: 2	We have renounced the **shameful**
Ph	3:19	looking to Jesus their **shame;**
He	12: 2	cross, disregarding its **shame,**
Ju	1:13	the foam of their own **shame;**
Re	3:18	and to keep the **shame** of your

153   GO5   AG25   LN7   B3:562   K1:189   R150
αισχυνω, I AM ASHAMED
Lk   16: 3   enough to dig, and I am **ashamed**
2C   10: 8   you down, I will not be **ashamed**
Ph   1:20   I will not be put to **shame**
1P   4:16   do not consider it a **disgrace,**
1J   2:28   and not be put to **shame** before

154   GO70   AG25   LN7   B2:855   K1:191
αιτεω, I ASK

Mt	5:42	Give to everyone who **begs** from
	6: 8	you need before you **ask** him.
	7: 7	"**Ask,** and it will be given you;
	7: 8	For everyone who **asks** receives,
	7: 9	if your child **asks** for bread,
	7:10	if the child **asks** for a fish,
	7:11	things to those who **ask** him!
	14: 7	her whatever she might **ask.**
	18:19	on earth about anything you **ask**
	20:20	before him, she **asked** a favor
	20:22	not know what you are **asking.**
	21:22	Whatever you **ask** for in prayer
	27:20	crowds to **ask** for Barabbas
	27:58	He went to Pilate and **asked**
Mk	6:22	"**Ask** me for whatever you wish,
	6:23	"Whatever you **ask** me, I will
	6:24	mother, "What should I **ask** for
	6:25	requested, "I want you to give."
	10:38	do not know what you are **asking.**
	11:24	So I tell you, whatever you **ask**
	15: 8	the crowd came and began to **ask**
	15:43	and **asked** for the body of Jesus
Lk	1:63	He **asked** for a writing tablet
	6:30	Give to everyone who **begs** from
	11: 9	"So I say to you, **Ask,** and it
	11:10	For everyone who **asks** receives,
	11:11	if your child **asks** for a fish,
	11:12	Or if the child **asks** for an egg
	11:13	Holy Spirit to those who **ask**
	12:48	even more will be **demanded.**
	23:23	they kept urgently **demanding**
	23:25	Jesus over as they **wished**
	23:52	**asked** for the body of Jesus

Jn	4: 9	**ask** a drink of me, a woman of
	4:10	you would have **asked** him,
	11:22	give you whatever you **ask**
	14:13	I will do whatever you **ask**
	14:14	**ask** me for anything I will do
	15: 7	**ask** for whatever you wish
	15:16	give you whatever you **ask**
	16:23	you will **ask** nothing of me
	16:24	Until now you have not **asked**
	16:24	**Ask** and you will receive
	16:26	you will **ask** in my name
Ac	3: 2	so that he could **ask** for alms
	3:14	and **asked** to have a murderer
	7:46	found favor with God and **asked**
	9: 2	and **asked** him for letters to
	12:20	they **asked** for a reconciliation
	13:21	Then they **asked** for a king;
	13:28	they **asked** Pilate to have him
	16:29	The jailer **called** for lights,
	25: 3	and **requested,** as a favor to
	25:15	**asked** for a sentence against
1C	1:22	For Jews **demand** signs and
Ep	3:13	I **pray** therefore that you may
	3:20	far more than all we can **ask** or
Co	1: 9	**asking** that you may be filled
Ja	1: 5	**ask** God, who gives to all
	1: 6	But **ask** in faith, never
	4: 2	have, because you do not **ask**.
	4: 3	You **ask** and do not receive,
	4: 3	not receive, because you **ask**
1P	3:15	defense to anyone who **demands**
1J	3:22	from him whatever we **ask,**
	5:14	if we **ask** anything according
	5:15	he hears us in whatever we **ask,**
	5:15	have obtained the requests **made**
	5:16	will **ask,** and God will give

155   ᴳᴼ3   ᴬᴳ26   ᴸᴺ7   ᴮ2:855   ᴷ1:193   ᴿ154
αιτημα, ASKING

Lk	23:24	his verdict that their **demand**
Ph	4: 6	thanksgiving let your **requests**
1J	5:15	we have obtained the **requests**

156   ᴳᴼ20   ᴬᴳ26   ᴸᴺ7   ᴮ2:137
αιτια, CAUSE

Mt	19: 3	divorce his wife for any **cause?**
	19:10	"If such is the **case** of a man
	27:37	his head they put the **charge**
Mk	15:26	of the **charge** against him read,

Lk	8:47	presence of all the people **why**
Jn	18:38	"I find no **case** against him.
	19: 4	I find no **case** against him."
	19: 6	I find no **case** against him."
Ac	10:21	what is the **reason** for your
	13:28	they found no **cause**
	22:24	to find out the **reason** for this
	23:28	to know the **charge** for which
	25:18	they did not **charge** him
	25:27	without indicating the **charges**
	28:18	because there was no **reason** for
	28:20	this **reason** therefore I have
2Ti	1: 6	For this **reason** I remind you
	1:12	for this **reason** I suffer
Ti	1:13	this **reason** rebuke them sharply
He	2:11	For this **reason** Jesus is not

159   ᴳᴼ5   ᴬᴳ26   ᴸᴺ7   ᴮ2:137
αιτιος, CAUSE

Lk	23: 4	crowds, "I find no **basis** for an
	23:14	guilty of any of your **charges**
	23:22	I have found in him no **ground**
Ac	19:40	since there is no **cause** that we
He	5: 9	he became the **source** of eternal

159a   ᴳᴼ1   ᴬᴳ26   ᴸᴺ7   ᴮ2:137
αιτιωμα, COMPLAINT

Ac	25: 7	bringing many serious **charges**

160   ᴳᴼ2   ᴬᴳ26   ᴸᴺ7
αιφνιδιος, SUDDEN

Lk	21:34	that day catch you **unexpectedly**
1Th	5: 3	**sudden** destruction will come

161   ᴳᴼ3   ᴬᴳ26   ᴸᴺ7   ᴮ3:590   ᴷ1:195   ᴿ164
αιχμαλωσια, CAPTIVITY

Ep	4: 8	made captivity itself a **captive**
Re	13:10	If you are to be taken **captive,**
	13:10	into **captivity** you go

162   ᴳᴼ1   ᴬᴳ26   ᴸᴺ7   ᴮ3:590   ᴷ1:195   ᴿ164
αιχμαλωτευω, I LEAD CAPTIVE

Ep	4: 8	he made **captivity** itself a

163   ᴳᴼ4   ᴬᴳ27   ᴸᴺ7   ᴮ3:590   ᴷ1:195   ᴿ164
αιχμαλωτιζω, I CAPTURE

Lk	21:24	be taken away as **captives** among
Ro	7:23	making me **captive** to the law
2C	10: 5	we take every thought **captive**
2Ti	3: 6	households and **captivate** silly

164   GO1   AG27   LN7   B3:590   K1:195
αιχμαλωτος, CAPTIVE
Lk   4:18   release to the **captives**

---

165   GO122   AG27   LN7   B3:826   K1:197
αιων, AGE

Mt	12:32	either in this **age** or in the
	13:22	but the cares of the **world**
	13:39	harvest is the end of the **age**,
	13:40	it be at the end of the **age**.
	13:49	will be at the end of the **age**.
	21:19	fruit ever come from you **again**
	24: 3	and of the end of the **age**?"
	28:20	always, to the end of the **age**."
Mk	3:29	is guilty of an **eternal** sin"
	4:19	but the cares of the **world**
	10:30	a hundredfold now in this **age**
	11:14	ever eat fruit from you **again**."
Lk	1:33	kingdom there will be no **end**."
	1:55	to his descendants **forever**.
	1:70	his holy prophets from of **old**,
	16: 8	for the children of this **age**
	18:30	this **age**, and in the age to
	20:34	"Those who belong to this **age**
	20:35	of a place in that **age**
Jn	4:14	I will give them will **never**
	6:51	this bread will live **forever**;
	6:58	this bread will live **forever**."
	8:35	have a **permanent** place
	8:35	son has a place there **forever**.
	8:51	keeps my word will **never** see
	8:52	keeps my word will **never** taste
	9:32	Never since the **world** began
	10:28	and they will **never** perish.
	11:26	and believes in me will **never**
	12:34	the Messiah remains **forever**.
	13: 8	"You will **never** wash my feet
	14:16	to be with you **forever**.
Ac	3:21	that God announced **long** ago
	15:18	known from **long ago**.
Ro	1:25	Creator, who is blessed **forever**
	9: 5	over all, God blessed **forever**.
	11:36	To him be the glory **forever**.
	12: 2	conformed to this **world**
	16:27	to whom be the glory **forever**!
1C	1:20	is the debater of this **age**?
	2: 6	is not a wisdom of this **age**
	2: 6	or of the rulers of this **age**,
	2: 7	God decreed before the **ages**
	2: 8	None of the rulers of this **age**
	3:18	that you are wise in this **age**,
	8:13	their falling, I will **never** eat
	10:11	the ends of the **ages** have come.
2C	4: 4	god of this **world** has blinded
	9: 9	righteousness endures **forever**
Ga	1: 4	free from the present evil **age**,
	1: 5	to whom be the glory **forever**
	1: 5	be the glory forever and **ever**.
Ep	1:21	not only in this **age** but also
	2: 2	following the **course** of this
	2: 7	so that in the **ages** to come
	3: 9	the mystery hidden for **ages**
	3:11	with the **eternal** purpose that
	3:21	to all generations, **forever**
	3:21	generations, forever and **ever**.
Ph	4:20	and Father be glory **forever**
	4:20	be glory forever and **ever**.
Co	1:26	been hidden throughout the **ages**
1Ti	1:17	To the King of the **ages**,
	1:17	be honor and glory **forever**
	1:17	and glory forever and **ever**.
	6:17	those who in the present **age**
2Ti	4:10	in love with this present **world**
	4:18	To him be the glory **forever** and
	4:18	be the glory forever and **ever**.
Ti	2:12	and in the present **age** to live
He	1: 2	whom he also created the **worlds**
	1: 8	O God, is **forever** and ever, and
	1: 8	O God, is forever and **ever**, and
	5: 6	"You are a priest **forever**,
	6: 5	the powers of the **age** to come,
	6:20	become a high priest **forever**
	7:17	him, "You are a priest **forever**,
	7:21	mind, 'You are a priest **forever**
	7:24	because he continues **forever**.
	7:28	has been made perfect **forever**.
	9:26	all at the end of the **age** to
	11: 3	that the **worlds** were prepared
	13: 8	yesterday and today and **forever**
	13:21	to whom be the glory **forever**
	13:21	be the glory forever and **ever**.
1P	1:25	of the Lord endures **forever**."
	4:11	glory and the power **forever**
	4:11	and the power forever and **ever**.
	5:11	be the power **forever** and ever.
2P	3:18	now and to the day of **eternity**.
1J	2:17	the will of God live **forever**.
2J	1: 2	and will be with us **forever**:

Ju	1:13	has been reserved **forever.**
	1:25	before all **time** and now and
	1:25	all time and now and **forever.**
Re	1: 6	glory and dominion **forever**
	1: 6	dominion forever and **ever.** Amen
	1:18	I am alive **forever** and ever;
	1:18	I am alive forever and **ever;**
	4: 9	who lives **forever** and ever,
	4: 9	who lives forever and **ever,**
	4:10	the one who lives **forever** and
	4:10	one who lives forever and **ever;**
	5:13	and glory and might **forever** and
	5:13	and might forever and **ever!"**
	7:12	might be to our God **forever**
	10: 6	by him who lives **forever**
	10: 6	him who lives forever and **ever,**
	11:15	he will reign **forever** and ever.
	11:15	he will reign forever and **ever.**
	14:11	their torment goes up **forever**
	14:11	goes up forever and **ever.** There
	15: 7	God, who lives **forever** and ever
	15: 7	God, who lives forever and **ever**
	19: 3	smoke goes up from her **forever**
	19: 3	up from her forever and **ever."**
	20:10	day and night **forever** and ever.
	20:10	day and night forever and **ever.**
	22: 5	and they will reign **forever**
	22: 5	will reign forever and **ever.**

166 ᴳᴼ71 ᴬᴳ28 ᴸᴺ7 ᴮ3:826 ᴷ1:208 ᴿ164
αιωνιος, ETERNAL

Mt	18: 8	be thrown into the **eternal** fire
	19:16	deed must I do to have **eternal**
	19:29	will inherit **eternal** life.
	25:41	from me into the **eternal** fire
	25:46	these will go away into **eternal**
	25:46	the righteous into **eternal** life
Mk	3:29	but is guilty of an **eternal** sin
	10:17	I do to inherit **eternal** life?"
	10:30	in the age to come **eternal**
Lk	10:25	must I do to inherit **eternal**
	16: 9	welcome you into the **eternal**
	18:18	do to inherit **eternal**
	18:30	in the age to come **eternal**
Jn	3:15	but may have **eternal** life.
	3:16	not perish but may have **eternal**
	3:36	believes in the Son has **eternal**
	4:14	gushing up to **eternal** life."

	4:36	fruit for **eternal** life
	5:24	him who sent me has **eternal**
	5:39	that in them you have **eternal**
	6:27	food that endures for **eternal**
	6:40	believe in him may have **eternal**
	6:47	whoever believes has **eternal**
	6:54	my blood have **eternal** life
	6:68	You have the words of **eternal**
	10:28	I give them **eternal** life
	12:25	world will keep it for **eternal**
	12:50	that his commandment is **eternal**
	17: 2	all people, to give **eternal**
	17: 3	this is **eternal** life
Ac	13:46	to be unworthy of **eternal** life,
	13:48	been destined for **eternal** life
Ro	2: 7	he will give **eternal** life;
	5:21	leading to **eternal** life
	6:22	The end is **eternal** life.
	6:23	free gift of God is **eternal**
	16:25	was kept secret for long **ages**
	16:26	the command of the **eternal** God,
2C	4:17	is preparing us for an **eternal**
	4:18	what cannot be seen is **eternal.**
	5: 1	not made with hands, **eternal**
Ga	6: 8	you will reap **eternal** life
2Th	1: 9	punishment of **eternal**
	2:16	grace gave us **eternal** comfort
1Ti	1:16	believe in him for **eternal** life
	6:12	take hold of the **eternal** life,
	6:16	to him be honor and **eternal**
2Ti	1: 9	in Christ Jesus before the **ages**
	2:10	in Christ Jesus, with **eternal**
Ti	1: 2	hope of **eternal** life that God,
	1: 2	promised before the **ages** began
	3: 7	to the hope of **eternal** life.
Pm	1:15	might have him back **forever,**
He	5: 9	he became the source of **eternal**
	6: 2	the dead, and **eternal** judgment.
	9:12	obtaining **eternal** redemption.
	9:14	who through the **eternal** Spirit
	9:15	receive the promised **eternal**
	13:20	by the blood of the **eternal**
1P	5:10	called you to his **eternal** glory
2P	1:11	entry into the **eternal** kingdom
1J	1: 2	and declare to you the **eternal**
	2:25	has promised us, **eternal** life.
	3:15	murderers do not have **eternal**
	5:11	God gave us **eternal** life

	5:13	that you have **eternal** life.
	5:20	He is the true God and **eternal**
Ju	1: 7	punishment of **eternal** fire.
	1:21	that leads to **eternal** life.
Re	14: 6	with an **eternal** gospel to

167　GO10　AG28　LN7　B3:102　K3:427　R169
ακαθαρσια, UNCLEANNESS

Mt	23:27	dead and of all kinds of **filth.**
Ro	1:24	of their hearts to **impurity**
	6:19	members as slaves to **impurity**
2C	12:21	repented of the **impurity,**
Ga	5:19	obvious: fornication, **impurity,**
Ep	4:19	practice every kind of **impurity**
	5: 3	But fornication and **impurity** of
Co	3: 5	earthly: fornication, **impurity,**
1Th	2: 3	deceit or **impure motives** or
	4: 7	God did not call us to **impurity**

169　GO32　AG29　LN7　B3:102　K3:427
ακαθαρτος, UNCLEAN

Mt	10: 1	authority over **unclean** spirits,
	12:43	"When the **unclean** spirit has
Mk	1:23	a man with an **unclean** spirit,
	1:26	And the **unclean** spirit,
	1:27	He commands even the **unclean**
	3:11	Whenever the **unclean** spirits
	3:30	"He has an **unclean** spirit."
	5: 2	an **unclean** spirit met him.
	5: 8	of the man, you **unclean** spirit!
	5:13	And the **unclean** spirits came
	6: 7	over the **unclean** spirits.
	7:25	daughter had an **unclean** spirit
	9:25	he rebuked the **unclean** spirit,
Lk	4:33	spirit of an **unclean** demon,
	4:36	he commands the **unclean** spirits
	6:18	troubled with **unclean** spirits
	8:29	**unclean** spirit to come out
	9:42	rebuked the **unclean** spirit,
	11:24	"When the **unclean** spirit has
Ac	5:16	tormented by **unclean** spirits,
	8: 7	for **unclean** spirits, crying
	10:14	that is profane or **unclean.**"
	10:28	call anyone profane or **unclean.**
	11: 8	profane or **unclean** has ever
1C	7:14	children would be **unclean**
2C	6:17	and touch nothing **unclean**
Ep	5: 5	that no fornicator or **impure**
Re	16:13	I saw three **foul** spirits
	17: 4	**impurities** of her fornication;

	18: 2	a haunt of every **foul** spirit,
	18: 2	a haunt of every **foul** bird,
	18: 2	a haunt of every **foul** and hateful beast

170　GO1　AG29　LN7　B3:833　K3:462　R2540
ακαιρεομαι, I HAVE SEASON

Ph	4:10	but had no **opportunity** to show

171　GO1　AG29　LN7　B3:837　K3:462　R2540
ακαιρως, UNSEAONABLLY

2Ti	4: 2	is favorable or **unfavorable;**

172　GO2　AG29　LN7　B1:561　K3:482　R2556
ακακος, UNBAD

Ro	16:18	hearts of the **simple-minded.**
He	7:26	high priest, holy, **blameless,**

173　GO14　AG29　LN8　B1:725
ακανθα, THORN

Mt	7:16	grapes gathered from **thorns,**
	13: 7	Other seeds fell among **thorns,**
	13: 7	the **thorns** grew up and choked
	13:22	what was sown among **thorns,**
	27:29	after twisting some **thorns** into
Mk	4: 7	Other seed fell among **thorns,**
	4: 7	the **thorns** grew up and choked
	4:18	those sown among the **thorns:**
Lk	6:44	not gathered from **thorns**
	8: 7	Some fell among **thorns**
	8: 7	**thorns** grew with it and choked
	8:14	what fell among the **thorns,**
Jn	19: 2	wove a crown of **thorns**
He	6: 8	But if it produces **thorns**

174　GO2　AG29　LN8　B1:725　R173
ακανθινος, THORN

Mk	15:17	twisting some **thorns**
Jn	19: 5	wearing the crown of **thorns**

175　GO7　AG29　LN8　B1:721　K3:616　R2590
ακαρπος, FRUITLESS

Mt	13:22	word, and it yields **nothing.**
Mk	4:19	word, and it yields **nothing.**
1C	14:14	but my mind is **unproductive.**
Ep	5:11	Take no part in the **unfruitful**
Ti	3:14	they may not be **unproductive.**
2P	1: 8	ineffective and **unfruitful**
Ju	1:12	autumn trees **without fruit,**

176 GO1 AG29 LN8 K1:714 R2607
ακαταγνωστος, NOT KNOWN AGAINST
Ti 2: 8 speech that cannot be **censured;**

177 GO2 AG29 LN8 R2619
ακατακαλυπτος, UNCOVERED OVER
1C 11: 5 her head **unveiled** disgraces
         her
    11:13 to God with her head **unveiled?**

178 GO2 AG29 LN8 K3:952 R1:2632
ακατακριτος, UNCONDEMNED
Ac 16:37 in public, **uncondemned**
    22:25 citizen who is **uncondemned?"**
1C 14:33 God is a God not of **disorder**
2C   6: 5 beatings, imprisonments, **riots,**
    12:20 gossip, conceit, and **disorder.**
Ja   3:16 will also be **disorder**

179 GO1 AG30 LN8 B3:177 K4:338 R2647
ακαταλυτος, INDESTRUCTIBLE
He   7:16 power of an **indestructible**

180 GO1 AG30 LN8 R2664
ακαταπαυστος, UNABLE TO STOP
2P   2:14 adultery, **insatiable** for sin.

181 GO5 AG30 LN8 B2:780 K3:446 R182
ακαταστασια, UNSTABLENESS
Lk 21: 9 hear of wars and **insurrections,**
1C 14:33 God is a God not of **disorder**
2C   6: 5 beatings, imprisonments,
           riots,
    12:20 gossip, conceit, and **disorder.**
Ja   3:16 will also be **disorder**

182 GO2 AG30 LN8 K3:447
ακαταστατος, UNSTABLE
Ja   1: 8 double-minded and **unstable**
     3: 8 the tongue—a **restless** evil,

184 GO1 AG30 LN8 B1:93
ακελδαμαχ, AKELDAMACH
Ac   1:19 in their language **Hakeldama,**

185 GO3 AG30 LN8 K1:209
ακεραιος, INNOCENT
Mt 10:16 **innocent** as doves.
Ro 16:19 **guileless** in what is evil.
Ph   2:15 may be blameless and **innocent,**

186 GO1 AG30 LN8 R2827
ακλινης, UNLEANING
He 10:23 our hope **without wavering,**

187 GO1 AG30 LN8
ακμαζω, I RIPEN
Re 14:18 for its grapes are **ripe."**

188 GO1 AG30 LN8
ακμην, EVEN NOW
Mt 15:16 **still** without understanding?

189 GO24 AG30 LN8 B2:172 K1:221 R191
ακοη, HEARING
Mt   4:24 his **fame** spread throughout all
    13:14 'You will indeed **listen,** but
    14: 1 heard **reports** about Jesus;
    24: 6 wars and **rumors** of wars
Mk   1:28 his **fame** began to spread
     7:35 **ears** were opened, his tongue
    13: 7 wars and **rumors** of wars,
Lk   7: 1 in the **hearing** of the people,
Jn 12:38 who has believed our **message,**
Ac 17:20 It **sounds** rather strange to us,
    28:26 You will indeed **listen,**
Ro 10:16 who has believed our **message?"**
    10:17 faith comes from what is **heard,**
    10:17 what is **heard** comes through
1C 12:17 where would the **hearing** be?
    12:17 If the whole body were **hearing,**
Ga   3: 2 by believing what you **heard?**
     3: 5 your believing what you **heard?**
1Th 2:13 word of God that you **heard**
2Ti 4: 3 to suit their own **desires,**
     4: 4 wander away to **myths.**
He   4: 2 the **message** they heard did not
     5:11 become dull in **understanding.**
2P   2: 8 deeds that he saw and **heard**

190 GO90 AG31 LN8 B1:480 K1:210
ακολουθεω, I FOLLOW
Mt   4:20 their nets and **followed** him.
     4:22 their father, and **followed** him.
     4:25 great crowds **followed** him
     8: 1 crowds **followed** him;
     8:10 said to those who **followed** him,
     8:19 "Teacher, I will **follow** you
     8:22 Jesus said to him, "**Follow** me
     8:23 his disciples **followed** him.
     9: 9 he said to him, "**Follow** me."

9: 9	he said to him, "**Follow** me."	
9:19	Jesus got up and **followed** him,	
9:27	two blind men **followed** him,	
10:38	take up the cross and **follow** me	
12:15	Many crowds **followed** him,	
14:13	they **followed** him on foot	
16:24	take up their cross and **follow**	
19: 2	Large crowds **followed** him,	
19:21	then come, **follow** me."	
19:27	left everything and **followed**	
19:28	you who have **followed** me	
20:29	a large crowd **followed** him.	
20:34	their sight and **followed** him.	
21: 9	that **followed** were shouting,	
26:58	But Peter was **following** him	
27:55	they had **followed** Jesus	

Mk
1:18	left their nets and **followed**
2:14	he said to him, "**Follow** me."
2:14	he got up and **followed** him
3: 7	multitude from Galilee **followed**;
5:24	a large crowd **followed** him
6: 1	his disciples **followed** him.
8:34	any want to become my **followers**,
8:34	take up their cross and **follow**
9:38	he was not **following** us."
10:21	then come, **follow** me."
10:28	left everything and **followed**
10:32	those who **followed** were afraid.
10:52	regained his sight and **followed**
11: 9	who **followed** were shouting,
14:13	will meet you; **follow** him,
14:54	Peter had **followed** him
15:41	These used to **follow** him

Lk
5:11	left everything and **followed**
5:27	said to him, "**Follow** me."
5:28	left everything, and **followed**
7: 9	to the crowd that **followed** him,
9:11	they **followed** him
9:23	their cross daily and **follow** me.
9:49	because he does not **follow**
9:57	"I will **follow** you wherever you
9:59	To another he said, "**Follow** me
9:61	"I will **follow** you, Lord;
18:22	heaven; then come, **follow** me."
18:28	left our homes and **followed**
18:43	his sight and **followed** him,
22:10	**follow** him into the house
22:39	the disciples **followed** him.
22:54	But Peter was **following**

| 23:27 | number of the people **followed** |
Jn
1:37	say this, and they **followed**
1:38	turned and saw them **following**,
1:40	and **followed** him was Andrew
1:43	to him, "**Follow** me."
6: 2	large crowd kept **following** him,
8:12	Whoever **follows** me will never
10: 4	and the sheep **follow** him
10: 5	will not **follow** a stranger
10:27	I know them, and they **follow**
11:31	They **followed** her because they
12:26	serves me must **follow** me,
13:36	you cannot **follow** me now;
13:36	but you will **follow** afterward."
13:37	why can I not **follow** you now?
18:15	and another disciple **followed**
20: 6	Simon Peter came, **following**
21:19	he said to him, "**Follow** me."
21:20	whom Jesus loved **following** them
21:22	what is that to you? **Follow** me!
Ac
12: 8	cloak around you and **follow** me.
12: 9	Peter went out and **followed** him
13:43	converts to Judaism **followed**
21:36	The crowd that **followed** kept
1C
10: 4	spiritual rock that **followed**
Re
6: 8	and Hades **followed** with him;
14: 4	these **follow** the Lamb wherever
14: 8	angel, a second, **followed**,
14: 9	angel, a third, **followed** them,
14:13	for their deeds **follow** them."
19:14	and pure, were **following** him

---

191   GO428 AG31 LN8 B2:172 K1:216
ακουω, I HEAR
Mt
2: 3	When King Herod **heard** this,
2: 9	When they had **heard** the king,
2:18	"A voice was **heard** in Ramah,
2:22	when he **heard** that Archelaus
4:12	when Jesus **heard** that John
5:21	"You have **heard** that it was
5:27	You have **heard** that it was said
5:33	you have **heard** that it was said
5:38	You have **heard** that it was said
5:43	You have **heard** that it was said
7:24	"Everyone then who **hears** these
7:26	everyone who **hears** these words
8:10	When Jesus **heard** him, he was
9:12	when he **heard** this, he said,
10:14	not welcome you or **listen** to

10:27	what you **hear** whispered,		2:17	When Jesus **heard** this, he said
11: 2	When John **heard** in prison what		3: 8	**hearing** all that he was doing,
11: 4	tell John what you **hear** and see		3:21	When his family **heard** it, they
11: 5	the deaf **hear,** the dead are		4: 3	**"Listen!** A sower went out
11:15	Let anyone with ears **listen!**		4: 9	anyone with ears to **hear**
12:19	nor will anyone **hear** his voice		4: 9	with ears to hear **listen!"**
12:24	But when the Pharisees **heard** it		4:12	perceive, and may indeed **listen,**
12:42	the ends of the earth to **listen**		4:12	perceive, and may indeed **listen,**
13: 9	Let anyone with ears **listen!"**		4:15	word is sown: when they **hear,**
13:13	**hearing** they do not listen,		4:16	when they **hear** the word,
13:13	hearing they do not **listen,**		4:18	these are the ones who **hear**
13:14	'You will indeed **listen,** but		4:20	they **hear** the word and accept
13:15	their ears are hard of **hearing,**		4:23	anyone with ears to **hear** listen
13:15	**listen** with their ears,		4:23	anyone with ears to hear **listen**
13:16	and your ears, for they **hear.**		4:24	"Pay attention to what you **hear**
13:17	to **hear** what you hear,		4:33	they were able to **hear** it;
13:17	to hear what you **hear,**		5:27	She **had heard** about Jesus
13:17	but did not **hear** it.		6: 2	who **heard** him were astounded
13:18	**"Hear** then the parable of the		6:11	they refuse to **hear** you
13:19	When anyone **hears** the word		6:14	King Herod **heard** of it
13:20	one who **hears** the word		6:16	But when Herod **heard** of it
13:22	one who **hears** the word,		6:20	When he **heard** him
13:23	one who **hears** the word		6:29	When his disciples **heard** about
13:43	Let anyone with ears **listen!**		6:55	to wherever they **heard** he was.
14: 1	Herod the ruler **heard** reports		7:14	**"Listen** to me, all of you,
14:13	Now when Jesus **heard** this		7:25	spirit immediately **heard**
14:13	when the crowds **heard** it,		7:37	he even makes the deaf to **hear**
15:10	**"Listen** and understand:		8:18	you have ears, and fail to **hear**
15:12	when they **heard** what you said?"		9: 7	Son, the Beloved; **listen** to him
17: 5	well pleased; **listen** to him!"		10:41	When the ten **heard** this, they
17: 6	When the disciples **heard** this,		10:47	When he **heard** that it was Jesus
18:15	If the member **listens** to you,		11:14	And his disciples **heard** it.
18:16	But if you are not **listened** to,		11:18	priests and scribes **heard** it
19:22	the young man **heard** this word,		12:28	and **heard** them disputing
19:25	When the disciples **heard** this,		12:29	**Hear,** O Israel: the Lord our
20:24	When the ten **heard** it, they		12:37	large crowd was **listening**
20:30	When they **heard** that Jesus was		13: 7	When you **hear** of wars
21:16	"Do you **hear** what these are		14:11	When they **heard** it, they were
21:33	**"Listen** to another parable.		14:58	We **heard** him say, I will
21:45	Pharisees **heard** his parables,		14:64	You have **heard** his blasphemy!
22:22	When they **heard** this, they were		15:35	**"Listen,** he is calling for
22:33	when the crowd **heard** it, they		16:11	when they **heard** that he was
22:34	When the Pharisees **heard** that	Lk 1:41	Elizabeth **heard** Mary's greeting
24: 6	you will **hear** of wars		1:58	neighbors and relatives **heard**
26:65	have now **heard** his blasphemy.		1:66	All who **heard** them pondered
27:13	"Do you not **hear** how many		2:18	all who **heard** it were amazed
27:47	some of the bystanders **heard** it		2:20	for all they had **heard** and seen
28:14	**comes to** the governor's **ears,**		2:46	**listening** to them and asking
Mk 2: 1	it was **reported** that he was		2:47	all who **heard** him were amazed

4:23	the things that we have **heard**
4:28	When they **heard** this, all in
5: 1	was pressing in on him to **hear**
5:15	crowds would gather to **hear** him
6:18	They had come to **hear** him
6:27	"But I say to you that **listen,**
6:47	**hears** my words, and acts
6:49	the one who **hears** and does not
7: 3	When he **heard** about Jesus,
7: 9	When Jesus **heard** this he was
7:22	what you have seen and **heard:**
7:22	the deaf **hear**
7:29	(And all the people who **heard**
8: 8	"Let anyone with ears to **hear**
8: 8	with ears to hear **listen!**"
8:10	perceive, and **listening** they
8:12	are those who have **heard;**
8:13	when they **hear** the word,
8:14	these are the ones who **hear;**
8:15	when they **hear** the word, hold it
8:18	pay attention to how you **listen**
8:21	my brothers are those who **hear**
8:50	Jesus **heard** this, he replied
9: 7	Herod the ruler **heard** about all
9: 9	who is this about whom I **hear**
9:35	Son, my Chosen; **listen** to him!"
10:16	"Whoever **listens** to you listens
10:16	"Whoever listens to you **listens**
10:24	and to **hear** what you hear
10:24	and to hear what you **hear**
10:24	you hear, but did not **hear** it."
10:39	feet and **listened** to what he was
11:28	those who **hear** the word of God
11:31	to **listen** to the wisdom of
12: 3	will be **heard** in the light,
14:15	guests, on **hearing** this, said
14:35	Let anyone with ears to **hear**
14:35	with ears to hear **listen!**"
15: 1	were coming near to **listen**
15:25	he **heard** music and dancing.
16: 2	What is this that I **hear** about
16:14	lovers of money, **heard** all this
16:29	they should **listen** to them.'
16:31	If they do not **listen** to Moses
18: 6	"**Listen** to what the unjust judge
18:22	When Jesus **heard** this, he said
18:23	when he **heard** this, he became
18:26	Those who **heard** it said,
18:36	When he **heard** a crowd going by,

19:11	As they were **listening** to this,
19:48	spellbound by what they **heard.**
20:16	When they **heard** this, they said
20:45	the **hearing** of all the people
21: 9	When you **hear** of wars
21:38	early in the morning to **listen**
22:71	We have **heard** it ourselves from
23: 6	When Pilate **heard** this,
23: 8	because he had **heard** about him
Jn 1:37	The two disciples **heard** him say
1:40	One of the two who **heard** John
3: 8	you **hear** the sound of it
3:29	who stands and **hears** him,
3:32	to what he has seen and **heard,**
4: 1	that the Pharisees had **heard,**
4:42	for we have **heard** for ourselves
4:47	he **heard** that Jesus had come
5:24	anyone who **hears** my word and
5:25	the dead will **hear** the voice
5:25	those who **hear** will live.
5:28	will **hear** his voice
5:30	As I **hear,** I judge; and my
5:37	You have never **heard** his voice
6:45	who has **heard** and learned from
6:60	many of his disciples **heard** it,
6:60	is difficult; who can **accept** it
7:32	The Pharisees **heard** the crowd
7:40	When they **heard** these words
7:51	giving them a **hearing** to find
8: 9	When they **heard** it, they went
8:26	what I have **heard** from him."
8:38	should do what you have **heard**
8:40	the truth that I **heard** from God
8:43	you cannot **accept** my word.
8:47	Whoever is from God **hears** the
8:47	The reason you do not **hear** them
9:27	and you would not **listen.**
9:27	do you want to **hear** it again?
9:31	God does not **listen** to sinners
9:31	does **listen** to one who worships
9:32	has it been **heard** that anyone
9:35	Jesus **heard** that they had
9:40	Pharisees near him **heard** this
10: 3	the sheep **hear** his voice.
10: 8	but the sheep did not **listen**
10:16	they will **listen** to my voice.
10:20	Why **listen** to him?"
10:27	My sheep **hear** my voice.
11: 4	when Jesus **heard** it, he said,

11: 6	after having **heard** that Lazarus	9:13	I have **heard** from many about
11:20	When Martha **heard** that Jesus	9:21	all who **heard** him were amazed
11:29	And when she **heard** it, she got	9:38	disciples, who **heard** that Peter
11:41	I thank you for having **heard** me	10:22	to **hear** what you have to say
11:42	I knew that you always **hear** me	10:33	presence of God to **listen** to
12:12	had come to the festival **heard**	10:44	upon all who **heard** the word.
12:18	It was also because they **heard**	10:46	for they **heard** them speaking
12:29	crowd standing there **heard** it	11: 1	the Gentiles had also **accepted**
12:34	"We have **heard** from the law	11: 7	also **heard** a voice saying to me
12:47	I do not judge anyone who **hears**	11:18	When they **heard** this, they were
14:24	and the word that you **hear**	11:22	News of this **came to** the ears
14:28	You **heard** me say to you,	13: 7	wanted to **hear** the word of God.
15:15	everything that I have **heard**.	13:16	others who fear God, **listen**.
16:13	will speak whatever he **hears**,	13:44	city gathered to **hear** the word
18:21	Ask those who **heard** what I said	13:48	When the Gentiles **heard** this
18:37	belongs to the truth **listens** to	14: 9	He **listened** to Paul as he was
19: 8	Now when Pilate **heard** this,	14:14	Barnabas and Paul **heard** of it
19:13	When Pilate **heard** these words,	15: 7	Gentiles would **hear** the message
21: 7	When Simon Peter **heard** that it	15:12	**listened** to Barbabas and Paul
Ac 1: 4	is what you have **heard** from me;	15:13	My brothers, **listen** to me
2: 6	because each one **heard** them	15:24	we have **heard** that certain
2: 8	And how is it that we **hear**,	16:14	Lord opened her heart to **listen**
2:11	in our own languages we **hear**	16:38	were afraid when they **heard**
2:22	**listen** to what I have to say:	17: 8	disturbed when they **heard** this,
2:33	this that you both see and **hear**	17:21	telling or **hearing** something
2:37	Now when they **heard** this, they	17:32	they **heard** of the resurrection
3:22	You must **listen** to whatever he	17:32	"We will **hear** you again about
3:23	everyone who does not **listen**	18: 8	Corinthians who **heard** Paul
4: 4	But many of those who **heard**	18:26	Priscilla and Acquila **heard**
4:19	right in God's sight to **listen**	19: 2	we have not even **heard** that
4:20	what we have seen and **heard**."	19: 5	On **hearing** this, they were
4:24	When they **heard** it	19:10	**heard** the word of the Lord
5: 5	when Ananias **heard** these words,	19:26	You also see and **hear**
5: 5	great fear seized all who **heard**	19:28	When they **heard** this
5:11	all who **heard** of these things.	21:12	When we **heard** this
5:21	When they **heard** this	21:20	When they **heard** it
5:24	the chief priests **heard** these	21:22	**hear** that you have come
5:33	When they **heard** this,	22: 1	**listen** to the defense that I
6:11	"We have **heard** him speak	22: 2	When they **heard** him addressing
6:14	for we have **heard** him say that	22: 7	**heard** a voice saying to me,
7: 2	**listen** to me. The God of glory	22: 9	but did not **hear** the voice
7:12	But when Jacob **heard** that there	22:14	to **hear** his own voice;
7:34	and have **heard** their groaning	22:15	what you have seen and **heard**.
7:54	When they **heard** these things,	22:22	Up to this point they **listened**
8: 6	one accord **listened** eagerly	22:26	When the centurion **heard** that,
8:14	**heard** that Samaria had accepted	23:16	the son of Paul's sister **heard**
8:30	**heard** him reading the prophet	24: 4	I beg you to **hear** us briefly
9: 4	**heard** a voice saying to him	24:24	he sent for Paul and **heard** him
9: 7	they **heard** the voice but saw	25:22	"I would like to **hear** the man

	25:22	he said, "you will **hear** him."
	26: 3	I beg of you to **listen** to me
	26:14	I **heard** a voice saying to me
	26:29	all who are **listening** to me
	28:15	when they **heard** of us, came
	28:22	we would like to **hear** from you
	28:26	You will indeed **listen**, but
	28:27	their ears are hard of **hearing**,
	28:27	and **listen** with their ears,
	28:28	the Gentiles; they will **listen**.
Ro	10:14	whom they have never **heard**?
	10:14	how are they to **hear** without
	10:18	But I ask, have they not **heard**?
	11: 8	ears that would not **hear**
	15:21	those who have never **heard**
1C	2: 9	no eye has seen, nor ear **heard**,
	5: 1	It is actually **reported** that
	11:18	I **hear** that there are divisions
	14: 2	for nobody **understands** them,
2C	12: 4	into Paradise and **heard** things
	12: 6	is seen in me or **heard** from me,
Ga	1:13	You have **heard**, no doubt, of
	1:23	they only **heard** it said, "The
	4:21	will you not **listen** to the law?
Ep	1:13	when you had **heard** the word of
	1:15	I have **heard** of your faith
	3: 2	surely you have already **heard**
	4:21	you have **heard** about him
	4:29	give grace to those who **hear**.
Ph	1:27	am absent and **hear** about you,
	1:30	I had and now **hear** that I still
	2:26	distressed because you **heard**
	4: 9	received and **heard** and seen
Co	1: 4	for we have **heard** of your faith
	1: 6	from the day you **heard** it
	1: 9	since the day we **heard** it,
	1:23	by the gospel that you **heard**,
2Th	3:11	For we **hear** that some of you
1Ti	4:16	both yourself and your **hearers**.
2Ti	1:13	you have **heard** from me,
	2: 2	and what you have **heard** from me
	2:14	ruins those who are **listening**.
	4:17	all the Gentiles might **hear** it.
Pm	1: 5	I **hear** of your love for all
He	2: 1	attention to what we have **heard**
	2: 3	to us by those who **heard** him,
	3: 7	Today, if you **hear** his voice,
	3:15	Today, if you **hear** his voice,
	3:16	Now who were they who **heard**

	4: 2	but the message they **heard**
	4: 7	Today, if you **hear** his voice,
	12:19	whose words made the **hearers**
Ja	1:19	let everyone be quick to **listen**
	2: 5	**Listen,** my beloved brothers
	5:11	You have **heard** of the endurance
2P	1:18	We ourselves **heard** this voice
1J	1: 1	what we have **heard,** what we
	1: 3	what we have seen and **heard**
	1: 5	message we have **heard** from him
	2: 7	the word that you have **heard**.
	2:18	you have **heard** that antichrist
	2:24	Let what you **heard** from the
	2:24	If what you **heard** from the
	3:11	the message you have **heard** from
	4: 3	of which you have **heard** that it
	4: 5	and the world **listens** to them.
	4: 6	Whoever knows God **listens** to us
	4: 6	not from God does not **listen** to
	5:14	according to his will, he **hears**
	5:15	And if we know that he **hears** us
2J	1: 6	just as you have **heard** it from
3J	1: 4	to **hear** that my children
Re	1: 3	blessed are those who **hear**
	1:10	I **heard** behind me a loud voice
	2: 7	anyone who has an ear **listen**
	2:11	anyone who has an ear **listen**
	2:17	anyone who has an ear **listen**
	2:29	anyone who has an ear **listen**
	3: 3	what you received and **heard**;
	3: 6	anyone who has an ear **listen**
	3:13	anyone who has an ear **listen**
	3:20	if you **hear** my voice
	3:22	anyone who has an ear **listen**
	4: 1	which I had **heard** speaking
	5:11	I **heard** the voice of many
	5:13	Then I **heard** every creature in
	6: 1	I **heard** one of the four living
	6: 3	I **heard** the second living
	6: 5	I **heard** the third living
	6: 6	I **heard** what seemed to be
	6: 7	I **heard** the voice of the fourth
	7: 4	I **heard** the number of those who
	8:13	I **heard** an eagle crying
	9:13	I **heard** a voice from the four
	9:16	I **heard** their number.
	9:20	cannot see or **hear** or walk.
	10: 4	I **heard** a voice from heaven
	10: 8	the voice that I had **heard**

11:12	Then they **heard** a loud voice
12:10	I **heard** a loud voice in heaven
13: 9	anyone who has an ear **listen:**
14: 2	I **heard** a voice from heaven
14: 2	the voice I **heard** was like the
14:13	I **heard** a voice from heaven
16: 1	Then I **heard** a loud voice
16: 5	I **heard** the angel of the waters
16: 7	I **heard** the altar respond, "Yes
18: 4	Then I **heard** another voice from
18:22	trumpeters will be **heard** in you
18:22	of the millstone will be **heard**
18:23	bride will be **heard** in you
19: 1	After this I **heard** what seemed
19: 6	Then I **heard** what seemed to be
21: 3	And I **heard** a loud voice from
22: 8	I, John, am the one who **heard**
22: 8	And when I **heard** and saw them,
22:17	let everyone who **hears** say,
22:18	everyone who **hears** the words

---

192   G02   AG33   LN8   B1:494   K2:339   R193
ακρασια, LACK OF STRENGTH
Mt 23:25   greed and **self-indulgence.**
1C 7: 5   of your lack of **self-control.**

---

193   G01   AG33   LN8   B1:494   K2:339   R2904
ακρατης, NO STRENGTH
2Ti 3: 3   slanderers, **profligates**

---

194   G01   AG33   LN8
ακρατος, UNDILUTED
Re 14:10   poured **unmixed** into the cup

---

195   G01   AG33   LN9   R196
ακριβεια, ACCURACY
Ac 22: 3   Gamaliel, educated **strictly**

---

196   G01   AG33   LN9
ακριβης, MOST ACCURATE
Ac 26: 5   have belonged to the **strictest**

---

198   G02   AG33   LN9   R196
ακριβοω, I DETERMINE ACCURATELY
Mt 2: 7   **learned** from them the **exact**
     2:16   to the time that he had **learned**

---

199   G09   AG33   LN9   R196
ακριβως, ACCURATELY
Mt 2: 8   "Go and search **diligently** for

Lk	1: 3	everything **carefully** from the
Ac	18:25	taught **accurately** the things
	18:26	God to him more **accurately.**
	23:15	want to make a more **thorough**
	23:20	to inquire more **thoroughly**
	24:22	who was rather **well informed**
Ep	5:15	Be **careful** then how you live
1Th	5: 2	you yourselves know **very well**

---

200   G04   AG33
ακρις, LOCUST
Mt 3: 4   food was **locusts** and wild honey
Mk 1: 6   he ate **locusts** and wild honey.
Re 9: 3   from the smoke came **locusts**
     9: 7   In appearance the **locusts** were

---

201   G01   AG33   LN9   R202
ακροατηριον, HEARING PLACE
Ac 25:23   they entered the **audience hall**

---

202   G04   AG33   LN9   B2:172   R191
ακροατης, HEARER
Ro 2:13   not the **hearers** of the law
Ja 1:22   not merely **hearers** who deceive
     1:23   if any are **hearers** of the word
     1:25   being not **hearers** who forget

---

203   G020   AG33   LN9   B1:307   K1:225
ακροβυστια, UNCIRCUMCISION
Ac 11: 3   did you go to **uncircumcised** men
Ro 2:25   has become **uncircumcision.**
     2:26   if those who are **uncircumcised**
     2:26   **uncircumcision** be regarded
     2:27   are physically **uncircumcised**
     3:30   faith and the **uncircumcised**
     4: 9   or also on the **uncircumcised?**
     4:10   **before** or . . . been **circumcised**
     4:10   **before** he was **circumcised.**
     4:11   he was still **uncircumcised.**
     4:11   **without being circumcised**
     4:12   **before** he was **circumcised.**
1C 7:18   of his call **uncircumcised?**
     7:19   and **uncircumcision** is nothing;
Ga 2: 7   gospel for the **uncircumcised,**
     5: 6   circumcision nor **uncircumcision**
     6:15   circumcision nor **uncircumcision**
Ep 2:11   called "the **uncircumcision**"
Co 2:13   **uncircumcision** of your flesh,
     3:11   circumcised and **uncircumcised,**

204 ᴳᴼ2 ᴬᴳ33 ᴸᴺ9 ᴮ3:388 ᴷ1:792 ᴿ206,1137
ακρογωνιαιος, CORNERSTONE
Ep   2:20   himself as the **cornerstone.**
1P   2: 6   **cornerstone** chosen and precious

---

205 ᴳᴼ1 ᴬᴳ33 ᴸᴺ9
ακροθινιον, SPOILS
He   7: 4   gave him a tenth of the **spoils.**

---

206 ᴳᴼ6 ᴬᴳ34 ᴸᴺ9
ακρον, TIP
Mt 24:31   winds, from one **end** of heaven
    24:31   one end of heaven to the **other.**
Mk 13:27   from the **ends** of the earth
    13:27   the earth to the **ends** of heaven
Lk 16:24   send Lazarus to dip the **tip**
He 11:21   bowing in worship over the **top**

---

207 ᴳᴼ6 ᴬᴳ34 ᴸᴺ9
ακυλας, ACQUILA
Ac 18: 2   he found a Jew named **Aquila,**
    18:18   by Priscilla and **Aquila.**
    18:26   but when Priscilla and **Aquila**
Ro 16: 3   Greet Prisca and **Aquila,**
1C 16:19   **Aquila** and Prisca, together
2Ti 4:19   Greet Prisca and **Aquila,**

---

208 ᴳᴼ3 ᴬᴳ34 ᴸᴺ9 ᴷ3:1099 ᴿ2964
ακυροω, I INVALIDATE
Mt 15: 6   you make **void** the word of God.
Mk   7:13   making **void** the word of God
Ga   3:17   so as to **nullify** the promise.

---

209 ᴳᴼ1 ᴬᴳ34 ᴸᴺ9 ᴿ2967
ακωλυτως, UNHINDEREDLY
Ac 28:31   boldness and **without hindrance.**

---

210 ᴳᴼ1 ᴬᴳ34 ᴸᴺ9 ᴷ2:469 ᴿ1635
ακων, UNWILLING
1C   9:17   but if **not of my own will**

---

211 ᴳᴼ4 ᴬᴳ34 ᴸᴺ9
αλαβαστρον, ALABASTER JAR
Mt 26: 7   to him with an **alabaster** jar
Mk 14: 3   **alabaster** jar of very costly
    14: 3   **alabaster** jar of very costly
Lk   7:37   an **alabaster** jar of ointment.

---

212 ᴳᴼ2 ᴬᴳ34 ᴸᴺ9 ᴮ3:28 ᴷ1:226 ᴿ213
αλαζονεια, BOAST

Ja   4:16   you boast in your **arrogance**
1J   2:16   the eyes, the **pride** in riches

---

213 ᴳᴼ2 ᴬᴳ34 ᴸᴺ9 ᴮ2:435 ᴷ1:226
αλαζων, BOASTER
Ro   1:30   insolent, haughty, **boastful**
2Ti 3: 2   lovers of money, **boasters**

---

214 ᴳᴼ2 ᴬᴳ34 ᴸᴺ9 ᴷ1:227
αλαλαζω, I WAIL
Mk   5:38   people weeping and **wailing**
1C 13: 1   noisy gong or a **clanging** cymbal

---

215 ᴳᴼ1 ᴬᴳ34 ᴸᴺ9 ᴿ2980
αλαλητος, UNSPEAKABLE
Ro   8:26   with sighs **too deep for words.**

---

216 ᴳᴼ3 ᴬᴳ9 ᴿ2980
αλαλος, SPEECHLESS
Mk   7:37   to hear and the **mute** to speak.
     9:17   makes him **unable to speak;**
     9:25   **keeps** this boy **from speaking**

---

217 ᴳᴼ8 ᴬᴳ35 ᴸᴺ9 ᴮ3:443 ᴷ1:228
'αλας, SALT
Mt   5:13   You are the **salt** of the earth;
     5:13   if **salt** has lost its taste,
Mk   9:50   **Salt** is good; but if salt
     9:50   Salt is good; but if **salt**
     9:50   Have **salt** in yourselves,
Lk 14:34   **Salt** is good; but if salt
    14:34   if **salt** has lost its taste,
Co   4: 6   seasoned with **salt,** so that you

---

218 ᴳᴼ9 ᴬᴳ35 ᴸᴺ9 ᴮ1:119 ᴷ1:229
αλειφω, I SMEAR (ANOINT)
Mt   6:17   **put** oil on your head and wash
Mk   6:13   and **anointed** with oil many who
    16: 1   they might go and **anoint** him.
Lk   7:38   kissing his feet and **anointing**
     7:46   not **anoint** my head with oil,
     7:46   but she has **anointed** my
Jn 11: 2   Mary was the one who **anointed**
    12: 3   nard, **anointed** Jesus' feet,
Ja   5:14   pray over them, **anointing** them

---

219 ᴳᴼ1 ᴬᴳ35 ᴸᴺ9 ᴿ220,5456
αλεκτοροφωνια, ROOSTER-SOUNDING
Mk 13:35   or at midnight, or at **cockcrow,**

220   GO12   AG35   LN9
αλεκτωρ, ROOSTER
Mt 26:34   night, before the **cock** crows,
    26:74   At that moment the **cock** crowed.
    26:75   Before the **cock** crows,
Mk 14:30   before the **cock** crows twice,
    14:68   Then the **cock** crowed.
    14:72   At that moment the **cock** crowed
    14:72   Before the **cock** crows twice,
Lk 22:34   the **cock** will not crow this day
    22:60   still speaking, the **cock** crowed.
    22:61   Before the **cock** crows today
Jn 13:38   tell you, before the **cock** crows
    18:27   that moment the **cock** crowed.

221   GO2   AG35   LN9
αλεξανδρευς, ALEXANDRIAN
Ac   6: 9   Cyrenians, **Alexandrians,**
    18:24   a native of **Alexandria.**

222   GO2   AG35   LN9
αλεξανδρινος, ALEXANDRIAN
Ac 27: 6   centurion found an **Alexandrian**
    28:11   **Alexandrian** ship with the Twin

223   GO6   AG35   LN9
αλεξανδρος, ALEXANDER
Mk 15:21   Cyrene, the father of **Alexander**
Ac   4: 6   Caiaphas, John, and **Alexander,**
    19:33   gave instructions to **Alexander,**
    19:33   **Alexander** motioned for silence
1Ti 1:20   are Hymenaeus and **Alexander,**
2Ti 4:14   **Alexander** the coppersmith

224   GO2   AG35   LN9
αλευρον, FLOUR
Mt 13:33   with three measures of **flour**
Lk 13:21   with three measures of **flour**

225   GO109   AG35   LN9   B3:874   K1:232   R227
αληθεια, TRUTH
Mt 22:16   of God in accordance with **truth**
Mk   5:33   and told him the whole **truth.**
    12:14   God in accordance with **truth.**
    12:32   You are **right,** Teacher;
Lk   4:25   But the **truth** is, there were
    20:21   of God in accordance with **truth.**
    22:59   **Surely** this man also was with
Jn   1:14   son, full of grace and **truth.**
     1:17   grace and **truth** came through

     3:21   those who do what is **true**
     4:23   the Father in spirit and **truth,**
     4:24   worship in spirit and **truth.**
     5:33   he testified to the **truth.**
     8:32   and you will know the **truth,**
     8:32   the **truth** will make you free.
     8:40   man who has told you the **truth**
     8:44   does not stand in the **truth,**
     8:44   because there is no **truth**
     8:45   But because I tell the **truth,**
     8:46   If I tell the **truth,** why do you
    14: 6   I am the way, and the **truth,**
    14:17   This is the Spirit of **truth,**
    15:26   the Spirit of **truth** who comes
    16: 7   I tell you the **truth:** it is to
    16:13   When the Spirit of **truth** comes
    16:13   guide you into all **truth**
    17:17   Sanctify them in the **truth;**
    17:17   your word is **truth.**
    17:19   also may be sanctified in **truth**
    18:37   world, to testify to the **truth.**
    18:37   belongs to the **truth** listens
    18:38   asked him, "What is **truth?**"
Ac   4:27   For in this city, in **fact,**
    10:34   I **truly** understand that God
    26:25   I am speaking the sober **truth.**
Ro   1:18   wickedness suppress the **truth.**
     1:25   they exchanged the **truth** about
     2: 2   is in accordance with **truth.**
     2: 8   not the **truth** but wickedness,
     2:20   of knowledge and **truth,**
     3: 7   God's **truthfulness** abounds
     9: 1   speaking the **truth** in Christ
    15: 8   on behalf of the **truth** of God
1C   5: 8   bread of sincerity and **truth.**
    13: 6   but rejoices in the **truth.**
2C   4: 2   the open statement of the **truth**
     6: 7   **truthful** speech, and the power
     7:14   we said to you was **true,**
     7:14   Titus has proved **true** as well.
    11:10   As the **truth** of Christ is in me,
    12: 6   I will be speaking the **truth.**
    13: 8   do anything against the **truth,**
    13: 8   but only for the **truth.**
Ga   2: 5   so that the **truth** of the gospel
     2:14   with the **truth** of the gospel,
     5: 7   you from obeying the **truth?**
Ep   1:13   had heard the word of **truth,**
     4:21   in him, as **truth** is in Jesus.

	4:24	the likeness of God in **true**
	4:25	let all of us speak the **truth**
	5: 9	that is good and right and **true**
	6:14	fasten the belt of **truth**
Ph	1:18	out of false motives or **true;**
Co	1: 5	before in the word of the **truth**
	1: 6	heard it and **truly** comprehended
2Th	2:10	they refused to love the **truth**
	2:12	who have not believed the **truth**
	2:13	through belief in the **truth.**
1Ti	2: 4	to the knowledge of the **truth.**
	2: 7	apostle (I am telling the **truth**
	2: 7	the Gentiles in faith and **truth**
	3:15	pillar and bulwark of the **truth**
	4: 3	believe and know the **truth.**
	6: 5	and bereft of the **truth,**
2Ti	2:15	explaining the word of **truth.**
	2:18	who have swerved from the **truth**
	2:25	and come to know the **truth,**
	3: 7	at a knowledge of the **truth.**
	3: 8	faith, also oppose the **truth.**
	4: 4	from listening to the **truth**
Ti	1: 1	the knowledge of the **truth**
	1:14	those who reject the **truth.**
He	10:26	the knowledge of the **truth,**
Ja	1:18	birth by the word of **truth,**
	3:14	false to the **truth.**
	5:19	wanders from the **truth**
1P	1:22	by your obedience to the **truth**
2P	1:12	are established in the **truth**
	2: 2	way of **truth** will be maligned.
1J	1: 6	and do not do what is **true;**
	1: 8	and the **truth** is not in us.
	2: 4	the **truth** does not exist;
	2:21	you do not know the **truth,** but
	2:21	no lie comes from the **truth.**
	3:18	in word or speech, but in **truth**
	3:19	know that we are from the **truth**
	4: 6	we know the spirit of **truth**
	5: 6	for the Spirit is the **truth.**
2J	1: 1	whom I love in the **truth,**
	1: 1	but also all who know the **truth**
	1: 2	the **truth** that abides in us
	1: 3	Father's Son, in **truth** and love
	1: 4	children walking in the **truth,**
3J	1: 1	Gaius, whom I love in **truth.**
	1: 3	your faithfulness to the **truth,**
	1: 3	how you walk in the **truth.**
	1: 4	are walking in the **truth.**

| | 1: 8 | co-workers with the **truth.** |
| | 1:12 | and so has the **truth** itself. |

226   GO2   AG36   LN10   B3:874   K1:251   R227
αληθευω, I TELL TRUTH
| Ga | 4:16 | enemy by **telling** you the **truth?** |
| Ep | 4:15 | But **speaking** the **truth** in love, |

227   GO26   AG36   LN10   B3:874   K1:247
αληθης, TRUE
Mt	22:16	of God in accordance with **truth**
Mk	12:14	of God in accordance with **truth**
Jn	3:33	this, that God is **true.**
	4:18	What you have said is **true!**
	5:31	my testimony is not **true.**
	5:32	his testimony to me is **true.**
	6:55	for my flesh is **true** food
	6:55	and my blood is **true** drink.
	7:18	of him who sent him is **true,**
	8:13	your testimony is not **valid.**
	8:14	behalf, my testimony is **valid**
	8:17	of two witnesses is **valid.**
	8:26	but the one who sent me is **true**
	10:41	said about this man was **true.**
	19:35	knows that he tells the **truth.)**
	21:24	know that his testimony is **true.**
Ac	12: 9	with the angel's help was **real**
Ro	3: 4	let God be proved **true,**
2C	6: 8	impostors, and yet are **true;**
Ph	4: 8	whatever is **true,** whatever is
Ti	1:13	That testimony is **true.**
1P	5:12	this is the **true** grace of God.
2P	2:22	according to the **true** proverb
1J	2: 8	a new commandment that is **true**
	2:27	and is **true** and is not a lie,
3J	1:12	know that our testimony is **true**

228   GO28   AG37   LN10   B3:874   K1:249   R227
αληθινος, TRUE
Lk	16:11	entrust to you the **true** riches?
Jn	1: 9	The **true** light
	4:23	**true** worshipers will worship
	4:37	For here the saying holds **true,**
	6:32	the **true** bread from heaven.
	7:28	But the one who sent me is **true**
	8:16	my judgment is **valid**
	15: 1	I am the **true** vine, and my
	17: 3	may know you, the only **true** God
	19:35	His testimony is **true,** and he
1Th	1: 9	to serve a living and **true** God,

He 8: 2   the **true** tent that the Lord
    9:24   a mere copy of the **true** one,
   10:22   us approach with a **true** heart
1J 2: 8   a new commandment that is **true**
    5:20   we may know him who is **true**;
    5:20   and we are in him who is **true**,
    5:20   He is the **true** God and eternal
Re 3: 7   the **true** one, who has the key
    3:14   the faithful and **true** witness,
    6:10   Sovereign Lord, holy and **true**,
   15: 3   Just and **true** are your ways,
   16: 7   your judgments are **true** and just
   19: 2   his judgments are **true** and just
   19: 9   These are **true** words of God.
   19:11   is called Faithful and **True**,
   21: 5   words are trustworthy and **true**.
   22: 6   words are trustworthy and **true**,

---

229   GO2   AG37   LN10   R224
αληθω, I GRIND
Mt 24:41   Two women will be **grinding** meal
Lk 17:35   will be two women **grinding** meal

---

230   GO18   AG37   LN10   B3:874   R227
αληθως, TRULY
Mt 14:33   **Truly** you are the Son of God.
   26:73   **Certainly** you are also one of
   27:54   **Truly** this man was God's Son!
Mk 14:70   **Certainly** you are one of them;
   15:39   **Truly** this man was God's Son!
Lk 9:27   But **truly** I tell you, there are
   12:44   **Truly** I tell you, he will put
   21: 3   **Truly** I tell you, this poor
Jn 1:47   Here is **truly** an Israelite in
    4:42   **truly** the Savior of the world.
    6:14   This is **indeed** the prophet.
    7:26   the authorities **really** know
    7:40   This is **really** the prophet.
    8:31   you are **truly** my disciples;
   17: 8   and know **in truth** that I came
Ac 12:11   Now I am **sure** that the Lord
1Th 2:13   but as what it **really** is,
1J 2: 5   **truly** in this person the love

---

231   GO5   AG37   LN10
'αλιευς, FISHERMAN
Mt 4:18   for they were **fishermen**.
    4:19   will make you **fish** for people.
Mk 1:16   for they were **fishermen**.
    1:17   will make you **fish** for people.

Lk 5: 2   **fishermen** had gone out of them

---

232   GO1   AG37   LN10   R231
'αλιευω, I FISH
Jn 21: 3   I am going **fishing**.

---

233   GO2   AG37   LN10
'αλιζω, I SALT
Mt 5:13   can its **saltiness** be restored?
Mk 9:49   For everyone will be **salted**

---

234   GO1   AG37   LN10
αλισγημα, POLLUTIONS
Ac 15:20   things **polluted** by idols

---

235   GO638   AG38   LN10
αλλα, BUT [MULTIPLE OCCURRENCES]

---

236   GO6   AG39   LN10   B3:166   K1:251
αλλασσω, I CHANGE
Ac 6:14   will **change** the customs that
Ro 1:23   and they **exchanged** the glory of
1C 15:51   die, but we will all be **changed**
   15:52   and we will be **changed**.
Ga 4:20   and could **change** my tone, for
He 1:12   clothing they will be **changed**.

---

237   GO1   AG39   LN10
αλλαχοθεν, FROM ANOTHER
Jn 10: 1   but climbs in **by another** way

237a   GO1   AG39   LN10
αλλαχου, ELSEWHERE
Mk 1:38   Let us go **on** to the

---

238   GO1   AG39   LN10   B2:743   K1:260
αλληγορεω, I ALLEGORIZE
Ga 4:24   Now this is an **allegory**

---

239   GO4   AG39   LN10   B1:99   K1:264
'αλληλουια, HALLELUJAH
Re 19: 1   **Hallelujah!** Salvation and glory
   19: 3   more they said, "**Hallelujah!**
   19: 4   saying, "Amen. **Hallelujah!**"
   19: 6   **Hallelujah!** For the Lord our

---

240   GO100   AG39   LN10
αλληλων, ONE ANOTHER
Mt 24:10   they will betray one **another**
   24:10   another and hate one **another**.

	25:32	people one from **another** as a
Mk	4:41	said to one **another**, "Who then
	8:16	They said to one **another**,
	9:34	had argued with one **another**
	9:50	be at peace with one **another**.
	15:31	mocking him **among themselves**
Lk	2:15	shepherds said to one **another**,
	4:36	kept saying to one **another**,
	6:11	discussed with one **another**
	7:32	and calling to one **another**,
	8:25	and said to one **another**,
	12: 1	they trampled on one **another**,
	20:14	discussed it **among themselves**
	23:12	became friends with **each other**;
	24:14	and talking with **each other**
	24:17	you discussing with **each other**
	24:32	They said to **each other**,
Jn	4:33	disciples said to one **another**,
	5:44	accept glory from one **another**
	6:43	not complain **among yourselves**.
	6:52	disputed **among themselves**,
	11:56	were asking one **another**
	13:14	to wash one **another's** feet.
	13:22	disciples looked at one **another**
	13:34	that you love one **another**.
	13:34	also should love one **another**.
	13:35	you have love for one **another**.
	15:12	that you love one **another**
	15:17	that you may love one **another**.
	16:17	disciples said to one **another**,
	16:19	you discussing **among yourselves**
	19:24	So they said to one **another**,
Ac	4:15	the matter with one **another**.
	7:26	why do you wrong **each other**?
	15:39	sharp that they **parted company**;
	19:38	there against one **another**.
	21: 6	said farewell to one **another**.
	26:31	they said to one **another**,
	28: 4	they said to one **another**,
	28:25	they disagreed with **each other**;
Ro	1:12	by each **other's** faith, both
	1:27	with passion for one **another**.
	2:15	**their** conflicting thoughts will
	12: 5	we are members one of **another**.
	12:10	love one **another** with mutual
	12:10	outdo one **another** in showing
	12:16	in harmony with one **another**;
	13: 8	for the one who loves **another**
	14:13	pass judgment on one **another**,
	14:19	makes for peace and for **mutual**
	15: 5	live in harmony with one **another**
	15: 7	Welcome one **another**, therefore,
	15:14	able to instruct one **another**.
	16:16	Greet one **another** with a holy
1C	7: 5	Do not deprive one **another**
	11:33	to eat, wait for one **another**.
	12:25	the same care for one **another**.
	16:20	Greet one **another** with a holy
2C	13:12	Greet one **another** with a holy
Ga	5:13	become slaves to one **another**.
	5:15	bite and devour one **another**,
	5:15	are not consumed by one **another**
	5:17	these are opposed to **each other**
	5:26	competing against one **another**,
	5:26	another, envying one **another**.
	6: 2	Bear one **another's** burdens,
Ep	4: 2	bearing with one **another** in
	4:25	we are members of one **another**.
	4:32	forgiving one **another**, as God
	5:21	Be subject to one **another** out
Ph	2: 3	in humility regard **others**
Co	3: 9	Do not lie to one **another**,
	3:13	Bear with one **another** and, if
1Th	3:12	abound in love for one **another**
	4: 9	by God to love one **another**;
	4:18	Therefore encourage one **another**
	5:11	Therefore encourage one **another**
	5:15	seek to do good to one **another**
2Th	1: 3	for one **another** is increasing.
Ti	3: 3	despicable, hating one **another**.
He	10:24	to provoke one **another** to love
Ja	4:11	speak evil against one **another**,
	5: 9	not grumble against one **another**
	5:16	sins to one **another**, and pray
	5:16	pray for one **another**, so that
1P	1:22	love, love one **another** deeply
	4: 9	Be hospitable to one **another**
	5: 5	your dealings with one **another**,
	5:14	Greet one **another** with a kiss
1J	1: 7	fellowship with one **another**,
	3:11	that we should love one **another**
	3:23	love one **another**, just as he
	4: 7	Beloved, let us love one **another**
	4:11	also ought to love one **another**.
	4:12	we love one **another**, God lives
2J	1: 5	let us love one **another**.
Re	6: 4	would slaughter one **another**;
	11:10	celebrate and **exchange** presents

241   GO1 AG39 LN10 B1:684 K1:266 R243,1085
αλλογενης, OTHER RACE
Lk   17:18   to God except this **foreigner?**

---

242   GO3 AG39 LN10
αλλομαι, I LEAP
Jn   4:14   spring of water **gushing** up to
Ac   3: 8   with them, walking and **leaping**
      14:10   the man **sprang up** and began to

---

243   GO155 AG39 LN10 B2:739 K1:264
αλλος, OTHER [MULTIPLE OCCURENCES]

---

244   GO1 AG40 LN10 B2:742 K2:620 R245,1985
αλλοτριεπισκοπος, OVERSEER OF
            OTHERS
1P   4:15   or even as a **mischief maker.**

---

245   GO14 AG40 LN10 B1:684 K1:265 R243
αλλοτριος, OF ANOTHER
Mt   17:25   their children or **from others?**
     17:26   When Peter said, **"From**
              others,"
Lk   16:12   with what **belongs to another,**
Jn   10: 5   They will not follow a **stranger**
     10: 5   not know the voice of **strangers**
Ac   7: 6   a country **belonging** to **others,**
Ro   14: 4   judgment on servants of **another**
     15:20   do not build on **someone else's**
2C   10:15   labors of **others;** but our hope
     10:16   done in **someone else's** sphere
1Ti   5:22   in the sins of **others;** keep
He   9:25   with blood that is **not his own;**
     11: 9   promised, as in a **foreign** land,
     11:34   put **foreign** armies to flight.

---

246   GO1 AG41 LN10 B1:684 K1:267 R243,5443
αλλοφυλος, OTHER TRIBE
Ac   10:28   or to visit a **Gentile;** but God

---

247   GO1 AG41 LN10 B2:739 R243
αλλως, OTHERWISE
1Ti   5:25   and even when **they** are not,

---

248   GO3 AG41 LN10
αλοαω, I THRESH
1C   9: 9   an ox while it is **treading** out
      9:10   whoever **threshes** should
              thresh
1Ti   5:18   an ox while it is **treading** out

---

249   GO3 AG41 LN10 B3:1081 K4:141 R3056
αλογος, UNSPEAKING
Ac   25:27   for it seems to me **unreasonable**
2P   2:12   are like **irrational** animals,
Ju   1:10   like **irrational** animals, they

---

250   GO1 AG41 LN11
αλοη, ALOE
Jn   19:39   a mixture of myrrh and **aloes,**

---

252   GO1 AG41 LN11 B3:443
'αλυκος, SALT
Ja   3:12   No more can **salt** water yield

---

253   GO1 AG41 LN11 K4:323 R3077
αλυπος, NO GRIEF
Ph   2:28   and that I may be **less anxious.**

---

254   GO11 AG41 LN11
'αλυσις, CHAIN
Mk   5: 3   him any more, even with a **chain**
      5: 4   with shackles and **chains,** but
      5: 4   but the **chains** he wrenched apart
Lk   8:29   bound with **chains** and shackles,
Ac   12: 6   Peter, bound with two **chains,**
     12: 7   the **chains** fell off his wrists.
     21:33   him to be bound with two **chains**
     28:20   that I am bound with this **chain**
Ep   6:20   I am an ambassador in **chains.**
2Ti   1:16   was not ashamed of my **chain;**
Re   20: 1   pit and a great **chain.**

---

255   GO1 AG41 LN11
αλυσιτελης, UNPROFITABLE
He   13:17   that would be **harmful** to you.

255a   GO3 AG41 LN11
αλφα, ALPHA
Re   1: 8   I am the **Alpha** and the Omega,
     21: 6   I am the **Alpha** and the Omega,
     22:13   I am the **Alpha** and the Omega,

---

256   GO5 AG41 LN11
αλφαιος, ALPHAEUS
Mt   10: 3   James son of **Alphaeus,**
Mk   2:14   he saw Levi son of **Alphaeus**
      3:18   James son of **Alphaeus,**
Lk   6:15   James son of **Alphaeus,**
Ac   1:13   James son of **Alphaeus,**

257　GO2　AG41　LN11
αλων, THRESHING FLOOR
Mt　3:12　will clear his **threshing floor**
Lk　3:17　to clear his **threshing floor**

258　GO3　AG41　LN11
αλωπηξ, FOX
Mt　8:20　**Foxes** have holes, and birds of
Lk　9:58　**Foxes** have holes, and birds of
　　13:32　Go and tell that **fox** for me,

259　GO1　AG42　LN11
αλωσις, CAPTURE
2P　2:12　born to be **caught** and killed.

260　GO10　AG42　LN11
'αμα, AT SAME TIME
Mt　13:29　would uproot the wheat **along**
　　20: 1　went out **early** in the morning
Ac　24:26　At the **same time** he hoped that
　　27:40　At the **same time** they loosened
Ro　3:12　All have turned aside, **together**
Co　4: 3　At the **same time** pray for us as
1Th　4:17　up in the clouds **together**
　　5:10　asleep we may live **with** him.
1Ti　5:13　**Besides that,** they learn to be
Pm　1:22　One thing **more**—prepare a

261　GO1　AG42　LN11　R3129
αμαθης, UNLEARNED
2P　3:16　which the **ignorant** and unstable

262　GO1　AG42　LN11　R263
αμαραντινος, UNFADING
1P　5: 4　glory that never **fades** away.

263　GO1　AG42　LN11　R3133
αμαραντος, UNFADING
1P　1: 4　undefiled, and **unfading,** kept

264　GO43　AG42　LN11　B3:577　K1:267
'αμαρτανω, I SIN
Mt　18:15　of the church **sins** against you,
　　18:21　of the church **sins** against me,
　　27: 4　I have **sinned** by betraying
Lk　15:18　to him, "Father, I have **sinned**
　　15:21　I have **sinned** against heaven
　　17: 3　If another disciple **sins,** you
　　17: 4　same person **sins** against you
Jn　5:14　Do not **sin** any more, so that

　　8:11　from now on do not **sin** again.
　　9: 2　Rabbi, who **sinned,** this man or
　　9: 3　this man nor his parents **sinned**
Ac　25: 8　**committed** an **offense** against
Ro　2:12　All who have **sinned** apart from
　　2:12　all who have **sinned** under the
　　3:23　since all have **sinned** and fall
　　5:12　to all because all have **sinned**
　　5:14　those whose **sins** were not like
　　5:16　effect of the one man's **sin.**
　　6:15　Should we **sin** because we are
1C　6:18　fornicator **sins** against the
　　7:28　if you marry, you do not **sin,**
　　7:28　marries, she does not **sin.**
　　7:36　as he wishes; it is no **sin.**
　　8:12　But when you thus **sin** against
　　8:12　you **sin** against Christ.
　　15:34　right mind, and **sin** no more;
Ep　4:26　Be angry but do not **sin;**
1Ti　5:20　As for those who persist in **sin**
Ti　3:11　person is perverted and **sinful,**
He　3:17　Was it not those who **sinned,**
　　10:26　if we willfully persist in **sin**
1P　2:20　you are beaten for **doing wrong,**
2P　2: 4　angels when they **sinned,** but
1J　1:10　we say that we have not **sinned,**
　　2: 1　to you so that you may not **sin.**
　　2: 1　But if anyone does **sin,** we have
　　3: 6　No one who abides in him **sins;**
　　3: 6　no one who **sins** has either seen
　　3: 8　for the devil has been **sinning**
　　3: 9　they cannot **sin,** because they
　　5:16　brother or sister **committing**
　　5:16　those whose **sin** is not mortal.
　　5:18　who are born of God do not **sin,**

265　GO4　AG42　LN11　B3:577　K1:267　R264
'αμαρτημα, SIN
Mk　3:28　will be forgiven for their **sins**
　　3:29　but is guilty of an eternal **sin**
Ro　3:25　passed over the **sins** previously
1C　6:18　Every **sin** that a person commits.

266　GO173　AG43　LN11　B3:573　K1:267　R264
'αμαρτια, SIN
Mt　1:21　save his people from their **sins**
　　3: 6　Jordan, confessing their **sins.**
　　9: 2　Take heart, son; your **sins**
　　9: 5　Your **sins** are forgiven,

	9: 6	on earth to forgive **sins**			5:12	just as **sin** came into the world
	12:31	will be forgiven for every **sin**			5:12	and death came through **sin,**
	26:28	many for the forgiveness of **sins**			5:13	**sin** was indeed in the world
Mk	1: 4	for the forgiveness of **sins**			5:13	but **sin** is not reckoned when
	1: 5	Jordan, confessing their **sins**			5:20	where **sin** increased, grace
	2: 5	Son, your **sins** are forgiven.			5:21	just as **sin** exercised dominion
	2: 7	Who can forgive **sins** but God			6: 1	Should we continue in **sin** in
	2: 9	Your **sins** are forgiven,			6: 2	How can we who died to **sin** go
	2:10	on earth to forgive **sins**			6: 6	body of **sin** might be destroyed,
Lk	1:77	the forgiveness of their **sins.**			6: 6	no longer be enslaved to **sin.**
	3: 3	for the forgiveness of **sins,**			6: 7	has died is freed from **sin.**
	5:20	Friend, your **sins** are forgiven			6:10	death he died, he died to **sin,**
	5:21	Who can forgive **sins** but God			6:11	dead to **sin** and alive to God
	5:23	Your **sins** are forgiven you,			6:12	not let **sin** exercise dominion
	5:24	on earth to forgive **sins**			6:13	members to **sin** as instruments
	7:47	her **sins,** which were many,			6:14	For **sin** will have no dominion
	7:48	to her, "Your **sins** are forgiven			6:16	**sin,** which leads to death,
	7:49	is this who even forgives **sins?**			6:17	having once been slaves of **sin,**
	11: 4	forgive us our **sins,** for we			6:18	from **sin,** have become slaves
	24:47	forgiveness of **sins** is to be			6:20	When you were slaves of **sin,**
Jn	1:29	God who takes away the **sin** of			6:22	you have been freed from **sin**
	8:21	but you will die in your **sin.**			6:23	For the wages of **sin** is death,
	8:24	that you would die in your **sins**			7: 5	our **sinful** passions, aroused by
	8:24	for you will die in your **sins**			7: 7	we say? That the law is **sin?**
	8:34	everyone who commits **sin** is a			7: 7	I would not have known **sin.**
	8:34	commits sin is a slave to **sin.**			7. 8	But **sin,** seizing an opportunity
	8:46	Which of you convicts me of **sin?**			7: 8	from the law **sin** lies dead.
	9:34	You were born entirely in **sins,**			7: 9	commandment came, **sin** revived
	9:41	you would not have **sin.** But now			7:11	**sin,** seizing an opportunity
	9:41	your **sin** remains.			7:13	It was **sin,** working death in me
	15:22	they would not have **sin;**			7:13	**sin** might be shown to be sin,
	15:22	have no excuse for their **sin.**			7:13	might be shown to be **sin**
	15:24	they would not have **sin.**			7:14	sold into slavery under **sin.**
	16: 8	the world wrong about **sin** and			7:17	but **sin** that dwells within me.
	16: 9	about **sin,** because they do not			7:20	but **sin** that dwells within me.
	19:11	is guilty of a greater **sin.**			7:23	law of **sin** that dwells in my
	20:23	If you forgive the **sins** of any,			7:25	I am a slave to the law of **sin.**
Ac	2:38	your **sins** may be forgiven;			8: 2	you free from the law of **sin**
	3:19	turn to God so that your **sins**			8: 3	in the likeness of **sinful** flesh
	5:31	Israel and forgiveness of **sins.**			8: 3	and to deal with **sin,**
	7:60	do not hold this **sin** against			8: 3	he condemned **sin** in the flesh,
	10:43	receives forgiveness of **sins**			8:10	body is dead because of **sin,**
	13:38	this man forgiveness of **sins**			11:27	when I take away their **sins.**
	22:16	and have your **sins** washed away,			14:23	not proceed from faith is **sin.**
	26:18	forgiveness of **sins** and a place		1C	15: 3	that Christ died for our **sins**
Ro	3: 9	are under the power of **sin,**			15:17	you are still in your **sins.**
	3:20	law comes the knowledge of **sin.**			15:56	The sting of death is **sin,**
	4: 7	and whose **sins** are covered;			15:56	the power of **sin** is the law.
	4: 8	the Lord will not reckon **sin.**		2C	5:21	he made him to be **sin** who knew

	5:21	who knew no **sin**, so that in him
	11: 7	**sin** by humbling myself
Ga	1: 4	for our **sins** to set us free
	2:17	Christ then a servant of **sin?**
	3:22	things under the power of **sin**,
Ep	2: 1	through the trespasses and **sins**
Co	1:14	the forgiveness of **sins.**
1Th	2:16	the measure of their **sins**;
1Ti	5:22	do not participate in the **sins**
	5:24	The **sins** of some people are
2Ti	3: 6	overwhelmed by their **sins** and
He	1: 3	had made purification for **sins**,
	2:17	atonement for the **sins** of the
	3:13	by the deceitfulness of **sin.**
	4:15	as we are, yet without **sin.**
	5: 1	gifts and sacrifices for **sins.**
	5: 3	sacrifice for his own **sins**
	7:27	first for his own **sins**, and
	8:12	I will remember their **sins** no
	9:26	to remove **sin** by the sacrifice
	9:28	offered once to bear the **sins**
	9:28	to deal with **sin,** but to save
	10: 2	have any consciousness of **sin?**
	10: 3	reminder of **sin** year after year
	10: 4	and goats to take away **sins.**
	10: 6	in burnt offerings and **sin**
	10: 8	burnt offerings and **sin**
	10:11	that can never take away **sins.**
	10:12	a single sacrifice for **sins,**
	10:17	I will remember their **sins**
	10:18	no longer any offering for **sin.**
	10:26	if we willfully persist in **sin**
	11:25	the fleeting pleasures of **sin.**
	12: 1	the **sin** that clings so closely,
	12: 4	In your struggle against **sin**
Ja	1:15	it gives birth to **sin,**
	1:15	**sin,** when it is fully grown,
	2: 9	show partiality, you commit **sin**
	4:17	and fails to do it, commits **sin**
	5:15	anyone who has committed **sins**
	5:16	Therefore confess your **sins** to
	5:20	will cover a multitude of **sins.**
1P	2:22	He committed no **sin,** and no
	2:24	He himself bore our **sins** in
	2:24	so that, free from **sins,** we
	3:18	Christ also suffered for **sins**
	4: 1	the flesh has finished with **sin**
	4: 8	love covers a multitude of **sins**
2P	1: 9	of the cleansing of past **sins.**

	2:14	adultery, insatiable for **sin.**
1J	1: 7	Son cleanses us from all **sin.**
	1: 8	If we say that we have no **sin,**
	1: 9	If we confess our **sins,**
	1: 9	forgive us our **sins** and cleanse
	2: 2	atoning sacrifice for our **sins,**
	2:12	**sins** are forgiven on account of
	3: 4	who commits **sin** is guilty of
	3: 4	lawlessness; **sin** is lawlessness
	3: 5	was revealed to take away **sins,**
	3: 5	and in him there is no **sin.**
	3: 8	who commits **sin** is a child of
	3: 9	born of God do not **sin,** because
	4:10	atoning sacrifice for our **sins.**
	5:16	not a mortal **sin,** you will ask,
	5:16	There is **sin** that is mortal;
	5:17	All wrongdoing is **sin,** but
	5:17	there is **sin** that is not mortal
Re	1: 5	freed us from our **sins** by his
	18: 4	do not take part in her **sins,**
	18: 5	for her **sins** are heaped high as

---

267   GO1   AG44   LN11   R3144
αμαρτυρος, WITHOUT WITNESS
Ac 14:17   left himself **without a witness**

---

268   GO47   AG44   LN11   B3:577   K1:317   R264
'αμαρτωλος, SINNER
Mt	9:10	many tax collectors and **sinners**
	9:11	with tax collectors and **sinners**
	9:13	not the righteous but **sinners.**
	11:19	tax collectors and **sinners**
	26:45	into the hands of **sinners.**
Mk	2:15	many tax collectors and **sinners**
	2:16	eating with **sinners** and tax
	2:16	eat with tax collectors and **sinners?"**
	2:17	not the righteous but **sinners.**
	8:38	adulterous and **sinful** generation,
	14:41	into the hands of **sinners.**
Lk	5: 8	Lord, for I am a **sinful** man!
	5:30	with tax collectors and **sinners**
	5:32	but **sinners** to repentance.
	6:32	For even **sinners** love those who
	6:33	For even **sinners** do the same.
	6:34	Even **sinners** lend to sinners,
	6:34	Even sinners lend to **sinners,**
	7:34	of tax collectors and **sinners!**
	7:37	who was a **sinner,**
	7:39	that she is a **sinner.**

13: 2 they were worse **sinners** than
15: 1 tax collectors and **sinners**
15: 2 This fellow welcomes **sinners**
15: 7 over one **sinner** who repents
15:10 over one **sinner** who repents.
18:13 be merciful to me, a **sinner!**
19: 7 guest of one who is a **sinner.**
24: 7 handed over to **sinners,** and be
Jn 9:16 How can a man who is a **sinner**
9:24 know that this man is a **sinner.**
9:25 not know whether he is a **sinner.**
9:31 God does not listen to **sinners,**
Ro 3: 7 being condemned as a **sinner?**
5: 8 while we still were **sinners**
5:19 the many were made **sinners,**
7:13 might become **sinful** beyond
Ga 2:15 birth and not Gentile **sinners;**
2:17 have been found to be **sinners,**
1Ti 1: 9 for the godless and **sinful,**
1:15 into the world to save **sinners**
He 7:26 separated from **sinners,**
12: 3 against himself from **sinners,**
Ja 4: 8 Cleanse your hands, you **sinners**
5:20 whoever brings back a **sinner**
1P 4:18 the ungodly and the **sinners?**
Ju 1:15 things that ungodly **sinners**

269 GO2 AG44 LN11 K4:527 R3163
αμαχος, NON-FIGHTER
1Ti 3: 3 not a drunkard, **not violent** but
Ti 3: 2 **avoid quarreling,** to be gentle,

270 GO1 AG44 LN11
αμαω, I REAP
Ja 5: 4 laborers who **mowed** your fields,

271 GO1 AG44 LN11 B3:396
αμεθυστος, AMEYTHYST
Re 21:20 jacinth, the twelfth **amethyst.**

272 GO4 AG44 LN11 R3199
αμελεω, I CARE NOT
Mt 22: 5 But they **made light** of it and
1Ti 4:14 Do not **neglect** the gift that
He 2: 3 how can we escape if we **neglect**
8: 9 so I **had no concern** for them,

273 GO5 AG45 LN11 B2:143 K4:571 R3201
αμεμπτος, FAULTLESS
Lk 1: 6 before God, living **blamelessly**

Ph 2:15 so that you may be **blameless**
3: 6 under the law, **blameless.**
1Th 3:13 that you may be **blameless**
He 8: 7 covenant had been **faultless,**

274 GO2 AG45 LN11 B2:143 R273
αμεμπτως, FAULTLESSLY
1Th 2:10 and **blameless** our conduct was
5:23 be kept sound and **blameless** at

275 GO2 AG45 LN11 K4:593 R3308
αμεριμνος, UNANXIOUS
Mt 28:14 **keep you out of trouble**
1C 7:32 I want you **to be free** from

276 GO2 AG45 LN11
αμεταθετος, IRREVOCABLE
He 6:17 the **unchangeable** character
6:18 that through two **unchangeable**

277 GO1 AG45 LN11
αμετακινητος, UNMOVEABLE
1C 15:58 **immovable,** always excelling

278 GO2 AG45 LN12 B1:356 K4:629
αμεταμελητως, I CARE NOT
Ro 11:29 calling of God are **irrevocable.**
2C 7:10 brings **no regret,** but worldly

279 GO1 AG45 LN12 B1:357 K4:1009
αμετανοητος, UNCHANGED MIND
Ro 2: 5 your hard and **impenitent** heart

280 GO2 AG45 LN12 K4:632 R3358
αμετρος, UNMEASUREABLE
2C 10:13 will not boast **beyond limits,**
10:15 We do not boast **beyond limits,**

281 GO129 AG45 LN12 B1:97 K1:335
αμην, AMEN [MULTIPLE OCCURRENCES]

282 GO1 AG46 LN12 R3384
αμητωρ, NO MOTHER
He 7: 3 Without father, **without**
mother,

283 GO4 AG46 LN12 B1:447 K4:647 R3392
αμιαντος, UNDEFILED
He 7:26 holy, blameless, **undefiled,**
13: 4 marriage bed be kept **undefiled;**

Ja　1:27　pure and **undefiled** before God,
1P　1: 4　**undefiled,** and unfading, kept

284　GO3　AG46　LN12
αμιναδαβ, AMINADAB
Mt　1: 4　and Aram the father of **Aminadab**
　　1: 4　**Aminadab** the father of Nahshon
Lk　3:33　son of **Amminadab,** son of Admin

285　GO5　AG46　LN12
αμμος, SAND
Mt　7:26　man who built his house on **sand**
Ro　9:27　were like the **sand** of the sea,
He　11:12　the innumerable grains of **sand**
Re　12:18　took his stand on the **sand** of
　　20: 8　as the **sands** of the sea.

286　GO4　AG46　LN12　B2:410　K1:338
αμνος, LAMB
Jn　1:29　**Lamb** of God who takes away the
　　1:36　Look, here is the **Lamb** of God!
Ac　8:32　**lamb** silent before its shearer,
1P　1:19　**lamb** without defect or blemish.

287　GO1　AG46　LN12
αμοιβη, RETURNS
1Ti　5: 4　some **repayment** to their parents

288　GO9　AG46　LN12　B3:918　K1:342
αμπελος, VINE
Mt　26:29　drink of this fruit of the **vine**
Mk　14:25　drink of the fruit of the **vine**
Lk　22:18　drink of the fruit of the **vine**
Jn　15: 1　I am the true **vine,** and my
　　15: 4　unless it abides in the **vine,**
　　15: 5　I am the **vine,** you are the
Ja　3:12　olives, or a **grapevine** figs?
Re　14:18　clusters of the **vine** of the
　　14:19　gathered the **vintage** of the

289　GO1　AG47　LN12　B3:919　R288,2041
αμπελουργος, VINEYARD WORKER
Lk　13: 7　So he said to the **gardener,**

290　GO23　AG47　LN12　B3:918　R288
αμπελων, VINEYARD
Mt　20: 1　hire laborers for his **vineyard.**
　　20: 2　he sent them into his **vineyard.**
　　20: 4　You also go into the **vineyard,**
　　20: 7　You also go into the **vineyard.**

20: 8　the owner of the **vineyard** said
21:28　and work in the **vineyard** today.
21:33　planted a **vineyard,** put a fence
21:39　threw him out of the **vineyard,**
21:40　when the owner of the **vineyard**
21:41　lease the **vineyard** to other
Mk　12: 1　A man planted a **vineyard,**
　　12: 2　of the produce of the **vineyard.**
　　12: 8　threw him out of the **vineyard.**
　　12: 9　will the owner of the **vineyard**
　　12: 9　give the **vineyard** to others.
Lk　13: 6　tree planted in his **vineyard;**
　　20: 9　A man planted a **vineyard,**
　　20:10　of the produce of the **vineyard;**
　　20:13　Then the owner of the **vineyard**
　　20:15　threw him out of the **vineyard**
　　20:15　will the owner of the **vineyard**
　　20:16　give the **vineyard** to others.
1C　9: 7　Who plants a **vineyard** and does

291　GO1　AG47　LN12
αμπλιατος, AMPLIATUS
Ro　16: 8　Greet **Ampliatus,** my beloved

292　GO1　AG47　LN12
αμυνομαι, I DEFEND
Ac　7:24　he **defended** the oppressed man

292a　GO1　AG47　LN12
αμφιβαλλω, I THROW AROUND
Mk　1:16　brother Andrew **casting** a net

293　GO1　AG47　LN12
αμφιβληστρον, THROWN AROUND (NET)
Mt　4:18　his brother, casting a **net** into

293a　GO1　AG47　LN12
αμφιαζω, I CLOTHE
Lk　12:28　much more will he **clothe** you—

294　GO3　AG47　LN12
αμφιεννυμι, I DRESS
Mt　6:30　he not much more **clothe** you
　　11: 8　Someone **dressed** in soft robes?
Lk　7:25　Someone **dressed** in soft robes?

295　GO1　AG47　LN12
αμφιπολις, AMPHIPOLIS
Ac　17: 1　had passed through **Amphipolis**

296 GO1 AG47 LN12
αμφοδον, STREET
Mk 11: 4 a door, outside in the **street.**

---

297 GO14 AG47 LN12
αμφοτεροι, BOTH
Mt   9:17 and so **both** are preserved.
      13:30 Let **both** of them grow together
      15:14 **both** will fall into a pit.
Lk   1: 6 **Both** of them were righteous
      1: 7 **both** were getting on in years.
      5: 7 they came and filled **both** boats
      6:39 Will not **both** fall into a pit?
      7:42 canceled the debts for **both** of
Ac   8:38 **both** of them, Philip and the
      19:16 and so overpowered **them** that
      23: 8 Pharisees acknowledge **all** three
Ep   2:14 he has made **both** groups into
      2:16 and might reconcile **both** groups
      2:18 for through him **both** of us have

---

298 GO1 AG47 LN12 B3:923 K4:831 R3469
αμωμητος, BLAMELESS
2P   3:14 without spot or **blemish;**

298a GO1 AG47 LN12
αμωμον, SPICE
Re 18:13 cinnamon, **spice,** incense, myrrh.

---

299 GO7 AG47 LN12 B3:923 K4:830 R3470
αμωμος, BLAMELESS
Ep   1: 4 holy and **blameless** before him
      5:27 may be holy and **without**
              blemish
Ph   2:15 children of God **without blemish**
Co   1:22 present you holy and **blameless**
He   9:14 offered himself **without blemish**
1P   1:19 lamb without defect or **blemish.**
Ju   1:24 make you stand **without blemish**
Re 14: 5 was found; they are **blameless.**

---

301 GO3 AG48 LN12
αμως, AMOS
Mt   1:10 and Manasseh the father of **Amos**
      1:10 and **Amos** the father of Josiah,
Lk   3:25 son of **Amos,** son of Nahum,

---

302 GO166 AG48 LN12
αν, "UNTRANSLATABLE PARTICLE"
[MULTIPLE OCCURRENCES]

303 GO13 AG49 LN13 B3:1172
ανα, AMONG, EACH
Mt 13:25 sowed weeds **among** the wheat,
      20: 9 received the **usual** daily wage.
      20:10 received the **usual** daily wage.
Mk   7:31 **in** the region of the Decapolis.
Lk   9: 3 not even an **extra** tunic.
      9:14 there were **about** five thousand
      10: 1 sent them on **ahead** of him in
Jn   2: 6 **each** holding twenty or thirty
1C   6: 5 to decide **between** one believer
      14:27 at most three, and **each** in turn
Re   4: 8 **each** of them with six wings,
      7:17 for the Lamb at the **center** of
      21:21 **each** of the gates is a single

---

304 GO2 AG50 LN13
αναβαθμος, STAIRS
Ac 21:35 When Paul came to the **steps,**
      21:40 Paul stood on the **steps** and

---

305 GO82 AG50 LN13 B2:42 K1:519
αναβαινω, I GO UP
Mt   3:16 as he **came** up from the water,
      5: 1 he **went** up the mountain; and
      13: 7 the thorns **grew** up and choked
      14:23 he **went** up the mountain by
      14:32 When they **got** into the boat,
      15:29 he **went** up the mountain
      17:27 take the first fish that **comes**
      20:17 While Jesus was **going** up to
      20:18 we are **going** up to Jerusalem,
Mk   1:10 just as he was **coming** up out
      3:13 He **went** up the mountain and
      4: 7 the thorns **grew** up and choked
      4: 8 **growing** up and increasing and
      4:32 when it is sown it **grows** up
      6:51 he **got** into the boat with them
      10:32 **going** up to Jerusalem, and
      10:33 we are **going** up to Jerusalem,
      15: 8 the crowd **came** and began to ask
Lk   2: 4 Joseph also **went** from the town
      2:42 they **went** up as usual for the
      5:19 they **went** up on the roof and
      9:28 and **went** up on the mountain to
      18:10 Two men **went** up to the temple
      18:31 we are **going** up to Jerusalem,
      19: 4 So he ran ahead and **climbed** a
      19:28 **going** up to Jerusalem.
      24:38 why do doubts **arise** in your

Jn	1:51	the angels of God **ascending** and
	2:13	and Jesus **went** up to Jerusalem.
	3:13	No one has **ascended** into heaven
	5: 1	Jesus **went** up to Jerusalem.
	6:62	see the Son of Man **ascending**
	7: 8	I am not **going** to this festival,
	7: 8	my time has not yet fully **come**
	7:10	But after his brothers had **gone**
	7:10	then he also **went,** not publicly
	7:14	Jesus **went** up into the temple
	10: 1	but **climbs** in by another way is
	11:55	many **went** up from the country
	12:20	Now among those who **went** up to
	20:17	I have not yet **ascended** to the
	20:17	I am **ascending** to my Father
	21:11	So Simon Peter **went aboard** and
Ac	1:13	they **went** to the room upstairs
	2:34	For David did not **ascend** into
	3: 1	Peter and John were **going** up to
	7:23	it **came** into his heart to visit
	8:31	he invited Philip to **get** in and
	8:39	they **came** up out of the water,
	10: 4	have **ascended** as a memorial
	10: 9	Peter **went** up on the roof to
	11: 2	when Peter **went** up to Jerusalem
	15: 2	others were appointed to **go** up
	18:22	he **went** up to Jerusalem and
	20:11	Then Paul **went** upstairs, and
	21: 6	Then we **went** on board the ship,
	21:12	urged him not to **go** up to
	21:15	started to **go** up to Jerusalem.
	21:31	word **came** to the tribune of the
	24:11	days since I **went** up to worship
	25: 1	he **went** up from Caesarea to
	25: 9	you wish to **go** up to Jerusalem
Ro	10: 6	Who will **ascend** into heaven?
1C	2: 9	nor the human heart **conceived,**
Ga	2: 1	I **went** up again to Jerusalem
	2: 2	I **went** up in response to a
Ep	4: 8	When he **ascended** on high he
	4: 9	When it says, "He **ascended,**"
	4:10	the same one who **ascended** far
Re	4: 1	**Come** up here, and I will show
	7: 2	another angel **ascending** from the
	8: 4	**rose** before God from the hand
	9: 2	from the shaft **rose** smoke like
	11: 7	the beast that **comes** up from
	11:12	saying to them, "**Come** up here!"
	11:12	And they **went** up to heaven in a

	13: 1	And I saw a beast **rising** out of
	13:11	saw another beast that **rose** out
	14:11	the smoke of their torment **goes**
	17: 8	and is about to **ascend** from the
	19: 3	.The smoke **goes** up from her
	20: 9	They **marched** up over the

306 GO1 AG50 LN13 R303,906
αναβαλλω, I SEND UP
Ac 24:22 **adjourned** the hearing with the

307 GO1 AG50 LN13
αναβιβαζω, I BRING UP
Mt 13:48 they **drew** it ashore, sat down,

308 GO25 AG50 LN13 R303,991
αναβλεπω, I LOOK UP, I SEE AGAIN

Mt	11: 5	the blind **receive** their **sight,**
	14:19	he **looked** up to heaven, and
	20:34	Immediately they **regained** their
Mk	6:41	he **looked** up to heaven, and
	7:34	Then **looking** up to heaven, he
	8:24	And the man **looked** up and said,
	10:51	My teacher, let me **see again.**
	10:52	he **regained** his **sight** and
	16: 4	When they **looked** up, they saw
Lk	7:22	the blind **receive** their **sight,**
	9:16	he **looked** up to heaven, and
	18:41	Lord, let me **see again.**
	18:42	**Receive** your **sight;** your
	18:43	he **regained** his **sight** and
	19: 5	he **looked** up and said to him,
	21: 1	He **looked** up and saw rich
Jn	9:11	washed and **received** my **sight**
	9:15	**received** his **sight.** He said to
	9:18	and had **received** his **sight**
	9:18	man who had **received** his **sight**
Ac	9:12	he might **regain** his **sight.**
	9:17	you may **regain** your **sight**
	9:18	and his **sight** was **restored.**
	22:13	Saul, **regain** your **sight!**
	22:13	Saul, **regain** your **sight!**

309 GO1 AG51 LN13 R308
αναβλεψις, SEE AGAIN
Lk 4:18 **recovery** of **sight** to the blind,

310 GO1 AG51 LN13 B1:410 R303,994
αναβοαω, I SHOUT OUT
Mt 27:46 Jesus **cried** with a loud voice,

311 GO1 AG51 LN13 R306
αναβολη, NO DELAY
Ac 25:17 I **lost no time,** but on the next

311a GO2 AG51 LN13
αναγαιον, UPSTAIRS ROOM
Mk 14:15 show you a **large room upstairs**
Lk 22:12 show you a **large room upstairs**

---

312 GO14 AG51 LN13 B3:44 K1:61 R303,31a
αναγγελλω, I DECLARE
Jn 4:25 When he comes, he will **proclaim**
    5:15 man went away and **told** the Jews
    16:13 he will **declare** to you
    16:14 is mine and **declare** it to you.
    16:15 is mine and **declare** it to you.
Ac 14:27 **related** all that God had done
    15: 4 they **reported** all that God had
    19:18 and **disclosed** their practices.
    20:20 **proclaiming** the message to you
    20:27 I did not shrink from **declaring**
Ro 15:21 been **told** of him shall see,
2C 7: 7 as he **told** us of your longing,
1P 1:12 have now been **announced** to you
1J 1: 5 heard from him and **proclaim** to

---

313 GO2 AG51 LN13 B1:176 K1:673 R303,1080
αναγεννναω, I GIVE BIRTH AGAIN
1P 1: 3 he has **given** us a **new birth**
    1:23 You have **been born anew,** not of

---

314 GO32 AG51 LN13 B1:245 K1:343
αναγινωσκω, I READ
Mt 12: 3 Have you not **read** what David
    12: 5 have you not **read** in the law
    19: 4 Have you not **read** that the one
    21:16 Yes; have you never **read,**
    21:42 Have you never **read** in the
    22:31 have you not **read** what was
    24:15 let the **reader** understand
Mk 2:25 Have you never **read** what
    12:10 Have you not **read** this
    12:26 have you not **read** in the book
    13:14 let the **reader** understand
Lk 4:16 He stood up to **read,**
    6: 3 Have you not **read** what David
    10:26 What do you **read** there?
Jn 19:20 Many of the Jews **read** this
Ac 8:28 he was **reading** the prophet
    8:30 heard him **reading** the prophet

    8:30 what you are **reading**
    8:32 scripture that he was **reading**
    13:27 prophets that are **read** every
    15:21 for he has been **read** aloud
    15:31 When its members **read** it,
    23:34 On **reading** the letter, he asked
2C 1:13 what you can **read** and also
    3: 2 to be known and **read** by all;
    3:15 whenever Moses is **read,** a veil
Ep 3: 4 a **reading** of which will enable
Co 4:16 when this letter has been **read**
    4:16 have it **read** also in the church
    4:16 that you **read** also the letter
1Th 5:27 letter be **read** to all of them.
Re 1: 3 Blessed is the one who **reads**

---

315 GO9 AG52 LN13 K1:344 R318
αναγκαζω, I COMPEL
Mt 14:22 he **made** the disciples get into
Mk 6:45 he **made** his disciples get into
Lk 14:23 and **compel** people to come in,
Ac 26:11 I tried to **force** them to
    28:19 I was **compelled** to appeal
2C 12:11 You **forced** me to it. Indeed you
Ga 2: 3 not **compelled** to be circumcised
    2:14 how can you **compel** the Gentiles
    6:12 flesh that try to **compel** you

---

316 GO8 AG52 LN13 B2:663 K1:344 R318
αναγκαιος, NECESSARY
Ac 10:24 his relatives and **close** friends
    13:46 It was **necessary** that the word
1C 12:22 to be weaker are **indispensable**
2C 9: 5 I thought it **necessary** to urge
Ph 1:24 in the flesh is more **necessary**
    2:25 I think it **necessary** to send to
Ti 3:14 in order to meet **urgent** needs,
He 8: 3 it is **necessary** for this priest

---

317 GO1 AG52 LN13 B2:663 R315
αναγκαστως, BY COMPULSION
1P 5: 2 not under **compulsion** but

---

318 GO17 AG52 LN13 B2:663 K1:344
αναγκη, NECESSITY
Mt 18: 7 for stumbling are **bound**
         to **come**
Lk 14:18 and I **must** go out and see it
    21:23 there will be great **distress**
Ro 13: 5 Therefore one **must** be subject

1C	7:26	in view of the impending **crisis**
	7:37	being under no **necessity** but
	9:16	for an **obligation** is laid on me
2C	6: 4	in afflictions, **hardships,**
	9: 7	reluctantly or under **compulsion**
	12:10	weaknesses, insults, **hardships,**
1Th	3: 7	during all our **distress**
Pm	1:14	and not something **forced.**
He	7:12	there is **necessarily** a change
	7:27	has no **need** to offer sacrifices
	9:16	who made it **must** be established
	9:23	Thus it was **necessary** for the
Ju	1: 3	I find it **necessary** to write

319   GO1   AG52   LN13   R303,1107
αναγνωριζω, I MAKE KNOWN
| Ac | 7:13 | Joseph **made** himself **known** to |

320   GO3   AG52   LN13   B1:245   K1:343   R314
αναγνωσις, READING
Ac	13:15	After the **reading** of the law
2C	3:14	when they hear the **reading** of
1Ti	4:13	to the public **reading** of

321   GO23   AG53   LN13   R303,71
αναγω, I LEAD/BRING UP
Mt	4: 1	Jesus was **led** up by the Spirit
Lk	2:22	they **brought** him up to
	4: 5	Then the devil **led** him up and
	8:22	So they **put** out,
Ac	7:41	**offered** a sacrifice to the idol
	9:39	they **took** him to the room
	12: 4	intending to **bring** him out to
	13:13	his companions **set sail** from
	16:11	We **set sail** from Troas and took
	16:34	**brought** them up into the house
	18:21	Then he **set sail** from Ephesus.
	20: 3	was about to **set sail** for Syria
	20:13	the ship and **set sail** for Assos
	21: 1	parted from them and **set sail,**
	21: 2	we went on board and **set sail.**
	27: 2	coast of Asia, we **put** to sea,
	27: 4	**Putting out to sea** from there,
	27:12	of **putting** to sea from there,
	27:21	not have **set sail** from Crete
	28:10	when we were about to **sail,**
	28:11	Three months later we **set sail**
Ro	10: 7	that is, to **bring** Christ up
He	13:20	who **brought** back from the
		dead

322   GO2   AG53   LN13   B3:569   K2:30   R303,1166
αναδεικνυμι, I SHOW UP
| Lk | 10: 1 | Lord **appointed** seventy others |
| Ac | 1:24 | **Show** us which one of these two |

323   GO1   AG53   LN14   B3:569   K2:31   R322
αναδειξις, SHOWING UP
| Lk | 1:80 | the day he **appeared publicly** |

324   GO2   AG53   LN14   R303,1209
αναδεχομαι, I WELCOME AGAIN
| Ac | 28: 7 | who **received** us and entertained |
| He | 11:17 | who had **received** the promises |

325   GO1   AG53   LN14   R303,1325
αναδιδωμι, I GIVE UP
| Ac | 23:33 | and **delivered** the letter to the |

326   GO2   AG53   LN14   B3:259   K2:872   R303,2198
αναζαω, I LIVE AGAIN
| Lk | 15:24 | was dead and is **alive again;** |
| Ro | 7: 9 | commandment came, sin **revived** |

327   GO3   AG53   LN14   R303,2212
αναζητεω, I SEEK AFTER
Lk	2:44	Then they started to **look** for
	2:45	returned to Jerusalem to **search**
Ac	11:25	Barnabas went to Tarsus to **look**

328   GO1   AG53   LN14   R303,2224
αναζωννυμι, I BIND UP
| 1P | 1:13 | **prepare** your minds for action |

329   GO1   AG54   LN14   R303,4442
αναζωπυρεω, I FIRE AGAIN TO LIFE
| 2Ti | 1: 6 | remind you to **rekindle** the gift |

330   GO1   AG54   LN14
αναθαλλω, I REVIVE
| Ph | 4:10 | you have **revived** your concern |

331   GO6   AG54   LN14   B1:413   K1:354
αναθεμα, CURSE
Ac	23:14	bound ourselves by an **oath** to
Ro	9: 3	myself were **accursed** and cut
1C	12: 3	Let Jesus be **cursed!**
	16:22	be **accursed** who has no love
Ga	1: 8	let that one be **accursed!**
	1: 9	let that one be **accursed!**

332 GO4 AG54 LN14 B1:413 K1:355 R331
αναθεματιζω, I SWEAR A CURSE
Mk 14:71 he began to **curse,** and he swore
Ac 23:12 **bound** themselves by an **oath**
    23:14 **bound** ourselves by an **oath**
    23:21 **bound** themselves by an **oath**

---

333 GO2 AG54 LN14 R303,2334
αναθεωρεω, I WATCH AGAIN
Ac 17:23 **looked carefully** at the objects
He 13: 7 **consider** the outcome of their

---

334 GO1 AG54 LN14 B1:413 K1:354
αναθημα, DEDICATION
Lk 21: 5 gifts **dedicated** to God, he said

---

335 GO1 AG54 LN14
αναιδεια, SHAMELESSNESS
Lk 11: 8 his **persistence** he will get up

---

336 GO1 AG54 LN14 R337
αναιρεσις, KILLING
Ac   8: 1 Saul approved of their **killing**

---

337 GO24 AG54 LN14
αναιρεω, I KILL
Mt   2:16 he sent and **killed** all the
Lk 22: 2 a way to **put Jesus to death**
    23:32 led away to be **put to death**
Ac   2:23 you crucified and **killed** by the
     5:33 and wanted to **kill** them
     5:36 joined him; but he was **killed**
     7:21 Pharaoh's daughter **adopted** him
     7:28 Do you want to **kill** me as you
     7:28 want to kill me as you **killed**
     9:23 the Jews plotted to **kill** him
     9:24 so that they might **kill** him;
     9:29 were attempting to **kill** him.
    10:39 **put** him **to death** by hanging
    12: 2 of John, **killed** with the sword
    13:28 asked Pilate to have him **killed**
    16:27 was about to **kill** himself,
    22:20 coats of those who **killed** him.
    23:15 And we are ready to **do away**
    23:21 eat nor drink until they **kill**
    23:27 was about to be **killed** by them,
    25: 3 planning an ambush to **kill** him
    26:10 were being **condemned** to **death.**
2Th 2: 8 the Lord Jesus will **destroy**
He 10: 9 He **abolishes** the first in order

338 GO2 AG55 LN14 B2:137
αναιτιος, BLAMELESS
Mt 12: 5 sabbath and yet are **guiltless?**
    12: 7 have condemned the **guiltless.**

---

339 GO2 AG55 LN14 R303,2523
ανακαθιζω, I SIT UP
Lk   7:15 The dead man **sat up** and began
Ac   9:40 and seeing Peter, she **sat up**

---

340 GO1 AG55 LN14 B2:670 K3:451 R303,2537
ανακαινιζω, I RENEW
He   6: 4 to **restore again**

---

341 GO2 AG55 LN14 B2:670 K3:452 R303,2537
ανακαινοω, I RENEW
2C   4:16 nature is being **renewed** day by
Co   3:10 self, which is being **renewed** in

---

342 GO2 AG55 LN14 K3:453 R341
ανακαινωσις, RENEWAL
Ro 12: 2 by the **renewing** of your minds,
Ti   3: 5 and **renewal** by the Holy Spirit.

---

343 GO2 AG55 LN14 B2:212 K3:560 R303,2572
ανακαλυπτω, I UNCOVER
2C   3:14 that same **veil** is still there,
     3:18 all of us, with **unveiled** faces

---

344 GO4 AG55 LN14 R303,2578
ανακαμπτω, I BEND AGAIN (I RETURN)
Mt   2:12 warned in a dream not to
                return
Lk 10: 6 if not, it will **return** to you.
Ac 18:21 I will **return** to you, if God
He 11:15 have had opportunity to **return.**

---

345 GO14 AG55 LN14 K3:654
ανακειμαι, I RECLINE
Mt   9:10 came and were **sitting** with him
    22:10 hall was filled with **guests.**
    22:11 king came in to see the **guests,**
    26: 7 his head as he **sat** at the table
    26:20 he **took** his **place** with the
Mk   6:26 his oaths and for the **guests**
    14:18 they had **taken** their **places**
    16:14 they were **sitting** at the table
Lk 22:27 the one who **is** at the **table**
    22:27 Is it not the one **at** the **table**
Jn   6:11 them to those who were **seated**

12: 2   those **at** the **table** with him.
13:23   was **reclining** next to him
13:28   no one **at** the **table** knew why

---

346   GO2 AG55 LN14 B2:156 K3:681 R303,2775
αυακεφαλαιοω, I HEAD UP
Ro   13: 9   are **summed** up in this word,
Ep   1:10   to **gather up** all things in him,

---

347   GO6 AG56 LN15 R303,2827
αυακλιυω, I RECLINE
Mt   8:11   will **eat** with Abraham and Isaac
      14:19   crowds to **sit down** on the grass
Mk   6:39   people to **sit down** in groups
Lk   2: 7   and **laid** him in a manger,
      12:37   and have them **sit down** to eat,
      13:29   will **eat** in the kingdom of God.

---

349   GO5 AG56 LN15 K3:898 R303,2896
αυακραζω, I SHOUT OUT
Mk   1:24   and he **cried** out, What
       6:49   it was a ghost and **cried** out;
Lk   4:33   he **cried** out with a loud voice
       8:28   **shouted** at the top of his voice
      23:18   they all **shouted** out together,

---

350   GO16 AG56 LN15 B2:362 K3:943 R303,2919
αυακριυω, I EXAMINE
Lk   23:14   I have **examined** him in your
Ac   4: 9   if we are **questioned** today
      12:19   he **examined** the guards and
      17:11   **examined** the scriptures every
      24: 8   By **examining** him yourself you
      28:18   When they had **examined** me,
1C   2:14   they are spiritually **discerned.**
       2:15   Those who are spiritual **discern**
       2:15   **subject** . . . one else's **scrutiny**
       4: 3   that I should be **judged** by you
       4: 3   I do not even **judge** myself.
       4: 4   It is the Lord who **judges** me.
       9: 3   to those who would **examine** me.
      10:25   **without raising** any **question**
      10:27   **without raising** any **question**
      14:24   and **called to account** by all.

---

351   GO1 AG56 LN15 K3:934 R350
αυακρισις, EXAMINATION
Ac   25:26   after we have **examined**
                     him,

---

352   GO4 AG56 LN15 R303,2955
αυακυπτω, I BEND UP (I STRAIGHTEN)
Lk   13:11   was quite unable to **stand up**
      21:28   **stand up** and raise your heads,
Jn   8: 7   he **straightened up** and said to
       8:10   Jesus **straightened up** and said

---

353   GO13 AG56 LN15 B3:747 K4:7 R303,2983
αυαλαμβαυω, I TAKE UP
Mk   16:19   was **taken up** into heaven and
Ac   1: 2   when he was **taken up** to heaven,
       1:11   who has been **taken up** from you
       1:22   when he was **taken up** from us
       7:43   **took** along the tent of Moloch,
      10:16   was suddenly **taken up** to
                     heaven
      20:13   to **take** Paul on board there
      20:14   we **took** him on board and went
      23:31   **took** Paul and brought him
Ep   6:13   **take up** the whole armor of
                     God,
       6:16   **take** the shield of faith, with
1Ti   3:16   **taken up** in glory.
2Ti   4:11   **Get** Mark and bring him with
                     you

---

354   GO1 AG57 LN15 B3:747 K4:7 R353
αυαλημψις, TAKEN UP
Lk   9:51   for him to be **taken up,** he set

---

355   GO2 AG57 LN15
αυαλισκω, I CONSUME
Lk   9:54   from heaven and **consume** them?
Ga   5:15   care that you are not **consumed**

---

356   GO1 AG57 LN15 K1:347 R303,3056
αυαλογια, PROPORTION
Ro   12: 6   in **proportion** to faith

---

357   GO1 AG57 LN15
αυαλογιζομαι, I REASON
He   12: 3   **Consider** him who endured such

---

358   GO1 AG57 LN15 B3:443
αυαλος, SALTLESS
Mk   9:50   if salt has **lost** its **saltiness**

---

359   GO1 AG57 LN15 K4:328 R360
αυαλυσις, DEPARTURE
2Ti   4: 6   time of my **departure** has come.

360 GO2 AG57 LN15 B2:925 K4:328 R303,3089
αναλυω, I DEPART
Lk 12:36 to **return** from the wedding
Ph 1:23 is to **depart** and be with Christ

---

361 GO1 AG57 LN15 K1:333 R264
αναμαρτητος, UNSINFUL
Jn 8: 7 who is **without sin** be the first

---

362 GO1 AG57 LN15 R303,3306
αναμενω, I STAY FOR
1Th 1:10 and to **wait for** his Son from

---

363 GO6 AG57 LN15 B3:230 R303,3403
αναμιμνησκω, I REMIND
Mk 11:21 Then Peter **remembered** and
said
14:72 Peter **remembered** that Jesus
had
1C 4:17 to **remind** you of my ways in
2C 7:15 **remembers** the obedience of all
2Ti 1: 6 For this reason I **remind** you
He 10:32 But **recall** those earlier days

---

364 GO4 AG58 LN15 B3:230 R363
αναμνησις, REMEMBRANCE
Lk 22:19 Do this in **remembrance** of me
1C 11:24 Do this in **remembrance** of me
11:25 drink it, in **remembrance** of me
He 10: 3 there is a **reminder** of sin year

---

365 GO1 AG58 LN15 B2:674 K4:899 R303,3501
ανανεοω, I RENEW
Ep 4:23 and to be **renewed** in the spirit

---

366 GO1 AG58 LN15 B1:514 R303,3525
ανανηφω, I AM WELL BALANCED AGAIN
2Ti 2:26 they may **escape** from the snare

---

367 GO11 AG58 LN15
ανανιας, ANANIAS
Ac 5: 1 But a man named **Ananias,** with
5: 3 **"Ananias,"** Peter asked, "why
5: 5 when **Ananias** heard these words
9:10 in Damascus named **Ananias.**
9:10 to him in a vision, **"Ananias**
9:12 a man named **Ananias** come in and
9:13 But **Ananias** answered, "Lord,
9:17 So **Ananias** went and entered
22:12 A certain **Ananias,** who was a

23: 2 the high priest **Ananias** ordered
24: 1 high priest **Ananias** came down

---

368 GO1 AG58 LN15
αναντιρρητος, WITHOUT CONTRADICTION
Ac 19:36 these things cannot be **denied,**

---

369 GO1 AG58 LN15 R368
αναντιρρητως, WITHOUT CONTRADICTION
Ac 10:29 I came **without objection.**

---

370 GO1 AG58 LN15 B3:348 K1:379 R514
αναξιος, UNWORTHY
1C 6: 2 **incompetent** to try trivial cases

---

371 GO1 AG58 LN15 B3:349 R370
αναξιως, UNWORTHILY
1C 11:27 in an **unworthy** manner will be

---

372 GO5 AG58 LN16 B3:254 K1:350 R373
αναπαυσις, REST
Mt 11:29 will find **rest** for your souls.
12:43 looking for a **resting** place,
Lk 11:24 looking for a **resting** place,
Re 4: 8 without **ceasing** they sing,
14:11 There is no **rest** day or night

---

373 GO12 AG58 LN16 B3:254 K1:350 R303,3973
αναπαυω, I REST
Mt 11:28 and I will give you **rest.**
26:45 sleeping and taking your **rest?**
Mk 6:31 by yourselves and **rest** a while
14:41 sleeping and taking your **rest?**
Lk 12:19 **relax,** eat, drink, be merry.
1C 16:18 for they **refreshed** my spirit
2C 7:13 his mind has been set at **rest**
Pm 1: 7 have been **refreshed** through you
1:20 **Refresh** my heart in Christ.
1P 4:14 Spirit of God, is **resting**
Re 6:11 told to **rest** a little longer,
14:13 will **rest** from their labors,

---

374 GO1 AG59 LN16 R303,3982
αναπειθω, I PERSUADE AGAIN
Ac 18:13 man is **persuading** people

374a GO2 AG59 LN16
αναπειρος, DISABLED
Lk 14:13 invite the poor, the **crippled,**
14:21 bring in the poor, the **crippled**

375 ᴳᴼ5 ᴬᴳ59 ᴸᴺ16 ᴿ303,3992

αναπεμπω, I SEND UP, I SEND BACK

Lk 23: 7 he **sent** him off to Herod, who

23:11 and **sent** him **back** to Pilate.

23:15 for he **sent** him **back** to us.

Ac 25:21 be held until I could **send** him

Pm 1:12 I am **sending** him, that is, my

375a ᴳᴼ1 ᴬᴳ59 ᴸᴺ16

αναπηδαω, I JUMP UP

Mk 10:50 he **sprang up** and came to Jesus.

---

377 ᴳᴼ12 ᴬᴳ59 ᴸᴺ16 ᴮ3:589 ᴿ303,4098

αναπιπτω, I RECLINE

Mt 15:35 ordering the crowd to **sit down**

Mk 6:40 So they **sat down** in groups of

8: 6 ordered the crowd to **sit down**

Lk 11:37 he went in and **took** his **place**

14:10 **sit down** at the lowest place,

17: 7 **take** your **place** at the table

22:14 he **took** his **place** at the table

Jn 6:10 Make the people **sit down.**

6:10 so they **sat down,** about five

13:12 and had **returned** to the table,

13:25 while **reclining** next to Jesus,

21:20 he was the one who had **reclined**

---

378 ᴳᴼ6 ᴬᴳ59 ᴸᴺ16 ᴮ1:733 ᴷ6:305 ᴿ303,4137

αναπληροω, I FILL UP

Mt 13:14 With them indeed is **fulfilled**

1C 14:16 how can anyone in the **position**

16:17 because they have **made up for**

Ga 6: 2 will **fulfill** the law of Christ.

Ph 2:30 risking his life to **make up** for

1Th 2:16 have constantly been **filling** up

---

379 ᴳᴼ2 ᴬᴳ60 ᴸᴺ16 ᴮ2:137 ᴿ626

αναπολογητος, WITHOUT DEFENSE

Ro 1:20 So they are **without excuse;**

2: 1 Therefore you **have no excuse,**

---

380 ᴳᴼ1 ᴬᴳ60 ᴸᴺ16 ᴿ303,4428

αναπτυσσω, I UNROLL

Lk 4:17 He **unrolled** the scroll and

---

381 ᴳᴼ2 ᴬᴳ60 ᴸᴺ16 ᴿ303,681

αναπτω, I IGNITE

Lk 12:49 it were already **kindled!**

Ja 3: 5 great a forest is **set ablaze**

---

382 ᴳᴼ1 ᴬᴳ60 ᴸᴺ16 ᴿ705

αναριθμητος, INNUMERABLE

He 11:12 the **innumerable** grains of sand

---

383 ᴳᴼ2 ᴬᴳ60 ᴸᴺ16 ᴮ3:556 ᴿ303,4579

ανασειω, I SHAKE UP

Mk 15:11 the chief priests **stirred up**

Lk 23: 5 He **stirs up** the people by

---

384 ᴳᴼ1 ᴬᴳ60 ᴸᴺ16 ᴿ303,4632

ανασκευαζω, I UNSETTLE

Ac 15:24 and have **unsettled** your minds,

---

385 ᴳᴼ2 ᴬᴳ60 ᴸᴺ16 ᴿ303,4685

ανασπαω, I DRAW UP

Lk 14: 5 not immediately **pull** it **out**

Ac 11:10 everything was **pulled up** again

---

386 ᴳᴼ42 ᴬᴳ60 ᴸᴺ16 ᴮ3:259 ᴷ1:371 ᴿ450

αναστασις, STANDING UP

Mt 22:23 there is no **resurrection;**

22:28 In the **resurrection,** then,

22:30 For in the **resurrection** they

22:31 the **resurrection** of the dead,

Mk 12:18 say there is no **resurrection,**

12:23 the **resurrection** whose wife

Lk 2:34 falling and the **rising** of many

14:14 **resurrection** of the righteous

20:27 say there is no **resurrection,**

20:33 In the **resurrection,** therefore,

20:35 the **resurrection** from the dead

20:36 children of the **resurrection.**

Jn 5:29 to the **resurrection** of life,

5:29 **resurrection** of condemnation.

11:24 rise again in the **resurrection**

11:25 I am the **resurrection** and the

Ac 1:22 with us to his **resurrection.**

2:31 David spoke of the **resurrection**

4: 2 the **resurrection** of the dead.

4:33 **resurrection** of the Lord Jesus,

17:18 Jesus and the **resurrection.)**

17:32 they heard of the **resurrection**

23: 6 the **resurrection** of the dead.

23: 8 that there is no **resurrection,**

24:15 there will be a **resurrection** of

24:21 the **resurrection** of the dead

26:23 the first to **rise** from the dead

Ro 1: 4 by **resurrection** from the dead,

6: 5 in a **resurrection** like his.

1C 15:12 no **resurrection** of the dead?

15:13   is no **resurrection** of the dead,
15:21   the **resurrection** of the dead
15:42   the **resurrection** of the dead.
Ph   3:10   the power of his **resurrection**
2Ti   2:18   the **resurrection** has already
He   6: 2   **resurrection** of the dead,
11:35   dead by **resurrection.** Others
11:35   to obtain a better **resurrection**
1P   1: 3   **resurrection** of Jesus Christ
3:21   **resurrection** of Jesus Christ
Re   20: 5   This is the first **resurrection**
20: 6   share in the first **resurrection**

---

387   GO3   AG61   LN16
ανασταtoω, I UPSET
Ac   17: 6   **turning** the world **upside down**
21:38   recently **stirred** up a revolt
Ga   5:12   I wish those who **unsettle** you

---

388   GO1   AG61   LN16   B1:391   K7:583   R303,4717
ανασταυροω, I CRUCIFY AGAIN
He   6: 6   **crucifying again** the Son of God

---

389   GO1   AG61   LN16   R303,4727
αναστεναζω, I GROAN
Mk   8:12   he **sighed deeply** in his spirit

---

390   GO9   AG61   LN17   B3:933   K7:715   R303,4762
αναστρεφω, I BEHAVE, I RETURN
Ac   5:22   so they **returned** and reported,
15:16   After this I will **return,** and
2C   1:12   we have **behaved** in the world
Ep   2: 3   All of us once **lived** among them
1Ti   3:15   how one ought to **behave** in the
He   10:33   partners with those so **treated.**
13:18   desiring to **act honorably** in
1P   1:17   **live** in reverent fear during
2P   2:18   from those who **live** in error.

---

391   GO13   AG61   LN17   B3:933   K7:715   R390
αναστροφη, BEHAVIOR
Ga   1:13   of my earlier **life** in Judaism.
Ep   4:22   away your former way of **life,**
1Ti   4:12   example in speech and **conduct**
He   13: 7   outcome of their way of **life,**
Ja   3:13   Show by your good **life** that
1P   1:15   yourselves in all your **conduct;**
1:18   ransomed from the futile **ways**
2:12   **Conduct** yourselves honorably
3: 1   a word by their wives' **conduct,**

3: 2   and reverence of your **lives.**
3:16   for your good **conduct** in Christ
2P   2: 7   distressed . . . **licentiousness**
3:11   leading **lives** of holiness and

---

392   GO1   AG61   LN17   K8:32   R303,5021
ανατασσομαι, I SET UP IN ORDER
Lk   1: 1   to set down an **orderly** account

---

393   GO9   AG62   LN17   K1:351
ανατελλω, I ARISE
Mt   4:16   of death light has **dawned.**
5:45   for he makes his sun **rise** on
13: 6   when the sun **rose,** they were
Mk   4: 6   And when the sun **rose,** it was
16: 2   when the sun had **risen,** they
Lk   12:54   When you see a cloud **rising**
He   7:14   Lord was **descended** from
Judah,
Ja   1:11   sun **rises** with its scorching
2P   1:19   star **rises** in your hearts.

---

394   GO2   AG62   LN17   K1:353   R303,5087
ανατιθημι, I SET UP
Ac   25:14   Festus **laid** Paul's case before
Ga   2: 2   Then I **laid** before them

---

395   GO11   AG62   LN17   K1:352
ανατολη, RISING (EAST)
Mt   2: 1   wise men from the **East** came to
2: 2   observed his star at its **rising**
2: 9   they had seen at its **rising,**
8:11   will come from **east** and west
24:27   lightning comes from the **east**
Mk   16: 8   from the **east** to west,
Lk   1:78   **dawn** from on high will break
13:29   people will come from **east** and
Re   7: 2   angel ascending from the **rising**
16:12   way for the kings from the **east**
21:13   on the **east** three gates, on the

---

396   GO3   AG62   LN17
ανατρεπω, I TURN UP
Jn   2:15   money changers and **overturned**
2Ti   2:18   They are **upsetting** the faith of
Ti   1:11   are **upsetting** whole families

---

397   GO3   AG62   LN17   B3:933   K7:714   R303,5142
ανατρεφω, I NOURISH
Ac   7:20   three months he was **brought** up

7:21　adopted him and **brought** him **up**
22: 3　but **brought up** in this city at

---

398 ᴳᴼ2 ᴬᴳ63 ᴸᴺ17 ᴿ303,5316
αναφαινω, I APPEAR AGAIN
Lk　19:11　kingdom of God was to **appear**
Ac　21: 3　We came in **sight** of Cyprus;

---

399 ᴳᴼ10 ᴬᴳ63 ᴸᴺ17 ᴮ3:1195 ᴷ9:60 ᴿ303,5342
αναφερω, I BRING UP
Mt　17: 1　**led** them **up** a high mountain
Mk　 9: 2　**led** them **up** a high mountain
Lk　24:51　was **carried up** into heaven.
He　 7:27　no need to **offer** sacrifices
　　 7:27　for all when he **offered** himself
　　 9:28　so Christ, having been **offered**
　　13:15　continually **offer** a sacrifice
Ja　 2:21　when he **offered** his son Isaac
1P　 2: 5　to **offer** spiritual sacrifices
　　 2:24　**bore** our sins in his body on

---

400 ᴳᴼ1 ᴬᴳ63 ᴸᴺ17 ᴿ303,5455
αναφωνεω, I SOUND OUT
Lk　 1:42　and **exclaimed** with a loud cry,

---

401 ᴳᴼ1 ᴬᴳ63 ᴸᴺ17
αναχυσις, POURING OUT
1P　 4: 4　same **excesses** of dissipation

---

402 ᴳᴼ14 ᴬᴳ63 ᴸᴺ17 ᴿ303,5562
αναχωρεω, I DEPART
Mt　 2:12　they **left** for their own country
　　 2:13　Now after they had **left,** an
　　 2:14　by night, and **went** to Egypt,
　　 2:22　he **went** away to the district
　　 4:12　he **withdrew** to Galilee.
　　 9:24　**Go away;** for the girl is not
　　12:15　aware of this, he **departed.**
　　14:13　he **withdrew** from there in a
　　15:21　left that place and **went away**
　　27: 5　he **departed;** and he went and
Mk　 3: 7　**departed** with his disciples to
Jn　 6:15　he **withdrew** again to the
Ac　23:19　**drew** him **aside** privately,
　　26:31　and as they **were leaving,**

---

403 ᴳᴼ1 ᴬᴳ63 ᴸᴺ17 ᴮ3:686 ᴷ9:664 ᴿ404
αναψυξις, REFRESHMENT
Ac　 3:20　times of **refreshing** may come

---

404 ᴳᴼ1 ᴬᴳ63 ᴸᴺ17 ᴮ3:686 ᴷ9:663 ᴿ303,5594
αναψυχω, I REFRESH
2Ti　 1:16　because he often **refreshed** me

---

405 ᴳᴼ1 ᴬᴳ63 ᴸᴺ17 ᴮ3:380
ανδραποδιστης, MAN-TRAPPER
1Ti　 1:10　sodomites, **slave traders,** liars

---

406 ᴳᴼ13 ᴬᴳ63 ᴸᴺ17
ανδρεας, ANDREW
Mt　 4:18　and **Andrew** his brother, casting
　　10: 2　Peter, and his brother **Andrew;**
Mk　 1:16　Simon and his brother **Andrew**
　　 1:29　the house of Simon and **Andrew,**
　　 3:18　and **Andrew,** and Philip,
　　13: 3　**Andrew** asked him privately,
Lk　 6:14　**Andrew,** Simon Peter's brother.
Jn　 1:44　the city of **Andrew** and Peter.
　　 6: 8　One of his disciples, **Andrew,**
　　12:22　Philip went and told **Andrew;**
　　12:22　then **Andrew** and Philip went
Ac　 1:13　James, and **Andrew,** Philip and

---

407 ᴳᴼ1 ᴬᴳ64 ᴸᴺ17 ᴮ2:562 ᴷ1:360 ᴿ435
ανδριζομαι, I AM LIKE A MAN
1C　16:13　**be courageous,** be strong.

---

408 ᴳᴼ1 ᴬᴳ64 ᴸᴺ17
ανδρονικος, ANDRONICUS
Ro　16: 7　Greet **Andronicus** and Junia, my

---

409 ᴳᴼ1 ᴬᴳ64 ᴸᴺ17 ᴿ435,5408
ανδροφονος, MAN-MURDERER
1Ti　 1: 9　father or mother, for **murderers,**

---

410 ᴳᴼ5 ᴬᴳ64 ᴸᴺ17 ᴷ1:356 ᴿ1458
ανεγκλητος, IRREPROACHABLE
1C　 1: 8　so that you may be **blameless**
Co　 1:22　**blameless** and irreproachable
1Ti　 3:10　they prove themselves **blameless**
Ti　 1: 6　**blameless,** married only once,
　　 1: 7　steward, must be **blameless;**

---

411 ᴳᴼ1 ᴬᴳ64 ᴸᴺ18 ᴿ1555
ανεκδιηγητος, INEXPRESSIBLE
2C　 9:15　God for his **indescribable** gift

---

412 ᴳᴼ1 ᴬᴳ64 ᴸᴺ18 ᴿ1583
ανεκλαλητος, UNSPEAKABLE
1P　 1: 8　**indescribable** and glorious joy,

413   GO1   AG64   LN18   R1587
ανεκλειπτος, UNFAILING
Lk 12:33   an **unfailing** treasure in heaven

---

414   GO5   AG64   LN18   B2:765   K1:359   R430
ανεκτος, ENDURABLE, TOLERABLE
Mt 10:15   will be more **tolerable** for the
     11:22   will be more **tolerable** for Tyre
     11:24   will be more **tolerable** for the
Lk 10:12   be more **tolerable** for Sodom
     10:14   it will be more **tolerable** for

---

415   GO1   AG64   LN18   B2:594   K2:487   R1655
ανελεημων, WITHOUT MERCY
Ro   1:31   faithless, heartless, **ruthless**

415a   GO1   AG64   LN18   B2:594   K2:487   R1656
ανελεος, WITHOUT MERCY
Ja   2:13   judgment will be **without mercy**

---

416   GO1   AG64   LN18   R417
ανεμιζω, I THROW BY WIND
Ja   1: 6   **driven** and tossed **by the wind;**

---

417   GO31   AG64   LN18   B3:1000
ανεμος, WIND
Mt   7:25   the **winds** blew and beat on that
      7:27   the **winds** blew and beat against
      8:26   rebuked the **winds** and the sea;
      8:27   even the **winds** and the sea obey
    11: 7   A reed shaken by the **wind?**
    14:24   for the **wind** was against them.
    14:30   when he noticed the strong **wind,**
    14:32   into the boat, the **wind** ceased.
    24:31   his elect from the four **winds,**
Mk   4:37   A great **windstorm** arose,
      4:39   He woke up and rebuked the
             wind
      4:39   Then the **wind** ceased, and there
      4:41   the **wind** and the sea obey him?
      6:48   against an adverse **wind,**
      6:51   the boat with them and the **wind**
    13:27   his elect from the four **winds,**
Lk   7:24   A reed shaken by the **wind?**
      8:23   A **windstorm** swept down on the
      8:24   he woke up and rebuked the
             wind
      8:25   that he commands even the **winds**
Jn   6:18   a strong **wind** was blowing.
Ac 27: 4   because the **winds** were against

    27: 7   as the **wind** was against us, we
    27:14   But soon a violent **wind,**
    27:15   be turned head-on into the **wind**
Ep   4:14   blown about by every **wind** of
Ja   3: 4   it takes strong **winds** to drive
Ju   1:12   carried along by the **winds;**
Re   6:13   fruit when shaken by a **gale.**
      7: 1   holding back the four **winds**
      7: 1   so that no **wind** could blow on

---

418   GO1   AG65   LN18   R1735
ανενδεκτος, UNACCEPTABLE
Lk 17: 1   for stumbling are **bound to come**

---

419   GO1   AG65   LN18   B3:532   K1:357   R1830
ανεξεραυνητος, UNSEARCHABLE
Ro 11:33   How **unsearchable** are his

---

420   GO1   AG65   LN18   K3:486   R430,2556
ανεξικακος, PUT UP WITH BAD
2Ti 2:24   an apt teacher, **patient,**

---

421   GO2   AG65   LN18   K1:358
ανεξιχνιαστος, UNTRACEABLE
Ro 11:33   and how **inscrutable** his ways
Ep   3: 8   news of the **boundless** riches

---

422   GO1   AG65   LN18
ανεπαισχυντος, UNASHAMED
2Ti 2:15   who has **no need to be ashamed,**

---

423   GO3   AG65   LN19   B3:750   K4:9   R1949
ανεπιλημπτος, UNIMPEACHABLE
1Ti 3: 2   a bishop must be **above reproach**
      5: 7   that they may be **above reproach**
      6:14   **without** spot or **blame** until the

---

424   GO3   AG65   LN19   R303,2064
ανερχομαι, I WENT UP
Jn   6: 3   Jesus **went up** the mountain and
Ga   1:17   nor did I **go up** to Jerusalem to
      1:18   after three years I did **go up**

---

425   GO5   AG65   LN19   K1:367   R447
ανεσις, RELIEF
Ac 24:23   to let him have some **liberty**
2C   2:13   but my mind could not **rest**
      7: 5   our bodies had no **rest,** but
      8:13   **relief** for others and pressure
2Th 1: 7   to give **relief** to the afflicted

426   GO2   AG65   LN19
ανεταζω, I EXAMINE
Ac   22:24   him to be **examined** by flogging,
      22:29   who were about to **examine** him

---

427   GO3   AG65   LN19
ανευ, WITHOUT
Mt   10:29   will fall to the ground **apart**
1P   3: 1   may be won over **without** a word
      4: 9   another **without** complaining.

---

428   GO1   AG65   LN19   R2111
ανευθετος, UNSUITABLE
Ac   27:12   the harbor was **not suitable**

---

429   GO2   AG65   LN19   R303,2147
ανευρισκω, I DISCOVER
Lk   2:16   went with haste and **found** Mary
Ac   21: 4   We **looked up** the disciples and

---

430   GO15   AG65   LN19   B2:764   K1:359   R303,2192
ανεχω, I ENDURE
Mt   17:17   How much longer must I **put up**
Mk   9:19   How much longer must I **put up**
Lk   9:41   I be with you and **bear with** you
Ac   18:14   would be **justified** in accepting
1C   4:12   when persecuted, we **endure;**
2C   11: 1   I wish you **would bear** with me
      11: 1   **Do bear** with me!
      11: 4   you **submit** to it readily enough
      11:19   you gladly **put up** with fools,
      11:20   you **put up** with it when someone
Ep   4: 2   **bearing with** one another in
            love,
Co   3:13   **Bear with** one another and, if
2Th   1: 4   that you are **enduring.**
2Ti   4: 3   people will not **put up** with
He   13:22   **bear with** my word of

---

431   GO1   AG66   LN19
ανεψιος, COUSIN
Co   4:10   Mark the **cousin** of Barnabas,

---

432   GO1   AG66   LN19   B2:210
ανηθον, ANISE
Mt   23:23   For you tithe mint, **dill,** and

---

433   GO3   AG66   LN19
ανηκω, IT IS PROPER
Ep   5: 4   but **instead,**

Co   3:18   as **is fitting** in the Lord.
Pm   1: 8   to command you to **do** your **duty,**

---

434   GO1   AG66   LN19
ανημερος, UNTAMED
2Ti   3: 3   **brutes,** haters of good,

---

435   GO216   AG66   LN19   B2:562   K1:360
ανηρ, MAN (MALE)
Mt   1:16   Joseph the **husband** of Mary,
      1:19   Her **husband** Joseph, being a
      7:24   will be like a wise **man** who
      7:26   will be like a foolish **man** who
      12:41   **people** of Nineveh will rise up
      14:21   were about five thousand **men,**
      14:35   After the **people** of that place
      15:38   eaten were four thousand **men,**
Mk   6:20   he was a righteous and holy **man**
      6:44   numbered five thousand **men.**
      10: 2   lawful for a **man** to divorce his
      10:12   and if she divorces her **husband**
Lk   1:27   engaged to a **man** whose name
            was
      1:34   since I am a **virgin?**
      2:36   lived with her **husband** seven
      5: 8   Lord, for I am a sinful **man!**
      5:12   was a **man** covered with leprosy.
      5:18   **men** came, carrying a paralyzed
      6: 8   the **man** who had the withered
      7:20   When the **men** had come to him,
      8:27   **man** of the city who had demons
      8:38   The **man** from whom the demons
      8:41   there came a **man** named Jairus,
      9:14   were about five thousand **men.**
      9:30   Suddenly they saw two **men,**
      9:32   two **men** who stood with him.
      9:38   a **man** from the crowd shouted,
      11:31   the **people** of this generation
      11:32   **people** of Nineveh will rise up
      14:24   none of **those** who were invited
      16:18   divorced from her **husband**
      17:12   ten **lepers** approached him.
      19: 2   A **man** was there named
            Zacchaeus
      19: 7   guest of **one** who is a sinner
      22:63   the **men** who were holding Jesus
      23:50   Now **there** was a good and
      23:50   righteous **man** named Joseph,
      24: 4   **men** in dazzling clothes stood
      24:19   was a **prophet** mighty in deed

Jn	1:13	flesh or of the will of **man,**
	1:30	comes a **man** who ranks ahead of
	4:16	call your **husband,** and come
	4:17	"I have no **husband."** Jesus said
	4:17	in saying, 'I have no **husband**
	4:18	for you have had five **husbands,**
	4:18	have now is not your **husband.**
	6:10	so **they** sat down, about
Ac	1:10	suddenly two **men** in white robes
	1:11	**Men** of Galilee, why do you
	1:16	**Friends,** the scripture had to
	1:21	the **men** who have accompanied us
	2: 5	Now there were **devout** Jews
	2:14	**Men** of Judea and all who live
	2:22	You that are **Israelites,**
	2:22	a **man** attested to you by God
	2:29	**Fellow** Israelites, I may say
	2:37	**Brothers,** what should we do?
	3: 2	a **man** lame from birth was being
	3:12	**Israelites,** why do you wonder
	3:14	asked to have a **murderer** given
	4: 4	and **they** numbered about five
	5: 1	But a **man** named Ananias, with
	5: 9	who have buried your **husband**
	5:10	buried her beside her **husband.**
	5:14	great numbers of both **men** and
	5:25	the **men** whom you put in prison
	5:35	**Fellow** Israelites, consider
	5:36	a number of **men,** about four
	6: 3	seven **men** of good standing,
	6: 5	Stephen, a **man** full of faith
	6:11	some **men** to say, "We have heard
	7: 2	Brothers and **fathers,** listen to
	7:26	**Men,** you are brothers; why do
	8: 2	Devout **men** buried Stephen and
	8: 3	dragging off both **men** and women
	8: 9	Now a certain **man** named Simon
	8:12	baptized, both **men** and women.
	8:27	there was an **Ethiopian** eunuch,
	9: 2	to the Way, **men** or women, he
	9: 7	**men** who were traveling with him
	9:12	a **man** named Ananias come in and
	9:13	heard from many about this **man,**
	9:38	sent two **men** to him with the
	10: 1	there was a **man** named Cornelius
	10: 5	send **men** to Joppa for a certain
	10:17	the **men** sent by Cornelius
	10:19	three **men** are searching for you
	10:21	So Peter went down to the **men**
	10:22	an upright and God-fearing **man,**
	10:28	unlawful for a **Jew** to associate
	10:30	a **man** in dazzling clothes stood
	11: 3	go to uncircumcised **men** and eat
	11:11	three **men,** sent to me from
	11:12	and we entered the **man's** house.
	11:20	some **men** of Cyprus and Cyrene
	11:24	for he was a good **man,** full of
	13: 6	they met a **certain** magician,
	13: 7	Paulus, an intelligent **man,**
	13:15	**Brothers,** if you have any word
	13:16	You **Israelites,** and others who
	13:21	a **man** of the tribe of Benjamin,
	13:22	to be a **man** after my heart, who
	13:26	My **brothers,** you descendants
	13:38	to you therefore, my **brothers,**
	14: 8	a **man** sitting who could not
	14:15	**Friends,** why are you doing
	15: 7	My **brothers,** you know that in
	15:13	My **brothers,** listen to me.
	15:22	to choose **men** from among their
	15:22	**leaders** among the brothers,
	15:25	to choose **representatives** and
	16: 9	a **man** of Macedonia pleading
	17: 5	with the help of some **ruffians**
	17:12	women and **men** of high standing.
	17:22	**Athenians,** I see how extremely
	17:31	a **man** whom he has appointed,
	17:34	But **some** of them joined him and
	18:24	He was an eloquent **man,**
	19: 7	there were about twelve of **them.**
	19:25	**Men,** you know that we get our
	19:35	**Citizens** of Ephesus, who is
	19:37	these **men** here who are neither
	20:30	**Some** even from your own group
	21:11	bind the **man** who owns this belt
	21:23	four **men** who are under a vow.
	21:26	Then Paul took the **men,** and
	21:28	**Fellow** Israelites, help! This
	21:38	led the four thousand **assassins**
	22: 1	Brothers and **fathers,** listen to
	22: 3	I am a **Jew,** born in Tarsus
	22: 4	binding both **men** and women and
	22:12	Ananias, who was a devout **man**
	23: 1	**Brothers,** up to this day I have
	23: 6	**Brothers,** I am a Pharisee,
	23:21	their **men** are lying in ambush
	23:27	This **man** was seized by the Jews

	23:30	would be a plot against the **man,**
	24: 5	found this **man** a pestilent
	25: 5	wrong about the **man,** let them
	25:14	is a **man** here who was left
	25:17	ordered the **man** to be brought.
	25:23	the prominent **men** of the city.
	25:24	this **man** about whom the whole
	27:10	**Sirs,** I can see that the voyage
	27:21	**Men,** you should have listened
	27:25	So keep up your courage, **men,**
	28:17	**Brothers,** though I had done
Ro	4: 8	blessed is the **one** against whom
	7: 2	her **husband** as long as he lives
	7: 2	but if her **husband** dies, she is
	7: 2	the law concerning the **husband.**
	7: 3	if she lives with another **man**
	7: 3	while her **husband** is alive.
	7: 3	But if her **husband** dies, she is
	7: 3	and if she marries another **man,**
	11: 4	seven thousand **who** have not
1C	7: 2	each **man** should have his own
	7: 3	The **husband** should give to his
	7: 3	the wife to her **husband.**
	7: 4	but the **husband** does; likewise
	7: 4	likewise the **husband** does not
	7:10	not separate from her **husband**
	7:11	be reconciled to her **husband**
	7:11	the **husband** should not divorce
	7:13	a **husband** who is an unbeliever
	7:13	she should not divorce **him.**
	7:14	**husband** is made holy through
	7:16	you might save your **husband.**
	7:16	**Husband,** for all you know, you
	7:34	how to please her **husband.**
	7:39	as long as her **husband** lives.
	7:39	if the **husband** dies, she is
	11: 3	Christ is the head of every **man**
	11: 3	the **husband** is the head of his
	11: 4	Any **man** who prays or prophesies
	11: 7	For a **man** ought not to have his
	11: 7	woman is the reflection of **man.**
	11: 8	**man** was not made from woman,
	11: 8	but woman from **man.**
	11: 9	Neither was **man** created for the
	11: 9	but woman for the sake of **man.**
	11:11	woman is not independent of **man**
	11:11	or **man** independent of woman.
	11:12	just as woman came from **man,**
	11:12	so **man** comes through woman;

	11:14	if a **man** wears long hair, it is
	13:11	when I became an **adult,** I put
	14:35	let them ask their **husbands** at
2C	11: 2	in marriage to one **husband,**
Ga	4:27	of the one who is **married.**
Ep	4:13	to **maturity,** to the measure of
	5:22	be subject to your **husbands**
	5:23	For the **husband** is the head
	5:24	everything, to their **husbands.**
	5:25	**Husbands,** love your wives,
	5:28	**husbands** should love their
	5:33	should respect her **husband.**
Co	3:18	be subject to your **husbands,**
	3:19	**Husbands,** love your wives
1Ti	2: 8	that in every place the **men**
	2:12	to have authority over a **man;**
	3: 2	**married** only once, temperate,
	3:12	deacons be **married** only once,
	5: 9	and has been **married** only once;
Ti	1: 6	blameless, **married** only once,
	2: 5	submissive to their **husbands,**
Ja	1: 8	for the **doubter**
	1:12	Blessed is **anyone** who endures
	1:20	for **your** anger does not produce
	1:23	those **who** look at themselves
	2: 2	For if a **person** with gold rings
	3: 2	**Anyone** who makes not mistakes
1P	3: 1	authority of your **husbands**
	3: 5	the authority of their **husbands**
	3: 7	**Husbands,** in the same way,
		show
Re	21: 2	bride adorned for her **husband.**

---

436   ᴳᴼ14   ᴬᴳ67   ᴸᴺ20   ᴿ473,2476
αντιστημι, I STAND AGAINST

Mt	5:39	Do not **resist** an evildoer.
Lk	21:15	will be able to **withstand** or
Ac	6:10	could not **withstand** the wisdom
	13: 8	**opposed** them and tried to turn
Ro	9:19	For who can **resist** his will?
	13: 2	whoever **resists** authority
	13: 2	those who **resist** will incur
Ga	2:11	I **opposed** him to his face,
Ep	6:13	you may be able to **withstand**
2Ti	3: 8	As Jannes and Jambres **opposed**
	3: 8	counterfeit faith, also **oppose**
	4:15	he strongly **opposed** our message
Ja	4: 7	**Resist** the devil, and he will
1P	5: 9	**Resist** him, steadfast in your

437 ᴳᴼ1 ᴬᴳ67 ᴸᴺ20 ᴷ5:199 ᴿ473,3670
ανθομολογεομαι, I CONFESS IN RESPONSE
Lk 2:38 she came, and began to **praise**

---

438 ᴳᴼ4 ᴬᴳ67 ᴸᴺ20
ανθος, FLOWER
Ja 1:10 will disappear like a **flower**
    1:11 its **flower** falls, and its
1P 1:24 glory like the **flower** of grass.
    1:24 and the **flower** falls,

---

439 ᴳᴼ2 ᴬᴳ67 ᴸᴺ20 ᴿ440
ανθρακια, COAL FIRE
Jn 18:18 made a **charcoal** fire because
    21: 9 they saw a **charcoal** fire there,

---

440 ᴳᴼ1 ᴬᴳ67 ᴸᴺ20 ᴮ3:396
ανθραξ, BURNING COALS
Ro 12:20 will heap burning **coals**

---

441 ᴳᴼ2 ᴬᴳ67 ᴸᴺ20 ᴮ2:815 ᴷ1:456 ᴿ444,700
ανθρωπαρεσκος, MAN-PLEASER
Ep 6: 6 and in order to **please** them
Co 3:22 and in order to **please** them

---

442 ᴳᴼ7 ᴬᴳ67 ᴸᴺ20 ᴮ2:564 ᴷ1:366 ᴿ444
ανθρωπινος, MAN-LIKE
Ac 17:25 nor is he served by **human** hands
Ro 6:19 I am speaking in **human** terms
1C 2:13 not taught by **human** wisdom but
    4: 3 by you or by any **human** court.
    10:13 that is not common to **everyone.**
Ja 3: 7 been tamed by the **human** species,
1P 2:13 authority of every **human**

---

443 ᴳᴼ3 ᴬᴳ68 ᴸᴺ20
ανθρωποκτονος, MAN-KILLER
Jn 8:44 He was a **murderer** from the
1J 3:15 brother or sister are **murderers**
    3:15 **murderers** do not have eternal

---

444 ᴳᴼ550 ᴬᴳ68 ᴸᴺ20 ᴮ2:562 ᴷ1:364
ανθρωπος, MAN (HUMAN)
Mt 4: 4 **One** does not live by bread
    4:19 I will make you fish for **people**
    5:13 and trampled under **foot.**
    5:16 your light shine before **others,**
    5:19 teaches **others** to do the same,
    6: 1 before **others** in order to be
    6: 2 they may be praised by **others.**

6: 5 they may be seen by **others.**
6:14 if you forgive **others** their
6:15 if you do not forgive **others,**
6:16 to show **others** that they are
6:18 by **others** but by your Father
7: 9 Is there **anyone** among you who,
7:12 do to **others** as you would have
8: 9 I also am a **man** under authority
8:20 but the Son of **Man** has nowhere
8:27 What sort of **man** is this,
9: 6 the Son of **Man** has authority on
9: 8 such authority to **human beings.**
9: 9 he saw a **man** called Matthew
9:32 a **demoniac** who was mute was
10:17 Beware of **them,** for they will
10:23 before the Son of **Man** comes.
10:32 acknowledges me before **others,**
10:33 whoever denies me before **others**
10:35 to set a **man** against his father
10:36 and **one's** foes will be members
11: 8 **Someone** dressed in soft robes?
11:19 the Son of **Man** came eating and
11:19 Look, a **glutton** and a drunkard,
12: 8 For the Son of **Man** is lord of
12:10 a **man** was there with a withered
12:11 Suppose **one** of you has only one
12:12 more valuable is a **human being**
12:13 said to the **man,** "Stretch out
12:31 **people** will be forgiven for
12:32 a word against the Son of **Man**
12:35 The good **person** brings good
12:35 evil **person** brings evil things
12:36 **you** will have to give an
12:40 Son of **Man** will be in the heart
12:43 spirit has gone out of a **person**
12:45 the last state of that **person**
13:24 may be compared to **someone** who
13:25 but while **everybody** was asleep,
13:28 An **enemy** has done this.
13:31 that **someone** took and sowed
13:37 the good seed is the Son of **Man**
13:41 Son of **Man** will send his angels
13:44 which **someone** found and hid;
13:45 a **merchant** in search of fine
13:52 the **master** of a household who
15: 9 teaching **human** precepts as
15:11 that defiles a **person,** but
15:11 this is what **defiles.**
15:20 These are what defile a **person,**

15:20	unwashed hands does not **defile.**
16:13	Who do **people** say that the Son
16:13	say that the Son of **Man** is?
16:23	on divine things but on **human**
16:26	what will **they** give in return
16:26	For what will it profit **them**
16:27	For the Son of **Man** is to come
16:28	before they see the Son of **Man**
17: 9	the Son of **Man** has been raised
17:12	Son of **Man** is about to suffer
17:14	a **man** came to him, knelt
17:22	The Son of **Man** is going to be
17:22	be betrayed into **human** hands,
18: 7	woe to the **one** by whom the
18:12	a **shepherd** has a hundred sheep,
18:23	compared to a **king** who wished
19: 3	lawful for a **man** to divorce his
19: 5	a **man** shall leave his father
19: 6	together, let no **one** separate.
19:10	case of a **man** with his wife,
19:12	been made eunuchs by **others,**
19:26	For **mortals** it is impossible,
19:28	Son of **Man** is seated on the
20: 1	a **landowner** who went out early
20:18	Son of **Man** will be handed over
20:28	the Son of **Man** came not to be
21:25	or was it of **human** origin?
21:26	if we say, 'Of **human** origin,
21:28	A **man** had two sons; he went to
21:33	a **landowner** who planted a
22: 2	a **king** who gave a wedding
22:11	a **man** there who was not wearing
22:16	regard **people** with partiality.
23: 4	them on the shoulders of **others**
23: 5	to be seen by **others;** for they
23: 7	have **people** call them rabbi.
23:13	lock **people** out of the kingdom
23:28	look righteous to **others,** but
24:27	be the coming of the Son of **Man**
24:30	Then the sign of the Son of **Man**
24:30	Son of **Man** coming on the clouds
24:37	be the coming of the Son of **Man**
24:39	be the coming of the Son of **Man**
24:44	the Son of **Man** is coming at an
25:14	For it is as if a **man,** going
25:24	knew that you were a harsh **man,**
25:31	Son of **Man** comes in his glory,
26: 2	Son of **Man** will be handed
26:24	The Son of **Man** goes as it is
26:24	woe to that **one** by whom the Son
26:24	the Son of **Man** is betrayed!
26:24	that **one** not to have been born.
26:45	the Son of **Man** is betrayed into
26:64	Son of **Man** seated at the right
26:72	I do not know the **man.**
26:74	I do not know the **man!**
27:32	came upon a **man** from Cyrene
27:57	a rich **man** from Arimathea,
Mk 1:17	will make you fish for **people**
1:23	a **man** with an unclean spirit,
2:10	the Son of **Man** has authority on
2:27	sabbath was made for **humankind,**
2:27	not **humankind** for the sabbath;
2:28	so the Son of **Man** is lord even
3: 1	**man** was there who had a
3: 3	And he said to the **man** who had
3: 5	said to the **man,** "Stretch out
3:28	**people** will be forgiven for
4:26	**someone** would scatter seed on
5: 2	a **man** out of the tombs with an
5: 8	Come out of the **man,** you
7: 7	teaching **human** precepts as
7: 8	hold to **human** tradition.
7:11	if **anyone** tells father or
7:15	nothing outside a **person** that
7:15	that come **out** are what defile.
7:15	that come out are what **defile.**
7:18	goes into a **person** from outside
7:20	what comes out of a **person** that
7:20	out of a person that **defiles.**
7:21	within, from the **human** heart,
7:23	and they defile a **person.**
8:24	And the **man** looked up and said,
8:27	Who do **people** say that I am?
8:31	Son of **Man** must undergo great
8:33	things but on **human** things.
8:36	For what will it profit **them**
8:37	what can **they** give in return
8:38	the Son of **Man** will also be
9: 9	the Son of **Man** had risen from
9:12	written about the Son of **Man,**
9:31	**Man** is to be betrayed into
9:31	be betrayed into **human** hands,
10: 7	For this reason a **man** shall
10: 9	let no **one** separate.
10:27	For **mortals** it is impossible,
10:33	Son of **Man** will be handed over
10:45	the Son of **Man** came not to be

	11: 2	never been ridden [by **men**]	11:24	spirit has gone out of a **person**
	11:30	or was it of **human** origin?	11:26	state of that **person** is worse
	11:32	Of **human** origin	11:30	the Son of **Man** will be to this
	12: 1	A **man** planted a vineyard, put	11:44	**people** walk over them without
	12:14	regard **people** with partiality,	11:46	load **people** with burdens hard
	13:26	the Son of **Man** coming in	12: 8	acknowledges me before **others,**
	13:34	like a **man** going on a journey,	12: 8	**Man** also will acknowledge
	14:13	a **man** carrying a jar of water	12: 9	whoever denies me before **others**
	14:21	For the Son of **Man** goes as it	12:10	word against the Son of **Man**
	14:21	but woe to that **one** by whom	12:14	**Friend,** who set me to be a
	14:21	the Son of **Man** is betrayed!	12:16	land of a rich **man** produced
	14:21	that **one** not to have been born.	12:36	be like **those** who are waiting
	14:41	the Son of **Man** is betrayed	12:40	the Son of **Man** is coming at an
	14:62	Son of **Man** seated at the right	13: 4	than all the **others** living in
	14:71	know this **man** you are talking	13:19	that **someone** took and sowed in
	15:39	Truly this **man** was God's Son!	14: 2	there was a **man** who had dropsy.
Lk	1:25	I have endured among my **people.**	14:16	**Someone** gave a great dinner
	2:14	among **those** whom he favors!	14:30	This **fellow** began to build
	2:25	there was a **man** in Jerusalem	15: 4	Which **one** of you, having a
	2:52	and in divine and **human** favor.	15:11	There was a **man** who had two
	4: 4	**One** does not live by bread	16: 1	a rich **man** who had a manager,
	4:33	a **man** who had the spirit of	16:15	in the sight of **others;** but God
	5:10	you will be catching **people.**	16:15	what is prized by **human** beings
	5:18	carrying a paralyzed **man**	16:19	There was a rich **man** who was
	5:20	**Friend,** your sins are	17:22	the days of the Son of **Man,**
	5:24	Son of **Man** has authority on	17:24	the Son of **Man** be in his day.
	6: 5	The Son of **Man** is lord of the	17:26	in the days of the Son of **Man.**
	6: 6	a **man** there whose right hand	17:30	the day that the Son of **Man**
	6:22	when **people** hate you, and when	18: 2	nor had respect for **people.**
	6:22	on account of the Son of **Man.**	18: 4	and no respect for **anyone,**
	6:26	Woe to you when **all** speak well	18: 8	when the Son of **Man** comes, will
	6:31	you would have **them** do to you.	18:10	Two **men** went up to the temple
	6:45	The good **person** out of the good	18:11	I am not like other **people**
	6:48	is like a **man** building a house,	18:27	What is impossible for **mortals**
	6:49	is like a **man** who built a house	18:31	written about the Son of **Man**
	7: 8	a **man** set under authority, with	19:10	the Son of **Man** came to seek out
	7:25	**Someone** dressed in soft robes?	19:12	A **nobleman** went to a distant
	7:31	the **people** of this generation,	19:21	because you are a harsh **man**
	7:34	the Son of **Man** has come eating	19:22	that I was a harsh **man,** taking
	7:34	Look, a **glutton** and a drunkard	19:30	never been ridden [by **men**]
	8:29	spirit to come out of the **man.**	20: 4	or was it of **human** origin?
	8:33	demons came out of the **man** and	20: 6	if we say, 'Of **human** origin
	8:35	they found the **man** from whom	20: 9	A **man** planted a vineyard, and
	9:22	The Son of **Man** must undergo	21:26	**People** will faint from fear and
	9:25	it profit **them** if they gain	21:27	Son of **Man** coming in a
	9:26	the Son of **Man** will be ashamed	21:36	to stand before the Son of **Man.**
	9:44	**Man** is going to be betrayed	22:10	a **man** carrying a jar of water
	9:58	Son of **Man** has nowhere to lay	22:22	For the Son of **Man** is going as
	10:30	A **man** was going down from	22:22	woe to that **one** by whom he is

22:48	are betraying the Son of **Man?**
22:58	But Peter said, **"Man,** I am not!
22:60	But Peter said, **"Man,** I do not
22:69	the Son of **Man** will be seated
23: 4	accusation against this **man.**
23: 6	whether the **man** was a Galilean
23:14	You brought me this **man** as one
23:14	have not found this **man** guilty
23:47	Certainly this **man** was innocent
24: 7	Son of **Man** must be handed over
24: 7	handed over to **sinners,** and be

Jn 1: 4 was the light of all **people.**
1: 6 There was a **man** sent from God
1: 9 which enlightens **everyone,**
1:51 descending upon the Son of **Man.**
2:10 **Everyone** serves the good wine
2:25 no one to testify about **anyone**
2:25 knew what was in **everyone.**
3: 1 a **Pharisee** named Nicodemus,
3: 4 How can **anyone** be born after
3:13 from heaven, the Son of **Man.**
3:14 the Son of **Man** be lifted up,
3:19 **people** loved darkness rather
3:27 No **one** can receive anything
4:28 She said to the **people,**
4:29 Come and see a **man** who told me
4:50 The **man** believed the word that
5: 5 One **man** was there who had been
5: 7 I have no **one** to put me into
5: 9 At once the **man** was made well,
5:12 Who is the **man** who said to you,
5:15 The **man** went away and told the
5:27 because he is the Son of **Man.**
5:34 I accept such **human** testimony,
5:41 accept glory from **human** beings.
6:10 Make the **people** sit down.
6:14 When the **people** saw the sign
6:27 the Son of **Man** will give you.
6:53 eat the flesh of the Son of **Man**
6:62 to see the Son of **Man** ascending
7:22 circumcise a **man** on the sabbath
7:23 If a **man** receives circumcision
7:23 I healed a **man's** whole body on
7:46 Never has **anyone** spoken like
7:51 Our law does not judge **people**
8:17 the testimony of two **witnesses**
8:28 have lifted up the Son of **Man,**
8:40 a **man** who has told you the
9: 1 he saw a **man** blind from birth.

9:11 The **man** called Jesus made mud,
9:16 This **man** is not from God, for
9:16 How can a **man** who is a sinner
9:24 the **man** who had been blind,
9:24 know that this **man** is a sinner
9:30 The **man** answered, "Here is an
9:35 you believe in the Son of **Man?**
10:33 though only a **human being,** are
11:47 **man** is performing many signs.
11:50 have one **man** die for the people
12:23 the Son of **Man** to be glorified.
12:34 Son of **Man** must be lifted up?
12:34 Who is this Son of **Man?**
12:43 for they loved **human** glory more
13:31 Now the Son of **Man** has been
16:21 brought a **human being** into the
17: 6 known to **those** whom you gave me
18:14 one **person** die for the people.
18:17 one of this **man's** disciples,
18:29 do you bring against this **man?**
19: 5 Here is the **man!**

Ac 4: 9 done to **someone** who was sick
4:12 given among **mortals** by which we
4:13 uneducated and ordinary **men,**
4:14 saw the **man** who had been cured
4:16 What will we do with **them?**
4:17 to speak no more to **anyone** in
4:22 For the **man** on whom this sign
5: 4 did not lie to **us** but to God!
5:28 bring this **man's** blood on us.
5:29 rather than any **human** authority
5:34 the **men** to be put outside for
5:35 you propose to do to these **men.**
5:38 these **men** and let them alone;
5:38 undertaking is of **human origin,**
6:13 **man** never stops saying things
7:56 **Man** standing at the right hand
9:33 he found a **man** named Aeneas,
10:26 Stand up; I am only a **mortal.**
10:28 call **anyone** profane or unclean.
12:22 of a god, and not of a **mortal!**
14:11 come down to us in **human** form!
14:15 We are **mortals** just like you,
15:17 other **peoples** may seek the Lord
15:26 **who** have risked their lives for
16:17 **men** are slaves of the Most High
16:20 **men** are disturbing our city;
16:35 Let those **men** go.
16:37 **men** who are Roman citizens,

17:26	he made all **nations** to inhabit	2:11	**human being** knows what is truly
17:29	art and imagination of **mortals.**	2:11	**human** except the human spirit
17:30	the times of **human** ignorance,	2:11	the **human** spirit that is within
18:13	This **man** is persuading people	3: 3	according to **human** inclinations
19:16	the **man** with the evil spirit	3: 4	are you not merely **human?**
19:35	**who** is there that does not know	3:21	one boast about **human** leaders.
21:28	This is the **man** who is teaching	4: 1	Think of **us** in this way,
21:39	Paul replied, "I am a **Jew,** from	4: 9	to angels and to **mortals.**
22:15	be his witness to all the **world**	6:18	a **person** commits is outside the
22:25	for you to flog a Roman **citizen**	7: 1	It is well for a **man** not to
22:26	This **man** is a Roman citizen.	7: 7	**all** were as I myself am.
23: 9	nothing wrong with this **man.**	7:23	become slaves of **human** masters.
24:16	toward God and all **people.**	7:26	for **you** to remain as you are.
25:16	to hand over **anyone** before the	9: 8	I say this on **human** authority?
25:22	I would like to hear the **man**	11:28	Examine **yourselves,** and only
26:31	This **man** is doing nothing to	13: 1	in the tongues of **mortals** and
26:32	**man** could have been set free if	14: 2	to other **people** but to God;
28: 4	This **man** must be a murderer;	14: 3	prophesy speak to other **people**
Ro 1:18	**those** who by their wickedness	15:19	of all **people** most to be pitied
1:23	resembling a mortal **human being**	15:21	came through a **human being,**
2: 1	**whoever** you are, when you judge	15:21	also come through a **human being**
2: 3	**whoever** you are, that when you	15:32	merely **human** hopes I fought
2: 9	for **everyone** who does evil,	15:39	is one flesh for **human beings,**
2:16	the secret thoughts of **all.**	15:45	The first **man,** Adam, became a
2:29	a **person** is a Jew who is one	15:47	first **man** was from the earth,
3: 4	Although **everyone** is a liar,	15:47	the second **man** is from heaven.
3: 5	(I speak in a **human** way.)	2C 3: 2	to be known and read by **all;**
3:28	a **person** is justified by faith	4: 2	**everyone** in the sight of God.
4: 6	**those** to whom God reckons	4:16	outer **nature** is wasting away,
5:12	through one **man,** and death came	5:11	we try to persuade **others;**
5:12	to **all** because all have sinned	8:21	but also in the sight of **others**
5:15	through the one **man's** trespass,	12: 2	I know a **person** in Christ who
5:18	one **man's** trespass led to	12: 3	And I know that such a **person**
5:18	one **man's** act of righteousness	12: 4	**mortal** is permitted to repeat.
5:19	one **man's** disobedience the many	Ga 1: 1	neither by **human** commission
6: 6	old **self** was crucified with him	1: 1	nor from **human** authorities,
7: 1	the law is binding on a **person**	1:10	I now seeking **human** approval,
7:22	law of God in my inmost **self,**	1:10	am I trying to please **people?**
7:24	Wretched **man** that I am!	1:10	I were still pleasing **people,**
9:20	**human being,** to argue with God?	1:11	by me is not of **human** origin;
10: 5	the **person** who does these	1:12	receive it from a **human** source,
12:17	is noble in the sight of **all.**	2: 6	God shows no **partiality**
12:18	live peaceably with **all.**	2:16	a **person** is justified not by
14:18	to God and has **human** approval.	3:15	**person's** will has been ratified
14:20	**others** fall by what you eat;	3:15	give an example from **daily life**
1C 1:25	is wiser than **human** wisdom,	5: 3	every **man** who lets himself be
1:25	stronger than **human** strength.	6: 1	if **anyone** is detected in a
2: 5	**human** wisdom but on the power	6: 7	for you reap whatever **you** sow.
2: 9	nor the **human** heart conceived,	Ep 2:15	**humanity** in place of the two,

	3: 5	not made known to **humankind,**
	3:16	in your inner **being** with power
	4: 8	he gave gifts to his **people.**
	4:14	by **people's** trickery, by their
	4:22	your old **self,** corrupt and
	4:24	with the new **self,** created
	5:31	a **man** will leave his father
	6: 7	to the Lord and not to **men** and
Ph	2: 7	being born in **human** likeness.
	2: 7	And being found in **human** form,
	4: 5	gentleness be known to **everyone**
Co	1:28	warning **everyone** and teaching
	1:28	teaching **everyone** in all wisdom
	1:28	**everyone** mature in Christ.
	2: 8	according to **human** tradition,
	2:22	they are simply **human** commands
	3: 9	stripped off the old **self** with
	3:23	and not for your **masters,**
1Th	2: 4	we speak, not to please **mortals**
	2: 6	we seek praise from **mortals,**
	2:13	as a **human** word but as what it
	2:15	God and oppose **everyone**
	4: 8	rejects not **human** authority but
2Th	2: 3	lawless **one** is revealed,
	3: 2	from wicked and evil **people;**
1Ti	2: 1	be made for **everyone,**
	2: 4	desires **everyone** to be saved
	2: 5	between God and **humankind,**
	2: 5	Christ Jesus, himself **human,**
	4:10	the Savior of all **people,**
	5:24	The sins of some **people** are
	6: 5	who are depraved in **mind** and
	6: 9	that plunge **people** into ruin
	6:11	But as for you, **man** of God,
	6:16	whom no **one** has ever seen or
2Ti	2: 2	entrust to faithful **people**
	3: 2	For **people** will be lovers of
	3: 8	so these **people,** of corrupt
	3:13	wicked **people** and impostors
	3:17	**everyone** who belongs to God
Ti	1:14	of **those** who reject the truth.
	2:11	bringing salvation to **all,**
	3: 2	show every courtesy to **everyone**
	3: 8	**those** who have come to believe
	3:10	**anyone** who causes divisions,
He	2: 6	What are **human beings** that you
	2: 6	**mortals,** that you care for them
	5: 1	chosen from among **mortals** is
	5: 1	to God on **their** behalf,

	6:16	**Human** beings, of course, swear
	7: 8	by those who are **mortal;**
	7:28	as high priests **those** who are
	8: 2	the Lord, and not any **mortal,**
	9:27	for **mortals** to die once, and
	13: 6	What can **anyone** do to me?
Ja	1: 7	**unstable** in every way, must not
	1:19	let **everyone** be quick to listen
	2:20	you senseless **person,**
	2:24	a **person** is justified by works
	3: 8	but no **one** can tame the tongue
	3: 9	we curse **those** who are made in
	5:17	was a **human being** like us,
1P	2: 4	**mortals** yet chosen and precious
	2:15	the ignorance of the **foolish.**
	3: 4	the inner **self** with the lasting
	4: 2	**human** desires but by the will
	4: 6	the flesh as **everyone** is judged,
2P	1:21	ever came by **human** will, but
	1:21	**men** and women moved by the Holy
	2:16	donkey spoke with a **human** voice
	3: 7	and destruction of the **godless.**
1J	5: 9	If we receive **human** testimony,
Ju	1: 4	certain **intruders** have stolen
Re	1:13	I saw one like the Son of **Man,**
	4: 7	with a face like a **human** face,
	8:11	and **many** died from the water,
	9: 4	**people** who do not have the seal
	9: 5	scorpion when it stings **someone**
	9: 6	**people** will seek death but will
	9: 7	faces were like **human** faces
	9:10	is their power to harm **people**
	9:15	to kill a third of **humankind.**
	9:18	a third of **humankind** was killed
	9:20	The rest of **humankind,** who were
	11:13	seven thousand **people** were
	13:13	to earth in the sight of **all;**
	13:18	it is the number of a **person.**
	14: 4	from **humankind** as first fruits
	14:14	was one like the Son of **Man,**
	16: 2	painful sore came on **those** who
	16: 8	was allowed to scorch **them** with
	16: 9	**they** were scorched by the
	16:18	**people** were upon the earth, so
	16:21	dropped from heaven on **people,**
	18:13	slaves—and **human** lives.
	21: 3	home of God is among **mortals.**
	21:17	cubits by **human** measurement,

446 GO5 AG69 LN20 B1:270
ανθυπατος, DEPUTY

Ac	13: 7	He was with the **proconsul,**
	13: 8	**proconsul** away from the faith.
	13:12	When the **proconsul** saw what had
	18:12	But when Gallio was **proconsul**
	19:38	and there are **proconsuls;** let

---

447 GO4 AG69 LN20 K1:367
ανιημι, I LEFT

Ac	16:26	chains were **unfastened.**
	27:40	they **loosened** the ropes that
Ep	6: 9	**Stop** threatening them, for you
He	13: 5	will never **leave** you or forsake

---

449 GO2 AG69 LN20 B1:153 K4:947 R3538
ανιπτος, UNWASHED

| Mt | 15:20 | but to eat with **unwashed** hands |
| Mk | 7: 2 | that is, **without washing** them. |

---

450 GO108 AG70 LN20 B3:259 K1:368 R303,2476
ανιστημι, I STAND UP

Mt	9: 9	And he **got up** and followed him.
	12:41	will **rise up** at the judgment
	22:24	**raise up** children for his
	26:62	high priest **stood up** and said,
Mk	1:35	he **got up** and went out to a
	2:14	And he **got up** and followed him.
	3:26	has **risen up** against himself
	5:42	**got up** and began to walk about
	7:24	he **set out** and went away to the
	8:31	and after three days **rise again**
	9: 9	of Man **had risen** from the dead.
	9:10	what this **rising** from the dead
	9:27	and he was able **to stand.**
	9:31	he will **rise again.**
	10: 1	He **left** that place and went to
	10:34	three days he will **rise again.**
	12:23	In the **resurrection** whose wife
	12:25	when they **rise** from the dead,
	14:57	Some **stood up** and gave false
	14:60	Then the high priest **stood up**
	16: 9	he **rose** early on the first day
Lk	1:39	**set out** and went with haste to
	4:16	He **stood up** to read,
	4:29	They **got up,** drove him out of
	4:38	After **leaving** the synagogue he
	4:39	**got up** and began to serve them.
	5:25	he **stood up** before them, took
	5:28	And he **got up,** left everything,
	6: 8	He **got up** and stood there.
	8:55	and she **got up** at once. Then he
	9: 8	the ancient prophets had **arisen.**
	9:19	the ancient prophets has **arisen**
	10:25	lawyer **stood up** to test Jesus.
	11: 7	I cannot **get up** and give you
	11: 8	**get up** and give him anything
	11:32	will **rise up** at the judgment
	15:18	**get up** and go to my father,
	15:20	**set off** and went to his father.
	16:31	if someone **rises** from the dead.
	17:19	**Get up** and go on your way;
	18:33	third day he will **rise again.**
	22:45	When he **got up** from prayer,
	22:46	**Get up** and pray that you may
	23: 1	the assembly **rose** as a body and
	24: 7	and on the third day **rise again**
	24:12	**got up** and ran to the tomb;
	24:33	That same hour they **got up** and
	24:46	and **to rise** from the dead
Jn	6:39	but **raise** it **up** on the last day
	6:40	I will **raise** them **up** on the
	6:44	I will **raise** that person **up** on
	6:54	will **raise** them **up** on the last
	11:23	Your brother will **rise again.**
	11:24	I know that he will **rise again**
	11:31	saw Mary **get up** quickly and go
	20: 9	that he must **rise** from the dead
Ac	1:15	**stood up** among the believers
	2:24	But God **raised** him **up,** having
	2:32	This Jesus God **raised up,** and
	3:22	your God will **raise up** for you
	3:26	When God **raised up** his servant,
	5: 6	The young men **came** and wrapped
	5:17	the high priest **took action;**
	5:34	**stood up** and ordered the men to
	5:36	some time ago Theudas **rose up,**
	5:37	Judas the Galilean **rose up** at
	6: 9	**stood up** and argued with
	7:18	had not known Joseph **ruled** over
	7:37	God will **raise up** a prophet for
	8:26	**Get up** and go toward the south
	8:27	So he **got up** and went.
	9: 6	But **get up** and enter the city,
	9:11	**Get up** and go to the street
	9:18	Then he **got up** and was baptized
	9:34	**get up** and make your bed!
	9:34	And immediately he **got up.**

9:39	Peter **got up** and went with them
9:40	"Tabitha, **get up**." Then she
9:41	his hand and **helped** her **up.**
10:13	**Get up,** Peter; kill and eat.
10:20	**get up,** go down, and go with
10:23	he **got up** and went with them
10:26	**Stand up;** I am only a mortal.
10:41	after he **rose** from the dead.
11: 7	**Get up,** Peter; kill and eat.
11:28	Agabus **stood up** and predicted
12: 7	**Get up** quickly.
13:16	Paul **stood up** and with a
13:33	by **raising** Jesus; as also it
13:34	his **raising** him from the dead,
14:10	**Stand** upright on your feet.
14:20	he **got up** and went into the
15: 7	Peter **stood up** and said to them
17: 3	and **to rise** from the dead,
17:31	by **raising** him from the dead.
20:30	**will come** distorting the truth
22:10	**Get up** and go to Damascus;
22:16	**Get up,** be baptized, and have
23: 9	group **stood up** and contended,
26:16	**get up** and stand on your feet;
26:30	Then the king **got up,** and with
Ro 15:12	who **rises** to rule the Gentiles;
1C 10: 7	and they **rose up** to play.
Ep 5:14	**Rise** from the dead, and Christ
1Th 4:14	that Jesus died and **rose again,**
4:16	dead in Christ will **rise** first.
He 7:11	**arising** according to the
7:15	**arises,** resembling Melchizedek,

---

451 GO1 AG70 LN21
αννα, ANNA
Lk 2:36 **Anna** the daughter of Phanuel,

---

452 GO4 AG70 LN21
αννας, ANNAS
Lk 3: 2 high priesthood of **Annas** and
Jn 18:13 First they took him to **Annas,**
18:24 Then **Annas** sent him bound to
Ac 4: 6 with **Annas** the high priest,

---

453 GO6 AG70 LN21 B3:122 K4:961 R3539
ανοητος, UNMINDFUL
Lk 24:25 Oh, how **foolish** you are,
Ro 1:14 to the wise and to the **foolish**
Ga 3: 1 You **foolish** Galatians! Who has
3: 3 Are you so **foolish?**

1Ti 6: 9 trapped by many **senseless** and
Ti 3: 3 we ourselves were once **foolish,**

---

454 GO2 AG70 LN21 B3:122 K4:962 R3563
ανοια, MINDLESS
Lk 6:11 But they were filled with **fury**
2Ti 3: 9 their **folly** will become plain

---

455 GO77 AG70 LN21 B2:726
ανοιγω, I OPEN
Mt 2:11 **opening** their treasure chests,
3:16 heavens were **opened** to him and
5: 2 he **began to speak,** and taught
7: 7 the door will be **opened** for you.
7: 8 the door will be **opened.**
9:30 And their eyes were **opened.**
13:35 I will **open** my mouth to speak
17:27 and when you **open** its mouth,
20:33 Lord, let our eyes be **opened.**
25:11 Lord, lord, **open** to us.
27:52 The tombs also were **opened,**
Mk 7:35 his ears were **opened,**
Lk 1:64 his mouth was **opened** and his
3:21 the heaven was **opened,**
11: 9 the door will be **opened** for you.
11:10 the door will be **opened.**
12:36 so that they may **open** the door
13:25 Lord, **open** to us,
Jn 1:51 you will see heaven **opened**
9:10 how were your eyes **opened?**
9:14 Jesus made the mud and **opened**
9:17 It was your eyes he **opened.**
9:21 do we know who **opened** his eyes.
9:26 How did he **open** your eyes?
9:30 and yet he **opened** my eyes.
9:32 that anyone **opened** the eyes of
10: 3 The gatekeeper **opens** the gate
10:21 **open** the eyes of the blind?
11:37 **opened** the eyes of the blind
Ac 5:19 **opened** the prison doors,
5:23 but when we **opened** them,
8:32 so he does not **open** his mouth.
8:35 Then Philip **began to speak,**
9: 8 and though his eyes were **open,**
9:40 Then she **opened** her eyes,
10:11 He saw the heaven **opened** and
10:34 Peter **began to speak** to them:
12:10 It **opened** for them of its own
12:14 instead of **opening** the gate,

	12:16	when they **opened** the gate,
	14:27	he had **opened** a door of faith
	16:26	all the doors were **opened** and
	16:27	saw the prison doors wide **open,**
	18:14	Just as Paul was **about to speak**
	26:18	to **open** their eyes so that they
Ro	3:13	throats are **opened** graves;
1C	16: 9	for effective work has **opened**
2C	2:12	a door was **opened** for me in the
	6:11	our heart is wide **open** to you.
Co	4: 3	God will **open** to us a door for
Re	3: 7	who **opens** and no one will shut,
	3: 7	who shuts and no one **opens:**
	3: 8	**open** door, which no one is able
	3:20	hear my voice and **open** the door
	4: 1	in heaven a door stood **open!**
	5: 2	to **open** the scroll and break
	5: 3	was able to **open** the scroll
	5: 4	to **open** the scroll or to look
	5: 5	so that he can **open** the scroll
	5: 9	to take the scroll and to **open**
	6: 1	**open** one of the seven seals,
	6: 3	When he **opened** the second seal,
	6: 5	When he **opened** the third seal,
	6: 7	When he **opened** the fourth seal,
	6: 9	When he **opened** the fifth seal,
	6:12	When he **opened** the sixth seal
	8: 1	Lamb **opened** the seventh seal,
	9: 2	he **opened** the shaft of the
	10: 2	He held a little scroll **open**
	10: 8	take the scroll that is **open**
	11:19	temple in heaven was **opened,**
	12:16	**opened** its mouth and swallowed
	13: 6	It **opened** its mouth to utter
	15: 5	of witness in heaven was **opened**
	19:11	Then I saw heaven **opened,** and
	20:12	books were **opened.** Also another
	20:12	another book was **opened,** the

456   GO2   AG71   LN21   R303,3618
ανοικοδομεω, I BUILD AGAIN
Ac	15:16	**rebuild** the dwelling of David,
	15:16	its ruins I will **rebuild** it,

457   GO1   AG71   LN21   B2:726   R455
ανοιξις, OPENING
Ep	6:19	so that when I **speak,**

458   GO15   AG71   LN21   B2:438   K4:1085   R459
ανομια, LAWLESSNESS

Mt	7:23	go away from me, you **evildoers**
	13:41	causes of sin and all **evildoers**
	23:28	of hypocrisy and **lawlessness.**
	24:12	of the increase of **lawlessness,**
Ro	4: 7	are those whose **iniquities**
	6:19	to greater and greater **iniquity**
	6:19	to greater and greater **iniquity**
2C	6:14	righteousness and **lawlessness?**
2Th	2: 3	the **lawless** one is revealed,
	2: 7	For the mystery of **lawlessness**
Ti	2:14	redeem us from all **iniquity**
He	1: 9	hated **wickedness;** therefore God,
	10:17	sins and their **lawless** deeds
1J	3: 4	sin is guilty of **lawlessness;**
	3: 4	sin is **lawlessness.**

459   GO9   AG72   LN21   B2:438   K4:1086   R3551
ανομος, LAWLESS
Lk	22:37	was counted among the **lawless**
Ac	2:23	hands of those **outside the law.**
1C	9:21	To those **outside the law**
	9:21	I became as one **outside the law**
	9:21	I am **not free from** God's **law**
	9:21	might win those **outside the law**
2Th	2: 8	then the **lawless** one will be
1Ti	1: 9	for the **lawless** and disobedient
2P	2: 8	by their **lawless** deeds that he

460   GO2   AG72   LN21   B2:446   R459
ανομως, LAWLESSLY
Ro	2:12	have sinned **apart from the law**
	2:12	also perish **apart from the law**

461   GO3   AG72   LN21   R303,3717
ανορθοω, I STRAIGHTEN UP
Lk	13:13	she **stood up straight** and began
Ac	15:16	and I will **set** it **up**
He	12:12	and **strengthen** your weak knees,

462   GO2   AG72   LN21   B2:236   K5:492   R3741
ανοσιος, UNHOLY
1Ti	1: 9	for the **unholy** and profane,
2Ti	3: 2	parents, ungrateful, **unholy,**

463   GO2   AG72   LN21   B2:765   K1:359   R430
ανοχη, RESTRAINT
Ro	2: 4	kindness and **forbearance** and
	3:26	in his divine **forbearance**

464 ᴳᴼ1 ᴬᴳ72 ᴸᴺ21 ᴮ1:644 ᴷ1:134 ᴿ473,75
ανταγωνιζομαι, I CONTEST AGAINST
He 12: 4   In your **struggle** against sin

---

465 ᴳᴼ2 ᴬᴳ72 ᴸᴺ21 ᴮ3:166 ᴷ1:252 ᴿ473,236
ανταλλαγμα, EXCHANGE
Mt 16:26   what will they give in **return**
Mk   8:37   what can they give in **return**

---

466 ᴳᴼ1 ᴬᴳ72 ᴸᴺ21 ᴮ1:741 ᴷ6:307 ᴿ473,378
ανταναπληροω, I FILL UP
Co   1:24   **I am completing** what is lacking

---

467 ᴳᴼ7 ᴬᴳ73 ᴸᴺ21 ᴮ3:134 ᴷ2:169 ᴿ473,591
ανταποδιδωμι, I GIVE BACK AGAIN
Lk 14:14   because they cannot **repay** you,
    14:14   **repaid** at the resurrection
Ro 11:35   to receive a gift in **return?**
    12:19   I will **repay,** says the Lord.
1Th 3: 9   in **return** for all the joy that
2Th 1: 6   to **repay** with affliction those
He 10:30   I will **repay**

---

468 ᴳᴼ2 ᴬᴳ73 ᴸᴺ21 ᴮ3:134 ᴷ2:169 ᴿ467
ανταποδομα, GIVEN BACK AGAIN
Lk 14:12   they may invite you in **return,**
Ro 11: 9   and a **retribution** for them;

---

469 ᴳᴼ1 ᴬᴳ73 ᴸᴺ21 ᴮ3:134 ᴷ2:169 ᴿ467
ανταποδοσις, REPAYMENT
Co   3:24   the inheritance as your **reward**

---

470 ᴳᴼ2 ᴬᴳ73 ᴸᴺ21 ᴷ3:944 ᴿ473,611
ανταποκρινομαι, I ANSWER BACK
Lk 14: 6   they could not **reply** to this.
Ro   9:20   human being, to **argue** with God?

---

472 ᴳᴼ4 ᴬᴳ73 ᴸᴺ22 ᴷ2:827 ᴿ473,2192
αντεχω, I HOLD ON
Mt   6:24   or be **devoted** to the one and
Lk 16:13   or be **devoted** to the one and
1Th 5:14   **help** the weak, be patient with
Ti   1: 9   have a **firm grasp** of the word

---

473 ᴳᴼ22 ᴬᴳ73 ᴸᴺ22 ᴮ3:1171 ᴷ1:372
αντι, IN PLACE OF, INSTEAD OF
Mt   2:22   **in place of** his father Herod,
     5:38   An eye **for** an eye and a tooth
     5:38   an eye and a tooth **for** a tooth.
    17:27   give it to them **for** you and me.

    20:28   give his life a ransom **for** many
Mk 10:45   give his life a ransom **for** many
Lk   1:20   **because** you did not believe my
    11:11   give a snake **instead** of a fish?
    12: 3   **Therefore** whatever you have
    19:44   **because** you did not recognize
Jn   1:16   grace **upon** grace
Ac 12:23   **because** he had not given the
Ro 12:17   not repay anyone evil **for** evil
1C 11:15   **For** her hair is given to her
Ep   5:31   **For** this reason a man will
1Th 5:15   of you repays evil **for** evil,
2Th 2:10   **because** they refused to love
He 12: 2   **for the sake** of the joy
    12:16   birthright **for** a single meal.
Ja   4:15   **Instead** you ought to say,
1P   3: 9   Do not repay evil **for** evil or
     3: 9   for evil or abuse **for** abuse;

---

474 ᴳᴼ1 ᴬᴳ74 ᴸᴺ22 ᴿ473,906
αντιβαλλω, I PUT AGAINST (DISPUTE)
Lk 24:17   What are you **discussing** with

---

475 ᴳᴼ1 ᴬᴳ74 ᴸᴺ22 ᴿ473,1303
αντιδιατιθημι, I SET FIRMLY AGAINST
2Ti 2:25   correcting **opponents** with

---

476 ᴳᴼ5 ᴬᴳ74 ᴸᴺ22 ᴮ1:553 ᴷ1:373 ᴿ473,1349
αντιδικος, OPPONENT
Mt   5:25   quickly with your **accuser** while
     5:25   or your **accuser** may hand you
Lk 12:58   when you go with your **accuser**
    18: 3   justice against my **opponent**
1P   5: 8   your **adversary** the devil prowls

---

477 ᴳᴼ1 ᴬᴳ74 ᴸᴺ22 ᴿ473,5087
αντιθεσις, OPPOSITION
1Ti 6:20   chatter and **contradictions**

---

478 ᴳᴼ1 ᴬᴳ74 ᴸᴺ22 ᴿ473,2525
αντικαθιστημι, I STAND UP AGAINST
He 12: 4   not yet **resisted** to the point

---

479 ᴳᴼ1 ᴬᴳ74 ᴸᴺ22 ᴷ3:496 ᴿ473,2564
αντικαλεω, I CALL BACK
Lk 14:12   they may **invite** you **in return,**

---

480 ᴳᴼ8 ᴬᴳ74 ᴸᴺ22 ᴷ3:655 ᴿ473,2749
αντικειμαι, I LIE AGAINST
Lk 13:17   his **opponents** were put to shame

	21:15	your **opponents** will be able to
1C	16: 9	and there are many **adversaries.**
Ga	5:17	these are **opposed** to each other
Ph	1:28	intimidated by your **opponents.**
2Th	2: 4	He **opposes** and exalts himself
1Ti	1:10	and whatever else **is contrary**
	5:14	so as to give the **adversary** no

481　GO1　AG74　LN22　R473
αντικρυς, OPPOSITE
Ac　20:15　we arrived **opposite** Chios.

482　GO3　AG74　LN22　K1:375　R473,2983
αντιλαμβανω, I TAKE PART
Lk　1:54　has **helped** his servant Israel,
Ac　20:35　we must **support** the weak,
1Ti　6: 2　who **benefit** by their service

483　GO11　AG74　LN22　R473,3004
αντιλεγω, I SPEAK AGAINST
Lk　2:34　be a sign that will be **opposed**
　　20:27　**say** there is **no** resurrection,
　　21:15　able to withstand or **contradict**
Jn　19:12　sets himself **against**
Ac　4:14　nothing to **say in opposition.**
　　13:45　**contradicted** what was spoken by
　　28:19　But when the Jews **objected,**
　　28:22　everywhere it is **spoken against**
Ro　10:21　disobedient and **contrary** people
Ti　1: 9　**refute** those who contradict it.
　　2: 9　they are not to **talk back,**

484　GO1　AG75　LN22　K1:375　R482
αντιλημψις, ASSISTANCE
1C　12:28　forms of **assistance,** forms of

485　GO4　AG75　LN22　R483
αντιλογια, WORD AGAINST
He　6:16　puts an end to all **dispute.**
　　7: 7　It is beyond **dispute** that the
　　12: 3　him who endured such **hostility**
Ju　1:11　and perish in Korah's **rebellion**

486　GO1　AG75　LN22　B3:346　K4:293　R473,3058
αντιλοιδορεω, I ABUSE BACK
1P　2:23　he did not **return abuse;**

487　GO1　AG75　LN22　B3:189　K4:349　R473,3083
αντιλυτρον, RANSOM
1Ti　2: 6　gave himself a **ransom** for all

488　GO1　AG75　LN22　R473,3354
αντιμετρεω, I MEASURE AGAINST
Lk　6:38　be the **measure** you get **back**

489　GO2　AG75　LN22　K4:695　R473,3408
αντιμισθια, RETURN WAGE
Ro　1:27　the **due penalty** for their error
2C　6:13　In **return**

490　GO18　AG75　LN22
αντιοχεια, ANTIOCH
Ac　11:19　and **Antioch,** and they spoke the
　　11:20　on coming to **Antioch,** spoke to
　　11:22　they sent Barnabas to **Antioch.**
　　11:26　he brought him to **Antioch.**
　　11:26　in **Antioch** that the disciples
　　11:27　down from Jerusalem to **Antioch.**
　　13: 1　Now in the church at **Antioch**
　　13:14　came to **Antioch** in Pisidia.
　　14:19　Jews came there from **Antioch**
　　14:21　then on to Iconium and **Antioch.**
　　14:26　they sailed back to **Antioch,**
　　15:22　send them to **Antioch** with Paul
　　15:23　of Gentile origin in **Antioch**
　　15:30　and went down to **Antioch.**
　　15:35　Barnabas remained in **Antioch,**
　　18:22　and then went down to **Antioch.**
Ga　2:11　But when Cephas came to **Antioch**
2Ti　3:11　that happened to me in **Antioch,**

491　GO1　AG75　LN22
αντιοχευς, ANTIOCHEAN
Ac　6: 5　a proselyte of **Antioch.**

492　GO2　AG75　LN22　R473,3928
αντιπαρερχομαι, I GO ALONG OPPOSITE
Lk　10:31　he **passed by** on the **other side.**
　　10:32　**passed by** on the **other side.**

493　GO1　AG75　LN22
αντιπας, ANTIPAS
Re　2:13　even in the days of **Antipas**

494　GO1　AG75　LN22
αντιπατρις, ANTIPATRIS
Ac　23:31　during the night to **Antipatris.**

495　GO1　AG75　LN22　R473,4008
αντιπερα, ACROSS AGAINST
Lk　8:26　which is **opposite** Galilee.

496　GO1　AG75　LN22　R473,4098
αντιπιπτω, I FALL AGAINST
Ac　7:51　**opposing** the Holy Spirit, just

497　GO1　AG75　LN22　R473,4754
αντιστρατευομαι, I SOLDIER AGAINST
Ro　7:23　another law **at war** with the law

498　GO5　AG76　LN22　R473,5021
αντιτασσω, I SET IN ORDER AGAINST
Ac　18: 6　they **opposed** and reviled him
Ro　13: 2　whoever **resists** authority
Ja　4: 6　God **opposes** the proud
　　5: 6　one, who does not **resist** you
1P　5: 5　God **opposes** the proud

499　GO2　AG76　LN22　B3:903　K8:246　R473,5179
αντιτυπος, ANTITYPE
He　9:24　a mere **copy** of the true one,
1P　3:21　baptism, which this **prefigured,**

500　GO5　AG76　LN23　B1:124　K9:493　R473,5547
αντιχριστος, ANTICHRIST
1J　2:18　heard that **antichrist** is coming
　　2:18　now many **antichrists** have
　　　　come.
　　2:22　This is the **antichrist,** the one
　　4: 3　the spirit of the **antichrist,**
2J　1: 7　the deceiver and the **antichrist**

501　GO4　AG76　LN23
αντλεω, I DRAW OUT
Jn　2: 8　Now **draw** some **out,** and take it
　　2: 9　who **had drawn** the water
　　4: 7　Samaritan woman came **to
　　　　draw**
　　4:15　keep coming here **to draw** water

502　GO1　AG76　LN23　R501
αντλημα, BUCKET
Jn　4:11　Sir, you have no **bucket**

503　GO1　AG76　LN23　R473,3788
αντοφθαλμεω, I LOOK DIRECTLY AT
Ac　27:15　could not be **turned head-on**

504　GO4　AG76　LN23　R5204
ανυδρος, WATERLESS
Mt　12:43　it wanders through **waterless**
Lk　11:24　it wanders through **waterless**

2P　2:17　**waterless** springs and mists
Ju　1:12　**waterless** clouds carried along

505　GO6　AG76　LN23　K8:570　R5271
ανυποκριτος, UNHYPOCRITICAL
Ro　12: 9　Let love be **genuine**
2C　6: 6　spirit, **genuine** love
1Ti　1: 5　conscience, and **sincere** faith
2Ti　1: 5　reminded of your **sincere** faith
Ja　3:17　of partiality or **hypocrisy**
1P　1:22　you have **genuine** mutual love

506　GO4　AG76　LN23　K8:47
ανυποτακτος, UNSUBMITTING
1Ti　1: 9　for the lawless and **disobedient**
Ti　1: 6　debauchery and not **rebellious**
　　1:10　are also many **rebellious** people
He　2: 8　nothing **outside their control**

507　GO9　AG77　LN23　B2:187　K1:376
ανω, UP
Jn　2: 7　they filled them up **to the brim**
　　8:23　from below, I am from **above**
　　11:41　Jesus looked **upward** and said
Ac　2:19　portents in the heaven **above**
Ga　4:26　to the Jerusalem **above**
Ph　3:14　**heavenly** call of God in Christ
Co　3: 1　seek the things that are **above**
　　3: 2　minds on things that are **above**
He　12:15　root of bitterness springs **up**

509　GO13　AG77　LN23　B2:187　K1:378　R507
ανωθεν, FROM ABOVE
Mt　27:51　torn in two, **from top** to bottom
Mk　15:38　torn in two, **from top** to bottom
Lk　1: 3　carefully **from the very first**
Jn　3: 3　without being born **from above**
　　3: 7　You must be born **from above**
　　3:31　The one who comes **from above**
　　19:11　had been given you **from above**
　　19:23　woven in one piece **from the top**
Ac　26: 5　They have known **for a long time**
Ga　4: 9　to be enslaved to them **again**
Ja　1:17　perfect gift, is **from above**
　　3:15　not come down **from above**
　　3:17　wisdom **from above** is first pure

510　GO1　AG77　LN23　R507
ανωτερικος, UPPERMOST
Ac　19: 1　through the **interior** regions

511 GO2 AG77 LN23 K1:376 R507
ανωτερος, UPPER
Lk 14:10 Friend, move up **higher**
He 10: 8 When he said **above,** "You have

512 GO2 AG77 LN23 R5624
ανωφελης, UNPROFITABLE
Ti 3: 9 for they are **unprofitable**
He 7:18 it was weak and **ineffectual**

513 GO2 AG77 LN23
αξινη, AXE
Mt 3:10 the **ax** is lying at the root
Lk 3: 9 the **ax** is lying at the root

514 GO41 AG78 LN23 B3:348 K1:379
αξιος, WORTHY
Mt 3: 8 Bear fruit **worthy** of repentance
    10:10 for laborers **deserve** their food
    10:11 find out who in it is **worthy,**
    10:13 If the house is **worthy,**
    10:13 but if it is not **worthy**
    10:37 than me is not **worthy** of me
    10:37 than me is not **worthy** of me
    10:38 follow me is not **worthy** of me
    22: 8 those invited were not **worthy**
Lk 3: 8 fruits **worthy** of repentance
    7: 4 He is **worthy** of having you do
    10: 7 the laborer **deserves** to be paid
    12:48 did what **deserved** a beating
    15:19 I am no longer **worthy**
    15:21 I am no longer **worthy**
    23:15 done nothing to **deserve** death
    23:41 what we **deserve** for our deeds
Jn 1:27 I am not **worthy** to untie
Ac 13:25 I am not **worthy** to untie
    13:46 to be **unworthy** of eternal life
    23:29 with nothing **deserving** death
    25:11 for which I **deserve** to die
    25:25 done nothing **deserving** death
    26:20 to God and do deeds **consistent**
    26:31 doing nothing to **deserve** death
Ro 1:32 such things **deserve** to die
    8:18 are not **worth** comparing with
1C 16: 4 **advisable** that I should go
2Th 1: 3 and sisters, as is **right**
1Ti 1:15 saying is sure and **worthy**
    4: 9 saying is sure and **worthy**
    5:18 laborer **deserves** to be paid
    6: 1 regard their masters as **worthy**

He 11:38 whom the world was not **worthy.**
Re 3: 4 in white, for they are **worthy**
    4:11 are **worthy,** our Lord and God
    5: 2 is **worthy** to open the scroll
    5: 4 found **worthy** to open the scroll
    5: 9 are **worthy** to take the scroll
    5:12 **Worthy** is the Lamb that was
    16: 6 It is what they **deserve**

515 GO7 AG78 LN23 B3:348 K1:380 R514
αξιοω, I AM WORTHY
Lk 7: 7 I did not **presume** to come
Ac 15:38 Paul **decided** not to take with
    28:22 we **would like** to hear from you
2Th 1:11 God will **make** you **worthy**
1Ti 5:17 **considered worthy** of double
He 3: 3 Jesus **is worthy** of more glory
    10:29 do you think **will be deserved**

516 GO6 AG78 LN23 B3:348 R514
αξιως, WORTHILY
Ro 16: 2 as is **fitting** for the saints,
Ep 4: 1 a life **worthy** of the calling
Ph 1:27 manner **worthy** of the gospel
Co 1:10 lead lives **worthy** of the Lord
1Th 2:12 lead a life **worthy** of God
3J 1: 6 in a manner **worthy** of God

517 GO5 AG79 LN23 B3:128 K5:368 R3707
αορατος, UNSEEN
Ro 1:20 **invisible** though they are
Co 1:15 the image of the **invisible** God
    1:16 things visible and **invisible**
1Ti 1:17 **invisible,** the only God
He 11:27 he saw him who is **invisible**

518 GO45 AG79 LN23 B3:44 K1:64 R575,31a
απαγγελλω, I TELL
Mt 2: 8 **bring** me **word** so that I may
    8:33 they **told** the whole story
    11: 4 Go and **tell** John what you hear
    12:18 he will **proclaim** justice
    14:12 then they went and **told** Jesus
    28: 8 ran to **tell** his disciples.
    28:10 go and **tell** my brothers
    28:11 **told** the chief priests
Mk 5:14 swineherds ran off and **told** it
    5:19 **tell** them how much the Lord
    6:30 **told** him all that they had
    16:10 She went out and **told** those

16:13　went back and **told** the rest

Lk　7:18　disciples of John **reported**

　　7:22　**tell** John what you have seen

　　8:20　And he was **told,** "Your mother

　　8:34　they ran off and **told** it

　　8:36　who had seen it **told** them how

　　8:47　she **declared** in the presence

　　9:36　**told** no one any of the things

　　13: 1　**told** him about the Galileans

　　14:21　slave returned and **reported**

　　18:37　They **told** him,

　　24: 9　they **told** all this

Jn　16:25　but will **tell** you plainly

Ac　4:23　**reported** what the chief priests

　　5:22　they returned and **reported**

　　5:25　someone arrived and **announced,**

　　11:13　He **told** us how he had seen

　　12:14　she ran in and **announced**

　　12:17　**Tell** this to James

　　15:27　who themselves will **tell** you

　　16:36　the jailer **reported** the message

　　16:38　police **reported** these words

　　22:26　to the tribune and **said** to him

　　23:16　to the barracks and **told** Paul

　　23:17　he has something to **report**

　　23:19　that you have to **report** to me

　　26:20　but **declared** first to those

　　28:21　coming here has **reported**

1C　14:25　**declaring,** "God is really

1Th　1: 9　**report** about us what kind of

He　2:12　I will **proclaim** your name

1J　1: 2　**declare** to you the eternal life

　　1: 3　we **declare** to you what we have

519　GO1　AG79　LN23
απαγχω, I CHOKE OFF
Mt　27: 5　in the temple, he **departed**

520　GO15　AG79　LN23　R575,71
απαγω, I LEAD OFF
Mt　7:13　the road is easy that **leads**

　　7:14　the road is hard that **leads**

　　26:57　**took** him to Caiaphas the high

　　27: 2　They bound him, **led** him **away,**

　　27:31　**led** him **away** to crucify him.

Mk　14:44　**lead** him **away** under guard

　　14:53　They **took** Jesus to the high

Lk　13:15　**lead** it **away** to give it water

　　21:12　**will be brought** before kings

22:66　**brought** him to their council

23:26　As they **led** him **away**

Ac　12:19　them **to be put to death**

23:17　**Take** this young man to the

1C　12: 2　led **astray** to idols

521　GO1　AG79　LN23　K5:596　R3811
απαιδευτος, UNINSTRUCTED AS A CHILD
2Ti　2:23　to do with stupid and **senseless**

522　GO3　AG79　LN23　R575,142
απαιρω, I LIFT UP
Mt　9:15　the bridegroom **is taken away**

Mk　2:20　the bridegroom **is taken away**

Lk　5:35　bridegroom **will be taken away**

523　GO2　AG80　LN23　B2:855　K1:193　R575,154
απαιτεω, I ASK BACK
Lk　6:30　**do** not **ask for** them again

　　12:20　your life **is being demanded**

524　GO1　AG80　LN24
απαλγεω, I AM CALLOUS
Ep　4:19　They have **lost** all **sensitivity**

525　GO3　AG80　LN24　B3:166　K1:252　R575,236
απαλλασσω, I RELEASE
Lk　12:58　an effort **to settle** the case

Ac　19:12　their diseases **left** them

He　2:15　**free** those who all their lives

526　GO3　AG80　LN24　B2:742　K1:265　R575,245
απαλλοτριοω, I ALIENATE
Ep　2:12　**aliens** from the commonwealth

　　4:18　**alienated** from the life of God

Co　1:21　you who were once **estranged**

527　GO2　AG80　LN24
απαλος, TENDER
Mt　24:32　as its branch becomes **tender**

Mk　13:28　as its branch becomes **tender**

528　GO2　AG80　LN24　B1:324
απανταω, I MEET
Mk　14:13　a jar of water **will meet** you,

Lk　17:12　ten lepers **approached** him

529　GO3　AG80　LN24　B1:324　K1:380　R528
απαντησις, MEETING
Mt　25: 6　Come out to **meet** him

Ac   28:15   and Three Taverns to **meet** us
1Th   4:17   to **meet** the Lord in the air

---

530   GO14   AG80   LN24   K1:381   R537
'απαξ, ONCE

2C   11:25   **Once** I received a stoning
Ph   4:16   for my needs more than **once.**
1Th   2:18   wanted to **again** and again
He   6: 4   who have **once** been enlightened
      9: 7   and he but **once** a year,
      9:26   has appeared **once** for all
      9:27   for mortals to die **once**
      9:28   having been offered **once**
      10: 2   cleansed **once** for all
      12:26   **once** more I will shake not only
      12:27   Yet **once** more,
1P   3:18   suffered for sins **once** for all
Ju   1: 3   faith that was **once** for all
      1: 5   who **once** for all saved a people

---

531   GO1   AG80   LN24   B3:583   K5:742   R3845
απαραβατος, UNTRANSFERABLE
He   7:24   his priesthood **permanently**

---

532   GO1   AG80   LN24   B3:119   R3903
απαρασκευαστος, UNPREPARED
2C   9: 4   find that you are **not ready**

---

533   GO11   AG81   LN24   B1:454   K1:471   R575,720
απαρνεομαι, I DENY THOROUGHLY
Mt   16:24   let them **deny** themselves
      26:34   you **will deny** me three times
      26:35   I **will** not **deny** you
      26:75   you **will deny** me three times
Mk   8:34   let them **deny** themselves
      14:30   you **will deny** me three times
      14:31   I **will** not **deny** you
      14:72   you **will deny** me three times
Lk   12: 9   whoever **denies** me before others
      22:34   you **have denied** three times
      22:61   you **will deny** me three times

---

535   GO1   AG81   LN24
απαρτισμος, WELL FIT
Lk   14:28   he has **enough to complete** it

---

536   GO9   AG81   LN24   B3:415   K1:484   R575,756
απαρχη, FROM BEGINNING (FIRST FRUITS)
Ro   8:23   the **first fruits** of the Spirit
      11:16   offered as **first fruits**

      16: 5   who was the **first** convert
1C   15:20   **first fruits** of those who have
      15:23   Christ the **first fruits**
      16:15   the **first** converts in Achaia
2Th   2:13   chose you as the **first fruits**
Ja   1:18   **first fruits** of his creatures
Re   14: 4   from humankind as **first**
                  fruits

---

537   GO34   AG81   LN24   K5:886   R3956
'απας, ALL

Mt   6:32   who strive for **all** these things
      24:39   came and swept them **all** away
      28:11   the chief priests **everything**
Mk   1:27   They were **all** amazed
      8:25   he saw **everything** clearly
      11:32   **all** regarded John as truly
      16:15   Go into **all** the world
Lk   3:21   **all** the people were baptized,
      4: 6   glory and **all** this authority
      4:40   **all** those who had any
      5:26   Amazement seized **all** of them
      8:37   Then **all** the people of the
      9:15   made them **all** sit down.
      19:37   the **whole** multitude of the
      19:48   for **all** the people were
      20: 6   **all** the people will stone us
      21:15   that **none** of your opponents
      23: 1   the assembly rose **as a body**
Jn   4:25   he will proclaim **all** things
Ac   2: 7   not **all** these who are speaking
      2:44   **All** who believed were together
      4:31   **all** filled with the Holy Spirit
      4:32   **everything** they owned was
                  held
      5:12   they were **all** together
      5:16   and they were **all** cured
      10: 8   after telling them **everything,**
      11:10   **everything** was pulled up again
      16: 3   they **all** knew that his father
      16:28   for we are **all** here
      25:24   Agrippa and **all** here present
      27:33   Paul urged **all** of them to take
Ep   6:13   day, and having done **everything**
1Ti   1:16   display the **utmost** patience,
Ja   3: 2   **all** of us make many mistakes.

537a   GO1   AG81   LN24   K1:496
απασπαζομαι, I TAKE LEAVE OF
Ac   21: 6   said **farewell** to one another.

538　ᴳᴏ3　ᴬᴳ81　ᴸɴ24　ᴮ2:457　ᴷ1:384
απαταω, I DECEIVE
Ep　5: 6　Let no one **deceive** you
1Ti　2:14　and Adam **was** not **deceived,**
Ja　1:26　but **deceive** their hearts

539　ᴳᴏ7　ᴬᴳ82　ᴸɴ24　ᴮ2:457　ᴷ1:385　ᴿ538
απατη, DECEPTION
Mt　13:22　**lure** of wealth choke the word
Mk　4:19　**lure** of wealth, and the desire
Ep　4:22　and **deluded** by its lusts
Co　2: 8　philosophy and empty **deceit,**
2Th　2:10　every kind of wicked **deception**
He　3:13　hardened by the **deceitfulness**
2P　2:13　reveling in their **dissipation**

540　ᴳᴏ1　ᴬᴳ82　ᴸɴ24　ᴮ1:615　ᴷ5:1019　ᴿ3962
απατωρ, NO FATHER
He　7: 3　**Without father,** without mother,

541　ᴳᴏ1　ᴬᴳ82　ᴸɴ24　ᴮ2:289　ᴷ1:508　ᴿ575,826
απαυγασμα, RADIANCE
He　1: 3　the **reflection** of God's glory

543　ᴳᴏ7　ᴬᴳ82　ᴸɴ24　ᴮ1:588　ᴷ6:11　ᴿ545
απειθεια, DISOBEDIENCE
Ro　11:30　because of their **disobedience**
　　11:32　imprisoned all in **disobedience**
Ep　2: 2　among those who are **disobedient**
　　5: 6　on those who are **disobedient**
Co　3: 6　on those who are **disobedient**
He　4: 6　because of **disobedience**
　　4:11　through such **disobedience**

544　ᴳᴏ14　ᴬᴳ82　ᴸɴ24　ᴮ1:588　ᴷ6:10　ᴿ545
απειθεω, I DISOBEY
Jn　3:36　whoever **disobeys** the Son
Ac　14: 2　the **unbelieving** Jews stirred up
　　19: 9　stubbornly **refused to believe**
Ro　2: 8　who **obey not** the truth
　　10:21　out my hands to a **disobedient**
　　11:30　you **were** once **disobedient**
　　11:31　they **have** now **been disobedient**
　　15:31　rescued from the **unbelievers**
He　3:18　to those who **were disobedient**
　　11:31　with those who **were disobedient**
1P　2: 8　stumble because they **disobey**
　　3: 1　if some of them do **not obey**
　　3:20　in former times did **not obey**
　　4:17　end for those who do **not obey**

545　ᴳᴏ6　ᴬᴳ82　ᴸɴ25　ᴮ1:588　ᴷ6:10　ᴿ3982
απειθης, DISOBEDIENT
Lk　1:17　the **disobedient** to the wisdom
Ac　26:19　I was not **disobedient**
Ro　1:30　**rebellious** toward parents,
2Ti　3: 2　**disobedient** to their parents,
Ti　1:16　are detestable, **disobedient,**
　　3: 3　**disobedient,** led astray,

546　ᴳᴏ2　ᴬᴳ82　ᴸɴ25
απειλεω, I THREATEN
Ac　4:17　**let** us **warn** them to speak no
1P　2:23　he **did** not **threaten;** but he

547　ᴳᴏ3　ᴬᴳ83　ᴸɴ25　ᴿ547
απειλη, THREATENING
Ac　4:29　look at their **threats,**
　　9: 1　Saul, still breathing **threats**
Ep　6: 9　Stop **threatening** them

548　ᴳᴏ7　ᴬᴳ83　ᴸɴ25　ᴿ575,1510
απειμι, I AM ABSENT
1C　5: 3　For though **absent** in body
2C　10: 1　bold toward you when I **am away**
　　10:11　we say by letter when **absent**
　　13: 2　I warn them now while **absent**
　　13:10　while I **am away** from you,
Ph　1:27　or **am absent** and hear about
　　　　　you
Co　2: 5　For though I **am absent** in body,

549　ᴳᴏ1　ᴬᴳ83　ᴸɴ25
απειμι, I GO OFF
Ac　17:10　**went to** the Jewish synagogue

550　ᴳᴏ1　ᴬᴳ83　ᴸɴ25　ᴿ575,2036
απειπον, I RENOUNCE
2C　4: 2　**renounced** the shameful things

551　ᴳᴏ1　ᴬᴳ83　ᴸɴ25　ᴮ3:798　ᴷ6:23　ᴿ3987
απειραστος, UNPRESSUREABLE
Ja　1:13　God **cannot be tempted** by evil

552　ᴳᴏ1　ᴬᴳ83　ᴸɴ25　ᴿ3984
απειρος, INEXPERIENCED
He　5:13　is **unskilled** in the word

553　ᴳᴏ8　ᴬᴳ83　ᴸɴ25　ᴮ2:244　ᴷ2:56　ᴿ575,1551
απεκδεχομαι, I AWAIT
Ro　8:19　**waits** with eager longing

	8:23	while we **wait** for adoption,
	8:25	we **wait** for it with patience.
1C	1: 7	as you **wait** for the revealing
Ga	5: 5	we eagerly **wait** for the hope
Ph	3:20	we **are expecting** a Savior
He	9:28	**are** eagerly **waiting** for him.
1P	3:20	when God **waited** patiently

---

554 GO2 AG83 LN25 B1:314 K2:318
R575,1562
απεκδυομαι, I PUT OFF FROM

Co	2:15	He **disarmed** the rulers
	3: 9	have **stripped off** the old self

---

555 GO1 AG83 LN25 B1:314 K2:321 R554
απεκδυσις, PUTTING OFF FROM

Co	2:11	by **putting off** the body

---

556 GO1 AG83 LN25 R575,1643
απελαυνω, I DRIVE AWAY

Ac	18:16	And he **dismissed** them from

---

557 GO1 AG83 LN25 R575,1651
απελεγμος, DISREPUTE

Ac	19:27	of ours may come into **disrepute**

---

558 GO1 AG83 LN25 B1:715 K2:487 R575,1658
απελευθερος, FREED MAN

1C	7:22	is a **freed person** belonging

---

559 GO1 AG83 LN25
απελλης, APELLES

Ro	16:10	Greet **Apelles,** who is approved

---

560 GO1 AG83 LN25 B2:238 K2:533 R575,1679
απελπιζω, I GIVE UP HOPE

Lk	6:35	**expecting nothing in return.**

---

561 GO5 AG84 LN25 R575,1725
απεναντι, OVER AGAINST

Mt	27:24	and washed his hands **before**
	27:61	sitting **opposite** the tomb.
Ac	3:16	perfect health **in the presence**
	17: 7	They are all acting **contrary**
Ro	3:18	fear of God **before** their eyes

---

562 GO1 AG84 LN26
απεραντος, ENDLESS

1Ti	1: 4	myths and **endless** genealogies

---

563 GO1 AG84 LN26
απερισπαστως, UNDISTRACTEDLY

1C	7:35	order and **unhindered** devotion

---

564 GO1 AG84 LN26 B1:307 K6:72
απεριτμητος, UNCIRCUMCISED

Ac	7:51	**uncircumcised** in heart and ears

---

565 GO117 AG84 LN26 B1:320 K2:675
R575,2064
απερχομαι, I GO OFF

Mt	2:22	he was afraid **to go** there.
	4:24	So his fame **spread throughout**
	5:30	whole body **to go** into hell.
	8:18	he gave orders **to go** over
	8:19	follow you wherever you **go**
	8:21	let me **go** and bury my father
	8:32	And he said to them, **"Go!"**
	8:33	on **going** into the town,
	9: 7	stood up and **went** to his home
	10: 5	**Go** nowhere among the Gentiles
	13:25	the wheat, and then **went away**
	13:28	Then do you want us **to go**
	13:46	he **went** and sold all
	14:15	they **may go** into the villages
	14.16	They need not **go away**
	16: 4	he left them and **went away**
	16:21	that he must **go** to Jerusalem
	18:30	then he **went** and threw him
	19:22	he **went away** grieving,
	20: 5	he **went out** again about noon
	21:29	he changed his mind and **went.**
	21:30	'I go, sir'; but he **did** not **go.**
	22: 5	made light of it and **went away**
	22:22	they left him and **went away.**
	25:10	And while they **went** to buy it,
	25:18	**went off** and dug a hole
	25:25	I **went** and hid your talent
	25:46	**go away** into eternal punishment
	26:36	**went** with them to a place
	26:42	**went away** for the second time
	26:44	he **went away** and prayed
	27: 5	he **went** and hanged himself.
	27:60	door of the tomb and **went away**
	28: 8	they **left** the tomb quickly
	28:10	my brothers to **go** to Galilee;
Mk	1:20	and **followed** him.
	1:35	**went out** to a deserted place
	1:42	the leprosy **left** him,
	3:13	and they **came** to him.

5:17	began to beg Jesus to **leave**	
5:20	**went away** and began to proclaim	
5:24	So he **went** with him.	
6:27	He **went** and beheaded him	
6:32	they **went away** in the boat	
6:36	them away so that **they may go**	
6:37	to **go** and buy two hundred	
6:46	he **went** up on the mountain	
7:24	**went away** to the region of Tyre	
7:30	So she **went** home	
8:13	**went** across to the other side	
9:43	two hands and **to go** to hell,	
10:22	shocked and **went away** grieving	
11: 4	They **went away** and found a colt	
12:12	So they left him and **went away.**	
14:10	**went** to the chief priests	
14:12	Where do you want us **to go**	
14:39	again he **went away** and prayed,	
16:13	**went** back and told the rest	
Lk 1:23	he **went** to his home.	
1:38	the angel **departed** from her.	
2:15	left them and **gone** into heaven,	
5:13	the leprosy **left** him.	
5:14	**"Go,"** he said, "and show	
5:25	**went** to his home, glorifying	
7:24	John's messengers **had gone**	
8:31	not to order them **to go** back	
8:37	asked Jesus **to leave** them;	
8:39	So he **went away,** proclaiming	
9:57	will follow you wherever you **go**	
9:59	first **let** me **go** and bury	
9:60	**go** and proclaim the kingdom	
10:30	beat him, and **went away,**	
17:23	**Do** not **go,** do not set off	
19:32	those who were sent **departed**	
22: 4	he **went away** and conferred	
22:13	So they **went** and found	
24:12	then he **went** home, amazed at	
24:24	**went** to the tomb and found it	
Jn 4: 3	he left Judea and **started** back	
4: 8	disciples **had gone** to the city	
4:28	and **went** back to the city.	
4:47	he **went** and begged him to come	
5:15	man **went away** and told the Jews	
6: 1	Jesus **went** to the other side	
6:22	disciples **had gone away** alone	
6:66	his disciples **turned** back	
6:68	Lord, to whom can we **go**	
9: 7	he **went** and washed and came	

9:11	I **went** and washed and received	
10:40	He **went** away again across the	
11:28	she **went** back and called her	
11:46	But some of them **went** to the	
11:54	**went** from there to a town	
12:19	the world **has gone after** him	
12:36	he **departed** and hid from them.	
16: 7	your advantage that I **go away**	
16: 7	for if I **do** not **go away,**	
18: 6	they **stepped back** and fell	
20:10	Then the disciples **returned**	
Ac 4:15	them **to leave** the council	
5:26	captain **went** with the temple	
9:17	So Ananias **went** and entered	
10: 7	angel who spoke to him **had left**	
16:39	out and asked them **to leave**	
23:32	they **let** the horsemen **go** on	
Ro 15:28	I **will set out** by way of you	
Ga 1:17	I **went away** at once into Arabia	
Ja 1:24	**going away,** immediately forget	
Ju 1: 7	and **pursued** unnatural lust,	
Re 9:12	The first woe **has passed.**	
10: 9	So I **went** to the angel	
11:14	The second woe **has passed.**	
12:17	**went off** to make war	
16: 2	angel **went** and poured his bowl	
18:14	your soul longed **has gone from**	
21: 1	the first earth **had passed away**	
21: 4	first things **have passed away**	

---

568 GO19 AG84 LN26 K2:828 R575,2192
αρεχω, I HOLD OFF, I RECEIVE

Mt 6: 2	they **have received** their reward.	
6: 5	they **have received** their reward.	
6:16	they **have received** their reward.	
14:24	**was far** from the land,	
15: 8	their hearts **are far** from me	
Mk 7: 6	their hearts **are far** from me	
14:41	**Enough!** The hour has come	
Lk 6:24	for you **have received** your	
7: 6	he **was** not **far** from the house,	
15:20	while he **was still far** off,	
24:13	Emmaus, **about** seven miles from	
Ac 15:20	to **abstain** only from things	
15:29	you **keep** yourselves **from** these	
Ph 4:18	I **have been paid in full**	
1Th 4: 3	you **abstain** from fornication;	
5:22	**abstain** from every form of evil	
1Ti 4: 3	demand **abstinence** from foods,	

| Pm | 1:15 | so that you **might have** him **back** |
| 1P | 2:11 | to **abstain** from the desires |

569 GO8 AG85 LN26 B1:594 K6:174 R571
απιστεω, I TRUST NOT

Mk	16:11	they would **not believe** it.
	16:16	the one who **does not believe**
Lk	24:11	they did **not believe** them.
	24:41	they **were disbelieving**
Ac	28:24	others **refused to believe.**
Ro	3: 3	What if some were **unfaithful**
2Ti	2:13	if we **are faithless,**
1P	2: 7	for those who **do not believe**

570 GO11 AG85 LN26 B1:594 K6:174 R571
απιστια, UNTRUST

Mt	13:58	because of their **unbelief.**
Mk	6: 6	he was amazed at their **unbelief**
	9:24	I believe; help my **unbelief**
	16:14	**lack of faith** and stubbornness,
Ro	3: 3	What if some were **unfaithful**
	4:20	No **distrust** made him waver
	11:20	because of their **unbelief,**
	11:23	they do not persist in **unbelief**
1Ti	1:13	acted ignorantly in **unbelief,**
He	3:12	have an evil, **unbelieving** heart
	3:19	to enter because of **unbelief.**

571 GO23 AG85 LN26 B1:594 K6:174
R4103
απιστος, UNTRUSTFUL, UNBELIEVING

Mt	17:17	You **faithless** and perverse
Mk	9:19	You **faithless** generation,
Lk	9:41	You **faithless** and perverse
	12:46	put him with the **unfaithful**
Jn	20:27	Do **not doubt** but believe.
Ac	26: 8	Why is it thought **incredible**
1C	6: 6	and before **unbelievers** at that
	7:12	a wife who is an **unbeliever,**
	7:13	a husband who is an **unbeliever,**
	7:14	the **unbelieving** husband is made
	7:14	**unbelieving** wife is made holy
	7:15	**unbelieving** partner separates,
	10:27	If an **unbeliever** invites you
	14:22	believers but for **unbelievers,**
	14:22	**unbelievers** but for believers
	14:23	outsiders or **unbelievers** enter
	14:24	an **unbeliever** or outsider
2C	4: 4	the minds of the **unbelievers,**
	6:14	be mismatched with **unbelievers**

	6:15	share with an **unbeliever**
1Ti	5: 8	and is worse than an **unbeliever**
Ti	1:15	**unbelieving** nothing is pure.
Re	21: 8	for the cowardly, the **faithless**

572 GO8 AG85 LN27 K1:386 R573
απλοτης, OPENNESS

Ro	12: 8	the giver, in **generosity;**
2C	1:12	**frankness** and godly sincerity,
	8: 2	in a wealth of **generosity**
	9:11	for your great **generosity,**
	9:13	the **generosity** of your sharing
	11: 3	a **sincere** and pure devotion
Ep	6: 5	**trembling,** singleness of heart,
Co	3:22	but **wholeheartedly,** fearing

573 GO2 AG86 LN27 K1:386
απλους, OPEN

| Mt | 6:22 | if your eye is **healthy,** |
| Lk | 11:34 | If your eye is **healthy,** |

574 GO1 AG86 LN27 R573
απλως, OPENLY

| Ja | 1: 5 | **generously** and ungrudgingly, |

575 GO646 AG86 LN27 B3:1180
απο, FROM [MULTIPLE OCCURRENCES]

576 GO4 AG88 LN27
αποβαινω, I GO OFF

Lk	5: 2	fishermen **had gone out** of them
	21:13	**will give** you an opportunity
Jn	21: 9	When they **had gone** ashore,
Ph	1:19	this **will turn out** for my

577 GO2 AG88 LN27 R575,906
αποβαλλω, I THROW OFF

| Mk | 10:50 | So **throwing off** his cloak, |
| He | 10:35 | **abandon** that confidence |

578 GO1 AG89 LN27 R575,991
αποβλεπω, I LOOK OFF

| He | 11:26 | **was looking ahead** to the reward |

579 GO1 AG89 LN27 R577
αποβλητος, THROWN OFF

| 1Ti | 4: 4 | nothing is to be **rejected,** |

580 GO2 AG89 LN27 R577
αποβολη, THROW OFF

Ac	27:22	there will be no **loss** of life
Ro	11:15	For if their **rejection** is the

581　GO1 AG89 LN27 B1:181 K1:686 R575,1096
απογινομαι, I COME AWAY

1P	2:24	so that, **free** from sins,

582　GO2 AG89 LN27 R583
απογραφη, ENROLLMENT

Lk	2: 2	This was the first **registration**
Ac	5:37	at the time of the **census**

583　GO4 AG89 LN27 R575,1125
απογραφω, I ENROLL

Lk	2: 1	In those days a **decree** went out
	2: 3	own towns to be **registered.**
	2: 5	went to be **registered** with Mary
He	12:23	the firstborn who are **enrolled**

584　GO4 AG89 LN27 B3:570 R575,1166
αποδεικνυμι, I SHOW OFF

Ac	2:22	a man **attested** to you by God
	25: 7	which they **could** not **prove**
1C	4: 9	I think that God has **exhibited**
2Th	2: 4	**declaring** himself to be God

585　GO1 AG89 LN27 B3:570 R584
αποδειξις, SHOW OFF

1C	2: 4	a **demonstration** of the Spirit

586　GO4 AG89 LN27 B2:693 R575,1183
αποδεκατοω, I GIVE TENTH

Mt	23:23	For you **tithe** mint, dill,
Lk	11:42	For you **tithe** mint and rue
	18:12	I **give** a **tenth** of all my income
He	7: 5	**collect tithes** from the people

587　GO2 AG90 LN27 B3:744 K2:58 R588
αποδεκτος, ACCEPTABLE

1Ti	2: 3	This is right and is **acceptable**
	5: 4	this is **pleasing** in God's sight

588　GO7 AG90 LN28 B3:744 K2:55 R575,1209
αποδεχομαι, I WELCOME THOROUGHLY

Lk	8:40	the crowd **welcomed** him
	9:11	and he **welcomed** them
Ac	2:41	those who **welcomed** his message
	18:27	to the disciples **to welcome** him
	21:17	the brothers **welcomed** us warmly

	24: 3	We **welcome** this in every way
	28:30	**welcomed** all who came to him

589　GO6 AG90 LN28 B2:790 R590
αποδημεω, I JOURNEY

Mt	21:33	and **went to another country**
	25:14	a man, **going on** a **journey**
	25:15	Then he **went away**
Mk	12: 1	and **went to another country**
Lk	15:13	**traveled** to a distant country,
	20: 9	and **went to another country**

590　GO1 AG90 LN28 R575,1218
αποδημος, JOURNEY

Mk	13:34	like a man going on a **journey,**

591　GO48 AG90 LN28 B3:134 K2:167 R575,1325
αποδιδωμι, I GIVE AWAY

Mt	5:26	you **have paid** the last penny
	5:33	but **carry out** the vows
	6: 4	sees in secret **will reward** you
	6: 6	sees in secret **will reward** you
	6:18	sees in secret **will reward** you
	12:36	**will have to give** an account
	16:27	he **will repay** everyone
	18:25	as he **could** not **pay**
	18:25	and **payment to be made**
	18:26	and I **will pay** you everything
	18:28	he said, '**Pay** what you owe.'
	18:29	with me, and I **will pay** you
	18:30	until he **would pay** the debt
	18:34	tortured until he **would pay**
	20: 8	**give** them their **pay,**
	21:41	who **will give** him the produce
	22:21	**Give** therefore to the emperor
	27:58	it **to be given** to him.
Mk	12:17	**Give to** the emperor the things
Lk	4:20	**gave** it **back** to the attendant,
	7:42	When they **could** not **pay,** he
	9:42	**gave** him **back** to his father.
	10:35	I **will repay** you whatever more
	12:59	you **have paid** the very last
	16: 2	**Give** me an accounting of your
	19: 8	I **will pay back** four times as
	20:25	Then **give** to the emperor the
Ac	4:33	apostles **gave** their testimony
	5: 8	**sold** the land for such and such
	7: 9	**sold** him into Egypt; but God
	19:40	we can **give** to justify this
Ro	2: 6	For he **will repay**

12:17	**Do** not **repay** anyone evil for
13: 7	**Pay** to all what is due them
1C 7: 3	husband **should give** to his wife
1Th 5:15	none of you **repays** evil for
1Ti 5: 4	**make** some **repayment** to their
2Ti 4: 8	**will give** me on that day, and
4:14	Lord **will pay** him **back** for his
He 12:11	it **yields** the peaceful fruit
12:16	who **sold** his birthright for a
13:17	souls and **will give** an account
1P 3: 9	Do not **repay** evil for evil
4: 5	But they **will have to give** an
Re 18: 6	**Render** to her as she herself
18: 6	she herself **has rendered,**
22: 2	**producing** its fruit each month;
22:12	**to repay** according to everyone

592 GO1 AG90 LN28 K5:455
αποδιοριζω, I DIVIDE OFF

Ju 1:19	people . . . **causing divisions**

593 GO9 AG90 LN28 B3:808 K2:255 R575,1381
αποδοκιμαζω, I REJECT

Mt 21:42	builders **rejected** has become
Mk 8:31	be **rejected** by the elders,
12:10	builders **rejected** has become
Lk 9:22	be **rejected** by the elders,
17:25	be **rejected** by this generation.
20:17	builders **rejected** has become
He 12:17	he was **rejected,** for he found
1P 2: 4	though **rejected** by mortals
2: 7	builders **rejected** has become

594 GO2 AG91 LN28 B3:744 K2:55 R588
αποδοχη, ACCEPTANCE

1Ti 1:15	worthy of full **acceptance,**
4: 9	worthy of full **acceptance.**

595 GO2 AG91 LN28 B1:314 R659
αποθεσις, SETTING OFF

1P 3:21	not as a **removal** of dirt from
2P 1:14	my **death** will come soon,

596 GO6 AG91 LN28
αποθηκη, STOREHOUSE

Mt 3:12	his wheat into the **granary;**
6:26	nor reap nor gather into **barns**
13:30	gather the wheat into my **barn.**
Lk 3:17	the wheat into his **granary;**

12:18	I will pull down my **barns**
12:24	neither storehouse nor **barn,**

597 GO1 AG91 LN28 R575,2343
αποθησαυριζω, I TREASURE UP

1Ti 6:19	thus **storing up** for themselves

598 GO1 AG91 LN28 R575,2346
αποθλιβω, I AFFLICT

Lk 8:45	surround you and **press in** on

599 GO111 AG91 LN28 B1:430 K3:7 R575,2348
αποθνησκω, I DIE

Mt 8:32	**perished** in the water.
9:24	the girl is not **dead** but
22:24	If a man **dies** childless,
22:27	the woman herself **died.**
26:35	Even though I must **die** with you
Mk 5:35	Your daughter is **dead.**
5:39	The child is not **dead** but
9:26	them said, "He is **dead.**"
12:19	if a man's brother **dies,**
12:20	when he **died,** left no children;
12:21	second married her and **died,**
12:22	the woman herself **died.**
15:44	he **had been dead** for some time.
Lk 8:42	who **was dying.** As he went,
8:52	she is not **dead** but sleeping
8:53	knowing that she **was dead.**
16:22	The poor man **died** and was
16:22	rich man also **died**
20:28	if a man's brother **dies,**
20:29	first married, and **died**
20:31	all seven **died** childless.
20:32	Finally the woman also **died.**
20:36	Indeed they cannot **die** anymore,
Jn 4:47	he was at the point of **death.**
4:49	before my little boy **dies.**
6:49	wilderness, and they **died.**
6:50	may eat of it and not **die.**
6:58	ate, and they **died.**
8:21	but you **will die** in your sin.
8:24	you **would die** in your sins,
8:24	for you will **die** in your sins
8:52	demon. Abraham **died,** and so did
8:53	our father Abraham, who **died?**
8:53	The prophets also **died.**
11:14	Lazarus is **dead.**
11:16	that we **may die** with him.
11:21	my brother would not **have died.**

	11:25	even though they **die**, will live
	11:26	believes in me will never **die**.
	11:32	my brother would not have **died**.
	11:37	have kept this man from **dying?**
	11:50	have one man **die** for the people
	11:51	Jesus was about to **die** for the
	12:24	falls into the earth and **dies**,
	12:24	but if it **dies**, it bears much
	12:33	kind of death he was to **die**.
	18:14	have one person **die** for the
	18:32	kind of death he was to **die**.
	19: 7	he ought to **die** because he has
	21:23	disciple would not **die**.
	21:23	he would not **die**, but, "If it
Ac	7: 4	After his father **died**, God had
	9:37	she became ill and **died**.
	21:13	even to **die** in Jerusalem
	25:11	for which I deserve to **die**,
Ro	5: 6	Christ **died** for the ungodly.
	5: 7	rarely will anyone **die** for a
	5: 7	might actually dare to **die**.
	5: 8	sinners Christ **died** for us.
	5:15	if the many **died** through the
	6: 2	How can we who **died** to sin go
	6: 7	For whoever has **died** is freed
	6: 8	But if we have **died** with Christ
	6: 9	**will** never **die** again; death no
	6:10	The death he **died**, he died to
	6:10	he **died** to sin, once for all;
	7: 2	but if her husband **dies**,
	7: 3	if her husband **dies**, she is
	7: 6	discharged from the law, **dead**
	7:10	and I **died**, and the very
	8:13	you **will die**; but if by the
	8:34	who **died**, yes, who was raised,
	14: 7	we do not **die** to ourselves.
	14: 8	if we **die**, we die to the Lord;
	14: 8	we **die** to the Lord; so then,
	14: 8	whether we **die**, we are the Lord
	14: 9	For to this end Christ **died** and
	14:15	for whom Christ **died**.
1C	8:11	believers for whom Christ **died**
	9:15	I would rather **die** than that
	15: 3	Christ **died** for our sins in
	15:22	for as all **die** in Adam, so all
	15:31	I **die** every day! That is as
	15:32	drink, for tomorrow we **die**.
	15:36	come to life unless it **dies**.
2C	5:14	one has **died** for all; therefore

	5:14	all; therefore all have **died.**
	5:15	And he **died** for all,
	5:15	for him who **died** and was raised
	6: 9	**dying**, and see—we are alive;
Ga	2:19	through the law I **died** to the
	2:21	then Christ **died** for nothing.
Ph	1:21	living is Christ and **dying** is
Co	2:20	If with Christ you **died** to the
	3: 3	for you **have died**, and your
1Th	4:14	Jesus **died** and rose again,
	5:10	who **died** for us, so that
He	7: 8	by those who are **mortal**;
	9:27	for mortals to **die** once,
	10:28	law of Moses **dies** without mercy
	11: 4	**died**, but through his faith he
	11:13	All of these **died** in faith
	11:21	By faith Jacob, when **dying**
	11:37	they **were killed** by the sword;
Ju	1:12	without fruit, twice **dead**,
Re	3: 2	is on the point of **death**,
	8: 9	creatures in the sea **died**,
	8:11	many **died** from the water,
	9: 6	they will long to **die**,
	14:13	dead who from now on **die** in
	16: 3	living thing in the sea **died**.

---

600   GO8 AG91 LN28 B3:146 K1:387 R575,2525
αποκαθιστημι, I RESTORE

Mt	12:13	it was **restored**, as sound as
	17:11	and **will restore** all things;
Mk	3: 5	his hand was **restored**.
	8:25	his sight **was restored**,
	9:12	coming first to **restore** all
Lk	6:10	and his hand was **restored**.
Ac	1: 6	when you **will restore** the
He	13:19	so that I may **be restored** to

---

601   GO26 AG92 LN28 B3:309 K3:563 R575,2572
αποκαλυπτω, I UNCOVER

Mt	10:26	that will not be **uncovered**,
	11:25	have **revealed** them to infants;
	11:27	the Son chooses to **reveal** him.
	16:17	and blood has not **revealed** this
Lk	2:35	of many will be **revealed**
	10:21	have **revealed** them to infants;
	10:22	the Son chooses to **reveal** him.
	12: 2	that will not be **uncovered**,
	17:30	the Son of Man is **revealed**.
Jn	12:38	arm of the Lord been **revealed?**

Ro	1:17	God is **revealed** through faith
	1:18	the wrath of God is **revealed**
	8:18	the glory about to be **revealed**
1C	2:10	these things God has **revealed**
	3:13	it will be **revealed** with fire,
	14:30	If a **revelation** is made to
Ga	1:16	to **reveal** his Son to me, so
	3:23	until faith would be **revealed**.
Ep	3: 5	has now been **revealed** to his
Ph	3:15	God will **reveal** to you.
2Th	2: 3	the lawless one is **revealed**,
	2: 6	may be **revealed** when his time
	2: 8	lawless one will be **revealed**,
1P	1: 5	salvation ready to be **revealed**
	1:12	It was **revealed** to them that
	5: 1	in the glory to be **revealed**,

602 GO18 AG92 LN28 B3:310 K3:563 R601
αποκαλυψις, UNCOVERING (REVELATION)

Lk	2:32	**revelation** to the Gentiles
Ro	2: 5	judgment will be **revealed**.
	8:19	longing for the **revealing** of
	16:25	the **revelation** of the mystery
1C	1: 7	as you wait for the **revealing**
	14: 6	in some **revelation** or knowledge
	14:26	lesson, a **revelation**, a tongue,
2C	12: 1	and **revelations** of the Lord.
	12: 7	character of the **revelations**.
Ga	1:12	through a **revelation** of Jesus
	2: 2	in response to a **revelation**.
Ep	1:17	spirit of wisdom and **revelation**
	3: 3	made known to me by **revelation**,
2Th	1: 7	when the Lord Jesus is **revealed**
1P	1: 7	when Jesus Christ is **revealed**.
	1:13	bring you when he is **revealed**.
	4:13	when his glory is **revealed**.
Re	1: 1	The **revelation** of Jesus Christ,

603 GO2 AG92 LN29 B2:238 K1:393
αποκαραδοκια, EAGER EXPECTATION

| Ro | 8:19 | waits with **eager longing** for |
| Ph | 1:20 | It is my **eager expectation** and |

604 GO3 AG92 LN29 B3:166 K1:258 R575,2644
αποκαταλλασσω, I RECONCILE
　　THOROUGHLY

Ep	2:16	and might **reconcile** both groups
Co	1:20	God was pleased to **reconcile** to
	1:22	**reconciled** in his fleshly body

605 GO1 AG92 LN29 B3:146 K1:389 R600
αποκαταστασις, RESTORATION

| Ac | 3:21 | **restoration** that God announced |

606 GO4 AG92 LN29 K3:655 R575,2749
αποκειμαι, I LAY OFF

Lk	19:20	I **wrapped** it up in a piece of
Co	1: 5	hope **laid** up for you in heaven.
2Ti	4: 8	is **reserved** for me the
He	9:27	as it is **appointed** for mortals

607 GO4 AG93 LN29 R575,2776
αποκεφαλιζω, I CUT OFF HEAD

Mt	14:10	he sent and had John **beheaded**
Mk	6:16	said, "John, whom I **beheaded**,
	6:27	He went and **beheaded** him in the
Lk	9: 9	Herod said, "John I **beheaded**;

608 GO1 AG93 LN29 R575,2808
αποκλειω, I CLOSE OFF

| Lk | 13:25 | has got up and **shut** the door, |

609 GO6 AG93 LN29 K3:852 R575,2875
αποκοπτω, I CUT OFF

Mk	9:43	you to stumble, **cut** it **off**;
	9:45	you to stumble, **cut** it **off**;
Jn	18: 1	and **cut off** his right ear.
	18:26	man whose ear Peter had **cut off**
Ac	27:32	soldiers **cut away** the ropes of
Ga	5:12	would **castrate** themselves!

610 GO1 AG93 LN29 K3:945 R611
αποκριμα, SENTENCE

| 2C | 1: 9 | received the **sentence** of death |

611 GO231 AG93 LN29 K3:944
αποκρινομαι, I ANSWER

Mt	3:15	Jesus **answered** him, "Let it be
	4: 4	he **answered**, "It is written,
	8: 8	The centurion **answered**, "Lord,
	11: 4	Jesus **answered** them, "Go and
	11:25	Jesus **said**, "I thank you,
	12:38	and Pharisees **said** to him,
	12:39	But he **answered** them, "An evil
	12:48	Jesus **replied**, "Who is my
	13:11	He **answered**, "To you it has
	13:37	He **answered**, "The one who sows
	14:28	Peter **answered** him, "Lord, if
	15: 3	He **answered** them, "And why do
	15:13	He **answered**, "Every plant

15:15	Peter **said** to him, "Explain
15:23	he did not **answer** her at all.
15:24	He **answered,** "I was sent only
15:26	He **answered,** "It is not fair
15:28	Jesus **answered** her, "Woman,
16: 2	He **answered** them, "When it is
16:16	**answered,** "You are the Messiah,
16:17	**answered** him, "Blessed are you,
17: 4	Peter **said** to Jesus, "Lord, it
17:11	He **replied,** "Elijah is indeed
17:17	Jesus **answered,** "You faithless
19: 4	He **answered,** "Have you not read
19:27	Peter said in **reply,** "Look, we
20:13	he **replied** to one of them,
20:22	Jesus **answered,** "You do not
21:21	Jesus **answered** them, "Truly I
21:24	Jesus **said** to them, "I will
21:27	**answered** Jesus, "We do not know
21:29	He **answered,** 'I will not';
21:30	and he **answered,** 'I go, sir'
22: 1	to them in parables, **saying:**
22:29	Jesus **answered** them, "You are
22:46	was able to give him an **answer,**
24: 2	**asked** them, "You see all these,
24: 4	Jesus **answered** them, "Beware
25: 9	But the wise **replied,** 'No!
25:12	he **replied,** 'Truly I tell you,
25:26	his master **replied,** 'You wicked
25:37	the righteous will **answer** him,
25:40	king will **answer** them,
25:44	Then they also will **answer,**
25:45	he will **answer** them, 'Truly I
26:23	He **answered,** "The one who has
26:25	Judas, who betrayed him, **said,**
26:33	Peter **said** to him, "Though all
26:62	Have you no **answer?** What is it
26:66	**answered,** "He deserves death."
27:12	and elders, he did not **answer.**
27:14	But he gave him no **answer,**
27:21	governor again **said** to them,
27:25	the people as a whole **answered,**
28: 5	But the angel **said** to the women
Mk 3:33	he **replied,** "Who are my mother
6:37	But he **answered** them, "You give
7:28	But she **answered** him, "Sir,
8: 4	His disciples **replied,** "How
8:29	Peter **answered** him, "You are
9: 5	Peter **said** to Jesus, "Rabbi,
9: 6	He did not know what to **say,**

9:17	Someone from the crowd **answered**
9:19	He **answered** them,
10: 3	He **answered** them,
10:24	But Jesus **said** to them again,
10:51	Then Jesus **said** to him, "What
11:14	He **said** to it, "May no one ever
11:22	Jesus **answered** them, "Have
11:29	**answer** me, and I will tell you
11:30	of human origin? **Answer** me.
11:33	So they **answered** Jesus, "We do
12:28	that he **answered** them well,
12:29	Jesus **answered,** "The first is,
12:34	saw that he **answered** wisely,
12:35	he **said,** "How can the scribes
14:40	did not know what to **say** to him
14:48	Jesus **said** to them, "Have you
14:60	Have you no **answer?** What is it
14:61	was silent and did not **answer.**
15: 2	He **answered** him, "You say so."
15: 4	Have you no **answer?** See how
15: 5	Jesus made no further **reply,**
15: 9	Then he **answered** them, "Do you
15:12	Pilate **spoke** to them again,
Lk 1:19	angel **replied,** "I am Gabriel.
1:35	angel **said** to her, "The Holy
1:60	his mother **said,** "No; he is to
3:11	In **reply** he said to them,
3:16	John **answered** all of them by
4: 4	Jesus **answered** him, "It is
4: 8	Jesus **answered** him, "It is
4:12	Jesus **answered** him, "It is
5: 5	Simon **answered,** "Master, we
5:22	he **answered** them, "Why do you
5:31	Jesus **answered,** "Those who are
6: 3	Jesus **answered,** "Have you not
7:22	he **answered** them, "Go and tell
7:40	Jesus **spoke** up and said to him,
7:43	Simon **answered,** "I suppose the
8:21	But he **said** to them, "My mother
8:50	he **replied,** "Do not fear. Only
9:19	**answered,** "John the Baptist;
9:20	Peter **answered,** "The Messiah of
9:41	Jesus **answered,** "You faithless
9:49	John **answered,** "Master, we saw
10:27	He **answered,** "You shall love
10:28	You have given the right **answer**
10:41	the Lord **answered** her, "Martha,
11: 7	And he **answers** from within,
11:45	lawyers **answered** him, "Teacher,

13: 2	He **asked** them, "Do you think
13: 8	He **replied,** 'Sir, let it alone
13:14	kept **saying** to the crowd,
13:15	Lord **answered** him and said,
13:25	in **reply** he will say to you,
14: 3	And Jesus **asked** the lawyers
15:29	But he **answered** his father,
17:17	Jesus **asked,** "Were not ten made
17:20	he **answered,** "The kingdom of
17:37	they **asked** him, "Where, Lord?"
19:40	He **answered,** "I tell you, if
20: 3	He **answered** them, "I will also
20: 7	they **answered** that they did not
20:39	the scribes **answered,** "Teacher,
22:51	Jesus **said,** "No more of this!"
22:68	you will not **answer.**
23: 3	He **answered,** "You say so."
23: 9	but Jesus **gave** him no **answer.**
23:40	**saying,** "Do you not fear God,
24:18	Cleopas, **answered** him, "Are you
Jn 1:21	He **answered,** "No."
1:26	John **answered** them, "I baptize
1:48	Jesus **answered,** "I saw you
1:49	Nathanael **replied,** "Rabbi, you
1:50	Jesus **answered,** "Do you believe
2:18	Jews then **said** to him,
2:19	Jesus **answered** them, "Destroy
3: 3	Jesus **answered** him, "Very
3: 5	Jesus **answered,** "Very truly,
3: 9	Nicodemus **said** to him, "How can
3:10	Jesus **answered** him, "Are you a
3:27	John **answered,** "No one can
4:10	Jesus **answered** her, "If you
4:13	Jesus **said** to her, "Everyone
4:17	woman **answered** him, "I have no
5: 7	sick man **answered** him, "Sir,
5:11	he **answered** them, "The man who
5:17	Jesus **answered** them, "My Father
5:19	Jesus **said** to them, "Very truly
6: 7	Philip **answered** him, "Six
6:26	Jesus **answered** them
6:29	Jesus **answered** them, "This is
6:43	Jesus **answered** them, "Do not
6:68	Simon Peter **answered** him, "Lord
6:70	Jesus **answered** them, "Did I not
7:16	**answered** them, "My teaching is
7:20	**answered,** "You have a demon!
7:21	**answered** them, "I performed one
7:46	**answered,** "Never has anyone

7:47	Then the Pharisees **replied,**
7:52	They **replied,** "Surely you are
8:14	Jesus **answered,** "Even if I
8:19	**answered,** "You know neither me
8:33	They **answered** him, "We are
8:34	Jesus **answered** them,
8:39	They **answered** him, "Abraham is
8:48	Jews **answered** him, "Are we not
8:49	Jesus **answered,** "I do not have
8:54	**answered,** "If I glorify myself,
9: 3	**answered,** "Neither this man nor
9:11	**answered,** "The man called Jesus
9:20	parents **answered,** "We know that
9:25	**answered,** "I do not know
9:27	**answered** them, "I have told you
9:30	The man **answered,** "Here is
9:34	**answered** him, "You were born
9:36	**answered,** "And who is he, sir?
10:25	**answered,** "I have told you,
10:32	**replied,** "I have shown you many
10:33	The Jews **answered,** "It is not
10:34	**answered,** "Is it not written in
11: 9	Jesus **answered,** "Are there not
12:23	Jesus **answered** them, "The hour
12:30	Jesus **answered,** "This voice has
12:34	**answered** him, "We have heard
13: 7	**answered,** "You do not know now
13: 8	**answered,** "Unless I wash you,
13:26	Jesus **answered,** "It is the one
13:36	**answered,** "Where I am going,
13:38	**answered,** "Will you lay down
14:23	**answered** him, "Those who love
16:31	**answered** them, "Do you now
18: 5	**answered,** "Jesus of Nazareth
18: 8	Jesus **answered,** "I told you that
18:20	**answered,** "I have spoken openly
18:23	**answered,** "If I have spoken
18:30	**answered,** "If this man were not
18:34	**answered,** "Do you ask this
18:35	Pilate **replied,** "I am not a Jew
18:36	**answered,** "My kingdom is not
18:37	**answered,** "You say that I am a
19: 7	**answered** him, "We have a law,
19:11	Jesus **answered** him, "You would
19:15	**answered,** "We have no king but
19:22	**answered,** "What I have written
20:28	Thomas **answered** him, "My Lord
21: 5	They **answered** him, "No."
Ac 3:12	he **addressed** the people,

	4:19	Peter and John **answered** them,
	5: 8	Peter **said** to her, "Tell me
	5:29	**answered,** "We must obey God
	8:24	Simon **answered,** "Pray for me
	8:34	The eunuch **asked** Philip,
	9:13	But Ananias **answered,** "Lord, I
	10:46	Then Peter **said,**
	11: 9	the voice **answered** from heaven,
	15:13	James **replied,** "My brothers,
	19:15	spirit said to them in **reply,**
	21:13	Then Paul **answered,** "What are
	22: 8	I **answered,** 'Who are you, Lord?
	22:28	tribune **answered,** "It cost me
	24:10	**replied:** "I cheerfully make my
	24:25	frightened and **said,** "Go away
	25: 4	Festus **replied** that Paul was
	25: 9	**asked** Paul, "Do you wish to go
	25:12	**replied,** "You have appealed to
	25:16	I **told** them that it was not
Co	4: 6	you ought to **answer** everyone.
Re	7:13	one of the elders **addressed** me,

612 ᴳᴼ4 ᴬᴳ93 ᴸᴺ29 ᴷ3:946 ᴿ611
απόκρισις, ANSWER

Lk	2:47	understanding and his **answers.**
	20:26	and being amazed by his **answer,**
Jn	1:22	an **answer** for those who sent us
	19: 9	But Jesus gave him no **answer.**

613 ᴳᴼ4 ᴬᴳ93 ᴸᴺ29 ᴷ3:957 ᴿ575,2928
αποκρύπτω, I HIDE AWAY

Lk	10:21	you have **hidden** these things
1C	2: 7	God's wisdom, secret and **hidden**
Ep	3: 9	mystery **hidden** for ages in God
Co	1:26	mystery that has been **hidden**

614 ᴳᴼ3 ᴬᴳ93 ᴸᴺ29 ᴮ2:214 ᴷ3:957 ᴿ613
απόκρυφος, HIDDEN AWAY

Mk	4:22	For there is nothing **hidden,**
Lk	8:17	nothing is **hidden** that will not
Co	2: 3	are **hidden** all the treasures

615 ᴳᴼ74 ᴬᴳ93 ᴸᴺ29 ᴮ1:429
αποκτείνω, I KILL

Mt	10:28	those who **kill** the body
	10:28	but cannot **kill** the soul;
	14: 5	wanted to **put** him to **death,**
	16:21	be **killed,** and on the third day
	17:23	**kill** him, and on the third day
	21:35	**killed** another, and stoned

	21:38	let us **kill** him and get his
	21:39	and **killed** him.
	22: 6	and **killed** them.
	23:34	you will **kill** and crucify,
	23:37	city that **kills** the prophets
	24: 9	and will **put** you to **death,**
	26: 4	by stealth and **kill** him.
Mk	3: 4	to save life or to **kill?**
	6:19	and wanted to **kill** him
	8:31	be **killed,** and after three days
	9:31	will **kill** him, and three days
	9:31	three days after being **killed,**
	10:34	**kill** him; and after three days
	12: 5	and that one they **killed.**
	12: 5	and others they **killed.**
	12: 7	come, let us **kill** him,
	12: 8	So they seized him, **killed** him,
	14: 1	by stealth and **kill** him;
Lk	9:22	be **killed,** and on the third day
	11:47	whom your ancestors **killed.**
	11:48	for they **killed** them,
	11:49	they will **kill** and persecute,
	12: 4	those who **kill** the body,
	12: 5	he has **killed,** has authority
	13: 4	those eighteen who were **killed**
	13:31	for Herod wants to **kill** you.
	13:34	city that **kills** the prophets
	18:33	will **kill** him, and on the third
	20:14	let us **kill** him so that the
	20:15	and **killed** him.
Jn	5:18	to **kill** him, because he was not
	7: 1	for an opportunity to **kill** him.
	7:19	for an opportunity to **kill** me?
	7:20	Who is trying to **kill** you
	7:25	whom they are trying to **kill?**
	8:22	Is he going to **kill** himself?
	8:37	look for an opportunity to **kill**
	8:40	now you are trying to **kill** me,
	11:53	planned to **put** him to **death.**
	12:10	planned to **put** Lazarus to **death**
	16: 2	when those who **kill** you
	18:31	to **put** anyone to **death.**
Ac	3:15	you **killed** the Author of life,
	7:52	They **killed** those who foretold
	21:31	While they were trying to **kill**
	23:12	nor drink until they had **killed**
	23:14	until we have **killed** Paul.
	27:42	The soldiers' plan was to **kill**
Ro	7:11	and through it **killed** me.

	11: 3	they have **killed** your prophets
2C	3: 6	for the letter **kills**
Ep	2:16	**putting** to **death** that hostility
1Th	2:15	who **killed** both the Lord Jesus
Re	2:13	who was **killed** among you,
	2:23	I will **strike** her children dead
	6: 8	to **kill** with sword, famine,
	6:11	they themselves had been **killed**
	9: 5	but not to **kill** them
	9:15	to **kill** a third of humankind.
	9:18	a third of humankind was **killed**
	9:20	who were not **killed** by these
	11: 5	must be **killed** in this manner.
	11: 7	and conquer them and **kill** them
	11:13	were **killed** in the earthquake
	13:10	if you **kill** with the sword,
	13:10	the sword you must be **killed**
	13:15	image of the beast to be **killed**
	19:21	rest were **killed** by the sword

616 GO2 AG94 LN29
απokυεω, I ENGENDER
| Ja | 1:15 | grown, **gives birth** to death. |
| | 1:18 | he **gave** us **birth** by the word of |

617 GO4 AG94 LN29 R575,2947
απokυλιω, I ROLL OFF
Mt	28: 2	**rolled** back the stone and sat
Mk	16: 3	Who will **roll** away the stone
	16: 4	had already been **rolled** back.
Lk	24: 2	found the stone **rolled** away

618 GO10 AG94 LN29 B3:747 R575,2983
απoλαμβανω, I TAKE BACK
Mk	7:33	He **took** him **aside** in private,
Lk	6:34	to **receive** as much again.
	15:27	because he has **got** him **back**
	16:25	you **received** your good things,
	18:30	**get back** very much more in this
	23:41	we are **getting** what we deserve
Ro	1:27	**received** in their own persons
Ga	4: 5	that we might **receive** adoption
Co	3:24	will **receive** the inheritance
2J	1: 8	but may **receive** a full reward.

619 GO2 AG94 LN29
απoλαυσις, ENJOYMENT
| 1Ti | 6:17 | everything for our **enjoyment**. |
| He | 11:25 | **enjoy** the fleeting pleasures |

620 GO7 AG94 LN29 R575,3007
απoλειπω, I LEFT OFF
2Ti	4:13	bring the cloak that I **left**
	4:20	I **left** ill in Miletus.
Ti	1: 5	I **left** you **behind** in Crete
He	4: 6	**failed** to enter because of
	4: 9	a sabbath rest still **remains**
	10:26	there no longer **remains**
Ju	1: 6	but **left** their proper dwelling

622 GO90 AG95 LN30 B1:462 K1:394
απoλλυμι, I DESTROY
Mt	2:13	to **destroy** him
	5:29	to **lose** one of your members
	5:30	to **lose** one of your members
	8:25	We are **perishing**
	9:17	and the skins are **destroyed**
	10: 6	go rather to the **lost** sheep
	10:28	can **destroy** both soul and body
	10:39	find their life will **lose** it
	10:39	who **lose** their life for my sake
	10:42	these will **lose** their reward
	12:14	how to **destroy** him.
	15:24	the **lost** sheep of the house of
	16:25	save their life will **lose** it
	16:25	and those who **lose** their life
	18:14	little ones should be **lost**.
	21:41	will **put** . . . to a miserable **death**
	22: 7	**destroyed** those murderers
	26:52	will **perish** by the sword.
	27:20	and to have Jesus **killed**.
Mk	1:24	Have you come to **destroy** us?
	2:22	and the wine is **lost**
	3: 6	against him, how to **destroy** him
	4:38	not care that we are **perishing?**
	8:35	to save their life will **lose** it
	8:35	**lose** their life for my sake
	9:22	to **destroy** him; but if you are
	9:41	by no means **lose** the reward.
	11:18	looking for a way to **kill** him;
	12: 9	**destroy** the tenants and give
Lk	4:34	Have you come to **destroy** us?
	5:37	and the skins will be **destroyed**
	6: 9	to save life or to **destroy** it?
	8:24	Master, we are **perishing**
	9:24	to save their life will **lose** it
	9:24	and those who **lose** their life
	9:25	but **lose** or forfeit themselves?
	11:51	who **perished** between the altar

	13: 3	you will all **perish** as they did
	13: 5	will all **perish** just as they did
	13:33	for a prophet to be **killed**
	15: 4	sheep and **losing** one of them,
	15: 4	go after the one that is **lost**
	15: 6	found my sheep that was **lost**
	15: 8	if she **loses** one of them
	15: 9	found the coin that I had **lost**
	15:17	but here I am **dying** of hunger!
	15:24	he was **lost** and is found!
	15:32	he was **lost** and has been found
	17:27	the flood came and **destroyed**
	17:29	from heaven and **destroyed** all
	17:33	their life secure will **lose** it
	17:33	**lose** their life will keep it.
	19:10	seek out and to save the **lost**
	19:47	looking for a way to **kill** him
	20:16	He will come and **destroy** those
	21:18	a hair of your head will **perish**
Jn	3:16	believes in him may not **perish**
	6:12	so that nothing may be **lost**
	6:27	for the food that **perishes**
	6:39	I should **lose** nothing of all
	10:10	to steal and kill and **destroy**
	10:28	and they will never **perish**
	11:50	have the whole nation **destroyed**
	12:25	who love their life **lose** it
	17:12	and not one of them was **lost**
	18: 9	I did not **lose** a single one
Ac	5:37	he also **perished,** and all who
	27:34	none of you will **lose** a hair
Ro	2:12	also **perish** apart from the law,
	14:15	being **injured** by what you eat
1C	1:18	to those who are **perishing**
	1:19	I will **destroy** the wisdom
	8:11	whom Christ died are **destroyed**
	10: 9	were **destroyed** by serpents.
	10:10	were **destroyed** by the destroyer
	15:18	died in Christ have **perished**
2C	2:15	among those who are **perishing;**
	4: 3	to those who are **perishing.**
	4: 9	struck down, but not **destroyed;**
2Th	2:10	for those who are **perishing,**
He	1:11	they will **perish**
Ja	1:11	and its beauty **perishes**
	4:12	is able to save and to **destroy**
1P	1: 7	though **perishable,** is tested by
2P	3: 6	deluged with water and **perished**
	3: 9	not wanting any to **perish**

2J	1: 8	so that you do not **lose**
Ju	1: 5	**destroyed** those who did not
	1:11	and **perish** in Korah's rebellion
Re	18:14	your splendor are **lost** to you

623   GO1   AG95   LN30   B1:462   K1:397
απολλυων, APOLLYON
Re   9:11   in Greek he is called **Apollyon.**

624   GO1   AG95   LN30
απολλωνια, APOLLONIA
Ac   17: 1   through Amphipolis and
                 Apollonia

625   GO10   AG95   LN30
απολλως, APOLLOS

Ac	18:24	to Ephesus a Jew named **Apollos**
	19: 1	While **Apollos** was in Corinth,
1C	1:12	or "I belong to **Apollos,**"
	3: 4	I belong to **Apollos,**
	3: 5	What then is **Apollos?**
	3: 6	I planted, **Apollos** watered
	3:22	**Apollos** or Cephas or the world
	4: 6	applied all this to **Apollos**
	16:12	concerning our brother **Apollos**
Ti	3:13	lawyer and **Apollos** on their way

626   GO10   AG95   LN30
απολογεομαι, I DEFEND

Lk	12:11	you are to **defend** yourselves
	21:14	not to prepare your **defense**
Ac	19:33	and tried to make a **defense**
	24:10	I cheerfully make my **defense,**
	25: 8	Paul said in his **defense,**
	26: 1	and began to **defend** himself:
	26: 2	I am to make my **defense** today
	26:24	he was making this **defense**
Ro	2:15	accuse or perhaps **excuse** them
2C	12:19	**defending** ourselves before you?

627   GO8   AG96   LN30   B1:51   R626
απολογια, DEFENSE

Ac	22: 1	the **defense** that I now make
	25:16	a **defense** against the charge
1C	9: 3	This is my **defense** to those who
2C	7:11	eagerness **to clear** yourselves,
Ph	1: 7	in the **defense** and confirmation
	1:16	put here for the **defense** of the
2Ti	4:16	At my first **defense** no one came
1P	3:15	be ready to make your **defense**

628   GO2 AG96 LN30 B1:150 K4:295 R575,3068
απολουω, I WASH OFF
Ac 22:16   and have your sins **washed** away
1C   6:11   But you were **washed,** you were

629   GO10 AG96 LN30 B3:189 K4:328 R575,3083
απολυτρωσις, REDEMPTION
Lk 21:28   your **redemption** is drawing near
Ro   3:24   through the **redemption** that is
     8:23   the **redemption** of our bodies.
1C   1:30   sanctification and **redemption**
Ep   1: 7   **redemption** through his blood
     1:14   **redemption** as God's own people
     4:30   for the day of **redemption**
Co   1:14   in whom we have **redemption**
He   9:15   death has occurred that **redeems**
    11:35   refusing to accept **release**

630   GO66 AG96 LN30 B1:505 R575,3089
απολυω, I LOOSE OFF
Mt   1:19   planned to **dismiss** her quietly
     5:31   Whoever **divorces** his wife
     5:32   anyone who **divorces** his wife
     5:32   **divorced** woman commits adultery
    14:15   **send** the crowds **away** so that
    14:22   while he **dismissed** the crowds.
    14:23   he had **dismissed** the crowds
    15:23   **Send** her **away,** for she keeps
    15:32   to **send** them **away** hungry,
    15:39   After **sending away** the crowds,
    18:27   **released** him and forgave him
    19: 3   **divorce** his wife for any cause
    19: 7   give a certificate of **dismissal**
    19: 8   Moses allowed you to **divorce**
    19: 9   whoever **divorces** his wife
    27:15   to **release** a prisoner for the
    27:17   **release** for you, Jesus Barabbas
    27:21   you want me to **release** for you
    27:26   he **released** Barabbas for them
Mk   6:36   **send** them **away** so that they may
     6:45   while he **dismissed** the crowd
     8: 3   If I **send** them **away** hungry
     8: 9   And he **sent** them **away**
    10: 2   for a man to **divorce** his wife
    10: 4   of dismissal and to **divorce** her
    10:11   Whoever **divorces** his wife and
    10:12   if she **divorces** her husband
    15: 6   to **release** a prisoner for them
    15: 9   Do you want me to **release**
    15:11   to have him **release** Barabbas

     15:15   **released** Barabbas for them
Lk   2:29   Master, now you are **dismissing**
     6:37   **Forgive,** and you will be
     6:37   and you will be **forgiven**
     8:38   but Jesus **sent** him **away**
     9:12   **Send** the crowd **away,** so that
    13:12   Woman, you are **set free** from
    14: 4   healed him, and **sent** him **away**
    16:18   Anyone who **divorces** his wife
    16:18   marries a woman **divorced** from
    23:16   him flogged and **release** him
    23:18   **Release** Barabbas for us!
    23:20   wanting to **release** Jesus
    23:22   flogged and then **release** him
    23:25   **released** the man they asked for
Jn 18:39   that I **release** someone for you
    18:39   to **release** for you the King of
    19:10   I have power to **release** you
    19:12   Pilate tried to **release** him
    19:12   If you **release** this man
Ac   3:13   he had decided to **release** him
     4:21   they **let** them **go**
     4:23   After they were **released**
     5:40   and **let** them **go**
    13: 3   and **sent** them **off**
    15:30   they **were sent off** and went
    15:33   they were **sent off** in peace
    16:35   **Let** those men **go.**
    16:36   sent word to **let** you **go**
    17: 9   they **let** them **go**
    19:40   he **dismissed** the assembly
    23:22   tribune **dismissed** the young
             man
    26:32   **set free** if he had not appealed
    28:18   the Romans wanted to **release** me
    28:25   and as they **were leaving**
He 13:23   Timothy has been **set free**

631   GO1 AG96 LN30
απομασσω, I WIPE OFF
Lk 10:11   we **wipe off** in protest against

632   GO1 AG97 LN30
απονεμω, I ASSIGN
1P   3: 7   **paying** honor to the woman as

633   GO1 AG97 LN30 R575,3538
απονιπτω, I WASH OFF
Mt 27:24   water and **washed** his hands

634 GO1 AG97 LN30 R575,4098
απopιπτω, I FALL OFF
Ac 9:18 scales **fell** from his eyes,

---

635 GO2 AG97 LN30 B2:457 R575,4105
αποπλαναω, I DECEIVE AWAY
Mk 13:22 omens, to **lead astray,**
1Ti 6:10 some have **wandered** away from

---

636 GO4 AG97 LN30 R575,4126
αποπλεω, I SAIL OFF
Ac 13: 4 **sailed** to Cyprus.
14:26 From there they **sailed** back
20:15 We **sailed** from there, and on
27: 1 we were to **sail** for Italy,

---

638 GO2 AG97 LN30 B1:226 K6:455 R575,4155
αποπνιγω, I CHOKE OFF
Lk 8: 7 thorns grew with it and **choked**
8:33 into the lake and was **drowned.**

---

639 GO6 AG97 LN30
απορεω, I DOUBT
Mk 6:20 he was greatly **perplexed;**
Lk 24: 4 While they were **perplexed** about
Jn 13:22 at one another, **uncertain** of
Ac 25:20 Since I **was** at a **loss** how to
2C 4: 8 but not crushed; **perplexed,** but
Ga 4:20 for I am **perplexed** about you.

---

640 GO1 AG97 LN30
απορια, DOUBT
Lk 21:25 distress among nations **confused**

---

641 GO1 AG97 LN30 K6:991 R575,4496
απoριπτω, I FLING OFF
Ac 27:43 to **jump overboard** first and

---

642 GO1 AG98 LN31 R575,3737
απορφανιζω, I ORPHAN OFF
1Th 2:17 we **were made orphans** by being

---

644 GO1 AG98 LN31 B3:553 K7:399 R575,4639
αποσκιασμα, OVERSHADOW
Ja 1:17 no variation or **shadow** due to

---

645 GO4 AG98 LN31 R575,4685
αποσπαω, I DRAW OFF
Mt 26:51 **drew** it, and struck the slave
Lk 22:41 he **withdrew** from them about a

Ac 20:30 order to **entice** the disciples
21: 1 When we had **parted** from them

---

646 GO2 AG98 LN31 B1:606 K1:513 R868
αποστασια, STAND OFF
Ac 21:21 **forsake** Moses, and that you
2Th 2: 3 the **rebellion** comes first and

---

647 GO3 AG98 LN31 B1:606 R868
αποστασιον, STANDING OFF
Mt 5:31 her a certificate of **divorce.**
19: 7 a **certificate** of dismissal and
Mk 10: 4 a man to write a **certificate** of

---

648 GO1 AG98 LN31 R575,4721
αποστεγαζω, I UNROOF
Mk 2: 4 they **removed** the roof above him

---

649 GO132 AG98 LN31 B1:126 K1:398 R575,4724
αποστελλω, I DELEGATE
Mt 2:16 **sent** and killed all the
8:31 If you cast us out, **send** us
10: 5 These twelve Jesus **sent** out
10:16 See, I am **sending** you out like
10:40 welcomes the one who **sent** me.
11:10 See, I am **sending** my messenger
13:41 Son of Man will **send** his angels,
14:35 they **sent** word throughout the
15:24 He answered, "I was **sent** only
20: 2 he **sent** them into his vineyard.
21: 1 Jesus **sent** two disciples,
21: 3 And he will **send** them
21:34 harvest time had come, he **sent**
21:36 Again he **sent** other slaves,
21:37 Finally he **sent** his son to them
22: 3 He **sent** his slaves to call
22: 4 Again he **sent** other slaves,
22:16 So they **sent** their disciples
23:34 Therefore I **send** you prophets,
23:37 those who are **sent** to it! How
24:31 And he will **send** out his angels
27:19 his wife **sent** word to him,
Mk 1: 2 See, I am **sending** my messenger
3:14 and to be **sent** out to proclaim
3:31 they **sent** to him and called him
4:29 at once he **goes in** with his
5:10 earnestly not to **send** them out
6: 7 began to **send** them out two by
6:17 For Herod himself had **sent** men
6:27 the king **sent** a soldier of the

	8:26	Then he **sent** him away to his		6:57	Just as the living Father **sent**
	9:37	not me but the one who **sent** me.		7:29	I am from him, and he **sent** me.
	11: 1	he **sent** two of his disciples		7:32	Pharisees **sent** temple police
	11: 3	needs it and will **send** it back		8:42	not come on my own, but he **sent**
	12: 2	**sent** a slave to the tenants to		9: 7	of Siloam" (which means **Sent**).
	12: 3	and **sent** him away empty-handed.		10:36	Father has sanctified and **sent**
	12: 4	And again he **sent** another slave		11: 3	So the sisters **sent** a message
	12: 5	Then he **sent** another, and that		11:42	believe that you **sent** me.
	12: 6	Finally he **sent** him to them,		17: 3	Jesus Christ whom you have **sent**
	12:13	Then they **sent** to him some		17: 8	believed that you **sent** me.
	13:27	he will **send** out the angels,		17:18	As you have **sent** me into the
	14:13	So he **sent** two of his disciples		17:18	so I have **sent** them into the
Lk	1:19	I have been **sent** to speak to		17:21	believe that you have **sent** me.
	1:26	angel Gabriel was **sent** by God		17:23	may know that you have **sent** me
	4:18	he has **anointed** me to bring		17:25	know that you have **sent** me.
	4:18	He has **sent** me to proclaim		18:24	Then Annas **sent** him bound to
	4:43	for I was **sent** for this purpose		20:21	the Father has **sent** me, so I
	7: 3	he heard about Jesus, he **sent**	Ac	3:20	that he may **send** the Messiah
	7:20	John the Baptist has **sent** us		3:26	he **sent** him first to you, to
	7:27	written, 'See, I am **sending** my		5:21	**sent** to the prison to have them
	9: 2	he **sent** them out to proclaim		7:14	Then Joseph **sent** and invited
	9:48	one who **sent** me; for the least		7:34	Come now, I will **send** you to
	9:52	And he **sent** messengers ahead of		7:35	and whom God now **sent** as both
	10: 1	seventy others and **sent** them on		8:14	they **sent** Peter and John to
	10: 3	See, I am **sending** you out like		9:17	has **sent** me so that you may
	10:16	me rejects the one who **sent** me.		9:38	Peter was there, **sent** two
	11:49	God said, 'I will **send** them		10: 8	he **sent** them to Joppa.
	13:34	stones those who are **sent** to it		10:17	men **sent** by Cornelius appeared.
	14:17	time for the dinner he **sent** his		10:20	for I have **sent** them.
	14:32	he **sends** a delegation and asks		10:36	You know the message he **sent** to
	19:14	hated him and **sent** a delegation		11:11	**sent** to me from Caesarea,
	19:29	he **sent** two of the disciples,		11:13	**Send** to Joppa and bring Simon,
	19:32	So those who were **sent** departed		11:30	this they did, **sending** it to
	20:10	When the season came, he **sent** a		13:15	synagogue **sent** them a message,
	20:20	**sent** spies who pretended to be		15:27	We have therefore **sent** Judas
	22: 8	So Jesus **sent** Peter and John,		15:33	they were **sent** off in peace by
	22:35	He said to them, "When I **sent**		16:35	the magistrates **sent** the police
	24:49	And see, I am **sending** upon you		16:36	The magistrates **sent** word to
Jn	1: 6	There was a man **sent** from God,		19:22	So he **sent** two of his helpers,
	1:19	when the Jews **sent** priests and		26:17	to whom I am **sending** you
	1:24	Now they had been **sent** from		28:28	has been **sent** to the Gentiles;
	3:17	Indeed, God did not **send** the	Ro	10:15	unless they are **sent**? As it is
	3:28	but I have been **sent** ahead of	1C	1:17	For Christ did not **send** me to
	3:34	He whom God has **sent** speaks the	2C	12:17	those whom I **sent** to you?
	4:38	I **sent** you to reap that for	2Ti	4:12	I have **sent** Tychicus to Ephesus
	5:33	You **sent** messengers to John,	He	1:14	**sent** to serve for the sake of
	5:36	behalf that the Father has **sent**	1P	1:12	Holy Spirit **sent** from heaven
	5:38	believe him whom he has **sent**.	1J	4: 9	God **sent** his only Son into the
	6:29	believe in him whom he has **sent**		4:10	but that he loved us and **sent**

	4:14	the Father has **sent** his Son as	
Re	1: 1	he made it known by **sending** his	
	5: 6	seven spirits of God **sent** out	
	22: 6	has **sent** his angel to show his	

---

650 GO6 AG99 LN31 B3:379 K7:719
αποστερεω, I DEPRIVE

Mk	10:19	You shall not **defraud;** Honor
1C	6: 7	Why not rather be **defrauded?**
	6: 8	yourselves wrong and **defraud—**
	7: 5	Do not **deprive** one another
1Ti	6: 5	depraved in mind and **bereft** of
Ja	5: 4	which you **kept back by fraud,**

---

651 GO4 AG99 LN31 B2:111,299 K1:446 R649
αποστολη, DELEGATESHIP (APOSTLESHIP)

Ac	1:25	ministry and **apostleship** from
Ro	1: 5	grace and **apostleship** to bring
1C	9: 2	are the seal of my **apostleship**
Ga	2: 8	making him an **apostle** to the

---

652 GO80 AG99 LN31 B1:126 K1:407 R649
αποστολος, DELEGATE (APOSTLE)

Mt	10: 2	twelve **apostles:** first, Simon,
Mk	3:14	named **apostles,** to be with him,
	6:30	**apostles** gathered around Jesus,
Lk	6:13	whom he also named **apostles:**
	9:10	On their return the **apostles**
	11:49	prophets and **apostles,** some of
	17: 5	The **apostles** said to the Lord,
	22:14	and the **apostles** with him.
	24:10	who told this to the **apostles.**
Jn	13:16	nor are **messengers** greater
Ac	1: 2	Spirit to the **apostles** whom he
	1:26	added to the eleven **apostles.**
	2:37	and to the other **apostles,**
	2:42	to the **apostles'** teaching and
	2:43	were being done by the **apostles**
	4:33	**apostles** gave their testimony
	4:35	They laid it at the **apostles**
	4:36	Joseph, to whom the **apostles**
	4:37	and laid it at the **apostles**
	5: 2	laid it at the **apostles'** feet.
	5:12	the people through the **apostles**
	5:18	arrested the **apostles** and put
	5:29	But Peter and the **apostles**
	5:40	**apostles,** they had them flogged
	6: 6	**apostles,** who prayed and laid
	8: 1	except the **apostles** were
	8:14	**apostles** at Jerusalem heard

	8:18	laying on of the **apostles**
	9:27	brought him to the **apostles,**
	11: 1	Now the **apostles** and the
	14: 4	and some with the **apostles.**
	14:14	When the **apostles** Barnabas
	15: 2	question with the **apostles** and
	15: 4	the church and the **apostles** and
	15: 6	The **apostles** and the elders met
	15:22	Then the **apostles** and the
	15:23	both the **apostles** and the
	16: 4	**apostles** and elders who were in
Ro	1: 1	called to be an **apostle,** set
	11:13	I am an **apostle** to the Gentiles
	16: 7	prominent among the **apostles,**
1C	1: 1	Paul, called to be an **apostle**
	4: 9	God has exhibited us **apostles**
	9: 1	free? Am I not an **apostle?**
	9: 2	If I am not an **apostle** to
	9: 5	as do the other **apostles** and
	12:28	first **apostles,** second prophets
	12:29	Are all **apostles?** Are all
	15: 7	then to all the **apostles.**
	15: 9	least of the **apostles,** unfit to
	15: 9	unfit to be called an **apostle**
2C	1: 1	Paul, an **apostle** of Christ
	8:23	they are **messengers** of the
	11: 5	to these super-**apostles.**
	11:13	themselves as **apostles** of Christ.
	12:11	to these super-**apostles,**
	12:12	The signs of a true **apostle**
Ga	1: 1	Paul an **apostle**—sent neither
	1:17	already **apostles** before me, but
	1:19	other **apostle** except James the
Ep	1: 1	Paul, an **apostle** of Christ
	2:20	foundation of the **apostles** and
	3: 5	revealed to his holy **apostles**
	4:11	**apostles,** some prophets, some
Ph	2:25	**messenger** and minister to my
Co	1: 1	Paul, an **apostle** of Christ
1Th	2: 7	demands as **apostles** of Christ.
1Ti	1: 1	Paul, an **apostle** of Christ
	2: 7	herald and an **apostle** (I am
2Ti	1: 1	Paul, an **apostle** of Christ
	1:11	herald and an **apostle** and a
Ti	1: 1	**apostle** of Jesus Christ, for
He	3: 1	the **apostle** and high priest of
1P	1: 1	Peter, an **apostle** of Jesus
2P	1: 1	a servant and **apostle** of Jesus
	3: 2	spoken through your **apostles.**

Ju   1:17   predictions of the **apostles** of
Re   2: 2   claim to be **apostles** but are
      18:20   **apostles** and prophets! For God
      21:14   twelve **apostles** of the Lamb.

---

653 ᴳᴼ1 ᴬᴳ100 ᴸᴺ31 ᴿ575,4750
αποστοματιζω, I SPEAK OFF
Lk   11:53   to **cross-examine** him about many

---

654 ᴳᴼ9 ᴬᴳ100 ᴸᴺ31 ᴮ1:354 ᴷ7:719 ᴿ575,4762
αποστρεφω, I TURN OFF
Mt   5:42   do not **refuse** anyone who wants
      26:52   **Put** your sword **back** into its
Lk   23:14   who was **perverting** the people;
Ac   3:26   to bless you by **turning** each of
Ro   11:26   he **will banish** ungodliness from
2Ti   1:15   have **turned away** from me,
      4: 4   and will **turn away** from
Ti   1:14   of those who **reject** the truth.
He   12:25   escape if we **reject** the one who

---

655 ᴳᴼ1 ᴬᴳ100 ᴸᴺ31
αποστυγεω, I ABHOR
Ro   12: 9   Let love be genuine; **hate** what

---

656 ᴳᴼ3 ᴬᴳ100 ᴸᴺ31 ᴷ7:848 ᴿ575,4864
αποσυναγωγος, FROM SYNAGOGUE
Jn   9:22   be **put out of the synagogue.**
      12:42   be **put out of the synagogue;**
      16: 2   **put you out of the synagogues.**

---

657 ᴳᴼ6 ᴬᴳ100 ᴸᴺ31 ᴷ8:33
αποτασσω, I SAY GOOD BYE
Mk   6:46   After **saying farewell** to them,
Lk   9:61   let me first **say farewell** to
      14:33   if you do not **give up** all your
Ac   18:18   Paul **said farewell** to the
      18:21   but on **taking leave** of them, he
2C   2:13   So I **said farewell** to them and

---

658 ᴳᴼ2 ᴬᴳ100 ᴸᴺ31 ᴿ575,5055
αποτελεω, I FINISH COMPLETELY
Lk   13:32   the third day I **finish** my work
Ja   1:15   sin, when it is **fully grown,**

---

659 ᴳᴼ9 ᴬᴳ101 ᴸᴺ31 ᴮ1:314 ᴿ575,5087
αποτιθημι, I SET OFF
Mt   14: 3   **put** him in prison on account of
Ac   7:58   witnesses **laid** their coats at
Ro   13:12   Let us then **lay aside** the works

Ep   4:22   **put away** your former way of
      4:25   So then, **putting away** falsehood
Co   3: 8   But now you must **get rid** of all
He   12: 1   let us also **lay aside** every
Ja   1:21   Therefore **rid** yourselves of all
1P   2: 1   **Rid** yourselves, therefore, of

---

660 ᴳᴼ2 ᴬᴳ101 ᴸᴺ31 ᴮ3:560
αποτινασσω, I SHAKE OFF
Lk   9: 5   **shake** the dust off your feet as
Ac   28: 5   **shook** off the creature into the

---

661 ᴳᴼ1 ᴬᴳ101 ᴸᴺ32 ᴿ575,5099
αποτινω, I PAY DAMAGES
Pm   1:19   I will **repay** it. I say nothing

---

662 ᴳᴼ1 ᴬᴳ101 ᴸᴺ32 ᴷ8:181 ᴿ575,5111
αποτολμαω, I DARE MORE
Ro   10:20   Then Isaiah **is so bold** as to

---

663 ᴳᴼ2 ᴬᴳ101 ᴸᴺ32 ᴷ8:106
αποτομια, SEVERITY
Ro   11:22   kindness and the **severity** of
      11:22   **severity** toward those who have

---

664 ᴳᴼ2 ᴬᴳ101 ᴵᴺ32 ᴷ8:106
αποτομως, SEVERELY
2C   13:10   **severe** in using the authority
Ti   1:13   rebuke them **sharply,** so that

---

665 ᴳᴼ1 ᴬᴳ101 ᴸᴺ32 ᴮ3:902
αποτρεπω, I TURN FROM
2Ti   3: 5   denying its power. **Avoid** them!

---

666 ᴳᴼ1 ᴬᴳ101 ᴸᴺ32 ᴿ548
απουσια, ABSENCE
Ph   2:12   much more now in my **absence,**

---

667 ᴳᴼ6 ᴬᴳ101 ᴸᴺ32 ᴿ575,5342
αποφερω, I CARRY OFF
Mk   15: 1   They bound Jesus, **led** him **away,**
Lk   16:22   **carried away** by the angels to
Ac   19:12   **touched** his skin were brought
1C   16: 3   to **take** your gift to Jerusalem.
Re   17: 3   So he **carried** me away in the
      21:10   in the spirit he **carried** me

---

668 ᴳᴼ3 ᴬᴳ101 ᴸᴺ32 ᴮ1:558 ᴿ575,5343
αποφευγω, I FLEE FROM
2P   1: 4   through them you may **escape**

2:18　people who have just **escaped**
2:20　For if, after they have **escaped**

669　GO3 AG102 LN32 B3:1080 K1:447
αποφθεγγομαι, I SPEAK OFF
Ac　2: 4　the Spirit **gave** them **ability.**
　　2:14　**addressed** them, "Men of Judea
　　26:25　I am **speaking** the sober truth.

670　GO1 AG102 LN32 R575,5412
αποφορτιζομαι, I PACK OFF
Ac　21: 3　ship was to **unload** its cargo

671　GO1 AG102 LN32 R575,5530
αποχρησις, FULL USE
Co　2:22　things that perish **with use;**

672　GO3 AG102 LN32 R575,5562
αποχωρεω, I MAKE ROOM OFF
Mt　7:23　I never knew you; **go away** from
Lk　9:39　will scarcely **leave** him.
Ac　13:13　John, however, **left** them and

673　GO2 AG102 LN32 R575,5563
αποχωριζω, I SEPARATE OFF
Ac　15:39　they **parted company;** Barnabas
Re　6:14　The sky **vanished** like a scroll

674　GO1 AG102 LN32
αποψυχω, I FAINT
Lk　21:26　People **will faint** from fear and

675　GO1 AG102 LN32
απποιος, APPIUS
Ac　28:15　Forum of **Appius** and Three

676　GO1 AG102 LN32
απροσιτος, UNAPPROACHABLE
1Ti　6:16　dwells in **unapproachable** light,

677　GO3 AG102 LN32 B2:705 K6:745 R4350
απροσκοπος, BLAMELESS
Ac　24:16　have a **clear** conscience toward
1C　10:32　Give no **offense** to Jews or to
Ph　1:10　you may be pure and **blameless,**

678　GO1 AG102 LN32 B1:585 K6:779 R4383,2983
απροσωπολημπτως, NOT RECEIVING
　　FACE (IMPARTIALLY)
1P　1:17　**impartially** according to their

679　GO1 AG102 LN32 R4417
απταιστος, WITHOUT STUMBLING
Ju　1:24　keep you **from falling,** and to

681　GO39 AG102 LN32 B3:859
'απτω, I TOUCH
Mt　8: 3　**touched** him, saying, "I do
　　8:15　he **touched** her hand, and the
　　9:20　**touched** the fringe of his cloak
　　9:21　If I only **touch** his cloak, I
　　9:29　Then he **touched** their eyes and
　　14:36　might **touch** even the fringe of
　　14:36　who **touched** it were
　　17: 7　But Jesus came and **touched** them
　　20:34　Jesus **touched** their eyes.
Mk　1:41　out his hand and **touched** him,
　　3:10　pressed upon him to **touch** him.
　　5:27　in the crowd and **touched** his
　　5:28　If I but **touch** his clothes, I
　　5:30　Who **touched** my clothes?
　　5:31　can you say, 'Who **touched** me?'
　　6:56　him that they might **touch** even
　　6:56　and all who **touched** it were
　　7:33　he spat and **touched** his tongue.
　　8:22　begged him to **touch** him.
　　10:13　in order that he might **touch**
Lk　5:13　**touched** him, and said, "I do
　　6:19　**touch** him, for power came out
　　7:14　**touched** the bier, and the
　　7:39　**touching** him—that she is a
　　8:16　No one after **lighting** a lamp
　　8:44　**touched** the fringe of his
　　8:45　Then Jesus asked, "Who **touched**
　　8:46　Jesus said, "Someone **touched** me
　　8:47　why she had **touched** him, and
　　11:33　No one after **lighting** a lamp
　　15: 8　does not **light** a lamp, sweep
　　18:15　that he might **touch** them; and
　　22:51　And he **touched** his ear and
Jn　20:17　Do not **hold on** to me, because
Ac　28: 2　**kindled** a fire and welcomed all
1C　7: 1　man not to **touch** a woman.
2C　6:17　**touch** nothing unclean; then I
Co　2:21　Do not taste, Do not **touch**"?
1J　5:18　and the evil one does not **touch**

682　GO1 AG103 LN32
απφια, APPHIA
Pm　1: 2　**Apphia** our sister, to Archippus

683 GO6 AG103 LN32 K1:448
απωθεω, I SHOVE OFF

Ac	7:27	**pushed** Moses **aside,** saying,
	7:39	instead, they **pushed** him **aside,**
	13:46	Since you **reject** it and judge
Ro	11: 1	has God **rejected** his people? By
	11: 2	God has not **rejected** his people
1Ti	1:19	By **rejecting** conscience,

684 GO18 AG103 LN32 B1:462 K1:396 R622
απωλεια, DESTRUCTION

Mt	7:13	leads to **destruction,** and there
	26: 8	angry and said, "Why this **waste**
Mk	14: 4	ointment **wasted** in this way?
Jn	17:12	the one **destined** to be **lost,** so
Ac	8:20	silver **perish** with you, because
Ro	9:22	that are made for **destruction;**
Ph	1:28	evidence of their **destruction,**
	3:19	Their end is **destruction;** their
2Th	2: 3	one destined for **destruction.**
1Ti	6: 9	into ruin and **destruction.**
He	10:39	who shrink back and so **are lost**
2P	2: 1	secretly bring in **destructive**
	2: 1	bringing swift **destruction** on
	2: 3	their **destruction** is not asleep
	3: 7	judgment and **destruction** of the
	3:16	twist to their own **destruction,**
Re	17: 8	pit and go to **destruction.** And
	17:11	and it goes to **destruction.**

685 GO1 AG103 LN33 B1:416 K1:448
αρα, OF CURSING

| Ro | 3:14 | mouths are full of **cursing** and |

686 GO49 AG103 LN33
αρα, THEN

Mt	7:20	**Thus** you will know them by
	12:28	**then** the kingdom of God has
	17:26	Jesus said to him, **"Then** the
	18: 1	**Who** is the greatest in the
	19:25	said, **"Then** who can be saved?"
	19:27	you. What **then** will we have?
	24:45	Who **then** is the faithful and
Mk	4:41	Who **then** is this, that even
	11:13	he went to see **whether** perhaps
Lk	1:66	What **then** will this child
	8:25	Who **then** is this, that he
	11:20	**then** the kingdom of God has
	11:48	**So** you are witnesses and
	12:42	Who **then** is the faithful and

	22:23	**Then** they began to ask one
Ac	8:22	if **possible,** the intent of your
	11:18	**Then** God has given even to the
	12:18	among the soldiers over **what**
	17:27	search for God and **perhaps**
	21:38	**Then** you are not the Egyptian
Ro	5:18	Therefore **just** as one man's
	7: 3	**Accordingly,** she will be called
	7:21	**So** I find it to be a law that
	7:25	So **then,** with my mind I am a
	8: 1	There is **therefore** now no
	8:12	So **then,** brothers and sisters,
	9:16	So it depends not on human will
	9:18	So **then** he has mercy on
	10:17	So faith comes from what is
	14:12	So then, each of us will be
	14:19	Let us **then** pursue what makes
1C	5:10	would **then** need to go out of
	7:14	**Otherwise,** your children would
	15:14	**then** our proclamation has been
	15:15	if it is true **that** the dead are
	15:18	**Then** those also who have died
2C	1:17	Was I vacillating **when** I wanted
	5:14	all; **therefore** all have died.
	7:12	So although I wrote to you, it
Ga	2:21	**then** Christ died for nothing.
	3: 7	**so,** you see, those who believe
	3:29	**then** you are Abraham's
	5:11	**In that case** the offense of the
	6:10	So **then,** whenever we have an
Ep	2:19	So **then** you are no longer
1Th	5: 6	So **then** let us not fall asleep
2Th	2:15	So **then,** brothers and sisters,
He	4: 9	So **then,** a sabbath rest still
	12: 8	**then** you are illegitimate and

687 GO3 AG104 LN33
αρα, THEN

Lk	18: 8	And **yet,** when the Son of Man
Ac	8:30	Do **you** understand what you are
Ga	2:17	is Christ **then** a servant of sin

688 GO2 AG104 LN33
αραβια, ARABIA

| Ga | 1:17 | went away at once into **Arabia,** |
| | 4:25 | Mount Sinai in **Arabia** and |

689 GO2 AG104 LN33
αραμ, ARAM

Mt 1: 3 Hezron the father of **Aram,**
    1: 4 and **Aram** the father of Aminadab

689a GO1 AG104 LN33
αραφος, WITHOUT SEWING
Jn 19:23 now the tunic was **seamless,**

---

690 GO1 AG104 LN33
αραψ, ARABIAN
Ac 2:11 Cretans and **Arabs**—in our own

---

691 GO1 AG104 LN33 K1:452 R692
αργεω, I AM IDLE
2P 2: 3 has not been **idle,** and their

---

692 GO8 AG104 LN33 K1:452 R2041
αργος, IDLE
Mt 12:36 account for every **careless** word
    20: 3 others standing **idle** in the
    20: 6 Why are you standing here **idle**
1Ti 5:13 they learn to be **idle,** gadding
     5:13 they are not merely **idle,** but
Ti 1:12 vicious brutes, **lazy** gluttons.
Ja 2:20 apart from works is **barren?**
2P 1: 8 you from being **ineffective**

---

693 GO3 AG105 LN33 B2:96
αργυρους, SILVER
Ac 19:24 made **silver** shrines of Artemis
2Ti 2:20 gold and **silver** but also of
Re 9:20 idols of gold and **silver** and

---

694 GO20 AG104 LN33 B2:96 R696
αργυριον, SILVER
Mt 25:18 and hid his master's **money.**
    25:27 invested my **money** with the
    26:15 thirty pieces of **silver.**
    27: 3 thirty pieces of **silver** to the
    27: 5 pieces of **silver** in the temple,
    27: 6 **silver,** said, "It is not lawful
    27: 9 **silver,** the price of the one on
    28:12 sum of **money** to the soldiers,
    28:15 So they took the **money** and did
Mk 14:11 promised to give him **money.**
Lk 9: 3 nor bag, nor bread, nor **money**
    19:15 whom he had given the **money,** to
    19:23 did you not put my **money** into
    22: 5 agreed to give him **money.**
Ac 3: 6 I have no **silver** or gold, but
    7:16 a sum of **silver** from the sons

19:19 come to fifty thousand **silver**
20:33 I coveted no one's **silver** or
1P 1:18 perishable things like **silver**

---

695 GO1 AG105 LN33 R696,2875
αργυροκοπος, SILVER LABORER
Ac 19:24 named Demetrius, a **silversmith**

---

696 GO5 AG105 LN33 B2:96
αργυρος, SILVER
Mt 10: 9 Take no gold, or **silver,** or
Ac 17:29 gold, or **silver,** or stone, an
1C 3:12 gold, **silver,** precious stones,
Ja 5: 3 gold and **silver** have rusted,
Re 18:12 cargo of gold, **silver,** jewels

---

697 GO2 AG105 LN33
αρειος παγος, AREOPAGUS
Ac 17:19 to the **Areopagus** and asked
                him
    17:22 **Areopagus** and said, "Athenians

---

698 GO1 AG105 LN33
αρεοπαγιτης, AEROPAGITE
Ac 17:34 Dionysius the **Areopagite** and a

---

699 GO1 AG105 LN33 B2:814 K1:456 R700
αρεσκεια, PLEASING
Co 1:10 **fully pleasing** to him, as you

---

700 GO17 AG105 LN33 B2:814 K1:455
αρεσκω, I PLEASE
Mt 14: 6 company, and she **pleased**
                Herod
Mk 6:22 danced, she **pleased** Herod and
Ac 6: 5 What they said **pleased** the
Ro 8: 8 in the flesh cannot **please** God.
    15: 1 not to **please** ourselves.
    15: 2 Each of us must **please** our
    15: 3 Christ did not **please** himself;
1C 7:32 Lord, how to **please** the Lord;
    7:33 world, how to **please** his wife,
    7:34 how to **please** her husband.
    10:33 try to **please** everyone in
Ga 1:10 Or am I trying to **please** people
    1:10 If I were still **pleasing** people
1Th 2: 4 not to **please** mortals, but to
    2:15 they **displease** God and oppose
    4: 1 to live and to **please** God (as,
2Ti 2: 4 aim is to **please** the enlisting

701   G04 AG105 LN33 B2:814 K1:456 R700
αρεστος, PLEASING
Jn   8:29   I always do what is **pleasing** to
Ac   6: 2   It is not **right** that we should
      12: 3   After he saw that it **pleased**
1J   3:22   and do what **pleases** him.

702   G01 AG105 LN33
αρετας, ARETAS
2C   11:32   King **Aretas** guarded the city of

703   G05 AG105 LN33 B3:925 K1:457
αρετη, VIRTUE
Ph   4: 8   if there is any **excellence** and
1P   2: 9   proclaim the **mighty acts** of him
2P   1: 3   by his own glory and **goodness.**
      1: 5   your faith with **goodness,**
      1: 5   and **goodness** with knowledge,

704   G01 AG106 LN33 B2:410 K1:340
αρην, SHEEP
Lk   10: 3   like **lambs** into the midst of

705   G03 AG106 LN33 B2:703 K1:461 R706
αριθμεω, I NUMBER
Mt   10:30   of your head are all **counted.**
Lk   12: 7   **counted.** Do not be afraid;
Re   7: 9   no one could **count,** from every

706   G018 AG106 LN33 B2:683 K1:461
αριθμος, NUMBER
Lk   22: 3   Iscariot, who was **one** of the
Jn   6:10   **about** five thousand in all.
Ac   4: 4   they **numbered** about five
      5:36   and a **number** of men, about four
      6: 7   **number** of the disciples
      11:21 **number** became believers and
      16: 5 increased in **numbers** daily.
Ro   9:27   Though the **number** of the
Re   5:11   **numbered** myriads of myriads and
      7: 4   And I heard the **number** of those
      9:16   The **number** of the troops of
      9:16   million; I heard their **number.**
      13:17 beast or the **number** of its name
      13:18 **number** of the beast, for it is
      13:18 **number** of a person. Its number
      13:18 **number** is six hundred sixty-six
      15: 2 **number** of its name, standing
      20: 8 as **numerous** as the sands of the

707   G04 AG106 LN33
αριμαθαια, ARIMATHEA
Mt   27:57   **Arimathea,** named Joseph, who
Mk   15:43   Joseph of **Arimathea,** a
Lk   23:51   town of **Arimathea,** and he was
Jn   19:38   Joseph of **Arimathea,** who was a

708   G05 AG106 LN34
αρισταρχος, ARISTARCHUS
Ac   19:29   Gaius and **Aristarchus,**
      20: 4   **Aristarchus** and Secundus from
      27: 2   **Aristarchus,** a Macedonian from
Co   4:10   **Aristarchus** my fellow prisoner
Pm   1:24   **Aristarchus,** Demas, and Luke,

709   G03 AG106 LN34 R712
αρισταω, I EAT A MEAL
Lk   11:37   a Pharisee invited him **to dine**
Jn   21:12   Come and **have breakfast.**
      21:15 **breakfast,** Jesus said to Simon

710   G04 AG106 LN34 B2:148
αριστερος, LEFT
Mt   6: 3   do not let your **left** hand know
Mk   10:37   right hand and one at your **left**
Lk   23:33   his right and one on his **left.**
2C   6: 7   right hand and for the **left;**

711   G01 AG106 LN34
αριστοβουλος, ARISTOBULUS
Ro   16:10   the family of **Aristobulus.**

712   G03 AG106 LN34
αριστον, MEAL
Mt   22: 4   I have prepared my **dinner,** my
Lk   11:38   not first wash before **dinner.**
      14:12 When you give a **luncheon** or a

713   G03 AG107 LN34 B3:727 K1:464 R714
αρκετος, SUFFICIENT
Mt   6:34   Today's trouble is **enough** for
      10:25 it is **enough** for the disciple
1P   4: 3   already spent **enough** time in

714   G08 AG107 LN34 B3:726 K1:464
αρκεω, I AM ENOUGH
Mt   25: 9   not be **enough** for you and for
Lk   3:14   be **satisfied** with your wages.
Jn   6: 7   not buy **enough** bread for each
      14: 8   we will be **satisfied.**

2C	12: 9	My grace is **sufficient** for you
1Ti	6: 8	we will be **content** with these.
He	13: 5	and be **content** with what you
3J	1:10	And not **content** with those

715 GO1 AG107 LN34
αρκος, BEAR

Re	13: 2	its feet were like a **bear's,**

716 GO4 AG107 LN34
αρμα, CHARIOT

Ac	8:28	seated in his **chariot,** he was
	8:29	Go over to this **chariot** and
	8:38	commanded the **chariot** to stop,
Re	9: 9	noise of many **chariots** with

717 GO1 AG107 LN34 B3:959 K1:468
'αρμαγεδων, HARMAGEDON

Re	16:16	in Hebrew is called **Harmagedon.**

718 GO1 AG107 LN34
'αρμοζω, I HARMONIZE, I JOIN

2C	11: 2	I **promised** you in marriage to

719 GO1 AG107 LN34
'αρμος, JOINT

He	4:12	soul from spirit, **joints** from

720 GO33 AG107 LN34 B1:454 K1:469
αρνεομαι, I DENY

Mt	10:33	but whoever **denies** me before
	10:33	I also will **deny** before my
	26:70	But he **denied** it before all of
	26:72	Again he **denied** it with an oath
Mk	14:68	But he **denied** it, saying, "I do
	14:70	But again he **denied** it. Then
Lk	8:45	When all **denied** it, Peter said,
	9: 2	let them **deny** themselves and
	12: 9	but whoever **denies** me before
	22:57	But he **denied** it, saying,
Jn	1:20	He confessed and did not **deny**
	13:38	you will have **denied** me three
	18:25	He **denied** it and said, "I am
	18:27	Again Peter **denied** it, and at
Ac	3:13	handed over and **rejected** in the
	3:14	But you **rejected** the Holy and
	4:16	through them; we cannot **deny** it
	7:35	Moses whom they **rejected** when
1Ti	5: 8	has **denied** the faith and is
2Ti	2:12	if we **deny** him, he will also

	2:12	**deny** him, he will also **deny** us;
	2:13	for he cannot **deny** himself.
	3: 5	godliness but **denying** its power
Ti	1:16	but they **deny** him by their
	2:12	training us to **renounce** impiety
He	11:24	**refused** to be called a son of
2P	2: 1	They will even **deny** the Master
1J	2:22	one who **denies** that Jesus is
	2:22	the one who **denies** the Father
	2:23	No one who **denies** the Son has
Ju	1: 4	licentiousness and **deny** our
Re	2:13	did not **deny** your faith in me
	3: 8	my word and have not **denied** my

720a GO1 AG108 LN34
αρνι, ARNI

Lk	3:33	son of Admin, son of **Arni,** son

721 GO30 AG108 LN34 B2:410 K1:340 R704
αρνιον, LAMB

Jn	21:15	said to him, "Feed my **lambs.**"
Re	5: 6	a **Lamb** standing as if it
	5: 8	fell before the **Lamb,** each
	5:12	Worthy is the **Lamb** that was
	5:13	to the **Lamb** be blessing and
	6: 1	Then I saw the **Lamb** open one
	6:16	from the wrath of the **Lamb;**
	7: 9	throne and before the **Lamb,**
	7:10	throne, and to the **Lamb!**
	7:14	white in the blood of the **Lamb.**
	7:17	for the **Lamb** at the center of
	12:11	by the blood of the **Lamb** and by
	13: 8	book of life of the **Lamb** that
	13:11	**lamb** and it spoke like a dragon
	14: 1	**Lamb,** standing on Mount Zion!
	14: 4	these follow the **Lamb** wherever
	14: 4	fruits for God and the **Lamb,**
	14:10	the presence of the **Lamb.**
	15: 3	the song of the **Lamb:** "Great
	17:14	they will make war on the **Lamb,**
	17:14	the **Lamb** will conquer them, for
	19: 7	marriage of the **Lamb** has come,
	19: 9	marriage supper of the **Lamb.**
	21: 9	bride, the wife of the **Lamb.**
	21:14	twelve apostles of the **Lamb.**
	21:22	God the Almighty and the **Lamb.**
	21:23	its lamp is the **Lamb.**
	21:27	written in the **Lamb's** book of

22: 1   throne of God and of the **Lamb**
22: 3   throne of God and of the **Lamb**

---

722 ᴳᴼ3 ᴬᴳ108 ᴸᴺ34 ᴿ723
αροτριαω, I PLOW
Lk 17: 7   **plowing** or tending sheep in
1C   9:10   whoever **plows** should plow in
     9:10   **plow** in hope and whoever

---

723 ᴳᴼ1 ᴬᴳ108 ᴸᴺ34
αροτρον, PLOW
Lk   9:62   puts a hand to the **plow** and

---

724 ᴳᴼ3 ᴬᴳ108 ᴸᴺ34 ᴮ3:601 ᴿ726
αρπαγη, SEIZURE
Mt 23:25   inside they are full of **greed**
Lk 11:39   full of **greed** and wickedness.
He 10:34   **plundering** of your possessions,

---

725 ᴳᴼ1 ᴬᴳ108 ᴸᴺ34 ᴮ3:601 ᴷ1:473
ʽαρπαγμος, SEIZURE
Ph   2: 6   as something to be **exploited,**

---

726 ᴳᴼ14 ᴬᴳ109 ᴸᴺ35 ᴮ3:601 ᴷ1:472
ʽαρπαζω, I SEIZE
Mt 11:12   the violent **take** it by **force.**
    12:29   **plunder** his property, without
    13:19   the evil one comes and **snatches**
Jn   6:15   **take** him by **force** to make him
    10:12   the wolf **snatches** them and
    10:28   No one will **snatch** them out of
    10:29   no one can **snatch** it out of the
Ac   8:39   the Spirit of the Lord **snatched**
    23:10   **take** him by **force,** and bring
2C 12: 2   **was caught up** to the third
    12: 4   **was caught up** into Paradise and
1Th 4:17   will be **caught up** in the clouds
Ju   1:23   save others by **snatching** them
Re 12: 5   But her child was **snatched** away

---

727 ᴳᴼ5 ᴬᴳ109 ᴸᴺ35 ᴮ3:601 ᴿ726
ʽαρπαξ, PLUNDERER
Mt   7:15   but inwardly are **ravenous**
Lk 18:11   not like other people: **thieves,**
1C   5:10   the greedy and **robbers,** or
     5:11   reviler, drunkard, or **robber.**
     6:10   **robbers**—none of these will

---

728 ᴳᴼ3 ᴬᴳ109 ᴸᴺ35 ᴮ2:39 ᴷ1:475
αρραβων, EARNEST

2C   1:22   hearts as a **first installment.**
     5: 5   us the Spirit as a **guarantee.**
Ep   1:14   this is the **pledge** of our

---

730 ᴳᴼ9 ᴬᴳ109 ᴸᴺ35 ᴮ2:569
αρσην, MALE
Mt 19: 4   made them **male** and female,
Mk 10: 6   God made them **male** and female.
Lk   2:23   Every firstborn **male** shall be
Ro   1:27   the **men,** giving up natural
     1:27   **Men** committed shameless acts
     1:27   **men** and received in their own
Ga   3:28   no longer **male** and female; for
Re 12: 5   a **male** child, who is to rule
    12:13   had given birth to the **male**

---

731 ᴳᴼ1 ᴬᴳ109 ᴸᴺ35
αρρητος, UNSPEAKABLE
2C 12: 4   things that are **not to be told,**

---

732 ᴳᴼ5 ᴬᴳ109 ᴸᴺ35
αρρωστος, FEEBLE
Mt 14:14   for them and cured their **sick.**
Mk   6: 5   laid his hands on a few **sick**
     6:13   many who were **sick** and cured
    16:18   lay their hands on the **sick,**
1C 11:30   weak and **ill,** and some have

---

733 ᴳᴼ2 ᴬᴳ109 ᴸᴺ35 ᴮ2:569 ᴿ730,2845
αρσενοκοιτης, MALE SEX PARTNER
1C   6: 9   male prostitutes, **sodomites,**
1Ti 1:10   **sodomites,** slave traders, liars

---

734 ᴳᴼ1 ᴬᴳ110 ᴸᴺ35
αρτεμας, ARTEMAS
Ti   3:12   When I send **Artemas** to you, or

---

735 ᴳᴼ5 ᴬᴳ110 ᴸᴺ35
αρτεμις, ARTEMIS
Ac 19:24   silver shrines of **Artemis,**
    19:27   goddess **Artemis** will be scorned
    19:28   Great is **Artemis** of the
    19:34   Great is **Artemis** of the
    19:35   **Artemis** and of the statue that

---

736 ᴳᴼ1 ᴬᴳ110 ᴸᴺ35
αρτεμων, SAIL
Ac 27:40   hoisting the **foresail** to the

737 ᴳᴼ36 ᴬᴳ110 ᴸᴺ35 ᴮ3:833 ᴷ4:1106
αρτι, NOW

Mt	3:15	Let it be so **now;** for it is
	9:18	My daughter has **just** died; but
	11:12	**now** the kingdom of heaven has
	23:39	**until** you say, 'Blessed is the
	26:29	I tell you, I will never **again**
	26:53	he will **at once** send me more
	26:64	I tell you, From **now** on you
Jn	2:10	kept the good wine until **now.**
	5:17	My Father is **still** working,
	9:19	How then does he **now** see?
	9:25	I was blind, **now** I see.
	13: 7	You do not know **now** what I am
	13:19	I tell you this **now,** before it
	13:33	**now** I say to you, 'Where I am
	13:37	can I not follow you **now?** I
	14: 7	From **now** on you do know him and
	16:12	you cannot bear them **now.**
	16:24	Until **now** you have not asked
	16:31	answered them, "Do you **now**
1C	4:11	To the **present** hour we are
	4:13	things, to **this very day.**
	8: 7	accustomed to idols until **now,**
	13:12	For **now** we see in a mirror,
	13:12	**Now** I know only in part; then
	15: 6	most of whom are **still** alive,
	16: 7	I do not want to see you **now**
Ga	1: 9	As we have said before, so **now**
	1:10	Am I **now** seeking human approval
	4:20	were present with you **now** and
1Th	3: 6	But Timothy has just **now** come
2Th	2: 7	the one who **now** restrains it is
1P	1: 6	this you rejoice, even if **now**
	1: 8	**now,** you believe in him and
1J	2: 9	sister, is **still** in the
Re	12:10	**Now** have come the salvation
	14:13	are the dead who from **now** on

---

738 ᴳᴼ1 ᴬᴳ110 ᴸᴺ35 ᴷ1:672 ᴿ737,1084
αρτιγεννητος, JUST BORN

1P	2: 2	Like **newborn** infants, long for

---

739 ᴳᴼ1 ᴬᴳ110 ᴸᴺ35 ᴮ3:349 ᴷ1:475
αρτιος, FIT

2Ti	3:17	**proficient,** equipped for every

---

740 ᴳᴼ97 ᴬᴳ110 ᴸᴺ35 ᴮ1:249 ᴷ1:477
αρτος, BREAD

Mt	4: 3	to become loaves of **bread.**

	4: 4	live by **bread** alone, but by
	6:11	us this day our daily **bread.**
	7: 9	if your child asks for **bread,**
	12: 4	ate the **bread** of the Presence
	14:17	but five **loaves** and two fish.
	14:19	Taking the five **loaves** and the
	14:19	broke the **loaves,** and gave them
	15: 2	their hands before they **eat.**
	15:26	children's **food** and throw it to
	15:33	**bread** in the desert to feed so
	15:34	How many **loaves** have you?
	15:36	he took the seven **loaves** and
	16: 5	forgotten to bring any **bread.**
	16: 7	we have brought no **bread.**
	16: 8	talking about having no **bread?**
	16: 9	remember the five **loaves** for
	16:10	Or the seven **loaves** for the
	16:11	**bread?** Beware of the yeast of
	16:12	**bread,** but of the teaching of
	26:26	Jesus took a loaf of **bread,** and
Mk	2:26	and ate the **bread** of the
	3:20	so that they could not even **eat**
	6: 8	no **bread,** no bag, no money in
	6:37	You give them something to **eat**
	6:38	How many **loaves** have you? Go
	6:41	Taking the five **loaves** and the
	6:41	blessed and broke the **loaves,**
	6:44	Those who had eaten the **loaves**
	6:52	not understand about the **loaves**
	7: 2	**eating** with defiled hands, that
	7: 5	but **eat** with defiled hands?
	7:27	children's **food** and throw it to
	8: 4	feed these people with **bread**
	8: 5	How many **loaves** do you have?
	8: 6	and he took the seven **loaves,**
	8:14	forgotten to bring any **bread;**
	8:14	they had only one **loaf** with
	8:16	It is because we have no **bread**
	8:17	**bread?** Do you still not
	8:19	When I broke the five **loaves**
	14:22	he took a loaf of **bread,** and
Lk	4: 3	stone to become a loaf of **bread**
	4: 4	One does not live by **bread**
	6: 4	took and ate the **bread** of the
	7:33	eating no **bread** and drinking no
	9: 3	nor bag, nor **bread,** nor money
	9:13	five **loaves** and two fish—
	9:16	And taking the five **loaves** and

	11: 3	us each day our daily **bread.**
	11: 5	lend me three loaves of **bread;**
	14: 1	eat a **meal** on the sabbath, they
	14:15	who will eat **bread** in the
	15:17	**bread** enough and to spare, but
	22:19	**bread,** and when he had given
	24:30	he took **bread,** blessed and
	24:35	in the breaking of the **bread.**
Jn	6: 5	Where are we to buy **bread** for
	6: 7	would not buy enough **bread** for
	6: 9	five barley **loaves** and two fish
	6:11	Then Jesus took the **loaves,** and
	6:13	five barley **loaves,** left by
	6:23	eaten the **bread** after the Lord
	6:26	you ate your fill of the **loaves**
	6:31	He gave them **bread** from heaven
	6:32	who gave you the **bread** from
	6:32	gives you the true **bread** from
	6:33	For the **bread** of God is that
	6:34	Sir, give us this **bread** always
	6:35	them, "I am the **bread** of life.
	6:41	I am the **bread** that came down
	6:48	I am the **bread** of life.
	6:50	This is the **bread** that comes
	6:51	I am the living **bread** that came
	6:51	Whoever eats of this **bread** will
	6:51	and the **bread** that I will give
	6:58	This is the **bread** that came
	6:58	the one who eats this **bread**
	13:18	The one who ate my **bread** has
	21: 9	with fish on it, and **bread.**
	21:13	Jesus came and took the **bread**
Ac	2:42	to the breaking of **bread** and
	2:46	they broke **bread** at home and
	20: 7	when we met to break **bread,**
	20:11	after he had broken **bread** and
	27:35	**bread;** and giving thanks to God
1C	10:16	The **bread** that we break, is it
	10:17	Because there is one **bread,** we
	10:17	we all partake of the one **bread**
	11:23	betrayed took a loaf of **bread,**
	11:26	as often as you eat this **bread**
	11:27	therefore, eats the **bread** or
	11:28	then eat of the **bread** and drink
2C	9:10	**bread** for food will supply and
2Th	3: 8	we did not eat anyone's **bread**
	3:12	and to earn their own **living.**
He	9: 2	the table, and the **bread** of the

741 GO3 AG111 LN35
αρτυω, I SEASON

Mk	9:50	how can you **season** it? Have
Lk	14:34	can its saltiness **be restored?**
Co	4: 6	be gracious, **seasoned** with salt

742 GO1 AG111 LN35
αρφαξαδ, ARPHAXAD

Lk	3:36	son of Cainan, son of **Arphaxad,**

743 GO2 AG111 LN35 B1:101 K1:87 R757,31a
αρχαγγελος, FIRST (CHIEF) MESSENGER

1Th	4:16	with the **archangel's** call and
Ju	1: 9	But when the **archangel** Michael

744 GO11 AG111 LN35 B1:164 K1:486 R746
αρχαιος, ANCIENT

Mt	5:21	those of **ancient** times, 'You
	5:33	**ancient** times, 'You shall not
Lk	9: 8	one of the **ancient** prophets had
	9:19	the **ancient** prophets has arisen
Ac	15: 7	in the **early** days God made a
	15:21	for generations **past,** Moses has
	21:16	an **early** disciple, with whom we
2C	5:17	everything **old** has passed away;
2P	2: 5	he did not spare the **ancient**
Re	12: 9	that **ancient** serpent, who is
	20: 2	seized the dragon, that **ancient**

745 GO1 AG111 LN35
αρχελαος, ARCHELAUS

Mt	2:22	**Archelaus** was ruling over Judea

746 GO55 AG111 LN35 B1:164 K1:479 R756
αρχη, BEGINNING, RULER

Mt	19: 4	made them at the **beginning**
	19: 8	but from the **beginning** it was
	24: 8	all this is but the **beginning**
	24:21	from the **beginning** of the world
Mk	1: 1	The **beginning** of the good news
	10: 6	**beginning** of creation, 'God
	13: 8	**beginning** of the birth pangs.
	13:19	has not been from the **beginning**
Lk	1: 2	those who from the **beginning**
	12:11	**rulers,** and the authorities,
	20:20	**jurisdiction** and authority of
Jn	1: 1	In the **beginning** was the Word,
	1: 2	He was in the **beginning** with

	2:11	Jesus did this, the **first**
	6:64	For Jesus knew from the **first**
	8:25	Jesus said to them, **"Why** do I
	8:44	a murderer from the **beginning**
	15:27	been with me from the **beginning**
	16: 4	**beginning,** because I was with
Ac	10:11	ground by its four **corners.**
	11: 5	lowered by its four **corners;**
	11:15	it had upon us at the **beginning**
	26: 4	a life spent from the **beginning**
Ro	8:38	life, nor angels, nor **rulers,**
1C	15:24	he has destroyed every **ruler**
Ep	1:21	far above all **rule** and
	3:10	made known to the **rulers** and
	6:12	but against the **rulers,** against
Ph	4:15	in the **early days** of the gospel
Co	1:16	thrones or dominions or **rulers**
	1:18	is the **beginning,** the firstborn
	2:10	who is the head of every **ruler**
	2:15	He disarmed the **rulers** and
Ti	3: 1	subject to **rulers** and
He	1:10	And, "In the **beginning,** Lord,
	2: 3	It was declared **at first**
	3:14	if only we hold our **first**
	5:12	teach you again the **basic**
	6: 1	leaving behind the **basic**
	7: 3	having neither **beginning** of
2P	3: 4	they were from the **beginning** of
1J	1: 1	what was from the **beginning,**
	2: 7	had from the **beginning;** the
	2:13	him who is from the **beginning.**
	2:14	him who is from the **beginning.**
	2:24	**beginning** abide in you. If what
	2:24	you heard from the **beginning**
	3: 8	sinning from the **beginning.** The
	3:11	from the **beginning,** that we
2J	1: 5	**beginning,** let us love one
	1: 6	**beginning**—you must walk in
Ju	1: 6	keep their **own position,** but
Re	3:14	the **origin** of God's creation:
	21: 6	the **beginning** and the end. To
	22:13	the **beginning** and the end.

747 GO3 AG112 LN35 B1:164 K1:487 R746,71
αρχηγος, BEGINNER

Ac	3:15	and you killed the **Author** of
	5:31	at his right hand as **Leader**
He	2:10	the **pioneer** of their salvation
	12: 2	looking to Jesus the **pioneer**

748 GO1 AG112 LN36 B3:32 R746,2413
αρχιερατικος, RULER PRIESTHOOD

Ac	4: 6	of the **high-priestly** family.

749 GO122 AG112 LN36 B2:232 K3:265 R746,2409
αρχιερευς, RULER PRIEST

Mt	2: 4	the **chief priests** and scribes
	16:21	**chief priests** and scribes, and
	20:18	over to the **chief priests** and
	21:15	But when the **chief priests** and
	21:23	**chief priests** and the elders of
	21:45	When the **chief priests** and the
	26: 3	Then the **chief priests** and the
	26: 3	palace of the **high priest,** who
	26:14	went to the **chief priests**
	26:47	from the **chief priests** and the
	26:51	slave of the **high priest,**
	26:57	Caiaphas the **high priest,** in
	26:58	courtyard of the **high priest;**
	26:59	Now the **chief priests** and the
	26:62	The **high priest** stood up and
	26:63	Then the **high priest** said to
	26:65	**high priest** tore his clothes
	27: 1	all the **chief priests** and the
	27: 3	silver to the **chief priests** and
	27: 6	But the **chief priests,** taking
	27:12	accused by the **chief priests**
	27:20	Now the **chief priests** and the
	27:41	the **chief priests** also, along
	27:62	**chief priests** and the Pharisees
	28:11	told the **chief priests**
Mk	2:26	Abiathar was **high priest,** and
	8:31	**chief priests,** and the scribes,
	10:33	over to the **chief priests** and
	11:18	And when the **chief priests** and
	11:27	the **chief priests,** the scribes,
	14: 1	The **chief priests** and the
	14:10	**chief priests** in order to
	14:43	**chief priests,** the scribes, and
	14:47	slave of the **high priest,**
	14:53	Jesus to the **high priest;** and
	14:53	and all the **chief priests,**
	14:54	courtyard of the **high priest;**
	14:55	Now the **chief priests** and the
	14:60	Then the **high priest** stood up
	14:61	Again the **high priest** asked him
	14:63	**high priest** tore his clothes
	14:66	servant-girl of the **high priest**
	15: 1	the **chief priests** held a

	15: 3	chief priests accused him of
	15:10	jealousy that the chief priests
	15:11	But the chief priests stirred
	15:31	chief priests, along with the
Lk	3: 2	high priesthood of Annas and
	9:22	chief priests, and scribes, and
	19:47	The chief priests, the scribes,
	20: 1	chief priests and the scribes
	20:19	chief priests realized that he
	22: 2	chief priests and the scribes
	22: 4	chief priests and officers of
	22:50	high priest and cut off his
	22:52	said to the chief priests, the
	22:54	high priest's house. But Peter
	22:66	chief priests and scribes,
	23: 4	chief priests and the crowds,
	23:10	The chief priests and the
	23:13	chief priests, the leaders, and
	24:20	and how our chief priests and
Jn	7:32	and the chief priests and
	7:45	chief priests and Pharisees,
	11:47	So the chief priests and the
	11:49	Caiaphas, who was high priest
	11:51	but being high priest that year
	11:57	Now the chief priests and the
	12:10	So the chief priests planned to
	18: 3	police from the chief priests
	18:10	struck the high priest's slave,
	18:13	the high priest that year.
	18:15	known to the high priest, he
	18:15	courtyard of the high priest,
	18:16	high priest, went out, spoke to
	18:19	Then the high priest questioned
	18:22	how you answer the high priest?
	18:26	high priest, a relative of the
	18:35	nation and the chief priests
	19: 6	When the chief priests and the
	19:15	The chief priests answered, "We
	19:21	Then the chief priests of the
Ac	4: 6	with Annas the high priest,
	4:23	reported what the chief priests
	5:17	the high priest took action;
	5:21	When the high priest and those
	5:24	chief priests heard these words
	5:27	The high priest questioned them
	7: 1	Then the high priest asked him,
	9: 1	went to the high priest
	9:14	from the chief priests to bind
	9:21	bound before the chief priests?

	19:14	Jewish high priest named Sceva
	22: 5	as the high priest and the
	22:30	ordered the chief priests and
	23: 2	Then the high priest Ananias
	23: 4	insult God's high priest?
	23: 5	high priest; for it is written,
	23:14	They went to the chief priests
	24: 1	high priest Ananias came down
	25: 2	where the chief priests and the
	25:15	chief priests and the elders
	26:10	chief priests, I not only
	26:12	commission of the chief priests
He	2:17	and faithful high priest in the
	3: 1	the apostle and high priest of
	4:14	we have a great high priest who
	4:15	we do not have a high priest
	5: 1	Every high priest chosen from
	5: 5	becoming a high priest, but was
	5:10	designated by God a high priest
	6:20	having become a high priest
	7:26	high priest, holy, blameless,
	7:27	Unlike the other high priests,
	7:28	appoints as high priests those
	8: 1	we have such a high priest, one
	8: 3	every high priest is appointed
	9: 7	but only the high priest goes
	9:11	Christ came as a high priest
	9:25	as the high priest enters the
	13:11	sanctuary by the high priest as

---

750   GO1 AG113 LN36 B3:564 K6:485 R746,4166
αρχιποιμην, RULER SHEPHERD
1P   5: 4   chief shepherd appears, you

---

751   GO2 AG113 LN36
αρχιππος, ARCHIPPUS
Co   4:17   And say to Archippus, "See
Pm   1: 2   to Archippus our fellow soldier

---

752   GO9 AG113 LN36 K7:844 R746,4864
αρχισυναγωγος, SYNAGOGUE RULER
Mk   5:22   leaders of the synagogue named
     5:35   leader's house to say, "Your
     5:36   leader of the synagogue, "Do
     5:38   the leader of the synagogue, he
Lk   8:49   someone came from the leader's
     13:14 But the leader of the synagogue
Ac   13:15 officials of the synagogue sent
     18: 8 the official of the synagogue,
     18:17 the official of the synagogue,

753 GO1 AG113 LN36 B1:279 R746,5045
αρχιτεκτων, FIRST CRAFTSMAN
1C   3:10   like a skilled **master builder** I

---

754 GO1 AG113 LN36 B3:755 R746,5057
αρχιτελωνης, CHIEF TAX COLLECTOR
Lk   19: 2   he was a **chief tax collector**

---

755 GO3 AG113 LN36
αρχιτρικλινος, CHIEF BANQUET STEWARD
Jn   2: 8   take it to the **chief steward.**
       2: 9   When the **steward** tasted the
       2: 9   **steward** called the bridegroom

---

757 GO86 AG113 LN36 B1:164 K1:478
αρχω, I BEGIN, I RULE
Mt   4:17   From that time Jesus **began** to
      11: 7   As they went away, Jesus **began**
      11:20   Then he **began** to reproach the
      12: 1   and they **began** to pluck heads
      14:30   **beginning** to sink, he cried out
      16:21   From that time on, Jesus **began**
      16:22   **began** to rebuke him, saying,
      18:24   When he **began** the reckoning,
      20: 8   give them their pay, **beginning**
      24:49   he **begins** to beat his fellow
      26:22   **began** to say to him one after
      26:37   and **began** to be grieved and
      26:74   Then he **began** to curse, and he
Mk   1:45   But he went out and **began** to
       2:23   his disciples **began** to pluck
       4: 1   Again he **began** to teach beside
       5:17   Then they **began** to beg Jesus to
       5:20   And he went away and **began** to
       6: 2   On the sabbath he **began** to
       6: 7   He called the twelve and **began**
       6:34   and he **began** to teach them many
       6:55   **began** to bring the sick on mats
       8:11   The Pharisees came and **began** to
       8:31   Then he **began** to teach them
       8:32   Peter took him aside and **began**
      10:28   Peter **began** to say to him,
      10:32   twelve aside again and **began**
      10:41   they **began** to be angry with
      10:42   recognize as their **rulers** lord
      10:47   he **began** to shout out and say,
      11:15   he entered the temple and **began**
      12: 1   Then he **began** to speak to them
      13: 5   Then Jesus **began** to say to them
      14:19   They **began** to be distressed and

14:33   and **began** to be distressed and
14:65   Some **began** to spit on him, to
14:69   **began** again to say to the
14:71   But he **began** to curse, and he
15: 8   So the crowd came and **began** to
15:18   And they **began** saluting him,
Lk   3: 8   Do not **begin** to say to
       3:23   he **began** his work. He was the
       4:21   Then he **began** to say to them,
       5:21   **began** to question, "Who is this
       7:15   The dead man sat up and **began**
       7:24   Jesus **began** to speak to the
       7:38   weeping, and **began** to bathe his
       7:49   **began** to say among themselves,
       9:12   The day **was drawing** to a close,
      11:29   he **began** to say, "This
      11:53   **began** to be very hostile toward
      12: 1   **began** to speak first to his
      12:45   if he **begins** to beat the other
      13:25   you **begin** to stand outside and
      13:26   Then you will **begin** to say, 'We
      14: 9   you would **start** to take the
      14:18   But they all alike **began** to
      14:29   all who see it will **begin** to
      14:30   saying, 'This fellow **began** to
      15:14   and he **began** to be in need.
      15:24   And they **began** to celebrate.
      19:37   **began** to praise God joyfully
      19:45   he entered the temple and **began**
      20: 9   He **began** to tell the people
      21:28   Now when these things **begin** to
      22:23   Then they **began** to ask one
      23: 2   They **began** to accuse him,
      23: 5   from Galilee where he **began**
      23:30   Then they will **begin** to say to
      24:27   Then **beginning** with Moses and
      24:47   **beginning** from Jerusalem.
Jn   8: 9   **beginning** with the elders; and
      13: 5   water into a basin and **began** to
Ac   1: 1   and taught from the **beginning**
       1:22   **beginning** from the baptism of
       2: 4   Holy Spirit and **began** to speak
       8:35   Then Philip **began** to speak, and
      10:37   **beginning** in Galilee after the
      11: 4   Then Peter **began** to explain it
      11:15   And as I **began** to speak, the
      18:26   He **began** to speak boldly in the
      24: 2   Tertullus **began** to accuse him,
      27:35   he broke it and **began** to eat.

Ro	15:12	the one who rises to **rule** the
2C	3: 1	Are we **beginning** to commend
1P	4:17	**begin** with the household of God

758 GO37 AG113 LN36 B1:164 K1:488 R757
αρχων, RULER

Mt	9:18	suddenly a **leader** of the
	9:23	the **leader's** house and saw the
	9:34	By the **ruler** of the demons he
	12:24	Beelzebul, the **ruler** of the
	20:25	the **rulers** of the Gentiles lord
Mk	3:22	by the **ruler** of the demons he
Lk	8:41	Jairus, a **leader** of the
	11:15	the **ruler** of the demons.
	12:58	accuser before a **magistrate,** on
	14: 1	**leader** of the Pharisees to eat
	18:18	A certain **ruler** asked him,
	23:13	the **leaders,** and the people,
	23:35	but the **leaders** scoffed at him,
	24:20	our chief priests and **leaders**
Jn	3: 1	Nicodemus, a **leader** of the Jews
	7:26	Can it be that the **authorities**
	7:48	Has any one of the **authorities**
	12:31	now the **ruler** of this world
	12:42	even of the **authorities,**
	14:30	for the **ruler** of this world is
	16:11	judgment, because the **ruler** of
Ac	3:17	as did also your **rulers.**
	4: 5	**rulers,** elders, and scribes
	4: 8	**Rulers** of the people and
	4:26	**rulers** have gathered together
	7:27	Who made you a **ruler** and a
	7:35	**ruler** and a judge?' and whom
	7:35	**ruler** and liberator through the
	13:27	their **leaders** did not recognize
	14: 5	**rulers,** to mistreat them and to
	16:19	before the **authorities.**
	23: 5	evil of a **leader** of your people
Ro	13: 3	For **rulers** are not a terror to
1C	2: 6	**rulers** of this age, who are
	2: 8	None of the **rulers** of this age
Ep	2: 2	following the **ruler** of the
Re	1: 5	the **ruler** of the kings of the

759 GO4 AG114 LN36
αρωμα, SPICE

Mk	16: 1	bought **spices,** so that they
Lk	23:56	and prepared **spices** and
	24: 1	taking the **spices** that they had

Jn	19:40	wrapped it with the **spices** in

760 GO2 AG114 LN36
ασαφ, ASAPH

Mt	1: 7	and Abijah the father of **Asaph,**
	1: 8	and **Asaph** the father of

761 GO2 AG114 LN36 B3:558 R4531
ασαλευτος, UNSHAKEABLE

Ac	27:41	remained **immovable,** but the
He	12:28	a kingdom that **cannot be shaken**

762 GO3 AG114 LN36 B3:110 R4570
ασβεστος, UNEXTINGUISHABLE

Mt	3:12	burn with **unquenchable** fire.
Mk	9:43	to the **unquenchable** fire.
Lk	3:17	burn with **unquenchable** fire.

763 GO6 AG114 LN36 B2:91 K7:185 R765
ασεβεια, IRREVERENCE

Ro	1:18	against all **ungodliness** and
	11:26	**ungodliness** from Jacob.
2Ti	2:16	into more and more **impiety,**
Ti	2:12	renounce **impiety** and worldly
Ju	1:15	the deeds of **ungodliness** that
	1:18	indulging their own **ungodly**

764 GO2 AG114 LN36 B2:93 K7:185 R765
ασεβεω, I AM IRREVERENT

2P	2: 6	what is coming to the **ungodly;**
Ju	1:15	in such an **ungodly** way, and of

765 GO8 AG114 LN36 B2:91 K7:185 R4576
ασεβης, IRREVERENT

Ro	4: 5	him who justifies the **ungodly,**
	5: 6	Christ died for the **ungodly.**
1Ti	1: 9	for the **godless** and sinful, for
1P	4:18	what will become of the **ungodly**
2P	2: 5	flood on a world of the **ungodly**
	3: 7	destruction of the **godless.**
Ju	1: 4	this condemnation as **ungodly,**
	1:15	harsh things that **ungodly**

766 GO10 AG114 LN36 B2:587 K1:490
ασελγεια, DEBAUCHERY

Mk	7:22	**licentiousness,** envy, slander,
Ro	13:13	debauchery and **licentiousness,**
2C	12:21	and **licentiousness** that they
Ga	5:19	impurity, **licentiousness,**
Ep	4:19	themselves to **licentiousness,**

1P	4: 3	living in **licentiousness,**
2P	2: 2	follow their **licentious** ways,
	2: 7	the **licentiousness** of the
	2:18	and with **licentious** desires of
Ju	1: 4	of our God into **licentiousness**

767 GO1 AG115 LN36 K7:267
ασημος, INSIGNIFICANT

| Ac | 21:39 | a citizen of an **important** city; |

768 GO2 AG115 LN36
ασηρ, ASHER

| Lk | 2:36 | of the tribe of **Asher.** |
| Re | 7: 6 | **Asher** twelve thousand, from the |

769 GO24 AG115 LN36 B3:993 K1:490 R772
ασθενεια, WEAKNESS

Mt	8:17	He took our **infirmities** and
Lk	5:15	be cured of their **diseases.**
	8: 2	evil spirits and **infirmities:**
	13:11	**crippled** her for eighteen years
	13:12	set free from your **ailment.**
Jn	5: 5	been **ill** for thirty-eight years
	11: 4	**illness** does not lead to death;
Ac	28: 9	**diseases** also came and were
Ro	6:19	of your natural **limitations.**
	8:26	Spirit helps us in our **weakness**
1C	2: 3	And I came to you in **weakness**
	15:43	It is sown in **weakness,** it is
2C	11:30	things that show my **weakness.**
	12: 5	except of my **weaknesses.**
	12: 9	is made perfect in **weakness.**
	12: 9	boast all the more gladly of my
	12:10	I am content with **weaknesses,**
	13: 4	he was crucified in **weakness,**
Ga	4:13	because of a physical **infirmity**
1Ti	5:23	and your frequent **ailments.**
He	4:15	sympathize with our **weaknesses,**
	5: 2	himself is subject to **weakness;**
	7:28	who are subject to **weakness,**
	11:34	won strength out of **weakness,**

770 GO33 AG115 LN36 B3:993 K1:490 R772
ασθενεω, I AM WEAK

Mt	10: 8	Cure the **sick,** raise the dead,
	25:36	I was **sick** and you took care of
	25:39	was it that we saw you **sick** or
Mk	6:56	they laid the **sick** in the
Lk	4:40	**sick** with various kinds of
Jn	4:46	whose son lay **ill** in Capernaum.

	5: 3	In these lay many **invalids**—
	5: 7	The **sick** man answered him,
	6: 2	that he was doing for the **sick.**
	11: 1	Now a certain man was **ill,**
	11: 2	her brother Lazarus was **ill.**
	11: 3	Lord, he whom you love is **ill.**
	11: 6	Lazarus was **ill,** he stayed two
Ac	9:37	At that time she became **ill** and
	19:12	skin were brought to the **sick,**
	20:35	we must support the **weak,**
Ro	4:19	He did not **weaken** in faith when
	8: 3	**weakened** by the flesh, could
	14: 1	Welcome those who are **weak** in
	14: 2	while the **weak** eat only
1C	8:11	those **weak** believers for whom
	8:12	conscience when it is **weak,** you
2C	11:21	we were too **weak** for that!
	11:29	Who is **weak,** and I am not weak?
	11:29	Who is weak, and I am not **weak?**
	12:10	I am content with **weaknesses,**
	13: 3	He is not **weak** in dealing with
	13: 4	he was crucified in **weakness,**
	13: 9	For we rejoice when we are **weak**
Ph	2:26	you heard that he was **ill.**
	2:27	He was indeed so **ill** that he
2Ti	4:20	Trophimus I left **ill** in Miletus
Ja	5:14	Are any among you **sick?** They

771 GO1 AG115 LN36 K1:490 R770
ασθενημα, WEAKNESS

| Ro | 15: 1 | with the failings of the **weak,** |

772 GO25 AG115 LN36 B3:993 K1:490 R4599
ασθενης, WEAK

Mt	25:43	**sick** and in prison and you did
	25:44	stranger or naked or **sick** or in
	26:41	willing, but the flesh is **weak.**
Mk	14:38	willing, but the flesh is **weak.**
Lk	9: 2	of God and to heal [the **sick**].
	10: 9	cure the **sick** who are there,
Ac	4: 9	done to someone who was **sick**
	5:15	**sick** into the streets, and laid
	5:16	bringing the **sick** and those
Ro	5: 6	For while we were still **weak,**
1C	1:25	and God's **weakness** is stronger
	1:27	chose what is **weak** in the world
	4:10	We are **weak,** but you are strong

8: 7	conscience, being **weak,** is
8: 9	a stumbling block to the **weak.**
8:10	since their conscience is **weak,**
9:22	To the **weak** I became weak, so
9:22	To the weak I became **weak,** so
11:30	many of you are **weak** and ill,
12:22	to be **weaker** are indispensable,
2C 10:10	his bodily presence is **weak,**
Ga 4: 9	turn back again to the **weak** and
1Th 5:14	help the **weak,** be patient with
He 7:18	it was **weak** and ineffectual
1P 3: 7	the woman as the **weaker** sex,

---

773 GO18 AG116 LN36
ασια, ASIA

Ac	2: 9	Cappadocia, Pontus and **Asia,**
	6: 9	those from Cilicia and **Asia,**
	16: 6	to speak the word in **Asia.**
	19:10	all the residents of **Asia,** both
	19:22	for some time longer in **Asia.**
	19:26	**Asia** this Paul has persuaded
	19:27	**Asia** and the world to worship
	20:16	not have to spend time in **Asia;**
	20:18	day that I set foot in **Asia,**
	21:27	the Jews from **Asia,** who had
	24:19	some Jews from **Asia**—they
	27: 2	along the coast of **Asia,** we put
Ro	16: 5	first convert in **Asia** for
1C	16:19	The churches of **Asia** send
2C	1: 8	we experienced in **Asia;** for we
2Ti	1:15	all who are in **Asia** have
1P	1: 1	Cappadocia, **Asia,** and Bithynia,
Re	1: 4	churches that are in **Asia:**

---

774 GO1 AG116 LN36
ασιανος, ASIAN
Ac 20: 4   and Trophimus from **Asia.**

---

775 GO1 AG116 LN36
ασιαρχης, ASIARCH
Ac 19:31   **officials . . . of Asia**

---

776 GO1 AG116 LN37 R777
ασιτια, ABSTINENCE
Ac 27:21   they had been **without food** for

---

777 GO1 AG116 LN37 R4621
ασιτος, ABSTAINING
Ac 27:33   remaining **without food,**

---

778 GO1 AG116 LN37 B1:494 K1:494
ασκεω, I ENGAGE
Ac 24:16   Therefore **I do my best** always

---

779 GO12 AG116 LN37
ασκος, WINESKIN

Mt	9:17	new wine put into old **wineskins**
	9:17	otherwise, the **skins** burst, and
	9:17	**skins** are destroyed; but new
	9:17	**wineskins,** and so both are
Mk	2:22	new wine into old **wineskins;**
	2:22	the wine will burst the **skins**
	2:22	is lost, and so are the **skins;**
	2:22	new wine into fresh **wineskins.**
Lk	5:37	new wine into old **wineskins;**
	5:37	new wine will burst the **skins**
	5:37	and the **skins** will be destroyed
	5:38	be put into fresh **wineskins.**

---

780 GO1 AG116 LN37
ασμενως, GLADLY
Ac 21:17   brothers welcomed us **warmly**

---

781 GO1 AG116 LN37 B3:1026 R4680
ασοφος, UNWISE
Ep 5:15   not as **unwise** people but as

---

782 GO57 AG116 LN37 B1:206 K1:496
ασπαζομαι, I GREET

Mt	5:47	And if you **greet** only your
	10:12	As you enter the house, **greet**
Mk	9:15	ran forward to **greet** him.
	15:18	And they began **saluting** him,
Lk	1:40	house of Zechariah and **greeted**
	10: 4	and **greet** no one on the road.
Ac	18:22	up to Jerusalem and **greeted** the
	20: 1	them and **saying farewell,** he
	21: 7	we **greeted** the believers and
	21:19	After **greeting** them, he related
	25:13	at Caesarea to **welcome** Festus.
Ro	16: 3	**Greet** Prisca and Aquila, who
	16: 5	**Greet** also the church in their
	16: 6	**Greet** Mary, who has worked
	16: 7	**Greet** Andronicus and Junia, my
	16: 8	**Greet** Ampliatus, my beloved in
	16: 9	**Greet** Urbanus, our co-worker in
	16:10	**Greet** Apelles, who is approved
	16:11	**Greet** my relative Herodion.
	16:11	**Greet** those in the Lord who
	16:12	**Greet** those workers in the Lord

	16:13	**Greet** Rufus, chosen in the Lord
	16:14	**Greet** Asyncritus, Phlegon,
	16:15	**Greet** Philologus, Julia, Nereus
	16:16	**Greet** one another with a holy
	16:16	churches of Christ **greet** you.
	16:21	Timothy, my co-worker, **greets**
	16:22	letter, **greet** you in the Lord.
	16:23	to the whole church, **greets** you
	16:23	and our brother Quartus, **greet**
1C	16:19	churches of Asia send **greetings**
	16:19	**greet** you warmly in the Lord.
	16:20	sisters send **greetings.**
	16:20	**Greet** one another with a holy
2C	13:12	**Greet** one another with a holy
	13:12	All the saints **greet** you.
Ph	4:21	**Greet** every saint in Christ
	4:21	friends who are with me **greet**
	4:22	All the saints **greet** you,
Co	4:10	**greets** you, as does Mark the
	4:12	servant of Christ Jesus, **greets**
	4:14	physician, and Demas **greet** you.
	4:15	Give my **greetings** to the
1Th	5:26	**Greet** all the brothers and
2Ti	4:19	**Greet** Prisca and Aquila, and
	4:21	Eubulus sends **greetings** to you,
Ti	3:15	who are with me send **greetings**
	3:15	**Greet** those who love us in the
Pm	1:23	Jesus, sends **greetings** to you,
He	11:13	they saw and **greeted** them. They
	13:24	**Greet** all your leaders and all
	13:24	from Italy send you **greetings.**
1P	5:13	sends you **greetings;** and so
	5:14	**Greet** one another with a kiss
2J	1:13	sister send you their **greetings**
3J	1:15	send you their **greetings.**
	1:15	**Greet** the friends there, each

783 ^{GO}10 ^{AG}117 ^{LN}37 ^B1:206 ^K1:496 ^R782
ασπασμος, GREETING

Mt	23: 7	and to be **greeted** with respect
Mk	12:38	**greeted** with respect in the
Lk	1:29	pondered what sort of **greeting**
	1:41	Elizabeth heard Mary's **greeting**
	1:44	the sound of your **greeting,** the
	11:43	be **greeted** with respect in the
	20:46	love to be **greeted** with respect
1C	16:21	I, Paul, write this **greeting**

Co	4:18	I, Paul, write this **greeting**
2Th	3:17	I, Paul, write this **greeting**

784 ^{GO}4 ^{AG}117 ^{LN}37 ^B3:923 ^K1:502 ^R4695
ασπιλος, WITHOUT STAIN

1Ti	6:14	the commandment **without spot** or
Ja	1:27	keep oneself **unstained** by the
1P	1:19	lamb **without defect** or blemish.
2P	3:14	**without spot** or blemish;

785 ^{GO}1 ^{AG}117 ^{LN}37
ασπις, SNAKE

Ro	3:13	The venom of **vipers** is under

786 ^{GO}1 ^{AG}117 ^{LN}37
ασπονδος, IRRECONCILABLE

2Ti	3: 3	inhuman, **implacable,**

787 ^{GO}2 ^{AG}117 ^{LN}37
ασσαριον, ASSARION

Mt	10:29	sparrows sold for a **penny?** Yet
Lk	12: 6	sparrows sold for two **pennies?**

788 ^{GO}1 ^{AG}117 ^{LN}37
ασσον, CLOSE

Ac	27:13	past Crete, **close** to the shore.

789 ^{GO}2 ^{AG}117 ^{LN}37
ασσος, ASSOS

Ac	20:13	ship and set sail for **Assos,**
	20:14	When he met us in **Assos,** we

790 ^{GO}1 ^{AG}117 ^{LN}37 ^K1:503
αστατεω, I DO NOT STAND

1C	4:11	clothed and beaten and **homeless**

791 ^{GO}2 ^{AG}117 ^{LN}37
αστειος, WELL FORMED

Ac	7:20	he was **beautiful** before God.
He	11:23	that the child was **beautiful;**

792 ^{GO}24 ^{AG}117 ^{LN}37 ^B3:734 ^K1:503
αστηρ, STAR

Mt	2: 2	observed his **star** at its rising
	2: 7	time when the **star** had appeared
	2: 9	went the **star** that they had
	2:10	When they saw that the **star** had
	24:29	the **stars** will fall from heaven
Mk	13:25	and the **stars** will be falling
1C	15:41	and another glory of the **stars;**

	15:41	indeed, **star** differs from star
	15:41	star differs from **star** in glory
Ju	1:13	wandering **stars,** for whom the
Re	1:16	right hand he held seven **stars,**
	1:20	mystery of the seven **stars**
	1:20	the seven **stars** are the angels
	2: 1	who holds the seven **stars** in
	2:28	also give the morning **star.**
	3: 1	of God and the seven **stars:**
	6:13	and the **stars** of the sky fell
	8:10	and a great **star** fell from
	8:11	The name of the **star** is
	8:12	a third of the **stars,** so
	9: 1	and I saw a **star** that had
	12: 1	head a crown of twelve **stars.**
	12: 4	down a third of the **stars** of
	22:16	David, the bright morning **star.**

793   G0 2   AG 118   LN 37   K 7:653
αστηρικτος, UNSTABLE

2P	2:14	adultery, **insatiable** for sin.
	3:16	which the ignorant and **unstable**

794   G0 2   AG 118   LN 37   B 2:538
αστοργος, WITHOUT FAMILY AFFECTION

Ro	1:31	foolish, faithless, **heartless,**
2Ti	3: 3	**inhuman,** implacable, slanderers

795   G0 3   AG 118   LN 37
αστοχεω, I MISS MARK

1Ti	1: 6	Some people have **deviated** from
	6:21	it some have **missed the mark** as
2Ti	2:18	who have **swerved** from the truth

796   G0 9   AG 118   LN 37   B 3:1000   K 1:505   R 797
αστραπη, LIGHTNING

Mt	24:27	For as the **lightning** comes from
	28: 3	appearance was like **lightning,**
Lk	10:18	like a flash of **lightning.**
	11:36	gives you light with its **rays.**
	17:24	For as the **lightning** flashes
Re	4: 5	throne are flashes of **lightning**
	8: 5	flashes of **lightning,** and an
	11:19	**lightning,** rumblings, peals of
	16:18	there came flashes of **lightning**

797   G0 2   AG 118   LN 37
αστραπτω, I FLASH

Lk	17:24	For as the lightning **flashes**
	24: 4	suddenly two men in **dazzling**

798   G0 4   AG 118   LN 37   B 3:734   K 1:503   R 792
αστρον, STAR

Lk	21:25	sun, the moon, and the **stars,**
Ac	7:43	**star** of your god Rephan, the
	27:20	When neither sun nor **stars**
He	11:12	as many as the **stars** of

799   G0 1   AG 118   LN 37
ασυγκριτος, ASYNCRITUS

Ro	16:14	Greet **Asyncritus,** Phlegon,

800   G0 1   AG 118   LN 37   R 1859
ασυμφωνος, DISAGREEMENT

Ac	28:25	So they **disagreed** with each

801   G0 5   AG 118   LN 37   B 3:131   K 7:888   R 4908
ασυνετος, NOT UNDERSTANDING

Mt	15:16	still **without understanding?**
Mk	7:18	also **fail** to **understand?** Do you
Ro	1:21	and their **senseless minds** were
	1:31	**foolish,** faithless, heartless,
	10:19	with a **foolish** nation I will

802   G0 1   AG 118   LN 37
ασυνθετος, DISLOYAL

Ro	1:31	foolish, **faithless,** heartless,

803   G0 3   AG 118   LN 37   B 1:663   K 1:506   R 804
ασφαλεια, SECURITY

Lk	1: 4	you may know the **truth**
Ac	5:23	We found the prison **securely**
1Th	5: 3	There is peace and **security,**

804   G0 5   AG 119   LN 37   B 1:663   K 1:506
ασφαλης, SECURE

Ac	21:34	could not learn the **facts**
	22:30	Since he wanted to **find out**
	25:26	I may have **something** to write
Ph	3: 1	for you it is a **safeguard.**
He	6:19	We have this hope, a **sure** and

805   G0 4   AG 119   LN 38   B 1:663   K 1:506   R 804
ασφαλιζω, I SECURE

Mt	27:64	tomb to be **made secure** until
	27:65	go, **make** it as **secure** as you
	27:66	**made** the tomb **secure** by sealing
Ac	16:24	**fastened** their feet in the

806   G0 3   AG 119   LN 38   B 1:663   K 1:506   R 804
ασφαλως, SECURELY

Mk 14:44   lead him away **under guard.**
Ac   2:36   of Israel know with **certainty**
     16:23   jailer to keep them **securely.**

---

807 GO2 AG119 LN38 R809
ασχημονεω, I AM SHAMEFUL
1C   7:36   not **behaving properly** toward
     13: 5   or **rude.** It does not insist on

---

808 GO2 AG119 LN38 R809
ασχημοσυνη, SHAMELESSNESS, SHAME
Ro   1:27   Men committed **shameless** acts
Re 16:15   naked and exposed to **shame."**

---

809 GO1 AG119 LN38
ασχημων, SHAMEFUL
1C 12:23   that we think **less honorable** we

---

810 GO3 AG119 LN38 K1:506
ασωτια, DISSIPATION
Ep   5:18   wine, for that is **debauchery;**
Ti   1: 6   not accused of **debauchery** and
1P   4: 4   excesses of **dissipation,** and so

---

811 GO1 AG119 LN38 K1:506
ασωτως, EXTRAVAGANTLY
Lk 15:13   his property in **dissolute**

---

812 GO1 AG119 LN38 K8:47 R813
αταχτεω, I AM IDLE
2Th 3: 7   we were not **idle** when we were

---

813 GO1 AG119 LN38 K8:47 R5021
αταχτος, IDLE
1Th 5:14   admonish the **idlers,** encourage

---

814 GO2 AG119 LN38 K8:47 R813
αταχτως, IDLY
2Th 3: 6   living in **idleness** and not
     3:11   **idleness,** mere busybodies, not

---

815 GO2 AG119 LN38 R5043
ατεχνος, CHILDLESS
Lk 20:28   leaving a wife but **no children,**
    20:29   married, and died **childless;**

---

816 GO14 AG119 LN38 B3:520
ατενιζω, I STARE
Lk   4:20   all in the synagogue were **fixed**
    22:56   **stared** at him and said, "This

Ac   1:10   they were **gazing** up toward
     3: 4   Peter **looked intently** at him,
     3:12   why do you **stare** at us, as
     6:15   **looked intently** at him, and
     7:55   **gazed** into heaven and saw
    10: 4   He **stared** at him in terror and
    11: 6   As I **looked** at it **closely** I saw
    13: 9   Holy Spirit, **looked intently** at
    14: 9   **looking** at him **intently** and
    23: 1   While Paul was **looking intently**
2C   3: 7   could not **gaze** at Moses' face
     3:13   people of Israel from **gazing** at

---

817 GO2 AG120 LN38
ατερ, WITHOUT
Lk 22: 6   them when **no** crowd was present.
    22:35   When I sent you out **without** a

---

818 GO7 AG120 LN38 B2:48 R820
ατιμαζω, I DISHONOR
Mk 12: 4   beat over the head and **insulted**
Lk 20:11   beat and **insulted** and sent away
Jn   8:49   my Father, and you **dishonor** me.
Ac   5:41   **dishonor** for the sake of the
Ro   1:24   to the **degrading** of their
     2:23   do you **dishonor** God by breaking
Ja   2: 6   But you have **dishonored** the

---

819 GO7 AG120 LN38 B2:48 R820
ατιμια, DISHONOR
Ro   1:26   God gave them up to **degrading**
     9:21   and another for **ordinary** use?
1C 11:14   hair, it is **degrading** to him,
    15:43   It is sown in **dishonor,** it is
2C   6: 8   in honor and **dishonor,** in ill
    11:21   To my **shame,** I must say, we
2Ti 2:20   special use, some for **ordinary.**

---

820 GO4 AG120 LN38 B2:48 R5092
ατιμος, DISHONORED
Mt 13:57   Prophets are not **without honor**
Mk   6: 4   **without honor,** except in their
1C   4:10   honor, but we in **disrepute.**
    12:23   **less honorable** we clothe with

---

822 GO2 AG120 LN38
ατμις, VAPOR
Ac   2:19   blood, and fire, and smoky **mist**
Ja   4:14   For you are a **mist** that appears

823 GO1 AG120 LN38
ατομος, INSTANT
1C   15:52   in a **moment,** in the twinkling

---

824 GO4 AG120 LN38 R5117
ατοπος, OUT OF PLACE
Lk   23:41   have been condemned **justly,** for
Ac   25: 5   if there is anything **wrong**
       28: 6   nothing **unusual** had happened to
2Th   3: 2   we may be rescued from **wicked**

---

825 GO1 AG120 LN38
ατταλεια, ATTALIA
Ac   14:25   they went down to **Attalia.**

---

826 GO1 AG120 LN38 B2:289 K1:507
αυγαζω, TO DAWN
2C   4: 4   keep them from **seeing** the light

---

827 GO1 AG120 LN38 B1:711, 2:289
αυγη, DAYBREAK
Ac   20:11   until **dawn;** then he left.

---

828 GO1 AG120 LN38
αυγουστος, AUGUSTUS
Lk   2: 1   went out from Emperor **Augustus**

---

829 GO2 AG120 LN38 K1:508
αυθαδης, SELF-WILLED
Ti   1: 7   he must not be **arrogant** or
2P   2:10   Bold and **willful,** they are not

---

830 GO2 AG121 LN38
αυθαιρετος, BY SELF CHOICE
2C   8: 3   they **voluntarily** gave according
       8:17   to you of his **own accord.**

---

831 GO1 AG121 LN38
αυθεντεω, I DOMINATE
1Ti   2:12   **have authority** over a man; she

---

832 GO3 AG121 LN38 B2:436 R836
αυλεω, I PLAY FLUTE
Mt   11:17   We **played** the **flute** for you,
Lk   7:32   We **played** the **flute** for you,
1C   14: 7   such as the **flute** or the harp.

---

833 GO12 AG38 B3:565
αυλη, COURTYARD
Mt   26: 3   gathered in the **palace** of the

       26:58   as far as the **courtyard** of the
       26:69   outside in the **courtyard.** A
Mk   14:54   right into the **courtyard** of the
       14:66   below in the **courtyard,** one of
       15:16   led him into the **courtyard** of
Lk   11:21   guards his **castle,** his property
       22:55   **courtyard** and sat down
                   together
Jn   10: 1   enter the **sheepfold** by the gate
       10:16   do not belong to this **fold.** I
       18:15   with Jesus into the **courtyard**
Re   11: 2   but do not measure the **court**

---

834 GO2 AG121 LN38 R832
αυλητης, FLUTIST
Mt   9:23   **flute players** and the crowd
Re   18:22   **flutists** and trumpeters will be

---

835 GO2 AG121 LN38
αυλιζομαι, I LODGE
Mt   21:17   Bethany, and **spent the night**
Lk   21:37   go out and **spend the night** on

---

836 GO1 AG121 LN38
αυλος, FLUTE
1C   14: 7   such as the **flute** or the harp.

---

837 GO23 AG121 LN39 B2:128 K8:517
αυξανω, I GROW
Mt   6:28   **grow;** they neither toil nor
       13:32   but when it has **grown** it is
Mk   4: 8   **growing** up and increasing and
Lk   1:80   The child **grew** and became
       2:40   The child **grew** and became
       12:27   the lilies, how they **grow:** they
       13:19   it **grew** and became a tree, and
Jn   3:30   He must **increase,** but I must
Ac   6: 7   of God **continued** to spread;
       7:17   our people in Egypt **increased**
       12:24   **continued** to **advance** and gain
       19:20   So the word of the Lord **grew**
1C   3: 6   but God gave the **growth.**
       3: 7   only God who gives the **growth.**
2C   9:10   **increase** the harvest of your
       10:15   as your faith **increases,** our
Ep   2:21   joined together and **grows** into
       4:15   we must **grow** up in every way
Co   1: 6   bearing fruit and **growing** in
       1:10   work and as you **grow** in the
       2:19   **grows** with a growth that is

1P 2: 2 so that by it you may **grow**
2P 3:18 But **grow** in the grace

---

838 GO2 AG122 LN39 B2:128 R837
αυξησις, GROWTH
Ep 4:16 promotes the body's **growth** in
Co 2:19 grows with a **growth** that is

---

839 GO14 AG122 LN39
αυριον, TOMORROW
Mt 6:30 alive today and **tomorrow** is
6:34 So do not worry about
tomorrow
6:34 for **tomorrow** will bring worries
Lk 10:35 The **next day** he took out two
12:28 and **tomorrow** is thrown into
the
13:32 **tomorrow,** and on the third day
13:33 Yet today, **tomorrow,** and the
Ac 4: 3 in custody until the **next day,**
4: 5 The **next day** their rulers,
23:20 **tomorrow,** as though they were
25:22 "**Tomorrow,**" he said, "you will
1C 15:32 drink, for **tomorrow** we die.
Ja 4:13 Today or **tomorrow** we will go
4:14 know what **tomorrow** will
bring.

---

840 GO2 AG122 LN39
αυστηρος, SEVERE, AUSTERE
Lk 19:21 because you are a **harsh** man;
19:22 that I was a **harsh** man, taking

---

841 GO2 AG122 LN39 B3:727 K1:466 R842
αυταρκεια, SELF- SUFFICIENT
2C 9: 8 **having enough** of everything,
1Ti 6: 6 combined with **contentment;**

---

842 GO1 AG122 LN39 B3:727 K1:466 R846,714
αυταρκης, SELF-SUFFICIENT
Ph 4:11 I have learned to be **content**

---

843 GO1 AG122 LN39 B2:365 K3:952 R846,2632
αυτοκατακριτος, SELF-CONDEMNED
Ti 3:11 sinful, being **self-condemned.**

---

844 GO2 AG122 LN39
αυτοματος, BY ITSELF
Mk 4:28 The earth produces of **itself,**
Ac 12:10 of its **own accord,** and they

---

845 GO1 AG122 LN39 K5:373 R846,3700
αυτοπτης, EYE WITNESS
Lk 1: 2 beginning were **eyewitnesses**

---

846 GO5601 AG122 LN39
αυτος, SELF [MULTIPLE OCCURRENCES]

---

847 GO4 AG124 LN39
αυτου, HERE, THERE
Mt 26:36 Sit **here** while I go over
Lk 9:27 there are some standing **here**
Ac 18:19 he left them **there,** but first
21: 4 and stayed **there** for seven days

848a GO1 AG124 LN39
αυτοφωρος, SELF ACT
Jn 8: 4 in the **very act** of committing

---

849 GO1 AG124 LN39 R846,5495
αυτοχειρ, OWN HAND
Ac 27:19 **own hands** they threw the ship's

849a GO1 AG124 LN39
αυχεω, I BOAST
Ja 3: 5 yet it **boasts** of great exploits

---

850 GO1 AG124 LN39 B3:153
αυχμηρος, DINGY
2P 1:19 as to a lamp shining in a **dark**

---

851 GO10 AG124 LN39
αφαιρεω, I LIFT OFF
Mt 26:51 priest, **cutting off** his ear.
Mk 14:47 priest, **cutting off** his ear.
Lk 1:25 **took away** the disgrace I have
10:42 will not be **taken away** from her
16: 3 **taking** the position **away** from
22:50 and **cut off** his right ear.
Ro 11:27 when I **take away** their sins.
He 10: 4 bulls and goats to **take away**
Re 22:19 if anyone **takes away** from the
22:19 will **take away** that person's

---

852 GO1 AG124 LN39 R5316
αφανης, DISAPPEARED
He 4:13 no creature is **hidden,** but all

---

853 GO5 AG124 LN39 R852 B2:831
αφανιζω, I CAUSE TO DISAPPEAR
Mt 6:16 for they **disfigure** their faces

6:19	where moth and rust **consume**
6:20	neither moth nor rust **consumes**
Ac 13:41	Be amazed and **perish,** for in
Ja 4:14	little while and then **vanishes.**

854 GO1 AG124 LN39 R853
αφανισμος, DISAPPEARANCE
He 8:13	growing old will soon **disappear**

855 GO1 AG124 LN39 R5316
αφαντος, DISAPPEARED
Lk 24:31	he **vanished** from their sight.

856 GO2 AG124 LN39
αφεδρων, LATRINE
Mt 15:17	goes out into the **sewer?**
Mk 7:19	**sewer?"** (Thus he declared all

857 GO1 AG124 LN40
αφειδια, UNSPARING
Co 2:23	**severe treatment** of the body,

858 GO1 AG124 LN40
αφελοτης, SIMPLICITY
Ac 2:46	with glad and **generous** hearts,

859 GO17 AG125 LN40 B1:697 K1:509 R863
αφεσις, SENDING OFF
Mt 26:28	for many for the **forgiveness** of
Mk 1: 4	for the **forgiveness** of sins.
3:29	can never have **forgiveness,** but
Lk 1:77	his people by the **forgiveness**
3: 3	repentance for the **forgiveness**
4:18	proclaim **release** to the
4:18	**release** to the captives and
24:47	that repentance and **forgiveness**
Ac 2:38	that your sins may be **forgiven;**
5:31	Israel and **forgiveness** of sins.
10:43	receives **forgiveness** of sins
13:38	through this man **forgiveness** of
26:18	they may receive **forgiveness** of
Ep 1: 7	**forgiveness** of our trespasses,
Co 1:14	the **forgiveness** of sins.
He 9:22	there is no **forgiveness** of sins
10:18	Where there is **forgiveness** of

860 GO2 AG125 LN40
αφη, LIGAMENT
Ep 4:16	together by every **ligament**
Co 2:19	**ligaments** and sinews, grows

861 GO7 AG125 LN40 B1:467 K9:93 R862
αφθαρσια, INCORRUPTION
Ro 2: 7	honor and **immortality,** he will
1C 15:42	what is raised is **imperishable.**
15:50	inherit the **imperishable.**
15:53	put on **imperishability,** and
15:54	puts on **imperishability,** and
Ep 6:24	an **undying** love for our Lord
2Ti 1:10	life and **immortality** to light

862 GO8 AG125 LN40 B1:467 K9:93 R5351
αφθαρτος, INCORRUPTIBLE
Mk 16: 8	spiritual and **imperishable**
Ro 1:23	glory of the **immortal** God for
1C 9:25	but we an **imperishable** one.
15:52	will be raised **imperishable,**
1Ti 1:17	**immortal,** invisible, the only
1P 1: 4	that is **imperishable,** undefiled
1:23	perishable but of **imperishable**
3: 4	the inner self with the **lasting**

862a GO1 AG125 LN40 K9:93
αφθορια, INCORRUPTIBLE
Ti 2: 7	your teaching show **integrity,**

863 GO143 AG125 LN40 B1:697 K1:509
αφιημι, I SEND OFF, I FORGIVE
Mt 3:15	Jesus answered him, **"Let it be**
3:15	Then he **consented.**
4:11	Then the devil **left** him, and
4:20	Immediately they **left** their
4:22	Immediately they **left** the boat
5:24	**leave** your gift there before
5:40	coat, **give** your cloak as well;
6:12	And **forgive** us our debts, as we
6:12	also have **forgiven** our debtors.
6:14	For if you **forgive** others their
6:14	Father will also **forgive** you;
6:15	but if you do not **forgive**
6:15	Father **forgive** your trespasses.
7: 4	**Let** me take the speck out of
8:15	the fever **left** her, and she got
8:22	Follow me, and **let** the dead
9: 2	son; your sins are **forgiven.**
9: 5	'Your sins are **forgiven,'** or to
9: 6	authority on earth to **forgive**
12:31	people will be **forgiven** for
12:31	the Spirit will not be **forgiven**
12:32	**forgiven,** but whoever speaks
12:32	**forgiven,** either in this age or

	13:30	**Let** both of them grow together		12:19	**leaving** a wife but no child,
	13:36	Then he **left** the crowds and		12:20	when he died, **left** no children;
	15:14	**Let** them alone; they are blind		12:22	none of the seven **left** children
	18:12	**leave** the ninety-nine on the		13: 2	Not one stone will be **left** here
	18:21	how often should I **forgive?** As		13:34	when he **leaves** home and puts
	18:27	released him and **forgave** him		14: 6	But Jesus said, "**Let** her alone;
	18:32	I **forgave** you all that debt		14:50	All of them **deserted** him and
	18:35	if you do not **forgive** your		15:36	**let** us see whether Elijah will
	19:14	Jesus said, "**Let** the little		15:37	loud cry and breathed his **last.**
	19:27	we **have left** everything and	Lk	4:39	the fever, and it **left** her.
	19:29	everyone who has **left** houses		5:11	they **left** everything and
	22:22	they **left** him and went away.		5:20	your sins are **forgiven** you.
	22:25	**leaving** the widow to his		5:21	Who can **forgive** sins but God
	23:13	are going in, you **stop** them.		5:23	Your sins are **forgiven** you,
	23:23	**neglected** the weightier		5:24	authority on earth to **forgive**
	23:23	without **neglecting** the others.		6:42	Friend, **let** me take out the
	23:38	your house is **left** to you,		7:47	**forgiven;** hence she has shown
	24: 2	not one stone will **be left**		7:47	one to whom little is **forgiven,**
	24:40	taken and one will be **left.**		7:48	her, "Your sins are **forgiven.**"
	24:41	taken and one will be **left.**		7:49	this who even **forgives** sins?
	26:44	So **leaving** them again, he went		8:51	he did not **allow** anyone to
	26:56	all the disciples **deserted** him		9:60	**Let** the dead bury their own
	27:49	**let** us see whether Elijah will		10:30	and went away, **leaving** him half
	27:50	voice and breathed his **last.**		11: 4	And **forgive** us our sins, for we
Mk	1:18	And immediately they **left** their		11: 4	for we ourselves **forgive**
	1:20	they **left** their father Zebedee		12:10	will be **forgiven;** but whoever
	1:31	Then the fever **left** her, and		12:10	Spirit will not be **forgiven.**
	1:34	he would not **permit** the demons		12:39	would not have **let** his house be
	2: 5	Son, your sins are **forgiven.**		13: 8	He replied, 'Sir, **let** it alone
	2: 7	Who can **forgive** sins but God		13:35	See, your house is **left** to you.
	2: 9	'Your sins are **forgiven,**' or to		17: 3	is repentance, you must **forgive**
	2:10	authority on earth to **forgive**		17: 4	'I repent,' you must **forgive.**"
	3:28	people will be **forgiven** for		17:34	be taken and the other **left.**
	4:12	not turn again and be **forgiven.**		17:35	be taken and the other **left.**
	4:36	And **leaving** the crowd behind,		18:16	**Let** the little children come
	5:19	But Jesus **refused,** and said to		18:28	Look, we have **left** our homes
	5:37	He **allowed** no one to follow him		18:29	there is no one who has **left**
	7: 8	You **abandon** the commandment of		19:44	and they will not **leave** within
	7:12	then you no longer **permit** doing		21: 6	not one stone will be **left**
	7:27	He said to her, "**Let** the		23:34	Father, **forgive** them; for
	8:13	And he **left** them, and getting	Jn	4: 3	he **left** Judea and started back
	10:14	**Let** the little children come		4:28	Then the woman **left** her water
	10:28	Look, we have **left** everything		4:52	afternoon the fever **left** him.
	10:29	there is no one who has **left**		8:29	he has not **left** me alone, for I
	11: 6	and they **allowed** them to take		10:12	**leaves** the sheep and runs away
	11:16	and he would not **allow** anyone		11:44	Unbind him, and **let** him go.
	11:25	**forgive,** if you have		11:48	If we **let** him go on like this,
	11:25	heaven may also **forgive** you		12: 7	**keep** it for the day of my
	12:12	So they **left** him and went away.		14:18	I **will** not **leave** you orphaned

	14:27	Peace I **leave** with you; my
	16:28	I am **leaving** the world and am
	16:32	you will **leave** me alone. Yet I
	18: 8	looking for me, **let** these men
	20:23	If you **forgive** the sins of any,
	20:23	they **are forgiven** them; if you
Ac	5:38	away from these men and **let**
	8:22	your heart may be **forgiven** you.
	14:17	yet he has not **left** himself
Ro	1:27	the men, **giving up** natural
	4: 7	iniquities are **forgiven,** and
1C	7:11	husband should not **divorce** his
	7:12	he should not **divorce** her.
	7:13	she should not **divorce** him.
He	2: 8	God **left** nothing outside their
	6: 1	**leaving** behind the basic
Ja	5:15	committed sins will be **forgiven**
1J	1: 9	**forgive** us our sins and cleanse
	2:12	sins are **forgiven** on account of
Re	2: 4	you have **abandoned** the love you
	2:20	you **tolerate** that woman Jezebel
	11: 9	refuse to **let** them be placed in

864 ᴳᴼ1 ᴬᴳ126 ᴸᴺ40
αφικνεομαι, I REACH
Ro 16:19   your obedience is **known** to all,

865 ᴳᴼ1 ᴬᴳ126 ᴸᴺ40 ᴷ1:18 ᴿ5358
αφιλαγαθος, NOT LOVER OF GOOD
2Ti 3: 3   brutes, **haters of good,**

866 ᴳᴼ2 ᴬᴳ126 ᴸᴺ40 ᴿ5366
αφιλαργυρος, NOT LOVER OF SILVER
1Ti 3: 3   and **not** a **lover of money.**
He 13: 5   free from the **love** of **money,**

867 ᴳᴼ1 ᴬᴳ126 ᴸᴺ41
αφιξις, DEPARTURE, I LEAVE
Ac 20:29   I know that after I have **gone,**

868 ᴳᴼ14 ᴬᴳ126 ᴸᴺ41 ᴮ1:606 ᴷ1:512 ᴿ575,2476
αφιστημι, I STAND OFF, I LEAVE

Lk	2:37	She never **left** the temple but
	4:13	he **departed** from him until an
	8:13	in a time of testing **fall away.**
	13:27	**go away** from me, all you
Ac	5:37	Judas the Galilean **rose up** at
	5:38	**keep away** from these men and
	12:10	suddenly the angel **left** him.
	15:38	one who had **deserted** them in

	19: 9	he **left** them, taking the
	22:29	examine him **drew back** from
		him;
2C	12: 8	about this, that it **would leave**
1Ti	4: 1	**renounce** the faith by paying
2Ti	2:19	Lord **turn away** from wickedness.
He	3:12	heart that **turns away** from the

869 ᴳᴼ3 ᴬᴳ127 ᴸᴺ41
αφνω, SUDDENLY
Ac   2: 2   And **suddenly** from heaven there
     16:26   **Suddenly** there was an
     28: 6   him to swell up or **drop** dead,

870 ᴳᴼ4 ᴬᴳ127 ᴸᴺ41 ᴿ5401
αφοβως, FEARLESSLY
Lk   1:74   might serve him **without fear,**
1C 16:10   he has **nothing** to **fear** among
Ph   1:14   boldness and **without fear.**
Ju   1:12   feast with you **without fear,**

871 ᴳᴼ1 ᴬᴳ127 ᴸᴺ41 ᴮ2:500 ᴷ5:198
αφομοιοω, I MAKE LIKE
He   7: 3   but **resembling** the Son of

872 ᴳᴼ2 ᴬᴳ127 ᴸᴺ41
αφοραω, I SEE OFF
Ph   2:23   as soon as I **see** how things go
He 12: 2   **looking to** Jesus the pioneer

873 ᴳᴼ10 ᴬᴳ127 ᴸᴺ41 ᴮ1:472 ᴷ5:454
αφοριζω, I SEPARATE

Mt	13:49	**separate** the evil from the
	25:32	he will **separate** people one
	25:32	as a shepherd **separates** the
Lk	6:22	when they **exclude** you, revile
Ac	13: 2	**Set apart** for me Barnabas and
	19: 9	**taking** the disciples with him,
Ro	1: 1	**set apart** for the gospel of God
2C	6:17	**be separate** from them, says the
Ga	1:15	God, who had **set me apart**
	2:12	kept himself **separate** for fear

874 ᴳᴼ7 ᴬᴳ127 ᴸᴺ41 ᴷ5:472
αφορμη, OPPORTUNITY
Ro   7: 8   But sin, seizing an **opportunity**
     7:11   **opportunity** in the commandment,
2C   5:12   giving you an **opportunity** to
     11:12   deny an **opportunity** to those
     11:12   who want an **opportunity** to be

Ga   5:13   freedom as an **opportunity** for
1Ti 5:14   the adversary no **occasion** to

---

875   GO2 AG127 LN41 R876
αφριζω, I FOAM
Mk   9:18   and he **foams** and grinds his
       9:20   about, **foaming** at the mouth.

---

876   GO1 AG127 LN41
αφρος, FOAM
Lk   9:39   convulses him until he **foams** at

---

877   GO4 AG127 LN41 B3:1023 K9:220 R878
αφροσυνη, THOUGHTLESSNESS
Mk   7:22   envy, slander, pride, **folly.**
2C 11: 1   **foolishness.** Do bear with me!
    11:17   Lord's authority, but as a **fool**
    11:21   I am speaking as a **fool**

---

878   GO11 AG127 LN41 B3:1023 K9:220 R5424
αφρων, UNTHINKING
Lk 11:40   You **fools!** Did not the one
             who
    12:20   But God said to him, 'You
             fool!
Ro   2:20   a corrector of the **foolish,** a
1C 15:36   **Fool!** What you sow does not
2C 11:16   think that I am a **fool;** but if
    11:16   then accept me as a **fool,** so
    11:19   gladly put up with **fools,**
    12: 6   I will not be a **fool,** for I
    12:11   I have been a **fool!** You forced
Ep   5:17   So do not be **foolish,** but
1P   2:15   the ignorance of the **foolish.**

---

879   GO1 AG127 LN41 K8:545 R575,5258
αφυπνοω, I FALL ASLEEP
Lk   8:23   were sailing he **fell asleep.** A

---

880   GO4 AG128 LN41 R5456
αφωνος, SOUNDLESS
Ac   8:32   and like a lamb **silent** before
1C 12: 2   astray to idols that **could not**
    14:10   and nothing is **without sound.**
2P   2:16   a **speechless** donkey spoke with

---

881   GO2 AG128 LN41
αχαζ, AHAZ
Mt   1: 9   Jotham the father of **Ahaz,** and
     1: 9   and **Ahaz** the father of Hezekiah

---

882   GO10 AG128 LN41
αχαια, ACHAIA
Ac 18:12   Gallio was proconsul of **Achaia,**
    18:27   cross over to **Achaia,** the
    19:21   through Macedonia and **Achaia,**
Ro 15:26   for Macedonia and **Achaia** have
1C 16:15   the first converts in **Achaia,**
2C   1: 1   the saints throughout **Achaia:**
     9: 2   saying that **Achaia** has been
    11:10   in the regions of **Achaia.**
1Th 1: 7   in Macedonia and in **Achaia.**
     1: 8   only in Macedonia and **Achaia,**

---

883   GO1 AG128 LN41
αχαικος, ACHAICUS
1C 16:17   and Fortunatus and **Achaicus,**

---

884   GO2 AG128 LN41 K9:372 R5483
αχαριστος, UNFAVORABLE
Lk   6:35   he is kind to the **ungrateful**
2Ti 3: 2   their parents, **ungrateful,**

---

885   GO2 AG128 LN41
αχιμ, ACHIM
Mt   1:14   Zadok the father of **Achim,** and
     1:14   **Achim** the father of Eliud,

---

886   GO3 AG128 LN41 K9:436 R5499
αχειροποιητος, UNHANDMADE
Mk 14:58   another, **not made with hands.**
2C   5: 1   a house **not made with hands,**
Co   2:11   circumcised with a **spiritual**

---

887   GO1 AG128 LN41
αχλυς, MISTINESS
Ac 13:11   Immediately **mist** and darkness

---

888   GO2 AG128 LN42 R5534
αχρειος, UNNEEDED
Mt 25:30   As for this **worthless** slave,
Lk 17:10   We are **worthless** slaves; we

---

889   GO1 AG128 LN42 R888
αχρειοω, I AM UNUSEFUL
Ro   3:12   they have **become worthless;**

---

890   GO1 AG128 LN42 R5543
αχρηστος, UNUSEFUL
Pm   1:11   Formerly he was **useless** to you,

891   GO49   AG128   LN42
αχρι, UNTIL

Mt	24:38	**until** the day Noah entered the
Mk	16: 8	from east **to** west, the sacred
Lk	1:20	**until** the day these things
	4:13	departed from him **until** an
	17:27	**until** the day Noah entered the
	21:24	**until** the times of the Gentiles
Ac	1: 2	**until** the day when he was taken
	2:29	his tomb is with us **to** this day
	3:21	who must remain in heaven **until**
	7:18	**until** another king who had not
	11: 5	corners; and it came **close** to
	13: 6	**as far as** Paphos, they met a
	13:11	you will be blind **for a while,**
	20: 6	**in** five days we joined them in
	20:11	converse with them **until** dawn;
	22: 4	**up to the point** of death by
	22:22	**Up to this point** they listened
	23: 1	Brothers, **up to** this day I
	26:22	**To this** day I have had help
	27:33	**Just before** daybreak, Paul
	28:15	came **as far as** the Forum of
Ro	1:13	but **thus far** have been
	5:13	**before** the law, but sin is not
	8:22	groaning in labor pains **until**
	11:25	**until** the full number of the
1C	4:11	**To** the present hour we are
	11:26	the Lord's death **until** he comes
	15:25	For he must reign **until** he has
2C	3:14	Indeed, **to this very** day, when
	10:13	to reach out even **as far as** you
	10:14	**all the way** to you with the
Ga	3:19	**until** the offspring would come
	4: 2	**until** the date set by the
Ph	1: 5	from the first day **until** now.
	1: 6	bring it to completion **by the**
He	3:13	**as long as** it is called "today,
	4:12	piercing **until** it divides soul
	6:11	assurance of hope **to the very**
Re	2:10	Be faithful **until** death, and I
	2:25	to what you have **until** I come.
	2:26	to do my works **to the** end,
	7: 3	**until** we have marked the
	12:11	life **even in the face** of death.
	14:20	**as high as** a horse's bridle,
	15: 8	**until** the seven plagues of the
	17:17	**until** the words of God will be
	18: 5	for her sins are heaped **high as**
	20: 3	**until** the thousand years were
	20: 5	dead did not come to life **until**

---

892   GO2   AG129   LN42
αχυρον, CHAFF

Mt	3:12	but the **chaff** he will burn with
Lk	3:17	but the **chaff** he will burn with

---

893   GO1   AG129   LN42   B2:470   K9:594   R5579
αψευδης, UNLYING

Ti	1: 2	**who never lies,** promised before

---

894   GO2   AG129   LN42   B2:27
αψινθος, WORMWOOD

Re	8:11	name of the star is **Wormwood.** A
	8:11	waters became **wormwood,** and

---

895   GO1   AG129   LN42   R5590
αψυχος, UNSOULED

1C	14: 7	is the same way with **lifeless**

β

896   GO1   AG129   LN42
βααλ, BAAL

Ro	11: 4	have not bowed the knee to **Baal**

---

897   GO12   AG129   LN42   B1:140   K1:514
βαβυλων, BABYLON

Mt	1:11	of the deportation to **Babylon.**
	1:12	the deportation to **Babylon:**
	1:17	**Babylon,** fourteen generations;
	1:17	**Babylon** to the Messiah,
Ac	7:43	will remove you beyond **Babylon.**
1P	5:13	Your sister church in **Babylon,**
Re	14: 8	Fallen, fallen is **Babylon** the
	16:19	God remembered great **Babylon**
	17: 5	**Babylon** the great, mother of
	18: 2	Fallen, fallen is **Babylon** the
	18:10	the great city, **Babylon,** the
	18:21	With such violence **Babylon** the

---

898   GO1   AG130   LN42
βαθμος, STEP

1Ti	3:13	deacons gain a good **standing**

---

899   GO8   AG130   LN42   B2:197   K1:517
βαθος, DEPTH

Mt	13: 5	since they had no **depth** of soil

Mk	4: 5	since it had no **depth** of soil.
Lk	5: 4	Put out into the **deep** water
Ro	8:39	nor height, nor **depth,** nor
	11:33	O the **depth** of the riches and
1C	2:10	even the **depths** of God.
2C	8: 2	abundant joy and their **extreme**
Ep	3:18	length and height and **depth,**

900　GO1 AG130 LN42 R899
βαθυνω, I DEEPEN
Lk　6:48　who dug **deeply** and laid the

901　GO4 AG130 LN42 B2:197 R900
βαθυς, DEEP

Lk	24: 1	of the week, at **early** dawn
Jn	4:11	no bucket, and the well is **deep**
Ac	20: 9	to sink off into a **deep** sleep
Re	2:24	the **deep** things of Satan

902　GO1 AG130 LN42
βαιον, BRANCH
Jn　12:13　took **branches** of palm trees

903　GO3 AG130 LN42 K1:524
βαλααμ, BALAAM

2P	2:15	the road of **Balaam** son of Bosor
Ju	1:11	abandon themselves to **Balaam's**
Re	2:14	to the teaching of **Balaam**

904　GO1 AG130 LN42
βαλακ, BALAK
Re　2:14　taught **Balak** to put a stumbling

905　GO4 AG130 LN42 B1:142 K1:525
βαλλαντιον, PURSE

Lk	10: 4	Carry no **purse**
	12:33	Make **purses** for yourselves
	22:35	I sent you out without a **purse**
	22:36	one who has a **purse** must take

906　GO122 AG130 LN42 K1:526
βαλλω, I THROW

Mt	3:10	down and **thrown** into the fire
	4: 6	**throw** yourself down; for it is
	4:18	**casting** a net into the sea
	5:13	but is **thrown** out and trampled
	5:25	you will be **thrown** into prison
	5:29	tear it out and **throw** it away;
	5:29	your whole body to be **thrown**
	5:30	cut it off and **throw** it away
	6:30	is **thrown** into the oven
	7: 6	**throw** your pearls before swine
	7:19	down and **thrown** into the fire
	8: 6	my servant is **lying** at home
	8:14	his mother-in-law **lying** in bed
	9: 2	a paralyzed man **lying** on a bed
	9:17	new wine **put** into old wineskins
	9:17	but new wine is **put** into fresh
	10:34	that I have come to **bring** peace
	10:34	I have not come to **bring** peace
	13:42	they will **throw** them into the
	13:47	that was **thrown** into the sea
	13:48	but **threw** out the bad
	13:50	and **throw** them into the furnace
	15:26	food and **throw** it to the dogs
	17:27	go to the sea and **cast** a hook
	18: 8	cut it off and **throw** it away
	18: 8	**thrown** into the eternal fire
	18: 9	tear it out and **throw** it away
	18: 9	to be **thrown** into the hell
	18:30	**threw** him into prison until
	21:21	up and **thrown** into the sea
	25:27	Then you ought to have **invested**
	26:12	By **pouring** this ointment on my
	27: 6	to **put** them into the treasury
	27:35	themselves by **casting** lots
Mk	2:22	no one **puts** new wine into old
	4:26	someone would **scatter** seed
	7:30	the child **lying** on the bed
	7:33	**put** his fingers into his ears
	9:22	often **cast** him into the fire
	9:42	you were **thrown** into the sea
	9:45	and to be **thrown** into hell
	9:47	and to be **thrown** into hell
	11:23	up and **thrown** into the sea
	12:41	**putting** money into the treasury
	12:41	rich people **put in** large sums
	12:42	**put in** two small copper coins
	12:43	this poor widow has **put in** more
	12:43	**contributing** to the treasury
	12:44	all of them have **contributed**
	12:44	has **put in** everything she had
	15:24	**casting** lots to decide what
Lk	3: 9	down and **thrown** into the fire
	4: 9	**throw** yourself down from here
	5:37	no one **puts** new wine into old

	12:28	is **thrown** into the oven
	12:49	came to **bring** fire to the earth
	12:58	the officer **throw** you in prison
	13: 8	around it and **put** manure on it
	13:19	took and **sowed** in the garden
	14:35	they **throw** it away
	16:20	And at his gate **lay** a poor man
	21: 1	rich people **putting** their gifts
	21: 2	widow **put** in two small copper
	21: 3	**put** in more than all of them
	21: 4	all of them have **contributed**
	21: 4	**put** in all she had to live on
	23:19	who had been **put** in prison
	23:25	who had been **put** in prison
	23:34	And they **cast** lots to divide
Jn	3:24	not yet been **thrown** into prison
	5: 7	no one to **put** me into the pool
	8: 7	first to **throw** a stone at her
	8:59	stones to **throw** at him
	12: 6	used to steal what was **put**
	13: 2	The devil had already **put** it
	13: 5	he **poured** water into a basin
	15: 6	abide in me is **thrown** away
	15: 6	**thrown** into the fire
	18:11	**Put** your sword back into its
	19:24	for my clothing they **cast** lots
	20:25	**put** my finger in the mark
	20:25	and **my hand in his side**
	20:27	**Put** your finger here and see
	21: 6	**Cast** the net to the right side
	21: 6	So they **cast** it, and now they
	21: 7	naked, and **jumped** into the sea
Ac	16:23	they **threw** them into prison
	16:24	he **put** them in the innermost
	16:37	have **thrown** us into prison
	22:23	and **tossing** dust into the air
	27:14	**rushed** down from Crete
Ja	3: 3	If we **put** bits into the mouths
1J	4:18	but perfect love **casts** out fear
Re	2:10	the devil is about to **throw**
	2:14	to **put** a stumbling block before
	2:22	I am **throwing** her on a bed
	2:24	I do not **lay** on you any other
	4:10	they **cast** their crowns before
	6:13	fig tree **drops** its winter fruit
	8: 5	and **threw** it on the earth
	8: 7	they were **hurled** to the earth
	8: 8	was **thrown** into the sea
	12: 4	and **threw** them to the earth

	12: 9	great dragon was **thrown down**
	12: 9	he was **thrown down** to the earth
	12: 9	were **thrown down** with him
	12:10	comrades has been **thrown down**
	12:13	been **thrown down** to the earth
	12:15	**poured** water like a river
	12:16	dragon had **poured** from his
	14:16	**swung** his sickle over the earth
	14:19	**swung** his sickle over the earth
	14:19	he **threw** it into the great wine
	18:19	they **threw** dust on their heads
	18:21	and **threw** it into the sea
	18:21	great city will be **thrown down**
	19:20	These two were **thrown** alive
	20: 3	and **threw** him into the pit
	20:10	was **thrown** into the lake
	20:14	Death and Hades were **thrown**
	20:15	was **thrown** into the lake

---

907 GO77 AG131 LN43 B1:143 K1:529
βαπτιζω, I IMMERSE

Mt	3: 6	**baptized** by him in the river
	3:11	I **baptize** you with water for
	3:11	He will **baptize** you with the
	3:14	I need to be **baptized** by you
	3:16	when Jesus had been **baptized**
	28:19	**baptizing** them in the name
Mk	1: 4	John the **baptizer** appeared
	1: 5	and were **baptized** by him
	1: 8	I have **baptized** you with water
	1: 8	but he will **baptize** you with
	1: 9	and was **baptized** by John
	6:14	the **baptizer** has been raised
	6:24	The head of John the **baptizer**
	7: 4	the market unless they **wash** it
	10:38	or be **baptized** with the baptism
	10:38	baptism that I am **baptized** with
	10:39	with which I am **baptized**
	10:39	baptized, you will be **baptized**
	16:16	who believes and is **baptized**
Lk	3: 7	came out to be **baptized** by him
	3:12	collectors came to be **baptized**
	3:16	I **baptize** you with water
	3:16	He will **baptize** you with the
	3:21	all the people were **baptized**
	3:21	Jesus also had been **baptized**
	7:29	had been **baptized** with John's
	7:30	refusing to be **baptized** by him
	11:38	that he did not first **wash**

	12:50	with which to be **baptized**
Jn	1:25	Why then are you **baptizing**
	1:26	I **baptize** with water
	1:28	where John was **baptizing**
	1:31	but I came **baptizing** with water
	1:33	to **baptize** with water said
	1:33	who **baptizes** with the Holy
	3:22	there with them and **baptized**
	3:23	also was **baptizing** at Aenon
	3:23	and were being **baptized**
	3:26	here he is **baptizing**
	4: 1	Jesus is making and **baptizing**
	4: 2	but his disciples who **baptized**
	10:40	where John had been **baptizing**
Ac	1: 5	for John **baptized** with water
	1: 5	but you will be **baptized** with
	2:38	be **baptized** every one of you
	2:41	his message were **baptized**
	8:12	Christ, they were **baptized**
	8:13	After being **baptized,** he stayed
	8:16	they had only been **baptized**
	8:36	prevent me from being **baptized**
	8:38	and Philip **baptized** him
	9:18	he got up and was **baptized**
	10:47	for **baptizing** these people
	10:48	ordered them to be **baptized**
	11:16	John **baptized** with water
	11:16	but you will be **baptized**
	16:15	her household were **baptized**
	16:33	his entire family were **baptized**
	18: 8	believers and were **baptized**
	19: 3	what then were you **baptized**
	19: 4	Paul said, "John **baptized** with
	19: 5	they were **baptized** in the name
	22:16	Get up, be **baptized,** and have
Ro	6: 3	who have been **baptized**
	6: 3	were **baptized** into his death
1C	1:13	were you **baptized** in the name
	1:14	that I **baptized** none of you
	1:15	you were **baptized** in my name
	1:16	I did **baptize** also the
	1:16	whether I **baptized** anyone else
	1:17	did not send me to **baptize**
	10: 2	all were **baptized** into Moses
	12:13	we were all **baptized** into one
	15:29	who **receive baptism** on behalf
	15:29	people **baptized** on their behalf
Ga	3:27	As many of you as were **baptized**

908 ᴳᴼ19 ᴬᴳ132 ᴸᴺ43 ᴮ1:144 ᴷ1:545 ᴿ907
βαπτισμα, IMMERSION

Mt	3: 7	Sadducees coming for **baptism**
	21:25	Did the **baptism** of John come
Mk	1: 4	**baptism** of repentance for the
	10:38	baptized with the **baptism**
	10:39	with the **baptism** with which
	11:30	Did the **baptism** of John come
Lk	3: 3	a **baptism** of repentance
	7:29	baptized with John's **baptism**
	12:50	I have a **baptism** with which
	20: 4	Did the **baptism** of John come
Ac	1:22	from the **baptism** of John until
	10:37	after the **baptism** that John
	13:24	a **baptism** of repentance to all
	18:25	knew only the **baptism** of John
	19: 3	Into John's **baptism.**
	19: 4	with the **baptism** of repentance
Ro	6: 4	with him by **baptism** into death
Ep	4: 5	Lord, one faith, one **baptism**
1P	3:21	**baptism,** which this prefigured

909 ᴳᴼ4 ᴬᴳ132 ᴸᴺ43 ᴮ1:144 ᴷ1:545 ᴿ907
βαπτισμος, IMMERSION

Mk	7: 4	the **washing** of cups, pots
Co	2:12	were buried with him in **baptism**
He	6: 2	instruction about **baptisms**
	9:10	and drink and various **baptisms**

910 ᴳᴼ12 ᴬᴳ132 ᴸᴺ43 ᴮ3:1208 ᴷ1:545 ᴿ907
βαπτιστης, IMMERSER

Mt	3: 1	In those days John the **Baptist**
	11:11	greater than John the **Baptist**
	11:12	the days of John the **Baptist**
	14: 2	This is John the **Baptist**
	14: 8	the head of John the **Baptist**
	16:14	Some say John the **Baptist**
	17:13	to them about John the **Baptist**
Mk	6:25	the head of John the **Baptist**
	8:28	John the **Baptist;** and others
Lk	7:20	John the **Baptist** has sent us
	7:33	For John the **Baptist** has come
	9:19	John the **Baptist;** but others

911 ᴳᴼ4 ᴬᴳ132 ᴸᴺ43 ᴮ1:143 ᴷ1:529
βαπτω, I DIP

Lk	16:24	to **dip** the tip of his finger
Jn	13:26	I have **dipped** it in the dish
	13:26	had **dipped** the piece of bread
Re	19:13	in a robe **dipped** in blood

912 GO11 AG133 LN43
βαραββας, BARABBAS

Mt	27:16	prisoner, called Jesus **Barabbas**
	27:17	Jesus **Barabbas** or Jesus who is
	27:20	the crowds to ask for **Barabbas**
	27:21	And they said, "**Barabbas.**"
	27:26	he released **Barabbas** for them
Mk	15: 7	**Barabbas** was in prison with the
	15:11	to have him release **Barabbas**
	15:15	released **Barabbas** for them
Lk	23:18	Release **Barabbas** for us!
Jn	18:40	Not this man, but **Barabbas!**
	18:40	Now **Barabbas** was a bandit

913 GO1 AG133 LN43
βαρακ, BARAK

| He | 11:32 | tell of Gideon, **Barak,** Samson |

914 GO1 AG133 LN43
βαραχιας, BARACHIAH

| Mt | 23:35 | Zechariah son of **Barachiah** |

915 GO6 AG133 LN43 B2:790 K1:546
βαρβαρος, BARBARIAN

Ac	28: 2	The **natives** showed us unusual
	28: 4	the **natives** saw the creature
Ro	1:14	to Greeks and to **barbarians**
1C	14:11	I will be a **foreigner** to the
	14:11	the speaker a **foreigner** to me
Co	3:11	**barbarian,** Scythian, slave

916 GO6 AG133 LN43 B1:260 K1:558 R926
βαρεω, I BURDEN

Mt	26:43	for their eyes **were heavy**
Lk	9:32	**were weighed down** with sleep
	21:34	**weighed down** with dissipation
2C	1: 8	so utterly, unbearably **crushed**
	5: 4	we groan **under our burden**
1Ti	5:16	let the church not **be burdened**

917 GO2 AG133 LN43 B1:261 R926
βαρεως, HEAVILY

| Mt | 13:15 | their ears are **hard** of hearing |
| Ac | 28:27 | their ears are **hard** of hearing |

918 GO4 AG133 LN43
βαρθολομαιος, BARTHOLOMEW

Mt	10: 3	Philip and **Bartholomew**
Mk	3:18	and Philip, and **Bartholomew**
Lk	6:14	and Philip, and **Bartholomew**

| Ac | 1:13 | Thomas, **Bartholomew** and Matthew |

919 GO1 AG133 LN43
βαριησους, BARJESUS

| Ac | 13: 6 | false prophet, named **Bar-Jesus** |

920 GO1 AG133 LN43
βαριωνας, BARJONAH

| Mt | 16:17 | are you, Simon **son of Jonah** |

921 GO28 AG133 LN43
βαρναβας, BARNABAS

Ac	4:36	apostles gave the name **Barnabas**
	9:27	**Barnabas** took him, brought him
	11:22	they sent **Barnabas** to Antioch
	11:30	by **Barnabas** and Saul
	12:25	**Barnabas** and Saul returned to
	13: 1	**Barnabas,** Simeon who was called
	13: 2	Set apart for me **Barnabas**
	13: 7	who summoned **Barnabas** and Saul
	13:43	followed Paul and **Barnabas**
	13:46	Then both Paul and **Barnabas**
	13:50	against Paul and **Barnabas**
	14:12	**Barnabas** they called Zeus
	14:14	the apostles **Barnabas** and Paul
	14:20	he went on with **Barnabas**
	15: 2	And after Paul and **Barnabas**
	15: 2	Paul and **Barnabas** and some
	15:12	listened to **Barnabas** and
	15:22	Antioch with Paul and **Barnabas**
	15:25	our beloved **Barnabas** and Paul
	15:35	But Paul and **Barnabas** remained
	15:36	Paul said to **Barnabas**
	15:37	**Barnabas** wanted to take with
	15:39	**Barnabas** took Mark with him
1C	9: 6	Or is it only **Barnabas** and I
Ga	2: 1	to Jerusalem with **Barnabas**
	2: 9	they gave to **Barnabas** and
	2:13	even **Barnabas** was led astray
Co	4:10	Mark the cousin of **Barnabas**

922 GO6 AG133 LN43 B1:260 K1:553
βαρος, BURDEN

Mt	20:12	borne the **burden** of the day
Ac	15:28	impose on you no further **burden**
2C	4:17	an eternal **weight** of glory
Ga	6: 2	Bear one another's **burdens**
1Th	2: 7	we might have made **demands**
Re	2:24	lay on you any other **burden**

923　GO2　AG134　LN43
βαρσαββας, BARSABBAS
Ac　1:23　Joseph called **Barsabbas**
　　　15:22　sent Judas called **Barsabbas**

924　GO1　AG134　LN43
βαρτιμαιος, BARTIMAEUS
Mk　10:46　**Bartimaeus** son of Timaeus

926　GO6　AG134　LN43　B1:260　K1:556　R922
βαρυς, BURDEN
Mt　23:4　They tie up heavy **burdens**
　　　23:23　**weightier matters** of the law
Ac　20:29　**savage** wolves will come in
　　　25:7　bringing many **serious** charges
2C　10:10　letters are **weighty** and strong
1J　5:3　commandments are not
　　　　　　　burdensome

927　GO1　AG134　LN44　B1:260
βαρυτιμος, HEAVY VALUE
Mt　26:7　jar of **very costly** ointment

928　GO12　AG134　LN44　B3:855　K1:561　R931
βασανιζω, I TORMENT
Mt　8:6　paralyzed, in terrible **distress**
　　　8:29　Have you come here to **torment**
　　　14:24　**battered** by the waves
Mk　5:7　by God, do not **torment** me
　　　6:48　were **straining** at the oars
Lk　8:28　I beg you, do not **torment** me
2P　2:8　**was tormented** in his righteous
Re　9:5　They were allowed to **torture**
　　　11:10　two prophets **had been a torment**
　　　12:2　**in the agony** of giving birth
　　　14:10　**will be tormented** with fire
　　　20:10　**will be tormented** day and night

929　GO6　AG134　LN44　B3:855　K1:561　R928
βασανισμος, TORMENT
Re　9:5　**torture** was like the torture
　　　9:5　torture was like the **torture**
　　　14:11　And the smoke of their **torment**
　　　18:7　a like measure of **torment**
　　　18:10　in fear of her **torment**
　　　18:15　in fear of her **torment**

930　GO1　AG134　LN44　B3:855　K1:561　R928
βασανιστης, TORMENTOR
Mt　18:34　handed him over to **be tortured**

931　GO3　AG134　LN44　B3:855　K1:561
βασανος, TORMENTS
Mt　4:24　with various diseases and **pains**
Lk　16:23　where he was being **tormented**
　　　16:28　come into this place of **torment**

932　GO162　AG134　LN44　B2:372　K1:564　R935
βασιλεια, KINGDOM
Mt　3:2　for the **kingdom** of heaven
　　　4:8　all the **kingdoms** of the world
　　　4:17　for the **kingdom** of heaven
　　　4:23　good news of the **kingdom**
　　　5:3　theirs is the **kingdom** of heaven
　　　5:10　theirs is the **kingdom** of heaven
　　　5:19　called least in the **kingdom**
　　　5:19　called great in the **kingdom**
　　　5:20　will never enter the **kingdom**
　　　6:10　Your **kingdom** come. Your will
　　　6:33　strive first for the **kingdom**
　　　7:21　enter the **kingdom** of heaven
　　　8:11　in the **kingdom** of heaven
　　　8:12　while the heirs of the **kingdom**
　　　9:35　the good news of the **kingdom**
　　　10:7　**kingdom** of heaven has come near
　　　11:11　yet the least in the **kingdom**
　　　11:12　**kingdom** of heaven has suffered
　　　12:25　Every **kingdom** divided against
　　　12:26　how then will his **kingdom** stand
　　　12:28　the **kingdom** of God has come
　　　13:11　know the secrets of the **kingdom**
　　　13:19　the word of the **kingdom**
　　　13:24　The **kingdom** of heaven may be
　　　13:31　The **kingdom** of heaven is like
　　　13:33　The **kingdom** of heaven is like
　　　13:38　are the children of the **kingdom**
　　　13:41　will collect out of his **kingdom**
　　　13:43　in the **kingdom** of their Father
　　　13:44　The **kingdom** of heaven is like
　　　13:45　the **kingdom** of heaven is like
　　　13:47　the **kingdom** of heaven is like
　　　13:52　for the **kingdom** of heaven
　　　16:19　the keys of the **kingdom**
　　　16:28　coming in his **kingdom**
　　　18:1　is the greatest in the **kingdom**
　　　18:3　enter the **kingdom** of heaven
　　　18:4　the greatest in the **kingdom**
　　　18:23　**kingdom** of heaven may be
　　　19:12　sake of the **kingdom** of heaven
　　　19:14　such as these that the **kingdom**

	19:23	person to enter the **kingdom**		11:20	demons, then the **kingdom** of God
	19:24	to enter the **kingdom** of God		12:31	Instead, strive for his **kingdom**
	20: 1	the **kingdom** of heaven is like		12:32	to give you the **kingdom**
	20:21	at your left, in your **kingdom**		13:18	What is the **kingdom** of God like
	21:31	are going into the **kingdom**		13:20	I compare the **kingdom** of God
	21:43	the **kingdom** of God will be		13:28	the prophets in the **kingdom**
	22: 2	The **kingdom** of heaven may be		13:29	will eat in the **kingdom** of God
	23:13	lock people out of the **kingdom**		14:15	will eat bread in the **kingdom**
	24: 7	and **kingdom** against kingdom		16:16	the good news of the **kingdom**
	24: 7	and kingdom against **kingdom**		17:20	the **kingdom** of God was coming
	24:14	this good news of the **kingdom**		17:20	The **kingdom** of God is not
	25: 1	Then the **kingdom** of heaven		17:21	the **kingdom** of God is among
	25:34	inherit the **kingdom** prepared		18:16	the **kingdom** of God belongs
Mk	1:15	**kingdom** of God has come near		18:17	receive the **kingdom** of God
	3:24	If a **kingdom** is divided against		18:24	to enter the **kingdom** of God
	3:24	that **kingdom** cannot stand		18:25	to enter the **kingdom** of God
	4:11	secret of the **kingdom** of God		18:29	sake of the **kingdom** of God
	4:26	The **kingdom** of God is as if		19:11	the **kingdom** of God was to
	4:30	we compare the **kingdom** of God		19:12	to get **royal power** for himself
	6:23	even half of my **kingdom**		19:15	having received **royal power**
	9: 1	see that the **kingdom** of God has		21:10	and **kingdom** against kingdom
	9:47	for you to enter the **kingdom**		21:10	and kingdom against **kingdom**
	10:14	that the **kingdom** of God belongs		21:31	the **kingdom** of God is near
	10:15	does not receive the **kingdom**		22:16	it is fulfilled in the **kingdom**
	10:23	to enter the **kingdom** of God		22:29	conferred on me, a **kingdom**
	10:24	to enter the **kingdom** of God		22:30	at my table in my **kingdom**
	10:25	to enter the **kingdom** of God		23:42	you come into your **kingdom**
	11:10	Blessed is the coming **kingdom**		23:51	expectantly for the **kingdom**
	12:34	far from the **kingdom** of God	Jn	3: 3	no one can see the **kingdom**
	13: 8	nation, and **kingdom** against		3: 5	no one can enter the **kingdom**
	13: 8	kingdom against **kingdom**		18:36	My **kingdom** is not from this
	14:25	I drink it new in the **kingdom**		18:36	If my **kingdom** were from this
	15:43	expectantly for the **kingdom**		18:36	my **kingdom** is not from here
Lk	1:33	and of his **kingdom** there will	Ac	1: 3	and speaking about the **kingdom**
	4: 5	all the **kingdoms** of the world		1: 6	you will restore the **kingdom**
	4:43	the good news of the **kingdom**		8:12	good news about the **kingdom**
	6:20	for yours is the **kingdom** of God		14:22	that we must enter the **kingdom**
	7:28	yet the least in the **kingdom**		19: 8	persuasively about the **kingdom**
	8: 1	good news of the **kingdom** of God		20:25	about proclaiming the **kingdom**
	8:10	secrets of the **kingdom** of God		28:23	testifying to the **kingdom**
	9: 2	to proclaim the **kingdom** of God		28:31	proclaiming the **kingdom** of God
	9:11	spoke to them about the **kingdom**	Ro	14:17	For the **kingdom** of God is not
	9:27	proclaim the **kingdom** of God	1C	4:20	For the **kingdom** of God depends
	9:62	is fit for the **kingdom** of God		6: 9	will not inherit the **kingdom**
	10: 9	The **kingdom** of God has come		6:10	will inherit the **kingdom** of God
	10:11	**kingdom** of God has come near		15:24	he hands over the **kingdom**
	11: 2	Your **kingdom** come		15:50	cannot inherit the **kingdom**
	11:17	Every **kingdom** divided against	Ga	5:21	will not inherit the **kingdom**
	11:18	how will his **kingdom** stand	Ep	5: 5	any inheritance in the **kingdom**

Co	1:13	transferred us into the **kingdom**
	4:11	co-workers for the **kingdom**
1Th	2:12	into his own **kingdom** and glory
2Th	1: 5	worthy of the **kingdom** of God
2Ti	4: 1	his appearing and his **kingdom**
	4:18	me for his heavenly **kingdom**
He	1: 8	is the scepter of your **kingdom**
	11:33	faith conquered **kingdoms**
	12:28	we are receiving a **kingdom**
Ja	2: 5	to be heirs of the **kingdom**
2P	1:11	into the eternal **kingdom**
Re	1: 6	and made us to be a **kingdom**
	1: 9	the persecution and the **kingdom**
	5:10	made them to be a **kingdom**
	11:15	The **kingdom** of the world
	12:10	and the **kingdom** of our God
	16:10	its **kingdom** was plunged into
	17:12	have not yet received a **kingdom**
	17:17	agreeing to give their **kingdom**
	17:18	is the great city that **rules**

---

934 ᴳᴼ2 ᴬᴳ136 ᴸᴺ44 ᴮ2:372 ᴷ1:591 ᴿ935
βασιλειος, KINGLY

| Lk | 7:25 | in luxury are in **royal palaces** |
| 1P | 2: 9 | chosen race, a **royal** priesthood |

---

935 ᴳᴼ115 ᴬᴳ136 ᴸᴺ44 ᴮ2:372 ᴷ1:564
βασιλευς, KING

Mt	1: 6	Jesse the father of **King** David
	2: 1	In the time of **King** Herod
	2: 2	who has been born **king** of the
	2: 3	When **King** Herod heard this
	2: 9	When they had heard the **king**
	5:35	the city of the great **King**
	10:18	before governors and **kings**
	11: 8	soft robes are in **royal** palaces
	14: 9	The **king** was grieved
	17:25	From whom do **kings** of the earth
	18:23	compared to a **king** who wished
	21: 5	your **king** is coming to you
	22: 2	to a **king** who gave a wedding
	22: 7	The **king** was enraged
	22:11	**king** came in to see the guests
	22:13	**king** said to the attendants
	25:34	the **king** will say to those
	25:40	And the **king** will answer them
	27:11	Are you the **King** of the Jews
	27:29	Hail, **King** of the Jews!
	27:37	Jesus, the **King** of the Jews

	27:42	He is the **King** of Israel
Mk	6:14	**King** Herod heard of it
	6:22	and the **king** said to the girl
	6:25	she rushed back to the **king**
	6:26	The **king** was deeply grieved
	6:27	the **king** sent a soldier of the
	13: 9	before governors and **kings**
	15: 2	Are you the **King** of the Jews
	15: 9	for you the **King** of the Jews
	15:12	with the man you call the **King**
	15:18	Hail, **King** of the Jews!
	15:26	The **King** of the Jews.
	15:32	Messiah, the **King** of Israel
Lk	1: 5	In the days of **King**
	10:24	that many prophets and **kings**
	14:31	Or what **king**, going out to
	14:31	war against another **king**
	19:38	Blessed is the **king** who comes
	21:12	will be brought before **kings**
	22:25	The **kings** of the Gentiles lord
	23: 2	is the Messiah, a **king**
	23: 3	Are you the **king** of the Jews?
	23:37	you are the **King** of the Jews
	23:38	This is the **King** of the Jews.
Jn	1:49	You are the **King** of Israel
	6:15	by force to make him **king**
	12:13	the **King** of Israel
	12:15	Look, your **king** is coming
	18:33	Are you the **King** of the Jews?
	18:37	So you are a **king**?
	18:37	You say that I am a **king**
	18:39	to release for you the **King**
	19: 3	Hail, **King** of the Jews!
	19:12	who claims to be a **king**
	19:14	Here is your **King**!
	19:15	Shall I crucify your **King**?
	19:15	have no **king** but the emperor
	19:19	Nazareth, the **King** of the Jews
	19:21	The **King** of the Jews,
	19:21	I am **King** of the Jews
Ac	4:26	The **kings** of the earth took
	7:10	before Pharaoh, **king** of Egypt
	7:18	another **king** who had not known
	9:15	before Gentiles and **kings**
	12: 1	About that time **King** Herod
	12:20	Blastus, the **king's** chamberlain
	13:21	Then they asked for a **king**
	13:22	he made David their **king**
	17: 7	is another **king** named Jesus

	25:13	**King** Agrippa and Bernice
	25:14	Paul's case before the **king**
	25:24	**King** Agrippa and all here
	25:26	before you, **King** Agrippa
	26: 2	is before you, **King** Agrippa
	26: 7	this hope, **your Excellency**
	26:13	the road, **your Excellency**
	26:19	After that, **King** Agrippa
	26:26	Indeed the **king** knows about
	26:27	**King** Agrippa, do you believe
	26:30	Then the **king** got up
2C	11:32	the governor under **King** Aretas
1Ti	1:17	To the **King** of the ages
	2: 2	for **kings** and all who are in
	6:15	the **King** of kings and Lord
He	7: 1	**King** Melchizedek of Salem
	7: 1	from defeating the **kings**
	7: 2	means **"king** of righteousness
	7: 2	he is also **king** of Salem
	7: 2	that is, **"king** of peace."
	11:23	not afraid of the **king's** edict
	11:27	unafraid of the **king's** anger
1P	2:13	whether of the **emperor** as
	2:17	Honor the **emperor.**
Re	1: 5	ruler of the **kings** of the earth
	6:15	Then the **kings** of the earth
	9:11	They have as **king** over them
	10:11	nations and languages and **kings**
	15: 3	**King** of the nations!
	16:12	prepare the way for the **kings**
	16:14	who go abroad to the **kings**
	17: 2	whom the **kings** of the earth
	17: 9	also, they are seven **kings**
	17:12	that you saw are ten **kings**
	17:12	to receive authority as **kings**
	17:14	Lord of lords and **King** of kings
	17:14	Lord of lords and King of **kings**
	17:18	city that rules over the **kings**
	18: 3	the **kings** of the earth have
	18: 9	And the **kings** of the earth
	19:16	**King** of kings and Lord of
	19:16	King of **kings** and Lord of
	19:18	to eat the flesh of **kings**
	19:19	**kings** of the earth with their
	21:24	**kings** of the earth will bring

936 GO21 AG136 LN44 B2:372 K1:590 R935
βασιλευω, I AM KING, I AM RULING
Mt   2:22   heard that Archelaus **was ruling**

Lk	1:33	He **will reign** over the house
	19:14	want this man **to rule** over us
	19:27	who did not want me **to be king**
Ro	5:14	Yet death **exercised dominion**
	5:17	death **exercised dominion** through
	5:17	**exercise dominion** in life
	5:21	just as sin **exercised dominion**
	5:21	**might** also **exercise dominion**
	6:12	let sin **exercise dominion**
1C	4: 8	from us you **have become kings**
	4: 8	that you **had become kings**
	15:25	For he must **reign** until he has
1Ti	6:15	the King of **kings** and Lord
Re	5:10	and they **will reign** on earth
	11:15	and he **will reign** forever
	11:17	power and **begun to reign**
	19: 6	our God the Almighty **reigns**
	20: 4	came to life and **reigned**
	20: 6	they **will reign** with him
	22: 5	they **will reign** forever and

937 GO5 AG136 LN44 B3:372 K1:591 R935
βασιλικος, KINGLY
Jn	4:46	Now there was a **royal official**
	4:49	The **official** said to him
Ac	12:20	depended on the **king's** country
	12:21	Herod put on his **royal robes**
Ja	2: 8	really fulfill the **royal law**

938 GO4 AG137 LN44 B2:372 K1:590 R936
βασιλισσα, QUEEN
Mt	12:42	**queen** of the South will rise up
Lk	11:31	**queen** of the South will rise
Ac	8:27	**queen** of the Ethiopians
Re	18: 7	I rule as a **queen;** I am no

939 GO1 AG137 LN44
βασις, FEET
Ac   3: 7   his **feet** and ankles were made

940 GO1 AG137 LN44 B2:552 K1:594
βασκαινω, I BEWITCH
Ga   3: 1   Who **has bewitched** you?

941 GO27 AG137 LN44 K1:596
βασταζω, I BEAR
Mt	3:11	not worthy **to carry** his sandals
	8:17	took our infirmities and **bore**
	20:12	who **have borne** the burden
Mk	14:13	a man **carrying** a jar of water

Lk　7:14　and the **bearers** stood still
　　10: 4　**Carry** no purse, no bag
　　11:27　Blessed is the womb that **bore**
　　14:27　not **carry** the cross and follow
　　22:10　a man **carrying** a jar of water
Jn　10:31　The Jews **took up** stones again
　　12: 6　and **used to steal** what was put
　　16:12　but you cannot **bear** them now
　　19:17　**carrying** the cross by himself
　　20:15　if you **have carried** him **away**
Ac　3: 2　from birth was being **carried in**
　　9:15　I have chosen **to bring** my name
　　15:10　nor we have been able **to bear**
　　21:35　that he had **to be carried**
Ro　11:18　not you that **support** the root
　　15: 1　**to put up with** the failings
Ga　5:10　that is confusing you **will pay**
　　6: 2　**Bear** one another's burdens
　　6: 5　all **must carry** their own loads
　　6:17　I **carry** the marks of Jesus
Re　2: 2　you cannot **tolerate** evildoers
　　2: 3　**bearing up** for the sake of my
　　17: 7　and ten horns that **carries** her

942 GO5 AG137 LN44
βατος, THORN BUSH
Mk　12:26　in the story about the **bush**
Lk　6:44　picked from a **bramble bush**
　　20:37　in the story about the **bush**
Ac　7:30　in the flame of a burning **bush**
　　7:35　appeared to him in the **bush**

943 GO1 AG137 LN44
βατος, BATH
Lk　16: 6　A hundred **jugs** of olive oil.

944 GO1 AG137 LN44
βατραχος, FROG
Re　16:13　three foul spirits like **frogs**

945 GO1 AG137 LN44 B1:795 K1:597
βατταλογεω, I BABBLE
Mt　6: 7　do not **heap up empty phrases**

946 GO6 AG137 LN44 K1:598 R948
βδελυγμα, ABOMINATION
Mt　24:15　see the desolating **sacrilege**
Mk　13:14　see the desolating **sacrilege**
Lk　16:15　is an **abomination** in the sight
Re　17: 4　cup full of **abominations**

　　17: 5　of earth's **abominations**
　　21:27　who practices **abomination**

947 GO1 AG138 LN44 K1:598 R948
βδελυκτος, ABOMINATORS
Ti　1:16　They are **detestable**

948 GO2 AG138 LN44 K1:598
βδελυσσομαι, I ABOMINATE
Ro　2:22　You that **abhor** idols, do you
Re　21: 8　the faithless, the **polluted**

949 GO8 AG138 LN45 B1:658 K1:600
βεβαιος, FIRM
Ro　4:16　**guaranteed** to all his
2C　1: 7　Our hope for you is **unshaken**
He　2: 2　through angels was **valid**
　　3:14　our first confidence **firm** to
　　6:19　a sure and **steadfast** anchor
　　9:17　will **takes effect** only at death
2P　1:10　eager to **confirm** your call
　　1:19　message **more fully confirmed**

950 GO8 AG138 LN45 B1:658 K1:600 R949
βεβαιοω, I CONFIRM
Mk　16:20　**confirmed** the message by the
Ro　15: 8　he might **confirm** the promises
1C　1: 6　**has been strengthened** among you
　　1: 8　He **will** also **strengthen** you
2C　1:21　it is God who **establishes** us
Co　2: 7　**established** in the faith,
He　2: 3　it **was attested** to us by those
　　13: 9　**to be strengthened** by grace

951 GO2 AG138 LN45 B1:658 K1:600 R950
βεβαιωσις, CONFIRMATION
Ph　1: 7　and **confirmation** of the gospel
He　6:16　an oath given as **confirmation**

952 GO5 AG138 LN45 K1:604
βεβηλος, DESECRATED, PROFANE
1Ti　1: 9　for the unholy and **profane**
　　4: 7　Have nothing to do with **profane**
　　6:20　Avoid the **profane** chatter
2Ti　2:16　Avoid **profane** chatter
He　12:16　an immoral and **godless** person

953 GO2 AG138 LN45 K1:605 R952
βεβηλοω, I DESECRATE
Mt　12: 5　in the temple **break** the sabbath

Ac   24: 6   tried **to profane** the temple

---

954   GO7 AG139 LN45 B3:468 K1:605
βεελζεβουλ, BEELZEBUL
Mt   10:25   master of the house **Beelzebul**
     12:24   It is only by **Beelzebul**
     12:27   I cast out demons by **Beelzebul**
Mk   3:22   He has **Beelzebul,** and by the
Lk   11:15   casts out demons by **Beelzebul**
     11:18   out the demons by **Beelzebul**
     11:19   out the demons by **Beelzebul**

---

955   GO1 AG139 LN45 B3:468 K1:607
βελιαρ, BELIAR
2C   6:15   does Christ have with **Beliar**

955a   GO1 AG139 LN45
βελονη, NEEDLE
Lk   18:25   go through the eye of a **needle**

---

956   GO1 AG139 LN45 B3:959 K1:608
βελος, DART
Ep   6:16   quench all the flaming **arrows**

---

957   GO1 AG139 LN45
βελτιων, BETTER
2Ti   1:18   you know **very well** how much

---

958   GO4 AG139 LN45
βενιαμειν, BENJAMIN
Ac   13:21   man of the tribe of **Benjamin**
Ro   11: 1   member of the tribe of **Benjamin**
Ph   3: 5   of the tribe of **Benjamin**
Re   7: 8   from the tribe of **Benjamin**

---

959   GO3 AG139 LN45
βερνικη, BERNICE
Ac   25:13   King Agrippa and **Bernice**
     25:23   Agrippa and **Bernice** came with
     26:30   the governor and **Bernice**

---

960   GO2 AG139 LN45
βεροια, BEROEA
Ac   17:10   Paul and Silas off to **Beroea**
     17:13   proclaimed by Paul in **Beroea**

---

961   GO1 AG139 LN45
βεροιαιος, BEROEAN
Ac   20: 4   son of Pyrrhus **from Beroea**

---

963   GO12 AG139 LN45
βηθανια, BETHANY
Mt   21:17   out of the city to **Bethany**
     26: 6   Now while Jesus was at **Bethany**
Mk   11: 1   at Bethphage and **Bethany**
     11:11   he went out to **Bethany**
     11:12   when they came from **Bethany**
     14: 3   While he was at **Bethany**
Lk   19:29   near Bethphage and **Bethany**
     24:50   led them out as far as **Bethany**
Jn   1:28   This took place in **Bethany**
     11: 1   **Bethany,** the village of Mary
     11:18   Now **Bethany** was near Jerusalem
     12: 1   Jesus came to **Bethany**

964a   GO1 AG140 LN45
βηθζαθα, BETHZATHA
Jn   5: 2   called in Hebrew **Beth-zatha**

---

965   GO8 AG140 LN45 B1:169
βηθλεεμ, BETHLEHEM
Mt   2: 1   Jesus was born in **Bethlehem**
      2: 5   In **Bethlehem** of Judea
      2: 6   **Bethlehem,** in the land of Judah
      2: 8   he sent them to **Bethlehem**
      2:16   in and around **Bethlehem**
Lk   2: 4   city of David called **Bethlehem**
      2:15   Let us go now to **Bethlehem**
Jn   7:42   and comes from **Bethlehem**

---

966   GO7 AG140 LN45
βηθσαιδα, BETHSAIDA
Mt   11:21   Woe to you, **Bethsaida!**
Mk   6:45   to the other side, to **Bethsaida**
      8:22   They came to **Bethsaida**
Lk   9:10   to a city called **Bethsaida**
     10:13   Woe to you, **Bethsaida!**
Jn   1:44   Now Philip was from **Bethsaida**
     12:21   who was from **Bethsaida**

---

967   GO3 AG140 LN45
βηθφαγη, BETHPHAGE
Mt   21: 1   and had reached **Bethphage**
Mk   11: 1   at **Bethphage** and Bethany
Lk   19:29   he had come near **Bethphage**

---

968   GO12 AG140 LN46 B2:369
βημα, TRIBUNAL
Mt   27:19   sitting on the **judgment seat**
Jn   19:13   and sat on the **judge's bench**

Ac	7: 5	not even a foot's **length**
	12:21	took his seat on the **platform**
	18:12	brought him before the **tribunal**
	18:16	them from the **tribunal**
	18:17	in front of the **tribunal**
	25: 6	his seat on the **tribunal**
	25:10	to the emperor's **tribunal**
	25:17	took my seat on the **tribunal**
Ro	14:10	stand before the **judgment seat**
2C	5:10	appear before the **judgment seat**

---

969   GO1   AG140   LN46   B3:396
βηρυλλος, BERYL

Re	21:20	chrysolite, the eighth **beryl**

---

970   GO3   AG140   LN46   B3:711
βια, VIOLENCE

Ac	5:26	them, but without **violence**
	21:35	the **violence** of the mob was so
	27:41	by the **force** of the waves

---

971   GO2   AG140   LN46   B3:711   K1:609   R970
βιαζω, I FORCE

Mt	11:12	of heaven **has suffered violence**
Lk	16:16	tries to **enter** it **by force**

---

972   GO1   AG141   LN46   B3:711   R970
βιαιος, VIOLENT

Ac	2: 2	like the rush of a **violent** wind

---

973   GO1   AG141   LN46   B3:711   K1:613   R971
βιαστης, VIOLENT ONE

Mt	11:12	the **violent** take it by force

---

974   GO3   AG141   LN46   R975
βιβλαριδιον, LITTLE BOOK

Re	10: 2	He held a **little scroll** open
	10: 9	to give me the **little scroll**
	10:10	So I took the **little scroll**

---

975   GO34   AG141   LN46   B1:243   K1:617   R976
βιβλιον, BOOK

Mt	19: 7	a **certificate** of dismissal
Mk	10: 4	a man to write a **certificate**
Lk	4:17	and the **scroll** of the prophet
	4:17	He unrolled the **scroll**
	4:20	And he rolled up the **scroll**
Jn	20:30	are not written in this **book**
	21:25	could not contain the **books**

Ga	3:10	things written in the **book**
2Ti	4:13	also the **books,** and above all
He	9:19	sprinkled both the **scroll**
	10: 7	in the scroll of the **book**
Re	1:11	Write in a **book** what you see
	5: 1	**scroll** written on the inside
	5: 2	is worthy to open the **scroll**
	5: 3	to open the **scroll** or to look
	5: 4	worthy to open the **scroll**
	5: 5	he can open the **scroll**
	5: 8	When he had taken the **scroll**
	5: 9	are worthy to take the **scroll**
	6:14	The sky vanished like a **scroll**
	10: 8	take the **scroll** that is open
	13: 8	in the **book** of life of the Lamb
	17: 8	written in the **book** of life
	20:12	throne, and **books** were opened
	20:12	Also another **book** was opened
	20:12	as recorded in the **books**
	21:27	written in the Lamb's **book**
	22: 7	of the prophecy of this **book**
	22: 9	keep the words of this **book**
	22:10	prophecy of this **book**
	22:18	of the prophecy of this **book**
	22:18	plagues described in this **book**
	22:19	from the words of the **book**
	22:19	are described in this **book**

---

976   GO10   AG141   LN46   B1:242   K1:615
βιβλος, BOOK

Mt	1: 1	An **account** of the genealogy
Mk	12:26	not read in the **book** of Moses
Lk	3: 4	as it is written in the **book**
	20:42	says in the **book** of Psalms
Ac	1:20	written in the **book** of Psalms
	7:42	it is written in the **book**
	19:19	collected their **books**
Ph	4: 3	names are in the **book** of life
Re	3: 5	your name out of the **book**
	20:15	not found written in the **book**

---

977   GO1   AG141   LN46
βιβρωσκω, I EAT

Jn	6:13	left by those who **had eaten**

---

978   GO2   AG141   LN46
βιθυνια, BITHYNIA

Ac	16: 7	attempted to go into **Bithynia**
1P	1: 1	Cappadocia, Asia, and **Bithynia**

979 GO10 AG141 LN46 B2:474 K2:832
βιος, LIFE
Mk 12:44   all she had **to live on**
Lk   8:14   riches and pleasures of **life**
       8:43   she had spent all **she had**
      15:12   he divided his **property** between
      15:30   who has devoured your **property**
      21: 4   in all she had **to live on**
1Ti   2: 2   a quiet and peaceable **life**
2Ti   2: 4   entangled in **everyday** affairs
1J   2:16   the eyes, the pride in **riches**
      3:17   who has the world's **goods**

---

980 GO1 AG142 LN46 B2:474 K2:832 R979
βιοω, I LIVE
1P   4: 2   so as **to live** for the rest

---

981 GO1 AG142 LN46 R980
βιωσις, TYPE OF LIFE
Ac 26: 4   the Jews know my **way of life**

---

982 GO3 AG142 LN46 B2:474 R980
βιωτικος, OF THIS LIFE
Lk 21:34   and the worries of **this life**
1C   6: 3   say nothing of **ordinary matters**
      6: 4   If you have **ordinary cases**

---

983 GO1 AG142 LN46
βλαβερος, HARMFUL
1Ti   6: 9   senseless and **harmful** desires

---

984 GO2 AG142 LN46
βλαπτω, I HURT
Mk 16:18   it **will** not **hurt** them
Lk   4:35   **having done** him any **harm**

---

985 GO4 AG142 LN46 B3:865
βλαστανω, I SPROUT
Mt 13:26   So when the plants **came up**
Mk   4:27   seed would **sprout** and grow
He   9: 4   and Aaron's rod that **budded**
Ja   5:18   the earth **yielded** its harvest

---

986 GO1 AG142 LN46
βλαστος, BLASTUS
Ac 12:20   after winning over **Blastus**

---

987 GO34 AG142 LN46 B3:340 K1:621 R989
βλασφημεω, I INSULT, I BLASPHEME
Mt   9: 3   This man **is blaspheming.**

26:65   He **has blasphemed!**
27:39   Those who passed by **derided** him
Mk   2: 7   It **is blasphemy!**
      3:28   whatever blasphemies they **utter**
      3:29   but whoever **blasphemes** against
     15:29   who passed by **derided** him
Lk 12:10   but whoever **blasphemes** against
     22:65   **heaping** many other **insults**
     23:39   hanged there **kept deriding** him
Jn 10:36   into the world **is blaspheming**
Ac 13:45   and **blaspheming,** they
     18: 6   When they opposed and **reviled**
     19:37   **blasphemers** of our goddess
     26:11   force them **to blaspheme**
Ro   2:24   name of God **is blasphemed**
      3: 8   as some people **slander** us
     14:16   your good **be spoken of as evil**
1C 10:30   why should I **be denounced**
1Ti   1:20   may learn not **to blaspheme**
      6: 1   teaching **may** not **be blasphemed**
Ti   2: 5   God **may** not **be discredited**
      3: 2   **to speak evil** of no one
Ja   2: 7   Is it not they who **blaspheme**
1P   4: 4   and so they **blaspheme**
2P   2: 2   way of truth **will be maligned**
      2:10   to **slander** the glorious ones
      2:12   They **slander** what they do not
Ju   1: 8   and **slander** the glorious ones
      1:10   these people **slander** whatever
Re 13: 6   **blaspheming** his name and his
     16: 9   but they **cursed** the name of God
     16:11   and **cursed** the God of heaven
     16:21   until they **cursed** God for the

---

988 GO18 AG143 LN46 B3:341 K1:621 R989
βλασφημια, INSULT, BLASPHEMY
Mt 12:31   for every sin and **blasphemy**
     12:31   **blasphemy** against the Spirit
     15:19   theft, false witness, **slander**
     26:65   have now heard his **blasphemy**
Mk   3:28   whatever **blasphemies** they utter
      7:22   envy, **slander,** pride, folly
     14:64   You have heard his **blasphemy**
Lk   5:21   who is speaking **blasphemies?**
Jn 10:33   but for **blasphemy,** because you
Ep   4:31   anger and wrangling and **slander**
Co   3: 8   wrath, malice, **slander**
1Ti   6: 4   **slander,** base suspicions
Ju   1: 9   condemnation of **slander** against

Re　2: 9　I know the **slander** on the part
　　13: 1　heads were **blasphemous** names
　　13: 5　haughty and **blasphemous words**
　　13: 6　its mouth to utter **blasphemies**
　　17: 3　that was full of **blasphemous**

989　G04　AG143　LN46　B3:341　K1:621
βλασφημος, INSULTING, BLASPHEMOUS
Ac　6:11　heard him speak **blasphemous**
1Ti　1:13　I was formerly a **blasphemer**
2Ti　3: 2　arrogant, **abusive**, disobedient
2P　2:11　against them a **slanderous**

990　G01　AG143　LN46　R991
βλεμμα, SEEING
2P　2: 8　lawless deeds **that he saw**

991　G0132　AG143　LN46　B3:511　K5:315
βλεπω, I SEE
Mt　5:28　everyone who **looks** at a woman
　　6: 4　your Father who **sees** in secret
　　6: 6　your Father who **sees** in secret
　　6:18　your Father who **sees** in secret
　　7: 3　Why **do** you **see** the speck
　　11: 4　what you hear and **see**
　　12:22　been mute could speak and **see**
　　13:13　**seeing** they do not perceive
　　13:13　seeing they do not **perceive**
　　13:14　and you will indeed **look**
　　13:14　indeed look, but never **perceive**
　　13:16　are your eyes, for they **see**
　　13:17　longed to see what you **see**
　　14:30　**when** he **noticed** the strong wind
　　15:31　crowd was amazed **when** they **saw**
　　15:31　walking, and the blind **seeing**
　　18:10　continually **see** the face of my
　　22:16　for you do not **regard** people
　　24: 2　You **see** all these, do you not?
　　24: 4　**Beware** that no one leads you
Mk　4:12　they may indeed **look,** but not
　　4:12　indeed look, but not **perceive**
　　4:24　**Pay attention to** what you hear
　　5:31　You **see** the crowd pressing in
　　8:15　**beware** of the yeast of the
　　8:18　have eyes, and fail **to see**
　　8:23　Can you **see** anything?
　　8:24　I **can see** people, but they
　　12:14　**show** deference to no one
　　12:38　**Beware** of the scribes
　　13: 2　**Do** you **see** these great

13: 5　**Beware** that no one leads you
13: 9　As for yourselves, **beware**
13:23　But **be alert;** I have already
13:33　**Beware,** keep alert; for you
Lk　6:41　Why **do** you **see** the speck
　　6:42　**do** not **see** the log in your own
　　7:21　**sight** to many who were blind
　　7:44　**Do** you **see** this woman?
　　8:10　**looking** they may not perceive
　　8:10　looking they **may** not **perceive**
　　8:16　who enter **may see** the light
　　8:18　Then **pay attention to** how you
　　9:62　and **looks** back is fit for the
　　10:23　eyes that **see** what you see
　　10:23　eyes that see what you **see**
　　10:24　desired to see what you **see**
　　11:33　who enter **may see** the light
　　21: 8　**Beware** that you are not led
　　21:30　you **can see** for yourselves
　　24:12　stooping and **looking in**
Jn　1:29　The next day he **saw** Jesus
　　5:19　what he **sees** the Father doing
　　9: 7　and came back **able to see**
　　9:15　Then I washed, and **now I see**
　　9:19　How then **does** he now **see?**
　　9:21　how it is that now he **sees**
　　9:25　I was blind, now I **see**
　　9:39　those who **do** not **see** may see
　　9:39　those who do not see **may see**
　　9:39　who **do see** may become blind
　　9:41　that you say, 'We **see,**'
　　11: 9　they **see** the light of this
　　13:22　disciples **looked** at one another
　　20: 1　and **saw** that the stone had been
　　20: 5　to look in and **saw** the linen
　　21: 9　they **saw** a charcoal fire there
　　21:20　Peter turned and **saw** the
Ac　1: 9　**as they were watching,** he was
　　2:33　that you both **see** and hear
　　3: 4　and said, "**Look** at us."
　　4:14　When they **saw** the man who had
　　8: 6　**seeing** the signs that he did
　　9: 8　he **could see** nothing; so they
　　9: 9　three days he was without **sight**
　　12: 9　thought he **was seeing** a vision
　　13:11　unable **to see** the sun
　　13:40　**Beware,** therefore, that what
　　27:12　**facing** southwest and northwest
　　28:26　and you will **indeed look**

	28:26	and you **will** indeed **look**
Ro	7:23	but I **see** in my members another
	8:24	Now hope that **is seen** is not
	8:24	who hopes for what **is seen**
	8:25	for what we **do** not **see**
	11: 8	eyes that **would** not **see**
	11:10	so that they cannot **see**
1C	1:26	**Consider** your own call
	3:10	builder **must choose with care**
	8: 9	But **take care** that this liberty
	10:12	**watch out** that you do not fall
	10:18	**Consider** the people of Israel
	13:12	For now we **see** in a mirror
	16:10	**see** that he has nothing to fear
2C	4:18	look not at what **can be seen**
	4:18	but at what **cannot be seen**
	4:18	what **can be seen** is temporary
	4:18	what **cannot be seen** is eternal
	7: 8	for I **see** that I grieved you
	10: 7	**Look at** what is before your
	12: 6	than what **is seen** in me
Ga	5:15	**take care** that you are not
Ep	5:15	**Be careful** then how you live
Ph	3: 2	**Beware** of the dogs, beware of
	3: 2	**beware** of the evil workers
	3: 2	**beware** of those who mutilate
Co	2: 5	I rejoice **to see** your morale
	2: 8	**See to it** that no one takes you
	4:17	**See** that you complete the task
He	2: 9	but we **do see** Jesus, who for
	3:12	**Take care,** brothers and
	3:19	So we **see** that they were unable
	10:25	as you **see** the Day approaching
	11: 1	conviction of things not **seen**
	11: 3	so that what **is seen** was made
	11: 7	about events as yet un**seen**
	12:25	**See** that you do not refuse
Ja	2:22	You **see** that faith was active
2J	1: 8	**Be on** your **guard,** so that you
Re	1:11	Write in a book what you **see**
	1:12	I turned **to see** whose voice
	3:18	your eyes so that you **may see**
	5: 3	the scroll or **to look into** it
	5: 4	the scroll or **to look into** it
	9:20	**cannot see** or hear or walk
	11: 9	nations **will gaze** at their dead
	16:15	going about naked and **exposed**
	17: 8	amazed when they **see** the beast
	18: 9	when they **see** the smoke of her

	18:18	cried out as they **saw** the smoke
	22: 8	who heard and **saw** these things
	22: 8	when I heard and **saw** them

992 GO1 AG144 LN47
βλητεος, MUST THROW
Lk 5:38 But new wine **must be put** into

993 GO1 AG144 LN47
βοανηργες, BOANERGES
Mk 3:17 whom he gave the name
              Boanerges

994 GO12 AG144 LN47 B1:410 K1:625
βοαω, I CRY ALOUD
Mt 3: 3 voice of **one crying out** in the
Mk 1: 3 voice of **one crying out** in the
      15:34 three o'clock Jesus **cried out**
Lk 3: 4 voice of **one crying out** in the
      9:38 a man from the crowd **shouted**
      18: 7 his chosen ones **who cry** to him
      18:38 Then he **shouted,** "Jesus, Son
Jn 1:23 the voice of **one crying out**
Ac 8: 7 **crying** with loud shrieks, came
      17: 6 the city authorities, **shouting**
      25:24 **shouting** that he ought not to
Ga 4:27 burst into song and **shout**

994a GO2 AG144 LN47
βοες, BOES (BOAZ)
Mt 1: 5 and Salmon the father of **Boaz**
      1: 5 **Boaz** the father of Obed by Ruth

995 GO1 AG144 LN47 B1:410 R994
βοη, LOUD CRIES
Ja 5: 4 the **cries** of the harvesters

996 GO2 AG144 LN47 K1:628 R998
βοηθεια, HELP
Ac 27:17 they took **measures** to undergird
He 4:16 to **help** in time of **need**

997 GO8 AG144 LN47 K1:628 R998
βοηθεω, I HELP
Mt 15:25 Lord, **help** me.
Mk 9:22 have pity on us and **help** us
      9:24 I believe; **help** my unbelief!
Ac 16: 9 to Macedonia and **help** us
      21:28 Fellow Israelites, **help!**
2C 6: 2 day of salvation I **have helped**

He   2:18   he is able **to help** those
Re 12:16   But the earth **came to the**

---

998   GO1 AG144 LN47 K1:628
βοηθος, HELPER
He 13: 6   The Lord is my **helper;** I will

---

999   GO3 AG144 LN47 R900
βοθυνος, DITCH
Mt 12:11   into a **pit** on the sabbath
    15:14   both will fall into a **pit**
Lk   6:39   Will not both fall into a **pit**

1000   GO1 AG144 LN47 R906
βολη, THROW
Lk 22:41   from them about a stone's **throw**

1001   GO2 AG144 LN47
βολιζω, I TAKE SOUNDING
Ac 27:28   they **took soundings** and found
    27:28   they **took soundings** again and

1003   GO1 AG145 LN47
βοος, BOOS (BOAZ)
Lk   3:32   son of **Boaz**

1004   GO1 AG145 LN47
βορβορος, FILTH
2P   2:22   only to wallow in the **mud**

1005   GO2 AG145 LN47
βορρας, NORTH
Lk 13:29   from **north** and south,
Re 21:13   on the **north** three gates,

1006   GO9 AG145 LN47
βοσκω, I GRAZE
Mt   8:30   large herd of swine was **feeding**
     8:33   The **swineherds** ran off
Mk   5:11   great herd of swine was **feeding**
     5:14   The **swineherds** ran off and told
Lk   8:32   large herd of swine was **feeding**
     8:34   When the **swineherds** saw what
    15:15   to his fields to **feed** the pigs
Jn 21:15   said to him, "**Feed** my lambs
    21:17   said to him, "**Feed** my sheep

1007   GO1 AG145 LN47
βοσορ, BOSOR
2P   2:15   Balaam son of **Bosor,** who loved

1008   GO1 AG145 LN47 B2:210
βοτανη, VEGETATION
He   6: 7   and that produces a **crop** useful

1009   GO1 AG145 LN47
βοτρυς, BUNCH OF GRAPES
Re 14:18   gather the **clusters** of the vine

1010   GO2 AG145 LN47 R1011
βουλευτης, COUNCILER
Mk 15:43   respected **member of the council**
Lk 23:50   though a **member of the council**

1011   GO6 AG145 LN47 R1012
βουλευω, I PLAN
Lk 14:31   and **consider** whether he is able
Jn 11:53   **planned** to put him to death.
    12:10   **planned** to put Lazarus to death
Ac 27:39   **planned** to run the ship ashore,
2C   1:17   when I **wanted** to do this?
     1:17   Do I **make** my **plans** according to

1012   GO12 AG145 LN47 B3:1015 K1:633 R1014
βουλη, PLAN
Lk   7:30   lawyers rejected God's **purpose**
    23:51   had not agreed to their **plan**
Ac   2:23   according to the definite **plan**
     4:28   your **plan** had predestined
     5:38   because if this **plan** or this
    13:36   had served the **purpose** of God
    20:27   the whole **purpose** of God.
    27:12   was **in favor** of putting to sea
    27:42   **plan** was to kill the prisoners
1C   4: 5   the **purposes** of the heart.
Ep   1:11   according to the **purpose** of him
He   6:17   character of his **purpose,**

1013   GO3 AG145 LN47 B3:1015 K1:636 R1014
βουλημα, PLAN
Ac 27:43   from carrying out their **plan.**
Ro   9:19   For who can resist his **will?**
1P   4: 3   doing **what** the Gentiles like

1014   GO37 AG146 LN47 B3:1015 K1:629
βουλομαι, I PLAN
Mt   1:19   **planned** to dismiss her quietly
    11:27   the Son chooses to reveal **him.**
Mk 15:15   **wishing** to satisfy the crowd

Lk	10:22	the Son chooses to reveal **him**
	22:42	Father, if you **are willing,**
Jn	18:39	Do you **want** me to release for
Ac	5:28	you are **determined** to bring
	5:33	enraged and **wanted** to kill
	12: 4	**intending** to bring him out to
	15:37	we **would like** to know what
	18:15	I do not **wish** to be a judge
	18:27	**wished** to cross over to Achaia,
	19:30	**wished** to go into the crowd,
	22:30	Since he **wanted** to find out
	23:28	I **wanted** to know the charge
	25:20	he **wished** to go to Jerusalem
	25:22	I **would like** to hear the man
	27:43	centurion, **wishing** to save Paul
	28:18	the Romans **wanted** to release me
1C	12:11	just as the Spirit **chooses**
2C	1:15	I **wanted** to come to you first,
	1:17	when I **wanted** to do this?
Ph	1:12	I **want** you to know, beloved,
1Ti	2: 8	I **desire,** then, that in every
	5:14	**would have** younger widows marry
	6: 9	those who **want** to be rich fall
Ti	3: 8	I **desire** that you insist
Pm	1:13	I **wanted** to keep him with me,
He	6:17	when God **desired** to show even
Ja	1:18	of his own **purpose** he gave us
	3: 4	the will of the pilot **directs**
	4: 4	whoever **wishes** to be a friend
2P	3: 9	not **wanting** any to perish,
2J	1:12	I **would** rather not **use** paper
3J	1:10	prevents those who **want** to do
Ju	1: 5	Now I **desire** to remind you,

1015   GO2 AG146 LN48
βουνος, MOUNT

Lk	3: 5	**hill** shall be made low,
	23:30	to the **hills,** 'Cover us.'

1016   GO8 AG146 LN48
βους, OX

Lk	13:15	untie his **ox** or his donkey from
	14: 5	one of you has a child or an **ox**
	14:19	I have bought five yoke of **oxen**
Jn	2:14	he found people selling **cattle**
	2:15	both the sheep and the **cattle.**
1C	9: 9	You shall not muzzle an **ox**
	9: 9	for **oxen** that God is concerned?
1Ti	5:18	You shall not muzzle an **ox**

1017   GO2 AG146 LN48 B1:647 K1:638
βραβειον, PRIZE

1C	9:24	but only one receives the **prize**
Ph	3:14	the **prize** of the heavenly call

1018   GO1 AG146 LN48 B1:648 K1:637
βραβευω, I PRESIDE

Co	3:15	let the peace of Christ **rule**

1019   GO2 AG147 LN48 R1021
βραδυνω, I AM SLOW

1Ti	3:15	if I **am delayed,** you may know
2P	3: 9	The Lord **is** not **slow** about his

1020   GO1 AG147 LN48 R1021,4126
βραδυπλοεω, I SAIL SLOWLY

Ac	27: 7	We **sailed slowly** for a number

1021   GO3 AG147 LN48
βραδυς, SLOW

Lk	24:25	how **slow** of heart to believe
Ja	1:19	**slow** to speak
	1:19	**slow** to anger

1022   GO1 AG147 LN48 R1021
βραδυτης, SLOWNESS

2P	3: 9	as some think of **slowness,** but

1023   GO3 AG147 LN48 K1:639
βραχιων, ARM

Lk	1:51	has shown strength with his **arm**
Jn	12:38	**arm** of the Lord been revealed?
Ac	13:17	with uplifted **arm** he led them

1024   GO7 AG147 LN48
βραχυς, LITTLE

Lk	22:58	A **little** later someone else,
Jn	6: 7	each of them to get a **little**
Ac	5:34	be put outside for a **short** time
	27:28	a **little** farther on they took
He	2: 7	for a **little** while lower than
	2: 9	a **little** while was made lower
	13:22	I have written to you **briefly**

1025   GO8 AG147 LN48 B1:283 K5:636
βρεφος, INFANT

Lk	1:41	the **child** leaped in her womb.
	1:44	the **child** in my womb leaped
	2:12	**child** wrapped in bands of cloth

	2:16	the **child** lying in the manger
	18:15	bringing even **infants** to him
Ac	7:19	their **infants** so that they
2Ti	3:15	from **childhood** you have known
1P	2: 2	Like newborn **infants,** long for

1026　GO7 AG147 LN48 B3:1000
βρεχω, I RAIN

Mt	5:45	and **sends rain** on the righteous
Lk	7:38	**to bathe** his feet with her
	7:44	**bathed** my feet with her tears
	17:29	it **rained** fire and sulfur from
Ja	5:17	that it **might** not **rain**
	5:17	it **did** not **rain** on the earth
Re	11: 6	so that no **rain** may fall

1027　GO12 AG147 LN48 B3:1000 K1:640
βροντη, THUNDER

Mk	3:17	that is, Sons of **Thunder**
Jn	12:29	and said that it was **thunder**
Re	4: 5	rumblings and peals of **thunder**
	6: 1	with a voice of **thunder,** "Come!
	8: 5	and there were peals of **thunder**
	10: 3	the seven **thunders** sounded
	10: 4	the seven **thunders** had sounded
	10: 4	the seven **thunders** have said,
	11:19	rumblings, peals of **thunder,**
	14: 2	like the sound of loud **thunder**
	16:18	peals of **thunder,** and a violent
	19: 6	sound of mighty **thunderpeals,**

1028　GO2 AG147 LN48 B3:1000 R1026
βροχη, RAIN

| Mt | 7:25 | The **rain** fell, the floods came, |
| | 7:27 | The **rain** fell, and the floods |

1029　GO1 AG147 LN48
βροχος, NOOSE

| 1C | 7:35 | to put any **restraint** upon you, |

1030　GO7 AG147 LN48 B2:421 K1:641 R1031
βρυγμος, GRINDING

Mt	8:12	weeping and **gnashing** of teeth
	13:42	weeping and **gnashing** of teeth
	13:50	weeping and **gnashing** of teeth
	22:13	weeping and **gnashing** of teeth
	24:51	weeping and **gnashing** of teeth
	25:30	weeping and **gnashing** of teeth
Lk	13:28	weeping and **gnashing** of teeth

1031　GO1 AG148 LN48 B2:421 K1:641
βρυχω, I GRIND

| Ac | 7:54 | enraged and **ground** their teeth |

1032　GO1 AG148 LN48
βρυω, I GUSH

| Ja | 3:11 | **pour forth** from the same opening |

1033　GO17 AG148 LN48 B2:268 K1:642
βρωμα, FOOD

Mt	14:15	into the villages and buy **food**
Mk	7:19	he declared all **foods** clean
Lk	3:11	whoever has **food** must do
	9:13	buy **food** for all these people
Jn	4:34	My **food** is to do the will of
Ro	14:15	being injured by **what** you eat
	14:15	**what** you eat cause the ruin
	14:20	for the sake of **food,** destroy
1C	3: 2	with milk, not solid **food,**
	6:13	**Food** is meant for the stomach
	6:13	and the stomach for **food,**
	8: 8	**Food** will not bring us close
	8:13	if **food** is a cause of their
	10: 3	all ate the same spiritual **food**
1Ti	4: 3	demand abstinence from **foods,**
He	9:10	deal only with **food** and drink
	13: 9	not by regulations about **food,**

1034　GO1 AG148 LN48 R1033
βρωσιμος, EDIBLE

| Lk | 24:41 | Have you **anything** here **to eat?** |

1035　GO11 AG148 LN48 B2:268 K1:642
βρωσις, FOOD

Mt	6:19	where moth and **rust** consume
	6:20	neither moth nor **rust** consumes
Jn	4:32	I have **food** to eat that you
	6:27	work for the **food** that perishes
	6:27	but for the **food** that endures
	6:55	for my flesh is true **food**
Ro	14:17	the kingdom of God is not **food**
1C	8: 4	as to the eating of **food** offered
2C	9:10	and bread for **food** will supply
Co	2:16	condemn you in matters of **food**
He	12:16	birthright for a single **meal**

1036　GO2 AG148 LN48
βυθιζω, I SINK

| Lk | 5: 7 | so that they began to **sink.** |
| 1Ti | 6: 9 | that **plunge** people into ruin |

1037 GO1 AG148 LN48
βυθος, DEEP
2C 11:25   and a day I was **adrift at sea**

1038 GO3 AG148 LN48
βυρσευς, TANNER
Ac 9:43   with a certain Simon, a **tanner**
     10: 6   is lodging with Simon, a **tanner**
     10:32   in the home of Simon, a **tanner**

1039 GO5 AG148 LN48 R1040
βυσσινος, LINEN
Re 18:12   jewels and pearls, **fine linen,**
     18:16   city, clothed in **fine linen,**
     19: 8   to be clothed with **fine linen**
     19: 8   the **fine linen** is the righteous
     19:14   wearing **fine linen,** white and

1040 GO1 AG148 LN48
βυσσος, LINEN
Lk 16:19   in purple and **fine linen**

1041 GO1 AG148 LN49 B3:418
βωμος, HIGH PLACE, ALTAR
Ac 17:23   **altar** with the inscription

γ

1042 GO1 AG149 LN49
γαββαθα, GABBATHA
Jn 19:13   Pavement, or in Hebrew
            Gabbatha

1043 GO2 AG149 LN49 B1:103
γαβριηλ, GABRIEL
Lk 1:19   angel replied, "I am **Gabriel**
     1:26   angel **Gabriel** was sent by God

1044 GO1 AG149 LN49
γαγγραινα, GANGRENE
2Ti 2:17   talk will spread like **gangrene**

1045 GO1 AG149 LN49
γαδ, GAD
Re 7: 5   tribe of **Gad** twelve thousand

1046 GO1 AG149 LN49
γαδαρηνος, GADARENE
Mt 8:28   to the country of the **Gadarenes**

1047 GO1 AG149 LN49
γαζα, TREASURE
Ac 8:27   charge of her entire **treasury**

1048 GO1 AG149 LN49
γαζα, GAZA
Ac 8:26   down from Jerusalem to **Gaza**

1049 GO5 AG149 LN49 B3:795 R1047,5438
γαζοφυλακειον, TREASURY BOX
Mk 12:41   sat down opposite the **treasury**
     12:41   putting money into the **treasury**
     12:43   contributing to the **treasury.**
Lk 21: 1   their gifts into the **treasury**
Jn 8:20   in the **treasury** of the temple

1050 GO5 AG149 LN49
γαιος, GAIUS
Ac 19:29   dragging with them **Gaius**
     20: 4   by **Gaius** from Derbe,
Ro 16:23   **Gaius,** who is host to me
1C 1:14   except Crispus and **Gaius,**
3J 1: 1   elder to the beloved **Gaius,**

1051 GO5 AG149 LN49 B2:268 K1:645
γαλα, MILK
1C 3: 2   I fed you with **milk,** not solid
     9: 7   does not get any of its **milk?**
He 5:12   You need **milk,** not solid food
     5:13   for everyone who lives on **milk**
1P 2: 2   for the pure, spiritual **milk**

1052 GO1 AG149 LN49
γαλατης, GALATIAN
Ga 3: 1   You foolish **Galatians!**

1053 GO4 AG149 LN49
γαλατια, GALATIA
1C 16: 1   gave to the churches of **Galatia**
Ga 1: 2   To the churches of **Galatia**
2Ti 4:10   Crescens has gone to **Galatia**
1P 1: 1   in Pontus, **Galatia,** Cappadocia

1054 GO2 AG150 LN49
γαλατικος, GALATIAN
Ac 16: 6   region of Phrygia and **Galatia**
     18:23   through the region of **Galatia**

1055 GO3 AG150 LN49
γαληνη, CALM

Mt	8:26	sea; and there was a dead **calm.**
Mk	4:39	and there was a dead **calm.**
Lk	8:24	ceased, and there was a **calm.**

1056 ᴳᴼ61 ᴬᴳ150 ᴸᴺ49
γαλιλαια, GALILEE

Mt	2:22	to the district of **Galilee.**
	3:13	Then Jesus came from **Galilee**
	4:12	he withdrew to **Galilee.**
	4:15	**Galilee** of the Gentiles
	4:18	he walked by the Sea of **Galilee**
	4:23	Jesus went throughout **Galilee,**
	4:25	followed him from **Galilee,**
	15:29	passed along the Sea of **Galilee**
	17:22	they were gathering in **Galilee,**
	19: 1	he left **Galilee** and went to the
	21:11	Jesus from Nazareth in **Galilee**
	26:32	will go ahead of you to **Galilee**
	27:55	had followed Jesus from **Galilee**
	28: 7	going ahead of you to **Galilee**
	28:10	my brothers to go to **Galilee;**
	28:16	disciples went to **Galilee**
Mk	1: 9	came from Nazareth of **Galilee**
	1:14	Jesus came to **Galilee**
	1:16	passed along the Sea of **Galilee**
	1:28	surrounding region of **Galilee**
	1:39	And he went throughout **Galilee**
	3: 7	great multitude from **Galilee**
	6:21	and for the leaders of **Galilee**
	7:31	towards the Sea of **Galilee**
	9:30	and passed through **Galilee**
	14:28	will go before you to **Galilee**
	15:41	when he was in **Galilee**
	16: 7	going ahead of you to **Galilee**
Lk	1:26	town in **Galilee** called Nazareth
	2: 4	the town of Nazareth in **Galilee**
	2:39	they returned to **Galilee**
	3: 1	Herod was ruler of **Galilee**
	4:14	returned to **Galilee**
	4:31	to Capernaum, a city in **Galilee**
	5:17	every village of **Galilee**
	8:26	which is opposite **Galilee**
	17:11	between Samaria and **Galilee**
	23: 5	from **Galilee** where he began
	23:49	had followed him from **Galilee**
	23:55	had come with him from **Galilee**
	24: 6	while he was still in **Galilee**
Jn	1:43	Jesus decided to go to **Galilee**
	2: 1	a wedding in Cana of **Galilee**

	2:11	his signs, in Cana of **Galilee**
	4: 3	and started back to **Galilee**
	4:43	went from that place to **Galilee**
	4:45	When he came to **Galilee**
	4:46	came again to Cana in **Galilee**
	4:47	had come from Judea to **Galilee**
	4:54	coming from Judea to **Galilee**
	6: 1	side of the Sea of **Galilee**
	7: 1	Jesus went about in **Galilee**
	7: 9	he remained in **Galilee**
	7:41	does not come from **Galilee**
	7:52	you are not also from **Galilee**
	7:52	is to arise from **Galilee**
	12:21	was from Bethsaida in **Galilee**
	21: 2	Nathanael of Cana in **Galilee**
Ac	9:31	Judea, **Galilee,** and Samaria
	10:37	beginning in **Galilee** after the
	13:31	came up with him from **Galilee**

1057 ᴳᴼ11 ᴬᴳ150 ᴸᴺ49
γαλιλαιος, GALILEAN

Mt	26:69	were with Jesus the **Galilean**
Mk	14:70	for you are a **Galilean.**
Lk	13: 1	told him about the **Galileans**
	13: 2	**Galileans** suffered in this way
	13: 2	than all other **Galileans?**
	22:59	for he is a **Galilean**
	23: 6	whether the man was a **Galilean**
Jn	4:45	the **Galileans** welcomed him,
Ac	1:11	They said, "Men of **Galilee,**
	2: 7	who are speaking **Galileans?**
	5:37	Judas the **Galilean** rose up

1058 ᴳᴼ3 ᴬᴳ150 ᴸᴺ49
γαλλιων, GALLIO

Ac	18:12	**Gallio** was proconsul of Achaia
	18:14	**Gallio** said to the Jews
	18:17	But **Gallio** paid no attention

1059 ᴳᴼ2 ᴬᴳ150 ᴸᴺ49
γαμαλιηλ, GAMALIEL

Ac	5:34	**Gamaliel,** a teacher of the law
	22: 3	at the feet of **Gamaliel**

1060 ᴳᴼ28 ᴬᴳ150 ᴸᴺ49 ᴮ2:575 ᴷ1:648 ᴿ1062
γαμεω, I MARRY

Mt	5:32	**marries** a divorced woman
	19: 9	and **marries** another commits
	19:10	it is better not to **marry**
	22:25	the first **married,** and died

	22:30	neither **marry** nor are given in
	24:38	**marrying** and giving in marriage
Mk	6:17	because Herod had **married** her
	10:11	divorces his wife and **marries**
	10:12	her husband and **marries** another
	12:25	neither **marry** nor are given in
Lk	14:20	I have just been **married**
	16:18	divorces his wife and **marries**
	16:18	**marries** a woman divorced from
	17:27	**marrying** and being given in
	20:34	**marry** and are given in marriage
	20:35	**marry** nor are given in marriage
1C	7: 9	self-control, they should **marry**
	7: 9	to **marry** than to be aflame
	7:10	the **married** I give this command
	7:28	**marry** will experience distress
	7:33	but the **married** man is anxious
	7:34	the **married** woman is anxious
	7:36	let him **marry** as he wishes
	7:39	she is free to **marry** anyone
1Ti	4: 3	They forbid **marriage** and demand
	5:11	from Christ, they want to **marry**
	5:14	widows **marry,** bear children

1060a   GO7 AG151 LN49 B2:575 R1062
γαμίζω, I MARRY

Mt	22:30	nor **are given in marriage**
	24:38	marrying and **giving in marriage**
Mk	12:25	marry nor are **given in marriage**
Lk	17:27	being **given in marriage**
	20:35	marry nor are **given in marriage**
1C	7:38	he who **marries** his fiancée
	7:38	he who refrains from **marriage**

1061   GO1 AG151 LN49 B2:575 R1062
γαμίσκω, I GIVE IN MARRIAGE

| Lk | 20:34 | marry and are **given in marriage** |

1062   GO16 AG151 LN49 B2:575 K1:648
γάμος, WEDDING

Mt	22: 2	a **wedding** banquet for his son
	22: 3	invited to the **wedding** banquet
	22: 4	come to the **wedding** banquet
	22: 8	The **wedding** is ready, but those
	22: 9	you find to the **wedding** banquet
	22:10	so the **wedding** hall was filled
	22:11	was not wearing a **wedding** robe
	22:12	here without a **wedding** robe?
	25:10	went with him into the **wedding**

Lk	12:36	return from the **wedding** banquet
	14: 8	invited by someone to a **wedding**
Jn	2: 1	there was a **wedding** in Cana
	2: 2	been invited to the **wedding.**
He	13: 4	**marriage** be held in honor
Re	19: 7	**marriage** of the Lamb has come
	19: 9	the **marriage** supper of the Lamb

1063   GO1042 AG151 LN49
γάρ, FOR [MULTIPLE OCCURRENCES]

1064   GO9 AG152 LN49
γαστήρ, WOMB

Mt	1:18	was **found** to be **with child**
	1:23	the virgin **shall conceive**
	24:19	Woe to those who **are pregnant**
Mk	13:17	Woe to those who **are pregnant**
Lk	1:31	you **will conceive** in your womb
	21:23	Woe to those who **are pregnant**
1Th	5: 3	come upon a **pregnant** woman
Ti	1:12	vicious brutes, lazy **gluttons**
Re	12: 2	She **was pregnant** and was

1065   GO25 AG152 LN49
γε, INDEED

Mt	6: 1	**for then** you have no reward
	7:20	**Thus** you will know them by
	9:17	**otherwise,** the skins burst
Lk	5:36	**otherwise** the new will be torn
	5:37	**otherwise** the new wine will
	10: 6	**but if** not, it will return to
	11: 8	**at least** because of his
	13: 9	**but if** not, you can cut it down
	14:32	**then,** while the other is still
	18: 5	**yet** because this widow keeps
	24:21	and **besides** all this, it is now
Ac	2:18	**Even** upon my slaves, both men
	8:30	**Do** you understand what you
	17:27	**perhaps** grope for him and find
	17:27	**indeed** he is not far from each
Ro	8:32	**He** who did not withhold his own
1C	4: 8	**Quite apart** from us you have
	9: 2	**at least** I am to you; for you
2C	5: 3	if **indeed,** when we have taken
	11:16	**but if** you do, then accept me
Ga	3: 4	if it **really** was for nothing
Ep	3: 2	**for surely** you have already
	4:21	**For surely** you have heard about
Co	1:23	provided **that** you continue

1066   GO1 AG153 LN50
γεδεων, GIDEON
He   11:32   to tell of **Gideon**

1067   GO12 AG153 LN50 B2:208 K1:657
γεεννα, GEHENNA
Mt   5:22   be liable to the **hell** of fire
     5:29   body to be thrown into **hell**
     5:30   your whole body to go into **hell**
    10:28   both soul and body in **hell**
    18: 9   be thrown into the **hell** of fire
    23:15   twice as much a child of **hell**
    23:33   escape being sentenced to **hell?**
Mk   9:43   two hands and to go to **hell**
     9:45   and to be thrown into **hell**
     9:47   and to be thrown into **hell**
Lk   12: 5   has authority to cast into **hell**
Ja   3: 6   is itself set on fire by **hell**

1068   GO2 AG153 LN50 B2:710
γεθσημανι, GETHSEMANE
Mt   26:36   to a place called **Gethsemane**
Mk   14:32   to a place called **Gethsemane**

1069   GO4 AG153 LN50
γειτων, NEIGHBOR
Lk   14:12   relatives or rich **neighbors**
    15: 6   his friends and **neighbors,**
    15: 9   her friends and **neighbors**
Jn   9: 8   The **neighbors** and those who had

1070   GO2 AG153 LN50 B2:429 K1:658
γελαω, I LAUGH
Lk   6:21   weep now, for you will **laugh.**
    6:25   Woe to you who are **laughing** now

1071   GO1 AG153 LN50 B2:429 K1:658 R1070
γελως, LAUGHTER
Ja   4: 9   Let your **laughter** be turned

1072   GO8 AG153 LN50 B1:742 R1073
γεμιζω, I FILL
Mk   4:37   boat was already **being swamped.**
    15:36   **filled** a sponge with sour wine
Lk   14:23   so that my house may be **filled**
Jn   2: 7   **Fill** the jars with water.
     2: 7   they **filled** them up to the brim
     6:13   they **filled** twelve baskets.
Re   8: 5   **filled** it with fire from the
    15: 8   temple was **filled** with smoke

1073   GO11 AG153 LN50 B1:742
γεμω, I AM FULL
Mt   23:25   inside they are **full** of greed
    23:27   **full** of the bones of the dead
Lk   11:39   **full** of greed and wickedness
Ro   3:14   **full** of cursing and bitterness
Re   4: 6   **full** of eyes in front and
     4: 8   are **full** of eyes all around
     5: 8   golden bowls **full** of incense
    15: 7   bowls **full** of the wrath of God
    17: 3   was **full** of blasphemous names
    17: 4   golden cup **full** of abominations
    21: 9   **full** of the seven last plagues

1074   GO43 AG153 LN50 B2:35 K1:662 R1085
γενεα, GENERATION
Mt   1:17   the **generations** from Abraham to
     1:17   David are fourteen **generations**
     1:17   Babylon, fourteen **generations**
     1:17   Messiah, fourteen **generations**
    11:16   will I compare this **generation?**
    12:39   **generation** asks for a sign,
    12:41   this **generation** and condemn it
    12:42   this **generation** and condemn it
    12:45   also with this evil **generation**
    16: 4   evil and adulterous **generation**
    17:17   and perverse **generation,** how
    23:36   will come upon this **generation**
    24:34   this **generation** will not pass
Mk   8:12   Why does this **generation** ask
     8:12   be given to this **generation**
     8:38   and sinful **generation,** of them
     9:19   You faithless **generation,**
    13:30   this **generation** will not pass
Lk   1:48   all **generations** will call me
     1:50   fear him from **generation** to
     1:50   from generation to **generation**
     7:31   the people of this **generation**
     9:41   perverse **generation,** how much
    11:29   This **generation** is an evil
    11:29   is an evil **generation;** it asks
    11:30   will be to this **generation**
    11:31   the people of this **generation**
    11:32   this **generation** and condemn it,
    11:50   this **generation** may be charged
    11:51   charged against this **generation**
    16: 8   with their own **generation** than
    17:25   be rejected by this **generation**
    21:32   **generation** will not pass away

Ac	2:40	from this corrupt **generation**
	8:33	Who can describe his **generation**
	13:36	of God in his own **generation,**
	14:16	In past **generations** he allowed
	15:21	for **generations** past
Ep	3: 5	former **generations** this mystery
	3:21	Christ Jesus to all **generations**
Ph	2:15	crooked and perverse **generation**
Co	1:26	the ages and **generations** but
He	3:10	was angry with that **generation**

1075   GO1 AG154 LN50 R1:665
γενεαλογεω, I HAVE GENEALOGY
He   7: 6   not belong to their **ancestry,**

1076   GO2 AG154 LN50 B2:35 K1:663 R1074,3056
γενεαλογια, GENEALOGY
1Ti   1: 4   endless **genealogies** that
Ti   3: 9   **genealogies,** dissensions, and

1077   GO2 AG154 LN50 R1078
γενεσια, BIRTHDAY
Mt   14: 6   But when Herod's **birthday** came,
Mk   6:21   when Herod on his **birthday** gave

1078   GO5 AG154 LN50 K1:682
γενεσις, ORIGIN
Mt   1: 1   **genealogy** of Jesus the Messiah
| | 1:18 | the **birth** of Jesus the Messiah |
Lk   1:14   many will rejoice at his **birth**
Ja   1:23   look at **themselves** in a mirror
| | 3: 6 | on fire the cycle of **nature** |

1079   GO1 AG155 LN50
γενετη, BIRTH
Jn   9: 1   he saw a man blind from **birth**

1079a   GO4 AG155 LN50 K1:685
γενημα, PRODUCE
Mt   26:29   this **fruit** of the vine until
Mk   14:25   the **fruit** of the vine until
Lk   22:18   the **fruit** of the vine until
2C   9:10   **harvest** of your righteousness

1080   GO97 AG155 LN50 B1:176 K1:665
γενναω, I GIVE BIRTH
Mt   1: 2   Abraham was the **father** of Isaac
	1: 2	Isaac the **father** of Jacob
	1: 2	Jacob the **father** of Judah and
	1: 3	Judah the **father** of Perez and

	1: 3	and Perez the **father** of Hezron
	1: 3	and Hezron the **father** of Aram
	1: 4	and Aram the **father** of Aminadab
	1: 4	Aminadab the **father** of Nahshon
	1: 4	Nahshon the **father** of Salmon
	1: 5	and Salmon the **father** of Boaz
	1: 5	Boaz the **father** of Obed by Ruth
	1: 5	Salmon the father of Boaz by
	1: 6	Jesse the **father** of King David
	1: 6	David was the **father** of Solomon
	1: 7	Solomon the **father** of Rehoboam
	1: 7	Rehoboam the **father** of Abijah
	1: 7	and Abijah the **father** of Asaph
	1: 8	Asaph the **father** of Jehoshaphat
	1: 8	Jehoshaphat the **father** of Joram
	1: 8	and Joram the **father** of Uzziah
	1: 9	Uzziah the **father** of Jotham
	1: 9	and Jotham the **father** of Ahaz
	1: 9	and Ahaz the **father** of Hezekiah
	1:10	Hezekiah the **father** of Manasseh
	1:10	and Manasseh the **father** of Amos
	1:10	and Amos the **father** of Josiah
	1:11	Josiah the **father** of Jechoniah
	1:12	was the **father** of Salathiel
	1:12	the **father** of Zerubbabel,
	1:13	Zerubbabel the **father** of Abiud
	1:13	Abiud the **father** of Eliakim
	1:13	and Eliakim the **father** of Azor
	1:14	and Azor the **father** of Zadok
	1:14	and Zadok the **father** of Achim
	1:14	and Achim the **father** of Eliud
	1:15	Eliud the **father** of Eleazar
	1:15	Eleazar the **father** of Matthan
	1:15	and Matthan the **father** of Jacob
	1:16	and Jacob the **father** of Joseph
	1:16	of whom Jesus **was born,** who is
	1:20	for the child **conceived** in her
	2: 1	after Jesus **was born**
	2: 4	the Messiah **was to be born**
	19:12	who have been so from **birth**
	26:24	that one not to **have been born**
Mk	14:21	that one not to **have been born**
Lk	1:13	Elizabeth **will bear** you a son
	1:35	**child to be born** will be holy
	1:57	give birth, and she **bore** a son
	23:29	and the wombs that never **bore**
Jn	1:13	who **were born,** not of blood
	3: 3	without **being born** from above
	3: 4	How can anyone **be born** after

3: 4	the mother's womb and **be born?**	
3: 5	**being born** of water and Spirit	
3: 6	What **is born** of the flesh is	
3: 6	what **is born** of the Spirit is	
3: 7	You must **be born** from above.	
3: 8	who **is born** of the Spirit	
8:41	are not **illegitimate** children	
9: 2	that he **was born** blind?	
9:19	who you say **was born** blind?	
9:20	and that he **was born** blind;	
9:32	the eyes of a person **born** blind	
9:34	You **were born** entirely in sins	
16:21	But when her child **is born,**	
16:21	joy of **having brought** a human	
18:37	For this I **was born,** and for	

Ac	2: 8	in our own **native** language?
	7: 8	became the **father** of Isaac
	7:20	At this time Moses **was born,**
	7:29	**became** the **father** of two sons
	13:33	today I **have begotten** you
	22: 3	I am a Jew, **born** in Tarsus
	22:28	But I **was born** a citizen.
Ro	9:11	Even before they **had been born**
1C	4:15	I **became** your **father** through
Ga	4:23	**was born** according to the flesh
	4:24	**bearing children** for slavery
	4:29	**was born** according to the flesh
2Ti	2:23	know that they **breed** quarrels
Pm	1:10	whose **father** I have **become**
He	1: 5	today I **have begotten** you
	5: 5	today I **have begotten** you
	11:12	descendants **were born**
	11:23	three months after his **birth**
2P	2:12	**born** to be caught and killed
1J	2:29	does right **has been born** of him
	3: 9	Those who **have been born** of God
	3: 9	they **have been born** of God
	4: 7	who loves **is born** of God
	5: 1	Christ has **been born** of God
	5: 1	everyone who loves the **parent**
	5: 1	the parent loves the **child**
	5: 4	whatever **is born** of God
	5:18	those who **are born** of God
	5:18	the one who **was born** of God

1081   GO4 AG155 LN50 K1:672 R1080
γεννημα, GENERATION

Mt	3: 7	You **brood** of vipers! Who warned
	12:34	You **brood** of vipers! How can
	23:33	You snakes, you **brood** of vipers
Lk	3: 7	You **brood** of vipers! Who

1082   GO3 AG156 LN50
γεννησαρετ, GENNESARET

Mt	14:34	they came to land at **Gennesaret**
Mk	6:53	they came to land at **Gennesaret**
Lk	5: 1	beside the lake of **Gennesaret**

1084   GO2 AG156 LN50 K1:672 R1080
γεννητος, BORN ONE

Mt	11:11	among those **born** of women
Lk	7:28	among those **born** of women

1085   GO20 AG156 LN51 K1:684 R1096
γενος, KIND

Mt	13:47	and caught fish of every **kind**
Mk	7:26	of Syrophoenician **origin.**
	9:29	This **kind** can come out only
Ac	4: 6	of the high-priestly **family.**
	4:36	a Levite, a **native** of Cyprus,
	7:13	Joseph's **family** became known
	7:19	He dealt craftily with our **race**
	13:26	**descendants** of Abraham's family
	17:28	For we too are his **offspring.**
	17:29	Since we are God's **offspring,**
	18: 2	Aquila, a **native** of Pontus,
	18:24	Apollos, a **native** of Alexandria
1C	12:10	various **kinds** of tongues, to
	12:28	various **kinds** of tongues.
	14:10	many different **kinds** of sounds
2C	11:26	danger from my **own people**
Ga	1:14	among **my people** of the same age
Ph	3: 5	**member** of the people of Israel
1P	2: 9	But you are a chosen **race,**
Re	22:16	am the root and the **descendant**

1086   GO3 AG156 LN51
γερασηνος, GERASENES

Mk	5: 1	to the country of the **Gerasenes**
Lk	8:26	the country of the **Gerasenes**
	8:37	country of the **Gerasenes**

1087   GO1 AG156 LN51 R1088
γερουσια, OLDER ONE

Ac	5:21	the **whole body** of the elders

1088   GO1 AG157 LN51
γερων, OLD MAN

Jn	3: 4	be born after having **grown old**

1089 GO15 AG157 LN51 B2:269 K1:675
γευομαι, I TASTE
Mt	16:28	who will not **taste** death before
	27:34	but when he **tasted** it, he would
Mk	9: 1	who will not **taste** death until
Lk	9:27	who will not **taste** death before
	14:24	invited will **taste** my dinner
Jn	2: 9	the steward **tasted** the water
	8:52	keeps my word will never **taste**
Ac	10:10	and wanted something **to eat**
	20:11	he had broken bread and **eaten,**
	23:14	by an oath to **taste** no food
Co	2:21	Do not handle, Do not **taste**
He	2: 9	he might **taste** death for
	6: 4	have **tasted** the heavenly gift
	6: 5	**tasted** the goodness of the word
1P	2: 3	**tasted** that the Lord is good

1090 GO1 AG157 LN51 R1092
γεωργεω, I FARM
He	6: 7	for whom it is **cultivated**

1091 GO1 AG157 LN51 R1092
γεωργιον, FARMLAND
1C	3: 9	you are God's **field**

1092 GO18 AG157 LN51 R2041,1093
γεωργος, FARMER
Mt	21:33	he leased it to **tenants**
	21:34	to the **tenants** to collect his
	21:35	the **tenants** seized his slaves
	21:38	when the **tenants** saw the son,
	21:40	will he do to those **tenants**
	21:41	to other **tenants** who will give
Mk	12: 1	then he leased it to **tenants**
	12: 2	When the season came, he sent
	12: 2	When the season came, he sent
	12: 7	**tenants** said to one another,
	12: 9	come and destroy the **tenants**
Lk	20: 9	and leased it to **tenants,**
	20:10	sent a slave to the **tenants**
	20:14	But when the **tenants** saw him,
	20:16	come and destroy those **tenants**
Jn	15: 1	and my Father is the **vinegrower**
2Ti	2: 6	the **farmer** who does the work
Ja	5: 7	**farmer** waits for the precious

1093 GO250 AG157 LN51 B1:517 K1:677
γη, LAND/EARTH
Mt	2: 6	Bethlehem, in the **land** of Judah
	2:20	and go to the **land** of Israel
	2:21	and went to the **land** of Israel.
	4:15	**Land** of Zebulun
	4:15	**land** of Naphtali
	5: 5	they will inherit the **earth**
	5:13	You are the salt of the **earth**
	5:18	heaven and **earth** pass away
	5:35	or by the **earth,** for it is his
	6:10	on **earth** as it is in heaven
	6:19	treasures on **earth,** where moth
	9: 6	authority on **earth** to forgive
	9:26	spread throughout that **district**
	9:31	throughout that **district**
	10:15	the **land** of Sodom and Gomorrah
	10:29	of them will fall to the **ground**
	10:34	to bring peace to the **earth**
	11:24	for the **land** of Sodom
	11:25	Lord of heaven and **earth**
	12:40	be in the heart of the **earth.**
	12:42	came from the ends of the **earth**
	13: 5	they did not have much **soil**
	13: 5	since they had no depth of **soil**
	13: 8	Other seeds fell on good **soil**
	13:23	for what was sown on good **soil**
	14:24	was far from the **land**
	14:34	came to **land** at Gennesaret
	15:35	crowd to sit down on the **ground**
	16:19	and whatever you bind on **earth**
	16:19	whatever you loose on **earth**
	17:25	kings of the **earth** take toll
	18:18	whatever you bind on **earth**
	18:18	whatever you loose on **earth**
	18:19	agree on **earth** about anything
	23: 9	no one your father on **earth,**
	23:35	blood shed on **earth**
	24:30	all the tribes of the **earth**
	24:35	Heaven and **earth** will pass away
	25:18	and dug a hole in the **ground**
	25:25	hid your talent in the **ground**
	27:45	came over the whole **land** until
	27:51	The **earth** shook, and the rocks
	28:18	in heaven and on **earth**
Mk	2:10	has authority on **earth**
	4: 1	beside the sea on the **land**
	4: 5	where it did not have much **soil**
	4: 5	it had no depth of **soil**
	4: 8	Other seed fell into good **soil**
	4:20	the ones sown on the good **soil**

	4:26	scatter seed on the **ground**
	4:28	The **earth** produces of itself
	4:31	when sown upon the **ground**
	4:31	of all the seeds on **earth**
	6:47	he was alone on the **land**
	6:53	came to **land** at Gennesaret
	8: 6	to sit down on the **ground**
	9: 3	no one on **earth** could bleach
	9:20	fell on the **ground** and rolled
	13:27	from the ends of the **earth**
	13:31	Heaven and **earth** will pass away
	14:35	threw himself on the **ground**
	15:33	came over the whole **land**
Lk	2:14	and on **earth** peace among those
	4:25	severe famine over all the **land**
	5: 3	a little way from the **shore**
	5:11	brought their boats to **shore**
	5:24	has authority on **earth**
	6:49	who built a house on the **ground**
	8: 8	Some fell into good **soil**
	8:15	as for that in the good **soil**
	8:27	As he stepped out on **land**
	10:21	Lord of heaven and **earth**
	11:31	came from the ends of the **earth**
	12:49	came to bring fire to the **earth**
	12:51	to bring peace to the **earth?**
	12:56	the appearance of **earth** and sky
	13: 7	should it be wasting the **soil?**
	14:35	It is fit neither for the **soil**
	16:17	is easier for heaven and **earth**
	18: 8	will he find faith on **earth?**
	21:23	great distress on the **earth**
	21:25	on the **earth** distress among
	21:33	Heaven and **earth** will pass away
	21:35	on the face of the whole **earth**
	22:44	falling down on the **ground**
	23:44	came over the whole **land**
	24: 5	bowed their faces to the **ground**
Jn	3:22	into the Judean **countryside**
	3:31	the one who is of the **earth**
	3:31	belongs to the **earth** and speaks
	3:31	and speaks about **earthly** things
	6:21	the boat reached the **land**
	8: 6	with his finger on the **ground**
	8: 8	and wrote on the **ground**
	12:24	falls into the **earth** and dies
	12:32	I am lifted up from the **earth**
	17: 4	I glorified you on **earth**
	21: 8	they were not far from the **land**

	21: 9	When they had gone **ashore**
	21:11	and hauled the net **ashore**
Ac	1: 8	and to the ends of the **earth**
	2:19	and signs on the **earth** below
	3:25	all the families of the **earth**
	4:24	made the heaven and the **earth**
	4:26	The kings of the **earth**
	7: 3	Leave your **country** and your
	7: 3	and go to the **land** that I
	7: 4	Then he left the **country**
	7: 4	move from there to this **country**
	7: 6	a **country** belonging to others
	7:29	alien in the **land** of Midian
	7:33	you are standing is holy **ground**
	7:36	wonders and signs in **Egypt**
	7:40	out from the **land** of Egypt
	7:49	and the **earth** is my footstool
	8:33	is taken away from the **earth**
	9: 4	He fell to the **ground**
	9: 8	Saul got up from the **ground**
	10:11	being lowered to the **ground**
	10:12	**reptiles** and birds of the air.
	11: 6	I saw four-footed **animals**
	13:17	their stay in the **land** of Egypt
	13:19	nations in the **land** of Canaan
	13:19	their **land** as an inheritance
	13:47	to the ends of the **earth**
	14:15	made the heaven and the **earth**
	17:24	who is Lord of heaven and **earth**
	17:26	to inhabit the whole **earth**
	22:22	such a fellow from the **earth**
	26:14	had all fallen to the **ground**
	27:39	they did not recognize the **land**
	27:43	and make for the **land**
	27:44	all were brought safely to **land**
Ro	9:17	be proclaimed in all the **earth**
	9:28	sentence on the **earth** quickly
	10:18	has gone out to all the **earth**
1C	8: 5	gods in heaven or on **earth**
	10:26	the **earth** and its fullness
	15:47	first man was from the **earth**
Ep	1:10	in heaven and things on **earth**
	3:15	family in heaven and on **earth**
	4: 9	the lower parts of the **earth**
	6: 3	may live long on the **earth**
Co	1:16	in heaven and on **earth**
	1:20	whether on **earth** or in heaven
	3: 2	not on things that are on **earth**
	3: 5	whatever in you is **earthly**

He	1:10	Lord, you founded the **earth**		10: 2	and his left foot on the **land**
	6: 7	**Ground** that drinks up the rain		10: 5	on the sea and the **land** raised
	8: 4	Now if he were on **earth**		10: 6	the **earth** and what is in it
	8: 9	out of the **land** of Egypt		10: 8	on the sea and on the **land**
	11: 9	as in a foreign **land**		11: 4	before the Lord of the **earth**
	11:13	and foreigners on the **earth**		11: 6	to strike the **earth**
	11:29	Red Sea as if it were dry **land**		11:10	inhabitants of the **earth** will
	11:38	caves and holes in the **ground**		11:10	to the inhabitants of the **earth**
	12:25	one who warned them on **earth**		11:18	those who destroy the **earth**
	12:26	his voice shook the **earth**		12: 4	and threw them to the **earth**
	12:26	the **earth** but also the heaven		12: 9	he was thrown down to the **earth**
Ja	5: 5	You have lived on the **earth**		12:12	woe to the **earth** and the sea
	5: 7	precious crop from the **earth**		12:13	been thrown down to the **earth**
	5:12	either by heaven or by **earth**		12:16	But the **earth** came to the help
	5:17	it did not rain on the **earth**		12:16	**it** opened its mouth and
	5:18	the **earth** yielded its harvest		13: 3	whole **earth** followed the beast
2P	3: 5	**earth** was formed out of water		13: 8	the inhabitants of the **earth**
	3: 7	the present heavens and **earth**		13:11	that rose out of the **earth**
	3:10	the **earth** and everything that		13:12	and it makes the **earth** and its
	3:13	for new heavens and a new **earth**		13:13	come down from heaven to **earth**
Ju	1: 5	out of the **land** of Egypt		13:14	the inhabitants of **earth**
Re	1: 5	of the kings of the **earth**		13:14	telling **them** to make an image
	1: 7	all the tribes of the **earth**		14: 3	been redeemed from the **earth**
	3:10	the inhabitants of the **earth**		14: 6	to those who live on the **earth**
	5: 3	no one in heaven or on **earth**		14: 7	him who made heaven and **earth**
	5: 3	on earth or under the **earth**		14:15	the harvest of the **earth**
	5: 6	sent out into all the **earth**		14:16	his sickle over the **earth**
	5:10	and they will reign on **earth**		14:16	and the **earth** was reaped
	5:13	on **earth** and under the earth		14:18	of the vine of the **earth**
	5:13	under the **earth** and in the sea		14:19	swung his sickle over the **earth**
	6: 4	to take peace from the **earth**		14:19	the vintage of the **earth**
	6: 8	over a fourth of the **earth**		16: 1	Go and pour out on the **earth**
	6: 8	the wild animals of the **earth**		16: 2	poured his bowl on the **earth**
	6:10	on the inhabitants of the **earth**		16:18	people were upon the **earth**
	6:13	of the sky fell to the **earth**		17: 2	whom the kings of the **earth**
	6:15	Then the kings of the **earth**		17: 2	the inhabitants of the **earth**
	7: 1	the four corners of the **earth,**		17: 5	and of **earth's** abominations
	7: 1	four winds of the **earth**		17: 8	the inhabitants of the **earth**
	7: 1	no wind could blow on **earth**		17:18	over the kings of the **earth**
	7: 2	power to damage **earth** and sea		18: 1	and the **earth** was made bright
	7: 3	not damage the **earth** or the sea		18: 3	and the kings of the **earth**
	8: 5	had fallen from heaven to **earth**		18: 3	and the merchants of the **earth**
	9: 3	and threw it on the **earth**		18: 9	And the kings of the **earth**
	8: 7	they were hurled to the **earth**		18:11	And the merchants of the **earth**
	8: 7	a third of the **earth** was burned		18:23	were the magnates of the **earth**
	8:13	to the inhabitants of the **earth**		18:24	have been slaughtered on **earth**
	9: 1	came locusts on the **earth**		19: 2	who corrupted the **earth**
	9: 3	of scorpions of the **earth**		19:19	and the kings of the **earth**
	9: 4	damage the grass of the **earth**		20: 8	the four corners of the **earth**

20: 9	over the breadth of the **earth**
20:11	the **earth** and the heaven fled
21: 1	a new heaven and a new **earth**
21: 1	heaven and the first **earth**
21:24	and the kings of the **earth**

1094   GO1 AG157 LN51 R1088
γηρας, OLD AGE
Lk   1:36   Elizabeth in her **old age**

1095   GO2 AG158 LN51 R1094
γηρασκω, I GROW OLD
Jn   21:18   But when you **grow old,** you will
He   8:13   is obsolete and **growing old**

1096   GO666 AG158 LN51 B1:181 K1:681
γινομαι, I BECOME
Mt   1:22   All this **took place** to fulfill
4: 3   these stones to **become** loaves
5:18   until all is **accomplished**
5:45   so that you **may be** children
6:10   Your will **be done,** on earth
6:16   **do** not **look** dismal, like the
7:28   **Now when** Jesus had finished
8:13   **let** it **be** done for you
8:16   **That** evening they brought to
8:24   A windstorm **arose** on the sea,
8:26   and there **was** a dead calm.
9:10   And **as** he sat at dinner in the
9:16   and a worse tear **is** made
9:29   faith **let** it **be** done to you
10:16   so **be** wise as serpents and
10:25   disciple to **be** like the teacher
11: 1   **Now** when Jesus had finished
11:20   deeds of power had **been done**
11:21   the deeds of power **done** in you
11:21   had **been done** in Tyre and Sidon
11:23   had **been done** in Sodom
11:23   the deeds of power **done** in you
11:26   for such **was** your gracious will.
12:45   state of that person **is** worse
13:21   trouble or persecution **arises**
13:22   and it **yields** nothing
13:32   of shrubs and **becomes** a tree
13:53   **When** Jesus had finished these
14: 6   But when Herod's birthday **came**
14:15   When it **was** evening
14:23   When evening **came,** he was
15:28   **Let** it **be** done for you as you
16: 2   When it **is** evening, you say,

17: 2   his clothes **became** dazzling
18: 3   and **become** like children,
18:12   a shepherd **has** a hundred sheep
18:13   And if he **finds** it
18:19   it **will be** done for you
18:31   slaves saw what **had happened**
18:31   all that **had taken place**
19: 1   **When** Jesus had finished saying
19: 8   from the beginning it **was** not
20: 8   When evening **came**
20:26   wishes to **be** great among you
21: 4   This **took place** to fulfill
21:19   no fruit ever **come** from you
21:21   it **will be** done
21:42   **has become** the cornerstone
23:15   **and** you make the new convert
23:26   outside also **may become** clean
24: 6   for this **must take place**
24:20   flight **may** not **be** in winter
24:21   **has** not **been** from the beginning
24:21   no, and never **will be**
24:32   its branch **becomes** tender
24:34   these things **have taken place**
24:44   you also must **be** ready,
25: 6   at midnight there **was** a shout
26: 1   **When** Jesus had finished saying
26: 2   the Passover **is** coming,
26: 5   or there **may be** a riot among
26: 6   Now while Jesus **was** at Bethany
26:20   When it **was** evening,
26:42   your **will be** done
26:54   it **must happen** in this way?
26:56   But all this **has taken place,**
27: 1   When morning **came,**
27:24   that a riot **was** beginning,
27:45   darkness **came** over the whole
27:54   earthquake and what **took place,**
27:57   When it **was** evening,
28: 2   there **was** a great earthquake;
28: 4   shook and **became** like dead men.
28:11   everything that **had happened.**
Mk   1: 4   John the baptizer **appeared** in
1: 9   **In** those days Jesus came from
1:11   And a voice **came** from heaven,
1:17   will make you **fish** for people
1:32   **That** evening, at sundown,
2:15   And **as** he sat at dinner in
2:21   and a worse tear **is** made.

2:23	**One** sabbath he was going	1: 5	**was** a priest named Zechariah
2:27	The sabbath **was** made for	1: 8	**Once** when he was serving as
4: 4	**And** as he sowed,	1:20	the day these things **occur**
4:10	When he **was** alone,	1:23	**When** his time of service was
4:11	everything **comes** in parables;	1:38	**let it be** with me according to
4:17	trouble or persecution **arises**	1:41	**When** Elizabeth heard Mary's
4:19	and it **yields** nothing.	1:44	as **soon** as I heard the sound
4:22	For there **is** nothing hidden,	1:59	**On** the eighth day they came to
4:32	it grows up and **becomes**	1:65	**came** over all their neighbors
4:35	when evening had **come,**	2: 1	**In** those days a decree went out
4:37	A great windstorm **arose,**	2: 2	**was taken** while Quirinius was
4:39	and there **was** a dead calm.	2: 6	**While** they were there
5:14	what it **was** that had happened.	2:13	there **was** with the angel
5:16	what had **happened** to the	2:15	**When** the angels had left them
5:33	what **had happened** to her,	2:15	this thing that has **taken place**
6: 2	**On** the sabbath he began to	2:42	when he **was** twelve years old
6: 2	deeds of power **are being** done	2:46	**After** three days they found him
6:14	Jesus' name **had become** known.	3: 2	the word of God **came** to John
6:21	But an opportunity **came** when	3:21	**Now** when all the people were
6:26	The king **was** deeply grieved	3:22	And a voice **came** from heaven
6:35	When it **grew** late	4: 3	to **become** a loaf of bread
6:47	When evening **came**	4:23	things that we have heard you **did**
9: 3	clothes **became** dazzling white	4:25	there **was** a severe famine
9: 6	for they **were** terrified.	4:36	They **were** all amazed
9: 7	**Then** a cloud overshadowed them	4:42	**At** daybreak he departed
9: 7	there **came** a voice	5: 1	**Once** while Jesus was standing
9:21	has this **been happening** to him	5:12	**Once,** when he was in one of the
9:26	and the boy **was** like a corpse	5:17	**One** day, while he was teaching
9:33	and when he **was** in the house	6: 1	**One** sabbath
9:50	if salt **has lost** its saltiness	6: 6	**On** another sabbath
10:43	whoever wishes to **become** great	6:12	**Now** during those days
11:19	And when evening **came**	6:13	And when day **came**
11:23	what you say **will come to pass**	6:16	who **became** a traitor
12:10	has **become** the cornerstone	6:36	**Be** merciful
12:11	this **was** the Lord's doing	6:48	when a flood **arose**
13: 7	this must **take place**	6:49	great **was** the ruin
13:18	that it **may** not **be** in winter	7:11	**Soon** afterwards
13:19	**has** not **been** from the beginning	8: 1	**Soon** afterwards
13:19	and never **will be.**	8:17	that **will** not **be** disclosed
13:28	as its branch **becomes** tender	8:22	**One** day he got into a boat
13:29	see these things **taking place**	8:24	there **was** a calm
13:30	these things **have taken place**	8:34	saw what **had happened**
14: 4	Why **was** the ointment wasted	8:35	to see what **had happened**
14:17	When it **was** evening	8:56	tell no one what **had happened**
15:33	When it **was** noon	9: 7	all that had **taken place**
15:33	darkness **came** over the whole	9:18	**Once** when Jesus was praying
15:42	When evening **had come**	9:28	**Now** about eight days after
16:10	those who **had been** with him	9:29	And **while** he was praying
Lk 1: 2	**were** eyewitnesses and servants	9:33	**Just as** they were leaving him

9:34	**came** and overshadowed them		21:28	things begin to **take place**
9:35	**came** a voice that said		21:31	these things **taking place**
9:36	**When** the voice had spoken		21:32	all things have **taken place**
9:37	**On** the next day		21:36	things that will **take place**
9:51	**When** the days drew near		22:14	When the hour **came**
10:13	**done** in you had been done		22:24	A dispute also **arose** among them
10:13	done in you had been **done**		22:26	must **become** like the youngest
10:21	such **was** your gracious will		22:40	**When** he reached the place
10:32	**So** likewise a Levite		22:42	not my will but yours **be done**
10:36	**was** a neighbor to the man		22:44	**In** his anguish he prayed
11: 1	**He** was praying		22:44	sweat **became** like great drops
11:14	**Now** he was casting out a demon		22:66	When day **came**
11:26	**is** worse than the first		23: 8	to see him **perform** some sign
11:27	**While** he was saying this		23:12	**became** friends with each other
11:30	just as Jonah **became** a sign		23:19	had **taken place** in the city
12:40	You also must **be** ready		23:24	their demand should **be granted**
12:54	and so it **happens**		23:31	**will happen** when it is dry
12:55	and it **happens**		23:44	**came** over the whole land
13: 2	they **were** worse sinners		23:47	saw what had **taken place**
13: 4	that they **were** worse offenders		23:48	saw what had **taken place**
13:17	things that he **was doing**		24: 4	**While** they were perplexed
13:19	it grew and **became** a tree		24: 5	The women **were** terrified
14: 1	**On one occasion** when Jesus		24:12	he went home, amazed at what **had**
14:12	and you **would be** repaid			**happened.**
14:22	what you ordered **has been**		24:15	**While** they were talking
	done		24:18	things that have **taken place**
15:10	there **is** joy in the presence		24:19	**was** a prophet mighty in deed
15:14	a severe famine **took place**		24:21	since these things **took place.**
16:11	you **have** not **been** faithful		24:22	They **were** at the tomb
16:12	if you **have** not **been** faithful		24:30	**When** he was at the table
16:22	[So] the poor man died		24:31	he **vanished** from their sight
17:11	**On** the way to Jerusalem		24:37	They **were** startled
17:14	And **as** they went		24:51	**While** he was blessing them
17:26	Just as it **was**	Jn	1: 3	All things **came** into **being**
17:28	as it **was** in the days of Lot,		1: 3	not one thing **came** into **being**
18:23	he heard this, he **became** sad		1: 3	What has **come** into **being**
18:35	**As** he approached Jericho		1: 6	There **was** a man sent from God
19: 9	salvation **has come**		1:10	world **came** into **being**
19:15	**When** he returned		1:12	to **become** children of God
19:17	**take** charge of ten cities		1:14	the Word **became** flesh
19:19	**rule** over five cities		1:15	because he **was** before me
19:29	**When** he had come near		1:17	truth **came** through Jesus Christ
	Bethphage		1:28	This **took place** in Bethany
20: 1	One day, **as** he **was** teaching		1:30	because he **was** before me
20:14	the inheritance **may be** ours		2: 1	there **was** a wedding in Cana
20:16	they said, "Heaven **forbid**		2: 9	water that **had become** wine
20:17	has **become** the cornerstone		3: 9	How can these things **be?**
20:33	whose wife will the woman **be?**		3:25	**arose** between John's disciples
21: 7	this is about to **take place?**		4:14	**will become** in them a spring
21: 9	things must **take place** first		5: 6	Do you want to **be made** well?

5: 9	At once the man **was made** well		4:28	had predestined to **take place.**
5:14	See, you **have been made** well!		4:30	**are performed** through the name
5:14	nothing worse **happens** to you		5: 5	fear **seized** all who heard of it
6:16	When evening **came**		5: 7	**After** an interval of about
6:17	It **was** now dark		5: 7	not knowing what **had happened.**
6:19	and **coming** near the boat		5:11	fear **seized** the whole church
6:21	the boat **reached** the land		5:12	wonders **were done**
6:25	when did you **come** here		5:24	what **might be** going on.
7:43	there **was** a division		5:36	followed him **were dispersed**
8:33	You will **be made** free		6: 1	**complained** against the Hebrews
8:58	before Abraham **was,** I am		7:13	family **became** known to
9:22	**be put** out of the synagogue			Pharaoh.
9:27	want to **become** his disciples		7:29	**became** a resident alien
9:39	who do see may **become** blind		7:31	**came** the voice of the Lord:
10:16	there **will be** one flock		7:32	Moses **began** to tremble
10:19	Again the Jews **were** divided		7:38	who **was** in the congregation
10:22	**took place** in Jerusalem.		7:39	**were** unwilling to obey him;
10:35	to whom the word of God **came**		7:40	know what **has happened** to him.
12:29	said that it **was** thunder		7:52	you have **become** his betrayers
12:30	This voice **has come** for your		8: 1	**began** against the church
12:36	**may become** children of light.		8: 8	So there **was** great joy
12:42	**be put** out of the synagogue;		8:13	great miracles that **took place.**
13: 2	And **during** supper		9: 3	**Now** as he was going along
13:19	before it **occurs,**		9:19	he **was** with the disciples
13:19	so that when it does **occur,**		9:32	**Now as** Peter went here
14:22	Lord, how **is** it that you will		9:37	**At** that time she became ill
14:29	told you this before it **occurs,**		9:42	**became** known throughout
14:29	so that when it does **occur,**			Joppa,
15: 7	and it **will be** done for you.		9:43	**Meanwhile** he stayed in Joppa
15: 8	and **become** my disciples.		10: 4	He stared at him **in** terror
16:20	your pain **will turn** into joy.		10:10	He **became** hungry and wanted
19:36	These things **occurred** so that		10:10	he **fell** into a trance.
20:27	**Do** not doubt but believe.		10:13	Then he **heard** a voice saying,
21: 4	**Just** after daybreak,		10:16	This **happened** three times,
Ac 1:16	who **became** a guide for those		10:25	**On** Peter's arrival
1:18	and **falling** headlong,		10:37	message **spread** throughout Judea
1:19	This **became** known to all		10:40	and allowed him **to** appear,
1:20	**Let** his homestead **become**		11:10	This **happened** three times;
1:22	must **become** a witness with us		11:19	persecution that **took place**
2: 2	there **came** a sound		11:26	it **was** that for an entire year
2: 6	**And at** this sound		11:28	**took place** during the reign
2:43	Awe **came** upon everyone,		12: 5	**prayed** fervently to God
2:43	**were being** done		12: 9	realize that what **was happening**
4: 4	**numbered** about five thousand.		12:11	Then Peter **came** to himself
4: 5	[So] the next day their rulers,		12:18	**When** morning came,
4:11	it **has become** the cornerstone.		12:18	over what **had become** of Peter.
4:16	**has been** done through them;		12:23	he **was eaten** by worms and died.
4:21	for what **had happened.**		13: 5	**When** they arrived at Salamis,
4:22	healing **had been performed**		13:12	proconsul saw what **had happened**
			13:32	God **promised** to our ancestors

14: 1	same thing **occurred** in Iconium	
14: 3	wonders **to be** done through them.	
14: 5	And when an attempt **was** made	
15: 2	And **after** Paul and Barnabas	
15: 7	there **had been** much debate,	
15:25	we have **decided** unanimously	
15:39	disagreement **became** so sharp	
16:16	**One day,** as we were going	
16:26	there **was** an earthquake,	
16:27	**When** the jailer woke up	
16:29	he **fell down** trembling	
16:35	When morning **came,**	
19: 1	While Apollos **was** in Corinth,	
19:10	This **continued** for two years,	
19:17	**became** known to all residents	
19:21	things **had been accomplished,**	
19:23	**broke** out concerning the Way.	
19:26	made with hands **are** not gods.	
19:28	they **were** enraged and shouted,	
19:34	all of them **shouted** in unison,	
20: 3	a plot **was** made against him	
20: 3	he **decided** to return through	
20:16	he **might** not have to spend time	
20:16	he was eager to **be** in Jerusalem,	
20:18	know how I **lived** among you	
20:37	There **was** much weeping among	
21: 1	**When** we had parted from them	
21: 5	When our days there **were** ended,	
21:14	The Lord's **will be** done.	
21:17	When we **arrived** in Jerusalem,	
21:30	and the people **rushed** together.	
21:35	When Paul **came** to the steps,	
21:40	and when there **was** a great hush	
22: 6	While I **was** on my way	
22:17	**After** I had returned	
22:17	I **fell** into a trance	
23: 7	**began** between the Pharisees	
23: 9	Then a great clamor **arose,**	
23:10	the dissension **became** violent,	
23:12	**In** the morning the Jews joined	
24: 2	reforms **have been** made	
24:25	Felix **became** frightened	
25:15	When I **was** in Jerusalem,	
25:26	I may have **something** to write	
26: 4	life **spent** from the beginning	
26: 6	in the promise **made** by God	
26:19	I **was** not disobedient	
26:22	Moses said would **take place:**	
26:29	might **become** such as I am	

27: 7	**arrived** with difficulty	
27:16	we were scarcely **able** to get	
27:27	as we **were** drifting	
27:29	and prayed for day **to come.**	
27:33	**Just** before daybreak,	
27:36	all of them **were** encouraged	
27:39	**In** the morning	
27:42	The soldiers' plan **was** to kill	
27:44	so it **was** that all were brought	
28: 6	nothing unusual **had happened**	
28: 8	It so **happened** that the father	
28: 9	After this **happened,** the rest	
28:17	Three days **later** he called	
Ro 1: 3	who was **descended** from David	
2:25	your circumcision **has become**	
3: 4	**By no means!** Although everyone	
3: 4	**let** God **be** proved true,	
3: 6	**By no means!** For then how	
3:19	the whole world **may be** held	
4:18	believed that he would **become**	
6: 2	**By no means!** How can we who	
6: 5	if we **have been** united with	
6:15	but under grace? **By no means!**	
7: 3	if she **lives with** another	
7: 3	if she **marries** another man,	
7: 4	so that you **may belong** to	
7: 7	law is sin? **By no means!**	
7:13	good, then, **bring** death to me?	
7:13	bring death to me? **By no means!**	
7:13	sin **might be** shown to be sin,	
9:14	on God's part? **By no means!**	
9:29	would **have fared** like Sodom	
10:20	I **have shown** myself to those	
11: 1	his people? **By no means!**	
11: 5	there **is** a remnant, chosen by	
11: 6	grace **would** no longer **be** grace	
11: 9	**Let** their table **become** a snare	
11:11	so as to fall? **By no means!**	
11:17	**were** grafted in their place	
11:25	a hardening **has come** upon part	
11:34	Or who **has been** his counselor?	
12:16	claim to be wiser than you **are**	
15: 8	Christ **has become** a servant	
15:16	**may be** acceptable, sanctified	
15:31	**may be** acceptable to the saints	
16: 2	for she **has been** a benefactor	
16: 7	they **were** in Christ	
1C 1:30	**became** for us wisdom from God,	

2: 3	And I **came** to you in weakness	
3:13	of each builder **will become**	
3:18	you **should become** fools	
3:18	so that you **may become** wise.	
4: 5	**will receive** commendation	
4: 9	we have **become** a spectacle	
4:13	We **have become** like the rubbish	
4:16	**be** imitators of me.	
6:15	of a prostitute? **Never!**	
7:21	if you **can gain** your freedom,	
7:23	**do** not **become** slaves of human	
7:36	so it has **to be,** let him marry	
8: 9	**become** a stumbling block	
9:15	they **may be** applied in my case.	
9:20	To the Jews I **became** as a Jew,	
9:22	To the weak I **became** weak,	
9:22	I have **become** all things	
9:23	I **may share** in its blessings.	
9:27	**should** not **be** disqualified.	
10: 6	Now these things **occurred**	
10: 7	Do not **become** idolaters as some	
10:20	you **to be** partners with demons.	
10:32	**Give** no offense to Jews or to	
11: 1	**Be** imitators of me, as I am	
11:19	**become** clear who among you	
13: 1	I **am** a noisy gong or a clanging	
13:11	when I **became** an adult,	
14:20	**do** not **be** children in your	
14:20	but in thinking **be** adults.	
14:25	heart **are** disclosed,	
14:26	**Let** all things **be** done	
14:40	should **be** done decently	
15:10	**has** not **been** in vain.	
15:37	the body that **is to be,**	
15:45	Adam, **became** a living being";	
15:54	is written **will be** fulfilled:	
15:58	**be** steadfast, immovable, always	
16: 2	not **be taken** when I come.	
16:10	**has** nothing to fear among you,	
16:14	**Let** all that you do **be** done	

2C	1: 8	the affliction we **experienced**
	1:19	**was** not "Yes and No"; but in
	1:19	but in him it **is** always "Yes."
	3: 7	**came** in glory so that the
	5:17	everything **has become** new!
	5:21	**might become** the righteousness
	6:14	**Do** not **be** mismatched
	7:14	**has proved** true as well.
	8:14	abundance **may be** for your need,

	8:14	there **may be** a fair balance.
	12:11	I **have been** a fool!
Ga	2:17	servant of sin? **Certainly** not!
	3:13	**becoming** a curse for us
	3:14	**might come** to the Gentiles,
	3:17	**came** four hundred thirty years
	3:21	promises of God? **Certainly** not!
	3:24	until Christ **came,** so that we
	4: 4	his Son, **born** of a woman,
	4: 4	**born** under the law,
	4:12	I beg you, **become** as I am,
	4:16	Have I now **become** your enemy
	5:26	**Let** us not **become** conceited,
	6:14	**May** I never boast of anything
Ep	2:13	**have been** brought near by the
	3: 7	I **have become** a servant
	4:32	and **be** kind to one another,
	5: 1	Therefore **be** imitators of God,
	5:12	it **is** shameful even to mention
	5:17	So **do** not **be** foolish,
	6: 3	it **may be** well with you
Ph	1:13	it **has become** known throughout
	2: 7	And **being** found in human form,
	2: 8	**became** obedient to the point
	2:15	so that you **may be** blameless
	3: 6	under the law, **blameless.**
	3:17	**join** in imitating me,
Co	1:18	so that he **might come**
	1:23	**became** a servant of this gospel
	1:25	I **became** its servant according
	3:15	And **be** thankful.
	4:11	**have been** a comfort to me.
1Th	1: 5	**came** to you not in word only,
	1: 5	**to be** among you for your sake.
	1: 6	you **became** imitators of us
	1: 7	so that you **became** an example
	2: 1	coming to you **was** not in vain,
	2: 5	**came** with words of flattery
	2: 7	But we **were** gentle among you,
	2: 8	you **have become** very dear
	2:10	blameless our conduct **was**
	2:14	**became** imitators . . . churches
	3: 4	so **it turned out,** as you know.
	3: 5	our labor **had been** in vain.
2Th	2: 7	who now restrains it **is** removed
1Ti	2:14	and **became** a transgressor.
	4:12	**set** the believers an example
	5: 9	she **is** not less than sixty
	6: 4	From these **come** envy,

2Ti	1:17	when he **arrived** in Rome,
	2:18	resurrection has ... **taken place**
	3: 9	**in the case** of those two men,
	3:11	the things that **happened** to me
Ti	3: 7	we **might become** heirs according
Pm	1: 6	your faith **may become** effective
He	1: 4	**having become** as much superior
	2: 2	through angels **was** valid,
	2:17	so that he **might be** a merciful
	3:14	**have become** partners of Christ,
	4: 3	though his works **were** finished
	5: 5	glorify himself in **becoming**
	5: 9	he **became** the source of eternal
	5:11	since you **have become** dull
	5:12	You **need** milk, not solid food;
	6: 4	**have** shared in the Holy Spirit,
	6:12	you **may** not **become** sluggish,
	6:20	**having become** a high priest
	7:12	there **is** necessarily a change
	7:16	one who **has become** a priest,
	7:18	There **is**, on the one hand,
	7:20	**took** their office without an
	7:22	**has** also **become** the guarantee
	7:23	the former priests **were** many
	7:26	and exalted **above** the heavens.
	9:11	the good things that **have come,**
	9:15	**has occurred** that redeems them
	9:22	there **is** no forgiveness of sins
	10:33	and sometimes **being** partners
	11: 3	things that **are** not visible.
	11: 6	he **rewards** those who seek him.
	11: 7	**became** an heir
	11:24	when he **was** grown up,
	11:34	**became** mighty in war,
	12: 8	in which all children **share,**
Ja	1:12	Such a one **has** stood the test
	1:22	But **be** doers of the word,
	1:25	**being** not hearers who forget
	2: 4	**become** judges with evil
	2:10	point **has become** accountable
	2:11	you **have become** a transgressor
	3: 1	**should become** teachers,
	3: 9	**are** made in the likeness of God
	3:10	this ought not **to be** so.
	5: 2	your clothes **are** moth-eaten.
1P	1:15	**be** holy yourselves in all your
	2: 7	**has become** the very head of the
	3: 6	You **have become** her daughters
	3:13	**are** eager to do what is good?

	4:12	**taking place** among you to test
	5: 3	but **be** examples to the flock.
2P	1: 4	**may become** participants of the
	1:16	we **had been** eyewitnesses
	1:20	scripture **is** a matter of one's
	2: 1	**will be** false teachers among
	2:20	**has become** worse for them
1J	2:18	many antichrists **have come.**
2J	1:12	I hope **to come** to you and talk
3J	1: 8	we **may become** co-workers
Re	1: 1	what must soon **take place;**
	1: 9	**was** on the island called Patmos
	1:10	I **was** in the spirit,
	1:18	I **was** dead, and see, I am alive
	1:19	to **take place** after this.
	2: 8	who **was** dead and came to life:
	2:10	**Be** faithful until death,
	3: 2	**Wake** up, and strengthen
	4: 1	what must **take place** after this
	4: 2	At once I **was** in the spirit,
	6:12	there **came** a great earthquake;
	6:12	sun **became** black as sackcloth,
	6:12	full moon **became** like blood,
	8: 1	there **was** silence in heaven
	8: 5	there **were** peals of thunder,
	8: 7	there **came** hail and fire,
	8: 9	A third of the sea **became** blood,
	8:11	the waters **became** wormwood,
	11:13	there **was** a great earthquake,
	11:13	the rest **were** terrified
	11:15	**were** loud voices in heaven,
	11:15	world **has become** the kingdom
	11:19	there **were** flashes of lightning,
	12: 7	And war **broke out** in heaven;
	12:10	Now have **come** the salvation
	16: 2	painful sore **came** on those
	16: 3	**became** like the blood,
	16: 4	and they **became** blood.
	16:10	**was plunged** into darkness;
	16:17	It **is done!**
	16:18	**came** flashes of lightning,
	16:18	such as had not **occurred** since
	16:18	people **were** upon the earth,
	16:19	**was** split into three parts,
	18: 2	It **has become** a dwelling place
	21: 6	he said to me, "It **is done!**
	22: 6	what must soon **take place**

1097   GO222   AG160   LN51   B2:390   K1:689

γινωσκω, I KNOW

Mt	1:25	no **marital relations** with her
	6: 3	**know** what your right hand
	7:23	I never **knew** you; go away
	9:30	See that no one **knows** of this
	10:26	that will not become **known.**
	12: 7	you had **known** what this means,
	12:15	When Jesus became **aware** of this,
	12:33	tree is **known** by its fruit.
	13:11	**know** the secrets of the kingdom
	16: 3	You **know** how to interpret
	16: 8	And becoming **aware** of it,
	21:45	**realized** that he was speaking
	22:18	Jesus, **aware** of their malice,
	24:32	you **know** that summer is near.
	24:33	you **know** that he is near,
	24:39	and they **knew** nothing
	24:43	owner of the house had **known**
	24:50	an hour that he does not **know.**
	25:24	I **knew** that you were a harsh
	26:10	But Jesus, **aware** of this,
Mk	4:13	Then how will you **understand**
	5:29	she **felt** in her body that she
	5:43	that no one should **know** this,
	6:38	When they **had found out,**
	7:24	want anyone to **know** he was
	8:17	And **becoming aware** of it,
	9:30	He did not want anyone to **know**
	12:12	When they **realized** that he had
	13:28	you **know** that summer is near.
	13:29	you **know** that he is near,
	15:10	For he **realized** that it was
	15:45	**learned** from the centurion
Lk	1:18	How will I **know** that this is so
	1:34	since I am a **virgin?**
	2:43	but his parents did not **know** it
	6:44	tree is **known** by its own fruit.
	7:39	he would have **known** who
	8:10	it has been given to **know**
	8:17	that will not become **known**
	8:46	I **noticed** that power had gone
	9:11	the crowds **found out** about it,
	10:11	Yet **know** this: the kingdom of
	10:22	no one **knows** who the Son is
	12: 2	that will not become **known.**
	12:39	But **know** this: if the owner
	12:46	an hour that he does not **know**
	12:47	**knew** what his master wanted,

	12:48	But the one who did not **know**
	16: 4	I have **decided** what to do
	16:15	but God **knows** your hearts
	18:34	did not **grasp** what was said.
	19:15	**find out** what they had gained
	19:42	**had** only **recognized** on this day
	19:44	you did not **recognize** the time
	20:19	**realized** that he had told this
	21:20	then **know** that its desolation
	21:30	see for yourselves and **know**
	21:31	**know** that the kingdom of God
	24:18	who does not **know** the things
	24:35	how he had been made **known**
Jn	1:10	yet the world did not **know** him
	1:48	Where did you get to **know** me?
	2:24	because he **knew** all people
	2:25	**knew** what was in everyone.
	3:10	do not **understand** these things?
	4: 1	Now when Jesus **learned** that the
	4:53	The father **realized** that this
	5: 6	and **knew** that he had been there
	5:42	I **know** that you do not have
	6:15	When Jesus **realized** that they
	6:69	have come to believe and **know**
	7:17	**know** whether the teaching is
	7:26	the authorities really **know**
	7:27	no one will **know** where he is
	7:49	does not **know** the law
	7:51	to **find out** what they are doing
	8:27	**understand** that he was speaking
	8:28	you will **realize** that I am he,
	8:32	and you will **know** the truth,
	8:43	you not **understand** what I say?
	8:52	we **know** that you have a demon.
	8:55	though you do not **know** him.
	10: 6	but they did not **understand**
	10:14	I **know** my own and my own know
	10:14	my own and my own **know** me,
	10:15	just as the Father **knows** me
	10:15	knows me and I **know** the Father
	10:27	I **know** them, and they follow me
	10:38	so that you may **know**
	10:38	you may know and **understand**
	11:57	should let them **know,** so that
	12: 9	Jews **learned** that he was there,
	12:16	disciples did not **understand**
	13: 7	You do not **know** now what I am
	13:12	**know** what I have done to you?
	13:28	Now no one at the table **knew**

	13:35	everyone will **know** that you
	14: 7	If you **know** me, you will know
	14: 7	you will **know** my Father also.
	14: 7	From now on you do **know** him
	14: 9	and you still do not **know** me?
	14:17	neither sees him nor **knows** him.
	14:17	You **know** him, because he
	14:20	**know** that I am in my Father,
	14:31	the world may **know** that I love
	15:18	be **aware** that it hated me
	16: 3	have not **known** the Father or me
	16:19	**knew** that they wanted to ask
	17: 3	that they may **know** you
	17: 7	Now they **know** that everything
	17: 8	received them and **know** in truth
	17:23	**know** that you have sent me
	17:25	the world does not **know** you,
	17:25	but I **know** you;
	17:25	**know** that you have sent me.
	19: 4	out to you to let you **know**
	21:17	Lord, you **know** everything;
Ac	1: 7	It is not for you to **know**
	2:36	**know** with certainty that God
	8:30	**understand** what you are reading
	9:24	their plot became **known** to Saul
	17:13	Jews of Thessalonica **learned**
	17:19	May we **know** what this new
	17:20	like to **know** what it means.
	19:15	Jesus I **know,** and Paul I know
	19:35	who is there that does not **know**
	20:34	You **know** for yourselves
	21:24	Thus all will **know** that there
	21:34	could not **learn** the facts
	21:37	Do you **know** Greek?
	22:14	chosen you to **know** his will,
	22:30	Since he wanted to **find out**
	23: 6	When Paul **noticed** that some
Ro	1:21	for though they **knew** God,
	2:18	**know** his will and determine
	3:17	peace they have not **known**
	6: 6	We **know** that our old self
	7: 1	speaking to those who **know**
	7: 7	I would not have **known** sin.
	7:15	not **understand** my own actions
	10:19	did Israel not **understand?**
	11:34	**known** the mind of the Lord?
1C	1:21	the world did not **know** God
	2: 8	rulers of this age **understood**
	2: 8	for if they **had,** they would

	2:11	**knows** what is truly human
	2:14	they are unable to **understand**
	2:16	**known** the mind of the Lord
	3:20	The Lord **knows** the thoughts
	4:19	I will **find out** not the talk
	8: 2	who claims to **know** something
	8: 2	to know something **does** not yet
	8: 2	have the necessary **knowledge;**
	8: 3	who loves God is **known** by him.
	13: 9	For we **know** only in part,
	13:12	Now I **know** only in part;
	14: 7	**know** what is being played?
	14: 9	**know** what is being said?
2C	2: 4	**know** the abundant love
	2: 9	**know** whether you are obedient
	3: 2	to be **known** and read by all;
	5:16	**knew** Christ from a human point
	5:16	**know** him no longer in that way.
	5:21	to be sin who **knew** no sin,
	8: 9	you **know** the generous act
	13: 6	I hope you will **find** out
Ga	3: 7	so, you **see,** those who believe
	4: 9	you have come to **know** God,
	4: 9	rather to be **known** by God,
Ep	3:19	to **know** the love of Christ
	5: 5	Be **sure** of this, that no
	6:22	to let you **know** how we are,
Ph	1:12	I want you to **know,** beloved,
	2:19	may be cheered by **news** of you
	2:22	But Timothy's worth you **know,**
	3:10	to **know** Christ and the power
	4: 5	Let your gentleness be **known**
Co	4: 8	that you may **know** how we are
1Th	3: 5	to **find out** about your faith;
2Ti	1:18	**know** very well how much service
	2:19	Lord **knows** those who are his
	3: 1	You must **understand** this,
He	3:10	they have not **known** my ways
	8:11	'Know the Lord,' for they shall
	10:34	**knowing** that you yourselves
	13:23	**know** that our brother Timothy
Ja	1: 3	you **know** that the testing
	2:20	Do you want to be **shown,**
	5:20	**know** that whoever brings back
2P	1:20	you must **understand** this,
	3: 3	you must **understand** this,
1J	2: 3	Now by this we may **be sure**
	2: 3	may be sure that we **know** him,
	2: 4	I have come to **know** him,

2: 5	may be **sure** that we are in him:
2:13	because you **know** him who is
2:14	because you **know** the Father.
2:14	because you **know** him who is
2:18	**know** that it is the last hour.
2:29	**know** that he is righteous,
3: 1	the world does not **know** us
3: 1	that it did not **know** him.
3: 6	has either seen him or **known** him.
3:16	We **know** love by this, that he
3:19	we will **know** that we are from
3:20	and he **knows** everything.
3:24	we **know** that he abides in us,
4: 2	you **know** the Spirit of God:
4: 6	Whoever **knows** God listens to us
4: 6	we **know** the spirit of truth
4: 7	is born of God and **knows** God.
4: 8	does not love does not **know** God
4:13	we **know** that we abide in him
4:16	have **known** and believe the love
5: 2	By this we **know** that we love
5:20	we **know** that the Son of God

2J 1: 1 also all who **know** the truth,
Re 2:23 all the churches will **know**
2:24 have not **learned** what some call
3. 3 you will not **know** at what hour
3: 9 **learn** that I have loved you.

1098   GO1 AG162 LN52 R1099
γλευκος, SWEET WINE
Ac   2:13   They are filled with **new wine**

1099   GO4 AG162 LN52
γλυκυς, SWEET
Ja   3:11   both **fresh** and brackish water?
3:12   can salt water yield **fresh.**
Re 10: 9   **sweet** as honey in your mouth,
10:10   **sweet** as honey in my mouth,

1100   GO49 AG162 LN52 B3:1078 K1:719
γλωσσα, TONGUE
Mk   7:33   he spat and touched his **tongue.**
7:35   his **tongue** was released,
16:17   they will speak in new **tongues;**
Lk   1:64   in water and cool my **tongue;**
Ac   2: 3   Divided **tongues,** as of fire,
2: 4   to speak in other **languages,**
2:11   in our own **languages** we hear
2:26   and my **tongue** rejoiced;
10:46   heard them speaking in **tongues**

	19: 6	they spoke in **tongues**
Ro	3:13	use their **tongues** to deceive
	14:11	every **tongue** shall give praise
1C	12:10	various kinds of **tongues,**
	12:10	the interpretation of **tongues.**
	12:28	various kinds of **tongues.**
	12:30	Do all speak in **tongues?**
	13: 1	speak in the **tongues** of mortals
	13: 8	as for **tongues,** they will cease
	14: 2	For those who speak in a **tongue**
	14: 4	Those who speak in a **tongue**
	14: 5	all of you to speak in **tongues,**
	14: 5	than one who speaks in **tongues,**
	14: 6	come to you speaking in **tongues**
	14: 9	if in a **tongue** you utter speech
	14:13	one who speaks in a **tongue**
	14:14	For if I pray in a **tongue,**
	14:18	that I speak in **tongues** more
	14:19	ten thousand words in a **tongue.**
	14:22	**Tongues,** then, are a sign
	14:23	and all speak in **tongues,**
	14:26	lesson, a revelation, a **tongue,**
	14:27	If anyone speaks in a **tongue,**
	14:39	not forbid speaking in **tongues;**
Ph	2:11	and every **tongue** should confess
Ja	1:26	do not bridle their **tongues**
	3: 5	the **tongue** is a small member,
	3: 6	And the **tongue** is a fire.
	3: 8	but no one can tame the **tongue**
1P	3:10	keep their **tongues** from evil
1J	3:18	not in word or **speech,**
Re	5: 9	from every tribe and **language**
	7: 9	and peoples and **languages,**
	10:11	and nations and **languages**
	11: 9	and tribes and **languages**
	13: 7	and people and **language**
	14: 6	tribe and **language** and people.
	16:10	gnawed their **tongues** in agony,
	17:15	and nations and **languages.**

1101   GO2 AG162 LN52 B1:142
γλωσσοκομον, TREASURE BOX
Jn 12: 6   he kept the **common purse**
13:29   Judas had the **common purse,**

1102   GO1 AG162 LN52
γναφευς, WOOL CLEANER
Mk   9: 3   no **one** on earth **could bleach**

1103   GO4 AG162 LN52 K1:727
γνησιος, LEGITIMATE
2C	8: 8	I am testing the **genuineness**
Ph	4: 3	ask you also, my **loyal**
1Ti	1: 2	my **loyal** child in the faith:
Ti	1: 4	my **loyal** child in the faith

1104   GO1 AG163 LN52 R1103
γνησιως, LEGITIMATELY
| Ph | 2:20 | will be **genuinely** concerned for |

1105   GO1 AG163 LN52
γνοφος, DARK
| He | 12:18 | and **darkness,** and gloom, |

1106   GO9 AG163 LN52 B2:397 K1:717
γνωμη, PURPOSE
Ac	20: 3	so he **decided** to return through
1C	1:10	same mind and the same **purpose.**
	7:25	but I give my **opinion** as one
	7:40	But in my **judgment** she is more
2C	8:10	I am giving my **advice:**
Pm	1:14	do nothing without your **consent**
Re	17:13	These are **united** in yielding
	17:17	to carry out his **purpose**
	17:17	**agreeing** to give their kingdom

1107   GO25 AG163 LN52 B3:314 K1:718 R1097
γνωριζω, I MAKE KNOWN
Lk	2:15	the Lord has **made known** to us.
	2:17	**made known** what had been told
Jn	15:15	**made known** to you everything
	17:26	I **made** your name **known** to them,
	17:26	I will **make** it **known,**
Ac	2:28	You have **made known** to me
Ro	9:22	and to **make known** his power,
	9:23	to **make known** the riches of his
	16:26	**made known** to all the Gentiles,
1C	12: 3	I want you to **understand**
	15: 1	Now I **would remind** you,
2C	8: 1	We **want** you **to know,**
Ga	1:11	For I **want** you **to know,**
Ep	1: 9	**made known** to us the mystery
	3: 3	how the mystery was **made known**
	3: 5	mystery was not **made known**
	3:10	be **made known** to the rulers
	6:19	to **make known** with boldness
	6:21	**will tell** you everything.
Ph	1:22	I **do** not **know** which I prefer
	4: 6	let your requests be **made known**

Co	1:27	To them God chose to **make known**
	4: 7	Tychicus **will tell** you all the
	4: 9	**will tell** you about everything
2P	1:16	we **made known** to you the power

1108   GO29 AG163 LN52 B2:392 K1:689 R1097
γνωσις, KNOWLEDGE
Lk	1:77	to give **knowledge** of salvation
	11:52	taken away the key of **knowledge;**
Ro	2:20	the embodiment of **knowledge**
	11:33	wisdom and **knowledge** of God!
	15:14	filled with all **knowledge,**
1C	1: 5	and **knowledge** of every kind
	8: 1	all of us possess **knowledge.**
	8: 1	**Knowledge** puffs up, but love
	8: 7	who has this **knowledge.**
	8:10	who possess **knowledge,**
	8:11	So by your **knowledge**
	12: 8	the utterance of **knowledge**
	13: 2	mysteries and all **knowledge,**
	13: 8	as for **knowledge,** it will come
	14: 6	that comes from **knowing** him
2C	4: 6	**knowledge** of the glory of God
	6: 6	by purity, **knowledge,** patience,
	8: 7	in speech, in **knowledge,**
	10: 5	up against the **knowledge** of God
	11: 6	but not in **knowledge;**
Ep	3:19	that surpasses **knowledge,**
Ph	3: 8	value of **knowing** Christ Jesus
Co	2: 3	of wisdom and **knowledge**
1Ti	6:20	is falsely called **knowledge**
1P	3: 7	wives in your **life together,**
2P	1: 5	and goodness with **knowledge**
	1: 6	**knowledge** with self-control,
	3:18	grow in the grace and **knowledge**

1109   GO1 AG164 LN52 R1097
γνωστης, KNOWLEDGEABLE
| Ac | 26: 3 | you are especially **familiar** |

1110   GO15 AG164 LN52 B2:392 K1:718 R1097
γνωστος, KNOWN
Lk	2:44	their relatives and **friends**
	23:49	But all his **acquaintances,**
Jn	18:15	Since that disciple was **known**
	18:16	was **known** to the high priest,
Ac	1:19	**known** to all the residents
	2:14	let this be **known** to you,

4:10	let it be **known** to all of you,	
4:16	a **notable** sign has been done	
9:42	became **known** throughout Joppa,	
13:38	Let it be **known** to you	
15:18	**known** from long ago	
19:17	became **known** to all residents	
28:22	we **know** that everywhere it is	
28:28	Let it be **known** to you then	
Ro 1:19	what can be **known** about God	

1111 GO8 AG164 LN52 K1:728
γογγυζω, I GRUMBLE

Mt	20:11	**grumbled** against the landowner
Lk	5:30	**complaining** to his disciples,
Jn	6:41	began to **complain** about him
	6:43	not **complain** among yourselves
	6:61	were **complaining** about it,
	7:32	the crowd **muttering** such things
1C	10:10	not **complain** as some of them
	10:10	complain as some of them **did,**

1112 GO4 AG164 LN52 K1:735 R1111
γογγυσμος, GRUMBLING

Jn	7:12	**complaining** about him among
Ac	6: 1	the Hellenists **complained**
Ph	2:14	without **murmuring** and arguing
1P	4: 9	another without **complaining**

1113 GO1 AG164 LN52 K1:737 R1111
γογγυστης, GRUMBLER

Ju	1:16	**grumblers** and malcontents;

1114 GO1 AG164 LN52 B2:552 K1:737
γοης, CHARLATAN

2Ti	3:13	wicked people and **impostors**

1115 GO3 AG164 LN53
γολγοθα, GOLGOTHA

Mt	27:33	to a place called **Golgotha**
Mk	15:22	the place called **Golgotha**
Jn	19:17	in Hebrew is called **Golgotha**

1116 GO4 AG164 LN53
γομορρα, GOMORRAH

Mt	10:15	land of Sodom and **Gomorrah**
Ro	9:29	been made like **Gomorrah.**
2P	2: 6	cities of Sodom and **Gomorrah**
Ju	1: 7	Likewise, Sodom and **Gomorrah**

1117 GO3 AG164 LN53
γομος, CARGO

Ac	21: 3	ship was to unload its **cargo**
Re	18:11	no one buys their **cargo** anymore
	18:12	**cargo** of gold, silver, jewels

1118 GO20 AG165 LN53
γονευς, PARENT

Mt	10:21	will rise against **parents**
Mk	13:12	will rise against **parents**
Lk	2:27	**parents** brought in the child
	2:41	his **parents** went to Jerusalem
	2:43	his **parents** did not know it
	8:56	Her **parents** were astounded
	18:29	**parents** or children,
	21:16	betrayed even by **parents** and
Jn	9: 2	this man or his **parents,**
	9: 3	this man nor his **parents**
	9:18	until they called the **parents**
	9:20	His **parents** answered,
	9:22	His **parents** said this because
	9:23	Therefore his **parents** said,
Ro	1:30	rebellious toward **parents**
2C	12:14	to lay up for their **parents,**
	12:14	but **parents** for their children
Ep	6: 1	Children, obey your **parents**
Co	3:20	Children, obey your **parents**
2Ti	3: 2	disobedient to their **parents,**

1119 GO12 AG165 LN53 B2:859 K1:738
γονυ, KNEE

Mk	15:19	**knelt** down in homage to him
Lk	5: 8	fell down at Jesus' **knees,**
	22:41	**knelt** down, and prayed
Ac	7:60	Then he **knelt** down and cried
	9:40	then he **knelt** down and prayed
	20:36	he **knelt** down with them all
	21: 5	we **knelt** down on the beach
Ro	11: 4	who have not bowed the **knee**
	14:11	every **knee** shall bow to me,
Ep	3:14	bow my **knees** before the Father
Ph	2:10	every **knee** should bend,
He	12:12	strengthen your weak **knees**

1120 GO4 AG165 LN53 B2:855 K1:738
γονυπετεω, I FALL ON KNEES

Mt	17:14	**knelt** before him
	27:29	**knelt** before him and mocked
Mk	1:40	**kneeling** he said to him,
	10:17	a man ran up and **knelt**

1121   GO14 AG165 LN53 B3:482 K1:761 R1125
γραμμα, LETTER

Lk	16: 6	He said to him, 'Take your **bill**
	16: 7	He said to him, 'Take your **bill**
Jn	5:47	do not believe what he **wrote**
	7:15	this man have such **learning,**
Ac	26:24	Too much **learning** is driving
	28:21	received no **letters** from Judea
Ro	2:27	you that have the **written** code
	2:29	it is spiritual and not **literal**
	7: 6	not under the old **written** code
2C	3: 6	not of **letter** but of spirit;
	3: 6	for the **letter** kills,
	3: 7	chiseled in **letters** on stone
Ga	6:11	See what large **letters** I make
2Ti	3:15	known the sacred **writings**

1122   GO63 AG165 LN53 B3:477 K1:740 R1121
γραμματευς, WRITER, SCRIBE

Mt	2: 4	chief priests and **scribes**
	5:20	exceeds that of the **scribes**
	7:29	and not as their **scribes.**
	8:19	A **scribe** then approached
	9: 3	the **scribes** said to themselves
	12:38	Then some of the **scribes**
	13:52	**scribe** who has been trained
	15: 1	**scribes** came to Jesus
	16:21	chief priests and **scribes,**
	17:10	do the **scribes** say that Elijah
	20:18	chief priests and **scribes,**
	21:15	chief priests and the **scribes**
	23: 2	**scribes** and the Pharisees sit
	23:13	**scribes** and Pharisees,
	23:15	**scribes** and Pharisees,
	23:23	**scribes** and Pharisees,
	23:25	**scribes** and Pharisees,
	23:27	**scribes** and Pharisees,
	23:29	**scribes** and Pharisees,
	23:34	prophets, sages, and **scribes,**
	26:57	the **scribes** and the elders
	27:41	with the **scribes** and elders,
Mk	1:22	and not as the **scribes.**
	2: 6	the **scribes** were sitting there
	2:16	the **scribes** of the Pharisees
	3:22	And the **scribes** who came down
	7: 1	**scribes** who had come from
	7: 5	the Pharisees and the **scribes**
	8:31	chief priests, and the **scribes,**
	9:11	the **scribes** say that Elijah

	9:14	some **scribes** arguing with them.
	10:33	chief priests and the **scribes,**
	11:18	the **scribes** heard it, they kept
	11:27	chief priests, the **scribes,**
	12:28	One of the **scribes** came near
	12:32	Then the **scribe** said to him,
	12:35	**scribes** say that the Messiah
	12:38	Beware of the **scribes,**
	14: 1	**scribes** were looking for a way
	14:43	the **scribes,** and the elders.
	14:53	the **scribes** were assembled.
	15: 1	with the elders and **scribes**
	15:31	along with the **scribes,**
Lk	5:21	the **scribes** and the Pharisees
	5:30	The Pharisees and their **scribes**
	6: 7	The **scribes** and the Pharisees
	9:22	chief priests, and **scribes,**
	11:53	the **scribes** and the Pharisees
	15: 2	the Pharisees and the **scribes**
	19:47	The chief priests, the **scribes**
	20: 1	**scribes** came with the elders
	20:19	the **scribes** and chief priests
	20:39	some of the **scribes** answered,
	20:46	Beware of the **scribes,**
	22: 2	chief priests and the **scribes**
	22:66	both chief priests and **scribes,**
	23:10	chief priests and the **scribes**
Jn	8: 3	The **scribes** and the Pharisees
Ac	4: 5	**scribes** assembled in Jerusalem,
	6:12	the elders and the **scribes;**
	19:35	the **town clerk** had quieted
	23: 9	and certain **scribes**
1C	1:20	Where is the **scribe?**

1123   GO1 AG166 LN53 R1125
γραπτος, WRITTEN

Ro	2:15	is **written** on their hearts,

1124   GO50 AG166 LN53 B3:482 K1:749 R1125
γραφη, WRITING

Mt	21:42	never read in the **scriptures**
	22:29	you know neither the **scriptures**
	26:54	the **scriptures** be fulfilled,
	26:56	**scriptures** of the prophets
Mk	12:10	you not read this **scripture**
	12:24	know neither the **scriptures**
	14:49	the **scriptures** be fulfilled.
Lk	4:21	**scripture** has been fulfilled
	24:27	in all the **scriptures.**

	24:32	opening the **scriptures** to us		11:10	about whom it is **written,**
	24:45	to understand the **scriptures,**		21:13	It is **written,**
Jn	2:22	they believed the **scripture**		26:24	goes as it is **written** of him,
	5:39	You search the **scriptures**		26:31	for it is **written,**
	7:38	As the **scripture** has said,		27:37	charge against him, which **read,**
	7:42	Has not the **scripture** said	Mk	1: 2	**written** in the prophet Isaiah,
	10:35	**scripture** cannot be annulled		7: 6	as it is **written,**
	13:18	it is to fulfill the **scripture,**		9:12	**written** about the Son of Man,
	17:12	**scripture** might be fulfilled.		9:13	as it is **written** about him.
	19:24	what the **scripture** says		10: 4	to **write** a certificate
	19:28	to fulfill the **scripture**		10: 5	he **wrote** this commandment
	19:36	**scripture** might be fulfilled,		11:17	Is it not **written,**
	19:37	another passage of **scripture**		12:19	Moses **wrote** for us
	20: 9	understand the **scripture,**		14:21	goes as it is **written** of him,
Ac	1:16	**scripture** had to be fulfilled,		14:27	for it is **written,**
	8:32	the passage of the **scripture**	Lk	1: 3	to **write** an orderly account
	8:35	starting with this **scripture,**		1:63	He asked for a **writing** tablet
	17: 2	with them from the **scriptures**		2:23	as it is **written** in the law
	17:11	examined the **scriptures**		3: 4	as it is **written** in the book
	18:24	well-versed in the **scriptures.**		4: 4	It is **written,**
	18:28	showing by the **scriptures**		4: 8	It is **written,**
Ro	1: 2	prophets in the holy **scriptures**		4:10	for it is **written,**
	4: 3	what does the **scripture** say?		4:17	the place where it was **written**
	9:17	the **scripture** says to Pharaoh,		7:27	one about whom it is **written,**
	10:11	The **scripture** says,		10:26	What is **written** in the law?
	11: 2	the **scripture** says of Elijah,		16: 6	and **make it** fifty.
	15: 4	encouragement of the **scriptures**		16: 7	and **make it** eighty
	16:26	the prophetic **writings**		18:31	everything that is **written**
1C	15: 3	accordance with the **scriptures**		19:46	It is **written**
	15: 4	accordance with the **scriptures**		20:17	What then does this **text** mean:
Ga	3: 8	And the **scripture,**		20:28	Moses **wrote** for us
	3:22	the **scripture** has imprisoned		21:22	of all that is **written.**
	4:30	what does the **scripture** say?		22:37	what is **written** about me
1Ti	5:18	for the **scripture** says,		24:44	everything **written** about me
2Ti	3:16	**scripture** is inspired by God		24:46	Thus it is **written,**
Ja	2: 8	according to the **scripture,**	Jn	1:45	and also the prophets **wrote,**
	2:23	the **scripture** was fulfilled		2:17	remembered that it was **written,**
	4: 5	that the **scripture** says,		5:46	for he **wrote** about me.
1P	2: 6	For it stands in **scripture:**		6:31	as it is **written,**
2P	1:20	no prophecy of **scripture**		6:45	It is **written** in the prophets,
	3:16	as they do the other **scriptures.**		8: 8	and **wrote** on the ground.

1125 GO191 AG166 LN53 B3:482 K1:742
γραφω, I WRITE

Mt	2: 5	has been **written** by the prophet		8:17	In your law it is **written**
	4: 4	It is **written,**		10:34	Is it not **written** in your law,
	4: 6	for it is **written,**		12:14	as it is **written:**
	4: 7	Again it is **written,**		12:16	these things had been **written**
	4:10	for it is **written,**		15:25	the word that is **written**
				19:19	had an inscription **written**
				19:19	It **read,** "Jesus of Nazareth,
				19:20	it was **written** in Hebrew,

	19:21	not **write** 'The King of the Jews
	19:22	have **written** I have written.
	19:22	have written I have **written**
	20:30	which are not **written**
	20:31	**written** so that you may come
	21:24	and has **written** them,
	21:25	one of them were **written** down,
	21:25	the books that would be **written**
Ac	1:20	For it is **written** in the book
	7:42	as it is **written** in the book
	13:29	that was **written** about him,
	13:33	is **written** in the second psalm
	15:15	the prophets, as it is **written**
	15:23	with the following **letter:**
	18:27	and **wrote** to the disciples
	23: 5	for it is **written,**
	23:25	**wrote** a letter to this effect
	24:14	or **written** in the prophets.
	25:26	have nothing definite to **write**
	25:26	I may have something to **write**
Ro	1:17	as it is **written,**
	2:24	For, as it is **written,**
	3: 4	as it is **written,**
	3:10	as it is **written:**
	4:17	as it is **written,**
	4:23	**written** not for his sake alone,
	8:36	As it is **written,**
	9:13	As it is **written,**
	9:33	as it is **written,**
	10: 5	Moses **writes** concerning
	10:15	As it is **written,**
	11: 8	as it is **written,**
	11:26	as it is **written,**
	12:19	for it is **written,**
	14:11	For it is **written,**
	15: 3	as it is **written,**
	15: 4	whatever was **written**
	15: 9	As it is **written,**
	15:15	**written** to you rather boldly
	15:21	but as it is **written,**
	16:22	the **writer** of this letter,
1C	1:19	For it is **written,**
	1:31	as it is **written,**
	2: 9	But, as it is **written,**
	3:19	For it is **written,**
	4: 6	Nothing beyond what is **written**
	4:14	I am not **writing** this
	5: 9	I **wrote** to you in my letter
	5:11	But now I am **writing** to you

	7: 1	matters about which you **wrote:**
	9: 9	For it is **written** in the law
	9:10	It was indeed **written**
	9:15	nor am I **writing** this
	10: 7	as it is **written,**
	10:11	and they were **written** down
	14:21	In the law it is **written,**
	14:37	that what I am **writing** to you
	15:45	Thus it is **written,**
	15:54	the saying that is **written**
2C	1:13	For we **write** you nothing other
	2: 3	And I **wrote** as I did,
	2: 4	**wrote** you out of much distress
	2: 9	I **wrote** for this reason:
	4:13	is in accordance with **scripture**
	7:12	So although I **wrote** to you,
	8:15	As it is **written,**
	9: 1	to **write** you about the ministry
	9: 9	As it is **written,**
	13:10	So I **write** these things
Ga	1:20	In what I am **writing** to you,
	3:10	for it is **written,**
	3:10	obey all the things **written**
	3:13	for it is **written,**
	4:22	For it is **written**
	4:27	For it is **written,**
	6:11	I am **writing** in my own hand!
Ph	3: 1	To **write** the same things
1Th	4: 9	to have anyone **write** to you,
	5: 1	have anything **written** to you.
2Th	3:17	I, Paul, **write** this greeting
1Ti	3:14	I am **writing** these instructions
Pm	1:19	I, Paul, am **writing** this
	1:21	I am **writing** to you,
He	10: 7	it is **written** of me
1P	1:16	for it is **written,**
	5:12	have **written** this short letter
2P	3: 1	the second letter I am **writing**
	3:15	Paul **wrote** to you
1J	1: 4	We are **writing** these things
	2: 1	I am **writing** these things
	2: 7	**writing** you no new commandment
	2: 8	**writing** you a new commandment
	2:12	I am **writing** to you,
	2:13	I am **writing** to you,
	2:13	I am **writing** to you,
	2:14	I **write** to you,
	2:14	I **write** to you,
	2:14	I **write** to you,

	2:21	I **write** to you,
	2:26	I **write** these things to you
	5:13	I **write** these things to you
2J	1: 5	**writing** you a new commandment,
	1:12	I have much to **write** to you,
3J	1: 9	I have **written** something
	1:13	I have much to **write** to you,
	1:13	I would rather not **write**
Ju	1: 3	eagerly preparing to **write**
	1: 3	I find it necessary to **write**
Re	1: 3	who keep what is **written** in it;
	1:11	**Write** in a book what you see
	1:19	Now **write** what you have seen,
	2: 1	the church in Ephesus **write:**
	2: 8	the church in Smyrna **write:**
	2:12	the church in Pergamum **write:**
	2:17	is **written** a new name
	2:18	the church in Thyatira **write:**
	3: 1	the church in Sardis **write:**
	3: 7	church in Philadelphia **write**
	3:12	I will **write** on you the name
	3:14	the church in Laodicea **write:**
	5: 1	a scroll **written** on the inside
	10: 4	about to **write,** but I heard
	10: 4	and do not **write** it down.
	13: 8	whose name has not been **written**
	14: 1	name **written** on their foreheads
	14:13	**Write** this:
	17: 5	on her forehead was **written**
	17: 8	names have not been **written**
	19: 9	**Write** this:
	19:12	and he has a name **inscribed**
	19:16	he has a name **inscribed,**
	20:12	as **recorded** in the books.
	20:15	not found **written** in the book
	21: 5	**Write** this,
	21:27	**written** in the Lamb's book
	22:18	plagues **described** in this book
	22:19	which are **described**

1126   GO1   AG167   LN53
γραωδης, OLD WOMAN
1Ti   4: 7   myths and **old wives'** tales

1127   GO22   AG167   LN53   B2:136   K2:338
γρηγορεω, I KEEP AWAKE

Mt	24:42	**Keep awake** therefore
	24:43	he would have stayed **awake**
	25:13	**Keep awake** therefore,

	26:38	and **stay awake** with me.
	26:40	could you not **stay awake**
	26:41	**Stay awake**
Mk	13:34	to **be on** the **watch.**
	13:35	Therefore, **keep awake**
	13:37	**Keep awake.**
	14:34	and **keep awake.**
	14:37	Could you not **keep awake**
	14:38	**Keep awake** and pray
Lk	12:37	whom the master finds **alert**
Ac	20:31	Therefore **be alert,**
1C	16:13	**Keep alert,**
Co	4: 2	**keeping alert** in it
1Th	5: 6	let us **keep awake** and be sober
	5:10	we **are awake** or asleep
1P	5: 8	**keep alert.**
Re	3: 3	If you do not **wake up,**
	16:15	the one who **stays awake**

1128   GO4   AG167   LN53   B1:312   K1:775
γυμναζω, I EXERCISE

1Ti	4: 7	**Train** yourself in godliness,
He	5:14	faculties have been **trained**
	12:11	to those who have been **trained**
2P	2:14	have hearts **trained** in greed.

1129   GO1   AG167   LN53   B1:312   K1:775   R1128
γυμνασια, EXERCISE
1Ti   4: 8   **physical training** is of some

1130   GO1   AG167   LN53   R1131
γυμνιτευω, I AM NAKED
1C   4:11   we are **poorly clothed**

1131   GO15   AG167   LN53   B1:312   K1:773
γυμνος, NAKED

Mt	25:36	I was **naked**
	25:38	or **naked** and gave you clothing?
	25:43	**naked** and you did not give me
	25:44	or **naked** or sick or in prison,
Mk	14:51	**wearing nothing** but a linen
	14:52	and ran off **naked.**
Jn	21: 7	for he was **naked,**
Ac	19:16	fled out of the house **naked**
1C	15:37	but a **bare** seed,
2C	5: 3	we will not be found **naked.**
He	4:13	all are **naked** and laid bare
Ja	2:15	is **naked** and lacks daily food,
Re	3:17	poor, blind, and **naked.**

16:15	not going about **naked**	
17:16	make her desolate and **naked;**	

1132 ᴳᴼ3 ᴬᴳ168 ᴸᴺ53 ᴮ1:312 ᴷ1:775 ᴿ1131
γυμνοτης, NAKEDNESS

Ro	8:35	or **nakedness,** or peril,
2C	11:27	without food, cold and **naked**
Re	3:18	the shame of your **nakedness**

1133 ᴳᴼ1 ᴬᴳ168 ᴸᴺ53 ᴮ3:1055 ᴿ1135
γυναικαριον, LITTLE WOMAN

2Ti	3: 6	and captivate silly **women,**

1134 ᴳᴼ1 ᴬᴳ168 ᴸᴺ53 ᴮ3:1055
γυναικειος, WOMAN

1P	3: 7	paying honor to the **woman**

1135 ᴳᴼ215 ᴬᴳ168 ᴸᴺ53 ᴮ3:1055 ᴷ1:776
γυνη, WOMAN

Mt	1:20	to take Mary as your **wife,**
	1:24	he took her as his **wife,**
	5:28	looks at a **woman** with lust
	5:31	Whoever divorces his **wife**
	5:32	anyone who divorces his **wife,**
	9:20	a **woman** who had been suffering
	9:22	the **woman** was made well.
	11:11	among those born of **women**
	13:33	that a **woman** took and mixed
	14: 3	his brother Philip's **wife,**
	14:21	besides **women** and children.
	15:22	Just then a Canaanite **woman**
	15:28	**Woman,** great is your faith!
	15:38	besides **women** and children.
	18:25	with his **wife** and children
	19: 3	for a man to divorce his **wife**
	19: 5	and be joined to his **wife,**
	19: 8	to divorce your **wives,**
	19: 9	whoever divorces his **wife,**
	19:10	case of a man with his **wife,**
	22:24	brother shall marry the **widow,**
	22:25	leaving the **widow**
	22:27	the **woman** herself died.
	22:28	whose **wife** of the seven
	26: 7	a **woman** came to him
	26:10	do you trouble the **woman?**
	27:19	his **wife** sent word to him,
	27:55	Many **women** were also there,
	28: 5	the angel said to the **women,**
Mk	5:25	Now there was a **woman**
	5:33	But the **woman,**

	6:17	his brother Philip's **wife,**
	6:18	to have your brother's **wife.**
	7:25	a **woman** whose little daughter
	7:26	the **woman** was a Gentile,
	10: 2	for a man to divorce his **wife?**
	10: 7	and be joined to his **wife,**
	10:11	divorces his **wife** and marries
	12:19	leaving a **wife** but no child,
	12:19	the man shall marry the **widow**
	12:20	the first **married**
	12:22	the **woman** herself died.
	12:23	whose **wife** will she be?
	12:23	For the seven had **married** her.
	14: 3	**woman** came with an alabaster
	15:40	There were also **women** looking
Lk	1: 5	**wife** was a descendant of Aaron,
	1:13	Your **wife** Elizabeth will bear
	1:18	my **wife** is getting on in years.
	1:24	his **wife** Elizabeth conceived,
	1:42	Blessed are you among **women,**
	3:19	Herodias, his brother's **wife,**
	4:26	a **widow** at Zarephath in Sidon.
	7:28	among those born of **women**
	7:37	And a **woman** in the city,
	7:39	what kind of **woman** this is
	7:44	turning toward the **woman,**
	7:44	Do you see this **woman?**
	7:50	And he said to the **woman,**
	8: 2	some **women** who had been cured
	8: 3	Joanna, the **wife** of Herod's
	8:43	a **woman** who had been suffering
	8:47	When the **woman** saw
	10:38	**woman** named Martha welcomed him
	11:27	a **woman** in the crowd raised
	13:11	appeared a **woman** with a spirit
	13:12	**Woman,** you are set free
	13:21	like yeast that a **woman** took
	14:20	I have just been **married,**
	14:26	mother, **wife** and children,
	15: 8	**woman** having ten silver coins,
	16:18	Anyone who divorces his **wife**
	17:32	Remember Lot's **wife.**
	18:29	one who has left house or **wife**
	20:28	leaving a **wife** but no children,
	20:28	the man shall marry the **widow**
	20:29	the first **married,**
	20:32	Finally the **woman** also died.
	20:33	whose **wife** will the woman be?
	20:33	whose wife will the **woman** be?

	20:33	the seven had **married** her	1C	5: 1	living with his father's **wife**
	22:57	**Woman,** I do not know him.		7: 1	for a man not to touch a **woman.**
	23:27	**women** who were beating their		7: 2	man should have his own **wife**
	23:49	the **women** who had followed him		7: 3	husband should give to his **wife**
	23:55	The **women** who had come with him		7: 3	the **wife** to her husband.
				7: 4	**wife** does not have authority
	24:22	some **women** of our group		7: 4	but the **wife** does.
	24:24	just as the **women** had said;		7:10	the **wife** should not separate
Jn	2: 4	**Woman,** what concern is that		7:11	should not divorce his **wife.**
	4: 7	A Samaritan **woman** came		7:12	a **wife** who is an unbeliever,
	4: 9	The Samaritan **woman** said		7:13	if any **woman** has a husband
	4: 9	of me, a **woman** of Samaria		7:14	is made holy through his **wife,**
	4:11	The **woman** said to him,		7:14	unbelieving **wife** is made holy
	4:15	The **woman** said to him,		7:16	**Wife,** for all you know,
	4:17	The **woman** answered him,		7:16	you might save your **wife.**
	4:19	The **woman** said to him,		7:27	Are you bound to a **wife?**
	4:21	**Woman,** believe me,		7:27	Are you free from a **wife?**
	4:25	The **woman** said to him,		7:27	Do not seek a **wife.**
	4:27	he was speaking with a **woman,**		7:29	let even those who have **wives**
	4:28	the **woman** left her water jar		7:33	how to please his **wife,**
	4:39	of the **woman's** testimony,		7:34	**woman** and the virgin
	4:42	They said to the **woman,**		7:39	A **wife** is bound
	8: 3	a **woman** who had been caught		9: 5	accompanied by a believing **wife**
	8: 4	this **woman** was caught		11: 3	husband is the head of his **wife,**
	8: 9	left alone with the **woman**		11: 5	**woman** who prays or prophesies
	8:10	**Woman,** where are they?		11: 6	a **woman** will not veil herself,
	16:21	When a **woman** is in labor,		11: 6	it is disgraceful for a **woman**
	19:26	**Woman,** here is your son.		11: 7	**woman** is the reflection of man.
	20:13	**Woman,** why are you weeping		11: 8	man was not made from **woman,**
	20:15	**Woman,** why are you weeping?		11: 8	but **woman** from man.
Ac	1:14	together with certain **women,**		11: 9	created for the sake of **woman,**
	5: 1	consent of his **wife** Sapphira,		11: 9	but **woman** for the sake of man.
	5: 2	with his **wife's** knowledge,		11:10	**woman** ought to have a symbol
	5: 7	his **wife** came in, not knowing		11:11	**woman** is not independent
	5:14	numbers of both men and **women,**		11:11	or man independent of **woman.**
	8: 3	dragging off both men and **women**		11:12	just as **woman** came from man,
	8:12	baptized, both men and **women.**		11:12	so man comes through **woman;**
	9: 2	to the Way, men or **women,**		11:13	a **woman** to pray to God
	13:50	incited the devout **women**		11:15	but if a **woman** has long hair,
	16: 1	Jewish **woman** who was a believer		14:34	**women** should be silent
	16:13	the **women** who had gathered		14:35	shameful for a **woman** to speak
	16:14	A certain **woman** named Lydia,	Ga	4: 4	his Son, born of a **woman,**
	17: 4	not a few of the leading **women.**	Ep	5:22	**Wives,** be subject to your
	17:12	not a few Greek **women** and men		5:23	husband is the head of the **wife**
	17:34	and a **woman** named Damaris,		5:24	so also **wives** ought to be,
	18: 2	with his **wife** Priscilla,		5:25	Husbands, love your **wives,**
	21: 5	with **wives** and children,		5:28	should love their **wives**
	22: 4	binding both men and **women**		5:28	He who loves his **wife**
	24:24	came with his **wife** Drusilla,		5:31	and be joined to his **wife,**
Ro	7: 2	**woman** is bound by the law			

	5:33	should love his **wife** as himself
	5:33	**wife** should respect her husband
Co	3:18	**Wives**, be subject to your
	3:19	Husbands, love your **wives**
1Ti	2: 9	**women** should dress themselves
	2:10	**women** who profess reverence
	2:11	Let a **woman** learn in silence
	2:12	I permit no **woman** to teach
	2:14	the **woman** was deceived
	3: 2	**married** only once,
	3:11	**Women** likewise must be serious,
	3:12	deacons be **married** only once
	5: 9	has been **married** only once;
Ti	1: 6	**married** only once,
He	11:35	**Women** received their dead
1P	3: 1	**Wives**, in the same way,
	3: 1	by their **wives'** conduct,
	3: 5	holy **women** who hoped in God
Re	2:20	you tolerate that **woman** Jezebel
	9: 8	their hair like **women's** hair
	12: 1	a **woman** clothed with the sun,
	12: 4	**woman** who was about to bear
	12: 6	**woman** fled into the wilderness,
	12:13	the **woman** who had given birth
	12:14	**woman** was given the two wings
	12:15	the **woman**, to sweep her away
	12:16	came to the help of the **woman**;
	12:17	dragon was angry with the **woman**
	14: 4	defiled themselves with **women**,
	17: 3	a **woman** sitting on a scarlet
	17: 4	**woman** was clothed in purple
Re	17: 6	**woman** was drunk with the blood
	17: 7	the mystery of the **woman**,
	17: 9	on which the **woman** is seated;
	17:18	**woman** you saw is the great city
	19: 7	and **his** bride has made herself
	21: 9	the **wife** of the Lamb.

1136   GO1   AG168   LN54   B3:959   K1:789
γωγ, GOG
Re   20: 8   **Gog** and Magog,

1137   GO9   AG168   LN54   B3:388   K1:791
γωνια, CORNER

Mt	6: 5	and at the street **corners**,
	21:42	has become the **cornerstone**
Mk	12:10	has become the **cornerstone**
Lk	20:17	has become the **cornerstone**
Ac	4:11	has become the **cornerstone**

	26:26	this was not done in a **corner**.
1P	2: 7	the very head of the **corner**,
Re	7: 1	standing at the four **corners**
	20: 8	four **corners** of the earth,

δ

1139   GO13   AG169   LN54   B1:450   K2:19   R1142
δαιμονιζομαι, I DEMONIZE

Mt	4:24	pains, **demoniacs**, epileptics,
	8:16	who were **possessed** with **demons**;
	8:28	two **demoniacs** coming out
	8:33	had happened to the **demoniacs**.
	9:32	a **demoniac** who was mute
	12:22	a **demoniac** who was blind
	15:22	is **tormented** by a **demon**.
Mk	1:32	sick or **possessed** with **demons**.
	5:15	saw the **demoniac** sitting there,
	5:16	had happened to the **demoniac**
	5:18	had been **possessed** by **demons**
Lk	8:36	had been **possessed** by **demons**
Jn	10:21	words of one who has a **demon**.

1140   GO63   AG169   LN54   B1:450   K2:1   R1142
δαιμονιον, DEMON

Mt	7:22	cast out **demons** in your name,
	9:33	the **demon** had been cast out,
	9:34	By the ruler of the **demons**
	9:34	he casts out the **demons**.
	10: 8	cast out **demons**.
	11:18	He has a **demon**
	12:24	the ruler of the **demons**,
	12:24	fellow casts out the **demons**.
	12:27	I cast out **demons** by Beelzebul,
	12:28	that I cast out **demons**,
	17:18	And Jesus rebuked the **demon**,
Mk	1:34	and cast out many **demons**;
	1:34	not permit the **demons** to speak,
	1:39	and casting out **demons**.
	3:15	authority to cast out **demons**.
	3:22	by the ruler of the **demons**
	3:22	he casts out **demons**.
	6:13	They cast out many **demons**,
	7:26	to cast the **demon** out
	7:29	**demon** has left your daughter.
	7:30	and the **demon** gone.
	9:38	someone casting out **demons**
	16: 9	he had cast out seven **demons**.

	16:17	they will cast out **demons**;
Lk	4:33	the spirit of an unclean **demon**
	4:35	When the **demon** had thrown him
	4:41	**Demons** also came out of many,
	7:33	and you say, 'He has a **demon**'
	8: 2	seven **demons** had gone out,
	8:27	who had **demons** met him.
	8:29	be driven by the **demon**
	8:30	many **demons** had entered him.
	8:33	the **demons** came out of the man
	8:35	from whom the **demons** had gone
	8:38	from whom the **demons** had gone
	9: 1	authority over all **demons**
	9:42	**demon** dashed him to the ground
	9:49	casting out **demons** in your name
	10:17	even the **demons** submit to us!
	11:14	he was casting out a **demon**
	11:14	when the **demon** had gone out,
	11:15	He casts out **demons**
	11:15	the ruler of the **demons**.
	11:18	say that I cast out the **demons**
	11:19	Now if I cast out the **demons**
	11:20	that I cast out the **demons**,
	13:32	I am casting out **demons**
Jn	7:20	You have a **demon**
	8:48	and have a **demon**
	8:49	I do not have a **demon**;
	8:52	we know that you have a **demon**
	10:20	He has a **demon**
	10:21	words of one who has a **demon**.
Ac	17:18	of foreign **divinities**
1C	10:20	they sacrifice to **demons**
	10:20	to be partners with **demons**.
	10:21	and the cup of **demons**.
	10:21	and the table of **demons**.
1Ti	4: 1	and teachings of **demons**
Ja	2:19	Even the **demons** believe
Re	9:20	give up worshiping **demons**
	16:14	These are **demonic** spirits,
	18: 2	a dwelling place of **demons**,

1141   GO1 AG169 LN54 K2:20 R1142
δαιμονιωδης, DEMONIC
Ja   3:15   earthly, unspiritual, **devilish**.

1142   GO1 AG169 LN54 B1:449 K2:1
δαιμων, DEMON
Mt   8:31   The **demons** begged him,

1143   GO1 AG169 LN54
δακνω, I BITE
Ga   5:15   you **bite** and devour one another

1144   GO10 AG170 LN54
δακρυον, TEAR
Lk	7:38	bathe his feet with her **tears**
	7:44	bathed my feet with her **tears**
Ac	20:19	all humility and with **tears**,
	20:31	to warn everyone with **tears**.
2C	2: 4	and with many **tears**,
2Ti	1: 4	Recalling your **tears**,
He	5: 7	with loud cries and **tears**,
	12:17	sought the blessing with **tears**.
Re	7:17	God will wipe away every **tear**
	21: 4	he will wipe every **tear**

1145   GO1 AG170 LN54 R1144
δακρυω, I CRY
Jn   11:35   Jesus began to **weep**.

1146   GO1 AG170 LN54 R1147
δακτυλιος, RING
Lk   15:22   put a **ring** on his finger

1147   GO8 AG170 LN54 B2:148 K2:20
δακτυλος, FINGER
Mt	23: 4	are unwilling to lift a **finger**
Mk	7:33	put his **fingers** into his ears,
Lk	11:20	it is by the **finger** of God
	11:46	do not lift a **finger**
	16:24	to dip the tip of his **finger**
Jn	8: 6	wrote with his **finger**
	20:25	put my **finger** in the mark
	20:27	Put your **finger** here and see

1148   GO1 AG170 LN54
δαλμανουθα, DALMANUTHA
Mk   8:10   to the district of **Dalmanutha**.

1149   GO1 AG170 LN54
δαλματια, DALMATIA
2Ti   4:10   Titus to **Dalmatia**.

1150   GO4 AG170 LN54
δαμαζω, I TAME
Mk	5: 4	had the strength to **subdue** him.
Ja	3: 7	can be **tamed** and has been tamed
	3: 7	can be tamed and has been **tamed**
	3: 8	but no one can **tame** the tongue

1151 GO1 AG170 LN54
δαμαλις, HEIFER
He   9:13   of the ashes of a **heifer,**

1152 GO1 AG170 LN54
δαμαρις, DAMARIS
Ac   17:34   a woman named **Damaris,**

1153 GO1 AG170 LN54
δαμασκηνος, OF DAMASCUS
2C   11:32   guarded the city of **Damascus**

1154 GO15 AG170 LN54
δαμασκος, DAMASCUS
Ac   9: 2   to the synagogues at **Damascus,**
    9: 3   along and approaching
       Damascus
    9: 8   and brought him into **Damascus.**
    9:10   **Damascus** named Ananias.
    9:19   with the disciples in **Damascus,**
    9:22   the Jews who lived in **Damascus**
    9:27   how in **Damascus** he had
       spoken
    22: 5   to the brothers in **Damascus,**
    22: 6   and approaching **Damascus,**
    22:10   Get up and go to **Damascus;**
    22:11   and led me to **Damascus.**
    26:12   I was traveling to **Damascus**
    26:20   first to those in **Damascus,**
2C   11:32   In **Damascus,**
Ga   1:17   I returned to **Damascus.**

1155 GO4 AG170 LN54 R1156
δανειζω, I LEND
Mt   5:42   anyone who wants to **borrow**
Lk   6:34   If you **lend** to those
    6:34   Even sinners **lend** to sinners,
    6:35   do good, and **lend,**

1156 GO1 AG170 LN54
δανειον, LOAN
Mt   18:27   and forgave him the **debt.**

1157 GO1 AG170 LN54 B2:667 R1155
δανειστης, LENDER
Lk   7:41   creditor had two **debtors;**

1158 GO1 AG170 LN54
δανιηλ, DANIEL
Mt   24:15   by the prophet **Daniel**

1159 GO5 AG171 LN54 R1160
δαπαναω, I SPEND
Mk   5:26   had **spent** all that she had;
Lk   15:14   When he had **spent** everything,
Ac   21:24   and **pay** for the shaving
2C   12:15   I will most gladly **spend**
Ja   4: 3   in order to **spend** what you get

1160 GO1 AG171 LN54
δαπανη, COST
Lk   14:28   sit down and estimate the **cost,**

1160a GO59 AG171 LN54 B1:425 K8:478
δαυιδ, DAVID
Mt   1: 1   the son of **David,**
    1: 6   Jesse the father of King **David.**
    1: 6   **David** was the father of Solomon
    1:17   from Abraham to **David**
    1:17   from **David** to the deportation
    1:20   Joseph, son of **David,**
    9:27   Have mercy on us, Son of **David**
    12: 3   not read what **David** did
    12:23   this be the Son of **David?**
    15:22   Lord, Son of **David;**
    20:30   Son of **David**
    20:31   Lord, Son of **David**
    21: 9   Hosanna to the Son of **David**
    21:15   Hosanna to the Son of **David**
    22:42   The son of **David.**
    22:43   that **David** by the Spirit calls
    22:45   If **David** thus calls him Lord,
Mk   2:25   you never read what **David** did
    10:47   Jesus, Son of **David,**
    10:48   Son of **David,** have mercy on me
    11:10   kingdom of our ancestor **David**
    12:35   Messiah is the son of **David?**
    12:36   **David** himself,
    12:37   **David** himself calls him Lord;
Lk   1:27   of the house of **David.**
    1:32   throne of his ancestor **David.**
    1:69   the house of his servant **David,**
    2: 4   city of **David** called Bethlehem,
    2: 4   house and family of **David.**
    2:11   in the city of **David** a Savior,
    3:31   son of **David,**
    6: 3   you not read what **David** did
    18:38   Jesus, Son of **David,**
    18:39   Son of **David,** have mercy on me
    20:41   the Messiah is **David's** son
    20:42   For **David** himself says

	20:44	**David** thus calls him Lord;
Jn	7:42	Messiah is descended from **David**
	7:42	the village where **David** lived
Ac	1:16	Spirit through **David** foretold
	2:25	For **David** says concerning him,
	2:29	of our ancestor **David**
	2:34	For **David** did not ascend
	4:25	through our ancestor **David**,
	7:45	there until the time of **David**,
	13:22	he made **David** their king.
	13:22	**David**, son of Jesse,
	13:34	holy promises made to **David**.
	13:36	For **David**,
	15:16	rebuild the dwelling of **David**,
Ro	1: 3	who was descended from **David**
	4: 6	**David** speaks of the blessedness
	11: 9	And **David** says,
2Ti	2: 8	a descendant of **David**
He	4: 7	through **David** much later,
	11:32	of **David** and Samuel
Re	3: 7	who has the key of **David**,
	5: 5	the Root of **David**,
	22:16	the descendant of **David**,

1161   GO2801 AG171 LN54
δε, BUT [MULTIPLE OCCURRENCES]

1162   GO18 AG171 LN55 B2:860 K2:40 R1189
δεησις, REQUEST

Lk	1:13	for your **prayer** has been heard.
	2:37	with fasting and **prayer**
	5:33	frequently fast and **pray**,
Ro	10: 1	and **prayer** to God for them
2C	1:11	in helping us by your **prayers**,
	9:14	long for you and **pray** for you
Ep	6:18	every prayer and **supplication**.
	6:18	persevere in **supplication**
Ph	1: 4	constantly **praying** with joy
	1: 4	every one of my **prayers** for all
	1:19	that through your **prayers**
	4: 6	by prayer and **supplication**
1Ti	2: 1	I urge that **supplications**,
	5: 5	and continues in **supplications**
2Ti	1: 3	constantly in my **prayers**
He	5: 7	prayers and **supplications**,
Ja	5:16	The **prayer** of the righteous
1P	3:12	ears are open to their **prayer**.

1163   GO101 AG172 LN55 B2:662 K2:21
δει, IT IS NECESSARY

Mt	16:21	he **must** go to Jerusalem
	17:10	that Elijah **must** come first
	18:33	**Should** you not have had mercy
	23:23	you **ought** to have practiced
	24: 6	for this **must** take place,
	25:27	Then you **ought** to have invested
	26:35	Even though I **must** die with you
	26:54	say it **must** happen in this way
Mk	8:31	**must** undergo great suffering,
	9:11	say that Elijah **must** come first
	13: 7	this **must** take place,
	13:10	news **must** first be proclaimed
	13:14	set up where it **ought** not to be
	14:31	Even though I **must** die with you
Lk	2:49	I **must** be in my Father's house
	4:43	I **must** proclaim the good news
	9:22	**must** undergo great suffering,
	11:42	you **ought** to have practiced,
	12:12	what you **ought** to say.
	13:14	work **ought** to be done
	13:16	And **ought** not this woman,
	13:33	I **must** be on my way,
	15:32	we **had** to celebrate
	17:25	he **must** endure much suffering
	18: 1	**about their need** to pray always
	19: 5	I **must** stay at your house today
	21: 9	these things **must** take place
	22: 7	lamb **had** to be sacrificed.
	22:37	scripture **must** be fulfilled
	24: 7	Son of Man **must** be handed over
	24:26	**Was it** not **necessary**
	24:44	the psalms **must** be fulfilled.
Jn	3: 7	You **must** be born from above.
	3:14	**must** the Son of Man be lifted
	3:30	He **must** increase,
	4: 4	he **had** to go through Samaria.
	4:20	place where people **must** worship
	4:24	**must** worship in spirit
	9: 4	We **must** work the works
	10:16	I **must** bring them also,
	12:34	Son of Man **must** be lifted up
	20: 9	he **must** rise from the dead.
Ac	1:16	scripture **had** to be fulfilled,
	1:22	**must** become a witness
	3:21	who **must** remain in heaven
	4:12	by which we **must** be saved.
	5:29	We **must** obey God
	9: 6	be told what you **are** to do.
	9:16	how much he **must** suffer

	14:22	we **must** enter the kingdom
	15: 5	**It is necessary** for them
	16:30	what **must** I do to be saved?
	17: 3	proving that **it was necessary**
	19:21	I **must** also see Rome.
	19:36	you **ought** to be quiet
	20:35	we **must** support the weak,
	23:11	you **must** bear witness
	24:19	they **ought** to be here before
	25:10	**this** is where I should be tried
	25:24	he **ought** not to live any longer
	26: 9	I **ought** to do many things
	27:21	you **should** have listened to me
	27:24	you **must** stand
	27:26	we will **have to** run aground
Ro	1:27	**received** in their own persons
	8:26	know how to pray as we **ought,**
	12: 3	more highly than you **ought** to
1C	8: 2	have the **necessary** knowledge;
	11:19	there **have to** be factions
	15:25	he **must** reign until he has
	15:53	**must** put on imperishability,
2C	2: 3	**that** my joy would be the joy
	5:10	**must** appear before the judgment
	11:30	If I **must** boast, I will boast
	12: 1	**It is necessary** to boast;
Ep	6:20	it boldly, as I **must** speak.
Co	4: 4	reveal it clearly, as I **should.**
	4: 6	know how you **ought** to answer
1Th	4: 1	how you **ought** to live
2Th	3: 7	how you **ought** to imitate us;
1Ti	3: 2	a bishop **must** be above reproach,
	3: 7	he **must** be well thought of
	3:15	know how one **ought** to behave
	5:13	saying what they **should** not say
2Ti	2: 6	**ought** to have the first share
	2:24	**must** not be quarrelsome
Ti	1: 7	steward, **must** be blameless;
	1:11	they **must** be silenced,
	1:11	what **it is** not **right** to teach.
He	2: 1	we **must** pay greater attention
	9:26	have **had to** suffer again
	11: 6	**must** believe that he exists
1P	1: 6	**had to** suffer various trials,
2P	3:11	sort of persons **ought** you to be
Re	1: 1	what **must** soon take place;
	4: 1	what **must** take place after this
	10:11	You **must** prophesy again
	11: 5	**must** be killed in this manner.

	17:10	**must** remain only a little while
	20: 3	he **must** be let out
	22: 6	what **must** soon take place.

1164   GO1   AG172   LN55   B3:570
δειγμα, SHOWING
| Ju | 1: 7 | serve as an **example** |

1165   GO2   AG172   LN55   B3:570   K2:31   R1164
δειγματιζω, I EXPOSE PUBLICLY
| Mt | 1:19 | **expose** her **to public disgrace,** |
| Co | 2:15 | **made** a **public example** of them, |

1166   GO33   AG172   LN55   B3:569   K2:25
δεικνυμι, I SHOW
Mt	4: 8	**showed** him all the kingdoms
	8: 4	**show** yourself to the priest,
	16:21	began to **show** his disciples
Mk	1:44	**show** yourself to the priest,
	14:15	He will **show** you a large room
Lk	4: 5	and **showed** him in an instant
	5:14	**show** yourself to the priest,
	20:24	**Show** me a denarius.
	22:12	He will **show** you a large room
	24:40	he **showed** them his hands
Jn	2:18	What sign can you **show** us
	5:20	**shows** him all that he himself
	5:20	he will **show** him greater works
	10:32	have **shown** you many good works
	14: 8	Lord, **show** us the Father,
	14: 9	**Show** us the Father
	20:20	he **showed** them his hands
Ac	7: 3	the land that I will **show** you.
	10:28	**shown** me that I should not call
1C	12:31	**show** you a still more excellent
1Ti	6:15	which he will **bring about**
He	8: 5	was **shown** you on the mountain.
Ja	2:18	**Show** me your faith apart from
	2:18	by my works will **show** you
	3:13	**Show** by your good life
Re	1: 1	**show** his servants what must
	4: 1	I will **show** you what must take
	17: 1	I will **show** you the judgment
	21: 9	I will **show** you the bride,
	21:10	and **showed** me the holy city
	22: 1	the angel **showed** me the river
	22: 6	angel to **show** his servants
	22: 8	angel who **showed** them to me

1167 GO1 AG173 LN55 R1169
δειλια, COWARDICE
2Ti 1: 7   give us a spirit of **cowardice,**

1168 GO1 AG173 LN55 R1167
δειλιαω, I AM COWARD
Jn 14:27   do not let them **be afraid.**

1169 GO3 AG173 LN55
δειλος, COWARD
Mt 8:26   Why are you **afraid,**
Mk 4:40   Why are you **afraid**
Re 21: 8   But as for the **cowardly,**

1170 GO1 AG173 LN55
δεινα, SUCH MAN
Mt 26:18   into the city to a **certain** man,

1171 GO2 AG173 LN55
δεινως, TERRIBLY
Mt 8: 6   paralyzed, in **terrible** distress
Lk 11:53   to be very **hostile** toward him

1172 GO4 AG173 LN55 B2:520 K2:34 R1173
δειπνεω, I DINE
Lk 17: 8   Prepare **supper** for me,
    22:20   with the cup after **supper,**
1C 11:25   took the cup also, after **supper**
Re 3:20   come in to you and **eat** with
            you

1173 GO16 AG173 LN55 B2:520 K2:34
δειπνον, DINNER
Mt 23: 6   the place of honor at **banquets**
Mk 6:21   gave a **banquet**
    12:39   places of honor at **banquets**
Lk 14:12   give a luncheon or a **dinner,**
    14:16   gave a great **dinner** and
            invited
    14:17   At the time for the **dinner**
    14:24   invited will taste my **dinner**
    20:46   places of honor at **banquets.**
Jn 12: 2   they gave a **dinner** for him.
    13: 2   And during **supper**
    13: 4   got up from the **table,**
    21:20   next to Jesus at the **supper**
1C 11:20   really to eat the Lord's **supper**
    11:21   ahead with your own **supper,**
Re 19: 9   marriage **supper** of the Lamb
    19:17   for the great **supper** of God,

1174 GO1 AG173 LN55 B1:450 K2:20
δεισιδαιμων, MORE DEMON FEARING
Ac 17:22   I see how extremely **religious**

1175 GO1 AG173 LN55 B1:450 K2:20 R1174
δεισιδαιμονια, DEMON FEARING
Ac 25:19   about their own **religion**

1176 GO25 AG173 LN55 B2:692 K2:36
δεκα, TEN
Mt 20:24   When the **ten** heard it,
    25: 1   **Ten** bridesmaids took their
    25:28   the one with the **ten** talents.
Mk 10:41   When the **ten** heard this,
Lk 13:16   bound for **eighteen** long years,
    14:31   with **ten** thousand to oppose
    15: 8   woman having **ten** silver coins,
    17:12   **ten** lepers approached him.
    17:17   Were not **ten** made clean
    19:13   He summoned **ten** of his slaves,
    19:13   gave them **ten** pounds,
    19:16   your pound has made **ten** more
    19:17   take charge of **ten** cities.
    19:24   to the one who has **ten** pounds.
    19:25   Lord, he has **ten** pounds
Ac 25: 6   more than eight or **ten** days,
Re 2:10   for **ten** days you will have
    12: 3   with seven heads and **ten** horns,
    13: 1   **ten** horns and seven heads;
    13: 1   on its horns were **ten** diadems,
    17: 3   had seven heads and **ten** horns.
    17: 7   with seven heads and **ten** horns
    17:12   And the **ten** horns that you saw
    17:12   that you saw are **ten** kings
    17:16   the **ten** horns that you saw,

1176a GO2 AG174 LN55 R1176,3638
δεκαοκτω, EIGHTEEN
Lk 13: 4   those **eighteen** who were killed
    13:11   crippled her for **eighteen** years

1178 GO3 AG174 LN55 R1176,4002
δεκαπεντε, FIFTEEN
Jn 11:18   some **two** miles away,
Ac 27:28   and found **fifteen** fathoms.
Ga 1:18   stayed with him **fifteen** days

1179 GO3 AG174 LN56
δεκαπολις, DECAPOLIS
Mt 4:25   the **Decapolis,**

Mk	5:20	to proclaim in the **Decapolis**
	7:31	in the region of the **Decapolis**

1180 GO5 AG174 LN56 R1176,5064
δεκατεσσαρες, FOURTEEN

Mt	1:17	David are **fourteen** generations;
	1:17	Babylon, **fourteen** generations;
	1:17	Messiah, **fourteen** generations.
2C	12: 2	**fourteen** years ago was caught
Ga	2: 1	Then after **fourteen** years

1181 GO4 AG174 LN56 B2:692 R1182
δεκατη, TENTH

He	7: 2	**one-tenth** of everything.
	7: 4	gave him a **tenth** of the spoils.
	7: 8	**tithes** are received by those
	7: 9	who receives **tithes,**

1182 GO3 AG174 LN56 B2:692 R1176
δεκατος, TENTH

Jn	1:39	**four** o'clock in the afternoon.
Re	11:13	and a **tenth** of the city fell;
	21:20	the **tenth** chrysoprase,

1183 GO2 AG174 LN56 B2:692 R1181
δεκατοω, I GIVE TENTH

He	7: 6	**collected tithes** from Abraham
	7: 9	**paid tithes** through Abraham,

1184 GO5 AG174 LN56 B3:744 K2:58
δεκτος, ACCEPTABLE

Lk	4:19	the year of the Lord's **favor.**
	4:24	no prophet is **accepted**
Ac	10:35	what is right is **acceptable**
2C	6: 2	At an **acceptable** time I have
Ph	4:18	a sacrifice **acceptable**

1185 GO3 AG174 LN56
δελεαζω, I ENSNARE

Ja	1:14	being lured and **enticed** by it;
2P	2:14	They **entice** unsteady souls.
	2:18	they **entice** people

1186 GO25 AG174 LN56 B3:865
δενδρον, TREE

Mt	3:10	lying at the root of the **trees;**
	3:10	every **tree** therefore that does
	7:17	every good **tree** bears
	7:17	bad **tree** bears bad fruit.
	7:18	good **tree** cannot bear bad

	7:18	can a bad **tree** bear good fruit.
	7:19	Every **tree** that does not bear
	12:33	Either make the **tree** good,
	12:33	or make the **tree** bad,
	12:33	the **tree** is known by its fruit.
	13:32	of shrubs and becomes a **tree,**
	21: 8	cut branches from the **trees**
Mk	8:24	but they look like **trees,**
Lk	3: 9	lying at the root of the **trees;**
	3: 9	every **tree** therefore that does
	6:43	No good **tree** bears bad fruit,
	6:43	does a bad **tree** bear good fruit
	6:44	each **tree** is known by its own
	13:19	it grew and became a **tree,**
	21:29	the fig tree and all the **trees**
Ju	1:12	autumn **trees** without fruit,
Re	7: 1	or sea or against any **tree.**
	7: 3	or the sea or the **trees,**
	8: 7	third of the **trees** were burned
	9: 4	any green growth or any **tree,**

1187 GO1 AG174 LN56
δεξιολαβος, SPEARMAN

Ac	23:23	and two hundred **spearmen.**

1188 GO54 AG174 LN56 B2:146 K2:37
δεξιος, RIGHT

Mt	5:29	If your **right** eye causes you
	5:30	if your **right** hand causes you
	5:39	strikes you on the **right** cheek
	6: 3	what your **right** hand is doing,
	20:21	one at your **right** hand
	20:23	but to sit at my **right** hand
	22:44	Sit at my **right** hand,
	25:33	the sheep at his **right** hand
	25:34	say to those at his **right** hand,
	26:64	at the **right** hand of Power
	27:29	put a reed in his **right** hand
	27:38	one on his **right**
Mk	10:37	one at your **right** hand
	10:40	but to sit at my **right** hand
	12:36	Sit at my **right** hand,
	14:62	seated at the **right** hand
	15:27	one on his **right**
	16: 5	sitting on the **right** side;
	16:19	sat down at the **right** hand
Lk	1:11	standing at the **right** side
	6: 6	whose **right** hand was withered.
	20:42	Sit at my **right** hand,

	22:50	and cut off his **right** ear.
	22:69	be seated at the **right** hand
	23:33	one on his **right**
Jn	18:10	and cut off his **right** ear.
	21: 6	Cast the net to the **right** side
Ac	2:25	for he is at my **right** hand
	2:33	at the **right** hand of God,
	2:34	Sit at my **right** hand,
	3: 7	he took him by the **right** hand
	5:31	exalted him at his **right** hand
	7:55	standing at the **right** hand
	7:56	standing at the **right** hand
Ro	8:34	who is at the **right** hand of God
2C	6: 7	for the **right** hand and for the
Ga	2: 9	the **right** hand of fellowship,
Ep	1:20	seated him at his **right** hand
Co	3: 1	seated at the **right** hand of God.
He	1: 3	he sat down at the **right** hand
	1:13	Sit at my **right** hand until I
	8: 1	who is seated at the **right** hand
	10:12	down at the **right** hand of God,
	12: 2	at the **right** hand of the throne
1P	3:22	is at the **right** hand of God,
Re	1:16	In his **right** hand he held seven
	1:17	he placed his **right** hand on me,
	1:20	that you saw in my **right** hand,
	2: 1	seven stars in his **right** hand,
	5: 1	Then I saw in the **right** hand
	5: 7	from the **right** hand of the one
	10: 2	his **right** foot on the sea
	10: 5	raised his **right** hand to heaven
	13:16	be marked on the **right** hand

1189   GO22 AG175 LN56 B2:860 K2:40
δεομαι, I BEG

Mt	9:38	**ask** the Lord of the harvest
Lk	5:12	face to the ground and **begged**
	8:28	I **beg** you, do not torment me
	8:38	**begged** that he might be with
	9:38	I **beg** you to look at my son;
	9:40	I **begged** your disciples to cast
	10: 2	**ask** the Lord of the harvest
	21:36	**praying** that you may have the
	22:32	but I have **prayed** for you
Ac	4:31	When they had **prayed,**
	8:22	**pray** to the Lord that,
	8:24	**Pray** for me to the Lord,
	8:34	About whom, may I **ask** you,
	10: 2	and **prayed** constantly to God.

	21:39	I **beg** you, let me speak
	26: 3	I **beg** of you to listen to me
Ro	1:10	**asking** that by God's will
2C	5:20	**entreat** you on behalf of Christ
	8: 4	**begging** us earnestly
	10: 2	I **ask** that when I am present
Ga	4:12	Friends, I **beg** you,
1Th	3:10	we **pray** most earnestly

1189a   GO1 AG175 LN56 K9:189
δεος, AWE

He	12:28	worship with reverence and **awe;**

1190   GO1 AG175 LN56
δερβαιος, DERBEAN

Ac	20: 4	by Gaius from **Derbe,**

1191   GO3 AG175 LN56
δερβη, DERBE

Ac	14: 6	and fled to Lystra and **Derbe,**
	14:20	went on with Barnabas to **Derbe.**
	16: 1	Paul went on also to **Derbe**

1192   GO1 AG175 LN56
δερμα, SKIN

He	11:37	went about in **skins** of sheep

1193   GO2 AG175 LN56 R1192
δερματινος, OF SKIN

Mt	3: 4	a **leather** belt around his waist,
Mk	1: 6	a **leather** belt around his waist,

1194   GO15 AG175 LN56 B1:161
δερω, I BEAT

Mt	21:35	seized his slaves and **beat** one,
Mk	12: 3	they seized him, and **beat** him,
	12: 5	some they **beat,** and others
	13: 9	will be **beaten** in synagogues;
Lk	12:47	will receive a severe **beating.**
	12:48	will receive a light **beating.**
	20:10	but the tenants **beat** him
	20:11	they **beat** and insulted
	22:63	to mock him and **beat** him;
Jn	18:23	why do you **strike** me?
Ac	5:40	they had them **flogged.**
	16:37	They have **beaten** us in public,
	22:19	I imprisoned and **beat** those
1C	9:26	box as though **beating** the air;
2C	11:20	**gives** you a **slap** in the face.

1195 GO3 AG175 LN56 B3:591
δεσμευω, I TIE UP
Mt 23: 4 They **tie up** heavy burdens,
Lk 8:29 **bound** with chains and shackles,
Ac 22: 4 by **binding** both men and women

1197 GO1 AG176 LN56 B3:591
δεσμη, BUNDLE
Mt 13:30 bind them in **bundles**

1198 GO16 AG176 LN56 B3:591 K2:43 R1199
δεσμιος, PRISONER
Mt 27:15 release a **prisoner**
27:16 they had a notorious **prisoner,**
Mk 15: 6 he used to release a **prisoner**
Ac 16:25 **prisoners** were listening
16:27 that the **prisoners** had escaped.
23:18 The **prisoner** Paul called me
25:14 who was **left in prison** by Felix
25:27 unreasonable to send a **prisoner**
28:17 I was **arrested** in Jerusalem
Ep 3: 1 I Paul am a **prisoner** for Christ
4: 1 the **prisoner** in the Lord,
2Ti 1: 8 or of me his **prisoner,**
Pm 1: 1 a **prisoner** of Christ Jesus,
1: 9 as a **prisoner** of Christ Jesus.
He 10:34 for those who were in **prison,**
13: 3 those who are in **prison,**

1199 GO18 AG176 LN56 B3:591 K2:43 R1210
δεσμος, CHAIN
Mk 7:35 his **tongue** was released,
Lk 8:29 but he would break the **bonds**
13:16 be set free from this **bondage**
Ac 16:26 **chains** were unfastened.
20:23 **imprisonment** and persecutions
23:29 deserving death or **imprisonment**
26:29 except for these **chains.**
26:31 deserve death or **imprisonment**
Ph 1: 7 both in my **imprisonment**
1:13 my **imprisonment** is for Christ;
1:14 in the Lord by my **imprisonment**
1:17 my suffering in my **imprisonment**
Co 4:18 Remember my **chains.**
2Ti 2: 9 being **chained** like a criminal.
Pm 1:10 become during my **imprisonment.**
1:13 during my **imprisonment**
He 11:36 even **chains** and imprisonment.
Ju 1: 6 kept in eternal **chains**

1200 GO3 AG176 LN56 B3:591 R1199,5441
δεσμοφυλαξ, CHAIN GUARD
Ac 16:23 ordered the **jailer** to keep them
16:27 When the **jailer** woke up and saw
16:36 the **jailer** reported the message

1201 GO4 AG176 LN56 B3:591 R1199
δεσμωτηριον, GUARD PLACE
Mt 11: 2 When John heard in **prison**
Ac 5:21 and sent to the **prison**
5:23 We found the **prison** securely
16:26 the foundations of the **prison**

1202 GO2 AG176 LN57 B3:591 R1199
δεσμωτης, PRISONER
Ac 27: 1 Paul and some other **prisoners**
27:42 was to kill the **prisoners**

1203 GO10 AG176 LN57 K2:44
δεσποτης, SUPERVISOR
Lk 2:29 **Master,** now you are dismissing
Ac 4:24 **Sovereign Lord,** who made
1Ti 6: 1 regard their **masters** as worthy
6: 2 who have believing **masters**
2Ti 2:21 to the **owner** of the house,
Ti 2: 9 be submissive to their **masters**
1P 2:18 the authority of your **masters**
2P 2: 1 even deny the **Master**
Ju 1: 4 deny our only **Master** and Lord,
Re 6:10 **Sovereign Lord,** holy and true,

1204 GO9 AG176 LN57
δευρο, COME
Mt 19:21 then **come,** follow me.
Mk 10:21 then **come,** follow me.
Lk 18:22 then **come,** follow me.
Jn 11:43 Lazarus, **come** out!
Ac 7: 3 and **go** to the land
7:34 **Come** now, I will send you
Ro 1:13 **thus far** have been prevented
Re 17: 1 **Come,** I will show you
21: 9 **Come,** I will show you the bride

1205 GO12 AG176 LN57
δευτε, COME
Mt 4:19 **Follow** me, and I will make you
11:28 **Come** to me, all you that are
21:38 **come,** let us kill him
22: 4 **come** to the wedding banquet.
25:34 **Come,** you that are blessed

	28: 6	**Come,** see the place where he
Mk	1:17	**Follow** me and I will make you
	6:31	**Come** away to a deserted place
	12: 7	**come,** let us kill him,
Jn	4:29	**Come** and see a man who told me
	21:12	**Come** and have breakfast.
Re	19:17	**Come,** gather for the great

1206 GO1 AG177 LN57 R1208
δευτεραιος, SECOND

Ac	28:13	and on the **second** day we came

1208 GO43 AG177 LN57 R1417
δευτερος, SECOND

Mt	22:26	The **second** did the same,
	22:39	And a **second** is like it:
	26:42	went away for the **second** time
Mk	12:21	and the **second** married her
	12:31	The **second** is this,
	14:72	crowed for the **second** time.
Lk	12:38	during the **middle** of the night,
	19:18	Then the **second** came,
	20:30	then the **second**
Jn	3: 4	Can one enter a **second** time
	4:54	Now this was the **second** sign
	9:24	So for the **second** time
	21:16	A **second** time he said to him,
Ac	7:13	On the **second** visit
	10:15	a **second** time,
	11: 9	But a **second** time
	12:10	the first and the **second** guard,
	13:33	written in the **second** psalm,
1C	12:28	first apostles, **second** prophets
	15:47	the **second** man is from heaven.
2C	1:15	you might have a **double** favor;
	13: 2	when present on my **second** visit
Ti	3:10	a first and **second** admonition,
He	8: 7	no need to look for a **second**
	9: 3	Behind the **second** curtain
	9: 7	priest goes into the **second,**
	9:28	will appear a **second** time,
	10: 9	to establish the **second.**
2P	3: 1	the **second** letter I am writing
Ju	1: 5	**afterward** destroyed those
Re	2:11	be harmed by the **second** death.
	4: 7	the **second** living creature
	6: 3	When he opened the **second** seal,
	6: 3	the **second** living creature
	8: 8	**second** angel blew his trumpet,

	11:14	The **second** woe has passed.
	14: 8	Then another angel, a **second,**
	16: 3	**second** angel poured his bowl
	19: 3	**Once more** they said,
	20: 6	Over these the **second** death
	20:14	This is the **second** death,
	21: 8	which is the **second** death.
	21:19	the **second** sapphire,

1209 GO56 AG177 LN57 B3:744 K2:50
δεχομαι, I WELCOME

Mt	10:14	If anyone will not **welcome** you
	10:40	Whoever **welcomes** you welcomes
	10:40	Whoever welcomes you **welcomes**
	10:40	whoever **welcomes** me welcomes
	10:40	**welcomes** the one who sent me.
	10:41	Whoever **welcomes** a prophet
	10:41	**welcomes** a righteous person
	11:14	if you are willing to **accept** it,
	18: 5	Whoever **welcomes** one such child
	18: 5	in my name **welcomes** me.
Mk	6:11	If any place will not **welcome**
	9:37	**welcomes** one such child
	9:37	child in my name **welcomes** me,
	9:37	whoever **welcomes** me welcomes
	9:37	welcomes me **welcomes** not me
	10:15	whoever does not **receive**
Lk	2:28	Simeon **took** him in his arms
	8:13	**receive** it with joy.
	9: 5	they do not **welcome** you,
	9:48	**welcomes** this child in my name
	9:48	child in my name **welcomes** me,
	9:48	whoever **welcomes** me welcomes
	9:48	**welcomes** the one who sent me;
	9:53	but they did not **receive** him,
	10: 8	its people **welcome** you,
	16: 4	people may **welcome** me
	16: 6	**Take** your bill,
	16: 7	**Take** your bill
	16: 9	**welcome** you into the eternal
	18:17	does not **receive** the kingdom
	22:17	Then he **took** a cup,
Jn	4:45	the Galileans **welcomed** him,
Ac	3:21	who must **remain** in heaven
	7:38	and he **received** living oracles
	7:59	Lord Jesus, **receive** my spirit.
	8:14	Samaria had **accepted** the word
	11: 1	the Gentiles had also **accepted**
	17:11	for they **welcomed** the message

	22: 5	I also **received** letters
	28:21	We have **received** no letters
1C	2:14	do not **receive** the gifts
2C	6: 1	not to **accept** the grace of God
	7:15	how you **welcomed** him with fear
	8:17	he not only **accepted** our appeal,
	11: 4	from the one you **accepted,**
	11:16	then **accept** me as a fool,
Ga	4:14	but **welcomed** me as an angel
Ep	6:17	**Take** the helmet of salvation,
Ph	4:18	now that I have **received**
Co	4:10	he comes to you, **welcome** him.
1Th	1: 6	you **received** the word with joy
	2:13	**accepted** it not as a human word
2Th	2:10	they **refused** to love the truth
He	11:31	she had **received** the spies
Ja	1:21	**welcome** with meekness

1210 GO43 AG177 LN57 B1:171 K2:60
δεω, I BIND

Mt	12:29	and **bind** them in bundles
	14: 3	arrested John, **bound** him,
	16:19	whatever you **bind** on earth
	16:19	earth will be **bound** in heaven,
	18:18	whatever you **bind** on earth
	18:18	earth will be **bound** in heaven,
	21: 2	you will find a donkey **tied,**
	22:13	**Bind** him hand and foot,
	27: 2	They **bound** him, led him away,
Mk	3:27	first **tying** up the strong man;
	5: 3	no one could **restrain** him
	5: 4	he had often been **restrained**
	6:17	arrested John, **bound** him,
	11: 2	you will find **tied** there a colt
	11: 4	found a colt **tied** near a door,
	15: 1	They **bound** Jesus, led him away,
	15: 7	Barabbas was in **prison**
Lk	13:16	**bound** for eighteen long years,
	19:30	will find **tied** there a colt
Jn	11:44	his hands and feet **bound**
	18:12	arrested Jesus and **bound** him.
	18:24	sent him **bound** to Caiaphas
	19:40	and **wrapped** it with the spices
Ac	9: 2	he might bring them **bound**
	9:14	to **bind** all who invoke
	9:21	of bringing them **bound**
	12: 6	Peter, **bound** with two chains,
	20:22	as a **captive** to the Spirit,
	21:11	**bound** his own feet and hands

	21:11	**bind** the man who owns this belt
	21:13	ready not only to be **bound**
	21:33	to be **bound** with two chains;
	22: 5	to **bind** those who were there
	22:29	and that he had **bound** him.
	24:27	Felix left Paul **in prison.**
Ro	7: 2	woman is **bound** by the law
1C	7:27	Are you **bound** to a wife?
	7:39	wife is **bound** as long as her
Co	4: 3	for which I am **in prison,**
2Ti	2: 9	word of God is not **chained.**
Re	9:14	the four angels who are **bound**
	20: 2	**bound** him for a thousand years,

1211 GO5 AG178 LN57
δη, INDEED

Mt	13:23	who **indeed** bears fruit
Lk	2:15	Let us go **now** to Bethlehem
Ac	13: 2	Set apart **for** me Barnabas
	15:36	**Come,** let us return and visit
1C	6:20	**therefore** glorify God

1212 GO3 AG178 LN57 B3:316
δηλος, CLEAR

Mt	26:73	for your accent **betrays** you.
1C	15:27	it is **plain** that this does not
Ga	3:11	Now it is **evident** that no one

1213 GO7 AG178 LN57 B3:316 K2:61 R1212
δηλοω, I MAKE CLEAR

1C	1:11	For it **has been reported** to me
	3:13	Day will **disclose** it,
Co	1: 8	he has made **known** to us
He	9: 8	the Holy Spirit **indicates**
	12:27	**indicates** the removal of what
1P	1:11	Christ within them **indicated**
2P	1:14	Jesus Christ **has made clear**

1214 GO3 AG178 LN57
δημας, DEMAS

Co	4:14	and **Demas** greet you.
2Ti	4:10	for **Demas,**
Pm	1:24	Aristarchus, **Demas,** and Luke,

1215 GO1 AG178 LN57
δημηγορεω, I MAKE A SPEECH
Ac 12:21　**delivered a public address**

1216 GO3 AG178 LN57
δημητριος, DEMETRIUS

Ac   19:24   A man named **Demetrius,**
      19:38   **Demetrius** and the artisans
3J   1:12   favorably about **Demetrius,**

1217   GO1 AG178 LN57 B1:387 K2:62
δημιουργος, CONSTRUCTOR
He   11:10   architect and **builder** is God.

1218   GO4 AG179 LN57 B2:788 K2:63
δημος, PUBLIC
Ac   12:22   The **people** kept shouting,
      17: 5   bring them out to the **assembly**
      19:30   wished to go into the **crowd,**
      19:33   a defense before the **people.**

1219   GO4 AG179 LN57 B2:788
δημοσιος, PUBLIC
Ac   5:18   put them in the **public** prison.
      16:37   They have beaten us in **public,**
      18:28   refuted the Jews in **public,**
      20:20   teaching you **publicly**

1220   GO16 AG179 LN57
δηναριον, DENARIUS
Mt   18:28   who owed him a hundred **denarii**
      20: 2   for the usual **daily wage,**
      20: 9   received the usual **daily wage.**
      20:10   received the usual **daily wage.**
      20:13   for the usual **daily wage**
      22:19   they brought him a **denarius.**
Mk   6:37   buy two hundred **denarii** worth
      12:15   Bring me a **denarius** and let me
      14: 5   more than three hundred **denarii**
Lk   7:41   one owed five hundred **denarii,**
      10:35   he took out two **denarii,**
      20:24   Show me a **denarius.**
Jn   6: 7   **Six months' wages** would not buy
      12: 5   sold for three hundred **denarii**
Re   6: 6   quart of wheat for a **day's pay,**
       6: 6   of barley for a **day's pay,**

1222   GO1 AG179 LN57
δηπου, SURELY
He   2:16   For it is **clear** that he did

1223   GO667 AG179 LN57 B3:1181 K2:65
δια, THROUGH [MULTIPLE OCCURRENCES]

1224   GO3 AG181 LN58
διαβαινω, I GO THROUGH

Lk   16:26   who might **want to pass**
Ac   16: 9   **Come over** to Macedonia
He   11:29   the people **passed through**

1225   GO1 AG181 LN58 B3:468 K2:71
διαβαλλω, I ACCUSE
Lk   16: 1   **charges were brought** to him

1226   GO2 AG181 LN58
διαβεβαιοομαι, I ASSERT FIRMLY
1Ti   1: 7   which they **make assertions.**
Ti   3: 8   that you **insist on** these things,

1227   GO3 AG181 LN58
διαβλεπω, I SEE CLEARLY
Mt   7: 5   and then you will **see clearly**
Mk   8:25   and his **sight was restored,**
Lk   6:42   and then you will **see clearly**

1228   GO37 AG182 LN58 B3:468 K2:72
διαβολος, SLANDERER
Mt   4: 1   to be tempted by the **devil.**
       4: 5   the **devil** took him to the holy
       4: 8   the **devil** took him to a very
       4:11   Then the **devil** left him,
      13:39   who sowed them is the **devil;**
      25:41   fire prepared for the **devil**
Lk   4: 2   he was tempted by the **devil.**
       4: 3   The **devil** said to him,
       4: 6   And the **devil** said to him,
       4:13   When the **devil** had finished
       8:12   the **devil** comes and takes away
Jn   6:70   Yet one of you is a **devil.**
       8:44   are from your father the **devil,**
      13: 2   **devil** had already put it
Ac   10:38   were oppressed by the **devil,**
      13:10   You son of the **devil,**
Ep   4:27   do not make room for the **devil.**
       6:11   condemnation of the **devil.**
1Ti   3: 7   the snare of the **devil.**
       3:11   must be serious, not **slanderers**
2Ti   2:26   the snare of the **devil,**
       3: 3   inhuman, implacable, **slanderers**
Ti   2: 3   not to be **slanderers** or slaves
He   2:14   of death, that is, the **devil,**
Ja   4: 7   Resist the **devil,**
1P   5: 8   the **devil** prowls around,
1J   3: 8   is a child of the **devil;**
       3: 8   for the **devil** has been sinning
       3: 8   destroy the works of the **devil.**

3:10   the children of the **devil**

Ju   1: 9   contended with the **devil**

Re   2:10   the **devil** is about to throw

12: 9   who is called the **Devil**

12:12   the **devil** has come down to you

20: 2   serpent, who is the **Devil**

20:10   the **devil** who had deceived them

1229   ᴳᴼ3   ᴬᴳ182   ᴸᴺ58   ᴷ1:67   ᴿ1223,31a

διαγγελλω, I BROADCAST

Lk   9:60   go and **proclaim** the kingdom

Ac   21:26   **making public** the completion

Ro   9:17   my name may be **proclaimed**

1230   ᴳᴼ3   ᴬᴳ182   ᴸᴺ58   ᴿ1223,1096

διαγινομαι, I BECOME THROUGH

Mk   16: 1   When the sabbath **was over,**

Ac   25:13   After several days **had passed,**

27: 9   Since much time **had been lost**

1231   ᴳᴼ2   ᴬᴳ182   ᴸᴺ58   ᴿ1223,1097

διαγινωσκω, I KNOW THOROUGHLY

Ac   23:15   **make** more **thorough examination**

24:22   **I will decide** your case

1233   ᴳᴼ1   ᴬᴳ182   ᴸᴺ58   ᴿ1231

διαγνωσις, DECISION

Ac   25:21   in custody for the **decision**

1234   ᴳᴼ2   ᴬᴳ182   ᴸᴺ58   ᴷ1:735   ᴿ1223,1111

διαγογγυζω, I GRUMBLE THOROUGHLY

Lk   15: 2   the scribes were **grumbling**

19: 7   who saw it began to **grumble**

1235   ᴳᴼ1   ᴬᴳ182   ᴸᴺ58   ᴿ1223,1127

διαγρηγορεω, I AWAKE THOROUGHLY

Lk   9:32   but since they had **stayed awake**

1236   ᴳᴼ2   ᴬᴳ182   ᴸᴺ58   ᴿ1223,71

διαγω, I LEAD THROUGH

1Ti   2: 2   **may lead** a quiet and peaceable

Ti   3: 3   **despicable,** hating one another.

1237   ᴳᴼ1   ᴬᴳ182   ᴸᴺ58   ᴿ1223,1209

διαδεχομαι, I WELCOME THOROUGHLY

Ac   7:45   **brought** it in with Joshua

1238   ᴳᴼ3   ᴬᴳ182   ᴸᴺ58   ᴮ1:405

διαδημα, DIADEM

Re   12: 3   and seven **diadems** on his heads.

13: 1   on its horns were ten **diadems,**

19:12   on his head are many **diadems;**

1239   ᴳᴼ4   ᴬᴳ182   ᴸᴺ58   ᴿ1223,1325

διαδιδωμι, I GIVE THOROUGHLY

Lk   11:22   and **divides** his plunder.

18:22   **distribute** the money

Jn   6:11   **distributed** them to those

Ac   4:35   it was **distributed** to each

1240   ᴳᴼ1   ᴬᴳ182   ᴸᴺ58   ᴿ1237

διαδοχος, SUCCESSOR

Ac   24:27   **succeeded** by Porcius Festus;

1241   ᴳᴼ3   ᴬᴳ182   ᴸᴺ58   ᴮ3:120   ᴷ5:302   ᴿ1223,2224

διαζωννυμι, I PUT ON A BELT

Jn   13: 4   **tied** a towel **around** himself.

13: 5   towel that was **tied around** him.

21: 7   he **put on** some clothes,

1242   ᴳᴼ33   ᴬᴳ183   ᴸᴺ58   ᴮ1:365   ᴷ2:106   ᴿ1303

διαθηκη, AGREEMENT

Mt   26:28   my blood of the **covenant,**

Mk   14:24   my blood of the **covenant,**

Lk   1:72   remembered his holy **covenant,**

22:20   new **covenant** in my blood.

Ac   3:25   the **covenant** that God gave

7: 8   Then he gave him the **covenant**

Ro   9: 4   the glory, the **covenants,**

11:27   this is my **covenant** with them,

1C   11:25   This cup is the new **covenant**

2C   3: 6   ministers of a new **covenant,**

3:14   the reading of the old **covenant**

Ga   3:15   **will** has been ratified,

3:17   does not annul a **covenant**

4:24   these women are two **covenants.**

Ep   2:12   to the **covenants** of promise,

He   7:22   guarantee of a better **covenant.**

8: 6   mediator of a better **covenant,**

8: 8   will establish a new **covenant**

8: 9   like the **covenant** that I made

8: 9   not continue in my **covenant,**

8:10   **covenant** that I will make

9: 4   the ark of the **covenant**

9: 4   the tablets of the **covenant;**

9:15   mediator of a new **covenant,**

9:15   under the first **covenant.**

9:16   Where a **will** is involved,

9:17   For a **will** takes effect

9:20   the blood of the **covenant**

	10:16	the **covenant** that I will make
	10:29	the blood of the **covenant**
	12:24	mediator of a new **covenant,**
	13:20	blood of the eternal **covenant,**
Re	11:19	the ark of his **covenant**

1243　GO3 AG183 LN58 K1:184 R1244
διαιρεσις, DIFFERENT SELECTIONS
1C	12: 4	there are **varieties** of gifts,
	12: 5	there are **varieties** of services
	12: 6	**varieties** of activities,

1244　GO2 AG183 LN58 K1:184 R1223,138
διαιρεω, I DIVIDE
Lk	15:12	So he **divided** his property
1C	12:11	who **allots** to each one

1244a　GO1 AG183 LN58
διακαθαιρω, I CLEAN THOROUGHLY
Lk	3:17	**to clear** his threshing floor

1245　GO1 AG183 LN58 R1223,2511
διακαθαριζω, I CLEAN THOROUGHLY
Mt	3:12	**will clear** his threshing floor

1246　GO1 AG184 LN59
διακατελεγχομαι, I REBUKE
THOROUGHLY
Ac	18:28	he **powerfully refuted** the Jews

1247　GO37 AG184 LN59 B3:544 K2:81 R1249
διακονεω, I SERVE
Mt	4:11	angels came and **waited** on him.
	8:15	got up and began to **serve** him.
	20:28	came not to be **served**
	20:28	not to be served but to **serve,**
	25:44	and **did** not **take care** of you
	27:55	had **provided** for him.
Mk	1:13	the angels **waited** on him.
	1:31	she began to **serve** them.
	10:45	not to be **served** but to serve,
	10:45	not to be served but to **serve,**
	15:41	and **provided** for him
Lk	4:39	got up and began to **serve** them.
	8: 3	who **provided** for them
	10:40	has left me to **do** all the **work**
	12:37	he will come and **serve** them.
	17: 8	**serve** me while I eat and drink;
	22:26	the leader like one who **serves.**
	22:27	or the one who **serves**

	22:27	am among you as one who **serves.**
Jn	12: 2	Martha **served,**
	12:26	**serves** me must follow me,
	12:26	Whoever **serves** me,
Ac	6: 2	in order to **wait on** tables.
	19:22	So he sent two of his **helpers,**
Ro	15:25	in a **ministry** to the saints;
2C	3: 3	**prepared** by us,
	8:19	while we are **administering**
	8:20	gift that we are **administering,**
1Ti	3:10	let them **serve** as deacons.
	3:13	those who **serve** well as deacons
2Ti	1:18	how much **service** he rendered
Pm	1:13	he might be of **service** to me
He	6:10	his sake in **serving** the saints,
	6:10	the saints, as you still **do.**
1P	1:12	**serving** not themselves but you,
	4:10	**serve** one another
	4:11	whoever **serves** must do so

1248　GO34 AG184 LN59 B3:544 K2:87 R1249
διακονια, SERVICE
Lk	10:40	distracted by her many **tasks;**
Ac	1:17	his share in this **ministry.**
	1:25	the place in this **ministry**
	6: 1	daily **distribution** of food.
	6: 4	prayer and to **serving** the word
	11:29	according to their **ability,**
	12:25	after completing their **mission**
	20:24	**ministry** that I received
	21:19	through his **ministry.**
Ro	11:13	I glorify my **ministry**
	12: 7	**ministry,** in ministering;
	12: 7	ministry, in **ministering;**
	15:31	that my **ministry** to Jerusalem
1C	12: 5	there are varieties of **services**
	16:15	to the **service** of the saints;
2C	3: 7	Now if the **ministry** of death,
	3: 8	will the **ministry** of the Spirit
	3: 9	the **ministry** of condemnation,
	3: 9	the **ministry** of justification
	4: 1	we are engaged in this **ministry**
	5:18	the **ministry** of reconciliation
	6: 3	may be found with our **ministry,**
	8: 4	sharing in this **ministry**
	9: 1	the **ministry** to the saints,
	9:12	the rendering of this **ministry**
	9:13	the testing of this **ministry**
	11: 8	in order to **serve** you.

Ep 4:12 for the work of **ministry,**
Co 4:17 the **task** that you have received
1Ti 1:12 and appointed me to his **service**
2Ti 4: 5 carry out your **ministry** fully.
4:11 he is useful in my **ministry.**
He 1:14 sent to **serve** for the sake
Re 2:19 your love, faith, **service**

1249 GO29 AG184 LN59 B3:544 K2:88
διακονος, SERVANT
Mt 20:26 must be your **servant,**
22:13 king said to the **attendants,**
23:11 will be your **servant.**
Mk 9:35 last of all and **servant** of all
10:43 among you must be your **servant,**
Jn 2: 5 mother said to the **servants,**
2: 9 **servants** who had drawn
12:26 there will my **servant** be also.
Ro 13: 4 it is God's **servant**
13: 4 It is the **servant** of God
15: 8 Christ has become a **servant**
16: 1 a **deacon** of the church
1C 3: 5 **Servants** through whom you
came
2C 3: 6 competent to be **ministers**
6: 4 but as **servants** of God we have
11:15 if his **ministers** also disguise
11:15 as **ministers** of righteousness.
11:23 Are they **ministers** of Christ?
Ga 2:17 is Christ then a **servant** of sin
Ep 3: 7 I have become a **servant**
6:21 faithful **minister** in the Lord.
Ph 1: 1 **servants** of Christ Jesus,
Co 1: 7 He is a faithful **minister**
1:23 became a **servant** of this gospel
1:25 I became its **servant**
4: 7 a faithful **minister,**
1Ti 3: 8 **Deacons** likewise must be
3:12 **deacons** be married only once,
4: 6 you will be a good **servant**

1250 GO8 AG185 LN59 R1364,1540
διακοσιοι, TWO HUNDRED
Mk 6:37 go and buy **two hundred** denarii
Jn 6: 7 **Six months' wages** would not
buy
21: 8 only about a **hundred** yards off.
Ac 23:23 with **two hundred** soldiers,
23:23 and **two hundred** spearmen.
27:37 **two hundred** seventy-six persons

Re 11: 3 thousand **two hundred** sixty days
12: 6 thousand **two hundred** sixty days

1251 GO1 AG185 LN59 R1223,191
διακουω, I HEAR THOROUGHLY
Ac 23:35 I will **give** you a **hearing**

1252 GO19 AG185 LN59 B1:503 K3:946
R1223,2919
διακρινω, I DOUBT
Mt 16: 3 You know how to **interpret**
21:21 you have faith and **do not doubt**
Mk 11:23 if you **do not doubt**
Ac 10:20 **go** with them **without hesitation**
11: 2 believers **criticized** him,
11:12 not **to make** a **distinction**
15: 9 he has **made** no **distinction**
Ro 4:20 No distrust **made** him **waver**
14:23 those who **have doubts**
1C 4: 7 who **sees** anything **different**
6: 5 without **discerning** the body,
11:31 But if we **judged** ourselves,
Ja 1: 6 ask in faith, never **doubting,**
1: 6 for the one who **doubts**
2: 4 not **made distinctions** among
Ju 1: 9 **contended** with the devil
1:22 mercy on some who are **wavering**

1253 GO3 AG185 LN59 B1:503 K3:949 R1252
διακρισις, DIFFERENTIATIONS
Ro 14: 1 of quarreling over **opinions.**
1C 12:10 the **discernment** of spirits,
He 5:14 to **distinguish** good from evil.

1254 GO1 AG185 LN59 R1223,2967
διακωλυω, I PREVENT
Mt 3:14 John would have **prevented** him,

1255 GO2 AG185 LN59 R1223,2980
διαλαλεω, I SPEAK THOROUGHLY
Lk 1:65 these things were **talked about**
6:11 **discussed** with one another what

1256 GO13 AG185 LN59 B3:820 K2:93 R1223,3004
διαλεγομαι, I DISPUTE
Mk 9:34 had **argued** with one another
Ac 17: 2 on three sabbath days **argued**
17:17 So he **argued** in the synagogue
18: 4 Every sabbath he would **argue**
18:19 a **discussion** with the Jews.

19: 8	and **argued** persuasively about
19: 9	**argued** daily in the lecture
20: 7	he **continued speaking** until
20: 9	while Paul **talked** still longer.
24:12	They did not find me **disputing**
24:25	And as he **discussed** justice,
He 12: 5	exhortation that **addresses** you
Ju 1: 9	**disputed** about the body

1257 GO1 AG185 LN59 B3:247 R1223,3007
διαλειπω, I LEAVE THOROUGHLY
Lk 7:45 she has not **stopped** kissing

1258 GO6 AG185 LN59
διαλεκτος, DIALECT
Ac	1:19	in their **language** Hakeldama,
	2: 6	the native **language** of each.
	2: 8	in our own native **language**
	21:40	in the Hebrew **language**,
	22: 2	addressing them in **Hebrew**,
	26:14	in the Hebrew **language**,

1259 GO1 AG186 LN59 B3:166 K1:253 R1223,236
διαλλασσομαι, I RECONCILE
Mt 5:24 **be reconciled** to your brother

1260 GO16 AG186 LN59 B3:820 K2:95 R1223,3049
διαλογιζομαι, I REASON
Mt	16: 7	They **said** to one another,
	16: 8	why **are** you **talking**
	21:25	they **argued** with one another,
Mk	2: 6	**questioning** in their hearts,
	2: 8	**were discussing** these questions
	2: 8	Why do you **raise** such **questions**
	8:16	They **said** to one another,
	8:17	Why **are** you **talking** about
	9:33	What were you **arguing** about
	11:31	They **argued** with one another,
Lk	1:29	**pondered** what sort of greeting
	3:15	all **were questioning**
	5:21	Pharisees began **to question**,
	5:22	Why do you **raise** such **questions**
	12:17	And he **thought** to himself,
	20:14	**discussed** it among themselves

1261 GO14 AG186 LN59 B3:820 K2:96 R1260
διαλογισμος, REASONING
Mt	15:19	come evil **intentions**,
Mk	7:21	that evil **intentions** come:
Lk	2:35	the inner **thoughts** of many

	5:22	perceived their **questionings**,
	6: 8	he knew what they were **thinking**
	9:46	An **argument** arose among them
	9:47	aware of their inner **thoughts**,
	24:38	do **doubts** arise in your hearts
Ro	1:21	futile in their **thinking**,
	14: 1	for the purpose of **quarreling**
1C	3:20	The Lord knows the **thoughts**
Ph	2:14	without murmuring and **arguing**,
1Ti	2: 8	without anger or **argument**;
Ja	2: 4	have you not made **distinctions**

1262 GO1 AG186 LN59 B2:33 R1223,3089
διαλυω, I LOOSE THOROUGHLY
Ac 5:36 were **dispersed** and disappeared.

1263 GO15 AG186 LN59 B3:1038 K4:510 R1223,3140
διαμαρτυρομαι, I TESTIFY THOROUGHLY
Lk	16:28	that he may **warn** them,
Ac	2:40	he **testified** with many other
	8:25	Peter and John had **testified**
	10:42	**testify** that he is the one
	18: 5	**testifying** to the Jews
	20:23	the Holy Spirit **testifies** to me
	20:24	to **testify** to the good news
	23:11	as you have **testified** for me
	28:23	**testifying** to the kingdom
1Th	4: 6	and **solemnly warned** you.
1Ti	5:21	I **warn** you to keep these
2Ti	2:14	and **warn** them before God
	4: 1	I **solemnly urge** you:
He	2: 6	someone has **testified** somewhere

1264 GO1 AG186 LN59 R1223,3164
διαμαχομαι, I FIGHT THOROUGHLY
Ac 23: 9 group stood up and **contended**,

1265 GO5 AG186 LN59 R1223,3306
διαμενω, I STAY THROUGH
Lk	1:22	**remained** unable to speak.
	22:28	might always **remain** with you.
He	1:11	but you **remain**;
2P	3: 4	things **continue** as they were

1266 GO11 AG186 LN59 R1223,3307
διαμεριζω, I DIVIDE COMPLETELY
Mt	27:35	they **divided** his clothes
Mk	15:24	**divided** his clothes among them,
Lk	11:17	kingdom **divided** against itself
	11:18	is **divided** against himself,

	12:52	one household will be **divided,**
	12:53	they will be **divided:**
	22:17	Take this and **divide** it
	23:34	they cast lots to **divide**
Jn	19:24	They **divided** my clothes
Ac	2: 3	**Divided** tongues, as of fire,
	2:45	**distribute** the proceeds to all

1267   GO1 AG186 LN60 R1266
διαμερισμος, THOROUGH DIVISION
Lk 12:51   I tell you, but rather **division**

1268   GO1 AG186 LN60
διανεμω, I SPREAD
Ac 4:17   keep it from **spreading further**

1269   GO1 AG187 LN60
διανευω, I NOD
Lk 1:22   He **kept motioning** to them

1270   GO1 AG187 LN60 B3:122 K4:968
διανοημα, THOROUGH THOUGHT
Lk 11:17   knew what they were **thinking**

1271   GO12 AG187 LN60 B3:122 K4:963
διανοια, INTELLIGENCE

Mt	22:37	and with all your **mind.**
Mk	12:30	and with all your **mind,**
Lk	1:51	in the **thoughts** of their hearts
	10:27	and with all your **mind;**
Ep	2: 3	desires of flesh and **senses,**
	4:18	darkened in their **understanding**
Co	1:21	and hostile in **mind,**
He	8:10	put my laws in their **minds,**
	10:16	write them on their **minds,**
1P	1:13	Therefore prepare your **minds**
2P	3: 1	arouse your sincere **intention**
1J	5:20	has given us **understanding**

1272   GO8 AG187 LN60 B2:726 R1223,455
διανοιγω, I OPEN COMPLETELY

Mk	7:34	that is, "**Be opened.**"
Lk	2:23	Every **firstborn** male shall be
	24:31	Then their eyes **were opened,**
	24:32	he **was opening** the scriptures
	24:45	Then he **opened** their minds
Ac	7:56	I see the heavens **opened**
	16:14	The Lord **opened** her heart
	17: 3	**explaining** and proving

1273   GO1 AG187 LN60 R1223,3571
διανυκτερευω, I STAY THROUGH NIGHT
Lk 6:12   and he **spent the night**

1274   GO1 AG187 LN60
διανυω, I COMPLETE
Ac 21: 7   When we **had finished** the voyage

1274a   GO1 AG187 LN60
διαπαρατριβη, CONSTANT IRRITATIONS
1Ti 6: 5   and **wrangling** among those

1276   GO6 AG187 LN60
διαπεραω, I CROSS OVER

Mt	9: 1	he **crossed** the sea
	14:34	When they had **crossed over,**
Mk	5:21	When Jesus had **crossed** again
	6:53	When they had **crossed over,**
Lk	16:26	no one can **cross** from there
Ac	21: 2	a ship **bound** for Phoenicia,

1277   GO1 AG187 LN60 R1223,4126
διαπλεω, I SAIL THROUGH
Ac 27: 5   we had **sailed across** the sea

1278   GO2 AG187 LN60
διαπονεομαι, I AM PAINED

| Ac | 4: 2 | much **annoyed** because they were |
| | 16:18 | Paul, very much **annoyed,** |

1279   GO5 AG187 LN60 R1223,4198
διαπορευομαι, I TRAVEL THROUGH

Lk	6: 1	while Jesus **was going through**
	13:22	Jesus **went through** one town
	18:36	When he heard a crowd **going by,**
Ac	16: 4	As they **went from** town to town,
Ro	15:24	when I **go** to Spain.

1280   GO4 AG187 LN60 R1223,639
διαπορεω, I DOUBT THOROUGHLY

Lk	9: 7	and he was **perplexed,**
Ac	2:12	All were amazed and **perplexed,**
	5:24	they were **perplexed** about them,
	10:17	Peter was greatly **puzzled**

1281   GO1 AG187 LN60 K6:641
διαπραγματευομαι, I PRACTICE BY
    TRADING
Lk 19:15   what they **had gained by trading**

1282   GO2 AG187 LN60
διαπριω, I SAW THROUGH
Ac   5:33   they **were enraged**
       7:54   they **became enraged**

1283   GO3 AG188 LN60 R1223,726
διαρπαζω, I SEIZE THOROUGHLY
Mt 12:29   and **plunder** his property,
Mk   3:27   and **plunder** his property
       3:27   the house can **be plundered.**

1284   GO5 AG188 LN60 R1223,4486
διαρρηγνυμι, I TEAR APART
Mt 26:65   high priest **tore** his clothes
Mk 14:63   high priest **tore** his clothes
Lk   5: 6   nets were beginning **to break.**
       8:29   but he **would break** the bonds
Ac 14:14   they **tore** their clothes

1285   GO2 AG188 LN60
διασαφεω, I TELL CLEARLY
Mt 13:36   **Explain** to us the parable
      18:31   **reported** to their lord

1286   GO1 AG188 LN60 B3:556 R1223,4579
διασειω, I SHAKE DOWN
Lk   3:14   **Do** not **extort** money from
                  anyone

1287   GO9 AG188 LN60 B2:33 K7:418
R1223,4650
διασκορπιζω, I SCATTER THOROUGHLY
Mt 25:24   where you **did** not **scatter** seed;
      25:26   gather where I **did** not **scatter?**
      26:31   flock **will be scattered.**
Mk 14:27   the sheep **will be scattered.**
Lk   1:51   he **has scattered** the proud
      15:13   he **squandered** his property
      16: 1   was **squandering** his property.
Jn 11:52   the **dispersed** children of God.
Ac   5:37   who followed him were **scattered**

1288   GO2 AG188 LN60 R1223,4685
διασπαω, I TEAR IN PIECES
Mk   5: 4   the shackles he **broke in pieces**
Ac 23:10   they would **tear** Paul **to pieces,**

1289   GO3 AG188 LN60 B2:33 R1223,4687
διασπειρω, I SOW THOROUGHLY
Ac   8: 1   were **scattered throughout**

       8: 4   those who were **scattered** went
      11:19   Now those who were **scattered**

1290   GO3 AG188 LN60 B1:685 K2:98 R1289
διασπορα, DISPERSION
Jn   7:35   the **Dispersion** among the
                  Greeks
Ja   1: 1   twelve tribes in the **Dispersion**
1P   1: 1   To the exiles of the **Dispersion**

1291   GO8 AG188 LN61 K7:591
διαστελλω, I COMMAND
Mt 16:20   Then he sternly **ordered**
Mk   5:43   He strictly **ordered** them
       7:36   Then Jesus **ordered** them to tell
       7:36   but the more he **ordered** them,
       8:15   And he **cautioned** them,
       9: 9   he **ordered** them to tell no one
Ac 15:24   with no **instructions** from us,
He 12:20   endure the **order** that was
                  given

1292   GO1 AG188 LN61
διαστημα, INTERVAL
Ac   5: 7   **interval** of about three hours

1293   GO3 AG188 LN61 K7:592
διαστολη, DIFFERENCE
Ro   3:22   For there is no **distinction,**
      10:12   For there is no **distinction**
1C 14: 7   do not give **distinct** notes,

1294   GO7 AG189 LN61 K7:717
διαστρεφω, I PERVERT
Mt 17:17   and **perverse** generation,
Lk   9:41   and **perverse** generation,
      23: 2   man **perverting** our nation,
Ac 13: 8   **to turn** the proconsul **away**
      13:10   you not stop **making crooked**
      20:30   group will come **distorting**
Ph   2:15   and **perverse** generation,

1295   GO8 AG189 LN61 B3:205 R1223,4982
διασωζω, I DELIVER THOROUGHLY
Mt 14:36   all who touched it **were healed.**
Lk   7: 3   to come and **heal** his slave.
Ac 23:24   **take** him **safely** to Felix
      27:43   wishing **to save** Paul,
      27:44   all **were brought safely** to land
      28: 1   After we **had reached safety,**

28: 4 he **has escaped** from the sea,
1P 3:20 **were saved** through water.

1296 GO2 AG189 LN61 K8:36 R1299
διαταγη, DIRECTION
Ac 7:53 the law as **ordained** by angels,
Ro 13: 2 resists what God has **appointed,**

1297 GO1 AG189 LN61 R1299
διαταγμα, DIRECTIVE
He 11:23 not afraid of the king's **edict.**

1298 GO1 AG189 LN61 R1223,5015
διαταρασσω, I TROUBLE
Lk 1:29 she **was much perplexed**

1299 GO16 AG189 LN61 K8:34 R1223,5021
διατασσω, I DIRECT
Mt 11: 1 Jesus had finished **instructing**
Lk 3:13 the **amount prescribed** for you
   8:55 he **directed** them to give her
   17: 9 for doing what was **commanded**
   17:10 all that you were **ordered** to do
Ac 7:44 as God **directed** when he spoke
   18: 2 **had ordered** all Jews to leave
   20:13 he had **made** this **arrangement,**
   23:31 according to their **instructions**
   24:23 Then he **ordered** the centurion
1C 7:17 my **rule** in all the churches.
   9:14 the Lord **commanded** that those
   11:34 I **will give instructions**
   16: 1 follow the **directions I gave**
Ga 3:19 it **was ordained** through angels
Ti 1: 5 as I **directed** you

1300 GO1 AG189 LN61 R1223,5055
διατελεω, I CONTINUE
Ac 27:33 been in suspense and **remaining**

1301 GO2 AG189 LN61 K8:151 R1223,5083
διατηρεω, I KEEP THOROUGHLY
Lk 2:51 **treasured** all these things
Ac 15:29 you **keep** yourselves from these,

1303 GO7 AG189 LN61 K2:104
διατιθημι, I AGREE
Lk 22:29 and I **confer** on you,
   22:29 my Father has **conferred** on me,
Ac 3:25 the covenant that God **gave**
He 8:10 the covenant that I **will make**

9:16 who made it **must be established**
9:17 the one who **made** it is alive.
10:16 the covenant that I **will make**

1304 GO9 AG190 LN61
διατριβω, I CONTINUE
Jn 3:22 he **spent some time** there
Ac 12:19 to Caesarea and **stayed** there.
   14: 3 they **remained** for a long time,
   14:28 **stayed** there with the disciples
   15:35 But Paul and Barnabas **remained**
   16:12 We **remained** in this city
   20: 6 where we **stayed** for seven days.
   25: 6 After he had **stayed** among them
   25:14 Since they **were staying** there

1305 GO1 AG190 LN61
διατροφη, SUSTENANCE
1Ti 6: 8 if we have **food** and clothing,

1306 GO1 AG190 LN61 B2:289
διαυγαζω, I DAWN
2P 1:19 until the day **dawns**

1306a GO1 AG190 LN61
διαυγης, TRANSPARENT
Re 21:21 **transparent** as glass.

1308 GO13 AG190 LN61 K9:62 R1223,5342
διαφερω, I DIFFER
Mt 6:26 **Are** you not of more **value**
   10:31 you **are** of more **value**
   12:12 much more **valuable is** a human
Mk 11:16 allow anyone to **carry** anything
Lk 12: 7 you **are** of more **value**
   12:24 how much more **value are** you
Ac 13:49 **spread throughout** the region
   27:27 we **were drifting** across the sea
Ro 2:18 and **determine** what is **best**
1C 15:41 star **differs** from star
Ga 2: 6 **makes** no **difference** to me;
   4: 1 **are** no **better** than slaves,
Ph 1:10 to determine what is **best,**

1309 GO1 AG190 LN61 R1223,5343
διαφευγω, I FLEE AWAY
Ac 27:42 none might swim away and **escape**

1310 GO3 AG190 LN61 R1223,5345
διαφημιζω, I SPEAK THOROUGHLY

Mt 9:31   went away and **spread** the **news**
    28:15   this story **is** still **told**
Mk 1:45   and **to spread** the word,

1311   GO6 AG190 LN61 K9:93 R1223,5351
διαφθειρω, I CORRUPT THOROUGHLY
Lk 12:33   and no moth **destroys.**
    4:16   outer nature **is wasting away,**
1Ti 6: 5   those who **are depraved** in mind
Re 8: 9   the ships **were destroyed.**
    11:18   **destroying** those who destroy
    11:18   destroying those who **destroy**

1312   GO6 AG190 LN61 K9:93 R1311
διαφθορα, CORRUPTION
Ac 2:27   Holy One experience **corruption**
    2:31   his flesh experience **corruption**
    13:34   no more to return to **corruption**
    13:35   Holy One experience **corruption**
    13:36   and experienced **corruption**
    13:37   experienced no **corruption.**

1313   GO4 AG190 LN61 R1308
διαφορος, DIFFERING
Ro 12: 6   We have gifts that **differ**
He 1: 4   as much **superior** to angels
    8: 6   obtained a **more excellent**
    9:10   **various** baptisms, regulations

1314   GO1 AG191 LN61 R1223,5442
διαφυλασσω, I GUARD THOROUGHLY
Lk 4:10   concerning you, to **protect** you

1315   GO2 AG191 LN62 R1223,5495
διαχειριζω, I HANDLE THOROUGHLY
Ac 5:30   you **had killed** by hanging him
    26:21   the temple and tried to **kill** me

1315a   GO1 AG191 LN62
διαχλευαζω, I JEER THOROUGHLY
Ac 2:13   But others **sneered** and said,

1316   GO1 AG191 LN62
διαχωριζω, I SEPARATE THOROUGHLY
Lk 9:33   Just as they **were leaving** him,

1317   GO2 AG191 LN62 B3:759 K2:165 R1318
διδακτικος, ABLE TO TEACH
1Ti 3: 2   hospitable, an **apt teacher,**
2Ti 2:24   an **apt teacher,** patient,

1318   GO3 AG191 LN62 B3:759 K2:165 R1321
διδακτος, TAUGHT
Jn 6:45   they shall all be **taught** by God
1C 2:13   things in words not **taught**
    2:13   but **taught** by the Spirit,

1319   GO21 AG191 LN62 B3:768 K2:160 R1320
διδασκαλια, TEACHING
Mt 15: 9   human precepts as **doctrines.**
Mk 7: 7   human precepts as **doctrines.**
Ro 12: 7   the teacher, in **teaching;**
    15: 4   written for our **instruction**
Ep 4:14   about by every wind of **doctrine,**
Co 2:22   human commands and **teachings.**
1Ti 1:10   contrary to the sound **teaching**
    4: 1   spirits and **teachings** of demons
    4: 6   **teaching** that you have followed.
    4:13   to exhorting, to **teaching.**
    4:16   yourself and to your **teaching;**
    5:17   labor in preaching and **teaching**
    6: 1   name of God and the **teaching**
    6: 3   Jesus Christ and the **teaching**
2Ti 3:10   you have observed my **teaching,**
    3:16   is useful for **teaching,**
    4: 3   not put up with sound **doctrine,**
Ti 1: 9   to preach with sound **doctrine**
    2: 1   consistent with sound **doctrine.**
    2: 7   in your **teaching** show integrity
    2:10   the **doctrine** of God our Savior.

1320   GO59 AG191 LN62 B3:765 K2:148 R1321
διδασκαλος, TEACHER
Mt 8:19   **Teacher,** I will follow you
    9:11   Why does your **teacher** eat
    10:24   is not above the **teacher,**
    10:25   to be like the **teacher,**
    12:38   **Teacher,** we wish to see a sign
    17:24   Does your **teacher** not pay
    19:16   **Teacher,** what good deed must
    22:16   **Teacher,** we know that you are
    22:24   **Teacher,** Moses said,
    22:36   **Teacher,** which commandment
    23: 8   for you have one **teacher,**
    26:18   The **Teacher** says, My time is
Mk 4:38   **Teacher,** do you not care
    5:35   Why trouble the **teacher**
    9:17   **Teacher,** I brought you my son;
    9:38   **Teacher,** we saw someone casting
    10:17   Good **Teacher,** what must I do
    10:20   **Teacher,** I have kept all these

	10:35	**Teacher,** we want you to do
	12:14	**Teacher,** we know that you are
	12:19	**Teacher,** Moses wrote for us
	12:32	You are right, **Teacher;**
	13: 1	**Teacher,** what large stones
	14:14	**Teacher** asks, Where is my guest
Lk	2:46	sitting among the **teachers,**
	3:12	**Teacher,** what should we do?
	6:40	is not above the **teacher,**
	6:40	will be like the **teacher.**
	7:40	"**Teacher,**" he replied, "Speak."
	8:49	do not trouble the **teacher**
	9:38	**Teacher,** I beg you to look at
	10:25	"**Teacher,**" he said, "what must
	11:45	**Teacher,** when you say these
	12:13	**Teacher,** tell my brother to
	18:18	Good **Teacher,** what must I do
	19:39	**Teacher,** order your disciples
	20:21	**Teacher,** we know that you are
	20:28	**Teacher,** Moses wrote for us
	20:39	**Teacher,** you have spoken well.
	21: 7	**Teacher,** when will this be,
	22:11	**teacher** asks you, "Where is the
Jn	1:38	which translated means **Teacher**
	3: 2	we know that you are a **teacher**
	3:10	Are you a **teacher** of Israel,
	8: 4	**Teacher,** this woman was caught
	11:28	**Teacher** is here and is calling
	13:13	You call me **Teacher** and Lord
	13:14	So if I, your Lord and **Teacher,**
	20:16	(which means **Teacher**)
Ac	13: 1	were prophets and **teachers:**
Ro	2:20	a **teacher** of children,
1C	12:28	second prophets, third **teachers**
	12:29	Are all **teachers?**
Ep	4:11	some pastors and **teachers,**
1Ti	2: 7	a **teacher** of the Gentiles
2Ti	1:11	apostle and a **teacher,**
	4: 3	**teachers** to suit their own
He	5:12	you ought to be **teachers,**
Ja	3: 1	should become **teachers,**

1321   GO97 AG192 LN62 B3:759 K2:135
διδασκω, I TEACH

Mt	4:23	**teaching** in their synagogues
	5: 2	began to speak, and **taught** them
	5:19	**teaches** others to do the same,
	5:19	does them and **teaches** them
	7:29	**taught** them as one having

	9:35	**teaching** in their synagogues,
	11: 1	**teach** and proclaim his message
	13:54	began to **teach** the people
	15: 9	**teaching** human precepts
	21:23	came to him as he **was teaching,**
	22:16	**teach** the way of God
	26:55	I sat in the temple **teaching,**
	28:15	did as they were **directed.**
	28:20	**teaching** them to obey
Mk	1:21	the synagogue and **taught.**
	1:22	**taught** them as one having
	2:13	around him, and he **taught** them.
	4: 1	began to **teach** beside the sea.
	4: 2	He began to **teach** them many
	6: 2	to **teach** in the synagogue,
	6: 6	among the villages **teaching.**
	6:30	that they had done and **taught.**
	6:34	began to **teach** them many things
	7: 7	**teaching** human precepts
	8:31	Then he began to **teach** them
	9:31	he was **teaching** his disciples,
	10: 1	custom, he again **taught** them.
	11:17	He was **teaching** and saying,
	12:14	but **teach** the way of God
	12:35	was **teaching** in the temple,
	14:49	with you in the temple **teaching**
Lk	4:15	He began to **teach** in their
	4:31	**teaching** them on the sabbath.
	5: 3	**taught** the crowds from the boat
	5:17	One day, while he was **teaching,**
	6: 6	the synagogue and **taught,**
	11: 1	Lord, **teach** us to pray,
	11: 1	Lord, **teach** us to pray,
	12:12	the Holy Spirit will **teach** you
	13:10	Now he was **teaching** in one
	13:22	**teaching** as he made his way
	13:26	and you **taught** in our streets.
	19:47	he **was teaching** in the temple.
	20: 1	as he **was teaching** the people
	20:21	right in what you say and **teach**
	20:21	but **teach** the way of God
	21:37	he **was teaching** in the temple,
	23: 5	by **teaching** throughout all
Jn	6:59	was **teaching** in the synagogue
	7:14	the temple and began to **teach.**
	7:28	he **was teaching** in the temple,
	7:35	the Greeks and **teach** the Greeks
	8: 2	and began to **teach** them.
	8:20	was **teaching** in the treasury

	8:28	as the Father **instructed** me.
	9:34	are you trying to **teach** us
	14:26	will **teach** you everything,
	18:20	always **taught** in synagogues
Ac	1: 1	all that Jesus did and **taught**
	4: 2	they **were teaching** the people
	4:18	not to speak or **teach** at all
	5:21	with their **teaching.**
	5:25	in the temple and **teaching**
	5:28	not to **teach** in this name,
	5:42	not cease to **teach** and proclaim
	11:26	**taught** a great many people,
	15: 1	**were teaching** the brothers,
	15:35	they **taught** and proclaimed
	18:11	**teaching** the word of God
	18:25	**taught** accurately the things
	20:20	**teaching** you publicly
	21:21	you **teach** all the Jews living
	21:28	**teaching** everyone everywhere
	28:31	**teaching** about the Lord Jesus
Ro	2:21	you, then, that **teach** others,
	2:21	will you not **teach** yourself?
	12: 7	the teacher, in **teaching;**
1C	4:17	as I **teach** them everywhere
	11:14	nature itself **teach** you
Ga	1:12	nor was I **taught** it,
Ep	4:21	him and were **taught** in him,
Co	1:28	**teaching** everyone in all wisdom
	2: 7	just as you were **taught,**
	3:16	**teach** and admonish one another
2Th	2:15	traditions that you were **taught**
1Ti	2:12	I permit no woman to **teach**
	4:11	you must insist on and **teach.**
	6: 2	**Teach** and urge these duties.
2Ti	2: 2	able to **teach** others as well.
Ti	1:11	by **teaching** for sordid gain
He	5:12	to **teach** you again the basic
	8:11	shall not **teach** one another
1J	2:27	not need anyone to **teach** you.
	2:27	anointing **teaches** you about all
	2:27	just as it has **taught** you,
Re	2:14	Balaam, who **taught** Balak
	2:20	**teaching** and beguiling

1322   GO30   AG192   LN62   B3:768   K2:163   R1321
διδαχη, TEACHING

Mt	7:28	were astounded at his **teaching,**
	16:12	the **teaching** of the Pharisees
	22:33	were astounded at his **teaching.**
Mk	1:22	were astounded at his **teaching,**
	1:27	What is this? A new **teaching**
	4: 2	in his **teaching** he said to them
	11:18	spellbound by his **teaching.**
	12:38	As he **taught,** he said,
Lk	4:32	were astounded at his **teaching,**
Jn	7:16	My **teaching** is not mine but his
	7:17	**teaching** is from God or whether
	18:19	and about his **teaching.**
Ac	2:42	**teaching** and fellowship,
	5:28	Jerusalem with your **teaching**
	13:12	was astonished at the **teaching**
	17:19	what this new **teaching** is
Ro	6:17	to the form of **teaching**
	16:17	in opposition to the **teaching**
1C	14: 6	prophecy or **teaching?**
	14:26	one has a hymn, a **lesson,**
2Ti	4: 2	the utmost patience in **teaching.**
Ti	1: 9	in accordance with the **teaching,**
He	6: 2	**instruction** about baptisms,
	13: 9	all kinds of strange **teachings;**
2J	1: 9	not abide in the **teaching**
	1: 9	abides in the **teaching**
	1:10	does not bring this **teaching;**
Re	2:14	hold to the **teaching** of Balaam,
	2:15	the **teaching** of the Nicolaitans
	2:24	who do not hold this **teaching,**

1323   GO2   AG192   LN62   B3:752   R1364,1406
διδραχμον, DIDRACHMA

Mt	17:24	collectors of the **temple tax**
	17:24	teacher not pay the **temple tax**

1324   GO3   AG192   LN62
διδυμος, DIDYMUS

Jn	11:16	Thomas, who was called the **Twin**
	20:24	Thomas (who was called the **Twin**
	21: 2	Thomas called the **Twin,**

1325   GO415   AG192   LN62   B2:40   K2:166
διδωμι, I GIVE

Mt	4: 9	All these I will **give** you,
	5:31	let him **give** her a certificate
	5:42	**Give** to everyone who begs
	6:11	**Give** us this day our daily
	7: 6	not **give** what is holy to dogs;
	7: 7	Ask, and it will **be given** you
	7:11	how to **give** good gifts
	7:11	heaven **give** good things
	9: 8	who **had given** such authority

	10: 1	**gave** them authority over		4: 7	and it **yielded** no grain.
	10: 8	**give** without payment.		4: 8	**yielding** thirty and sixty
	10:19	will be **given** to you		4:11	**has been given** the secret
	12:39	no sign will be **given** to it		4:25	who have, more will be **given;**
	13: 8	soil and **brought forth** grain,		5:43	to **give** her something to eat.
	13:11	it **has been given** to know		6: 2	wisdom that has been **given**
	13:11	to them it **has** not **been given.**		6: 7	**gave** them authority over the
	13:12	more will be **given,**		6:22	you wish, and I will **give** it
	14: 7	**grant** her whatever she might		6:23	I will **give** you, even half
	14: 8	**Give** me the head of John		6:25	I want you to **give** me at once
	14: 9	he commanded it to **be given;**		6:28	**gave** it to the girl.
	14:11	**given** to the girl, who brought		6:28	girl **gave** it to her mother.
	14:16	you **give** them something to eat		6:37	**give** them something to eat
	14:19	**gave** them to the disciples,		6:37	and **give** it to them to eat
	15:36	**gave** them to the disciples,		6:41	**gave** them to his disciples
	16: 4	no sign will be **given** to it		8: 6	**gave** them to his disciples
	16:19	I will **give** you the keys		8:12	no sign will be **given**
	16:26	what will they **give** in return		8:37	what can they **give** in return
	17:27	**give** it to them for you and me		10:21	**give** the money to the poor,
	19: 7	**give** a certificate of dismissal		10:37	**Grant** us to sit, one at your
	19:11	only those to whom it **is given.**		10:40	my left is not mine to **grant,**
	19:21	**give** the money to the poor,		10:45	to **give** his life a ransom
	20: 4	I will **pay** you whatever is right		11:28	Who **gave** you this authority
	20:14	I choose to **give** to this last		12: 9	**give** the vineyard to others.
	20:23	this is not mine to **grant,**		12:14	**pay** taxes to the emperor,
	20:28	to **give** his life a ransom		12:14	taxes to the emperor, or **not**
	21:23	who **gave** you this authority?		12:14	taxes to the emperor, or **not**
	21:43	**given** to a people that produces		13:11	is **given** you at that time,
	22:17	to **pay** taxes to the emperor,		13:22	**produce** signs and omens,
	24:24	**produce** great signs and omens,		13:24	moon will not **give** its light,
	24:29	moon will not **give** its light;		13:34	**puts** his slaves in charge,
	24:45	to **give** the other slaves		14: 5	the money **given** to the poor
	25: 8	**Give** us some of your oil,		14:11	promised to **give** him money.
	25:15	to one he **gave** five talents,		14:22	broke it, **gave** it to them,
	25:28	**give** it to the one with the		14:23	**gave** it to them,
	25:29	who have, more will be **given,**		14:44	**given** them a sign,
	25:35	hungry and you **gave** me food,		15:23	they **offered** him wine
	25:42	hungry and you **gave** me no food,	Lk	1:32	Lord God will **give** to him
	26: 9	the money **given** to the poor.		1:73	ancestor Abraham, to **grant** us
	26:15	you **give** me if I betray him		1:77	to **give** knowledge of salvation
	26:26	**gave** it to the disciples,		2:24	they **offered** a sacrifice
	26:27	he **gave** it to them, saying,		4: 6	I will **give** their glory
	26:48	betrayer **had given** them a sign,		4: 6	I **give** it to anyone I please.
	27:10	they **gave** them for the potter's		6: 4	**gave** some to his companions
	27:34	they **offered** him wine to drink,		6:30	**Give** to everyone who begs
	28:12	to **give** a large sum of money		6:38	**give,** and it will be given
	28:18	on earth **has been given** to me.		6:38	and it will be **given** to you.
Mk	2:26	he **gave** some to his companions		6:38	the measure you **give** will be
	3: 6	**conspired** with the Herodians		7:15	Jesus **gave** him to his mother.

7:44	**gave** me no water for my feet,
7:45	You **gave** me no kiss,
8:10	it has been **given** to know
8:18	more will be **given**
8:55	to **give** her something to eat.
9: 1	**gave** them power and authority
9:13	**give** them something to eat
9:16	**gave** them to the disciples
10:19	I have **given** you authority
10:35	**gave** them to the innkeeper,
11: 3	**Give** us each day our daily
11: 7	get up and **give** you anything.
11: 8	get up and **give** him anything
11: 8	**give** him whatever he needs.
11: 9	it will be **given** you;
11:13	how to **give** good gifts to your
11:13	heavenly Father **give** the Holy
11:29	but no sign will be **given**
11:41	So **give** for alms those things
12:32	to **give** you the kingdom.
12:33	your possessions, and **give** alms.
12:42	**give** them their allowance
12:48	to whom much has been **given,**
12:51	to **bring** peace to the earth?
12:58	**make** an effort to settle
14: 9	**Give** this person your place,
15:12	**give** me the share of the
15:16	no one **gave** him anything.
15:22	**put** a ring on his finger
15:29	you have never **given** me
16:12	will **give** you what is your own
17:18	**give** praise to God except
18:43	when they saw it, **praised** God.
19: 8	I will **give** to the poor;
19:13	**gave** them ten pounds, and said
19:15	to whom he had **given** the money,
19:23	**put** my money into the bank?
19:24	**give** it to the one who has ten
19:26	more will be **given;**
20: 2	who **gave** you this authority
20:10	they might **give** him his share
20:16	**give** the vineyard to others
20:22	lawful for us to **pay** taxes
21:15	I will **give** you words
22: 5	agreed to **give** him money.
22:19	which is **given** for you.
22:19	broke it and **gave** it to them,
23: 2	forbidding us to **pay** taxes
Jn 1:12	**gave** power to become children

1:17	indeed was **given** through Moses
1:22	Let us **have** an answer for those
3:16	he **gave** his only Son,
3:27	has been **given** from heaven.
3:34	he **gives** the Spirit
3:35	loves the Son and has **placed**
4: 5	had **given** to his son Joseph.
4: 7	**Give** me a drink.
4:10	**Give** me a drink,
4:10	have **given** you living water.
4:12	Jacob, who **gave** us the well,
4:14	I will **give** them will never
4:14	The water that I will **give**
4:15	**give** me this water,
5:22	**given** all judgment to the Son,
5:26	**granted** the Son also to have
5:27	he has **given** him authority
5:36	has **given** me to complete,
6:27	Son of Man will **give** you.
6:31	He **gave** them bread from heaven
6:32	Moses who **gave** you the bread
6:32	who **gives** you the true bread
6:33	**gives** life to the world
6:34	**give** us this bread always
6:37	the Father **gives** me will come
6:39	of all that he has **given** me,
6:51	**give** for the life of the world
6:52	**give** us his flesh to eat
6:65	it is **granted** by the Father.
7:19	Did not Moses **give** you the law
7:22	Moses **gave** you circumcision
9:24	**Give** glory to God! We know
10:28	I **give** them eternal life,
10:29	What my Father has **given** me
11:22	I know that God will **give** you
11:57	Pharisees had **given** orders
12: 5	the money **given** to the poor
12:49	**given** me a commandment
13: 3	the Father had **given** all things
13:15	For I have **set** you an example,
13:26	one to whom I **give** this piece
13:26	he **gave** it to Judas
13:29	**give** something to the poor.
13:34	I **give** you a new commandment,
14:16	will **give** you another Advocate,
14:27	my peace I **give** to you.
14:27	I do not **give** to you as the
14:27	**give** to you as the world **gives.**
15:16	Father will **give** you whatever

	16:23	he will **give** it to you.		13:21	God **gave** them Saul son of Kish,
	17: 2	you have **given** him authority.		13:34	**give** you the holy promises
	17: 2	to **give** eternal life to all		13:35	will not **let** your Holy One
	17: 2	to all whom you have **given** him.		14: 3	by **granting** signs and wonders
	17: 4	work that you **gave** me to do.		14:17	**giving** you rains from heaven
	17: 6	you **gave** me from the world.		15: 8	by **giving** them the Holy Spirit,
	17: 6	yours, and you **gave** them to me,		17:25	he himself **gives** to all mortals
	17: 7	you have **given** me is from you;		19:31	not to **venture** into the theater
	17: 8	words that you **gave** to me		20:32	to **give** you the inheritance
	17: 8	I have **given** to them, and they		20:35	It is more blessed to **give**
	17: 9	behalf of those whom you **gave**		24:26	hoped that money would be **given**
	17:11	name that you have **given** me,	Ro	4:20	faith as he **gave** glory to God,
	17:12	name that you have **given** me.		5: 5	that has been **given** to us.
	17:14	I have **given** them your word,		11: 8	God **gave** them a sluggish spirit
	17:22	glory that you have **given** me		12: 3	For by the grace **given** to me
	17:22	given me I have **given** them,		12: 6	to the grace **given** to us:
	17:24	whom you have **given** me,		12:19	**leave** room for the wrath of God
	17:24	which you have **given** me		14:12	each of us will **be** accountable
	18: 9	one of those whom you **gave** me		15: 5	**grant** you to live in harmony
	18:11	that the Father has **given** me		15:15	because of the grace **given** me
	18:22	nearby **struck** Jesus on the face	1C	1: 4	has been **given** you in Christ
	19: 3	and **striking** him on the face.		3: 5	as the Lord **assigned** to each.
	19: 9	But Jesus **gave** him no answer.		3:10	the grace of God **given** to me,
	19:11	had been **given** you from above;		7:25	but I **give** my opinion as one
	21:13	the bread and **gave** it to them,		9:12	rather than **put** an obstacle
Ac	1:26	And they **cast** lots for them,		11:15	her hair is **given** to her
	2: 4	as the Spirit **gave** them ability.		12: 7	each is **given** the manifestation
	2:19	**show** portents in the heaven		12: 8	one is **given** through the Spirit
	2:27	you will not **abandon** my soul		12:24	**giving** the greater honor
	3: 6	but what I have I **give** you;		14: 7	instruments that **produce** sound,
	3:16	**given** him this perfect health		14: 7	they do not **give** distinct notes
	4:12	**given** among mortals by which		14: 8	the bugle **gives** an indistinct
	4:29	**grant** to your servants to speak		14: 9	in a tongue you **utter** speech
	5:31	**give** repentance to Israel		15:38	But God **gives** it a body as he
	5:32	Spirit whom God has **given**		15:57	who **gives** us the victory
	7: 5	He did not **give** him any of it	2C	1:22	his seal on us and **giving** us
	7: 5	but promised to **give** it to him		5: 5	who has **given** us the Spirit
	7: 8	he **gave** him the covenant		5:12	but **giving** you an opportunity
	7:10	**enabled** him to win favor		5:18	has **given** us the ministry
	7:25	through him was **rescuing** them,		6: 3	We are **putting** no obstacle
	7:38	living oracles **to give** to us.		8: 1	that has been **granted** to the
	8:18	**given** through the laying on		8: 5	they **gave** themselves first
	8:19	**Give** me also this power		8:10	I am **giving** my advice:
	9:41	**gave** her his hand and helped		8:16	who **put** in the heart of Titus
	10:40	and **allowed** him to appear,		9: 9	he **gives** to the poor;
	11:17	God **gave** them the same gift		10: 8	the Lord **gave** for building you
	11:18	**given** even to the Gentiles		12: 7	thorn was **given** me in the flesh
	12:23	he had not **given** the glory		13:10	Lord has **given** me for building
	13:20	he **gave** them judges until	Ga	1: 4	who **gave** himself for our sins

	2: 9	grace that had been **given** to me
	2: 9	they **gave** to Barnabas and me
	3:21	**given** that could make alive,
	3:22	be **given** to those who believe.
	4:15	your eyes and **given** them to me.
Ep	1:17	may **give** you a spirit of wisdom
	1:22	has **made** him the head over all
	3: 2	grace that was **given** me for you,
	3: 7	**given** me by the working.
	3: 8	this grace was **given** to me
	3:16	he may **grant** that you may be
	4: 7	But each of us was **given** grace
	4: 8	he **gave** gifts to his people.
	4:11	The gifts he **gave** were that
	4:27	do not **make** room for the devil.
	4:29	your words may **give** grace
	6:19	message may be **given** to me
Co	1:25	God's commission that was **given**
1Th	4: 2	know what instructions we **gave**
	4: 8	who also **gives** his Holy Spirit
2Th	1: 8	**inflicting** vengeance on those
	2:16	**gave** us eternal comfort
	3: 9	in order to **give** you an example
	3:16	**give** you peace at all times
1Ti	2: 6	who **gave** himself a ransom
	4:14	**given** to you through prophecy
	5:14	so as to **give** the adversary
2Ti	1: 7	God did not **give** us a spirit
	1: 9	This grace was **given** to us
	1:16	May the Lord **grant** mercy
	1:18	**grant** that he will find mercy
	2: 7	will **give** you understanding
	2:25	**grant** that they will repent
Ti	2:14	He it is who **gave** himself
He	2:13	the children whom God has **given**
	7: 4	**gave** him a tenth of the spoils.
	8:10	will **put** my laws in their minds,
	10:16	**put** my laws in their hearts,
Ja	1: 5	who **gives** to all generously
	1: 5	and it will be **given** you.
	2:16	not **supply** their bodily needs,
	4: 6	he **gives** all the more grace;
	4: 6	but **gives** grace to the humble
	5:18	**gave** rain and the earth yielded
1P	1:21	the dead and **gave** him glory,
	5: 5	but **gives** grace to the humble
2P	3:15	according to the wisdom **given**
1J	3: 1	love the Father has **given** us,
	3:23	just as he has **commanded** us.
	3:24	Spirit that he has **given** us.
	4:13	he has **given** us of his Spirit.
	5:11	God **gave** us eternal life,
	5:16	God will **give** life to such
	5:20	has **given** us understanding
Re	1: 1	**gave** him to show his servants
	2: 7	I will **give** permission to eat
	2:10	will **give** you the crown of life.
	2:17	**give** some of the hidden manna,
	2:17	I will **give** a white stone,
	2:21	I **gave** her time to repent,
	2:23	I will **give** to each of you
	2:26	**give** authority over the nations
	2:28	also **give** the morning star.
	3: 8	I have **set** before you an open
	3: 9	**make** those of the synagogue
	3:21	I will **give** a place with me
	4: 9	living creatures **give** glory
	6: 2	a crown was **given** to him,
	6: 4	**was permitted** to take peace
	6: 4	he was **given** a great sword.
	6: 8	they were **given** authority
	6:11	They were each **given** a white
	7: 2	four angels who had been **given**
	8: 2	seven trumpets were **given**
	8: 3	he was **given** a great quantity
	8: 3	to **offer** with the prayers
	9: 1	**given** the key to the shaft
	9: 5	They were **allowed** to torture
	10: 9	to **give** me the little scroll;
	11: 1	I was **given** a measuring rod
	11: 2	**given** over to the nations,
	11: 3	**grant** my two witnesses
	11:13	**gave** glory to the God of heaven
	11:18	for **rewarding** your servants,
	12:14	woman was **given** the two wings
	13: 2	the dragon **gave** it his power
	13: 4	he had **given** his authority
	13: 5	The beast was **given** a mouth
	13: 5	**allowed** to exercise authority
	13: 7	it was **allowed** to make war
	13: 7	It was **given** authority
	13:14	that it is **allowed** to perform
	13:15	it was **allowed** to give breath
	13:15	it was allowed to **give** breath
	13:16	to **be** marked on the right hand
	14: 7	Fear God and **give** him glory,
	15: 7	**gave** the seven angels seven
	16: 6	have **given** them blood to drink.

16: 8	it was **allowed** to scorch them
16: 9	not repent and **give** him glory.
16:19	**gave** her the wine-cup of the
17:13	These are united in **yielding**
17:17	has **put** it into their hearts
17:17	agreeing to **give** their kingdom
18: 7	so **give** her a like measure
19: 7	exult and **give** him the glory,
19: 8	to her it has been **granted**
20: 4	were **given** authority to judge.
20:13	And the sea **gave** up the dead
20:13	Hades **gave** up the dead
21: 6	I will **give** water as a gift

1326   G06 AG193 LN62 R1223,1453
διεγειρω, I RAISE THOROUGHLY

Mk	4:39	He **woke up** and rebuked the wind
Lk	8:24	went to him and **woke** him **up,**
	8:24	he **woke up** and rebuked the wind
Jn	6:18	The sea **became rough** because
2P	1:13	to **refresh** your memory,
	3: 1	trying to **arouse** your sincere

1326a   G01 AG194 LN63
διενθυμεομαι, I REFLECT
Ac   10:19   While Peter was still **thinking**

1327   G01 AG194 LN63 B3:940 K5:103 R1223,1841
διεξοδος, THROUGHWAYS
Mt   22: 9   Go therefore into the **main**

1328   G01 AG194 LN63 B1:579 K2:661 R1329
διερμηνευτης, TRANSLATOR
1C   14:28   if there is no one to **interpret**

1329   G06 AG194 LN63 B1:579 K2:661 R1223,2059
διερμηνευω, I TRANSLATE

Lk	24:27	he **interpreted** to them
Ac	9:36	**which in** Greek is Dorcas.
1C	12:30	Do all **interpret?**
	14: 5	unless someone **interprets,**
	14:13	pray for the power to **interpret**
	14:27	and let one **interpret.**

1330   G043 AG194 LN63 B1:320 K2:676 R1223,2064
διερχομαι, I GO THROUGH

Mt	12:43	it **wanders** through waterless
	19:24	a camel to **go through** the eye
Mk	4:35	Let us **go** across to the other
	10:25	a camel to **go through** the eye

Lk	2:15	Let us **go** now to Bethlehem
	2:35	**will pierce** your own soul too
	4:30	But he **passed through** the midst
	5:15	word about Jesus **spread abroad;**
	8:22	Let us **go** across to the other
	9: 6	They departed and **went through**
	11:24	it **wanders** through waterless
	17:11	**was going through** the region
	19: 1	and was **passing through** it.
	19: 4	he **was going** to pass that way.
Jn	4: 4	he had to **go through** Samaria.
	4:15	or have to keep **coming** here
Ac	8: 4	were scattered **went** from place
	8:40	**was passing through** the region,
	9:32	as Peter **went** here and there
	9:38	Please **come** to us without delay
	10:38	how he **went about** doing good
	11:19	**traveled** as far as Phoenicia,
	11:22	they sent Barnabas **to** Antioch.
	12:10	After they **had passed** the first
	13: 6	**gone through** the whole island
	13:14	but they **went on** from Perga
	14:24	they **passed through** Pisidia
	15: 3	**passed through** both Phoenicia
	15:41	**went through** Syria and Cilicia,
	16: 6	They **went through** the region
	17:23	For as I **went through** the city
	18:23	**went** from place to place
	18:27	when he wished to **cross over**
	19: 1	**passed through** the interior
	19:21	**go through** Macedonia and Achaia,
	20: 2	had **gone through** those regions
	20:25	**gone about** proclaiming
Ro	5:12	so death **spread** to all because
1C	10: 1	all **passed through** the sea,
	16: 5	after **passing through** Macedonia
	16: 5	to **pass through** Macedonia
2C	1:16	**come back** to you from Macedonia
He	4:14	**passed through** the heavens,

1331   G01 AG194 LN63 R1223,2065
διερωταω, I ASK
Ac   10:17   **were asking** for Simon's house

1332   G01 AG194 LN63 R1364,2094
διετης, TWO YEARS
Mt   2:16   were **two years** old or under,

1333   G02 AG194 LN63 R1332
διετια, TWO YEARS

Ac 24:27 After **two years** had passed,
    28:30 He lived there **two** whole **years**

1334 ᴳᴼ8 ᴬᴳ195 ᴸᴺ63 ᴮ1:573 ᴿ1223,2233
διηγεομαι, I NARRATE
Mk 5:16 to the swine **reported** it.
    9: 9 to **tell** no one about what they
Lk 8:39 **declare** how much God has done
    9:10 the apostles **told** Jesus all
Ac 8:33 Who can **describe** his generation
    9:27 **described** for them how on the
   12:17 **described** for them how the
He 11:32 to **tell** of Gideon, Barak,

1335 ᴳᴼ1 ᴬᴳ195 ᴸᴺ63 ᴮ1:573 ᴷ2:909 ᴿ1334
διηγησις, NARRATIVE
Lk 1: 1 set down an orderly **account**

1336 ᴳᴼ4 ᴬᴳ195 ᴸᴺ63
διηνεκης, PERPETUITY
He 7: 3 he remains a priest **forever.**
   10: 1 offered **year after year,**
   10:12 **for all time** a single sacrifice
   10:14 perfected **for all time** those

1337 ᴳᴼ1 ᴬᴳ195 ᴸᴺ64 ᴿ1364,2281
διθαλασσος, TWO SEAS
Ac 27:41 But striking a **reef,** they ran

1338 ᴳᴼ1 ᴬᴳ195 ᴸᴺ64
διικνεομαι, I PIERCE THOROUGHLY
He 4:12 it **divides** soul from spirit,

1339 ᴳᴼ3 ᴬᴳ195 ᴸᴺ64
διιστημι, I STAND THROUGH
Lk 22:59 Then about an hour **later** still
    24:51 he **withdrew** from them
Ac 27:28 a little **farther on** they took

1340 ᴳᴼ2 ᴬᴳ195 ᴸᴺ64
διισχυριζομαι, I INSIST
Lk 22:59 still another kept **insisting,**
Ac 12:15 she **insisted** that it was so.

1341 ᴳᴼ1 ᴬᴳ195 ᴸᴺ64 ᴷ2:174 ᴿ1342,2920
δικαιοκρισια, RIGHT JUDGMENT
Ro 2: 5 when God's **righteous judgment**

1342 ᴳᴼ79 ᴬᴳ195 ᴸᴺ64 ᴮ3:352 ᴷ2:174 ᴿ1349
δικαιος, RIGHT

Mt 1:19 Joseph, being a **righteous** man
    5:45 sends rain on the **righteous**
    9:13 not the **righteous** but sinners.
   10:41 welcomes a **righteous** person
   10:41 name of a **righteous** person
   10:41 the reward of the **righteous;**
   13:17 prophets and **righteous** people
   13:43 Then the **righteous** will shine
   13:49 the evil from the **righteous**
   20: 4 pay you whatever is **right**
   23:28 look **righteous** to others,
   23:29 graves of the **righteous,**
   23:35 the blood of **righteous** Abel
   23:35 all the **righteous** blood shed
   25:37 the **righteous** will answer him,
   25:46 the **righteous** into eternal life
   27:19 with that **innocent** man,
Mk 2:17 to call not the **righteous**
    6:20 a **righteous** and holy man,
Lk 1: 6 Both of them were **righteous**
    1:17 to the wisdom of the **righteous,**
    2:25 this man was **righteous**
    5:32 to call not the **righteous**
   12:57 yourselves what is **right**
   14:14 resurrection of the **righteous**
   15: 7 ninety-nine **righteous** persons
   18: 9 that they were **righteous**
   20:20 who pretended to be **honest,**
   23:47 Certainly this man was **innocent**
   23:50 **righteous** man named Joseph,
Jn 5:30 and my judgment is **just,**
    7:24 but judge with **right** judgment
   17:25 **Righteous** Father, the world
Ac 3:14 the Holy and **Righteous** One
    4:19 it is **right** in God's sight
    7:52 coming of the **Righteous** One,
   10:22 an **upright** and God-fearing man,
   22:14 to see the **Righteous** One
   24:15 **righteous** and the unrighteous.
Ro 1:17 The one who is **righteous**
    2:13 **righteous** in God's sight,
    3:10 no one who is **righteous,**
    3:26 that he himself is **righteous**
    5: 7 die for a **righteous** person
    5:19 many will be made **righteous.**
    7:12 is holy and **just** and good.
Ga 3:11 one who is **righteous** will live
Ep 6: 1 in the Lord, for this is **right.**
Ph 1: 7 It is **right** for me to think

	4: 8	is honorable, whatever is **just,**
Co	4: 1	treat your slaves **justly**
2Th	1: 5	the **righteous** judgment of God,
	1: 6	For it is indeed **just** of God
1Ti	1: 9	not for the **innocent** but for
2Ti	4: 8	the crown of **righteousness,**
Ti	1: 8	prudent, **upright,** devout,
He	10:38	but my **righteous** one will live
	11: 4	received approval as **righteous,**
	12:23	spirits of the **righteous**
Ja	5: 6	murdered the **righteous** one
	5:16	prayer of the **righteous**
1P	3:12	Lord are on the **righteous,**
	3:18	**righteous** for the unrighteous,
	4:18	it is hard for the **righteous**
2P	1:13	I think it **right,**
	2: 7	Lot, a **righteous** man greatly
	2: 8	for that **righteous** man,
	2: 8	tormented in his **righteous** soul
1J	1: 9	who is faithful and **just**
	2: 1	Jesus Christ the **righteous;**
	2:29	you know that he is **righteous,**
	3: 7	does what is right is **righteous**
	3: 7	just as he is **righteous.**
	3:12	and his brother's **righteous.**
Re	15: 3	**Just** and true are your ways,
	16: 5	You are **just,** O Holy One,
	16: 7	judgments are true and **just**
	19: 2	judgments are true and **just;**
	22:11	the **righteous** still do right,

1343   GO92 AG196 LN64 B3:352 K1:174 R1342
δικαιοσυνη, RIGHTNESS

Mt	3:15	to fulfill all **righteousness**
	5:10	persecuted for **righteousness'**
	5:20	your **righteousness** exceeds
	6: 1	practicing your **piety** before
	6:33	God and his **righteousness,**
	21:32	the way of **righteousness**
Lk	1:75	holiness and **righteousness**
Jn	16: 8	about sin and **righteousness**
	16:10	about **righteousness,** because
Ac	10:35	and does what is **right**
	13:10	enemy of all **righteousness,**
	17:31	world judged in **righteousness**
	24:25	And as he discussed **justice,**
Ro	1:17	the **righteousness** of God
	3: 5	to confirm the **justice** of God,
	3:21	the **righteousness** of God

	3:22	the **righteousness** of God
	3:25	to show his **righteousness,**
	3:26	that he himself is **righteous**
	4: 3	to him as **righteousness**
	4: 5	is reckoned as **righteousness.**
	4: 6	God reckons **righteousness**
	4: 9	to Abraham as **righteousness.**
	4:11	a seal of the **righteousness**
	4:11	have **righteousness** reckoned
	4:13	but through the **righteousness**
	4:22	to him as **righteousness**
	5:17	free gift of **righteousness**
	5:21	dominion through **justification**
	6:13	instruments of **righteousness**
	6:16	which leads to **righteousness**
	6:18	become slaves of **righteousness**
	6:19	as slaves to **righteousness**
	6:20	in regard to **righteousness.**
	8:10	life because of **righteousness.**
	9:30	not strive for **righteousness,**
	9:30	righteousness, have attained **it**
	9:30	**righteousness** through faith;
	9:31	strive for the **righteousness**
	10: 3	ignorant of the **righteousness**
	10: 3	seeking to establish their **own,**
	10: 3	to God's **righteousness.**
	10: 4	be **righteousness** for everyone
	10: 5	concerning the **righteousness**
	10: 6	the **righteousness** that comes
	10:10	the heart and so is **justified,**
	14:17	but **righteousness** and peace
1C	1:30	from God, and **righteousness**
2C	3: 9	the ministry of **justification**
	5:21	become the **righteousness**
	6: 7	weapons of **righteousness**
	6:14	**righteousness** and lawlessness
	9: 9	his **righteousness** endures
	9:10	harvest of your **righteousness.**
	11:15	as ministers of **righteousness.**
Ga	2:21	**justification** comes through the
	3: 6	to him as **righteousness,**
	3:21	then **righteousness** would indeed
	5: 5	for the hope of **righteousness.**
Ep	4:24	of God in true **righteousness**
	5: 9	that is good and **right** and true
	6:14	breastplate of **righteousness.**
Ph	1:11	the harvest of **righteousness**
	3: 6	to **righteousness** under the law,
	3: 9	not having a **righteousness**

	3: 9	the **righteousness** from God
1Ti	6:11	pursue **righteousness**,
2Ti	2:22	and pursue **righteousness**,
	3:16	for training in **righteousness**,
	4: 8	crown of **righteousness**,
Ti	3: 5	any works of **righteousness**
He	1: 9	You have loved **righteousness**
	5:13	in the word of **righteousness**.
	7: 2	means "king of **righteousness**
	11: 7	heir to the **righteousness**
	11:33	kingdoms, administered **justice**,
	12:11	peaceful fruit of **righteousness**
Ja	1:20	produce God's **righteousness**.
	2:23	to him as **righteousness**
	3:18	harvest of **righteousness**
1P	2:24	might live for **righteousness**;
	3:14	suffer for doing what is **right**,
2P	1: 1	ours through the **righteousness**
	2: 5	Noah, a herald of **righteousness**,
	2:21	known the way of **righteousness**
	3:13	where **righteousness** is at home.
1J	2:29	that everyone who does **right**
	3: 7	who does what is **right**
	3:10	who do not do what is **right**
Re	19:11	in **righteousness** he judges
	22:11	the righteous still do **right**,

1344   GO39 AG197 LN64 B3:352 K2:174 R1342
δικαιοω, I MAKE RIGHT

Mt	11:19	Yet wisdom is **vindicated**
	12:37	words you will be **justified**,
Lk	7:29	**acknowledged** the **justice**
	7:35	wisdom is **vindicated** by all
	10:29	But wanting to **justify** himself,
	16:15	those who **justify** yourselves
	18:14	**justified** rather than the other
Ac	13:39	**freed** by the law of Moses
	13:39	who believes is **set free** from
Ro	2:13	the law who will be **justified**.
	3: 4	you may be **justified** in your
	3:20	human being will be **justified**
	3:24	now **justified** by his grace
	3:26	that he **justifies** the one
	3:28	a person is **justified** by faith
	3:30	he will **justify** the circumcised
	4: 2	Abraham was **justified** by works,
	4: 5	him who **justifies** the ungodly,
	5: 1	since we are **justified** by faith,
	5: 9	been **justified** by his blood,

	6: 7	has died is **freed** from sin.
	8:30	he called he also **justified**;
	8:30	he **justified** he also glorified.
	8:33	It is God who **justifies**.
1C	4: 4	I am not thereby **acquitted**.
	6:11	you were **justified** in the name
Ga	2:16	know that a person is **justified**
	2:16	**justified** by faith in Christ,
	2:16	no one will be **justified**
	2:17	to be **justified** in Christ,
	3: 8	**justify** the Gentiles by faith,
	3:11	no one is **justified** before God
	3:24	we might be **justified** by faith.
	5: 4	to be **justified** by the law
1Ti	3:16	in flesh, **vindicated** in spirit,
Ti	3: 7	been **justified** by his grace,
Ja	2:21	Abraham **justified** by works
	2:24	a person is **justified** by works
	2:25	prostitute also **justified** by

1345   GO10 AG198 LN64 B3:352 K2:174 R1344
δικαιωμα, RIGHT ACTS

Lk	1: 6	**regulations** of the Lord.
Ro	1:32	They know God's **decree**,
	2:26	keep the **requirements**
	5:16	brings **justification**.
	5:18	one man's **act** of **righteousness**
	8: 4	**just** requirement of the law
He	9: 1	first covenant had **regulations**
	9:10	**regulations** for the body
Re	15: 4	**judgments** have been revealed.
	19: 8	linen is the **righteous deeds**

1346   GO5 AG198 LN64 B3:352 R1342
δικαιως, RIGHTLY

Lk	23:41	have been condemned **justly**,
1C	15:34	Come to a sober and **right** mind,
1Th	2:10	**upright**, and blameless our
Ti	2:12	are self-controlled, **upright**,
1P	2:23	to the one who judges **justly**.

1347   GO2 AG198 LN64 B3:352 K2:174 R1344
δικαιωσις, MAKING RIGHT

| Ro | 4:25 | raised for our **justification**. |
| | 5:18 | leads to **justification** and life |

1348   GO2 AG198 LN64 R1349
δικαστης, ONE MAKING RIGHT

| Ac | 7:27 | made you a ruler and a **judge** |
| | 7:35 | made you a ruler and a **judge** |

1349 GO3 AG198 LN64 B3:92 K2:174
δικη, RIGHT
Ac 28: 4 **justice** has not allowed him
2Th 1: 9 will suffer the **punishment**
Ju 1: 7 a **punishment** of eternal fire.

1350 GO12 AG198 LN64
δικτυον, NET
Mt 4:20 they left their **nets**
     4:21 mending their **nets,**
Mk 1:18 left their **nets** and followed
     1:19 in their boat mending the **nets.**
Lk 5: 2 and were washing their **nets.**
     5: 4 let down your **nets** for a catch
     5: 5 I will let down the **nets**
     5: 6 **nets** were beginning to break
Jn 21: 6 Cast the **net** to the right side
     21: 8 dragging the **net** full of fish,
     21:11 hauled the **net** ashore, full of
     21:11 so many, the **net** was not torn.

1351 GO1 AG198 LN64 R1364,3056
διλογος, DOUBLE-WORDED
1Ti 3: 8 serious, not **double-tongued,**

1352 GO53 AG198 LN64
διο, WHEREFORE
Mt 27: 8 **For this reason** that field
Lk 1:35 **therefore** the child to be born
     7: 7 **therefore** I did not presume to
Ac 10:29 **So when** I was sent for,
     15:19 **Therefore** I have reached the
     20:31 **Therefore** be alert,
     24:26 and **for that reason** he used
     25:26 **Therefore** I have brought him
     26: 3 **therefore** I beg of you to
     27:25 **So** keep up your courage, men,
     27:34 **Therefore** I urge you to take
Ro 1:24 **Therefore** God gave them up
     2: 1 **Therefore** you have no excuse,
     4:22 **Therefore** his faith
     13: 5 **Therefore** one must be subject,
     15: 7 Welcome one another,
           therefore,
     15:22 **This is the reason** that I have
1C 12: 3 **Therefore** I want you to
     14:13 **Therefore,** one who speaks in
2C 1:20 **For this reason** it is through
     2: 8 **So** I urge you to reaffirm
     4:13 I believed, and **so** I spoke

     4:13 also believe, and **so** we speak,
     4:16 **So** we do not lose heart.
     5: 9 **So** whether we are at home
     6:17 **Therefore** come out from them,
     12: 7 **Therefore,** to keep me from
     12:10 **Therefore** I am content with
Ga 4:31 **So then,** friends,
Ep 2:11 **So then,** remember that at one
     3:13 I pray **therefore** that you may
     4: 8 **Therefore** it is said,
     4:25 **So then,** putting away
     5:14 **Therefore** it says, "Sleeper,
Ph 2: 9 **Therefore** God also highly
1Th 3: 1 **Therefore** when we could bear
     5:11 **Therefore** encourage one
           another
Pm 1: 8 **For this reason,** though I am
He 3: 7 **Therefore,** as the Holy Spirit
     3:10 **Therefore** I was angry with that
     6: 1 **Therefore** let us go on toward
     10: 5 **Consequently,** when Christ came
     11:12 **Therefore** from one person,
     11:16 **Therefore** God is not ashamed
     12:12 **Therefore** lift your drooping
     12:28 **Therefore,** since we are
     13:12 **Therefore** Jesus also suffered
Ja 1:21 **Therefore** rid yourselves of all
     4: 6 **therefore** it says, "God opposes
1P 1:13 **Therefore** prepare your minds
2P 1:10 **Therefore,** brothers and sisters
     1:12 **Therefore** I intend to keep on
     3:14 **Therefore,** beloved, while you

1353 GO2 AG198 LN64 R1223,3593
διοδευω, I MAKE WAY THROUGH
Lk 8: 1 he **went on** through cities and
Ac 17: 1 had **passed through** Amphipolis

1354 GO1 AG199 LN64
διονυσιος, DIONYSIUS
Ac 17:34 **Dionysius** the Areopagite

1355 GO2 AG199 LN64
διοπερ, THEREFORE
1C 8:13 **Therefore,** if food is a cause
     10:14 **Therefore,** my dear friends,

1356 GO1 AG199 LN64
διοπετης, FALLEN GOD
Ac 19:35 statue that **fell from heaven**

1356a GO1 AG199 LN64
διορθωμα, CORRECTION
Ac 24: 2 and **reforms** have been made

1357 GO1 AG199 LN64 B3:351 K5:450
διορθωσις, CORRECTION
He 9:10 **regulations** for the body

1358 GO4 AG199 LN64 R1223,3736
διορυσσω, I DIG THROUGH
Mt 6:19 thieves **break in** and steal
 6:20 thieves do not **break in** and
 24:43 let his house be **broken into.**
Lk 12:39 let his house **be broken into.**

1359 GO1 AG199 LN64
διοσκουροι, DIOSCURI
Ac 28:11 with the **Twin Brothers**

1360 GO23 AG199 LN65
διοτι, BECAUSE
Lk 1:13 **for** your prayer has been heard
 2: 7 **because** there was no place
 21:28 **because** your redemption
Ac 13:35 **Therefore** he has also said in
 18:10 **for** I am with you, and no one
 18:10 **for** there are many in this city
 20:26 **Therefore** I declare to you
 22:18 **because** they will not accept
Ro 1:19 **For** what can be known about
 1:21 **for though** they knew God,
 3:20 **For** "no human being will be
 8: 7 **For this reason** the mind that
1C 15: 9 **because** I persecuted the
 church
Ph 2:26 **because** you heard that he was
1Th 2: 8 **because** you have become very
 2:18 **For** we wanted to come to you
 4: 6 **because** the Lord is an avenger
He 11: 5 **because** God had taken him
 11:23 **because** they saw that the
 child
Ja 4:3 **because** you ask wrongly,
1P 1:16 **for** it is written, "You shall
 1:24 **For** "All flesh is like grass
 2: 6 **For** it stands in scripture

1361 GO1 AG199 LN65
διοτρεφης, DIOTREPHES
3J 1: 9 but **Diotrephes,** who likes

1362 GO4 AG199 LN65
διπλους, DOUBLE
Mt 23:15 **twice** as much a child of hell
1Ti 5:17 worthy of **double** honor,
Re 18: 6 repay her **double** for her
 deeds
 18: 6 mix a **double** draught for her

1363 GO1 AG199 LN65 R1362
διπλοω, I DOUBLE
Re 18: 6 **repay** her double for her deeds

1364 GO6 AG199 LN65 R1417
δις, TWICE
Mk 14:30 before the cock crows **twice,**
 14:72 cock crowed for the **second**
 time
Lk 18:12 I fast **twice** a week
Ph 4:16 for my needs **more than once.**
1Th 2:18 wanted to again and **again**
Ju 1:12 **twice** dead, uprooted

1364a GO1 AG199 LN65 R3461
δισμυριας, TWO TEN THOUSANDS
Re 9:16 was **two hundred [million]**

1365 GO2 AG200 LN65
δισταζω, I DOUBT
Mt 14:31 little faith, why did you **doubt**
 28:17 worshiped him; but some
 doubted

1366 GO3 AG200 LN65 R1364,4750
διστομος, TWO-MOUTHED
He 4:12 than any **two-edged** sword,
Re 1:16 came a sharp, **two-edged**
 sword,
 2:12 has the sharp **two-edged** sword

1367 GO1 AG200 LN65 B2:699 R1364,5507
δισχιλιοι, TWO THOUSAND
Mk 5:13 numbering about **two thousand**

1368 GO1 AG200 LN65
διυλιζω, I FILTER
Mt 23:24 **strain out** a gnat but swallow

1369 GO1 AG200 LN65
διχαζω, I SPLIT APART
Mt 10:35 to **set** a man **against** his father

1370　GO2 AG200 LN65 K1:514
διχοστασια, DIVISIONS
Ro　16:17　cause **dissensions** and offenses,
Ga　5:20　anger, quarrels, **dissensions,**

1371　GO2 AG200 LN65 K2:225
διχοτομεω, I CUT IN TWO
Mt　24:51　He will **cut** him **in pieces**
Lk　12:46　will **cut** him **in pieces,**

1372　GO16 AG200 LN65 B2:264 K2:226 R1373
διψαω, I THIRST
Mt　5: 6　**thirst** for righteousness,
　　25:35　I was **thirsty** and you gave me
　　25:37　or **thirsty** and gave you
　　25:42　I was **thirsty** and you gave me
　　25:44　we saw you hungry or **thirsty**
Jn　4:13　water will be **thirsty** again,
　　4:14　them will never be **thirsty.**
　　4:15　that I may never be **thirsty**
　　6:35　in me will never be **thirsty.**
　　7:37　who is **thirsty** come to me
　　19:28　I am **thirsty.**
Ro　12:20　if they are **thirsty,** give them
1C　4:11　hour we are hungry and
　　　　thirsty
Re　7:16　no more, and **thirst** no more
　　21: 6　the **thirsty** I will give water
　　22:17　everyone who is **thirsty** come.

1373　GO1 AG200 LN65 B2:265 K2:226
διψος, THIRST
2C　11:27　hungry and **thirsty,**

1374　GO2 AG201 LN65 B3:686 K9:665 R1364,5590
διψυχος, TWO-SOULED
Ja　1: 8　being **double-minded**
　　4: 8　your hearts, you **double-**
　　　　minded.

1375　GO10 AG201 LN65 B2:805 R1377
διωγμος, PERSECUTION
Mt　13:21　trouble or **persecution** arises
Mk　4:17　trouble or **persecution** arises
　　10:30　and fields with **persecutions**
Ac　8: 1　That day a severe **persecution**
　　13:50　stirred up **persecution**
Ro　8:35　or distress, or **persecution,**
2C　12:10　hardships, **persecutions,**
2Th　1: 4　during all your **persecutions**

2Ti　3:11　my **persecutions** and suffering
　　3:11　What **persecutions** I endured!

1376　GO1 AG201 LN65 R1377
διωκτης, PERSECUTOR
1Ti　1:13　blasphemer, a **persecutor,**

1377　GO45 AG201 LN65 B2:805 K2:229
διωκω, I PURSUE
Mt　5:10　those who are **persecuted**
　　5:11　revile you and **persecute** you
　　5:12　they **persecuted** the prophets
　　5:44　pray for those who **persecute**
　　10:23　they **persecute** you in one town
　　23:34　and **pursue** from town to town,
Lk　11:49　will kill and **persecute,**
　　17:23　do not set off in **pursuit.**
　　21:12　arrest you and **persecute** you;
Jn　5:16　Jews started **persecuting** Jesus
　　15:20　If they **persecuted** me,
　　15:20　will of the prophets **persecute**
Ac　7:52　your ancestors not **persecute**
　　9: 4　Saul, why do you **persecute** me
　　9: 5　whom you are **persecuting.**
　　22: 4　I **persecuted** this Way up to the
　　22: 7　why are you **persecuting** me
　　22: 8　whom you are **persecuting.**
　　26:11　I **pursued** them even to foreign
　　26:14　why are you **persecuting** me
　　26:15　Jesus whom you are **persecuting.**
Ro　9:30　Gentiles, who did not **strive**
　　9:31　but Israel, who did **strive**
　　12:13　**extend** hospitality
　　12:14　Bless those who **persecute** you
　　14:19　**pursue** what makes for peace
1C　4:12　when **persecuted,** we endure
　　14: 1　**Pursue** love and strive for the
　　15: 9　I **persecuted** the church of God.
2C　4: 9　**persecuted,** but not forsaken
Ga　1:13　I was violently **persecuting**
　　1:23　who formerly was **persecuting** us
　　4:29　**persecuted** the child who was
　　5:11　why am I still being **persecuted**
　　6:12　that they may not be **persecuted**
Ph　3: 6　a **persecutor** of the church;
　　3:12　I **press on** to make it my own,
　　3:14　I **press on** toward the goal
1Th　5:15　but always **seek** to do good
1Ti　6:11　**pursue** righteousness,

2Ti	2:22	and **pursue** righteousness,
	3:12	will be **persecuted.**
He	12:14	**Pursue** peace with everyone
1P	3:11	seek peace and **pursue** it
Re	12:13	he **pursued** the woman who had

1378　ᴳᴼ5　ᴬᴳ201　ᴸᴺ65　ᴮ1:330　ᴷ2:230
δογμα, DECREE

Lk	2: 1	a **decree** went out from Emperor
Ac	16: 4	**decisions** that had been reached
	17: 7	acting contrary to the **decrees**
Ep	2:15	its commandments and **ordinances**
Co	2:14	erasing the **record** that stood

1379　ᴳᴼ1　ᴬᴳ201　ᴸᴺ65　ᴮ1:330　ᴷ2:230　ᴿ1379
δογματιζω, I DECREE

Co	2:20	do you **submit to regulations,**

1380　ᴳᴼ62　ᴬᴳ201　ᴸᴺ65　ᴮ3:821　ᴷ2:232
δοκεω, I THINK

Mt	3: 9	Do not **presume** to say
	6: 7	for they **think** that they will
	17:25	What do you **think,** Simon?
	18:12	What do you **think?**
	21:28	What do you **think?**
	22:17	Tell us, then, what you **think.**
	22:42	do you **think** of the Messiah?
	24:44	coming at an **unexpected** hour.
	26:53	Do you **think** that I cannot
	26:66	What is your **verdict**
Mk	6:49	they **thought** it was a ghost
	10:42	they **recognize** as their rulers
Lk	1: 3	I too **decided,**
	8:18	what they **seem** to have will be
	10:36	of these three, do you **think,**
	12:40	coming at an **unexpected** hour
	12:51	Do you **think** that I have come
	13: 2	Do you **think** that because
	13: 4	do you **think** that they were
	19:11	they **supposed** that the kingdom
	22:24	to be **regarded** as the greatest.
	24:37	**thought** that they were seeing
Jn	5:39	you **think** that in them you have
	5:45	Do not **think** that I will accuse
	11:13	but they **thought** that he was
	11:31	they **thought** that she was going
	11:56	What do you **think?** Surely he
	13:29	Some **thought** that, because
	16: 2	you will **think** that by doing so
	20:15	**Supposing** him to be the

Ac	12: 9	**thought** he was seeing a vision.
	15:22	**decided** to choose men
	15:25	we have **decided** unanimously
	15:28	**seemed** good to the Holy Spirit
	17:18	He **seems** to be a proclaimer
	25:27	**seems** to me unreasonable
	26: 9	I myself **was convinced**
	27:13	they **thought** they could achieve
1C	3:18	If you **think** that you are wise
	4: 9	I **think** that God has exhibited
	7:40	And I **think** that I too have
	8: 2	Anyone who **claims** to know
	10:12	if you **think** you are standing,
	11:16	if anyone is **disposed** to be
	12:22	the body that **seem** to be weaker
	12:23	that we **think** less honorable
	14:37	who **claims** to be a prophet,
2C	10: 9	I do not want to **seem** as though
	11:16	no one **think** that I am a fool;
	12:19	you been **thinking** all along
Ga	2: 2	with the **acknowledged** leaders
	2: 6	**supposed** to be acknowledged
	2: 6	**leaders** contributed nothing
	2: 9	who were **acknowledged** pillars,
	6: 3	**think** they are something,
Ph	3: 4	If anyone else has **reason**
He	4: 1	none of you should **seem** to have
	10:29	do you **think** will be deserved
	12:10	time as **seemed** best to them,
	12:11	discipline always **seems** painful
Ja	1:26	If any **think** they are religious
	4: 5	**suppose** that it is for nothing

1381　ᴳᴼ22　ᴬᴳ202　ᴸᴺ66　ᴮ3:808　ᴷ2:255　ᴿ1384
δοκιμαζω, I APPROVE

Lk	12:56	You know how to **interpret**
	12:56	to **interpret** the present time
	14:19	I am going to **try** them **out;**
Ro	1:28	since they **did** not **see fit**
	2:18	know his will and **determine**
	12: 2	so that you may **discern**
	14:22	because of what they **approve.**
1C	3:13	the fire **will test** what sort
	16: 3	any whom you **approve**
2C	8: 8	**am testing** the genuineness
	8:22	whom we **have** often **tested**
	13: 5	**Test** yourselves. Do you not
Ga	6: 4	All must **test** their own work;
Ep	5:10	**Try to find out** what is

Ph	1:10	to **determine** what is best,
1Th	2: 4	just as we **have been approved**
	2: 4	God who **tests** our hearts.
	5:21	but **test** everything;
1Ti	3:10	let them first **be tested;**
1P	1: 7	perishable, **is tested** by fire
1J	4: 1	but **test** the spirits to see

1381a   GO1 AG202 LN66 B3:808 K2:255 R1384
δοκιμασια, PROVING
| He | 3: 9 | ancestors put me to the **test,** |

1382   GO7 AG202 LN66 B3:808 K2:255 R1384
δοκιμη, APPROVAL
Ro	5: 4	endurance produces **character,**
	5: 4	and **character** produces hope,
2C	2: 9	to **test** you and to know
	8: 2	for during a severe **ordeal**
	9:13	the **testing** of this ministry
	13: 3	you desire **proof** that Christ
Ph	2:22	But Timothy's **worth** you know,

1383   GO2 AG203 LN66 B3:808 K2:255
δοκιμιον, PROOF
| Ja | 1: 3 | you know that the **testing** |
| 1P | 1: 7 | perishable, **is tested** by fire |

1384   GO7 AG203 LN66 B3:808 K2:255
δοκιμος, PROVED
Ro	14:18	to God and has human **approval.**
	16:10	who is **approved** in Christ.
1C	11:19	clear who among you are **genuine**
2C	10:18	themselves that are **approved,**
	13: 7	may appear to have **met** the test
2Ti	2:15	to God as one **approved** by him,
Ja	1:12	Such a one **has stood** the test

1385   GO6 AG203 LN66
δοκος, LOG
Mt	7: 3	notice the **log** in your own eye
	7: 4	the **log** is in your own eye
	7: 5	the **log** out of your own eye,
Lk	6:41	notice the **log** in your own eye
	6:42	not see the **log** in your own eye
	6:42	first take the **log** out of your

1386   GO1 AG203 LN66 R1388
δολιος, BEGUILING
| 2C | 11:13 | apostles, **deceitful** workers, |

1387   GO1 AG203 LN66 R1386
δολιοω, I BEGUILE
| Ro | 3:13 | use their tongues to **deceive** |

1388   GO11 AG203 LN66
δολος, GUILE
Mt	26: 4	to arrest Jesus by **stealth**
Mk	7:22	avarice, wickedness, **deceit,**
	14: 1	to arrest Jesus by **stealth**
Jn	1:47	in whom there is no **deceit**
Ac	13:10	full of all **deceit** and villainy
Ro	1:29	envy, murder, strife, **deceit,**
2C	12:16	I took you in by **deceit.**
1Th	2: 3	does not spring from **deceit**
1P	2: 1	of all malice, and all **guile,**
	2:22	**deceit** was found in his mouth
	3:10	their lips from speaking **deceit**

1389   GO1 AG203 LN66 R1388
δολοω, I BEGUILE
| 2C | 4: 2 | practice cunning or to **falsify** |

1390   GO4 AG203 LN66 R1325
δομα, GIFT
Mt	7:11	know how to give good **gifts**
Lk	11:13	know how to give good **gifts**
Ep	4: 8	he gave **gifts** to his people
Ph	4:17	Not that I seek the **gift,**

1391   GO166 AG203 LN66 B2:44 K2:233
δοξα, SPLENDOR, GLORY
Mt	4: 8	of the world and their **splendor**
	6:29	Solomon in all his **glory**
	16:27	in the **glory** of his Father,
	19:28	on the throne of his **glory,**
	24:30	with power and great **glory.**
	25:31	Son of Man comes in his **glory,**
	25:31	sit on the throne of his **glory.**
Mk	8:38	in the **glory** of his Father
	10:37	at your left, in your **glory**
	13:26	with great power and **glory**
Lk	2: 9	the **glory** of the Lord shone
	2:14	**Glory** to God in the highest
	2:32	**glory** to your people Israel
	4: 6	I will give their **glory**
	9:26	when he comes in his **glory**
	9:31	They appeared in **glory**
	9:32	they saw his **glory**
	12:27	Solomon in all his **glory**
	14:10	be **honored** in the presence

	17:18	return and give **praise** to God
	19:38	**glory** in the highest heaven
	21:27	with power and great **glory**
	24:26	and then enter into his **glory**
Jn	1:14	we have seen his **glory,**
	1:14	**glory** as of a father's only son
	2:11	and revealed his **glory;**
	5:41	I do not accept **glory**
	5:44	when you accept **glory** from one
	5:44	and do not seek the **glory** that
	7:18	own seek their own **glory;**
	7:18	the one who seeks the **glory**
	8:50	I do not seek my own **glory;**
	8:54	myself, my **glory** is nothing.
	9:24	Give **glory** to God! We know that
	11: 4	rather it is for God's **glory,**
	11:40	you would see the **glory** of God
	12:41	because he saw his **glory**
	12:43	for they loved human **glory** more
	12:43	the **glory** that comes from God.
	17: 5	with the **glory** that I had
	17:22	The **glory** that you have given
	17:24	where I am, to see my **glory,**
Ac	7: 2	The God of **glory** appeared
	7:55	heaven and saw the **glory** of God
	12:23	he had not given the **glory**
	22:11	of the **brightness** of that light
Ro	1:23	and they exchanged the **glory**
	2: 7	seek for **glory** and honor
	2:10	but **glory** and honor and peace
	3: 7	abounds to his **glory,** why am I
	3:23	fall short of the **glory** of God
	4:20	faith as he gave **glory** to God,
	5: 2	our hope of sharing the **glory**
	6: 4	by the **glory** of the Father,
	8:18	worth comparing with the **glory**
	8:21	obtain the freedom of the **glory**
	9: 4	belong the adoption, the **glory,**
	9:23	known the riches of his **glory**
	9:23	prepared beforehand for **glory**
	11:36	To him be the **glory** forever.
	15: 7	for the **glory** of God.
	16:27	to whom be the **glory** forever
1C	2: 7	before the ages for our **glory.**
	2: 8	crucified the Lord of **glory.**
	10:31	everything for the **glory** of God
	11: 7	he is the image and **reflection**
	11: 7	woman is the **reflection** of man.
	11:15	it is her **glory**

	15:40	but the **glory** of the heavenly
	15:41	There is one **glory** of the sun,
	15:41	and another **glory** of the moon,
	15:41	and another **glory** of the stars;
	15:41	differs from star in **glory.**
	15:43	it is raised in **glory.**
2C	1:20	"Amen," to the **glory** of God.
	3: 7	came in **glory** so that the
	3: 7	of the **glory** of his face,
	3: 8	of the Spirit come in **glory**
	3: 9	was **glory** in the ministry
	3: 9	justification abound in **glory**
	3:10	because of the greater **glory**
	3:11	set aside came through **glory,**
	3:11	has the permanent come in **glory**
	3:18	seeing the **glory** of the Lord
	3:18	one degree of **glory** to another
	3:18	one degree of glory to **another;**
	4: 4	gospel of the **glory** of Christ,
	4: 6	knowledge of the **glory** of God
	4:15	to the **glory** of God.
	4:17	for an eternal weight of **glory**
	6: 8	in **honor** and dishonor,
	8:19	the **glory** of the Lord himself
	8:23	churches, the **glory** of Christ.
Ga	1: 5	to whom be the **glory** forever
Ep	1: 6	to the praise of his **glorious**
	1:12	for the praise of his **glory.**
	1:14	the praise of his **glory.**
	1:17	the Father of **glory,**
	1:18	his **glorious** inheritance among
	3:13	they are your **glory.**
	3:16	to the riches of his **glory,**
	3:21	to him be **glory** in the church
Ph	1:11	for the **glory** and praise of God
	2:11	the **glory** of God the Father.
	3:19	their **glory** is in their shame;
	3:21	to the body of his **glory,**
	4:19	his riches in **glory** in Christ
	4:20	To our God and Father be **glory**
Co	1:11	comes from his **glorious** power,
	1:27	of the **glory** of this mystery,
	1:27	in you, the hope of **glory.**
	3: 4	be revealed with him in **glory.**
1Th	2: 6	nor did we seek **praise**
	2:12	into his own kingdom and **glory**
	2:20	Yes, you are our **glory** and joy
2Th	1: 9	from the **glory** of his might,
	2:14	**glory** of our Lord Jesus Christ.

1Ti	1:11	conforms to the **glorious** gospel		**1392**	GO61 AG204 LN66 B2:44 K2:253 R1391	
	1:17	be honor and **glory** forever and		δοξαζω, I GIVE SPLENDOR, I GLORIFY		
	3:16	the world, taken up in **glory**.		Mt	5:16	**give glory** to your Father
2Ti	2:10	Jesus, with eternal **glory**.			6: 2	they **may be praised** by others
	4:18	To him be the **glory** forever			9: 8	and they **glorified** God,
Ti	2:13	the **glory** of our great God			15:31	they **praised** the God of Israel
He	1: 3	the reflection of God's **glory**		Mk	2:12	all amazed and **glorified** God,
	2: 7	have crowned them with **glory**		Lk	2:20	**glorifying** and praising God
	2: 9	now crowned with **glory**			4:15	and was **praised** by everyone.
	2:10	bringing many children to **glory**			5:25	to his home, **glorifying** God.
	3: 3	Jesus is worthy of more **glory**			5:26	**glorified** God and were filled
	9: 5	were the cherubim of **glory**			7:16	them; and they **glorified** God
	13:21	to whom be the **glory** forever			13:13	and began **praising** God
Ja	2: 1	believe in our **glorious** Lord			17:15	**praising** God with a loud voice
1P	1: 7	to result in praise and **glory**			18:43	followed him, **glorifying** God
	1:11	Christ and the subsequent **glory**			23:47	he **praised** God and said
	1:21	the dead and gave him **glory,**		Jn	7:39	Jesus was not yet **glorified.**
	1:24	like grass and all its **glory**			8:54	If I **glorify** myself, my glory
	4:11	To him belong the **glory** and			8:54	It is my Father who **glorifies**
	4:13	when his **glory** is revealed.			11: 4	Son of God may be **glorified**
	4:14	because the spirit of **glory,**			12:16	but when Jesus was **glorified,**
	5: 1	one who shares in the **glory**			12:23	the Son of Man to be **glorified**
	5: 4	will win the crown of **glory**			12:28	Father, **glorify** your name.
	5:10	to his eternal **glory** in Christ			12:28	I have **glorified** it, and I will
2P	1: 3	by his own **glory** and goodness.			12:28	and I will **glorify** it again.
	1:17	For he received honor and **glory**			13:31	Son of Man has been **glorified,**
	1:17	by the Majestic **Glory,** saying,			13:31	God has been **glorified** in him.
	2:10	afraid to slander the **glorious**			13:32	God has been **glorified** in him
	3:18	To him be the **glory** both now			13:32	God will also **glorify** him in
Ju	1: 8	and slander the **glorious** ones.			13:32	and will **glorify** him at once.
	1:24	in the presence of his **glory**			14:13	the Father may be **glorified**
	1:25	be **glory,** majesty, power,			15: 8	Father is **glorified** by this,
Re	1: 6	to him be **glory** and dominion			16:14	He will **glorify** me,
	4: 9	living creatures give **glory**			17: 1	has come; **glorify** your Son
	4:11	to receive **glory** and honor			17: 1	that the Son may **glorify** you,
	5:12	honor and **glory** and blessing			17: 4	I **glorified** you on earth
	5:13	**glory** and might forever			17: 5	**glorify** me in your own presence
	7:12	Blessing and **glory** and wisdom			17:10	I have been **glorified** in them.
	11:13	**glory** to the God of heaven.			21:19	by which he would **glorify** God
	14: 7	Fear God and give him **glory,**		Ac	3:13	**glorified** his servant Jesus,
	15: 8	smoke from the **glory** of God			4:21	for all of them **praised** God
	16: 9	not repent and give him **glory**.			11:18	they **praised** God, saying,
	18: 1	made bright with his **splendor.**			13:48	were glad and **praised** the word
	19: 1	**glory** and power to our God			21:20	they heard it, they **praised** God
	19: 7	and give him the **glory,**		Ro	1:21	they did not **honor** him as God
	21:11	It has the **glory** of God			8:30	he justified he also **glorified**
	21:23	the **glory** of God is its light,			11:13	I **glorify** my ministry
	21:24	earth will bring their **glory**.			15: 6	with one voice **glorify** the God
	21:26	**glory** and the honor of the			15: 9	the Gentiles might **glorify** God

1C	6:20	**glorify** God in your body.
	12:26	if one member is **honored,**
2C	3:10	what once **had glory** has lost
	3:10	has **lost** its **glory** because
	9:13	**glorify** God by your obedience
Ga	1:24	**glorified** God because of me.
2Th	3: 1	be **glorified** everywhere,
He	5: 5	Christ did not **glorify** himself
1P	1: 8	indescribable and **glorious** joy
	2:12	**glorify** God when he comes to
	4:11	may be **glorified** in all things
	4:16	**glorify** God because you bear
Re	15: 4	who will not fear and **glorify**
	18: 7	she **glorified** herself and lived

1393　　GO2 AG204 LN66
δορκας, DORCAS

Ac	9:36	which in Greek is **Dorcas.**
	9:39	clothing that **Dorcas** had made

1394　　GO2 AG204 LN66 R1325
δοσις, GIVING

Ph	4:15	matter of **giving** and receiving,
Ja	1:17	Every generous act of **giving,**

1395　　GO1 AG205 LN66 R1325
δοτης, GIVER

2C	9: 7	for God loves a cheerful **giver.**

1396　　GO1 AG205 LN66 K2:279 R1401,71
δουλαγωγεω, I LEAD INTO SLAVERY

1C	9:27	I punish my body and **enslave** it

1397　　GO5 AG205 LN66 B3:592 K2:261 R1398
δουλεια, SLAVERY

Ro	8:15	receive a spirit of **slavery**
	8:21	be set free from its **bondage**
Ga	4:24	bearing children for **slavery**
	5: 1	again to a yoke of **slavery.**
He	2:15	**slavery** by the fear of death

1398　　GO25 AG205 LN66 B3:592 K2:261 R1401
δουλευω, I SLAVE

Mt	6:24	No one can **serve** two masters
	6:24	You cannot **serve** God and wealth
Lk	15:29	have been **working like a slave**
	16:13	No slave can **serve** two masters
	16:13	You cannot **serve** God and wealth
Jn	8:33	never **been slaves** to anyone
Ac	7: 7	the nation that they **serve**

	20:19	**serving** the Lord with all
Ro	6: 6	no longer **be enslaved** to sin
	7: 6	so that we **are slaves** not under
	7:25	with my mind I **am** a **slave**
	9:12	elder **shall serve** the younger
	12:11	in spirit, **serve** the Lord
	14:18	The one who thus **serves** Christ
	16:18	do not **serve** our Lord Christ
Ga	4: 8	you **were enslaved** to beings
	4: 9	How can you want to **be enslaved**
	4:25	**is in slavery** with her children
	5:13	but through love **become slaves**
Ep	6: 7	**Render** service with enthusiasm
Ph	2:22	he **has served** with me
Co	3:24	you **serve** the Lord Christ
1Th	1: 9	to **serve** a living and true God
1Ti	6: 2	**must serve** them all the more,
Ti	3: 3	**slaves** to various passions

1399　　GO3 AG205 LN66 K2:261 R1401
δουλη, WOMAN SLAVE

Lk	1:38	the **servant** of the Lord;
	1:48	on the lowliness of his **servant**
Ac	2:18	my **slaves,** both men and women,

1400　　GO2 AG205 LN67 R1401
δουλος, SLAVE

Ro	6:19	members as **slaves** to impurity
	6:19	present your members as **slaves**

1401　　GO124 AG205 LN67 B3:292 K2:261
δουλος, SLAVE

Mt	8: 9	to my **slave,** 'Do this
	10:24	nor a **slave** above the master
	10:25	the **slave** like the master
	13:27	the **slaves** of the householder
	13:28	The **slaves** said to him,
	18:23	settle accounts with his **slaves**
	18:26	So the **slave** fell on his knees
	18:27	the lord of that **slave**
	18:28	But that same **slave,**
	18:32	You wicked **slave**
	20:27	among you must be your **slave**
	21:34	sent his **slaves** to the tenants
	21:35	the tenants seized his **slaves**
	21:36	Again he sent other **slaves**
	22: 3	He sent his **slaves** to call
	22: 4	Again he sent other **slaves,**
	22: 6	the rest seized his **slaves,**

	22: 8	Then he said to his **slaves,**		15:20	**Servants** are not greater than
	22:10	Those **slaves** went out into the		18:10	struck the high priest's **slave,**
	24:45	is the faithful and wise **slave**		18:10	The **slave's** name was Malchus.
	24:46	Blessed is that **slave**		18:18	Now the **slaves** and the police
	24:48	But if that wicked **slave**		18:26	One of the **slaves** of the high
	24:50	the master of that **slave**	Ac	2:18	Even upon my **slaves,** both men
	25:19	master of those **slaves** came		16:17	men are **slaves** of the Most High
	25:21	good and trustworthy **slave**	Ro	1: 1	Paul, a **servant** of Jesus Christ
	25:23	good and trustworthy **slave**		6:16	to anyone as obedient **slaves,**
	25:26	You wicked and lazy **slave!**		6:16	you are **slaves** of the one whom
	25:30	As for this worthless **slave,**		6:17	having once been **slaves** of sin
	26:51	the **slave** of the high priest		6:20	When you were **slaves** of sin,
Mk	10:44	among you must be **slave** of all	1C	7:21	Were you a **slave** when called?
	12: 2	he sent a **slave** to the tenants		7:22	called in the Lord as a **slave**
	12: 4	he sent another **slave** to them		7:22	free when called is a **slave**
	13:34	puts his **slaves** in charge		7:23	become **slaves** of human masters
	14:47	the **slave** of the high priest		12:13	Jews or Greeks, **slaves** or free
Lk	2:29	you are dismissing your **servant**	2C	4: 5	and ourselves as your **slaves**
	7: 2	had a **slave** whom he valued	Ga	1:10	not be a **servant** of Christ
	7: 3	to come and heal his **slave.**		3:28	is no longer **slave** or free,
	7: 8	to my **slave,** 'Do this,'		4: 1	are no better than **slaves,**
	7:10	found the **slave** in good health		4: 7	So you are no longer a **slave**
	12:37	Blessed are those **slaves** whom	Ep	6: 5	**Slaves,** obey your earthly
	12:43	Blessed is that **slave** whom		6: 6	but as **slaves** of Christ,
	12:45	if that **slave** says to himself		6: 8	whether we are **slaves** or free.
	12:46	master of that **slave** will come	Ph	1: 1	and Timothy, **servants** of Christ
	12:47	**slave** who knew what his master		2: 7	taking the form of a **slave,**
	14:17	he sent his **slave** to say	Co	3:11	Scythian, **slave** and free;
	14:21	the **slave** returned and reported		3:22	**Slaves,** obey your earthly
	14:21	angry and said to his **slave,**		4: 1	treat your **slaves** justly and
	14:22	And the **slave** said, 'Sir,		4:12	a **servant** of Christ Jesus,
	14:23	the master said to the **slave,**	1Ti	6: 1	under the yoke of **slavery**
	15:22	the father said to his **slaves,**	2Ti	2:24	And the Lord's **servant** must not
	17: 7	would say to your **slave** who has	Ti	1: 1	**servant** of God and an apostle
	17: 9	Do you thank the **slave** for		2: 9	Tell **slaves** to be submissive
	17:10	We are worthless **slaves;**	Pm	1:16	no longer as a **slave** but more
	19:13	He summoned ten of his **slaves,**		1:16	but more than a **slave**
	19:15	he ordered these **slaves,**	Ja	1: 1	James, a **servant** of God
	19:17	Well done, good **slave!**	1P	2:16	As **servants** of God, live as
	19:22	own words, you wicked **slave!**	2P	1: 1	Simeon Peter, a **servant**
	20:10	he sent a **slave** to the tenants		2:19	are **slaves** of corruption;
	20:11	Next he sent another **slave;**	Ju	1: 1	Jude, a **servant** of Jesus Christ
	22:50	one of them struck the **slave**	Re	1: 1	to show his **servants** what must
Jn	4:51	his **slaves** met him and told him		1: 1	his angel to his **servant** John,
	8:34	commits sin is a **slave** to sin.		2:20	beguiling my **servants**
	8:35	The **slave** does not have		6:15	everyone, **slave** and free,
	13:16	**servants** are not greater than		7: 3	marked the **servants** of our God
	15:15	I do not call you **servants** any		10: 7	announced to his **servants**
	15:15	because the **servant** does not		11:18	for rewarding your **servants,**

13:16 and poor, both free and **slave,**
15: 3 the **servant** of God,
19: 2 the blood of his **servants**
19: 5 our God, all you his **servants,**
19:18 both free and **slave,** both small
22: 3 his **servants** will worship him
22: 6 show his **servants** what must

1402 GO8 AG206 LN67 K2:279 R1401
δουλοω, I SLAVE

Ac   7: 6 would **enslave** them and mistreat
Ro   6:18 **become slaves** of righteousness.
       6:22 freed from sin and **enslaved**
1C   7:15 brother or sister **is** not **bound.**
       9:19 I have **made** myself a **slave**
Ga   4: 3 were minors, we **were enslaved**
Ti   2: 3 slanderers or **slaves** to drink;
2P   2:19 for people **are slaves**

1403 GO2 AG206 LN67 K2:54 R1209
δοχη, RECEPTION

Lk   5:29 Then Levi gave a great **banquet**
      14:13 But when you give a **banquet,**

1404 GO13 AG206 LN67 B1:507 K2:281
δρακων, DRAGON

Re   12: 3 a great red **dragon,** with seven
      12: 4 **dragon** stood before the woman
      12: 7 fought against the **dragon.**
      12: 7 The **dragon** and his angels
      12: 9 great **dragon** was thrown down,
      12:13 So when the **dragon** saw that he
      12:16 **dragon** had poured from his
      12:17 **dragon** was angry with the
              woman
      13: 2 the **dragon** gave it his power
      13: 4 They worshiped the **dragon,**
      13:11 and it spoke like a **dragon.**
      16:13 from the mouth of the **dragon,**
      20: 2 He seized the **dragon,**

1405 GO1 AG206 LN67
δρασσομαι, I TRAP

1C   3:19 He **catches** the wise in their

1406 GO3 AG206 LN67
δραχμη, DRACHMA

Lk   15: 8 woman having ten silver **coins,**
      15: 8 if she loses **one** of them,
      15: 9 found the **coin** that I had lost

1407 GO8 AG206 LN67
δρεπανον, SICKLE

Mk   4:29 he goes in with his **sickle,**
Re   14:14 a sharp **sickle** in his hand
      14:15 Use your **sickle** and reap,
      14:16 his **sickle** over the earth,
      14:17 he too had a sharp **sickle.**
      14:18 him who had the sharp **sickle**
      14:18 Use your sharp **sickle**
      14:19 So the angel swung his **sickle**

1408 GO3 AG206 LN67 B3:945 K8:233
δρομος, RACE

Ac   13:25 as John was finishing his **work,**
      20:24 if only I may finish my **course**
2Ti   4: 7 I have finished the **race,**

1409 GO1 AG207 LN67
δρουσιλλα, DRUSILLA

Ac   24:24 came with his wife **Drusilla,**

1410 GO210 AG207 LN67 B2:601 K2:284
δυναμαι, I AM ABLE

Mt   3: 9 God **is able** from these stones
       5:14 built on a hill **cannot be** hid.
       5:36 you **cannot** make one hair white
       6:24 No one **can** serve two masters;
       6:24 You **cannot** serve God and wealth
       6:27 **can** any of you by worrying
       7:18 A good tree **cannot** bear bad
       8: 2 choose, you **can** make me clean
       9:15 The wedding guests **cannot** mourn
       9:28 you believe that I **am able**
      10:28 but **cannot** kill the soul;
      10:28 **can** destroy both soul and body
      12:29 **one** enter a strong man's house
      12:34 How **can** you speak good things,
      16: 3 you **cannot** interpret the signs
      17:16 but they **could** not cure him
      17:19 Why **could** we not cast it out
      19:12 anyone accept this who **can.**
      19:25 Then who **can** be saved?
      20:22 Are you **able** to drink the cup
      20:22 said to him, "We **are able.**"
      22:46 No one **was able** to give him
      26: 9 ointment **could** have been sold
      26:42 **cannot** pass unless I drink it
      26:53 you think that I **cannot** appeal
      26:61 I **am able** to destroy the temple
      27:42 he **cannot** save himself.

Mk	1:40	you **can** make me clean
	1:45	Jesus **could** no longer go into
	2: 4	when they **could** not bring him
	2: 7	Who **can** forgive sins but God
	2:19	wedding guests **cannot** fast
	2:19	with them, they **cannot** fast
	3:20	they **could** not even eat
	3:23	How **can** Satan cast out Satan?
	3:24	that kingdom **cannot** stand
	3:25	will not **be able to stand.**
	3:26	divided, he **cannot** stand,
	3:27	But no one **can** enter a strong
	4:32	**can** make nests in its shade.
	4:33	as they **were able** to hear it
	5: 3	one **could** restrain him any more
	6: 5	he **could** do no deed of power
	6:19	But she **could** not
	7:15	that by going in **can** defile,
	7:18	from outside **cannot** defile
	7:24	Yet he **could** not escape notice
	8: 4	How **can** one feed these people
	9: 3	one on earth **could** bleach them
	9:22	but if you **are able** to do
	9:23	If you **are able**
	9:28	Why **could** we not cast it out
	9:29	This kind **can** come out only
	9:39	will **be able** soon afterward
	10:26	Then who **can** be saved
	10:38	**Are** you **able** to drink the cup
	10:39	We **are able.**
	14: 5	ointment **could** have been sold
	14: 7	you **can** show kindness to them
	15:31	he **cannot** save himself
Lk	1:20	become mute, **unable** to speak
	1:22	he **could** not speak to them
	3: 8	God **is able** from these stones
	5:12	you **can** make me clean
	5:21	Who **can** forgive sins but God
	5:34	You **cannot** make wedding guests
	6:39	**Can** a blind person guide
	6:42	**can** you say to your neighbor
	8:19	they **could** not reach him
	9:40	cast it out, but they **could** not
	11: 7	I **cannot** get up and give you
	12:25	**can** any of you by worrying add
	12:26	you **are** not **able** to do so small
	13:11	**unable** to stand up straight.
	14:20	and therefore I **cannot** come
	14:26	**cannot** be my disciple.

	14:27	follow me **cannot** be my disciple
	14:33	of you **can** become my disciple
	16: 2	**cannot** be my manager any longer
	16:13	No slave **can** serve two masters
	16:13	You **cannot** serve God and wealth
	16:26	from here to you **cannot** do so,
	18:26	Then who **can** be saved?
	19: 3	of the crowd he **could** not
	20:36	Indeed they **cannot** die anymore
	21:15	**will be able** to withstand
Jn	1:46	**Can** anything good come out
	3: 2	for no one **can** do these signs
	3: 3	no one **can** see the kingdom
	3: 4	How **can** anyone be born after
	3: 4	**Can** one enter a second time
	3: 5	no one **can** enter the kingdom
	3: 9	How **can** these things be
	3:27	No one **can** receive anything
	5:19	Son **can** do nothing on his own,
	5:30	I **can** do nothing on my own.
	5:44	How **can** you believe when you
	6:44	No one **can** come to me unless
	6:52	How **can** this man give us his
	6:60	is difficult; who **can** accept it
	6:65	no one **can** come to me unless
	7: 7	The world **cannot** hate you,
	7:34	where I am, you **cannot** come
	7:36	Where I am, you **cannot** come
	8:21	I am going, you **cannot** come
	8:22	I am going, you **cannot** come
	8:43	you **cannot** accept my word.
	9: 4	is coming when no one **can** work
	9:16	How **can** a man who is a sinner
	9:33	from God, he **could** do nothing
	10:21	**Can** a demon open the eyes
	10:29	no one **can** snatch it out
	10:35	scripture **cannot** be annulled
	11:37	**Could** not he who opened
	12:39	so they **could** not believe,
	13:33	Where I am going, you **cannot**
	13:36	I am going, you **cannot** follow
	13:37	why **can** I not follow you now
	14: 5	How **can** we know the way
	14:17	whom the world **cannot** receive
	15: 4	**cannot** bear fruit by itself
	15: 5	from me you **can** do nothing.
	16:12	but you **cannot** bear them now.
Ac	4:16	through them; we **cannot** deny it
	4:20	we **cannot** keep from speaking

5:39	will not **be able** to overthrow		1Th	2: 7	we might **have made** demands
8:31	How **can** I, unless someone			3: 9	How **can** we thank God enough
10:47	**Can** anyone withhold the water		1Ti	5:25	they **cannot** remain hidden.
13:39	**could** not be freed by law			6: 7	we **can** take nothing out
15: 1	of Moses, you **cannot** be saved			6:16	no one has ever seen or **can** see
17:19	**May** we know what this new		2Ti	2:13	for he **cannot** deny himself
19:40	no cause that we **can** give			3: 7	instructed and **can** never arrive
20:32	a message that **is able** to build			3:15	that **are able** to instruct you
21:34	as he **could** not learn the facts		He	2:18	he **is able** to help those
24: 8	you **will be able** to learn			3:19	we see that they **were unable**
24:11	As you **can** find out,			4:15	who **is unable** to sympathize
24:13	Neither **can** they prove to you			5: 2	He **is able** to deal gently
25:11	no one **can** turn me over to them			5: 7	**was able** to save him from death
26:32	man **could** have been set free			7:25	he **is able** for all time to save
27:12	they **could** spend the winter			9: 9	**cannot** perfect the conscience
27:15	caught and **could** not be turned			10: 1	it **can** never, by the same
27:31	the ship, you **cannot** be saved			10:11	that **can** never take away sins
27:39	the ship ashore, if they **could**		Ja	1:21	that **has the power** to save
27:43	those who **could** swim to jump			2:14	**Can** faith save you?
Ro 8: 7	God's law—indeed it **cannot**			3: 8	no one **can** tame the tongue
8: 8	in the flesh **cannot** please God			3:12	**Can** a fig tree,
8:39	will **be able** to separate us			4: 2	something and **cannot** obtain it
15:14	**able** to instruct one another.			4:12	judge who **is able** to save
16:25	God who **is able** to strengthen		1J	3: 9	abides in them; they **cannot** sin
1C 2:14	**are unable** to understand them			4:20	**cannot** love God whom they have
3: 1	I **could** not speak to you		Ju	1:24	to him who **is able** to keep you
3: 2	for you **were** not **ready**		Re	2: 2	I know that you **cannot** tolerate
3: 2	now you **are** still not **ready**			3: 8	which no one **is able** to shut
3:11	no one **can** lay any foundation			5: 3	**was able** to open the scroll
6: 5	**Can** it be that there is no one			6:17	and who **is able** to stand
7:21	if you **can** gain your freedom,			7: 9	that no one **could** count,
10:13	be tested **beyond** your strength,			9:20	which **cannot** see or hear
10:13	you **may be able** to endure it.			13: 4	who **can** fight against it
10:21	You **cannot** drink the cup of the			13:17	so that no one **can** buy or sell
10:21	**cannot** partake of the table			14: 3	No one **could** learn that song
12: 3	no one **can** say "Jesus is Lord"			15: 8	no one **could** enter the temple
12:21	eye **cannot** say to the hand,				
14:31	For you **can** all prophesy one				
15:50	flesh and blood **cannot** inherit			**1411** GO119 AG207 LN67 B2:601 K2:284 R1410	
2C 1: 4	**may be able** to console those			δυναμις, POWER	
3: 7	**could** not gaze at Moses' face		Mt	7:22	deeds of **power** in your name
13: 8	we **cannot** do anything against			11:20	deeds of **power** had been done,
Ga 3:21	that **could** make alive,			11:21	the deeds of **power** done in you
Ep 3: 4	will **enable** you to perceive			11:23	deeds of **power** done in you
3:20	within us **is able** to accomplish			13:54	wisdom and these deeds of **power**
6:11	**may be able** to stand against			13:58	did not do many deeds of **power**
6:13	you **may be able** to withstand			14: 2	**powers** are at work in him
6:16	you **will be able** to quench			22:29	nor the **power** of God.
Ph 3:21	**enables** him to make all things			24:29	**powers** of heaven will be
				24:30	with **power** and great glory.

	25:15	each according to his **ability.**
Mk	5:30	aware that **power** had gone forth
	6: 2	deeds of **power** are being done
	6: 5	could do no deed of **power** there
	6:14	these **powers** are at work in him
	9: 1	of God has come with **power**
	9:39	one who does a deed of **power**
	12:24	scriptures nor the **power** of God
	13:25	the **powers** in the heavens
	13:26	with great **power** and glory.
	14:62	the right hand of the **Power**
Lk	1:17	spirit and **power** of Elijah
	1:35	the **power** of the Most High
	4:14	with the **power** of the Spirit,
	4:36	For with authority and **power**
	5:17	**power** of the Lord was with him
	6:19	**power** came out from him
	8:46	I noticed that **power** had gone
	9: 1	gave them **power** and authority
	10:13	the deeds of **power** done in you
	10:19	all the **power** of the enemy;
	19:37	for all the deeds of **power**
	21:26	for the **powers** of the heavens
	21:27	with **power** and great glory.
	22:69	right hand of the **power** of God
	24:49	have been clothed with **power**
Ac	1: 8	But you will receive **power**
	2:22	by God with deeds of **power,**
	3:12	as though by our own **power**
	4: 7	By what **power** or by what name
	4:33	With great **power** the apostles
	6: 8	full of grace and **power,**
	8:10	This man is the **power** of God
	8:13	the signs and great **miracles**
	10:38	the Holy Spirit and with **power**
	19:11	God did extraordinary **miracles**
Ro	1: 4	to be Son of God with **power**
	1:16	it is the **power** of God for
	1:20	eternal **power** and divine nature
	8:38	nor things to come, nor **powers**
	9:17	purpose of showing my **power**
	15:13	by the **power** of the Holy Spirit
	15:19	the **power** of signs and wonders,
	15:19	the **power** of the Spirit of God,
1C	1:18	saved it is the **power** of God
	1:24	Christ the **power** of God.
	2: 4	of the Spirit and of **power**
	2: 5	wisdom but on the **power** of God
	4:19	arrogant people but their **power**

	4:20	not on talk but on **power**
	5: 4	with the **power** of our Lord
	6:14	also raise us by his **power**
	12:10	another the working of **miracles**
	12:28	teachers; then deeds of **power,**
	12:29	Do all work **miracles?**
	14:11	I do not know the **meaning**
	15:24	and every authority and **power**
	15:43	weakness, it is raised in **power**
	15:56	the **power** of sin is the law
2C	1: 8	**unbearably** crushed that we
	4: 7	**power** belongs to God and does
	6: 7	speech, and the **power** of God
	8: 3	gave according to their **means,**
	8: 3	and even beyond their **means**
	12: 9	for **power** is made perfect
	12: 9	**power** of Christ may dwell in me
	12:12	wonders and **mighty works.**
	13: 4	but lives by the **power** of God.
	13: 4	with him by the **power** of God.
Ga	3: 5	work **miracles** among you
Ep	1:19	greatness of his **power** for us
	1:21	**power** and dominion, and above
	3: 7	me by the working of his **power**
	3:16	with **power** through his Spirit,
	3:20	to him who by the **power** at work
Ph	3:10	to know Christ and the **power**
Co	1:11	comes from his glorious **power,**
	1:29	that he **powerfully** inspires
1Th	1: 5	in **power** and in the Holy Spirit
2Th	1: 7	heaven with his **mighty** angels
	1:11	will fulfill by his **power**
	2: 9	Satan, who uses all **power,**
2Ti	1: 7	but rather a spirit of **power**
	1: 8	relying on the **power** of God,
	3: 5	godliness but denying its **power**
He	1: 3	all things by his **powerful** word.
	2: 4	wonders and various **miracles,**
	6: 5	the **powers** of the age to come,
	7:16	but through the **power**
	11:11	By faith he received **power**
	11:34	weakness, became **mighty** in war
1P	1: 5	protected by the **power** of God
	3:22	and **powers** made subject to him
2P	1: 3	His divine **power** has given us
	1:16	**power** and coming of our Lord
	2:11	greater in might and **power,**
Re	1:16	the sun shining with full **force**
	3: 8	you have but little **power,**

4:11	glory and honor and **power,**	
5:12	to receive **power** and wealth	
7:12	honor and **power** and might be	
11:17	have taken your great **power**	
12:10	the **power** and the kingdom	
13: 2	the dragon gave it his **power**	
15: 8	glory of God and from his **power**	
17:13	united in yielding their **power**	
18: 3	from the **power** of her luxury	
19: 1	glory and **power** to our God	

1412   GO2 AG208 LN67 B2:601 K2:284 R1411
δυναμοω, I EXERT POWER

Co	1:11	May you **be made strong** with all
He	11:34	**won strength** out of weakness,

1413   GO3 AG208 LN67 B2:601 K2:284 R1410
δυναστης, POWER ONE

Lk	1:52	has brought down the **powerful**
Ac	8:27	a **court official** of the Candace
1Ti	6:15	the blessed and only **Sovereign**

1414   GO3 AG208 LN67 B2:601 K2:284 R1415
δυνατεω, I EXERT POWER

Ro	14: 4	Lord **is able** to make them stand
2C	9: 8	God **is able** to provide you
	13: 3	but is **powerful** in you

1415   GO32 AG208 LN67 B2:601 K2:284 R1410
δυνατος, POWER

Mt	19:26	for God all things are **possible**
	24:24	to lead astray, if **possible**
	26:39	My Father, if it is **possible,**
Mk	9:23	All things **can be** done
	10:27	God all things are **possible**
	13:22	lead astray, if **possible,**
	14:35	if it were **possible,**
	14:36	you all things are **possible;**
Lk	1:49	has done **great** things for me
	14:31	consider whether he **is able**
	18:27	for mortals is **possible** for God
	24:19	was a prophet **mighty** in deed
Ac	2:24	because it **was impossible**
	7:22	**was powerful** in his words
	11:17	that I **could** hinder God
	18:24	**well-versed** in the scriptures.
	20:16	to be in Jerusalem, if **possible**
	25: 5	you who have the **authority**
Ro	4:21	that God **was able** to do
	9:22	to make known his **power,**

11:23	God has the **power** to graft them	
12:18	If it is **possible,**	
15: 1	who are **strong** ought to put up	
1C	1:26	not many were **powerful,**
2C	10: 4	but they have divine **power**
	12:10	I am weak, then I am **strong.**
	13: 9	we are weak and you are **strong**
Ga	4:15	had it been **possible,**
2Ti	1:12	I am sure that he **is able**
Ti	1: 9	he may **be able** both to preach
He	11:19	God **is able** even to raise
Ja	3: 2	**able** to keep the whole body

1416   GO2 AG209 LN67 B1:314 K2:318
δυνω, IT IS SET

Mk	1:32	That evening, at **sundown,**
Lk	4:40	As the sun **was setting,**

1417   GO135 AG209 LN67
δυο, TWO

Mt	4:18	he saw **two** brothers, Simon,
	4:21	he saw **two** other brothers,
	5:41	go also the **second** mile.
	6:24	No one can serve **two** masters
	8:28	**two** demoniacs coming out of
	9:27	**two** blind men followed him,
	10:10	for your journey, or **two** tunics
	10:29	Are not **two** sparrows sold
	14:17	but five loaves and **two** fish
	14:19	five loaves and the **two** fish
	18: 8	to have **two** hands or two feet
	18: 8	to have two hands or **two** feet
	18: 9	one eye than to have **two** eyes
	18:16	take one or **two** others along
	18:16	the evidence of **two** or three
	18:19	if **two** of you agree on earth
	18:20	**two** or three are gathered
	19: 5	**two** shall become one flesh
	19: 6	So they are no longer **two,**
	20:21	Declare that these **two** sons
	20:24	angry with the **two** brothers.
	20:30	There were **two** blind men
	21: 1	Jesus sent **two** disciples,
	21:28	A man had **two** sons;
	21:31	Which of the **two** did the will
	22:40	On these **two** commandments hang
	24:40	Then **two** will be in the field;
	24:41	**Two** women will be grinding meal

	25:15	five talents, to another **two,**	16:13	No slave can serve **two** masters
	25:17	one who had the **two** talents	17:34	there will be **two** in one bed
	25:17	made **two** more talents.	17:35	will be **two** women grinding
	25:22	the one with the **two** talents	18:10	**Two** men went up to the temple
	25:22	handed over to me **two** talents	19:29	he sent **two** of the disciples
	25:22	I have made **two** more talents	21: 2	widow put in **two** small copper
	26: 2	You know that after **two** days	22:38	look, here are **two** swords
	26:37	the **two** sons of Zebedee,	23:32	**Two** others also, who were
	26:60	At last **two** came forward	24: 4	**two** men in dazzling clothes
	27:21	Which of the **two** do you want	24:13	**two** of them were going
	27:38	**two** bandits were crucified	Jn 1:35	with **two** of his disciples
	27:51	temple was torn in **two,**	1:37	The **two** disciples heard him
Mk	6: 7	to send them out **two** by two,	1:40	One of the **two** who heard John
	6: 7	to send them out two by **two,**	2: 6	each holding **twenty** or thirty
	6: 9	not to put on **two** tunics.	4:40	he stayed there **two** days.
	6:38	they said, "Five, and **two** fish	4:43	When the **two** days were over
	6:41	five loaves and the **two** fish,	6: 9	five barley loaves and **two** fish
	6:41	he divided the **two** fish	8:17	the testimony of **two** witnesses
	9:43	**two** hands and to go to hell,	11: 6	he stayed **two** days longer
	9:45	have **two** feet and to be thrown	19:18	and with him **two** others,
	9:47	one eye than to have **two** eyes	20: 4	The **two** were running together
	10: 8	the **two** shall become one flesh.	20:12	she saw **two** angels in white,
	10: 8	So they are no longer **two,**	21: 2	**two** others of his disciples.
	11: 1	he sent **two** of his disciples	Ac 1:10	**two** men in white robes stood
	12:42	widow came and put in **two**	1:23	So they proposed **two,**
	14: 1	**two** days before the Passover	1:24	which one of these **two**
	14:13	he sent **two** of his disciples,	7:29	became the father of **two** sons
	15:27	him they crucified **two** bandits,	9:38	sent **two** men to him with the
	15:38	of the temple was torn in **two,**	10: 7	he called **two** of his slaves
	16:12	in another form to **two** of them,	12: 6	Peter, bound with **two** chains,
Lk	2:24	or **two** young pigeons	12: 6	sleeping between **two** soldiers,
	3:11	has **two** coats must share	19:10	This continued for **two** years,
	5: 2	he saw **two** boats there	19:22	So he sent **two** of his helpers,
	7:18	summoned **two** of his disciples	19:34	for about **two** hours all of them
	7:41	creditor had **two** debtors	21:33	him to be bound with **two** chains
	9: 3	not even an **extra** tunic	23:23	summoned **two** of the centurions
	9:13	five loaves and **two** fish	1C 6:16	The **two** shall be one flesh
	9:16	five loaves and the **two** fish	14:27	be only **two** or at most three,
	9:30	Suddenly they saw **two** men	14:29	Let **two** or three prophets speak
	9:32	the **two** men who stood with him	2C 13: 1	by the evidence of **two** or three
	10: 1	Lord appointed **seventy** others	Ga 4:22	that Abraham had **two** sons,
	10: 1	on ahead of him in **pairs**	4:24	these women are **two** covenants.
	10: 1	in **pairs** to every town and	Ep 2:15	humanity in place of the **two,**
	10:17	The **seventy** returned with joy,	5:31	the **two** will become one flesh
	10:35	he took out **two** denarii,	Ph 1:23	hard pressed between the **two**
	12: 6	sparrows sold for **two** pennies	1Ti 5:19	the evidence of **two** or three
	12:52	be divided, three against **two**	He 6:18	**two** unchangeable things,
	12:52	two and **two** against three	10:28	testimony of **two** or three
	15:11	was a man who had **two** sons	Re 9:12	are still **two** woes to come.

11: 2　holy city for forty-**two** months
11: 3　I will grant my **two** witnesses
11: 4　These are the **two** olive trees
11: 4　**two** lampstands that stand
11:10　because these **two** prophets
12:14　woman was given the **two** wings
13: 5　authority for forty-**two** months
13:11　it had **two** horns like a lamb
19:20　These **two** were thrown alive

1419　GO2 AG209 LN68
δυσβαστακτος, DOUBLY HEAVY
Mt 23: 4　heavy burdens, **hard to bear,**
Lk 11:46　with burdens **hard to bear,**

1420　GO1 AG209 LN68
δυσεντεριον, DYSENTERY
Ac 28: 8　in bed with fever and **dysentery**

1421　GO1 AG209 LN68
δυσερμηνευτος, DIFFICULT
INTERPRETATION
He 5:11　that is **hard to explain,**

1421a　GO1 AG209 LN68
δυσις, WEST
Mk 16: 8　from east to **west,** the

1422　GO1 AG209 LN68
δυσκολος, DIFFICULT
Mk 10:24　how **hard** it is to enter

1423　GO3 AG209 LN68 R1422
δυσκολως, DIFFICULTLY
Mt 19:23　**hard** for a rich person to enter
Mk 10:23　How **hard** it will be for those
Lk 18:24　How **hard** it is for those who

1424　GO5 AG209 LN68 R1416
δυσμη, WEST
Mt 8:11　will come from east and **west**
　　24:27　flashes as far as the **west**
Lk 12:54　a cloud rising in the **west**
　　13:29　will come from east and **west**
Re 21:13　and on the **west** three gates

1425　GO1 AG209 LN68 B3:122 K4:963
δυσνοητος, HARD TO UNDERSTAND
2P 3:16　in them **hard to understand,**

1425a　GO1 AG209 LN68
δυσφημεω, I VILIFY
1C 4:13　when **slandered,** we speak kindly

1426　GO1 AG209 LN68
δυσφημια, BAD REPORT
2C 6: 8　in **ill repute** and good repute

1427　GO75 AG210 LN68 B2:694 K2:321 R1417,1176
δωδεκα, TWELVE
Mt 9:20　hemorrhages for **twelve** years
　　10: 1　Then Jesus summoned his **twelve**
　　10: 2　names of the **twelve** apostles
　　10: 5　These **twelve** Jesus sent out
　　11: 1　finished instructing his **twelve**
　　14:20　broken pieces, **twelve** baskets
　　19:28　will also sit on **twelve** thrones
　　19:28　the **twelve** tribes of Israel
　　20:17　the **twelve** disciples aside
　　26:14　Then one of the **twelve,**
　　26:20　his place with the **twelve**
　　26:47　Judas, one of the **twelve,**
　　26:53　more than **twelve** legions
Mk 3:14　And he appointed **twelve,** whom
　　3:16　So he appointed the **twelve**
　　4:10　along with the **twelve** asked him
　　5:25　hemorrhages for **twelve** years
　　5:42　she was **twelve** years of age
　　6: 7　He called the **twelve** and began
　　6:43　they took up **twelve** baskets
　　8:19　They said to him, **"Twelve."**
　　9:35　He sat down, called the **twelve**
　　10:32　He took the **twelve** aside again
　　11:11　out to Bethany with the **twelve**
　　14:10　who was one of the **twelve,**
　　14:17　he came with the **twelve.**
　　14:20　It is one of the **twelve**
　　14:43　Judas, one of the **twelve**
Lk 2:42　when he was **twelve** years old,
　　6:13　his disciples and chose **twelve**
　　8: 1　The **twelve** were with him,
　　8:42　about **twelve** years old,
　　8:43　hemorrhages for **twelve** years
　　9: 1　Jesus called the **twelve**
　　9:12　the **twelve** came to him and said
　　9:17　**twelve** baskets of broken pieces
　　18:31　Then he took the **twelve** aside
　　22: 3　who was one of the **twelve;**
　　22:30　judging the **twelve** tribes
　　22:47　Judas, one of the **twelve,**

Jn	6:13	they filled **twelve** baskets.
	6:67	So Jesus asked the **twelve,**
	6:70	not choose you, the **twelve**
	6:71	he, though one of the **twelve**
	11: 9	Are there not **twelve** hours of
	20:24	the Twin), one of the **twelve,**
Ac	6: 2	And the **twelve** called together
	7: 8	Jacob of the **twelve** patriarchs.
	19: 7	were about **twelve** of them.
	24:11	it is not more than **twelve** days
1C	15: 5	to Cephas, then to the **twelve.**
Ja	1: 1	To the **twelve** tribes in the
Re	7: 5	tribe of Judah **twelve** thousand
	7: 5	tribe of Reuben **twelve** thousand
	7: 5	tribe of Gad **twelve** thousand,
	7: 6	tribe of Asher **twelve** thousand,
	7: 6	of Naphtali **twelve** thousand
	7: 6	of Manasseh **twelve** thousand,
	7: 7	tribe of Simeon **twelve** thousand
	7: 7	tribe of Levi **twelve** thousand,
	7: 7	of Issachar **twelve** thousand,
	7: 8	of Zebulun **twelve** thousand,
	7: 8	tribe of Joseph **twelve** thousand
	7: 8	of Benjamin **twelve** thousand
	12: 1	head a crown of **twelve** stars.
	21:12	high wall with **twelve** gates
	21:12	at the gates **twelve** angels
	21:12	the names of the **twelve** tribes
	21:14	city has **twelve** foundations,
	21:14	the **twelve** names of the twelve
	21:14	names of the **twelve** apostles
	21:16	**fifteen hundred** miles
	21:21	**twelve** gates are twelve pearls
	21:21	twelve gates are **twelve** pearls
	22: 2	with its **twelve** kinds of fruit

1428   GO1 AG210 LN68 K2:321 R1427
δωδεκατος, TWELFTH
Re	21:20	jacinth, the **twelfth** amethyst

1429   GO1 AG210 LN68 K2:321 R1427,5443
δωδεκαφυλον, TWELVE TRIBE
Ac	26: 7	promise that our **twelve tribes**

1430   GO7 AG210 LN68
δωμα, ROOF
Mt	10:27	proclaim from the **housetops.**
	24:17	the one on the **housetop**
Mk	13:15	the one on the **housetop**
Lk	5:19	they went up on the **roof**

	12: 3	proclaimed from the **housetops**
	17:31	anyone on the **housetop**
Ac	10: 9	Peter went up on the **roof**

1431   GO11 AG210 LN68 B2:40 K2:166 R1435
δωρεα, GIFT
Jn	4:10	If you knew the **gift** of God,
Ac	2:38	you will receive the **gift**
	8:20	you could obtain God's **gift**
	10:45	the **gift** of the Holy Spirit
	11:17	God gave them the same **gift**
Ro	5:15	But the free **gift** is not like
	5:17	**gift** of righteousness exercise
2C	9:15	God for his indescribable **gift**
Ep	3: 7	servant according to the **gift**
	4: 7	the measure of Christ's **gift**
He	6: 4	have tasted the heavenly **gift**

1432   GO9 AG210 LN68 B2:40 K2:167 R1431
δωρεαν, AS A GIFT
Mt	10: 8	You received **without payment**
	10: 8	give **without payment**
Jn	15:25	They hated me **without a cause**
Ro	3:24	by his grace as a **gift,**
2C	11: 7	good news to you **free of charge**
Ga	2:21	then Christ died **for nothing**
2Th	3: 8	bread **without paying for** it
Re	21: 6	I will give water as a **gift**
	22:17	the water of life as a **gift**

1433   GO3 AG210 LN68 B2:40 K2:166 R1435
δωρεομαι, I GIFT
Mk	15:45	he **granted** the body to Joseph
2P	1: 3	His divine power has **given** us
	1: 4	Thus he has **given** us,

1434   GO2 AG210 LN68 B2:40 K2:166 R1433
δωρημα, GIFT
Ro	5:16	And the free **gift** is not like
Ja	1:17	with every perfect **gift,**

1435   GO19 AG210 LN68 B2:40 K2:166
δωρον, GIFT
Mt	2:11	they offered him **gifts** of gold
	5:23	you are offering your **gift**
	5:24	leave your **gift** there before
	5:24	then come and offer your **gift**
	8: 4	offer the **gift** that Moses
	15: 5	had from me is **given** to God
	23:18	but whoever swears by the **gift**

23:19   the **gift** or the altar
23:19   that makes the **gift** sacred
Mk   7:11   (that is, an **offering** to God)
Lk   21: 1   their **gifts** into the treasury
21: 4   has put in **all** she had
Ep   2: 8   it is the **gift** of God
He   5: 1   to offer **gifts** and sacrifices
8: 3   is appointed to offer **gifts**
8: 4   priests who offer **gifts**
9: 9   time, during which **gifts**
11: 4   giving approval to his **gifts**
Re   11:10   celebrate and exchange **presents**

ε

1436   GO1 AG211 LN68
εα, AH
Lk   4:34   **Let** us alone! What have you?

1437   GO333 AG211 LN68 R1487,302
εαν, IF [MULTIPLE OCCURRENCES]

1437a   GO3 AG211 LN68
εανπερ, IF INDEED
He   3: 6   we are his house **if** we hold
3:14   **if** only we hold our first
6: 3   will do this, **if** God permits

1438   GO319 AG211 LN68
εαυτου, OF HIMSELF [MULTIPLE
OCCURRENCES]

1439   GO11 AG212 LN69
εαω, I ALLOW
Mt   24:43   would not have **let** his house
Lk   4:41   would not **allow** them to speak
22:51   Jesus said, "No **more** of this!"
Ac   14:16   he **allowed** all the nations
16: 7   Spirit of Jesus did not **allow**
19:30   disciples would not **let** him
23:32   they **let** the horsemen go on
27:32   the boat and **set** it adrift
27:40   **left** them in the sea.
28: 4   has not **allowed** him to live
1C   10:13   he will not **let** you be tested

1440   GO5 AG212 LN69 B2:696 K2:627 R1442,1176
ἑβδομηκοντα, SEVENTY
Lk   10: 1   Lord appointed **seventy** others

10:17   **seventy** returned with joy
Ac   7:14   to him, **seventy**-five in all
23:23   soldiers, **seventy** horsemen,
27:37   hundred **seventy**-six persons

1441   GO1 AG213 LN69 K2:627 R1440
ἑβδομηκοντακις, SEVENTY TIMES
Mt   18:22   tell you, **seventy**-seven times

1442   GO9 AG213 LN69 K2:627 R2033
ἑβδομος, SEVENTH
Jn   4:52   at **one** in the afternoon
He   4: 4   it speaks about the **seventh** day
4: 4   God rested on the **seventh** day
Ju   1:14   in the **seventh** generation from
Re   8: 1   Lamb opened the **seventh** seal
10: 7   the **seventh** angel is to blow
11:15   **seventh** angel blew his trumpet
16:17   **seventh** angel poured his bowl
21:20   the **seventh** chrysolite,

1443   GO1 AG213 LN69
Ἑβερ, EBER
Lk   3:35   son of Peleg, son of **Eber,**

1445   GO4 AG213 LN69 B2:304 K3:356
Ἑβραιος, HEBREW
Ac   6: 1   complained against the **Hebrews**
2C   11:22   Are they **Hebrews?**
Ph   3: 5   a **Hebrew** born of Hebrews
3: 5   a Hebrew born of **Hebrews**

1446   GO3 AG213 LN69 B2:304 K3:356
Ἑβραις, HEBREW
Ac   21:40   addressed them in the **Hebrew**
22: 2   him addressing them in **Hebrew,**
26:14   to me in the **Hebrew** language

1447   GO7 AG213 LN69 K3:356
Ἑβραιστι, HEBREW
Jn   5: 2   called in **Hebrew** Beth-zatha
19:13   or in **Hebrew** Gabbatha
19:17   in **Hebrew** is called Golgotha
19:20   it was written in **Hebrew,**
20:16   said to him in **Hebrew**
Re   9:11   his name in **Hebrew** is Abaddon
16:16   at the place that in **Hebrew**

1448   GO42 AG213 LN69 K2:330 R1451
εγγιζω, I NEAR

Mt	3: 2	kingdom of heaven has **come near**
	4:17	kingdom of heaven has **come near**
	10: 7	kingdom of heaven has **come near**
	21: 1	they had **come near** Jerusalem
	21:34	When the harvest time had **come**
	26:45	See, the hour **is at hand,**
	26:46	See, my betrayer **is at hand**
Mk	1:15	kingdom of God has **come near**
	11: 1	they were **approaching** Jerusalem
	14:42	See, my betrayer **is at hand**
Lk	7:12	As he **approached** the gate
	10: 9	kingdom of God has **come near**
	10:11	kingdom of God has **come near**
	12:33	where no thief **comes near**
	15: 1	sinners were **coming near**
	15:25	when he came and **approached**
	18:35	As he **approached** Jericho,
	18:40	and when he **came near,**
	19:29	he had **come near** Bethphage
	19:37	As he was now **approaching**
	19:41	he **came near** and saw the city
	21: 8	The time **is near!**
	21:20	its desolation has **come near**
	21:28	redemption **is drawing near**
	22: 1	called the Passover, **was near**
	22:47	He **approached** Jesus to kiss him
	24:15	**came near** and went with them,
	24:28	As they **came near** the village
Ac	7:17	But as the time **drew near**
	9: 3	going along and **approaching**
	10: 9	their journey and **approaching**
	21:33	Then the tribune **came,**
	22: 6	I was on my way and **approaching**
	23:15	away with him before he **arrives**
Ro	13:12	is far gone, the day **is near**
Ph	2:30	because he **came close** to death
He	7:19	through which we **approach** God
	10:25	as you see the Day **approaching**
Ja	4: 8	**Draw near** to God, and he will
	4: 8	he **will draw near** to you.
	5: 8	the coming of the Lord **is near**
1P	4: 7	The end of all things **is near**

1449   GO3   AG213   LN69   K1:769   R1722,1125
εγγραφω, I WRITE IN

Lk	10:20	names are **written** in heaven
2C	3: 2	**written** on our hearts,
	3: 3	**written** not with ink but with

1450   GO1   AG214   LN69   K2:329
εγγυος, BOND

He	7:22	**guarantee** of a better covenant

1451   GO31   AG214   LN69   K2:330
εγγυς, NEAR

Mt	24:32	you know that summer is **near**
	24:33	you know that he is **near**
	26:18	My time is **near;** I will keep
Mk	13:28	you know that summer is **near**
	13:29	you know that he is **near**
Lk	19:11	because he was **near** Jerusalem
	21:30	that summer is already **near**
	21:31	the kingdom of God is **near**
Jn	2:13	Passover of the Jews was **near**
	3:23	baptizing at Aenon **near** Salim
	6: 4	festival of the Jews, was **near**
	6:19	the sea and coming **near** the boat
	6:23	boats from Tiberias came **near**
	7: 2	festival of Booths was **near.**
	11:18	Now Bethany was **near** Jerusalem
	11:54	the region **near** the wilderness
	11:55	Passover of the Jews was **near,**
	19:20	Jesus was crucified was **near**
	19:42	and the tomb was **nearby,**
Ac	1:12	which is **near** Jerusalem,
	9:38	Since Lydda was **near** Joppa,
	27: 8	Havens, **near** the city of Lasea
Ro	10: 8	The word is **near** you,
	13:11	For salvation is **nearer** to us
Ep	2:13	far off have been brought **near**
	2:17	peace to those who were **near**
Ph	4: 5	The Lord is **near.**
He	6: 8	worthless and **on the verge**
	8:13	growing old will **soon** disappear
Re	1: 3	for the time is **near.**
	22:10	for the time is **near**

1453   GO144   AG214   LN69   B3:279   K2:333
εγειρω, I RISE

Mt	1:24	When Joseph **awoke** from sleep
	2:13	**Get up,** take the child and his
	2:14	Joseph **got up,** took the child
	2:20	**Get up,** take the child
	2:21	Joseph **got up,** took the child
	3: 9	from these stones **to raise up**
	8:15	she **got up** and began to serve
	8:25	they went and **woke** him **up,**
	8:26	Then he **got up** and rebuked
	9: 5	**Stand up** and walk

9: 6	**Stand up,** take your bed	
9: 7	**stood up** and went to his home	
9:19	Jesus **got up** and followed him,	
9:25	the hand, and the girl **got up**	
10: 8	Cure the sick, **raise** the dead,	
11: 5	the dead **are raised,**	
11:11	no one **has arisen** greater	
12:11	lay hold of it and **lift** it **out**	
12:42	queen of the South **will rise up**	
14: 2	**has been raised** from the dead	
16:21	on the third day **be raised**	
17: 7	**Get up** and do not be afraid	
17: 9	Son of Man has been **raised**	
17:23	third day he will be **raised**	
20:19	third day he will be **raised**	
24: 7	nation **will rise** against nation	
24:11	many false prophets **will arise**	
24:24	false prophets **will appear**	
25: 7	all those bridesmaids **got up**	
26:32	But after I **am raised up,**	
26:46	**Get up,** let us be going.	
27:52	had fallen asleep **were raised.**	
27:63	three days I **will rise** again	
27:64	**has been raised** from the dead	
28: 6	for he **has been raised,**	
28: 7	has **been raised** from the dead,	
Mk 1:31	by the hand and **lifted** her **up**	
2: 9	**Stand up** and take your mat	
2:11	I say to you, **stand up,**	
2:12	And he **stood up,**	
3: 3	withered hand, **"Come** forward."	
4:27	sleep and **rise** night and day,	
4:38	they **woke** him **up** and said	
5:41	Little girl, **get up!**	
6:14	**has been raised** from the dead	
6:16	I beheaded, **has been raised.**	
9:27	the hand and **lifted** him **up**	
10:49	**get up,** he is calling you.	
12:26	as for the dead **being raised,**	
13: 8	nation **will rise** against nation,	
13:22	false prophets **will appear**	
14:28	But after I **am raised up,**	
14:42	**Get up,** let us be going.	
16: 6	He has **been raised;**	
16:14	who saw him after he **had risen.**	
Lk 1:69	**has raised up** a mighty savior	
3: 8	from these stones **to raise up**	
5:23	or to say, **'Stand up** and walk'	
5:24	**stand up** and take your bed	

6: 8	He **got up** and stood there.	
7:14	man, I say to you, **rise!**	
7:16	prophet **has risen** among us	
7:22	deaf hear, the dead **are raised**	
8:54	Child, **get up!**	
9: 7	**had been raised** from the dead,	
9:22	on the third day **be raised.**	
11: 8	he **will get up** and give him	
11:31	**will rise** at the judgment	
13:25	**has got up** and shut the door,	
20:37	fact that the dead **are raised**	
21:10	Nation **will rise** against	
24: 7	on the third day **rise**	
24:34	The Lord **has risen** indeed,	
Jn 2:19	three days I **will raise** it **up.**	
2:20	you **raise** it **up** in three days	
2:22	he **was raised** from the dead,	
5: 8	**Stand up,** take your mat	
5:21	the Father **raises** the dead	
7:52	is to **arise** from Galilee.	
11:29	she **got up** quickly and went.	
12: 1	he **had raised** from the dead.	
12: 9	he **had raised** from the dead	
12:17	**raised** him from the dead	
13: 4	**got up** from the table,	
14:31	**Rise,** let us be on our way	
21:14	he **was raised** from the dead.	
Ac 3: 6	**stand up** and walk.	
3: 7	hand and **raised** him **up;**	
3:15	God **raised** from the dead	
4:10	God **raised** from the dead	
5:30	our ancestors **raised up** Jesus,	
9: 8	Saul **got up** from the ground,	
10:26	But Peter made him **get up,**	
10:40	God **raised** him on the third day	
12: 7	Peter on the side and **woke** him,	
13:22	he **made** David their king.	
13:30	God **raised** him from the dead;	
13:37	but he whom God **raised up**	
26: 8	that God **raises** the dead	
Ro 4:24	believe in him who **raised** Jesus	
4:25	**raised** for our justification.	
6: 4	just as Christ **was raised**	
6: 9	**being raised** from the dead	
7: 4	to him who **has been raised**	
8:11	the Spirit of him who **raised**	
8:11	**raised** Christ from the dead	
8:34	who was **raised,** who is at the	
10: 9	God **raised** him from the dead	

	13:11	for you to **wake** from sleep
1C	6:14	And God **raised** the Lord
	15: 4	he was **raised** on the third day
	15:12	Christ is proclaimed as **raised**
	15:13	Christ has not **been raised**
	15:14	if Christ has not **been raised,**
	15:15	of God that he **raised** Christ
	15:15	whom he did not **raise**
	15:15	that the dead are not **raised.**
	15:16	if the dead are not **raised,**
	15:16	Christ has not been **raised.**
	15:17	If Christ has not **been raised,**
	15:20	in fact Christ has **been raised**
	15:29	If the dead **are** not **raised**
	15:32	If the dead **are** not **raised,**
	15:35	How are the dead **raised?**
	15:42	what is **raised** is imperishable
	15:43	it is **raised** in glory
	15:43	it is **raised** in power
	15:44	it is **raised** a spiritual body
	15:52	the dead will **be raised**
2C	1: 9	but on God who **raises** the dead
	4:14	one who **raised** the Lord Jesus
	4:14	Jesus **will raise** us also
	5:15	who died and **was raised**
Ga	1: 1	who **raised** him from the dead
Ep	1:20	he **raised** him from the dead
	5:14	**Rise** from the dead, and Christ
Ph	1:17	**increase** my suffering
Co	2:12	who **raised** him from the dead
1Th	1:10	whom he **raised** from the dead
2Ti	2: 8	Christ, **raised** from the dead
He	11:19	that God is able even to **raise**
Ja	5:15	the Lord **will raise** them up
1P	1:21	who **raised** him from the dead
Re	11: 1	**Come** and measure the temple

1454   ᴳᴼ1   ᴬᴳ215   ᴸᴺ70   ᴮ3:279   ᴷ2:337   ᴿ1453
εγερσις, RESURRECTION
Mt 27:53   After his **resurrection**

1455   ᴳᴼ1   ᴬᴳ215   ᴸᴺ70
εγκαθετος, SPY
Lk 20:20   they watched him and sent **spies**

1456   ᴳᴼ1   ᴬᴳ215   ᴸᴺ70
εγκαινια, FESTIVAL OF DEDICATIONS
Jn 10:22   the festival of the **Dedication**

1457   ᴳᴼ2   ᴬᴳ215   ᴸᴺ70   ᴷ3:453
εγκαινιζω, I MAKE NEW
He 9:18   first covenant **was inaugurated**
    10:20   living way that he **opened**

1457a   ᴳᴼ6   ᴬᴳ215   ᴸᴺ70   ᴷ3:486
εγκακεω, I GIVE IN TO BAD
Lk 18: 1   always and not to **lose heart**
2C 4: 1   ministry, we do not **lose heart**
    4:16   So we do not **lose heart.**
Ga 6: 9   time, if we **do** not **give up.**
Ep 3:13   you may not **lose heart**
2Th 3:13   not **be weary** in doing what is

1458   ᴳᴼ7   ᴬᴳ215   ᴸᴺ70   ᴷ3:496   ᴿ1722,2564
εγκαλεω, I CALL IN
Ac 19:38   let them **bring charges** there
    19:40   **being charged** with rioting
    23:28   for which they **accused** him,
    23:29   I found that he **was accused**
    26: 2   all the **accusations** of the Jews
    26: 7   that I **am accused** by Jews
Ro 8:33   Who **will bring** any **charge**

1459   ᴳᴼ10   ᴬᴳ215   ᴸᴺ70   ᴿ1722,2641
εγκαταλειπω, I LEAVE BEHIND
Mt 27:46   God, why have you **forsaken** me
Mk 15:34   God, why have you **forsaken** me
Ac 2:27   you **will** not **abandon** my soul
    2:31   He **was** not **abandoned** to Hades
Ro 9:29   had not **left** survivors to us,
2C 4: 9   persecuted, but not **forsaken;**
2Ti 4:10   world, has **deserted** me and gone
    4:16   support, but all **deserted** me.
He 10:25   not **neglecting** to meet together
    13: 5   never leave you or **forsake** you

1460   ᴳᴼ1   ᴬᴳ216   ᴸᴺ70   ᴿ1722,2730
εγκατοικεω, I DWELL IN (AMONG)
2P 2: 8   **living** among them day after day

1460a   ᴳᴼ1   ᴬᴳ216   ᴸᴺ70   ᴷ3:653
εγκαυχαομαι, I BRAG IN
2Th 1: 4   we ourselves **boast** of you

1461   ᴳᴼ6   ᴬᴳ216   ᴸᴺ70
εγκεντριζω, I GRAFT IN
Ro 11:17   were **grafted in** their place
    11:19   I **might be grafted in**
    11:23   power to **graft** them **in** again

11:23   unbelief, **will be grafted in**
11:24   a wild olive tree and **grafted,**
11:24   branches **be grafted** back into

1462   GO2 AG216 LN70 K3:496
εγκλημα, CHARGE
Ac   23:29   but was **charged** with nothing
     25:16   a defense against the **charge.**

1463   GO1 AG216 LN70 K2:339
εγκομβοομαι, I AM CLOTHED
1P   5: 5   **must clothe** yourselves with

1464   GO1 AG216 LN70 K3:855 R1465
εγκοπη, HINDRANCE
1C   9:12   put an **obstacle** in the way

1465   GO5 AG216 LN70 K3:855 R1722,2875
εγκοπτω, I HINDER
Ac   24: 4   to **detain** you no further,
Ro   15:22   **hindered** from coming to you.
Ga   5: 7   who **prevented** you from obeying
1Th   2:18   but Satan **blocked** our way.
1P   3: 7   **may hinder** your prayers.

1466   GO4 AG216 LN70 K2:339 R1468
εγκρατεια, INNER STRENGTH
Ac   24:25   discussed justice, **self-control**
Ga   5:23   gentleness, and **self-control.**
2P   1: 6   knowledge with **self-control,**
      1: 6   knowledge with **self-control,**

1467   GO2 AG216 LN70 K2:339 R1468
εγκρατευομαι, I HAVE INNER STRENGTH
1C   7: 9   are not **practicing self-control**
      9:25   Athletes **exercise self-control**

1468   GO1 AG216 LN70 K2:339 R1722,2904
εγκρατης, INNER STRENGTH
Ti   1: 8   devout, and **self-controlled.**

1469   GO1 AG216 LN70 K3:951 R1722,2919
εγκρινω, I JUDGE
2C   10:12   We do not dare to **classify**

1470   GO2 AG216 LN70 R1722,2928
εγκρυπτω, I HIDE IN
Mt   13:33   **mixed in** with three measures
Lk   13:21   **mixed in** with three measures

1471   GO1 AG216 LN70
εγκυος, PREGNANT
Lk   2: 5   was expecting a child

1472   GO1 AG217 LN70 R1722,5548
εγχριω, I ANOINT ON
Re   3:18   salve to **anoint** your eyes

1473   GO2868 AG217 LN70 B2:278 K2:343
εγω, I [MULTIPLE OCCURRENCES]

1474   GO1 AG217 LN70 R1475
εδαφιζω, I GRIND TO GROUND
Lk   19:44   **will crush** you to the ground,

1475   GO1 AG217 LN71
εδαφος, GROUND
Ac   22: 7   I fell **to the ground** and heard

1476   GO3 AG217 LN71 B1:660 K2:362
'εδραιος, STABLE
1C   7:37   stands **firm** in his resolve
     15:58   be **steadfast,** immovable,
Co   1:23   and **steadfast** in the faith,

1477   GO1 AG218 LN71 B1:660 K2:362 R1476
'εδραιωμα, FIRMNESS
1Ti   3:15   pillar and **bulwark** of the truth

1478   GO2 AG218 LN71
'εζεκιας, HEZEKIAH
Mt   1: 9   Ahaz the father of **Hezekiah**
      1:10   **Hezekiah** the father of Manasseh

1479   GO1 AG218 LN71 K3:155
εθελοθρησκια, SELF-CHOSEN PIETY
Co   2:23   in promoting **self-imposed piety**

1480   GO1 AG218 LN71 R1485
εθιζω, I ACCUSTOM
Lk   2:27   **was customary** under the law

1481   GO1 AG218 LN71 R1484,746
εθναρχης, ETHNARCH
2C   11:32   the **governor** under King Aretas

1482   GO4 AG218 LN71 B2:790 K2:372 R1484
εθνικος, NATION
Mt   5:47   even the **Gentiles** do the same
      6: 7   phrases as the **Gentiles** do

18:17   be to you as a **Gentile**
3J   1: 7   no support from **non-believers**

1483   GO1 AG218 LN71 B2:790 R1482
εθνικως, NATIONALLY
Ga   2:14   can you compel the **Gentiles**

1484   GO162 AG218 LN71 B2:790 K2:364
εθνος, NATION
Mt   4:15   Galilee of the **Gentiles**
6:32   the **Gentiles** who strive
10: 5   Go nowhere among the **Gentiles**,
10:18   to them and the **Gentiles.**
12:18   justice to the **Gentiles.**
12:21   his name the **Gentiles** will hope
20:19   hand him over to the **Gentiles**
20:25   the rulers of the **Gentiles**
21:43   from you and given to a **people**
24: 7   **nation** will rise against nation
24: 7   nation will rise against **nation**
24: 9   will be hated by all **nations**
24:14   testimony to all the **nations;**
25:32   the **nations** will be gathered
28:19   make disciples of all **nations,**
Mk 10:33   hand him over to the **Gentiles**
10:42   know that among the **Gentiles**
11:17   prayer for all the **nations**
13: 8   **nation** will rise against
13: 8   will rise against **nation,**
13:10   proclaimed to all **nations.**
Lk   2:32   revelation to the **Gentiles**
7: 5   for he loves our **people**
12:30   the **nations** of the world
18:32   handed over to the **Gentiles;**
21:10   **Nation** will rise against
21:10   will rise against **nation,**
21:24   as captives among all **nations;**
21:24   be trampled on by the **Gentiles,**
21:24   the times of the **Gentiles**
21:25   distress among **nations** confused
22:25   The kings of the **Gentiles**
23: 2   this man perverting our **nation,**
24:47   in his name to all **nations,**
Jn 11:48   our holy place and our **nation**
11:50   have the whole **nation** destroyed
11:51   about to die for the **nation,**
11:52   and not for the **nation** only,
18:35   Your own **nation** and the chief
Ac   2: 5   Jews from every **nation**

4:25   Why did the **Gentiles** rage,
4:27   Pilate, with the **Gentiles**
7: 7   But I will judge the **nation**
7:45   they dispossessed the **nations**
8: 9   amazed the **people** of Samaria,
9:15   bring my name before **Gentiles**
10:22   by the whole Jewish **nation**
10:35   every **nation** anyone who fears
10:45   poured out even on the **Gentiles**
11: 1   the **Gentiles** had also accepted
11:18   has given even to the **Gentiles**
13:19   he had destroyed seven **nations**
13:46   are now turning to the **Gentiles**
13:47   be a light for the **Gentiles,**
13:48   When the **Gentiles** heard this,
14: 2   Jews stirred up the **Gentiles**
14: 5   made by both **Gentiles** and Jews
14:16   **nations** to follow their own
14:27   door of faith for the **Gentiles**
15: 3   the conversion of the **Gentiles**
15: 7   **Gentiles** would hear the message
15:12   through them among the **Gentiles**
15:14   favorably on the **Gentiles,**
15:17   even all the **Gentiles**
15:19   those **Gentiles** who are turning
15:23   believers of **Gentile** origin
17:26   he made all **nations** to inhabit
18: 6   I will go to the **Gentiles**
21:11   hand him over to the **Gentiles**
21:19   among the **Gentiles**
21:21   Jews living among the **Gentiles**
21:25   But as for the **Gentiles** who
22:21   you far away to the **Gentiles**
24: 2   have been made for this **people**
24:10   a judge over this **nation.**
24:17   came to bring alms to my **nation**
26: 4   among my own **people** and in
26:17   people and from the **Gentiles**
26:20   and also to the **Gentiles,**
26:23   our people and to the **Gentiles**
28:19   to bring against my **nation.**
28:28   has been sent to the **Gentiles;**
Ro   1: 5   of faith among all the **Gentiles**
1:13   among the rest of the **Gentiles.**
2:14   When **Gentiles,** who do not
2:24   blasphemed among the **Gentiles**
3:29   not the God of **Gentiles** also
3:29   Yes, of **Gentiles** also,
4:17   the father of many **nations**

4:18	the father of many **nations**,
9:24	but also from the **Gentiles**
9:30	**Gentiles**, who did not strive
10:19	who are not a **nation**;
10:19	with a foolish **nation** I will
11:11	has come to the **Gentiles**,
11:12	means riches for **Gentiles**,
11:13	I am speaking to you **Gentiles**.
11:13	am an apostle to the **Gentiles**,
11:25	the full number of the **Gentiles**
15: 9	the **Gentiles** might glorify God
15: 9	confess you among the **Gentiles**
15:10	Rejoice, O **Gentiles**,
15:11	the Lord, all you **Gentiles**
15:12	who rises to rule the **Gentiles**;
15:12	in him the **Gentiles** shall hope.
15:16	Christ Jesus to the **Gentiles**
15:16	the offering of the **Gentiles**
15:18	obedience from the **Gentiles**,
15:27	**Gentiles** have come to share
16: 4	the churches of the **Gentiles**.
16:26	made known to all the **Gentiles**,
1C 1:23	and foolishness to **Gentiles**,
5: 1	not found even among **pagans**;
12: 2	know that when you were **pagans**,
2C 11:26	danger from **Gentiles**,
Ga 1:16	him among the **Gentiles**,
2: 2	I proclaim among the **Gentiles**
2: 8	in sending me to the **Gentiles**
2: 9	we should go to the **Gentiles**
2:12	used to eat with the **Gentiles**.
2:14	how can you compel the **Gentiles**
2:15	birth and not **Gentile** sinners;
3: 8	God would justify the **Gentiles**
3: 8	the **Gentiles** shall be blessed
3:14	might come to the **Gentiles**,
Ep 2:11	one time you **Gentiles** by birth,
3: 1	for the sake of you **Gentiles**
3: 6	the **Gentiles** have become fellow
3: 8	to bring to the **Gentiles**
4:17	no longer live as the **Gentiles**
Co 1:27	how great among the **Gentiles**
1Th 2:16	from speaking to the **Gentiles**
4: 5	like the **Gentiles** who do not
1Ti 2: 7	a teacher of the **Gentiles**
3:16	proclaimed among **Gentiles**,
2Ti 4:17	all the **Gentiles** might hear it
1P 2: 9	priesthood, a holy **nation**,
2:12	honorably among the **Gentiles**,

4: 3	time in doing what the **Gentiles**
Re 2:26	give authority over the **nations**
5: 9	language and people and **nation**
7: 9	could count, from every **nation**,
10:11	about many peoples and **nations**
11: 2	is given over to the **nations**,
11: 9	**nations** will gaze at their dead
11:18	The **nations** raged, but your
12: 5	rule all the **nations** with a rod
13: 7	people and language and **nation**
14: 6	to every **nation** and tribe and
14: 8	all **nations** drink of the wine
15: 3	your ways, King of the **nations**
15: 4	**nations** will come and worship
16:19	cities of the **nations** fell.
17:15	**nations** and languages
18: 3	For all the **nations** have drunk
18:23	all **nations** were deceived
19:15	to strike down the **nations**,
20: 3	deceive the **nations** no more,
20: 8	to deceive the **nations** at the
21:24	**nations** will walk by its light
21:26	and the honor of the **nations**
22: 2	for the healing of the **nations**

1485   GO12 AG218 LN71 B2:436 K2:372
εθος, CUSTOM

Lk 1: 9	to the **custom** of the priesthood
2:42	they went up **as usual** for the
22:39	went, as was his **custom**,
Jn 19:40	according to the burial **custom**
Ac 6:14	will change the **customs**
15: 1	according to the **custom**
16:21	and are advocating **customs**
21:21	children or observe the **customs**
25:16	it was not the **custom**
26: 3	**customs** and controversies
28:17	the **customs** of our ancestors,
He 10:25	as is the **habit** of some,

1487   GO507 AG219 LN71
ει, IF [MULTIPLE OCCURRENCES]

1489a   GO1 AG220 LN72 K2:373
ειδεα, APPEARANCE
Mt   28: 3   **appearance** was like lightning,

1491   GO5 AG221 LN72 B1:703 K2:373
ειδος, VISIBLE FORM
Lk   3:22   upon him in bodily **form**

9:29 **appearance** of his face changed
Jn 5:37 his voice or seen his **form**
2C 5: 7 we walk by faith, not by **sight**
1Th 5:22 abstain from every **form** of evil

1493 GO1 AG221 LN72 B2:284 K2:379 R1497
ειδωλειον, IDOL TEMPLE
1C 8:10 eating in the **temple of an idol**

1494 GO9 AG221 LN72 B2:284 K2:378 R1497,2380
ειδωλοθυτος, IDOL SACRIFICES
Ac 15:29 has been **sacrificed to idols**
21:25 has been **sacrificed to idols**
1C 8: 1 **food sacrificed to idols:**
8: 4 of **food offered to idols,**
8: 7 as **food offered to an idol**
8:10 eating **food sacrificed to idols**
10:19 That **food sacrificed to idols**
Re 2:14 eat **food sacrificed to idols**
2:20 to eat **food sacrificed to idols**

1495 GO4 AG221 LN72 B2:284 K2:379 R1497,2999
ειδωλολατρια, IDOL SERVICE
1C 10:14 flee from the **worship of idols**
Ga 5:20 **idolatry,** sorcery, enmities,
Co 3: 5 and greed (which is **idolatry**)
1P 4: 3 carousing, and lawless **idolatry**

1496 GO7 AG221 LN72 B2:284 K2:379 R1495
ειδωλολατρης, IDOL SERVERS
1C 5:10 and robbers, or **idolaters,**
5:11 or is an **idolater,** reviler,
6: 9 **idolaters,** adulterers, male
10: 7 Do not become **idolaters** as some
Ep 5: 5 greedy (that is, an **idolater**
Re 21: 8 the sorcerers, the **idolaters,**
22:15 and murderers and **idolaters,**

1497 GO11 AG221 LN72 B2:284 K2:375
ειδωλον, IDOL
Ac 7:41 offered a sacrifice to the **idol**
15:20 from things polluted by **idols**
Ro 2:22 You that abhor **idols**
1C 8: 4 **idol** in the world really exists
8: 7 accustomed to **idols** until now
10:19 or that an **idol** is anything
12: 2 enticed and led astray to **idols**
2C 6:16 the temple of God with **idols**
1Th 1: 9 you turned to God from **idols**

1J 5:21 keep yourselves from **idols**
Re 9:20 up worshiping demons and **idols**

1500 GO5 AG221 LN72 K2:380
εικη, WITHOUT CAUSE
Ro 13: 4 does not bear the sword **in vain**
1C 15: 2 have come to believe **in vain**
Ga 3: 4 experience so much **for nothing**
3: 4 if it really was **for nothing**
4:11 for you may have been **wasted**
Co 2:18 puffed up **without cause**

1501 GO11 AG222 LN72
εικοσι, TWENTY
Lk 14:31 against him with **twenty**
Jn 6:19 they had rowed about **three** or
Ac 1:15 one hundred **twenty** persons
27:28 found **twenty** fathoms;
1C 10: 8 **twenty**-three thousand fell
Re 4: 4 throne are **twenty**-four thrones,
4: 4 thrones are **twenty**-four elders,
4:10 **twenty**-four elders fall before
5: 8 **twenty**-four elders fell before
11:16 Then the **twenty**-four elders who
19: 4 And the **twenty**-four elders and

1502 GO1 AG222 LN72 B2:256
εικω, I YIELD
Ga 2: 5 we did not **submit** to them even

1504 GO23 AG222 LN72 B2:286 K2:381
εικων, IMAGE
Mt 22:20 Whose **head** is this, and whose
Mk 12:16 Whose **head** is this, and whose
Lk 20:24 Whose **head** and whose title
Ro 1:23 immortal God for **images**
8:29 be conformed to the **image**
1C 11: 7 **image** and reflection of God;
15:49 we have borne the **image** of the
15:49 we will also bear the **image**
2C 3:18 transformed into the same **image**
4: 4 who is the **image** of God.
Co 1:15 is the **image** of the invisible
3:10 according to the **image** of its
He 10: 1 **true form** of these realities,
Re 13:14 make an **image** for the beast
13:15 **image** of the beast could even
13:15 to give breath to the **image**
13:15 not worship the **image** of the
14: 9 worship the beast and its **image**

14:11	worship the beast and its **image**
15: 2	**image** and the number of its
16: 2	who worshiped its **image.**
19:20	those who worshiped its **image.**
20: 4	the beast or its **image** and had

1505   GO3   AG222   LN72   K2:397   R1506

ειλικρινεια, UNMIXEDNESS

1C	5: 8	unleavened bread of **sincerity**
2C	1:12	frankness and godly **sincerity,**
	2:17	speak as persons of **sincerity,**

1506   GO2   AG222   LN72   K2:397

ειλικρινης, UNMIXED

Ph	1:10	you may be **pure** and blameless,
2P	3: 1	arouse your **sincere** intention

1510   GO2461   AG222   LN73   B2:278   K2:398

ειμι, I AM [MULTIPLE OCCURRENCES]

1511a   GO3   AG226   LN73

εινεκεν, ON ACCOUNT

Lk	4:18	**because** he has anointed me
Ac	28:20	it is **for the sake** of the hope
2C	3:10	**because** of the greater glory

1512   GO6   AG226   LN73

ειπερ, IF INDEED

Ro	3:30	**since** God is one;
	8: 9	**since** the Spirit of God dwells
	8:17	**if, in fact,** we suffer with
1C	8: 5	**Indeed,** even **though** there
	15:15	did not raise **if it is true**
2Th	1: 6	it is **indeed** just of God

1514   GO4   AG227   LN73   B2:776   K2:417   R1515

ειρηνευω, I AM AT PEACE

Mk	9:50	**be at peace** with one another
Ro	12:18	**live peaceably** with all
2C	13:11	one another, **live in peace**
1Th	5:13	**Be at peace** among yourselves

1515   GO92   AG227   LN73   B2:776   K2:400

ειρηνη, PEACE

Mt	10:13	let your **peace** come upon it
	10:13	let your **peace** return to you.
	10:34	I have come to bring **peace**
	10:34	have not come to bring **peace,**
Mk	5:34	go in **peace,** and be healed
Lk	1:79	into the way of **peace**

	2:14	on earth **peace** among those
	2:29	your servant in **peace,**
	7:50	has saved you; go in **peace**
	8:48	has made you well; go in **peace**
	10: 5	**Peace** to this house!
	10: 6	there who shares in **peace,**
	10: 6	your **peace** will rest on that
	11:21	his property is **safe.**
	12:51	I have come to bring **peace**
	14:32	asks for the terms of **peace.**
	19:38	**Peace** in heaven,
	19:42	the things that make for **peace**
	24:36	**Peace** be with you.
Jn	14:27	**Peace** I leave with you;
	14:27	my **peace** I give to you.
	16:33	in me you may have **peace.**
	20:19	**Peace** be with you.
	20:21	**Peace** be with you.
	20:26	**Peace** be with you.
Ac	7:26	tried to **reconcile** them,
	9:31	Samaria had **peace** and was built
	10:36	preaching **peace** by Jesus Christ
	12:20	asked for a **reconciliation,**
	15:33	they were sent off in **peace**
	16:36	come out now and go in **peace.**
	24: 2	we have long enjoyed **peace,**
Ro	1: 7	Grace to you and **peace** from God
	2:10	glory and honor and **peace**
	3:17	way of **peace** they have not
	5: 1	we have **peace** with God through
	8: 6	on the Spirit is life and **peace.**
	14:17	righteousness and **peace** and joy
	14:19	pursue what makes for **peace**
	15:13	with all joy and **peace**
	15:33	The God of **peace** be with all
	16:20	The God of **peace** will shortly
1C	1: 3	Grace to you and **peace**
	7:15	It is to **peace** that God has
	14:33	not of disorder but of **peace.**
	16:11	Send him on his way in **peace,**
2C	1: 2	Grace to you and **peace** from God
	13:11	live in **peace;** and the God
Ga	1: 3	Grace to you and **peace**
	5:22	love, joy, **peace,** patience,
	6:16	**peace** be upon them, and mercy,
Ep	1: 2	Grace to you and **peace** from God
	2:14	For he is our **peace;**
	2:15	the two, thus making **peace,**
	2:17	So he came and proclaimed **peace**

	2:17	**peace** to those who were near;
	4: 3	the Spirit in the bond of **peace.**
	6:15	to proclaim the gospel of **peace.**
	6:23	**Peace** be to the whole community,
Ph	1: 2	Grace to you and **peace** from God
	4: 7	And the **peace** of God,
	4: 9	God of **peace** will be with you.
Co	1: 2	Grace to you and **peace** from God
	3:15	let the **peace** of Christ rule
1Th	1: 1	Grace to you and **peace.**
	5: 3	There is **peace** and security
	5:23	May the God of **peace** himself
2Th	1: 2	Grace to you and **peace** from
	3:16	may the Lord of **peace** himself
	3:16	give you **peace** at all times
1Ti	1: 2	**peace** from God the Father
2Ti	1: 2	**peace** from God the Father
	2:22	faith, love, and **peace,** along
Ti	1: 4	Grace and **peace** from God
Pm	1: 3	Grace to you and **peace**
He	7: 2	that is, "king of **peace.**
	11:31	received the spies in **peace.**
	12:14	Pursue **peace** with everyone,
	13:20	Now may the God of **peace,**
Ja	2:16	Go in **peace;** keep warm
	3:18	righteousness is sown in **peace**
	3:18	for those who make **peace.**
1P	1: 2	May grace and **peace** be yours
	3:11	let them seek **peace** and pursue
	5:14	**Peace** to all of you
2P	1: 2	May grace and **peace** be yours
	3:14	to be found by him at **peace,**
2J	1: 3	Grace, mercy, and **peace** will be
3J	1:15	**Peace** to you.
Ju	1: 2	May mercy, **peace,** and love
Re	1: 4	Grace to you and **peace** from him
	6: 4	to take **peace** from the earth,

1516   GO2 AG228 LN73 B3:776 K2:418 R1515
ειρηνικος, PEACEABLE
He 12:11   it yields the **peaceful** fruit
Ja   3:17   is first pure, then **peaceable,**

1517   GO1 AG228 LN73 B2:776 K2:419 R1515,4160
ειρηνοποιεω, I MAKE PEACE
Co   1:20   **making peace** through the blood

1518   GO1 AG228 LN73 B2:776 K2:419
ειρηνοποιος, PEACEMAKER
Mt   5: 9   Blessed are the **peacemakers,**

1519   GO1768 AG228 LN73 K2:420
εις, INTO

1520   GO345 AG230 LN74 B2:719 K2:434
`εις, ONE [MULTIPLE OCCURRENCES]

1521   GO11 AG232 LN74 R1519,71
εισαγω, I LEAD INTO
Lk   2:27   parents **brought in** the child
| | 14:21 | the town and **bring in** the poor |
| | 22:54 | **bringing** him **into** the high |
Jn 18:16   gate, and **brought** Peter **in.**
Ac   7:45   **brought** it **in** with Joshua
	9: 8	and **brought** him **into** Damascus.
	21:28	**brought** Greeks **into** the temple
	21:29	**brought** him **into** the temple.
	21:37	was about **to be brought into**
	22:24	that he was **to be brought into**
He   1: 6   he **brings** the firstborn **into**

1522   GO5 AG232 LN74 B2:172 K1:222 R1519,191
εισακουω, I HEAR
Mt   6: 7   think that they **will be heard**
Lk   1:13   for your prayer **has been heard.**
Ac 10:31   your prayer **has been heard**
1C 14:21   they **will** not **listen** to me
He   5: 7   he **was heard** because of his

1523   GO1 AG232 LN74 B3:744 K2:57 R1519,1209
εισδεχομαι, I WELCOME IN
2C   6:17   then I **will welcome** you,

1524   GO4 AG232 LN74
εισειμι, I GO INTO
Ac   3: 3   about **to go into** the temple,
| | 21:18 | The next day Paul **went** with us |
| | 21:26 | he **entered** the temple with them |
He   9: 6   priests **go** continually

1525   GO194 AG232 LN75 B1:320 K2:676 R1519,2064
εισερχομαι, I GO INTO
Mt   2:21   **went to** the land of Israel.
	5:20	**enter** the kingdom of heaven.
	6: 6	**go into** your room and shut
	7:13	**Enter** through the narrow gate
	7:13	there are many who **take** it.
	7:21	**enter** the kingdom of heaven,
	8: 5	When he **entered** Capernaum,
	8: 8	have you **come** under my roof;
	9:25	he **went in** and took her by the

	10: 5	enter no town of the Samaritans	10:24	to enter the kingdom of God
	10:11	town or village you enter,	10:25	to enter the kingdom of God
	10:12	As you enter the house,	11:11	Then he entered Jerusalem
	12: 4	He entered the house of God	11:15	And he entered the temple
	12:29	one enter a strong man's house	13:15	or enter the house to take
	12:45	they enter and live there;	14:14	and wherever he enters,
	15:11	not what goes into the mouth	15:43	went boldly to Pilate
	18: 3	will never enter the kingdom	16: 5	As they entered the tomb,
	18: 8	better for you to enter life	Lk 1: 9	to enter the sanctuary
	18: 9	better for you to enter life	1:28	And he came to her
	19:17	If you wish to enter into life,	1:40	where she entered the house
	19:23	for a rich person to enter	4:16	he went to the synagogue
	19:24	someone who is rich to enter	4:38	he entered Simon's house.
	21:10	When he entered Jerusalem,	6: 4	He entered the house of God
	21:12	Jesus entered the temple	6: 6	he entered the synagogue
	22:11	the king came in to see	7: 1	he entered Capernaum.
	22:12	how did you get in here	7: 6	to have you come under my roof
	23:13	For you do not go in yourselves	7:36	went into the Pharisee's house
	23:13	and when others are going in,	7:44	I entered your house
	23:13	going in, you stop them.	7:45	but from the time I came in
	24:38	the day Noah entered the ark,	8:30	many demons had entered him.
	25:10	went with him into the wedding	8:32	Jesus to let them enter these.
	25:21	enter into the joy of your	8:33	the man and entered the swine,
	25:23	enter into the joy of your	8:41	begged him to come to his house,
	26:41	come into the time of trial;	8:51	did not allow anyone to enter
	26:58	and going inside, he sat with	9: 4	Whatever house you enter,
	27:53	and entered the holy city	9:34	as they entered the cloud.
Mk 1:21	he entered the synagogue	9:46	An argument arose among them
	1:45	could no longer go into a town	9:52	they entered a village
	2: 1	When he returned to Capernaum	10: 5	Whatever house you enter,
	2:26	He entered the house of God,	10: 8	Whenever you enter a town
	3: 1	he entered the synagogue,	10:10	whenever you enter a town
	3:27	enter a strong man's house	10:38	he entered a certain village,
	5:12	the swine; let us enter them	11:26	and they enter and live there
	5:13	out and entered the swine;	11:37	he went in and took his place
	5:39	When he had entered,	11:52	you did not enter yourselves,
	6:10	Wherever you enter a house,	11:52	those who were entering.
	6:22	Herodias came in and danced,	13:24	enter through the narrow door
	6:25	she rushed back to the king	13:24	will try to enter and will not
	7:17	crowd and entered the house,	14:23	and compel people to come in,
	7:24	He entered a house and did not	15:28	angry and refused to go in.
	8:26	even go into the village	17: 7	has just come in from plowing
	9:25	and never enter him again	17:12	As he entered a village,
	9:28	When he had entered the house,	17:27	the day Noah entered the ark,
	9:43	for you to enter life maimed	18:17	little child will never enter
	9:45	for you to enter life lame	18:25	camel to go through the eye of
	9:47	for you to enter the kingdom	18:25	is rich to enter the kingdom
	10:15	little child will never enter	19: 1	He entered Jericho
	10:23	who have wealth to enter		

	19:45	Then he **entered** the temple
	21:21	in the country must not **enter**
	22: 3	Then Satan **entered** into Judas
	22:10	when you have **entered** the city
	22:40	**come into** the time of trial
	22:46	**come into** the time of trial
	24: 3	but when they **went in,**
	24:26	then **enter** into his glory
	24:29	he **went in** to stay with them.
Jn	3: 4	Can one **enter** a second time
	3: 5	no one can **enter** the kingdom
	4:38	have **entered** into their labor
	10: 1	does not **enter** the sheepfold
	10: 2	one who **enters** by the gate
	10: 9	Whoever **enters** by me will be
	10: 9	**will come in** and go out and
	13:27	Satan **entered** into him.
	18: 1	he and his disciples **entered.**
	18:28	did not **enter** the headquarters,
	18:33	Pilate **entered** the headquarters
	19: 9	He **entered** his headquarters
	20: 5	but he did not **go in.**
	20: 6	and **went into** the tomb.
	20: 8	the tomb first, also **went in,**
Ac	1:13	When they had **entered** the city,
	1:21	the Lord Jesus **went in** and out
	3: 8	**entered** the temple with them,
	5: 7	his wife **came in,**
	5:10	When the young men **came in**
	5:21	**entered** the temple at daybreak
	9: 6	But get up and **enter** the city,
	9:12	a man named Ananias **come in**
	9:17	So Ananias went and **entered**
	10: 3	saw an angel of God **coming in**
	10:24	they **came to** Caesarea.
	10:25	On Peter's **arrival**
	10:27	he **went in** and found that many
	11: 3	Why did you **go to** uncircumcised
	11: 8	has ever **entered** my mouth
	11:12	and we **entered** the man's house.
	13:14	they **went into** the synagogue
	14: 1	**went into** the Jewish synagogue
	14:20	got up and **went into** the city.
	14:22	that we must **enter** the kingdom
	16:15	**come** and stay at my home
	16:40	they **went to** Lydia's home;
	17: 2	And Paul **went in,** as was his
	18: 7	**went to** the house of a man
	18:19	himself **went into** the synagogue

	19: 8	He **entered** the synagogue
	19:30	wished **to go into** the crowd,
	20:29	savage wolves will **come in**
	21: 8	we **went into** the house of Philip
	23:16	**gained entrance** to the barracks
	23:33	When they **came to** Caesarea
	25:23	they **entered** the audience hall
	28: 8	Paul **visited** him and cured him
	28:16	When we **came into** Rome,
Ro	5:12	sin **came into** the world
	11:25	of the Gentiles has **come in.**
1C	14:23	outsiders or unbelievers **enter**
	14:24	They will not **enter** my rest.
He	3:18	they would not **enter** his rest,
	3:19	that they were unable to **enter**
	4: 1	while the promise of **entering**
	4: 3	have believed **enter** that rest,
	4: 3	They shall not **enter** my rest,
	4: 5	They shall not **enter** my rest.
	4: 6	open for some to **enter** it,
	4: 6	failed to **enter** because of
	4:10	those who **enter** God's rest
	4:11	make every effort to **enter**
	6:19	a hope that **enters** the inner
	6:20	on our behalf, has **entered,**
	9:12	he **entered** once for all into
	9:24	For Christ did not **enter**
	9:25	priest **enters** the Holy Place
	10: 5	when Christ **came into** the world
Ja	2: 2	**comes into** your assembly,
	2: 2	dirty clothes also **comes in,**
	5: 4	**have reached** the ears of the
Re	3:20	I **will come in** to you and eat
	11:11	of life from God **entered** them,
	15: 8	no one could **enter** the temple
	21:27	But nothing unclean will **enter**
	22:14	may **enter** the city by the gates

1528 GO1 AG233 LN75 K3:496 R1519,2564
εισκαλεομαι, I CALL IN
Ac 10:23 So Peter **invited** them in

1529 GO5 AG233 LN75 B3:935 K5:103 R1519,3598
εισοδος, ENTRANCE

Ac	13:24	before his **coming** John had
1Th	1: 9	what kind of **welcome** we had
	2: 1	that our **coming** to you was not
He	10:19	to **enter** the sanctuary by the
2P	1:11	**entry** into the eternal kingdom

1530   GO1   AG233   LN75
εισπηδαω, I RUSH IN
Ac   16:29   and **rushing in,** he fell down

1531   GO18   AG233   LN75   K6:578   R1519,4198
εισπορευομαι, I TRAVEL INTO
Mt   15:17   whatever **goes into** the mouth
Mk   1:21   he **entered** the synagogue
    4:19   other things **come in** and choke
    5:40   **went in** where the child was.
    6:56   And wherever he **went,**
    7:15   by **going in** can defile,
    7:18   **goes into** a person from
            outside
    7:19   since it **enters,**
   11: 2   immediately as you **enter** it,
Lk   8:16   those who **enter** may see
   11:33   those who **enter** may see
   18:24   to **enter** the kingdom of God
   19:30   you **enter** it you will find
   22:10   him into the house he **enters**
Ac   3: 2   from those **entering** the temple
    8: 3   by **entering** house after house
    9:28   So he **went in** and out
   28:30   welcomed all who **came to** him,

1532   GO1   AG233   LN75   R1519,5143
ειστρεχω, I RUN IN
Ac   12:14   she **ran in** and announced

1533   GO8   AG233   LN75   K9:64   R1519,5342
εισφερω, I CARRY IN
Mt   6:13   do not **bring** us **to** the time
Lk   5:18   were trying to **bring** him **in**
    5:19   finding no way to **bring** him **in**
   11: 4   do not **bring** us **to** the time
   12:11   When they **bring** you before the
Ac   17:20   to know what it **means.**
1Ti   6: 7   **brought** nothing **into** the
            world,
He   13:11   is **brought into** the sanctuary

1534   GO15   AG233   LN75
ειτα, THEN
Mk   4:17   **when** trouble or persecution
    4:28   **then** the head, then the full
    4:28   **then** the full grain in the head
    8:25   **Then** Jesus laid his hands
Lk   8:12   **then** the devil comes and takes
Jn   13: 5   **Then** he poured water into a

   19:27   **Then** he said to the disciple,
   20:27   **Then** he said to Thomas,
1C   15: 5   **then** to the twelve.
   15: 7   **Then** he appeared to James,
   15:24   **Then** comes the end,
1Ti   2:13   formed first, **then** Eve;
    3:10   **then,** if they prove themselves
He   12: 9   **Moreover,** we had human parents
Ja   1:15   **then,** when that desire has

1535   GO65   AG234   LN75
ειτε, WHETHER [MULTIPLE OCCURRENCES]

1536a   GO4   AG234   LN75
ειωθα, CUSTOM
Mt   27:15   the governor was **accustomed**
Mk   10: 1   as was his **custom,** he again
Lk   4:16   as was his **custom.** He stood up
Ac   17: 2   Paul went in, as was his **custom**

1537   GO916   AG234   LN75
εκ, FROM [MULTIPLE OCCURRENCES]

1538   GO82   AG236   LN76
ἑκαστος, EACH [MULTIPLE OCCURRENCES]

1539   GO1   AG236   LN76
ἑκαστοτε, ALWAYS
2P   1:15   And I will make **every** effort

1540   GO17   AG236   LN76,
ἑκατον, HUNDRED
Mt   13: 8   grain, some a **hundredfold,**
   13:23   in one case a **hundredfold,**
   18:12   shepherd has a **hundred** sheep,
   18:28   who owed him a **hundred** denarii
Mk   4: 8   and sixty and a **hundredfold**
    4:20   and sixty and a **hundredfold**
    6:40   sat down in groups of **hundreds**
Lk   15: 4   having a **hundred** sheep
   16: 6   A **hundred** jugs of olive oil.
   16: 7   A **hundred** containers of wheat
Jn   19:39   weighing about a **hundred** pounds
   21:11   a **hundred** fifty-three of them;
Ac   1:15   one **hundred** twenty persons
Re   7: 4   one **hundred** forty-four thousand
   14: 1   one **hundred** forty-four thousand
   14: 3   one **hundred** forty-four thousand
   21:17   one **hundred** forty-four cubits

1541 ᴳᴼ1 ᴬᴳ236 ᴸᴺ76 ᴿ1540,2097
ἑκατονταετης, HUNDRED YEARS
Ro 4:19 was about a **hundred years old**

1542 ᴳᴼ3 ᴬᴳ237 ᴸᴺ76
ἑκατονταπλασιων, HUNDRED TIMES
Mt 19:29 will receive a **hundredfold**,
Mk 10:30 will not receive a **hundredfold**
Lk 8: 8 produced a **hundredfold**

1543 ᴳᴼ20 ᴬᴳ237 ᴸᴺ76 ᴿ1540,757
ἑκατονταρχης, RULER OF HUNDRED
Mt 8: 5 a **centurion** came to him
 8: 8 The **centurion** answered, "Lord,
 8:13 And to the **centurion** Jesus said
 27:54 when the **centurion** and those
Lk 7: 2 A **centurion** there had a slave
 7: 6 the **centurion** sent friends
 23:47 **centurion** saw what had taken
Ac 10: 1 **centurion** of the Italian Cohort
 10:22 Cornelius, a **centurion**,
 21:32 he took soldiers and **centurions**
 22:25 Paul said to the **centurion**
 22:26 When the **centurion** heard that,
 23:17 called one of the **centurions**
 23:23 summoned two of the **centurions**
 24:23 Then he ordered the **centurion**
 27: 1 to a **centurion** of the Augustan
 27: 6 **centurion** found an Alexandrian
 27:11 **centurion** paid more attention
 27:31 Paul said to the **centurion**
 27:43 but the **centurion**,

1543a ᴳᴼ1 ᴬᴳ237 ᴸᴺ76,
εκβαινω, I COME OUT
He 11:15 land that they **had left behind,**

1544 ᴳᴼ81 ᴬᴳ237 ᴸᴺ76 ᴮ1:453 ᴷ1:527 ᴿ1537,906
εκβαλλω, I THROW OUT
Mt 7: 4 **take** the speck **out** of your eye
 7: 5 **take** the log **out** of your own
 7: 5 **take** the speck **out** of your
 7:22 **cast out** demons in your name,
 8:12 **thrown into** the outer darkness
 8:16 he **cast out** the spirits
 8:31 If you **cast us out,**
 9:25 crowd **had been put outside,**
 9:33 the demon had been **cast out,**
 9:34 he **casts out** the demons.
 9:38 to **send out** laborers into

10: 1 spirits, to **cast** them **out,**
10: 8 the lepers, **cast out** demons
12:20 he **brings** justice to victory.
12:24 fellow **casts out** the demons.
12:26 If Satan **casts out** Satan,
12:27 **cast out** demons by Beelzebul,
12:27 own exorcists **cast** them **out**
12:28 of God that I **cast out** demons,
12:35 **brings** good things **out** of a
12:35 **brings** evil things **out** of an
13:52 who **brings out** of his treasure
15:17 and **goes out** into the sewer
17:19 Why could we not **cast** it **out**
21:12 **drove out** all who were selling
21:39 threw him **out** of the vineyard,
22:13 **throw** him into the outer
25:30 **throw** him into the outer
Mk 1:12 immediately **drove** him **out** into
 1:34 **cast out** many demons;
 1:39 synagogues and **casting out** demons.
 1:43 he **sent** him **away** at once,
 3:15 authority to **cast out** demons.
 3:22 demons he **casts out** demons.
 3:23 How can Satan **cast out** Satan
 5:40 Then he **put** them all **outside,**
 6:13 They **cast out** many demons,
 7:26 **to cast** the demon **out** of her
 9:18 your disciples to **cast** it **out,**
 9:28 Why could we not **cast** it **out**
 9:38 someone **casting out** demons
 9:47 you to stumble, **tear** it **out;**
 11:15 began to **drive out** those who
 12: 8 **threw** him **out** of the vineyard.
 16: 9 he had **cast out** seven demons.
 16:17 they will **cast out** demons;
Lk 4:29 **drove** him **out** of the town,
 6:22 and **defame** you on account
 6:42 **take out** the speck in your eye
 6:42 **take** the log **out** of your own
 9:40 your disciples to **cast** it **out,**
 9:49 someone **casting out** demons
 10: 2 **send out** laborers into his
 10:35 day he **took out** two denarii,
 11:14 he was **casting out** a demon
 11:15 He **casts out** demons by
 11:18 for you say that I **cast out**
 11:19 Now if I **cast out** the demons
 11:19 your exorcists **cast** them **out**
 11:20 that I **cast out** the demons,

	13:28	you yourselves **thrown out.**
	13:32	I am **casting out** demons
	19:45	**drive out** those who were
	20:12	they wounded and **threw out.**
	20:15	So they **threw** him **out** of the
Jn	2:15	he **drove** all of them **out**
	6:37	I **will** never **drive away;**
	9:34	And they **drove** him **out.**
	9:35	that they **had driven** him **out,**
	10: 4	When he **has brought out** all
	12:31	this world **will be driven out.**
Ac	7:58	**dragged** him **out** of the city
	9:40	Peter **put** all of them **outside,**
	13:50	**drove** them **out** of their region
	16:37	to **discharge** us in secret
	27:38	**throwing** the wheat **into** the
Ga	4:30	**Drive out** the slave and her
Ja	2:25	**sent** them **out** by another road
3J	1:10	**expels** them from the church.
Re	11: 2	**leave** that **out,** for it is given

1545 ᴳᴼ2 ᴬᴳ237 ᴸᴺ76
εκβασις, GOING OUT

1C	10:13	will also provide the **way out**
He	13: 7	consider the **outcome** of their

1546 ᴳᴼ1 ᴬᴳ238 ᴸᴺ76 ᴿ1544
εκβολη, THROW OUT

Ac	27:18	to **throw** the cargo **overboard,**

1549 ᴳᴼ1 ᴬᴳ238 ᴸᴺ76
εκγονος, DESCENDANTS

1Ti	5: 4	has children or **grandchildren,**

1550 ᴳᴼ1 ᴬᴳ238 ᴸᴺ76 ᴿ1537,1159
εκδαπαναω, I SPEND OUT

2C	12:15	**be spent for** you. If I love

1551 ᴳᴼ6 ᴬᴳ238 ᴸᴺ76 ᴮ2:244 ᴷ2:56
εκδεχομαι, I WAIT FOR

Ac	17:16	Paul **was waiting** for them in
1C	11:33	**wait** for one another.
	16:11	I **am expecting** him with the
He	10:13	since then **has been waiting**
	11:10	**looked forward** to the city
Ja	5: 7	farmer **waits** for the precious

1552 ᴳᴼ1 ᴬᴳ238 ᴸᴺ76 ᴿ1537,1212
εκδηλος, VERY CLEAR

2Ti	3: 9	their folly will become **plain**

1553 ᴳᴼ3 ᴬᴳ238 ᴸᴺ76 ᴮ2:788 ᴷ2:63
εκδημεω, I AM OUT OF HOME

2C	5: 6	we **are away** from the Lord
	5: 8	rather **be away from** the body
	5: 9	whether we **are** at home
		or **away,**

1554 ᴳᴼ4 ᴬᴳ238 ᴸᴺ76 ᴿ1537,1325
εκδιδωμι, I GIVE OUT

Mt	21:33	Then he **leased** it to tenants
	21:41	**lease** the vineyard to other
Mk	12: 1	then he **leased** it to tenants
Lk	20: 9	**leased** it to tenants, and went

1555 ᴳᴼ2 ᴬᴳ238 ᴸᴺ76 ᴿ1537,1223,2233
εκδιηγεομαι, I NARRATE OUT

Ac	13:41	even if someone **tells** you
	15: 3	they **reported** the conversion

1556 ᴳᴼ6 ᴬᴳ238 ᴸᴺ77 ᴮ3:92 ᴷ2:442 ᴿ1558
εκδικεω, I BRING OUT RIGHT

Lk	18: 3	**Grant** me **justice** against my
	18: 5	I will **grant** her **justice,**
Ro	12:19	never **avenge** yourselves,
2C	10: 6	to **punish** every disobedience
Re	6:10	before you judge and **avenge**
	19: 2	he **has avenged** on her the
		blood

1557 ᴳᴼ9 ᴬᴳ238 ᴸᴺ77 ᴮ3:92 ᴷ2:445 ᴿ1556
εκδικησις, BRING OUT RIGHT

Lk	18: 7	**grant justice** to his chosen
	18: 8	quickly **grant justice** to them.
	21:22	these are days of **vengeance,**
Ac	7:24	**avenged** him by striking down
Ro	12:19	**Vengeance** is mine, I will repay
2C	7:11	what zeal, what **punishment**
2Th	1: 8	inflicting **vengeance** on those
He	10:30	**Vengeance** is mine, I will repay
1P	2:14	sent by him to **punish** those

1558 ᴳᴼ2 ᴬᴳ238 ᴸᴺ77 ᴮ3:92 ᴷ2:444 ᴿ1537,1349
εκδικος, BRING OUT RIGHT

Ro	13: 4	**execute wrath** on the wrong-
		doer.
1Th	4: 6	because the Lord is an **avenger**

1559 ᴳᴼ1 ᴬᴳ239 ᴸᴺ77 ᴮ2:805 ᴿ1537,1377
εκδιωκω, I PERSECUTE

1Th	2:15	the prophets, and **drove** us **out**

1560   GO1   AG239   LN77   R1537,1325
εκδοτος, GIVEN OUT
Ac   2:23   this man, **handed over** to you

1561   GO1   AG239   LN77   B2:244   R1551
εκδοχη, AWAITING
He   10:27   fearful **prospect** of judgment

1562   GO6   AG239   LN77   B1:313   K2:318
εκδυω, I PUT OFF
Mt   27:28   They **stripped** him
     27:31   they **stripped** him of the robe
Mk   15:20   they **stripped** him of the purple
Lk   10:30   who **stripped** him, beat him,
2C   5: 3   when we have **taken** it **off**
     5: 4   we wish not **to be unclothed**

1563   GO95   AG239   LN77
εκει, THERE
Mt   2:13   remain **there** until I tell you;
     2:15   remained **there** until the death
     2:22   he was afraid to go **there.**
     5:24   leave your gift **there**
     6:21   **there** your heart will be also.
     8:12   where **there** will be weeping
     12:45   they enter and live **there;**
     13:42   **there** will be weeping
     13:50   **there** will be weeping
     13:58   do many deeds of power **there**
     14:23   When evening came, he was **there**
     15:29   **where** he sat down.
     17:20   Move from here to **there**
     18:20   I am **there** among them
     19: 2   and he cured them **there.**
     21:17   and spent the night **there.**
     22:11   **there** who was not wearing
     22:13   where **there** will be weeping
     24:28   **there** the vultures will gather.
     24:51   where **there** will be weeping
     25:30   where **there** will be weeping
     26:36   while I go over **there** and pray
     26:71   she said to the **bystanders,**
     27:36   then they sat down **there**
     27:47   some of the **bystanders** heard
     27:55   Many women were also **there,**
     27:61   and the other Mary were **there,**
     28: 7   **there** you will see him.
Mk   1:38   proclaim the message **there**
     2: 6   the scribes were sitting **there,**
     3: 1   was **there** who had a withered

     5:11   Now **there** on the hillside
     6: 5   could do no deed of power **there**
     6:10   stay **there** until you leave
     6:33   they hurried **there** on foot
     11: 5   some of the **bystanders** said
     13:21   or 'Look! **There** he is!
     14:15   Make preparations for us **there**
     16: 7   **there** you will see him,
Lk   2: 6   While they were **there,**
     6: 6   **there** was a man there whose
     8:32   Now **there** on the hillside
     9: 4   house you enter, stay **there,**
     10: 6   anyone is **there** who shares
     11:26   they enter and live **there;**
     12:18   **there** I will store all my
     12:34   **there** your heart will be also
     13:28   **There** will be weeping
     15:13   **there** he squandered
     17:21   **There** it is!
     17:23   Look **there!**
     17:37   **there** the vultures will gather.
     21: 2   **put** in two small copper coins.
     22:12   Make preparations for us **there**
     23:33   they crucified Jesus **there**
Jn   2: 1   the mother of Jesus was **there.**
     2: 6   Now standing **there** were six
     2:12   they remained **there** a few days.
     3:22   he spent some time **there**
     3:23   water was abundant **there;**
     4: 6   Jacob's well was **there,**
     4:40   he stayed **there** two days.
     5: 5   One man was **there** who had been
     6: 3   **there** with his disciples.
     6:22   **there** had been only one boat
     6:24   nor his disciples were **there,**
     10:40   and he remained **there.**
     10:42   And many believed in him **there.**
     11: 8   are you going **there** again
     11:15   I am glad I was not **there,**
     11:31   to the tomb to weep **there.**
     12: 2   **There** they gave a dinner
     12: 9   Jews learned that he was **there**
     12:26   **there** will my servant be also.
     18: 2   because Jesus often met **there**
     18: 3   they came **there** with lanterns
     19:42   they laid Jesus **there.**
Ac   9:33   **There** he found a man named
     16: 1   **there** was a disciple named
     17:14   and Timothy remained **behind.**

	19:21	After I have gone **there**
	25: 9	be tried **there** before me
	25:14	Since they were staying **there**
Ro	9:26	**there** they shall be called
	15:24	journey and to be sent **on**
Ti	3:12	to spend the winter **there.**
He	7: 8	in the **other,** by one of whom
Ja	2: 3	Stand **there,**
	3:16	For where **there** is envy
	4:13	a town and spend a year **there,**
Re	2:14	you have some **there** who hold
	12: 6	**where** she has a place prepared
	12: 6	**there** she can be nourished for
	12:14	to her **place** where she is
	21:25	there will be no night **there.**

1564   GO27   AG239   LN77   R1563
ἐκεῖθεν, FROM THERE

Mt	4:21	As he went **from there,**
	5:26	you will never get **out** until
	9: 9	As Jesus was walking **along,**
	9:27	As Jesus went on **from there,**
	11: 1	he went on **from there** to teach
	12: 9	He left that **place** and entered
	12:15	aware of this, he **departed.**
	13:53	he left **that place.**
	14:13	withdrew **from there** in a boat
	15:21	Jesus left **that place**
	15:29	Jesus had left **that place,**
	19:15	and went on **his way.**
Mk	6: 1	He left **that place** and came
	6:10	there until you leave **the place**
	6:11	to hear you, as you **leave,**
	7:24	**From there** he set out and went
	10: 1	He left **that place**
Lk	9: 4	there, and leave **from there.**
	12:59	you will never get **out**
	16:26	no one can cross **from there**
Jn	4:43	went **from that place**
	11:54	but went **from there** to a town
Ac	13: 4	and **from there** they sailed
	18: 7	Then he **left** the synagogue
	20:13	to take Paul on board **there**
	27:12	putting to sea **from there,**
Re	22: 2	**and** the leaves of the tree

1565   GO243   AG239   LN77
ἐκεῖνος, THAT

Mt	3: 1	In **those** days John the Baptist

	7:22	On **that** day many will say to me
	7:25	beat on **that** house, but it did
	7:27	beat against **that** house
	8:13	servant was healed in **that** hour
	8:28	that no one could pass **that** way
	9:22	**instantly** the woman was made
	9:26	spread throughout **that** district
	9:31	throughout **that** district.
	10:14	as you leave **that** house or town
	10:15	judgment than for **that** town.
	10:19	be given to you at **that** time;
	11:25	At **that** time Jesus said,
	12: 1	At **that** time Jesus went
	12:45	the last state of **that** person
	13: 1	**That** same day Jesus went out
	13:11	to **them** it has not been given.
	13:44	and sells all **that** he has
	14: 1	At **that** time Herod the ruler
	14:35	the people of **that** place
	14:35	word throughout **the** region
	15:22	woman from **that** region came out
	15:28	daughter was healed **instantly.**
	17:18	the boy was cured **instantly.**
	17:27	take **that** and give it to them
	18: 1	At **that** time the disciples
	18:27	the lord of **that** slave released
	18:28	But **that** same slave,
	18:32	I forgave you all **that** debt
	20: 4	and he said to **them,**
	21:40	will he do to **those** tenants
	22: 7	destroyed **those** murderers,
	22:10	**Those** slaves went out into the
	22:23	**same** day some Sadducees came
	22:46	nor from **that** day did anyone
	24:19	nursing infants in **those** days
	24:22	if **those** days had not been cut
	24:22	**those** days will be cut short.
	24:29	the suffering of **those** days
	24:36	But about **that** day and hour
	24:38	For as in **those** days before
	24:43	But understand **this:**
	24:46	Blessed is **that** slave whom his
	24:48	But if **that** wicked slave says
	24:50	the master of **that** slave
	25: 7	all **those** bridesmaids got up
	25:19	the master of **those** slaves came
	26:24	but woe to **that** one by whom
	26:24	have been better for **that** one
	26:29	until **that** day when I drink it

	26:55	At **that** hour Jesus said to the
	27: 8	For this reason **that** field
	27:19	to do with **that** innocent man,
	27:63	remember what **that** impostor
Mk	1: 9	In **those** days Jesus came
	2:20	**that** kingdom cannot stand.
	3:25	**that** house will not be able
	4:11	but for **those** outside,
	4:20	And **these** are the ones sown
	4:35	On **that** day, when evening
	6:55	and rushed about **that** whole
	7:20	out of a person **that** defiles.
	8: 1	In **those** days when there was
	12: 7	But **those** tenants said to one
	13:11	is given you at **that** time,
	13:17	nursing infants in **those** days
	13:19	For in **those** days there will
	13:24	But in **those** days, after that
	13:24	after **that** suffering,
	13:32	But about **that** day or hour
	14:21	but woe to **that** one by whom
	14:21	for **that** one not to have been
	14:25	until **that** day when I drink it
	16:10	**She** went out and told those
	16:13	**they** went back and told the rest
	16:13	but **they** did not believe them.
	16:20	**they** went out and proclaimed
Lk	2: 1	In **those** days a decree went
	4: 2	nothing at all during **those**
	5:35	they will fast in **those** days
	6:23	Rejoice in **that** day and leap
	6:48	river burst against **that** house
	6:49	was the ruin of **that** house
	7:21	Jesus had **just** then cured many
	8:32	Jesus to let them enter **these.**
	9: 5	as you are leaving **that** town
	9:36	in **those** days told no one
	10:12	I tell you, on **that** day
	10:12	for Sodom than for **that** town.
	10:31	was going down **that** road;
	11:26	last state of **that** person
	12:37	Blessed are **those** slaves
	12:38	blessed are **those** slaves.
	12:43	Blessed is **that** slave whom his
	12:45	if **that** slave says to himself,
	12:46	master of **that** slave will come
	12:47	**That** slave who knew what his
	13: 4	**those** eighteen who were killed
	14:24	none of **those** who were invited

	15:14	place throughout **that** country,
	15:15	citizens of **that** country,
	17:31	On **that** day, anyone on the
	18: 3	In **that** city there was a widow
	18:14	justified rather than the **other**
	19: 4	because **he** was going to pass
	20:18	who falls on **that** stone will be
	20:35	worthy of a place in **that** age
	21:23	nursing infants in **those** days
	21:34	and **that** day catch you
	22:22	but woe to **that** one by whom
Jn	1: 8	**He** himself was not the light
	1:18	**who** has made him known.
	1:33	but the **one** who sent me
	1:39	they remained with him **that** day
	2:21	**he** was speaking of the temple
	3:28	I have been sent ahead of **him**
	3:30	**He** must increase, but I must
	4:25	When **he** comes
	4:39	Samaritans from **that** city
	4:53	**this** was the hour when Jesus
	5: 9	Now **that** day was a sabbath.
	5:11	The man **who** made me well
	5:19	for whatever the **Father** does
	5:35	**He** was a burning and shining
	5:37	has **himself** testified on my
	5:38	believe him whom **he** has sent.
	5:39	it is **they** that testify
	5:43	you will accept **him.**
	5:46	for **he** wrote about me.
	5:47	do not believe **what** he wrote,
	6:29	believe in him whom **he** has sent
	7:11	Where is **he?**
	7:45	Pharisees, **who** asked them,
	8:42	my own, but **he** sent me.
	8:44	**He** was a murderer from the
	9: 9	**He** kept saying, "I am the man
	9:12	Where is **he?**
	9:11	**He** answered, "The man called
	9:25	**He** answered, "I do not know
	9:28	You are **his** disciple, but we
	9:36	**He** answered, "And who is he,
	9:37	one speaking with you is **he**
	10: 1	**anyone** who does not enter
	10: 6	but **they** did not understand
	10:35	If **those** to whom the word
	11:13	but **they** thought that he was
	11:29	And when **she** heard it,
	11:49	who was high priest **that** year,

11:51	being high priest **that** year		19:23	About **that** time
11:53	So from **that** day on		20: 2	had gone through **those** regions
12:48	the word **that** I have spoken		21: 6	and **they** returned home.
13:25	**he** asked him, "Lord, who is it?		22:11	**those** who were with me
13:26	It is the **one** to whom I give		28: 7	Now in the neighborhood of **that**
13:27	bread, Satan entered into **him.**	Ro	6:21	end of **those** things is death.
13:30	**he** immediately went out.		14:14	anyone **who** thinks it unclean.
14:20	On **that** day you will know		14:15	cause the ruin of **one** for whom
14:21	are **those** who love me;	1C	9:25	**they** do it to receive
14:26	**whom** the Father will send		10:11	**These** things happened to them
15:26	**he** will testify on my behalf.		10:28	the **one** who informed you,
16: 8	And when **he** comes,		15:11	then it was I or **they,**
16:13	**he** will guide you into all	2C	7: 8	grieved you with **that** letter,
16:14	**He** will glorify me,		8: 9	so that by **his** poverty
16:23	On **that** day you will ask		8:14	abundance and **their** need,
16:26	On **that** day you will ask		8:14	abundance may be for **your** need
18:13	the high priest **that** year.		10:18	For it is not **those** who commend
18:15	Since **that** disciple was known	Ep	2:12	that you were at **that** time
18:17	are you?" **He** said, "I am not."	2Th	1:10	be marveled at on **that** day
18:25	**He** denied it	2Ti	1:12	to guard until **that** day
19:15	**They** cried out,		1:18	from the Lord on **that** day
19:21	**This** man said, I am King		2:13	**he** remains faithful
19:27	from **that** hour the disciple		2:26	captive by him to do **his** will.
19:31	because **that** sabbath was a day		3: 9	in the case of **those** two men,
19:35	and **he** knows that he tells		4: 8	will give me on **that** day,
20:13	**They** said to her, "Woman,	Ti	3: 7	been justified by **his** grace,
20:15	to be the gardener, **she** said	He	4: 2	faith with **those** who listened.
20:16	**She** turned and said to him		4:11	to enter **that** rest,
20:19	it was evening on **that** day,		6: 7	a crop useful to **those**
21: 3	**that** night they caught nothing.		8: 7	For if **that** first covenant
21: 7	**That** disciple whom Jesus loved		8:10	of Israel after **those** days,
21:23	**this** disciple would not die.		10:16	make with them after **those** days
Ac 1:19	so that **the** field was called		11:15	the land **that** they had left
2:18	in **those** days I will pour out		12:25	for if **they** did not escape
2:41	**that** day about three thousand	Ja	1: 7	for **the** doubter, being
3:13	he had decided to release **him**		4:15	will live and do this or **that**
3:23	not listen to **that** prophet	2P	1:16	eyewitnesses of **his** majesty.
7:41	At **that** time they made a calf	1J	2: 6	to walk just as **he** walked.
8: 1	**That** day a severe persecution		3: 3	ust as **he** is pure.
8: 8	was great joy in **that** city.		3: 5	You know that **he** was revealed
9:37	At **that** time she became ill		3: 7	just as **he** is righteous.
10: 9	as **they** were on their journey		3:16	**he** laid down his life for us
12: 1	About that **time** King Herod		4:17	because as **he** is, so are we
12: 6	The **very** night before Herod		5:16	you should pray about **that.**
14:21	the good news to **that** city	Re	9: 6	And in **those** days people
16: 3	Jews who were in **those** places,		11:13	At **that** moment there was
16:33	At the **same** hour of the night			
16:35	Let **those** men go.			
19:16	they fled out of **the** house			

1566   GO2 AG240 LN77

εκειcε, THERE

Ac 21: 3　　was to unload its cargo **there.**
　　 22: 5　　to bind those who were **there**

1567　 ᴳᴼ7 ᴬᴳ240 ᴸᴺ77 ᴮ3:530 ᴷ2:894 ᴿ1537,2212
εκζητεω, I SEEK OUT
Lk 11:50　　this generation **may be charged**
　　 11:51　　it **will be charged** against
Ac 15:17　　other peoples **may seek** the Lord
Ro   3:11　　there is no one who **seeks** God.
He 11: 6　　he rewards those who **seek** him.
　　 12:17　　**sought** the blessing with tears.
1P   1:10　　made careful search and **inquiry**

1567a　 ᴳᴼ1 ᴬᴳ240 ᴸᴺ77 ᴮ3:532
εκζητησις, SPECULATIONS
1Ti 1: 4　　that promote **speculations**

1568　 ᴳᴼ4 ᴬᴳ240 ᴸᴺ77 ᴮ2:621 ᴷ3:4 ᴿ1569
εκθαμβεω, I AM GREATLY ASTONISHED
Mk   9:15　　immediately **overcome with awe,**
　　 14:33　　began **to be distressed**
　　 16: 5　　and they **were alarmed.**
　　 16: 6　　Do not **be alarmed;**

1569　 ᴳᴼ1 ᴬᴳ240 ᴸᴺ77 ᴮ2:621 ᴷ3:4 ᴿ1537,2285
εκθαμβος, GREATLY ASTONISHED
Ac   3:11　　Portico, utterly **astonished.**

1569a　 ᴳᴼ1 ᴬᴳ240 ᴸᴺ77 ᴮ2:621
εκθαυμαζω, I AM GREATLY ASTONISHED
Mk 12:17　　they **were utterly amazed**

1570　 ᴳᴼ1 ᴬᴳ240 ᴸᴺ77
εκθετος, SET OUT
Ac   7:19　　to **abandon** their infants

1571　 ᴳᴼ2 ᴬᴳ240 ᴸᴺ77 ᴮ3:102 ᴷ3:430 ᴿ1537,2508
εκκαθαιρω, I CLEAN OUT
1C   5: 7　　**Clean out** the old yeast
2Ti 2:21　　All who **cleanse** themselves

1572　 ᴳᴼ1 ᴬᴳ240 ᴸᴺ77 ᴿ1537,2545
εκκαιω, I BURN THOROUGHLY
Ro   1:27　　**were consumed** with passion

1574　 ᴳᴼ2 ᴬᴳ240 ᴸᴺ77 ᴷ2:446
εκκεντεω, I PIERCE
Jn 19:37　　the one whom they **have pierced**
Re   1: 7　　even those who **pierced** him

1575　 ᴳᴼ3 ᴬᴳ240 ᴸᴺ77 ᴿ1537,2806
εκκλαω, I BREAK OFF
Ro 11:17　　the branches **were broken off,**
　　 11:19　　Branches **were broken off**
　　 11:20　　They **were broken off**

1576　 ᴳᴼ2 ᴬᴳ240 ᴸᴺ77 ᴿ1537,2808
εκκλειω, I CLOSE OUT
Ro   3:27　　boasting? It is **excluded.**
Ga   4:17　　they want to **exclude** you,

1577　 ᴳᴼ114 ᴬᴳ240 ᴸᴺ77 ᴮ1:291 ᴷ3:501
εκκλησια, ASSEMBLY
Mt 16:18　　I will build my **church,**
　　 18:17　　tell it to the **church;**
　　 18:17　　to listen even to the **church,**
Ac   5:11　　fear seized the whole **church**
　　 7:38　　who was in the **congregation**
　　 8: 1　　began against the **church**
　　 8: 3　　Saul was ravaging the **church**
　　 9:31　　the **church** throughout Judea,
　　 11:22　　came to the ears of the **church**
　　 11:26　　they met with the **church**
　　 12: 1　　some who belonged to the **church.**
　　 12: 5　　the **church** prayed fervently
　　 13: 1　　Now in the **church** at Antioch
　　 14:23　　elders for them in each **church,**
　　 14:27　　they called the **church** together
　　 15: 3　　sent on their way by the **church,**
　　 15: 4　　were welcomed by the **church**
　　 15:22　　the consent of the whole **church**
　　 15:41　　strengthening the **churches.**
　　 16: 5　　the **churches** were strengthened
　　 18:22　　and greeted the **church,**
　　 19:32　　the **assembly** was in confusion,
　　 19:39　　settled in the regular **assembly**
　　 19:41　　he dismissed the **assembly**
　　 20:17　　asking the elders of the **church**
　　 20:28　　to shepherd the **church** of God
Ro 16: 1　　Phoebe, a deacon of the **church**
　　 16: 4　　the **churches** of the Gentiles.
　　 16: 5　　Greet also the **church** in their
　　 16:16　　**churches** of Christ greet you.
　　 16:23　　and to the whole **church,**
1C   1: 2　　To the **church** of God that is
　　 4:17　　everywhere in every **church.**
　　 6: 4　　have no standing in the **church**
　　 7:17　　my rule in all the **churches.**
　　 10:32　　Greeks or to the **church** of God,
　　 11:16　　nor do the **churches** of God.

	11:18	come together as a **church**,
	11:22	show contempt for the **church**
	12:28	has appointed in the **church**
	14: 4	prophesy build up the **Church**
	14: 5	so that the **church** may be built
	14:12	for building up the **church**.
	14:19	in **church** I would rather speak
	14:23	the whole **church** comes together
	14:28	let them be silent in **church**
	14:33	all the **churches** of the saints,
	14:34	be silent in the **churches**.
	14:35	for a woman to speak in **church**.
	15: 9	I persecuted the **church** of God.
	16: 1	I gave to the **churches**
	16:19	The **churches** of Asia send
	16:19	together with the **church**
2C	1: 1	To the **church** of God that is
	8: 1	to the **churches** of Macedonia;
	8:18	famous among all the **churches**
	8:19	appointed by the **churches**
	8:23	are messengers of the **churches**,
	8:24	openly before the **churches**,
	11: 8	I robbed other **churches**
	11:28	anxiety for all the **churches**.
	12:13	than the other **churches**,
Ga	1: 2	To the **churches** of Galatia:
	1:13	persecuting the **church** of God
	1:22	to the **churches** of Judea
Ep	1:22	over all things for the **church**,
	3:10	so that through the **church**
	3:21	to him be glory in the **church**
	5:23	is the head of the **church**,
	5:24	**church** is subject to Christ,
	5:25	as Christ loved the **church**
	5:27	present the **church** to himself
	5:29	as Christ does for the **church**,
	5:32	to Christ and the **church**.
Ph	3: 6	a persecutor of the **church**;
	4:15	no **church** shared with me
Co	1:18	head of the body, the **church**
	1:24	his body, that is, the **church**
	4:15	and to Nympha and the **church**
	4:16	it read also in the **church**
1Th	1: 1	the **church** of the Thessalonians
	2:14	imitators of the **churches**
2Th	1: 1	the **church** of the Thessalonians
	1: 4	boast of you among the **churches**
1Ti	3: 5	he take care of God's **church**
	3:15	the **church** of the living God

	5:16	let the **church** not be burdened
Pm	1: 2	to the **church** in your house:
He	2:12	the midst of the **congregation**
	12:23	the **assembly** of the firstborn
Ja	5:14	for the elders of the **church**
3J	1: 6	your love before the **church**.
	1: 9	written something to the **church**
	1:10	and expels them from the **church**
Re	1: 4	John to the seven **churches**
	1:11	send it to the seven **churches**,
	1:20	angels of the seven **churches**,
	1:20	are the seven **churches**.
	2: 1	To the angel of the **church**
	2: 7	is saying to the **churches**.
	2: 8	to the angel of the **church**
	2:11	is saying to the **churches**.
	2:12	to the angel of the **church**
	2:17	is saying to the **churches**.
	2:18	to the angel of the **church**
	2:23	**churches** will know that I am
	2:29	is saying to the **churches**.
	3: 1	to the angel of the **church**
	3: 6	is saying to the **churches**.
	3: 7	to the angel of the **church**
	3:13	is saying to the **churches**.
	3:14	to the angel of the **church**
	3:22	is saying to the **churches**
	22:16	testimony for the **churches**

1578 GO3 AG241 LN78 R1537,2827
εκκλινω, I BOW OUT
Ro   3:12   All have **turned aside**,
     16:17   you have learned; **avoid** them.
1P   3:11   **let** them **turn away** from evil

1579 GO1 AG241 LN78 R1537,2860
εκκολυμβαω, I SWIM OUT
Ac 27:42   **might swim** away and escape;

1580 GO1 AG241 LN78
εκκομιζω, I CARRY OUT
Lk   7:12   had died was **being carried out**

1581 GO10 AG241 LN78 K3:857 R1537,2875
εκκοπτω, I CUT OFF
Mt   3:10   bear good fruit is **cut down**
     5:30   causes you to sin, **cut it off**
     7:19   bear good fruit is **cut down**
     18: 8   you to stumble, **cut it off**
Lk   3: 9   bear good fruit is **cut down**

	13: 7	**Cut** it **down!** Why should it be
	13: 9	but if not, you can **cut** it **down**
Ro	11:22	you also **will be cut off.**
	11:24	if you **have been cut** from what
2C	11:12	to **deny** an opportunity to those

1582　GO1 AG242 LN78 K3:915
εκκρεμαννυμι, I HANG ON
Lk　19:48　all the people **were spellbound**

1583　GO1 AG242 LN78 R1537,2980
εκλαλεω, I SPEAK OUT
Ac　23:22　**Tell** no one that you have

1584　GO1 AG242 LN78 B2:484 K4:16 R1537,2989
εκλαμπω, I SHINE OUT
Mt　13:43　Then the righteous **will shine**

1585　GO1 AG242 LN78 R1537,2990
εκλανθανομαι, I FORGET
He　12: 5　**have forgotten** the exhortation

1586　GO22 AG242 LN78 B1:536 K4:144
εκλεγομαι, I SELECT
Mk	13:20	the elect, whom he **chose,**
Lk	6:13	and **chose** twelve of them,
	9:35	my **Chosen;** listen to him
	10:42	Mary **has chosen** the better part
	14: 7	how the guests **chose** the places
Jn	6:70	I not **choose** you, the twelve
	13:18	I know whom I have **chosen.**
	15:16	You did not **choose** me
	15:16	choose me but I **chose** you.
	15:19	I **have chosen** you out of the
Ac	1: 2	the apostles whom he **had chosen**
	1:24	of these two you **have chosen**
	6: 5	they **chose** Stephen, a man full
	13:17	**chose** our ancestors and made
	15: 7	decided to **choose** men
	15:25	decided unanimously to **choose**
1C	1:27	But God **chose** what is foolish
	1:27	God **chose** what is weak in the
	1:28	God **chose** what is low
Ep	1: 4	just as he **chose** us in Christ
Ja	2: 5	Has not God **chosen** the poor

1587　GO4 AG242 LN78 B3:248 R1537,3007
εκλειπω, I LEFT OFF
Lk　16: 9　wealth so that when it **is gone,**

	22:32	your own faith **may** not **fail;**
	23:45	while the sun's light **failed;**
He	1:12	your years **will** never **end.**

1588　GO22 AG242 LN78 B1:536 K4:181 R1586
εκλεκτος, SELECT
Mt	22:14	are called, but few are **chosen**
	24:22	for the sake of the **elect**
	24:24	if possible, even the **elect.**
	24:31	they will gather his **elect**
Mk	13:20	for the sake of the **elect,**
	13:22	if possible, the **elect.**
	13:27	and gather his **elect**
Lk	18: 7	God grant justice to his **chosen**
	23:35	Messiah of God, his **chosen** one
Ro	8:33	any charge against God's **elect**
	16:13	Greet Rufus, **chosen** in the Lord
Co	3:12	As God's **chosen** ones
1Ti	5:21	Jesus and of the **elect** angels
2Ti	2:10	for the sake of the **elect,**
Ti	1: 1	of the faith of God's **elect**
1P	1: 1	To the **exiles** of the Dispersion
	2: 4	rejected by mortals yet **chosen**
	2: 6	a cornerstone **chosen**
	2: 9	But you are a **chosen** race,
2J	1: 1	The elder to the **elect** lady
	1:13	children of your **elect** sister
Re	17:14	called and **chosen** and faithful

1589　GO7 AG243 LN78 B1:536 K4:176 R1586
εκλογη, SELECT
Ac	9:15	instrument whom I have **chosen**
Ro	9:11	that God's purpose of **election**
	11: 5	is a remnant, **chosen** by grace.
	11: 7	The **elect** obtained it,
	11:28	**election** they are beloved,
1Th	1: 4	by God, that he has **chosen** you
2P	1:10	confirm your call and **election**

1590　GO5 AG243 LN78 B3:177 R1537,3089
εκλυω, I LOOSE OUT
Mt	15:32	for they **might faint** on the way
Mk	8: 3	they **will faint** on the way
Ga	6: 9	if we **do** not **give up.**
He	12: 3	not grow weary or **lose heart.**
	12: 5	**lose heart** when you are punished

1591　GO5 AG243 LN78
εκμασσω, I WIPE DRY
Lk　7:38　and to **dry** them with her hair.

	7:44	and **dried** them with her hair.
Jn	11: 2	**wiped** his feet with her hair
	12: 3	and **wiped** them with her hair.
	13: 5	to **wipe** them with the towel

1592   G02   AG243   LN78   K4:796   R1537,3456
εκμυκτηριζω, I MOCK AT
Lk	16:14	and they **ridiculed** him.
	23:35	the leaders **scoffed** at him,

1593   G01   AG243   LN78
εκνευω, I WITHDRAW
Jn	5:13	for Jesus **had disappeared**

1594   G01   AG243   LN78   B1:514   K4:941
εκνηφω, I AM SOBER
1C	15:34	Come to a **sober** and right mind

1595   G01   AG243   LN78   K2:470   R1635
εκουσιος, WILLINGNESS
Pm	1:14	good deed might be **voluntary**

1596   G02   AG243   LN78   R1635
εκουσιως, WILLINGLY
He	10:26	For if we **willfully** persist
1P	5: 2	under compulsion but **willingly,**

1597   G02   AG243   LN78   R1537,3819
εκπαλαι, FROM OLD
2P	2: 3	against them **long ago,**
	3: 5	heavens existed **long ago**

1598   G04   AG243   LN78   B3:798   K6:23   R1537,3985
εκπειραζω, I TEST
Mt	4: 7	**put** . . . Lord your God **to the test**
Lk	4:12	**put** . . . Lord your God **to the test**
	10:25	lawyer stood up **to test** Jesus
1C	10: 9	not **put** Christ **to the test**

1599   G02   AG243   LN78   R1537,3992
εκπεμπω, I SEND OUT
Ac	13: 4	**being sent out** by the Holy
	17:10	believers **sent** Paul and Silas

1599a   G01   AG243   LN78
εκπερισσως, EXCESSIVELY
Mk	14:31	But he said **vehemently,**

1600   G01   AG243   LN79
εκπετaννυμι, I STRETCH OUT
Ro	10:21	I **have held out** my hands

1600a   G01   AG243   LN79
εκπηδαω, I RUSH OUT
Ac	14:14	and **rushed out** into the crowd

1601   G010   AG243   LN79   B1:608   K6:167   R1537,4098
εκπιπτω, I FALL OUT
Ac	12: 7	the chains **fell off** his wrists
	27:17	they **would run on** the Syrtis,
	27:26	we will have to **run aground**
	27:29	that we **might run on** the rocks,
	27:32	the boat and set it **adrift.**
Ro	9: 6	the word of God **had failed.**
Ga	5: 4	you have **fallen away** from grace
Ja	1:11	the field; its flower **falls,**
1P	1:24	and the flower **falls,**
2P	3:17	and **lose** your own stability.

1602   G03   AG244   LN79   R1537,4126
εκπλεω, I SAIL OUT
Ac	15:39	and **sailed away** to Cyprus.
	18:18	**sailed** for Syria, accompanied
	20: 6	but we **sailed** from Philippi

1603   G01   AG244   LN79   K6:307   R1537,4137
εκπληροω, I FILL OUT
Ac	13:33	he **has fulfilled** for us,

1604   G01   AG244   LN79   K6:308   R1603
εκπληρωσις, FILLING OUT
Ac	21:26	making public the **completion**

1605   G013   AG244   LN79   B1:529   R1537,4141
εκπλησσω, I AM ASTONISHED
Mt	7:28	the crowds **were astounded**
	13:54	so that they were **astounded**
	19:25	they were greatly **astounded**
	22:33	were **astounded** at his teaching
Mk	1:22	were **astounded** at his teaching
	6: 2	who heard him were **astounded.**
	7:37	were **astounded** beyond measure,
	10:26	They were greatly **astounded**
	11:18	the whole crowd was **spellbound**
Lk	2:48	saw him they were **astonished**
	4:32	were **astounded** at his teaching
	9:43	And all were **astounded**
Ac	13:12	for he was **astonished**

1606 ᴳᴼ3 ᴬᴳ244 ᴸᴺ79 ᴮ3:689 ᴷ6:452 ᴿ1537,4154
εκπνεω, I BREATHE OUT
Mk 15:37 loud cry and **breathed** his last.
    15:39 this way he **breathed** his last,
Lk 23:46 said this, he **breathed** his last

1607 ᴳᴼ33 ᴬᴳ244 ᴸᴺ79 ᴷ6:578 ᴿ1537,4198
εκπορευομαι, I TRAVEL OUT
Mt   3: 5 all Judea were **going out** to him
     4: 4 word that **comes from** the mouth
    15:11 what **comes out** of the mouth
    15:18 what **comes out** of the mouth
    20:29 As they **were leaving** Jericho,
Mk   1: 5 **were going out** to him,
     6:11 as you **leave,** shake off the
     7:15 that **come out** are what defile
     7:19 and **goes out** into the sewer
     7:20 what **comes out** of a person
     7:21 that evil intentions **come**
     7:23 evil things **come from** within
    10:17 was **setting out** on a journey
    10:46 large crowd **were leaving**
    11:19 disciples **went out** of the city
    13: 1 As he **came out** of the temple,
Lk   3: 7 to the crowds that **came out**
     4:22 **began to reach** every place
Jn   5:29 and will **come out**—those who
    15:26 truth who **comes from** the Father
Ac   9:28 he **went** in and **out** among them
    19:12 evil spirits **came out** of them.
    25: 4 that he himself intended **to go**
Ep   4:29 Let no evil talk **come out** of
Re   1:16 **came** a sharp, two-edged sword
     4: 5 **Coming** from the throne
     9:17 sulfur **came out** of their mouths
     9:18 sulfur **coming out** of their
    11: 5 fire **pours from** their mouth
    16:14 who **go abroad** to the kings
    19:15 From his mouth **comes** a sharp
    22: 1 **flowing from** the throne of God

1608 ᴳᴼ1 ᴬᴳ244 ᴸᴺ79 ᴷ6:579 ᴿ1537,4203
εκπορνευω, I AM COMPLETELY SEXUALLY IMMORAL
Ju   1: 7 **indulged in sexual immorality**

1609 ᴳᴼ1 ᴬᴳ244 ᴸᴺ79 ᴷ2:448 ᴿ1537,4429
εκπτυω, I SPIT OUT
Ga   4:14 you did not **scorn** or despise me

1610 ᴳᴼ4 ᴬᴳ244 ᴸᴺ79 ᴮ3:865 ᴷ6:991 ᴿ1537,4492
εκριζοω, I ROOT OUT
Mt 13:29 you **would uproot** the wheat
    15:13 not planted will be **uprooted.**
Lk 17: 6 Be **uprooted** and planted in the
Ju   1:12 fruit, twice dead, **uprooted**

1611 ᴳᴼ7 ᴬᴳ245 ᴸᴺ79 ᴮ1:527 ᴷ2:449 ᴿ1839
εκστασις, AMAZEMENT
Mk   5:42 were overcome with **amazement.**
    16: 8 for terror and **amazement**
Lk   5:26 **Amazement** seized all of them,
Ac   3:10 with wonder and **amazement**
    10:10 he fell into a **trance.**
    11: 5 and in a **trance** I saw a vision
    22:17 I fell into a **trance**

1612 ᴳᴼ1 ᴬᴳ245 ᴸᴺ79 ᴿ1537,4762
εκστρεφω, I TURN OUT
Ti   3:11 such a person is **perverted**

1613 ᴳᴼ1 ᴬᴳ245 ᴸᴺ79 ᴿ1537,5015
εκταρασσω, I TROUBLE THOROUGHLY
Ac 16:20 These men are **disturbing**

1614 ᴳᴼ16 ᴬᴳ245 ᴸᴺ79 ᴷ2:460
εκτεινω, I STRETCH OUT
Mt   8: 3 He **stretched out** his hand
    12:13 **Stretch out** your hand.
    12:13 He **stretched** it **out,**
    12:49 **pointing** to his disciples,
    14:31 **reached out** his hand and caught
    26:51 **put** his hand **on** his sword,
Mk   1:41 Jesus **stretched out** his hand
     3: 5 **Stretch out** your hand.
     3: 5 He **stretched** it **out,**
Lk   5:13 Jesus **stretched out** his hand,
     6:10 **Stretch out** your hand.
    22:53 you **did** not **lay** hands on me.
Jn 21:18 will **stretch out** your hands,
Ac   4:30 while you **stretch out** your hand
    26: 1 Paul **stretched out** his hand
    27:30 **putting out** anchors from the

1615 ᴳᴼ2 ᴬᴳ245 ᴸᴺ79 ᴿ1537,5055
εκτελεω, I FINISH
Lk 14:29 and is not able to **finish,**
    14:30 was not able to **finish.**

1616   GO1 AG245 LN79 K2:464
εκτενεια, PERSEVERANCE
Ac 26: 7   **earnestly** worship day and night

1618   GO1 AG245 LN79 K2:463
εκτενης, INTENSE
1P   4: 8   **constant** love for one another,

1619   GO3 AG245 LN79
εκτενως, INTENSELY
Lk 22:44   he prayed more **earnestly,**
Ac 12: 5   the church prayed **fervently**
1P   1:22   love one another **deeply**

1620   GO4 AG245 LN80 R1537,5087
εκτιθημι, I SET OUT
Ac   7:21   and when he **was abandoned,**
    11: 4   Then Peter began to **explain** it
    18:26   **explained** the Way of God
    28:23   he **explained** the matter to
            them

1621   GO4 AG245 LN80 B3:560
εκτινασσω, I SWING OUT
Mt 10:14   **shake off** the dust from your
Mk   6:11   **shake off** the dust that is on
Ac 13:51   **shook** the dust **off** their feet
    18: 6   in protest he **shook** the dust

1622   GO8 AG246 LN80
εκτος, OUTSIDE
Mt 23:26   **outside** also may become clean.
Ac 26:22   nothing **but** what the prophets
1C   6:18   commits is **outside** the body
    14: 5   **unless** someone interprets,
    15: 2   **unless** you have come to believe
    15:27   that this **does not include**
2C 12: 2   in the body or **out** of the body
1Ti 5:19   **except** on the evidence of two

1623   GO14 AG246 LN80
εκτος, SIXTH
Mt 20: 5   he went out again about **noon**
    27:45   From **noon** on, darkness came
Mk 15:33   When it was **noon,** darkness
            came
Lk   1:26   In the **sixth** month the angel
     1:36   is the **sixth** month for her
    23:44   It was now about **noon,**
Jn   4: 6   It was about **noon.**

    19:14   and it was about **noon.**
Ac 10: 9   About **noon** the next day,
Re   6:12   When he opened the **sixth** seal,
     9:13   **sixth** angel blew his trumpet,
     9:14   saying to the **sixth** angel
    16:12   The **sixth** angel poured his bowl
    21:20   fifth onyx, the **sixth** carnelian

1624   GO5 AG246 LN80 B3:902
εκτρεπω, I TURN OUT
1Ti 1: 6   and **turned** to meaningless talk,
     5:15   some have already **turned away**
     6:20   **Avoid** the profane chatter
2Ti 4: 4   truth and **wander away** to myths
He 12:13   may not be **put out** of joint

1625   GO2 AG246 LN80 R1537,5142
εκτρεφω, I NOURISH
Ep   5:29   **nourishes** and tenderly cares
     6: 4   **bring** them **up** in the discipline

1626   GO1 AG246 LN80 B1:182 K2:465
εκτρωμα, PREMATURE
1C 15: 8   as to one **untimely born,**

1627   GO8 AG246 LN80 R1537,5342
εκφερω, I CARRY OUT
Mk   8:23   by the hand and **led** him **out**
Lk 15:22   Quickly, **bring out** a robe
Ac   5: 6   **carried** him **out** and buried him
     5: 9   and they **will carry you** out.
     5:10   they **carried** her **out** and buried
     5:15   they even **carried out** the
1Ti 6: 7   we can **take** nothing **out** of it
He   6: 8   But if it **produces** thorns

1628   GO8 AG246 LN80 R1537,5343
εκφευγω, I FLEE OUT
Lk 21:36   the strength to **escape** all
Ac 16:27   that the prisoners **had escaped.**
    19:16   that they **fled out** of the house
Ro   2: 3   you **will escape** the judgment
2C 11:33   and **escaped** from his hands.
1Th 5: 3   and there will be no **escape**
He   2: 3   can we **escape** if we neglect
    12:25   for if they did not **escape**

1629   GO1 AG247 LN80 R1537,5399
εκφοβεω, I AM FEARFUL
2C 10: 9   to **frighten** you with my letters

1630 ᴳᴼ2 ᴬᴳ247 ᴸᴺ80 ᴿ1629
εκφοβος, VERY FEARFUL
Mk　9: 6　for they were **terrified.**
He　12:21　so **terrifying** was the sight

1631 ᴳᴼ2 ᴬᴳ247 ᴸᴺ80 ᴿ1537,5453
εκφυω, I SPROUT OUT
Mt　24:32　and **puts forth** its leaves
Mk　13:28　and **puts forth** its leaves

1632 ᴳᴼ16 ᴬᴳ247 ᴸᴺ80 ᴮ2:853 ᴷ2:467
εκχεω, I POUR OUT
Mt　9:17　burst, and the wine **is spilled,**
Jn　2:15　He also **poured out** the coins
Ac　2:17　I will **pour out** my Spirit.
　　2:18　I will **pour out** my Spirit
　　2:33　he has **poured out** this that
Ro　3:15　feet are swift to **shed** blood
Ti　3: 6　Spirit he **poured out** on us
Re　16: 1　Go and **pour out** on the earth
　　16: 2　first angel went and **poured**
　　16: 3　second angel **poured** his bowl
　　16: 4　third angel **poured** his bowl
　　16: 6　they **shed** the blood of saints
　　16: 8　fourth angel **poured** his bowl
　　16:10　fifth angel **poured** his bowl
　　16:12　sixth angel **poured** his bowl
　　16:17　seventh angel **poured** his bowl

1632a ᴳᴼ11 ᴬᴳ247 ᴸᴺ80 ᴮ2:853 ᴷ2:467
εκχυννω, I POUR OUT
Mt　23:35　righteous blood **shed** on earth
　　26:28　which is **poured out** for many
Mk　14:24　which is **poured out** for many
Lk　5:37　the skins and **will be spilled,**
　　11:50　blood of all the prophets **shed**
　　22:20　This cup that is **poured out**
Ac　1:18　and all his bowels **gushed out.**
　　10:45　Spirit had been **poured out**
　　22:20　your witness Stephen was **shed**
Ro　5: 5　has been **poured** into our hearts
Ju　1:11　**abandon** themselves to Balaam's

1633 ᴳᴼ1 ᴬᴳ247 ᴸᴺ80 ᴿ1537,5562
εκχωρεω, I MAKE ROOM OUT
Lk　21:21　inside the city **must leave** it

1634 ᴳᴼ3 ᴬᴳ247 ᴸᴺ80
εκψυχω, I EXPIRE
Ac　5: 5　he fell down and **died.**

　　5:10　fell down at his feet and **died**
　　12:23　he was eaten by worms and **died.**

1635 ᴳᴼ2 ᴬᴳ247 ᴸᴺ80 ᴷ2:469
εκων, WILLING
Ro　8:20　of its **own will** but by the will
1C　9:17　For if I do this of my **own will**

1636 ᴳᴼ15 ᴬᴳ247 ᴸᴺ81 ᴮ2:710
ελαια, OLIVE
Mt　21: 1　at the Mount of **Olives,**
　　24: 3　sitting on the Mount of **Olives**
　　26:30　out to the Mount of **Olives.**
Mk　11: 1　near the Mount of **Olives,**
　　13: 3　on the Mount of **Olives**
　　14:26　out to the Mount of **Olives.**
Lk　19:37　from the Mount of **Olives,**
　　22:39　to the Mount of **Olives;**
Jn　8: 1　went to the Mount of **Olives.**
Ro　11:17　rich root of the **olive** tree,
　　11:24　back into their own **olive** tree
Ja　3:12　yield **olives,** or a grapevine
Re　11: 4　These are the two **olive** trees

1637 ᴳᴼ11 ᴬᴳ247 ᴸᴺ81 ᴮ2:710 ᴷ2:470 ᴿ1636
ελαιον, OIL
Mt　25: 3　they took no **oil** with them
　　25: 4　but the wise took flasks of **oil**
　　25: 8　Give us some of your **oil,**
Mk　6:13　and anointed with **oil** many who
Lk　7:46　not anoint my head with **oil,**
　　10:34　having poured **oil** and wine
　　16: 6　A hundred jugs of **olive oil.**
He　1: 9　has anointed you with the **oil**
Ja　5:14　anointing them with **oil**
Re　6: 6　do not damage the **olive oil**
　　18:13　frankincense, wine, **olive oil,**

1638 ᴳᴼ1 ᴬᴳ248 ᴸᴺ81 ᴮ2:710 ᴿ1636
ελαιων, OF OLIVES
Lk　19:29　called the Mount **of Olives,**
　　21:37　on the Mount **of Olives,**
Ac　1:12　from the mount called **Olivet**

1639 ᴳᴼ1 ᴬᴳ248 ᴸᴺ81
ελαμιτης, ELAMITES
Ac　2: 9　Parthians, Medes, **Elamites,**

1640 ᴳᴼ4 ᴬᴳ248 ᴸᴺ81 ᴮ2:427 ᴷ4:648
ελασσων, LESSER

Jn	2:10	and then the **inferior** wine
Ro	9:12	elder shall serve the **younger**
1Ti	5: 9	not **less** than sixty years old
He	7: 7	dispute that the **inferior**

1641 GO1 AG248 LN81 R1640
ελαττονεω, I MAKE LESS
| 2C | 8:15 | little did not **have** too **little** |

1642 GO3 AG248 LN81 R1640
ελαττοω, I AM LESSENED
Jn	3:30	increase, but I must **decrease**
He	2: 7	for a little while **lower** than
	2: 9	was made **lower** than the angels

1643 GO5 AG248 LN81
ελαυνω, I DRIVE
Mk	6:48	were straining at the **oars**
Lk	8:29	and **be driven** by the demon
Jn	6:19	they **had rowed** about three or
Ja	3: 4	strong winds **to drive** them
2P	2:17	and mists **driven** by a storm

1644 GO1 AG248 LN81 R1645
ελαφρια, LIGHTNESS
| 2C | 1:17 | Was I **vacillating** when I wanted |

1645 GO2 AG248 LN81
ελαφρος, LIGHT
| Mt | 11:30 | and my burden is **light** |
| 2C | 4:17 | an eternal **weight** of glory |

1646 GO14 AG248 LN81 B2:427 K4:648
ελαχιστος, LEAST
Mt	2: 6	by no means **least** among the
	5:19	whoever breaks one of the **least**
	5:19	be called **least** in the kingdom
	25:40	to one of the **least** of these
	25:45	to one of the **least** of these
Lk	12:26	are not able to do so **small**
	16:10	is faithful in a very **little**
	16:10	is dishonest in a very **little**
	19:17	trustworthy in a very **small**
1C	4: 3	it is a very **small** thing
	6: 2	incompetent to try **trivial**
	15: 9	I am the **least** of the apostles
Ep	3: 8	Although I am the very **least**
Ja	3: 4	guided by a very **small** rudder

1648 GO2 AG249 LN81
ελεαζαρ, ELEAZAR
| Mt | 1:15 | and Eliud the father of **Eleazar** |
| | 1:15 | **Eleazar** the father of Matthan |

1648a GO4 AG249 LN81 B2:594
ελεαω, I SHOW MERCY
Ro	9:16	but on God who shows **mercy.**
	12: 8	diligence; the **compassionate**
Ju	1:22	And have **mercy** on some
	1:23	have **mercy** on still others

1648b GO1 AG249 LN81 B2:140
ελεγμος, REBUKING
| 2Ti | 3:16 | for **reproof,** for correction, |

1649 GO1 AG249 LN81 R1651
ελεγξις, REBUKE
| 2P | 2:16 | but was **rebuked** for his own |

1650 GO1 AG249 LN81 K2:476 R1651
ελεγχος, REBUKE
| He | 11: 1 | **conviction** of things not seen |

1651 GO17 AG249 LN81 K2:473
ελεγχω, I REBUKE
Mt	18:15	go and **point out the fault**
Lk	3:19	who **had been rebuked** by him
Jn	3:20	their deeds **may not be exposed.**
	8:46	Which of you **convicts** me of sin
	16: 8	he **will prove** the world wrong
1C	14:24	outsider who enters is **reproved**
Ep	5:11	but instead **expose** them.
	5:13	everything **exposed** by the light
1Ti	5:20	**rebuke** them in the presence
2Ti	4: 2	**rebuke,** and encourage,
Ti	1: 9	to **refute** those who contradict
	1:13	this reason **rebuke** them sharply
	2:15	**reprove** with all authority
He	12: 5	when you are **punished** by him
Ja	2: 9	commit sin and are **convicted**
Ju	1:15	and to **convict** everyone of all
Re	3:19	I **reprove** and discipline those

1652 GO2 AG249 LN81 B2:594
ελεεινος, MORE IN NEED OF MERCY
| 1C | 15:19 | all people most **to be pitied.** |
| Re | 3:17 | **pitiable,** poor, blind, |

1653 GO28 AG249 LN81 B2:594 K2:477 R1656
ελεεω, I SHOW MERCY
Mt 5: 7 for they will **receive mercy.**
9:27 **Have mercy** on us,
15:22 **Have mercy** on me, Lord,
17:15 Lord, **have mercy** on my son,
18:33 Should you not **have had mercy**
18:33 as I **had mercy** on you
20:30 Lord, **have mercy** on us,
20:31 **Have mercy** on us, Lord
Mk 5:19 and what **mercy** he **has shown** you
10:47 Son of David, **have mercy** on me
10:48 Son of David, **have mercy** on me
Lk 16:24 Abraham, **have mercy** on me,
17:13 Master, **have mercy** on us
18:38 Son of David, **have mercy** on me
18:39 Son of David, **have mercy** on me
Ro 9:15 I **will have mercy** on whom
9:15 mercy on whom I **have mercy,**
9:18 then he **has mercy** on whomever
11:30 but have now **received mercy**
11:31 they too **may** now **receive mercy**
11:32 that he **may be merciful** to all
1C 7:25 as one who by the Lord's **mercy**
2C 4: 1 since it is by God's **mercy**
Ph 2:27 But God **had mercy** on him,
1Ti 1:13 But I **received mercy**
1:16 very reason I **received mercy**
1P 2:10 once you had not **received mercy**
2:10 but now you have **received mercy**

1654 GO13 AG249 LN81 B2:594 K2:485 R1656
ελεημοσυνη, MERCIFULNESS
Mt 6: 2 So whenever you give **alms**
6: 3 But when you give **alms,**
6: 4 your **alms** may be done in secret
Lk 11:41 So give for **alms** those things
12:33 your possessions, and give **alms**
Ac 3: 2 so that he could ask for **alms**
3: 3 temple, he asked them for **alms.**
3:10 used to sit and ask for **alms**
9:36 good works and **acts of charity**
10: 2 he gave **alms** generously to the
10: 4 Your prayers and your **alms**
10:31 your **alms** have been remembered
24:17 to bring **alms** to my nation

1655 GO2 AG250 LN81 B2:594 K2:485 R1653
ελεημων, MERCIFUL

Mt 5: 7 Blessed are the **merciful,**
He 2:17 be a **merciful** and faithful high

1656 GO27 AG250 LN81 B2:593 K2:477
ελεος, MERCY
Mt 9:13 I desire **mercy,** not sacrifice
12: 7 I desire **mercy** and not sacrifice
23:23 justice and **mercy** and faith.
Lk 1:50 His **mercy** is for those who fear
1:54 in remembrance of his **mercy,**
1:58 shown his great **mercy** to her
1:72 Thus he has shown the **mercy**
1:78 By the tender **mercy** of our God,
10:37 The one who showed him **mercy**
Ro 9:23 glory for the objects of **mercy**
11:31 by the **mercy** shown to you,
15: 9 might glorify God for his **mercy**
Ga 6:16 peace be upon them, and **mercy**
Ep 2: 4 But God, who is rich in **mercy**
1Ti 1: 2 Grace, **mercy,** and peace
2Ti 1: 2 Grace, **mercy,** and peace
1:16 May the Lord grant **mercy**
1:18 grant that he will find **mercy**
Ti 3: 5 but according to his **mercy,**
He 4:16 so that we may receive **mercy**
Ja 2:13 anyone who has shown no **mercy**
2:13 **mercy** triumphs over judgment.
3:17 full of **mercy** and good fruits
1P 1: 3 By his great **mercy** he has given
2J 1: 3 Grace, **mercy,** and peace will be
Ju 1: 2 May **mercy,** peace, and love be
1:21 the **mercy** of our Lord Jesus

1657 GO11 AG250 LN81 B1:715 K2:487 R1658
ελευθερια, FREEDOM
Ro 8:21 and will obtain the **freedom**
1C 10:29 should my **liberty** be subject
2C 3:17 the Lord is, there is **freedom.**
Ga 2: 4 to spy on the **freedom** we have
5: 1 **freedom** Christ has set us free
5:13 For you were called to **freedom**
5:13 do not use your **freedom** as an
Ja 1:25 perfect law, the law of **liberty**
2:12 be judged by the law of **liberty**
1P 2:16 use your **freedom** as a pretext
2P 2:19 They promise them **freedom,**

1658 GO23 AG250 LN81 B1:715 K2:487
ελευθερος, FREE
Mt 17:26 Then the children are **free**

Jn	8:33	You will be made **free**
	8:36	you will be **free** indeed.
Ro	6:20	**free** in regard to righteousness
	7: 3	she is **free** from that law,
1C	7:21	if you can gain your **freedom,**
	7:22	whoever was **free** when called
	7:39	she is **free** to marry anyone
	9: 1	Am I not **free?**
	9:19	I am **free** with respect to all
	12:13	Jews or Greeks, slaves or **free**
Ga	3:28	is no longer slave or **free,**
	4:22	and the other by a **free** woman.
	4:23	the child of the **free** woman,
	4:26	Jerusalem above; she is **free**
	4:30	the child of the **free** woman
	4:31	but of the **free** woman.
Ep	6: 8	whether we are slaves or **free.**
Co	3:11	Scythian, slave and **free;**
1P	2:16	live as **free** people,
Re	6:15	and everyone, slave and **free,**
	13:16	both **free** and slave,
	19:18	both **free** and slave,

1659   GO7 AG250 LN81 B1:715 K2:487 R1658
ελευθεροω, I FREE

Jn	8:32	the truth will **make** you **free**
	8:36	So if the Son **makes** you **free**
Ro	6:18	having been **set free** from sin
	6:22	you have been **freed** from sin
	8: 2	has **set** you **free** from the law
	8:21	itself will be **set free** from
Ga	5: 1	freedom Christ has **set** us **free**

1660   GO1 AG251 LN81 B1:320 K2:675
ελευσις, COMING

Ac	7:52	the **coming** of the Righteous One

1661   GO1 AG251 LN82
ελεφαντινος, IVORY

Re	18:12	all articles of **ivory,**

1662   GO3 AG251 LN82
ελιακιμ, ELIAKIM

Mt	1:13	Abiud the father of **Eliakim**
	1:13	**Eliakim** the father of Azor
Lk	3:30	son of Jonam, son of **Eliakim**

1663   GO1 AG251 LN82
ελιεζερ, ELIEZER

Lk	3:29	son of Joshua, son of **Eliezer**

1664   GO2 AG251 LN82
ελιουδ, ELIUD

Mt	1:14	Achim the father of **Eliud,**
	1:15	**Eliud** the father of Eleazar

1665   GO9 AG251 LN82
ελισαβετ, ELIZABETH

Lk	1: 5	and her name was **Elizabeth.**
	1: 7	because **Elizabeth** was barren
	1:13	Your wife **Elizabeth** will bear
	1:24	his wife **Elizabeth** conceived,
	1:36	**Elizabeth** in her old age
	1:40	Zechariah and greeted **Elizabeth**
	1:41	**Elizabeth** heard Mary's greeting
	1:41	**Elizabeth** was filled with the
	1:57	for **Elizabeth** to give birth,

1666   GO1 AG251 LN82
ελισαιος, ELISHA

Lk	4:27	the time of the prophet **Elisha**

1667   GO2 AG251 LN82
ελισσω, I ROLL

He	1:12	a cloak you will **roll** them **up,**
Re	6:14	like a scroll **rolling** itself **up,**

1668   GO3 AG251 LN82
ελκος, SORE

Lk	16:21	would come and lick his **sores.**
Re	16: 2	a foul and painful **sore** came on
	16:11	of their pains and **sores,**

1669   GO1 AG251 LN82 R1668
ελκοω, I ROLL

Lk	16:20	Lazarus, **covered with sores,**

1670   GO8 AG251 LN82 K2:503
ελκω, I HAUL

Jn	6:44	unless **drawn** by the Father
	12:32	will **draw** all people to myself
	18:10	who had a sword, **drew** it,
	21: 6	they were not able to **haul** it
	21:11	and **hauled** the net ashore,
Ac	16:19	Paul and Silas and **dragged** them
	21:30	Paul and **dragged** him out of the
Ja	2: 6	they who **drag** you into court

1671   GO1 AG251 LN82 K2:504
ελλας, GREECE

Ac	20: 2	he came to **Greece,**

1672 GO25 AG251 LN82 K2:504
ἑλλην, GREEK
Jn   7:35   Dispersion among the **Greeks**
       7:35   the Greeks and teach the **Greeks**
      12:20   the festival were some **Greeks.**
Ac   17: 4   many of the devout **Greeks**
      18: 4   to convince Jews and **Greeks.**
      19:10   of Asia, both Jews and **Greeks**
      19:17   Ephesus, both Jews and **Greeks**
      20:21   to both Jews and **Greeks**
      21:28   he has actually brought **Greeks**
Ro   1:14   I am a debtor both to **Greeks**
       1:16   Jew first and also to the **Greek**
       2: 9   Jew first and also the **Greek**
       2:10   Jew first and also the **Greek**
       3: 9   both Jews and **Greeks,** are under
      10:12   between Jew and **Greek;** the same
1C   1:22   signs and **Greeks** desire wisdom,
       1:24   both Jews and **Greeks,**
      10:32   offense to Jews or to **Greeks**
      12:13   Jews or **Greeks,** slaves or free
Ga   2: 3   though he was a **Greek.**
       3:28   There is no longer Jew or **Greek**
Co   3:11   is no longer **Greek** and Jew,

1673 GO1 AG252 LN82 K2:504
ἑλληνικος, GREEK
Re   9:11   in **Greek** he is called Apollyon.

1674 GO2 AG252 LN82 K2:504
ἑλληνις, GREEK
Mk   7:26   Now the woman was a **Gentile,**
Ac   17:12   including not a few **Greek**
                  women

1675 GO3 AG252 LN82 K2:504
ἑλληνιστης, HELLENIST
Ac   6: 1   **Hellenists** complained against
       9:29   argued with the **Hellenists**
      11:20   spoke to the **Hellenists** also

1676 GO2 AG252 LN82 K2:504
ἑλληνιστι, IN GREEK
Jn   19:20   Hebrew, in Latin, and in
                  Greek.
Ac   21:37   replied, "Do you know **Greek?**

1676a GO1 AG252 LN82
ελλογαω, I CHARGE
Pm   1:18   **charge** that to my **account.**

1677 GO1 AG252 LN82 K2:516
ελλογεω, I CHARGE
Ro   5:13   but sin **is** not **reckoned**

1678 GO1 AG252 LN82
ελμαδαμ, ELMADAM
Lk   3:28   son of **Elmadam,**

1679 GO31 AG252 LN82 B2:238 K2:517 R1680
ελπιζω, I HOPE
Mt   12:21   his name the Gentiles **will hope**
Lk   6:34   from whom you **hope** to receive,
      23: 8   **was hoping** to see him perform
      24:21   we had **hoped** that he was the
                  one
Jn   5:45   on whom you have set your
                  hope.
Ac   24:26   he **hoped** that money would be
      26: 7   twelve tribes **hope** to attain
Ro   8:24   For who **hopes** for what is seen?
       8:25   we **hope** for what we do not see
      15:12   the Gentiles shall **hope**
      15:24   For I do **hope** to see you on my
1C   13: 7   all things, **hopes** all things
      15:19   only we have **hoped** in Christ
      16: 7   for I **hope** to spend some time
2C   1:10   on him we have set our **hope**
       1:13   I **hope** you will understand
       5:11   I **hope** that we are also well
       8: 5   not merely as we **expected;**
      13: 6   I **hope** you will find out
Ph   2:19   I **hope** in the Lord Jesus
       2:23   I **hope** therefore to send him
1Ti   3:14   I **hope** to come to you soon,
       4:10   our **hope** set on the living God
       5: 5   has set her **hope** on God
       6:17   or to set their **hopes** on the
Pm   1:22   am **hoping** through your prayers
He   11: 1   assurance of things **hoped** for,
1P   1:13   set all your **hope** on the grace
       3: 5   holy women who **hoped** in God
2J   1:12   instead I **hope** to come to you
3J   1:14   instead I **hope** to see you soon

1680 GO53 AG252 LN82 B2:238 K2:517
ελπις, HOPE
Ac   2:26   my flesh will live in **hope.**
      16:19   their **hope** of making money
      23: 6   am on trial concerning the **hope**
      24:15   I have a **hope** in God

	26: 6	**hope** in the promise made by God
	26: 7	It is for this **hope,**
	27:20	all **hope** of our being saved
	28:20	sake of the **hope** of Israel
Ro	4:18	**Hoping** against hope,
	4:18	Hoping against **hope,**
	5: 2	our **hope** of sharing the glory
	5: 4	and character produces **hope**
	5: 5	**hope** does not disappoint us,
	8:20	who subjected it, in **hope**
	8:24	For in **hope** we were saved.
	8:24	**hope** that is seen is not hope
	8:24	hope that is seen is not **hope**
	12:12	Rejoice in **hope,** be patient
	15: 4	scriptures we might have **hope.**
	15:13	God of **hope** fill you with all
	15:13	you may abound in **hope** by the
1C	9:10	plows should plow in **hope.**
	9:10	should thresh in **hope**
	13:13	now faith, **hope,** and love abide
2C	1: 7	Our **hope** for you is unshaken
	3:12	we have such a **hope,** we act
	10:15	others; but our **hope** is that
Ga	5: 5	we eagerly wait for the **hope**
Ep	1·18	you may know what is the **hope**
	2:12	having no **hope** and without God
	4: 4	the one **hope** of your calling
Ph	1:20	my eager expectation and **hope**
Co	1: 5	because of the **hope** laid up
	1:23	without shifting from the **hope**
	1:27	in you, the **hope** of
1Th	1: 3	love and steadfastness of **hope**
	2:19	For what is our **hope** or joy
	4:13	as others do who have no **hope**
	5: 8	a helmet the **hope** of salvation
2Th	2:16	eternal comfort and good **hope**
1Ti	1: 1	and of Christ Jesus our **hope**
Ti	1: 2	in the **hope** of eternal life
	2:13	we wait for the blessed **hope**
	3: 7	heirs according to the **hope**
He	3: 6	the pride that belong to **hope**
	6:11	the full assurance of **hope**
	6:18	encouraged to seize the **hope**
	7:19	introduction of a better **hope**
	10:23	to the confession of our **hope**
1P	1: 3	new birth into a living **hope**
	1:21	that your faith and **hope**
	3:15	for the **hope** that is in you
1J	3: 3	all who have this **hope** in him

1681   GO1 AG253 LN82
ελυμας, ELYMAS
Ac 13: 8   But the magician **Elymas**

1682   GO2 AG253 LN82
ελωι, ELOI
Mk 15:34   with a loud voice, "**Eloi, Eloi**

1683   GO37 AG253 LN83
εμαυτου, OF MYSELF

Mt	8: 9	with soldiers under **me**
Lk	7: 7	I did not **presume** to come
	7: 8	with soldiers under **me**
Jn	5:30	I can do nothing on **my own**
	5:31	If I testify about **myself**
	7:17	I am speaking on **my own**
	7:28	I have not come on **my own**
	8:14	if I testify on **my own** behalf
	8:18	I testify on **my own** behalf
	8:28	I do nothing on **my own,**
	8:42	I did not come on **my own**
	8:54	If I glorify **myself,**
	10:18	lay it down **of my own accord**
	12:32	will draw all people to **myself**
	12:49	I have not spoken on **my own**
	14. 3	and will take you to **myself**
	14:10	I do not speak on **my own**
	14:21	them and reveal **myself** to them
	17:19	their sakes I sanctify **myself**
Ac	20:24	life of any value to **myself**
	24:10	I cheerfully make **my** defense
	26: 2	I consider **myself** fortunate
	26: 9	I **myself** was convinced
Ro	11: 4	I have kept for **myself**
1C	4: 3	judge **myself**
	4: 4	of anything against **myself**
	4: 6	this to Apollos and **myself**
	7: 7	all were as I **myself** am.
	9:19	I have made **myself** a slave
	10:33	not seeking **my own** advantage
2C	2: 1	So I made up **my** mind
	11: 7	commit a sin by humbling **myself**
	11: 9	I refrained and will continue
	12: 5	but on **my own** behalf I will
Ga	2:18	that I am a transgressor
Ph	3:13	that I have made it **my own**
Pm	1:13	I wanted to keep him with **me**

1684   GO16 AG254 LN83
εμβαινω, I GO INTO

Mt	8:23	And when he **got into** the boat
	9: 1	And after **getting into** a boat
	13: 2	that he **got into** a boat and sat
	14:22	the disciples **get into** the boat
	15:39	he **got into** the boat and went
Mk	4: 1	he **got into** a boat on the sea
	5:18	As he was **getting into** the boat
	6:45	his disciples **get into** the boat
	8:10	he **got into** the boat with his
	8:13	and **getting into** the boat again
Lk	5: 3	He **got into** one of the boats
	8:22	One day he **got into** a boat
	8:37	So he **got into** the boat
Jn	6:17	**got into** a boat, and started
	6:24	themselves **got into** the boats
	21: 3	went out and **got into** the boat

1685 GO1 AG254 LN83 R1722,906
εμβαλλω, I THROW IN
Lk 12: 5 has authority to **cast into** hell

1686 GO2 AG254 LN83 R1722,911
εμβαπτω, I DIP IN
Mt 26:23 **dipped** his hand **into** the bowl
Mk 14:20 **is dipping** bread **into** the bowl

1687 GO1 AG254 LN83 K2:535
εμβατευω, I PENETRATE
Co 2:18 **dwelling** on visions, puffed up

1688 GO1 AG254 LN83
εμβιβαζω, I BOARD
Ac 27: 6 for Italy and **put** us **on board**

1689 GO12 AG254 LN83 B3:519 R1722,991
εμβλεπω, I LOOK IN
Mt 6:26 **Look at** the birds of the air
19:26 Jesus **looked at** them and said
Mk 8:25 and he **saw** everything clearly
10:21 **looking at** him, loved him
10:27 Jesus **looked at** them and said
14:67 she **stared at** him and said
Lk 20:17 But he **looked at** them and said
22:61 Lord turned and **looked at** Peter
Jn 1:36 as he **watched** Jesus walk by
1:42 who **looked at** him and said
Ac 1:11 why do you stand **looking up**
22:11 Since I could not **see** because

1690 GO5 AG254 LN83
εμβριμαομαι, I AM INDIGNANT
Mt 9:30 Then Jesus **sternly ordered** them
Mk 1:43 After **sternly warning** him
14: 5 And they **scolded** her.
Jn 11:33 he was **greatly disturbed**
11:38 Jesus, again **greatly disturbed**

1692 GO1 AG254 LN83
εμεω, I VOMIT
Re 3:16 I am about to **spit** you out

1693 GO1 AG255 LN83 R1722,3105
εμμαινομαι, I AM MAD AGAINST
Ac 26:11 I was so **furiously enraged**

1694 GO1 AG255 LN83 B2:86
εμμανουηλ, EMMANUEL
Mt 1:23 they shall name him **Emmanuel**

1695 GO1 AG255 LN83
εμμαους, EMMAUS
Lk 24:13 to a village called **Emmaus**

1696 GO4 AG255 LN83 B3:223 K4:576 R1722,3306
εμμενω, I STAY IN
Ac 14:22 and encouraged them **to continue**
28:30 He **lived** there two whole years
Ga 3:10 everyone who does not **observe**
He 8: 9 they **did** not **continue** in my

1697 GO1 AG255 LN83
'εμμωρ, HAMOR
Ac 7:16 the sons of **Hamor** in Shechem

1699 GO74 AG255 LN83
εμος, MINE
Mt 18:20 three are gathered in **my** name
20:15 choose with what belongs to **me**
20:23 this is not **mine** to grant,
25:27 what was **my own** with interest.
Mk 8:38 ashamed of me and of **my** words
10:40 at my left is not **mine** to grant
Lk 9:26 ashamed of me and of **my** words
15:31 and all that is **mine** is yours
22:19 Do this in remembrance **of me**
Jn 3:29 **my** joy has been fulfilled
4:34 **My** food is to do the will
5:30 and **my** judgment is just
5:30 I seek to do not **my own** will

5:47	how will you believe what **I** say	
6:38	not to do **my own** will	
7: 6	**My** time has not yet come	
7: 8	**my** time has not yet fully come	
7:16	**My** teaching is not mine but	
7:16	My teaching is not **mine** but	
8:16	**my** judgment is valid	
8:31	If you continue in **my** word	
8:37	no place in you for **my** word	
8:43	you not understand what **I** say	
8:43	you cannot accept **my** word.	
8:51	**my** word will never see death	
8:56	that he would see **my** day	
10:14	I know **my own** and my own know	
10:14	I know my own and **my own** know	
10:26	you do not belong to **my** sheep	
10:27	My sheep hear **my** voice.	
12:26	there will **my** servant be also	
14:15	you will keep **my** commandments	
14:24	word that you hear is not **mine**	
14:27	**my** peace I give to you	
15:11	that **my** joy may be in you	
15:12	This is **my** commandment	
16:14	will take what is **mine**	
16:15	All that the Father has is **mine**	
16:15	that he will take what is **mine**	
17:10	All **mine** are yours, and yours	
17:10	are yours, and yours are **mine**	
17:13	that they may have **my** joy made	
17:24	where I am, to see **my** glory	
18:36	**My** kingdom is not from this	
18:36	If **my** kingdom were from this	
18:36	**my** followers would be fighting	
18:36	**my** kingdom is not from here	
Ro 3: 7	But if through **my** falsehood	
10: 1	**my** heart's desire and prayer	
1C 1:15	you were baptized in **my** name	
5: 4	and **my** spirit is present	
7:40	that **I** too have the Spirit	
9: 3	This is **my** defense to those	
11:24	Do this in remembrance of **me**	
11:25	is the new covenant in **my** blood	
11:25	drink it, in remembrance of **me**	
16:18	for they refreshed **my** spirit	
16:21	this greeting with **my own** hand.	
2C 1:23	on God as witness against **me**	
2: 3	**my** joy would be the joy of all	
8:23	As for Titus, he is **my** partner	
Ga 1:13	of **my** earlier life in Judaism.	

Ph 1:26	when **I** come to you again.
3: 9	righteousness of **my own** that
Co 4:18	this greeting with **my own** hand
2Th 3:17	this greeting with **my own** hand
Pm 1:10	appealing to you for **my** child
1:12	him, that is, **my** own heart
1:19	writing this with **my own** hand
2P 1:15	after **my** departure you may be
3J 1: 4	that **my** children are walking
Re 2:20	beguiling **my** servants

1700a GO1 AG255 LN83 K5:635
εμπαιγμονη, IN MOCKERY
2P 3: 3 the last days **scoffers** will come

1701 GO1 AG255 LN83 K5:635 R1702
εμπαιγμος, MOCKING
He 11:36 suffered **mocking** and flogging

1702 GO13 AG255 LN83 K5:630 R1722,3815
εμπαιζω, I MOCK
Mt 2:16	he had been **tricked** by the wise
20:19	to be **mocked** and flogged
27:29	knelt before him and **mocked** him
27:31	After **mocking** him
27:41	**were mocking** him,
Mk 10:34	they **will mock** him
15:20	After **mocking** him
15:31	were also **mocking** him
Lk 14:29	will begin to **ridicule** him
18:32	he will be **mocked** and insulted
22:63	began to **mock** him and beat him
23:11	with contempt and **mocked** him
23:36	The soldiers also **mocked** him

1703 GO2 AG255 LN83 K5:635 R1703
εμπαικτης, MOCKER
2P 3: 3 **scoffers** will come, scoffing
Ju 1:18 there will be **scoffers**

1704 GO1 AG256 LN83 B3:943 K5:940 R1722,4043
εμπεριπατεω, I WALK AMONG
2C 6:16 in them and **walk among** them

1705 GO5 AG256 LN84 B1:733 K6:128
εμπιπλημι, I FILL IN
Lk 1:53	he has **filled** the hungry
6:25	Woe to you who **are full** now,
Jn 6:12	When they **were satisfied**,

Ac 14:17   and **filling** you with food
Ro 15:24   I **have enjoyed** your **company**

1705a   GO1 AG256 LN84
εμπιπρημι, I BURN UP
Mt 22: 7   and **burned** their city.

1706   GO7 AG256 LN84 R1722,4098
εμπιπτω, I FALL IN
Mt 12:11   it **falls into** a pit
Lk   6:39   Will not both **fall into** a pit?
    10:36   the man who **fell into** the hands
1Ti 3: 6   **fall into** the condemnation
     3: 7   he may not **fall into** disgrace
     6: 9   **fall into** temptation and are
He 10:31   to **fall into** the hands

1707   GO2 AG256 LN84 R1722,4120
εμπλεκω, I INWEAVE
2Ti 2: 4   **gets entangled** in everyday
2P   2:20   they **are** again **entangled**

1708   GO1 AG256 LN84
εμπλοκη, BRAIDING
1P   3: 3   outwardly by **braiding** your hair

1709   GO1 AG256 LN84 B3:689 K6:452 R1722,4154
εμπνεω, I BLOW IN
Ac   9: 1   Saul, still **breathing** threats

1710   GO2 AG256 LN84 B1:268 R1722,4198
εμπορευομαι, I EXPLOIT
Ja   4:13   **doing business** and making money
2P   2: 3   **will exploit** you with deceptive

1711   GO1 AG256 LN84 R1713
εμπορια, MERCHANDISE
Mt 22: 5   another to his **business**

1712   GO1 AG257 LN84 R1713
εμποριον, OF MERCHANDISE
Jn   2:16   my Father's house a **marketplace**

1713   GO5 AG257 LN84
εμπορος, MERCHANTS
Mt 13:45   is like a **merchant** in search of
Re 18: 3   the **merchants** of the earth
    18:11   the **merchants** of the earth weep
    18:15   The **merchants** of these wares
    18:23   **merchants** were the magnates

1715   GO48 AG257 LN84 B3:1205
εμπροσθεν, IN FRONT OF
Mt   5:16   let your light shine **before**
     5:24   **before** the altar and go
     6: 1   piety **before** others in order
     6: 2   not sound a trumpet **before** you
     7: 6   throw your pearls **before** swine
    10:32   acknowledges me **before** others
    10:32   acknowledge **before** my Father in
    10:33   whoever denies me **before** others
    10:33   deny **before** my Father in heaven
    11:10   sending my messenger **ahead** of
    11:26   for such was **your** gracious will
    17: 2   was transfigured **before** them,
    18:14   is not the will **of** your Father
    23:13   lock **people** out of the kingdom
    25:32   will be gathered **before** him
    26:70   he denied it **before** all of them
    27:11   Jesus stood **before** the governor
    27:29   and **before** him and mocked him
Mk   2:12   And went out **before** all of them
     9: 2   was transfigured **before** them,
Lk   5:19   middle of the crowd **in front of**
     7:27   prepare your way **before** you
    10:21   for such was **your** gracious will
    12: 8   acknowledges me **before** others
    12: 8   **before** the angels of God;
    14: 2   Just then, **in front of** him,
    19: 4   So he ran **ahead** and climbed
    19:27   slaughter them **in my presence**
    19:28   he went **on ahead,** going up to
    21:36   to stand **before** the Son of Man
Jn   1:15   because he was **before** me
     1:30   because he was **before** me
     3:28   I have been sent **ahead** of him
    10: 4   he goes **ahead** of them
    12:37   so many signs **in their presence**
Ac 10: 4   ascended as a memorial **before**
    18:17   him **in front of** the tribunal
2C   5:10   all of us must appear **before**
Ga   2:14   I said to Cephas **before** them
Ph   3:13   forward **to what** lies **ahead,**
1Th 1: 3   remembering **before** our God
                  and
     2:19   **before** our Lord Jesus at his
     3: 9   that we feel **before** our God
     3:13   be blameless **before** our God
1J   3:19   reassure our hearts **before** him
Re   4: 6   of eyes **in front** and behind
    19:10   down **at** his feet to worship him

22: 8　**at** the feet of the angel who

1716　GO6 AG257 LN84 R1722,4429
εμπτυω, I SPIT IN
Mt　26:67　Then they **spat in** his face
　　27:30　They **spat on** him, and took the
Mk　10:34　mock him, and **spit upon** him,
　　14:65　Some began to **spit on** him,
　　15:19　with a reed, **spat upon** him,
Lk　18:32　and insulted and **spat upon.**

1717　GO2 AG257 LN84 B2:488 R1722,5316
εμφανης, VISIBLE
Ac　10:40　and allowed him **to appear,**
Ro　10:20　I have **shown** myself to those

1718　GO10 AG257 LN84 B2:488 K9:7 R1717
εμφανιζω, I MAKE VISIBLE
Mt　27:53　holy city and **appeared** to many.
Jn　14:21　love them and **reveal** myself
　　14:22　you will **reveal** yourself to us
Ac　23:15　council must **notify** the tribune
　　23:22　that you have **informed** me
　　24: 1　**reported** their case against
　　25: 2　gave him a **report** against Paul
　　25:15　the Jews **informed** me about him
He　 9:24　now to **appear** in the presence
　　11:14　**make it clear** that they are

1719　GO5 AG257 LN84 R1722,5401
εμφοβος, IN FEAR
Lk　24: 5　The women were **terrified**
　　24:37　were startled and **terrified**
Ac　10: 4　He stared at him in **terror**
　　24:25　Felix **became frightened**
Re　11:13　the rest **were terrified**

1720　GO1 AG258 LN84 K2:536
εμφυσαω, I BLOW IN
Jn　20:22　he **breathed on** them and said

1721　GO1 AG258 LN84 B3:865 R1722,5453
εμφυτος, IMPLANTED
Ja　 1:21　the **implanted** word that has

1722　GO2752 AG258 LN84 B3:1190 K2:537
εν, IN [MULTIPLE OCCURRENCES]

1723　GO2 AG261 LN85 R1722,43
εναγκαλιζομαι, I EMBRACE

Mk　 9:36　and **taking** it **in** his **arms,**
　　10:16　he **took** them **up in** his **arms**

1724　GO1 AG261 LN85
εναλιος, SEA LIFE
Ja　 3: 7　of reptile and **sea creature**

1725　GO2 AG261 LN85
εναντι, IN PRESENCE
Lk　 1: 8　serving as priest **before** God
Ac　 8:21　heart is not right **before** God

1726　GO5 AG261 LN85 R1727
εναντιον, IN PRESENCE
Lk　 1: 6　them were righteous **before** God
　　20:26　in the **presence of** the people
　　24:19　**before** God and all the people,
Ac　 7:10　when he stood **before** Pharaoh
　　 8:32　lamb silent **before** its shearer

1727　GO8 AG262 LN85 R1725
εναντιος, AGAINST
Mt　14:24　for the wind was **against** them.
Mk　 6:48　**against** an adverse wind
　　15:39　centurion, who stood **facing**
　　　　　him
Ac　26: 9　do many things **against** the
　　　　　name
　　27: 4　because the winds were **against**
　　28:17　done nothing **against** our people
1Th　 2:15　displease God and **oppose**
Ti　 2: 8　then any **opponent** will be put

1728　GO2 AG262 LN85 R1722,756
εναρχομαι, I BEGIN IN
Ga　 3: 3　**Having started** with the Spirit
Ph　 1: 6　the one who **began** a good work

1728a　GO10 AG262 LN85
ενατος, NINTH
Mt　20: 5　**three** o'clock, he did the same
　　27:45　until **three** in the afternoon
　　27:46　And about **three** o'clock Jesus
Mk　15:33　until **three** in the afternoon.
　　15:34　At **three** o'clock Jesus cried
Lk　23:44　until **three** in the afternoon,
Ac　 3: 1　of prayer, at **three** o'clock
　　10: 3　at about **three** o'clock he had
　　10:30　very hour, at **three** o'clock
Re　21:20　eighth beryl, the **ninth** topaz,

1729　GO1 AG262 LN85
ενδεης, IN NEED
Ac　4:34　There was not a **needy** person

1730　GO1 AG262 LN85 R1731
ενδειγμα, EVIDENCE
2Th　1: 5　is **evidence** of the righteous

1731　GO11 AG262 LN85 R1722,1166
ενδεικνυμι, I DEMONSTRATE
Ro　2:15　They **show** that what the law
　　9:17　of **showing** my power in you,
　　9:22　desiring to **show** his wrath
2C　8:24　**show** them the proof of your
Ep　2: 7　the ages to come he might **show**
1Ti　1:16　Jesus Christ might **display** the
2Ti　4:14　coppersmith **did** me great harm
Ti　2:10　to pilfer, but to **show** complete
　　3: 2　and to **show** every courtesy
He　6:10　love that you **showed** for his
　　6:11　want each one of you to **show**

1732　GO4 AG262 LN85 R1731
ενδειξις, DEMONSTRATION
Ro　3:25　this to **show** his righteousness
　　3:26　it was to **prove** at the present
2C　8:24　**show** them the proof of your
Ph　1:28　them this is **evidence** of their

1733　GO6 AG262 LN85 R1520,1176
ενδεκα, ELEVEN
Mt　28:16　Now the **eleven** disciples went
Mk　16:14　Later he appeared to the **eleven**
Lk　24: 9　told all this to the **eleven**
　　24:33　and they found the **eleven**
Ac　1:26　he was added to the **eleven**
　　2:14　Peter, standing with the **eleven**

1734　GO3 AG262 LN85 R1733
ενδεκατος, ELEVENTH
Mt　20: 6　And about **five** o'clock he went
　　20: 9　hired about **five** o'clock came,
Re　21:20　the **eleventh** jacinth,

1735　GO1 AG262 LN86
ενδεχομαι, IT IS POSSIBLE
Lk　13:33　**it is impossible** for a prophet

1736　GO3 AG263 LN86 B2:788 K2:63
ενδημεω, I AM AT HOME

2C　5: 6　we **are at home** in the body
　　5: 8　and **at home** with the Lord.
　　5: 9　whether we **are at home** or away

1737　GO2 AG263 LN86 R1746
ενδιδυσκω, I PUT ON
Mk　15:17　they **clothed** him in a purple
Lk　16:19　man who was **dressed** in purple

1738　GO2 AG263 LN86 R1722,1349
ενδικος, IN RIGHT
Ro　3: 8　Their condemnation is **deserved**
He　2: 2　received a **just** penalty

1740　GO2 AG263 LN86 K2:254 R1741
ενδοξαζομαι, I GIVE SPLENDOR
2Th　1:10　when he comes **to be glorified**
　　1:12　our Lord Jesus **may be glorified**

1741　GO4 AG263 LN86 B2:44 K2:254 R1722,1391
ενδοξος, IN SPLENDOR
Lk　7:25　those who put on **fine** clothing
　　13:17　rejoicing at all the **wonderful**
1C　4:10　You are held in **honor,** but we
Ep　5:27　in **splendor,** without a spot

1742　GO8 AG263 LN86 B2:579 R1746
ενδυμα, CLOTHES
Mt　3: 4　wore **clothing** of camel's hair
　　6:25　the body more than **clothing**
　　6:28　why do you worry about **clothing**
　　7:15　come to you in sheep's **clothing**
　　22:11　was not wearing a wedding **robe**
　　22:12　in here without a wedding **robe**
　　28: 3　his **clothing** white as snow
Lk　12:23　the body more than **clothing.**

1743　GO7 AG263 LN86 B2:601 K2:284 R1722,1412
ενδυναμοω, I EMPOWER
Ac　9:22　**became** increasingly . . . **powerful**
Ro　4:20　but he **grew strong** in his faith
Ep　6:10　Finally, **be strong** in the Lord
Ph　4:13　through him who **strengthens** me
1Ti　1:12　Lord, who has **strengthened** me
2Ti　2: 1　**be strong** in the grace that is
　　4:17　by me and **gave** me **strength**

1744　GO1 AG263 LN86 B1:314
ενδυνω, I CREEP
2Ti　3: 6　**make** their **way** into households

1745　^{GO}1　^{AG}263　^{LN}86　^R1746
ενδυσις, DRESSING
1P　3: 3　gold ornaments or fine **clothing**

1746　^{GO}27　^{AG}264　^{LN}86　^B1:314　^K2:319
ενδυω, I PUT ON
Mt　6:25　your body, what you **will wear**
　　22:11　man there who **was** not **wearing**
　　27:31　and **put** his own **clothes** on him
Mk　1: 6　**was clothed** with camel's hair
　　6: 9　but to **wear** sandals and not to
　　15:20　**put** his own **clothes** on him
Lk　8:27　he **had worn** no clothes
　　12:22　your body, what you **will wear**
　　15:22　and **put** it **on** him; put a ring
　　24:49　**clothed** with power from on high
Ac　12:21　Herod **put on** his royal robes,
Ro　13:12　**put on** the armor of light;
　　13:14　**put on** the Lord Jesus Christ,
1C　15:53　must **put on** imperishability,
　　15:53　must **put on** immortality.
　　15:54　**puts on** imperishability,
　　15:54　mortal body **puts on** immortality
Ga　3:27　**clothed** yourselves with Christ.
Ep　4:24　**to clothe** yourselves with the
　　6:11　**Put on** the whole armor of God,
　　6:14　**put on** the breastplate of
Co　3:10　and **have clothed** yourselves
　　3:12　and beloved, **clothe** yourselves
1Th　5: 8　**put on** the breastplate of faith
Re　1:13　**clothed** with a long robe
　　15: 6　**robed** in pure bright linen,
　　19:14　**wearing** fine linen, white

1746a　^{GO}1　^{AG}264　^{LN}86
ενδωμησις, CONSTRUCTION
Re　21:18　The wall is **built** of jasper,

1747　^{GO}2　^{AG}264　^{LN}86
ενεδρα, AMBUSH
Ac　23:16　heard about the **ambush**
　　25: 3　planning an **ambush** to kill him

1748　^{GO}2　^{AG}264　^{LN}86
ενεδρευω, I LIE IN WAIT
Lk　11:54　**lying in wait** for him
Ac　23:21　their men **are lying in ambush**

1750　^{GO}1　^{AG}264　^{LN}86
ενειλεω, I WRAP

Mk　15:46　**wrapped** it in the linen cloth

1751　^{GO}1　^{AG}264　^{LN}86
ενειμι, I AM IN
Lk　11:41　those things that **are within**

1752　^{GO}23　^{AG}264　^{LN}86
ενεκα, ON ACCOUNT OF
Mt　5:10　**for** righteousness' sake
　　5:11　you falsely **on** my **account**
　　10:18　**because of** me, as a testimony
　　10:39　life **for** my **sake** will find it
　　16:25　lose their life **for** my **sake**
　　19: 5　**For this reason** a man shall
　　19:29　or fields, **for** my name's **sake**
Mk　8:35　who lose their life **for** my **sake**
　　10: 7　**For this reason** a man shall
　　10:29　**for** my **sake** and for the sake
　　10:29　**for** the **sake** of the good news
　　13: 9　and kings **because of** me
Lk　6:22　**on account of** the Son of Man
　　9:24　lose their life **for** my **sake**
　　18:29　**for** the **sake** of the kingdom
　　21:12　governors **because of** my name
Ac　19:32　**why** they had come together
　　26:21　**For** this **reason** the Jews
Ro　8:36　**For** your **sake** we are being
　　14:20　**for** the **sake** of food, destroy
2C　7:12　not **on account of** the one
　　7:12　nor **on account of** the one who
　　7:12　but **in order that** your zeal

1752a　^{GO}4　^{AG}265　^{LN}86
ενενηκοντα, NINETY
Mt　18:12　he not leave the **ninety**-nine
　　18:13　than over the **ninety**-nine
Lk　15: 4　**ninety**-nine in the wilderness
　　15: 7　**ninety**-nine righteous persons

1752b　^{GO}1　^{AG}265　^{LN}86
ενεος, SPEECHLESS
Ac　9: 7　stood **speechless** because they

1753　^{GO}8　^{AG}265　^{LN}87　^B3:1147　^K2:652　^R1756
ενεργεια, OPERATION
Ep　1:19　the **working** of his great power
　　3: 7　the **working** of his power
　　4:16　each part is **working** properly
Ph　3:21　by the **power** that also enables
Co　1:29　struggle with all the **energy**

2:12   faith in the **power** of God,

2Th   2: 9   in the **working** of Satan

2:11   sends them a **powerful** delusion

1754   GO21 AG265 LN87 B3:1147 K2:652 R1756
ενεργεω, I OPERATE

Mt   14: 2   reason these powers **are at work**

Mk   6:14   these powers **are at work** in him

Ro   7: 5   **were at work** in our members

1C   12: 6   the same God who **activates** all

12:11   All these **are activated** by one

2C   1: 6   **experience** when you patiently

4:12   So death **is at work** in us,

Ga   2: 8   for he who **worked** through
Peter

2: 8   **worked** through me in sending me

3: 5   **work** miracles among you by
your

5: 6   is faith **working** through love

Ep   1:11   who **accomplishes** all things

1:20   spirit that is now **at work**

3:20   who by the power **at work**

Ph   2:13   for it is God who is **at work**

2:13   to **work** for his good pleasure

Co   1:29   that he **powerfully** inspires

1Th   2:13   also **at work** in you believers

2Th   2: 7   lawlessness is already **at work**

Ja   5:16   is powerful and **effective.**

1755   GO2 AG265 LN87 B3:1147 K2:652 R1754
ενεργημα, OPERATION

1C   12: 6   are varieties of **activities**

12:10   the **working** of miracles

1756   GO3 AG265 LN87 B3:1147 K2:652 R1722,2041
ενεργης, OPERATIONAL

1C   16: 9   wide door for effective **work**

Pm   1: 6   faith may become **effective**

He   4:12   of God is living and **active**

1757   GO2 AG265 LN87 B1:206 K2:765 R1722,2127
ενευλογεω, I SPEAK WELL IN

Ac   3:25   of the earth shall be **blessed**

Ga   3: 8   the Gentiles shall be **blessed**

1758   GO3 AG265 LN87 B2:142 K2:828
ενεχω, I HOLD IN

Mk   6:19   **had** a **grudge** against him

Lk   11:53   to **be** very **hostile** toward him

Ga   5: 1   **do** not **submit** again to a yoke

1759   GO8 AG266 LN87
ενθαδε, IN THIS PLACE

Lk   24:41   keep coming **here** to draw
water

Jn   4:16   your husband, and come **back**

Ac   10:18   called Peter, was staying **there**

16:28   yourself, for we are all **here**

17: 6   upside down have come **here**

25:17   So when they met **here**

25:24   both in Jerusalem and **here**

1759a   GO2 AG266 LN87
ενθεν, FROM HERE

Mt   17:20   Move **from here** to there

Lk   16:26   want to pass **from here** to you

1760   GO2 AG266 LN87 B1:105 K3:172
ενθυμεομαι, I REFLECT

Mt   1:20   But just when he **had resolved**

9: 4   Why do you **think** evil in your

1761   GO4 AG266 LN87 B1:105 K3:172 R1760
ενθυμησις, REFLECTIONS

Mt   9: 4   perceiving their **thoughts,**

12:25   He knew what they were **thinking**

Ac   17:29   we ought not **to think** that the

He   4:12   the **thoughts** and intentions

1762   GO6 AG266 LN87
ενι, THERE IS

1C   6: 5   **there is** no one among you wise

Ga   3:28   **There is** no longer Jew or Greek

3:28   **there is** no longer slave

3:28   **there is** no longer male

Co   3:11   **there is** no longer Greek

Ja   1:17   **there is** no variation or shadow

1763   GO14 AG266 LN87 B2:688
ενιαυτος, YEAR

Lk   4:19   proclaim the **year** of the Lord's

Jn   11:49   who was high priest that **year**

11:51   being high priest that **year**

18:13   the high priest that **year.**

Ac   11:26   was that for an entire **year**

18:11   He stayed there a **year** and six

Ga   4:10   months, and seasons, and **years**

He   9: 7   he but once a **year**

9:25   the Holy Place **year** after year

10: 1   offered **year** after year

10: 3   reminder of sin **year** after year

Ja 4:13 a town and spend a **year** there
    5:17 for three **years** and six months
Re 9:15 day, the month, and the **year**

1764 GO7 AG266 LN87 K2:543
ενιστημι, I AM PRESENT
Ro 8:38 nor rulers, nor **things present**
1C 3:22 life or death or the **present**
    7:26 in view of the **impending** crisis
Ga 1: 4 free from the **present** evil age
2Th 2: 2 day of the Lord is already **here**
2Ti 3: 1 distressing times **will come**
He 9: 9 a symbol of the **present** time

1765 GO2 AG266 LN87 R1722,2480
ενισχυω, I STRENGTHEN IN
Lk 22:43 to him and **gave** him **strength**
Ac 9:19 he **regained** his **strength**

1767 GO5 AG267 LN87
εννεα, NINE
Mt 18:12 leave the ninety-**nine** on the
    18:13 than over the ninety-**nine** that
Lk 15: 4 not leave the ninety-**nine**
    15: 7 ninety-**nine** righteous persons
    17:17 But the other **nine,** where are

1770 GO1 AG267 LN87 R1722,3506
εννευω, I NOD IN
Lk 1:62 Then they began **motioning**

1771 GO2 AG267 LN87 B3:122 K4:968 R1722,3563
εννοια, INSIGHT
He 4:12 and **intentions** of the heart
1P 4: 1 also with the same **intention**

1772 GO2 AG267 LN88 B2:446 K4:1087 R1722,3551
εννομος, IN LAW
Ac 19:39 settled in the **regular** assembly
1C 9:21 but am **under** Christ's **law**

1773 GO1 AG267 LN88 R1722,3571
εννυχος, IN NIGHT
Mk 1:35 while it was still **very dark**

1774 GO5 AG267 LN88 B2:247 R1722,3611
ενοικεω, I HOUSE IN
Ro 8:11 his Spirit that **dwells** in you
2C 6:16 I will **live in** them and walk
Co 3:16 word of Christ **dwell in** you

2Ti 1: 5 a faith that **lived** first in
    1:14 of the Holy Spirit **living** in us

1774a GO1 AG267 LN88 K5:464
ενορκιζω, I PUT UNDER OATH
1Th 5:27 I **solemnly command** you by the

1775 GO2 AG267 LN88 R1520
ενοτης, ONENESS
Ep 4: 3 the **unity** of the Spirit
    4:13 come to the **unity** of the faith

1776 GO2 AG267 LN88
ενοχλεω, I ANNOY
Lk 6:18 who **were troubled** with unclean
He 12:15 springs up and **causes trouble**

1777 GO10 AG267 LN88 B2:142 K2:828
ενοχος, GUILTY
Mt 5:21 shall be **liable** to judgment
    5:22 you will be **liable** to judgment
    5:22 will be **liable** to the council
    5:22 be **liable** to the hell of fire
    26:66 He **deserves** death.
Mk 3:29 is **guilty** of an eternal sin
    14:64 him as **deserving** death
1C 11:27 will be **answerable** for the body
He 2:15 lives were **held in** slavery
Ja 2:10 become **accountable** for all

1778 GO3 AG268 LN88 R1781
ενταλμα, COMMAND
Mt 15: 9 teaching human **precepts**
Mk 7: 7 teaching human **precepts**
Co 2:22 they are simply human **commands**

1779 GO2 AG268 LN88 B1:263 R1722,5028
ενταφιαζω, I BURY
Mt 26:12 she has prepared me for **burial.**
Jn 19:40 according to the **burial** custom

1780 GO2 AG268 LN88 B1:263 R1779
ενταφιασμος, BURIAL
Mk 14: 8 body beforehand for its **burial**
Jn 12: 7 for the day of my **burial**

1781 GO15 AG268 LN88 B1:331 K2:544
εντελλω, I COMMAND
Mt 4: 6 He **will command** his angels
    17: 9 Jesus **ordered** them

	19: 7	Why then did Moses **command** us
	28:20	that I have **commanded** you
Mk	10: 3	What did Moses **command** you?
	13:34	**commands** the doorkeeper to be
Lk	4:10	He will **command** his angels
Jn	8: 5	Moses **commanded** us to stone
	14:31	as the Father has **commanded** me
	15:14	if you do what I **command** you
	15:17	I am giving you these **commands**
Ac	1: 2	after **giving instructions**
	13:47	so the Lord has **commanded** us
He	9:20	that God has **ordained** for you
	11:22	**gave instructions** about his

1782　 GO10 AG268 LN88
εντευθεν, FROM HERE

Lk	4: 9	throw yourself down **from here**
	13:31	Get away **from here,** for Herod
Jn	2:16	Take these things **out of here**
	7: 3	Leave **here** and go to Judea
	14:31	Rise, let us be **on our way**
	18:36	my kingdom is not **from here**
	19:18	two others, one **on** either **side**
	19:18	two others, one on **either side**
Ja	4: 1	where do they come **from**
Re	22: 2	**On either** side of the river

1783　 GO2 AG268 LN88 B2:860 K8:244 R1793
εντευξις, APPEAL

1Ti	2: 1	prayers, **intercessions**
	4: 5	by God's word and by **prayer**

1784　 GO5 AG268 LN88 B2:48 R1722,5092
εντιμος, IN HONOR

Lk	7: 2	a slave whom he **valued** highly
	14: 8	sit down at the **place of honor**
Ph	2:29	all joy, and **honor** such people
1P	2: 4	and **precious** in God's sight,
	2: 6	chosen and **precious;**

1785　 GO67 AG269 LN88 B1:331 K2:545 R1781
εντολη, COMMAND

Mt	5:19	least of these **commandments**
	15: 3	do you break the **commandment**
	19:17	keep the **commandments**
	22:36	which **commandment** in the law
	22:38	greatest and first **commandment**
	22:40	On these two **commandments** hang
Mk	7: 8	abandon the **commandment** of God

	7: 9	rejecting the **commandment**
	10: 5	wrote this **commandment** for you
	10:19	You know the **commandments**
	12:28	Which **commandment** is the first
	12:31	no other **commandment** greater
Lk	1: 6	to all the **commandments** and
	15:29	never disobeyed your **command**
	18:20	You know the **commandments**
	23:56	according to the **commandment**
Jn	10:18	I have received this **command**
	11:57	the Pharisees had given **orders**
	12:49	himself given me a **commandment**
	12:50	I know that his **commandment**
	13:34	I give you a new **commandment**
	14:15	you will keep my **commandments**
	14:21	They who have my **commandments**
	15:10	If you keep my **commandments**
	15:10	kept my Father's **commandments**
	15:12	This is my **commandment**
Ac	17:15	after receiving **instructions**
Ro	7: 8	opportunity in the **commandment**
	7: 9	but when the **commandment** came
	7:10	**commandment** that promised life
	7:11	opportunity in the **commandment**
	7:12	the **commandment** is holy
	7:13	through the **commandment** might
	13: 9	any other **commandment,** are
1C	7:19	but obeying the **commandments**
	14:37	writing to you is a **command**
Ep	2:15	law with its **commandments**
	6: 2	first **commandment** with a promise
Co	4:10	you have received **instructions**
1Ti	6:14	the **commandment** without spot
Ti	1:14	or to **commandments** of those
He	7: 5	have a **commandment** in the law
	7:16	through a legal **requirement**
	7:18	of an earlier **commandment**
	9:19	**commandment** had been told
2P	2:21	**commandment** that was passed
	3: 2	the **commandment** of the Lord
1J	2: 3	if we obey his **commandments**
	2: 4	does not obey his **commandments**
	2: 7	writing you no new **commandment**
	2: 7	but an old **commandment** that
	2: 7	the old **commandment** is the word
	2: 8	writing you a new **commandment**
	3:22	we obey his **commandments**

3:23 And this is his **commandment,**
3:23 just as he has **commanded** us.
3:24 who obey his **commandments** abide
4:21 **commandment** we have from him
5: 2 God and obey his **commandments**
5: 3 that we obey his **commandments**
5: 3 And his **commandments** are not
2J 1: 4 been **commanded** by the Father
1: 5 writing you a new **commandment**
1: 6 **commandment** just as you have
1: 6 according to his **commandments**
Re 12:17 keep the **commandments** of God
14:12 keep the **commandments** of God

1786 ᴳᴼ1 ᴬᴳ269 ᴸᴺ88
εντοπιος, LOCAL ONE
Ac 21:12 we and the **people** there urged

1787 ᴳᴼ2 ᴬᴳ269 ᴸᴺ88
εντος, WITHIN
Mt 23:26 clean the **inside** of the cup,
Lk 17:21 the kingdom of God is **among** you

1788 ᴳᴼ9 ᴬᴳ269 ᴸᴺ88
εντρεπω, I REGARD
Mt 21:37 They will **respect** my son.
Mk 12: 6 They will **respect** my son.
Lk 18: 2 nor had **respect** for people
18: 4 and no **respect** for anyone
20:13 perhaps they will **respect** him
1C 4:14 this **to make** you **ashamed**
2Th 3:14 so that they **may be ashamed**
Ti 2: 8 opponent will be **put to shame**
He 12: 9 and we **respected** them

1789 ᴳᴼ1 ᴬᴳ269 ᴸᴺ88 ᴿ1722,5142
εντρεφω, I NOURISH
1Ti 4: 6 **nourished** on the words of the

1790 ᴳᴼ3 ᴬᴳ269 ᴸᴺ88 ᴿ1722,5156
εντρομος, TREMBLING
Ac 7:32 Moses began **to tremble**
16:29 he fell down **trembling** before
He 12:21 I **tremble** with fear.

1791 ᴳᴼ2 ᴬᴳ269 ᴸᴺ88
εντροπη, SHAME
1C 6: 5 I say this to your **shame**
15:34 I say this to your **shame**

1792 ᴳᴼ1 ᴬᴳ270 ᴸᴺ88 ᴿ1722,5171
εντρυφαω, I INDULGE
2P 2:13 **reveling** in their dissipation

1793 ᴳᴼ5 ᴬᴳ270 ᴸᴺ88 ᴷ8:242 ᴿ1722,5177
εντυγχανω, I APPEAL
Ac 25:24 Jewish community **petitioned** me
Ro 8:27 because the Spirit **intercedes**
8:34 who indeed **intercedes** for us
11: 2 how he **pleads** with God
He 7:25 lives to make **intercession**

1794 ᴳᴼ3 ᴬᴳ270 ᴸᴺ88
εντυλισσω, I WRAP
Mt 27:59 took the body and **wrapped** it
Lk 23:53 **wrapped** it in a linen cloth
Jn 20: 7 lying with the linen **wrappings**

1795 ᴳᴼ1 ᴬᴳ270 ᴸᴺ89 ᴿ1722,5179
εντυπow, I ENGRAVE
2C 3: 7 **chiseled** in letters on stone

1796 ᴳᴼ1 ᴬᴳ270 ᴸᴺ89 ᴷ8:295
ενυβριζω, I ABUSE
He 10:29 **outraged** the Spirit of grace

1797 ᴳᴼ2 ᴬᴳ270 ᴸᴺ89 ᴷ8:545 ᴿ1798
ενυπνιαζομαι, I DREAM
Ac 2:17 your old men **shall dream** dreams
Ju 1: 8 in the same way these **dreamers**

1798 ᴳᴼ1 ᴬᴳ270 ᴸᴺ89 ᴷ8:545 ᴿ1722,5258
ενυπνιον, IN DREAM
Ac 2:17 your old men shall dream **dreams**

1799 ᴳᴼ94 ᴬᴳ270 ᴸᴺ89
ενωπιον, BEFORE
Lk 1:15 great **in the sight** of the Lord
1:17 he will go **before** him, to turn
1:19 I stand **in the presence** of God
1:75 **before** him all our days.
1:76 you will go **before** the Lord
4: 7 If you, then, will worship **me**
5:18 in and lay him **before** Jesus
5:25 he stood up **before** them
8:47 and falling down **before** him
12: 6 is forgotten **in** God's **sight.**
12: 9 whoever denies me **before** others
12: 9 **before** the angels of God
13:26 We ate and drank **with** you

	14:10	honored **in the presence** of all
	15:10	there is joy **in the presence**
	15:18	against heaven and **before** you
	15:21	against heaven and **before** you
	16:15	**in the sight** of others; but God
	16:15	abomination **in the sight** of God
	23:14	examined him **in your presence**
	24:11	seemed **to** them an idle tale
	24:43	it and ate **in** their **presence.**
Jn	20:30	other signs **in the presence**
Ac	2:25	the Lord always **before** me
	4:10	this man is standing **before** you
	4:19	it is right **in** God's **sight**
	6: 5	pleased **the** whole community
	6: 6	men stand **before** the apostles
	7:46	who found favor **with** God
	9:15	bring my name **before** Gentiles
	10:30	stood **before** me.
	10:31	been remembered **before** God
	10:33	here **in the presence** of God
	19: 9	**before** the congregation,
	19:19	books and burned them **publicly**
	27:35	thanks to God **in the presence**
Ro	3:20	be justified **in his sight**
	12:17	for what is noble **in the sight**
	14:22	your own conviction **before** God
1C	1:29	boast **in the presence** of God
2C	4: 2	everyone **in the sight** of God
	7:12	made known to you **before** God
	8:21	not only **in** the Lord's **sight**
	8:21	also **in the sight** of others
Ga	1:20	**before** God, I do not lie
1Ti	2: 3	**in the sight** of God
	5: 4	this is pleasing **in** God's **sight**
	5:20	rebuke them **in the presence** of
	5:21	**In the presence** of God
	6:12	**in the presence** of many
	6:13	**In the presence** of God,
2Ti	2:14	and warn them **before** God
	4: 1	**In the presence** of God
He	4:13	And **before** him no creature is
	13:21	which is pleasing **in his sight**
Ja	4:10	yourselves **before** the Lord
1P	3: 4	very precious **in** God's **sight**
1J	3:22	and do what pleases **him**
3J	1: 6	your love **before** the church
Re	1: 4	who are **before** his throne
	2:14	**before** the people of Israel
	3: 2	perfect **in the sight** of my God

3: 5	**before** my Father and before
3: 5	before my Father and **before**
3: 8	I have set **before** you an open
3: 9	and bow down **before** your feet
4: 5	and **in front** of the throne
4: 6	and **in front** of the throne
4:10	elders fall **before** the one
4:10	crowns **before** the throne
5: 8	elders fell **before** the Lamb
7: 9	standing **before** the throne
7: 9	throne and **before** the Lamb
7:11	**before** the throne and worshiped
7:15	**before** the throne of God
8: 2	angels who stand **before** God
8: 3	the golden altar that is **before**
8: 4	rose **before** God from the hand
9:13	the golden altar **before** God
11: 4	lampstands that stand **before**
11:16	on their thrones **before** God
12: 4	dragon stood **before** the woman
12:10	day and night **before** our God
13:12	the first beast **on** its **behalf**
13:13	to earth **in the sight** of all
13:14	allowed to perform **on behalf**
14: 3	a new song **before** the throne
14: 3	and **before** the four living
14:10	**in the presence** of the Lamb
14:10	**in the presence** of the holy
15: 4	come and worship **before** you
16:19	**God** remembered great Babylon
19:20	had performed **in** its **presence**
20:12	standing **before** the throne

1800   GO1 AG271 LN89
ενως, ENOS (ENOCH)
Lk   3:38   son of **Enos,** son of Seth

1801   GO1 AG271 LN89 K5:559 R1722,3775
ενωτιζομαι, I GIVE EAR TO
Ac   2:14   and **listen** to what I say.

1802   GO3 AG271 LN89 K2:556
ενωχ, ENOS (ENOCH)
Lk   3:37   son of Methuselah, son of **Enoch**
He   11: 5   By faith **Enoch** was taken
Ju   1:14   was also about these that **Enoch**

1803   GO13 AG271 LN89
'εξ, SIX
Mt   17: 1   **Six** days later, Jesus took with

Mk	9: 2	**Six** days later, Jesus took with
Lk	4:25	three years and **six** months
	13:14	There are **six** days on which
Jn	2: 6	there were **six** stone water jars
	2:20	for forty-**six** years
	12: 1	**Six** days before the Passover
Ac	11:12	These **six** brothers
	18:11	there a year and **six** months
	27:37	two hundred seventy-**six** persons
Ja	5:17	for three years and **six** months
Re	4: 8	each of them with **six** wings
	13:18	number is six hundred sixty-**six**

1804   GO2 AG271 LN89 B3:44 K1:69 R1537,31a
εξαγγελλω, I ANNOUNCE OUT
Mk	16:20	they went out and **proclaimed**
1P	2: 9	in order that you may **proclaim**

1805   GO4 AG271 LN89 B1:267 K1:124 R1537,39
εξαγοραζω, I BUY OUT
Ga	3:13	**redeemed** us from the curse
	4: 5	in order **to redeem** those
Ep	5:16	**making the most** of the time
Co	4: 5	**making the most** of the time

1806   GO12 AG271 LN89 R1537,71
εξαγω, I LEAD OUT
Mk	15:20	they **led** him **out** to crucify him
Lk	24:50	**led** them **out** as far as Bethany
Jn	10: 3	by name and **leads** them **out**
Ac	5:19	doors, **brought** them **out**
	7:36	He **led** them **out**
	7:40	this Moses who **led** us **out**
	12:17	the Lord had **brought** him **out**
	13:17	uplifted arm he **led** them **out**
	16:37	come and **take** us **out** themselves
	16:39	they **took** them **out** and asked
	21:38	**led** the four thousand assassins
He	8: 9	to **lead** them **out** of the land

1807   GO8 AG271 LN89
εξαιρεω, I PICK OUT
Mt	5:29	**tear** it **out** and throw it away
	18: 9	**tear** it **out** and throw it away
Ac	7:10	and **rescued** him from all his
	7:34	have come down to **rescue** them
	12:11	**rescued** me from the hands
	23:27	with the guard and **rescued** him
	26:17	I **will rescue** you from your
Ga	1: 4	**to set** us **free** from the present

1808   GO1 AG272 LN89 R1537,142
εξαιρω, I LIFT UP OUT
1C	5:13	**Drive out** the wicked person

1809   GO1 AG272 LN89 B2:855 K1:194
R1537,154
εξαιτεω, I ASK OUT
Lk	22:31	Satan **has demanded** to sift

1810   GO5 AG272 LN89
εξαιφνης, SUDDENLY
Mk	13:36	asleep when he comes **suddenly**
Lk	2:13	And **suddenly** there was with the
	9:39	**Suddenly** a spirit seizes him,
Ac	9: 3	**suddenly** a light from heaven
	22: 6	**suddenly** shone about me

1811   GO3 AG272 LN89 B1:480 K1:215 R1537,190
εξακολουθεω, I FOLLOW AFTER
2P	1:16	For we did not **follow** cleverly
	2: 2	**will follow** their licentious
	2:15	**following** the road of Balaam

1812   GO2 AG272 LN89 R1803,342
Ἑξακοσιοι, SIX HUNDRED
Re	13:18	number is **six hundred** sixty-six
	14:20	of about **two hundred** miles

1813   GO5 AG272 LN89 B1:471 R1537,218
εξαλειφω, I WIPE OFF
Ac	3:19	your sins **may be wiped out**
Co	2:14	**erasing** the record that stood
Re	3: 5	I will not **blot** your name out
	7:17	God **will wipe away** every tear
	21: 4	he **will wipe** every tear

1814   GO1 AG272 LN89 R1537,242
εξαλλομαι, I LEAP OUT
Ac	3: 8	**Jumping up,** he stood and began

1815   GO1 AG272 LN89 B3:259 K1:371 R1817
εξαναστασις, STANDING UP OUT
Ph	3:11	I may attain the **resurrection**

1816   GO2 AG272 LN89
εξανατελλω, I SPRING UP OUT
Mt	13: 5	and they **sprang up** quickly
Mk	4: 5	and it **sprang up** quickly

1817 GO3 AG272 LN90 B3:259 K1:368 R1537,450
εξανιστημι, I STAND UP OUT

Mk	12:19	**raise up** children for his
Lk	20:28	**raise up** children for his
Ac	15: 5	of the Pharisees **stood up**

1818 GO6 AG273 LN90 B2:457 K1:384 R1537,538
εξαπαταω, I DECEIVE THOROUGHLY

Ro	7:11	**deceived** me and through it
	16:18	they **deceive** the hearts
1C	3:18	Do not **deceive** yourselves
2C	11: 3	as the serpent **deceived** Eve
2Th	2: 3	Let no one **deceive** you
1Ti	2:14	and Adam was not **deceived**

1819 GO1 AG273 LN90
εξαπινα, SUDDENLY

| Mk | 9: 8 | **Suddenly** when they looked |

1820 GO2 AG273 LN90 R1537,639
εξαπορεω, I DOUBT GREATLY

| 2C | 1: 8 | that we **despaired** of life itself |
| | 4: 8 | but not **driven to despair;** |

1821 GO13 AG273 LN90 B1:126 K1:406 R1537,649
εξαποστελλω, I DELEGATE OUT

Mk	16: 8	Jesus himself **sent out** through
Lk	1:53	and **sent** the rich away empty
	20:10	**sent** him **away** empty-handed
	20:11	and **sent away** empty-handed
Ac	7:12	he **sent** our ancestors there
	9:30	and **sent** him **off** to Tarsus
	11:22	they **sent** Barnabas to Antioch
	12:11	that the Lord has **sent** his angel
	13:26	this salvation **has been sent**
	17:14	immediately **sent** Paul **away**
	22:21	for I will **send** you far away
Ga	4: 4	God **sent** his Son
	4: 6	God has **sent** the Spirit of his

1822 GO2 AG273 LN90 B3:349 K1:475 R1537,739
εξαρτιζω, I FINISH

| Ac | 21: 5 | When our days there **were ended** |
| 2Ti | 3:17 | **equipped** for every good work |

1823 GO1 AG273 LN90
εξαστραπτω, I GLITTER

| Lk | 9:29 | clothes became **dazzling** white |

1824 GO6 AG273 LN90
εξαυτης, AT ONCE

Mk	6:25	I want you to give me **at once**
Ac	10:33	I sent for you **immediately**
	11:11	**At that very moment** three men
	21:32	**Immediately** he took soldiers
	23:30	I sent him to you **at once**
Ph	2:23	to send him **as soon as** I see

1825 GO2 AG273 LN90 K2:338 R1537,1453
εξεγειρω, I RAISE OUT

| Ro | 9:17 | I have **raised** you **up** for the |
| 1C | 6:14 | will also **raise** us by his power |

1826 GO4 AG273 LN90 B2:606
εξειμι, I GO OUT

Ac	13:42	and Barnabas **were going out**
	17:15	soon as possible, they **left** him
	20: 7	intended to **leave** the next day
	27:43	first and **make for** the land

1828 GO1 AG274 LN90 R1537,1670
εξελκω, I DRAG OUT

| Ja | 1:14 | **being lured** and enticed by it |

1829 GO1 AG274 LN91
εξεραμα, VOMIT

| 2P | 2:22 | turns back to its own **vomit** |

1830 GO1 AG274 LN91 B3:532 K2:655
εξεραυναω, I SEARCH OUT

| 1P | 1:10 | yours **made careful search** and |

1831 GO218 AG274 LN91 B1:320 K2:678 R1537,2064
εξερχομαι, I GO OUT

Mt	2: 6	from you **shall come** a ruler
	5:26	you **will** never **get out** until
	8:28	demoniacs **coming out** of the
	8:32	So they **came out** and entered
	8:34	Then the whole town **came out**
	9:26	of this **spread throughout** that
	9:31	But they **went away** and spread
	9:32	After they **had gone away,**
	10:11	and stay there until you **leave**
	10:14	as you **leave** that house or town
	11: 7	you **go out** into the wilderness
	11: 8	What then did you **go out** to see
	11: 9	What then did you **go out** to see
	12:14	**went out** and conspired against
	12:43	unclean spirit **has gone out**

12:44	to my house from which I **came**	6:54	When they **got out** of the boat
13: 1	That same day Jesus **went out**	7:29	demon **has left** your daughter
13: 3	A sower **went out** to sow	7:30	on the bed, and the demon **gone**
13:49	The angels **will come out**	7:31	he **returned** from the region
14:14	When he **went ashore**	8:11	The Pharisees **came** and began
15:18	what **comes out** of the mouth	8:27	**went on** with his disciples
15:19	For out of the heart **come**	9:25	I command you, **come out** of him
15:21	left that place and **went away**	9:26	him terribly, it **came out**
15:22	woman from that region **came out**	9:29	This kind can **come out** only
17:18	it **came out** of him, and the boy	9:30	They **went on** from there
18:28	that same slave, as he **went out**	11:11	and **went into** the temple
20: 1	**went out** early in the morning	11:12	when they **came from** Bethany
20: 3	When he **went out** about nine	14:16	So the disciples **set out**
20: 5	When he **went out** again about	14:26	they **went out** to the Mount
20: 6	about five o'clock he **went out**	14:48	Have you **come out** with swords
21:17	**went out** of the city to Bethany	14:68	he **went out** into the forecourt
22:10	**went out** into the streets	16: 8	So they **went out** and fled
24: 1	Jesus **came out** of the temple	16:20	they **went out** and proclaimed
24:26	do not **go out**	Lk 1:22	When he did **come out**
24:27	lightning **comes** from the east	2: 1	In those days a decree **went out**
25: 1	**went** to meet the bridegroom	4:14	about him **spread** through all
25: 6	**Come out** to meet him	4:35	Be silent, and **come out** of him
26:30	they **went out** to the Mount	4:35	he **came out** of him without
26:55	Have you **come out** with swords	4:36	spirits, and **out** they **come**
26:71	When he **went out** to the porch	4:41	Demons also **came out** of many
26:75	he **went out** and wept bitterly	4:42	At daybreak he **departed**
27:32	As they **went out,** they came	5: 8	**Go away** from me, Lord, for I am
27:53	they **came out** of the tombs	5:27	After this he **went out** and saw
Mk 1:25	Be silent, and **come out** of him	6:12	during those days he **went out**
1:26	a loud voice, **came out** of him	6:19	for power **came out** from him
1:28	fame began to **spread throughout**	7:17	**spread** throughout Judea
1:29	soon as they **left** the synagogue	7:24	**go out** into the wilderness
1:35	**went out** to a deserted place	7:25	then did you **go out** to see
1:38	that is what I **came out** to do	7:26	did you **go out** to see?
1:45	**went out** and began to proclaim	8: 2	whom seven demons **had gone out**
2:12	took the mat and **went out**	8: 5	sower **went out** to sow his seed
2:13	Jesus **went out** again beside	8:27	As he **stepped out** on land
3: 6	The Pharisees **went out**	8:29	spirit to **come out** of the man
3:21	they **went out** to restrain him	8:33	demons **came out** of the man
4: 3	A sower **went out** to sow.	8:35	Then people **came out** to see
5: 2	he had **stepped out** of the boat	8:35	from whom the demons had **gone**
5: 8	**Come out** of the man	8:38	from whom the demons **had gone**
5:13	unclean spirits **came out**	8:46	power **had gone out** from me
5:30	aware that power had **gone forth**	9: 4	there, and **leave** from there
6: 1	He **left** that place and came	9: 5	as you **are leaving** that town
6:10	stay there until you **leave**	9: 6	They **departed** and went through
6:12	So they **went out**	11:14	when the demon **had gone out**
6:24	**went out** and said to her mother	11:24	unclean spirit **has gone out**
6:34	As he **went ashore**	11:24	the unclean spirit **has gone out**

	11:53	When he **went outside**
	12:59	you will never **get out** until
	13:31	**Get away** from here, for Herod
	14:18	I must **go out** and see it
	14:21	**Go out** at once into the streets
	14:23	**Go out** into the roads and lanes
	15:28	His father **came out** and began
	17:29	on the day that Lot **left** Sodom
	21:37	at night he would **go out**
	22:39	He **came out** and went, as was
	22:52	Have you **come out** with swords
	22:62	he **went out** and wept bitterly.
Jn	1:43	Jesus decided **to go** to Galilee
	4:30	They **left** the city and were
	4:43	he **went** from that place
	8: 9	they heard it, they **went away**
	8:42	for I **came from** God and now
	8:59	and **went out** of the temple
	10: 9	will come in and **go out**
	10:39	he **escaped** from their hands
	11:31	get up quickly and **go out**
	11:44	The dead man **came out**
	12:13	and **went out** to meet him
	13: 3	and that he had **come from** God
	13:30	he immediately **went out**
	13:31	When he had **gone out**
	16:27	believed that I **came from** God
	16:28	I **came from** the Father
	16:30	believe that you **came from** God
	17: 8	that I **came from** you
	18: 1	he **went out** with his disciples
	18: 4	**came forward** and asked them
	18:16	to the high priest, **went out**
	18:29	So Pilate went **out** to them
	18:38	he **went out** to the Jews again
	19: 4	Pilate **went out** again and said
	19: 5	So Jesus **came out**, wearing the
	19:17	he **went out** to what is called
	19:34	once blood and water **came out**
	20: 3	the other disciple **set out**
	21: 3	**went out** and got into the boat
	21:23	rumor **spread** in the community
Ac	1:21	Lord Jesus **went** in and **out**
	7: 3	**Leave** your country and your
	7: 4	Then he **left** the country
	7: 7	they shall **come out**
	8: 7	**came out** of many who were
	10:23	he got up and **went** with them
	11:25	Then Barnabas **went** to Tarsus

	12: 9	Peter **went out** and followed him
	12:10	they **went outside** and walked
	12:17	**left** and went to another place
	14:20	he **went on** with Barnabas
	15:24	who have **gone out** from us
	15:40	Paul chose Silas and **set out**
	16: 3	wanted Timothy to **accompany** him
	16:10	**to cross over** to Macedonia
	16:13	the sabbath day we **went outside**
	16:18	Jesus Christ to **come out** of her
	16:18	it **came out** that very hour
	16:19	hope of making money **was gone**
	16:36	therefore **come out** now and go
	16:40	After **leaving** the prison
	16:40	sisters there, they **departed**
	17:33	At that point Paul **left** them
	18:23	he **departed** and went from place
	20: 1	he **left** for Macedonia
	20:11	until dawn; then he **left**
	21: 5	we **left** and proceeded on our
	21: 8	The next day we **left** and came
	22:18	Hurry and **get out** of Jerusalem
	28: 3	**driven out** by the heat
Ro	10:18	Their voice has **gone out** to all
1C	5:10	need to **go out** of the world
	14:36	the word of God **originate**
2C	2:13	**went on** to Macedonia
	6:17	Therefore **come out** from them
	8:17	he is **going** to you of his own
Ph	4:15	when I **left** Macedonia
1Th	1: 8	faith in God **has become known**
He	3:16	not all those who **left** Egypt
	7: 5	these also are **descended** from
	11: 8	he was called to **set out**
	11: 8	and he **set out,** not knowing
	13:13	Let us then **go** to him outside
Ja	3:10	the same mouth **come** blessing
1J	2:19	They **went out** from us,
	4: 1	false prophets have **gone out**
2J	1: 7	Many deceivers have **gone out**
3J	1: 7	for they **began their journey**
Re	3:12	you will never **go out** of it
	6: 2	he **came out** conquering
	6: 4	And **out came** another horse
	9: 3	from the smoke **came** locusts
	14:15	angel **came out** of the temple
	14:17	angel **came out** of the temple
	14:18	angel **came out** from the altar
	14:20	blood **flowed from** the wine

15: 6	and out of the temple **came** the
16:17	voice **came out** of the temple
18: 4	**Come out** of her, my people
19: 5	from the throne **came** a voice
19:21	sword that **came from** his mouth
20: 8	and **will come out** to deceive

1832   GO31   AG275   LN91   B2:606   K2:560
εξεστι, IT IS POSSIBLE

Mt	12: 2	what **is** not **lawful** to do
	12: 4	it **was** not **lawful** for him
	12:10	**Is** it **lawful** to cure on the
	12:12	So it **is lawful** to do good
	14: 4	It **is** not **lawful** for you
	19: 3	**Is** it **lawful** for a man to
	20:15	**Am** I not **allowed** to do what
	22:17	**Is** it **lawful** to pay taxes
	27: 6	It **is** not **lawful** to put them
Mk	2:24	doing what **is** not **lawful**
	2:26	which it is not **lawful** for any
	3: 4	**Is** it **lawful** to do good
	6:18	It is not **lawful** for you
	10: 2	**Is** it **lawful** for a man
	12:14	**Is** it **lawful** to pay taxes
Lk	6: 2	what **is** not **lawful** on the
	6: 4	which it is not **lawful** for any
	6: 9	I ask you, is it **lawful** to do
	14: 3	**Is** it **lawful** to cure people
	20:22	**Is** it **lawful** for us to pay
Jn	5:10	it is not **lawful** for you to
	18:31	We **are** not **permitted** to put
Ac	2:29	I **may** say to you confidently
	16:21	customs that **are** not **lawful**
	21:37	**May** I say something to you
	22:25	**Is** it **legal** for you to flog
1C	6:12	All things **are lawful** for me
	6:12	All things **are lawful** for me
	10:23	All things **are lawful,**
	10:23	All things **are lawful,**
2C	12: 4	mortal **is permitted** to repeat

1833   GO3   AG275   LN91
εξεταζω, I INQUIRE

Mt	2: 8	Go and **search** diligently
	10:11	**find out** who in it is worthy
Jn	21:12	the disciples dared to **ask** him

1834   GO6   AG275   LN91   B1:573   K2:908   R1537,2233
εξηγεομαι, I EXPLAIN

Lk	24:35	what **had happened** on the road

Jn	1:18	who **has made** him **known.**
Ac	10: 8	after **telling** them everything
	15:12	as they **told** of all the signs
	15:14	Simeon has **related** how God
	21:19	**related** one by one the things

1835   GO9   AG276   LN91   R1803
ἐξηκοντα, SIXTY

Mt	13: 8	some a hundredfold, some **sixty**
	13:23	in another **sixty**
Mk	4: 8	and **sixty** and a hundredfold
	4:20	and **sixty** and a hundredfold
Lk	24:13	**seven** miles from Jerusalem
1Ti	5: 9	if she is not less than **sixty**
Re	11: 3	thousand two hundred **sixty** days
	12: 6	thousand two hundred **sixty** days
	13:18	number is six hundred **sixty**-six

1836   GO5   AG276   LN92
ἐξης, NEXT

Lk	7:11	**afterwards** he went to a town
	9:37	On the **next** day, when they had
Ac	21: 1	and the **next** day to Rhodes
	25:17	on the **next** day took my seat
	27:18	that on the **next** day they began

1837   GO1   AG276   LN92
εξηχεω, I SOUND OUT

1Th	1: 8	the Lord **has sounded forth**

1838   GO1   AG276   LN92
ἐξις, HABIT

He	5:14	have been trained by **practice**

1839   GO17   AG276   LN92   K2:459   R1537,2476
εξιστημι, I AM AMAZED

Mt	12:23	All the crowds **were amazed**
Mk	2:12	that they **were** all **amazed**
	3:21	He **has gone out of his mind**
	5:42	**overcome** with **amazement**
	6:51	they **were** utterly **astounded**
Lk	2:47	all who heard him **were amazed**
	8:56	Her parents **were astounded**
	24:22	women of our group **astounded**
Ac	2: 7	**Amazed** and astonished
	2:12	All were **amazed** and perplexed
	8: 9	**amazed** the people of Samaria
	8:11	had **amazed** them with his magic
	8:13	with Philip and **was amazed**
	9:21	All who heard him **were amazed**

	10:45	**were astounded** that the gift
	12:16	they saw him and **were amazed.**
2C	5:13	For if we **are beside** ourselves

1840　GO1　AG276　LN92
εξισχυω, I MAKE THOROUGHLY STRONG
Ep　3:18　that you **may have the power** to

1841　GO3　AG276　LN92　K5:103　R1537,3598
εξοδος, WAY OUT
Lk　9:31　were speaking of his **departure**
He　11:22　made mention of the **exodus**
2P　1:15　so that after my **departure**

1842　GO1　AG276　LN92　B1:465　K5:170
εξολεθρευω, I RUIN COMPLETELY
Ac　3:23　**will be utterly rooted out** of

1843　GO10　AG277　LN92　B1:344　K5:199　R1537,3670
εξομολογεω, I CONFESS OUT
Mt　3: 6　Jordan, **confessing** their sins
　　11:25　I **thank** you, Father, Lord of
Mk　1: 5　Jordan, **confessing** their sins
Lk　10:21　I **thank** you, Father, Lord of
　　22: 6　he **consented** and began to look
Ac　19:18　who became believers **confessed**
Ro　14:11　every tongue **shall give praise**
　　15: 9　Therefore I **will confess** you
Ph　2:11　every tongue **should confess**
Ja　5:16　Therefore **confess** your sins

1844　GO1　AG277　LN92　B3:737　K5:464　R1537,3726
εξορκιζω, I PUT UNDER OATH
Mt　26:63　I **put** you **under oath** before the

1845　GO1　AG277　LN92　B3:737　K5:464　R1844
εξορκιστης, EXORCIST
Ac　19:13　some itinerant Jewish **exorcists**

1846　GO2　AG277　LN92　R1537,3736
εξορυσσω, I DIG OUT
Mk　2: 4　and after **having dug through** it
Ga　4:15　would **have torn out** your eyes

1847　GO1　AG277　LN92　B1:74
εξουδενεω, I SET TO NOTHING
Mk　9:12　and **be treated with contempt**

1848　GO11　AG277　LN92　B1:74
εξουθενεω, I DISPISE

Lk	18: 9	**regarded others with contempt**
	23:11	**treated** him **with contempt** and
Ac	4:11	stone that **was rejected** by you
Ro	14: 3	Those who eat **must** not **despise**
	14:10	why **do** you **despise** your brother
1C	1:28	chose what **is low and despised**
	6: 4	**have no standing** in the church
	16:11	**let** no one **despise** him
2C	10:10	and his speech **contemptible**
Ga	4:14	you did not scorn or **despise** me
1Th	5:20	**Do** not **despise** the words of

1849　GO102　AG277　LN92　B2:606　K2:562
εξουσια, AUTHORITY
Mt　7:29　as one having **authority**
　　8: 9　I also am a man under **authority**
　　9: 6　Son of Man has **authority**
　　9: 8　who had given such **authority**
　　10: 1　**authority** over unclean spirits
　　21:23　By what **authority** are you doing
　　21:23　and who gave you this **authority**
　　21:24　by what **authority** I do these
　　21:27　by what **authority** I am doing
　　28:18　All **authority** in heaven and on
Mk　1:22　them as one having **authority**
　　1:27　new teaching—with **authority**
　　2:10　**authority** on earth to forgive
　　3:15　**authority** to cast out demons
　　6: 7　**authority** over the unclean
　　11:28　By what **authority** are you doing
　　11:28　Who gave you this **authority**
　　11:29　by what **authority** I do these
　　11:33　by what **authority** I am doing
　　13:34　and puts his slaves **in charge**
Lk　4: 6　glory and all this **authority**
　　4:32　because he spoke with **authority**
　　4:36　For with **authority** and power
　　5:24　the Son of Man has **authority**
　　7: 8　a man set under **authority**
　　9: 1　gave them power and **authority**
　　10:19　I have given you **authority**
　　12: 5　has **authority** to cast into hell
　　12:11　rulers, and the **authorities**
　　19:17　**take charge** of ten cities
　　20: 2　by what **authority** are you doing
　　20: 2　who gave you this **authority**
　　20: 8　by what **authority** I am doing
　　20:20　and **authority** of the governor.
　　22:53　and the **power** of darkness

	23: 7	was under Herod's **jurisdiction**
Jn	1:12	gave **power** to become children
	5:27	he has given him **authority**
	10:18	I have **power** to lay it down
	10:18	I have **power** to take it up
	17: 2	**authority** over all people
	19:10	I have **power** to release you
	19:10	and **power** to crucify you
	19:11	You would have no **power** over me
Ac	1: 7	has set by his own **authority.**
	5: 4	the proceeds at your **disposal**
	8:19	Give me also this **power**
	9:14	he has **authority** from the chief
	26:10	**authority** received from the
	26:12	with the **authority**
	26:18	from the **power** of Satan to God
Ro	9:21	Has the potter no **right** over
	13: 1	to the governing **authorities**
	13: 1	no **authority** except from God
	13: 2	whoever resists **authority**
	13: 3	have no fear of the **authority**
1C	7:37	his own desire under **control**
	8: 9	that this **liberty** of yours
	9: 4	Do we not have the **right** to our
	9: 5	Do we not have the **right** to he
	9: 6	I who have no **right** to refrain
	9:12	If others share this **rightful**
	9:12	not made use of this **right**
	9:18	to make full use of my **rights**
	11:10	to have a symbol of **authority**
	15:24	every **authority** and power.
2C	10: 8	too much of our **authority**
	13:10	severe in using the **authority**
Ep	1:21	all rule and **authority**
	2: 2	ruler of the **power** of the air
	3:10	**authorities** in the heavenly
	6:12	against the **authorities**
Co	1:13	from the **power** of darkness
	1:16	dominions or rulers or **powers**
	2:10	of every ruler and **authority**
	2:15	the rulers and **authorities**
2Th	3: 9	we do not have that **right,**
Ti	3: 1	to rulers and **authorities,**
He	13:10	have no **right** to eat
1P	3:22	with angels, **authorities,**
Ju	1:25	majesty, power, and **authority**
Re	2:26	**authority** over the nations
	6: 8	**authority** over a fourth of the
	9: 3	they were given **authority** like

	9: 3	like the **authority** of scorpions
	9:10	is their **power** to harm people
	9:19	For the **power** of the horses
	11: 6	They have **authority** to shut
	11: 6	have **authority** over the waters
	12:10	the **authority** of his Messiah
	13: 2	his throne and great **authority.**
	13: 4	his **authority** to the beast,
	13: 5	to exercise **authority**
	13: 7	**authority** over every tribe
	13:12	It exercises all the **authority**
	14:18	who has **authority** over fire,
	16: 9	**authority** over these plagues
	17:12	to receive **authority** as kings
	17:13	their power and **authority**
	18: 1	heaven, having great **authority**
	20: 6	the second death has no **power**
	22:14	they will have the **right**

1850   GO4 AG279 LN92 K2:574 R1849
εξουσιαζω, I HAVE AUTHORITY

Lk	22:25	those in **authority** over them
1C	6:12	but I will not **be dominated**
	7: 4	wife does not **have authority**
	7: 4	**have authority** over his own

1851   GO1 AG279 LN92
εξοχη, PROMINENCE

| Ac | 25:23 | the **prominent** men of the city |

1852   GO1 AG279 LN93 K8:545 R1853
εξυπνιζω, I AWAKE

| Jn | 11:11 | going there **to awaken** him |

1853   GO1 AG279 LN93 K8:545 R1537,5258
εξυπνος, AWAKE

| Ac | 16:27 | When the jailer **woke up** and saw |

1854   GO63 AG279 LN93 K2:575
εξω, OUTSIDE

Mt	5:13	is thrown **out** and trampled
	10:14	as you **leave** that house
	12:46	brothers were standing **outside**
	12:47	brothers are standing **outside**
	13:48	baskets but threw **out** the bad
	21:17	went **out** of the city to Bethany
	21:39	threw him **out** of the vineyard,
	26:69	Now Peter was sitting **outside**
	26:75	he went **out** and wept bitterly
Mk	1:45	but stayed **out** in the country

	3:31	and standing **outside,**
	3:32	are **outside,** asking for you
	4:11	but for those **outside,**
	5:10	send them **out** of the country
	8:23	led him **out** of the village
	11: 4	**outside** in the street
	11:19	went **out** of the city.
	12: 8	threw him **out** of the vineyard
	14:68	he went **out** into the forecourt
Lk	1:10	the people was praying **outside**
	4:29	drove him **out** of the town,
	8:20	brothers are standing **outside**
	13:25	you begin to stand **outside**
	13:28	you yourselves thrown **out**
	13:33	prophet to be killed **outside**
	14:35	they throw it **away**
	20:15	threw him **out** of the vineyard
	22:62	he went **out** and wept bitterly
	24:50	led them **out** as far as Bethany
Jn	6:37	I will never drive **away**
	9:34	And they drove him **out**
	9:35	that they had driven him **out**
	11:43	loud voice, "Lazarus, come **out**
	12:31	this world will be driven **out**
	15: 6	not abide in me is thrown **away**
	18:16	but Peter was standing **outside**
	18:29	So Pilate went **out** to them
	19: 4	Pilate went **out** again and said
	19: 4	I am bringing him **out** to you
	19: 5	So Jesus came **out**
	19:13	he brought Jesus **outside**
	20:11	Mary stood weeping **outside** the
Ac	4:15	So they ordered them to **leave**
	5:34	the men to be put **outside**
	7:58	dragged him **out** of the city
	9:40	Peter put all of them **outside**
	14:19	dragged him **out** of the city,
	16:13	we went **outside** the gate
	16:30	Then he brought them **outside**
	21: 5	escorted us **outside** the city
	21:30	dragged him **out** of the temple
	26:11	pursued them even to **foreign**
1C	5:12	with judging those **outside**
	5:13	God will judge those **outside**
2C	4:16	Even though our **outer** nature
Co	4: 5	wisely toward **outsiders**
1Th	4:12	properly toward **outsiders**
He	13:11	are burned **outside** the camp
	13:12	Jesus also suffered **outside**

	13:13	go to him **outside** the camp
1J	4:18	perfect love casts **out** fear
Re	3:12	you will never go **out** of it
	22:15	**Outside** are the dogs

1855   GO13   AG279   LN93
εξωθεν, FROM OUTSIDE

Mt	23:25	clean the **outside** of the cup
	23:27	on the **outside** look beautiful,
	23:28	So you also on the **outside** look
Mk	7:15	is nothing **outside** a person
	7:18	**from outside** cannot defile
Lk	11:39	clean the **outside** of the cup
	11:40	the one who made the **outside**
2C	7: 5	**without** and fears within
1Ti	3: 7	well thought of by **outsiders**
1P	3: 3	not adorn yourselves **outwardly**
Re	11: 2	the court **outside** the temple
	11: 2	the temple; leave that **out,**
	14:20	was trodden **outside** the city

1856   GO2   AG280   LN93
εξωθεω, I PUSH OUT

| Ac | 7:45 | that God **drove out** before our |
| | 27:39 | planned to **run** the ship **ashore** |

1857   GO3   AG280   LN93
εξωτερος, OUTERMOST

Mt	8:12	thrown into the **outer** darkness
	22:13	him into the **outer** darkness
	25:30	him into the **outer** darkness

1857a   GO2   AG280   LN93
εοικα, IT RESEMBLES

| Ja | 1: 6 | **is like** a wave of the sea, |
| | 1:23 | they **are like** those who look |

1858   GO1   AG280   LN93   R1859
ἑορταζω, I KEEP FESTIVAL

| 1C | 5: 8 | **let** us **celebrate** the **festival** |

1859   GO25   AG280   LN93
ἑορτη, FESTIVAL

Mt	26: 5	Not during the **festival**
	27:15	Now at the **festival**
Mk	14: 2	Not during the **festival**
	15: 6	Now at the **festival** he used
Lk	2:41	the **festival** of the Passover
	2:42	as usual for the **festival**
	22: 1	Now the **festival** of Unleavened

Jn	2:23	during the Passover **festival**
	4:45	in Jerusalem at the **festival**
	4:45	had gone to the **festival**
	5: 1	a **festival** of the Jews,
	6: 4	the **festival** of the Jews
	7: 2	Jewish **festival** of Booths
	7: 8	Go to the **festival** yourselves
	7: 8	not going to this **festival**
	7:10	had gone to the **festival**
	7:11	for him at the **festival**
	7:14	the middle of the **festival**
	7:37	On the last day of the **festival**
	11:56	will not come to the **festival**
	12:12	that had come to the **festival**
	12:20	the **festival** were some Greeks
	13: 1	the **festival** of the Passover
	13:29	what we need for the **festival**
Co	2:16	or of observing **festivals**,

1860   ᴳᴼ52 ᴬᴳ280 ᴸᴺ93 ᴮ3:68 ᴷ2:576 ᴿ1861
επαγγελια, PROMISE

Lk	24:49	you what my Father **promised**
Ac	1: 4	for the **promise** of the Father
	2:33	**promise** of the Holy Spirit
	2:39	For the **promise** is for you
	7:17	fulfillment of the **promise**
	13:23	a Savior, Jesus, as he **promised**
	13:32	God **promised** to our ancestors
	23:21	are waiting for your **consent**
	26: 6	in the **promise** made by God
Ro	4:13	For the **promise** that he would
	4:14	null and the **promise** is void
	4:16	the **promise** may rest on grace
	4:20	concerning the **promise** of God
	9: 4	the worship, and the **promises**
	9: 8	the children of the **promise**
	9: 9	this is what the **promise** said
	15: 8	might confirm the **promises**
2C	1:20	every one of God's **promises**
	7: 1	Since we have these **promises**
Ga	3:14	we might receive the **promise**
	3:16	**promises** were made to Abraham
	3:17	so as to nullify the **promise**
	3:18	longer comes from the **promise**
	3:18	to Abraham through the **promise**
	3:21	opposed to the **promises** of God
	3:22	what was **promised** through faith
	3:29	heirs according to the **promise**
	4:23	was born through the **promise**

	4:28	are children of the **promise,**
Ep	1:13	of the **promised** Holy Spirit
	2:12	to the covenants of **promise**
	3: 6	and sharers in the **promise**
	6: 2	commandment with a **promise**
1Ti	4: 8	holding **promise** for both the
2Ti	1: 1	for the sake of the **promise**
He	4: 1	while the **promise** of entering
	6:12	patience inherit the **promises**
	6:15	endured, obtained the **promise**
	6:17	to the heirs of the **promise**
	7: 6	who had received the **promises**
	8: 6	enacted through better **promises**
	9:15	**promised** eternal inheritance
	10:36	may receive what was **promised**
	11: 9	the land he had been **promised**
	11: 9	with him of the same **promise**
	11:13	having received the **promises,**
	11:17	had received the **promises**
	11:33	obtained **promises,** shut the
	11:39	not receive what was **promised**
2P	3: 4	Where is the **promise** of his
	3: 9	not slow about his **promise**
1J	2:25	is what he has **promised** us,

1861   ᴳᴼ15 ᴬᴳ280 ᴵᴺ93 ᴮ3:68 ᴷ2:576
επαγγελλομαι, I PROMISE

Mk	14:11	and **promised** to give him money
Ac	7: 5	but **promised** to give it to him
Ro	4:21	able to do what he had **promised**
Ga	3:19	whom the **promise** had been made
1Ti	2:10	for women who **profess** reverence
	6:21	by **professing** it some have
Ti	1: 2	**promised** before the ages began
He	6:13	When God **made** a promise
	10:23	he who **has promised** is faithful
	11:11	him faithful who **had promised.**
	12:26	but now he has **promised,**
Ja	1:12	that the Lord has **promised**
	2: 5	that he has **promised** to those
2P	2:19	They **promise** them freedom,
1J	2:25	what he has **promised** us

1862   ᴳᴼ2 ᴬᴳ281 ᴸᴺ93 ᴮ3:68 ᴷ2:585 ᴿ1861
επαγγελμα, PROMISE

2P	1: 4	and very great **promises,**
	3:13	in accordance with his **promise**

1863   ᴳᴼ3 ᴬᴳ281 ᴸᴺ93 ᴿ1909,71
επαγω, I BRING ON

Ac　5:28　you are determined to **bring**
2P　2: 1　who will secretly **bring** in
　　2: 5　when he **brought** a flood

1864　GO1　AG281　LN93　B1:644
επαγωνιζομαι, I CONTEND FOR
Ju　1: 3　to **contend** for the faith that

1865　GO1　AG281　LN93
επαθροιζω, I AM THRONGED
Lk　11:29　When the crowds **were increasing**

1866　GO1　AG281　LN93
επαινετος, EPAENETUS
Ro　16: 5　Greet my beloved **Epaenetus,**

1867　GO6　AG281　LN93　B3:816　R1909,134
επαινεω, I PRAISE
Lk　16: 8　**commended** the dishonest
　　　　　　manager
Ro　15:11　**let** all the peoples **praise** him
1C　11: 2　I **commend** you because you
　　11:17　I do not **commend** you,
　　11:22　Should I **commend** you?
　　11:22　In this matter I do not **commend**

1868　GO11　AG281　LN93　B2:874　K2:586　R1867
επαινος, PRAISE
Ro　2:29　Such a person receives **praise**
　　13: 3　you will receive its **approval**
1C　4: 5　one will receive **commendation**
2C　8:18　the brother who is **famous**
Ep　1: 6　to the **praise** of his glorious
　　1:12　for the **praise** of his glory
　　1:14　to the **praise** of his glory
Ph　1:11　the glory and **praise** of God
　　4: 8　is anything worthy of **praise**
1P　1: 7　to result in **praise** and glory
　　2:14　to **praise** those who do right

1869　GO19　AG281　LN93　K1:186　R1909,142
επαιρω, I LIFT UP ON
Mt　17: 8　And when they **looked up**
Lk　6:20　he **looked up** at his disciples
　　11:27　**raised** her voice and said
　　16:23　he **looked up** and saw Abraham
　　18:13　would not even **look up**
　　21:28　stand up and **raise** your heads,
　　24:50　**lifting up** his hands,
Jn　4:35　I tell you, **look around** you,

　　6: 5　When he **looked up** and saw
　　13:18　**has lifted** his heel against me
　　17: 1　he **looked up** to heaven and said
Ac　1: 9　he **was lifted up,**
　　2:14　**raised** his voice and addressed
　　14:11　**shouted** in the Lycaonian
　　22:22　but then they **shouted,**
　　27:40　**hoisting** the foresail to the
2C　10: 5　**raised up** against the knowledge
　　11:20　of you, or **puts on airs,**
1Ti　2: 8　**lifting up** holy hands without

1870　GO11　AG282　LN94　B3:562　K1:189　R1909,153
επαισχυνομαι, I AM ASHAMED
Mk　8:38　Those who **are ashamed** of me
　　8:38　will also **be ashamed** when he
Lk　9:26　Those who **are ashamed** of me
　　9:26　Son of Man will **be ashamed**
Ro　1:16　I **am** not **ashamed** of the gospel
　　6:21　of which you now **are ashamed**
2Ti　1: 8　Do not **be ashamed**
　　1:12　But I **am** not **ashamed**
　　1:16　and was not **ashamed** of my
　　　　　　chain
He　2:11　Jesus is not **ashamed** to call
　　11:16　God is not **ashamed** to be called

1871　GO2　AG282　LN94　R1909,154
επαιτεω, I ASK
Lk　16: 3　and I am ashamed **to beg**
　　18:35　sitting by the roadside **begging**

1872　GO4　AG282　LN94　B1:480　K1:215　R1909,190
επακολουθεω, I FOLLOW ON
Mk　16:20　the signs that **accompanied** it
1Ti　5:10　**devoted** herself to doing good
　　5:24　sins of others **follow** them
1P　2:21　you should **follow** in his steps

1873　GO1　AG282　LN94　B2:172　K1:222　R1909,191
επακουω, I HEARD
2C　6: 2　I have **listened** to you,

1874　GO1　AG282　LN94　B2:172
επακροαομαι, I LISTEN
Ac　16:25　the prisoners **were listening**

1875　GO3　AG282　LN94
επαν, WHEN
Mt　2: 8　**when** you have found him,

Lk   11:22   But **when** one stronger than he
      11:34   **but if** it is not healthy,

1876   ᴳᴼ1   ᴬᴳ282 ᴸᴺ94
επαναγκες, NECESSARY
Ac   15:28   burden than these **essentials**

1877   ᴳᴼ3 ᴬᴳ282 ᴸᴺ94
επαναγω, I LEAD UP
Mt   21:18   when he **returned** to the city,
Lk   5: 3   to **put out** a little way from
       5: 4   **Put out** into the deep water

1878   ᴳᴼ1 ᴬᴳ282 ᴸᴺ94
επαναμιμνησκω, I REMIND AGAIN
Ro   15:15   boldly **by way of reminder,**

1879   ᴳᴼ2 ᴬᴳ282 ᴸᴺ94 ᴮ3:254 ᴷ1:351 ᴿ1909,373
επαναπαυομαι, I REST ON
Lk   10: 6   your peace **will rest on** that
Ro   2:17   a Jew and **rely on** the law

1880   ᴳᴼ2 ᴬᴳ283 ᴸᴺ94 ᴿ1909,424
επανερχομαι, I COME UP ON
Lk   10:35   and when I **come back**
      19:15   When he **returned,**

1881   ᴳᴼ2 ᴬᴳ283 ᴸᴺ94 ᴿ1909,450
επανιστημι, I STAND UP
Mt   10:21   children **will rise** against
Mk   13:12   children **will rise** against

1882   ᴳᴼ1 ᴬᴳ283 ᴸᴺ94 ᴮ3:351 ᴷ5:450 ᴿ1909,461
επανορθωσις, STRAIGHTENING
2Ti   3:16   for reproof, for **correction**

1883   ᴳᴼ19 ᴬᴳ283 ᴸᴺ94 ᴿ1909,507
επανω, UPON
Mt   2: 9   it stopped **over** the place
       5:14   A city built **on** a hill cannot
      21: 7   on them, and he sat **on** them
      23:18   the gift that is **on** the altar
      23:20   by it and by everything **on** it
      23:22   the one who is seated **upon** it
      27:37   **Over** his head they put the
      28: 2   back the stone and sat **on** it
Mk   14: 5   have been sold for **more than**
Lk   4:39   stood **over** her and rebuked the
      10:19   tread **on** snakes and scorpions,
      11:44   people walk **over** them without

      19:17   take charge **of** ten cities
      19:19   rule **over** five cities
Jn   3:31   comes from above is **above** all
       3:31   comes from heaven is **above** all
1C   15: 6   to **more than** five hundred
Re   6: 8   Its **rider's** name was Death,
      20: 3   locked and sealed it **over** him

1883a   ᴳᴼ1 ᴬᴳ283 ᴸᴺ94 ᴮ1:416 ᴷ1:451
επαρατος, CURSED ONES
Jn   7:49   they are **accursed**

1884   ᴳᴼ3 ᴬᴳ283 ᴸᴺ94
επαρκεω, I GIVE RELIEF
1Ti   5:10   **helped** the afflicted
       5:16   let her **assist** them
       5:16   so that it can **assist** those

1885   ᴳᴼ2 ᴬᴳ283 ᴸᴺ94
επαρχεια, PROVINCE
Ac   23:34   what **province** he belonged to
      25: 1   had arrived in the **province**

1886   ᴳᴼ1 ᴬᴳ283 ᴸᴺ94
επαυλις, COTTAGE
Ac   1:20   his **homestead** become desolate

1887   ᴳᴼ17 ᴬᴳ283 ᴸᴺ94 ᴿ1909,839
επαυριον, TOMORROW
Mt   27:62   The **next day,** that is, after
Mk   11:12   On the **following day,** when they
Jn   1:29   The **next day** he saw Jesus
       1:35   The **next day** John again was
       1:43   The **next day** Jesus decided
       6:22   The **next day** the crowd that had
      12:12   The **next day** the great crowd
Ac   10: 9   About noon the **next day,**
      10:23   The **next day** he got up and went
      10:24   The **following day** they came
      14:20   The **next day** he went on with
      20: 7   intended to leave the **next day,**
      21: 8   The **next day** we left and came
      22:30   the **next day** he released him
      23:32   The **next day** they let the
      25: 6   the **next day** he took his seat
      25:23   So on the **next day** Agrippa

1889   ᴳᴼ3 ᴬᴳ283 ᴸᴺ94
επαφρας, EPAPHRAS
Co   1: 7   This you learned from **Epaphras**

| | 4:12 | **Epaphras,** who is one of you |
| Pm | 1:23 | **Epaphras,** my fellow prisoner |

1890   GO1 AG283 LN94 R1909,875
επαφριζω, I FOAM UP
| Ju | 1:13 | **casting up** the **foam** of their |

1891   GO2 AG284 LN94
επαφροδιτος, EPAPHRODITUS
| Ph | 2:25 | to send to you **Epaphroditus** |
| | 4:18 | received from **Epaphroditus** |

1892   GO2 AG284 LN95 R1909,1453
επεγειρω, I RAISE UP
| Ac | 13:50 | **stirred up** persecution against |
| | 14: 2 | the unbelieving Jews **stirred up** |

1893   GO26 AG284 LN95
επει, SINCE
Mt	18:32	**because** you pleaded with me.
	21:46	**because** they regarded him
	27: 6	**since** they are blood money
Mk	15:42	**since** it was the day of
Lk	1:34	**since** I am a virgin
Jn	13:29	**because** Judas had the common
	19:31	**Since** it was the day of
Ro	3: 6	For **then** how could God judge
	11: 6	**otherwise** grace would no longer
	11:22	**otherwise** you also will be cut
1C	5:10	**since** you would then need to
	7:14	**Otherwise,** your children would
	14:12	**since** you are eager for
	14:16	**Otherwise,** if you say a
	15:29	**Otherwise,** what will those
2C	11:18	**since** many boast according
	13: 3	**since** you desire proof that
He	2:14	**Since,** therefore, the children
	4: 6	**Since** therefore it remains open
	5: 2	**since** he himself is subject
	5:11	**since** you have become dull in
	6:13	**because** he had no one greater
	9:17	**since** it is not in force as
	9:26	**since** the foundation of the
	10: 2	**Otherwise,** would they not have
	11:11	**because** he considered him

1894   GO10 AG284 LN95
επειδη, SINCE
| Lk | 7: 1 | **After** Jesus had finished all |

	11: 6	**for** a friend of mine has
Ac	13:46	**Since** you reject it and judge
	14:12	**because** he was the chief
	15:24	**Since** we have heard that
1C	1:21	**since,** in the wisdom of God
	1:22	**For** Jews demand signs and
	14:16	**Otherwise,** if you say a
	15:21	For **since** death came through
Ph	2:26	**for** he has been longing for all

1895   GO1 AG284 LN95
επειδηπερ, SINCE INDEED
| Lk | 1: 1 | **Since** many have undertaken |

1897a   GO1 AG284
επειμι, I COME ON
Ac	7:26	The **next** day he came to some
	16:11	the **following** day to Neapolis
	20:15	on the **following** day we arrived
	21:18	The **next** day Paul went with us
	23:11	That **night** the Lord stood near

1898   GO1 AG284 LN95
επεισαγωγη, BRINGING IN ON
| He | 7:19 | **introduction** of a better hope |

1898a   GO1 AG284 LN95
επεισερχομαι, I COME IN ON
| Lk | 21:35 | For it **will come upon** all |

1899   GO16 AG284 LN95
επειτα, THEN
Lk	16: 7	**Then** he asked another
Jn	11: 7	**Then** after this he said to the
1C	12:28	**then** deeds of power
	12:28	**then** gifts of healing
	15: 6	**Then** he appeared to more than
	15: 7	**Then** he appeared to James
	15:23	**then** at his coming those who
	15:46	and **then** the spiritual
Ga	1:18	**Then** after three years I did go
	1:21	**Then** I went into the regions
	2: 1	**Then** after fourteen years
1Th	4:17	**Then** we who are alive
He	7: 2	**next** he is also king of Salem
	7:27	**then** for those of the people
Ja	3:17	**then** peaceable, gentle, willing
	4:14	little while and **then** vanishes

1900   GO1   AG284   LN95
επεκεινα, BEYOND
Ac   7:43   will remove you **beyond** Babylon

1901   GO1   AG284   LN95   R1909,1614
επεκτεινομαι, STRETCH FORWARD
Ph   3:13   and **straining forward** to what

1902   GO2   AG284   LN95   B1:313   K2:320   R1909,1746
επενδυομαι, I PUT ON
2C   5: 2   longing **to be clothed** with our
     5: 4   but **to be** further **clothed,**

1903   GO1   AG285   LN95   R1902
επενδυτης, OUTER COAT
Jn   21: 7   he put on some **clothes,** for he

1904   GO9   AG285   LN96   B1:320   K2:680   R1909,2064
επερχομαι, I COME ON
Lk   1:35   Holy Spirit **will** come **upon** you
     11:22   one stronger than he **attacks**
     21:26   what **is coming upon** the world
Ac   1: 8   Holy Spirit **has come upon** you
     8:24   what you have said **may happen**
     13:40   said **does** not **happen** to you
     14:19   Jews **came** there from Antioch
Ep   2: 7   so that in the ages **to come**
Ja   5: 1   miseries that **are coming** to you

1905   GO56   AG285   LN96   B2:879   K2:687   R1909,2064
επερωταω, I ASK
Mt   12:10   hand, and they **asked** him
     16: 1   to test Jesus they **asked** him
     17:10   And the disciples **asked** him
     22:23   they **asked** him a **question**
     22:35   **asked** him a **question** to test
     22:41   Jesus **asked** them this **question**
     22:46   to **ask** him any more **questions**
     27:11   and the governor **asked** him
Mk   5: 9   Then Jesus **asked** him
     7: 5   Pharisees and the scribes **asked**
     7:17   his disciples **asked** him about
     8:23   hands on him, he **asked** him
     8:27   he **asked** his disciples
     8:29   He **asked** them, "But who do
     9:11   Then they **asked** him
     9:16   He **asked** them, "What are you
     9:21   Jesus **asked** the father,
     9:28   disciples **asked** him privately
     9:32   and were afraid to **ask** him

     9:33   was in the house he **asked** them
     10: 2   and to test him they **asked**
     10:10   the disciples **asked** him again
     10:17   knelt before him, and **asked**
     11:29   I **will ask** you one question
     12:18   and **asked** him a **question,**
     12:28   answered them well, he **asked**
     12:34   dared **to ask** him any **question**
     13: 3   Andrew **asked** him privately
     14:60   before them and **asked** Jesus
     14:61   Again the high priest **asked** him
     15: 2   Pilate **asked** him, "Are you the
     15: 4   Pilate **asked** him again, "Have
     15:44   he **asked** him whether he had
Lk   2:46   and **asking** them **questions**
     3:10   And the crowds **asked** him
     3:14   Soldiers also **asked** him
     6: 9   I **ask** you, is it lawful to do
     8: 9   Then his disciples **asked** him
     8:30   Jesus then **asked** him
     9:18   disciples near him, he **asked**
     17:20   Once Jesus **was asked** by the
     18:18   A certain ruler **asked** him
     18:40   when he came near, he **asked** him
     20:21   So they **asked** him, "Teacher,
     20:28   **asked** him a **question**
     20:40   to **ask** him another **question**
     21: 7   They **asked** him, "Teacher,
     22:64   kept **asking** him, "Prophesy!
     23: 6   he **asked** whether the man
     23: 9   He **questioned** him at some
Jn   9:23   He is of age; **ask** him.
     18: 7   Again he **asked** them, "Whom
Ac   5:27   The high priest **questioned** them
     23:34   he **asked** what province he
Ro   10:20   those who did not **ask** for me
1C   14:35   **ask** their husbands at home.

1906   GO1   AG285   LN96   B2:879   K2:688   R1905
επερωτημα, ASKING
1P   3:21   but as an **appeal** to God for a

1907   GO5   AG285   LN96   R1909,2192
επεχω, I HOLD ON
Lk   14: 7   When he **noticed** how the guests
Ac   3: 5   he **fixed** his **attention** on them
     19:22   he himself **stayed** for some time
Ph   2:16   your **holding fast** to the word
1Ti   4:16   **Pay close attention** to yourself

1908 GO2 AG285 LN96
επηρεαζω, I MISTREAT
Lk　6:28　pray for those who **abuse** you
1P　3:16　those who **abuse** you for your

1909 GO891 AG285 LN96
επι, ON, UPON [MULTIPLE OCCURRENCES]

1910 GO6 AG289 LN97
επιβαινω, I GO ON
Mt　21: 5　and **mounted on** a donkey
Ac　20:18　day that I **set foot** in Asia,
　　21: 2　we **went on board** and set sail
　　21: 4　not **to go on** to Jerusalem.
　　25: 1　days after Festus **had arrived**
　　27: 2　**Embarking** on a ship

1911 GO18 AG289 LN97 K1:528 R1909,916
επιβαλλω, I THROW ON
Mt　9:16　No one **sews** a piece of unshrunk
　　26:50　they came and **laid** hands on
Mk　4:37　the waves **beat** into the boat
　　11: 7　and **threw** their cloaks on it
　　14:46　Then they **laid** hands on him
　　14:72　he **broke down** and wept
Lk　5:36　and **sews** it on an old garment
　　9:62　who **puts** a hand to the plow
　　15:12　the **share** of the property
　　20:19　they wanted **to lay** hands on him
　　21:12　they **will arrest** you
Jn　7:30　but no one **laid** hands on him
　　7:44　but no one **laid** hands on him
Ac　4: 3　So they **arrested** them and put
　　5:18　**arrested** the apostles and put
　　12: 1　King Herod **laid** violent hands
　　21:27　They **seized** him
1C　7:35　not to **put** any restraint

1912 GO3 AG290 LN97 R1909,916
επιβαρεω, I PUT BURDEN ON
2C　2: 5　not to **exaggerate** it
1Th　2: 9　we **might** not **burden** any of you
2Th　3: 8　we **might** not **burden** any of you

1913 GO3 AG290 LN97
επιβιβαζω, I MOUNT
Lk　10:34　he **put** him on his own animal
　　19:35　the colt, they **set** Jesus on it
Ac　23:24　provide mounts for Paul **to ride**

1914 GO3 AG290 LN97 R1909,991
επιβλεπω, I LOOK ON
Lk　1:48　for he has **looked** with favor
　　9:38　I beg you **to look** at my son
Ja　2: 3　if you **take notice** of the one

1915 GO4 AG290 LN97
επιβλημα, PATCH
Mt　9:16　No one sews a **piece** of unshrunk
Mk　2:21　No one sews a **piece** of unshrunk
Lk　5:36　No one tears a **piece** from a new
　　5:36　**piece** from the new will not

1917 GO4 AG290 LN97 R1909,994
επιβουλη, PLAN AGAINST
Ac　9:24　but their **plot** became known
　　20: 3　when a **plot** was made against
　　20:19　through the **plots** of the Jews
　　23:30　would be a **plot** against the
　　　　　man

1918 GO1 AG290 LN97
επιγαμβρευω, I MARRY
Mt　22:24　brother **shall marry** the widow

1919 GO7 AG290 LN97 B1:517 K1:680 R1909,1093
επιγειος, ON EARTH
Jn　3:12　told you about **earthly** things
1C　15:40　heavenly bodies and **earthly**
　　15:40　that of the **earthly** is another.
2C　5: 1　For we know that if the **earthly**
Ph　2:10　bend, in heaven and **on earth**
　　3:19　minds are set on **earthly** things
Ja　3:15　but is **earthly**, unspiritual,

1920 GO1 AG290 LN98 R1909,1096
επιγινομαι, I BECOME ON
Ac　28:13　there a south wind **sprang up**

1921 GO44 AG291 LN98 B2:392 K1:689 R1909,1097
επιγινωσκω, I PERCEIVE
Mt　7:16　You **will know** them by their
　　7:20　Thus you **will know** them by
　　11:27　no one **knows** the Son except
　　11:27　no one **knows** the Father except
　　14:35　people of that place **recognized**
　　17:12　they did not **recognize** him
Mk　2: 8　At once Jesus **perceived** in his
　　5:30　Immediately **aware** that power
　　6:33　saw them going and **recognized**

	6:54	people at once **recognized** him
Lk	1: 4	so that you may **know** the truth
	1:22	they **realized** that he had seen
	5:22	When Jesus **perceived** their
	7:37	**having learned** that he was
	23: 7	when he **learned** that he was
	24:16	were kept from **recognizing** him
	24:31	and they **recognized** him
Ac	3:10	they **recognized** him as the one
	4:13	**recognized** them as companions
	9:30	the believers **learned** of it
	12:14	On **recognizing** Peter's voice
	19:34	**recognized** that he was a Jew
	22:24	**to find out** the reason for
	22:29	**realized** that Paul was a Roman
	23:28	I wanted **to know** the charge
	24: 8	you will be able **to learn** from
	24:11	As you can **find out,** it is not
	25:10	the Jews, as you very well **know**
	27:39	they did not **recognize** the land
	28: 1	we then **learned** that the island
Ro	1:32	They **know** God's decree
1C	13:12	then I will **know** fully, even as
	13:12	even as I **have been fully known**
	14:37	must **acknowledge** that what I am
	16:18	So **give recognition** to such
2C	1:13	can read and also **understand**
	1:13	I hope you will **understand**
	1:14	you have already **understood** us
	6: 9	and yet **are** well **known;**
	13: 5	Do you not **realize** that Jesus
Co	1: 6	truly **comprehended** the grace
1Ti	4: 3	those who believe and **know**
2P	2:21	never to **have known** the way
	2:21	after **knowing** it, to turn back

1922 GO20 AG291 LN98 B2:392 K1:689 R1921
επιγνωσις, PERCEPTION

Ro	1:28	not see fit to **acknowledge** God
	3:20	law comes the **knowledge** of sin
	10: 2	but it is not **enlightened**
Ep	1:17	revelation as you come to **know**
	4:13	the **knowledge** of the Son of God
Ph	1: 9	with **knowledge** and full insight
Co	1: 9	the **knowledge** of God's will
	1:10	grow in the **knowledge** of God.
	2: 2	have the **knowledge** of God's
	3:10	is being renewed in **knowledge**
1Ti	2: 4	to come to the **knowledge**

2Ti	2:25	will repent and come to **know**
	3: 7	can never arrive at a **knowledge**
Ti	1: 1	the **knowledge** of the truth
Pm	1: 6	when you **perceive** all the good
He	10:26	the **knowledge** of the truth
2P	1: 2	abundance in the **knowledge**
	1: 3	through the **knowledge** of him
	1: 8	unfruitful in the **knowledge**
	2:20	through the **knowledge** of our

1923 GO5 AG291 LN98 B3:489 R1924
επιγραφη, WRITTEN ON

Mt	22:20	head is this, and whose **title**
Mk	12:16	head is this, and whose **title**
	15:26	The **inscription** of the charge
Lk	20:24	Whose head and whose **title**
	23:38	There was also an **inscription**

1924 GO5 AG291 LN98 B3:489 R1909,1125
επιγραφω, I WRITE ON

Mk	15:26	The **inscription** of the charge
Ac	17:23	an altar with the **inscription**
He	8:10	**write** them on their hearts
	10:16	**will write** them on their minds
Re	21:12	on the gates are **inscribed**

1925 GO7 AG291 LN98 R1909,1166
επιδεικνυμι, I SHOW ON

Mt	16: 1	they asked him to **show** them
	22:19	**Show** me the coin used for the
	24: 1	came **to point out** to him
Lk	17:14	Go and **show** yourselves to the
Ac	9:39	weeping and **showing** tunics and
	18:28	**showing** by the scriptures
He	6:17	to **show** even more clearly

1926 GO2 AG292 LN98 R1909,1209
επιδεχομαι, I WELCOME

3J	1: 9	does not **acknowledge** our
	1:10	refuses to **welcome** the friends

1927 GO2 AG292 LN98
επιδημεω, I LIVE TEMPORARILY

Ac	2:10	Cyrene, and **visitors** from Rome
	17:21	Athenians and the **foreigners**

1928 GO1 AG292 LN98
επιδιατασσομαι, I ADD

Ga	3:15	no one adds to it or **annuls** it

1929 GO9 AG292 LN98 R1909,1325
επιδιδωμι, I GIVE ON

Mt	7: 9	for bread, **will give** a stone
	7:10	for a fish, **will give** a snake
Lk	4:17	of the prophet Isaiah **was given**
	11:11	**will give** a snake instead
	11:12	an egg, **will give** a scorpion
	24:30	broke it, and **gave** it to them
	24:42	**gave** him a piece of broiled
Ac	15:30	they **delivered** the letter
	27:15	we **gave way** to it and were

1930 GO1 AG292 LN98
επιδιορθοω, I SET STRAIGHT

| Ti | 1: 5 | you **should put in order** what |

1931 GO1 AG292 LN98
επιδυω, I SET

| Ep | 4:26 | **do** not **let** the sun **go down** |

1932 GO2 AG292 LN98 B2:256 K2:588 R1933
επιεικεια, GENTLENESS

| Ac | 24: 4 | your customary **graciousness.** |
| 2C | 10: 1 | by the meekness and **gentleness** |

1933 GO5 AG292 LN98 B2:256 K2:588
επιεικης, GENTLE

Ph	4: 5	Let your **gentleness** be known
1Ti	3: 3	not violent but **gentle,**
Ti	3: 2	quarreling, to be **gentle**
Ja	3:17	**gentle,** willing to yield
1P	2:18	those who are kind and **gentle**

1934 GO13 AG292 LN98 B3:530 K2:895 R1909,2212
επιζητεω, I SEEK AFTER

Mt	6:32	the Gentiles who **strive for** all
	12:39	generation **asks for** a sign
	16: 4	generation **asks for** a sign
Lk	4:42	the crowds **were looking for** him
	12:30	that **strive after** all these
Ac	12:19	Herod **had searched for** him
	13: 7	**wanted** to hear the word of God
	19:39	anything further you **want**
Ro	11: 7	to obtain what it **was seeking**
Ph	4:17	Not that I **seek** the gift
	4:17	but I **seek** the profit that
He	11:14	they **are seeking** a homeland
	13:14	we **are looking for** the city

1935 GO1 AG292 LN98 R1909,2288
επιθανατιος, DEATH SENTENCE

| 1C | 4: 9 | as **though sentenced to death** |

1936 GO4 AG293 LN98 K8:159 R2007
επιθεσις, SETTING ON

Ac	8:18	through the **laying on** of the
1Ti	4:14	with the **laying on** of hands
2Ti	1: 6	through the **laying on** of my
He	6: 2	baptisms, **laying on** of hands

1937 GO17 AG293 LN98 B1:456 K3:168
επιθυμεω, I DESIRE

Mt	5:28	looks at a woman with **lust**
	13:17	righteous people **longed** to see
Lk	15:16	He would **gladly** have filled
	16:21	**longed** to satisfy his hunger
	17:22	when you **will long** to see one
	22:15	I **have** eagerly **desired** to eat
Ac	20:33	I **coveted** no one's silver
Ro	7: 7	You **shall** not **covet.**
	13: 9	You shall not **covet**
1C	10: 6	not desire evil as they **did**
Ga	5:17	For what the flesh **desires**
1Ti	3: 1	of bishop **desires** a noble task
He	6:11	we **want** each one of you to show
Ja	4: 2	You **want** something and do not
1P	1:12	things into which angels **long**
Re	9: 6	they **will long** to die

1938 GO1 AG293 LN99 K3:172 R1937
επιθυμητης, DESIRER

| 1C | 10: 6 | that we might not **desire** evil |

1939 GO38 AG293 LN99 B1:456 K3:168 R1937
επιθυμια, DESIRE

Mk	4:19	**desire** for other things come in
Lk	22:15	I have **eagerly** desired to eat
Jn	8:44	to do your father's **desires**
Ro	1:24	God gave them up in the **lusts**
	6:12	to make you obey their **passions**
	7: 7	known what it is to **covet**
	7: 8	in me all kinds of **covetousness**
	13:14	to gratify its **desires**
Ga	5:16	do not gratify the **desires**
	5:24	with its passions and **desires**
Ep	2: 3	following the **desires** of flesh
	4:22	and deluded by its **lusts**
Ph	1:23	my **desire** is to depart and be
Co	3: 5	impurity, passion, evil **desire**

1Th	2:17	we longed with great **eagerness**		25:21	Paul **had appealed** to be kept
	4: 5	not with **lustful** passion		25:25	he **appealed** to his Imperial
1Ti	6: 9	senseless and harmful **desires**		26:32	if he had not **appealed** to the
2Ti	2:22	Shun youthful **passions**		28:19	I was compelled **to appeal**
	3: 6	swayed by all kinds of **desires**	Ro	10:12	to all who **call on** him
	4: 3	to suit their own **desires**		10:13	Everyone who **calls on** the name
Ti	2:12	impiety and worldly **passions**		10:14	But how are they to **call on** one
	3: 3	slaves to various **passions**	1C	1: 2	**call on** the name of our Lord
Ja	1:14	is tempted by one's own **desire**	2C	1:23	But I **call on** God as witness
	1:15	when that **desire** has conceived	2Ti	2:22	who **call on** the Lord from a
1P	1:14	**desires** that you formerly had	He	11:16	**to be called** their God;
	2:11	to abstain from the **desires**	Ja	2: 7	name that was **invoked** over you
	4: 2	no longer by human **desires**	1P	1:17	If you **invoke** as Father the one
	4: 3	**passions,** drunkenness, revels			
2P	1: 4	in the world because of **lust**			

1942   GO1 AG294 LN99
επικαλυμμα, COVER OVER
1P   2:16   use your freedom as a **pretext**

	2:10	their flesh in depraved **lust**
	2:18	and with licentious **desires**
	3: 3	indulging their own **lusts**

1943   GO1 AG294 LN99 R1909,2572
επικαλυπτω, I COVER OVER
Ro   4: 7   and whose sins **are covered**

1J	2:16	the **desire** of the flesh
	2:16	the **desire** of the eyes
	2:17	And the world and its **desire**
Ju	1:16	they indulge their own **lusts**
	1:18	their own ungodly **lusts**
Re	18:14	for which your soul **longed**

1944   GO2 AG294 LN99 B1:416 K1:451 R1909,2672
επικαταρατος, CURSE ON
Ga   3:10   **Cursed** is everyone who does not
   3:13   **Cursed** is everyone who hangs

1940   GO1 AG293 LN99 R1909,2523
επικαθιζω, I SIT ON
Mt   21: 7   on them, and he **sat on** them

1945   GO7 AG294 LN99 K3:655 R1909,2749
επικειμαι, I LIE ON

Lk	5: 1	while Jesus **was standing beside**
	23:23	But **they** kept urgently demanding
Jn	11:38	a stone **was lying against** it
	21: 9	with fish **on** it, and bread
Ac	27:20	and no small tempest **raged**
1C	9:16	for an obligation **is laid on** me
He	9:10	time comes **to set** things right

1941   GO30 AG294 LN99 B2:874 K3:496 R1909,2564
επικαλεω, I CALL ON

Mt	10:25	If they **have called** the master
Ac	1:23	who **was** also **known** as Justus,
	2:21	everyone who **calls on** the name
	4:36	the apostles **gave** the **name**
	7:59	stoning Stephen, he **prayed**
	9:14	to bind all who **invoke** your
	9:21	those who **invoked** this name
	10: 5	Simon who **is called** Peter
	10:18	Simon, who **was called** Peter
	10:32	Simon, who **is called** Peter
	11:13	Simon, who **is called** Peter
	12:12	John whose **other name was** Mark
	12:25	John, whose **other name was** Mark
	15:17	whom my name **has been called**
	22:16	**calling on** his name
	25:11	I **appeal** to the emperor
	25:12	You **have appealed** to the

1945a   GO1 AG294 LN99
επικελλω, I GROUND
Ac   27:41   they **ran** the ship **aground**

1946   GO1 AG294 LN99
επικουρειος, EPICUREAN
Ac   17:18   Also some **Epicurean** and Stoic

1947   GO1 AG294 LN99
επικουρια, HELP
Ac   26:22   I have had **help** from God

1948   GO1 AG295 LN99 R1909,2919
επικρινω, I JUDGE ON
Lk   23:24   So Pilate **gave** his **verdict**

1949   GO19 AG295 LN99 B3:747 K4:9 R1909,2983
επιλαμβανομαι, I TAKE ON
Mt   14:31   out his hand and **caught** him
Mk   8:23   He **took** the blind man by the
Lk   9:47   **took** a little child and put it
    14: 4   Jesus **took** him and healed him
    20:20   in order **to trap** him by what
    20:26   **to trap** him by what he said
    23:26   they **seized** a man, Simon of
Ac   9:27   But Barnabas **took** him, brought
    16:19   they **seized** Paul and Silas
    17:19   So they **took** him and brought
    18:17   all of them **seized** Sosthenes
    21:30   They **seized** Paul and dragged
    21:33   the tribune came, **arrested** him
    23:19   tribune **took** him by the hand
1Ti   6:12   **take hold** of the eternal life
    6:19   so that they **may take hold**
He   2:16   he **did** not **come to help** angels
    2:16   **but** the descendants of Abraham
    8: 9   when I **took** them by the hand

1950   GO8 AG295 LN99 R1909,2990
επιλανθανομαι, I FORGET
Mt   16: 5   they **had forgotten** to bring
Mk   8:14   Now the disciples **had forgotten**
Lk   12: 6   not one of them **is forgotten**
Ph   3:13   **forgetting** what lies behind
He   6:10   he **will** not **overlook** your work
    13: 2   **Do** not **neglect** to show
    13:16   **Do** not **neglect** to do good
Ja   1:24   **forget** what they were like

1951   GO2 AG295 LN99 R1909,3004
επιλεγω, I CALL ON
Jn   5: 2   **called in** Hebrew Beth-zatha
Ac   15:40   Paul **chose** Silas and set out

1952   GO1 AG295 LN99 R1909,3007
επιλειπω, I LEAVE
He   11:32   For time **would fail** me to tell

1952a   GO1 AG295 LN99
επιλειχω, I LICK
Lk   16:21   the dogs would come and **lick**

1953   GO1 AG295 LN99 R1950
επιλησμονη, FORGETFULNESS
Ja   1:25   being not hearers who **forget**

1954   GO1 AG295 LN99 R1909,3062
επιλοιπος, REMAINING
1P   4: 2   so as to live for the **rest** of

1955   GO1 AG295 LN99 B1:576 K4:328 R1956
επιλυσις, RELEASE
2P   1:20   of one's own **interpretation**

1956   GO2 AG295 LN100 B1:576 K4:328 R1909,3089
επιλυω, I LOOSE, I UNRAVEL
Mk   4:34   but he **explained** everything
Ac   19:39   **must be settled** in the regular

1957   GO1 AG296 LN100 B3:1042 K4:508 R1909,3140
επιμαρτυρεω, I TESTIFY
1P   5:12   **testify** that this is the true

1958   GO1 AG296 LN100 R1959
επιμελεια, CARE
Ac   27: 3   to his friends to be **cared** for

1959   GO3 AG296 LN100
επιμελεομαι, I TAKE CARE
Lk   10:34   an inn, and **took care** of him
    10:35   **Take care** of him; and when I
1Ti   3: 5   how can he **take care** of God's

1960   GO1 AG296 LN100 R1959
επιμελως, CAREFULLY
Lk   15: 8   search **carefully** until she finds

1961   GO16 AG296 LN100 B3:223 R1909,3306
επιμενω, I STAY ON
Jn   8: 7   they **kept on** questioning him
Ac   10:48   invited him **to stay** for several
    12:16   Peter **continued** knocking
    21: 4   **stayed** there for seven days
    21:10   While we **were staying** there
    28:12   **stayed** there for three days
    28:14   were invited **to stay** with them
Ro   6: 1   Should we **continue** in sin
    11:22   provided you **continue** in his
    11:23   they do not **persist** in unbelief
1C   16: 7   hope to **spend** some time with
    16: 8   But I will **stay** in Ephesus
Ga   1:18   **stayed** with him fifteen days

Ph　1:24　but to **remain** in the flesh
Co　1:23　that you **continue** securely
1Ti　4:16　**continue** in these things

1962　ᴳᴼ1　ᴬᴳ296　ᴸᴺ100
επινευω, I NOD ON
Ac　18:20　him to stay longer, he **declined**

1963　ᴳᴼ1　ᴬᴳ296　ᴸᴺ100
επινοια, THOUGHT ON
Ac　8:22　the **intent** of your heart may

1964　ᴳᴼ1　ᴬᴳ296　ᴸᴺ100　ᴷ5:466　ᴿ1965
επιορκεω, I PERJURE
Mt　5:33　You **shall** not **swear falsely**

1965　ᴳᴼ1　ᴬᴳ296　ᴸᴺ100　ᴷ5:466　ᴿ1909,3727
επιορκος, PERJURER
1Ti　1:10　traders, liars, **perjurers**

1967　ᴳᴼ2　ᴬᴳ296　ᴸᴺ100　ᴮ1:251　ᴷ2:590
επιουσιος, SUSTAINING
Mt　6:11　us this day our **daily** bread
Lk　11: 3　us each day our **daily** bread

1968　ᴳᴼ11　ᴬᴳ297　ᴸᴺ100　ᴿ1909,4098
επιπιπτω, I FALL ON
Mk　3:10　**pressed upon** him to touch him
Lk　1:12　and fear **overwhelmed** him
　　15:20　**put his arms around** him
Ac　8:16　the Spirit **had** not **come upon**
　　10:44　Holy Spirit **fell upon** all
　　11:15　Holy Spirit **fell upon** them
　　19:17　everyone **was** awestruck
　　20:10　**bending over** him took him
　　20:37　they **embraced** Paul and kissed
Ro　15: 3　insult you **have fallen on** me
Re　11:11　who saw them **were** terrified

1969　ᴳᴼ1　ᴬᴳ297　ᴸᴺ100
επιπλησσω, I STRIKE AT
1Ti　5: 1　Do not **speak harshly** to an

1971　ᴳᴼ9　ᴬᴳ297　ᴸᴺ100
επιποθεω, I DESIRE LONGINGLY
Ro　1:11　For I **am longing** to see you
2C　5: 2　**longing** to be clothed
　　9:14　**long for** you and pray for you
Ph　1: 8　how I **long** for all of you
　　2:26　he **has been longing** for all

1Th　3: 6　remember us kindly and **long** to
2Ti　1: 4　I **long** to see you so that I
Ja　4: 5　God **yearns** jealously for the
1P　2: 2　infants, **long** for the pure

1972　ᴳᴼ2　ᴬᴳ298　ᴸᴺ100　ᴿ1971
επιποθησις, LONGING DESIRE
2C　7: 7　he told us of your **longing**
　　7:11　what alarm, what **longing**

1973　ᴳᴼ1　ᴬᴳ298　ᴸᴺ100　ᴿ1971
επιποθητος, DESIRED ONES
Ph　4: 1　whom I love and **long for**

1974　ᴳᴼ1　ᴬᴳ298　ᴸᴺ100　ᴿ1971
επιποθια, DESIRE
Ro　15:23　I **desire,** as I have for many

1975　ᴳᴼ1　ᴬᴳ298　ᴸᴺ100　ᴿ1909,4198
επιπορευομαι, I TRAVEL ON
Lk　8: 4　town after town **came** to him

1976　ᴳᴼ1　ᴬᴳ298　ᴸᴺ100
επιραπτω, I SEW ON
Mk　2:21　No one **sews** a piece of unshrunk

1977　ᴳᴼ2　ᴬᴳ298　ᴸᴺ100　ᴷ6:991　ᴿ1909,4496
επιριπτω, I THROW ON
Lk　19:35　and after **throwing** their cloaks
1P　5: 7　**Cast** all your anxiety on him

1978　ᴳᴼ2　ᴬᴳ298　ᴸᴺ100　ᴷ7:267
επισημος, PROMINENT
Mt　27:16　they had a **notorious** prisoner
Ro　16: 7　**prominent** among the apostles

1979　ᴳᴼ1　ᴬᴳ298　ᴸᴺ101
επισιτισμος, PROVISIONS
Lk　9:12　to lodge and get **provisions**

1980　ᴳᴼ11　ᴬᴳ298　ᴸᴺ101　ᴮ1:188　ᴷ2:599
επισκεπτομαι, I LOOK ON
Mt　25:36　in prison and you **visited** me
　　25:43　in prison and you did not **visit**
Lk　1:68　he has **looked favorably** on his
　　1:78　from on high **will break** upon us
　　7:16　God has **looked favorably** on his
Ac　6: 3　**select** from among yourselves
　　7:23　to **visit** his relatives.
　　15:14　God first **looked favorably**

	15:36	**visit** the believers in every
He	2: 6	mortals, that you **care for** them
Ja	1:27	**to care for** orphans and widows

1980a GO1 AG298 LN101
επισκευαζομαι, I PREPARE
| Ac | 21:15 | we **got ready** and started to go |

1981 GO1 AG298 LN101 B3:814 K7:386
επισκηνοω, I SET UP TENT
| 2C | 12: 9 | power of Christ **may dwell** in me |

1982 GO5 AG298 LN101 B3:553 K7:399 R1909,4639
επισκιαζω, I OVERSHADOW
Mt	17: 5	bright cloud **overshadowed** them
Mk	9: 7	Then a cloud **overshadowed** them
Lk	1:35	Most High **will overshadow** you
	9:34	a cloud came and **overshadowed**
Ac	5:15	that Peter's **shadow might fall**

1983 GO2 AG298 LN101 B1:188 K2:599 R1909,4648
επισκοπεω, I OVERSEE
| He | 12:15 | **See to** it that no one fails |
| 1P | 5: 2 | **exercising** the oversight, not |

1984 GO4 AG299 LN101 B1:188 K2:606 R1980
επισκοπη, OVERSIGHT
Lk	19:44	the time of your **visitation**
Ac	1:20	take his **position** of **overseer**
1Ti	3: 1	God when he comes to **judge**

1985 GO5 AG299 LN101 B1:188 K2:608 R1983
επισκοπος, OVERSEER
Ac	20:28	Spirit has made you **overseers**
Ph	1: 1	with the **bishops** and deacons
1Ti	3: 2	**bishop** must be above reproach
Ti	1: 7	For a **bishop,** as God's steward
1P	2:25	and **guardian** of your souls

1986 GO1 AG299 LN101
επισπαομαι, I PULL OVER
| 1C | 7:18 | to **remove** the marks of circumcision. |

1986a GO1 AG300 LN101
επισπειρω, I SOW ON
| Mt | 13:25 | **sowed** weeds among the wheat |

1987 GO14 AG300 LN101
επισταμαι, I UNDERSTAND
| Mk | 14:68 | I do not know or **understand** |

Ac	10:28	**know** that it is unlawful
	15: 7	**know** that in the early days
	18:25	**knew** only the baptism of John
	19:15	Jesus I know, and Paul I **know**
	19:25	**know** that we get our wealth
	20:18	**know** how I lived among you
	22:19	they themselves **know** that in
	24:10	**knowing** that for many years
	26:26	Indeed the king **knows** about
1Ti	6: 4	**understanding** nothing, and has
He	11: 8	not **knowing** where he was going
Ja	4:14	Yet you do not even **know** what
Ju	1:10	whatever they do not **understand**

1987a GO2 AG300 LN101
επιστασις, ATTENTION
| Ac | 24:12 | temple or **stirring up** a crowd |
| 2C | 11:28 | I am under daily **pressure** |

1988 GO7 AG300 LN101 K2:622
επιστατης, MASTER TEACHER
Lk	5: 5	Simon answered, "**Master,** we
	8:24	**Master,** Master, we are
	8:24	**Master,** we are perishing
	8:45	**Master,** the crowds surround
	9:33	**Master,** it is good for us to
	9:49	John answered, "**Master,** we saw
	17:13	Jesus, **Master,** have mercy on us

1989 GO3 AG300 LN101 B1:246 K7:593
επιστελλω, I WRITE LETTER
Ac	15:20	but we **should write** to them
	21:25	we **have sent** a **letter** with our
He	13:22	I **have written** to you briefly

1990 GO1 AG300 LN101
επιστημων, UNDERSTANDING
| Ja | 3:13 | Who is wise and **understanding** |

1991 GO4 AG300 LN101 K7:653 R1909,4741
επιστηριζω, I STRENGTHEN
Ac	14:22	they **strengthened** the souls
	15:32	and **strengthen** the believers
	15:41	**strengthening** the churches
	18:23	**strengthening** all the disciples

1992 GO24 AG300 LN101 B1:246 K7:593 R1989
επιστολη, LETTER
| Ac | 9: 2 | asked him for **letters** to the |

	15:30	they delivered the **letter**
	22: 5	I also received **letters** to the
	23:25	wrote a **letter** to this effect
	23:33	delivered the **letter** to the
Ro	16:22	the writer of this **letter**
1C	5: 9	I wrote to you in my **letter**
	16: 3	whom you approve with **letters**
2C	3: 1	**letters** of recommendation
	3: 2	You yourselves are our **letter**
	3: 3	you are a **letter** of Christ
	7: 8	made you sorry with my **letter**
	7: 8	made you sorry with my **letter**
	10: 9	frighten you with my **letters**
	10:10	His **letters** are weighty
	10:11	what we say by **letter**
Co	4:16	when this **letter** has been read
1Th	5:27	this **letter** be read to all
2Th	2: 2	or by word or by **letter**
	2:15	of mouth or by our **letter**
	3:14	what we say in this **letter**
	3:17	mark in every **letter** of mine
2P	3: 1	beloved, the **second** letter
	3:16	as he does in all his **letters**

1993   GO1 AG301 LN101 R1909,4750
επιστομιζω, I MUZZLE MOUTH

Ti	1:11	they **must be silenced,** since

1994   GO36 AG301 LN101 B1:353 K7:722 R1909,4762
επιστρεφω, I RETURN

Mt	10:13	I **will return** to my house
	13:15	with their heart and **turn**
	24:18	must not **turn** back to get
Mk	4:12	they may not **turn** again
	5:30	**turned** about in the crowd
	8:33	But **turning** and looking at his
	13:16	in the field **must** not **turn** back
Lk	1:16	He **will turn** many of the people
	1:17	to **turn** the hearts of parents
	2:39	they **returned** to Galilee
	8:55	Her spirit **returned,** and she
	17: 4	**turns** back to you seven times
	17:31	in the field **must** not **turn** back
	22:32	when once you **have turned** back
Jn	21:20	Peter **turned** and saw the
Ac	3:19	**turn** to God so that your sins
	9:35	saw him and **turned** to the Lord
	9:40	He **turned** to the body and said
	11:21	became believers and **turned**

	14:15	you should **turn** from these
	15:19	those Gentiles who are **turning**
	15:36	**return** and visit the believers
	16:18	**turned** and said to the spirit
	26:18	they may **turn** from darkness
	26:20	**turn** to God and do deeds
	28:27	with their heart and **turn**
2C	3:16	when one **turns** to the Lord
Ga	4: 9	how can you **turn** back again
1Th	1: 9	you **turned** to God from idols
Ja	5:19	is **brought back** by another
	5:20	whoever **brings back** a sinner
1P	2:25	have **returned** to the shepherd
2P	2:22	dog **turns** back to its own vomit
Re	1:12	I **turned** to see whose voice
	1:12	on **turning** I saw seven golden

1995   GO1 AG301 LN102 B1:354 K7:722 R1994
επιστροφη, RETURN

Ac	15: 3	the **conversion** of the Gentiles

1996   GO8 AG301 LN102 B2:33 R1909,4863
επισυναγω, I BRING TOGETHER

Mt	23:37	**gather** your children together
	23.37	as a hen **gathers** her brood
	24:31	they will **gather** his elect
Mk	1:33	And the whole city was **gathered**
	13:27	**gather** his elect from the four
Lk	12: 1	crowd **gathered** by the thousands
	13:34	**gather** your children together
	17:37	there the vultures will **gather**

1997   GO2 AG301 LN102 B2:33 K7:841 R1996
επισυναγωγη, BRING TOGETHER

2Th	2: 1	**being gathered together** to him,
He	10:25	not neglecting **to meet together**

1998   GO1 AG301 LN102 R1909,4936
επισυντρεχω, I RUN ON TOGETHER

Mk	9:25	a crowd **came running together**

2000   GO1 AG302 LN102
επισφαλης, UNSECURE

Ac	27: 9	and sailing was now **dangerous**

2001   GO1 AG302 LN102
επισχυω, I AM STRONG

Lk	23: 5	But they were **insistent**

2002 ᴳᴼ1 ᴬᴳ302 ᴸᴺ102 ᴷ7:1094 ᴿ1909,4987
επισωρευω, I HEAP ON
2Ti 4: 3 **will accumulate** for themselves

2003 ᴳᴼ7 ᴬᴳ302 ᴸᴺ102 ᴷ8:36 ᴿ2004
επιταγη, ORDER
Ro 16:26 the **command** of the eternal God
1C 7: 6 of concession, not of **command**
    7:25 I have no **command** of the Lord
2C 8: 8 I do not say this as a **command**
1Ti 1: 1 the **command** of God our Savior
Ti 1: 3 the **command** of God our Savior
    2:15 reprove with all **authority**

2004 ᴳᴼ10 ᴬᴳ302 ᴸᴺ102 ᴿ1909,5021
επιτασσω, I ORDER
Mk 1:27 He **commands** even the unclean
    6:27 **sent** a soldier . . . **with orders**
    6:39 Then he **ordered** them to get all
    9:25 I **command** you, come out of him,
Lk 4:36 he **commands** the unclean spirits
    8:25 he **commands** even the winds
    8:31 begged him not **to order** them
    14:22 what you **ordered** has been done
Ac 23: 2 high priest Ananias **ordered**
Pm 1: 8 to **command** you to do your duty

2005 ᴳᴼ10 ᴬᴳ302 ᴸᴺ102 ᴷ8:61 ᴿ1909,5055
επιτελεω, I COMPLETE THOROUGHLY
Ro 15:28 So, when I **have completed** this
2C 7: 1 **making** holiness **perfect** in the
    8: 6 so he **should** also **complete**
    8:11 now **finish** doing it
    8:11 by **completing** it according to
Ga 3: 3 are you now **ending** with the
Ph 1: 6 will **bring** it **to completion**
He 8: 5 he was about to **erect** the tent
    9: 6 the first tent **to carry out**
1P 5: 9 are **undergoing** the same kinds

2006 ᴳᴼ1 ᴬᴳ302 ᴸᴺ102
επιτηδειος, NEEDFUL
Ja 2:16 not supply their bodily **needs**

2007 ᴳᴼ39 ᴬᴳ302 ᴸᴺ102 ᴮ2:146 ᴷ8:159 ᴿ1909,5087
επιτιθημι, I SET ON
Mt 9:18 come and **lay** your hand **on** her
    19:13 he **might lay** his hands **on** them
    19:15 And he **laid** his hands **on** them
    21: 7 and **put** their cloaks **on** them

23: 4 and **lay** them **on** the shoulders
27:29 they **put** it **on** his head.
27:37 **put** the charge against him,
Mk 3:16 to whom he **gave** the name Peter
    3:17 he **gave** the name Boanerges
    5:23 Come and **lay** your hands **on** her
    6: 5 he **laid** his hands **on** a few
    7:32 begged him **to lay** his hand **on**
    8:23 and **laid** his hands **on** him
    8:25 Jesus **laid** his hands **on** his
    16:18 **will lay** their hands **on** the
Lk 4:40 he **laid** his hands **on** each
    10:30 who stripped him, **beat** him
    13:13 When he **laid** his hands **on** her
    15: 5 he **lays** it **on** his shoulders
    23:26 and they **laid** the cross **on** him
Jn 9:15 He **put** mud **on** my eyes
    19: 2 crown of thorns and **put** it **on**
Ac 6: 6 and **laid** their hands **on** them.
    8:17 John **laid** their hands **on** them
    8:19 anyone on whom I **lay** my hands
    9:12 **lay** his hands **on** him so that
    9:17 He **laid** his hands **on** Saul
    13: 3 they **laid** their hands **on** them
    15:10 by **placing** on the neck of the
    15:28 to **impose** on you no further
    16:23 After they had **given** them
    18:10 no one **will lay** a hand **on** you
    19: 6 Paul **had laid** his hands **on** them
    28: 3 **was putting** it **on** the fire
    28: 8 and **putting** his hands **on** him
    28:10 they **put on** board all the
1Ti 5:22 Do not **ordain** anyone hastily
Re 22:18 if anyone **adds** to them
    22:18 God **will add** to that person

2008 ᴳᴼ29 ᴬᴳ303 ᴸᴺ102 ᴮ1:572 ᴷ2:623
επιτιμαω, I ADMONISH
Mt 8:26 **rebuked** the winds and the sea
    12:16 he **ordered** them not to make
    16:22 aside and began to **rebuke** him
    17:18 Jesus **rebuked** the demon
    19:13 **spoke sternly** to those who
    20:31 crowd **sternly ordered** them
Mk 1:25 But Jesus **rebuked** him
    3:12 But he **sternly ordered** them
    4:39 woke up and **rebuked** the wind
    8:30 he **sternly ordered** them not to
    8:32 aside and began to **rebuke** him

	8:33	**rebuked** Peter and said
	9:25	he **rebuked** the unclean spirit
	10:13	the disciples **spoke sternly**
	10:48	Many **sternly ordered** him to be
Lk	4:35	But Jesus **rebuked** him
	4:39	stood over her and **rebuked**
	4:41	But he **rebuked** them and would
	8:24	woke up and **rebuked** the wind
	9:21	**ordered** and commanded them
	9:42	**rebuked** the unclean spirit
	9:55	But he turned and **rebuked** them
	17: 3	you must **rebuke** the offender
	18:15	they **sternly ordered** them not
	18:39	**sternly ordered** him to be quiet
	19:39	**order** your disciples to stop
	23:40	But the other **rebuked** him
2Ti	4: 2	convince, **rebuke,** and encourage
Ju	1: 9	The Lord **rebuke** you!

2009   GO1 AG303 LN102 B1:572 K2:627
επιτιμια, ADMONISHMENT
2C   2: 6   **punishment** by the majority

2010   GO18 AG303 LN102
επιτρεπω, I ALLOW
Mt	8:21	**let** me go and bury my father
	19: 8	Moses **allowed** you to divorce
Mk	5:13	So he **gave** them **permission**
	10: 4	Moses **allowed** a man to write
Lk	8:32	begged Jesus to **let** them enter
	8:32	So he **gave** them **permission**
	9:59	**let** me go and bury my father
	9:61	**let** me first say farewell
Jn	19:38	Pilate **gave** him **permission**
Ac	21:39	**let** me speak to the people
	21:40	he had **given** him **permission**
	26: 1	You **have permission** to speak
	27: 3	**allowed** him to go to his
	28:16	Paul was **allowed** to live by
1C	14:34	For they **are** not **permitted**
	16: 7	with you, if the Lord **permits**
1Ti	2:12	I **permit** no woman to teach
He	6: 3	will do this, if God **permits**

2011   GO1 AG303 LN102 R2010
επιτροπη, ALLOWANCE
Ac 26:12   the authority and **commission**

2012   GO3 AG303 LN102
επιτροπος, GOVERNOR

Mt	20: 8	vineyard said to his **manager**
Lk	8: 3	wife of Herod's **steward** Chuza
Ga	4: 2	they remain under **guardians**

2013   GO5 AG303 LN102 R1909,5177
επιτυγχανω, I OBTAIN
Ro	11: 7	Israel failed **to obtain**
	11: 7	The elect **obtained** it,
He	6:15	endured, **obtained** the promise
	11:33	**obtained** promises, shut the
Ja	4: 2	something and cannot **obtain** it

2014   GO4 AG304 LN103 B3:317 K9:7 R1909,5316
επιφαινω, I APPEAR
Lk	1:79	to **give light** to those who sit
Ac	27:20	neither sun nor stars **appeared**
Ti	2:11	the grace of God **has appeared,**
	3: 4	of God our Savior **appeared**

2015   GO6 AG304 LN103 B3:317 K9:7 R2016
επιφανεια, APPEARANCE
2Th	2: 8	the **manifestation** of his coming
1Ti	6:14	the **manifestation** of our Lord
2Ti	1:10	**appearing** of our Savior Christ
	4: 1	in view of his **appearing**
	4: 8	have longed for his **appearing**
Ti	2:13	the **manifestation** of the glory

2016   GO1 AG304 LN103 B3:317 K9:7 R2014
επιφανης, APPEARANCE
Ac   2:20   Lord's great and **glorious** day

2017   GO1 AG304 LN103 K9:310 R2014
επιφαυσκω, I SHINE ON
Ep   5:14   Christ **will shine** on you

2018   GO2 AG304 LN103 R1909,5342
επιφερω, I CARRY ON
| Ro | 3: 5 | That God is unjust **to inflict** |
| Ju | 1: 9 | dare **to bring** a condemnation |

2019   GO4 AG304 LN103 B1:408 R1909,5455
επιφωνεω, I SOUND ON
Lk	23:21	but they kept **shouting**
Ac	12:22	The people kept **shouting**
	21:34	in the crowd **shouted** one thing
	22:24	for this **outcry** against him

2020   GO2 AG304 LN103 K9:310 R2017
επιφωσκω, I DAWN ON

Mt 28: 1 day of the week **was dawning**
Lk 23:54 the sabbath **was beginning**

2021 GO3 AG304 LN103
επιχειρεω, I SET HANDS ON
Lk 1: 1 Since many **have undertaken**
Ac 9:29 but they **were attempting**
  19:13 Jewish exorcists **tried** to use

2022 GO1 AG305 LN103
επιχεω, I POUR ON
Lk 10:34 **having poured** oil and wine on

2023 GO5 AG305 LN103 R1909,5524
επιχορηγεω, I SUPPLY FURTHER
2C 9:10 **supplies** seed to the sower
Ga 3: 5 **does** God **supply** you with the
Co 2:19 **nourished** and held together
2P 1: 5 make every effort to **support**
  1:11 will be richly **provided** for you

2024 GO2 AG305 LN103 R2023
επιχορηγια, SUPPORT
Ep 4:16 with which it is **equipped**
Ph 1:19 and the **help** of the Spirit

2025 GO2 AG305 LN103 R1909,5548
επιχριω, I ANOINT ON
Jn 9: 6 the saliva and **spread** the mud
  9:11 Jesus made mud, **spread** it on

2026 GO7 AG305 LN103 B2:251 K5:147
R1909,3618
εποικοδομεω, I BUILD ON
1C 3:10 someone else **is building on** it
  3:10 with care how **to build on** it
  3:12 anyone **builds on** the foundation
  3:14 If what **has been built** on the
Ep 2:20 **built upon** the foundation
Co 2: 7 rooted and **built up** in him
Ju 1:20 **build** yourselves up on your

2028 GO1 AG305 LN103 B2:648 K5:282 R1909,3687
επονομαζω, I NAME
Ro 2:17 But if you **call** yourself a Jew

2029 GO2 AG305 LN103 B3:512 K5:373
εποπτευω, I OBSERVE
1P 2:12 **may see** your honorable deeds
  3: 2 **see** the purity and reverence

2030 GO1 AG305 LN103 K5:373
εποπτης, EYEWITNESS
2P 1:16 **eyewitnesses** of his majesty.

2031 GO1 AG305 LN103
επος, SO
He 7: 9 One might **even** say that Levi

2032 GO19 AG305 LN103 B2:188 K5:538 R1909,3772
επουρανιος, ON HEAVENLY
Jn 3:12 if I tell you about **heavenly**
1C 15:40 There are both **heavenly** bodies
  15:40 but the glory of the **heavenly**
  15:48 as is the man **of heaven**
  15:48 so are those who are **of heaven**
  15:49 the image of the man **of heaven**
Ep 1: 3 blessing in the **heavenly** places
  1:20 hand in the **heavenly** places
  2: 6 **heavenly** places in Christ Jesus
  3:10 authorities in the **heavenly**
  6:12 evil in the **heavenly** places
Ph 2:10 **in heaven** and on earth
2Ti 4:18 me for his **heavenly** kingdom
He 3: 1 partners in a **heavenly** calling
  6: 4 have tasted the **heavenly** gift
  8: 5 shadow of the **heavenly** one
  9:23 **heavenly** things themselves
  11:16 that is, a **heavenly** one.
  12:22 the **heavenly** Jerusalem

2033 GO88 AG306 LN103 B2:690 K2:627
'επτα, SEVEN
Mt 12:45 **seven** other spirits more evil
  15:34 **Seven,** and a few small fish
  15:36 he took the **seven** loaves
  15:37 left over, **seven** baskets full
  16:10 Or the **seven** loaves for the
  18:22 Not **seven** times
  22:25 Now there were **seven** brothers
  22:26 down to the **seventh**
  22:28 wife of the **seven** will she be
Mk 8: 5 They said, "**Seven.**"
  8: 6 he took the **seven** loaves
  8: 8 left over, **seven** baskets full
  8:20 And the **seven** for the four
  8:20 they said to him, "**Seven.**"
  12:20 There were **seven** brothers
  12:22 none of the **seven** left children
  12:23 For the **seven** had married her
  16: 9 he had cast out **seven** demons

Lk	2:36	with her husband **seven** years
	8: 2	whom **seven** demons had gone out
	11:26	brings **seven** other spirits
	20:29	Now there were **seven** brothers
	20:31	all **seven** died childless
	20:33	For the **seven** had married her
Ac	6: 3	**seven** men of good standing
	13:19	had destroyed **seven** nations
	19:14	**Seven** sons of a Jewish high
	20: 6	where we stayed for **seven** days
	21: 4	stayed there for **seven** days
	21: 8	one of the **seven**
	21:27	the **seven** days were almost
	28:14	stay with them for **seven** days
He	11:30	been encircled for **seven** days
Re	1: 4	John to the **seven** churches
	1: 4	from the **seven** spirits who are
	1:11	send it to the **seven** churches
	1:12	I saw **seven** golden lampstands
	1:16	right hand he held **seven** stars
	1:20	the mystery of the **seven** stars
	1:20	the **seven** golden lampstands
	1:20	the **seven** stars are the angels
	1:20	angels of the **seven** churches
	1:20	**seven** lampstands are the seven
	1:20	seven lampstands are the **seven**
	2: 1	**seven** stars in his right hand
	2: 1	the **seven** golden lampstands
	3: 1	has the **seven** spirits of God
	3: 1	of God and the **seven** stars
	4: 5	burn **seven** flaming torches
	4: 5	the **seven** spirits of God
	5: 1	back, sealed with **seven** seals
	5: 5	scroll and its **seven** seals
	5: 6	**seven** horns and seven eyes
	5: 6	seven horns and **seven** eyes
	5: 6	**seven** spirits of God sent out
	6: 1	open one of the **seven** seals
	8: 2	And I saw the **seven** angels who
	8: 2	**seven** trumpets were given to
	8: 6	Now the **seven** angels who had
	8: 6	who had the **seven** trumpets
	10: 3	the **seven** thunders sounded
	10: 4	the **seven** thunders had sounded
	10: 4	the **seven** thunders had sounded
	11:13	**seven** thousand people were
	12: 3	with **seven** heads and ten horns
	12: 3	**seven** diadems on his heads
	13: 1	ten horns and **seven** heads

	15: 1	**seven** angels with seven plagues
	15: 1	seven angels with **seven** plagues
	15: 6	**seven** angels with the seven
	15: 6	with the **seven** plagues
	15: 7	creatures gave the **seven** angels
	15: 7	seven angels **seven** golden bowls
	15: 8	**seven** plagues of the seven
	15: 8	the **seven** angels were ended
	16: 1	temple telling the **seven** angels
	16: 1	pour out on the earth the **seven**
	17: 1	Then one of the **seven** angels
	17: 1	angels who had the **seven** bowls
	17: 3	had **seven** heads and ten horns
	17: 7	the beast with **seven** heads
	17: 9	**seven** heads are seven mountains
	17: 9	seven heads are **seven** mountains
	17: 9	also, they are **seven** kings
	17:11	but it belongs to the **seven**
	21: 9	Then one of the **seven** angels
	21: 9	who had the **seven** bowls full
	21: 9	full of the **seven** last plagues

2034 GO4 AG306 LN103 B2:690 K2:627 R2033
επτακις, SEVEN TIMES

Mt	18:21	As many as **seven times?**
	18:22	said to him, "Not **seven times**
Lk	17: 4	sins against you **seven times**
	17: 4	turns back to you **seven times**

2035 GO1 AG306 LN103 K2:627 R2034,5507
επτακισχιλιοι, SEVEN THOUSAND

Ro	11: 4	kept for myself **seven thousand**

2037 GO3 AG306 LN104
εραστος, ERASTUS

Ac	19:22	helpers, Timothy and **Erastus**
Ro	16:23	**Erastus,** the city treasurer
2Ti	4:20	**Erastus** remained in Corinth

2037a GO6 AG306 LN104 B3:532
εραυναω, I SEARCH

Jn	5:39	You **search** the scriptures
	7:52	**Search** and you will see
Ro	8:27	God, who **searches** the heart
1C	2:10	the Spirit **searches** everything
1P	1:11	**inquiring** about the person
Re	2:23	the one who **searches** minds

2038 GO41 AG306 LN104 B3:1147 K2:635 R2041
εργαζομαι, I WORK

Mt	7:23	away from me, you **evildoers**
	21:28	go and **work** in the vineyard
	25:16	at once and **traded** with them
	26:10	has **performed** a good service
Mk	14: 6	has **performed** a good service
Lk	13:14	on which **work** ought to be done
Jn	3:21	deeds **have been done** in God
	5:17	My Father is still **working**
	5:17	and I also **am working**
	6:27	Do not **work** for the food
	6:28	What must we do to **perform**
	6:30	What work are you **performing?**
	9: 4	We must **work** the works of him
	9: 4	is coming when no one can **work**
Ac	10:35	him and **does** what is right
	13:41	your days I **am doing** a **work**
	18: 3	and they **worked** together
Ro	2:10	for everyone who **does** good
	4: 4	Now to one who **works,** wages
	4: 5	But to one who without **works**
	13:10	**does** no wrong to a neighbor
1C	4:12	from the **work** of our own hands
	9: 6	right to refrain from **working**
	9:13	who **are employed** in the temple
	16:10	for he is **doing** the work
2C	7:10	grief **produces** a repentance
Ga	6:10	let us **work** for the good
Ep	4:28	**work** honestly with their own
Co	3:23	as **done** for the Lord and not
1Th	2: 9	we **worked** night and day
	4:11	to **work** with your hands
2Th	3: 8	labor we **worked** night and day
	3:10	Anyone unwilling **to work** should
	3:11	busybodies, not **doing** any **work**
	3:12	to **do** their **work** quietly
He	11:33	**administered** justice, obtained
Ja	1:20	for your anger does not **produce**
	2: 9	**commit** sin and are convicted
2J	1: 8	lose what we **have worked** for
3J	1: 5	whatever you **do** for the friends
Re	18:17	all whose **trade** is on the sea

2039   GO6 AG307 LN104 B3:1147 R2040

εργασια, WORKING

Lk	12:58	an **effort** to settle the case
Ac	16:16	owners a great deal of **money**
	16:19	their hope of **making money**
	19:24	brought no little **business**

| | 19:25 | our wealth from this **business** |
| Ep | 4:19 | greedy to **practice** every kind |

2040   GO16 AG307 LN104 B3:1147 R2041

εργατης, WORKER

Mt	9:37	but the **laborers** are few
	9:38	**laborers** into his harvest
	10:10	for **laborers** deserve their food
	20: 1	hire **laborers** for his vineyard
	20: 2	agreeing with the **laborers**
	20: 8	Call the **laborers** and give
Lk	10: 2	but the **laborers** are few;
	10: 2	send out **laborers** into his
	10: 7	**laborer** deserves to be paid
	13:27	from me, all you evil**doers**
Ac	19:25	the **workers** of the same trade
2C	11:13	deceitful **workers,** disguising
Ph	3: 2	beware of the evil **workers**
1Ti	5:18	**laborer** deserves to be paid
2Ti	2:15	**worker** who has no need to be
Ja	5: 4	The wages of the **laborers** who

2041   GO169 AG307 LN104 B3:1147 K2:635

εργον, WORK

Mt	5:16	they may see your good **works**
	11: 2	what the Messiah was **doing**
	11:19	is vindicated by her **deeds**
	23: 3	do not **practice** what they teach
	23: 5	all their **deeds** to be seen
	26:10	performed a good **service** for me
Mk	13:34	in charge, each with his **work**
	14: 6	performed a good **service** for me
Lk	11:48	the **deeds** of your ancestors
	24:19	prophet mighty in **deed** and word
Jn	3:19	because their **deeds** were evil
	3:20	their **deeds** may not be exposed
	3:21	**deeds** have been done in God
	4:34	me and to complete his **work**
	5:20	he will show him greater **works**
	5:36	**works** that the Father has given
	5:36	the very **works** that I am doing
	6:28	to perform the **works** of God
	6:29	This is the **work** of God
	7: 3	see the **works** you are doing
	7: 7	that its **works** are evil
	7:21	I performed one **work,**
	8:39	be doing what Abraham **did**
	8:41	doing what your father **does**
	9: 3	God's **works** might be revealed

	9: 4	We must work the **works** of him		2:16	not by doing the **works** of the
	10:25	The **works** that I do in my		2:16	justified by the **works** of the
	10:32	shown you many good **works**		3: 2	by doing the **works** of the law
	10:32	which of **these** are you going		3: 5	doing the **works** of the law
	10:33	It is not for a good **work**		3:10	For all who rely on the **works**
	10:37	If I am not doing the **works**		5:19	Now the **works** of the flesh
	10:38	believe me, believe the **works**		6: 4	All must test their own **work**
	14:10	dwells in me does his **works**	Ep	2: 9	not the result of **works**
	14:11	because of the **works** themselves		2:10	Christ Jesus for good **works,**
	14:12	also do the **works** that I do		4:12	equip the saints for the **work**
	15:24	the **works** that no one else did		5:11	unfruitful **works** of darkness
	17: 4	**work** that you gave me to do	Ph	1: 6	began a good **work** among you
Ac	5:38	this plan or this **undertaking**		1:22	means fruitful **labor** for me
	7:22	powerful in his words and **deeds**		2:30	to death for the **work** of Christ
	7:41	in the **works** of their hands	Co	1:10	bear fruit in every good **work**
	9:36	She was devoted to good **works**		1:21	in mind, doing evil **deeds**
	13: 2	for the **work** to which I have		3:17	in word or **deed,** do everything
	13:41	your days I am doing a **work**	1Th	1: 3	your **work** of faith and labor
	13:41	a **work** that you will never		5:13	because of their **work**
	14:26	**work** that they had completed	2Th	1:11	good resolve and **work** of faith
	15:38	accompanied them in the **work**		2:17	in every good **work** and word
	26:20	turn to God and do **deeds**	1Ti	2:10	but with good **works**
Ro	2: 6	according to each one's **deeds**		3: 1	of bishop desires a noble **task**
	2: 7	by patiently **doing** good seek		5:10	attested for her good **works**
	2:15	that what the law **requires**		5:10	to **doing** good in every way
	3:20	by **deeds** prescribed by the law		5:25	also good **works** are conspicuous
	3:27	By that of **works?**		6:18	to be rich in good **works**
	3:28	**works** prescribed by the law	2Ti	1: 9	not according to our **works**
	4: 2	Abraham was justified by **works**		2:21	ready for every good **work**
	4: 6	righteousness apart from **works**		3:17	equipped for every good **work**
	9:12	not by **works** but by his call		4: 5	the **work** of an evangelist
	9:32	if it were based on **works**		4:14	pay him back for his **deeds**
	11: 6	longer on the basis of **works**		4:18	from every evil **attack**
	13: 3	not a terror to good **conduct**	Ti	1:16	they deny him by their **actions**
	13:12	**works** of darkness and put on		1:16	unfit for any good **work**
	14:20	destroy the **work** of God		2: 7	a model of good **works**
	15:18	the Gentiles, by word and **deed**		2:14	who are zealous for good **deeds**
1C	3:13	the **work** of each builder		3: 1	be ready for every good **work**
	3:13	will test what sort of **work**		3: 5	not because of any **works** of
	3:14	been built on the **foundation**		3: 8	devote themselves to good **works**
	3:15	If the **work** is burned up		3:14	devote themselves to good **works**
	5: 2	so that he who has **done** this	He	1:10	and the heavens are the **work**
	9: 1	Are you not my **work** in the Lord		3: 9	though they had seen my **works**
	15:58	in the **work** of the Lord		4: 3	though his **works** were finished
	16:10	doing the **work** of the Lord		4: 4	seventh day from all his **works**
2C	9: 8	abundantly in every good **work**		4:10	also cease from their **labors**
	10:11	we will also **do** when present		6: 1	repentance from dead **works**
	11:15	end will match their **deeds**		6:10	he will not overlook your **work**
Ga	2:16	by the **works** of the law		9:14	our conscience from dead **works**

	10:24	another to love and good **deeds**
Ja	1: 4	endurance have its full **effect**
	1:25	who forget but doers who **act**
	2:14	faith but do not have **works**
	2:17	if it has no **works,** is dead
	2:18	have faith and I have **works**
	2:18	faith apart from your **works**
	2:18	I by my **works** will show you my
	2:20	apart from **works** is barren?
	2:21	Abraham justified by **works**
	2:22	active along with his **works**
	2:22	to completion by the **works**
	2:24	a person is justified by **works**
	2:25	by **works** when she welcomed
	2:26	so faith without **works** is also
	3:13	your good life that your **works**
1P	1:17	according to their **deeds**
	2:12	may see your honorable **deeds**
2P	2: 8	by their lawless **deeds** that he
	3:10	everything that is **done** on it
1J	3: 8	destroy the **works** of the devil
	3:12	Because his own **deeds** were evil
	3:18	speech, but in truth and **action.**
2J	1:11	participate in the evil **deeds**
3J	1:10	what he is **doing** in spreading
Ju	1:15	of all the **deeds** of ungodliness
Re	2: 2	I know your **works,** your toil
	2: 5	do the **works** you did at first
	2: 6	the **works** of the Nicolaitans
	2:19	I know your **works**—your love
	2:19	I know that your last **works**
	2:22	they repent of her **doings**
	2:23	each of you as your **works**
	2:26	to do my **works** to the end
	3: 1	I know your **works;** you have
	3: 2	not found your **works** perfect
	3: 8	I know your **works**
	3:15	I know your **works.**
	9:20	did not repent of the **works**
	14:13	for their **deeds** follow them
	15: 3	and amazing are your **deeds**
	16:11	did not repent of their **deeds**
	18: 6	repay her double for her **deeds**
	20:12	according to their **works**
	20:13	to **what they had done**
	22:12	according to everyone's **work**

2042　GO2 AG308 LN104
ερεθιζω, I PROVOKE

| | 9: 2 | your zeal has **stirred** up most |
| Co | 3:21 | do not **provoke** your children |

2043　GO1 AG308 LN104
ερειδω, I STICK
| Ac | 27:41 | **stuck** and remained immovable |

2044　GO1 AG308 LN104
ερευγομαι, I SPEAK OUT LOUD
| Mt | 13:35 | **will proclaim** what has been |

2047　GO4 AG308 LN104 B3:1004 K2:657 R2048
ερημια, DESERT
Mt	15:33	enough bread in the **desert**
Mk	8: 4	with bread here in the **desert**
2C	11:26	danger in the **wilderness**
He	11:38	They wandered in **deserts**

2048　GO48 AG309 LN104 B3:1004 K2:657
ερημος, DESERT
Mt	3: 1	appeared in the **wilderness**
	3: 3	crying out in the **wilderness**
	4: 1	the **wilderness** to be tempted
	11: 7	the **wilderness** to look at
	14:13	to a **deserted** place by himself
	14:15	This is a **deserted** place
	23:38	house is left to you, **desolate**
	24:26	He is in the **wilderness**
Mk	1: 3	crying out in the **wilderness**
	1: 4	appeared in the **wilderness**
	1:12	out into the **wilderness**
	1:13	in the **wilderness** forty days
	1:35	went out to a **deserted** place
	1:45	but stayed out in the **country**
	6:31	Come away to a **deserted** place
	6:32	in the boat to a **deserted** place
	6:35	This is a **deserted** place
Lk	1:80	he was in the **wilderness**
	3: 2	in the **wilderness**
	3: 4	crying out in the **wilderness**
	4: 1	by the Spirit in the **wilderness**
	4:42	went into a **deserted** place
	5:16	withdraw to **deserted** places
	7:24	you go out into the **wilderness**
	8:29	by the demon into the **wilds**
	9:12	are here in a **deserted** place
	15: 4	ninety-nine in the **wilderness**
Jn	1:23	crying out in the **wilderness**
	3:14	the serpent in the **wilderness**

	6:31	ate the manna in the **wilderness**
	6:49	ate the manna in the **wilderness**
	11:54	the region near the **wilderness**
Ac	1:20	his homestead become **desolate**
	7:30	the **wilderness** of Mount Sinai
	7:36	the **wilderness** for forty years
	7:38	the **wilderness** with the angel
	7:42	forty years in the **wilderness**
	7:44	testimony in the **wilderness**
	8:26	This is a **wilderness** road
	13:18	with them in the **wilderness**
	21:38	out into the **wilderness**
1C	10: 5	struck down in the **wilderness**
Ga	4:27	children of the **desolate** woman
He	3: 8	of testing in the **wilderness**
	3:17	bodies fell in the **wilderness**
Re	12: 6	fled into the **wilderness**
	12:14	serpent into the **wilderness**
	17: 3	the spirit into a **wilderness**

2049   GO5 AG309 LN104 B3:1004 K2:657 R2049
ερημοω, I DESOLATE

Mt	12:25	against itself **is laid waste**
Lk	11:17	against itself **becomes** a **desert**
Re	17:16	they will **make** her **desolate**
	18:17	wealth **has been laid waste**
	18:19	hour she **has been laid waste**

2050   GO3 AG309 LN104 B3:1004 K2:660 R2049
ερημωσις, DESOLATION

Mt	24:15	when you see the **desolating**
Mk	13:14	when you see the **desolating**
Lk	21:20	its **desolation** has come near

2051   GO1 AG309 LN104 R2054
εριζω, I STRIVE

Mt	12:19	He will not **wrangle** or cry

2052   GO7 AG309 LN104 K2:660
εριθεια, SELFISH AMBITION

Ro	2: 8	for those who are **self-seeking**
2C	12:20	anger, **selfishness,** slander,
Ga	5:20	anger, **quarrels,** dissensions,
Ph	1:17	Christ out of **selfish ambition**
	2: 3	nothing from **selfish ambition**
Ja	3:14	envy and **selfish ambition**
	3:16	is envy and **selfish ambition**

2053   GO2 AG309 LN104
εριον, OF WOOL

He	9:19	with water and scarlet **wool**
Re	1:14	hair were white as white **wool**

2054   GO9 AG309 LN104
ερις, STRIFE

Ro	1:29	Full of envy, murder, **strife,**
	13:13	not in **quarreling** and jealousy
1C	1:11	there are **quarrels** among you,
	3: 3	jealousy and **quarreling** among
2C	12:20	may perhaps be **quarreling**
Ga	5:20	sorcery, enmities, **strife**
Ph	1:15	Christ from envy and **rivalry**
1Ti	6: 4	envy, **dissension,** slander, base
Ti	3: 9	and **quarrels** about the law

2055   GO1 AG309 LN104 R2056
εριφιον, GOAT

Mt	25:33	hand and the **goats** at the left

2056   GO2 AG309 LN104
εριφος, GOAT

Mt	25:32	the sheep from the **goats**
Lk	15:29	given me even a young **goat**

2057   GO1 AG309 LN104
῾ερμας, HERMAS

Ro	16:14	Hermes, Patrobas, **Hermas**

2058   GO2 AG310 LN104 B1:579 K2:661 R2059
ερμηνεια, INTERPRETATION

1C	12:10	to another the **interpretation**
	14:26	tongue, or an **interpretation**

2059   GO3 AG310 LN104 B1:579 K2:661
ερμηνευω, I INTERPRET

Jn	1:42	which is **translated** Peter
	9: 7	of Siloam" (which **means** Sent
He	7: 2	**means** "king of righteousness

2060   GO2 AG310 LN104
ερμης, HERMES

Ac	14:12	and Paul they called **Hermes**
Ro	16:14	Asyncritus, Phlegon, **Hermes**

2061   GO1 AG310 LN105
ερμογενης, HERMOGENES

2Ti	1:15	Phygelus and **Hermogenes**

2062   GO4 AG310 LN105
ερπετον, REPTILE

Ac	10:12	creatures and **reptiles**
	11: 6	beasts of prey, **reptiles,**
Ro	1:23	animals or **reptiles**
Ja	3: 7	of **reptile** and sea creature

2063   GO2 AG310 LN105
ερυθρος, RED

Ac	7:36	signs in Egypt, at the **Red Sea**
He	11:29	passed through the **Red Sea**

2064   GO632 AG310 LN105 B1:319 K2:666
ερχομαι, I COME, GO

Mt	2: 2	**have come** to pay him homage
	2: 8	that I **may** also **go** and pay
	2: 9	**went** the star that they had
	2:11	On **entering** the house
	2:23	he **made** his home in a town
	3: 7	Pharisees and Sadducees **coming**
	3:11	than I **is coming** after me
	3:14	and **do** you **come** to me
	3:16	and **alighting** on him
	4:13	He left Nazareth and **made** his
	5:17	Do not think that I **have come**
	5:17	I **have come** not to abolish
	5:24	then **come** and offer your gift
	6:10	Your kingdom **come.** Your will
	7:15	who **come** to you in sheep's
	7:25	rain fell, the floods **came**
	7:27	rain fell, and the floods **came**
	8: 7	I **will come** and cure him.
	8: 9	and to another, '**Come,**' and he
	8: 9	another, 'Come,' and he **comes**
	8:14	Jesus **entered** Peter's house
	8:28	When he **came** to the other side
	8:29	Have you **come** here to torment
	9: 1	and **came** to his own town
	9:10	sinners **came** and were sitting
	9:13	For I have **come** to call not
	9:15	The days **will come** when the
	9:18	**came** in and knelt before him
	9:18	but **come** and lay your hand
	9:23	Jesus **came** to the leader's
	9:28	When he **entered** the house
	10:13	let your peace **come** upon it
	10:23	before the Son of Man **comes**
	10:34	Do not think that I have **come**
	10:34	I have not **come** to bring peace
	10:35	For I have **come** to set a man
	11: 3	the one who is to **come**

	11:14	he is Elijah who is to **come**
	11:18	For John **came** neither eating
	11:19	the Son of Man **came** eating and
	12: 9	He left that place and **entered**
	12:42	**came** from the ends of the earth
	12:44	When it **comes,** it finds it
	13: 4	the birds **came** and ate them up
	13:19	the evil one **comes** and snatches
	13:25	an enemy **came** and sowed weeds
	13:32	the birds of the air **come**
	13:36	he left the crowds and **went**
	13:54	He **came** to his hometown
	14:12	then they **went** and told Jesus
	14:25	he **came** walking toward them
	14:28	to **come** to you on the water
	14:29	He said, "**Come.**" So Peter got
	14:29	on the water, and **came** toward
	14:34	they **came** to land at Gennesaret
	15:25	But she **came** and knelt before
	15:29	**passed** along the Sea of Galilee
	15:39	**went** to the region of Magadan
	16: 5	When the disciples **reached** the
	16:13	Now when Jesus **came** into the
	16:24	want to become my **followers**
	16:27	For the Son of Man is to **come**
	16:28	they see the Son of Man **coming**
	17:10	that Elijah must **come** first
	17:11	Elijah is indeed **coming**
	17:12	that Elijah has already **come**
	17:14	When they **came** to the crowd
	17:24	**came** to Peter and said
	17:25	And when he **came** home, Jesus
	18: 7	for stumbling are bound to **come**
	18: 7	whom the stumbling block **comes**
	18:31	they **went** and reported to their
	19: 1	**went** to the region of Judea
	19:14	the little children **come** to me
	20: 9	hired about five o'clock **came**
	20:10	Now when the first **came**
	20:28	just as the Son of Man **came**
	21: 1	and had **reached** Bethphage
	21: 5	Look, your king **is coming**
	21: 9	Blessed is the one who **comes**
	21:19	he **went** to it and found nothing
	21:23	When he **entered** the temple
	21:32	For John **came** to you in the way
	21:40	the owner of the vineyard **comes**
	22: 3	but they would not **come**
	23:35	so that upon you may **come** all

23:39	the one who **comes** in the name	5:14	people **came** to see what it was
24: 5	For many will **come** in my name	5:15	They **came** to Jesus and saw
24:30	the Son of Man **coming** on the	5:22	**came** and, when he saw him, fell
24:39	until the flood **came** and swept	5:23	**Come** and lay your hands on her
24:42	on what day your Lord is **coming**	5:26	but rather **grew** worse
24:43	the night the thief was **coming**	5:27	**came** up behind him in the crowd
24:44	is **coming** at an unexpected hour	5:33	**came** in fear and trembling
24:46	find at work when he **arrives**	5:35	**came** from the leader's house
25:10	to buy it, the bridegroom **came**	5:38	When they **came** to the house
25:11	other bridesmaids **came** also	6: 1	**came** to his hometown, and his
25:19	the master of those slaves **came**	6:29	they **came** and took his body
25:27	and on my **return** I would have	6:31	For many **were coming** and going
25:31	Son of Man **comes** in his glory	6:48	he **came** towards them early
25:36	in prison and you **visited** me	6:53	**came** to land at Gennesaret
25:39	or in prison and **visited** you	7: 1	who **had come** from Jerusalem
26:36	Then Jesus **went** with them	7:25	**came** and bowed down at his feet
26:40	Then he **came** to the disciples	7:31	he **returned** from the region
26:43	Again he **came** and found them	8:10	**went** to the district
26:45	Then he **came** to the disciples	8:22	They **came** to Bethsaida
26:47	one of the twelve, **arrived**	8:38	when he **comes** in the glory
26:64	**coming** on the clouds of heaven	9: 1	the kingdom of God **has come**
27:33	And when they **came** to a place	9:11	that Elijah must **come** first
27:49	Elijah **will come** to save him	9:12	Elijah is indeed **coming** first
27:57	**came** a rich man from Arimathea	9:13	I tell you that Elijah **has come**
27:64	his disciples may **go** and steal	9:14	When they **came** to the disciples
28: 1	other Mary **went** to see the tomb	9:33	Then they **came** to Capernaum
28:11	of the guard **went** into the city	10: 1	and **went** to the region of Judea
28:13	**came** by night and stole him	10:14	the little children **come** to me
Mk 1: 7	than I is **coming** after me	10:30	in the age to **come** eternal life
1: 9	Jesus **came** from Nazareth	10:45	**came** not to be served but
1:14	Jesus **came** to Galilee	10:46	They **came** to Jericho
1:24	Have you **come** to destroy us	10:50	he sprang up and **came** to Jesus
1:29	they **entered** the house of Simon	11: 9	the one who **comes** in the name
1:39	And he **went** throughout Galilee	11:10	Blessed is the **coming** kingdom
1:40	A leper **came** to him begging	11:13	he **went** to see whether perhaps
1:45	people **came** to him from every	11:13	he **came** to it, he found nothing
2: 3	Then some people **came**	11:15	Then they **came** to Jerusalem
2:13	whole crowd **gathered** around him	11:27	Again they **came** to Jerusalem
2:17	**come** to call not the righteous	11:27	and the elders **came** to him
2:18	people **came** and said to him	12: 9	He will **come** and destroy
2:20	The days **will come** when the	12:14	And they **came** and said to him
3: 8	**came** to him in great numbers	12:18	**came** to him and asked him
3:20	the crowd **came** together again	12:42	A poor widow **came** and put in
3:31	mother and his brothers **came**	13: 6	Many will **come** in my name
4: 4	the birds **came** and ate it up	13:26	the Son of Man **coming** in
4:15	Satan immediately **comes**	13:35	master of the house **will come**
4:21	**Is** a lamp **brought** in to be put	13:36	find you asleep when he **comes**
4:22	except to **come** to light	14: 3	woman **came** with an alabaster
5: 1	They **came** to the other side	14:16	set out and **went** to the city

	14:17	he **came** with the twelve.
	14:32	They **went** to a place called
	14:37	**came** and found them sleeping
	14:38	you may not **come** into the time
	14:40	he **came** and found them sleeping
	14:41	He **came** a third time and said
	14:41	The hour has **come**
	14:45	So when he **came**
	14:62	**coming** with the clouds of
	14:66	of the high priest **came** by
	15:21	**was coming** in from the country
	15:36	**will come** to take him down
	15:43	**went** boldly to Pilate and asked
	16: 1	they **might go** and anoint him
	16: 2	they **went to** the tomb
Lk	1:43	mother of my Lord **comes** to me
	1:59	**came** to circumcise the child,
	2:16	So they **went** with haste
	2:27	Simeon **came** into the temple
	2:44	they **went** a day's journey
	2:51	with them and **came** to Nazareth
	3: 3	He **went** into all the region
	3:12	collectors **came** to be baptized
	3:16	more powerful than I is **coming**
	4:16	When he **came** to Nazareth
	4:34	Have you **come** to destroy us
	4:42	when they **reached** him
	5: 7	to **come** and help them
	5: 7	**came** and filled both boats
	5:17	**had come** from every village
	5:32	I have **come** to call not the
	5:35	The days will **come** when the
	6:18	They had **come** to hear him
	6:47	is like who **comes** to me
	7: 3	asking him to **come** and heal
	7: 7	not presume to **come** to you
	7: 8	'**Come**,' and he comes
	7: 8	'**Come**,' and he **comes**
	7:19	the one who is to **come**
	7:20	the one who is to **come**
	7:33	John the Baptist has **come**
	7:34	Son of Man has **come** eating
	8:12	then the devil **comes** and takes
	8:17	become known and **come** to light
	8:35	and when they **came** to Jesus
	8:41	there **came** a man named Jairus
	8:47	she **came** trembling
	8:49	someone **came** from the leader's
	8:51	When he **came** to the house

9:23	want to become my **followers**
9:26	when he **comes** in his glory
10: 1	where he himself intended to **go**
10:32	when he **came** to the place
10:33	Samaritan while traveling **came**
11: 2	be your name. Your kingdom **come**
11:25	When it **comes**, it finds it
12:36	soon as he **comes** and knocks
12:37	finds alert when he **comes**
12:38	If he **comes** during the middle
12:39	what hour the thief was **coming**
12:40	the Son of Man **is coming**
12:43	find at work when he **arrives**
12:45	master is delayed **in coming**
12:49	I **came** to bring fire
12:54	It **is going** to rain
13: 6	he **came** looking for fruit on it
13: 7	I have **come** looking for fruit
13:14	**come** on those days and be cured
13:35	the one who **comes** in the name
14: 1	Jesus **was going** to the house
14: 9	both of you may **come** and say
14:10	so that when your host **comes**
14:17	**Come;** for everything is ready
14:20	and therefore I cannot **come**
14:26	Whoever **comes** to me and does
14:27	and **follow** me cannot be my
14:31	to oppose the one who **comes**
15: 6	And when he **comes** home
15:17	But when he **came** to himself
15:20	So he set off and **went** to his
15:25	and when he **came** and approached
15:30	But when this son of yours **came**
16:21	even the dogs would **come**
16:28	that they will not also **come**
17: 1	for stumbling are bound to **come**
17: 1	to anyone by whom they **come**
17:20	the kingdom of God **was coming**
17:20	kingdom of God is not **coming**
17:22	The days **are coming** when you
17:27	the flood **came** and destroyed
18: 3	was a widow who kept **coming**
18: 5	me out by continually **coming**
18: 8	when the Son of Man **comes**
18:16	Let the little children **come**
18:30	and in the age to **come** eternal
19: 5	When Jesus **came** to the place
19:10	the Son of Man **came** to seek out
19:13	with these until I **come** back

19:18	Then the second **came,** saying
19:20	Then the other **came,** saying
19:23	Then when I **returned,** I could
19:38	Blessed is the king who **comes**
20:16	He **will come** and destroy those
21: 6	the days **will come** when not
21: 8	for many **will come** in my name
21:27	Son of Man **coming** in a
22: 7	Then **came** the day of Unleavened
22:18	until the kingdom of God **comes**
22:45	he **came** to the disciples
23:26	Cyrene, who **was coming** from the
23:29	For the days are surely **coming**
23:33	When they **came** to the place
23:42	remember me when you **come**
24: 1	they **came** to the tomb
24:23	they **came** back and told us

Jn 1: 7 He **came** as a witness to testify
1: 9 **was coming** into the world
1:11 He **came** to what was his own
1:15 He who **comes** after me ranks
1:27 one who is **coming** after me
1:29 he saw Jesus **coming** toward him
1:30 After me **comes** a man who ranks
1:31 but I **came** baptizing with water
1:39 said to them, **"Come** and see."
1:39 They **came** and saw where he was
1:46 said to him, **"Come** and see."
1:47 When Jesus saw Nathanael **coming**
3: 2 He **came** to Jesus by night
3: 2 a teacher who **has come** from God
3: 8 where it **comes** from or where
3:19 light **has come** into the world
3:20 do not **come** to the light
3:21 who do what is true **come** to the
3:22 Jesus and his disciples **went**
3:26 They **came** to John and said
3:26 baptizing, and all **are going**
3:31 The one who **comes** from above
3:31 The one who **comes** from heaven
4: 5 So he **came** to a Samaritan city
4: 7 A Samaritan woman **came** to draw
4:16 your husband, and **come** back
4:21 the hour is **coming** when you
4:23 But the hour is **coming,** and is
4:25 I know that Messiah **is coming**
4:25 When he **comes,** he will
4:27 Just then his disciples **came**
4:30 the city and **were on their way**

4:35 more, then **comes** the harvest
4:40 So when the Samaritans **came**
4:45 When he **came** to Galilee
4:45 for they too **had gone** to the
4:46 Then he **came** again to Cana
4:54 **coming** from Judea to Galilee
5: 7 while I **am making** my way
5:24 **does** not **come** under judgment
5:25 the hour **is coming,** and is now
5:28 for the hour **is coming** when all
5:40 Yet you refuse **to come** to me
5:43 I **have come** in my Father's
5:43 if another **comes** in his own
6: 5 a large crowd **coming** toward him
6:14 who is to **come** into the world
6:15 they were about **to come**
6:17 and **started** across the sea
6:17 Jesus had not yet **come** to them
6:23 boats from Tiberias **came** near
6:24 **went** to Capernaum looking for
6:35 Whoever **comes** to me will never
6:37 and anyone who **comes** to me
6:44 No one can **come** to me unless
6:45 from the Father **comes** to me
6:65 no one can **come** to me unless
7:27 but when the Messiah **comes**
7:28 I **have** not **come** on my own
7:30 his hour **had** not yet **come**
7:31 When the Messiah **comes**
7:34 where I am, you cannot **come**
7:36 Where I am, you cannot **come**
7:37 Let anyone who is thirsty **come**
7:41 Messiah **does** not **come** from
7:42 David and **comes** from Bethlehem
7:45 the temple police **went** back
7:50 who **had gone** to Jesus before
8: 2 All the people **came** to him
8:14 I know where I **have come** from
8:14 not know where I **come** from or
8:20 his hour had not yet **come**
8:21 I **am going,** you cannot **come**
8:22 I am going, you cannot **come**
8:42 I did not **come** on my own
9: 4 night is **coming** when no one
9: 7 washed and **came** back able to
9:39 I **came** into this world for
10: 8 who **came** before me are thieves
10:10 The thief **comes** only to steal
10:10 I **came** that they may have life

10:12	sees the wolf **coming** and leaves
10:41	Many **came** to him, and they were
11:17	When Jesus **arrived,** he found
11:19	the Jews **had come** to Martha
11:20	heard that Jesus **was coming**
11:27	the one **coming** into the world
11:29	quickly and **went** to him
11:30	had not yet **come** to the village
11:32	When Mary **came** where Jesus was
11:34	to him, "Lord, **come** and see."
11:38	disturbed, **came** to the tomb
11:45	who **had come** with Mary
11:48	Romans **will come** and destroy
11:56	will not **come** to the festival
12: 1	Jesus **came** to Bethany, the home
12: 9	they **came** not only because of
12:12	that had **come** to the festival
12:12	heard that Jesus was **coming**
12:13	Blessed is the one who **comes**
12:15	Look, your king is **coming**
12:22	Philip **went** and told Andrew
12:22	Philip **went** and told Jesus
12:23	has **come** for the Son of Man
12:27	that I have **come** to this hour
12:28	Then a voice **came** from heaven
12:46	I have **come** as light into the
12:47	I **came** not to judge the world
13: 1	his hour had **come** to depart
13: 6	He **came** to Simon Peter
13:33	I am going, you cannot **come**
14: 3	I will **come** again and will
14: 6	No one **comes** to the Father
14:18	orphaned; I am **coming** to you.
14:23	we will **come** to them and make
14:28	and I am **coming** to you
14:30	ruler of this world is **coming**
15:22	If I had not **come** and spoken
15:26	When the Advocate **comes**
16: 2	an hour is **coming** when those
16: 4	that when their hour **comes**
16: 7	Advocate will not **come** to you
16: 8	when he **comes,** he will prove
16:13	the Spirit of truth **comes**
16:13	When the Spirit of truth **comes**
16:21	because her hour has **come**
16:25	The hour is **coming** when I will
16:28	and have **come** into the world
16:32	The hour is **coming,** indeed it
16:32	indeed it has **come,** when you

	17: 1	Father, the hour has **come**
	17:11	and I am **coming** to you
	17:13	But now I am **coming** to you
	18: 3	all that was to **happen** to him
	18:37	for this I **came** into the world
	19: 3	They kept **coming** up to him
	19:32	the soldiers **came** and broke
	19:33	But when they **came** to Jesus
	19:38	so he **came** and removed his body
	19:39	to Jesus by night, also **came**
	19:39	who had at first **come** to Jesus
	20: 1	Mary Magdalene **came** to the tomb
	20: 2	So she ran and **went** to Simon
	20: 3	set out and **went** toward the
	20: 4	and **reached** the tomb first
	20: 6	Then Simon Peter **came**
	20: 8	who **reached** the tomb first
	20:18	Magdalene **went** and announced
	20:19	Jesus **came** and stood among them
	20:24	not with them when Jesus **came**
	20:26	Jesus **came** and stood among them
	21: 3	We will **go** with you.
	21: 8	But the other disciples **came**
	21:13	Jesus **came** and took the bread
	21:22	that he remain until I **come**
	21:23	that he remain until I **come**
Ac	1:11	will **come** in the same way
	2:20	the **coming** of the Lord's great
	3:20	may **come** from the presence
	4:23	they **went** to their friends
	5:15	on some of them as he **came** by
	7:11	there **came** a famine throughout
	8:27	He had **come** to Jerusalem
	8:36	they **came** to some water
	8:40	until he **came** to Caesarea
	9:17	appeared to you **on your way**
	9:21	has he not **come** here for the
	10:29	I **came** without objection
	11: 5	and it **came** close to me.
	11:12	brothers also **accompanied** me
	11:20	on **coming** to Antioch, spoke to
	12:10	they **came** before the iron gate
	12:12	he **went** to the house of Mary,
	13:13	and **came** to Perga in Pamphylia
	13:25	No, but one is **coming** after me
	13:44	The **next** sabbath almost the
	13:51	protest against them, and **went**
	14:24	Pisidia and **came** to Pamphylia
	16: 7	they had **come** opposite Mysia

	16:37	Let them **come** and take us	
	16:39	so they **came** and apologized	
	17: 1	they **came** to Thessalonica	
	17:13	they **came** there too, to stir	
	17:15	Silas and Timothy **join** him	
	18: 1	Paul left Athens and **went**	
	18: 2	recently **come** from Italy	
	19: 4	one who was to **come** after him	
	19: 6	the Holy Spirit **came** upon them	
	19:18	who **became** believers confessed	
	19:27	of ours may **come** into disrepute	
	20: 2	he **came** to Greece	
	20: 6	we **joined** them in Troas	
	20:14	on board and **went** to Mitylene	
	20:15	after that we **came** to Miletus	
	21: 1	we **came** by a straight course	
	21: 8	we left and **came** to Caesarea	
	21:11	He **came** to us and took Paul's	
	21:22	hear that you have **come**	
	22:11	me took my hand and **led** me	
	22:13	**came** to me; and standing	
	25:23	Bernice **came** with great pomp	
	27: 8	we **came** to a place called Fair	
	28:13	second day we **came** to Puteoli	
	28:14	And so we **came** to Rome	
	28:15	**came** as far as the Forum of	
	28:23	**came** to him at his lodgings	
Ro	1:10	succeed in **coming** to you	
	1:13	often intended to **come** to you	
	3: 8	do evil so that good may **come**	
	7: 9	but when the commandment **came**	
	9: 9	I will **return** and Sarah shall	
	15:22	hindered from **coming** to you	
	15:23	for many years, to **come** to you	
	15:29	I know that when I **come** to you	
	15:29	I will **come** in the fullness	
	15:32	by God's will I may **come** to you	
1C	2: 1	When I **came** to you, brothers	
	2: 1	I did not **come** proclaiming the	
	4: 5	before the Lord **comes,** who will	
	4:18	that I am not **coming** to you	
	4:19	But I will **come** to you soon	
	4:21	I to **come** to you with a stick	
	11:26	the Lord's death until he **comes**	
	11:34	give instructions when I **come**	
	13:10	but when the complete **comes**	
	14: 6	if I **come** to you speaking	
	15:35	what kind of body do they **come**	
	16: 2	need not be taken when I **come**	

	16: 5	I will **visit** you after passing	
	16:10	If Timothy **comes,** see that	
	16:11	so that he may **come** to me	
	16:12	I strongly urged him to **visit**	
	16:12	not at all willing to **come** now	
	16:12	He **will come** when he has the	
2C	1:15	I wanted to **come** to you first	
	1:16	**come** back to you from Macedonia	
	1:23	I did not **come** again to Corinth	
	2: 1	make you another painful **visit**	
	2: 3	as I did, so that when I **came**	
	2:12	I **came** to Troas to proclaim	
	7: 5	when we **came** into Macedonia	
	9: 4	some Macedonians **come** with me	
	11: 4	if someone **comes** and proclaims	
	11: 9	friends who **came** from Macedonia	
	12: 1	but I will **go** on to visions	
	12:14	ready to **come** to you this third	
	12:20	For I fear that when I **come**	
	12:21	I fear that when I **come** again	
	13: 1	third time I **am coming** to you	
	13: 2	visit, that if I **come** again	
Ga	1:21	I **went** into the regions of	
	2:11	when Cephas **came** to Antioch	
	2:12	certain people **came** from James	
	2:12	But after they **came,** he drew	
	3:19	until the offspring would **come**	
	3:23	Now before faith **came,**	
	3:25	But now that faith **has come**	
	4: 4	the fullness of time **had come**	
Ep	2:17	So he **came** and proclaimed peace	
	5: 6	the wrath of God **comes** on those	
Ph	1:12	that what has **happened** to me	
	1:27	whether I **come** and see you	
	2:24	that I will also **come** soon	
Co	3: 6	the wrath of God **is coming**	
	4:10	if he **comes** to you, welcome him	
1Th	1:10	from the wrath that **is coming**	
	2:18	For we wanted to **come** to you	
	3: 6	has just now **come** to us from	
	5: 2	the day of the Lord **will come**	
2Th	1:10	when he **comes** to be glorified	
	2: 3	for that day will not **come**	
1Ti	1:15	**came** into the world to save	
	2: 4	to **come** to the knowledge	
	3:14	I hope to **come** to you soon	
	4:13	Until I **arrive,** give attention	
2Ti	3: 7	can never **arrive** at a knowledge	
	4: 9	Do your best **to come** to me soon	

	4:13	When you **come,** bring the cloak
	4:21	Do your best **to come** before
Ti	3:12	**to come** to me at Nicopolis,
He	6: 7	drinks up the rain **falling** on
	8: 8	The days are surely **coming**
	10:37	one who is **coming** will come
	11: 8	not knowing where he **was going**
	13:23	and if he **comes** in time
2P	3: 3	last days scoffers **will come**
1J	2:18	that antichrist **is coming**
	4: 2	Christ **has come** in the flesh
	4: 3	have heard that it **is coming**
	5: 6	the one who **came** by water and
2J	1: 7	Christ **has come** in the flesh
	1:10	welcome anyone who **comes** to you
3J	1: 3	some of the friends **arrived**
	1:10	So if I **come,** I will call
Ju	1:14	the Lord **is coming** with ten
Re	1: 4	who was and who is **to come**
	1: 7	He **is coming** with the clouds
	1: 8	who was and who is **to come**
	2: 5	I **will come** to you and remove
	2:16	I **will come** to you soon and
	3:10	**is coming** on the whole world
	3:11	I **am coming** soon; hold fast
	4: 8	who was and is and is **to come**
	5: 7	He **went** and took the scroll
	6: 1	a voice of thunder, **"Come!"**
	6: 3	creature call out, **"Come!"**
	6: 5	creature call out, **"Come!"**
	6: 7	creature call out, **"Come!"**
	6:17	day of their wrath has **come**
	7:13	where have they **come** from
	7:14	**come** out of the great ordeal
	8: 3	**came** and stood at the altar
	9:12	are still two woes to **come**
	11:14	third woe **is coming** very soon
	11:18	but your wrath **has come**
	14: 7	hour of his judgment has **come**
	14:15	for the hour to reap has **come**
	16:15	I **am coming** like a thief
	17: 1	who had the seven bowls **came**
	17:10	the other **has** not yet **come**
	17:10	and when he **comes,** he must
	18:10	hour your judgment **has come**
	19: 7	marriage of the Lamb **has come**
	21: 9	the seven last plagues **came**
	22: 7	See, I **am coming** soon!
	22:12	See, I **am coming** soon

	22:17	the bride say, **"Come."**
	22:17	who hears say, **"Come."**
	22:17	everyone who is thirsty **come**
	22:20	Surely I **am coming** soon.
	22:20	Amen. **Come,** Lord Jesus

2065 GO63 AG311 LN105 B2:879 K2:685
ερωταω, I ASK

Mt	15:23	disciples came and **urged** him
	16:13	he **asked** his disciples
	19:17	Why do you **ask** me about what
	21:24	will also **ask** you one question
Mk	4:10	**asked** him about the parables
	7:26	**begged** him to cast the demon
	8: 5	He **asked** them, "How many
Lk	4:38	and they **asked** him about her
	5: 3	**asked** him to put out a little
	7: 3	**asking** him to come and heal
	7:36	One of the Pharisees **asked**
	8:37	**asked** Jesus to leave them
	9:45	they were afraid to **ask** him
	11:37	a Pharisee **invited** him to dine
	14:18	**please** accept my regrets
	14:19	**please** accept my regrets
	14:32	**asks** for the terms of peace
	16:27	I **beg** you to send him to my
	19:31	If anyone **asks** you
	20: 3	will also **ask** you a question
	22:68	if I **question** you, you will
	23: 3	Then Pilate **asked** him
Jn	1:19	from Jerusalem to **ask** him
	1:21	And they **asked** him
	1:25	They **asked** him
	4:31	the disciples **were urging** him
	4:40	**asked** him to stay with them
	4:47	he went and **begged** him to come
	5:12	They **asked** him
	8: 7	they kept on **questioning** him
	9: 2	His disciples **asked** him
	9:15	Pharisees also began to **ask** him
	9:19	**asked** them, "Is this your son
	9:21	**Ask** him; he is of age.
	12:21	and **said** to him, "Sir, we wish
	14:16	And I **will ask** the Father
	16: 5	yet none of you **asks** me
	16:19	that they wanted **to ask** him
	16:23	you **will ask** nothing of me
	16:26	you **will ask** in my name
	16:30	to have anyone **question** you

	17: 9	I **am asking** on their behalf		15:27	even the dogs **eat** the crumbs
	17: 9	I **am** not **asking** on behalf		15:32	days and have nothing to **eat**
	17:15	I **am** not **asking** you to take		15:37	all of them **ate** and were filled
	17:20	I **ask** not only on behalf of		15:38	Those who **had eaten** were four
	18:19	high priest **questioned** Jesus		24:49	**eats** and drinks with drunkards
	18:21	Why do you **ask** me		25:35	was hungry and you gave me
	18:21	**Ask** those who heard what			**food**
	19:31	So they **asked** Pilate to have		25:42	hungry and you gave me no **food**
	19:38	**asked** Pilate to let him take		26:17	for you to **eat** the Passover
Ac	1: 6	they **asked** him, "Lord, is this		26:21	and while they **were eating**
	3: 3	he **asked** them for alms		26:26	While they **were eating**
	10:48	Then they **invited** him to stay		26:26	Take, **eat;** this is my body.
	16:39	**asked** them to leave the city	Mk	1: 6	he **ate** locusts and wild honey
	18:20	they **asked** him to stay longer		2:16	he **was eating** with sinners
	23:18	**asked** me to bring this young		2:16	**does** he **eat** with tax collectors
	23:20	Jews have agreed **to ask** you		2:26	**ate** the bread of the Presence
Ph	4: 3	Yes, and I **ask** you also		2:26	any but the priests to **eat**
1Th	4: 1	we **ask** and urge you in the Lord		3:20	they could not even **eat**
	5:12	But we **appeal** to you, brothers		5:43	to give her something to **eat**
2Th	2: 1	we **beg** you, brothers and		6:31	had no leisure even to **eat**
1J	5:16	you **will ask,** and God will		6:36	for themselves to **eat**
2J	1: 5	But now, dear lady, I **ask** you		6:37	You give them something
					to **eat**
				6:37	and give it to them to **eat**
2066	GO8 AG312 LN105			6:42	And all **ate** and were filled
εσθης, CLOTHES				6:44	Those who **had eaten** the loaves
Lk	23:11	he put an elegant **robe** on him		7: 2	**were eating** with defiled hands
	24: 4	two men in dazzling **clothes**		7: 3	do not **eat** unless they
Ac	1:10	two men in white **robes** stood		7: 4	they do not **eat** anything
	10:30	a man in dazzling **clothes**		7: 5	but **eat** with defiled hands
	12:21	Herod put on his royal **robes**		7:28	the dogs under the table **eat**
Ja	2: 2	gold rings and in fine **clothes**		8: 1	crowd without anything to **eat**
	2: 2	a poor person in dirty **clothes**		8: 2	days and have nothing to **eat**
	2: 3	one wearing the fine **clothes**		8: 8	They **ate** and were filled
				11:14	May no one ever **eat** fruit
				14:12	for you to **eat** the Passover
2068	GO158 AG312 LN105 B2:271 K2:689			14:14	where I may **eat** the Passover
εσθιω, I EAT				14:18	their places and **were eating**
Mt	6:25	what you will **eat** or what you		14:18	one who **is eating** with me
	6:31	What will we **eat?**		14:22	While they **were eating**
	9:11	Why does your teacher **eat**	Lk	4: 2	He **ate** nothing at all during
	11:18	For John came neither **eating**		5:30	Why **do** you **eat** and drink with
	11:19	the Son of Man came **eating**		5:33	your disciples **eat** and drink
	12: 1	pluck heads of grain and to **eat**		6: 1	in their hands, and **ate** them
	12: 4	**ate** the bread of the Presence		6: 4	**ate** the bread of the Presence
	12: 4	him or his companions to **eat**		6: 4	for any but the priests to **eat**
	14:16	you give them something **to eat**		7:33	has come **eating** no bread and
	14:20	And all **ate** and were filled		7:34	Son of Man has come **eating**
	14:21	those who **ate** were about five		7:36	asked Jesus **to eat** with him
	15: 2	their hands before they **eat**		8:55	to give her something **to eat**
	15:20	but to **eat** with unwashed hands			

	9:13	give them something to **eat**
	9:17	And all **ate** and were filled
	10: 7	**eating** and drinking whatever
	10: 8	**eat** what is set before you
	12:19	relax, **eat,** drink, be merry
	12:22	what you **will eat**
	12:29	for what you are **to eat**
	12:45	to **eat** and drink and get drunk
	13:26	We **ate** and drank with you
	14: 1	to **eat** a **meal** on the sabbath,
	14:15	is anyone who will **eat** bread
	15:16	pods that the pigs **were eating**
	15:23	let us **eat** and celebrate
	17: 8	serve me while I **eat** and drink
	17: 8	later you **may eat** and drink
	17:27	They were **eating** and drinking
	17:28	they were **eating** and drinking
	22: 8	where I may **eat** the Passover
	22:15	I have eagerly desired to **eat**
	22:16	I will not **eat** it until it is
	22:30	so that you may **eat** and drink
	24:43	he took it and **ate** in their
Jn	4:31	Rabbi, **eat** something.
	4:32	I have food to **eat** that you do
	4:33	brought him something to **eat**
	6: 5	bread for these people to **eat**
	6:23	where they **had eaten** the bread
	6:26	you **ate** your fill of the loaves
	6:31	Our ancestors **ate** the manna
	6:31	them bread from heaven to **eat**
	6:49	Your ancestors **ate** the manna
	6:50	one may **eat** of it and not die
	6:51	Whoever **eats** of this bread
	6:52	man give us his flesh to **eat**
	6:53	unless you **eat** the flesh
	6:58	that which your ancestors **ate**
	18:28	to be able to **eat** the Passover
Ac	9: 9	For three days he was without
	10:13	Get up, Peter; kill and **eat.**
	10:14	for I have never **eaten** anything
	11: 7	Get up, Peter; kill and **eat.**
	23:12	neither to **eat** nor drink until
	23:21	neither to **eat** nor drink until
	27:35	he broke it and began to **eat**
Ro	14: 2	believe in **eating** anything
	14: 2	the weak **eat** only vegetables
	14: 3	Those who **eat** must not despise
	14: 3	not despise those who **abstain,**
	14: 3	**abstain** must not pass judgment

	14: 3	pass judgment on those who **eat;**
	14: 6	Also those who **eat**
	14: 6	**eat** in honor of the Lord
	14: 6	while those who **abstain**
	14: 6	**abstain** in honor of the Lord
	14:20	others fall by what you **eat**
	14:21	it is good not to **eat** meat
	14:23	are condemned if they **eat**
1C	8: 7	think of the food they **eat**
	8: 8	no worse off if we do not **eat**
	8: 8	and no better off if we **do.**
	8:10	to the point of **eating** food
	8:13	I will never **eat** meat
	9: 4	not have the right to our **food**
	9: 7	does not **eat** any of its fruit?
	9: 7	does not **get** any of its milk?
	9:13	get their **food** from the temple
	10: 3	all **ate** the same spiritual food
	10: 7	sat down to **eat** and drink
	10:18	those who **eat** the sacrifices
	10:25	**Eat** whatever is sold in the
	10:27	**eat** whatever is set before you
	10:28	then do not **eat** it
	10:31	So, whether you **eat** or drink
	11:20	really to **eat** the Lord's supper
	11:21	For when the time comes to **eat**
	11:22	Do you not have homes to **eat**
	11:26	as often as you **eat** this bread
	11:27	**eats** the bread or drinks the
	11:28	only then **eat** of the bread
	11:29	all who **eat** and drink without
	11:29	**eat** and drink judgment against
	11:33	when you come together to **eat**
	11:34	If you are hungry, **eat** at home
	15:32	Let us **eat** and drink
2Th	3: 8	we did not **eat** anyone's bread
	3:10	to work should not **eat**
	3:12	to **earn** their own living
He	10:27	fury of fire that will **consume**
	13:10	the tent have no right to **eat**
Ja	5: 3	**will eat** your flesh like fire
Re	2: 7	to **eat** from the tree of life
	2:14	they would **eat** food sacrificed
	2:20	**eat** food sacrificed to idols
	10:10	but when I **had eaten** it
	17:16	they will **devour** her flesh
	19:18	to **eat** the flesh of kings

2069 GO1 AG313 LN105
εσλι, ESLI
Lk   3:25   son of **Esli**, son of Naggai

2072 GO2 AG313 LN105 K1:178
εσοπτρον, MIRROR
1C 13:12   For now we see in a **mirror**
Ja   1:23   look at themselves in a **mirror**

2073 GO3 AG313 LN106
εσπερα, EVENING
Lk 24:29   because it is almost **evening**
Ac   4: 3   for it was already **evening**
    28:23   From morning until **evening**

2074 GO3 AG313 LN106
εσρωμ, ESROM (HEZRON)
Mt   1: 3   and Perez the father of **Hezron**
     1: 3   and **Hezron** the father of Aram
Lk   3:33   son of **Hezron,** son of Perez

2074a GO1 AG313 LN106
εσσοομαι, I AM LESSENED
2C 12:13   How have you **been worse off**

2078 GO52 AG313 LN106 B2:55 K2:697
εσχατος, LAST
Mt   5:26   until you have paid the **last**
    12:45   the **last** state of that person
    19:30   many who are first will be **last**
    19:30   the **last** will be first
    20: 8   beginning with the **last**
    20:12   These **last** worked only one hour
    20:14   I choose to give to this **last**
    20:16   So the **last** will be first
    20:16   the first will be **last**
    27:64   the **last** deception would be
Mk   9:35   wants to be first must be **last**
    10:31   many who are first will be **last**
    10:31   and the **last** will be first
    12: 6   **Finally** he sent him to them
    12:22   **Last** of all the woman herself
Lk 11:26   the **last** state of that person
    12:59   you have paid the very **last**
    13:30   some are **last** who will be first
    13:30   some are first who will be **last**
    14: 9   would start to take the **lowest**
    14:10   sit down at the **lowest** place
Jn   6:39   but raise it up on the **last** day
     6:40   raise them up on the **last** day

6:44   that person up on the **last** day
6:54   raise them up on the **last** day
7:37   the **last** day of the festival
11:24   resurrection on the **last** day
12:48   on the **last** day the word
Ac   1: 8   to the **ends** of the earth
     2:17   In the **last** days it will be
    13:47   to the **ends** of the earth
1C   4: 9   us apostles as **last** of all
    15: 8   **Last** of all, as to one untimely
    15:26   The **last** enemy to be destroyed
    15:45   **last** Adam became a life-giving
    15:52   of an eye, at the **last** trumpet
2Ti 3: 1   in the **last** days distressing
He   1: 2   these **last** days he has spoken
Ja   5: 3   laid up treasure for the **last**
1P   1: 5   to be revealed in the **last** time
     1:20   revealed at the **end** of the ages
2P   2:20   the **last** state has become worse
     3: 3   in the **last** days scoffers will
1J   2:18   Children, it is the **last** hour
     2:18   know that it is the **last** hour
Ju   1:18   In the **last** time there will be
Re   1:17   I am the first and the **last**
     2: 8   words of the first and the **last**
     2:19   I know that your **last** works
    15: 1   plagues, which are the **last**
    21: 9   full of the seven **last** plagues
    22:13   Omega, the first and the **last**

2079 GO1 AG314 LN106 B2:55 R2078
εσχατως, LASTLY
Mk   5:23   is at the **point of death**

2080 GO9 AG314 LN106 K2:698
εσω, INSIDE
Mt 26:58   and going **inside,** he sat with
Mk 14:54   **right** into the courtyard of the
    15:16   led him **into** the courtyard
Jn 20:26   disciples were again **in** the
Ac   5:23   them, we found no one **inside**
Ro   7:22   law of God in my **inmost** self
1C   5:12   Is it not those who are **inside**
2C   4:16   **inner** nature is being renewed
Ep   3:16   in your **inner** being with power

2081 GO12 AG314 LN106 R2080
εσωθεν, FROM INSIDE
Mt   7:15   **inwardly** are ravenous wolves
    23:25   but **inside** they are full of

	23:27	but **inside** they are full of the	5: 7	in the **other** boat to come
	23:28	but **inside** you are full of	6: 6	On **another** sabbath he entered
Mk	7:21	For it is **from within**	7:41	denarii, and the **other** fifty
	7:23	evil things come **from within**	8: 3	and Susanna, and many **others**
Lk	11: 7	And he answers **from within**	8: 6	**Some** fell on the rock
	11:39	**inside** you are full of greed	8: 7	**Some** fell among thorns
	11:40	outside make the **inside** also	8: 8	**Some** fell into good soil
2C	7: 5	without and fears **within**	9:29	appearance of his face **changed**
Re	4: 8	of eyes all around and **inside**	9:56	they went on to **another** village
	5: 1	scroll written on the **inside**	9:59	To **another** he said

2082 GO2 AG314 LN106 B3:794 R2080
εσωτερος, INNER

Ac	16:24	put them in the **innermost** cell	11:16	**Others,** to test him, kept
He	6:19	that enters the **inner** shrine	11:26	seven **other** spirits more evil

2083 GO3 AG314 LN106 B1:259 K2:699
'εταιρος, COMRADE

Mt	20:13	**Friend,** I am doing you no wrong	14:31	to wage war against **another**
	22:12	**Friend,** how did you get in here	16: 7	Then he asked **another**
	26:50	**Friend,** do what you are here to	16:13	the one and love the **other**

2084 GO1 AG314 LN106 B 2:739 K1:726 R2087,1100
'ετερογλωσσος, OTHER TONGUE

1C	14:21	By people of **strange tongues**	17:35	be taken and the **other** left

2085 GO2 AG314 LN107 B3:766 K2:163 R2087,1320
'ετεροδιδασκαλεω, I TEACH OTHER

1Ti	1: 3	not to **teach** any **different**	19:20	Then the **other** came, saying
	6: 3	Whoever **teaches otherwise**	20:11	Next he sent **another** slave

2086 GO1 AG314 LN107 B2:739 K2:901 R2087,2218
'ετεροζυγεω, I YOKE OTHER

2C	6:14	Do not be **mismatched** with	23:40	But the **other** rebuked him

2087 GO98 AG315 LN107 B2:739 K2:702
'ετερος, OTHER

Mt	6:24	hate the one and love the **other**		
	6:24	the one and despise the **other**		
	8:21	**Another** of his disciples said		
	10:23	flee to the **next;** for truly		
	11: 3	or are we to wait for **another**		
	11:16	and calling to one **another**		
	12:45	seven **other** spirits more evil		
	15:30	the mute, and many **others**		
	16:14	and still **others** Jeremiah or		
	21:30	The father went to the **second**		
Mk	16:12	he appeared in **another** form		
Lk	3:18	with many **other** exhortations		
	4:43	the kingdom of God to the **other**		

	9:61	**Another** said, "I will follow
	10: 1	Lord appointed seventy **others**
	14:19	**Another** said, 'I have bought
	14:20	**Another** said, 'I have just
	16:13	the one and despise the **other**
	16:18	his wife and marries **another**
	17:34	be taken and the **other** left
	18:10	and the **other** a tax collector
	22:58	A little later **someone** else
	22:65	heaping many **other** insults
	23:32	Two **others** also, who were
Jn	19:37	**another** passage of scripture
Ac	1:20	Let **another** take his position
	2: 4	to speak in **other** languages
	2:13	But **others** sneered and said
	2:40	with many **other** arguments
	4:12	for there is no **other** name
	7:18	until **another** king who had not
	8:34	himself or about **someone** else
	12:17	left and went to **another** place
	13:35	has also said in **another** psalm
	15:35	with many **others,** they taught
	17: 7	is **another** king named Jesus
	17:21	nothing **but** telling or hearing
	17:34	Damaris, and **others** with them
	20:15	The **next day** we touched at
	23: 6	and **others** were Pharisees
	27: 1	Paul and some **other** prisoners
	27: 3	The **next day** we put in at Sidon
Ro	2: 1	in passing judgment on **another**

	2:21	you, then, that teach **others**		26:65	Why do we **still** need witnesses
	7: 3	if she lives with **another** man		27:63	said while he was **still** alive
	7: 3	if she marries **another** man	Mk	5:35	While he was **still** speaking
	7: 4	that you may belong to **another**		5:35	trouble the teacher **any further**
	7:23	but I see in my members **another**		12: 6	He had **still** one other
	8:39	height, nor depth, nor **anything**		14:43	while he was **still** speaking
	13: 8	for the one who loves **another**		14:63	Why do we **still** need witnesses
	13: 9	and any **other** commandment	Lk	1:15	**even** before his birth he will
1C	3: 4	"I belong to Paul," and **another**		8:49	While he was **still** speaking
	4: 6	in favor of one against **another**		9:42	**While** he was coming, the demon
	6: 1	has a grievance against **another**		14:22	done, and there is **still** room
	10:24	but that of the **other.**		14:26	yes, and **even** life itself
	10:29	I mean the **other's** conscience		14:32	the other is **still** far away
	12: 9	to **another** gifts of healing		15:20	while he was **still** far off
	12:10	to **another** various kinds of		16: 2	cannot be my manager **any longer**
	14:17	the **other** person is not built		18:22	There is **still** one thing
	14:21	by the lips of **foreigners**		20:36	**Indeed** they cannot die anymore
	15:40	of the heavenly is **one thing**		22:47	While he was **still** speaking
	15:40	that of the earthly is **another.**		22:60	while he was **still** speaking
2C	8: 8	the earnestness of **others**		22:71	What **further** testimony do we
	11: 4	you receive a **different** spirit		24: 6	while he was **still** in Galilee
	11: 4	or a **different** gospel from the		24:41	and **still** wondering, he said
Ga	1: 6	turning to a **different** gospel		24:44	while I was **still** with you
	1:19	I did not see any **other** apostle	Jn	4:35	Four months **more,** then comes
	6: 4	**rather than** their neighbor's		7:33	with you a little while **longer**
Ep	3: 5	In **former** generations		11:30	but was **still** at the place
Ph	2: 4	but to the interests of **others**		12:35	with you for a little **longer**
1Ti	1:10	and whatever **else** is contrary		13:33	with you only a little **longer**
2Ti	2: 2	able to teach **others** as well		14:19	In a **little while** the world
He	5: 6	he says also in **another** place		16:12	I **still** have many things to say
	7:11	to speak of **another** priest		20: 1	while it was **still** dark, Mary
	7:13	belonged to **another** tribe	Ac	2:26	**moreover** my flesh will live in
	7:15	when **another** priest arises		9: 1	Saul, **still** breathing threats
	11:36	**Others** suffered mocking and		10:44	While Peter was **still** speaking
Ja	2:25	sent them out by **another** road		18:18	**After** staying there for a
Ju	1: 7	and pursued **unnatural** lust		21:28	he has **actually** brought Greeks
			Ro	3: 7	why am I **still** being condemned

2088   GO1 AG315 LN107 B1:739 R2087
ἑτέρως, OTHERWISE
Ph   3:15   if you think **differently** about

		5: 6	For while we were **still** weak
		5: 6	at the **right** time Christ died
		5: 8	while we **still** were sinners
		6: 2	died to sin **go on** living in it
		9:19	does he **still** find fault
1C	3: 2	now you are **still** not ready

2089   GO93 AG315 LN107
ἔτι, STILL

Mt	5:13	**no longer** good for anything		3: 3	for you are **still** of the flesh
	12:46	While he was **still** speaking		12:31	a **still** more excellent way
	17: 5	While he was **still** speaking		15:17	and you are **still** in your sins
	18:16	take one or two **others** along	2C	1:10	that he will rescue us **again**
	19:20	what do I **still** lack	Ga	1:10	If I were **still** pleasing people
	26:47	While he was **still** speaking		5:11	why am I **still** being persecuted

	5:11	if I am **still** preaching
Ph	1: 9	your love may overflow **more**
2Th	2: 5	when I was **still** with you
He	7:10	for he was **still** in the loins
	7:11	what **further** need would there
	7:15	It is **even** more obvious when
	8:12	remember their sins no **more**
	9: 8	first tent is **still** standing
	10: 2	would **no longer** have any
	10:17	and their lawless deeds no **more**
	10:37	For yet "in a very little **while**
	11: 4	but through his faith he **still**
	11:32	And what **more** should I say
	11:36	**even** chains and imprisonment
	12:26	**Yet** once more I will shake not
	12:27	This phrase, **"Yet** once more,"
Re	3:12	you will **never** go out of it
	6:11	told to rest a little **longer**
	7:16	They will hunger no **more**
	7:16	no more, and thirst no **more**
	9:12	There are **still** two woes to
	12: 8	there was no **longer** any place
	18:21	and will be found no **more**
	18:22	will be heard in you no **more**
	18:22	will be found in you no **more**
	18:22	will be heard in you no **more**
	18:23	will shine in you no **more**
	18:23	will be heard in you no **more**
	20: 3	deceive the nations no **more**
	21: 1	and the sea was no **more**
	21: 4	Death will be no **more**
	21: 4	crying and pain will be no **more**
	22: 3	will be found there any **more**
	22: 5	And there will be no **more** night
	22:11	Let the evildoer **still** do evil
	22:11	and the filthy **still** be filthy
	22:11	the righteous **still** do right
	22:11	and the holy **still** be holy

2090   GO40 AG316 LN107 B3:116 K2:704
ἑτοιμαζω, I PREPARE

Mt	3: 3	**Prepare** the way of the Lord
	20:23	it **has been prepared** by my
	22: 4	I **have prepared** my dinner
	25:34	the kingdom **prepared** for you
	25:41	into the eternal fire **prepared**
	26:17	**to make** the **preparations**
	26:19	and they **prepared** the Passover
Mk	1: 3	**Prepare** the way of the Lord

	10:40	for whom it **has been prepared**
	14:12	to go and **make** the **preparations**
	14:15	**Make preparations** for us there
	14:16	and they **prepared** the Passover
Lk	1:17	a people **prepared** for the Lord
	1:76	before the Lord **to prepare** his
	2:31	which you **have prepared** in the
	3: 4	**Prepare** the way of the Lord
	9:52	to **make ready** for him
	12:20	the things you **have prepared**
	12:47	but did not **prepare** himself
	17: 8	**Prepare** supper for me, put on
	22: 8	Go and **prepare** the Passover
	22: 9	want us to **make preparations**
	22:12	**Make preparations** for us there
	22:13	they **prepared** the Passover meal
	23:56	**prepared** spices and ointments
	24: 1	spices that they **had prepared**
Jn	14: 2	that I go to **prepare** a place
	14: 3	And if I go and **prepare** a place
Ac	23:23	**Get ready** to leave by nine
1C	2: 9	what God has **prepared** for those
2Ti	2:21	**ready** for every good work
Pm	1:22	**prepare** a guest room for me
He	11:16	he **has prepared** a city for them
Re	8: 6	**made ready** to blow them
	9: 7	like horses **equipped** for battle
	9:15	who **had been held ready** for the
	12: 6	where she has a place **prepared**
	16:12	in order to **prepare** the way
	19: 7	bride has **made** herself **ready**
	21: 2	**prepared** as a bride adorned

2091   GO1 AG316 LN107 B3:166 K2:704 R2090
ἑτοιμασια, PREPARATION

| Ep | 6:15 | whatever will make you **ready** |

2092   GO17 AG316 LN107 B3:166 K2:704 R2090
ἑτοιμος, PREPARED

Mt	22: 4	Look, I have **prepared** my dinner
	22: 8	The wedding is **ready**
	24:44	you also must be **ready**
	25:10	who were **ready** went with him
Mk	14:15	upstairs, furnished and **ready**
Lk	12:40	You also must be **ready**
	14:17	for everything is **ready** now
	22:33	I am **ready** to go with you
Jn	7: 6	but your time is always **here**
Ac	23:15	are **ready** to do away with him

	23:21	are **ready** now and are waiting
2C	9: 5	so that it may be **ready** as a
	10: 6	We are **ready** to punish every
	10:16	boasting of work **already** done
Ti	3: 1	to be **ready** for every good work
1P	1: 5	salvation **ready** to be revealed
	3:15	be **ready** to make your defense

2093   GO3 AG316 LN107 R2092
ἑτοίμως, READILY

Ac	21:13	I am **ready** not only to be bound
2C	12:14	**ready** to come to you this third
1P	4: 5	him who stands **ready** to judge

2094   GO49 AG316 LN107
ετος, YEAR

Mt	9:20	hemorrhages for twelve **years**
Mk	5:25	hemorrhages for twelve **years**
	5:42	she was twelve **years of age**
Lk	2:36	seven **years** after her marriage
	2:37	to the **age** of eighty-four
	2:41	Now every **year** his parents went
	2:42	when he was twelve **years** old
	3: 1	fifteenth **year** of the reign
	3:23	Jesus was about thirty **years**
	4:25	shut up three **years** and six
	8:42	for he had an only daughter
	8:43	hemorrhages for twelve **years**
	12:19	goods laid up for many **years**
	13: 7	For three **years** I have come
	13: 8	alone for one more **year**
	13:11	her for eighteen **years**
	13:16	bound for eighteen long **years**
	15:29	For all these **years** I have been
Jn	2:20	for forty-six **years,** and will
	5: 5	ill for thirty-eight **years.**
	8:57	You are not yet fifty **years** old
Ac	4:22	was more than forty **years** old
	7: 6	them during four hundred **years**
	7:30	Now when forty **years** had passed
	7:36	wilderness for forty **years**
	7:42	sacrifices forty **years** in the
	9:33	bedridden for eight **years**
	13:20	about four hundred fifty **years**
	13:21	who reigned for forty **years**
	19:10	This continued for two **years**
	24:10	knowing that for many **years**
	24:17	Now after some **years** I came
Ro	15:23	as I have for many **years**

2C	12: 2	who fourteen **years** ago was
Ga	1:18	after three **years** I did go up
	2: 1	after fourteen **years** I went up
	3:17	four hundred thirty **years** later
1Ti	5: 9	is not less than sixty **years**
He	1:12	your **years** will never end
	3:10	for forty **years**
	3:17	was he angry forty **years**
2P	3: 8	day is like a thousand **years**
	3: 8	thousand **years** are like one day
Re	20: 2	bound him for a thousand **years**
	20: 3	the thousand **years** were ended
	20: 4	with Christ a thousand **years**
	20: 5	the thousand **years** were ended
	20: 6	with him a thousand **years**
	20: 7	the thousand **years** are ended

2095   GO6 AG317 LN107
ευ, WELL

Mt	25:21	**Well** done, good and trustworthy
	25:23	**Well** done, good and trustworthy
Mk	14: 7	you can show **kindness** to them
Lk	19:17	**Well** done, good slave!
Ac	15:29	you will do **well.**
Ep	6: 3	it may be **well** with you

2096   GO2 AG317 LN107
ευα, EVE

2C	11: 3	as the serpent deceived **Eve**
1Ti	2:13	Adam was formed first, then **Eve**

2097   GO54 AG317 LN107 B2:107 K2:707 R2095,31a
ευαγγελιζω, I TELL GOOD MESSAGE

Mt	11: 5	the poor **have good news** brought
Lk	1:19	to **bring** you this **good news**
	2:10	I am **bringing** you **good news**
	3:18	he **proclaimed** the **good news**
	4:18	to **bring good news** to the poor
	4:43	I must **proclaim** the **good news**
	7:22	the poor **have good news brought**
	8: 1	**bringing the good news** of the
	9: 6	**bringing the good news** and
	16:16	**good news . . . is proclaimed,**
	20: 1	and **telling the good news**
Ac	5:42	not cease to teach and **proclaim**
	8: 4	to place, **proclaiming** the word
	8:12	was **proclaiming the good news**
	8:25	**proclaiming the good news** to
	8:35	**proclaimed** to him **the good news**
	8:40	he **proclaimed the good news** to

	10:36	**preaching** peace by Jesus Christ
	11:20	**proclaiming** the Lord Jesus
	13:32	we **bring** you **the good news**
	14: 7	**proclaiming the good news**
	14:15	and we **bring** you **good news**
	14:21	had **proclaimed the good news**
	15:35	they taught and **proclaimed**
	16:10	**proclaim the good news** to them
	17:18	he **was telling the good news**
Ro	1:15	to **proclaim the gospel** to you
	10:15	of those who **bring good news**
	15:20	to **proclaim the good news**
1C	1:17	but to **proclaim the gospel**
	9:16	If I **proclaim the gospel**
	9:16	if I do not **proclaim the gospel**
	9:18	**make the gospel** free of charge
	15: 1	news that I **proclaimed** to you
	15: 2	that I **proclaimed** to you
2C	10:16	we may **proclaim the good news**
	11: 7	I **proclaimed** God's **good news**
Ga	1: 8	**proclaim** to you a **gospel**
	1: 8	contrary to what we **proclaimed**
	1: 9	**proclaims** to you a **gospel**
	1:11	the gospel that was **proclaimed**
	1:16	so that I might **proclaim** him
	1:23	is now **proclaiming** the faith
	4:13	I first **announced the gospel**
Ep	2:17	So he came and **proclaimed** peace
	3: 8	**bring** to the Gentiles **the news**
1Th	3: 6	**has brought** us **the good news**
He	4: 2	the **good news came** to us
	4: 6	formerly **received the good news**
1P	1:12	those who **brought** you **good news**
	1:25	**good news** that **was announced**
	4: 6	the **gospel was proclaimed** even
Re	10: 7	as he **announced** to his servants
	14: 6	an eternal gospel **to proclaim**

2098   G076 AG317 LN107 B2:107 K2:721 R2097

ευαγγελιον, GOOD MESSAGE

Mt	4:23	proclaiming the **good news**
	9:35	proclaiming the **good news**
	24:14	this **good news** of the kingdom
	26:13	this **good news** is proclaimed
Mk	1: 1	the **good news** of Jesus Christ
	1:14	the **good news** of God
	1:15	believe in the **good news**
	8:35	for the sake of the **gospel**
	10:29	for the sake of the **good news**

	13:10	And the **good news** must first be
	14: 9	the **good news** is proclaimed
	16:15	proclaim the **good news** to the
Ac	15: 7	the message of the **good news**
	20:24	the **good news** of God's grace
Ro	1: 1	set apart for the **gospel**
	1: 9	by announcing the **gospel** of his
	1:16	I am not ashamed of the **gospel**
	2:16	according to my **gospel**
	10:16	all have obeyed the **good news**
	11:28	As regards the **gospel** they are
	15:16	service of the **gospel** of God
	15:19	the **good news** of Christ
	16:25	according to my **gospel**
1C	4:15	your father through the **gospel**
	9:12	in the way of the **gospel**
	9:14	those who proclaim the **gospel**
	9:14	get their living by the **gospel**
	9:18	I may make the **gospel** free
	9:18	use of my rights in the **gospel**
	9:23	for the sake of the **gospel**
	15: 1	the **good news** that I proclaimed
2C	2:12	to proclaim the **good news**
	4: 3	even if our **gospel** is veiled
	4: 4	the light of the **gospel**
	8:18	his proclaiming the **good news**
	9:13	the confession of the **gospel**
	10:14	with the **good news** of Christ
	11: 4	or a different **gospel** from the
	11: 7	God's **good news** to you free
Ga	1: 6	turning to a different **gospel**
	1: 7	want to pervert the **gospel**
	1:11	the **gospel** that was proclaimed
	2: 2	the **gospel** that I proclaim
	2: 5	so that the truth of the **gospel**
	2: 7	been entrusted with the **gospel**
	2:14	with the truth of the **gospel**
Ep	1:13	the **gospel** of your salvation
	3: 6	Christ Jesus through the **gospel**
	6:15	ready to proclaim the **gospel**
	6:19	the mystery of the **gospel**
Ph	1: 5	the **gospel** from the first day
	1: 7	and confirmation of the **gospel**
	1:12	helped to spread the **gospel**
	1:16	for the defense of the **gospel**
	1:27	worthy of the **gospel** of Christ
	1:27	for the faith of the **gospel**
	2:22	in the work of the **gospel**
	4: 3	in the work of the **gospel**

	4:15	the early days of the **gospel**
Co	1: 5	word of the truth, the **gospel**
	1:23	the hope promised by the **gospel**
1Th	1: 5	our message of the **gospel** came
	2: 2	to declare to you the **gospel**
	2: 4	with the message of the **gospel**
	2: 8	not only the **gospel** of God but
	2: 9	to you the **gospel** of God
	3: 2	in proclaiming the **gospel**
2Th	1: 8	who do not obey the **gospel**
	2:14	proclamation of the **good news**
1Ti	1:11	conforms to the glorious **gospel**
2Ti	1: 8	in suffering for the **gospel**
	1:10	to light through the **gospel**
	2: 8	that is my **gospel**
Pm	1:13	my imprisonment for the **gospel**
1P	4:17	who do not obey the **gospel**
Re	14: 6	with an eternal **gospel**

2099   GO3   AG318   LN107   B2:107   K2:736   R2097
ευαγγελιστης, GOOD MESSAGE TELLER

Ac	21: 8	house of Philip the **evangelist**
Ep	4:11	some prophets, some **evangelists**
2Ti	4: 5	do the work of an **evangelist**

2100   GO3   AG318   LN107   B2:814   K1:456   R2101
ευαρεστεω, I AM WELL PLEASED

He	11: 5	that "he **had pleased** God."
	11: 6	it is impossible **to please** God
	13:16	such sacrifices **are pleasing**

2101   GO9   AG318   LN107   B2:814 K 1:456   R2095,701
ευαρεστος, WELL-PLEASING

Ro	12: 1	holy and **acceptable** to God
	12: 2	what is good and **acceptable**
	14:18	serves Christ is **acceptable**
2C	5: 9	we make it our aim to **please**
Ep	5:10	what is **pleasing** to the Lord
Ph	4:18	acceptable and **pleasing** to God
Co	3:20	this is your **acceptable** duty
Ti	2: 9	and to give **satisfaction**
He	13:21	which is **pleasing** in his sight

2102   GO1   AG318   LN107   R2101
ευαρεστως, WELL-PLEASINGLY

He	12:28	to God an **acceptable** worship

2103   GO1   AG319   LN107
ευβουλος, EUBULUS

2Ti	4:21	**Eubulus** sends greetings to you

2104   GO3   AG319   LN107   B1:187   R2095,1096
ευγενης, WELL BORN

Lk	19:12	A **nobleman** went to a distant
Ac	17:11	These Jews were **more receptive**
1C	1:26	not many were of **noble birth**

2105   GO1   AG319   LN107   B3:1000
ευδια, GOOD WEATHER

Mt	16: 2	It will be **fair weather**

2106   GO21   AG319   LN108   B2:383   K2:738   R2095,1380
ευδοκεω, I THINK WELL

Mt	3:17	with whom I **am well pleased**
	12:18	whom my soul **is well pleased**
	17: 5	with him I **am well pleased**
Mk	1:11	with you I **am well pleased**
Lk	3:22	with you I **am well pleased**
	12:32	your Father's **good pleasure**
Ro	15:26	**have been pleased** to share
	15:27	They **were pleased** to do this
1C	1:21	God **decided,** through the
	10: 5	God **was** not **pleased** with most
2C	5: 8	Yes, we do have **confidence**
	12:10	I **am content** with weaknesses
Ga	1:15	through his grace, **was pleased**
Co	1:19	fullness of God **was pleased**
1Th	2: 8	that we **are determined** to share
	3: 1	we **decided** to be left alone
2Th	2:12	the truth but **took pleasure** in
He	10: 6	you **have taken** no **pleasure**
	10: 8	desired nor **taken pleasure**
	10:38	My soul **takes** no **pleasure**
2P	1:17	with whom I **am well pleased**

2107   GO9   AG319   LN108   B2:817   K2:742   R2106
ευδοκια, GOOD THOUGHT

Mt	11:26	for such was your **gracious** will
Lk	2:14	among those whom he **favors**
	10:21	for such was your **gracious** will
Ro	10: 1	my heart's **desire** and prayer
Ep	1: 5	according to the **good pleasure**
	1: 9	according to his **good pleasure**
Ph	1:15	but others from **goodwill**
	2:13	to work for his **good pleasure**
2Th	1:11	every **good resolve** and work

2108   GO2   AG319   LN108   B3:1152   K2:654   R2110
ευεργεσια, GOOD WORK

Ac	4: 9	because of a **good deed** done
1Ti	6: 2	who benefit by their **service**

2109 GO1 AG320 LN108 B3:1147 R2110
ευεργετεω, I WORK WELL
Ac 10:38 how he went about **doing good**

2110 GO1 AG320 LN108 B3:1147 K2:654 R2095,2038
ευεργετης, GOOD WORKER
Lk 22:25 them are called **benefactors**

2111 GO3 AG320 LN108
ευθετος, SUITABLE
Lk 9:62 is **fit** for the kingdom of God
    14:35 It is **fit** neither for the soil
He 6: 7 produces a crop **useful** to those

2112 GO36 AG320 LN108 B3:833
ευθεως, IMMEDIATELY
Mt 4:20 **Immediately** they left their
    4:22 **Immediately** they left the boat
    8: 3 **Immediately** his leprosy was
    13: 5 and they sprang up **quickly**
    14:22 **Immediately** he made the
    14:31 Jesus **immediately** reached out
    20:34 **Immediately** they regained their
    21: 2 **immediately** you will find a
    24:29 **Immediately** after the suffering
    25:15 went off **at once** and traded
    26:49 **At once** he came up to Jesus
    26:74 **At that moment** the cock crowed
    27:48 **At once** one of them ran
Mk 7:35 And **immediately** his ears were
Lk 5:13 **Immediately** the leprosy left
    12:36 **as soon as** he comes and knocks
    12:54 you **immediately** say, 'It is
    14: 5 will you not **immediately** pull
    17: 7 Come here **at once** and take
    21: 9 end will not follow **immediately**
Jn 5: 9 **At once** the man was made well
    6:21 **immediately** the boat reached
    18:27 **at that moment** the cock crowed
Ac 9:18 And **immediately** something like
    9:20 and **immediately** he began to
    9:34 And **immediately** he got up
    12:10 when **suddenly** the angel left
    16:10 we **immediately** tried to cross
    17:10 That **very** night the
    17:14 believers **immediately** sent Paul
    21:30 **immediately** the doors were shut
    22:29 **Immediately** those who were
Ga 1:16 did not confer with **any** human
Ja 1:24 **immediately** forget what they

3J 1:14 instead I hope to see you **soon**
Re 4: 2 **At once** I was in the spirit

2113 GO2 AG320 LN108 R2117,1408
ευθυδρομεω, I RUN STRAIGHT
Ac 16:11 **took** a **straight course** to
    21: 1 we **came by** a **straight course** to

2114 GO3 AG320 LN108 R2115
ευθυμεω, I AM CHEERFUL
Ac 27:22 to **keep up** your **courage**
    27:25 So **keep up** your **courage,** men,
Ja 5:13 **Are any cheerful?** They should

2115 GO1 AG320 LN108
ευθυμος, CHEERFUL
Ac 27:36 all of them were **encouraged**

2115a GO1 AG320 LN108
ευθυμως, CHEERFULLY
Ac 24:10 I **cheerfully** make my defense

2116 GO2 AG320 LN108 R2117
ευθυνω, I STRAIGHTEN
Jn 1:23 **Make straight** the way of the
Ja 3: 4 the will of the **pilot** directs

2117 GO51 AG321 LN108 B3:833 R2112
ευθυς, IMMEDIATELY
Mt 3:16 **suddenly** the heavens were
    13:20 **immediately** receives it with
    13:21 person **immediately** falls away
    14:27 **immediately** Jesus spoke to them
    21: 3 he will send them **immediately**
Mk 1:10 **just as** he was coming up out
    1:12 Spirit **immediately** drove him
    1:18 **immediately** they left their
    1:20 **Immediately** he called them
    1:21 and **when** the sabbath came
    1:23 **Just then** there was in their
    1:28 **At once** his fame began to
    1:29 **As soon as** they left the
    1:30 told him about her **at once**
    1:42 **Immediately** the leprosy left
    1:43 he sent him away **at once**
    2: 8 **At once** Jesus perceived in his
    2:12 **immediately** took the mat
    3: 6 **immediately** conspired with the
    4: 5 and it sprang up **quickly,** since
    4:15 Satan **immediately** comes

4:16	they **immediately** receive it
4:17	**immediately** they fall away
4:29	**at once** he goes in with his
5: 2	**immediately** a man out of the
5:29	**Immediately** her hemorrhage
5:30	**Immediately** aware that power
5:42	**immediately** the girl got up
5:42	**At this** they were overcome
6:25	**Immediately** she rushed back to
6:27	**Immediately** the king sent a
6:45	**Immediately** he made his
6:50	**immediately** he spoke to them
6:54	people **at once** recognized him
7:25	**immediately** heard about him
8:10	**immediately** he got into the
9:15	they were **immediately** overcome
9:20	**immediately** it convulsed the
9:24	**Immediately** the father of the
10:52	**Immediately** he regained his
11: 2	**immediately** as you enter it
11: 3	send it back here **immediately**
14:43	**Immediately,** while he was still
14:45	he went up to him **at once**
14:72	**At that moment** the cock crowed
15: 1	**As soon as** it was morning
Lk 6:49	**immediately** it fell, and great
Jn 13:30	he **immediately** went out
13:32	and will glorify him **at once**
19:34	and **at once** blood and water
Ac 10:16	**suddenly** taken up to heaven

2117a   GO8 AG321 LN108
ευθυς, STRAIGHT

Mt 3: 3	make his paths **straight**
Mk 1: 3	make his paths **straight**
Lk 3: 4	make his paths **straight**
3: 5	crooked shall be made **straight**
Ac 8:21	heart is not **right** before God
9:11	the street called **Straight**
13:10	the **straight** paths of the Lord
2P 2:15	have left the **straight** road

2118   GO1 AG321 LN108 R2117
ευθυτης, STRAIGHTNESS

He 1: 8	the **righteous** scepter is the

2119   GO3 AG321 LN108 B3:833 R2121
ευκαιρεω, I HAVE GOOD SEASON

Mk 6:31	they **had no leisure** even to eat

Ac 17:21	there **would spend** their **time**
1C 16:12	when he **has** the **opportunity**

2120   GO2 AG321 LN108 B3:833 K3:462 R2121
ευκαιρια, GOOD SEASON

Mt 26:16	for an **opportunity** to betray
Lk 22: 6	to look for an **opportunity**

2121   GO2 AG321 LN108 B3:833 K3:462 R2095,2540
ευκαιρος, GOOD SEASON

Mk 6:21	But an **opportunity** came when
He 4:16	grace to help **in time** of need

2122   GO2 AG321 LN108 B3:833 R2121
ευκαιρως, GOOD SEASONALLY

Mk 14:11	to look for an **opportunity**
2Ti 4: 2	whether the time is **favorable**

2123   GO7 AG321 LN108 R2095,2873
ευκοπος, EASIER LABOR

Mt 9: 5	For which is **easier,** to say
19:24	it is **easier** for a camel to go
Mk 2: 9	Which is **easier,** to say to the
10:25	It is **easier** for a camel to go
Lk 5:23	Which is **easier,** to say
16:17	But it is **easier** for heaven
18:25	it is **easier** for a camel to go

2124   GO2 AG321 LN108 B2:90 K2:751 R2126
ευλαβεια, REVERENCE

He 5: 7	of his **reverent** submission
12:28	worship with **reverence** and awe

2125   GO1 AG321 LN108 B2:90 K2:751 R2126
ευλαβεομαι, I AM REVERENT

He 11: 7	**respected** the warning and built

2126   GO4 AG322 LN108 B2:90 K2:751
ευλαβης, REVERENT

Lk 2:25	man was righteous and **devout**
Ac 2: 5	Now there were **devout** Jews
8: 2	**Devout** men buried Stephen
22:12	Ananias, who was a **devout** man

2127   GO41 AG322 LN108 B1:206 K2:754 R2095,3056
ευλογεω, I SPEAK WELL

Mt 14:19	**blessed** and broke the loaves
21: 9	**Blessed** is the one who comes
23:39	**Blessed** is the one who comes

	25:34	that are **blessed** by my Father
	26:26	after **blessing** it he broke it
Mk	6:41	**blessed** and broke the loaves
	8: 7	and after **blessing** them
	11: 9	**Blessed** is the one who comes
	11:10	**Blessed** is the coming kingdom
	14:22	after **blessing** it he broke it
Lk	1:42	**Blessed** are you among women
	1:42	**blessed** is the fruit of your
	1:64	began to speak, **praising** God
	2:28	in his arms and **praised** God,
	2:34	Then Simeon **blessed** them
	6:28	**bless** those who curse you
	9:16	and **blessed** and broke them
	13:35	**Blessed** is the one who
	19:38	**Blessed** is the king who comes
	24:30	bread, **blessed** and broke it
	24:50	up his hands, he **blessed** them
	24:51	While he **was blessing** them
	24:53	in the temple **blessing** God
Jn	12:13	**Blessed** is the one who comes
Ac	3:26	to **bless** you by turning each
Ro	12:14	**Bless** those who persecute you
	12:14	**bless** and do not curse them
1C	4:12	When reviled, we **bless**
	10:16	cup of blessing that we **bless**
	14:16	if you say a **blessing** with the
Ga	3: 9	those who believe **are blessed**
Ep	1: 3	who **has blessed** us in Christ
He	6:14	I will **surely** bless you and
	6:14	I will **surely** bless you and
	7: 1	defeating the kings and **blessed**
	7: 6	**blessed** him who had received
	7: 7	that the inferior **is blessed**
	11:20	Isaac **invoked blessings**
	11:21	**blessed** each of the sons of
Ja	3: 9	we **bless** the Lord and Father
1P	3: 9	repay with a **blessing**

2128　GO8 AG322 LN108 B1:206 K2:764 R2127
ευλογητος, WELL SPOKEN

Mk	14:61	the Son of the **Blessed** One
Lk	1:68	**Blessed** be the Lord God of
Ro	1:25	the Creator, who is **blessed**
	9: 5	over all, God **blessed** forever
2C	1: 3	**Blessed** be the God and Father
	11:31	**blessed** be he forever
Ep	1: 3	**Blessed** be the God and Father
1P	1: 3	**Blessed** be the God and Father

2129　GO16 AG322 LN108 B1:206 K2:754 R2127
ευλογια, GOOD WORD

Ro	15:29	fullness of the **blessing**
	16:18	by smooth talk and **flattery**
1C	10:16	The cup of **blessing** that we
2C	9: 5	for this **bountiful gift** that
	9: 5	be ready as a **voluntary gift**
	9: 6	the one who sows **bountifully**
	9: 6	will also reap **bountifully**
Ga	3:14	the **blessing** of Abraham might
Ep	1: 3	with every spiritual **blessing**
He	6: 7	receives a **blessing** from God
	12:17	wanted to inherit the **blessing**
Ja	3:10	the same mouth come **blessing**
1P	3: 9	you might inherit a **blessing**
Re	5:12	honor and glory and **blessing**
	5:13	**blessing** and honor and glory
	7:12	**Blessing** and glory and wisdom

2130　GO1 AG323 LN108 R2095,3330
ευμεταδοτος, GOOD EXCHANGER

1Ti	6:18	**generous,** and ready to share

2131　GO1 AG323 LN109
ευνικη, EUNICE

2Ti	1: 5	Lois and your mother **Eunice**

2132　GO1 AG323 LN109 K4:971 R2095,3539
ευνοεω, I AM WELL MINDED

Mt	5:25	**Come to terms** quickly with

2133　GO1 AG323 LN109 K4:971
ευνοια, GOOD MIND

Ep	6: 7	Render service with **enthusiasm**

2134　GO2 AG323 LN109 B1:559 K2:765 R2135
ευνουχιζω, I MAKE EUNUCH

Mt	19:12	who **have been made eunuchs** by
	19:12	**have made themselves eunuchs**

2135　GO8 AG323 LN109 B1:559 K2:765
ευνουχος, EUNUCH

Mt	19:12	For there are **eunuchs** who have
	19:12	**eunuchs** who have been made
	19:12	and there are **eunuchs** who have
Ac	8:27	there was an Ethiopian **eunuch**
	8:34	The **eunuch** asked Philip
	8:36	and the **eunuch** said, "Look,
	8:38	the **eunuch,** went down into the
	8:39	the **eunuch** saw him no more

2136 GO1 AG323 LN109
ευοδια, EUODIA
Ph   4: 2   I urge **Euodia** and I urge

2137 GO4 AG323 LN109 K5:109 R2095,3598
ευοδοω, I TRAVEL WELL
Ro   1:10   **succeed** in coming to you
1C 16: 2   save whatever **extra you earn**
3J   1: 2   I pray that all **may go well**
      1: 2   as **it is well** with your soul

2137a GO1 AG324 LN109
ευπαρεδρος, CONSISTENT
1C   7:35   **unhindered** devotion to the Lord

2138 GO1 AG324 LN109 R2095,3982
ευπειθης, WELL-PERSUADED
Ja   3:17   gentle, willing to **yield**

2139 GO1 AG324 LN109 R2095,4012,2476
ευπεριστατος, WELL-WRAPPED
He 12: 1   the sin that **clings so closely**

2140 GO1 AG324 LN109 R2095,4160
ευποιια, DOING WELL
He 13:16   Do not neglect **to do good**

2141 GO1 AG324 LN109
ευπορεω, I PROSPER
Ac 11:29   that according **to their ability**

2142 GO1 AG324 LN109
ευπορια, PROSPERITY
Ac 19:25   you know that we get our **wealth**

2143 GO1 AG324 LN109
ευπρεπεια, GOOD APPEARANCE
Ja   1:11   falls, and its **beauty** perishes

2144 GO5 AG324 LN109 B3:744 K2:58 R2095,4327
ευπροσδεκτος, WELL-ACCEPTED
Ro 15:16   the Gentiles may be **acceptable**
      15:31   may be **acceptable** to the saints
2C   6: 2   now is the **acceptable** time
      8:12   the gift is **acceptable**
1P   2: 5   spiritual sacrifices **acceptable**

2146 GO1 AG324 LN109 K6:779
ευπροσωπεω, I PUT ON A GOOD FACE
Ga   6:12   who want to **make** a **good showing**

2146a GO1 AG324 LN109
ευρακυλων, NORTHEAST
Ac 27:14   called the **northeaster**

2147 GO176 AG324 LN109 B3:527 K2:769
ευρισκω, I FIND
Mt   1:18   she **was found** to be with child
      2: 8   and when you **have found** him
      7: 7   search, and you **will find**
      7: 8   and everyone who searches **finds**
      7:14   and there are few who **find** it
      8:10   Israel have I **found** such faith
      10:39   Those who **find** their life will
      10:39   life for my sake will **find** it
      11:29   will **find** rest for your souls
      12:43   place, but it **finds** none
      12:44   it comes, it **finds** it empty
      13:44   which someone **found** and hid
      13:46   **finding** one pearl of great
      16:25   for my sake **will find** it
      17:27   you **will find** a coin
      18:13   And if he **finds** it
      18:28   **came upon** one of his fellow
      20: 6   **found** others standing around
      21: 2   you **will find** a donkey tied
      21:19   **found** nothing at all on it
      22: 9   and invite everyone you **find**
      22:10   gathered all whom they **found**
      24:46   his master **will find** at work
      26:40   and **found** them sleeping
      26:43   Again he came and **found** them
      26:60   but they **found** none
      27:32   **came upon** a man from Cyrene
Mk   1:37   When they **found** him, they said
      7:30   **found** the child lying on the
      11: 2   you **will find** tied there a colt
      11: 4   They went away and **found** a colt
      11:13   perhaps he **would find** anything
      11:13   he **found** nothing but leaves
      13:36   or else he **may find** you asleep
      14:16   **found** everything as he had told
      14:37   He came and **found** them sleeping
      14:40   he came and **found** them sleeping
      14:55   to death; but they **found** none
Lk   1:30   you **have found** favor with God
      2:12   you **will find** a child wrapped
      2:45   When they **did** not **find** him
      2:46   After three days they **found** him
      4:17   **found** the place where it

	5:19	but **finding** no way to bring him
	6: 7	they **might find** an accusation
	7: 9	Israel have I **found** such faith
	7:10	**found** the slave in good health
	8:35	they **found** the man from whom
	9:12	to lodge and **get** provisions
	9:36	Jesus **was found** alone
	11: 9	search, and you **will find**
	11:10	and everyone who searches **finds**
	11:24	but not **finding** any, it says
	11:25	**finds** it swept and put in order
	12:37	whom the master **finds** alert
	12:38	near dawn, and **finds** them so
	12:43	his master **will find** at work
	13: 6	for fruit on it and **found** none
	13: 7	fig tree, and still I **find** none
	15: 4	one that is lost until he **finds**
	15: 5	When he **has found** it
	15: 6	I **have found** my sheep that was
	15: 8	carefully until she **finds** it
	15: 9	When she **has found** it
	15: 9	for I **have found** the coin
	15:24	he was lost and **is found**
	15:32	he was lost and **has been found**
	17:18	none of them **found** to return
	18: 8	**will** he **find** faith on earth
	19:30	you **will find** tied there a colt
	19:32	**found** it as he had told them
	19:48	but they did not **find** anything
	22:13	they went and **found** everything
	22:45	**found** them sleeping because of
	23: 2	We **found** this man perverting
	23: 4	I **find** no basis for
	23:14	**have** not **found** this man guilty
	23:22	I **have found** in him no ground
	24: 2	**found** the stone rolled away
	24: 3	they **did** not **find** the body
	24:23	when they **did** not **find** his body
	24:24	**found** it just as the women had
	24:33	they **found** the eleven and their
Jn	1:41	first **found** his brother Simon
	1:41	We have **found** the Messiah
	1:43	He **found** Philip and said to
	1:45	Philip **found** Nathanael and said
	1:45	We have **found** him about whom
	2:14	In the temple he **found** people
	5:14	Jesus **found** him in the temple
	6:25	they **found** him on the other
	7:34	but you **will** not **find** me

	7:35	that we **will** not **find** him
	7:36	me and you **will** not **find**
	9:35	and when he **found** him, he said
	10: 9	in and go out and **find** pasture
	11:17	he **found** that Lazarus had
	12:14	Jesus **found** a young donkey
	18:38	I **find** no case against him
	19: 4	that I **find** no case against him
	19: 6	I **find** no case against him
	21: 6	and you will **find** some
Ac	4:21	**finding** no way to punish them
	5:10	men came in they **found** her dead
	5:22	did not **find** them in the prison
	5:23	We **found** the prison securely
	5:23	we **found** no one inside
	5:39	you **may** even **be found** fighting
	7:11	ancestors could **find** no food.
	7:46	who **found** favor with God
	7:46	he **might find** a dwelling place
	8:40	Philip **found** himself at Azotus
	9: 2	if he **found** any who belonged
	9:33	he **found** a man named Aeneas
	10:27	went in and **found** that many
	11:26	and when he had **found** him
	12:19	for him and could not **find** him
	13: 6	they **met** a certain magician
	13:22	I **have found** David, son of
	13:28	though they **found** no cause
	17: 6	When they could not **find** them
	17:23	I **found** among them an altar
	17:27	grope for him and **find** him
	18: 2	he **found** a Jew named Aquila
	19: 1	where he **found** some disciples
	19:19	it **was found** to come to fifty
	21: 2	When we **found** a ship bound for
	23: 9	We **find** nothing wrong with
	23:29	I **found** that he was accused
	24: 5	**found** this man a pestilent
	24:12	They did not **find** me disputing
	24:18	they **found** me in the temple
	24:20	tell what crime they had **found**
	27: 6	**found** an Alexandrian ship bound
	27:28	took soundings and **found** twenty
	27:28	again and **found** fifteen fathoms
	28:14	There we **found** believers
Ro	4: 1	we to say **was gained** by Abraham
	7:10	life **proved to be** death to me
	7:21	So I **find** it to be a law

	10:20	I **have been found** by those who
1C	4: 2	that they be **found** trustworthy
	15:15	We **are** even **found** to be
2C	2:13	I did not **find** my brother Titus
	5: 3	we will not **be found** naked
	9: 4	**find** that you are not ready
	11:12	to **be recognized** as our equals
	12:20	that you **may find** me not as you
	12:20	I **may find** you not as I wish
Ga	2:17	we ourselves **have been found**
Ph	2: 7	And **being found** in human form
	3: 9	**be found** in him, not having
2Ti	1:17	searched for me and **found** me
	1:18	will **find** mercy from the Lord
He	4:16	**find** grace to help in time of
	9:12	**obtaining** eternal redemption
	11: 5	he **was** not **found,** because God
	12:17	he **found** no chance to repent
1P	1: 7	**may be found** to result in
	2:22	no deceit **was found** in his
2P	3:10	is done on it **will be disclosed**
	3:14	strive **to be found** by him
2J	1: 4	I was overjoyed **to find** some
Re	2: 2	and **have found** them to be false
	3: 2	I **have** not **found** your works
	5: 4	because no one **was found** worthy
	9: 6	seek death but will not **find** it
	12: 8	there **was** no longer any place
	14: 5	in their mouth no lie **was found**
	16:20	no mountains **were to be found**
	18:14	never **to be found** again
	18:21	and **will be found** no more
	18:22	any trade **will be found** in you
	18:24	And in you **was found** the blood
	20:11	and no place **was found** for them
	20:15	name **was** not **found** written

2149 GO1 AG326 LN109
ευρυχωρος, BROADSPACED
Mt 7:13   the road is **easy** that leads to

2150 GO15 AG326 LN109 B2:91 K7:175 R2152
ευσεβεια, REVERENCE
Ac 3:12   by our own power or **piety**
1Ti 2: 2   in all **godliness** and dignity
     3:16   the mystery of our **religion**
     4: 7   Train yourself in **godliness**
     4: 8   **godliness** is valuable in every
     6: 3   in accordance with **godliness**

	6: 5	**godliness** is a means of gain
	6: 6	is great gain in **godliness**
	6:11	**godliness,** faith, love
2Ti	3: 5	outward form of **godliness**
Ti	1: 1	is in accordance with **godliness**
2P	1: 3	needed for life and **godliness**
	1: 6	and endurance with **godliness**
	1: 7	**godliness** with mutual affection
	3:11	lives of holiness and **godliness**

2151 GO2 AG326 LN109 B2:91 K7:175 R2152
ευσεβεω, I REVERE
Ac 17:23 What therefore you **worship** as
1Ti 5: 4   first learn their **religious duty**

2152 GO3 AG326 LN109 K7:175 R2095,4576
ευσεβης, REVERENT
Ac 10: 2 He was a **devout** man who feared
     10: 7 a **devout** soldier from the ranks
2P 2: 9   knows how to rescue the **godly**

2153 GO2 AG326 LN110 R2152
ευσεβως, REVERENTLY
2Ti 3:12 who want to live a **godly** life
Ti 2:12 upright, and **godly**

2154 GO1 AG326 LN110 K2:770
ευσημος, WELL-DEFINED
1C 14: 9 that is not **intelligible**

2155 GO2 AG326 LN110 B2:599 K7:548 R2095,4698
ευσπλαγχνος, WELL-AFFECTIONED
Ep 4:32 to one another, **tenderhearted**
1P 3: 8 for one another, a **tender heart**

2156 GO3 AG327 LN110 R2158
ευσχημονως, PROPERLY
Ro 13:13 let us live **honorably** as in
1C 14:40 should be done **decently** and in
1Th 4:12 so that you may behave **properly**

2157 GO1 AG327 LN110 R2158
ευσχημοσυνη, APPROPRIATENESS
1C 12:23 treated with greater **respect**

2158 GO5 AG327 LN110 K2:770
ευσχημων, PROPER
Mk 15:43 a **respected** member of the
Ac 13:50 devout women of **high standing**
     17:12 women and men of **high standing**

1C   7:35   but to promote **good order**
    12:24   our more **respectable** members

2159   GO2 AG327 LN110
ευτονως, INTENSELY
Lk   23:10   stood by, **vehemently** accusing
Ac   18:28   he **powerfully** refuted the Jews

2160   GO1 AG327 LN110
ευτραπελια, COARSE JOKING
Ep   5: 4   obscene, silly, and **vulgar talk**

2161   GO1 AG327 LN110
ευτυχος, EUTYCHUS
Ac   20: 9   A young man named **Eutychus**

2162   GO1 AG327 LN110 R2163
ευφημια, GOOD REPORT
2C   6: 8   in ill repute and **good repute**

2163   GO1 AG327 LN110 R2095,5345
ευφημος, GOOD SAYING
Ph   4: 8   whatever is **commendable**

2164   GO1 AG327 LN110
ευφορεω, I WEAR WELL
Lk   12:16   rich man **produced abundantly.**

2165   GO14 AG327 LN110 B2:354 K2:772
ευφραινω, I AM MERRY
Lk   12:19   relax, eat, drink, **be merry**
    15:23   and let us eat and **celebrate**
    15:24   And they began to **celebrate**
    15:29   goat so that I **might celebrate**
    15:32   we had to **celebrate** and rejoice
    16:19   and who **feasted** sumptuously
Ac   2:26   therefore my heart **was glad**
    7:41   **reveled** in the works of their
Ro   15:10   **Rejoice,** O Gentiles, with his
2C   2: 2   who is there to **make** me **glad**
Ga   4:27   **Rejoice,** you childless one
Re   11:10   **celebrate** and exchange presents
    12:12   **Rejoice** then, you heavens and
    18:20   **Rejoice** over her, O heaven

2166   GO2 AG328 LN110
ευφρατης, EUPHRATES
Re   9:14   at the great river **Euphrates**
    16:12   on the great river **Euphrates**

2167   GO2 AG328 LN110 B2:354 K2:772
ευφροσυνη, MERRIMENT
Ac   2:28   will make me full of **gladness**
    14:17   food and your hearts with **joy**

2168   GO38 AG328 LN110 B2:855 K9:407 R2170
ευχαριστεω, I GIVE GOOD FAVOR
Mt   15:36   **giving thanks** he broke them
    26:27   and after **giving thanks** he gave
Mk   8: 6   after **giving thanks** he broke
    14:23   after **giving thanks** he gave it
Lk   17:16   at Jesus' feet and **thanked** him
    18:11   God, I **thank** you that I am not
    22:17   after **giving thanks** he said
    22:19   when he had **given thanks**
Jn   6:11   when he had **given thanks**
    6:23   after the Lord **had given thanks**
    11:41   Father, I **thank** you for having
Ac   27:35   **giving thanks** to God in the
    28:15   Paul **thanked** God and took
Ro   1: 8   First, I **thank** my God through
    1:21   honor him as God or **give thanks**
    14: 6   since they **give thanks** to God
    14: 6   the Lord and **give thanks** to God
    16: 4   whom not only I **give thanks**
1C   1: 4   I **give thanks** to my God always
    1:14   I **thank** God that I baptized
    10:30   of that for which I **give thanks**
    11:24   and when he had **given thanks**
    14:17   you may **give thanks** well enough
    14:18   I **thank** God that I speak
2C   1:11   **will give thanks** on our behalf
Ep   1:16   I do not cease **to give thanks**
    5:20   **giving thanks** to God the Father
Ph   1: 3   I **thank** my God every time
Co   1: 3   we always **thank** God, the Father
    1:12   **giving thanks** to the Father
    3:17   **giving thanks** to God the Father
1Th   1: 2   We always **give thanks** to God
    2:13   We also constantly **give thanks**
    5:18   **give thanks** in all
2Th   1: 3   must always **give thanks** to God
    2:13   But we must always **give thanks**
Pm   1: 4   I always **thank** my God
Re   11:17   We **give** you **thanks,** Lord God

2169   GO15 AG328 LN110 B3:817 K9:407 R2170
ευχαριστια, GOOD FAVOR
Ac   24: 3   with utmost **gratitude**
1C   14:16   "Amen" to your **thanksgiving**

2C	4:15	may increase **thanksgiving**
	9:11	which will produce **thanksgiving**
	9:12	with many **thanksgivings** to God
Ep	5: 4	let there be **thanksgiving**
Ph	4: 6	supplication with **thanksgiving**
Co	2: 7	abounding in **thanksgiving**
	4: 2	alert in it with **thanksgiving**
1Th	3: 9	we **thank** God enough for you
1Ti	2: 1	and **thanksgivings** be made
	4: 3	be received with **thanksgiving**
	4: 4	is received with **thanksgiving**
Re	4: 9	**thanks** to the one who is seated
	7:12	wisdom and **thanksgiving**

2170 ᴳᴼ1 ᴬᴳ329 ᴸᴺ110 ᴮ2:874 ᴷ9:407 ᴿ2095,5483
ευχαριστος, WELL FAVORED
| Co | 3:15 | And be **thankful.** |

2171 ᴳᴼ3 ᴬᴳ329 ᴸᴺ110 ᴮ2:861 ᴷ2:775 ᴿ2172
ευχη, VOW
Ac	18:18	for he was under a **vow**
	21:23	four men who are under a **vow**
Ja	5:15	The **prayer** of faith will save

2172 ᴳᴼ7 ᴬᴳ329 ᴸᴺ110 ᴮ2:861 ᴷ2:775
ευχομαι, I WISH
Ac	26:29	I **pray** to God that not only you
	27:29	**prayed** for day to come.
Ro	9: 3	For I could **wish** that I myself
2C	13: 7	we **pray** to God that you may not
	13: 9	This is what we **pray** for
Ja	5:16	and **pray** for one another
3J	1: 2	I **pray** that all may go well

2173 ᴳᴼ3 ᴬᴳ329 ᴸᴺ110
ευχρηστος, GOOD USE
2Ti	2:21	utensils, dedicated and **useful**
	4:11	for he is **useful** in my ministry
Pm	1:11	he is indeed **useful** both to you

2174 ᴳᴼ1 ᴬᴳ329 ᴸᴺ110 ᴮ3:687
ευψυχεω, I HAVE GOOD SOUL
| Ph | 2:19 | I **may be cheered** by news of you |

2175 ᴳᴼ3 ᴬᴳ329 ᴸᴺ110 ᴮ3:599 ᴷ2:808
ευωδια, GOOD SMELL
2C	2:15	For we are the **aroma** of Christ
Ep	5: 2	**fragrant** offering and sacrifice
Ph	4:18	**fragrant** offering, a sacrifice

2176 ᴳᴼ9 ᴬᴳ329 ᴸᴺ110 ᴮ2:148
ευωνυμος, LEFT
Mt	20:21	right hand and one at your **left**
	20:23	at my right hand and at my **left**
	25:33	and the goats at the **left**
	25:41	say to those at his **left** hand
	27:38	his right and one on his **left**
Mk	10:40	at my right hand or at my **left**
	15:27	his right and one on his **left**
Ac	21: 3	and leaving it on our **left**
Re	10: 2	and his **left** foot on the land

2177 ᴳᴼ1 ᴬᴳ330 ᴸᴺ110 ᴿ1909,242
εφαλλομαι, I LEAP ON
| Ac | 19:16 | the evil spirit **leaped** on them |

2178 ᴳᴼ5 ᴬᴳ330 ᴸᴺ111 ᴮ2:716 ᴷ1:383 ᴿ1909,530
εφαπαξ, ONCE FOR ALL
Ro	6:10	he died to sin, **once for all**
1C	15: 6	and sisters **at one time,** most
He	7:27	this he did **once for all** when
	9:12	entered **once for all** into the
	10:10	of Jesus Christ **once for all**

2180 ᴳᴼ5 ᴬᴳ330 ᴸᴺ111
εφεσιος, EPHESIAN
Ac	19:28	is Artemis of the **Ephesians**
	19:34	is Artemis of the **Ephesians**
	19:35	Citizens of **Ephesus,** who is
	19:35	city of the **Ephesians** is the
	21:29	Trophimus the **Ephesian** with him

2181 ᴳᴼ16 ᴬᴳ330 ᴸᴺ111
εφεσος, EPHESUS
Ac	18:19	When they reached **Ephesus**
	18:21	Then he set sail from **Ephesus**
	18:24	there came to **Ephesus** a Jew
	19: 1	regions and came to **Ephesus**
	19:17	to all residents of **Ephesus**
	19:26	hear that not only in **Ephesus**
	20:16	decided to sail past **Ephesus**
	20:17	he sent a message to **Ephesus**
1C	15:32	with wild animals at **Ephesus**
	16: 8	But I will stay in **Ephesus**
Ep	1: 1	the saints who are in **Ephesus**
1Ti	1: 3	to remain in **Ephesus** so that
2Ti	1:18	service he rendered in **Ephesus**
	4:12	I have sent Tychicus to **Ephesus**
Re	1:11	the seven churches, to **Ephesus**
	2: 1	angel of the church in **Ephesus**

2182　GO1 AG330 LN111
εφευρετης, INVENTOR
Ro　1:30　**inventors** of evil, rebellious

2183　GO2 AG330 LN111 R2184
εφημερια, DIVISION
Lk　1: 5　belonged to the **priestly order**
　　1: 8　and his **section** was on duty

2184　GO1 AG330 LN111 R1909,2250
εφημερος, DAILY
Ja　2:15　is naked and lacks **daily** food

2185　GO2 AG330 LN111
εφικνεομαι, I REACH
2C　10:13　to **reach out** even as far as
　　10:14　when we **reached** you; we were

2186　GO21 AG330 LN111 R1909,2476
εφιστημι, I STAND ON
Lk　2: 9　angel of the Lord **stood before**
　　2:38　At that moment she **came**
　　4:39　Then he **stood over** her
　　10:40　so she **came** to him and asked
　　20: 1　scribes **came** with the elders
　　21:34　day **catch** you unexpectedly
　　24: 4　men in dazzling clothes
Ac　4: 1　the Sadducees **came** to them
　　6:12　they suddenly **confronted** him
　　10:17　and **were standing** by the gate
　　11:11　**arrived** at the house where we
　　12: 7　an angel of the Lord **appeared**
　　17: 5　they **attacked** Jason's house
　　22:13　and **standing beside** me, he said
　　22:20　I myself **was standing by**
　　23:11　That night the Lord **stood near**
　　23:27　I **came** with the guard
　　28: 2　Since it **had begun** to rain
1Th　5: 3　destruction **will come upon** them
2Ti　4: 2　**be persistent** whether the time
　　4: 6　time of my departure **has come**

2186a　GO2 AG331 LN111
εφοραω, I LOOK ON
Lk　1:25　when he **looked** favorably **on** me
Ac　4:29　Lord, **look at** their threats

2187　GO1 AG331 LN111
εφραιμ, EPHRAIM
Jn　11:54　to a town called **Ephraim** in the

2188　GO1 AG331 LN111 B2:560
εφφαθα, EPHPHATHA
Mk　7:34　said to him, "**Ephphatha**,"

2188a　GO3 AG331 LN111
εχθες, YESTERDAY
Jn　4:52　**Yesterday** at one in the
Ac　7:28　killed the Egyptian **yesterday**
He　13: 8　Christ is the same **yesterday**

2189　GO6 AG331 LN111 B1:553 K2:815 R2190
εχθρα, HOSTILITY
Lk　23:12　this they had been **enemies**
Ro　8: 7　on the flesh is **hostile** to God
Ga　5:20　idolatry, sorcery, **enmities**
Ep　2:14　the **hostility** between us
　　2:16　putting to death that **hostility**
Ja　4: 4　the world is **enmity** with God

2190　GO32 AG331 LN111 B1:553 K2:811
εχθρος, HOSTILE ONE
Mt　5:43　neighbor and hate your **enemy**
　　5:44　Love your **enemies** and pray for
　　10:36　and one's **foes** will be members
　　13:25　an **enemy** came and sowed weeds
　　13:28　An **enemy** has done this.
　　13:39　and the **enemy** who sowed them
　　22:44　your **enemies** under your feet
Mk　12:36　your **enemies** under your feet
Lk　1:71　would be saved from our **enemies**
　　1:74　from the hands of our **enemies**
　　6:27　Love your **enemies**, do good
　　6:35　But love your **enemies**, do good
　　10:19　over all the power of the **enemy**
　　19:27　as for these **enemies** of mine
　　19:43　**enemies** will set up ramparts
　　20:43　your **enemies** your footstool
Ac　2:35　your **enemies** your footstool
　　13:10　you **enemy** of all righteousness
Ro　5:10　For if while we were **enemies**
　　11:28　**enemies** of God for your sake
　　12:20　if your **enemies** are hungry
1C　15:25　all his **enemies** under his feet
　　15:26　The last **enemy** to be destroyed
Ga　4:16　Have I now become your **enemy**
Ph　3:18　For many live as **enemies**
Co　1:21　once estranged and **hostile**
2Th　3:15　Do not regard them as **enemies**
He　1:13　until I make your **enemies**
　　10:13　until his **enemies** would be made

Ja	4: 4	becomes an **enemy** of God
Re	11: 5	mouth and consumes their **foes**
	11:12	their **enemies** watched them

2191 GO5 AG331 LN111 K2:815

εχιδνα, POISON SNAKE

Mt	3: 7	to them, "You brood of **vipers!**
	12:34	You brood of **vipers!**
	23:33	You snakes, you brood of **vipers**
Lk	3: 7	You brood of **vipers!** Who warned
Ac	28: 3	when a **viper,** driven out by the

2192 GO711 AG331 LN111 R2:816

εχω, I HAVE

Mt	1:18	to **be** with child from the Holy
	1:23	virgin shall **conceive** and bear
	3: 4	John **wore** clothing of camel's
	3: 9	**have** Abraham as our ancestor
	3:14	I **need** to be baptized by you,
	4:24	who **were** afflicted with
	5:23	sister **has** something against
	5:46	what reward do you **have?** Do
	6: 1	then you **have** no reward from
	6: 8	what you **need** before you ask
	7:29	as one **having** authority, and
	8: 9	**with** soldiers under me; and I
	8:16	and cured all who **were** sick.
	8:20	Foxes **have** holes, and birds
	8:20	the Son of Man **has** nowhere to
	9: 6	Son of Man **has** authority on
	9:12	who are well **have** no need of a
	9:12	but those who **are** sick.
	9:36	like sheep **without** a shepherd.
	11:15	Let anyone **with** ears listen!
	11:18	they say, 'He **has** a demon';
	12:10	man was there **with** a withered
	12:11	one of you **has** only one sheep
	13: 5	they did not **have** much soil,
	13: 5	since they **had** no depth of
	13: 6	they **had** no root, they
	13: 9	Let anyone with **ears** listen!
	13:12	to those who **have,** more will
	13:12	from those who **have** nothing,
	13:12	they **have** will be taken away.
	13:21	yet such a person **has** no root,
	13:27	then, did these weeds **come**
	13:43	Let anyone with **ears** listen!
	13:44	sells all that he **has** and buys
	13:46	sold all that he **had** and

	14: 4	not lawful for you to **have** her
	14: 5	they **regarded** him as a prophet
	14:16	They **need** not go away; you
	14:17	We **have** nothing here but five
	14:35	all who were **sick** to him,
	15:30	with them the **lame,** the maimed
	15:32	and **have** nothing to eat; and I
	15:34	How many loaves **have** you?
	16: 8	talking about **having** no bread?
	17:20	if you **have** faith the size of
	18: 8	to **have** two hands or two feet
	18: 9	to **have** two eyes and to be
	18:25	he **could** not pay, his lord
	18:25	his **possessions,** and payment
	19:16	must I do to **have** eternal life
	19:21	you will **have** treasure in
	19:22	for he **had** many possessions.
	21: 3	'The Lord **needs** them.' And he
	21:21	**have** faith and do not doubt,
	21:26	all **regard** John as a prophet.
	21:28	A man **had** two sons; he went to
	21:38	him and **get** his inheritance.
	21:46	they **regarded** him as a prophet.
	22:12	in here **without** a wedding robe
	22:24	man dies **childless,** his
	22:25	and died **childless,** leaving
	22:28	all of them **had** married her.
	24:19	Woe to those who are **pregnant**
	25:25	Here you **have** what is yours.
	25:28	give it to the one **with** the
	25:29	who **have,** more will be given,
	25:29	from those who **have** nothing,
	25:29	they **have** will be taken away.
	26: 7	**with** an alabaster jar of very
	26:11	For you always **have** the poor
	26:11	but you will not always **have**
	26:65	Why do we still **need** witnesses
	27:16	they **had** a notorious prisoner,
	27:65	You **have** a guard of soldiers;
Mk	1:22	as one **having** authority, and
	1:32	were **sick** or possessed with
	1:34	he cured many who were **sick**
	1:38	go on to the **neighboring** towns
	2:10	the Son of Man **has** authority
	2:17	who are well **have** no need of a
	2:17	but those who are **sick;** I have
	2:19	they **have** the bridegroom with
	2:25	hungry and in **need** of food?
	3: 1	there who **had** a withered hand.

3: 3	man who **had** the withered hand,
3:10	all who **had** diseases pressed
3:15	to **have** authority to cast out
3:22	He **has** Beelzebul, and by the
3:26	stand, but his end **has** come.
3:29	can never **have** forgiveness,
3:30	He **has** an unclean spirit.
4: 5	where it did not **have** much
4: 5	since it **had** no depth of soil.
4: 6	since it **had** no root, it
4: 9	Let anyone **with** ears to hear
4:17	But they **have** no root,
4:23	Let anyone **with** ears to hear
4:25	those who **have,** more will be
4:25	from those who **have** nothing,
4:25	what they **have** will be taken
4:40	afraid? **Have** you still no
5: 3	He **lived** among the tombs; and
5:15	very man who **had had** the
5:23	daughter **is** at the point of
6:18	for you to **have** your brother's
6:34	like sheep **without** a shepherd;
6:38	How many loaves **have** you?
6:55	began to bring the **sick** on
7:25	daughter **had** an unclean spirit
8: 1	crowd **without** anything to eat,
8: 2	three days and **have** nothing to
8: 5	How many loaves do you **have**
8: 7	They **had** also a few small fish
8:14	and they **had** only one loaf
8:16	because we **have** no bread.
8:17	talking about **having** no bread?
8:17	understand? **Are** your hearts
8:18	Do you **have** eyes, and fail to
8:18	Do you **have** ears, and fail to
9:17	my son; he **has** a spirit that
9:43	maimed than to **have** two hands
9:45	lame than to **have** two feet and
9:47	one eye than to **have** two eyes
9:50	**Have** salt in yourselves, and
10:21	sell what you **own,** and give
10:21	you **will have** treasure in
10:22	for he **had** many possessions.
10:23	those who **have** wealth to enter
11: 3	The Lord **needs** it and will
11:13	a fig tree **in** leaf, he went to
11:22	them, "**Have** faith in God.
11:25	forgive, if you **have** anything
11:32	for all **regarded** John as truly

12: 6	He **had** still one other, a
12:23	For the seven **had** married her.
12:44	has put in everything she **had,**
13:17	Woe to those who are **pregnant**
14: 3	a woman came **with** an alabaster
14: 7	For you always **have** the poor
14: 7	but you will not always **have**
14: 8	She **has** done what she could;
14:63	Why do we still **need**
16: 8	terror and amazement **had**
16:18	sick, and they will **recover**
Lk 3: 8	**have** Abraham as our ancestor';
3:11	Whoever **has** two coats must
3:11	must share with anyone who **has**
3:11	and whoever **has** food must do
4:33	there was a man who **had** the
4:40	all those who **had** any who were
5:24	the Son of Man **has** authority on
5:31	Those who are well **have** no need
5:31	but those who **are** sick;
6: 8	said to the man who **had** the
7: 2	and who was **ill** and close to
7: 8	**with** soldiers under me; and I
7:33	and you say, 'He **has** a demon';
7:40	I **have** something to say to you
7:42	When they **could** not pay, he
8: 6	withered for **lack** of moisture.
8: 8	Let anyone **with** ears to hear
8:13	But these **have** no root; they
8:18	for to those who **have,** more
8:18	and from those who do not **have**
8:18	even what they seem to **have**
8:27	man of the city who **had** demons
9: 3	not **even** an extra tunic.
9:11	healed those who **needed** to be
9:58	Foxes **have** holes, and birds
9:58	the Son of Man **has** nowhere to
11: 5	Suppose one of you **has** a
11: 6	I **have** nothing to set before
11:36	**with** no part of it in darkness
12: 4	after that **can** do nothing more
12: 5	**has** authority to cast into
12:17	What should I do, for I **have**
12:19	Soul, you **have** ample goods
12:50	I **have** a baptism with which to
13: 6	A man **had** a fig tree planted
13:11	there appeared a woman **with** a
13:33	the **next** day I must be on my
14:14	they **cannot** repay you, for you

14:18	and I **must** go out and see it;	4:18	for you **have** had five husbands
14:18	it; please **accept** my regrets.	4:18	and the one you **have** now is
14:19	out; please **accept** my regrets.	4:32	I **have** food to eat that you
14:28	to see whether he **has** enough	4:44	a prophet **has** no honor in the
14:35	Let anyone **with** ears to hear	4:52	afternoon the fever **left** him.
15: 4	Which one of you, **having** a	5: 2	which **has** five porticoes.
15: 7	righteous persons who **need** no	5: 5	One man was there who **had** been
15: 8	Or what woman **having** ten	5: 6	knew that he **had** been there a
15:11	There was a man who **had** two	5: 7	Sir, I **have** no one to put me
16: 1	who **had** a manager, and charges	5:24	believes him who sent me **has**
16:28	for I **have** five brothers	5:26	For just as the Father **has**
16:29	**have** Moses and the prophets;	5:26	granted the Son also **to have**
17: 6	The Lord replied, "If you **had**	5:36	But I **have** a testimony greater
17: 7	would say to **your** slave who	5:38	and you do not **have** his word
17: 9	Do you **thank** the slave for	5:39	in them you **have** eternal life;
18:22	Sell all that you **own** and	5:40	refuse to come to me to **have**
18:22	and you **will have** treasure in	5:42	I know that you do not **have**
18:24	those who have **wealth** to enter	6: 9	There is a boy here who **has**
19:17	**take** charge of ten cities.	6:40	believe in him **may have**
19:20	I **wrapped** it up in a piece of	6:47	whoever believes **has** eternal
19:24	to the one who **has** ten pounds.	6:53	his blood, you **have** no life in
19:25	Lord, he **has** ten pounds!	6:54	drink my blood **have** eternal
19:26	to all those who **have,** more	6:68	You **have** the words of eternal
19:26	but from those who **have**	7:20	The crowd answered, "You **have**
19:26	even what they **have** will be	8: 6	so that they **might have** some
19:31	say this, 'The Lord **needs** it.'	8:12	walk in darkness but **will have**
19:34	They said, "The Lord **needs** it.	8:26	I **have** much to say about you
20:24	whose title does it **bear?**	8:41	we **have** one father, God
20:28	**leaving** a wife but no children	8:48	a Samaritan and **have** a demon?
20:33	For the seven **had** married her.	8:49	I do not **have** a demon; but I
21: 4	has put in all she **had** to live	8:52	Now we know that you **have** a
21:23	Woe to those who are **pregnant**	8:57	You **are** not yet fifty years
22:36	the one who **has** a purse must	9:21	Ask him; he **is** of age. He will
22:36	And the one who **has** no sword	9:23	He is **of** age; ask him.
22:37	is written about me is **being**	9:41	you would not **have** sin. But
22:71	further testimony do we **need?**	10:10	I came that they **may have** life
24:39	a ghost does not **have** flesh	10:10	life, and **have** it abundantly.
24:39	bones as you see that I **have.**	10:16	I **have** other sheep that do not
24:41	**Have** you anything here to eat	10:18	I **have** power to lay it down,
Jn 2: 3	said to him, "They **have** no	10:18	I **have** power to take it up
2:25	and **needed** no one to testify	10:20	He **has** a demon and is out of
3:15	believes in him **may have**	11:17	found that Lazarus **had** already
3:16	may not perish but **may have**	12: 6	he **kept** the common purse and
3:29	He who **has** the bride is the	12: 8	You always **have** the poor with
3:36	believes in the Son **has**	12: 8	but you do not always **have** me.
4:11	Sir, you **have** no bucket, and	12:35	Walk while you **have** the light,
4:11	Where do you **get** that living	12:36	While you **have** the light,
4:17	I **have** no husband.	12:48	does not receive my word **has** a
4:17	I **have** no husband	13: 8	Unless I wash you, you **have**

13:10	bathed does not **need** to wash,		19:38	**have** a complaint against
13:29	Judas **had** the common purse,		20:15	and the **day after** that we came
13:29	Buy what we **need** for the		21:13	For I **am** ready not only to be
13:35	you **have** love for one another.		21:23	We **have** four men who are under
14:21	They who **have** my commandments		21:26	the **next** day, having purified
14:30	He **has** no power over me;		23:17	for he **has** something to report
15:13	No one **has** greater love than		23:18	he **has** something to tell you.
15:22	they would not **have** sin; but		23:19	What is it that you **have** to
15:22	now they **have** no excuse for		23:25	wrote a letter to this **effect:**
15:24	they would not **have** sin. But		23:29	death or **imprisonment.**
16:12	I still **have** many things to		24: 9	asserting that all **this** was
16:15	All that the Father **has** is		24:15	I **have** a hope in God—a hope
16:21	she **has** pain, because her hour		24:16	to **have** a clear conscience
16:22	So you **have** pain now; but I		24:19	if they **have** anything against
16:30	and do not **need** to have anyone		24:23	but to let him **have** some
16:33	that in me you **may have** peace.		24:25	when I **have** an opportunity, I
16:33	the world you **face** persecution		25:16	before the accused **had** met the
17: 5	the glory that I **had** in your		25:19	Instead they **had** certain
17:13	so that they **may have** my joy		25:26	But I **have** nothing definite to
18:10	who **had** a sword, drew it,		25:26	I **may have** something to write
19: 7	We **have** a law, and according		27:39	but they noticed a bay **with** a
19:10	Do you not know that I **have**		28: 9	who **had** diseases also came and
19:10	you, and **power** to crucify you?		28:19	even though I **had** no charge to
19:11	You would **have** no power over	Ro	1:13	in order that I may **reap** some
19:11	me over to you is **guilty** of a		1:28	And since they did not see **fit**
19:15	**have** no king but the emperor.		2:14	who do not **possess** the law, do
20:31	through believing you **may have**		2:14	though not **having** the law, are
21: 5	Children, you **have** no fish,		2:20	a teacher of children, **having**
Ac 1:12	a sabbath day's journey **away.**		4: 2	he **has** something to boast
2:44	and **had** all things in common;		5: 1	we **have** peace with God through
2:45	to all, as any **had** need.		5: 2	through whom we **have** obtained
2:47	praising God and **having** the		6:21	**get** from the things of which
3: 6	but what I **have** I give you; in		6:22	the advantage you **get** is
4:14	they **had** nothing to say in		8: 9	Anyone who does not **have** the
4:35	distributed to each as any **had**		8:23	but we ourselves, who **have** the
7: 1	asked him, "**Are** these things		9:10	when she **had** conceived
8: 7	out of many who were **possessed**		9:21	**Has** the potter no right over
9:14	and here he **has** authority from		10: 2	I can testify that they **have** a
9:31	**had** peace and was built up.		12: 4	For as in one body we **have**
11: 3	did you go to **uncircumcised**		12: 4	not all the members **have** the
12:15	But she insisted that it **was**		12: 6	We **have** gifts that differ
13: 5	they **had** John also to assist		13: 3	Do you wish to **have** no fear of
14: 9	seeing that he **had** faith to be		14:22	The faith that you **have,** have
15:21	Moses **has had** those who		14:22	The faith that you have, **have**
15:36	and see how they **are doing**		15: 4	scriptures we **might have** hope.
16:16	we met a slave-girl who **had** a		15:17	In Christ Jesus, then, I **have**
17:11	see whether these things **were**		15:23	But now, **with** no further place
18:18	cut, for he **was** under a vow.		15:23	I desire, as I **have** for many
19:13	over those who **had** evil	1C	2:16	But we **have** the mind of Christ

4: 7	What do you **have** that you did
4:15	For though you **might have** ten
5: 1	for a man is **living** with his
6: 1	When any of you **has** a
6: 4	If you **have** ordinary cases,
6: 7	In fact, to **have** lawsuits at
6:19	which you **have** from God, and
7: 2	each man should **have** his own
7: 2	each woman **her** own husband.
7: 7	But each **has** a particular gift
7:12	that if any believer **has** a
7:13	And if any woman **has** a husband
7:25	Now concerning virgins, I **have**
7:28	who marry **will experience**
7:29	let even those who **have** wives
7:29	be as though they **had** none,
7:37	**being** under no necessity but
7:37	**having** his own desire under
7:40	that I too **have** the Spirit of
8: 1	all of us **possess** knowledge.
8:10	who **possess** knowledge, eating
9: 4	**have** the right to our food and
9: 5	**have** the right to be
9: 6	who **have** no right to refrain
9:17	I **have** a reward; but if not of
11: 4	prophesies **with** something on
11:10	ought to **have** a symbol of
11:16	we **have** no such custom, nor do
11:22	What! Do you not **have** homes
11:22	who **have** nothing? What should
12:12	one and **has** many members, and
12:21	"I **have** no need of you," nor
12:21	feet, "I **have** no need of you."
12:23	**are treated** with greater
12:24	members do not **need** this.
12:30	Do all **possess** gifts of healing
13: 1	do not **have** love, I am a noisy
13: 2	And if I **have** prophetic powers,
13: 2	if I **have** all faith, so as to
13: 2	but do not **have** love, I am
13: 3	but do not **have** love, I gain
14:26	each one **has** a hymn, a lesson,
14:26	a **lesson,** a revelation,
14:26	a **revelation,** a tongue, or an
14:26	a **tongue,** or an interpretation.
14:26	an **interpretation.** Let all
15:31	I **make** in Christ Jesus our Lord
15:34	people **have** no knowledge of God
2C 1: 9	we **had** received the sentence of

1:15	that you **might have** a double
2: 3	I **might** not **suffer** pain from
2: 4	love that I **have** for you.
2:13	but my mind **could** not rest
3: 4	that we **have** through Christ
3:12	we **have** such a hope, we act
4: 1	we **are engaged** in this
4: 7	But we **have** this treasure in
4:13	But just as we **have** the same
5: 1	we **have** a building from God,
5:12	that you **may be able** to answer
6:10	as **having** nothing, and yet
7: 1	Since we **have** these promises,
7: 5	our bodies **had** no rest, but we
8:11	your eagerness may be **matched**
8:12	according to what one **has**
8:12	to what one does not **have.**
9: 8	by always **having** enough of
10: 6	We **are** ready to punish every
10:15	but our hope **is** that, as your
12:14	**Here** I am, ready to come to
Ga 2: 4	the freedom we **have** in Christ
4:22	Abraham **had** two sons, one by a
4:27	of the one who **is married.**
6: 4	will become a **cause** for pride.
6:10	we **have** an opportunity, let us
Ep 1: 7	In him we **have** redemption
2:12	**having** no hope and without God
2:18	both of us **have** access in one
3:12	in whom we **have** access to God
4:28	as to **have** something to share
4:28	to share **with** the needy.
5: 5	**has** any inheritance in the
5:27	**without** a spot or wrinkle or
Ph 1: 7	you **hold** me in your heart, for
1:23	my desire is to depart and be
1:30	you are **having** the same
2: 2	**having** the same love, being in
2:20	I **have** no one like him who
2:27	God **had** mercy on him, and not
2:29	all joy, and **honor** such people
3: 4	anyone else **has** reason to be
3: 9	not **having** a righteousness of
3:17	example you **have** in us.
Co 1: 4	you **have** for all the saints,
1:14	in whom we **have** redemption,
2: 1	know how **much** I am struggling
2:23	These **have** indeed an
3:13	anyone **has** a complaint against

	4: 1	also **have** a Master in heaven.
	4:13	he **has** worked hard for you and
1Th	1: 8	so that we **have** no need to
	1: 9	welcome we **had** among you, and
	3: 6	you **always** remember us kindly
	4: 9	you do not need **to have** anyone
	4:12	outsiders and **be** dependent on
	4:13	others do who **have** no hope.
	5: 1	do not **need** to have anything
	5: 3	pains come upon a **pregnant**
2Th	3: 9	we do not **have** that right, but
1Ti	1:12	I am **grateful** to Christ Jesus
	1:19	**having** faith and a good
	3: 4	**keeping** his children
	3: 7	he must **be** well thought of by
	3: 9	they must **hold** fast to the
	4: 8	**holding** promise for both the
	5: 4	If a widow **has** children or
	5:12	for **having** violated their
	5:16	woman **has** relatives who are
	5:20	the rest also **may stand** in
	5:25	they **cannot** remain hidden.
	6: 2	who **have** believing masters
	6: 8	if we **have** food and clothing,
	6:16	who **has** immortality and dwells
2Ti	1: 3	I am **grateful** to God—whom I
	1: 3	when I **remember** you constantly
	1:13	**Hold** to the standard of sound
	2:17	talk will **spread** like gangrene
	2:19	**bearing** this inscription: "The
	3: 5	**holding** to the outward form of
Ti	1: 6	whose children **are** believers,
	2: 8	**having** nothing evil to say of
Pm	1: 5	your love **for** all the saints
	1: 7	I have indeed **received** much
	1: 8	though I **am** bold enough in
	1:17	So if you **consider** me your
He	2:14	destroy the one who **has** the
	3: 3	builder of a house **has** more
	4:14	we **have** a great high priest
	4:15	we do not **have** a high priest
	5:12	you **need** someone to teach you
	5:12	You **need** milk, not solid food;
	5:14	faculties **have** been trained by
	6: 9	things that **belong** to
	6:13	because he **had** no one greater
	6:18	might **be** strongly encouraged
	6:19	We **have** this hope, a sure and
	7: 3	**having** neither beginning of

	7: 5	**have** a commandment in the law
	7: 6	blessed him who **had** received
	7:24	but he **holds** his priesthood
	7:27	he **has** no need to offer
	7:28	who are **subject** to weakness,
	8: 1	we **have** such a high priest,
	8: 3	also to **have** something to
	9: 1	first covenant **had** regulations
	9: 4	In it stood the **golden** altar
	9: 4	a golden urn **holding** the manna
	9: 8	first tent is still **standing.**
	10: 1	Since the law **has** only a
	10: 2	would they not **have** ceased
	10:19	we **have** confidence to enter
	10:34	you yourselves **possessed**
	10:35	it **brings** a great reward.
	10:36	For you **need** endurance, so
	11:10	city that **has** foundations,
	11:15	they would **have** had
	11:25	to **enjoy** the fleeting
	12: 1	we **are** surrounded by so great
	12: 9	we **had** human parents to
	12:28	let us **give** thanks, by which
	13:10	We **have** an altar from which
	13:10	who **officiate** in the tent have
	13:14	here we **have** no lasting city,
	13:18	we **have** a clear conscience,
Ja	1: 4	and let endurance **have** its
	2: 1	do you **with** your acts of
	2:14	if you say you **have** faith but
	2:14	but do not **have** works? Can
	2:17	if it **has** no works, is dead.
	2:18	You **have** faith and I have
	2:18	I **have** works." Show me your
	3:14	But if you **have** bitter envy
	4: 2	do not **have** it; so you commit
	4: 2	You do not **have,** because you
1P	2:12	yourselves **honorably** among the
	2:16	freedom as a **pretext** for evil.
	3:16	**Keep** your conscience clear, so
	4: 5	him who **stands** ready to judge
	4: 8	**maintain** constant love for one
2P	1:15	you **may** be able at any time
	1:19	we **have** the prophetic message
	2:14	They **have** eyes full of
	2:14	They **have** hearts trained in
	2:16	but **was** rebuked for his own
1J	1: 3	also **may have** fellowship with
	1: 6	we **have** fellowship with him

	1: 7	we **have** fellowship with one		2:24	who do not **hold** this teaching,
	1: 8	If we say that we **have** no sin,		2:25	only **hold** fast to what you
	2: 1	we **have** an advocate with the		2:29	anyone who **has** an ear listen
	2: 7	that you **have had** from the		3: 1	who **has** the seven spirits of
	2:20	But you **have** been anointed by		3: 1	you **have** a name of being alive
	2:23	who denies the Son **has** the		3: 4	you **have** still a few persons
	2:23	confesses the Son **has** the		3: 6	anyone who **has** an ear listen
	2:27	you do not **need** anyone to		3: 7	who **has** the key of David, who
	2:28	we **may have** confidence and not		3: 8	you **have** but little power, and
	3: 3	And all who **have** this hope in		3:11	hold fast to what you **have,** so
	3:15	do not **have** eternal life		3:13	anyone who **has** an ear listen
	3:17	in anyone who **has** the world's		3:17	and I **need** nothing.' You do
	3:17	sister **in** need and yet refuses		3:22	anyone who **has** an ear listen
	3:21	we **have** boldness before God;		4: 7	living creature **with** a face
	4:16	God **has** for us. God is love,		4: 8	of them **with** six wings, are
	4:17	that we **may have** boldness on		4: 8	night **without** ceasing they
	4:18	fears **has** not reached		5: 6	**having** seven horns and seven
	4:21	The commandment we **have** from		5: 8	each **holding** a harp and
	5:10	in the Son of God **have** the		6: 2	Its rider **had** a bow; a crown
	5:12	Whoever **has** the Son has life;		6: 5	Its rider **held** a pair of
	5:12	Son **has** life; whoever does not		6: 9	the testimony they **had** given;
	5:12	whoever does not **have** the Son		7: 2	**having** the seal of the living
	5:12	of God does not **have** life.		8: 3	he **was** given a great quantity
	5:13	know that you **have** eternal		8: 6	seven angels who **had** the
	5:14	boldness we **have** in him, that		8: 9	a third of the **living**
	5:15	we **have** obtained the requests		9: 3	authority **like** the authority
2J	1: 5	but one we **have had** from the		9: 4	do not **have** the seal of God on
	1: 9	does not **have** God; whoever		9: 8	their hair **like** women's hair,
	1: 9	teaching **has** both the Father		9: 9	they **had** scales like iron
	1:12	Although I **have** much to write		9:10	They **have** tails like scorpions
3J	1: 4	I **have** no greater joy than		9:11	They **have** as king over them
	1:13	I **have** much to write to you,		9:11	in Greek he **is** called Apollyon
Ju	1: 3	I **find** it necessary to write		9:14	sixth angel who **had** the
	1:19	these worldly people, **devoid**		9:17	the riders **wore** breastplates
Re	1:16	right hand he **held** seven stars		9:19	**having** heads; and with them
	1:18	I **have** the keys of Death and		10: 2	He **held** a little scroll open
	2: 3	that you **have** not grown weary.		11: 6	They **have** authority to shut
	2: 4	But I **have** this against you,		11: 6	they **have** authority over the
	2: 6	Yet this **is** to your credit:		12: 2	She was **pregnant** and was
	2: 7	anyone who **has** an ear listen		12: 3	**with** seven heads and ten horns
	2:10	for ten days you **will have**		12: 6	where she **has** a place prepared
	2:11	anyone who **has** an ear listen		12:12	you **with** great wrath, because
	2:12	words of him who **has** the sharp		12:12	his time **is** short!
	2:14	But I **have** a few things		12:17	and **hold** the testimony of
	2:14	you **have** some there who hold		13: 1	**having** ten horns and seven
	2:15	So you also **have** some who hold		13: 9	anyone who **has** an ear listen:
	2:17	anyone who **has** an ear listen		13:11	it **had** two horns like a lamb
	2:18	who **has** eyes like a flame of		13:14	beast that **had** been wounded by
	2:20	But I **have** this against you:		13:17	who does not **have** the mark,

13:18	anyone **with** understanding		5:26	get out **until** you have paid
14: 1	**had** his name and his Father's		10:11	and stay there **until** you leave
14: 6	**with** an eternal gospel to		10:23	Israel **before** the Son of Man
14:11	There **is** no rest day or night		11:12	**until** now the kingdom of
14:14	**with** a golden crown on his head		11:13	law prophesied **until** John came
14:17	and he too **had** a sharp sickle.		11:23	**will** you be exalted to heaven?
14:18	angel who **has** authority over		11:23	would have remained **until** this
14:18	to him who **had** the sharp		12:20	**until** he brings justice to
15: 1	seven angels **with** seven		13:30	**until** the harvest; and at
15: 2	sea of glass **with** harps of God		13:33	**until** all of it was leavened.
15: 6	seven angels **with** the seven		14:22	**while** he dismissed the crowds.
16: 2	who **had** the mark of the beast		16:28	taste death **before** they see
16: 9	who **had** authority over these		17: 9	**until** after the Son of Man has
17: 1	**had** the seven bowls came and		17:17	**how much** longer must I be with
17: 3	**had** seven heads and ten horns.		17:17	**How much** longer must I put up
17: 4	**holding** in her hand a golden		18:21	forgive? **As many as** seven
17: 7	**with** seven heads and ten horns		18:22	**Not** seven times, but, I tell
17: 9	mind that **has** wisdom: the		18:22	**but,** I tell you, seventy-seven
17:13	These are **united** in yielding		18:30	threw him into prison **until** he
17:18	great city **that** rules over the		18:34	**until** he would pay his entire
18: 1	**having** great authority; and		20: 8	and **then** going to the first.
18:19	where all who **had** ships at sea		22:26	third, **down to** the seventh.
19:10	who **hold** the testimony of		22:44	Sit at my right hand, **until** I
19:12	he **has** a name inscribed that		23:35	**to** the blood of Zechariah son
19:16	he **has** a name inscribed, "King		23:39	**until** you say, 'Blessed is the
20: 1	**holding** in his hand the key to		24:21	**until** now, no, and never will
20: 6	those who **share** in the first		24:27	**as far as** the west, so will be
20: 6	second death **has** no power, but		24:31	from one end of heaven **to** the
21: 9	seven angels who **had** the seven		24:34	**until** all these things have
21:11	It **has** the glory of God and a		24:39	and they knew nothing **until**
21:12	It **has** a great, high wall with		26:29	**until** that day when I drink it
21:12	wall **with** twelve gates, and		26:36	Sit here **while** I go over
21:14	city **has** twelve foundations,		26:38	**even to** death; remain here,
21:15	who talked to me **had** a		26:58	**as far as** the courtyard of the
21:23	the city **has** no need of sun or		27: 8	the Field of Blood **to** this day
22: 5	they **need** no light of lamp or		27:45	**until** three in the afternoon.
			27:51	from top **to** bottom. The earth

2193　　ᴳᴼ146　ᴬᴳ334　ᴸᴺ112

εως, UNTIL

Mt	1:17	Abraham **to** David are fourteen		27:64	made secure **until** the third
	1:17	from David **to** the deportation		28:20	always, **to** the end of the age.
	1:17	**to** the Messiah, fourteen	Mk	6:10	stay there **until** you leave the
	1:25	with her **until** she had borne a		6:23	you, **even** half of my kingdom.
	2: 9	**until** it stopped over the		6:45	**while** he dismissed the crowd.
	2:13	remain there **until** I tell you;		9: 1	death **until** they see that the
	2:15	**until** the death of Herod. This		9:19	**how much** longer must I be
	5:18	you, **until** heaven and earth		9:19	**How much** longer must I put up
	5:18	law **until** all is accomplished.		12:36	**until** I put your enemies under
	5:25	your accuser **while** you are on		13:19	God created **until** now, no, and
				13:27	from the ends of the earth **to**
				14:25	**until** that day when I drink it

	14:32	Sit here **while** I pray.
	14:34	**even to** death; remain here,
	14:54	**right into** the courtyard of
	15:33	**until** three in the afternoon.
	15:38	in two, from top **to** bottom.
Lk	1:80	**until** the day he appeared
	2:15	Let us go now **to** Bethlehem
	2:37	then as a widow **to** the age of
	4:29	led him **to** the brow of the
	4:42	and **when** they reached him,
	9:27	will not taste death **before**
	9:41	**how much** longer must I be with
	10:15	will you be exalted **to** heaven?
	10:15	will be brought down **to** Hades.
	11:51	from the blood of Abel **to** the
	12:50	what stress I am under **until**
	12:59	**until** you have paid the very
	13: 8	**until** I dig around it and put
	13:21	**until** all of it was leavened.
	13:35	you will not see me **until** the
	15: 4	that is lost **until** he finds it
	15: 8	search carefully **until** she
	17: 8	serve me **while** I eat and drink
	20:43	**until** I make your enemies your
	21:32	**until** all things have taken
	22:16	I will not eat it **until** it is
	22:18	**until** the kingdom of God comes
	22:34	**until** you have denied three
	22:51	**"No more** of this!" And he
	23: 5	where he began **even to** this
	23:44	**until** three in the afternoon,
	24:49	**until** you have been clothed
	24:50	**as far as** Bethany, and,
Jn	2: 7	And they filled them up **to** the
	2:10	kept the good wine **until** now.
	5:17	My Father is **still** working,
	9: 4	**while** it is day; night is
	9:18	**until** they called the parents
	10:24	**How long** will you keep us in
	13:38	**before** the cock crows, you
	16:24	**Until** now you have not asked
	21:22	**until** I come, what is that to
	21:23	**until** I come, what is that to
Ac	1: 8	and **to** the ends of the earth.
	1:22	**until** the day when he was
	2:35	**until** I make your enemies your
	7:45	**until** the time of David,
	8:10	All of them, from the least **to**
	8:40	all the towns **until** he came to

	9:38	come **to** us without delay.
	11:19	traveled **as far as** Phoenicia,
	11:22	they sent Barnabas **to** Antioch.
	13:20	**until** the time of the prophet
	13:47	bring salvation **to** the ends of
	17:14	sent Paul away **to** the coast,
	17:15	brought him **as far as** Athens;
	21: 5	escorted us **outside** the city.
	21:26	**when** the sacrifice would be
	23:12	neither to eat nor drink **until**
	23:14	taste no food **until** we have
	23:21	**until** they kill him. They are
	23:23	**for** Caesarea with two hundred
	25:21	I ordered him to be held **until**
	26:11	I pursued them **even** to foreign
	28:23	From morning **until** evening he
Ro	3:12	there is not **even** one.
	11: 8	hear, **down to this** very day.
1C	1: 8	blameless **on** the day of our
	4: 5	**before** the Lord comes, who
	4:13	all things, **to this** very day.
	8: 7	**until** now, they still think of
	15: 6	most of whom are **still** alive,
	16: 8	I will stay in Ephesus **until**
2C	1:13	will understand **until** the end
	3:15	Indeed, **to this very** day
	12: 2	caught up **to** the third heaven
2Th	2: 7	but only **until** the one who now
1Ti	4:13	**Until** I arrive, give attention
He	1:13	Sit at my right hand **until** I
	8:11	from the least of them **to** the
	10:13	**until** his enemies would be
Ja	5: 7	**until** the coming of the Lord.
	5: 7	being patient with it **until** it
2P	1:19	**until** the day dawns and the
1J	2: 9	is **still** in the darkness.
Re	6:10	**how long** will it be before you
	6:11	**until** the number would be

ζ

2194 GO3 AG335 LN112
ζχαβουλων, ZEBULUN

Mt	4:13	territory of **Zebulun** and
	4:15	**Zebulun**, land of Naphtali, on
Re	7: 8	from the tribe of **Zebulun**

2195 GO3 AG335
ζακχαιος, ZACCHAEUS

Lk	19: 2	man was there named **Zacchaeus;**
	19: 5	**Zacchaeus,** hurry and come
	19: 8	**Zacchaeus** stood there and said

2196   ᴳᴼ1 ᴬᴳ335
ζαρα, ZARA (ZERAH)

Mt	1: 3	**Zerah** by Tamar, and Perez the

2197   ᴳᴼ11 ᴬᴳ335 ᴸᴺ112
ζαχαριας, ZACHARIAS (ZECHARIAH)

Mt	23:35	blood of **Zechariah** son of
Lk	1: 5	a priest named **Zechariah,** who
	1:12	When **Zechariah** saw him, he was
	1:13	Do not be afraid, **Zechariah,**
	1:18	**Zechariah** said to the angel,
	1:21	were waiting for **Zechariah,**
	1:40	house of **Zechariah** and greeted
	1:59	name him **Zechariah** after his
	1:67	Then his father **Zechariah** was
	3: 2	John son of **Zechariah** in the
	11:51	blood of **Zechariah,** who

2198   ᴳᴼ135 ᴬᴳ336 ᴸᴺ112 ᴮ2:476 ᴷ2:832
ζαω, I LIVE

Mt	4: 4	One **does** not **live** by bread
	9:18	on her, and she **will live.**
	16:16	the Son of the **living** God.
	22:32	the dead, but of the **living.**
	26:63	oath before the **living** God,
	27:63	while he **was** still **alive,**
Mk	5:23	may be made well, and **live.**
	12:27	but of the **living;** you are
	16:11	he was **alive** and had been seen
Lk	2:36	**having lived** with her husband
	4: 4	One does not **live** by bread
	10:28	do this, and you **will live.**
	15:13	property in dissolute **living.**
	15:32	has come to **life;** he was lost
	20:38	but of the **living;** for to him
	20:38	to him all of them are **alive.**
	24: 5	do you look for the **living**
	24:23	who said that he was **alive.**
Jn	4:10	would have given you **living**
	4:11	Where do you get that **living**
	4:50	Go; your son **will live.**
	4:51	him that his child **was alive.**
	4:53	"Your son **will live.**" So he
	5:25	and those who hear **will live.**
	6:51	I am the **living** bread that
	6:51	eats of this bread **will live**

	6:57	Just as the **living** Father sent
	6:57	I **live** because of the Father,
	6:57	whoever eats me **will live**
	6:58	who eats this bread **will live**
	7:38	flow rivers of **living** water.
	11:25	though they die, **will live,**
	11:26	and everyone who **lives** and
	14:19	because I **live,** you also will
	14:19	I live, you also **will live.**
Ac	1: 3	himself **alive** to them by many
	7:38	he received **living** oracles to
	9:41	he showed her **to be alive.**
	10:42	judge of the **living** and the
	14:15	to the **living** God, who made
	17:28	For 'In him we **live** and move
	20:12	taken the boy away **alive** and
	22:22	should not be allowed **to live.**
	25:19	whom Paul asserted **to be alive**
	25:24	ought not **to live** any longer.
	26: 5	religion and **lived** as a
	28: 4	has not allowed him **to live.**
Ro	1:17	one who is righteous **will live**
	6: 2	who died to sin **go on** living
	6:10	but the life he **lives,** he
	6:10	life he lives, he **lives** to God
	6:11	**alive** to God in Christ Jesus.
	6:13	from death to **life,** and
	7: 1	during that person's **lifetime?**
	7: 2	husband as long as he **lives;**
	7: 3	if she **lives** with another man
	7: 9	I **was** once **alive** apart from
	8:12	**to live** according to the flesh
	8:13	for if you **live** according to
	8:13	of the body, you **will live.**
	9:26	children of the **living** God.
	10: 5	does these things **will live** by
	12: 1	your bodies as a **living**
	14: 7	We **do** not **live** to ourselves,
	14: 8	If we **live,** we live to the
	14: 8	If we live, we **live** to the
	14: 8	whether we **live** or whether we
	14: 9	Christ died and **lived** again,
	14: 9	both the dead and the **living.**
	14:11	For it is written, "As I **live,**
1C	7:39	as long as her husband **lives.**
	9:14	get their **living** by the gospel
	15:45	became a **living** being"; the
2C	1: 8	we despaired of **life** itself.
	3: 3	Spirit of the **living** God, not

	4:11	For while we **live,** we are
	5:15	so that those who **live** might
	5:15	**might live** no longer for
	6: 9	we are **alive;** as punished, and
	6:16	are the temple of the **living**
	13: 4	but **lives** by the power of God.
	13: 4	we **will live** with him by the
Ga	2:14	**live** like a Gentile and not
	2:19	so that I **might live** to God.
	2:20	it is no longer I who **live,**
	2:20	but it is Christ who **lives** in
	2:20	the life I now **live** in the
	2:20	I **live** by faith in the Son of
	3:11	righteous **will live** by faith.
	3:12	works of the law **will live** by
	5:25	If we **live** by the Spirit, let
Ph	1:21	For to me, **living** is Christ
	1:22	If I **am to live** in the flesh,
Co	2:20	why do you **live** as if you
	3: 7	when you **were living** that life
1Th	1: 9	to serve a **living** and true God
	3: 8	For we now **live,** if you
	4:15	that we who **are alive,** who are
	4:17	Then we who **are alive,** who are
	5:10	or asleep we **may live** with him
1Ti	3:15	the church of the **living** God,
	4:10	hope set on the **living** God,
	5: 6	but the widow who **lives** for
2Ti	3:12	Indeed, all who want **to live**
	4: 1	who is to judge the **living** and
Ti	2:12	present age to **live** lives that
He	2:15	all their **lives** were held in
	3:12	turns away from the **living** God
	4:12	the word of God is **living** and
	7: 8	it is testified that he **lives.**
	7:25	since he always **lives** to make
	9:14	works to worship the **living**
	9:17	the one who made it **is alive.**
	10:20	by the new and **living** way that
	10:31	the hands of the **living** God
	12: 9	Father of spirits and **live?**
	12:22	to the city of the **living** God,
Ja	4:15	we **will live** and do this or
1P	1: 3	into a **living** hope through the
	1:23	the **living** and enduring word
	2: 4	Come to him, a **living** stone,
	2: 5	like **living** stones, let
	2:24	free from sins, we **might live**
	4: 5	judge the **living** and the dead.

	4: 6	they **might live** in the spirit
1J	4: 9	that we **might live** through him
Re	1:18	and the **living** one. I was dead
	1:18	I **am alive** forever and ever;
	2: 8	who was dead and came to **life:**
	3: 1	you have a name of **being alive**
	4: 9	whenever the **living** creatures
	4:10	worship the one who **lives**
	7: 2	the seal of the **living** God,
	10: 6	and swore by him who **lives**
	13:14	by the sword and yet **lived;**
	15: 7	Then one of the four **living**
	19:20	These two were thrown **alive**
	20: 4	They came **to life** and reigned
	20: 5	did not come **to life** until the

2199   GO12 AG337 LN112
ζεβεδαιος, ZEBEDEE

Mt	4:21	James son of **Zebedee** and his
	4:21	with their father **Zebedee,**
	10: 2	James son of **Zebedee,** and his
	20:20	mother of the sons of **Zebedee**
	26:37	the two sons of **Zebedee,** and
	27:56	mother of the sons of **Zebedee.**
Mk	1:19	James son of **Zebedee** and his
	1.20	they left their father **Zebedee**
	3:17	James son of **Zebedee** and John
	10:35	the sons of **Zebedee,** came
Lk	5:10	sons of **Zebedee,** who were
Jn	21: 2	the sons of **Zebedee,** and two

2200   GO3 AG337 LN112 B1:317 R2204
ζεστος, BOILING

Re	3:15	you are neither cold nor **hot.**
	3:15	you were either cold or **hot.**
	3:16	neither cold nor **hot,** I am

2201   GO2 AG337 LN112 B3:1160
ζευγος, YOKE

| Lk | 2:24 | a **pair** of turtledoves or two |
| | 14:19 | I have bought five **yoke** of |

2202   GO1 AG337 LN112
ζευκτηρια, BANDS

| Ac | 27:40 | they loosened the **ropes** that |

2203   GO2 AG337 LN112
ζευς, ZEUS

| Ac | 14:12 | Barnabas they called **Zeus,** and |
| | 14:13 | The priest of **Zeus,** whose |

2204   GO2 AG337 LN112 B2:875
ζεω, I BOIL
Ac 18:25   spoke with **burning** enthusiasm
Ro 12:11   Do not lag in zeal, be **ardent**

2204a   GO1 AG337 LN112
ζηλευω, I AM JEALOUS
Re   3:19   **Be earnest,** therefore, and

2205   GO16 AG337 LN112 B3:1166 K2:877 R2204
ζηλος, JEALOUSY
Jn   2:17   **Zeal** for your house will
Ac   5:17   being filled with **jealousy,**
     13:45 they were filled with **jealousy;**
Ro 10: 2   they have a **zeal** for God, but
     13:13 not in quarreling and **jealousy.**
1C   3: 3   as long as there is **jealousy**
2C   7: 7   your **zeal** for me, so that I
     7:11   what longing, what **zeal,** what
     9: 2   and your **zeal** has stirred up
     11: 2 I feel a divine **jealousy** for
     12:20 quarreling, **jealousy,** anger,
Ga   5:20   **jealousy,** anger, quarrels,
Ph   3: 6   as to **zeal,** a persecutor of the
He 10:27   **fury** of fire that will consume
Ja   3:14   But if you have bitter **envy** and
     3:16   where there is **envy** and selfish

2206   GO11 AG338 LN113 B3:1166 K2:882 R2205
ζηλοω, I AM JEALOUS
Ac   7: 9   The patriarchs, **jealous** of
     17: 5 But the Jews **became jealous,**
1C 12:31   **strive** for the greater gifts.
     13: 4 love **is** not **envious** or boastful
     14: 1 Pursue love and **strive** for the
     14:39 So, my friends, be **eager** to
2C 11: 2   I feel a divine **jealousy** for
Ga   4:17   They **make much** of you, but for
     4:17   that you **may make much** of them.
     4:18   It is good **to be made much** of
Ja   4: 2   And you **covet** something and

2207   GO8 AG338 LN113 B3:1166 K2:882 R2206
ζηλωτης, JEALOUS ONE
Lk   6:15   who was called the **Zealot,**
Ac   1:13   Simon the **Zealot,** and Judas son
     21:20 they are all **zealous** for the
     22: 3 being **zealous** for God, just as
1C 14:12   you are **eager** for spiritual
Ga   1:14   I was far more **zealous** for the

Ti   2:14   who are **zealous** for good deeds.
1P   3:13   are **eager** to do what is good?

2209   GO4 AG338 LN113 B3:136 K2:888
ζημια, LOSS
Ac 27:10   with danger and much heavy **loss**
     27:21 avoided this damage and **loss.**
Ph   3: 7   I have come to regard as **loss**
     3: 8   everything as **loss** because of

2210   GO6 AG338 LN113 K2:888 R2209
ζημιοω, I LOSE
Mt 16:26   world but **forfeit** their life?
Mk   8:36   the whole world and **forfeit**
Lk   9:25   but lose or **forfeit** themselves?
1C   3:15   the builder will **suffer loss;**
2C   7: 9   so that you **were** not **harmed** in
Ph   3: 8   I have **suffered** the **loss** of all

2211   GO1 AG338 LN113
ζηνας, ZENAS
Ti   3:13   Make every effort to send **Zenas**

2212   GO117 AG338 LN113 B3:530 K2:892
ζητεω, I SEEK
Mt   2:13   Herod is about **to search** for
     2:20   **were seeking** the child's life
     6:33   But **strive** first for the
     7: 7   **search,** and you will find;
     7: 8   everyone who **searches** finds,
     12:43 waterless regions **looking** for a
     12:46 **wanting** to speak to him.
     12:47 **wanting** to speak to you.
     13:45 merchant in **search** of fine
     18:12 go in **search** of the one that
     21:46 They **wanted** to arrest him, but
     26:16 **look for** an opportunity to
     26:59 council **were looking** for false
     28: 5 I know that you **are looking** for
Mk   1:37   Everyone is **searching** for you.
     3:32   sisters are outside, **asking** for
     8:11   **asking** him for a sign from
     8:12   Why does this generation **ask**
     11:18 they **kept looking** for a way to
     12:12 they **wanted** to arrest him, but
     14: 1 **were looking** for a way
     14:11 So he began **to look** for an
     14:55 **were looking** for testimony
     16: 6 you **are looking** for Jesus of
Lk   2:48   **have been searching** for you in

2:49	Why **were** you **searching** for me?
5:18	They **were trying** to bring him
6:19	all in the crowd **were trying** to
9: 9	And he **tried** to see him.
11: 9	**search,** and you will find;
11:10	everyone who **searches** finds,
11:16	**kept demanding** from him a sign
11:24	**looking** for a resting place,
11:29	it **asks** for a sign, but no sign
12:29	And do not **keep striving** for
12:31	Instead, **strive** for his kingdom
12:48	much **will be required;** and from
13: 6	he came **looking** for fruit on it
13: 7	I have come **looking** for fruit
13:24	**will try** to enter and will not
15: 8	and **search** carefully until she
17:33	Those who **try** to make their
19: 3	He **was trying** to see who Jesus
19:10	Son of Man came to **seek** out and
19:47	the people **kept looking** for a
20:19	they **wanted** to lay hands on him
22: 2	**were looking** for a way to put
22: 6	he consented and began **to look**
24: 5	said to them, "Why **do** you **look**
Jn 1:38	What are you **looking** for?
4:23	the Father **seeks** such as these
4:27	"What do you **want?**" or, "Why
5:18	the Jews **were seeking** all the
5:30	because I **seek** to do not my own
5:44	do not **seek** the glory that
6:24	to Capernaum **looking** for Jesus.
6:26	you **are looking** for me, not
7: 1	the Jews **were looking** for an
7: 4	for no one who **wants** to be
7:11	The Jews **were looking** for him
7:18	on their own **seek** their own
7:18	the one who **seeks** the glory of
7:19	you **looking** for an opportunity
7:20	Who **is trying** to kill you?
7:25	whom they **are trying** to kill?
7:30	Then they **tried** to arrest him,
7:34	You **will search** for me, but you
7:36	You **will search** for me and you
8:21	you **will search** for me, but you
8:37	yet you **look for** an opportunity
8:40	now you **are trying** to kill me,
8:50	Yet I do not **seek** my own glory;
8:50	there is one who **seeks** it and
10:39	Then they **tried** to arrest him

11: 8	the Jews **were** just now **trying**
11:56	They were **looking for** Jesus
13:33	You **will look for** me; and as
16:19	**discussing** among yourselves
18: 4	Whom are you **looking for?**
18: 7	Whom are you **looking for?**
18: 8	if you are **looking for** me,
19:12	Pilate **tried** to release him,
20:15	Whom are you **looking for?**
Ac 9:11	**look for** a man of Tarsus named
10:19	three men are **searching** for you
10:21	the one you are **looking for;**
13: 8	opposed them and **tried** to turn
13:11	he went about **groping** for
16:10	we immediately **tried** to cross
17: 5	While they **were searching** for
17:27	so that they **would search** for
21:31	While they **were trying** to kill
27:30	But when the sailors **tried** to
Ro 2: 7	doing good **seek** for glory and
10: 3	**seeking** to establish their own,
10:20	those who did not **seek** me; I
11: 3	and they are **seeking** my life.
1C 1:22	signs and Greeks **desire** wisdom,
4: 2	it is **required** of stewards that
7:27	a wife? Do not **seek** to be free.
7:27	from a wife? Do not **seek** a wife
10:24	Do not **seek** your own advantage,
10:33	not **seeking** my own advantage,
13: 5	or rude. It does not **insist** on
14:12	**strive** to excel in them for
2C 12:14	because I do not **want** what is
13: 3	since you **desire** proof that
Ga 1:10	Am I now **seeking** human approval
2:17	in our **effort** to be justified
Ph 2:21	All of them are **seeking** their
Co 3: 1	**seek** the things that are above,
1Th 2: 6	nor did we **seek** praise from
2Ti 1:17	he eagerly **searched** for me and
He 8: 7	no need to **look for** a second
1P 3:11	let them **seek** peace and pursue
5: 8	**looking for** someone to devour.
Re 9: 6	people **will seek** death but will

2213   GO5   AG339   LN113   R2212

ζητημα, QUESTION

Ac 15: 2	discuss this **question** with the
18:15	it is a matter of **questions**
23:29	**questions** of their law, but was

25:19 **disagreement** with him about

26: 3 customs and **controversies** of

2214 GO7 AG339 LN113 B3:530 K2:893 R2212

ζητησις, SPECULATION

Jn 3:25 Now a **discussion** about

Ac 15: 2 dissension and **debate** with them

15: 7 there had been much **debate,**

25:20 investigate these **questions,** I

1Ti 6: 4 morbid craving for **controversy**

2Ti 2:23 senseless **controversies; you**

Ti 3: 9 But avoid stupid **controversies,**

2215 GO8 AG339 LN113

ζιζανιον, WEED

Mt 13:25 an enemy came and sowed **weeds**

13:26 then the **weeds** appeared as well

13:27 then, did these **weeds** come from

13:29 gathering the **weeds** you would

13:30 Collect the **weeds** first and

13:36 parable of the **weeds** of the

13:38 the **weeds** are the children of

13:40 Just as the **weeds** are collected

2216 GO3 AG339 LN113

ζοροβαβελ, ZOROBABEL (ZERUBBABEL)

Mt 1:12 the father of **Zerubbabel,**

1:13 and **Zerubbabel** the father of

Lk 3:27 son of **Zerubbabel,** son of

2217 GO5 AG339 LN113

ζοφος, GLOOM

He 12:18 and **gloom,** and a tempest,

2P 2: 4 chains of **deepest darkness** to

2:17 the **deepest darkness** has been

Ju 1: 6 in **deepest darkness** for the

1:13 for whom the **deepest darkness**

2218 GO6 AG339 LN113 B3:1160 K2:896

ζυγος, YOKE

Mt 11:29 Take my **yoke** upon you, and

11:30 For my **yoke** is easy, and my

Ac 15:10 **yoke** that neither our ancestors

Ga 5: 1 again to a **yoke** of slavery.

1Ti 6: 1 Let all who are under the **yoke**

Re 6: 5 Its rider held a **pair** of scales

2219 GO13 AG340 LN113 B2:461 K2:902

ζυμη, YEAST

Mt 13:33 **yeast** that a woman took and

16: 6 beware of the **yeast** of the

16:11 Beware of the **yeast** of the

16:12 beware of the **yeast** of bread,

Mk 8:15 **yeast** of the Pharisees and the

8:15 **yeast** of the Pharisees and the

Lk 12: 1 Beware of the **yeast** of the

13:21 It is like **yeast** that a woman

1C 5: 6 little **yeast** leavens the whole

5: 7 Clean out the old **yeast** so that

5: 8 not with the old **yeast,** the

5: 8 the **yeast** of malice and evil,

Ga 5: 9 little **yeast** leavens the whole

2220 GO4 AG340 LN113 B2:461 K2:902 R2219

ζυμοω, I YEAST (LEAVEN)

Mt 13:33 until all of it was **leavened.**

Lk 13:21 until all of it was **leavened.**

1C 5: 6 little yeast **leavens** the whole

Ga 5: 9 **leavens** the whole batch of

2221 GO2 AG340 LN113

ζωγρεω, I CAPTURE ALIVE

Lk 5:10 now on you **will be catching**

2Ti 2:26 **having been held captive** by him

2222 GO135 AG340 LN113 B2:476 K2:832 R2198

ζωη, LIFE

Mt 7:14 road is hard that leads to **life**

18: 8 better for you to enter **life**

18: 9 better for you to enter **life**

19:16 must I do to have eternal **life?**

19:17 If you wish to enter into **life,**

19:29 and will inherit eternal **life.**

25:46 the righteous into eternal **life**

Mk 9:43 better for you to enter **life**

9:45 better for you to enter **life**

10:17 I do to inherit eternal **life?**

10:30 the age to come eternal **life.**

Lk 10:25 I do to inherit eternal **life?**

12:15 for one's **life** does not consist

16:25 during your **lifetime** you

18:18 I do to inherit eternal **life?**

18:30 in the age to come eternal **life**

Jn 1: 4 in him was **life,** and the life

1: 4 **life** was the light of all

3:15 in him may have eternal **life.**

3:16 but may have eternal **life.**

3:36 in the Son has eternal **life;**

3:36 the Son will not see **life,**

4:14 gushing up to eternal **life.**

	4:36	fruit for eternal **life,** so that
	5:24	who sent me has eternal **life,**
	5:24	passed from death to **life.**
	5:26	the Father has **life** in himself;
	5:26	to have **life** in himself;
	5:29	to the resurrection of **life,**
	5:39	in them you have eternal **life;**
	5:40	to come to me to have **life.**
	6:27	that endures for eternal **life,**
	6:33	and gives **life** to the world.
	6:35	I am the bread of **life.**
	6:40	in him may have eternal **life;**
	6:47	believes has eternal **life.**
	6:48	I am the bread of **life.**
	6:51	**life** of the world is my flesh.
	6:53	blood, you have no **life** in you.
	6:54	my blood have eternal **life,** and
	6:63	the spirit that gives **life;**
	6:68	have the words of eternal **life.**
	8:12	but will have the light of **life**
	10:10	I came that they may have **life,**
	10:28	I give them eternal **life,**
	11:25	the resurrection and the **life.**
	12:25	will keep it for eternal **life.**
	12:50	commandment is eternal **life.**
	14: 6	and the truth, and the **life.** No
	17: 2	to give eternal **life** to all
	17: 3	And this is eternal **life,** that
	20:31	you may have **life** in his name.
Ac	2:28	known to me the ways of **life;**
	3:15	you killed the Author of **life,**
	5:20	whole message about this **life.**
	8:33	For his **life** is taken away from
	11:18	repentance that leads to **life.**
	13:46	to be unworthy of eternal **life,**
	13:48	destined for eternal **life**
	17:25	all mortals **life** and breath and
Ro	2: 7	he will give eternal **life;**
	5:10	will we be saved by his **life.**
	5:17	exercise dominion in **life**
	5:18	justification and **life** for all.
	5:21	leading to eternal **life** through
	6: 4	might walk in newness of **life.**
	6:22	The end is eternal **life.**
	6:23	eternal **life** in Christ Jesus
	7:10	promised **life** proved to be
	8: 2	law of the Spirit of **life** in
	8: 6	on the Spirit is **life** and peace
	8:10	the Spirit is **life** because of

	8:38	neither death, nor **life,** nor
	11:15	be but **life** from the dead!
1C	3:22	or the world or **life** or death
	15:19	If for this **life** only we have
2C	2:16	a fragrance from **life** to life.
	2:16	**life.** Who is sufficient for
	4:10	the **life** of Jesus may also be
	4:11	the **life** of Jesus may be made
	4:12	work in us, but **life** in you.
	5: 4	may be swallowed up by **life.**
Ga	6: 8	reap eternal **life** from the
Ep	4:18	alienated from the **life** of God
Ph	1:20	whether by **life** or by death.
	2:16	fast to the word of **life** that I
	4: 3	names are in the book of **life.**
Co	3: 3	your **life** is hidden with Christ
	3: 4	When Christ who is your **life** is
1Ti	1:16	believe in him for eternal **life**
	4: 8	present **life** and the life to
	6:12	take hold of the eternal **life,**
	6:19	take hold of the **life** that
2Ti	1: 1	sake of the promise of **life**
	1:10	death and brought **life** and
Ti	1: 2	in the hope of eternal **life**
	3. 7	to the hope of eternal **life.**
He	7: 3	of days nor end of **life,** but
	7:16	power of an indestructible **life**
Ja	1:12	receive the crown of **life** that
	4:14	will bring. What is your **life?**
1P	3: 7	of the gracious gift of **life**—
	3:10	For "Those who desire **life** and
2P	1: 3	needed for **life** and godliness,
1J	1: 1	concerning the word of **life**—
	1: 2	this **life** was revealed, and we
	1: 2	the eternal **life** that was with
	2:25	has promised us, eternal **life.**
	3:14	have passed from death to **life**
	3:15	not have eternal **life** abiding
	5:11	God gave us eternal **life,** and
	5:11	and this **life** is in his Son.
	5:12	Whoever has the Son has **life;**
	5:12	Son of God does not have **life.**
	5:13	know that you have eternal **life**
	5:16	and God will give **life** to such
	5:20	the true God and eternal **life.**
Ju	1:21	that leads to eternal **life.**
Re	2: 7	eat from the tree of **life** that
	2:10	give you the crown of **life.**
	3: 5	out of the book of **life;**

7:17	springs of the water of **life,**	
11:11	breath of **life** from God entered	
13: 8	in the book of **life** of the Lamb	
16: 3	every **living** thing in the sea	
17: 8	written in the book of **life**	
20:12	the book of **life.** And the dead	
20:15	written in the book of **life**	
21: 6	the spring of the water of **life**	
21:27	in the Lamb's book of **life.**	
22: 1	river of the water of **life,**	
22: 2	tree of **life** with its twelve	
22:14	tree of **life** and may enter the	
22:17	the water of **life** as a gift.	
22:19	share in the tree of **life** and	

2223   GO8 AG341 LN113 B3:120 K5:302
ζωνη, BELT

Mt	3: 4	leather **belt** around his waist,
	10: 9	silver, or copper in your **belts**
Mk	1: 6	leather **belt** around his waist,
	6: 8	no bag, no money in their **belts**
Ac	21:11	took Paul's **belt,** bound his own
	21:11	bind the man who owns this **belt**
Re	1:13	a golden **sash** across his chest.
	15: 6	**sashes** across their chests.

2224   GO3 AG341 LN113 B3:120 K5:302 R2223
ζωννυμι, I BELT

Jn	21:18	used to **fasten your own belt**
	21:18	**will fasten** a **belt** around you
Ac	12: 8	**Fasten your belt** and put on

2225   GO3 AG341 LN113 B2:476 K2:873
ζωογονεω, I PRESERVE LIVE

Lk	17:33	lose their **life will keep** it.
Ac	7:19	infants so that they **would die.**
1Ti	6:13	God, who **gives life** to all

2226   GO23 AG341 LN113 K2:873 R2198
ζωον, LIVING ONE, LIVING THINGS

He	13:11	bodies of those **animals** whose
2P	2:12	irrational **animals,** mere
Ju	1:10	irrational **animals,** they know
Re	4: 6	are four **living creatures,** full
	4: 7	**living creature** like a lion,
	4: 7	**living creature** like an ox, the
	4: 7	**living creature** with a face
	4: 7	**living creature** like a flying
	4: 8	four **living creatures,** each of
	4: 9	**living creatures** give glory and

5: 6	**living creatures** and among the
5: 8	the four **living creatures** and
5:11	**living creatures** and the elders
5:14	**living creatures** said, "Amen!"
6: 1	**living creatures** call out, as
6: 3	**living creature** call out, "Come
6: 5	**living creature** call out, "Come
6: 6	**living creatures** saying, "A
6: 7	**living creature** call out, "Come
7:11	four **living creatures,** and they
14: 3	**living creatures** and before the
15: 7	**living creatures** gave the seven
19: 4	**living creatures** fell down and

2227   GO11 AG341 LN114 B2:476 K2:874 R2198,4160
ζωοποιεω, I MAKE ALIVE

Jn	5:21	the dead and **gives** them **life,**
	5:21	the Son **gives life** to whomever
	6:63	is the spirit that **gives life;**
Ro	4:17	who **gives life** to the dead and
	8:11	**give life** to your mortal bodies
1C	15:22	will be **made alive** in Christ.
	15:36	**come to life** unless it dies.
	15:45	became a **life-giving** spirit.
2C	3: 6	but the Spirit **gives life.**
Ga	3:21	given that could **make alive,**
1P	3:18	but **made alive** in the spirit,

η

2228   GO343 AG342 LN114
η, OR [MULTIPLE OCCURRENCES]

2230   GO2 AG343 LN114
ἡγεμονευω, I LEAD

Lk	2: 2	Quirinius **was governor** of Syria
	3: 1	**was governor** of Judea, and

2231   GO1 AG343 LN114 R2232
ἡγεμονια, LEADERSHIP

Lk	3: 1	fifteenth year of the **reign** of

2232   GO20 AG343 LN114 B1:270 R2233
ἡγεμων, LEADER

Mt	2: 6	least among the **rulers** of Judah
	10:18	**governors** and kings because of
	27: 2	him over to Pilate the **governor**
	27:11	Jesus stood before the **governor**
	27:11	the **governor** asked him, "Are

	27:14	the **governor** was greatly amazed
	27:15	at the festival the **governor**
	27:21	The **governor** again said to them
	27:27	the soldiers of the **governor**
	28:14	to the **governor's** ears, we will
Mk	13: 9	**governors** and kings because of
Lk	20:20	and authority of the **governor.**
	21:12	before kings and **governors**
Ac	23:24	safely to Felix the **governor.**
	23:26	his Excellency the **governor**
	23:33	letter to the **governor,** they
	24: 1	against Paul to the **governor.**
	24:10	When the **governor** motioned to
	26:30	with him the **governor** and
1P	2:14	or of **governors,** as sent by him

2233   GO28 AG343 LN114 K2:907
ἡγέομαι, I LEAD/CONSIDER

Mt	2: 6	from you shall come a **ruler** who
Lk	22:26	the **leader** like one who serves.
Ac	7:10	appointed him **ruler** over Egypt
	14:12	because he was the **chief**
	15:22	**leaders** among the brothers,
	26: 2	I **consider** myself fortunate
2C	9: 5	So I **thought** it necessary to
Ph	2: 3	in humility **regard** others as
	2: 6	did not **regard** equality with
	2:25	Still, I **think** it necessary to
	3: 7	these I have come to **regard** as
	3: 8	I **regard** everything as loss
	3: 8	I **regard** them as rubbish, in
1Th	5:13	**esteem** them very highly in love
2Th	3:15	Do not **regard** them as enemies,
1Ti	1:12	he **judged** me faithful and
	6: 1	**regard** their masters as worthy
He	10:29	**profaned** the blood of the
	11:11	he **considered** him faithful who
	11:26	He **considered** abuse suffered
	13: 7	**consider** the outcome of their
	13:17	Obey your **leaders** and submit to
	13:24	Greet all your **leaders** and all
Ja	1: 2	**consider** it nothing but joy,
2P	1:13	I **think** it right, as long as I
	2:13	They **count** it a pleasure to
	3: 9	as some **think** of slowness, but
	3:15	and **regard** the patience of

2234   GO5 AG343 LN114
ἡδέως, GLADLY

Mk	6:20	he **liked** to listen to him.
	12:37	listening to him with **delight.**
2C	11:19	For you **gladly** put up with
	12: 9	boast all the more **gladly** of my
	12:15	I will most **gladly** spend and be

2235   GO61 AG344 LN114
ἤδη, ALREADY

Mt	3:10	**Even now** the ax is lying at the
	5:28	**already** committed adultery with
	14:15	the hour is **now late;** send the
	14:24	but **by this time** the boat,
	15:32	been with me **now** for three days
	17:12	Elijah has **already** come, and
	24:32	**as soon as** its branch becomes
Mk	4:37	so that the boat was **already**
	6:35	it grew late, his disciples
	6:35	the hour is **now** very late;
	8: 2	they have been with me **now** for
	11:11	it was **already** late, he went
	13:28	**as soon as** its branch becomes
	15:42	**When** evening had come, and
	15:44	if he were **already** dead; and
Lk	3: 9	**Even now** the ax is lying at the
	7: 6	but **when** he was not far from
	11: 7	door has **already** been locked,
	12:49	I wish it were **already** kindled!
	14:17	Come; for everything is **ready**
	19:37	As he was **now** approaching the
	21:30	**as soon as** they sprout leaves
	21:30	know that summer is **already**
	23:44	It was **now** about noon, and
	24:29	the day is **now nearly** over." So
Jn	3:18	are condemned **already,** because
	4:36	reaper is **already** receiving
	4:51	As he was going down, his
	5: 6	knew that he had been **there** a
	6:17	It was **now** dark, and Jesus had
	7:14	**About** the middle of the
	9:22	the Jews had **already** agreed
	9:27	I have told you **already,** and
	11:17	Lazarus had **already** been in the
	11:39	Lord, **already** there is a stench
	13: 2	The devil had **already** put it
	15: 3	You have **already** been cleansed
	19:28	Jesus knew that all was **now**
	19:33	saw that he was **already** dead,
	21: 4	Just **after** daybreak, Jesus
	21:14	This was **now** the third time

Ac	4: 3	for it was **already** evening.
	27: 9	and sailing was **now** dangerous,
	27: 9	even the Fast had **already** gone
Ro	1:10	**at last** succeed in coming to
	4:19	which was **already** as good as
	13:11	how it is **now** the moment for
1C	4: 8	**Already** you have all you want!
	4: 8	**Already** you have become rich!
	5: 3	**already** pronounced judgment
	6: 7	**already** a defeat for you. Why
Ph	3:12	Not that I have **already**
	3:12	**already** reached the goal; but I
	4:10	**now** at last you have revived
2Th	2: 7	**already** at work, but only until
1Ti	5:15	For some have **already** turned
2Ti	2:18	resurrection has **already** taken
	4: 6	As for me, I am **already** being
2P	3: 1	This is **now**, beloved, the
1J	2: 8	the true light is **already**
	4: 3	and now it is **already** in the

2237 GO5 AG344 LN114 B1:458 K2:909
'ηδονη, PLEASURE

Lk	8:14	**pleasures** of life, and their
Ti	3: 3	various passions and **pleasures**,
Ja	4: 1	come from your **cravings** that
	4: 3	what you get on your **pleasures**.
2P	2:13	count it a **pleasure** to revel in

2238 GO2 AG344 LN114 B2:210
'ηδυοσμον, MINT

Mt	23:23	For you tithe **mint**, dill, and
Lk	11:42	you tithe **mint** and rue and

2239 GO1 AG344 LN114
ηθος, CUSTOM

1C	15:33	Bad company ruins good **morals**.

2240 GO26 AG344 LN114 B1:320 K2:926
'ηκω, I COME

Mt	8:11	many **will come** from east and
	23:36	all this **will come** upon this
	24:14	and then the end **will come**.
	24:50	master of that slave **will come**
Mk	8: 3	some of them **have come** from a
Lk	12:46	**will come** on a day when he does
	13:29	Then people **will come** from east
	13:35	until the time **comes** when you
	15:27	Your brother **has come**, and
	19:43	Indeed, the days **will come** upon

Jn	2: 4	My hour **has** not yet **come**.
	4:47	he heard that Jesus **had come**
	6:37	**will come** to me, and anyone who
	8:42	now I **am here**. I did not come
Ro	11:26	Out of Zion **will come** the
He	10: 7	See, God, I **have come** to do
	10: 9	See, I **have come** to do your
	10:37	the one who is coming **will come**
2P	3:10	the day of the Lord **will come**
1J	5:20	the Son of God **has come** and has
Re	2:25	to what you have until I **come**.
	3: 3	I **will come** like a thief, and
	3: 3	at what hour I **will come** to you
	3: 9	I **will make** them **come** and bow
	15: 4	All nations **will come** and
	18: 8	therefore her plagues **will come**

2241 GO2 AG345 LN115
ηλι, ELI

Mt	27:46	**Eli, Eli,** lema sabachthani?

2242 GO1 AG345 LN115
ηλι, ELI

Lk	3:23	thought) of Joseph son of **Heli,**

2243 GO29 AG345 LN115 B1:543 K2:928
ηλιας, ELIJAH

Mt	11:14	it, he is **Elijah** who is to come
	16:14	but others **Elijah,** and still
	17: 3	to them Moses and **Elijah,**
	17: 4	for Moses, and one for **Elijah.**
	17:10	the scribes say that **Elijah**
	17:11	**Elijah** is indeed coming and
	17:12	but I tell you that **Elijah** has
	27:47	This man is calling for **Elijah**
	27:49	let us see whether **Elijah** will
Mk	6:15	But others said, "It is **Elijah**
	8:28	the Baptist; and others, **Elijah**
	9: 4	there appeared to them **Elijah**
	9: 5	for Moses, and one for **Elijah.**
	9:11	the scribes say that **Elijah**
	9:12	**Elijah** is indeed coming first
	9:13	But I tell you that **Elijah** has
	15: 3	he is calling for **Elijah.**
	15:36	let us see whether **Elijah** will
Lk	1:17	spirit and power of **Elijah** he
	4:25	in Israel in the time of **Elijah**
	4:26	yet **Elijah** was sent to none of
	9: 8	some that **Elijah** had appeared,
	9:19	**Elijah;** and still others, that

	9:30	two men, Moses and **Elijah,**
	9:33	Moses, and one for **Elijah"**—
Jn	1:21	"What then? Are you **Elijah?"** He
	1:25	nor **Elijah,** nor the prophet?
Ro	11: 2	scripture says of **Elijah,** how
Ja	5:17	**Elijah** was a human being like

2244   G08 AG345 LN115 B1:92 K2:941
ἡλικια, STATURE

Mt	6:27	add a single hour to your **span**
Lk	2:52	in wisdom and in **years,** and in
	12:25	single hour to your **span** of
	19: 3	because he was short in **stature**
Jn	9:21	Ask him; he is **of age.** He will
	9:23	He is **of age;** ask him.
Ep	4:13	the full **stature** of Christ.
He	11:11	even though he was **too old**—

2245   G03 AG345 LN115
ἡλικος, HOW GREAT

Co	2: 1	For I want you to know **how much**
Ja	3: 5	**How great** a forest is set
	3: 5	is set ablaze by a **small** fire!

2246   G032 AG345 LN115 B3:730
ἡλιος, SUN

Mt	5:45	for he makes his **sun** rise on
	13: 6	But when the **sun** rose, they
	13:43	shine like the **sun** in the
	17: 2	his face shone like the **sun,**
	24:29	the **sun** will be darkened, and
Mk	1:32	That evening, at **sun**down, they
	4: 6	And when the **sun** rose, it was
	13:24	the **sun** will be darkened, and
	16: 2	when the **sun** had risen, they
Lk	4:40	As the **sun** was setting, all
	21:25	There will be signs in the **sun**
	23:45	while the **sun's** light failed;
Ac	2:20	The **sun** shall be turned to
	13:11	a while, unable to see the **sun**
	26:13	brighter than the **sun,** shining
	27:20	When neither **sun** nor stars
1C	15:41	There is one glory of the **sun,**
Ep	4:26	do not let the **sun** go down on
Ja	1:11	For the **sun** rises with its
Re	1:16	his face was like the **sun**
	6:12	the **sun** became black as
	7: 2	from the rising of the **sun,**
	7:16	the **sun** will not strike them,
	8:12	a third of the **sun** was struck,

	9: 2	and the **sun** and the air were
	10: 1	his face was like the **sun,** and
	12: 1	a woman clothed with the **sun,**
	16: 8	poured his bowl on the **sun,**
	16:12	way for the kings from the **east**
	19:17	an angel standing in the **sun,**
	21:23	has no need of **sun** or moon to
	22: 5	need no light of lamp or **sun,**

2247   G02 AG345 LN115
ἡλος, NAIL

Jn	20:25	mark of the **nails** in his hands,
	20:25	**nails** and my hand in his side,

2250   G0389 AG345 LN115 B2:887 K2:943
ἡμερα, DAY

Mt	2: 1	In the **time** of King Herod,
	3: 1	In those **days** John the Baptist
	4: 2	He fasted forty **days** and forty
	6:34	**Today's** trouble is enough for
	7:22	On that **day** many will say to me
	9:15	The **days** will come when the
	10:15	on the **day** of judgment than
	11:12	From the **days** of John the
	11:22	But I tell you, on the **day**
	11:24	But I tell you that on the **day**
	12:36	on the **day** of judgment you will
	12:40	just as Jonah was three **days**
	12:40	for three **days** and three nights
	13: 1	That same **day** Jesus went out of
	15:32	for three **days** and have
	16:21	and on the third **day** be raised.
	17: 1	Six **days** later, Jesus took with
	17:23	on the third **day** he will be
	20: 2	for the usual **daily** wage, he
	20: 6	you standing here idle all **day?**
	20:12	the **day** and the scorching heat.
	20:19	on the third **day** he will be
	22:23	The same **day** some Sadducees
	22:46	nor from that **day** did anyone
	23:30	If we had lived in the **days** of
	24:19	nursing infants in those **days!**
	24:22	And if those **days** had not been
	24:22	sake of the elect those **days**
	24:29	the suffering of those **days** the
	24:36	But about that **day** and hour no
	24:37	For as the **days** of Noah were,
	24:38	For as in those **days** before the
	24:38	until the **day** Noah entered the

24:42	do not know on what **day** your
24:50	will come on a **day** when he does
25:13	you know neither the **day** nor
26: 2	You know that after two **days**
26:29	until that **day** when I drink it
26:55	**Day** after day I sat in the
26:61	and to build it in three **days.**
27:40	build it in three **days,** save
27:63	After three **days** I will rise
27:64	secure until the third **day;**
28:15	told among the Jews to this **day**
28:20	remember, I am with you **always,**
Mk 1: 9	In those **days** Jesus came from
1:13	in the wilderness forty **days,**
2: 1	**days,** it was reported that he
2:20	The **days** will come when the
2:20	then they will fast on that **day**
4:27	sleep and rise night and **day,**
4:35	On that **day,** when evening had
5: 5	Night and **day** among the tombs
6:21	But an **opportunity** came when
8: 1	In those **days** when there was
8: 2	been with me now for three **days**
8:31	be killed, and after three **days**
9: 2	Six **days** later, Jesus took with
9:31	three **days** after being killed,
10:34	after three **days** he will rise
13:17	nursing infants in those **days!**
13:19	For in those **days** there will be
13:20	cut short those **days,** no one
13:20	he has cut short those **days.**
13:24	But in those **days,** after that
13:32	But about that **day** or hour no
14: 1	It was two **days** before the
14:12	On the first **day** of Unleavened
14:25	until that **day** when I drink it
14:49	**Day** after day I was with you in
14:58	in three **days** I will build
15:29	and build it in three **days,**
Lk 1: 5	In the **days** of King Herod of
1: 7	both were getting on in **years.**
1:18	my wife is getting on in **years.**
1:20	the **day** these things occur.
1:23	When his **time** of service was
1:24	After those **days** his wife
1:25	**when** he looked favorably on me
1:39	In those **days** Mary set out and
1:59	On the eighth **day** they came to
1:75	before him all our **days.**

1:80	**day** he appeared publicly to
2: 1	In those **days** a decree went out
2: 6	While they were there, the **time**
2:21	it was **time** to circumcise the
2:22	When the **time** came for their
2:36	She was of a great **age,** having
2:37	and prayer night and **day.**
2:43	When the **festival** was ended
2:44	they went a **day's** journey.
2:46	After three **days** they found him
4: 2	where for forty **days** he was
4: 2	at all during those **days,** and
4:16	on the sabbath **day,** as was his
4:25	in the **time** of Elijah, when the
4:42	At **day**break he departed and
5:17	One **day,** while he was teaching,
5:35	The **days** will come when the
5:35	they will fast in those **days.**
6:12	Now during those **days** he went
6:13	And when **day** came, he called
6:23	Rejoice in that **day** and leap
8:22	One **day** he got into a boat with
9:12	The **day** was drawing to a close,
9:22	and on the third **day** be raised.
9:23	take up their cross **daily** and
9:28	Now about eight **days** after
9:36	in those **days** told no one any
9:37	On the next **day,** when they had
9:51	When the **days** drew near for
	him
10:12	I tell you, on that **day** it will
11: 3	Give us each **day** our daily
12:46	will come on a **day** when he does
13:14	There are six **days** on which
13:14	come on those **days** and be cured
13:16	this bondage on the sabbath **day**
14: 5	pull it out on a sabbath **day?**
15:13	A few **days** later the younger
16:19	feasted sumptuously every **day.**
17: 4	seven times a **day,** and turns
17:22	The **days** are coming when you
17:22	see one of the **days** of the Son
17:24	the Son of Man be in his **day.**
17:26	Just as it was in the **days** of
17:26	it will be in the **days** of the
17:27	until the **day** Noah entered the
17:28	it was in the **days** of Lot: they
17:29	but on the **day** that Lot left
17:30	on the **day** that the Son of
	Man

	17:31	On that **day,** anyone on the
	18: 7	chosen ones who cry to him **day**
	18:33	on the third **day** he will rise
	19:42	recognized on this **day** the
	19:43	Indeed, the **days** will come upon
	19:47	Every **day** he was teaching in
	20: 1	One **day,** as he was teaching the
	21: 6	the **days** will come when not one
	21:22	for these are **days** of vengeance
	21:23	nursing infants in those **days!**
	21:34	that **day** catch you unexpectedly
	21:37	Every **day** he was teaching in
	22: 7	Then came the **day** of Unleavened
	22:53	When I was with you **day** after
	22:66	When **day** came, the assembly of
	23: 7	in Jerusalem at that **time.**
	23:12	That same **day** Herod and Pilate
	23:29	For the **days** are surely coming
	23:54	It was the **day** of Preparation,
	24: 7	on the third **day** rise again.
	24:13	Now on that same **day** two of
	24:18	taken place there in these **days**
	24:21	it is now the third **day** since
	24:29	almost evening and the **day** is
	24:46	from the dead on the third **day,**
Jn	1:39	they remained with him that **day**
	2: 1	**day** there was a wedding in Cana
	2:12	they remained there a few **days.**
	2:19	three **days** I will raise it up.
	2:20	you raise it up in three **days?**
	4:40	and he stayed there two **days.**
	4:43	When the two **days** were over, he
	5: 9	Now that **day** was a sabbath.
	6:39	raise it up on the last **day.**
	6:40	raise them up on the last **day.**
	6:44	that person up on the last **day.**
	6:54	raise them up on the last **day;**
	7:37	On the last **day** of the festival
	8:56	he would see my **day;** he saw it
	9: 4	while it is **day;** night is
	9:14	Now it was a sabbath **day** when
	11: 6	he stayed two **days** longer in
	11: 9	twelve hours of **day**light? Those
	11: 9	who walk during the **day** do not
	11:17	been in the tomb four **days.**
	11:24	resurrection on the last **day.**
	11:53	from that **day** on they planned
	12: 1	Six **days** before the Passover
	12: 7	she might keep it for the **day**

	12:48	on the last **day** the word that
	14:20	On that **day** you will know that
	16:23	On that **day** you will ask
	16:26	On that **day** you will ask in my
	19:31	Since it was the **day** of
	20:19	When it was evening on that **day**
	20:26	A **week** later his disciples were
Ac	1: 2	until the **day** when he was taken
	1: 3	forty **days** and speaking about
	1: 5	Spirit not many **days** from now.
	1:15	In those **days** Peter stood up
	1:22	until the **day** when he was taken
	2: 1	When the **day** of Pentecost had
	2:15	nine o'clock in the **morning.**
	2:17	In the last **days** it will be,
	2:18	in those **days** I will pour out
	2:20	Lord's great and glorious **day.**
	2:29	his tomb is with us to this **day**
	2:41	that **day** about three thousand
	2:46	**Day** by day, as they spent much
	2:47	And **day** by day the Lord added
	3: 2	People would lay him **daily** at
	3:24	him, also predicted these **days.**
	5:36	For some **time** ago Theudas rose
	5:37	at the **time** of the census and
	5:42	And every **day** in the temple and
	6: 1	Now during those **days,** when the
	7: 8	him on the eighth **day;** and
	7:26	The next **day** he came to some of
	7:41	At that **time** they made a calf,
	7:45	it was there until the **time** of
	8: 1	That **day** a severe persecution
	9: 9	For three **days** he was without
	9:19	For several **days** he was with
	9:23	After some **time** had passed, the
	9:24	were watching the gates **day** and
	9:37	At that **time** she became ill and
	9:43	some **time** with a certain Simon,
	10: 3	One **afternoon** at about three
	10:30	Four **days** ago at this very
	10:40	God raised him on the third **day**
	10:48	him to stay for several **days.**
	11:27	At that **time** prophets came down
	12: 3	(This was during the **festival**
	12:18	When **morning** came, there was no
	12:21	On an appointed **day** Herod put
	13:14	And on the sabbath **day** they
	13:31	and for many **days** he appeared
	13:41	in your **days** I am doing a work,

15: 7	in the early **days** God made a		28:14	stay with them for seven **days.**
15:36	After some **days** Paul said to		28:17	Three **days** later he called
16: 5	and increased in numbers **daily.**		28:23	After they had set a **day** to
16:12	in this city for some **days.**	Ro	2: 5	wrath for yourself on the **day**
16:13	On the sabbath **day** we went		2:16	on the **day** when, according to
16:18	doing this for many **days.** But		8:36	being killed all **day** long; we
16:35	When **morning** came, the		10:21	All **day** long I have held out
17:11	the scriptures every **day** to		11: 8	hear, down to this very **day.**
17:17	in the marketplace every **day**		13:12	the night is far gone, the **day**
17:31	because he has fixed a **day** on		13:13	live honorably as in the **day,**
18:18	for a considerable **time,** Paul		14: 5	Some judge one **day** to be better
19: 9	and argued **daily** in the lecture		14: 5	better than **another,** while
20: 6	after the **days** of Unleavened		14: 5	others judge all **days** to be
20: 6	in five **days** we joined them		14: 6	Those who observe the **day,**
20: 6	where we stayed for seven **days.**	1C	1: 8	may be blameless on the **day** of
20:16	if possible, on the **day** of		3:13	the **Day** will disclose it,
20:18	from the first **day** that I set		4: 3	by you or by any human **court.**
20:26	**day** that I am not responsible		5: 5	may be saved in the **day** of the
20:31	night or **day** to warn everyone		10: 8	thousand fell in a single **day.**
21: 4	stayed there for seven **days.**		15: 4	he was raised on the third **day**
21: 5	When our **days** there were ended,		15:31	I die every **day!** That is as
21: 7	stayed with them for one **day.**	2C	1:14	that on the **day** of the Lord
21:10	staying there for several **days,**		3:14	to this very **day,** when they
21:15	After these **days** we got ready		4:16	nature is being renewed **day** by
21:26	and the next **day,** having		4:16	is being renewed day by **day.**
21:26	completion of the **days** of		6: 2	on a **day** of salvation I have
21:27	When the seven **days** were almost		6: 2	now is the **day** of salvation!
21:38	**recently** stirred up a revolt		11:28	I am under **daily** pressure
23: 1	Brothers, up to this **day** I	Ga	1:18	stayed with him fifteen **days;**
23:12	In the **morning** the Jews joined		4:10	You are observing special **days,**
24: 1	Five **days** later the high priest	Ep	4:30	seal for the **day** of redemption.
24:11	twelve **days** since I went up to		5:16	because the **days** are evil.
24:24	Some **days** later when Felix came		6:13	withstand on that evil **day,**
25: 1	Three **days** after Festus had	Ph	1: 5	from the first **day** until now.
25: 6	more than eight or ten **days,** he		1: 6	completion by the **day** of Jesus
25:13	After several **days** had passed,		1:10	so that in the **day** of Christ
25:14	staying there several **days,**		2:16	I can boast on the **day** of
26: 7	earnestly worship **day** and	Co	1: 6	from the **day** you heard it and
26:13	when at mid**day** along the road,		1: 9	since the **day** we heard it, we
26:22	To this **day** I have had help	1Th	2: 9	we worked night and **day,** so
27: 7	number of **days** and arrived		3:10	Night and **day** we pray most
27:20	many **days,** and no small tempest		5: 2	the **day** of the Lord will come
27:29	prayed for **day** to come.		5: 4	for that **day** to surprise you
27:33	Just before **day**break, Paul		5: 5	light and children of the **day;**
27:33	Today is the fourteenth **day**		5: 8	But since we belong to the **day,**
27:39	In the **morning** they did not	2Th	1:10	on that **day** among all who have
28: 7	us hospitably for three **days.**		2: 2	to the effect that the **day** of
28:12	stayed there for three **days;**		3: 8	we worked night and **day,** so
28:13	After one **day** there a south	1Ti	5: 5	and prayers night and **day;**

2Ti	1: 3	in my prayers night and **day.**
	1:12	until that **day** what I have
	1:18	from the Lord on that **day!** And
	3: 1	that in the last **days**
	4: 8	will give me on that **day,** and
He	1: 2	but in these last **days** he has
	3: 8	as on the **day** of testing in the
	3:13	exhort one another every **day,**
	4: 4	the seventh **day** as follows,
	4: 7	again he sets a certain **day**—
	4: 8	speak later about another **day.**
	5: 7	In the **days** of his flesh, Jesus
	7: 3	neither beginning of **days** nor
	7:27	no need to offer sacrifices **day**
	8: 8	The **days** are surely coming,
	8: 9	on the **day** when I took them by
	8:10	of Israel after those **days,**
	10:11	And every priest stands **day**
	10:16	after those **days,** says the
	10:25	more as you see the **Day**
	10:32	But recall those earlier **days**
	11:30	been encircled for seven **days.**
	12:10	short **time** as seemed best to
Ja	5: 3	up treasure for the last **days.**
	5: 5	fattened your hearts in a **day**
1P	2:12	God when he comes to **judge.**
	3:10	desire to see good **days,** let
	3:20	in the **days** of Noah, during the
2P	1:19	until the **day** dawns and the
	2: 8	living among them **day** after day
	2: 8	among them day after **day,** was
	2: 9	punishment until the **day**
	2:13	to revel in the **day**time. They
	3: 3	that in the last **days** scoffers
	3: 7	kept until the **day** of judgment
	3: 8	with the Lord one **day** is like a
	3: 8	thousand years are like one **day**
	3:10	But the **day** of the Lord will
	3:12	hastening the coming of the **day**
	3:18	now and to the **day** of eternity.
1J	4:17	we may have boldness on the **day**
Ju	1: 6	the judgment of the great **Day.**
Re	1:10	in the spirit on the Lord's **day**
	2:10	for ten **days** you will have
	2:13	even in the **days** of Antipas my
	4: 8	**Day** and night without ceasing
	6:17	for the great **day** of their
	7:15	and worship him **day** and night
	8:12	a third of the **day** was kept

	9: 6	And in those **days** people will
	9:15	the **day,** the month, and the
	10: 7	but in the **days** when the
	11: 3	two hundred sixty **days,** wearing
	11: 6	during the **days** of their
	11: 9	For three and a half **days**
	11:11	**days,** the breath of life from
	12: 6	thousand two hundred sixty **days**
	12:10	who accuses them **day** and night
	14:11	There is no rest **day** or night
	16:14	battle on the great **day** of God
	18: 8	will come in a single **day**—
	20:10	they will be tormented **day** and
	21:25	never be shut by **day**

2251   GO7 AG347 LN115
ἡμέτερος, OUR

Ac	2:11	in **our** own languages we hear
	26: 5	strictest sect of **our** religion
Ro	15: 4	written for **our** instruction,
2Ti	4:15	he strongly opposed **our** message
Ti	3:14	And let **people** learn to devote
1J	1: 3	truly **our** fellowship is with
	2: 2	not for **ours** only but also for

2253   GO1 AG348 LN115
ἡμιθανής, HALF-DEAD

Lk	10:30	away, leaving him **half dead.**

2255   GO5 AG348 LN115
ἥμισυς, HALF

Mk	6:23	you, even **half** of my kingdom.
Lk	19: 8	Look, **half** of my possessions,
Re	11: 9	For three and a **half** days
	11:11	But after the three and a **half**
	12:14	and times, and **half** a time.

2256   GO1 AG348 LN115 R2255,5610
ἡμίωρον, HALF HOUR

Re	8: 1	heaven for about **half an hour.**

2259   GO2 AG348 LN116
ἡνίκα, WHEN

2C	3:15	to this very day **whenever**
	3:16	but **when** one turns to the

2260   GO1 AG348 LN116
ἤπερ, THAN

Jn	12:43	human glory more **than** the

2261 GO1 AG348 LN116
ηπιος, GENTLE
2Ti 2:24 but **kindly** to everyone, an apt

2262 GO1 AG348 LN116
ηρ, ER
Lk 3:28 son of Elmadam, son of **Er,**

2263 GO1 AG348 LN116
ηρεμος, TRANQUIL
1Ti 2: 2 we may lead a **quiet** and

2264 GO43 AG348 LN116
ηρωδης, HEROD
Mt 2: 1 In the time of King **Herod,**
   2: 3 When King **Herod** heard this, he
   2: 7 Then **Herod** secretly called for
   2:12 dream not to return to **Herod,**
   2:13 for **Herod** is about to search
   2:15 there until the death of **Herod.**
   2:16 When **Herod** saw that he had been
   2:19 When **Herod** died, an angel of
   2:22 in place of his father **Herod,**
   14: 1 At that time **Herod** the ruler
   14: 3 For **Herod** had arrested John,
   14: 6 But when **Herod's** birthday came,
   14: 6 company, and she pleased **Herod**
Mk 6:14 King **Herod** heard of it, for
   6:16 But when **Herod** heard of it, he
   6:17 For **Herod** himself had sent men
   6:18 For John had been telling **Herod**
   6:20 for **Herod** feared John, knowing
   6:21 when **Herod** on his birthday gave
   6:22 pleased **Herod** and his guests;
   8:15 and the yeast of **Herod.**
Lk 1: 5 In the days of King **Herod** of
   3: 1 governor of Judea, and **Herod**
   3:19 But **Herod** the ruler, who had
   3:19 all the evil things that **Herod**
   8: 3 and Joanna, the wife of **Herod's**
   9: 7 Now **Herod** the ruler heard
   9: 9 **Herod** said, "John I beheaded;
   13:31 Get away from here, for **Herod**
   23: 7 he was under **Herod's**
   23: 7 he sent him off to **Herod,** who
   23: 8 When **Herod** saw Jesus, he was
   23:11 Even **Herod** with his soldiers
   23:12 That same day **Herod** and Pilate
   23:15 Neither has **Herod,** for he sent
Ac 4:27 both **Herod** and Pontius Pilate,

   12: 1 About that time King **Herod** laid
   12: 6 The very night before **Herod** was
   12:11 me from the hands of **Herod** and
   12:19 When **Herod** had searched for him
   12:21 On an appointed day **Herod** put
   13: 1 member of the court of **Herod**
   23:35 kept under guard in **Herod's**

2265 GO3 AG348 LN116
ηρωδιανοι, HERODIANS
Mt 22:16 along with the **Herodians,**
Mk 3: 6 conspired with the **Herodians**
   12:13 some **Herodians** to trap him in

2266 GO6 AG348 LN116
ηρωδιας, HERODIAS
Mt 14: 3 **Herodias,** his brother Philip's
   14: 6 the daughter of **Herodias** danced
Mk 6:17 prison on account of **Herodias,**
   6:19 And **Herodias** had a grudge
   6:22 When his daughter **Herodias** came
Lk 3:19 because of **Herodias,** his

2267 GO1 AG348 LN116
ηρωδιων, HERODIAN
Ro 16:11 Greet my relative **Herodion.**

2268 GO22 AG348 LN116
ησαιας, ISAIAH
Mt 3: 3 prophet **Isaiah** spoke when he
   4:14 the prophet **Isaiah** might be
   8:17 through the prophet **Isaiah,**
   12:17 through the prophet **Isaiah:**
   13:14 the prophecy of **Isaiah** that
   15: 7 You hypocrites! **Isaiah**
Mk 1: 2 **Isaiah,** "See, I am sending my
   7: 6 **Isaiah** prophesied rightly
Lk 3: 4 words of the prophet **Isaiah,**
   4:17 scroll of the prophet **Isaiah**
Jn 1:23 as the prophet **Isaiah** said.
   12:38 spoken by the prophet **Isaiah:**
   12:39 believe, because **Isaiah** also
   12:41 **Isaiah** said this because he
Ac 8:28 was reading the prophet **Isaiah.**
   8:30 reading the prophet **Isaiah.** He
   28:25 through the prophet **Isaiah,**
Ro 9:27 And **Isaiah** cries out concerning
   9:29 And as **Isaiah** predicted, "If
   10:16 for **Isaiah** says, "Lord, who has

10:20 Then **Isaiah** is so bold as to
15:12 and again **Isaiah** says, "The

2269 GO3 AG349 LN116 K2:953
ησαυ, ESAU
Ro 9:13 Jacob, but I have hated **Esau.**
He 11:20 the future on Jacob and **Esau.**
12:16 no one becomes like **Esau,** an

2269a GO2 AG349 LN116
'ησσων, WORSE
1C 11:17 the better but for the **worse.**
2C 12:15 more, am I to be loved **less?**

2270 GO5 AG349 LN116 B3:111
'ησυχαζω, I AM QUIET
Lk 14: 4 But they **were silent.** So Jesus
23:56 On the sabbath they **rested**
Ac 11:18 they **were silenced.** And they
21:14 we **remained silent** except to
1Th 4:11 to aspire to **live quietly,** to

2271 GO4 AG349 LN116 B3:111 R2272
'ησυχια, QUIET
Ac 22: 2 they became even more **quiet.**
2Th 3:12 do their work **quietly** and to
1Ti 2:11 Let a woman learn in **silence**
2:12 man; she is to keep **silent.**

2272 GO2 AG349 LN116 B3:111
'ησυχιος, QUIET
1Ti 2: 2 that we may lead a **quiet** and
1P 3: 4 beauty of a gentle and **quiet**

2273 GO1 AG349 LN116
ητοι, WHETHER
Ro 6:16 **either** of sin, which leads to

2274 GO2 AG349 LN116
'ητταομαι, I DEFEAT
2P 2:19 slaves to whatever **masters** them
2:20 **overpowered,** the last state has

2275 GO2 AG349 LN116 R2274
'ηττημα, DEFEAT
Ro 11:12 if their **defeat** means riches
1C 6: 7 already a **defeat** for you. Why

2278 GO1 AG349 LN117 K2:954 R2279
ηχεω, I RESOUND

1C 13: 1 I am a **noisy** gong or a clanging

2279 GO4 AG349 LN117
ηχος, SOUND
Lk 4:37 And a **report** about him began to
21:25 confused by the **roaring** of the
Ac 2: 2 came a **sound** like the rush of a
He 12:19 and the **sound** of a trumpet, and

θ

2279a GO1 AG491 LN117
θα, THA
1C 16:22 for the Lord. Our Lord, **come!**

2280 GO2 AG350 LN117
θαδδαιος, THADDEUS
Mt 10: 3 son of Alphaeus, and **Thaddaeus;**
Mk 3:18 son of Alphaeus, and **Thaddaeus,**

2281 GO91 AG350 LN117 B3:982
θαλασσα, SEA
Mt 4:15 on the road by the **sea,** across
4:18 As he walked by the **Sea** of
4:18 casting a net into the **sea**—
8:24 A windstorm arose on the **sea,**
8:26 rebuked the winds and the **sea;**
8:27 even the winds and the **sea** obey
8:32 steep bank into the **sea** and
13: 1 house and sat beside the **sea.**
13:47 that was thrown into the **sea**
14:25 walking toward them on the **sea.**
14:26 saw him walking on the **sea,**
15:29 he passed along the **Sea** of
17:27 go to the **sea** and cast a hook;
18: 6 drowned in the depth of the **sea**
21:21 thrown into the **sea,**' it will
23:15 For you cross **sea** and land to
Mk 1:16 As Jesus passed along the **Sea**
1:16 casting a net into the **sea**—
2:13 beside the **sea;** the whole crowd
3: 7 **sea,** and a great multitude from
4: 1 began to teach beside the **sea.**
4: 1 got into a boat on the **sea** and
4: 1 was beside the **sea** on the land.
4:39 and said to the **sea,** "Peace! Be
4:41 even the wind and the **sea** obey
5: 1 other side of the **sea,** to the
5:13 the steep bank into the **sea,**

	5:13	and were drowned in the **sea.**
	5:21	him; and he was by the **sea.**
	6:47	the boat was out on the **sea,**
	6:48	morning, walking on the **sea.** He
	6:49	saw him walking on the **sea,**
	7:31	towards the **Sea** of Galilee, in
	9:42	you were thrown into the **sea.**
	11:23	up and thrown into the **sea,**
Lk	17: 2	you were thrown into the **sea**
	17: 6	uprooted and planted in the **sea**
	21:25	of the **sea** and the waves.
Jn	6: 1	also called the **Sea** of Tiberias
	6:16	disciples went down to the **sea,**
	6:17	and started across the **sea** to
	6:18	The **sea** became rough because a
	6:19	saw Jesus walking on the **sea**
	6:22	on the other side of the **sea**
	6:25	other side of the **sea,** they
	21: 1	to the disciples by the **Sea** of
	21: 7	naked, and jumped into the **sea.**
Ac	4:24	the **sea,** and everything in them
	7:36	at the Red **Sea,** and in the
	10: 6	whose house is by the **seaside.**
	10:32	of Simon, a tanner, by the **sea.**
	14:15	and the **sea** and all that is in
	17:14	sent Paul away to the **coast,**
	27:30	lowered the boat into the **sea,**
	27:38	throwing the wheat into the **sea**
	27:40	and left them in the **sea.** At
	28: 4	he has escaped from the **sea,**
Ro	9:27	were like the sand of the **sea,**
1C	10: 1	and all passed through the **sea,**
	10: 2	in the cloud and in the **sea,**
2C	11:26	danger at **sea,** danger from
He	11:12	grains of sand by the **seashore.**
	11:29	through the Red **Sea** as if it
Ja	1: 6	is like a wave of the **sea,**
Ju	1:13	wild waves of the **sea,** casting
Re	4: 6	something like a **sea** of glass,
	5:13	and in the **sea,** and all that is
	7: 1	blow on earth or **sea** or against
	7: 2	power to damage earth and **sea,**
	7: 3	damage the earth or the **sea** or
	8: 8	fire, was thrown into the **sea.**
	8: 8	A third of the **sea** became
	8: 9	living creatures in the **sea**
	10: 2	his right foot on the **sea** and
	10: 5	standing on the **sea** and the
	10: 6	and the **sea** and what is in it:

	10: 8	who is standing on the **sea** and
	12:12	woe to the earth and the **sea,**
	12:18	on the sand of the **seashore.**
	13: 1	beast rising out of the **sea,**
	14: 7	**sea** and the springs of water.
	15: 2	a **sea** of glass mixed with fire,
	15: 2	standing beside the **sea** of
	16: 3	his bowl into the **sea,** and it
	16: 3	living thing in the **sea** died.
	18:17	all whose trade is on the **sea,**
	18:19	all who had ships at **sea** grew
	18:21	threw it into the **sea,** saying,
	20: 8	as the sands of the **sea.**
	20:13	And the **sea** gave up the dead
	21: 1	and the **sea** was no more.

2282   GO2 AG350 LN117
θαλπω, I CHERISH
| Ep | 5:29 | nourishes and **tenderly cares** |
| 1Th | 2: 7 | like a nurse **tenderly caring** |

2283   GO1 AG350 LN117 K3:1
θαμαρ, THAMAR (TAMAR)
| Mt | 1: 3 | by **Tamar,** and Perez the father |

2284   GO3 AG350 LN117 B2:621 K3:4 R2285
θαμβεω, I AM ASTONISHED
Mk	1:27	They were all **amazed,** and they
	10:24	the disciples **were perplexed** at
	10:32	they **were amazed,** and those who

2285   GO3 AG350 LN117 B2:621 K3:4
θαμβος, ASTONISHMENT
Lk	4:36	They were all **amazed** and kept
	5: 9	who were with him were **amazed**
Ac	3:10	wonder and **amazement** at what

2286   GO1 AG350 LN117 R2288
θανασιμος, DEADLY
| Mk | 16:18 | if they drink any **deadly** thing, |

2287   GO1 AG350 LN117
θανατηφορος, CARRYING DEATH
| Ja | 3: 8 | restless evil, full of **deadly** |

2288   GO120 AG350 LN117 B1:429 K3:7 R2348
θανατος, DEATH
| Mt | 4:16 | shadow of **death** light has |

	10:21	betray brother to **death,** and a		7: 5	members to bear fruit for **death**
	15: 4	or mother must surely **die.**		7:10	life proved to be **death** to me.
	16:28	who will not taste **death**		7:13	bring **death** to me? By no means!
	20:18	they will condemn him to **death;**		7:13	working **death** in me through
	26:38	even to **death;** remain here, and		7:24	me from this body of **death?**
	26:66	answered, "He deserves **death.**"		8: 2	the law of sin and of **death.**
Mk	7:10	or mother must surely **die.**		8: 6	flesh is **death,** but to set the
	9: 1	who will not taste **death** until		8:38	convinced that neither **death,**
	10:33	they will condemn him to **death;**	1C	3:22	or life or **death** or the present
	13:12	brother to **death,** and a father		11:26	you proclaim the Lord's **death**
	14:34	even to **death;** remain here, and		15:21	For since **death** came through a
	14:64	him as deserving **death.**		15:26	enemy to be destroyed is **death.**
Lk	1:79	in the shadow of **death,** to		15:54	**Death** has been swallowed up in
	2:26	he would not see **death** before		15:55	Where, O **death,** is your
	9:27	who will not taste **death** before		15:55	Where, O **death,** is your sting?
	22:33	with you to prison and to **death**		15:56	The sting of **death** is sin, and
	23:15	done nothing to deserve de ath.	2C	1: 9	received the sentence of **death**
	23:22	the sentence of **death;** I will		1:10	rescued us from so **deadly** a
	24:20	be condemned to **death** and		2:16	a fragrance from **death** to death
Jn	5:24	has passed from **death** to life.		2:16	fragrance from death to **death,**
	8:51	my word will never see **death.**		3: 7	Now if the ministry of **death,**
	8:52	word will never taste **death.**		4:11	being given up to **death** for
	11: 4	illness does not lead to **death;**		4:12	So **death** is at work in us, but
	11·13	been speaking about his **death,**		7:10	worldly grief produces **death.**
	12:33	the kind of **death** he was to die		11:23	floggings, and often near **death**
	18:32	indicated the kind of **death** he	Ph	1:20	whether by life or by **death.**
	21:19	indicate the kind of **death** by		2: 8	obedient to the point of **death**
Ac	2:24	having freed him from **death,**		2: 8	death—even **death** on a cross.
	13:28	cause for a sentence of **death,**		2:27	he nearly **died.** But God had
	22: 4	up to the point of **death** by		2:30	because he came close to **death**
	23:29	nothing deserving **death** or		3:10	becoming like him in his **death,**
	25:11	am not trying to escape **death;**	Co	1:22	fleshly body through **death,** so
	25:25	done nothing deserving **death;**	2Ti	1:10	abolished **death** and brought
	26:31	doing nothing to deserve **death**	He	2: 9	suffering of **death,** so that by
	28:18	no reason for the **death** penalty		2: 9	might taste **death** for everyone.
Ro	1:32	deserve to **die**—yet they not		2:14	so that through **death** he might
	5:10	through the **death** of his Son,		2:14	who has the power of **death,**
	5:12	and **death** came through sin, and		2:15	in slavery by the fear of **death**
	5:12	**death** spread to all because all		5: 7	was able to save him from **death**
	5:14	Yet **death** exercised dominion		7:23	prevented by **death** from
	5:17	**death** exercised dominion		9:15	because a **death** has occurred
	5:21	sin exercised dominion in **death**		9:16	the **death** of the one who made
	6: 3	were baptized into his **death?**		11: 5	he did not experience **death;**
	6: 4	by baptism into **death,** so that,	Ja	1:15	grown, gives birth to **death.**
	6: 5	united with him in a **death** like		5:20	the sinner's soul from **death**
	6: 9	**death** no longer has dominion	1J	3:14	passed from **death** to life
	6:16	which leads to **death,** or of		3:14	does not love abides in **death.**
	6:21	end of those things is **death.**		5:16	what is not a **mortal** sin, you
	6:23	For the wages of sin is **death,**		5:16	whose sin is not **mortal.** There

	5:16	There is sin that is **mortal;**
	5:17	there is sin that is not **mortal**
Re	1:18	I have the keys of **Death** and
	2:10	Be faithful until **death,** and I
	2:11	be harmed by the second **death.**
	2:23	will strike her children **dead.**
	6: 8	Its rider's name was **Death,** and
	6: 8	famine, and **pestilence,** and by
	9: 6	people will seek **death** but will
	9: 6	but **death** will flee from them.
	12:11	life even in the face of **death.**
	13: 3	received a **death**-blow, but its
	13: 3	but its **mortal** wound had been
	13:12	whose **mortal** wound had been
	18: 8	**pestilence** and mourning and
	20: 6	Over these the second **death** has
	20:13	**Death** and Hades gave up the
	20:14	Then **Death** and Hades were
	20:14	This is the second **death,** the
	21: 4	**Death** will be no more;
	21: 8	which is the second **death.**

2289 GO11 AG351 LN117 B1:430 K3:21 R2288
θανατοω, I PUT TO DEATH

Mt	10:21	and have them **put to death;**
	26:59	they might **put** him **to death,**
	27: 1	order to **bring about** his **death.**
Mk	13:12	and have them **put to death;**
	14:55	Jesus to **put** him **to death;**
Lk	21:16	will **put** some of you **to death.**
Ro	7: 4	you **have died** to the law
	8:13	you **put to death** the deeds of
	8:36	we **are being killed** all day
2C	6: 9	as punished, and yet not **killed**
1P	3:18	He was **put to death** in the

2290 GO11 AG351 LN117 B1:263
θαπτω, I BURY

Mt	8:21	let me go and **bury** my father.
	8:22	let the dead **bury** their own
	14:12	took the body and **buried** it;
Lk	9:59	first let me go and **bury** my
	9:60	Let the dead **bury** their own
	16:22	man also died and was **buried.**
Ac	2:29	died and **was buried,** and his
	5: 6	then carried him out and **buried**
	5: 9	feet of those who **have buried**
	5:10	carried her out and **buried** her
1C	15: 4	and that he **was buried,** and

2291 GO1 AG351 LN117
θαρα, THARA (TERAH)

Lk	3:34	Abraham, son of **Terah,** son of

2292 GO6 AG352 LN117 B1:327 K3:25
θαρρεω, I AM CONFIDENT

2C	5: 6	So we **are** always **confident;**
	5: 8	Yes, we **do have confidence,**
	7:16	I **have complete confidence** in
	10: 1	but **bold** toward you when I am
	10: 2	I need not **show boldness** by
He	13: 6	So we can **say** with **confidence,**

2293 GO7 AG352 LN117 B1:327 K3:25 R2294
θαρσεω, I TAKE COURAGE

Mt	9: 2	**Take heart,** son; your sins
	9:22	**Take heart,** daughter; your
	14:27	**Take heart,** it is I; do not
Mk	6:50	**Take heart,** it is I; do not be
	10:49	**Take heart;** get up, he is
Jn	16:33	But **take courage;** I have
Ac	23:11	**Keep** up your **courage!** For just

2294 GO1 AG352 LN117
θαρσος, COURAGE

Ac	28:15	thanked God and took **courage.**

2295 GO2 AG352 LN117 B2:621 K3:27 R2296
θαυμα, MARVEL

2C	11:14	And no **wonder!** Even Satan
Re	17: 6	When I saw her, I was **greatly**

2296 GO43 AG352 LN118 B2:621 K3:27
θαυμαζω, I MARVEL

Mt	8:10	he **was amazed** and said to
	8:27	They **were amazed,** saying,
	9:33	the crowds **were amazed** and said
	15:31	so that the crowd **was amazed**
	21:20	they **were amazed,** saying, "How
	22:22	they **were amazed;** and they left
	27:14	the governor **was** greatly **amazed**
Mk	5:20	him; and everyone **was amazed.**
	6: 6	And he **was amazed** at their
	15: 5	so that Pilate **was amazed.**
	15:44	Then Pilate **wondered** if he were
Lk	1:21	Zechariah, and **wondered** at his
	1:63	And all of them **were amazed.**
	2:18	all who heard it **were amazed** at
	2:33	**were amazed** at what was being
	4:22	**were amazed** at the gracious

	7: 9	**was amazed** at him, and turning
	8:25	They were afraid and **amazed,**
	9:43	While everyone **was amazed** at
	11:14	and the crowds **were amazed.**
	11:38	The Pharisee **was amazed** to see
	20:26	and **being amazed** by his answer,
	24:12	**amazed** at what had happened.
	24:41	**wondering,** he said to them,
Jn	3: 7	**Do** not **be astonished** that I
	4:27	They **were astonished** that
	5:20	so that you **will be astonished.**
	5:28	**Do** not **be astonished** at this;
	7:15	The Jews **were astonished** at it,
	7:21	and all of you **are astonished.**
Ac	2: 7	Amazed and **astonished,** they
	3:12	why **do** you **wonder** at this, or
	4:13	they **were amazed** and recognized
	7:31	he **was amazed** at the sight; and
	13:41	**Be amazed** and perish, for in
Ga	1: 6	I **am astonished** that you are so
2Th	1:10	to **be marveled** at on that day
1J	3:13	**Do** not **be astonished,** brothers
Ju	1:16	**flattering** people to their own
Re	13: 3	In **amazement** the whole earth
	17: 6	her, I **was greatly amazed.**
	17: 7	Why **are** you so **amazed?** I will
	17: 8	**will be amazed** when they see

2297 GO1 AG352 LN118 B2:621 K3:27 R2296
θαυμασιος, MARVEL

Mt	21:15	saw the **amazing** things that he

2298 GO6 AG352 LN118 B2:621 K3:27 R2296
θαυμαστος, MARVELOUS

Mt	21:42	doing, and it is **amazing** in
Mk	12:11	it is **amazing** in our eyes
Jn	9:30	Here is an **astonishing** thing!
1P	2: 9	into his **marvelous** light.
Re	15: 1	in heaven, great and **amazing:**
	15: 3	Great and **amazing** are your

2299 GO1 AG353 LN118 R2316
θεα, GODDESS

Ac	19:27	the great **goddess** Artemis will

2300 GO22 AG353 LN118 B3:511 K5:315
θεαομαι, I WATCH

Mt	6: 1	order **to be seen** by them; for
	11: 7	**to look at?** A reed shaken by
	22:11	came in **to see** the guests, he

	23: 5	**to be seen** by others; for they
Mk	16:11	**had been seen** by her, they
	16:14	believed those who **saw** him
Lk	5:27	he went out and **saw** a tax
	7:24	into the wilderness **to look at?**
	23:55	they **saw** the tomb and how his
Jn	1:14	and we **have seen** his glory, the
	1:32	And John testified, "I **saw** the
	1:38	When Jesus turned and **saw** them
	4:35	and **see** how the fields are ripe
	6: 5	When he **looked** up and saw a
	11:45	and **had seen** what Jesus did,
Ac	1:11	in the same way as you **saw** him
	21:27	who **had seen** him in the temple,
	22: 9	**saw** the light but did not
Ro	15:24	For I do hope **to see** you on my
1J	1: 1	what we **have looked at** and
	4:12	No one **has** ever **seen** God; if we
	4:14	And we **have seen** and do testify

2301 GO1 AG353 LN118 B3:521 K3:42
θεατριζω, I STARE AT

He	10:33	**being publicly exposed** to abuse

2302 GO3 AG353 LN118 B3:520 K3:42 R2300
θεατρον, THEATER

Ac	19:29	to the **theater,** dragging with
	19:31	not to venture into the **theater**
1C	4: 9	we have become a **spectacle** to

2303 GO7 AG353 LN118
θειον, SULPHUR

Lk	17:29	rained fire and **sulfur** from
Re	9:17	sapphire and of **sulfur;** the
	9:18	**sulfur** coming out of their
	14:10	tormented with fire and **sulfur**
	19:20	fire that burns with **sulfur.**
	20:10	**sulfur,** where the beast and the
	21: 8	fire and **sulfur,** which is the

2304 GO3 AG353 LN118 B2:66 K3:122 R2316
θειος, GODLY

Ac	17:29	not to think that the **deity** is
2P	1: 3	His **divine** power has given us
	1: 4	participants of the **divine**

2305 GO1 AG354 LN118 B2:66 K3:123 R2304
θειοτης, DIETY

Ro	1:20	eternal power and **divine nature**

2306　 GO1　AG354　LN118
θειωδης, SULPHUROUS
Re　　9:17　　and of sapphire and of **sulfur**

2307　 GO62　AG354　LN118　B3:1018　K3:52　R2309
θελημα, WANT
Mt　　6:10　　Your **will** be done, on earth as
　　　　7:21　　the one who does the **will** of my
　　　　12:50　　For whoever does the **will** of my
　　　　18:14　　So it is not the **will** of your
　　　　21:31　　Which of the two did the **will**
　　　　26:42　　I drink it, your **will** be done.
Mk　　3:35　　Whoever does the **will** of God is
Lk　　12:47　　who knew what his master **wanted**
　　　　12:47　　or do what was **wanted,** will
　　　　22:42　　yet, not my **will** but yours be
　　　　23:25　　Jesus over as they **wished.**
Jn　　1:13　　of blood or of the **will** of the
　　　　1:13　　flesh or of the **will** of man,
　　　　4:34　　My food is to do the **will** of
　　　　5:30　　I seek to do not my own **will**
　　　　5:30　　but the **will** of him who sent me
　　　　6:38　　not to do my own **will,** but the
　　　　6:38　　but the **will** of him who sent me
　　　　6:39　　And this is the **will** of him who
　　　　6:40　　the **will** of my Father, that all
　　　　7:17　　do the **will** of God will know
　　　　9:31　　worships him and obeys his **will**
Ac　　13:22　　will carry out all my **wishes.**
　　　　21:14　　say, "The Lord's **will** be done."
　　　　22:14　　chosen you to know his **will,** to
Ro　　1:10　　asking that by God's **will** I may
　　　　2:18　　and know his **will** and determine
　　　　12: 2　　may discern what is the **will** of
　　　　15:32　　so that by God's **will** I may
1C　　1: 1　　by the **will** of God, and our
　　　　7:37　　having his own **desire** under
　　　　16:12　　but he was not at all **willing**
2C　　1: 1　　by the **will** of God, and Timothy
　　　　8: 5　　Lord and, by the **will** of God,
Ga　　1: 4　　according to the **will** of our
Ep　　1: 1　　by the **will** of God, To the
　　　　1: 5　　the good pleasure of his **will,**
　　　　1: 9　　mystery of his **will,** according
　　　　1:11　　to his counsel and **will,**
　　　　2: 3　　following the **desires** of flesh
　　　　5:17　　understand what the **will** of the
　　　　6: 6　　doing the **will** of God from the
Co　　1: 1　　by the **will** of God, and Timothy

　　　　1: 9　　God's **will** in all spiritual
　　　　4:12　　in everything that God **wills.**
1Th　　4: 3　　For this is the **will** of God,
　　　　5:18　　for this is the **will** of God in
2Ti　　1: 1　　by the **will** of God, for the
　　　　2:26　　captive by him to do his **will.**
He　　10: 7　　I have come to do your **will,** O
　　　　10: 9　　I have come to do your **will.**
　　　　10:10　　And it is by God's **will** that
　　　　10:36　　when you have done the **will** of
　　　　13:21　　so that you may do his **will,**
1P　　2:15　　For it is God's **will** that by
　　　　3:17　　suffering should be God's **will,**
　　　　4: 2　　human desires but by the **will**
　　　　4:19　　**will** entrust themselves to a
2P　　1:21　　ever came by human **will,** but
1J　　2:17　　those who do the **will** of God
　　　　5:14　　anything according to his **will,**
Re　　4:11　　and by your **will** they existed

2308　 GO1　AG354　LN118　B3:1018　K3:62
θελησις, WANT
He　　2: 4　　according to his **will.**

2309　 GO209　AG354　LN118　B3:1018　K3:44　R2309
θελω, I WANT
Mt　　1:19　　**unwilling** to expose her to
　　　　2:18　　she **refused** to be consoled,
　　　　5:40　　and if anyone **wants** to sue you
　　　　5:42　　do not refuse anyone who **wants**
　　　　7:12　　do to others as you **would have**
　　　　8: 2　　Lord, if you **choose,** you can
　　　　8: 3　　I **do choose.** Be made clean!
　　　　9:13　　I **desire** mercy, not sacrifice.
　　　　11:14　　and if you **are willing** to
　　　　12: 7　　I **desire** mercy and not
　　　　12:38　　Teacher, we **wish** to see a sign
　　　　13:28　　Then do you **want** us to go and
　　　　14: 5　　Though Herod **wanted** to put him
　　　　15:28　　**wish."** And her daughter was
　　　　15:32　　I **do** not **want** to send them away
　　　　16:24　　If any **want** to become my
　　　　16:25　　For those who **want** to save
　　　　17: 4　　if you **wish,** I will make
　　　　17:12　　to him whatever they **pleased.**
　　　　18:23　　a king who **wished** to settle
　　　　18:30　　But he **refused;** then he went
　　　　19:17　　If you **wish** to enter into life,
　　　　19:21　　Jesus said to him, "If you **wish**

	20:14	I **choose** to give to this last	8:20	standing outside, **wanting** to
	20:15	what I **choose** with what belongs	9:23	If any **want** to become my
	20:21	"What do you **want?**" She said to	9:24	For those who **want** to save
	20:26	whoever **wishes** to be great	9:54	Lord, do you **want** us to
	20:27	and whoever **wishes** to be first	10:24	many prophets and kings **desired**
	20:32	What do you **want** me to do for	10:29	But **wanting** to justify himself,
	21:29	He answered, 'I **will** not'; but	12:49	I **wish** it were already kindled!
	22: 3	banquet, but they **would** not	13:31	for Herod **wants** to kill you.
	23: 4	they themselves are un**willing**	13:34	How often have I **desired** to
	23:37	How often have I **desired** to	13:34	wings, and you **were** not **willing**
	23:37	wings, and you **were** not **willing**	14:28	For which of you, **intending** to
	26:15	and said, "What **will** you give	15:28	he became angry and **refused** to
	26:17	Where do you **want** us to make	16:26	those who **might want** to pass
	26:39	yet not what I **want** but what	18: 4	For a while he **refused;** but
	27:15	crowd, anyone whom they **wanted.**	18:13	**would** not even look up to
	27:17	Whom do you **want** me to release	18:41	What do you **want** me to do for
	27:21	Which of the two do you **want**	19:14	We do not **want** this man to
	27:34	tasted it, he **would** not drink	19:27	who did not **want** me to be king
Mk	1:40	If you **choose,** you can make me	20:46	of the scribes, who **like**
	1:41	I **do choose.** Be made clean!	22: 9	asked him, "Where do you **want**
	3:13	those whom he **wanted,** and they	23: 8	he **had been wanting** to see him
	6:19	**wanted** to kill him. But she	23:20	**wanting** to release Jesus,
	6:22	Ask me for whatever you **wish,**	Jn 1:43	next day Jesus **decided** to go
	6:25	I **want** you to give me at once	3: 8	The wind blows where it **chooses**
	6:26	he did not **want** to refuse her.	5: 6	Do you **want** to be made well?
	6:48	sea. He **intended** to pass them	5:21	life to whomever he **wishes**.
	7:24	did not **want** anyone to know he	5:35	you **were willing** to rejoice for
	8:34	If any **want** to become my	5:40	Yet you **refuse** to come to me to
	8:35	For those who **want** to save	6:11	fish, as much as they **wanted.**
	9:13	to him whatever they **pleased,**	6:21	Then they **wanted** to take him
	9:30	He did not **want** anyone to know	6:67	Do you also **wish** to go away?
	9:35	Whoever **wants** to be first must	7: 1	He did not **wish** to go about in
	10:35	Teacher, we **want** you to do for	7:17	Anyone who **resolves** to do the
	10:36	What is it you **want** me to do	7:44	Some of them **wanted** to arrest
	10:43	whoever **wishes** to become great	8:44	you **choose** to do your father's
	10:44	and whoever **wishes** to be first	9:27	Why do you **want** to hear it
	10:51	What do you **want** me to do for	9:27	Do you also **want** to become his
	12:38	scribes, who **like** to walk	12:21	him, "Sir, we **wish** to see Jesus
	14: 7	to them whenever you **wish;** but	15: 7	ask for whatever you **wish,** and
	14:12	Where do you **want** us to go and	16:19	Jesus knew that they **wanted** to
	14:36	yet, not what I **want,** but what	17:24	Father, I **desire** that those
	15: 9	Do you **want** me to release for	21:18	go wherever you **wished.** But
	15:12	what do you **wish** me to do with	21:18	you where you **do** not **wish** to go
Lk	1:62	what name he **wanted** to give him	21:22	If it **is** my **will** that he
	4: 6	I give it to anyone I **please.**	21:23	is my **will** that he remain until
	5:12	Lord, if you **choose,** you can	Ac 2:12	another, "What **does** this mean?"
	5:13	I **do choose.** Be made clean.	7:28	Do you **want** to kill me as you
	5:39	**desires** new wine,	7:39	Our ancestors **were** un**willing** to
	6:31	Do to others as you **would** have	10:10	He became hungry and **wanted**

	14:13	**wanted** to offer sacrifice.
	16: 3	Paul **wanted** Timothy to
	17:18	What does this babbler **want** to
	17:20	like to know what it **means.**
	18:21	return to you, if God **wills.**
	19:33	**tried** to make a defense before
	24:27	he **wanted** to grant the Jews a
	25: 9	But Festus, **wishing** to do the
	25: 9	Do you **wish** to go up to
	26: 5	if they **are willing** to testify,
Ro	1:13	I **want** you to know, brothers
	7:15	For I do not do what I **want,**
	7:16	Now if I do what I do not **want,**
	7:18	I **can will** what is right, but I
	7:19	For I do not do the good I **want**
	7:19	the evil I do not **want** is what
	7:20	Now if I do what I do not **want,**
	7:21	when I **want** to do what is good,
	9:16	So it **depends** not **on** human **will**
	9:18	mercy on whomever he **chooses,**
	9:18	heart of whomever he **chooses.**
	9:22	What if God, **desiring** to show
	11:25	I **want** you to understand this
	13: 3	Do you **wish** to have no fear of
	16:19	I **want** you to be wise in what
1C	4:19	if the Lord **wills,** and I will
	4:21	What **would** you **prefer?** Am I to
	7: 7	I **wish** that all were as I
	7:32	I **want** you to be free from
	7:36	let him marry as he **wishes;** it
	7:39	free to marry anyone she **wishes**
	10: 1	I do not **want** you to be unaware
	10:20	I do not **want** you to be
	10:27	you are **disposed** to go, eat
	11: 3	But I **want** you to understand
	12: 1	I do not **want** you to be
	12:18	each one of them, as he **chose.**
	14: 5	Now I **would like** all of you to
	14:19	in church I **would** rather speak
	14:35	there is anything they **desire**
	15:38	body as he **has chosen,** and to
	16: 7	I do not **want** to see you now
2C	1: 8	We do not **want** you to be
	5: 4	we **wish** not to be unclothed
	8:10	but even to **desire** to do
	8:11	your eagerness may be **matched**
	11:12	those who **want** an opportunity
	12: 6	But if I **wish** to boast, I will
	12:20	I may find you not as I **wish,**

	12:20	**wish;** I fear that there may
Ga	1: 7	**want** to pervert the gospel of
	3: 2	The only thing I **want** to learn
	4: 9	How can you **want** to be enslaved
	4:17	they **want** to exclude you, so
	4:20	I **wish** I were present with you
	4:21	Tell me, you who **desire** to be
	5:17	you from doing what you **want.**
	6:12	It is those who **want** to make a
	6:13	they **want** you to be circumcised
Ph	2:13	enabling you both **to will** and
Co	1:27	To them God **chose** to make known
	2: 1	For I **want** you to know how much
	2:18	**insisting** on self-abasement and
1Th	2:18	For we **wanted** to come to you—
	4:13	But we do not **want** you to be
2Th	3:10	Anyone un**willing** to work
1Ti	1: 7	**desiring** to be teachers of the
	2: 4	**desires** everyone to be saved
	5:11	from Christ, they **want** to marry
2Ti	3:12	Indeed, all who **want** to live a
Pm	1:14	but I **preferred** to do nothing
He	10: 5	not **desired,** but a body you
	10: 8	neither **desired** nor taken
	12:17	when he **wanted** to inherit the
	13:18	**desiring** to act honorably in
Ja	2:20	Do you **want** to be shown, you
	4:15	If the Lord **wishes,** we will
1P	3:10	For "Those who **desire** life and
	3:17	if suffering **should** be God's
2P	3: 5	They **deliberately** ignore this
3J	1:13	I **would** rather not write with
Re	2:21	she **refuses** to repent of her
	11: 5	And if anyone **wants** to harm
	11: 5	anyone who **wants** to harm them
	11: 6	plague, as often as they **desire**
	22:17	Let anyone who **wishes** take the

2310   GO16 AG355 LN118 B1:660 K3:63
θεμελιος, FOUNDATION

Lk	6:48	laid the **foundation** on rock;
	6:49	without a **foundation.** When the
	14:29	**foundation** and is not able to
Ac	16:26	the **foundations** of the prison
Ro	15:20	on someone else's **foundation,**
1C	3:10	**foundation,** and someone else is
	3:11	no one can lay any **foundation**
	3:12	anyone builds on the **foundation**
Ep	2:20	built upon the **foundation** of

1Ti	6:19	good **foundation** for the future,
2Ti	2:19	God's firm **foundation** stands,
He	6: 1	not laying again the **foundation**
	11:10	city that has **foundations**,
Re	21:14	twelve **foundations**, and on them
	21:19	The **foundations** of the wall of
	21:19	The **foundations** of the wall of

2311   ᴳᴼ5 ᴬᴳ356 ᴸᴺ118 ᴮ1:660 ᴷ3:63 ᴿ2310
θεμελιοω, I FOUND

Mt	7:25	it **had been founded** on rock.
Ep	3:17	rooted and **grounded** in love.
Co	1:23	**established** and steadfast in
He	1:10	you **founded** the earth, and the
1P	5:10	strengthen, and **establish** you.

2312   ᴳᴼ1 ᴬᴳ356 ᴸᴺ118 ᴷ3:121 ᴿ2316,1321
θεοδιδακτος, GOD-TAUGHT

1Th	4: 9	**taught by God** to love one

2314   ᴳᴼ1 ᴬᴳ356 ᴸᴺ118 ᴮ3:963 ᴷ4:528 ᴿ2316,3164
θεομαχος, GOD-FIGHTER

Ac	5:39	found **fighting against God!**

2315   ᴳᴼ1 ᴬᴼ356 ᴸᴺ118 ᴮ3:689 ᴷ6:453 ᴿ2316,4154
θεοπνευστος, GOD-BREATHED

2Ti	3:16	scripture is **inspired by God**

2316   ᴳᴼ1318 ᴬᴳ356 ᴸᴺ118 ᴮ2:66 ᴷ3:65
θεος, GOD

Mt	1:23	means, **"God** is with us."
	3: 9	**God** is able from these stones
	3:16	Spirit of **God** descending like a
	4: 3	If you are the Son of **God,**
	4: 4	comes from the mouth of **God.**
	4: 6	**God,** throw yourself down; for
	4: 7	Do not put the Lord your **God**
	4:10	Worship the Lord your **God,** and
	5: 8	for they will see **God.**
	5: 9	will be called children of **God.**
	5:34	for it is the throne of **God,**
	6:24	You cannot serve **God** and wealth
	6:30	But if **God** so clothes the grass
	6:33	first for the kingdom of **God**
	8:29	**God?** Have you come here to
	9: 8	they glorified **God,** who had
	12: 4	He entered the house of **God**
	12:28	it is by the Spirit of **God** that
	12:28	the kingdom of **God** has come to
	14:33	Truly you are the Son of **God.**

	15: 3	commandment of **God** for the sake
	15: 4	For **God** said, 'Honor your
	15: 6	you make void the word of **God.**
	15:31	And they praised the **God** of
	16:16	the Son of the living **God.**
	16:23	setting your mind not on **divine**
	19: 6	Therefore what **God** has joined
	19:24	to enter the kingdom of **God.**
	19:26	for **God** all things are possible
	21:31	into the kingdom of **God** ahead
	21:43	**God** will be taken away from you
	22:16	teach the way of **God** in
	22:21	and to **God** the things that are
	22:21	God the things that are **God's.**
	22:29	scriptures nor the power of **God**
	22:31	what was said to you by **God,**
	22:32	I am the **God** of Abraham, the
	22:32	**God** of Isaac, and the God of
	22:32	**God** of Jacob'? He is God not of
	22:32	He is **God** not of the dead, but
	22:37	love the Lord your **God** with all
	23:22	swears by the throne of **God** and
	26:61	temple of **God** and to build it
	26:63	oath before the living **God,**
	26:63	the Messiah, the Son of **God.**
	27:40	you are the Son of **God,** come
	27:43	He trusts in **God;** let God
	27:43	for he said, 'I am **God's** Son.'
	27:46	My **God,** my God, why have you
	27:46	my **God,** why have you forsaken
	27:54	said, "Truly this man was **God's**
Mk	1: 1	Jesus Christ, the Son of **God.**
	1:14	the good news of **God,**
	1:15	the kingdom of **God** has come
	1:24	you are, the Holy One of **God.**
	2: 7	Who can forgive sins but **God**
	2:12	glorified **God,** saying, "We have
	2:26	He entered the house of **God,**
	3:11	You are the Son of **God!**
	3:35	Whoever does the will of **God** is
	4:11	secret of the kingdom of **God,**
	4:26	The kingdom of **God** is as if
	4:30	kingdom of **God,** or what parable
	5: 7	Son of the Most High **God?** I
	5: 7	you by **God,** do not torment me.
	7: 8	the commandment of **God** and hold
	7: 9	commandment of **God** in order to
	7:13	making void the word of **God**
	8:33	setting your mind not on **divine**

	9: 1	the kingdom of **God** has come
	9:47	**God** with one eye than to have
	10: 9	Therefore what **God** has joined
	10:14	that the kingdom of **God** belongs
	10:15	**God** as a little child will
	10:18	No one is good but **God** alone.
	10:23	is to enter the kingdom of **God**!
	10:24	is to enter the kingdom of **God**!
	10:25	to enter the kingdom of **God**.
	10:27	not for **God**; for God all things
	10:27	**God** all things are possible.
	11:22	them, "Have faith in **God**.
	12:14	the way of **God** in accordance
	12:17	**God** the things that are God's.
	12:17	that are **God's**." And they were
	12:24	scriptures nor the power of **God**
	12:26	**God** said to him, 'I am the God
	12:26	I am the **God** of Abraham, the
	12:26	the **God** of Isaac, and the God
	12:26	Isaac, and the **God** of Jacob'?
	12:27	He is **God** not of the dead, but
	12:29	Lord our **God**, the Lord is one;
	12:30	shall love the Lord your **God**
	12:34	not far from the kingdom of **God**
	13:19	the creation that **God** created
	14:25	it new in the kingdom of **God**.
	15:34	My **God**, my God, why have you
	15:34	My God, my **God**, why have you
	15:39	Truly this man was God's **Son**!
	15:43	kingdom of **God**, went boldly to
	16:19	down at the right hand of **God**.
Lk	1: 6	righteous before **God**, living
	1: 8	priest before **God** and his
	1:16	Israel to the Lord their **God**.
	1:19	I stand in the presence of **God**,
	1:26	Gabriel was sent by **God** to a
	1:30	you have found favor with **God**.
	1:32	the Lord **God** will give to him
	1:35	he will be called Son of **God**.
	1:37	will be impossible with **God**.
	1:47	and my spirit rejoices in **God**
	1:64	he began to speak, praising **God**
	1:68	Blessed be the Lord **God** of
	1:78	By the tender mercy of our **God**,
	2:13	host, praising **God** and saying,
	2:14	Glory to **God** in the highest
	2:20	glorifying and praising **God** for
	2:28	in his arms and praised **God**,
	2:38	and began to praise **God** and to

2:40	the favor of **God** was upon him.
2:52	years, and in **divine** and human
3: 2	the word of **God** came to John
3: 6	shall see the salvation of **God**.
3: 8	**God** is able from these stones
3:38	Seth, son of Adam, son of **God**.
4: 3	If you are the Son of **God**,
4: 8	Worship the Lord your **God**, and
4: 9	**God**, throw yourself down from
4:12	Do not put the Lord your **God**
4:34	you are, the Holy One of **God**.
4:41	**God**!" But he rebuked them and
4:43	good news of the kingdom of **God**
5: 1	on him to hear the word of **God**,
5:21	Who can forgive sins but **God**
5:25	to his home, glorifying **God**.
5:26	they glorified **God** and were
6: 4	He entered the house of **God** and
6:12	the night in prayer to **God**.
6:20	for yours is the kingdom of **God**
7:16	they glorified **God**, saying, "A
7:16	and **"God** has looked favorably
7:28	least in the kingdom of **God** is
7:29	acknowledged the justice of **God**
7:30	rejected **God's** purpose for
8: 1	good news of the kingdom of **God**
8:10	secrets of the kingdom of **God**;
8:11	The seed is the word of **God**.
8:21	those who hear the word of **God**
8:28	**God**? I beg you, do not torment
8:39	declare how much **God** has done
9: 2	proclaim the kingdom of **God** and
9:11	kingdom of **God**, and healed
9:20	answered, "The Messiah of **God**."
9:27	they see the kingdom of **God**.
9:43	at the greatness of **God**. While
9:60	proclaim the kingdom of **God**.
9:62	fit for the kingdom of **God**.
10: 9	The kingdom of **God** has come
10:11	kingdom of **God** has come near.
10:27	love the Lord your **God** with all
11:20	by the finger of **God** that I
11:20	the kingdom of **God** has come to
11:28	hear the word of **God** and obey
11:42	justice and the love of **God**; it
11:49	Wisdom of **God** said, 'I will
12: 6	of them is forgotten in **God's**
12: 8	before the angels of **God**;
12: 9	denied before the angels of **God**

12:20	But **God** said to him, 'You fool!
12:21	but are not rich toward **God.**
12:24	and yet **God** feeds them. Of how
12:28	But if **God** so clothes the grass
13:13	straight and began praising **God**
13:18	What is the kingdom of **God**
13:20	I compare the kingdom of **God?**
13:28	prophets in the kingdom of **God,**
13:29	eat in the kingdom of **God.**
14:15	bread in the kingdom of **God!**
15:10	presence of the angels of **God**
16:13	You cannot serve **God** and wealth
16:15	**God** knows your hearts; for what
16:15	abomination in the sight of **God**
16:16	good news of the kingdom of **God**
17:15	praising **God** with a loud voice.
17:18	give praise to **God** except this
17:20	kingdom of **God** was coming, and
17:20	The kingdom of **God** is not
17:21	the kingdom of **God** is among you
18: 2	judge who neither feared **God**
18: 4	I have no fear of **God** and no
18: 7	And will not **God** grant justice
18:11	praying thus, **'God,** I thank you
18:13	**God,** be merciful to me, a
18:16	that the kingdom of **God** belongs
18:17	**God** as a little child will
18:19	No one is good but **God** alone.
18:24	to enter the kingdom of **God!**
18:25	to enter the kingdom of **God.**
18:27	mortals is possible for **God.**
18:29	the sake of the kingdom of **God,**
18:43	**God;** and all the people, when
18:43	when they saw it, praised **God.**
19:11	kingdom of **God** was to appear
19:37	began to praise **God** joyfully
20:21	teach the way of **God** in
20:25	to **God** the things that are
20:25	**God** the things that are **God's.**
20:36	children of **God,** being children
20:37	the **God** of Abraham, the God
20:37	the **God** of Isaac, and the God
20:37	of Isaac, and the **God** of Jacob.
20:38	Now he is **God** not of the dead,
21:31	know that the kingdom of **God** is
22:16	fulfilled in the kingdom of **God**
22:18	until the kingdom of **God** comes.
22:69	right hand of the power of **God.**
22:70	Are you, then, the Son of **God?**

23:35	if he is the Messiah of **God,**
23:40	Do you not fear **God,** since you
23:47	he praised **God** and said,
23:51	for the kingdom of **God.**
24:19	before **God** and all the people,
24:53	in the temple blessing **God.**
Jn 1: 1	and the Word was with **God,** and
1: 1	with God, and the Word was **God.**
1: 2	was in the beginning with **God.**
1: 6	There was a man sent from **God,**
1:12	power to become children of **God**
1:13	of the will of man, but of **God.**
1:18	No one has ever seen **God.** It is
1:18	It is **God** the only Son, who is
1:29	Here is the Lamb of **God** who
1:34	that this is the Son of **God.**
1:36	Look, here is the Lamb of **God!**
1:49	Rabbi, you are the Son of **God!**
1:51	the angels of **God** ascending and
3: 2	a teacher who has come from **God**
3: 2	apart from the presence of **God.**
3: 3	one can see the kingdom of **God**
3: 5	can enter the kingdom of **God**
3:16	For **God** so loved the world
3:17	Indeed, **God** did not send the
3:18	the name of the only Son of **God**
3:21	deeds have been done in **God.**
3:33	this, that **God** is true.
3:34	He whom **God** has sent speaks the
3:34	**God,** for he gives the Spirit
3:36	see life, but must endure **God's**
4:10	If you knew the gift of **God,**
4:24	**God** is spirit, and those who
5:18	calling **God** his own Father,
5:18	making himself equal to **God.**
5:25	the voice of the Son of **God,**
5:42	you do not have the love of **God**
5:44	from the one who alone is **God?**
6:27	For it is on him that **God** the
6:28	do to perform the works of **God?**
6:29	This is the work of **God,** that
6:33	For the bread of **God** is that
6:45	all be taught by **God.'** Everyone
6:46	the one who is from **God;** he has
6:69	you are the Holy One of **God.**
7:17	do the will of **God** will know
8:40	the truth that I heard from **God**
8:41	we have one father, **God** himself
8:42	If **God** were your Father, you

8:42	I came from **God** and now I am	2:33	right hand of **God,** and having
8:47	Whoever is from **God** hears the	2:36	know with certainty that **God**
8:47	hears the words of **God.** The	2:39	everyone whom the Lord our **God**
8:47	is that you are not from **God.**	2:47	praising **God** and having the
8:54	of whom you say, 'He is our **God**	3: 8	and leaping and praising **God.**
9: 3	blind so that **God's** works might	3: 9	walking and praising **God,**
9:16	This man is not from **God,** for	3:13	The **God** of Abraham, the God of
9:24	Give glory to **God!** We know	3:13	the **God** of Isaac, and the God
9:29	We know that **God** has spoken to	3:13	**God** of Jacob, the God of our
9:31	**God** does not listen to sinners,	3:13	**God** of our ancestors has
9:33	If this man were not from **God,**	3:15	whom **God** raised from the dead.
10:33	being, are making yourself **God.**	3:18	In this way **God** fulfilled what
10:34	your law, 'I said, you are **gods**	3:21	**God** announced long ago through
10:35	those to whom the word of **God**	3:22	Moses said, 'The Lord your **God**
10:35	came were called **'gods'**—and the	3:25	**God** gave to your ancestors,
10:36	because I said, 'I am **God's** Son	3:26	When **God** raised up his servant,
11: 4	rather it is for **God's** glory,	4:10	whom **God** raised from the dead.
11: 4	so that the Son of **God** may be	4:19	in **God's** sight to listen to you
11:22	But even now I know that **God**	4:19	rather than to **God,** you must
11:22	you whatever you ask of **him.**	4:21	all of them praised **God** for
11:27	the Son of **God,** the one coming	4:24	their voices together to **God**
11:40	you would see the glory of **God?**	4:31	spoke the word of **God** with
11:52	the dispersed children of **God.**	5: 4	did not lie to us but to **God!**
12:43	the glory that comes from **God.**	5:29	We must obey **God** rather than
13: 3	he had come from **God** and was	5:30	The **God** of our ancestors raised
13: 3	from God and was going to **God,**	5:31	**God** exalted him at his right
13:31	and **God** has been glorified in	5:32	the Holy Spirit whom **God** has
13:32	If **God** has been glorified in	5:39	but if it is of **God,** you will
13:32	**God** will also glorify him in	6: 2	neglect the word of **God** in
14: 1	Believe in **God,** believe also in	6: 7	The word of **God** continued to
16: 2	are offering worship to **God.**	6:11	words against Moses and **God.**
16:27	believed that I came from **God.**	7: 2	The **God** of glory appeared to
16:30	believe that you came from **God.**	7: 6	And **God** spoke in these terms,
17: 3	the only true **God,** and Jesus	7: 7	that they serve,' said **God,**
19: 7	claimed to be the Son of **God.**	7: 9	Egypt; but **God** was with him,
20:17	and your Father, to my **God** and	7:17	promise that **God** had made to
20:17	Father, to my God and your **God.**	7:20	he was beautiful before **God.**
20:28	him, "My Lord and my **God!**"	7:25	**God** through him was rescuing
20:31	Son of **God,** and that through	7:32	I am the **God** of your ancestors
21:19	glorify **God.**) After this he	7:32	the **God** of Abraham, Isaac, and
Ac 1: 3	about the kingdom of **God.**	7:35	whom **God** now sent as both ruler
2:11	hear them speaking about **God's**	7:37	**God** will raise up a prophet
2:17	**God** declares, that I will pour	7:40	saying to Aaron, 'Make **gods** for
2:22	attested to you by **God** with	7:42	But **God** turned away from them
2:22	signs that **God** did through him	7:43	your **god** Rephan, the images
2:23	**God,** you crucified and killed	7:45	the nations that **God** drove out
2:24	But **God** raised him up, having	7:46	who found favor with **God** and
2:30	he knew that **God** had sworn with	7:55	saw the glory of **God** and Jesus
2:32	This Jesus **God** raised up, and	7:55	at the right hand of **God.**

7:56	at the right hand of **God!**	14:22	must enter the kingdom of **God.**
8:10	This man is the power of **God**	14:26	grace of **God** for the work that
8:12	**God** and the name of Jesus	14:27	related all that **God** had done
8:14	had accepted the word of **God,**	15: 4	reported all that **God** had done
8:20	obtain **God's** gift with money!	15: 7	in the early days **God** made a
8:21	heart is not right before **God.**	15: 8	And **God,** who knows the human
9:20	saying, "He is the Son of **God.**"	15:10	why are you putting **God** to the
10: 2	was a devout man who feared **God**	15:12	signs and wonders that **God** had
10: 2	and prayed constantly to **God.**	15:14	Simeon has related how **God**
10: 3	he clearly saw an angel of **God**	15:19	Gentiles who are turning to **God**
10: 4	as a memorial before **God.**	16:10	being convinced that **God** had
10:15	What **God** has made clean, you	16:14	worshiper of **God,** was listening
10:22	an upright and **God**-fearing man,	16:17	slaves of the Most High **God,**
10:28	but **God** has shown me that I	16:25	**God,** and the prisoners were
10:31	have been remembered before **God**	16:34	he had become a believer in **God**
10:33	the presence of **God** to listen	17:13	word of **God** had been proclaimed
10:34	I truly understand that **God**	17:23	'To an unknown **god.**' What
10:38	how **God** anointed Jesus of	17:24	The **God** who made the world and
10:38	the devil, for **God** was with him	17:27	they would search for **God** and
10:40	but **God** raised him on the third	17:29	Since we are **God's** offspring,
10:41	to us who were chosen by **God** as	17:30	While **God** has overlooked the
10:42	the one ordained by **God** as	18: 7	a worshiper of **God;** his house
10:46	in tongues and extolling **God.**	18:11	teaching the word of **God** among
11: 1	also accepted the word of **God.**	18:13	worship **God** in ways that are
11: 9	What **God** has made clean, you	18:21	I will return to you, if **God**
11:17	If then **God** gave them the same	18:26	explained the Way of **God** to him
11:17	was I that I could hinder **God?**	19: 8	about the kingdom of **God.**
11:18	they praised **God,** saying, "Then	19:11	**God** did extraordinary miracles
11:18	Then **God** has given even to the	19:26	made with hands are not **gods.**
11:23	of **God,** he rejoiced, and he	19:37	nor blasphemers of our **goddess.**
12: 5	church prayed fervently to **God**	20:21	repentance toward **God** and faith
12:22	The voice of a **god,** and not of	20:24	to the good news of **God's** grace
12:23	had not given the glory to **God,**	20:27	to you the whole purpose of **God**
12:24	But the word of **God** continued	20:28	shepherd the church of **God**
13: 5	they proclaimed the word of **God**	20:32	And now I commend you to **God**
13: 7	wanted to hear the word of **God.**	21:19	things that **God** had done among
13:16	and others who fear **God,** listen	21:20	they praised **God.** Then they
13:17	The **God** of this people Israel	22: 3	being zealous for **God,** just as
13:21	**God** gave them Saul son of Kish,	22:14	Then he said, 'The **God** of our
13:23	Of this man's posterity **God** has	23: 1	a clear conscience before **God.**
13:26	and others who fear **God,** to us	23: 3	At this Paul said to him, "**God**
13:30	But **God** raised him from the	23: 4	Do you dare to insult **God's**
13:33	**he** has fulfilled for us, their	24:14	I worship the **God** of our
13:36	served the purpose of **God** in	24:15	have a hope in **God**—a hope that
13:37	whom **God** raised up experienced	24:16	a clear conscience toward **God**
13:43	continue in the grace of **God.**	26: 6	the promise made by **God** to our
13:46	necessary that the word of **God**	26: 8	of you that **God** raises the dead
14:11	The **gods** have come down to us	26:18	the power of Satan to **God,** so
14:15	living **God,** who made the heaven	26:20	repent and turn to **God** and do

26:22	I have had help from **God,** and	3: 7	if through my falsehood **God's**
26:29	I pray to **God** that not only you	3:11	there is no one who seeks **God.**
27:23	angel of the **God** to whom	3:18	There is no fear of **God** before
27:24	**God** has granted safety to all	3:19	may be held accountable to **God.**
27:25	for I have faith in **God** that it	3:21	righteousness of **God** has been
27:35	giving thanks to **God** in	3:22	the righteousness of **God**
28: 6	began to say that he was a **god.**	3:23	fall short of the glory of **God;**
28:15	thanked **God** and took courage.	3:25	whom **God** put forward as a
28:23	to the kingdom of **God** and	3:26	is **divine** forbearance
28:28	salvation of **God** has been sent	3:29	Or is God the **God** of Jews only?
28:31	proclaiming the kingdom of **God**	3:30	since **God** is one; and he will
Ro 1: 1	set apart for the gospel of **God**	4: 2	boast about, but not before **God**
1: 4	declared to be Son of **God** with	4: 3	Abraham believed **God,** and it
1: 7	To all **God's** beloved in Rome,	4: 6	of those to whom **God** reckons
1: 7	Grace to you and peace from **God**	4:17	presence of the **God** in whom he
1: 8	First, I thank my **God** through	4:20	the promise of **God,** but he grew
1: 9	For **God,** whom I serve with my	4:20	faith as he gave glory to **God,**
1:10	asking that by **God's** will I may	5: 1	we have peace with **God** through
1:16	it is the power of **God** for	5: 2	of sharing the glory of **God.**
1:17	the righteousness of **God** is	5: 5	because **God's** love has been
1:18	the wrath of **God** is revealed	5: 8	But **God** proves his love for us
1:19	For what can be known about **God**	5:10	we were reconciled to **God**
1:19	**God** has shown it to them.	5:11	we even boast in **God** through
1:21	for though they knew **God,** they	5:15	**God** and the free gift in the
1:21	honor him as **God** or give thanks	6:10	life he lives, he lives to **God.**
1:23	immortal **God** for images	6:11	alive to **God** in Christ Jesus.
1:24	Therefore **God** gave them up in	6:13	present yourselves to **God** as
1:25	exchanged the truth about **God**	6:13	present your members to **God** as
1:26	For this reason **God** gave them	6:17	But thanks be to **God** that you,
1:28	not see fit to acknowledge **God,**	6:22	from sin and enslaved to **God,**
1:28	**God** gave them up to a debased	6:23	but the free gift of **God** is
1:32	They know **God's** decree, that	7: 4	that we may bear fruit for **God.**
2: 2	You say, "We know that **God's**	7:22	For I delight in the law of **God**
2: 3	will escape the judgment of **God**	7:25	Thanks be to **God** through Jesus
2: 4	Do you not realize that **God's**	7:25	slave to the law of **God,** but
2: 5	**God's** righteous judgment will	8: 3	For **God** has done what the law,
2:11	For **God** shows no partiality.	8: 7	is hostile to **God;** it does not
2:13	**God's** sight, but the doers of	8: 7	it does not submit to **God's**
2:16	**God,** through Jesus Christ, will	8: 8	in the flesh cannot please **God.**
2:17	boast of your relation to **God**	8: 9	the Spirit of **God** dwells in you
2:23	do you dishonor **God** by breaking	8:14	led by the Spirit of **God** are
2:24	The name of **God** is blasphemed	8:14	of God are children of **God.**
2:29	not from others but from **God.**	8:16	that we are children of **God,**
3: 2	with the oracles of **God.**	8:17	heirs of **God** and joint heirs
3: 3	the faithfulness of **God?**	8:19	of the children of **God;**
3: 4	let **God** be proved true, as it	8:21	glory of the children of **God.**
3: 5	confirm the justice of **God,**	8:27	according to the will of **God.**
3: 5	That **God** is unjust to	8:28	**God,** who are called according
3: 6	how could **God** judge the world?	8:31	If **God** is for us, who is

8:33	charge against **God's** elect? It
8:33	It is **God** who justifies.
8:34	at the right hand of **God,** who
8:39	us from the love of **God** in
9: 5	all, **God** blessed forever. Amen.
9: 6	the word of **God** had failed. For
9: 8	who are the children of **God,**
9:11	so that **God's** purpose of
9:14	Is there injustice on **God's**
9:16	but on **God** who shows mercy.
9:20	to argue with **God?** Will what
9:22	What if **God,** desiring to show
9:26	children of the living **God.**
10: 1	prayer to **God** for them is that
10: 2	they have a zeal for **God,** but
10: 3	that comes from **God,** and
10: 3	have not submitted to **God's**
10: 9	believe in your heart that **God**
11: 1	I ask, then, has **God** rejected
11: 2	**God** has not rejected his people
11: 2	how he pleads with **God** against
11: 8	as it is written, **"God** gave
11:21	For if **God** did not spare the
11:22	and the severity of **God:**
11:22	but **God's** kindness toward you,
11:23	for **God** has the power to graft
11:29	gifts and the calling of **God**
11:30	disobedient to **God** but have now
11:32	For **God** has imprisoned all in
11:33	wisdom and knowledge of **God!**
12: 1	**God,** to present your bodies as
12: 1	holy and acceptable to **God,**
12: 2	what is the will of **God**—what is
12: 3	measure of faith that **God** has
13: 1	no authority except from **God,**
13: 1	have been instituted by **God.**
13: 2	resists what **God** has appointed,
13: 4	it is **God's** servant for your
13: 4	It is the servant of **God** to
13: 6	authorities are **God's** servants,
14: 3	eat; for **God** has welcomed them.
14: 6	since they give thanks to **God;**
14: 6	the Lord and give thanks to **God**
14:10	before the judgment seat of **God**
14:11	tongue shall give praise to **God**
14:12	us will be accountable to **God.**
14:17	For the kingdom of **God** is not
14:18	acceptable to **God** and has human
14:20	**God.** Everything is indeed clean

	14:22	your own conviction before **God.**
	15: 5	May the **God** of steadfastness
	15: 6	glorify the **God** and Father of
	15: 7	you, for the glory of **God.**
	15: 8	of the truth of **God** in order
	15: 9	glorify **God** for his mercy. As
	15:13	May the **God** of hope fill you
	15:15	of the grace given me by **God**
	15:16	service of the gospel of **God,**
	15:17	to boast of my work for **God.**
	15:19	power of the Spirit of **God,** so
	15:30	me in earnest prayer to **God** on
	15:32	so that by **God's** will I may
	15:33	The **God** of peace be with all of
	16:20	The **God** of peace will shortly
	16:26	command of the eternal **God,** to
	16:27	to the only wise **God,** through
1C	1: 1	by the will of **God,** and our
	1: 2	To the church of **God** that is in
	1: 3	Grace to you and peace from **God**
	1: 4	I give thanks to my **God** always
	1: 4	grace of **God** that has been
	1: 9	**God** is faithful; by him you
	1:14	I thank **God** that I baptized
	1:18	saved it is the power of **God.**
	1:20	Has not **God** made foolish the
	1:21	For since, in the wisdom of **God**
	1:21	the world did not know **God**
	1:21	For since, in the wisdom of God
	1:24	Christ the power of **God** and the
	1:24	of God and the wisdom of **God.**
	1:25	For **God's** foolishness is wiser
	1:25	and **God's** weakness is stronger
	1:27	But **God** chose what is foolish
	1:27	**God** chose what is weak in the
	1:28	**God** chose what is low and
	1:29	boast in the presence of **God.**
	1:30	for us wisdom from **God,** and
	2: 1	proclaiming the mystery of **God**
	2: 5	wisdom but on the power of **God.**
	2: 7	But we speak **God's** wisdom,
	2: 7	which **God** decreed before the
	2: 9	what **God** has prepared for those
	2:10	these things **God** has revealed
	2:10	even the depths of **God.**
	2:11	comprehends what is truly **God's**
	2:11	God's except the Spirit of **God.**
	2:12	but the Spirit that is from **God**
	2:12	the gifts bestowed on us by **God**

2:14	the gifts of **God's** Spirit, for
3: 6	but **God** gave the growth.
3: 7	but only **God** who gives the
3: 9	For we are **God's** servants,
3: 9	are **God's** field, God's building
3: 9	God's field, **God's** building.
3:10	According to the grace of **God**
3:16	you not know that you are **God's**
3:16	temple and that **God's** Spirit
3:17	If anyone destroys **God's** temple
3:17	**God** will destroy that person.
3:17	For **God's** temple is holy, and
3:19	foolishness with **God.** For it is
3:23	and Christ belongs to **God.**
4: 1	of Christ and stewards of **God's**
4: 5	receive commendation from **God.**
4: 9	For I think that **God** has
4:20	For the kingdom of **God** depends
5:13	**God** will judge those outside.
6: 9	not inherit the kingdom of **God?**
6:10	will inherit the kingdom of **God**
6:11	and in the Spirit of our **God.**
6:13	and **God** will destroy both one
6:14	And **God** raised the Lord and
6:19	which you have from **God,** and
6:20	therefore glorify **God** in your
7: 7	a particular gift from **God,** one
7:15	It is to peace that **God** has
7:17	to which **God** called you. This
7:19	obeying the commandments of **God**
7:24	sisters, there remain with **God.**
7:40	I too have the Spirit of **God.**
8: 3	but anyone who loves **God** is
8: 4	that "there is no **God** but one."
8: 5	so-called **gods** in heaven or on
8: 5	many **gods** and many lords—
8: 6	yet for us there is one **God,**
8: 8	bring us close to **God.**" We are
9: 9	Is it for oxen that **God** is
9:21	I am not free from **God's** law
10: 5	Nevertheless, **God** was not
10:13	**God** is faithful, and he will
10:20	demons and not to **God.** I do not
10:31	everything for the glory of **God**
10:32	Greeks or to the church of **God,**
11: 3	and **God** is the head of Christ.
11: 7	image and reflection of **God;**
11:12	but all things come from **God.**
11:13	woman to pray to **God** with her

	11:16	nor do the churches of **God.**
	11:22	contempt for the church of **God**
	12: 3	**God** ever says "Let Jesus be
	12: 6	but it is the same **God** who
	12:18	But as it is, **God** arranged the
	12:24	But **God** has so arranged the
	12:28	And **God** has appointed in the
	14: 2	to other people but to **God;** for
	14:18	I thank **God** that I speak in
	14:25	bow down before **God** and worship
	14:25	declaring, **"God** is really among
	14:28	speak to themselves and to **God.**
	14:33	for God is a **God** not of
	14:36	Or did the word of **God**
	15: 9	I persecuted the church of **God.**
	15:10	But by the grace of **God** I am
	15:10	but the grace of **God** that is
	15:15	misrepresenting **God,** because
	15:15	we testified of **God** that he
	15:24	hands over the kingdom to **God**
	15:28	so that **God** may be all in all.
	15:34	people have no knowledge of **God**
	15:38	But **God** gives it a body as he
	15:50	inherit the kingdom of **God,** nor
	15:57	But thanks be to **God,** who gives
2C	1: 1	**God,** and Timothy our brother,
	1: 1	To the church of **God** that is in
	1: 2	Grace to you and peace from **God**
	1: 3	Blessed be the **God** and Father
	1: 3	of mercies and the **God** of all
	1: 4	ourselves are consoled by **God.**
	1: 9	not on ourselves but on **God** who
	1:12	frankness and **godly** sincerity,
	1:12	wisdom but by the grace of **God**—
	1:18	As surely as **God** is faithful,
	1:19	For the Son of **God,** Jesus
	1:20	For in him every one of **God's**
	1:20	the "Amen," to the glory of **God**
	1:21	But it is **God** who establishes
	1:23	But I call on **God** as witness
	2:14	But thanks be to **God,** who in
	2:15	the aroma of Christ to **God**
	2:17	we are not peddlers of **God's**
	2:17	as persons sent from **God** and
	2:17	from God and standing in **his**
	3: 3	Spirit of the living **God,** not
	3: 4	have through Christ toward **God.**
	3: 5	our competence is from **God,**
	4: 2	falsify **God's** word; but by the

4: 2	of everyone in the sight of **God**	
4: 4	In their case the **god** of this	
4: 4	Christ, who is the image of **God**	
4: 6	it is the **God** who said,	
4: 6	glory of **God** in the face of	
4:15	to the glory of **God**	
5: 1	have a building from **God**	
5: 5	**God,** who has given us the	
5:11	ourselves are well known to **God**	
5:13	it is for **God;** if we are in	
5:18	All this is from **God**	
5:19	in Christ **God** was reconciling	
5:20	**God** is making his appeal	
5:20	be reconciled to **God**	
5:21	become the righteousness of **God**	
6: 1	not to accept the grace of **God**	
6: 4	but as servants of **God** we have	
6: 7	power of **God;** with the weapons	
6:16	agreement has the temple of **God**	
6:16	the temple of the living **God;**	
6:16	as **God** said, "I will live in	
6:16	I will be their **God,** and they	
7: 1	perfect in the fear of **God.**	
7: 6	But **God,** who consoles the	
7: 9	for you felt a **godly** grief, so	
7:10	For **godly** grief produces a	
7:11	**godly** grief has produced in you	
7:12	be made known to you before **God**	
8: 1	about the grace of **God** that has	
8: 5	by the will of **God,** to us,	
8:16	But thanks be to **God** who put in	
9: 7	for **God** loves a cheerful giver.	
9: 8	And **God** is able to provide you	
9:11	produce thanksgiving to **God**	
9:12	with many thanksgivings to **God.**	
9:13	glorify **God** by your obedience	
9:14	surpassing grace of **God** that he	
9:15	Thanks be to **God** for his	
10: 4	but they have **divine** power to	
10: 5	up against the knowledge of **God**	
10:13	keep within the field that **God**	
11: 2	I feel a **divine** jealousy for	
11: 7	I proclaimed **God's** good news to	
11:11	Because I do not love you? **God**	
11:31	The **God** and Father of the Lord	
12: 2	body I do not know; **God** knows.	
12: 3	of the body I do not know; **God**	
12:19	speaking in Christ before **God.**	
12:21	my **God** may humble me before you	

	13: 4	lives by the power of **God.** For
	13: 4	with him by the power of **God.**
	13: 7	But we pray to **God** that you may
	13:11	and the **God** of love and peace
	13:13	love of **God,** and the communion
Ga	1: 1	through Jesus Christ and **God**
	1: 3	Grace to you and peace from **God**
	1: 4	the will of our **God** and Father,
	1:10	or **God's** approval? Or am I
	1:13	persecuting the church of **God**
	1:15	But when **God,** who had set me
	1:20	before **God,** I do not lie!
	1:24	And they glorified **God** because
	2: 6	**God** shows no partiality)—
	2:19	so that I might live to **God.** I
	2:20	by faith in the Son of **God,** who
	2:21	do not nullify the grace of **God**
	3: 6	Just as Abraham "believed **God,**
	3: 8	foreseeing that **God** would
	3:11	no one is justified before **God**
	3:17	previously ratified by **God,** so
	3:18	but **God** granted it to Abraham
	3:20	more than one party; but **God** is
	3:21	opposed to the promises of **God?**
	3:26	are all children of **God** through
	4: 4	**God** sent his Son, born of a
	4: 6	**God** has sent the Spirit of his
	4: 7	then also an heir, through **God.**
	4: 8	when you did not know **God,** you
	4: 8	that by nature are not **gods.**
	4: 9	you have come to know **God,** or
	4: 9	rather to be known by **God,** how
	4:14	welcomed me as an angel of **God,**
	5:21	inherit the kingdom of **God.**
	6: 7	Do not be deceived; **God** is not
	6:16	and upon the Israel of **God.**
Ep	1: 1	**God,** To the saints who are in
	1: 2	peace from **God** our Father and
	1: 3	Blessed be the **God** and Father
	1:17	I pray that the **God** of our Lord
	2: 4	But **God,** who is rich in mercy,
	2: 8	doing; it is the gift of **God**—
	2:10	which **God** prepared beforehand
	2:16	reconcile both groups to **God** in
	2:19	members of the household of **God**
	2:22	into a dwelling place for **God.**
	3: 2	the commission of **God's** grace
	3: 7	according to the gift of **God's**
	3: 9	mystery hidden for ages in **God**

	3:10	the church the wisdom of **God** in
	3:19	with all the fullness of **God.**
	4: 6	one **God** and Father of all, who
	4:13	knowledge of the Son of **God,** to
	4:18	alienated from the life of **God**
	4:24	to the likeness of **God** in true
	4:30	grieve the Holy Spirit of **God,**
	4:32	as **God** in Christ has forgiven
	5: 1	Therefore be imitators of **God,**
	5: 2	offering and sacrifice to **God.**
	5: 5	kingdom of Christ and of **God.**
	5: 6	wrath of **God** comes on those who
	5:20	giving thanks to **God** the Father
	6: 6	doing the will of **God** from the
	6:11	Put on the whole armor of **God,**
	6:13	whole armor of **God,** so that you
	6:17	which is the word of **God.**
	6:23	from **God** the Father and the
Ph	1: 2	peace from **God** our Father and
	1: 3	I thank my **God** every time I
	1: 8	For **God** is my witness, how I
	1:11	for the glory and praise of **God**
	1:28	And this is **God's** doing.
	2: 6	in the form of **God,** did not
	2: 6	not regard equality with **God** as
	2: 9	Therefore **God** also highly
	2:11	to the glory of **God** the Father.
	2:13	for it is **God** who is at work in
	2:15	children of **God** without blemish
	2:27	But **God** had mercy on him, and
	3: 3	worship in the Spirit of **God**
	3: 9	righteousness from **God** based on
	3:14	of the heavenly call of **God** in
	3:15	this too **God** will reveal to you
	3:19	their **god** is the belly; and
	4: 6	requests be made known to **God.**
	4: 7	And the peace of **God,** which
	4: 9	and the **God** of peace will be
	4:18	acceptable and pleasing to **God.**
	4:19	And my **God** will fully satisfy
	4:20	To our **God** and Father be glory
Co	1: 1	by the will of **God,** and Timothy
	1: 2	and peace from **God** our Father.
	1: 3	we always thank **God,** the Father
	1: 6	comprehended the grace of **God.**
	1:10	grow in the knowledge of **God.**
	1:15	image of the invisible **God,** the
	1:25	according to **God's** commission
	1:25	to make the word of **God** fully

	1:27	To them **God** chose to make known
	2: 2	have the knowledge of **God's**
	2:12	faith in the power of **God,** who
	2:19	with a growth that is from **God.**
	3: 1	seated at the right hand of **God**
	3: 3	hidden with Christ in **God**
	3: 6	the wrath of **God** is coming
	3:12	As **God's** chosen ones, holy
	3:16	spiritual songs to **God**
	3:17	giving thanks to **God** the
	4: 3	**God** will open to us a door
	4:11	kingdom of **God,** and they have
	4:12	assured in everything that **God**
1Th	1: 1	Thessalonians in **God** the Father
	1: 2	We always give thanks to **God**
	1: 3	remembering before our **God** and
	1: 4	beloved by **God,** that he has
	1: 8	every place your faith in **God**
	1: 9	how you turned to **God** from
	1: 9	to serve a living and true **God,**
	2: 2	we had courage in our **God** to
	2: 2	gospel of **God** in spite of great
	2: 4	approved by **God** to be entrusted
	2: 4	but to please **God** who tests our
	2: 5	As you know and as **God** is our
	2: 8	gospel of **God** but also our own
	2: 9	to you the gospel of **God.**
	2:10	You are witnesses, and **God** also
	2:12	lead a life worthy of **God,** who
	2:13	give thanks to **God** for this,
	2:13	received the word of **God** that
	2:13	**God's** word, which is also at
	2:14	**God** in Christ Jesus that are in
	2:15	they displease **God** and oppose
	3: 2	**God** in proclaiming the gospel
	3: 9	How can we thank **God** enough for
	3: 9	joy that we feel before our **God**
	3:11	Now may our **God** and Father
	3:13	blameless before our **God** and
	4: 1	ought to live and to please **God**
	4: 3	For this is the will of **God,**
	4: 5	Gentiles who do not know **God;**
	4: 7	For **God** did not call us to
	4: 8	not human authority but **God,**
	4:14	through Jesus, **God** will bring
	4:16	the sound of **God's** trumpet,
	5: 9	For **God** has destined us not for
	5:18	this is the will of **God** in
	5:23	May the **God** of peace himself

2Th	1: 1	**God** our Father and the Lord		2:19	But **God's** firm foundation
	1: 2	Grace to you and peace from **God**		2:25	**God** may perhaps grant that they
	1: 3	We must always give thanks to **God**		3:17	everyone who belongs to **God** may
	1: 4	**God** for your steadfastness and		4: 1	In the presence of **God** and of
	1: 5	righteous judgment of **God,** and	Ti	1: 1	Paul, a servant of **God** and an
	1: 5	worthy of the kingdom of **God,**		1: 1	the faith of **God's** elect and
	1: 6	For it is indeed just of **God** to		1: 2	hope of eternal life that **God,**
	1: 8	**God** and on those who do not		1: 3	entrusted by the command of **God**
	1:11	asking that our **God** will make		1: 4	Grace and peace from **God** the
	1:12	grace of our **God** and the Lord		1: 7	For a bishop, as **God's** steward,
	2: 4	**god** or object of worship, so		1:16	They profess to know **God,** but
	2: 4	his seat in the temple of **God,**		2: 5	so that the word of **God** may not
	2: 4	declaring himself to be **God.**		2:10	ornament to the doctrine of **God**
	2:11	For this reason **God** sends them		2:11	For the grace of **God** has
	2:13	thanks to **God** for you, brothers		2:13	glory of our great **God** and
	2:13	because **God** chose you as the		3: 4	loving kindness of **God** our
	2:16	**God** our Father, who loved us		3: 8	who have come to believe in **God**
	3: 5	your hearts to the love of **God**	Pm	1: 3	Grace to you and peace from **God**
1Ti	1: 1	**God** our Savior and of Christ		1: 4	prayers, I always thank my **God**
	1: 2	and peace from **God** the Father	He	1: 1	Long ago **God** spoke to our
	1: 4	rather than the **divine** training		1: 6	Let all **God's** angels worship
	1:11	gospel of the blessed **God,**		1: 8	Your throne, O **God,** is forever
	1:17	invisible, the only **God,** be		1: 9	therefore **God,** your God, has
	2: 3	acceptable in the sight of **God**		1: 9	your **God,** has anointed you with
	2: 5	For there is one **God;** there is		2: 4	while **God** added his testimony
	2: 5	one mediator between **God** and		2: 9	by the grace of **God** he might
	3: 5	can he take care of **God's**		2:13	the children whom **God** has given
	3:15	behave in the household of **God,**		2:17	**God,** to make a sacrifice of
	3:15	the church of the living **God,**		3: 4	builder of all things is **God.**)
	4: 3	which **God** created to be		3:12	turns away from the living **God.**
	4: 4	For everything created by **God**		4: 4	And **God** rested on the seventh
	4: 5	for it is sanctified by **God's**		4: 9	remains for the people of **God;**
	4:10	our hope set on the living **God,**		4:10	cease from their labors as **God**
	5: 4	this is pleasing in **God's** sight		4:12	Indeed, the word of **God** is
	5: 5	set her hope on **God** and		4:14	Jesus, the Son of **God,** let us
	5:21	In the presence of **God** and of		5: 1	pertaining to **God** on
	6: 1	so that the name of **God** and the		5: 4	only when called by **God,** just
	6:11	But as for you, man of **God,**		5:10	having been designated by **God**
	6:13	In the presence of **God,** who		5:12	elements of the oracles of **God.**
	6:17	but rather on **God** who richly		6: 1	dead works and faith toward **God**
2Ti	1: 1	the will of **God,** for the sake		6: 3	we will do this, if **God** permits
	1: 2	mercy, and peace from **God** the		6: 5	**God** and the powers of the age
	1: 3	I am grateful to **God**—whom I		6: 6	Son of **God** and are holding him
	1: 6	rekindle the gift of **God** that		6: 7	receives a blessing from **God.**
	1: 7	for **God** did not give us a		6:10	For **God** is not unjust; he will
	1: 8	relying on the power of **God,**		6:13	When **God** made a promise to
	2: 9	the word of **God** is not chained.		6:17	In the same way, when **God**
	2:14	warn them before **God** that they		6:18	it is impossible that **God** would
	2:15	present yourself to **God** as one		7: 1	priest of the Most High **God,**

7: 3	resembling the Son of **God,** he	
7:19	through which we approach **God.**	
7:25	save those who approach **God**	
8:10	and I will be their **God,** and	
9:14	without blemish to **God,** purify	
9:14	works to worship the living **God**	
9:20	blood of the covenant that **God**	
9:24	appear in the presence of **God**	
10: 7	O **God'** (in the scroll of the	
10:12	down at the right hand of **God,**	
10:21	priest over the house of **God,**	
10:29	spurned the Son of **God,**	
10:31	the hands of the living **God.**	
10:36	you have done the will of **God,**	
11: 3	prepared by the word of **God,** so	
11: 4	By faith Abel offered to **God** a	
11: 4	**God** himself giving approval to	
11: 5	because **God** had taken him." For	
11: 5	away that "he had pleased **God."**	
11: 6	it is impossible to please **God,**	
11:10	architect and builder is **God.**	
11:16	Therefore **God** is not ashamed	
11:16	to be called their **God;** indeed,	
11:19	**God** is able even to raise	
11:25	people of **God** than to enjoy the	
11:40	since **God** had provided	
12: 2	right hand of the throne of **God**	
12: 7	**God** is treating you as children	
12:15	to obtain the grace of **God;**	
12:22	city of the living **God,** the	
12:23	and to **God** the judge of all,	
12:28	by which we offer to **God** an	
12:29	indeed our **God** is a consuming	
13: 4	for **God** will judge fornicators	
13: 7	those who spoke the word of **God**	
13:15	sacrifice of praise to **God,**	
13:16	sacrifices are pleasing to **God.**	
13:20	Now may the **God** of peace, who	

Ja	1: 1	James, a servant of **God** and of
	1: 5	ask **God,** who gives to all
	1:13	I am being tempted by **God**
	1:13	for **God** cannot be tempted by
	1:20	anger does not produce **God's**
	1:27	pure and undefiled before **God,**
	2: 5	Has not **God** chosen the poor in
	2:19	You believe that **God** is one;
	2:23	Abraham believed **God,** and it
	2:23	he was called the friend of **God**
	3: 9	made in the likeness of **God.**

4: 4	enmity with **God?** Therefore	
4: 4	world becomes an enemy of **God.**	
4: 6	**God** opposes the proud	
4: 7	**God.** Resist the devil	
4: 8	Draw near to **God**	

1P	1: 2	destined by **God** the Father
	1: 3	Blessed be the **God** and Father
	1: 5	protected by the power of **God**
	1:21	have come to trust in **God**
	1:21	hope are set on **God**
	1:23	enduring word of **God**
	2: 4	chosen and precious in **God's**
	2: 5	sacrifices acceptable to **God**
	2:10	now you are **God's** people; once
	2:12	glorify **God** when he comes to
	2:15	For it is **God's** will that by
	2:16	As servants of **God,** live as
	2:17	Fear **God.** Honor the emperor.
	2:19	being aware of **God,** you endure
	2:20	it, you have **God's** approval.
	3: 4	which is very precious in **God's**
	3: 5	holy women who hoped in **God**
	3:17	if suffering should be **God's**
	3:18	in order to bring you to **God.**
	3:20	when **God** waited patiently in
	3:21	appeal to **God** for a good
	3:22	right hand of **God,** with angels,
	4: 2	desires but by the will of **God.**
	4: 6	live in the spirit as **God** does.
	4:10	manifold grace of **God,** serve
	4:11	speaking the very words of **God;**
	4:11	the strength that **God** supplies,
	4:11	so that **God** may be glorified in
	4:14	which is the Spirit of **God,** is
	4:16	glorify **God** because you bear
	4:17	begin with the household of **God**
	4:17	do not obey the gospel of **God?**
	4:19	in accordance with **God's** will
	5: 2	to tend the flock of **God** that
	5: 2	as **God** would have you do it
	5: 5	for "**God** opposes the proud, but
	5: 6	under the mighty hand of **God,**
	5:10	the **God** of all grace, who has
	5:12	this is the true grace of **God.**

2P	1: 1	righteousness of our **God** and
	1: 2	knowledge of **God** and of Jesus
	1:17	honor and glory from **God** the
	1:21	the Holy Spirit spoke from **God.**
	2: 4	if **God** did not spare the angels

3: 5	that by the word of **God** heavens
3:12	the coming of the day of **God,**
1J 1: 5	that **God** is light and in him
2: 5	in this person the love of **God**
2:14	the word of **God** abides in you,
2:17	do the will of **God** live forever
3: 1	be called children of **God;** and
3: 2	Beloved, we are **God's** children
3: 8	The Son of **God** was revealed for
3: 9	Those who have been born of **God**
3: 9	they have been born of **God.**
3:10	The children of **God** and the
3:10	what is right are not from **God,**
3:17	does **God's** love abide in anyone
3:20	for **God** is greater than our
3:21	we have boldness before **God;**
4: 1	whether they are from **God;** for
4: 2	you know the Spirit of **God:**
4: 2	come in the flesh is from **God,**
4: 3	confess Jesus is not from **God.**
4: 4	you are from **God,** and have
4: 6	We are from **God.** Whoever knows
4: 6	**God** listens to us, and whoever
4: 6	is not from **God** does not listen
4: 7	love is from **God;** everyone who
4: 7	loves is born of **God** and knows
4: 7	is born of God and knows **God.**
4: 8	does not know **God,** for God is
4: 8	know God, for **God** is love.
4: 9	**God's** love was revealed among
4: 9	**God** sent his only Son into the
4:10	not that we loved **God** but that
4:11	Beloved, since **God** loved us so
4:12	No one has ever seen **God;** if we
4:12	**God** lives in us, and his love
4:15	**God** abides in those who confess
4:15	Jesus is the Son of **God,** and
4:15	of God, and they abide in **God.**
4:16	believe the love that **God** has
4:16	**God** is love, and those who
4:16	abide in **God,** and God abides in
4:16	in God, and **God** abides in them.
4:20	Those who say, "I love **God,**"
4:20	cannot love **God** whom they have
4:21	those who love **God** must love
5: 1	born of **God,** and everyone who
5: 2	love the children of **God,** when
5: 2	**God** and obey his commandments.
5: 3	For the love of **God** is this

5: 4	whatever is born of **God**
5: 5	that Jesus is the Son of **God?**
5: 9	testimony of **God** is greater;
5: 9	testimony of **God** that he has
5:10	believe in the Son of **God**
5:10	do not believe in **God** have
5:10	testimony that **God** has given
5:11	this is the testimony: **God**
5:12	does not have the Son of **God**
5:13	in the name of the Son of **God,**
5:18	who are born of **God** do not sin,
5:18	the one who was born of **God**
5:19	know that we are **God's** children
5:20	And we know that the Son of **God**
5:20	the true **God** and eternal life.
2J 1: 3	peace will be with us from **God**
1: 9	beyond it, does not have **God;**
3J 1: 6	in a manner worthy of **God;**
1:11	Whoever does good is from **God;**
1:11	does evil has not seen **God.**
Ju 1: 1	are beloved in **God** the Father
1: 4	pervert the grace of our **God**
1:21	yourselves in the love of **God;**
1:25	to the only **God** our Savior,
Re 1: 1	which **God** gave him to show his
1: 2	testified to the word of **God**
1: 6	serving his **God** and Father,
1: 8	the Omega," says the Lord **God,**
1: 9	because of the word of **God** and
2: 7	that is in the paradise of **God.**
2:18	are the words of the Son of **God**
3: 1	the seven spirits of **God** and
3: 2	perfect in the sight of my **God.**
3:12	pillar in the temple of my **God;**
3:12	write on you the name of my **God**
3:12	of my **God,** the new Jerusalem
3:12	my **God** out of heaven, and my
3:14	witness, the origin of **God's**
4: 5	are the seven spirits of **God;**
4: 8	Holy, holy, holy, the Lord **God,**
4:11	are worthy, our Lord and **God,**
5: 6	the seven spirits of **God** sent
5: 9	blood you ransomed for **God**
5:10	serving our **God,** and they will
6: 9	slaughtered for the word of **God**
7: 2	the seal of the living **God,** and
7: 3	servants of our **God** with a seal
7:10	Salvation belongs to our **God**
7:11	the throne and worshiped **God,**

7:12	power and might be to our **God**
7:15	before the throne of **God,** and
7:17	**God** will wipe away every tear
8: 2	angels who stand before **God,**
8: 4	before **God** from the hand of the
9: 4	not have the seal of **God** on
9:13	the golden altar before **God,**
10: 7	the mystery of **God** will be
11: 1	the temple of **God** and the altar
11:11	the breath of life from **God**
11:13	gave glory to the **God** of heaven
11:16	their thrones before **God** fell
11:16	their faces and worshiped **God,**
11:17	We give you thanks, Lord **God**
11:19	Then **God's** temple in heaven was
12: 5	snatched away and taken to **God**
12: 6	she has a place prepared by **God**
12:10	the kingdom of our **God** and the
12:10	day and night before our **God.**
12:17	keep the commandments of **God**
13: 6	blasphemies against **God,**
14: 4	as first fruits for **God**
14: 7	Fear **God** and give him glory,
14:10	the wine of **God's** wrath, poured
14:12	commandments of **God** and hold
14:19	wine press of the wrath of **God.**
15: 1	the wrath of **God** is ended
15: 2	harps of **God** in their hands
15: 3	Moses, the servant of **God**
15: 3	Lord **God** the Almighty
15: 7	bowls full of the wrath of **God,**
15: 8	smoke from the glory of **God**
16: 1	seven bowls of the wrath of **God**
16: 7	Yes, O Lord **God,** the Almighty,
16: 9	they cursed the name of **God,**
16:11	and cursed the **God** of heaven
16:14	great day of **God** the Almighty.
16:19	**God** remembered great Babylon
16:21	they cursed **God** for the plague
17:17	For **God** has put it into their
17:17	until the words of **God** will be
18: 5	heaped high as heaven, and **God**
18: 8	is the Lord **God** who judges her.
18:20	For **God** has given judgment for
19: 1	and glory and power to our **God,**
19: 4	down and worshiped **God** who
19: 5	Praise our **God,** all you his
19: 6	the Lord our **God** the Almighty
19: 9	These are true words of **God.**

19:10	Worship **God!** For the testimony
19:13	name is called The Word of **God.**
19:15	the wrath of **God** the Almighty.
19:17	for the great supper of **God,**
20: 4	Jesus and for the word of **God.**
20: 6	priests of **God** and of Christ,
21: 2	of heaven from **God,** prepared as
21: 3	See, the home of **God** is among
21: 3	dwell with them as their **God;**
21: 3	**God** himself will be with them;
21: 7	I will be their **God** and they
21:10	down out of heaven from **God.**
21:11	It has the glory of **God** and a
21:22	is the Lord **God** the Almighty
21:23	the glory of **God** is its light,
22: 1	flowing from the throne of **God**
22: 3	throne of **God** and of the Lamb
22: 5	Lord **God** will be their light,
22: 6	the **God** of the spirits of the
22: 9	words of this book. Worship **God**
22:18	**God** will add to that person the
22:19	prophecy, **God** will take away

2317　GO1　AG358　LN119　B2:91　K3:123　R2318
θεοσεβεια, GODLY REVERENCE
1Ti　2:10　who profess **reverence for God.**

2318　GO1　AG358　LN119　B2:91　K3:123　R2316,4576
θεοσεβης, GOD-WORSHIPER
Jn　9:31　listen to one who **worships** him

2319　GO1　AG358　LN119
θεοστυγης, GOD-HATER
Ro　1:30　**God-haters,** insolent,

2320　GO1　AG358　LN119　B2:66　K3:119　R2316
θεοτης, GODNESS
Co　2: 9　fullness of **deity** dwells bodily

2321　GO2　AG358　LN119
θεοφιλος, THEOPHILUS
Lk　1: 3　you, most excellent **Theophilus,**
Ac　1: 1　In the first book, **Theophilus,**

2322　GO3　AG358　LN119　B2:164　K3:131　R2323
θεραπεια, HEALING
Lk　9:11　**healed** those who needed to be
　　12:42　in charge of his **slaves,** to
Re　22: 2　of the tree are for the **healing**

2323   GO43 AG359 LN119 B2:164 K3:128
θεραπευω, I HEAL

Mt	4:23	**curing** every disease and every
	4:24	paralytics, and he **cured** them.
	8: 7	I will come and **cure** him
	8:16	and **cured** all who were sick
	9:35	**curing** every disease and every
	10: 1	**cure** every disease and every
	10: 8	**Cure** the sick, raise the dead,
	12:10	lawful to **cure** on the sabbath?
	12:15	and he **cured** all of them,
	12:22	and mute; and he **cured** him,
	14:14	for them and **cured** their sick.
	15:30	at his feet, and he **cured** them,
	17:16	but they could not **cure** him.
	17:18	and the boy **was cured** instantly
	19: 2	followed him, and he **cured** them
	21:14	the temple, and he **cured** them.
Mk	1:34	And he **cured** many who were sick
	3: 2	would **cure** him on the sabbath,
	3:10	for he had **cured** many, so that
	6: 5	few sick people and **cured** them.
	6:13	who were sick and **cured** them.
Lk	4:23	proverb, 'Doctor, **cure** yourself
	4:40	on each of them and **cured** them.
	5:15	to be **cured** of their diseases.
	6: 7	he **would cure** on the sabbath,
	6:18	with unclean spirits were **cured**
	7:21	**cured** many people of diseases,
	8: 2	been **cured** of evil spirits
	8:43	no one could **cure** her.
	9: 1	all demons and to **cure** diseases
	9: 6	and **curing** diseases everywhere.
	10: 9	**cure** the sick who are there,
	13:14	Jesus **had cured** on the sabbath
	13:14	come on those days and be **cured**
	14: 3	**cure** people on the sabbath,
Jn	5:10	been **cured**, "It is the sabbath;
Ac	4:14	who **had been cured** standing
	5:16	and they **were** all **cured.**
	8: 7	paralyzed or lame **were cured.**
	17:25	nor is he **served** by human hands
	28: 9	also came and **were cured.**
Re	13: 3	mortal wound **had been healed.**
	13:12	mortal wound **had been healed.**

2324   GO1 AG359 LN119 B2:164 K3:132
θεραπων, SERVANT

He	3: 5	as a **servant,** to testify to the

2325   GO21 AG359 LN119 B3:525 K3:132 R2330
θεριζω, I HARVEST

Mt	6:26	neither sow nor **reap** nor gather
	25:24	**reaping** where you did not sow,
	25:26	You knew, did you, that I **reap**
Lk	12:24	they neither sow nor **reap,**
	19:21	and **reap** what you did not sow.
	19:22	**reaping** what I did not sow?
Jn	4:36	The **reaper** is already receiving
	4:36	sower and **reaper** may rejoice
	4:37	One sows and another **reaps.**
	4:38	I sent you to **reap** that for
1C	9:11	we **reap** your material benefits?
2C	9: 6	will also **reap** sparingly, and
	9: 6	will also **reap** bountifully.
Ga	6: 7	for you **reap** whatever you sow.
	6: 8	flesh, you will **reap** corruption
	6: 8	**reap** eternal life from the
	6: 9	we **will reap** at harvest time,
Ja	5: 4	the cries of the **harvesters**
Re	14:15	Use your sickle and **reap,** for
	14:15	the hour to **reap** has come,
	14:16	and the earth **was reaped.**

2326   GO13 AG359 LN119 B3:525 K3:133 R2325
θεριομος, HARVEST

Mt	9:37	The **harvest** is plentiful, but
	9:38	Lord of the **harvest** to send
	9:38	out laborers into his **harvest.**
	13:30	together until the **harvest;**
	13:30	at **harvest** time I will tell
	13:39	**harvest** is the end of the age,
Mk	4:29	because the **harvest** has come.
Lk	10: 2	The **harvest** is plentiful, but
	10: 2	Lord of the **harvest** to send
	10: 2	out laborers into his **harvest.**
Jn	4:35	then comes the **harvest'**? But I
	4:35	fields are ripe for **harvesting.**
Re	14:15	**harvest** of the earth is fully

2327   GO2 AG359 LN119 B3:525 R2325
θεριστης, HARVESTER

Mt	13:30	will tell the **reapers,** Collect
	13:39	age, and the **reapers** are angels

2328   GO6 AG359 LN119 R2329
θερμαινω, I WARM

Mk	14:54	**warming** himself at the fire.
	14:67	she saw Peter **warming** himself,
Jn	18:18	**warming** themselves. Peter also

	18:18	standing with them and **warming**
	18:25	standing and **warming** himself.
Ja	2:16	Go in peace; **keep warm** and eat

2329   GO1 AG359 LN119 B1:317
θερμη, HEAT

Ac	28: 3	out by the **heat,** fastened

2330   GO3 AG359 LN119
θερος, SUMMER

Mt	24:32	leaves, you know that **summer** is
Mk	13:28	leaves, you know that **summer** is
Lk	21:30	that **summer** is already near.

2331   GO4 AG359 LN119
θεσσαλονικευς, THESSALONIAN

Ac	20: 4	Secundus from **Thessalonica,** by
	27: 2	a Macedonian from **Thessalonica.**
1Th	1: 1	church of the **Thessalonians** in
2Th	1: 1	**Thessalonians** in God our Father

2332   GO5 AG359 LN119
θεσσαλονικη, THESSALONICA

Ac	17: 1	they came to **Thessalonica,**
	17:11	**Thessalonica,** for they welcomed
	17:13	Jews of **Thessalonica** learned
Ph	4:16	when I was in **Thessalonica,** you
2Ti	4:10	gone to **Thessalonica;** Crescens

2333   GO1 AG359 LN119
θευδας, THEUDAS

Ac	5:36	For some time ago **Theudas** rose

2334   GO58 AG360 LN119 B3:511 K5:315 R2300
θεωρεω, I WATCH

Mt	27:55	**looking on** from a distance;
	28: 1	other Mary went **to see** the tomb
Mk	3:11	unclean spirits **saw** him, they
	5:15	They came to Jesus and **saw** the
	5:38	he **saw** a commotion, people
	12:41	**watched** the crowd putting money
	15:40	**looking on** from a distance;
	15:47	**saw** where the body was laid.
	16: 4	they **saw** that the stone, which
Lk	10:18	He said to them, "I **watched**
	14:29	all who **see** it will begin to
	21: 6	these things that you **see,** the
	23:35	the people stood by, **watching;**
	23:48	**saw** what had taken place, they
	24:37	thought that they **were seeing** a

	24:39	bones as you **see** that I have.
Jn	2:23	because they **saw** the signs that
	4:19	I **see** that you are a prophet.
	6: 2	they **saw** the signs that he was
	6:19	**saw** Jesus walking on the sea
	6:40	all who **see** the Son and believe
	6:62	Then what if you were to **see**
	7: 3	also **may see** the works you are
	8:51	my word **will** never **see** death.
	9: 8	**had seen** him before as a beggar
	10:12	**sees** the wolf coming and leaves
	12:19	You **see,** you can do nothing.
	12:45	And whoever **sees** me sees him
	12:45	And whoever sees me **sees** him
	14:17	it neither **sees** him nor knows
	14:19	the world will no longer **see** me
	14:19	but you will **see** me; because I
	16:10	and you **will see** me no longer;
	16:16	and you **will** no longer **see** me,
	16:17	you **will** no longer **see** me, and
	16:19	**will** no longer **see** me, and
	17:24	**to see** my glory, which you have
	20: 6	**saw** the linen wrappings lying
	20:12	and she **saw** two angels in white
	20:14	she turned around and **saw** Jesus
Ac	3:16	whom you **see** and know; and the
	4:13	Now when they **saw** the boldness
	7:56	"Look," he said, "I **see** the
	8:13	amazed when he **saw** the signs
	9: 7	heard the voice but **saw** no one.
	10:11	He **saw** the heaven opened and
	17:16	distressed **to see** that the city
	17:22	Athenians, I **see** how extremely
	19:26	You also **see** and hear that not
	20:38	they **would** not **see** him again.
	21:20	You **see,** brother, how many
	25:24	you **see** this man about whom the
	27:10	saying, "Sirs, I can **see** that
	28: 6	**saw** that nothing unusual had
He	7: 4	**See** how great he is! Even
1J	3:17	**sees** a brother or sister in
Re	11:11	who **saw** them were terrified.
	11:12	while their enemies **watched**

2335   GO1 AG360 LN119
θεωρια, THING WATCHED

Lk	23:48	for this **spectacle** saw what had

2336   GO1 AG360 LN119
θηκη, PLACE
Jn   18:11   sword back into its **sheath.**

2337   GO5 AG360 LN119
θηλαζω, I NURSE
Mt   21:16   infants and **nursing babies** you
      24:19   **nursing infants** in those days!
Mk   13:17   **nursing infants** in those days!
Lk   11:27   and the breasts that **nursed** you
      21:23   those who are **nursing infants**

2338   GO5 AG360 LN119 B2:569 R2337
θηλυς, FEMALE
Mt   19: 4   made them male and **female,**
Mk   10: 6   God made them male and **female.**
Ro   1:26   Their **women** exchanged natural
      1:27   natural intercourse with **women,**
Ga   3:28   no longer male and **female;** for

2339   GO1 AG360 LN119
θηρα, NET
Ro   11: 9   snare and a **trap,** a stumbling

2340   GO1 AG360 LN119
θηρευω, I SNARE
Lk   11:54   **catch** him in something he might

2341   GO1 AG360 LN119 R2342,3164
θηριομαχεω, I FIGHT WILD ANIMALS
1C   15:32   I **fought** with **wild animals** at

2342   GO46 AG361 LN119 B1:113 K3:133
θηριον, WILD ANIMAL
Mk   1:13   he was with the **wild beasts;**
Ac   11: 6   **beasts** of prey, reptiles, and
      28: 4   **creature** hanging from his hand,
      28: 5   shook off the **creature** into the
Ti   1:12   vicious **brutes,** lazy gluttons.
He   12:20   If even an **animal** touches the
Ja   3: 7   For every species of **beast** and
Re   6: 8   the **wild animals** of the earth.
      11: 7   **beast** that comes up from the
      13: 1   And I saw a **beast** rising out of
      13: 2   And the **beast** that I saw was
      13: 3   whole earth followed the **beast.**
      13: 4   his authority to the **beast,** and
      13: 4   and they worshiped the **beast,**
      13: 4   Who is like the **beast,** and who
      13:11   Then I saw another **beast** that

      13:12   the first **beast** on its behalf,
      13:12   worship the first **beast,** whose
      13:14   **beast,** it deceives the
      13:14   make an image for the **beast**
      13:15   image of the **beast** so that the
      13:15   image of the **beast** could even
      13:15   of the **beast** to be killed.
      13:17   name of the **beast** or the number
      13:18   the number of the **beast,** for it
      14: 9   Those who worship the **beast**
      14:11   those who worship the **beast** and
      15: 2   conquered the **beast** and its
      16: 2   mark of the **beast** and who
      16:10   on the throne of the **beast,** and
      16:13   from the mouth of the **beast,**
      17: 3   sitting on a scarlet **beast** that
      17: 7   the **beast** with seven heads and
      17: 8   The **beast** that you saw was, and
      17: 8   amazed when they see the **beast,**
      17:11   As for the **beast** that was and
      17:12   hour, together with the **beast.**
      17:13   and authority to the **beast;**
      17:16   **beast** will hate the whore; they
      17:17   their kingdom to the **beast,**
      18: 2   of every foul and hateful **beast**
      19:19   Then I saw the **beast** and the
      19:20   And the **beast** was captured, and
      19:20   received the mark of the **beast**
      20: 4   worshiped the **beast** or its
      20:10   where the **beast** and the false

2343   GO8 AG361 LN119 B2:829 K3:138 R2344
θησαυριζω, I TREASURE
Mt   6:19   Do not **store up** for yourselves
      6:20   but **store up** for yourselves
Lk   12:21   it is with those who **store up**
Ro   2: 5   you are **storing up** wrath for
1C   16: 2   **save** whatever extra you earn,
2C   12:14   children ought not **to lay up**
Ja   5: 3   You **have laid up** treasure for
2P   3: 7   **have been reserved** for fire,

2344   GO17 AG361 LN120 B2:829 K3:136
θησαυρος, TREASURE
Mt   2:11   opening their **treasure** chests,
      6:19   **treasures** on earth, where moth
      6:20   **treasures** in heaven, where
      6:21   For where your **treasure** is,
      12:35   things out of a good **treasure,**

	12:35	things out of an evil **treasure.**
	13:44	**treasure** hidden in a field,
	13:52	out of his **treasure** what is new
	19:21	you will have **treasure** in
Mk	10:21	**treasure** in heaven; then come,
Lk	6:45	**treasure** of the heart produces
	12:33	an unfailing **treasure** in heaven
	12:34	For where your **treasure** is,
	18:22	you will have **treasure** in
2C	4: 7	But we have this **treasure** in
Co	2: 3	hidden all the **treasures** of
He	11:26	wealth than the **treasures** of

2345   G03   AG361   LN120
θιγγανω, I HANDLE

Co	2:21	Do not taste, Do not **touch**"?
He	11:28	firstborn **would** not **touch** the
	12:20	If even an animal **touches** the

2346   G010   AG362   LN120   B2:807   K3:139
θλιβω, I AFFLICT

Mt	7:14	the road is **hard** that leads to
Mk	3: 9	so that they **would** not **crush**
2C	1: 6	If we are **being afflicted,** it
	4: 8	We **are afflicted** in every way,
	7: 5	but we **were afflicted** in every
1Th	3: 4	we were to **suffer persecution;**
2Th	1: 6	affliction those who **afflict**
	1: 7	relief to the **afflicted** as well
1Ti	5:10	helped the **afflicted,** and
He	11:37	**persecuted,** tormented—

2347   G045   AG362   LN120   B2:807   K3:139   R2346
θλιψις, AFFLICTION

Mt	13:21	when **trouble** or persecution
	24: 9	hand you over **to be tortured**
	24:21	there will be great **suffering,**
	24:29	after the **suffering** of those
Mk	4:17	when **trouble** or persecution
	13:19	there will be **suffering,** such
	13:24	after that **suffering,** the sun
Jn	16:21	no longer remembers the **anguish**
	16:33	the world you face **persecution.**
Ac	7:10	him from all his **afflictions,**
	7:11	and great **suffering,** and our
	11:19	because of the **persecution** that
	14:22	through many **persecutions** that
	20:23	imprisonment and **persecutions**
Ro	2: 9	There will be **anguish** and

	5: 3	we also boast in our **sufferings**
	5: 3	knowing that **suffering** produces
	8:35	Will **hardship,** or distress, or
	12:12	be patient in **suffering,**
1C	7:28	experience **distress** in this
2C	1: 4	**affliction,** so that we may be
	1: 4	**affliction** with the consolation
	1: 8	the **affliction** we experienced
	2: 4	**distress** and anguish of heart
	4:17	slight momentary **affliction** is
	6: 4	in **afflictions,** hardships,
	7: 4	overjoyed in all our **affliction**
	8: 2	ordeal of **affliction,** their
	8:13	**pressure** on you, but it is a
Ep	3:13	lose heart over my **sufferings**
Ph	1:17	increase my **suffering** in my
	4:14	of you to share my **distress.**
Co	1:24	**afflictions** for the sake of his
1Th	1: 6	for in spite of **persecution** you
	3: 3	be shaken by these **persecutions**
	3: 7	**persecution** we have been
2Th	1: 4	**afflictions** that you are
	1: 6	repay with **affliction** those who
He	10:33	abuse and **persecution,** and
Ja	1:27	and widows in their **distress,**
Re	1: 9	in Jesus the **persecution** and
	2: 9	I know your **affliction** and
	2:10	you will have **affliction.** Be
	2:22	throwing into great **distress,**
	7:14	come out of the great **ordeal;**

2348   G09   AG362   LN120   B1:430   K3:7
θνησκω, I DIE

Mt	2:20	the child's life **are dead.**
Mk	15:44	if he **were** already **dead;** and
Lk	7:12	a man who **had died** was being
	8:49	Your daughter **is dead;** do not
Jn	11:44	The **dead** man came out, his
	19:33	saw that he **was** already **dead,**
Ac	14:19	supposing that he **was dead.**
	25:19	a certain Jesus, who **had died,**
1Ti	5: 6	lives for pleasure **is dead**

2349   G06   AG362   LN120   B1:430   K3:21   R2348
θνητος, DEATH-LIKE

Ro	6:12	dominion in your **mortal** bodies,
	8:11	give life to your **mortal** bodies
1C	15:53	this **mortal** body must put on
	15:54	and this **mortal** body puts on

2C   4:11   visible in our **mortal** flesh.
    5: 4   what is **mortal** may be swallowed

2349a   GO1   AG362   LN120   B2:621
θορυβαζω, UPROAR
Lk   10:41   worried and **distracted** by many

2350   GO4   AG362   LN120   B2:621   R2351
θορυβεω, I MAKE AN UPROAR
Mt   9:23   the crowd **making** a **commotion,**
Mk   5:39   Why do you **make** a **commotion**
Ac   17: 5   and **set** the city **in an uproar.**
    20:10   **Do** not **be alarmed,** for his

2351   GO7   AG363   LN120   B2:621
θορυβος, UPROAR
Mt   26: 5   there may be a **riot** among the
    27:24   a **riot** was beginning, he took
Mk   5:38   he saw a **commotion,** people
    14: 2   there may be a **riot** among the
Ac   20: 1   After the **uproar** had ceased,
    21:34   facts because of the **uproar,**
    24:18   any crowd or **disturbance.**

2352   GO1   AG363   LN120
θραυω, I CRUSH
Lk   4:18   **to let** the **oppressed** go free,

2353   GO1   AG363   LN120
θρεμμα, LIVESTOCK
Jn   4:12   and his **flocks** drank from it

2354   GO4   AG363   LN120   B2:416   K3:148
θρηνεω, I LAMENT
Mt   11:17   **wailed,** and you did not mourn.
Lk   7:32   **wailed,** and you did not weep.
    23:27   their breasts and **wailing** for
Jn   16:20   you will weep and **mourn,** but

2356   GO4   AG363   LN120   B3:549   K3:155
θρησκεια, PIETY
Ac   26: 5   strictest sect of our **religion**
Co   2:18   self-abasement and **worship** of
Ja   1:26   If any think they are **religious**
    1:27   **Religion** that is pure and

2357   GO1   AG363   LN120   B3:549   K3:155   R2356
θρησκος, PIOUS
Ja   1:26   If any think they are **religious**

2358   GO2   AG363   LN120   B1:649   K3:159
θριαμβευω, I LEAD IN TRIUMPH
2C   2:14   **leads in triumphal procession**
Co   2:15   **triumphing** over them in it.

2359   GO15   AG363   LN120
θριξ, HAIR
Mt   3: 4   clothing of camel's **hair** with a
    5:36   you cannot make one **hair**
      white
    10:30   And even the **hairs** of your
      head
Mk   1: 6   clothed with camel's **hair,** with
Lk   7:38   and to dry them with her **hair.**
    7:44   and dried them with her **hair.**
    12: 7   But even the **hairs** of your head
    21:18   But not a **hair** of your head
Jn   11: 2   wiped his feet with her **hair;**
    12: 3   **hair.** The house was filled with
Ac   27:34   none of you will lose a **hair**
1P   3: 3   braiding your **hair,** and by
Re   1:14   head and his **hair** were white as
    9: 8   their **hair** like women's hair,
    9: 8   their hair like women's **hair,**

2360   GO3   AG364   LN120
θροεω, I DISTURB
Mt   24: 6   see that you **are** not **alarmed;**
Mk   13: 7   **do** not **be alarmed;** this must
2Th   2: 2   **alarmed,** either by spirit or by

2361   GO1   AG364   LN120
θρομβος, CLOT
Lk   22:44   sweat became like **great drops**

2362   GO62   AG364   LN120   B2:611   K3:160
θρονος, THRONE
Mt   5:34   for it is the **throne** of God,
    19:28   seated on the **throne** of his
    19:28   sit on twelve **thrones,** judging
    23:22   swears by the **throne** of God
    25:31   he will sit on the **throne** of
Lk   1:32   give to him the **throne** of his
    1:52   powerful from their **thrones,**
    22:30   and you will sit on **thrones**
Ac   2:30   his descendants on his **throne.**
    7:49   Heaven is my **throne,** and the
Co   1:16   whether **thrones** or dominions or
He   1: 8   Your **throne,** O God, is forever
    4:16   approach the **throne** of grace

	8: 1	right hand of the **throne** of the
	12: 2	right hand of the **throne** of God
Re	1: 4	who are before his **throne,**
	2:13	where Satan's **throne** is. Yet
	3:21	a place with me on my **throne,**
	3:21	with my Father on his **throne.**
	4: 2	there in heaven stood a **throne,**
	4: 2	with one seated on the **throne!**
	4: 3	and around the **throne** is a
	4: 4	Around the **throne** are
	4: 4	twenty-four **thrones,** and seated
	4: 4	on the **thrones** are twenty-four
	4: 5	Coming from the **throne** are
	4: 5	in front of the **throne** burn
	4: 6	in front of the **throne** there is
	4: 6	Around the **throne,** and on each
	4: 6	side of the **throne,** are four
	4: 9	who is seated on the **throne,**
	4:10	**throne** and worship the one who
	4:10	their crowns before the **throne,**
	5: 1	**throne** a scroll written on
	5: 6	Then I saw between the **throne**
	5: 7	who was seated on the **throne.**
	5:11	angels surrounding the **throne**
	5:13	**throne** and to the Lamb be
	6:16	seated on the **throne** and from
	7: 9	standing before the **throne** and
	7:10	on the **throne,** and to the Lamb!
	7:11	stood around the **throne** and
	7:11	their faces before the **throne**
	7:15	before the **throne** of God, and
	7:15	seated on the **throne** will
	7:17	center of the **throne** will be
	8: 3	altar that is before the **throne**
	11:16	**thrones** before God fell on
	12: 5	taken to God and to his **throne;**
	13: 2	power and his **throne** and great
	14: 3	before the **throne** and before
	16:10	**throne** of the beast, and its
	16:17	from the **throne,** saying, "It is
	19: 4	God who is seated on the **throne**
	19: 5	And from the **throne** came a
	20: 4	Then I saw **thrones,** and those
	20:11	Then I saw a great white **throne**
	20:12	standing before the **throne,** and
	21: 3	voice from the **throne** saying,
	21: 5	seated on the **throne** said, "See
	22: 1	flowing from the **throne** of God
	22: 3	But the **throne** of God and of

2363   GO4 AG364 LN120
θυατειρα, THYATIRA

Ac	16:14	from the city of **Thyatira** and a
Re	1:11	to Pergamum, to **Thyatira,** to
	2:18	angel of the church in **Thyatira**
	2:24	the rest of you in **Thyatira,**

2364   GO28 AG364 LN120
θυγατηρ, DAUGHTER

Mt	9:18	My **daughter** has just died; but
	9:22	Take heart, **daughter;** your
	10:35	and a **daughter** against her
	10:37	son or **daughter** more than me is
	14: 6	the **daughter** of Herodias danced
	15:22	my **daughter** is tormented by a
	15:28	And her **daughter** was healed
	21: 5	Tell the **daughter** of Zion,
Mk	5:34	He said to her, "**Daughter,** your
	5:35	Your **daughter** is dead. Why
	6:22	When his **daughter** Herodias came
	7:26	the demon out of her **daughter.**
	7:29	demon has left your **daughter.**
Lk	1: 5	wife was a **descendant** of Aaron,
	2:36	Anna the **daughter** of Phanuel,
	8:42	for he had an only **daughter,**
	8:48	He said to her, "**Daughter,** your
	8:49	Your **daughter** is dead; do not
	12:53	mother against **daughter** and
	12:53	**daughter** against mother,
	13:16	a **daughter** of Abraham whom
	23:28	**Daughters** of Jerusalem, do not
Jn	12:15	**daughter** of Zion. Look, your
Ac	2:17	sons and your **daughters** shall
	7:21	Pharaoh's **daughter** adopted him
	21: 9	He had four unmarried **daughters**
2C	6:18	my sons and **daughters,** says the
He	11:24	a son of Pharaoh's **daughter,**

2365   GO2 AG365 LN121 R2364
θυγατριον, SMALL DAUGHTER

Mk	5:23	My **little daughter** is at the
	7:25	a woman whose **little daughter**

2366   GO1 AG365 LN121
θυελλα, STORM

He	12:18	and gloom, and a **tempest,**

2367   GO1 AG365 LN121
θυινος, CITRON

Re	18:12	all kinds of **scented** wood, all

2368 GO6 AG365 LN121 B2:293 R2370
θυμιαμα, INCENSE
Lk 1:10 **incense** offering, the whole
    1:11 side of the altar of **incense.**
Re 5: 8 golden bowls full of **incense,**
    8: 3 great quantity of **incense** to
    8: 4 And the smoke of the **incense,**
    18:13 cinnamon, spice, **incense,** myrrh

2369 GO1 AG365 LN121 B2:293 R2369
θυμιατηριον, PLACE OF INCENSE
He 9: 4 golden **altar of incense** and the

2370 GO1 AG365 LN121 B2:293 R2380
θυμιαω, I BURN INCENSE
Lk 1: 9 of the Lord and **offer incense.**

2371 GO1 AG365 LN121 R2372,3164
θυμομαχεω, I FIGHT FURIOUSLY
Ac 12:20 Now Herod **was angry** with the

2372 GO18 AG365 LN121 B1:105 K3:167
θυμος, FURY
Lk 4:28 synagogue were filled with **rage**
Ac 19:28 they were **enraged** and shouted,
Ro 2: 8 there will be wrath and **fury.**
2C 12:20 quarreling, jealousy, **anger,**
Ga 5:20 strife, jealousy, **anger,**
Ep 4:31 bitterness and **wrath** and anger
Co 3: 8 all such things—anger, **wrath,**
He 11:27 unafraid of the king's **anger;**
Re 12:12 great **wrath,** because he knows
    14: 8 drink of the wine of the **wrath**
    14:10 drink the wine of God's **wrath,**
    14:19 great wine press of the **wrath**
    15: 1 with them the **wrath** of God is
    15: 7 bowls full of the **wrath** of God,
    16: 1 the seven bowls of the **wrath** of
    16:19 of the fury of his **wrath.**
    18: 3 the wine of the **wrath** of her
    19:15 fury of the **wrath** of God the

2373 GO1 AG365 LN121 B1:105
θυμοω, I AM ANGRY
Mt 2:16 he **was infuriated,** and he sent

2374 GO39 AG365 LN121 B2:30 K3:173
θυρα, DOOR
Mt 6: 6 shut the **door** and pray to your
    24:33 he is near, at the very **gates.**

    25:10 banquet; and the **door** was shut.
    27:60 to the **door** of the tomb and
Mk 1:33 was gathered around the **door.**
    2: 2 not even in front of the **door;**
    11: 4 found a colt tied near a **door,**
    13:29 he is near, at the very **gates.**
    15:46 against the **door** of the tomb.
    16: 3 from the **entrance** to the tomb?
Lk 11: 7 Do not bother me; the **door** has
    13:24 through the narrow **door;** for
    13:25 got up and shut the **door,** and
    13:25 knock at the **door,** saying,
Jn 10: 1 enter the sheepfold by the **gate**
    10: 2 The one who enters by the **gate**
    10: 7 I am the **gate** for the sheep.
    10: 9 I am the **gate.** Whoever enters
    18:16 standing outside at the **gate.**
    20:19 the **doors** of the house where
    20:26 Although the **doors** were shut,
Ac 3: 2 lay him daily at the **gate** of
    5: 9 **door,** and they will carry you
    5:19 opened the prison **doors,**
    5:23 guards standing at the **doors,**
    12: 6 guards in front of the **door**
    12:13 knocked at the outer **gate,** a
    14:27 opened a **door** of faith for the
    16:26 immediately all the **doors** were
    16:27 prison **doors** wide open, he drew
    21:30 immediately the **doors** were shut
1C 16: 9 for a wide **door** for effective
2C 2:12 a **door** was opened for me in the
Co 4: 3 open to us a **door** for the word,
Ja 5: 9 Judge is standing at the **doors!**
Re 3: 8 set before you an open **door,**
    3:20 I am standing at the **door,**
    3:20 hear my voice and open the **door**
    4: 1 and there in heaven a **door**

2375 GO1 AG366 LN121 B3:959 K5:312 R2374
θυρεος, SHIELD
Ep 6:16 take the **shield** of faith, with

2376 GO2 AG366 LN121 R2374
θυρις, WINDOW
Ac 20: 9 who was sitting in the **window,**
2C 11:33 through a **window** in the wall,

2377 GO4 AG366 LN121
θυρωρος, DOORKEEPER
Mk 13:34 commands the **doorkeeper** to be

Jn   10: 3   The **gatekeeper** opens the gate
     18:16   **woman who guarded the gate,**
     18:17   The **woman** said to Peter, "You

2378   ᴳᴼ28 ᴬᴳ366 ᴸᴺ121 ᴮ3:417 ᴷ3:180 ᴿ2380
θυσια, SACRIFICE

Mt   9:13   I desire mercy, not **sacrifice.**
     12: 7   burnt offerings and **sacrifices.**
Lk   2:24   and they offered a **sacrifice**
     13: 1   mingled with their **sacrifices.**
Ac   7: 4   offered a **sacrifice** to the idol
      7:42   slain victims and **sacrifices**
Ro   12: 1   bodies as a living **sacrifice,**
1C   10:18   those who eat the **sacrifices**
Ep   5: 2   offering and **sacrifice** to God.
Ph   2:17   libation over the **sacrifice**
He   5: 1   to offer gifts and **sacrifices**
      7:27   no need to offer **sacrifices** day
      8: 3   offer gifts and **sacrifices;**
      9: 9   gifts and **sacrifices** are
      9:23   need better **sacrifices** than
      9:26   sin by the **sacrifice** of himself
     10: 1   by the same **sacrifices** that are
     10: 5   **Sacrifices** and offerings you
     10: 8   taken pleasure in **sacrifices**
     10:11   the same **sacrifices** that can
     10:12   a single **sacrifice** for sins,
     10:26   no longer remains a **sacrifice**
     11: 4   a more acceptable **sacrifice**
     13:15   continually offer a **sacrifice**
     13:16   such **sacrifices** are pleasing to
1P   2: 5   to offer spiritual **sacrifices**

2379   ᴳᴼ23 ᴬᴳ366 ᴸᴺ121 ᴮ3:417 ᴷ3:180 ᴿ2378
θυσιαστηριον, SACRIFICE PLACE

Mt   5:23   offering your gift at the **altar**
      5:24   before the **altar** and go; first
     23:18   Whoever swears by the **altar** is
     23:19   the gift or the **altar** that
     23:20   So whoever swears by the
             altar,
     23:35   the sanctuary and the **altar.**
Lk   1:11   the right side of the **altar** of
     11:51   perished between the **altar** and
Ro   11: 3   have demolished your **altars;**
1C   9:13   those who serve at the **altar**
      9:13   what is sacrificed on the **altar**
     10:18   partners in the **altar?**
He   7:13   has ever served at the **altar.**
     13:10   We have an **altar** from which

Ja   2:21   his son Isaac on the **altar?**
Re   6: 9   I saw under the **altar** the souls
      8: 3   came and stood at the **altar;** he
      8: 3   saints on the golden **altar** that
      8: 5   fire from the **altar** and threw
      9:13   horns of the golden **altar**
     11: 1   temple of God and the **altar** and
     14:18   came out from the **altar,** the
     16: 7   And I heard the **altar** respond,

2380   ᴳᴼ14 ᴬᴳ367 ᴸᴺ121 ᴮ3:417 ᴷ3:180
θυω, I SACRIFICE

Mt   22: 4   calves **have been slaughtered,**
Mk   14:12   Passover lamb **is sacrificed,**
Lk   15:23   get the fatted calf and **kill** it
     15:27   your father **has killed** the
     15:30   you **killed** the fatted calf for
     22: 7   lamb **had to be sacrificed.**
Jn   10:10   to steal and **kill** and destroy.
Ac   10:13   Get up, Peter; **kill** and eat.
     11: 7   Get up, Peter; **kill** and eat.
     14:13   wanted to **offer sacrifice.**
     14:18   from **offering sacrifice** to them
1C   5: 7   Christ, **has been sacrificed.**
     10:20   what pagans **sacrifice,** they
     10:20   **sacrifice** to demons and not to

2381   ᴳᴼ11 ᴬᴳ367 ᴸᴺ121
θωμας, THOMAS

Mt   10: 3   Philip and Bartholomew;
             Thomas
Mk   3:18   and **Thomas,** and James son of
Lk   6:15   and Matthew, and **Thomas,** and
Jn   11:16   **Thomas,** who was called the Twin
     14: 5   **Thomas** said to him, "Lord, we
     20:24   But **Thomas** (who was called the
     20:26   in the house, and **Thomas** was
     20:27   Then he said to **Thomas,** "Put
     20:28   **Thomas** answered him, "My
             Lord
     21: 2   **Thomas** called the Twin
Ac   1:13   Philip and **Thomas,** Bartholomew

2382   ᴳᴼ5 ᴬᴳ367 ᴸᴺ121 ᴮ3:959 ᴷ5:308
θωραξ, BREASTPLATE

Ep   6:14   **breastplate** of righteousness.
1Th   5: 8   **breastplate** of faith and love,
Re   9: 9   scales like iron **breastplates,**
      9: 9   iron **breastplates,** and the
      9:17   the riders wore **breastplates**

ι

2383   GO2 AG367 LN121
ιαιρος, JAIRUS

Mk	5:22	**Jairus** came and, when he saw
Lk	8:41	there came a man named **Jairus,**

2384   GO27 AG367 LN121 B2:316 K3:191
ιακωβ, JACOB

Mt	1: 2	and Isaac the father of **Jacob,**
	1: 2	and **Jacob** the father of Judah
	1:15	and Matthan the father of **Jacob**
	1:16	and **Jacob** the father of Joseph
	8:11	Abraham and Isaac and **Jacob** in
	22:32	Isaac, and the God of **Jacob'**?
Mk	12:26	Isaac, and the God of **Jacob'**?
Lk	1:33	the house of **Jacob** forever, and
	3:34	son of **Jacob,** son of Isaac, son
	13:28	**Jacob** and all the prophets in
	20:37	Isaac, and the God of **Jacob.**
Jn	4: 5	plot of ground that **Jacob** had
	4: 6	**Jacob's** well was there, and
	4:12	greater than our ancestor **Jacob**
Ac	3:13	**Jacob,** the God of our ancestors
	7: 8	became the father of **Jacob,** and
	7: 8	**Jacob** of the twelve patriarchs.
	7:12	But when **Jacob** heard that there
	7:14	his father **Jacob** and all his
	7:15	so **Jacob** went down to Egypt. He
	7:32	Isaac, and **Jacob.**
	7:46	place for the house of **Jacob.**
Ro	9:13	I have loved **Jacob,** but I have
	11:26	banish ungodliness from **Jacob.**
He	11: 9	**Jacob,** who were heirs with him
	11:20	the future on **Jacob** and Esau.
	11:21	By faith **Jacob,** when dying,

2385   GO42 AG367 LN121 B2:316
ιακωβος, JACOB (JAMES)

Mt	4:21	**James** son of Zebedee and his
	10: 2	**James** son of Zebedee, and his
	10: 3	**James** son of Alphaeus, and
	13:55	are not his brothers **James** and
	17: 1	**James** and his brother John and
	27:56	Mary the mother of **James** and
Mk	1:19	he saw **James** son of Zebedee and
	1:29	Andrew, with **James** and John.
	3:17	**James** son of Zebedee and John
	3:17	John the brother of **James** (to

	3:18	and **James** son of Alphaeus, and
	5:37	Peter, **James,** and John, the
	5:37	John, the brother of **James.**
	6: 3	of Mary and brother of **James**
	9: 2	Peter and **James** and John, and
	10:35	**James** and John, the sons of
	10:41	to be angry with **James** and John
	13: 3	Peter, **James,** John, and Andrew
	14:33	Peter and **James** and John, and
	15:40	mother of **James** the younger and
	16: 1	Mary the mother of **James,** and
Lk	5:10	and so also were **James** and John
	6:14	his brother Andrew, and **James,**
	6:15	**James** son of Alphaeus, and
	6:16	and Judas son of **James,** and
	8:51	except Peter, John, and **James,**
	9:28	Peter and John and **James,** and
	9:54	When his disciples **James** and
	24:10	Mary the mother of **James,** and
Ac	1:13	**James,** and Andrew, Philip and
	1:13	**James** son of Alphaeus, and
	1:13	Zealot, and Judas son of **James.**
	12: 2	Tell this to **James** and to the
	15:13	**James** replied, "My brothers,
	21:18	went with us to visit **James;**
1C	15: 7	Then he appeared to **James,**
Ga	1:19	except **James** the Lord's brother
	2: 9	and when **James** and Cephas and
	2:12	certain people came from **James,**
Ja	1: 1	**James,** a servant of God and of
Ju	1: 1	brother of **James,** To those who

2386   GO3 AG368 LN121 B2:166 K3:194 R2390
ιαμα, CURE

1C	12: 9	gifts of **healing** by the one
	12:28	then gifts of **healing,** forms of
	12:30	Do all possess gifts of **healing**

2387   GO1 AG368 LN121 K3:192
ιαμβρης, JAMBRES

2Ti	3: 8	As Jannes and **Jambres** opposed

2388   GO1 AG368 LN121
ιανναι, JANNAI

Lk	3:24	son of Melchi, son of **Jannai,**

2389   GO1 AG368 LN121 K3:192
ιαννης, JANNES

2Ti	3: 8	As **Jannes** and Jambres opposed

2390　GO26 AG368 LN121 B2:166 K3:194
ιαομαι, I CURE
Mt　8: 8　and my servant **will be healed.**
　　8:13　And the servant **was healed** in
　　13:15　and turn—and I **would heal** them.
　　15:28　And her daughter **was healed**
Mk　5:29　she **was healed** of her disease.
Lk　5:17　the Lord was with him **to heal.**
　　6:18　to hear him and **to be healed** of
　　6:19　came out from him and **healed**
　　7: 7　and let my servant **be healed.**
　　8:47　she **had been** immediately **healed**
　　9: 2　the kingdom of God and **to heal.**
　　9:11　and **healed** those who needed to
　　9:42　**healed** the boy, and gave him
　　14: 4　Jesus took him and **healed** him,
　　17:15　when he saw that he **was healed,**
　　22:51　he touched his ear and **healed**
Jn　4:47　come down and **heal** his son, for
　　5:13　Now the man who **had been healed**
　　12:40　turn—and I **would heal** them.
Ac　9:34　Aeneas, Jesus Christ **heals** you
　　10:38　doing good and **healing** all who
　　28: 8　Paul visited him and **cured** him
　　28:27　heart and turn—and I **would heal**
He　12:13　of joint, but rather **be healed.**
Ja　5:16　so that you **may be healed.** The
1P　2:24　his wounds you **have been healed**

2391　GO1 AG368 LN121
ιαρετ, JARET (JARED)
Lk　3:37　son of **Jared,** son of Mahalaleel

2392　GO3 AG368 LN122 B2:166 K3:194 R2390
ιασις, CURE
Lk　13:32　out demons and performing **cures**
Ac　4:22　this sign of **healing** had been
　　4:30　stretch out your hand to **heal,**

2393　GO4 AG368 LN122 B3:395
ιασπις, JASPER
Re　4: 3　looks like **jasper** and carnelian
　　21:11　like **jasper,** clear as crystal.
　　21:18　The wall is built of **jasper,**
　　21:19　the first was **jasper,** the

2394　GO5 AG368 LN122
ιασων, JASON
Ac　17: 5　they attacked **Jason's** house.

17: 6　they dragged **Jason** and some
17: 7　and **Jason** has entertained them
17: 9　they had taken bail from **Jason**
Ro　16:21　Lucius and **Jason** and Sosipater,

2395　GO7 AG368 LN122 B2:166 K3:194 R2390
ιατρος, PHYSICIAN
Mt　9:12　have no need of a **physician,**
Mk　2:17　**physician,** but those who are
　　5:26　much under many **physicians,**
Lk　4:23　'**Doctor,** cure yourself!' And
　　5:31　have no need of a **physician,**
　　8:43　spent all she had on **physicians**
Co　4:14　Luke, the beloved **physician,**

2396　GO34 AG369 LN122
ιδε, LOOK
Mt　25:20　**see,** I have made five more
　　25:22　**see,** I have made two more
　　25:25　**Here** you have what is yours.
　　26:65　**You** have now heard his
Mk　2:24　Pharisees said to him, "**Look,**
　　3:34　**Here** are my mother and my
　　11:21　Rabbi, **look!** The fig tree that
　　13: 1　**Look,** Teacher, what large
　　13:21　'**Look!** Here is the Messiah!' or
　　13:21　'**Look!** There he is!'—do not
　　15: 4　**See** how many charges they bring
　　15:35　**Listen,** he is calling for
　　16: 6　**Look,** there is the place they
Jn　1:29　**Here** is the Lamb of God who
　　1:36　**Look,** here is the Lamb of God!
　　1:46　said to him, "Come and **see.**"
　　1:47　**Here** is truly an Israelite in
　　3:26　**here** he is baptizing, and all
　　5:14　**See,** you have been made well!'
　　7:26　And **here** he is, speaking openly
　　7:52　Search and you will **see** that no
　　11: 3　sent a message **to** Jesus, "Lord,
　　11:34　to him, "Lord, come and **see.**"
　　11:36　So the Jews said, "**See** how he
　　12:19　**Look,** the world has gone after
　　16:29　**Yes,** now you are speaking
　　18:21　**they** know what I said.
　　19: 4　**Look,** I am bringing him out to
　　19:14　to the Jews, "**Here** is your King
　　19:26　Woman, **here** is your son.
　　19:27　"**Here** is your mother." And from

	20:27	Put your finger here and **see**
Ro	11:22	**Note** then the kindness and the
Ga	5: 2	**Listen!** I, Paul, am telling you

2398   GO114 AG369 LN122 B2:839
ιδιος, OWN

Mt	9: 1	sea and came to his **own** town.
	14:13	to a deserted place by **himself.**
	14:23	up the mountain by **himself** to
	17: 1	a high mountain, by **themselves.**
	17:19	to Jesus **privately** and said,
	20:17	disciples aside by **themselves,**
	22: 5	one to **his** farm, another to his
	24: 3	disciples came to him **privately**
	25:14	summoned **his** slaves and
	25:15	to each according to **his**
Mk	4:34	in **private** to his disciples.
	4:34	in private to **his** disciples.
	6:31	**all by yourselves** and rest a
	6:32	a deserted place by **themselves.**
	7:33	He took him aside in **private,**
	9: 2	by **themselves.** And he was
	9:28	disciples asked him **privately,**
	13: 3	and Andrew asked him **privately,**
Lk	6:41	notice the log in your **own** eye?
	6:44	each tree is known by its **own**
	9:10	withdrew **privately** to a city
	10:23	Jesus said to them **privately,**
	10:34	he put him on his **own** animal,
	18:28	Look, we have left **our homes**
Jn	1:11	He came to what was **his own,**
	1:11	and **his own** people did not
	1:41	He first found **his** brother
	4:44	in the prophet's **own** country).
	5:18	calling God his **own** Father,
	5:43	another comes in his **own** name,
	7:18	Those who speak on their **own**
	8:44	according to his **own nature,**
	10: 3	He calls his **own** sheep by name
	10: 4	all his **own,** he goes ahead of
	10:12	does not **own** the sheep, sees
	13: 1	Having loved his **own** who were
	15:19	would love you as its **own.**
	16:32	each one to **his home,** and you
	19:27	took her into his **own** home.
Ac	1: 7	Father has set by his **own**
	1:19	the field was called in **their**
	1:25	aside to go to his **own** place.
	2: 6	speaking in the **native** language

	2: 8	each of us, in our **own** native
	3:12	as though by our **own** power or
	4:23	they went to **their friends** and
	4:32	everything they **owned** was held
	13:36	in his **own** generation, died,
	20:28	with the blood of his **own** Son.
	21: 6	ship, and they returned **home.**
	23:19	drew him aside **privately,** and
	24:23	**his friends** from taking care of
	24:24	Felix came with **his** wife
	25:19	their **own** religion and about a
	28:30	at his **own** expense and welcomed
Ro	8:32	He who did not withhold his **own**
	10: 3	seeking to establish their **own,**
	11:24	grafted back into their **own**
	14: 4	It is before their **own** lord
	14: 5	fully convinced in their **own**
1C	3: 8	and **each** will receive wages
	3: 8	according to the labor **of each.**
	4:12	the work of our **own** hands.
	6:18	sins against the body **itself.**
	7: 2	each man should have his **own**
	7: 4	authority over her **own** body,
	7: 4	authority over his **own** body,
	7: 7	But each has a **particular** gift
	7:37	necessity but having his **own**
	7:37	determined in his **own** mind to
	9: 7	Who at any time pays **the** [his own] expenses
	11:21	with your **own** supper, and one
	12:11	to each one **individually** just
	14:35	let them ask **their** husbands at
	15:23	But each in his **own** order:
	15:38	to each kind of seed its **own**
Ga	2: 2	though only in a **private**
	6: 5	For all must carry their **own**
	6: 9	we will reap at **harvest** time,
Ep	4:28	work honestly with their **own**
	5:22	Wives, be subject to **your**
1Th	2:14	the same things from your **own**
	4:11	mind your **own** affairs, and to
	4:11	work with **your** hands, as we
1Ti	2: 6	was attested at the **right** time.
	3: 4	must manage his **own** household
	3: 5	know how to manage his **own**
	3:12	manage their children and **their**
	4: 2	liars **whose** consciences are
	5: 4	duty to their **own** family and
	5: 8	provide for **relatives,** and

	6: 1	**their** masters as worthy of all
	6:15	bring about at the **right** time
2Ti	1: 9	according to his **own** purpose
	4: 3	teachers to suit their **own**
Ti	1: 3	in **due** time he revealed his
	1:12	their very **own** prophet, who
	2: 5	submissive to **their** husbands,
	2: 9	submissive to **their** masters and
He	4:10	labors as God did from **his.**
	7:27	first for his **own** sins, and
	9:12	with his **own** blood, thus
	13:12	the people by his **own** blood.
Ja	1:14	tempted by one's **own** desire,
1P	3: 1	the authority of **your** husbands,
	3: 5	the authority of **their** husbands
2P	1: 3	called us by his **own** glory and
	1:20	of one's **own** interpretation,
	2:16	but was rebuked for his **own**
	2:22	dog turns back to its **own** vomit
	3: 3	and indulging their **own** lusts
	3:16	twist to their **own** destruction,
	3:17	and lose your **own** stability.
Ju	1: 6	did not keep their **own** position

2399 GO5 AG370 LN122 B2:456 K3:215
ιδιωτης, UNLEARNED

Ac	4:13	uneducated and **ordinary** men,
1C	14:16	position of an **outsider** say the
	14:23	and **outsiders** or unbelievers
	14:24	an unbeliever or **outsider** who
2C	11: 6	I may be **untrained** in speech,

2400 GO200 AG370 LN122 B3:516
ιδου, LOOK [MULTIPLE OCCURRENCES]

2401 GO1 AG371 LN122
ιδουμαια, IDUMEA

Mk	3: 8	from Judea, Jerusalem, **Idumea**

2402 GO1 AG371 LN122
ιδρως, SWEAT

Lk	22:44	his **sweat** became like great

2403 GO1 AG371 LN122 K3:217
ιεζαβελ, JEZABEL

Re	2:20	tolerate that woman **Jezebel**

2404 GO1 AG371 LN122
ιεραπολις, HIERAPOLIS

Co	4:13	in Laodicea and in **Hierapolis**

2405 GO2 AG371 LN122 B2:232 K3:251 R2409
ιερατεια, PRIESTHOOD

Lk	1: 9	to the custom of the **priesthood**
He	7: 5	who receive the **priestly office**

2406 GO2 AG371 LN122 B2:232 K3:249 R2409
ιερατευμα, PRIESTHOOD

1P	2: 5	to be a holy **priesthood**
	2: 9	chosen race, a royal **priesthood**

2407 GO1 AG371 LN122 B2:232 K3:248 R2409
ιερατευω, I SERVE AS PRIEST

Lk	1: 8	when he was **serving as priest**

2408 GO3 AG371 LN122 K3:218
ιερεμιας, JEREMIAH

Mt	2:17	through the prophet **Jeremiah**
	16:14	**Jeremiah** or one of the prophets
	27: 9	through the prophet **Jeremiah**

2409 GO31 AG372 LN122 B2:232 K3:257
ιερευς, PRIEST

Mt	8: 4	show yourself to the **priest**
	12: 4	but only for the **priests**
	12: 5	the **priests** in the temple
Mk	1:44	show yourself to the **priest**
	2:26	when Abiathar was high **priest**
Lk	1: 5	a **priest** named Zechariah
	5:14	show yourself to the **priest**
	6: 4	but the **priests** to eat
	10:31	Now by chance a **priest** was
	17:14	show yourselves to the **priests**
Jn	1:19	when the Jews sent **priests**
Ac	4: 1	the **priests,** the captain of
	6: 7	the **priests** became obedient
	14:13	The **priest** of Zeus
He	5: 6	You are a **priest** forever
	7: 1	**priest** of the Most High God
	7: 3	he remains a **priest** forever
	7:11	to speak of another **priest**
	7:14	said nothing about **priests**
	7:15	when another **priest** arises
	7:17	You are a **priest** forever
	7:20	for others who became **priests**
	7:21	You are a **priest** forever
	7:23	the former **priests** were many
	8: 4	he would not be a **priest** at all
	9: 6	the **priests** go continually
	10:11	**priest** stands day after day
	10:21	since we have a great **priest**

Re	1: 6	**priests** serving his God
	5:10	and **priests** serving our God
	20: 6	they will be **priests** of God

2410   GO7 AG372 LN122

ιεριχω, JERICHO

Mt	20:29	As they were leaving **Jericho**
Mk	10:46	They came to **Jericho.**
	10:46	crowd were leaving **Jericho**
Lk	10:30	from Jerusalem to **Jericho**
	18:35	As he approached **Jericho**
	19: 1	He entered **Jericho** and was
He	11:30	By faith the walls of **Jericho**

2410a   GO1 AG372 LN122 B2:232 K3:252

ἱεροθυτος, TEMPLE SACRIFICE

| 1C | 10:28 | has been **offered in sacrifice** |

2411   GO72 AG372 LN122 B2:232 K3:230 R2413

ἱερον, TEMPLE

Mt	4: 5	on the pinnacle of the **temple**
	12: 5	the priests in the **temple**
	12: 6	greater than the **temple**
	21:12	Then Jesus entered the **temple**
	21:12	and buying in the **temple**
	21:14	came to him in the **temple**
	21:15	crying out in the **temple**
	21:23	When he entered the **temple**
	24: 1	As Jesus came out of the **temple**
	24: 1	the buildings of the **temple.**
	26:55	I sat in the **temple** teaching
Mk	11:11	and went into the **temple**
	11:15	he entered the **temple**
	11:15	who were buying in the **temple**
	11:16	anything through the **temple**
	11:27	he was walking in the **temple**
	12:35	was teaching in the **temple**
	13: 1	As he came out of the **temple**
	13: 3	of Olives opposite the **temple**
	14:49	I was with you in the **temple**
Lk	2:27	Simeon came into the **temple**
	2:37	She never left the **temple**
	2:46	they found him in the **temple**
	4: 9	on the pinnacle of the **temple**
	18:10	men went up to the **temple**
	19:45	Then he entered the **temple**
	19:47	he was teaching in the **temple**
	20: 1	the people in the **temple**
	21: 5	were speaking about the **temple**

	21:37	he was teaching in the **temple**
	21:38	listen to him in the **temple**
	22:52	officers of the **temple** police
	22:53	day after day in the **temple**
	24:53	were continually in the **temple**
Jn	2:14	In the **temple** he found people
	2:15	all of them out of the **temple**
	5:14	Jesus found him in the **temple**
	7:14	went up into the **temple**
	7:28	was teaching in the **temple**
	8: 2	he came again to the **temple**
	8:20	in the treasury of the **temple**
	8:59	and went out of the **temple**
	10:23	Jesus was walking in the **temple**
	11:56	as they stood in the **temple**
	18:20	in synagogues and in the **temple**
Ac	2:46	time together in the **temple**
	3: 1	were going up to the **temple**
	3: 2	daily at the gate of the **temple**
	3: 2	from those entering the **temple.**
	3: 3	about to go into the **temple**
	3: 8	entered the **temple** with them
	3:10	Beautiful Gate of the **temple**
	4: 1	the captain of the **temple**
	5:20	stand in the **temple** and tell
	5:21	they entered the **temple**
	5:24	when the captain of the **temple**
	5:25	are standing in the **temple**
	5:42	And every day in the **temple**
	19:27	**temple** of the great goddess
	21:26	entered the **temple** with them
	21:27	who had seen him in the **temple**
	21:28	brought Greeks into the **temple**
	21:29	had brought him into the **temple**
	21:30	dragged him out of the **temple**
	22:17	I was praying in the **temple**
	24:12	with anyone in the **temple**
	24:18	they found me in the **temple**
	25: 8	or against the **temple**
	26:21	Jews seized me in the **temple**
1C	9:13	employed in the **temple** service
	9:13	get their food from the **temple**

2412   GO1 AG372 LN122 K3:253

ἱεροπρεπης, BEFITTING SACRED

| Ti | 2: 3 | the older women to be **reverent** |

2413   GO2 AG372 LN122 B2:232 K3:221 R2409

ἱερος, SACRED

Mk	16: 8	**sacred** and imperishable
2Ti	3:15	have known the **sacred** writings

2414　GO62　AG372　LN122　B2:324　K7:292
ἱεροσολυμα, JERUSALEM

Mt	2: 1	the East came to **Jerusalem**
	2: 3	and all **Jerusalem** with him
	3: 5	Then the people of **Jerusalem**
	4:25	Decapolis, **Jerusalem**, Judea
	5:35	or by **Jerusalem**, for it is the
	15: 1	came to Jesus from **Jerusalem**
	16:21	that he must go to **Jerusalem**
	20:17	Jesus was going up to **Jerusalem**
	20:18	we are going up to **Jerusalem**
	21: 1	they had come near **Jerusalem**
	21:10	When he entered **Jerusalem**
Mk	3: 8	from Judea, **Jerusalem**, Idumea
	3:22	who came down from **Jerusalem**
	7: 1	who had come from **Jerusalem**
	10:32	going up to **Jerusalem**
	10:33	we are going up to **Jerusalem**,
	11: 1	they were approaching **Jerusalem**
	11:11	Then he entered **Jerusalem**
	11:15	Then they came to **Jerusalem**
	11:27	Again they came to **Jerusalem**
	15:41	come up with him to **Jerusalem**
Lk	2:22	brought him up to **Jerusalem**
	13:22	he made his way to **Jerusalem**
	19:28	going up to **Jerusalem**
	23: 7	who was himself in **Jerusalem**
Jn	1:19	Levites from **Jerusalem** to ask
	2:13	Jesus went up to **Jerusalem**
	2:23	When he was in **Jerusalem**
	4:20	must worship is in **Jerusalem**
	4:21	this mountain nor in **Jerusalem**
	4:45	that he had done in **Jerusalem**
	5: 1	Jesus went up to **Jerusalem**
	5: 2	Now in **Jerusalem** by the Sheep
	10:22	took place in **Jerusalem**
	11:18	Bethany was near **Jerusalem**
	11:55	the country to **Jerusalem**
	12:12	Jesus was coming to **Jerusalem**
Ac	1: 4	not to leave **Jerusalem**
	8: 1	against the church in **Jerusalem**
	8:14	when the apostles at **Jerusalem**
	8:25	they returned to **Jerusalem**
	11:27	came down from **Jerusalem**
	13:13	them and returned to **Jerusalem**
	16: 4	elders who were in **Jerusalem**

	19:21	then to go on to **Jerusalem**
	20:16	was eager to be in **Jerusalem**
	21: 4	Paul not to go on to **Jerusalem**
	21:15	started to go up to **Jerusalem**
	21:17	When we arrived in **Jerusalem**
	25: 1	up from Caesarea to **Jerusalem**
	25: 7	had gone down from **Jerusalem**
	25: 9	you wish to go up to **Jerusalem**
	25:15	When I was in **Jerusalem**
	25:20	he wished to go to **Jerusalem**
	25:24	both in **Jerusalem** and here
	26: 4	own people and in **Jerusalem**
	26:10	is what I did in **Jerusalem**
	26:20	then in **Jerusalem**
	28:17	I was arrested in **Jerusalem**
Ga	1:17	nor did I go up to **Jerusalem**
	1:18	I did go up to **Jerusalem**
	2: 1	I went up again to **Jerusalem**

2415　GO2　AG373　LN122　B2:324　K7:292
ιεροσολυμιτης, JERUSALEMITE

Mk	1: 5	all the **people of Jerusalem**
Jn	7:25	of the **people of Jerusalem** were

2416　GO1　AG373　LN122　B2:232　K3:255
ἱεροσυλεω, I ROB TEMPLE

Ro	2:22	do you **rob temples**

2417　GO1　AG373　LN122　B2:235　K3:256
R2411,4813
ἱεροσυλος, TEMPLE ROBBER

Ac	19:37	who are neither **temple robbers**

2418　GO1　AG373　LN123　B2:232
ἱερουργεω, I SERVE AS PRIEST

Ro	15:16	in the **priestly service** of the

2419　GO77　AG373　LN123　B2:324　K7:292
ἱερουσαλημ, JERUSALEM

Mt	23:37	**Jerusalem**, Jerusalem, the city
	23:37	Jerusalem, **Jerusalem**, the city
Lk	2:25	there was a man in **Jerusalem**
	2:38	for the redemption of **Jerusalem**
	2:41	his parents went to **Jerusalem**
	2:43	stayed behind in **Jerusalem**
	2:45	they returned to **Jerusalem**
	4: 9	devil took him to **Jerusalem**
	5:17	and Judea and from **Jerusalem**
	6:17	from all Judea, **Jerusalem**
	9:31	to accomplish at **Jerusalem**

	9:51	his face to go to **Jerusalem**
	9:53	was set toward **Jerusalem**
	10:30	was going down from **Jerusalem**
	13: 4	the others living in **Jerusalem**
	13:33	be killed outside of **Jerusalem**
	13:34	**Jerusalem,** Jerusalem, the city
	13:34	Jerusalem, **Jerusalem,** the city
	17:11	On the way to **Jerusalem** Jesus
	18:31	we are going up to **Jerusalem**
	19:11	because he was near **Jerusalem**
	21:20	When you see **Jerusalem**
	21:24	**Jerusalem** will be trampled on
	23:28	Daughters of **Jerusalem,** do not
	24:13	seven miles from **Jerusalem**
	24:18	only stranger in **Jerusalem** who
	24:33	up and returned to **Jerusalem**
	24:47	beginning from **Jerusalem**
	24:52	returned to **Jerusalem**
Ac	1: 8	be my witnesses in **Jerusalem**
	1:12	they returned to **Jerusalem**
	1:12	which is near **Jerusalem**
	1:19	the residents of **Jerusalem**
	2: 5	heaven living in **Jerusalem**
	2:14	all who live in **Jerusalem**
	4: 5	scribes assembled in **Jerusalem**
	4:16	all who live in **Jerusalem**
	5:16	the towns around **Jerusalem**
	5:28	here you have filled **Jerusalem**
	6: 7	increased greatly in **Jerusalem**
	8:26	that goes down from **Jerusalem**
	8:27	come to **Jerusalem** to worship
	9: 2	bring them bound to **Jerusalem**
	9:13	to your saints in **Jerusalem**
	9:21	who made havoc in **Jerusalem**
	9:26	When he had come to **Jerusalem**
	9:28	out among them in **Jerusalem**
	10:39	in Judea and in **Jerusalem**
	11: 2	Peter went up to **Jerusalem**
	11:22	of the church in **Jerusalem**
	12:25	Saul returned to **Jerusalem**
	13:27	the residents of **Jerusalem**
	13:31	him from Galilee to **Jerusalem**
	15: 2	up to **Jerusalem** to discuss
	15: 4	When they came to **Jerusalem**
	20:22	on my way to **Jerusalem**
	21:11	Jews in **Jerusalem** will bind
	21:12	him not to go up to **Jerusalem**
	21:13	but even to die in **Jerusalem**
	21:31	all **Jerusalem** was in an uproar

	22: 5	bring them back to **Jerusalem**
	22:17	I had returned to **Jerusalem**
	22:18	get out of **Jerusalem** quickly
	23:11	testified for me in **Jerusalem**
	24:11	went up to worship in **Jerusalem**
	25: 3	him transferred to **Jerusalem**
Ro	15:19	from **Jerusalem** and as far
	15:25	I am going to **Jerusalem**
	15:26	among the saints at **Jerusalem**
	15:31	that my ministry to **Jerusalem**
1C	16: 3	take your gift to **Jerusalem**
Ga	4:25	to the present **Jerusalem**
	4:26	corresponds to the **Jerusalem**
He	12:22	the heavenly **Jerusalem**
Re	21: 2	the new **Jerusalem** that comes
	21: 2	holy city, the new **Jerusalem**
	21:10	**Jerusalem** coming down out of

2420   GO3 AG373 LN123 B2:232 K3:247 R2413
ἱερωσυνη, PRIESTHOOD

He	7:11	the levitical **priesthood**
	7:12	is a change in the **priesthood**
	7:24	but he holds his **priesthood**

2421   GO5 AG373 LN123
ιεσσαι, JESSE

Mt	1: 5	and Obed the father of **Jesse**
	1: 6	**Jesse** the father of King David
Lk	3:32	son of **Jesse**
Ac	13:22	David, son of **Jesse**
Ro	15:12	The root of **Jesse** shall come

2422   GO1 AG373 LN123
ιεφθαε, JEPHTHA

He	11:32	Barak, Samson, **Jephthah**

2423   GO2 AG373 LN123
ιεχονιας, JECONIAS (JECHONIAH)

Mt	1:11	Josiah the father of **Jechoniah**
	1:12	**Jechoniah** was the father

2424   GO917 AG373 LN123 B2:330 K3:284
ιησους, JESUS

Mt	1: 1	of the genealogy of **Jesus**
	1:16	Mary, of whom **Jesus** was born
	1:18	birth of **Jesus** the Messiah
	1:21	you are to name him **Jesus**
	1:25	and he named him **Jesus**
	2: 1	**Jesus** was born in Bethlehem
	3:13	Then **Jesus** came from Galilee

3:15	But **Jesus** answered him	15:32	Then **Jesus** called his disciples
3:16	when **Jesus** had been baptized	15:34	**Jesus** asked them
4: 1	Then **Jesus** was led up by the	16: 6	**Jesus** said to them
4: 7	**Jesus** said to him	16: 8	**Jesus** said, "You of little
4:10	**Jesus** said to him	16:13	Now when **Jesus** came into the
4:17	**Jesus** began to proclaim	16:17	And **Jesus** answered him
7:28	Now when **Jesus** had finished	16:21	**Jesus** began to show his
8: 4	Then **Jesus** said to him	16:24	**Jesus** told his disciples
8:10	When **Jesus** heard him	17: 1	**Jesus** took with him Peter
8:13	to the centurion **Jesus** said	17: 4	Then Peter said to **Jesus**
8:14	**Jesus** entered Peter's house	17: 7	But **Jesus** came and touched
8:18	when **Jesus** saw great crowds	17: 8	no one except **Jesus** himself
8:20	And **Jesus** said to him	17: 9	**Jesus** ordered them
8:22	But **Jesus** said to him	17:17	**Jesus** answered
8:34	came out to meet **Jesus**	17:18	And **Jesus** rebuked the demon
9: 2	When **Jesus** saw their faith	17:19	disciples came to **Jesus**
9: 4	But **Jesus,** perceiving their	17:22	**Jesus** said to them
9: 9	As **Jesus** was walking along	17:25	**Jesus** spoke of it first
9:10	came and were sitting with **him**	17:26	**Jesus** said to him
9:15	And **Jesus** said to them	18: 1	the disciples came to **Jesus**
9:19	And **Jesus** got up and followed	18:22	**Jesus** said to him
9:22	**Jesus** turned, and seeing her	19: 1	When **Jesus** had finished saying
9:23	When **Jesus** came to the leader's	19:14	but **Jesus** said
9:27	As **Jesus** went on from there	19:18	And **Jesus** said
9:28	and **Jesus** said to them	19:21	**Jesus** said to him,
9:30	Then **Jesus** sternly ordered	19:23	**Jesus** said to his disciples
9:35	Then **Jesus** went about all the	19:26	But **Jesus** looked at them
10: 5	These twelve **Jesus** sent out	19:28	**Jesus** said to them
11: 1	Now when **Jesus** had finished	20:17	While **Jesus** was going up to
11: 4	**Jesus** answered them	20:22	But **Jesus** answered
11: 7	**Jesus** began to speak to the	20:25	**Jesus** called them to him
11:25	At that time **Jesus** said	20:30	that **Jesus** was passing by
12: 1	**Jesus** went through the	20:32	**Jesus** stood still and called
12:15	**Jesus** became aware of this	20:34	**Jesus** touched their eyes
13: 1	That same day **Jesus** went out	21: 1	**Jesus** sent two disciples
13:34	**Jesus** told the crowds all	21: 6	did as **Jesus** had directed
13:53	When **Jesus** had finished these	21:11	This is the prophet **Jesus**
13:57	But **Jesus** said to them	21:12	Then **Jesus** entered the temple
14: 1	heard reports about **Jesus**	21:16	**Jesus** said to them
14:12	then they went and told **Jesus**	21:21	**Jesus** answered them
14:13	Now when **Jesus** heard this	21:24	**Jesus** said to them
14:16	**Jesus** said to them	21:27	So they answered **Jesus**
14:27	But immediately **Jesus** spoke	21:31	**Jesus** said to them
14:29	and came toward **Jesus**	21:42	**Jesus** said to them,
14:31	**Jesus** immediately reached out	22: 1	Once more **Jesus** spoke to them
15: 1	came to **Jesus** from Jerusalem	22:29	**Jesus** answered them
15:21	**Jesus** left that place and went	22:41	**Jesus** asked them this question
15:28	Then **Jesus** answered her	23: 1	Then **Jesus** said to the crowds
15:29	**Jesus** had left that place	24: 1	**Jesus** came out of the temple

24: 4	**Jesus** answered them	1:17	And **Jesus** said to them
26: 1	When **Jesus** had finished saying	1:24	**Jesus** of Nazareth
26: 4	they conspired to arrest **Jesus**	1:25	But **Jesus** rebuked him
26: 6	Now while **Jesus** was at Bethany	2: 5	When **Jesus** saw their faith
26:10	But **Jesus,** aware of this, said	2: 8	At once **Jesus** perceived
26:17	the disciples came to **Jesus**	2:15	sitting with **Jesus** and his
26:19	did as **Jesus** had directed them	2:17	When **Jesus** heard this
26:26	**Jesus** took a loaf of bread	2:19	**Jesus** said to them
26:31	Then **Jesus** said to them	3: 7	**Jesus** departed with his
26:34	**Jesus** said to him	5: 6	he saw **Jesus** from a distance
26:36	Then **Jesus** went with them	5: 7	**Jesus,** Son of the Most High
26:49	At once he came up to **Jesus**	5:15	They came to **Jesus** and saw
26:50	**Jesus** said to him, "Friend,	5:20	how much **Jesus** had done for
26:50	hands on **Jesus** and arrested him	5:21	When **Jesus** had crossed again
26:51	one of those with **Jesus** put	5:27	She had heard about **Jesus**
26:52	Then **Jesus** said to him	5:30	**Jesus** turned about in the crowd
26:55	At that hour **Jesus** said	5:36	**Jesus** said to the leader
26:57	Those who had arrested **Jesus**	6: 4	Then **Jesus** said to them
26:59	false testimony against **Jesus**	6:30	apostles gathered around **Jesus**
26:63	But **Jesus** was silent.	8:27	**Jesus** went on with his
26:64	**Jesus** said to him	9: 2	**Jesus** took with him Peter
26:69	were with **Jesus** the Galilean	9: 4	who were talking with **Jesus**
26:71	man was with **Jesus** of Nazareth	9: 5	Then Peter said to **Jesus**
26:75	remembered what **Jesus** had said	9: 8	them any more, but only **Jesus**
27: 1	against **Jesus** in order to bring	9:23	**Jesus** said to him
27:11	**Jesus** stood before the governor	9:25	When **Jesus** saw that a crowd
27:11	**Jesus** said, "You say so."	9:27	But **Jesus** took him by the hand
27:16	called **Jesus** Barabbas	9:39	But **Jesus** said
27:17	**Jesus** Barabbas or Jesus	10: 5	But **Jesus** said to them
27:17	**Jesus** who is called	10:14	But when **Jesus** saw this
27:20	and to have **Jesus** killed	10:18	**Jesus** said to him
27:22	should I do with **Jesus**	10:21	**Jesus,** looking at him, loved
27:26	and after flogging **Jesus**	10:23	Then **Jesus** looked around
27:27	took **Jesus** into the governor's	10:24	But **Jesus** said to them again
27:37	This is **Jesus,** the King	10:27	**Jesus** looked at them and said
27:46	**Jesus** cried with a loud voice	10:29	**Jesus** said, "Truly I tell you
27:50	Then **Jesus** cried again	10:32	**Jesus** was walking ahead of
27:54	were keeping watch over **Jesus**	10:38	But **Jesus** said to them
27:55	they had followed **Jesus**	10:39	Then **Jesus** said to them
27:57	was also a disciple of **Jesus**	10:42	So **Jesus** called them and said
27:58	asked for the body of **Jesus**	10:47	that it was **Jesus** of Nazareth
28: 5	that you are looking for **Jesus**	10:47	**Jesus,** Son of David
28: 9	**Jesus** met them and said	10:49	**Jesus** stood still and said
28:10	Then **Jesus** said to them	10:50	he sprang up and came to **Jesus**
28:16	to which **Jesus** had directed	10:51	Then **Jesus** said to him
28:18	**Jesus** came and said to them	10:52	**Jesus** said to him
Mk 1: 1	the good news of **Jesus** Christ	11: 6	told them what **Jesus** had said
1: 9	**Jesus** came from Nazareth	11: 7	they brought the colt to **Jesus**
1:14	**Jesus** came to Galilee	11:22	**Jesus** answered them

11:29	**Jesus** said to them	5:31	**Jesus** answered
11:33	So they answered **Jesus**	5:34	**Jesus** said to them
11:33	And **Jesus** said to them	6: 3	**Jesus** answered
12:17	**Jesus** said to them	6: 9	Then **Jesus** said to them
12:24	**Jesus** said to them	6:11	what they might do to **Jesus**
12:29	**Jesus** answered	7: 3	When he heard about **Jesus**
12:34	**Jesus** saw that he answered	7: 4	When they came to **Jesus**
12:35	While **Jesus** was teaching	7: 6	And **Jesus** went with them
13: 2	Then **Jesus** asked him	7: 9	When **Jesus** heard this he was
13: 5	Then **Jesus** began to say to	7:40	**Jesus** spoke up and said to him
14: 6	But **Jesus** said	8:28	When he saw **Jesus,** he fell down
14:18	and were eating, **Jesus** said	8:28	you to do with me, **Jesus**
14:27	And **Jesus** said to them	8:30	**Jesus** then asked him
14:30	**Jesus** said to him	8:35	and when they came to **Jesus**
14:48	Then **Jesus** said to them	8:35	sitting at the feet of **Jesus**
14:53	They took **Jesus** to the high	8:39	how much **Jesus** had done for
14:55	against **Jesus** to put him to	8:40	Now when **Jesus** returned
14:60	up before them and asked **Jesus**	8:41	He fell at **Jesus'** feet
14:62	**Jesus** said, "I am; and	8:45	Then **Jesus** asked
14:67	You also were with **Jesus**	8:46	But **Jesus** said
14:72	remembered that **Jesus** had said	8:50	When **Jesus** heard this
15: 1	They bound **Jesus,** led him away	9:33	Peter said to **Jesus**
15: 5	But **Jesus** made no further reply	9:36	**Jesus** was found alone
15:15	and after flogging **Jesus**	9:41	**Jesus** answered
15:34	At three o'clock **Jesus** cried	9:42	But **Jesus** rebuked the unclean
15:37	Then **Jesus** gave a loud cry	9:47	But **Jesus,** aware of their inner
15:43	asked for the body of **Jesus**	9:50	But **Jesus** said to him
16: 6	looking for **Jesus** of Nazareth	9:58	And **Jesus** said to him
16:19	So then the Lord **Jesus**	9:62	**Jesus** said to him
Lk 1:31	and you will name him **Jesus**	10:29	justify himself, he asked **Jesus**
2:21	and he was called **Jesus**	10:30	**Jesus** replied
2:27	brought in the child **Jesus**	10:37	**Jesus** said to him
2:43	the boy **Jesus** stayed behind	13:12	When **Jesus** saw her
2:52	And **Jesus** increased in wisdom	13:14	**Jesus** had cured on the sabbath
3:21	**Jesus** also had been baptized	14: 3	And **Jesus** asked the lawyers
3:23	**Jesus** was about thirty years	17:13	**Jesus,** Master, have mercy on us
3:29	son of **Joshua,** son of Eliezer	17:17	Then **Jesus** asked
4: 1	**Jesus,** full of the Holy Spirit	18:16	But **Jesus** called for them
4: 4	**Jesus** answered him	18:19	**Jesus** said to him
4: 8	**Jesus** answered him	18:22	When **Jesus** heard
4:12	**Jesus** answered him	18:24	**Jesus** looked at him and said
4:14	Then **Jesus,** filled with the	18:37	**Jesus** of Nazareth is passing by
4:34	do with us, **Jesus** of Nazareth	18:38	**Jesus,** Son of David, have mercy
4:35	But **Jesus** rebuked him	18:40	**Jesus** stood still and ordered
5: 8	he fell down at **Jesus'** knees	18:42	**Jesus** said to him
5:10	Then **Jesus** said to Simon	19: 3	trying to see who **Jesus** was
5:12	When he saw **Jesus,** he bowed	19: 5	When **Jesus** came to the place
5:19	of the crowd in front of **Jesus**	19: 9	Then **Jesus** said to him
5:22	When **Jesus** perceived their	19:35	Then they brought it to **Jesus**

19:35	the colt, they set **Jesus** on it		4: 7	**Jesus** said to her,
20: 8	Then **Jesus** said to them		4:10	**Jesus** answered her
20:34	**Jesus** said to them		4:13	**Jesus** said to her
22:47	He approached **Jesus** to kiss him		4:17	**Jesus** said to her
22:48	but **Jesus** said to him		4:21	**Jesus** said to her
22:51	But **Jesus** said		4:26	**Jesus** said to her
22:52	Then **Jesus** said to the chief		4:34	**Jesus** said to them
23: 8	When Herod saw **Jesus**		4:44	for **Jesus** himself had testified
23:20	wanting to release **Jesus**		4:47	that **Jesus** had come from Judea
23:25	he handed **Jesus** over as they		4:48	Then **Jesus** said to him
23:26	made him carry it behind **Jesus**		4:50	**Jesus** said to him
23:28	But **Jesus** turned to them		4:50	word that **Jesus** spoke to him
23:34	Then **Jesus** said		4:53	hour when **Jesus** had said to him
23:42	**Jesus,** remember me when you		4:54	the second sign that **Jesus** did
23:46	Then **Jesus,** crying with a loud		5: 1	**Jesus** went up to Jerusalem
23:52	asked for the body of **Jesus**		5: 6	When **Jesus** saw him lying there
24: 3	they did not find the **body**		5: 8	**Jesus** said to him
24:15	**Jesus** himself came near		5:13	for **Jesus** had disappeared
24:19	things about **Jesus** of Nazareth		5:14	Later **Jesus** found him in the
Jn 1:17	truth came through **Jesus** Christ		5:15	it was **Jesus** who had made him
1:29	he saw **Jesus** coming toward him		5:16	Jews started persecuting **Jesus**
1:36	as he watched **Jesus** walk by		5:17	But **Jesus** answered them
1:37	and they followed **Jesus**		5:19	**Jesus** said to them
1:38	When **Jesus** turned and saw them		6: 1	After this **Jesus** went to the
1:42	He brought Simon to **Jesus**		6: 3	**Jesus** went up the mountain
1:42	Jesus, **who** looked at him		6: 5	**Jesus** said to Philip
1:43	**Jesus** decided to go to Galilee		6:10	**Jesus** said
1:45	**Jesus** son of Joseph from		6:11	Then **Jesus** took the loaves
1:47	When **Jesus** saw Nathanael		6:15	When **Jesus** realized that they
1:48	**Jesus** answered		6:17	**Jesus** had not yet come to them
1:50	**Jesus** answered		6:19	they saw **Jesus** walking on the
2: 1	the mother of **Jesus** was there		6:22	that **Jesus** had not got into
2: 2	**Jesus** and his disciples had		6:24	neither **Jesus** nor his disciples
2: 3	mother of **Jesus** said to him		6:24	to Capernaum looking for **Jesus**
2: 4	And **Jesus** said to her		6:26	**Jesus** answered them
2: 7	**Jesus** said to them		6:29	**Jesus** answered them
2:11	**Jesus** did this, the first of		6:32	Then **Jesus** said to them
2:13	**Jesus** went up to Jerusalem		6:35	**Jesus** said to them
2:19	**Jesus** answered them		6:42	Is not this **Jesus,** the son of
2:22	the word that **Jesus** had spoken		6:43	**Jesus** answered them
2:24	But **Jesus** on his part would		6:53	So **Jesus** said to them
3: 3	**Jesus** answered him		6:61	**Jesus,** being aware that his
3: 5	**Jesus** answered		6:64	For **Jesus** knew from the first
3:10	**Jesus** answered him		6:67	So **Jesus** asked the twelve
3:22	**Jesus** and his disciples went		6:70	**Jesus** answered them
4: 1	**Jesus** learned that the		7: 1	After this **Jesus** went about
4: 1	**Jesus** is making and baptizing		7: 6	**Jesus** said to them
4: 2	it was not **Jesus** himself but		7:14	**Jesus** went up into the temple
4: 6	**Jesus,** tired out by his journey		7:16	Then **Jesus** answered them

7:21	**Jesus** answered them	11:38	Then **Jesus**
7:28	Then **Jesus** cried out as he was	11:39	**Jesus** said
7:33	**Jesus** then said	11:40	**Jesus** said to her
7:37	while **Jesus** was standing there	11:41	**Jesus** looked upward and said
7:39	**Jesus** was not yet glorified	11:44	**Jesus** said to them
8: 1	**Jesus** went to the Mount	11:46	and told them what **he** had done
8: 6	**Jesus** bent down and wrote with	11:51	that **Jesus** was about to die
8:10	**Jesus** straightened up and said	11:54	**Jesus** therefore no longer
8:11	And **Jesus** said	11:56	They were looking for **Jesus**
8:12	Again **Jesus** spoke to them	12: 1	**Jesus** came to Bethany,
8:14	**Jesus** answered	12: 1	**he** had raised from the dead.
8:19	**Jesus** answered	12: 3	pure nard, anointed **Jesus'** feet
8:25	**Jesus** said to them	12: 7	**Jesus** said
8:28	So **Jesus** said	12: 9	not only because of **Jesus**
8:31	Then **Jesus** said to the Jews	12:11	and were believing in **Jesus**
8:34	**Jesus** answered them	12:12	**Jesus** was coming to Jerusalem
8:39	**Jesus** said to them	12:14	**Jesus** found a young donkey
8:42	**Jesus** said to them	12:16	but when **Jesus** was glorified
8:49	**Jesus** answered	12:21	Sir, we wish to see **Jesus.**
8:54	**Jesus** answered	12:22	Philip went and told **Jesus**
8:58	**Jesus** said to them	12:23	**Jesus** answered them
8:59	but **Jesus** hid himself and went	12:30	**Jesus** answered
9: 3	**Jesus** answered	12:35	**Jesus** said to them
9:11	The man called **Jesus** made mud	12:36	After **Jesus** had said this
9:14	when **Jesus** made the mud	12:44	Then **Jesus** cried aloud
9:35	**Jesus** heard that they had	13: 1	**Jesus** knew that his hour had
9:37	**Jesus** said to him	13: 7	**Jesus** answered
9:39	**Jesus** said	13: 8	**Jesus** answered
9:41	**Jesus** said to them	13:10	**Jesus** said to him
10: 6	**Jesus** used this figure of	13:21	**Jesus** was troubled in spirit
10: 7	So again **Jesus** said to them	13:23	the one whom **Jesus** loved
10:23	**Jesus** was walking in the temple	13:23	was reclining next to **him**
10:25	**Jesus** answered	13:25	while reclining next to **Jesus**
10:32	**Jesus** replied	13:26	**Jesus** answered
10:34	**Jesus** answered	13:27	**Jesus** said to him
11: 4	But when **Jesus** heard it	13:29	**Jesus** was telling him
11: 5	though **Jesus** loved Martha	13:31	he had gone out, **Jesus** said
11: 9	**Jesus** answered	13:36	**Jesus** answered
11:13	**Jesus**, however, had been	13:38	**Jesus** answered
11:14	Then **Jesus** told them plainly	14: 6	**Jesus** said to him
11:17	When **Jesus** arrived, he found	14: 9	**Jesus** said to him
11:20	When Martha heard that **Jesus**	14:23	**Jesus** answered him
11:21	Martha said to **Jesus**	16:19	**Jesus** knew that they wanted
11:23	**Jesus** said to her	16:31	**Jesus** answered them
11:25	**Jesus** said to her	17: 1	**Jesus** had spoken these words
11:30	Now **Jesus** had not yet come	17: 3	**Jesus** Christ whom you have sent
11:32	When Mary came where **Jesus** was	18: 1	**Jesus** had spoken these words
11:33	When **Jesus** saw her weeping	18: 2	because **Jesus** often met there
11:35	**Jesus** began to weep.	18: 4	Then **Jesus,** knowing all that

18: 5	**Jesus** of Nazareth.		20:30	Now **Jesus** did many other signs
18: 7	**Jesus** of Nazareth.		20:31	that **Jesus** is the Messiah
18: 8	**Jesus** answered		21: 1	After these things **Jesus** showed
18:11	**Jesus** said to Peter		21: 4	**Jesus** stood on the beach
18:12	Jewish police arrested **Jesus**		21: 4	did not know that it was **Jesus**
18:15	another disciple followed **Jesus**		21: 5	**Jesus** said to them
18:15	he went with **Jesus** into the		21: 7	That disciple whom **Jesus** loved
18:19	high priest questioned **Jesus**		21:10	**Jesus** said to them
18:20	**Jesus** answered		21:12	**Jesus** said to them
18:22	struck **Jesus** on the face		21:13	**Jesus** came and took the bread
18:23	**Jesus** answered		21:14	**Jesus** appeared to the disciples
18:28	they took **Jesus** from Caiaphas		21:15	**Jesus** said to Simon Peter
18:32	to fulfill what **Jesus** had said		21:17	**Jesus** said to him
18:33	summoned **Jesus,** and asked him		21:20	the disciple whom **Jesus** loved
18:34	**Jesus** answered		21:21	saw him, he said to **Jesus**
18:36	**Jesus** answered		21:22	**Jesus** said to him
18:37	**Jesus** answered		21:23	Yet **Jesus** did not say to him
19: 1	Then Pilate took **Jesus**		21:25	other things that **Jesus** did
19: 5	So **Jesus** came out, wearing	Ac	1: 1	about all that **Jesus** did
19: 9	again and asked **Jesus**		1:11	**Jesus,** who has been taken up
19: 9	But **Jesus** gave him no answer		1:14	Mary the mother of **Jesus**
19:11	**Jesus** answered him		1:16	for those who arrested **Jesus**
19:13	he brought **Jesus** outside		1:21	**Jesus** went in and out among us
19:16	So they took **Jesus**		2:22	**Jesus** of Nazareth, a man
19:18	with **Jesus** between them		2:32	This **Jesus** God raised up
19:19	**Jesus** of Nazareth, the King		2:36	this **Jesus** whom you crucified
19:20	place where **Jesus** was crucified		2:38	in the name of **Jesus** Christ
19:23	soldiers had crucified **Jesus**		3: 6	in the name of **Jesus** Christ
19:25	near the cross of **Jesus** were		3:13	has glorified his servant **Jesus**
19:26	When **Jesus** saw his mother		3:20	for you, that is, **Jesus**
19:28	**Jesus** knew that all was now		4: 2	and proclaiming that in **Jesus**
19:30	**Jesus** had received the wine		4:10	by the name of **Jesus** Christ
19:33	But when they came to **Jesus**		4:13	them as companions of **Jesus**
19:38	who was a disciple of **Jesus**		4:18	at all in the name of **Jesus**
19:38	take away the body of **Jesus**		4:27	your holy servant **Jesus**
19:40	They took the body of **Jesus**		4:30	of your holy servant **Jesus**
19:42	they laid **Jesus** there		4:33	resurrection of the Lord **Jesus**
20: 2	the one whom **Jesus** loved		5:30	our ancestors raised up **Jesus**
20:12	body of **Jesus** had been lying		5:40	to speak in the name of **Jesus**
20:14	saw **Jesus** standing there		5:42	proclaim **Jesus** as the Messiah
20:14	not know that it was **Jesus**		6:14	that this **Jesus** of Nazareth
20:15	**Jesus** said to her		7:45	brought it in with **Joshua**
20:16	**Jesus** said to her, "Mary!"		7:55	saw the glory of God and **Jesus**
20:17	**Jesus** said to her		7:59	Lord **Jesus,** receive my spirit
20:19	**Jesus** came and stood among		8:12	and the name of **Jesus** Christ
20:21	**Jesus** said to them again		8:16	in the name of the Lord **Jesus**
20:24	not with them when **Jesus** came		8:35	him the good news about **Jesus**
20:26	**Jesus** came and stood among them		9: 5	I am **Jesus,** whom you are
20:29	**Jesus** said to him		9:17	the Lord **Jesus,** who appeared

	9:20	he began to proclaim **Jesus**		5:11	in God through our Lord **Jesus**
	9:27	boldly in the name of **Jesus**		5:15	grace of the one man, **Jesus**
	9:34	**Jesus** Christ heals you		5:17	through the one man, **Jesus**
	10:36	preaching peace by **Jesus**		5:21	to eternal life through **Jesus**
	10:38	how God anointed **Jesus** of		6: 3	baptized into Christ **Jesus**
	10:48	in the name of **Jesus** Christ		6:11	alive to God in Christ **Jesus**
	11:17	believed in the Lord **Jesus**		6:23	is eternal life in Christ **Jesus**
	11:20	proclaiming the Lord **Jesus**		7:25	Thanks be to God through **Jesus**
	13:23	to Israel a Savior, **Jesus**		8: 1	those who are in Christ **Jesus**
	13:33	children, by raising **Jesus**		8: 2	Spirit of life in Christ **Jesus**
	15:11	the grace of the Lord **Jesus**		8:11	Spirit of him who raised **Jesus**
	15:26	for the sake of our Lord **Jesus**		8:34	It is Christ **Jesus,** who died
	16: 7	but the Spirit of **Jesus**		8:39	love of God in Christ **Jesus**
	16:18	in the name of **Jesus** Christ		10: 9	with your lips that **Jesus**
	16:31	Believe on the Lord **Jesus**		13:14	put on the Lord **Jesus** Christ
	17: 3	the Messiah, **Jesus** whom I am		14:14	am persuaded in the Lord **Jesus**
	17: 7	is another king named **Jesus**		15: 5	in accordance with Christ **Jesus**
	17:18	the good news about **Jesus**		15: 6	Father of our Lord **Jesus** Christ
	18: 5	that the Messiah was **Jesus**		15:16	be a minister of Christ **Jesus**
	18:25	the things concerning **Jesus**		15:17	In Christ **Jesus,** then, I have
	18:28	that the Messiah is **Jesus**		15:30	by our Lord **Jesus** Christ
	19: 4	after him, that is, in **Jesus**		16: 3	work with me in Christ **Jesus**
	19: 5	in the name of the Lord **Jesus.**		16:20	The grace of our Lord **Jesus**
	19:13	name of the Lord **Jesus** over		16:25	the proclamation of **Jesus**
	19:13	**Jesus** whom Paul proclaims.		16:27	through **Jesus** Christ, to whom
	19:15	**Jesus** I know, and Paul I know	1C	1: 1	an apostle of Christ **Jesus**
	19:17	the name of the Lord **Jesus** was		1: 2	are sanctified in Christ **Jesus**
	20:21	faith toward our Lord **Jesus**		1: 2	the name of our Lord **Jesus**
	20:24	I received from the Lord **Jesus**		1: 3	our Father and the Lord **Jesus**
	20:35	the words of the Lord **Jesus**		1: 4	been given you in Christ **Jesus**
	21:13	for the name of the Lord **Jesus**		1: 7	the revealing of our Lord **Jesus**
	22: 8	I am **Jesus** of Nazareth whom		1: 8	the day of our Lord **Jesus**
	24:24	faith in Christ **Jesus**		1: 9	his Son, **Jesus** Christ our Lord
	25:19	and about a certain **Jesus**		1:10	by the name of our Lord **Jesus**
	26: 9	the name of **Jesus** of Nazareth		1:30	of your life in Christ **Jesus**
	26:15	I am **Jesus** whom you are		2: 2	nothing among you except **Jesus**
	28:23	to convince them about **Jesus**		3:11	that foundation is **Jesus** Christ
	28:31	teaching about the Lord **Jesus**		4:15	in Christ **Jesus** I became your
Ro	1: 1	Paul, a servant of **Jesus** Christ		4:17	of my ways in Christ **Jesus**
	1: 4	from the dead, **Jesus** Christ		5: 4	in the name of the Lord **Jesus**
	1: 6	called to belong to **Jesus**		5: 4	the power of our Lord **Jesus**
	1: 7	our Father and the Lord **Jesus**		6:11	in the name of the Lord **Jesus**
	1: 8	I thank my God through **Jesus**		8: 6	and one Lord, **Jesus** Christ
	2:16	God, through **Jesus** Christ		9: 1	Have I not seen **Jesus** our Lord
	3:22	through faith in **Jesus** Christ		11:23	the Lord **Jesus** on the night
	3:24	that is in Christ **Jesus**		12: 3	Let **Jesus** be cursed
	3:26	the one who has faith in **Jesus**		12: 3	no one can say "**Jesus** is Lord"
	4:24	in him who raised **Jesus**		15:31	make in Christ **Jesus** our Lord
	5: 1	with God through our Lord **Jesus**		15:57	through our Lord **Jesus** Christ

16:23	The grace of the Lord **Jesus**
16:24	all of you in Christ **Jesus**
2C 1: 1	an apostle of Christ **Jesus**
1: 2	our Father and the Lord **Jesus**
1: 3	Father of our Lord **Jesus** Christ
1:14	on the day of the Lord **Jesus**
1:19	For the Son of God, **Jesus**
4: 5	proclaim **Jesus** Christ as Lord
4: 5	as your slaves for **Jesus'** sake
4: 6	in the face of **Jesus** Christ
4:10	in the body the death of **Jesus**
4:10	so that the life of **Jesus**
4:11	given up to death for **Jesus**
4:11	the life of **Jesus** may be made
4:14	who raised the Lord **Jesus**
4:14	will raise us also with **Jesus**
8: 9	generous act of our Lord **Jesus**
11: 4	proclaims another **Jesus** than
11:31	Father of the Lord **Jesus**
13: 5	Do you not realize that **Jesus**
13:13	grace of the Lord **Jesus** Christ
Ga 1: 1	but through **Jesus** Christ and
1: 3	and the Lord **Jesus** Christ
1:12	through a revelation of **Jesus**
2: 4	we have in Christ **Jesus**
2:16	through faith in **Jesus** Christ
2:16	to believe in Christ **Jesus**
3: 1	before your eyes that **Jesus**
3:14	in order that in Christ **Jesus**
3:22	through faith in **Jesus** Christ
3:26	for in Christ **Jesus** you are
3:28	of you are one in Christ **Jesus**
4:14	angel of God, as Christ **Jesus**
5: 6	For in Christ **Jesus** neither
5:24	who belong to Christ **Jesus**
6:14	cross of our Lord **Jesus** Christ
6:17	I carry the marks of **Jesus**
6:18	May the grace of our Lord **Jesus**
Ep 1: 1	an apostle of Christ **Jesus**
1: 1	are faithful in Christ **Jesus**
1: 2	our Father and the Lord **Jesus**
1: 3	and Father of our Lord **Jesus**
1: 5	of your faith in the Lord **Jesus**
1:17	that the God of our Lord **Jesus**
2: 6	heavenly places in Christ **Jesus**
2: 7	toward us in Christ **Jesus**
2:10	created in Christ **Jesus**
2:13	But now in Christ **Jesus**
2:20	with Christ **Jesus** himself

3: 1	am a prisoner for Christ **Jesus**
3: 6	in the promise in Christ **Jesus**
3:11	has carried out in Christ **Jesus**
3:21	the church and in Christ **Jesus**
4:21	in him, as truth is in **Jesus**
5:20	name of our Lord **Jesus** Christ
6:23	the Father and the Lord **Jesus**
6:24	undying love for our Lord **Jesus**
Ph 1: 1	servants of Christ **Jesus**
1: 1	the saints in Christ **Jesus**
1: 2	our Father and the Lord **Jesus**
1: 6	completion by the day of **Jesus**
1: 8	the compassion of Christ **Jesus**
1:11	that comes through **Jesus** Christ
1:19	help of the Spirit of **Jesus**
1:26	your boasting in Christ **Jesus**
2: 5	that was in Christ **Jesus**
2:10	so that at the name of **Jesus**
2:11	should confess that **Jesus**
2:19	I hope in the Lord **Jesus**
2:21	not those of **Jesus** Christ
3: 3	boast in Christ **Jesus**
3: 8	knowing Christ **Jesus** my Lord
3:12	**Jesus** has made me his own
3:14	call of God in Christ **Jesus**
3:20	a Savior, the Lord **Jesus** Christ
4: 7	your minds in Christ **Jesus**
4:19	in glory in Christ **Jesus**
4:21	every saint in Christ **Jesus**
4:23	The grace of the Lord **Jesus**
Co 1: 1	an apostle of Christ **Jesus**
1: 3	the Father of our Lord **Jesus**
1: 4	your faith in Christ **Jesus**
2: 6	have received Christ **Jesus**
3:17	in the name of the Lord **Jesus**
4:11	**Jesus** who is called Justus
4:12	a servant of Christ **Jesus**
1Th 1: 1	the Father and the Lord **Jesus**
1: 3	hope in our Lord **Jesus** Christ
1:10	**Jesus,** who rescues us from the
2:14	of God in Christ **Jesus** that are
2:15	who killed both the Lord **Jesus**
2:19	boasting before our Lord **Jesus**
3:11	our Lord **Jesus** direct our way
3:13	the coming of our Lord **Jesus**
4: 1	urge you in the Lord **Jesus**
4: 2	gave you through the Lord **Jesus**
4:14	since we believe that **Jesus**

	4:14	again, even so, through **Jesus**
	5: 9	through our Lord **Jesus** Christ
	5:18	will of God in Christ **Jesus**
	5:23	at the coming of our Lord **Jesus**
	5:28	The grace of our Lord **Jesus**
2Th	1: 1	our Father and the Lord **Jesus**
	1: 2	our Father and the Lord **Jesus**
	1: 7	the Lord **Jesus** is revealed
	1: 8	the gospel of our Lord **Jesus**
	1:12	the name of our Lord **Jesus**
	1:12	of our God and the Lord **Jesus**
	2: 1	the coming of our Lord **Jesus**
	2: 8	the Lord **Jesus** will destroy
	2:14	glory of our Lord **Jesus** Christ
	2:16	Now may our Lord **Jesus** Christ
	3: 6	the name of our Lord **Jesus**
	3:12	and exhort in the Lord **Jesus**
	3:18	grace of our Lord **Jesus** Christ
1Ti	1: 1	an apostle of Christ **Jesus**
	1: 1	and of Christ **Jesus** our hope
	1: 2	the Father and Christ **Jesus**
	1:12	I am grateful to Christ **Jesus**
	1:14	love that are in Christ **Jesus**
	1:15	Christ **Jesus** came into the
	1:16	**Jesus** Christ might display
	2: 5	Christ **Jesus,** himself human
	3:13	faith that is in Christ **Jesus**
	4: 6	a good servant of Christ **Jesus**
	5:21	of God and of Christ **Jesus**
	6: 3	words of our Lord **Jesus** Christ
	6:13	things, and of Christ **Jesus**
	6:14	manifestation of our Lord **Jesus**
2Ti	1: 1	an apostle of Christ **Jesus** by
	1: 1	life that is in Christ **Jesus**
	1: 2	the Father and Christ **Jesus**
	1: 9	given to us in Christ **Jesus**
	1:10	of our Savior Christ **Jesus**
	1:13	love that are in Christ **Jesus**
	2: 1	grace that is in Christ **Jesus**
	2: 3	good soldier of Christ **Jesus**
	2: 8	Remember **Jesus** Christ, raised
	2:10	that is in Christ **Jesus**
	3:12	Christ **Jesus** will be persecuted
	3:15	through faith in Christ **Jesus**
	4: 1	of God and of Christ **Jesus**
Ti	1: 1	an apostle of **Jesus** Christ
	1: 4	the Father and Christ **Jesus**
	2:13	God and Savior, **Jesus** Christ
	3: 6	**Jesus** Christ our Savior

Pm	1: 1	a prisoner of Christ **Jesus**
	1: 3	Father and the Lord **Jesus**
	1: 5	faith toward the Lord **Jesus**
	1: 9	as a prisoner of Christ **Jesus**
	1:23	prisoner in Christ **Jesus**
	1:25	The grace of the Lord **Jesus**
He	2: 9	but we do see **Jesus,** who for
	3: 1	that **Jesus,** the apostle and
	4: 8	For if **Joshua** had given them
	4:14	**Jesus,** the Son of God
	6:20	where **Jesus,** a forerunner
	7:22	accordingly **Jesus** has also
	10:10	of the body of **Jesus** Christ
	10:19	sanctuary by the blood of **Jesus**
	12: 2	looking to **Jesus** the pioneer
	12:24	and to **Jesus,** the mediator
	13: 8	**Jesus** Christ is the same
	13:12	**Jesus** also suffered outside
	13:20	from the dead our Lord **Jesus**
	13:21	through **Jesus** Christ, to whom
Ja	1: 1	of the Lord **Jesus** Christ
	2: 1	in our glorious Lord **Jesus**
1P	1: 1	Peter, an apostle of **Jesus**
	1: 2	to be obedient to **Jesus** Christ
	1: 3	Father of our Lord **Jesus** Christ
	1: 3	resurrection of **Jesus** Christ
	1: 7	when **Jesus** Christ is revealed
	1:13	that **Jesus** Christ will bring
	2: 5	to God through **Jesus** Christ
	3:21	resurrection of **Jesus** Christ
	4:11	things through **Jesus** Christ
	5:10	his eternal glory in **Christ**
2P	1: 1	servant and apostle of **Jesus**
	1: 1	of our God and Savior **Jesus**
	1: 2	of God and of **Jesus** our Lord
	1: 8	of our Lord **Jesus** Christ
	1:11	our Lord and Savior **Jesus**
	1:14	**Jesus** Christ has made clear
	1:16	coming of our Lord **Jesus**
	2:20	of our Lord and Savior **Jesus**
	3:18	of our Lord and Savior **Jesus**
1J	1: 3	with his Son **Jesus** Christ
	1: 7	and the blood of **Jesus** his Son
	2: 1	**Jesus** Christ the righteous
	2:22	one who denies that **Jesus**
	3:23	in the name of his Son **Jesus**
	4: 2	**Jesus** Christ has come in the
	4: 3	that does not confess **Jesus**
	4:15	that **Jesus** is the Son of God

5: 1	**Jesus** is the Christ has been
5: 5	**Jesus** is the Son of God
5: 6	water and blood, **Jesus** Christ
5:20	in his Son **Jesus** Christ
2J 1: 3	Father and from **Jesus** Christ
1: 7	who do not confess that **Jesus**
Ju 1: 1	a servant of **Jesus**
1: 1	kept safe for **Jesus** Christ
1: 4	Master and Lord, **Jesus** Christ
1:17	of our Lord **Jesus** Christ
1:21	the mercy of our Lord **Jesus**
1:25	through **Jesus** Christ our Lord
Re 1: 1	The revelation of **Jesus** Christ
1: 2	testimony of **Jesus** Christ
1: 5	and from **Jesus** Christ
1: 9	who share with you in **Jesus**
1: 9	and the testimony of **Jesus**
12:17	hold the testimony of **Jesus**
14:12	fast to the faith of **Jesus**
17: 6	of the witnesses to **Jesus**
19:10	hold the testimony of **Jesus**
19:10	For the testimony of **Jesus**
20: 4	for their testimony to **Jesus**
22:16	I, **Jesus,** who sent my angel
22:20	Amen. Come, Lord **Jesus!**
22:21	The grace of the Lord **Jesus**

2425   GO39 AG374 LN123 B3:728 K3:293
ἱκανος, ENOUGH

Mt	3:11	I am not **worthy** to carry his
	8: 8	I am not **worthy** to have you
	28:12	to give a **large sum** of money
Mk	1: 7	I am not **worthy** to stoop down
	10:46	and a **large** crowd were leaving
	15:15	wishing to **satisfy** the crowd
Lk	3:16	I am not **worthy** to untie
	7: 6	I am not **worthy** to have you
	7:12	with her was a **large** crowd
	8:27	For a **long** time he had worn no
	8:32	**large** herd of swine was feeding
	20: 9	another country for a **long** time
	22:38	He replied, "It is **enough.**"
	23: 8	to see him for a **long** time
	23: 9	questioned him at **some** length
Ac	8:11	because for a **long** time he had
	9:23	After **some** time had passed
	9:43	stayed in Joppa for **some** time
	11:24	**great** many people were brought

	11:26	taught a **great** many people
	12:12	where **many** had gathered
	14: 3	they remained for a **long** time
	14:21	had made **many** disciples
	17: 9	after they had taken **bail**
	18:18	there for a **considerable** time
	19:19	**number** of those who practiced
	19:26	**considerable** number of people
	20: 8	**many** lamps in the room upstairs
	20:11	he **continued** to converse with
	20:37	There was **much** weeping among
	22: 6	a **great** light from heaven
	27: 7	We sailed slowly for a **number**
	27: 9	Since **much** time had been lost
1C	11:30	and **some** have died
	15: 9	**unfit** to be called an apostle
2C	2: 6	by the majority is **enough**
	2:16	Who is **sufficient** for these
	3: 5	we are **competent** of ourselves
2Ti	2: 2	will be **able** to teach others

2426   GO1 AG374 LN123 B3:728 K3:293 R2425
ἱκανοτης, ENOUGHNESS

2C	3: 5	our **competence** is from God

2427   GO2 AG374 LN123 B3:728 K3:293 R2425
ἱκανοω, I MAKE ENOUGH

2C	3: 6	who **has made** us **competent**
Co	1:12	who **has enabled** you to share

2428   GO1 AG375 LN123 B2:860 K3:296
ἱκετηρια, PETITIONS

He	5: 7	prayers and **supplications**

2429   GO1 AG375 LN123
ἱκμας, MOISTURE

Lk	8: 6	withered for lack of **moisture**

2430   GO6 AG375 LN123
ἱκονιον, ICONIUM

Ac	13:51	and went to **Iconium**
	14: 1	same thing occurred in **Iconium**
	14:19	from Antioch and **Iconium**
	14:21	then on to **Iconium** and Antioch
	16: 2	in Lystra and **Iconium**
2Ti	3:11	Antioch, **Iconium,** and Lystra

2431   GO1 AG375 LN123 K3:297
ἱλαρος, CHEERFUL

2C	9: 7	God loves a **cheerful** giver

2432 GO1 AG375 LN123 K3:297 R2431
'ιλαροτης, CHEERFULNESS
Ro 12: 8 compassionate, in **cheerfulness**

2433 GO2 AG375 LN123 B3:148 K3:301
'ιλασκομαι, I EXPIATE
Lk 18:13 **be merciful** to me, a sinner
He 2:17 **make a sacrifice of atonement**

2434 GO2 AG375 LN123 B3:148 K3:301
'ιλασμος, EXPIATION
1J 2: 2 he is the **atoning sacrifice**
 4:10 to be the **atoning sacrifice**

2435 GO2 AG375 LN123 B3:148 K3:318 R2433
'ιλαστηριον, PLACE OF EXPIATION
Ro 3:25 as a **sacrifice of atonement**
He 9: 5 overshadowing the **mercy seat**

2436 GO2 AG376 LN123 B3:148 K3:300
'ιλεως, MERCIFUL
Mt 16:22 **God forbid it,** Lord!
He 8:12 For I will be **merciful** toward

2437 GO1 AG376 LN123
ιλλυρικον, ILLYRICUM
Ro 15:19 as far around as **Illyricum**

2438 GO4 AG376 LN123
'ιμας, STRAP
Mk 1: 7 untie the **thong** of his sandals
Lk 3:16 untie the **thong** of his sandals
Jn 1:27 not worthy to untie the **thong**
Ac 22:25 tied him up with **thongs**

2439 GO2 AG376 LN123 R2440
'ιματιζω, I CLOTHE
Mk 5:15 **clothed** and in his right mind
Lk 8:35 **clothed** and in his right mind

2440 GO60 AG376 LN123 B1:316
'ιματιον, CLOTHES
Mt 5:40 give your **cloak** as well
 9:16 cloth on an old **cloak**
 9:16 pulls away from the **cloak**
 9:20 the fringe of his **cloak**
 9:21 I only touch his **cloak**
 14:36 even the fringe of his **cloak**
 17: 2 his **clothes** became dazzling
 21: 7 put their **cloaks** on them

21: 8 crowd spread their **cloaks**
24:18 turn back to get a **coat**
26:65 priest tore his **clothes**
27:31 put his own **clothes** on him
27:35 they divided his **clothes**
Mk 2:21 cloth on an old **cloak**
 5:27 crowd and touched his **cloak**
 5:28 If I but touch his **clothes**
 5:30 Who touched my **clothes**
 6:56 even the fringe of his **cloak**
 9: 3 his **clothes** became dazzling
 10:50 So throwing off his **cloak**
 11: 7 Jesus and threw their **cloaks**
 11: 8 Many people spread their **cloaks**
 13:16 turn back to get a **coat**
 15:20 put his own **clothes** on him
 15:24 divided his **clothes** among them
Lk 5:36 a piece from a new **garment**
 5:36 sews it on an old **garment**
 6:29 anyone who takes away your **coat**
 7:25 Someone dressed in soft **robes**
 8:27 he had worn no **clothes**
 8:44 the fringe of his **clothes**
 19:35 after throwing their **cloaks**
 19:36 their **cloaks** on the road
 22:36 must sell his **cloak** and buy
 23:34 lots to divide his **clothing**
Jn 13: 4 took off his **outer robe**
 13:12 had put on his **robe**
 19: 2 dressed him in a purple **robe**
 19: 5 of thorns and the purple **robe**
 19:23 took his **clothes** and divided
 19:24 They divided my **clothes** among
Ac 7:58 witnesses laid their **coats**
 9:39 **clothing** that Dorcas had made
 12: 8 Wrap your **cloak** around you
 14:14 they tore their **clothes**
 16:22 stripped of their **clothing**
 18: 6 the dust from his **clothes**
 22:20 keeping the **coats** of those
 22:23 throwing off their **cloaks**
He 1:11 all wear out like **clothing**
 1:12 like **clothing** they will be
Ja 5: 2 your **clothes** are moth-eaten
1P 3: 3 gold ornaments or fine **clothing**
Re 3: 4 have not soiled their **clothes**
 3: 5 like them in white **robes**
 3:18 white **robes** to clothe you
 4: 4 dressed in white **robes**

	16:15	who stays awake and is **clothed**
	19:13	in a **robe** dipped in blood
	19:16	On his **robe** and on his thigh

2441 GO5 AG376 LN123 R2439
'ιματισμος, CLOTHING

Lk	7:25	those who put on fine **clothing**
	9:29	his **clothes** became dazzling
Jn	19:24	for my **clothing** they cast lots
Ac	20:33	silver or gold or **clothing**
1Ti	2: 9	pearls, or expensive **clothes**

2443 GO663 AG376 LN123 K3:323
'ινα, IN ORDER THAT [MULTIPLE OCCURRENCES]

2444 GO6 AG378 LN123
'ινατι, WHY

Mt	9: 4	**Why** do you think evil in your
	27:46	**why** have you forsaken me
Lk	13: 7	**Why** should it be wasting
Ac	4:25	**Why** did the Gentiles rage
	7:26	**why** do you wrong each other
1C	10:29	For **why** should my liberty

2445 GO10 AG378 LN124
ιοππη, JOPPA

Ac	9:36	in **Joppa** there was a disciple
	9:38	Since Lydda was near **Joppa**
	9:42	became known throughout **Joppa**
	9:43	Meanwhile he stayed in **Joppa**
	10: 5	Now send men to **Joppa**
	10: 8	he sent them to **Joppa**
	10:23	from **Joppa** accompanied him
	10:32	Send therefore to **Joppa**
	11: 5	I was in the city of **Joppa**
	11:13	Send to **Joppa** and bring Simon

2446 GO15 AG378 LN124 B3:991 K6:608
ιορδανης, JORDAN

Mt	3: 5	all the region along the **Jordan**
	3: 6	by him in the river **Jordan**
	3:13	to John at the **Jordan**
	4:15	by the sea, across the **Jordan**
	4:25	and from beyond the **Jordan**
	19: 1	of Judea beyond the **Jordan**
Mk	1: 5	by him in the river **Jordan**
	1: 9	baptized by John in the **Jordan**
	3: 8	Idumea, beyond the **Jordan**
	10: 1	of Judea and beyond the **Jordan**
Lk	3: 3	the region around the **Jordan**

	4: 1	returned from the **Jordan**
Jn	1:28	in Bethany across the **Jordan**
	3:26	was with you across the **Jordan**
	10:40	away again across the **Jordan**

2447 GO3 AG378 LN124 B2:27 K3:334
ιος, POISON

Ro	3:13	The **venom** of vipers is under
Ja	3: 8	evil, full of deadly **poison**
	5: 3	their **rust** will be evidence

2449 GO44 AG379 LN124 B2:305 K3:356
ιουδαια, JUDEA

Mt	2: 1	born in Bethlehem of **Judea**
	2: 5	In Bethlehem of **Judea**
	2:22	Archelaus was ruling over **Judea**
	3: 1	in the wilderness of **Judea**
	3: 5	of Jerusalem and all **Judea**
	4:25	Decapolis, Jerusalem, **Judea**
	19: 1	went to the region of **Judea**
	24:16	then those in **Judea** must
Mk	1: 5	the whole **Judean** countryside
	3: 8	great numbers from **Judea**
	10: 1	went to the region of **Judea**
	13:14	then those in **Judea** must flee
Lk	1: 5	days of King Herod of **Judea**
	1:65	entire hill country of **Judea**
	2: 4	Nazareth in Galilee to **Judea**
	3: 1	Pilate was governor of **Judea**
	4:44	in the synagogues of **Judea**
	5:17	village of Galilee and **Judea**
	6:17	of people from all **Judea**
	7:17	spread throughout **Judea**
	21:21	Then those in **Judea** must flee
	23: 5	teaching throughout all **Judea**
Jn	3:22	into the **Judean** countryside
	4: 3	he left **Judea** and started
	4:47	Jesus had come from **Judea**
	4:54	after coming from **Judea**
	7: 1	not wish to go about in **Judea**
	7: 3	Leave here and go to **Judea**
	11: 7	Let us go to **Judea** again.
Ac	1: 8	in all **Judea** and Samaria
	2: 9	residents of Mesopotamia, **Judea**
	8: 1	the countryside of **Judea**
	9:31	the church throughout **Judea**
	10:37	message spread throughout **Judea**
	11: 1	who were in **Judea** heard that
	11:29	the believers living in **Judea**

	12:19	Then he went down from **Judea**		5: 1	was a festival of the **Jews**
	15: 1	came down from **Judea** and were		5:10	So the **Jews** said to the man
	21:10	Agabus came down from **Judea**		5:15	went away and told the **Jews**
	26:20	the countryside of **Judea**		5:16	Therefore the **Jews** started
	28:21	received no letters from **Judea**		5:18	the **Jews** were seeking all the
Ro	15:31	from the unbelievers in **Judea**		6: 4	the festival of the **Jews**
2C	1:16	have you send me on to **Judea**		6:41	the **Jews** began to complain
Ga	1:22	to the churches of **Judea**		6:52	The **Jews** then disputed among
1Th	2:14	Christ Jesus that are in **Judea**		7: 1	because the **Jews** were looking

2450 GO1 AG379 LN124 B2:310 K3:356 R2453
ιουδαιζω, I JUDAIZE
Ga 2:14   the Gentiles **to live like Jews**

2451 GO1 AG379 LN124 B2:310 K3:356
ιουδαικος, JUDAIC (JEWISH)
Ti 1:14   not paying attention to **Jewish**

2452 GO1 AG379 LN124 B2:304
ιουδαικως, JUDAICALLY
Ga 2:14   a Gentile and not **like** a **Jew**

2453 GO194 AG379 LN124 B2:304 K3:356
ιουδαιος, JUDEAN (JEWS)

Mt	2: 2	has been born king of the **Jews**		7: 2	**Jewish** festival of Booths
	27:11	Are you the King of the **Jews?**		7:11	The **Jews** were looking for him
	27:29	Hail, King of the **Jews!**		7:13	about him for fear of the **Jews**
	27:37	Jesus, the King of the **Jews**		7:15	The **Jews** were astonished at it
	28:15	is still told among the **Jews**		7:35	The **Jews** said to one another
Mk	7: 3	the Pharisees, and all the **Jews**		8:22	Then the **Jews** said
	15: 2	Are you the King of the **Jews?**		8:31	Then Jesus said to the **Jews**
	15: 9	the King of the **Jews**		8:48	The **Jews** answered him
	15:12	you call the King of the **Jews**		8:52	The **Jews** said to him
	15:18	Hail, King of the **Jews!**		8:57	Then the **Jews** said to him
	15:26	The King of the **Jews.**		9:18	The **Jews** did not believe
Lk	7: 3	he sent some **Jewish** elders		9:22	they were afraid of the **Jews**
	23: 3	Are you the king of the **Jews?**		9:22	for the **Jews** had already agreed
	23:37	you are the King of the **Jews**		10:19	Again the **Jews** were divided
	23:38	This is the King of the **Jews.**		10:24	the **Jews** gathered around him
	23:51	He came from the **Jewish** town		10:31	The **Jews** took up stones again
Jn	1:19	when the **Jews** sent priests		10:33	The **Jews** answered
	2: 6	**Jewish** rites of purification		11: 8	the **Jews** were just now trying
	2:13	Passover of the **Jews** was near		11:19	and many of the **Jews** had come
	2:18	The **Jews** then said to him		11:31	The **Jews** who were with her
	2:20	The **Jews** then said		11:33	the **Jews** who came with her
	3: 1	Nicodemus, a leader of the **Jews**		11:36	So the **Jews** said
	3:25	John's disciples and a **Jew**		11:45	Many of the **Jews** therefore
	4: 9	you, a **Jew,** ask a drink of		11:54	about openly among the **Jews**
	4: 9	**Jews** do not share		11:55	Now the Passover of the **Jews**
	4:22	for salvation is from the **Jews**		12: 9	the great crowd of the **Jews**
				12:11	the **Jews** were deserting
				13:33	as I said to the **Jews** so now I
				18:12	and the **Jewish** police arrested
				18:14	who had advised the **Jews**
				18:20	all the **Jews** come together
				18:31	The **Jews** replied
				18:33	Are you the King of the **Jews?**
				18:35	I am not a **Jew,** am I?
				18:36	being handed over to the **Jews**
				18:38	he went out to the **Jews** again
				18:39	for you the King of the **Jews?**
				19: 3	Hail, King of the **Jews!**
				19: 7	The **Jews** answered him
				19:12	but the **Jews** cried out

19:14	He said to the **Jews**	
19:19	the King of the **Jews**	
19:20	Many of the **Jews** read this	
19:21	chief priests of the **Jews**	
19:21	The King of the **Jews,**	
19:21	I am King of the **Jews**	
19:31	**Jews** did not want the bodies	
19:38	of his fear of the **Jews**	
19:40	the burial custom of the **Jews**	
19:42	**Jewish** day of Preparation	
20:19	locked for fear of the **Jews**	

Ac	2: 5	devout **Jews** from every nation
	2:10	both **Jews** and proselytes
	2:14	Men of **Judea** and all who live
	9:22	confounded the **Jews** who lived
	9:23	the **Jews** plotted to kill him
	10:22	by the whole **Jewish** nation
	10:28	for a **Jew** to associate with
	10:39	in **Judea** and in Jerusalem
	11:19	to no one except **Jews**
	12: 3	that it pleased the **Jews**
	12:11	from all that the **Jewish** people
	13: 5	in the synagogues of the **Jews**
	13: 6	a **Jewish** false prophet
	13:43	devout converts to **Judaism**
	13:45	when the **Jews** saw the crowds
	13:50	the **Jews** incited the devout
	14: 1	into the **Jewish** synagogue
	14: 1	great number of both **Jews**
	14: 2	unbelieving **Jews** stirred up
	14: 4	some sided with the **Jews**
	14: 5	by both Gentiles and **Jews**
	14:19	But **Jews** came there from
	16: 1	the son of a **Jewish** woman
	16: 3	because of the **Jews** who were
	16:20	our city; they are **Jews**
	17: 1	synagogue of the **Jews**
	17: 5	But the **Jews** became jealous
	17:10	went to the **Jewish** synagogue.
	17:13	when the **Jews** of Thessalonica
	17:17	in the synagogue with the **Jews**
	18: 2	he found a **Jew** named Aquila
	18: 2	Claudius had ordered all **Jews**
	18: 4	would try to convince **Jews**
	18: 5	testifying to the **Jews**
	18:12	the **Jews** made a united attack
	18:14	Gallio said to the **Jews**
	18:14	the complaint of you **Jews**
	18:19	had a discussion with the **Jews**

18:24	to Ephesus a **Jew** named Apollos	
18:28	refuted the **Jews** in public	
19:10	of Asia, both **Jews** and Greeks	
19:13	itinerant **Jewish** exorcists	
19:14	sons of a **Jewish** high priest	
19:17	Ephesus, both **Jews** and Greeks	
19:33	the **Jews** had pushed forward	
19:34	recognized that he was a **Jew**	
20: 3	against him by the **Jews**	
20:19	through the plots of the **Jews**	
20:21	to both **Jews** and Greeks about	
21:11	**Jews** in Jerusalem will bind	
21:20	there are among the **Jews**	
21:21	that you teach all the **Jews**	
21:27	completed, the **Jews** from Asia	
21:39	I am a **Jew,** from Tarsus in	
22: 3	I am a **Jew,** born in Tarsus	
22:12	by all the **Jews** living there	
22:30	being accused of by the **Jews**	
23:12	In the morning the **Jews** joined	
23:20	The **Jews** have agreed to ask	
23:27	This man was seized by the **Jews**	
24: 5	an agitator among all the **Jews**	
24: 9	The **Jews** also joined in the	
24:19	there were some **Jews** from Asia	
24:24	wife Drusilla, who was **Jewish**	
24:27	he wanted to grant the **Jews**	
25: 2	the leaders of the **Jews** gave	
25: 7	When he arrived, the **Jews** who	
25: 8	against the law of the **Jews**	
25: 9	wishing to do the **Jews** a favor	
25:10	done no wrong to the **Jews**	
25:15	and the elders of the **Jews**	
25:24	**Jewish** community petitioned me	
26: 2	all the accusations of the **Jews**	
26: 3	and controversies of the **Jews**	
26: 4	the **Jews** know my way of life	
26: 7	that I am accused by **Jews**	
26:21	For this reason the **Jews** seized	
28:17	the local leaders of the **Jews**	
28:19	But when the **Jews** objected	

Ro	1:16	to the **Jew** first and also
	2: 9	**Jew** first and also the Greek
	2:10	**Jew** first and also the Greek
	2:17	if you call yourself a **Jew**
	2:28	For a person is not a **Jew**
	2:29	a person is a **Jew** who is one
	3: 1	what advantage has the **Jew**
	3: 9	that all, both **Jews** and Greeks

	3:29	Or is God the God of **Jews** only
	9:24	from the **Jews** only but also
	10:12	is no distinction between **Jew**
1C	1:23	a stumbling block to **Jews**
	1:24	called, both **Jews** and Greeks
	9:20	To the **Jews** I became as a Jew
	9:20	To the Jews I became as a **Jew**
	9:20	in order to win **Jews**
	10:32	Give no offense to **Jews**
	12:13	**Jews** or Greeks, slaves or free
2C	11:24	I have received from the **Jews**
Ga	2:13	And the other **Jews** joined him
	2:14	If you, though a **Jew,** live like
	2:15	We ourselves are **Jews** by birth
	3:28	is no longer **Jew** or Greek
Co	3:11	is no longer Greek and **Jew**
1Th	2:14	as they did from the **Jews**
Re	2: 9	who say that they are **Jews**
	3: 9	who say that they are **Jews**

2454   GO2 AG379 LN124 B2:310 K3:356 R2450
ιουδαισμος, JUDAISM

| Ga | 1:13 | my earlier life in **Judaism** |
| | 1:14 | I advanced in **Judaism** |

2455   GO44 AG379 LN124 B2:316
ιουδας, JUDAS

Mt	1: 2	and Jacob the father of **Judah**
	1: 3	and **Judah** the father of Perez
	2: 6	Bethlehem, in the land of **Judah**
	2: 6	least among the rulers of **Judah**
	10: 4	**Judas** Iscariot, the one who
	13:55	Joseph and Simon and **Judas**
	26:14	who was called **Judas** Iscariot
	26:25	**Judas,** who betrayed him, said
	26:47	**Judas,** one of the twelve
	27: 3	When **Judas,** his betrayer, saw
Mk	3:19	**Judas** Iscariot, who betrayed
	6: 3	James and Joses and **Judas**
	14:10	Then **Judas** Iscariot, who was
	14:43	**Judas,** one of the twelve
Lk	1:39	with haste to a **Judean** town
	3:30	son of Simeon, son of **Judah**
	3:33	son of Perez, son of **Judah**
	6:16	and **Judas** son of James
	6:16	and **Judas** Iscariot, who
	22: 3	Then Satan entered into **Judas**
	22:47	and the one called **Judas**
	22:48	**Judas,** is it with a kiss that

Jn	6:71	He was speaking of **Judas**
	12: 4	But **Judas** Iscariot, one of his
	13: 2	it into the heart of **Judas**
	13:26	he gave it to **Judas** son of
	13:29	because **Judas** had the common
	14:22	**Judas** (not Iscariot) said to
	18: 2	Now **Judas,** who betrayed him
	18: 3	So **Judas** brought a detachment
	18: 5	**Judas,** who betrayed him, was
Ac	1:13	Zealot, and **Judas** son of James
	1:16	David foretold concerning **Judas**
	1:25	from which **Judas** turned aside
	5:37	After him **Judas** the Galilean
	9:11	and at the house of **Judas** look
	15:22	sent **Judas** called Barsabbas
	15:27	We have therefore sent **Judas**
	15:32	**Judas** and Silas, who were
He	7:14	Lord was descended from **Judah**
	8: 8	with the house of **Judah**
Ju	1: 1	**Jude,** a servant of Jesus Christ
Re	5: 5	the Lion of the tribe of **Judah**
	7: 5	From the tribe of **Judah** twelve

2456   GO1 AG380 LN124
ιουλια, JULIA

| Ro | 16:15 | **Julia,** Nereus and his sister |

2457   GO2 AG380 LN124
ιουλιος, JULIUS

| Ac | 27: 1 | Augustan Cohort, named **Julius** |
| | 27: 3 | and **Julius** treated Paul kindly |

2458   GO1 AG380 LN124
ιουνιας, JUNIAS

| Ro | 16: 7 | Greet Andronicus and **Junia** |

2459   GO3 AG380 LN124
ιουστος, JUSTUS

Ac	1:23	who was also known as **Justus**
	18: 7	a man named Titius **Justus**
Co	4:11	Jesus who is called **Justus**

2460   GO2 AG380 LN124 R2462
ιππευς, HORSEMAN

| Ac | 23:23 | soldiers, seventy **horsemen** |
| | 23:32 | they let the **horsemen** go on |

2461   GO1 AG380 LN124 R2462
ιππικος, HORSEMAN

| Re | 9:16 | of the troops of **cavalry** |

2462 GO17 AG380 LN124 K3:336
ἱππος, HORSE

Ja	3: 3	into the mouths of **horses**
Re	6: 2	and there was a white **horse**
	6: 4	And out came another **horse**
	6: 5	and there was a black **horse**
	6: 8	there was a pale green **horse**
	9: 7	the locusts were like **horses**
	9: 9	with **horses** rushing into battle
	9:17	this was how I saw the **horses**
	9:17	the heads of the **horses** were
	9:19	For the power of the **horses**
	14:20	as high as a **horse's** bridle
	18:13	cattle and sheep, **horses** and
	19:11	and there was a white **horse**
	19:14	following him on white **horses**
	19:18	the flesh of **horses** and their
	19:19	rider on the **horse** and against
	19:21	the rider on the **horse**

2463 GO2 AG380 LN124 B3:1000 K3:339
ιρις, RAINBOW

Re	4: 3	around the throne is a **rainbow**
	10: 1	with a **rainbow** over his head;

2464 GO20 AG380 LN124 B1:81
ισαακ, ISAAC

Mt	1: 2	Abraham was the father of **Isaac**
	1: 2	**Isaac** the father of Jacob
	8:11	will eat with Abraham and **Isaac**
	22:32	the God of **Isaac**, and the God
Mk	12:26	the God of **Isaac**, and the God
Lk	3:34	son of Jacob, son of **Isaac**
	13:28	you see Abraham and **Isaac**
	20:37	the God of **Isaac**, and the God
Ac	3:13	the God of **Isaac**, and the God
	7: 8	became the father of **Isaac** and
	7: 8	**Isaac** became the father of
	7:32	Abraham, **Isaac**, and Jacob
Ro	9: 7	through **Isaac** that descendants
	9:10	husband, our ancestor **Isaac**
Ga	4:28	of the promise, like **Isaac**
He	11: 9	as did **Isaac** and Jacob
	11:17	to the test, offered up **Isaac**
	11:18	through **Isaac** that descendants
	11:20	**Isaac** invoked blessings for
Ja	2:21	when he offered his son **Isaac**

2465 GO1 AG380 LN124 B1:101 K1:87 R2470,32
ισαγγελος, EQUAL MESSENGER

Lk	20:36	because they are **like angels**

2465a GO3 AG380 LN124
ισκαριωθ, ISCARIOTH

Mk	3:19	Judas **Iscariot**, who betrayed
	14:10	Judas **Iscariot**, who was one
Lk	6:16	Judas **Iscariot**, who became a

2469 GO8 AG380 LN124
ισκαριοτης, ISCARIOT

Mt	10: 4	Judas **Iscariot**, the one who
	26:14	who was called Judas **Iscariot**
Lk	22: 3	into Judas called **Iscariot**
Jn	6:71	Judas son of Simon **Iscariot**
	12: 4	But Judas **Iscariot**, one of his
	13: 2	Judas son of Simon **Iscariot**
	13:26	to Judas son of Simon **Iscariot**
	14:22	Judas (not **Iscariot**) said to

2470 GO8 AG381 LN124 B2:497 K3:343
ισος, EQUAL

Mt	20:12	you have made them **equal** to us
Mk	14:56	their testimony did not **agree**
	14:59	their testimony did not **agree**
Lk	6:34	to receive **as much again**
Jn	5:18	making himself **equal** to God
Ac	11:17	God gave them the **same** gift
Ph	2: 6	not regard **equality** with God
Re	21:16	and width and height are **equal**

2471 GO3 AG381 LN124 B2:497 K3:343
ισοτης, EQUALITY

2C	8:13	a question of a **fair balance**
	8:14	there may be a **fair balance**
Co	4: 1	your slaves justly and **fairly**

2472 GO1 AG381 LN124 B2:497 K3:343 R2470,5092
ισοτιμος, EQUAL VALUE

2P	1: 1	a faith as **precious as ours**

2473 GO1 AG381 LN124 B2:497
ισοψυχος, EQUAL SOUL

Ph	2:20	I have no one **like him** who will

2474 GO68 AG381 LN125 B2:304 K3:356
ισραηλ, ISRAEL

Mt	2: 6	is to shepherd my people **Israel**
	2:20	and go to the land of **Israel**

	2:21	and went to the land of **Israel**
	8:10	in no one in **Israel** have I
	9:33	like this been seen in **Israel**
	10: 6	sheep of the house of **Israel**
	10:23	through all the towns of **Israel**
	15:24	sheep of the house of **Israel**
	15:31	they praised the God of **Israel**
	19:28	the twelve tribes of **Israel**
	27: 9	people of **Israel** had set a
	27:42	He is the King of **Israel**
Mk	12:29	The first is, 'Hear, O **Israel:**
	15:32	King of **Israel,** come down from
Lk	1:16	many of the people of **Israel**
	1:54	has helped his servant **Israel**
	1:68	be the Lord God of **Israel**
	1:80	he appeared publicly to **Israel**
	2:25	to the consolation of **Israel**
	2:32	glory to your people **Israel**
	2:34	the rising of many in **Israel**
	4:25	were many widows in **Israel**
	4:27	were also many lepers in **Israel**
	7: 9	not even in **Israel** have I found
	22:30	the twelve tribes of **Israel**
	24:21	was the one to redeem **Israel**
Jn	1:31	he might be revealed to **Israel**
	1:49	You are the King of **Israel**
	3:10	Are you a teacher of **Israel**
	12:13	the Lord—the King of **Israel**
Ac	1: 6	restore the kingdom to **Israel**
	2:36	let the entire house of **Israel**
	4:10	to all the people of **Israel**
	4:27	and the peoples of **Israel**
	5:21	body of the elders of **Israel**
	5:31	might give repentance to **Israel**
	7:23	his relatives, the **Israelites**
	7:37	who said to the **Israelites**
	7:42	wilderness, O house of **Israel**
	9:15	before the people of **Israel**
	10:36	he sent to the people of **Israel**
	13:17	The God of this people **Israel**
	13:23	has brought to **Israel** a Savior
	13:24	to all the people of **Israel**
	28:20	the sake of the hope of **Israel**
Ro	9: 6	not all **Israelites** truly belong
	9: 6	truly belong to **Israel**
	9:27	cries out concerning **Israel**
	9:27	children of **Israel** were like
	9:31	but **Israel,** who did strive for
	10:19	did **Israel** not understand

	10:21	But of **Israel** he says
	11: 2	pleads with God against **Israel**
	11: 7	**Israel** failed to obtain what
	11:25	has come upon part of **Israel**
	11:26	And so all **Israel** will be saved
1C	10:18	Consider the people of **Israel**
2C	3: 7	so that the people of **Israel**
	3:13	to keep the people of **Israel**
Ga	6:16	and upon the **Israel** of God
Ep	2:12	from the commonwealth of **Israel**
Ph	3: 5	member of the people of **Israel**
He	8: 8	with the house of **Israel**
	8:10	make with the house of **Israel**
	11:22	of the exodus of the **Israelites**
Re	2:14	before the people of **Israel**
	7: 4	tribe of the people of **Israel**
	21:12	twelve tribes of the **Israelites**

2475 G09 AG381 LN125 B2:304 K3:356
ισραηλιτης, ISRAELITE

Jn	1:47	an **Israelite** in whom there is
Ac	2:22	You that are **Israelites,** listen
	3:12	You **Israelites,** why do you
	5:35	Fellow **Israelites,** consider
	13:16	You **Israelites,** and others
	21:28	Fellow **Israelites,** help!
Ro	9: 4	They are **Israelites,** and to
	11: 1	I myself am an **Israelite**
2C	11:22	Are they **Israelites?**

2475a G01 AG381 LN125
ισσαχαρ, ISSACHAR

Re	7: 7	from the tribe of **Issachar**

2476 G0155 AG381 LN125 K7:638
ιστημι, I STAND

Mt	2: 9	until it **stopped** over the place
	4: 5	**placed** him on the pinnacle
	6: 5	for they love to **stand** and pray
	12:25	against itself **will stand.**
	12:26	then **will** his kingdom **stand**
	12:46	brothers **were standing** outside
	12:47	brothers **are standing** outside
	13: 2	whole crowd **stood** on the beach
	16:28	there are some **standing** here
	18: 2	whom he **put** among them
	18:16	every word **may be confirmed**
	20: 3	he saw others **standing** idle
	20: 6	found others **standing** around
	20: 6	Why are you **standing** here idle

20:32   Jesus **stood** still and called
24:15   **standing** in the holy place
25:33   and he **will put** the sheep
26:15   They **paid** him thirty pieces
26:73   the **bystanders** came up and said
27:11   Jesus **stood** before the governor
27:47   some of the **bystanders** heard it

Mk   3:24   that kingdom cannot **stand**
3:25   house will not be able **to stand**
3:26   and is divided, he cannot **stand**
7: 9   in order to **keep** your tradition
9: 1   there are some **standing** here
9:36   child and **put** it among them
10:49   Jesus **stood** still and said
11: 5   the **bystanders** said to them
13: 9   you **will stand** before governors
13:14   sacrilege **set up** where it ought

Lk   1:11   **standing** at the right side
4: 9   and **placed** him on the pinnacle
5: 1   Once while Jesus **was standing**
5: 2   two boats **there** at the shore
6: 8   Come and **stand** here.
6: 8   He got up and **stood** there
6:17   and **stood** on a level place
7:14   and the bearers **stood** still
7:38   **stood** behind him at his feet
8:20   brothers **are standing** outside
8:44   her hemorrhage **stopped**
9:27   there are some **standing** here
9:47   child and **put** it by his side
11:18   how will his kingdom **stand**
13:25   and you begin **to stand** outside
17:12   **Keeping** their distance
18:11   Pharisee, **standing** by himself
18:13   collector, **standing** far off
18:40   Jesus **stood** still and ordered
19: 8   Zacchaeus **stood** there and
21:36   to **stand** before the Son of Man
23:10   priests and the scribes **stood**
23:35   And the people **stood** by
23:49   **stood** at a distance, watching
24:17   They **stood** still, looking sad.
24:36   Jesus himself **stood** among them

Jn   1:26   **stands** one whom you do not
know
1:35   John again **was standing** with
3:29   who **stands** and hears him
6:22   the crowd that **had stayed**
7:37   while Jesus **was standing** there
8: 3   and making her **stand** before all

8:44   does not **stand** in the truth
11:56   as they **stood** in the temple
12:29   The crowd **standing** there heard
18: 5   **was standing** with them
18:16   but Peter **was standing** outside
18:18   they **were standing** around it
18:18   Peter also **was standing** with
18:25   Now Simon Peter **was standing**
19:25   **standing** near the cross of
20:11   But Mary **stood** weeping outside
20:14   and saw Jesus **standing** there
20:19   Jesus came and **stood** among
them
20:26   Jesus came and **stood** among
them
21: 4   Jesus **stood** on the beach

Ac   1:11   why **do** you **stand** looking up
1:23   So they **proposed** two, Joseph
2:14   **standing** with the eleven
3: 8   he **stood** and began to walk
4: 7   had made the prisoners **stand**
4:14   man who had been cured **standing**
5:20   **stand** in the temple and tell
5:23   guards **standing** at the doors
5:25   **are standing** in the temple
5:27   they **had** them **stand** before the
6: 6   They had these men **stand** before
6:13   They **set up** false witnesses
7:33   you **are standing** is holy ground
7:55   Jesus **standing** at the right
7:56   **standing** at the right hand of
7:60   do not **hold** this sin against
8:38   commanded the chariot **to stop**
9: 7   **stood** speechless because they
10:30   **stood** before me
11:13   angel **standing** in his house
12:14   Peter **was standing** at the gate
16: 9   there **stood** a man of Macedonia
17:22   Then Paul **stood** in front of
17:31   because he **has fixed** a day
21:40   Paul **stood** on the steps and
22:25   centurion who **was standing** by
22:30   **had** him **stand** before them
24:20   when I **stood** before the council
24:21   while **standing** before them
25:10   am **appealing** to the emperor's
25:18   When the accusers **stood** up
26: 6   And now I **stand** here on trial
26:16   get up and **stand** on your feet
26:22   and so I **stand** here

	27:21	Paul then **stood** up among them
Ro	3:31	contrary, we **uphold** the law
	5: 2	to this grace in which we **stand**
	10: 3	seeking **to establish** their own
	11:20	you **stand** only through faith
	14: 4	that they **stand** or fall
	14: 4	is able to make them **stand**
1C	7:37	**stands** firm in his resolve
	10:12	you think you **are standing**
	15: 1	in which also you **stand**
2C	1:24	you **stand** firm in the faith
	13: 1	charge **must be sustained**
Ep	6:11	able **to stand** against the
	6:13	done everything, to **stand** firm
	6:14	**Stand** therefore, and fasten
Co	4:12	so that you **may stand** mature
2Ti	2:19	God's firm foundation **stands**
He	10: 9	in order to **establish** the
	10:11	every priest **stands** day after
Ja	2: 3	you say, "**Stand** there,"
	5: 9	Judge **is standing** at the doors
1P	5:12	**Stand** fast in it
Ju	1:24	make you **stand** without blemish
Re	3:20	I **am standing** at the door
	5: 6	Lamb **standing** as if it had been
	6:17	and who is able to **stand**
	7: 1	I saw four angels **standing**
	7: 9	**standing** before the throne
	7:11	all the angels **stood** around
	8: 2	angels who **stand** before God
	8: 3	came and **stood** at the altar .
	10: 5	angel whom I saw **standing**
	10: 8	angel who **is standing** on the
	11: 4	lampstands that **stand** before
	11:11	they **stood** on their feet
	12: 4	dragon **stood** before the woman
	12:18	Then the dragon **took** his **stand**
	14: 1	Lamb, **standing** on Mount Zion
	15: 2	**standing** beside the sea of
	18:10	they will **stand** far off
	18:15	**will stand** far off
	18:17	is on the sea, **stood** far off
	19:17	an angel **standing** in the sun
	20:12	**standing** before the throne

2477　GO1 AG383 LN125 K3:391
'ιστορεω, I VISIT WITH

Ga	1:18	to Jerusalem **to visit** Cephas

2478　GO29 AG383 LN125 B3:712 K3:397 R2479
ισχυρος, STRONG

Mt	3:11	but one who is **more powerful**
	12:29	enter a **strong** man's house
	12:29	first tying up the **strong** man
	14:30	when he noticed the **strong** wind
Mk	1: 7	one who is **more powerful** than I
	3:27	can enter a **strong** man's house
	3:27	first tying up the **strong** man
Lk	3:16	one who is **more powerful** than I
	11:21	When a **strong** man, fully armed
	11:22	But when one **stronger** than he
	15:14	a **severe** famine took place
1C	1:25	and God's weakness is **stronger**
	1:27	the world to shame the **strong**
	4:10	are weak, but you are **strong**
	10:22	Are we **stronger** than he?
2C	10:10	letters are weighty and **strong**
He	5: 7	with **loud** cries and tears
	6:18	might be **strongly** encouraged
	11:34	became **mighty** in war
1J	2:14	because you are **strong**
Re	5: 2	a **mighty** angel proclaiming
	6:15	the rich and the **powerful**
	10: 1	I saw another **mighty** angel
	18: 2	called out with a **mighty** voice
	18: 8	for **mighty** is the Lord God
	18:10	Babylon, the **mighty** city!
	18:21	**mighty** angel took up a stone
	19: 6	sound of **mighty** thunderpeals
	19:18	the flesh of the **mighty**

2479　GO10 AG383 LN125 B3:712 K3:397
ισχυς, STRENGTH

Mk	12:30	with all your **strength**
	12:33	with all the **strength**
Lk	10:27	with all your **strength**
Ep	1:19	working of his **great** power
	6:10	in the **strength** of his power
2Th	1: 9	from the glory of his **might**
1P	4:11	the **strength** that God supplies
2P	2:11	greater in **might** and power
Re	5:12	wisdom and **might** and honor
	7:12	honor and power and **might**

2480　GO28 AG383 LN125 B3:712 K3:397 R2479
ισχυω, I AM STRONG

Mt	5:13	It **is no longer good** for
	8:28	no one **could pass** that way
	9:12	Those who **are well** have no need

	26:40	**could** you not **stay** awake
Mk	2:17	Those who **are well** have no need
	5: 4	one **had** the **strength** to subdue
	9:18	but they **could** not **do** so
	14:37	**Could** you not keep awake one
Lk	6:48	house but **could** not shake it
	8:43	no one **could** cure her
	13:24	to enter and **will** not **be able**
	14: 6	they **could** not reply to this.
	14:29	and **is** not **able** to finish
	14:30	and **was** not **able** to finish
	16: 3	I **am** not **strong** enough to dig
	20:26	And they **were** not **able** in the
Jn	21: 6	they **were** not **able** to haul it
Ac	6:10	**could** not withstand the wisdom
	15:10	nor we **have been able** to bear
	19:16	so **overpowered** them that they
	19:20	grew mightily and **prevailed**
	25: 7	which they **could** not prove
	27:16	we **were** scarcely **able** to get
Ga	5: 6	**counts** for anything
Ph	4:13	I **can do** all things through
He	9:17	it **is** not **in force** as long
Ja	5:16	of the righteous is **powerful**
Re	12: 8	but they **were defeated**

2481   ᴳᴼ1 ᴬᴳ384 ᴸᴺ125
ισως, LIKELY
| Lk | 20:13 | **perhaps** they will respect him |

2482   ᴳᴼ4 ᴬᴳ384 ᴸᴺ125
ιταλια, ITALY
Ac	18: 2	had recently come from **Italy**
	27: 1	we were to sail for **Italy**
	27: 6	ship bound for **Italy**
He	13:24	Those from **Italy** send you

2483   ᴳᴼ1 ᴬᴳ384 ᴸᴺ125
ιταλικος, ITALIAN
| Ac | 10: 1 | centurion of the **Italian** Cohort |

2484   ᴳᴼ1 ᴬᴳ384 ᴸᴺ125
ιτουραιος, ITUREA
| Lk | 3: 1 | ruler of the region of **Ituraea** |

2485   ᴳᴼ2 ᴬᴳ384 ᴸᴺ125 ᴮ1:670 ᴿ2486
ιχθυδιον, SMALL FISH
| Mt | 15:34 | Seven, and a few **small fish.** |
| Mk | 8: 7 | They had also a few **small fish** |

2486   ᴳᴼ20 ᴬᴳ384 ᴸᴺ125 ᴮ1:670
ιχθυς, FISH
Mt	7:10	if the child asks for a **fish**
	14:17	but five loaves and two **fish**
	14:19	five loaves and the two **fish**
	15:36	seven loaves and the **fish**
	17:27	take the first **fish** that comes
Mk	6:38	Five, and two **fish.**
	6:41	five loaves and the two **fish**
	6:41	divided the two **fish** among them
	6:43	broken pieces and of the **fish**
Lk	5: 6	they caught so many **fish**
	5: 9	amazed at the catch of **fish**
	9:13	than five loaves and two **fish**
	9:16	five loaves and the two **fish**
	11:11	if your child asks for a **fish**
	11:11	give a snake instead of a **fish**
	24:42	him a piece of broiled **fish**
Jn	21: 6	because there were so many **fish**
	21: 8	dragging the net full of **fish**
	21:11	net ashore, full of large **fish**
1C	15:39	for birds, and another for **fish**

2487   ᴳᴼ3 ᴬᴳ384 ᴸᴺ125 ᴷ3:402
ιχνος, FOOTPRINT
Ro	4:12	but who also follow the **example**
2C	12:18	Did we not take the same **steps**
1P	2:21	you should follow in his **steps**

2488   ᴳᴼ2 ᴬᴳ384 ᴸᴺ125
ιωαθαμ, JOATHAM
| Mt | 1: 9 | and Uzziah the father of **Jotham** |
| | 1: 9 | and **Jotham** the father of Ahaz |

2488a   ᴳᴼ1 ᴬᴳ384 ᴸᴺ125
ιωαναν, JOANAN
| Lk | 3:27 | son of **Joanan,** son of Rhesa |

2489   ᴳᴼ2 ᴬᴳ384 ᴸᴺ126
ιωαννα, JOANNA
| Lk | 8: 3 | and **Joanna,** the wife of Herod's |
| | 24:10 | it was Mary Magdalene, **Joanna** |

2491   ᴳᴼ135 ᴬᴳ384 ᴸᴺ126
ιωαννης, JOHN
Mt	3: 1	In those days **John** the Baptist
	3: 4	**John** wore clothing of camel's
	3:13	came from Galilee to **John**
	3:14	**John** would have prevented him
	4:12	when Jesus heard that **John**

	4:21	of Zebedee and his brother **John**	
	9:14	Then the disciples of **John** came	
	10: 2	and his brother **John**	
	11: 2	When **John** heard in prison what	
	11: 4	tell **John** what you hear and see	
	11: 7	speak to the crowds about **John**	
	11:11	greater than **John** the Baptist	
	11:12	the days of **John** the Baptist	
	11:13	law prophesied until **John** came	
	11:18	**John** came neither eating nor	
	14: 2	This is **John** the Baptist	
	14: 3	For Herod had arrested **John**	
	14: 4	**John** had been telling him	
	14: 8	the head of **John** the Baptist	
	14:10	he sent and had **John** beheaded	
	16:14	Some say **John** the Baptist, but	
	17: 1	James and his brother **John**	
	17:13	to them about **John** the Baptist	
	21:25	Did the baptism of **John** come	
	21:26	all regard **John** as a prophet	
	21:32	For **John** came to you in the way	
Mk	1: 4	**John** the baptizer appeared	
	1: 6	**John** was clothed with camel's	
	1: 9	was baptized by **John** in the	
	1:14	Now after **John** was arrested	
	1:19	Zebedee and his brother **John**	
	1:29	and Andrew, with James and **John**	
	2:18	Now **John's** disciples and the	
	2:18	Why do **John's** disciples and the	
	3:17	**John** the brother of James	
	5:37	except Peter, James, and **John**	
	6:14	**John** the baptizer has been	
	6:16	**John,** whom I beheaded	
	6:17	had sent men who arrested **John**	
	6:18	For **John** had been telling Herod	
	6:20	for Herod feared **John,** knowing	
	6:24	The head of **John** the baptizer	
	6:25	the head of **John** the Baptist	
	8:28	**John** the Baptist; and others	
	9: 2	Peter and James and **John,**	
	9:38	**John** said to him	
	10:35	James and **John,** the sons of	
	10:41	to be angry with James and **John**	
	11:30	Did the baptism of **John** come	
	11:32	for all regarded **John** as truly	
	13: 3	Peter, James, **John,** and Andrew	
	14:33	Peter and James and **John**	
Lk	1:13	and you will name him **John**	
	1:60	he is to be called **John**	

1:63	His name is **John.**
3: 2	the word of God came to **John**
3:15	in their hearts concerning **John**
3:16	**John** answered all of them
3:20	by shutting up **John** in prison
5:10	so also were James and **John**
5:33	**John's** disciples, like the
6:14	Andrew, and James, and **John**
7:18	The disciples of **John** reported
7:18	So **John** summoned two of his
7:20	**John** the Baptist has sent us
7:22	tell **John** what you have seen
7:24	When **John's** messengers had gone
7:24	speak to the crowds about **John**
7:28	no one is greater than **John**
7:29	baptized with **John's** baptism
7:33	For **John** the Baptist has come
8:51	except Peter, **John,** and James
9: 7	that **John** had been raised from
9: 9	**John** I beheaded; but who is this
9:19	**John** the Baptist; but others
9:28	took with him Peter and **John**
9:49	**John** answered, "Master, we saw
9:54	his disciples James and **John**
11: 1	as **John** taught his disciples
16:16	were in effect until **John** came
20: 4	Did the baptism of **John** come
20: 6	that **John** was a prophet
22: 8	So Jesus sent Peter and **John**

Jn	1: 6	from God, whose name was **John**
	1:15	**John** testified to him and cried
	1:19	the testimony given by **John**
	1:26	**John** answered them
	1:28	where **John** was baptizing
	1:32	And **John** testified
	1:35	**John** again was standing with
	1:40	One of the two who heard **John**
	1:42	You are Simon son of **John**
	3:23	**John** also was baptizing
	3:24	**John,** of course, had not yet
	3:25	between **John's** disciples and a
	3:26	came to **John** and said to him
	3:27	**John** answered
	4: 1	more disciples than **John**
	5:33	You sent messengers to **John**
	5:36	testimony greater than **John's**
	10:40	where **John** had been baptizing
	10:41	**John** performed no sign
	10:41	but everything that **John** said

21:15 Simon son of **John,** do you love
21:16 Simon son of **John,** do you love
21:17 Simon son of **John,** do you love
Ac   1: 5 for **John** baptized with water
1:13 Peter, and **John,** and James
1:22 from the baptism of **John** until
3: 1 Peter and **John** were going up
3: 3 Peter and **John** about to go
3: 4 intently at him, as did **John**
3:11 he clung to Peter and **John**
4: 6 the high priest, Caiaphas, **John**
4:13 the boldness of Peter and **John**
4:19 Peter and **John** answered them
8:14 they sent Peter and **John**
10:37 the baptism that **John** announced
11:16 **John** baptized with water
12: 2 James, the brother of **John**
12:12 Mary, the mother of **John**
12:25 and brought with them **John**
13: 5 they had **John** also to assist
13:13 **John,** however, left them
13:24 **John** had already proclaimed
13:25 as **John** was finishing his work
15:37 take with them **John** called Mark
18:25 knew only the baptism of **John**
19: 3 Into **John's** baptism.
19: 4 **John** baptized with the baptism
Ga   2: 9 when James and Cephas and **John**
Re   1: 1 his angel to his servant **John**
1: 4 **John** to the seven churches
1: 9 I, **John,** your brother
22: 8 I, **John,** am the one who heard

2492   GO1 AG385 LN126
ιωβ, JOB
Ja   5:11 heard of the endurance of **Job**

2492a   GO3 AG385 LN126
ιωβηδ, JOBED (OBED)
Mt   1: 5 Boaz the father of **Obed** by Ruth
1: 5 **Obed** the father of Jesse
Lk   3:32 son of Jesse, son of **Obed**

2492b   GO1 AG385 LN126
ιωδα, JODA
Lk   3:26 son of Josech, son of **Joda**

2493   GO1 AG385 LN126
ιωηλ, JOEL
Ac   2:16 spoken through the prophet **Joel**

2494   GO1 AG385 LN126
ιωναμ, JONAM
Lk   3:30 son of Joseph, son of **Jonam**

2495   GO9 AG385 LN126 B2:350 K3:406
ιωνας, JONAH
Mt 12:39 the sign of the prophet **Jonah**
12:40 just as **Jonah** was three days
12:41 at the proclamation of **Jonah**
12:41 something greater than **Jonah**
16: 4 to it except the sign of **Jonah**
Lk 11:29 to it except the sign of **Jonah**
11:30 For just as **Jonah** became a sign
11:32 at the proclamation of **Jonah**
11:32 something greater than **Jonah**

2496   GO2 AG385 LN126
ιωραμ, JORAM
Mt   1: 8 Jehoshaphat the father of **Joram**
1: 8 **Joram** the father of Uzziah

2497   GO1 AG385 LN126
ιωριμ, JORIM
Lk   3:29 son of Eliezer, son of **Jorim**

2498   GO2 AG385 LN126
ιωσαφατ, JOSAPHAT
Mt   1: 8 Asaph the father of **Jehoshaphat**
1: 8 **Jehoshaphat** the father of Joram

2500   GO3 AG385 LN126
ιωσης, JOSES
Mk   6: 3 brother of James and **Joses**
15:40 James the younger and of **Joses**
15:47 Mary the mother of **Joses** saw

2501   GO35 AG385 LN126
ιωσηφ, JOSEPH
Mt   1:16 Jacob the father of **Joseph**
1:18 had been engaged to **Joseph**
1:19 Her husband **Joseph**
1:20 **Joseph,** son of David, do not
1:24 When **Joseph** awoke from sleep
2:13 appeared to **Joseph** in a dream
2:19 appeared in a dream to **Joseph**
13:55 his brothers James and **Joseph**
27:56 the mother of James and **Joseph**
27:57 from Arimathea, named **Joseph**
27:59 So **Joseph** took the body
Mk 15:43 **Joseph** of Arimathea

	15:45	he granted the body to **Joseph**
Lk	1:27	to a man whose name was **Joseph**
	2: 4	**Joseph** also went from the town
	2:16	and found Mary and **Joseph**
	3:23	son (as was thought) of **Joseph**
	3:24	son of Jannai, son of **Joseph**
	3:30	son of Judah, son of **Joseph**
	4:22	Is not this **Joseph's** son?
	23:50	righteous man named **Joseph**
Jn	1:45	son of **Joseph** from Nazareth
	4: 5	had given to his son **Joseph**
	6:42	Jesus, the son of **Joseph**
	19:38	**Joseph** of Arimathea, who was
Ac	1:23	**Joseph** called Barsabbas, who
	4:36	a native of Cyprus, **Joseph**
	7: 9	patriarchs, jealous of **Joseph**
	7:13	**Joseph** made himself known to
	7:13	**Joseph's** family became known
	7:14	Then **Joseph** sent and invited
	7:18	who had not known **Joseph**
He	11:21	each of the sons of **Joseph**
	11:22	By faith **Joseph,** at the end
Re	7: 8	from the tribe of **Joseph**

2501a GO1 AG385 LN126
ιωσηχ, JOSECH
Lk　　3:26　　son of Semein, son of **Josech**

2502 GO2 AG386 LN126
ιωσιας, JOSIAS (JOSIAH)
Mt　　1:10　　and Amos the father of **Josiah**
　　　　1:11　　**Josiah** the father of Jechoniah

2503 GO1 AG386 LN126
ιωτα, IOTA
Mt　　5:18　　earth pass away, not one **letter**

Κ

2504 GO84 AG386 LN126 R2532,1473
καγω, AND I

Mt	2: 8	so that **I** may **also** go and pay
	10:32	**I also** will acknowledge before
	10:33	**I also** will deny before my
	11:28	**and I** will give you rest
	16:18	**And I** tell you, you are Peter
	18:33	as **I** had mercy on you
	21:24	**I** will **also** ask you one
	21:24	then **I** will **also** tell you

	26:15	if **I** betray him to you
Lk	1: 3	**I too** decided
	2:48	your father **and I** have been
	11: 9	So **I** say to you, Ask, and it
	19:23	**I** could have collected it
	20: 3	**I** will **also** ask you a
	22:29	**and I** confer on you, just as
Jn	1:31	**I** myself did not know him;
	1:33	**I** myself did not know him,
	1:34	**I** myself have seen and have
	5:17	working, and **I** also am working
	6:44	**and I** will raise that person
	6:54	**and I** will raise them up on the
	6:56	abide in me, **and I** in them
	6:57	**and I** live because of the
	7:28	You know **me,** and you know where
	8:26	**and I** declare to the world
	10:15	knows me **and I** know the Father
	10:27	**I** know them, and they follow me
	10:28	**I** give them eternal life
	10:38	**and I** am in the Father
	12:32	**And I,** when I am lifted up
	14:16	**And I** will ask the Father
	14:20	and you in me, **and I** in you
	14:21	Father, **and I** will love them
	15: 4	Abide in me as **I** abide in you
	15: 5	abide in me **and I** in them bear
	15: 9	so **I** have loved you
	16:32	**and** you will leave **me** alone
	17: 6	**and** you gave them to me
	17:11	**and I** am coming to you
	17:18	so **I** have sent them into the
	17:21	are in me **and I** am in you
	17:22	have given me **I** have given them
	17:26	may be in them, **and I** in them
	20:15	**and I** will take him away
	20:21	has sent me, **so I** send you
Ac	8:19	Give **me also** this power so
	10:28	but God has shown **me** that I
	22:13	**I** regained my sight
	22:19	**And I** said, 'Lord, they
Ro	3: 7	why am **I** still being condemned
	11: 3	**I** alone am left, and they are
1C	2: 1	When **I** came to you, brothers
	2: 3	**And I** came to you in weakness
	3: 1	**I** could not speak to you
	7: 8	to remain unmarried as **I** am
	7:40	that **I too** have the Spirit
	10:33	as **I** try to please everyone

	11: 1	**as I** am of Christ
	15: 8	he appeared **also to me**
	16: 4	advisable that **I** should go **also**
	16:10	work of the Lord just as **I** am
2C	2:10	you forgive, **I also** forgive
	6:17	**then I** will welcome you
	11:16	that **I too** may boast a little
	11:18	**I** will **also** boast
	11:21	**I also** dare to boast of that
	11:22	Are they Hebrews? **So am I.**
	11:22	Are they Israelites? **So am I**
	11:22	of Abraham? **So am I**
	12:20	**I** may find you not **as I** wish
Ga	4:12	I beg you, become **as I** am
	6:14	to me, **and I** to the world
Ep	1:15	I have heard of your faith
Ph	2:19	so that **I** may be cheered
	2:28	**and** that **I** may be less anxious
1Th	3: 5	when **I** could bear it no longer
He	8: 9	**and** so **I** had no concern
Ja	2:18	You have faith **and I** have works
	2:18	**and I** by my works will show
Re	2: 6	Nicolaitans, which **I also** hate
	2:28	as **I also** received authority
	3:10	**I** will keep you from the hour
	3:21	just **as I** myself conquered
	22: 8	**I,** John, am the one who heard

2505   ᴳᴼ1 ᴬᴳ386 ᴸᴺ126
καθα, JUST AS

Mt	27:10	**as** the Lord commanded me

2506   ᴳᴼ3 ᴬᴳ386 ᴸᴺ126 ᴷ3:412 ᴿ2507
καθαιρεσις, TAKING DOWN

2C	10: 4	power to **destroy** strongholds
	10: 8	up and not for **tearing** you **down**
	13:10	up and not for **tearing down**

2507   ᴳᴼ9 ᴬᴳ386 ᴸᴺ126 ᴷ3:411
καθαιρεω, I TAKE DOWN

Mk	15:36	will come **to take** him **down**
	15:46	and **taking down** the body
Lk	1:52	He **has brought** down the
	12:18	I **will pull down** my barns
	23:53	Then he **took** it **down,** wrapped
Ac	13:19	After he **had destroyed** seven
	13:29	they **took** him **down** from the
	19:27	she **will be deprived** of her
2C	10: 4	have divine power **to destroy**

2508   ᴳᴼ1 ᴬᴳ386 ᴸᴺ126 ᴮ3:102 ᴷ3:413 ᴿ2513
καθαιρω, I CLEAN

Jn	15: 2	he **prunes** to make it bear more

2509   ᴳᴼ13 ᴬᴳ387 ᴸᴺ126
καθαπερ, JUST AS INDEED

Ro	4: 6	**So also** David speaks of the
	12: 4	**For as** in one body we have many
1C	10:10	complain **as** some of them did
	12:12	For **just as** the body is one
2C	1:14	**that** on the day of the Lord
	3:13	not **like** Moses, who put a veil
	3:18	**for this** comes from the Lord
	8:11	so **that** your eagerness may be
1Th	2:11	**As** you know, we dealt with
	3: 6	**just as** we long to see you
	3:12	**just as** we abound in love
	4: 5	**like** the Gentiles who do not
He	4: 2	came to us **just as** to them

2510   ᴳᴼ1 ᴬᴳ387 ᴸᴺ126
καθαπτω, I TOUCH ONTO (I FASTEN)

Ac	28: 3	**fastened itself** on his hand

2511   ᴳᴼ31 ᴬᴳ387 ᴸᴺ126 ᴮ3:102 ᴷ3:413 ᴿ2513
καθαριζω, I CLEAN

Mt	8: 2	you **can make** me **clean**
	8: 3	I do choose. **Be made clean!**
	8: 3	his leprosy was **cleansed**
	10: 8	**cleanse** the lepers, cast out
	11: 5	the lepers are **cleansed**
	23:25	**clean** the outside of the cup
	23:26	**clean** the inside of the cup
Mk	1:40	you can **make me clean**
	1:41	I do choose. **Be made clean!**
	1:42	left him, and he **was made clean**
	7:19	he declared all foods **clean**
Lk	4:27	none of them **was cleansed**
	5:12	you **can make** me **clean**
	5:13	I do choose. **Be made clean.**
	7:22	the lepers **are cleansed**
	11:39	**clean** the outside of the cup
	17:14	they went, they **were made clean**
	17:17	Were not ten **made clean**
Ac	10:15	What God **has made clean**
	11: 9	What God **has made clean**
	15: 9	**cleansing** their hearts by faith
2C	7: 1	let us **cleanse ourselves** from
Ep	5:26	**cleansing** her with the washing
Ti	2:14	**purify** for himself a people

He	9:14	**purify** our conscience from dead
	9:22	almost everything **is purified**
	9:23	**to be purified** with these rites
	10: 2	**cleansed** once for all
Ja	4: 8	**Cleanse** your hands
1J	1: 7	Son **cleanses** us from all sin
	1: 9	us our sins and **cleanse** us

2512 ᴳᴼ7 ᴬᴳ387 ᴸᴺ126 ᴮ3:102 ᴷ3:429 ᴿ2511
καθαρισμος, CLEANING

Mk	1:44	**cleansing** what Moses commanded
Lk	2:22	came for their **purification**
	5:14	an offering for your **cleansing**
Jn	2: 6	Jewish rites of **purification**
	3:25	discussion about **purification**
He	1: 3	When he had made **purification**
2P	1: 9	is forgetful of the **cleansing**

2513 ᴳᴼ27 ᴬᴳ388 ᴸᴺ126 ᴮ3:162 ᴷ3:413
καθαρος, CLEAN

Mt	5: 8	Blessed are the **pure** in heart
	23:26	outside also may become **clean**
	27:59	wrapped it in a **clean** linen
Lk	11:41	will be **clean** for you
Jn	13:10	but is entirely **clean**
	13:10	And you are **clean**
	13:11	Not all of you are **clean.**
	15: 3	You have already been **cleansed**
Ac	18: 6	your own heads! I am **innocent.**
	20:26	that I am **not responsible**
Ro	14:20	Everything is indeed **clean**
1Ti	1: 5	that comes from a **pure** heart
	3: 9	faith with a **clear** conscience
2Ti	1: 3	worship with a **clear** conscience
	2:22	on the Lord from a **pure** heart
Ti	1:15	To the **pure** all things are pure
	1:15	To the pure all things are **pure**
	1:15	and unbelieving nothing is **pure**
He	10:22	bodies washed with **pure** water
Ja	1:27	that is **pure** and undefiled
1P	1:22	another **deeply** from the heart
Re	15: 6	robed in **pure** bright linen
	19: 8	fine linen, bright and **pure**
	19:14	fine linen, white and **pure**
	21:18	the city is **pure** gold
	21:18	pure gold, **clear** as glass
	21:21	the city is **pure** gold

2514 ᴳᴼ1 ᴬᴳ388 ᴸᴺ127 ᴮ3:102 ᴷ3:413 ᴿ2513
καθαροτης, CLEANING

| He | 9:13 | so that their flesh is **purified** |

2515 ᴳᴼ3 ᴬᴳ388 ᴸᴺ127 ᴮ3:587 ᴿ2516
καθεδρα, SEAT

Mt	21:12	**seats** of those who sold doves
	23: 2	Pharisees sit on Moses' **seat**
Mk	11:15	**seats** of those who sold doves

2516 ᴳᴼ7 ᴬᴳ388 ᴸᴺ127 ᴮ3:587 ᴷ3:440
καθεζομαι, I SIT

Mt	26:55	I **sat** in the temple teaching
Lk	2:46	**sitting** among the teachers
Jn	4: 6	**was sitting** by the well
	11:20	while Mary **stayed** at home
	20:12	**sitting** where the body of Jesus
Ac	6:15	And all who **sat** in the council
	20: 9	who **was sitting** in the window

2517 ᴳᴼ5 ᴬᴳ388 ᴸᴺ127
καθεξης, IN ORDER

Lk	1: 3	to write an **orderly** account
	8: 1	Soon **afterwards** he went on
Ac	3:24	from Samuel and **those after** him
	11: 4	to them, **step by step,** saying
	18:23	went from **place to place**

2518 ᴳᴼ22 ᴬᴳ388 ᴸᴺ127 ᴮ1:441 ᴷ3:431
καθευδω, I SLEEP

Mt	8:24	by the waves; but he **was asleep**
	9:24	girl is not dead but **sleeping**
	13:25	but while everybody **was asleep**
	25: 5	them became drowsy and **slept**
	26:40	and found them **sleeping**
	26:43	he came and found them **sleeping**
	26:45	Are you still **sleeping**
Mk	4:27	and would **sleep** and rise night
	4:38	**asleep** on the cushion
	5:39	child is not dead but **sleeping**
	13:36	or else he may find you **asleep**
	14:37	He came and found them **sleeping**
	14:37	Simon, are you **asleep**
	14:40	he came and found them **sleeping**
	14:41	Are you still **sleeping**
Lk	8:52	she is not dead but **sleeping**
	22:46	Why are you **sleeping**
Ep	5:14	**Sleeper,** awake! Rise from the
1Th	5: 6	So then let us not **fall asleep**
	5: 7	those who **sleep** sleep at night
	5: 7	those who sleep **sleep** at night
	5:10	whether we are awake or **asleep**

2519 ᴳᴼ2 ᴬᴳ388 ᴸᴺ127 ᴿ2727
καθηγητης, TEACHER
Mt 23:10   you to be called **instructors**
      23:10   have one **instructor**

2520 ᴳᴼ2 ᴬᴳ389 ᴸᴺ127 ᴷ3:437
καθηκω, I AM PROPER
Ac 22:22   **should** not **be allowed** to live
Ro   1:28   things that **should** not **be done**

2521 ᴳᴼ91 ᴬᴳ389 ᴸᴺ127 ᴮ2:615 ᴷ3:440
καθημαι, I SIT
Mt   4:16   the people who **sat** in darkness
      4:16   for those who **sat** in the region
      9: 9   **sitting** at the tax booth
     11:16   **sitting** in the marketplaces
     13: 1   house and **sat** beside the sea
     13: 2   into a boat and **sat** there
     15:29   the mountain, where he **sat** down
     19:28   **will** also **sit** on twelve thrones
     20:30   were two blind men **sitting**
     22:44   **Sit** at my right hand, until I
     23:22   by the one who **is seated** upon it
     24: 3   When he **was sitting** on the Mount
     26:58   he **sat** with the guards in order
     26:64   Son of Man **seated** at the right
     26:69   Now Peter **was sitting** outside
     27:19   While he **was sitting** on the
     27:36   then they **sat** down there
     27:61   **sitting** opposite the tomb
     28: 2   rolled back the stone and **sat**
Mk   2: 6   the scribes **were sitting** there
      2:14   Levi son of Alphaeus **sitting**
      3:32   A crowd **was sitting** around him
      3:34   looking at those who **sat** around
      4: 1   into a boat on the sea and **sat**
      5:15   saw the demoniac **sitting** there
     10:46   **was sitting** by the roadside
     12:36   **Sit** at my right hand, until I
     13: 3   he **was sitting** on the Mount of
     14:62   **seated** at the right hand of the
     16: 5   **sitting** on the right side
Lk   1:79   to give light to those who **sit**
      5:17   of the law **were sitting** near by
      5:27   **sitting** at the tax booth
      7:32   They are like children **sitting**
      8:35   **sitting** at the feet of Jesus
     10:13   **sitting** in sackcloth and ashes
     18:35   **was sitting** by the roadside
     20:42   **Sit** at my right hand

     21:35   it will come upon all who **live**
     22:30   you **will sit** on thrones judging
     22:55   Peter **sat** among them
     22:56   **seeing** him in the firelight
     22:69   the Son of Man **will be seated**
Jn   2:14   and the money changers **seated**
      6: 3   up the mountain and **sat** down
      9: 8   not the man who used to **sit**
     12:15   **sitting** on a donkey's colt
Ac   2: 2   house where they **were sitting**
      2:34   **Sit** at my right hand
      3:10   as the one who used to **sit**
      8:28   **seated** in his chariot
     14: 8   there was a man **sitting**
     23: 3   **Are** you **sitting** there to judge
1C 14:30   to someone else **sitting** nearby
Co   3: 1   **seated** at the right hand of God
He   1:13   **Sit** at my right hand until I
Ja   2: 3   Have a **seat** here, please,
      2: 3   **Sit** at my feet,
Re   4: 2   with one **seated** on the throne
      4: 3   **seated** there looks like jasper
      4: 4   **seated** on the thrones are
      4: 9   one who **is seated** on the throne
      4:10   one who is **seated** on the throne
      5: 1   one **seated** on the throne
      5: 7   one who **was seated** on the throne
      5:13   To the one **seated** on the throne
      6: 2   Its **rider** had a bow; a crown
      6: 4   its **rider** was permitted to take
      6: 5   Its **rider** held a pair of scales
      6: 8   Its **rider's** name was Death
      6:16   one **seated** on the throne
      7:10   God who **is seated** on the throne
      7:15   one who **is seated** on the throne
      9:17   the **riders** wore breastplates
     11:16   elders who **sit** on their thrones
     14: 6   to those who **live** on the earth
     14:14   **seated** on the cloud was one
     14:15   the one who **sat** on the cloud
     14:16   So the one who **sat** on the cloud
     17: 1   the great whore who **is seated**
     17: 3   **sitting** on a scarlet beast
     17: 9   on which the woman **is seated**
     17:15   where the whore **is seated**
     18: 7   I **rule** as a queen; I am no
     19: 4   worshiped God who **is seated**
     19:11   Its **rider** is called Faithful
     19:18   of horses and their **riders**

19:19　　to make war against the **rider**
19:21　　by the sword of the **rider**
20:11　　and the one who **sat** on it
21: 5　　who was **seated** on the throne

2522　GO1　AG389　LN127　R2596,2250
καθημερινος, DAILY
Ac　6: 1　　the **daily** distribution of food

2523　GO46　AG389　LN127　B3:587　K3:440　R2516
καθιζω, I SIT
Mt　5: 1　　after he **sat down**
　　13:48　　drew it ashore, **sat down**
　　19:28　　when the Son of Man **is seated**
　　20:21　　these two sons of mine **will sit**
　　20:23　　but **to sit** at my right hand
　　23: 2　　Pharisees **sit** on Moses' seat
　　25:31　　then he **will sit** on the throne
　　26:36　　**Sit** here while I go over there
Mk　9:35　　He **sat** down, called the twelve
　　10:37　　Grant us **to sit,** one at your
　　10:40　　but **to sit** at my right hand
　　11: 2　　colt that has never been **ridden**
　　11: 7　　cloaks on it; and he **sat** on it
　　12:41　　He **sat** down opposite the
　　14:32　　**Sit** here while I pray.
　　16:19　　**sat** down at the right hand of
Lk　4:20　　back to the attendant, and **sat**
　　5: 3　　Then he **sat** down and taught
　　14:28　　does not first **sit** down and
　　14:31　　**will** not **sit** down first and
　　16: 6　　your bill, **sit** down quickly
　　19:30　　colt that has never been **ridden**
　　24:49　　so **stay** here in the city
Jn　8: 2　　he **sat** down and began to teach
　　12:14　　found a young donkey and **sat**
　　19:13　　**sat** on the judge's bench
Ac　2: 3　　and a tongue **rested** on each
　　2:30　　**put** one of his descendants on
　　8:31　　Philip to get in and **sit** beside
　　12:21　　took his **seat** on the platform
　　13:14　　into the synagogue and **sat** down
　　16:13　　**sat** down and spoke to the women
　　18:11　　He **stayed** there a year and six
　　25: 6　　After he **had stayed** among them
　　25:17　　**took** my **seat** on the tribunal
1C　6: 4　　do you **appoint as judges** those
　　10: 7　　The people **sat** down to eat
Ep　1:20　　**seated** him at his right hand

2Th　2: 4　　he takes his **seat** in the temple
He　1: 3　　he **sat** down at the right hand
　　8: 1　　one who **is seated** at the right
　　10:12　　he **sat** down at the right hand
　　12: 2　　**has taken** his **seat** at the right
Re　3:21　　I will give a **place** with me
　　3:21　　**sat** down with my Father on his
　　20: 4　　those **seated** on them were given

2524　GO4　AG390　LN127
καθιημι, I LET DOWN
Lk　5:19　　and **let** him **down** with his bed
Ac　9:25　　**let** him **down** through an opening
　　10:11　　**being lowered** to the ground
　　11: 5　　**being lowered** by its four

2525　GO21　AG390　LN127　B1:471　K3:444
καθιστημι, I APPOINT
Mt　24:45　　**put in charge** of his household
　　24:47　　he will **put** that one **in charge**
　　25:21　　I **will put** you **in charge**
　　25:23　　I **will put** you **in charge**
Lk　12:14　　who **set** me to be a judge
　　12:42　　his master will **put in charge**
　　12:44　　he will **put** that one **in charge**
Ac　6: 3　　we **may appoint** to this task
　　7:10　　who **appointed** him ruler over
　　7:27　　**made** you a ruler and a judge
　　7:35　　**made** you a ruler and a judge
　　17:15　　who **conducted** Paul brought him
Ro　5:19　　the many **were made** sinners
　　5:19　　many **will be made** righteous
Ti　1: 5　　**appoint** elders in every town
He　5: 1　　is **put in charge** of things
　　7:28　　**appoints** a Son who has been
　　8: 3　　every high priest **is appointed**
Ja　3: 6　　The tongue **is placed** among
　　4: 4　　of the world **becomes** an enemy
2P　1: 8　　**keep** you from being ineffective

2526　GO4　AG390　LN127
καθο, BY WHAT
Ro　8:26　　know how to pray **as we ought**
2C　8:12　　**according to** what one has
　　8:12　　not **according to** what one does
1P　4:13　　But rejoice **insofar as** you are

2527　GO1　AG391　LN127　R2596,3650
καθολου, BY WHOLE
Ac　4:18　　not to speak or teach **at all**

2528 GO1 AG391 LN127 R2596,3695
καθοπλιζω, I ARM THOROUGHLY
Lk 11:21 When a strong man, **fully armed**

2529 GO1 AG391 LN127 B3:511 K5:379
καθοραω, I SEE THOROUGHLY
Ro 1:20 **seen** through the things he has

2530 GO6 AG391 LN128
καθοτι, ACCORDING THAT
Lk 1: 7 **because** Elizabeth was barren
    19: 9 **because** he too is a son of
Ac 2:24 **because** it was impossible for
    2:45 to all, **as** any had need
    4:35 to each **as** any had need
    17:31 **because** he has fixed a day

2531 GO182 AG391 LN128 R2596,5613
καθως, JUST AS [MULTIPLE OCCURRENCES]

2531a GO1 AG391 LN128
καθωσπερ, JUST AS INDEED
He 5: 4 by God, **just as** Aaron was

2532 GO9164 AG391 LN128
και, AND/ALSO [MULTIPLE OCCURRENCES]

2533 GO9 AG393 LN128
καιαφας, CAIAPHAS
Mt 26: 3 priest, who was called **Caiaphas**
    26:57 took him to **Caiaphas** the high
Lk 3: 2 of Annas and **Caiaphas,** the word
Jn 11:49 **Caiaphas,** who was high priest
    18:13 the father-in-law of **Caiaphas**
    18:14 **Caiaphas** was the one who had
    18:24 sent him bound to **Caiaphas**
    18:28 they took Jesus from **Caiaphas**
Ac 4: 6 the high priest, **Caiaphas**

2535 GO3 AG394 LN128 K1:6
καιν, CAIN
He 11: 4 sacrifice than **Cain's.**
1J 3:12 We must not be like **Cain**
Ju 1:11 For they go the way of **Cain**

2536 GO2 AG394 LN128
καιναμ, CAINAN
Lk 3:36 son of **Cainan,** son of Arphaxad
    3:37 of Mahalaleel, son of **Cainan**

2537 GO42 AG394 LN128 B2:669 K3:447
καινος, NEW
Mt 9:17 is put into **fresh** wineskins
    13:52 what is **new** and what is old
    26:29 when I drink it **new** with you
    27:60 laid it in his own **new** tomb
Mk 1:27 A **new** teaching
    2:21 the **new** from the old
    2:22 new wine into **fresh** wineskins
    14:25 that day when I drink it **new**
    16:17 they will speak in **new** tongues
Lk 5:36 No one tears a piece from a **new**
    5:36 otherwise the **new** will be torn
    5:36 the piece from the **new** will not
    5:38 must be put into **fresh** wineskins
    22:20 the **new** covenant in my blood
Jn 13:34 I give you a **new** commandment
    19:41 there was a **new** tomb in which
Ac 17:19 what this **new** teaching is that
    17:21 or hearing something **new**
1C 11:25 This cup is the **new** covenant
2C 3: 6 be ministers of a **new** covenant
    5:17 there is a **new** creation
    5:17 everything has become **new**
Ga 6:15 a **new** creation is everything
Ep 2:15 one **new** humanity in place of
    4:24 yourselves with the **new** self
He 8: 8 I will establish a **new** covenant
    8:13 speaking of "a **new** covenant,"
    9:15 mediator of a **new** covenant
2P 3:13 **new** heavens and a **new** earth
    3:13 new heavens and a **new** earth
1J 2: 7 writing you no **new** commandment
    2: 8 writing you a **new** commandment
2J 1: 5 I were writing you a **new**
Re 2:17 **new** name that no one knows
    3:12 the **new** Jerusalem that comes
    3:12 of heaven, and my own **new** name
    5: 9 They sing a **new** song
    14: 3 they sing a **new** song before
    21: 1 I saw a **new** heaven and a new
    21: 1 I saw a new heaven and a **new**
    21: 2 holy city, the **new** Jerusalem
    21: 5 I am making all things **new**

2538 GO2 AG394 LN128 B2:670 K3:450 R2537
καινοτης, NEWNESS
Ro 6: 4 might walk in **newness** of life
    7: 6 in the **new** life of the Spirit

2539   GO5 AG394 LN128
καιπερ, AND INDEED

Ph	3: 4	**even though** I, too, have reason
He	5: 8	**Although** he was a Son
	7: 5	**though** these also are descended
	12:17	**even though** he sought the
2P	1:12	**though** you know them already

2540   GO85 AG394 LN128 B3:833 K3:455
καιρος, SEASON, TIME

Mt	8:29	to torment us before the **time**
	11:25	At that **time** Jesus said
	12: 1	At that **time** Jesus went through
	13:30	and at harvest **time** I will tell
	14: 1	At that **time** Herod the ruler
	16: 3	the signs of the **times**
	21:34	the harvest **time** had come
	21:41	produce at the harvest **time**
	24:45	of food at the proper **time**
	26:18	Teacher says, My **time** is near
Mk	1:15	The **time** is fulfilled
	10:30	hundredfold now in this **age**
	11:13	it was not the **season** for figs
	12: 2	When the **season** came, he sent
	13:33	when the **time** will come
Lk	1:20	be fulfilled in their **time**
	4:13	until an opportune **time**
	8:13	they believe only for a **while**
	8:13	in a **time** of testing fall away
	12:42	of food at the proper **time**
	12:56	to interpret the present **time**
	13: 1	At that very **time** there were
	18:30	very much more in this **age**
	19:44	you did not recognize the **time**
	20:10	When the **season** came, he sent
	21: 8	The **time** is near!
	21:24	until the **times** of the Gentiles
	21:36	Be alert at all **times**
Jn	7: 6	My **time** has not yet come
	7: 6	but your **time** is always here
	7: 8	for my **time** has not yet fully
Ac	1: 7	to know the times or **periods**
	3:20	so that **times** of refreshing
	7:20	At this **time** Moses was born
	12: 1	About that **time** King Herod
	13:11	you will be blind for a **while**
	14:17	heaven and fruitful **seasons**
	17:26	he allotted the **times** of their
	19:23	About that **time** no little
	24:25	when I have an **opportunity**
Ro	3:26	to prove at the present **time**
	5: 6	at the right **time** Christ died
	8:18	sufferings of this present **time**
	9: 9	About this **time** I will return
	11: 5	So too at the present **time**
	13:11	you know what **time** it is
1C	4: 5	judgment before the **time**
	7: 5	by agreement for a set **time**
	7:29	appointed **time** has grown short
2C	6: 2	At an acceptable **time** I have
	6: 2	now is the acceptable **time**
	8:14	**present** abundance and their
Ga	4:10	days, and months, and **seasons**
	6: 9	we will reap at harvest **time**
	6:10	whenever we have an **opportunity**
Ep	1:10	for the fullness of **time**
	2:12	that you were at that **time**
	5:16	making the most of the **time**
	6:18	in the Spirit at all **times**
Co	4: 5	making the most of the **time**
1Th	2:17	for a short **time,** we were made
	5: 1	the times and the **seasons**
2Th	2: 6	revealed when his **time** comes
1Ti	2: 6	attested at the right **time**
	4: 1	that in later **times** some will
	6:15	bring about at the right **time**
2Ti	3: 1	distressing **times** will come
	4: 3	For the **time** is coming when
	4: 6	the **time** of my departure
Ti	1: 3	in due **time** he revealed his
He	9: 9	a symbol of the present **time**
	9:10	until the **time** comes to set
	11:11	even though he was too **old**
	11:15	they would have had **opportunity**
1P	1: 5	to be revealed in the last **time**
	1:11	about the person or **time** that
	4:17	the **time** has come for judgment
	5: 6	he may exalt you in due **time**
Re	1: 3	in it; for the **time** is near
	11:18	the **time** for judging the dead
	12:12	he knows that his **time** is short
	12:14	she is nourished for a **time**
	12:14	nourished for a time, and **times**
	12:14	and times, and half a **time**
	22:10	for the **time** is near

2541 G029 AG395 LN128 B1:269
καισαρ, CAESAR

Mt	22:17	to pay taxes to the **emperor**
	22:21	They answered, "The **emperor's**."
	22:21	Give therefore to the **emperor**
	22:21	things that are the **emperor's**
Mk	12:14	to pay taxes to the **emperor**
	12:16	They answered, "The **emperor's**."
	12:17	Give to the **emperor** the things
	12:17	things that are the **emperor's**
Lk	2: 1	went out from **Emperor** Augustus
	3: 1	the reign of **Emperor** Tiberius
	20:22	to pay taxes to the **emperor**
	20:24	They said, "The **emperor's**."
	20:25	give to the **emperor** the things
	20:25	things that are the **emperor's**
	23: 2	pay taxes to the **emperor**
Jn	19:12	are no friend of the **emperor**
	19:12	himself against the **emperor**
	19:15	no king but the **emperor**
Ac	17: 7	to the decrees of the **emperor**
	25: 8	or against the **emperor**
	25:10	am appealing to the **emperor's**
	25:11	I appeal to the **emperor**
	25:12	have appealed to the **emperor**
	25:12	to the **emperor** you will go
	25:21	could send him to the **emperor**
	26:32	not appealed to the **emperor**
	27:24	must stand before the **emperor**
	28:19	to appeal to the **emperor**
Ph	4:22	of the **emperor's** household

2542 G017 AG396 LN128
καισαρεια, CAESAREA

Mt	16:13	into the district of **Caesarea**
Mk	8:27	to the villages of **Caesarea**
Ac	8:40	until he came to **Caesarea**
	9:30	brought him down to **Caesarea**
	10: 1	In **Caesarea** there was a man
	10:24	they came to **Caesarea**
	12:19	down from Judea to **Caesarea**
	18:22	he had landed at **Caesarea**
	21: 8	we left and came to **Caesarea**
	21:16	of the disciples from **Caesarea**
	23:23	tonight for **Caesarea** with two
	23:33	When they came to **Caesarea**
	25: 1	he went up from **Caesarea**
	25: 4	was being kept at **Caesarea**

	25: 6	he went down to **Caesarea**
	25:13	Bernice arrived at **Caesarea**

2543 G02 AG396 LN128
καιτοι, AND INDEED

Ac	14:17	**yet** he has not left himself
He	4: 3	**though** his works were finished

2544 G01 AG396 LN128
καιτοιγε, EVEN THOUGH INDEED

Jn	4: 2	**although** it was not Jesus

2545 G011 AG396 LN128 K3:464
καιω, I BURN

Mt	5:15	No one after **lighting** a lamp
Lk	12:35	and have your lamps **lit**
	24:32	our hearts **burning** within us
Jn	5:35	He was a **burning** and shining
	15: 6	into the fire, and **burned**
He	12:18	be touched, a **blazing** fire
Re	4: 5	**burn** seven flaming torches
	8: 8	mountain, **burning** with fire
	8:10	**blazing** like a torch, and it
	19:20	fire that **burns** with sulfur
	21: 8	that **burns** with fire and sulfur

2546 G010 AG396 LN128 R2532,1563
κακει, AND THERE

Mt	5:23	**if** you remember that your
	10:11	**and** stay **there** until you leave
	28:10	**there** they will see me
Mk	1:35	**and there** he prayed
Jn	11:54	**and** he remained **there** with the
Ac	14: 7	**and there** they continued
	17:13	they came **there** too
	22:10	**there** you will be told
	25:20	**and** be tried **there** on these
	27: 6	**There** the centurion found an

2547 G010 AG396 LN128 R2532,1563
κακειθεν, AND FROM THERE

Mk	9:30	They went on **from there**
Lk	11:53	**When** he went outside
Ac	7: 4	God had him move **from there**
	13:21	**Then** they asked for a king
	14:26	**From there** they sailed back
	16:12	and **from there** to Philippi
	20:15	We sailed **from there**
	21: 1	and **from there** to Patara

| 27: 4 | Putting out to sea **from there** |
| 28:15 | The believers **from there** |

2548　GO22 AG396 LN128 R2532,1565
κακεινος, AND THAT

Mt	15:18	**and this** is what defiles
	23:23	practiced **without** neglecting
Mk	12: 4	**this one** they beat over the
	12: 5	**and that one** they killed
	16:11	**But when they** heard that he was
	16:13	**And they** went back and told the
Lk	11: 7	**And he** answers from within
	11:42	**without** neglecting the others
	20:11	**that one** also they beat
	22:12	**He** will show you a large room
Jn	6:57	so **whoever** eats me will live
	7:29	I am from him, **and he** sent me
	10:16	I must bring **them also**
	14:12	**and,** in fact, will do greater
	17:24	I desire that **those also**
Ac	5:37	**he also** perished, and all
	15:11	**just as they** will
	18:19	he left **them** there, but first
Ro	11:23	And **even those** of Israel
1C	10: 6	not desire evil **as they** did
2Ti	2:12	**he** will **also** deny us
He	4: 2	came to us **just as** to them

2549　GO11 AG397 LN128 B1:561 K3:482 R2556
κακια, BADNESS

Mt	6:34	Today's **trouble** is enough for
Ac	8:22	of this **wickedness** of yours
Ro	1:29	evil, covetousness, **malice**
1C	5: 8	the yeast of **malice** and evil
	14:20	rather, be infants in **evil**
Ep	4:31	together with all **malice**
Co	3: 8	anger, wrath, **malice,** slander
Ti	3: 3	passing our days in **malice**
Ja	1:21	rank growth of **wickedness**
1P	2: 1	of all **malice,** and all guile
	2:16	freedom as a pretext for **evil**

2550　GO1 AG397 LN129 K3:485
κακοηθεια, MALICE

| Ro | 1:29 | strife, deceit, **craftiness** |

2551　GO4 AG397 LN129 K3:468 R2556,3806
κακολογεω, I SPEAK BAD

| Mt | 15: 4 | Whoever **speaks evil** of father |
| Mk | 7:10 | Whoever **speaks evil** of father |

| 9:39 | soon afterward to **speak evil** |
| Ac | 19: 9 | to believe and **spoke evil** |

2552　GO1 AG397 LN129 B3:724 K5:936 R2556,3806
κακοπαθεια, BAD SUFFERING

| Ja | 5:10 | As an example of **suffering** |

2553　GO3 AG397 LN129 B3:719 K5:936 R2552
κακοπαθεω, I SUFFER BAD

2Ti	2: 9	for which I **suffer hardship**
	4: 5	be sober, **endure suffering**
Ja	5:13	**Are** any among you **suffering**

2554　GO4 AG397 LN129 B1:561 K3:485 R2555
κακοποιεω, I DO BAD

Mk	3: 4	or to **do harm** on the sabbath
Lk	6: 9	or to **do harm** on the sabbath
1P	3:17	to suffer for **doing evil**
3J	1:11	whoever **does evil** has not seen

2555　GO3 AG397 LN129 B1:561 K3:485 R2556,4160
κακοποιος, BAD DOER

1P	2:12	they malign you as **evildoers**
	2:14	to punish those who **do wrong**
	4:15	murderer, a thief, a **criminal**

2556　GO50 AG397 LN128 B1:561 K3:469
κακος, BAD

Mt	21:41	He will put those **wretches**
	24:48	if that **wicked** slave says
	27:23	Why, what **evil** has he done?
Mk	7:21	that **evil** intentions come
	15:14	Why, what **evil** has he done?
Lk	16:25	in like manner **evil** things
	23:22	Why, what **evil** has he done?
Jn	18:23	testify to the **wrong**
	18:30	this man were not a **criminal**
Ac	9:13	how much **evil** he has done
	16:28	Do not **harm** yourself, for we
	23: 9	We find nothing **wrong** with this
	28: 5	the fire and suffered no **harm**
Ro	1:30	boastful, inventors of **evil**
	2: 9	for everyone who does **evil**
	3: 8	Let us do **evil** so that good
	7:19	but the **evil** I do not want
	7:21	**evil** lies close at hand
	12:17	Do not repay anyone **evil**
	12:17	repay anyone evil for **evil**
	12:21	Do not be overcome by **evil**
	12:21	but overcome **evil** with good

	13: 3	to good conduct, but to **bad**
	13: 4	But if you do what is **wrong**
	13: 4	execute wrath on the **wrongdoer**
	13:10	does no **wrong** to a neighbor
	14:20	but it is **wrong** for you
	16:19	guileless in what is **evil**
1C	10: 6	we might not desire **evil**
	13: 5	not irritable or **resentful**
	15:33	**Bad** company ruins good morals
2C	13: 7	you may not do anything **wrong**
Ph	3: 2	beware of the **evil** workers
Co	3: 5	impurity, passion, **evil** desire
1Th	5:15	of you repays **evil** for evil
	5:15	of you repays evil for **evil**
1Ti	6:10	coppersmith did me great **harm**
Ti	1:12	always liars, **vicious** brutes
He	5:14	to distinguish good from **evil**
Ja	1:13	God cannot be tempted by **evil**
	3: 8	**evil**, full of deadly poison
1P	3: 9	Do not repay **evil** for evil
	3: 9	Do not repay evil for **evil**
	3:10	keep their tongues from **evil**
	3:11	let them turn away from **evil**
	3:12	is against those who do **evil**
3J	1:11	do not imitate what is **evil**
Re	2: 2	you cannot tolerate **evildoers**
	16: 2	a **foul** and painful sore came on

2557 GO4 AG398 LN129 B1:561 K3:484
κακουργος, WORKER OF BAD

Lk	23:32	who were **criminals,** were led
	23:33	there with the **criminals**
	23:39	One of the **criminals** who were
2Ti	2: 9	being chained like a **criminal**

2558 GO2 AG398 LN129
κακουχεω, I TREAT BADLY

He	11:37	persecuted, **tormented**
	13: 3	those who are being **tortured**

2559 GO6 AG398 LN129 B1:561 K3:484 R2556
κακοω, I DO BAD

Ac	7: 6	enslave them and **mistreat** them
	7:19	King Herod laid **violent** hands
	14: 2	and **poisoned** their minds
	18:10	a hand on you to **harm** you
1P	3:13	Now who **will harm** you if you

2560 GO16 AG398 LN129 K4:1091 R2556
κακως, BADLY

Mt	4:24	those who were **afflicted** with
	8:16	and cured all who were **sick**
	9:12	but those who are **sick**
	14:35	all who were **sick** to him
	15:22	my daughter is **tormented**
	17:15	and he suffers **terribly**
	21:41	wretches to a **miserable** death
Mk	1:32	to him all who were **sick**
	1:34	he cured many who were **sick**
	2:17	but those who are **sick**
	6:55	began to bring the **sick** on mats
Lk	5:31	but those who are **sick**
	7: 2	who was **ill** and close to death
Jn	18:23	If I have spoken **wrongly**
Ac	23: 5	You shall not speak **evil**
Ja	4: 3	because you ask **wrongly**

2561 GO1 AG398 LN129 R2559
κακωσις, BADNESS

Ac	7:34	surely seen the **mistreatment**

2562 GO1 AG398 LN129 R2563
καλαμη, STRAW

1C	3:12	stones, wood, hay, **straw**

2563 GO12 AG398 LN129
καλαμος, REED

Mt	11: 7	A **reed** shaken by the wind?
	12:20	will not break a bruised **reed**
	27:29	They put a **reed** in his right
	27:30	took the **reed** and struck him
	27:48	wine, put it on a **stick**
Mk	15:19	struck his head with a **reed**
	15:36	sour wine, put it on a **stick**
Lk	7:24	A **reed** shaken by the wind?
3J	1:13	rather not write with **pen**
Re	11: 1	I was given a measuring **rod**
	21:15	had a measuring **rod** of gold
	21:16	measured the city with his **rod**

2564 GO148 AG398 LN129 B1:270 K3:487
καλεω, I CALL

Mt	1:21	you are to **name** him Jesus
	1:23	they **shall name** him Emmanuel
	1:25	and he **named** him Jesus
	2: 7	Then Herod secretly **called** for
	2:15	of Egypt I **have called** my son
	2:23	He **will be called** a Nazorean.
	4:21	their nets, and he **called** them
	5: 9	they **will be called** children

	5:19	**will be called** least in the
	5:19	**will be called** great in the
	9:13	For I have come **to call** not
	20: 8	**Call** the laborers and give
	21:13	house **shall be called** a house
	22: 3	He sent his slaves **to call**
	22: 3	those who **had been invited**
	22: 4	those who **have been invited**
	22: 8	those **invited** were not worthy
	22: 9	**invite** everyone you find
	22:43	David by the Spirit **calls** him
	22:45	If David thus **calls** him Lord
	23: 7	to have people **call** them rabbi
	23: 8	you **are** not **to be called** rabbi
	23: 9	And **call** no one your father
	23:10	Nor **are** you **to be called**
	25:14	a journey, **summoned** his slaves
	27: 8	that field **has been called**
Mk	1:20	Immediately he **called** them
	2:17	I have come **to call** not the
	3:31	sent to him and **called** him
	11:17	house **shall be called** a house
Lk	1:13	and you **will name** him John
	1:31	and you **will name** him Jesus
	1:32	and **will be called** the Son
	1:35	he **will be called** Son of God
	1:36	who **was said to be** barren
	1:59	they **were going to name** him
	1:60	he **is to be called** John
	1:61	None of your relatives **has**
	1:62	find out what **name** he wanted
	1:76	city of David **called** Bethlehem
	2:21	and he **was called** Jesus
	2:21	the **name given** by the angel
	2:23	**shall be designated** as holy
	5:32	I have come to **call** not the
	6:15	who **was called** the Zealot
	6:46	Why do you **call** me
	7:11	he went to a town **called** Nain
	7:39	who **had invited** him saw it
	8: 2	Mary, **called** Magdalene
	9:10	to a city **called** Bethsaida
	10:39	She had a sister **named** Mary
	14: 7	he noticed how the **guests** chose
	14: 8	When you **are invited** by someone
	14: 8	**has been invited** by your host
	14: 9	host who **invited** both of you
	14:10	But when you **are invited**
	14:10	when your **host** comes, he may
	14:12	the one who **had invited** him
	14:13	**invite** the poor, the crippled
	14:16	gave a great dinner and **invited**
	14:17	to those who **had been invited**
	14:24	of those who **were invited**
	15:19	worthy **to be called** your son
	15:21	worthy **to be called** your son
	19: 2	A man was there **named** Zacchaeus
	19:13	He **summoned** ten of his slaves
	19:29	**called** the Mount of Olives
	20:44	David thus **calls** him Lord
	21:37	of Olives, as it **was called**
	22: 3	into Judas **called** Iscariot
	22:25	are **called** benefactors
	23:33	that **is called** The Skull
Jn	1:42	You are **to be called** Cephas
	2: 2	**had** also **been invited** to the
Ac	1:12	from the mount **called** Olivet
	1:19	so that the field **was called**
	1:23	Joseph **called** Barsabbas
	3:11	the portico **called** Solomon's
	4:18	So they **called** them and ordered
	7:58	a young man **named** Saul
	8:10	God that **is called** Great
	9:11	the street **called** Straight
	10: 1	Cohort, as it **was called**
	13: 1	Simeon who **was called** Niger
	14:12	Barnabas they **called** Zeus
	15:22	sent Judas **called** Barsabbas
	15:37	with them John **called** Mark
	24: 2	When Paul **had been summoned**
	27: 8	to a place **called** Fair Havens
	27:14	**called** the northeaster
	27:16	small island **called** Cauda
	28: 1	the island **was called** Malta
Ro	4:17	and **calls** into existence the
	8:30	he predestined he also **called**
	8:30	those whom he **called** he also
	9: 7	that descendants **shall be named**
	9:12	not by works but by his **call**
	9:24	us whom he **has called**
	9:25	I **will call** 'my people,'
	9:26	they **shall be called** children
1C	1: 9	by him you **were called** into
	7:15	to peace that God **has called**
	7:17	to which God **called** you
	7:18	at the time of his **call**
	7:18	at the time of his **call**
	7:20	in which you **were called**

	7:21	Were you a slave when **called**
	7:22	whoever **was called** in the Lord
	7:22	when **called** is a slave of
	7:24	condition you **were called**
	10:27	If an unbeliever **invites** you
	15: 9	unfit **to be called** an apostle
Ga	1: 6	one who **called** you in the grace
	1:15	born and **called** me through his
	5: 8	come from the one who **calls** you
	5:13	For you **were called** to freedom
Ep	4: 1	to which you **have been called**
	4: 4	just as you **were called** to the
Co	3:15	you **were called** in the one body
1Th	2:12	who **calls** you into his own
	4: 7	For God did not **call** us to
	5:24	one who **calls** you is faithful
2Th	2:14	For this purpose he **called** you
1Ti	6:12	to which you **were called**
2Ti	1: 9	who saved us and **called** us
He	2:11	Jesus is not ashamed **to call**
	3:13	it **is called** "today," so that
	5: 4	it only when **called** by God
	9:15	so that those who **are called**
	11: 8	obeyed when he **was called**
	11·18	that descendants **shall be named**
Ja	2:23	he **was called** the friend of God
1P	1:15	as he who **called** you is holy
	2: 9	acts of him who **called** you out
	2:21	to this you **have been called**
	3: 6	obeyed Abraham and **called** him
	3: 9	for this that you **were called**
	5:10	who **has called** you to his
2P	1: 3	who **called** us by his own glory
1J	3: 1	we **should be called** children
Re	1: 9	was on the island **called** Patmos
	11: 8	prophetically **called** Sodom
	12: 9	who **is called** the Devil
	16:16	in Hebrew **is called** Harmagedon
	19: 9	are those who **are invited** to
	19:11	Its rider **is called** Faithful
	19:13	name **is called** The Word of God

2565   GO1 AG400 LN129 B2:710 R2570,1636
καλλιελαιος, CULTIVATED OLIVE
Ro 11:24 into a **cultivated olive tree**

2567   GO1 AG400 LN129 B3:765 K2:159 R2570,1320
καλοδιδασκαλος, TEACHER OF GOOD
Ti 2: 3 they are to **teach** what is **good**

2569   GO1 AG400 LN129 B2:102 R2570,4160
καλοποιεω, I DO GOOD
2Th 3:13 be weary in **doing** what is **right**

2570   GO101 AG400 LN129 B2:102 K3:536
καλος, GOOD

Mt	3:10	that does not bear **good** fruit
	5:16	they may see your **good** works
	7:17	every **good** tree bears good
	7:18	bad tree bear **good** fruit
	7:19	that does not bear **good** fruit
	12:33	Either make the tree **good**
	12:33	tree good, and its fruit **good**
	13: 8	Other seeds fell on **good** soil
	13:23	for what was sown on **good** soil
	13:24	to someone who sowed **good** seed
	13:27	did you not sow **good** seed
	13:37	The one who sows the **good** seed
	13:38	the **good** seed are the children
	13:45	in search of **fine** pearls
	13:48	and put the **good** into baskets
	15:26	It is not **fair** to take the
	17: 4	Lord, it is **good** for us to be
	18: 8	it is **better** for you to enter
	18: 9	it is **better** for you to enter
	26:10	has performed a **good** service
	26:24	It would have been **better** for
Mk	4: 8	Other seed fell into **good** soil
	4:20	the ones sown on the **good** soil
	7:27	it is not **fair** to take the
	9: 5	Rabbi, it is **good** for us to be
	9:42	it would be **better** for you
	9:43	it is **better** for you to enter
	9:45	it is **better** for you to enter
	9:47	it is **better** for you to enter
	9:50	Salt is **good;** but if salt
	14: 6	has performed a **good** service
	14:21	been **better** for that one not
Lk	3: 9	that does not bear **good** fruit
	6:38	A **good** measure, pressed down
	6:43	No **good** tree bears bad fruit
	6:43	a bad tree bear **good** fruit
	8:15	as for that in the **good** soil
	8:15	in an honest and **good** heart
	9:33	it is **good** for us to be here
	14:34	Salt is **good;** but if salt has
	21: 5	adorned with **beautiful** stones
Jn	2:10	serves the **good** wine first
	2:10	you have kept the **good** wine

	10:11	I am the **good** shepherd
	10:11	The **good** shepherd lays down
	10:14	I am the **good** shepherd
	10:32	have shown you many **good** works
	10:33	It is not for a **good** work
Ac	27: 8	to a place called **Fair** Havens
Ro	7:16	I agree that the law is **good**
	7:18	nothing **good** dwells within me
	7:21	I want to do what is **good**
	12:17	for what is **noble** in the sight
	14:21	it is **good** not to eat meat
1C	5: 6	Your boasting is not a **good**
	7: 1	It is **well** for a man not to
	7: 8	it is **well** for them to remain
	7:26	it is **well** for you to remain
	7:26	for you to remain as you **are**
	9:15	I would **rather** die than that
2C	8:21	intend to do what is **right**
	13: 7	that you may do what is **right**
Ga	4:18	It is **good** to be made much of
	4:18	for a **good** purpose at all
	6: 9	weary in doing what is **right**
1Th	5:21	hold fast to what is **good**
1Ti	1: 8	we know that the law is **good**
	1:18	you may fight the **good** fight
	2: 3	This is **right** and is acceptable
	3: 1	of bishop desires a **noble** task
	3: 7	he must be **well thought** of by
	3:13	a **good** standing for themselves
	4: 4	created by God is **good**
	4: 6	you will be a **good** servant
	4: 6	and of the **sound** teaching
	5:10	attested for her **good** works
	5:25	**good** works are conspicuous
	6:12	Fight the **good** fight of the
	6:12	you made the **good** confession
	6:13	made the **good** confession
	6:18	They are to do **good,** to be rich
	6:19	treasure of a **good** foundation
2Ti	1:14	Guard the **good** treasure
	2: 3	suffering like a **good** soldier
	4: 7	I have fought the **good** fight
Ti	2: 7	respects a model of **good** works
	2:14	who are zealous for **good** deeds
	3: 8	devote themselves to **good** works
	3: 8	these things are **excellent**
	3:14	to devote themselves to **good**
He	5:14	to distinguish **good** from evil
	6: 5	and have tasted the **goodness**

	10:24	to love and **good** deeds
	13: 9	for it is **well** for the heart
	13:18	sure that we have a **clear**
Ja	2: 7	blaspheme the **excellent** name
	3:13	Show by your **good** life that
	4:17	who knows the **right** thing to do
1P	2:12	Conduct yourselves **honorably**
	2:12	may see your **honorable** deeds
	4:10	Like **good** stewards of the

2571   GO4   AG400   LN129   B2:212   K3:558   R2572
καλυμμα, VEIL

2C	3:13	not like Moses, who put a **veil**
	3:14	that same **veil** is still there
	3:15	a **veil** lies over their minds
	3:16	the Lord, the **veil** is removed

2572   GO8   AG401   LN129   B2:211
καλυπτω, I COVER, I VEIL

Mt	8:24	that the boat **was being swamped**
	10:26	for nothing **is covered up**
Lk	8:16	after lighting a lamp **hides** it
	23:30	and to the hills, '**Cover** us.'
2C	4: 3	even if our gospel **is veiled**
	4: 3	it **is veiled** to those who are
Ja	5:20	**will cover** a multitude of sins
1P	4: 8	love **covers** a multitude of sins

2573   GO37   AG401   LN129   R2570
καλως, WELL

Mt	12:12	So it is lawful to do **good**
	15: 7	Isaiah prophesied **rightly**
Mk	7: 6	Isaiah prophesied **rightly**
	7: 9	have a **fine** way of rejecting
	7:37	He has done everything **well**
	12:28	that he answered them **well**
	12:32	You are **right,** Teacher
	16:18	the sick, and they will **recover**
Lk	6:26	when all speak **well** of you
	6:27	do **good** to those who hate you
	6:48	because it had been **well** built
	20:39	Teacher, you have spoken **well**
Jn	4:17	You are **right** in saying
	8:48	Are we not **right** in saying
	13:13	and you are **right,** for that
	18:23	But if I have spoken **rightly**
Ac	10:33	have been **kind** enough to come
	25:10	the Jews, as you very **well** know
	28:25	The Holy Spirit was **right**
Ro	11:20	That is **true.**

1C	7:37	his fiancée, he will do **well**
	7:38	marries his fiancée does **well**
	14:17	you may give thanks **well** enough
2C	11: 4	you submit to it **readily** enough
Ga	4:17	but for no **good** purpose
	5: 7	You were running **well**
Ph	4:14	it was **kind** of you to share
1Ti	3: 4	manage his own household **well**
	3:12	and their households **well**
	3:13	deacons gain a **good** standing
	5:17	Let the elders who rule **well**
He	13:18	desiring to act **honorably**
Ja	2: 3	Have a seat here, **please,**
	2: 8	You do **well** if you really
	2:19	that God is one; you do **well**
2P	1:19	You will do **well** to be
3J	1: 6	You will do **well** to send them

2574   GO6 AG401 LN130 K3:592
καμηλος, CAMEL

Mt	3: 4	John wore clothing of **camel's**
	19:24	it is easier for a **camel** to go
	23:24	out a gnat but swallow a **camel**
Mk	1: 6	John was clothed with **camel's**
	10:25	It is easier for a **camel** to go
Lk	18:25	it is easier for a **camel** to go

2575   GO4 AG401 LN130
καμινος, FURNACE

Mt	13:42	into the **furnace** of fire
	13:50	throw them into the **furnace**
Re	1:15	refined as in a **furnace**
	9: 2	the smoke of a great **furnace**

2576   GO2 AG402 LN130
καμμυω, I SHUT

Mt	13:15	they **have shut** their eyes
Ac	28:27	they **have shut** their eyes

2577   GO2 AG402 LN130
καμνω, I AM WEARY

He	12: 3	that you may not **grow weary**
Ja	5:15	of faith will save the **sick**

2578   GO4 AG402 LN130 K3:594
καμπτω, I BOW

Ro	11: 4	who **have** not **bowed** the knee
	14:11	every knee **shall bow** to me
Ep	3:14	For this reason I **bow** my knees
Ph	2:10	every knee **should bend**

2579   GO17 AG402 LN130 R2532,1437
καν, AND IF

Mt	21:21	but **even if** you say to this
	26:35	**Even though** I must die with you
Mk	5:28	**If** I but touch his clothes
	6:56	might touch **even** the fringe
	16:18	**and if** they drink any deadly
Lk	12:38	**If** he comes during the middle
	12:38	**or** near dawn, and finds them
	13: 9	**but if** not, you can cut it
Jn	8:14	**Even if** I testify on my own
	8:55	**if** I would say that I do not
	10:38	**even though** you do not believe
	11:25	**even though** they die, will live
Ac	5:15	Peter's shadow **might** fall on
1C	13: 3	**If** I give away all my
2C	11:16	**then** accept me as a fool
He	12:20	**If even** an animal touches the
Ja	5:15	**and** anyone who has committed

2580   GO4 AG402 LN130
κανα, CANA

Jn	2: 1	there was a wedding in **Cana**
	2:11	in **Cana** of Galilee
	4:46	Then he came again to **Cana**
	21. 2	Nathanael of **Cana** in Galilee

2581   GO2 AG402 LN130 B3:1167
κανααιος, CANANEAN

Mt	10: 4	Simon the **Cananaean**
Mk	3:18	and Simon the **Cananaean**

2582   GO1 AG402 LN130
κανδακη, CANDACE

Ac	8:27	court official of the **Candace**

2583   GO4 AG403 LN130 B3:399 K3:596
κανων, RULE

2C	10:13	but will keep within the **field**
	10:15	our **sphere of action** among you
	10:16	someone else's **sphere of action**
Ga	6:16	those who will follow this **rule**

2585   GO1 AG403 LN130 K3:603
καπηλευω, I TRADE ON

2C	2:17	are not **peddlers** of God's word

2586   GO13 AG403 LN130
καπνος, SMOKE

Ac	2:19	blood, and fire, and **smoky** mist

Re	8: 4	And the **smoke** of the incense
	9: 2	and from the shaft rose **smoke**
	9: 2	rose smoke like the **smoke**
	9: 2	with the **smoke** from the shaft
	9: 3	from the **smoke** came locusts
	9:17	fire and **smoke** and sulfur
	9:18	fire and **smoke** and sulfur
	14:11	And the **smoke** of their torment
	15: 8	temple was filled with **smoke**
	18: 9	see the **smoke** of her burning
	18:18	the **smoke** of her burning
	19: 3	The **smoke** goes up from her

2587　GO2 AG403 LN130
καππαδοκια, CAPPADOCIA

Ac	2: 9	Judea and **Cappadocia,** Pontus
1P	1: 1	**Cappadocia,** Asia, and Bithynia

2588　GO156 AG403 LN130 B2:180 K3:605
καρδια, HEART

Mt	5: 8	Blessed are the pure in **heart**
	5:28	adultery with her in his **heart**
	6:21	there your **heart** will be also
	9: 4	you think evil in your **hearts**
	11:29	I am gentle and humble in **heart**
	12:34	of the abundance of the **heart**
	12:40	be in the **heart** of the earth
	13:15	people's **heart** has grown dull
	13:15	understand with their **heart**
	13:19	what is sown in the **heart**
	15: 8	their **hearts** are far from me
	15:18	proceeds from the **heart**
	15:19	For out of the **heart** come evil
	18:35	or sister from your **heart**
	22:37	your God with all your **heart**
	24:48	wicked slave says to **himself**
Mk	2: 6	questioning in their **hearts**
	2: 8	such questions in your **hearts**
	3: 5	at their hardness of **heart**
	6:52	but their **hearts** were hardened
	7: 6	their **hearts** are far from me
	7:19	not the **heart** but the stomach
	7:21	from the human **heart**
	8:17	Are your **hearts** hardened
	11:23	you do not doubt in your **heart**
	12:30	your God with all your **heart**
	12:33	love him with all the **heart**
Lk	1:17	to turn the **hearts** of parents
	1:51	in the thoughts of their **hearts**

	1:66	who heard them **pondered** them
	2:19	pondered them in her **heart**
	2:35	so that the **inner** thoughts
	2:51	all these things in her **heart**
	3:15	questioning in their **hearts**
	5:22	such questions in your **hearts**
	6:45	the good treasure of the **heart**
	6:45	the abundance of the **heart**
	8:12	the word from their **hearts**
	8:15	in an honest and good **heart**
	9:47	aware of their **inner** thoughts
	10:27	your God with all your **heart**
	12:34	there your **heart** will be also
	12:45	that slave says to **himself**
	16:15	but God knows your **hearts**
	21:14	So make up your **minds** not to
	21:34	on guard so that your **hearts**
	24:25	how slow of **heart** to believe
	24:32	Were not our **hearts** burning
	24:38	do doubts arise in your **hearts**
Jn	12:40	eyes and hardened their **heart**
	12:40	understand with their **heart**
	13: 2	put it into the **heart**
	14: 1	let your **hearts** be troubled
	14:27	let your **hearts** be troubled
	16: 6	sorrow has filled your **hearts**
	16:22	your **hearts** will rejoice
Ac	2:26	therefore my **heart** was glad
	2:37	they were cut to the **heart**
	2:46	with glad and generous **hearts**
	4:32	who believed were of one **heart**
	5: 3	why has Satan filled your **heart**
	5: 4	this deed in your **heart**
	7:23	came into his **heart** to visit
	7:39	in their **hearts** they turned
	7:51	uncircumcised in **heart** and ears
	7:54	they became **enraged** and ground
	8:21	for your **heart** is not right
	8:22	the intent of your **heart** may
	11:23	with steadfast **devotion**
	13:22	to be a man after my **heart**
	14:17	and your **hearts** with joy
	15: 9	and in cleansing their **hearts**
	16:14	The Lord opened her **heart**
	21:13	weeping and breaking my **heart**
	28:27	people's **heart** has grown dull
	28:27	understand with their **heart**
Ro	1:21	senseless **minds** were darkened
	1:24	in the lusts of their **hearts**

	2: 5	your hard and impenitent **heart**
	2:15	is written on their **hearts**
	2:29	is a matter of the **heart**
	5: 5	has been poured into our **hearts**
	6:17	become obedient from the **heart**
	8:27	And God, who searches the **heart**
	9: 2	unceasing anguish in my **heart**
	10: 1	my **heart's** desire and prayer
	10: 6	Do not say in your **heart**
	10: 8	on your lips and in your **heart**
	10: 9	believe in your **heart** that
	10:10	For one believes with the **heart**
	16:18	they deceive the **hearts** of the
1C	2: 9	nor the human **heart** conceived
	4: 5	the purposes of the **heart**
	7:37	stands firm in his **resolve**
	7:37	has determined in his own **mind**
	14:25	of the unbeliever's **heart**
2C	1:22	his Spirit in our **hearts**
	2: 4	distress and anguish of **heart**
	3: 2	written on our **hearts**
	3: 3	but on tablets of human **hearts**
	3:15	veil lies over their **minds**
	4: 6	who has shone in our **hearts**
	5:12	and not in the **heart**
	6:11	our **heart** is wide open to you
	7: 3	that you are in our **hearts**
	8:16	who put in the **heart** of Titus
	9: 7	you have made up your **mind**
Ga	4: 6	his Son into our **hearts**
Ep	1:18	with the eyes of your **heart**
	3:17	may dwell in your **hearts**
	4:18	ignorance and hardness of **heart**
	5:19	to the Lord in your **hearts**
	6: 5	in singleness of **heart**
	6:22	and to encourage your **hearts**
Ph	1: 7	you hold me in your **heart**
	4: 7	your **hearts** and your minds
Co	2: 2	I want their **hearts** to be
	3:15	rule in your **hearts,** to which
	3:16	with gratitude in your **hearts**
	3:22	please them, but whole**heartedly**
	4: 8	he may encourage your **hearts**
1Th	2: 4	please God who tests our **hearts**
	2:17	in person, not in **heart**
	3:13	he so strengthen your **hearts**
2Th	2:17	comfort your **hearts**
	3: 5	May the Lord direct your **hearts**
1Ti	1: 5	comes from a pure **heart**

2Ti	2:22	on the Lord from a pure **heart**
He	3: 8	do not harden your **hearts**
	3:10	go astray in their **hearts**
	3:12	**heart** that turns away from
	3:15	do not harden your **hearts**
	4: 7	do not harden your **hearts**
	4:12	and intentions of the **heart**
	8:10	write them on their **hearts**
	10:16	put my laws in their **hearts**
	10:22	approach with a true **heart**
	10:22	our **hearts** sprinkled clean
	13: 9	for it is well for the **heart**
Ja	1:26	but deceive their **hearts**
	3:14	ambition in your **hearts**
	4: 8	and purify your **hearts**
	5: 5	you have fattened your **hearts**
	5: 8	Strengthen your **hearts**
1P	1:22	another deeply from the **heart**
	3: 4	adornment be the inner **self**
	3:15	but in your **hearts** sanctify
2P	1:19	star rises in your **hearts**
	2:14	have **hearts** trained in greed
1J	3:19	and will reassure our **hearts**
	3:20	whenever our **hearts** condemn us
	3:20	God is greater than our **hearts**
	3:21	if our **hearts** do not condemn
Re	2:23	who searches minds and **hearts**
	17:17	has put it into their **hearts**
	18: 7	Since in her **heart** she says

2589   GO2 AG404 LN130 B2:180 K3:613 R2588,1097
καρδιογνωστης, HEART-KNOWER

Ac	1:24	you **know** everyone's **heart**
	15: 8	who **knows** the human **heart**

2590   GO66 AG404 LN131 B1:721 K3:614
καρπος, FRUIT

Mt	3: 8	Bear **fruit** worthy of repentance
	3:10	does not bear good **fruit** is cut
	7:16	will know them by their **fruits**
	7:17	good tree bears good **fruit**
	7:17	the bad tree bears bad **fruit**
	7:18	good tree cannot bear bad **fruit**
	7:18	bad tree bear good **fruit**
	7:19	that does not bear good **fruit**
	7:20	will know them by their **fruits**
	12:33	tree good, and its **fruit** good
	12:33	tree bad, and its **fruit** bad
	12:33	tree is known by its **fruit**

	13: 8	and brought forth **grain**
	13:26	plants came up and bore **grain**
	21:19	May no **fruit** ever come from
	21:34	When the **harvest** time had come
	21:34	tenants to collect his **produce**
	21:41	will give him the **produce**
	21:43	the **fruits** of the kingdom
Mk	4: 7	and it yielded no **grain**
	4: 8	and brought forth **grain**
	4:29	But when the **grain** is ripe
	11:14	May no one ever eat **fruit**
	12: 2	his share of the **produce**
Lk	1:42	and blessed is the **fruit**
	3: 8	**fruits** worthy of repentance
	3: 9	that does not bear good **fruit**
	6:43	No good tree bears bad **fruit**
	6:43	bad tree bear good **fruit**
	6:44	is known by its own **fruit**
	8: 8	it **produced** a hundredfold
	12:17	no place to store my **crops**
	13: 6	he came looking for **fruit**
	13: 7	I have come looking for **fruit**
	13: 9	If it bears **fruit** next year
	20:10	his share of the **produce**
Jn	4:36	gathering **fruit** for eternal
	12:24	it dies, it bears much **fruit**
	15: 2	in me that bears no **fruit**
	15: 2	Every branch that bears **fruit**
	15: 2	to make it bear more **fruit**
	15: 4	cannot bear **fruit** by itself
	15: 5	I in them bear much **fruit**
	15: 8	that you bear much **fruit**
	15:16	you to go and bear **fruit**
	15:16	fruit, **fruit** that will last
Ac	2:30	put one of his **descendants**
Ro	1:13	I may reap some **harvest** among
	6:21	So what **advantage** did you then
	6:22	the **advantage** you get is
	15:28	to them what has been **collected**
1C	9: 7	does not eat any of its **fruit**
Ga	5:22	**fruit** of the Spirit is love
Ep	5: 9	for the **fruit** of the light
Ph	1:11	the **harvest** of righteousness
	1:22	means **fruitful** labor for me
	4:17	**profit** that accumulates to
2Ti	2: 6	the first share of the **crops**
He	12:11	it yields the peaceful **fruit**
	13:15	the **fruit** of lips that confess
Ja	3:17	full of mercy and good **fruits**

	3:18	And a **harvest** of righteousness
	5: 7	waits for the precious **crop**
	5:18	the earth yielded its **harvest**
Re	22: 2	with its twelve kinds of **fruit**
	22: 2	producing its **fruit** each month

2591 GO1 AG404 LN131
καρπος, CARPUS
2Ti 4:13 cloak that I left with **Carpus**

2592 GO8 AG405 LN131 B1:721 K3:616 R2593
καρποφορεω, I BEAR FRUIT
Mt 13:23 who indeed **bears fruit**
Mk 4:20 accept it and **bear fruit**
    4:28 The earth **produces** of itself
Lk 8:15 **bear fruit** with patient
Ro 7: 4 that we may **bear fruit** for God
    7: 5 to **bear fruit** for death
Co 1: 6 Just as it is **bearing fruit**
    1:10 as you **bear fruit** in every

2593 GO1 AG405 LN131 R2590,5342
καρποφορος, FRUIT-BEARING
Ac 14:17 heaven and **fruitful** seasons

2594 GO1 AG405 LN131 B2:767 K3:617
καρτερεω, I PERSEVERE
He 11:27 for he **persevered** as though

2595 GO6 AG405 LN131
καρφος, SPLINTER
Mt 7: 3 Why do you see the **speck**
    7: 4 take the **speck** out of your eye
    7: 5 see clearly to take the **speck**
Lk 6:41 Why do you see the **speck**
    6:42 let me take out the **speck**
    6:42 clearly to take the **speck**

2596 GO473 AG405 LN131 B3:1172
κατα, BY/ACCORDING TO [MULTIPLE
OCCURRENCES]

2597 GO81 AG408 LN131 B2:184 K1:522
καταβαινω, I GO DOWN
Mt 3:16 the Spirit of God **descending**
    7:25 The rain **fell**
    7:27 The rain **fell**
    8: 1 When Jesus **had come down**
    11:23 you **will be brought down**
    14:29 So Peter **got out** of the boat

	17: 9	As they **were coming down**
	24:17	must not **go down** to take
	27:40	**come down** from the cross
	27:42	**let** him **come down** from the
	28: 2	Lord, **descending** from heaven
Mk	1:10	**descending** like a dove on him
	3:22	who **came down** from Jerusalem
	9: 9	**were coming down** the mountain
	13:15	must not **go down** or enter
	15:30	**come down** from the cross
	15:32	**come down** from the cross now
Lk	2:51	Then he **went down** with them
	3:22	Holy Spirit **descended** upon him
	6:17	**came down** with them and stood
	8:23	windstorm **swept down** on the
	9:54	fire **to come down** from heaven
	10:15	**will be brought down** to Hades
	10:30	A man **was going down** from
	10:31	**was going down** that road
	17:31	must not **come down** to take
	18:14	this man **went down** to his home
	19: 5	Zacchaeus, hurry and **come down**
	19: 6	he **hurried down** and was happy
	22:44	drops of blood **falling down**
Jn	1:32	**descending** from heaven like
	1:33	you see the Spirit **descend**
	1:51	**descending** upon the Son of Man
	2:12	he **went down** to Capernaum
	3:13	except the one who **descended**
	4:47	begged him **to come down**
	4:49	**come down** before my little boy
	4:51	As he **was going down**
	5: 7	someone else **steps down** ahead
	6:16	disciples **went down** to the sea
	6:33	which **comes down** from heaven
	6:38	I **have come down** from heaven
	6:41	that **came down** from heaven
	6:42	I **have come down** from heaven
	6:50	that **comes down** from heaven
	6:51	that **came down** from heaven
	6:58	that **came down** from heaven
Ac	7:15	so Jacob **went down** to Egypt
	7:34	I **have come down** to rescue
	8:15	The two **went down** and prayed
	8:26	**goes down** from Jerusalem to
	8:38	**went down** into the water
	10:11	like a large sheet **coming down**
	10:20	Now get up, **go down,** and go
	10:21	So Peter **went down** to the men

	11: 5	like a large sheet **coming down**
	14:11	The gods **have come down** to us
	14:25	they **went down** to Attalia
	16: 8	they **went down** to Troas
	18:22	and then **went down** to Antioch
	20:10	But Paul **went down**
	23:10	the soldiers **to go down**
	24: 1	high priest Ananias **came down**
	24:22	Lysias the tribune **comes down**
	25: 6	he **went down** to Caesarea
	25: 7	**had gone down** from Jerusalem
Ro	10: 7	Who **will descend** into the abyss
Ep	4: 9	**descended** into the lower parts
	4:10	who **descended** is the same one
1Th	4:16	**will descend** from heaven
Ja	1:17	**coming down** from the Father
Re	3:12	new Jerusalem that **comes down**
	10: 1	angel **coming down** from heaven
	12:12	the devil **has come down** to you
	13:13	fire **come down** from heaven
	16:21	**dropped** from heaven on people
	18: 1	angel **coming down** from heaven
	20: 1	angel **coming down** from heaven
	20: 9	fire **came down** from heaven
	21: 2	**coming down** out of heaven
	21:10	**coming down** out of heaven

2598   GO2   AG408   LN132   B1:376   R2596,906
καταβαλλω, I THROW DOWN
2C   4: 9   but not forsaken; **struck down**
He   6: 1   **laying** again the foundation

2599   GO1   AG408   LN132   R2596,916
καταβαρεω, I BURDEN DOWN
2C   12:16   that I **did** not **burden** you

2599a   GO1   AG408   LN132
καταβαρυνω, I BURDEN DOWN
Mk   14:40   for their eyes **were very heavy**

2600   GO1   AG409   LN132   R2597
καταβασις, GOING DOWN
Lk   19:37   **path down** from the Mount of

2602   GO11   AG409   LN132   B1:376   K3:620   R2598
καταβολη, FOUNDATION
Mt   13:35   hidden from the **foundation** of
| 25:34   from the **foundation** of the
Lk   11:50   shed since the **foundation** of
Jn   17:24   before the **foundation** of the

Ep 1: 4 before the **foundation** of the
He 4: 3 finished at the **foundation** of
    9:26 since the **foundation** of the
    11:11 power of **procreation,** even
1P 1:20 before the **foundation** of the
Re 13: 8 **foundation** of the world in the
    17: 8 of life from the **foundation** of

2603 GO1 AG409 LN132 B1:648
καταβραβευω, I DECIDE AGAINST
Co   2:18 Do not let anyone **disqualify**

2604 GO1 AG409 LN132 K1:70 R2605
καταγγελευς, PROCLAIMER
Ac 17:18 He seems to be a **proclaimer** of

2605 GO18 AG409 LN132 K1:70 R2596,31a
καταγγελλω, I PROCLAIM
Ac 3:24 him, also **predicted** these days.
    4: 2 **proclaiming** that in Jesus there
    13: 5 they **proclaimed** the word of God
    13:38 of sins is **proclaimed** to you;
    15:36 we **proclaimed** the word of the
    16:17 who **proclaim** to you a way of
    16:21 and **are advocating** customs that
    17: 3 Jesus whom I **am proclaiming** to
    17:13 God **had been proclaimed**
            by Paul
    17:23 unknown, this I **proclaim** to you
    26:23 he would **proclaim** light both to
Ro 1: 8 faith **is proclaimed** throughout
1C 2: 1 I did not come **proclaiming** the
    9:14 those who **proclaim** the gospel
    11:26 you **proclaim** the Lord's death
Ph 1:17 the others **proclaim** Christ out
    1:18 Christ is **proclaimed** in every
Co 1:28 It is he whom we **proclaim,**

2606 GO3 AG409 LN132 B2:429 K1:658
καταγελαω, I LAUGH
Mt 9:24 And they **laughed at** him.
Mk 5:40 **laughed at** him. Then he put
Lk 8:53 **laughed at** him, knowing that

2607 GO3 AG409 LN132 B2:362 K1:714 R2596,1097
καταγινωσκω, I KNOW AGAINST
Ga 2:11 because he stood self-**condemned**
1J 3:20 whenever our hearts **condemn** us;
    3:21 hearts do not **condemn** us, we

2608 GO4 AG409 LN132
καταγνυμι, I BREAK
Mt 12:20 He **will** not **break** a bruised
Jn 19:31 of the crucified men **broken**
    19:32 the soldiers came and **broke** the
    19:33 they **did** not **break** his legs.

2608a GO1 AG410 LN132 R2596,1125
καταγραφω, I WRITE DOWN
Jn 8: 6 Jesus bent down and **wrote** with

2609 GO9 AG410 LN132 R2596,71
καταγω, I LEAD DOWN
Lk 5:11 When they **had brought** their
Ac 9:30 **brought** him **down** to Caesarea
    22:30 He **brought** Paul **down** and had
    23:15 **bring** him **down** to you, on the
    23:20 ask you to **bring** Paul **down** to
    23:28 I **had** him **brought** to their
    27: 3 The next day we **put in** at Sidon
    28:12 We **put in** at Syracuse and
Ro 10: 6 that is, to **bring** Christ **down**

2610 GO1 AG410 LN132 B1:644 R2596,75
καταγωνιζομαι, I CONTEND OVER
He 11:33 who through faith **conquered**

2611 GO1 AG410 LN132 R2596,1210
καταδεω, I BIND DOWN
Lk 10:34 He went to him and **bandaged** his

2612 GO1 AG410 LN132 R2596,1212
καταδηλος, VERY CLEAR
He 7:15 It is even **more obvious** when

2613 GO5 AG410 LN132 B2:370 K3:621
καταδικαζω, I CONDEMN
Mt 12: 7 you would not **have condemned**
    12:37 words you **will be condemned.**
Lk 6:37 **do** not **condemn,** and you will
    6:37 and you **will** not **be condemned.**
Ja 5: 6 You have **condemned** and murdered

2613a GO1 AG410 LN132 B2:370 K3:622
καταδικη, JUDGMENT
Ac 25:15 asked for a **sentence** against

2614 GO1 AG410 LN132 B2:805 R2596,1377
καταδιωκω, I PURSUE AFTER
Mk 1:36 his companions **hunted** for him.

2615 GO2 AG410 LN132 K2:279 R2596,153
καταδουλοω, I ENSLAVE THOROUGHLY
2C 11:20 someone **makes slaves** of you, or
Ga 2: 4 so that they **might enslave** us

2616 GO2 AG410 LN132 R2596,1413
καταδυναστευω, I EXERCISE POWER
AGAINST
Ac 10:38 healing all who **were oppressed**
Ja 2: 6 Is it not the rich who **oppress**

2616a GO1 AG410 LN132 B1:413 K1:354
καταθεμα, CURSE
Re 22: 3 **accursed** will be found

2616b GO1 AG410 LN133 B1:413 K1:355
καταθεματιζω, I CURSE THOROUGHLY
Mt 26:74 Then he began to **curse,** and he

2617 GO13 AG410 LN133 B3:562 K1:189 R2596,153
καταισχυνω, I SHAME
Lk 13:17 his opponents **were put to shame**
Ro 5: 5 and hope **does** not **disappoint** us
9:33 in him **will** not **be put to shame**
10:11 in him **will be put to shame.**
1C 1:27 foolish in the world to **shame**
1:27 weak in the world to **shame** the
11: 4 on his head **disgraces** his head,
11: 5 her head unveiled **disgraces** her
11:22 **humiliate** those who have
2C 7:14 I **was** not **disgraced;** but just
9: 4 we **would be humiliated**
1P 2: 6 him **will** not **be put to shame.**
3:16 in Christ **may be put to shame.**

2618 GO12 AG411 LN133 R2596,2545
κατακαιω, I BURN DOWN
Mt 3:12 the chaff he **will burn** with
13:30 bundles **to be burned,** but
13:40 **burned up** with fire, so will it
Lk 3:17 **will burn** with unquenchable
Ac 19:19 **burned** them publicly; when the
1C 3:15 If the work **is burned up,** the
He 13:11 for sin **are burned** outside the
Re 8: 7 of the earth **was burned up,** and
8: 7 of the trees **were burned up,**
8: 7 all green grass **was burned up.**
17:16 flesh and **burn** her **up** with fire
18: 8 she **will be burned** with fire;

2619 GO3 AG411 LN133 B2:212 K3:561 R2596,2572
κατακαλυπτω, I COVER OVER
1C 11: 6 For if a woman **will** not **veil**
11: 6 shaved, she **should wear** a **veil.**
11: 7 not **to have** his head **veiled,**

2620 GO4 AG411 LN133 B1:227 K3:653 R2596,2744
κατακαυχαομαι, I BRAG AGAINST
Ro 11:18 **do** not **boast over** the branches.
11:18 If you **do boast,** remember that
Ja 2:13 mercy **triumphs** over judgment.
3:14 **do** not **be boastful** and false to

2621 GO12 AG411 LN133 K3:655 R2596,2749
κατακειμαι, I LIE DOWN
Mk 1:30 mother-in-law **was in bed** with a
2: 4 mat on which the paralytic **lay.**
2:15 And as he **sat at dinner** in
14: 3 as he **sat at** the **table,** a woman
Lk 5:25 took what he **had been lying on,**
5:29 others **sitting at the table**
7:37 learned that he **was eating** in
Jn 5: 3 In these **lay** many invalids
5: 6 When Jesus saw him **lying** there
Ac 9:33 who **had been bedridden** for
28: 8 Publius **lay** sick **in bed** with
1C 8:10 **eating** in the temple of an idol

2622 GO2 AG411 LN133 R2596,2806
κατακλαω, I BREAK OFF
Mk 6:41 blessed and **broke** the loaves,
Lk 9:16 and blessed and **broke** them, and

2623 GO2 AG411 LN133 R2596,2808
κατακλειω, I CLOSE UP
Lk 3:20 by **shutting up** John in prison.
Ac 26:10 I not only **locked up** many of

2624 GO1 AG411 LN133 K3:767
κατακληρονομεω, I GIVE INHERITANCE
Ac 13:19 **gave** them . . . **as an inheritance**

2625 GO5 AG411 LN133 R2596,2827
κατακλινω, I RECLINE
Lk 7:36 and **took** his **place at the table**
9:14 **Make** them **sit down** in groups
9:15 so and **made** them all **sit down.**
14: 8 you **are invited** by someone to a
24:30 When he **was at the table** with

2626　GO1　AG411　LN133
κατακλυζω, I FLOOD
2P　　3: 6　　world of that time **was deluged**

2627　GO4　AG411　LN133　B3:991　R2626
κατακλυσμος, FLOOD
Mt　24:38　　before the **flood** they were
　　24:39　　knew nothing until the **flood**
Lk　17:27　　the **flood** came and destroyed
2P　　2: 5　　when he brought a **flood** on a

2628　GO2　AG412　LN133　R2596,190
κατακολουθεω, I FOLLOW AFTER
Lk　23:55　　with him from Galilee **followed,**
Ac　16:17　　While she **followed** Paul and us,

2629　GO1　AG412　LN133　R2596,2875
κατακοπτω, I CUT IN PIECES
Mk　　5: 5　　was always howling and **bruising**

2630　GO1　AG412　LN133
κατακρημνιζω, I HURL DOWN
Lk　　4:29　　that they **might hurl** him **off**

2631　GO3　AG412　LN133　B2:362　K3:951　R2632
κατακριμα, CONDEMNATION
Ro　　5:16　　trespass brought **condemnation,**
　　5:18　　led to **condemnation** for all, so
　　8: 1　　no **condemnation** for those who

2632　GO18　AG412　LN133　B2:362　K3:951　R2596,2919
κατακρινω, I CONDEMN
Mt　12:41　　this generation and **condemn** it,
　　12:42　　**condemn** it, because she came
　　20:18　　and they **will condemn** him to
　　27: 3　　saw that Jesus **was condemned,**
Mk　10:33　　and they **will condemn** him to
　　14:64　　All of them **condemned** him as
　　16:16　　not believe will be **condemned.**
Lk　11:31　　and **condemn** them, because she
　　11:32　　this generation and **condemn** it,
Jn　　8:10　　**Has** no one **condemned** you?"
　　8:11　　Neither **do I condemn** you. Go
Ro　　2: 1　　you **condemn** yourself, because
　　8: 3　　to deal with sin, he **condemned**
　　8:34　　Who is **to condemn?** It is Christ
　　14:23　　**are condemned** if they eat,
1C　11:32　　so that we may not **be condemned**
He　11: 7　　by this he **condemned** the world
2P　　2: 6　　he **condemned** them to extinction

2633　GO2　AG412　LN133　B2:362　K3:951　R2632
κατακρισις, CONDEMNATION
2C　　3: 9　　in the ministry of **condemnation,**
　　7: 3　　I do not say this to **condemn**

2633a　GO1　AG412　LN133　R2596,2955
κατακυπτω, I BEND DOWN
Jn　　8: 8　　And once again he **bent down** and

2634　GO4　AG412　LN133　B2:510　K3:1098　R2596,2961
κατακυριευω, I MASTER OVER
Mt　20:25　　**lord** it **over** them, and their
Mk　10:42　　**lord** it **over** them, and their
Ac　19:16　　**mastered** them all, and so
1P　　5: 3　　**Do** not **lord** it **over** those in

2635　GO5　AG412　LN133　B3:345　K4:3　R2637
καταλαλεω, I TALK AGAINST
Ja　　4:11　　Do not **speak evil against** one
　　4:11　　Whoever **speaks evil against**
　　4:11　　**speaks evil against** the law and
1P　　2:12　　though they **malign** you as
　　3:16　　when you **are maligned,** those

2636　GO2　AG412　LN133　B3:345　K4:3　R2637
καταλαλια, SPEECHES AGAINST
2C　12:20　　**slander,** gossip, conceit, and
1P　　2: 1　　envy, and all **slander.**

2637　GO1　AG412　LN133　B3:345　K4:3　R2596,2980
καταλαλος, SPEAKER AGAINST
Ro　　1:30　　**slanderers,** God-haters,

2638　GO15　AG412　LN133　B3:747　K4:9　R2596,2983
καταλαμβανω, I OVERTAKE
Mk　　9:18　　and whenever it **seizes** him, it
Jn　　1: 5　　darkness **did** not **overcome** it.
　　8: 3　　a woman who **had been caught** in
　　8: 4　　Teacher, this woman **was caught**
　　12:35　　the darkness **may** not **overtake**
Ac　　4:13　　and **realized** that they were
　　10:34　　I truly **understand** that God
　　25:25　　But I **found** that he had done
Ro　　9:30　　**have attained** it, that is,
1C　　9:24　　such a way that you **may win** it.
Ep　　3:18　　have the power to **comprehend,**
Ph　　3:12　　I press on **to make** it **my own,**
　　3:12　　Jesus **has made** me his **own.**
　　3:13　　I **have made** it **my own;** but this
1Th　5: 4　　for that day **to surprise** you

2639 GO1 AG413 LN134
καταλεγω, I ENROLL
1Ti 5: 9 Let a widow **be put on the list**

2641 GO24 AG413 LN134 B3:247 K4:194 R2596,3007
καταλειπω, I LEAVE BEHIND
Mt 4:13 He **left** Nazareth and made his
16: 4 Then he **left** them and went away
19: 5 a man **shall leave** his father
21:17 He **left** them, went out of the
Mk 10: 7 **shall leave** his father and
12:19 **leaving** a wife but no child,
12:21 **leaving** no children; and the
14:52 but he **left** the linen cloth and
Lk 5:28 And he got up, **left** everything,
10:40 my sister has **left** me to do all
15: 4 **does** not **leave** the ninety-nine
20:31 way all seven died **childless.**
Jn 8: 9 and Jesus **was left** alone with
Ac 6: 2 that we should **neglect** the word
18:19 he **left** them there, but first
21: 3 and **leaving** it on our left, we
24:27 Felix **left** Paul in prison.
25:14 here who **was left** in prison by
Ro 11: 4 I **have kept** for myself seven
Ep 5:31 this reason a man **will leave**
1Th 3: 1 we decided **to be left** alone in
He 4: 1 seem to have **failed** to reach it
11:27 By faith he **left** Egypt,
2P 2:15 They **have left** the straight

2642 GO1 AG413 LN134 K4:267 R2596
καταλιθαζω, I STONE THOROUGHLY
Lk 20: 6 all the people **will stone** us;

2643 GO4 AG414 LN134 B3:166 K1:258 R2644
καταλλαγη, RECONCILIATION
Ro 5:11 now received **reconciliation.**
11:15 **reconciliation** of the world,
2C 5:18 ministry of **reconciliation;**
5:19 message of **reconciliation** to us

2644 GO6 AG414 LN134 B3:166 K1:254 R2596,236
καταλλασσω, I RECONCILE
Ro 5:10 we **were reconciled** to God
5:10 **having been reconciled,** will we
1C 7:11 **be reconciled** to her husband
2C 5:18 who **reconciled** us to himself
5:19 in Christ God **was reconciling**
5:20 Christ, **be reconciled** to God.

2645 GO1 AG414 LN134 B3:247 R2596,3062
καταλοιπος, REST BEHIND
Ac 15:17 so that **all other peoples** may

2646 GO3 AG414 LN134 B3:177 K4:328
καταλυμα, GUEST LODGE
Mk 14:14 Where is my **guest room** where
Lk 2: 7 no place for them in the **inn.**
22:11 Where is the **guest room,** where

2647 GO17 AG414 LN134 B3:177 K4:328 R2596,3089
καταλυω, I UNLOOSE
Mt 5:17 I have come **to abolish** the law
5:17 I have come not **to abolish** but
24: 2 all **will be thrown down.**
26:61 I am able **to destroy** the
27:40 You who **would destroy** the
Mk 13: 2 all **will be thrown down.**
14:58 I **will destroy** this temple
15:29 Aha! You who **would destroy** the
Lk 9:12 **to lodge** and get provisions;
19: 7 He has gone **to be the guest** of
21: 6 all **will be thrown down.**
Ac 5:38 human origin, **it will fail;**
5:39 not be able **to overthrow** them
6:14 Jesus of Nazareth **will destroy**
Ro 14:20 **destroy** the work of God.
2C 5: 1 **is destroyed,** we have a
Ga 2:18 things that I once **tore down,**

2648 GO1 AG414 LN134 K4:414 R2596
καταμανθανω, I LEARN THOROUGHLY
Mt 6:28 **Consider** the lilies of the

2649 GO3 AG414 LN134 B3:1038 K4:508 R2596,3140
καταμαρτυρεω, I TESTIFY THOROUGHLY
Mt 26:62 that they **testify against** you?"
27:13 **accusations** they **make against**
Mk 14:60 that they **testify against** you?"

2650 GO1 AG414 LN134 R2596,3306
καταμενω, I STAY DOWN
Ac 1:13 where they were **staying,** Peter,

2654 GO1 AG414 LN134
καταναλισκω, I CONSUME ALL
He 12:29 indeed our God is a **consuming**

2655　G03 AG414 LN134
καταναρκαω, I BURDEN
2C　11: 9　I **did** not **burden** anyone, for
　　12:13　I myself **did** not **burden** you?
　　12:14　And I **will** not **be a burden,**

2656　G01 AG415 LN134 R2596,3506
κατανευω, I NOD TOWARD
Lk　5: 7　So they **signaled** their

2657　G014 AG415 LN134 B3:122 K4:973 R2596,3539
κατανοεω, I THINK CAREFULLY
Mt　7: 3　but do not **notice** the log in
Lk　6:41　but do not **notice** the log in
　　12:24　**Consider** the ravens: they
　　12:27　**Consider** the lilies, how they
　　20:23　But he **perceived** their
Ac　7:31　there **came** the voice of the
　　7:32　and did not dare **to look.**
　　11: 6　As I **looked** at it **closely** I saw
　　27:39　but they **noticed** a bay with a
Ro　4:19　when he **considered** his own body
He　3: 1　**consider** that Jesus, the apostle
　　10:24　And **let** us **consider** how to
Ja　1:23　those who **look at** themselves in
　　1:24　for they **look at** themselves and

2658　G013 AG415 LN134 B1:324 K3:623
καταντaω, I ARRIVE
Ac　16: 1　Paul **went on** also to Derbe and
　　18:19　When they **reached** Ephesus, he
　　18:24　Now there **came** to Ephesus a Jew
　　20:15　the following day we **arrived**
　　21: 7　we **arrived** at Ptolemais; and we
　　25:13　Bernice **arrived** at Caesarea to
　　26: 7　twelve tribes hope **to attain,**
　　27:12　somehow they could **reach**
　　28:13　then we weighed anchor and **came**
1C　10:11　the ends of the ages **have come.**
　　14:36　the only ones it **has reached?**
Ep　4:13　until all of us **come** to the
Ph　3:11　if somehow I **may attain** the

2659　G01 AG415 LN134 K3:626
κατανυξις, STUPOR
Ro　11: 8　God gave them a **sluggish**

2660　G01 AG415 LN134 K3:626 R2596,3572
κατανυσσομαι, I STAB THOROUGHLY
Ac　2:37　they **were cut** to the heart and

2661　G03 AG415 LN134 B3:348 K1:380 R2596,515
καταξιοω, I AM WORTHY
Lk　20:35　**are considered worthy** of a
Ac　5:41　they **were considered worthy** to
2Th　1: 5　intended **to make** you **worthy** of

2662　G05 AG415 LN134 B3:943 K5:940 R2596,3961
καταπατεω, I WALK OVER
Mt　5:13　thrown out and **trampled** under
　　7: 6　they **will trample** them under
Lk　8: 5　on the path and **was trampled on**
　　12: 1　they **trampled on** one another,
He　10:29　**profaned** the blood of the

2663　G09 AG415 LN134 B3:254 K3:628 R2664
καταπαυσις, COMPLETE STOP, REST
Ac　7:49　or what is the place of my **rest**
He　3:11　They will not enter my **rest.**
　　3:18　they would not enter his **rest,**
　　4: 1　promise of entering his **rest** is
　　4: 3　enter that **rest,** just as God
　　4: 3　They shall not enter my **rest,**
　　4: 5　They shall not enter my **rest.**
　　4:10　for those who enter God's **rest**
　　4:11　enter that **rest,** so that no one

2664　G04 AG416 LN134 B3:254 K3:627 R2596,3973
καταπαυω, I STOP (REST) COMPLETELY
Ac　14:18　they scarcely **restrained** the
He　4: 4　And God **rested** on the seventh
　　4: 8　if Joshua **had given** them **rest,**
　　4:10　their labors as God **did** from

2665　G06 AG416 LN134 B3:794 K3:628
καταπετασμα, VEIL
Mt　27:51　At that moment the **curtain** of
Mk　15:38　And the **curtain** of the temple
Lk　23:45　and the **curtain** of the temple
He　6:19　inner shrine behind the **curtain**
　　9: 3　Behind the **second curtain** was a
　　10:20　for us through the **curtain**

2666　G07 AG416 LN135 K6:158 R2596,4095
καταπινω, I SWALLOW
Mt　23:24　out a gnat but **swallow** a camel!
1C　15:54　Death **has been swallowed**
　　　　　　up in
2C　2: 7　he **may** not **be overwhelmed** by
　　5: 4　**may be swallowed up** by life.
He　11:29　to do so they **were drowned.**

1P	5: 8	looking for someone **to devour.**
Re	12:16	**swallowed** the river that the

2667 GO3 AG416 LN135 B1:608 K6:169 R2596,4098
καταπιπτω, I FALL DOWN

Lk	8: 6	Some **fell on** the rock; and as
Ac	26:14	When we **had** all **fallen** to the
	28: 6	swell up or **drop** dead, but

2668 GO1 AG416 LN135 R2596,4126
καταπλεω, I SAIL DOWN

Lk	8:26	they **arrived** at the country of

2669 GO2 AG416 LN135
καταπονεω, I WEAR DOWN

Ac	7:24	he defended the **oppressed** man
2P	2: 7	man greatly **distressed** by the

2670 GO2 AG417 LN135
καταποντιζω, I DROWN

Mt	14:30	beginning **to sink,** he cried out
	18: 6	you **were drowned** in the depth

2671 GO6 AG417 LN135 B1:416 K1:449
καταρα, CURSE

Ga	3:10	under a **curse;** for it is
	3:13	by becoming a **curse** for us—
	3:13	**curse** for us—for it is
He	6: 8	on the verge of being **cursed;**
Ja	3:10	mouth come blessing and **cursing**
2P	2:14	in greed. **Accursed** children!

2672 GO5 AG417 LN135 B1:416 K1:448 R2671
καταραομαι, I CURSE

Mt	25:41	You that **are accursed,** depart
Mk	11:21	The fig tree that you **cursed**
Lk	6:28	bless those who **curse** you, pray
Ro	12:14	you; bless and do not **curse**
Ja	3: 9	with it we **curse** those who are

2673 GO27 AG417 LN135 B1:73 K1:452
καταργεω, I ABOLISH

Lk	13: 7	Why should it **be wasting** the
Ro	3: 3	their faithlessness **nullify** the
	3:31	Do we then **overthrow** the law by
	4:14	is null and the promise **is void**
	6: 6	body of sin **might be destroyed,**
	7: 2	she **is discharged** from the law
	7: 6	But now we **are discharged** from

1C	1:28	**to reduce to nothing** things
	2: 6	age, who **are doomed to perish.**
	6:13	God **will destroy** both one and
	13: 8	they **will come to an end;** as
	13: 8	it **will come to an end.**
	13:10	the partial **will come to an end**
	13:11	I **put an end** to childish ways.
	15:24	he **has destroyed** every ruler
	15:26	The last enemy **to be destroyed**
2C	3: 7	his face, a glory now **set aside**
	3:11	for if what **was set aside** came
	3:13	glory that **was being set aside.**
	3:14	only in Christ is it **set aside.**
Ga	3:17	so as **to nullify** the promise.
	5: 4	**have cut** yourselves **off** from
	5:11	of the cross **has been removed.**
Ep	2:15	He **has abolished** the law with
2Th	2: 8	the Lord Jesus **will destroy**
2Ti	1:10	who **abolished death** and brought
He	2:14	through death he **might destroy**

2674 GO1 AG417 LN135
καταριθμεω, I NUMBER

Ac	1:17	for he **was numbered** among us

2675 GO13 AG417 LN135 B3:349 K1:475
καταρτιζω, I PUT IN ORDER

Mt	4:21	**mending** their nets, and he
	21:16	you have **prepared** praise for
Mk	1:19	in their boat **mending** the nets.
Lk	6:40	who **is fully qualified** will be
Ro	9:22	objects of wrath that **are made**
1C	1:10	you **be united** in the same mind
2C	13:11	**Put things in order,** listen to
Ga	6: 1	**restore** such a one in a spirit
1Th	3:10	**restore** whatever is lacking in
He	10: 5	a body you **have prepared** for me
	11: 3	the worlds **were prepared** by the
	13:21	**make** you **complete** in everything
1P	5:10	will himself **restore,** support,

2676 GO1 AG418 LN135 B3:349 K1:475 R2675
καταρτισις, PUTTING IN ORDER

2C	13: 9	that you **may become perfect.**

2677 GO1 AG418 LN135 B3:349 K1:475 R2675
καταρτισμος, PUTTING IN ORDER

Ep	4:12	to **equip** the saints for the

2678　GO4 AG418 LN135 B3:556 R2596,4579
κατασειω, I MOTION
Ac　12:17　He **motioned** to them with his
　　13:16　with a **gesture** began to speak:
　　19:33　Alexander **motioned** for silence
　　21:40　**motioned** to the people for

2679　GO2 AG418 LN135 R2596,4626
κατασκαπτω, I DUG DOWN
Ac　15:16　which **has fallen;** from its
Ro　11: 3　they **have demolished** your

2680　GO11 AG418 LN135 B3:118
κατασκευαζω, I PREPARE
Mt　11:10　**will prepare** your way before
Mk　 1: 2　who **will prepare** your way;
Lk　 1:17　make ready a people **prepared**
　　 7:27　who **will prepare** your way
He　 3: 3　just as the **builder** of a house
　　 3: 4　For every house **is built** by
　　 3: 4　the **builder** of all things is
　　 9: 2　For a tent **was constructed,** the
　　 9: 6　Such **preparations** having been
　　11: 7　and **built** an ark to save his
1P　 3:20　during the **building** of the ark,

2681　GO4 AG418 LN135 B3:813 K7:387 R2596,4637
κατασκηνοω, I SET UP TENT
Mt　13:32　air come and **make nests** in its
Mk　 4:32　air **can make nests** in its shade
Lk　13:19　air **made nests** in its branches.
Ac　 2:26　moreover my flesh **will live** in

2682　GO2 AG418 LN135 B3:813 R2681
κατασκηνωσις, SET UP TENTS
Mt　 8:20　birds of the air have **nests;**
Lk　 9:58　**nests;** but the Son of Man has

2683　GO1 AG418 LN135 R2596,4639
κατασκιαζω, I SHADOW OVER
He　 9: 5　cherubim of glory **over-
　　　　　　shadowing**

2684　GO1 AG418 LN136 K7:416 R2685
κατασκοπεω, I LOOK CAREFULLY
Ga　 2: 4　who slipped in **to spy on** the

2685　GO1 AG418 LN136 K7:417 R2596,4648
κατασκοπος, SPY
He　11:31　she had received the **spies** in

2686　GO1 AG418 LN136
κατασοφιζομαι, HAVING USED WISDOM
　　　　TO GO AGAIN
Ac　 7:19　He **dealt craftily** with our race

2687　GO2 AG419 LN136 K7:595
καταστελλω, I CALM
Ac　19:35　the town clerk **had quieted** the
　　19:36　you ought **to be quiet** and do

2688　GO1 AG419 LN136
καταστημα, DEMEANOR
Ti　 2: 3　be reverent in **behavior,** not to

2689　GO1 AG419 LN136 K7:595
καταστολη, APPAREL
1Ti　 2: 9　that the women **should dress**

2690　GO2 AG419 LN136 K7:715 R2596,4762
καταστρεφω, I TURN OVER
Mt　21:12　he **overturned** the tables of the
Mk　11:15　he **overturned** the tables of the

2691　GO1 AG419 LN136 K3:631
καταστρηνιαω, I HAVE SEXUAL DESIRES
　　　　AGAINST
1Ti　 5:11　their **sensual desires alienate**

2692　GO2 AG419 LN136 K7:715 R2690
καταστροφη, OVERTURN
2Ti　 2:14　but only **ruins** those who are
2P　 2: 6　he condemned them to
　　　　　　extinction

2693　GO1 AG419 LN136
καταστρωννυμι, I THROW DOWN
1C　10: 5　they **were struck down** in the

2694　GO1 AG419 LN136 R2596,4951
κατασυρω, I DRAG DOWN
Lk　12:58　you **may be dragged** before the

2695　GO1 AG419 LN136 R2596,4969
κατασφαζω, I SLAUGHTER
　　　　THOROUGHLY
Lk　19:27　**slaughter** them in my presence.

2696　GO1 AG419 LN136 B3:497 K7:939 R2596
κατασφραγιζω, I SEAL THOROUGHLY
Re　 5: 1　back, **sealed** with seven seals;

2697 GO2 AG419 LN136
κατασχεσις, POSSESSION
Ac 7: 5 as his **possession** and to his
  7:45 they **dispossessed** the nations

2698 GO2 AG419 LN136 R2596,5087
κατατιθημι, I SET DOWN
Ac 24:27 he wanted **to grant** the Jews a
  25: 9 But Festus, wishing **to do** the

2699 GO1 AG419 LN136 B1:307 K8:109
κατατομη, I CUT DOWN
Ph 3: 2 those who **mutilate the flesh!**

2701 GO1 AG419 LN136 R2596,5143
κατατρεχω, I RUN DOWN
Ac 21:32 **ran down** to them. When they
       saw

2702 GO4 AG419 LN136
καταφερω, I BRING DOWN
Ac 20: 9 **began to sink off** into a deep
  20: 9 **Overcome** by sleep, he fell to
  25: 7 **bringing** many . . . charges
       against
  26:10 also **cast** my vote **against** them

2703 GO2 AG420 LN136 R2596,5343
καταφευγω, I FLEE AWAY
Ac 14: 6 learned of it and **fled** to
He 6:18 we who **have taken refuge** might

2704 GO1 AG420 LN136 K9:93 R2596,5351
καταφθειρω, I RUIN COMPLETELY
2Ti 3: 8 **corrupt** mind and counterfeit

2705 GO6 AG420 LN136 B2:547 K9:114 R2596,5368
καταφιλεω, I KISS
Mt 26:49 "Greetings, Rabbi!" and **kissed**
Mk 14:45 said, "Rabbi!" and **kissed** him.
Lk 7:38 she **continued kissing** his feet
  7:45 has not stopped **kissing** my feet
  15:20 arms around him and **kissed** him.
Ac 20:37 they embraced Paul and **kissed**

2706 GO9 AG420 LN137 B1:461 K3:631 R2596,5426
καταφρονεω, I THINK DOWN (I DESPISE)
Mt 6:24 devoted to the one and **despise**
  18:10 do not **despise** one of these
Lk 16:13 devoted to the one and **despise**

Ro 2: 4 Or do you **despise** the riches of
1C 11:22 do you **show contempt** for the
1Ti 4:12 **Let** no one **despise** your youth,
  6: 2 must not **be disrespectful** to
He 12: 2 **disregarding** its shame, and has
2P 2:10 who **despise** authority. Bold and

2707 GO1 AG420 LN137 B1:461 K3:632 R2706
καταφρονητης, ONE THINKING DOWN
Ac 13:41 Look, you **scoffers!** Be amazed

2708 GO2 AG420 LN137
καταχεω, I POUR DOWN
Mt 26: 7 she **poured** it **on** his head as he
Mk 14: 3 **poured** the ointment **on** his
       head

2709 GO1 AG420 LN137 K3:633
καταχθονιος, SUBTERRANEAN
Ph 2:10 on earth and **under the earth,**

2710 GO2 AG420 LN137 R2596,5530
καταχραομαι, I USE THOROUGHLY
1C 7:31 they **had no dealings** with it.
  9:18 **to make full use** of my rights

2711 GO1 AG421 LN137 R2596,5594
καταψυχω, I COOL
Lk 16:24 **cool** my tongue; for I am in

2712 GO1 AG421 LN137 B2:284 K2:379
κατειδωλος, FULL OF IDOLS
Ac 17:16 that the city was **full of idols**

2713 GO8 AG421 LN137
κατεναντι, OVER AGAINST
Mt 21: 2 into the village **ahead** of you,
Mk 11: 2 **ahead** of you, and immediately
  12:41 sat down **opposite** the treasury,
  13: 3 **opposite** the temple, Peter,
Lk 19:30 **ahead** of you, and as you enter
Ro 4:17 in the presence of the God in
2C 2:17 and standing **in his presence.**
  12:19 speaking in Christ **before** God.

2714 GO3 AG421 LN137 R2596,1799
κατενωπιον, DOWN BEFORE
Ep 1: 4 holy and blameless **before** him
Co 1:22 irreproachable **before** him
Ju 1:24 without blemish **in the presence**

2715 GO2 AG421 LN137 B2:606 K2:575 R2596,1850
κατεξουσιαζω, I EXERCISE AUTHORITY
OVER

| Mt | 20:25 | **lord** it **over** them, and their |
| Mk | 10:42 | their rulers **lord** it **over** them, |

2716 GO22 AG421 LN138 K3:634 R2596,2038
κατεργαζομαι, I WORK THOROUGHLY

Ro	1:27	Men **committed** shameless acts
	2: 9	everyone who **does** evil, the Jew
	4:15	For the law **brings** wrath; but
	5: 3	knowing that suffering **produces**
	7: 8	**produced** in me all kinds of
	7:13	Did what is good, then, **bring**
	7:15	not understand my own **actions.**
	7:17	I that **do** it, but sin that
	7:18	is right, but I cannot **do** it.
	7:20	it is no longer I that **do** it,
	15:18	Christ **has accomplished** through
1C	5: 4	who **has done** such a thing
2C	4:17	**is preparing** us for an eternal
	5: 5	He who **has prepared** us for this
	7:10	but worldly grief **produces**
	7:11	godly grief has **produced** in you
	9:11	which **will produce** thanksgiving
	12:12	**were performed** among you with
Ep	6:13	and **having done** everything, to
Ph	2:12	**work out** your own salvation
Ja	1: 3	testing of your faith **produces**
1P	4: 3	**doing** what the Gentiles like to

2718 GO16 AG422 LN138 R2596,2064
κατερχομαι, I GO DOWN

Lk	4:31	He **went down** to Capernaum, a
	9:37	when they **had come down** from
Ac	8: 5	Philip **went down** to the city
	9:32	he **came down** also to the saints
	11:27	**came down** from Jerusalem to
	12:19	Then he **went down** from Judea to
	13: 4	they **went down** to Seleucia; and
	15: 1	**came down** from Judea and were
	15:30	**went down** to Antioch. When they
	18: 5	When Silas and Timothy **arrived**
	18:22	and then **went down** to Antioch.
	19: 1	**came** to Ephesus, where he found
	21: 3	**landed** at Tyre, because the
	21:10	Agabus **came down** from Judea.
	27: 5	we **came** to Myra in Lycia.
Ja	3:15	does not **come down** from above,

2719 GO14 AG422 LN138 R2596,2068
κατεσθιω, I EAT UP

Mt	13: 4	the birds came and **ate** them **up.**
Mk	4: 4	the birds came and **ate** it **up.**
	12:40	They **devour** widows' houses and
Lk	8: 5	the birds of the air **ate** it **up.**
	15:30	who **has devoured** your property
	20:47	They **devour** widows' houses and
Jn	2:17	for your house **will consume** me.
2C	11:20	or **preys** upon you, or takes
Ga	5:15	you bite and **devour** one another
Re	10: 9	Take it, and **eat;** it will be
	10:10	**ate** it; it was sweet as honey
	11: 5	**consumes** their foes; anyone
	12: 4	so that he **might devour** her
	20: 9	from heaven and **consumed** them.

2720 GO3 AG422 LN138 R2596,2116
κατευθυνω, I MAKE STRAIGHT

Lk	1:79	**to guide** our feet into the way
1Th	3:11	Jesus **direct** our way to you.
2Th	3: 5	**May** the Lord **direct** your hearts

2720a GO1 AG422 LN138 R2596,2127
κατευλογεω, I COMPLETELY SPEAK WELL

| Mk | 10:16 | hands on them, and **blessed** them |

2721 GO1 AG422 LN138
κατεφισταμαι, I STAND UP AGAINST

| Ac | 18:12 | **made** a united **attack** on Paul |

2722 GO17 AG422 LN138 K2:829 R2596,2192
κατεχω, I HOLD DOWN

Lk	4:42	they wanted **to prevent** him from
	8:15	**hold** it **fast** in an honest and
	14: 9	start **to take** the lowest place.
Ac	27:40	wind, they **made for** the beach.
Ro	1:18	wickedness **suppress** the truth.
	7: 6	to that which **held us captive,**
1C	7:30	though they **had no possessions,**
	11: 2	**maintain** the traditions just as
	15: 2	**hold firmly** to the message that
2C	6:10	and yet **possessing** everything.
1Th	5:21	**hold fast** to what is good;
2Th	2: 6	what **is** now **restraining** him, so
	2: 7	until the one who now **restrains**
Pm	1:13	I wanted **to keep** him with me,
He	3: 6	if we **hold firm** the confidence
	3:14	we **hold** our first confidence
	10:23	**Let** us **hold fast** to the

2723 GO23 AG423 LN138 B1:82 K3:637 R2725
κατηγορεω, I ACCUSE
Mt	12:10	so that they **might accuse** him.
	27:12	But when he **was accused** by the
Mk	3: 2	so that they **might accuse** him.
	15: 3	chief priests **accused** him of
	15: 4	charges they **bring against** you.
Lk	6: 7	they might find **an accusation**
	23: 2	They began to **accuse** him,
	23:10	stood by, vehemently **accusing**
	23:14	guilty of any of your **charges**
Jn	5:45	Do not think that I **will accuse**
	5:45	your **accuser** is Moses, on whom
	8: 6	some **charge** to bring against
Ac	22:30	Paul **was being accused** of by
	24: 2	began to **accuse** him, saying:
	24: 8	everything of which we **accuse**
	24:13	prove to you the **charge** that
	24:19	**make** an accusation, if they
	25: 5	the man, **let** them **accuse** him.
	25:11	to their **charges against** me, no
	25:16	before the **accused** had met the
	28:19	even though I **had** no **charge** to
Ro	2:15	**will accuse** or perhaps excuse
Re	12:10	who **accuses** them day and night

2724 GO3 AG423 LN139 B1:82 K3:637 R2724
κατηγορια, ACCUSATION
Jn	18:29	What **accusation** do you bring
1Ti	5:19	Never accept any **accusation**
Ti	1: 6	not **accused** of debauchery and

2725 GO4 AG423 LN139 B1:82 K3:636
κατηγορος, ACCUSER
Ac	23:30	ordering his **accusers** also to
	23:35	a hearing when your **accusers**
	25:16	**accusers** face to face and had
	25:18	When the **accusers** stood up,

2725a GO1 AG423 LN139 B1:82 K3:636
κατηγωρ, ACCUSER
| Re | 12:10 | the **accuser** of our comrades |

2726 GO1 AG423 LN139
κατηφεια, DEJECTION
| Ja | 4: 9 | and your joy into **dejection.** |

2727 GO8 AG423 LN139 B3:771 K3:638
κατηχεω, I INSTRUCT
| Lk | 1: 4 | which you **have been instructed.** |

Ac	18:25	He **had been instructed** in the
	21:21	They **have been told** about you
	21:24	**have been told** about you, but
Ro	2:18	because you **are instructed** in
1C	14:19	order **to instruct** others also,
Ga	6: 6	Those who **are taught** the word
	6: 6	good things with their **teacher.**

2728 GO1 AG424 LN139 K3:334
κατιοω, I COVER WITH RUST
| Ja | 5: 3 | gold and silver **have rusted,** |

2729 GO3 AG424 LN139 B3:712 K3:397 R2596,2480
κατισχυω, I AM STRONG AGAINST
Mt	16:18	gates of Hades **will** not **prevail**
Lk	21:36	**may have** the **strength** to escape
	23:23	and their voices **prevailed.**

2730 GO44 AG424 LN139 B2:247 K5:153 R2596,3611
κατοικεω, I RESIDE
Mt	2:23	There he **made** his **home** in a
	4:13	**made** his **home** in Capernaum by
	12:45	they enter and **live** there; and
	23:21	and by the one who **dwells** in it
Lk	11:26	they enter and **live** there; and
	13: 4	the others **living** in Jerusalem?
Ac	1:19	known to all the **residents** of
	1:20	**let** there be no one to **live** in
	2: 5	heaven **living** in Jerusalem.
	2: 9	**residents** of Mesopotamia, Judea
	2:14	all who **live** in Jerusalem, let
	4:16	all who **live** in Jerusalem that
	7: 2	before he **lived** in Haran,
	7: 4	**settled** in Haran. After his
	7: 4	in which you **are** now **living.**
	7:48	the Most High **does** not **dwell**
	9:22	confounded the Jews who **lived**
	9:32	to the saints **living** in Lydda.
	9:35	And all the **residents** of Lydda
	11:29	the believers **living** in Judea;
	13:27	Because the **residents** of
	17:24	**does** not **live** in shrines made
	17:26	**to inhabit** the whole earth, and
	19:10	so that all the **residents** of
	19:17	to all **residents** of Ephesus,
	22:12	of by all the Jews **living** there
Ep	3:17	and that Christ **may dwell** in
Co	1:19	of God was pleased **to dwell,**
	2: 9	fullness of deity **dwells** bodily
He	11: 9	**living** in tents, as did Isaac

2P	3:13	where righteousness **is at home.**
Re	2:13	I know where you **are living,**
	2:13	among you, where Satan **lives.**
	3:10	to test the **inhabitants** of the
	6:10	on the **inhabitants** of the earth
	8:13	woe to the **inhabitants** of the
	11:10	**inhabitants** of the earth will
	11:10	torment to the **inhabitants** of
	13: 8	and all the **inhabitants** of the
	13:12	the earth and its **inhabitants**
	13:14	deceives the **inhabitants** of
	13:14	telling **them** to make an image
	17: 2	**inhabitants** of the earth have
	17: 8	**inhabitants** of the earth, whose

2731　GO1 AG424 LN139 R2730
κατοικησις, RESIDENCE
Mk　5: 3　He **lived** among the tombs; and

2732　GO2 AG424 LN139 B2:247 K5:155 R2730
κατοικητηριον, RESIDENCE PLACE
Ep　2:22　into a **dwelling place** for God.
Re　18: 2　It has become a **dwelling place**

2733　GO1 AG424 LN139
κατοικια, RESIDENCE
Ac　17:26　places where they would **live,**

2733a　GO1 AG424 LN139 B2:247 K5:156
κατοικιζω, I RESIDE
Ja　4: 5　that he has made **to dwell** in us

2734　GO1 AG424 LN139 K2:696
κατοπτριζω, I REFLECT
2C　3:18　as though **reflected in** a **mirror**

2736　GO9 AG425 LN139 B2:187 K3:640
κατω, DOWN

Mt	4: 6	throw yourself **down;** for it is
	27:51	torn in two, from top to **bottom**
Mk	14:66	While Peter was **below** in the
	15:38	torn in two, from top to **bottom**
Lk	4: 9	throw yourself **down** from here,
Jn	8: 6	Jesus bent **down** and wrote with
	8:23	You are from **below,** I am from
Ac	2:19	signs on the earth **below,** blood,
	20: 9	floors **below** and was picked up

2737　GO2 AG425 LN139 B2:209 K3:640
κατωτερος, DOWN UNDER

Mt	2:16	were two years old or **under,**
Ep	4: 9	descended into the **lower** parts

2737a　GO1 AG425 LN139
καυδα, CAUDA
Ac　27:16　a small island called **Cauda** we

2738　GO2 AG425 LN139 B1:652 K3:642 R2545
καυμα, BURN
Re　7:16　them, nor any **scorching heat;**
　　16: 9　scorched by the **fierce heat,**

2739　GO4 AG425 LN139 B1:652 K3:643 R2738
καυματιζω, I BURN
Mt　13: 6　they **were scorched;** and since
Mk　4: 6　it **was scorched;** and since it
Re　16: 8　was allowed to **scorch** them with
　　16: 9　**were scorched** by the fierce

2740　GO1 AG425 LN139 K3:643 R2745
καυσις, BURNING
He　6: 8　its end is **to be burned over.**

2741　GO2 AG425 LN139 K3:644 R2740
καυσοω, I BURN
2P　3:10　dissolved **with fire,** and the
　　3:12　elements will melt **with fire?**

2741a　GO1 AG425 LN140 B2:574 K3:644
καυστηριαζω, I AM SEARED BY FIRE
1Ti　4: 2　**are seared with** a **hot iron.**

2742　GO3 AG425 LN140 K3:644 R2741
καυσων, BURNING HEAT
Mt　20:12　the day and the **scorching heat.**
Lk　12:55　There will be **scorching heat**
Ja　1:11　**scorching heat** and withers the

2744　GO37 AG425 LN140 B1:227 K3:645
καυχαομαι, I BRAG

Ro	2:17	and **boast** of your relation to
	2:23	You that **boast** in the law, do
	5: 2	we **boast** in our hope of
	5: 3	we also **boast** in our sufferings
	5:11	we even **boast** in God through
1C	1:29	so that no one **might boast** in
	1:31	Let the one who boasts, **boast**
	3:21	So let no one **boast** about human
	4: 7	why do you **boast** as if it were
	13: 3	so that I **may boast,** but do not

2C	5:12	those who **boast** in outward
	7:14	**have been** somewhat **boastful**
	9: 2	the subject of my **boasting**
	10: 8	Now, even if I **boast** a
	10:13	We, however, **will** not **boast**
	10:15	We **do** not **boast** beyond limits,
	10:16	without **boasting** of work
	10:17	Let the one who **boasts, boast**
	10:17	Let the one who boasts, **boast**
	11:12	equals in what they **boast** about
	11:16	that I too **may boast** a little.
	11:18	since many **boast** according to
	11:18	standards, I **will** also **boast.**
	11:30	If I **must boast,** I will boast
	11:30	If I must boast, I **will boast**
	12: 1	It is necessary to **boast;**
	12: 5	I **will boast,** but on my own
	12: 5	own behalf I **will** not **boast,**
	12: 6	But if I wish **to boast,** I will
	12: 9	So, I **will boast** all the more
Ga	6:13	they **may boast** about your flesh
	6:14	**May** I never **boast** of anything
Ep	2: 9	works, so that no one **may boast**
Ph	3: 3	**boast** in Christ Jesus and have
Ja	1: 9	is lowly **boast** in being raised
	4:16	As it is, you **boast** in your

2745   GO11 AG426 LN140 B1:227 K3:645 R2744
καυχημα, BRAG

Ro	4: 2	he has something to **boast** about
1C	5: 6	Your **boasting** is not a good
	9:15	me of my ground for **boasting!**
	9:16	no ground for **boasting,** for an
2C	1:14	we are your **boast** even as you
	5:12	an opportunity to **boast** about
	9: 3	our **boasting** about you may not
Ga	6: 4	will become a cause for **pride.**
Ph	1:26	**boasting** in Christ Jesus when
	2:16	I can **boast** on the day of
He	3: 6	and the **pride** that belong to

2746   GO11 AG426 LN140 B1:227 K3:645 R2744
καυχησις, BRAG

Ro	3:27	Then what becomes of **boasting?**
	15:17	I have reason to **boast** of my
1C	15:31	as my **boasting** of you—a
2C	1:12	Indeed, this is our **boast,** the
	7: 4	I often **boast** about you; I have
	7:14	so our **boasting** to Titus has

	8:24	reason for **boasting** about you.
	11:10	this **boast** of mine will not be
	11:17	this **boastful** confidence, I am
1Th	2:19	**boasting** before our Lord Jesus
Ja	4:16	all such **boasting** is evil.

2746a   GO16 AG426 LN140
καφαρναουμ, CAPERNAUM

Mt	4:13	**Capernaum** by the sea, in the
	8: 5	When he entered **Capernaum,** a
	11:23	And you, **Capernaum,** will you be
	17:24	When they reached **Capernaum,**
Mk	1:21	They went to **Capernaum;** and
	2: 1	When he returned to **Capernaum**
	9:33	Then they came to **Capernaum;**
Lk	4:23	heard you did at **Capernaum.**
	4:31	He went down to **Capernaum,**
	7: 1	people, he entered **Capernaum.**
	10:15	And you, **Capernaum,** will you be
Jn	2:12	he went down to **Capernaum** with
	4:46	whose son lay ill in **Capernaum.**
	6:17	across the sea to **Capernaum.** It
	6:24	went to **Capernaum** looking for
	6:59	in the synagogue at **Capernaum.**

2747   GO2 AG426 LN140
κεγχρεαι, CENCHREAE

| Ac | 18:18 | At **Cenchreae** he had his hair |
| Ro | 16: 1 | of the church at **Cenchreae,** |

2748   GO1 AG426 LN140
κεδρων, KEDRON (KIDRON)

| Jn | 18: 1 | across the **Kidron** valley to a |

2749   GO24 AG426 LN140 K3:654
κειμαι, I LIE

Mt	3:10	Even now the ax **is lying** at the
	5:14	A city **built** on a hill cannot
	28: 6	see the place where he **lay.**
Lk	2:12	of cloth and **lying** in a manger.
	2:16	the child **lying** in the manger.
	2:34	This child **is destined** for the
	3: 9	Even now the ax **is lying** at the
	12:19	you have ample goods **laid up**
	23:53	and **laid** it in a rock-hewn tomb
Jn	2: 6	Now **standing** there were six
	19:29	**was standing** there. So they put
	20: 5	saw the linen wrappings **lying**
	20: 6	the linen wrappings **lying** there
	20: 7	head, not **lying** with the linen

	20:12	body of Jesus **had been lying,**
	21: 9	saw a charcoal fire **there,** with
1C	3:11	the one that **has been laid;**
2C	3:15	a veil **lies** over their minds;
Ph	1:16	knowing that I **have been put**
1Th	3: 3	this is what we **are destined**
1Ti	1: 9	the law **is laid down** not for
1J	5:19	the whole world **lies** under the
Re	4: 2	there in heaven **stood** a throne,
	21:16	The city **lies** foursquare, its

2750 G01 AG427 LN140
κειρια, IN WRAPPINGS
Jn 11:44 bound with **strips of cloth,** and

2751 G04 AG427 LN140
κειρω, I SHREAR MYSELF
Ac	8:32	silent before its **shearer,** so
	18:18	he had his hair **cut,** for he was
1C	11: 6	she should **cut off** her hair;
	11: 6	have her hair **cut off** or to be

2752 G01 AG427 LN140 B1:341 K3:656 R2753
κελευσμα, COMMAND
1Th 4:16 with a cry of **command,** with the

2753 G025 AG427 LN140 B1:341
κελευω, I COMMAND
Mt	8:18	he **gave orders** to go over to
	14: 9	he **commanded** it to be given;
	14:19	Then he **ordered** the crowds to
	14:28	**command** me to come to you on
	18:25	his lord **ordered** him to be sold
	27:58	Pilate **ordered** it to be given
	27:64	Therefore **command** the tomb to
Lk	18:40	**ordered** the man to be brought
Ac	4:15	So they **ordered** them to leave
	5:34	and **ordered** the men to be put
	8:38	**commanded** the chariot to stop,
	12:19	**ordered** them to be put to death
	16:22	**ordered** them to be beaten with
	21:33	**ordered** him to be bound with
	21:34	**ordered** him to be brought into
	22:24	the tribune **directed** that he
	22:30	**ordered** the chief priests and
	23: 3	law you **order** me to be struck?
	23:10	**ordered** the soldiers to go down
	23:35	Then he **ordered** that he be kept
	25: 6	and **ordered** Paul to be brought.
	25:17	**ordered** the man to be brought.

	25:21	I **ordered** him to be held until
	25:23	Then Festus **gave the order** and
	27:43	He **ordered** those who could swim

2754 G01 AG427 LN140 B1:546 K3:662
κενοδοξια, EMPTY SPLENDOR
Ph 2: 3 selfish ambition or **conceit,**

2755 G01 AG427 LN140 B1:546 K3:662 R2756,5456
κενοδοξος, EMPTY SPLENDOR
Ga 5:26 Let us not become **conceited,**

2756 G018 AG427 LN140 B1:546 K3:659
κενος, EMPTY
Mk	12: 3	and sent him away **empty**-handed.
Lk	1:53	and sent the rich away **empty.**
	20:10	and sent him away **empty**-handed.
	20:11	insulted and sent away **empty**-
Ac	4:25	the peoples imagine **vain** things
1C	15:10	has not been in **vain.** On the
	15:14	been in **vain** and your faith
	15:14	your faith has been in **vain.**
	15:58	Lord your labor is not in **vain.**
2C	6: 1	accept the grace of God in **vain**
Ga	2: 2	or had not run, in **vain.**
Ep	5: 6	deceive you with **empty** words,
Ph	2:16	I did not run in **vain** or labor
	2:16	run in vain or labor in **vain.**
Co	2: 8	philosophy and **empty** deceit,
1Th	2: 1	coming to you was not in **vain,**
	3: 5	our labor had been in **vain.**
Ja	2:20	you **senseless** person, that

2757 G02 AG428 LN140 R2756,5456
κενοφωνια, EMPTY SOUND
1Ti	6:20	Avoid the profane **chatter** and
2Ti	2:16	Avoid profane **chatter,** for it

2758 G05 AG428 LN140 B1:546 K3:661 R2756
κενοω, I EMPTY
Ro	4:14	faith **is null** and the promise
1C	1:17	**might** not **be emptied** of its
	9:15	no one **will deprive** me of my
2C	9: 3	**to have been empty** in this case
Ph	2: 7	but **emptied** himself, taking the

2759 G04 AG428 LN140 B1:511 K3:663
κεντρον, STING
Ac	26:14	you to kick against the **goads.**
1C	15:55	Where, O death, is your **sting?**

15:56　The **sting** of death is sin, and
Re　9:10　**stingers,** and in their tails is

2760　GO3 AG428 LN141 B3:958
κεντυριων, CENTURION
Mk 15:39　Now when the **centurion,** who
　　15:44　summoning the **centurion,** he
　　15:45　**centurion** that he was dead, he

2761　GO1 AG428 LN141 R2756
κενως, EMPTILY
Ja　4: 5　it is **for nothing** that the

2762　GO2 AG428 LN141
κεραια, POINT
Mt　5:18　not one **stroke** of a letter,
Lk 16:17　than for one **stroke** of a letter

2763　GO3 AG428 LN141 B3:910 R2766
κεραμευς, POTTER
Mt 27: 7　the **potter's** field as a place
　　27:10　**potter's** field, as the Lord
Ro　9:21　Has the **potter** no right over

2764　GO1 AG428 LN141 B3:910 R2766
κεραμικυς, CERAMIC
Re　2:27　as when **clay** pots are shattered

2765　GO2 AG428 LN141 B3:910 R2766
κεραμιον, CERAMIC POT
Mk 14:13　a man carrying a **jar** of water
Lk 22:10　**jar** of water will meet you;

2766　GO1 AG429 LN141 B3:910
κεραμος, CERAMIC TILE
Lk　5:19　through the **tiles** into the

2767　GO3 AG429 LN141 B3:910
κεραννυμι, I MIX
Re 14:10　poured un**mixed** into the cup of
　　18: 6　**mix** a double draught for her
　　18: 6　for her in the cup she **mixed.**

2768　GO11 AG429 LN141 B3:714 K3:669
κερας, HORN
Lk　1:69　He has raised up a **mighty**
Re　5: 6　having seven **horns** and seven
　　9:13　four **horns** of the golden altar
　　12: 3　seven heads and ten **horns,** and
　　13: 1　ten **horns** and seven heads; and

13: 1　on its **horns** were ten diadems,
13:11　had two **horns** like a lamb and
17: 3　had seven heads and ten **horns.**
17: 7　and ten **horns** that carries her.
17:12　And the ten **horns** that you saw
17:16　And the ten **horns** that you saw,

2769　GO1 AG429 LN141
κερατιον, POD
Lk 15:16　the **pods** that the pigs were

2770　GO17 AG429 LN141 B3:136 K3:672 R2771
κερδαινω, I GAIN
Mt 16:26　**gain** the whole world but
　　18:15　you have **regained** that one.
　　25:16　and **made** five more talents.
　　25:17　two talents **made** two more
　　25:20　I **have made** five more talents.
　　25:22　I **have made** two more talents.
Mk　8:36　**to gain** the whole world and
Lk　9:25　if they **gain** the whole world,
Ac 27:21　thereby **avoided** this damage and
1C　9:19　so that I **might win** more of
　　9:20　in order **to win** Jews. To those
　　9:20　so that I **might win** those under
　　9:21　so that I **might win** those
　　9:22　so that I **might win** the weak. I
Ph　3: 8　in order that I **may gain** Christ
Ja　4:13　doing business and **making money**
1P　3: 1　they **may be won over** without a

2771　GO3 AG429 LN141 B3:136 K3:672
κερδος, GAIN
Ph　1:21　is Christ and dying is **gain.**
　　3: 7　Yet whatever **gains** I had, these
Ti　1:11　sordid **gain** what it is not

2772　GO1 AG429 LN141
κερμα, COIN
Jn　2:15　He also poured out the **coins** of

2773　GO1 AG429 LN141 R2772
κερματιστης, MONEY CHANGER
Jn　2:14　the **money changers** seated at

2774　GO2 AG429 LN141 R2776
κεφαλαιον, SUM
Ac 22:28　cost me a large **sum of money** to
He　8: 1　Now the **main point** in what we

2775 GO1 AG430 LN141 R2776
κεφαλιοω, I WOUND IN HEAD
Mk 12: 4 they **beat over the head** and

2776 GO75 AG430 LN141 B2:156 K3:673
κεφαλη, HEAD
Mt 5:36 And do not swear by your **head,**
6:17 put oil on your **head** and wash
8:20 Man has nowhere to lay his **head**
10:30 And even the hairs of your **head**
14: 8 Give me the **head** of John the
14:11 The **head** was brought on a
21:42 become the **cornerstone**; this
26: 7 she poured it on his **head** as he
27:29 they put it on his **head.** They
27:30 reed and struck him on the **head**
27:37 Over his **head** they put the
27:39 him, shaking their **heads**
Mk 6:24 The **head** of John the baptizer.
6:25 the **head** of John the Baptist on
6:27 orders to bring John's **head.** He
6:28 brought his **head** on a platter,
12:10 has become the **cornerstone;**
14: 3 poured the ointment on his **head**
15:19 They struck his **head** with a
15:29 shaking their **heads** and saying,
Lk 7:38 and to dry them with her **hair.**
7:46 You did not anoint my **head** with
9:58 Man has nowhere to lay his **head**
12: 7 But even the hairs of your **head**
20:17 has become the **cornerstone'?**
21:18 But not a hair of your **head**
21:28 stand up and raise your **heads,**
Jn 13: 9 but also my hands and my **head!**
19: 2 thorns and put it on his **head,**
19:30 Then he bowed his **head** and gave
20: 7 been on Jesus' **head,** not lying
20:12 one at the **head** and the other
Ac 4:11 it has become the **cornerstone.**
18: 6 blood be on your own **heads!**
18:18 he had his **hair** cut, for he was
21:24 the shaving of their **heads.**
27:34 lose a hair from your **heads.**
Ro 12:20 burning coals on their **heads.**
1C 11: 3 Christ is the **head** of every man,
11: 3 husband is the **head** of his wife,
11: 3 and God is the **head** of Christ.
11: 4 with something on his **head**
11: 4 his head disgraces his **head,**

11: 5 her **head** unveiled disgraces
11: 5 **head**—it is one and the same
11: 7 man ought not to have his **head**
11:10 symbol of authority on her **head**
12:21 nor again the **head** to the feet,
Ep 1:22 him the **head** over all things
4:15 into him who is the **head,** into
5:23 For the husband is the **head** of
5:23 just as Christ is the **head** of
Co 1:18 He is the **head** of the body, the
2:10 who is the **head** of every ruler
2:19 not holding fast to the **head,**
1P 2: 7 has become the very **head** of the
Re 1:14 **head** and his hair were white as
4: 4 golden crowns on their **heads.**
9: 7 On their **heads** were what looked
9:17 the **heads** of the horses were
9:17 like lions' **heads,** and fire and
9:19 like serpents, having **heads;**
10: 1 with a rainbow over his **head;**
12: 1 and on her **head** a crown of
12: 3 with seven **heads** and ten horns,
12: 3 and seven diadems on his **heads.**
13: 1 ten horns and seven **heads;** and
13: 1 on its **heads** were blasphemous
13: 3 One of its **heads** seemed to have
14:14 golden crown on his **head,** and a
17: 3 had seven **heads** and ten horns.
17: 7 seven **heads** and ten horns that
17: 9 seven **heads** are seven mountains
18:19 threw dust on their **heads,** as
19:12 on his **head** are many diadems;

2777 GO1 AG430 LN141 R2776
κεφαλις, HEADING
He 10: 7 (in the **scroll** of the book it

2777a GO1 AG430 LN141
κημοω, I MUZZLE
1C 9: 9 You shall not **muzzle** an ox

2778 GO4 AG430 LN141 B3:752
κηνσος, TRIBUTE
Mt 17:25 take toll or **tribute?** From
22:17 Is it lawful to pay **taxes** to
22:19 the coin used for the **tax."** And
Mk 12:14 Is it lawful to pay **taxes** to

2779 GO5 AG430 LN141
κηπος, GARDEN

Lk	13:19	took and sowed in the **garden;**
Jn	18: 1	place where there was a **garden,**
	18:26	see you in the **garden** with him?
	19:41	Now there was a **garden** in the
	19:41	in the **garden** there was a new

2780　GO1 AG430 LN141
κηπουρος, GARDEN KEEPER
Jn　20:15　to be the **gardener,** she said

2782　GO9 AG430 LN141 B3:48 K3:714 R2784
κηρυγμα, ANNOUNCEMENT

Mt	12:41	the **proclamation** of Jonah, and
Mk	16: 8	imperishable **proclamation** of
Lk	11:32	**proclamation** of Jonah, and see,
Ro	16:25	**proclamation** of Jesus Christ,
1C	1:21	our **proclamation,** to save those
	2: 4	My speech and my **proclamation**
	15:14	then our **proclamation** has been
2Ti	4:17	fully **proclaimed** and all the
Ti	1: 3	through the **proclamation** with

2783　GO3 AG431 LN142 B3:48 K3:683 R2784
κηρυξ, ANNOUNCER

1Ti	2: 7	I was appointed a **herald** and an
2Ti	1:11	**herald** and an apostle and a
2P	2: 5	a **herald** of righteousness, with

2784　GO61 AG431 LN142 B3:48 K3:697
κηρυσσω, I ANNOUNCE

Mt	3: 1	of Judea, **proclaiming,**
	4:17	began to **proclaim,** "Repent, for
	4:23	**proclaiming** the good news of
	9:35	**proclaiming** the good news of
	10: 7	As you go, **proclaim** the good
	10:27	**proclaim** from the housetops.
	11: 1	**proclaim** his message in their
	24:14	**proclaimed** throughout the world
	26:13	this good news is **proclaimed** in
Mk	1: 4	**proclaiming** a baptism of
	1: 7	He **proclaimed,** "The one who is
	1:14	**proclaiming** the good news of
	1:38	that I **may proclaim** the message
	1:39	**proclaiming** the message in
	1:45	began to **proclaim** it freely,
	3:14	out to **proclaim** the message,
	5:20	**proclaim** in the Decapolis how
	6:12	So they went out and **proclaimed**
	7:36	more zealously they **proclaimed**
	13:10	be **proclaimed** to all nations.

	14: 9	**proclaimed** in the whole world,
	16:15	into all the world and **proclaim**
	16:20	they went out and **proclaimed**
Lk	3: 3	around the Jordan, **proclaiming**
	4:18	He has sent me to **proclaim**
	4:19	to **proclaim** the year of the
	4:44	So he continued **proclaiming** the
	8: 1	**proclaiming** and bringing the
	8:39	**proclaiming** throughout the
	9: 2	**proclaim** the kingdom of God and
	12: 3	closed doors will be **proclaimed**
	24:47	**to be proclaimed** in his name to
Ac	8: 5	**proclaimed** the Messiah to them.
	9:20	began to **proclaim** Jesus in the
	10:37	the baptism that John **announced**
	10:42	He commanded us to **preach** to
	15:21	had those who **proclaim** him, for
	19:13	the Jesus whom Paul **proclaims.**
	20:25	**proclaiming** the kingdom, will
	28:31	**proclaiming** the kingdom of God
Ro	2:21	**preach** against stealing, do you
	10: 8	word of faith that we **proclaim)**
	10:14	without someone to **proclaim** him
	10:15	And how are they to **proclaim**
1C	1:23	we **proclaim** Christ crucified,
	9:27	so that after **proclaiming** to
	15:11	we **proclaim** and so you have
	15:12	Now if Christ is **proclaimed** as
2C	1:19	whom we **proclaimed** among you,
	4: 5	we do not **proclaim** ourselves;
	11: 4	someone comes and **proclaims**
	11: 4	**proclaimed,** or if you receive
Ga	2: 2	the gospel that I **proclaim**
	5:11	am still **preaching** circumcision
Ph	1:15	Some **proclaim** Christ from envy
Co	1:23	which has been **proclaimed** to
1Th	2: 9	while we **proclaimed** to you the
1Ti	3:16	**proclaimed** among Gentiles,
2Ti	4: 2	**proclaim** the message; be
1P	3:19	and **made** a **proclamation** to the
Re	5: 2	mighty angel **proclaiming** with a

2785　GO1 AG431 LN142 B1:670
κητος, SEA CREATURE
Mt　12:40　belly of the **sea monster,** so

2786　GO9 AG431 LN142 B3:381 K6:100
κηφας, CEPHAS
Jn　1:42　You are to be called **Cephas**

1C	1:12	"I belong to **Cephas**," or "I
	3:22	or **Cephas** or the world or life
	9: 5	brothers of the Lord and **Cephas**
	15: 5	and that he appeared to **Cephas**,
Ga	1:18	to visit **Cephas** and stayed with
	2: 9	and when James and **Cephas** and
	2:11	But when **Cephas** came to Antioch
	2:14	I said to **Cephas** before them

2787   G06 AG431 LN142
κιβωτος, BOX

Mt	24:38	the day Noah entered the **ark,**
Lk	17:27	**ark,** and the flood came and
He	9: 4	**ark** of the covenant overlaid on
	11: 7	built an **ark** to save his
1P	3:20	building of the **ark,** in which a
Re	11:19	the **ark** of his covenant was

2788   G04 AG432 LN142
κιθαρα, HARP

1C	14: 7	such as the flute or the **harp.**
Re	5: 8	holding a **harp** and golden bowls
	14: 2	harpists playing on their **harps**
	15: 2	**harps** of God in their hands.

2789   G02 AG432 LN142 R2788
κιθαριζω, I PLAY HARP

| 1C | 14: 7 | such as the flute or the **harp.** |
| Re | 14: 2 | sound of harpists **playing** on |

2790   G02 AG432 LN142
κιθαρωδος, HARPIST

| Re | 14: 2 | sound of **harpists** playing on |
| | 18:22 | and the sound of **harpists** and |

2791   G08 AG432 LN142
κιλικια, CILICIA

Ac	6: 9	from **Cilicia** and Asia, stood up
	15:23	Syria and **Cilicia**, greetings.
	15:41	went through Syria and **Cilicia,**
	21:39	Tarsus in **Cilicia**, a citizen
	22: 3	born in Tarsus in **Cilicia**, but
	23:34	that he was from **Cilicia,**
	27: 5	off **Cilicia** and Pamphylia, we
Ga	1:21	regions of Syria and **Cilicia,**

2792   G01 AG432 LN142
κινναμωμον, CINNAMON

| Re | 18:13 | **cinnamon**, spice, incense, myrrh |

2793   G04 AG432 LN142 B1:419 R2794
κινδυνευω, I AM IN DANGER

Lk	8:23	and they **were in danger.**
Ac	19:27	And there **is danger** not only
	19:40	For we **are in danger** of being
1C	15:30	**putting** ourselves **in danger**

2794   G09 AG432 LN142 B1:419
κινδυνος, DANGER

Ro	8:35	famine, or nakedness, or **peril,**
2C	11:26	on frequent journeys, in **danger**
	11:26	**danger** from bandits, danger
	11:26	**danger** from my own people,
	11:26	**danger** from Gentiles, danger
	11:26	**danger** in the city, danger in
	11:26	**danger** in the wilderness,
	11:26	**danger** at sea, danger from
	11:26	**danger** from false brothers and

2795   G08 AG432 LN142 K3:718
κινεω, I MOVE

Mt	23: 4	unwilling **to lift** a finger to
	27:39	him, **shaking** their heads
Mk	15:29	**shaking** their heads and saying,
Ac	17:28	In him we live and **move** and
	21:30	Then all the city was **aroused,**
	24: 5	an **agitator** among all the Jews
Re	2: 5	**remove** your lampstand from its
	6:14	island **was removed** from its

2797   G01 AG432 LN142
κις, KISH

| Ac | 13:21 | God gave them Saul son |
| | | of **Kish,** |

2797a   G01 AG433 LN142
κιχρημι, I LEND

| Lk | 11: 5 | **lend** me three loaves of bread; |

2798   G011 AG433 LN142 B3:865 K3:720 R2806
κλαδος, BRANCH

Mt	13:32	and make nests in its **branches.**
	21: 8	cut **branches** from the trees
	24:32	as its **branch** becomes tender
Mk	4:32	puts forth large **branches,** so
	13:28	as soon as its **branch** becomes
Lk	13:19	air made nests in its **branches.**
Ro	11:16	then the **branches** also are holy
	11:17	if some of the **branches** were
	11:18	do not boast over the **branches.**

	11:19	**Branches** were broken off so	Lk	24:35	in the **breaking** of the bread.
	11:21	natural **branches**, perhaps he	Ac	2:42	to the **breaking** of bread and

2799   GO40 AG433 LN142 B2:416 K3:722
κλαιω, I CRY

Mt	2:18	Rachel **weeping** for her children
	26:75	And he went out and **wept**
Mk	5:38	people **weeping** and wailing
	5:39	make a commotion and **weep**? The
	14:72	And he broke down and **wept**.
	16:10	they were mourning and **weeping**.
Lk	6:21	Blessed are you who **weep** now,
	6:25	for you will mourn and **weep**.
	7:13	and said to her, "Do not **weep**."
	7:32	wailed, and you did not **weep**.
	7:38	**weeping**, and began to bathe his
	8:52	They were all **weeping** and
	8:52	Do not **weep**; for she is not
	19:41	and saw the city, he **wept** over
	22:62	he went out and **wept** bitterly.
	23:28	do not **weep** for me, but weep
	23:28	but **weep** for yourselves and for
Jn	11:31	going to the tomb to **weep** there
	11:33	When Jesus saw her **weeping**, and
	11:33	came with her also **weeping**, he
	16:20	you will **weep** and mourn, but
	20:11	But Mary stood **weeping** outside
	20:11	As she **wept**, she bent over to
	20:13	Woman, why are you **weeping**?
	20:15	Woman, why are you **weeping**?
Ac	9:39	**weeping** and showing tunics and
	21:13	**weeping** and breaking my heart?
Ro	12:15	**weep** with those who weep.
	12:15	weep with those who **weep**.
1C	7:30	and those who **mourn** as though
	7:30	were not **mourning**, and those
Ph	3:18	I tell you even with **tears**.
Ja	4: 9	Lament and mourn and **weep**. Let
	5: 1	Come now, you rich people, **weep**
Re	5: 4	And I began to **weep** bitterly
	5: 5	Do not **weep**. See, the Lion of
	18: 9	**will weep** and wail over her
	18:11	merchants of the earth **weep** and
	18:15	**weeping** and mourning aloud,
	18:19	as they **wept** and mourned,

2800   GO2 AG433 LN142 B2:520 K3:726 R2806
κλασις, BREAKING

2801   GO9 AG433 LN142 K3:726 R2806
κλασμα, FRAGMENT

Mt	14:20	left over of the **broken pieces**,
	15:37	took up the **broken pieces** left
Mk	6:43	**broken pieces** and of the fish.
	8: 8	took up the **broken pieces** left
	8:19	baskets full of **broken pieces**
	8:20	baskets full of **broken pieces**
Lk	9:17	twelve baskets of **broken pieces**
Jn	6:12	Gather up the **fragments** left
	6:13	from the **fragments** of the five

2803   GO1 AG433 LN142
κλαυδια, CLAUDIA

2Ti	4:21	**Claudia** and all the brothers

2804   GO3 AG433 LN142
κλαυδιος, CLAUDIUS

Ac	11:28	during the reign of **Claudius**.
	18: 2	because **Claudius** had ordered
	23:26	**Claudius** Lysias to his

2805   GO9 AG433 LN142 B2·416 K3:725
κλαυθμος, CRYING

Mt	2:18	**wailing** and loud lamentation,
	8:12	where there will be **weeping** and
	13:42	where there will be **weeping** and
	13:50	where there will be **weeping** and
	22:13	**weeping** and gnashing of teeth.
	24:51	**weeping** and gnashing of teeth.
	25:30	**weeping** and gnashing of teeth.
Lk	13:28	There will be **weeping**
Ac	20:37	There was much **weeping** among

2806   GO14 AG433 LN142 B2:524 K3:726
κλαω, I BREAK

Mt	14:19	blessed and **broke** the loaves,
	15:36	after giving thanks he **broke**
	26:26	after blessing it he **broke** it,
Mk	8: 6	he **broke** them and gave them to
	8:19	When I **broke** the five loaves
	14:22	after blessing it he **broke** it,
Lk	22:19	he **broke** it and gave it to them
	24:30	blessed and **broke** it, and gave
Ac	2:46	they **broke** bread at home and
	20: 7	when we met to **break** bread,
	20:11	after he **had broken** bread and

	27:35	he **broke** it and began to eat.
1C	10:16	The bread that we **break**, is it
	11:24	he **broke** it and said, "This is

2807　GO6 AG433 LN142 B2:729 K3:744 R2808
κλεις, KEY

Mt	16:19	I will give you the **keys** of the
Lk	11:52	you have taken away the **key** of
Re	1:18	I have the **keys** of Death and of
	3: 7	who has the **key** of David, who
	9: 1	he was given the **key** to the
	20: 1	holding in his hand the **key** to

2808　GO16 AG434 LN143 B2:729
κλειω, I CLOSE

Mt	6: 6	go into your room and **shut** the
	23:13	For you **lock** people **out** of the
	25:10	banquet; and the door **was shut**.
Lk	4:25	when the heaven **was shut** up
	11: 7	door **has** already **been locked**,
Jn	20:19	**were locked** for fear of the
	20:26	Although the doors **were shut**,
Ac	5:23	prison securely **locked** and the
	21:30	immediately the doors **were shut**
1J	3:17	in need and yet **refuses** help?
Re	3: 7	who opens and no one **will shut**,
	3: 7	who **shuts** and no one opens:
	3: 8	which no one is able **to shut**.
	11: 6	They have authority **to shut** the
	20: 3	**locked** and sealed it over him,
	21:25	Its gates **will** never **be shut** by

2809　GO1 AG434 LN143 R2813
κλεμμα, THEFT

Re	9:21	fornication or their **thefts**.

2810　GO1 AG435 LN143
κλεοπας, CLEOPAS

Lk	24:18	name was **Cleopas**, answered him,

2811　GO1 AG434 LN143
κλεος, FAME

1P	2:20	what **credit** is that? But if you

2812　GO16 AG434 LN143 B3:377 K3:754 R2813
κλεπτης, THIEF

Mt	6:19	where **thieves** break in and
	6:20	where **thieves** do not break in
	24:43	part of the night the **thief** was
Lk	12:33	where no **thief** comes near and

	12:39	what hour the **thief** was coming,
Jn	10: 1	way is a **thief** and a bandit.
	10: 8	**thieves** and bandits; but the
	10:10	The **thief** comes only to steal
	12: 6	because he was a **thief**; he kept
1C	6:10	**thieves,** the greedy, drunkards,
1Th	5: 2	will come like a **thief** in the
	5: 4	to surprise you like a **thief;**
1P	4:15	a **thief**, a criminal, or even as
2P	3:10	will come like a **thief,** and
Re	3: 3	I will come like a **thief,** and
	16:15	("See, I am coming like a **thief**

2813　GO13 AG434 LN143 B3:377 K3:754
κλεπτω, I THIEVE

Mt	6:19	thieves break in and **steal;**
	6:20	do not break in and **steal.**
	19:18	You **shall** not **steal;** You shall
	27:64	disciples may go and **steal** him
	28:13	**stole** him away while we were
Mk	10:19	You **shall** not **steal;** You shall
Lk	18:20	You **shall** not **steal;** You shall
Jn	10:10	The thief comes only **to steal**
Ro	2:21	you preach against **stealing,** do
	2:21	against stealing, **do** you **steal?**
	13: 9	You **shall** not **steal;** You shall
Ep	4:28	Thieves must give up **stealing;**
	4:28	Thieves must give up **stealing;**

2814　GO4 AG434 LN143 B3:865 K3:757
κλημα, BRANCH

Jn	15: 2	He removes every **branch** in me
	15: 4	Just as the **branch** cannot bear
	15: 5	you are the **branches.** Those who
	15: 6	**branch** and withers; such

2815　GO1 AG434 LN143
κλημης, CLEMENT

Ph	4: 3	together with **Clement** and the

2816　GO18 AG434 LN143 B2:295 K3:767 R2818
κληρονομεω, I INHERIT

Mt	5: 5	for they **will inherit** the earth
	19:29	and **will inherit** eternal life.
	25:34	**inherit** the kingdom prepared
Mk	10:17	must I do **to inherit** eternal
Lk	10:25	I do **to inherit** eternal life?
	18:18	I do **to inherit** eternal life?
1C	6: 9	wrongdoers **will** not **inherit** the
	6:10	none of these **will inherit** the

	15:50	flesh and blood cannot **inherit**
	15:50	**inherit** the imperishable.
Ga	4:30	**share** the **inheritance** with the
	5:21	do such things **will not inherit**
He	1: 4	name he **has inherited** is more
	1:14	of those who are **to inherit**
	6:12	faith and patience **inherit** the
	12:17	when he wanted **to inherit** the
1P	3: 9	that you **might inherit** a
Re	21: 7	Those who conquer **will inherit**

2817   GO14 AG435 LN143 B2:295 K3:767 R2818
κληρονομια, INHERITANCE

Mt	21:38	him and get his **inheritance.**
Mk	12: 7	and the **inheritance** will be
Lk	12:13	divide the family **inheritance**
	20:14	so that the **inheritance** may be
Ac	7: 5	a **heritage,** not even a foot's
	20:32	give you the **inheritance** among
Ga	3:18	For if the **inheritance** comes
Ep	1:14	**inheritance** toward redemption
	1:18	glorious **inheritance** among the
	5: 5	has any **inheritance** in the
Co	3:24	receive the **inheritance** as your
He	9:15	promised eternal **inheritance,**
	11: 8	receive as an **inheritance;** and
1P	1: 4	and into an **inheritance** that is

2818   GO15 AG435 LN143 B2:295 K3:767
κληρονομος, INHERITOR

Mt	21:38	This is the **heir; come, let us**
Mk	12: 7	This is the **heir; come, let us**
Lk	20:14	This is the **heir; let us kill**
Ro	4:13	he would **inherit** the world did
	4:14	law who are to be the **heirs,**
	8:17	and if children, then **heirs,**
	8:17	then heirs, **heirs** of God and
Ga	3:29	**heirs** according to the promise.
	4: 1	My point is this: **heirs,** as
	4: 7	if a child then also an **heir,**
Ti	3: 7	we might become **heirs** according
He	1: 2	whom he appointed **heir** of all
	6:17	clearly to the **heirs** of the
	11: 7	an **heir** to the righteousness
Ja	2: 5	to be **heirs** of the kingdom that

2819   GO11 AG435 LN143 B2:295 K3:758
κληρος, LOT

Mt	27:35	themselves by casting **lots;**
Mk	15:24	casting **lots** to decide what

Jn	19:24	my clothing they cast **lots.**
Ac	1:17	was **allotted** his share in this
	1:26	And they cast **lots** for them,
	1:26	the **lot** fell on Matthias; and
	8:21	You have no part or **share** in
	26:18	a **place** among those who are
Co	1:12	share in the **inheritance** of
1P	5: 3	those in your **charge,** but be

2820   GO1 AG435 LN143 B2:295 K3:764 R2819
κληροω, I APPOINT

Ep	1:11	**have obtained** an inheritance,

2821   GO11 AG435 LN143 B1:270 K3:491 R2564
κλησις, CALL

Ro	11:29	gifts and the **calling** of God
1C	1:26	Consider your own **call,**
	7:20	in which you were **called.**
Ep	1:18	hope to which he has **called** you
	4: 1	worthy of the **calling** to which
	4: 4	to the one hope of your **calling**
Ph	3:14	the prize of the heavenly **call**
2Th	1:11	worthy of his **call** and will
2Ti	1: 9	called us with a holy **calling,**
He	3: 1	partners in a heavenly **calling,**
2P	1:10	confirm your **call** and election,

2822   GO10 AG436 LN143 B1:270 K3:494 R2821
κλητος, CALLED

Mt	22:14	For many are **called,** but few
Ro	1: 1	**called** to be an apostle, set
	1: 6	who are **called** to belong to
	1: 7	who are **called** to be saints:
	8:28	who are **called** according to his
1C	1: 1	Paul, **called** to be an apostle
	1: 2	Jesus, **called** to be saints,
	1:24	but to those who are the **called**
Ju	1: 1	To those who are **called,** who
Re	17:14	those with him are **called** and

2823   GO2 AG436 LN143
κλιβανος, FURNACE

Mt	6:30	thrown into the **oven,** will he
Lk	12:28	is thrown into the **oven,** how

2824   GO3 AG436 LN143
κλιμα, REGION

Ro	15:23	place for me in these **regions,**
2C	11:10	be silenced in the **regions** of
Ga	1:21	Then I went into the **regions** of

2824a GO1 AG436 LN143
κλιναριον, SMALL BED
Ac 5:15 laid them on **cots** and mats, in

2825 GO9 AG436 LN143 R2827
κλινη, BED
Mt 9: 2 paralyzed man lying on a **bed.**
    9: 6 Stand up, take your **bed** and
Mk 4:21 or under the **bed,** and not on
    7: 4 and bronze kettles.) [and **beds**]
    7:30 the child lying on the **bed,** and
Lk 5:18 a paralyzed man on a **bed.** They
    8:16 or puts it under a **bed,** but
    17:34 there will be two in one **bed;**
Re 2:22 I am throwing her on a **bed,** and

2826 GO22 AG436 LN143 R2825
κλινιδιον, BED
Lk 5:19 let him down with his **bed**
    5:24 stand up and take your **bed** and

2827 GO7 AG436 LN143
κλινω, I BOW
Mt 8:20 Son of Man has nowhere **to lay**
Lk 9:12 The day **was drawing** to a close,
    9:58 Son of Man has nowhere **to lay**
    24: 5 **bowed** their faces to the ground
    24:29 the day **is now nearly over."** So
Jn 19:30 Then he **bowed** his head and
            gave
He 11:34 **put** foreign armies **to flight.**

2828 GO1 AG436 LN143
κλισια, GROUP
Lk 9:14 sit down in **groups** of about

2829 GO2 AG436 LN144 R2813
κλοπη, THEFT
Mt 15:19 fornication, **theft,** false
Mk 7:21 fornication, **theft,** murder,

2830 GO2 AG436 LN144
κλυδων, WAVE
Lk 8:24 wind and the raging **waves;**
            they
Ja 1: 6 doubts is like a **wave** of the

2831 GO1 AG436 LN144 R2830
κλυδωνιζομαι, I TOSS BY WAVE
Ep 4:14 **tossed to and fro** and blown

2832 GO1 AG436 LN144
κλωπας, CLOPAS
Jn 19:25 Mary the wife of **Clopas,** and

2833 GO1 AG437 LN144
κνηθω, I TICKLE
2Ti 4: 3 teachers **to suit** their own

2834 GO1 AG437 LN144
κνιδος, CNIDUS
Ac 27: 7 off **Cnidus,** and as the wind was

2835 GO2 AG437 LN144
κοδραντης, CODRANTES
Mt 5:26 you have paid the last **penny.**
Mk 12:42 coins, which are worth a **penny.**

2836 GO22 AG437 LN144 B1:169 K3:786
κοιλια, STOMACH
Mt 12:40 in the **belly** of the sea monster
    15:17 enters the **stomach,** and goes
    19:12 who have been so from **birth,**
Mk 7:19 not the heart but the **stomach,**
Lk 1:15 even before his **birth** he will
    1:41 child leaped in her **womb.**
    1:42 is the fruit of your **womb.**
    1:44 the child in my **womb** leaped for
    2:21 he was conceived in the **womb.**
    11:27 Blessed is the **womb** that bore
    23:29 and the **wombs** that never bore,
Jn 3: 4 into the mother's **womb** and be
    7:38 Out of the believer's **heart**
Ac 3: 2 And a man lame from **birth** was
    14: 8 he had been crippled from **birth**
Ro 16:18 but their own **appetites,** and by
1C 6:13 Food is meant for the **stomach**
    6:13 and the **stomach** for food," and
Ga 1:15 before I was **born** and called me
Ph 3:19 their god is the **belly;** and
Re 10: 9 bitter to your **stomach,** but
    10:10 it, my **stomach** was made bitter.

2837 GO18 AG437 LN144 B1:441
κοιμαω, I SLEEP
Mt 27:52 who **had fallen asleep** were
    28:13 him away while we **were asleep.**
Lk 22:45 found them **sleeping** because of
Jn 11:11 **has fallen asleep,** but I am
    11:12 if he **has fallen asleep,** he
Ac 7:60 When he had said this, he **died.**

	12: 6	**was sleeping** between two
	13:36	**died,** was laid beside his
1C	7:39	But if the husband **dies,** she is
	11:30	ill, and some have **died.**
	15: 6	alive, though some **have died.**
	15:18	Then those also who **have died**
	15:20	fruits of those who **have died.**
	15:51	We **will** not all **die,** but we
1Th	4:13	about those who **have died,** so
	4:14	with him those who **have died.**
	4:15	precede those who **have died.**
2P	3: 4	ever since our ancestors **died,**

2838   GO1 AG437 LN144 R2837
κοιμησις, SLEEP

| Jn | 11:13 | was referring merely to **sleep.** |

2839   GO14 AG438 LN144 B1:639 K3:789
κοινος, COMMON

Mk	7: 2	eating with **defiled** hands, that
	7: 5	but eat with **defiled** hands?
Ac	2:44	and had all things in **common;**
	4:32	they owned was held in **common.**
	10:14	that is **profane** or unclean.
	10:28	should not call anyone **profane**
	11: 8	nothing **profane** or unclean has
Ro	14:14	nothing is **unclean** in itself;
	14:14	it is **unclean** for anyone who
	14:14	anyone who thinks it **unclean.**
Ti	1: 4	child in the faith we **share:**
He	10:29	**profaned** the blood of the
Ju	1: 3	salvation we **share,** I find it
Re	21:27	But nothing **unclean** will enter

2840   GO14 AG438 LN144 B1:639 K3:809 R2839
κοινοω, I MAKE COMMON, I DEFILE

Mt	15:11	into the mouth that **defiles** a
	15:11	out of the mouth that **defiles.**
	15:18	heart, and this is what **defiles**
	15:20	These are what **defile** a person,
	15:20	unwashed hands does not **defile.**
Mk	7:15	that by going in can **defile,**
	7:15	that come out **are** what **defile.**
	7:18	from outside cannot **defile,**
	7:20	out of a person that **defiles.**
	7:23	and they **defile** a person.
Ac	10:15	you must not call **profane.**
	11: 9	you must not call **profane.**
	21:28	the temple and **has defiled** this
He	9:13	those who **have been defiled** so

2841   GO8 AG438 LN144 B1:636 K3:797 R2844
κοινωνεω, I AM PARTNER

Ro	12:13	**Contribute** to the needs of the
	15:27	Gentiles have come **to share** in
Ga	6: 6	**share** in all good things with
Ph	4:15	no church **shared** with me in the
1Ti	5:22	**do** not **participate** in the sins
He	2:14	children **share** flesh and blood
1P	4:13	**are sharing** Christ's sufferings
2J	1:11	to welcome is **to participate** in

2842   GO19 AG438 LN144 B1:639 K3:797 R2844
κοινωνια, PARTNERSHIP

Ac	2:42	teaching and **fellowship,** to the
Ro	15:26	**share** their **resources** with the
1C	1: 9	called into the **fellowship** of
	10:16	it not a **sharing** in the blood
	10:16	is it not a **sharing** in the body
2C	6:14	Or what **fellowship** is there
	8: 4	privilege of **sharing** in this
	9:13	your **sharing** with them and with
	13:13	and the **communion** of the Holy
Ga	2: 9	the right hand of **fellowship,**
Ph	1: 5	because of your **sharing** in the
	2: 1	any **sharing** in the Spirit, any
	3:10	the **sharing** of his sufferings
Pm	1: 6	I pray that the **sharing** of your
He	13:16	to do good and **to share** what
1J	1: 3	have **fellowship** with us; and
	1: 3	truly our **fellowship** is with
	1: 6	we say that we have **fellowship**
	1: 7	we have **fellowship** with one

2843   GO1 AG439 LN144 B1:639 K3:809 R2844
κοινωνικος, PARTNER

| 1Ti | 6:18 | generous, and **ready to share,** |

2844   GO10 AG439 LN144 B1:639 K3:797 R2839
κοινωνος, PARTNER

Mt	23:30	taken **part** with them in
Lk	5:10	who were **partners** with Simon
1C	10:18	eat the sacrifices **partners** in
	10:20	want you to be **partners** with
2C	1: 7	as you **share** in our sufferings,
	8:23	As for Titus, he is my **partner**
Pm	1:17	if you consider me your **partner**
He	10:33	sometimes being **partners** with
1P	5: 1	one who **shares** in the glory to
2P	1: 4	may become **participants** of the

2845   GO4 AG440 LN144 B2:586 R2849
κοιτη, BED
Lk   11: 7   my children are with me in **bed;**
Ro   9:10   when she had **conceived**
             children
     13:13   **debauchery** and licentiousness,
He   13: 4   let the marriage **bed** be kept

2846   GO1 AG440 LN144 R2845
κοιτων, BEDROOM
Ac   12:20   Blastus, the king's **chamberlain**

2847   GO6 AG440 LN144 K3:812
κοκκινος, SCARLET
Mt   27:28   and put a **scarlet** robe on him,
He   9:19   with water and **scarlet** wool and
Re   17: 3   sitting on a **scarlet** beast that
     17: 4   purple and **scarlet,** and adorned
     18:12   silk and **scarlet,** all kinds of
     18:16   purple and **scarlet,** adorned

2848   GO7 AG440 LN144 K3:810
κοκκος, GRAIN
Mt   13:31   heaven is like a mustard **seed**
     17:20   the size of a mustard **seed,** you
Mk   4:31   It is like a mustard **seed,**
Lk   13:19   It is like a mustard **seed** that
     17: 6   the size of a mustard **seed,** you
Jn   12:24   unless a **grain** of wheat falls
1C   15:37   a bare **seed,** perhaps of wheat

2849   GO2 AG440 LN144 B3:98 K3:814
κολαζω, I PUNISH
Ac   4:21   finding no way **to punish** them
2P   2: 9   unrighteous under **punishment**

2850   GO1 AG440 LN144 K3:817
κολακεια, FLATTERY
1Th   2: 5   with words of **flattery** or with

2851   GO2 AG440 LN144 B3:98 K3:816 R2849
κολασις, PUNISHMENT
Mt   25:46   eternal **punishment,** but the
1J   4:18   fear has to do with **punishment,**

2852   GO5 AG441 LN145 B1:161 K3:818 R2849
κολαφιζω, I KNOCK ABOUT
Mt   26:67   spat in his face and **struck** him
Mk   14:65   and to **strike** him, saying to
1C   4:11   are poorly clothed and **beaten**

2C   12: 7   a messenger of Satan to
             torment
1P   2:20   when you **are beaten** for doing

2853   GO12 AG441 LN145 B2:348 K3:822
κολλαω, I JOIN
Mt   19: 5   and **be joined** to his wife, and
Lk   10:11   **clings** to our feet, we wipe off
     15:15   So he went and **hired** himself
Ac   5:13   None of the rest dared **to join**
      8:29   to this chariot and **join** it.
      9:26   attempted **to join** the disciples
     10:28   a Jew **to associate** with or to
     17:34   But some of them **joined**
             him and
Ro   12: 9   evil, **hold fast** to what is good
1C   6:16   **is united** to a prostitute
      6:17   But anyone **united** to the Lord
Re   18: 5   for her sins **are heaped** high as

2854   GO1 AG441 LN145 B3:518
κολλουριον, EYE SALVE
Re   3:18   and **salve** to anoint your eyes

2855   GO3 AG442 LN145
κολλυβιστης, MONEY CHANGERS
Mt   21:12   tables of the **money changers**
Mk   11:15   tables of the **money changers**
Jn   2:15   coins of the **money changers**

2856   GO4 AG442 LN145 K3:823
κολοβοω, I SHORTEN
Mt   24:22   days had not **been cut short,** no
     24:22   those days **will be cut short.**
Mk   13:20   had not **cut short** those days,
     13:20   he **has cut short** those days.

2857   GO1 AG442 LN145
κολοσσαι, COLOSSAE
Co   1: 2   in Christ in **Colossae:** Grace to

2859   GO6 AG442 LN145 K3:824
κολπος, LAP
Lk   6:38   will be put into your **lap;** for
     16:22   the angels to **be with** Abraham.
     16:23   away with Lazarus **by his side.**
Jn   1:18   who is **close** to the Father's
     13:23   was reclining **next** to him;
Ac   27:39   they noticed a **bay** with a
             beach

2860 GO1 AG442 LN145
κολυμβαω, I SWIM
Ac 27:43 jump overboard first and **make**

2861 GO3 AG442 LN145 R2860
κολυμβηθρα, POOL
Jn   5: 2 there is a **pool,** called in
      5: 7 put me into the **pool** when the
      9: 7 Go, wash in the **pool** of

2862 GO1 AG442 LN145
κολωνια, COLONY
Ac 16:12 Macedonia and a Roman **colony.**

2863 GO2 AG442 LN145 R2864
κομαω, I WEAR LONG HAIR
1C 11:14 a man **wears long hair,** it is
      11:15 but if a woman **has long hair,**

2864 GO1 AG442 LN145
κομη, LONG HAIR
1C 11:15 but if a woman has **long hair,**

2865 GO10 AG442 LN145
κομιζω, I OBTAIN
Mt 25:27 my return I **would have received**
Lk   7:37 **brought** an alabaster jar of
2C   5:10 so that each **may receive**
Ep   6: 8 we **will receive** the same again
Co   3:25 **will be paid back** for whatever
He 10:36 **may receive** what was promised.
      11:19 he **did receive** him **back.**
      11:39 **did** not **receive** what was
1P   1: 9 for you **are receiving** the
      5: 4 you **will win** the crown of glory

2866 GO1 AG443 LN145
κομψοτερον, MORE FINE
Jn   4:52 when he began **to recover,** and

2867 GO2 AG443 LN145 K3:827
κονιαω, I WHITEWASH
Mt 23:27 you are like **whitewashed** tombs,
Ac 23: 3 you **whitewashed** wall! Are you

2868 GO5 AG443 LN145
κονιορτος, BLOWING DUST
Mt 10:14 shake off the **dust** from your
Lk   9: 5 shake the **dust** off your feet as
      10:11 Even the **dust** of your town

Ac 13:51 So they shook the **dust** off
      22:23 and tossing **dust** into the air,

2869 GO3 AG443 LN145
κοπαζω, I CEASE
Mt 14:32 into the boat, the wind **ceased**
Mk   4:39 Then the wind **ceased,** and
      6:51 with them and the wind **ceased.**

2870 GO1 AG443 LN145 B2:417 K3:830 R2875
κοπετος, MOURNING
Ac   8: 2 made loud **lamentation** over him.

2871 GO1 AG443 LN145
κοπη, SLAUGHTER
He   7: 1 returning from **defeating** the

2872 GO23 AG443 LN145 B1:262 K3:827 R2873
κοπιαω, I LABOR
Mt   6:28 they neither **toil** nor spin,
      11:28 all you that **are weary** and are
Lk   5: 5 Master, we **have worked** all
      12:27 they neither **toil** nor spin; yet
Jn   4: 6 **tired out** by his journey, was
      4:38 you **did** not **labor.** Others have
      4:38 Others have **labored,** and you
Ac 20:35 work we **must support** the weak
Ro 16: 6 Greet Mary, who has **worked**
      16:12 Greet those **workers** in the Lord
      16:12 who has **worked** hard in the
              Lord
1C   4:12 grow weary from the **work** of our
      15:10 I **worked** harder than any of
      16:16 who works and **toils** with them.
Ga   4:11 I am afraid that my **work** for
Ep   4:28 rather let them **labor** and work
Ph   2:16 did not run in vain or **labor** in
Co   1:29 For this I **toil** and struggle
1Th 5:12 respect those who **labor** among
1Ti 4:10 For to this end we **toil** and
      5:17 those who **labor** in preaching
2Ti 2: 6 the farmer who **does** the **work**
Re   2: 3 that you **have** not **grown**
              weary.

2873 GO18 AG443 LN145 B1:262 K3:827
κοπος, LABOR
Mt 26:10 Why do you **trouble** the woman?
Mk 14: 6 why do you **trouble** her? She has
Lk 11: 7 Do not **bother** me; the door has

	18: 5	this widow keeps **bothering** me,
Jn	4:38	have entered into their **labor.**
1C	3: 8	wages according to the **labor** of
	15:58	in the Lord your **labor** is not
2C	6: 5	imprisonments, riots, **labors,**
	10:15	in the **labors** of others; but
	11:23	with far greater **labors,**
	11:27	in **toil** and hardship, through
Ga	6:17	let no one make **trouble** for me;
1Th	1: 3	your work of faith and **labor** of
	2: 9	You remember our **labor** and toil
	3: 5	that our **labor** had been in vain
2Th	3: 8	but with **toil** and labor we
Re	2: 2	I know your works, your **toil**
	14:13	will rest from their **labors,**

2874   GO2 AG443 LN145 B1:480
κοπρια, MANURE

Lk	13: 8	dig around it and put **manure** on
	14:35	nor for the **manure** pile; they

2875   GO8 AG444 LN145 B2:417 K3:830
κοπτω, I MOURN, I CUT

Mt	11:17	wailed, and you did not **mourn.**
	21: 8	and others **cut** branches from
	24:30	tribes of the earth **will mourn,**
Mk	11: 8	that they **had cut** in the fields
Lk	8:52	were all weeping and **wailing**
	23:27	their breasts and **wailing** for
Re	1: 7	even those who **pierced** him; and
	18: 9	will weep and **wail** over her

2876   GO1 AG444 LN146
κοραξ, RAVEN

Lk	12:24	Consider the **ravens:** they

2877   GO8 AG444 LN146
κορασιον, YOUNG GIRL

Mt	9:24	Go away; for the **girl** is not
	9:25	the hand, and the **girl** got up.
	14:11	platter and given to the **girl,**
Mk	5:41	which means, "**Little girl,** get
	5:42	And immediately the **girl** got up
	6:22	the king said to the **girl,** "Ask
	6:28	and gave it to the **girl.** Then
	6:28	Then the **girl** gave it to her

2878   GO1 AG444 LN146 B2:43 K3:860
κορβαν, CORBAN

Mk	7:11	have had from me is **Corban**

2878a   GO1 AG444 LN146 B2:43 K3:860
κορβανας, CORBAN

Mt	27: 6	put them into the **treasury,**

2879   GO1 AG444 LN146
κορε, KORAH

Ju	1:11	perish in **Korah's** rebellion.

2880   GO2 AG444 LN146
κορεννυμι, I AM FULL

Ac	27:38	**had satisfied their hunger,**
1C	4: 8	Already **you have become rich!**

2881   GO2 AG444 LN146
κορινθιος, CORINTHIAN

Ac	18: 8	many of the **Corinthians** who
2C	6:11	frankly to you **Corinthians;** our

2882   GO6 AG444 LN146
κορινθος, CORINTH

Ac	18: 1	left Athens and went to **Corinth**
	19: 1	While Apollos was in **Corinth,**
1C	1: 2	of God that is in **Corinth,** to
2C	1: 1	of God that is in **Corinth,**
	1:23	I did not come again to **Corinth**
2Ti	4:20	Erastus remained in **Corinth;**

2883   GO8 AG444 LN146
κορνηλιος, CORNELIUS

Ac	10: 1	was a man named **Cornelius,** a
	10: 3	saying to him, "**Cornelius.**"
	10:17	the men sent by **Cornelius**
	10:22	They answered, "**Cornelius,** a
	10:24	**Cornelius** was expecting them
	10:25	On Peter's arrival **Cornelius**
	10:30	**Cornelius** replied, "Four days
	10:31	**Cornelius,** your prayer has

2884   GO1 AG444 LN146
κορος, KOR (MEASURE)

Lk	16: 7	A hundred **containers** of wheat.

2885   GO10 AG445 LN146 B1:521 K3:867
κοσμεω, I ADORN

Mt	12:44	empty, swept, and **put in order.**
	23:29	and **decorate** the graves of the
	25: 7	got up and **trimmed** their lamps.
Lk	11:25	finds it swept and **put in order**
	21: 5	it **was adorned** with beautiful
1Ti	2: 9	women **should dress** themselves

Ti	2:10	they may be an **ornament** to the
1P	3: 5	used **to adorn** themselves by
Re	21: 2	prepared as a bride **adorned** for
	21:19	**are adorned** with every jewel;

2886   ᴳᴼ2 ᴬᴳ445 ᴸᴺ146 ᴮ1:521 ᴷ3:897 ᴿ2889
κοσμικος, WORLDLY

Ti	2:12	renounce impiety and **worldly**
He	9: 1	and an **earthly** sanctuary.

2887   ᴳᴼ2 ᴬᴳ445 ᴸᴺ146 ᴮ1:521 ᴷ3:895 ᴿ2885
κοσμιος, RESPECTABLE

1Ti	2: 9	dress themselves **modestly** and
	3: 2	sensible, **respectable,**

2888   ᴳᴼ1 ᴬᴳ445 ᴸᴺ146 ᴮ2:514 ᴷ3:913 ᴿ2889,2902
κοσμοκρατωρ, WORLD STRENGTH

Ep	6:12	against the **cosmic powers** of

2889   ᴳᴼ186 ᴬᴳ445 ᴸᴺ146 ᴮ1:521 ᴷ3:868
κοσμος, WORLD

Mt	4: 8	kingdoms of the **world** and their
	5:14	You are the light of the **world**
	13:35	the foundation of the **world.**
	13:38	the field is the **world,** and the
	16:26	gain the whole **world** but
	18: 7	Woe to the **world** because of
	24:21	beginning of the **world** until
	25:34	the foundation of the **world;**
	26:13	proclaimed in the whole **world,**
Mk	8:36	gain the whole **world** and
	14: 9	proclaimed in the whole **world,**
	16:15	Go into all the **world** and
Lk	9:25	gain the whole **world,** but lose
	11:50	the foundation of the **world,**
	12:30	nations of the **world** that
Jn	1: 9	was coming into the **world.**
	1:10	He was in the **world,** and the
	1:10	the **world** came into being
	1:10	yet the **world** did not know him.
	1:29	takes away the sin of the **world**
	3:16	For God so loved the **world**
	3:17	send the Son into the **world** to
	3:17	to condemn the **world,** but in
	3:17	**world** might be saved through
	3:19	light has come into the **world,**
	4:42	the Savior of the **world.**
	6:14	who is to come into the **world.**
	6:33	and gives life to the **world.**
	6:51	life of the **world** is my flesh.

7: 4	show yourself to the **world.**
7: 7	The **world** cannot hate you, but
8:12	I am the light of the **world.**
8:23	you are of this **world,** I am not
8:23	I am not of this **world.**
8:26	I declare to the **world** what I
9: 5	As long as I am in the **world,** I
9: 5	I am the light of the **world.**
9:39	I came into this **world** for
10:36	and sent into the **world** is
11: 9	see the light of this **world.**
11:27	the one coming into the **world.**
12:19	Look, the **world** has gone after
12:25	hate their life in this **world**
12:31	judgment of this **world;** now
12:31	the ruler of this **world** will be
12:46	as light into the **world,** so
12:47	I came not to judge the **world,**
12:47	world, but to save the **world.**
13: 1	depart from this **world** and go
13: 1	his own who were in the **world,**
14:17	whom the **world** cannot receive,
14:19	the **world** will no longer see me
14:22	to us, and not to the **world?**
14:27	not give to you as the **world**
14:30	ruler of this **world** is coming.
14:31	the **world** may know that I love
15:18	If the **world** hates you, be
15:19	If you belonged to the **world,**
15:19	the **world** would love you as
15:19	you do not belong to the **world,**
15:19	chosen you out of the **world**
15:19	therefore the **world** hates you.
16: 8	he will prove the **world** wrong
16:11	the ruler of this **world** has
16:20	but the **world** will rejoice; you
16:21	a human being into the **world.**
16:28	come into the **world;** again, I
16:28	leaving the **world** and am going
16:33	the **world** you face persecution.
16:33	I have conquered the **world!**
17: 5	before the **world** existed.
17: 6	whom you gave me from the **world**
17: 9	asking on behalf of the **world,**
17:11	I am no longer in the **world,**
17:11	but they are in the **world,** and
17:13	speak these things in the **world**
17:14	the **world** has hated them
17:14	do not belong to the **world,**

	17:14	I do not belong to the **world.**
	17:15	take them out of the **world,** but
	17:16	They do not belong to the **world**
	17:16	as I do not belong to the **world**
	17:18	sent me into the **world,** so I
	17:18	I have sent them into the **world**
	17:21	that the **world** may believe that
	17:23	the **world** may know that you
	17:24	the foundation of the **world.**
	17:25	the **world** does not know you,
	18:20	have spoken openly to the **world**
	18:36	kingdom is not from this **world.**
	18:36	from this **world,** my followers
	18:37	came into the **world,** to testify
	21:25	**world** itself could not contain
Ac	17:24	The God who made the **world**
Ro	1: 8	proclaimed throughout the **world**
	1:20	creation of the **world** his
	3: 6	how could God judge the **world?**
	3:19	the whole **world** may be held
	4:13	inherit the **world** did not come
	5:12	sin came into the **world** through
	5:13	sin was indeed in the **world**
	11:12	riches for the **world,** and if
	11:15	reconciliation of the **world,**
1C	1:20	foolish the wisdom of the **world**
	1:21	the **world** did not know God
	1:27	foolish in the **world** to shame
	1:27	weak in the **world** to shame the
	1:28	low and despised in the **world,**
	2:12	the spirit of the **world,** but
	3:19	For the wisdom of this **world** is
	3:22	or Cephas or the **world** or life
	4: 9	a spectacle to the **world,** to
	4:13	rubbish of the **world,** the dregs
	5:10	immoral of this **world,** or the
	5:10	need to go out of the **world.**
	6: 2	saints will judge the **world?**
	6: 2	if the **world** is to be judged by
	7:31	deal with the **world** as though
	7:31	present form of this **world** is
	7:33	the affairs of the **world,** how
	7:34	the affairs of the **world,** how
	8: 4	no idol in the **world** really
	11:32	condemned along with the **world.**
	14:10	kinds of sounds in the **world,**
2C	1:12	behaved in the **world** with
	5:19	reconciling the **world** to

	7:10	**worldly** grief produces death.
Ga	4: 3	elemental spirits of the **world.**
	6:14	the **world** has been crucified
	6:14	to me, and I to the **world.**
Ep	1: 4	the foundation of the **world** to
	2: 2	the course of this **world,**
	2:12	and without God in the **world.**
Ph	2:15	shine like stars in the **world.**
Co	1: 6	growing in the whole **world,** so
	2: 8	spirits of the **universe,** and
	2:20	spirits of the **universe,** why do
	2:20	still belonged to the **world?**
1Ti	1:15	came into the **world** to save
	3:16	in throughout the **world,** taken
	6: 7	brought nothing into the **world,**
He	4: 3	at the foundation of the **world.**
	9:26	the foundation of the **world.**
	10: 5	when Christ came into the **world**
	11: 7	he condemned the **world** and
	11:38	whom the **world** was not worthy.
Ja	1:27	oneself unstained by the **world.**
	2: 5	chosen the poor in the **world** to
	3: 6	members as a **world** of iniquity;
	4: 4	friendship with the **world** is
	4: 4	friend of the **world** becomes an
1P	1:20	foundation of the **world,** but
	3: 3	Do not **adorn** yourselves
	5: 9	in all the **world** are undergoing
2P	1: 4	that is in the **world** because of
	2: 5	ancient **world,** even though he
	2: 5	brought a flood on a **world** of
	2:20	defilements of the **world**
	3: 6	through which the **world** of that
1J	2: 2	for the sins of the whole **world**
	2:15	Do not love the **world** or the
	2:15	or the things in the **world.** The
	2:15	not in those who love the **world**
	2:16	for all that is in the **world**—
	2:16	the Father but from the **world.**
	2:17	And the **world** and its desire
	3: 1	The reason the **world** does not
	3:13	sisters, that the **world** hates
	3:17	anyone who has the **world's**
	4: 1	have gone out into the **world.**
	4: 3	now it is already in the **world.**
	4: 4	the one who is in the **world.**
	4: 5	They are from the **world;**
	4: 5	what they say is from the **world**
	4: 5	and the **world** listens to them.

4: 9   his only Son into the **world** so
4:14   Son as the Savior of the **world.**
4:17   he is, so are we in this **world.**
5: 4   born of God conquers the **world.**
5: 4   victory that conquers the **world**
5: 5   conquers the **world** but the one
5:19   and that the whole **world** lies
2J   1: 7   have gone out into the **world,**
Re   11:15   The kingdom of the **world** has
13: 8   foundation of the **world** in the
17: 8   foundation of the **world,** will

2890   GO1 AG447 LN146
κουαρτος, QUARTUS
Ro   16:23   our brother **Quartus,** greet you.

2891   GO1 AG447 LN146
κουμ, CUM
Mk   5:41   "Talitha **cum,**" which means,

2892   GO3 AG447 LN146
κουστωδια, CUSTODIAN
Mt   27:65   you have a **guard of soldiers;**
27:66   So they went with the **guard** and
28:11   some of the **guard** went into the

2893   GO1 AG447 LN146
κουφιζω, I LIGHTEN
Ac   27:38   **lightened** the ship by throwing

2894   GO6 AG447 LN146
κοφινος, WICKER BASKET
Mt   14:20   pieces, twelve **baskets** full.
16: 9   how many **baskets** you gathered?
Mk   6:43   they took up twelve **baskets**
8:19   how many **baskets** full of broken
Lk   9:17   twelve **baskets** of broken pieces
Jn   6:13   they filled twelve **baskets.**

2895   GO11 AG447 LN146
κραβαττος, MAT
Mk   2: 4   they let down the **mat** on which
2: 9   Stand up and take your **mat** and
2:11   take your **mat** and go to your
2:12   immediately took the **mat** and
6:55   began to bring the sick on **mats**
Jn   5: 8   Stand up, take your **mat** and
5: 9   he took up his **mat** and began to
5:10   for you to carry your **mat.**
5:11   Take up your **mat** and walk.

Ac   5:15   and laid them on cots and **mats,**
9:33   had been **bed**ridden for eight

2896   GO55 AG447 LN146 B1:408 K3:898
κραζω, I SHOUT
Mt   8:29   Suddenly they **shouted,** "What
9:27   **crying loudly,** "Have mercy on
14:26   is a ghost!" And they **cried out**
14:30   he **cried out,** "Lord, save me!"
15:22   started **shouting,** "Have mercy
15:23   away, for she keeps **shouting**
20:30   they **shouted,** "Lord, have mercy
20:31   they **shouted** even more loudly,
21: 9   were **shouting,** "Hosanna to the
21:15   heard the children **crying out**
27:23   But they **shouted** all the more,
27:50   Then Jesus **cried** again with a
Mk   3:11   **shouted,** "You are the Son of
5: 5   was always **howling** and bruising
5: 7   and he **shouted** at the top of
9:24   **cried out,** "I believe; help my
9:26   After **crying out** and convulsing
10:47   he began **to shout out** and say,
10:48   he **cried out** even more loudly,
11: 9   who followed were **shouting,**
15:13   They **shouted** back, "Crucify
15:14   But they **shouted** all the more,
Lk   9:39   all at once he **shrieks.** It
18:39   but he **shouted** even more loudly
19:40   the stones would **shout out.**
Jn   1:15   **cried out,** "This was he of whom
7:28   Then Jesus **cried out** as he was
7:37   he **cried out,** "Let anyone who
12:44   Then Jesus **cried aloud:**
Ac   7:57   with a **loud shout** all rushed
7:60   he knelt down and **cried out** in
14:14   out into the crowd, **shouting,**
16:17   she would **cry out,** "These men
19:28   they were enraged and **shouted,**
19:32   Meanwhile, some were **shouting**
19:34   all of them **shouted** in unison,
21:28   **shouting,** "Fellow Israelites,
21:36   kept **shouting,** "Away with him!"
23: 6   he **called out** in the council,
24:21   I **called out** while standing
Ro   8:15   When we **cry,** "Abba! Father!"
9:27   And Isaiah **cries out** concerning
Ga   4: 6   hearts, **crying,** "Abba! Father!"
Ja   5: 4   kept back by fraud, **cry out,**

Re   6:10   they **cried out** with a loud
     7: 2   he **called** with a loud voice to
     7:10   They **cried out** in a loud voice,
    10: 3   he **gave** a great shout, like a
    10: 3   And when he **shouted,** the seven
    12: 2   and **was crying out** in birth
    14:15   **calling** with a loud voice to
    18: 2   He **called out** with a mighty
    18:18   and **cried out** as they saw the
    18:19   **crying out,** "Alas, alas, the
    19:17   with a loud voice he **called** to

2897   GO1 AG448 LN146
κραιπαλη, DISSIPATION
Lk   21:34   weighed down with **dissipation**

2898   GO4 AG448 LN146
κρανιον, SKULL
Mt   27:33   (which means Place of a **Skull),**
Mk   15:22   means the place of a **skull).**
Lk   23:33   place that is called The **Skull,**
Jn   19:17   The Place of the **Skull,** which

2899   GO5 AG448 LN146 K3:904
κρασπεδον, EDGE, FRINGE
Mt   9:20   touched the **fringe** of his cloak
     14:36   touch even the **fringe** of his
     23: 5   broad and their **fringes** long.
Mk   6:56   even the **fringe** of his cloak;
Lk   8:44   touched the **fringe** of his

2900   GO1 AG448 LN146 B3:716 K3:912 R2900
κραταιος, STRONG
1P   5: 6   under the **mighty** hand of God,

2901   GO4 AG448 LN146 B3:716 K3:912 R2900
κραταιοω, I BECOME STRONG
Lk   1:80   child grew and **became strong** in
     2:40   child grew and **became strong,**
1C   16:13   faith, be courageous, **be strong**
Ep   3:16   you **may be strengthened** in your

2902   GO47 AG448 LN146 B3:716 K3:910 R2904
κρατεω, I HOLD
Mt   9:25   he went in and **took** her by the
     12:11   **will** you not **lay hold** of it and
     14: 3   For Herod **had arrested** John,
     18:28   **seizing** him by the throat, he
     21:46   They wanted **to arrest** him, but
     22: 6   while the rest **seized** his

26: 4   and they conspired **to arrest**
26:48   kiss is the man; **arrest** him.
26:50   hands on Jesus and **arrested** him
26:55   and you did not **arrest** me.
26:57   Those who **had arrested** Jesus
28: 9   **took hold** of his feet, and
Mk   1:31   He came and **took** her by the
     3:21   they went out **to restrain** him,
     5:41   He **took** her by the hand and
     6:17   **arrested** John, bound him, and
     7: 3   thus **observing** the tradition of
     7: 4   traditions that they **observe,**
     7: 8   and **hold** to human tradition.
     9:10   So they **kept** the matter to
     9:27   But Jesus **took** him by the hand
     12:12   they wanted **to arrest** him, but
     14: 1   **to arrest** Jesus by stealth and
     14:44   **arrest** him and lead him away
     14:46   hands on him and **arrested** him.
     14:49   you **did** not **arrest** me. But let
     14:51   cloth. They **caught hold** of him,
Lk   8:54   But he **took** her by the hand and
     24:16   but their eyes **were kept** from
Jn   20:23   if you **retain** the sins of any,
     20:23   of any, they **are retained.**
Ac   2:24   for him **to be held** in its power
     3:11   While he **clung** to Peter and
     24: 6   the temple, and so we **seized**
     27:13   thought they **could achieve**
Co   2:19   and not **holding** fast to the
2Th   2:15   stand firm and **hold** fast to the
He   4:14   let us **hold** fast to our
     6:18   **to seize** the hope set before us
Re   2: 1   words of him who **holds** the
     2:13   Yet you **are holding** fast to
     2:14   you have some there who **hold** to
     2:15   So you also have some who **hold**
     2:25   only **hold** fast to what you have
     3:11   I am coming soon; **hold** fast to
     7: 1   **holding** back the four winds of
     20: 2   **seized** the dragon, that ancient

2903   GO4 AG449 LN147 B3:716 R2904
κρατιστος, MOST STRONG
Lk   1: 3   you, **most excellent** Theophilus,
Ac   23:26   Lysias to his **Excellency** the
     24: 2   Your **Excellency,** because of
     26:25   **most excellent** Festus, but I am

2904   GO12 AG449 LN147 B3:716 K3:905
κρατος, STRENGTH

Lk	1:51	He has shown **strength** with his
Ac	19:20	word of the Lord grew **mightily**
Ep	1:19	the working of his **great** power.
	6:10	and in the **strength** of his
Co	1:11	with all the **strength** that
1Ti	6:16	honor and eternal **dominion.**
He	2:14	the one who has the **power** of
1P	4:11	glory and the **power** forever and
	5:11	To him be the **power** forever and
Ju	1:25	**power,** and authority, before
Re	1: 6	glory and **dominion** forever and
	5:13	glory and **might** forever and

2905   GO9 AG449 LN147 K3:898 R2906
κραυγαζω, I SHOUT

Mt	12:19	will not wrangle or **cry aloud,**
Lk	4:41	**shouting,** "You are the Son of
Jn	11:43	When he had said this, he **cried**
	12:13	**shouting,** "Hosanna! Blessed is
	18:40	They **shouted** in reply, "Not
	19: 6	**shouted,** "Crucify him! Crucify
	19:12	**cried out,** "If you release this
	19:15	They **cried out,** "Away with him!
Ac	22:23	And while they **were shouting,**

2906   GO6 AG449 LN147 K3:898 R2896
κραυγη, SHOUT

Mt	25: 6	at midnight there was a **shout,**
Lk	1:42	and exclaimed with a loud **cry,**
Ac	23: 9	Then a great **clamor** arose, and
Ep	4:31	anger and **wrangling** and slander
He	5: 7	loud **cries** and tears, to the
Re	21: 4	mourning and **crying** and pain

2907   GO2 AG449 LN147 B1:671
κρεας, MEAT

| Ro | 14:21 | it is good not to eat **meat** or |
| 1C | 8:13 | I will never eat **meat,** so that |

2909   GO19 AG449 LN147
κρειττων, BETTER

1C	7: 9	For it is **better** to marry than
	7:38	from marriage will do **better.**
	11:17	it is not for the **better** but
Ph	1:23	Christ, for that is far **better;**
He	1: 4	having become as much **superior**
	6: 9	confident of **better** things in
	7: 7	is blessed by the **superior.**

	7:19	introduction of a **better** hope
	7:22	guarantee of a **better** covenant.
	8: 6	mediator of a **better** covenant,
	8: 6	enacted through **better** promises
	9:23	need **better** sacrifices than
	10:34	something **better** and more
	11:16	they desire a **better** country,
	11:35	to obtain a **better** resurrection
	11:40	**better** so that they would not,
	12:24	speaks a **better** word than the
1P	3:17	For it is **better** to suffer for
2P	2:21	For it would have been **better**

2910   GO7 AG450 LN147 B1:391 K3:915
κρεμαννυμι, I HANG

Mt	18: 6	a great millstone **were fastened**
	22:40	On these two commandments **hang**
Lk	23:39	**were hanged** there kept deriding
Ac	5:30	killed by **hanging** him on a tree
	10:39	death by **hanging** him on a tree;
	28: 4	**hanging** from his hand, they
Ga	3:13	Cursed is everyone who **hangs**

2911   GO3 AG450 LN147
κρημνος, STEEP SLOPE

Mt	8:32	herd rushed down the **steep bank**
Mk	5:13	**steep bank** into the sea, and
Lk	8:33	herd rushed down the **steep bank**

2912   GO2 AG450 LN147
κρης, CRETAN

| Ac | 2:11 | **Cretans** and Arabs—in our own |
| Ti | 1:12 | **Cretans** are always liars, |

2913   GO1 AG450 LN147
κρησκης, CRESCENS

| 2Ti | 4:10 | **Crescens** has gone to Galatia, |

2914   GO5 AG450 LN147
κρητη, CRETE

Ac	27: 7	the lee of **Crete** off Salmone.
	27:12	It was a harbor of **Crete,**
	27:13	began to sail past **Crete,** close
	27:21	set sail from **Crete** and thereby
Ti	1: 5	I left you behind in **Crete** for

2915   GO1 AG450 LN147
κριθη, BARLEY

| Re | 6: 6 | three quarts of **barley** for a |

2916 GO2 AG450 LN147 R2915
κρίθινος, BARLEY

| Jn | 6: 9 | five **barley** loaves and two fish |
| | 6:13 | five **barley** loaves, left by |

2917 GO27 AG450 LN147 B2:362 K3:942 R2919
κρίμα, JUDGMENT

Mt	7: 2	For with the **judgment** you make
Mk	12:40	the greater **condemnation.**
Lk	20:47	the greater **condemnation.**
	23:40	sentence of **condemnation?**
	24:20	him over to be **condemned** to
Jn	9:39	for **judgment** so that those who
Ac	24:25	the coming **judgment,** Felix
Ro	2: 2	We know that God's **judgment** on
	2: 3	you will escape the **judgment** of
	3: 8	Their **condemnation** is deserved!
	5:16	For the **judgment** following one
	11:33	unsearchable are his **judgments**
	13: 2	who resist will incur **judgment.**
1C	6: 7	In fact, to have **lawsuits** at
	11:29	**judgment** against themselves.
	11:34	not be for your **condemnation.**
Ga	5:10	you will pay the **penalty.**
1Ti	3: 6	fall into the **condemnation** of
	5:12	and so they incur **condemnation**
He	6: 2	the dead, and eternal **judgment.**
Ja	3: 1	we who teach will be **judged**
1P	4:17	the time has come for **judgment**
2P	2: 3	Their **condemnation,** pronounced
Ju	1: 4	**condemnation** as ungodly, who
Re	17: 1	I will show you the **judgment** of
	18:20	God has given **judgment** for you
	20: 4	given authority to **judge.**

2918 GO2 AG451 LN147
κρίνον, LILY

| Mt | 6:28 | Consider the **lilies** of the |
| Lk | 12:27 | Consider the **lilies,** how they |

2919 GO114 AG451 LN147 B2:361 K3:921
κρίνω, I JUDGE

Mt	5:40	and if anyone wants to **sue** you
	7: 1	Do not **judge,** so that you may
	7: 1	so that you may not **be judged.**
	7: 2	For with the judgment you **make**
	7: 2	you make you **will be judged,**
	19:28	**judging** the twelve tribes of
Lk	6:37	Do not **judge,** and you will not
	6:37	not **be judged;** do not condemn,

	7:43	You **have judged** rightly.
	12:57	And why do you not **judge** for
	19:22	I **will judge** you by your own
	22:30	sit on thrones **judging** the
Jn	3:17	to **condemn** the world, but in
	3:18	**are** not **condemned;** but those
	3:18	do not believe **are condemned**
	5:22	The Father **judges** no one but
	5:30	As I hear, I **judge;** and my
	7:24	Do not **judge** by appearances,
	7:24	but **judge** with right judgment.
	7:51	Our law does not **judge** people
	8:15	You **judge** by human standards;
	8:15	I **judge** no one.
	8:16	Yet even if I do **judge,** my
	8:26	much **to condemn;** but the one
	8:50	seeks it and he **is** the **judge.**
	12:47	I do not **judge** anyone who hears
	12:47	I came not **to judge** the world,
	12:48	has a **judge;** on the last day
	12:48	have spoken **will serve** as **judge**
	16:11	this world **has been condemned.**
	18:31	**judge** him according to your law
Ac	3:13	though he **had decided** to
	4:19	than to God, you **must judge;**
	7: 7	But I **will judge** the nation
	13:27	those words by **condemning** him.
	13:46	Since you reject it and **judge**
	15:19	I **have reached** the **decision**
	16: 4	that **had been reached** by the
	16:15	If you **have judged** me to be
	17:31	**judged** in righteousness by a
	20:16	For Paul **had decided** to sail
	21:25	with our **judgment** that they
	23: 3	Are you sitting there **to judge**
	23: 6	I **am on trial** concerning the
	24:21	that I **am on trial** before you
	25: 9	**be tried** there before me on
	25:10	this is where I **should be tried**
	25:20	**be tried** there on these charges
	25:25	Majesty, I **decided** to send him.
	26: 6	And now I stand here **on trial**
	26: 8	Why **is** it **thought** incredible by
	27: 1	When it **was decided** that we
Ro	2: 1	**whoever** you are, when you judge
	2: 1	when you **judge** others; for in
	2: 1	you, the **judge,** are doing the
	2: 3	that when you **judge** those who
	2:12	under the law **will be judged** by

	2:16	**will judge** the secret thoughts
	2:27	**will condemn** you that have the
	3: 4	and prevail in your **judging.**
	3: 6	how could God **judge** the world?
	3: 7	why am I still **being condemned**
	14: 3	must not **pass judgment** on those
	14: 4	Who are you to **pass judgment** on
	14: 5	Some **judge** one day to be better
	14: 5	while others **judge** all days to
	14:10	Why do you **pass judgment** on
	14:13	**pass judgment** on one another,
	14:13	but **resolve** instead never to
	14:22	no reason to **condemn** themselves
1C	2: 2	For I **decided** to know nothing
	4: 5	do not **pronounce judgment**
	5: 3	already **pronounced judgment**
	5:12	do with **judging** those outside?
	5:12	inside that you are **to judge?**
	5:13	God **will judge** those outside.
	6: 1	take it **to court** before the
	6: 2	saints **will judge** the world?
	6: 2	if the world is **to be judged** by
	6: 3	we are **to judge** angels—to
	6: 6	but a believer **goes to court**
	7:37	**has determined** in his own mind
	10:15	**judge** for yourselves what I say
	10:29	**be subject to the judgment** of
	11:13	**Judge** for yourselves: is it
	11:31	we would not be **judged.**
	11:32	But when we **are judged** by the
2C	2: 1	So I **made up my mind** not to
	5:14	because we **are convinced** that
Co	2:16	do not let anyone **condemn** you
2Th	2:12	**will be condemned.**
2Ti	4: 1	who is **to judge** the living and
Ti	3:12	for I **have decided** to spend the
He	10:30	The Lord **will judge** his people
	13: 4	for God **will judge** fornicators
Ja	2:12	who are **to be judged** by the law
	4:11	or **judges** another, speaks evil
	4:11	**judges** the law; but if you
	4:11	but if you **judge** the law, you
	4:12	are you to **judge** your neighbor?
	5: 9	you may not **be judged.** See, the
1P	1:17	the one who **judges** all people
	2:23	to the one who **judges** justly.
	4: 5	who stands ready **to judge** the
	4: 6	though they **had been judged** in
Re	6:10	before you **judge** and avenge our

	11:18	**judging** the dead, for rewarding
	16: 5	for you **have judged** these
	18: 8	the Lord God who **judges** her.
	18:20	For God **has given judgment** for
	19: 2	he **has judged** the great whore
	19:11	in righteousness he **judges** and
	20:12	the dead **were judged** according
	20:13	all **were judged** according to

2920   GO47 AG452 LN147 B2:362 K3:941
κρισις, JUDGMENT

Mt	5:21	shall be liable to **judgment.**
	5:22	you will be liable to **judgment;**
	10:15	Gomorrah on the day of **judgment**
	11:22	on the day of **judgment** it will
	11:24	on the day of **judgment** it will
	12:18	he will proclaim **justice** to the
	12:20	until he brings **justice** to
	12:36	**judgment** you will have to
	12:41	rise up at the **judgment** with
	12:42	rise up at the **judgment** with
	23:23	**justice** and mercy and faith. It
	23:33	escape **being sentenced** to hell?
Lk	10:14	But at the **judgment** it will be
	11:31	rise at the **judgment** with the
	11:32	rise up at the **judgment** with
	11:42	neglect **justice** and the love of
Jn	3:19	And this is the **judgment,** that
	5:22	given all **judgment** to the Son,
	5:24	does not come under **judgment,**
	5:27	authority to execute **judgment,**
	5:29	resurrection of **condemnation.**
	5:30	and my **judgment** is just,
	7:24	but judge with right **judgment.**
	8:16	my **judgment** is valid; for it is
	12:31	Now is the **judgment** of this
	16: 8	and righteousness and **judgment:**
	16:11	about **judgment,** because the
Ac	8:33	In his humiliation **justice** was
2Th	1: 5	righteous **judgment** of God, and
1Ti	5:24	precede them to **judgment,** while
He	9:27	and after that the **judgment,**
	10:27	fearful prospect of **judgment,**
Ja	2:13	For **judgment** will be
	2:13	mercy triumphs over **judgment.**
	5:12	may not fall under **condemnation**
2P	2: 4	to be kept until the **judgment;**
	2: 9	until the day of **judgment**
	2:11	slanderous **judgment** from the

	3: 7	until the day of **judgment** and
1J	4:17	boldness on the day of **judgment**
Ju	1: 6	the **judgment** of the great Day.
	1: 9	**condemnation** of slander against
	1:15	to execute **judgment** on all, and
Re	14: 7	the hour of his **judgment** has
	16: 7	your **judgments** are true and
	18:10	in one hour your **judgment** has
	19: 2	for his **judgments** are true and

2921   GO2 AG453 LN148
κρισπος, CRISPUS

Ac	18: 8	**Crispus,** the official of the
1C	1:14	of you except **Crispus** and Gaius

2922   GO3 AG453 LN148 K3:943 R2923
κριτηριον, JUDGE COURT

1C	6: 2	to try trivial **cases?**
	6: 4	If you have ordinary **cases,**
Ja	2: 6	they who drag you into **court?**

2923   GO19 AG453 LN148 B2:362 K3:942 R2919
κριτης, JUDGE

Mt	5:25	hand you over to the **judge,** and
	5:25	the **judge** to the guard, and you
	12:27	they will be your **judges.**
Lk	11:19	they will be your **judges.**
	12:14	who set me to be a **judge** or
	12:58	dragged before the **judge,** and
	12:58	the **judge** hand you over to the
	18: 2	there was a **judge** who neither
	18: 6	to what the unjust **judge** says.
Ac	10:42	as **judge** of the living and the
	13:20	gave them **judges** until the time
	18:15	I do not wish to be a **judge** of
	24:10	you have been a **judge** over this
2Ti	4: 8	the Lord, the righteous **judge,**
He	12:23	to God the **judge** of all, and to
Ja	2: 4	become **judges** with evil
	4:11	a doer of the law but a **judge.**
	4:12	There is one lawgiver and **judge**
	5: 9	See, the **Judge** is standing at

2924   GO1 AG453 LN148 B2:362 K3:943 R2923
κριτικος, JUDGE

He	4:12	is **able to judge** the thoughts

2925   GO9 AG453 LN148 B2:881 K3:954
κρουω, I KNOCK

Mt	7: 7	**knock,** and the door will be

	7: 8	for everyone who **knocks,** the
Lk	11: 9	**knock,** and the door will be
	11:10	for everyone who **knocks,** the
	12:36	as soon as he comes and **knocks.**
	13:25	to **knock** at the door, saying,
Ac	12:13	When he **knocked** at the outer
	12:16	Peter continued **knocking;** and
Re	3:20	standing at the door, **knocking;**

2926   GO1 AG454 LN148 K3:957 R2928
κρυπτη, HIDDEN

Lk	11:33	lamp puts it in a **cellar,** but

2927   GO17 AG454 LN148 B2:214 K3:957 R2928
κρυπτος, HIDDEN

Mt	6: 4	alms may be done in **secret;** and
	6: 4	your Father who sees in **secret**
	6: 6	your Father who is in **secret;**
	6: 6	your Father who sees in **secret**
	10:26	nothing **secret** that will not
Mk	4:22	nor is anything **secret,** except
Lk	8:17	nor is anything **secret** that
	12: 2	and nothing **secret** that will
Jn	7: 4	widely known acts in **secret.** If
	7:10	but as it were in **secret.**
	18:20	I have said nothing in **secret.**
Ro	2:16	judge the **secret** thoughts of
	2:29	Jew who is one **inwardly,** and
1C	4: 5	things now **hidden** in darkness
	14:25	After the **secrets** of the
2C	4: 2	shameful things **that one hides;**
1P	3: 4	adornment be the **inner self**

2928   GO18 AG454 LN148 B2:214 K3:957
κρυπτω, I HIDE

Mt	5:14	built on a hill cannot be **hid.**
	11:25	because you **have hidden** these
	13:35	proclaim what **has been hidden**
	13:44	like treasure **hidden** in a field
	13:44	which someone found and **hid;**
	25:18	a hole in the ground and **hid**
	25:25	I went and **hid** your talent in
Lk	18:34	what he said was **hidden** from
	19:42	But now they **are hidden** from
Jn	8:59	but Jesus **hid** himself and went
	12:36	he departed and **hid** from them.
	19:38	**though** a secret one because of
Co	3: 3	your life **is hidden** with Christ
1Ti	5:25	not, they cannot remain **hidden.**
He	11:23	By faith Moses **was hidden** by

Re 2:17 give some of the **hidden** manna,
    6:15 **hid** in the caves and among the
    6:16 Fall on us and **hide** us from

2929 GO1 AG454 LN148 R2930
κρυσταλλιζω, I SPARKLE LIKE CRYSTAL
Re 21:11 like jasper, **clear as crystal.**

2930 GO2 AG454 LN148 B3:398
κρυσταλλος, CRYSTAL
Re   4: 6 a sea of glass, like **crystal.**
     22: 1 bright as **crystal,** flowing from

2930a GO2 AG454 LN148 B2:214 K3:957
κρυφαιος, HIDING
Mt 6:18 by your Father who is in **secret**
    6:18 your Father who sees in **secret**

2931 GO1 AG454 LN148 K3:957 R2928
κρυφη, HIDING
Ep 5:12 what such people do **secretly;**

2932 GO7 AG455 LN148
κταομαι, I ACQUIRE
Mt 10: 9 **Take** no gold, or silver, or
Lk 18:12 give a tenth of all my **income.**
    21:19 By your endurance you **will gain**
Ac   1:18 (Now this man **acquired** a field
     8:20 you thought you **could obtain**
    22:28 It **cost** me a large sum of
1Th 4: 4 know how **to control** your own

2933 GO4 AG455 LN148 B2:845 R2932
κτημα, ACQUISITION
Mt 19:22 for he had many **possessions.**
Mk 10:22 for he had many **possessions.**
Ac   2:45 sell their **possessions** and
     5: 1 sold a piece of **property;**

2934 GO4 AG455 LN148
κτηνος, ANIMAL
Lk 10:34 put him on his own **animal,**
Ac 23:24 Also provide **mounts** for Paul
1C 15:39 another for **animals,** another
Re 18:13 **cattle** and sheep, horses and

2935 GO1 AG455 LN148 R2932
κτητωρ, ACQUISITION
Ac   4:34 as many as **owned** lands or

2936 GO15 AG455 LN148 B1:378 K3:1000
κτιζω, I CREATE
Mt 19: 4 the one who **made** them at the
Mk 13:19 creation that God **created** until
Ro   1:25 rather than the **Creator,** who is
1C 11: 9 Neither **was** man **created** for the
Ep   2:10 **created** in Christ Jesus for
     2:15 that he **might create** in himself
     3: 9 in God who **created** all things;
     4:24 **created** according to the
Co   1:16 all things have been **created**
     1:16 all things have been **created**
     3:10 to the image of its **creator.**
1Ti 4: 3 foods, which God **created** to be
Re   4:11 for you **created** all things, and
     4:11 they existed and **were created.**
    10: 6 who **created** heaven and what is

2937 GO19 AG455 LN148 B1:378 K3:1000 R2936
κτισις, CREATION
Mk 10: 6 from the beginning of **creation,**
    13:19 **creation** that God created until
    16:15 good news to the whole **creation**
Ro   1:20 Ever since the **creation** of the
     1:25 served the **creature** rather than
     8:19 the **creation** waits with eager
     8:20 for the **creation** was subjected
     8:21 that the **creation** itself will
     8:22 the whole **creation** has been
     8:39 anything else in all **creation,**
2C   5:17 new **creation:** everything old
Ga   6:15 a new **creation** is everything!
Co   1:15 firstborn of all **creation;**
     1:23 proclaimed to every **creature**
He   4:13 And before him no **creature** is
     9:11 that is, not of this **creation),**
1P   2:13 of every human **institution,**
2P   3: 4 from the beginning of **creation!**
Re   3:14 the origin of God's **creation:**

2938 GO4 AG456 LN148 B1:378 K3:1000 R2936
κτισμα, CREATION
1Ti 4: 4 For everything **created** by God
Ja   1:18 first fruits of his **creatures.**
Re   5:13 Then I heard every **creature** in
     8: 9 a third of the living **creatures**

2939 GO1 AG456 LN148 B1:378 K3:1000 R2936
κτιστης, CREATOR
1P   4:19 a faithful **Creator,** while

2940 ᴳᴼ1 ᴬᴳ456 ᴸᴺ148
κυβεια, TRICKERY
Ep 4:14 by people's **trickery,** by their

2941 ᴳᴼ1 ᴬᴳ456 ᴸᴺ148 ᴮ1:192 ᴷ3:1035
κυβερνησις, ADMINISTRATION
1C 12:28 forms of **leadership,** various

2942 ᴳᴼ2 ᴬᴳ456 ᴸᴺ148
κυβερνητης, HELMSMAN
Ac 27:11 **pilot** and to the owner of the
Re 18:17 all **shipmasters** and seafarers,

2942a ᴳᴼ1 ᴬᴳ456 ᴸᴺ148
κυκλευω, I CIRCLE
Re 20: 9 and **surrounded** the camp

2943 ᴳᴼ3 ᴬᴳ456 ᴸᴺ148 ᴿ2945
κυκλοθεν, CIRCLED
Re 4: 3 **around** the throne is a rainbow
4: 4 **Around** the throne are
4: 8 eyes all **around** and inside.

2944 ᴳᴼ4 ᴬᴳ456 ᴸᴺ149 ᴿ2945
κυκλοω, I ENCIRCLE
Lk 21:20 Jerusalem **surrounded** by
armies,
Jn 10:24 So the Jews **gathered around**
him
Ac 14:20 the disciples **surrounded** him,
He 11:30 after they **had been encircled**

2945 ᴳᴼ8 ᴬᴳ456 ᴸᴺ149
κυκλω, IN CIRCLE
Mk 3:34 sat **around** him, he said, "Here
6: 6 Then he went about **among** the
6:36 into the **surrounding** country
Lk 9:12 into the **surrounding** villages
Ro 15:19 as far **around** as Illyricum I
Re 4: 6 **Around** the throne, and on each
5:11 many angels **surrounding** the
7:11 **around** the elders and the four

2946 ᴳᴼ1 ᴬᴳ457 ᴸᴺ149 ᴿ2947
κυλισμος, ROLLING
2P 2:22 sow is washed only to **wallow** in

2947 ᴳᴼ1 ᴬᴳ457 ᴸᴺ149
κυλιω, I ROLL
Mk 9:20 on the ground and **rolled about,**

2948 ᴳᴼ4 ᴬᴳ457 ᴸᴺ149 ᴮ2:414
κυλλος, CRIPPLED
Mt 15:30 the **maimed,** the blind, the mute
15:31 the **maimed** whole, the lame
18: 8 enter life **maimed** or lame than
Mk 9:43 enter life **maimed** than to have

2949 ᴳᴼ5 ᴬᴳ457 ᴸᴺ149
κυμα, WAVE
Mt 8:24 swamped by the **waves;** but he
14:24 battered by the **waves,** was far
Mk 4:37 **waves** beat into the boat, so
Ac 27:41 up by the force of the **waves.**
Ju 1:13 wild **waves** of the sea, casting

2950 ᴳᴼ1 ᴬᴳ457 ᴸᴺ149 ᴷ3:1037
κυμβαλον, CYMBAL
1C 13: 1 noisy gong or a clanging
cymbal.

2951 ᴳᴼ1 ᴬᴳ457 ᴸᴺ149 ᴮ2:210
κυμινον, CUMMIN
Mt 23:23 tithe mint, dill, and **cummin,**

2952 ᴳᴼ4 ᴬᴳ457 ᴸᴺ149 ᴷ3:1104 ᴿ2965
κυναριον, PUPPY
Mt 15:26 food and throw it to the **dogs.**
15:27 even the **dogs** eat the crumbs
Mk 7:27 food and throw it to the **dogs.**
7:28 even the **dogs** under the table

2953 ᴳᴼ3 ᴬᴳ457 ᴸᴺ149
κυπριος, CYPRIOT
Ac 4:36 a native of **Cyprus,** Joseph
11:20 men of **Cyprus** and Cyrene who,
21:16 Mnason of **Cyprus,** an early

2954 ᴳᴼ5 ᴬᴳ457 ᴸᴺ149
κυπρος, CYPRUS
Ac 11:19 **Cyprus,** and Antioch, and they
13: 4 him and sailed away to **Cyprus**
15:39 sailed away to **Cyprus**
21: 3 We came in sight of **Cyprus;**
27: 4 sailed under the lee of **Cyprus,**

2955 ᴳᴼ2 ᴬᴳ458 ᴸᴺ149
κυπτω, I BEND
Mk 1: 7 I am not worthy **to stoop down**
Jn 8: 6 Jesus **bent down** and wrote
with

2956　GO6 AG458 LN149
κυρηναιος, CYRENEAN
Mt　27:32　a man from **Cyrene** named Simon;
Mk　15:21　it was Simon of **Cyrene,** the
Lk　23:26　Simon of **Cyrene,** who was coming
Ac　6: 9　**Cyrenians,** Alexandrians, and
　　11:20　men of Cyprus and **Cyrene** who,
　　13: 1　Lucius of **Cyrene,** Manaen a

2957　GO1 AG458 LN149
κυρηνη, CYRENE
Ac　2:10　Libya belonging to **Cyrene,** and

2958　GO1 AG458 LN149
κυρηνιος, CYRENIUS
Lk　2: 2　and was taken while **Quirinius**

2959　GO2 AG458 LN149 B2:510 K3:1095 R2962
κυρια, LADY
2J　1: 1　The elder to the elect **lady** and
　　1: 5　But now, dear **lady,** I ask you,

2960　GO2 AG458 LN149 B2:510 K3:1095 R2962
κυριακος, OF MASTER, OF LORD
1C　11:20　not really to eat the **Lord's**
Re　1:10　was in the spirit on the **Lord's**

2961　GO7 AG458 LN149 B2:510 K3:1097 R2962
κυριευω, I MASTER, I LORD OVER
Lk　22:25　**lord** it **over** them; and those in
Ro　6: 9　death no longer **has dominion**
　　6:14　For sin **will have** no **dominion**
　　7: 1　the law **is binding** on a person
　　14: 9　so that he **might be Lord** of
2C　1:24　we **lord** it **over** your faith;
1Ti　6:15　King of kings and Lord of **lords**

2962　GO717 AG458 LN149 B2:508 K3:1039
κυριος, MASTER, LORD
Mt　1:20　an angel of the **Lord** appeared
　　1:22　had been spoken by the **Lord**
　　1:24　he did as the angel of the **Lord**
　　2:13　an angel of the **Lord** appeared
　　2:15　spoken by the **Lord** through the
　　2:19　an angel of the **Lord** suddenly
　　3: 3　Prepare the way of the **Lord,**
　　4: 7　Do not put the **Lord** your God
　　4:10　Worship the **Lord** your God, and
　　5:33　vows you have made to the **Lord.**
　　6:24　No one can serve two **masters;**

7:21　'**Lord,** Lord,' will enter the
7:21　'Lord, **Lord,**' will enter the
7:22　**Lord,** Lord, did we not
7:22　Lord, **Lord,** did we not
8: 2　**Lord,** if you choose, you can
8: 6　and saying, "**Lord,** my servant
8: 8　The centurion answered, "**Lord,**
8:21　**Lord,** first let me go and bury
8:25　**Lord,** save us! We are
9:28　They said to him, "Yes, **Lord.**"
9:38　therefore ask the **Lord** of the
10:24　nor a slave above the **master;**
10:25　and the slave like the **master.**
11:25　I thank you, Father, **Lord** of
12: 8　For the Son of Man is **lord** of
13:27　**Master,** did you not sow good
14:28　Peter answered him, "**Lord,** if
14:30　he cried out, "**Lord,** save me!"
15:22　Have mercy on me, **Lord,** Son of
15:25　him, saying, "**Lord,** help me."
15:27　She said, "Yes, **Lord,** yet even
15:27　that fall from their **masters**
16:22　God forbid it, **Lord!** This
17: 4　**Lord,** it is good for us to be
17:15　**Lord,** have mercy on my son,
18:21　**Lord,** if another member of the
18:25　his **lord** ordered him to be sold
18:27　the **lord** of that slave released
18:31　their **lord** all that had taken
18:32　Then his **lord** summoned him and
18:34　And in anger his **lord** handed
20: 8　the **owner** of the vineyard said
20:30　**Lord,** have mercy on us, Son of
20:31　Have mercy on us, **Lord,** Son of
20:33　**Lord,** let our eyes be opened.
21: 3　'The **Lord** needs them.' And he
21: 9　comes in the name of the **Lord!**
21:30　'I go, **sir**'; but he did not go.
21:40　**owner** of the vineyard comes,
21:42　this was the **Lord's** doing, and
22:37　You shall love the **Lord** your
22:43　Spirit calls him **Lord,** saying,
22:44　The **Lord** said to my Lord, "Sit
22:44　**Lord,** "Sit at my right hand,
22:45　If David thus calls him **Lord,**
23:39　comes in the name of the **Lord.**
24:42　on what day your **Lord** is coming
24:45　whom his **master** has put in
24:46　whom his **master** will find at

	24:48	himself, 'My **master** is delayed,	1:45	was spoken to her by the **Lord.**
	24:50	the **master** of that slave will	1:46	My soul magnifies the **Lord,**
	25:11	saying, **'Lord,** lord, open to us	1:58	heard that the **Lord** had shown
	25:11	saying, 'Lord, **lord,** open to us	1:66	hand of the **Lord** was with him.
	25:18	and hid his **master's** money.	1:68	Blessed be the **Lord** God of
	25:19	After a long time the **master** of	1:76	go before the **Lord** to prepare
	25:20	**Master,** you handed over to me	2: 9	Then an angel of the **Lord** stood
	25:21	His **master** said to him, 'Well	2: 9	the glory of the **Lord** shone
	25:21	into the joy of your **master.**	2:11	who is the Messiah, the **Lord.**
	25:22	**Master,** you handed over to me	2:15	which the **Lord** has made known
	25:23	His **master** said to him, 'Well	2:22	to present him to the **Lord**
	25:23	into the joy of your **master.**	2:23	written in the law of the **Lord,**
	25:24	**Master,** I knew that you were a	2:23	designated as holy to the **Lord**
	25:26	But his **master** replied, 'You	2:24	stated in the law of the **Lord,**
	25:37	**Lord,** when was it that we saw	2:26	he had seen the **Lord's** Messiah.
	25:44	**Lord,** when was it that we saw	2:39	required by the law of the **Lord**
	26:22	another, "Surely not I, **Lord?"**	3: 4	Prepare the way of the **Lord,**
	27:10	field, as the **Lord** commanded me	4: 8	Worship the **Lord** your God, and
	27:63	and said, **"Sir,** we remember	4:12	Do not put the **Lord** your God
	28: 2	angel of the **Lord,** descending	4:18	The Spirit of the **Lord** is upon
Mk	1: 3	Prepare the way of the **Lord,**	4:19	proclaim the year of the **Lord's**
	2:28	so the Son of Man is **lord** even	5: 8	Go away from me, **Lord,** for I
	5:19	tell them how much the **Lord** has	5:12	**Lord,** if you choose, you can
	7:28	**Sir,** even the dogs under the	5:17	the power of the **Lord** was with
	11: 3	The **Lord** needs it and will	6: 5	The Son of Man is **lord** of the
	11: 9	comes in the name of the **Lord!**	6:46	Why do you call me **'Lord,** Lord
	12: 9	What then will the **owner** of the	6:46	Why do you call me 'Lord, **Lord**
	12:11	this was the **Lord's** doing, and	7: 6	**Lord,** do not trouble yourself,
	12:29	Hear, O Israel: the **Lord** our	7:13	When the **Lord** saw her, he had
	12:29	Lord our God, the **Lord** is one;	7:19	and sent them to the **Lord** to
	12:30	you shall love the **Lord** your	9:54	**Lord,** do you want us to
	12:36	The **Lord** said to my Lord, "Sit	9:59	**Lord,** first let me go and bury
	12:36	**Lord,** "Sit at my right hand,	9:61	**Lord;** but let me first say
	12:37	David himself calls him **Lord;**	10: 1	After this the **Lord** appointed
	13:20	And if the **Lord** had not cut	10: 2	therefore ask the **Lord** of the
	13:35	when the **master** of the house	10:17	**Lord,** in your name even the
	16:19	So then the **Lord** Jesus, after	10:21	I thank you, Father, **Lord** of
	16:20	while the **Lord** worked with them	10:27	You shall love the **Lord** your
Lk	1: 6	and regulations of the **Lord.**	10:39	who sat at the **Lord's** feet and
	1: 9	sanctuary of the **Lord** and offer	10:40	**Lord,** do you not care that my
	1:11	angel of the **Lord,** standing at	10:41	But the **Lord** answered her,
	1:15	great in the sight of the **Lord.**	11: 1	**Lord,** teach us to pray, as
	1:16	people of Israel to the **Lord**	11:39	Then the **Lord** said to him,
	1:17	a people prepared for the **Lord.**	12:36	waiting for their **master** to
	1:25	This is what the **Lord** has done	12:37	slaves whom the **master** finds
	1:28	one! The **Lord** is with you.	12:41	**Lord,** are you telling this
	1:32	the **Lord** God will give to him	12:42	And the **Lord** said, "Who then
	1:38	the servant of the **Lord;** let it	12:42	prudent manager whom his **master**
	1:43	that the mother of my **Lord**	12:43	whom his **master** will find at

12:45	My **master** is delayed in coming		5: 7	**Sir,** I have no one to put me
12:46	the **master** of that slave will		6:23	after the **Lord** had given thanks
12:47	slave who knew what his **master**		6:34	**Sir,** give us this bread always
13: 8	He replied, '**Sir,** let it alone		6:68	**Lord,** to whom can we go? You
13:15	But the **Lord** answered him and		8:11	"No one, **sir.**" And Jesus said,
13:23	**Lord,** will only a few be saved		9:36	And who is he, **sir?** Tell me,
13:25	'**Lord,** open to us,' then in		9:38	He said, "**Lord,** I believe."
13:35	comes in the name of the **Lord.**		11: 2	anointed the **Lord** with perfume
14:21	Then the **owner** of the house		11: 3	**Lord,** he whom you love is ill.
14:22	**Sir,** what you ordered has been		11:12	**Lord,** if he has fallen asleep,
14:23	Then the **master** said to the		11:21	**Lord,** if you had been here, my
16: 3	now that my **master** is taking		11:27	Yes, **Lord,** I believe that you
16: 5	summoning his **master's** debtors		11:32	**Lord,** if you had been here, my
16: 5	How much do you owe my **master?**		11:34	They said to him, "**Lord,** come
16: 8	And his **master** commended the		11:39	**Lord,** already there is a
16:13	No slave can serve two **masters;**		12:13	in the name of the **Lord**—the
17: 5	The apostles said to the **Lord,**		12:21	**Sir,** we wish to see Jesus.
17: 6	The **Lord** replied, "If you had		12:38	**Lord,** who has believed our
17:37	"Where, **Lord?**" He said to them,		12:38	to whom has the arm of the **Lord**
18: 6	And the **Lord** said, "Listen to		13: 6	**Lord,** are you going to wash my
18:41	said, "**Lord,** let me see again."		13: 9	**Lord,** not my feet only but
19: 8	said to the **Lord,** "Look, half		13:13	You call me Teacher and **Lord**
19: 8	**Lord,** I will give to the poor;		13:14	So if I, your **Lord** and Teacher,
19:16	**Lord,** your pound has made ten		13:16	**master,** nor are messengers
19:18	**Lord,** your pound has made five		13:25	he asked him, "**Lord,** who is it?
19:20	**Lord,** here is your pound. I		13:36	**Lord,** where are you going?
19:25	(And they said to him, '**Lord,**		13:37	**Lord,** why can I not follow you
19:31	say this, 'The **Lord** needs it.'		14: 5	**Lord,** we do not know where you
19:33	its **owners** asked them, "Why are		14: 8	**Lord,** show us the Father, and
19:34	They said, "The **Lord** needs it."		14:22	**Lord,** how is it that you will
19:38	comes in the name of the **Lord!**		15:15	does not know what the **master**
20:13	Then the **owner** of the vineyard		15:20	not greater than their **master.**
20:15	What then will the **owner** of the		20: 2	They have taken the **Lord** out
20:37	where he speaks of the **Lord** as		20:13	They have taken away my **Lord,**
20:42	The **Lord** said to my Lord, "Sit		20:15	**Sir,** if you have carried him
20:42	The Lord said to my **Lord,** "Sit		20:18	"I have seen the **Lord**"; and she
20:44	David thus calls him **Lord;** so		20:20	rejoiced when they saw the **Lord**
22:33	And he said to him, "**Lord,** I am		20:25	"We have seen the **Lord.**" But he
22:38	They said, "**Lord,** look, here		20:28	him, "My **Lord** and my God!"
22:49	**Lord,** should we strike with		21: 7	"It is the **Lord!**" When Simon
22:61	The **Lord** turned and looked at		21: 7	heard that it was the **Lord,** he
22:61	remembered the word of the **Lord**		21:12	they knew it was the **Lord.**
24: 3	find the body of the **Lord** Jesus		21:15	Yes, **Lord;** you know that I
24:34	The **Lord** has risen indeed,		21:16	Yes, **Lord;** you know that I
Jn 1:23	straight the way of the **Lord,**		21:17	**Lord,** you know everything; you
4:11	**Sir,** you have no bucket, and		21:20	**Lord,** who is it that is going
4:15	**Sir,** give me this water, so		21:21	Jesus, "**Lord,** what about him?"
4:19	**Sir,** I see that you are a		Ac 1: 6	**Lord,** is this the time when
4:49	**Sir,** come down before my		1:21	all the time that the **Lord**

1:24	**Lord,** you know everyone's	11:21	The hand of the **Lord** was with
2:20	before the coming of the **Lord's**	11:21	and turned to the **Lord.**
2:21	calls on the name of the **Lord**	11:23	remain faithful to the **Lord**
2:25	I saw the **Lord** always before	11:24	people were brought to the **Lord**
2:34	The **Lord** said to my Lord,	12: 7	Suddenly an angel of the **Lord**
2:34	**Lord,** "Sit at my right hand,	12:11	Now I am sure that the **Lord**
2:36	made him both **Lord** and Messiah,	12:17	described for them how the **Lord**
2:39	everyone whom the **Lord** our God	12:23	an angel of the **Lord** struck him
2:47	And day by day the **Lord** added	13: 2	worshiping the **Lord** and fasting
3:20	the presence of the **Lord,** and	13:10	the straight paths of the **Lord?**
3:22	The **Lord** your God will raise	13:11	the hand of the **Lord** is against
4:26	together against the **Lord** and	13:12	at the teaching about the **Lord.**
4:29	And now, **Lord,** look at their	13:44	to hear the word of the **Lord.**
4:33	to the resurrection of the **Lord**	13:47	For so the **Lord** has commanded
5: 9	put the Spirit of the **Lord** to	13:48	praised the word of the **Lord;**
5:14	**Lord,** great numbers of both men	13:49	the word of the **Lord** spread
5:19	an angel of the **Lord** opened the	14: 3	speaking boldly for the **Lord,**
7:31	came the voice of the **Lord:**	14:23	entrusted them to the **Lord** in
7:33	Then the **Lord** said to him,	15:11	through the grace of the **Lord**
7:49	says the **Lord,** or what is the	15:17	peoples may seek the **Lord**—
7:59	**Lord** Jesus, receive my spirit.	15:17	peoples may seek the **Lord**—
7:60	**Lord,** do not hold this sin	15:26	for the sake of our **Lord** Jesus
8:16	in the name of the **Lord**	15:35	proclaimed the word of the **Lord**
8:22	pray to the **Lord** that, if	15:36	proclaimed the word of the **Lord**
8:24	Pray for me to the **Lord,** that	15:40	him to the grace of the **Lord.**
8:25	spoken the word of the **Lord,**	16:14	The **Lord** opened her heart to
8:26	Then an angel of the **Lord** said	16:15	to be faithful to the **Lord,**
8:39	the Spirit of the **Lord** snatched	16:16	brought her **owners** a great deal
9: 1	disciples of the **Lord,** went to	16:19	But when her **owners** saw that
9: 5	He asked, "Who are you, **Lord?"**	16:30	**Sirs,** what must I do to be
9:10	Ananias. The **Lord** said to him	16:31	Believe on the **Lord** Jesus, and
9:10	He answered, "Here I am, **Lord."**	16:32	They spoke the word of the **Lord**
9:11	The **Lord** said to him, "Get up	17:24	he who is **Lord** of heaven and
9:13	But Ananias answered, **"Lord,** I	18: 8	became a believer in the **Lord,**
9:15	But the **Lord** said to him, "Go,	18: 9	One night the **Lord** said to Paul
9:17	Brother Saul, the **Lord** Jesus,	18:25	in the Way of the **Lord;** and he
9:27	the road he had seen the **Lord,**	19: 5	in the name of the **Lord** Jesus.
9:28	boldly in the name of the **Lord.**	19:10	heard the word of the **Lord.**
9:31	Living in the fear of the **Lord**	19:13	to use the name of the **Lord**
9:35	saw him and turned to the **Lord.**	19:17	the name of the **Lord** Jesus was
9:42	and many believed in the **Lord.**	19:20	So the word of the **Lord** grew
10: 4	"What is it, **Lord?"** He answered	20:19	serving the **Lord** with all
10:14	By no means, **Lord;** for I have	20:21	faith toward our **Lord** Jesus.
10:33	listen to all that the **Lord** has	20:24	I received from the **Lord** Jesus,
10:36	Jesus Christ—he is **Lord** of	20:35	words of the **Lord** Jesus, for he
11: 8	By no means, **Lord;** for nothing	21:13	for the name of the **Lord** Jesus.
11:16	remembered the word of the **Lord**	21:14	say, "The **Lord's** will be done."
11:17	believed in the **Lord** Jesus	22: 8	I answered, 'Who are you, **Lord?**
11:20	proclaiming the **Lord** Jesus.	22:10	'What am I to do, **Lord?'** The

	22:10	The **Lord** said to me, 'Get up	16:22	letter, greet you in the **Lord.**
	22:19	**Lord,** they themselves know	1C	1: 2	call on the name of our **Lord**
	23:11	That night the **Lord** stood near		1: 3	our Father and the **Lord** Jesus
	25:26	to write to our **sovereign** about		1: 7	revealing of our **Lord** Jesus
	26:15	I asked, 'Who are you, **Lord?'**		1: 8	on the day of our **Lord** Jesus
	26:15	The **Lord** answered, 'I am Jesus		1: 9	his Son, Jesus Christ our **Lord.**
	28:31	teaching about the **Lord** Jesus		1:10	by the name of our **Lord** Jesus
Ro	1: 4	the dead, Jesus Christ our **Lord**		1:31	who boasts, boast in the **Lord.**
	1: 7	God our Father and the **Lord**		2: 8	crucified the **Lord** of glory.
	4: 8	against whom the **Lord** will not		2:16	the mind of the **Lord** so as to
	4:24	who raised Jesus our **Lord** from		3: 5	as the **Lord** assigned to each.
	5: 1	peace with God through our **Lord**		3:20	The **Lord** knows the thoughts of
	5:11	boast in God through our **Lord**		4: 4	It is the **Lord** who judges me.
	5:21	through Jesus Christ our **Lord.**		4: 5	before the **Lord** comes, who will
	6:23	life in Christ Jesus our **Lord.**		4:17	faithful child in the **Lord,** to
	7:25	through Jesus Christ our **Lord!**		4:19	if the **Lord** wills, and I will
	8:39	of God in Christ Jesus our **Lord**		5: 4	in the name of the **Lord** Jesus
	9:28	for the **Lord** will execute his		5: 4	with the power of our **Lord**
	9:29	If the **Lord** of hosts had not		5: 5	be saved in the day of the **Lord**
	10: 9	your lips that Jesus is **Lord**		6:11	in the name of the **Lord** Jesus
	10:12	the same Lord is **Lord** of all		6:13	but for the **Lord,** and the Lord
	10:13	calls on the name of the **Lord**		6:13	and the **Lord** for the body.
	10:16	**Lord,** who has believed our		6:14	And God raised the **Lord** and
	11: 3	**Lord,** they have killed your		6:17	But anyone united to the **Lord**
	11:34	known the mind of the **Lord?**		7:10	not I but the **Lord**—that the
	12:11	in spirit, serve the **Lord.**		7:12	I and not the **Lord**—that if
	12:19	I will repay, says the **Lord.**		7:17	lead the life that the **Lord**
	13:14	Instead, put on the **Lord** Jesus		7:22	whoever was called in the **Lord**
	14: 4	It is before their own **lord**		7:22	person belonging to the **Lord,**
	14: 4	for the **Lord** is able to make		7:25	I have no command of the **Lord,**
	14: 6	observe it in honor of the **Lord**		7:25	as one who by the **Lord's** mercy
	14: 6	eat in honor of the **Lord,** since		7:32	the affairs of the **Lord,** how to
	14: 6	abstain in honor of the **Lord**		7:32	how to please the **Lord;**
	14: 8	If we live, we live to the **Lord**		7:34	about the affairs of the **Lord,**
	14: 8	if we die, we die to the **Lord;**		7:35	unhindered devotion to the **Lord**
	14: 8	we die, we are the **Lord's.**		7:39	she wishes, only in the **Lord.**
	14:11	I live, says the **Lord,** every		8: 5	are many gods and many **lords**—
	14:14	persuaded in the **Lord** Jesus		8: 6	one **Lord,** Jesus Christ, through
	15: 6	God and Father of our **Lord**		9: 1	Are you not my work in the **Lord**
	15:11	and again, "Praise the **Lord,**		9: 1	Jesus our **Lord?**
	15:30	by our **Lord** Jesus Christ and by		9: 2	of my apostleship in the **Lord.**
	16: 2	welcome her in the **Lord** as is		9: 5	brothers of the **Lord** and Cephas
	16: 8	my beloved in the **Lord.**		9:14	In the same way, the **Lord**
	16:11	Greet those in the **Lord** who		10:21	drink the cup of the **Lord** and
	16:12	Greet those workers in the **Lord**		10:21	table of the **Lord** and the table
	16:12	who has worked hard in the **Lord**		10:22	Or are we provoking the **Lord** to
	16:13	Greet Rufus, chosen in the **Lord**		10:26	its fullness are the **Lord's.**
	16:18	do not serve our **Lord** Christ,		11:11	Nevertheless, in the **Lord** woman
	16:20	The grace of our **Lord** Jesus		11:23	For I received from the **Lord**

	11:23	that the **Lord** Jesus on the		4: 1	though they are the **owners** of
	11:26	you proclaim the **Lord's** death		5:10	in the **Lord** that you will not
	11:27	or drinks the cup of the **Lord**		6:14	the cross of our **Lord** Jesus
	11:27	the body and blood of the **Lord.**		6:18	May the grace of our **Lord** Jesus
	11:32	when we are judged by the **Lord,**	Ep	1: 2	God our Father and the **Lord**
	12: 3	no one can say "Jesus is **Lord**"		1: 3	God and Father of our **Lord**
	12: 5	of services, but the same **Lord;**		1:15	faith in the **Lord** Jesus and
	14:21	listen to me," says the **Lord.**		1:17	God of our **Lord** Jesus Christ,
	14:37	to you is a command of the **Lord**		2:21	into a holy temple in the **Lord;**
	15:31	I make in Christ Jesus our **Lord**		3:11	out in Christ Jesus our **Lord,**
	15:57	through our **Lord** Jesus Christ.		4: 1	the prisoner in the **Lord,** beg
	15:58	in the work of the **Lord,**		4: 5	one **Lord,** one faith, one
	15:58	in the **Lord** your labor is not		4:17	insist on in the **Lord:** you must
	16: 7	with you, if the **Lord** permits.		5: 8	but now in the **Lord** you are
	16:10	doing the work of the **Lord** just		5:10	what is pleasing to the **Lord.**
	16:19	greet you warmly in the **Lord.**		5:17	what the will of the **Lord** is.
	16:22	no love for the Lord. Our **Lord,**		5:19	making melody to the **Lord** in
	16:23	The grace of the **Lord** Jesus be		5:20	in the name of our **Lord** Jesus
2C	1: 2	God our Father and the **Lord**		5:22	husbands as you are to the **Lord**
	1: 3	Father of our **Lord** Jesus Christ		6: 1	obey your parents in the **Lord,**
	1:14	on the day of the **Lord** Jesus we		6: 4	and instruction of the **Lord.**
	2:12	was opened for me in the **Lord;**		6: 5	obey your earthly **masters** with
	3:16	but when one turns to the **Lord,**		6: 7	as to the **Lord** and not to men
	3:17	Now the **Lord** is the Spirit, and		6: 8	the same again from the **Lord,**
	3:17	Spirit of the **Lord** is, there is		6: 9	And, **masters,** do the same to
	3:18	the glory of the **Lord** as though		6: 9	have the same **Master** in heaven,
	3:18	this comes from the **Lord,** the		6:10	Finally, be strong in the **Lord**
	4: 5	proclaim Jesus Christ as **Lord**		6:21	a faithful minister in the **Lord**
	4:14	one who raised the **Lord** Jesus		6:23	Father and the **Lord** Jesus
	5: 6	we are away from the **Lord**—		6:24	undying love for our **Lord** Jesus
	5: 8	body and at home with the **Lord.**	Ph	1: 2	God our Father and the **Lord**
	5:11	knowing the fear of the **Lord,**		1:14	made confident in the **Lord** by
	6:17	**Lord,** and touch nothing unclean		2:11	Jesus Christ is **Lord,** to the
	6:18	daughters, says the **Lord**		2:19	I hope in the **Lord** Jesus to
	8: 5	themselves first to the **Lord**		2:24	and I trust in the **Lord** that I
	8: 9	the generous act of our **Lord**		2:29	Welcome him then in the **Lord**
	8:19	for the glory of the **Lord**		3: 1	rejoice in the **Lord.** To write
	8:21	not only in the **Lord's** sight		3: 8	knowing Christ Jesus my **Lord.**
	10: 8	which the **Lord** gave for		3:20	a Savior, the **Lord** Jesus Christ
	10:17	who boasts, boast in the **Lord.**		4: 1	stand firm in the **Lord** in this
	10:18	those whom the **Lord** commends.		4: 2	be of the same mind in the **Lord**
	11:17	not with the **Lord's** authority,		4: 4	Rejoice in the **Lord** always;
	11:31	The God and Father of the **Lord**		4: 5	to everyone. The **Lord** is near.
	12: 1	and revelations of the **Lord.**		4:10	I rejoice in the **Lord** greatly
	12: 8	I appealed to the **Lord** about		4:23	The grace of the **Lord** Jesus
	13:10	authority that the **Lord** has	Co	1: 3	the Father of our **Lord** Jesus
	13:13	The grace of the **Lord** Jesus		1:10	lead lives worthy of the **Lord,**
Ga	1: 3	God our Father and the **Lord**		2: 6	received Christ Jesus the **Lord,**
	1:19	except James the **Lord's** brother		3:13	just as the **Lord** has forgiven

3:17	name of the **Lord** Jesus, giving
3:18	as is fitting in the **Lord.**
3:20	acceptable duty in the **Lord.**
3:22	obey your earthly **masters** in
3:22	fearing the **Lord.**
3:23	Lord and not for your **masters,**
3:24	you know that from the **Lord** you
3:24	you serve the **Lord** Christ.
4: 1	**Masters,** treat your slaves
4: 1	you also have a **Master** in
4: 7	a fellow servant in the **Lord.**
4:17	you have received in the **Lord.**

1Th 1: 1　the **Lord** Jesus Christ: Grace to
　　1: 3　hope in our **Lord** Jesus Christ.
　　1: 6　imitators of us and of the **Lord**
　　1: 8　For the word of the **Lord** has
　　2:15　who killed both the **Lord** Jesus
　　2:19　boasting before our **Lord** Jesus
　　3: 8　to stand firm in the **Lord.**
　　3:11　**Lord** Jesus direct our way to
　　3:12　And may the **Lord** make you
　　3:13　the coming of our **Lord** Jesus
　　4: 1　urge you in the **Lord** Jesus that
　　4: 2　gave you through the **Lord** Jesus
　　4: 6　because the **Lord** is an avenger
　　4:15　by the word of the **Lord,** that
　　4:15　until the coming of the **Lord,**
　　4:16　For the **Lord** himself, with a
　　4:17　meet the **Lord** in the air; and
　　4:17　will be with the **Lord** forever.
　　5: 2　the day of the **Lord** will come
　　5: 9　salvation through our **Lord**
　　5:12　charge of you in the **Lord** and
　　5:23　coming of our **Lord** Jesus Christ
　　5:27　command you by the **Lord** that
　　5:28　The grace of our **Lord** Jesus
2Th 1: 1　and the **Lord** Jesus Christ:
　　1: 2　Father and the **Lord** Jesus
　　1: 7　when the **Lord** Jesus is revealed
　　1: 8　the gospel of our **Lord** Jesus.
　　1: 9　presence of the **Lord** and from
　　1:12　so that the name of our **Lord**
　　1:12　God and the **Lord** Jesus Christ.
　　2: 1　As to the coming of our **Lord**
　　2: 2　effect that the day of the **Lord**
　　2: 8　**Lord** Jesus will destroy with
　　2:13　sisters beloved by the **Lord,**
　　2:14　obtain the glory of our **Lord**
　　2:16　Now may our **Lord** Jesus Christ

　　3: 1　word of the **Lord** may spread
　　3: 3　But the **Lord** is faithful; he
　　3: 4　have confidence in the **Lord**
　　3: 5　May the **Lord** direct your hearts
　　3: 6　in the name of our **Lord** Jesus
　　3:12　exhort in the **Lord** Jesus Christ
　　3:16　may the **Lord** of peace himself
　　3:16　The **Lord** be with all of you.
　　3:18　The grace of our **Lord** Jesus
1Ti 1: 2　and Christ Jesus our **Lord.**
　　1:12　Christ Jesus our **Lord,** who has
　　1:14　and the grace of our **Lord**
　　6: 3　sound words of our **Lord** Jesus
　　6:14　manifestation of our **Lord** Jesus
　　6:15　King of kings and **Lord** of lords
2Ti 1: 2　and Christ Jesus our **Lord.**
　　1: 8　the testimony about our **Lord** or
　　1:16　May the **Lord** grant mercy to the
　　1:18　—may the **Lord** grant that he
　　1:18　mercy from the **Lord** on that day
　　2: 7　for the **Lord** will give you
　　2:19　The **Lord** knows those who are
　　2:19　name of the **Lord** turn away from
　　2:22　call on the **Lord** from a pure
　　2:24　And the **Lord's** servant must not
　　3:11　Yet the **Lord** rescued me from
　　4: 8　which the **Lord,** the righteous
　　4:14　the **Lord** will pay him back for
　　4:17　But the **Lord** stood by me and
　　4:18　The **Lord** will rescue me from
　　4:22　The **Lord** be with your spirit.
Pm 1: 3　Father and the **Lord** Jesus
　　1: 5　faith toward the **Lord** Jesus.
　　1:16　in the flesh and in the **Lord.**
　　1:20　from you in the **Lord!** Refresh
　　1:25　The grace of the **Lord** Jesus
He 1:10　And, "In the beginning, **Lord,**
　　2: 3　through the **Lord,** and it was
　　7:14　For it is evident that our **Lord**
　　7:21　The **Lord** has sworn and will
　　8: 2　the true tent that the **Lord,**
　　8: 8　surely coming, says the **Lord,**
　　8: 9　concern for them, says the **Lord**
　　8:10　after those days, says the **Lord**
　　8:11　'Know the **Lord,'** for they shall
　10:16　says the **Lord:** I will put my
　10:30　The **Lord** will judge his people
　12: 5　discipline of the **Lord,** or lose
　12: 6　for the **Lord** disciplines those

	12:14	which no one will see the **Lord.**
	13: 6	The **Lord** is my helper; I will
	13:20	back from the dead our **Lord**
Ja	1: 1	servant of God and of the **Lord**
	1: 7	receive anything from the **Lord.**
	2: 1	believe in our glorious **Lord**
	3: 9	With it we bless the **Lord** and
	4:10	yourselves before the **Lord,** and
	4:15	If the **Lord** wishes, we will
	5: 4	the ears of the **Lord** of hosts.
	5: 7	until the coming of the **Lord.**
	5: 8	for the coming of the **Lord** is
	5:10	spoke in the name of the **Lord.**
	5:11	seen the purpose of the **Lord,**
	5:11	how the **Lord** is compassionate
	5:14	oil in the name of the **Lord.**
	5:15	the **Lord** will raise them up;
1P	1: 3	Father of our **Lord** Jesus Christ
	1:25	the word of the **Lord** endures
	2: 3	tasted that the **Lord** is good.
	2:13	For the **Lord's** sake accept the
	3: 6	Abraham and called him **lord.**
	3:12	For the eyes of the **Lord** are on
	3:12	the face of the **Lord** is against
	3:15	sanctify Christ as **Lord.** Always
2P	1: 2	of God and of Jesus our **Lord.**
	1: 8	knowledge of our **Lord** Jesus
	1:11	eternal kingdom of our **Lord** and
	1:14	as indeed our **Lord** Jesus Christ
	1:16	power and coming of our **Lord**
	2: 9	then the **Lord** knows how to
	2:11	judgment from the **Lord.**
	2:20	the knowledge of our **Lord** and
	3: 2	commandment of the **Lord** and
	3: 8	with the **Lord** one day is like a
	3: 9	The **Lord** is not slow about his
	3:10	But the day of the **Lord** will
	3:15	regard the patience of our **Lord**
	3:18	knowledge of our **Lord** and
Ju	1: 4	deny our only Master and **Lord,**
	1: 5	that the **Lord,** who once for all
	1: 9	but said, "The **Lord** rebuke you!
	1:14	See, the **Lord** is coming with
	1:17	the apostles of our **Lord** Jesus
	1:21	mercy of our **Lord** Jesus Christ
	1:25	through Jesus Christ our **Lord,**
Re	1: 8	says the **Lord** God, who is and
	4: 8	Holy, holy, holy, the **Lord** God
	4:11	You are worthy, our **Lord** and

	7:14	I said to him, "**Sir,** you are
	11: 4	stand before the **Lord** of the
	11: 8	also their **Lord** was crucified.
	11:15	become the kingdom of our **Lord**
	11:17	We give you thanks, **Lord** God
	14:13	who from now on die in the **Lord**
	15: 3	**Lord** God the Almighty! Just and
	15: 4	**Lord,** who will not fear and
	16: 7	Yes, O **Lord** God, the Almighty,
	17:14	he is **Lord** of lords and King of
	17:14	he is Lord of **lords** and King of
	18: 8	mighty is the **Lord** God who
	19: 6	the **Lord** our God the Almighty
	19:16	King of kings and **Lord** of
	19:16	of kings and Lord of **lords.**
	21:22	its temple is the **Lord** God the
	22: 5	**Lord** God will be their light,
	22: 6	for the **Lord,** the God of the
	22:20	Amen. Come, **Lord** Jesus!
	22:21	The grace of the **Lord** Jesus be

2963　ᴳᴼ4　ᴬᴳ460　ᴸᴺ149　ᴮ2:510　ᴷ3:1096　ᴿ2962
κυριοτης, MASTERSHIP, LORDSHIP

Ep	1:21	power and **dominion,** and above
Co	1:16	whether thrones or **dominions** or
2P	2:10	and who despise **authority.**
Ju	1: 8	reject **authority,** and slander

2964　ᴳᴼ2　ᴬᴳ461　ᴸᴺ149　ᴮ1:664　ᴷ3:1098
κυροω, I AUTHENTICATE

2C	2: 8	So I urge you to **reaffirm** your
Ga	3:15	person's will **has been ratified**

2965　ᴳᴼ5　ᴬᴳ461　ᴸᴺ149　ᴷ3:1101
κυων, DOG

Mt	7: 6	not give what is holy to **dogs;**
Lk	16:21	even the **dogs** would come and
Ph	3: 2	Beware of the **dogs,** beware of
2P	2:22	The **dog** turns back to its own
Re	22:15	Outside are the **dogs** and

2966　ᴳᴼ1　ᴬᴳ461　ᴸᴺ149
κωλον, CORPSE

He	3:17	sinned, whose **bodies** fell in

2967　ᴳᴼ23　ᴬᴳ461　ᴸᴺ149　ᴮ2:220
κωλυω, I HINDER

Mt	19:14	do not **stop** them; for it is to
Mk	9:38	we tried to **stop** him, because
	9:39	Do not **stop** him; for no one

	10:14	do not **stop** them; for it is to
Lk	6:29	coat do not **withhold** even your
	9:49	we tried to **stop** him, because
	9:50	Do not **stop** him; for whoever
	11:52	and you **hindered** those who were
	18:16	do not **stop** them; for it is to
	23: 2	**forbidding** us to pay taxes to
Ac	8:36	What is **to prevent** me from
	10:47	Can anyone **withhold** the water
	11:17	who was I that I could **hinder**
	16: 6	**having been forbidden** by the
	24:23	**to prevent** any of his friends
	27:43	**kept** them from carrying out
Ro	1:13	thus far **have been prevented**),
1C	14:39	and do not **forbid** speaking in
1Th	2:16	by **hindering** us from speaking
1Ti	4: 3	They **forbid** marriage and demand
He	7:23	because they **were prevented** by
2P	2:16	and **restrained** the prophet's
3J	1:10	even **prevents** those who want to

2968   GO27 AG461 LN149
κωμη, VILLAGE

Mt	9:35	cities and **villages,** teaching
	10:11	Whatever town or **village** you
	14:15	they may go into the **villages**
	21: 2	Go into the **village** ahead of
Mk	6: 6	went about among the **villages**
	6:36	country and **villages** and buy
	6:56	into **villages** or cities or
	8:23	led him out of the **village;** and
	8:26	not even go into the **village.**
	8:27	to the **villages** of Caesarea
	11: 2	Go into the **village** ahead of
Lk	5:17	every **village** of Galilee and
	8: 1	through cities and **villages,**
	9: 6	went through the **villages,**
	9:12	surrounding **villages** and
	9:52	way they entered a **village** of
	9:56	they went on to another **village**
	10:38	he entered a certain **village,**
	13:22	one town and **village** after
	17:12	As he entered a **village,** ten
	19:30	Go into the **village** ahead of
	24:13	to a **village** called Emmaus,
	24:28	As they came near the **village**
Jn	7:42	the **village** where David lived?
	11: 1	the **village** of Mary and her
	11:30	come to the **village,** but was
Ac	8:25	good news to many **villages** of

2969   GO1 AG461 LN149 R2968,4172
κωμοπολις, CITY, TOWN

Mk	1:38	on to the neighboring **towns,** so

2970   GO3 AG461 LN149
κωμος, CAROUSING

Ro	13:13	not in **reveling** and drunkenness
Ga	5:21	envy, drunkenness, **carousing,**
1P	4: 3	**revels,** carousing, and lawless

2971   GO1 AG462 LN149
κωνωψ, GNAT

Mt	23:24	strain out a **gnat** but swallow

2972   GO1 AG462 LN150
κως, KOS (COS)

Ac	21: 1	came by a straight course to **Cos**

2973   GO1 AG462 LN150
κωσαμ, KOSAM

Lk	3:28	son of **Cosam,** son of Elmadam,

2974   GO14 AG462 LN150 B1:428
κωφος, DEAF

Mt	9:32	a demoniac who was **mute** was
	9:33	the one who had been **mute** spoke
	11: 5	the **deaf** hear, the dead are
	12:22	demoniac who was blind and **mute**
	12:22	who had been **mute** could speak
	15:30	the maimed, the blind, the **mute**
	15:31	when they saw the **mute** speaking
Mk	7:32	They brought to him a **deaf** man
	7:37	he even makes the **deaf** to hear
	9:25	**hearing,** I command you, come
Lk	1:22	remained **unable to speak.**
	7:22	the **deaf** hear, the dead are
	11:14	a demon that was **mute;** when the
	11:14	who had been **mute** spoke, and

λ

2975   GO4 AG462 LN150 K4:1
λαγχανω, I OBTAIN

Lk	1: 9	he was **chosen by lot,** according
Jn	19:24	but **cast lots** for it to see who
Ac	1:17	**was allotted** his share in this
2P	1: 1	To those who **have received** a

2976　GO15 AG462 LN150
λαζαρος, LAZARUS
Lk　16:20　lay a poor man named **Lazarus,**
　　16:23　Abraham far away with **Lazarus**
　　16:24　send **Lazarus** to dip the tip of
　　16:25　and **Lazarus** in like manner evil
Jn　11: 1　man was ill, **Lazarus** of Bethany
　　11: 2　her brother **Lazarus** was ill.
　　11: 5　and her sister and **Lazarus,**
　　11:11　Our friend **Lazarus** has fallen
　　11:14　them plainly, "**Lazarus** is dead.
　　11:43　loud voice, "**Lazarus,** come out!
　　12: 1　the home of **Lazarus,** whom he
　　12: 2　Martha served, and **Lazarus** was
　　12: 9　but also to see **Lazarus,** whom
　　12:10　planned to put **Lazarus** to death
　　12:17　when he called **Lazarus** out of

2977　GO4 AG462 LN150
λαθρα, PRIVATELY
Mt　1:19　planned to dismiss her **quietly.**
　　2: 7　Then Herod **secretly** called for
Jn　11:28　her **privately,** "The Teacher
Ac　16:37　us **in secret?** Certainly not!

2978　GO3 AG462 LN150 B3:1000
λαιλαψ, STORM
Mk　4:37　A great **windstorm** arose, and
Lk　8:23　A **windstorm** swept down on the
2P　2:17　mists driven by a **storm;** for

2978a　GO1 AG463 LN150
λακαω, I BURST OPEN
Ac　1:18　he **burst open** in the middle

2979　GO1 AG463 LN150 K4:3
λακτιζω, I KICK
Ac　26:14　It hurts you to **kick against**

2980　GO296 AG463 LN150 B3:1081 K4:3
λαλεω, I SPEAK, SAY
Mt　9:18　he **was saying** these things to
　　9:33　the one who had been mute
　　　　　　spoke
　　10:19　about how you are **to speak** or
　　10:19　what you are **to say** will be
　　10:20　for it is not you who **speak,**
　　10:20　Father **speaking** through you.
　　12:22　who had been mute could **speak**
　　12:34　How can you **speak** good things,

12:34　of the heart the mouth **speaks.**
12:36　every careless word you **utter;**
12:46　While he was still **speaking** to
12:46　outside, wanting **to speak** to
12:47　outside, wanting **to speak** to
13: 3　And he **told** them many things in
13:10　Why do you **speak** to them in
13:13　The reason I **speak** to them in
13:33　He **told** them another parable:
13:34　Jesus **told** the crowds all these
13:34　without a parable he **told** them
14:27　But immediately Jesus **spoke** to
15:31　mute **speaking,** the maimed whole
17: 5　While he was still **speaking,**
23: 1　Then Jesus **said** to the crowds
26:13　what she has done **will be told**
26:47　While he was still **speaking,**
28:18　And Jesus came and **said** to them
Mk　1:34　not permit the demons to **speak,**
　　2: 2　and he was **speaking** the word to
　　2: 7　Why does this fellow **speak** in
　　4:33　many such parables he **spoke**
　　4:34　he did not **speak** to them except
　　5:35　While he was still **speaking,**
　　5:36　But overhearing what they **said,**
　　6:50　But immediately he **spoke** to
　　7:35　released, and he **spoke** plainly.
　　7:37　to hear and the mute to **speak.**
　　8:32　He **said** all this quite openly.
　　11:23　believe that what you **say** will
　　12: 1　Then he began to **speak** to them
　　13:11　about what you are to **say;** but
　　13:11　but **say** whatever is given you
　　13:11　it is not you who **speak,** but
　　14: 9　she has done **will be told** in
　　14:31　But he **said** vehemently, "Even
　　14:43　while he was still **speaking,**
　　16:17　they **will speak** in new tongues;
　　16:19　after he **had spoken** to them,
Lk　1:19　I have been sent to **speak** to
　　1:20　become mute, unable to **speak,**
　　1:22　he could not **speak** to them, and
　　1:45　fulfillment of what **was spoken**
　　1:55　to the promise he **made**
　　1:64　and he began to **speak,** praising
　　1:70　as he **spoke** through the mouth
　　2:15　**said** to one another, "Let us go
　　2:17　what had been **told** them about
　　2:18　at what the shepherds **told** them

2:20	seen, as it had **been told** them.	
2:33	amazed at what **was being said**	
2:38	to praise God and to **speak**	
2:50	understand what he **said** to them	
4:41	would not allow them to **speak,**	
5: 4	When he had finished **speaking,**	
5:21	Who is this who is **speaking**	
6:45	the heart that the mouth **speaks**	
7:15	sat up and began to **speak,** and	
8:49	While he was still **speaking,**	
9:11	and **spoke** to them about the	
11:14	one who had been mute **spoke,**	
11:37	While he **was speaking,** a	
12: 3	whatever you **have said** in the	
22:47	While he was still **speaking,**	
22:60	still **speaking,** the cock crowed	
24: 6	Remember how he **told** you, while	
24:25	Then he **said** to them, "Oh, how	
24:32	while he **was talking** to us on	
24:36	While they **were talking** about	
24:44	my words that I **spoke** to you	

Jn	1:37	The two disciples heard him **say**
	3:11	we **speak** of what we know and
	3:31	**speaks** about earthly things.
	3:34	He whom God has sent **speaks** the
	4:26	he, the one who is **speaking** to
	4:27	he **was speaking** with a woman,
	4:27	Why are you **speaking** with her?
	6:63	The words that I **have spoken** to
	7:13	Yet no one would **speak** openly
	7:17	whether I **am speaking** on my own
	7:18	Those who **speak** on their own
	7:26	And here he is, **speaking** openly
	7:46	Never has anyone **spoken** like
	8:12	Again Jesus **spoke** to them,
	8:20	He **spoke** these words while
	8:25	Why do I **speak** to you at all?
	8:26	I have much **to say** about you
	8:26	and I **declare** to the world what
	8:28	but I **speak** these things as the
	8:30	As he **was saying** these things,
	8:38	I **declare** what I have seen in
	8:40	a man who has **told** you the
	8:44	no truth in him. When he **lies,**
	8:44	he **speaks** according to his own
	9:21	age. He **will speak** for himself.
	9:29	We know that God **has spoken** to
	9:37	the one **speaking** with you is he
	10: 6	understand what he **was saying**

12:29	An angel **has spoken** to him.	
12:36	After Jesus **had said** this, he	
12:41	his glory and **spoke** about him.	
12:48	the word that I **have spoken**	
12:49	for I **have** not **spoken** on my own	
12:49	what to say and what to **speak.**	
12:50	What I **speak,** therefore, I	
12:50	I **speak** just as the Father has	
14:10	I do not **speak** on my own; but	
14:25	I **have said** these things to	
14:30	I will no longer **talk** much with	
15: 3	by the word that I **have spoken**	
15:11	I **have said** these things to you	
15:22	If I had not come and **spoken** to	
16: 1	I **have said** these things to	
16: 4	But I **have said** these things to	
16: 6	But because I **have said** these	
16:13	for he **will** not **speak** on his	
16:13	but **will speak** whatever he	
16:18	not know what he **is talking**	
16:25	I **have said** these things to	
16:25	I **will** no longer **speak** to you	
16:29	now you **are speaking** plainly,	
16:33	I **have said** this to you, so	
17: 1	After Jesus **had spoken** these	
17:13	and I **speak** these things in the	
18:20	I **have spoken** openly to the	
18:20	I **have said** nothing in secret.	
18:21	heard what I **said** to them; they	
18:23	If I **have spoken** wrongly,	
19:10	Do you refuse to **speak** to me?	

Ac	2: 4	**to speak** in other languages, as
	2: 6	each one heard them **speaking** in
	2: 7	not all these who **are speaking**
	2:11	hear them **speaking** about God's
	2:31	**saying,** 'He was not abandoned
	3:21	that God **announced** long ago
	3:22	listen to whatever he **tells** you
	3:24	as many as **have spoken,** from
	4: 1	Peter and John **were speaking** to
	4:17	warn them to **speak** no more to
	4:20	cannot keep from **speaking** about
	4:29	**to speak** your word with all
	4:31	**spoke** the word of God with
	5:20	**tell** the people the whole
	5:40	ordered them not **to speak** in
	6:10	the Spirit with which he **spoke.**
	6:11	heard him **speak** blasphemous
	6:13	This man never stops **saying**

7: 6	And God **spoke** in these terms,		12: 3	no one **speaking** by the Spirit
7:38	the angel who **spoke** to him at		12:30	Do all **speak** in tongues? Do all
7:44	God directed when he **spoke** to		13: 1	If I **speak** in the tongues of
8:25	testified and **spoken** the word		13:11	When I was a child, I **spoke**
8:26	an angel of the Lord **said** to		14: 2	For those who **speak** in a tongue
9: 6	and you **will be told** what you		14: 2	do not **speak** to other people
9:27	who **had spoken** to him, and how		14: 2	they are **speaking** mysteries in
9:29	He **spoke** and argued with the		14: 3	those who prophesy **speak** to
10: 7	When the angel who **spoke** to		14: 4	Those who **speak** in a tongue
10:44	While Peter was still **speaking**,		14: 5	**speak** in tongues, but even more
10:46	for they heard them **speaking**		14: 5	greater than one who **speaks** in
11:14	he will **give** you a message by		14: 6	if I come to you **speaking** in
11:15	And as I began **to speak**, the		14: 6	unless I **speak** to you in some
11:19	they **spoke** the word to no one		14: 9	anyone know what **is being said?**
11:20	**spoke** to the Hellenists also,		14: 9	you will be **speaking** into the
13:42	the people urged them **to speak**		14:11	foreigner to the **speaker** and
13:45	contradicted what was **spoken** by		14:11	the **speaker** a foreigner to me.
13:46	word of God **should be spoken**		14:13	Therefore, one who **speaks** in a
14: 1	**spoke** in such a way that a		14:18	I thank God that I **speak** in
14: 9	Paul as he **was speaking.** And		14:19	I would rather **speak** five words
14:25	When they **had spoken** the word		14:21	I **will speak** to this people;
16:14	listen eagerly to what **was said**		14:23	and all **speak** in tongues, and
16: 6	Spirit **to speak** the word in		14:27	If anyone **speaks** in a tongue,
16:13	sat down and **spoke** to the women		14:28	silent in church and **speak** to
16:32	They **spoke** the word of the Lord		14:29	Let two or three prophets **speak**
17:19	is that you are **presenting?**		14:34	not permitted **to speak,** but
18: 9	Do not be afraid, but **speak**		14:35	shameful for a woman **to speak**
18:25	**spoke** with burning enthusiasm		14:39	not forbid **speaking** in tongues;
19: 6	they **spoke** in tongues and		15:34	I **say** this to your shame.
20:30	will come **distorting** the truth	2C	2:17	in Christ we **speak** as persons
21:39	**let** me **speak** to the people.		4:13	I believed, and so I **spoke**
22: 9	the one who **was speaking** to me.		4:13	also believe, and so we **speak,**
22:10	you **will be told** everything		7:14	everything we **said** to you was
23: 9	a spirit or an angel **has spoken**		11:17	What I **am saying** in regard to
23:18	he has something **to tell** you.		11:17	I **am saying** not with the Lord's
26:22	prophets and Moses **said** would		11:23	I **am talking** like a madman
26:26	to him I **speak** freely; for I am		12: 4	things that are not **to be told,**
26:31	they **said** to one another, "This		12:19	We **are speaking** in Christ
27:25	be exactly as I **have been told.**		13: 3	proof that Christ **is speaking**
28:21	**spoken** anything evil about you.	Ep	4:25	let all of us **speak** the truth
28:25	in **saying** to your ancestors		5:19	as you **sing** psalms and hymns
Ro 3:19	**speaks** to those who are under		6:20	it boldly, as I must **speak.**
7: 1	for I **am speaking** to those who	Ph	1:14	dare **to speak** the word with
15:18	For I will not venture **to speak**	Co	4: 3	that we **may declare** the mystery
1C 2: 6	among the mature we **do speak**		4: 4	reveal it clearly, as I **should.**
2: 7	But we **speak** God's wisdom,	1Th	1: 8	have no need **to speak** about it.
2:13	And we **speak** of these things in		2: 2	courage in our God **to declare**
3: 1	I could not **speak** to you as		2: 4	even so we **speak,** not to please
9: 8	I **say** this on human authority?		2:16	by hindering us from **speaking**

1Ti	5:13	**saying** what they should not say
Ti	2: 1	But as for you, **teach** what is
	2:15	**Declare** these things; exhort
He	1: 1	Long ago God **spoke** to our
	1: 2	he **has spoken** to us by a Son,
	2: 2	For if the message **declared**
	2: 3	It **was declared** at first
	2: 5	about which we **are speaking,** to
	3: 5	things that **would be spoken**
	4: 8	God **would** not **speak** later about
	5: 5	the one who **said** to him, "You
	6: 9	Even though we **speak** in this
	7:14	Moses **said** nothing about
	9:19	**had been told** to all the people
	11: 4	his faith he still **speaks.**
	11:18	of whom he **had been told,** "It
	12:24	the sprinkled blood that **speaks**
	12:25	refuse the one who **is speaking;**
	13: 7	those who **spoke** the word of God
Ja	1:19	quick to listen, slow **to speak,**
	2:12	So **speak** and so act as those
	5:10	take the prophets who **spoke** in
1P	3:10	their lips from **speaking** deceit
	4:11	Whoever **speaks** must do so as
2P	1:21	the Holy Spirit **spoke** from God,
	3:16	**speaking** of this as he does in
1J	4: 5	what they **say** is from the world
2J	1:12	come to you and **talk** with you
3J	1:14	we **will talk** together face to
Ju	1:15	ungodly sinners **have spoken**
	1:16	they are bombastic in **speech,**
Re	1:12	voice it was that **spoke** to me,
	4: 1	which I had heard **speaking** to
	10: 3	the seven thunders **sounded.**
	10: 4	thunders had **sounded,** I was
	10: 4	seven thunders **have said,** and
	10: 8	**spoke** to me again, saying, "Go,
	13: 5	a mouth **uttering** haughty and
	13:11	like a lamb and it **spoke** like a
	13:15	**speak** and cause those who would
	17: 1	came and **said** to me, "Come, I
	21: 9	came and **said** to me, "Come, I
	21:15	The angel who **talked** to me had

2981 ᴳᴼ3 ᴬᴳ464 ᴸᴺ150 ᴿ2980
λαλια, SPEECH

Mt	26:73	for your **accent** betrays you.
Jn	4:42	what you **said** that we believe,
	8:43	not understand what I **say?** It

2982 ᴳᴼ1 ᴬᴳ464
λαμα, LAMA (LEMA)

Mk	15:34	Eloi, Eloi, **lema** sabachthani?

2983 ᴳᴼ258 ᴬᴳ464 ᴸᴺ150 ᴮ3:747 ᴷ4:5
λαμβανω, I TAKE, RECEIVE

Mt	5:40	**take** your coat, give your cloak
	7: 8	For everyone who asks **receives,**
	8:17	He **took** our infirmities and
	10: 8	You **received** without payment;
	10:38	and whoever does not **take** up
	10:41	will **receive** a prophet's
	10:41	will **receive** the reward of the
	12:14	**conspired** against him, how to
	13:20	immediately **receives** it with
	13:31	someone **took** and sowed in his
	13:33	yeast that a woman **took** and
	14:19	**Taking** the five loaves and the
	15:26	**take** the children's food and
	15:36	he **took** the seven loaves and
	16: 5	forgotten **to bring** any bread.
	16: 7	we have **brought** no bread.
	16: 9	how many baskets you **gathered?**
	16:10	how many baskets you **gathered?**
	17:24	the **collectors** of the temple
	17:25	**take** toll or tribute? From
	17:27	**take** the first fish that comes
	19:29	**will receive** a hundredfold,
	20: 9	each of them **received** the usual
	20:10	they thought they would **receive**
	20:10	also **received** the usual daily
	20:11	And when they **received** it, they
	21:22	with faith, you will **receive.**
	21:34	tenants to **collect** his produce.
	21:35	the tenants **seized** his slaves
	21:39	So they **seized** him, threw him
	22:15	**plotted** to entrap him in what
	25: 1	Ten bridesmaids **took** their
	25: 3	When the foolish **took** their
	25: 3	they **took** no oil with them;
	25: 4	but the wise **took** flasks of
	25:16	The one who **had received** the
	25:18	But the one who **had received**
	25:20	Then the one who **had received**
	25:24	Then the one who **had received**
	26:26	Jesus **took** a loaf of bread, and
	26:26	**Take,** eat; this is my body.
	26:27	Then he **took** a cup, and after
	26:52	all who **take** the sword will

	27: 1	**conferred** together against
	27: 6	**taking** the pieces of silver,
	27: 7	After **conferring** together, they
	27: 9	And they **took** the thirty
	27:24	he **took** some water and washed
	27:30	**took** the reed and struck him on
	27:48	At once one of them ran and **got**
	27:59	So Joseph **took** the body and
	28:12	they **devised** a plan to give a
	28:15	So they **took** the money and did
Mk	4:16	immediately **receive** it with joy
	6:41	**Taking** the five loaves and the
	7:27	it is not fair **to take** the
	8: 6	he **took** the seven loaves, and
	8:14	forgotten to **bring** any bread;
	9:36	Then he **took** a little child and
	10:30	will not **receive** a hundredfold
	11:24	believe that you **have received**
	12: 2	**collect** from them his share of
	12: 3	But they **seized** him, and beat
	12: 8	So they **seized** him, killed him,
	12:19	the man shall **marry** the widow
	12:20	the first **married** and, when he
	12:21	and the second **married** her and
	12:40	They **will receive** the greater
	14:22	he **took** a loaf of bread, and
	14:22	said, **"Take;** this is my body."
	14:23	Then he **took** a cup, and after
	14:65	The guards also **took** him over
	15:23	myrrh; but he did not **take** it.
Lk	5: 5	but have **caught** nothing. Yet if
	5:26	Amazement **seized** all of them,
	6: 4	**took** and ate the bread of the
	6:34	to **receive** as much again.
	7:16	Fear **seized** all of them; and
	9:16	And **taking** the five loaves and
	9:39	Suddenly a spirit **seizes** him,
	11:10	For everyone who asks **receives,**
	13:19	someone **took** and sowed in the
	13:21	yeast that a woman **took** and
	19:12	a distant country to **get** royal
	19:15	**having received** royal power, he
	20:21	you **show deference** to no one,
	20:28	man shall **marry** the widow and
	20:29	the first **married,** and died
	20:31	and the third **married** her, and
	20:47	They **will receive** the greater
	22:17	**Take** this and divide it among
	22:19	Then he **took** a loaf of bread,

	24:30	he **took** bread, blessed and
	24:43	and he **took** it and ate in their
Jn	1:12	But to all who **received** him,
	1:16	have all **received,** grace upon
	3:11	yet you do not **receive** our
	3:27	No one can **receive** anything
	3:32	no one **accepts** his testimony.
	3:33	**accepted** his testimony has
	4:36	The reaper is already **receiving**
	5:34	Not that I **accept** such human
	5:41	I do not **accept** glory from
	5:43	you do not **accept** me; if
	5:43	name, you **will accept** him.
	5:44	when you **accept** glory from one
	6: 7	each of them to **get** a little.
	6:11	Then Jesus **took** the loaves,
	6:21	Then they wanted **to take** him
	7:23	If a man **receives** circumcision
	7:39	in him were to **receive;** for as
	10:17	in order **to take** it up again.
	10:18	I have power **to take** it up
	10:18	I **have received** this command
	12: 3	Mary **took** a pound of costly
	12:13	So they **took** branches of palm
	12:48	does not **receive** my word has
	13: 4	and **tied** a towel around himself
	13:12	**had put** on his robe, and had
	13:20	whoever **receives** one whom I
	13:20	send **receives** me; and whoever
	13:20	**receives** me receives him who
	13:20	whoever receives me **receives**
	13:26	he **gave** it to Judas son of
	13:30	So, after **receiving** the piece
	14:17	whom the world cannot **receive,**
	16:14	because he **will take** what is
	16:15	he **will take** what is mine and
	16:24	Ask and you **will receive,** so
	17: 8	they **have received** them and
	18: 3	So Judas **brought** a detachment
	18:31	**Take** him yourselves and judge
	19: 1	Then Pilate **took** Jesus and had
	19: 6	**Take** him yourselves and
	19:23	**took** his clothes and divided
	19:27	the disciple **took** her into his
	19:30	When Jesus **had received** the
	19:40	They **took** the body of Jesus and
	20:22	them, **"Receive** the Holy Spirit.
	21:13	Jesus came and **took** the bread
Ac	1: 8	But you **will receive** power when

	1:20	**Let** another **take** his position
	1:25	to **take** the place in this
	2:33	and **having received** from the
	2:38	you **will receive** the gift of
	3: 3	temple, he asked them **for** alms.
	3: 5	expecting **to receive** something
	7:53	You are the ones that **received**
	8:15	that they **might receive** the
	8:17	and they **received** the Holy
	8:19	I lay my hands **may receive** the
	9:19	and after **taking** some food, he
	9:25	but his disciples **took** him by
	10:43	**receives** forgiveness of sins
	10:47	**have received** the Holy Spirit
	15:14	to **take** from among them a
	16: 3	he **took** him and had him
	16:24	he **put** them in the innermost
	17: 9	and after they **had taken** bail
	17:15	after **receiving** instructions to
	19: 2	Did you **receive** the Holy
	20:24	ministry that I **received** from
	20:35	blessed to give than to **receive**
	24:27	Felix **was succeeded** by Porcius
	25:16	**had been given** an opportunity
	26:10	with authority **received** from
	26:18	they **may receive** forgiveness of
	27:35	**took** bread; and giving thanks
	28:15	Paul thanked God and **took**
Ro	1: 5	through whom we have **received**
	4:11	He **received** the sign of
	5:11	now **received** reconciliation.
	5:17	those who **receive** the abundance
	7: 8	But sin, **seizing** an opportunity
	7:11	For sin, **seizing** an opportunity
	8:15	For you did not **receive** a
	8:15	you **have received** a spirit of
	13: 2	who resist **will incur** judgment.
1C	2:12	Now we **have received** not the
	3: 8	each **will receive** wages
	3:14	builder will **receive** a reward.
	4: 7	that you did not **receive**? And
	4: 7	And if you **received** it, why do
	4: 7	boast as if it were not a **gift**?
	9:24	only one **receives** the prize?
	9:25	do it to **receive** a perishable
	10:13	No testing **has overtaken** you
	11:23	For I **received** from the Lord
	14: 5	so that the church **may be built**
2C	11: 4	or if you **receive** a different

	11: 4	from the one you **received,** or
	11: 8	by **accepting** support from them
	11:20	or **takes** advantage of you, or
	11:24	Five times I **have received** from
	12:16	crafty, I **took** you in by deceit
Ga	2: 6	to me; God shows no **partiality**)
	3: 2	Did you **receive** the Spirit by
	3:14	so that we **might receive** the
Ph	2: 7	**taking** the form of a slave,
	3:12	I have already **obtained** this or
Co	4:10	you have **received** instructions
1Ti	4: 4	provided it is **received** with
2Ti	1: 5	I am **reminded** of your sincere
He	2: 2	disobedience **received** a just
	2: 3	**was declared** at first through
	4:16	so that we **may receive** mercy
	5: 1	Every high priest **chosen** from
	5: 4	presume **to take** this honor, but
	7: 5	**receive** the priestly office
	7: 8	tithes **are received** by those
	7: 9	who **receives** tithes, paid
	9:15	called **may receive** the promised
	9:19	he **took** the blood of calves and
	10:26	sin after **having received** the
	11: 8	**to receive** as an inheritance;
	11:11	By faith he **received** power of
	11:13	**having received** the promises,
	11:29	the Egyptians **attempted** to do
	11:35	Women **received** their dead by
	11:36	**even** chains and imprisonment.
Ja	1: 7	must not expect **to receive**
	1:12	**will receive** the crown of life
	3: 1	we who teach will be **judged**
	4: 3	You ask and do not **receive,**
	5: 7	until it **receives** the early and
	5:10	**As** an example of suffering and
1P	4:10	gift each of you **has received.**
2P	1: 9	**forgetful** of the cleansing of
	1:17	For he **received** honor and glory
1J	2:27	the anointing that you **received**
	3:22	we **receive** from him whatever
	5: 9	If we **receive** human testimony,
2J	1: 4	just as we **have been commanded**
	1:10	Do not **receive** into the house
3J	1: 7	**accepting** no support from
Re	2:17	except the one who **receives** it.
	2:28	even as I also **received**
	3: 3	Remember then what you **received**

3:11　　no one **may seize** your crown.
4:11　　to **receive** glory and honor and
5: 7　　went and **took** the scroll from
5: 8　　When he **had taken** the scroll,
5: 9　　You are worthy **to take** the
5:12　　slaughtered to **receive** power
6: 4　　permitted to **take** peace from
8: 5　　Then the angel **took** the censer
10: 8　　Go, **take** the scroll that is
10: 9　　**Take** it, and eat; it will be
10:10　　So I **took** the little scroll
11:17　　for you **have taken** your great
14: 9　　and **receive** a mark on their
14:11　　anyone who **receives** the
　　　　　　mark of
17:12　　not yet **received** a kingdom, but
17:12　　they are to **receive** authority
18: 4　　do not **take** part in her sins,
19:20　　**had received** the mark of the
20: 4　　**had** not **received** its mark on
22:17　　Let anyone who wishes **take** the

2984　　ᴳᴼ1 ᴬᴳ465 ᴸᴺ150
λαμεχ, LAMECH
Lk　3:36　　son of Noah, son of **Lamech,**

2985　　ᴳᴼ9 ᴬᴳ465 ᴸᴺ150 ᴮ2:484 ᴷ4:16 ᴿ2989
λαμπας, LAMP
Mt　25: 1　　bridesmaids took their **lamps**
　　25: 3　　the foolish took their **lamps,**
　　25: 4　　flasks of oil with their **lamps.**
　　25: 7　　got up and trimmed their
　　　　　　　lamps.
　　25: 8　　for our **lamps** are going out.
Jn　18: 3　　lanterns and **torches** and
Ac　20: 8　　There were many **lamps** in the
Re　4: 5　　seven flaming **torches,** which
　　8:10　　blazing like a **torch,** and it

2986　　ᴳᴼ9 ᴬᴳ465 ᴸᴺ150 ᴮ2:484 ᴷ4:16 ᴿ2985
λαμπρος, BRIGHT
Lk　23:11　　he put an **elegant** robe on him,
Ac　10:30　　a man in **dazzling** clothes stood
Ja　2: 2　　with gold rings and in **fine**
　　2: 3　　wearing the **fine** clothes and
Re　15: 6　　robed in pure **bright** linen,
　　18:14　　your **splendor** are lost to you,
　　19: 8　　**bright** and pure"—for the
　　22: 1　　**bright** as crystal, flowing from
　　22:16　　David, the **bright** morning star.

2987　　ᴳᴼ1 ᴬᴳ466 ᴸᴺ150 ᴮ2:484 ᴿ2986
λαμπροτης, BRIGHTNESS
Ac　26:13　　**brighter** than the sun, shining

2988　　ᴳᴼ1 ᴬᴳ466 ᴸᴺ151 ᴮ2:484 ᴿ2986
λαμπρως, BRIGHTLY
Lk　16:19　　feasted **sumptuously** every day.

2989　　ᴳᴼ7 ᴬᴳ466 ᴸᴺ151 ᴮ2:484 ᴷ4:16
λαμπω, I SHINE
Mt　5:15　　and it **gives light** to all in
　　5:16　　**let** your light **shine** before
　　17: 2　　his face **shone** like the sun,
Lk　17:24　　lightning flashes and **lights** up
Ac　12: 7　　light **shone** in the cell. He
2C　4: 6　　light **shine** out of darkness,
　　4: 6　　who has **shone** in our hearts to

2990　　ᴳᴼ6 ᴬᴳ466 ᴸᴺ151
λανθανω, I ESCAPE NOTICE
Mk　7:24　　Yet he could not **escape**
　　　　　　　notice,
Lk　8:47　　she could not **remain hidden,**
Ac　26:26　　**has escaped** his **notice,** for
He　13: 2　　angels **without knowing** it.
2P　3: 5　　They **deliberately ignore** this
　　3: 8　　But **do** not **ignore** this one fact

2991　　ᴳᴼ1 ᴬᴳ466 ᴸᴺ151
λαξευτος, CUT STONE
Lk　23:53　　laid it in a **rock-hewn** tomb

2992　　ᴳᴼ142 ᴬᴳ466 ᴸᴺ151 ᴮ2:795 ᴷ4:29
λαος, PEOPLE
Mt　1:21　　he will save his **people** from
　　2: 4　　of the **people,** he inquired of
　　2: 6　　who is to shepherd my **people**
　　4:16　　the **people** who sat in darkness
　　4:23　　every sickness among the **people**
　　13:15　　For this **people's** heart has
　　15: 8　　This **people** honors me with
　　21:23　　elders of the **people** came to
　　26: 3　　elders of the **people** gathered
　　26: 5　　may be a riot among the **people.**
　　26:47　　and the elders of the **people.**
　　27: 1　　elders of the **people** conferred
　　27:25　　Then the **people** as a whole
　　27:64　　tell the **people,** 'He has been
Mk　7: 6　　This **people** honors me with
　　14: 2　　may be a riot among the **people.**

Lk	1:10	whole assembly of the **people**
	1:17	to make ready a **people** prepared
	1:21	Meanwhile the **people** were
	1:68	favorably on his **people** and
	1:77	his **people** by the forgiveness
	2:10	great joy for all the **people:**
	2:31	in the presence of all **peoples,**
	2:32	for glory to your **people** Israel
	3:15	As the **people** were filled with
	3:18	the good news to the **people.**
	3:21	Now when all the **people** were
	6:17	a great multitude of **people**
	7: 1	in the hearing of the **people,**
	7:16	looked favorably on his **people!**
	7:29	(And all the **people** who heard
	8:47	all the **people** why she had
	9:13	buy food for all these **people.**
	18:43	all the **people,** when they saw
	19:47	the leaders of the **people** kept
	19:48	the **people** were spellbound by
	20: 1	teaching the **people** in the
	20: 6	all the **people** will stone us;
	20: 9	He began to tell the **people**
	20:19	but they feared the **people.**
	20:26	in the presence of the **people**
	20:45	hearing of all the **people** he
	21:23	and wrath against this **people;**
	21:38	And all the **people** would get up
	22: 2	they were afraid of the **people.**
	22:66	the elders of the **people,** both
	23: 5	He stirs up the **people** by
	23:13	the leaders, and the **people,**
	23:14	who was perverting the **people;**
	23:27	A great number of the **people**
	23:35	And the **people** stood by,
	24:19	before God and all the **people,**
Jn	8: 2	All the **people** came to him and
	11:50	one man die for the **people**
	18:14	one person die for the **people.**
Ac	2:47	goodwill of all the **people.** And
	3: 9	All the **people** saw him walking
	3:11	all the **people** ran together to
	3:12	he addressed the **people,** "You
	3:23	rooted out of the **people.**
	4: 1	speaking to the **people,** the
	4: 2	they were teaching the **people**
	4: 8	Rulers of the **people** and
	4:10	and to all the **people** of Israel
	4:17	further among the **people,** let

	4:21	because of the **people,** for all
	4:25	and the **peoples** imagine vain
	4:27	the Gentiles and the **peoples** of
	5:12	were done among the **people**
	5:13	but the **people** held them in
	5:20	tell the **people** the whole
	5:25	temple and teaching the **people!**
	5:26	of being stoned by the **people.**
	5:34	respected by all the **people,**
	5:37	got **people** to follow him; he
	6: 8	and signs among the **people.**
	6:12	They stirred up the **people** as
	7:17	our **people** in Egypt increased
	7:34	mistreatment of my **people** who
	10: 2	to the **people** and prayed
	10:41	not to all the **people** but to us
	10:42	preach to the **people** and to
	12: 4	bring him out to the **people**
	12:11	all that the Jewish **people** were
	13:15	exhortation for the **people,**
	13:17	The God of this **people** Israel
	13:17	made the **people** great during
	13:24	to all the **people** of Israel.
	13:31	his witnesses to the **people.**
	15:14	take from among them a **people**
	18:10	in this city who are my **people.**
	19: 4	telling the **people** to believe
	21:28	everywhere against our **people,**
	21:30	the **people** rushed together.
	21:36	The **crowd** that followed kept
	21:39	let me speak to the **people.**
	21:40	motioned to the **people** for
	23: 5	evil of a leader of your **people**
	26:17	rescue you from your **people** and
	26:23	both to our **people** and to the
	28:17	nothing against our **people** or
	28:26	Go to this **people** and say, You
	28:27	For this **people's** heart has
Ro	9:25	Those who were not my **people** I
	9:25	will call 'my **people,'** and her
	9:26	'You are not my **people,'** there
	10:21	disobedient and contrary **people**
	11: 1	has God rejected his **people?** By
	11: 2	God has not rejected his **people**
	15:10	O Gentiles, with his **people";**
	15:11	and let all the **peoples** praise
1C	10: 7	The **people** sat down to eat and
	14:21	By **people** of strange tongues
2C	6:16	and they shall be my **people.**

Ti　2:14　purify for himself a **people** of
He　2:17　for the sins of the **people.**
　　4: 9　still remains for the **people** of
　　5: 3　well as for those of the **people**
　　7: 5　collect tithes from the **people,**
　　7:11　for the **people** received the law
　　7:27　then for those of the **people;**
　　8:10　and they shall be my **people.**
　　9: 7　unintentionally by the **people.**
　　9:19　itself and all the **people,**
　　9:19　been told to all the **people** by
　　10:30　The Lord will judge his **people**
　　11:25　ill-treatment with the **people**
　　13:12　sanctify the **people** by his own
1P　2: 9　God's own **people,** in order that
　　2:10　Once you were not a **people,**
　　2:10　but now you are God's **people;**
2P　2: 1　arose among the **people,** just as
Ju　1: 5　saved a **people** out of the land
Re　5: 9　tribe and language and **people**
　　7: 9　all tribes and **peoples** and
　　10:11　again about many **peoples** and
　　11: 9　of the **peoples** and tribes and
　　13: 7　tribe and **people** and language
　　14: 6　tribe and language and **people.**
　　17:15　are **peoples** and multitudes and
　　18: 4　Come out of her, my **people,** so
　　21: 3　they will be his **peoples,** and

2993　GO6 AG466 LN151
λαοδικεια, LAODICEA
Co　2: 1　for those in **Laodicea,** and for
　　4:13　in **Laodicea** and in Hierapolis.
　　4:15　and sisters in **Laodicea,** and to
　　4:16　also the letter from **Laodicea.**
Re　1:11　Philadelphia, and to **Laodicea.**
　　3:14　angel of the church in **Laodicea**

2994　GO1 AG466 LN151
λαοδικευς, LAODICEAN
Co　4:16　church of the **Laodiceans;** and

2995　GO1 AG467 LN151 K4:57
λαρυγξ, THROAT
Ro　3:13　Their **throats** are opened

2996　GO1 AG467 LN151
λασαια, LASEA
Ac　27: 8　Havens, near the city of
　　　　　Lasea.

2998　GO2 AG467 LN151 R2991
λατομεω, I CUT
Mt　27:60　which he **had hewn** in the rock.
Mk　15:46　tomb that **had been hewn** out of

2999　GO5 AG467 LN151 B3:549 K4:58 R3000
λατρεια, SERVICE
Jn　16: 2　are offering **worship** to God.
Ro　9: 4　the **worship,** and the promises;
　　12: 1　which is your spiritual **worship**
He　9: 1　regulations for **worship** and an
　　9: 6　carry out their **ritual duties;**

3000　GO21 AG467 LN151 B3:549 K4:58
λατρευω, I SERVE
Mt　4:10　your God, and **serve** only him.
Lk　1:74　might **serve** him without fear,
　　2:37　**worshiped** there with fasting
　　4: 8　your God, and **serve** only him.
Ac　7: 7　come out and **worship** me in this
　　7:42　handed them over to **worship** the
　　24:14　sect, I **worship** the God of our
　　26: 7　earnestly **worship** day and night
　　27:23　I belong and whom I **worship,**
Ro　1: 9　For God, whom I **serve** with my
　　1:25　**served** the creature rather than
Ph　3: 3　who **worship** in the Spirit of
2Ti　1: 3　whom I **worship** with a clear
He　8: 5　They offer **worship** in a
　　9: 9　the conscience of the **worshiper**
　　9:14　from dead works **to worship** the
　　10: 2　since the **worshipers,** cleansed
　　12:28　God an acceptable **worship** with
　　13:10　those who **officiate** in the tent
Re　7:15　**worship** him day and night
　　22: 3　his servants **will worship** him;

3001　GO4 AG467 LN151 B2:210 K4:65
λαχανον, VEGETABLE
Mt　13:32　it is the greatest of **shrubs**
Mk　4:32　the greatest of all **shrubs,** and
Lk　11:42　tithe mint and rue and **herbs** of
Ro　14: 2　the weak eat only **vegetables.**

3003　GO4 AG467 LN151 K4:68
λεγιων, LEGION
Mt　26:53　than twelve **legions** of angels?
Mk　5: 9　"My name is **Legion;** for we are
　　5:15　man who had had the **legion;** and
Lk　8:30　"**Legion**"; for many demons had

3004 ᴳᴼ2353 ᴬᴳ468 ᴸᴺ151 ᴮ3:1081 ᴷ4:69
λεγω, I SAY, SPEAK, TELL

Mt	1:16	who **is called** the Messiah.
	1:20	and **said,** "Joseph, son of David
	1:22	what **had been spoken** by the
	1:22	what had been **spoken** by the
	2: 2	**asking,** "Where is the child who
	2: 5	They **told** him, "In Bethlehem of
	2: 8	sent them to Bethlehem, **saying,**
	2:13	Joseph in a dream and **said,**
	2:13	remain there until I **tell** you
	2:15	**had been spoken** by the Lord
	2:15	**spoken** by the Lord through the
	2:17	fulfilled what **had been spoken**
	2:17	**spoken** through the prophet
	2:19	to Joseph in Egypt and **said**
	2:23	what **had been spoken** through
	2:23	**spoken** through the prophets
		might
	3: 1	of Judea, **proclaiming**
	3: 3	prophet Isaiah **spoke** when he
	3: 3	**said,** "The voice of one crying
	3: 7	he **said** to them, "You brood of
	3: 9	presume to **say** to yourselves,
	3: 9	for I **tell** you, God is able
	3:14	prevented him, **saying,** "I need
	3:15	But Jesus **answered** him, "Let it
	3:17	And a voice from heaven **said,**
	4: 3	The tempter came and **said** to
	4: 3	**command** these stones to
		become
	4: 4	But he **answered,** "It is written
	4: 6	**saying** to him, "If you are the
	4: 9	and he **said** to him, "All these
	4:10	Jesus **said** to him, "Away with
	4:14	so that what **had been spoken**
	4:14	so that what had been **spoken**
	4:17	Jesus began to **proclaim,**
	4:18	Simon, who **is called** Peter, and
	4:19	And he **said** to them, "Follow me
	5: 2	speak, and taught them, **saying:**
	5:11	**utter** all kinds of evil against
	5:18	For truly I **tell** you, until
	5:20	For I **tell** you, unless your
	5:21	have heard that it **was said** to
	5:22	But I **say** to you that if you
	5:22	and if you **insult** a brother or
	5:22	and if you **say,** 'You fool,' you
	5:26	Truly I **tell** you, you will
	5:27	have heard that it **was said,**

	5:28	But I **say** to you that everyone
	5:31	"It **was** also **said,** 'Whoever
	5:32	But I **say** to you that anyone
	5:33	that **it was said** to those of
	5:34	But I **say** to you, Do not swear
	5:38	have heard that it **was said,**
	5:39	But I **say** to you, Do not resist
	5:43	have heard that it **was said,**
	5:44	But I **say** to you, Love your
	6: 2	Truly I **tell** you, they have
	6: 5	Truly I **tell** you, they have
	6:16	Truly I **tell** you, they have
	6:25	"Therefore I **tell** you, do not
	6:29	yet I **tell** you, even Solomon in
	6:31	Therefore do not worry, **saying,**
	7: 4	Or how can you **say** to your
	7:21	"Not everyone who **says** to me,
	7:22	On that day many **will say** to me
	8: 2	**saying,** "Lord, if you choose,
	8: 3	**saying,** "I do choose. Be made
	8: 4	Then Jesus **said** to him, "See
	8: 4	"See that you **say** nothing to
	8: 6	and **saying,** "Lord, my servant
	8: 7	And he **said** to him, "I will
	8: 8	but only **speak** the word, and my
	8: 9	and I **say** to one, 'Go,' and he
	8:10	he was amazed and **said** to those
	8:10	"Truly I **tell** you, in no one in
	8:11	I **tell** you, many will come from
	8:13	And to the centurion Jesus **said**
	8:17	fulfill what **had been spoken**
	8:17	**spoken** through the prophet Isaiah
	8:19	approached and **said,** "Teacher,
	8:20	And Jesus **said** to him, "Foxes
	8:21	Another of his disciples **said**
	8:22	But Jesus **said** to him, "Follow
	8:25	**saying,** "Lord, save us! We are
	8:26	And he **said** to them, "Why are
	8:27	They were amazed, **saying,**
	8:29	Suddenly they **shouted,** "What
	8:31	The demons **begged** him, "If you
	8:32	And he **said** to them, "Go!" So
	9: 2	he **said** to the paralytic, "Take
	9: 3	Then some of the scribes **said**
	9: 4	**said,** "Why do you think evil in
	9: 5	For which is easier, **to say,**
	9: 5	or **to say,** 'Stand up and walk'?
	9: 6	he then **said** to the paralytic
	9: 9	he saw a man **called** Matthew

9: 9	and he **said** to him, "Follow me.	12:32	**speaks** against the Holy Spirit
9:11	they **said** to his disciples,	12:36	I **tell** you, on the day of
9:12	he **said,** "Those who are well	12:38	scribes and Pharisees **said** to
9:14	came to him, **saying,** "Why do we	12:39	But he **answered** them, "An evil
9:15	And Jesus **said** to them, "The	12:44	Then it **says,** 'I will return to
9:18	and knelt before him, **saying,**	12:47	Someone **told** him, "Look, your
9:21	for she **said** to herself, "If I	12:48	who **had told** him this, Jesus
9:22	seeing her he **said,** "Take heart	12:48	Jesus **replied,** "Who is my
9:24	he **said,** "Go away; for the girl	12:49	he **said,** "Here are my mother
9:27	**crying loudly,** "Have mercy on	13: 3	in parables, **saying:** "Listen!
9:28	Jesus **said** to them, "Do you	13:10	disciples came and **asked** him,
9:28	They **said** to him, "Yes, Lord."	13:11	He **answered,** "To you it has
9:29	he touched their eyes and **said,**	13:14	prophecy of Isaiah that **says:**
9:30	Then Jesus sternly **ordered** them	13:17	Truly I **tell** you, many prophets
9:33	the crowds were amazed and **said**	13:24	**put before** them another parable
9:34	But the Pharisees **said,** "By the	13:27	came and **said** to him, 'Master,
9:37	Then he **said** to his disciples,	13:28	The slaves **said** to him, 'Then
10: 2	also **known** as Peter, and his	13:30	I **will tell** the reapers,
10: 5	with the following **instructions**	13:31	He **put before** them another
10: 7	As you go, **proclaim** the good	13:35	to fulfill what **had been spoken**
10:15	Truly I **tell** you, it will be	13:35	**spoken** through the prophet
10:23	truly I **tell** you, you will not	13:36	**saying,** "Explain to us the
10:27	What I **say** to you in the dark,	13:37	He **answered,** "The one who sows
10:27	**tell** in the light; and what you	13:51	all this?" They **answered,** "Yes.
10:42	truly I **tell** you, none of these	13:52	And he **said** to them, "Therefore
11: 3	**said** to him, "Are you the one	13:54	astounded and **said,** "Where did
11: 4	Jesus **answered** them, "Go and	13:55	Is not his mother **called** Mary?
11: 7	Jesus began **to speak** to the	13:57	Jesus **said** to them, "Prophets
11: 9	Yes, I **tell** you, and more than	14: 2	and he **said** to his servants,
11:11	Truly I **tell** you, among those	14: 4	John **had been telling** him, "It
11:16	**calling** to one	14:15	disciples came to him and **said,**
11:18	and they **say,** 'He has a demon';	14:16	Jesus **said** to them, "They need
11:19	and they **say,** 'Look, a glutton	14:17	They **replied,** "We have nothing
11:22	But I **tell** you, on the day of	14:18	And he **said,** "Bring them here
11:24	But I **tell** you that on the day	14:26	**saying,** "It is a ghost!" And
11:25	At that time Jesus **said,** "I	14:27	But immediately Jesus **spoke** to
12: 2	they **said** to him, "Look, your	14:28	Peter **answered** him, "Lord, if
12: 3	He **said** to them, "Have you not	14:29	He **said,** "Come." So Peter got
12: 6	I **tell** you, something greater	14:30	beginning to sink, he **cried out**
12:10	and they **asked** him, "Is it	14:31	**saying** to him, "You of little
12:11	He **said** to them, "Suppose one	14:33	worshiped him, **saying,** "Truly
12:13	Then he **said** to the man,	15: 1	Jesus from Jerusalem and **said,**
12:17	to fulfill what **had been spoken**	15: 3	He **answered** them, "And why do
12:17	**spoken** through the prophet	15: 4	God **said,** 'Honor your father
12:23	crowds were amazed and **said,**	15: 5	But you **say** that whoever tells
12:24	Pharisees heard it, they **said,**	15: 5	whoever **tells** father or mother,
12:25	they were thinking and **said** to	15: 7	rightly about you when he **said:**
12:31	Therefore I **tell** you, people	15:10	and **said** to them, "Listen and
12:32	Whoever **speaks** a word against	15:12	and **said** to him, "Do you know

15:13	He **answered,** "Every plant that
15:15	But Peter **said** to him, "Explain
15:16	Then he **said,** "Are you also
15:22	started **shouting,** "Have mercy
15:23	urged him, **saying,** "Send her
15:24	He **answered,** "I was sent only
15:25	before him, **saying,** "Lord, help
15:26	He **answered,** "It is not fair to
15:27	She **said,** "Yes, Lord, yet even
15:28	Then Jesus **answered** her, "Woman
15:32	and **said,** "I have compassion
15:33	The disciples **said** to him,
15:34	Jesus **asked** them, "How many
15:34	They **said,** "Seven, and a few
16: 2	He **answered** them, "When it is
16: 2	"When it is evening, you **say,**
16: 6	Jesus **said** to them, "Watch out
16: 7	They **said** to one another, "It
16: 8	Jesus **said,** "You of little
16:11	that I **was** not **speaking** about
16:12	that he **had** not **told** them to
16:13	he **asked** his disciples, "Who do
16:13	"Who do people **say** that the Son
16:14	And they **said,** "Some say John
16:15	He **said** to them, "But who do
16:15	But who do you **say** that I am?
16:16	**answered,** "You are the Messiah,
16:17	Jesus **answered** him, "Blessed
16:18	And I **tell** you, you are Peter,
16:20	not **to tell** anyone that he was
16:22	him, **saying,** "God forbid it,
16:23	But he turned and **said** to Peter
16:24	Then Jesus **told** his disciples,
16:28	Truly I **tell** you, there are
17: 4	Then Peter **said** to Jesus, "Lord
17: 5	and from the cloud a voice **said**
17: 7	touched them, **saying,** "Get up
17: 9	mountain, Jesus **ordered** them,
17: 9	**Tell** no one about the vision
17:10	And the disciples **asked** him,
17:10	**say** that Elijah must come first
17:11	He **replied,** "Elijah is indeed
17:12	but I **tell** you that Elijah has
17:13	understood that he **was speaking**
17:15	and **said,** "Lord, have mercy on
17:17	Jesus **answered,** "You faithless
17:19	and **said,** "Why could we not
17:20	He **said** to them, "Because of
17:20	For truly I **tell** you, if you
17:20	you **will say** to this mountain,
17:22	Jesus **said** to them, "The Son of
17:24	and **said,** "Does your teacher
17:25	He **said,** "Yes, he does." And
17:25	Jesus **spoke** of it first, asking
17:26	When Peter **said,** "From others,
18: 1	and **asked,** "Who is the greatest
18: 3	and **said,** "Truly I tell you,
18: 3	"Truly I **tell** you, unless you
18:10	I **tell** you, in heaven their
18:13	truly I **tell** you, he rejoices
18:17	listen to them, **tell** it to the
18:18	Truly I **tell** you, whatever you
18:19	Again, truly I **tell** you, if two
18:21	Then Peter came and **said** to him
18:22	Jesus **said** to him, "Not seven
18:22	but, I **tell** you, seventy-seven
18:26	**saying,** 'Have patience with me,
18:28	he **said,** 'Pay what you owe.'
18:29	and **pleaded** with him, 'Have
18:32	**said** to him, 'You wicked slave!
19: 3	**asked,** "Is it lawful for a man
19: 4	He **answered,** "Have you not read
19: 5	**said,** 'For this reason a man
19: 7	They **said** to him, "Why then
19: 8	He **said** to them, "It was
19: 9	And I **say** to you, whoever
19:10	His disciples **said** to him, "If
19:11	But he **said** to them, "Not
19:14	Jesus **said,** "Let the little
19:16	**said,** "Teacher, what good deed
19:17	And he **said** to him, "Why do you
19:18	He **said** to him, "Which ones?"
19:18	Jesus **said,** "You shall not
19:20	man **said** to him, "I have kept
19:23	Jesus **said** to his disciples,
19:23	"Truly I **tell** you, it will be
19:24	Again I **tell** you, it is easier
19:25	astounded and **said,** "Then who
19:26	Jesus looked at them and **said,**
19:27	Then Peter **said** in reply,
19:28	Jesus **said** to them, "Truly I
19:28	I **tell** you, at the renewal of
20: 4	and he **said** to them, 'You also
20: 6	he **said** to them, 'Why are you
20: 7	They **said** to him, 'Because no
20: 7	He **said** to them, 'You also go
20: 8	owner of the vineyard **said** to
20:12	**saying,** 'These last worked only

20:13	But he **replied** to one of them,
20:17	and **said** to them on the way,
20:21	And he **said** to her, "What do
20:21	She **said** to him, "Declare that
20:21	**Declare** that these two sons of
20:22	But Jesus **answered,** "You do not
20:22	They **said** to him, "We are able.
20:23	He **said** to them, "You will
20:25	**said,** "You know that the rulers
20:30	they **shouted,** "Lord, have mercy
20:31	they **shouted** even more loudly,
20:32	**saying,** "What do you want me to
20:33	They **said** to him, "Lord, let
21: 2	**saying** to them, "Go into the
21: 3	If anyone **says** anything to you,
21: 3	just **say** this, 'The Lord needs
21: 4	what **had been spoken** through
21: 4	through the prophet, **saying,**
21: 5	**Tell** the daughter of Zion,
21: 9	**shouting,** "Hosanna to the Son
21:10	turmoil, **asking,** "Who is this?"
21:11	The crowds **were saying,** "This
21:13	He **said** to them, "It is written
21:15	the children **crying** out in the
21:16	and **said** to him, "Do you hear
21:16	you hear what these are **saying**
21:16	Jesus **said** to them, "Yes; have
21:19	he **said** to it, "May no fruit
21:20	they were amazed, **saying,** "How
21:21	Jesus **answered** them, "Truly I
21:21	"Truly I **tell** you, if you have
21:21	if you **say** to this mountain,
21:23	**said,** "By what authority are
21:24	Jesus **said** to them, "I will
21:24	if you **tell** me the answer, then
21:24	then I **will** also **tell** you by
21:25	they **argued** with one another,
21:25	"If we **say,** 'From heaven,' he
21:25	he **will say** to us, 'Why then
21:26	But if we **say,** 'Of human origin
21:27	So they **answered** Jesus, "We do
21:27	Neither **will I tell** you by what
21:28	**said,** 'Son, go and work in the
21:29	He **answered,** 'I will not'; but
21:30	**said** the same; and he answered,
21:30	he **answered,** 'I go, sir'; but
21:31	They **said,** "The first." Jesus
21:31	Jesus **said** to them, "Truly I
21:31	"Truly I **tell** you, the tax
21:37	**saying,** 'They will respect my
21:38	they **said** to themselves, 'This
21:41	They **said** to him, "He will put
21:42	Jesus **said** to them, "Have you
21:43	I **tell** you, the kingdom of God
21:45	that he **was speaking** about them
22: 1	Jesus **spoke** to them in parables
22: 1	to them in parables, **saying:**
22: 4	**saying,** 'Tell those who have
22: 4	**Tell** those who have been
22: 8	Then he **said** to his slaves,
22:12	and he **said** to him, 'Friend,
22:13	king **said** to the attendants,
22:16	**saying,** "Teacher, we know that
22:17	**Tell** us, then, what you think.
22:18	**said,** "Why are you putting me
22:20	**said** to them, "Whose head is
22:21	They **answered,** "The emperor's."
22:21	**said** to them, "Give therefore
22:23	**saying** there is no resurrection
22:23	asked him a question, **saying**
22:24	"Teacher, Moses **said,** 'If a man
22:29	Jesus **answered** them, "You are
22:31	what **was said** to you by God,
22:31	what was **said** to you by God,
22:42	**What** do you think of the
22:42	They **said** to him, "The son of
22:43	He **said** to them, "How is it
22:43	Spirit calls him Lord, **saying,**
22:44	The Lord **said** to my Lord,
23: 1	Jesus **said** to the crowds
23: 3	do whatever they **teach** you and
23: 3	not practice what they **teach.**
23:16	guides, who **say,** 'Whoever
23:30	and you **say,** 'If we had lived
23:36	Truly I **tell** you, all this will
23:39	I **tell** you, you will not see me
23:39	you **say,** 'Blessed is the one
24: 2	Then he **asked** them, "You see
24: 2	Truly I **tell** you, not one stone
24: 3	**saying,** "Tell us, when will
24: 3	**Tell** us, when will this be,
24: 4	Jesus **answered** them, "Beware
24: 5	**saying,** 'I am the Messiah!'
24:15	as **was spoken** of by the prophet
24:23	Then if anyone **says** to you,
24:26	So, if they **say** to you, 'Look!
24:34	I **tell** you, this generation
24:47	Truly I **tell** you, he will put

24:48	if that wicked slave **says** to
25: 8	The foolish **said** to the wise,
25: 9	But the wise **replied**, 'No!
25:11	**saying**, 'Lord, lord, open to us
25:12	he **replied**, 'Truly I tell you,
25:12	I **tell** you, I do not know you.'
25:20	**saying**, 'Master, you handed
25:22	**saying**, 'Master, you handed
25:24	**saying**, 'Master, I knew that
25:26	master **replied**, 'You wicked
25:34	Then the king **will say** to those
25:37	Then the righteous **will answer**
25:40	And the king **will answer** them,
25:40	Truly I **tell** you, just as you
25:41	Then he **will say** to those at
25:44	they also **will answer**, 'Lord,
25:45	Then he **will answer** them,
25:45	Truly I **tell** you, just as you
26: 1	he **said** to his disciples,
26: 3	priest, who **was called** Caiaphas
26: 5	But they **said**, "Not during the
26: 8	angry and **said**, "Why this waste
26:10	**said** to them, "Why do you
26:13	Truly I **tell** you, wherever
26.14	twelve, who **was called** Judas
26:15	**said**, "What will you give me if
26:17	**saying**, "Where do you want us
26:18	He **said**, "Go into the city to
26:18	**say** to him, 'The Teacher says,
26:18	The Teacher **says**, My time is
26:21	he **said**, "Truly I tell you, one
26:21	"Truly I **tell** you, one of you
26:22	distressed and began **to say** to
26:23	He **answered**, "The one who has
26:25	Judas, who betrayed him, **said**,
26:25	He **replied**, "You have said so."
26:25	replied, "You **have said** so."
26:26	**said**, "Take, eat; this is my
26:27	**saying**, "Drink from it, all of
26:29	I **tell** you, I will never again
26:31	Then Jesus **said** to them, "You
26:33	Peter **said** to him, "Though all
26:34	Jesus **said** to him, "Truly
26:35	Peter **said** to him, "Even though
26:35	And so **said** all the disciples.
26:36	to a place **called** Gethsemane;
26:36	he **said** to his disciples, "Sit
26:38	he **said** to them, "I am deeply
26:39	**prayed**, "My Father, if it is

26:40	he **said** to Peter, "So, could
26:42	and **prayed**, "My Father, if this
26:44	time, **saying** the same words.
26:45	**said** to them, "Are you still
26:48	**saying**, "The one I will kiss
26:49	**said**, "Greetings, Rabbi!" and
26:50	Jesus **said** to him, "Friend, do
26:52	Jesus **said** to him, "Put your
26:55	Jesus **said** to the crowds, "Have
26:61	and **said**, "This fellow said
26:62	**said**, "Have you no answer?
26:63	**said** to him, "I put you under
26:63	**tell** us if you are the Messiah,
26:64	Jesus **said** to him, "You have
26:64	"You **have said** so. But I tell
26:64	But I **tell** you, From now on you
26:65	**said**, "He has blasphemed! Why
26:66	**answered**, "He deserves death."
26:68	**saying**, "Prophesy to us, you
26:69	**said**, "You also were with Jesus
26:70	**saying**, "I do not know what you
26:70	know what you are **talking** about
26:71	**said** to the bystanders, "This
26:73	**said** to Peter, "Certainly you
26:75	**had said**: "Before the cock
27: 4	He **said**, "I have sinned by
27: 4	They **said**, "What is that to us?
27: 6	**said**, "It is not lawful to put
27: 9	fulfilled what **had been spoken**
27: 9	**spoken** through the prophet
27:11	**asked** him, "Are you the King of
27:11	Jesus said, "You **say** so."
27:13	Pilate **said** to him, "Do you not
27:16	prisoner, **called** Jesus Barabbas
27:17	Pilate **said** to them, "Whom do
27:17	Jesus who **is called** the Messiah
27:19	wife sent **word** to him, "Have
27:21	again **said** to them, "Which
27:21	And they **said**, "Barabbas."
27:22	Pilate **said** to them, "Then what
27:22	Jesus who **is called** the Messiah
27:22	All of them **said**, "Let him be
27:23	But they **shouted** all the more,
27:24	**saying**, "I am innocent of this
27:25	the people as a whole **answered**,
27:29	**saying**, "Hail, King of the Jews
27:33	a place **called** Golgotha (which
27:33	(which **means** Place of a Skull),
27:40	**saying**, "You who would destroy

27:41	were mocking him, **saying,**
27:43	for he **said,** 'I am God's Son.'
27:46	Jesus **cried** with a loud voice,
27:47	they **said,** "This man is calling
27:49	But the others **said,** "Wait, let
27:54	**said,** "Truly this man was
27:63	**said,** "Sir, we remember what
27:63	**said** while he was still alive,
27:64	**tell** the people, 'He has been
28: 5	the angel **said** to the women,
28: 6	as he **said.** Come, see the place
28: 7	Then go quickly and **tell** his
28: 7	This is my **message** for you.
28: 9	met them and **said,** "Greetings!"
28:10	Then Jesus **said** to them, "Do
28:13	**telling** them, "You must say,
28:13	must **say,** 'His disciples came
28:18	And Jesus came and **said** to them

Mk	1: 7	He **proclaimed,** "The one who is
	1:15	**saying,** "The time is fulfilled,
	1:17	And Jesus **said** to them, "Follow
	1:24	he **cried** out, "What have you to
	1:25	But Jesus rebuked him, **saying,**
	1:27	kept on **asking** one another,
	1:30	they **told** him about her at once
	1:37	they **said** to him, "Everyone is
	1:38	He **answered,** "Let us go on to
	1:40	kneeling he **said** to him, "If
	1:41	and **said** to him, "I do choose.
	1:44	**saying** to him, "See that you
	1:44	you **say** nothing to anyone; but
	2: 5	he **said** to the paralytic, "Son,
	2: 8	he **said** to them, "Why do you
	2: 9	Which is easier, to **say** to the
	2: 9	or to **say,** 'Stand up and take
	2:10	he **said** to the paralytic—
	2:11	"I **say** to you, stand up, take
	2:12	glorified God, **saying,** "We have
	2:14	he **said** to him, "Follow me."
	2:16	they **said** to his disciples,
	2:17	he **said** to them, "Those who are
	2:18	**said** to him, "Why do John's
	2:19	**said** to them, "The wedding
	2:24	The Pharisees **said** to him,
	2:25	And he **said** to them, "Have you
	2:27	he **said** to them, "The sabbath
	3: 3	And he **said** to the man who had
	3: 4	Then he **said** to them, "Is it
	3: 5	**said** to the man, "Stretch out

3: 9	He **told** his disciples to have a
3:11	**shouted,** "You are the Son of
3:21	**were saying,** "He has gone out
3:22	**said,** "He has Beelzebul, and
3:23	**spoke** to them in parables, "How
3:28	"Truly I **tell** you, people will
3:30	for they had **said,** "He has an
3:32	they **said** to him, "Your mother
3:33	he **replied,** "Who are my mother
3:34	he **said,** "Here are my mother
4: 2	in his teaching he **said** to them
4: 9	he **said,** "Let anyone with ears
4:11	he **said** to them, "To you has
4:13	And he **said** to them, "Do you
4:21	He **said** to them, "Is a lamp
4:24	And he **said** to them, "Pay
4:26	He also **said,** "The kingdom of
4:30	He also **said,** "With what can we
4:35	he **said** to them, "Let us go
4:38	**said** to him, "Teacher, do you
4:39	**said** to the sea, "Peace! Be
4:40	He **said** to them, "Why are you
4:41	**said** to one another, "Who then
5: 7	he **shouted** at the top of his
5: 8	he **had said** to him, "Come out
5: 9	He **replied,** "My name is Legion;
5:12	unclean spirits **begged** him,
5:19	**said** to him, "Go home to your
5:23	and **begged** him repeatedly, "My
5:28	for she **said,** "If I but touch
5:30	**said,** "Who touched my clothes?"
5:31	**said** to him, "You see the crowd
5:31	how can you **say,** 'Who touched
5:33	and **told** him the whole truth.
5:34	He **said** to her, "Daughter, your
5:35	to **say,** "Your daughter is dead.
5:36	But overhearing what they **said**
5:39	he **said** to them, "Why do you
5:41	**said** to her, "Talitha cum,"
5:41	which **means,** "Little girl, get
5:43	**told** them to give her something
6: 2	They **said,** "Where did this man
6: 4	Jesus **said** to them, "Prophets
6:10	He **said** to them, "Wherever you
6:14	**were saying,** "John the baptizer
6:15	But others **said,** "It is Elijah
6:15	others **said,** "It is a prophet,
6:16	he **said,** "John, whom I beheaded
6:18	For John **had been telling** Herod

6:22	king **said** to the girl, "Ask me
6:24	**said** to her mother, "What
6:24	She **replied,** "The head of John
6:25	and **requested,** "I want you to
6:31	He **said** to them, "Come away to
6:35	**said,** "This is a deserted place
6:37	But he **answered** them, "You give
6:37	They **said** to him, "Are we to go
6:38	And he **said** to them, "How many
6:38	they **said,** "Five, and two fish.
6:50	**said,** "Take heart, it is I; do
7: 6	He **said** to them, "Isaiah
7: 9	Then he **said** to them, "You have
7:10	For Moses **said,** 'Honor your
7:11	But you **say** that if anyone
7:11	anyone **tells** father or mother,
7:14	**said** to them, "Listen to me,
7:18	He **said** to them, "Then do you
7:20	he **said,** "It is what comes out
7:27	**said** to her, "Let the children
7:28	she **answered** him, "Sir, even
7:29	**said** to her, "For saying that,
7:34	**said** to him, "Ephphatha," that
7:36	ordered them to **tell** no one;
7:37	**saying**, "He has done everything
8: 1	disciples and **said** to them,
8: 5	you have?" They **said,** "Seven."
8: 7	he **ordered** that these too
8:12	and **said,** "Why does this
8:12	Truly I **tell** you, no sign will
8:15	**saying,** "Watch out—beware of
8:17	Jesus **said** to them, "Why are
8:19	They **said** to him, "Twelve."
8:20	And they **said** to him, "Seven."
8:21	he **said** to them, "Do you not
8:24	looked up and **said,** "I can see
8:26	**saying,** "Do not even go into
8:27	he **asked** his disciples, "Who do
8:27	Who do people **say** that I am?
8:28	they **answered** him, "John the
8:28	And they **answered** him, "John
8:29	But who do you **say** that I am?
8:29	Peter **answered** him, "You are
8:30	not to **tell** anyone about him.
8:33	he rebuked Peter and **said,** "Get
8:34	**said** to them, "If any want to
9: 1	he **said** to them, "Truly I tell
9: 1	"Truly I **tell** you, there are
9: 5	Peter **said** to Jesus, "Rabbi, it

9:11	Then they **asked** him, "Why do
9:11	scribes **say** that Elijah must
9:13	But I **tell** you that Elijah has
9:18	I **asked** your disciples to cast
9:19	**answered** them, "You faithless
9:21	And he **said,** "From childhood.
9:23	**said** to him, "If you are able!
9:24	father of the child **cried** out,
9:25	unclean spirit, **saying** to it,
9:26	most of them **said,** "He is dead.
9:29	He **said** to them, "This kind can
9:31	**saying** to them, "The Son of Man
9:35	**said** to them, "Whoever wants to
9:36	it in his arms, he **said** to them
9:39	Jesus **said,** "Do not stop him;
9:41	For truly I **tell** you, whoever
10: 3	He **answered** them, "What did
10: 4	They **said,** "Moses allowed a man
10: 5	But Jesus **said** to them,
10:11	He **said** to them, "Whoever
10:14	**said** to them, "Let the little
10:15	Truly I **tell** you, whoever does
10:18	Jesus **said** to him, "Why do you
10:18	you **call** me good? No one is
10:21	loved him and **said,** "You lack
10:23	**said** to his disciples, "How
10:24	But Jesus **said** to them again,
10:26	**said** to one another, "Then who
10:27	**said,** "For mortals it is
10:28	Peter began **to say** to him,
10:29	I **tell** you, there is no one who
10:32	and began to **tell** them what was
10:35	**said** to him, "Teacher, we want
10:36	**said** to them, "What is it you
10:37	**said** to him, "Grant us to sit,
10:38	**said** to them, "You do not
10:39	They **replied,** "We are able."
10:39	Jesus **said** to them, "The cup
10:42	**said** to them, "You know that
10:47	and **say,** "Jesus, Son of David,
10:49	**said,** "Call him here." And
10:49	**saying** to him, "Take heart; get
10:51	Then Jesus **said** to him, "What
10:51	The blind man **said** to him, "My
10:52	Jesus **said** to him, "Go; your
11: 2	and **said** to them, "Go into the
11: 3	If anyone **says** to you, 'Why are
11: 3	just **say** this, 'The Lord needs
11: 5	some of the bystanders **said** to

11: 6	They **told** them what Jesus had
11: 6	had **said;** and they allowed them
11:14	He **said** to it, "May no one
11:17	and **saying,** "Is it not written,
11:21	**said** to him, "Rabbi, look! The
11:22	**answered** them, "Have faith in
11:23	**tell** you, if you say to this
11:23	if you **say** to this mountain,
11:24	So I **tell** you, whatever you
11:28	and **said,** "By what authority
11:29	Jesus **said** to them, "I will ask
11:29	**will tell** you by what authority
11:31	They **argued** with one another,
11:31	"If we **say,** 'From heaven,' he
11:31	he **will say,** 'Why then did you
11:32	**shall** we **say,** 'Of human origin'
11:33	**answered** Jesus, "We do not know
11:33	**said** to them, "Neither will I
11:33	"Neither will I **tell** you by
12: 6	he sent him to them, **saying,**
12: 7	But those tenants **said** to one
12:12	**had told** this parable against
12:14	And they came and **said** to him,
12:15	he **said** to them, "Why are you
12:16	**said** to them, "Whose head is
12:16	They **answered,** "The emperor's."
12:17	Jesus **said** to them, "Give to
12:18	**say** there is no resurrection,
12:18	asked him a question, **saying,**
12:26	how God **said** to him, 'I am the
12:26	**said** to him, 'I am the God of
12:32	the scribe **said** to him, "You
12:32	truly **said** that 'he is one, and
12:34	he **said** to him, "You are not
12:35	he **said,** "How can the scribes
12:35	scribes **say** that the Messiah is
12:36	by the Holy Spirit, **declared,**
12:36	The Lord **said** to my Lord, "Sit
12:37	David himself **calls** him Lord;
12:38	As he taught, he **said,** "Beware
12:43	his disciples and **said** to them,
12:43	I **tell** you, this poor widow
13: 1	**said** to him, "Look, Teacher,
13: 2	Then Jesus **asked** him, "Do you
13: 4	**Tell** us, when will this be,
13: 5	Jesus began **to say** to them,
13: 6	will come in my name and **say,**
13:21	if anyone **says** to you at that
13:30	I **tell** you, this generation
13:37	And what I **say** to you I say to
13:37	And what I say to you I **say** to
14: 2	**said,** "Not during the festival,
14: 6	But Jesus **said,** "Let her alone;
14: 9	Truly I **tell** you, wherever the
14:12	**said** to him, "Where do you want
14:13	**saying** to them, "Go into the
14:14	**say** to the owner of the house,
14:14	The Teacher **asks,** Where is my
14:16	as he **had told** them; and they
14:18	Jesus **said,** "Truly I tell you,
14:18	I **tell** you, one of you will
14:19	distressed and **to say** to him
14:20	He **said** to them, "It is one of
14:22	**said,** "Take; this is my body."
14:24	He **said** to them, "This is my
14:25	Truly I **tell** you, I will never
14:27	And Jesus **said** to them, "You
14:30	Jesus **said** to him, "Truly I
14:30	I **tell** you, this day, this
14:31	But he **said** vehemently, "Even
14:32	he **said** to his disciples, "Sit
14:34	And he **said** to them, "I am
14:36	He **said,** "Abba, Father, for you
14:37	he **said** to Peter, "Simon, are
14:39	prayed, **saying** the same words.
14:41	third time and **said** to them,
14:44	**saying,** "The one I will kiss is
14:45	**said,** "Rabbi!" and kissed him.
14:48	**said** to them, "Have you come
14:57	testimony against him, **saying,**
14:58	him **say,** 'I will destroy this
14:60	**asked** Jesus, "Have you no
14:61	**asked** him, "Are you the Messiah
14:62	Jesus **said,** "I am; and 'you
14:63	tore his clothes and **said,**
14:65	and to strike him, **saying** to
14:67	**said,** "You also were with Jesus
14:68	he denied it, **saying,** "I do not
14:68	what you are **talking** about.
14:69	again **to say** to the bystanders,
14:70	again **said** to Peter, "Certainly
14:71	this man you are **talking** about.
14:72	Jesus **had said** to him, "Before
15: 2	He **answered** him, "You say so."
15: 2	He answered him, "You **say** so."
15: 4	Pilate **asked** him again, "Have
15: 7	Now a man **called** Barabbas was
15: 9	Then he **answered** them, "Do you

15:12	Pilate **spoke** to them again,	4: 6	And the devil **said** to him, "To
15:12	you **call** the King of the Jews?	4: 8	**answered** him, "It is written,
15:14	Pilate **asked** them, "Why,	4: 9	**saying** to him, "If you are the
15:29	**saying,** "Aha! You who would	4:12	Jesus **answered** him, "It is said
15:31	and **saying,** "He saved others;	4:12	"It **is said,** 'Do not put the
15:35	**said,** "Listen, he is calling	4:21	Then he began to **say** to them,
15:36	**saying,** "Wait, let us see	4:22	**said,** "Is not this Joseph's son
15:39	**said,** "Truly this man was God's	4:23	He **said** to them, "Doubtless you
16: 3	**saying** to one another, "Who	4:23	you **will say,** 'Do here also in
16: 6	But he **said** to them, "Do not be	4:24	And he **said,** "Truly I tell you,
16: 7	But go, **tell** his disciples and	4:24	I **tell** you, no prophet is
16: 7	see him, just as he **told** you.	4:25	But the truth **is,** there were
16: 8	they **said** nothing to anyone, for	4:35	But Jesus rebuked him, **saying,**
16:15	And he **said** to them, "Go into	4:36	kept **saying** to one another,
Lk 1:13	But the angel **said** to him,	4:41	**shouting,** "You are the Son of
1:18	Zechariah **said** to the angel,	4:43	But he **said** to them, "I must
1:19	angel **replied,** "I am Gabriel.	5: 4	he **said** to Simon, "Put out into
1:24	in seclusion. She **said,**	5: 5	Simon **answered,** "Master, we
1:28	**said,** "Greetings, favored one!	5: 8	**saying,** "Go away from me,
1:30	**said** to her, "Do not be afraid,	5:10	Jesus **said** to Simon, "Do not
1:34	Mary **said** to the angel, "How	5:12	and **begged** him, "Lord, if you
1:35	**said** to her, "The Holy Spirit	5:13	**said,** "I do choose. Be made
1:38	Then Mary **said,** "Here am I, the	5:14	he ordered him to **tell** no one.
1:42	and **exclaimed** with a loud cry,	5:20	he saw their faith, he **said,**
1·46	Mary **said,** "My soul magnifies	5:21	began to **question,** "Who is
1:60	mother **said,** "No; he is to be	5:22	he **answered** them, "Why do you
1:61	They **said** to her, "None of your	5:23	easier, to **say,** 'Your sins are
1:63	and **wrote,** "His name is John."	5:23	or to **say,** 'Stand up and walk'?
1:66	them pondered them and **said,**	5:24	he **said** to the one who was
1:67	the Holy Spirit and **spoke** this	5:24	"I **say** to you, stand up and
2:10	angel **said** to them, "Do not be	5:26	**saying,** "We have seen strange
2:13	host, praising God and **saying,**	5:27	and he **said** to him, "Follow me.
2:24	what **is stated** in the law of	5:30	**saying,** "Why do you eat and
2:28	arms and praised God, **saying,**	5:31	Jesus **answered,** "Those who are
2:34	Simeon blessed them and **said**	5:33	Then they **said** to him, "John's
2:48	his mother **said** to him, "Child,	5:34	Jesus **said** to them, "You
2:49	He **said** to them, "Why were you	5:36	He also **told** them a parable:
3: 7	John **said** to the crowds that	5:39	new wine, but **says,** 'The old
3: 8	not begin to **say** to yourselves,	6: 2	**said,** "Why are you doing what
3: 8	I **tell** you, God is able from	6: 3	Jesus **answered,** "Have you not
3:10	crowds **asked** him, "What then	6: 5	**said** to them, "The Son of Man
3:11	**said** to them, "Whoever has two	6: 8	**said** to the man who had the
3:12	**asked** him, "Teacher, what	6: 9	Jesus **said** to them, "I ask you,
3:13	He **said** to them, "Collect no	6:10	**said** to him, "Stretch out your
3:14	Soldiers also **asked** him, "And	6:20	disciples and **said:** "Blessed
3:14	He **said** to them, "Do not	6:26	"Woe to you when all **speak** well
3:16	by **saying,** "I baptize you with	6:27	"But I **say** to you that listen,
4: 3	The devil **said** to him, "If you	6:39	He also **told** them a parable:
4: 3	Son of God, **command** this stone	6:42	Or how can you **say** to your

6:46	and do not do what I **tell** you?
7: 4	**saying,** "He is worthy of having
7: 6	sent friends to **say** to him,
7: 7	But only **speak** the word, and
7: 8	I **say** to one, 'Go,' and he
7: 9	he **said,** "I tell you, not even
7: 9	"I **tell** you, not even in Israel
7:13	and **said** to her, "Do not weep."
7:14	And he **said,** "Young man, I say
7:14	"Young man, I **say** to you, rise!
7:16	they glorified God, **saying,**
7:19	**ask,** "Are you the one who is to
7:20	**said,** "John the Baptist has
7:20	to **ask,** 'Are you the one who is
7:22	And he **answered** them, "Go and
7:24	**speak** to the crowds about John:
7:26	Yes, I **tell** you, and more than
7:28	I **tell** you, among those born of
7:32	**calling** to one another, 'We
7:33	you **say,** 'He has a demon';
7:34	you **say,** 'Look, a glutton and
7:39	he **said** to himself, "If this
7:39	he **said** to himself, "If this
7:40	Jesus spoke up and **said** to him,
7:40	I have something to **say** to you.
7:40	"Teacher," he **replied,** "Speak."
7:43	Simon **answered,** "I suppose the
7:43	Jesus **said** to him, "You have
7:47	Therefore, I **tell** you, her sins
7:48	Then he **said** to her, "Your sins
7:49	**say** among themselves, "Who is
7:50	**said** to the woman, "Your faith
8: 4	he **said** in a parable:
8: 8	As he **said** this, he called out,
8:10	He **said,** "To you it has been
8:21	But he **said** to them, "My mother
8:22	he **said** to them, "Let us go
8:24	woke him up, **shouting,** "Master,
8:25	He **said** to them, "Where is your
8:25	and **said** to one another, "Who
8:28	**shouted** at the top of his voice
8:30	**said,** "Legion"; for many demons
8:38	but Jesus sent him away, **saying**
8:45	Jesus **asked,** "Who touched me?"
8:45	Peter **said,** "Master, the crowds
8:46	Jesus **said,** "Someone touched me
8:48	**said** to her, "Daughter, your
8:49	leader's house to **say,** "Your
8:52	but he **said,** "Do not weep; for
8:54	and **called** out, "Child, get up!
8:56	he ordered them to **tell** no one
9: 3	He **said** to them, "Take nothing
9: 7	it **was said** by some that John
9: 9	Herod **said,** "John I beheaded;
9:12	**said,** "Send the crowd away, so
9:13	But he **said** to them, "You give
9:13	They **said,** "We have no more
9:14	he **said** to his disciples, "Make
9:18	**asked** them, "Who do the crowds
9:18	the crowds **say** that I am?
9:19	**answered,** "John the Baptist;
9:20	He **said** to them, "But who do
9:20	you **say** that I am?" Peter
9:20	**answered,** "The Messiah of God."
9:21	them not to **tell** anyone,
9:22	**saying,** "The Son of Man must
9:23	Then he **said** to them all, "If
9:27	But truly I **tell** you, there are
9:31	**were speaking** of his departure,
9:33	Peter **said** to Jesus, "Master,
9:33	not knowing what he **said.**
9:34	While he **was saying** this,
9:35	voice that **said,** "This is my
9:38	**shouted,** "Teacher, I beg you to
9:41	Jesus **answered,** "You faithless
9:43	doing, he **said** to his disciples
9:48	**said** to them, "Whoever welcomes
9:49	John **answered,** "Master, we saw
9:50	But Jesus **said** to him, "Do not
9:54	**said,** "Lord, do you want us to
9:54	want us to **command** fire to
9:57	**said** to him, "I will follow you
9:58	And Jesus **said** to him, "Foxes
9:59	To another he **said,** "Follow me.
9:59	he **said,** "Lord, first let me go
9:60	Jesus **said** to him, "Let the
9:61	Another **said,** "I will follow
9:62	Jesus **said** to him, "No one who
10: 2	He **said** to them, "The harvest
10: 5	first **say,** 'Peace to this house
10: 9	and **say** to them, 'The kingdom
10:10	go out into its streets and **say**
10:12	I **tell** you, on that day it will
10:17	returned with joy, **saying,**
10:18	**said** to them, "I watched Satan
10:21	Holy Spirit and **said,** "I thank
10:23	Jesus **said** to them privately,
10:24	For I **tell** you that many

10:25	he **said**, "what must I do to
10:26	**said** to him, "What is written
10:27	He **answered**, "You shall love
10:28	And he **said** to him, "You have
10:29	he **asked** Jesus, "And who is my
10:30	Jesus **replied**, "A man was going
10:35	**said**, 'Take care of him; and
10:37	He **said**, "The one who showed
10:37	Jesus **said** to him, "Go and do
10:40	came to him and **asked**, "Lord,
10:40	**Tell** her then to help me.
10:41	the Lord **answered** her, "Martha,
11: 1	**said** to him, "Lord, teach us to
11: 2	He **said** to them, "When you pray
11: 2	**say**: Father, hallowed be your
11: 5	And he **said** to them, "Suppose
11: 5	**say** to him, 'Friend, lend me
11: 7	And he **answers** from within, 'Do
11: 8	I **tell** you, even though he will
11: 9	"So I **say** to you, Ask, and it
11:15	some of them **said**, "He casts
11:17	**said** to them, "Every kingdom
11:18	you **say** that I cast out the
11:24	it **says**, 'I will return to my
11:27	he **was saying** this, a woman in
11:27	**said** to him, "Blessed is the
11:28	But he **said**, "Blessed rather
11:29	began to **say**, "This generation
11:39	Then the Lord **said** to him, "Now
11:45	One of the lawyers **answered** him
11:45	"Teacher, when you **say** these
11:46	**said**, "Woe also to you lawyers!
11:49	Wisdom of God **said**, 'I will
11:51	Yes, I **tell** you, it will be
12: 1	began **to speak** first to his
12: 3	you **have said** in the dark will
12: 4	"I **tell** you, my friends, do not
12: 5	Yes, I **tell** you, fear him!
12: 8	"And I **tell** you, everyone who
12:10	And everyone who **speaks** a word
12:11	or what you are **to say**;
12:12	very hour what you ought **to say**
12:13	**said** to him, "Teacher, tell my
12:13	"Teacher, **tell** my brother to
12:14	But he **said** to him, "Friend,
12:15	And he **said** to them, "Take care
12:16	Then he **told** them a parable
12:16	**told** them a parable: "The land
12:17	he **thought** to himself, 'What
12:18	Then he **said**, 'I will do this:
12:19	And I **will say** to my soul,
12:20	But God **said** to him, 'You fool!
12:22	He **said** to his disciples,
12:22	"Therefore I **tell** you, do not
12:27	yet I **tell** you, even Solomon in
12:37	I **tell** you, he will fasten his
12:41	Peter **said**, "Lord, are you
12:41·	**telling** this parable for us or
12:42	And the Lord **said**, "Who then
12:44	Truly I **tell** you, he will put
12:45	if that slave **says** to himself,
12:51	No, I **tell** you, but rather
12:54	He also **said** to the crowds,
12:54	you immediately **say**, 'It is
12:55	**say**, 'There will be scorching
12:59	I **tell** you, you will never get
13: 2	He **asked** them, "Do you think
13: 3	**tell** you; but unless you repent
13: 5	No, I **tell** you; but unless you
13: 6	**told** this parable: "A man had a
13: 7	So he **said** to the gardener,
13: 8	He **replied**, 'Sir, let it alone
13:12	**said**, "Woman, you are set free
13:14	kept **saying** to the crowd,
13:15	and **said**, "You hypocrites! Does
13:17	When he **said** this, all his
13:18	He **said** therefore, "What is the
13:20	And again he **said**, "To what
13:23	Someone **asked** him, "Lord, will
13:23	a few be saved?" He **said** to
13:24	I **tell** you, will try to enter
13:25	**saying**, 'Lord, open to us,'
13:25	reply he **will say** to you, 'I do
13:26	Then you will begin to **say**, 'We
13:27	But he **will say**, 'I do not know
13:27	**say**, 'I do not know where you
13:31	**said** to him, "Get away from
13:32	He **said** to them, "Go and tell
13:32	**tell** that fox for me, 'Listen,
13:35	I **tell** you, you will not see me
13:35	you **say**, 'Blessed is the one
14: 3	And Jesus **asked** the lawyers and
14: 3	**asked** the lawyers and Pharisees
14: 5	**said** to them, "If one of you
14: 7	he **told** them a parable.
14: 7	he **told** them a parable.
14: 9	**say** to you, 'Give this person
14:10	he **may say** to you, 'Friend,

14:12	He **said** also to the one who had
14:15	**said** to him, "Blessed is anyone
14:16	Jesus **said** to him, "Someone
14:17	sent his slave **to say** to those
14:18	The first **said** to him, 'I have
14:19	**said,** 'I have bought five yoke
14:20	**said,** 'I have just been married
14:21	**said** to his slave, 'Go out at
14:22	And the slave **said,** 'Sir, what
14:23	the master **said** to the slave,
14:24	For I **tell** you, none of those
14:25	and he turned and **said** to them,
14:30	**saying,** 'This fellow began to
15: 2	**saying,** "This fellow welcomes
15: 3	So he **told** them this parable:
15: 3	So he **told** them this parable:
15: 6	**saying** to them, 'Rejoice with
15: 7	**tell** you, there will be more
15: 9	**saying,** 'Rejoice with me, for I
15:10	I **tell** you, there is joy in the
15:11	**said,** "There was a man who had
15:12	**said** to his father, 'Father,
15:18	I **will say** to him, "Father, I
15:21	Then the son **said** to him,
15:22	But the father **said** to his
15:27	He **replied,** 'Your brother has
15:29	But he **answered** his father,
16: 1	Jesus **said** to the disciples,
16: 2	summoned him and **said** to him,
16: 3	the manager **said** to himself,
16: 5	**asked** the first, 'How much do
16: 6	He **answered,** 'A hundred jugs
16: 6	**said** to him, 'Take your bill,
16: 7	**asked** another, 'And how much do
16: 7	**replied,** 'A hundred containers
16: 7	He **said** to him, 'Take your bill
16: 9	And I **tell** you, make friends
16:15	So he **said** to them, "You are
16:24	He **called** out, 'Father Abraham,
16:25	But Abraham **said,** 'Child,
16:27	He **said,** 'Then, father, I beg
16:29	Abraham **replied,** 'They have
16:30	He **said,** 'No, father Abraham;
16:31	He **said** to him, 'If they do not
17: 1	Jesus **said** to his disciples,
17: 4	**says,** 'I repent,' you must
17: 5	The apostles **said** to the Lord,
17: 6	The Lord **replied,** "If you had
17: 6	you **could say** to this mulberry

17: 7	you **would say** to your slave who
17: 8	Would you not rather **say** to him
17:10	**say,** 'We are worthless slaves;
17:13	called out, **saying,** "Jesus,
17:14	he **said** to them, "Go and show
17:17	Jesus **asked,** "Were not ten made
17:19	Then he **said** to him, "Get up
17:20	he **answered,** "The kingdom of
17:21	nor **will** they **say,** 'Look, here
17:22	Then he **said** to the disciples,
17:23	They **will say** to you, 'Look
17:34	I **tell** you, on that night there
17:37	they **asked** him, "Where, Lord?"
17:37	He **said** to them, "Where the
18: 1	Then Jesus **told** them a parable
18: 2	He **said,** "In a certain city
18: 3	**saying,** 'Grant me justice
18: 4	he **said** to himself, 'Though I
18: 6	And the Lord **said,** "Listen to
18: 6	what the unjust judge **says.**
18: 8	I **tell** you, he will quickly
18: 9	He also **told** this parable to
18:13	**saying,** 'God, be merciful to me
18:14	I **tell** you, this man went down
18:16	**said,** "Let the little children
18:17	Truly I **tell** you, whoever does
18:18	**asked** him, "Good Teacher, what
18:19	**said** to him, "Why do you call
18:19	**call** me good? No one is good
18:21	He **replied,** "I have kept all
18:22	**said** to him, "There is still
18:24	**said,** "How hard it is for those
18:26	Those who heard it **said,** "Then
18:27	**replied,** "What is impossible
18:28	Then Peter **said,** "Look, we have
18:29	And he **said** to them, "Truly
18:29	"Truly I **tell** you, there is no
18:31	took the twelve aside and **said**
18:34	what he **said** was hidden from
18:38	Then he **shouted,** "Jesus, Son of
18:41	**said,** "Lord, let me see again."
18:42	Jesus **said** to him, "Receive
19: 5	he looked up and **said** to him,
19: 7	began to grumble and **said,** "He
19: 8	Zacchaeus stood there and **said**
19: 9	Then Jesus **said** to him, "Today
19:11	he went on to **tell** a parable,
19:12	So he **said,** "A nobleman went to
19:13	**said** to them, 'Do business with

19:14	**saying,** 'We do not want this
19:15	he **ordered** these slaves, to
19:16	The first came forward and **said**
19:17	He **said** to him, 'Well done,
19:18	Then the second came, **saying,**
19:19	He **said** to him, 'And you, rule
19:20	Then the other came, **saying,**
19:22	He **said** to him, 'I will judge
19:24	He **said** to the bystanders,
19:25	(And they **said** to him, 'Lord,
19:28	After he had **said** this, he went
19:30	**saying,** "Go into the village
19:31	**say** this, 'The Lord needs it.'
19:32	found it as he **had told** them.
19:33	its owners **asked** them, "Why are
19:34	They **said,** "The Lord needs it."
19:38	**saying,** "Blessed is the king
19:39	**said** to him, "Teacher, order
19:40	He **answered,** "I tell you, if
19:40	He answered, "I **tell** you, if
19:42	**saying,** "If you, even you, had
19:46	and he **said,** "It is written,
20: 2	and **said** to him, "Tell us, by
20: 2	and **said** to him, "Tell us, by
20: 2	**Tell** us, by what authority are
20: 3	He **answered** them, "I will also
20: 3	you a question, and you **tell** me
20: 5	**saying,** "If we say, 'From
20: 5	"If we **say,** 'From heaven,' he
20: 5	he **will say,** 'Why did you not
20: 6	But if we **say,** 'Of human origin
20: 8	Then Jesus **said** to them,
20: 8	"Neither will I **tell** you
20: 9	He began to **tell** the people
20:13	the owner of the vineyard **said,**
20:14	it among themselves and **said,**
20:16	they **said,** "Heaven forbid!"
20:17	But he looked at them and **said,**
20:19	**had told** this parable against
20:21	So they **asked** him, "Teacher, we
20:21	right in what you **say** and teach
20:23	their craftiness and **said** to
20:24	bear?" They **said,** "The emperor
20:25	He **said** to them, "Then give to
20:28	and **asked** him a question,
20:34	Jesus **said** to them, "Those who
20:37	where he **speaks** of the Lord as
20:39	some of the scribes **answered,**
20:39	"Teacher, you **have spoken** well.
20:41	Then he **said** to them, "How can
20:41	"How can they **say** that the
20:42	For David himself **says** in the
20:42	The Lord **said** to my Lord, "Sit
20:45	people he **said** to the disciples
21: 3	He **said,** "Truly I tell you,
21: 3	He said, "Truly I **tell** you,
21: 5	When some **were speaking** about
21: 5	gifts dedicated to God, he **said**
21: 7	They **asked** him, "Teacher, when
21: 8	And he **said,** "Beware that you
21: 8	come in my name and **say,** 'I am
21:10	Then he **said** to them, "Nation
21:29	Then he **told** them a parable:
21:32	Truly I **tell** you, this
22: 1	which is **called** the Passover,
22: 8	**saying,** "Go and prepare the
22: 9	They **asked** him, "Where do you
22:10	"Listen," he **said** to them,
22:11	and **say** to the owner of the
22:11	The teacher **asks** you, "Where
22:13	found everything as he **had told**
22:15	He **said** to them, "I have
22:16	for I **tell** you, I will not eat
22:17	after giving thanks he **said,**
22:18	for I **tell** you that from now
22:19	**saying,** "This is my body, which
22:20	**saying,** "This cup that is
22:25	But he **said** to them, "The kings
22:33	And he **said** to him, "Lord, I am
22:34	Jesus **said,** "I tell you, Peter,
22:34	Jesus said, "I **tell** you, Peter,
22:35	He **said** to them, "When I sent
22:35	They **said,** "No, not a thing."
22:36	He **said** to them, "But now, the
22:37	For I **tell** you, this scripture
22:38	They **said,** "Lord, look, here
22:38	He **replied,** "It is enough."
22:40	he **said** to them, "Pray that you
22:41	knelt down, and **prayed**
22:46	and he **said** to them, "Why are
22:47	one **called** Judas, one of the
22:48	but Jesus **said** to him, "Judas,
22:49	they **asked,** "Lord, should we
22:51	But Jesus **said,** "No more of
22:52	Then Jesus **said** to the chief
22:56	**said,** "This man also was with
22:57	**saying,** "Woman, I do not know
22:59	still another kept **insisting,**

22:60	But Peter **said,** "Man, I do not		24:36	**said** to them, "Peace be with
22:60	know what you are **talking** about		24:38	He **said** to them, "Why are you
22:61	how he **had said** to him, "Before		24:40	And when he **had said** this, he
22:64	kept **asking** him, "Prophesy! Who		24:41	he **said** to them, "Have you
22:65	heaping many other **insults** on		24:44	Then he **said** to them, "These
22:67	They **said,** "If you are the		24:46	and he **said** to them, "Thus it
22:67	**tell** us." He replied, "If I	Jn	1:15	**cried** out, "This was he of whom
22:67	He **replied,** "If I tell you, you		1:15	I **said,** 'He who comes after me
22:67	"If I **tell** you, you will not		1:21	prophet?" He **answered,** "No."
22:70	All of them **asked,** "Are you,		1:22	Then they **said** to him, "Who are
22:70	to them, "You **say** that I am."		1:22	What do you **say** about yourself?
22:71	Then they **said,** "What further		1:23	He **said,** "I am the voice of one
23: 2	**saying,** "We found this man		1:25	They **asked** him, "Why then are
23: 2	and **saying** that he himself is		1:26	John **answered** them, "I baptize
23: 3	Then Pilate **asked** him, "Are you		1:29	coming toward him and **declared,**
23: 3	Jews?" He answered, "You **say** so		1:30	This is he of whom I **said,**
23: 4	Then Pilate **said** to the chief		1:32	And John **testified,** "I saw the
23: 5	**said,** "He stirs up the people		1:33	baptize with water **said** to me
23:14	and **said** to them, "You brought		1:36	he **exclaimed,** "Look, here is
23:18	Then they all **shouted** out		1:38	he **said** to them, "What are you
23:21	**shouting,** "Crucify, crucify him		1:38	They **said** to him, "Rabbi"
23:22	A third time he **said** to them,		1:38	(which translated **means** Teacher
23:28	**said,** "Daughters of Jerusalem,		1:39	He **said** to them, "Come and see
23:29	when they **will say,** 'Blessed		1:41	**said** to him, "We have found the
23:30	Then they will begin **to say** to		1:42	who looked at him and **said,**
23:34	Then Jesus **said,** "Father,		1:43	Philip and **said** to him, "Follow
23:35	**saying,** "He saved others; let		1:45	Philip found Nathanael and **said**
23:37	and **saying,** "If you are the		1:46	Nathanael **said** to him, "Can
23:39	**saying,** "Are you not the		1:46	Philip **said** to him, "Come and
23:42	Then he **said,** "Jesus, remember		1:47	he **said** of him, "Here is truly
23:43	He **replied,** "Truly I tell you,		1:48	Nathanael **asked** him, "Where did
23:43	"Truly I **tell** you, today you		1:48	Jesus **answered,** "I saw you
23:46	**said,** "Father, into your hands		1:50	Jesus **answered,** "Do you believe
23:46	**Having said** this, he breathed		1:50	because I **told** you that I saw
23:47	**said,** "Certainly this man was		1:51	And he **said** to him, "Very truly
24: 5	the men **said** to them, "Why do		1:51	I **tell** you, you will see heaven
24: 7	Remember how he told **you**		2: 3	**said** to him, "They have no wine
24:10	**told** this to the apostles.		2: 4	And Jesus **said** to her, "Woman,
24:17	And he **said** to them, "What are		2: 5	His mother **said** to the servants
24:18	**answered** him, "Are you the only		2: 5	Do whatever he **tells** you.
24:19	He **asked** them, "What things?"		2: 7	Jesus **said** to them, "Fill the
24:19	They **replied,** "The things about		2: 8	He **said** to them, "Now draw some
24:23	they came back and **told** us that		2:10	and **said** to him, "Everyone
24:23	who **said** that he was alive.		2:16	He **told** those who were selling
24:24	just as the women had **said;** but		2:18	The Jews then **said** to him,
24:25	Then he **said** to them, "Oh, how		2:19	Jesus **answered** them, "Destroy
24:29	**saying,** "Stay with us, because		2:20	The Jews then **said,** "This
24:32	They **said** to each other, "Were		2:21	But he **was** speaking of the
24:34	They **were saying,** "The Lord has		2:22	that he **had said** this; and they

2:22	the word that Jesus **had spoken.**
3: 2	**said** to him, "Rabbi, we know
3: 3	Jesus **answered** him, "Very truly
3: 3	"Very truly, I **tell** you, no one
3: 4	Nicodemus **said** to him, "How can
3: 5	Jesus **answered,** "Very truly, I
3: 7	I **said** to you, 'You must be
3: 9	Nicodemus **said** to him, "How can
3:10	Jesus **answered** him, "Are you a
3:11	"Very truly, I **tell** you, we
3:12	If I **have told** you about
3:12	how can you believe if I **tell**
3:26	They came to John and **said** to
3:27	John **answered,** "No one can
3:28	that I **said,** 'I am not the
4: 5	Samaritan city **called** Sychar,
4: 7	Jesus **said** to her, "Give me a
4: 9	The Samaritan woman **said** to him
4:10	Jesus **answered** her, "If you
4:10	who it is that **is saying** to
4:11	The woman **said** to him, "Sir,
4:13	Jesus **said** to her, "Everyone
4:15	The woman **said** to him, "Sir,
4:16	Jesus **said** to her, "Go, call
4:17	The woman **answered** him, "I have
4:17	Jesus **said** to her, "You are
4:17	"You are right in **saying,** 'I
4:18	What you **have said** is true!
4:19	The woman **said** to him, "Sir,
4:20	but you **say** that the place
4:21	Jesus **said** to her, "Woman,
4:25	The woman **said** to him, "I
4:25	(who is **called** Christ). "When
4:26	Jesus **said** to her, "I am he,
4:27	no one **said,** "What do you want
4:28	city. She **said** to the people,
4:29	"Come and see a man who **told** me
4:31	disciples were **urging** him,
4:32	But he **said** to them, "I have
4:33	So the disciples **said** to one
4:34	Jesus **said** to them, "My food
4:35	Do you not **say,** 'Four months
4:35	But I **tell** you, look around you
4:39	"He **told** me everything I have
4:42	They **said** to the woman, "It is
4:48	Then Jesus **said** to him, "Unless
4:49	The official **said** to him, "Sir,
4:50	Jesus **said** to him, "Go; your
4:50	the word that Jesus **spoke** to
4:51	**told** him that his child was
4:52	recover, and they **said** to him,
4:53	the hour when Jesus **had said** to
5: 6	he **said** to him, "Do you want to
5: 8	Jesus **said** to him, "Stand up,
5:10	So the Jews **said** to the man who
5:11	"The man who made me well **said**
5:12	"Who is the man who **said** to you
5:14	**said** to him, "See, you have
5:18	but was also **calling** God his
5:19	Jesus **said** to them, "Very truly
5:19	"Very truly, I **tell** you, the
5:24	Very truly, I **tell** you, anyone
5:25	"Very truly, I **tell** you, the
5:34	but I **say** these things so that
6: 5	Jesus **said** to Philip, "Where
6: 6	He **said** this to test him, for
6: 8	Simon Peter's brother, **said** to
6:10	Jesus **said,** "Make the people
6:12	he **told** his disciples, "Gather
6:14	they began **to say,** "This is
6:20	But he **said** to them, "It is I;
6:25	they **said** to him, "Rabbi, when
6:26	Jesus **answered** them, "Very
6:26	I **tell** you, you are looking for
6:28	Then they **said** to him, "What
6:29	Jesus **answered** them, "This is
6:30	So they **said** to him, "What sign
6:32	Then Jesus **said** to them, "Very
6:32	"Very truly, I **tell** you, it was
6:34	They **said** to him, "Sir, give us
6:35	Jesus **said** to them, "I am the
6:36	But I **said** to you that you have
6:41	about him because he **said,** "I
6:42	They **were saying,** "Is not this
6:42	How can he now **say,** 'I have
6:43	Jesus **answered** them, "Do not
6:47	Very truly, I **tell** you,
6:52	**saying,** "How can this man give
6:53	So Jesus **said** to them, "Very
6:53	So Jesus **said** to them, "Very
6:59	He **said** these things while he
6:60	they **said,** "This teaching is
6:61	**said** to them, "Does this offend
6:65	And he **said,** "For this reason I
6:65	And he **said,** "For this reason
6:67	So Jesus **asked** the twelve,
6:71	He **was speaking** of Judas son
7: 3	So his brothers **said** to him,

7: 6	Jesus **said** to them, "My time
7: 9	After **saying** this, he remained
7:11	festival and **saying,** "Where is
7:12	While some **were saying,** "He is
7:12	others **were saying,** "No, he is
7:15	**saying,** "How does this man have
7:16	Then Jesus **answered** them, "My
7:21	Jesus **answered** them, "I
7:25	people of Jerusalem **were saying**
7:26	but they **say** nothing to him!
7:28	Then Jesus **cried** out as he was
7:31	**were saying,** "When the Messiah
7:33	Jesus then **said,** "I will be
7:35	The Jews **said** to one another,
7:36	What does he mean by **saying,**
7:37	he **cried** out, "Let anyone who
7:38	As the scripture **has said,** 'Out
7:39	Now he **said** this about the
7:40	some in the crowd **said,** "This
7:41	Others **said,** "This is the
7:41	But some **asked,** "Surely the
7:42	Has not the scripture **said** that
7:45	who **asked** them, "Why did you
7:50	and who was one of them, **asked,**
7:52	They **replied,** "Surely you are
8: 4	they **said** to him, "Teacher,
8: 5	such women. Now what do you **say**
8: 6	They **said** this to test him, so
8: 7	**said** to them, "Let anyone among
8:10	Jesus straightened up and **said**
8:11	She **said,** "No one, sir." And
8:11	**said,** "Neither do I condemn you
8:12	**saying,** "I am the light of the
8:13	Then the Pharisees **said** to him,
8:14	Jesus **answered,** "Even if I
8:19	Then they **said** to him, "Where
8:21	Again he **said** to them, "I am
8:22	Then the Jews **said,** "Is he
8:22	Is that what he means by **saying**
8:23	He **said** to them, "You are from
8:24	I **told** you that you would
8:25	They **said** to him, "Who are
8:25	Jesus **said** to them, "Why do I
8:27	he **was speaking** to them about
8:28	So Jesus **said,** "When you have
8:31	Then Jesus **said** to the Jews who
8:33	What do you mean by **saying,**
8:34	truly, I **tell** you, everyone
8:39	They **answered** him, "Abraham is

8:39	Jesus **said** to them, "If you
8:41	They **said** to him, "We are not
8:42	Jesus **said** to them, "If God
8:45	But because I **tell** the truth,
8:46	If I **tell** the truth, why do you
8:48	The Jews **answered** him, "Are we
8:48	not right in **saying** that you
8:51	Very truly, I **tell** you, whoever
8:52	The Jews **said** to him, "Now we
8:52	yet you **say,** 'Whoever keeps my
8:54	he of whom you **say,** 'He is our
8:55	if I would **say** that I do not
8:57	Then the Jews **said** to him, "You
8:58	Jesus **said** to them, "Very truly
8:58	I **tell** you, before Abraham was,
9: 2	His disciples **asked** him, "Rabbi
9: 6	When he **had said** this, he spat
9: 7	**saying** to him, "Go, wash in the
9: 8	a beggar began to **ask,** "Is this
9: 9	Some **were saying,** "It is he."
9: 9	Others **were saying,** "No, but it
9: 9	He kept **saying,** "I am the man."
9:10	But they kept **asking** him, "Then
9:11	He answered, "The man **called**
9:11	and **said** to me, 'Go to Siloam
9:12	They **said** to him, "Where is he?
9:12	He **said,** "I do not know."
9:15	He **said** to them, "He put mud on
9:16	Some of the Pharisees **said,**
9:16	But others **said,** "How can a man
9:17	So they **said** again to the blind
9:17	"What do you **say** about him? It
9:17	He **said,** "He is a prophet."
9:19	and **asked** them, "Is this your
9:19	and **asked** them, "Is this your
9:20	His parents **answered,** "We know
9:22	His parents **said** this because
9:23	Therefore his parents **said,**
9:24	and they **said** to him, "Give
9:26	They **said** to him, "What did he
9:27	"I have **told** you already, and
9:28	Then they reviled him, **saying,**
9:30	The man **answered,** "Here is an
9:34	They **answered** him, "You were
9:35	he **said,** "Do you believe in the
9:36	He **answered,** "And who is he,
9:37	Jesus **said** to him, "You have
9:39	Jesus **said,** "I came into this
9:40	**said** to him, "Surely we are not

9:41	Jesus **said** to them, "If you
9:41	But now that you **say**, 'We see,'
10: 1	"Very truly, I **tell** you, anyone
10: 6	Jesus **used** this figure of
10: 7	So again Jesus **said** to them,
10: 7	I **tell** you, I am the gate for
10:20	Many of them **were saying**, "He
10:21	Others **were saying**, "These are
10:24	**said** to him, "How long will you
10:24	If you are the Messiah, **tell** us
10:25	Jesus answered, "I **have told**
10:34	your law, 'I **said**, you are gods
10:35	**were called** 'gods'—and the
10:36	can you **say** that the one whom
10:36	because I **said**, 'I am God's Son
10:41	and they **were saying**, "John
10:41	everything that John **said** about
11: 3	So the sisters sent a **message**
11: 4	he **said**, "This illness does not
11: 7	Then after this he **said** to the
11: 8	The disciples **said** to him,
11:11	After **saying** this, he told them
11:11	After saying this, he **told** them
11:12	The disciples **said** to him,
11:13	**had been speaking** about his
11:13	he **was referring** merely to
11:14	Then Jesus **told** them plainly,
11:16	Thomas, who **was called** the Twin
11:16	**said** to his fellow disciples,
11:21	Martha **said** to Jesus, "Lord,
11:23	Jesus **said** to her, "Your
11:24	Martha **said** to him, "I know
11:25	Jesus **said** to her, "I am the
11:27	She **said** to him, "Yes, Lord,
11:28	When she **had said** this, she
11:28	**told** her privately, "The
11:32	she knelt at his feet and **said**
11:34	He **said**, "Where have you laid
11:34	They **said** to him, "Lord, come
11:36	So the Jews **said**, "See how he
11:37	But some of them **said**, "Could
11:39	Jesus **said**, "Take away the
11:39	**said** to him, "Lord, already
11:40	Jesus **said** to her, "Did I not
11:40	**tell** you that if you believed,
11:41	**said**, "Father, I thank you for
11:42	but I **have said** this for the
11:43	When he **had said** this, he cried
11:44	Jesus **said** to them, "Unbind him
11:47	**said**, "What are we to do? This
11:49	**said** to them, "You know nothing
11:51	He **did** not say this on his own,
11:54	to a town **called** Ephraim in the
11:56	**were asking** one another as they
12: 4	was about to betray him), **said**,
12: 6	(He **said** this not because he
12: 7	Jesus **said**, "Leave her alone.
12:19	The Pharisees then **said** to one
12:21	and **said** to him, "Sir, we wish
12:22	Philip went and **told** Andrew;
12:22	Andrew and Philip went and **told**
12:23	Jesus **answered** them, "The
12:24	Very truly, I **tell** you, unless
12:27	what should I **say**—'Father,
12:29	heard it and **said** that it was
12:29	An angel **has spoken** to him.
12:30	Jesus **answered**, "This voice has
12:33	He **said** this to indicate the
12:34	How can you **say** that the Son of
12:35	Jesus **said** to them, "The light
12:38	fulfill the word **spoken** by the
12:39	because Isaiah also **said**,
12:41	Isaiah **said** this because he saw
12:44	Then Jesus **cried** aloud:
12:49	about what to **say** and what to
12:50	just as the Father **has told** me.
13: 6	who **said** to him, "Lord, are you
13: 7	Jesus **answered**, "You do not
13: 8	Peter **said** to him, "You will
13: 9	Simon Peter **said** to him, "Lord,
13:10	Jesus **said** to him, "One who has
13:11	for this reason he **said**, "Not
13:12	he **said** to them, "Do you know
13:13	and you are **right**, for that is
13:16	Very truly, I **tell** you,
13:18	I **am** not **speaking** of all of you
13:19	I **tell** you this now, before it
13:20	Very truly, I **tell** you, whoever
13:21	After **saying** this Jesus was
13:21	and **declared**, "Very truly, I
13:21	I **tell** you, one of you will
13:22	of whom he **was speaking**.
13:24	Jesus of whom he **was speaking**.
13:25	he **asked** him, "Lord, who is it?
13:27	Jesus **said** to him, "Do quickly
13:28	knew why he **said** this to him.
13:29	Jesus **was telling** him, "Buy
13:31	Jesus **said**, "Now the Son of Man

13:33	as I **said** to the Jews so now I
13:33	**say** to you, 'Where I am going,
13:36	Simon Peter **said** to him, "Lord,
13:37	Peter **said** to him, "Lord, why
13:38	I **tell** you, before the cock
14: 2	would I **have told** you that I go
14: 5	Thomas **said** to him, "Lord, we
14: 6	Jesus **said** to him, "I am the
14: 8	Philip **said** to him, "Lord, show
14: 9	Jesus **said** to him, "Have I been
14: 9	How can you **say**, 'Show us the
14:10	The words that I **say** to you I
14:12	Very truly, I **tell** you, the one
14:22	Judas (not Iscariot) **said** to
14:23	Jesus **answered** him, "Those who
14:26	of all that I **have said** to you.
14:28	You heard me **say** to you, 'I am
14:29	And now I **have told** you this
15:15	I do not **call** you servants any
15:15	but I **have called** you friends,
15:20	Remember the word that I **said**
16: 4	remember that I **told** you about
16: 4	"I **did** not **say** these things to
16: 7	Nevertheless I **tell** you the
16:12	many things to **say** to you, but
16:15	For this reason I **said** that he
16:17	some of his disciples **said** to
16:17	"What does he mean by **saying** to
16:18	They **said**, "What does he mean
16:18	**mean** by this 'a little while'?
16:19	so he **said** to them, "Are you
16:19	when I **said**, 'A little while,
16:20	Very truly, I **tell** you, you
16:23	Very truly, I **tell** you, if you
16:26	I do not **say** to you that I will
16:29	His disciples **said**, "Yes, now
16:29	"Yes, now you are **speaking**
17: 1	**said**, "Father, the hour has
18: 1	After Jesus **had spoken** these
18: 4	came forward and **asked** them,
18: 5	Jesus **replied**, "I am he." Judas
18: 6	When Jesus **said** to them, "I am
18: 7	And they **said**, "Jesus of
18: 8	Jesus answered, "I **told** you
18: 9	that he **had spoken**, "I did not
18:11	Jesus **said** to Peter, "Put your
18:16	**spoke** to the woman who guarded
18:17	The woman **said** to Peter, "You
18:17	are you?" He **said**, "I am not."
18:21	to them; they know what I **said.**
18:22	When he **had said** this, one of
18:22	**saying**, "Is that how you answer
18:25	They **asked** him, "You are not
18:25	denied it and **said**, "I am not."
18:26	**asked**, "Did I not see you in
18:30	They **answered**, "If this man
18:31	Pilate **said** to them, "Take him
18:31	The Jews **replied**, "We are not
18:32	fulfill what Jesus **had said**
18:33	and **asked** him, "Are you the
18:34	Jesus answered, "Do you **ask**
18:34	or did others **tell** you about me
18:37	Pilate **asked** him, "So you are a
18:37	"You **say** that I am a king. For
18:38	Pilate **asked** him, "What is
18:38	After he **had said** this, he went
18:38	and **told** them, "I find no case
18:40	They shouted in **reply**, "Not
19: 3	**saying**, "Hail, King of the Jews
19: 4	Pilate went out again and **said**
19: 5	Pilate **said** to them, "Here is
19: 6	they **shouted**, "Crucify him!
19: 6	Pilate **said** to them, "Take him
19: 9	**asked** Jesus, "Where are you
19:10	Pilate therefore **said** to him,
19:12	but the Jews **cried** out, "If you
19:13	place **called** The Stone Pavement
19:14	He **said** to the Jews, "Here is
19:15	Pilate **asked** them, "Shall
19:17	he went out to what is **called**
19:17	in Hebrew is **called** Golgotha.
19:21	**said** to Pilate, "Do not write,
19:21	This man **said,** I am King of
19:24	So they **said** to one another,
19:24	fulfill what the scripture **says**
19:26	he **said** to his mother, "Woman,
19:27	Then he **said** to the disciple,
19:28	he **said** (in order to fulfill
19:30	he **said**, "It is finished." Then
19:35	knows that he **tells** the truth.)
19:37	passage of scripture **says,**
20: 2	and **said** to them, "They have
20:13	They **said** to her, "Woman, why
20:13	She **said** to them, "They have
20:14	When she **had said** this, she
20:15	Jesus **said** to her, "Woman, why
20:15	she **said** to him, "Sir, if you
20:15	**tell** me where you have laid him

20:16	Jesus **said** to her, "Mary!" She
20:16	She turned and **said** to him in
20:16	"Rabbouni!" (which **means**
20:17	Jesus **said** to her, "Do not hold
20:17	go to my brothers and **say** to
20:18	she **told** them that he had said
20:19	and **said**, "Peace be with you."
20:20	After he **said** this, he showed
20:21	Jesus **said** to them again,
20:22	When he **had said** this, he
20:22	he breathed on them and **said** to
20:24	But Thomas (who **was called** the
20:25	So the other disciples **told** him
20:25	But he **said** to them, "Unless I
20:26	and **said**, "Peace be with you."
20:27	Then he **said** to Thomas, "Put
20:28	Thomas **answered** him, "My Lord
20:29	Jesus **said** to him, "Have you
21: 2	Thomas **called** the Twin,
21: 3	Simon Peter **said** to them, "I
21: 3	They **said** to him, "We will go
21: 5	Jesus **said** to them, "Children,
21: 6	He **said** to them, "Cast the net
21: 7	**said** to Peter, "It is the Lord!
21:10	Jesus **said** to them, "Bring some
21:12	Jesus **said** to them, "Come and
21:15	Jesus **said** to Simon Peter,
21:15	He **said** to him, "Yes, Lord; you
21:15	Jesus **said** to him, "Feed my
21:16	A second time he **said** to him,
21:16	He **said** to him, "Yes, Lord;
21:16	Jesus **said** to him, "Tend my
21:17	He **said** to him the third time,
21:17	he **said** to him the third time,
21:17	And he **said** to him, "Lord, you
21:17	Jesus **said** to him, "Feed my
21:18	Very truly, I **tell** you, when
21:19	(He **said** this to indicate the
21:19	After this he **said** to him,
21:19	After this he **said** to him,
21:20	and had **said**, "Lord, who is it
21:21	When Peter saw him, he **said** to
21:22	Jesus **said** to him, "If it is
21:23	Yet Jesus did not **say** to him
Ac 1: 3	**speaking** about the kingdom of
1: 6	they **asked** him, "Lord, is this
1: 7	He **replied**, "It is not for you
1: 9	When he **had said** this, as they
1:11	They **said**, "Men of Galilee, why

1:15	twenty persons) and **said**,
1:24	Then they prayed and **said**,
2: 7	they **asked**, "Are not all these
2:12	**saying** to one another, "What
2:13	But others sneered and **said**,
2:16	No, this is what **was spoken**
2:17	God **declares**, that I will pour
2:25	For David **says** concerning him,
2:29	"Fellow Israelites, I may **say**
2:34	but he himself **says**, 'The Lord
2:34	The Lord **said** to my Lord, "Sit
2:37	cut to the heart and **said** to
2:40	**saying**, "Save yourselves from
3: 2	the gate of the temple **called**
3: 4	John, and **said**, "Look at us."
3: 6	But Peter **said**, "I have no
3:22	Moses **said**, 'The Lord your God
3:25	**saying** to Abraham, 'And in your
4: 8	**said** to them, "Rulers of the
4:16	They **said**, "What will we do
4:19	But Peter and John **answered**
4:23	priests and the elders **had said**
4:24	**said**, "Sovereign Lord, who made
4:25	it is you who **said** by the Holy
4:32	no one **claimed** private
5: 3	"Ananias," Peter **asked**, "why
5: 8	Peter said to her, "**Tell** me
5: 8	And she **said**, "Yes, that was
5:19	brought them out, and **said**,
5:22	returned and **reported**
5:28	**saying**, "We gave you strict
5:29	**answered**, "We must obey God
5:35	Then he **said** to them, "Fellow
5:36	**claiming** to be somebody, and a
5:38	So in the present case, I **tell**
6: 2	**said**, "It is not right that we
6: 9	(as it **was called**), Cyrenians,
6:11	instigated some men to **say**, "We
6:13	false witnesses who **said**, "This
6:14	for we have heard him **say** that
7: 1	Then the high priest **asked** him,
7: 3	and **said** to him, 'Leave your
7: 7	**said** God, 'and after that they
7:26	**saying**, 'Men, you are brothers;
7:27	**saying**, 'Who made you a ruler
7:33	Then the Lord **said** to him,
7:35	rejected when they **said**, 'Who
7:37	This is the Moses who **said** to
7:40	**saying** to Aaron, 'Make gods for

7:48	hands; as the prophet **says,**
7:49	**says** the Lord, or what is the
7:56	"Look," he **said,** "I see the
7:59	he **prayed,** "Lord Jesus, receive
7:60	When he **had said** this, he died.
8: 6	to what **was said** by Philip,
8: 9	**saying** that he was someone
8:10	**saying,** "This man is the power
8:19	**saying,** "Give me also this
8:20	But Peter **said** to him, "May
8:24	Simon **answered,** "Pray for me to
8:24	nothing of what you **have said**
8:26	Then an angel of the Lord **said**
8:29	Then the Spirit **said** to Philip,
8:30	He **asked,** "Do you understand
8:31	He **replied,** "How can I, unless
8:34	The eunuch **asked** Philip, "About
8:34	does the prophet **say** this,
9: 4	heard a voice **saying** to him,
9: 5	He **asked,** "Who are you, Lord?"
9:10	The Lord **said** to him in a
9:10	He **answered,** "Here I am, Lord."
9:15	But the Lord **said** to him, "Go,
9:17	laid his hands on Saul and **said**
9:21	were amazed and **said,** "Is not
9:34	Peter **said** to him, "Aeneas,
9:36	which in Greek **is** Dorcas. She
9:40	**said,** "Tabitha, get up." Then
10: 3	coming in and **saying** to him,
10: 4	**said,** "What is it, Lord?" He
10: 4	He **answered,** "Your prayers and
10:14	But Peter **said,** "By no means,
10:19	the Spirit **said** to him, "Look,
10:21	**said,** "I am the one you are
10:22	They **answered,** "Cornelius, a
10:26	**saying,** "Stand up; I am only a
10:28	and he **said** to them, "You
10:34	Then Peter began **to speak** to
11: 3	**saying,** "Why did you go to
11: 4	to them, step by step, **saying,**
11: 7	I also heard a voice **saying** to
11: 8	But I **replied,** 'By no means,
11:12	The Spirit **told** me to go with
11:13	in his house and **saying,** 'Send
11:16	how he **had said,** 'John baptized
11:18	**saying,** "Then God has given
12: 7	**saying,** "Get up quickly." And
12: 8	The angel **said** to him, "Fasten
12: 8	Then he **said** to him, "Wrap your
12:11	**said,** "Now I am sure that the
12:15	They **said** to her, "You are out
12:15	They **said,** "It is his angel."
12:17	And he **added,** "Tell this to
13: 2	Spirit **said,** "Set apart for me
13:10	and **said,** "You son of the devil
13:15	**saying,** "Brothers, if you have
13:15	for the people, **give** it.
13:16	**speak:** "You Israelites, and
13:22	testimony about him he **said,**
13:25	he **said,** 'What do you suppose
13:34	he **has spoken** in this way,
13:35	Therefore he has also **said**
13:40	that what the prophets **said**
13:46	**saying,** "It was necessary that
14:10	**said** in a loud voice, "Stand
14:11	they **shouted** in the Lycaonian
14:14	into the crowd, **shouting**
14:18	Even with these **words,** they
15: 5	**said,** "It is necessary for them
15: 7	Peter stood up and **said** to them
15:13	James **replied,** "My brothers,
15:17	Thus **says** the Lord, who has
15:36	After some days Paul **said** to
16: 9	**saying,** "Come over to Macedonia
16:15	**saying,** "If you have judged me
16:17	she would **cry** out, "These men
16:18	turned and **said** to the spirit,
16:20	they **said,** "These men are
16:28	But Paul **shouted** in a loud
16:31	They **answered,** "Believe on the
16:35	police, **saying,** "Let those men
17: 7	**saying** that there is another
17:18	Some **said,** "What does this
17:18	does this babbler want to **say?**
17:19	and **asked** him, "May we know
17:21	nothing but **telling** or hearing
17:28	**have said,** 'For we too are his
17:32	but others **said,** "We will hear
18: 6	**said** to them, "Your blood be on
18: 9	One night the Lord **said** to Paul
18:13	They **said,** "This man is
18:14	Gallio **said** to the Jews, "If it
18:21	he **said,** "I will return to you,
19: 2	He **said** to them, "Did you
19: 3	Then he **said,** "Into what then
19: 3	They **answered,** "Into John's
19: 4	Paul **said,** "John baptized with
19: 4	**telling** the people to believe

19:13	**saying,** "I adjure you by the		23:20	He **answered,** "The Jews have
19:15	But the evil spirit **said** to		23:23	**said,** "Get ready to leave by
19:21	He **said,** "After I have gone		23:30	to **state** before you what they
19:25	and **said,** "Men, you know that		24: 2	**saying:** "Your Excellency,
19:26	people by **saying** that gods made		24:10	Paul **replied:** "I cheerfully
19:28	they were enraged and **shouted,**		24:14	**call** a sect, I
19:41	When he **had said** this		24:20	Or let these men here **tell**
20:10	and **said,** "Do not be alarmed,		24:22	with the **comment,** "When Lysias
20:18	When they came to him, he **said**		25: 9	**asked** Paul, "Do you wish to go
20:23	the Holy Spirit **testifies** to me		25:10	Paul **said,** "I am appealing to
20:35	for he himself **said,** 'It is		25:14	**saying,** "There is a man here
20:36	When he had finished **speaking,**		25:20	I **asked** whether he wished to go
20:38	because of what he **had said,**		26: 1	"You have permission **to speak**
21: 4	Through the Spirit they **told**		26:14	I heard a voice **saying** to me in
21:11	and **said,** "Thus says the Holy		26:15	I **asked,** 'Who are you, Lord?'
21:11	"Thus **says** the Holy Spirit,		26:15	The Lord **answered,** 'I am Jesus
21:14	remained silent except to **say,**		26:22	**saying** nothing but what the
21:20	Then they **said** to him, "You see		26:31	they **said** to one another,
21:21	and that you **tell** them not to		27:10	**saying,** "Sirs, I can see that
21:23	So do what we **tell** you. We have		27:11	the ship than to what Paul **said**
21:37	he **said** to the tribune, "May I		27:21	among them and **said,** "Men, you
21:37	May I **say** something to you?		27:24	and he **said,** 'Do not be afraid,
21:39	Paul **replied,** "I am a Jew, from		27:31	Paul **said** to the centurion and
21:40	in the Hebrew language, **saying:**		27:33	take some food, **saying,** "Today
22: 7	heard a voice **saying** to me,		27:35	After he **had said** this, he took
22: 8	Then he **said** to me, 'I am Jesus		28: 4	they **said** to one another, "This
22:10	I **asked,** 'What am I to do, Lord		28: 6	began **to say** that he was a god.
22:10	The Lord **said** to me, 'Get up		28:17	he **said** to them, "Brothers,
22:13	he **said,** 'Brother Saul, regain		28:21	They **replied,** "We have received
22:14	Then he **said,** 'The God of our		28:24	convinced by what he **had said,**
22:18	and saw Jesus **saying** to me,		28:25	Paul **made** one further statement
22:19	And I **said,** 'Lord, they		28:25	was right in **saying** to your
22:21	Then he **said** to me, 'Go, for I		28:26	Go to this people and **say,** You
22:22	but then they **shouted,** "Away	Ro	2:22	You that **forbid** adultery, do
22:24	and **ordered** him to be examined		3: 5	what **should we say?** That God is
22:25	Paul **said** to the centurion who		3: 5	us? (I **speak** in a human way.)
22:26	**said** to him, "What are you		3: 8	us by saying that we **say**), "Let
22:27	The tribune came and **asked** Paul		3:19	law **says,** it speaks to those
22:27	**Tell** me, are you a Roman		4: 1	What then are we **to say** was
23: 1	**said,** "Brothers, up to this day		4: 3	For what does the scripture **say**
23: 3	At this Paul **said** to him, "God		4: 6	So also David **speaks** of the
23: 4	Those standing nearby **said,** "Do		4: 9	We **say,** "Faith was reckoned to
23: 5	And Paul **said,** "I did not		4:18	according to what **was said,**
23: 7	When he **said** this, a dissension		6: 1	What then are we **to say?** Should
23: 8	(The Sadducees **say** that there		6:19	I **am speaking** in human terms
23: 9	**contended,** "We find nothing		7: 7	What then **should** we **say?** That
23:11	**said,** "Keep up your courage!		7: 7	if the law had not **said,**
23:12	**bound** themselves by an oath		8:31	What then **are we to say** about
23:14	**said,** "We have strictly bound		9: 1	I **am speaking** the truth in

9:12	she **was told,** "The elder shall	
9:14	What then **are we to say?** Is	
9:15	For he **says** to Moses, "I will	
9:17	For the scripture **says** to	
9:19	You **will say** to me then, "Why	
9:20	Will what is molded **say** to the	
9:25	As indeed he **says** in Hosea,	
9:26	where it **was** said to them, 'You	
9:30	What then **are we to say?**	
10: 6	that comes from faith **says,** "Do	
10: 6	"Do not **say** in your heart, 'Who	
10: 8	But what **does** it **say?** "The word	
10:11	The scripture **says,** "No one who	
10:16	for Isaiah **says,** "Lord, who has	
10:18	But I **ask,** have they not heard?	
10:19	Again I **ask,** did Israel not	
10:19	First Moses **says,** "I will make	
10:20	Isaiah is so bold as **to say,**	
10:21	But of Israel he **says,** "All day	
11: 1	I **ask,** then, has God rejected	
11: 2	the scripture **says** of Elijah,	
11: 4	But what is the divine **reply** to	
11: 9	And David **says,** "Let their	
11:11	So I **ask,** have they stumbled so	
11:13	Now I **am speaking** to you	
11:19	You **will say,** "Branches were	
12: 3	I **say** to everyone among you not	
12:19	I will repay, **says** the Lord.	
14:11	**says** the Lord, every knee shall	
15: 8	For I **tell** you that Christ has	
15:10	and again he **says,** "Rejoice, O	
15:12	and again Isaiah **says,** "The	
1C 1:10	all of you be in **agreement** and	
1:12	What I **mean** is that each of you	
1:12	each of you **says,** "I belong to	
1:15	so that no one can **say** that you	
3: 4	For when one **says,** "I belong to	
6: 5	I **say** this to your shame. Can	
7: 6	This I **say** by way of concession	
7: 8	I **say** that it is well for them	
7:12	To the rest I **say**—I and not	
7:35	I **say** this for your own benefit	
8: 5	there may be so-**called** gods in	
9: 8	Does not the law also **say** the	
9:10	Or does he not **speak** entirely	
10:15	I **speak** as to sensible people;	
10:28	But if someone **says** to you,	
10:29	I **mean** the other's conscience,	
11:22	What **should** I **say** to you?	

11:24	he broke it and **said,** "This is	
11:25	after supper, **saying,** "This cup	
12: 3	ever **says** "Let Jesus be cursed!	
12: 3	no one can **say** "Jesus is Lord"	
12:15	If the foot would **say,** "Because	
12:16	And if the ear would **say,**	
12:21	The eye cannot **say** to the hand,	
14:16	outsider **say** the "Amen" to your	
14:16	not know what you are **saying?**	
14:21	listen to me," **says** the Lord.	
14:23	**will** they not **say** that you are	
14:34	as the law also **says.**	
15:12	how can some of you **say** there	
15:27	But when it **says,** "All things	
15:35	But someone **will ask,** "How are	
15:51	Listen, I **will tell** you a	
2C 4: 6	For it is the God who **said,**	
6: 2	For he **says,** "At an acceptable	
6:13	In return—I **speak** as to	
6:16	as God **said,** "I will live in	
6:17	be separate from them, **says** the	
6:18	**says** the Lord Almighty.	
7: 3	I do not **say** this to condemn	
8: 8	I do not **say** this as a command,	
9: 3	ready, as I **said** you would be;	
9: 4	**say** nothing of you—in this	
11:16	I **repeat,** let no one think that	
11:21	To my shame, I must **say,**	
11:21	I **am speaking** as a fool—I	
12: 6	I **will be speaking** the truth.	
12: 9	but he **said** to me, "My grace is	
Ga 1: 9	so now I **repeat,** if anyone	
2:14	I **said** to Cephas before them	
3:15	Brothers and sisters, I **give** an	
3:16	Now the promises **were made** to	
3:16	offspring; it **does** not **say,**	
3:17	My **point** is this: the law,	
4: 1	My **point** is this: heirs, as	
4:21	**Tell** me, you who desire to be	
4:30	But what does the scripture **say**	
5: 2	Listen! I, Paul, **am telling** you	
5:16	Live by the Spirit, I **say,** and	
Ep 2:11	**called** "the uncircumcision" by	
2:11	by those who are **called** "the	
4: 8	Therefore it **is said,** "When he	
4:17	Now this I **affirm** and insist on	
5:12	it is shameful even to **mention**	
5:14	Therefore it **says,** "Sleeper,	
5:32	I **am applying** it to Christ and	

Ph	3:18	I have often **told** you of them,
	3:18	now I **tell** you even with tears.
	4: 4	again I **will say**, Rejoice.
	4:11	Not that I am **referring** to
Co	2: 4	I **am saying** this so that no
	4:11	And Jesus who **is called** Justus
	4:17	And **say** to Archippus, "See that
1Th	4:15	For this we **declare** to you by
	5: 3	When they **say**, "There is peace
2Th	2: 4	above every so-**called** god or
	2: 5	Do you not remember that I **told**
1Ti	1: 7	what they are **saying** or the
	2: 7	(I **am telling** the truth, I am
	4: 1	Now the Spirit expressly **says**
	5:18	for the scripture **says**, "You
2Ti	2: 7	Think over what I **say**, for the
	2:18	from the truth by **claiming** that
Ti	1:12	who **said**, "Cretans are always
	2: 8	having nothing evil **to say** of
Pm	1:19	I **say** nothing about your owing
	1:21	will do even more than I **say**.
He	1: 5	did God ever **say**, "You are my
	1: 6	he **says**, "Let all God's angels
	1: 7	Of the angels he **says**, "He
	1:13	angels **has** he ever **said**, "Sit
	2: 6	someone has **testified** somewhere
	2:12	**saying**, "I will proclaim your
	3: 7	as the Holy Spirit **says**, "Today
	3:10	and I **said**, 'They always go
	3:15	As it **is said**, "Today, if you
	4: 3	just as God has **said**, "As in my
	4: 4	For in one place it **speaks**
	4: 7	**saying** through David much later
	5: 6	as he **says** also in another
	5:11	About this we have much **to say**
	6:14	**saying**, "I will surely bless
	7: 9	One **might** even **say** that Levi
	7:11	to **speak** of another priest
	7:13	of whom these things **are spoken**
	7:21	the one who **said** to him, "The
	8: 1	in what we **are saying** is this:
	8: 8	when he **says**: "The days are
	8: 8	**says** the Lord, when I will
	8: 9	no concern for them, **says** the
	8:10	**says** the Lord: I will put my
	8:11	or **say** to each other, 'Know the
	8:13	In **speaking** of "a new covenant
	9: 2	this is **called** the Holy Place.
	9: 3	tent **called** the Holy of Holies.
	9: 5	we cannot **speak** now in detail.
	9:20	**saying**, "This is the blood of
	10: 5	**said**, "Sacrifices and offerings
	10: 7	Then I **said**, 'See, God, I have
	10: 8	When he **said** above, "You have
	10: 9	then he **added**, "See, I have
	10:15	to us, for after **saying**,
	10:16	**says** the Lord: I will put my
	10:30	For we know the one who **said**,
	11:14	for people who **speak** in this
	11:24	refused to be **called** a son of
	11:32	And what more should I **say**?
	12:21	Moses **said**, "I tremble with
	12:26	but now he has **promised**, "Yet
	13: 5	he **has said**, "I will never
	13: 6	So we can **say** with confidence,
Ja	1:13	should **say**, "I am being tempted
	2: 3	**say**, "Have a seat here, please,
	2: 3	**say**, "Stand there," or, "Sit at
	2:11	the one who **said**, "You shall
	2:11	also **said**, "You shall not
	2:14	if you **say** you have faith but
	2:16	and one of you **says** to them,
	2:18	But someone **will say**, "You have
	2:23	**says**, "Abraham believed God,
	4: 5	the scripture **says**, "God yearns
	4: 6	therefore it **says**, "God opposes
	4:13	Come now, you who **say**, "Today
	4:15	Instead you ought to **say**, "If
2P	3: 4	and **saying**, "Where is the
1J	1: 6	If we **say** that we have
	1: 8	If we **say** that we have no sin,
	1:10	If we **say** that we have not
	2: 4	Whoever **says**, "I have come to
	2: 6	whoever **says**, "I abide in him,"
	2: 9	Whoever **says**, "I am in the
	4:20	Those who **say**, "I love God,"
	5:16	I **do** not **say** that you should
2J	1:10	or **welcome** anyone who comes to
	1:11	for to **welcome** is to
Ju	1: 9	but **said**, "The Lord rebuke you!
	1:14	**saying**, "See, the Lord is
	1:18	for they **said** to you, "In the
Re	1: 8	**says** the Lord God, who is and
	1:11	**saying**, "Write in a book what
	1:17	**saying**, "Do not be afraid; I am
	2: 1	These are the **words** of him who
	2: 2	those who **claim** to be apostles

2: 7	to what the Spirit **is saying** to	10:11	Then they **said** to me, "You must
2: 8	These are the **words** of the	11: 1	and I **was told,** "Come and
2: 9	of those who **say** that they are	11:12	**saying** to them, "Come up here!"
2:11	what the Spirit **is saying** to	11:15	**saying,** "The kingdom of the
2:12	These are the **words** of him who	11:17	**singing,** "We give you thanks,
2:17	the Spirit **is saying** to the	12:10	**proclaiming,** "Now have come the
2:18	These are the **words** of the Son	13: 4	**saying,** "Who is like the beast,
2:20	who **calls** herself a prophet	13:14	**telling** them to make an image
2:24	to you I **say,** I do not lay on	14: 7	He **said** in a loud voice, "Fear
2:24	not learned what some **call** 'the	14: 8	**saying,** "Fallen, fallen is
2:29	what the Spirit **is saying** to	14: 9	**crying** with a loud voice,
3: 1	These are the **words** of him who	14:13	**saying,** "Write this: Blessed
3: 6	to what the Spirit **is saying** to	14:13	"Yes," **says** the Spirit, "they
3: 7	These are the **words** of the holy	14:18	he **called** with a loud voice to
3: 9	who **say** that they are Jews and	15: 3	And they **sing** the song of Moses
3:13	the Spirit **is saying** to the	16: 1	**telling** the seven angels, "Go
3:14	The **words** of the Amen, the	16: 5	angel of the waters **say,** "You
3:17	For you **say,** 'I am rich, I have	16: 7	And I heard the altar **respond,**
3:22	what the Spirit **is saying** to	16:17	from the throne, **saying,** "It is
4: 1	**said,** "Come up here, and I will	17: 1	**said** to me, "Come, I will show
4: 8	without ceasing they **sing,**	17: 7	But the angel **said** to me, "Why
4:10	before the throne, **singing,**	17: 7	But the angel **said** to me, "Why
5: 5	Then one of the elders **said** to	17:15	And he **said** to me, "The waters
5: 9	They **sing** a new song: "You are	18: 2	He **called** out with a mighty
5:12	**singing** with full voice,	18: 4	from heaven **saying,** "Come out
5:13	**singing,** "To the one seated on	18: 7	**says,** 'I rule as a queen; I am
5:14	living creatures **said,** "Amen!"	18:15	weeping and **mourning** aloud
6: 1	**call out,** as with a voice of	18:10	and **say,** "Alas, alas, the great
6: 3	living creature **call out,** "Come	18:18	and **cried** out as they saw the
6: 5	third living creature **call out,**	18:19	**crying** out, "Alas, alas, the
6: 6	four living creatures **saying,**	18:21	**saying,** "With such violence
6: 7	fourth living creature **call out**	19: 1	in heaven, **saying,** "Hallelujah!
6:10	**cried** out with a loud voice,	19: 3	more they **said,** "Hallelujah!
6:11	**told** to rest a little longer,	19: 4	**saying,** "Amen. Hallelujah!"
6:16	**calling** to the mountains and	19: 5	came a voice **saying,** "Praise
7: 3	**saying,** "Do not damage	19: 6	**crying** out, "Hallelujah! For
7:10	**saying,** "Salvation belongs to	19: 9	And the angel **said** to me,
7:12	**singing,** "Amen! Blessing and	19: 9	And he **said** to me, "These are
7:13	**saying,** "Who are these, robed	19:10	but he **said** to me, "You must
7:14	I **said** to him, "Sir, you are	19:17	with a loud voice he **called** to
7:14	Then he **said** to me, "These are	21: 3	voice from the throne **saying,**
8:11	name of the star **is** Wormwood.	21: 5	throne **said,** "See, I am making
8:13	I heard an eagle **crying** with a	21: 5	Also he **said,** "Write this, for
9: 4	They **were told** not to damage	21: 6	Then he **said** to me, "It is done
9:14	**saying** to the sixth angel who	21: 9	**said** to me, "Come, I will show
10: 4	a voice from heaven **saying,**	22: 6	And he **said** to me, "These
10: 8	**saying,** "Go, take the scroll	22: 9	but he **said** to me, "You must
10: 9	**told** him to give me the little	22:10	And he **said** to me, "Do not
10: 9	he **said** to me, "Take it, and	22:17	The Spirit and the bride **say,**

22:17   let everyone who hears **say,**
22:20   **says,** "Surely I am coming soon

3005   ᴳᴼ1 ᴬᴳ470 ᴸᴺ151 ᴮ3:247 ᴷ4:194
λειμμα, REMNANT
Ro   11: 5   there is a **remnant,** chosen by

3006   ᴳᴼ1 ᴬᴳ470 ᴸᴺ151 ᴷ4:193
λειος, SMOOTH
Lk   3: 5   and the rough ways made **smooth;**

3007   ᴳᴼ6 ᴬᴳ470 ᴸᴺ151 ᴮ3:247
λειπω, I LEAVE
Lk   18:22   is still one thing **lacking.**
Ti   1: 5   what **remained** to be done, and
        3:13   and see that they **lack** nothing.
Ja   1: 4   complete, **lacking** in nothing.
        1: 5   If any of you is **lacking** in
        2:15   is naked and **lacks** daily food,

3008   ᴳᴼ3 ᴬᴳ470 ᴸᴺ151 ᴮ1:551 ᴷ4:215 ᴿ3011
λειτουργεω, I SERVE
Ac   13: 2   While they were **worshiping** the
Ro   15:27   ought also **to be of service** to
He   10:11   **offering** again and again the

3009   ᴳᴼ6 ᴬᴳ471 ᴸᴺ151 ᴮ3:551 ᴷ4:215 ᴿ3008
λειτουργια, SERVICE
Lk   1:23   When his time of **service** was
2C   9:12   this **ministry** not only supplies
Ph   2:17   the **offering** of your faith, I
        2:30   those **services** that you could
He   8: 6   a more excellent **ministry,** and
        9:21   all the vessels **used in worship**

3010   ᴳᴼ1 ᴬᴳ471 ᴸᴺ152 ᴮ3:551 ᴷ4:231 ᴿ3008
λειτουργικος, SERVING
He   1:14   spirits in the **divine** service,

3011   ᴳᴼ5 ᴬᴳ471 ᴸᴺ152 ᴮ3:551 ᴷ4:229 ᴿ3008
λειτουργος, SERVANT
Ro   13: 6   authorities are God's **servants,**
        15:16   to be a **minister** of Christ
Ph   2:25   your messenger and **minister** to
He   1: 7   and his **servants** flames of fire
        8: 2   a **minister** in the sanctuary and

3011a   ᴳᴼ1 ᴬᴳ471 ᴸᴺ152
λεμα, LEMA
Mt   27:46   Eli, Eli, **lema** sabachthani?

3012   ᴳᴼ2 ᴬᴳ471 ᴸᴺ152
λεντιον, TOWEL
Jn   13: 4   and tied a **towel** around himself
        13: 5   wipe them with the **towel** that

3013   ᴳᴼ1 ᴬᴳ471 ᴸᴺ152 ᴷ4:232 ᴿ3014
λεπις, FLAKE
Ac   9:18   something like **scales** fell from

3014   ᴳᴼ4 ᴬᴳ471 ᴸᴺ152 ᴮ2:464 ᴷ4:233
λεπρα, LEPROSY
Mt   8: 3   Immediately his **leprosy** was
Mk   1:42   Immediately the **leprosy** left
Lk   5:12   was a man covered with **leprosy.**
        5:13   Immediately the **leprosy** left

3015   ᴳᴼ9 ᴬᴳ472 ᴸᴺ152 ᴮ2:463 ᴷ4:233 ᴿ3014
λεπρος, LEPER
Mt   8: 2   and there was a **leper** who came
        10: 8   cleanse the **lepers,** cast out
        11: 5   the **lepers** are cleansed, the
        26: 6   in the house of Simon the **leper**
Mk   1:40   A **leper** came to him begging him
        14: 3   in the house of Simon the **leper**
Lk   4:27   There were also many **lepers** in
        7:22   the **lepers** are cleansed, the
        17:12   ten **lepers** approached him.

3016   ᴳᴼ3 ᴬᴳ472 ᴸᴺ152 ᴮ2:850
λεπτος, LEPTA
Mk   12:42   two small **copper coins,** which
Lk   12:59   have paid the very last **penny.**
        21: 2   put in two small **copper coins.**

3017   ᴳᴼ5 ᴬᴳ472 ᴸᴺ152 ᴮ2:466 ᴷ4:234
λευι, LEVI
Lk   3:24   son of Matthat, son of **Levi,**
        3:29   son of Matthat, son of **Levi,**
He   7: 5   And those descendants of **Levi**
        7: 9   One might even say that **Levi**
Re   7: 7   from the tribe of **Levi** twelve

3018   ᴳᴼ3 ᴬᴳ472 ᴸᴺ152 ᴮ2:466 ᴷ4:234
λευις, LEVI
Mk   2:14   he saw **Levi** son of Alphaeus
Lk   5:27   a tax collector named **Levi,**
        5:29   Then **Levi** gave a great banquet

3019   ᴳᴼ3 ᴬᴳ472 ᴸᴺ152 ᴮ2:466 ᴷ4:239
λευιτης, LEVITE

Lk   10:32   So likewise a **Levite,** when he
Jn   1:19   Jews sent priests and **Levites**
Ac   4:36   There was a **Levite,** a native

3020   GO1 AG472 LN152 B2:466
λευιτικος, LEVITICAL
He   7:11   **levitical** priesthood—for the

3021   GO2 AG472 LN152 K4:241 R3022
λευκαινω, I WHITEN
Mk   9: 3   clothes **became** dazzling **white,**
Re   7:14   **made** them **white** in the blood of

3022   GO25 AG472 LN152 B1:204 K4:241
λευκος, WHITE
Mt   5:36   make one hair **white** or black.
     17: 2   clothes became dazzling **white.**
     28: 3   and his clothing **white** as snow.
Mk   9: 3   dazzling **white,** such as no one
     16: 5   dressed in a **white** robe,
Lk   9:29   clothes became dazzling **white.**
Jn   4:35   see how the fields are **ripe** for
     20:12   and she saw two angels in **white**
Ac   1:10   two men in **white** robes stood by
Re   1:14   head and his hair were **white** as
     1:14   **white** wool, white as snow; his
     2:17   I will give a **white** stone, and
     3: 4   dressed in **white,** for they are
     3: 5   clothed like them in **white**
     3:18   **white** robes to clothe you and
     4: 4   dressed in **white** robes, with
     6: 2   and there was a **white** horse!
     6:11   They were each given a **white**
     7: 9   robed in **white,** with palm
     7:13   robed in **white,** and where have
     14:14   there was a **white** cloud, and
     19:11   and there was a **white** horse!
     19:14   wearing fine linen, **white** and
     19:14   were following him on **white**
     20:11   Then I saw a great **white** throne

3023   GO9 AG472 LN152 K4:251
λεων, LION
2Ti   4:17   I was rescued from the **lion's**
He   11:33   shut the mouths of **lions,**
1P   5: 8   Like a roaring **lion** your
Re   4: 7   living creature like a **lion,**
     5: 5   the **Lion** of the tribe of Judah,
     9: 8   their teeth like **lions'** teeth;
     9:17   horses were like **lions'** heads,

10: 3   like a **lion** roaring. And when
13: 2   its mouth was like a **lion's**

3024   GO1 AG472 LN152 R2990
ληθη, FORGETFULNESS
2P   1: 9   is **forgetful** of the cleansing

3024a   GO1 AG473 LN152
λημψις, RECEIVING
Ph   4:15   matter of giving and **receiving,**

3025   GO5 AG473 LN152 K4:254
ληνος, WINE PRESS
Mt   21:33   dug a **wine press** in it, and
Re   14:19   into the great **wine press** of
     14:20   And the **wine press** was
             trodden
     14:20   flowed from the **wine press,** as
     19:15   will tread the **wine press** of

3026   GO1 AG473 LN152
ληρος, NONSENSE
Lk   24:11   seemed to them an **idle** tale,

3027   GO15 AG473 LN152 B3:377 K4:257
ληστης, ROBBER
Mt   21:13   are making it a den of **robbers.**
     26:55   as though I were a **bandit?** Day
     27:38   Then two **bandits** were crucified
     27:44   The **bandits** who were crucified
Mk   11:17   have made it a den of **robbers.**
     14:48   me as though I were a **bandit?**
     15:27   they crucified two **bandits,** one
Lk   10:30   fell into the hands of **robbers,**
     10:36   into the hands of the **robbers?**
     19:46   have made it a den of **robbers.**
     22:52   and clubs as if I were a **bandit**
Jn   10: 1   way is a thief and a **bandit.**
     10: 8   are thieves and **bandits;** but
     18:40   Now Barabbas was a **bandit.**
2C   11:26   danger from **bandits,** danger

3029   GO12 AG473 LN152
λιαν, VERY
Mt   2:16   he was **infuriated,** and he sent
     4: 8   devil took him to a **very** high
     8:28   They were **so** fierce that no one
     27:14   the governor was **greatly** amazed
Mk   1:35   while it was still **very** dark,
     6:51   And they were **utterly** astounded

9: 3 and his clothes became **dazzling**
16: 2 And **very** early on the first day
Lk 23: 8 he was **very** glad, for he had
2Ti 4:15 he **strongly** opposed our message
2J 1: 4 I was **overjoyed** to find some of
3J 1: 3 I was **overjoyed** when some of

3030 GO2 AG473 LN152 B2:293 K4:263
λιβανος, FRANKINCENSE
Mt 2:11 gold, **frankincense,** and myrrh.
Re 18:13 **frankincense,** wine, olive oil,

3031 GO2 AG473 LN152 B2:293 K4:263
λιβανωτος, INCENSE HOLDER
Re 8: 3 angel with a golden **censer** came
8: 5 Then the angel took the **censer**

3032 GO1 AG473 LN152 B3:598 K4:265
λιβερτινος, LIBERTINE
Ac 6: 9 synagogue of the **Freedmen** (as

3033 GO1 AG473 LN152
λιβυη, LIBYA
Ac 2:10 the parts of **Libya** belonging to

3034 GO9 AG473 LN152 K4:267 R3037
λιθαζω, I STONE
Jn 8: 5 commanded us **to stone** such
10:31 up stones again **to stone** him.
10:32 these are you **going to stone** me
10:33 we are going **to stone** you, but
11: 8 just now trying **to stone** you,
Ac 5:26 afraid of **being stoned** by the
14:19 they **stoned** Paul and dragged
2C 11:25 Once I received a **stoning.**
He 11:37 They were **stoned** to death, they

3035 GO3 AG474 LN152 B3:390 K4:268 R3037
λιθινος, OF STONE
Jn 2: 6 standing there were six **stone**
2C 3: 3 not on tablets of **stone** but on
Re 9:20 and bronze and **stone** and wood,

3036 GO7 AG474 LN153 K4:267 R3037,907
λιθοβολεω, I THROW STONE
Mt 21:35 killed another, and **stoned**
23:37 kills the prophets and **stones**
Lk 13:34 **stones** those who are sent to it
Ac 7:58 and began to **stone** him; and the
7:59 While they **were stoning** Stephen

14: 5 to mistreat them and to **stone**
He 12:20 it **shall be stoned** to death.

3037 GO59 AG474 LN153 B3:390 K4:268
λιθος, STONE
Mt 3: 9 God is able from these **stones**
4: 3 command these **stones** to become
4: 6 dash your foot against a **stone.**
7: 9 for bread, will give a **stone?**
21:42 The **stone** that the builders
21:44 The one who falls on this **stone**
24: 2 not one **stone** will be left here
24: 2 left here upon **another;** all
27:60 He then rolled a great **stone** to
27:66 secure by sealing the **stone.**
28: 2 came and rolled back the **stone**
Mk 5: 5 bruising himself with **stones.**
12:10 The **stone** that the builders
13: 1 what large **stones** and what
13: 2 Not one **stone** will be left here
13: 2 upon **another;** all will be
15:46 He then rolled a **stone** against
16: 3 Who will roll away the **stone**
16: 4 they saw that the **stone,** which
Lk 3: 8 God is able from these **stones**
4: 3 command this **stone** to become a
4:11 dash your foot against a **stone.**
17: 2 if a mill **stone** were hung
19:40 the **stones** would shout out.
19:44 one **stone** upon another; because
19:44 **another;** because you did not
20:17 The **stone** that the builders
20:18 falls on that **stone** will be
21: 5 adorned with beautiful **stones**
21: 6 not one **stone** will be left upon
21: 6 **another;** all will be thrown
22:41 about a **stone's** throw, knelt
24: 2 They found the **stone** rolled
Jn 8: 7 first to throw a **stone** at her.
8:59 So they picked up **stones** to
10:31 The Jews took up **stones** again
11:38 and a **stone** was lying against it
11:39 "Take away the **stone.**" Martha,
11:41 So they took away the **stone.**
20: 1 saw that the **stone** had been
Ac 4:11 This Jesus is 'the **stone** that
17:29 or **stone,** an image formed by
Ro 9:32 over the stumbling **stone,**
9:33 **stone** that will make people

1C 3:12 precious **stones,** wood, hay,
2C 3: 7 chiseled in letters on **stone**
1P 2: 4 Come to him, a living **stone,**
    2: 5 like living **stones,** let
    2: 6 I am laying in Zion a **stone,** a
    2: 7 The **stone** that the builders
    2: 8 and "A **stone** that makes them
Re 4: 3 looks like **jasper** and carnelian
    17: 4 adorned with gold and **jewels**
    18:12 cargo of gold, silver, **jewels**
    18:16 with **jewels,** and with pearls!
    18:21 took up a **stone** like a great
    21:11 radiance like a very rare **jewel**
    21:11 like **jasper,** clear as crystal.
    21:19 adorned with every **jewel;** the

3038 GO1 AG474 LN153
λιθοστρωτος, STONE PAVEMENT
Jn 19:13 place called The **Stone Pavement**

3039 GO2 AG474 LN153 K4:280
λικμαω, I PULVERIZE
Mt 21:44 it **will crush** anyone on whom it
Lk 20:18 it **will crush** anyone on whom it

3040 GO3 AG475 LN153
λιμην, HARBOR
Ac 27: 8 to a place called Fair **Havens,**
    27:12 the **harbor** was not suitable for
    27:12 It was a **harbor** of Crete,

3041 GO11 AG475 LN153 B3:992
λιμνη, LAKE
Lk 5: 1 standing beside the **lake** of
    5: 2 there at the shore of the **lake;**
    8:22 the other side of the **lake.**" So
    8:23 swept down on the **lake,** and the
    8:33 into the **lake** and was drowned.
Re 19:20 thrown alive into the **lake** of
    20:10 thrown into the **lake** of fire
    20:14 thrown into the **lake** of fire.
    20:14 second death, the **lake** of fire;
    20:15 life was thrown into the **lake**
    21: 8 their place will be in the **lake**

3042 GO12 AG475 LN153 B2:264 K6:12
λιμος, FAMINE
Mt 24: 7 and there will be **famines** and
Mk 13: 8 there will be **famines.** This is
Lk 4:25 there was a severe **famine** over

    15:14 a severe **famine** took place
    15:17 but here I am dying of **hunger!**
    21:11 in various places **famines** and
Ac 7:11 there came a **famine** throughout
    11:28 there would be a severe **famine**
Ro 8:35 **famine,** or nakedness, or peril,
2C 11:27 **hungry** and thirsty, often
Re 6: 8 **famine,** and pestilence, and by
    18: 8 mourning and **famine**—and she

3043 GO2 AG475 LN153
λινον, LINEN
Mt 12:20 quench a smoldering **wick** until
Re 15: 6 robed in pure bright **linen,**

3044 GO1 AG475 LN153
λινος, LINUS
2Ti 4:21 as do Pudens and **Linus** and

3045 GO1 AG475 LN153
λιπαρος, SLEEK
Re 18:14 and all your **dainties** and your

3046 GO2 AG475 LN153
λιτρα, LITRE
Jn 12: 3 Mary took a **pound** of costly
    19:39 weighing about a hundred **pounds**

3047 GO1 AG475 LN153
λιψ, SOUTHWEST
Ac 27:12 facing **southwest** and northwest

3048 GO2 AG475 LN153 B3:751 K4:282 R3056
λογεια, COLLECTION
1C 16: 1 Now concerning the **collection**
    16: 2 so that **collections** need not be

3049 GO40 AG475 LN153 B3:822 K4:284 R3056
λογιζομαι, I REASON
Lk 22:37 And he **was counted** among the
Jn 11:50 You do not **understand** that it
Ac 19:27 goddess Artemis will be **scorned**
Ro 2: 3 Do you **imagine,** whoever you are
    2:26 **be regarded** as circumcision?
    3:28 For we **hold** that a person is
    4: 3 it was **reckoned** to him as
    4: 4 wages are not **reckoned** as a
    4: 5 such faith is **reckoned** as
    4: 6 those to whom God **reckons**
    4: 8 the Lord will not **reckon** sin.

	4: 9	Faith **was reckoned** to Abraham
	4:10	How then was it **reckoned** to him
	4:11	have righteousness **reckoned** to
	4:22	faith **"was reckoned** to him as
	4:23	Now the words, "it **was reckoned**
	4:24	It **will be reckoned** to us who
	6:11	So you also must **consider**
	8:18	I **consider** that the sufferings
	8:36	we **are accounted** as sheep to be
	9: 8	of the promise **are counted** as
	14:14	unclean for anyone who **thinks**
1C	4: 1	**Think** of us in this way, as
	13: 5	not irritable or **resentful**
	13:11	I **reasoned** like a child; when I
2C	3: 5	competent of ourselves to **claim**
	5:19	not **counting** their trespasses
	10: 2	daring to **oppose** those who
	10: 2	those who **think** we are acting
	10: 7	**remind** yourself of this, that
	10:11	Let such people **understand** that
	11: 5	I **think** that I am not in the
	12: 6	so that no one may **think** better
Ga	3: 6	and it was **reckoned** to him as
Ph	3:13	Beloved, I do not **consider** that
	4: 8	**think** about these things.
2Ti	4:16	May it not be **counted** against
He	11:19	He **considered** the fact that God
Ja	2:23	and it **was reckoned** to him as
1P	5:12	whom I **consider** a faithful

3050　GO2 AG476 LN153 B3:1081 K4:142 R3056
λογικος, REASONABLE
Ro 12: 1　which is your **spiritual** worship
1P　2: 2　**spiritual** milk, so that by it

3051　GO4 AG476 LN153 B3:1081 K4:137 R3052
λογιον, SAYING
Ac　7:38　he received living **oracles** to
Ro　3: 2　entrusted with the **oracles** of
He　5:12　basic elements of the **oracles**
1P　4:11　as one speaking the very **words**

3052　GO1 AG476 LN153 B3:1081 K4:136 R3056
λογιος, WORDY
Ac 18:24　He was an **eloquent** man,

3053　GO2 AG476 LN153 B3:822 K4:284 R3049
λογισμος, REASONING
Ro　2:15　their conflicting **thoughts** will
2C 10: 4　We destroy **arguments**

3054　GO1 AG477 LN153 B3:1119 K4:143 R3056
λογομαχεω, I BATTLE WITH WORDS
2Ti　2:14　avoid **wrangling over words,**

3055　GO1 AG477 LN153 B3:1119 K4:143 R3054
λογομαχια, WORD-FIGHT
1Ti　6: 4　and for **disputes about words.**

3056　GO330 AG477 LN153 B3:1081 K4:69 R3004
λογος, WORD

Mt	5:32	on the **ground** of unchastity,
	5:37	Let your **word** be 'Yes, Yes' or
	7:24	who hears these **words** of mine
	7:26	who hears these **words** of mine
	7:28	finished saying these **things,**
	8: 8	but only speak the **word,** and my
	8:16	out the spirits with a **word,**
	10:14	or listen to your **words,** shake
	12:32	Whoever speaks a **word** against
	12:36	account for every careless **word**
	12:37	for by your **words** you will be
	12:37	and by your **words** you will be
	13:19	When anyone hears the **word** of
	13:20	hears the **word** and immediately
	13:21	on account of the **word,** that
	13:22	the one who hears the **word,** but
	13:22	lure of wealth choke the **word,**
	13:23	one who hears the **word** and
	15: 6	you make void the **word** of God.
	15:12	when they heard **what** you said?
	15:23	he did not answer her at **all.**
	18:23	wished to settle **accounts** with
	19: 1	finished saying these **things,**
	19:11	can accept this **teaching,** but
	19:22	man heard this **word,** he went
	21:24	ask you one **question;** if you
	22:15	entrap him in what he **said.**
	22:46	give him an **answer,** nor from
	24:35	my **words** will not pass away.
	25:19	and settled **accounts** with them.
	26: 1	saying all these **things,** he
	26:44	time, saying the same **words.**
	28:15	And this **story** is still told
Mk	1:45	and to spread the **word,** so that
	2: 2	was speaking the **word** to them.
	4:14	The sower sows the **word.**
	4:15	where the **word** is sown: when
	4:15	takes away the **word** that is
	4:16	when they hear the **word,** they
	4:17	arises on account of the **word,**

4:18	the ones who hear the **word,**
4:19	choke the **word,** and it yields
4:20	they hear the **word** and accept
4:33	he spoke the **word** to them, as
5:36	But overhearing what they **said,**
7:13	thus making void the **word** of
7:29	For saying **that,** you may go
8:32	He said all **this** quite openly.
8:38	of my **words** in this adulterous
9:10	So they kept the **matter** to
10:22	When he heard **this,** he was
10:24	perplexed at these **words.** But
11:29	I will ask you one **question;**
12:13	to trap him in what he **said.**
13:31	but my **words** will not pass away
14:39	prayed, saying the same **words.**
16:20	confirmed the **message** by the

Lk 1: 2 and servants of the **word,**
1: 4 concerning the **things** about
1:20 you did not believe my **words,**
1:29 much perplexed by his **words** and
3: 4 of the **words** of the prophet
4:22 amazed at the gracious **words**
4:32 because he **spoke** with authority
4:36 What kind of **utterance** is this
5: 1 on him to hear the **word** of God,
5:15 But now more than ever the **word**
6:47 hears my **words,** and acts on
7: 7 But only speak the **word,** and
7:17 This **word** about him spread
8:11 The seed is the **word** of God.
8:12 takes away the **word** from their
8:13 when they hear the **word,**
8:15 when they hear the **word,** hold
8:21 those who hear the **word** of God
9:26 of my **words,** of them the Son of
9:28 eight days after these **sayings**
9:44 Let these **words** sink into your
10:39 listened to what he was **saying.**
11:28 those who hear the **word** of God
12:10 And everyone who speaks a **word**
16: 2 Give me an **accounting** of your
20: 3 I will also ask you a **question**
20:20 trap him by what he **said,** so as
21:33 but my **words** will not pass away
23: 9 questioned him at some **length,**
24:17 What are you **discussing** with
24:19 mighty in deed and **word** before
24:44 These are my **words** that I

Jn 1: 1 In the beginning was the **Word,**
1: 1 and the **Word** was with God, and
1: 1 with God, and the **Word** was God.
1:14 And the **Word** became flesh and
2:22 the **word** that Jesus had spoken.
4:37 For here the **saying** holds true,
4:39 the woman's **testimony,** "He told
4:41 believed because of his **word.**
4:50 The man believed the **word** that
5:24 anyone who hears my **word** and
5:38 and you do not have his **word**
6:60 This **teaching** is difficult;
7:36 What does he mean by **saying,**
7:40 When they heard these **words,**
8:31 If you continue in my **word,**
8:37 no place in you for my **word.**
8:43 you cannot accept my **word.**
8:51 whoever keeps my **word** will
8:52 Whoever keeps my **word** will
8:55 know him and I keep his **word.**
10:19 divided because of these **words.**
10:35 If those to whom the **word** of
12:38 This was to fulfill the **word**
12:48 does not receive my **word** has a
14:23 love me will keep my **word,** and
14:24 does not keep my **words;** and the
14:24 and the **word** that you hear is
15: 3 been cleansed by the **word** that
15:20 Remember the **word** that I said
15:20 Remember the **word** that I said
15:25 It was to fulfill the **word** that
17: 6 and they have kept your **word.**
17:14 I have given them your **word,**
17:17 truth; your **word** is truth.
17:20 in me through their **word,**
18: 9 This was to fulfill the **word**
18:32 fulfill what Jesus had **said**
19: 8 Now when Pilate heard **this,** he
19:13 When Pilate heard these **words,**
21:23 So the **rumor** spread in the

Ac 1: 1 In the first **book,** Theophilus,
2:22 listen to what I have to **say:**
2:40 with many other **arguments** and
2:41 those who welcomed his **message**
4: 4 of those who heard the **word**
4:29 your **word** with all boldness,
4:31 spoke the **word** of God with
5: 5 Ananias heard these **words,** he
5:24 chief priests heard these **words**

6: 2	we should neglect the **word** of		20: 2	had given the believers **much**
6: 4	prayer and to serving the **word.**		20: 7	he continued **speaking** until
6: 5	What they **said** pleased the		20:24	But I do not **count** my life of
6: 7	The **word** of God continued to		20:32	to the **message** of his grace, a
7:22	powerful in his **words** and deeds		20:35	remembering the **words** of the
7:29	When he heard **this**, Moses fled		20:38	because of what he had **said,**
8: 4	to place, proclaiming the **word.**		22:22	Up to this **point** they listened
8:14	accepted the **word** of God, they	Ro	3: 4	justified in your **words,** and
8:21	no part or share in **this,** for		9: 6	It is not as though the **word** of
8:25	spoken the **word** of the Lord,		9: 9	this is what the promise **said,**
10:29	Now may I ask **why** you sent for		9:28	Lord will execute his **sentence**
10:36	You know the **message** he sent to		13: 9	are summed up in this **word,**
10:44	upon all who heard the **word.**		14:12	each of us will be **accountable**
11: 1	also accepted the **word** of God.		15:18	the Gentiles, by **word** and deed,
11:19	they spoke the **word** to no one	1C	1: 5	**speech** and knowledge of every
11:22	News of **this** came to the ears		1:17	and not with **eloquent** wisdom,
12:24	But the **word** of God continued		1:18	For the **message** about the cross
13: 5	they proclaimed the **word** of God		2: 1	to you in lofty **words** or wisdom
13: 7	wanted to hear the **word** of God.		2: 4	My **speech** and my proclamation
13:15	Brothers, if you have any **word**		2: 4	plausible **words** of wisdom, but
13:26	fear God, to us the **message** of		2:13	in **words** not taught by human
13:44	gathered to hear the **word** of		4:19	I will find out not the **talk** of
13:46	It was necessary that the **word**		4:20	depends not on **talk** but on
13;48	were glad and praised the **word**		12: 8	the **utterance** of wisdom, and to
13:49	Thus the **word** of the Lord		12: 8	the **utterance** of knowledge
14: 3	who testified to the **word** of		14: 9	if in a tongue you utter **speech**
14:12	he was the chief **speaker.**		14:19	I would rather speak five **words**
14:25	When they had spoken the **word**		14:19	than ten thousand **words** in a
15: 6	to consider this **matter.**		14:36	Or did the **word** of God
15: 7	would hear the **message** of the		15: 2	hold firmly to the **message** that
15:15	This agrees with the **words** of		15:54	then the **saying** that is written
15:24	have said **things** to disturb you	2C	1:18	our **word** to you has not been
15:27	same things by **word** of mouth.		2:17	peddlers of God's **word** like so
15:32	**said** much to encourage and		4: 2	or to falsify God's **word;** but
15:35	proclaimed the **word** of the Lord		5:19	and entrusting the **message** of
15:36	we proclaimed the **word** of the		6: 7	truthful **speech,** and the power
16: 6	to speak the **word** in Asia.		8: 7	faith, in **speech,** in knowledge,
16:32	They spoke the **word** of the Lord		10:10	and his **speech** contemptible.
16:36	reported the **message** to Paul,		10:11	what we **say** by letter when
17:11	they welcomed the **message** very		11: 6	I may be untrained in **speech,**
17:13	learned that the **word** of God	Ga	5:14	up in a single **commandment,**
18: 5	with proclaiming the **word,**		6: 6	Those who are taught the **word**
18:11	teaching the **word** of God among	Ep	1:13	when you had heard the **word** of
18:14	accepting the **complaint** of you		4:29	that your **words** may give grace
18:15	questions about **words** and names		5: 6	deceive you with empty **words,**
19:10	heard the **word** of the Lord.		6:19	a **message** may be given to me to
19:20	So the **word** of the Lord grew	Ph	1:14	dare to speak the **word** with
19:38	have a **complaint** against anyone		2:16	holding fast to the **word** of
19:40	there is no **cause** that we can		4:15	shared with me in the **matter** of

	4:17	accumulates to your **account.**
Co	1: 5	in the **word** of the truth, the
	1:25	to make the **word** of God fully
	2:23	**These** have indeed an appearance
	3:16	Let the **word** of Christ dwell in
	3:17	And whatever you do, in **word** or
	4: 3	open to us a door for the **word,**
	4: 6	Let your **speech** always be
1Th	1: 5	came to you not in **word** only,
	1: 6	you received the **word** with joy
	1: 8	For the **word** of the Lord has
	2: 5	we never came with **words** of
	2:13	when you received the **word** of
	2:13	not as a human **word** but as what
	2:13	God's **word,** which is also at
	4:15	by the **word** of the Lord, that
	4:18	one another with these **words.**
2Th	2: 2	either by spirit or by **word** or
	2:15	either by **word** of mouth or by
	2:17	in every good work and **word.**
	3: 1	so that the **word** of the Lord
	3:14	do not obey what we **say** in this
1Ti	1:15	The **saying** is sure and worthy
	3: 1	The **saying** is sure: whoever
	4: 5	sanctified by God's **word** and by
	4: 6	nourished on the **words** of the
	4: 9	The **saying** is sure and worthy
	4:12	example in **speech** and conduct,
	5:17	who labor in **preaching** and
	6: 3	the sound **words** of our Lord
2Ti	1:13	standard of sound **teaching** that
	2: 9	But the **word** of God is not
	2:11	The **saying** is sure: If we have
	2:15	rightly explaining the **word** of
	2:17	and their **talk** will spread like
	4: 2	proclaim the **message;** be
	4:15	strongly opposed our **message.**
Ti	1: 3	he revealed his **word** through
	1: 9	a firm grasp of the **word** that
	2: 5	so that the **word** of God may not
	2: 8	and sound **speech** that cannot be
	3: 8	The **saying** is sure. I desire
He	2: 2	For if the **message** declared
	4: 2	but the **message** they heard did
	4:12	Indeed, the **word** of God is
	4:13	whom we must render an **account.**
	5:11	About this we have much to **say**
	5:13	is unskilled in the **word** of
	6: 1	basic **teaching** about Christ,

	7:28	but the **word** of the oath, which
	12:19	and a voice whose **words** made
	13: 7	those who spoke the **word** of God
	13:17	souls and will give an **account.**
	13:22	my **word** of exhortation, for I
Ja	1:18	he gave us birth by the **word** of
	1:21	the implanted **word** that has the
	1:22	But be doers of the **word,** and
	1:23	if any are hearers of the **word**
	3: 2	makes no mistakes in **speaking**
1P	1:23	living and enduring **word** of God
	2: 8	they disobey the **word,** as they
	3: 1	do not obey the **word,** they may
	3: 1	be won over without a **word** by
	3:15	an **accounting** for the hope that
	4: 5	give an **accounting** to him who
2P	1:19	prophetic **message** more fully
	2: 3	you with deceptive **words.** Their
	3: 5	that by the **word** of God heavens
	3: 7	by the same **word** the present
1J	1: 1	concerning the **word** of life
	1:10	liar, and his **word** is not in us
	2: 5	whoever obeys his **word,** truly
	2: 7	old commandment is the **word**
	2:14	you are strong and the **word** of
	3:18	not in **word** or speech, but in
3J	1:10	spreading false **charges** against
Re	1: 2	who testified to the **word** of
	1: 3	reads aloud the **words** of the
	1: 9	because of the **word** of God and
	3: 8	yet you have kept my **word** and
	3:10	slaughtered for the **word** of God
	12:11	by the **word** of their testimony,
	17:17	until the **words** of God will be
	19: 9	These are true **words** of God.
	19:13	his name is called The **Word** of
	20: 4	Jesus and for the **word** of God.
	21: 5	for these **words** are trustworthy
	22: 6	These **words** are trustworthy
	22: 7	the one who keeps the **words** of
	22: 9	with those who keep the **words**
	22:10	Do not seal up the **words** of
	22:18	everyone who hears the **words** of
	22:19	takes away from the **words** of

3057   GO1 AG479 LN153

λογχη, SPEAR

Jn 19:34 pierced his side with a **spear,**

3058 GO4 AG479 LN153 B3:346 K4:293 R3060
λοιδορεω, I ABUSE

Jn	9:28	Then they **reviled** him, saying,
Ac	23: 4	Do you dare to **insult** God's
1C	4:12	When **reviled,** we bless; when
1P	2:23	When he **was abused,** he did not

3059 GO3 AG479 LN153 B3:346 K4:293 R3060
λοιδορια, ABUSE

1Ti	5:14	adversary no occasion to **revile**
1P	3: 9	repay evil for evil or **abuse**
	3: 9	for **abuse;** but, on the contrary

3060 GO2 AG479 LN154 B3:346 K4:293
λοιδορος, ABUSER

| 1C | 5:11 | an idolater, **reviler,** drunkard, |
| | 6:10 | **revilers,** robbers—none of |

3061 GO2 AG479 LN154
λοιμος, PLAGUE

| Lk | 21:11 | places famines and **plagues;** and |
| Ac | 24: 5 | this man a **pestilent** fellow, an |

3062 GO55 AG479 LN154 B3:247
λοιπος, REMAINING

Mt	22: 6	while the **rest** seized his
	25:11	Later the **other** bridesmaids
	26:45	Are you **still** sleeping and
	27:49	But the **others** said, "Wait, let
Mk	4:19	the desire for **other** things
	14:41	Are you **still** sleeping and
	16:13	went back and told the **rest,**
Lk	8:10	but to **others** I speak in
	12:26	do you worry about the **rest?**
	18: 9	regarded **others** with contempt:
	18:11	that I am not like **other** people
	24: 9	the eleven and to all the **rest.**
	24:10	the **other** women with them who
Ac	2:37	Peter and to the **other** apostles
	5:13	None of the **rest** dared to join
	17: 9	from Jason and the **others,** they
	27:20	saved was **at last** abandoned.
	27:44	and the **rest** to follow, some on
	28: 9	After this happened, the **rest**
Ro	1:13	as I have among the **rest** of the
	11: 7	but the **rest** were hardened,
1C	1:16	**beyond that,** I do not know
	4: 2	**Moreover,** it is required of
	7:12	To the **rest** I say—I and
	7:29	**from now on,** let even those who

	9: 5	as do the **other** apostles and
	11:34	About the **other things** I will
	15:37	of wheat or of some **other** grain
2C	12:13	worse off than the **other**
	13: 2	previously and all the **others,**
	13:11	**Finally,** brothers and sisters,
Ga	2:13	And the **other** Jews joined him
	6:17	**From now on,** let no one make
Ep	2: 3	of wrath, like **everyone** else.
	6:10	**Finally,** be strong in the Lord
Ph	1:13	and to **everyone else** that my
	3: 1	**Finally,** my brothers and
	4: 3	and the **rest** of my co-workers,
	4: 8	**Finally,** beloved, whatever is
1Th	4: 1	**Finally,** brothers and sisters,
	4:13	you may not grieve as **others** do
	5: 6	not fall asleep as **others** do,
2Th	3: 1	**Finally,** brothers and sisters,
1Ti	5:20	so that the **rest** also may stand
2Ti	4: 8	**From now on** there is reserved
He	10:13	and **since then** has been waiting
2P	3:16	as they do the **other** scriptures
Re	2:24	But to the **rest** of you in
	3: 2	strengthen what **remains** and is
	8:13	at the blasts of the **other**
	9:20	The **rest** of humankind, who were
	11:13	and the **rest** were terrified and
	12:17	make war on the **rest** of her
	19:21	And the **rest** were killed by the
	20: 5	(The **rest** of the dead did not

3065 GO3 AG480 LN154
λουκας, LUKE

Co	4:14	**Luke,** the beloved physician,
2Ti	4:11	Only **Luke** is with me. Get Mark
Pm	1:24	Demas, and **Luke,** my fellow

3066 GO2 AG480 LN154
λουκιος, LUCIUS

| Ac | 13: 1 | **Lucius** of Cyrene, Manaen a |
| Ro | 16:21 | so do **Lucius** and Jason and |

3067 GO2 AG480 LN154 B1:150 K4:295 R3068
λουτρον, WASHING

| Ep | 5:26 | cleansing her with the **washing** |
| Ti | 3: 5 | through the **water** of rebirth |

3068 GO5 AG480 LN154 B1:150 K4:295
λουω, I WASH

| Jn | 13:10 | One who has **bathed** does not |

Ac	9:37	When they had **washed** her, they
	16:33	he took them and **washed** their
He	10:22	our bodies **washed** with pure
2P	2:22	The sow is **washed** only to

3069   GO3   AG481   LN154
λυδδα, LYDDA

Ac	9:32	to the saints living in **Lydda.**
	9:35	And all the residents of **Lydda**
	9:38	Since **Lydda** was near Joppa, the

3070   GO2   AG481   LN154
λυδια, LYDIA

Ac	16:14	A certain woman named **Lydia,** a
	16:40	they went to **Lydia's** home; and

3071   GO1   AG481   LN154
λυκαονια, LYCAONIA

Ac	14: 6	cities of **Lycaonia,** and to the

3072   GO1   AG481   LN154
λυκαονιστι, IN LYCAONIAN [LANGUAGE]

Ac	14:11	they shouted **in the Lycaonian language**

3073   GO1   AG481   LN154
λυκια, LYCIA

Ac	27: 5	we came to Myra in **Lycia.**

3074   GO6   AG481   LN154   K4:308
λυκος, WOLF

Mt	7:15	inwardly are ravenous **wolves.**
	10:16	sheep into the midst of **wolves;**
Lk	10: 3	lambs into the midst of **wolves.**
Jn	10:12	sees the **wolf** coming and leaves
	10:12	and the **wolf** snatches them and
Ac	20:29	savage **wolves** will come in

3075   GO1   AG481   LN154   K4:312
λυμαινομαι, I RAVAGE

Ac	8: 3	Saul **was ravaging** the church

3076   GO26   AG481   LN154   B2:419   K4:313   R3077
λυπεω, I GRIEVE

Mt	14: 9	The king was **grieved,** yet out
	17:23	they were greatly **distressed.**
	18:31	they were greatly **distressed,**
	19:22	he went away **grieving,** for he
	26:22	they became greatly **distressed**
	26:37	began to be **grieved** and

Mk	10:22	shocked and went away **grieving,**
	14:19	They began to be **distressed** and
Jn	16:20	you will **have pain,** but your
	21:17	Peter **felt hurt** because he said
Ro	14:15	**is being injured** by what you
2C	2: 2	For if I **cause** you **pain,** who is
	2: 2	but the one whom I **have pained?**
	2: 4	not **to cause** you **pain,** but to
	2: 5	But if anyone **has caused pain,**
	2: 5	he has **caused** it not to me, but
	6:10	as **sorrowful,** yet always
	7: 8	For even if I **made** you **sorry**
	7: 8	I see that I **grieved** you with
	7: 9	not because you **were grieved,**
	7: 9	but because your **grief** led to
	7: 9	for you felt a godly **grief,** so
	7:11	this godly **grief** has produced
Ep	4:30	And do not **grieve** the Holy
1Th	4:13	so that you may not **grieve** as
1P	1: 6	you have had to **suffer** various

3077   GO16   AG482   LN154   K4:313
λυπη, GRIEF

Lk	22:45	them sleeping because of **grief,**
Jn	16: 6	**sorrow** has filled your hearts.
	16:20	your **pain** will turn into joy.
	16:21	she has **pain,** because her hour
	16:22	So you have **pain** now; but I
Ro	9: 2	I have great **sorrow** and
2C	2: 1	to make you another **painful**
	2: 3	I might not suffer **pain** from
	2: 7	overwhelmed by excessive **sorrow**
	7:10	For godly **grief** produces a
	7:10	worldly **grief** produces death.
	9: 7	**reluctantly** or under compulsion
Ph	2:27	I would not have one **sorrow**
	2:27	have one sorrow after **another.**
He	12:11	discipline always seems **painful**
1P	2:19	you endure **pain** while suffering

3078   GO1   AG482   LN154
λυσανιας, LYSANIAS

Lk	3: 1	and **Lysanias** ruler of Abilene,

3079   GO2   AG482   LN154
λυσιας, LYSIAS

Ac	23:26	Claudius **Lysias** to his
	24:22	When **Lysias** the tribune comes

3080 ^{GO}1 ^{AG}482 ^{LN}154 ^B3:177 ^R3089
λυσις, LOOSENING
1C 7:27 Do not seek to be **free.**

3081 ^{GO}1 ^{AG}482 ^{LN}154
λυσιτελεω, IT IS MORE ADVANTAGEOUS
Lk 17: 2 It **would be better** for you if a

3082 ^{GO}6 ^{AG}482 ^{LN}154
λυστρα, LYSTRA
Ac 14: 6 In **Lystra** there was a man
    14:21 they returned to **Lystra,** then
    16: 1 to Derbe and to **Lystra,** where
    16: 2 by the believers in **Lystra** and
2Ti 3:11 Antioch, Iconium, and **Lystra.**

3083 ^{GO}2 ^{AG}482 ^{LN}154 ^B3:189 ^K4:328
λυτρον, RANSOM
Mt 20:28 give his life a **ransom** for many
Mk 10:45 give his life a **ransom** for many

3084 ^{GO}3 ^{AG}482 ^{LN}154 ^B3:189 ^K4:328 ^R3083
λυτροω, I REDEEM
Lk 24:21 **redeem** Israel. Yes, and besides
Ti 2:14 that he might **redeem** us from
1P 1:18 You know that you **were**
                ransomed

3085 ^{GO}3 ^{AG}483 ^{LN}154 ^B2:189 ^K4:328 ^R3084
λυτρωσις, RANSOM
Lk 1:68 on his people and **redeemed** them
    2:38 looking for the **redemption** of
He 9:12 obtaining eternal **redemption.**

3086 ^{GO}1 ^{AG}483 ^{LN}154 ^B3:189 ^K4:328 ^R3084
λυτρωτης, REDEEMER
Ac 7:35 ruler and **liberator** through the

3087 ^{GO}12 ^{AG}483 ^{LN}154 ^B2:486 ^K4:324 ^R3088
λυχνια, LAMPSTAND
Mt 5:15 on the **lampstand,** and it gives
Mk 4:21 bed, and not on the **lampstand?**
Lk 8:16 puts it on a **lampstand,** so that
    11:33 but on the **lampstand** so that
He 9: 2 in which were the **lampstand,**
Re 1:12 I saw seven golden **lampstands,**
    1:13 in the midst of the **lampstands**
    1:20 seven golden **lampstands:** the
    1:20 the seven **lampstands** are the
    2: 1 the seven golden **lampstands:**

    2: 5 remove your **lampstand** from its
    11: 4 two **lampstands** that stand

3088 ^{GO}14 ^{AG}483 ^{LN}154 ^B2:486 ^K4:324
λυχνος, LAMP
Mt 5:15 No one after lighting a **lamp**
    6:22 The eye is the **lamp** of the
Mk 4:21 He said to them, "Is a **lamp**
Lk 8:16 No one after lighting a **lamp**
    11:33 No one after lighting a **lamp**
    11:34 Your eye is the **lamp** of your
    11:36 as when a **lamp** gives you light
    12:35 action and have your **lamps** lit;
    15: 8 does not light a **lamp,** sweep
Jn 5:35 a burning and shining **lamp,** and
2P 1:19 to this as to a **lamp** shining in
Re 18:23 and the light of a **lamp** will
    21:23 and its **lamp** is the Lamb.
    22: 5 need no light of **lamp** or sun,

3089 ^{GO}42 ^{AG}483 ^{LN}154 ^B3:177 ^K4:328
λυω, I LOOSE
Mt 5:19 Therefore, whoever **breaks** one
    16:19 whatever you **loose** on earth
    16;19 **will be loosed** in heaven.
    18:18 whatever you **loose** on earth
    18:18 loose on earth **will be loosed**
    21: 2 **untie** them and bring them to me
Mk 1: 7 stoop down and **untie** the thong
    7:35 his tongue **was released,** and he
    11: 2 ridden; **untie** it and bring it.
    11: 4 street. As they **were untying** it
    11: 5 you doing, **untying** the colt?
Lk 3:16 I am not worthy to **untie** the
    13:15 **untie** his ox or his donkey from
    13:16 be **set free** from this bondage
    19:30 ridden. **Untie** it and bring it
    19:31 'Why are you **untying** it?' just
    19:33 As they **were untying** the colt,
    19:33 Why are you **untying** the colt?
Jn 1:27 I am not worthy to **untie** the
    2:19 Jesus answered them, **"Destroy**
    5:18 he was not only **breaking** the
    7:23 may not **be broken,** are you
    10:35 scripture cannot **be annulled**
    11:44 **Unbind** him, and let him go.
Ac 2:24 having **freed** him from death,
    7:33 **Take off** the sandals from your
    13:25 I am not worthy to **untie** the

	13:43	of the synagogue **broke up,** many
	22:30	the next day he **released** him
	27:41	the stern was being **broken up**
1C	7:27	**Are** you **free** from a wife? Do
Ep	2:14	**has broken down** the dividing
2P	3:10	the elements **will be dissolved**
	3:11	**are to be dissolved** in this way
	3:12	be set ablaze and **dissolved,**
1J	3: 8	to **destroy** the works of the
Re	1: 5	To him who loves us and **freed**
	5: 2	open the scroll and **break** its
	9:14	**Release** the four angels who
	9:15	four angels **were released,** who
	20: 3	he must be **let out** for a little
	20: 7	Satan will be **released** from his

3090   GO1 AG484 LN155
λωις, LOIS
2Ti 1: 5   your grandmother **Lois** and your

3091   GO4 AG484 LN155
λωτ, LOT
Lk 17:28   in the days of **Lot:** they were
   17:29   but on the day that **Lot** left
   17:32   Remember **Lot's** wife.
2P 2: 7   and if he rescued **Lot,** a

μ

3092   GO1 AG484 LN155
μααθ, MAATH
Lk 3:26   son of **Maath,** son of Mattathias

3093   GO1 AG484 LN155
μαγαδαν, MAGADAN
Mt 15:39   went to the region of **Magadan.**

3094   GO12 AG484 LN155
μαγδαληνη, MAGDALENE
Mt 27:56   Among them were Mary
      Magdalene,
   27:61   Mary **Magdalene** and the other
   28: 1   Mary **Magdalene** and the other
Mk 15:40   among them were Mary
      Magdalene,
   15:47   Mary **Magdalene** and Mary the
   16: 1   Mary **Magdalene,** and Mary the
   16: 9   first to Mary **Magdalene,** from
Lk 8: 2   Mary, called **Magdalene,** from

   24:10   Now it was Mary **Magdalene,**
Jn 19:25   of Clopas, and Mary **Magdalene.**
   20: 1   Mary **Magdalene** came to the
      tomb
   20:18   Mary **Magdalene** went and

3095   GO1 AG484 LN155 B2:552 K4:359 R3096
μαγεια, MAGIC
Ac 8:11   had amazed them with his **magic.**

3096   GO1 AG484 LN155 B2:552 K4:359 R3097
μαγευω, I PRACTICE MAGIC
Ac 8: 9   had previously **practiced magic**

3097   GO6 AG484 LN155 B2:552 K4:356
μαγος, MAGICIAN
Mt 2: 1   **wise men** from the East came to
   2: 7   called for the **wise men** and
   2:16   tricked by the **wise men,** he was
   2:16   had learned from the **wise men.**
Ac 13: 6   they met a certain **magician,** a
   13: 8   But the **magician** Elymas (for

3098   GO1 AG485 LN155 K1:789
μαγωγ, MAGOG
Re 20: 8   Gog and **Magog,** in order to

3099   GO1 AG485 LN155
μαδιαμ, MADIAM
Ac 7:29   alien in the land of **Midian.**

3100   GO4 AG485 LN155 K4:461 R3101
μαθητευω, I LEARN
Mt 13:52   scribe who **has been trained** for
   27:57   was also a **disciple** of Jesus.
   28:19   Go therefore and **make disciples**
Ac 14:21   **had made** many **disciples,** they

3101   GO261 AG485 LN155 B1:483 K4:415 R3129
μαθητης, LEARNER
Mt 5: 1   his **disciples** came to him
   8:21   Another of his **disciples** said
   8:23   his **disciples** followed him
   9:10   with him and his **disciples**
   9:11   they said to his **disciples**
   9:14   Then the **disciples** of John came
   9:14   but your **disciples** do not fast
   9:19   with his **disciples**
   9:37   Then he said to his **disciples**
   10: 1   summoned his twelve **disciples**

10:24	A **disciple** is not above the		26:18	at your house with my **disciples**
10:25	it is enough for the **disciple**		26:19	So the **disciples** did as Jesus
10:42	ones in the name of a **disciple**		26:26	gave it to the **disciples**
11: 1	his twelve **disciples,** he went		26:35	And so said all the **disciples**
11: 2	he sent word by his **disciples**		26:36	he said to his **disciples**
12: 1	his **disciples** were hungry		26:40	Then he came to the **disciples**
12: 2	your **disciples** are doing what		26:45	Then he came to the **disciples**
12:49	And pointing to his **disciples**		26:56	all the **disciples** deserted him
13:10	Then the **disciples** came		27:64	his **disciples** may go and steal
13:36	his **disciples** approached him		28: 7	quickly and tell his **disciples**
14:12	His **disciples** came and took		28: 8	ran to tell his **disciples**
14:15	the **disciples** came to him		28:13	His **disciples** came by night
14:19	and gave them to the **disciples**		28:16	Now the eleven **disciples** went
14:19	and gave them to the **disciples**	Mk	2:15	with Jesus and his **disciples**
14:22	he made the **disciples** get into		2:16	they said to his **disciples**
14:26	But when the **disciples** saw him		2:18	Now John's **disciples** and the
15: 2	Why do your **disciples** break		2:18	Why do John's **disciples**
15:12	Then the **disciples** approached		2:18	the **disciples** of the Pharisees
15:23	his **disciples** came and urged		2:18	but your **disciples** do not fast
15:32	Jesus called his **disciples**		2:23	his **disciples** began to pluck
15:33	The **disciples** said to him		3: 7	departed with his **disciples**
15:36	**disciples** gave them to the		3: 9	He told his **disciples** to have
15:36	gave them to the **disciples**		4:34	in private to his **disciples**
16: 5	When the **disciples** reached the		5:31	And his **disciples** said to him
16.13	he asked his **disciples**		6: 1	and his **disciples** followed him
16:20	sternly ordered the **disciples**		6:29	When his **disciples** heard about
16:21	began to show his **disciples**		6:35	his **disciples** came to him
16:24	Then Jesus told his **disciples**		6:41	gave them to his **disciples**
17: 6	When the **disciples** heard this		6:45	he made his **disciples** get into
17:10	And the **disciples** asked him		7: 2	that some of his **disciples**
17:13	Then the **disciples** understood		7: 5	Why do your **disciples** not live
17:16	I brought him to your **disciples**		7:17	his **disciples** asked him about
17:19	the **disciples** came to Jesus		8: 1	he called his **disciples**
18: 1	At that time the **disciples**		8: 4	His **disciples** replied
19:10	His **disciples** said to him		8: 6	gave them to his **disciples**
19:13	The **disciples** spoke sternly		8:10	with his **disciples** and went
19:23	Jesus said to his **disciples**		8:27	with his **disciples** to the
19:25	When the **disciples** heard this		8:27	the way he asked his **disciples**
20:17	he took the twelve **disciples**		8:33	and looking at his **disciples**
21: 1	Jesus sent two **disciples**		8:34	the crowd with his **disciples**
21: 6	The **disciples** went and did		9:14	they came to the **disciples**
21:20	When the **disciples** saw it		9:18	your **disciples** to cast it out
22:16	sent their **disciples** to him		9:28	his **disciples** asked him
23: 1	crowds and to his **disciples**		9:31	he was teaching his **disciples**
24: 1	his **disciples** came to point out		10:10	the **disciples** asked him again
24: 3	**disciples** came to him privately		10:13	the **disciples** spoke sternly .
26: 1	he said to his **disciples**		10:23	and said to his **disciples**
26: 8	But when the **disciples** saw it		10:24	the **disciples** were perplexed
26:17	the **disciples** came to Jesus		10:46	As he and his **disciples**

	11: 1	he sent two of his **disciples**	2: 2	Jesus and his **disciples** had

	11: 1	he sent two of his **disciples**	2: 2	Jesus and his **disciples** had
	11:14	And his **disciples** heard it	2:11	his **disciples** believed in him
	12:43	Then he called his **disciples**	2:12	his brothers, and his **disciples**
	13: 1	one of his **disciples** said to	2:17	His **disciples** remembered that
	14:12	his **disciples** said to him	2:22	his **disciples** remembered that
	14:13	he sent two of his **disciples**	3:22	Jesus and his **disciples** went
	14:14	the Passover with my **disciples**	3:25	John's **disciples** and a Jew
	14:16	So the **disciples** set out and	4: 1	baptizing more **disciples**
	14:32	he said to his **disciples**	4: 2	but his **disciples** who baptized
	16: 7	But go, tell his **disciples**	4: 8	His **disciples** had gone to
Lk	5:30	complaining to his **disciples**	4:27	Just then his **disciples** came
	5:33	John's **disciples,** like the	4:31	the **disciples** were urging him
	6: 1	his **disciples** plucked some	4:33	**disciples** said to one another
	6:13	he called his **disciples**	6: 3	there with his **disciples**
	6:17	great crowd of his **disciples**	6: 8	One of his **disciples,** Andrew
	6:20	looked up at his **disciples**	6:12	he told his **disciples**
	6:40	A **disciple** is not above the	6:16	his **disciples** went down to
	7:11	his **disciples** and a large	6:22	his **disciples** had gone away
	7:18	The **disciples** of John reported	6:22	the boat with his **disciples**
	7:18	summoned two of his **disciples**	6:24	neither Jesus nor his **disciples**
	8: 9	Then his **disciples** asked him	6:60	When many of his **disciples**
	8:22	with his **disciples,** and he said	6:61	his **disciples** were complaining
	9:14	And he said to his **disciples**	6:66	many of his **disciples** turned
	9:16	gave them to the **disciples**	7: 3	your **disciples** also may see
	9:18	with only the **disciples** near	8:31	you are truly my **disciples**
	9:40	I begged your **disciples** to cast	9: 2	His **disciples** asked him
	9:43	he said to his **disciples**	9:27	want to become his **disciples**
	9:54	When his **disciples** James	9:28	You are his **disciple**
	10:23	Then turning to the **disciples**	9:28	but we are **disciples** of Moses
	11: 1	one of his **disciples** said to	11: 7	he said to the **disciples**
	11: 1	as John taught his **disciples**	11: 8	The **disciples** said to him
	12: 1	speak first to his **disciples**	11:12	The **disciples** said to him
	12:22	He said to his **disciples**	11:54	there with the **disciples**
	14:26	cannot be my **disciple**	12: 4	one of his **disciples**
	14:27	cannot be my **disciple**	12:16	**disciples** did not understand
	14:33	can become my **disciple** if you	13: 5	to wash the **disciples'** feet
	16: 1	Jesus said to the **disciples**	13:22	**disciples** looked at one another
	17: 1	Jesus said to his **disciples**	13:23	One of his **disciples**
	17:22	Then he said to the **disciples**	13:35	that you are my **disciples**
	18:15	and when the **disciples** saw it	15: 8	fruit and become my **disciples**
	19:29	sent two of the **disciples**	16:17	some of his **disciples**
	19:37	multitude of the **disciples**	16:29	His **disciples** said
	19:39	order your **disciples** to stop	18: 1	**disciples** across the Kidron
	20:45	he said to the **disciples**	18: 1	he and his **disciples** entered.
	22:11	the Passover with my **disciples**	18: 2	met there with his **disciples**
	22:39	and the **disciples** followed him	18:15	Peter and another **disciple**
	22:45	he came to the **disciples**	18:15	Since that **disciple** was known
Jn	1:35	with two of his **disciples**	18:16	So the other **disciple**
	1:37	The two **disciples** heard him	18:17	one of this man's **disciples**

18:19	Jesus about his **disciples**
18:25	also one of his **disciples**
19:26	the **disciple** whom he loved
19:27	Then he said to the **disciple**
19:27	from that hour the **disciple**
19:38	who was a **disciple** of Jesus
20: 2	Peter and the other **disciple**
20: 3	Peter and the other **disciple**
20: 4	the other **disciple** outran Peter
20: 8	Then the other **disciple**
20:10	Then the **disciples** returned
20:18	announced to the **disciples**
20:19	where the **disciples** had met
20:20	Then the **disciples** rejoiced .
20:25	the other **disciples** told him
20:26	A week later his **disciples**
20:30	the presence of his **disciples**
21: 1	again to the **disciples** by the
21: 2	two others of his **disciples**
21: 4	but the **disciples** did not know
21: 7	That **disciple** whom Jesus loved
21: 8	the other **disciples** came in the
21:12	none of the **disciples** dared
21:14	Jesus appeared to the **disciples**
21:20	turned and saw the **disciple**
21:23	this **disciple** would not die
21:24	This is the **disciple** who is
Ac 6: 1	the **disciples** were increasing
6: 2	community of the **disciples**
6: 7	the number of the **disciples**
9: 1	against the **disciples** of the
9:10	Now there was a **disciple**
9:19	he was with the **disciples**
9:25	but his **disciples** took him
9:26	attempted to join the **disciples**
9:26	believe that he was a **disciple.**
9:38	the **disciples,** who heard that
11:26	in Antioch that the **disciples**
11:29	The **disciples** determined that
13:52	**disciples** were filled with joy
14:20	when the **disciples** surrounded
14:22	the souls of the **disciples**
14:28	stayed there with the **disciples**
15:10	on the neck of the **disciples**
16: 1	where there was a **disciple**
18:23	strengthening all the **disciples**
18:27	and wrote to the **disciples**
19: 1	he found some **disciples**
19: 9	taking the **disciples** with him

19:30	but the **disciples** would not let
20: 1	Paul sent for the **disciples**
20:30	to entice the **disciples**
21: 4	We looked up the **disciples**
21:16	the **disciples** from Caesarea
21:16	of Cyprus, an early **disciple**

3102   ᴳᴼ1 ᴬᴳ486 ᴸᴺ155 ᴷ4:460 ᴿ3101
μαθητρια, LEARNER
Ac   9:36   in Joppa there was a **disciple**

3102a   ᴳᴼ5 ᴬᴳ486 ᴸᴺ155
μαθθαιος, MATTHEW
Mt   9: 9   saw a man called **Matthew**
      10: 3   **Matthew** the tax collector
Mk   3:18   Bartholomew, and **Matthew**
Lk   6:15   **Matthew,** and Thomas, and James
Ac   1:13   Bartholomew and **Matthew,** James

3102b   ᴳᴼ2 ᴬᴳ486 ᴸᴺ155
μαθθατ, MATTHAT
Lk   3:24   son of **Matthat,** son of Levi
      3:29   son of Jorim, son of **Matthat**

3102c   ᴳᴼ2 ᴬᴳ486 ᴸᴺ155
μαθθιας, MATTHIAS
Ac   1:23   known as Justus, and **Matthias**
      1:26   the lot fell on **Matthias**

3103   ᴳᴼ1 ᴬᴳ486 ᴸᴺ155
μαθουσαλα, MATHUSALA (METHUSALA)
Lk   3:37   son of **Methuselah**

3105   ᴳᴼ5 ᴬᴳ486 ᴸᴺ155 ᴮ1:527 ᴷ4:360
μαινομαι, I AM CRAZY
Jn   10:20   demon and **is out of his mind**
Ac   12:15   You **are out of your mind**
      26:24   You **are out of your mind**
      26:25   I am not **out of my mind**
1C   14:23   that you **are out of your mind**

3106   ᴳᴼ2 ᴬᴳ486 ᴸᴺ155 ᴮ1:215 ᴷ4:362 ᴿ3107
μακαριζω, I CALL FORTUNATE
Lk   1:48   **will call me blessed**
Ja   5:11   Indeed we **call blessed** those

3107   ᴳᴼ50 ᴬᴳ486 ᴸᴺ155 ᴮ1:215 ᴷ4:362
μακαριος, FORTUNATE
Mt   5: 3   **Blessed** are the poor in spirit
      5: 4   **Blessed** are those who mourn

	5: 5	**Blessed** are the meek
	5: 6	**Blessed** are those who hunger
	5: 7	**Blessed** are the merciful
	5: 8	**Blessed** are the pure in heart
	5: 9	**Blessed** are the peacemakers
	5:10	**Blessed** are those who are
	5:11	**Blessed** are you when people
	11: 6	**blessed** is anyone who takes no
	13:16	But **blessed** are your eyes
	16:17	**Blessed** are you, Simon son
	24:46	**Blessed** is that slave whom his
Lk	1:45	**blessed** is she who believed
	6:20	**Blessed** are you who are poor
	6:21	**Blessed** are you who are hungry
	6:21	**Blessed** are you who weep now
	6:22	**Blessed** are you when people
	7:23	**blessed** is anyone who takes
	10:23	**Blessed** are the eyes that see
	11:27	**Blessed** is the womb that bore
	11:28	**Blessed** rather are those who
	12:37	**Blessed** are those slaves whom
	12:38	**blessed** are those slaves
	12:43	**Blessed** is that slave whom his
	14:14	And you will be **blessed**
	14:15	**Blessed** is anyone who will eat
	23:29	**Blessed** are the barren
Jn	13:17	you are **blessed** if you do them
	20:29	**Blessed** are those who have not
Ac	20:35	It is more **blessed** to give than
	26: 2	I consider myself **fortunate**
Ro	4: 7	**Blessed** are those whose
	4: 8	**blessed** is the one against
	14:22	**Blessed** are those who have
1C	7:40	she is more **blessed** if she
1Ti	1:11	gospel of the **blessed** God
	6:15	he who is the **blessed** and only
Ti	2:13	we wait for the **blessed** hope
Ja	1:12	**Blessed** is anyone who endures
	1:25	will be **blessed** in their doing
1P	3:14	what is right, you are **blessed**
	4:14	name of Christ, you are **blessed**
Re	1: 3	**Blessed** is the one who reads
	14:13	**Blessed** are the dead who from
	16:15	**Blessed** is the one who stays
	19: 9	**Blessed** are those who are
	20: 6	**Blessed** and holy are those
	22: 7	**Blessed** is the one who keeps
	22:14	**Blessed** are those who wash

3108 GO3 AG487 LN155 B1:215 K4:362 R3106
μακαρισμος, FORTUNATENESS

Ro	4: 6	David speaks of the **blessedness**
	4: 9	Is this **blessedness**
Ga	4:15	What has become of the **goodwill**

3109 GO22 AG487 LN155
μακεδονια, MACEDONIA

Ac	16: 9	there stood a man of **Macedonia**
	16:10	to cross over to **Macedonia**
	16:12	of the district of **Macedonia**
	18: 5	Timothy arrived from **Macedonia**
	19:21	to go through **Macedonia**
	19:22	and Erastus, to **Macedonia**
	20: 1	he left for **Macedonia**
	20: 3	to return through **Macedonia**
Ro	15:26	for **Macedonia** and Achaia
1C	16: 5	after passing through **Macedonia**
	16: 5	to pass through **Macedonia**—
2C	1:16	on my way to **Macedonia**
	1:16	back to you from **Macedonia**
	2:13	and went on to **Macedonia**
	7: 5	when we came into **Macedonia**
	8: 1	to the churches of **Macedonia**
	11: 9	friends who came from **Macedonia**
Ph	4:15	when I left **Macedonia**
1Th	1: 7	all the believers in **Macedonia**
	1: 8	not only in **Macedonia**
	4:10	sisters throughout **Macedonia**
1Ti	1: 3	was on my way to **Macedonia**

3110 GO5 AG487 LN155
μακεδων, MACEDONIAN

Ac	16: 9	stood a man of **Macedonia**
	19:29	**Macedonians** who were Paul's
	27: 2	a **Macedonian** from Thessalonica
2C	9: 2	to the people of **Macedonia**
	9: 4	some **Macedonians** come with me

3111 GO1 AG487 LN156 K4:370
μακελλον, MEAT MARKET

1C	10:25	is sold in the **meat market**

3112 GO10 AG487 LN156 B2:52 K4:372 R3117
μακραν, FAR

Mt	8:30	at some **distance** from them
Mk	12:34	You are not **far** from the
Lk	7: 6	when he was not **far** from the
	15:20	while he was still **far** off
Jn	21: 8	they were not **far** from the land

Ac	2:39	for all who are **far** away
	17:27	he is not **far** from each one
	22:21	I will send you **far** away
Ep	2:13	you who once were **far** off
	2:17	to you who were **far** off

3113　GO14 AG487 LN156 K4:372 R3117
μακροθεν, FROM FAR

Mt	26:58	as **far** as the courtyard
	27:55	looking on **from** a **distance**
Mk	5: 6	he saw Jesus **from** a **distance**
	8: 3	come **from** a great **distance**
	11:13	Seeing in the **distance**
	14:54	had followed him at a **distance**
	15:40	looking on **from** a **distance**
Lk	16:23	and saw Abraham **far** away
	18:13	collector, standing **far** off
	22:54	was following at a **distance**
	23:49	stood at a **distance**
Re	18:10	they will stand **far** off
	18:15	will stand **far** off
	18:17	stood **far** off

3114　GO10 AG488 LN156 B2:768 K4:374 R2373
μακροθυμεω, I AM LONG-TEMPERED

Mt	18:26	**Have patience** with me
	18:29	**Have patience** with me
Lk	18: 7	**Will** he **delay long** in helping
1C	13: 4	Love **is patient**
1Th	5:14	**be patient** with all of them
He	6:15	**having patiently endured**
Ja	5: 7	**Be patient,** therefore, beloved
	5: 7	**being patient** with it until it
	5: 8	You also must **be patient**
2P	3: 9	but **is patient** with you

3115　GO14 AG488 LN156 B2:768 K4:374 R3114
μακροθυμια, LONG TEMPER

Ro	2: 4	and forbearance and **patience**
	9:22	has endured with much **patience**
2C	6: 6	by purity, knowledge, **patience**
Ga	5:22	love, joy, peace, **patience**
Ep	4: 2	gentleness, with **patience**
Co	1:11	everything with **patience**
	3:12	meekness, and **patience**
1Ti	1:16	display the utmost **patience**
2Ti	3:10	my faith, my **patience,** my love
	4: 2	with the utmost **patience**
He	6:12	who through faith and **patience**
Ja	5:10	of suffering and **patience**

1P	3:20	when God waited **patiently**
2P	3:15	the **patience** of our Lord

3116　GO1 AG488 LN156 B2:768 K4:387 R3114
μακροθυμως, LONG-TEMPEREDLY

Ac	26: 3	you to listen to me **patiently**

3117　GO4 AG488 LN156 R3372
μακρος, FAR

Mk	12:40	of appearance say **long** prayers
Lk	15:13	traveled to a **distant** country
	19:12	went to a **distant** country
	20:47	of appearance say **long** prayers

3118　GO1 AG488 LN156 R3117,5550
μακροχρονιος, LONG TIME

Ep	6: 3	you may live **long** on the earth

3119　GO3 AG488 LN156 B3:996 K4:1091
μαλακια, SICKNESS

Mt	4:23	every **sickness** among the people
	9:35	disease and every **sickness**
	10: 1	disease and every **sickness**

3120　GO4 AG488 LN156
μαλακος, SOFT

Mt	11: 8	Someone dressed in **soft** robes?
	11: 8	those who wear **soft** robes
Lk	7:25	Someone dressed in **soft** robes?
1C	6: 9	**male prostitutes,** sodomites

3121　GO1 AG488 LN156
μαλελεηλ, MALELEEL (MAHALALEEL)

Lk	3:37	son of **Mahalaleel**

3122　GO12 AG488 LN156
μαλιστα, ESPECIALLY

Ac	20:38	grieving **especially** because of
	25:26	and **especially** before you
	26: 3	you are **especially** familiar
Ga	6:10	and **especially** for those
Ph	4:22	**especially** those of the
1Ti	4:10	**especially** of those who believe
	5: 8	**especially** for family members
	5:17	**especially** those who labor
2Ti	4:13	and **above all** the parchments
Ti	1:10	**especially** those of the
Pm	1:16	**especially** to me but how much
2P	2:10	**especially** those who indulge

3123 GO81 AG489 LN156
μαλλον, MORE

Mt	6:26	Are you not of **more** value
	6:30	will he not much **more** clothe
	7:11	how much **more** will your Father
	10: 6	but go **rather** to the lost sheep
	10:25	how much **more** will they malign
	10:28	**rather** fear him who can destroy
	18:13	he rejoices over it **more**
	25: 9	**better** go to the dealers
	27:24	but **rather** that a riot was
Mk	5:26	but **rather** grew worse
	7:36	but the **more** he ordered them
	9:42	it would be **better** for you
	10:48	he cried out even **more** loudly
	15:11	Barabbas for them **instead**
Lk	5:15	But now **more** than ever
	11:13	how much **more** will the
	12:24	Of how much **more** value
	12:28	how much **more** will he clothe
	18:39	he shouted even **more** loudly
Jn	3:19	**rather** than light because.
	5:18	were seeking all the **more**
	12:43	**more** than the glory that comes
	19: 8	he was **more** afraid than ever
Ac	4:19	listen to you **rather** than to
	5:14	Yet **more** than ever believers
	5:29	We must obey God **rather** than
	9:22	Saul became increasingly **more**
	20:35	It is **more** blessed to give
	22: 2	they became even **more** quiet
	27:11	paid **more** attention to the
Ro	5: 9	Much **more** surely then
	5:10	his Son, much **more** surely
	5:15	much **more** surely have the grace
	5:17	much **more** surely will those
	8:34	**yes,** who was raised, who is
	11:12	how much **more** will their full
	11:24	how much **more** will these
	14:13	but resolve **instead** never to
1C	5: 2	Should you not **rather** have
	6: 7	Why not **rather** be wronged?
	6: 7	Why not **rather** be defrauded?
	7:21	condition now **more** than ever
	9:12	do not we still **more?**
	9:15	I would **rather** die than that
	12:22	On the **contrary,** the members
	14: 1	**especially** that you may
	14: 5	but even **more** to prophesy

	14:18	I speak in tongues **more**
2C	2: 7	so now **instead** you should
	3: 8	how much **more** will the
	3: 9	much **more** does the ministry
	3:11	much **more** has the permanent
	5: 8	we would **rather** be away from
	7: 7	so that I rejoiced still **more**
	7:13	we rejoiced still **more** at the
	12: 9	boast all the **more** gladly
Ga	4: 9	or **rather** to be known by God
	4:27	are **more** numerous than the
Ep	4:28	**rather** let them labor and work
	5: 4	but **instead,** let there be
	5:11	but **instead** expose them
Ph	1: 9	your love may overflow **more**
	1: 9	may overflow more and **more**
	1:12	has **actually** helped to spread
	1:23	for that is **far** better
	2:12	but much **more** now in my
	3: 4	in the flesh, I have **more**
1Th	4: 1	should do so **more** and more
	4:10	to do so **more** and more
1Ti	1: 4	**rather** than the divine
	6: 2	must serve them all the **more**
2Ti	3: 4	**rather** than lovers of God
Pm	1: 9	I would **rather** appeal to you
	1:16	how much **more** to you
He	9:14	how much **more** will the blood
	10:25	and all the **more** as you see
	11:25	choosing **rather** to share
	12: 9	not be even **more** willing to be
	12:13	but **rather** be healed
	12:25	how **much** less will we escape
2P	1:10	be all the **more** eager

3124 GO1 AG489 LN156
μαλχος, MALCHUS

| Jn | 18:10 | The slave's name was **Malchus.** |

3125 GO1 AG490 LN156
μαμμη, GRANDMOTHER

| 2Ti | 1: 5 | lived first in your **grandmother** |

3126 GO4 AG490 LN156 B2:836 K4:388
μαμωνας, MAMMON

Mt	6:24	You cannot serve God and **wealth**
Lk	16: 9	by means of dishonest **wealth**
	16:11	with the dishonest **wealth**
	16:13	You cannot serve God and **wealth**

3127 ᴳᴼ1 ᴬᴳ490 ᴸᴺ156
μαναην, MANAEN
Ac 13: 1 **Manaen** a member of the court

3128 ᴳᴼ3 ᴬᴳ490 ᴸᴺ156
μανασσης, MANASSES (MANASSEH)
Mt 1:10 Hezekiah the father of **Manasseh**
    1:10 **Manasseh** the father of Amos,
Re 7: 6 from the tribe of **Manasseh**

3129 ᴳᴼ25 ᴬᴳ490 ᴸᴺ156 ᴮ1:483 ᴷ4:390
μανθανω, I LEARN
Mt   9:13 Go and **learn** what this means
    11:29 upon you, and **learn** from me
    24:32 From the fig tree **learn** its
Mk 13:28 From the fig tree **learn** its
Jn   6:45 who has heard and **learned**
     7:15 this man have such **learning**
Ac 23:27 but when I **had learned**
Ro 16:17 teaching that you **have learned**
1C   4: 6 so that you **may learn** through
    14:31 so that all may **learn**
    14:35 anything they desire to **know**
Ga   3: 2 The only thing I want **to
               learn**
Ep   4:20 That is not the way you **learned**
Ph   4: 9 that you **have learned**
     4:11 I **have learned** to be content
Co   1: 7 This you **learned** from
               Epaphras
1Ti 2:11 Let a woman **learn** in silence
     5: 4 they should first **learn**
     5:13 they **learn** to be idle
2Ti 3: 7 are always being **instructed**
     3:14 in what you **have learned**
     3:14 from whom you **learned** it
Ti   3:14 let people **learn** to devote
He   5: 8 he **learned** obedience through
Re 14: 3 No one could **learn** that song

3130 ᴳᴼ1 ᴬᴳ490 ᴸᴺ156 ᴮ1:528 ᴿ3105
μανια, CRAZINESS
Ac 26:24 learning is driving you **insane**

3131 ᴳᴼ4 ᴬᴳ490 ᴸᴺ156 ᴮ1:252 ᴷ4:462
μαννα, MANNA
Jn   6:31 Our ancestors ate the **manna**
     6:49 Your ancestors ate the **manna**
He   9: 4 golden urn holding the **manna**
Re   2:17 give some of the hidden **manna**

3132 ᴳᴼ1 ᴬᴳ491 ᴸᴺ156 ᴮ3:74
μαντευομαι, I TELL FORTUNE
Ac 16:16 of money by **fortune-telling**

3133 ᴳᴼ1 ᴬᴳ491 ᴸᴺ156
μαραινω, I WASTE AWAY
Ja   1:11 they **will wither away**

3134 ᴳᴼ1 ᴬᴳ491 ᴸᴺ156 ᴮ2:895
μαρανα θα, MARANA THA
1C 16:22 for the Lord. **Our Lord, come**

3135 ᴳᴼ9 ᴬᴳ491 ᴸᴺ156 ᴮ3:394 ᴷ4:472
μαργαριτης, PEARL
Mt   7: 6 throw your **pearls** before swine
    13:45 in search of fine **pearls**
    13:46 one **pearl** of great value
1Ti 2: 9 with gold, **pearls,** or expensive
Re 17: 4 gold and jewels and **pearls**
    18:12 silver, jewels and **pearls**
    18:16 with jewels, and with **pearls**
    21:21 twelve gates are twelve **pearls**
    21:21 the gates is a single **pearl,**

3136 ᴳᴼ13 ᴬᴳ491 ᴸᴺ156
μαρθα, MARTHA
Lk 10:38 a woman named **Martha** welcomed
    10:40 But **Martha** was distracted
    10:41 **Martha,** Martha, you are worried
    10:41 Martha, **Martha,** you are worried
Jn 11: 1 Mary and her sister **Martha**
    11: 5 though Jesus loved **Martha**
    11:19 the Jews had come to **Martha**
    11:20 When **Martha** heard that Jesus
    11:21 **Martha** said to Jesus
    11:24 **Martha** said to him
    11:30 place where **Martha** had met him
    11:39 **Martha,** the sister of the dead
    12: 2 dinner for him. **Martha** served

3137 ᴳᴼ27 ᴬᴳ491 ᴸᴺ156
μαρια, MARIA
Mt   1:16 Joseph the husband of **Mary**
     1:18 When his mother **Mary** had been
     1:20 do not be afraid to take **Mary**
     2:11 they saw the child with **Mary**
    27:56 Among them were **Mary**
               Magdalene
    27:56 and **Mary** the mother of James
    27:61 and the other **Mary** were there

	28: 1	Magdalene and the other **Mary**
Mk	6: 3	the son of **Mary** and brother
	15:40	among them were **Mary** Magdalene
	15:40	and **Mary** the mother of James
	15:47	**Mary** Magdalene and Mary the
	15:47	Mary Magdalene and **Mary** the
	16: 1	**Mary** Magdalene, and Mary the
	16: 1	**Mary** the mother of James
	16: 9	he appeared first to **Mary**
Lk	1:41	Elizabeth heard **Mary's** greeting,
	8: 2	**Mary**, called Magdalene, from
	24:10	Now it was **Mary** Magdalene
	24:10	**Mary** the mother of James
Jn	11: 1	the village of **Mary** and her
	19:25	**Mary** the wife of Clopas
	19:25	of Clopas, and **Mary** Magdalene
	20: 1	**Mary** Magdalene came to the tomb
	20:11	But **Mary** stood weeping outside
Ac	12:12	to the house of **Mary**
Ro	16: 6	Greet **Mary**, who has worked

3137a　GO27 AG492 LN156
μαριαμ, MARIAM

Mt	13:55	Is not his mother called **Mary?**
	27:61	**Mary** Magdalene and the other
	28: 1	**Mary** Magdalene and the other
Lk	1:27	The virgin's name was **Mary.**
	1:30	Do not be afraid, **Mary**
	1:34	**Mary** said to the angel
	1:38	Then **Mary** said
	1:39	In those days **Mary** set out
	1:46	And **Mary** said
	1:56	And **Mary** remained with her
	2: 5	to be registered with **Mary**
	2:16	and found **Mary** and Joseph
	2:19	But **Mary** treasured all these
	2:34	said to his mother **Mary**
	10:39	She had a sister named **Mary**
	10:42	**Mary** has chosen the better part
Jn	11: 2	**Mary** was the one who anointed
	11:19	Martha and **Mary** to console them
	11:20	while **Mary** stayed at home
	11:28	and called her sister **Mary**
	11:31	saw **Mary** get up quickly
	11:32	When **Mary** came where Jesus was
	11:45	who had come with **Mary** and had
	12: 3	**Mary** took a pound of costly
	20:16	Jesus said to her, **"Mary!"**

	20:18	**Mary** Magdalene went
Ac	1:14	**Mary** the mother of Jesus

3138　GO8 AG492 LN156
μαρκος, MARK

Ac	12:12	John whose other name was **Mark**
	12:25	whose other name was **Mark**
	15:37	with them John called **Mark**
	15:39	Barnabas took **Mark** with him
Co	4:10	**Mark** the cousin of Barnabas
2Ti	4:11	Get **Mark** and bring him with
Pm	1:24	and so do **Mark,** Aristarchus
1P	5:13	and so does my son **Mark**

3139　GO1 AG492 LN156
μαρμαρος, MARBLE

Re	18:12	bronze, iron, and **marble**

3140　GO77 AG492 LN157 B3:1038 K4:474 R3144
μαρτυρεω, I TESTIFY

Mt	23:31	you **testify** against yourselves
Lk	4:22	All **spoke well** of him and were
Jn	1: 7	He came as a witness **to testify**
	1: 8	but he came **to testify** to the
	1:15	John **testified** to him
	1:32	And John **testified**
	1:34	have seen and **have testified**
	2:25	and needed no one to **testify**
	3:11	**testify** to what we have seen
	3:26	to whom you **testified**
	3:28	You yourselves **are** my **witnesses**
	3:32	He **testifies** to what he has
	4:39	of the woman's **testimony**
	4:44	for Jesus himself **had testified**
	5:31	If I **testify** about myself
	5:32	There is another who **testifies**
	5:32	his **testimony** to me is true
	5:33	and he **testified** to the truth
	5:36	**testify** on my behalf that the
	5:37	has himself **testified** on my
	5:39	it is they that **testify**
	7: 7	I **testify** against it that its
	8:13	You are **testifying** on your own
	8:14	Even if I **testify** on my own
	8:18	I **testify** on my own behalf,
	8:18	sent me **testifies** on my behalf
	10:25	in my Father's name **testify** to
	12:17	the dead continued to **testify**
	13:21	**declared,** "Very truly, I tell
	15:26	he **will testify** on my behalf

	15:27	You also are to **testify**
	18:23	**testify** to the wrong
	18:37	to **testify** to the truth
	19:35	He who saw this **has testified**
	21:24	the disciple who **is testifying**
Ac	6: 3	seven men **of good standing**
	10:22	who **is well spoken** of by the
	10:43	All the prophets **testify**
	13:22	In his **testimony** about him
	14: 3	who **testified** to the word
	15: 8	**testified** to them by giving
	16: 2	He **was well spoken** of by the
	22: 5	council of elders can **testify**
	22:12	**well spoken** of by all the Jews
	23:11	just as you **have testified**
	26: 5	they are willing to **testify**
Ro	3:21	**is attested** by the law
	10: 2	I can **testify** that they have
1C	15:15	because we **testified** of God
2C	8: 3	For, as I can **testify,** they
Ga	4:15	For I **testify** that, had it been
Co	4:13	For I **testify** for him
1Ti	5:10	she must be well **attested**
	6:13	in his **testimony** before Pontius
He	7: 8	by one of whom it is **testified**
	7:17	For it **is attested** of him
	10:15	the Holy Spirit also **testifies**
	11: 2	our ancestors **received approval**
	11: 4	**received approval** as righteous
	11: 4	God himself **giving approval**
	11: 5	For it **was attested** before he
	11:39	though they **were commended**
1J	1: 2	have seen it and **testify** to it
	4:14	we have seen and do **testify**
	5: 6	is the one that **testifies**
	5: 7	There are three that **testify**
	5: 9	he has **testified** to his Son
	5:10	testimony that God **has given**
3J	1: 3	friends arrived and **testified**
	1: 6	**have testified** to your love
	1:12	Everyone **has testified**
	1:12	We also **testify** for him
Re	1: 2	**testified** to the word of God
	22:16	this **testimony** for the churches
	22:18	I **warn** everyone who hears
	22:20	The one who **testifies** to these

3141   GO37 AG493 LN157 B3:1038 K4:474 R3144
μαρτυρια, TESTIMONY

Mk	14:55	were looking for **testimony**
	14:56	their **testimony** did not agree
	14:59	their **testimony** did not agree
Lk	22:71	What further **testimony** do we
Jn	1: 7	He came as a **witness**
	1:19	This is the **testimony** given
	3:11	do not receive our **testimony**
	3:32	one accepts his **testimony**
	3:33	has accepted his **testimony**
	5:31	my **testimony** is not true
	5:32	his **testimony** to me is true
	5:34	I accept such human **testimony**
	5:36	But I have a **testimony** greater
	8:13	your **testimony** is not valid
	8:14	my **testimony** is valid
	8:17	**testimony** of two witnesses
	19:35	His **testimony** is true
	21:24	that his **testimony** is true
Ac	22:18	accept your **testimony** about
1Ti	3: 7	he must be **well thought** of
Ti	1:13	That **testimony** is true
1J	5: 9	If we receive human **testimony**
	5: 9	**testimony** of God is greater
	5: 9	for this is the **testimony**
	5:10	have the **testimony** in their
	5:10	believing in the **testimony**
	5:11	And this is the **testimony**
3J	1:12	that our **testimony** is true
Re	1: 2	**testimony** of Jesus Christ
	1: 9	word of God and the **testimony**
	6: 9	the **testimony** they had given
	11: 7	have finished their **testimony**
	12:11	by the word of their **testimony**
	12:17	hold the **testimony** of Jesus
	19:10	who hold the **testimony** of Jesus
	19:10	**testimony** of Jesus is the
	20: 4	beheaded for their **testimony**

3142   GO19 AG493 LN157 B3:1038 K4:474 R3144
μαρτυριον, TESTIMONY

Mt	8: 4	as a **testimony** to them
	10:18	as a **testimony** to them
	24:14	a **testimony** to all the nations
Mk	1:44	as a **testimony** to them
	6:11	as a **testimony** against them
	13: 9	as a **testimony** to them
Lk	5:14	for a **testimony** to them
	9: 5	as a **testimony** against them
	21:13	you an opportunity to **testify**

Ac	4:33	apostles gave their **testimony**
	7:44	had the tent of **testimony**
1C	1: 6	just as the **testimony** of Christ
2C	1:12	the **testimony** of our conscience
2Th	1:10	because our **testimony** to you
1Ti	2: 6	this was **attested** at the right
2Ti	1: 8	of the **testimony** about our Lord
He	3: 5	to **testify** to the things
Ja	5: 3	will be **evidence** against you
Re	15: 5	the tent of **witness** in heaven

3143 GO4 AG494 LN157 B3:1038 K4:510 R3144
μαρτυρομαι, I TESTIFY

Ac	20:26	**I declare** to you this day
	26:22	**testifying** to both small
Ga	5: 3	I **testify** to every man
Ep	4:17	I affirm and **insist on**
1Th	2:12	**pleading** that you lead a life

3144 GO35 AG494 LN157 B3:1038 K4:474
μαρτυς, TESTIFIER

Mt	18:16	of two or three **witnesses**
	26:65	do we still need **witnesses**
Mk	14:63	Why do we still need **witnesses**
Lk	11:48	you are **witnesses** and approve
	24:48	are **witnesses** of these things
Ac	1: 8	you will be my **witnesses**
	1:22	must become a **witness** with us
	2:32	all of us are **witnesses**
	3:15	To this we are **witnesses.**
	5:32	**witnesses** to these things
	6:13	They set up false **witnesses**
	7:58	the **witnesses** laid their coats
	10:39	We are **witnesses** to all
	10:41	were chosen by God as **witnesses**
	13:31	his **witnesses** to the people
	22:15	for you will be his **witness**
	22:20	while the blood of your **witness**
	26:16	**testify** to the things in which
Ro	1: 9	is my **witness** that without
2C	1:23	But I call on God as **witness**
	13: 1	of two or three **witnesses**
Ph	1: 8	For God is my **witness**
1Th	2: 5	and as God is our **witness**
	2:10	You are **witnesses**, and God also
1Ti	5:19	of two or three **witnesses**
	6:12	the presence of many **witnesses**
2Ti	2: 2	from me through many **witnesses**

He	10:28	of two or three **witnesses**
	12: 1	great a cloud of **witnesses**
1P	5: 1	a **witness** of the sufferings
Re	1: 5	Christ, the faithful **witness**
	2:13	days of Antipas my **witness**
	3:14	the faithful and true **witness**
	11: 3	will grant my two **witnesses**
	17: 6	the blood of the **witnesses**

3145 GO1 AG495 LN157 K4:514
μασαομαι, I CHEW

Re	16:10	people **gnawed** their tongues

3146 GO7 AG495 LN157 B1:161 K4:515 R3148
μαστιγοω, I SCOURGE

Mt	10:17	**flog** you in their synagogues
	20:19	**flogged** and crucified
	23:34	**flog** in your synagogues
Mk	10:34	and **flog** him, and kill him
Lk	18:33	After they have **flogged** him
Jn	19: 1	took Jesus and **had** him **flogged**
He	12: 6	**chastises** every child whom he

3147 GO1 AG495 LN157 B1:161 K4:515 R3148
μαστιζω, I SCOURGE

Ac	22:25	to **flog** a Roman citizen who is

3148 GO6 AG495 LN157 B1:161 K4:518
μαστιξ, SCOURGE

Mk	3:10	that all who had **diseases**
	5:29	she was healed of her **disease**
	5:34	and be healed of your **disease**
Lk	7:21	cured many people of **diseases**
Ac	22:24	to be examined by **flogging**
He	11:36	suffered mocking and **flogging**

3149 GO3 AG495 LN157
μαστος, BREAST

Lk	11:27	the **breasts** that nursed you
	23:29	the **breasts** that never nursed
Re	1:13	a golden sash across his **chest**

3150 GO1 AG495 LN157 B1:550 K4:524 R3151
ματαιολογια, FUTILE TALK

1Ti	1: 6	and turned to **meaningless talk**

3151 GO1 AG495 LN157 B1:550 K4:524 R3152,3004
ματαιολογος, FUTILE WORD

Ti	1:10	**idle talkers** and deceivers

3152 GO6 AG495 LN157 B1:549 K4:519
ματαιος, FUTILE
Ac 14:15 from these **worthless things**
1C 3:20 wise, that they are **futile**
15:17 your faith is **futile** and you
Ti 3: 9 are unprofitable and **worthless**
Ja 1:26 their religion is **worthless**
1P 1:18 were ransomed from the **futile**

3153 GO3 AG495 LN157 B1:549 K4:523
ματαιοτης, FUTILITY
Ro 8:20 was subjected to **futility**
Ep 4:17 in the **futility** of their minds
2P 2:18 they speak bombastic **nonsense**

3154 GO1 AG495 LN157 B1:549 K4:523 R3152
ματαιοω, I AM FUTILE
Ro 1:21 but they **became futile** in their

3155 GO2 AG495 LN157 B1:549 K4:523
ματην, FUTILITY
Mt 15: 9 **in vain** do they worship me
Mk 7: 7 **in vain** do they worship me

3157 GO2 AG496 LN157
ματθαν, MATTHAN
Mt 1:15 Eleazar the father of **Matthan**
1:15 **Matthan** the father of Jacob

3160 GO1 AG496 LN157
ματταθα, MATTATHA
Lk 3:31 son of **Mattatha**

3161 GO2 AG496 LN157
ματταθιας, MATTATHIAS
Lk 3:25 son of **Mattathias**
3:26 son of **Mattathias**

3162 GO29 AG496 LN157 B3:958 K4:524 R3163
μαχαιρα, SWORD
Mt 10:34 to bring peace, but a **sword**
26:47 a large crowd with **swords**
26:51 put his hand on his **sword**
26:52 Put your **sword** back into its
26:52 all who take the **sword** will
26:52 will perish by the **sword.**
26:55 Have you come out with **swords**
Mk 14:43 a crowd with **swords** and clubs
14:47 drew his **sword** and struck the
14:48 Have you come out with **swords**

Lk 21:24 by the edge of the **sword**
22:36 the one who has no **sword**
22:38 here are two **swords**
22:49 we strike with the **sword**
22:52 Have you come out with **swords**
Jn 18:10 Peter, who had a **sword**
18:11 Put your **sword** back into its
Ac 12: 2 killed with the **sword**
16:27 he drew his **sword** and was about
Ro 8:35 nakedness, or peril, or **sword**
13: 4 does not bear the **sword** in vain
Ep 6:17 and the **sword** of the Spirit
He 4:12 than any two-edged **sword**
11:34 the edge of the **sword**
11:37 they were killed by the **sword**
Re 6: 4 he was given a great **sword**
13:10 with the **sword** you must be
13:10 if you kill with the **sword**
13:14 had been wounded by the **sword**

3163 GO4 AG496 LN157 B3:958 K4:527 R3164
μαχη, BATTLE
2C 7: 5 **disputes** without and fears
2Ti 2:23 know that they breed **quarrels**
Ti 3: 9 and **quarrels** about the law
Ja 4: 1 Those conflicts and **disputes**

3164 GO4 AG496 LN157 B3:959 K4:527
μαχομαι, I BATTLE
Jn 6:52 The Jews then **disputed** among
Ac 7:26 them as they were **quarreling**
2Ti 2:24 must not be **quarrelsome**
Ja 4: 2 so you engage in **disputes**

3167 GO1 AG496 LN157 K4:541 R3173
μεγαλειος, GREATNESS
Ac 2:11 about God's **deeds of power**

3168 GO3 AG496 LN157 B2:424 K4:541 R3167
μεγαλειοτης, GREATNESS
Lk 9:43 were astounded at the **greatness**
Ac 19:27 temple of the **great** goddess
2P 1:16 eyewitnesses of his **majesty**

3169 GO1 AG497 LN158 K4:542
μεγαλοπρεπης, GREATLY FITTING
2P 1:17 conveyed to him by the **Majestic**

3170 GO8 AG497 LN158 B2:424 K4:543 R3173
μεγαλυνω, I MAKE GREAT

Mt	23: 5	**make** their phylacteries **broad**
Lk	1:46	My soul **magnifies** the Lord
	1:58	**shown** his **great** mercy to her
Ac	5:13	**held** them **in high esteem**
	10:46	in tongues and **extolling** God
	19:17	of the Lord Jesus **was praised**
2C	10:15	you may be **greatly enlarged**
Ph	1:20	Christ will be **exalted** now as

3171　GO1 AG497 LN158 R3173
μεγαλως, GREATLY

Ph	4:10	I rejoice in the Lord **greatly**

3172　GO3 AG497 LN158 B2:424 K4:544 R3173
μεγαλωσυνη, GREATNESS

He	1: 3	the right hand of the **Majesty**
	8: 1	the **Majesty** in the heavens
Ju	1:25	**majesty,** power, and authority

3173　GO243 AG497 LN158 B2:424 K4:529
μεγας, GREAT

Mt	2:10	were **overwhelmed** with joy
	4:16	have seen a **great** light
	5:19	will be called **great** in the
	5:35	the city of the **great** King
	7:27	and **great** was its fall
	8:24	so **great** that the boat was
	8:26	and there was a **dead** calm
	11:11	no one has arisen **greater**
	11:11	of heaven is **greater** than he
	12: 6	something **greater** than the
	13:32	it is the **greatest** of shrubs
	15:28	Woman, **great** is your faith
	18: 1	Who is the **greatest** in the
	18: 4	is the **greatest** in the kingdom
	20:25	their **great** ones are tyrants
	20:26	whoever wishes to be **great**
	20:31	they shouted even more **loudly**
	22:36	in the law is the **greatest**
	22:38	This is the **greatest** and first
	23:11	The **greatest** among you will be
	23:17	For which is **greater,** the gold
	23:19	For which is **greater,** the gift
	24:21	there will be **great** suffering
	24:24	produce **great** signs and omens
	24:31	with a **loud** trumpet call
	27:46	Jesus cried with a **loud** voice
	27:50	cried again with a **loud** voice
	27:60	He then rolled a **great** stone
	28: 2	And suddenly there was a **great**

	28: 8	quickly with fear and **great** joy
Mk	1:26	crying with a **loud** voice
	4:32	the **greatest** of all shrubs,
	4:32	puts forth **large** branches,
	4:37	A **great** windstorm arose,
	4:39	and there was a **dead** calm
	4:41	they were filled with **great** awe
	5: 7	shouted at the **top** of his voice
	5:11	a **great** herd of swine was
	5:42	were **overcome** with amazement
	9:34	another who was the **greatest**
	10:42	their **great** ones are tyrants
	10:43	whoever wishes to become **great**
	12:31	no other commandment **greater**
	13: 2	you see these **great** buildings
	14:15	He will show you a **large** room
	15:34	cried out with a **loud** voice
	15:37	Then Jesus gave a **loud** cry
	16: 4	the stone, which was very **large**
Lk	1:15	he will be **great** in the sight
	1:32	He will be **great,** and will be
	1:42	and exclaimed with a **loud** cry
	1:49	has done **great** things for me
	2: 9	and they were **terrified**
	2:10	good news of **great** joy for all
	4:25	there was a **severe** famine
	4:33	cried out with a **loud** voice
	4:38	suffering from a **high** fever
	5:29	Then Levi gave a **great** banquet
	6:49	**great** was the ruin of that
	7:16	A **great** prophet has risen
	7:28	no one is **greater** than John
	7:28	of God is **greater** than he
	8:28	at the **top** of his voice
	8:37	were seized with **great** fear
	9:46	one of them was the **greatest**
	9:48	all of you is the **greatest**
	12:18	my barns and build **larger** ones
	14:16	Someone gave a **great** dinner
	16:26	a **great** chasm has been fixed
	17:15	praising God with a **loud** voice
	19:37	joyfully with a **loud** voice
	21:11	will be **great** earthquakes
	21:11	and **great** signs from heaven
	21:23	there will be **great** distress
	22:12	He will show you a **large** room
	22:24	be regarded as the **greatest**
	22:26	the **greatest** among you must
	22:27	For who is **greater,** the one

	23:23	demanding with **loud** shouts		26:22	to both small and **great**
	23:46	crying with a **loud** voice		26:24	this defense, Festus **exclaimed**
	24:52	to Jerusalem with **great** joy		26:29	Whether quickly or **not**, I pray
Jn	1:50	You will see **greater** things	Ro	9: 2	I have **great** sorrow
	4:12	**greater** than our ancestor Jacob		9:12	The **elder** shall serve the
	5:20	he will show him **greater** works	1C	9:11	is it too **much** if we reap
	5:36	But I have a testimony **greater**		12:31	But strive for the **greater**
	6:18	a **strong** wind was blowing		13:13	the **greatest** of these is love
	7:37	of the festival, the **great** day		14: 5	One who prophesies is **greater**
	8:53	**greater** than our father		16: 9	for a **wide** door for effective
	10:29	has given me is **greater**	2C	11:15	So it is not **strange** if his
	11:43	he cried with a **loud** voice	Ep	5:32	This is a **great** mystery
	13:16	servants are not **greater** than	1Ti	3:16	of our religion is **great**
	13:16	nor are messengers **greater**		6: 6	**great** gain in godliness
	14:12	do **greater** works than these	2Ti	2:20	In a **large** house there are
	14:28	the Father is **greater** than I	Ti	2:13	the glory of our **great** God
	15:13	has **greater** love than this	He	4:14	we have a **great** high priest
	15:20	Servants are not **greater** than		6:13	he had no one **greater** by
	19:11	is guilty of a **greater** sin		6:16	someone **greater** than themselves
	19:31	was a day of **great** solemnity		8:11	least of them to the **greatest**
	21:11	net ashore, full of **large** fish		9:11	then through the **greater**
Ac	2:20	Lord's **great** and glorious day		10:21	since we have a **great** priest
	4:33	With **great** power the apostles		10:35	it brings a **great** reward
	4:33	and **great** grace was upon them		11:24	Moses, when he was **grown up**
	5: 5	And **great** fear seized all who		11:26	to be **greater** wealth than the
	5:11	**great** fear seized the whole		13:20	the **great** shepherd of the sheep
	6: 8	did **great** wonders and signs	Ja	3: 1	judged with **greater** strictness
	7:11	Canaan, and **great** suffering		3: 5	yet it boasts of **great** exploits
	7:57	with a **loud** shout all rushed		4: 6	But he gives all the **more** grace
	7:60	cried out in a **loud** voice	2P	1: 4	and very **great** promises
	8: 1	That day a **severe** persecution		2:11	**greater** in might and power
	8: 2	made **loud** lamentation over him	1J	3:20	God is **greater** than our hearts
	8: 7	crying with **loud** shrieks		4: 4	is **greater** than the one who is
	8: 9	that he was someone **great.**		5: 9	testimony of God is **greater**
	8:10	the least to the **greatest**	3J	1: 4	I have no **greater** joy than this
	8:10	of God that is called **Great**	Ju	1: 6	the judgment of the **great** Day
	8:13	**great** miracles that took place	Re	1:10	a **loud** voice like a trumpet
	10:11	something like a **large** sheet		2:22	am throwing into **great** distress
	11: 5	something like a **large** sheet		5: 2	proclaiming with a **loud** voice
	11:28	would be a **severe** famine over		5:12	singing with **full** voice
	14:10	said in a **loud** voice		6: 4	he was given a **great** sword
	15: 3	brought **great** joy to all		6:10	cried out with a **loud** voice
	16:26	so **violent** that the foundations		6:12	there came a **great** earthquake
	16:28	Paul shouted in a **loud** voice		6:13	fruit when shaken by a **gale**
	19:27	the temple of the **great** goddess		6:17	the **great** day of their wrath
	19:28	**Great** is Artemis of the		7: 2	he called with a **loud** voice
	19:34	**Great** is Artemis of the		7:10	They cried out in a **loud** voice
	19:35	keeper of the **great** Artemis		7:14	come out of the **great** ordeal
	23: 9	Then a **great** clamor arose		8: 8	like a **great** mountain

8:10	a **great** star fell from heaven
8:13	crying with a **loud** voice
9: 2	the smoke of a **great** furnace
9:14	at the **great** river Euphrates
10: 3	he gave a **great** shout
11: 8	the street of the **great** city
11:11	who saw them were **terrified**
11:12	Then they heard a **loud** voice
11:13	there was a **great** earthquake
11:15	were **loud** voices in heaven
11:17	have taken your **great** power
11:18	your name, both small and **great**
11:19	an earthquake, and **heavy** hail
12: 1	A **great** portent appeared in
12: 3	a **great** red dragon, with seven
12: 9	**great** dragon was thrown down
12:10	Then I heard a **loud** voice
12:12	down to you with **great** wrath
12:14	two wings of the **great** eagle
13: 2	his throne and **great** authority
13: 5	**haughty** and blasphemous words
13:13	It performs **great** signs
13:16	both small and **great**
14: 2	like the sound of **loud** thunder
14: 7	He said in a **loud** voice
14: 8	fallen is Babylon the **great**
14: 9	crying with a **loud** voice
14:15	calling with a **loud** voice
14:18	he called with a **loud** voice
14:19	into the **great** wine press
15: 1	**great** and amazing: seven angels
15: 3	**Great** and amazing are your
16: 1	Then I heard a **loud** voice
16: 9	scorched by the **fierce** heat
16:12	on the **great** river Euphrates
16:14	battle on the **great** day of God
16:17	a **loud** voice came out of the
16:18	and a **violent** earthquake
16:18	so **violent** was that earthquake
16:19	The **great** city was split into
16:19	God remembered **great** Babylon
16:21	**huge** hailstones, each weighing
16:21	so **fearful** was that plague
17: 1	judgment of the **great** whore
17: 5	Babylon the **great**, mother of
17: 6	I was **greatly** amazed
17:18	is the **great** city that rules
18: 1	having **great** authority
18: 2	fallen is Babylon the **great**

18:10	the **great** city, Babylon
18:16	Alas, alas, the **great** city
18:18	What city was like the **great**
18:19	Alas, alas, the **great** city
18:21	like a **great** millstone
18:21	Babylon the **great** city will be
19: 1	**loud** voice of a great multitude
19: 2	he has judged the **great** whore
19: 5	who fear him, small and **great**
19:17	and with a **loud** voice he called
19:17	gather for the **great** supper
19:18	both small and **great**
20: 1	pit and a **great** chain
20:11	I saw a **great** white throne
20:12	the dead, **great** and small
21: 3	And I heard a **loud** voice
21:10	away to a **great,** high mountain
21:12	It has a **great,** high wall

3174   GO1 AG498 LN158 K4:544 R3173
μεγεθος, GREATNESS
Ep   1:19   is the immeasurable **greatness**

3175   GO3 AG498 LN158 R3173
μεγισταν, GREAT ONE

Mk	6:21	a banquet for his **courtiers**
Re	6:15	the **magnates** and the generals
	18:23	the **magnates** of the earth

3177   GO8 AG498 LN158 R3326,2059
μεθερμηνευω, I TRANSLATE

Mt	1:23	which **means**, "God is with us."
Mk	5:41	**means**, "Little girl, get up!"
	15:22	**means** the place of a skull
	15:34	**means**, "My God, my God, why
Jn	1:38	which **translated** means Teacher
	1:41	which is **translated** Anointed
Ac	4:36	**means** "son of encouragement
	13: 8	for that is the **translation**

3178   GO3 AG498 LN158 B1:513 K4:545
μεθη, DRUNKENNESS

Lk	21:34	dissipation and **drunkenness**
Ro	13:13	reveling and **drunkenness**
Ga	5:21	envy, **drunkenness,** carousing

3179   GO5 AG498 LN158
μεθιστημι, I TRANSFER

Lk	16: 4	when I **am dismissed** as manager
Ac	13:22	When he **had removed** him

	19:26	**drawn** away a considerable
1C	13: 2	so as to **remove** mountains
Co	1:13	**transferred** us into the kingdom

3180   GO2 AG499 LN158 B3:935 K5:102
μεθοδεια, SCHEMING

Ep	4:14	their **craftiness** in deceitful
	6:11	to stand against the **wiles**

3182   GO4 AG499 LN158 B1:513 K4:545 R3184
μεθυσκω, I AM DRUNK

Lk	12:45	eat and drink and **get drunk**
Ep	5:18	Do not **get drunk** with wine
1Th	5: 7	those who **are drunk** get drunk

3183   GO2 AG499 LN158 B1:513 K4:545 R3184
μεθυσος, DRUNKARD

1C	5:11	idolater, reviler, **drunkard**
	6:10	thieves, the greedy, **drunkards**

3184   GO6 AG499 LN158 B1:513 K4:545 R3178
μεθυω, I AM DRUNK

Mt	24:49	eats and drinks with **drunkards**
Jn	2:10	guests **have become drunk**
Ac	2:15	these **are** not **drunk**
1C	11:21	and another **becomes drunk**
1Th	5: 7	those who are drunk **get drunk**
Re	17: 2	of the earth **have become drunk**
	17: 6	I saw that the woman **was drunk**

3189   GO6 AG499 LN158 B1:203 K4:549
μελας, BLACK

Mt	5:36	make one hair white or **black**
2C	3: 3	written not with **ink** but with
2J	1:12	rather not use paper and **ink**
3J	1:13	not write with pen and **ink**
Re	6: 5	there was a **black** horse!
	6:12	sun became **black** as sackcloth

3190   GO1 AG500 LN158
μελεα, MELEA

Lk	3:31	son of **Melea**

3190a   GO10 AG500 LN158
μελει, IT IS A CARE

Mt	22:16	and **show deference** to no one
Mk	4:38	Teacher, **do** you not **care**
	12:14	and **show deference** to no one
Lk	10:40	Lord, **do** you not **care**
Jn	10:13	a hired hand **does** not **care**

	12: 6	he **cared** about the poor
Ac	18:17	Gallio **paid** no **attention**
1C	7:21	**Do** not **be concerned** about it
	9: 9	oxen that God **is concerned**
1P	5: 7	because he **cares** for you

3191   GO2 AG500 LN159
μελεταω, I TAKE CARE

Ac	4:25	the peoples **imagine** vain things
1Ti	4:15	**Put** these things **into practice**

3192   GO4 AG500 LN159 K4:552
μελι, HONEY

Mt	3: 4	food was locusts and wild **honey**
Mk	1: 6	he ate locusts and wild **honey**
Re	10: 9	sweet as **honey** in your mouth
	10:10	it was sweet as **honey**

3194   GO1 AG500 LN159
μελιτη, MELITA

Ac	28: 1	the island was called **Malta**

3195   GO109 AG500 LN159 B1:325
μελλω, I AM ABOUT TO

Mt	2:13	for Herod **is about to** search
	3: 7	flee from the wrath **to come**
	11:14	he is Elijah who is **to come**
	12:32	or in the age **to come**
	16:27	For the Son of Man is **to come**
	17:12	Son of Man **is about** to suffer
	17:22	The Son of Man **is going** to be
	20:22	that I **am about** to drink
	24: 6	**will** hear of wars and rumors
Mk	10:32	began to tell them **what was to**
	13: 4	**are about** to be accomplished
Lk	3: 7	to flee from the wrath **to come**
	7: 2	who was ill and **close** to death
	9:31	he **was about** to accomplish
	9:44	**is going** to be betrayed into
	10: 1	where he himself **intended** to go
	13: 9	If it bears fruit **next year**
	19: 4	he **was going** to pass that way
	19:11	kingdom of God **was to** appear
	21: 7	this **is about** to take place
	21:36	things that **will** take place
	22:23	which one of them it **could be**
	24:21	he was the one **to** redeem Israel
Jn	4:47	he was **at the point** of death
	6: 6	knew what he **was going** to do
	6:15	that they **were about** to come

	6:71	**was going** to betray him
	7:35	does this man **intend** to go
	7:35	Does he **intend** to go to the
	7:39	in him **were** to receive
	11:51	that Jesus **was about** to die
	12: 4	who **was about** to betray him
	12:33	kind of death he **was** to die
	14:22	that you **will** reveal yourself
	18:32	the kind of death he **was** to die
Ac	3: 3	**about** to go into the temple
	5:35	you **propose** to do to these men
	11:28	there **would be** a severe famine
	12: 6	before Herod **was going** to bring
	13:34	**no more** to return to corruption
	16:27	**was about** to kill himself
	17:31	he **will** have the world judged
	18:14	Just as Paul **was about** to speak
	19:27	ours **may come** into disrepute
	20: 3	He **was about** to set sail for
	20: 7	since he **intended** to leave the
	20:13	**intending** to take Paul on board
	20:13	**intending** to go by land himself
	20:38	they **would** not see him again
	21:27	days were **almost** completed
	21:37	Paul **was about** to be brought
	22:16	And now why **do** you **delay?**
	22:26	What **are** you **about** to do?
	22:29	those who **were about** to examine
	23: 3	God **will** strike you
	23:15	you **want** to make a more
	23:20	**as though** they were going to
	23:27	and **was about** to be killed
	24:15	there **will be** a resurrection
	24:25	Felix **became** frightened
	25: 4	that he himself **intended** to go
	26: 2	I **am** to make my defense today
	26:22	Moses said **would** take place
	26:23	he **would** proclaim light both
	27: 2	that **was about** to set sail
	27:10	the voyage **will** be with danger
	27:30	the sailors **tried** to escape
	27:33	Just **before** daybreak
	28: 6	were **expecting** him to swell up
Ro	4:24	It **will** be reckoned to us who
	5:14	of the one who **was to come**
	8:13	to the flesh, you **will** die
	8:18	the glory **about** to be revealed
	8:38	nor things **to come,** nor powers

1C	3:22	or the present or the **future**
Ga	3:23	until faith **would** be revealed
Ep	1:21	but also in the age **to come**
Co	2:17	a shadow of what is **to come**
1Th	3: 4	we **were** to suffer persecution
1Ti	1:16	who **would come** to believe
	4: 8	life and the life **to come.**
	6:19	good foundation **for the future**
2Ti	4: 1	who **is** to judge the living
He	1:14	who **are** to inherit salvation
	2: 5	not subject the **coming** world
	6: 5	the powers of the age **to come**
	8: 5	he **was about** to erect the tent
	10: 1	the good things **to come**
	10:27	fury of fire that **will** consume
	11: 8	place that he **was** to receive
	11:20	blessings **for the future**
	13:14	the city that is **to come**
Ja	2:12	as those who **are** to be judged
1P	5: 1	in the glory **to be** revealed
2P	1:12	Therefore I **intend** to keep
	2: 6	an example of what **is coming**
Re	1:19	and **what is to take place** after
	2:10	what you **are about** to suffer
	2:10	the devil is **about** to throw
	3: 2	and is **on the point** of death
	3:10	hour of trial that **is coming**
	3:16	I **am about** to spit you out
	6:11	who **were soon** to be killed
	8:13	three angels **are about** to blow
	10: 4	I **was about** to write
	10: 7	angel **is** to blow his trumpet
	12: 4	the woman who **was about** to bear
	12: 5	who **is** to rule all the nations
	17: 8	**is about** to ascend from the

3196   GO34 AG501 LN159 B1:229 K4:555
μελος, MEMBER

Mt	5:29	to lose one of your **members**
	5:30	to lose one of your **members**
Ro	6:13	present your **members** to sin
	6:13	present your **members** to God
	6:19	your **members** as slaves
	6:19	so now present your **members**
	7: 5	at work in our **members** to
	7:23	but I see in my **members** another
	7:23	that dwells in my **members**
	12: 4	one body we have many **members**

	12: 4	**members** have the same function
	12: 5	we are **members** one of another
1C	6:15	that your bodies are **members**
	6:15	take the **members** of Christ
	6:15	**members** of a prostitute? Never!
	12:12	is one and has many **members**
	12:12	and all the **members** of the body
	12:14	does not consist of one **member**
	12:18	God arranged the **members**
	12:19	If all were a single **member**
	12:20	there are many **members**
	12:22	**members** of the body that seem
	12:25	**members** may have the same care
	12:26	If one **member** suffers
	12:26	**all** suffer together with it
	12:26	if one **member** is honored
	12:26	**all** rejoice together with it
	12:27	individually **members** of it
Ep	4:25	we are **members** of one another
	5:30	we are **members** of his body
Co	3: 5	whatever in **you** is earthly
Ja	3: 5	the tongue is a small **member**
	3: 6	is placed among our **members**
	4: 1	that are at war within **you**

3197   GO2 AG502 LN159
μελχι, MELCHI
Lk   3:24   son of Levi, son of **Melchi**
     3:28   son of **Melchi,** son of Addi

3198   GO8 AG502 LN159 B2:590 K4:568
μελχισεδεκ, MELCHISEDEK
He   5: 6   to the order of **Melchizedek**
     5:10   to the order of **Melchizedek**
     6:20   to the order of **Melchizedek**
     7: 1   King **Melchizedek** of Salem
     7:10   when **Melchizedek** met him
     7:11   to the order of **Melchizedek**
     7:15   arises, resembling **Melchizedek**
     7:17   to the order of **Melchizedek**

3200   GO502 AG159
μεμβρανα, PARCHMENTS
2Ti   4:13   and above all the **parchments**

3201   GO2 AG502 LN159 B2:143 K4:571
μεμφομαι, I FIND FAULT
Ro   9:19   then does he still **find fault**
He   8: 8   God **finds fault** with them

3202   GO1 AG502 LN159 B2:143 K4:571
μεμψιμοιρος, COMPLAINERS
Ju   1:16   are grumblers and **malcontents**

3303   GO179 AG502 LN159
μεν, INDEED [MULTIPLE OCCURRENCES]

3303a   GO1 AG503 LN159
μεννα, MENNA
Lk   3:31   son of Melea, son of **Menna**

3303b   GO1 AG503 LN159
μενουν, INDEED THEN
Lk   11:28   Blessed **rather** are those

3304   GO3 AG503 LN159
μενουνγε, ON THE CONTRARY
Ro   9:20   But who **indeed** are you
     10:18   not heard? **Indeed** they have
Ph   3: 8   **More than that,** I regard

3305   GO8 AG503 LN159
μεντοι, HOWEVER
Jn   4:27   with a woman, **but** no one said
     7:13   **Yet** no one would speak openly
     12:42   **Nevertheless** many, even of the
     20: 5   lying there, **but** he did not go
     21: 4   **but** the disciples did not know
2Ti   2:19   **But** God's firm foundation
Ja   2: 8   if you **really** fulfill the royal
Ju   1: 8   **Yet** in the same way these

3306   GO118 AG503 LN159 B3:223 K4:574
μενω, I STAY
Mt   10:11   **stay** there until you leave
     11:23   have **remained** until this day
     26:38   **remain** here, and stay awake
Mk   6:10   **stay** there until you leave the
     14:34   **remain** here, and keep awake
Lk   1:56   And Mary **remained** with her
     8:27   and he **did** not **live** in a house
     9: 4   **stay** there, and leave from
     10: 7   **Remain** in the same house
     19: 5   for I must **stay** at your house
     24:29   **Stay** with us, because it is
     24:29   he went in to **stay** with them
Jn   1:32   like a dove, and it **remained**
     1:33   the Spirit descend and **remain**
     1:38   where **are** you **staying**
     1:39   saw where he **was staying**

1:39	they **remained** with him that day
2:12	they **remained** there a few days
3:36	but must **endure** God's wrath
4:40	asked him to **stay** with them;
4:40	and he **stayed** there two days
5:38	have his word **abiding** in you
6:27	but for the food that **endures**
6:56	**abide** in me, and I in them
7: 9	After saying this, he **remained**
8:31	If you **continue** in my word
8:35	does not **have** a **permanent place**
8:35	son **has** a **place** there forever
9:41	'We see,' your sin **remains**
10:40	and he **remained** there
11: 6	he **stayed** two days longer
11:54	he **remained** there with the
12:24	it **remains** just a single grain
12:34	the Messiah **remains** forever
12:46	not **remain** in the darkness
14:10	but the Father who **dwells** in me
14:17	because he **abides** with you
14:25	while I **am still with** you
15: 4	**Abide** in me as I abide in you.
15: 4	unless it **abides** in the vine
15: 4	can you unless you **abide** in me
15: 5	Those who **abide** in me and I in
15: 6	Whoever does not **abide** in me
15: 7	If you **abide** in me, and my
15: 7	and my words **abide** in you
15: 9	loved you; **abide** in my love
15:10	you will **abide** in my love
15:10	and **abide** in his love
15:16	fruit, fruit that **will last**
19:31	the bodies **left** on the cross
21:22	If it is my will that he **remain**
21:23	If it is my will that he **remain**
Ac 5: 4	While it **remained** unsold
5: 4	did it not **remain** your own
9:43	Meanwhile he **stayed** in Joppa
16:15	come and **stay** at my home
18: 3	he **stayed** with them
18:20	went ahead and **were waiting**
20:23	persecutions **are waiting for** me
21: 7	**stayed** with them for one day
21: 8	the seven, and **stayed** with him
27:31	these men **stay** in the ship
27:41	stuck and **remained** immovable
28:16	was allowed **to live** by himself
Ro 9:11	of election might **continue**

1C 3:14	on the foundation **survives**
7: 8	to **remain** unmarried as I am
7:11	let her **remain** unmarried
7:20	**remain** in the condition
7:24	there **remain** with God
7:40	if she **remains** as she is
13:13	faith, hope, and love **abide**
15: 6	most of whom **are still alive**
2C 3:11	**has the permanent come** in glory
3:14	that same veil **is still there**
9: 9	righteousness **endures** forever
Ph 1:25	I know that I will **remain**
1Ti 2:15	provided they **continue** in faith
2Ti 2:13	faithless, he **remains** faithful
3:14	**continue** in what you have
4:20	Erastus **remained** in Corinth
He 7: 3	he **remains** a priest forever
7:24	because he **continues** forever
10:34	better and more **lasting**
12:27	cannot be shaken may **remain**
13: 1	Let mutual love **continue.**
13:14	here we have no **lasting** city
1P 1:23	the living and **enduring** word
1:25	word of the Lord **endures**
1J 2: 6	says, "I **abide** in him,"
2:10	or sister **lives** in the light
2:14	word of God **abides** in you
2:17	the will of God **live** forever
2:19	they would **have remained**
2:24	the beginning **abide** in you
2:24	the beginning **abides** in you
2:24	then you will **abide** in the Son
2:27	received from him **abides** in you
2:27	it has taught you, **abide** in him
2:28	little children, **abide** in him
3: 6	No one who **abides** in him sins
3: 9	God's seed **abides** in them
3:14	does not love **abides** in death
3:15	eternal life **abiding** in them
3:17	How does God's love **abide**
3:24	his commandments **abide** in him
3:24	we know that he **abides** in us
4:12	one another, God **lives** in us
4:13	By this we know that we **abide**
4:15	**abides** in those who confess
4:16	those who **abide** in love abide
4:16	those who abide in love **abide**
4:16	and God **abides** in them

2J	1: 2	the truth that **abides** in us
	1: 9	Everyone who does not **abide**
	1: 9	whoever **abides** in the teaching
Re	17:10	must **remain** only a little while

3307   GO14 AG504 LN160 R3313
μερίζω, I DIVIDE

Mt	12:25	kingdom **divided** against itself
	12:25	city or house **divided** against
	12:26	he is **divided** against himself
Mk	3:24	If a kingdom is **divided** against
	3:25	house is **divided** against itself
	3:26	himself and is **divided**
	6:41	**divided** the two fish among them
Lk	12:13	**divide** the family inheritance
Ro	12: 3	of faith that God **has assigned**
1C	1:13	Has Christ **been divided**?
	7:17	that the Lord **has assigned**
	7:34	and his interests **are divided**
2C	10:13	that God **has assigned** to us
He	7: 2	and to him Abraham **apportioned**

3308   GO6 AG504 LN160 B1:276 K4:589
μέριμνα, ANXIETY

Mt	13:22	but the **cares** of the world
Mk	4:19	but the **cares** of the world
Lk	8:14	by the **cares** and riches
	21:34	and the **worries** of this life
2C	11:28	because of my **anxiety** for
1P	5: 7	Cast all your **anxiety** on him

3309   GO19 AG505 LN160 B1:276 K4:589
μεριμνάω, I AM ANXIOUS

Mt	6:25	**do** not **worry** about your
	6:27	can any of you by **worrying** add
	6:28	why **do** you **worry** about clothing
	6:31	Therefore **do** not **worry**
	6:34	So **do** not **worry** about tomorrow
	6:34	for tomorrow will **bring worries**
	10:19	**do** not **worry** about how you are
Lk	10:41	Martha, you **are worried**
	12:11	**do** not **worry** about how you are
	12:22	I tell you, **do** not **worry** about
	12:25	And can any of you by **worrying**
	12:26	why **do** you **worry** about the rest
1C	7:32	The unmarried man **is anxious**
	7:33	but the married man **is anxious**
	7:34	**are anxious** about the affairs
	7:34	the married woman **is anxious**
	12:25	members may **have** the same **care**

Ph	2:20	**concerned** for your welfare
	4: 6	**Do** not **worry** about anything

3310   GO5 AG505 LN160 B2:303 R3313
μερίς, PART

Lk	10:42	Mary has chosen the better **part**
Ac	8:21	You have no **part** or share
	16:12	of the **district** of Macedonia
2C	6:15	Or what does a believer **share**
Co	1:12	who has enabled you to **share**

3311   GO2 AG505 LN160
μερισμός, DIVISION

He	2: 4	**distributed** according to his
	4:12	piercing until it **divides** soul

3312   GO1 AG505 LN160 B1:372 R3307
μεριστής, DIVIDER

Lk	12:14	to be a judge or **arbitrator**

3313   GO42 AG505 LN160 B2:303 K4:594
μέρος, PART

Mt	2:22	he went away to the **district**
	15:21	went away to the **district**
	16:13	Jesus came into the **district**
	24:51	put him **with** the hypocrites
Mk	8:10	and went to the **district** of
Lk	11:36	no **part** of it in darkness
	12:46	put him **with** the unfaithful
	15:12	the **share** of the property
	24:42	They gave him a **piece**
Jn	13: 8	you have no **share** with me
	19:23	divided them into four **parts**
	19:23	**one** for each soldier
	21: 6	to the right **side** of the boat
Ac	2:10	Egypt and the **parts** of Libya
	5: 2	only a **part** and laid it
	19: 1	through the interior **regions**
	19:27	this **trade** of ours may come
	20: 2	gone through those **regions**
	23: 6	that **some** were Sadducees
	23: 9	scribes of the Pharisees' **group**
Ro	11:25	has come upon **part** of Israel
	15:15	Nevertheless on some **points**
	15:24	your company for a **little while**
1C	11:18	to some **extent** I believe it
	12:27	individually members of **it**
	13: 9	For we know only in **part**
	13: 9	we prophesy only in **part**
	13:10	the **partial** will come to an end

	13:12	Now I know only in **part**
	14:27	and each in **turn**
2C	1:14	already understood us in **part**
	2: 5	not to me, but to some **extent**
	3:10	**because** of the greater glory
	9: 3	been empty in this **case**
Ep	4: 9	descended into the lower **parts**
	4:16	each **part** is working properly
Co	2:16	or of **observing** festivals
He	9: 5	cannot speak now in **detail**
Re	16:19	was split into three **parts**
	20: 6	holy are those who **share**
	21: 8	their **place** will be in the lake
	22:19	take away that person's **share**

3314　GO2 AG506 LN160 R3319,2250
μεσημβρια, MIDDAY

Ac	8:26	Get up and go toward the **south**
	22: 6	about **noon** a great light from

3315　GO1 AG506 LN160 K4:598 R3316
μεσιτευω, I MEDIATE

He	6:17	he **guaranteed** it by an oath

3316　GO6 AG506 LN160 K4:598
μεσιτης, MEDIATOR

Ga	3:19	through angels by a **mediator**
	3:20	Now a **mediator** involves more
1Ti	2: 5	there is also one **mediator**
He	8: 6	that degree he is the **mediator**
	9:15	he is the **mediator** of a new
	12:24	the **mediator** of a new covenant

3317　GO4 AG507 LN160 R3319,3571
μεσονυκτιον, MIDDLE NIGHT

Mk	13:35	or at **midnight**
Lk	11: 5	you go to him at **midnight**
Ac	16:25	About **midnight** Paul and Silas
	20: 7	speaking until **midnight**

3318　GO2 AG507 LN160
μεσοποταμια, MESOPOTAMIA

Ac	2: 9	residents of **Mesopotamia**
	7: 2	when he was in **Mesopotamia**

3319　GO58 AG507 LN160
μεσος, MIDDLE

Mt	10:16	into the **midst** of wolves
	13:25	sowed weeds **among** the wheat
	13:49	the evil **from** the righteous

	14: 6	danced **before** the company
	18: 2	whom he put **among** them
	18:20	I am there **among** them
	25: 6	But at **midnight** there was a
Mk	3: 3	Come **forward.**
	6:47	the boat was out **on** the sea
	7:31	**in** the region of the Decapolis
	9:36	child and put it **among** them
	14:60	priest stood up **before** them
Lk	2:46	sitting **among** the teachers
	4:30	he passed through the **midst**
	4:35	had thrown him down **before** them
	5:19	into the **middle** of the crowd
	6: 8	Come and stand **here.**
	8: 7	Some fell **among** thorns
	10: 3	lambs into the **midst** of wolves
	17:11	**between** Samaria and Galilee
	21:21	those **inside** the city
	22:27	But I am **among** you as one
	22:55	kindled a fire in the **middle**
	22:55	Peter sat **among** them.
	23:45	of the temple was torn in **two**
	24:36	Jesus himself stood **among** them
Jn	1:26	**Among** you stands one whom you
	8: 3	making her stand **before** all
	8: 9	the woman standing **before** him
	19:18	with Jesus **between** them
	20:19	Jesus came and stood **among** them
	20:26	Jesus came and stood **among** them
Ac	1:15	stood up **among** the believers
	1:18	he burst open in the **middle**
	2:22	God did through him **among** you
	4: 7	prisoners stand in their **midst**
	17:22	stood in **front** of the Areopagus
	17:33	At that point Paul left **them**
	23:10	go down, **take** him by force
	26:13	when at **midday** along the road
	27:21	Paul then stood up **among** them
	27:27	about **midnight** the sailors
1C	5: 2	been removed from **among** you
	6: 5	there is no one **among** you
2C	6:17	Therefore come out **from** them
Ph	2:15	in the **midst** of a crooked
Co	2:14	He set this **aside**
1Th	2: 7	But we were gentle **among** you
2Th	2: 7	who now restrains it is **removed**
He	2:12	the **midst** of the congregation
Re	1:13	the **midst** of the lampstands
	2: 1	who walks **among** the seven

4: 6	and in **front** of the throne
5: 6	Then I saw **between** the throne
5: 6	and **among** the elders a Lamb
6: 6	in the **midst** of the four living
7:17	at the **center** of the throne
22: 2	the **middle** of the street

3320 ᴳᴼ1 ᴬᴳ508 ᴸᴺ160 ᴮ3:795 ᴷ4:625 ᴿ3319,5109
μεσοτοιχον, MIDDLE WALL
Ep 2:14   broken down the **dividing wall**

3321 ᴳᴼ3 ᴬᴳ508 ᴸᴺ160 ᴿ3319,3772
μεσουρανημα, MIDDLE HEAVEN
Re 8:13   as it flew in **midheaven**
14: 6   angel flying in **midheaven**
19:17   birds that fly in **midheaven**

3322 ᴳᴼ1 ᴬᴳ508 ᴸᴺ160 ᴿ3319
μεσοω, I AM IN MIDDLE
Jn 7:14   the **middle** of the festival

3323 ᴳᴼ2 ᴬᴳ508 ᴸᴺ160 ᴮ2:334
μεσσιας, MESSIAH
Jn 1:41   We have found the **Messiah**
4:25   I know that **Messiah** is coming

3324 ᴳᴼ9 ᴬᴳ508 ᴸᴺ160
μεστος, FULL
Mt 23:28   you are **full of** hypocrisy
Jn 19:29   A jar **full of** sour wine
19:29   put a sponge **full of** the wine
21:11   **full of** large fish,
Ro 1:29   were **filled** with every kind
15:14   yourselves are **full of** goodness
Ja 3: 8   **full of** deadly poison
3:17   **full of** mercy and good fruits
2P 2:14   have eyes **full of** adultery

3325 ᴳᴼ1 ᴬᴳ508 ᴸᴺ160 ᴿ3324
μεστοω, I AM FULL
Ac 2:13   They are **filled** with new wine

3326 ᴳᴼ469 ᴬᴳ508 ᴸᴺ160 ᴮ3:1206 ᴷ7:766
μετα, WITH, AFTER [MULTIPLE OCCURRENCES]

3327 ᴳᴼ12 ᴬᴳ510 ᴸᴺ161 ᴮ2:184 ᴷ1:523
μεταβαινω, I GO ACROSS
Mt 8:34   to **leave** their neighborhood
11: 1   he **went on** from there to teach

12: 9	He **left** that place and entered
15:29	After Jesus **had left** that place
17:20	**Move** from here to there,
17:20	and it **will move**
Lk 10: 7	Do not **move** about from house
Jn 5:24	**has passed** from death to life
7: 3	**Leave here** and go to Judea
13: 1	had come to **depart** from this
Ac 18: 7	Then he **left** the synagogue
1J 3:14	we **have passed** from death

3328 ᴳᴼ1 ᴬᴳ510 ᴸᴺ161 ᴿ3326,906
μεταβαλλω, I CHANGE
Ac 28: 6   they **changed their minds**

3329 ᴳᴼ2 ᴬᴳ510 ᴸᴺ161 ᴿ3326,71
μεταγω, I LEAD ABOUT
Ja 3: 3   we **guide** their whole bodies
3: 4   yet they **are guided** by a very

3330 ᴳᴼ5 ᴬᴳ510 ᴸᴺ161 ᴿ3326,1325
μεταδιδωμι, I SHARE
Lk 3:11   **share** with anyone who has none
Ro 1:11   so that I **may share** with you
12: 8   the **giver,** in generosity
Ep 4:28   to **share** with the needy
1Th 2: 8   we are determined to **share**

3331 ᴳᴼ3 ᴬᴳ511 ᴸᴺ161 ᴷ8:161
μεταθεσις, CHANGE
He 7:12   a **change** in the law as well
11: 5   before he **was taken away**
12:27   the **removal** of what is shaken

3332 ᴳᴼ2 ᴬᴳ511 ᴸᴺ161
μεταιρω, I MOVE ACROSS
Mt 13:53   he **left** that place
19: 1   he **left** Galilee and went

3333 ᴳᴼ4 ᴬᴳ511 ᴸᴺ161 ᴷ3:496 ᴿ3326,2564
μετακαλεω, I CALL FOR
Ac 7:14   sent and **invited** his father
10:32   to Joppa and **ask** for Simon
20:17   **asking** the elders of the church
24:25   I **will send for** you

3334 ᴳᴼ1 ᴬᴳ511 ᴸᴺ161 ᴷ3:720 ᴿ3326,2795
μετακινεω, I MOVE ABOUT
Co 1:23   without **shifting** from the hope

3335 GO7 AG511 LN161 B3:747 K4:10 R3326,2983
μεταλαμβανω, I TAKE WITH
Ac　2:46　　and **ate** their food with glad
　　24:25　　when I have **an opportunity**
　　27:33　　all of them to **take** some food
　　27:34　　I urge you to **take** some food
2Ti　2: 6　　ought to **have** the first **share**
He　6: 7　　**receives** a blessing from God
　　12:10　　that we may **share** his holiness

3336 GO1 AG511 LN161 B3:747 K4:10 R3335
μεταλημψις, SHARING
1Ti　4: 3　　God created **to be received**

3337 GO2 AG511 LN161 B3:166 K1:259 R3326,236
μεταλλασσω, I CHANGE ACROSS
Ro　1:25　　they **exchanged** the truth
　　1:26　　**exchanged** natural intercourse

3338 GO6 AG511 LN161 B1:356 K4:626
μεταμελομαι, I AM SORRY
Mt　21:29　　he **changed his mind** and went
　　21:32　　you **did** not **change your minds**
　　27: 3　　he **repented** and brought back
2C　7: 8　　I do not **regret** it
　　7: 8　　though I did **regret** it
He　7:21　　and **will** not **change his mind**

3339 GO4 AG511 LN161 B3:861 K4:755 R3326,3445
μεταμορφοω, I TRANSFORM
Mt　17: 2　　was **transfigured** before them
Mk　9: 2　　was **transfigured** before them
Ro　12: 2　　**transformed** by the renewing
2C　3:18　　are being **transformed** into the

3340 GO34 AG511 LN161 B1:357 K4:975 R3326,3539
μετανοεω, I CHANGE MIND
Mt　3: 2　　**Repent,** for the kingdom of
　　4:17　　**Repent,** for the kingdom of
　　11:20　　because they did not **repent**
　　11:21　　would have **repented** long ago
　　12:41　　**repented** at the proclamation
Mk　1:15　　**repent,** and believe in the
　　6:12　　that all should **repent**
Lk　10:13　　would have **repented** long
　　　　　　ago
　　11:32　　**repented** at the proclamation
　　13: 3　　but unless you **repent**
　　13: 5　　but unless you **repent**
　　15: 7　　one sinner who **repents** than

　　15:10　　over one sinner who **repents**
　　16:30　　the dead, they will **repent**
　　17: 3　　and if there is **repentance**
　　17: 4　　'**I repent,**' you must forgive
Ac　2:38　　**Repent,** and be baptized
　　3:19　　**Repent** therefore, and turn
　　8:22　　**Repent** therefore of this
　　17:30　　all people everywhere to
　　　　　　repent
　　26:20　　**repent** and turn to God
2C　12:21　　**repented** of the impurity
Re　2: 5　　**repent,** and do the works
　　2: 5　　**repent,** and do the works
　　2:16　　**Repent** then
　　2:21　　I gave her time to **repent**
　　2:21　　but she refuses to **repent**
　　2:22　　they **repent** of her doings
　　3: 3　　obey it, and **repent**
　　3:19　　earnest, therefore, and
　　　　　　repent
　　9:20　　did not **repent** of the works
　　9:21　　they did not **repent** of their
　　16: 9　　they did not **repent** and give
　　16:11　　did not **repent** of their
　　　　　　deeds

3341 GO22 AG512 LN161 B1:357 K4:975 R3340
μετανοια, CHANGE OF MIND
Mt　3: 8　　fruit worthy of **repentance**
　　3:11　　with water for **repentance**
Mk　1: 4　　a baptism of **repentance** for
Lk　3: 3　　a baptism of **repentance** for
　　3: 8　　fruits worthy of **repentance**
　　5:32　　but sinners to **repentance**
　　15: 7　　persons who need no **repentance**
　　24:47　　that **repentance** and forgiveness
Ac　5:31　　give **repentance** to Israel
　　11:18　　**repentance** that leads to life
　　13:24　　a baptism of **repentance**
　　19: 4　　the baptism of **repentance**
　　20:21　　about **repentance** toward God
　　26:20　　consistent with **repentance**
Ro　2: 4　　meant to lead you to **repentance**
2C　7: 9　　your grief led to **repentance**
　　7:10　　grief produces a **repentance**
2Ti　2:25　　they will **repent** and come
He　6: 1　　**repentance** from dead works
　　6: 6　　restore again to **repentance**
　　12:17　　he found no chance to **repent**
2P　3: 9　　but all to come to **repentance**

3342   GO9 AG512 LN161
μεταξυ, BETWEEN
Mt	18:15	when the **two** of you are alone
	23:35	**between** the sanctuary and the
Lk	11:51	who perished **between** the altar
	16:26	**between** you and us a great
Jn	4:31	**Meanwhile** the disciples were
Ac	12: 6	sleeping **between** two soldiers
	13:42	things again the **next** sabbath
	15: 9	no distinction **between** them
Ro	2:15	and their **conflicting** thoughts

3343   GO9 AG513 LN161 R3326,3992
μεταπεμπω, I SEND FOR
Ac	10: 5	Now **send** men to Joppa
	10:22	to **send for** you to come to his
	10:29	So when I **was sent for**
	10:29	I ask why you **sent for** me
	11:13	Send to Joppa and **bring** Simon
	20: 1	Paul **sent for** the disciples
	24:24	he **sent for** Paul and heard him
	24:26	he used to **send for** him
	25: 3	to have him **transferred**

3344   GO2 AG513 LN161 K7:729 R3326,4762
μεταστρεφω, I TURN
Ac	2:20	**shall be turned** to darkness
Ga	1: 7	and want to **pervert** the gospel

3345   GO5 AG513 LN161 B1:708 K7:957 R3326,4976
μετασχηματιζω, I RESHAPE
1C	4: 6	I **have applied** all this to
2C	11:13	**disguising** themselves as
	11:14	Even Satan **disguises** himself
	11:15	if his ministers also **disguise**
Ph	3:21	He **will transform** the body

3346   GO6 AG513 LN162 B3:601 K8:161 R3326,5087
μετατιθημι, I CHANGE
Ac	7:16	their bodies **were brought back**
Ga	1: 6	you are so quickly **deserting**
He	7:12	a **change** in the priesthood
	11: 5	By faith Enoch **was taken**
	11: 5	before he **was taken away**
Ju	1: 4	**pervert** the grace of our God

3346a   GO1 AG513 LN162
μετατρεπω, I TURN
Ja	4: 9	Let your laughter **be turned**

3347   GO1 AG514 LN162
μετεπειτα, AFTERWARD
He	12:17	You know that **later**

3348   GO8 AG514 LN162 B1:635 K2:830 R3326,2192
μετεχω, I HOLD WITH
1C	9:10	in hope of a **share** in the crop
	9:12	**share** this rightful claim
	10:17	for we all **partake** of the one
	10:21	You cannot **partake** of the table
	10:30	If I **partake** with thankfulness
He	2:14	likewise **shared** the same things
	5:13	for everyone who **lives on** milk
	7:13	**belonged** to another tribe

3349   GO1 AG514 LN162 K4:630
μετεωριζομαι, I AM RESTLESS
Lk	12:29	and do not **keep worrying**

3350   GO4 AG514 LN162 R3326,3624
μετοικεσια, CHANGE OF HOME
Mt	1:11	the time of the **deportation**
	1:12	the **deportation** to Babylon
	1:17	to the **deportation** to Babylon
	1:17	the **deportation** to Babylon

3351   GO2 AG514 LN162 R3350
μετοικιζω, I CHANGE HOME
Ac	7: 4	God **had** him **move** from there
	7:43	so I **will remove** you beyond

3352   GO1 AG514 LN162 B1:635 K2:830 R3348
μετοχη, COMMONALITY
2C	6:14	For what **partnership** is there

3353   GO6 AG514 LN162 B1:635 K2:830 R3348
μετοχος, SHARER
Lk	5: 7	So they signaled their **partners**
He	1: 9	gladness beyond your **companions**
	3: 1	**partners** in a heavenly calling
	3:14	For we have become **partners**
	6: 4	and have **shared** in the Holy
	12: 8	in which all children **share**

3354   GO11 AG514 LN162 B3:402 K4:632 R3358
μετρεω, I MEASURE
Mt	7: 2	and the **measure** you **give**
	7: 2	will be the **measure** you **get**

Mk	4:24	the **measure** you **give** will be
	4:24	will be the **measure** you **get**
Lk	6:38	for the **measure** you **give** will
2C	10:12	when they **measure** themselves
Re	11: 1	Come and **measure** the temple
	11: 2	but do not **measure** the court
	21:15	rod of gold to **measure** the city
	21:16	**measured** the city with his rod
	21:17	He also **measured** its wall

3355   GO1 AG514 LN162 B3:403 R3354
μετρητης, MEASURE

Jn	2: 6	twenty or thirty **gallons**

3356   GO1 AG514 LN162 K5:938
μετριοπαθεω, I SUFFER IN MEASURE

He	5: 2	He is able to **deal gently**

3357   GO1 AG515 LN162
μετριως, MEASUREABLY

Ac	20:12	were **not a little** comforted

3358   GO14 AG515 LN162 B3:402 K4:632
μετρον, MEASURE

Mt	7: 2	and the **measure** you give
	23:32	the **measure** of your ancestors
Mk	4:24	the **measure** you give will be
Lk	6:38	A good **measure,** pressed down
	6:38	the **measure** you give will be
Jn	3:34	the Spirit without **measure**
Ro	12: 3	the **measure** of faith that God
2C	10:13	but will keep within the **field**
	10:13	keep within the field **that** God
Ep	4: 7	to the **measure** of Christ's gift
	4:13	**measure** of the full stature
	4:16	each part is working **properly**
Re	21:15	had a **measuring** rod of gold
	21:17	cubits by human **measurement**

3359   GO8 AG515 LN162 K4:635
μετωπον, FOREHEAD

Re	7: 3	with a seal on their **foreheads**
	9: 4	seal of God on their **foreheads**
	13:16	right hand or the **forehead**
	14: 1	name written on their **foreheads**
	14: 9	a mark on their **foreheads**
	17: 5	on her **forehead** was written
	20: 4	its mark on their **foreheads**
	22: 4	name will be on their **foreheads**

3360   GO17 AG515 LN162
μεχρι, UNTIL

Mt	11:23	have remained **until** this day
	28:15	among the Jews **to** this day
Mk	13:30	away **until** all these things
Lk	16:16	in effect **until** John came
Ac	10:30	days ago **at** this very hour
	20: 7	speaking **until** midnight
Ro	5:14	dominion from Adam **to** Moses
	15:19	**as far around as** Illyricum
Ga	4:19	**until** Christ is formed in you
Ep	4:13	**until** all of us come to the
Ph	2: 8	became obedient **to the point**
	2:30	because he came **close** to death
1Ti	6:14	**until** the manifestation of our
2Ti	2: 9	even **to the point** of being
He	3:14	confidence firm **to** the end
	9:10	**until** the time comes to set
	12: 4	not yet resisted **to the point**

3361   GO1042 AG515 LN162
μη, NOT [MULTIPLE OCCURRENCES]

3365   GO2 AG517 LN163
μηδαμως, CERTAINLY NOT

Ac	10:14	**By no means,** Lord; for I have
	11: 8	**By no means,** Lord; for nothing

3366   GO56 AG517 LN163 R3361,1161
μηδε, BUT NOT, NOT EVEN

Mt	6:25	will drink, **or** about your body
	7: 6	**and** do not throw your pearls
	10: 9	Take no gold, **or** silver
	10: 9	**or** copper in your belts
	10:10	**or** two tunics, or sandals
	10:10	**or** sandals, or a staff
	10:10	or sandals, **or** a staff
	10:14	welcome you **or** listen to your
	22:29	the scriptures **nor** the power
	23:10	**Nor** are you to be called
	24:20	in winter **or** on a sabbath
Mk	2: 2	**not even** in front of the door
	3:20	so that they could **not even** eat
	6:11	**and** they refuse to hear you
	8:26	Do **not even** go into the village
	12:24	scriptures **nor** the power of God
	13:15	go down **or** enter the house
Lk	3:14	threats **or** false accusation
	12:22	**or** about your body
	14:12	**or** your brothers or your

	14:12	brothers **or** your relatives		7:36	ordered them to tell **no one**
	14:12	relatives **or** rich neighbors		8:30	not to tell **anyone** about him
	16:26	**and** no one can cross from		9: 9	he ordered them to tell **no one**
	17:23	do **not** set off in pursuit		11:14	May **no one** ever eat fruit
Jn	4:15	**or** have to keep coming here	Lk	3:13	Collect **no** more than the
	14:27	**and** do **not** let them be afraid		3:14	Do not extort money from **anyone**
Ac	4:18	not to speak **or** teach at all		4:35	having done him **any harm**
	21:21	circumcise their children **or**		5:14	he ordered him to tell **no one**
Ro	6:13	**No longer** present your members		6:35	expecting **nothing** in return
	9:11	**or** had done anything good or		8:56	tell **no one** what had happened
	14:21	not to eat meat **or** drink wine		9: 3	Take **nothing** for your journey
	14:21	or drink wine **or** do anything		9:21	not to tell **anyone**
1C	5: 8	**the** yeast of malice and evil		10: 4	greet **no one** on the road
	5:11	Do **not even** eat with such a	Ac	4:17	to speak no more to **anyone**
	10: 7	Do **not** become idolaters as some		4:21	finding **no way** to punish them
	10: 8	We must **not** indulge in sexual		8:24	that **nothing** of what you have
	10: 9	We must **not** put Christ to the		9: 7	heard the voice but saw **no one**
	10:10	**And** do **not** complain as some		10:20	go with them **without hesitation**
2C	4: 2	refuse to practice cunning **or**		10:28	I should not call **anyone**
Ep	4:27	**and** do **not** make room for the		11:12	**not** to make a distinction
	5: 3	must **not even** be mentioned		11:19	spoke the word to **no one**
Ph	2: 3	selfish ambition **or** conceit		13:28	Even though they found **no** cause
Co	2:21	Do **not** taste, Do not touch		15:28	on you **no** further burden
	2:21	Do not taste, Do **not** touch		16:28	Do **not** harm yourself
2Th	2: 2	shaken in mind **or** alarmed		19:36	be quiet and do **nothing** rash
	3:10	to work should **not** eat		19:40	since there is **no** cause that
1Ti	1: 4	**and not** to occupy themselves		23:14	by an oath to taste **no** food
	5:22	**and** do **not** participate in the		23:22	Tell **no one** that you have
	6:17	**or** to set their hopes on the		23:29	but was charged with **nothing**
2Ti	1: 8	testimony about our Lord **or**		24:23	**not** to prevent **any** of his
He	12: 5	**or** lose heart when you are		25:17	I lost **no** time
1P	3:14	**and** do **not** be intimidated		25:25	he had done **nothing** deserving
	5: 2	**not** for sordid gain but eagerly		28: 6	saw that **nothing** unusual
	5: 3	Do **not** lord it over those in		28:18	because there was **no** reason
1J	2:15	love the world **or** the things	Ro	12:17	Do not repay **anyone** evil for
	3:18	not in word **or** speech		13: 8	Owe **no one** anything

---

3367   GO90 AG518 LN163 R3361,1520
μηδεις, NOTHING

				13: 8	Owe no one **anything**
Mt	8: 4	that you say nothing to **anyone**	1C	1: 7	lacking in **any** spiritual gift
	9:30	See that **no one** knows of this		3:18	Do **not** deceive yourselves
	16:20	not to tell **anyone** that he was		3:21	So let **no one** boast about human
	17: 9	Tell **no one** about the vision		10:24	Do **not** seek your own advantage
	27:19	Have **nothing** to do with that		10:25	in the meat market **without**
Mk	1:44	See that you say **nothing**		10:27	**without** raising any question
	1:44	you say nothing to **anyone**	2C	6: 3	We are putting **no** obstacle
	5:26	and she was **no better**		6: 3	no obstacle in **anyone's** way
	5:43	that **no one** should know this		6:10	many rich; as having **nothing**
	6: 8	ordered them to take **nothing**		7: 9	so that you were **not** harmed
				11: 5	I am **not** in the least inferior
				13: 7	you may not do **anything** wrong

Ga	6: 3	For if those who are **nothing**
	6:17	let **no one** make trouble for me
Ep	5: 6	Let **no one** deceive you with
Ph	1:28	and are in **no way** intimidated
	2: 3	Do **nothing** from selfish
	4: 6	Do not worry about **anything**
Co	2: 4	that **no one** may deceive you
	2:18	Do not let **anyone** disqualify
1Th	3: 3	that **no one** would be shaken
	4:12	and be dependent on **no one**
2Th	2: 3	Let **no one** deceive you in any
	3:11	busybodies, **not** doing any work
1Ti	4:12	Let **no one** despise your youth
	5:14	give the adversary **no** occasion
	5:21	doing **nothing** on the basis of
	5:22	Do not ordain **anyone** hastily
	6: 4	understanding **nothing**
Ti	2: 8	having **nothing** evil to say
	2:15	Let **no one** look down on you
	3: 2	to speak evil of **no one**
	3:13	and see that they lack **nothing**
He	10: 2	would **no longer** have any
Ja	1: 4	lacking in **nothing**
	1: 6	in faith, **never** doubting
	1:13	**No one,** when tempted
1P	3: 6	**never** let fears alarm you
1J	3: 7	let **no one** deceive you
3J	1: 7	accepting **no** support from
Re	2:10	Do **not** fear what you are about
	3:11	**no one** may seize your crown

Mk	1:45	Jesus could **no longer** go
	2: 2	was **no longer** room for them
	9:25	and **never** enter him again
	11:14	May no one **ever** eat fruit
Lk	8:49	trouble the teacher **any longer**
Jn	5:14	Do not sin **any more**
	8:11	and **from now on** do not sin
Ac	4:17	to speak **no more** to anyone
	13:34	**no more** to return to corruption
	25:24	he ought not to live **any longer**
Ro	6: 6	we might **no longer** be enslaved
	14:13	**no longer** pass judgment on one
	15:23	with **no further** place for me
2C	5:15	who live might live **no longer**
Ep	4:14	We must **no longer** be children
	4:17	you must **no longer** live as the
	4:28	Thieves must **give up** stealing
1Th	3: 1	we could bear it **no longer**
	3: 5	I could bear it **no longer**
1Ti	5:23	**No longer** drink only water
1P	4: 2	**no longer** by human desires

3372 GO3 AG518 LN163
μηκος, LENGTH

Ep	3:18	what is the breadth and **length**
Re	21:16	**length** the same as its width
	21:16	**length** and width and height

3373 GO1 AG518 LN163
μηκυνω, I LENGTHEN

Mk	4:27	seed would sprout and **grow**

3374 GO1 AG518 LN163
μηλωτη, SHEEPSKIN

He	11:37	in **skins** of **sheep** and goats

3375 GO1 AG518 LN163
μην, YET

He	6:14	I will **surely** bless you

3368 GO1 AG518 LN163
μηδεποτε, BUT NOT YET

2Ti	3: 7	can **never** arrive at a knowledge

3369 GO1 AG518 LN163
μηδεπω, BUT NOT YET

He	11: 7	about events **as yet** unseen

3370 GO1 AG518 LN163
μηδος, MEDES

Ac	2: 9	Parthians, **Medes,** Elamites

3370a GO1
μηθεις, NOTHING

Ac	27:33	food, having eaten **nothing**

3371 GO22 AG518 LN163 R3361,2089
μηκετι, NO LONGER

Mt	21:19	May no fruit **ever** come from you

3376 GO18 AG518 LN163 K4:638
μην, MONTH

Lk	1:24	for five **months** she remained
	1:26	In the sixth **month** the angel
	1:36	this is the sixth **month** for her
	1:56	about three **months** and then
	4:25	three years and six **months**
Ac	7:20	For three **months** he was brought
	18:11	there a year and six **months**
	19: 8	and for three **months** spoke out

	20: 3	he stayed for three **months**
	28:11	Three **months** later we set sail
Ga	4:10	special days, and **months**
Ja	5:17	three years and six **months**
Re	9: 5	to torture them for five **months**
	9:10	to harm people for five **months**
	9:15	hour, the day, the **month**
	11: 2	holy city for forty-two **months**
	13: 5	authority for forty-two **months**
	22: 2	producing its fruit each **month**

3377   GO4 AG519 LN163

μηνυω, I REPORT

Lk	20:37	are raised Moses himself **showed**
Jn	11:57	Jesus was should **let** them **know**
Ac	23:30	When I **was informed** that there
1C	10:28	for the one who **informed** you

3379   GO25 AG519 LN163

μηποτε, NOT THEN

Mt	4: 6	**so that** you will not dash your
	5:25	**or** your accuser may hand you
	7: 6	**or** they will trample them under
	13:15	**so that** they might not look
	13:29	**for** in gathering the weeds
	15:32	**for** they might faint on the
	25: 9	**No!** there will not be enough
	27:64	**otherwise** his disciples may go
Mk	4:12	**so that** they may not turn again
	14: 2	**or** there may be a riot among
Lk	3:15	**whether** he might be the Messiah
	4:11	**so that** you will not dash your
	12:58	**or** you may be dragged before
	14: 8	**in case** someone more
	14:12	**in case** they may invite you
	14:29	**Otherwise,** when he has laid
	21:34	**so that** your hearts are not
Jn	7:26	Can it be **that** the authorities
Ac	5:39	**in that case** you may even be
	28:27	**so that** they might not look
2Ti	2:25	God may **perhaps** grant that
He	2: 1	**so that** we do not drift away
	3:12	**that** none of you may have an
	4: 1	**while** the promise of entering
	9:17	**since** it is not in force

3380   GO2 AG519 LN163

μηπω, NOT YET

Ro	9:11	**Even before** they had been born
He	9: 8	has **not yet** been disclosed

3382   GO1 AG519 LN163

μηρος, THIGH

Re	19:16	On his robe and on his **thigh**

3383   GO34 AG519 LN163

μητε, NOR

Mt	5:34	**either** by heaven, for it is the
	5:35	**or** by the earth, for it is his
	5:35	**or** by Jerusalem, for it is the
	5:36	**And** do **not** swear by your head
	11:18	For John came **neither** eating
	11:18	neither eating **nor** drinking
Lk	7:33	no bread and drinking **no** wine
	9: 3	**no** staff, nor bag, nor bread
	9: 3	**nor** bag, nor bread, nor money
	9: 3	nor bag, **nor** bread, nor money
	9: 3	nor bag, nor bread, **nor** money
	9: 3	**not even** an extra tunic
Ac	23: 8	**or** angel, or spirit; but the
	23: 8	or angel, **or** spirit; but the
	23:12	**neither** to eat nor drink until
	23:12	neither to eat **nor** drink until
	23:21	**neither** to eat nor drink until
	23:21	neither to eat **nor** drink until
	27:20	When **neither** sun nor stars
	27:20	When neither sun **nor** stars
2Th	2: 2	**either** by spirit or by word
	2: 2	either by spirit **or** by word
	2: 2	spirit or by word **or** by letter
1Ti	1: 7	**either** what they are saying
	1: 7	they are saying **or** the things
He	7: 3	**neither** beginning of days nor
	7: 3	beginning of days **nor** end of
Ja	5:12	**either** by heaven or by earth
	5:12	either by heaven **or** by earth
	5:12	by earth **or** by any other oath
Re	7: 1	wind could blow on earth **or** sea
	7: 1	blow on earth or sea **or** against
	7: 3	damage the earth **or** the sea
	7: 3	earth or the sea **or** the trees

3384   GO83 AG520 LN163 B3:1068 K4:642

μητηρ, MOTHER

Mt	1:18	When his **mother** Mary had been
	2:11	the child with Mary his **mother**
	2:13	take the child and his **mother**
	2:14	took the child and his **mother**
	2:20	take the child and his **mother**
	2:21	took the child and his **mother**
	10:35	a daughter against her **mother**

	10:37	Whoever loves father or **mother**
	12:46	his **mother** and his brothers
	12:47	your **mother** and your brothers
	12:48	Who is my **mother,** and who are
	12:49	Here are my **mother** and my
	12:50	brother and sister and **mother**
	13:55	Is not his **mother** called Mary
	14: 8	Prompted by her **mother**
	14:11	who brought it to her **mother**
	15: 4	your father and your **mother**
	15: 4	evil of father or **mother**
	15: 5	whoever tells father or **mother**
	19: 5	leave his father and **mother**
	19:12	who have been so from **birth**
	19:19	Honor your father and **mother**
	19:29	sisters or father or **mother**
	20:20	Then the **mother** of the sons
	27:56	and Mary the **mother** of James
	27:56	**mother** of the sons of Zebedee
Mk	3:31	his **mother** and his brothers
	3:32	Your **mother** and your brothers
	3:33	Who are my **mother** and my
	3:34	Here are my **mother** and my
	3:35	brother and sister and **mother**
	5:40	the child's father and **mother**
	6:24	and said to her **mother**
	6:28	the girl gave it to her **mother**
	7:10	your father and your **mother**
	7:10	speaks evil of father or **mother**
	7:11	anyone tells father or **mother**
	7:12	anything for a father or **mother**
	10: 7	leave his father and **mother**
	10:19	Honor your father and **mother**
	10:29	brothers or sisters or **mother**
	10:30	sisters, **mothers** and children
	15:40	and Mary the **mother** of James
Lk	1:15	even before his **birth** he will
	1:43	that the **mother** of my Lord
	1:60	But his **mother** said
	2:33	the child's father and **mother**
	2:34	and said to his **mother** Mary
	2:48	and his **mother** said to him
	2:51	His **mother** treasured all these
	7:12	He was his **mother's** only son
	7:15	Jesus gave him to his **mother**
	8:19	his **mother** and his brothers
	8:20	Your **mother** and your brothers
	8:21	My **mother** and my brothers
	8:51	the child's father and **mother**

	12:53	**mother** against daughter
	12:53	daughter against **mother**
	14:26	does not hate father and **mother**
	18:20	Honor your father and **mother**
Jn	2: 1	the **mother** of Jesus was there
	2: 3	the wine gave out, the **mother** of
	2: 5	His **mother** said to the servants
	2:12	to Capernaum with his **mother**
	3: 4	into the **mother's** womb and be
	6:42	whose father and **mother** we know
	19:25	cross of Jesus were his **mother**
	19:25	and his **mother's** sister
	19:26	When Jesus saw his **mother**
	19:26	he said to his **mother**
	19:27	Here is your **mother**
Ac	1:14	Mary the **mother** of Jesus
	3: 2	And a man lame from **birth**
	12:12	the **mother** of John whose other
	14: 8	been crippled from **birth**
Ro	16:13	and greet his **mother**
Ga	1:15	before I was **born** and called me
	4:26	and she is our **mother**
Ep	5:31	leave his father and **mother**
	6: 2	Honor your father and **mother**
1Ti	5: 2	to older women as **mothers**
2Ti	1: 5	Lois and your **mother** Eunice
Re	17: 5	**mother** of whores and of earth's

3385 ᴳᴼ17 ᴬᴳ520 ᴸᴺ163

μητι, NOT SOME

Mt	7:16	**Are** grapes gathered from thorns
	12:23	**Can** this be the Son of David
	26:22	**Surely not** I, Lord?
	26:25	**Surely not** I, Rabbi?
Mk	4:21	**Is** a lamp brought in to be put
	14:19	**Surely, not** I?
Lk	6:39	**Can** a blind person guide a
	9:13	**unless** we are to go and buy
Jn	4:29	He **cannot** be the Messiah
	8:22	**Is** he going to kill himself
	18:35	I am not a Jew, am I
Ac	10:47	**Can** anyone withhold the water
1C	6: 3	judge angels—**to say nothing**
	7: 5	not deprive one another **except**
2C	1:17	**when** I wanted to do this?
	12:18	take advantage of you, **did** he
	13: 5	**unless,** indeed, you fail
Ja	3:11	**Does** a spring pour forth

3388 GO2 AG520 LN163 R3384
μητρα, MOTHERHOOD
Lk   2:23   Every **firstborn** male shall be
Ro   4:19   the barrenness of Sarah's **womb**

3389 GO1 AG520 LN163
μητρολωας, MOTHER-KILLER
1Ti   1: 9   **kill** their father or **mother**

3392 GO5 AG520 LN163 B1:447 K4:644
μιαινω, I DEFILE
Jn   18:28   to **avoid ritual defilement**
Ti   1:15   the **corrupt** and unbelieving
      1:15   consciences are **corrupted**
He 12:15   through it many **become defiled**
Ju   1: 8   these dreamers also **defile**

3393 GO1 AG521 LN164 B1:447 K4:646 R3392
μιασμα, POLLUTION
2P   2:20   have escaped the **defilements**

3394 GO1 AG521 LN164 B1:447 K4:647 R3392
μιασμος, POLLUTION
2P   2:10   indulge their flesh in **depraved**

3395 GO1 AG521 LN164 R3396
μιγμα, MIXTURE
Jn 19:39   bringing a **mixture** of myrrh

3396 GO4 AG521 LN164
μιγνυμι, I MIX
Mt 27:34   **mixed** with gall; but when he
Lk 13: 1   whose blood Pilate had **mingled**
Re   8: 7   **mixed** with blood, and they were
     15: 2   a sea of glass **mixed** with fire

3398 GO46 AG521 LN164 B2:427 K4:648
μικρος, LITTLE
Mt 10:42   to one of these **little** ones
     11:11   yet the **least** in the kingdom
     13:32   it is the **smallest** of all the
     18: 6   before one of these **little** ones
     18:10   one of these **little** ones
     18:14   one of these **little** ones
     26:39   And going a **little** farther
     26:73   After a **little** while the
Mk   4:31   is the **smallest** of all the
      9:42   these **little** ones who believe
     14:35   And going a **little** farther
     14:70   Then after a **little** while

     15:40   the mother of James the **younger**
Lk   7:28   yet the **least** in the kingdom
      9:48   for the **least** among all of you
     12:32   Do not be afraid, **little** flock
     17: 2   cause one of these **little** ones
     19: 3   because he was **short** in stature
Jn   7:33   with you a **little** while longer
     12:35   is with you for a **little** longer
     13:33   with you only a **little** longer
     14:19   In a **little** while the world
     16:16   A **little** while, and you will
     16:16   and again a **little** while
     16:17   A **little** while, and you will no
     16:17   and again a **little** while
     16:18   a **little** while'? We do not
     16:19   A **little** while, and you will
     16:19   and again a **little** while
Ac   8:10   from the **least** to the greatest
     26:22   testifying to both **small** and
1C   5: 6   that a **little** yeast leavens
2C   11: 1   with me in a **little** foolishness
     11:16   I too may boast a **little**
Ga   5: 9   A **little** yeast leavens the
He   8:11   from the **least** of them to the
     10:37   in a very **little** while
Ja   3: 5   the tongue is a **small** member
Re   3: 8   I know that you have but **little**
      6:11   told to rest a **little** longer
     11:18   name, both **small** and great
     13:16   all, both **small** and great
     19: 5   who fear him, **small** and great
     19:18   slave, both **small** and great
     20: 3   let out for a **little** while
     20:12   saw the dead, great and **small**

3399 GO3 AG521 LN164
μιλητος, MILETUS
Ac 20:15   after that we came to **Miletus**
     20:17   From **Miletus** he sent a
             message
2Ti   4:20   Trophimus I left ill in **Miletus**

3400 GO1 AG521 LN164
μιλιον, MILE
Mt   5:41   forces you to go one **mile**

3401 GO4 AG521 LN164 B1:490 K4:659
μιμεομαι, I IMITATE
2Th 3: 7   how you ought to **imitate** us
      3: 9   give you an example to **imitate**

He 13: 7 and **imitate** their faith
3J 1:11 do not **imitate** what is evil

3402 ᴳᴼ6 ᴬᴳ522 ᴸᴺ164 ᴮ1:490 ᴷ4:659 ᴿ3401
μιμητης, IMITATOR
1C 4:16 you, then, be **imitators** of me
11: 1 Be **imitators** of me
Ep 5: 1 Therefore be **imitators** of God
1Th 1: 6 And you became **imitators** of us
2:14 **imitators** of the churches
He 6:12 but **imitators** of those who

3403 ᴳᴼ23 ᴬᴳ522 ᴸᴺ164 ᴮ3:230 ᴷ4:675
μιμνησκομαι, I REMEMBER
Mt 5:23 you **remember** that your brother
26:75 Peter **remembered** what Jesus
27:63 we **remember** what that impostor
Lk 1:54 in **remembrance** of his mercy
1:72 **remembered** his holy covenant
16:25 **remember** that during your
23:42 **remember** me when you come into
24: 6 **Remember** how he told you
24: 8 Then they **remembered** his words
Jn 2:17 **remembered** that it was written
2:22 **remembered** that he had said
12:16 **remembered** that these things
Ac 10:31 have been **remembered** before God
11:16 And I **remembered** the word
1C 11: 2 **remember** me in everything
2Ti 1: 4 **Recalling** your tears
He 2: 6 that you **are mindful** of them
8:12 I **will remember** their sins
10:17 I **will remember** their sins
13: 3 **Remember** those who are in
2P 3: 2 **remember** the words spoken in
Ju 1:17 you, beloved, must **remember**
Re 16:19 God **remembered** great Babylon

3404 ᴳᴼ40 ᴬᴳ522 ᴸᴺ164 ᴮ1:555 ᴷ4:683
μισεω, I HATE
Mt 5:43 love your neighbor and **hate**
6:24 slave will either **hate** the one
10:22 and you will be **hated** by all
24: 9 will be **hated** by all nations
24:10 another and **hate** one another
Mk 13:13 you will be **hated** by all
Lk 1:71 the hand of all who **hate** us
6:22 are you when people **hate** you
6:27 do good to those who **hate** you
14:26 not **hate** father and mother

16:13 either **hate** the one and love
19:14 **hated** him and sent a delegation
21:17 You will be **hated** by all
Jn 3:20 who do evil **hate** the light
7: 7 The world cannot **hate** you
7: 7 it **hates** me because I testify
12:25 **hate** their life in this world
15:18 If the world **hates** you
15:18 it hated me before it **hated** you
15:19 therefore the world **hates** you
15:23 Whoever **hates** me hates my
15:23 hates me **hates** my Father also
15:24 **hated** both me and my Father
15:25 They **hated** me without a cause
17:14 world has **hated** them because
Ro 7:15 I do the very thing I **hate**
9:13 Jacob, but I have **hated** Esau.
Ep 5:29 no one ever **hates** his own body
Ti 3: 3 despicable, **hating** one another
He 1: 9 **hated** wickedness; therefore God
1J 2: 9 **hating** a brother or sister
2:11 whoever **hates** another believer
3:13 that the world **hates** you
3:15 who **hate** a brother or sister
4:20 **hate** their brothers or sisters
Ju 1:23 **hating** even the tunic defiled
Re 2: 6 you **hate** the works of the
2: 6 Nicolaitans, which I also **hate**
17:16 the beast will **hate** the whore
18: 2 of every foul and **hateful** beast

3405 ᴳᴼ3 ᴬᴳ523 ᴸᴺ164 ᴮ3:138 ᴷ4:695 ᴿ3406
μισθαποδοσια, WAGE GIVEN
He 2: 2 received a just **penalty**
10:35 it brings a great **reward**
11:26 looking ahead to the **reward**

3406 ᴳᴼ1 ᴬᴳ523 ᴸᴺ164 ᴮ3:138 ᴷ4:695 ᴿ3409,591
μισθαποδοτης, WAGE GIVER
He 11: 6 he exists and that he **rewards**

3407 ᴳᴼ2 ᴬᴳ523 ᴸᴺ164 ᴮ3:138 ᴷ4:695 ᴿ3408
μισθιος, WAGE-EARNER
Lk 15:17 **hired hands** have bread enough
15:19 like one of your **hired hands**

3408 ᴳᴼ29 ᴬᴳ523 ᴸᴺ164 ᴮ3:138 ᴷ4:695
μισθος, WAGE
Mt 5:12 your **reward** is great in heaven
5:46 what **reward** do you have

6: 1	for then you have no **reward**
6: 2	they have received their **reward**
6: 5	they have received their **reward**
6:16	they have received their **reward**
10:41	will receive a prophet's **reward**
10:41	the **reward** of the righteous
10:42	these will lose their **reward**
20: 8	and give them their **pay**
Mk 9:41	by no means lose the **reward**
Lk 6:23	surely your **reward** is great
6:35	Your **reward** will be great
10: 7	the laborer deserves to be **paid**
Jn 4:36	is already receiving **wages**
Ac 1:18	the **reward** of his wickedness
Ro 4: 4	**wages** are not reckoned as a
1C 3: 8	will receive **wages** according
3:14	builder will receive a **reward**
9:17	own will, I have a **reward**
9:18	What then is my **reward**
1Ti 5:18	laborer deserves to be **paid**
Ja 5: 4	The **wages** of the laborers
2P 2:13	suffering the **penalty** for doing
2:15	loved the **wages** of doing wrong
2J 1: 8	but may receive a full **reward**
Ju 1:11	error for the **sake of gain**
Re 11:18	for **rewarding** your servants
22:12	my **reward** is with me

3409   GO2 AG523 LN164 B3:138 K4:695 R3408
μισθοω, I HIRE FOR WAGES

Mt 20: 1	to **hire** laborers for his
20: 7	no one **has hired** us

3410   GO1 AG523 LN164 B3:138
μισθωμα, HIRED PLACE

Ac 28:30	years at **his own expense**

3411   GO3 AG523 LN164 B3:138 K4:695 R3409
μισθωτος, WAGE EARNER

Mk 1:20	the boat with the **hired men**
Jn 10:12	The **hired hand,** who is not
10:13	The **hired hand** runs away

3412   GO1 AG524 LN164
μιτυληνη, MITYLENE

Ac 20:14	on board and went to **Mitylene**

3413   GO2 AG524 LN164 B1:104
μιχαηλ, MICHAEL

Ju 1: 9	But when the archangel **Michael**
Re 12: 7	**Michael** and his angels fought

3414   GO9 AG524 LN164
μνα, MINA

Lk 19:13	and gave them ten **pounds**
19:16	your **pound** has made ten more
19:16	has made ten more **pounds**
19:18	your **pound** has made five pounds
19:18	your pound has made five **pounds**
19:20	Lord, here is your **pound**
19:24	Take the **pound** from him
19:24	to the one who has ten **pounds**
19:25	Lord, he has ten **pounds**

3416   GO1 AG524 LN164
μνασων, MNASON

Ac 21:16	the house of **Mnason** of Cyprus

3417   GO7 AG524 LN164 B3:230 K4:678
μνεια, MEMORY

Ro 1: 9	I **remember** you always in my
Ep 1:16	I **remember** you in my prayers
Ph 1: 3	every time I **remember** you
1Th 1: 2	for all of you and **mention** you
3: 6	you always **remember** us kindly
2Ti 1: 3	when I **remember** you constantly
Pm 1: 4	I **remember** you in my prayers

3418   GO8 AG524 LN164 B1:263 K4:679
μνημα, GRAVE

Mk 5: 3	He lived among the **tombs**
5: 5	Night and day among the **tombs**
Lk 8:27	in a house but in the **tombs**
23:53	laid it in a rock-hewn **tomb**
24: 1	they came to the **tomb**
Ac 2:29	**tomb** is with us to this day
7:16	laid in the **tomb** that Abraham
Re 11: 9	let them be placed in a **tomb**

3419   GO40 AG524 LN164 B1:263 K4:680
μνημειον, GRAVE

Mt 8:28	coming out of the **tombs** met him
23:29	build the **tombs** of the prophets
27:52	The **tombs** also were opened
27:53	they came out of the **tombs**
27:60	laid it in his own new **tomb**
27:60	to the door of the **tomb**
28: 8	So they left the **tomb** quickly
Mk 5: 2	a man out of the **tombs** with an

6:29	body, and laid it in a **tomb**
15:46	and laid it in a **tomb**
15:46	against the door of the **tomb**
16: 2	they went to the **tomb**
16: 3	from the entrance to the **tomb**
16: 5	As they entered the **tomb**
16: 8	went out and fled from the **tomb**
Lk 11:44	you are like unmarked **graves**
11:47	For you build the **tombs**
23:55	and they saw the **tomb** and how
24: 2	rolled away from the **tomb**
24: 9	and returning from the **tomb**
24:12	got up and ran to the **tomb**
24:22	They were at the **tomb** early
24:24	with us went to the **tomb**
Jn 5:28	all who are in their **graves**
11:17	already been in the **tomb**
11:31	that she was going to the **tomb**
11:38	disturbed, came to the **tomb**
12:17	called Lazarus out of the **tomb**
19:41	garden there was a new **tomb**
19:42	and the **tomb** was nearby
20: 1	Mary Magdalene came to the **tomb**
20: 1	had been removed from the **tomb**
20: 2	taken the Lord out of the **tomb**
20: 3	and went toward the **tomb**
20: 4	and reached the **tomb** first
20: 6	him, and went into the **tomb**
20: 8	who reached the **tomb** first
20:11	stood weeping outside the **tomb**
20:11	bent over to look into the **tomb**
Ac 13:29	the tree and laid him in a **tomb**

3420   GO1 AG524 LN164 B3:230 K4:679 R3403
μνημη, MEMORIAL
2P   1:15   any time to **recall** these things

3421   GO21 AG525 LN164 B3:230 K4:682
μνημονευω, I REMEMBER

Mt 16: 9	not **remember** the five loaves
Mk 8:18	And do you not **remember**?
Lk 17:32	**Remember** Lot's wife.
Jn 15:20	**Remember** the word that I said
16: 4	you may **remember** that I told
16:21	no longer **remembers** the anguish
Ac 20:31	**remembering** that for three
20:35	**remembering** the words of the
Ga 2:10	that we **remember** the poor
Ep 2:11	**remember** that at one time

Co 4:18	**Remember** my chains
1Th 1: 3	**remembering** before our God
2: 9	**remember** our labor and toil
2Th 2: 5	not **remember** that I told you
2Ti 2: 8	**Remember** Jesus Christ, raised
He 11:15	**had been thinking** of the land
11:22	made **mention** of the exodus
13: 7	**Remember** your leaders
Re 2: 5	**Remember** then from what you
3: 3	**Remember** then what you received
18: 5	has **remembered** her iniquities

3422   GO3 AG525 LN165 B3:230 R3421
μνημοσυνον, MEMORIAL
Mt 26:13   will be told in **remembrance**
Mk 14: 9   will be told in **remembrance**
Ac 10: 4   have ascended as a **memorial**

3423   GO3 AG525 LN165
μνηστευω, I AM ENGAGED
Mt 1:18   Mary **had been engaged** to Joseph
Lk 1:27   to a virgin **engaged** to a man
2: 5   Mary, to whom he **was engaged**

3424   GO1 AG525 LN165 R3425,2980
μογιλαλος, SPEECH DIFFICULTY
Mk 7:32   had an **impediment in** his **speech**

3425   GO1 AG525 LN165 K4:735
μογις, HARDLY
Lk 9:39   it mauls him and will **scarcely**

3426   GO3 AG525 LN165
μοδιος, MEASURING SCOOP
Mt 5:15   puts it under the **bushel basket**
Mk 4:21   be put under the **bushel basket**
Lk 11:33   a lamp puts it in a **cellar**

3428   GO7 AG526 LN165 B2:582 K4:729 R3432
μοιχαλις, ADULTEROUS
Mt 12:39   evil and **adulterous** generation
16: 4   evil and **adulterous** generation
Mk 8:38   in this **adulterous** and
Ro 7: 3   will be called an **adulteress**
7: 3   she is not an **adulteress**
Ja 4: 4   **Adulterers!** Do you not know
2P 2:14   They have eyes full of **adultery**

3429   GO4 AG526 LN165 K4:729 R3432
μοιχαω, I COMMIT ADULTERY

Mt	5:32	divorced woman **commits adultery**
	19: 9	another **commits adultery**
Mk	10:11	**commits adultery** against her
	10:12	she **commits adultery**

3430   GO3 AG526 LN165 B2:582 K4:729 R3431
μοιχεια, ADULTERY

Mt	15:19	**adultery**, fornication, theft
Mk	7:22	**adultery**, avarice, wickedness
Jn	8: 3	had been caught in **adultery**

3431   GO15 AG526 LN165 B2:582 K4:729 R3432
μοιχευω, I COMMIT ADULTERY

Mt	5:27	You **shall** not **commit adultery**
	5:28	has already **committed adultery**
	5:32	causes her to **commit adultery**
	19:18	You shall not **commit adultery**
Mk	10:19	You shall not **commit adultery**
Lk	16:18	another **commits adultery**
	16:18	her husband **commits adultery**
	18:20	You shall not **commit adultery**
Jn	8: 4	very act of **committing adultery**
Ro	2:22	You that forbid **adultery**
	2:22	do you **commit adultery**
	13· 9	You shall not **commit adultery**
Ja	2:11	You shall not **commit adultery**
	2:11	if you do not **commit adultery**
Re	2:22	and those who **commit adultery**

3432   GO3 AG526 LN165 B2:582 K4:729
μοιχος, ADULTERER

Lk	18:11	thieves, rogues, **adulterers**
1C	6: 9	**adulterers**, male prostitutes
He	13: 4	fornicators and **adulterers**

3433   GO6 AG526 LN165 K4:735
μολις, SCARCELY

Ac	14:18	**scarcely** restrained the crowds
	27: 7	with **difficulty** off Cnidus
	27: 8	past it with **difficulty**
	27:16	we were **scarcely** able to get
Ro	5: 7	**rarely** will anyone die for a
1P	4:18	it is **hard** for the righteous

3434   GO1 AG526 LN165
μολοχ, MOLOCH

Ac	7:43	took along the tent of **Moloch**

3435   GO3 AG526 LN165 B1:448 K4:736
μολυνω, I STAIN

1C	8: 7	being weak, **is defiled**
Re	3: 4	**have** not **soiled** their clothes
	14: 4	who **have** not **defiled** themselves

3436   GO1 AG527 LN165 B1:448 K4:737 R3435
μολυσμος, STAINNESS

2C	7: 1	from every **defilement** of body

3437   GO1 AG527 LN165 K4:571 R3201
μομφη, COMPLAINT

Co	3:13	has a **complaint** against another

3438   GO2 AG527 LN165 B3:224 K4:579 R3306
μονη, ROOM TO STAY

Jn	14: 2	there are many **dwelling places**
	14:23	and make our **home** with them

3439   GO9 AG527 LN165 B2:723 K4:737
μονογενης, ONLY BORN, UNIQUE

Lk	7:12	He was his mother's **only** son
	8:42	for he had an **only** daughter
	9:38	he is my **only** child
Jn	1:14	as of a father's **only** son
	1:18	It is God the **only** Son
	3:16	that he gave his **only** Son
	3:18	name of the **only** Son of God
He	11:17	ready to offer up his **only** son
1J	4: 9	his **only** Son into the world

3441   GO114 AG527 LN165 B2:723
μονος, ALONE

Mt	4: 4	does not live by bread **alone**
	4:10	your God, and serve **only** him
	5:47	**only** your brothers and sisters
	8: 8	but **only** speak the word
	9:21	If I **only** touch his cloak
	10:42	gives **even** a cup of cold water
	12: 4	but **only** for the priests
	14:23	he was there **alone**
	14:36	**even** the fringe of his cloak
	17: 8	except Jesus himself **alone**
	18:15	when the two of you are **alone**
	21:19	nothing at all on it **but** leaves
	21:21	not **only** will you do what has
	24:36	but **only** the Father
Mk	4:10	When he was **alone**
	5:36	Do not fear, **only** believe
	6: 8	their journey **except** a staff
	6:47	and he was **alone** on the land
	9: 2	mountain apart, by **themselves**

	9: 8	them any more, but **only** Jesus
Lk	4: 4	not live by bread **alone**
	4: 8	God, and serve **only** him
	5:21	forgive sins but God **alone**
	6: 4	for any **but** the priests to eat
	8:50	**Only** believe, and she will
	9:18	**only** the disciples near him
	9:36	Jesus was found **alone**
	10:40	to do all the work **by myself**
	24:12	the linen cloths **by themselves**
	24:18	Are you the **only** stranger
Jn	5:18	not **only** breaking the sabbath
	5:44	from the one who **alone** is God
	6:15	to the mountain **by himself**
	6:22	disciples had gone away **alone**
	8: 9	Jesus was left **alone** with
	8:16	I **alone** who judge, but I
	8:29	he has not left me **alone**
	11:52	and not for the nation **only**
	12: 9	came not **only** because of Jesus
	12:24	it remains just a **single** grain
	13: 9	my feet **only** but also my hands
	16:32	and you will leave me **alone**
	16:32	not **alone** because the Father
	17: 3	know you, the **only** true God
	17:20	not **only** on behalf of these
Ac	8:16	they had **only** been baptized
	11:19	the word to no one **except** Jews
	18:25	though he knew **only** the baptism
	19:26	not **only** in Ephesus but in
	19:27	danger not **only** that this trade
	21:13	not **only** to be bound but even
	26:29	that not **only** you but also all
	27:10	not **only** of the cargo and the
Ro	1:32	yet they not **only** do them but
	3:29	Or is God the God of Jews **only**
	4:12	who are not **only** circumcised
	4:16	not **only** to the adherents
	4:23	written not for his sake **alone**
	5: 3	And not **only** that, but we also
	5:11	**But** more than that, we even
	8:23	and not **only** the creation
	9:10	**Nor** is that all; something
	9:24	not from the Jews **only** but also
	11: 3	your altars; I **alone** am left
	13: 5	not **only** because of wrath
	16: 4	to whom not **only** I give thanks
	16:27	to the **only** wise God

1C	7:39	wishes, **only** in the Lord
	9: 6	Or is it **only** Barnabas and I
	14:36	Or are you the **only** ones
	15:19	If for this life **only** we have
2C	7: 7	and not **only** by his coming
	8:10	not **only** to do something but
	8:19	and not **only** that, but he
	8:21	not **only** in the Lord's sight
	9:12	not **only** supplies the needs
Ga	1:23	they **only** heard it said
	2:10	They asked **only** one thing
	3: 2	**only** thing I want to learn
	4:18	and not **only** when I am present
	5:13	**only** do not use your freedom
	6: 4	All must test their **own** work
	6:12	**only** that they may not be
Ep	1:21	not **only** in this age but also
Ph	1:27	**Only,** live your life in a
	1:29	privilege not **only** of believing
	2:12	not **only** in my presence
	2:27	not **only** on him but on me also
	4:15	and receiving, except you **alone**
Co	4:11	These are the **only** ones of the
1Th	1: 5	came to you not in word **only**
	1: 8	from you not **only** in Macedonia
	2: 8	not **only** the gospel of God
	3: 1	we decided to be left **alone**
2Th	2: 7	but **only** until the one who now
1Ti	1:17	the **only** God, be honor
	5:13	and they are not **merely** idle
	6:15	the blessed and **only** Sovereign
	6:16	he **alone** who has immortality
2Ti	2:20	utensils not **only** of gold
	4: 8	and not **only** to me but also
	4:11	**Only** Luke is with me
He	9: 7	but **only** the high priest goes
	9:10	deal **only** with food and drink
	12:26	shake not **only** the earth
Ja	1:22	not **merely** hearers who deceive
	2:24	by works and not by faith **alone**
1P	2:18	not **only** those who are kind
1J	2: 2	and not for ours **only** but also
	5: 6	the water **only** but with the
2J	1: 1	and not **only** I but also all
Ju	1: 4	deny our **only** Master and Lord
	1:25	to the **only** God our Savior
Re	15: 4	For you **alone** are holy

3442 GO2 AG528 LN165 R3441,3788
μονοφθαλμος, ONE EYE
Mt 18: 9   to enter life with **one eye**
Mk   9:47   with **one eye** than to have two

3443 GO1 AG528 LN165 R3440
μονοω, I LEAVE ALONE
1Ti 5: 5   widow, **left alone,** has set her

3444 GO3 AG528 LN165 B1:705 K4:742
μορφη, FORM
Mk 16:12   he appeared in another **form**
Ph   2: 6   he was in the **form** of God
     2: 7   taking the **form** of a slave

3445 GO1 AG528 LN165 B1:705 K4:752 R3444
μορφοω, I FORM
Ga   4:19   until Christ **is formed** in you

3446 GO2 AG528 LN165 B1:705 K4:754 R3445
μορφωσις, FORM
Ro   2:20   the **embodiment** of knowledge
2Ti 3: 5   the outward **form** of godliness

3447 GO1 AG528 LN165 R3448,4160
μοσχοποιεω, I MAKE A CALF
Ac   7:41   At that time they **made** a **calf**

3448 GO6 AG528 LN165 K4:760
μοσχος, CALF
Lk 15:23   get the fatted **calf** and kill it
    15:27   has killed the fatted **calf**
    15:30   you killed the fatted **calf**
He   9:12   the blood of goats and **calves**
     9:19   he took the blood of **calves**
Re   4: 7   living creature like an **ox**

3449 GO3 AG528 LN166 B1:262
μοχθος, TOIL
2C 11:27   in toil and **hardship**
1Th 2: 9   You remember our labor and **toil**
2Th 3: 8   with toil and **labor** we worked

3451 GO1 AG528 LN166
μουσικος, MUSICIAN
Re 18:22   sound of harpists and **minstrels**

3452 GO1 AG528 LN166
μυελος, MARROW
He   4:12   spirit, joints from **marrow;**

3453 GO1 AG529 LN166 B3:501 K4:828
μυεω, I LEARN SECRET
Ph   4:12   I **have learned the secret** of

3454 GO5 AG529 LN166 B2:643 K4:762
μυθος, MYTH
1Ti 1: 4   to occupy themselves with **myths**
     4: 7   to do with profane **myths**
2Ti 4: 4   truth and wander away to **myths**
Ti   1:14   attention to Jewish **myths**
2P   1:16   follow cleverly devised **myths**

3455 GO1 AG529 LN166
μυκαομαι, I ROAR
Re 10: 3   shout, like a lion **roaring**

3456 GO1 AG529 LN166 K4:796
μυκτηριζω, I MOCK
Ga   6: 7   deceived; God is not **mocked**

3457 GO1 AG529 LN166 B3:390 R3458
μυλικος, OF MILL (MILLSTONE)
Lk 17: 2   if a **millstone** were hung

3457a GO1 AG529 LN166 B3:390
μυλινος, OF MILL (MILLSTONE)
Re 18:21   stone like a great **millstone**

3458 GO4 AG529 LN166 B3:390
μυλος, MILLSTONE
Mt 18: 6   for you if a great **millstone**
    24:41   Two women will be **grinding** meal
Mk   9:42   if a great **millstone** were hung
Re 18:22   the sound of the **millstone**

3460 GO1 AG529 LN166
μυρα, MYRA
Ac 27: 5   we came to **Myra** in Lycia

3461 GO8 AG529 LN166 R3463
μυριας, TEN THOUSAND
Lk 12: 1   crowd gathered by the **thousands**
Ac 19:19   to fifty **thousand** silver coins
    21:20   how many **thousands** of believers
He 12:22   and to **innumerable** angels
Ju   1:14   **ten thousands** of his holy ones
Re   5:11   numbered **myriads** of myriads
     5:11   numbered myriads of **myriads**
     9:16   was two hundred **million**

3462　GO1 AG529 LN166 K4:800 R3464
μυριζω, I ANOINT WITH PERFUME
Mk 14: 8　she **has anointed** my body

3463　GO3 AG529 LN166
μυριος, TEN THOUSAND
Mt 18:24　owed him **ten thousand** talents
1C　4:15　have **ten thousand** guardians
　　14:19　**ten thousand** words in a tongue

3464　GO14 AG529 LN166 B2:294 K4:800
μυρον, PERFUME
Mt 26: 7　jar of very costly **ointment**
　　26:12　pouring this **ointment** on my
Mk 14: 3　jar of very costly **ointment**
　　14: 4　Why was the **ointment** wasted
　　14: 5　this **ointment** could have been
Lk　7:37　an alabaster jar of **ointment**
　　7:38　them with the **ointment**
　　7:46　anointed my feet with **ointment**
　　23:56　prepared spices and **ointments**
Jn　11: 2　anointed the Lord with **perfume**
　　12: 3　took a pound of costly **perfume**
　　12: 3　the fragrance of the **perfume**
　　12: 5　Why was this **perfume** not sold
Re　18:13　cinnamon, spice, incense, **myrrh**

3465　GO2 AG530 LN166
μυσια, MYSIA
Ac　16: 7　they had come opposite **Mysia**
　　16: 8　so, passing by **Mysia,** they went

3466　GO28 AG530 LN166 B3:501 K4:802
μυστηριον, MYSTERY
Mt 13:11　to know the **secrets** of the
Mk　4:11　given the **secret** of the kingdom
Lk　8:10　to know the **secrets** of the
Ro 11:25　to understand this **mystery**
　　16:25　revelation of the **mystery**
1C　2: 1　proclaiming the **mystery** of God
　　2: 7　God's wisdom, **secret** and
　　　　　hidden
　　4: 1　stewards of God's **mysteries**
　　13: 2　understand all **mysteries**
　　14: 2　they are speaking **mysteries**
　　15:51　I will tell you a **mystery**
Ep　1: 9　made known to us the **mystery**
　　3: 3　the **mystery** was made known
　　3: 4　understanding of the **mystery**
　　3: 9　the plan of the **mystery** hidden

　　5:32　This is a great **mystery**
　　6:19　the **mystery** of the gospel
Co　1:26　**mystery** that has been hidden
　　1:27　the glory of this **mystery**
　　2: 2　the knowledge of God's
　　　　　mystery
　　4: 3　we may declare the **mystery**
2Th 2: 7　For the **mystery** of lawlessness
1Ti 3: 9　must hold fast to the **mystery**
　　3:16　the **mystery** of our religion
Re　1:20　As for the **mystery** of the seven
　　10: 7　the **mystery** of God will be
　　17: 5　written a name, a **mystery**
　　17: 7　the **mystery** of the woman

3467　GO1 AG531 LN166
μυωπαζω, I AM SHORT SIGHTED
2P　1: 9　is **nearsighted** and blind

3468　GO1 AG531 LN166 K4:829
μωλωψ, WOUND
1P　2:24　by his **wounds** you have been

3469　GO2 AG531 LN166 R3470
μωμαομαι, I STAIN
2C　6: 3　so that no **fault** may be **found**
　　8:20　that no one should **blame** us

3470　GO1 AG531 LN166 K4:829 R3201
μωμος, BLEMISH
2P　2:13　They are blots and **blemishes**

3471　GO4 AG531 LN166 B3:1023 K4:832 R3474
μωραινω, I AM FOOLISH
Mt　5:13　but if salt **has lost its taste**
Lk 14:34　but if salt **has lost its taste**
Ro　1:22　to be wise, they **became fools**
1C　1:20　Has not God **made foolish**

3472　GO5 AG531 LN166 B3:1023 K4:832 R3474
μωρια, FOOLISHNESS
1C　1:18　about the cross is **foolishness**
　　1:21　through the **foolishness** of our
　　1:23　and **foolishness** to Gentiles
　　2:14　they are **foolishness** to them
　　3:19　is **foolishness** with God

3473　GO1 AG531 LN166 B3:1026 K4:832 R3474,3004
μωρολογια, FOOLISH WORD
Ep　5: 4　obscene, **silly**, and vulgar **talk**

3474 GO12 AG531 LN166 B3:1023 K4:832
μωρος, FOOL

Mt   5:22   if you say, 'You **fool**,'
      7:26   like a **foolish** man who built
    23:17   You blind **fools!**
    25: 2   Five of them were **foolish**
    25: 3   the **foolish** took their lamps
    25: 8   The **foolish** said to the wise
1C   1:25   For God's **foolishness** is wiser
    1:27   But God chose what is **foolish**
    3:18   you should become **fools**
    4:10   **fools** for the sake of Christ
2Ti   2:23   Have nothing to do with **stupid**
Ti   3: 9   But avoid **stupid** controversies

3475 GO80 AG531 LN166 B2:635 K4:848
μωυσης, MOSES

Mt   8: 4   the gift that **Moses** commanded
    17: 3   there appeared to them **Moses**
    17: 4   one for **Moses,** and one for
    19: 7   Why then did **Moses** command us
    19: 8   **Moses** allowed you to divorce
    22:24   Teacher, **Moses** said, 'If a man
    23: 2   Pharisees sit on **Moses'** seat
Mk   1:44   cleansing what **Moses** commanded
    7:10   For **Moses** said, 'Honor your
    9: 4   to them Elijah with **Moses**
    9: 5   one for **Moses,** and one for
    10: 3   What did **Moses** command you?
    10: 4   **Moses** allowed a man to write
    12:19   **Moses** wrote for us that
    12:26   not read in the book of **Moses**
Lk   2:22   according to the law of **Moses**
    5:14   as **Moses** commanded, make an
    9:30   saw two men, **Moses** and Elijah
    9:33   one for you, one for **Moses**
    16:29   have **Moses** and the prophets
    16:31   they do not listen to **Moses**
    20:28   **Moses** wrote for us that if a
    20:37   are raised **Moses** himself showed
    24:27   Then beginning with **Moses**
    24:44   about me in the law of **Moses**
Jn   1:17   was given through **Moses**
    1:45   **Moses** in the law and also the
    3:14   And just as **Moses** lifted
    5:45   your accuser is **Moses**
    5:46   If you believed **Moses**
    6:32   it was not **Moses** who gave you
    7:19   Did not **Moses** give you the law

    7:22   **Moses** gave you circumcision
    7:22   not from **Moses,** but from the
    7:23   law of **Moses** may not be broken
    8: 5   **Moses** commanded us to stone
    9:28   but we are disciples of **Moses**
    9:29   God has spoken to **Moses**
Ac   3:22   **Moses** said, 'The Lord your God
    6:11   blasphemous words against **Moses**
    6:14   the customs that **Moses** handed
    7:20   At this time **Moses** was born
    7:22   So **Moses** was instructed in all
    7:29   **Moses** fled and became a
    7:31   When **Moses** saw it
    7:32   **Moses** began to tremble and did
    7:35   **Moses** whom they rejected
    7:37   This is the **Moses** who said
    7:40   as for this **Moses** who led us
    7:44   directed when he spoke to **Moses**
  13:39   freed by the law of **Moses**
  15: 1   to the custom of **Moses**
  15: 5   to keep the law of **Moses**
  15:21   **Moses** has had those who
  21:21   the Gentiles to forsake **Moses**
  26:22   the prophets and **Moses** said
  28:23   both from the law of **Moses**
Ro   5:14   dominion from Adam to **Moses**
    9:15   For he says to **Moses**
  10: 5   **Moses** writes concerning the
  10:19   First **Moses** says, "I will make
1C   9: 9   written in the law of **Moses**
  10: 2   all were baptized into **Moses**
2C   3: 7   could not gaze at **Moses'** face
    3:13   not like **Moses,** who put a veil
    3:15   day whenever **Moses** is read
2Ti   3: 8   and Jambres opposed **Moses**
He   3: 2   **Moses** also "was faithful in
    3: 3   worthy of more glory than **Moses**
    3: 5   Now **Moses** was faithful in all
    3:16   under the leadership of **Moses**
    7:14   that tribe **Moses** said nothing
    8: 5   for **Moses,** when he was about
    9:19   told to all the people by **Moses**
  10:28   has violated the law of **Moses**
  11:23   By faith **Moses** was hidden by
  11:24   **Moses,** when he was grown up
  12:21   was the sight that **Moses** said
Ju   1: 9   about the body of **Moses**
Re   15: 3   they sing the song of **Moses**

ν

3476   GO3   AG532   LN167
ναασσων, NAASSON

Mt	1: 4	Aminadab the father of **Nahshon**
	1: 4	**Nahshon** the father of Salmon
Lk	3:32	son of Sala, son of **Nahshon**

3477   GO1   AG532   LN167
ναγγαι, NAGGAI

| Lk | 3:25 | son of Esli, son of **Naggai** |

3477a   GO2   AG532   LN167
ναζαρα, NAZARA

| Mt | 4:13 | He left **Nazareth** and made his |
| Lk | 4:16 | When he came to **Nazareth** |

3478   GO6   AG532   LN167
ναζαρεθ, NAZARETH

Mt	21:11	Jesus from **Nazareth** in Galilee
Lk	1:26	town in Galilee called **Nazareth**
	2: 4	from the town of **Nazareth**
	2:39	to their own town of **Nazareth**
	2:51	with them and came to **Nazareth**
Ac	10:38	anointed Jesus of **Nazareth**

3478a   GO4   AG532   LN167
ναζαρετ, NAZARET

Mt	2:23	in a town called **Nazareth**
Mk	1: 9	came from **Nazareth** of Galilee
Jn	1:45	son of Joseph from **Nazareth**
	1:46	good come out of **Nazareth**

3479   GO6   AG532   LN167   B2:332   K4:874
ναζαρηνος, NAZARENE

Mk	1:24	do with us, Jesus **of Nazareth**
	10:47	that it was Jesus **of Nazareth**
	14:67	Jesus, the man **from Nazareth**
	16: 6	looking for Jesus **of Nazareth**
Lk	4:34	do with us, Jesus **of Nazareth**
	24:19	things about Jesus **of Nazareth**

3480   GO13   AG532   LN167   B2:332   K4:874
ναζωραιος, NAZOREAN

Mt	2:23	He will be called a **Nazorean.**
	26:71	man was with Jesus **of Nazareth**
Lk	18:37	Jesus **of Nazareth** is passing
Jn	18: 5	Jesus **of Nazareth.**
	18: 7	Jesus **of Nazareth.**
	19:19	Jesus **of Nazareth,** the King

Ac	2:22	Jesus **of Nazareth,** a man
	3: 6	of Jesus Christ **of Nazareth**
	4:10	of Jesus Christ **of Nazareth**
	6:14	that this Jesus **of Nazareth**
	22: 8	I am Jesus **of Nazareth** whom
	24: 5	of the sect of the **Nazarenes**
	26: 9	the name of Jesus **of Nazareth**

3481   GO1   AG532   LN167
ναθαμ, NATHAM (NATHAN)

| Lk | 3:31 | son of **Nathan,** son of David |

3482   GO6   AG532   LN167
ναθαναηλ, NATHANAEL

Jn	1:45	Philip found **Nathanael** and said
	1:46	**Nathanael** said to him
	1:47	When Jesus saw **Nathanael** coming
	1:48	**Nathanael** asked him
	1:49	**Nathanael** replied
	21: 2	**Nathanael** of Cana in Galilee

3483   GO33   AG532   LN167
ναι, YES

Mt	5:37	Let your word be '**Yes,** Yes'
	5:37	Let your word be 'Yes, **Yes**'
	9:28	They said to him, "**Yes,** Lord."
	11: 9	**Yes,** I tell you, and more
	11:26	**yes,** Father, for such
	13:51	They answered, "**Yes.**"
	15:27	**Yes,** Lord, yet even the dogs
	17:25	He said, "**Yes,** he does."
	21:16	**Yes;** have you never read
Lk	7:26	**Yes,** I tell you, and more
	10:21	**yes,** Father, for such was your
	11:51	**Yes,** I tell you, it will be
	12: 5	**Yes,** I tell you, fear him
Jn	11:27	**Yes,** Lord, I believe that
	21:15	**Yes,** Lord; you know that I love
	21:16	**Yes,** Lord; you know that I love
Ac	5: 8	**Yes,** that was the price.
	22:27	And he said, "**Yes.**"
Ro	3:29	**Yes,** of Gentiles also
2C	1:17	ready to say "**Yes,** yes"
	1:17	ready to say "Yes, **yes**"
	1:18	to you has not been "**Yes** and No
	1:19	was not "**Yes** and No"; but in
	1:19	but in him it is always "**Yes.**"
	1:20	God's promises is a "**Yes.**"

Ph	4: 3	**Yes,** and I ask you also
Pm	1:20	**Yes,** brother, let me have
Ja	5:12	but let your **"Yes"** be yes
	5:12	but let your "Yes" be **yes**
Re	1: 7	**So it is to be.** Amen
	14:13	**"Yes,"** says the Spirit
	16: 7	altar respond, **"Yes,** O Lord
	22:20	**Amen.** Come, Lord Jesus!

3483a GO1 AG533 LN167
ναιμαν, NAAMAN
Lk   4:27   was cleansed except **Naaman**

3484 GO1 AG533 LN167
ναιν, NAIN
Lk   7:11   he went to a town called **Nain**

3485 GO45 AG533 LN167 B3:781 K4:880
ναος, TEMPLE

Mt	23:16	Whoever swears by the **sanctuary**
	23:16	the gold of the **sanctuary**
	23:17	or the **sanctuary** that has made
	23:21	whoever swears by the **sanctuary**
	23:35	murdered between the **sanctuary**
	26:61	to destroy the **temple** of God
	27: 5	pieces of silver in the **temple**
	27:40	who would destroy the **temple**
	27:51	curtain of the **temple** was torn
Mk	14:58	I will destroy this **temple**
	15:29	who would destroy the **temple**
	15:38	And the curtain of the **temple**
Lk	1: 9	the **sanctuary** of the Lord
	1:21	at his delay in the **sanctuary**
	1:22	seen a vision in the **sanctuary**
	23:45	curtain of the **temple** was torn
Jn	2:19	Destroy this **temple,** and in
	2:20	This **temple** has been under
	2:21	he was speaking of the **temple**
Ac	17:24	in **shrines** made by human hands
	19:24	made silver **shrines** of Artemis
1C	3:16	that you are God's **temple**
	3:17	If anyone destroys God's **temple**
	3:17	For God's **temple** is holy
	6:19	that your body is a **temple**
2C	6:16	What agreement has the **temple**
	6:16	the **temple** of the living God
Ep	2:21	and grows into a holy **temple**
2Th	2: 4	takes his seat in the **temple**
Re	3:12	make you a pillar in the **temple**
	7:15	day and night within his **temple**

	11: 1	Come and measure the **temple**
	11: 2	the court outside the **temple**
	11:19	Then God's **temple** in heaven
	11:19	was seen within his **temple**
	14:15	angel came out of the **temple**
	14:17	angel came out of the **temple**
	15: 5	**temple** of the tent of witness
	15: 6	and out of the **temple** came
	15: 8	**temple** was filled with smoke
	15: 8	no one could enter the **temple**
	16: 1	a loud voice from the **temple**
	16:17	voice came out of the **temple**
	21:22	I saw no **temple** in the city,
	21:22	its **temple** is the Lord God

3486 GO1 AG534 LN167
ναουμ, NAUM
Lk   3:25   son of Amos, son of **Nahum**

3487 GO2 AG534 LN167
ναρδος, OF NARD
Mk 14: 3   very costly ointment of **nard**
Jn 12: 3   perfume made of pure **nard**

3488 GO1 AG534 LN167
ναρκισσος, NARCISSUS
Ro 16:11   to the family of **Narcissus.**

3489 GO2 AG534 LN167 K4:891
ναυαγεω, I SHIPWRECK
2C 11:25   Three times I **was shipwrecked**
1Ti 1:19   persons **have suffered shipwreck**

3490 GO1 AG534 LN167
ναυκληρος, OWNER
Ac 27:11   and to the **owner of the ship**

3491 GO1 AG534 LN167
ναυς, SHIP
Ac 27:41   they ran the **ship** aground

3492 GO3 AG534 LN167 R3491
ναυτης, SAILOR
Ac 27:27   the **sailors** suspected that they
   27:30   the **sailors** tried to escape
Re 18:17   **sailors** and all whose trade

3493 GO1 AG534 LN167
ναχωρ, NACHOR
Lk   3:34   son of Terah, son of **Nahor**

3494   GO3 AG534 LN167 R3501
νεανιας, YOUNG MAN

Ac	7:58	at the feet of a **young man**
	20: 9	A **young man** named Eutychus
	23:17	Take this **young man** to the

3495   GO11 AG534 LN167 R3494
νεανισκος, YOUNG MAN

Mt	19:20	The **young man** said to him
	19:22	the **young man** heard this word
Mk	14:51	**young man** was following him
	16: 5	they saw a **young man**
Lk	7:14	**Young man,** I say to you, rise!
Ac	2:17	**young men** shall see visions,
	5:10	When the **young men** came in
	23:18	to bring this **young man** to you
	23:22	tribune dismissed the **young man**
1J	2:13	writing to you, **young people**
	2:14	I write to you, **young people**

3496   GO1 AG534 LN167
νεαπολις, NEAPOLIS

| Ac | 16:11 | the following day to **Neapolis** |

3498   GO128 AG534 LN167 B1:443 K4:892
νεκρος, DEAD

Mt	8:22	let the **dead** bury their own
	8:22	the dead bury their own **dead**
	10: 8	Cure the sick, raise the **dead**
	11: 5	deaf hear, the **dead** are raised
	14: 2	has been raised from the **dead**
	17: 9	has been raised from the **dead**
	22:31	the resurrection of the **dead**
	22:32	He is God not of the **dead**
	23:27	of the bones of the **dead**
	27:64	has been raised from the **dead**
	28: 4	shook and became like **dead** men
	28: 7	been raised from the **dead**
Mk	6:14	has been raised from the **dead**
	9: 9	had risen from the **dead.**
	9:10	rising from the **dead** could mean
	9:26	of them said, "He is **dead.**"
	12:25	they rise from the **dead**
	12:26	as for the **dead** being raised
	12:27	He is God not of the **dead**
Lk	7:15	The **dead** man sat up and began
	7:22	the **dead** are raised, the poor
	9: 7	had been raised from the **dead**
	9:60	Let the **dead** bury their own
	9:60	the dead bury their own **dead**

	15:24	for this son of mine was **dead**
	15:32	this brother of yours was **dead**
	16:30	goes to them from the **dead**
	16:31	someone rises from the **dead**
	20:35	resurrection from the **dead**
	20:37	that the **dead** are raised
	20:38	Now he is God not of the **dead**
	24: 5	for the living among the **dead**
	24:46	and to rise from the **dead**
Jn	2:22	he was raised from the **dead**
	5:21	the Father raises the **dead**
	5:25	the **dead** will hear the voice
	12: 1	he had raised from the **dead**
	12: 9	he had raised from the **dead**
	12:17	and raised him from the **dead**
	20: 9	he must rise from the **dead**
	21:14	whom God raised from the **dead**
Ac	4: 2	is the resurrection of the **dead**
	4:10	whom God raised from the **dead**
	5:10	came in they found her **dead**
	10:41	after he rose from the **dead**
	10:42	of the living and the **dead**
	13:30	God raised him from the **dead**
	13:34	his raising him from the **dead**
	17: 3	and to rise from the **dead**
	17:31	by raising him from the **dead**
	17:32	the resurrection of the **dead**
	20: 9	below and was picked up **dead**
	23: 6	the resurrection of the **dead**
	24:21	the resurrection of the **dead**
	26: 8	that God raises the **dead**
	26:23	first to rise from the **dead**
	28: 6	to swell up or drop **dead**
Ro	1: 4	by resurrection from the **dead**
	4:17	who gives life to the **dead**
	4:24	Jesus our Lord from the **dead**
	6: 4	Christ was raised from the **dead**
	6: 9	being raised from the **dead**
	6:11	must consider yourselves **dead**
	6:13	been brought from **death** to life
	7: 4	has been raised from the **dead**
	7: 8	from the law sin lies **dead**
	8:10	though the body is **dead**
	8:11	raised Jesus from the **dead**
	8:11	raised Christ from the **dead**
	10: 7	bring Christ up from the **dead**
	10: 9	God raised him from the **dead**
	11:15	be but life from the **dead**
	14: 9	be Lord of both the **dead**

1C	15:12	as raised from the **dead**
	15:12	is no resurrection of the **dead**
	15:13	is no resurrection of the **dead**
	15:15	that the **dead** are not raised
	15:16	For if the **dead** are not raised
	15:20	has been raised from the **dead**
	15:21	the resurrection of the **dead**
	15:29	baptism on behalf of the **dead**
	15:29	If the **dead** are not raised
	15:32	If the **dead** are not raised
	15:35	How are the **dead** raised
	15:42	the resurrection of the **dead**
	15:52	the **dead** will be raised
2C	1: 9	on God who raises the **dead**
Ga	1: 1	who raised him from the **dead**
Ep	1:20	he raised him from the **dead**
	2: 1	**dead** through the trespasses
	2: 5	even when we were **dead** through
	5:14	Rise from the **dead**
Ph	3:11	the resurrection from the **dead**
Co	1:18	the firstborn from the **dead**
	2:12	who raised him from the **dead**
	2:13	you were **dead** in trespasses
1Th	1:10	whom he raised from the **dead**
	4:16	the **dead** in Christ will rise
2Ti	2: 8	Christ, raised from the **dead**
	4: 1	judge the living and the **dead**
He	6: 1	repentance from **dead** works
	6: 2	resurrection of the **dead**
	9:14	from **dead** works to worship the
	9:17	will takes effect only at **death**
	11:19	raise someone from the **dead**
	11:35	their **dead** by resurrection
	13:20	brought back from the **dead**
Ja	2:17	it has no works, is **dead**
	2:26	without the spirit is **dead**
	2:26	without works is also **dead**
1P	1: 3	of Jesus Christ from the **dead,**
	1:21	raised him from the **dead**
	4: 5	judge the living and the **dead**
	4: 6	proclaimed even to the **dead**
Re	1: 5	the firstborn of the **dead**
	1:17	fell at his feet as though **dead**
	1:18	I was **dead,** and see, I am alive
	2: 8	who was **dead** and came to life
	3: 1	being alive, but you are **dead**
	11:18	the time for judging the **dead**
	14:13	Blessed are the **dead** who from
	16: 3	like the blood of a **corpse**

	20: 5	The rest of the **dead** did not
	20:12	the **dead,** great and small
	20:12	**dead** were judged according
	20:13	And the sea gave up the **dead**
	20:13	gave up the **dead** that were

3499   GO3 AG535 LN168 B1:443 K4:894 R34798
νεκροω, I AM DEAD

Ro	4:19	was already as good **as dead**
Co	3: 5	**Put to death**
He	11:12	and this one as good **as dead**

3500   GO2 AG535 LN168 B1:443 K4:895 R3499
νεκρωσις, DEADNESS

| Ro | 4:19 | was already as good as **dead** |
| 2C | 4:10 | carrying in the body the **death** |

3500a   GO1 AG535 LN168 K4:638
νεομηνια, NEW MOON

| Co | 2:16 | observing festivals, **new moons** |

3501   GO23 AG535 LN168 B2:674 K4:896
νεος, NEW

Mt	9:17	Neither is **new** wine put into
	9:17	but **new** wine is put into fresh
Mk	2:22	no one puts **new** wine into old
	2:22	but one puts **new** wine into
Lk	5:37	no one puts **new** wine into old
	5:37	otherwise the **new** wine will
	5:38	But **new** wine must be put into
	15:12	The **younger** of them said
	15:13	**younger** son gathered all he had
	22:26	must become like the **youngest**
Jn	21:18	when you were **younger**
Ac	5: 6	The **young** men came and wrapped
1C	5: 7	so that you may be a **new** batch
Co	3:10	yourselves with the **new** self
1Ti	5: 1	to **younger** men as brothers
	5: 2	to **younger** women as sisters
	5:11	refuse to put **younger** widows
	5:14	So I would have **younger** widows
Ti	2: 4	encourage the **young** women
	2: 6	urge the **younger** men to be
He	12:24	the mediator of a **new** covenant
1P	5: 5	you who are **younger** must accept

3503   GO4 AG536 LN168 B2:674 R3501
νεοτης, NEWNESS

| Mk | 10:20 | kept all these since my **youth** |
| Lk | 18:21 | kept all these since my **youth** |

Ac 26: 4   my way of life from my **youth**
1Ti 4:12   Let no one despise your **youth**

3504   GO1 AG536 LN168 B2:674 R3501,5453
νεοφυτος, NEW PLANT
1Ti 3: 6   He must not be a **recent convert**

3506   GO2 AG536 LN168
νευω, I NOD
Jn 13:24   Simon Peter therefore **motioned**
Ac 24:10   When the governor **motioned**

3507   GO25 AG536 LN168 B3:1000 K4:902 R3509
νεφελη, CLOUD
Mt 17: 5   bright **cloud** overshadowed them
     17: 5   and from the **cloud** a voice said
     24:30   coming on the **clouds** of heaven
     26:64   coming on the **clouds** of heaven
Mk   9: 7   Then a **cloud** overshadowed them
      9: 7   from the **cloud** there came
     13:26   Son of Man coming in **clouds**
     14:62   with the **clouds** of heaven
Lk   9:34   **cloud** came and overshadowed
      9:34   as they entered the **cloud**
      9:35   Then from the **cloud** came
     12:54   When you see a **cloud** rising
     21:27   Son of Man coming in a **cloud**
Ac   1: 9   and a **cloud** took him out of
1C 10: 1   were all under the **cloud**
     10: 2   in the **cloud** and in the sea
1Th 4:17   caught up in the **clouds**
Ju   1:12   They are waterless **clouds**
Re   1: 7   He is coming with the **clouds**
     10: 1   from heaven, wrapped in a **cloud**
     11:12   up to heaven in a **cloud**
     14:14   and there was a white **cloud**
     14:14   and seated on the **cloud** was one
     14:15   the one who sat on the **cloud**
     14:16   So the one who sat on the **cloud**

3508   GO3 AG537 LN168
νεφθαλιμ, NEPHTHALIM (NAPHTHALI)
Mt   4:13   of Zebulun and **Naphtali**
      4:15   land of **Naphtali,** on the road
Re   7: 6   from the tribe of **Naphtali**

3509   GO1 AG537 LN168 B3:1003 K4:902 R3507
νεφος, CLOUD
He 12: 1   surrounded by so great a **cloud**

3510   GO1 AG537 LN168 K4:911
νεφρος, KIDNEY
Re   2:23   who searches **minds** and hearts

3511   GO1 AG537 LN168 B3:796
νεωκορος, TEMPLE KEEPER
Ac 19:35   **temple keeper** of the great

3512   GO1 AG537 LN168 R3501
νεωτερικος, YOUTHFUL
2Ti 2:22   Shun **youthful** passions

3513   GO1 AG537 LN168 R3483
νη, YEA
1C 15:31   That is **as certain,** brothers

3514   GO2 AG537 LN168
νηθω, I SPIN
Mt   6:28   they neither toil nor **spin**
Lk 12:27   they neither toil nor **spin**

3515   GO1 AG537 LN168 K4:912 R3516
νηπιαζω, I AM INFANT
1C 14:20   rather, **be infants** in evil

3516   GO15 AG537 LN168 B1:280 K4:912
νηπιος, INFANT
Mt 11:25   have revealed them to **infants**
     21:16   Out of the mouths of **infants**
Lk 10:21   have revealed them to **infants**
Ro   2:20   a teacher of **children**
1C   3: 1   as **infants** in Christ
     13:11   When I was a **child,** I spoke
     13:11   child, I spoke like a **child**
     13:11   I thought like a **child**
     13:11   I reasoned like a **child**
     13:11   I put an end to **childish** ways
Ga   4: 1   as long as they are **minors**
      4: 3   while we were **minors**
Ep   4:14   We must no longer be **children**
1Th 2: 7   caring for her own **children**
He   5:13   being still an **infant**

3517   GO1 AG538 LN168
νηρευς, NEREUS
Ro 16:15   Julia, **Nereus** and his sister

3518   GO1 AG538 LN168
νηρι, NERI
Lk   3:27   son of Shealtiel, son of **Neri**

3519   GO1   AG538   LN168   R3520
νησιον, SMALL ISLAND
Ac   27:16   under the lee of a **small island**

3520   GO9   AG538   LN168
νησος, ISLAND
Ac   13: 6   gone through the whole **island**
     27:26   to run aground on some **island**
     28: 1   the **island** was called Malta.
     28: 7   the leading man of the **island**
     28: 9   the people on the **island**
     28:11   had wintered at the **island**
Re   1: 9   was on the **island** called Patmos
     6:14   mountain and **island** was removed
     16:20   And every **island** fled away

3521   GO5   AG538   LN168   B1:611   K4:924   R3522
νηστεια, FASTING
Lk   2:37   worshiped there with **fasting**
Ac   14:23   with prayer and **fasting**
     27: 9   the **Fast** had already gone by
2C   6: 5   sleepless nights, **hunger**
     11:27   night, **hungry** and thirsty

3522   GO20   AG538   LN168   B1:611   K4:924   R3523
νηστευω, I FAST
Mt   4: 2   He **fasted** forty days and forty
     6:16   And whenever you **fast**
     6:16   others that they **are fasting**
     6:17   But when you **fast,** put oil on
     6:18   that your **fasting** may be seen
     9:14   do we and the Pharisees **fast**
     9:14   but your disciples do not **fast**
     9:15   and then they will **fast**
Mk   2:18   and the Pharisees **were fasting**
     2:18   disciples of the Pharisees **fast**
     2:18   but your disciples do not **fast**
     2:19   wedding guests cannot **fast**
     2:19   with them, they cannot **fast**
     2:20   they **will fast** on that day
Lk   5:33   frequently **fast** and pray
     5:34   and then they **will fast**
     18:12   I **fast** twice a week
Ac   13: 2   the Lord and **fasting**
     13: 3   Then after **fasting** and praying

3523   GO2   AG538   LN168   B1:611   K4:924
νηστις, FASTING
Mt   15:32   want to send them away **hungry**
Mk   8: 3   If I send them away **hungry**

3524   GO3   AG538   LN168   B1:513   K4:939   R3525
νηφαλιος, TEMPERATE
1Ti   3: 2   married only once, **temperate**
     3:11   not slanderers, but **temperate**
Ti   2: 2   the older men to be **temperate**

3525   GO6   AG538   LN168   B1:514   K4:936
νηφω, I AM WELL-BALANCED
1Th   5: 6   let us keep awake and **be sober**
     5: 8   to the day, let us **be sober**
2Ti   4: 5   As for you, always **be sober**
1P   1:13   **discipline yourselves;** set all
     4: 7   **be serious** and discipline
     5: 8   **Discipline yourselves,** keep

3526   GO1   AG539   LN168
νιγερ, NIGER
Ac   13: 1   Simeon who was called **Niger**

3527   GO1   AG539   LN168
νικανωρ, NICANOR
Ac   6: 5   with Philip, Prochorus, **Nicanor**

3528   GO28   AG539   LN168   B1:650   K4:942   R3529
νικαω, I CONQUER
Lk   11:22   attacks him and **overpowers** him
Jn   16:33   I **have conquered** the world
Ro   3: 4   and **prevail** in your judging
     12:21   Do not be **overcome** by evil
     12:21   but **overcome** evil with good
1J   2:13   **have conquered** the evil one
     2:14   you **have overcome** the evil one
     4: 4   and **have conquered** them
     5: 4   born of God **conquers** the world
     5: 4   that **conquers** the world
     5: 5   that **conquers** the world
Re   2: 7   To everyone who **conquers**
     2:11   Whoever **conquers** will not be
     2:17   To everyone who **conquers** I will
     2:26   To everyone who **conquers**
     3: 5   If you **conquer,** you will be
     3:12   If you **conquer,** I will make you
     3:21   To the one who **conquers** I will
     3:21   just as I myself **conquered**
     5: 5   Root of David, **has conquered**
     6: 2   out **conquering** and to conquer
     6: 2   out conquering and **to conquer**
     11: 7   make war on them and **conquer**
     12:11   But they **have conquered** him
     13: 7   the saints and to **conquer** them

15: 2	who **had conquered** the beast
17:14	and the Lamb **will conquer** them
21: 7	Those who **conquer** will inherit

3529   GO1 AG539 LN169 B1:650 K4:942
νικη, CONQUEST
1J   5: 4   **victory** that conquers the world

3530   GO5 AG539 LN169
νικοδημος, NICODEMUS
Jn   3: 1   was a Pharisee named **Nicodemus**
    3: 4   **Nicodemus** said to him
    3: 9   **Nicodemus** said to him
    7:50   **Nicodemus,** who had gone to
    19:39   **Nicodemus,** who had at first

3531   GO2 AG539 LN169 B2:676
νικολαιτης, NICOLAITAN
Re   2: 6   the works of the **Nicolaitans**
    2:15   the teaching of the **Nicolaitans**

3532   GO1 AG539 LN169 B2:676
νικολαος, NICOLAOS
Ac   6: 5   Timon, Parmenas, and **Nicolaus**

3533   GO1 AG539 LN169
νικοπολις, NICOPOLIS
Ti   3:12   to come to me at **Nicopolis**

3534   GO4 AG539 LN169 B1:650 K4:942 R3529
νικος, CONQUEST
Mt   12:20   he brings justice to **victory**
1C   15:54   been swallowed up in **victory**
    15:55   O death, is your **victory**
    15:57   who gives us the **victory**

3536   GO3 AG540 LN169 B2:678
νινευιτης, NINEVITE
Mt   12:41   people **of Nineveh** will rise
Lk   11:30   a sign to the people **of Nineveh**
    11:32   people **of Nineveh** will rise up

3537   GO1 AG540 LN169 R3538
νιπτηρ, WASH BOWL
Jn   13: 5   he poured water into a **basin**

3538   GO17 AG540 LN169 B1:153 K4:946
νιπτω, I WASH
Mt   6:17   put oil on your head and **wash**
    15: 2   they do not **wash** their hands

Mk   7: 3   unless they thoroughly **wash**
Jn   9: 7   Go, **wash** in the pool of Siloam
    9: 7   Then he went and **washed**
    9:11   Go to Siloam and **wash.**
    9:11   **washed** and received my sight
    9:15   Then I **washed,** and now I see
    13: 5   began to **wash** the disciples
    13: 6   you going to **wash** my feet
    13: 8   You will never **wash** my feet
    13: 8   Unless I **wash** you, you have
    13:10   does not need to **wash**
    13:12   After he had **washed** their feet
    13:14   **have washed** your feet
    13:14   to **wash** one another's feet
1Ti   5:10   **washed** the saints' feet

3539   GO14 AG540 LN169 B3:122 K4:948 R3563
νοεω, I GIVE THOUGHT
Mt   15:17   Do you not **see** that whatever
    16: 9   Do you still not **perceive?**
    16:11   How could you fail to **perceive**
    24:15   **let** the reader **understand**
Mk   7:18   do you also fail to **understand**
    8:17   Do you still not **perceive**
    13:14   **let** the reader **understand**
Jn   12:40   **understand** with their heart
Ro   1:20   **have been understood** and seen
Ep   3: 4   will enable you to **perceive**
    3:20   than all we can ask or **imagine**
1Ti   1: 7   without **understanding** either
2Ti   2: 7   **Think over** what I say
He   11: 3   we **understand** that the worlds

3540   GO6 AG540 LN169 B3:122 K4:960 R3539
νοημα, THOUGHT
2C   2:11   are not ignorant of his **designs**
    3:14   But their **minds** were hardened
    4: 4   the **minds** of the unbelievers
    10: 5   take every **thought** captive
    11: 3   **thoughts** will be led astray
Ph   4: 7   your hearts and your **minds**

3541   GO1 AG540 LN169 B1:187
νοθος, ILLEGITIMATE
He   12: 8   then you are **illegitimate**

3542   GO2 AG541 LN169
νομη, GRAZING
Jn   10: 9   and go out and find **pasture**
2Ti   2:17   talk will **spread** like gangrene

3543   GO15 AG541 LN169
νομιζω, I THINK

Mt	5:17	Do not **think** that I have come
	10:34	Do not **think** that I have come
	20:10	they **thought** they would receive
Lk	2:44	**Assuming** that he was in the
	3:23	son (as **was thought**) of Joseph
Ac	7:25	He **supposed** that his kinsfolk
	8:20	you **thought** you could obtain
	14:19	**supposing** that he was dead
	16:13	where we **supposed** there was
	16:27	he **supposed** that the prisoners
	17:29	we ought not to **think** that the
	21:29	and they **supposed** that Paul
1C	7:26	I **think** that, in view of the
	7:36	If anyone **thinks** that he is not
1Ti	6: 5	**imagining** that godliness is a

3544   GO9 AG541 LN169 B2:438 K4:1088 R3551
νομικος, LAWYER

Mt	22:35	one of them, a **lawyer,** asked
Lk	7:30	the **lawyers** rejected God's
	10:25	a **lawyer** stood up to test Jesus
	11:45	the **lawyers** answered him
	11.46	Woe also to you **lawyers!**
	11:52	Woe to you **lawyers!**
	14: 3	asked the **lawyers** and Pharisees
Ti	3: 9	and quarrels about the **law**
	3:13	to send Zenas the **lawyer**

3545   GO2 AG541 LN169 B2:438 K4:1088 R3551
νομιμως, LAWFULLY

| 1Ti | 1: 8 | if one uses it **legitimately** |
| 2Ti | 2: 5 | **according to the rules** |

3546   GO1 AG541 LN169
νομισμα, COINAGE

| Mt | 22:19 | Show me the **coin** used for the |

3547   GO3 AG541 LN169 B2:438 K2:159 R3551,1320
νομοδιδασκαλος, LAW-TEACHER

Lk	5:17	**teachers of the law** were
Ac	5:34	Gamaliel, a **teacher of the law**
1Ti	1: 7	to be **teachers of the law**

3548   GO1 AG541 LN169 B2:438 K4:1089 R3550
νομοθεσια, LAW-GIVING

| Ro | 9: 4 | the **giving of the law** |

3549   GO2 AG541 LN169 B2:438 K4:1090 R3550
νομοθετεω, I AM GIVEN LAW

| He | 7:11 | for the people **received the law** |
| | 8: 6 | **has been enacted** through better |

3550   GO1 AG542 LN169 B2:438 K4:1089
R3551,5087
νομοθετης, LAW-SETTER

| Ja | 4:12 | There is one **lawgiver** and judge |

3551   GO194 AG542 LN169 B2:437 K4:1022
νομος, LAW

Mt	5:17	have come to abolish the **law**
	5:18	will pass from the **law** until
	7:12	for this is the **law** and the
	11:13	all the prophets and the **law**
	12: 5	have you not read in the **law**
	22:36	which commandment in the **law**
	22:40	hang all the **law** and the
	23:23	weightier matters of the **law**
Lk	2:22	according to the **law** of Moses
	2:23	written in the **law** of the Lord
	2:24	to what is stated in the **law**
	2:27	was customary under the **law**
	2:39	required by the **law** of the Lord
	10:26	What is written in the **law**
	16:16	The **law** and the prophets
	16:17	stroke of a letter in the **law**
	24:44	about me in the **law** of Moses
Jn	1:17	**law** indeed was given through
	1:45	about whom Moses in the **law**
	7:19	Did not Moses give you the **law**
	7:19	Yet none of you keeps the **law**
	7:23	in order that the **law** of Moses
	7:49	which does not know the **law**
	7:51	Our **law** does not judge people
	8: 5	Now in the **law** Moses commanded
	8:17	In your **law** it is written
	10:34	it not written in your **law**
	12:34	We have heard from the **law**
	15:25	that is written in their **law**
	18:31	judge him according to your **law**
	19: 7	We have a **law,** and according
	19: 7	and according to that **law**
Ac	6:13	this holy place and the **law**
	7:53	the ones that received the **law**
	13:15	After the reading of the **law**
	13:39	freed by the **law** of Moses
	15: 5	to keep the **law** of Moses
	18:13	that are contrary to the **law**

	18:15	and names and your own **law**		6:14	since you are not under **law**
	21:20	are all zealous for the **law**		6:15	we are not under **law**
	21:24	observe and guard the **law**		7: 1	to those who know the **law**
	21:28	against our people, our **law**		7: 1	the **law** is binding on a person
	22: 3	according to our ancestral **law**		7: 2	woman is bound by the **law**
	22:12	according to the **law**		7: 2	discharged from the **law**
	23: 3	according to the **law**		7: 3	she is free from that **law**
	23:29	questions of their **law**		7: 4	have died to the **law**
	24:14	laid down according to the **law**		7: 5	aroused by the **law**
	25: 8	an offense against the **law**		7: 6	are discharged from the **law**
	28:23	about Jesus both from the **law**		7: 7	That the **law** is sin?
Ro	2:12	have sinned apart from the **law**		7: 7	it had not been for the **law**
	2:12	will be judged by the **law.**		7: 7	if the **law** had not said
	2:13	not the hearers of the **law**		7: 8	Apart from the **law** sin lies
	2:13	but the doers of the **law**		7: 9	once alive apart from the **law**
	2:14	who do not possess the **law**		7:12	So the **law** is holy
	2:14	what the **law** requires		7:14	that the **law** is spiritual
	2:14	though not having the **law**		7:16	I agree that the **law** is good
	2:14	are a **law** to themselves		7:21	So I find it to be a **law**
	2:15	what the **law** requires		7:22	For I delight in the **law** of God
	2:17	and rely on the **law** and boast		7:23	another **law** at war with the law
	2:18	you are instructed in the **law**		7:23	law at war with the **law** of my
	2:20	in the **law** the embodiment		7:23	making me captive to the **law**
	2:23	You that boast in the **law**		7:25	I am a slave to the **law** of God
	2:23	by breaking the **law**		7:25	I am a slave to the **law** of sin
	2:25	if you obey the **law**		8: 2	the **law** of the Spirit of life
	2:25	but if you break the **law**		8: 2	has set you free from the **law**
	2:26	requirements of the **law**		8: 3	For God has done what the **law**
	2:27	uncircumcised but keep the **law**		8: 4	the just requirement of the **law**
	2:27	circumcision but break the **law**		8: 7	it does not submit to God's **law**
	3:19	that whatever the **law** says		9:31	that is based on the **law**
	3:19	to those who are under the **law**		9:31	succeed in fulfilling that **law**
	3:20	by deeds prescribed by the **law**		10: 4	Christ is the end of the **law**
	3:20	for through the **law** comes the		10: 5	that comes from the **law**
	3:21	But now, apart from **law**		13: 8	another has fulfilled the **law**
	3:21	and is attested by the **law**		13:10	is the fulfilling of the **law**
	3:27	By what **law?**	1C	9: 8	Does not the **law** also say the
	3:27	No, but by the **law** of faith		9: 9	it is written in the **law**
	3:28	works prescribed by the **law**		9:20	To those under the **law**
	3:31	Do we then overthrow the **law**		9:20	I became as one under the **law**
	3:31	the contrary, we uphold the **law**		9:20	I myself am not under the **law**
	4:13	descendants through the **law**		9:20	I might win those under the **law**
	4:14	the adherents of the **law**		14:21	In the **law** it is written
	4:15	For the **law** brings wrath		14:34	as the **law** also says
	4:15	where there is no **law**		15:56	the power of sin is the **law**
	4:16	the adherents of the **law**	Ga	2:16	not by the works of the **law**
	5:13	in the world before the **law**		2:16	by doing the works of the **law**
	5:13	reckoned when there is no **law**		2:16	by the works of the **law**
	5:20	But **law** came in		2:19	For through the **law** I died

	2:19	the law I died to the **law**
	2:21	comes through the **law**
	3: 2	by doing the works of the **law**
	3: 5	doing the works of the **law**
	3:10	rely on the works of the **law**
	3:10	in the book of the **law**
	3:11	justified before God by the **law**
	3:12	the **law** does not rest on faith
	3:13	from the curse of the **law**
	3:17	My point is this: the **law**
	3:18	inheritance comes from the **law**
	3:19	Why then the **law?**
	3:21	Is the **law** then opposed to the
	3:21	For if a **law** had been given
	3:21	indeed come through the **law**
	3:23	and guarded under the **law**
	3:24	Therefore the **law** was our
	4: 4	born under the **law**
	4: 5	who were under the **law**
	4:21	to be subject to the **law**
	4:21	will you not listen to the **law**
	5: 3	obliged to obey the entire **law**
	5: 4	to be justified by the **law**
	5:14	For the whole **law** is summed up
	5:18	you are not subject to the **law**
	5:23	There is no **law** against such
	6: 2	will fulfill the **law** of Christ
	6:13	not themselves obey the **law**
Ep	2:15	He has abolished the **law**
Ph	3: 5	as to the **law,** a Pharisee
	3: 6	under the **law,** blameless
	3: 9	my own that comes from the **law**
1Ti	1: 8	we know that the **law** is good
	1: 9	understanding that the **law**
He	7: 5	have a commandment in the **law**
	7:12	a change in the **law** as well
	7:16	not through a **legal** requirement
	7:19	for the **law** made nothing
	7:28	For the **law** appoints as high
	7:28	which came later than the **law**
	8: 4	gifts according to the **law**
	8:10	I will put my **laws** in their
	9:19	in accordance with the **law**
	9:22	under the **law** almost everything
	10: 1	Since the **law** has only a shadow
	10: 8	offered according to the **law**
	10:16	put my **laws** in their hearts
	10:28	who has violated the **law**
Ja	1:25	who look into the perfect **law**

	2: 8	really fulfill the royal **law**
	2: 9	and are convicted by the **law**
	2:10	whoever keeps the whole **law**
	2:11	a transgressor of the **law**
	2:12	judged by the **law** of liberty
	4:11	speaks evil against the **law**
	4:11	the law and judges the **law**
	4:11	but if you judge the **law**
	4:11	are not a doer of the **law**

3552   GO1 AG543 LN169 B3:996 K4:1091 R3554
νοσεω, I AIL
1Ti 6: 4   **morbid craving** for controversy

3554   GO11 AG543 LN169 B3:996 K4:1091
νοσος, ILLNESS
Mt	4:23	and curing every **disease**
	4:24	with various **diseases** and pains
	8:17	and bore our **diseases**
	9:35	curing every **disease** and every
	10: 1	to cure every **disease** and every
Mk	1:34	were sick with various **diseases**
Lk	4:40	with various kinds of **diseases**
	6:18	to be healed of their **diseases**
	7:21	cured many people of **diseases**
	9: 1	all demons and to cure **diseases**
Ac	19:12	their **diseases** left them,

3555   GO1 AG543 LN169 R3502
νοσσια, YOUNG ONE
Lk 13:34   as a hen gathers her **brood**

3556   GO1 AG543 LN170 R3502
νοσσιον, YOUNG
Mt 23:37   as a hen gathers her **brood**

3556a   GO1 AG543 LN170
νοσσος, YOUNG
Lk 2:24   or two **young** pigeons

3557   GO3 AG543 LN170
νοσφιζω, I MISAPPROPRIATE
Ac	5: 2	**kept back** some of the proceeds
	5: 3	**keep back** part of the proceeds
Ti	2:10	not to **pilfer,** but to show

3558   GO7 AG544 LN170 B3:1000
νοτος, SOUTH
Mt	12:42	queen of the **South** will rise up
Lk	11:31	queen of the **South** will rise at

	12:55	And when you see the **south** wind
	13:29	west, from north and **south**
Ac	27:13	When a moderate **south** wind
	28:13	a **south** wind sprang up
Re	21:13	on the **south** three gates

3559   GO3 AG544 LN170 B1:568 K4:1019
R3560
νουθεσια, WARNING

1C	10:11	to them to serve as an **example**
Ep	6: 4	discipline and **instruction** of
Ti	3:10	a first and second **admonition**

3560   GO8 AG544 LN170 B1:567 K4:1019
νουθετεω, I WARN

Ac	20:31	night or day to **warn** everyone
Ro	15:14	able to **instruct** one another
1C	4:14	**admonish** you as my beloved
Co	1:28	**warning** everyone and teaching
	3:16	teach and **admonish** one another
1Th	5:12	in the Lord and **admonish** you
	5:14	to **admonish** the idlers
2Th	3:15	but **warn** them as believers

3562   GO1 AG544 LN170 K2:816
νουνεχως, THOUGHTFULLY

Mk	12:34	saw that he answered **wisely**

3563   GO24 AG544 LN170 B3:122 K4:951
νους, MIND

Lk	24:45	Then he opened their **minds**
Ro	1:28	gave them up to a debased **mind**
	7:23	at war with the law of my **mind**
	7:25	with my **mind** I am a slave
	11:34	For who has known the **mind**
	12: 2	by the renewing of your **minds**
	14: 5	convinced in their own **minds**
1C	1:10	be united in the same **mind**
	2:16	For who has known the **mind**
	2:16	But we have the **mind** of Christ
	14:14	but my **mind** is unproductive
	14:15	but I will pray with the **mind**
	14:15	sing praise with the **mind** also
	14:19	speak five words with my **mind**
Ep	4:17	in the futility of their **minds**
	4:23	in the spirit of your **minds**
Ph	4: 7	your hearts and your **minds**
Co	2:18	by a human way of **thinking**
2Th	2: 2	to be quickly shaken in **mind**
1Ti	6: 5	who are depraved in **mind**

2Ti	3: 8	these people, of corrupt **mind**
Ti	1:15	very **minds** and consciences
Re	13:18	let anyone with **understanding**
	17: 9	This calls for a **mind** that has

3564   GO1 AG545 LN170
νυμφα, NYMPHA

Co	4:15	and to **Nympha** and the church

3565   GO8 AG545 LN170 B2:584 K4:1099
νυμφη, BRIDE

Mt	10:35	and a **daughter-in-law** against
Lk	12:53	against her **daughter-in-law**
	12:53	and **daughter-in-law** against
Jn	3:29	the **bride** is the bridegroom
Re	18:23	**bride** will be heard in you no
	21: 2	prepared as a **bride** adorned
	21: 9	I will show you the **bride**
	22:17	The Spirit and the **bride** say

3566   GO16 AG545 LN170 B2:584 K4:1099 R3565
νυμφιος, BRIDEGROOM

Mt	9:15	mourn as long as the **bridegroom**
	9:15	when the **bridegroom** is taken
	25: 1	went to meet the **bridegroom**
	25: 5	As the **bridegroom** was delayed
	25: 6	Here is the **bridegroom**!
	25:10	the **bridegroom** came
Mk	2:19	the **bridegroom** is with them
	2:19	as they have the **bridegroom**
	2:20	when the **bridegroom** is taken
Lk	5:34	while the **bridegroom** is with
	5:35	will come when the **bridegroom**
Jn	2: 9	steward called the **bridegroom**
	3:29	the bride is the **bridegroom**
	3:29	The friend of the **bridegroom**
	3:29	at the **bridegroom's** voice
Re	18:23	and the voice of **bridegroom**

3567   GO3 AG545 LN170 B2:584 R3565
νυμφων, BRIDAL CHAMBER

Mt	9:15	The **wedding** guests cannot mourn
Mk	2:19	The **wedding** guests cannot fast
Lk	5:34	You cannot make **wedding** guests

3568   GO147 AG545 LN170 B3:833 K4:1106
νυν, NOW

Mt	24:21	of the world until **now**
	26:65	have **now** heard his blasphemy
	27:42	down from the cross **now**

	27:43	let God deliver him **now**
Mk	10:30	not receive a hundredfold **now**
	13:19	that God created until **now**
	15:32	come down from the cross **now**
Lk	1:48	from **now** on all generations
	2:29	**now** you are dismissing
	5:10	from **now** on you will be
	6:21	are you who are hungry **now**
	6:21	Blessed are you who weep **now**
	6:25	Woe to you who are full **now**
	6:25	to you who are laughing **now**
	11:39	**Now** you Pharisees clean the
	12:52	From **now** on five in one
	16:25	but **now** he is comforted here
	19:42	But **now** they are hidden from
	22:18	I tell you that from **now** on
	22:36	But **now**, the one who has
	22:69	But from **now** on the Son of Man
Jn	2: 8	**Now** draw some out, and take it
	4:18	and the one you have **now**
	4:23	is coming, and is **now** here
	5:25	is coming, and is **now** here
	6:42	How can he **now** say
	8:11	and from **now** on do not sin
	8:40	but **now** you are trying to
	8:52	**Now** we know that you have a
	9:21	how it is that **now** he sees
	9:41	But **now** that you say
	11: 8	the Jews were just **now** trying
	11:22	But even **now** I know that God
	12:27	**Now** my soul is troubled
	12:31	**Now** is the judgment of this
	12:31	**now** the ruler of this world
	13:31	**Now** the Son of Man has been
	13:36	you cannot follow me **now**
	14:29	And **now** I have told you this
	15:22	but **now** they have no excuse
	15:24	But **now** they have seen and
	16: 5	But **now** I am going to him
	16:22	So you have pain **now**
	16:29	**now** you are speaking plainly
	16:30	**Now** we know that you know
	17: 5	So **now**, Father, glorify me
	17: 7	**Now** they know that everything
	17:13	But **now** I am coming to you
	18:36	But **as it is,** my kingdom is not
	21:10	that you have **just** caught
Ac	3:17	And **now**, friends, I know that
	4:29	And **now**, Lord, look at their
	5:38	So in the **present** case
	7: 4	in which you are **now** living
	7:34	Come **now**, I will send you
	7:52	and **now** you have become his
	10: 5	**Now** send men to Joppa for a
	10:33	So **now** all of us are here
	12:11	**Now** I am sure that the Lord
	13:11	And **now** listen—the hand of
	13:31	they are **now** his witnesses
	15:10	**Now** therefore why are you
	16:36	come out **now** and go in peace
	16:37	and **now** are they going to
	17:30	**now** he commands all people
	18: 6	From **now** on I will go to the
	20:22	And **now,** as a captive to the
	20:25	And **now** I know that none of
	20:32	And **now** I commend you to God
	22:16	And **now** why do you delay?
	23:15	**Now** then, you and the council
	23:21	They are ready **now** and
	24:25	Go away for the **present**
	26: 6	And **now** I stand here on trial
	27:22	I urge you **now** to keep up your
Ro	3:26	to prove at the **present** time
	5: 9	**now** that we have been
	5:11	through whom we have **now**
	6:19	so **now** present your members
	6:21	of which you **now** are ashamed?
	8: 1	therefore **now** no condemnation
	8:18	sufferings of this **present** time
	8:22	in labor pains until **now**
	11: 5	So too at the **present** time
	11:30	but have **now** received mercy
	11:31	they have **now** been disobedient
	11:31	they too may **now** receive mercy
	13:11	salvation is nearer to us **now**
	16:26	but is **now** disclosed
1C	3: 2	Even **now** you are still not
	5:11	But **now** I am writing to you
	7:14	but **as it is,** they are holy
	12:20	**As it is,** there are many
	14: 6	**Now,** brothers and sisters
	16:12	not at all willing to come **now**
2C	5:16	From **now** on, therefore, we
	5:16	know him no longer **in that way**
	6: 2	**now** is the acceptable time
	6: 2	**now** is the day of salvation

	7: 9	**Now** I rejoice, not because you
	8:14	your **present** abundance
	13: 2	I warn them **now** while absent
Ga	1:23	is **now** proclaiming the faith
	2:20	I **now** live in the flesh I live
	3: 3	you **now** ending with the flesh
	4: 9	**Now,** however, that you have
	4:25	**Now** Hagar is Mount Sinai
	4:29	the Spirit, so it is **now** also
Ep	2: 2	that is **now** at work among those
	3: 5	as it has **now** been revealed
	3:10	might **now** be made known to the
	5: 8	**now** in the Lord you are light
Ph	1: 5	from the first day until **now**
	1:20	Christ will be exalted **now**
	1:30	and **now** hear that I still have
	2:12	but much more **now** in my absence
	3:18	and **now** I tell you even with
Co	1:24	I am **now** rejoicing in my
	1:26	but has **now** been revealed
1Th	3: 8	we **now** live, if you continue
2Th	2: 6	what is **now** restraining him
1Ti	4: 8	for both the **present** life
	6:17	those who in the **present** age
2Ti	1:10	but it has **now** been revealed
	4:10	love with this **present** world
Ti	2:12	and in the **present** age to live
He	2: 8	**Now** in subjecting all things
	9: 5	we cannot speak **now** in detail
	9:24	**now** to appear in the presence
	11:16	But **as it is,** they desire
	12:26	but **now** he has promised
Ja	4:13	Come **now,** you who say
	4:16	**As it is,** you boast in your
	5: 1	Come **now,** you rich people
1P	1:12	that have **now** been announced
	2:10	but **now** you are God's people
	2:10	**now** you have received mercy
	2:25	but **now** you have returned
	3:21	prefigured, **now** saves you
2P	3: 7	the **present** heavens and earth
	3:18	To him be the glory both **now**
1J	2:18	so **now** many antichrists have
	2:28	And **now,** little children
	3: 2	we are God's children **now**
	4: 3	**now** it is already in the world
2J	1: 5	But **now,** dear lady, I ask you
Ju	1:25	all time and **now** and forever

3570 GO20 AG546 LN170 B3:833 R3568
νυνί, NOW

Ac	22: 1	that I **now** make before you
	24:13	that they **now** bring against me
Ro	3:21	But **now,** apart from law
	6:22	**now** that you have been freed
	7: 6	**now** we are discharged from the
	7:17	**in fact** it is no longer I that
	15:23	**now,** with no further place for
	15:25	At **present,** however, I am going
1C	12:18	But **as it is,** God arranged the
	13:13	And **now** faith, hope, and love
	15:20	But **in fact** Christ has been
2C	8:11	**now** finish doing it, so that
	8:22	but who is **now** more eager
Ep	2:13	But **now** in Christ Jesus
Co	1:22	he has **now** reconciled in his
	3: 8	**now** you must get rid of all
Pm	1: 9	**now** also as a prisoner of
	1:11	**now** he is indeed useful both
He	8: 6	But Jesus has **now** obtained
	9:26	But **as it is,** he has appeared

3571 GO61 AG546 LN170 B1:420 K4:1123
νύξ, NIGHT

Mt	2:14	child and his mother by **night**
	4: 2	forty days and forty **nights**
	12:40	three days and three **nights**
	12:40	three days and three **nights**
	14:25	early in the **morning** he came
	25: 6	But at **midnight** there was a
	26:31	because of me this **night**
	26:34	this very **night,** before the
	28:13	His disciples came by **night**
Mk	4:27	sleep and rise **night** and day
	5: 5	**Night** and day among the tombs
	6:48	them early in the **morning**
	14:30	this day, this very **night**
Lk	2: 8	over their flock by **night**
	2:37	and prayer **night** and day
	5: 5	we have worked all **night**
	12:20	This very **night** your life
	17:34	on that **night** there will be
	18: 7	who cry to him day and **night**
	21:37	and at **night** he would go out
Jn	3: 2	He came to Jesus by **night**
	9: 4	**night** is coming when no one
	11:10	those who walk at **night** stumble
	13:30	And it was **night**

	19:39	at first come to Jesus by **night**
	21: 3	but that **night** they caught
Ac	5:19	But during the **night** an angel
	9:24	the gates day and **night**
	9:25	disciples took him by **night**
	12: 6	The very **night** before Herod
	16: 9	During the **night** Paul had a
	16:33	At the same hour of the **night**
	17:10	That very **night** the believers
	18: 9	One **night** the Lord said to Paul
	20:31	years I did not cease **night**
	23:11	That **night** the Lord stood
	23:23	leave by nine o'clock **tonight**
	23:31	brought him during the **night**
	26: 7	earnestly worship day and **night**
	27:23	last **night** there stood by me
	27:27	the fourteenth **night** had come
	27:27	about **midnight** the sailors
Ro	13:12	the **night** is far gone
1C	11:23	the **night** when he was betrayed
1Th	2: 9	we worked **night** and day,
	3:10	**Night** and day we pray most
	5: 2	come like a thief in the **night**
	5: 5	of the **night** or of darkness
	5: 7	those who sleep sleep at **night**
	5: 7	are drunk get drunk at **night**
2Th	3: 8	labor we worked **night** and day
1Ti	5: 5	and prayers **night** and day
2Ti	1: 3	in my prayers **night** and day
Re	4: 8	Day and **night** without ceasing
	7:15	and worship him day and **night**
	8:12	and likewise the **night**
	12:10	accuses them day and **night**
	14:11	There is no rest day or **night**
	20:10	be tormented day and **night**
	21:25	and there will be no **night**
	22: 5	there will be no more **night**

3572　GO1　AG547　LN170
νυσσω, I STAB
Jn　19:34　one of the soldiers **pierced**

3573　GO2　AG547　LN170
νυσταζω, I DOZE
Mt　25: 5　all of them became **drowsy** and
2P　 2: 3　their destruction is not **asleep**

3574　GO1　AG547　LN170　R3571,2250
νυχθημερον, NIGHT-DAY
2C　11:25　a **night and a day** I was adrift

3575　GO8　AG547　LN170　B2:681
νεω, NOAH
Mt　24:37　For as the days of **Noah** were
	24:38	the day **Noah** entered the ark
Lk	3:36	son of Shem, son of **Noah**
	17:26	as it was in the days of **Noah**
	17:27	the day **Noah** entered the ark
He	11: 7	By faith **Noah,** warned by God
1P	3:20	patiently in the days of **Noah**
2P	2: 5	even though he saved **Noah**

3576　GO2　AG547　LN170　K4:1126
νωθρος, DULL
He　5:11　since you have become **dull**
　　6:12　you may not become **sluggish**

3577　GO1　AG547　LN170　B3:1000
νωτος, BACK
Ro　11:10　keep their **backs** forever bent

ξ

3578　GO2　AG547　LN170　K5:1　R3581
ξενια, STRANGER'S ROOM
Ac　28:23　came to him at his **lodgings**
Pm　 1:22　prepare a **guest room** for me

3579　GO10　AG547　LN171　K5:1　R3581
ξενιζω, I ENTERAIN A STRANGER
Ac	10: 6	he is **lodging** with Simon
	10:18	called Peter, **was staying** there
	10:23	in and **gave** them **lodging**
	10:32	he **is staying** in the home
	17:20	It **sounds** rather **strange** to us
	21:16	with whom we **were to stay**
	28: 7	and **entertained** us **hospitably**
He	13: 2	some **have entertained** angels
1P	4: 4	They **are surprised** that you
	4:12	Beloved, **do** not **be surprised**

3580　GO1　AG548　LN171　B1:686　K5:1　R3581,1209
ξενοδοχεω, I WELCOME STRANGER
1Ti　5:10　**shown hospitality,** washed the

3581　GO14　AG548　LN171　B1:686　K5:1
ξενος, STRANGER
Mt　25:35　I was a **stranger** and you
　　25:38　we saw you a **stranger**
　　25:43　I was a **stranger** and you did

	25:44	hungry or thirsty or a **stranger**
	27: 7	as a place to bury **foreigners**
Ac	17:18	to be a proclaimer of **foreign**
	17:21	and the **foreigners** living there
Ro	16:23	Gaius, who is **host** to me and to
Ep	2:12	**strangers** to the covenants
	2:19	you are no longer **strangers**
He	11:13	that they were **strangers**
	13: 9	all kinds of **strange** teachings
1P	4:12	as though something **strange**
3J	1: 5	they are **strangers** to you

3582　GO1 AG548 LN171
ξεστης, JUG

Mk	7: 4	cups, **pots,** and bronze kettles

3583　GO15 AG548 LN171 B1:515 R3584
ξηραινω, I DRY OUT

Mt	13: 6	no root, they **withered** away
	21:19	the fig tree **withered** at once
	21:20	How did the fig tree **wither**
Mk	3: 1	there who had a **withered** hand
	4: 6	no root, it **withered** away
	5:29	her hemorrhage **stopped**
	9:18	his teeth and **becomes rigid**
	11:20	they saw the fig tree **withered**
	11:21	that you cursed **has withered**
Lk	8: 6	it **withered** for lack of
Jn	15: 6	like a branch and **withers**
Ja	1:11	heat and **withers** the field
1P	1:24	The grass **withers**
Re	14:15	of the earth is **fully ripe**
	16:12	and its water **was dried up**

3584　GO8 AG548 LN171 B1:515
ξηρος, DRIED OUT

Mt	12:10	was there with a **withered** hand
	23:15	For you cross sea and **land**
Mk	3: 3	man who had the **withered** hand
Lk	6: 6	whose right hand was **withered**
	6: 8	man who had the **withered** hand
	23:31	what will happen when it is **dry**
Jn	5: 3	blind, lame, and **paralyzed**
He	11:29	Red Sea as if it were **dry** land

3585　GO2 AG549 LN171 R3586
ξυλινος, WOODEN

2Ti	2:20	but also **of wood** and clay
Re	9:20	bronze and stone and **wood**

3586　GO20 AG549 LN171 B1:389 K5:37
ξυλον, WOOD

Mt	26:47	crowd with swords and **clubs**
	26:55	come out with swords and **clubs**
Mk	14:43	crowd with swords and **clubs**
	14:48	come out with swords and **clubs**
Lk	22:52	come out with swords and **clubs**
	23:31	do this when the **wood** is green
Ac	5:30	by hanging him on a **tree**
	10:39	by hanging him on a **tree**
	13:29	took him down from the **tree**
	16:24	their feet in the **stocks**
1C	3:12	stones, **wood,** hay, straw
Ga	3:13	everyone who hangs on a **tree**
1P	2:24	in his body on the **cross**
Re	2: 7	permission to eat from the **tree**
	18:12	all kinds of scented **wood**
	18:12	all articles of costly **wood**
	22: 2	is the **tree** of life with its
	22: 2	and the leaves of the **tree**
	22:14	the right to the **tree** of
	22:19	share in the **tree** of life

3587　GO3 AG549 LN171
ξυραω, I SHAVE

Ac	21:24	for the **shaving** of their heads
1C	11: 5	thing as **having** her head **shaved**
	11: 6	hair cut off or **to be shaved**

O

3588　GO19904 AG549 LN171
'ο, 'η, το, THE [MULTIPLE OCCURRENCES]

3589　GO2 AG552 LN171 R3590
ογδοηκοντα, EIGHTY

Lk	2:37	widow to the age of **eighty-four**
	16: 7	your bill and make it **eighty**

3590　GO5 AG552 LN171 R3638
ογδοος, EIGHTH

Lk	1:59	On the **eighth** day they came
Ac	7: 8	circumcised him on the **eighth**
2P	2: 5	with **seven** others, when he
Re	17:11	it is an **eighth** but it belongs
	21:20	chrysolite, the **eighth** beryl

3591   GO1 AG553 LN171 K5:41
ογκος, WEIGHT
He 12: 1   us also lay aside every **weight**

3592   GO10 AG553 LN171
ὁδε, BUT THESE
Lk 10:39   She **had** a sister named Mary
Ac 21:11   **Thus** says the Holy Spirit
Ja   4:13   go to **such and such** a town
Re   2: 1   **These** are the words of him
     2: 8   **These** are the words of the
     2:12   **These** are the words of him
     2:18   **These** are the words of the Son
     3: 1   **These** are the words of him
     3: 7   **These** are the words of the
     3:14   **The** words of the Amen

3593   GO1 AG553 LN171 R3598
ὁδευω, I JOURNEY
Lk 10:33   But a Samaritan while **traveling**

3594   GO5 AG553 LN171 B3:935 K5:97 R3595
ὁδηγεω, I GUIDE
Mt 15:14   And if one blind person **guides**
Lk   6·39   blind person **guide** a blind
Jn 16:13   he **will guide** you into all
Ac   8:31   unless someone **guides** me
Re   7:17   he **will guide** them to springs

3595   GO5 AG553 LN171 B3:935 K5:97
ὁδηγος, GUIDE
Mt 15:14   blind **guides** of the blind
    23:16   Woe to you, blind **guides**
    23:24   You blind **guides**!
Ac   1:16   who became a **guide** for those
Ro   2:19   are sure that you are a **guide**

3596   GO1 AG553 LN171 B3:941 R3598,4198
ὁδοιπορεω, I WALK A JOURNEY
Ac 10: 9   as they **were on** their **journey**

3597   GO2 AG553 LN171 R3596
ὁδοιπορια, WALKING JOURNEY
Jn   4: 6   tired out by his **journey**
2C 11:26   on frequent **journeys**

3598   GO101 AG553 LN171 B3:935 K5:42
ὁδος, WAY
Mt   2:12   own country by another **road**
     3: 3   Prepare the **way** of the Lord

     4:15   on the **road** by the sea
     5:25   you are on the **way** to court
     7:13   and the **road** is easy that
     7:14   and the **road** is hard
     8:28   no one could pass that **way**
    10: 5   Go nowhere **among** the Gentiles
    10:10   no bag for your **journey**
    11:10   prepare your **way** before you
    13: 4   some seeds fell on the **path**
    13:19   is what was sown on the **path**
    15:32   they might faint on the **way**
    20:17   and said to them on the **way**
    20:30   men sitting by the **roadside**
    21: 8   spread their cloaks on the **road**
    21: 8   and spread them on the **road**
    21:19   by the side of the **road**
    21:32   in the **way** of righteousness
    22: 9   therefore into the main **streets**
    22:10   went out into the **streets**
    22:16   and teach the **way** of God
Mk   1: 2   who will prepare your **way**
     1: 3   Prepare the **way** of the Lord
     2:23   and as they made their **way**
     4: 4   some seed fell on the **path**
     4·15   These are the ones on the **path**
     6: 8   take nothing for their **journey**
     8: 3   they will faint on the **way**
     8:27   and on the **way** he asked his
     9:33   arguing about on the **way**
     9:34   for on the **way** they had argued
    10:17   was setting out on a **journey**
    10:32   They were on the **road**
    10:46   was sitting by the **roadside**
    10:52   and followed him on the **way**
    11: 8   spread their cloaks on the **road**
    12:14   but teach the **way** of God
Lk   1:76   the Lord to prepare his **ways**
     1:79   to guide our feet into the **way**
     2:44   they went a day's **journey**
     3: 4   Prepare the **way** of the Lord
     3: 5   and the rough **ways** made smooth
     7:27   prepare your **way** before you
     8: 5   some fell on the **path** and was
     8:12   The ones on the **path** are those
     9: 3   Take nothing for your **journey**
     9:57   they were going along the **road**
    10: 4   greet no one on the **road**
    10:31   priest was going down that **road**
    11: 6   a friend of mine has **arrived**

	12:58	on the **way** make an effort
	14:23	Go out into the **roads** and lanes
	18:35	man was sitting by the **roadside**
	19:36	their cloaks on the **road**
	20:21	but teach the **way** of God
	24:32	was talking to us on the **road**
	24:35	what had happened on the **road**
Jn	1:23	Make straight the **way** of the
	14: 4	know the **way** to the place
	14: 5	How can we know the **way**
	14: 6	I am the **way,** and the truth
Ac	1:12	a sabbath day's **journey** away
	2:28	known to me the **ways** of life
	8:26	This is a wilderness **road**
	8:36	were going along the **road**
	8:39	and went on his **way** rejoicing
	9: 2	any who belonged to the **Way**
	9:17	appeared to you on your **way**
	9:27	how on the **road** he had seen
	13:10	the straight **paths** of the Lord
	14:16	to follow their own **ways**
	16:17	to you a **way** of salvation
	18:25	in the **Way** of the Lord
	18:26	explained the **Way** of God to
	19: 9	spoke evil of the **Way** before
	19:23	broke out concerning the **Way**
	22: 4	I persecuted this **Way** up to
	24:14	that according to the **Way**
	24:22	well informed about the **Way**
	25: 3	to kill him along the **way**
	26:13	when at midday along the **road**
Ro	3:16	and misery are in their **paths**
	3:17	the **way** of peace they have not
	11:33	and how inscrutable his **ways**
1C	4:17	to remind you of my **ways**
	12:31	you a still more excellent **way**
1Th	3:11	our Lord Jesus direct our **way**
He	3:10	and they have not known my **ways**
	9: 8	Spirit indicates that the **way**
	10:20	by the new and living **way**
Ja	1: 8	and unstable in every **way**
	2:25	sent them out by another **road**
	5:20	back a sinner from **wandering**
2P	2: 2	follow their licentious **ways**
	2:15	have left the straight **road**
	2:15	following the **road** of Balaam
	2:21	never to have known the **way**
Ju	1:11	For they go the **way** of Cain

Re	15: 3	Just and true are your **ways**
	16:12	in order to prepare the **way**

3599 GO12 AG555 LN172

οδους, TOOTH

Mt	5:38	eye and a **tooth** for a tooth
	5:38	eye and a tooth for a **tooth**
	8:12	weeping and gnashing of **teeth**
	13:42	weeping and gnashing of **teeth**
	13:50	weeping and gnashing of **teeth**
	22:13	weeping and gnashing of **teeth**
	24:51	weeping and gnashing of **teeth**
	25:30	weeping and gnashing of **teeth**
Mk	9:18	he foams and grinds his **teeth**
Lk	13:28	weeping and gnashing of **teeth**
Ac	7:54	ground their **teeth** at Stephen
Re	9: 8	their **teeth** like lions' teeth

3600 GO4 AG555 LN172 K5:115 R3601

οδυναω, I AM IN TORMENT

Lk	2:48	for you **in great anxiety**
	16:24	for I **am in agony** in these
	16:25	and you **are in agony**
Ac	20:38	**grieving** especially because

3601 GO2 AG555 LN172 K5:115

οδυνη, IN PAIN

Ro	9: 2	sorrow and unceasing **anguish**
1Ti	6:10	themselves with many **pains**

3602 GO2 AG555 LN172 K5:116

οδυρμος, LAMENTING

Mt	2:18	wailing and **loud lamentation**
2C	7: 7	your **mourning,** your zeal for me

3604 GO2 AG555 LN172

οζιας, OZIAS (UZZIAH)

Mt	1: 8	Joram the father of **Uzziah**
	1: 9	**Uzziah** the father of Jotham

3605 GO1 AG555 LN172

οζω, I STINK

Jn	11:39	there **is a stench** because he

3606 GO15 AG555 LN172

'οθεν, FROM WHERE

Mt	12:44	to my house **from which** I came
	14: 7	**so much** that he promised on
	25:24	gathering **where** you did not
	25:26	gather **where** I did not scatter

Lk 11:24   to my house **from which** I came
Ac 14:26   **where** they had been commended
    26:19   **After that,** King Agrippa
    28:13   **then** we weighed anchor and came
He   2:17   **Therefore** he had to become like
     3: 1   **Therefore,** brothers and sisters
     7:25   **Consequently** he is able for all
     8: 3   **hence** it is necessary for this
     9:18   **Hence** not even the first
    11:19   **and** figuratively speaking
1J   2:18   **From this** we know that it is

3607   ᴳᴼ2 ᴬᴳ555 ᴸᴺ172
οθονη, SHEET
Ac 10:11   something like a large **sheet**
    11: 5   something like a large **sheet**

3608   ᴳᴼ5 ᴬᴳ555 ᴸᴺ172
οθονιον, LINEN STRIPS
Lk 24:12   he saw the **linen cloths**
Jn 19:40   with the spices in **linen cloths**
    20: 5   saw the **linen wrappings** lying
    20: 6   He saw the **linen wrappings** lying
    20: 7   lying with the **linen wrappings**

3609   ᴳᴼ3 ᴬᴳ556 ᴸᴺ172 ᴮ2:247 ᴷ5:134 ᴷ3609
οικειος, HOUSEHOLD
Ga   6:10   those of the **family** of faith
Ep   2:19   members of the **household** of God
1Ti 5: 8   especially for **family members**

3609a   ᴳᴼ318 ᴬᴳ555 ᴸᴺ172 ᴷ5:116
οιδα, I KNOW
Mt   6: 8   your Father **knows** what you need
     6:32   your heavenly Father **knows** that
     7:11   **know** how to give good gifts
     9: 6   **know** that the Son of Man has
    12:25   He **knew** what they were thinking
    15:12   Do you **know** that the Pharisees
    20:22   not **know** what you are asking
    20:25   You **know** that the rulers of the
    21:27   answered Jesus, "We do not **know**
    22:16   we **know** that you are sincere
    22:29   you **know** neither the scriptures
    24:36   day and hour no one **knows**
    24:42   you do not **know** on what day
    24:43   owner of the house **had known**
    25:12   I do not **know** you
    25:13   for you **know** neither the day
    25:26   You **knew,** did you, that I reap

    26: 2   You **know** that after two days
    26:70   **know** what you are talking about
    26:72   I do not **know** the man
    26:74   I do not **know** the man
    27:18   For he **realized** that it was out
    27:65   make it as secure as you **can**
    28: 5   I **know** that you are looking for
Mk   1:24   I **know** who you are, the Holy
     1:34   speak, because they **knew** him
     2:10   But so that you may **know** that
     4:13   not **understand** this parable
     4:27   he does not **know** how
     5:33   **knowing** what had happened to
     6:20   **knowing** that he was a righteous
     9: 6   He did not **know** what to say
    10:19   You **know** the commandments
    10:38   You do not **know** what you are
    10:42   **know** that among the Gentiles
    11:33   We do not **know**
    12:14   we **know** that you are sincere
    12:15   But **knowing** their hypocrisy
    12:24   you **know** neither the scriptures
    13:32   that day or hour no one **knows**
    13:33   do not **know** when the time
    13:35   do not **know** when the master
    14:40   they did not **know** what to say
    14:68   I do not **know** or understand
    14:71   I do not **know** this man you are
Lk   2:49   Did you not **know** that I must be
     4:34   I **know** who you are, the Holy
     4:41   **knew** that he was the Messiah
     5:24   **know** that the Son of Man has
     6: 8   Even though he **knew** what they
     8:53   **knowing** that she was dead
     9:33   not **knowing** what he said
     9:47   **aware** of their inner thoughts
    11:13   **know** how to give good gifts
    11:17   **knew** what they were thinking
    11:44   over them without **realizing** it
    12:30   your Father **knows** that you need
    12:39   owner of the house **had known**
    12:56   You **know** how to interpret the
    12:56   but why do you not **know** how to
    13:25   I do not **know** where you come
    13:27   I do not **know** where you come
    18:20   You **know** the commandments
    19:22   You **knew,** did you, that I was
    20: 7   not **know** where it came from
    20:21   we **know** that you are right in

	22:34	three times that you **know** me
	22:57	I do not **know** him
	22:60	**know** what you are talking about
	23:34	not **know** what they are doing
Jn	1:26	stands one whom you do not **know**
	1:31	I myself did not **know** him
	1:33	I myself did not **know** him
	2: 9	did not **know** where it came from
	2: 9	who had drawn the water **knew**
	3: 2	we **know** that you are a teacher
	3: 8	**know** where it comes from
	3:11	we speak of what we **know**
	4:10	If you **knew** the gift of God
	4:22	worship what you do not **know**
	4:22	we worship what we **know**
	4:25	I **know** that Messiah is coming
	4:32	that you do not **know** about
	4:42	we **know** that this is truly
	5:13	did not **know** who it was
	5:32	I **know** that his testimony to me
	6: 6	**knew** what he was going to do
	6:42	whose father and mother we **know**
	6:61	**being aware** that his disciples
	6:64	For Jesus **knew** from the first
	7:15	this man have such **learning**
	7:27	we **know** where this man is from
	7:28	You **know** me, and you know where
	7:28	and you **know** where I am from
	7:28	and you do not **know** him
	7:29	I **know** him, because I am from
	8:14	I **know** where I have come from
	8:14	you do not **know** where I come
	8:19	**know** neither me nor my Father
	8:19	If you **knew** me, you would know
	8:19	you would **know** my Father also
	8:37	I **know** that you are descendants
	8:55	though you do not **know** him
	8:55	say that I do not **know** him
	8:55	But I do **know** him and I keep
	9:12	He said, "I do not **know**."
	9:20	We **know** that this is our son
	9:21	but we do not **know** how it is
	9:21	nor do we **know** who opened his
	9:24	**know** that this man is a sinner
	9:25	I do not **know** whether he is a
	9:25	I do **know,** that though I was
	9:29	We **know** that God has spoken to
	9:29	we do not **know** where he comes
	9:30	You do not **know** where he comes
	9:31	**know** that God does not listen
	10: 4	because they **know** his voice
	10: 5	they do not **know** the voice
	11:22	But even now I **know** that God
	11:24	I **know** that he will rise again
	11:42	I **knew** that you always hear me
	11:49	You **know** nothing at all!
	12:35	do not **know** where you are going
	12:50	And I **know** that his commandment
	13: 1	**knew** that his hour had come
	13: 3	**knowing** that the Father had
	13: 7	not **know** now what I am doing
	13:11	For he **knew** who was to betray
	13:17	If you **know** these things
	13:18	I **know** whom I have chosen
	14: 4	you **know** the way to the place
	14: 5	do not **know** where you are going
	14: 5	How can we **know** the way
	15:15	does not **know** what the master
	15:21	because they do not **know** him
	16:18	**know** what he is talking about
	16:30	**know** that you know all things
	16:30	Now we know that you **know** all
	18: 2	also **knew** the place
	18: 4	**knowing** all that was to happen
	18:21	to them; they **know** what I said
	19:10	you not **know** that I have power
	19:28	**knew** that all was now finished
	19:35	**knows** that he tells the truth
	20: 2	we do not **know** where they have
	20: 9	not **understand** the scripture
	20:13	I do not **know** where they have
	20:14	did not **know** that it was Jesus
	21: 4	but the disciples did not **know**
	21:12	they **knew** it was the Lord
	21:15	you **know** that I love you
	21:16	you **know** that I love you
	21:17	you **know** that I love you
	21:24	we **know** that his testimony
Ac	2:22	as you yourselves **know**
	2:30	he **knew** that God had sworn with
	3:16	whom you see and **know**
	3:17	I **know** that you acted
	5: 7	not **knowing** what had happened
	7:18	king who **had** not **known** Joseph
	7:40	not **know** what has happened
	10:36	You know the **message**
	12: 9	he did not **realize** that what
	12:11	Now I am **sure** that the Lord

	16: 3	knew that his father was a		16:15	you know that members of the
	19:32	did not know why they had come	2C	1: 7	we know that as you share in
	20:22	not knowing what will happen		4:14	we know that the one who raised
	20:25	And now I know that none of you		5: 1	For we know that if the earthly
	20:29	I know that after I have gone		5: 6	know that while we are at home
	23: 5	I did not realize, brothers		5:11	knowing the fear of the Lord
	24:22	who was rather well informed		5:16	know him no longer in that way
	26: 4	the Jews know my way of life		9: 2	for I know your eagerness
	26:27	I know that you believe		11:11	love you? God knows I do!
Ro	2: 2	We know that God's judgment		11:31	knows that I do not lie
	3:19	know that whatever the law		12: 2	I know a person in Christ
	5: 3	knowing that suffering produces		12: 2	out of the body I do not know
	6: 9	know that Christ, being raised		12: 2	body I do not know; God knows
	6:16	Do you not know that if you		12: 2	body I do not know; God knows
	7: 7	have known what it is to covet		12: 3	And I know that such a person
	7:14	know that the law is spiritual		12: 3	of the body I do not know
	7:18	For I know that nothing good		12: 3	I do not know; God knows
	8:22	We know that the whole creation	Ga	2:16	know that a person is justified
	8:26	we do not know how to		4: 8	when you did not know God
	8:27	knows what is the mind of the		4:13	You know that it was because
	8:28	We know that all things work	Ep	1:18	you may know what is the hope
	11: 2	know what the scripture says		5: 5	Be sure of this, that no
	13:11	you know what time it is		6: 8	knowing that whatever good we
	14:14	I know and am persuaded in the		6: 9	you know that both of you have
	15:29	know that when I come to you		6:21	know how I am and what I am
1C	1:16	do not know whether I baptized	Ph	1:16	knowing that I have been put
	2: 2	know nothing among you except		1:19	know that through your prayers
	2:11	For what human being knows		1:25	I know that I will remain and
	2:12	we may understand the gifts		4:12	know what it is to have little
	3:16	know that you are God's temple		4:12	know what it is to have plenty
	5: 6	know that a little yeast		4:15	know that in the early days
	6: 2	Do you not know that the saints	Co	2: 1	know how much I am struggling
	6: 3	Do you not know that we are to		3:24	you know that from the Lord
	6: 9	you not know that wrongdoers		4: 1	for you know that you also have
	6:15	you not know that your bodies		4: 6	know how you ought to answer
	6:16	know that whoever is united	1Th	1: 4	For we know, brothers and
	6:19	know that your body is a temple		1: 5	know what kind of persons we
	7:16	Wife, for all you know		2: 1	You yourselves know, brothers
	7:16	Husband, for all you know		2: 2	at Philippi, as you know
	8: 1	we know that "all of us possess		2: 5	As you know and as God is our
	8: 4	we know that "no idol in the		2:11	As you know, we dealt with
	9:13	Do you not know that those		3: 3	know that this is what we are
	9:24	Do you not know that in a		3: 4	so it turned out, as you know
	11: 3	But I want you to understand		4: 2	For you know what instructions
	12: 2	know that when you were pagans		4: 4	know how to control your own
	13: 2	and understand all mysteries		4: 5	Gentiles who do not know God
	14:11	not know the meaning of a sound		5: 2	you yourselves know very well
	14:16	the outsider does not know what		5:12	to respect those who labor
	15:58	you know that in the	2Th	1: 8	those who do not know God

	2: 6	**know** what is now restraining
	3: 7	**know** how you ought to imitate
1Ti	1: 8	we **know** that the law is good
	1: 9	**understanding** that the law is
	3: 5	if someone does not **know** how
	3:15	**know** how one ought to behave
2Ti	1:12	I **know** the one in whom I have
	1:15	You are **aware** that all who are
	2:23	**know** that they breed quarrels
	3:14	**knowing** from whom you learned
	3:15	**have known** the sacred writings
Ti	1:16	They profess to **know** God
	3:11	you **know** that such a person
Pm	1:21	**knowing** that you will do even
He	8:11	to each other, '**Know** the Lord,'
	10:30	For we **know** the one who said
	12:17	You **know** that later, when he
Ja	1:19	You must **understand** this
	3: 1	you **know** that we who teach
	4: 4	**know** that friendship with the
	4:17	who **knows** the right thing to do
1P	1:18	You **know** that you were ransomed
	5: 9	you **know** that your brothers
2P	1:12	though you **know** them already
	1:14	since I **know** that my death
	2: 9	**knows** how to rescue the godly
1J	2:11	and does not **know** the way to go
	2:20	all of you have **knowledge**
	2:21	not because you do not **know**
	2:21	truth, but because you **know** it
	2:29	you **know** that he is righteous
	3: 2	What we do **know** is this
	3: 5	You **know** that he was revealed
	3:14	We **know** that we have passed
	3:15	you **know** that murderers do not
	5:13	so that you may **know** that you
	5:15	And if we **know** that he hears
	5:15	we **know** that we have obtained
	5:18	We **know** that those who are born
	5:19	**know** that we are God's children
	5:20	And we **know** that the Son of God
3J	1:12	**know** that our testimony is true
Ju	1: 5	though you are **fully informed**
	1:10	whatever they do not **understand**
Re	2: 2	I **know** your works, your toil
	2: 9	I **know** your affliction and your
	2:13	I **know** where you are living
	2:17	new name that no one **knows**
	2:19	I **know** your works—your love

	3: 1	I **know** your works; you have a
	3: 8	I **know** your works. Look, I have
	3:15	I **know** your works; you are
	3:17	You do not **realize** that you
	7:14	you are the one that **knows**
	12:12	because he **knows** that his time
	19:12	no one **knows** but himself

3609b　ᴳᴼ1　ᴬᴳ556　ᴸᴺ172　ᴿ3624
οικετεια, HOUSEHOLD
Mt　24:45　put in charge of his **household**

3610　ᴳᴼ4　ᴬᴳ557　ᴸᴺ172　ᴿ3611
οικετης, HOUSE SERVANT
Lk	16:13	No **slave** can serve two masters
Ac	10: 7	he called two of his **slaves**
Ro	14: 4	to pass judgment on **servants**
1P	2:18	**Slaves,** accept the authority

3611　ᴳᴼ9　ᴬᴳ557　ᴸᴺ172　ᴮ2:247　ᴷ5:135　ᴿ3624
οικεω, I HOUSE, I DWELL
Ro	7:17	sin that **dwells** within me
	7:18	nothing good **dwells** within me
	7:20	but sin that **dwells** within me
	8: 9	Spirit of God **dwells** in you
	8:11	his Spirit that **dwells** in you
1C	3:16	God's Spirit **dwells** in you
	7:12	consents **to live** with him
	7:13	he consents **to live** with her
1Ti	6:16	**dwells** in unapproachable light

3612　ᴳᴼ1　ᴬᴳ557　ᴸᴺ172　ᴿ3611
οικημα, BUILDING
Ac　12: 7　and a light shone in the **cell**

3613　ᴳᴼ2　ᴬᴳ557　ᴸᴺ172　ᴷ5:155　ᴿ3611
οικητηριον, HOUSE PLACE
2C	5: 2	with our heavenly **dwelling**
Ju	1: 6	but left their proper **dwelling**

3614　ᴳᴼ93　ᴬᴳ557　ᴸᴺ172　ᴮ2:247　ᴷ5:131　ᴿ3624
οικια, HOUSE
Mt	2:11	On entering the **house**
	5:15	gives light to all in the **house**
	7:24	wise man who built his **house**
	7:25	blew and beat on that **house**
	7:26	who built his **house** on sand
	7:27	and beat against that **house**
	8: 6	my servant is lying at **home**
	8:14	Jesus entered Peter's **house**

	9:10	he sat at dinner in the **house**
	9:23	came to the leader's **house**
	9:28	When he entered the **house**
	10:12	As you enter the **house**
	10:13	If the **house** is worthy
	10:14	as you leave that **house** or town
	12:25	**house** divided against itself
	12:29	enter a strong man's **house**
	12:29	the **house** can be plundered
	13: 1	Jesus went out of the **house**
	13:36	crowds and went into the **house**
	13:57	country and in their own **house**
	17:25	And when he came **home,** Jesus
	19:29	everyone who has left **houses**
	24:17	to take what is in the **house**
	24:43	would not have let his **house**
	26: 6	in the **house** of Simon the leper
Mk	1:29	they entered the **house** of Simon
	2:15	sat at dinner in Levi's **house**
	3:25	**house** is divided against itself
	3:25	**house** will not be able to stand
	3:27	can enter a strong man's **house**
	3:27	the **house** can be plundered
	6: 4	and in their own **house**
	6:10	Wherever you enter a **house**
	7:24	He entered a **house** and did not
	9:33	when he was in the **house**
	10:10	Then in the **house** the disciples
	10:29	no one who has left **house**
	10:30	**houses,** brothers and sisters
	12:40	They devour widows' **houses**
	13:15	not go down or enter the **house**
	13:34	when he leaves **home** and puts
	13:35	master of the **house** will come
	14: 3	he was at Bethany in the **house**
Lk	4:38	he entered Simon's **house**
	5:29	banquet for him in his **house**
	6:48	like a man building a **house**
	6:48	river burst against that **house**
	6:49	like a man who built a **house**
	6:49	was the ruin of that **house**
	7: 6	he was not far from the **house**
	7:37	eating in the Pharisee's **house**
	7:44	I entered your **house**
	8:27	he did not live in a **house**
	8:51	When he came to the **house**
	9: 4	Whatever **house** you enter
	10: 5	Whatever **house** you enter
	10: 7	Remain in the same **house**

	10: 7	move about from **house** to house
	10: 7	move about from house to **house**
	15: 8	light a lamp, sweep the **house**
	15:25	came and approached the **house**
	17:31	has belongings in the **house**
	18:29	no one who has left **house**
	20:47	They devour widows' **houses**
	22:10	follow him into the **house**
	22:11	say to the owner of the **house**
	22:54	into the high priest's **house**
Jn	4:53	along with his whole **household**
	8:35	place in the **household**
	11:31	who were with her in the **house**
	12: 3	The **house** was filled with the
	14: 2	In my Father's **house** there are
Ac	4:34	many as owned lands or **houses**
	9:11	and at the **house** of Judas look
	9:17	went and entered the **house**
	10: 6	whose **house** is by the seaside
	10:17	were asking for Simon's **house**
	10:32	he is staying in the **home**
	11:11	arrived at the **house** where we
	12:12	he went to the **house** of Mary
	16:32	all who were in his **house**
	17: 5	they attacked Jason's **house**
	18: 7	and went to the **house** of a man
	18: 7	his **house** was next door to the
1C	11:22	**homes** to eat and drink in
	16:15	that members of the **household**
2C	5: 1	know that if the earthly **tent**
	5: 1	a **house** not made with hands
Ph	4:22	of the emperor's **household**
1Ti	5:13	about from **house** to house
2Ti	2:20	In a large **house** there are
	3: 6	make their way into **households**
2J	1:10	Do not receive into the **house**

3615   GO2 AG557 LN172 R3614
οικιακος, HOUSEHOLD
Mt 10:25 malign those of his **household**
      10:36 members of one's own **household**

3616   GO1 AG558 LN172 B2:508 K2:49 R3617
οικοδεσποτεω, I SUPERVISE HOUSE
1Ti 5:14 and **manage** their **households**

3617   GO12 AG558 LN172 B2:508 K2:49 R3624,1203
οικοδεσποτης, HOUSE SUPERVISOR
Mt 10:25 called the **master of the house**
      13:27 the slaves of the **householder**

	13:52	the **master of a household** who
	20: 1	heaven is like a **landowner** who
	20:11	grumbled against the **landowner**
	21:33	was a **landowner** who planted
	24:43	**owner of the house** had known
Mk	14:14	say to the **owner of the house**
Lk	12:39	**owner of the house** had known
	13:25	**owner of the house** has got up
	14:21	**owner of the house** became angry
	22:11	say to the **owner of the house**

3618　GO41 AG558 LN172 B2:251 K5:136 R3619
οικοδομεω, I BUILD

Mt	7:24	like a wise man who **built**
	7:26	who **built** his house on sand
	16:18	I **will build** my church
	21:33	and **built** a watchtower
	21:42	that the **builders** rejected
	23:29	**build** the tombs of the prophets
	26:61	and to **build** it in three days
	27:40	and **build** it in three days
Mk	12: 1	and **built** a watchtower; then he
	12:10	that the **builders** rejected
	14:58	three days I **will build** another
	15:29	and **build** it in three days
Lk	4:29	on which their town **was built**
	6:48	like a man **building** a house
	6:48	because it had been well **built**
	6:49	like a man who **built** a house
	7: 5	is he who **built** our synagogue
	11:47	For you **build** the tombs of the
	11:48	and you **build** their tombs
	12:18	my barns and **build** larger ones
	14:28	intending to **build** a tower
	14:30	This fellow began to **build**
	17:28	selling, planting and **building**
	20:17	that the **builders** rejected
Jn	2:20	**has been under construction** for
Ac	4:11	rejected by you, the **builders**
	7:47	Solomon who **built** a house for
	7:49	house will you **build** for me
	9:31	had peace and **was built** up
	20:32	message that is able to **build**
Ro	15:20	not **build** on someone else's
1C	8: 1	puffs up, but love **builds** up
	8:10	**be encouraged** to the point of
	10:23	but not all things **build** up
	14: 4	in a tongue **build** up themselves
	14: 5	that the church **may be built** up

	14:17	other person is not **built** up
Ga	2:18	But if I **build** up again
1Th	5:11	another and **build** up each other
1P	2: 5	**be built** into a spiritual house
	2: 7	that the **builders** rejected

3619　GO18 AG558 LN172 B2:251 K5:144
οικοδομη, BUILDING

Mt	24: 1	the **buildings** of the temple
Mk	13: 1	stones and what large **buildings**
	13: 2	you see these great **buildings**
Ro	14:19	peace and for mutual **upbuilding**
	15: 2	the good purpose of **building** up
1C	3: 9	God's field, God's **building**
	14: 3	people for their **upbuilding**
	14: 5	that the church may be **built** up
	14:12	excel in them for **building** up
	14:26	things be done for **building** up
2C	5: 1	we have a **building** from God
	10: 8	Lord gave for **building** you up
	12:19	the sake of **building** you up
	13:10	for **building** up and not for
Ep	2:21	the whole **structure** is joined
	4:12	**building** up the body of Christ
	4:16	growth in **building** itself up
	4:29	what is useful for **building** up

3621　GO1 AG559 LN173 B2:253 R3623
οικονομεω, I MANAGE

Lk	16: 2	cannot **be** my **manager** any longer

3622　GO9 AG559 LN173 B2:253 K5:151 R3623
οικονομια, MANAGEMENT

Lk	16: 2	accounting of your **management**
	16: 3	is taking the **position** away
	16: 4	I am dismissed as **manager**
1C	9:17	am entrusted with a **commission**
Ep	1:10	as a **plan** for the fullness
	3: 2	the **commission** of God's grace
	3: 9	what is the **plan** of the mystery
Co	1:25	according to God's **commission**
1Ti	1: 4	rather than the divine **training**

3623　GO10 AG560 LN173 B2:253 K5:149 R3624,3551
οικονομος, MANAGER

Lk	12:42	faithful and prudent **manager**
	16: 1	a rich man who had a **manager**
	16: 3	the **manager** said to himself
	16: 8	commended the dishonest **manager**
Ro	16:23	Erastus, the city **treasurer**

1C	4: 1	**stewards** of God's mysteries		11:24	I will return to my **house**
	4: 2	it is required of **stewards**		11:51	the altar and the **sanctuary**
Ga	4: 2	under guardians and **trustees**		12:39	owner of the **house** had known
Ti	1: 7	For a bishop, as God's **steward**		12:52	now on five in one **household**
1P	4:10	good **stewards** of the manifold		13:35	See, your **house** is left to you
				14: 1	Jesus was going to the **house**

3624   GO114 AG560 LN173 B2:247 K5:119
οἶκος, HOUSE

Mt	9: 6	your bed and go to your **home**		14:23	so that my **house** may be filled
	9: 7	stood up and went to his **home**		15: 6	And when he comes **home**
	10: 6	sheep of the **house** of Israel		16: 4	welcome me into their **homes**
	11: 8	robes are in royal **palaces**		16:27	send him to my father's **house**
	12: 4	He entered the **house** of God		18:14	man went down to his **home**
	12:44	I will return to my **house**		19: 5	I must stay at your **house**
	15:24	sheep of the **house** of Israel		19: 9	has come to this **house**
	21:13	My **house** shall be called a		19:46	My **house** shall be a house
	21:13	be called a **house** of prayer		19:46	My house shall be a **house**
	23:38	your **house** is left to you	Jn	2:16	Father's **house** a marketplace
Mk	2: 1	reported that he was at **home**		2:16	Father's house a **marketplace**
	2:11	your mat and go to your **home**		2:17	for your **house** will consume me
	2:26	He entered the **house** of God		7:53	Then each of them went **home**
	3:19	Then he went **home**		11:20	while Mary stayed at **home**
	5:19	Go **home** to your friends	Ac	2: 2	it filled the entire **house**
	5:38	When they came to the **house**		2:36	Therefore let the entire **house**
	7:17	the crowd and entered the **house**		2:46	they broke bread at **home**
	7:30	So she went **home**		5:42	in the temple and at **home**
	8: 3	away hungry to their **homes**		7:10	and over all his **household**
	8:26	he sent him away to his **home**		7:20	up in his father's **house**
	9:28	When he had entered the **house**		7:42	wilderness, O **house** of Israel
	11:17	**house** shall be called a house		7:46	place for the **house** of Jacob
	11:17	house shall be called a **house**		7:47	Solomon who built a **house**
Lk	1:23	he went to his **home**		7:49	What kind of **house** will you
	1:27	Joseph, of the **house** of David		8: 3	by entering **house** after house
	1:33	reign over the **house** of Jacob		10: 2	with all his **household**
	1:40	the **house** of Zechariah		10:22	for you to come to his **house**
	1:56	and then returned to her **home**		10:30	I was praying in my **house**
	1:69	savior for us in the **house**		11:12	and we entered the man's **house**
	2: 4	was descended from the **house**		11:13	angel standing in his **house**
	5:24	your bed and go to your **home**		11:14	you and your entire **household**
	5:25	lying on, and went to his **home**		16:15	she and her **household** were
	6: 4	He entered the **house** of God		16:15	Lord, come and stay at my **home**
	7:10	sent returned to the **house**		16:31	saved, you and your **household**
	7:36	into the Pharisee's **house**		16:34	brought them up into the **house**
	8:39	Return to your **home**		18: 8	together with all his **household**
	8:41	begged him to come to his **house**		19:16	fled out of the **house** naked
	9:61	farewell to those at my **home**		20:20	and from **house** to house
	10: 5	Peace to this **house**		21: 8	went into the **house** of Philip
	11:17	and **house** falls on house	Ro	16: 5	also the church in their **house**
	11:17	and house falls on **house**	1C	1:16	did baptize also the **household**
				11:34	If you are hungry, eat at **home**
				14:35	them ask their husbands at **home**

	16:19	with the church in their **house**
Co	4:15	and the church in her **house**
1Ti	3: 4	must manage his own **household**
	3: 5	how to manage his own **household**
	3:12	children and their **households**
	3:15	to behave in the **household**
	5: 4	duty to their own **family**
2Ti	1:16	grant mercy to the **household**
	4:19	the **household** of Onesiphorus
Ti	1:11	are upsetting whole **families**
Pm	1: 2	to the church in your **house**
He	3: 2	was faithful in all God's **house**
	3: 3	honor than the **house** itself
	3: 4	For every **house** is built by
	3: 5	was faithful in all God's **house**
	3: 6	was faithful over God's **house**
	3: 6	and we are his **house** if we hold
	8: 8	a new covenant with the **house**
	8: 8	with the **house** of Judah
	8:10	make with the **house** of Israel
	10:21	priest over the **house** of God
	11: 7	an ark to save his **household**
1P	2: 5	be built into a spiritual **house**
	4:17	to begin with the **household**

3625   GO15 AG561 LN173 B1:517 K5:157 R3611
οικουμενη, INHABITED WORLD

Mt	24:14	proclaimed throughout the **world**
Lk	2: 1	the **world** should be registered
	4: 5	all the kingdoms of the **world**
	21:26	what is coming upon the **world**
Ac	11:28	famine over all the **world**
	17: 6	turning the **world** upside down
	17:31	he will have the **world** judged
	19:27	and the **world** to worship her
	24: 5	the Jews throughout the **world**
Ro	10:18	words to the ends of the **world**
He	1: 6	the firstborn into the **world**
	2: 5	not subject the coming **world**
Re	3:10	is coming on the whole **world**
	12: 9	deceiver of the whole **world**
	16:14	the kings of the whole **world**

3626   GO1 AG561 LN173
οικουργος, HOUSE-WORKER

Ti	2: 5	good **managers of the household**

3627   GO2 AG561 LN173 B2:598
οικτιρω, I HAVE COMPASSION

Ro	9:15	I **will have compassion** on whom
	9:15	on whom I **have compassion**

3628   GO5 AG561 LN173 B2:598 K5:159 R3627
οικτιρμος, COMPASSION

Ro	12: 1	the **mercies** of God, to present
2C	1: 3	Christ, the Father of **mercies**
Ph	2: 1	any compassion and **sympathy**
Co	3:12	yourselves with **compassion**
He	10:28	dies without **mercy**

3629   GO3 AG561 LN173 B2:598 K5:159 R3627
οικτιρμων, COMPASSIONATE

Lk	6:36	Be **merciful,** just as your
	6:36	just as your Father is **merciful**
Ja	5:11	is compassionate and **merciful**

3630   GO2 AG562 LN173 B3:918 R3631,4095
οινοποτης, WINE DRINKER

Mt	11:19	a glutton and a **drunkard**
Lk	7:34	a glutton and a **drunkard**

3631   GO34 AG562 LN173 B3:918 K5:162
οινος, WINE

Mt	9:17	Neither is new **wine** put into
	9:17	burst, and the **wine** is spilled
	9:17	but new **wine** is put into fresh
	27:34	they offered him **wine** to drink
Mk	2:22	new **wine** into old wineskins
	2:22	the **wine** will burst the skins
	2:22	and the **wine** is lost
	2:22	puts new **wine** into fresh
	15:23	offered him **wine** mixed with
Lk	1:15	He must never drink **wine** or
	5:37	And no one puts new **wine**
	5:37	the new **wine** will burst the
	5:38	But new **wine** must be put into
	7:33	no bread and drinking no **wine**
	10:34	having poured oil and **wine** on
Jn	2: 3	When the **wine** gave out
	2: 3	They have no **wine.**
	2: 9	the water that had become **wine**
	2:10	Everyone serves the good **wine**
	2:10	you have kept the good **wine**
	4:46	had changed the water into **wine**
Ro	14:21	not to eat meat or drink **wine**
Ep	5:18	Do not get drunk with **wine**
1Ti	3: 8	not indulging in much **wine**
	5:23	take a little **wine** for the sake
Ti	2: 3	slanderers or slaves to **drink**

Re   6: 6   the olive oil and the **wine**
      14: 8   drink of the **wine** of the wrath
      14:10   they will also drink the **wine**
      16:19   the **wine**-cup of the fury
      17: 2   **wine** of whose fornication
      18: 3   the **wine** of the wrath of her
      18:13   **wine,** olive oil, choice flour
      19:15   he will tread the **wine** press

3632   GO1 AG562 LN173 B3:918
οινοφλυγια, DRUNKENNESS
1P   4: 3   **drunkenness,** revels, carousing

3633   GO3 AG562 LN173
οιομαι, I EXPECT
Jn   21:25   I **suppose** that the world itself
Ph   1:17   but **intending** to increase my
Ja   1: 7   must not **expect** to receive

3634   GO14 AG562 LN173
οιος, SUCH
Mt   24:21   **such as** has not been from the
Mk   9: 3   **such as** no one on earth could
      13:19   **such as** has not been from the
Ro   9: 6   It is not **as** though the word
1C   15:48   As was the man of dust, so are
      15:48   **as** is the man of heaven, so are
2C   10:11   that **what** we say by letter
      12:20   I may find you not **as** I wish
      12:20   may find me not **as** you wish
Ph   1:30   struggle **that** you saw I had
1Th   1: 5   **what kind** of persons we proved
2Ti   3:11   things **that** happened to me in
      3:11   **What** persecutions I endured!
Re   16:18   **such as** had not occurred since

3635   GO1 AG563 LN173
οκνεω, I DELAY
Ac   9:38   Please come to us without **delay**

3636   GO3 AG563 LN173 K5:166 R3635
οκνηρος, TROUBLESOME
Mt   25:26   You wicked and **lazy** slave!
Ro   12:11   Do not **lag** in zeal, be ardent
Ph   3: 1   is not **troublesome** to me

3637   GO1 AG563 LN173 R3638,2250
οκταημερος, EIGHTH DAY
Ph   3: 5   circumcised on the **eighth day**

3638   GO8 AG563 LN173 B2:692
οκτω, EIGHT
Lk   2:21   After **eight** days had passed
      9:28   about **eight** days after these
      13:16   bound for **eighteen** long years
Jn   5: 5   ill for thirty-**eight** years
      20:26   A **week** later his disciples
Ac   9:33   been bedridden for **eight** years
      25: 6   among them not more than
                eight
1P   3:20   a few, that is, **eight** persons

3639   GO4 AG563 LN173 B1:465 K5:168
ολεθρος, RUIN
1C   5: 5   the **destruction** of the flesh
1Th   5: 3   sudden **destruction** will come
2Th   1: 9   of eternal **destruction**
1Ti   6: 9   into ruin and **destruction**

3639a   GO1 AG563 LN173 K6:174 R3641,4102
ολιγοπιστια, LITTLE TRUST
Mt   17:20   Because of your **little faith**

3640   GO5 AG563 LN173 K6:174 R3641,4102
ολιγοπιστος, LITTLE TRUSTING
Mt   6:30   you of **little faith**
      8:26   you afraid, you of **little faith**
      14:31   You of **little faith,** why did
      16: 8   You of **little faith,** why are
Lk   12:28   you of **little faith**

3641   GO40 AG563 LN173 B2:427 K5:171
ολιγος, FEW
Mt   7:14   there are **few** who find it
      9:37   but the laborers are **few**
      15:34   Seven, and a **few** small fish.
      22:14   called, but **few** are chosen
      25:21   trustworthy in a **few** things
      25:23   trustworthy in a **few** things
Mk   1:19   As he went a **little** farther
      6: 5   laid his hands on a **few** sick
      6:31   by yourselves and rest a **while**
      8: 7   They had also a **few** small fish
Lk   5: 3   a **little** way from the shore
      7:47   But the one to whom **little**
      7:47   is forgiven, loves **little**
      10: 2   but the laborers are **few**
      12:48   will receive a **light** beating.
      13:23   Lord, will only a **few** be saved
Ac   12:18   there was no **small** commotion

	14:28	the disciples for **some** time
	15: 2	no **small** dissension and debate
	17: 4	not a **few** of the leading women
	17:12	including not a **few** Greek women
	19:23	no **little** disturbance broke out
	19:24	brought no **little** business to
	26:28	Are you so **quickly** persuading
	26:29	Whether **quickly** or not, I pray
	27:20	and no **small** tempest raged
2C	8:15	and the one who had **little** did
Ep	3: 3	as I wrote above in a **few** words
1Ti	4: 8	training is of **some** value
	5:23	a **little** wine for the sake
He	12:10	disciplined us for a **short** time
Ja	4:14	that appears for a **little** while
1P	1: 6	if now for a **little** while
	3:20	a **few**, that is, eight persons
	5:10	suffered for a **little** while
	5:12	have written this **short** letter
Re	2:14	have a **few** things against you
	3: 4	you have still a **few** persons
	12:12	he knows that his time is **short**
	17:10	must remain only a **little** while

3642 GO1 AG564 LN174 B3:687 K9:665 R3641,5590
ολιγοψυχος, LITTLE-SOULED
1Th 5:14 encourage the **faint hearted**

3643 GO1 AG564 LN174 B1:462
ολιγωρεω, I THINK LITTLE
He 12: 5 **regard lightly** the discipline

3643a GO1 AG564 LN174 R3641
ολιγως, SCARCELY
2P 2:18 people who have **just** escaped

3644 GO1 AG564 LN174 B1:465 K5:169 R3645
ολοθρευτης, DESTROYER
1C 10:10 were destroyed by the **destroyer**

3645 GO1 AG564 LN174 B1:465 R3639
ολοθρευω, I DESTROY
He 11:28 the **destroyer** of the firstborn

3646 GO3 AG564 LN174 B3:417 R3650,2545
ὁλοκαυτωμα, WHOLE BURNT OFFERING
Mk 12:33 than all **whole burnt offerings**
He 10: 6 in **burnt offerings** and sin
10: 8 and **burnt offerings** and sin

3647 GO1 AG564 LN174 K3:767 R3648
ὁλοκληρια, WHOLE SHARE
Ac 3:16 given him this **perfect health**

3648 GO2 AG564 LN174 K3:766
ὁλοκληρος, WHOLLY CALLED
1Th 5:23 sanctify you **entirely;** and may
Ja 1: 4 may be mature and **complete**

3649 GO1 AG564 LN174 K5:173
ολολυζω, I WAIL
Ja 5: 1 you rich people, weep and **wail**

3650 GO109 AG564 LN174 K5:174
ὁλος, WHOLE

Mt	1:22	**All** this took place to fulfill
	4:23	Jesus went **throughout** Galilee
	4:24	spread **throughout** all Syria
	5:29	than for your **whole** body to be
	5:30	than for your **whole** body to go
	6:22	your **whole** body will be full
	6:23	your **whole** body will be full
	9:26	spread **throughout** that district
	9:31	him **throughout** that district
	13:33	until **all** of it was leavened
	14:35	sent word **throughout** the region
	16:26	if they gain the **whole** world
	20: 6	standing here idle **all** day
	22:37	your God with **all** your heart
	22:37	heart, and with **all** your soul
	22:37	and with **all** your mind
	22:40	hang **all** the law and the
	24:14	a testimony to **all** the nations
	26:13	proclaimed in the **whole** world
	26:56	But **all** this has taken place
	26:59	the **whole** council were looking
	27:27	they gathered the **whole** cohort
Mk	1:28	fame began to spread **throughout**
	1:33	And the **whole** city was gathered
	1:39	And he went **throughout** Galilee
	6:55	rushed about that **whole** region
	8:36	to gain the **whole** world
	12:30	your God with **all** your heart
	12:30	heart, and with **all** your soul
	12:30	soul, and with **all** your mind
	12:30	and with **all** your strength.
	12:33	to love him with **all** the heart
	12:33	with **all** the understanding
	12:33	with **all** the strength,' and

	12:44	**all** she had to live on
	14: 9	proclaimed in the **whole** world
	14:55	priests and the **whole** council
	15: 1	scribes and the **whole** council
	15:16	together the **whole** cohort
	15:33	came over the **whole** land
Lk	1:65	were talked about **throughout**
	4:14	**all** the surrounding country
	5: 5	we have worked **all** night long
	7:17	spread **throughout** Judea
	8:39	proclaiming **throughout** the city
	8:43	she had spent **all** she had
	9:25	if they gain the **whole** world
	10:27	your God with **all** your heart
	10:27	heart, and with **all** your soul
	10:27	and with **all** your strength
	10:27	and with **all** your mind
	11:34	**whole** body is full of light
	11:36	**whole** body is full of light
	11:36	it will be as **full** of
	13:21	until **all** of it was leavened
	23: 5	teaching throughout **all** Judea
	23:44	came over the **whole** land
Jn	4:53	along with his **whole** household
	7:23	I healed a man's **whole** body
	9:34	You were born **entirely** in sins
	11:50	have the **whole** nation destroyed
	13:10	the feet, but is **entirely** clean
	19:23	woven **in one piece** from the top
Ac	2: 2	and it filled the **entire** house
	2:47	the goodwill of **all** the people
	5:11	fear seized the **whole** church
	7:10	and over **all** his household
	7:11	a famine **throughout** Egypt
	9:31	the church **throughout** Judea
	9:42	became known **throughout** Joppa
	10:22	by the **whole** Jewish nation
	10:37	message spread **throughout** Judea
	11:26	that for an **entire** year
	11:28	famine over **all** the world
	13: 6	gone through the **whole** island
	13:49	spread **throughout** the region
	15:22	the consent of the **whole** church
	18: 8	together with **all** his household
	19:27	majesty that brought **all** Asia
	21:30	Then **all** the city was aroused
	21:31	**all** Jerusalem was in an uproar
	28:30	He lived there two **whole** years

Ro	1: 8	proclaimed **throughout** the world
	8:36	are being killed **all** day long
	10:21	**All** day long I have held out
	16:23	to me and to the **whole** church
1C	5: 6	the **whole** batch of dough
	12:17	If the **whole** body were an eye
	12:17	If the **whole** body were hearing
	14:23	the **whole** church comes together
2C	1: 1	the saints **throughout** Achaia
Ga	5: 3	obliged to obey the **entire** law
	5: 9	yeast leavens the **whole** batch
Ph	1:13	throughout the **whole** imperial
1Th	4:10	sisters **throughout** Macedonia
Ti	1:11	upsetting **whole** families
He	3: 2	faithful in **all** God's house
	3: 5	was faithful in **all** God's house
Ja	2:10	whoever keeps the **whole** law
	3: 2	able to keep the **whole** body
	3: 3	we guide their **whole** bodies
	3: 6	it stains the **whole** body
1J	2: 2	for the sins of the **whole** world
	5:19	that the **whole** world lies under
Re	3:10	is coming on the **whole** world
	6:12	the **full** moon became like blood
	12: 9	deceiver of the **whole** world
	13: 3	**whole** earth followed the beast
	16:14	the kings of the **whole** world

3651   GO1 AG565 LN174 K5:175 R3650,5056
ὁλοτελης, WHOLLY COMPLETED
1Th 5:23   himself sanctify you **entirely**

3652   GO1 AG565 LN174
ολυμπας, OLYMPAS
Ro 16:15   and his sister, and **Olympas**

3653   GO1 AG565 LN174 K7:751
ολυνθος, UNRIPE ONE
Re 6:13   fig tree drops its **winter fruit**

3654   GO4 AG565 LN174 R3650
ὁλως, WHOLLY
Mt 5:34   Do not swear **at all,** either by
1C 5: 1   It is **actually** reported that
    6: 7   to have lawsuits **at all** with
    15:29   the dead are not raised **at all**

3655   GO1 AG565 LN174 B3:1000
ομβρος, RAIN STORM
Lk 12:54   It is going to **rain**

3655a　GO1 AG565 LN174 K5:176
ὀμειρομαι, I YEARN
1Th　2: 8　So **deeply do we care** for you

3656　GO4 AG565 LN174
ὁμιλεω, I CONVERSE
Lk　24:14　and **talking** with each other
　　24:15　were **talking** and discussing
Ac　20:11　continued to **converse** with them
　　24:26　for him very often and **converse**

3657　GO1 AG565 LN174 R3656
ὁμιλια, CONVERSATION
1C　15:33　Bad **company** ruins good morals

3657a　GO1 AG565 LN174 B3:1000
ὁμιχλη, MIST
2P　2:17　and **mists** driven by a storm

3659　GO2 AG565 LN174 R3700
ομμα, EYE
Mt　20:34　Jesus touched their **eyes**
Mk　8:23　he had put saliva on his **eyes**

3660　GO26 AG565 LN174 B3:737 K5:176
ομνυω, I TAKE OATH
Mt　5:34　Do not **swear** at all
　　5:36　And do not **swear** by your head
　　23:16　Whoever **swears** by the sanctuary
　　23:16　but whoever **swears** by the gold
　　23:18　Whoever **swears** by the altar
　　23:18　but whoever **swears** by the gift
　　23:20　So whoever **swears** by the altar
　　23:20　**swears** by it and by everything
　　23:21　whoever **swears** by the sanctuary
　　23:21　**swears** by it and by the one
　　23:22　and whoever **swears** by heaven
　　23:22　**swears** by the throne of God
　　26:74　to curse, and he **swore** an oath
Mk　6:23　And he solemnly **swore** to her
　　14:71　to curse, and he **swore** an oath
Lk　1:73　the oath that he **swore** to our
Ac　2:30　that God had **sworn** with an oath
He　3:11　As in my anger I **swore**
　　3:18　And to whom did he **swear** that
　　4: 3　As in my anger I **swore**
　　6:13　one greater by whom to **swear**
　　6:13　to swear, he **swore** by himself
　　6:16　**swear** by someone greater than
　　7:21　The Lord has **sworn** and will not

Ja　5:12　my beloved, do not **swear**
Re　10: 6　**swore** by him who lives forever

3661　GO11 AG566 LN174 B3:908 K5:185
ὁμοθυμαδον, WITH ONE MIND
Ac　1:14　**together** with certain women
　　2:46　they spent much time **together**
　　4:24　raised their voices **together**
　　5:12　And they were all **together**
　　7:57　rushed **together** against him
　　8: 6　The crowds **with one accord**
　　12:20　they came to him **in a body**
　　15:25　we have decided **unanimously**
　　18:12　the Jews made a **united** attack
　　19:29　rushed **together** to the theater
Ro　15: 6　**together** you may with one voice

3663　GO2 AG566 LN174 B2:500 K5:938 R3664,3806
ὁμοιοπαθης, LIKE SUFFERING
Ac　14:15　We are **mortals** just like you
Ja　5:17　was a **human being** like us

3664　GO45 AG566 LN174 B2:500 K5:186
ὁμοιος, LIKE
Mt　11:16　It is **like** children sitting in
　　13:31　kingdom of heaven is **like** a
　　13:33　kingdom of heaven is **like** yeast
　　13:44　of heaven is **like** treasure
　　13:45　of heaven is **like** a merchant
　　13:47　kingdom of heaven is **like** a net
　　13:52　of heaven is **like** the master
　　20: 1　of heaven is **like** a landowner
　　22:39　And a second is **like** it
Lk　6:47　what someone is **like** who comes
　　6:48　That one is **like** a man building
　　6:49　and does not act is **like** a man
　　7:31　and what are they **like**
　　7:32　They are **like** children sitting
　　12:36　be **like** those who are waiting
　　13:18　What is the kingdom of God **like**
　　13:19　It is **like** a mustard seed
　　13:21　It is **like** yeast that a woman
Jn　8:55　I would be a liar **like** you
　　9: 9　but it is someone **like** him
Ac　17:29　that the deity is **like** gold
Ga　5:21　and things **like** these
1J　3: 2　revealed, we will be **like** him
Ju　1: 7　**Likewise,** Sodom and Gomorrah
Re　1:13　I saw one **like** the Son of Man
　　1:15　his feet were **like** burnished

	2:18	who has eyes **like** a flame
	4: 3	seated there looks **like** jasper
	4: 3	that looks **like** an emerald
	4: 6	something **like** a sea of glass
	4: 7	living creature **like** a lion
	4: 7	**like** an ox, the third living
	4: 7	with a face **like** a human face
	9: 7	the locusts were **like** horses
	9: 7	what looked **like** crowns of gold
	9:10	They have tails **like** scorpions
	9:19	their tails are **like** serpents
	11: 1	measuring **rod** like a staff
	13: 2	that I saw was **like** a leopard
	13: 4	Who is **like** the beast
	13:11	and it spoke **like** a dragon
	14:14	was one **like** the Son of Man
	18:18	city was **like** the great city
	21:11	radiance **like** a very rare jewel
	21:18	is pure gold, clear **as** glass

3665   ᴳᴼ2 ᴬᴳ567 ᴸᴺ174 ᴮ2:500 ᴷ5:189 ᴿ3664
ʽομοιοτης, LIKENESS

He	4:15	have one who in **every respect**
	7:15	arises, **resembling** Melchizedek

3666   ᴳᴼ15 ᴬᴳ567 ᴸᴺ174 ᴮ2:500 ᴷ5:188 ᴿ3664
ʽομοιοω, I LIKEN

Mt	6: 8	Do not **be like** them, for your
	7:24	**will be like** a wise man who
	7:26	**will be like** a foolish man who
	11:16	But to what **will I compare**
	13:24	**may be compared** to someone who
	18:23	**may be compared** to a king who
	22: 2	**may be compared** to a king who
	25: 1	of heaven **will be like** this
Mk	4:30	what can we **compare** the kingdom
Lk	7:31	**will I compare** the people
	13:18	to what **should I compare** it
	13:20	To what **should I compare**
Ac	14:11	down to us **in human form**
Ro	9:29	and **been made like** Gomorrah
He	2:17	he had **to become like** his

3667   ᴳᴼ6 ᴬᴳ567 ᴸᴺ174 ᴮ2:500 ᴷ5:191 ᴿ3666
ʽομοιωμα, LIKENESS

Ro	1:23	for images **resembling** a mortal
	5:14	**like** the transgression of Adam
	6: 5	with him in a death **like** his
	8: 3	in the **likeness** of sinful flesh

Ph	2: 7	being born in human **likeness**
Re	9: 7	faces were **like** human faces

3668   ᴳᴼ30 ᴬᴳ567 ᴸᴺ174 ᴮ2:500 ᴿ3664
ʽομοιως, LIKEWISE

Mt	22:26	The second did the **same**
	26:35	And **so** said all the disciples
	27:41	In the **same way** the chief
Mk	15:31	In the **same way** the chief
Lk	3:11	has food must do **likewise**
	5:10	**so** also were James and John
	5:33	**like** the disciples of the
	6:31	Do to others **as** you would have
	10:32	So **likewise** a Levite, when he
	10:37	to him, "Go and do **likewise**."
	13: 3	you will all perish **as** they did
	16:25	in **like** manner evil things
	17:28	**Likewise,** just as it was in the
	17:31	**likewise** anyone in the field
	22:36	take it, and **likewise** a bag
Jn	5:19	the Son does **likewise**
	6:11	**so** also the fish, as much as
	21:13	and did the **same** with the fish
Ro	1:27	in the **same way** also the men
1C	7: 3	**likewise** the wife to her
	7: 4	**likewise** the husband does not
	7:22	just **as** whoever was free when
He	9:21	in the **same way** he sprinkled
Ja	2:25	**Likewise,** was not Rahab the
1P	3: 1	Wives, in the **same way,** accept
	3: 7	Husbands, in the **same way,** show
	5: 5	In the **same way,** you who are
Ju	1: 8	in the **same way** these dreamers
Re	2:15	So you **also** have some who hold
	8:12	shining, and **likewise** the night

3669   ᴳᴼ1 ᴬᴳ568 ᴸᴺ175 ᴮ2:500 ᴷ5:190 ᴿ3666
ʽομοιωσις, LIKENESS

Ja	3: 9	are made in the **likeness** of God

3670   ᴳᴼ26 ᴬᴳ568 ᴸᴺ175 ᴮ1:344 ᴷ5:199 ᴿ3674,3056
ʽομολογεω, I CONFESS

Mt	7:23	Then I **will declare** to them
	10:32	therefore who **acknowledges** me
	10:32	**acknowledge** before my Father
	14: 7	he **promised** on oath to grant
Lk	12: 8	everyone who **acknowledges** me
	12: 8	also will **acknowledge** before
Jn	1:20	He **confessed** and did not deny
	1:20	not deny it, but **confessed**

	9:22	that anyone who **confessed** Jesus
	12:42	Pharisees they did not **confess**
Ac	7:17	that God **had made** to Abraham
	23: 8	but the Pharisees **acknowledge**
	24:14	But this I **admit** to you
Ro	10: 9	if you **confess** with your lips
	10:10	one **confesses** with the mouth
1Ti	6:12	you **made** the good confession
Ti	1:16	They **profess** to know God
He	11:13	They **confessed** that they were
	13:15	the fruit of lips that **confess**
1J	1: 9	If we **confess** our sins, he who
	2:23	everyone who **confesses** the Son
	4: 2	**confesses** that Jesus Christ
	4: 3	that does not **confess** Jesus
	4:15	abides in those who **confess**
2J	1: 7	not **confess** that Jesus Christ
Re	3: 5	I **will confess** your name before

3671   GO6 AG568 LN175 B1:344 K5:199 R3670
ὁμολογια, CONFESSION

2C	9:13	to the **confession** of the gospel
1Ti	6:12	you made the good **confession**
	6:13	Pilate made the good **confession**
He	3: 1	high priest of our **confession**
	4:14	hold fast to our **confession**
	10:23	to the **confession** of our hope

3672   GO1 AG569 LN175 K5:199 R3670
ὁμολογουμενως, CONFESSIONALLY

1Ti	3:16	**Without any doubt,** the mystery

3673   GO1 AG569 LN175 R3674,5078
ὁμοτεχνος, SAME CRAFT

Ac	18: 3	he was of the **same trade**

3674   GO4 AG569 LN175
ὁμου, SAME

Jn	4:36	reaper may rejoice **together**
	20: 4	The two were running **together**
	21: 2	Gathered there **together** were
Ac	2: 1	were all **together** in one place

3675   GO1 AG569 LN175 R3674,5424
ὁμοθρων, SAME THINKING

1P	3: 8	of you, have **unity of spirit**

3676   GO3 AG569 LN175 R3674
ὁμως, LIKEWISE

Jn	12:42	**Nevertheless** many, even of the

1C	14: 7	**is the same way** with lifeless
Ga	3:15	**once** a person's will has been

3677   GO6 AG569 LN175 B1:511 K5:220
οναρ, DREAM

Mt	1:20	appeared to him in a **dream**
	2:12	having been warned in a **dream**
	2:13	appeared to Joseph in a **dream**
	2:19	suddenly appeared in a **dream**
	2:22	after being warned in a **dream**
	27:19	because of a **dream** about him

3678   GO1 AG570 LN175 K5:283 R3688
οναριον, SMALL DONKEY

Jn	12:14	Jesus found a **young donkey**

3679   GO9 AG570 LN175 K5:239 R3681
ονειδιζω, I REVILE

Mt	5:11	are you when people **revile** you
	11:20	he began to **reproach** the cities
	27:44	**taunted** him in the same way
Mk	15:32	with him also **taunted** him
	16:14	**upbraided** them for their lack
Lk	6:22	**revile** you, and defame you
Ro	15: 3	The insults of those who **insult**
Ja	1: 5	all generously and **ungrudgingly**
1P	4:14	you **are reviled** for the name

3680   GO5 AG570 LN175 K5:241 R3679
ονειδισμος, REVILING

Ro	15: 3	The **insults** of those who insult
1Ti	3: 7	he may not fall into **disgrace**
He	10:33	being publicly exposed to **abuse**
	11:26	He considered **abuse** suffered
	13:13	and bear the **abuse** he endured

3681   GO1 AG570 LN175 K5:238
ονειδος, REPROACH

Lk	1:25	the **disgrace** I have endured

3682   GO2 AG570 LN175
ονησιμος, ONESIMUS

Co	4: 9	he is coming with **Onesimus**
Pm	1:10	to you for my child, **Onesimus**

3683   GO2 AG570 LN175
ονησιφορος, ONESIPHORUS

2Ti	1:16	the household of **Onesiphorus**
	4:19	the household of **Onesiphorus**

3684   GO2 AG570 LN175 R3688
ονικος, [POWERED BY] DONKEY (MILLSTONE)
Mt 18: 6   great **millstone** were fastened
Mk   9:42   great **millstone** were hung

3685   GO1 AG570 LN175
ονινημι, I BENEFIT
Pm   1:20   let me **have** this **benefit** from

3686   GO230 AG570 LN175 B2:648 K5:242
ονομα, NAME
Mt   1:21   and you are to **name** him Jesus
      1:23   they shall **name** him Emmanuel
      1:25   and he **named** him Jesus
      6: 9   heaven, hallowed be your **name**
      7:22   we not prophesy in your **name**
      7:22   cast out demons in your **name**
      7:22   deeds of power in your **name**
     10: 2   **names** of the twelve apostles
     10:22   hated by all because of my **name**
     10:41   welcomes a prophet in the **name**
     10:41   a righteous person in the **name**
     10:42   ones in the **name** of a disciple
     12:21   And in his **name** the Gentiles
     18: 5   one such child in my **name**
     18:20   three are gathered in my **name**
     19:29   or fields, for my **name's** sake
     21: 9   comes in the **name** of the Lord
     23:39   the one who comes in the **name**
     24: 5   For many will come in my **name**
     24: 9   all nations because of my **name**
     27:32   a man from Cyrene **named** Simon
     28:19   them in the **name** of the Father
Mk   3:16   to whom he gave the **name** Peter
      3:17   he gave the **name** Boanerges
      5: 9   What is your **name?**
      5: 9   My **name** is Legion; for we
      5:22   of the synagogue **named** Jairus
      6:14   Jesus' **name** had become known
      9:37   one such child in my **name**
      9:38   casting out demons in your **name**
      9:39   does a deed of power in my **name**
      9:41   you bear the **name** of Christ
     11: 9   comes in the **name** of the Lord
     13: 6   Many will come in my **name**
     13:13   hated by all because of my **name.**
     14:32   to a place **called** Gethsemane
     16:17   by using my **name** they will cast
Lk   1: 5   was a priest **named** Zechariah
      1: 5   and her **name** was Elizabeth

      1:13   and you will **name** him John
      1:26   town in Galilee **called** Nazareth
      1:27   a man whose **name** was Joseph
      1:27   The virgin's **name** was Mary
      1:31   and you will **name** him Jesus
      1:49   for me, and holy is his **name**
      1:59   going to **name** him Zechariah
      1:61   your relatives has this **name**
      1:63   His **name** is John
      2:21   the **name** given by the angel
      2:25   a man in Jerusalem whose **name**
      5:27   saw a tax collector **named** Levi
      6:22   revile you, and **defame** you
      8:30   What is your **name?**
      8:41   there came a man **named** Jairus
      9:48   welcomes this child in my **name**
      9:49   casting out demons in your **name**
     10:17   in your **name** even the demons
     10:20   but rejoice that your **names**
     10:38   where a woman **named** Martha
     11: 2   Father, hallowed be your **name**
     13:35   comes in the **name** of the Lord
     16:20   a poor man **named** Lazarus
     19: 2   man was there **named** Zacchaeus
     19:38   comes in the **name** of the Lord
     21: 8   for many will come in my **name**
     21:12   governors because of my **name**
     21:17   hated by all because of my **name**
     23:50   and righteous man **named** Joseph
     24:13   to a village **called** Emmaus
     24:18   whose **name** was Cleopas
     24:47   in his **name** to all nations
Jn   1: 6   from God, whose **name** was John
      1:12   who believed in his **name**
      2:23   many believed in his **name**
      3: 1   was a Pharisee **named** Nicodemus
      3:18   have not believed in the **name**
      5:43   have come in my Father's **name**
      5:43   another comes in his own **name**
     10: 3   calls his own sheep by **name**
     10:25   that I do in my Father's **name**
     12:13   comes in the **name** of the Lord
     12:28   Father, glorify your **name**
     14:13   whatever you ask in my **name**
     14:14   If in my **name** you ask me for
     14:26   the Father will send in my **name**
     15:16   whatever you ask him in my **name**
     15:21   to you on account of my **name**
     16:23   of the Father in my **name**

	16:24	asked for anything in my **name**		16: 1	was a disciple **named** Timothy
	16:26	day you will ask in my **name**		16:14	A certain woman **named** Lydia
	17: 6	I have made your **name** known to		16:18	order you in the **name** of Jesus
	17:11	protect them in your **name**		17:34	and a woman **named** Damaris
	17:12	protected them in your **name**		18: 2	he found a Jew **named** Aquila
	17:26	I made your **name** known to them		18: 7	of a man **named** Titius Justus
	18:10	The slave's **name** was Malchus		18:15	questions about words and **names**
	20:31	you may have life in his **name**		18:24	to Ephesus a Jew **named** Apollos
Ac	1:15	the crowd **numbered** about one		19: 5	in the **name** of the Lord Jesus
	2:21	everyone who calls on the **name**		19:13	use the **name** of the Lord Jesus
	2:38	in the **name** of Jesus Christ		19:17	and the **name** of the Lord Jesus
	3: 6	in the **name** of Jesus Christ		19:24	A man **named** Demetrius
	3:16	And by faith in his **name**		20: 9	A young man **named** Eutychus
	3:16	his **name** itself has made this		21:10	a prophet **named** Agabus came
	4: 7	or by what **name** did you do this		21:13	for the **name** of the Lord Jesus
	4:10	by the **name** of Jesus Christ		22:16	away, calling on his **name**
	4:12	for there is no other **name**		26: 9	many things against the **name**
	4:17	no more to anyone in this **name**		27: 1	Augustan Cohort, **named** Julius
	4:18	at all in the **name** of Jesus		28: 7	of the island, **named** Publius
	4:30	through the **name** of your holy	Ro	1: 5	for the sake of his **name**
	5: 1	But a man **named** Ananias		2:24	The **name** of God is blasphemed
	5:28	not to teach in this **name**		9:17	that my **name** may be proclaimed
	5:34	in the council **named** Gamaliel		10:13	Everyone who calls on the **name**
	5:40	to speak in the **name** of Jesus		15: 9	and sing praises to your **name**
	5:41	for the sake of the **name**	1C	1: 2	call on the **name** of our Lord
	8: 9	Now a certain man **named** Simon		1:10	by the **name** of our Lord Jesus
	8:12	and the **name** of Jesus Christ		1:13	baptized in the **name** of Paul
	8:16	in the **name** of the Lord Jesus		1:15	you were baptized in my **name**
	9:10	in Damascus **named** Ananias		5: 4	in the **name** of the Lord Jesus
	9:11	for a man of Tarsus **named** Saul		6:11	in the **name** of the Lord Jesus
	9:12	a vision a man **named** Ananias	Ep	1:21	above every name that is **named**
	9:14	bind all who invoke your **name**		5:20	in the **name** of our Lord Jesus
	9:15	I have chosen to bring my **name**	Ph	2: 9	gave him the **name** that is above
	9:16	for the sake of my **name**		2: 9	name that is above every **name**
	9:21	those who invoked this **name**		2:10	so that at the **name** of Jesus
	9:27	boldly in the **name** of Jesus		4: 3	whose **names** are in the book
	9:28	speaking boldly in the **name**	Co	3:17	in the **name** of the Lord Jesus
	9:33	he found a man **named** Aeneas	2Th	1:12	so that the **name** of our Lord
	9:36	whose **name** was Tabitha		3: 6	in the **name** of our Lord Jesus
	10: 1	there was a man **named** Cornelius	1Ti	6: 1	so that the **name** of God and the
	10:43	of sins through his **name**	2Ti	2:19	everyone who calls on the **name**
	10:48	baptized in the **name** of Jesus	He	1: 4	the **name** he has inherited
	11:28	One of them **named** Agabus stood		2:12	I will proclaim your **name** to my
	12:13	maid **named** Rhoda came to		6:10	that you showed for his **sake**
		answer		13:15	of lips that confess his **name**
	13: 6	false prophet, **named** Bar-Jesus	Ja	2: 7	blaspheme the excellent **name**
	13: 8	is the translation of his **name**		5:10	prophets who spoke in the **name**
	15:14	them a people for his **name**		5:14	oil in the **name** of the Lord
	15:17	whom my **name** has been called	1P	4:14	reviled for the **name** of Christ
	15:26	for the **sake** of our Lord Jesus			

	4:16	God because you bear this **name**
1J	2:12	forgiven on account of his **name**
	3:23	in the **name** of his Son Jesus
	5:13	in the **name** of the Son of God
3J	1: 7	journey for the **sake** of Christ
	1:15	friends there, each by **name**
Re	2: 3	up for the sake of my **name**
	2:13	are holding fast to my **name**
	2:17	stone is written a new **name**
	3: 1	you have a **name** of being alive
	3: 4	you have still a few **persons**
	3: 5	not blot your **name** out of the
	3: 5	I will confess your **name** before
	3: 8	and have not denied my **name**
	3:12	the **name** of the city of my God
	3:12	I will write on you the **name**
	3:12	the **name** of the city of my God
	6: 8	Its rider's **name** was Death
	8:11	**name** of the star is Wormwood
	9:11	his **name** in Hebrew is Abaddon
	9:11	in Greek he is **called** Apollyon
	11:13	thousand **people** were killed
	11:18	and all who fear your **name**
	13: 1	heads were blasphemous **names**
	13: 6	God, blaspheming his **name**
	13: 8	whose **name** has not been written
	13:17	the **name** of the beast or the
	13:17	beast or the number of its **name**
	14: 1	had his **name** and his Father's
	14: 1	name and his Father's **name**
	14:11	receives the mark of its **name**
	15: 2	and the number of its **name**
	15: 4	not fear and glorify your **name**
	16: 9	they cursed the **name** of God
	17: 3	was full of blasphemous **names**
	17: 5	her forehead was written a **name**
	17: 8	**names** have not been written
	19:12	and he has a **name** inscribed
	19:13	and his **name** is called The Word
	19:16	on his thigh he has a **name**
	21:12	gates are inscribed the **names**
	21:12	**names** of the twelve tribes of
	21:14	on them are the twelve **names**
	22: 4	and his **name** will be on their

3687 GO10 AG573 LN175 B2:648 K5:282 R3686
ονομαζω, I NAME

Mk	3:14	whom he also **named** apostles
Lk	6:13	whom he also **named** apostles

	6:14	Simon, whom he **named** Peter,
Ac	19:13	to **use** the **name** of the Lord
Ro	15:20	Christ has already **been named**
1C	5:11	with anyone who **bears** the **name**
Ep	1:21	above every name that **is named**
	3:15	and on earth **takes** its **name**
	5: 3	not even **be mentioned** among you
2Ti	2:19	**calls on** the name of the Lord

3688 GO5 AG574 LN175 K5:283
ονος, DONKEY

Mt	21: 2	you will find a **donkey** tied
	21: 5	humble, and mounted on a **donkey**
	21: 7	they brought the **donkey** and the
Lk	13:15	untie his ox or his **donkey**
Jn	12:15	sitting on a **donkey's** colt

3689 GO10 AG574 LN175
οντως, REALLY

Mk	11:32	John as **truly** a prophet
Lk	23:47	**Certainly** this man was innocent
	24:34	The Lord has risen **indeed**
Jn	8:36	you will be free **indeed**
1C	14:25	God is **really** among you.
Ga	3:21	righteousness would **indeed** come
1Ti	5: 5	The **real** widow, left alone
	5:16	those who are **real** widows
	6:19	of the life that **really** is life

3690 GO6 AG574 LN176 K5:288
οξος, SOUR WINE

Mt	27:48	filled it with **sour wine**
Mk	15:36	filled a sponge with **sour wine**
Lk	23:36	and offering him **sour wine**
Jn	19:29	A jar full of **sour wine** was
	19:29	**wine** on a branch of hyssop
	19:30	Jesus had received the **wine**

3691 GO8 AG574 LN176
οξυς, SHARP

Ro	3:15	Their feet are **swift** to shed
Re	1:16	came a **sharp,** two-edged sword
	2:12	has the **sharp** two-edged sword
	14:14	a **sharp** sickle in his hand
	14:17	he too had a **sharp** sickle
	14:18	him who had the **sharp** sickle
	14:18	to him who had the **sharp** sickle
	19:15	his mouth comes a **sharp** sword

3692 ᴳᴼ2 ᴬᴳ574 ᴸᴺ176
οπη, HOLE

| He | 11:38 | caves and **holes** in the ground |
| Ja | 3:11 | forth from the same **opening** |

3693 ᴳᴼ7 ᴬᴳ574 ᴸᴺ176 ᴮ1:492 ᴷ5:289
οπισθεν, FROM BEHIND

Mt	9:20	for twelve years came up **behind**
	15:23	she keeps shouting **after** us
Mk	5:27	came up **behind** him in the crowd
Lk	8:44	came up **behind** him and touched
	23:26	made him carry it **behind** Jesus
Re	4: 6	of eyes in front and **behind**
	5: 1	the inside and **on the back**

3694 ᴳᴼ35 ᴬᴳ575 ᴸᴺ177 ᴮ1:492 ᴷ5:289
οπισω, AFTER

Mt	3:11	than I is coming **after** me
	4:19	**Follow** me, and I will make you
	10:38	take up the cross and **follow** me
	16:23	Get **behind** me, Satan! You are
	16:24	any want to become my **followers**
	24:18	the field must not turn **back**
Mk	1: 7	than I is coming **after** me
	1:17	**Follow** me and I will make you
	1:20	hired men, and **followed** him
	8:33	Get **behind** me, Satan! For you
	8:34	any want to become my **followers**
	13:16	in the field must not turn **back**
Lk	7:38	stood **behind** him at his feet
	9:23	any want to become my **followers**
	9:62	to the plow and looks **back**
	14:27	carry the cross and **follow** me
	17:31	in the field must not turn **back**
	19:14	and sent a delegation **after** him
	21: 8	Do not go **after** them.
Jn	1:15	He who comes **after** me ranks
	1:27	the one who is coming **after** me
	1:30	**After** me comes a man who ranks
	6:66	turned **back** and no longer went
	12:19	the world has gone **after** him
	18: 6	they stepped **back** and fell
	20:14	she turned **around** and saw Jesus
Ac	5:37	and got people to **follow** him
	20:30	the disciples to **follow** them
Ph	3:13	forgetting what lies **behind**
1Ti	5:15	turned away **to follow** Satan
2P	2:10	those who **indulge** their flesh
Ju	1: 7	and **pursued** unnatural lust
Re	1:10	I heard **behind** me a loud voice

| | 12:15 | like a river **after** the woman |
| | 13: 3 | whole earth **followed** the beast |

3695 ᴳᴼ1 ᴬᴳ575 ᴸᴺ176 ᴮ3:959 ᴷ5:294 ᴿ3696
οπλιζω, I ARM

| 1P | 4: 1 | **arm yourselves** also with the |

3696 ᴳᴼ6 ᴬᴳ575 ᴸᴺ176 ᴮ3:959 ᴷ5:292
οπλον, WEAPON

Jn	18: 3	and torches and **weapons**
Ro	6:13	members to sin as **instruments**
	6:13	**instruments** of righteousness
	13:12	and put on the **armor** of light
2C	6: 7	**weapons** of righteousness
	10: 4	the **weapons** of our warfare

3697 ᴳᴼ5 ᴬᴳ575 ᴸᴺ176
οποιος, OF WHAT SORT

Ac	26:29	today might become **such** as I am
1C	3:13	will test **what sort** of work
Ga	2: 6	what they **actually** were makes
1Th	1: 9	**what kind** of welcome we had
Ja	1:24	forget **what** they were like

3699 ᴳᴼ82 ᴬᴳ576 ᴸᴺ176
οπου, WHERE

Mt	6:19	**where** moth and rust consume
	6:19	**where** thieves break in and
	6:20	**where** neither moth nor rust
	6:20	**where** thieves do not break in
	6:21	For **where** your treasure is
	8:19	I will follow you **wherever**
	13: 5	**where** they did not have much
	24:28	**Wherever** the corpse is
	25:24	reaping **where** you did not sow
	25:26	I reap **where** I did not sow,
	26:13	**wherever** this good news is
	26:57	**in whose house** the scribes
	28: 6	see the place **where** he lay
Mk	2: 4	they removed the roof **above** him
	2: 4	mat on **which** the paralytic lay.
	4: 5	**where** it did not have much soil
	4:15	**where** the word is sown
	5:40	went in **where** the child was
	6:10	**Wherever** you enter a house
	6:55	**wherever** they heard he was
	6:56	And **wherever** he went
	9:18	and **whenever** it seizes him
	9:48	**where** their worm never dies
	13:14	set up **where** it ought to be

	14: 9	**wherever** the good news is
	14:14	and **wherever** he enters, say to
	14:14	**Where** is my guest room where
	16: 6	**there** is the place they laid
Lk	9:57	I will follow you **wherever**
	12:33	**where** no thief comes near
	12:34	For **where** your treasure is
	17:37	**Where** the corpse is, there the
	22:11	**Where** is the guest room
Jn	1:28	**where** John was baptizing
	3: 8	wind blows **where** it chooses
	4:20	place **where** people must worship
	4:46	**where** he had changed the water
	6:23	**where** they had eaten the bread
	6:62	to **where** he was before
	7:34	and **where** I am, you cannot come
	7:36	**Where** I am, you cannot come
	7:42	the village **where** David lived
	8:21	**Where** I am going, you cannot
	8:22	**Where** I am going, you cannot
	10:40	**where** John had been baptizing
	11:30	place **where** Martha had met him
	11:32	When Mary came **where** Jesus was
	12: 1	Bethany, the **home** of Lazarus
	12:26	**where** I am, there will my
	13:33	**Where** I am going, you cannot
	13:36	**Where** I am going, you cannot
	14: 3	so that **where** I am, there you
	14: 4	to the place **where** I am going
	17:24	may be with me **where** I am
	18: 1	**where** there was a garden
	18:20	**where** all the Jews come
	19:18	**There** they crucified him
	19:20	place **where** Jesus was crucified
	19:41	place **where** he was crucified
	20:12	sitting **where** the body of
	20:19	**where** the disciples had met
	21:18	and to go **wherever** you wished
	21:18	take you **where** you do not wish
Ac	17: 1	**where** there was a synagogue
	20: 6	**where** we stayed for seven days
Ro	15:20	**where** Christ has already been
1C	3: 3	as long as **there** is jealousy
Co	3:11	that renewal **there** is no longer
He	6:20	**where** Jesus, a forerunner
	9:16	**Where** a will is involved
	10:18	**Where** there is forgiveness
Ja	3: 4	**wherever** the will of the pilot
	3:16	For **where** there is envy

2P	2:11	**whereas** angels, though greater
Re	2:13	I know **where** you are living
	2:13	**where** Satan's throne is
	11: 8	**where** also their Lord was
	12: 6	**where** she has a place prepared
	12:14	**where** she is nourished for a
	14: 4	follow the Lamb **wherever** he
	17: 9	mountains **on which** the woman
	20:10	**where** the beast and the false

3700   GO1 AG576 LN176 B3:516 K5:315
οπτανομαι, I SEE
Ac   1: 3   **appearing** to them during forty

3701   GO4 AG576 LN176 B3:511 K5:372 R3700
οπτασια, VISION
Lk   1:22   he had seen a **vision** in the
| 24:23   seen a **vision** of angels who
Ac   26:19   the heavenly **vision,**
2C   12: 1   I will go on to **visions** and

3702   GO1 AG576 LN176
οπτος, GRILLED
Lk   24:42   him a piece of **broiled** fish

3703   GO1 AG576 LN176
οπωρα, FRUIT
Re   18:14   The **fruit** for which your soul

3704   GO53 AG576 LN176
'οπως, SO THAT
Mt   2: 8   bring me word **so that** I may
| 2:23   **so that** what had been spoken
| 5:16   **so that** they may see your good
| 5:45   **so that** you may be children
| 6: 2   **so that** they may be praised
| 6: 4   **so that** your alms may be done
| 6: 5   **so that** they may be seen .
| 6:16   **so as** to show others that they
| 6:18   **so that** your fasting may be
| 8:17   **This was** to fulfill what had
| 8:34   and **when** they saw him
| 9:38   **to** send out laborers into his
| 12:14   against him, **how to** destroy him
| 13:35   **This was** to fulfill what had
| 22:15   went and plotted **to** entrap him
| 23:35   **so that** upon you may come all
| 26:59   **so that** they might put him to
Mk   3: 6   against him, **how** to destroy him
Lk   2:35   **so that** the inner thoughts of

	7: 3	asking him **to** come and heal
	10: 2	Lord of the harvest **to** send out
	11:37	invited him **to** dine with him
	16:26	**so that** those who might want
	16:28	**so that** they will not also come
	24:20	and **how** our chief priests and
Jn	11:57	**so that** they might arrest him
Ac	3:20	**so that** times of refreshing
	8:15	prayed for them **that** they might
	8:24	**that** nothing of what you have
	9: 2	**so that** if he found any who
	9:12	lay his hands on him **so that**
	9:17	sent me **so that** you may regain
	9:24	**so that** they might kill him
	15:17	**so that** all other peoples
	20:16	**so that** he might not have
	23:15	on the pretext **that** you want
	23:20	agreed to ask you **to** bring
	23:23	**for** Caesarea with two hundred
	25: 3	**to** have him transferred to
	25:26	**so that,** after we have
Ro	3: 4	**So that** you may be justified
	9:17	**for the very purpose** of showing
	9:17	**so that** my name may be
1C	1:29	**so that** no one might boast
2C	8:11	**so that** your eagerness may be
	8:14	**so that** their abundance may be
Ga	1: 4	for our sins **to** set us free
2Th	1:12	**so that** the name of our Lord
Pm	1: 6	I pray **that** the sharing of your
He	2: 9	**so that** by the grace of God
	9:15	**so that** those who are called
Ja	5:16	**so that** you may be healed
1P	2: 9	**in order that** you may proclaim

3705   GO12 AG577 LN176 B3:511 K5:371 R3708
῾οραμα, SIGHT

Mt	17: 9	Tell no one about the **vision**
Ac	7:31	he was amazed at the **sight**
	9:10	Lord said to him in a **vision**
	9:12	and he has seen in a **vision**
	10: 3	he had a **vision** in which he
	10:17	what to make of the **vision**
	10:19	still thinking about the **vision**
	11: 5	and in a trance I saw a **vision**
	12: 9	thought he was seeing a **vision**
	16: 9	the night Paul had a **vision**
	16:10	When he had seen the **vision**
	18: 9	Lord said to Paul in a **vision**

3706   GO4 AG577 LN176 B3:512 K5:370 R3708
῾ορασις, SIGHT

Ac	2:17	young men shall see **visions**
Re	4: 3	seated there **looks** like jasper
	4: 3	that **looks** like an emerald
	9:17	I saw the horses in my **vision**

3707   GO1 AG577 LN176 B3:511 K5:368 R3708
῾ορατος, SEEN

Co	1:16	things **visible** and invisible

3708   GO449 AG577 LN176 B3:511 K5:315
῾οραω, I SEE

Mt	2: 2	For we **observed** his star at its
	2: 9	they **had seen** at its rising
	2:10	When they **saw** that the star
	2:11	they **saw** the child with Mary
	2:16	When Herod **saw** that he had been
	3: 7	But when he **saw** many Pharisees
	3:16	and he **saw** the Spirit of God
	4:16	who sat in darkness **have seen**
	4:18	he **saw** two brothers, Simon
	4:21	he **saw** two other brothers
	5: 1	When Jesus **saw** the crowds
	5: 8	for they **will see** God
	5:16	so that they may **see** your good
	8: 4	**See** that you say nothing to
	8:14	he **saw** his mother-in-law lying
	8:18	Now when Jesus **saw** great crowds
	8:34	and when they **saw** him
	9: 2	When Jesus **saw** their faith
	9: 4	**perceiving** their thoughts
	9: 8	When the crowds **saw** it
	9: 9	he **saw** a man called Matthew
	9:11	When the Pharisees **saw** this
	9:22	and **seeing** her he said
	9:23	and **saw** the flute players
	9:30	**See** that no one knows of this
	9:36	When he **saw** the crowds
	11: 8	then did you go out to **see**
	11: 9	then did you go out to **see?**
	12: 2	When the Pharisees **saw** it
	12:38	we wish to **see** a sign from you
	13:14	indeed look, but never **perceive**
	13:15	might not **look** with their eyes
	13:17	longed to **see** what you see
	13:17	you see, but did not **see** it
	14:14	he **saw** a great crowd
	14:26	the disciples **saw** him walking
	16: 6	Jesus said to them, **"Watch** out

16:28	taste death before they **see**	
17: 3	Suddenly there **appeared** to them	
17: 8	they **saw** no one except Jesus	
18:10	their angels continually **see**	
18:31	slaves **saw** what had happened	
20: 3	he **saw** others standing idle	
21:15	priests and the scribes **saw**	
21:19	And **seeing** a fig tree by the	
21:20	When the disciples **saw** it	
21:32	and even after you **saw** it	
21:38	when the tenants **saw** the son	
22:11	king came in to **see** the guests	
23:39	you will not **see** me again	
24: 6	**see** that you are not alarmed	
24:15	So when you **see** the desolating	
24:30	they **will see** 'the Son of	
24:33	when you **see** all these things	
25:37	that we **saw** you hungry and gave	
25:38	that we **saw** you a stranger	
25:39	that we **saw** you sick or in	
25:44	we **saw** you hungry or thirsty	
26: 8	But when the disciples **saw** it	
26:58	in order to **see** how this would	
26:64	you **will see** the Son of Man	
26:71	another servant-girl **saw** him	
27: 3	**saw** that Jesus was condemned	
27: 4	**See** to it yourself	
27:24	Pilate **saw** that he could do	
27:24	**see** to it yourselves	
27:49	let us **see** whether Elijah	
27:54	over Jesus, **saw** the earthquake	
28: 6	**see** the place where he lay	
28: 7	there you **will see** him	
28:10	there they **will see** me	
28:17	When they **saw** him	
Mk 1:10	he **saw** the heavens torn apart	
1:16	he **saw** Simon and his brother	
1:19	he **saw** James son of Zebedee	
1:44	**See** that you say nothing to	
2: 5	When Jesus **saw** their faith	
2:12	We **have** never **seen** anything	
2:14	he **saw** Levi son of Alphaeus	
2:16	scribes of the Pharisees **saw**	
4:12	indeed look, but not **perceive**	
5: 6	he **saw** Jesus from a distance	
5:14	Then people came to **see** what	
5:16	Those who **had seen** what had	
5:22	he **saw** him, fell at his feet	
5:32	He looked all around to **see**	

6:33	Now many **saw** them going and	
6:34	he **saw** a great crowd	
6:38	loaves have you? Go and **see**	
6:48	When he **saw** that they were	
6:49	But when they **saw** him walking	
6:50	for they all **saw** him and were	
7: 2	they **noticed** that some of his	
8:15	**Watch** out—beware of the	
8:24	but they **look** like trees	
8:33	But turning and **looking** at his	
9: 1	until they **see** that the kingdom	
9: 4	And there **appeared** to them	
9: 8	they **saw** no one with them	
9: 9	no one about what they **had seen**	
9:14	they **saw** a great crowd around	
9:15	When the whole crowd **saw** him	
9:20	When the spirit **saw** him	
9:25	When Jesus **saw** that a crowd	
9:38	**saw** someone casting out demons	
10:14	But when Jesus **saw** this	
11:13	**Seeing** in the distance a fig	
11:20	they **saw** the fig tree withered	
12:15	a denarius and let me **see** it	
12:28	**seeing** that he answered them	
12:34	When Jesus **saw** that he answered	
13:14	when you **see** the desolating	
13:26	Then they **will see**	
13:29	when you **see** these things	
14:62	**will see** the Son of Man seated	
14:67	she **saw** Peter warming himself	
14:69	servant-girl, on **seeing** him	
15:32	that we may **see** and believe	
15:36	Wait, **let** us **see** whether Elijah	
15:39	**saw** that in this way he	
16: 5	they **saw** a young man	
16: 7	there you **will see** him	
Lk 1:11	**appeared** to him an angel of the	
1:12	When Zechariah **saw** him	
1:22	that he **had seen** a vision	
2:15	**see** this thing that has taken	
2:17	When they **saw** this	
2:20	all they had heard and **seen**	
2:26	that he would not **see** death	
2:26	see death before he **had seen**	
2:30	eyes **have seen** your salvation	
2:48	When his parents **saw** him	
3: 6	and all flesh **shall see**	
5: 2	he **saw** two boats there at the	
5: 8	But when Simon Peter **saw** it	

5:12	When he **saw** Jesus, he bowed
5:20	When he **saw** their faith
5:26	We **have seen** strange things
7:13	When the Lord **saw** her
7:22	what you **have seen** and heard
7:25	What then did you go out to **see**
7:26	What then did you go out to **see**
7:39	who had invited him **saw** it
8:20	outside, wanting to **see** you
8:28	When he **saw** Jesus,
8:34	When the swineherds **saw** what
8:35	Then people came out to **see**
8:36	Those who **had seen** it told them
8:47	When the woman **saw** that she
9: 9	And he tried to **see** him
9:27	before they **see** the kingdom
9:31	They **appeared** in glory
9:32	they **saw** his glory and the two
9:36	any of the things they **had seen**
9:49	**saw** someone casting out demons
9:54	disciples James and John **saw** it
10:24	desired to **see** what you see
10:24	you see, but did not **see** it
10:31	that road; and when he **saw** him
10:32	the place and **saw** him
10:33	near him; and when he **saw** him
11:38	The Pharisee was amazed to **see**
12:15	**Take care!** Be on your guard
12:54	When you **see** a cloud rising
13:12	When Jesus **saw** her
13:28	when you **see** Abraham and Isaac
13:35	you **will** not **see** me until the
14:18	I must go out and **see** it
15:20	father **saw** him and was filled
16:23	he **looked** up and saw Abraham
17:14	When he **saw** them, he said to
17:15	when he **saw** that he was healed
17:22	when you will long to **see** one
17:22	and you **will** not **see** it
18:15	and when the disciples **saw** it
18:24	Jesus **looked** at him and said
18:43	the people, when they **saw** it
19: 3	was trying to **see** who Jesus was
19: 4	climbed a sycamore tree to **see**
19: 7	All who **saw** it began to grumble
19:37	of power that they **had seen**
19:41	he came near and **saw** the city
20:14	But when the tenants **saw** him
21: 1	looked up and **saw** rich people

	21: 2	he also **saw** a poor widow put in
	21:20	you **see** Jerusalem surrounded
	21:27	they **will see** 'the Son of Man
	21:29	**Look** at the fig tree and all
	21:31	when you **see** these things
	22:43	an angel from heaven **appeared**
	22:49	those who were around him **saw**
	22:56	**seeing** him in the firelight
	22:58	someone else, on **seeing** him
	23: 8	When Herod **saw** Jesus
	23: 8	he had been wanting to **see** him
	23: 8	was hoping to **see** him perform
	23:47	When the centurion **saw** what
	23:49	**watching** these things
	24:23	that they **had** indeed **seen**
	24:24	but they did not **see** him
	24:34	and he **has appeared** to Simon
	24:39	**Look** at my hands and my feet
	24:39	Touch me and **see**
Jn	1:18	No one **has** ever **seen** God
	1:33	He on whom you **see** the Spirit
	1:34	**have seen** and have testified
	1:39	He said to them, "Come and **see**
	1:39	They came and **saw** where he was
	1:47	Jesus **saw** Nathanael coming
	1:48	I **saw** you under the fig tree
	1:50	I told you that I **saw** you
	1:50	You **will see** greater things
	1:51	you **will see** heaven opened
	3: 3	no one can **see** the kingdom
	3:11	testify to what we **have seen**
	3:32	testifies to what he **has seen**
	3:36	the Son **will** not **see** life
	4:29	Come and **see** a man who told me
	4:45	since they **had seen** all that
	4:48	you **see** signs and wonders
	5: 6	When Jesus **saw** him lying there
	5:37	his voice or **seen** his form
	6:14	When the people **saw** the sign
	6:22	**saw** that there had been only
	6:24	the crowd **saw** that neither
	6:26	not because you **saw** signs
	6:30	so that we **may see** it and
	6:36	that you **have seen** me
	6:46	anyone **has seen** the Father
	6:46	he **has seen** the Father
	8:38	I declare what I **have seen**
	8:56	that he would **see** my day
	8:56	he **saw** it and was glad

8:57	and **have** you **seen** Abraham	7:35	the angel who **appeared** to him
9: 1	he **saw** a man blind from birth	7:44	to the pattern he **had seen**
9:37	You **have seen** him	7:55	**saw** the glory of God and Jesus
11:31	**saw** Mary get up quickly and go	8:18	when Simon **saw** that the Spirit
11:32	where Jesus was and **saw** him	8:23	I **see** that you are in the gall
11:33	When Jesus **saw** her weeping	8:39	the eunuch **saw** him no more
11:40	you would **see** the glory of God	9:12	and he **has seen** in a vision
12: 9	but also to **see** Lazarus	9:17	who **appeared** to you on your way
12:21	Sir, we wish to **see** Jesus.	9:27	he **had seen** the Lord
12:40	they might not **look** with their	9:35	**saw** him and turned to the Lord
12:41	because he **saw** his glory	9:40	her eyes, and **seeing** Peter
14: 7	know him and **have seen** him	10: 3	vision in which he clearly **saw**
14: 9	Whoever **has seen** me has seen	10:17	of the vision that he **had seen**
14: 9	Whoever has seen me **has seen**	11: 5	and in a trance I **saw** a vision
15:24	they **have seen** and hated both	11: 6	I **saw** four-footed animals
16:16	while, and you **will see** me	11:13	how he **had seen** the angel
16:17	and you **will see** me	11:23	came and **saw** the grace of God
16:19	while, and you **will see** me	12: 3	After he **saw** that it pleased
16:22	but I **will see** you again	12:16	they **saw** him and were amazed
18:26	Did I not **see** you in the garden	13:12	proconsul **saw** what had happened
19: 6	priests and the police **saw** him	13:31	he **appeared** to those who came
19:26	When Jesus **saw** his mother	13:35	**let** your Holy One **experience**
19:33	they came to Jesus and **saw**	13:36	and **experienced** corruption
19:35	He who **saw** this has testified	13:37	whom God raised up **experienced**
19:37	They **will look** on the one whom	13:41	**Look,** you scoffers!
20: 8	and he **saw** and believed	13:45	when the Jews **saw** the crowds
20:18	I **have seen** the Lord	14: 9	**seeing** that he had faith to be
20:20	rejoiced when they **saw** the Lord	14:11	When the crowds **saw** what Paul
20:25	We **have seen** the Lord.	15: 6	met together to **consider** this
20:25	I **see** the mark of the nails	16: 9	During the night Paul **had** a
20:29	because you **have seen** me	16:10	When he **had seen** the vision
20:29	those who **have** not **seen** and yet	16:19	But when her owners **saw** that
21:21	When Peter **saw** him, he said	16:27	the jailer woke up and **saw**
Ac 2: 3	**appeared** among them	16:40	they **had seen** and encouraged
2:17	young men **shall see** visions	18:15	**see** to it yourselves
2:27	or **let** your Holy One **experience**	19:21	I must also **see** Rome
2:31	nor did his flesh **experience**	20:25	**will** ever **see** my face again
3: 3	When he **saw** Peter and John	21:32	When they **saw** the tribune
3: 9	All the people **saw** him walking	22:14	to **see** the Righteous One
3:12	When Peter **saw** it	22:15	of what you **have seen** and heard
4:20	what we **have seen** and heard	22:18	and **saw** Jesus saying to me
6:15	they **saw** that his face was like	26:13	I **saw** a light from heaven
7: 2	God of glory **appeared** to our	26:16	for I have **appeared** to you
7:24	When he **saw** one of them being	26:16	in which you **have seen** me
7:26	The next day he **came** to some	26:16	in which I will **appear** to you
7:30	an angel **appeared** to him in the	28: 4	the natives **saw** the creature
7:31	When Moses **saw** it	28:15	On **seeing** them, Paul thanked
7:34	I have surely **seen** the	28:20	I have asked to **see** you
7:34	**seen** the mistreatment of my	28:26	indeed look, but never **perceive**

	28:27	might not **look** with their eyes
Ro	1:11	For I am longing to **see** you
	15:21	been told of him **shall see**
1C	2: 9	What no eye **has seen**
	8:10	For if others **see** you
	9: 1	**Have** I not **seen** Jesus our Lord
	15: 5	and that he **appeared** to Cephas
	15: 6	he **appeared** to more than five
	15: 7	Then he **appeared** to James
	15: 8	he **appeared** also to me
	16: 7	I do not want to **see** you now
Ga	1:19	I did not **see** any other apostle
	2: 7	when they **saw** that I had been
	2:14	But when I **saw** that they were
	6:11	**See** what large letters I make
Ph	1:27	whether I come and **see** you
	1:30	that you **saw** I had and now
	2:28	you may rejoice at **seeing** him
	4: 9	received and heard and **seen**
Co	2: 1	for all who **have** not **seen** me
	2:18	of angels, dwelling on **visions**
1Th	2:17	with great eagerness to **see** you
	3: 6	us kindly and long to **see** us
	3:10	we may **see** you face to face
	5:15	**See** that none of you repays
1Ti	3:16	**seen** by angels, proclaimed
	6:16	whom no one **has** ever **seen**
	6:16	has ever seen or can **see**
2Ti	1: 4	I long to **see** you so that I
He	2: 8	we do not yet **see** everything
	3: 9	though they **had seen** my works
	8: 5	**See** that you make everything
	9:28	**will appear** a second time
	11: 5	he did not **experience** death
	11:13	a distance they **saw** and greeted
	11:23	they **saw** that the child was
	11:27	persevered as though he **saw**
	12:14	which no one **will see** the Lord
	13:23	will be with me when I **see** you
Ja	2:24	**see** that a person is justified
	5:11	and you **have seen** the purpose
1P	1: 8	Although you **have** not **seen** him
	1: 8	you **do** not **see** him now
	3:10	and desire to **see** good days
1J	1: 1	what we **have seen** with our eyes
	1: 2	**have seen** it and testify to it
	1: 3	what we **have seen** and heard
	3: 1	**See** what love the Father has
	3: 2	for we **will see** him as he is

	3: 6	who sins **has** either **seen** him
	4:20	or sister whom they **have seen**
	4:20	God whom they **have** not **seen**
	5:16	If you **see** your brother
3J	1:11	does evil **has** not **seen** God
	1:14	I hope to **see** you soon
Re	1: 2	even to all that he **saw**
	1: 7	every eye **will see** him
	1:12	to **see** whose voice it was
	1:17	When I **saw** him, I fell at his
	1:19	Now write what you **have seen**
	1:20	seven stars that you **saw**
	4: 1	After this I **looked**
	5: 1	Then I **saw** in the right hand
	5: 2	and I **saw** a mighty angel
	5: 6	Then I **saw** between the throne
	5:11	Then I **looked,** and I heard
	6: 1	Then I **saw** the Lamb open one
	6: 2	I **looked,** and there was a
	6: 5	I **looked,** and there was a
	6: 8	I **looked** and there was a
	6: 9	I **saw** under the altar the souls
	6:12	I **looked,** and there came a
	7: 1	After this I **saw** four angels
	7: 2	I **saw** another angel ascending
	7: 9	After this I **looked,** and there
	8: 2	**saw** the seven angels who stand
	8:13	Then I **looked,** and I heard an
	9: 1	I **saw** a star that had fallen
	9:17	this was how I **saw** the horses
	10: 1	And I **saw** another mighty angel
	10: 5	I **saw** standing on the sea
	11:19	ark of his covenant **was seen**
	12: 1	portent **appeared** in heaven
	12: 3	Then another portent **appeared**
	12:13	dragon **saw** that he had been
	13: 1	I **saw** a beast rising out of the
	13: 2	the beast that I **saw** was like
	13:11	Then I **saw** another beast that
	14: 1	Then I **looked,** and there was
	14: 6	I **saw** another angel flying
	14:14	Then I **looked,** and there was
	15: 1	I **saw** another portent in heaven
	15: 2	**saw** what appeared to be a sea
	15: 5	I **looked,** and the temple of the
	16:13	**saw** three foul spirits like
	17: 3	I **saw** a woman sitting on a
	17: 6	I **saw** that the woman was drunk
	17: 6	When I **saw** her, I was greatly

17: 8   The beast that you **saw** was
17:12   And the ten horns that you **saw**
17:15   The waters that you **saw**
17:16   And the ten horns that you **saw**
17:18   The woman you **saw** is the great
18: 1   After this I **saw** another angel
18: 7   and I **will** never **see** grief
19:10   **You** must not do that!
19:11   Then I **saw** heaven opened
19:17   Then I **saw** an angel standing
19:19   **saw** the beast and the kings
20: 1   Then I **saw** an angel coming
20: 4   Then I **saw** thrones, and those
20:11   I **saw** a great white throne
20:12   And I **saw** the dead, great and
21: 1   Then I **saw** a new heaven and a
21: 2   And I **saw** the holy city
21:22   I **saw** no temple in the city
22: 4   they will **see** his face
22: 9   **You** must not do that

3709   GO36 AG578 LN176 B1:107 K5:382
οργη, ANGER
Mt   3: 7   to flee from the **wrath** to come
Mk   3: 5   around at them with **anger**
Lk   3: 7   to flee from the **wrath** to come
     21:23   and **wrath** against this people
Jn   3:36   but must endure God's **wrath**
Ro   1:18   the **wrath** of God is revealed
     2: 5   you are storing up **wrath**
     2: 5   yourself on the day of **wrath**
     2: 8   there will be **wrath** and fury
     3: 5   God is unjust to inflict **wrath**
     4:15   For the law brings **wrath**
     5: 9   through him from the **wrath**
     9:22   desiring to show his **wrath**
     9:22   patience the objects of **wrath**
     12:19   but leave room for the **wrath**
     13: 4   execute **wrath** on the wrongdoer
     13: 5   not only because of **wrath**
Ep   2: 3   by nature children of **wrath**
     4:31   bitterness and wrath and **anger**
     5: 6   the **wrath** of God comes on those
Co   3: 6   the **wrath** of God is coming on
     3: 8   **anger,** wrath, malice, slander
1Th 1:10   who rescues us from the **wrath**
     2:16   but God's **wrath** has overtaken
     5: 9   has destined us not for **wrath**
1Ti 2: 8   up holy hands without **anger**

He   3:11   As in my **anger** I swore
     4: 3   As in my **anger** I swore
Ja   1:19   slow to speak, slow to **anger**
     1:20   for your **anger** does not produce
Re   6:16   and from the **wrath** of the Lamb
     6:17   day of their **wrath** has come
     11:18   but your **wrath** has come
     14:10   into the cup of his **anger**
     16:19   of the fury of his **wrath**
     19:15   of the **wrath** of God

3710   GO8 AG579 LN177 B1:107 K5:382 R3709
οργιζω, I AM ANGRY
Mt   5:22   you **are angry** with a brother
     18:34   And in **anger** his lord handed
     22: 7   The king was **enraged**
Lk   14:21   owner of the house **became angry**
     15:28   he **became angry** and refused
Ep   4:26   **Be angry** but do not sin
Re   11:18   but your **wrath** has come
     12:17   Then the dragon **was angry**

3711   GO1 AG579 LN177 B1:107 K5:382 R3709
οργιλος, QUICK TEMPERED
Ti   1: 7   he arrogant or **quick-tempered**

3712   GO2 AG579 LN177
οργυια, FATHOM
Ac   27:28   and found twenty **fathoms**
     27:28   again and found fifteen **fathoms**

3713   GO3 AG579 LN177 K5:447
ορεγω, I STRIVE
1Ti 3: 1   whoever **aspires** to the office
     6:10   in their **eagerness** to be rich
He   11:16   they **desire** a better country

3714   GO2 AG580 LN177 B3:1008 R3735
ορεινος, HILL COUNTRY
Lk   1:39   Judean town in the **hill country**
     1:65   entire **hill country** of Judea

3715   GO1 AG580 LN177 B1:460 K5:447 R3713
ορεξις, LUST
Ro   1:27   were **consumed** with passion for

3716   GO1 AG580 LN177 B3:351 K5:451 R3717,4228
ορθοποδεω, I WALK STRAIGHT
Ga   2:14   **were** not **acting consistently**

3717　GO2 AG580 LN177 B3:351 K5:449
ορθος, STRAIGHT
Ac　14:10　Stand **upright** on your feet.
He　12:13　**straight** paths for your feet

3718　GO1 AG580 LN177 B3:351 K8:111
ορθοτομεω, I CUT STRAIGHT
2Ti　2:15　**rightly explaining** the word of

3719　GO1 AG580 LN177 R3722
ορθριζω, I COME EARLY IN MORNING
Lk　21:38　the people would **get up early**

3720　GO1 AG580 LN177 R3722
ορθρινος, IN DAWN
Lk　24:22　at the tomb **early** this morning

3722　GO3 AG580 LN177
ορθρος, OF DAWN
Lk　24: 1　of the week, at **early** dawn
Jn　8: 2　**Early** in the **morning** he came
Ac　5:21　entered the temple at **daybreak**

3723　GO4 AG580 LN177 B3:351 R3717
ορθως, STRAIGHTLY
Mk　7:35　released, and he spoke **plainly**
Lk　7:43　You have judged **rightly.**
　　10:28　You have given the **right** answer
　　20:21　we know that you are **right**

3724　GO8 AG580 LN177 B1:472 K5:452
'οριζω, I DESIGNATE
Lk　22:22　going as it **has been determined**
Ac　2:23　according to the **definite** plan
　　10:42　he is the one **ordained** by God
　　11:29　The disciples **determined** that
　　17:26　he **allotted** the times of their
　　17:31　by a man whom he **has appointed**
Ro　1: 4　**was declared** to be Son of God
He　4: 7　again he **sets** a certain day

3725　GO12 AG581 LN177
'οριον, TERRITORY
Mt　2:16　all the children in and **around**
　　4:13　in the **territory** of Zebulun
　　8:34　him to leave their **neighborhood**
　　15:22　woman from that **region** came out
　　15:39　went to the **region** of Magadan
　　19: 1　and went to the **region** of Judea
Mk　5:17　to leave their **neighborhood**

7:24　went away to the **region** of Tyre
7:31　from the **region** of Tyre
7:31　in the **region** of the Decapolis
10: 1　and went to the **region** of Judea
Ac　13:50　drove them out of their **region**

3726　GO2 AG581 LN177 B3:737 K5:462 R3727
'ορκιζω, I PUT UNDER OATH
Mk　5: 7　I **adjure** you by God, do not
Ac　19:13　I **adjure** you by the Jesus whom

3727　GO10 AG581 LN177 B3:737 K5:457
'ορκος, OATH
Mt　5:33　**vows** you have made to the
　　　　　　Lord
　　14: 7　much that he promised on **oath**
　　14: 9　out of regard for his **oaths**
　　26:72　Again he denied it with an **oath**
Mk　6:26　out of regard for his **oaths**
Lk　1:73　the **oath** that he swore to our
Ac　2:30　God had sworn with an **oath**
He　6:16　an **oath** given as confirmation
　　6:17　he guaranteed it by an **oath**
Ja　5:12　by earth or by any other **oath**

3728　GO4 AG581 LN177 B3:737 K5:463
'ορκωμοσια, OATH-TAKING
He　7:20　This was confirmed with an **oath**
　　7:20　their office without an **oath**
　　7:21　became a priest with an **oath**
　　7:28　but the word of the **oath**

3729　GO5 AG581 LN177 K5:467
'ορμαω, I RUSH
Mt　8:32　herd **rushed** down the steep
　　　　　　bank
Mk　5:13　**rushed** down the steep bank
Lk　8:33　herd **rushed** down the steep
　　　　　　bank
Ac　7:57　with a loud shout all **rushed**
　　19:29　people **rushed** together to the

3730　GO2 AG581 LN177 K5:467
'ορμη, IMPULSE
Ac　14: 5　And when an **attempt** was made
Ja　3: 4　the **will** of the pilot directs

3731　GO1 AG581 LN177 K5:467 R3730
'ορμημα, IN RUSH
Re　18:21　such **violence** Babylon the great

3732 GO3 AG581 LN177 R3733
ορνεον, BIRD
Re 18: 2   a haunt of every foul **bird**
    19:17   he called to all the **birds**
    19:21   **birds** were gorged with their

3733 GO2 AG582 LN177
ορνις, HEN
Mt 23:37   **hen** gathers her brood under her
Lk 13:34   **hen** gathers her brood under her

3734 GO1 AG582 LN177
'οροθεσια, SET TERRITORIES
Ac 17:26   the **boundaries** of the places

3735 GO63 AG582 LN177 B3:1009 K5:475
ορος, HILL
Mt 4: 8   high **mountain** and showed him
     5: 1   he went up the **mountain**
     5:14   A city built on a **hill** cannot
     8: 1   come down from the **mountain**
    14:23   he went up the **mountain**
    15:29   and he went up the **mountain**
    17: 1   led them up a high **mountain**
    17: 9   coming down the **mountain**,
    17:20   you will say to this **mountain**
    18:12   ninety-nine on the **mountains**
    21: 1   at the **Mount** of Olives, Jesus
    21:21   if you say to this **mountain**
    24: 3   on the **Mount** of Olives
    24:16   must flee to the **mountains**
    26:30   to the **Mount** of Olives
    28:16   to the **mountain** to which Jesus
Mk 3:13   He went up the **mountain**
     5: 5   on the **mountains** he was always
     5:11   Now there on the **hillside**
     6:46   he went up on the **mountain** to
     9: 2   led them up a high **mountain**
     9: 9   were coming down the **mountain**
    11: 1   near the **Mount** of Olives
    11:23   if you say to this **mountain**
    13: 3   sitting on the **Mount** of Olives
    13:14   must flee to the **mountains**
    14:26   to the **Mount** of Olives
Lk 3: 5   every **mountain** and hill shall
     4:29   to the brow of the **hill**
     6:12   he went out to the **mountain**
     8:32   Now there on the **hillside**
     9:28   went up on the **mountain**
               to pray

     9:37   come down from the **mountain**
    19:29   called the **Mount** of Olives
    19:37   down from the **Mount** of Olives
    21:21   must flee to the **mountains**
    21:37   spend the night on the **Mount**
    22:39   to the **Mount** of Olives
    23:30   to say to the **mountains**
Jn 4:20   worshiped on this **mountain**
     4:21   neither on this **mountain** nor
     6: 3   Jesus went up the **mountain**
     6:15   withdrew again to the **mountain**
     8: 1   while Jesus went to the **Mount**
Ac 1:12   to Jerusalem from the **mount**
     7:30   the wilderness of **Mount** Sinai
     7:38   spoke to him at **Mount** Sinai
1C 13: 2   so as to remove **mountains**
Ga 4:24   is Hagar, from **Mount** Sinai
     4:25   Now Hagar is **Mount** Sinai in
He 8: 5   was shown you on the **mountain**
    11:38   in deserts and **mountains**
    12:20   an animal touches the **mountain**
    12:22   you have come to **Mount** Zion
2P 1:18   with him on the holy **mountain**
Re 6:14   and every **mountain** and island
     6:15   the rocks of the **mountains**
     6:16   to the **mountains** and rocks
     8: 8   something like a great **mountain**
    14: 1   standing on **Mount** Zion
    16:20   no **mountains** were to be found
    17: 9   seven heads are seven **mountains**
    21:10   to a great, high **mountain**

3736 GO3 AG582 LN177
ορυσσω, I DIG
Mt 21:33   **dug** a wine press in it
    25:18   and **dug** a hole in the ground
Mk 12: 1   **dug** a pit for the wine press

3737 GO2 AG583 LN177 B2:737 K5:487
ορφανος, ORPHAN
Jn 14:18   I will not leave you **orphaned**
Ja 1:27   to care for **orphans** and widows

3738 GO4 AG583 LN177
ορχεομαι, I DANCE
Mt 11:17   and you did not **dance**
    14: 6   the daughter of Herodias
               danced
Mk 6:22   Herodias came in and **danced**
Lk 7:32   and you did not **dance**

3739　GO1406　AG583　LN178
'ος, WHO, WHICH, THAT [MULTIPLE OCCURRENCES]

3740　GO3　AG585　LN178
'οσακις, AS OFTEN AS
1C	11:25	Do this, **as often as** you drink
	11:26	**as often as** you eat this bread
Re	11: 6	**as often as** they desire

3741　GO8　AG585　LN178　B2:236　K5:489
'οσιος, HOLY
Ac	2:27	**Holy** One experience corruption
	13:34	**holy** promises made to David
	13:35	**Holy** One experience corruption
1Ti	2: 8	lifting up **holy** hands without
Ti	1: 8	**devout,** and self-controlled
He	7:26	**holy,** blameless, undefiled
Re	15: 4	For you alone are **holy**
	16: 5	You are just, O **Holy** One

3742　GO2　AG585　LN178　B2:236　K5:493　R3741
'οσιοτης, HOLINESS
Lk	1:75	in **holiness** and righteousness
Ep	4:24	righteousness and **holiness**

3743　GO1　AG585　LN178　K5:489　R3741
'οσιως, HOLILY
1Th	2:10	**pure,** upright, and blameless

3744　GO6　AG586　LN178　B3:599　K5:493　R3605
οσμη, ODOR
Jn	12: 3	was filled with the **fragrance**
2C	2:14	the **fragrance** that comes from
	2:16	a **fragrance** from death to death
	2:16	a **fragrance** from life to life
Ep	5: 2	**fragrant** offering and sacrifice
Ph	4:18	a **fragrant** offering

3745　GO110　AG586　LN178
'οσος, AS MUCH AS
Mt	7:12	**as** you would have them do to
	9:15	guests cannot mourn **as long as**
	13:44	and sells all **that** he has
	13:46	sold all **that** he had and bought
	14:36	**all** who touched it were healed
	17:12	but they did to him **whatever**
	18:18	**whatever** you bind on earth
	18:18	**whatever** you loose on earth
	18:25	and all **his** possessions
	21:22	**Whatever** you ask for in prayer
	22: 9	and invite **everyone** you find
	23: 3	do **whatever** they teach you
	25:40	**just as** you did it to one
	25:45	**just as** you did not do it
	28:20	**that** I have commanded you
Mk	2:19	**As long as** they have the
	3: 8	hearing **all that** he was doing
	3:10	**all** who had diseases pressed
	3:28	**whatever** blasphemies they utter
	5:19	**how much** the Lord has done
	5:20	**how much** Jesus had done for him
	6:30	**all** that they had done
	6:30	**all** that they had done
	6:56	**all** who touched it were healed
	7:36	but the **more** he ordered them
	9:13	to him **whatever** they pleased
	10:21	go, sell **what** you own, and give
	11:24	**whatever** you ask for in prayer
	12:44	has put in **everything** she had
Lk	4:23	**that** we have heard you did
	4:40	all **those** who had any who were
	8:39	declare **how much** God has done
	8:39	city **how much** Jesus had done
	9: 5	**Wherever** they do not welcome
	9:10	told Jesus **all** they had done
	11: 8	give him **whatever** he needs
	12: 3	**whatever** you have said in the
	18:12	a tenth of **all** my income
	18:22	Sell **all** that you own
Jn	1:12	But to **all** who received him
	4:29	a man who told me **everything**
	4:45	had seen **all** that he had done
	6:11	**as much as** they wanted
	10: 8	**All** who came before me are
	10:41	but **everything** that John said
	11:22	God will give you **whatever**
	16:13	will speak **whatever** he hears
	16:15	**All** that the Father has is mine
	17: 7	**everything** you have given me
Ac	2:39	**everyone** whom the Lord our God
	3:22	listen to **whatever** he tells you
	3:24	**as many as** have spoken
	4: 6	and **all** who were of the
	4:23	reported **what** the chief priests
	4:28	**whatever** your hand and your
	4:34	for **as many as** owned lands
	5:36	**who** followed him were dispersed
	5:37	**who** followed him were scattered

	9:13	**how much** evil he has done
	9:16	**how much** he must suffer for
	9:39	clothing **that** Dorcas had made
	10:45	**who** had come with Peter were
	13:48	**as many as** had been destined
	14:27	**all** that God had done with them
	15: 4	**all** that God had done with them
	15:12	and wonders **that** God had done
Ro	2:12	**All** who have sinned apart from
	2:12	**all** who have sinned under the
	3:19	that **whatever** the law says
	6: 3	that **all** of us who have been
	7: 1	**only during** that person's
	8:14	**all** who are led by the Spirit
	11:13	**Inasmuch** then as I am an
	15: 4	For **whatever** was written in
1C	7:39	A wife is bound **as long as** her
2C	1:20	For in him **every one** of God's
Ga	3:10	For **all** who rely on the works
	3:27	**As many** of you **as** were baptized
	4: 1	**as long as** they are minors
	6:12	It is those **who** want to make
	6:16	As for those **who** will follow
Ph	3:15	those of us then **who** are mature
	4: 8	beloved, **whatever** is true
	4: 8	**whatever** is honorable, **whatever**
	4: 8	**whatever** is just, whatever is
	4: 8	**whatever** is pure, whatever is
	4: 8	**whatever** is pleasing,
	4: 8	**whatever** is commendable
Co	2: 1	for **all** who have not seen me
1Ti	6: 1	Let **all** who are under the yoke
2Ti	1:18	**how much** service he rendered
He	1: 4	**more** excellent than theirs
	2:15	free those who **all** their lives
	3: 3	**more** honor than the house
	7:20	**who** became priests took their
	8: 6	enacted **through** better promises
	9:27	And **just as** it is appointed
	10:25	all the more **as** you see the Day
	10:37	For yet "in a very **little** while
	10:37	For yet "in a very little **while**
2P	1:13	**as long as** I am in this body
Ju	1:10	**whatever** they do not understand
	1:10	**that,** like irrational animals
Re	1: 2	even to **all** that he saw
	2:24	**who** do not hold this teaching
	3:19	discipline those **whom** I love
	13:15	**who** would not worship the image

	18: 7	**As** she glorified herself
	18:17	**all** whose trade is on the sea
	21:16	and width and height are **equal**

3747   GO4 AG586 LN178
οστεον, BONE

Mt	23:27	they are full of the **bones**
Lk	24:39	does not have flesh and **bones**
Jn	19:36	None of his **bones** shall be
He	11:22	instructions about his **burial**

3748   GO139 AG586 LN178
'οστις, WHO

Mt	2: 6	**who** is to shepherd my people
	5:39	**anyone** strikes you on the right
	5:41	**anyone** forces you to go one
	7:15	**who** come to you in sheep's
	7:24	**who** hears these words of mine
	7:24	**who** built his house on rock
	7:26	**who** built his house on sand
	10:32	**who** acknowledges me before
	10:33	**whoever** denies me before others
	12:50	**whoever** does the will of my
	13:12	For to those **who** have
	13:12	from those **who** have nothing
	13:52	**who** brings out of his treasure
	16:28	**who** will not taste death before
	18: 4	**Whoever** becomes humble
	19:12	**who** have been so from birth
	19:12	**who** have been made eunuchs
	19:12	**who** have made themselves
	19:29	**who** has left houses or
	20: 1	**who** went out early in the
	21:33	**who** planted a vineyard
	21:41	**who** will give him the produce
	22: 2	**who** gave a wedding banquet for
	23:12	**who** exalt themselves will be
	23:12	**who** humble themselves will be
	23:27	**which** on the outside look
	25: 1	**Ten** bridesmaids took their
	27:55	**they** had followed Jesus from
	27:62	The next day, **that is,** after
Mk	4:20	**they** hear the word and accept
	9: 1	**who** will not taste death until
	12:18	**who** say there is no
	15: 7	rebels **who** had committed murder
Lk	1:20	**which** will be fulfilled
	2: 4	city of David **called** Bethlehem
	2:10	great joy **for** all the people

	7:37	who was a sinner	1C	3:17	and **you** are that temple
	7:39	woman this is **who** is touching		5: 1	and of a kind **that** is not found
	8: 3	who provided for them out of	2C	8:10	who began last year not only
	8:15	the ones **who,** when they hear		9:11	which will produce thanksgiving
	8:26	which is opposite Galilee	Ga	2: 4	who slipped in to spy on the
	8:43	a woman **who** had been suffering		4:24	Now **this** is an allegory
	9:30	saw two men, **Moses** and Elijah,		4:24	One woman, in fact, **is** Hagar
	10:42	which will not be taken away		4:26	is free, and **she** is our mother
	12: 1	**that is,** their hypocrisy		5: 4	You **who** want to be justified
	14:15	who will eat bread in the		5:10	whoever it is that is confusing
	14:27	**Whoever** does not carry		5:19	works of the flesh are **obvious**
	15: 7	persons **who** need no repentance	Ep	1:23	which is his body
	23:19	who had been put in prison		3:13	for you; **they** are your glory
	23:55	The women **who** had come with		4:19	**They** have lost all sensitivity
		him		6: 2	**this** is the first commandment
Jn	8:53	our father Abraham, **who** died	Ph	1:28	**this** is evidence of their
	21:25	if **every** one of them were		2:20	who will be genuinely concerned
Ac	3:23	**everyone** who does not listen		3: 7	Yet **whatever** gains I had
	5:16	and **they** were all cured		4: 3	for **they** have struggled beside
	7:53	You are the **ones** that received	Co	2:23	**These** have indeed an appearance
	8:15	**The** two went down and prayed		3: 5	and greed (**which** is idolatry)
	9:35	saw him **and** turned to the Lord		4:11	they have been a comfort to me
	10:41	who ate and drank with him	2Th	1: 9	**These** will suffer the
	10:47	who have received the Holy	1Ti	1: 4	**that** promote speculations
	11:20	who, on coming to Antioch		3:15	which is the church of the
	11:28	**this** took place during the		6: 9	**that** plunge people into ruin
	12:10	**It** opened for them of its own	2Ti	1: 5	**that** lived first in your
	13:31	they are now his witnesses		2: 2	who will be able to teach
	13:43	who spoke to them and urged		2:18	who have swerved from the truth
	16:12	which is a leading city of the	Ti	1:11	they are upsetting whole
	16:16	**and** brought her owners a great	He	2: 3	**It** was declared at first
	16:17	who proclaim to you a way		8: 5	**that** is a sketch and shadow
	17:10	when **they** arrived, they went		8: 6	which has been enacted through
	17:11	they welcomed the message very		9: 2	**this** is called the Holy Place
	21: 4	they told Paul not to go on to		9: 9	**This** is a symbol of the present
	23:14	**They** went to the chief priests		10: 8	**these** are offered according
	23:21	**They** have bound themselves		10:11	**that** can never take away sins
	23:33	When **they** came to Caesarea		10:35	**it** brings a great reward
	24: 1	they reported their case		12: 5	**that** addresses you as children
	28:18	When **they** had examined me		13: 7	those **who** spoke the word of God
Ro	1:25	they exchanged the truth about	Ja	2:10	For **whoever** keeps the whole law
	1:32	**They** know God's decree		4:14	Yet **you** do not even know what
	2:15	**They** show that what the law	1P	2:11	**that** wage war against the soul
	6: 2	How can we **who** died to sin	2P	2: 1	who will secretly bring in
	9: 4	**They** are Israelites	1J	1: 2	**that** was with the Father
	11: 4	who have not bowed the knee	Re	1: 7	see him, even those **who** pierced
	16: 4	who risked their necks for my		1:12	it was **that** spoke to me
	16: 6	who has worked very hard among		2:24	who have not learned what some
	16: 7	who were in prison with me;		9: 4	who do not have the seal of God
	16:12	who has worked hard in the Lord		11: 8	**that** is prophetically called

12:13	the woman who had given birth
17:12	kings **who** have not yet received
19: 2	whore **who** corrupted the earth
20: 4	**They** had not worshiped the

3749   GO2 AG587 LN178 B3:913
οστρακινος, CLAY

2C	4: 7	have this treasure in **clay** jars
2Ti	2:20	but also of wood and **clay**

3750   GO1 AG587 LN178
οσφρησις, SMELLING

1C	12:17	would the **sense of smell** be

3751   GO8 AG587 LN178 K5:496
οσφυς, HIP

Mt	3: 4	leather belt around his **waist**
Mk	1: 6	leather belt around his **waist**
Lk	12:35	Be **dressed** for action and have
Ac	2:30	put one of his **descendants**
Ep	6:14	belt of truth around your **waist**
He	7: 5	also are **descended** from Abraham
	7:10	in the **loins** of his ancestor
1P	1:13	prepare your minds for **action**

3752   GO123 AG587 LN178
'οταν, WHEN

Mt	5:11	**when** people revile you
	6: 2	So **whenever** you give alms
	6: 5	And **whenever** you pray
	6: 6	But **whenever** you pray,
	6:16	And **whenever** you fast
	9:15	**when** the bridegroom is taken
	10:19	**When** they hand you over
	10:23	**When** they persecute you in one
	12:43	**When** the unclean spirit has
	13:32	but **when** it has grown it is
	15: 2	their hands **before** they eat
	19:28	**when** the Son of Man is seated
	21:40	**when** the owner of the vineyard
	23:15	**and** you make the new convert
	24:15	**when** you see the desolating
	24:32	**as soon as** its branch becomes
	24:33	**when** you see all these things
	25:31	**When** the Son of Man comes in
	26:29	until that day **when** I drink it
Mk	2:20	**when** the bridegroom is taken
	3:11	**Whenever** the unclean spirits
	4:15	**when** they hear, Satan
	4:16	**when** they hear the word

4:29	But **when** the grain is ripe
4:31	**when** sown upon the ground
4:32	yet **when** it is sown it grows up
8:38	**when** he comes in the glory
9: 9	until **after** the Son of Man
11:25	**Whenever** you stand praying
12:23	In the **resurrection** whose wife
12:25	**when** they rise from the dead
13: 4	**when** will this be, and what
13: 7	**When** you hear of wars and
13:11	**When** they bring you to trial
13:14	But **when** you see the desolating
13:28	**as soon as** its branch becomes
13:29	**when** you see these things
14: 7	to them **whenever** you wish
14:25	that day **when** I drink it new

Lk	5:35	**when** the bridegroom will be
	6:22	**when** people hate you
	6:26	Woe to you **when** all speak well
	8:13	**when** they hear the word
	9:26	**when** he comes in his glory
	11: 2	**When** you pray, say: Father
	11:21	**When** a strong man, fully armed
	11:24	**When** the unclean spirit has
	11:34	**If** your eye is healthy
	11:36	as full of light as **when** a lamp
	12:11	**When** they bring you before the
	12:54	**When** you see a cloud rising
	12:55	**when** you see the south wind
	13:28	**when** you see Abraham and Isaac
	14: 8	**When** you are invited by someone
	14:10	But **when** you are invited
	14:10	so that **when** your host comes
	14:12	**When** you give a luncheon
	14:13	But **when** you give a banquet
	16: 4	**when** I am dismissed as manager
	16: 9	so that **when** it is gone
	17:10	**when** you have done all that you
	21: 7	**when** will this be, and what
	21: 9	**When** you hear of wars and
	21:20	**When** you see Jerusalem
	21:30	**as soon as** they sprout leaves
	21:31	**when** you see these things
	23:42	remember me **when** you come into
Jn	2:10	inferior wine **after** the guests
	4:25	**When** he comes, he will proclaim
	5: 7	**when** the water is stirred up
	7:27	but **when** the Messiah comes
	7:31	**When** the Messiah comes, will he

	8:28	**When** you have lifted up the Son
	8:44	**When** he lies, he speaks
	9: 5	**As long as** I am in the world
	10: 4	**When** he has brought out all
	13:19	so that **when** it does occur
	14:29	so that **when** it does occur
	15:26	**When** the Advocate comes
	16: 4	so that **when** their hour comes
	16:13	**When** the Spirit of truth comes
	16:21	**When** a woman is in labor
	16:21	But **when** her child is born
	21:18	**when** you were younger
Ac	23:35	**when** your accusers arrive
	24:22	**When** Lysias the tribune comes
Ro	2:14	**When** Gentiles, who do not
	11:27	**when** I take away their sins
1C	3: 4	For **when** one says, "I belong
	13:10	but **when** the complete comes
	14:26	**When** you come together
	15:24	**when** he hands over the kingdom
	15:24	**after** he has destroyed every
	15:27	But **when** it says, "All things
	15:28	**When** all things are subjected
	15:54	**When** this perishable body puts
	16: 2	need not be taken **when** I come
	16: 3	And **when** I arrive, I will send
	16: 5	for I **intend** to pass through
	16:12	He will come **when** he has the
2C	10: 6	**when** your obedience is complete
	12:10	for **whenever** I am weak
	13: 9	we rejoice **when** we are weak
Co	3: 4	**When** Christ who is your life
	4:16	**when** this letter has been read
1Th	5: 3	**When** they say, "There is peace
2Th	1:10	**when** he comes to be glorified
1Ti	5:11	for **when** their sensual desires
Ti	3:12	**When** I send Artemas to you
He	1: 6	**when** he brings the firstborn
Ja	1: 2	**whenever** you face trials of any
1J	5: 2	**when** we love God and obey his
Re	4: 9	**whenever** the living creatures
	8: 1	**When** the Lamb opened the
	9: 5	of a scorpion **when** it stings
	10: 7	**when** the seventh angel is to
	11: 7	**When** they have finished their
	12: 4	devour her child **as soon as**
	17:10	**when** he comes, he must remain
	18: 9	**when** they see the smoke of her
	20: 7	**When** the thousand years are

3753   ᴳᴼ103   ᴬᴳ588   ᴸᴺ178

ὅτε, WHEN

Mt	7:28	Now **when** Jesus had finished
	9:25	**when** the crowd had been put
	11: 1	Now **when** Jesus had finished
	13:26	So **when** the plants came up
	13:48	**when** it was full, they drew
	13:53	**When** Jesus had finished these
	19: 1	**When** Jesus had finished saying
	21: 1	**When** they had come near
	21:34	**When** the harvest time had come
	26: 1	**When** Jesus had finished saying
	27:31	**After** mocking him
Mk	1:32	That evening, **at** sundown
	2:25	**when** he and his companions
	4: 6	And **when** the sun rose
	4:10	**When** he was alone, those who
	6:21	**when** Herod on his birthday
	7:17	**When** he had left the crowd
	8:19	**When** I broke the five loaves
	8:20	**And** the seven for the four
	11: 1	**When** they were approaching
	14:12	**when** the Passover lamb is
	15:20	**After** mocking him
	15:41	**when** he was in Galilee
Lk	2:21	**After** eight days had passed
	2:22	**When** the time came for their
	2:42	**when** he was twelve years old
	4:25	**when** the heaven was shut up
	6: 3	**when** he and his companions
	6:13	And **when** day came, he called
	13:35	the time comes **when** you say
	15:30	But **when** this son of yours came
	17:22	**when** you will long to see one
	22:14	**When** the hour came, he took his
	22:35	**When** I sent you out without a
	23:33	**When** they came to the place
Jn	1:19	**when** the Jews sent priests
	2:22	**After** he was raised from the
	4:21	coming **when** you will worship
	4:23	**when** the true worshipers will
	4:45	**When** he came to Galilee
	5:25	**when** the dead will hear the
	6:24	**when** the crowd saw that neither
	9: 4	is coming **when** no one can work
	12:16	**when** Jesus was glorified
	12:17	**when** he called Lazarus out of
	13:12	**After** he had washed their feet
	13:31	**When** he had gone out

	16:25	**when** I will no longer speak
	17:12	**While** I was with them
	19: 6	**When** the chief priests and the
	19: 8	Now **when** Pilate heard this
	19:23	**When** the soldiers had crucified
	19:30	**When** Jesus had received the
	20:24	not with them **when** Jesus came
	21:15	**When** they had finished
	21:18	But **when** you grow old
Ac	1:13	**When** they had entered the city
	8:12	But **when** they believed Philip
	8:39	**When** they came up out of the
	11: 2	**when** Peter went up to Jerusalem
	12: 6	**before** Herod was going to bring
	21: 5	**When** our days there were ended
	21:35	**When** Paul came to the steps
	22:20	**while** the blood of your witness
	27:39	**In** the morning they did not
	28:16	**When** we came into Rome
Ro	2:16	**when,** according to my gospel
	6:20	**When** you were slaves of sin
	7: 5	**While** we were living in the
	13:11	**when** we became believers
1C	12: 2	know that **when** you were pagans
	13:11	**When** I was a child, I spoke
	13:11	**when** I became an adult
Ga	1:15	But **when** God, who had set me
	2:11	But **when** Cephas came to Antioch
	2:12	**after** they came, he drew back
	2:14	**when** I saw that they were not
	4: 3	**while** we were minors
	4: 4	**when** the fullness of time had
Ph	4:15	**when** I left Macedonia
Co	3: 7	**when** you were living that life
1Th	3: 4	**when** we were with you, we told
2Th	3:10	For even **when** we were with you
2Ti	4: 3	**when** people will not put up
Ti	3: 4	**when** the goodness and loving
He	7:10	**when** Melchizedek met him
	9:17	**as long as** the one who made it
1P	3:20	**when** God waited patiently in
Ju	1: 9	But **when** the archangel Michael
Re	1:17	**When** I saw him, I fell at his
	5: 8	**When** he had taken the scroll
	6: 1	**Then** I saw the Lamb open one
	6: 3	**When** he opened the second seal
	6: 5	**When** he opened the third seal
	6: 7	**When** he opened the fourth seal
	6: 9	**When** he opened the fifth seal

	6:12	**When** he opened the sixth seal
	10: 3	And **when** he shouted, the seven
	10: 4	And **when** the seven thunders had
	10:10	but **when** I had eaten it
	12:13	**when** the dragon saw that he had
	22: 8	**when** I heard and saw them

3754   GO1297   AG588   LN178
ὅτι, BECAUSE, THAT [MULTIPLE OCCURRENCES]

3755   GO5   AG589   LN178
ὅτου, WHEN

Mt	5:25	**while** you are on the way to
Lk	12:50	what stress I am under **until**
	13: 8	**until** I dig around it and put
	22:16	I will not eat it **until** it is
Jn	9:18	**until** they called the parents

3756   GO1613   AG590   LN179
οὖ, WHERE [MULTIPLE OCCURRENCES]

3756a   GO17   AG589   LN178
οὖ, NO, NOT

Mt	5:37	word be 'Yes, Yes' or '**No,** No'
	5:37	word be 'Yes, Yes' or 'No, **No**'
	13:29	**No;** for in gathering the weeds
	22:17	taxes to the emperor, or **not**
Mk	12:14	taxes to the emperor, or **not**
Lk	14: 3	people on the sabbath, or **not**
	20:22	to the emperor, or **not**
Jn	1:21	He answered, **"No."**
	7:12	**No,** he is deceiving the crowd
	21: 5	They answered him, **"No."**
Ro	7:18	but I **cannot** do it
2C	1:17	and **"No,** no" at the same time
	1:17	"No, **no"** at the same time
	1:18	has not been "Yes and **No."**
	1:19	was not "Yes and **No"**; but in
Ja	5:12	be yes and your **"No"** be no
	5:12	be yes and your "No" be **no**

3757   GO24   AG590   LN179
οὖ, WHERE

Mt	2: 9	the place **where** the child was
	18:20	**where** two or three are gathered
	28:16	**which** Jesus had directed them
Lk	4:16	**where** he had been brought up
	4:17	the place **where** it was written
	10: 1	**where** he himself intended to go
	23:53	**where** no one had ever been laid

	24:28	to **which** they were going
Ac	1:13	room upstairs **where** they were
	2: 2	house **where** they were sitting
	7:29	**There** he became the father of
	12:12	**where** many had gathered
	16:13	**where** we supposed there was a
	20: 8	room upstairs **where** we were
	25:10	this is **where** I should be tried
	28:14	**There** we found believers
Ro	4:15	but **where** there is no law
	5:20	but **where** sin increased
	9:26	**where** it was said to them
1C	16: 6	me on my way, **wherever** I go
2C	3:17	**where** the Spirit of the Lord is
Co	3: 1	**where** Christ is, seated at the
He	3: 9	**where** your ancestors put me to
Re	17:15	**where** the whore is seated

3758   GO1   AG591   LN179

ουα, AHA!

Mk	15:29	their heads and saying, **"Aha!**

3759   GO46   AG591   LN179   B3:1051

ουαι, WOE

Mt	11:21	**Woe** to you, Chorazin! Woe to
	11:21	**Woe** to you, Bethsaida!
	18: 7	**Woe** to the world because of
	18: 7	but **woe** to the one by whom the
	23:13	But **woe** to you, scribes and
	23:15	**Woe** to you, scribes and
	23:16	**Woe** to you, blind guides
	23:23	**Woe** to you, scribes and
	23:25	**Woe** to you, scribes
	23:27	**Woe** to you, scribes and
	23:29	**Woe** to you, scribes and
	24:19	**Woe** to those who are pregnant
	26:24	but **woe** to that one by
Mk	13:17	**Woe** to those who are pregnant
	14:21	but **woe** to that one by
Lk	6:24	But **woe** to you who are rich
	6:25	**Woe** to you who are full now
	6:25	**Woe** to you who are laughing
	6:26	**Woe** to you when all speak well
	10:13	**Woe** to you, Chorazin!
	10:13	**Woe** to you, Bethsaida!
	11:42	But **woe** to you Pharisees!
	11:43	**Woe** to you Pharisees!
	11:44	**Woe** to you! For you are like
	11:46	**Woe** also to you lawyers!

	11:47	**Woe** to you! For you build
	11:52	**Woe** to you lawyers!
	17: 1	**woe** to anyone by whom they come
	21:23	**Woe** to those who are pregnant
	22:22	**woe** to that one by whom he is
1C	9:16	**woe** to me if I do not proclaim
Ju	1:11	**Woe** to them! For they go the
Re	8:13	**Woe,** woe, woe to the
	8:13	Woe, **woe,** woe to the
	8:13	Woe, woe, **woe** to the
	9:12	The first **woe** has passed
	9:12	are still two **woes** to come
	11:14	The second **woe** has passed
	11:14	The third **woe** is coming very
	12:12	**woe** to the earth and the sea
	18:10	**Alas,** alas, the great city
	18:10	Alas, **alas,** the great city
	18:16	**Alas,** alas, the great city
	18:16	Alas, **alas,** the great city
	18:19	**Alas,** alas, the great city
	18:19	Alas, **alas,** the great city

3760   GO1   AG591   LN179

ουδαμως, NOT AT ALL

Mt	2: 6	are **by no means** least among the

3761   GO143   AG591   LN179   R3756,1161

ουδε, BUT NOT

Mt	5:15	**No one** after lighting a lamp
	6:15	**neither** will your Father
	6:20	do not break in **and** steal.
	6:26	they neither sow **nor** reap
	6:26	neither sow nor reap **nor** gather
	6:28	they neither toil **nor** spin
	6:29	**even** Solomon in all his glory
	7:18	**nor** can a bad tree bear good
	9:17	**but** new wine is put into fresh
	10:24	**nor** a slave above the master
	11:27	and **no one** knows the Father
	12: 4	**or** his companions to eat
	12:19	will not wrangle **or** cry aloud
	12:19	**nor** will anyone hear his voice
	13:13	**nor** do they understand
	16: 9	Do you **not** remember the five
	16:10	**Or** the seven loaves for the
	21:27	**Neither** will I tell you by what
	21:32	and **even** after you saw it
	22:46	**nor** from that day did anyone
	23:13	**and** when others are going in

	24:21	now, no, and **never** will be
	24:36	**neither** the angels of heaven
	24:36	angels of heaven, **nor** the Son
	25:13	neither the day **nor** the hour
	25:45	you did **not** do it to me
	27:14	**not even** to a single charge
Mk	4:22	**nor** is anything secret
	5: 3	any more, **even** with a chain
	6:31	had **no** leisure even to eat
	8:17	not perceive **or** understand
	11:33	**Neither** will I tell you by what
	12:10	you **not** read this scripture
	13:32	**neither** the angels in heaven
	13:32	angels in heaven, **nor** the Son
	14:59	**But even** on this point their
	16:13	**but** they did **not** believe them
Lk	6: 3	Have you **not** read what David
	6:43	**nor** again does a bad tree bear
	6:44	**nor** are grapes picked from a
	7: 7	I did **not** presume to come to
	7: 9	**not even** in Israel have I found
	8:17	**nor** is anything secret that
	11:33	a lamp puts it in a **cellar**
	12:24	they neither sow **nor** reap
	12:24	neither storehouse **nor** barn
	12:26	If then you are **not** able to do
	12:27	they neither toil **nor** spin
	12:27	**even** Solomon in all his glory
	12:33	comes near **and no** moth destroys
	16:31	**neither** will they be convinced
	17:21	**nor** will they say, 'Look, here
	18: 4	and **no** respect for anyone
	18:13	**not even** look up to heaven
	20: 8	**Neither** will I tell you by what
	20:36	**Indeed** they cannot die anymore
	23:15	**Neither** has Herod, for he sent
	23:40	Do **you** not fear God, since you
Jn	1: 3	not of blood **or** of the will of
	1:13	the flesh **or** of the will of man
	1:25	**nor** Elijah, nor the prophet
	1:25	nor Elijah, **nor** the prophet
	3:27	**except** what has been given from
	5:22	**The** Father judges no one but
	6:24	neither Jesus **nor** his disciples
	7: 5	**not even** his brothers believed
	8:11	**Neither** do I condemn you
	8:42	I did **not** come on my own
	11:50	You do **not** understand that it
	13:16	**nor** are messengers greater

	14:17	neither sees him **nor** knows him
	15: 4	**neither** can you unless you
	16: 3	have not known the Father **or** me
	21:25	could **not** contain the books
Ac	2:27	**or** let your Holy One experience
	4:12	there is **no** other name under
	4:32	and **no** one claimed private
	4:34	many as owned lands **or** houses
	7: 5	**not even** a foot's length
	8:21	have no part **or** share in this
	9: 9	and neither ate **nor** drank
	16:21	as Romans to adopt **or** observe
	17:25	**nor** is he served by human
	19: 2	we have **not even** heard that
	24:13	**Neither** can they prove to you
	24:18	any crowd **or** disturbance
Ro	2:28	**nor** is true circumcision
	3:10	who is righteous, **not even** one
	4:15	**neither** is there violation
	8: 7	God's law—**indeed** it cannot
	9: 7	**and not** all of Abraham's
	9:16	on human will **or** exertion
	11:21	**perhaps** he will not spare you
1C	2: 6	**or** of the rulers of this age
	3: 2	**Even** now you are still not
	4: 3	I do **not even** judge myself
	5: 1	is not found **even** among pagans
	11:14	Does **not** nature itself teach
	11:16	**nor** do the churches of God
	14:21	**even** then they will not listen
	15:13	**then** Christ has not been raised
	15:16	**then** Christ has not been raised
	15:50	**nor** does the perishable inherit
2C	7:12	**nor** on account of the one
Ga	1: 1	**nor** from human authorities
	1:12	**for** I did **not** receive it from
	1:17	**nor** did I go up to Jerusalem
	2: 3	But **even** Titus, who was with me
	2: 5	to them **even** for a moment
	3:28	There is no longer Jew **or** Greek
	3:28	is no longer slave **or** free
	4:14	not scorn **or** despise me
	6:13	**Even** the circumcised do not
Ph	2:16	run in vain **or** labor in vain
1Th	2: 3	does **not** spring **from** deceit
	2: 3	impure motives **or** trickery
	5: 5	the night **or** of darkness
2Th	3: 8	**and** we did **not** eat anyone's
1Ti	2:12	to teach **or** to have authority

	6: 7	so that we can take **nothing**
	6:16	no one has ever seen **or** can see
He	8: 4	he would **not** be a priest at all
	9:12	**not** with the blood of goats
	9:18	**not even** the first covenant
	9:25	**Nor** was it to offer himself
	10: 8	desired **nor** taken pleasure
	13: 5	leave you **or** forsake you
1P	2:22	**and** no deceit was found in his
2P	1: 8	ineffective **and** unfruitful
1J	2:23	**No** one who denies the Son
	3: 6	either seen him **or** known him
Re	5: 3	no one in heaven **or** on earth
	5: 3	on earth **or** under the earth
	7:16	**and** thirst no more; the sun
	7:16	the sun will **not** strike them
	7:16	**nor** any scorching heat
	9: 4	earth **or** any green growth
	9: 4	any green growth **or** any tree
	9:20	did **not** repent of the works
	12: 8	**and** there was **no** longer any
	20: 4	not worshiped the beast **or** its
	21:23	has no need of sun **or** moon

3762　ᴳᴼ234 ᴬᴳ591 ᴸᴺ179 ᴿ3761,1520
ουδεις, NO ONE

Mt	5:13	is no longer good for **anything**
	6:24	**No one** can serve two masters
	8:10	in **no one** in Israel have I
	9:16	**No one** sews a piece of unshrunk
	10:26	for **nothing** is covered up
	11:27	**no one** knows the Son except the
	13:34	parable he told them **nothing**
	17: 8	they saw **no one** except Jesus
	17:20	and **nothing** will be impossible
	20: 7	Because **no one** has hired us
	21:19	and found **nothing** at all on it
	22:16	and show deference to **no one**
	22:46	**No one** was able to give him an
	23:16	sanctuary is bound by **nothing**
	23:18	the altar is bound by **nothing**
	24:36	that day and hour **no one** knows
	26:62	Have you **no** answer
	27:12	elders, he did **not** answer
	27:24	saw that he could do **nothing**
Mk	2:21	**No one** sews a piece of unshrunk
	2:22	**no one** puts new wine into old
	3:27	**no one** can enter a strong man's
	5: 3	**no one** could restrain him any

	5: 4	**no one** had the strength to
	5:37	He allowed **no one** to follow
	6: 5	he could do **no** deed of power
	7:12	no longer permit doing **anything**
	7:15	is **nothing** outside a person
	7:24	did not want **anyone** to know
	9: 8	they saw **no one** with them any
	9:29	come out **only** through prayer
	9:39	for **no one** who does a deed of
	10:18	**No one** is good but God alone
	10:29	**no one** who has left house or
	11: 2	colt that has **never** been ridden
	11:13	he found **nothing** but leaves
	12:14	and show deference to **no one**
	12:34	**no one** dared to ask him any
	13:32	that day or hour **no one** knows
	14:60	Have you **no** answer?
	14:61	was silent and did **not** answer
	15: 4	Have you **no** answer?
	15: 5	Jesus made **no** further reply
	16: 8	and they said **nothing** to anyone
	16: 8	they said nothing to **anyone**
Lk	1:61	**None** of your relatives has this
	4: 2	He ate **nothing** at all during
	4:24	**no** prophet is accepted in the
	4:26	was sent to **none** of them
	4:27	and **none** of them was cleansed
	5: 5	long but have caught **nothing**
	5:36	**No one** tears a piece from a
	5:37	**no one** puts new wine into old
	5:39	**no one** after drinking old wine
	7:28	**no one** is greater than John
	8:16	**No one** after lighting a lamp
	8:43	**no one** could cure her
	9:36	in those days told **no one** any
	9:36	in those days told **no one** any
	9:62	**No one** who puts a hand to the
	10:19	and **nothing** will hurt you
	10:22	and **no one** knows who the Son
	11:33	**No one** after lighting a lamp
	12: 2	**Nothing** is covered up that will
	14:24	**none** of those who were invited
	15:16	and no one gave him **anything**
	16:13	**No** slave can serve two masters
	18:19	**No one** is good but God alone
	18:29	**no one** who has left house
	18:34	But they understood **nothing**
	19:30	colt that has **never** been ridden
	20:40	to ask him **another question**

	23: 4	**no** basis for an accusation
	23: 9	but Jesus gave him **no** answer
	23:15	he has done **nothing** to deserve
	23:22	I have found in him **no** ground
	23:41	this man has done **nothing** wrong
	23:53	where **no one** had ever been laid
Jn	1:18	**No one** has ever seen God
	3: 2	for **no one** can do these signs
	3:13	**No one** has ascended into heaven
	3:32	**no one** accepts his testimony
	4:27	with a woman, but **no one** said
	5:19	Son can do **nothing** on his own
	5:22	Father judges **no one** but has
	5:30	I can do **nothing** on my own.
	6:44	**No one** can come to me unless
	6:63	the flesh is **useless**
	6:65	**no one** can come to me unless
	7: 4	**no one** who wants to be widely
	7:13	Yet **no one** would speak openly
	7:19	Yet **none** of you keeps the law
	7:26	but they say **nothing** to him
	7:27	**no one** will know where he is
	7:30	but **no one** laid hands on him
	7:44	but **no one** laid hands on him
	8:10	Has **no one** condemned you
	8:11	She said, "**No one**, sir."
	8:15	I judge **no one**
	8:20	but **no one** arrested him
	8:28	that I do **nothing** on my own
	8:33	never been slaves to **anyone**
	8:54	my glory is **nothing**
	9: 4	is coming when **no one** can work
	9:33	he could do **nothing**
	10:18	**No one** takes it from me
	10:29	**no one** can snatch it out of the
	10:41	John performed **no** sign
	11:49	You know **nothing** at all!
	12:19	You see, you can do **nothing**
	13:28	Now **no one** at the table knew
	14: 6	**No one** comes to the Father
	14:30	He has **no** power over me
	15: 5	from me you can do **nothing**
	15:13	**No one** has greater love than
	15:24	the works that **no one** else did
	16: 5	yet **none** of you asks me
	16:22	**no one** will take your joy
	16:23	that day you will ask **nothing**
	16:24	you have not asked for **anything**
	16:29	**not** in any figure of speech

	17:12	and **not one** of them was lost
	18: 9	not lose a single **one** of those
	18:20	I have said **nothing** in secret
	18:31	to put **anyone** to death
	18:38	I find **no** case against him
	19: 4	you know that I find **no** case
	19:11	would have **no** power over me
	19:41	**no one** had ever been laid
	21: 3	that night they caught **nothing**
	21:12	Now **none** of the disciples dared
Ac	4:12	for there is **no** other name
	4:14	they had **nothing** to say in
	5:13	**None** of the rest dared to join
	5:23	we found **no one** inside
	5:36	were **dispersed** and disappeared
	8:16	the Spirit had **not** come upon
	9: 8	he could see **nothing**
	17:21	spend their time in **nothing**
	18:10	and **no one** will lay a hand
	18:17	Gallio paid **no** attention to **any** of these things
	20:20	not shrink from doing **anything**
	20:24	**not** count my life of any value
	20:33	**no one's** silver or gold
	21:24	there is **nothing** in what they
	23: 9	We find **nothing** wrong with this
	25:10	have done **no** wrong to the Jews
	25:11	if there is **nothing** to their
	25:11	**no one** can turn me over to them
	25:18	they did **not** charge him with
	26:22	saying **nothing** but what the
	26:31	This man is doing **nothing** to
	27:22	will be **no** loss of life among
	27:34	**none** of you will lose a hair
	28: 5	the fire and suffered **no** harm
	28:17	I had done **nothing** against our
Ro	8: 1	now **no** condemnation for those
	14: 7	We do **not** live to ourselves
	14: 7	and we do **not** die to ourselves
	14:14	**nothing** is unclean in itself
1C	1:14	that I baptized **none** of you
	2: 8	**None** of the rulers of this age
	2:11	So also **no one** comprehends
	2:15	to **no one** else's scrutiny
	3:11	**no one** can lay any foundation
	4: 4	I am not aware of **anything**
	6: 5	Can it be that there is **no one**
	7:19	Circumcision is **nothing**
	7:19	and uncircumcision is **nothing**
	8: 4	**no** idol in the world really

	8: 4	there is **no** God but one
	9:15	But I have made **no** use of any
	9:15	**no one** will deprive me of my
	12: 3	**no one** speaking by the Spirit
	12: 3	**no one** can say "Jesus is Lord"
	13: 3	have love, I gain **nothing**
	14: 2	for **nobody** understands them
	14:10	and **nothing** is without sound
2C	5:16	we regard **no one** from a human
	7: 2	we have wronged **no one**
	7: 2	we have corrupted **no one**
	7: 2	taken advantage of **no one**
	7: 5	our bodies had **no** rest
	12:11	for I am **not** at all inferior
	12:11	even though I am **nothing**
Ga	2: 6	were makes **no** difference to me
	2: 6	contributed **nothing** to me
	3:11	that **no one** is justified
	3:15	**no one** adds to it or annuls it
	4: 1	are **no** better than slaves
	4:12	You have done me **no** wrong
	5: 2	Christ will be of **no** benefit
	5:10	you will **not** think otherwise
Ep	5:29	**no one** ever hates his own body
Ph	1:20	I will **not** be put to shame
	2:20	I have **no one** like him
	4:15	**no** church shared with me
1Ti	4: 4	and **nothing** is to be rejected
	6: 7	brought **nothing** into the world
	6:16	whom **no one** has ever seen
2Ti	2: 4	**No one** serving in the army
	2:14	which does **no** good but only
	4:16	**no one** came to my support
Ti	1:15	unbelieving **nothing** is pure
Pm	1:14	but I preferred to do **nothing**
He	2: 8	God left **nothing** outside their
	6:13	because he had **no one** greater
	7:13	**no one** has ever served at the
	7:14	said **nothing** about priests
	7:19	the law made **nothing** perfect
	12:14	**no one** will see the Lord
Ja	1:13	**No one,** when tempted, should
	3: 8	**no one** can tame the tongue
1J	1: 5	there is **no** darkness at all
	4:12	**No one** has ever seen God
Re	2:17	written a new name that **no one**
	3: 7	who opens and **no one** will shut
	3: 7	who shuts and **no one** opens
	3: 8	which **no one** is able to shut

	3:17	prospered, and I need **nothing**
	5: 3	**no one** in heaven or on earth
	5: 4	because **no one** was found worthy
	7: 9	that **no one** could count
	14: 3	**No one** could learn that song
	15: 8	**no one** could enter the temple
	18:11	**no one** buys their cargo anymore
	19:12	that **no one** knows but himself

3763　GO16　AG592　LN179
ουδεποτε, BUT NOT EVER

Mt	7:23	I **never** knew you; go away from
	9:33	**Never** has anything like this
	21:16	Yes; have you **never** read
	21:42	**never** read in the scriptures
	26:33	I will **never** desert you
Mk	2:12	We have **never** seen anything
	2:25	Have you **never** read what David
Lk	15:29	and I have **never** disobeyed
	15:29	yet you have **never** given me
Jn	7:46	**Never** has anyone spoken like
Ac	10:14	for I have **never** eaten anything
	11: 8	has **ever** entered my mouth
	14: 8	his feet and had **never** walked
1C	13: 8	Love **never** ends
He	10: 1	it can **never,** by the same
	10:11	that can **never** take away sins

3764　GO4　AG592　LN179
ουδεπω, BUT NOT YET

Jn	7:39	Jesus was **not yet** glorified
	19:41	no one had **ever** been laid
	20: 9	**as yet** they did not understand
Ac	8:16	**as yet** the Spirit had not come

3764a　GO7　AG592　LN179
ουθεις, NOTHING

Lk	22:35	They said, "No, **not a thing.**"
	23:14	have **not** found this man guilty
Ac	15: 9	he has made **no** distinction
	19:27	goddess Artemis will be **scorned**
	26:26	**none** of these things has
1C	13: 2	not have love, I am **nothing**
2C	11: 9	I did not burden **anyone**

3765　GO47　AG592　LN179　R3756,2089
ουκετι, NO LONGER

Mt	19: 6	So they are **no longer** two
	22:46	to ask him **any more** questions
Mk	5: 3	could restrain him **any more**

	7:12	**no longer** permit doing anything
	9: 8	saw no one with them **any more**
	10: 8	they are **no longer** two
	12:34	dared to ask him **any** question
	14:25	I will **never** again drink
	15: 5	Jesus made **no** further reply
Lk	15:19	**no longer** worthy to be called
	15:21	**no longer** worthy to be called
	20:40	they **no longer** dared to ask
Jn	4:42	It is **no longer** because of what
	6:66	**no longer** went about with him
	11:54	**no longer** walked about openly
	14:19	world will **no longer** see me
	14:30	I will **no longer** talk much
	15:15	call you servants **any longer**
	16:10	you will see me **no longer**
	16:16	and you will **no longer** see me
	16:21	she **no longer** remembers the
	16:25	when I will **no longer** speak
	17:11	I am **no longer** in the world
	21: 6	they were **not** able to haul it
Ac	8:39	the eunuch saw him **no more**
	20:25	will **ever** see my face again
	20:38	they would **not** see him again
Ro	6: 9	will **never** die again
	6: 9	death **no longer** has dominion
	7:17	But in fact it is **no longer**
	7:20	it is **no longer** I that do it
	11: 6	it is **no longer** on the basis
	11: 6	grace would **no longer** be grace
	14:15	you are **no longer** walking in
2C	1:23	that I did **not** come again
	5:16	we know him **no longer** in that
Ga	2:20	it is **no longer** I who live
	3:18	it **no longer** comes from the
	3:25	we are **no longer** subject
	4: 7	So you are **no longer** a slave
Ep	2:19	you are **no longer** strangers
Pm	1:16	**no longer** as a slave but more
He	10:18	there is **no longer** any offering
	10:26	there **no longer** remains
Re	10: 6	There will be **no more** delay
	18:11	no one buys their cargo **anymore**
	18:14	**never** to be found again

3766　GO1　AG592　LN179
ουκουν, NOT THEN

Jn	18:37	**So you are a king?**

3767　GO501　AG592　LN179
ουν, THEN, THEREFORE [MULTIPLE OCCURRENCES]

3768　GO26　AG593　LN179
ουπω, NOT YET

Mt	16: 9	Do you **still not** perceive?
	24: 6	but the end is **not yet**
Mk	4:40	Have you **still no** faith?
	8:17	Do you **still not**
	8:21	Do you **not yet** understand?
	11: 2	that has **never** been ridden
	13: 7	but the end is **still** to come
Lk	23:53	where no one had **ever** been
Jn	2: 4	My hour has **not yet** come
	3:24	had **not yet** been thrown into
	6:17	Jesus had **not yet** come to them
	7: 6	My time has **not yet** come
	7: 8	for my time has **not yet** fully
	7:30	his hour had **not yet** come
	7:39	Jesus was **not yet** glorified
	8:20	his hour had **not yet** come
	8:57	You are **not yet** fifty years
	11:30	Now Jesus had **not yet** come
	20:17	I have **not yet** ascended
1C	3: 2	now you are **still not** ready
	8: 2	does **not yet** have the necessary
He	2: 8	we do **not yet** see everything
	12: 4	you have **not yet** resisted
1J	3: 2	has **not yet** been revealed
Re	17:10	the other has **not yet** come
	17:12	**not yet** received a kingdom

3769　GO5　AG593　LN179
ουρα, TAIL

Re	9:10	They have **tails** like scorpions
	9:10	in their **tails** is their power
	9:19	mouths and in their **tails**
	9:19	their **tails** are like serpents
	12: 4	His **tail** swept down a third

3770　GO9　AG593　LN179　B2:188　R3772
ουρανιος, HEAVENLY

Mt	5:48	your **heavenly** Father is perfect
	6:14	your **heavenly** Father will also
	6:26	and yet your **heavenly** Father
	6:32	your **heavenly** Father knows
	15:13	**heavenly** Father has not planted
	18:35	So my **heavenly** Father will also
	23: 9	the one in **heaven**

Lk	2:13	multitude of the **heavenly**
Ac	26:19	disobedient to the **heavenly**

3771   GO2 AG593 LN179 B2:188 K5:542 R3772
ουρανοθεν, FROM HEAVEN

Ac	14:17	giving you rains **from heaven**
	26:13	I saw a light **from heaven**

3772   GO273 AG593 LN179 B2:188 K5:497
ουρανος, HEAVEN

Mt	3: 2	for the kingdom of **heaven**
	3:16	the **heavens** were opened to him
	3:17	And a voice from **heaven** said
	4:17	kingdom of **heaven** has come
	5: 3	theirs is the kingdom of **heaven**
	5:10	theirs is the kingdom of **heaven**
	5:12	your reward is great in **heaven**
	5:16	to your Father in **heaven**
	5:18	until **heaven** and earth pass
	5:19	least in the kingdom of **heaven**
	5:19	in the kingdom of **heaven**
	5:20	enter the kingdom of **heaven**
	5:34	either by **heaven**
	5:45	of your Father in **heaven**
	6: 1	from your Father in **heaven**
	6: 9	Our Father in **heaven,** hallowed
	6:10	on earth as it is in **heaven**
	6:20	yourselves treasures in **heaven**
	6:26	Look at the birds of the **air**
	7:11	will your Father in **heaven**
	7:21	enter the kingdom of **heaven**
	7:21	will of my Father in **heaven**
	8:11	in the kingdom of **heaven**
	8:20	birds of the **air** have nests
	10: 7	The kingdom of **heaven** has come
	10:32	before my Father in **heaven**
	10:33	deny before my Father in **heaven**
	11:11	kingdom of **heaven** is greater
	11:12	kingdom of **heaven** has suffered
	11:23	you be exalted to **heaven**
	11:25	Lord of **heaven** and earth
	12:50	my Father in **heaven**
	13:11	of the kingdom of **heaven**
	13:24	The kingdom of **heaven** may be
	13:31	The kingdom of **heaven** is like
	13:32	the birds of the **air** come
	13:33	The kingdom of **heaven** is like
	13:44	The kingdom of **heaven** is like
	13:45	the kingdom of **heaven** is like

	13:47	the kingdom of **heaven** is like
	13:52	for the kingdom of **heaven**
	14:19	he looked up to **heaven**
	16: 1	show them a sign from **heaven**
	16: 2	weather, for the **sky** is red
	16: 3	for the **sky** is red
	16: 3	the appearance of the **sky**
	16:17	but my Father in **heaven**
	16:19	keys of the kingdom of **heaven**
	16:19	will be bound in **heaven**
	16:19	will be loosed in **heaven**
	18: 1	in the kingdom of **heaven**
	18: 3	enter the kingdom of **heaven**
	18: 4	in the kingdom of **heaven**
	18:10	in **heaven** their angels
	18:10	face of my Father in **heaven**
	18:14	of your Father in **heaven**
	18:18	earth will be bound in **heaven**
	18:18	earth will be loosed in **heaven**
	18:19	for you by my Father in **heaven**
	18:23	the kingdom of **heaven** may be
	19:12	sake of the kingdom of **heaven**
	19:14	the kingdom of **heaven** belongs
	19:21	will have treasure in **heaven**
	19:23	to enter the kingdom of **heaven**
	20: 1	For the kingdom of **heaven**
	21:25	of John come from **heaven**
	21:25	If we say, 'From **heaven,**'
	22: 2	The kingdom of **heaven** may be
	22:30	are like angels in **heaven**
	23:13	out of the kingdom of **heaven**
	23:22	and whoever swears by **heaven**
	24:29	stars will fall from **heaven**
	24:29	powers of **heaven** will be shaken
	24:30	will appear in **heaven**
	24:30	on the clouds of **heaven**
	24:31	from one end of **heaven** to the
	24:35	**Heaven** and earth will pass away
	24:36	neither the angels of **heaven**
	25: 1	the kingdom of **heaven** will be
	26:64	on the clouds of **heaven**
	28: 2	descending from **heaven**
	28:18	All authority in **heaven**
Mk	1:10	he saw the **heavens** torn apart
	1:11	And a voice came from **heaven**
	4:32	so that the birds of the **air**
	6:41	he looked up to **heaven**
	7:34	Then looking up to **heaven**
	8:11	him for a sign from **heaven**

	10:21	will have treasure in **heaven**		3:13	has ascended into **heaven**
	11:25	so that your Father in **heaven**		3:13	one who descended from **heaven**
	11:30	of John come from **heaven**		3:27	what has been given from **heaven**
	11:31	If we say, 'From **heaven**,'		3:31	The one who comes from **heaven**
	12:25	are like angels in **heaven**		6:31	gave them bread from **heaven**
	13:25	will be falling from **heaven**		6:32	you the bread from **heaven**
	13:25	the powers in the **heavens**		6:32	you the true bread from **heaven**
	13:27	earth to the ends of **heaven**		6:33	which comes down from **heaven**
	13:31	**Heaven** and earth will pass away		6:38	I have come down from **heaven**
	13:32	neither the angels in **heaven**		6:41	that came down from **heaven**
	14:62	with the clouds of **heaven**		6:42	I have come down from **heaven**
	16:19	was taken up into **heaven**		6:50	that comes down from **heaven**
Lk	2:15	left them and gone into **heaven**		6:51	that came down from **heaven**
	3:21	the **heaven** was opened		6:58	that came down from **heaven**
	3:22	And a voice came from **heaven**		12:28	Then a voice came from **heaven**
	4:25	when the **heaven** was shut up		17: 1	he looked up to **heaven**
	6:23	your reward is great in **heaven**	Ac	1:10	were gazing up toward **heaven**
	8: 5	the birds of the **air** ate it up		1:11	stand looking up toward **heaven**
	9:16	he looked up to **heaven**		1:11	taken up from you into **heaven**
	9:54	fire to come down from **heaven**		1:11	as you saw him go into **heaven**
	9:58	birds of the **air** have nests		2: 2	suddenly from **heaven** there came
	10:15	will you be exalted to **heaven**		2: 5	from every nation under **heaven**
	10:18	watched Satan fall from **heaven**		2:19	show portents in the **heaven**
	10:20	names are written in **heaven**		2:34	did not ascend into the **heavens**
	10:21	Lord of **heaven** and earth		3:21	who must remain in **heaven** until
	11:13	how much more will the **heavenly**		4:12	no other name under **heaven**
	11:16	from him a sign from **heaven**		4:24	made the **heaven** and the earth
	12:33	unfailing treasure in **heaven**		7:42	to worship the host of **heaven**
	12:56	the appearance of earth and **sky**		7:49	**Heaven** is my throne, and the
	13:19	birds of the **air** made nests		7:55	he gazed into **heaven** and saw
	15: 7	be more joy in **heaven** over one		7:56	I see the **heavens** opened and
	15:18	I have sinned against **heaven**		9: 3	suddenly a light from **heaven**
	15:21	I have sinned against **heaven**		10:11	He saw the **heaven** opened and
	16:17	But it is easier for **heaven**		10:12	reptiles and birds of the **air**
	17:24	lights up the **sky** from one side		10:16	suddenly taken up to **heaven**
	17:24	from one side to the **other**		11: 5	sheet coming down from **heaven**
	17:29	fire and sulfur from **heaven**		11: 6	reptiles, and birds of the **air**
	18:13	not even look up to **heaven**		11: 9	the voice answered from **heaven**
	18:22	will have treasure in **heaven**		11:10	was pulled up again to **heaven**
	19:38	Peace in **heaven,** and glory		14:15	made the **heaven** and the earth
	20: 4	of John come from **heaven**		17:24	he who is Lord of **heaven** and
	20: 5	If we say, 'From **heaven**,'		22: 6	a great light from **heaven**
	21:11	and great signs from **heaven**	Ro	1:18	is revealed from **heaven** against
	21:26	the powers of the **heavens**		10: 6	Who will ascend into **heaven**
	21:33	**Heaven** and earth will pass away	1C	8: 5	be so-called gods in **heaven**
	22:43	Then an angel from **heaven**		15:47	the second man is from **heaven**
	24:51	and was carried up into **heaven**	2C	5: 1	eternal in the **heavens**
Jn	1:32	Spirit descending from **heaven**		5: 2	with our **heavenly** dwelling
	1:51	you will see **heaven** opened		12: 2	caught up to the third **heaven**

Ga	1: 8	we or an angel from **heaven**
Ep	1:10	things in **heaven** and things
	3:15	whom every family in **heaven**
	4:10	far above all the **heavens**
	6: 9	the same Master in **heaven**
Ph	3:20	our citizenship is in **heaven**
Co	1: 5	laid up for you in **heaven**
	1:16	in him all things in **heaven**
	1:20	whether on earth or in **heaven**
	1:23	to every creature under **heaven**
	4: 1	also have a Master in **heaven**
1Th	1:10	wait for his Son from **heaven**
	4:16	will descend from **heaven**
2Th	1: 7	Jesus is revealed from **heaven**
He	1:10	**heavens** are the work of your
	4:14	passed through the **heavens**
	7:26	and exalted above the **heavens**
	8: 1	of the Majesty in the **heavens**
	9:23	sketches of the **heavenly** things
	9:24	he entered into **heaven** itself
	11:12	many as the stars of **heaven**
	12:23	who are enrolled in **heaven**
	12:25	the one who warns from **heaven**
	12:26	the earth but also the **heaven**
Ja	5:12	either by **heaven** or by earth
	5:18	and the **heaven** gave rain
1P	1: 4	kept in **heaven** for you
	1:12	Holy Spirit sent from **heaven**
	3:22	who has gone into **heaven**
2P	1:18	this voice come from **heaven**
	3: 5	**heavens** existed long ago
	3: 7	present **heavens** and earth have
	3:10	**heavens** will pass away with a
	3:12	**heavens** will be set
	3:13	we wait for new **heavens**
Re	3:12	from my God out of **heaven**
	4: 1	in **heaven** a door stood open
	4: 2	in **heaven** stood a throne
	5: 3	no one in **heaven** or on earth
	5:13	heard every creature in **heaven**
	6:13	and the stars of the **sky** fell
	6:14	The **sky** vanished like a scroll
	8: 1	there was silence in **heaven**
	8:10	great star fell from **heaven**
	9: 1	that had fallen from **heaven**
	10: 1	coming down from **heaven**
	10: 4	I heard a voice from **heaven**
	10: 5	raised his right hand to **heaven**
	10: 6	who created **heaven** and what is

	10: 8	I had heard from **heaven** spoke
	11: 6	authority to shut the **sky**
	11:12	heard a loud voice from **heaven**
	11:12	went up to **heaven** in a cloud
	11:13	gave glory to the God of **heaven**
	11:15	were loud voices in **heaven**
	11:19	temple in **heaven** was opened
	12: 1	portent appeared in **heaven**
	12: 3	portent appeared in **heaven**
	12: 4	third of the stars of **heaven**
	12: 7	And war broke out in **heaven**
	12: 8	any place for them in **heaven**
	12:10	I heard a loud voice in **heaven**
	12:12	you **heavens** and those who dwell
	13: 6	those who dwell in **heaven**
	13:13	fire come down from **heaven**
	14: 2	I heard a voice from **heaven**
	14: 7	him who made **heaven** and earth
	14:13	I heard a voice from **heaven**
	14:17	out of the temple in **heaven**
	15: 1	I saw another portent in **heaven**
	15: 5	tent of witness in **heaven**
	16:11	and cursed the God of **heaven**
	16:21	dropped from **heaven** on people
	18: 1	coming down from **heaven**
	18: 4	heard another voice from **heaven**
	18: 5	sins are heaped high as **heaven**
	18:20	Rejoice over her, O **heaven**
	19: 1	of a great multitude in **heaven**
	19:11	Then I saw **heaven** opened
	19:14	And the armies of **heaven**
	20: 1	angel coming down from **heaven**
	20: 9	And fire came down from **heaven**
	20:11	the earth and the **heaven** fled
	21: 1	I saw a new **heaven** and a new
	21: 1	for the first **heaven** and the
	21: 2	coming down out of **heaven**
	21:10	coming down out of **heaven**

3773   GO1 AG595 LN179
ουρβανος, URBANUS
Ro 16: 9 Greet **Urbanus,** our co-worker

3774   GO1 AG595 LN179 K3:1
ουριας, OURIAS (URIAH)
Mt   1: 6 of Solomon by the wife of **Uriah**

3775   GO36 AG595 LN179 K5:543
ους, EAR
Mt 10:27 and what you hear **whispered**

	11:15	Let anyone with **ears** listen!
	13: 9	Let anyone with **ears** listen!
	13:15	their **ears** are hard of hearing
	13:15	and listen with their **ears**
	13:16	and your **ears,** for they hear
	13:43	Let anyone with **ears** listen!
Mk	4: 9	anyone with **ears** to hear listen
	4:23	anyone with **ears** to hear listen
	7:33	put his fingers into his **ears**
	8:18	have **ears,** and fail to hear
Lk	1:44	as soon as I **heard** the sound
	4:21	been fulfilled in your **hearing**
	8: 8	Let anyone with **ears** to hear
	9:44	words sink into your **ears**
	12: 3	**whispered** behind closed doors
	14:35	Let anyone with **ears** to hear
	22:50	cut off his right **ear**
Ac	7:51	in heart and **ears,** you are
	7:57	But they covered their **ears**
	11:22	News of this came to the **ears**
	28:27	**ears** are hard of hearing
	28:27	and listen with their **ears**
Ro	11: 8	and **ears** that would not hear
1C	2: 9	no eye has seen, nor **ear**
	12:16	And if the **ear** would say
Ja	5: 4	reached the **ears** of the Lord
1P	3:12	his **ears** are open to their
Re	2: 7	Let anyone who has an **ear**
	2:11	Let anyone who has an **ear**
	2:17	Let anyone who has an **ear**
	2:29	Let anyone who has an **ear**
	3: 6	Let anyone who has an **ear**
	3:13	Let anyone who has an **ear**
	3:22	Let anyone who has an **ear**
	13: 9	Let anyone who has an **ear**

3776   GO2 AG596 LN180 B2:845
ουσια, SUBSTANCE

Lk	15:12	the share of the **property**
	15:13	he squandered his **property**

3777   GO87 AG596 LN180
ουτε, NOR

Mt	6:20	where **neither** moth nor rust
	6:20	where neither moth **nor** rust
	12:32	**either** in this age or in the
	12:32	either in this age **or** in the
	22:30	they **neither** marry nor are
	22:30	neither marry **nor** are given

Mk	12:25	they **neither** marry nor are
	12:25	they neither marry **nor** are
	14:68	But he denied it, **saying**
	14:68	I do not know **or** understand
Lk	14:35	fit **neither** for the soil
	14:35	neither for the soil **nor** for
	20:35	from the dead **neither** marry nor
	20:35	**nor** are given in marriage
Jn	4:11	you have **no** bucket
	4:21	**neither** on this mountain nor
	4:21	neither on this mountain **nor**
	5:37	You have **never** heard his voice
	5:37	his voice **or** seen his form
	8:19	know **neither** me nor my Father
	8:19	know neither me **nor** my Father
	9: 3	**Neither** this man nor his
	9: 3	this man **nor** his parents sinned
Ac	2:31	He was **not** abandoned to Hades
	2:31	**nor** did his flesh experience
	15:10	that **neither** our ancestors nor
	15:10	our ancestors **nor** we have been
	19:37	are **neither** temple robbers nor
	19:37	are neither temple robbers **nor**
	24:12	They did **not** find me disputing
	24:12	stirring up a crowd **either** in
	24:12	either in the synagogues **or**
	25: 8	I have in **no** way committed an
	25: 8	**or** against the temple
	25: 8	**or** against the emperor
	28:21	have received **no** letters from
	28:21	**none** of the brothers coming
Ro	8:38	convinced that **neither** death
	8:38	that neither death, **nor** life
	8:38	death, nor life, **nor** angels
	8:38	life, nor angels, **nor** rulers
	8:38	nor rulers, **nor** things present
	8:38	**nor** things to come, nor powers
	8:38	things to come, **nor** powers
	8:39	**nor** height, nor depth,
	8:39	nor height, **nor** depth
	8:39	**nor** anything else in all
1C	3: 7	So **neither** the one who plants
	3: 7	**nor** the one who waters is
	6: 9	Fornicators, **[nor]** idolaters
	6: 9	Fornicators, **[nor]** idolaters
	6: 9	adulterers, **[nor]** male prostitutes
	6: 9	male prostitutes, **[nor]** sodomites
	6: 9	male prostitutes, **[nor]** sodomites
	6:10	thieves, **[nor]** the greedy,

	6:10	thieves, **[nor]** the greedy,
	8: 8	We are **no** worse off if we do
	8: 8	and **no** better off if we do
	11:11	woman is **not** independent of
	11:11	**or** man independent of woman
Ga	1:12	**nor** was I taught it, but I
	5: 6	For in Christ Jesus **neither**
	5: 6	**nor** uncircumcision counts for
	6:15	For **neither** circumcision nor
	6:15	**nor** uncircumcision is anything
1Th	2: 5	**or** with a pretext for greed
	2: 6	**nor** did we seek praise from
	2: 6	**whether** from you or from others
	2: 6	whether from you **or** from others
Ja	3:12	**No more** can salt water yield
3J	1:10	**even** prevents those who want
Re	3:15	you are **neither** cold nor hot
	3:15	you are neither cold **nor** hot
	3:16	and **neither** cold nor hot
	3:16	and neither cold **nor** hot
	5: 3	open the scroll **or** to look into
	5: 4	open the scroll **or** to look into
	9:20	**which** cannot see or hear or
	9:20	which cannot see **or** hear or
	9:20	which cannot see or hear **or**
	9:21	murders **or** their sorceries
	9:21	**or** their fornication or their
	9:21	fornication **or** their thefts
	21: 4	Death will be **no more**
	21: 4	and pain will be **no more**
	21: 4	and pain will be **no more**

3778   ᴳᴼ1391   ᴬᴳ596   ᴸᴺ180
ουτος, THIS [MULTIPLE OCCURRENCES]

3779   ᴳᴼ208   ᴬᴳ597   ᴸᴺ180
ουτως, THUSLY

Mt	1:18	took place **in this way**
	2: 5	for **so** it has been written by
	3:15	for us **in this way** to fulfill
	5:12	heaven, for **in the same way**
	5:16	**In the same way,** let your light
	5:19	teaches others to do **the same**
	6: 9	Pray then **in this way**
	6:30	will he not **much more** clothe
	7:12	do to others **as** you would have
	7:17	**In the same way,** every good
	9:33	anything **like this** been seen

	11:26	for **such** was your gracious will
	12:40	**so** for three days and three
	12:45	**So** will it be also with this
	13:40	**so** will it be at the end of the
	13:49	**So** it will be at the end of the
	17:12	**So** also the Son of Man is about
	18:14	**So** it is not the will of your
	18:35	**So** my heavenly Father will also
	19: 8	the beginning it was not **so**
	19:10	If **such** is the case of a man
	19:12	who have been **so** from birth
	20:16	**So** the last will be first
	20:26	It will not be **so** among you
	23:28	**So** you also on the outside
	24:27	**so** will be the coming of the
	24:33	**So** also, when you see all
	24:37	**so** will be the coming of the
	24:39	**so** too will be the coming
	24:46	**at** work when he arrives
	26:40	**So,** could you not stay awake
	26:54	it must happen **in this way**
Mk	2: 7	this fellow speak **in this way**
	2: 8	were discussing **these** questions
	2:12	never seen anything **like this**
	4:26	He also **said,** "The kingdom of
	7:18	**Then** do you also fail to
	9: 3	**such as** no one on earth could
	10:43	But it is not **so** among you
	13:29	**So** also, when you see these
	14:59	But **even** on this point their
	15:39	**in this way** he breathed his
Lk	1:25	**This** is what the Lord has done
	2:48	have you treated us **like this**
	9:15	They did **so** and made them all
	10:21	for **such** was your gracious will
	11:30	**so** the Son of Man will be to
	12:21	**So** it is with those who store
	12:28	**how much more** will he clothe
	12:38	near dawn, and finds them **so**
	12:43	find at work when he **arrives**
	12:54	to rain'; and **so** it happens
	14:33	**So** therefore, none of you can
	15: 7	**Just so,** I tell you, there
	15:10	**Just so,** I tell you, there
	17:10	**So** you also, when you have done
	17:24	**so** will the Son of Man be in
	17:26	**so** too it will be in the days
	19:31	**just** say this, 'The Lord needs
	21:31	**So** also, when you see these

	22:26	But not **so** with you		5:21	**so** grace might also exercise
	24:24	**just** as the women had said		6: 4	**so** we too might walk in newness
	24:46	**Thus** it is written		6:11	**So** you also must consider
Jn	3: 8	**So** it is with everyone who is		6:19	**so** now present your members
	3:14	**so** must the Son of Man be		9:20	Why have you made me **like this**
	3:16	For God **so** loved the world		10: 6	**that** comes from faith says
	4: 6	was sitting **by** the well		11: 5	**So** too at the present time
	5:21	**so** also the Son gives life to		11:26	And **so** all Israel will be saved
	5:26	**so** he has granted the Son also		11:31	**so** they have now been
	7:46	has anyone spoken **like this**		12: 5	**so** we, who are many, are one
	11:48	If we let him go on **like this**		15:20	**Thus** I make it my ambition
	12:50	I speak, **therefore,** I speak	1C	2:11	**So** also no one comprehends
	13:25	**So** while reclining next to		3:15	but **only** as through fire
	14:31	but I do **as** the Father has		4: 1	Think of us **in this way**
	15: 4	**neither** can you unless you		5: 3	I **have** already pronounced
	18:22	Is that **how** you answer the high		6: 5	**Can it be** that there is no one
	21: 1	he showed himself **in this way**		7: 7	one **having one kind** and another
Ac	1:11	will come **in the same way**		7: 7	and another a **different kind**
	3:18	**In this way** God fulfilled		7:17	**that** the Lord has assigned
	7: 1	Are these things **so?**		7:17	**This** is my rule in all the
	7: 6	And God spoke **in these terms**		7:26	for you to remain **as** you are
	7: 8	**so** Abraham became the father		7:36	and **so** it has to be
	8:32	**so** he does not open his mouth		7:40	if she remains **as** she is
	12: 8	He did **so.** Then he said to him		8:12	you **thus** sin against members
	12.15	she insisted that it was **so**		9:14	**In the same way,** the Lord
	13: 8	for **that is** the translation		9:15	**so that** they may be applied
	13:34	he has spoken **in this way**		9:24	Run **in such a way** that you may
	13:47	For **so** the Lord has commanded		9:26	**So** I do not run aimlessly
	14: 1	spoke **in such a way** that a		9:26	**nor** do I box as though beating
	17:11	these things were **so**		11:12	**so** man comes through woman
	17:33	**At that point** Paul left them		11:28	and **only then** eat of the bread
	19:20	**So** the word of the Lord grew		12:12	one body, **so** it is with Christ
	20:11	them until dawn; **then** he left		14: 9	**So** with yourselves; if in a
	20:13	for he had made **this** arrangement		14:12	**So** with yourselves; since you
	20:35	that **by such** work we		14:21	yet **even** then they will not
	21:11	**This is the way** the Jews		14:25	**that** person will bow down
	22:24	**for this** outcry against him		15:11	**so** we proclaim and so you have
	23:11	**so** you must bear witness also		15:11	**so** you have come to believe
	24: 9	that all **this** was true		15:22	**so** all will be made alive in
	24:14	**[thus]** I worship the God of our		15:42	**So** it is with the resurrection
	27:17	sea anchor and **so** were driven		15:45	**Thus** it is written, "The first
	27:25	it will be **exactly** as I have		16: 1	**follow** the directions I gave
	27:44	And **so** it was that all were	2C	1: 5	**so** also our consolation is
Ro	1:15	**hence** my eagerness to proclaim		1: 7	**so** also you share in our
	4:18	**So** numerous shall your		7:14	**so** our boasting to Titus has
	5:12	and **so** death spread to all		8: 6	**so** he should also
	5:15	much more **surely** have the grace		8:11	**so that** your eagerness may be
	5:18	**so** one man's act of		9: 5	**So** I thought it necessary
	5:19	**so** by the one man's obedience		10: 7	belong to Christ, **so** also do we

Ga	1: 6	you are **so** quickly deserting
	3: 3	Are you **so** foolish?
	4: 3	**So** with us; while we were
	4:29	the Spirit, **so** it is now also
	6: 2	**in this way** you will fulfill
Ep	4:20	That is not **the way** you learned
	5:24	**so** also wives ought to be
	5:28	**In the same way,** husbands
	5:33	Each of you, **however,** should
Ph	3:17	**those** who live according to the
	4: 1	firm in the Lord **in this way**
Co	3:13	**so** you also must forgive
1Th	2: 4	**even so** we speak, not to please
	2: 8	**So** deeply do we care for you
	4:14	again, **even so,** through Jesus
	4:17	**so** we will be with the Lord
	5: 2	Lord will come **like** a thief
2Th	3:17	**it is the way** I write
2Ti	3: 8	**so** these people, of corrupt
He	4: 4	the seventh day **as follows**
	5: 3	**as well as** for those of the
	5: 5	**So** also Christ did not glorify
	6: 9	**Even** though we speak in this
	6:15	And **thus** Abraham
	9: 6	**Such** preparations having been
	9:28	**so** Christ, having been offered
	10:33	partners with those **so** treated
	12:21	**so** terrifying was the sight
Ja	1:11	**It is the same way** with the
	2:12	**So** speak and so act as those
	2:12	So speak and **so** act as those
	2:17	**So** faith by itself, if it has
	3: 5	**So** also the tongue is a small
	3:10	this ought not to be **so**
1P	2:15	**For** it is God's will that by
	3: 5	It was **in this way** long ago
2P	1:11	For **in this way,** entry into
	3: 4	things continue **as they were**
	3:11	**Since** all these things are to
1J	2: 6	ought to walk **just as** he walked
	4:11	we **also** ought to love one
Re	2:15	**So** you also have some who hold
	3: 5	you will be clothed **like** them
	3:16	**So,** because you are lukewarm
	9:17	**this was how** I saw the horses
	11: 5	must be killed **in this manner**
	16:18	**so** violent was that earthquake
	18:21	**With such** violence Babylon

3780 GO54 AG598 LN180 R3756

ουχι, NOT

Mt	5:46	Do **not** even the tax collectors
	5:47	Do **not** even the Gentiles do the
	6:25	do **not** worry about your life
	10:29	Are **not** two sparrows sold for
	12:11	will you **not** lay hold of it
	13:27	did you **not** sow good seed
	13:56	And are **not** all his sisters
	18:12	he **not** leave the ninety-nine
	20:13	did you **not** agree with me for
Lk	1:60	**No;** he is to be called John.
	4:22	Is **not** this Joseph's son?
	6:39	Will **not** both fall into a pit?
	12: 6	Are **not** five sparrows sold for
	12:51	**No,** I tell you, but rather
	13: 3	**No,** I tell you; but unless you
	13: 5	**No,** I tell you; but unless you
	14:28	does **not** first sit down
	14:31	will **not** sit down first
	15: 8	does **not** light a lamp
	16:30	**No,** father Abraham; but if
	17: 8	you **not** rather say to him
	17:17	Were **not** ten made clean?
	18:30	**not** get back very much more
	22:27	Is it **not** the one at the table
	23:39	Are you **not** the Messiah?
	24:26	Was it **not** necessary that the
	24:32	Were **not** our hearts burning
Jn	9: 9	**No,** but it is someone like him
	11: 9	Are there **not** twelve hours
	13:10	you are clean, though **not** all
	13:11	**Not** all of you are clean.
	14:22	to us, and **not** to the world
Ac	5: 4	did it **not** remain your own?
	7:50	Did **not** my hand make all these
Ro	3:27	**No,** but by the law of faith
	3:29	Is he **not** the God of Gentiles
	8:32	will he **not** with him also give
1C	1:20	Has **not** God made foolish the
	3: 3	are you **not** of the flesh
	5: 2	Should you **not** rather have
	5:12	Is it **not** those who are inside
	6: 1	**instead of** taking it before the
	6: 7	Why **not** rather be wronged?
	6: 7	Why **not** rather be defrauded?
	8:10	might they **not,** since their
	10:16	is it **not** a sharing in the
	10:16	is it **not** a sharing in the body

	10:29	conscience, **not** your own
2C	3: 8	how **much** more will the ministry
Ga	2:14	like a Gentile and **not** like a
1Th	2:19	at his coming? Is it **not** you?
He	1:14	Are **not** all angels spirits
	3:17	Was it **not** those who sinned

3781   GO7 AG598 LN180 B2:666 K5:565 R3784
οφειλετης, DEBTOR

Mt	6:12	And forgive us our **debts**
	18:24	one **who owed** him ten thousand
Lk	13: 4	they were **worse offenders** than
Ro	1:14	I am a **debtor** both to Greeks
	8:12	**debtors,** not to the flesh
	15:27	do this, and indeed **they owe**
Ga	5: 3	that he is **obliged** to obey

3782   GO3 AG598 LN180 B2:666 K5:564 R3784
οφειλη, DEBT

Mt	18:32	I forgave you all that **debt**
Ro	13: 7	Pay to all what **is due** them
1C	7: 3	his wife her conjugal **rights**

3783   GO2 AG598 LN180 B2:666 K5:565 R3784
οφειλημα, DEBT

| Mt | 6:12 | And forgive us our **debts** |
| Ro | 4: 4 | as a gift but as something **due** |

3784   GO35 AG598 LN180 B2:666 K5:559
οφειλω, I OWE

Mt	18:28	who **owed** him a hundred denarii
	18:28	Pay what you **owe.**
	18:30	until he would pay the **debt**
	18:34	he would pay his entire **debt**
	23:16	sanctuary **is bound** by the oath
	23:18	the altar **is bound** by the oath
Lk	7:41	one **owed** five hundred denarii
	11: 4	forgive everyone **indebted** to us
	16: 5	How much **do** you **owe** my master?
	16: 7	And how much **do** you **owe?**
	17:10	only what we **ought** to have done
Jn	13:14	**ought** to wash one another's
	19: 7	he **ought** to die because he has
Ac	17:29	we **ought** not to think that the
Ro	13: 8	**Owe** no one anything, except to
	15: 1	who are strong **ought** to put up
	15:27	**ought** also to be of service
1C	5:10	**need** to go out of the world
	7:36	and so it **has** to be, let him
	9:10	plows **should** plow in hope

	11: 7	a man **ought** not to have his
	11:10	woman **ought** to have a symbol
2C	12:11	you **should** have been the ones
	12:14	children **ought** not to lay up
Ep	5:28	husbands **should** love their
2Th	1: 3	**must** always give thanks to God
	2:13	But we **must** always give thanks
Pm	1:18	any way, or **owes** you anything
He	2:17	Therefore he **had** to become like
	5: 3	he **must** offer sacrifice for
	5:12	you **ought** to be teachers
1J	2: 6	**ought** to walk just as he walked
	3:16	we **ought** to lay down our lives
	4:11	also **ought** to love one another
3J	1: 8	Therefore we **ought** to support

3785   GO4 AG599 LN180 B2:666
οφελον, I WISH

1C	4: 8	**wish that** you had become kings
2C	11: 1	I **wish** you would bear with me
Ga	5:12	I **wish** those who unsettle you
Re	3:15	**wish that** you were either cold

3786   GO3 AG599 LN180
οφελος, ADVANTAGE

1C	15:32	what would I have **gained** by it
Ja	2:14	**What good** is it, my brothers
	2:16	what is the **good** of that

3787   GO2 AG599 LN180 K2:280 R3788,1397
οφθαλμοδουλια, EYE SLAVERY

| Ep | 6: 6 | not only while **being watched** |
| Co | 3:22 | **being watched** and in order to |

3788   GO100 AG599 LN180 B3:511 K5:375
οφθαλμος, EYE

Mt	5:29	If your right **eye** causes you
	5:38	An **eye** for an eye and a tooth
	5:38	An eye for an **eye** and a tooth
	6:22	The **eye** is the lamp of the body
	6:22	if your **eye** is healthy
	6:23	but if your **eye** is unhealthy
	7: 3	speck in your neighbor's **eye**
	7: 3	notice the log in your own **eye**
	7: 4	take the speck out of your **eye**
	7: 4	the log is in your own **eye**
	7: 5	log out of your own **eye**
	7: 5	out of your neighbor's **eye**
	9:29	Then he touched their **eyes**
	9:30	And their **eyes** were opened

	13:15	they have shut their **eyes**
	13:15	might not look with their **eyes**
	13:16	But blessed are your **eyes**
	17: 8	And when they **looked** up
	18: 9	if your **eye** causes you to
	18: 9	than to have two **eyes** and to be
	20:15	Or are you **envious** because I
	20:33	let our **eyes** be opened
	21:42	and it is amazing in our **eyes**
	26:43	for their **eyes** were heavy
Mk	7:22	**envy,** slander, pride, folly
	8:18	Do you have **eyes,** and fail to
	8:25	laid his hands on his **eyes**
	9:47	if your **eye** causes you to
	9:47	than to have two **eyes** and to be
	12:11	it is amazing in our **eyes**
	14:40	their **eyes** were very heavy
Lk	2:30	for my **eyes** have seen your
	4:20	The **eyes** of all in the
	6:20	Then he **looked** up at
	6:41	speck in your neighbor's **eye**
	6:41	notice the log in your own **eye**
	6:42	take out the speck in your **eye**
	6:42	see the log in your own **eye**
	6:42	the log out of your own **eye**
	6:42	out of your neighbor's **eye**
	10:23	Blessed are the **eyes** that see
	11:34	**eye** is the lamp of your body
	11:34	If your **eye** is healthy
	16:23	he **looked** up and saw Abraham
	18:13	would not even **look** up to
	19:42	they are hidden from your **eyes**
	24:16	but their **eyes** were kept
	24:31	Then their **eyes** were opened
Jn	4:35	But I tell you, **look** around
	6: 5	When he **looked** up and saw a
	9: 6	the mud on the man's **eyes**
	9:10	how were your **eyes** opened
	9:11	spread it on my **eyes,** and said
	9:14	the mud and opened his **eyes**
	9:15	He put mud on my **eyes**
	9:17	It was your **eyes** he opened
	9:21	do we know who opened his **eyes**
	9:26	How did he open your **eyes?**
	9:30	and yet he opened my **eyes**
	9:32	opened the **eyes** of a person
	10:21	Can a demon open the **eyes**
	11:37	opened the **eyes** of the blind
	11:41	And Jesus **looked** upward

	12:40	He has blinded their **eyes**
	12:40	not look with their **eyes**
	17: 1	he **looked** up to heaven and said
Ac	1: 9	took him out of their **sight**
	9: 8	and though his **eyes** were open
	9:18	like scales fell from his **eyes**
	9:40	Then she opened her **eyes**
	26:18	open their **eyes** so that they
	28:27	and they have shut their **eyes**
	28:27	might not look with their **eyes**
Ro	3:18	fear of God before their **eyes**
	11: 8	**eyes** that would not see
	11:10	let their **eyes** be darkened
1C	2: 9	What no **eye** has seen, nor ear
	12:16	Because I am not an **eye**
	12:17	If the whole body were an **eye**
	12:21	The **eye** cannot say to the hand
	15:52	in the twinkling of an **eye**
Ga	3: 1	It was before your **eyes** that
	4:15	would have torn out your **eyes**
Ep	1:18	with the **eyes** of your heart
He	4:13	bare to the **eyes** of the one
1P	3:12	For the **eyes** of the Lord
2P	2:14	have **eyes** full of adultery
1J	1: 1	we have seen with our **eyes**
	2:11	has brought on **blindness**
	2:16	the desire of the **eyes**
Re	1: 7	every **eye** will see him
	1:14	his **eyes** were like a flame
	2:18	who has **eyes** like a flame
	3:18	anoint your **eyes** so that you
	4: 6	of **eyes** in front and behind
	4: 8	full of **eyes** all around
	5: 6	seven horns and seven **eyes**
	7:17	every tear from their **eyes**
	19:12	His **eyes** are like a flame of
	21: 4	every tear from their **eyes**

3789   GO14 AG600 LN181 B1:508 K5:566
οφις, SNAKE, SERPENT

Mt	7:10	for a fish, will give a **snake**
	10:16	so be wise as **serpents**
	23:33	You **snakes,** you brood of vipers
Mk	16:18	they will pick up **snakes**
Lk	10:19	authority to tread on **snakes**
	11:11	give a **snake** instead of a fish
Jn	3:14	Moses lifted up the **serpent**
1C	10: 9	and were destroyed by **serpents**
2C	11: 3	I am afraid that as the **serpent**

Re   9:19   their tails are like **serpents**
    12: 9   that ancient **serpent,** who is
    12:14   could fly from the **serpent** into
    12:15   **serpent** poured water like a
    20: 2   dragon, that ancient **serpent**

3790   ᴳᴼ1   ᴬᴳ600   ᴸᴺ181
οφρυς, BROW
Lk   4:29   led him to the **brow** of the hill

3791   ᴳᴼ1   ᴬᴳ600   ᴸᴺ181
οχλεω, I CROWD
Ac   5:16   **tormented** by unclean spirits

3792   ᴳᴼ1   ᴬᴳ600   ᴸᴺ181   ᴿ3793,4160
οχλοποιεω, I FORM CROWD
Ac 17: 5   they **formed a mob** and set the

3793   ᴳᴼ175   ᴬᴳ600   ᴸᴺ181   ᴮ2:800   ᴷ5:582
οχλος, CROWD
Mt   4:25   And great **crowds** followed him
     5: 1   When Jesus saw the **crowds**
     7:28   the **crowds** were astounded
     8: 1   great **crowds** followed him
     8:18   Now when Jesus saw great
             crowds
     9: 8   When the **crowds** saw it
     9:23   the **crowd** making a commotion
     9:25   **crowd** had been put outside
     9:33   and the **crowds** were amazed
     9:36   When he saw the **crowds**
    11: 7   speak to the **crowds** about John
    12:15   Many **crowds** followed him
    12:23   All the **crowds** were amazed
    12:46   still speaking to the **crowds**
    13: 2   Such great **crowds** gathered
    13: 2   whole **crowd** stood on the beach
    13:34   told the **crowds** all these
    13:36   Then he left the **crowds**
    14: 5   he feared the **crowd,** because
    14:13   But when the **crowds** heard it
    14:14   he saw a great **crowd**
    14:15   send the **crowds** away so that
    14:19   he ordered the **crowds** to sit
    14:19   gave them to the **crowds**
    14:22   while he dismissed the **crowds**
    14:23   he had dismissed the **crowds**
    15:10   Then he called the **crowd** to him
    15:30   Great **crowds** came to him
    15:31   so that the **crowd** was amazed

    15:32   have compassion for the **crowd**
    15:33   desert to feed so great a **crowd**
    15:35   ordering the **crowd** to sit down
    15:36   gave them to the **crowds**
    15:39   After sending away the **crowds**
    17:14   When they came to the **crowd**
    19: 2   Large **crowds** followed him
    20:29   a large **crowd** followed him
    20:31   The **crowd** sternly ordered them
    21: 8   large **crowd** spread their cloaks
    21: 9   The **crowds** that went ahead
    21:11   The **crowds** were saying
    21:26   we are afraid of the **crowd**
    21:46   but they feared the **crowds**
    22:33   And when the **crowd** heard it
    23: 1   Then Jesus said to the **crowds**
    26:47   with him was a large **crowd**
    26:55   Jesus said to the **crowds**
    27:15   a prisoner for the **crowd,**
    27:20   elders persuaded the **crowds**
    27:24   his hands before the **crowd**
Mk   2: 4   to Jesus because of the **crowd**
     2:13   the whole **crowd** gathered
             around
     3: 9   because of the **crowd**
     3:20   the **crowd** came together again
     3:32   A **crowd** was sitting around him
     4: 1   large **crowd** gathered around him
     4: 1   the whole **crowd** was beside
     4:36   And leaving the **crowd** behind
     5:21   great **crowd** gathered around
     5:24   And a large **crowd** followed him
     5:27   came up behind him in the **crowd**
     5:30   Jesus turned about in the **crowd**
     5:31   You see the **crowd** pressing in
     6:34   he saw a great **crowd**
     6:45   while he dismissed the **crowd**
     7:14   Then he called the **crowd** again
     7:17   When he had left the **crowd**
     7:33   away from the **crowd**
     8: 1   there was again a great **crowd**
     8: 2   I have compassion for the **crowd**
     8: 6   he ordered the **crowd** to sit
     8: 6   distributed them to the **crowd.**
     8:34   He called the **crowd** with his
     9:14   saw a great **crowd** around them
     9:15   When the whole **crowd** saw him
     9:17   Someone from the **crowd**
             answered
     9:25   saw that a **crowd** came running

	10: 1	**crowds** again gathered around		22:47	suddenly a **crowd** came
	10:46	disciples and a large **crowd**		23: 4	chief priests and the **crowds**
	11:18	whole **crowd** was spellbound		23:48	**crowds** who had gathered there
	11:32	they were afraid of the **crowd**	Jn	5:13	had disappeared in the **crowd**
	12:12	but they feared the **crowd**		6: 2	large **crowd** kept following him
	12:37	the large **crowd** was listening		6: 5	looked up and saw a large **crowd**
	12:41	and watched the **crowd** putting		6:22	the **crowd** that had stayed
	14:43	with him there was a **crowd**		6:24	when the **crowd** saw that neither
	15: 8	**crowd** came and began to ask		7:12	about him among the **crowds**
	15:11	stirred up the **crowd** to have		7:12	he is deceiving the **crowd**
	15:15	wishing to satisfy the **crowd**		7:20	The **crowd** answered, "You have
Lk	3: 7	the **crowds** that came out to be		7:31	Yet many in the **crowd** believed
	3:10	And the **crowds** asked him		7:32	The Pharisees heard the **crowd**
	4:42	**crowds** were looking for him		7:40	some in the **crowd** said
	5: 1	the **crowd** was pressing in on		7:43	was a division in the **crowd**
	5: 3	taught the **crowds** from the boat		7:49	But this **crowd,** which does not
	5:15	many **crowds** would gather		11:42	for the sake of the **crowd**
	5:19	in because of the **crowd**		12: 9	**crowd** of the Jews learned
	5:29	there was a large **crowd** of tax		12:12	The next day the great **crowd**
	6:17	**crowd** of his disciples and a		12:17	So the **crowd** that had been with
	6:19	And all in the **crowd** were		12:18	the **crowd** went to meet him
	7: 9	the **crowd** that followed him		12:29	The **crowd** standing there heard
	7:11	a large **crowd** went with him		12:34	The **crowd** answered him
	7:12	with her was a large **crowd**	Ac	1:15	the **crowd** numbered about one
	7:24	began to speak to the **crowds**		6: 7	great **many** of the priests
	8: 4	When a great **crowd** gathered		8: 6	The **crowds** with one
	8:19	reach him because of the **crowd**		11:24	And a great many **people** were
	8:40	when Jesus returned, the **crowd**		11:26	taught a great many **people**
	8:42	the **crowds** pressed in on him		13:45	when the Jews saw the **crowds**
	8:45	the **crowds** surround you		14:11	When the **crowds** saw what Paul
	9:11	When the **crowds** found out about		14:13	he and the **crowds** wanted to
	9:12	Send the **crowd** away, so that		14:14	rushed out into the **crowd**
	9:16	to set before the **crowd**		14:18	scarcely restrained the **crowds**
	9:18	Who do the **crowds** say that I am		14:19	Iconium and won over the
	9:37	mountain, a great **crowd** met him			**crowds**
	9:38	Just then a man from the **crowd**		16:22	The **crowd** joined in attacking
	11:14	and the **crowds** were amazed		17: 8	**people** and the city officials
	11:27	the **crowd** raised her voice		17:13	stir up and incite the **crowds**
	11:29	the **crowds** were increasing		19:26	considerable number of **people**
	12: 1	**crowd** gathered by the thousands		19:33	Some of the **crowd** gave
	12:13	Someone in the **crowd** said		19:35	clerk had quieted the **crowd**
	12:54	He also said to the **crowds**		21:27	stirred up the whole **crowd**
	13:14	kept saying to the **crowd**		21:34	Some in the **crowd** shouted one
	13:17	entire **crowd** was rejoicing		21:35	violence of the **mob** was so
	14:25	large **crowds** were traveling		24:12	stirring up a **crowd** either
	18:36	When he heard a **crowd** going by		24:18	any **crowd** or disturbance
	19: 3	but on account of the **crowd**	Re	7: 9	there was a great **multitude**
	19:39	of the Pharisees in the **crowd**		17:15	are peoples and **multitudes**
	22: 6	when no **crowd** was present		19: 1	of a great **multitude** in heaven
				19: 6	the voice of a great **multitude**

3794   GO1 AG601 LN181 K5:590
οχυρωμα, FORTRESS
2C 10: 4   power to destroy **strongholds**

3795   GO5 AG601 LN181 B1:670
οψαριον, SMALL FISH
Jn   6: 9   five barley loaves and two **fish**
     6:11   so also the **fish,** as much as
     21: 9   fire there, with **fish** on it
     21:10   Bring some of the **fish** that
     21:13   and did the same with the **fish**

3796   GO3 AG601 LN181
οψε, EVENING
Mt 28: 1   **After** the sabbath, as the first
Mk 11:19   And when **evening** came, Jesus
     13:35   in the **evening,** or at midnight

3797   GO1 AG601 LN181 B3:1000 R3796
οψιμος, EVENING
Ja   5: 7   the early and the **late** rains

3798   GO15 AG601 LN181 R3796
οψιος, EVENING
Mt   8:16   That **evening** they brought to
     14:15   When it was **evening**
     14:23   When **evening** came, he was
     16: 2   When it is **evening,** you say
     20: 8   When **evening** came, the owner
     26:20   When it was **evening,** he took
     27:57   When it was **evening**
Mk   1:32   That **evening,** at sundown
     4:35   when **evening** had come
     6:47   When **evening** came, the boat
     11:11   as it was already **late,** he went
     14:17   When it was **evening,** he came
     15:42   When **evening** had come
Jn   6:16   When **evening** came
     20:19   When it was **evening** on that day

3799   GO3 AG601 LN181 R3700
οψις, SIGHT
Jn   6:16   When **evening** came
     7:24   Do not judge by **appearances**
     11:44   and his **face** wrapped in a cloth
Re   1:16   and his **face** was like the sun

3800   GO4 AG602 LN181 B3:144 K5:591
οψωνιον, SALARY, PROVISIONS
Lk   3:14   be satisfied with your **wages**

Ro   6:23   For the **wages** of sin is death
1C   9: 7   pays the **expenses** for doing
2C 11: 8   by accepting **support** from them

π

3802   GO1 AG602 LN181 K5:595 R3803
παγιδευω, I TRAP
Mt 22:15   and plotted to **entrap** him

3803   GO5 AG602 LN181 K5:593
παγις, TRAP
Lk 21:35   like a **trap.** For it will come
Ro 11: 9   become a **snare** and a trap
1Ti 3: 7   and the **snare** of the devil
     6: 9   **trapped** by many senseless
2Ti 2:26   they may escape from the **snare**

3803a   GO2 AG602 LN181 R697
παγος, PAGUS
Ac 17:19   brought him to the Areo **pagus**
     17:22   in front of the Areo **pagus**

3804   GO16 AG602 LN181 B3:719 K5:930 R3806
παθημα, SUFFERING
Ro   7: 5   the flesh, our sinful **passions**
     8:18   I consider that the **sufferings**
2C   1: 5   as the **sufferings** of Christ
     1: 6   endure the same **sufferings**
     1: 7   you share in our **sufferings**
Ga   5:24   with its **passions** and desires
Ph   3:10   the sharing of his **sufferings**
Co   1:24   rejoicing in my **sufferings**
2Ti 3:11   persecutions and **suffering**
He   2: 9   because of the **suffering**
     2:10   perfect through **sufferings**
     10:32   hard struggle with **sufferings**
1P   1:11   in advance to the **sufferings**
     4:13   sharing Christ's **sufferings**
     5: 1   the **sufferings** of Christ
     5: 9   the same kinds of **suffering**

3805   GO1 AG602 LN181 B3:719 K5:924 R3806
παθητος, SUFFERING
Ac 26:23   that the Messiah must **suffer**

3806   GO3 AG602 LN181 B3:719 K5:926
παθος, PASSION
Ro   1:26   them up to degrading **passions**

Co   3: 5   impurity, **passion,** evil desire
1Th   4: 5   not with lustful **passion**

3807   GO3 AG603 LN181 B1:370 K5:596 R3816,71
παιδαγωγος, TUTOR
1C   4:15   have ten thousand **guardians**
Ga   3:24   law was our **disciplinarian**
      3:25   subject to a **disciplinarian**

3808   GO1 AG603 LN181 B1:283 K5:636 R3816
παιδαριον, SMALL CHILD
Jn   6: 9   There is a **boy** here who has

3809   GO6 AG603 LN181 B3:775 K5:596 R3811
παιδεια, CHILD INSTRUCTION, DISCIPLINE
Ep   6: 4   bring them up in the **discipline**
2Ti   3:16   for **training** in righteousness
He   12: 5   the **discipline** of the Lord
     12: 7   for the sake of **discipline**
     12: 8   do not have that **discipline**
     12:11   **discipline** always seems painful

3810   GO2 AG603 LN181 B3:775 K5:596 R3811
παιδευτης, CHILD INSTRUCTOR
Ro   2:20   a **corrector** of the foolish
He   12: 9   parents to **discipline** us

3811   GO13 AG603 LN182 B3:775 K5:596 R3816
παιδευω, I DISCIPLINE
Lk   23:16   therefore have him **flogged**
     23:22   therefore have him **flogged**
Ac   7:22   So Moses **was instructed** in all
     22: 3   **educated** strictly according
1C   11:32   we **are disciplined** so that we
2C   6: 9   we are alive; as **punished**
1Ti   1:20   they may **learn** not to blaspheme
2Ti   2:25   **correcting** opponents with
Ti   2:12   **training** us to renounce
He   12: 6   **disciplines** those whom he loves
     12: 7   parent does not **discipline**
     12:10   **disciplined** us for a short time
Re   3:19   I reprove and **discipline** those

3812   GO1 AG604 LN182 R3813
παιδιοθεν, FROM CHILDHOOD
Mk   9:21   And he said, "From **childhood.**

3813   GO52 AG604 LN182 B1:283 K5:636 R3816
παιδιον, SMALL CHILD
Mt   2: 8   search diligently for the **child**

2: 9   the place where the **child** was
2:11   they saw the **child** with Mary
2:13   take the **child** and his mother
2:13   about to search for the **child**
2:14   took the **child** and his mother
2:20   take the **child** and his mother
2:20   the **child's** life are dead
2:21   Joseph got up, took the **child**
11:16   It is like **children** sitting in
14:21   besides women and **children**
15:38   besides women and **children**
18: 2   He called a **child,** whom he put
18: 3   change and become like **children**
18: 4   becomes humble like this **child**
18: 5   one such **child** in my name
19:13   **children** were being brought
19:14   Let the little **children** come
Mk   5:39   The **child** is not dead but
5:40   and took the **child's** father
5:40   went in where the **child** was
5:41   He took **her** by the hand
7:28   eat the **children's** crumbs
7:30   the **child** lying on the bed
9:24   father of the **child** cried out
9:36   Then he took a little **child**
9:37   **child** in my name welcomes me
10:13   were bringing little **children**
10:14   Let the little **children** come
10:15   as a little **child** will never
Lk   1:59   to circumcise the **child**
1:66   then will this **child** become
1:76   And you, **child,** will be called
1:80   **child** grew and became strong
2:17   told them about this **child**
2:27   brought in the **child** Jesus
2:40   **child** grew and became strong
7:32   They are like **children** sitting
9:47   took a little **child** and put it
9:48   Whoever welcomes this **child**
11: 7   my **children** are with me in bed
18:16   Let the little **children** come to
18:17   as a little **child** will never
Jn   4:49   down before my little **boy** dies
16:21   But when her **child** is born
21: 5   **Children,** you have no fish
1C   14:20   be **children** in your thinking
He   2:13   **children** whom God has given me
2:14   **children** share flesh and blood
11:23   that the **child** was beautiful

1J	2:14	I write to you, **children**
	2:18	**Children,** it is the last hour

3814   GO13 AG604 LN182 R3816
παιδισκη, SERVANT GIRL

Mt	26:69	**servant-girl** came to him
Mk	14:66	one of the **servant-girls**
	14:69	And the **servant-girl**
Lk	12:45	other slaves, men and **women**
	22:56	Then a **servant-girl**
Jn	18:17	The **woman** said to Peter
Ac	12:13	a **maid** named Rhoda came to
	16:16	we met a **slave-girl** who had
Ga	4:22	one by a **slave woman** and the
	4:23	One, the **child** of the **slave**
	4:30	Drive out the **slave** and her
	4:30	for the child of the **slave**
	4:31	the **slave** but of the free woman

3815   GO1 AG604 LN182 K5:625
παιζω, I PLAY

1C	10: 7	and they rose up to **play**

3816   GO24 AG604 LN182 B1:283 K5:636
παις, SERVANT BOY

Mt	2:16	killed all the **children** in and
	8: 6	my **servant** is lying at home
	8: 8	and my **servant** will be healed
	8:13	And the **servant** was healed
	12:18	Here is my **servant,** whom I have
	14: 2	and he said to his **servants**
	17:18	the **boy** was cured instantly
	21:15	heard the **children** crying out
Lk	1:54	has helped his **servant** Israel
	1:69	house of his **servant** David
	2:43	the **boy** Jesus stayed behind in
	7: 7	and let my **servant** be healed
	8:51	the **child's** father and mother
	8:54	called out, **"Child,** get up!"
	9:42	healed the **boy,** and gave him
	12:45	the other **slaves, men** and women
	15:26	He called one of the **slaves**
Jn	4:51	him that his **child** was alive
Ac	3:13	has glorified his **servant** Jesus
	3:26	When God raised up his **servant**
	4:25	ancestor David, your **servant**
	4:27	against your holy **servant** Jesus
	4:30	the name of your holy **servant**
	20:12	had taken the **boy** away alive

3817   GO5 AG605 LN182
παιω, I STRIKE

Mt	26:68	Who is it that **struck** you?
Mk	14:47	his sword and **struck** the slave
Lk	22:64	Who is it that **struck** you?
Jn	18:10	**struck** the high priest's slave
Re	9: 5	scorpion when it **stings** someone

3819   GO7 AG605 LN182 B2:713 K5:717
παλαι, OF OLD

Mt	11:21	would have repented **long ago**
Mk	15:44	he had been dead **for some time**
Lk	10:13	would have repented **long ago**
2C	12:19	you been thinking **all along**
He	1: 1	**Long ago** God spoke to our
2P	1: 9	of the cleansing of **past** sins
Ju	1: 4	who **long ago** were designated

3820   GO19 AG605 LN182 B2:713 K5:717 R3819
παλαιος, OLD

Mt	9:16	unshrunk cloth on an **old** cloak
	9:17	new wine put into **old** wineskins
	13:52	what is new and what is **old**
Mk	2:21	unshrunk cloth on an **old** cloak
	2:21	the new from the **old**
	2:22	new wine into **old** wineskins
Lk	5:36	sews it on an **old** garment
	5:36	the new will not match the **old**
	5:37	new wine into **old** wineskins
	5:39	after drinking **old** wine desires
	5:39	The **old** is good.
Ro	6: 6	We know that our **old** self
1C	5: 7	Clean out the **old** yeast so that
	5: 8	not with the **old** yeast
2C	3:14	the reading of the **old** covenant
Ep	4:22	way of life, your **old** self
Co	3: 9	stripped off the **old** self
1J	2: 7	but an **old** commandment that
	2: 7	the **old** commandment is the word

3821   GO1 AG606 LN182 B2:713 K5:720 R3820
παλαιοτης, OLDNESS

Ro	7: 6	not under the **old** written code

3822   GO4 AG606 LN182 B2:713 K5:720 R3820
παλαιοω, I AM OLD

Lk	12:33	that do not **wear out**
He	1:11	all **wear out** like clothing
	8:13	made the first one **obsolete**
	8:13	is **obsolete** and growing old

3823　^{GO}1　^{AG}606　^{LN}182
παλη, WRESTLING
Ep　6:12　For our **struggle** is not against

3824　^{GO}2　^{AG}606　^{LN}182　^B1:184　^K1:686　^R3825,1078
παλιγγενεσια, BORN AGAIN
Mt　19:28　at the **renewal** of all things
Ti　　3: 5　through the water of **rebirth**

3825　^{GO}141　^{AG}606　^{LN}182
παλιν, AGAIN
Mt　4: 7　**Again** it is written
　　4: 8　**Again,** the devil took him to a
　　5:33　**Again,** you have heard that it
　　13:45　**Again,** the kingdom of heaven
　　13:47　**Again,** the kingdom of heaven
　　18:19　**Again,** truly I tell you, if two
　　19:24　**Again** I tell you, it is easier
　　20: 5　he went out **again** about noon
　　21:36　**Again** he sent other slaves
　　22: 1　**Once more** Jesus spoke to them
　　22: 4　**Again** he sent other slaves
　　26:42　**Again** he went away for the
　　26:43　**Again** he came and found them
　　26:44　So leaving them **again,** he went
　　26:44　time, saying the **same** words
　　26:72　**Again** he denied it with an
　　27:50　cried **again** with a loud voice
Mk　2: 1　he returned **to** Capernaum
　　2:13　Jesus went out **again** beside
　　3: 1　**Again** he entered the synagogue
　　3:20　the crowd came together **again**
　　4: 1　**Again** he began to teach beside
　　5:21　had crossed **again** in the boat
　　7:14　Then he called the crowd **again**
　　7:31　returned **from** the region
　　8: 1　there was **again** a great crowd
　　8:13　getting into the boat **again**
　　8:25　his hands on his eyes **again**
　　10: 1　crowds **again** gathered around
　　10: 1　he **again** taught them
　　10:10　the disciples asked him **again**
　　10:24　But Jesus said to them **again**
　　10:32　He took the twelve aside **again**
　　11: 3　and will send it **back** here
　　11:27　Again they came **to** Jerusalem
　　12: 4　**again** he sent another slave
　　14:39　**again** he went away and prayed
　　14:40　**once more** he came and found
　　14:61　**Again** the high priest asked

　　14:69　began **again** to say to the
　　14:70　But **again** he denied it
　　14:70　bystanders **again** said to Peter
　　15: 4　Pilate asked him **again**
　　15:12　Pilate spoke to them **again**
　　15:13　shouted **back,** "Crucify him!"
Lk　6:43　nor **again** does a bad tree bear
　　13:20　And **again** he said
　　23:20　addressed them **again**
Jn　1:35　John **again** was standing with
　　4: 3　left Judea and started **back**
　　4:13　water will be thirsty **again**
　　4:46　Then he came **again** to Cana
　　4:54　Now this was **the** second sign
　　6:15　he withdrew **again** to the
　　8: 2　in the morning he came **again**
　　8: 8　And once **again** he bent down
　　8:12　**Again** Jesus spoke to them
　　8:21　**Again** he said to them
　　9:15　**Then** the Pharisees also began
　　9:17　said **again** to the blind man
　　9:27　do you want to hear it **again**
　　10: 7　So **again** Jesus said to them
　　10:17　in order to take it up **again**
　　10:18　have power to take it up **again**
　　10:19　**Again** the Jews were divided
　　10:31　took up stones **again** to stone
　　10:39　tried to arrest him **again**
　　10:40　went away **again** across the
　　11: 7　Let us go to Judea **again.**
　　11: 8　are you going there **again**
　　11:38　Jesus, **again** greatly disturbed
　　12:28　and I will glorify it **again**
　　12:39　because Isaiah **also** said
　　13:12　and had **returned** to the table
　　14: 3　I will come **again** and will take
　　16:16　and **again** a little while
　　16:17　and **again** a little while
　　16:19　and **again** a little while
　　16:22　but I will see you **again**
　　16:28　**again,** I am leaving the world
　　18: 7　**Again** he asked them
　　18:27　**Again** Peter denied it
　　18:33　entered the headquarters **again**
　　18:38　went out to the Jews **again**
　　18:40　They shouted in **reply**
　　19: 4　Pilate went out **again** and
　　19: 9　entered his headquarters **again**
　　19:37　And **again** another passage

	20:10	Then the disciples **returned**
	20:21	Jesus said to them **again**
	20:26	disciples were **again** in the
	21: 1	Jesus showed himself **again**
	21:16	A **second** time he said to him,
Ac	10:15	The voice said to him **again**
	11:10	everything was pulled up **again**
	17:32	We will hear you **again** about
	18:21	I will **return** to you
	27:28	they took soundings **again**
Ro	8:15	to fall **back** into fear
	11:23	power to graft them in **again.**
	15:10	and **again** he says
	15:11	and **again,** "Praise the Lord
	15:12	and **again** Isaiah says
1C	3:20	and **again,** "The Lord knows the
	7: 5	and then come together **again,**
	12:21	**again** the head to the feet
2C	1:16	and to come **back** to you from
	2: 1	not to make you **another** painful
	3: 1	to commend ourselves **again**
	5:12	ourselves to you **again**
	10: 7	**remind** yourself of this
	11:16	I **repeat,** let no one think
	12:21	I fear that when I come **again**
	13: 2	visit, that if I come **again**
Ga	1: 9	before, so now I **repeat**
	1:17	**afterwards** I returned to
	2: 1	fourteen years I went up **again**
	2:18	But if I build up **again**
	4: 9	how can you turn back **again**
	4: 9	be enslaved to them **again**
	4:19	for whom I am **again** in the pain
	5: 1	not submit **again** to a yoke
	5: 3	Once **again** I testify to every
Ph	1:26	when I come to you **again**
	2:28	rejoice at seeing him **again**
	4: 4	**again** I will say, Rejoice
He	1: 5	Or **again,** "I will be his Father
	1: 6	And **again,** when he brings the
	2:13	And **again,** "I will put my trust
	2:13	And **again,** "Here am I and the
	4: 5	**again** in this place it says
	4: 7	**again** he sets a certain day
	5:12	someone to teach you **again**
	6: 1	not laying **again** the foundation
	6: 6	they are crucifying **again**
	10:30	And **again,** "The Lord will judge
Ja	5:18	Then he prayed **again**

2P	2:20	they are **again** entangled
1J	2: 8	**Yet** I am writing you a new
Re	10: 8	from heaven spoke to me **again**
	10:11	**again** about many peoples

3826 GO1 AG607 LN182
παμπληθει, ALL QUANTITY, ALL TOGETHER
Lk 23:18 they all shouted out **together**

3828 GO5 AG607 LN182
παμφυλια, PAMPHYLIA
Ac 2:10 Phrygia and **Pamphylia,** Egypt
13:13 and came to Perga in **Pamphylia**
14:24 Pisidia and came to **Pamphylia**
15:38 deserted them in **Pamphylia**
27: 5 is off Cilicia and **Pamphylia**

3829 GO1 AG607 LN182
πανδοχειον, INN
Lk 10:34 brought him to an **inn**

3830 GO1 AG607 LN182
πανδοχευς, INNKEEPER
Lk 10:35 gave them to the **innkeeper**

3831 GO1 AG607 LN182 K5;722
πανηγυρις, FESTIVE GROUP
He 12:22 angels in **festal gathering**

3832 GO1 AG607 LN182 R3956,3624
πανοικει, ENTIRE HOUSE
Ac 16:34 he and his **entire household**

3833 GO3 AG607 LN182 B3:959 K5:295 R3956,3696
πανοπλια, ALL WEAPONRY
Lk 11:22 his **armor** in which he trusted
Ep 6:11 Put on the **whole armor** of God
6:13 take up the **whole armor** of God

3834 GO5 AG608 LN182 B1:412 K5:722 R3835
πανουργια, TRICKERY
Lk 20:23 he perceived their **craftiness**
1C 3:19 the wise in their **craftiness**
2C 4: 2 we refuse to practice **cunning**
11: 3 deceived Eve by its **cunning**
Ep 4:14 their **craftiness** in deceitful

3835 GO1 AG608 LN182 B1:412 K5:722
πανουργος, TRICKSTER
2C 12:16 since I was **crafty**

3835a   GO1   AG608   LN182
πανταχη, EVERY PLACE
Ac   21:28   teaching everyone **everywhere**

3837   GO7   AG608   LN182
πανταχου, EVERY PLACE
Mk   1:28   began to spread **throughout**
     16:20   the good news **everywhere**
Lk   9: 6   and curing diseases **everywhere**
Ac   17:30   commands all people **everywhere**
     24: 3   and **everywhere** with utmost
     28:22   **everywhere** it is spoken against
1C   4:17   as I teach them **everywhere**

3838   GO2   AG608   LN183   K8:66   R3956,5056
παντελης, ALL COMPLETE
Lk   13:11   unable to stand up **straight**
He   7:25   he is able **for all time** to save

3839   GO1   AG608   LN183,3956
παντη, IN ALL
Ac   24: 3   We welcome this in **every way**

3840   GO3   AG608   LN183   R3956
παντοθεν, FROM EVERYWHERE
Mk   1:45   came to him **from every quarter**
Lk   19:43   and hem you in **on every side**
He   9: 4   overlaid **on all sides** with gold

3841   GO10   AG608   LN183   B3:716   K3:914   R3956,2904
παντοκρατωρ, ALL STRENGTH, ALMIGHTY
2C   6:18   says the Lord **Almighty**
Re   1: 8   who is to come, the **Almighty**
     4: 8   holy, the Lord God the **Almighty**
     11:17   Lord God **Almighty,** who are
     15: 3   deeds, Lord God the **Almighty**
     16: 7   Yes, O Lord God, the **Almighty**
     16:14   great day of God the **Almighty**
     19: 6   the Lord our God the **Almighty**
     19:15   wrath of God the **Almighty**
     21:22   is the Lord God the **Almighty**

3842   GO41   AG609   LN183
παντοτε, ALWAYS
Mt   26:11   For you **always** have the poor
     26:11   but you will not **always** have me
Mk   14: 7   For you **always** have the poor
     14: 7   but you will not **always** have me
Lk   15:31   Son, you are **always** with me
     18: 1   their need to pray **always**

Jn   6:34   give us this bread **always**
     7: 6   but your time is **always** here
     8:29   **always** do what is pleasing
     11:42   I knew that you **always** hear me
     12: 8   **always** have the poor with you
     12: 8   but you do not **always** have me
     18:20   **always** taught in synagogues
Ro   1:10   may somehow **at last** succeed
1C   1: 4   I give thanks to my God **always**
     15:58   **always** excelling in the work
2C   2:14   who in Christ **always** leads us
     4:10   **always** carrying in the body
     5: 6   So we are **always** confident
     9: 8   so that by **always** having enough
Ga   4:18   for a good purpose **at all times**
Ep   5:20   God the Father **at all times**
Ph   1: 4   **constantly** praying with joy
     1:20   now as **always** in my body
     2:12   just as you have **always** obeyed
     4: 4   Rejoice in the Lord **always**
Co   1: 3   **always** thank God, the Father
     4: 6   your speech **always** be gracious
     4:12   He is **always** wrestling in his
1Th   1: 2   We **always** give thanks to God
     2:16   have **constantly** been filling up
     3: 6   you **always** remember us kindly
     4:17   will be with the Lord **forever**
     5:15   but **always** seek to do good
     5:16   Rejoice **always,**
2Th   1: 3   We must **always** give thanks
     1:11   we **always** pray for you
     2:13   But we must **always** give thanks
2Ti   3: 7   who are **always** being instructed
Pm   1: 4   I **always** thank my God
He   7:25   since he **always** lives to make

3843   GO8   AG609   LN183   R3956
παντως, ALTOGETHER
Lk   4:23   **Doubtless** you will quote to me
Ac   21:22   They will **certainly** hear that
     28: 4   This man **must** be a murderer
Ro   3: 9   better off? No, **not at all**
1C   5:10   not **at all** meaning the immoral
     9:10   Or does he not speak **entirely**
     9:22   that I might **by all means** save
     16:12   not **at all** willing to come now

3844   GO194   AG609   LN183   B3:1171   K5:727
παρα, FROM [MULTIPLE OCCURRENCES]

3845   GO3 AG611 LN183 B3:583 K5:736
παραβαινω, I GO ACROSS
Mt 15: 2   **break** the tradition of the
     15: 3   **break** the commandment of God
Ac   1:25   Judas **turned aside** to go to his

3846   GO1 AG611 LN183 R3844,906
παραβαλλω, I THROW ALONG
Ac 20:15   next day we **touched** at Samos

3847   GO7 AG611 LN183 B3:583 K5:739 R3845
παραβασις, TRANSGRESSION
Ro   2:23   by **breaking** the law
     4:15   law, neither is there **violation**
     5:14   like the **transgression** of Adam
Ga   3:19   because of **transgressions**
1Ti 2:14   and became a **transgressor**
He   2: 2   valid, and every **transgression**
     9:15   from the **transgressions** under

3848   GO5 AG612 LN183 B3:583 K5:740 R3845
παραβατης, TRANSGRESSOR
Ro   2:25   but if you **break** the law
     2:27   circumcision but **break** the law
Ga   2:18   that I am a **transgressor**
Ja   2: 9   by the law as **transgressors**
     2:11   a **transgressor** of the law

3849   GO2 AG612 LN183 R3844,971
παραβιαζομαι, I PRESS ALONG
Lk 24:29   But they **urged** him **strongly**
Ac 16:15   she **urged** us, saying, "If you

3850   GO50 AG612 LN183 B2:743 K5:744 R3846
παραβολη, PARALLEL STORY (PARABLE)
Mt 13: 3   them many things in **parables**
     13:10   you speak to them in **parables**
     13:13   I speak to them in **parables**
     13:18   Hear then the **parable** of the
     13:24   before them another **parable**
     13:31   before them another **parable**
     13:33   He told them another **parable**
     13:34   all these things in **parables**
     13:34   without a **parable** he told them
     13:35   my mouth to speak in **parables**
     13:36   the **parable** of the weeds
     13:53   had finished these **parables**
     15:15   Explain this **parable** to us
     21:33   Listen to another **parable**
     21:45   Pharisees heard his **parables**

     22: 1   Jesus spoke to them in **parables**
     24:32   fig tree learn its **lesson**
Mk   3:23   and spoke to them in **parables**
     4: 2   them many things in **parables**
     4:10   asked him about the **parables**
     4:11   everything comes in **parables**
     4:13   not understand this **parable**
     4:13   you understand all the **parables**
     4:30   what **parable** will we use for it
     4:33   many such **parables** he spoke
     4:34   to them except in **parables**
     7:17   asked him about the **parable**
     12: 1   to speak to them in **parables**
     12:12   that he had told this **parable**
     13:28   the fig tree learn its **lesson**
Lk   4:23   will quote to me this **proverb**
     5:36   He also told them a **parable**
     6:39   He also told them a **parable**
     8: 4   he said in a **parable**
     8: 9   what this **parable** meant
     8:10   to others I speak in **parables**
     8:11   Now the **parable** is this
     12:16   Then he told them a **parable**
     12:41   are you telling this **parable**
     13: 6   Then he told this **parable**
     14: 7   he told them a **parable**
     15: 3   So he told them this **parable**
     18: 1   Then Jesus told them a **parable**
     18: 9   He also told this **parable**
     19:11   he went on to tell a **parable**
     20: 9   to tell the people this **parable**
     20:19   that he had told this **parable**
     21:29   Then he told them a **parable**
He   9: 9   a **symbol** of the present time
     11:19   and **figuratively** speaking

3851   GO1 AG613 LN183
παραβολευομαι, I RISK
Ph   2:30   **risking** his life to make up

3852   GO5 AG613 LN183 B1:340 K5:761
παραγγελια, COMMAND
Ac   5:28   We gave you strict **orders** not
     16:24   Following these **instructions**
1Th 4: 2   For you know what **instructions**
1Ti 1: 5   the aim of such **instruction**
     1:18   giving you these **instructions**

3853   GO32 AG613 LN183 B1:340 K5:761
παραγγελλω, I COMMAND

Mt	10: 5	with the following **instructions**
	15:35	**ordering** the crowd to sit down
Mk	6: 8	**ordered** them to take nothing
	8: 6	**ordered** the crowd to sit down
	16: 8	that had been **commanded** them
Lk	5:14	he **ordered** him to tell no one
	8:29	**commanded** the unclean spirit
	8:56	**ordered** them to tell no one
	9:21	ordered and **commanded** them
Ac	1: 4	he **ordered** them not to leave
	4:18	**ordered** them not to speak
	5:28	We **gave** you **strict orders** not
	5:40	**ordered** them not to speak
	10:42	He **commanded** us to preach
	15: 5	**ordered** to keep the law of
	16:18	I **order** you in the name of
	16:23	**ordered** the jailer to keep them
	17:30	now he **commands** all people
	23:22	the young man, **ordering** him
	23:30	**ordering** his accusers also to
1C	7:10	married I **give** this **command**
	11:17	the **following instructions**
1Th	4:11	with your hands, as we **directed**
2Th	3: 4	the things that we **command**
	3: 6	Now we **command** you, beloved
	3:10	we gave you this **command**
	3:12	Now such persons we **command**
1Ti	1: 3	you **may instruct** certain people
	4:11	things you **must insist on**
	5: 7	**Give** these **commands** as well
	6:13	good confession, I **charge** you
	6:17	**command** them not to be haughty

3854　G037 AG613 LN183 R3844,1096
παραγινομαι, I ARRIVE

Mt	2: 1	wise men from the East **came**
	3: 1	**appeared** in the wilderness
	3:13	Then Jesus **came** from Galilee
Mk	14:43	one of the twelve, **arrived**
Lk	7: 4	When they **came** to Jesus
	7:20	When the men **had come** to him
	8:19	mother and his brothers **came**
	11: 6	a friend of mine **has arrived**
	12:51	Do you think that I **have come**
	14:21	**returned** and reported this
	19:16	first **came** forward and said
	22:52	the elders who **had come** for him
Jn	3:23	people **kept coming** and were
	8: 2	he **came** again to the temple

Ac	5:21	and those with him **arrived**
	5:22	the temple police **went** there
	5:25	someone **arrived** and announced
	9:26	When he **had come** to Jerusalem
	9:39	and when he **arrived,** they took
	10:33	have been kind enough **to come**
	11:23	When he **came** and saw the grace
	13:14	and **came** to Antioch in Pisidia
	14:27	When they **arrived,** they called
	15: 4	When they **came** to Jerusalem
	17:10	and when they **arrived**
	18:27	On his **arrival** he greatly
	20:18	When they **came** to him
	21:18	all the elders **were present**
	23:16	so he **went** and gained entrance
	23:35	when your accusers **arrive**
	24:17	**came** to bring alms to my nation
	24:24	when Felix **came** with his wife
	25: 7	When he **arrived,** the Jews
	28:21	**coming** here has reported or
1C	16: 3	And when I **arrive,** I will send
2Ti	4:16	no one **came** to my support
He	9:11	Christ **came** as a high priest

3855　G010 AG613 LN183 K1:129 R3844,71
παραγω, I LEAD ALONG

Mt	9: 9	As Jesus **was walking along**
	9:27	As Jesus **went on** from there
	20:30	heard that Jesus **was passing by**
Mk	1:16	As Jesus **passed along** the Sea
	2:14	As he **was walking along**
	15:21	They compelled a **passer-by**
Jn	9: 1	As he **walked along,** he saw
1J	2: 8	the darkness **is passing away**
	2:17	and its desire **are passing away**

3856　G01 AG614 LN184 B2:291 K2:32 R3844,1165
παραδειγματιζω, I EXPOSE PUBLICLY

He	6: 6	**are holding him up to contempt**

3857　G03 AG614 LN184 B2:760 K5:765
παραδεισος, PARADISE

Lk	23:43	will be with me in **Paradise**
2C	12: 4	was caught up into **Paradise**
Re	2: 7	that is in the **paradise** of God

3858　G06 AG614 LN184 R3844,1209
παραδεχομαι, I ACCEPT

Mk	4:20	and **accept** it and bear fruit
Ac	15: 4	**were welcomed** by the church

	16:21	for us as Romans **to adopt**		14:11	an opportunity to **betray** him.
	22:18	they **will** not **accept** your		14:18	one of you **will betray** me, one
1Ti	5:19	Never **accept** any accusation		14:21	the Son of Man **is betrayed!** It
He	12: 6	every child whom he **accepts**		14:41	the Son of Man **is betrayed** into
				14:42	See, my **betrayer** is at hand.

3860 ^{GO}119 ^{AG}614 ^{LN}184 ^B2:361 ^K2:169 ^R3844,1325
παραδιδωμι, I GIVE OVER

				14:44	Now the **betrayer** had given them
				15: 1	and **handed** him **over** to Pilate.
Mt	4:12	that John **had been arrested**		15:10	priests **had handed** him **over.**
	5:25	**may hand** you **over** to the judge		15:15	he **handed** him **over** to be
	10: 4	the one who **betrayed** him	Lk	1: 2	they **were handed** on to us by
	10:17	for they **will hand** you **over**		4: 6	for it **has been given over** to
	10:19	When they **hand** you **over**		9:44	is going **to be betrayed** into
	10:21	Brother **will betray** brother		10:22	things have **been handed over** to
	11:27	things **have been handed over**		12:58	the judge **hand** you **over** to the
	17:22	is going to **be betrayed**		18:32	For he **will be handed over** to
	18:34	his lord **handed** him **over** to be		20:20	so as to **hand** him **over** to the
	20:18	Man **will be handed over** to the		21:12	they will **arrest** you and
	20:19	then they **will hand** him **over**		21:16	You **will be betrayed** even by
	24: 9	Then they **will hand** you **over**		22: 4	how he **might betray** him to them
	24:10	they **will betray** one another		22: 6	opportunity to **betray** him to
	25:14	and **entrusted** his property		22:21	one who **betrays** me is with me,
	25:20	Master, you **handed over** to me		22:22	one by whom he **is betrayed!**
	25:22	Master, you **handed over** to me		22:48	you **are betraying** the Son of
	26: 2	Son of Man **will be handed over**		23:25	and he **handed** Jesus **over** as
	26:15	give me if I **betray** him to you?		24: 7	of Man must **be handed over** to
	26:16	an opportunity to **betray** him.		24:20	leaders **handed** him **over** to be
	26:21	you, one of you will **betray** me.	Jn	6:64	the one that would **betray** him.
	26:23	the bowl with me will **betray** me		6:71	twelve, was going to **betray** him
	26:24	the Son of Man is **betrayed!** It		12: 4	one who was about to **betray** him
	26:25	Judas, who **betrayed** him, said,		13: 2	Simon Iscariot to **betray** him.
	26:45	the Son of Man is **betrayed** into		13:11	he knew who was to **betray** him;
	26:46	See, my **betrayer** is at hand.		13:21	one of you **will betray** me.
	26:48	the **betrayer** had given them a		18: 2	Now Judas, who **betrayed** him,
	27: 2	and **handed** him **over** to Pilate		18: 5	Judas, who **betrayed** him, was
	27: 3	When Judas, his **betrayer,** saw		18:30	not **have handed** him **over** to you
	27: 4	by **betraying** innocent blood.		18:35	priests **have handed** you **over** to
	27:18	that they **had handed** him **over.**		18:36	keep me from **being handed over**
	27:26	he **handed** him **over** to be		19:11	one who **handed** me **over** to you
Mk	1:14	Now after John **was arrested,**		19:16	Then he **handed** him **over** to them
	3:19	Iscariot, who **betrayed** him.		19:30	his head and **gave up** his spirit
	4:29	But when the grain **is ripe,** at		21:20	that is going to **betray** you?
	7:13	that you **have handed on.** And	Ac	3:13	whom you **handed over** and
	9:31	of Man is **to be betrayed** into		6:14	customs that Moses **handed on** to
	10:33	of Man **will be handed over** to		7:42	and **handed** them **over** to worship
	10:33	then they will **hand** him **over** to		8: 3	**committed** them to prison.
	13: 9	they **will hand** you **over** to		12: 4	**handed** him **over** to four squads
	13:11	to trial and **hand** you **over,** do		14:26	they **had been commended** to the
	13:12	Brother **will betray** brother to		15:26	who **have risked** their lives for
	14:10	in order **to betray** him to them.		15:40	believers **commending** him to the

	16: 4	they **delivered** to them for
	21:11	and **will hand** him **over** to the
	22: 4	and **putting** them in prison,
	27: 1	they **transferred** Paul and some
	28:17	and **handed over** to the Romans.
Ro	1:24	Therefore God **gave** them **up** in
	1:26	this reason God **gave** them **up** to
	1:28	God **gave** them **up** to a debased
	4:25	who **was handed over** to death
	6:17	to which you **were entrusted,**
	8:32	but **gave** him **up** for all of us,
1C	5: 5	are to **hand** this man **over** to
	11: 2	as I **handed** them **on** to you.
	11:23	I also **handed on** to you, that
	11:23	when he was **betrayed** took a
	13: 3	if I **hand over** my body so that
	15: 3	For I **handed on** to you as of
	15:24	end, when he **hands over** the
2C	4:11	always **being given up** to death
Ga	2:20	and **gave** himself for me.
Ep	4:19	and **have abandoned** themselves
	5: 2	us and **gave** himself **up** for us,
	5:25	church and **gave** himself **up** for
1Ti	1:20	I **have turned over** to Satan, so
1P	2:23	he **entrusted** himself to the one
2P	2: 4	hell and **committed** them to
	2:21	that **was passed on** to them.
Ju	1: 3	for all **entrusted** to the saints

3861 ᴳᴼ1 ᴬᴳ615 ᴸᴺ184 ᴷ2:255
παραδοξος, PARADOX
Lk   5:26   have seen **strange things** today.

3862 ᴳᴼ13 ᴬᴳ615 ᴸᴺ184 ᴮ2:367 ᴷ2:172 ᴿ3860
παραδοσις, TRADITION

Mt	15: 2	the **tradition** of the elders?
	15: 3	for the sake of your **tradition?**
	15: 6	for the sake of your **tradition,**
Mk	7: 3	the **tradition** of the elders
	7: 5	the **tradition** of the elders
	7: 8	and hold to human **tradition**
	7: 9	to keep your **tradition!**
	7:13	through your **tradition** that
1C	11: 2	maintain the **traditions** just as
Ga	1:14	the **traditions** of my ancestors
Co	2: 8	according to human **tradition**
2Th	2:15	the **traditions** that you were
	3: 6	the **tradition** that they

3863 ᴳᴼ4 ᴬᴳ616 ᴸᴺ184 ᴿ3844,2206
παραζηλοω, I MAKE JEALOUS

Ro	10:19	I **will make** you **jealous** of
	11:11	so as to **make** Israel **jealous**
	11:14	to **make** my own people **jealous**
1C	10:22	**provoking** the Lord **to jealousy?**

3864 ᴳᴼ1 ᴬᴳ616 ᴸᴺ184 ᴿ3864,2281
παραθαλασσιος, ALONG SEA
Mt   4:13   in Capernaum **by the sea,** in the

3865 ᴳᴼ1 ᴬᴳ616 ᴸᴺ184 ᴿ3844,2334
παραθεωρεω, I OVERLOOK
Ac   6: 1   widows **were being neglected** in

3866 ᴳᴼ3 ᴬᴳ616 ᴸᴺ184 ᴷ8:162 ᴿ3908
παραθηκη, COMMITMENT

1Ti	6:20	guard **what has been entrusted**
2Ti	1:12	that day **what** I **have entrusted**
	1:14	good treasure **entrusted** to you,

3867 ᴳᴼ2 ᴬᴳ616 ᴸᴺ184
παραινεω, I ADVISE

Ac	27: 9	gone by, Paul **advised** them,
	27:22	I **urge** you now to keep up your

3868 ᴳᴼ12 ᴬᴳ616 ᴸᴺ184 ᴮ2:855 ᴷ1:195
παραιτεομαι, I REJECT

Mk	15: 6	anyone for whom they **asked.**
Lk	14:18	all alike began **to make excuses**
	14:18	it; please **accept** my **regrets.**
	14:19	out; please **accept** my **regrets.**
Ac	25:11	I **am** not **trying to escape** death
1Ti	4: 7	**Have nothing to do** with profane
	5:11	But **refuse** to put younger
2Ti	2:23	**Have nothing to do** with stupid
Ti	3:10	**have nothing** more **to do** with
He	12:19	the hearers **beg** that not
	12:25	See that you do not **refuse** the
	12:25	when they **refused** the one who

3869 ᴳᴼ1 ᴬᴳ616 ᴸᴺ184 ᴿ3844,2523
παρακαθεζομαι, I SIT BESIDE
Lk   10:39   who **sat** at the Lord's feet and

3870 ᴳᴼ109 ᴬᴳ617 ᴸᴺ185 ᴮ1:569 ᴷ5:773 ᴿ3844,2564
παρακαλεω, I ENCOURAGE

Mt	2:18	she refused to **be consoled,**
	5: 4	for they **will be comforted.**
	8: 5	came to him, **appealing** to him

	8:31	The demons **begged** him, "If you		4:13	when slandered, we **speak kindly**
	8:34	they **begged** him to leave their		4:16	I **appeal** to you, then, be
	14:36	and **begged** him that they might		14:31	may learn and all **be encouraged.**
	18:29	fell down and **pleaded** with him,		16:12	I strongly **urged** him to visit
	18:32	because you **pleaded** with me.		16:16	I **urge** you to put yourselves
	26:53	I cannot **appeal** to my Father,	2C	1: 4	who **consoles** us in all our
Mk	1:40	A leper came to him **begging** him		1: 4	able to **console** those who are
	5:10	He **begged** him earnestly not to		1: 4	ourselves **are consoled** by God.
	5:12	unclean spirits **begged** him,		1: 6	if we **are being consoled,** it is
	5:17	began to **beg** Jesus to leave		2: 7	and **console** him, so that he may
	5:18	demons **begged** him that he might		2: 8	So I **urge** you to reaffirm your
	5:23	and **begged** him repeatedly, "My		5:20	we **entreat** you on behalf of
	6:56	and **begged** him that they might		6: 1	we **urge** you also not to accept
	7:32	they **begged** him to lay his hand		7: 6	God, who **consoles** the downcast,
	8:22	and **begged** him to touch him.		7: 6	**consoled** us by the arrival of
Lk	3:18	many other **exhortations,** he		7: 7	he **was consoled** about you, as
	7: 4	they **appealed** to him earnestly,		7:13	In this we **find comfort.** In
	8:31	They **begged** him not to order		8: 6	so that we **might urge** Titus
	8:32	demons **begged** Jesus to let them		9: 5	necessary to **urge** the brothers
	8:41	and **begged** him to come to his		10: 1	I myself, Paul, **appeal** to you
	15:28	and began to **plead** with him.		12: 8	Three times I **appealed** to the
	16:25	but now he **is comforted** here,		12:18	I **urged** Titus to go, and sent
Ac	2:40	and **exhorted** them, saying,		13:11	**listen to my appeal,** agree with
	8:31	And he **invited** Philip to get in	Ep	4: 1	**beg** you to lead a life worthy
	9:38	with the **request,** "Please come		6:22	and to **encourage** your hearts.
	11:23	and he **exhorted** them all to	Ph	4: 2	I **urge** Euodia and I urge
	13:42	the people **urged** them to speak		4: 2	I **urge** Syntyche to be of the
	14:22	and **encouraged** them to continue	Co	2: 2	hearts **to be encouraged** and
	15:32	to **encourage** and strengthen the		4: 8	that he may **encourage** your
	16: 9	Macedonia **pleading** with him and	1Th	2:12	**urging** and encouraging you and
	16:15	she **urged** us, saying, "If you		3: 2	strengthen and **encourage** you
	16:39	so they came and **apologized** to		3: 7	we **have been encouraged** about
	16:40	and **encouraged** the brothers and		4: 1	we ask and **urge** you in the Lord
	19:31	a message **urging** him not to		4:10	But we **urge** you, beloved, to do
	20: 1	after **encouraging** them and		4:18	Therefore **encourage** one another
	20: 2	much **encouragement,** he came to		5:11	Therefore **encourage** one another
	20:12	and were not a little **comforted**		5:14	And we **urge** you, beloved, to
	21:12	the people there **urged** him not	2Th	2:17	**comfort** your hearts and
	24: 4	I **beg** you to hear us briefly		3:12	and **exhort** in the Lord Jesus
	25: 2	Paul. They **appealed** to him	1Ti	1: 3	I **urge** you, as I did when I was
	27:33	Paul **urged** all of them to take		2: 1	I **urge** that supplications,
	27:34	Therefore I **urge** you to take		5: 1	but **speak** to him as to a father
	28:14	and were **invited** to stay with		6: 2	Teach and **urge** these duties.
	28:20	therefore I **have asked** to see	2Ti	4: 2	and **encourage,** with the utmost
Ro	12: 1	I **appeal** to you therefore,	Ti	1: 9	to **preach** with sound doctrine
	12: 8	the **exhorter,** in exhortation;		2: 6	Likewise, **urge** the younger men
	15:30	I **appeal** to you, brothers and		2:15	**exhort** and reprove with all
	16:17	I **urge** you, brothers and	Pm	1: 9	I would rather **appeal** to you on
1C	1:10	Now I **appeal** to you, brothers		1:10	I **am appealing** to you for my

He　3:13　But **exhort** one another every
　　10:25　but **encouraging** one another,
　　13:19　I **urge** you all the more to do
　　13:22　I **appeal** to you, brothers and
1P　2:11　Beloved, I **urge** you as aliens
　　5: 1　I **exhort** the elders among you
　　5:12　to **encourage** you and to testify
Ju　1: 3　to write and **appeal** to you to

3871　ᴳᴼ1　ᴬᴳ617　ᴸᴺ185　ᴿ3844,2572
παρακαλυπτω, I COVER ALONG
Lk　9:45　its meaning **was concealed** from

3873　ᴳᴼ2　ᴬᴳ617　ᴸᴺ185　ᴷ3:656
παρακειμαι, I LIE BESIDE
Ro　7:18　I can will what **is** right, but
　　7:21　good, evil **lies close at hand.**

3874　ᴳᴼ29　ᴬᴳ618　ᴸᴺ185　ᴮ1:569　ᴷ5:773　ᴿ3870
παρακλησις, ENCOURAGEMENT
Lk　2:25　to the **consolation** of Israel,
　　6:24　have received your **consolation.**
Ac　4:36　means "son of **encouragement**").
　　9:31　the **comfort** of the Holy Spirit,
　　13:15　any word of **exhortation** for the
　　15:31　rejoiced at the **exhortation.**
Ro　12: 8　the exhorter, in **exhortation;**
　　15: 4　and by the **encouragement** of the
　　15: 5　and **encouragement** grant you to
1C　14: 3　and **encouragement** and
2C　1: 3　God of all **consolation,**
　　1: 4　the **consolation** with which we
　　1: 5　our **consolation** is abundant
　　1: 6　your **consolation** and salvation;
　　1: 6　your **consolation,** which you
　　1: 7　share in our **consolation.**
　　7: 4　I am filled with **consolation;** I
　　7: 7　by the **consolation** with which
　　7:13　own **consolation,** we rejoiced
　　8: 4　begging us **earnestly** for the
　　8:17　accepted our **appeal,** but since
Ph　2: 1　any **encouragement** in Christ,
1Th　2: 3　For our **appeal** does not spring
2Th　2:16　gave us eternal **comfort** and
1Ti　4:13　to **exhorting,** to teaching.
Pm　1: 7　much joy and **encouragement**
　　　　　from
He　6:18　might be strongly **encouraged** to
　　12: 5　forgotten the **exhortation** that
　　13:22　with my word of **exhortation,**

3875　ᴳᴼ5　ᴬᴳ618　ᴸᴺ185　ᴮ1:88　ᴷ5:800　ᴿ3870
παρακλητος, ENCOURAGER
Jn　14:16　give you another **Advocate,** to
　　14:26　the **Advocate,** the Holy Spirit,
　　15:26　When the **Advocate** comes, whom
　　16: 7　the **Advocate** will not come to
1J　2: 1　an **advocate** with the Father,

3876　ᴳᴼ3　ᴬᴳ618　ᴸᴺ185　ᴮ2:172　ᴷ1:223　ᴿ3878
παρακοη, DISOBEDIENCE
Ro　5:19　one man's **disobedience** the many
2C　10: 6　punish every **disobedience** when
He　2: 2　or **disobedience** received a just

3877　ᴳᴼ4　ᴬᴳ618　ᴸᴺ185　ᴮ1:480　ᴷ1:215　ᴿ3844,190
παρακολουθεω, I FOLLOW ALONG
Mk　16:17　signs **will accompany** those who
Lk　1: 3　after **investigating** everything
1Ti　4: 6　teaching that you **have followed**
2Ti　3:10　you **have observed** my teaching,

3878　ᴳᴼ3　ᴬᴳ619　ᴸᴺ185　ᴮ2:172　ᴷ1:223　ᴿ3844,191
παρακουω, I IGNORE HEARING
Mt　18:17　**refuses to listen** to them, tell
　　18:17　offender **refuses to listen** even
Mk　5:36　But **overhearing** what they said,

3879　ᴳᴼ5　ᴬᴳ619　ᴸᴺ185　ᴷ5:814　ᴿ3844,2955
παρακυπτω, I STOOP DOWN
Lk　24:12　**stooping** and looking in, he saw
Jn　20: 5　He **bent down** to look in and saw
　　20:11　she **bent over** to look into the
Ja　1:25　who **look into** the perfect law,
1P　1:12　into which angels long to **look!**

3880　ᴳᴼ49　ᴬᴳ619　ᴸᴺ185　ᴮ3:747　ᴷ4:11　ᴿ3844,2983
παραλαμβανω, I TAKE ALONG
Mt　1:20　**to take** Mary as your wife, for
　　1:24　he **took** her as his wife,
　　2:13　Get up, **take** the child and his
　　2:14　Joseph got up, **took** the child
　　2:20　Get up, **take** the child and his
　　2:21　Joseph got up, **took** the child
　　4: 5　Then the devil **took** him to the
　　4: 8　Again, the devil **took** him to a
　　12:45　and **brings along** seven other
　　17: 1　Jesus **took** with him Peter and
　　18:16　**take** one or two others **along**
　　20:17　disciples **aside** by themselves,
　　24:40　one **will be taken** and one will

	24:41	one **will be taken** and one will
	26:37	He **took** with him Peter and the
	27:27	governor **took** Jesus into the
Mk	4:36	they **took** him with them in the
	5:40	and **took** the child's father and
	7: 4	traditions that they **observe,**
	9: 2	Jesus **took** with him Peter and
	10:32	He **took** the twelve **aside** again
	14:33	He **took** with him Peter and
Lk	9:10	He **took** them with him and
	9:28	Jesus **took** with him Peter and
	11:26	and **brings** seven other spirits
	17:34	one **will be taken** and the other
	17:35	one **will be taken** and the other
	18:31	Then he **took** the twelve aside
Jn	1:11	own people did not **accept** him.
	14: 3	and **will take** you to myself, so
	19:16	crucified. So they **took** Jesus;
Ac	15:39	Barnabas **took** Mark with him
	16:33	he **took** them and washed their
	21:24	**Join** these men, go through the
	21:26	Then Paul **took** the men, and the
	21:32	Immediately he **took** soldiers
	23:18	So he **took** him, brought him to
1C	11:23	For I **received** from the Lord
	15: 1	which you in turn **received,** in
	15: 3	what I in turn **had received:**
Ga	1: 9	to what you **received,** let that
	1:12	for I did not **receive** it from
Ph	4: 9	you have learned and **received**
Co	2: 6	As you therefore **have received**
	4:17	you **have received** in the Lord.
1Th	2:13	you **received** the word of God
	4: 1	as you **learned** from us how you
2Th	3: 6	tradition that they **received**
He	12:28	we **are receiving** a kingdom that

3881   GO2 AG619 LN185
παραλεγομαι, I COAST ALONG

Ac	27: 8	**Sailing past** it with difficulty
	27:13	began **to sail past** Crete, close

3882   GO1 AG620 LN185
παραλιος, ALONG SEA (COAST)

Lk	6:17	the **coast** of Tyre and Sidon.

3883   GO1 AG620 LN185 R3844,236
παραλλαγη, CHANGE

Ja	1:17	no **variation** or shadow due to

3884   GO2 AG620 LN185 B2:457 R3844,3049
παραλογιζομαι, I REASON SO AS TO DECEIVE

Co	2: 4	no one **may deceive** you with
Ja	1:22	hearers who **deceive** themselves.

3885   GO10 AG620 LN185 B3:999 R3886
παραλυτικος, PARALYZED ONE

Mt	4:24	**paralytics,** and he cured them.
	8: 6	lying at home **paralyzed,** in
	9: 2	were carrying a **paralyzed** man
	9: 2	he said to the **paralytic,**
	9: 6	he then said to the **paralytic**
Mk	2: 3	a **paralyzed** man, carried by
	2: 4	mat on which the **paralytic** lay.
	2: 5	to the **paralytic,** "Son, your
	2: 9	to the **paralytic,** 'Your sins
	2:10	he said to the **paralytic**

3886   GO5 AG620 LN185 B3:999
παραλυω, I PARALYZE

Lk	5:18	carrying a **paralyzed** man on a
	5:24	one who was **paralyzed**
Ac	8: 7	were **paralyzed** or lame were
	9:33	years, for he was **paralyzed.**
He	12:12	and strengthen your **weak** knees,

3887   GO4 AG620 LN185 B3:223 K4:577 R3844,3306
παραμενω, I STAY ALONG

1C	16: 6	perhaps I **will stay** with you or
Ph	1:25	I **will remain** and continue with
He	7:23	death from **continuing** in office
Ja	1:25	**persevere,** being not hearers

3888   GO4 AG620 LN185 B1:328 K5:816
παραμυθεομαι, I COMFORT

Jn	11:19	to **console** them about their
	11:31	**consoling** her, saw Mary get up
1Th	2:12	urging and **encouraging** you and
	5:14	**encourage** the faint hearted,

3889   GO1 AG620 LN185 B1:328 K5:816 R3888
παραμυθια, COMFORT

1C	14: 3	encouragement and **consolation.**

3890   GO1 AG620 LN185 B1:328 K5:816 R3889
παραμυθιον, COMFORT

Ph	2: 1	any **consolation** from love, any

3891 ᴳᴼ1 ᴬᴳ621 ᴸᴺ185 ᴮ2:438 ᴷ4:1091 ᴿ3844,3551
παρανομεω, AGAINST LAW
Ac   23: 3   yet **in violation** of the law you

3892   ᴳᴼ1 ᴬᴳ621 ᴸᴺ185 ᴷ4:1090 ᴿ3891
παρανομια, LAWLESSNESS
2P   2:16   for his own **transgression;** a

3893   ᴳᴼ1 ᴬᴳ621 ᴸᴺ185 ᴮ1:202 ᴷ6:125
ᴿ3844,4087
παραπικραινω, I AM EMBITTERED
He   3:16   heard and yet **were rebellious**

3894   ᴳᴼ2 ᴬᴳ621 ᴸᴺ186 ᴮ1:203 ᴷ6:125 ᴿ3893
παραπικρασμος, EMBITTERMENT
He   3: 8   as in the **rebellion,** as on the
        3:15   your hearts as in the **rebellion**

3895   ᴳᴼ1 ᴬᴳ621 ᴸᴺ186 ᴮ1:608 ᴷ6:170
ᴿ3844,4098
παραπιπτω, I FALL FROM
He   6: 6   then **have fallen away,** since on

3896   ᴳᴼ1 ᴬᴳ621 ᴸᴺ186 ᴿ3844,4126
παραπλεω, I SAIL ALONG
Ac   20:16   decided to **sail past** Ephesus,

3897   ᴳᴼ1 ᴬᴳ621 ᴸᴺ186
παραπλησιος, NEIGHBOR ALONG
Ph   2:27   so ill that he **nearly** died. But

3898   ᴳᴼ1 ᴬᴳ621 ᴸᴺ186 ᴿ3897
παραπλησιως, NEARLY
He   2:14   he himself **likewise** shared the

3899   ᴳᴼ5 ᴬᴳ621 ᴸᴺ186 ᴿ3844,4198
παραπορευομαι, I TRAVEL ALONG
Mt   27:39   Those who **passed by** derided him
Mk   2:23   sabbath he **was going through**
        9:30   and **passed through** Galilee.
    11:20   as they **passed by,** they saw the
    15:29   Those who **passed by** derided him

3900   ᴳᴼ19 ᴬᴳ621 ᴸᴺ186 ᴮ3:585 ᴷ6:170 ᴿ3895
παραπτωμα, TRESPASS
Mt   6:14   others their **trespasses,** your
        6:15   Father forgive your **trespasses.**
Mk 11:25   forgive you your **trespasses.**
Ro   4:25   to death for our **trespasses** and
        5:15   not like the **trespass.** For if

        5:15   the one man's **trespass,** much
        5:16   gift following many **trespasses**
        5:17   the one man's **trespass,** death
        5:18   just as one man's **trespass** led
        5:20   the **trespass** multiplied; but
   11:11   their **stumbling** salvation has
   11:12   Now if their **stumbling** means
2C   5:19   counting their **trespasses**
Ga   6: 1   is detected in a **transgression,**
Ep   1: 7   forgiveness of our **trespasses,**
        2: 1   through the **trespasses** and sins
        2: 5   our **trespasses,** made us alive
Co   2:13   you were dead in **trespasses** and
        2:13   forgave us all our **trespasses,**

3901   ᴳᴼ1 ᴬᴳ621 ᴸᴺ186
παραρρεω, I DRIFT
He   2: 1   we **do** not **drift away** from it

3902   ᴳᴼ1 ᴬᴳ622 ᴸᴺ186
παρασημος, SIGNED BY (INSIGNIA)
Ac   28:11   Twin Brothers as its **figurehead**

3903   ᴳᴼ4 ᴬᴳ622 ᴸᴺ186 ᴮ3:118
παρασκευαζω, I PREPARE
Ac   10:10   and while it **was being prepared**
1C   14: 8   who **will get ready** for battle?
2C   9: 2   Achaia **has been ready** since
        9: 3   so that you **may be ready**

3904   ᴳᴼ6 ᴬᴳ622 ᴸᴺ186 ᴮ3:119 ᴷ7:1 ᴿ3903
παρασκευη, PREPARATION
Mt   27:62   after the day of **Preparation**
Lk   23:54   It was the day of **Preparation**
Jn   19:14   it was the day of **Preparation**
    19:31   it was the day of **Preparation**
    19:42   Jewish day of **Preparation**

3905   ᴳᴼ1 ᴬᴳ622 ᴸᴺ186
παρατεινω, I STRETCH ALONG
Ac   20: 7   he **continued speaking** until

3906   ᴳᴼ6 ᴬᴳ622 ᴸᴺ186 ᴮ2:132 ᴷ8:146 ᴿ3844,5083
παρατηρεω, I KEEP WATCH
Mk   3: 2   They **watched** him to see whether
Lk   6: 7   and the Pharisees **watched** him
    14: 1   they were **watching** him closely
    20:20   So they **watched** him and sent
Ac   9:24   They were **watching** the gates
Ga   4:10   You are **observing** special days

3907 GO1 AG622 LN186 B2:132 K8:148 R3906
παρατηρησις, WATCHING, OBSERVING
Lk 17:20 **things that can be observed**

3908 GO19 AG622 LN186 K8:162 R3844,5087
παρατιθημι, I SET ALONGSIDE
Mt 13:24 He **put before** them another
 13:31 He **put before** them another
Mk 6:41 disciples **to set before** the
 8: 6 to his disciples to **distribute**
 8: 6 they **distributed** them to the
 8: 7 these too should be **distributed**
Lk 9:16 disciples to **set before** the
 10: 8 eat what **is set before** you
 11: 6 have nothing **to set before** him
 12:48 to whom much **has been
 entrusted**
 23:46 your hands I **commend** my spirit
Ac 14:23 they **entrusted** them to the Lord
 16:34 and **set** food **before** them; and
 17: 3 explaining and **proving** that it
 20:32 And now I **commend** you to God
1C 10:27 eat whatever **is set before** you
1Ti 1:18 I **am giving** you these
2Ti 2: 2 **entrust** to faithful people who
1P 4:19 **will entrust** themselves to a

3909 GO1 AG623 LN186 R3844,5177
παρατυγχανω, I HAPPEN ALONG
Ac 17:17 those who **happened to be there**

3910 GO1 AG623 LN186
παραυτικα, MOMENTARY
2C 4:17 slight **momentary** affliction is

3911 GO4 AG623 LN186 R3844,5342
παραφερω, I CARRY ALONG
Mk 14:36 **remove** this cup from me
Lk 22:42 if you are willing, **remove** this
He 13: 9 **Do** not **be carried away** by all
Ju 1:12 clouds **carried along** by the

3912 GO1 AG623 LN186 R3844,5426
παραφρονεω, I THINK (ACT) BESIDE
(MYSELF)
2C 11:23 I **am talking like a madman**

3913 GO1 AG623 LN186 R3912
παραφρονια, BEYOND REASON (MADNESS)
2P 2:16 the prophet's **madness**

3914 GO4 AG623 LN186
παραχειμαζω, I WINTER
Ac 27:12 they **could spend the winter**
 28:11 on a ship that **had wintered** at
1C 16: 6 or even **spend the winter**
Ti 3:12 decided **to spend the winter**

3915 GO1 AG623 LN187 R3914
παραχειμασια, WINTERING
Ac 27:12 for **spending the winter**

3916 GO18 AG623 LN187
παραχρημα, SUDDENLY
Mt 21:19 the fig tree withered **at once**
 21:20 the fig tree wither **at once?**
Lk 1:64 **Immediately** his mouth was
 4:39 **Immediately** she got up
 5:25 **Immediately** he stood up before
 8:44 **immediately** her hemorrhage
 8:47 had been **immediately** healed
 8:55 and she got up **at once**
 13:13 **immediately** she stood up
 18:43 **Immediately** he regained his
 19:11 was to appear **immediately**
 22:60 **At that moment,** while he was
Ac 3: 7 **immediately** his feet and
 ankles
 5:10 **Immediately** she fell down
 12:23 And **immediately,** because he
 13:11 **Immediately** mist and darkness
 16:26 **immediately** all the doors
 16:33 were baptized **without delay**

3917 GO1 AG623 LN187
παρδαλις, LEOPARD
Re 13: 2 I saw was like a **leopard**

3917a GO1 AG624 LN187
παρεδρευω, I SIT BESIDE, I WAIT ON
1C 9:13 those who **serve** at the altar

3918 GO24 AG624 LN187 B2:898 K5:858 R3844,1510
παρειμι, I AM PRESENT
Mt 26:50 do what you **are here** to do
Lk 13: 1 there **were** some **present**
Jn 7: 6 My time **has** not yet **come**
 11:28 The Teacher **is here** and is
Ac 10:21 the reason for your **coming**
 10:33 So now all of us **are here**
 12:20 So they **came** to him in a

	17: 6	upside down **have come here** also
	24:19	they ought **to be here** before
1C	5: 3	I **am present** in spirit
	5: 3	as if **present** I have already
2C	10: 2	I ask that when I **am present**
	10:11	we will also do when **present**
	11: 9	when I **was** with you and was in
	13: 2	when **present** on my second visit
	13:10	so that when I **come**
Ga	4:18	when I **am present** with you
	4:20	I wish I **were present** with you
Co	1: 6	that **has come** to you
He	12:11	than pleasant **at the time**
	13: 5	be content with what you **have**
2P	1: 9	anyone who **lacks** these things
	1:12	**are established** in the truth
Re	17: 8	**is about** to ascend from the

3919 ᴳᴼ1 ᴬᴳ624 ᴸᴺ187 ᴷ5:824 ᴿ3844,1521
παρεισαγω, I BRING IN ALONG
2P 2: 1 who **will secretly bring in**

3920 ᴳᴼ1 ᴬᴳ624 ᴸᴺ187 ᴷ5:824
παρεισακτος, BROUGHT IN SECRETLY
Ga 2: 4 believers **secretly brought in**

3921 ᴳᴼ1 ᴬᴳ624 ᴸᴺ187
παρεισδυω, I SLIP IN BESIDE
Ju 1: 4 intruders **have stolen in** among

3922 ᴳᴼ2 ᴬᴳ624 ᴸᴺ187 ᴮ1:320 ᴷ2:682 ᴿ3844,1525
παρεισερχομαι, I COME/GO IN ALONG
Ro 5:20 law **came in,** with the result
Ga 2: 4 who **slipped in** to spy on the

3923 ᴳᴼ1 ᴬᴳ625 ᴸᴺ187 ᴿ3844,1533
παρεισφερω, I BRING IN ALONG
2P 1: 5 you **must make every effort** to

3924 ᴳᴼ3 ᴬᴳ625 ᴸᴺ187
παρεκτος, EXCEPT
Mt 5:32 **except** on the ground of
Ac 26:29 **except** for these chains
2C ˜11:28 **besides** other things

3924a ᴳᴼ1 ᴬᴳ625 ᴸᴺ188 ᴮ3:959
παρεμβαλλω, I ENCAMP
Lk 19:43 enemies **will set up** ramparts

3925 ᴳᴼ10 ᴬᴳ625 ᴸᴺ188 ᴮ3:959
παρεμβολη, BARRACKS
Ac 21:34 be brought into the **barracks**
     21:37 be brought into the **barracks**
     22:24 be brought into the **barracks**
     23:10 bring him into the **barracks**
     23:16 gained entrance to the **barracks**
     23:32 they returned to the **barracks**
He 11:34 put foreign **armies** to flight
     13:11 are burned outside the **camp**
     13:13 go to him outside the **camp**
Re 20: 9 the **camp** of the saints

3926 ᴳᴼ1 ᴬᴳ625 ᴸᴺ188
παρενοχλεω, I ANNOY
Ac 15:19 we **should** not **trouble** those

3927 ᴳᴼ3 ᴬᴳ625 ᴸᴺ188 ᴮ1:690 ᴷ2:64
παρεπιδημος, TRANSIENTS
He 11:13 were strangers and **foreigners**
1P 1: 1 To the **exiles** of the Dispersion
    2:11 I urge you as aliens and **exiles**

3928 ᴳᴼ29 ᴬᴳ625 ᴸᴺ188 ᴮ1:320 ᴷ2:681 ᴿ3844,2064
παρερχομαι, I COME/GO ALONG
Mt 5:18 heaven and earth **pass away**
    5:18 **will pass** from the law until
    8:28 no one **could pass** that way
    14:15 and the hour **is now late**
    24:34 generation **will** not **pass away**
    24:35 Heaven and earth **will pass away**
    24:35 my words will not **pass away**
    26:39 let this cup **pass** from me
    26:42 cannot **pass** unless I drink it
Mk 6:48 He intended to **pass** them **by**
    13:30 generation **will** not **pass away**
    13:31 Heaven and earth **will pass away**
    13:31 but my words **will** not **pass away**
    14:35 the hour **might pass** from him
Lk 11:42 without **neglecting** the others
    12:37 he **will come** and serve them
    15:29 never **disobeyed** your command
    16:17 heaven and earth **to pass away**
    17: 7 **Come** here at once and take your
    18:37 of Nazareth **is passing by**
    21:32 generation **will** not **pass away**
    21:33 Heaven and earth **will pass away**
    21:33 but my words **will** not **pass** away
Ac 16: 8 **passing by** Mysia, they went
    27: 9 the Fast **had** already **gone by**

2C	5:17	everything old **has passed away**
Ja	1:10	**will disappear** like a flower
1P	4: 3	**have** already **spent** enough time
2P	3:10	the heavens **will pass away**

3929　GO1 AG626 LN188 B1:697 K1:509
παρεσις, PASSING OVER

Ro	3:25	he **had passed over** the sins

3930　GO16 AG626 LN188 R3844,2192
παρεχω, I HOLD BESIDE

Mt	26:10	Why **do** you trouble the woman?
Mk	14: 6	why **do** you trouble her
Lk	6:29	**offer** the other also
	7: 4	worthy of having you **do** this
	11: 7	**Do** not bother me; the door has
	18: 5	this widow **keeps** bothering me
Ac	16:16	**brought** her owners a great
	17:31	of this he **has given** assurance
	19:24	**brought** no little business
	22: 2	they **became** even more quiet
	28: 2	The natives **showed** us unusual
Ga	6:17	let no one **make** trouble for me
Co	4: 1	**treat** your slaves justly
1Ti	1: 4	and not **to occupy** themselves
	6:17	on God who richly **provides** us
Ti	2: 7	**Show** yourself in all respects

3931　GO1 AG626 LN188
παρηγορια, COMFORT

Co	4:11	they have been a **comfort** to me

3932　GO1 AG626 LN188 B3:1072 R3933
παρθενια, VIRGINITY

Lk	2:36	seven years after her **marriage**

3933　GO15 AG627 LN188 B3:1071 K5:826
παρθενος, VIRGIN

Mt	1:23	the **virgin** shall conceive
	25: 1	**bridesmaids** took their lamps
	25: 7	all those **bridesmaids** got up
	25:11	the other **bridesmaids** came also
Lk	1:27	to a **virgin** engaged to a man
	1:27	The **virgin's** name was Mary
Ac	21: 9	had four **unmarried** daughters
1C	7:25	Now concerning **virgins**
	7:28	and if a **virgin** marries
	7:34	unmarried woman and the
		virgin
	7:36	properly toward his **fiancée**

	7:37	to keep her as his **fiancée**
	7:38	he who marries his **fiancée**
2C	11: 2	present you as a chaste **virgin**
Re	14: 4	for they are **virgins**

3934　GO1 AG627 LN188
παρθοι, PARTHIAN

Ac	2: 9	**Parthians,** Medes, Elamites

3935　GO2 AG627 LN189 K1:509
παριημι, LET FALL BESIDE, I NEGLECT

Lk	11:42	without **neglecting** the others
He	12:12	**drooping** hands and strengthen

3936　GO41 AG627 LN189 B1:474 K5:837 R3844,2476
παριστημι, I STAND BESIDE

Mt	26:53	he will at once **send** me more
Mk	4:29	because the harvest **has come**
	14:47	one of those who **stood near**
	14:69	to say to the **bystanders**
	14:70	the **bystanders** again said
	15:35	some of the **bystanders** heard
	15:39	who **stood facing** him
Lk	1:19	I **stand** in the presence of God
	2:22	to **present** him to the Lord
	19:24	He said to the **bystanders**
Jn	18:22	police **standing nearby** struck
	19:26	he loved **standing beside** her
Ac	1: 3	he **presented** himself alive
	1:10	in white robes **stood by** them
	4:10	this man **is standing before** you
	4:26	of the earth **took** their **stand**
	9:39	the widows **stood beside** him
	9:41	her his hand and **helped** her **up**
	23: 2	ordered those **standing near** him
	23: 4	Those **standing nearby** said
	23:24	Also **provide** mounts for Paul
	23:33	they **presented** Paul also before
	24:13	Neither can they **prove** to you
	27:23	For last night there **stood by**
	27:24	must **stand before** the emperor
Ro	6:13	**present** your members to sin
	6:13	but **present** yourselves to God
	6:16	not know that if you **present**
	6:19	you once **presented** your members
	6:19	so now **present** your members
	12: 1	**present** your bodies as a living
	14:10	**stand before** the judgment seat
	16: 2	**help** her in whatever she may
1C	8: 8	Food will not **bring us close**

2C 4:14 **will bring** us with you into his

11: 2 **present** you as a chaste virgin

Ep 5:27 **to present** the church to

Co 1:22 **to present** you holy and

1:28 we **may present** everyone mature

2Ti 2:15 your best **to present** yourself

4:17 But the Lord **stood by** me

3937 GO1 AG628 LN189
παρμενας, PARMENAS

Ac 6: 5 Timon, **Parmenas,** and Nicolaus,

3938 GO1 AG628 LN189 R3844,3598
παροδος, PASSAGE

1C 16: 7 see you now just in **passing**

3939 GO2 AG628 LN189 B1:690 K5:841 R3844,3611
παροικεω, I LIVE TRANSIENTLY

Lk 24:18 Are you the only **stranger**

He 11: 9 By faith he **stayed** for a time

3940 GO2 AG629 LN189 B1:690 K5:841 R3941
παροικια, TRANSIENCY

Ac 13:17 during their **stay** in the land

1P 1:17 during the time of your **exile**

3941 GO4 AG629 LN189 B1:690 K5:841 R3844,3624
παροικος, TRANSIENT

Ac 7: 6 would be **resident aliens**

7:29 became a **resident alien**

Ep 2:19 no longer strangers and **aliens**

1P 2:11 Beloved, I urge you as **aliens**

3942 GO5 AG629 LN189 B2:743 K5:854
παροιμια, PROVERB

Jn 10: 6 used this **figure of** speech

16:25 to you in **figures of speech.**

16:25 longer speak to you **in figures**

16:29 not in any **figure of speech**

2P 2:22 according to the true **proverb**

3943 GO2 AG629 LN189
παροινος, (DRUNK) WITH WINE

1Ti 3: 3 not a **drunkard,** not violent

Ti 1: 7 or **addicted to wine** or violent

3944 GO1 AG629 LN189
παροιχομαι, I PASS

Ac 14:16 In **past** generations he allowed

3945 GO1 AG629 LN189 B2:500 K5:199 R3946
παρομοιαζω, I AM LIKE

Mt 23:27 **you are like** whitewashed tombs

3946 GO1 AG629 LN189 B2:500 K5:198 R3844,3664
παρομοιος, SIMILAR

Mk 7:13 you do many things **like** this

3947 GO2 AG629 LN189 B1:107 K5:857 R3844,3631
παροξυνω, I PROVOKE

Ac 17:16 he was **deeply distressed** to see

1C 13: 5 is not **irritable** or resentful

3948 GO2 AG629 LN189 B1:107 K5:857 R3947
παροξυσμος, STIMULATION

Ac 15:39 **disagreement** became so sharp

He 10:24 how to **provoke** one another

3949 GO2 AG629 LN189 B1:107 K5:382 R3844,3710
παροργιζω, I MAKE ANGRY

Ro 10:19 nation I **will make** you **angry**

Ep 6: 4 **provoke** your children to anger

3950 GO1 AG629 LN189 B1:107 K5:382 R3849
παροργισμος, ANGRY MOOD

Ep 4:26 the sun go down on your **anger**

3951 GO1 AG629 LN189
παροτρυνω, I STIR UP

Ac 13:50 Jews **incited** the devout women

3952 GO24 AG629 LN189 B2:887 K5:858 R3918
παρουσια, PRESENCE

Mt 24: 3 will be the sign of your **coming**

24:27 the **coming** of the Son of Man

24:37 the **coming** of the Son of Man

24:39 the **coming** of the Son of Man

1C 15:23 then at his **coming** those who

16:17 I rejoice at the **coming**

2C 7: 6 consoled us by the **arrival**

7: 7 and not only by his **coming**

10:10 but his bodily **presence** is weak

Ph 1:26 when I **come** to you again

2:12 not only in my **presence**

1Th 2:19 Lord Jesus at his **coming**

3:13 the **coming** of our Lord Jesus

4:15 until the **coming** of the Lord

5:23 blameless at the **coming** of our

2Th 2: 1 the **coming** of our Lord Jesus

2: 8 manifestation of his **coming**

	2: 9	The **coming** of the lawless one
Ja	5: 7	until the **coming** of the Lord
	5: 8	the **coming** of the Lord is near
2P	1:16	**coming** of our Lord Jesus Christ
	3: 4	is the promise of his **coming**
	3:12	hastening the **coming** of the day
1J	2:28	shame before him at his **coming**

3953   GO1 AG630 LN189
παροψις, DISH
Mt 23:25   of the cup and of the **plate**

3954   GO31 AG630 LN190 B2:734 K5:871
παρρησια, BOLDNESS

Mk	8:32	He said all this quite **openly**
Jn	7: 4	who wants to be **widely**
	7:13	Yet no one would speak **openly**
	7:26	And here he is, speaking **openly**
	10:24	the Messiah, tell us **plainly**
	11:14	Then Jesus told them **plainly**
	11:54	no longer walked about **openly**
	16:25	but will tell you **plainly**
	16:29	you are speaking **plainly**
	18:20	spoken **openly** to the world
Λc	2:29	I may say to you **confidently**
	4:13	they saw the **boldness** of Peter
	4:29	your word with all **boldness**
	4:31	the word of God with **boldness**
	28:31	**boldness** and without hindrance
2C	3:12	act with great **boldness**
	7: 4	I often **boast** about you
Ep	3:12	access to God in **boldness**
	6:19	to make known with **boldness**
Ph	1:20	my speaking with all **boldness**
Co	2:15	made a **public** example of them
1Ti	3:13	and great **boldness** in the faith
Pm	1: 8	I am **bold** enough in Christ
He	3: 6	we hold firm the **confidence**
	4:16	throne of grace with **boldness**
	10:19	we have **confidence** to enter
	10:35	that **confidence** of yours
1J	2:28	we may have **confidence**
	3:21	we have **boldness** before God
	4:17	that we may have **boldness**
	5:14	this is the **boldness** we have

3955   GO9 AG631 LN190 B2:734 K5:871 R3954
παρρησιαζομαι, I AM BOLD
Ac 9:27   **had spoken boldly** in the name
     9:28   **speaking boldly** in the name

13:46	and Barnabas **spoke out boldly**
14: 3	**speaking boldly** for the Lord
18:26	He began to **speak boldly**
19: 8	**spoke out boldly,** and argued
26:26	and to him I speak **freely**
Ep 6:20	I may **declare** it **boldly**
1Th 2: 2	we **had courage** in our God

3956   GO1243 AG631 LN190 B1:94 K5:886
πας, ALL [MULTIPLE OCCURRENCES]

3957   GO29 AG633 LN190 B1:632 K5:896
πασχα, PASSOVER

Mt	26: 2	the **Passover** is coming
	26:17	for you to eat the **Passover**
	26:18	I will keep the **Passover**
	26:19	they prepared the **Passover** meal
Mk	14: 1	two days before the **Passover**
	14:12	**Passover** lamb is sacrificed
	14:12	for you to eat the **Passover**
	14:14	I may eat the **Passover**
	14:16	they prepared the **Passover** meal
Lk	2:41	the festival of the **Passover**
	22: 1	which is called the **Passover**
	22: 7	on which the **Passover** lamb
	22: 8	Go and prepare the **Passover**
	22:11	where I may eat the **Passover**
	22:13	they prepared the **Passover** meal
	22:15	desired to eat this **Passover**
Jn	2:13	**Passover** of the Jews was near
	2:23	during the **Passover** festival
	6: 4	Now the **Passover,** the festival
	11:55	Now the **Passover** of the Jews
	11:55	Jerusalem before the **Passover**
	12: 1	Six days before the **Passover**
	13: 1	the festival of the **Passover**
	18:28	be able to eat the **Passover**
	18:39	someone for you at the **Passover**
	19:14	Preparation for the **Passover**
Ac	12: 4	the people after the **Passover.**
1C	5: 7	For our **paschal** lamb, Christ
He	11:28	By faith he kept the **Passover**

3958   GO42 AG633 LN190 B3:719 K5:904
πασχω, I SUFFER

Mt	16:21	great **suffering** at the hands
	17:12	about to **suffer** at their hands
	17:15	epileptic and he **suffers**
	27:19	I **have suffered** a great deal
Mk	5:26	She had **endured** much

	8:31	must undergo great **suffering**
	9:12	go through many **sufferings**
Lk	9:22	must undergo great **suffering**
	13: 2	these Galileans **suffered**
	17:25	he must endure much **suffering**
	22:15	with you before I **suffer**
	24:26	should **suffer** these things
	24:46	is to **suffer** and to rise
Ac	1: 3	his **suffering** he presented
	3:18	that his Messiah would **suffer**
	9:16	**suffer** for the sake of my name
	17: 3	for the Messiah to **suffer**
	28: 5	the fire and **suffered** no harm
1C	12:26	one member **suffers,** all suffer
2C	1: 6	that we are also **suffering**
Ga	3: 4	Did you **experience** so much
Ph	1:29	of **suffering** for him as well
1Th	2:14	you **suffered** the same things
2Th	1: 5	which you **are** also **suffering**
2Ti	1:12	this reason I **suffer** as I do
He	2:18	tested by what he **suffered**
	5: 8	through what he **suffered**
	9:26	he would have had to **suffer**
	13:12	**suffered** outside the city gate
1P	2:19	endure pain while **suffering**
	2:20	you do right and **suffer** for it
	2:21	because Christ also **suffered**
	2:23	when he **suffered,** he did not
	3:14	But even if you do **suffer**
	3:17	than to **suffer** for doing evil
	3:18	Christ also **suffered** for sins
	4: 1	Christ **suffered** in the flesh
	4: 1	**has suffered** in the flesh
	4:15	of you **suffer** as a murderer
	4:19	**suffering** in accordance
	5:10	And after you **have suffered**
Re	2:10	what you are about to **suffer**

3959　GO1　AG634　LN190
πατ αρα, PATARA
Ac　21: 1　and from there to **Patara**

3960　GO10　AG634　LN190　B1:161　K5:939
πατασσω, I HIT
Mt	26:31	I **will strike** the shepherd
	26:51	**struck** the slave of the high
Mk	14:27	I **will strike** the shepherd
Lk	22:49	should we **strike** with the sword
	22:50	**struck** the slave of the high

Ac	7:24	avenged him by **striking** down
	12: 7	He **tapped** Peter on the side
	12:23	angel of the Lord **struck** him
Re	11: 6	**strike** the earth with every
	19:15	to **strike** down the nations

3961　GO5　AG634　LN190　B3:943　K5:940
πατεω, I WALK
Lk	10:19	authority to **tread** on snakes
	21:24	and Jerusalem will **be trampled**
Re	11: 2	**will trample** over the holy city
	14:20	And the wine press **was trodden**
	19:15	he **will tread** the wine press

3962　GO413　AG635　LN190　B1:615　K5:945
πατηρ, FATHER
Mt	2:22	in place of his **father** Herod
	3: 9	We have Abraham as our **ancestor**
	4:21	in the boat with their **father**
	4:22	the boat and their **father**
	5:16	give glory to your **Father**
	5:45	be children of your **Father**
	5:48	your heavenly **Father** is perfect
	6: 1	have no reward from your **Father**
	6: 4	your **Father** who sees in secret
	6: 6	pray to your **Father** who is in
	6: 6	your **Father** who sees in secret
	6: 8	for your **Father** knows what
	6: 9	Our **Father** in heaven, hallowed
	6:14	your heavenly **Father** will also
	6:15	**Father** forgive your trespasses
	6:18	your **Father** who is in secret
	6:26	your heavenly **Father** feeds them
	6:32	your heavenly **Father** knows
	7:11	your **Father** in heaven give
	7:21	does the will of my **Father**
	8:21	let me go and bury my **father**
	10:20	the Spirit of your **Father**
	10:21	and a **father** his child
	10:29	ground apart from your **Father**
	10:32	acknowledge before my **Father**
	10:33	will deny before my **Father**
	10:35	set a man against his **father**
	10:37	loves **father** or mother more
	11:25	I thank you, **Father,** Lord of
	11:26	yes, **Father,** for such was
	11:27	over to me by my **Father**
	11:27	the Son except the **Father**
	11:27	no one knows the **Father** except

	12:50	does the will of my **Father**	1:55	he made to our **ancestors**
	13:43	in the kingdom of their **Father**	1:59	Zechariah after his **father**
	15: 4	Honor your **father** and your	1:62	began motioning to his **father**
	15: 4	Whoever speaks evil of **father**	1:67	Then his **father** Zechariah
	15: 5	that whoever tells **father**	1:72	promised to our **ancestors**
	15: 6	need not honor the **father**	1:73	he swore to our **ancestor**
	15:13	**Father** has not planted will be	2:33	And the child's **father**
	16:17	but my **Father** in heaven	2:48	your **father** and I have been
	16:27	in the glory of his **Father**	2:49	I must be in my **Father's** house
	18:10	face of my **Father** in heaven	3: 8	have Abraham as our **ancestor**
	18:14	of your **Father** in heaven	6:23	**ancestors** did to the prophets
	18:19	by my **Father** in heaven	6:26	is what their **ancestors** did to
	18:35	my heavenly **Father** will also do	6:36	as your **Father** is merciful
	19: 5	a man shall leave his **father**	8:51	the child's **father** and mother
	19:19	Honor your **father** and mother	9:26	the glory of the **Father**
	19:29	brothers or sisters or **father**	9:42	gave him back to his **father**
	20:23	has been prepared by my **Father**	9:59	let me go and bury my **father**
	21:31	did the will of his **father**	10:21	**Father**, Lord of heaven and
	23: 9	And call no one your **father**	10:21	**Father**, for such was your
	23: 9	for you have one **Father**	10:22	handed over to me by my **Father**
	23:30	in the days of our **ancestors**	10:22	the Son is except the **Father**
	23:32	the measure of your **ancestors**	10:22	the **Father** is except the Son
	24:36	the Son, but only the **Father**	11: 2	When you pray, say: **Father**
	25:34	that are blessed by my **Father**	11:11	Is there any [**father**] among you
	26:29	with you in my **Father's** kingdom	11:13	will the heavenly **Father** give
	26:39	My **Father**, if it is possible	11:47	whom your **ancestors** killed
	26:42	My **Father**, if this cannot pass	11:48	the deeds of your **ancestors**
	26:53	I cannot appeal to my **Father**	12:30	your **Father** knows that you need
	28:19	in the name of the **Father**	12:32	your **Father's** good pleasure
Mk	1:20	they left their **father** Zebedee	12:53	**father** against son and son
	5:40	and took the child's **father**	12:53	and son against **father**
	7:10	Honor your **father** and your	14:26	and does not hate **father**
	7:10	Whoever speaks evil of **father**	15:12	of them said to his **father**
	7:11	say that if anyone tells **father**	15:12	**Father**, give me the share
	7:12	doing anything for a **father**	15:17	How many of my **father's** hired
	8:38	in the glory of his **Father**	15:18	get up and go to my **father**
	9:21	Jesus asked the **father**	15:18	**Father**, I have sinned against
	9:24	**father** of the child cried out	15:20	set off and went to his **father**
	10: 7	a man shall leave his **father**	15:20	**father** saw him and was filled
	10:19	Honor your **father** and mother	15:21	**Father**, I have sinned against
	10:29	sisters or mother or **father**	15:22	the **father** said to his slaves
	11:10	coming kingdom of our **ancestor**	15:27	**father** has killed the fatted
	11:25	so that your **Father** in heaven	15:28	His **father** came out and began
	13:12	and a **father** his child	15:29	But he answered his **father**
	13:32	the Son, but only the **Father**	16:24	**Father** Abraham, have mercy
	14:36	He said, "Abba, **Father,** for you	16:27	**father**, I beg you to send him
	15:21	**father** of Alexander and Rufus	16:27	send him to my **father's** house
Lk	1:17	to turn the hearts of **parents**	16:30	He said, 'No, **father** Abraham
	1:32	the throne of his **ancestor**	18:20	Honor your **father** and mother

	22:29	my **Father** has conferred on me	8:19	you would know my **Father** also
	22:42	**Father,** if you are willing	8:27	to them about the **Father**
	23:34	**Father,** forgive them; for they	8:28	as the **Father** instructed me
	23:46	**Father,** into your hands	8:38	seen in the **Father's** presence
	24:49	what my **Father** promised	8:38	you have heard from the **Father**
Jn	1:14	as of a **father's** only son	8:39	Abraham is our **father.**
	1:18	is close to the **Father's** heart	8:41	doing what your **father** does
	2:16	Stop making my **Father's** house	8:41	we have one **father**
	3:35	The **Father** loves the Son	8:42	If God were your **Father**
	4:12	greater than our **ancestor** Jacob	8:44	from your **father** the devil
	4:20	Our **ancestors** worshiped on this	8:44	to do your **father's** desires
	4:21	you will worship the **Father**	8:44	he is a liar and the **father**
	4:23	worship the **Father** in spirit	8:49	but I honor my **Father**
	4:23	the **Father** seeks such as these	8:53	greater than our **father** Abraham
	4:53	The **father** realized that this	8:54	is my **Father** who glorifies me
	5:17	My **Father** is still working	8:56	Your **ancestor** Abraham rejoiced
	5:18	also calling God his own **Father**	10:15	just as the **Father** knows me
	5:19	what he sees the **Father** doing	10:15	knows me and I know the **Father**
	5:20	The **Father** loves the Son	10:17	this reason the **Father** loves me
	5:21	as the **Father** raises the dead	10:18	this command from my **Father**
	5:22	The **Father** judges no one	10:25	that I do in my **Father's** name
	5:23	just as they honor the **Father**	10:29	What my **Father** has given me
	5:23	does not honor the **Father**	10:29	it out of the **Father's** hand
	5:26	For just as the **Father** has life	10:30	The **Father** and I are one
	5:36	**Father** has given me to complete	10:32	many good works from the **Father**
	5:36	that the **Father** has sent me	10:36	whom the **Father** has sanctified
	5:37	And the **Father** who sent me	10:37	doing the works of my **Father**
	5:43	I have come in my **Father's** name	10:38	that the **Father** is in me
	5:45	accuse you before the **Father**	10:38	in me and I am in the **Father**
	6:27	the **Father** has set his seal	11:41	**Father,** I thank you for having
	6:31	Our **ancestors** ate the manna	12:26	the **Father** will honor
	6:32	but it is my **Father** who gives	12:27	**Father,** save me from this hour
	6:37	that the **Father** gives me	12:28	**Father,** glorify your name
	6:40	indeed the will of my **Father**	12:49	but the **Father** who sent me
	6:42	whose **father** and mother we know	12:50	I speak just as the **Father**
	6:44	unless drawn by the **Father**	13: 1	this world and go to the **Father**
	6:45	from the **Father** comes to me	13: 3	that the **Father** had given
	6:46	anyone has seen the **Father**	14: 2	In my **Father's** house there are
	6:46	he has seen the **Father**	14: 6	No one comes to the **Father**
	6:49	Your **ancestors** ate the manna	14: 7	you will know my **Father** also
	6:57	the living **Father** sent me	14: 8	Lord, show us the **Father**
	6:57	I live because of the **Father**	14: 9	seen me has seen the **Father**
	6:58	that which your **ancestors** ate	14: 9	Show us the **Father**
	6:65	it is granted by the **Father**	14:10	that I am in the **Father**
	7:22	but from the **patriarchs**	14:10	and the **Father** is in me
	8:16	I and the **Father** who sent me	14:10	but the **Father** who dwells in me
	8:18	the **Father** who sent me	14:11	that I am in the **Father**
	8:19	Where is your **Father?**	14:11	the **Father** is in me
	8:19	know neither me nor my **Father**	14:12	I am going to the **Father**

14:13	the **Father** may be glorified		5:30	The God of our **ancestors**
14:16	And I will ask the **Father**		7: 2	Brothers and **fathers**
14:20	that I am in my **Father**		7: 2	appeared to our **ancestor**
14:21	will be loved by my **Father**		7: 4	After his **father** died
14:23	and my **Father** will love them		7:11	**ancestors** could find no food
14:24	is from the **Father** who sent me		7:12	he sent our **ancestors** there
14:26	whom the **Father** will send		7:14	sent and invited his **father**
14:28	that I am going to the **Father**		7:15	there as well as our **ancestors**
14:28	because the **Father** is greater		7:19	race and forced our **ancestors**
14:31	as the **Father** has commanded me		7:20	up in his **father's** house;
14:31	know that I love the **Father**		7:32	am the God of your **ancestors**
15: 1	and my **Father** is the vinegrower		7:38	Sinai, and with our **ancestors**
15: 8	My **Father** is glorified by this		7:39	Our **ancestors** were unwilling
15: 9	As the **Father** has loved me		7:44	Our **ancestors** had the tent
15:10	kept my **Father's** commandments		7:45	Our **ancestors** in turn brought
15:15	I have heard from my **Father**		7:45	drove out before our **ancestors**
15:16	that the **Father** will give you		7:51	as your **ancestors** used to do
15:23	hates me hates my **Father** also		7:52	your **ancestors** not persecute
15:24	and hated both me and my **Father**		13:17	Israel chose our **ancestors**
15:26	send to you from the **Father**		13:32	promised to our **ancestors**
15:26	who comes from the **Father**		13:36	was laid beside his **ancestors**
16: 3	they have not known the **Father**		15:10	that neither our **ancestors**
16:10	I am going to the **Father**		16: 1	but his **father** was a Greek
16:15	All that the **Father** has is mine		16: 3	that his **father** was a Greek
16:17	I am going to the **Father**		22: 1	Brothers and **fathers**
16:23	you ask anything of the **Father**		22:14	The God of our **ancestors**
16:25	tell you plainly of the **Father**		26: 6	made by God to our **ancestors**
16:26	ask the **Father** on your behalf		28: 8	that the **father** of Publius
16:27	the **Father** himself loves you		28:25	in saying to your **ancestors**
16:28	I came from the **Father**	Ro	1: 7	peace from God our **Father**
16:28	and am going to the **Father**		4:11	the **ancestor** of all who believe
16:32	because the **Father** is with me		4:12	the **ancestor** of the circumcised
17: 1	**Father,** the hour has come		4:12	**ancestor** Abraham had before he
17: 5	So now, **Father,** glorify me		4:16	he is the **father** of all of us
17:11	I am coming to you. Holy **Father**		4:17	I have made you the **father**
17:21	**Father,** are in me and I am in		4:18	the **father** of many nations
17:24	**Father,** I desire that those		6: 4	by the glory of the **Father**
17:25	**Father,** the world does not know		8:15	When we cry, "Abba! **Father!**"
18:11	that the **Father** has given me		9: 5	to them belong the **patriarchs**
20:17	not yet ascended to the **Father**		9:10	our **ancestor** Isaac
20:17	I am ascending to my **Father**		11:28	for the sake of their **ancestors**
20:17	to my Father and your **Father**		15: 6	glorify the God and **Father**
20:21	As the **Father** has sent me		15: 8	given to the **patriarchs**
Ac 1: 4	for the promise of the **Father**	1C	1: 3	peace from God our **Father**
1: 7	the **Father** has set by his own		4:15	you do not have many **fathers**
2:33	received from the **Father**		5: 1	living with his **father's** wife
3:13	the God of our **ancestors**		8: 6	is one God, the **Father**
3:25	that God gave to your **ancestors**		10: 1	our **ancestors** were all under
4:25	through our **ancestor** David		15:24	the kingdom to God the **Father**

2C	1: 2	peace from God our **Father**
	1: 3	Blessed be the God and **Father**
	1: 3	the **Father** of mercies
	6:18	and I will be your **father**
	11:31	The God and **Father** of the Lord
Ga	1: 1	Jesus Christ and God the **Father**
	1: 3	peace from God our **Father**
	1: 4	will of our God and **Father**
	4: 2	the date set by the **father**
	4: 6	hearts, crying, "Abba! **Father!**"
Ep	1: 2	peace from God our **Father**
	1: 3	God and **Father** of our Lord
	1:17	the **Father** of glory, may give
	2:18	in one Spirit to the **Father**
	3:14	bow my knees before the **Father**
	4: 6	one God and **Father** of all
	5:20	thanks to God the **Father**
	5:31	a man will leave his **father** and
	6: 2	Honor your **father** and mother
	6: 4	And, **fathers,** do not provoke
	6:23	from God the **Father** and the
Ph	1: 2	from God our **Father** and the
	2:11	to the glory of God the **Father.**
	2:22	like a son with a **father** he
	4:20	To our God and **Father** be glory
Co	1: 2	peace from God our **Father.**
	1: 3	the **Father** of our Lord Jesus
	1:12	giving thanks to the **Father,**
	3:17	to God the **Father** through him.
	3:21	**Fathers,** do not provoke your
1Th	1: 1	in God the **Father** and the Lord
	1: 3	before our God and **Father** your
	2:11	like a **father** with his children
	3:11	our God and **Father** himself and
	3:13	our God and **Father** at the
2Th	1: 1	in God our **Father** and the Lord
	1: 2	from God our **Father** and the
	2:16	and God our **Father,** who loved
1Ti	1: 2	from God the **Father** and Christ
	5: 1	speak to him as to a **father,**
2Ti	1: 2	from God the **Father** and Christ
Ti	1: 4	from God the **Father** and Christ
Pm	1: 3	from God our **Father** and the
He	1: 1	our **ancestors** in many and
	1: 5	I will be his **Father,** and he
	3: 9	where your **ancestors** put me to
	7:10	loins of his **ancestor** when
	8: 9	made with their **ancestors,** on
	11:23	hidden by his **parents** for three

	12: 7	there whom a **parent** does not
	12: 9	Moreover, we had human **parents**
	12: 9	subject to the **Father** of
Ja	1:17	down from the **Father** of lights,
	1:27	before God, the **Father,** is this
	2:21	Was not our **ancestor** Abraham
	3: 9	bless the Lord and **Father,** and
1P	1: 2	destined by God the **Father** and
	1: 3	Blessed be the God and **Father**
	1:17	If you invoke as **Father** the one
2P	1:17	glory from God the **Father** when
	3: 4	since our **ancestors** died, all
1J	1: 2	was with the **Father** and was
	1: 3	is with the **Father** and with his
	2: 1	advocate with the **Father,** Jesus
	2:13	I am writing to you, **fathers,**
	2:14	you know the **Father.** I write to
	2:14	I write to you, **fathers,**
	2:15	The love of the **Father** is not
	2:16	from the **Father** but from the
	2:22	denies the **Father** and the Son.
	2:23	denies the Son has the **Father;**
	2:23	the Son has the **Father** also.
	2:24	in the Son and in the **Father.**
	3: 1	See what love the **Father** has
	4:14	testify that the **Father** has
2J	1: 3	from God the **Father** and from
	1: 3	the **Father's** Son, in truth and
	1: 4	commanded by the **Father.**
	1: 9	has both the **Father** and the Son
Ju	1: 1	in God the **Father** and kept safe
Re	1: 6	his God and **Father,** to him be
	2:28	authority from my **Father.** To
	3: 5	before my **Father** and before his
	3:21	sat down with my **Father** on his
	14: 1	his **Father's** name written on

3963 GO1 AG636 LN190
πατμος, PATMOS
Re 1: 9 on the island called **Patmos**

3965 GO3 AG636 LN190 B1:615 K5:1015 R3962
πατρια, FATHERHOOD
Lk 2: 4 the house and **family** of David.
Ac 3:25 all the **families** of the earth
Ep 3:15 every **family** in heaven and on

3966 GO4 AG636 LN190 R3965,757
πατριαρχης, FATHER-RULERS
Ac 2:29 our **ancestor** David that he both

7: 8   Jacob of the twelve **patriarchs.**
7: 9   The **patriarchs,** jealous of
He   7: 4   Abraham the **patriarch** gave him

3967   GO1 AG636 LN190 K5:1021 R3962
πατρικος, OF FATHER
Ga   1:14   traditions of my **ancestors.**

3968   GO8 AG636 LN190 B1:615 R3962
πατρις, FATHERLAND
Mt   13:54   He came to his **hometown** and
      13:57   except in their own **country** and in
Mk   6: 1   came to his **hometown,** and his
      6: 4   in their **hometown,** and among
Lk   4:23   in your **hometown** the things
      4:24   in the prophet's **hometown.**
Jn   4:44   in the prophet's **own country**).
He   11:14   they are seeking a **homeland.**

3969   GO1 AG637 LN190
πατροβας, PATROBAS
Ro   16:14   **Patrobas,** Hermas, and the

3969a   GO1 AG637 LN191
πατρολωας, FATHER-KILLER
1Ti   1: 9   who **kill** their **father** or mother

3970   GO1 AG637 LN191 R3962,3860
πατροπαραδοτος, GIVEN OVER BY
FATHER
1P   1:18   **inherited from your ancestors**

3971   GO3 AG637 LN191 K5:1014 R3962
πατρωος, FATHER
Ac   22: 3   according to our **ancestral** law,
      24:14   the God of our **ancestors,**
      28:17   customs of our **ancestors,** yet

3972   GO158 AG637 LN191
παυλος, PAUL
Ac   13: 7   Sergius **Paulus,** an intelligent
      13: 9   But Saul, also known as **Paul,**
      13:13   Then **Paul** and his companions
      13:16   So **Paul** stood up and with a
      13:43   to Judaism followed **Paul** and
      13:45   what was spoken by **Paul.**
      13:46   Then both **Paul** and Barnabas
      13:50   against **Paul** and Barnabas, and
      14: 9   He listened to **Paul** as he was
      14:11   When the crowds saw what **Paul**

14:12   and **Paul** they called Hermes,
14:14   apostles Barnabas and **Paul**
14:19   Then they stoned **Paul** and
15: 2   And after **Paul** and Barnabas
15: 2   **Paul** and Barnabas and some of
15:12   listened to Barnabas and **Paul**
15:22   with **Paul** and Barnabas. They
15:25   our beloved Barnabas and **Paul,**
15:35   But **Paul** and Barnabas
         remained
15:36   After some days **Paul** said to
15:38   But **Paul** decided not to take
15:40   But **Paul** chose Silas and set
16: 3   **Paul** wanted Timothy to
16: 9   During the night **Paul** had a
16:14   to what was said by **Paul.**
16:17   While she followed **Paul** and us,
16:18   But **Paul,** very much annoyed,
16:19   they seized **Paul** and Silas and
16:25   About midnight **Paul** and Silas
16:28   But **Paul** shouted in a loud
16:29   trembling before **Paul** and Silas
16:36   message to **Paul,** saying, "The
16:37   But **Paul** replied, "They have
17: 2   And **Paul** went in, as was his
17: 4   and joined **Paul** and Silas, as
17.10   believers sent **Paul** and Silas
17:13   proclaimed by **Paul** in Beroea as
17:14   immediately sent **Paul** away to
17:15   who conducted **Paul** brought
         him
17:16   While **Paul** was waiting for them
17:22   Then **Paul** stood in front of the
17:33   At that point **Paul** left them.
18: 5   **Paul** was occupied with
18: 9   the Lord said to **Paul** in a
18:12   attack on **Paul** and brought him
18:14   Just as **Paul** was about to speak
18:18   **Paul** said farewell to the
19: 1   in Corinth, **Paul** passed through
19: 4   **Paul** said, "John baptized with
19: 6   When **Paul** had laid his hands on
19:11   miracles through **Paul,**
19:13   the Jesus whom **Paul** proclaims.
19:15   and **Paul** I know; but who are
19:21   **Paul** resolved in the Spirit to
19:26   this **Paul** has persuaded and
19:29   Macedonians who were **Paul's**
19:30   **Paul** wished to go into the
20: 1   **Paul** sent for the disciples;

20: 7	**Paul** was holding a discussion
20: 9	sleep while **Paul** talked still
20:10	But **Paul** went down, and bending
20:13	to take **Paul** on board there;
20:16	For **Paul** had decided to sail
20:37	they embraced **Paul** and kissed
21: 4	they told **Paul** not to go on to
21:11	took **Paul's** belt, bound his own
21:13	Then **Paul** answered, "What are
21:18	The next day **Paul** went with us
21:26	Then **Paul** took the men, and the
21:29	supposed that **Paul** had brought
21:30	They seized **Paul** and dragged
21:32	they stopped beating **Paul.**
21:37	Just as **Paul** was about to be
21:39	**Paul** replied, "I am a Jew, from
21:40	**Paul** stood on the steps and
22:25	**Paul** said to the centurion who
22:28	**Paul** said, "But I was born a
22:30	He brought **Paul** down and had
23: 1	While **Paul** was looking intently
23: 3	At this **Paul** said to him, "God
23: 5	And **Paul** said, "I did not
23: 6	When **Paul** noticed that some
23:10	they would tear **Paul** to pieces,
23:12	until they had killed **Paul.**
23:14	food until we have killed **Paul.**
23:16	Now the son of **Paul's** sister
23:16	the barracks and told **Paul.**
23:17	**Paul** called one of the
23:18	The prisoner **Paul** called me
23:20	bring **Paul** down to the council
23:24	Also provide mounts for **Paul** to
23:31	took **Paul** and brought him
23:33	presented **Paul** also before him.
24: 1	their case against **Paul** to the
24:10	**Paul** replied: "I cheerfully
24:24	he sent for **Paul** and heard him
24:26	given him by **Paul,** and for that
24:27	Felix left **Paul** in prison.
25: 2	gave him a report against **Paul.**
25: 4	Festus replied that **Paul** was
25: 6	and ordered **Paul** to be brought.
25: 8	**Paul** said in his defense, "I
25: 9	asked **Paul,** "Do you wish to go
25:10	**Paul** said, "I am appealing to
25:14	Festus laid **Paul's** case before
25:19	but whom **Paul** asserted to be
25:21	But when **Paul** had appealed to

25:23	order and **Paul** was brought in.
26: 1	Agrippa said to **Paul,** "You have
26: 1	Then **Paul** stretched out his
26:24	You are out of your mind, **Paul**
26:25	But **Paul** said, "I am not out of
26:28	Agrippa said to **Paul,** "Are you
26:29	**Paul** replied, "Whether quickly
27: 1	they transferred **Paul** and some
27: 3	Julius treated **Paul** kindly, and
27: 9	already gone by, **Paul** advised
27:11	ship than to what **Paul** said.
27:21	**Paul** then stood up among them
27:24	Do not be afraid, **Paul;** you
27:31	**Paul** said to the centurion and
27:33	**Paul** urged all of them to take
27:43	wishing to save **Paul,** kept them
28: 3	**Paul** had gathered a bundle of
28: 8	**Paul** visited him and cured him
28:15	**Paul** thanked God and took
28:16	**Paul** was allowed to live by
28:25	**Paul** made one further statement
Ro 1: 1	**Paul,** a servant of Jesus Christ
1C 1: 1	**Paul,** called to be an apostle
1:12	belong to **Paul,"** or "I belong
1:13	Was **Paul** crucified for you? Or
1:13	baptized in the name of **Paul?**
3: 4	"I belong to **Paul,"** and another
3: 5	What is **Paul?** Servants through
3:22	whether **Paul** or Apollos or
16:21	I, **Paul,** write this greeting
2C 1: 1	**Paul,** an apostle of Christ
10: 1	I myself, **Paul,** appeal to you
Ga 1: 1	**Paul** an apostle—sent neither
5: 2	Listen! I, **Paul,** am telling you
Ep 1: 1	**Paul,** an apostle of Christ
3: 1	I **Paul** am a prisoner for Christ
Ph 1: 1	**Paul** and Timothy, servants of
Co 1: 1	**Paul,** an apostle of Christ
1:23	I, **Paul,** became a servant of
4:18	I, **Paul,** write this greeting
1Th 1: 1	**Paul,** Silvanus, and Timothy,
2:18	I, **Paul,** wanted to again and
2Th 1: 1	**Paul,** Silvanus, and Timothy,
3:17	I, **Paul,** write this greeting
1Ti 1: 1	**Paul,** an apostle of Christ
2Ti 1: 1	**Paul,** an apostle of Christ
Ti 1: 1	**Paul,** a servant of God and an
Pm 1: 1	**Paul,** a prisoner of Christ
1: 9	I, **Paul,** do this as an old man,

1:19   I, **Paul,** am writing this with
2P   3:15   beloved brother **Paul** wrote to

3973   GO15   AG638   LN191
παυω, I STOP
Lk   5: 4   When he had **finished** speaking,
     8:24   they **ceased,** and there was a
     11: 1   and after he **had finished,** one
Ac   5:42   they did not **cease** to teach and
     6:13   This man never **stops** saying
     13:10   **will** you not **stop** making
     20: 1   After the uproar **had ceased,**
     20:31   I did not **cease** night or day to
     21:32   they **stopped** beating Paul.
1C   13: 8   tongues, they **will cease;** as
Ep   1:16   I do not **cease** to give thanks
Co   1: 9   we **have** not **ceased** praying for
He   10: 2   not have **ceased** being offered,
1P   3:10   let them **keep** their tongues
     4: 1   in the flesh **has finished** with

3974   GO2   AG638   LN191
παφος, PAPHOS
Ac   13: 6   whole island as far as **Paphos,**
     13:13   set sail from **Paphos** and came

3975   GO2   AG638   LN191   B2:153   K5:1022
παχυνω, I THICKEN
Mt   13:15   people's heart **has grown dull,**
Ac   28:27   people's heart **has grown dull,**

3976   GO3   AG638   LN191   R4228
πεδη, IN FOOT SHACKLES
Mk   5: 4   restrained with **shackles** and
     5: 4   and the **shackles** he broke in
Lk   8:29   chains and **shackles,** but he

3977   GO1   AG638   LN191   B3:1009
πεδινος, LEVEL
Lk   6:17   stood on a **level** place, with a

3978   GO1   AG638   LN191   R3979
πεζευω, I GO ON FOOT
Ac   20:13   intending **to go by land** himself

3979   GO2   AG638   LN191   R4228
πεζος, ON FOOT
Mt   14:13   they followed him **on foot** from
Mk   6:33   hurried there **on foot** from all

3980   GO4   AG638   LN191   B3:588   K6:9
πειθαρχεω, I OBEY
Ac   5:29   We must **obey** God rather than
     5:32   given to those who **obey** him.
     27:21   you **should have listened** to me
Ti   3: 1   to be **obedient,** to be ready for

3981   GO1   AG639   LN191   B1:588   K6:8   R3982
πειθος, PERSUASIVE
1C   2: 4   not with **plausible** words of

3982   GO52   AG639   LN191   B1:588   K6:1
πειθω, I PERSUADE
Mt   27:20   **persuaded** the crowds to ask for
     27:43   He **trusts** in God; let God
     28:14   we **will satisfy** him and keep
Lk   11:22   armor in which he **trusted** and
     16:31   will they **be convinced** even if
     18: 9   to some who **trusted** in
     20: 6   for they **are convinced** that
Ac   5:36   about four hundred, **joined** him;
     5:37   all who **followed** him were
     5:39   They **were convinced** by him,
     12:20   and after **winning over** Blastus,
     13:43   and **urged** them to continue in
     14:19   and **won over** the crowds. Then
     17: 4   Some of them **were persuaded** and
     18: 4   try to **convince** Jews and Greeks
     19: 8   and argued **persuasively** about
     19:26   Paul **has persuaded** and drawn
     21:14   would not **be persuaded,** we
     23:21   But do not **be persuaded** by them
     26:26   I **am certain** that none of these
     26:28   **Are** you so quickly **persuading**
     27:11   centurion **paid** more **attention**
     28:23   trying to **convince** them about
     28:24   Some **were convinced** by what he
Ro   2: 8   and who **obey** not the truth but
     2:19   and if you **are sure** that you
     8:38   For I **am convinced** that neither
     14:14   I know and **am persuaded** in the
     15:14   I myself **feel confident** about
2C   1: 9   we would **rely** not on ourselves
     2: 3   for I **am confident** about all of
     5:11   we try to **persuade** others; but
     10: 7   If you **are confident** that you
Ga   1:10   Am I now **seeking** human
             approval
     5: 7   you from **obeying** the truth?
     5:10   I **am confident** about you in the

Ph	1: 6	I **am confident** of this, that
	1:14	**having been made confident** in
	1:25	Since I **am convinced** of this,
	2:24	and I **trust** in the Lord that I
	3: 3	and **have** no **confidence** in the
	3: 4	**have reason** for **confidence** in
2Th	3: 4	And we **have confidence** in the
2Ti	1: 5	now, I **am sure**, lives in you.
	1:12	and I **am sure** that he is able
Pm	1:21	**Confident** of your obedience,
He	2:13	I **will put** my **trust** in him.
	6: 9	beloved, we **are confident** of
	13:17	**Obey** your leaders and submit to
	13:18	Pray for us; we **are sure** that
Ja	3: 3	them **obey** us, we guide their
1J	3:19	**will reassure** our hearts before

3983 GO23 AG640 LN191 B2:264 K6:12
πειναω, I HUNGER

Mt	4: 2	afterwards he **was famished.**
	5: 6	those who **hunger** and thirst
	12: 1	his disciples **were hungry,** and
	12: 3	and his companions **were hungry?**
	21:18	to the city, he **was hungry.**
	25:35	I **was hungry** and you gave me
	25:37	we saw you **hungry** and gave you
	25:42	for I **was hungry** and you gave
	25:44	we saw you **hungry** or thirsty or
Mk	2:25	and his companions **were hungry**
	11:12	from Bethany, he **was hungry.**
Lk	1:53	filled the **hungry** with good
	4: 2	they were over, he **was famished**
	6: 3	and his companions **were hungry?**
	6:21	Blessed are you who **are hungry**
	6:25	for you **will be hungry.** "Woe to
Jn	6:35	to me **will** never **be hungry,** and
Ro	12:20	No, "if your enemies **are hungry**
1C	4:11	hour we **are hungry** and thirsty,
	11:21	one **goes hungry** and another
	11:34	If you **are hungry,** eat at home
Ph	4:12	well-fed and **of going hungry,**
Re	7:16	They **will hunger** no more, and

3984 GO2 AG640 LN191 B3:798 K6:23
πειρα, TRIAL

He	11:29	the Egyptians **attempted** to do
	11:36	Others **suffered** mocking and

3985 GO38 AG640 LN191 B3:798 K6:23
πειραζω, I TEST

Mt	4: 1	to **be tempted** by the devil.
	4: 3	The **tempter** came and said to
	16: 1	and **to test** Jesus they asked
	19: 3	and **to test** him they asked, "Is
	22:18	are you **putting** me **to the test,**
	22:35	him a question to **test** him.
Mk	1:13	forty days, **tempted** by Satan;
	8:11	a sign from heaven, to **test** him
	10: 2	and to **test** him they asked, "Is
	12:15	are you **putting** me **to the test?**
Lk	4: 2	forty days he **was tempted** by
	11:16	Others, to **test** him, kept
Jn	6: 6	He said this to **test** him, for
	8: 6	They said this to **test** him,
Ac	5: 9	Spirit of the Lord to the **test?**
	9:26	he **attempted** to join the
	15:10	are you **putting** God **to the test**
	16: 7	**attempted** to go into Bithynia,
	24: 6	He even **tried** to profane the
1C	7: 5	so that Satan may not **tempt** you
	10: 9	not **put** Christ **to the test,** as
	10:13	not **let** you **be tested** beyond
2C	13: 5	**Test** yourselves. Do you not
Ga	6: 1	you yourselves **are** not **tempted.**
1Th	3: 5	somehow the **tempter** had tempted
	3: 5	somehow the tempter **had tempted**
He	2:18	Because he himself **was tested**
	2:18	help those who **are being tested**
	3: 9	ancestors **put** me **to the test,**
	4:15	**has been tested** as we are, yet
	11:17	Abraham, when **put to the test,**
Ja	1:13	No one, when **tempted,** should
	1:13	"I **am being tempted** by God";
	1:13	God cannot **be tempted** by evil
	1:14	But one **is tempted** by one's own
Re	2: 2	you **have tested** those who claim
	2:10	so that you **may be tested,** and
	3:10	to **test** the inhabitants of the

3986 GO21 AG640 LN191 B3:798 K6:23 R3985
πειρασμος, TEST, TRIAL

Mt	6:13	the time of **trial,** but rescue
	26:41	the time of **trial;** the spirit
Mk	14:38	into the time of **trial;** the
Lk	4:13	had finished every **test,** he
	8:13	in a time of **testing** fall away.
	11: 4	bring us to the time of **trial.**
	22:28	stood by me in my **trials;**
	22:40	come into the time of **trial.**

	22:46	come into the time of **trial.**
Ac	20:19	enduring the **trials** that came
1C	10:13	No **testing** has overtaken you
	10:13	but with the **testing** he will
Ga	4:14	put you to the **test,** you did
1Ti	6: 9	rich fall into **temptation** and
He	3: 8	as on the day of **testing** in the
Ja	1: 2	whenever you face **trials** of any
	1:12	anyone who endures **temptation.**
1P	1: 6	had to suffer various **trials,**
	4:12	fiery **ordeal** that is taking
2P	2: 9	rescue the godly from **trial,**
Re	3:10	the hour of **trial** that is

3987 GO1 AG641 LN191 B3:798 K6:23 R3985
πειραω, I TEST
Ac 26:21 the temple and **tried** to kill me

3988 GO1 AG641 LN192 B1:588 K6:9 R3982
πεισμονη, PERSUASION
Ga 5: 8 Such **persuasion** does not come

3989 GO2 AG641 LN192
πελαγος, OPEN SEA
Mt 18: 6 drowned in the **depth** of the sea
Ac 27: 5 sailed across the **sea** that is

3990 GO1 AG641 LN192
πελεκιζω, I BEHEAD
Re 20: 4 of those who **had been beheaded**

3991 GO4 AG641 LN192 R4002
πεμπτος, FIFTH
Re 6: 9 When he opened the **fifth** seal,
   9: 1 And the **fifth** angel blew his
   16:10 The **fifth** angel poured his bowl
   21:20 the **fifth** onyx, the sixth

3992 GO79 AG641 LN192 B1:126 K1:398
πεμπω, I SEND
Mt	2: 8	Then he **sent** them to Bethlehem,
	11: 2	he **sent** word by his disciples
	14:10	he **sent** and had John beheaded
	22: 7	He **sent** his troops, destroyed
Mk	5:12	**Send** us into the swine; let us
Lk	4:26	yet Elijah was **sent** to none of
	7: 6	the centurion **sent** friends to
	7:10	who **had been sent** returned to
	7:19	**sent** them to the Lord to ask
	15:15	who **sent** him to his fields to

	16:24	mercy on me, and **send** Lazarus
	16:27	I beg you to **send** him to my
	20:11	Next he **sent** another slave;
	20:12	And he **sent** still a third; this
	20:13	I will **send** my beloved son;
Jn	1:22	answer for those who **sent** us.
	1:33	the one who **sent** me to baptize
	4:34	do the will of him who **sent** me
	5:23	honor the Father who **sent** him.
	5:24	believes him who **sent** me has
	5:30	but the will of him who **sent** me
	5:37	the Father who **sent** me has
	6:38	but the will of him who **sent** me
	6:39	the will of him who **sent** me,
	6:44	by the Father who **sent** me; and
	7:16	not mine but his who **sent** me.
	7:18	the glory of him who **sent** him
	7:28	But the one who **sent** me is true
	7:33	I am going to him who **sent** me.
	8:16	I and the Father who **sent** me.
	8:18	Father who **sent** me testifies
	8:26	but the one who **sent** me is true
	8:29	And the one who **sent** me is with
	9: 4	the works of him who **sent** me
	12:44	in me but in him who **sent** me.
	12:45	sees me sees him who **sent** me.
	12:49	but the Father who **sent** me has
	13:16	than the one who **sent** them.
	13:20	whom I **send** receives me; and
	13:20	me receives him who **sent** me.
	14:24	is from the Father who **sent** me.
	14:26	whom the Father **will send** in my
	15:21	do not know him who **sent** me.
	15:26	whom I **will send** to you from
	16: 5	I am going to him who **sent** me;
	16: 7	if I go, I **will send** him to you
	20:21	has sent me, so I **send** you.
Ac	10: 5	Now **send** men to Joppa for a
	10:32	**Send** therefore to Joppa and ask
	10:33	I **sent** for you immediately, and
	11:29	each would **send** relief to the
	15:22	and to **send** them to Antioch
	15:25	and **send** them to you, along
	19:31	**sent** him a message urging him
	20:17	From Miletus he **sent** a message
	23:30	I **sent** him to you at once,
	25:25	Majesty, I decided to **send** him.
	25:27	unreasonable to **send** a prisoner
Ro	8: 3	by **sending** his own Son in the

1C	4:17	this reason I **sent** you Timothy,
	16: 3	I **will send** any whom you
2C	9: 3	But I **am sending** the brothers
Ep	6:22	I **am sending** him to you for
Ph	2:19	**to send** Timothy to you soon, so
	2:23	I hope therefore to **send** him as
	2:25	to **send** to you Epaphroditus—
	2:28	I am the more eager to **send** him
	4:16	you **sent** me help for my needs
Co	4: 8	I **have sent** him to you for this
1Th	3: 2	we **sent** Timothy, our brother
	3: 5	I **sent** to find out about your
2Th	2:11	For this reason God **sends** them
Ti	3:12	When I **send** Artemas to you, or
1P	2:14	or of governors, as **sent** by him
Re	1:11	**send** it to the seven churches,
	11:10	celebrate and **exchange** presents
	14:15	**Use** your sickle and reap, for
	14:18	**Use** your sharp sickle and
	22:16	Jesus, who **sent** my angel to you

3993   GO1   AG642   LN192   B2:820   K6:37
πενης, POOR
2C   9: 9   he gives to the **poor;** his

3994   GO6   AG642   LN192
πενθερα, MOTHER-IN-LAW

Mt	8:14	**mother-in-law** lying in bed with
	10:35	against her **mother-in-law;**
Mk	1:30	Now Simon's **mother-in-law**
Lk	4:38	Now Simon's **mother-in-law** was
	12:53	**mother-in-law** against her
	12:53	against **mother-in-law.**

3995   GO1   AG642   LN192
πενθερος, FATHER-IN-LAW
Jn   18:13   the **father-in-law** of Caiaphas,

3996   GO10   AG642   LN192   B2:421   K6:40   R3997
πενθεω, I MOURN

Mt	5: 4	Blessed are those who **mourn,**
	9:15	wedding guests cannot **mourn** as
Mk	16:10	they were **mourning** and weeping.
Lk	6:25	for you **will mourn** and weep.
1C	5: 2	not rather **have mourned,** so
2C	12:21	I may have to **mourn** over many
Ja	4: 9	Lament and **mourn** and weep. Let
Re	18:11	earth weep and **mourn** for her,
	18:15	weeping and **mourning** aloud,
	18:19	they wept and **mourned,** crying

3997   GO5   AG642   LN192   B2:421   K6:40
πενθος, MOURNING

Ja	4: 9	be turned into **mourning** and
Re	18: 7	measure of torment and **grief.**
	18: 7	and I will never see **grief,**
	18: 8	and **mourning** and famine—
	21: 4	**mourning** and crying and pain

3998   GO1   AG642   LN192   B2:820   K6:40
πενιχρος, VERY POOR
Lk   21: 2   he also saw a **poor** widow put

3999   GO1   AG643   LN192   R4002
πεντακις, FIVE TIMES
2C   11:24   **Five times** I have received from

4000   GO6   AG643   LN192   B2:699   R4002,5507
πεντακισχιλιοι, FIVE THOUSAND

Mt	14:21	were about **five thousand** men,
	16: 9	loaves for the **five thousand,**
Mk	6:44	numbered **five thousand** men.
	8:19	loaves for the **five thousand,**
Lk	9:14	there were about **five thousand**
Jn	6:10	sat down, about **five thousand**

4001   GO2   AG643   LN192   R4002,1540
πεντακοσιοι, FIVE HUNDRED

Lk	7:41	one owed **five hundred** denarii,
1C	15: 6	more than **five hundred** brothers

4002   GO38   AG643   LN192   B2:689
πεντε, FIVE

Mt	14:17	but **five** loaves and two fish.
	14:19	Taking the **five** loaves and the
	16: 9	not remember the **five** loaves
	25: 2	**Five** of them were foolish,
	25: 2	foolish, and **five** were wise.
	25:15	to one he gave **five** talents,
	25:16	had received the **five** talents
	25:16	and made **five** more talents.
	25:20	had received the **five** talents
	25:20	bringing **five** more talents,
	25:20	over to me **five** talents; see,
	25:20	I have made **five** more talents.
Mk	6:38	they said, "**Five,** and two fish.
	6:41	Taking the **five** loaves and the
	8:19	When I broke the **five** loaves
Lk	1:24	for **five** months she remained in
	9:13	no more than **five** loaves and
	9:16	And taking the **five** loaves and

	12: 6	Are not **five** sparrows sold for
	12:52	**five** in one household will be
	14:19	have bought **five** yoke of oxen,
	16:28	for I have **five** brothers—
	19:18	your pound has made **five** pounds
	19:19	And you, rule over **five** cities
Jn	4:18	for you have had **five** husbands,
	5: 2	which has **five** porticoes.
	6: 9	has **five** barley loaves and two
	6:13	fragments of the **five** barley
	6:19	rowed about **three** or four miles
Ac	4: 4	numbered about **five** thousand.
	7:14	seventy-**five** in all;
	19:19	to **fifty** thousand silver coins.
	20: 6	in **five** days we joined them in
	24: 1	**Five** days later the high priest
1C	14:19	I would rather speak **five** words
Re	9: 5	torture them for **five** months,
	9:10	harm people for **five** months.
	17:10	of whom **five** have fallen, one

4003   GO1 AG643 LN192 R4002,2532,1182
πεντεκαιδεκατος, FIFTEENTH
Lk	3: 1	In the **fifteenth** year of the

4004   GO7 AG643 LN192 R4002
πεντηκοντα, FIFTY
Mk	6:40	of hundreds and of **fifties.**
Lk	7:41	denarii, and the other **fifty.**
	9:14	in groups of about **fifty** each.
	16: 6	quickly, and make it **fifty.**
Jn	8:57	are not yet **fifty** years old,
	21:11	a hundred **fifty**-three of them;
Ac	13:20	about four hundred **fifty** years.

4005   GO3 AG643 LN192 B2:783 K6:44 R4004
πεντηκοστη, FIFTIETH
Ac	2: 1	When the day of **Pentecost** had
	20:16	on the day of **Pentecost.**
1C	16: 8	in Ephesus until **Pentecost,**

4006   GO6 AG643 LN192 B1:588 K6:7 R3982
πεποιθησις, PERSUASION
2C	1:15	Since I **was sure** of this, I
	3: 4	Such is the **confidence** that
	8:22	of his great **confidence** in you.
	10: 2	I need not **show** boldness by
Ep	3:12	in boldness and **confidence**
Ph	3: 4	for **confidence** in the flesh.

4006a   GO1 AG643 LN192
περαιτερω, MORE BEYOND
Ac	19:39	If there is anything **further**

4008   GO23 AG643 LN192
περαν, ACROSS
Mt	4:15	**across** the Jordan, Galilee of
	4:25	and from **beyond** the Jordan.
	8:18	to go over to the **other side.**
	8:28	When he came to the **other side,**
	14:22	go on ahead to the **other side,**
	16: 5	reached the **other side,** they
	19: 1	region of Judea **beyond** the
Mk	3: 8	**beyond** the Jordan, and the
	4:35	us go across to the **other side.**
	5: 1	came to the **other side** of the
	5:21	the boat to the **other side,** a
	6:45	ahead to the **other side,** to
	8:13	went across to the **other side.**
	10: 1	of Judea and **beyond** the Jordan.
Lk	8:22	go across to the **other side** of
Jn	1:28	in Bethany **across** the Jordan
	3:26	with you **across** the Jordan,
	6: 1	went to the **other side** of the
	6:17	started **across** the sea to
	6:22	had stayed on the **other side** of
	6:25	him on the **other side** of the
	10:40	away again **across** the Jordan
	18: 1	**across** the Kidron valley to a

4009   GO4 AG644 LN193
περας, LIMIT
Mt	12:42	came from the **ends** of the earth
Lk	11:31	the **ends** of the earth to listen
Ro	10:18	words to the **ends** of the world.
He	6:16	puts an **end** to all dispute.

4010   GO2 AG644 LN193
περγαμος, PERGAMUM
Re	1:11	to Smyrna, to **Pergamum,** to
	2:12	of the church in **Pergamum** write

4011   GO3 AG644 LN193
περγη, PERGA
Ac	13:13	and came to **Perga** in Pamphylia.
	13:14	but they went on from **Perga** and
	14:25	had spoken the word in **Perga,**

4012 GO333 AG644 LN193 B3:1172 K6:53
περι, AROUND, ABOUT [MULTIPLE OCCURRENCES]

4013 GO6 AG645 LN193 R4012,71
περιαγω, I LEAD AROUND

Mt	4:23	Jesus **went throughout** Galilee,
	9:35	Then Jesus **went about** all the
	23:15	For you **cross** sea and land to
Mk	6: 6	Then he **went about** among the
Ac	13:11	and he **went about** groping for
1C	9: 5	the right to **be accompanied** by

4014 GO5 AG645 LN193
περιαιρεω, I LIFT UP

Ac	27:20	saved **was** at last **abandoned.**
	27:40	then **hoisting** the foresail to
2C	3:16	Lord, the veil **is removed.**
He	10:11	that can never **take away** sins.

4014a GO1 AG645 LN193
περιαπτω, I LIGHT

Lk	22:55	When they **had kindled** a fire

4015 GO2 AG645 LN193 R4012,797
περιαστραπτω, I SHINE AROUND

Ac	9: 3	from heaven **flashed around** him.
	22: 6	heaven suddenly **shone about** me.

4016 GO23 AG646 LN193 R4012,906
περιβαλλω, I THROW AROUND (I CLOTHE)

Mt	6:29	not **clothed** like one of these.
	6:31	drink?' or 'What will we **wear?'**
	25:36	you **gave** me **clothing,** I was
	25:38	or naked and **gave** you **clothing?**
	25:43	you did not **give** me **clothing,**
Mk	14:51	**wearing** nothing but a linen
	16: 5	young man, **dressed** in a white
Lk	12:27	glory **was** not **clothed** like one
	23:11	he **put** an elegant robe **on** him,
Jn	19: 2	they **dressed** him in a purple
Ac	12: 8	**Wrap** your cloak around you and
Re	3: 5	conquer, you **will be clothed**
	3:18	and white robes **to clothe** you
	4: 4	elders, **dressed** in white robes,
	7: 9	the Lamb, **robed** in white, with
	7:13	**robed** in white, and where have
	10: 1	**wrapped** in a cloud, with a
	11: 3	sixty days, **wearing** sackcloth.
	12: 1	a woman **clothed** with the sun,

	17: 4	The woman **was clothed** in purple
	18:16	**clothed** in fine linen, in
	19: 8	granted **to be clothed** with
	19:13	He **is clothed** in a robe dipped

4017 GO7 AG646 LN193 R4012,991
περιβλεπω, I LOOK AROUND

Mk	3: 5	He **looked around** at them with
	3:34	And **looking at** those who sat
	5:32	He **looked all around** to see
	9: 8	when they **looked around,** they
	10:23	Then Jesus **looked around** and
	11:11	**looked around** at everything,
Lk	6:10	After **looking around** at all

4018 GO2 AG646 LN193 R4016
περιβολαιον, ROBE

1C	11:15	is given to her for a **covering.**
He	1:12	like a **cloak** you will roll them

4019 GO1 AG646 LN193 R4012,1210
περιδεω, I BIND AROUND

Jn	11:44	and his face **wrapped** in a cloth

4020 GO1 AG646 LN193 B1:266 R4012,2038
περιεργαζομαι, I WORK AROUND

2Th	3:11	mere **busybodies,** not doing any

4021 GO2 AG646 LN193 B1:266 R4012,2041
περιεργος, WORKER AROUND

Ac	19:19	who practiced **magic** collected
1Ti	5:13	also gossips and **busybodies,**

4022 GO4 AG646 LN193 B1:320 K2:682 R4012,2064
περιερχομαι, I COME/GO AROUND

Ac	19:13	**itinerant** Jewish exorcists
	28:13	and **came** to Rhegium. After one
1Ti	5:13	to be idle, **gadding about** from
He	11:37	they **went about** in skins of

4023 GO2 AG647 LN194 R4012,2192
περιεχω, I CONTAIN

Lk	5: 9	**were** amazed at the catch of
1P	2: 6	For it **stands** in scripture:

4024 GO6 AG647 LN194 B3:120 K5:302 R4012,2224
περιζωννυμι, I ENCIRCLE (I CLOTHE)

Lk	12:35	**Be dressed** for action and
	12:37	he **will fasten his belt** and
	17: 8	**put on your apron** and serve me

Ep   6:14   **fasten the belt** of truth **around**
Re   1:13   **clothed** with a long robe and
       15: 6   **with** golden sashes across their

4025   GO1 AG647 LN194 R4060
περιθεσις, I SET AROUND
1P   3: 3   and by **wearing** gold ornaments

4026   GO4 AG647 LN194 R4012,2476
περιιστημι, I STAND AROUND
Jn   11:42   sake of the crowd **standing** here
Ac   25: 7   **surrounded** him, bringing many
2Ti   2:16   **Avoid** profane chatter, for it
Ti   3: 9   But **avoid** stupid controversies,

4027   GO1 AG647 LN194 B1:479 K3:430
περικαθαρμα, FILTH
1C   4:13   like the **rubbish** of the world,

4028   GO3 AG647 LN194 R4012,2572
περικαλυπτω, I COVER AROUND
Mk   14:65   spit on him, **to blindfold** him,
Lk   22:64   they also **blindfolded** him and
He   9: 4   covenant **overlaid** on all sides

4029   GO5 AG647 LN194 K3:656 R4012,2749
περικειμαι, I SET AROUND
Mk   9:42   millstone **were hung around** your
Lk   17: 2   millstone **were hung around** your
Ac   28:20   that I **am bound** with this chain
He   5: 2   himself **is subject** to weakness;
       12: 1   since we **are surrounded** by so

4030   GO2 AG648 LN194 B3:959 K5:314 R4012,2776
περικεφαλαια, HELMET
Ep   6:17   Take the **helmet** of salvation,
1Th   5: 8   **helmet** the hope of salvation.

4031   GO1 AG648 LN194
περικρατης, IN CONTROL
Ac   27:16   the ship's boat **under control.**

4032   GO1 AG648 LN194 R4012,2928
περικρυβω, I HIDE ABOUT
Lk   1:24   she **remained in seclusion.** She

4033   GO1 AG648 LN194 R4012,2944
περικυκλοω, I ENCIRCLE AROUND
Lk   19:43   and **surround** you, and
                       hem you

4034   GO2 AG648 LN194 B2:484 K4:16 R4012,2989
περιλαμπω, I SHINE AROUND
Lk   2: 9   glory of the Lord **shone around**
Ac   26:13   than the sun, **shining around** me

4035   GO2 AG648 LN194 B3:247 R4012,3007
περιλειπομαι, I LEAVE AROUND
1Th   4:15   who **are left** until the coming
        4:17   who **are left,** will be caught

4036   GO5 AG648 LN194 K4:323
περιλυπος, GREATLY GRIEVED
Mt   26:38   I am **deeply grieved,** even to
Mk   6:26   The king was **deeply grieved;**
       14:34   I am **deeply grieved,** even to
Lk   18:23   became **sad;** for he was very
       18:24   Jesus looked **at** him and said,

4037   GO1 AG648 LN194 B3:224 K4:578
R4012,3306
περιμενω, I STAY AROUND
Ac   1: 4   but **to wait there** for the

4038   GO1 AG648 LN194
περιξ, AROUND
Ac   5:16   from the towns **around** Jerusalem

4039   GO1 AG648 LN194 R4012,3611
περιοικεω, I LIVE AROUND
Lk   1:65   all their **neighbors,** and all

4040   GO1 AG648 LN194 R4012,3624
περιοικος, HOUSEHOLD AROUND
Lk   1:58   Her **neighbors** and relatives

4041   GO1 AG648 LN194 B2:838 K6:57
περιουσιος, SPECIAL
Ti   2:14   purify for **himself** a people of

4042   GO1 AG648 LN194
περιοχη, SECTION
Ac   8:32   the **passage** of the scripture

4043   GO95 AG649 LN194 B3:935 K5:940
R4012,3961
περιπατεω, I WALK AROUND
Mt   4:18   As he **walked** by the Sea of
        9: 5   or to say, 'Stand up and **walk'?**
       11: 5   their sight, the lame **walk,**
       14:25   he **came walking** toward them on
       14:26   saw him **walking** on the sea,
       14:29   started **walking** on the water,
       15:31   the lame **walking,** and the blind

Mk	2: 9	up and take your mat and **walk'?**
	5:42	began to **walk** about (she was
	6:48	**walking** on the sea. He intended
	6:49	they saw him **walking** on the sea
	7: 5	not **live** according to the
	8:24	they look like trees, **walking.**"
	11:27	As he **was walking** in the temple
	12:38	to **walk around** in long robes,
	16:12	as they **were walking** into the
Lk	5:23	or to say, 'Stand up and **walk'?**
	7:22	the lame **walk,** the lepers are
	11:44	people **walk** over them without
	20:46	like to **walk around** in long
	24:17	while you **walk along?**" They
Jn	1:36	as he watched Jesus **walk** by,
	5: 8	take your mat and **walk.**"
	5: 9	and began to **walk.** Now that day
	5:11	Take up your mat and **walk.**
	5:12	'Take it up and **walk'?**"
	6:19	Jesus **walking** on the sea and
	6:66	and no longer **went about** with
	7: 1	After this Jesus **went about** in
	7: 1	not wish to **go about** in Judea
	8:12	follows me **will** never **walk** in
	10:23	and Jesus **was walking** in the
	11: 9	Those who **walk** during the day
	11:10	But those who **walk** at night
	11:54	no longer **walked about** openly
	12:35	**Walk** while you have the light,
	12:35	If you **walk** in the darkness,
	21:18	own belt and to **go** wherever you
Ac	3: 6	Nazareth, stand up and **walk.**"
	3: 8	he stood and began to **walk,** and
	3: 8	**walking** and leaping and
	3: 9	saw him **walking** and praising
	3:12	piety we had made him **walk?**
	14: 8	and **had** never **walked,** for he
	14:10	man sprang up and began to **walk**
	21:21	children or **observe** the customs
Ro	6: 4	too might **walk** in newness of
	8: 4	who **walk** not according to the
	13:13	let us **live** honorably as in
	14:15	you **are** no longer **walking** in
1C	3: 3	and **behaving** according to human
	7:17	each of you **lead the life** that
2C	4: 2	we **refuse to practice** cunning
	5: 7	we **walk** by faith, not by sight.
	10: 2	we **are acting** according to
	10: 3	we **live** as human beings, but

	12:18	Did we not **conduct** ourselves
Ga	5:16	**Live** by the Spirit, I say, and
Ep	2: 2	in which you once **lived,**
	2:10	to be **our way of life.**
	4: 1	to **lead** a life worthy of the
	4:17	no longer **live** as the Gentiles
	4:17	as the Gentiles **live,** in the
	5: 2	and **live** in love, as Christ
	5: 8	you are light. **Live** as children
	5:15	Be careful then how you **live,**
Ph	3:17	those who **live** according to the
	3:18	For many **live** as enemies of the
Co	1:10	you may **lead lives** worthy of
	2: 6	continue to **live your lives** in
	3: 7	when you **were living that life.**
	4: 5	**Conduct** yourselves wisely
1Th	2:12	that you **lead a life** worthy of
	4: 1	you ought **to live** and to please
	4: 1	(as, in fact, you **are doing**),
	4:12	so that you **may behave** properly
2Th	3: 6	who are **living** in idleness and
	3:11	of you **are living** in idleness,
He	13: 9	those who **observe** them.
1P	5: 8	the devil **prowls around,**
1J	1: 6	we **are walking** in darkness, we
	1: 7	but if we **walk** in the light as
	2: 6	ought to **walk** just as he walked
	2: 6	ought to walk just as he **walked**
	2:11	**walks** in the darkness, and does
2J	1: 4	**walking** in the truth, just as
	1: 6	that we **walk** according to his
	1: 6	beginning—you must **walk** in
3J	1: 3	how you **walk** in the truth.
	1: 4	my children **are walking** in the
Re	2: 1	who **walks** among the seven
	3: 4	they **will walk** with me, dressed
	9:20	cannot see or hear or **walk.**
	16:15	not **going about** naked and
	21:24	The nations **will walk** by its

4044　GO1 AG649 LN194
περιπειρω, I PIERCE

1Ti	6:10	faith and **pierced** themselves

4045　GO3 AG649 LN195 B1:608 K6:173 R4012,4098
περιπιπτω, I FALL

Lk	10:30	and **fell** into the hands of
Ac	27:41	But **striking** a reef, they ran
Ja	1: 2	whenever you **face** trials of any

4046 G03 AG650 LN195 R4012,4160
περιποιεω, I ACQUIRE
Lk 17:33 try to **make** their life **secure**
Ac 20:28 that he **obtained** with the blood
1Ti 3:13 as deacons **gain** a good standing

4047 G05 AG650 LN195 B2:838 R4046
περιποιησις, POSSESSION
Ep 1:14 redemption as God's **own** people,
1Th 5: 9 for **obtaining** salvation through
2Th 2:14 you may **obtain** the glory of our
He 10:39 who have faith and so **are** saved
1P 2: 9 God's **own** people, in order that

4048 G01 AG650 LN195 R4012,4486
περιρηγνυμι, I RIP OFF (ALL AROUND)
Ac 16:22 had them **stripped** of their

4049 G01 AG650 LN195 R4012,4685
περισπαω, I BECOME BUSY WITH
Lk 10:40 But Martha was **distracted** by

4050 G04 AG650 LN195 B1:728 K6:63 R4052
περισσεια, EXCESS
Ro 5:17 receive the **abundance** of grace
2C 8: 2 their **abundant** joy and their
10:15 you may be **greatly enlarged,**
Ja 1:21 sordidness and **rank growth** of

4051 G05 AG650 LN195 B1:728 K6:63 R4052
περισσευμα, EXCESS
Mt 12:34 out of the **abundance** of the
Mk 8: 8 the broken pieces **left over,**
Lk 6:45 out of the **abundance** of the
2C 8:14 your present **abundance** and
8:14 their **abundance** may be for your

4052 G039 AG650 LN195 B1:728 K6:58 R4053
περισσευω, I EXCEED
Mt 5:20 your righteousness **exceeds** that
13:12 and they **will have** an **abundance**
14:20 what **was left over** of the
15:37 broken pieces **left over,** seven
25:29 they **will have** an **abundance;**
Mk 12:44 out of their **abundance;** but she
Lk 9:17 What was **left over** was gathered
12:15 in the **abundance** of possessions
15:17 have bread enough and **to spare,**
21: 4 out of their **abundance,** but she
Jn 6:12 up the fragments **left over,** so

6:13 barley loaves, **left** by those
Ac 16: 5 faith and **increased** in numbers
Ro 3: 7 God's truthfulness **abounds** to
5:15 Jesus Christ, **abounded** for the
15:13 so that you may **abound** in hope
1C 8: 8 and no **better off** if we do.
14:12 strive to **excel** in them for
15:58 always **excelling** in the work of
2C 1: 5 Christ are **abundant** for us, so
1: 5 our consolation is **abundant**
3: 9 justification **abound** in glory!
4:15 may **increase** thanksgiving, to
8: 2 extreme poverty **have overflowed**
8: 7 Now as you **excel** in everything
8: 7 we want you to **excel** also in
9: 8 every blessing **in abundance,**
9: 8 you may share **abundantly** in
9:12 but also **overflows** with many
Ep 1: 8 that he **lavished** on us. With
Ph 1: 9 that your love may **overflow**
1:26 so that I may share **abundantly**
4:12 know what it is to **have plenty.**
4:12 of **having plenty** and of being
4:18 and **have more than enough;** I am
Co 2: 7 **abounding** in thanksgiving.
1Th 3:12 increase and **abound** in love for
4: 1 you should **do so more** and more.
4:10 beloved, to **do so more** and more

4053 G06 AG651 LN195 B1:728 K6:61
περισσος, EXCESS
Mt 5:37 anything **more than** this comes
5:47 what **more** are you doing than
Mk 6:51 And they **were** utterly astounded
Jn 10:10 life, and have it **abundantly.**
Ro 3: 1 Then what **advantage** has the Jew
2C 9: 1 Now it is not **necessary** for me

4055 G016 AG651 LN195 B1:728 R4053
περισσοτερος, MORE EXCESSIVE
Mt 11: 9 you, and **more than** a prophet.
Mk 7:36 more **zealously** they proclaimed
12:33 this is much **more important**
12:40 the **greater** condemnation.
Lk 7:26 you, and **more than** a prophet.
12: 4 after that can do nothing **more.**
12:48 entrusted, **even more** will be
20:47 the **greater** condemnation.
1C 12:23 we clothe with **greater** honor,

	12:23	treated with **greater** respect;
	12:24	the **greater** honor to the
	15:10	I worked **harder** than any of
2C	2: 7	overwhelmed by **excessive** sorrow
	10: 8	a little **too much** of our
He	6:17	to show **even more** clearly to
	7:15	It is **even more** obvious when

4056　GO12　AG651　LN195　B1:728　R4053
περισσοτερως, MORE EXCEEDINGLY

2C	1:12	and **all the more** toward you.
	2: 4	the **abundant** love that I have
	7:13	we rejoiced **still more** at the
	7:15	out **all the more** to you, as he
	11:23	with far **greater** labors, far
	11:23	**far more** imprisonments, with
	12:15	If I love you **more,** am I to be
Ga	1:14	for I was **far more** zealous for
Ph	1:14	with **greater** boldness and
1Th	2:17	we longed with **great** eagerness
He	2: 1	must pay **greater** attention to
	13:19	I urge you **all the more** to do

4057　GO4　AG651　LN195　B1:728　R4053
περισσως, EXCEEDINGLY

Mt	27:23	they shouted **all the more,** "Let
Mk	10:26	They were **greatly** astounded and
	15:14	they shouted **all the more,**
Ac	26:11	I was so **furiously** enraged at

4058　GO10　AG651　LN195
περιστερα, DOVE

Mt	3:16	descending like a **dove** and
	10:16	serpents and innocent as **doves.**
	21:12	seats of those who sold **doves.**
Mk	1:10	Spirit descending like a **dove**
	11:15	seats of those who sold **doves;**
Lk	2:24	or two young **pigeons.**"
	3:22	him in bodily form like a **dove.**
Jn	1:32	from heaven like a **dove,** and it
	2:14	cattle, sheep, and **doves,** and
	2:16	who were selling the **doves,**

4059　GO17　AG652　LN195　B1:307　K6:72
περιτεμνω, I CIRCUMCISE

Lk	1:59	came to **circumcise** the child,
	2:21	time to **circumcise** the child;
Jn	7:22	you **circumcise** a man on the
Ac	7: 8	and **circumcised** him on the
	15: 1	Unless you are **circumcised**

	15: 5	to be **circumcised** and ordered
	16: 3	**had** him **circumcised** because of
	21:21	to **circumcise** their children
1C	7:18	already **circumcised?** Let him
	7:18	time of his call **uncircumcised?**
Ga	2: 3	not compelled to be **circumcised**
	5: 2	let yourselves be **circumcised,**
	5: 3	who lets himself be **circumcised**
	6:12	compel you to be **circumcised**—
	6:13	Even the **circumcised** do not
	6:13	want you to be **circumcised** so
Co	2:11	you were **circumcised** with a

4060　GO8　AG652　LN195　R4012,5087
περιτιθημι, I SET AROUND

Mt	21:33	vineyard, **put** a fence **around** it
	27:28	and **put** a scarlet robe **on** him,
	27:48	wine, **put** it **on** a stick, and
Mk	12: 1	vineyard, **put** a fence **around** it
	15:17	crown, they **put** it **on** him.
	15:36	wine, **put** it **on** a stick, and
Jn	19:29	So they **put** a sponge full of
1C	12:23	we **clothe** with greater honor,

4061　GO36　AG652　LN195　B1:307　K6:72　R4059
περιτομη, CIRCUMCISION

Jn	7:22	Moses gave you **circumcision** (it
	7:23	If a man receives **circumcision**
Ac	7: 8	the covenant of **circumcision.**
	10:45	The **circumcised** believers who
	11: 2	the **circumcised** believers
Ro	2:25	**Circumcision** indeed is of value
	2:25	your **circumcision** has become
	2:26	be regarded as **circumcision?**
	2:27	and **circumcision** but break the
	2:28	is true **circumcision** something
	2:29	real **circumcision** is a matter
	3: 1	is the value of **circumcision?**
	3:30	he will justify the **circumcised**
	4: 9	on the **circumcised,** or also on
	4:10	after he had been **circumcised?**
	4:10	but before he was **circumcised.**
	4:11	the sign of **circumcision** as a
	4:12	ancestor of the **circumcised**
	4:12	not only **circumcised** but who
	15: 8	a servant of the **circumcised** on
1C	7:19	**Circumcision** is nothing, and
Ga	2: 7	gospel for the **circumcised**
	2: 8	apostle to the **circumcised** also

	2: 9	and they to the **circumcised.**
	2:12	of the **circumcision** faction.
	5: 6	neither **circumcision** nor
	5:11	still preaching **circumcision?**
	6:15	For neither **circumcision** nor
Ep	2:11	are called "the **circumcision**"
Ph	3: 3	who are the **circumcision,** who
	3: 5	**circumcised** on the eighth day,
Co	2:11	with a spiritual **circumcision,**
	2:11	in the **circumcision** of Christ;
	3:11	Greek and Jew, **circumcised** and
	4:11	ones of the **circumcision** among
Ti	1:10	those of the **circumcision;**

4062   GO1 AG653 LN195
περιτρεπω, I TURN AROUND
Ac   26:24   learning **is driving** you insane!

4063   GO1 AG653 LN195 R4012,5143
περιτρεχω, I RUN AROUND
Mk   6:55   and **rushed** about that whole

4064   GO3 AG653 LN195 R4012,5342
περιφερω, I BRING AROUND
Mk   6:55   began to **bring** the sick on mats
2C   4:10   always **carrying** in the body the
Ep   4:14   and **blown about** by every wind

4065   GO1 AG653 LN196 B1:461 K3:633 R4012,5426
περιφρονεω, I DISREGARD
Ti   2:15   Let no one **look down on** you.

4066   GO9 AG653 LN196 R4012,5561
περιχωρος, SURROUNDING COUNTRY
Mt   3: 5   and all the **region** along the
     14:35   throughout the **region** and
Mk   1:28   the **surrounding region** of
Lk   3: 3   all the **region** around the
     4:14   all the **surrounding country.**
     4:37   every place in the **region.**
     7:17   and all the **surrounding country**
     8:37   of the **surrounding country** of
Ac   14: 6   to the **surrounding country;**

4067   GO1 AG653 LN196 B1:479 K6:84
περιψημα, SCUM
1C   4:13   the **dregs** of all things, to

4068   GO1 AG653 LN196 K6:93
περπερευομαι, I PUT FORWARD

1C   13: 4   not envious or **boastful** or

4069   GO1 AG653 LN196
περσις, PERSIS
Ro   16:12   Greet the beloved **Persis,** who

4070   GO2 AG653 LN196
περυσι, LAST YEAR
2C   8:10   who began **last year** not only to
     9: 2   has been ready since **last year;**

4071   GO14 AG654 LN196 B1:172 R4072
πετεινον, BIRD
Mt   6:26   Look at the **birds** of the air;
     8:20   and **birds** of the air have nests
     13: 4   and the **birds** came and ate them
     13:32   the **birds** of the air come and
Mk   4: 4   and the **birds** came and ate it
     4:32   so that the **birds** of the air
Lk   8: 5   and the **birds** of the air ate it
     9:58   and **birds** of the air have nests
     12:24   value are you than the **birds!**
     13:19   the **birds** of the air made nests
Ac   10:12   reptiles and **birds** of the air.
     11: 6   reptiles, and **birds** of the air.
Ro   1:23   or **birds** or four-footed animals
Ja   3: 7   of beast and **bird,** of reptile

4072   GO5 AG654 LN196
πετομαι, I FLY
Re   4: 7   creature like a **flying** eagle.
     8:13   as it **flew** in midheaven, "Woe,
     12:14   so that she could **fly** from the
     14: 6   another angel **flying** in
     19:17   birds that **fly** in midheaven,

4073   GO15 AG654 LN196 B3:381 K6:95
πετρα, ROCK
Mt   7:24   who built his house on **rock.**
     7:25   it had been founded on **rock.**
     16:18   Peter, and on this **rock** I will
     27:51   shook, and the **rocks** were split
     27:60   he had hewn in the **rock.** He
Mk   15:46   had been hewn out of the **rock.**
Lk   6:48   and laid the foundation on **rock**
     8: 6   Some fell on the **rock;** and as
     8:13   The ones on the **rock** are those
Ro   9:33   a **rock** that will make them fall
1C   10: 4   drank from the spiritual **rock**
     10: 4   them, and the **rock** was Christ.

1P　2: 8　and a **rock** that makes them fall
Re　6:15　the **rocks** of the mountains,
　　　6:16　mountains and **rocks**, "Fall on

4074　ᴳᴼ156 ᴬᴳ654 ᴸᴺ196 ᴮ3:381 ᴷ6:100 ᴿ4073
πετρος, PETER

Mt　4:18　Simon, who is called **Peter,** and
　　8:14　Jesus entered **Peter's** house, he
　10: 2　Simon, also known as **Peter,** and
　14:28　**Peter** answered him, "Lord, if
　14:29　He said, "Come." So **Peter** got
　15:15　But **Peter** said to him, "Explain
　16:16　Simon **Peter** answered, "You are
　16:18　And I tell you, you are **Peter,**
　16:22　And **Peter** took him aside and
　16:23　turned and said to **Peter,** "Get
　17: 1　Jesus took with him **Peter** and
　17: 4　Then **Peter** said to Jesus, "Lord
　17:24　came to **Peter** and said, "Does
　18:21　Then **Peter** came and said to
　19:27　Then **Peter** said in reply, "Look
　26:33　**Peter** said to him, "Though all
　26:35　**Peter** said to him, "Even though
　26:37　He took with him **Peter** and the
　26:40　he said to **Peter,** "So, could
　26:58　But **Peter** was following him at
　26:69　Now **Peter** was sitting outside
　26:73　came up and said to **Peter,**
　26:75　Then **Peter** remembered what
Mk　3:16　to whom he gave the name **Peter)**
　　5:37　to follow him except **Peter,**
　　8:29　say that I am?" **Peter** answered
　　8:32　And **Peter** took him aside and
　　8:33　he rebuked **Peter** and said, "Get
　　9: 2　Jesus took with him **Peter** and
　　9: 5　Then **Peter** said to Jesus,
　10:28　**Peter** began to say to him,
　11:21　Then **Peter** remembered and said
　13: 3　**Peter,** James, John, and Andrew
　14:29　**Peter** said to him, "Even though
　14:33　He took with him **Peter** and
　14:37　he said to **Peter,** "Simon, are
　14:54　**Peter** had followed him at a
　14:66　While **Peter** was below in the
　14:67　When she saw **Peter** warming
　14:70　again said to **Peter,** "Certainly
　14:72　**Peter** remembered that Jesus had
　16: 7　tell his disciples and **Peter**
　16: 8　briefly to those around **Peter**

Lk　5: 8　But when Simon **Peter** saw it,
　　6:14　Simon, whom he named **Peter,**
　　8:45　**Peter** said, "Master, the crowds
　　8:51　except **Peter,** John, and James,
　　9:20　**Peter** answered, "The Messiah of
　　9:28　**Peter** and John and James, and
　　9:32　Now **Peter** and his companions
　　9:33　**Peter** said to Jesus, "Master,
　12:41　**Peter** said, "Lord, are you
　18:28　Then **Peter** said, "Look, we have
　22: 8　So Jesus sent **Peter** and John,
　22:34　Jesus said, "I tell you, **Peter,**
　22:54　But **Peter** was following at a
　22:55　together, **Peter** sat among them.
　22:58　But **Peter** said, "Man, I am not!
　22:60　But **Peter** said, "Man, I do not
　22:61　Lord turned and looked at **Peter**
　22:61　Then **Peter** remembered the word
　24:12　But **Peter** got up and ran to the
Jn　1:40　Andrew, Simon **Peter's** brother.
　　1:42　(which is translated **Peter**).
　　1:44　the city of Andrew and **Peter.**
　　6: 8　Andrew, Simon **Peter's** brother,
　　6:68　Simon **Peter** answered him, "Lord
　13: 6　He came to Simon **Peter,** who
　13: 8　**Peter** said to him, "You will
　13: 9　Simon **Peter** said to him, "Lord
　13:24　Simon **Peter** therefore motioned
　13:36　Simon **Peter** said to him, "Lord
　13:37　**Peter** said to him, "Lord, why
　18:10　Simon **Peter,** who had a sword,
　18:11　Jesus said to **Peter,** "Put your
　18:15　Simon **Peter** and another
　18:16　but **Peter** was standing outside
　18:16　the gate, and brought **Peter** in.
　18:17　The woman said to **Peter,** "You
　18:18　**Peter** also was standing with
　18:25　Now Simon **Peter** was standing
　18:26　whose ear **Peter** had cut off,
　18:27　Again **Peter** denied it, and at
　20: 2　ran and went to Simon **Peter** and
　20: 3　Then **Peter** and the other
　20: 4　other disciple outran **Peter** and
　20: 6　Then Simon **Peter** came,
　21: 2　together were Simon **Peter,**
　21: 3　Simon **Peter** said to them,
　21: 7　said to **Peter,** "It is the Lord!"
　21: 7　When Simon **Peter** heard that it
　21:11　So Simon **Peter** went aboard and

21:15	Jesus said to Simon **Peter,**
21:17	**Peter** felt hurt because he said
21:20	**Peter** turned and saw the
21:21	When **Peter** saw him, he said to
Ac 1:13	**Peter,** and John, and James, and
1:15	In those days **Peter** stood up
2:14	But **Peter,** standing with the
2:37	said to **Peter** and to the other
2:38	**Peter** said to them, "Repent,
3: 1	One day **Peter** and John were
3: 3	When he saw **Peter** and John
3: 4	**Peter** looked intently at him,
3: 6	But **Peter** said, "I have no
3:11	While he clung to **Peter** and
3:12	When **Peter** saw it, he addressed
4: 8	Then **Peter,** filled with the
4:13	boldness of **Peter** and John and
4:19	But **Peter** and John answered
5: 3	"Ananias," **Peter** asked, "why
5: 8	**Peter** said to her, "Tell me
5: 9	Then **Peter** said to her, "How
5:15	in order that **Peter's** shadow
5:29	But **Peter** and the apostles
8:14	they sent **Peter** and John to
8:20	But **Peter** said to him, "May
9:32	Now as **Peter** went here and
9:34	**Peter** said to him, "Aeneas,
9:38	**Peter** was there, sent two men
9:39	So **Peter** got up and went with
9:40	**Peter** put all of them outside,
9:40	and seeing **Peter,** she sat up.
10: 5	Simon who is called **Peter;**
10: 9	**Peter** went up on the roof to
10:13	Get up, **Peter;** kill and eat.
10:14	But **Peter** said, "By no means,
10:17	Now while **Peter** was greatly
10:18	was called **Peter,** was staying
10:19	While **Peter** was still thinking
10:21	So **Peter** went down to the men
10:25	On **Peter's** arrival Cornelius
10:26	But **Peter** made him get up,
10:32	for Simon, who is called **Peter;**
10:34	Then **Peter** began to speak to
10:44	While **Peter** was still speaking,
10:45	who had come with **Peter** were
10:46	extolling God. Then **Peter** said,
11: 2	So when **Peter** went up to
11: 4	Then **Peter** began to explain it
11: 7	Get up, **Peter;** kill and eat.

11:13	Simon, who is called **Peter;**
12: 3	he proceeded to arrest **Peter**
12: 5	While **Peter** was kept in prison
12: 6	**Peter,** bound with two chains,
12: 7	He tapped **Peter** on the side
12:11	Then **Peter** came to himself and
12:14	On recognizing **Peter's** voice,
12:14	that **Peter** was standing at the
12:16	Meanwhile **Peter** continued
12:18	over what had become of **Peter.**
15: 7	**Peter** stood up and said to them
Ga 2: 7	as **Peter** had been entrusted
2: 8	through **Peter** making him an
1P 1: 1	**Peter,** an apostle of Jesus
2P 1: 1	Simeon **Peter,** a servant and

4075 GO4 AG655 LN196 R4073
πετρωδης, ROCKY

Mt 13: 5	seeds fell on **rocky** ground,
13:20	what was sown on **rocky** ground,
Mk 4: 5	Other seed fell on **rocky** ground
4:16	the ones sown on **rocky** ground:

4076 GO1 AG655 LN196 B2:210
πηγανον, RUE

Lk 11:42	For you tithe mint and **rue** and

4077 GO11 AG655 LN196 B3:985 K6:112
πηγη, SPRING

Mk 5:29	her **hemorrhage** stopped; and she
Jn 4: 6	Jacob's **well** was there, and
4: 6	sitting by the **well.** It was
4:14	them a **spring** of water gushing
Ja 3:11	Does a **spring** pour forth from
2P 2:17	These are waterless **springs** and
Re 7:17	guide them to **springs** of the
8:10	rivers and on the **springs** of
14: 7	sea and the **springs** of water
16: 4	and the **springs** of water, and
21: 6	the **spring** of the water of life

4078 GO1 AG656 LN196
πηγνυμι, I AFFIX

He 8: 2	and not any mortal, **has set up.**

4079 GO2 AG656 LN196
πηδαλιον, RUDDER

Ac 27:40	that tied the **steering-oars;**
Ja 3: 4	guided by a very small **rudder**

4080 ᴳᴼ2 ᴬᴳ656 ᴸᴺ196
πηλικος, HOW GREAT
Ga 6:11 See **what large** letters I make
He 7: 4 See **how great** he is! Even

4081 ᴳᴼ6 ᴬᴳ656 ᴸᴺ196 ᴮ3:915 ᴷ6:118
πηλος, CLAY
Jn 9: 6 on the ground and made **mud** with
9: 6 the **mud** on the man's eyes,
9:11 The man called Jesus made **mud,**
9:14 Jesus made the **mud** and opened
9:15 He put **mud** on my eyes. Then I
Ro 9:21 over the **clay,** to make out of

4082 ᴳᴼ6 ᴬᴳ656 ᴸᴺ196 ᴮ1:143 ᴷ6:119
πηρα, BAG
Mt 10:10 no **bag** for your journey, or two
Mk 6: 8 no **bag,** no money in their belts
Lk 9: 3 nor **bag,** nor bread, nor money
10: 4 no **bag,** no sandals; and greet
22:35 without a purse, **bag,** or
22:36 and likewise a **bag.** And the one

4083 ᴳᴼ4 ᴬᴳ656 ᴸᴺ196
πηχυς, CUBIT
Mt 6:27 add a single **hour** to your span
Lk 12:25 add a single **hour** to your span
Jn 21: 8 only about a hundred **yards** off.
Re 21:17 hundred forty-four **cubits** by

4084 ᴳᴼ12 ᴬᴳ657 ᴸᴺ196
πιαζω, I CAPTURE
Jn 7:30 Then they tried to **arrest** him,
7:32 temple police to **arrest** him.
7:44 of them wanted to **arrest** him,
8:20 no one **arrested** him, because
10:39 Then they tried to **arrest** him
11:57 so that they might **arrest** him.
21: 3 that night they **caught** nothing.
21:10 that you **have** just **caught."**
Ac 3: 7 And he **took** him by the right
12: 4 When he **had seized** him, he put
2C 11:32 Damascus in order to **seize** me,
Re 19:20 And the beast **was captured,**

4085 ᴳᴼ1 ᴬᴳ657 ᴸᴺ196
πιεζω, I PRESS DOWN
Lk 6:38 A good measure, **pressed down,**

4086 ᴳᴼ1 ᴬᴳ657 ᴸᴺ196 ᴮ1:588 ᴿ3982,3056
πιθανολογια, PERSUASIVE WORD
Co 2: 4 you with **plausible arguments.**

4087 ᴳᴼ4 ᴬᴳ657 ᴸᴺ197 ᴮ1:202 ᴷ6:122 ᴿ4089
πικραινω, I AM BITTER
Co 3:19 and never **treat** them **harshly.**
Re 8:11 because it **was made bitter.**
10: 9 it **will be bitter** to your
10:10 my stomach **was made bitter.**

4088 ᴳᴼ4 ᴬᴳ657 ᴸᴺ197 ᴮ1:202 ᴷ6:122 ᴿ4089
πικρια, BITTERNESS
Ac 8:23 are in the gall of **bitterness**
Ro 3:14 full of cursing and **bitterness**
Ep 4:31 you all **bitterness** and wrath
He 12:15 no root of **bitterness** springs

4089 ᴳᴼ2 ᴬᴳ657 ᴸᴺ197 ᴮ1:201 ᴷ6:122
πικρος, BITTER
Ja 3:11 both fresh and **brackish** water?
3:14 But if you have **bitter** envy

4090 ᴳᴼ2 ᴬᴳ657 ᴸᴺ197 ᴮ1:201 ᴿ4089
πικρως, BITTERLY
Mt 26:75 he went out and wept **bitterly.**
Lk 22:62 he went out and wept **bitterly.**

4091 ᴳᴼ55 ᴬᴳ657 ᴸᴺ197
πιλατος, PILATE
Mt 27: 2 him over to **Pilate** the governor.
27:13 Then **Pilate** said to him, "Do
27:17 **Pilate** said to them, "Whom do
27:22 **Pilate** said to them, "Then what
27:24 So when **Pilate** saw that he
27:58 He went to **Pilate** and asked
27:58 **Pilate** ordered it to be given
27:62 gathered before **Pilate**
27:65 **Pilate** said to them, "You have
Mk 15: 1 and handed him over to **Pilate.**
15: 2 **Pilate** asked him, "Are you the
15: 4 **Pilate** asked him again, "Have
15: 5 so that **Pilate** was amazed.
15: 9 Then **he** answered them, "Do you
15:12 **Pilate** spoke to them again,
15:14 **Pilate** asked them, "Why, what
15:15 So **Pilate,** wishing to satisfy
15:43 went boldly to **Pilate** and asked
15:44 Then **Pilate** wondered if he were
Lk 3: 1 Pontius **Pilate** was governor of

	13: 1	whose blood **Pilate** had mingled
	23: 1	and brought Jesus before **Pilate**
	23: 3	**Pilate** asked him, "Are you the
	23: 4	Then **Pilate** said to the chief
	23: 6	When **Pilate** heard this, he
	23:11	and sent him back to **Pilate.**
	23:12	day Herod and **Pilate** became
	23:13	**Pilate** then called together
	23:20	**Pilate,** wanting to release
	23:24	So **Pilate** gave his verdict
	23:52	This man went to **Pilate** and
Jn	18:29	So **Pilate** went out to them and
	18:31	**Pilate** said to them, "Take him
	18:33	Then **Pilate** entered the
	18:35	**Pilate** replied, "I am not a Jew
	18:37	**Pilate** asked him, "So you are a
	18:38	**Pilate** asked him, "What is
	19: 1	Then **Pilate** took Jesus and had
	19: 4	**Pilate** went out again and said
	19: 6	**Pilate** said to them, "Take him
	19: 8	Now when **Pilate** heard this, he
	19:10	**Pilate** therefore said to him,
	19:12	From then on **Pilate** tried to
	19:13	When **Pilate** heard these words,
	19:15	**Pilate** asked them, "Shall I
	19:19	**Pilate** also had an inscription
	19:21	said to **Pilate,** "Do not write,
	19:22	**Pilate** answered, "What I have
	19:31	So they asked **Pilate** to have
	19:38	asked **Pilate** to let him take
	19:38	**Pilate** gave him permission; so
Ac	3:13	in the presence of **Pilate,**
	4:27	both Herod and Pontius **Pilate,**
	13:28	they asked **Pilate** to have him
1Ti	6:13	Pontius **Pilate** made the good

4092   GO24 AG658 LN197 B1:733
πιμπλημι, I FILL

Mt	22:10	wedding hall **was filled** with
	27:48	**filled** it with sour wine, put
Lk	1:15	he **will be filled** with the Holy
Lk	1:23	time of service **was ended,** he
	1:41	**was filled** with the Holy Spirit
	1:57	time **came** for Elizabeth to give
	1:67	**was filled** with the Holy Spirit
	2: 6	time **came** for her to deliver
	2:21	After eight days **had passed,**
	2:22	When the time **came** for their
	4:28	synagogue **were filled** with rage

	5: 7	and **filled** both boats, so that
	5:26	and **were filled** with awe,
	6:11	But they **were filled** with fury
	21:22	as a **fulfillment** of all that is
Ac	2: 4	**were filled** with the Holy
	3:10	they **were filled** with wonder
	4: 8	Peter, **filled** with the Holy
	4:31	they **were** all **filled** with the
	5:17	Sadducees), **being filled** with
	9:17	**be filled** with the Holy Spirit.
	13: 9	Paul, **filled** with the Holy
	13:45	they **were filled** with jealousy;
	19:29	The city **was filled** with

4092a   GO1 AG658 LN197
πιμπρημι, I SWELL

Ac	28: 6	were expecting him **to swell up**

4093   GO1 AG658 LN197
πινακιδιον, LITTLE TABLET

Lk	1:63	He asked for a **writing tablet**

4094   GO5 AG658 LN197 R4109
πιναξ, PLATTER

Mt	14: 8	Baptist here on a **platter**
	14:11	head was brought on a **platter**
Mk	6:25	John the Baptist on a **platter**
	6:28	brought his head on a **platter**
Lk	11:39	the cup and of the **dish**

4095   GO73 AG658 LN197 B2:274 K6:135
πινω, I DRINK

Mt	6:25	or what you **will drink,** or
	6:31	What **will** we **drink?**
	11:18	neither eating nor **drinking**
	11:19	came eating and **drinking**
	20:22	Are you able to **drink** the cup
	20:22	that I am about to **drink**
	20:23	You **will** indeed **drink** my cup
	24:38	they were eating and **drinking**
	24:49	eats and **drinks** with drunkards
	26:27	**Drink** from it, all of you;
	26:29	I **will** never again **drink** of
	26:29	when I **drink** it new with you
	26:42	unless I **drink** it, your will
	27:34	they offered him wine to **drink**
	27:34	he would not **drink** it.
Mk	10:38	Are you able to **drink** the cup
	10:38	that I **drink,** or be baptized
	10:39	that I **drink** you will drink

	10:39	**will drink;** and with the
	14:23	all of them **drank** from it.
	14:25	I **will** never again **drink**
	14:25	when I **drink** it new in the
	16:18	they **drink** any deadly thing
Lk	1:15	must never **drink** wine or strong
	5:30	Why do you eat and **drink** with
	5:33	your disciples eat and **drink.**
	5:39	after **drinking** old wine desires
	7:33	no bread and **drinking** no wine,
	7:34	has come eating and **drinking,**
	10: 7	eating and **drinking** whatever
	12:19	relax, eat, **drink,** be merry.
	12:29	what you are to **drink,** and do
	12:45	to eat and **drink** and get drunk,
	13:26	We ate and **drank** with you, and
	17: 8	serve me while I eat and **drink;**
	17: 8	later you may eat and **drink'?**
	17:27	They were eating and **drinking,**
	17:28	they were eating and **drinking,**
	22:18	from now on I **will** not **drink** of
	22:30	may eat and **drink** at my table
Jn	4: 7	said to her, **"Give** me a **drink."**
	4: 9	ask a **drink** of me, a woman of
	4:10	**'Give** me a **drink,'** you would
	4:12	and his flocks **drank** from it?
	4:13	who **drinks** of this water will
	4:14	**drink** of the water that I will
	6:53	Son of Man and **drink** his blood,
	6:54	eat my flesh and **drink** my blood
	6:56	eat my flesh and **drink** my blood
	7:38	who believes in me **drink**
	18:11	Am I not to **drink** the cup that
Ac	9: 9	and neither ate nor **drank.**
	23:12	neither to eat nor **drink** until
	23:21	neither to eat nor **drink** until
Ro	14:21	to eat meat or **drink** wine or do
1C	9: 4	right to our food and **drink?**
	10: 4	**drank** the same spiritual drink.
	10: 4	**drank** from the spiritual rock
	10: 7	sat down to eat and **drink,** and
	10:21	**drink** the cup of the Lord and
	10:31	whether you eat or **drink,** or
	11:22	have homes to eat and **drink** in?
	11:25	as often as you **drink** it, in
	11:26	this bread and **drink** the cup,
	11:27	the bread or **drinks** the cup of
	11:28	the bread and **drink** of the cup.
	11:29	and **drink** without discerning

	11:29	eat and **drink** judgment against
	15:32	Let us eat and **drink,** for
He	6: 7	Ground that **drinks** up the rain
Re	14:10	they **will** also **drink** the wine
	16: 6	have given them blood **to drink.**
	18: 3	nations have **drunk** of the

4096　GO1　AG659　LN197
πιοτης, FATNESS, RICHNESS
Ro　11:17　the **rich** root of the olive

4097　GO9　AG659　LN197　B1:268　K6:160
πιπρασκω, I SELL

Mt	13:46	went and **sold** all that he had
	18:25	him to be **sold,** together with
	26: 9	ointment could **have been sold**
Mk	14: 5	ointment could **have been sold**
Jn	12: 5	perfume not **sold** for three
Ac	2:45	**sell** their possessions and
	4:34	lands or houses **sold** them and
	5: 4	And after it **was sold,** were not
Ro	7:14	**sold** into slavery under sin.

4098　GO90　AG659　LN197　B1:608　K6:161
πιπτω, I FALL

Mt	2:11	**knelt** down and paid him homage.
	4: 9	if you **will fall down** and
	7:25	but it **did** not **fall,** because it
	7:27	and it **fell**—and great was
	10:29	them **will fall** to the ground
	13: 4	some seeds **fell** on the path,
	13: 5	seeds **fell** on rocky ground,
	13: 7	Other seeds **fell** among thorns,
	13: 8	Other seeds **fell** on good soil
	15:14	both **will fall** into a pit.
	15:27	that **fall** from their masters
	17: 6	they **fell** to the ground and
	17:15	he often **falls** into the fire
	18:26	slave **fell** on his knees before
	18:29	slave **fell** down and pleaded
	21:44	The one who **falls** on this stone
	21:44	crush anyone on whom it **falls."**
	24:29	the stars **will fall** from heaven
	26:39	he **threw** himself on the ground
Mk	4: 4	some seed **fell** on the path, and
	4: 5	Other seed **fell** on rocky ground
	4: 7	Other seed **fell** among thorns,
	4: 8	Other seed **fell** into good soil
	5:22	he saw him, **fell** at his feet
	9:20	and he **fell** on the ground and

	13:25	stars **will be falling** from
	14:35	he **threw** himself on the ground
Lk	5:12	he **bowed** with his face to the
	8: 5	he sowed, some **fell** on the path
	8: 7	Some **fell** among thorns, and the
	8: 8	Some **fell** into good soil,
	8:14	what **fell** among the thorns,
	8:41	He **fell** at Jesus' feet and
	10:18	watched Satan **fall** from heaven
	11:17	and house **falls** on house.
	13: 4	tower of Siloam **fell** on them—
	14: 5	ox that **has fallen** into a well,
	16:17	letter in the law to **be dropped**
	16:21	**fell** from the rich man's table;
	17:16	He **prostrated** himself at Jesus
	20:18	who **falls** on that stone will be
	20:18	crush anyone on whom it **falls.**"
	21:24	they **will fall** by the edge of
	23:30	to the mountains, '**Fall** on us';
Jn	11:32	she **knelt** at his feet and said
	12:24	unless a grain of wheat **falls**
	18: 6	stepped back and **fell** to the
Ac	1:26	and the lot **fell** on Matthias;
	5: 5	he **fell** down and died. And
	5.10	**fell** down at his feet and died.
	9: 4	He **fell** to the ground and heard
	10:25	**falling** at his feet, worshiped
	13:11	mist and darkness **came** over him
	15:16	of David, which **has fallen;**
	20: 9	sleep, he **fell** to the ground
	22: 7	I **fell** to the ground and heard
Ro	11:11	stumbled so as to **fall?** By no
	11:22	who **have fallen,** but God's
	14: 4	that they stand or **fall.** And
1C	10: 8	thousand **fell** in a single day.
	10:12	watch out that you do not **fall.**
	13: 8	Love never **ends.** But as for
	14:25	person will **bow** down before God
He	3:17	bodies **fell** in the wilderness?
	4:11	**fall** through such disobedience
	11:30	walls of Jericho **fell** after
Ja	5:12	may not **fall** under condemnation
Re	1:17	I **fell** at his feet as though
	2: 5	what you **have fallen;** repent,
	4:10	elders **fall** before the one who
	5: 8	elders **fell** before the Lamb,
	5:14	elders **fell** down and worshiped.
	6:13	of the sky **fell** to the earth
	6:16	**Fall** on us and hide us from

	7:11	**fell** on their faces before the
	7:16	the sun **will** not **strike** them,
	8:10	a great star **fell** from heaven,
	8:10	**fell** on a third of the rivers
	9: 1	star that **had fallen** from
	11:13	and a tenth of the city **fell;**
	11:16	**fell** on their faces and
	14: 8	**Fallen,** fallen is Babylon the
	14: 8	**fallen** is Babylon the great!
	16:19	cities of the nations **fell.** God
	17:10	five **have fallen,** one is living
	18: 2	**Fallen,** fallen is Babylon the
	18: 2	**fallen** is Babylon the great! It
	19: 4	**fell** down and worshiped God who
	19:10	Then I **fell** down at his feet to
	22: 8	I **fell** down to worship at the

4099   GO2 AG660 LN198
πισιδια, PISIDIA

Ac	13:14	came to Antioch in **Pisidia.** And
	14:24	through **Pisidia** and came to

4100   GO241 AG660 LN198 B1:593 K6:174 R4102
πιστευω, I TRUST, I BELIEVE

Mt	8:13	according to your **faith.**" And
	9:28	Do you **believe** that I am able
	18: 6	little ones who **believe** in me,
	21:22	ask for in prayer with **faith,**
	21:25	then did you not **believe** him?
	21:32	you did not **believe** him, but
	21:32	the prostitutes **believed** him;
	21:32	your minds and **believe** him.
	24:23	he is!'—do not **believe** it.
	24:26	inner rooms,' do not **believe** it
	27:42	and we will **believe** in him.
Mk	1:15	repent, and **believe** in the good
	5:36	Do not fear, only **believe.**
	9:23	for the one who **believes.**"
	9:24	I **believe;** help my unbelief!
	9:42	little ones who **believe** in me,
	11:23	but **believe** that what you say
	11:24	**believe** that you have received
	11:31	then did you not **believe** him?
	13:21	he is!'—do not **believe** it.
	15:32	so that we may see and **believe.**
	16:13	but they did not **believe** them.
	16:14	not **believed** those who saw him
	16:16	**believes** and is baptized will
	16:17	accompany those who **believe:** by

Lk	1:20	did not **believe** my words,
	1:45	And blessed is she who **believed**
	8:12	may not **believe** and be saved.
	8:13	they **believe** only for a while
	8:50	Only **believe,** and she will be
	16:11	**entrust** to you the true riches?
	20: 5	Why did you not **believe** him?
	22:67	tell you, you will not **believe;**
	24:25	how slow of heart to **believe**
Jn	1: 7	all might **believe** through him.
	1:12	who **believed** in his name, he
	1:50	Do you **believe** because I told
	2:11	his disciples **believed** in him.
	2:22	they **believed** the scripture and
	2:23	many **believed** in his name
	2:24	would not **entrust** himself to
	3:12	you do not **believe,** how can you
	3:12	how can you **believe** if I tell
	3:15	**believes** in him may have
	3:16	**believes** in him may not perish
	3:18	who **believe** in him are not
	3:18	not **believe** are condemned
	3:18	have not **believed** in the name
	3:36	Whoever **believes** in the Son has
	4:21	Woman, **believe** me, the hour is
	4:39	**believed** in him because of the
	4:41	**believed** because of his word.
	4:42	you said that we **believe,** for
	4:48	wonders you will not **believe.**"
	4:50	The man **believed** the word that
	4:53	So he himself **believed,** along
	5:24	hears my word and **believes** him
	5:38	you do not **believe** him whom he
	5:44	How can you **believe** when you
	5:46	If you **believed** Moses, you
	5:46	would **believe** me, for he wrote
	5:47	do not **believe** what he wrote,
	5:47	how will you **believe** what I say
	6:29	that you **believe** in him whom he
	6:30	we may see it and **believe** you?
	6:35	whoever **believes** in me will
	6:36	seen me and yet do not **believe.**
	6:40	and **believe** in him may have
	6:47	whoever **believes** has eternal
	6:64	are some who do not **believe.**"
	6:64	the ones that did not **believe,**
	6:69	come to **believe** and know that
	7: 5	not even his brothers **believed**
	7:31	many in the crowd **believed** in

	7:38	one who **believes** in me drink.
	7:39	Spirit, which **believers** in him
	7:48	the Pharisees **believed** in him?
	8:24	unless you **believe** that I am he
	8:30	things, many **believed** in him.
	8:31	Jews who had **believed** in him,
	8:45	truth, you do not **believe** me.
	8:46	why do you not **believe** me?
	9:18	The Jews did not **believe** that
	9:35	you **believe** in the Son of Man?
	9:36	so that I may **believe** in him.
	9:38	He said, "Lord, I **believe.**" And
	10:25	you, and you do not **believe.**
	10:26	you do not **believe,** because
	10:37	Father, then do not **believe** me.
	10:38	you do not **believe** me, believe
	10:38	believe me, **believe** the works,
	10:42	And many **believed** in him there.
	11:15	so that you may **believe.** But
	11:25	Those who **believe** in me, even
	11:26	lives and **believes** in me will
	11:26	never die. Do you **believe** this?
	11:27	I **believe** that you are the
	11:40	that if you **believed,** you would
	11:42	they may **believe** that you sent
	11:45	what Jesus did, **believed** in him
	11:48	everyone will **believe** in him,
	12:11	and were **believing** in Jesus.
	12:36	**believe** in the light, so that
	12:37	they did not **believe** in him.
	12:38	who has **believed** our message,
	12:39	And so they could not **believe,**
	12:42	authorities, **believed** in him.
	12:44	**believes** in me believes not in
	12:44	**believes** not in me but in him
	12:46	everyone who **believes** in me
	13:19	occur, you may **believe** that I
	14: 1	**Believe** in God, believe also in
	14: 1	in God, **believe** also in me.
	14:10	Do you not **believe** that I am in
	14:11	**Believe** me that I am in the
	14:11	then **believe** me because of the
	14:12	who **believes** in me will also do
	14:29	it does occur, you may **believe.**
	16: 9	they do not **believe** in me;
	16:27	**believed** that I came from God.
	16:30	**believe** that you came from God.
	16:31	them, "Do you now **believe?**
	17: 8	have **believed** that you sent me.

	17:20	who **will believe** in me through		4: 3	Abraham **believed** God, and it
	17:21	the world may **believe** that you		4: 5	without works **trusts** him who
	19:35	that you also may **believe.** His		4:11	ancestor of all who **believe**
	20: 8	in, and he saw and **believed;**		4:17	the God in whom he **believed,**
	20:25	his side, I will not **believe."**		4:18	against hope, he **believed** that
	20:29	**believed** because you have seen		4:24	who **believe** in him who raised
	20:29	and yet have come to **believe."**		6: 8	we **believe** that we will also
	20:31	**believe** that Jesus is the		9:33	**believes** in him will not be put
	20:31	through **believing** you may have		10: 4	for everyone who **believes.**
Ac	2:44	All who **believed** were together		10: 9	**believe** in your heart that God
	4: 4	heard the word **believed;** and		10:10	For one **believes** with the heart
	4:32	who **believed** were of one heart		10:11	No one who **believes** in him
	5:14	Yet more than ever **believers**		10:14	in whom they have not **believed?**
	8:12	But when they **believed** Philip,		10:14	how are they to **believe** in one
	8:13	Even Simon himself **believed.**		10:16	who has **believed** our message?
	9:26	they did not **believe** that he		13:11	when we became **believers;**
	9:42	and many **believed** in the Lord.		14: 2	Some **believe** in eating anything
	10:43	everyone who **believes** in him		15:13	all joy and peace in **believing,**
	11:17	**believed** in the Lord Jesus	1C	1:21	to save those who **believe.**
	11:21	became **believers** and turned to		3: 5	came to **believe,** as the Lord
	13:12	he **believed,** for he was		9:17	am **entrusted** with a commission.
	13:39	who **believes** is set free from		11:18	and to some extent I **believe** it
	13:41	you will never **believe,** even		13: 7	**believes** all things, hopes all
	13:48	eternal life became **believers.**		14:22	sign not for **believers** but for
	14: 1	and Greeks became **believers.**		14:22	unbelievers but for **believers.**
	14:23	whom they **had come to believe.**		15: 2	have come to **believe** in vain.
	15: 5	some **believers** who belonged to		15:11	so you have come to **believe.**
	15: 7	good news and become **believers.**	2C	4:13	I **believed,** and so I spoke
	15:11	**believe** that we will be saved		4:13	also **believe,** and so we speak,
	16:31	**Believe** on the Lord Jesus, and	Ga	2: 7	**entrusted** with the gospel for
	16:34	he had become a **believer** in God		2:16	come to **believe** in Christ
	17:12	Many of them therefore **believed**		3: 6	Just as Abraham **"believed** God,
	17:34	joined him and became **believers**		3:22	be given to those who **believe.**
	18: 8	became a **believer** in the Lord,	Ep	1:13	and **had believed** in him, were
	18: 8	became **believers** and were		1:19	power for us who **believe,**
	18:27	the **believers** encouraged him	Ph	1:29	not only of **believing** in Christ
	19: 2	when you became **believers?**	1Th	1: 7	an example to all the **believers**
	19: 4	to **believe** in the one who was		2: 4	**entrusted** with the message of
	19:18	became **believers** confessed and		2:10	was toward you **believers.**
	21:20	thousands of **believers** there		2:13	also at work in you **believers.**
	21:25	who have become **believers,** we		4:14	we **believe** that Jesus died and
	22:19	beat those who **believed** in you.	2Th	1:10	among all who have **believed,**
	24:14	**believing** everything laid down		1:10	testimony to you was **believed.**
	26:27	do you **believe** the prophets?		2:11	them to **believe** what is false,
	26:27	I know that you **believe.**		2:12	have not **believed** the truth but
	27:25	I **have faith** in God that it	1Ti	1:11	God, which he **entrusted** to me.
Ro	1:16	who **has faith,** to the Jew first		1:16	**believe** in him for eternal life
	3: 2	**entrusted** with the oracles of		3:16	**believed** in throughout the
	3:22	Christ for all who **believe.** For	2Ti	1:12	one in whom I **have put** my **trust**

Ti	1: 3	**entrusted** by the command of God
	3: 8	come to **believe** in God may be
He	4: 3	**believed** enter that rest, just
	11: 6	must **believe** that he exists
Ja	2:19	You **believe** that God is one;
	2:19	Even the demons **believe**—and
	2:23	Abraham **believed** God, and it
1P	1: 8	you **believe** in him and rejoice
	2: 6	whoever **believes** in him will
	2: 7	To you then who **believe,** he is
1J	3:23	should **believe** in the name of
	4: 1	do not **believe** every spirit,
	4:16	known and **believe** the love that
	5: 1	**believes** that Jesus is the
	5: 5	**believes** that Jesus is the Son
	5:10	Those who **believe** in the Son of
	5:10	do not **believe** in God have made
	5:10	not **believing** in the testimony
	5:13	**believe** in the name of the Son
Ju	1: 5	those who did not **believe.**

4101 GO2 AG662 LN198
πιστικος, GENUINE

Mk	14: 3	very **costly** ointment of nard,
Jn	12: 3	a pound of **costly** perfume made

4102 GO243 AG662 LN198 B1:593 K6:174
πιστις, TRUST, FAITH

Mt	8:10	Israel have I found such **faith.**
	9: 2	When Jesus saw their **faith,** he
	9:22	your **faith** has made you well.
	9:29	According to your **faith** let it
	15:28	Woman, great is your **faith!**
	17:20	**faith** the size of a mustard
	21:21	if you have **faith** and do not
	23:23	justice and mercy and **faith.** It
Mk	2: 5	When Jesus saw their **faith,** he
	4:40	Have you still no **faith?**
	5:34	Daughter, your **faith** has made
	10:52	Go; your **faith** has made you
	11:22	them, "Have **faith** in God.
Lk	5:20	When he saw their **faith,** he
	7: 9	Israel have I found such **faith.**
	7:50	Your **faith** has saved you; go
	8:25	Where is your **faith?**
	8:48	Daughter, your **faith** has made
	17: 5	the Lord, "Increase our **faith!**"
	17: 6	If you had **faith** the size of a
	17:19	your **faith** has made you well.

	18: 8	will he find **faith** on earth?
	18:42	sight; your **faith** has saved you
	22:32	your own **faith** may not fail;
Ac	3:16	And by **faith** in his name, his
	3:16	And by **faith** in his name, his
	6: 5	a man full of **faith** and the
	6: 7	became obedient to the **faith.**
	11:24	the Holy Spirit and of **faith.**
	13: 8	proconsul away from the **faith.**
	14: 9	seeing that he had **faith** to be
	14:22	continue in the **faith,** saying,
	14:27	he had opened a door of **faith**
	15: 9	cleansing their hearts by **faith**
	16: 5	strengthened in the **faith** and
	17:31	he has given **assurance** to all
	20:21	repentance toward God and **faith**
	24:24	speak concerning **faith** in
	26:18	are sanctified by **faith** in me.
Ro	1: 5	the obedience of **faith** among
	1: 8	your **faith** is proclaimed
	1:12	by each other's **faith,** both
	1:17	God is revealed through **faith**
	1:17	for **faith;** as it is written,
	1:17	is righteous will live by **faith**
	3: 3	nullify the **faithfulness** of God
	3:22	through **faith** in Jesus Christ
	3:25	effective through **faith.** He did
	3:26	the one who has **faith** in Jesus.
	3:27	No, but by the law of **faith.**
	3:28	justified by **faith** apart from
	3:30	on the ground of **faith** and the
	3:30	through that same **faith.**
	3:31	overthrow the law by this **faith**
	4: 5	such **faith** is reckoned as
	4: 9	We say, "**Faith** was reckoned to
	4:11	he had by **faith** while he was
	4:12	follow the example of the **faith**
	4:13	the righteousness of **faith.**
	4:14	**faith** is null and the promise
	4:16	depends on **faith,** in order that
	4:16	those who share the **faith** of
	4:19	He did not weaken in **faith** when
	4:20	he grew strong in his **faith** as
	5: 1	since we are justified by **faith**
	5: 2	we have obtained **access** to this
	9:30	righteousness through **faith;**
	9:32	for it on the basis of **faith,**
	10: 6	that comes from **faith** says, "Do
	10: 8	(that is, the word of **faith**

	10:17	So **faith** comes from what is		4:13	come to the unity of the **faith**
	11:20	you stand only through **faith.**		6:16	take the shield of **faith,** with
	12: 3	the measure of **faith** that God		6:23	and love with **faith,** from God
	12: 6	in proportion to **faith;**	Ph	1:25	your progress and joy in **faith,**
	14: 1	those who are weak in **faith,**		1:27	for the **faith** of the gospel,
	14:22	The **faith** that you have, have		2:17	the offering of your **faith,** I
	14:23	they do not act from **faith;** for		3: 9	comes through **faith** in Christ,
	14:23	does not proceed from **faith** is		3: 9	from God based on **faith.**
	16:26	about the obedience of **faith**—	Co	1: 4	for we have heard of your **faith**
1C	2: 5	so that your **faith** might rest		1:23	steadfast in the **faith,** without
	12: 9	to another **faith** by the same		2: 5	of your **faith** in Christ.
	13: 2	if I have all **faith,** so as to		2: 7	established in the **faith,** just
	13:13	And now **faith,** hope, and love		2:12	raised with him through **faith**
	15:14	your **faith** has been in vain.	1Th	1: 3	your work of **faith** and labor of
	15:17	your **faith** is futile and you		1: 8	in every place your **faith** in
	16:13	stand firm in your **faith,** be		3: 2	you for the sake of your **faith,**
2C	1:24	that we lord it over your **faith**		3: 5	to find out about your **faith;** I
	1:24	you stand firm in the **faith.**		3: 6	good news of your **faith** and
	4:13	the same spirit of **faith** that		3: 7	about you through your **faith.**
	5: 7	for we walk by **faith,** not by		3:10	is lacking in your **faith.**
	8: 7	in **faith,** in speech, in knowledge		5: 8	put on the breastplate of **faith**
	10:15	as your **faith** increases, our	2Th	1: 3	because your **faith** is growing
	13: 5	you are living in the **faith.**		1: 4	steadfastness and **faith** during
Ga	1:23	now proclaiming the **faith** he		1:11	good resolve and work of **faith,**
	2:16	but through **faith** in Jesus		2:13	and through **belief** in the truth
	2:16	we might be justified by **faith**		3: 2	people; for not all have **faith.**
	2:20	I live by **faith** in the Son of	1Ti	1: 2	my loyal child in the **faith:**
	3: 2	by **believing** what you heard?		1: 4	training that is known by **faith**
	3: 5	your **believing** what you heard?		1: 5	conscience, and sincere **faith.**
	3: 7	so, you see, those who **believe**		1:14	for me with the **faith** and love
	3: 8	justify the Gentiles by **faith,**		1:19	**faith** and a good conscience. By
	3: 9	those who **believe** are blessed		1:19	suffered shipwreck in the **faith**
	3:11	righteous will live by **faith.**		2: 7	of the Gentiles in **faith** and
	3:12	law does not rest on **faith;** on		2:15	provided they continue in **faith**
	3:14	of the Spirit through **faith.**		3: 9	the mystery of the **faith** with a
	3:22	promised through **faith** in Jesus		3:13	great boldness in the **faith**
	3:23	Now before **faith** came, we were		4: 1	renounce the **faith** by paying
	3:23	under the law until **faith** would		4: 6	words of the **faith** and of the
	3:24	we might be justified by **faith.**		4:12	in love, in **faith,** in purity.
	3:25	But now that **faith** has come, we		5: 8	denied the **faith** and is worse
	3:26	children of God through **faith.**		5:12	violated their first **pledge.**
	5: 5	by **faith,** we eagerly wait for		6:10	wandered away from the **faith**
	5: 6	generosity, **faithfulness,**		6:11	**faith,** love, endurance,
	6:10	those of the family of **faith.**		6:12	the good fight of the **faith;**
Ep	1:15	I have heard of your **faith** in		6:21	regards the **faith.** Grace be
	2: 8	have been saved through **faith,**	2Ti	1: 5	reminded of your sincere **faith**
	3:12	confidence through **faith** in him		1:13	in the **faith** and love that are
	3:17	in your hearts through **faith,**		2:18	They are upsetting the **faith** of
	4: 5	one Lord, one **faith,** one		2:22	pursue righteousness, **faith,**

	3: 8	counterfeit **faith,** also oppose		2:14	works? Can **faith** save you?
	3:10	my **faith,** my patience, my love,		2:17	So **faith** by itself, if it has
	3:15	salvation through **faith** in		2:18	Show me your **faith** apart from
	4: 7	race, I have kept the **faith.**		2:18	my works will show you my **faith**
Ti	1: 1	for the sake of the **faith** of		2:20	that **faith** apart from works is
	1: 4	my loyal child in the **faith** we		2:22	You see that **faith** was active
	1:13	may become sound in the **faith,**		2:22	works, and **faith** was brought to
	2: 2	and sound in **faith,** in love,		2:24	by works and not by **faith** alone
	2:10	complete and perfect **fidelity,**		2:26	so **faith** without works is also
	3:15	those who love us in the **faith.**		5:15	The prayer of **faith** will save
Pm	1: 5	all the saints and your **faith**	1P	1: 5	the power of God through **faith**
	1: 6	sharing of your **faith** may		1: 7	the genuineness of your **faith**
He	4: 2	they were not united by **faith**		1: 9	the outcome of your **faith,** the
	6: 1	dead works and **faith** toward God		1:21	your **faith** and hope are set on
	6:12	those who through **faith** and		5: 9	steadfast in your **faith,** for
	10:22	in full assurance of **faith,**	2P	1: 1	received a **faith** as precious as
	10:38	one will live by **faith.** My soul		1: 5	effort to support your **faith**
	10:39	among those who have **faith** and	1J	5: 4	conquers the world, our **faith.**
	11: 1	Now **faith** is the assurance of	Ju	1: 3	the **faith** that was once for all
	11: 3	By **faith** we understand that the		1:20	up on your most holy **faith;**
	11: 4	By **faith** Abel offered to God a	Re	2:13	you did not deny your **faith** in
	11: 5	By **faith** Enoch was taken so		2:19	your love, **faith,** service, and
	11: 6	And without **faith** it is		13:10	endurance and **faith** of the
	11: 7	By **faith** Noah, warned by God		14:12	hold fast to the **faith** of Jesus
	11: 7	is in accordance with **faith.**			
	11: 8	By **faith** Abraham obeyed when he	**4103**		ᴳᴼ67 ᴬᴳ664 ᴸᴺ198 ᴮ1:593 ᴷ6:174 ᴿ4102
	11: 9	By **faith** he stayed for a time	πιστος, TRUSTFUL, FAITHFUL		
	11:11	By **faith** he received power of	Mt	24:45	Who then is the **faithful** and
	11:13	All of these died in **faith**		25:21	done, good and **trustworthy**
	11:17	By **faith** Abraham, when put to		25:21	you have been **trustworthy** in a
	11:20	By **faith** Isaac invoked		25:23	done, good and **trustworthy**
	11:21	By **faith** Jacob, when dying,		25:23	you have been **trustworthy** in a
	11:22	By **faith** Joseph, at the end of	Lk	12:42	Who then is the **faithful** and
	11:23	By **faith** Moses was hidden by		16:10	Whoever is **faithful** in a very
	11:24	By **faith** Moses, when he was		16:10	is **faithful** also in much; and
	11:27	By **faith** he left Egypt,		16:11	you have not been **faithful** with
	11:28	By **faith** he kept the Passover		16:12	you have not been **faithful** with
	11:29	By **faith** the people passed		19:17	you have been **trustworthy** in a
	11:30	By **faith** the walls of Jericho	Jn	20:27	Do not doubt but **believe.**
	11:31	By **faith** Rahab the prostitute	Ac	10:45	The circumcised **believers** who
	11:33	who through **faith** conquered		13:34	give you the holy **promises** made
	11:39	commended for their **faith,** did		16: 1	Jewish woman who was a **believer**
	12: 2	perfecter of our **faith,** who for		16:15	judged me to be **faithful** to the
	13: 7	life, and imitate their **faith.**	1C	1: 9	God is **faithful;** by him you
Ja	1: 3	testing of your **faith** produces		4: 2	that they be found **trustworthy.**
	1: 6	But ask in **faith,** never		4:17	who is my beloved and **faithful**
	2: 1	really **believe** in our glorious		7:25	the Lord's mercy is **trustworthy**
	2: 5	rich in **faith** and to be heirs		10:13	God is **faithful,** and he will
	2:14	if you say you have **faith** but	2C	1:18	As surely as God is **faithful,**

	6:15	Or what does a **believer** share
Ga	3: 9	with Abraham who **believed.**
Ep	1: 1	are **faithful** in Christ Jesus:
	6:21	a **faithful** minister in the Lord
Co	1: 2	To the saints and **faithful**
	1: 7	He is a **faithful** minister of
	4: 7	a **faithful** minister, and a
	4: 9	**faithful** and beloved brother,
1Th	5:24	one who calls you is **faithful,**
2Th	3: 3	But the Lord is **faithful;** he
1Ti	1:12	because he judged me **faithful**
	1:15	The saying is **sure** and worthy
	3: 1	The saying is **sure:** whoever
	3:11	**faithful** in all things.
	4: 3	those who **believe** and know the
	4: 9	The saying is **sure** and worthy
	4:10	especially of those who **believe**
	4:12	set the **believers** an example in
	5:16	If any **believing** woman has
	6: 2	who have **believing** masters must
	6: 2	**believers** and beloved. Teach
2Ti	2: 2	entrust to **faithful** people who
	2:11	The saying is **sure:** If we have
	2:13	he remains **faithful**—for he
Ti	1: 6	whose children are **believers,**
	1: 9	is **trustworthy** in accordance
	3: 8	The saying is **sure.** I desire
He	2:17	a merciful and **faithful** high
	3: 2	was **faithful** to the one who
	3: 5	Now Moses was **faithful** in all
	10:23	he who has promised is **faithful**
	11:11	he considered him **faithful** who
1P	1:21	you have come to **trust** in God,
	4:19	to a **faithful** Creator, while
	5:12	I consider a **faithful** brother,
1J	1: 9	he who is **faithful** and just
3J	1: 5	Beloved, you do **faithfully**
Re	1: 5	**faithful** witness, the firstborn
	2:10	Be **faithful** until death, and I
	2:13	my **faithful** one, who was killed
	3:14	the **faithful** and true witness,
	17:14	called and chosen and **faithful.**
	19:11	Its rider is called **Faithful**
	21: 5	these words are **trustworthy** and
	22: 6	These words are **trustworthy**

4104   GO1 AG665 LN198 B1:594 K6:174
πιστοω, I TRUST, I BELIEVE

2Ti	3:14	firmly **believed,** knowing from

4105   GO39 AG665 LN198 B2:457 K6:228 R4106
πλαναω, I DECEIVE

Mt	18:12	one of them **has gone astray,**
	18:12	of the one that **went astray?**
	18:13	that never **went astray.**
	22:29	You **are wrong,** because you
	24: 4	that no one **leads** you **astray.**
	24: 5	and they **will lead** many **astray.**
	24:11	will arise and **lead many astray**
	24:24	**to lead astray,** if possible,
Mk	12:24	the reason you **are wrong,** that
	12:27	the living; **you are** quite **wrong**
	13: 5	that no one **leads** you **astray.**
	13: 6	and they **will lead** many **astray.**
Lk	21: 8	that you **are** not **led astray;**
Jn	7:12	No, he is **deceiving** the crowd.
	7:47	you **have** not **been deceived** too,
1C	6: 9	Do not **be deceived!** Fornicators
	15:33	Do not **be deceived:** "Bad
Ga	6: 7	Do not **be deceived;** God is not
2Ti	3:13	**deceiving** others and being
	3:13	others and **being deceived.**
Ti	3: 3	disobedient, **led astray,** slaves
He	3:10	They always **go astray** in their
	5: 2	the ignorant and **wayward,** since
	11:38	They **wandered** in deserts and
Ja	1:16	Do not be **deceived,** my beloved.
	5:19	if anyone among you **wanders**
1P	2:25	For you **were going astray** like
2P	2:15	have gone **astray,** following the
1J	1: 8	we **deceive** ourselves, and the
	2:26	those who would **deceive** you.
	3: 7	no one **deceive** you. Everyone
Re	2:20	**beguiling** my servants to
	12: 9	the **deceiver** of the whole world
	13:14	it **deceives** the inhabitants of
	18:23	all nations **were deceived** by
	19:20	**deceived** those who had received
	20: 3	so that he would **deceive** the
	20: 8	and will come out to **deceive**
	20:10	And the devil who **had deceived**

4106   GO10 AG665 LN198 B2:457 K6:228 R4108
πλανη, DECEIT

Mt	27:64	last **deception** would be worse
Ro	1:27	the due penalty for their **error**
Ep	4:14	in **deceitful** scheming.
1Th	2: 3	does not spring from **deceit** or
2Th	2:11	a powerful **delusion,** leading

Ja	5:20	from **wandering** will save the
2P	2:18	from those who live in **error.**
	3:17	with the **error** of the lawless
1J	4: 6	truth and the spirit of **error.**
Ju	1:11	Balaam's **error** for the sake of

4107 ᴳᴼ1 ᴬᴳ666 ᴸᴺ198 ᴮ2:457 ᴷ6:228 ᴿ4108
πλανητης, DECEPTIVE

Ju	1:13	**wandering** stars, for whom the

4108 ᴳᴼ5 ᴬᴳ666 ᴸᴺ198 ᴮ2:457 ᴷ6:228
πλανος, DECEIVER

Mt	27:63	what that **impostor** said while
2C	6: 8	We are treated as **impostors,**
1Ti	4: 1	paying attention to **deceitful**
2J	1: 7	Many **deceivers** have gone out
	1: 7	any such person is the **deceiver**

4109 ᴳᴼ3 ᴬᴳ666 ᴸᴺ198
πλαξ, TABLET

2C	3: 3	not on **tablets** of stone but on
	3: 3	but on **tablets** of human hearts.
He	9: 4	and the **tablets** of the covenant

4110 ᴳᴼ1 ᴬᴳ666 ᴸᴺ198 ᴷ6:254 ᴿ4111
πλασμα, MOLDED

Ro	9:20	Will what is **molded** say to the

4111 ᴳᴼ2 ᴬᴳ666 ᴸᴺ198 ᴷ6:254
πλασσω, I MOLD

Ro	9:20	say to the one who **molds** it,
1Ti	2:13	For Adam **was formed** first, then

4112 ᴳᴼ1 ᴬᴳ666 ᴸᴺ198 ᴷ6:262 ᴿ4111
πλαστος, MOLDED

2P	2: 3	you with **deceptive** words.

4113 ᴳᴼ10 ᴬᴳ666 ᴸᴺ198
πλατεια, WIDE PLACE (STREET)

Mt	6: 5	at the **street** corners, so that
	12:19	hear his voice in the **streets.**
Lk	10:10	go out into its **streets** and say
	13:26	and you taught in our **streets.**
	14:21	out at once into the **streets**
Ac	5:15	the sick into the **streets,** and
Re	11: 8	lie in the **street** of the great
	21:21	the **street** of the city is pure
	22: 2	the middle of the **street** of the

4114 ᴳᴼ4 ᴬᴳ666 ᴸᴺ198 ᴮ1:253 ᴿ4116
πλατος, WIDTH

Ep	3:18	what is the **breadth** and length
Re	20: 9	marched up over the **breadth** of
	21:16	length the same as its **width;**
	21:16	length the same as its **width;**

4115 ᴳᴼ3 ᴬᴳ667 ᴸᴺ198 ᴮ1:253 ᴿ4116
πλατυνω, I WIDEN

Mt	23: 5	**make** their phylacteries **broad**
2C	6:11	our heart **is wide open** to you.
	6:13	**open wide** your hearts also.

4116 ᴳᴼ1 ᴬᴳ667 ᴸᴺ198 ᴮ1:253
πλατυς, WIDE

Mt	7:13	for the gate is **wide** and the

4117 ᴳᴼ1 ᴬᴳ667 ᴸᴺ198 ᴿ4120
πλεγμα, BRAID

1Ti	2: 9	not with their hair **braided,** or

4120 ᴳᴼ3 ᴬᴳ667 ᴸᴺ199
πλεκω, I BRAID

Mt	27:29	and after **twisting** some thorns
Mk	15:17	and after **twisting** some thorns
Jn	19: 2	And the soldiers **wove** a crown

4121 ᴳᴼ9 ᴬᴳ667 ᴸᴺ199 ᴮ2:130 ᴷ6:263
πλεοναζω, I INCREASE

Ro	5:20	the trespass **multiplied;** but
	5:20	but where sin **increased,** grace
	6: 1	in order that grace **may abound?**
2C	4:15	may **increase** thanksgiving, to
	8:15	The one who **had much** did not
Ph	4:17	the profit that **accumulates** to
1Th	3:12	**make** you **increase** and abound in
2Th	1: 3	for one another **is increasing.**
2P	1: 8	**are increasing** among you, they

4122 ᴳᴼ5 ᴬᴳ667 ᴸᴺ199 ᴮ1:137 ᴷ6:266 ᴿ4123
πλεονεκτεω, I TAKE MORE

2C	2:11	**may** not **be outwitted** by Satan;
	7: 2	we **have taken advantage of** no
	12:17	**Did I take advantage** of you
	12:18	Titus **did** not **take advantage** of
1Th	4: 6	that no one wrong or **exploit** a

4123 ᴳᴼ4 ᴬᴳ667 ᴸᴺ199 ᴮ1:137 ᴷ6:266
πλεονεκτης, GREEDY

1C	5:10	or the **greedy** and robbers, or

	5:11	sexually immoral or **greedy,** or
	6:10	thieves, the **greedy,** drunkards,
Ep	5: 5	one who is **greedy** (that is, an

4124   GO10   AG667   LN199   B1:137   K6:266   R4123
πλεονεξια, GREEDINESS

Mk	7:22	adultery, **avarice,** wickedness,
Lk	12:15	against all kinds of **greed;** for
Ro	1:29	evil, **covetousness,** malice.
2C	9: 5	gift and not as an **extortion.**
Ep	4:19	**greedy** to practice every kind
	5: 3	or **greed,** must not even be
Co	3: 5	evil desire, and **greed** (which
1Th	2: 5	or with a pretext for **greed;**
2P	2: 3	And in their **greed** they will
	2:14	have hearts trained in **greed.**

4125   GO5   AG668   LN199
πλευρα, SIDE

Jn	19:34	pierced his **side** with a spear,
	20:20	them his hands and his **side.**
	20:25	my hand in his **side,** I will not
	20:27	put it in my **side.** Do not doubt
Ac	12: 7	He tapped Peter on the **side** and

4126   GO6   AG668   LN199
πλεω, I SAIL

Lk	8:23	and while they **were sailing** he
Ac	21: 3	we **sailed** to Syria and landed
	27: 2	about to **set sail** to the ports
	27: 6	ship **bound** for Italy and put us
	27:24	to all those who **are sailing**
Re	18:17	**seafarers,** sailors and all

4127   GO22   AG668   LN199   B1:161   R4141
πληγη, BLOW

Lk	10:30	**beat** him, and went away,
	12:48	**beating** will receive a light
Ac	16:23	given them a severe **flogging,**
	16:33	them and washed their **wounds;**
2C	6: 5	**beatings,** imprisonments, riots,
	11:23	countless **floggings,** and often
Re	9:18	By these three **plagues** a third
	9:20	killed by these **plagues,** did
	11: 6	with every kind of **plague,** as
	13: 3	mortal **wound** had been healed.
	13:12	whose mortal **wound** had been
	13:14	**wounded** by the sword and yet
	15: 1	seven angels with seven **plagues**
	15: 6	angels with the seven **plagues,**

	15: 8	until the seven **plagues** of the
	16: 9	authority over these **plagues,**
	16:21	cursed God for the **plague** of
	16:21	so fearful was that **plague.**
	18: 4	do not share in her **plagues;**
	18: 8	therefore her **plagues** will come
	21: 9	full of the seven last **plagues**
	22:18	add to that person the **plagues**

4128   GO31   AG668   LN199   B1:731   K6:274
πληθος, QUANTITY

Mk	3: 7	a great **multitude** from Galilee
	3: 8	came to him in great **numbers**
Lk	1:10	whole **assembly** of the people
	2:13	**multitude** of the heavenly host,
	5: 6	they caught so **many** fish that
	6:17	a great **multitude** of people
	8:37	Then **all** the people of the
	19:37	**multitude** of the disciples
	23: 1	Then the **assembly** rose as a
	23:27	A great **number** of the people
Jn	5: 3	In these lay **many** invalids—
	21: 6	because there were so **many** fish
Ac	2: 6	And at this sound the **crowd**
	4:32	Now the **whole group** of those
	5:14	**great numbers** of both men and
	5:16	A **great number** of people would
	6: 2	together the whole **community** of
	6: 5	pleased the whole **community,**
	14: 1	a great **number** of both Jews and
	14: 4	But the **residents** of the city
	15:12	The whole **assembly** kept silence
	15:30	they gathered the **congregation**
	17: 4	did a great **many** of the devout
	19: 9	before the **congregation,** he
	21:36	The **crowd** that followed kept
	23: 7	and the **assembly** was divided.
	25:24	the whole Jewish **community**
	28: 3	Paul had gathered a **bundle** of
He	11:12	as **many** as the stars of heaven
Ja	5:20	will cover a **multitude** of sins.
1P	4: 8	love covers a **multitude** of sins

4129   GO12   AG669   LN199   B1:732   K6:279
πληθυνω, I MULTIPLY

Mt	24:12	And because of the **increase** of
Ac	6: 1	the disciples were **increasing**
	6: 7	the disciples **increased** greatly
	7:17	Egypt increased and **multiplied**

	9:31	Spirit, it **increased** in numbers
	12:24	advance and **gain** adherents.
2C	9:10	**multiply** your seed for sowing
He	6:14	bless you and **multiply** you.
	6:14	bless you and **multiply** you.
1P	1: 2	and peace be yours in **abundance**
2P	1: 2	and peace be yours in **abundance**
Ju	1: 2	and love be yours in **abundance.**

4131　ᴳᴼ2　ᴬᴳ669　ᴸᴺ199　ᴿ4141
πλήκτης, HITTER
| 1Ti | 3: 3 | not a drunkard, not **violent** but |
| Ti | 1: 7 | or **violent** or greedy for gain; |

4132　ᴳᴼ1　ᴬᴳ669　ᴸᴺ199
πλημμύρα, FLOOD
| Lk | 6:48 | when a **flood** arose, the river |

4133　ᴳᴼ31　ᴬᴳ669　ᴸᴺ199
πλήν, EXCEPT
Mt	11:22	**But** I tell you, on the day of
	11:24	**But** I tell you that on the day
	18: 7	**but** woe to the one by whom the
	26:39	**yet** not what I want but what
	26:64	**But** I tell you, From now on you
Mk	12:32	he is one, and **besides** him
Lk	6:24	**But** woe to you who are rich,
	6:35	**But** love your enemies, do good,
	10:11	**Yet** know this: the kingdom of
	10:14	**But** at the judgment it will be
	10:20	**Nevertheless,** do not rejoice at
	11:41	**So** give for alms those things
	12:31	**Instead,** strive for his kingdom
	13:33	**Yet** today, tomorrow, and the
	17: 1	**but** woe to anyone by whom they
	18: 8	And **yet,** when the Son of Man
	19:27	**But** as for these enemies of
	22:21	**But** see, the one who betrays me
	22:22	**but** woe to that one by whom he
	22:42	**yet,** not my will but yours be
	23:28	**but** weep for yourselves and for
Ac	8: 1	and all **except** the apostles
	15:28	no further burden **than** these
	20:23	**except** that the Holy Spirit
	27:22	you, **but** only of the ship.
1C	11:11	**Nevertheless,** in the Lord woman
Ep	5:33	Each of you, **however,** should
Ph	1:18	What does it matter? **Just this,**
	3:16	**Only** let us hold fast to what

| | 4:14 | **In any case,** it was kind of |
| Re | 2:25 | **only** hold fast to what you have |

4134　ᴳᴼ16　ᴬᴳ669　ᴸᴺ199　ᴮ1:733　ᴷ6:283　ᴿ4130
πλήρης, FULL
Mt	14:20	pieces, twelve baskets **full.**
	15:37	left over, seven baskets **full.**
Mk	4:28	then the **full** grain in the head
	8:19	how many baskets **full** of broken
Lk	4: 1	Jesus, **full** of the Holy Spirit,
	5:12	man **covered with** leprosy. When
Jn	1:14	son, **full** of grace and truth.
Ac	6: 3	**full** of the Spirit and of
	6: 5	a man **full** of faith and the
	6: 8	Stephen, **full** of grace and
	7:55	But **filled** with the Holy Spirit
	9:36	She was **devoted** to good works
	11:24	for he was a good man, **full** of
	13:10	**full** of all deceit and villainy
	19:28	they were **enraged** and shouted,
2J	1: 8	but may receive a **full** reward.

4135　ᴳᴼ6　ᴬᴳ670　ᴸᴺ199　ᴮ1:733　ᴷ6:309
πληροφορέω, I AM FULLY PERSUADED
Lk	1: 1	that **have been fulfilled** among
Ro	4:21	**being fully convinced** that God
	14: 5	Let all **be fully convinced** in
Co	4:12	stand mature and **fully assured**
2Ti	4: 5	**carry out** your ministry **fully.**
	4:17	**might be fully proclaimed**

4136　ᴳᴼ4　ᴬᴳ670　ᴸᴺ199　ᴮ1:733　ᴷ6:310　ᴿ4135
πληροφορία, FULL PERSUASION
Co	2: 2	riches of **assured** understanding
1Th	1: 5	Spirit and with **full conviction**
He	6:11	realize the **full assurance** of
	10:22	in **full assurance** of faith,

4137　ᴳᴼ86　ᴬᴳ670　ᴸᴺ199　ᴮ1:733　ᴷ6:286　ᴿ4134
πληρόω, I FILL
Mt	1:22	All this took place to **fulfill**
	2:15	This was to **fulfill** what had
	2:17	Then **was fulfilled** what had
	2:23	the prophets might be **fulfilled**
	3:15	**fulfill** all righteousness.
	4:14	Isaiah might be **fulfilled:**
	5:17	not to abolish but **to fulfill.**
	8:17	This was **to fulfill** what had
	12:17	This was **to fulfill** what had

	13:35	This was **to fulfill** what had
	13:48	when it **was full,** they drew it
	21: 4	This took place to **fulfill** what
	23:32	**Fill** up, then, the measure of
	26:54	scriptures **be fulfilled,** which
	26:56	the prophets **may be fulfilled.**
	27: 9	Then **was fulfilled** what had
Mk	1:15	The time **is fulfilled,** and the
	14:49	let the scriptures **be fulfilled**
Lk	1:20	which **will be fulfilled** in
	2:40	**filled** with wisdom; and the
	3: 5	Every valley **shall be filled,**
	4:21	**has been fulfilled** in your
	7: 1	After Jesus **had finished** all
	9:31	he was about **to accomplish** at
	21:24	of the Gentiles **are fulfilled.**
	22:16	until it **is fulfilled** in the
	24:44	the psalms must **be fulfilled.**
Jn	3:29	my joy **has been fulfilled.**
	7: 8	time has not yet **fully come.**
	12: 3	**was filled** with the fragrance
	12:38	This was to **fulfill** the word
	13:18	it is to **fulfill** the scripture,
	15:11	that your joy **may be complete.**
	15:25	It was to **fulfill** the word that
	16: 6	sorrow **has filled** your hearts.
	16:24	that your joy **may be complete.**
	17:12	scripture **might be fulfilled.**
	17:13	have my joy **made complete** in
	18: 9	This was to **fulfill** the word
	18:32	(This was to **fulfill** what Jesus
	19:24	This was to **fulfill** what the
	19:36	scripture **might be fulfilled,**
Ac	1:16	scripture had **to be fulfilled,**
	2: 2	it **filled** the entire house
	2:28	**will make** me **full** of gladness
	3:18	In this way God **fulfilled** what
	5: 3	has Satan **filled** your heart to
	5:28	here you **have filled** Jerusalem
	7:23	When he **was** forty years old,
	7:30	when forty years **had passed,** an
	9:23	After some time **had passed,** the
	12:25	Then after **completing** their
	13:25	And as John **was finishing** his
	13:27	they **fulfilled** those words by
	13:52	And the disciples **were filled**
	14:26	work that they **had completed.**
	19:21	**had been accomplished,** Paul
	24:27	After two years **had passed,**

Ro	1:29	They **were filled** with every
	8: 4	**might be fulfilled** in us, who
	13: 8	loves another **has fulfilled** the
	15:13	so that you **may abound** in hope
	15:14	**filled** with all knowledge, and
	15:19	I **have fully proclaimed** the
2C	7: 4	I **am filled** with consolation; I
	10: 6	when your obedience **is complete**
Ga	5:14	For the whole law **is summed up**
Ep	1:23	the fullness of him who **fills**
	3:19	so that you **may be filled** with
	4:10	so that he **might fill** all
	5:18	but **be filled** with the Spirit,
Ph	1:11	**having produced** the harvest of
	2: 2	**make** my joy **complete:** be of the
	4:18	I **am fully satisfied,** now that
	4:19	And my God **will fully satisfy**
Co	1: 9	asking that you **may be filled**
	1:25	the word of God **fully known,**
	2:10	you have come to **fullness** in
	4:17	See that you **complete** the task
2Th	1:11	**will fulfill** by his power every
2Ti	1: 4	so that I **may be filled** with
Ja	2:23	the scripture **was fulfilled**
1J	1: 4	so that our joy **may be complete**
2J	1:12	so that our joy **may be complete**
Re	3: 2	found your works **perfect** in the
	6:11	the number **would be complete**

4138   GO17 AG672 LN200 B1:733 K6:298 R4137
πληρωμα, FULLNESS

Mt	9:16	the **patch** pulls away from the
Mk	2:21	the **patch** pulls away from it,
	6:43	twelve baskets **full** of broken
	8:20	how many baskets **full** of broken
Jn	1:16	From his **fullness** we have all
Ro	11:12	how much more will their **full**
	11:25	until the **full** number of the
	13:10	love is the **fulfilling** of the
	15:29	I will come in the **fullness** of
1C	10:26	for "the earth and its **fullness**
Ga	4: 4	But when the **fullness** of time
Ep	1:10	as a plan for the **fullness** of
	1:23	the **fullness** of him who fills
	3:19	filled with all the **fullness** of
	4:13	measure of the **full** stature of
Co	1:19	For in him all the **fullness** of
	2: 9	For in him the whole **fullness**

4139   GO17 AG672 LN200 B1:258 K6:311
πλησιον, NEIGHBOR
Mt	5:43	You shall love your **neighbor**
	19:19	love your **neighbor** as yourself.
	22:39	You shall love your **neighbor**
Mk	12:31	You shall love your **neighbor**
	12:33	and 'to love one's **neighbor** as
Lk	10:27	and your **neighbor** as yourself.
	10:29	Jesus, "And who is my **neighbor?**
	10:36	was a **neighbor** to the man who
Jn	4: 5	**near** the plot of ground that
Ac	7:27	wronging his **neighbor** pushed
Ro	13: 9	Love your **neighbor** as yourself
	13:10	does no wrong to a **neighbor;**
	15: 2	please our **neighbor** for the
Ga	5:14	You shall love your **neighbor**
Ep	4:25	the truth to our **neighbors,** for
Ja	2: 8	You shall love your **neighbor**
	4:12	are you to judge your **neighbor?**

4140   GO1 AG673 LN200 K6:131
πλησμονη, FILLING UP
Co	2:23	in checking self-**indulgence.**

4141   GO1 AG673 LN200
πλησσω, I STRIKE
Re	8:12	a third of the sun **was struck,**

4142   GO5 AG673 LN200 R4143
πλοιαριον, SMALL BOAT
Mk	3: 9	to have a **boat** ready for him
Jn	6:22	there had been only one **boat**
	6:23	Then some **boats** from Tiberias
	6:24	themselves got into the **boats**
	21: 8	came in the **boat,** dragging the

4143   GO67 AG673 LN200 R4126
πλοιον, BOAT
Mt	4:21	in the **boat** with their father
	4:22	Immediately they left the **boat**
	8:23	And when he got into the **boat,**
	8:24	great that the **boat** was being
	9: 1	And after getting into a **boat**
	13: 2	he got into a **boat** and sat
	14:13	withdrew from there in a **boat**
	14:22	get into the **boat** and go on
	14:24	but by this time the **boat,**
	14:29	So Peter got out of the **boat,**
	14:32	When they got into the **boat,**
	14:33	those in the **boat** worshiped

	15:39	got into the **boat** and went to
Mk	1:19	who were in their **boat** mending
	1:20	in the **boat** with the hired men,
	4: 1	he got into a **boat** on the sea
	4:36	took him with them in the **boat,**
	4:36	Other **boats** were with him.
	4:37	waves beat into the **boat,** so
	4:37	that the **boat** was already being
	5: 2	he had stepped out of the **boat,**
	5:18	As he was getting into the **boat**
	5:21	had crossed again in the **boat**
	6:32	And they went away in the **boat**
	6:45	get into the **boat** and go on
	6:47	When evening came, the **boat** was
	6:51	Then he got into the **boat** with
	6:54	When they got out of the **boat,**
	8:10	got into the **boat** with his
	8:14	one loaf with them in the **boat.**
Lk	5: 2	he saw two **boats** there at the
	5: 3	He got into one of the **boats,**
	5: 3	taught the crowds from the **boat**
	5: 7	partners in the other **boat** to
	5: 7	filled both **boats,** so that they
	5:11	brought their **boats** to shore,
	8:22	One day he got into a **boat** with
	8:37	So he got into the **boat** and
Jn	6:17	got into a **boat,** and started
	6:19	coming near the **boat,** and they
	6:21	take him into the **boat,** and
	6:21	immediately the **boat** reached
	6:22	not got into the **boat** with his
	21: 3	got into the **boat,** but that
	21: 6	right side of the **boat,** and you
Ac	20:13	We went ahead to the **ship** and
	20:38	they brought him to the **ship.**
	21: 2	When we found a **ship** bound for
	21: 3	because the **ship** was to unload
	21: 6	Then we went on board the **ship,**
	27: 2	Embarking on a **ship** of
	27: 6	an Alexandrian **ship** bound for
	27:10	the **ship,** but also of our lives
	27:15	Since the **ship** was caught and
	27:17	measures to undergird the **ship;**
	27:19	they threw the **ship's** tackle
	27:22	among you, but only of the **ship.**
	27:30	tried to escape from the **ship**
	27:31	these men stay in the **ship,** you
	27:37	seventy-six persons in the **ship**
	27:38	they lightened the **ship** by

	27:39	planned to run the **ship** ashore,
	27:44	others on pieces of the **ship.**
	28:11	we set sail on a **ship** that had
Ja	3: 4	Or look at **ships:** though they
Re	8: 9	a third of the **ships** were
	18:19	where all who had **ships** at sea

4144 GO3 AG673 LN200 R4126
πλους, SAILING

Ac	21: 7	When we had finished the **voyage**
	27: 9	**sailing** was now dangerous,
	27:10	I can see that the **voyage** will

4145 GO28 AG673 LN200 B2:840 K6:318 R4149
πλουσιος, RICH

Mt	19:23	will be hard for a **rich** person
	19:24	than for someone who is **rich** to
	27:57	there came a **rich** man from
Mk	10:25	than for someone who is **rich** to
	12:41	Many **rich** people put in large
Lk	6:24	But woe to you who are **rich,**
	12:16	The land of a **rich** man
	14:12	relatives or **rich** neighbors, in
	16: 1	There was a **rich** man who had a
	16:19	There was a **rich** man who was
	16:21	fell from the **rich** man's table;
	16:22	The **rich** man also died and was
	18:23	sad; for he was very **rich.**
	18:25	someone who is **rich** to enter
	19: 2	tax collector and was **rich.**
	21: 1	He looked up and saw **rich**
2C	8: 9	though he was **rich,** yet
Ep	2: 4	But God, who is **rich** in mercy,
1Ti	6:17	in the present age are **rich,**
Ja	1:10	and the **rich** in being brought
	1:11	is the same way with the **rich;**
	2: 5	to be **rich** in faith and to be
	2: 6	Is it not the **rich** who oppress
	5: 1	Come now, you **rich** people, weep
Re	2: 9	even though you are **rich.** I
	3:17	For you say, 'I am **rich,** I have
	6:15	and the **rich** and the powerful,
	13:16	both **rich** and poor, both free

4146 GO4 AG673 LN200 B2:840 R4145
πλουσιως, RICHLY

Co	3:16	of Christ dwell in you **richly;**
1Ti	6:17	but rather on God who **richly**

Ti	3: 6	poured out on us **richly** through
2P	1:11	will be **richly** provided for you

4147 GO12 AG673 LN200 B2:840 K6:318 R4148
πλουτεω, I AM RICH

Lk	1:53	and sent the **rich** away empty.
	12:21	but **are** not **rich** toward God.
Ro	10:12	**is generous** to all who call on
1C	4: 8	Already you have **become rich!**
2C	8: 9	poverty you **might become rich.**
1Ti	6: 9	But those who want **to be rich**
	6:18	They are to do good, **to be rich**
Re	3:17	For you say, 'I am rich, I have
	3:18	by fire so that you **may be rich**
	18: 3	of the earth **have grown rich**
	18:15	who **gained wealth** from her,
	18:19	who had ships at sea **grew rich**

4148 GO3 AG674 LN200 B2:840 K6:318 R4149
πλουτιζω, I MADE RICH

1C	1: 5	you **have been enriched** in him,
2C	6:10	as poor, yet **making** many **rich;**
	9:11	You **will be enriched** in every

4149 GO22 AG674 LN200 B2:840 K6:318
πλουτος, RICH

Mt	13:22	the lure of **wealth** choke the
Mk	4:19	the lure of **wealth,** and the
Lk	8:14	cares and **riches** and pleasures
Ro	2: 4	Or do you despise the **riches** of
	9:23	make known the **riches** of his
	11:12	their stumbling means **riches**
	11:12	if their defeat means **riches**
	11:33	O the depth of the **riches** and
2C	8: 2	overflowed in a **wealth** of
Ep	1: 7	according to the **riches** of his
	1:18	what are the **riches** of his
	2: 7	show the immeasurable **riches** of
	3: 8	news of the boundless **riches** of
	3:16	according to the **riches** of his
Ph	4:19	according to his **riches** in
Co	1:27	are the **riches** of the glory of
	2: 2	they may have all the **riches** of
1Ti	6:17	the uncertainty of **riches,** but
He	11:26	to be greater **wealth** than the
Ja	5: 2	Your **riches** have rotted, and
Re	5:12	**wealth** and wisdom and might
	18:17	For in one hour all this **wealth**

4150   ^{GO}3 ^{AG}674 ^{LN}200

πλυνω, I WASH

Lk	5: 2	and **were washing** their nets.
Re	7:14	they **have washed** their robes
	22:14	Blessed are those who **wash**

4151   ^{GO}379 ^{AG}674 ^{LN}200 ^B3:689 ^K6:332

πνευμα, SPIRIT, WIND

Mt	1:18	with child from the Holy **Spirit**
	1:20	in her is from the Holy **Spirit.**
	3:11	with the Holy **Spirit** and fire.
	3:16	and he saw the **Spirit** of God
	4: 1	Jesus was led up by the **Spirit**
	5: 3	Blessed are the poor in **spirit**
	8:16	he cast out the **spirits** with a
	10: 1	authority over unclean **spirits,**
	10:20	but the **Spirit** of your Father
	12:18	I will put my **Spirit** upon him,
	12:28	But if it is by the **Spirit** of
	12:31	blasphemy against the **Spirit**
	12:32	speaks against the Holy **Spirit**
	12:43	When the unclean **spirit** has
	12:45	seven other **spirits** more evil
	22:43	David by the **Spirit** calls him
	26:41	the **spirit** indeed is willing,
	27:50	with a loud voice and **breathed**
	28:19	the Son and of the Holy **Spirit,**
Mk	1: 8	you with the Holy **Spirit.**
	1:10	the **Spirit** descending like a
	1:12	And the **Spirit** immediately
	1:23	a man with an unclean **spirit,**
	1:26	And the unclean **spirit,**
	1:27	even the unclean **spirits,** and
	2: 8	perceived in his **spirit** that
	3:11	Whenever the unclean **spirits**
	3:29	against the Holy **Spirit** can
	3:30	said, "He has an unclean **spirit**
	5: 2	with an unclean **spirit** met him.
	5: 8	of the man, you unclean **spirit!**
	5:13	And the unclean **spirits** came
	6: 7	over the unclean **spirits.**
	7:25	daughter had an unclean **spirit**
	8:12	sighed deeply in his **spirit** and
	9:17	he has a **spirit** that makes him
	9:20	When the **spirit** saw him,
	9:25	he rebuked the unclean **spirit,**
	9:25	You **spirit** that keeps this boy
	12:36	by the Holy **Spirit,** declared,
	13:11	who speak, but the Holy **Spirit.**

	14:38	the **spirit** indeed is willing,
Lk	1:15	be filled with the Holy **Spirit.**
	1:17	With the **spirit** and power of
	1:35	The Holy **Spirit** will come upon
	1:41	was filled with the Holy **Spirit**
	1:47	and my **spirit** rejoices in God
	1:67	filled with the Holy **Spirit** and
	1:80	became strong in **spirit,** and he
	2:25	the Holy **Spirit** rested on him.
	2:26	Holy **Spirit** that he would not
	2:27	Guided by the **Spirit,** Simeon
	3:16	with the Holy **Spirit** and fire.
	3:22	and the Holy **Spirit** descended
	4: 1	Jesus, full of the Holy **Spirit,**
	4: 1	was led by the **Spirit** in the
	4:14	with the power of the **Spirit,**
	4:18	The **Spirit** of the Lord is upon
	4:33	a man who had the **spirit** of an
	4:36	he commands the unclean **spirits**
	6:18	troubled with unclean **spirits**
	7:21	evil **spirits,** and had given
	8: 2	been cured of evil **spirits** and
	8:29	commanded the unclean **spirit** to
	8:55	Her **spirit** returned, and she
	9:39	Suddenly a **spirit** seizes him,
	9:42	rebuked the unclean **spirit,**
	10:20	that the **spirits** submit to you,
	10:21	rejoiced in the Holy **Spirit** and
	11:13	give the Holy **Spirit** to those
	11:24	When the unclean **spirit** has
	11:26	seven other **spirits** more evil
	12:10	against the Holy **Spirit** will
	12:12	for the Holy **Spirit** will teach
	13:11	a woman with a **spirit** that had
	23:46	your hands I commend my **spirit.**
	24:37	that they were seeing a **ghost.**
	24:39	for a **ghost** does not have flesh
Jn	1:32	I saw the **Spirit** descending
	1:33	He on whom you see the **Spirit**
	1:33	baptizes with the Holy **Spirit.**
	3: 5	being born of water and **Spirit.**
	3: 6	what is born of the **Spirit** is
	3: 6	is born of the Spirit is **spirit**
	3: 8	The **wind** blows where it chooses
	3: 8	who is born of the **Spirit.**
	3:34	he gives the **Spirit** without
	4:23	worship the Father in **spirit**
	4:24	God is **spirit,** and those who
	4:24	worship in **spirit** and truth.

	6:63	is the **spirit** that gives life;
	6:63	to you are **spirit** and life.
	7:39	he said this about the **Spirit,**
	7:39	as yet there was no **Spirit,**
	11:33	greatly disturbed in **spirit**
	13:21	Jesus was troubled in **spirit,**
	14:17	This is the **Spirit** of truth,
	14:26	the Holy **Spirit,** whom the
	15:26	the **Spirit** of truth who comes
	16:13	When the **Spirit** of truth comes,
	19:30	his head and gave up his **spirit**
	20:22	them, "Receive the Holy **Spirit.**
Ac	1: 2	through the Holy **Spirit** to the
	1: 5	baptized with the Holy **Spirit**
	1: 8	power when the Holy **Spirit** has
	1:16	which the Holy **Spirit** through
	2: 4	filled with the Holy **Spirit** and
	2: 4	as the **Spirit** gave them ability
	2:17	I will pour out my **Spirit** upon
	2:18	I will pour out my **Spirit;** and
	2:33	the promise of the Holy **Spirit,**
	2:38	the gift of the Holy **Spirit.**
	4: 8	filled with the Holy **Spirit,**
	4:25	by the Holy **Spirit** through our
	4:31	filled with the Holy **Spirit** and
	5: 3	lie to the Holy **Spirit** and to
	5: 9	together to put the **Spirit** of
	5:16	tormented by unclean **spirits,**
	5:32	so is the Holy **Spirit** whom God
	6: 3	full of the **Spirit** and of
	6: 5	of faith and the Holy **Spirit,**
	6:10	and the **Spirit** with which he
	7:51	opposing the Holy **Spirit,** just
	7:55	But filled with the Holy **Spirit**
	7:59	Lord Jesus, receive my **spirit.**
	8: 7	for unclean **spirits,** crying
	8:15	might receive the Holy **Spirit**
	8:17	they received the Holy **Spirit.**
	8:18	Simon saw that the **Spirit** was
	8:19	may receive the Holy **Spirit.**
	8:29	Then the **Spirit** said to Philip,
	8:39	the **Spirit** of the Lord snatched
	9:17	be filled with the Holy **Spirit.**
	9:31	the comfort of the Holy **Spirit,**
	10:19	the **Spirit** said to him, "Look,
	10:38	with the Holy **Spirit** and with
	10:44	the Holy **Spirit** fell upon all

	10:45	the gift of the Holy **Spirit** had
	10:47	received the Holy **Spirit** just
	11:12	The **Spirit** told me to go with
	11:15	the Holy **Spirit** fell upon them
	11:16	baptized with the Holy **Spirit.**
	11:24	full of the Holy **Spirit** and of
	11:28	predicted by the **Spirit** that
	13: 2	Holy **Spirit** said, "Set apart
	13: 4	sent out by the Holy **Spirit,**
	13: 9	filled with the Holy **Spirit,**
	13:52	joy and with the Holy **Spirit.**
	15: 8	giving them the Holy **Spirit,**
	15:28	good to the Holy **Spirit** and to
	16: 6	forbidden by the Holy **Spirit** to
	16: 7	but the **Spirit** of Jesus did not
	16:16	slave-girl who had a **spirit** of
	16:18	turned and said to the **spirit,**
	17:16	he was deeply **distressed** to see
	18:25	spoke with burning **enthusiasm**
	19: 2	you receive the Holy **Spirit**
	19: 2	that there is a Holy **Spirit.**
	19: 6	the Holy **Spirit** came upon them,
	19:12	the evil **spirits** came out of
	19:13	those who had evil **spirits,**
	19:15	But the evil **spirit** said to
	19:16	the man with the evil **spirit**
	19:21	Paul resolved in the **Spirit** to
	20:22	as a captive to the **Spirit,** I
	20:23	except that the Holy **Spirit**
	20:28	of which the Holy **Spirit** has
	21: 4	Through the **Spirit** they told
	21:11	Thus says the Holy **Spirit,**
	23: 8	or **spirit;** but the Pharisees
	23: 9	What if a **spirit** or an angel
	28:25	The Holy **Spirit** was right in
Ro	1: 4	according to the **spirit** of
	1: 9	whom I serve with my **spirit** by
	2:29	it is **spiritual** and not literal
	5: 5	through the Holy **Spirit** that
	7: 6	in the new life of the **Spirit.**
	8: 2	For the law of the **Spirit** of
	8: 4	but according to the **Spirit.**
	8: 5	live according to the **Spirit**
	8: 5	on the things of the **Spirit.**
	8: 6	mind on the **Spirit** is life and
	8: 9	you are in the **Spirit,** since
	8: 9	since the **Spirit** of God dwells
	8: 9	does not have the **Spirit** of
	8:10	the **Spirit** is life because of

8:11	If the **Spirit** of him who raised
8:11	also through his **Spirit** that
8:13	by the **Spirit** you put to death
8:14	all who are led by the **Spirit**
8:15	you did not receive a **spirit**
8:15	you have received a **spirit** of
8:16	it is that very **Spirit** bearing
8:16	bearing witness with our **spirit**
8:23	first fruits of the **Spirit,**
8:26	Likewise the **Spirit** helps us in
8:26	but that very **Spirit** intercedes
8:27	mind of the **Spirit,** because the
9: 1	confirms it by the Holy **Spirit**
11: 8	gave them a sluggish **spirit,**
12:11	be ardent in **spirit,** serve the
14:17	and joy in the Holy **Spirit.**
15:13	by the power of the Holy **Spirit**
15:16	sanctified by the Holy **Spirit.**
15:19	by the power of the **Spirit** of
15:30	by the love of the **Spirit,** to

1C
2: 4	a demonstration of the **Spirit**
2:10	through the **Spirit;** for the
2:10	**Spirit** searches everything,
2:11	except the human **spirit** that is
2:11	God's except the **Spirit** of God.
2:12	received not the **spirit** of the
2:12	but the **Spirit** that is from God
2:13	wisdom but taught by the **Spirit**
2:14	the gifts of God's **Spirit,** for
3:16	that God's **Spirit** dwells in you
4:21	love in a **spirit** of gentleness?
5: 3	I am present in **spirit;** and as
5: 4	my **spirit** is present with the
5: 5	so that his **spirit** may be saved
6:11	and in the **Spirit** of our God.
6:17	becomes one **spirit** with him.
6:19	a temple of the Holy **Spirit**
7:34	holy in body and **spirit;** but
7:40	I too have the **Spirit** of God.
12: 3	speaking by the **Spirit** of God
12: 3	Lord" except by the Holy **Spirit**
12: 4	of gifts, but the same **Spirit;**
12: 7	manifestation of the **Spirit** for
12: 8	is given through the **Spirit** the
12: 8	according to the same **Spirit,**
12: 9	faith by the same **Spirit,** to
12: 9	of healing by the one **Spirit,**
12:10	the discernment of **spirits,** to
12:11	one and the same **Spirit,** who

12:13	For in the one **Spirit** we were
12:13	all made to drink of one **Spirit**
14: 2	mysteries in the **Spirit.**
14:12	are eager for **spiritual** gifts,
14:14	my **spirit** prays but my mind is
14:15	I will pray with the **spirit,**
14:15	sing praise with the **spirit,**
14:16	say a blessing with the **spirit,**
14:32	And the **spirits** of prophets are
15:45	became a life-giving **spirit.**
16:18	for they refreshed my **spirit** as

2C
1:22	giving us his **Spirit** in our
2:13	but my **mind** could not rest
3: 3	but with the **Spirit** of the
3: 6	not of letter but of **spirit;**
3: 6	but the **Spirit** gives life.
3: 8	ministry of the **Spirit** come in
3:17	Now the Lord is the **Spirit,**
3:17	where the **Spirit** of the Lord
3:18	comes from the Lord, the **Spirit**
4:13	the same **spirit** of faith that
5: 5	us the **Spirit** as
6: 6	kindness, holiness of **spirit,**
7: 1	of body and of **spirit,** making
7:13	because his **mind** has been set
11: 4	receive a different **spirit** from
12:18	ourselves with the same **spirit?**
13:13	communion of the Holy **Spirit** be

Ga
3: 2	Did you receive the **Spirit** by
3: 3	Having started with the **Spirit,**
3: 5	supply you with the **Spirit** and
3:14	promise of the **Spirit** through
4: 6	God has sent the **Spirit** of his
4:29	according to the **Spirit,** so it
5: 5	For through the **Spirit,** by
5:16	Live by the **Spirit,** I say, and
5:17	opposed to the **Spirit,** and what
5:17	the **Spirit** desires is opposed
5:18	led by the **Spirit,** you are not
5:22	fruit of the **Spirit** is love,
5:25	If we live by the **Spirit,** let
5:25	also be guided by the **Spirit.**
6: 1	received the **Spirit** should
6: 8	sow to the **Spirit,** you will
6: 8	eternal life from the **Spirit.**
6:18	be with your **spirit,** brothers

Ep
1:13	of the promised Holy **Spirit;**
1:17	give you a **spirit** of wisdom

	2: 2	the **spirit** that is now at work
	2:18	access in one **Spirit** to the
	2:22	built together **spiritually** into
	3: 5	and prophets by the **Spirit:**
	3:16	with power through his **Spirit,**
	4: 3	unity of the **Spirit** in the bond
	4: 4	is one body and one **Spirit,**
	4:23	and to be renewed in the **spirit**
	4:30	do not grieve the Holy **Spirit**
	5:18	but be filled with the **Spirit,**
	6:17	the sword of the **Spirit,** which
	6:18	Pray in the **Spirit** at all times
Ph	1:19	help of the **Spirit** of Jesus
	1:27	standing firm in one **spirit,**
	2: 1	sharing in the **Spirit,** any
	3: 3	worship in the **Spirit** of God
	4:23	Christ be with your **spirit.**
Co	1: 8	to us your love in the **Spirit.**
	2: 5	yet I am with you in **spirit,**
1Th	1: 5	power and in the Holy **Spirit**
	1: 6	joy inspired by the Holy **Spirit**
	4: 8	also gives his Holy **Spirit** to
	5:19	Do not quench the **Spirit.**
	5:23	may your **spirit** and soul and
2Th	2: 2	either by **spirit** or by word or
	2: 8	destroy with the **breath** of his
	2:13	the **Spirit** and through belief
1Ti	3:16	vindicated in **spirit,** seen by
	4: 1	Now the **Spirit** expressly says
	4: 1	deceitful **spirits** and teachings
2Ti	1: 7	God did not give us a **spirit** of
	1:14	help of the Holy **Spirit** living
	4:22	The Lord be with your **spirit.**
Ti	3: 5	and renewal by the Holy **Spirit.**
Pm	1:25	Christ be with your **spirit.**
He	1: 7	He makes his angels **winds,**
	1:14	Are not all angels **spirits** in
	2: 4	and by gifts of the Holy **Spirit**
	3: 7	as the Holy **Spirit** says, "Today
	4:12	soul from **spirit,** joints from
	6: 4	have shared in the Holy **Spirit,**
	9: 8	this the Holy **Spirit** indicates
	9:14	who through the eternal **Spirit**
	10:15	the Holy **Spirit** also testifies
	10:29	outraged the **Spirit** of grace?
	12: 9	the Father of **spirits** and live?
	12:23	to the **spirits** of the righteous
Ja	2:26	body without the **spirit** is dead

	4: 5	jealously for the **spirit** that
1P	1: 2	sanctified by the **Spirit** to be
	1:11	time that the **Spirit** of Christ
	1:12	good news by the Holy **Spirit**
	3: 4	gentle and quiet **spirit,** which
	3:18	but made alive in the **spirit,**
	3:19	proclamation to the **spirits** in
	4: 6	might live in the **spirit** as God
	4:14	because the **spirit** of glory,
2P	1:21	moved by the Holy **Spirit** spoke
1J	3:24	by the **Spirit** that he has given
	4: 1	do not believe every **spirit,**
	4: 1	test the **spirits** to see whether
	4: 2	By this you know the **Spirit** of
	4: 2	every **spirit** that confesses
	4: 3	and every **spirit** that does not
	4: 6	we know the **spirit** of truth
	4: 6	truth and the **spirit** of error.
	4:13	he has given us of his **Spirit.**
	5: 6	And the **Spirit** is the one that
	5: 6	for the **Spirit** is the truth.
	5: 8	the **Spirit** and the water and
Ju	1:19	devoid of the **Spirit,** who are
	1:20	faith; pray in the Holy **Spirit;**
Re	1: 4	from the seven **spirits** who are
	1:10	I was in the **spirit** on the
	2: 7	listen to what the **Spirit** is
	2:11	listen to what the **Spirit** is
	2:17	listen to what the **Spirit** is
	2:29	listen to what the **Spirit** is
	3: 1	seven **spirits** of God and the
	3: 6	listen to what the **Spirit** is
	3:13	listen to what the **Spirit** is
	3:22	listen to what the **Spirit** is
	4: 2	At once I was in the **spirit,**
	4: 5	which are the seven **spirits** of
	5: 6	the seven **spirits** of God sent
	11:11	the **breath** of life from God
	13:15	allowed to give **breath** to the
	14:13	"Yes," says the **Spirit,** "they
	16:13	And I saw three foul **spirits**
	16:14	These are demonic **spirits,**
	17: 3	carried me away in the **spirit**
	18: 2	a haunt of every foul **spirit,**
	19:10	Jesus is the **spirit** of prophecy
	21:10	And in the **spirit** he carried me
	22: 6	the God of the **spirits** of the
	22:17	The **Spirit** and the bride say,

4152　GO26 AG678 LN200 B3:689 K6:332 R4151
πνευματικος, SPIRITUAL
Ro　1:11　share with you some **spiritual**
　　7:14　the law is **spiritual;** but I am
　　15:27　to share in their **spiritual**
1C　2:13　interpreting **spiritual** things
　　2:13　to those who are **spiritual.**
　　2:15　Those who are **spiritual** discern
　　3: 1　speak to you as **spiritual**
　　9:11　If we have sown **spiritual** good
　　10: 3　and all ate the same **spiritual**
　　10: 4　all drank the same **spiritual**
　　10: 4　they drank from the **spiritual**
　　12: 1　Now concerning **spiritual** gifts,
　　14: 1　strive for the **spiritual** gifts,
　　14:37　have **spiritual** powers, must
　　15:44　it is raised a **spiritual** body.
　　15:44　there is also a **spiritual** body.
　　15:46　But it is not the **spiritual**
　　15:46　and then the **spiritual.**
Ga　6: 1　received the **Spirit** should
Ep　1: 3　every **spiritual** blessing in the
　　5:19　psalms and hymns and **spiritual**
　　6:12　against the **spiritual** forces of
Co　1: 9　God's will in all **spiritual**
　　3:16　psalms, hymns, and **spiritual**
1P　2: 5　built into a **spiritual** house,
　　2: 5　to offer **spiritual** sacrifices

4153　GO2 AG679 LN201 B3:689 R4152
πνευματικως, SPIRITUALLY
1C　2:14　because they are **spiritually**
Re　11: 8　**prophetically** called Sodom and

4154　GO7 AG679 LN201 B3:689 K6:452
πνεω, I BLOW
Mt　7:25　and the winds **blew** and beat on
　　7:27　and the winds **blew** and beat
Lk　12:55　south wind **blowing,** you say,
Jn　3: 8　The wind **blows** where it chooses
　　6:18　a strong wind **was blowing.**
Ac　27:40　foresail to the **wind,** they made
Re　7: 1　no wind could **blow** on earth or

4155　GO3 AG679 LN201 B1:226 K6:455
πνιγω, I CHOKE
Mt　13: 7　the thorns grew up and **choked**
　　18:28　seizing him by the **throat,** he
Mk　5:13　into the sea, and **were drowned**

4156　GO3 AG679 LN201 B1:226 K6:455 R4155
πνικτος, CHOKED
Ac　15:20　been **strangled** and from blood.
　　15:29　**strangled** and from fornication.
　　21:25　from what is **strangled** and from

4157　GO2 AG680 LN201 B3:689 K6:453 R4154
πνοη, WIND
Ac　2: 2　like the rush of a violent **wind**
　　17:25　life and **breath** and all things.

4158　GO1 AG680 LN201
ποδηρης, (REACHING) TO THE FEET
Re　1:13　clothed with a **long** robe and

4159　GO29 AG680 LN201
ποθεν, FROM WHERE
Mt　13:27　then, did these weeds come **from**
　　13:54　**Where** did this man get this
　　13:56　**Where** then did this man get all
　　15:33　**Where** are we to get enough
　　21:25　come **from** heaven, or was it of
Mk　6: 2　**Where** did this man get all
　　8: 4　His disciples replied, "**How** can
　　12:37　so **how** can he be his son?" And
Lk　1:43　And **why** has this happened to me
　　13:25　do not know **where** you come **from**
　　13:27　not know **where** you come **from;**
　　20: 7　did not know **where** it came **from**
Jn　1:48　Nathanael asked him, "**Where** did
　　2: 9　did not know **where** it came **from**
　　3: 8　not know **where** it comes **from** or
　　4:11　**Where** do you get that living
　　6: 5　**Where** are we to buy bread for
　　7:27　know **where** this man is **from;**
　　7:27　one will know **where** he is **from.**
　　7:28　you know **where** I am **from.** I
　　8:14　I know **where** I have come **from**
　　8:14　do not know **where** I come **from**
　　9:29　not know **where** he comes **from.**
　　9:30　do not know **where** he comes **from**
　　19: 9　"**Where** are you **from?**" But Jesus
Ja　4: 1　**where** do they come **from?** Do
　　4: 1　**where** do they come **from?** Do
Re　2: 5　Remember then **from what** you
　　7:13　and **where** have they come **from?**

4160　GO568 AG680 LN201 B3:1152 K6:458
ποιεω, I DO, I MAKE
Mt　1:24　he **did** as the angel of the Lord

3: 3	Lord, **make** his paths straight.		20:12	you have **made** them equal to us
3: 8	**Bear** fruit worthy of repentance		20:15	Am I not allowed to **do** what I
3:10	**does** not bear good fruit is cut		20:32	What do you want me to **do** for
4:19	I **will make** you fish for people		21: 6	The disciples went and **did** as
5:19	whoever **does** them and teaches		21:13	but you are **making** it a den of
5:32	**causes** her to commit adultery;		21:15	amazing things that he **did,** and
5:36	you cannot **make** one hair white		21:21	not only will you **do** what has
5:46	the tax collectors **do** the same?		21:23	what authority **are** you **doing**
5:47	what more **are** you **doing** than		21:24	by what authority I **do** these
5:47	even the Gentiles **do** the same?		21:27	I **am doing** these things.
6: 1	Beware of **practicing** your		21:31	Which of the two **did** the will
6: 2	So whenever you **give** alms, do		21:36	and they **treated** them in the
6: 2	as the hypocrites **do** in the		21:40	comes, what **will** he **do** to
6: 3	But when you **give** alms, do not		21:43	**produces** the fruits of the
6: 3	what your right hand **is doing,**		22: 2	who **gave** a wedding banquet for
7:12	In everything **do** to others as		23: 3	**do** whatever they teach you
7:12	you would have them **do** to you;		23: 3	do not **do** as they do, for they
7:17	every good tree **bears** good		23: 3	for they **do** not practice what
7:17	but the bad tree **bears** bad		23: 5	They **do** all their deeds to be
7:18	A good tree cannot **bear** bad		23:15	**make** a single convert, and you
7:18	can a bad tree **bear** good fruit.		23:15	**make** the new convert twice as
7:19	Every tree that does not **bear**		23:23	**practiced** without neglecting
7:21	only the one who **does** the will		24:46	find **at work** when he arrives.
7:22	and **do** many deeds of power in		25:40	just as you **did** it to one of
7:24	**acts on** them will be like a		25:40	of my family, you **did** it to me.
7:26	does not **act on** them will be		25:45	just as you did not **do** it to
8: 9	'**Do** this,' and the slave does		25:45	these, you did not **do** it to me.
8: 9	'**Do** this,' and the slave **does**		26:12	she has **prepared** me for burial.
9:28	I am able to **do** this?" They		26:13	what she **has done** will be told
12: 2	Look, your disciples **are doing**		26:18	I will **keep** the Passover at
12: 2	what is not lawful **to do** on the		26:19	So the disciples **did** as Jesus
12: 3	what David **did** when he and his		26:73	for your accent **betrays** you.
12:12	it is lawful **to do** good on the		27:22	Then what should I **do** with
12:16	and he ordered them not to **make**		27:23	Why, what evil **has** he **done?**
12:33	Either **make** the tree good, and		28:14	will satisfy him and **keep** you
12:33	or **make** the tree bad, and its		28:15	So they took the money and **did**
12:50	For whoever **does** the will of my	Mk	1: 3	Lord, **make** his paths straight,
13:23	indeed bears fruit and **yields,**		1:17	Follow me and I **will make** you
13:26	plants came up and **bore** grain,		2:23	as they **made** their way his
13:28	He answered, 'An enemy **has done**		2:24	why are they **doing** what is not
13:41	causes of sin and all evil**doers**		2:25	you never read what David **did**
13:58	And he did not **do** many deeds of		3: 4	Is it lawful to **do** good or to
17: 4	I **will make** three dwellings		3: 8	hearing all that he **was doing,**
17:12	they **did** to him whatever they		3:12	them not to **make** him known.
18:35	will also **do** to every one of		3:14	And he **appointed** twelve, whom
19: 4	**made** them male and female,		3:16	So he **appointed** the twelve:
19:16	must I **do** to have eternal life?		3:35	Whoever **does** the will of God
20: 5	three o'clock, he **did** the same.		4:32	**puts forth** large branches, so
20:12	saying, 'These last **worked** only		5:19	how much the Lord **has done** for

5:20	how much Jesus **had done** for him
5:32	all around to see who **had done**
6: 5	he could **do** no deed of power
6:21	Herod on his birthday **gave** a
6:30	told him all that they **had done**
7:12	then you no longer permit **doing**
7:13	you **do** many things like this.
7:37	He **has done** everything well;
7:37	he even **makes** the deaf to hear
9: 5	let us **make** three dwellings,
9:13	they **did** to him whatever they
9:39	for no one who **does** a deed of
10: 6	God **made** them male and female.
10:17	what must I **do** to inherit
10:35	Teacher, we want you to **do** for
10:36	What is it you want me to **do**
10:51	What do you want me **to do** for
11: 3	'Why **are** you **doing** this?' just
11: 5	What **are** you **doing**, untying
11:17	But you **have made** it a den of
11:28	what authority **are** you **doing**
11:28	you this authority to **do** them?
11:29	by what authority I **do** these
11:33	by what authority I **am doing**
12: 9	owner of the vineyard **do**? He
14: 7	you can **show** kindness to them
14: 8	She **has done** what she could;
14: 9	what she **has done** will be told
15: 1	the chief priests **held** a
15: 7	rebels who had **committed** murder
15: 8	began to ask Pilate to **do** for
15:12	do you wish me to **do** with the
15:14	Why, what evil has he **done**?
15:15	So Pilate, wishing **to** satisfy
Lk 1:25	This is what the Lord **has done**
1:49	for the Mighty One **has done**
1:51	**shown** strength with his arm;
1:68	on his people and **redeemed** them
1:72	Thus he has **shown** the mercy
2:27	child Jesus, to **do** for him what
2:48	Child, why have you **treated** us
3: 4	Lord, **make** his paths straight.
3: 8	**Bear** fruits worthy of
3: 9	that does not **bear** good fruit
3:10	him, "What then should we **do**?"
3:11	has food must **do** likewise.
3:12	Teacher, what should we **do**?
3:14	And we, what should we **do**?
3:19	evil things that Herod **had done**

4:23	And you will say, '**Do** here also
5: 6	When they **had done** this, they
5:29	Then Levi **gave** a great banquet
5:33	frequently fast and **pray,** but
5:34	You cannot **make** wedding guests
6: 2	Why **are** you **doing** what is not
6: 3	what David **did** when he and his
6:10	He **did** so, and his hand was
6:11	what they **might do** to Jesus.
6:23	ancestors **did** to the prophets.
6:26	ancestors **did** to the false
6:27	Love your enemies, **do** good to
6:31	**Do** to others as you would have
6:31	you would have them **do** to you.
6:33	For even sinners **do** the same.
6:43	No good tree **bears** bad fruit,
6:43	does a bad tree **bear** good fruit
6:46	and do not **do** what I tell you?
6:47	hears my words, and **acts** on
6:49	hears and does not **act** is like
7: 8	to my slave, '**Do** this,' and the
7: 8	'Do this,' and the slave **does**
8: 8	and when it grew, it **produced** a
8:21	hear the word of God and **do** it.
8:39	declare how much God **has done**
8:39	how much Jesus **had done** for him
9:10	told Jesus all they **had done.**
9:15	They **did** so and made them all
9:33	let us **make** three dwellings,
9:43	all that he **was doing,** he said
10:25	what must I **do** to inherit
10:28	**do** this, and you will live.
10:37	The one who **showed** him mercy.
10:37	to him, "Go and **do** likewise."
11:40	Did not the one who **made** the
11:40	who made the outside **make** the
11:42	you ought to have **practiced,**
12: 4	and after that can **do** nothing
12:17	What should I **do,** for I have
12:18	Then he said, 'I **will do** this:
12:33	**Make** purses for yourselves that
12:43	master will find **at work** when
12:47	or **do** what was wanted, will
12:48	**did** what deserved a beating
13: 9	If it **bears** fruit next year,
13:22	teaching as he **made** his way to
14:12	When you **give** a luncheon or a
14:13	But when you **give** a banquet,
14:16	Someone **gave** a great dinner

15:19	**treat** me like one of your hired
16: 3	What will I **do,** now that my
16: 4	I have decided what to **do** so
16: 8	because he had **acted** shrewdly;
16: 9	**make** friends for yourselves by
17: 9	thank the slave for **doing** what
17:10	So you also, when you **have done**
17:10	we **have done** only what we ought
17:10	only what we ought to **have done**
18: 7	And will not God **grant** justice
18: 8	he **will** quickly **grant** justice
18:18	what must I **do** to inherit
18:41	What do you want me to **do** for
19:18	Lord, your pound has **made** five
19:46	but you have **made** it a den of
19:48	anything they could **do,** for all
20: 2	by what authority **are** you **doing**
20: 8	by what authority I **am doing**
20:13	What **shall** I **do?** I will send
20:15	owner of the vineyard **do** to
22:19	**Do** this in remembrance of me.
23:22	Why, what evil **has** he **done?**
23:31	For if they **do** this when the
23:34	not know what they **are doing.**"

Jn	2: 5	**Do** whatever he tells you.
	2:11	Jesus **did** this, the first of
	2:15	**Making** a whip of cords, he
	2:16	Stop **making** my Father's house a
	2:18	can you show us for **doing** this?
	2:23	saw the signs that he **was doing**
	3: 2	for no one can **do** these signs
	3: 2	signs that you **do** apart from
	3:21	But those who **do** what is true
	4: 1	Jesus is **making** and baptizing
	4:29	everything I **have** ever **done!** He
	4:34	My food is to **do** the will of
	4:39	me everything I **have** ever **done.**
	4:45	that he **had done** in Jerusalem
	4:46	where he **had changed** the water
	4:54	that Jesus **did** after coming
	5:11	The man who **made** me well said
	5:15	was Jesus who **had made** him well
	5:16	because he **was doing** such
	5:18	thereby **making** himself equal to
	5:19	Son can **do** nothing on his own,
	5:19	what he sees the Father **doing;**
	5:19	whatever the Father **does,** the
	5:19	does, the Son **does** likewise.
	5:20	all that he himself **is doing;**

5:27	authority to **execute** judgment,
5:29	those who **have done** good, to
5:30	I can **do** nothing on my own.
5:36	very works that I **am doing,**
6: 2	signs that he **was doing** for the
6: 6	knew what he was going to **do.**
6:10	Jesus said, "**Make** the people
6:14	the sign that he **had done,** they
6:15	take him by force to **make** him
6:28	What must we **do** to perform the
6:30	sign are you **going to give** us
6:38	not to **do** my own will, but the
7: 3	may see the works you **are doing**
7: 4	wants to be widely known **acts**
7: 4	If you **do** these things, show
7:17	Anyone who resolves **to do** the
7:19	Yet none of you **keeps** the law.
7:21	I **performed** one work, and all
7:23	I **healed** a man's whole body on
7:31	will he **do** more signs than this
7:31	signs than this man **has done?**
7:51	find out what they **are doing,**
8:28	I am he, and that I **do** nothing
8:29	I always **do** what is pleasing to
8:34	everyone who **commits** sin is a
8:38	you should **do** what you have
8:39	you would **be doing** what Abraham
8:40	This is not what Abraham **did.**
8:41	doing what your father **does.**
8:44	you choose to **do** your father's
8:53	died. Who do you **claim** to be?
9: 6	he spat on the ground and **made**
9:11	The man called Jesus **made** mud,
9:14	when Jesus **made** the mud and
9:16	a man who is a sinner **perform**
9:26	What did he **do** to you? How did
9:31	worships him and **obeys** his will.
9:33	from God, he could **do** nothing.
10:25	works that I **do** in my Father's
10:33	being, **are making** yourself God.
10:37	If I **am** not **doing** the works of
10:38	But if I **do** them, even though
10:41	John **performed** no sign, but
11:37	eyes of the blind man have **kept**
11:45	seen what Jesus **did,** believed
11:46	and told them what he **had done.**
11:47	What are we to **do?** This man is
11:47	man is **performing** many signs.
12: 2	There they **gave** a dinner for

12:16	of him and **had been done** to him
12:18	heard that he had **performed**
12:37	Although he had **performed** so
13: 7	do not know now what I **am doing**
13:12	know what I **have done** to you?
13:15	that you also should **do** as I
13:15	should do as I **have done** to you
13:17	you are blessed if you **do** them.
13:27	**Do** quickly what you are going
13:27	what you **are going to do.**
14:10	who dwells in me **does** his works
14:12	**will** also **do** the works that I
14:12	that I **do** and, in fact, will do
14:12	that I do and, in fact, **will do**
14:13	I **will do** whatever you ask in
14:14	ask me for anything, I **will do**
14:23	come to them and **make** our home
14:31	**do** as the Father has commanded
15: 5	from me you can **do** nothing.
15:14	You are my friends if you **do**
15:15	know what the master **is doing**
15:21	But they will **do** all these
15:24	If I **had** not **done** among them
15:24	that no one else **did,** they
16: 2	They will **put** you out of the
16: 3	And they **will do** this because
17: 4	the work that you gave me to **do**
18:18	slaves and the police **had made**
18:30	this man were not a **criminal,**
18:35	over to me. What **have** you **done?**
19: 7	to die because he **has claimed**
19:12	Everyone who **claims** to be a
19:23	**divided** them into four parts,
19:25	is what the soldiers **did**
20:30	Now Jesus **did** many other signs
21:25	other things that Jesus **did;**
Ac 1: 1	**wrote** about all that Jesus did
1: 1	all that Jesus **did** and taught
2:22	signs that God **did** through him
2:36	God **has made** him both Lord and
2:37	Brothers, what should we **do?**
3:12	power or piety we **had made** him
4: 7	power or by what name **did** you
4:16	They said, "What will we **do**
4:24	Sovereign Lord, who **made** the
4:28	to **do** whatever your hand and
5:34	the men to be **put** outside for a
6: 8	**did** great wonders and signs
7:19	**abandon** their infants so that
7:24	**avenged** him by striking down
7:36	**having performed** wonders and
7:40	**Make** gods for us who will lead
7:43	images that you **made** to worship
7:44	him to **make** it according to the
7:50	Did not my hand **make** all these
8: 2	buried Stephen and **made** loud
8: 6	seeing the signs that he **did,**
9: 6	be told what you are to **do.**
9:13	how much evil he **has done** to
9:36	good works and **acts** of charity.
9:39	Dorcas had **made** while she was
10: 2	he **gave** alms generously to the
10:33	you **have been** kind enough to
10:39	that he **did** both in Judea and
11:30	this they **did,** sending it to
12: 8	He **did** so. Then he said to him,
13:22	**will carry out** all my wishes.
14:11	Paul **had done,** they shouted in
14:15	why **are you doing** this? We are
14:15	who **made** the heaven and the
14:27	related all that God **had done**
15: 3	and **brought** great joy to all
15: 4	reported all that God **had done**
15:12	God **had done** through them among
15:17	**has been making** these things
15:33	After they **had been** there for
16:18	She kept **doing** this for many
16:21	as Romans to adopt or **observe.**
16:30	what must I **do** to be saved?
17:24	The God who **made** the world and
17:26	From one ancestor he **made** all
18:23	After **spending** some time there
19:11	God **did** extraordinary miracles
19:14	priest named Sceva **were doing**
19:24	a silversmith who **made** silver
20: 3	where he **stayed** for three
20:24	But I **do** not **count** my life of
21:13	What **are** you **doing,** weeping
21:19	God **had done** among the Gentiles
21:23	So **do** what we tell you. We have
21:33	who he was and what he **had done**
22:10	I asked, 'What am I to **do,** Lord
22:10	has been assigned to you to **do.**
22:26	What are you about to **do?** This
23:12	In the morning the Jews **joined**
23:13	more than forty who **joined** in
24:12	**stirring** up a crowd either in
24:17	came to **bring** alms to my nation

	25: 3	They were, in fact, **planning** an
	25:17	So when they met here, I **lost**
	26:10	And that is what I **did** in
	26:28	persuading me to **become** a
	27:18	they began to **throw** the cargo
	28:17	though I **had done** nothing
Ro	1: 9	without ceasing I **remember** you
	1:28	things that should not **be done.**
	1:32	yet they not only **do** them but
	2: 3	yet **do** them yourself, you will
	2:14	**do** instinctively what the law
	3: 8	Let us **do** evil so that good
	3:12	is no one who **shows** kindness,
	4:21	God was able to **do** what he had
	7:15	For I do not **do** what I want,
	7:16	Now if I **do** what I do not want,
	7:19	For I do not **do** the good I want,
	7:20	Now if I **do** what I do not want,
	7:21	when I want to **do** what is good,
	9:20	Why have you **made** me like this
	9:21	to **make** out of the same lump
	9:28	for the Lord **will execute** his
	10: 5	person who **does** these things
	12:20	for by **doing** this you will heap
	13: 3	Then **do** what is good, and you
	13: 4	But if you **do** what is wrong,
	13:14	and **make** no provision for the
	15:26	been pleased to **share** their
	16:17	keep an eye on those who **cause**
1C	6:15	members of Christ and **make** them
	6:18	Every sin that a person **commits**
	7:36	it is no sin. Let them **marry.**
	7:37	as his fiancée, he **will do** well
	7:38	marries his fiancée **does** well;
	7:38	refrains from marriage **will do**
	9:23	I **do** it all for the sake of the
	10:13	testing he **will** also **provide**
	10:31	whatever you **do,** do everything
	10:31	**do** everything for the glory of
	11:24	**Do** this in remembrance of me.
	11:25	**Do** this, as often as you drink
	15:29	what **will** those people **do** who
	16: 1	should **follow** the directions I
2C	5:21	For our sake he **made** him to be
	8:10	began last year not only to **do**
	8:11	now finish **doing** it, so that
	11: 7	Did I **commit** a sin by humbling
	11:12	And what I **do** I will also
	11:12	I **will** also **continue to do,** in

	11:25	and a day I was **adrift** at sea;
	13: 7	you may not **do** anything wrong
	13: 7	may **do** what is right, though we
Ga	2:10	actually what I was eager to **do**
	3:10	Cursed is everyone who **does**
	3:12	Whoever **does** the works of the
	5: 3	is obliged to **obey** the entire
	5:17	prevent you from **doing** what you
	6: 9	let us not grow weary in **doing**
Ep	1:16	for you as I **remember** you in my
	2: 3	**following** the desires of flesh
	2:14	in his flesh he **has made** both
	2:15	place of the two, thus **making**
	3:11	he **has carried** out in Christ
	3:20	who by the power **at work** within
	4:16	**promotes** the body's growth in
	6: 6	**doing** the will of God from the
	6: 8	whatever good we **do,** we will
	6: 9	And, masters, **do** the same to
Ph	1: 4	constantly **praying** with joy in
	2:14	**Do** all things without murmuring
	4:14	In any case, it **was** kind of you
Co	3:17	And whatever you **do,** in word or
	3:23	Whatever your **task,** put
	4:16	**have** it read also in the church
1Th	1: 2	**mention** you in our prayers,
	4:10	beloved, to **do** so more and more
	5:11	other, as indeed you **are doing.**
	5:24	faithful, and he **will do** this.
2Th	3: 4	that you **are doing** and will go
	3: 4	**will go on doing** the things
1Ti	1:13	because I had **acted** ignorantly
	2: 1	and thanksgivings **be made** for
	4:16	for in **doing** this you will save
	5:21	**doing** nothing on the basis of
2Ti	4: 5	**carry out** your ministry fully.
Ti	3: 5	righteousness that we **had done,**
Pm	1: 4	I **remember** you in my prayers,
	1:14	but I preferred to **do** nothing
	1:21	knowing that you **will do** even
He	1: 2	through whom he also **created**
	1: 3	When he **had made** purification
	1: 7	He **makes** his angels winds, and
	3: 2	to the one who **appointed** him,
	6: 3	And we **will do** this, if God
	7:27	this he **did** once for all when
	8: 5	See that you **make** everything
	8: 9	the covenant that I **made** with
	10: 7	See, God, I have come to **do**

	10: 9	See, I have come to **do** your
	10:36	that when you **have done** the
	11:28	By faith he **kept** the Passover
	12:13	and **make** straight paths for
	12:27	that is, **created** things
	13: 6	What can anyone **do** to me?
	13:17	Let them **do** this with joy and
	13:19	I urge you all the more to **do**
	13:21	so that you may **do** his will,
	13:21	**working** among us that which is
Ja	2: 8	You **do** well if you really
	2:12	So speak and so **act** as those
	2:13	anyone who **has shown** no mercy;
	2:19	you **do** well. Even the demons
	3:12	**yield** olives, or a grapevine
	3:12	No more can salt water **yield**
	3:18	peace for those who **make** peace
	4:13	**doing** business and making money
	4:15	will live and **do** this or that.
	4:17	the right thing to **do** and fails
	4:17	and fails to **do** it, commits sin
	5:15	anyone who **has committed** sins
1P	2:22	He **committed** no sin, and no
	3:11	**do** good; let them seek peace
	3:12	is against those who **do** evil.
2P	1:10	all the more eager to **confirm**
	1:10	for if you **do** this, you will
	1:15	be able at any time to **recall**
	1:19	will **do** well to be attentive to
1J	1: 6	lie and do not **do** what is true;
	1:10	we **make** him a liar, and his
	2:17	but those who **do** the will of
	2:29	everyone who **does** right has
	3: 4	Everyone who **commits** sin is
	3: 4	Everyone who commits sin **is**
	3: 7	Everyone who **does** what is right
	3: 8	Everyone who **commits** sin is a
	3: 9	born of God **do** not sin, because
	3:10	all who do not **do** what is right
	3:22	we obey his commandments and **do**
	5: 2	God, when we love God and **obey**
	5:10	believe in God **have made** him a
3J	1: 5	Beloved, you **do** faithfully
	1: 6	You **will do** well to send them
	1:10	what he is **doing** in spreading
Ju	1: 3	while eagerly **preparing** to
	1:15	to **execute** judgment on all, and
Re	1: 6	and **made** us to be a kingdom,
	2: 5	repent, and **do** the works you

	3: 9	I **will make** those of the
	3:12	If you conquer, I **will make** you
	5:10	you **have made** them to be a
	11: 7	bottomless pit **will make** war on
	12:15	**sweep** her away with the flood.
	12:17	went off to **make** war on the
	13: 5	allowed to **exercise** authority
	13: 7	Also it was allowed **to make** war
	13:12	It **exercises** all the authority
	13:12	and it **makes** the earth and its
	13:13	It **performs** great signs, even
	13:13	even **making** fire come down from
	13:14	is allowed to **perform** on behalf
	13:14	telling them to **make** an image
	13:15	speak and **cause** those who would
	13:16	Also it **causes** all, both small
	14: 7	worship him who **made** heaven and
	16:14	**performing** signs, who go abroad
	17:16	they **will make** her desolate and
	17:17	their hearts to **carry out** his
	17:17	purpose by **agreeing** to give
	19:19	gathered to **make** war against
	19:20	false prophet who **had performed**
	21: 5	See, I **am making** all things
	21:27	who **practices** abomination or
	22: 2	**producing** its fruit each month;
	22:11	righteous still **do** right, and
	22:15	who loves and **practices**

4161   GO2   AG683   LN201   B3:1152   K6:458   R4160
ποίημα, THING MADE
Ro	1:20	the things he has **made.** So they
Ep	2:10	For we are what he has **made** us,

4162   GO1   AG683   LN201   B3:1152   K6:458   R4160
ποίησις, DOING
Ja	1:25	will be blessed in their **doing.**

4163   GO6   AG683   LN201   B3:1150   K6:458   R4160
ποιητής, DOER
Ac	17:28	as even some of your own **poets**
Ro	2:13	but the **doers** of the law who
Ja	1:22	But be **doers** of the word, and
	1:23	word and not **doers,** they are
	1:25	hearers who forget but **doers**
	4:11	you are not a **doer** of the law

4164   GO10   AG683   LN201   K6:484
ποικίλος, VARIOUS
Mt	4:24	afflicted with **various** diseases

Mk	1:34	sick with **various** diseases, and
Lk	4:40	sick with **various** kinds of
2Ti	3: 6	sins and swayed by all **kinds** of
Ti	3: 3	slaves to **various** passions and
He	2: 4	signs and wonders and **various**
	13: 9	carried away by all **kinds** of
Ja	1: 2	you face trials of any **kind,**
1P	1: 6	you have had to suffer **various**
	4:10	stewards of the **manifold** grace

4165   GO11 AG683 LN201 B3:564 K6:485 R4166
ποιμαινω, I SHEPHERD

Mt	2: 6	a ruler who is to **shepherd** my
Lk	17: 7	plowing or **tending sheep** in the
Jn	21:16	Jesus said to him, "**Tend** my
Ac	20:28	to **shepherd** the church of God
1C	9: 7	Or who **tends** a flock and does
1P	5: 2	to **tend** the flock of God that
Ju	1:12	**feeding** themselves. They are
Re	2:27	to **rule** them with an iron rod,
	7:17	throne **will** be their **shepherd,**
	12: 5	who is to **rule** all the nations
	19:15	he will **rule** them with a rod of

4166   GO18 AG684 LN201 B3:564 K6:485
ποιμην, SHEPHERD

Mt	9:36	like sheep without a **shepherd.**
	25:32	a **shepherd** separates the sheep
	26:31	I will strike the **shepherd,**
Mk	6:34	like sheep without a **shepherd;**
	14:27	I will strike the **shepherd,**
Lk	2: 8	there were **shepherds** living in
	2:15	the **shepherds** said to one
	2:18	amazed at what the **shepherds**
	2:20	**shepherds** returned, glorifying
Jn	10: 2	by the gate is the **shepherd** of
	10:11	I am the good **shepherd.** The
	10:11	The good **shepherd** lays down his
	10:12	not the **shepherd** and does not
	10:14	I am the good **shepherd.** I know
	10:16	will be one flock, one **shepherd**
Ep	4:11	some evangelists, some **pastors**
He	13:20	the great **shepherd** of the sheep
1P	2:25	returned to the **shepherd** and

4167   GO5 AG684 LN201 B3:564 K6:499 R4165
ποιμνη, FLOCK

Mt	26:31	the sheep of the **flock** will be
Lk	2: 8	keeping watch over their **flock**
Jn	10:16	So there will be one **flock,** one

1C	9: 7	Or who tends a **flock** and does
	9: 7	does not get any of **its** milk?

4168   GO5 AG684 LN201 B3:564 K6:499 R4167
ποιμνιον, LITTLE FLOCK

Lk	12:32	Do not be afraid, little **flock**
Ac	20:28	over all the **flock,** of which
	20:29	you, not sparing the **flock.**
1P	5: 2	to tend the **flock** of God that
	5: 3	but be examples to the **flock.**

4169   GO33 AG684 LN201
ποιος, WHAT KIND

Mt	19:18	He said to him, "**Which ones?**"
	21:23	**By what** authority are you
	21:24	I will also tell you **by what**
	21:27	I tell you **by what** authority I
	22:36	Teacher, **which** commandment in
	24:42	you do not know on **what** day
	24:43	known in **what** part of the night
Mk	11:28	**what** authority are you doing
	11:29	I will tell you by **what**
	11:33	by **what** authority I am doing
	12:28	**Which** commandment is the first
Lk	5:19	but finding no **way** to bring him
	6:32	**what** credit is that to you? For
	6:33	**what** credit is that to you? For
	6:34	**what** credit is that to you?
	12:39	known at **what** hour the thief
	20: 2	by **what** authority are you doing
	20: 8	by **what** authority I am doing
	24:19	He asked them, "**What** things?"
Jn	10:32	For **which** of these are you
	12:33	indicate the **kind** of death he
	18:32	indicated the **kind** of death he
	21:19	the **kind** of death by which he
Ac	4: 7	By **what** power or by what name
	4: 7	By what power or by **what** name
	7:49	**What kind** of house will you
	23:34	asked **what** province he belonged
Ro	3:27	By **what** law? By that of works?
1C	15:35	With **what kind** of body do they
Ja	4:14	**What** is your life? For you are
1P	1:11	person or **time** that the Spirit
	2:20	**what** credit is that? But if you
Re	3: 3	you will not know at **what** hour

4170   GO7 AG685 LN202 B3:958 K6:502 R4171
πολεμεω, I WAR

Ja	4: 2	**engage** in disputes . . . **conflicts**

Re	2:16	**make war** against them with the
	12: 7	Michael and his angels **fought**
	12: 7	dragon and his angels **fought**
	13: 4	who can **fight** against it?
	17:14	they will **make war** on the Lamb,
	19:11	he judges and **makes war.**

4171 GO18 AG685 LN202 B3:958 K6:502

πολεμος, WAR

Mt	24: 6	And you will hear of **wars** and
	24: 6	rumors of **wars;** see that you
Mk	13: 7	When you hear of **wars** and
	13: 7	rumors of **wars,** do not be
Lk	14:31	going out to wage **war** against
	21: 9	When you hear of **wars** and
1C	14: 8	who will get ready for **battle?**
He	11:34	became mighty in **war,** put
Ja	4: 1	Those **conflicts** and disputes
Re	9: 7	like horses equipped for **battle**
	9: 9	with horses rushing into **battle**
	11: 7	make **war** on them and conquer
	12: 7	And **war** broke out in heaven;
	12:17	went off to make **war** on the
	13: 7	allowed to make **war** on the
	16:14	assemble them for **battle** on the
	19:19	make **war** against the rider on
	20: 8	gather them for **battle;** they

4172 GO162 AG685 LN202 B2:801 K6:516

πολις, CITY

Mt	2:23	he made his home in a **town**
	4: 5	took him to the holy **city** and
	5:14	A **city** built on a hill cannot
	5:35	it is the **city** of the great
	8:33	on going into the **town,** they
	8:34	Then the whole **town** came out
	9: 1	sea and came to his own **town.**
	9:35	went about all the **cities** and
	10: 5	enter no **town** of the Samaritans
	10:11	Whatever **town** or village you
	10:14	as you leave that house or **town**
	10:15	of judgment than for that **town.**
	10:23	persecute you in one **town,** flee
	10:23	gone through all the **towns** of
	11: 1	his message in their **cities.**
	11:20	reproach the **cities** in which
	12:25	no **city** or house divided
	14:13	him on foot from the **towns.**
	21:10	the whole **city** was in turmoil,

	21:17	went out of the **city** to Bethany
	21:18	when he returned to the **city,**
	22: 7	and burned their **city.**
	23:34	and pursue from **town** to town,
	23:34	and pursue from town to **town,**
	26:18	He said, "Go into the **city** to a
	27:53	entered the holy **city** and
	28:11	went into the **city** and told the
Mk	1:33	And the whole **city** was gathered
	1:45	go into a **town** openly, but
	5:14	told it in the **city** and in the
	6:33	from all the **towns** and arrived
	6:56	villages or **cities** or farms,
	11:19	disciples went out of the **city.**
	14:13	Go into the **city,** and a man
	14:16	went to the **city,** and found
Lk	1:26	by God to a **town** in Galilee
	1:39	with haste to a Judean **town** in
	2: 3	All went to their own **towns** to
	2: 4	Joseph also went from the **town**
	2: 4	to the **city** of David called
	2:11	born this day in the **city** of
	2:39	to their own **town** of Nazareth.
	4:29	drove him out of the **town,** and
	4:29	on which their **town** was built,
	4:31	a **city** in Galilee, and was
	4:43	to the other **cities** also; for I
	5:12	he was in one of the **cities,**
	7:11	he went to a **town** called Nain,
	7:12	gate of the **town,** a man who had
	7:12	was a large crowd from the **town**
	7:37	And a woman in the **city,** who
	8: 1	he went on through **cities** and
	8: 4	people from **town** after town
	8:27	man of the **city** who had demons
	8:34	told it in the **city** and in the
	8:39	proclaiming throughout the **city**
	9: 5	as you are leaving that **town**
	9:10	withdrew privately to a **city**
	10: 1	to every **town** and place where
	10: 8	Whenever you enter a **town** and
	10:10	But whenever you enter a **town**
	10:11	Even the dust of your **town**
	10:12	for Sodom than for that **town.**
	13:22	Jesus went through one **town** and
	14:21	lanes of the **town** and bring in
	18: 2	In a certain **city** there was a
	18: 3	In that **city** there was a widow

19:17	take charge of ten **cities.**	
19:19	and you, rule over five **cities.**	
19:41	he came near and saw the **city**	
22:10	when you have entered the **city**	
23:19	had taken place in the **city,**	
23:51	He came from the Jewish **town** of	
24:49	stay here in the **city** until you	
Jn 1:44	Bethsaida, the **city** of Andrew	
4: 5	So he came to a Samaritan **city**	
4: 8	disciples had gone to the **city**	
4:28	jar and went back to the **city.**	
4:30	They left the **city** and were on	
4:39	Many Samaritans from that **city**	
11:54	from there to a **town** called	
19:20	crucified was near the **city;**	
Ac 4:27	For in this **city,** in fact, both	
5:16	gather from the **towns** around	
7:58	dragged him out of the **city** and	
8: 5	Philip went down to the **city** of	
8: 8	was great joy in that **city.**	
8: 9	practiced magic in the **city** and	
8:40	the good news to all the **towns**	
9: 6	But get up and enter the **city,**	
10: 9	and approaching the **city,** Peter	
11: 5	I was in the **city** of Joppa	
12:10	iron gate leading into the **city**	
13:44	almost the whole **city** gathered	
13:50	and the leading men of the **city**	
14: 4	But the residents of the **city**	
14: 6	**cities** of Lycaonia, and to the	
14:13	was just outside the **city,**	
14:19	dragged him out of the **city,**	
14:20	got up and went into the **city.**	
14:21	the good news to that **city** and	
15:21	For in every **city,**	
15:36	believers in every **city** where	
16: 4	As they went from **town** to town,	
16:12	which is a leading **city** of the	
16:12	We remained in this **city** for	
16:14	was from the **city** of Thyatira	
16:20	men are disturbing our **city;**	
16:39	asked them to leave the **city.**	
17: 5	formed a mob and set the **city**	
17:16	see that the **city** was full of	
18:10	many in this **city** who are my	
19:29	The **city** was filled with the	
19:35	does not know that the **city** of	
20:23	testifies to me in every **city**	

21: 5	escorted us outside the **city.**	
21:29	Ephesian with him in the **city,**	
21:30	Then all the **city** was aroused,	
21:39	a citizen of an important **city;**	
22: 3	but brought up in this **city** at	
24:12	or throughout the **city.**	
25:23	prominent men of the **city.**	
26:11	them even to foreign **cities.**	
27: 8	Fair Havens, near the **city** of	
Ro 16:23	the **city** treasurer, and our	
2C 11:26	Gentiles, danger in the **city,**	
11:32	guarded the **city** of Damascus in	
Ti 1: 5	appoint elders in every **town,**	
He 11:10	he looked forward to the **city**	
11:16	he has prepared a **city** for them	
12:22	to the **city** of the living God,	
13:14	here we have no lasting **city,**	
Ja 4:13	such a **town** and spend a year	
2P 2: 6	and if by turning the **cities**	
Ju 1: 7	surrounding **cities,** which, in	
Re 3:12	the name of the **city** of my God,	
11: 2	trample over the holy **city** for	
11: 8	street of the great **city** that	
11:13	and a tenth of the **city** fell;	
14:20	trodden outside the **city,** and	
16:19	The great **city** was split into	
16:19	the **cities** of the nations fell.	
17:18	is the great **city** that rules	
18:10	Alas, alas, the great **city,**	
18:10	Babylon, the mighty **city!**	
18:16	Alas, alas, the great **city,**	
18:18	city was like the great **city?**	
18:19	alas, the great **city,** where all	
18:21	violence Babylon the great **city**	
20: 9	saints and the beloved **city.**	
21: 2	And I saw the holy **city,** the	
21:10	me the holy **city** Jerusalem	
21:14	And the wall of the **city** has	
21:15	measure the **city** and its gates	
21:16	The **city** lies foursquare, its	
21:16	he measured the **city** with his	
21:18	while the **city** is pure gold,	
21:19	wall of the **city** are adorned	
21:21	the street of the **city** is pure	
21:23	And the **city** has no need of sun	
22:14	may enter the **city** by the gates	
22:19	and in the holy **city,** which are	

4173 ᴳᴼ2 ᴬᴳ686 ᴸᴺ202 ᴮ2:801 ᴿ4172,757
πολιταρχης, CITY RULERS

Ac   17: 6   before the **city authorities,**
     17: 8   people and the **city officials**

4174 ᴳᴼ2 ᴬᴳ686 ᴸᴺ202 ᴮ2:801 ᴷ6:516 ᴿ4177
πολιτεια, CITIZENSHIP

Ac   22:28   money to get my **citizenship.**
Ep   2:12   aliens from the **commonwealth** of

4175 ᴳᴼ1 ᴬᴳ686 ᴸᴺ202 ᴮ2:801 ᴷ6:516 ᴿ4176
πολιτευμα, CITIZENSHIP

Ph   3:20   our **citizenship** is in heaven,

4176 ᴳᴼ2 ᴬᴳ686 ᴸᴺ202 ᴮ2:801 ᴷ6:516 ᴿ4177
πολιτευομαι, I AM A CITIZEN

Ac   23: 1   **I have lived my life** with a
Ph   1:27   Only, **live your life** in a

4177 ᴳᴼ4 ᴬᴳ686 ᴸᴺ202 ᴮ2:801 ᴷ6:516 ᴿ4172
πολιτης, CITIZEN

Lk   15:15   one of the **citizens** of that
     19:14   But the **citizens** of his country
Ac   21:39   a **citizen** of an important city;
He   8:11   shall not teach one **another** or

4178 ᴳᴼ18 ᴬᴳ686 ᴸᴺ202
πολλακις, FREQUENTLY

Mt   17:15   he **often** falls into the fire
     17:15   falls into the fire and **often**
Mk   5: 4   he had **often** been restrained
     9:22   It has **often** cast him into the
Jn   18: 2   because Jesus **often** met there
Ac   26:11   By punishing them **often** in all
Ro   1:13   that I have **often** intended to
2C   8:22   whom we have **often** tested and
     11:23   floggings, and **often** near death
     11:26   on **frequent** journeys, in danger
     11:27   through **many** a sleepless night,
     11:27   **often** without food, cold and
Ph   3:18   I have **often** told you of them,
2Ti   1:16   because he **often** refreshed me
He   6: 7   rain falling on it **repeatedly,**
     9:25   **again and again,** as the high
     9:26   suffer **again and again** since
     10:11   offering **again and again** the

4179 ᴳᴼ1 ᴬᴳ686 ᴸᴺ202
πολλαπλασιων, MANY TIMES

Lk   18:30   **very much more** in this age, and

4180 ᴳᴼ1 ᴬᴳ687 ᴸᴺ202 ᴷ6:545 ᴿ4183,3056
πολυλογια, MANY WORDS

Mt   6: 7   because of their **many words.**

4181 ᴳᴼ1 ᴬᴳ687 ᴸᴺ202 ᴿ4183,3313
πολυμερως, IN MANY PARTS

He   1: 1   ancestors in **many** and various

4182 ᴳᴼ1 ᴬᴳ687 ᴸᴺ202 ᴷ6:485
πολυποικιλος, MUCH VARIETY

Ep   3:10   in its **rich variety** might now

4183 ᴳᴼ418 ᴬᴳ687 ᴸᴺ202 ᴮ1:94 ᴷ6:536
πολυς, MUCH [MULTIPLE OCCURRENCES]

4184 ᴳᴼ1 ᴬᴳ689 ᴸᴺ202 ᴮ2:598 ᴷ7:548 ᴿ4183,4698
πολυσπλαγχνος, MUCH AFFECTIONED

Ja   5:11   how the Lord is **compassionate**

4185 ᴳᴼ3 ᴬᴳ690 ᴸᴺ202 ᴮ3:388
πολυτελης, MUCH COST

Mk   14: 3   alabaster jar of **very costly**
1Ti   2: 9   pearls, or **expensive** clothes,
1P   3: 4   spirit, which is **very precious**

4186 ᴳᴼ1 ᴬᴳ690 ᴸᴺ202 ᴿ4183,5092
πολυτιμος, MUCH VALUE

Mt   13:46   one pearl of **great value,** he
Jn   12: 3   Mary took a pound of **costly**
1P   1: 7   being **more precious** than gold

4187 ᴳᴼ1 ᴬᴳ690 ᴸᴺ202 ᴿ4183,5158
πολυτροπως, IN MANY WAYS

He   1: 1   in many and **various ways** by the

4188 ᴳᴼ2 ᴬᴳ690 ᴸᴺ202 ᴮ2:274 ᴷ6:145
πομα, DRINK

1C   10: 4   drank the same spiritual **drink.**
He   9:10   deal only with food and **drink**

4189 ᴳᴼ7 ᴬᴳ690 ᴸᴺ202 ᴮ1:564 ᴷ6:562 ᴿ4190
πονηρια, EVIL

Mt   22:18   aware of their **malice,** said,
Mk   7:22   adultery, avarice, **wickedness,**
Lk   11:39   full of greed and **wickedness.**
Ac   3:26   of you from your **wicked** ways.
Ro   1:29   **wickedness, evil,** covetousness,
1C   5: 8   the yeast of malice and **evil,**
Ep   6:12   the spiritual forces of **evil** in

4190   ᴳᴼ78 ᴬᴳ690 ᴸᴺ202 ᴮ1:564 ᴷ6:546
πονηρός, EVIL

Mt	5:11	utter all kinds of **evil** against
	5:37	this comes from the **evil** one.
	5:39	Do not resist an **evil**doer. But
	5:45	makes his sun rise on the **evil**
	6:13	but rescue us from the **evil** one
	6:23	but if your eye is **unhealthy,**
	7:11	If you then, who are **evil,** know
	7:17	the bad tree bears **bad** fruit.
	7:18	A good tree cannot bear **bad**
	9: 4	Why do you think **evil** in your
	12:34	when you are **evil?** For out of
	12:35	**evil** person brings evil things
	12:35	the evil person brings **evil**
	12:35	evil things out of an **evil**
	12:39	But he answered them, "An **evil**
	12:45	seven other spirits more **evil**
	12:45	also with this **evil** generation.
	13:19	the **evil** one comes and snatches
	13:38	the children of the **evil** one,
	13:49	separate the **evil** from the
	15:19	For out of the heart come **evil**
	16: 4	An **evil** and adulterous
	18:32	You **wicked** slave! I forgave
	20:15	Or are you **envious** because I am
	22:10	both good and **bad;** so the
	25:26	You **wicked** and lazy slave!
Mk	7:22	licentiousness, **envy,** slander,
	7:23	All these **evil** things come from
Lk	3:19	the **evil** things that Herod had
	6:22	and **defame** you on account of
	6:35	the ungrateful and the **wicked.**
	6:45	the **evil** person out of evil
	6:45	the evil person out of **evil**
	6:45	evil treasure produces **evil;**
	7:21	and **evil** spirits, and had given
	8: 2	cured of **evil** spirits and
	11:13	If you then, who are **evil,**
	11:26	seven other spirits more **evil**
	11:29	This generation is an **evil**
	11:34	but if it is **not healthy,** your
	19:22	you **wicked** slave!
Jn	3:19	because their deeds were **evil.**
	7: 7	it that its works are **evil.**
	17:15	protect them from the **evil** one.
Ac	17: 5	with the help of some **ruffians**
	18:14	crime or **serious** villainy, I

	19:12	**evil** spirits came out of them.
	19:13	over those who had **evil** spirits
	19:15	But the **evil** spirit said to
	19:16	Then the man with the **evil**
	25:18	him with any of the **crimes** that
	28:21	spoken anything **evil** about you.
Ro	12: 9	hate what is **evil,** hold fast to
1C	5:13	Drive out the **wicked** person
Ga	1: 4	us free from the present **evil**
Ep	5:16	days, because the days are **evil**
	6:13	withstand on that **evil** day, and
	6:16	flaming arrows of the **evil** one.
Co	1:21	in mind, doing **evil** deeds,
1Th	5:22	abstain from every form of **evil**
2Th	3: 2	rescued from wicked and **evil**
	3: 3	and guard you from the **evil** one.
1Ti	6: 4	slander, **base** suspicions,
2Ti	3:13	But **wicked** people and impostors
	4:18	rescue me from every **evil**
He	3:12	none of you may have an **evil,**
	10:22	sprinkled clean from an **evil**
Ja	2: 4	become judges with **evil**
	4:16	all such boasting is **evil.**
1J	2:13	you have conquered the **evil** one
	2:14	you have overcome the **evil** one.
	3:12	from the **evil** one and murdered
	3:12	Because his own deeds were **evil**
	5:18	**evil** one does not touch them.
	5:19	under the power of the **evil** one
2J	1:11	participate in the **evil** deeds
3J	1:10	spreading **false** charges against
Re	16: 2	a foul and **painful** sore came on

4192   ᴳᴼ4 ᴬᴳ691 ᴸᴺ203 ᴮ1:262
πόνος, PAIN

Co	4:13	he has **worked** hard for you and
Re	16:10	gnawed their tongues in **agony,**
	16:11	because of their **pains** and
	21: 4	mourning and crying and **pain**

4193   ᴳᴼ1 ᴬᴳ691 ᴸᴺ203
Ποντικός, PONTUS

Ac	18: 2	Aquila, a native of **Pontus,** who

4194   ᴳᴼ3 ᴬᴳ691 ᴸᴺ203
Πόντιος, PONTIUS

Lk	3: 1	**Pontius** Pilate was governor of
Ac	4:27	Herod and **Pontius** Pilate, with
1Ti	6:13	testimony before **Pontius** Pilate

4195   GO2 AG691 LN203
πоντος, OF PONTUS
Ac   2: 9   and Cappadocia, **Pontus** and Asia
1P   1: 1   Dispersion in **Pontus,** Galatia,

4196   GO2 AG692 LN203
ποπλιος, POPLIUS (PUBLIUS)
Ac   28: 7   named **Publius,** who received us
      28: 8   the father of **Publius** lay sick

4197   GO2 AG692 LN203 R4198
πορεια, JOURNEY
Lk   13:22   teaching as he made his **way** to
Ja   1:11   the midst of a **busy life,** they

4198   GO153 AG692 LN203 B3:945 K6:566
πορευομαι, I TRAVEL
Mt   2: 8   **Go** and search diligently for
       2: 9   they **set** out; and there, ahead
       2:20   **go** to the land of Israel, for
       8: 9   '**Go,**' and he goes, and to
       8: 9   '**Go,**' and he **goes,** and to
       9:13   **Go** and learn what this means,
      10: 6   but **go** rather to the lost sheep
      10: 7   As you **go,** proclaim the good
      11: 4   **Go** and tell John what you hear
      11: 7   As they **went** away, Jesus began
      12: 1   At that time Jesus **went** through
      12:45   Then it **goes** and brings along
      17:27   **go** to the sea and cast a hook;
      18:12   **go** in search of the one that
      19:15   hands on them and **went** on his
      21: 2   saying to them, "**Go** into the
      21: 6   The disciples **went** and did as
      22: 9   **Go** therefore into the main
      22:15   Then the Pharisees **went** and
      24: 1   **was going** away, his disciples
      25: 9   better **go** to the dealers and
      25:16   received the five talents **went**
      25:41   **depart** from me into the eternal
      26:14   Judas Iscariot, **went** to the
      27:66   So they **went** with the guard and
      28: 7   Then **go** quickly and tell his
      28:11   While they **were going,** some of
      28:16   Now the eleven disciples **went**
      28:19   **Go** therefore and make disciples
Mk   16:10   She **went** out and told those who
      16:12   as they **were walking** into the
      16:15   And he said to them, "**Go** into
Lk   1: 6   **living** blamelessly according to

1:39   Mary set out and **went** with
2: 3   All **went** to their own towns to
2:41   Now every year his parents **went**
4:30   the midst of them and **went** on
4:42   he departed and **went** into a
4:42   prevent him from **leaving** them.
5:24   up and take your bed and **go** to
7: 6   And Jesus **went** with them, but
7: 8   '**Go,**' and he goes, and to
7: 8   '**Go,**' and he **goes,** and to
7:11   Soon afterwards he **went** to a
7:22   And he answered them, "**Go** and
7:50   Your faith has saved you; **go**
8:14   but as they **go** on their way,
8:48   has made you well; **go** in peace.
9:12   so that they may **go** into the
9:13   unless we are to **go** and buy
9:51   set his face to **go** to Jerusalem
9:52   On their **way** they entered a
9:53   face was **set** toward Jerusalem.
9:56   Then they **went** on to another
9:57   As they **were going** along the
10:37   Jesus said to him, "**Go** and do
10:38   Now as they **went** on their way,
11: 5   you **go** to him at midnight and
11:26   Then it **goes** and brings seven
13:31   **Get** away from here, for Herod
13:32   He said to them, "**Go** and tell
13:33   I must **be on my way,** because it
14:10   **go** and sit down at the lowest
14:19   and I **am going** to try them out;
14:31   Or what king, **going** out to wage
15: 4   **go** after the one that is lost
15:15   So he **went** and hired himself
15:18   I will get up and **go** to my
16:30   but if someone **goes** to them
17:11   Jesus **was going** through the
17:14   **Go** and show yourselves to the
17:19   Get up and **go** on your way;
19:12   So he said, "A nobleman **went** to
19:28   After he had said this, he **went**
19:36   As he **rode** along, people kept
21: 8   time is near!' Do not **go** after
22: 8   **Go** and prepare the Passover
22:22   For the Son of Man **is going** as
22:33   Lord, I am ready **to go** with
22:39   He came out and **went,** as was
24:13   **were going** to a village called
24:28   to which they **were going,** he

24:28   ahead as if he **were going** on.

Jn   4:50   Jesus said to him, **"Go;** your
4:50   Jesus spoke to him and **started**
7:35   does this man intend to **go** that
7:35   Does he intend to **go** to the
7:53   Then each of them **went** home,
8: 1   while Jesus **went** to the Mount
8:11   **Go** your way, and from now on do
10: 4   he **goes** ahead of them, and the
11:11   but I **am going** there to awaken
14: 2   told you that I **go** to prepare
14: 3   And if I **go** and prepare a place
14:12   because I **am going** to the
14:28   would rejoice that I **am going**
16: 7   if I **go,** I will send him to you
16:28   leaving the world and **am going**
20:17   But **go** to my brothers and say

Ac   1:10   While he **was going** and they
1:11   same way as you saw him **go** into
1:25   Judas turned aside to **go** to his
5:20   **Go,** stand in the temple and
5:41   As they **left** the council, they
8:26   Get up and **go** toward the south
8:27   So he got up and **went.** Now
8:36   As they **were going** along the
8:39   and **went** on his way rejoicing.
9: 3   Now as he **was going** along and
9:11   Get up and **go** to the street
9:15   **Go,** for he is an instrument
9:31   **Living** in the fear of the Lord
10:20   Now get up, go down, and **go**
12:17   he left and **went** to another
14:16   all the nations to **follow** their
16: 7   attempted to **go** into Bithynia,
16:16   One day, as we **were going** to
16:36   word to let you **go;** therefore
17:14   sent Paul away **to** the coast,
18: 6   From now on I **will go** to the
19:21   and then to **go** on to Jerusalem.
20: 1   farewell, he left **for** Macedonia
20:22   I am **on my way** to Jerusalem,
21: 5   we left and **proceeded** on our
22: 5   and I **went** there in order to
22: 6   While I was **on my way** and
22:10   Get up and **go** to Damascus;
22:21   Then he said to me, '**Go,** for I
23:23   Get ready to **leave** by nine
24:25   **Go** away for the present; when
25:12   to the emperor you **will go.**

25:20   whether he wished **to go** to
26:12   **was traveling** to Damascus with
26:13   around me and my **companions.**
27: 3   him to **go** to his friends to be
28:26   **Go** to this people and say,

Ro   15:24   when I **go** to Spain. For I do
15:25   I **am going** to Jerusalem in a

1C   10:27   disposed to **go,** eat whatever is
16: 4   advisable that I should **go** also
16: 4   go also, they **will accompany** me
16: 6   me on my way, wherever I **go.**

1Ti   1: 3   I was **on my way** to Macedonia,
2Ti   4:10   has deserted me and **gone** to
Ja   4:13   Today or tomorrow we **will go**
1P   3:19   in which also he **went** and made
3:22   who **has gone** into heaven and is
4: 3   **living** in licentiousness,
2P   2:10   especially those who **indulge**
3: 3   scoffing and **indulging** their
Ju   1:11   Woe to them! For they **go** the
1:16   they **indulge** their own lusts;
1:18   **indulging** their own ungodly

4199   GO3   AG693   LN203
πορθεω, I RAVAGE
Ac   9:21   this the man who **made havoc** in
Ga   1:13   and was trying to **destroy** it.
1:23   faith he once tried to **destroy.**

4200   GO2   AG693   LN203
πορισμος, MEANS OF GAIN
1Ti   6: 5   godliness is a means of **gain.**
6: 6   Of course, there is great **gain**

4201   GO1   AG693   LN203
πορκιος, PORCIUS
Ac   24:27   Felix was succeeded by **Porcius**

4202   GO25   AG693   LN203   B1:497   K6:579   R4203
πορνεια, SEXUAL IMMORALITY
Mt   5:32   on the ground of **unchastity,**
15:19   murder, adultery, **fornication,**
19: 9   except for **unchastity,** and
Mk   7:21   **fornication,** theft, murder,
Jn   8:41   We are not **illegitimate**
Ac   15:20   from **fornication** and from
15:29   strangled and from **fornication.**
21:25   strangled and from **fornication.**
1C   5: 1   **sexual immorality** among you,
5: 1   and of a **kind** that is not found

	6:13	not for **fornication** but for the
	6:18	Shun **fornication!** Every sin
	7: 2	cases of **sexual immorality,**
2C	12:21	the impurity, **sexual immorality**
Ga	5:19	obvious: **fornication,** impurity,
Ep	5: 3	But **fornication** and impurity of
Co	3: 5	**fornication,** impurity, passion,
1Th	4: 3	you abstain from **fornication;**
Re	2:21	to repent of her **fornication.**
	9:21	the wrath of her **fornication.**
	17: 2	have committed **fornication,** and
	17: 4	impurities of her **fornication;**
	18: 3	the wrath of her **fornication,**
	19: 2	earth with her **fornication,** and

4203   GO8 AG693 LN203 B1:497 K6:579 R4204
πορνευω, I COMMIT SEXUAL IMMORALITY

1C	6:18	but the **fornicator** sins against
	10: 8	**indulge in sexual immorality** as
	10: 8	of them **did,** and twenty-three
Re	2:14	idols and **practice fornication.**
	2:20	**practice fornication** and to eat
	17: 2	have **committed fornication,** and
	18: 3	**committed fornication** with her,
	18: 9	who **committed fornication** and

4204   GO12 AG693 LN203 B1:497 K6:579 R4205
πορνη, PROSTITUTE

Mt	21:31	**prostitutes** are going into the
	21:32	collectors and the **prostitutes**
Lk	15:30	property with **prostitutes,** you
1C	6:15	them members of a **prostitute?**
	6:16	united to a **prostitute** becomes
He	11:31	By faith Rahab the **prostitute**
Ja	2:25	was not Rahab the **prostitute**
Re	17: 1	great **whore** who is seated on
	17: 5	mother of **whores** and of earth's
	17:15	where the **whore** is seated, are
	17:16	beast will hate the **whore;** they
	19: 2	he has judged the great **whore**

4205   GO10 AG693 LN203 B1:497 K6:579
πορνος, SEXUALLY IMMORAL

1C	5: 9	with **sexually immoral persons**
	5:10	not at all meaning the **immoral**
	5:11	**sexually immoral** or greedy, or
	6: 9	**Fornicators,** idolaters,
Ep	5: 5	that no **fornicator** or impure
1Ti	1:10	**fornicators,** sodomites, slave
He	12:16	an **immoral** and godless person,

	13: 4	God will judge **fornicators** and
Re	21: 8	the **fornicators,** the sorcerers,
	22:15	**fornicators** and murderers and

4206   GO4 AG693 LN203 B2:53
πορρω, FAR

Mt	15: 8	their hearts are **far** from me;
Mk	7: 6	their hearts are **far** from me;
Lk	14:32	while the other is still **far**
	24:28	ahead as if he were going **on.**

4207   GO2 AG693 LN203 R4206
πορρωθεν, FROM FAR

| Lk | 17:12 | him. Keeping their **distance,** |
| He | 11:13 | but **from a distance** they saw |

4209   GO4 AG694 LN203 B1:205
πορφυρα, PURPLE

Mk	15:17	clothed him in a **purple** cloak;
	15:20	they stripped him of the **purple**
Lk	16:19	dressed in **purple** and fine
Re	18:12	**purple,** silk and scarlet, all

4210   GO4 AG694 LN203 B1:205 R4209
πορφυρους, PURPLE

Jn	19: 2	dressed him in a **purple** robe.
	19: 5	crown of thorns and the **purple**
Re	17: 4	The woman was clothed in **purple**
	18:16	in fine linen, in **purple** and

4211   GO1 AG694 LN203 R4209,4453
πορφυροπωλις, PURPLE-SELLER

| Ac | 16:14 | and a **dealer in purple cloth.** |

4212   GO3 AG694 LN203
ποσακις, HOW OFTEN

Mt	18:21	**how often** should I forgive?
	23:37	**How often** have I desired to
Lk	13:34	**How often** have I desired to

4213   GO3 AG694 LN203 B2:274 K6:135 R4095
ποσις, DRINK

Jn	6:55	food and my blood is true **drink**
Ro	14:17	of God is not food and **drink**
Co	2:16	matters of food and **drink** or of

4214   GO27 AG694 LN203
ποσος, HOW MUCH

| Mt | 6:23 | in you is darkness, **how great** |
| | 7:11 | **how much** more will your Father |

	10:25	**how much** more will they malign
	12:12	**How much** more valuable is a
	15:34	Jesus asked them, **"How many**
	16: 9	**how many** baskets you gathered?
	16:10	**how many** baskets you gathered?
	27:13	Do you not hear **how many**
Mk	6:38	**How many** loaves have you? Go
	8: 5	**How many** loaves do you have?
	8:19	**how many** baskets full of broken
	8:20	**how many** baskets full of broken
	9:21	**How long** has this been
	15: 4	you no answer? See **how many**
Lk	11:13	**how much** more will the heavenly
	12:24	Of **how much** more value are you
	12:28	**how much** more will he clothe
	15:17	**How many** of my father's hired
	16: 5	**How much** do you owe my master?
	16: 7	'And **how much** do you owe?'
Ac	21:20	You see, brother, **how many**
Ro	11:12	**how much** more will their full
	11:24	**how much** more will these
2C	7:11	For see **what** earnestness this
Pm	1:16	especially to me but **how much**
He	9:14	**how much** more will the blood of
	10:29	**How much** worse punishment do

4215   GO17 AG694 LN203 B3:985 K6:595
ποταμος, RIVER

Mt	3: 6	baptized by him in the **river**
	7:25	The rain fell, the **floods** came
	7:27	and the **floods**
Mk	1: 5	baptized by him in the **river**
Lk	6:48	when a flood arose, the **river**
	6:49	When the **river** burst against it
Jn	7:38	heart shall flow **rivers** of
Ac	16:13	outside the gate by the **river,**
2C	11:26	in danger from **rivers,** danger
Re	8:10	fell on a third of the **rivers**
	9:14	at the great **river** Euphrates.
	12:15	poured water like a **river** after
	12:16	swallowed the **river** that the
	16: 4	poured his bowl into the **rivers**
	16:12	on the great **river** Euphrates,
	22: 1	angel showed me the **river** of
	22: 2	On either side of the **river,**

4216   GO1 AG694 LN203 K6:607
ποταμοφορητος, CARRIED AWAY
   BY RIVER

Re	12:15	**sweep** her away **with** the **flood.**

4217   GO7 AG694 LN203
ποταπος, WHAT SORT

Mt	8:27	**What sort of** man is this, that
Mk	13: 1	**what large** stones and what
	13: 1	large stones and **what large**
Lk	1:29	pondered **what sort of** greeting
	7:39	**what kind of** woman this is who
2P	3:11	**what sort of** persons ought you
1J	3: 1	See **what** love the Father has

4218   GO29 AG695 LN204
ποτε, THEN, ONCE, FORMERLY

Lk	22:32	**when** once you have turned back,
Jn	9:13	man who had **formerly** been blind
Ro	1:10	I may somehow **at last** succeed
	7: 9	I was **once** alive apart from the
	11:30	as you were **once** disobedient to
1C	9: 7	Who **at any time** pays the
Ga	1:13	of my **earlier** life in Judaism.
	1:23	The one who **formerly** was
	1:23	proclaiming the faith he **once**
	2: 6	(what they **actually** were makes
Ep	2: 2	in which you **once** lived,
	2: 3	All of us **once** lived among them
	2:11	remember that **at one time** you
	2:13	you who **once** were far off have
	5: 8	For **once** you were darkness, but
	5:29	For no one **ever** hates his own
Ph	4:10	now **at last** you have revived
Co	1:21	And you who were **once** estranged
	3: 7	the ways you also **once** followed
1Th	2: 5	we **never** came with words of
Ti	3: 3	For we ourselves were **once**
Pm	1:11	**Formerly** he was useless to you,
He	1: 5	did God **ever** say, "You are my
	1:13	has he **ever** said, "Sit at my
1P	2:10	**Once** you were not a people, but
	3: 5	It was in this way **long ago**
	3:20	who in **former times** did not
2P	1:10	if you do this, you will **never**
	1:21	because no prophecy **ever** came

4219   GO19 AG695 LN203
ποτε, WHEN

Mt	17:17	**how much** longer must I be with
	17:17	**How much** longer must I put up
	24: 3	Tell us, **when** will this be,
	25:37	Lord, **when** was it that we saw
	25:38	And **when** was it that we saw you
	25:39	And **when** was it that we saw you

	25:44	Lord, **when** was it that we saw
Mk	9:19	**how much** longer must I be among
	9:19	**How much** longer must I put up
	13: 4	Tell us, **when** will this be,
	13:33	you do not know **when** the time
	13:35	you do not know **when** the master
Lk	9:41	**how much** longer must I be with
	12:36	waiting for their master **to**
	17:20	**when** the kingdom of God was
	21: 7	Teacher, **when** will this be,
Jn	6:25	Rabbi, **when** did you come here?
	10:24	**How long** will you keep us in
Re	6:10	**how long** will it be before you

4220   GO1   AG695   LN204
ποτερος, WHETHER
Jn   7:17   will of God will know **whether**

4221   GO31   AG695   LN204   B2:274   K6:148
ποτηριον, CUP

Mt	10:42	and whoever gives even a **cup**
	20:22	Are you able to drink the **cup**
	20:23	You will indeed drink my **cup,**
	23:25	clean the outside of the **cup**
	23:26	clean the inside of the **cup,** so
	26:27	Then he took a **cup,** and after
	26:39	let this **cup** pass from me; yet
Mk	7: 4	the washing of **cups,** pots, and
	9:41	gives you a **cup** of water to
	10:38	Are you able to drink the **cup**
	10:39	The **cup** that I drink you will
	14:23	Then he took a **cup,** and after
	14:36	remove this **cup** from me; yet,
Lk	11:39	clean the outside of the **cup**
	22:17	Then he took a **cup,** and after
	22:20	he did the same with the **cup**
	22:20	This **cup** that is poured out
	22:42	remove this **cup** from me; yet,
Jn	18:11	Am I not to drink the **cup** that
1C	10:16	The **cup** of blessing that we
	10:21	You cannot drink the **cup** of the
	10:21	the **cup** of demons. You cannot
	11:25	In the same way he took the **cup**
	11:25	This **cup** is the new covenant
	11:26	this bread and drink the **cup,**
	11:27	drinks the **cup** of the Lord in
	11:28	the bread and drink of the **cup.**
Re	14:10	poured unmixed into the **cup** of
	16:19	gave her the wine-**cup** of the

| | 17: 4 | in her hand a golden **cup** full |
| | 18: 6 | draught for her in the **cup** she |

4222   GO15   AG695   LN204   B2:274   K6:159
ποτιζω, I GIVE DRINK

Mt	10:42	and whoever **gives** even a cup of
	25:35	you **gave** me something **to drink,**
	25:37	and **gave** you something **to drink**
	25:42	you **gave** me nothing **to drink,**
	27:48	and **gave** it to him **to drink.**
Mk	9:41	**gives** you a cup . . . **to drink**
	15:36	**gave** it to him **to drink,** saying
Lk	13:15	lead it away to **give** it **water?**
Ro	12:20	**give** them something **to drink**
1C	3: 2	I **fed** you with milk, not solid
	3: 6	I planted, Apollos **watered,** but
	3: 7	nor the one who **waters** is
	3: 8	one who **waters** have a common
	12:13	we **were** all **made to drink** of
Re	14: 8	She **has made** all nations **drink**

4223   GO1   AG696   LN204
ποτιολοι, POTIOLOI (PUTEOLI)
Ac   28:13   second day we came to **Puteoli.**

4224   GO1   AG696   LN204   B2:274   K6:145
ποτος, DRINKING
1P   4: 3   **carousing,** and lawless idolatry

4225   GO4   AG696   LN204
που, WHERE

Ac	27:29	Fearing that we **might** run on
Ro	4:19	(for he was **about** a hundred
He	2: 6	testified **somewhere,** "What are
	4: 4	For **in one place** it speaks

4226   GO48   AG696   LN204
που, WHERE

Mt	2: 2	asking, **"Where** is the child who
	2: 4	he inquired of them **where** the
	8:20	but the Son of Man has no**where**
	26:17	**Where** do you want us to make
Mk	14:12	**Where** do you want us to go and
	14:14	**Where** is my guest room where I
	15:47	saw **where** the body was laid.
Lk	8:25	He said to them, **"Where** is your
	9:58	the Son of Man has no**where** to
	12:17	have no **place** to store my crops
	17:17	But the other nine, **where** are
	17:37	Then they asked him, **"Where,**

	22: 9	They asked him, **"Where** do you		18: 8	two hands or two **feet** and to be
	22:11	**Where** is the guest room, where		22:13	Bind him hand and **foot,** and
Jn	1:38	**where** are you staying?		22:44	your enemies under your **feet**
	1:39	They came and saw **where** he was		28: 9	took hold of his **feet,** and
	3: 8	where it comes from or **where** it	Mk	5:22	he saw him, fell at his **feet**
	7:11	festival and saying, **"Where** is		6:11	dust that is on your **feet** as a
	7:35	**Where** does this man intend to		7:25	came and bowed down at his **feet**
	8:10	Woman, **where** are they? Has no		9:45	And if your **foot** causes you to
	8:14	**where** I am going, but you do		9:45	than to have two **feet** and to be
	8:14	where I come from or **where** I am		12:36	your enemies under your **feet.**
	8:19	**"Where** is your Father?" Jesus	Lk	1:79	to guide our **feet** into the way
	9:12	They said to him, **"Where** is he?		4:11	dash your **foot** against a stone.
	11:34	He said, **"Where** have you laid		7:38	behind him at his **feet,** weeping
	11:57	who knew **where** Jesus was should		7:38	began to bathe his **feet** with
	12:35	do not know **where** you are going		7:38	kissing his **feet** and anointing
	13:36	Lord, **where** are you going?		7:44	gave me no water for my **feet,**
	14: 5	Lord, we do not know **where** you		7:44	she has bathed my **feet** with her
	16: 5	asks me, **'Where** are you going?'		7:45	has not stopped kissing my **feet**
	20: 2	we do not know **where** they have		7:46	she has anointed my **feet** with
	20:13	I do not know **where** they have		8:35	sitting at the **feet** of Jesus,
	20:15	tell me **where** you have laid him		8:41	He fell at Jesus' **feet** and
Ro	3:27	Then **what** becomes of boasting?		9: 5	shake the dust off your **feet** as
1C	1:20	**Where** is the one who is wise?		10:11	clings to our **feet,** we wipe off
	1:20	**Where** is the scribe? Where is		10:39	who sat at the Lord's **feet** and
	1:20	**Where** is the debater of this		15:22	finger and sandals on his **feet.**
	12:17	**where** would the hearing be? If		17:16	at Jesus' **feet** and thanked him.
	12:17	**where** would the sense of smell		20:43	your enemies your **foot**stool.
	12:19	**where** would the body be?		24:39	Look at my hands and my **feet;**
	15:55	**Where,** O death, is your		24:40	them his hands and his **feet.**
	15:55	**Where,** O death, is your sting?	Jn	11: 2	wiped his **feet** with her hair;
Ga	4:15	**What** has become of the goodwill		11:32	she knelt at his **feet** and said
He	11: 8	not knowing **where** he was going.		11:44	his hands and **feet** bound with
1P	4:18	**what** will become of the ungodly		12: 3	anointed Jesus' **feet,** and wiped
2P	3: 4	**Where** is the promise of his		12: 3	wiped **them** with her hair. The
1J	2:11	does not know **the way** to go,		13: 5	wash the disciples' **feet** and to
Re	2:13	I know **where** you are living,		13: 6	are you going to wash my **feet?**
				13: 8	You will never wash my **feet.**
				13: 9	Lord, not my **feet** only but

4227 GO1 AG696 LN204
πουδης, POUDES (PUDENS)
2Ti 4:21   as do **Pudens** and Linus and

4228 GO93 AG696 LN204 B1:239 K6:624
πους, FOOT

Mt	4: 6	dash your **foot** against a stone.		13:10	except for the **feet,** but is
	5:35	for it is his **foot**stool, or by		13:12	After he had washed their **feet,**
	7: 6	trample them under **foot** and		13:14	have washed your **feet,** you also
	10:14	off the dust from your **feet** as		13:14	to wash one another's **feet.**
	15:30	They put them at his **feet,** and		20:12	head and the other at the **feet.**
	18: 8	If your hand or your **foot**	Ac	2:35	your enemies your **foot**stool.
				4:35	the apostles' **feet,** and it was
				4:37	laid it at the apostles' **feet.**
				5: 2	laid it at the apostles' **feet.**
				5: 9	**feet** of those who have buried
				5:10	**feet** and died. When the young

7: 5	not even a **foot's** length, but
7:33	sandals from your **feet,** for the
7:49	the earth is my **foot**stool. What
7:58	laid their coats at the **feet** of
10:25	falling at his **feet,** worshiped
13:25	of the sandals on his **feet.**
13:51	shook the dust off their **feet**
14: 8	who could not use his **feet** and
14:10	Stand upright on your **feet.**
16:24	fastened their **feet** in the
21:11	bound his own **feet** and hands
22: 3	city at the **feet** of Gamaliel,
26:16	stand on your **feet;** for I have
Ro 3:15	Their **feet** are swift to shed
10:15	How beautiful are the **feet** of
16:20	crush Satan under your **feet.**
1C 12:15	If the **foot** would say, "Because
12:21	the head to the **feet,** "I have
15:25	all his enemies under his **feet.**
15:27	subjection under his **feet.**" But
Ep 1:22	all things under his **feet** and
6:15	As shoes for your **feet** put on
1Ti 5:10	washed the saints' **feet,** helped
He 1:13	a footstool for your **feet**"?
2: 8	all things under their **feet.**
10:13	made a footstool for his **feet.**
12:13	straight paths for your **feet,**
Re 1:15	his **feet** were like burnished
1:17	I fell at his **feet** as though
2:18	whose **feet** are like burnished
3: 9	bow down before your **feet,** and
10: 1	his **legs** like pillars of fire.
10: 2	Setting his right **foot** on the
11:11	they stood on their **feet,** and
12: 1	with the moon under her **feet,**
13: 2	its **feet** were like a bear's,
19:10	Then I fell down at his **feet**
22: 8	down to worship at the **feet** of

4229 GO11 AG697 LN204 B3:1155 K6:638 R4238
πραγμα, PRACTICE

Mt 18:19	agree on earth about **anything**
Lk 1: 1	orderly account of the **events**
Ac 5: 4	contrived this **deed** in your
Ro 16: 2	help her in **whatever** she may
1C 6: 1	When any of you has a **grievance**
2C 7:11	guiltless in the **matter.**
1Th 4: 6	in this **matter,** because the
He 6:18	through two unchangeable **things**

10: 1	true form of these **realities,**
11: 1	conviction of **things** not seen.
Ja 3:16	and wickedness of **every kind.**

4230 GO1 AG697 LN204 B3:1155 K6:640 R4231
πραγματεια, PRACTICE

2Ti 2: 4	entangled in everyday **affairs;**

4231 GO1 AG697 LN204 B3:1155 K6:641 R4229
πραγματευομαι, I PRACTICE TRADE

Lk 19:13	**Do business** with these until I

4232 GO8 AG697 LN204
πραιτωριον, PRAETORIUM

Mt 27:27	governor's **headquarters,** and
Mk 15:16	the governor's **headquarters);**
Jn 18:28	Pilate's **headquarters.** It was
18:28	did not enter the **headquarters,**
18:33	Pilate entered the **headquarters**
19: 9	He entered his **headquarters**
Ac 23:35	guard in Herod's **headquarters.**
Ph 1:13	the whole **imperial guard** and to

4233 GO2 AG697 LN204 B3:1157 K6:642
πρακτωρ, COURT OFFICER

Lk 12:58	hand you over to the **officer,**
12:58	the **officer** throw you in prison

4234 GO6 AG697 LN204 B3:1155 K6:642 R4238
πραξις, PRACTICE

Mt 16:27	everyone for what **has been done**
Lk 23:51	to their plan and **action.** He
Ac 19:18	and disclosed their **practices.**
Ro 8:13	put to death the **deeds** of the
12: 4	members have the same **function,**
Co 3: 9	the old self with its **practices**

4237 GO2 AG698 LN205
πρασια, BLOCK, PLOT, GROUP

Mk 6:40	So they sat down in **groups** of
6:40	So they sat down in **groups** of

4238 GO39 AG698 LN205 B3:1155 K6:632
πρασσω, I PRACTICE

Lk 3:13	**Collect** no more than the
19:23	I **could have collected** it with
22:23	it could be who would **do** this.
23:15	he **has done** nothing to deserve
23:41	what we deserve for our **deeds,**
23:41	this man has **done** nothing wrong

Jn 3:20 For all who **do** evil hate the
    5:29 those who **have done** evil, to
Ac 3:17 you **acted** in ignorance, as did
    5:35 what you propose to **do** to these
    15:29 you **will do** well. Farewell.
    16:28 **Do** not harm yourself, for we
    17: 7 They **are** all **acting** contrary to
    19:19 A number of those who **practiced**
    19:36 to be quiet and **do** nothing rash
    25:11 **have committed** something for
    25:25 But I found that he **had done**
    26: 9 ought to **do** many things against
    26:20 turn to God and **do** deeds
    26:26 this **was** not **done** in a corner.
    26:31 This man **is doing** nothing to
Ro 1:32 that those who **practice** such
    1:32 applaud others who **practice**
    2: 1 you, the judge, **are doing** the
    2: 2 judgment on those who **do** such
    2: 3 when you judge those who **do**
    2:25 if you **obey** the law; but if you
    7:15 For I do not **do** what I want,
    7:19 evil I do not want is what I **do**
    9:11 they had been born or **had done**
    13: 4 But if you **do** what is wrong,
1C 5: 2 so that he who **has done** this
    9:17 For if I **do** this of my own will
2C 5:10 for what **has been done** in the
    12:21 that they have **practiced.**
Ga 5:21 those who **do** such things will
Ep 6:21 what I **am doing,** Tychicus will
Ph 4: 9 **Keep on doing** the things that
1Th 4:11 to **mind** your own **affairs,** and

4238a   GO1 AG698 LN205 B2:256 K5:939
πραυπαθεια, GENTLE PASSION
1Ti 6:11 love, endurance, **gentleness.**

4239   GO4 AG698 LN205 B2:256 K6:645
πραυς, GENTLE
Mt 5: 5 Blessed are the **meek,** for they
    11:29 for I am **gentle** and humble in
    21: 5 **humble,** and mounted on a donkey
1P 3: 4 beauty of a **gentle** and quiet

4240   GO11 AG699 LN205 B2:256 K6:645 R4239
πραυτης, GENTLENESS
1C 4:21 love in a spirit of **gentleness?**
2C 10: 1 appeal to you by the **meekness**
Ga 5:23 **gentleness,** and self-control.

    6: 1 in a spirit of **gentleness.** Take
Ep 4: 2 all humility and **gentleness,**
Co 3:12 kindness, humility, **meekness,**
2Ti 2:25 opponents with **gentleness.** God
Ti 3: 2 and to show every **courtesy** to
Ja 1:21 welcome with **meekness** the
    3:13 works are done with **gentleness**
1P 3:16 yet do it with **gentleness** and

4241   GO7 AG699 LN205 B2:668
πρεπω, IT IS FITTING
Mt 3:15 for it is **proper** for us in this
1C 11:13 is it **proper** for a woman to
Ep 5: 3 as is **proper** among saints.
1Ti 2:10 as is **proper** for women who
Ti 2: 1 teach what is **consistent** with
He 2:10 It was **fitting** that God, for
    7:26 For it was **fitting** that we

4242   GO2 AG699 LN205 B1:192 R4243
πρεσβεια, ENVOY
Lk 14:32 he sends a **delegation** and asks
    19:14 sent a **delegation** after him,

4243   GO2 AG699 LN205 B1:192 K6:681
πρεσβευω, I AM AN ENVOY
2C 5:20 So we **are ambassadors** for
Ep 6:20 for which I **am** an **ambassador** in

4244   GO3 AG699 LN205 B1:192 K6:651 R4245
πρεσβυτεριον, GROUP OF OLDER MEN
Lk 22:66 the **assembly of the elders** of
Ac 22: 5 the whole **council of elders** can
1Ti 4:14 hands by the **council of elders.**

4245   GO66 AG699 LN205 B1:192 K6:651
πρεσβυτερος, OLDER MAN
Mt 15: 2 the tradition of the **elders?**
    16:21 hands of the **elders** and chief
    21:23 chief priests and the **elders**
    26: 3 chief priests and the **elders** of
    26:47 and the **elders** of the people.
    26:57 and the **elders** had gathered.
    27: 1 chief priests and the **elders** of
    27: 3 chief priests and the **elders.**
    27:12 chief priests and **elders,** he
    27:20 chief priests and the **elders**
    27:41 with the scribes and **elders**
    28:12 assembled with the **elders,** they
Mk 7: 3 the tradition of the **elders;**

	7: 5	tradition of the **elders,** but
	8:31	be rejected by the **elders,** the
	11:27	scribes, and the **elders** came to
	14:43	the scribes, and the **elders.**
	14:53	chief priests, the **elders,** and
	15: 1	consultation with the **elders**
Lk	7: 3	he sent some Jewish **elders** to
	9:22	be rejected by the **elders,**
	15:25	Now his **elder** son was in the
	20: 1	scribes came with the **elders**
	22:52	the **elders** who had come for him
Jn	8: 9	beginning with the **elders;** and
Ac	2:17	your **old men** shall dream dreams
	4: 5	next day their rulers, **elders,**
	4: 8	of the people and **elders,**
	4:23	chief priests and the **elders**
	6:12	as well as the **elders** and the
	11:30	sending it to the **elders** by
	14:23	appointed **elders** for them in
	15: 2	the apostles and the **elders.**
	15: 4	the apostles and the **elders,**
	15: 6	The apostles and the **elders** met
	15:22	the apostles and the **elders,**
	15:23	the apostles and the **elders,** to
	16: 4	by the apostles and **elders** who
	20:17	asking the **elders** of the church
	21:18	and all the **elders** were present
	23:14	the chief priests and **elders**
	24: 1	came down with some **elders** and
	25:15	chief priests and the **elders** of
1Ti	5: 1	speak harshly to an **older man,**
	5: 2	to **older women** as mothers, to
	5:17	Let the **elders** who rule well be
	5:19	against an **elder** except on the
Ti	1: 5	and should appoint **elders** in
He	11: 2	Indeed, by faith our **ancestors**
Ja	5:14	They should call for the **elders**
1P	5: 1	I exhort the **elders** among you
	5: 5	the authority of the **elders.**
2J	1: 1	The **elder** to the elect lady and
3J	1: 1	The **elder** to the beloved Gaius,
Re	4: 4	twenty-four **elders,** dressed in
	4:10	the twenty-four **elders** fall
	5: 5	Then one of the **elders** said to
	5: 6	the **elders** a Lamb standing
	5: 8	twenty-four **elders** fell before
	5:11	living creatures and the **elders**
	5:14	And the **elders** fell down and
	7:11	around the **elders** and the four

	7:13	one of the **elders** addressed me,
	11:16	Then the twenty-four **elders** who
	14: 3	creatures and before the **elders**
	19: 4	And the twenty-four **elders** and

4246   ᴳᴼ3   ᴬᴳ700   ᴸᴺ205   ᴮ1:192   ᴷ6:683
πρεσβυτης, OLD MAN

Lk	1:18	For I am an **old man,** and my
Ti	2: 2	the **older men** to be temperate,
Pm	1: 9	do this as an **old man,** and now

4247   ᴳᴼ1   ᴬᴳ700   ᴸᴺ205   ᴮ1:192   ᴿ4246
πρεσβυτις, OLD WOMAN

Ti	2: 3	Likewise, tell the **older women**

4248   ᴳᴼ1   ᴬᴳ700   ᴸᴺ205   ᴮ1:94
πρηνης, HEAD FIRST

Ac	1:18	and falling **headlong,** he burst

4249   ᴳᴼ1   ᴬᴳ701   ᴸᴺ205
πριζω, I SAW

He	11:37	they were **sawn in** two, they

4250   ᴳᴼ13   ᴬᴳ701   ᴸᴺ205
πριν, BEFORE

Mt	1:18	engaged to Joseph, but **before**
	26:34	**before** the cock crows, you will
	26:75	**Before** the cock crows, you
Mk	14:30	**before** the cock crows twice,
	14:72	**Before** the cock crows twice,
Lk	2:26	he would not see death **before**
	22:61	**Before** the cock crows today,
Jn	4:49	Sir, come down **before** my
	8:58	I tell you, **before** Abraham was
	14:29	I have told you this **before** it
Ac	2:20	**before** the coming of the Lord's
	7: 2	Mesopotamia, **before** he lived in
	25:16	hand over anyone **before** the

4251   ᴳᴼ3   ᴬᴳ701   ᴸᴺ205
πρισκα, PRISCA

Ro	16: 3	Greet **Prisca** and Aquila, who
1C	16:19	Aquila and **Prisca,** together
2Ti	4:19	Greet **Prisca** and Aquila, and

4252   ᴳᴼ3   ᴬᴳ701   ᴸᴺ205
πρισκιλλα, PRISCILLA

Ac	18: 2	Italy with his wife **Priscilla,**
	18:18	by **Priscilla** and Aquila. At
	18:26	but when **Priscilla** and Aquila

4253　GO47 AG701 LN205 B3:1172 K6:683
πρo, BEFORE

Mt	5:12	prophets who were **before** you.
	6: 8	you need **before** you ask him.
	8:29	to torment us **before** the time?
	11:10	prepare your way **before** you.
	24:38	For as in those days **before** the
Mk	1: 2	I am sending my messenger **ahead**
Lk	2:21	name given by the angel **before**
	7:27	I am sending my messenger **ahead**
	9:52	And he sent messengers **ahead** of
	10: 1	sent them on **ahead** of him in
	11:38	he did not first wash **before**
	21:12	But **before** all this occurs,
	22:15	with you **before** I suffer;
Jn	1:48	tree **before** Philip called you.
	5: 7	someone else steps down **ahead**
	10: 8	All who came **before** me are
	11:55	Jerusalem **before** the Passover
	12: 1	Six days **before** the Passover
	13: 1	Now **before** the festival of the
	13:19	I tell you this now, **before** it
	17: 5	I had in your presence **before**
	17:24	because you loved me **before** the
Ac	5:36	**For** some time ago Theudas rose
	12: 6	while guards **in front of** the
	12:14	Peter was standing **at the gate.**
	13:24	**before** his coming John had
	14:13	whose temple was just **outside**
	21:38	Egyptian who **recently** stirred
	23:15	away with him **before** he arrives
Ro	16: 7	they were in Christ **before** I
1C	2: 7	decreed **before** the ages for our
	4: 5	pronounce judgment **before** the
2C	12: 2	fourteen years **ago** was caught
Ga	1:17	already apostles **before** me, but
	2:12	for **until** certain people came
	3:23	Now **before** faith came, we were
Ep	1: 4	chose us in Christ **before** the
Co	1:17	He himself is **before** all things
2Ti	1: 9	in Christ Jesus **before** the ages
	4:21	Do your best to come **before**
Ti	1: 2	promised **before** the ages began
He	11: 5	For it was attested **before** he
Ja	5: 9	the Judge is standing **at** the
	5:12	**Above** all, my beloved, do not
1P	1:20	He was destined **before** the
	4: 8	**Above** all, maintain constant
Ju	1:25	**before** all time and now and

4254　GO20 AG702 LN205 K1:130 R4253,71
προαγω, I LEAD BEFORE

Mt	2: 9	**ahead** of them, **went** the star
	14:22	**go on ahead** to the other side,
	21: 9	The crowds that **went ahead** of
	21:31	prostitutes **are going** into the
	26:32	I **will go ahead** of you to
	28: 7	indeed he **is going ahead** of you
Mk	6:45	**go on ahead** to the other side,
	10:32	Jesus **was walking ahead** of them
	11: 9	Then those who **went ahead** and
	14:28	I **will go before** you to Galilee
	16: 7	he **is going ahead** of you to
Lk	18:39	Those who **were in front** sternly
Ac	12: 6	was going **to bring** him **out,**
	16:30	Then he **brought** them outside
	17: 5	**bring them out** to the assembly,
	25:26	I **have brought** him **before** all
1Ti	1:18	prophecies **made earlier** about
	5:24	conspicuous and **precede** them to
He	7:18	abrogation of an **earlier**
2J	1: 9	but **goes beyond** it, does not

4255　GO1 AG702 LN205 R4253,138
προαιρεω, I CHOOSE BEFORE

| 2C | 9: 7 | give as you **have made up** your |

4256　GO1 AG702 LN205
προαιτιαομαι, I ACCUSE BEFORE

| Ro | 3: 9 | for we **have already charged** |

4257　GO1 AG702 LN205 R4253,191
προακουω, I HEAR BEFORE

| Co | 1: 5 | **have heard** of this hope **before** |

4258　GO2 AG702 LN206 R4253,264
προαμαρτανω, I SIN BEFORE

| 2C | 12:21 | over many who **previously sinned** |
| | 13: 2 | those who **sinned previously** and |

4259　GO1 AG702 LN206 R4253,833
προαυλιον, FORECOURT

| Mk | 14:68 | He went out into the **forecourt.** |

4260　GO5 AG702 LN206
προβαινω, I GO BEFORE

Mt	4:21	As he **went** from there, he saw
Mk	1:19	As he **went** a little farther, he
Lk	1: 7	both **were getting on** in years.

| 1:18 | and my wife **is getting on** in |
| 2:36 | She **was of a great** age, having |

4261　ᴳᴼ2 ᴬᴳ702 ᴸᴺ206 ᴿ4253,906
προβαλλω, I THROW BEFORE

| Lk | 21:30 | as soon as they **sprout** leaves |
| Ac | 19:33 | the Jews **had pushed forward.** |

4262　ᴳᴼ1 ᴬᴳ703 ᴸᴺ206 ᴿ4263
προβατικος, SHEEP PLACE

| Jn | 5: 2 | In Jerusalem by the **Sheep Gate** |

4263　ᴳᴼ39 ᴬᴳ703 ᴸᴺ206 ᴮ2:412 ᴷ6:689
προβατον, SHEEP

Mt	7:15	who come to you in **sheep's**
	9:36	like **sheep** without a shepherd.
	10: 6	but go rather to the lost **sheep**
	10:16	I am sending you out like **sheep**
	12:11	has only one **sheep** and it falls
	12:12	a human being than a **sheep!** So
	15:24	to the lost **sheep** of the house
	18:12	shepherd has a hundred **sheep,**
	25:32	shepherd separates the **sheep**
	25:33	and he will put the **sheep** at
	26:31	and the **sheep** of the flock will
Mk	6:34	because they were like **sheep**
	14:27	and the **sheep** will be scattered
Lk	15: 4	having a hundred **sheep** and
	15: 6	I have found my **sheep** that was
Jn	2:14	people selling cattle, **sheep,**
	2:15	both the **sheep** and the cattle.
	10: 1	does not enter the **sheepfold** by
	10: 2	is the shepherd of the **sheep.**
	10: 3	gate for him, and the **sheep**
	10: 3	He calls his own **sheep** by name
	10: 4	the **sheep** follow him because
	10: 7	I am the gate for the **sheep.**
	10: 8	but the **sheep** did not listen to
	10:11	down his life for the **sheep.**
	10:12	does not own the **sheep,** sees
	10:12	coming and leaves the **sheep** and
	10:13	does not care for the **sheep.**
	10:15	lay down my life for the **sheep.**
	10:16	I have other **sheep** that do not
	10:26	you do not belong to my **sheep.**
	10:27	My **sheep** hear my voice. I know
	21:16	said to him, "Tend my **sheep."**
	21:17	said to him, "Feed my **sheep.**
Ac	8:32	Like a **sheep** he was led to the
Ro	8:36	we are accounted as **sheep** to be

He	13:20	the great shepherd of the **sheep**
1P	2:25	going astray like **sheep,** but
Re	18:13	cattle and **sheep,** horses and

4264　ᴳᴼ1 ᴬᴳ703 ᴸᴺ206
προβιβαζω, I LEAD FORWARD

| Mt | 14: 8 | **Prompted** by her mother, she |

4265　ᴳᴼ1 ᴬᴳ703 ᴸᴺ206 ᴿ4253,991
προβλεπω, I SEE BEFORE

| He | 11:40 | God **had provided** something |

4266　ᴳᴼ1 ᴬᴳ703 ᴸᴺ206 ᴮ2:767 ᴿ4253,1096
προγινομαι, I BECOME BEFORE

| Ro | 3:25 | the sins **previously committed;** |

4267　ᴳᴼ5 ᴬᴳ703 ᴸᴺ206 ᴮ1:692 ᴷ1:715 ᴿ4253,1097
προγινωσκω, I KNOW BEFORE

Ac	26: 5	They **have known** for a long time
Ro	8:29	For those whom he **foreknew** he
	11: 2	his people whom he **foreknew.** Do
1P	1:20	He **was destined** before the
2P	3:17	you **are forewarned,** beware

4268　ᴳᴼ2 ᴬᴳ703 ᴸᴺ206 ᴮ1:692 ᴷ1:715 ᴿ4267
προγνωσις, FOREKNOWLEDGE

| Ac | 2:23 | definite plan and **foreknowledge** |
| 1P | 1: 2 | chosen and **destined** by God the |

4269　ᴳᴼ2 ᴬᴳ704 ᴸᴺ206
προγονος, PARENT

| 1Ti | 5: 4 | repayment to their **parents;** for |
| 2Ti | 1: 3 | as my **ancestors** did—when I |

4270　ᴳᴼ4 ᴬᴳ704 ᴸᴺ206 ᴮ3:482 ᴷ1:770 ᴿ4253,1125
προγραφω, I WRITE BEFORE

Ro	15: 4	**was written in former** days was
Ga	3: 1	Christ **was publicly exhibited**
Ep	3: 3	as I **wrote above** in a few words
Ju	1: 4	who **long ago were designated**

4271　ᴳᴼ3 ᴬᴳ704 ᴸᴺ206 ᴿ4253,1212
προδηλος, CLEAR BEFORE

1Ti	5:24	are **conspicuous** and precede
	5:25	good works are **conspicuous;** and
He	7:14	For it is **evident** that our Lord

4272　ᴳᴼ1 ᴬᴳ704 ᴸᴺ206 ᴿ4253,1325
προδιδωμι, I GIVE BEFORE

| Ro | 11:35 | Or who **has given** a gift to him |

4273 GO3 AG704 LN206 R4272
προδοτης, TRAITOR
Lk   6:16   Iscariot, who became a **traitor.**
Ac   7:52   you have become his **betrayers**
2Ti   3: 4   **treacherous,** reckless, swollen

4274 GO1 AG704 LN206 B3:945 K8:235 R4253,1408
προδρομος, FORERUNNER
He   6:20   where Jesus, a **forerunner** on

4276 GO1 AG705 LN207 B2:238 K2:534 R4253,1679
προελπιζω, I HOPE BEFORE
Ep   1:12   the first to **set our hope on**

4278 GO2 AG705 LN207 R4253,1728
προεναρχομαι, I BEGIN BEFORE
2C   8: 6   **had already made a beginning,**
      8:10   for you who **began** last year not

4279 GO2 AG705 LN207 B3:68 K2:586
προεπαγγελλω, I PROMISE BEFORE
Ro   1: 2   which he **promised beforehand**
2C   9: 5   gift that you **have promised,** so

4281 GO9 AG705 LN207 B1:320 R4253,2064
προερχομαι, I COME/GO BEFORE
Mt   26:39   And **going** a little farther, he
Mk   6:33   all the towns and **arrived ahead**
     14:35   And **going** a little farther, he
Lk   1:17   he **will go before** him, to turn
     22:47   one of the twelve, **was leading**
Ac   12:10   they **came before** the iron gate
     20: 5   They **went ahead** and were
     20:13   We **went ahead** to the ship and
2C   9: 5   the brothers to **go on ahead** to

4282 GO2 AG705 LN207 B3:116 K2:704 R4253,2090
προετοιμαζω, I PREPARE BEFORE
Ro   9:23   he **has prepared beforehand** for
Ep   2:10   which God **prepared beforehand**

4283 GO1 AG705 LN207 K2:737 R4253,2097
προευαγγελιζομαι, I TOLD GOOD
MESSAGE BEFORE
Ga   3: 8   **declared** the gospel beforehand

4284 GO1 AG705 LN207 K6:692 R4253,2192
προεχω, I HOLD BEFORE, I HAVE FIRST
(PLACE)
Ro   3: 9   then? **Are we any better off?**

4285 GO1 AG706 LN207 K2:908 R4253,2233
προηγεομαι, I LEAD BEFORE
Ro   12:10   **outdo** one another in showing

4286 GO12 AG706 LN207 B1:696 K8:164 R4287
προθεσις, PURPOSE
Mt   12: 4   ate the bread of the **Presence,**
Mk   2:26   ate the bread of the **Presence,**
Lk   6: 4   ate the bread of the **Presence,**
Ac   11:23   Lord with steadfast **devotion;**
     27:13   achieve their **purpose;** so they
Ro   8:28   called according to his **purpose**
      9:11   (so that God's **purpose** of
Ep   1:11   according to the **purpose** of him
      3:11   eternal **purpose** that he has
2Ti   1: 9   according to his own **purpose**
      3:10   my **aim** in life, my faith, my
He   9: 2   and the bread of the **Presence;**

4287 GO1 AG706 LN207 B1:471 R4253,5087
προθεσμια, PURPOSE
Ga   4: 2   the **date set** by the father.

4288 GO5 AG706 LN207 B1:188 K6:697 R4289
προθυμια, EAGERNESS
Ac   17:11   the message very **eagerly** and
2C   8:11   your **eagerness** may be matched
      8:12   For if the **eagerness** is there,
      8:19   and to show our **goodwill.**
      9: 2   for I know your **eagerness,**

4289 GO3 AG706 LN207 K6:694
προθυμος, EAGER
Mt   26:41   the spirit indeed is **willing,**
Mk   14:38   the spirit indeed is **willing,**
Ro   1:15   —hence my **eagerness** to

4290 GO1 AG706 LN207 R4289
προθυμως, EAGERLY
1P   5: 2   not for sordid gain but **eagerly**

4290a GO1 AG706 LN207 B3:1000
προιμος, EARLY
Ja   5: 7   the **early** and the late rains.

4291 GO8 AG707 LN207 B1:192 K6:700 R4253,2476
προιστημι, I STAND BEFORE
Ro   12: 8   the **leader,** in diligence; the
1Th   5:12   **have charge** of you in the Lord
1Ti   3: 4   **manage** his own household well,

3: 5	does not know how to **manage** his
3:12	let them **manage** their children
5:17	Let the elders who **rule** well be
Ti 3: 8	**to devote** themselves to good
3:14	And let people learn **to devote**

4292   GO1   AG707   LN207   K3:496   R4253,2564
προκαλεω, I PROVOKE
| Ga   5:26 | **competing against** one another, |

4293   GO2   AG707   LN207   B3:44   K1:70   R4253,2605
προκαταγγελλω, I PROCLAIM BEFORE
| Ac   3:18 | what he had **foretold** through |
| 7:52 | They killed those who **foretold** |

4294   GO1   AG707   LN207   B3:349   R4253,2675
προκαταρτιζω, I ORGANIZE BEFORE
| 2C   9: 5 | **arrange in advance** for this |

4295   GO5   AG707   LN207   B1:400   K3:656   R4253,2749
προκειμαι, I LIE BEFORE
2C 8:12	For if the eagerness **is there,**
He 6:18	to seize the hope **set before** us
12: 1	the race that **is set before** us,
12: 2	the joy that **was set before** him
Ju 1: 7	by **undergoing** a punishment of

4296   GO1   AG707   LN208   K3:717   R4253,2784
προκηρυσσω, I ANNOUNCE BEFORE
| Ac   13:24 | already **proclaimed** a baptism of |

4297   GO3   AG707   LN208   B2:128   K6:703   R4298
προκοπη, PROGRESS
Ph 1:12	actually helped to **spread** the
1:25	for your **progress** and joy in
1Ti 4:15	that all may see your **progress.**

4298   GO6   AG707   LN208   B2:128   K6:703   R4253,2875
προκοπτω, I PROGRESS
Lk 2:52	And Jesus **increased** in wisdom
Ro 13:12	the night **is far gone,** the day
Ga 1:14	I **advanced** in Judaism beyond
2Ti 2:16	for it **will lead** people into
3: 9	**will** not **make much progress,**
3:13	impostors **will go from** bad to

4299   GO1   AG708   LN208   B2:363   K3:953
προκριμα, PREJUDGMENT (PREJUDICE)
| 1Ti   5:21 | instructions without **prejudice,** |

4300   GO1   AG708   LN208   B1:664   K3:1100   R4253,2964
προκυροω, I VALIDATE BEFORE
| Ga   3:17 | **does** not **annul . . . previously** |

4301   GO3   AG708   LN208   B3:747   K4:14   R4523,2983
προλαμβανω, I TAKE BEFORE
Mk 14: 8	**has anointed** my body **beforehand**
1C 11:21	each of you **goes ahead** with
Ga 6: 1	if anyone **is detected** in a

4302   GO15   AG708   LN208   B3:75   R4253,3004
προλεγω, I SAY BEFORE
Mt 24:25	**I have told** you **beforehand.**
Mk 13:23	**I have already told** you
Ac 1:16	**foretold** concerning Judas, who
Ro 9:29	And as Isaiah **predicted,** "If
2C 7: 3	for I **said before** that you are
13: 2	I **warned** those who sinned
13: 2	I **warn** them now while absent,
Ga 1: 9	As we **have said before,** so now
5:21	I **am warning** you, as I warned
5:21	I **warned** you before: those who
1Th 3: 4	we **told** you **beforehand** that we
4: 6	**have . . . told** you **beforehand**
He 4: 7	in the words **already quoted,**
2P 3: 2	words **spoken in the past** by the
Ju 1:17	remember the **predictions** of the

4303   GO1   AG708   LN208   K4:510   R4253,3143
προμαρτυρομαι, I TESTIFY BEFORE
| 1P   1:11 | when it **testified in advance** to |

4304   GO1   AG708   LN208   R4253,3191
προμελεταω, I TAKE CARE BEFORE
| Lk   21:14 | **prepare** your defense **in advance** |

4305   GO1   AG708   LN208   B1:276   K4:589   R4253,3309
προμεριμναω, I AM ANXIOUS
| Mk   13:11 | do not **worry beforehand** about |

4306   GO3   AG708   LN208   B1:692   K4:1009   R4253,3539
προνοεω, I THINK BEFORE
Ro 12:17	but **take thought** for what is
2C 8:21	for we **intend** to do what is
1Ti 5: 8	And whoever **does** not **provide**

4307   GO2   AG708   LN208   B1:692   K4:1009   R4306
προνοια, PROVISION
| Ac   24: 2 | and **reforms** have been made for |
| Ro   13:14 | make no **provision** for the flesh |

4308 GO4 AG709 LN208 K5:381 R4253,3708
προοραω, I SEE BEFORE
Ac 2:25 I **saw** the Lord always **before**
2:31 **Foreseeing** this, David spoke
21:29 For they **had previously seen**
Ga 3: 8 And the scripture, **foreseeing**

4309 GO6 AG709 LN208 K5:456 R4253,3724
προοριζω, I SET BOUNDS BEFORE
Ac 4:28 your plan had **predestined** to
Ro 8:29 **predestined** to be conformed to
8:30 And those whom he **predestined**
1C 2: 7 which God **decreed before** the
Ep 1: 5 He **destined** us for adoption as
1:11 having been **destined** according

4310 GO1 AG709 LN208 K5:924 R4253,3958
προπασχω, I SUFFER BEFORE
1Th 2: 2 **had already suffered** and been

4310a GO1 AG709 LN208 R4253,3962
προπατωρ, FOREFATHER
Ro 4: 1 our **ancestor** according to the

4311 GO9 AG709 LN208 R4253,3992
προπεμπω, I SEND BEFORE
Ac 15: 3 So they **were sent on** their way
20:38 they **brought** him to the ship.
21: 5 **escorted** us outside the city
Ro 15:24 and **to be sent on** by you, once
1C 16: 6 you **may send** me **on** my way,
16:11 **Send** him **on** his way in peace,
2C 1:16 **have** you **send** me **on** to Judea.
Ti 3:13 **send** Zenas . . . and Apollos **on**
3J 1: 6 **send** them **on** in a manner
worthy

4312 GO2 AG709 LN208
προπετης, RECKLESS
Ac 19:36 to be quiet and do nothing **rash**
2Ti 3: 4 treacherous, **reckless,** swollen

4313 GO2 AG709 LN208 R4253,4198
προπορευομαι, I TRAVEL BEFORE
Lk 1:76 for you **will go before** the
Lord
Ac 7:40 Make gods for us who **will lead**

4314 GO699 AG709 LN208 K6:720
προς, TOWARD [MULTIPLE OCCURRENCES]

4315 GO1 AG711 LN209 R4253,4521
προσαββατον, FORESABBATH
Mk 15:42 is, the day **before the sabbath,**

4316 GO1 AG711 LN209
προσαγορευω, I GIVE TITLE
He 5:10 **having been designated** by
God a

4317 GO4 AG711 LN209 K1:131 R4314,71
προσαγω, I LEAD TO
Lk 9:41 with you? **Bring** your son here.
Ac 16:20 they had **brought** them **before**
27:27 that they **were nearing** land.
1P 3:18 in order to **bring** you to God.

4318 GO3 AG711 LN209 B1:592 K1:133 R4317
προσαγωγη, ACCESS
Ro 5: 2 obtained **access** to this grace
Ep 2:18 both of us have **access** in one
3:12 in whom we have **access** to
God

4319 GO1 AG711 LN209
προσαιτεω, I BEG
Jn 9: 8 man who used to sit and **beg?**

4319a GO1 AG711 LN209 R4319
προσαιτης, BEGGAR
Mk 10:46 a blind **beggar,** was sitting by
Jn 9: 8 before as a **beggar** began to ask

4320 GO1 AG711 LN209 R4314,305
προσαναβαινω, I GO UP TO
Lk 14:10 'Friend, **move up** higher';

4321 GO1 AG711 LN209 R4314,355
προσαναλισκω, I SPEND
Lk 8:43 and though she **had spent** all

4322 GO2 AG711 LN209 B1:734 R4314,378
προσαναπληρω, I FILL UP TO
2C 9:12 not only **supplies** the needs of
11: 9 my needs **were supplied** by the

4323 GO2 AG711 LN209 K1:353
προσανατιθημι, I CONFER
Ga 1:16 I **did** not **confer** with any
human
2: 6 leaders **contributed** nothing to

4324 GO1 AG711 LN209 R4314,546
προσαπειλεω, I THOROUGHLY THREATEN
Ac 4:21 After **threatening** them **again,**

4325 GO1 AG712 LN209 R4314,1159
προσδαπαναω, I SPEND MORE
Lk 10:35 whatever **more** you **spend.**

4326 GO1 AG712 LN209 B2:860 K2:41
προσδεομαι, I NEED IN ADDITION TO
Ac 17:25 as though he **needed** anything,

4327 GO14 AG712 LN209 B2:238 K2:57
προσδεχομαι, I AWAIT
Mk 15:43 **waiting expectantly for** the
Lk 2:25 devout, **looking forward to** the
2:38 all who were **looking for** the
12:36 **are waiting for** their master
15: 2 This fellow **welcomes** sinners
23:51 he **was waiting expectantly for**
Ac 23:21 ready now and **are waiting for**
24:15 they themselves also **accept**—
Ro 16: 2 so that you may **welcome** her in
Ph 2:29 **Welcome** him then in the Lord
Ti 2:13 while we **wait for** the blessed
He 10:34 you cheerfully **accepted** the
11:35 refusing to **accept** release, in
Ju 1:21 **look forward to** the mercy of

4328 GO16 AG712 LN209 B2:238 K6:725
προσδοκαω, I WAIT EXPECTANTLY
Mt 11: 3 or are we to **wait for** another?
24:50 **does** not **expect** him and at an
Lk 1:21 the people **were waiting** for
3:15 **were filled with expectation,**
7:19 or are we **to wait for** another?
7:20 or are we **to wait for** another?
8:40 they were all **waiting for** him.
12:46 he **does** not **expect** him and at
Ac 3: 5 **expecting** to receive something
10:24 Cornelius **was expecting** them
27:33 **remaining** without food, having
28: 6 They **were expecting** him to
28: 6 after they **had waited** a long
2P 3:12 **waiting for** and hastening the
3:13 we **wait for** new heavens and a
3:14 while you **are waiting for** these

4329 GO2 AG712 LN209 K6:725 R4328
προσδοκια, EXPECTATION

Lk 21:26 fear and **foreboding** of what is
Ac 12:11 Jewish people **were expecting.**

4330 GO1 AG712 LN209 R4314,1439
προσεαω, I ALLOW TO GO FURTHER
Ac 27: 7 as the wind **was against** us, we

4333 GO1 AG713 LN209 R4314,2038
προσεργαζομαι, I EARN MORE
Lk 19:16 Lord, your pound **has made** ten

4334 GO86 AG713 LN210 B1:320 K2:683 R4314,2064
προσερχομαι, I COME TOWARD
Mt 4: 3 The tempter **came** and said to
4:11 suddenly angels **came** and waited
5: 1 his disciples **came to** him.
8: 2 there was a leper who **came to**
8: 5 a centurion **came to** him,
8:19 A scribe then **approached** and
8:25 And they **went** and woke him up,
9:14 **came to** him, saying, "Why do we
9:20 **came up** behind him and touched
9:28 the blind men **came to** him; and
13:10 Then the disciples **came** and
13:27 **came** and said to him, 'Master,
13:36 And his disciples **approached**
14:12 His disciples **came** and took the
14:15 the disciples **came to** him and
15: 1 **came to** Jesus from Jerusalem
15:12 Then the disciples **approached**
15:23 his disciples **came** and urged
15:30 Great crowds **came to** him,
16: 1 Pharisees and Sadducees **came,**
17: 7 But Jesus **came** and touched them
17:14 a man **came to** him, knelt before
17:19 Then the disciples **came to**
17:24 temple tax **came to** Peter and
18: 1 the disciples **came to** Jesus and
18:21 Then Peter **came** and said to him
19: 3 Some Pharisees **came to** him, and
19:16 Then someone **came to** him and
20:20 sons of Zebedee **came to** him
21:14 The blind and the lame **came to**
21:23 **came to** him as he was teaching,
21:28 he **went to** the first and said,
21:30 The father **went to** the second
22:23 some Sadducees **came to** him,
24: 1 his disciples **came to** point out
24: 3 the disciples **came to** him
25:20 five talents **came forward,**

	25:22	two talents also **came forward,**
	25:24	one talent also **came forward,**
	26: 7	a woman **came to** him with an
	26:17	the disciples **came to** Jesus,
	26:49	At once he **came up** to Jesus
	26:50	Then they **came** and laid hands
	26:60	false witnesses **came forward.**
	26:60	At last two **came forward**
	26:69	A servant-girl **came to** him and
	26:73	the bystanders **came up** and said
	27:58	He **went to** Pilate and asked for
	28: 2	**came** and rolled back the stone
	28: 9	And they **came** to him, took hold
	28:18	And Jesus **came** and said to them
Mk	1:31	He **came** and took her by the
	6:35	his disciples **came to** him and
	10: 2	Some Pharisees **came,** and to
	12:28	One of the scribes **came near**
	14:45	So when he came, he **went up** to
Lk	7:14	Then he **came forward** and
	8:24	They **went to** him and woke him
	8:44	She **came up** behind him and
	9:12	the twelve **came to** him and said
	9:42	While he **was coming,** the demon
	10:34	He **went to** him and bandaged his
	13:31	some Pharisees **came** and said to
	20:27	no resurrection, **came to** him
	23:36	**coming up** and offering him sour
	23:52	This man **went to** Pilate and
Jn	12:21	They **came to** Philip, who was
Ac	7:31	and as he **approached** to look,
	8:29	**Go over** to this chariot and
	9: 1	Lord, **went to** the high priest
	10:28	associate with or **to visit** a
	12:13	maid named Rhoda **came to** answer
	18: 2	Rome. Paul **went to** see them,
	22:26	he **went to** the tribune and said
	22:27	The tribune **came** and asked Paul
	23:14	They **went to** the chief priests
	28: 9	also **came** and were cured.
1Ti	6: 3	**does** not **agree** with the sound
He	4:16	Let us therefore **approach** the
	7:25	save those who **approach** God
	10: 1	make perfect those who **approach**
	10:22	**let** us **approach** with a true
	11: 6	whoever would **approach** him must
	12:18	You **have** not **come to** something
	12:22	But you **have come to** Mount Zion
1P	2: 4	**Come to** him, a living stone,

4335   GO37 AG713 LN210 B2:861 K2:807 R4336
προσευχη, PRAYER

Mt	21:13	be called a house of **prayer';**
	21:22	Whatever you ask for in **prayer**
Mk	9:29	come out only through **prayer.**
	11:17	called a house of **prayer** for
Lk	6:12	spent the night in **prayer** to
	19:46	shall be a house of **prayer';**
	22:45	When he got up from **prayer,**
Ac	1:14	devoting themselves to **prayer,**
	2:42	of bread and the **prayers.**
	3: 1	temple at the hour of **prayer,**
	6: 4	will devote ourselves to **prayer**
	10: 4	Your **prayers** and your alms
	10:31	your **prayer** has been heard and
	12: 5	the church **prayed** fervently to
	16:13	there was a place of **prayer;**
	16:16	going to the place of **prayer,**
Ro	1: 9	you always in my **prayers**
	12:12	suffering, persevere in **prayer.**
	15:30	join me in earnest **prayer** to
1C	7: 5	devote yourselves to **prayer,**
Ep	1:16	I remember you in my **prayers.**
	6:18	every **prayer** and supplication.
Ph	4· 6	in everything by **prayer** and
Co	4: 2	Devote yourselves to **prayer,**
	4:12	wrestling in his **prayers** on
1Th	1: 2	mention you in our **prayers,**
1Ti	2: 1	**prayers,** intercessions, and
	5: 5	supplications and **prayers** night
Pm	1: 4	remember you in my **prayers,** I
	1:22	am hoping through your **prayers**
Ja	5:17	he **prayed** fervently that it
1P	3: 7	nothing may hinder your **prayers**
	4: 7	for the sake of your **prayers.**
Re	5: 8	are the **prayers** of the saints.
	8: 3	offer with the **prayers** of all
	8: 4	with the **prayers** of the saints,

4336   GO86 AG713 LN210 B2:861 K2:807
προσευχομαι, I PRAY

Mt	5:44	Love your enemies and **pray** for
	6: 5	And whenever you **pray,** do not
	6: 5	they love to stand and **pray** in
	6: 6	But whenever you **pray,** go into
	6: 6	**pray** to your Father who is in
	6: 7	When you **are praying,** do not
	6: 9	**Pray** then in this way: Our
	14:23	the mountain by himself to **pray**

	19:13	lay his hands on them and **pray.**
	24:20	**Pray** that your flight may not
	26:36	while I go over there and **pray.**
	26:39	on the ground and **prayed,** "My
	26:41	Stay awake and **pray** that you
	26:42	**prayed,** "My Father, if this
	26:44	he went away and **prayed** for the
Mk	1:35	place, and there he **prayed.**
	6:46	went up on the mountain to **pray**
	11:24	whatever you ask for in **prayer,**
	11:25	Whenever you stand **praying,**
	12:40	**say** long **prayers.** They will
	13:18	**Pray** that it may not be in
	14:32	Sit here while I **pray.**
	14:35	and **prayed** that, if it were
	14:38	Keep awake and **pray** that you
	14:39	again he went away and **prayed,**
Lk	1:10	the people was **praying** outside.
	3:21	**was praying,** the heaven was
	5:16	to deserted places and **pray.**
	6:12	out to the mountain to **pray;**
	6:28	**pray** for those who abuse you.
	9:18	Once when Jesus was **praying**
	9:28	went up on the mountain to **pray**
	9:29	And while he **was praying,** the
	11: 1	He was **praying** in a certain
	11: 1	Lord, teach us to **pray,** as
	11: 2	He said to them, "When you **pray**
	18: 1	about their need to **pray** always
	18:10	up to the temple to **pray,** one a
	18:11	**was praying** thus, 'God, I thank
	20:47	of appearance say long **prayers.**
	22:40	**Pray** that you may not come
	22:41	throw, knelt down, and **prayed,**
	22:44	In his anguish he **prayed** more
	22:46	Get up and **pray** that you may
Ac	1:24	Then they **prayed** and said,
	6: 6	who **prayed** and laid their hands
	8:15	The two went down and **prayed**
	9:11	At this moment he is **praying,**
	9:40	then he knelt down and **prayed.**
	10: 9	went up on the roof **to pray.**
	10:30	I **was praying** in my house when
	11: 5	city of Joppa **praying,** and in a
	12:12	had gathered and **were praying.**
	13: 3	Then after fasting and **praying**
	14:23	with **prayer** and fasting they
	16:25	Paul and Silas **were praying** and
	20:36	down with them all and **prayed.**

	21: 5	down on the beach and **prayed**
	22:17	while I was **praying** in the
	28: 8	cured him by **praying** and
Ro	8:26	we do not know how **to pray** as
1C	11: 4	Any man who **prays** or prophesies
	11: 5	but any woman who **prays** or
	11:13	it proper for a woman to **pray**
	14:13	**pray** for the power to interpret
	14:14	For if I **pray** in a tongue, my
	14:14	my spirit **prays** but my mind is
	14:15	I will **pray** with the spirit,
	14:15	but I will **pray** with the mind
Ep	6:18	**Pray** in the Spirit at all times
Ph	1: 9	And this is my **prayer,** that
Co	1: 3	In our **prayers** for you we
	1: 9	we have not ceased **praying** for
	4: 3	At the same time **pray** for us as
1Th	5:17	**pray** without ceasing,
	5:25	Beloved, **pray** for us.
2Th	1:11	To this end we always **pray** for
	3: 1	**pray** for us, so that the word
1Ti	2: 8	the men should **pray,** lifting up
He	13:18	**Pray** for us; we are sure that
Ja	5:13	They should **pray.** Are any
	5:14	and have them **pray** over them,
	5:17	he **prayed** fervently that it
	5:18	Then he **prayed** again, and the
Ju	1:20	faith; **pray** in the Holy Spirit;

4337   ᴳᴼ24 ᴬᴳ714 ᴸᴺ210 ᴮ3:908 ᴿ4314,2192
προσεχω, I HOLD TO, I KEEP WATCH

Mt	6: 1	**Beware** of practicing your
	7:15	**Beware** of false prophets, who
	10:17	**Beware** of them, for they will
	16: 6	Watch out, and **beware** of the
	16:11	**Beware** of the yeast of the
	16:12	told them to **beware** of the
Lk	12: 1	**Beware** of the yeast of the
	17: 3	**Be on your guard!** If another
	20:46	**Beware** of the scribes, who
	21:34	**Be on guard** so that your
Ac	5:35	**consider carefully** what you
	8: 6	accord **listened** eagerly to what
	8:10	**listened** to him eagerly, saying
	8:11	And they **listened** eagerly to
	16:14	Lord opened her heart **to listen**
	20:28	**Keep watch** over yourselves and
1Ti	1: 4	and not **to occupy** themselves
	3: 8	not **indulging** in much wine, not

	4: 1	faith by **paying attention** to
	4:13	Until I arrive, **give attention**
Ti	1:14	not **paying attention** to Jewish
He	2: 1	**pay** greater **attention** to what
	7:13	which no one **has** ever **served** at
2P	1:19	will do well **to be attentive** to

4338   GO1 AG714 LN210 R4314,2247
προσηλοω, I NAIL
Co   2:14   He set this aside, **nailing** it

4339   GO4 AG715 LN210 B1:359 K6:727
προσηλυτος, CONVERT
Mt 23:15   make a single **convert,** and you
Ac   2:10   both Jews and **proselytes**
     6: 5   a **proselyte** of Antioch.
    13:43   many Jews and devout **converts**

4340   GO4 AG715 LN211 B3:833 K3:463 R4314,2540
προσκαιρος, TO SEASON
Mt 13:21   but endures only **for a while,**
Mk   4:17   endure **only for a while;** then,
2C   4:18   what can be seen is **temporary,**
He 11:25   God than to enjoy the **fleeting**

4341   GO29 AG715 LN211 B1:272 K3:500 R4314,2564
προσκαλεω, I CALL TO
Mt 10: 1   Then Jesus **summoned** his twelve
    15:10   Then he **called** the crowd to him
    15:32   Then Jesus **called** his disciples
    18: 2   He **called** a child, whom he put
    18:32   Then his lord **summoned** him and
    20:25   But Jesus **called** them to him
Mk   3:13   and **called** to him those whom he
     3:23   And he **called** them to him, and
     6: 7   He **called** the twelve and began
     7:14   Then he **called** the crowd again
     8: 1   he **called** his disciples and
     8:34   He **called** the crowd with his
    10:42   So Jesus **called** them and said
    12:43   Then he **called** his disciples
    15:44   **summoning** the centurion, he
Lk   7:18   So John **summoned** two of his
    15:26   He **called** one of the slaves and
    16: 5   So, **summoning** his master's
    18:16   But Jesus **called** for them and
Ac   2:39   whom the Lord our God **calls** to
     5:40   and when they **had called** in the
     6: 2   And the twelve **called** together
    13: 2   to which I **have called** them.

	13: 7	who **summoned** Barnabas
		and Saul
	16:10	convinced that God **had called**
	23:17	Paul **called** one of the
	23:18	The prisoner Paul **called** me
	23:23	Then he **summoned** two of the
Ja	5:14	They should **call** for the elders

4342   GO10 AG715 LN211 B2:767 K3:618 R4314,2594
προσκαρτερεω, I REMAIN CONSTANT
Mk   3: 9   **have** a boat **ready** for him
Ac   1:14   **devoting** themselves to prayer,
     2:42   They **devoted** themselves to the
     2:46   they **spent much time** together
     6: 4   **will devote** ourselves to prayer
     8:13   he **stayed constantly** with
    10: 7   ranks of those who **served** him,
Ro 12:12   suffering, **persevere** in prayer.
    13: 6   **busy with this very thing.**
Co   4: 2   **Devote** yourselves to prayer,

4343   GO1 AG715 LN211 B2:767 K3:619 R4342
προσκαρτερησις, CONSTANCY
Ep   6:18   **persevere** in supplication for

4344   GO1 AG715 LN211
προσκεφαλαιον, HEAD REST
Mk   4:38   asleep on the **cushion;** and they

4345   GO1 AG716 LN211 B2:300 K3:765
προσκληροω, I THREW LOT
Ac 17: 4   **joined** Paul and Silas, as did a

4345a   GO1 AG716 LN211
προσκλινω, I INCLINE
Ac   5:36   **joined** him; but he was killed,

4346   GO1 AG716 LN211 B1:271
προσκλισις, INCLINATION
1Ti 5:21   on the **basis of partiality.**

4347   GO2 AG716 LN211 B2:350 K3:823 R4314,2853
προσκολλαω, I JOIN
Mk 10: 7   and **be joined** to his wife,
Ep   5:31   and **be joined** to his wife, and

4348   GO6 AG716 LN211 B2:705 K6:745 R4350
προσκομμα, STUMBLING
Ro   9:32   stumbled over the **stumbling**
     9:33   will make people **stumble,** a

	14:13	never to put a **stumbling** block
	14:20	for you to **make** others **fall** by
1C	8: 9	become a **stumbling** block to the
1P	2: 8	stone that makes them **stumble,**

4349   GO1 AG716 LN211 B2:705 K6:745 R4350
προσκοπη, STUMBLE

2C	6: 3	We are putting no **obstacle** in

4350   GO8 AG716 LN211 B2:705 K6:745
προσκοπτω, I STUMBLE

Mt	4: 6	**dash** your foot against a stone.
	7:27	the winds blew and **beat** against
Lk	4:11	**dash** your foot against a stone.
Jn	11: 9	do not **stumble,** because they
	11:10	those who walk at night **stumble**
Ro	9:32	They **have stumbled** over the
	14:21	your brother or sister **stumble.**
1P	2: 8	They **stumble** because they

4351   GO2 AG716 LN211 R4314,2947
προσκυλιω, I ROLL

Mt	27:60	He then **rolled** a great stone to
Mk	15:46	He then **rolled** a stone against

4352   GO60 AG716 LN211 B2:875 K6:758
προσκυνεω, I WORSHIP

Mt	2: 2	and have come **to pay** him **homage**
	2: 8	may also go and **pay** him **homage.**
	2:11	knelt down and **paid** him **homage.**
	4: 9	will fall down and **worship** me.
	4:10	**Worship** the Lord your God, and
	8: 2	came to him and **knelt before**
	9:18	came in and **knelt before** him,
	14:33	And those in the boat **worshiped**
	15:25	**knelt before** him, saying, "Lord
	18:26	fell **on** his **knees before** him,
	20:20	**kneeling before** him, she asked
	28: 9	of his feet, and **worshiped** him.
	28:17	they saw him, they **worshiped**
Mk	5: 6	ran and **bowed down before** him;
	15:19	and **knelt down in homage** to him
Lk	4: 7	If you, then, **will worship** me,
	4: 8	**Worship** the Lord your God, and
	24:52	And they **worshiped** him, and
Jn	4:20	Our ancestors **worshiped** on this
	4:20	where people must **worship** is in
	4:21	is coming when you **will worship**
	4:22	You **worship** what you do not
	4:22	we **worship** what we know, for

	4:23	true worshipers **will worship**
	4:23	such as these to **worship** him.
	4:24	those who **worship** him must
	4:24	who worship him must **worship** in
	9:38	believe." And he **worshiped** him.
	12:20	up to **worship** at the festival
Ac	7:43	images that you made to **worship**
	8:27	come to Jerusalem to **worship**
	10:25	falling at his feet, **worshiped**
	24:11	went up to **worship** in Jerusalem
1C	14:25	**worship** him, declaring, "God is
He	1: 6	Let all God's angels **worship**
	11:21	bowing in **worship** over the top
Re	3: 9	make them come and **bow down**
	4:10	and **worship** the one who lives
	5:14	elders fell down and **worshiped.**
	7:11	before the throne and **worshiped**
	9:20	give up **worshiping** demons and
	11: 1	the altar and those who **worship**
	11:16	their faces and **worshiped** God,
	13: 4	**worshiped** the beast, saying,
	13: 4	They **worshiped** the dragon, for
	13: 8	of the earth **will worship** it,
	13:12	**worship** the first beast, whose
	13:15	those who would not **worship** the
	14: 7	**worship** him who made heaven and
	14: 9	Those who **worship** the beast
	14:11	for those who **worship** the beast
	15: 4	come and **worship** before you,
	16: 2	beast and who **worshiped** its
	19: 4	**worshiped** God who is seated on
	19:10	down at his feet to **worship** him
	19:10	**Worship** God! For the testimony
	19:20	those who **worshiped** its image.
	20: 4	They had not **worshiped** the
	22: 8	I fell down to **worship** at the
	22: 9	of this book. **Worship** God!

4353   GO1 AG717 LN211 B2:875 K6:766 R4352
προσκυνητης, WORSHIPER

Jn	4:23	when the true **worshipers** will

4354   GO2 AG717 LN211 R4314,2980
προσλαλεω, I SPEAK TO

Ac	13:43	who **spoke to** them and urged
	28:20	see you and **speak with** you,

4355   GO12 AG717 LN211 B3:747 K4:15 R4314,2983
προσλαμβανω, I TAKE TO

Mt	16:22	And Peter **took** him **aside** and

Mk	8:32	And Peter **took** him **aside** and
Ac	17: 5	**with the help of** some ruffians
	18:26	**took** him **aside** and explained
	27:33	food, **having eaten** nothing.
	27:36	and **took** food for themselves.
	28: 2	**welcomed** all of us around it.
Ro	14: 1	**Welcome** those who are weak in
	14: 3	eat; for God **has welcomed** them.
	15: 7	**Welcome** one another, therefore,
	15: 7	just as Christ **has welcomed** you
Pm	1:17	**welcome** him as you would

4356   GO1   AG717   LN211   B3:747   K4:15   R4355
προσλημψις, ACCEPTANCE

Ro	11:15	what will their **acceptance** be

4357   GO7   AG717   LN211   B3:223   K4:579   R4314,3306
προσμενω, I STAY TO

Mt	15:32	because they **have been with** me
Mk	8: 2	they **have been with** me now for
Ac	11:23	**to remain** faithful to the Lord
	13:43	urged them **to continue** in the
	18:18	After **staying** there for a
1Ti	1: 3	**to remain** in Ephesus so that
	5: 5	**continues** in supplications and

4358   GO1   AG717   LN211
προσορμιζω, I ANCHOR

Mk	6:53	Gennesaret and **moored** the boat.

4359   GO1   AG717   LN211   R4314,3784
προσοφειλω, I OWE TO

Pm	1:19	nothing about your **owing** me

4360   GO2   AG717   LN211
προσοχθιζω, I AM VEXED

He	3:10	Therefore I **was angry** with that
	3:17	But with whom **was he angry**

4361   GO1   AG718   LN211   R4314,3983
προσπεινος, TO HUNGER

Ac	10:10	He became **hungry** and wanted

4362   GO1   AG718   LN211   R4314,4078
προσπηγνυμι, I AFFIX

Ac	2:23	you **crucified** and killed by the

4363   GO8   AG718   LN212   R4314,4098
προσπιπτω, I FALL TO

Mt	7:25	the winds blew and **beat** on that

Mk	3:11	they **fell down** before him and
	5:33	**fell down** before him, and told
	7:25	she came and **bowed down** at his
Lk	5: 8	he **fell down** at Jesus' knees,
	8:28	When he saw Jesus, he **fell down**
	8:47	**falling down** before him, she
Ac	16:29	he **fell down** trembling before

4364   GO1   AG718   LN212   R4314,4160
προσποιεω, I MAKE TOWARD

Lk	24:28	ahead as if he **were going on.**

4365   GO1   AG718   LN212   R4314,4198
προσπορευομαι, I TRAVEL TOWARD

Mk	10:35	**came forward** to him and said to

4366   GO2   AG718   LN212   R4314,4486
προσρησσω, I BREAK TOWARD

Lk	6:48	river **burst against** that house
	6:49	When the river **burst against** it

4367   GO7   AG718   LN212   B1:477   K8:37   R4314,5021
προστασσω, I COMMAND

Mt	1:24	angel of the Lord **commanded** him
	8: 4	gift that Moses **commanded,** as a
Mk	1:44	cleansing what Moses **commanded,**
Lk	5:14	as Moses **commanded,** make an
Ac	10:33	all that the Lord has **commanded**
	10:48	he **ordered** them to be baptized
	17:26	he **allotted** the times of their

4368   GO1   AG718   LN212
προστατις, HELPER

Ro	16: 2	she has been a **benefactor** of

4369   GO18   AG718   LN212   B1:600   K8:167   R4314,5087
προστιθημι, I PUT FORTH (I ADD)

Mt	6:27	by worrying **add** a single hour
	6:33	these things **will be given** to
Mk	4:24	still more **will be given** you.
Lk	3:20	**added** to them all by shutting
	12:25	**add** a single hour to your span
	12:31	these things **will be given** to
	17: 5	the Lord, "**Increase** our faith!"
	19:11	he **went on** to tell a parable,
	20:11	**Next** he sent another slave;
	20:12	And he sent **still** a third; this
Ac	2:41	thousand persons **were added.**
	2:47	And day by day the Lord **added**

	5:14	**were added** to the Lord, great
	11:24	many people **were brought** to the
	12: 3	he **proceeded** to arrest Peter
	13:36	**was laid beside** his ancestors,
Ga	3:19	Why then the law? It **was added**
He	12:19	that not **another** word be spoken

4370   GO3 AG719 LN212 R4314,5143
προστρεχω, I RUN TOWARD

Mk	9:15	and they **ran forward** to greet
	10:17	a man **ran up** and knelt before
Ac	8:30	Philip **ran up** to it and heard

4371   GO1 AG719 LN212
προσφαγιον, THING TO EAT

Jn	21: 5	Children, you have no **fish,**

4372   GO1 AG719 LN212 B2:674 K6:766
προσφατος, FRESH

He	10:20	by the **new** and living way that

4373   GO1 AG719 LN212 K6:766
προσφατως, FRESHLY

Ac	18: 2	who had **recently** come from

4374   GO47 AG719 LN212 B2:41 K9:65 R4314,5342
προσφερω, I OFFER

Mt	2:11	they **offered** him gifts of gold,
	4:24	they **brought to** him all the
	5:23	So when you **are offering** your
	5:24	then come and **offer** your gift.
	8: 4	and **offer** the gift that Moses
	8:16	That evening they **brought to**
	9: 2	some people **were carrying** a
	9:32	who was mute **was brought** to him
	12:22	Then they **brought to** him a
	14:35	**brought** all who were sick to
	17:16	And I **brought** him to your
	18:24	talents **was brought** to him;
	19:13	children **were being brought** to
	22:19	And they **brought** him a denarius
	25:20	**bringing** five more talents,
Mk	1:44	**offer** for your cleansing what
	2: 4	And when they could not **bring**
	10:13	People **were bringing** little
Lk	5:14	**make** an **offering** for your
	18:15	People **were bringing** even
	23:14	You **brought** me this man as one
	23:36	coming up and **offering** him sour
Jn	16: 2	by doing so they **are offering**

	19:29	hyssop and **held** it to his mouth
Ac	7:42	Did you **offer** to me slain
	8:18	hands, he **offered** them money,
	21:26	the sacrifice **would be made** for
He	5: 1	to **offer** gifts and sacrifices
	5: 3	he must **offer sacrifice** for his
	5: 7	Jesus **offered** up prayers and
	8: 3	appointed to **offer** gifts and
	8: 3	also to have something to **offer**
	8: 4	are priests who **offer** gifts
	9: 7	he **offers** for himself and for
	9: 9	and sacrifices **are offered** that
	9:14	eternal Spirit **offered** himself
	9:25	Nor was it to **offer** himself
	9:28	so Christ, **having been offered**
	10: 1	continually **offered** year
	10: 2	ceased **being offered,** since the
	10: 8	(these **are offered** according to
	10:11	**offering** again and again the
	10:12	But when Christ **had offered** for
	11: 4	By faith Abel **offered** to God a
	11:17	**offered** up Isaac. He who had
	11:17	ready to **offer** up his only son,
	12: 7	God **is treating** you as children

4375   GO1 AG720 LN212
προσφιλης, PLEASING

Ph	4: 8	whatever is **pleasing,** whatever

4376   GO9 AG720 LN212 B2:40 K9:68 R4374
προσφορα, OFFERING

Ac	21:26	when the **sacrifice** would be
	24:17	nation and to offer **sacrifices.**
Ro	15:16	the **offering** of the Gentiles
Ep	5: 2	fragrant **offering** and sacrifice
He	10: 5	Sacrifices and **offerings** you
	10: 8	**offerings** and burnt offerings
	10:10	through the **offering** of the
	10:14	For by a single **offering** he has
	10:18	there is no longer any **offering**

4377   GO7 AG720 LN212 R4314,5455
προσφωνεω, I CALL TOWARD

Mt	11:16	and **calling to** one another,
Lk	6:13	he **called** his disciples and
	7:32	and **calling to** one another, 'We
	13:12	When Jesus saw her, he **called**
	23:20	release Jesus, **addressed** them
Ac	21:40	he **addressed** them in the Hebrew
	22: 2	When they heard him **addressing**

4378　GO1　AG720　LN212　B2:853
προσχυσις, POURING
He　11:28　and the **sprinkling** of blood, so

4379　GO1　AG720　LN213
προσψαυω, I TOUCH TOWARD
Lk　11:46　not lift a finger **to ease** them.

4380　GO1　AG720　LN213　B1:585　K6:779　R4381
προσωπολημπτεω, I RECEIVE FACE
Ja　2: 9　But if you **show partiality,** you

4381　GO1　AG720　LN213　B1:585　K6:779　R4382
προσωπολημπτης, RECEIVER OF FACE
Ac　10:34　that God shows no **partiality,**

4382　GO4　AG720　LN213　B1:585　K6:779　R4383,2983
προσωπολημψια, FACE RECEIVING
Ro　2:11　For God shows no **partiality.**
Ep　6: 9　with him there is no **partiality**
Co　3:25　and there is no **partiality.**
Ja　2: 1　with your acts of **favoritism**

4383　GO76　AG720　LN213　B1:585　K6:768
προσωπον, FACE
Mt　6:16　they disfigure their **faces** so
　　6:17　your head and wash your **face,**
　　11:10　prepare your way before **you.**
　　16: 3　how to interpret the **appearance**
　　17: 2　his **face** shone like the sun,
　　17: 6　they fell to the **ground** and
　　18:10　continually see the **face** of my
　　22:16　regard people with **partiality.**
　　26:39　he threw himself on the **ground**
　　26:67　Then they spat in his **face** and
Mk　1: 2　my messenger ahead of **you,** who
　　12:14　regard people with **partiality,**
　　14:65　to blindfold **him,** and to strike
Lk　2:31　prepared in the **presence** of all
　　5:12　he bowed with his **face** to the
　　7:27　my messenger ahead of **you,** who
　　9:29　the appearance of his **face**
　　9:51　he set his **face** to go to
　　9:52　sent messengers ahead of **him.**
　　9:53　because his **face** was set toward
　　10: 1　sent them on ahead of **him** in
　　12:56　how to interpret the **appearance**
　　17:16　He **prostrated** himself at Jesus
　　20:21　teach, and you show **deference**
　　21:35　all who live on the **face** of the

　　24: 5　bowed their **faces** to the ground
Ac　2:28　of gladness with your **presence.**
　　3:13　rejected in the **presence** of
　　3:20　come from the **presence** of the
　　5:41　As they **left** the council, they
　　6:15　they saw that his **face** was like
　　6:15　was like the **face** of an angel.
　　7:45　that God drove out **before** our
　　13:24　before **his** coming John had
　　17:26　nations to inhabit the **whole**
　　20:25　will ever see my **face** again.
　　20:38　they would not see **him** again.
　　25:16　met the accusers **face** to face
1C　13:12　but then we will see **face** to
　　13:12　then we will see face to **face.**
　　14:25　that person will bow **down**
2C　1:11　so that **many** will give thanks
　　2:10　for your sake in the **presence**
　　3: 7　gaze at Moses' **face** because of
　　3: 7　the glory of his **face,** a glory
　　3:13　a veil over his **face** to keep
　　3:18　with unveiled **faces,** seeing the
　　4: 6　glory of God in the **face** of
　　5:12　boast in outward **appearance** and
　　8:24　Therefore openly **before** the
　　10: 1　I who am humble when **face** to
　　10: 7　at what is before your **eyes.** If
　　11:20　or gives you a slap in the **face**
Ga　1:22　I was still unknown by **sight**
　　2: 6　to me; God shows no **partiality**
　　2:11　I opposed him to his **face,**
Co　2: 1　who have not seen me **face** to
1Th　2:17　when, for a short **time,** we were
　　2:17　eagerness to see you **face** to
　　3:10　that we may see you **face** to
2Th　1: 9　separated from the **presence** of
He　9:24　now to appear in the **presence**
Ja　1:11　its **beauty** perishes. It is the
　　1:23　look at **themselves** in a mirror;
1P　3:12　But the **face** of the Lord is
Ju　1:16　flattering **people** to their own
Re　4: 7　living creature with a **face**
　　6:16　on us and hide us from the **face**
　　7:11　they fell on their **faces** before
　　9: 7　**faces** were like human faces,
　　9: 7　faces were like human **faces,**
　　10: 1　his **face** was like the sun, and
　　11:16　their **faces** and worshiped God,
　　12:14　fly from the **serpent** into the

20:11　fled from his **presence,** and no
22: 4　they will see his **face,** and his

4385　GO1 AG721 LN213
προτεινω, I STRETCH BEFORE
Ac　22:25　But when they **had tied** him up

4387　GO11 AG721 LN213 B1:664
προτερος, FORMER
Jn　6:62　to where he was **before?**
　　7:50　who had gone to Jesus **before,**
　　9: 8　those who had seen him **before**
2C　1:15　I wanted to come to you **first,**
Ga　4:13　physical infirmity that I **first**
Ep　4:22　put away your **former** way of
1Ti　1:13　even though I was **formerly** a
He　4: 6　those who **formerly** received the
　　7:27　**first** for his own sins, and
　　10:32　But recall those **earlier** days
1P　1:14　desires that you **formerly** had

4388　GO3 AG722 LN213 B1:696 K8:164 R4253,5087
προτιθημι, I SET FORWARD
Ro　1:13　I **have** often **intended** to come
　　3:25　whom God **put forward** as a
Ep　1: 9　pleasure that he **set forth** in

4389　GO1 AG722 LN213
προτρεπω, I URGE
Ac　18:27　the believers **encouraged** him

4390　GO2 AG722 LN213 R4253,5143
προτρεχω, I RUN BEFORE
Lk　19: 4　So he **ran ahead** and climbed a
Jn　20: 4　The two **were running** together,

4391　GO2 AG722 LN213
προυπαρχω, I EXIST BEFORE
Lk　23:12　**before** this they **had been**
Ac　8: 9　Simon **had previously** practiced

4392　GO7 AG722 LN213
προφασις, PRETEXT
Mk　12:40　for the **sake of appearance** say
Lk　20:47　for the **sake of appearance** say
Jn　15:22　they have no **excuse** for their
Ac　27:30　the **pretext** of putting out
Ph　1:18　whether out of **false motives** or
1Th　2: 5　or with a **pretext** for greed;

4393　GO2 AG722 LN213 R4253,5342
προφερω, I BRING FORWARD
Lk　6:45　treasure of the heart **produces**
　　6:45　out of evil treasure **produces**

4394　GO19 AG722 LN213 B3:74 K6:781 R4396
προφητεια, SPEAKING BEFORE (PROPHECY)
Mt　13:14　fulfilled the **prophecy** of
Ro　12: 6　**prophecy,** in proportion to
1C　12:10　to another **prophecy,** to another
　　13: 2　And if I have **prophetic** powers,
　　13: 8　But as for **prophecies,** they
　　14: 6　knowledge or **prophecy** or
　　14:22　while **prophecy** is not for
1Th　5:20　despise the words of **prophets,**
1Ti　1:18　accordance with the **prophecies**
　　4:14　given to you through **prophecy**
2P　1:20　that no **prophecy** of scripture
　　1:21　because no **prophecy** ever came
Re　1: 3　aloud the words of the **prophecy**
　　11: 6　days of their **prophesying,** and
　　19:10　Jesus is the spirit of **prophecy**
　　22: 7　words of the **prophecy** of this
　　22:10　up the words of the **prophecy** of
　　22:18　hears the words of the **prophecy**
　　22:19　of the book of this **prophecy,**

4395　GO28 AG723 LN213 B3:74 K6:781 R4253,5346
προφητευω, I SPEAK BEFORE (PROPHESY)
Mt　7:22　Lord, did we not **prophesy** in
　　11:13　the law **prophesied** until John
　　15: 7　hypocrites! Isaiah **prophesied**
　　26:68　saying, "**Prophesy** to us, you
Mk　7: 6　Isaiah **prophesied** rightly
　　14:65　"**Prophesy!**" The guards also
Lk　1:67　Spirit and **spoke** this **prophecy:**
　　22:64　**Prophesy!** Who is it that
Jn　11:51　he **prophesied** that Jesus was
Ac　2:17　your daughters **shall prophesy,**
　　2:18　Spirit; and they **shall prophesy**
　　19: 6　spoke in tongues and **prophesied**
　　21: 9　who had the gift of **prophecy.**
1C　11: 4　Any man who prays or **prophesies**
　　11: 5　woman who prays or **prophesies**
　　13: 9　and we **prophesy** only in part;
　　14: 1　that you may **prophesy.**
　　14: 3　who **prophesy** speak to other
　　14: 4　who **prophesy** build up the
　　14: 5　but even more to **prophesy.** One
　　14: 5　One who **prophesies** is greater

14:24   if all **prophesy,** an unbeliever
14:31   For you can all **prophesy** one by
14:39   be eager to **prophesy,** and do
1P   1:10   the prophets who **prophesied** of
Ju   1:14   **prophesied,** saying, "See, the
Re   10:11   You must **prophesy** again about
11: 3   authority to **prophesy** for one

4396   GO144 AG723 LN213 B3:74 K6:781 R4395
προφητης, SPOKESMAN (PROPHET)
Mt   1:22   by the Lord through the **prophet**
2: 5   has been written by the **prophet**
2:15   by the Lord through the **prophet**
2:17   through the **prophet** Jeremiah:
2:23   spoken through the **prophets**
3: 3   the one of whom the **prophet**
4:14   spoken through the **prophet**
5:12   persecuted the **prophets** who
5:17   abolish the law or the **prophets**
7:12   is the law and the **prophets.**
8:17   through the **prophet** Isaiah,
10:41   Whoever welcomes a **prophet** in
10:41   in the name of a **prophet** will
10:41   will receive a **prophet's** reward
11: 9   A **prophet?** Yes, I tell you, and
11: 9   you, and more than a **prophet.**
11:13   For all the **prophets** and the
12:17   through the **prophet** Isaiah:
12:39   the sign of the **prophet** Jonah.
13:17   Truly I tell you, many **prophets**
13:35   spoken through the **prophet:**
13:57   **Prophets** are not without honor
14: 5   they regarded him as a **prophet.**
16:14   Jeremiah or one of the **prophets**
21: 4   spoken through the **prophet,**
21:11   This is the **prophet** Jesus from
21:26   all regard John as a **prophet.**
21:46   they regarded him as a **prophet.**
22:40   all the law and the **prophets.**
23:29   build the tombs of the **prophets**
23:30   the blood of the **prophets.**
23:31   those who murdered the **prophets**
23:34   Therefore I send you **prophets,**
23:37   city that kills the **prophets**
24:15   spoken of by the **prophet** Daniel
26:56   the scriptures of the **prophets**
27: 9   through the **prophet** Jeremiah,
Mk   1: 2   As it is written in the **prophet**
6: 4   **Prophets** are not without honor

6:15   It is a **prophet,** like one of
6:15   like one of the **prophets** of old
8:28   others, one of the **prophets.**
11:32   John as truly a **prophet.**
Lk   1:70   mouth of his holy **prophets** from
1:76   will be called the **prophet** of
3: 4   words of the **prophet** Isaiah,
4:17   and the scroll of the **prophet**
4:24   in the **prophet's** hometown.
4:27   time of the **prophet** Elisha,
6:23   ancestors did to the **prophets.**
7:16   A great **prophet** has risen
7:26   A **prophet?** Yes, I tell you,
7:26   you, and more than a **prophet.**
7:39   If this man were a **prophet,** he
9: 8   one of the ancient **prophets** had
9:19   ancient **prophets** has arisen.
10:24   many **prophets** and kings desired
11:47   build the tombs of the **prophets**
11:49   I will send them **prophets** and
11:50   blood of all the **prophets** shed
13:28   all the **prophets** in the kingdom
13:33   impossible for a **prophet** to be
13:34   city that kills the **prophets**
16:16   The law and the **prophets** were
16:29   have Moses and the **prophets;**
16:31   Moses and the **prophets,** neither
18:31   Son of Man by the **prophets** will
20: 6   that John was a **prophet.**
24:19   who was a **prophet** mighty in
24:25   all that the **prophets** have
24:27   Moses and all the **prophets,** he
24:44   the **prophets,** and the psalms
Jn   1:21   "Are you the **prophet?**" He
1:23   as the **prophet** Isaiah said.
1:25   nor Elijah, nor the **prophet?**
1:45   also the **prophets** wrote, Jesus
4:19   I see that you are a **prophet.**
4:44   testified that a **prophet** has no
6:14   This is indeed the **prophet** who
6:45   It is written in the **prophets,**
7:40   This is really the **prophet.**
7:52   you will see that no **prophet** is
8:52   and so did the **prophets;** yet
8:53   The **prophets** also died. Who do
9:17   He said, "He is a **prophet.**"
12:38   the word spoken by the **prophet**
Ac   2:16   spoken through the **prophet** Joel
2:30   Since he was a **prophet,** he knew

3:18	through all the **prophets,** that
3:21	ago through his holy **prophets.**
3:22	your own people a **prophet** like
3:23	does not listen to that **prophet**
3:24	And all the **prophets,** as many
3:25	descendants of the **prophets** and
7:37	God will raise up a **prophet**
7:42	in the book of the **prophets:**
7:48	hands; as the **prophet** says,
7:52	Which of the **prophets** did your
8:28	was reading the **prophet** Isaiah.
8:30	reading the **prophet** Isaiah. He
8:34	the **prophet** say this, about
10:43	All the **prophets** testify about
11:27	At that time **prophets** came down
13: 1	were **prophets** and teachers:
13:15	the law and the **prophets,** the
13:20	until the time of the **prophet**
13:27	words of the **prophets** that are
13:40	that what the **prophets** said
15:15	words of the **prophets,** as it is
15:32	who were themselves **prophets,**
21:10	a **prophet** named Agabus came
24:14	law or written in the **prophets.**
26:22	nothing but what the **prophets**
26:27	do you believe the **prophets?** I
28:23	of Moses and from the **prophets.**
28:25	through the **prophet** Isaiah,
Ro　1: 2	through his **prophets** in the
3:21	by the law and the **prophets,**
11: 3	they have killed your **prophets,**
1C 12:28	first apostles, second **prophets**
12:29	Are all **prophets?** Are all
14:29	Let two or three **prophets** speak
14:32	And the spirits of **prophets** are
14:32	are subject to the **prophets,**
14:37	who claims to be a **prophet,** or
Ep　2:20	the apostles and **prophets,** with
3: 5	holy apostles and **prophets** by
4:11	be apostles, some **prophets,**
1Th 2:15	Lord Jesus and the **prophets,**
Ti　1:12	their very own **prophet,** who
He　1: 1	various ways by the **prophets,**
11:32	and Samuel and the **prophets**—
Ja　5:10	beloved, take the **prophets** who
1P　1:10	the **prophets** who prophesied of
2P　2:16	restrained the **prophet's**
3: 2	past by the holy **prophets,** and
Re 10: 7	to his servants the **prophets.**

11:10	because these two **prophets** had
11:18	the **prophets** and saints and all
16: 6	blood of saints and **prophets,**
18:20	and apostles and **prophets!** For
18:24	blood of **prophets** and of saints
22: 6	spirits of the **prophets,** has
22: 9	comrades the **prophets,** and with

4397　GO2　AG724　LN213　B3:74　K6:781　R4395
προφητικος, OF SPEAKING BEFORE (PROPHETIC)

Ro 16:26	through the **prophetic** writings
2P　1:19	we have the **prophetic** message

4398　GO2　AG724　LN213　B3:74　K6:781　R4395
προφητις, SPOKESWOMAN (PROPHET)

Lk　2:36	There was also a **prophet,** Anna
Re　2:20	who calls herself a **prophet** and

4399　GO1　AG724　LN214　K9:88
προφθανω, I ANTICIPATE

Mt 17:25	Jesus **spoke** of it **first,** asking

4400　GO3　AG724　LN214　B1:475　K6:862
προχειριζω, I SET BEFOREHAND

Ac　3:20	send the Messiah **appointed** for
22:14	God of our ancestors **has chosen**
26:16	to **appoint** you to serve and

4401　GO1　AG724　LN214　B1:478　R4253,5500
προχειροτονεω, I STRETCH OUT HAND

Ac 10:41	us who **were chosen** by God as

4402　GO1　AG724　LN214
προχορος, PROCHORUS

Ac　6: 5	Philip, **Prochorus,** Nicanor,

4403　GO3　AG724　LN214
πρυμνα, STERN

Mk　4:38	he was in the **stern,** asleep
Ac 27:29	four anchors from the **stern**
27:41	**stern** was being broken up by

4404　GO12　AG724　LN214　B2:136
πρωι, MORNING

Mt 16: 3	And in the **morning,** 'It will be
20: 1	early in the **morning** to hire
21:18	the **morning,** when he returned
Mk　1:35	In the **morning,** while it was
11:20	In the **morning** as they passed

	13:35	or at cockcrow, or at **dawn,**	
	15: 1	As soon as it was **morning,** the	
	16: 2	And very **early** on the first day	
	16: 9	[Now after he rose **early** on the	
Jn	18:28	It was early in the **morning.**	
	20: 1	**Early** on the first day of the	
Ac	28:23	From **morning** until evening he	

4405 GO2 AG724 LN214 R4404
πρωια, MORNING

Mt	27: 1	When **morning** came, all the
Jn	21: 4	disciples did not **know** that it

4407 GO2 AG725 LN214 R4404
πρωινος, MORNING

Re	2:28	will also give the **morning** star
	22:16	David, the bright **morning** star.

4408 GO2 AG725 LN214
πρωρα, BOW

Ac	27:30	out anchors from the **bow,**
	27:41	the **bow** stuck and remained

4409 GO1 AG725 LN214 B1:664 K6:881
πρωτευω, I AM FIRST

Co	1:18	might come to **have first place**

4410 GO4 AG725 LN214 B1:664 K6:870 R4413,2515
πρωτοκαθεδρια, FIRST CHAIR

Mt	23: 6	**best seats** in the synagogues,
Mk	12:39	have the **best seats** in the
Lk	11:43	have the **seat of honor** in the
	20:46	to have the **best seats** in the

4411 GO5 AG725 LN214 B1:664 K6:870 R4413,2828
πρωτοκλισια, FIRST RECLINING PLACE

Mt	23: 6	have the **place of honor** at
Mk	12:39	synagogues and **places of honor**
Lk	14: 7	chose the **places of honor,**
	14: 8	sit down at the **place of honor,**
	20:46	synagogues and **places of honor**

4413 GO156 AG725 LN214 B1:664 K6:865
πρωτος, FIRST

Mt	5:24	**first** be reconciled to your
	6:33	But strive **first** for the
	7: 5	You hypocrite, **first** take the
	8:21	Lord, **first** let me go and bury
	10: 2	twelve apostles: **first,** Simon,
	12:29	without **first** tying up the

	12:45	worse than the **first.** So will
	13:30	weeds **first** and bind them in
	17:10	say that Elijah must come **first**
	17:27	take the **first** fish that comes
	19:30	But many who are **first** will be
	19:30	and the last will be **first.**
	20: 8	and then going to the **first.**
	20:10	Now when the **first** came, they
	20:16	So the last will be **first,** and
	20:16	and the **first** will be last.
	20:27	and whoever wishes to be **first**
	21:28	he went to the **first** and said,
	21:31	"The **first.**" Jesus said to them
	21:36	more than the **first;** and they
	22:25	the **first** married, and died
	22:38	This is the greatest and **first**
	23:26	You blind Pharisee! **First** clean
	26:17	On the **first** day of Unleavened
	27:64	would be worse than the **first.**
Mk	3:27	without **first** tying up the
	4:28	**first** the stalk, then the head,
	6:21	officers and for the **leaders** of
	7:27	Let the children be fed **first,**
	9:11	say that Elijah must come **first**
	9:12	Elijah is indeed coming **first**
	9:35	Whoever wants to be **first** must
	10:31	But many who are **first** will be
	10:31	and the last will be **first.**
	10:44	and whoever wishes to be **first**
	12:20	the **first** married and, when he
	12:28	Which commandment is the **first**
	12:29	Jesus answered, "The **first** is,
	13:10	And the good news must **first** be
	14:12	On the **first** day of Unleavened
	16: 9	early on the **first** day of the
	16: 9	he appeared **first** to Mary
Lk	2: 2	This was the **first** registration
	6:42	You hypocrite, **first** take the
	9:59	Lord, **first** let me go and bury
	9:61	but let me **first** say farewell
	10: 5	Whatever house you enter, **first**
	11:26	person is worse than the **first.**
	11:38	see that he did not **first** wash
	12: 1	he began to speak **first** to his
	13:30	last who will be **first,** and
	13:30	some are **first** who will be last
	14:18	The **first** said to him, 'I have
	14:28	does not **first** sit down and
	14:31	will not sit down **first** and

	15:22	the **best one**—and put it on
	16: 5	he asked the **first,** 'How much
	17:25	But **first** he must endure much
	19:16	The **first** came forward and said
	19:47	and the **leaders** of the people
	20:29	the **first** married, and died
	21: 9	must take place **first,** but the
Jn	1:15	of me because he was **before** me.
	1:30	of me because he was **before** me.
	1:41	He **first** found his brother
	2:10	serves the good wine **first,** and
	7:51	judge people without **first**
	8: 7	is without sin be the **first** to
	10:40	John had been baptizing **earlier**
	12:16	these things at **first;** but when
	15:18	it hated me **before** it hated you
	18:13	**First** they took him to Annas,
	19:32	broke the legs of the **first** and
	19:39	who had at **first** come to Jesus
	20: 4	and reached the tomb **first.**
	20: 8	reached the tomb **first,** also
Ac	1: 1	In the **first** book, Theophilus,
	3:26	sent him **first** to you, to
	7:12	ancestors there on their **first**
	12:10	After they had passed the **first**
	13:46	of God should be spoken **first**
	13:50	the **leading** men of the city,
	15:14	God **first** looked favorably on
	16:12	which is a **leading** city of the
	17: 4	not a few of the **leading** women.
	20:18	the entire time from the **first**
	25: 2	**leaders** of the Jews gave him a
	26:20	but declared **first** to those in
	26:23	by being the **first** to rise from
	27:43	jump overboard **first** and make
	28: 7	**leading** man of the island,
	28:17	local **leaders** of the Jews. When
Ro	1: 8	**First,** I thank my God through
	1:16	to the Jew **first** and also to
	2: 9	Jew **first** and also the Greek,
	2:10	Jew **first** and also the Greek.
	3: 2	For in the **first** place the Jews
	10:19	**First** Moses says, "I will make
	15:24	**once** I have enjoyed your
1C	11:18	For, **to begin with,** when you
	12:28	appointed in the church **first**
	14:30	let the **first** person be silent.
	15: 3	handed on to you as of **first**
	15:45	Thus it is written, "The **first**

	15:46	spiritual that is **first,** but
	15:47	The **first** man was from the
2C	8: 5	they gave themselves **first** to
Ep	6: 2	this is the **first** commandment
Ph	1: 5	gospel from the **first** day until
1Th	4:16	dead in Christ will rise **first.**
2Th	2: 3	the rebellion comes **first** and
1Ti	1:15	of whom I am the **foremost.**
	1:16	as the **foremost,** Jesus Christ
	2: 1	**First** of all, then, I urge that
	2:13	For Adam was formed **first,** then
	3:10	And let them **first** be tested;
	5: 4	they should **first** learn their
	5:12	for having violated their **first**
2Ti	1: 5	faith that lived **first** in your
	2: 6	ought to have the **first** share
	4:16	At my **first** defense no one came
He	7: 2	in the **first** place, means "king
	8: 7	For if that **first** covenant had
	8:13	has made the **first** one obsolete
	9: 1	Now even the **first** covenant had
	9: 2	the **first** one, in which were
	9: 6	go continually into the **first**
	9: 8	as long as the **first** tent is
	9:15	under the **first** covenant.
	9:18	not even the **first** covenant was
	10: 9	He abolishes the **first** in order
Ja	3:17	**first** pure, then peaceable,
1P	4:17	if it **begins** with us, what will
2P	1:20	**First** of all you must
	2:20	worse for them than the **first.**
	3: 3	**First** of all you must
1J	4:19	We love because he **first** loved
Re	1:17	afraid; I am the **first** and the
	2: 4	the love you had at **first.**
	2: 5	do the works you did at **first.**
	2: 8	the words of the **first** and the
	2:19	are greater than the **first.**
	4: 1	And the **first** voice, which I
	4: 7	the **first** living creature like
	8: 7	**first** angel blew his trumpet,
	13:12	authority of the **first** beast on
	13:12	**first** beast, whose mortal wound
	16: 2	So the **first** angel went and
	20: 5	This is the **first** resurrection.
	20: 6	those who share in the **first**
	21: 1	for the **first** heaven and the
	21: 1	the **first** earth had passed away
	21: 4	the **first** things have passed

21:19   **first** was jasper, the second
22:13   the **first** and the last, the

4414   GO1 AG726 LN214 B1:535
πρωτοστατης, CHIEF REVOLUTIONARY
Ac   24: 5   **ringleader** of the sect of the

4415   GO1 AG726 LN214 K6:871 R4416
πρωτοτοκια, FIRST CHILD RIGHT
He   12:16   **birthright** for a single meal.

4416   GO8 AG726 LN214 B1:667 K6:871
πρωτοτοκος, FIRSTBORN
Lk   2: 7   her **firstborn** son and wrapped
Ro   8:29   **firstborn** within a large family
Co   1:15   the **firstborn** of all creation;
       1:18   the **firstborn** from the dead, so
He   1: 6   when he brings the **firstborn**
      11:28   destroyer of the **firstborn**
      12:23   assembly of the **firstborn** who
Re   1: 5   the **firstborn** of the dead, and

4416a   GO1 AG727 LN214
πρωτως, FIRSTLY
Ac   11:26   the disciples were **first** called

4417   GO5 AG727 LN214 B3:573 K6:883
πταιω, I STUMBLE
Ro   11:11   So I ask, have they **stumbled** so
Ja   2:10   **fails** in one point has become
       3: 2   all of us **make** many **mistakes.**
       3: 2   Anyone who **makes** no **mistakes** in
2P   1:10   do this, you **will** never **stumble**

4418   GO1 AG727 LN214 B1:241
πτερνα, HEEL
Jn   13:18   has lifted his **heel** against me.

4419   GO2 AG727 LN214 B3:796 R4420
πτερυγιον, WING
Mt   4: 5   placed him on the **pinnacle** of
Lk   4: 9   placed him on the **pinnacle** of

4420   GO5 AG727 LN214 B3:796 R4072
πτερυξ, WING
Mt   23:37   her brood under her **wings,** and
Lk   13:34   her brood under her **wings,** and
Re   4: 8   each of them with six **wings,**
       9: 9   the noise of their **wings** was
      12:14   given the two **wings** of the

4421   GO1 AG727 LN214 R4071
πτηνος, BIRD
1C   15:39   another for **birds,** and another

4422   GO2 AG727 LN214
πτοεω, I AM TERRIFIED
Lk   21: 9   do not **be terrified;** for these
      24:37   were startled and **terrified,**

4423   GO1 AG727 LN214 R4422
πτοησις, TERROR
1P   3: 6   and never let fears **alarm** you.

4424   GO1 AG727 LN214
πτολεμαις, PTOLEMAIS
Ac   21: 7   we arrived at **Ptolemais;** and

4425   GO2 AG727 LN214 B3:527
πτυον, WINNOWING SHOVEL
Mt   3:12   His **winnowing fork** is in his
Lk   3:17   His **winnowing fork** is in his

4426   GO1 AG727 LN214
πτυρω, I FRIGHTEN
Ph   1:28   and are in no way **intimidated**

4427   GO1 AG727 LN214 R4429
πτυσμα, SPIT
Jn   9: 6   made mud with the **saliva** and

4428   GO1 AG727 LN214
πτυσσω, I ROLL
Lk   4:20   And he **rolled up** the scroll,

4429   GO3 AG727 LN215
πτυω, I SPIT
Mk   7:33   he **spat** and touched his tongue.
       8:23   when he had **put saliva** on his
Jn   9: 6   he **spat** on the ground and made

4430   GO7 AG727 LN215 B1:608 K6:166
πτωμα, CORPSE
Mt   14:12   took the **body** and buried it;
      24:28   Wherever the **corpse** is, there
Mk   6:29   came and took his **body,** and
      15:45   he granted the **body** to Joseph.
Re   11: 8   and their dead **bodies** will lie
      11: 9   gaze at their dead **bodies** and
      11: 9   refuse to let **them** be placed in

4431   ᴳᴼ2 ᴬᴳ728 ᴸᴺ215 ᴮ1:608 ᴷ6:167
πτωσις, FALL
Mt   7:27   fell—and great was its **fall!**
Lk   2:34   destined for the **falling** and

4432   ᴳᴼ3 ᴬᴳ728 ᴸᴺ215 ᴮ2:821 ᴷ6:885 ᴿ4433
πτωχεια, POVERTY
2C   8: 2   extreme **poverty** have overflowed
    8: 9   so that by his **poverty** you
Re   2: 9   your **poverty,** even though you

4433   ᴳᴼ1 ᴬᴳ728 ᴸᴺ215 ᴮ2:821 ᴷ6:885 ᴿ4434
πτωχευω, I BECOME POOR
2C   8: 9   he **became poor,** so that by his

4434   ᴳᴼ34 ᴬᴳ728 ᴸᴺ215 ᴮ2:821 ᴷ6:885
πτωχος, POOR
Mt   5: 3   Blessed are the **poor** in spirit
   11: 5   the **poor** have good news brought
   19:21   give the money to the **poor,** and
   26: 9   and the money given to the **poor**
   26:11   For you always have the **poor**
Mk   10:21   give the money to the **poor,** and
   12:42   A **poor** widow came and put in
   12:43   this **poor** widow has put in more
   14: 5   money given to the **poor.**" And
   14: 7   For you always have the **poor**
Lk   4:18   bring good news to the **poor.** He
   6:20   Blessed are you who are **poor,**
   7:22   the **poor** have good news brought
   14:13   invite the **poor,** the crippled,
   14:21   bring in the **poor,** the crippled
   16:20   And at his gate lay a **poor** man
   16:22   The **poor** man died and was
   18:22   money to the **poor,** and you will
   19: 8   I will give to the **poor;** and if
   21: 3   this **poor** widow has put in more
Jn   12: 5   and the money given to the **poor**
   12: 6   he cared about the **poor,** but
   12: 8   You always have the **poor** with
   13:29   give something to the **poor.**
Ro   15:26   resources with the **poor** among
2C   6:10   as **poor,** yet making many rich;
Ga   2:10   we remember the **poor,** which
        was
   4: 9   the weak and **beggarly** elemental
Ja   2: 2   if a **poor** person in dirty
   2: 3   to the one who is **poor** you say,
   2: 5   Has not God chosen the **poor** in
   2: 6   you have dishonored the **poor.**

Re   3:17   **poor,** blind, and naked.
   13:16   both rich and **poor,** both free

4435   ᴳᴼ1 ᴬᴳ728 ᴸᴺ215 ᴮ2:148 ᴷ6:915
πυγμη, IN FIST
Mk   7: 3   **thoroughly** wash their hands,

4436   ᴳᴼ1 ᴬᴳ728 ᴸᴺ215 ᴷ6:917
πυθων, PYTHON
Ac   16:16   a spirit of **divination** and

4437   ᴳᴼ3 ᴬᴳ729 ᴸᴺ215
πυκνος, FREQUENT
Lk   5:33   **frequently** fast and pray, but
Ac   24:26   send for him **very often** and
1Ti   5:23   and your **frequent** ailments.

4438   ᴳᴼ1 ᴬᴳ729 ᴸᴺ215 ᴷ6:915
πυκτευω, I BOX
1C   9:26   nor do I **box** as though beating

4439   ᴳᴼ10 ᴬᴳ729 ᴸᴺ215 ᴮ2:29 ᴷ6:921
πυλη, GATE
Mt   7:13   Enter through the narrow **gate;**
   7:13   for the **gate** is wide and the
   7:14   For the **gate** is narrow and the
   16:18   the **gates** of Hades will not
Lk   7:12   As he approached the **gate** of
Ac   3:10   Beautiful **Gate** of the temple;
   9:24   were watching the **gates** day and
   12:10   before the iron **gate** leading
   16:13   outside the **gate** by the river,
He   13:12   outside the city **gate** in order

4440   ᴳᴼ18 ᴬᴳ729 ᴸᴺ215 ᴮ2:29 ᴷ6:921 ᴿ4439
πυλων, GATE
Mt   26:71   When he went out to the **porch,**
Lk   16:20   And at his **gate** lay a poor man
Ac   10:17   and were standing by the **gate.**
   12:13   knocked at the outer **gate,** a
   12:14   instead of opening the **gate,**
   12:14   Peter was standing at the **gate.**
   14:13   oxen and garlands to the **gates;**
Re   21:12   wall with twelve **gates,** and at
   21:12   at the **gates** twelve angels, and
   21:13   on the east three **gates,** on the
   21:13   on the north three **gates,** on
   21:13   on the south three **gates,** and
   21:13   and on the west three **gates.**
   21:15   city and its **gates** and walls.

21:21	And the twelve **gates** are twelve
21:21	each of the **gates** is a single
21:25	Its **gates** will never be shut by
22:14	may enter the city by the **gates**

4441   GO12 AG729 LN215
πυνθανομαι, I INQUIRE

Mt	2: 4	he **inquired** of them where the
Lk	15:26	and **asked** what was going on.
	18:36	he **asked** what was happening.
Jn	4:52	So he **asked** them the hour when
	13:24	motioned to him to **ask** Jesus of
Ac	4: 7	they **inquired**, "By what power
	10:18	They called out to **ask** whether
	10:29	Now may I **ask** why you sent for
	21:33	he **inquired** who he was and what
	23:19	and **asked**, "What is it that you
	23:20	to **inquire** more thoroughly into
	23:34	On reading the letter, he **asked**

4442   GO73 AG729 LN215 B1:652 K6:928
πυρ, FIRE

Mt	3:10	down and thrown into the **fire.**
	3:11	with the Holy Spirit and **fire.**
	3:12	burn with unquenchable **fire.**
	5:22	be liable to the hell of **fire.**
	7:19	down and thrown into the **fire.**
	13:40	burned up with **fire,** so will it
	13:42	into the furnace of **fire,** where
	13:50	into the furnace of **fire,** where
	17:15	falls into the **fire** and often
	18: 8	be thrown into the eternal **fire**
	18: 9	thrown into the hell of **fire.**
	25:41	into the eternal **fire** prepared
Mk	9:22	cast him into the **fire** and into
	9:43	hell, to the unquenchable **fire.**
	9:48	and the **fire** is never quenched.
	9:49	will be salted with **fire.**
Lk	3: 9	down and thrown into the **fire.**
	3:16	with the Holy Spirit and **fire.**
	3:17	burn with unquenchable **fire.**
	9:54	do you want us to command **fire**
	12:49	I came to bring **fire** to the
	17:29	it rained **fire** and sulfur from
	22:55	When they had kindled a **fire** in
Jn	15: 6	into the **fire,** and burned.
Ac	2: 3	Divided tongues, as of **fire,**
	2:19	blood, and **fire,** and smoky mist
	7:30	in the flame of a **burning** bush.

	28: 5	into the **fire** and suffered no
Ro	12:20	heap **burning** coals on their
1C	3:13	will be revealed with **fire,** and
	3:13	the **fire** will test what sort of
	3:15	saved, but only as through **fire**
2Th	1: 8	in flaming **fire,** inflicting
He	1: 7	and his servants flames of **fire**
	10:27	fury of **fire** that will consume
	11:34	quenched raging **fire,** escaped
	12:18	a blazing **fire,** and darkness,
	12:29	our God is a consuming **fire.**
Ja	3: 5	is set ablaze by a small **fire!**
	3: 6	And the tongue is a **fire.** The
	5: 3	will eat your flesh like **fire.**
1P	1: 7	is tested by **fire**—may be
2P	3: 7	have been reserved for **fire,**
Ju	1: 7	a punishment of eternal **fire.**
	1:23	snatching them out of the **fire;**
Re	1:14	eyes were like a flame of **fire,**
	2:18	eyes like a flame of **fire,** and
	3:18	gold refined by **fire** so that
	4: 5	throne burn seven **flaming**
	8: 5	filled it with **fire** from the
	8: 7	there came hail and **fire,** mixed
	8: 8	burning with **fire,** was thrown
	9:17	color of **fire** and of sapphire
	9:18	the **fire** and smoke and sulfur
	10: 1	his legs like pillars of **fire.**
	11: 5	**fire** pours from their mouth and
	13:13	even making **fire** come down from
	14:10	tormented with **fire** and sulfur
	14:18	who has authority over **fire,**
	15: 2	a sea of glass mixed with **fire,**
	16: 8	to scorch them with **fire;**
	17:16	flesh and burn her up with **fire**
	18: 8	she will be burned with **fire;**
	19:12	eyes are like a flame of **fire,**
	19:20	into the lake of **fire** that
	20: 9	And **fire** came down from heaven
	20:10	thrown into the lake of **fire**
	20:14	thrown into the lake of **fire.**
	20:14	second death, the lake of **fire;**
	20:15	thrown into the lake of **fire.**
	21: 8	lake that burns with **fire** and

4443   GO2 AG730 LN215 B1:653
πυρα, FIRE

| Ac | 28: 2 | kindled a **fire** and welcomed |
| | 28: 3 | was putting it on the **fire,** |

4444　GO4 AG730 LN215 K6:953
πυργος, TOWER
Mt 21:33　built a **watchtower.** Then he
Mk 12: 1　built a **watchtower;** then he
Lk 13: 4　killed when the **tower** of Siloam
　 14:28　intending to build a **tower,**

4445　GO2 AG730 LN215 B1:653 K6:956 R4443
πυρεσσω, I BURN
Mt 8:14　lying in bed **with a fever;**
Mk 1:30　was in bed **with a fever,** and

4446　GO6 AG730 LN215 B1:653 K6:956 R4445
πυρετος, FEVER
Mt 8:15　and the **fever** left her, and she
Mk 1:31　Then the **fever** left her, and
Lk 4:38　suffering from a high **fever,**
　 4:39　rebuked the **fever,** and it left
Jn 4:52　one in the afternoon the **fever**
Ac 28: 8　sick in bed with **fever** and

4447　GO1 AG731 LN215 B1:653 K6:951 R4443
πυρινος, OF FIRE
Re 9:17　breastplates the **color of fire**

4448　GO6 AG731 LN215 B1:653 K6:948 R4442
πυροω, I SET ON FIRE
1C 7: 9　than **to be aflame with passion.**
2C 11:29　stumble, and I **am** not **indignant**
Ep 6:16　quench all the **flaming** arrows
2P 3:12　heavens will be set **ablaze** and
Re 1:15　**refined** as in a furnace, and
　 3:18　gold **refined** by fire so that

4449　GO2 AG731 LN216 B1:653
πυρραζω, I REDDEN
Mt 16: 2　weather, for the sky **is red.**
　 16: 3　the sky **is red** and threatening.

4449a　GO1 AG731 LN216
πυρρος, OF PYRRUS
Ac 20: 4　son **of Pyrrhus** from Beroea, by

4450　GO1 AG731 LN216 B1:205 K6:952 R4449
πυρρος, RED
Re 6: 4　came another horse, bright **red;**
　 12: 3　a great **red** dragon, with seven

4451　GO3 AG731 LN216 B1:653 K6:950 R4448
πυρωσις, BURNING

1P 4:12　surprised at the **fiery** ordeal
Re 18: 9　see the smoke of her **burning;**
　 18:18　saw the smoke of her **burning,**

4453　GO22 AG731 LN216 B1:268
πωλεω, I SELL
Mt 10:29　Are not two sparrows **sold** for
　 13:44　goes and **sells** all that he has
　 19:21　go, **sell** your possessions, and
　 21:12　drove out all who were **selling**
　 21:12　seats of those who **sold** doves.
　 25: 9　better go to the **dealers** and
Mk 10:21　go, **sell** what you own, and give
　 11:15　who **were selling** and those who
　 11:15　seats of those who **sold** doves;
Lk 12: 6　Are not five sparrows **sold** for
　 12:33　**Sell** your possessions, and give
　 17:28　buying and **selling,** planting
　 18:22　**Sell** all that you own and
　 19:45　those who **were selling** things
　 22:36　one who has no sword must **sell**
Jn 2:14　he found people **selling** cattle,
　 2:16　He told those who were **selling**
Ac 4:34　owned lands or houses **sold** them
　 4:37　He **sold** a field that belonged
　 5: 1　**sold** a piece of property;
1C 10:25　Eat whatever **is sold** in the
Re 13:17　so that no one can buy or **sell**

4454　GO12 AG731 LN216 B1:117 K6:959
πωλος, COLT
Mt 21: 2　and a **colt** with her; untie them
　 21: 5　and on a **colt,** the foal of a
　 21: 7　brought the donkey and the **colt**
Mk 11: 2　tied there a **colt** that has
　 11: 4　They went away and found a **colt**
　 11: 5　are you doing, untying the **colt**
　 11: 7　Then they brought the **colt** to
Lk 19:30　you will find tied there a **colt**
　 19:33　As they were untying the **colt,**
　 19:33　Why are you untying the **colt?**
　 19:35　their cloaks on the **colt,** they
Jn 12:15　sitting on a donkey's **colt!**

4455　GO6 AG732 LN216 B3:521
πωποτε, EVER YET (NEVER)
Lk 19:30　colt that has **never** been ridden
Jn 1:18　No one has **ever** seen God. It is
　 5:37　You have **never** heard his voice
　 6:35　believes in me will **never** be

| | 8:33 | **never** been slaves to anyone. |
| 1J | 4:12 | No one has **ever** seen God; if we |

4456 G05 AG732 LN216 B2:153 K5:1022
πωροω, I HARDEN

Mk	6:52	but their hearts **were hardened.**
	8:17	**Are** your hearts **hardened?**
Jn	12:40	**hardened** their heart, so that
Ro	11: 7	it, but the rest **were hardened,**
2C	3:14	But their minds **were hardened.**

4457 G03 AG732 LN216 B2:153 K5:1022 R4456
πωρωσις, HARDNESS

Mk	3: 5	grieved at their **hardness** of
Ro	11:25	a **hardening** has come upon part
Ep	4:18	ignorance and **hardness** of heart

4458 G015 AG732
πως, PERHAPS

Ac	27:12	on the chance that **somehow** they
Ro	1:10	I may **somehow** at last succeed
	11:14	**in order to** make my own
	11:21	natural branches, **perhaps** he
1C	8: 9	does not **somehow** become a
	9:27	**so that** after proclaiming to
2C	2: 7	console him, **so that** he may not
	9: 4	**otherwise,** if some Macedonians
	11: 3	But I am afraid **that** as the
	12:20	For I fear **that** when I come,
	12:20	there may **perhaps** be quarreling
Ga	2: 2	**in order to** make sure that I
	4:11	I am afraid **that** my work for
Ph	3:11	if **somehow** I may attain the
1Th	3: 5	I was afraid that **somehow** the

4459 G0103 AG732 LN216
πως, HOW

Mt	6:28	lilies of the field, **how** they
	7: 4	Or **how** can you say to your
	10:19	do not worry about **how** you are
	12: 4	**He** entered the house of God and
	12:26	**how** then will his kingdom stand
	12:29	Or **how** can one enter a strong
	12:34	You brood of vipers! **How** can
	16:11	**How** could you fail to perceive
	21:20	**How** did the fig tree wither
	22:12	Friend, **how** did you get in
	22:43	**How** is it then that David by
	22:45	him Lord, **how** can he be his son
	23:33	you brood of vipers! **How** can

	26:54	But **how** then would the
Mk	2:26	**He** entered the house of God,
	3:23	**How** can Satan cast out Satan?
	4:13	Then **how** will you understand
	4:30	He also said, **"With what** can we
	5:16	Those who had seen **what** had
	9:12	**How** then is it written about
	10:23	**How** hard it will be for those
	10:24	Children, **how** hard it is to
	11:18	they kept looking **for a way** to
	12:26	**how** God said to him, 'I am the
	12:35	**How** can the scribes say that
	12:41	watched **the** crowd putting money
	14: 1	scribes were looking **for a way**
	14:11	So he began **to look for** an
Lk	1:34	**How** can this be, since I am a
	6:42	Or **how** can you say to your
	8:18	Then pay attention to **how** you
	8:36	had seen it told them **how** the
	10:26	the law? **What** do you read there
	11:18	**how** will his kingdom stand?—
	12:11	do not worry about **how** you are
	12:27	Consider the lilies, **how** they
	12:50	**what** stress I am under until it
	12:56	You hypocrites! You know **how** to
	14: 7	When he noticed **how** the guests
	18:24	**How** hard it is for those who
	20:41	Then he said to them, **"How** can
	20:44	Lord; so **how** can he be his son?
	22: 2	looking **for a way** to put Jesus
	22: 4	about **how** he might betray him
Jn	3: 4	**How** can anyone be born after
	3: 9	him, **"How** can these things be?"
	3:12	**how** can you believe if I tell
	4: 9	**How** is it that you, a Jew, ask
	5:44	**How** can you believe when you
	5:47	**how** will you believe what I say
	6:42	**How** can he now say, 'I have
	6:52	**How** can this man give us his
	7:15	**How** does this man have such
	8:33	**What do you mean** by saying,
	9:10	Then **how** were your eyes opened
	9:15	began to ask him **how** he had
	9:16	**How** can a man who is a sinner
	9:19	**How** then does he now see?
	9:21	but we do not know **how** it is
	9:26	you? **How** did he open your eyes?
	11:36	said, "See **how** he loved him!"
	12:34	**How** can you say that the Son of

	14: 5	going. **How** can we know the way?
	14: 9	**How** can you say, 'Show us the
Ac	2: 8	And **how** is it that we hear,
	4:21	finding no way **to** punish them
	8:31	**How** can I, unless someone
	9:27	described for them **how** on the
	9:27	**how** in Damascus he had spoken
	11:13	He told us **how** he had seen the
	12:17	described for them **how** the Lord
	15:36	Lord and see **how** they are doing
	20:18	yourselves know **how** I lived
Ro	3: 6	By no means! For then **how** could
	4:10	**How** then was it reckoned to him
	6: 2	By no means! **How** can we who
	8:32	**will** he not with him also give
	10:14	But **how** are they to call on one
	10:14	And **how** are they to believe in
	10:14	**how** are they to hear without
	10:15	And **how** are they to proclaim
1C	3:10	choose with care **how** to build
	7:32	Lord, **how** to please the Lord;
	7:33	world, **how** to please his wife,
	7:34	**how** to please her husband.
	14: 7	**how** will anyone know what is
	14: 9	**how** will anyone know what is
	14:16	**how** can anyone in the position
	15:12	**how** can some of you say there
	15:35	**How** are the dead raised?
2C	3: 8	**how** much more will the ministry
Ga	2:14	**how** can you compel the Gentiles
	4: 9	**how** can you turn back again to
Ep	5:15	Be careful then **how** you live,
Co	4: 6	you may know **how** you ought to
1Th	1: 9	**how** you turned to God from
	4: 1	learned from us **how** you ought
2Th	3: 7	For you yourselves know **how** you
1Ti	3: 5	if someone does not know **how**
	3:15	I am delayed, you may know **how**
He	2: 3	**how** can we escape if we neglect
1J	3:17	**How** does God's love abide in
Re	3: 3	Remember then **what** you received

ρ

4460   ᴳᴼ2 ᴬᴳ733 ᴸᴺ216
ῥααβ, RAHAB

He	11:31	By faith **Rahab** the prostitute
Ja	2:25	Likewise, was not **Rahab** the

4461   ᴳᴼ15 ᴬᴳ733 ᴸᴺ216 ᴮ3:115 ᴷ6:961
ῥαββι, RABBI

Mt	23: 7	to have people call them **rabbi.**
	23: 8	you are not to be called **rabbi,**
	26:25	said, "Surely not I, **Rabbi?**" He
	26:49	"Greetings, **Rabbi!**" and kissed
Mk	9: 5	Peter said to Jesus, **"Rabbi,** it
	11:21	**Rabbi,** look! The fig tree that
	14:45	said, **"Rabbi!"** and kissed him.
Jn	1:38	**"Rabbi"** (which translated means
	1:49	Nathanael replied, **"Rabbi,** you
	3: 2	**Rabbi,** we know that you are a
	3:26	**Rabbi,** the one who was with
	4:31	him, **"Rabbi,** eat something."
	6:25	**Rabbi,** when did you come here?
	9: 2	**Rabbi,** who sinned, this man or
	11: 8	**Rabbi,** the Jews were just now

4462   ᴳᴼ2 ᴬᴳ733 ᴸᴺ216 ᴮ3:115 ᴷ6:961 ᴿ4461
ῥαββουνι, RABBONI

Mk	10:51	My **teacher,** let me see again.
Jn	20:16	**"Rabbouni!"** (which means

4463   ᴳᴼ2 ᴬᴳ733 ᴸᴺ216 ᴮ1:407 ᴷ6:970 ᴿ4464
ῥαβδιζω, I BEAT WITH A ROD

Ac	16:22	them **to be beaten with rods.**
2C	11:25	times I **was beaten with rods.**

4464   ᴳᴼ12 ᴬᴳ733 ᴸᴺ216 ᴮ1:161 ᴷ6:966
ῥαβδος, ROD

Mt	10:10	or sandals, or a **staff;** for
Mk	6: 8	their journey except a **staff;**
Lk	9: 3	no **staff,** nor bag, nor bread,
1C	4:21	I to come to you with a **stick,**
He	1: 8	the righteous **scepter** is the
	1: 8	the **scepter** of your kingdom.
	9: 4	and Aaron's **rod** that budded,
	11:21	over the top of his **staff.**
Re	2:27	to rule them with an iron **rod,**
	11: 1	measuring rod like a **staff,** and
	12: 5	rule all the nations with a **rod**
	19:15	rule them with a **rod** of iron;

4465   ᴳᴼ2 ᴬᴳ733 ᴸᴺ216 ᴮ1:407 ᴷ6:971
ῥαβδουχος, ROD-BEARERS

Ac	16:35	the magistrates sent the **police**
	16:38	The **police** reported these words

4466   GO1 AG733 LN216
ῥαγαυ, RHAGAU (REU)
Lk   3:35   son of Serug, son of **Reu,** son

4467   GO1 AG733 LN216 K6:972
ῥαδιουργημα, FRAUD
Ac 18:14   crime or serious **villainy,** I

4468   GO1 AG733 LN216 K6:972
ῥαδιουργια, FRAUD
Ac 13:10   full of all deceit and **villainy**

4468a   GO1 AG733 LN216
ῥαιφαν, RAIPHAN (REPHAN)
Ac   7:43   the star of your god **Rephan,**

4469   GO1 AG733 LN216 B1:417 K6:973
ῥακα, RACA
Mt   5:22   you **insult** a brother or sister,

4470   GO2 AG734 LN216
ῥακος, CLOTH
Mt   9:16   sews a piece of unshrunk **cloth**
Mk   2:21   sews a piece of unshrunk **cloth**

4471   GO1 AG734 LN216
ῥαμα, RAMA (RAMAH)
Mt   2:18   A voice was heard in **Ramah,**

4472   GO4 AG734 LN216 B1:224 K6:976
ῥαντιζω, I SPRINKLE
He   9:13   the **sprinkling** of the ashes of
     9:19   and **sprinkled** both the scroll
     9:21   in the same way he **sprinkled**
    10:22   with our hearts **sprinkled** clean

4473   GO2 AG734 LN216 B1:224 R4472
ῥαντισμος, SPRINKLING
He 12:24   the **sprinkled** blood that
            speaks
1P   1: 2   to be **sprinkled** with his blood:

4474   GO2 AG734 LN216 B1:162
ῥαπιζω, I SLAP
Mt   5:39   But if anyone **strikes** you on
    26:67   him; and some **slapped** him,

4475   GO3 AG734 LN216 B1:162 R4474
ῥαπισμα, SLAP
Mk 14:65   **strike** him, saying to him,

Jn 18:22   **struck** Jesus on the face,
    19: 3   Jews!" and **striking** him on the

4476   GO2 AG734 LN216
ῥαφις, NEEDLE
Mt 19:24   through the eye of a **needle**
Mk 10:25   through the eye of a **needle**

4477   GO1 AG734 LN217 K3:1
ῥαχαβ, RACHAB (RAHAB)
Mt   1: 5   the father of Boaz by **Rahab,** and

4478   GO1 AG734 LN217
ῥαχηλ, RACHEL
Mt   2:18   **Rachel** weeping for her children

4479   GO1 AG734 LN217
ῥεβεκκα, REBECCA
Ro   9:10   happened to **Rebecca** when she

4480   GO1 AG734 LN217
ῥεδη, CHARIOT
Re 18:13   **chariots,** slaves—and human

4482   GO1 AG735 LN217 B1:682
ῥεω, I FLOW
Jn   7:38   believer's heart **shall flow**

4484   GO1 AG735 LN217
ῥηγιον, RHEGIUM
Ac 28:13   anchor and came to **Rhegium.**

4485   GO1 AG735 LN217 R4486
ῥηγμα, BREAK UP
Lk   6:49   and great was the **ruin** of that

4486   GO7 AG735 LN217
ῥηγνυμι, I RIP
Mt   7: 6   under foot and turn and **maul**
     9:17   the skins **burst,** and the wine
Mk   2:22   the wine **will burst** the skins,
     9:18   it **dashes** him down; and he
Lk   5:37   new wine **will burst** the skins
     9:42   the demon **dashed** him to the
Ga   4:27   **burst** into song and shout, you

4487   GO68 AG735 LN217 B3:1119 K4:69
ῥημα, WORD
Mt   4: 4   but by every **word** that comes
    12:36   for every careless **word** you

	18:16	so that every **word** may be		28:25	Paul made one further **statement**
	26:75	Then Peter remembered **what**	Ro	10: 8	But what does it say? "The **word**
	27:14	But he gave him no **answer,**		10: 8	**word** of faith that we proclaim)
Mk	9:32	what he was **saying** and were		10:17	heard comes through the **word** of
	14:72	Then Peter remembered **that**		10:18	their **words** to the ends of the
Lk	1:37	For **nothing** will be impossible	2C	12: 4	heard **things** that are not to be
	1:38	according to your **word.**" Then		13: 1	Any **charge** must be sustained
	1:65	all these **things** were talked	Ep	5:26	washing of water by the **word,**
	2:15	see this **thing** that has taken		6:17	Spirit, which is the **word** of
	2:17	they made known **what** had been	He	1: 3	all things by his powerful **word**
	2:19	treasured all these **words** and		6: 5	tasted the goodness of the **word**
	2:29	peace, according to your **word;**		11: 3	prepared by the **word** of God, so
	2:50	they did not understand **what**		12:19	a voice whose **words** made the
	2:51	treasured all these **things** in	1P	1:25	the **word** of the Lord endures
	3: 2	the **word** of God came to John		1:25	That **word** is the good news that
	5: 5	Yet if you **say** so, I will let	2P	3: 2	remember the **words** spoken in
	7: 1	finished all his **sayings** in the	Ju	1:17	remember the **predictions** of the
	9:45	did not understand this **saying;**			
	9:45	to ask him about this **saying.**			

4488   G0 1   AG735   LN217
ῥησα, RHESA
Lk   3:27   son of Joanan, son of **Rhesa,**

4489   G0 1   AG735   LN217   B3:1119
ῥητωρ, SPEAKER
Ac   24: 1   some elders and an **attorney,**

4490   G0 1   AG736   LN217
ῥητως, EXPRESSLY
1Ti   4: 1   Now the Spirit **expressly** says

4491   G0 17   AG736   LN217   B3:865   K6:985
ῥιζα, ROOT

	18:34	what he **said** was hidden from
	20:26	trap him by what he **said;** and
	22:61	Peter remembered the **word** of
	24: 8	Then they remembered his **words,**
	24:11	But these **words** seemed to them
Jn	3:34	speaks the **words** of God, for he
	5:47	how will you believe what I **say**
	6:63	The **words** that I have spoken to
	6:68	You have the **words** of eternal
	8:20	He spoke these **words** while he
	8:47	hears the **words** of God. The
	10:21	These are not the **words** of one
	12:47	anyone who hears my **words** and
	12:48	does not receive my **word** has a
	14:10	The **words** that I say to you I
	15: 7	and my **words** abide in you, ask
	17: 8	for the **words** that you gave to
Ac	2:14	listen to what I **say.**
	5:20	whole **message** about this life.
	5:32	witnesses to these **things,** and
	6:11	speak blasphemous **words** against
	6:13	stops saying **things** against
	10:22	to hear **what** you have to say.
	10:37	That **message** spread throughout
	10:44	upon all who heard the **word.**
	11:14	he will give you a **message** by
	11:16	And I remembered the **word** of
	13:42	speak about these **things** again
	16:38	The police reported these **words**
	26:25	I am **speaking** the sober truth.

Mt	3:10	the ax is lying at the **root** of
	13: 6	since they had no **root,** they
	13:21	yet such a person has no **root,**
Mk	4: 6	and since it had no **root,** it
	4:17	But they have no **root,** and
	11:20	tree withered away to its **roots**
Lk	3: 9	the ax is lying at the **root** of
	8:13	But these have no **root;** they
Ro	11:16	if the **root** is holy, then the
	11:17	share the rich **root** of the
	11:18	support the **root,** but the root
	11:18	but the **root** that supports you.
	15:12	The **root** of Jesse shall come,
1Ti	6:10	For the love of money is a **root**
He	12:15	that no **root** of bitterness
Re	5: 5	**Root** of David, has conquered,
	22:16	am the **root** and the descendant

4492　ᴳᴼ2 ᴬᴳ736 ᴸᴺ217 ᴮ3:865 ᴷ6:990 ᴿ4491
ῥιζόω, I ROOT
Ep　3:17　are being **rooted** and grounded
Co　2: 7　**rooted** and built up in him and

4493　ᴳᴼ1 ᴬᴳ736 ᴸᴺ217 ᴮ2:925 ᴿ4496
ῥιπή, BLINK
1C　15:52　in a moment, in the **twinkling**

4494　ᴳᴼ1 ᴬᴳ736 ᴸᴺ217 ᴮ3:1000 ᴿ4496
ῥιπίζω, I TOSS
Ja　1: 6　driven and **tossed** by the wind;

4495　ᴳᴼ1 ᴬᴳ736 ᴸᴺ217
ῥιπτέω, I FLING
Ac　22:23　**throwing off** their cloaks, and

4496　ᴳᴼ7 ᴬᴳ736 ᴸᴺ217 ᴷ6:991
ῥίπτω, I FLING
Mt　9:36　harassed and **helpless,** like
　　15:30　They **put** them at his feet, and
　　27: 5　**Throwing down** the pieces of
Lk　4:35　the demon **had thrown** him **down**
　　17: 2　you **were thrown** into the sea
Ac　27:19　they **threw** the ship's tackle
　　27:29　they **let down** four anchors from

4497　ᴳᴼ2 ᴬᴳ736 ᴸᴺ217
ῥοβοαμ, ROBOAM (REHOBOAM)
Mt　1: 7　the father of **Rehoboam,** and
　　1: 7　**Rehoboam** the father of Abijah,

4498　ᴳᴼ1 ᴬᴳ736 ᴸᴺ217
ῥοδη, RHODA
Ac　12:13　maid named **Rhoda** came to
　　　　　　answer

4499　ᴳᴼ1 ᴬᴳ736 ᴸᴺ217
ῥοδος, RHODE
Ac　21: 1　and the next day to **Rhodes,** and

4500　ᴳᴼ1 ᴬᴳ737 ᴸᴺ217
ῥοιζηδόν, CRACKING SOUND
2P　3:10　pass away with a **loud noise,**

4501　ᴳᴼ7 ᴬᴳ737 ᴸᴺ217 ᴮ3:959 ᴷ6:993
ῥομφαία, SWORD
Lk　2:35　**sword** will pierce your own soul
Re　1:16　sharp, two-edged **sword,** and his
　　2:12　has the sharp two-edged **sword:**

　　2:16　them with the **sword** of my
　　　　　　mouth
　　6: 8　to kill with **sword,** famine, and
　　19:15　comes a sharp **sword** with which
　　19:21　killed by the **sword** of the

4502　ᴳᴼ1 ᴬᴳ737 ᴸᴺ218
ῥουβην, REUBEN
Re　7: 5　tribe of **Reuben** twelve thousand

4503　ᴳᴼ1 ᴬᴳ737 ᴸᴺ218 ᴷ3:1
ῥουθ, RUTH
Mt　1: 5　Boaz the father of Obed by **Ruth,**

4504　ᴳᴼ2 ᴬᴳ737 ᴸᴺ218
ῥουφος, RUFUS
Mk　15:21　father of Alexander and **Rufus.**
Ro　16:13　Greet **Rufus,** chosen in the Lord

4505　ᴳᴼ4 ᴬᴳ737 ᴸᴺ218
ῥύμη, LANE
Mt　6: 2　synagogues and in the **streets,**
Lk　14:21　Go out at once into the **streets**
Ac　9:11　Get up and go to the **street**
　　12:10　walked along a **lane,** when

4506　ᴳᴼ17 ᴬᴳ737 ᴸᴺ218 ᴮ3:200 ᴷ6:998
ῥύομαι, I RESCUE
Mt　6:13　but **rescue** us from the evil one
　　27:43　let God **deliver** him now, if he
Lk　1:74　we, **being rescued** from the
Ro　7:24　Who **will rescue** me from this
　　11:26　Zion will come the **Deliverer;**
　　15:31　that I **may be rescued** from the
2C　1:10　He who **rescued** us from so
　　1:10　peril will continue to **rescue**
　　1:10　hope that he will **rescue** us
Co　1:13　He has **rescued** us from the
1Th　1:10　who **rescues** us from the wrath
2Th　3: 2　and that we may be **rescued**
　　　　　　from
2Ti　3:11　Yet the Lord **rescued** me from
　　4:17　So I **was rescued** from the
　　4:18　The Lord **will rescue** me from
2P　2: 7　and if he **rescued** Lot, a
　　2: 9　the Lord knows how to **rescue**

4506a　ᴳᴼ1 ᴬᴳ737 ᴸᴺ218 ᴮ1:479
ῥυπαίνω, I AM DIRTY
Re　22:11　and the filthy still **be filthy,**

4507 GO1 AG738 LN218 B1:479 R4508
ρυπαρια, DIRTINESS
Ja　1:21　of all **sordidness** and rank

4508 GO2 AG738 LN218 B1:479 R4509
ρυπαρος, DIRTY
Ja　2: 2　if a poor person in **dirty**
Re　22:11　the **filthy** still be filthy, and

4509 GO1 AG738 LN218 B1:479
ρυπος, DIRT
1P　3:21　not as a removal of **dirt** from

4511 GO3 AG738 LN218 B1:682
ρυσις, FLOW
Mk　5:25　suffering from **hemorrhages** for
Lk　8:43　suffering from **hemorrhages** for
　　8:44　immediately her **hemorrhage**

4512 GO1 AG738 LN218
ρυτις, WRINKLE
Ep　5:27　without a spot or **wrinkle** or

4514 GO12 AG738 LN218
ρωμαιος, ROMAN
Jn　11:48　**Romans** will come and destroy
Ac　2:10　visitors from **Rome,** both Jews
　　16:21　lawful for us as **Romans** to
　　16:37　men who are **Roman** citizens,
　　　　and
　　16:38　that they were **Roman** citizens;
　　22:25　flog a **Roman** citizen who is
　　22:26　This man is a **Roman** citizen.
　　22:27　are you a **Roman** citizen?" And
　　22:29　realized that Paul was a **Roman**
　　23:27　learned that he was a **Roman**
　　25:16　custom of the **Romans** to hand
　　28:17　and handed over to the **Romans.**

4515 GO1 AG738 LN218
ρωμαιστι, IN ROMAN (LATIN)
Jn　19:20　written in Hebrew, in **Latin,**

4516 GO8 AG738 LN218
ρωμη, ROME
Ac　18: 2　ordered all Jews to leave **Rome.**
　　19:21　there, I must also see **Rome.**
　　23:11　must bear witness also in **Rome.**
　　28:14　days. And so we came to **Rome.**
　　28:16　When we came into **Rome,** Paul

Ro　1: 7　To all God's beloved in **Rome,**
　　1:15　to you also who are in **Rome.**
2Ti　1:17　when he arrived in **Rome,** he

4517 GO1 AG738 LN218
ρωννυμι, BE STRONG, FAREWELL
Ac　15:29　you will do well. **Farewell.**

σ, ς

4518 GO2 AG738 LN218
σαβαχθανι, SABACHTHANI
Mt　27:46　Eli, Eli, lema **sabachthani?**
Mk　15:34　Eloi, Eloi, lema **sabachthani?**

4519 GO1 AG738 LN218 B2:69
σαβαωθ, SABAOTH
Ro　9:29　the ears of the Lord of **hosts.**

4520 GO1 AG739 LN218 B3:411 K7:34 R4521
σαββατισμος, SABBATH OBSERVANCE
He　4: 9　So then, a **sabbath** rest still

4521 GO68 AG739 LN218 B3:405 K7:1
σαββατον, SABBATH
Mt　12: 1　grainfields on the **sabbath;** his
　　12: 2　not lawful to do on the **sabbath**
　　12: 5　that on the **sabbath** the priests
　　12: 5　break the **sabbath** and yet are
　　12: 8　of Man is lord of the **sabbath.**
　　12:10　cure on the **sabbath?"** so that
　　12:11　a pit on the **sabbath;** will you
　　12:12　to do good on the **sabbath.**
　　24:20　be in winter or on a **sabbath.**
　　28: 1　After the **sabbath,** as the first
　　28: 1　day of the **week** was dawning,
Mk　1:21　and when the **sabbath** came, he
　　2:23　One **sabbath** he was going
　　2:24　is not lawful on the **sabbath?**
　　2:27　The **sabbath** was made for
　　2:27　not humankind for the **sabbath;**
　　2:28　Man is lord even of the **sabbath**
　　3: 2　cure him on the **sabbath,** so
　　3: 4　to do harm on the **sabbath,** to
　　6: 2　**sabbath** he began to teach in
　　16: 1　When the **sabbath** was over,
　　　　Mary
　　16: 2　on the first day of the **week,**
　　16: 9　the first day of the **week,** he

Lk	4:16	on the **sabbath** day, as was his
	4:31	teaching them on the **sabbath.**
	6: 1	One **sabbath** while Jesus was
	6: 2	is not lawful on the **sabbath?**
	6: 5	of Man is lord of the **sabbath.**
	6: 6	On another **sabbath** he entered
	6: 7	he would cure on the **sabbath,**
	6: 9	to do harm on the **sabbath,** to
	13:10	the synagogues on the **sabbath.**
	13:14	Jesus had cured on the **sabbath,**
	13:14	and not on the **sabbath** day.
	13:15	not each of you on the **sabbath**
	13:16	this bondage on the **sabbath** day
	14: 1	eat a meal on the **sabbath,** they
	14: 3	cure people on the **sabbath,** or
	14: 5	pull it out on a **sabbath** day?
	18:12	I fast twice a **week;** I give a
	23:54	and the **sabbath** was beginning.
	23:56	On the **sabbath** they rested
	24: 1	on the first day of the **week,**
Jn	5: 9	Now that day was a **sabbath.**
	5:10	It is the **sabbath;** it is not
	5:16	such things on the **sabbath.**
	5:18	not only breaking the **sabbath,**
	7:22	circumcise a man on the **sabbath**
	7:23	circumcision on the **sabbath** in
	7:23	man's whole body on the **sabbath**
	9:14	Now it was a **sabbath** day when
	9:16	he does not observe the **sabbath**
	19:31	on the cross during the **sabbath**
	19:31	especially because that **sabbath**
	20: 1	the first day of the **week,**
	20:19	the first day of the **week,**
Ac	1:12	a **sabbath** day's journey away.
	13:14	on the **sabbath** day they went
	13:27	that are read every **sabbath,**
	13:42	things again the next **sabbath.**
	13:44	The next **sabbath** almost the
	15:21	read aloud every **sabbath** in the
	16:13	On the **sabbath** day we went
	17: 2	on three **sabbath** days argued
	18: 4	Every **sabbath** he would argue
	20: 7	On the first day of the **week,**
1C	16: 2	On the first day of every **week,**
Co	2:16	new moons, or **sabbaths.**

4522 GO1 AG739 LN218
σαγηνη, FISHING NET
Mt 13:47 is like a **net** that was thrown

4523 GO14 AG739 LN218 B3:439 K7:35
σαδδουκαιος, SADDUCEE

Mt	3: 7	Pharisees and **Sadducees** coming
	16: 1	Pharisees and **Sadducees** came,
	16: 6	of the Pharisees and **Sadducees.**
	16:11	of the Pharisees and **Sadducees!**
	16:12	of the Pharisees and **Sadducees.**
	22:23	The same day some **Sadducees**
	22:34	he had silenced the **Sadducees,**
Mk	12:18	Some **Sadducees,** who say there
Lk	20:27	Some **Sadducees,** those who say
Ac	4: 1	temple, and the **Sadducees** came
	5:17	the sect of the **Sadducees),**
	23: 6	some were **Sadducees** and others
	23: 7	Pharisees and the **Sadducees,**
	23: 8	(The **Sadducees** say that there

4524 GO2 AG739 LN218
σαδωκ, SADOK (ZADOK)

| Mt | 1:14 | and Azor the father of **Zadok,** |
| | 1:14 | and **Zadok** the father of Achim, |

4525 GO1 AG740 LN218 K7:54
σαινω, I SHAKE
1Th 3: 3 so that no one would **be shaken**

4526 GO4 AG740 LN218 K7:56
σακκος, SACKCLOTH

Mt	11:21	repented long ago in **sackcloth**
Lk	10:13	sitting in **sackcloth** and ashes.
Re	6:12	sun became black as **sackcloth,**
	11: 3	sixty days, wearing **sackcloth.**

4527 GO2 AG740 LN218
σαλα, SALA, SHELAH

| Lk | 3:32 | son of Boaz, son of **Sala,** son |
| | 3:35 | son of Eber, son of **Shelah,** |

4528 GO3 AG740 LN219
σαλαθιηλ, SALATHIEL

Mt	1:12	was the father of **Salathiel,**
	1:12	and **Salathiel** the father of
Lk	3:27	son of **Shealtiel,** son of Neri,

4529 GO1 AG740 LN219
σαλαμις, SALAMIS
Ac 13: 5 When they arrived at **Salamis,**

4530   GO1 AG740 LN219
σαλιμ, SALIM
Jn   3:23   baptizing at Aenon near **Salim**

4531   GO15 AG740 LN219 B3:558 K7:65
σαλευω, I SHAKE
Mt   11: 7   A reed **shaken** by the wind?
     24:29   powers of heaven **will be shaken**
Mk   13:25   in the heavens **will be shaken.**
Lk   6:38   pressed down, **shaken** together,
      6:48   but could not **shake** it, because
      7:24   A reed **shaken** by the wind?
     21:26   of the heavens **will be shaken.**
Ac   2:25   so that I **will** not **be shaken;**
      4:31   gathered together **was shaken;**
     16:26   of the prison **were shaken;** and
     17:13   to **stir up** and incite the
2Th   2: 2   not to be quickly **shaken** in
He   12:26   At that time his voice **shook**
     12:27   removal of what **is shaken**—
     12:27   what cannot **be shaken** may

4532   GO1 AG740 LN219 B2:592
σαλημ, SALEM
He   7: 1   This "King Melchizedek of **Salem**
      7: 2   king of **Salem,** that is, "king

4533   GO2 AG740 LN219
σαλμων, SALMON
Mt   1: 4   Nahshon the father of **Salmon,**
      1: 5   and **Salmon** the father of Boaz

4534   GO1 AG740 LN219
σαλμωνη, SALMONE
Ac   27: 7   the lee of Crete off **Salmone.**

4535   GO2 AG741 LN219 B3:558 K7:65
σαλος, SHAKING
Lk   21:25   of the sea and the **waves.**

4536   GO11 AG741 LN219 B3:873 K7:71
σαλπιγξ, TRUMPET
Mt   24:31   with a loud **trumpet** call, and
1C   14: 8   And if the **bugle** gives an
     15:52   at the last **trumpet.** For the
1Th   4:16   with the sound of God's **trumpet**
He   12:19   and the sound of a **trumpet,** and
Re   1:10   me a loud voice like a **trumpet**
      4: 1   speaking to me like a **trumpet,**
      8: 2   seven **trumpets** were given to

      8: 6   who had the seven **trumpets** made
      8:13   blasts of the other **trumpets**
      9:14   who had the **trumpet,** "Release

4537   GO12 AG741 LN219 B3:873 K7:71 R4536
σαλπιζω, I TRUMPET
Mt   6: 2   do not **sound a trumpet** before
1C   15:52   For the **trumpet will sound,** and
Re   8: 6   trumpets made ready **to blow**
      8: 7   first angel **blew** his **trumpet,**
      8: 8   second angel **blew** his **trumpet,**
      8:10   third angel **blew** his **trumpet,**
      8:12   fourth angel **blew** his **trumpet,**
      8:13   three angels are about **to blow!**
      9: 1   fifth angel **blew** his **trumpet,**
      9:13   sixth angel **blew** his **trumpet,**
     10: 7   angel is to **blow** his **trumpet,**
     11:15   seventh angel **blew** his **trumpet,**

4538   GO1 AG741 LN219 B3:874 K7:71 R4537
σαλπιστης, TRUMPETER
Re   18:22   flutists and **trumpeters** will be

4539   GO2 AG741 LN219
σαλωμη, SALOME
Mk   15:40   and of Joses, and **Salome.**
     16: 1   and **Salome** bought spices, so

4540   GO11 AG741 LN219 B3:449 K7:88
σαμαρεια, SAMARIA
Lk   17:11   between **Samaria** and Galilee.
Jn   4: 4   he had to go through **Samaria.**
      4: 5   So he came to a **Samaritan** city
      4: 7   A **Samaritan** woman came to draw
Ac   1: 8   in all Judea and **Samaria,** and
      8: 1   of Judea and **Samaria.**
      8: 5   city of **Samaria** and proclaimed
      8: 9   amazed the people of **Samaria,**
      8:14   heard that **Samaria** had accepted
      9:31   Judea, Galilee, and **Samaria** had
     15: 3   Phoenicia and **Samaria,** they

4541   GO9 AG741 LN219 B3:450 K7:88
σαμαριτης, SAMARITAN
Mt   10: 5   enter no town of the **Samaritans**
Lk   9:52   a village of the **Samaritans** to
     10:33   But a **Samaritan** while traveling
     17:16   him. And he was a **Samaritan.**
Jn   4: 9   The **Samaritan** woman said to him
      4: 9   in common with **Samaritans.**)

	4:39	Many **Samaritans** from that city
	4:40	So when the **Samaritans** came to
	8:48	you are a **Samaritan** and have a
Ac	8:25	many villages of the **Samaritans**

4542   GO1 AG741 LN219 B3:449 K7:88
σαμαριτις, SAMARITAN
Jn   4: 9   a woman of **Samaria?**" (Jews do

4543   GO1 AG741 LN219
σαμοθρακη, SAMOTHRACE
Ac   16:11   a straight course to **Samothrace**

4544   GO1 AG741 LN219
σαμος, SAMOS
Ac   20:15   next day we touched at **Samos**,

4545   GO3 AG741 LN219
σαμουηλ, SAMUEL
Ac   3:24   from **Samuel** and those after him
       13:20   the time of the prophet **Samuel.**
He   11:32   of David and **Samuel** and the

4546   GO1 AG742 LN219
σαμψων, SAMSON
He   11:32   tell of Gideon, Barak, **Samson,**

4547   GO2 AG742 LN219 K5:310
σανδαλιον, SANDAL
Mk   6: 9   but to wear **sandals** and not to
Ac   12: 8   belt and put on your **sandals.**

4548   GO1 AG742 LN219
σανις, BOARD
Ac   27:44   some on **planks** and others on

4549   GO9 AG742 LN219
σαουλ, SAUL
Ac   9: 4   **Saul,** Saul, why do you
     9: 4   Saul, **Saul,** why do you
     9:17   Brother **Saul,** the Lord Jesus,
     13:21   and God gave them **Saul** son of
     22: 7   **Saul,** Saul, why are you
     22: 7   Saul, **Saul,** why are you
     22:13   Brother **Saul,** regain your
     26:14   **Saul,** Saul, why are you
     26:14   Saul, **Saul,** why are you

4550   GO8 AG742 LN219 B1:565 K7:94
σαπρος, ROTTEN

Mt	7:17	the **bad** tree bears bad fruit.
	7:18	nor can a **bad** tree bear good
	12:33	or make the tree **bad,** and its
	12:33	and its fruit **bad;** for the tree
	13:48	baskets but threw out the **bad.**
Lk	6:43	No good tree bears **bad** fruit,
	6:43	nor again does a **bad** tree bear
Ep	4:29	Let no **evil** talk come out of

4551   GO1 AG742 LN219
σαπφιρη, SAPPHIRA
Ac   5: 1   consent of his wife **Sapphira,**

4552   GO1 AG742 LN219 B3:396
σαπφιρος, SAPPHIRE
Re   21:19   the second **sapphire,** the third

4553   GO1 AG742 LN219
σαργανη, ROPE BASKET
2C   11:33   but I was let down in a **basket**

4554   GO4 AG742 LN219
σαρδεις, SARDIS
Re   1:11   to **Sardis,** to Philadelphia, and
     3: 1   of the church in **Sardis** write:
     3: 4   few persons in **Sardis** who have
     4: 3   looks like jasper and **carnelian**

4556   GO1 AG742 LN219 B3:396
σαρδιον, SARDIS
Re   21:20   sixth **carnelian,** the seventh

4557   GO1 AG742 LN219 B3:396
σαρδονυξ, SARDONYX
Re   21:20   fifth **onyx,** the sixth carnelian

4558   GO1 AG742 LN219
σαρεπτα, SAREPTA (ZAREPHATH)
Lk   4:26   except to a widow at **Zarephath**

4559   GO7 AG742 LN220 B1:671 K7:98 R4561
σαρκικος, FLESHLY
Ro   15:27   to them in **material** things.
1C   3: 3   for you are still **of the flesh.**
     3: 3   are you not **of the flesh,** and
     9:11   we reap your **material** benefits?
2C   1:12   not by **earthly** wisdom but by
     10: 4   are not merely **human,** but they
1P   2:11   from the desires **of the flesh**

4560 GO4 AG743 LN220 B1:671 K7:98 R4561
σαρκινος, OF FLESH

Ro	7:14	but I am **of** the **flesh,** sold
1C	3: 1	rather as people **of** the **flesh,**
2C	3: 3	but on tablets **of human** hearts
He	7:16	concerning **physical** descent,

4561 GO147 AG743 LN220 B1:671 K7:98
σαρξ, FLESH

Mt	16:17	For **flesh** and blood has not
	19: 5	the two shall become one **flesh**
	19: 6	no longer two, but one **flesh.**
	24:22	no **one** would be saved; but for
	26:41	willing, but the **flesh** is weak.
Mk	10: 8	two shall become one **flesh.'** So
	10: 8	no longer two, but one **flesh.**
	13:20	no **one** would be saved; but for
	14:38	willing, but the **flesh** is weak.
Lk	3: 6	and all **flesh** shall see the
	24:39	a ghost does not have **flesh** and
Jn	1:13	the will of the **flesh** or of the
	1:14	And the Word became **flesh** and
	3: 6	What is born of the **flesh** is
	3: 6	born of the flesh is **flesh,** and
	6:51	life of the world is my **flesh.**
	6:52	man give us his **flesh** to eat?
	6:53	unless you eat the **flesh** of the
	6:54	Those who eat my **flesh** and
	6:55	for my **flesh** is true food and
	6:56	Those who eat my **flesh** and
	6:63	the **flesh** is useless. The words
	8:15	You judge by **human** standards;
	17: 2	authority over all **people,** to
Ac	2:17	out my Spirit upon all **flesh,**
	2:26	moreover my **flesh** will live in
	2:31	nor did his **flesh** experience
Ro	1: 3	David according to the **flesh**
	2:28	something external and **physical**
	3:20	For "no **human being** will be
	4: 1	ancestor according to the **flesh**
	6:19	terms because of your **natural**
	7: 5	we were living in the **flesh,**
	7:18	that is, in my **flesh.** I can
	7:25	my **flesh** I am a slave to the
	8: 3	weakened by the **flesh,** could
	8: 3	likeness of sinful **flesh,** and
	8: 3	he condemned sin in the **flesh,**
	8: 4	not according to the **flesh** but
	8: 5	live according to the **flesh** set
	8: 5	on the things of the **flesh,** but
	8: 6	To set the mind on the **flesh** is
	8: 7	mind that is set on the **flesh**
	8: 8	and those who are in the **flesh**
	8: 9	But you are not in the **flesh;**
	8:12	debtors, not to the **flesh,** to
	8:12	to live according to the **flesh**
	8:13	live according to the **flesh,**
	9: 3	kindred according to the **flesh.**
	9: 5	them, according to the **flesh,**
	9: 8	not the children of the **flesh**
	11:14	in order to make my own **people**
	13:14	make no provision for the **flesh**
1C	1:26	many of you were wise by **human**
	1:29	so that no **one** might boast in
	5: 5	the destruction of the **flesh,**
	6:16	The two shall be one **flesh.**
	7:28	distress in this **life,** and I
	10:18	Consider the **people** of Israel;
	15:39	Not all **flesh** is alike, but
	15:39	but there is one **flesh** for
	15:39	**another** for animals, another
	15:39	**another** for birds, and another
	15:50	**flesh** and blood cannot inherit
2C	1:17	according to ordinary **human**
	4:11	visible in our mortal **flesh.**
	5:16	we regard no one from a **human**
	5:16	once knew Christ from a **human**
	7: 1	from every defilement of **body**
	7: 5	our **bodies** had no rest, but we
	10: 2	acting according to **human**
	10: 3	Indeed, we live as **human** beings
	10: 3	according to **human** standards;
	11:18	according to **human** standards,
	12: 7	thorn was given me in the **flesh**
Ga	1:16	I did not confer with any **human**
	2:16	no **one** will be justified by the
	2:20	I now live in the **flesh** I live
	3: 3	you now ending with the **flesh?**
	4:13	because of a **physical** infirmity
	4:14	though my **condition** put you to
	4:23	born according to the **flesh;**
	4:29	born according to the **flesh**
	5:13	opportunity for **self-indulgence**
	5:16	the desires of the **flesh.**
	5:17	For what the **flesh** desires is
	5:17	opposed to the **flesh;** for these
	5:19	Now the works of the **flesh** are
	5:24	have crucified the **flesh** with

	6: 8	If you sow to your own **flesh,**
	6: 8	reap corruption from the **flesh;**
	6:12	good showing in the **flesh** that
	6:13	they may boast about your **flesh**
Ep	2: 3	in the passions of our **flesh,**
	2: 3	following the desires of **flesh**
	2:11	one time you Gentiles by **birth,**
	2:11	made in the **flesh** by human
	2:14	in his **flesh** he has made both
	5:29	hates his own **body,** but he
	5:31	the two will become one **flesh.**
	6: 5	obey your **earthly** masters with
	6:12	enemies of blood and **flesh,** but
Ph	1:22	If I am to live in the **flesh,**
	1:24	but to remain in the **flesh** is
	3: 3	have no confidence in the **flesh**
	3: 4	for confidence in the **flesh.** If
	3: 4	for confidence in the **flesh.** If
Co	1:22	now reconciled in his **fleshly**
	1:24	and in my **flesh** I am completing
	2: 1	who have not seen me **face** to
	2: 5	For though I am absent in **body,**
	2:11	the body of the **flesh** in the
	2:13	uncircumcision of your **flesh,**
	2:18	up without cause by a **human** way
	2:23	in checking **self-indulgence.**
	3:22	obey your **earthly** masters in
1Ti	3:16	He was revealed in **flesh,**
Pm	1:16	both in the **flesh** and in the
He	2:14	the children share **flesh** and
	5: 7	In the days of his **flesh,** Jesus
	9:10	regulations for the **body**
	9:13	defiled so that their **flesh** is
	10:20	(that is, through his **flesh),**
	12: 9	Moreover, we had **human** parents
Ja	5: 3	and it will eat your **flesh** like
1P	1:24	For "All **flesh** is like grass
	3:18	put to death in the **flesh,** but
	3:21	removal of dirt from the **body,**
	4: 1	Christ suffered in the **flesh,**
	4: 1	has suffered in the **flesh** has
	4: 2	no longer by **human** desires but
	4: 6	judged in the **flesh** as everyone
2P	2:10	indulge their **flesh** in depraved
	2:18	licentious desires of the **flesh**
1J	2:16	the desire of the **flesh,** the
	4: 2	Christ has come in the **flesh** is
2J	1: 7	Christ has come in the **flesh;**

Ju	1: 7	pursued **unnatural** lust, serve
	1: 8	also defile the **flesh,** reject
	1:23	tunic defiled by their **bodies.**
Re	17:16	they will devour her **flesh** and
	19:18	to eat the **flesh** of kings, the
	19:18	**flesh** of captains, the flesh
	19:18	the **flesh** of the mighty, the
	19:18	the **flesh** of horses and their
	19:18	**flesh** of all, both free and
	19:21	were gorged with their **flesh.**

4563   GO3 AG744 LN220
σαροω, I SWEEP

Mt	12:44	it finds it empty, **swept,** and
Lk	11:25	it finds it **swept** and put in
	15: 8	does not light a lamp, **sweep**

4564   GO4 AG744 LN220 B1:80
σαρρα, SARAH

Ro	4:19	the barrenness of **Sarah's** womb.
	9: 9	I will return and **Sarah** shall
He	11:11	and **Sarah** herself was barren
1P	3: 6	Thus **Sarah** obeyed Abraham and

4565   GO1 AG744 LN220
σαρων, SHARON

| Ac | 9:35 | Lydda and **Sharon** saw him and |

4567   GO36 AG744 LN220 B3:468 K7:151
σαταν, ADVERSARY, SATAN

Mt	4:10	Away with you, **Satan!** for it
	12:26	If **Satan** casts out Satan, he is
	12:26	If Satan casts out **Satan,** he is
	16:23	Get behind me, **Satan!** You are
Mk	1:13	tempted by **Satan;** and he was
	3:23	How can **Satan** cast out Satan?
	3:23	How can Satan cast out **Satan?**
	3:26	And if **Satan** has risen up
	4:15	**Satan** immediately comes and
	8:33	Get behind me, **Satan!** For you
Lk	10:18	I watched **Satan** fall from
	11:18	**Satan** also is divided against
	13:16	whom **Satan** bound for eighteen
	22: 3	Then **Satan** entered into Judas
	22:31	Simon, Simon, listen! **Satan**
Jn	13:27	**Satan** entered into him. Jesus
Ac	5: 3	why has **Satan** filled your
	26:18	from the power of **Satan** to God,
Ro	16:20	crush **Satan** under your feet.

1C	5: 5	hand this man over to **Satan** for
	7: 5	so that **Satan** may not tempt you
2C	2:11	may not be outwitted by **Satan;**
	11:14	And no wonder! Even **Satan**
	12: 7	a messenger of **Satan** to torment
1Th	2:18	again—but **Satan** blocked our
2Th	2: 9	in the working of **Satan,** who
1Ti	1:20	I have turned over to **Satan,** so
	5:15	turned away to follow **Satan.**
Re	2: 9	but are a synagogue of **Satan.**
	2:13	where **Satan's** throne is. Yet
	2:13	among you, where **Satan** lives.
	2:24	'the deep things of **Satan,**' to
	3: 9	the synagogue of **Satan** who say
	12: 9	called the Devil and **Satan,** the
	20: 2	who is the Devil and **Satan,** and
	20: 7	**Satan** will be released from his

4568 GO2 AG745 LN220
σατον, SATA (MEASURE)

Mt	13:33	mixed in with three **measures** of
Lk	13:21	mixed in with three **measures** of

4569 GO15 AG745 LN220
σαυλος, SAUL

Ac	7:58	feet of a young man named **Saul.**
	8: 1	And **Saul** approved of their
	8: 3	But **Saul** was ravaging the
	9: 1	Meanwhile **Saul,** still breathing
	9: 8	**Saul** got up from the ground,
	9:11	a man of Tarsus named **Saul.** At
	9:22	**Saul** became increasingly more
	9:24	plot became known to **Saul.** They
	11:25	went to Tarsus to look for **Saul**
	11:30	the elders by Barnabas and **Saul**
	12:25	Barnabas and **Saul** returned to
	13: 1	of Herod the ruler, and **Saul.**
	13: 2	Barnabas and **Saul** for the work
	13: 7	summoned Barnabas and **Saul** and
	13: 9	But **Saul,** also known as Paul,

4570 GO6 AG745 LN220 B3:109 K7:165
σβεννυμι, I QUENCH

Mt	12:20	**quench** a smoldering wick until
	25: 8	for our lamps **are going out.**
Mk	9:48	the fire is never **quenched.**
Ep	6:16	you will be able to **quench** all
1Th	5:19	Do not **quench** the Spirit.
He	11:34	**quenched** raging fire, escaped

4572 GO43 AG745 LN220
σεαυτου, YOURSELF

Mt	4: 6	throw **yourself** down; for it is
	8: 4	show **yourself** to the priest,
	19:19	love your neighbor as **yourself.**
	22:39	love your neighbor as **yourself.**
	27:40	it in three days, save **yourself**
Mk	1:44	show **yourself** to the priest,
	12:31	love your neighbor as **yourself.**
	15:30	save **yourself,** and come down
Lk	4: 9	throw **yourself** down from here,
	4:23	'Doctor, cure **yourself!**' And
	5:14	and show **yourself** to the
	10:27	and your neighbor as **yourself.**
	23:37	King of the Jews, save **yourself**
	23:39	not the Messiah? Save **yourself**
Jn	1:22	What do you say about **yourself?**
	7: 4	show **yourself** to the world.
	8:13	testifying on **your own behalf;**
	8:53	died. Who do **you** claim to be?
	10:33	being, are making **yourself** God.
	14:22	reveal **yourself** to us, and not
	17: 5	that I had in **your** presence
	18:34	Do you ask this on **your own,**
	21:18	fasten **your own** belt and to go
Ac	9:34	get up and make **your** bed!" And
	16:28	Do not harm **yourself,** for we
	26: 1	speak for **yourself.**" Then Paul
Ro	2: 1	you condemn **yourself,** because
	2: 5	storing up wrath for **yourself**
	2:19	if you are sure that **you** are a
	2:21	will you not teach **yourself?**
	13: 9	Love your neighbor as **yourself**
	14:22	have as **your own** conviction
Ga	5:14	love your neighbor as **yourself.**
	6: 1	Take care that you **yourselves**
1Ti	4: 7	Train **yourself** in godliness,
	4:16	Pay close attention to **yourself**
	4:16	Pay close attention to **yourself**
	5:22	of others; keep **yourself** pure.
2Ti	2:15	present **yourself** to God as one
	4:11	Get Mark and bring him with **you**
Ti	2: 7	Show **yourself** in all respects a
Pm	1:19	owing me even **your own self.**
Ja	2: 8	love your neighbor as **yourself.**

4573 GO1 AG745 LN220 B2:91 K7:172 R4576
σεβαζομαι, I REVERE

Ro	1:25	**worshiped** and served the

4574   GO2 AG745 LN220 B2:91 K7:173 R4573
σεβασμα, OBJECT OF WORSHIP
Ac 17:23   at the **objects of** your **worship,**
2Th 2: 4   god or **object of worship,** so

4575   GO3 AG745 LN220 B2:93 K7:174 R4573
σεβαστος, SEBASTUS
Ac 25:21   **Imperial Majesty,** I ordered him
     25:25   to his **Imperial Majesty,** I
     27: 1   the **Augustan** Cohort, named

4576   GO10 AG746 LN220 B2:91 K7:169
σεβω, I WORSHIP
Mt 15: 9   in vain do they **worship** me,
Mk   7: 7   in vain do they **worship** me,
Ac 13:43   many Jews and **devout** converts
     13:50   But the Jews incited the **devout**
     16:14   **worshiper** of God, was listening
     17: 4   many of the **devout** Greeks and
     17:17   Jews and the **devout** persons,
     18: 7   a **worshiper** of God; his house
     18:13   persuading people to **worship**
     19:27   Asia and the world to **worship**

4577   GO1 AG746 LN220
σειρα, PIT
2P   2: 4   committed them **to chains** of

4578   GO14 AG746 LN220 B3:556 K7:196 R4579
σεισμος, SHAKE
Mt   8:24   A **windstorm** arose on the sea,
     24: 7   famines and **earthquakes** in
     27:54   saw the **earthquake** and what
     28: 2   there was a great **earthquake;**
Mk 13: 8   there will be **earthquakes** in
Lk 21:11   there will be great **earthquakes**
Ac 16:26   there was an **earthquake,** so
Re   6:12   there came a great **earthquake;**
      8: 5   of lightning, and an **earthquake**
     11:13   there was a great **earthquake,**
     11:13   killed in the **earthquake,** and
     11:19   peals of thunder, an **earthquake**
     16:18   a violent **earthquake,** such as
     16:18   so violent was that **earthquake.**

4579   GO5 AG746 LN221 B3:556 K7:196
σειω, I SHAKE
Mt 21:10   the whole city was in **turmoil,**
     27:51   The earth **shook,** and the rocks
     28: 4   fear of him the guards **shook**

He 12:26   Yet once more I will **shake** not
Re   6:13   winter fruit when **shaken** by a

4580   GO1 AG746 LN221
σεκουνδος, SECUNDUS
Ac 20: 4   by Aristarchus and **Secundus**

4581   GO1 AG746 LN221
σελευκεια, SELEUCIA
Ac 13: 4   went down to **Seleucia;** and
                 from

4582   GO9 AG746 LN221 B3:733
σεληνη, MOON
Mt 24:29   **moon** will not give its light;
Mk 13:24   **moon** will not give its light,
Lk 21:25   the **moon,** and the stars, and on
Ac   2:20   the **moon** to blood, before the
1C 15:41   another glory of the **moon,** and
Re   6:12   the full **moon** became like blood
      8:12   third of the **moon,** and a third
     12: 1   with the **moon** under her feet,
     21:23   no need of sun or **moon** to shine

4583   GO2 AG746 LN221 B3:733 R4582
σεληνιαζομαι, I AM MOONSTRUCK
Mt   4:24   **epileptics,** and paralytics,
     17:15   for he is an **epileptic** and he

4584   GO1 AG746 LN221
σεμειν, SEMEIN
Lk   3:26   son of **Semein,** son of Josech,

4585   GO1 AG746 LN221
σεμιδαλις, FINE FLOUR
Re 18:13   **choice flour** and wheat, cattle

4586   GO4 AG746 LN221 B2:91 K7:191
σεμνος, GRAVE
Ph   4: 8   whatever is **honorable,**
1Ti 3: 8   likewise must be **serious,** not
      3:11   Women likewise must be
                 serious,
Ti   2: 2   **serious,** prudent, and sound in

4587   GO3 AG747 LN221 B2:91 K7:191 R4586
σεμνοτης, GRAVITY
1Ti 2: 2   in all godliness and **dignity.**
      3: 4   and **respectful** in every way—
Ti   2: 7   show integrity, **gravity,**

4588   GO1 AG747 LN221
σεργιος, SERGIUS
Ac 13: 7 **Sergius** Paulus, an intelligent

4588a   GO1 AG747 LN221
σερουχ, SERUCH (SERUG)
Lk 3:35 son of **Serug,** son of Reu, son

4589   GO1 AG747 LN221
σηθ, SETH
Lk 3:38 son of Enos, son of **Seth,** son

4590   GO1 AG747 LN221
σημ, SHEM
Lk 3:36 son of **Shem,** son of Noah, son

4591   GO6 AG747 LN221 K7:262
σημαινω, I SIGNIFY
Jn 12:33 He said this to **indicate** the
    18:32 said when he **indicated** the kind
    21:19 (He said this to **indicate** the
Ac 11:28 stood up and **predicted** by the
    25:27 **indicating** the charges against
Re   1: 1 he **made** it **known** by sending his

4592   GO77 AG747 LN221 B2:626 K7:200 R4591
σημειον, SIGN
Mt 12:38 we wish to see a **sign** from you.
    12:39 asks for a **sign,** but no sign
    12:39 but no **sign** will be given to it
    12:39 except the **sign** of the prophet
    16: 1 show them a **sign** from heaven.
    16: 3 interpret the **signs** of the
    16: 4 asks for a **sign,** but no sign
    16: 4 but no **sign** will be given to it
    16: 4 except the **sign** of Jonah." Then
    24: 3 what will be the **sign** of your
    24:24 produce great **signs** and omens,
    24:30 Then the **sign** of the Son of Man
    26:48 given them a **sign,** saying, "The
Mk   8:11 asking him for a **sign** from
     8:12 this generation ask for a **sign?**
     8:12 Truly I tell you, no **sign** will
    13: 4 what will be the **sign** that all
    13:22 appear and produce **signs** and
    16:17 And these **signs** will accompany
    16:20 the **signs** that accompanied it.]
Lk   2:12 This will be a **sign** for you:
     2:34 and to be a **sign** that will be
    11:16 demanding from him a **sign** from
    11:29 it asks for a **sign,** but no sign
    11:29 but no **sign** will be given to it
    11:29 to it except the **sign** of Jonah.
    11:30 For just as Jonah became a **sign**
    21: 7 what will be the **sign** that this
    21:11 portents and great **signs** from
    21:25 There will be **signs** in the sun
    23: 8 to see him perform some **sign.**
Jn   2:11 the first of his **signs,** in Cana
     2:18 What **sign** can you show us for
     2:23 because they saw the **signs** that
     3: 2 no one can do these **signs** that
     4:48 Unless you see **signs** and
     4:54 Now this was the second **sign**
     6: 2 because they saw the **signs** that
     6:14 When the people saw the **sign**
     6:26 not because you saw **signs,** but
     6:30 So they said to him, "What **sign**
     7:31 will he do more **signs** than this
     9:16 sinner perform such **signs?**" And
    10:41 John performed no **sign,** but
    11:47 man is performing many **signs.**
    12:18 performed this **sign** that the
    12:37 performed so many **signs** in
    20:30 Now Jesus did many other **signs**
Ac   2:19 heaven above and **signs** on the
     2:22 **signs** that God did through him
     2:43 many wonders and **signs** were
     4:16 a notable **sign** has been done
     4:22 For the man on whom this **sign**
     4:30 **signs** and wonders are performed
     5:12 Now many **signs** and wonders were
     6: 8 great wonders and **signs** among
     7:36 wonders and **signs** in Egypt, at
     8: 6 hearing and seeing the **signs**
     8:13 **signs** and great miracles that
    14: 3 granting **signs** and wonders to
    15:12 the **signs** and wonders that God
Ro   4:11 **sign** of circumcision as a seal
    15:19 the power of **signs** and wonders,
1C   1:22 Jews demand **signs** and Greeks
    14:22 Tongues, then, are a **sign** not
2C 12:12 The **signs** of a true apostle
    12:12 **signs** and wonders and mighty
2Th 2: 9 all power, **signs,** lying wonders
     3:17 This is the **mark** in every
He   2: 4 testimony by **signs** and wonders
Re 12: 1 **portent** appeared in heaven: a
    12: 3 Then another **portent** appeared

13:13	It performs great **signs,** even
13:14	and by the **signs** that it is
15: 1	Then I saw another **portent** in
16:14	performing **signs,** who go abroad
19:20	presence the **signs** by which he

4593 GO1 AG748 LN221 K7:265 R4592
σημειοω, I SIGNIFY
2Th 3:14 **have nothing** to do with them,

4594 GO41 AG749 LN221 B3:833 K7:269
σημερον, TODAY

Mt	6:11	us this **day** our daily bread.
	6:30	alive **today** and tomorrow is
	11:23	have remained until this **day.**
	16: 3	It will be stormy **today,** for
	21:28	work in the vineyard **today.**
	27: 8	the Field of Blood to this **day.**
	27:19	**today** I have suffered a great
	28:15	told among the Jews to this **day**
Mk	14:30	Truly I tell you, this **day,**
Lk	2:11	to you is born this **day** in the
	4:21	**Today** this scripture has been
	5:26	have seen strange things **today.**
	12:28	alive **today** and tomorrow is
	13:32	performing cures **today** and
	13:33	Yet **today,** tomorrow, and the
	19: 5	must stay at your house **today.**
	19: 9	Then Jesus said to him, "**Today**
	22:34	cock will not crow this **day,**
	22:61	Before the cock crows **today,**
	23:43	**today** you will be with me in
Ac	4: 9	if we are questioned **today**
	13:33	Son; **today** I have begotten you.
	19:40	charged with rioting **today,**
	20:26	declare to you this **day** that I
	22: 3	just as all of you are **today.**
	24:21	I am on trial before you **today.**
	26: 2	I am to make my defense **today**
	26:29	who are listening to me **today**
	27:33	**Today** is the fourteenth day
Ro	11: 8	not hear, down to this very **day**
2C	3:14	Indeed, to this very **day,** when
	3:15	to this very **day** whenever Moses
He	1: 5	**today** I have begotten you"? Or
	3: 7	**Today,** if you hear his voice,
	3:13	as long as it is called "**today,**
	3:15	As it is said, "**Today,** if you
	4: 7	sets a certain day—"**today**"

4: 7	**Today,** if you hear his voice,
5: 5	You are my Son, **today** I have
13: 8	same yesterday and **today** and
Ja	4:13	Come now, you who say, "**Today**

4595 GO1 AG749 LN221 K7:94
σηπω, I ROT
Ja 5: 2 Your riches **have rotted,** and

4597 GO3 AG749 LN221 B1:119 K7:275
σης, MOTH

Mt	6:19	treasures on earth, where **moth**
	6:20	where neither **moth** nor rust
Lk	12:33	comes near and no **moth** destroys

4598 GO1 AG749 LN221 K7:275
σητοβρωτος, MOTH-EATEN
Ja 5: 2 and your clothes are **moth-eaten**

4599 GO1 AG749 LN221
σθενοω, I INVIGORATE
1P 5:10 restore, support, **strengthen,**

4600 GO2 AG749 LN221
σιαγων, CHEEK

| Mt | 5·39 | strikes you on the right **cheek,** |
| Lk | 6:29 | strikes you on the **cheek,** offer |

4601 GO10 AG749 LN221 R4602
σιγαω, I AM SILENT

Lk	9:36	they **kept silent** and in those
	18:39	ordered him to **be quiet;** but he
	20:26	his answer, they **became silent.**
Ac	12:17	to **be silent,** and described for
	15:12	The whole assembly **kept silence**
	15:13	After they **finished** speaking,
Ro	16:25	mystery that was **kept secret**
1C	14:28	let them **be silent** in church
	14:30	let the first person **be silent.**
	14:34	women should **be silent** in the

4602 GO2 AG749 LN221
σιγη, SILENCE

| Ac | 21:40 | to the people for **silence;** and |
| Re | 8: 1 | there was **silence** in heaven |

4603 GO5 AG750 LN221 B2:97 R4604
σιδηρους, IRON

| Ac | 12:10 | they came before the **iron** gate |
| Re | 2:27 | to rule them with an **iron** rod, |

9: 9 they had scales like **iron**
12: 5 the nations with a rod of **iron.**
19:15 rule them with a rod of **iron;**

4604 GO1 AG750 LN221 B2:97
σιδηρος, IRON
Re 18:12 costly wood, bronze, **iron,** and

4605 GO9 AG750 LN221
σιδων, SIDON
Mt 11:21 had been done in Tyre and **Sidon**
11:22 tolerable for Tyre and **Sidon**
15:21 the district of Tyre and **Sidon.**
Mk 3: 8 region around Tyre and **Sidon.**
7:31 went by way of **Sidon** towards
Lk 6:17 the coast of Tyre and **Sidon.**
10:13 had been done in Tyre and **Sidon**
10:14 tolerable for Tyre and **Sidon**
Ac 27: 3 The next day we put in at **Sidon**

4606 GO2 AG750 LN221
σιδωνιος, SIDONIAN
Lk 4:26 a widow at Zarephath in **Sidon.**
Ac 12:20 the people of Tyre and **Sidon.**

4607 GO1 AG750 LN222 K7:278
σικαριος, ASSASSIN
Ac 21:38 led the four thousand **assassins**

4608 GO1 AG750 LN222
σικερα, INTOXICANT
Lk 1:15 drink wine or **strong drink;**

4609 GO13 AG750 LN222
σιλας, SILAS
Ac 15:22 and **Silas,** leaders among the
15:27 sent Judas and **Silas,** who
15:32 Judas and **Silas,** who were
15:40 But Paul chose **Silas** and set
16:19 they seized Paul and **Silas** and
16:25 About midnight Paul and **Silas**
16:29 trembling before Paul and **Silas**
17: 4 joined Paul and **Silas,** as did a
17:10 believers sent Paul and **Silas**
17:14 but **Silas** and Timothy remained
17:15 instructions to have **Silas** and
18: 5 When **Silas** and Timothy arrived

4610 GO4 AG750 LN222
σιλουανος, SILVANUS

2C 1:19 **Silvanus** and Timothy and I, was
1Th 1: 1 Paul, **Silvanus,** and Timothy, To
2Th 1: 1 Paul, **Silvanus,** and Timothy, To
1P 5:12 Through **Silvanus,** whom I

4611 GO3 AG750 LN222
σιλωαμ, SILOAM
Lk 13: 4 tower of **Siloam** fell on them—
Jn 9: 7 Go, wash in the pool of **Siloam**
9:11 'Go to **Siloam** and wash.' Then I

4612 GO1 AG751 LN222
σμικινθιον, APRON
Ac 19:12 handkerchiefs or **aprons** that

4613 GO75 AG751 LN222
σιμων, SIMON
Mt 4:18 **Simon,** who is called Peter, and
10: 2 first, **Simon,** also known as
10: 4 **Simon** the Cananaean, and Judas
13:55 Joseph and **Simon** and Judas?
16:16 **Simon** Peter answered, "You are
16:17 Blessed are you, **Simon** son of
17:25 What do you think, **Simon?** From
26: 6 in the house of **Simon** the leper
27:32 a man from Cyrene named **Simon;**
Mk 1:16 he saw **Simon** and his brother
1:16 he saw **Simon** and his brother
1:29 entered the house of **Simon** and
1:30 Now **Simon's** mother-in-law was
1:36 And **Simon** and his companions
3:16 **Simon** (to whom he gave the name
3:18 and **Simon** the Cananaean,
6: 3 Joses and Judas and **Simon,** and
14: 3 in the house of **Simon** the leper
14:37 **Simon,** are you asleep? Could
15:21 **Simon** of Cyrene, the father of
Lk 4:38 he entered **Simon's** house. Now
4:38 Now **Simon's** mother-in-law was
5: 3 the one belonging to **Simon,** and
5: 4 he said to **Simon,** "Put out into
5: 5 **Simon** answered, "Master, we
5: 8 But when **Simon** Peter saw it,
5:10 who were partners with **Simon.**
5:10 Then Jesus said to **Simon,** "Do
6:14 **Simon,** whom he named Peter, and
6:15 **Simon,** who was called the
7:40 **Simon,** I have something to say
7:43 **Simon** answered, "I suppose the
7:44 he said to **Simon,** "Do you see

	22:31	**Simon,** Simon, listen! Satan
	22:31	Simon, **Simon,** listen! Satan
	23:26	**Simon** of Cyrene, who was coming
	24:34	and he has appeared to **Simon!**
Jn	1:40	Andrew, **Simon** Peter's brother.
	1:41	found his brother **Simon** and
	1:42	You are **Simon** son of John.
	6: 8	Andrew, **Simon** Peter's brother,
	6:68	**Simon** Peter answered him, "Lord
	6:71	Judas son of **Simon** Iscariot,
	13: 2	Judas son of **Simon** Iscariot to
	13: 6	He came to **Simon** Peter, who
	13: 9	**Simon** Peter said to him, "Lord,
	13:24	**Simon** Peter therefore motioned
	13:26	gave it to Judas son of **Simon**
	13:36	**Simon** Peter said to him, "Lord,
	18:10	Then **Simon** Peter, who had a
	18:15	**Simon** Peter and another
	18:25	Now **Simon** Peter was standing
	20: 2	So she ran and went to **Simon**
	20: 6	**Simon** Peter came, following him
	21: 2	there together were **Simon** Peter
	21: 3	**Simon** Peter said to them, "I am
	21: 7	When **Simon** Peter heard that it
	21:11	So **Simon** Peter went aboard and
	21:15	Jesus said to **Simon** Peter,
	21:15	**Simon** son of John, do you love
	21:16	**Simon** son of John, do you love
	21:17	**Simon** son of John, do you love
Ac	1:13	and **Simon** the Zealot, and Judas
	8: 9	Now a certain man named **Simon**
	8:13	Even **Simon** himself believed.
	8:18	Now when **Simon** saw that the
	8:24	**Simon** answered, "Pray for me
	9:43	with a certain **Simon,** a tanner.
	10: 5	a certain **Simon** who is called
	10: 6	he is lodging with **Simon,** a
	10:17	They were asking for **Simon's**
	10:18	ask whether **Simon,** who was
	10:32	ask for **Simon,** who is called
	10:32	staying in the home of **Simon,**
	11:13	Send to Joppa and bring **Simon,**

4614 GO4 AG751 LN222 B3:1013 K7:282

σινα, SINAI

Ac	7:30	wilderness of Mount **Sinai,** in
	7:38	who spoke to him at Mount **Sinai**
Ga	4:24	is Hagar, from Mount **Sinai,**
	4:25	Now Hagar is Mount **Sinai** in

4615 GO5 AG751 LN222 B3:523 K7:287

σιναπι, MUSTARD

Mt	13:31	heaven is like a **mustard** seed
	17:20	faith the size of a **mustard**
Mk	4:31	It is like a **mustard** seed,
Lk	13:19	It is like a **mustard** seed that
	17: 6	faith the size of a **mustard**

4616 GO6 AG751 LN222 B3:296

σινδων, LINEN

Mt	27:59	wrapped it in a clean **linen**
Mk	14:51	wearing nothing but a **linen**
	14:52	but he left the **linen** cloth
	15:46	Then Joseph bought a **linen**
	15:46	wrapped it in the **linen** cloth,
Lk	23:53	wrapped it in a **linen** cloth,

4617 GO1 AG751 LN222 B3:804 K7:291

σινιαζω, I SIFT

Lk	22:31	Satan has demanded to **sift** all

4617a GO1 AG751 LN222

σιρικος, SILK

Re	18:12	linen, purple, **silk** and scarlet

4618 GO3 AG752 LN222 B1:116 R4621

σιτευτος, WHEAT-FED

Lk	15:23	get the **fatted** calf and kill it
	15:27	father has killed the **fatted**
	15:30	you killed the **fatted** calf for

4618a GO1 AG752 LN222

σιτιον, WHEAT

Ac	7:12	heard that there was **grain** in

4619 GO1 AG752 LN222 R4621

σιτιστος, FATTENED ONE

Mt	22: 4	my oxen and my **fat calves** have

4620 GO1 AG752 LN222 R4621,3358

σιτομετριον, WHEAT MEASURE

Lk	12:42	their **allowance of food** at the

4621 GO14 AG752 LN222 B3:523

σιτος, WHEAT

Mt	3:12	gather his **wheat** into the
	13:25	sowed weeds among the **wheat,**
	13:29	you would uproot the **wheat**
	13:30	but gather the **wheat** into my
Mk	4:28	then the full **grain** in the head

Lk	3:17	gather the **wheat** into his
	12:18	I will store all my **grain** and
	16: 7	A hundred containers of **wheat.**
	22:31	to sift all of you like **wheat,**
Jn	12:24	unless a grain of **wheat** falls
Ac	27:38	throwing the **wheat** into the sea
1C	15:37	perhaps of **wheat** or of some
Re	6: 6	A quart of **wheat** for a day's
	18:13	choice flour and **wheat,** cattle

4622 GO7 AG752 LN222 K7:292
σιων, SION (ZION)

Mt	21: 5	Tell the daughter of **Zion,**
Jn	12:15	daughter of **Zion.** Look, your
Ro	9:33	See, I am laying in **Zion** a
	11:26	Out of **Zion** will come the
He	12:22	But you have come to Mount **Zion**
1P	2: 6	See, I am laying in **Zion** a
Re	14: 1	Lamb, standing on Mount **Zion!**

4623 GO10 AG752 LN222
σιωπαω, I AM SILENT

Mt	20:31	them **to be quiet;** but they
	26:63	But Jesus **was silent.** Then the
Mk	3: 4	to kill?" But they **were silent.**
	4:39	"Peace! **Be still!**" Then the
	9:34	But they **were silent,** for on
	10:48	sternly ordered him **to be quiet**
	14:61	But he **was silent** and did not
Lk	1:20	you **will become mute,** unable to
	19:40	tell you, if these **were silent,**
Ac	18: 9	but speak and do not **be silent;**

4624 GO29 AG752 LN222 B2:707 K7:339 R4625
σκανδαλιζω, I CAUSE TO STUMBLE,
I OFFEND

Mt	5:29	**causes** you **to sin,** tear it out
	5:30	**causes** you **to sin,** cut it off
	11: 6	anyone who **takes** no **offense** at
	13:21	person immediately **falls away.**
	13:57	And they **took offense** at him.
	15:12	the Pharisees **took offense** when
	17:27	so that we **do** not **give offense**
	18: 6	**put** a **stumbling block** before
	18: 8	your foot **causes** you **to stumble**
	18: 9	your eye **causes** you **to stumble,**
	24:10	Then many **will fall away,** and
	26:31	You **will** all **become deserters**
	26:33	Though all **become deserters**
	26:33	of you, I **will** never **desert** you
Mk	4:17	immediately they **fall away.**

	6: 3	us?" And they **took offense** at
	9:42	**put** a **stumbling block** before
	9:43	**causes** you **to stumble,** cut it
	9:45	**causes** you **to stumble,** cut it
	9:47	**causes** you **to stumble,** tear it
	14:27	You **will** all **become deserters;**
	14:29	though all **become deserters,** I
Lk	7:23	anyone who **takes** no **offense** at
	17: 2	**to cause** . . . little **to stumble.**
Jn	6:61	said to them, "Does this **offend**
	16: 1	you to **keep** you **from stumbling.**
1C	8:13	is a **cause** of their **falling**
	8:13	**cause** one of them **to fall.**
2C	11:29	Who **is made to stumble,** and I

4625 GO15 AG753 LN222 B2:707 K7:339
σκανδαλον, STUMBLING BLOCK, OFFENSE

Mt	13:41	all **causes of sin** and all
	16:23	You are a **stumbling block** to me
	18: 7	because of **stumbling blocks!**
	18: 7	Occasions for **stumbling** are
	18: 7	whom the **stumbling block** comes!
Lk	17: 1	Occasions for **stumbling** are
Ro	9:33	rock that will make them **fall,**
	11: 9	a **stumbling block** and a
	14:13	never to put a **stumbling block**
	16:17	cause dissensions and **offenses,**
1C	1:23	a **stumbling block** to Jews and
Ga	5:11	In that case the **offense** of the
1P	2: 8	a rock that makes them **fall.**
1J	2:10	there is no **cause for stumbling**
Re	2:14	put a **stumbling block**

4626 GO3 AG753 LN222
σκαπτω, I DIG

Lk	6:48	who **dug** deeply and laid the
	13: 8	until I **dig** around it and put
	16: 3	I am not strong enough to **dig,**

4627 GO3 AG753 LN223
σκαφη, SMALL BOAT

Ac	27:16	the ship's **boat** under control.
	27:30	lowered the **boat** into the sea,
	27:32	cut away the ropes of the **boat**

4628 GO3 AG753 LN223
σκελος, LEG

Jn	19:31	**legs** of the crucified men
	19:32	broke the **legs** of the first and
	19:33	they did not break his **legs.**

4629   GO1 AG753 LN223
σκεπασμα, COVERING
1Ti   6: 8   if we have food and **clothing,**

4630   GO1 AG753 LN223
σκευας, SCEVA
Ac   19:14   high priest named **Sceva** were

4631   GO1 AG754 LN223
σκευη, TACKLING
Ac   27:19   they threw the ship's **tackle**

4632   GO23 AG754 LN223 B3:912 K7:358
σκευος, POT, VESSEL
Mt   12:29   plunder his **property,** without
Mk   3:27   plunder his **property** without
         11:16   to carry **anything** through the
Lk   8:16   a lamp hides it under a **jar,** or
         17:31   who has **belongings** in the house
Jn   19:29   A **jar** full of sour wine was
Ac   9:15   Go, for he is an **instrument**
         10:11   **something** like a large sheet
         10:16   the **thing** was suddenly taken up
         11: 5   There was **something** like a
         27:17   they lowered the **sea anchor** and
Ro   9:21   of the same lump one **object** for
         9:22   patience the **objects** of wrath
         9:23   for the **objects** of mercy, which
2C   4: 7   treasure in clay **jars,** so that
1Th   4: 4   your own **body** in holiness and
2Ti   2:20   there are **utensils** not only of
         2:21   will become special **utensils,**
He   9:21   tent and all the **vessels** used
1P   3: 7   woman as the weaker **sex,** since
Re   2:27   as when clay **pots** are shattered
         18:12   all **articles** of ivory, all
         18:12   all **articles** of costly wood,

4633   GO20 AG754 LN223 B3:811 K7:368
σκηνη, TENT
Mt   17: 4   I will make three **dwellings**
Mk   9: 5   let us make three **dwellings,**
Lk   9:33   let us make three **dwellings,**
         16: 9   you into the eternal **homes.**
Ac   7:43   No; you took along the **tent** of
         7:44   Our ancestors had the **tent** of
         15:16   I will rebuild the **dwelling** of
He   8: 2   and the true **tent** that the Lord
         8: 5   about to erect the **tent,** was
         9: 2   For a **tent** was constructed,

9: 3   was a **tent** called the Holy of
9: 6   into the first **tent** to carry
9: 8   first **tent** is still standing.
9:11   greater and perfect **tent** (not
9:21   both the **tent** and all the
11: 9   living in **tents,** as did Isaac
13:10   officiate in the **tent** have no
Re   13: 6   his name and his **dwelling,** that
15: 5   temple of the **tent** of witness
21: 3   **home** of God is among mortals.

4634   GO1 AG754 LN223 B3:813 K7:390 R4633,4078
σκηνοπηγια, TENT PITCHING
Jn   7: 2   the Jewish festival of **Booths**

4635   GO1 AG755 LN223 B3:811 K7:393 R4633,4160
σκηνοποιος, TENTMAKER
Ac   18: 3   by trade they were **tentmakers.**

4636   GO2 AG755 LN223 B3:811 K7:381 R4633
σκηνος, TENT
2C   5: 1   if the earthly **tent** we live in
5: 4   we are still in this **tent,** we

4637   GO5 AG755 LN223 B3:811 K7:385 R4633
σκηνοω, I TENT
Jn   1:14   became flesh and **lived** among us
Re   7:15   on the throne **will shelter** them
12:12   those who **dwell** in them! But
13: 6   is, those who **dwell** in heaven.
21: 3   He **will dwell** with them as

4638   GO3 AG755 LN223 B3:811 K7:383 R4633
σκηνωμα, TENT
Ac   7:46   find a **dwelling place** for the
2P   1:13   as long as I am in this **body,**
1:14   since I know that my **death** will

4639   GO7 AG755 LN223 B3:533 K7:394
σκια, SHADOW
Mt   4:16   sat in the region and **shadow** of
Mk   4:32   can make nests in its **shade.**
Lk   1:79   in darkness and in the **shadow**
Ac   5:15   in order that Peter's **shadow**
Co   2:17   These are only a **shadow** of what
He   8: 5   that is a sketch and **shadow** of
10: 1   Since the law has only a **shadow**

4640   GO3 AG755 LN223 K7:401
σκιρταω, I SKIP

Lk	1:41	the child **leaped** in her womb.
	1:44	the child in my womb **leaped** for
	6:23	Rejoice in that day and **leap**

4641 GO3 AG756 LN223 B2:153 K3:613 R4642,2588
σκληροκαρδια, HARD HEART

Mt	19: 8	you were so **hard-hearted** that
Mk	10: 5	your **hardness of heart** he wrote
	16:14	lack of faith and **stubbornness,**

4642 GO5 AG756 LN223 B2:153 K5:1022
σκληρος, HARD

Mt	25:24	I knew that you were a **harsh**
Jn	6:60	This teaching is **difficult;**
Ac	26:14	It **hurts** you to kick against
Ja	3: 4	it takes **strong** winds to drive
Ju	1:15	of all the **harsh** things that

4643 GO1 AG756 LN223 B2:153 K5:1022 R4642
σκληροτης, HARDNESS

Ro	2: 5	But by your **hard** and impenitent

4644 GO1 AG756 LN223 B2:153 K5:1022 R4642,5137
σκληροτραχηλος, HARD-NECKED

Ac	7:51	You **stiff-necked** people,

4645 GO6 AG756 LN223 B2:153 K5:1022 R4642
σκληρυνω, I HARDEN

Ac	19: 9	When some **stubbornly** refused
Ro	9:18	**hardens** the heart of whomever
He	3: 8	do not **harden** your hearts as in
	3:13	none of you **may be hardened** by
	3:15	**do** not **harden** your hearts as in
	4: 7	voice, **do** not **harden** your

4646 GO4 AG756 LN223 K7:403
σκολιος, CROOKED

Lk	3: 5	the **crooked** shall be made
Ac	2:40	yourselves from this **corrupt**
Ph	2:15	in the midst of a **crooked** and
1P	2:18	but also those who are **harsh.**

4647 GO1 AG756 LN223 B1:726 K7:409
σκολοψ, THORN

2C	12: 7	**thorn** was given me in the flesh

4648 GO6 AG756 LN223 B1:188 K7:414
σκοπεω, I LOOK CAREFULLY

Lk	11:35	Therefore **consider** whether the
Ro	16:17	to **keep an eye on** those who

2C	4:18	because we **look** not **at** what can
Ga	6: 1	**Take care** that you **yourselves**
Ph	2: 4	Let each of you **look** not to
	3:17	and **observe** those who live

4649 GO1 AG756 LN223 B1:188 K7:413
σκοπος, GOAL

Ph	3:14	I press on toward the **goal** for

4650 GO5 AG757 LN224 B2:32 K7:418
σκορπιζω, I SCATTER

Mt	12:30	not gather with me **scatters.**
Lk	11:23	not gather with me **scatters.**
Jn	10:12	snatches them and **scatters** them
	16:32	when you **will be scattered,**
2C	9: 9	He **scatters** abroad, he gives

4651 GO5 AG757 LN224 B1:510
σκορπιος, SCORPION

Lk	10:19	tread on snakes and **scorpions,**
	11:12	an egg, will give a **scorpion?**
Re	9: 3	authority of **scorpions** of the
	9: 5	torture of a **scorpion** when it
	9:10	They have tails like **scorpions,**

4652 GO3 AG757 LN224 B1:421 K7:423 R4655
σκοτεινος, DARKENED

Mt	6:23	body will be **full of darkness.**
Lk	11:34	your body is **full of darkness.**
	11:36	with no part of it in **darkness,**

4653 GO16 AG757 LN224 B1:420 K7:423 R4655
σκοτια, DARK

Mt	10:27	What I say to you in the **dark,**
Lk	12: 3	you have said in the **dark** will
Jn	1: 5	light shines in the **darkness,**
	1: 5	**darkness** did not overcome it.
	6:17	It was now **dark,** and Jesus had
	8:12	never walk in **darkness** but will
	12:35	so that the **darkness** may not
	12:35	If you walk in the **darkness,**
	12:46	not remain in the **darkness.**
	20: 1	while it was still **dark,** Mary
1J	1: 5	in him there is no **darkness** at
	2: 8	because the **darkness** is passing
	2: 9	is still in the **darkness.**
	2:11	believer is in the **darkness,**
	2:11	walks in the **darkness,** and does
	2:11	because the **darkness** has

4654   GO5 AG757 LN224 B1:421 K7:423 R4655
σκοτιζω, I DARKEN
Mt 24:29   days the sun **will be darkened,**
Mk 13:24   the sun **will be darkened,** and
Ro   1:21   senseless minds **were darkened.**
     11:10   let their eyes **be darkened** so
Re   8:12   of their light **was darkened;** a

4655   GO31 AG757 LN224 B1:420 K7:423
σκοτος, DARK
Mt   4:16   the people who sat in **darkness**
      6:23   the light in you is **darkness,**
      6:23   how great is the **darkness!**
      8:12   thrown into the outer **darkness,**
     22:13   him into the outer **darkness,**
     25:30   him into the outer **darkness,**
     27:45   From noon on, **darkness** came
Mk 15:33   When it was noon, **darkness**
Lk   1:79   those who sit in **darkness** and
     11:35   light in you is not **darkness.**
     22:53   hour, and the power of
            darkness
     23:44   and **darkness** came over the
Jn   3:19   people loved **darkness** rather
Ac   2:20   turned to **darkness** and the
            moon
     13:11   Immediately mist and **darkness**
     26:18   they may turn from **darkness** to
Ro   2:19   to those who are in **darkness,**
     13:12   lay aside the works of **darkness**
1C   4: 5   things now hidden in **darkness**
2C   4: 6   light shine out of **darkness,**
      6:14   between light and **darkness?**
Ep   5: 8   For once you were **darkness,**
            but
      5:11   unfruitful works of **darkness,**
      6:12   this present **darkness,** against
Co   1:13   from the power of **darkness** and
1Th 5: 4   not in **darkness,** for that day
      5: 5   not of the night or of **darkness**
1P   2: 9   called you out of **darkness** into
2P   2:17   them the deepest **darkness** has
1J   1: 6   we are walking in **darkness,** we
Ju   1:13   whom the deepest **darkness** has

4656   GO3 AG758 LN224 B1:421 K7:423 R4655
σκοτοω, I DARKEN
Ep   4:18   They **are darkened** in their
Re   9: 2   the air **were darkened** with the
     16:10   **was plunged into darkness;**

4657   GO1 AG758 LN224 B1:480 K7:445
σκυβαλον, GARBAGE
Ph   3: 8   I regard them as **rubbish,** in

4658   GO1 AG758 LN224 K7:447
σκυθης, SCYTHIAN
Co   3:11   **Scythian,** slave and free; but

4659   GO2 AG758 LN224 K7:450
σκυθρωπος, SAD FACED
Mt   6:16   do not look **dismal,** like the
Lk 24:17   They stood still, looking **sad.**

4660   GO4 AG758 LN224
σκυλλω, I ANNOY
Mt   9:36   because they were **harassed** and
Mk   5:35   Why **trouble** the teacher any
Lk   7: 6   Lord, do not **trouble** yourself,
      8:49   do not **trouble** the teacher any

4661   GO1 AG758 LN224 R4660
σκυλον, SPOILS
Lk 11:22   trusted and divides his **plunder**

4662   GO1 AG758 LN224 K7:456
σκωληκοβρωτος, FOOD FOR WORMS
Ac 12:23   he **was eaten by worms** and died

4663   GO1 AG758 LN224 K7:452
σκωληξ, WORM
Mk   9:48   where their **worm** never dies,

4664   GO1 AG758 LN224 B3:398 R4665
σμαραγδινος, EMERALD
Re   4: 3   that looks like an **emerald.**

4665   GO1 AG758 LN224 B3:396
σμαραγδος, EMERALD
Re 21:19   third agate, the fourth **emerald**

4666   GO2 AG758 LN224 B2:294 K7:457
σμυρνα, MYRRH
Mt   2:11   gold, frankincense, and **myrrh.**
Jn 19:39   bringing a mixture of **myrrh** and

4667   GO2 AG759 LN224
σμυρνα, SMYRNA
Re   1:11   Ephesus, to **Smyrna,** to Pergamum
      2: 8   church in **Smyrna** write: These

4669   GO1 AG759 LN224 B2:295 K7:458
σμυρνιζω, I SPICE WITH MYRRH
Mk 15:23   offered him wine **mixed with**

4670   GO9 AG759 LN224
σοδομα, SODOM
Mt 10:15   tolerable for the land of **Sodom**
    11:23   been done in **Sodom,** it would
    11:24   for the land of **Sodom** than for
Lk 10:12   more tolerable for **Sodom** than
    17:29   Lot left **Sodom,** it rained fire
Ro   9:29   we would have fared like **Sodom**
2P   2: 6   cities of **Sodom** and Gomorrah
Ju   1: 7   Likewise, **Sodom** and Gomorrah
Re 11: 8   prophetically called **Sodom** and

4672   GO12 AG759 LN224 B3:605 K7:459
σολομων, SOLOMON
Mt   1: 6   was the father of **Solomon** by
     1: 7   and **Solomon** the father of
     6:29   yet I tell you, even **Solomon**
    12:42   listen to the wisdom of **Solomon**
    12:42   something greater than **Solomon**
Lk 11:31   listen to the wisdom of **Solomon**
    11:31   something greater than **Solomon**
    12:27   even **Solomon** in all his glory
Jn 10:23   in the portico of **Solomon.**
Ac   3:11   called **Solomon's** Portico,
     5:12   were all together in **Solomon's**
     7:47   But it was **Solomon** who built a

4673   GO1 AG759 LN225
σορος, CASKET
Lk   7:14   touched the **bier,** and the

4674   GO27 AG759 LN225
σος, YOUR
Mt   7: 3   see the speck in **your** neighbor
     7:22   prophesy in **your** name, and cast
     7:22   cast out demons in **your** name,
     7:22   do many deeds of power in **your**
    13:27   sow good seed in **your** field?
    20:14   Take what belongs **to you** and
    24: 3   what will be the sign of **your**
    25:25   Here you have what is **yours.**
Mk   2:18   but **your** disciples do not fast?
     5:19   Go home to **your** friends, and
Lk   5:33   **your** disciples eat and drink.
     6:30   if anyone takes away **your** goods
    15:31   and all that is mine is **yours.**

    22:42   yet, not my will but **yours** be
Jn   4:42   longer because of what **you** said
    17:10   All mine are **yours,** and yours
    17:10   All mine are yours, and **yours**
    17:17   the truth; **your** word is truth.
    18:35   **Your** own nation and the chief
Ac   5: 4   were not the proceeds at **your**
    24: 2   **and** reforms have been made for
    24: 4   hear us briefly with **your**
1C   8:11   So by **your** knowledge those weak
    14:16   outsider say the "Amen" to **your**
Pm   1:14   nothing without **your** consent,

4676   GO4 AG759 LN225
σουδαριον, HANDKERCHIEF
Lk 19:20   it up in a **piece of cloth,**
Jn 11:44   his face wrapped **in a cloth.**
    20: 7   and the **cloth** that had been on
Ac 19:12   so that when the **handkerchiefs**

4677   GO1 AG759 LN225
σουσαννα, SUSANNA
Lk   8: 3   steward Chuza, and **Susanna,** and

4678   GO51 AG759 LN225 B3:1026 K7:465 R4680
σοφια, WISDOM
Mt 11:19   Yet **wisdom** is vindicated by her
    12:42   listen to the **wisdom** of Solomon
    13:54   get this **wisdom** and these deeds
Mk   6: 2   What is this **wisdom** that has
Lk   2:40   strong, filled with **wisdom;** and
     2:52   And Jesus increased in **wisdom**
     7:35   **wisdom** is vindicated by all her
    11:31   listen to the **wisdom** of Solomon
    11:49   Therefore also the **Wisdom** of
    21:15   words and a **wisdom** that none of
Ac   6: 3   of the Spirit and of **wisdom,**
     6:10   withstand the **wisdom** and the
     7:10   win favor and to show **wisdom**
     7:22   instructed in all the **wisdom**
Ro 11:33   riches and **wisdom** and knowledge
1C   1:17   not with eloquent **wisdom,** so
     1:19   I will destroy the **wisdom** of
     1:20   foolish the **wisdom** of the world
     1:21   For since, in the **wisdom** of God
     1:21   did not know God through
            wisdom
     1:22   signs and Greeks desire **wisdom,**
     1:24   power of God and the **wisdom** of
     1:30   became for us **wisdom** from God,

	2: 1	to you in lofty words or **wisdom**
	2: 4	with plausible words of **wisdom,**
	2: 5	rest not on human **wisdom** but on
	2: 6	we do speak **wisdom,** though it
	2: 6	though it is not a **wisdom** of
	2: 7	But we speak God's **wisdom,**
	2:13	not taught by human **wisdom**
	3:19	For the **wisdom** of this world is
	12: 8	the utterance of **wisdom,** and to
2C	1:12	not by earthly **wisdom** but by
Ep	1: 8	With all **wisdom** and insight
	1:17	may give you a spirit of **wisdom**
	3:10	through the church the **wisdom**
Co	1: 9	in all spiritual **wisdom** and
	1:28	teaching everyone in all **wisdom**
	2: 3	all the treasures of **wisdom** and
	2:23	appearance of **wisdom** in
	3:16	one another in all **wisdom;** and
	4: 5	Conduct yourselves **wisely**
Ja	1: 5	lacking in **wisdom,** ask God,
	3:13	with gentleness born of **wisdom.**
	3:15	Such **wisdom** does not come down
	3:17	But the **wisdom** from above is
2P	3:15	according to the **wisdom** given
Rc	5:12	power and wealth and **wisdom** and
	7:12	Blessing and glory and **wisdom**
	13:18	This calls for **wisdom:** let
	17: 9	a mind that has **wisdom:** the

4679　GO2　AG760　LN225　B3:1026　K7:527　R4680
σοφιζω, I MAKE WISE

2Ti	3:15	that are able **to instruct** you
2P	1:16	follow **cleverly devised** myths

4680　GO20　AG760　LN225　B3:1026　K7:465
σοφος, WISE

Mt	11:25	these things from the **wise** and
	23:34	prophets, **sages,** and scribes,
Lk	10:21	the **wise** and the intelligent
Ro	1:14	both to the **wise** and to the
	1:22	Claiming to be **wise,** they
	16:19	I want you to be **wise** in what
	16:27	to the only **wise** God, through
1C	1:19	destroy the wisdom of the **wise,**
	1:20	Where is the one who is **wise?**
	1:25	For God's foolishness is **wiser**
	1:26	not many of you were **wise** by
	1:27	to shame the **wise;** God chose
	3:10	like a **skilled** master builder

	3:18	If you think that you are **wise**
	3:18	so that you may become **wise.**
	3:19	He catches the **wise** in their
	3:20	thoughts of the **wise,** that they
	6: 5	no one among you **wise** enough to
Ep	5:15	as unwise people but as **wise,**
Ja	3:13	Who is **wise** and understanding

4681　GO2　AG760　LN225
σπανια, SPAIN

Ro	15:24	when I go to **Spain.** For I do
	15:28	out by way of you to **Spain;**

4682　GO3　AG760　LN225
σπαρασσω, I CONVULSE

Mk	1:26	**convulsing** him and crying with
	9:26	After crying out and **convulsing**
Lk	9:39	It **convulses** him until he foams

4683　GO2　AG760　LN225
σπαργανοω, I WRAP IN CLOTH

Lk	2: 7	**wrapped** him **in bands of cloth,**
	2:12	**wrapped in bands of cloth** and

4684　GO2　AG761　LN225
σπαταλαω, I INDULGE

1Ti	5: 6	lives **for pleasure** is dead even
Ja	5: 5	in **luxury and in pleasure;** you

4685　GO2　AG761　LN225
σπαω, I DRAW

Mk	14:47	stood near **drew** his sword and
Ac	16:27	he **drew** his sword and was about

4686　GO7　AG761　LN225
σπειρα, SQUADRON

Mt	27:27	gathered the whole **cohort**
Mk	15:16	together the whole **cohort.**
Jn	18: 3	So Judas brought a **detachment**
	18:12	So the **soldiers,** their officer
Ac	10: 1	centurion of the Italian **Cohort**
	21:31	tribune of the **cohort** that all
	27: 1	of the Augustan **Cohort,** named

4687　GO52　AG761　LN225　B3:521　K7:536
σπειρω, I SOW

Mt	6:26	they neither **sow** nor reap nor
	13: 3	Listen! A **sower** went out to
	13: 3	A sower went out **to sow.**
	13: 4	And as he **sowed,** some seeds

	13:18	then the parable of the **sower.**
	13:19	snatches away what **is sown** in
	13:19	this is what **was sown** on the
	13:20	As for what **was sown** on rocky
	13:22	As for what **was sown** among
	13:23	But as for what **was sown** on
	13:24	compared to someone who **sowed**
	13:27	Master, did you not **sow** good
	13:31	someone took and **sowed** in his
	13:37	He answered, "The one who **sows**
	13:39	and the enemy who **sowed** them
	25:24	reaping where you did not **sow,**
	25:26	I reap where I did not **sow,** and
Mk	4: 3	A **sower** went out to sow.
	4: 3	A sower went out **to sow.**
	4: 4	And as he **sowed,** some seed fell
	4:14	The **sower** sows the word.
	4:14	The sower **sows** the word.
	4:15	where the word **is sown:** when
	4:15	the word that **is sown** in them.
	4:16	And these **are** the ones **sown** on
	4:18	And others **are** those **sown** among
	4:20	And these **are** the ones **sown** on
	4:31	when **sown** upon the ground,
	4:32	yet when it is **sown** it grows up
Lk	8: 5	**sower** went out to sow his seed;
	8: 5	sower went out to **sow** his seed;
	8: 5	and as he **sowed,** some fell on
	12:24	they neither **sow** nor reap, they
	19:21	and reap what you did not **sow.**
	19:22	and reaping what I did not **sow?**
Jn	4:36	so that **sower** and reaper may
	4:37	One **sows** and another reaps.
1C	9:11	If we **have sown** spiritual good
	15:36	Fool! What you **sow** does not
	15:37	And as for what you **sow,** you
	15:37	you do not **sow** the body that is
	15:42	What **is sown** is perishable,
	15:43	It **is sown** in dishonor, it is
	15:43	It **is sown** in weakness, it is
	15:44	It **is sown** a physical body, it
2C	9: 6	the one who **sows** sparingly will
	9: 6	the one who **sows** bountifully
	9:10	supplies seed to the **sower** and
Ga	6: 7	for you reap whatever you **sow.**
	6: 8	If you **sow** to your own flesh,
	6: 8	but if you **sow** to the Spirit,
Ja	3:18	**is sown** in peace for those who

4688   GO1   AG761   LN225

σπεκουλατωρ, EXECUTIONER

Mk	6:27	sent a **soldier of the guard**

4689   GO2   AG761   LN225   B2:853   K7:528

σπενδω, I POUR OUT AS A LIBATION

Ph	2:17	**being poured out as a libation**
2Ti	4: 6	**being poured out as a libation,**

4690   GO43   AG761   LN225   B3:521   K7:536   R4687

σπερμα, SEED

Mt	13:24	someone who sowed good **seed** in
	13:27	did you not sow good **seed** in
	13:32	smallest of all the **seeds,** but
	13:37	sows the good **seed** is the Son
	13:38	the good **seed** are the children
	22:24	raise up **children** for his
	22:25	died **childless,** leaving the
Mk	4:31	smallest of all the **seeds** on
	12:19	raise up **children** for his
	12:20	when he died, left no **children;**
	12:21	leaving no **children;** and the
	12:22	none of the seven left **children**
Lk	1:55	and to his **descendants** forever.
	20:28	raise up **children** for his
Jn	7:42	the Messiah is **descended** from
	8:33	We are **descendants** of Abraham
	8:37	I know that you are **descendants**
Ac	3:25	And in your **descendants** all
	7: 5	to his **descendants** after him,
	7: 6	that his **descendants** would be
	13:23	Of this man's **posterity** God has
Ro	1: 3	who was **descended** from David
	4:13	to his **descendants** through the
	4:16	to all his **descendants,** not
	4:18	numerous shall your **descendants**
	9: 7	are his true **descendants;** but
	9: 7	through Isaac that **descendants**
	9: 8	are counted as **descendants.**
	9:29	not left **survivors** to us, we
	11: 1	**descendant** of Abraham, a member
1C	15:38	each kind of **seed** its own body.
2C	11:22	Are they **descendants** of Abraham
Ga	3:16	Abraham and to his **offspring;**
	3:16	"And to **offsprings,**" as of many
	3:16	"And to your **offspring,**" that
	3:19	until the **offspring** would come
	3:29	you are Abraham's **offspring,**
2Ti	2: 8	a **descendant** of David—that
He	2:16	but the **descendants** of Abraham.

	11:11	By faith he received **power** of
	11:18	through Isaac that **descendants**
1J	3: 9	because God's **seed** abides in
Re	12:17	war on the rest of her **children**

4691 GO1 AG762 LN225 B3:525 R4690,3004
σπερμολογος, SEED COLLECTOR
Ac 17:18 What does this **babbler** want to

4692 GO6 AG762 LN225 B2:245
σπευδω, I HURRY

Lk	2:16	So they went **with haste** and
	19: 5	Zacchaeus, **hurry** and come down
	19: 6	So he **hurried** down and was
Ac	20:16	he **was eager** to be in Jerusalem
	22:18	**Hurry** and get out of Jerusalem
2P	3:12	waiting for and **hastening** the

4693 GO6 AG762 LN225 B3:380
σπηλαιον, CAVE

Mt	21:13	you are making it a **den** of
Mk	11:17	have made it a **den** of robbers.
Lk	19:46	have made it a **den** of robbers.
Jn	11:38	It was a **cave**, and a stone was
He	11:38	**caves** and holes in the ground.
Re	6:15	hid in the **caves** and among the

4694 GO1 AG762 LN225
σπιλας, SPOT
Ju 1:12 These are **blemishes** on your

4695 GO2 AG762 LN225
σπιλοω, I SPOT

Ja	3: 6	it **stains** the whole body, sets
Ju	1:23	hating even the tunic **defiled**

4696 GO2 AG762 LN225
σπιλος, BLOT

Ep	5:27	without a **spot** or wrinkle or
2P	2:13	They are **blots** and blemishes,

4697 GO12 AG762 LN226 B2:599 K7:548 R4698
σπλαγχνιζομαι, I HAVE AFFECTION

Mt	9:36	he **had compassion** for them,
	14:14	and he **had compassion** for them
	15:32	**have compassion** for the crowd,
	18:27	And **out of pity** for him, the
	20:34	**Moved with compassion,** Jesus
Mk	1:41	**Moved with pity,** Jesus
	6:34	and he **had compassion** for them,

	8: 2	I **have compassion** for the
	9:22	**have pity** on us and help us.
Lk	7:13	he **had compassion** for her and
	10:33	saw him, he **was moved with pity**
	15:20	**was filled with compassion;** he

4698 GO11 AG763 LN226 B2:599 K7:548
σπλαγχνον, BOWELS, AFFECTION

Lk	1:78	By the **tender** mercy of our God,
Ac	1:18	and all his **bowels** gushed out.
2C	6:12	restriction in our **affections**,
	7:15	And his **heart** goes out all the
Ph	1: 8	with the **compassion** of Christ
	2: 1	any **compassion** and sympathy,
Co	3:12	yourselves with **compassion**,
Pm	1: 7	because the **hearts** of the
	1:12	my own **heart**, back to you.
	1:20	Refresh my **heart** in Christ.
1J	3:17	in need and yet **refuses** help?

4699 GO3 AG763 LN226
σπογγος, SPONGE

Mt	27:48	ran and got a **sponge,** filled it
Mk	15:36	someone ran, filled a **sponge**
Jn	19:29	So they put a **sponge** full of

4700 GO3 AG763 LN226
σποδος, ASH

Mt	11:21	long ago in sackcloth and **ashes**
Lk	10:13	sitting in sackcloth and **ashes.**
He	9:13	sprinkling of the **ashes** of a

4701 GO1 AG763 LN226 B3:527 K7:536 R4687
σπορα, SEED
1P 1:23 but of imperishable **seed,**

4702 GO3 AG763 LN226 K7:536 R4703
σποριμος, SOWN FIELD

Mt	12: 1	through the **grainfields** on the
Mk	2:23	going through the **grainfields;**
Lk	6: 1	going through the **grainfields,**

4703 GO6 AG763 LN226 B3:521 K7:536 R4687
σπορος, SEED

Mk	4:26	scatter **seed** on the ground,
	4:27	the **seed** would sprout and grow,
Lk	8: 5	went out to sow his **seed;** and
	8:11	The **seed** is the word of God.
2C	9:10	He who supplies **seed** to the
	9:10	multiply your **seed** for sowing

4704 GO11 AG763 LN226 B3:1168 K7:559 R4710
σπουδαζω, I AM DILIGENT

Ga	2:10	actually what I **was eager** to do
Ep	4: 3	**making every effort** to maintain
1Th	2:17	we **longed** with great eagerness
2Ti	2:15	**Do your best** to present
	4: 9	**Do your best** to come to me soon
	4:21	**Do your best** to come before
Ti	3:12	**do your best** to come to me at
He	4:11	**make every effort** to enter that
2P	1:10	**be** all the more **eager** to
	1:15	And I **will make every effort**
	3:14	**strive** to be found by him at

4705 GO3 AG763 LN226 B3:1168 K7:559 R4710
σπουδαιος, MORE DILIGENT

2C	8:17	since he is **more eager** than
	8:22	found **eager** in many matters,
	8:22	is now **more eager** than ever

4709 GO4 AG763 LN226
σπουδαιως, DILIGENTLY

Lk	7: 4	appealed to him **earnestly,**
Ph	2:28	I am the **more eager** to send
2Ti	1:17	he **eagerly** searched for me and
Ti	3:13	**Make every effort** to send Zenas

4710 GO12 AG763 LN226 B3:1168 K7:559 R4692
σπουδη, DILIGENCE

Mk	6:25	Immediately she **rushed** back to
Lk	1:39	went with **haste** to a Judean
Ro	12: 8	the leader, in **diligence;** the
	12:11	Do not lag in **zeal,** be ardent
2C	7:11	For see what **earnestness** this
	7:12	your **zeal** for us might be made
	8: 7	in utmost **eagerness,** and in our
	8: 8	love against the **earnestness** of
	8:16	the same **eagerness** for you that
He	6:11	show the same **diligence** so as
2P	1: 5	you must **make every effort** to
Ju	1: 3	while **eagerly** preparing to

4711 GO5 AG764 LN226
σπυρις, MAT BASKET

Mt	15:37	left over, seven **baskets** full.
	16:10	how many **baskets** you gathered?
Mk	8: 8	left over, seven **baskets** full.
	8:20	how many **baskets** full of broken
Ac	9:25	wall, lowering him in a **basket.**

4712 GO7 AG764 LN226
σταδιον, STADIA

Mt	14:24	was **far** from the land, for the
Lk	24:13	seven **miles** from Jerusalem,
Jn	6:19	three or four **miles,** they saw
	11:18	Jerusalem, some two **miles** away,
1C	9:24	Do you not know that in a **race**
Re	14:20	of about two hundred **miles.**
	21:16	his rod, fifteen hundred **miles;**

4713 GO1 AG764 LN226
σταμνος, JAR

| He | 9: 4 | there were a golden **urn** holding |

4713a GO1 AG764 LN226
στασιαστης, REVOLUTIONARY

| Mk | 15: 7 | was in prison with the **rebels** |

4714 GO9 AG764 LN226 B1:377 K7:568
στασις, REVOLUTION

Mk	15: 7	murder during the **insurrection.**
Lk	23:19	in prison for an **insurrection**
	23:25	prison for **insurrection** and
Ac	15: 2	had no small **dissension** and
	19:40	with **rioting** today, since there
	23: 7	When he said this, a **dissension**
	23:10	the **dissension** became violent,
	24: 5	an **agitator** among all the Jews
He	9: 8	first tent is still **standing.**

4715 GO1 AG764 LN226 B2:851
στατηρ, STATER

| Mt | 17:27 | you will find a **coin;** take that |

4716 GO27 AG764 LN226 B1:391 K7:572
σταυρος, CROSS

Mt	10:38	take up the **cross** and follow me
	16:24	take up their **cross** and follow
	27:32	this man to carry his **cross.**
	27:40	God, come down from the **cross.**
	27:42	come down from the **cross** now,
Mk	8:34	take up their **cross** and follow
	15:21	to carry his **cross;** it was
	15:30	and come down from the **cross!**
	15:32	come down from the **cross** now,
Lk	9:23	take up their **cross** daily and
	14:27	does not carry the **cross** and
	23:26	they laid the **cross** on him, and
Jn	19:17	carrying the **cross** by himself,
	19:19	written and put on the **cross.**

	19:25	standing near the **cross** of
	19:31	left on the **cross** during the
1C	1:17	that the **cross** of Christ might
	1:18	For the message about the **cross**
Ga	5:11	offense of the **cross** has been
	6:12	persecuted for the **cross** of
	6:14	except the **cross** of our Lord
Ep	2:16	one body through the **cross,**
Ph	2: 8	—even death on a **cross.**
	3:18	enemies of the **cross** of Christ;
Co	1:20	through the blood of his **cross.**
	2:14	aside, nailing it to the **cross.**
He	12: 2	endured the **cross,** disregarding

	19:23	When the soldiers **had crucified**
	19:41	place where he **was crucified,**
Ac	2:36	this Jesus whom you **crucified.**
	4:10	whom you **crucified,** whom God
1C	1:13	Was Paul **crucified** for you? Or
	1:23	we proclaim Christ **crucified,** a
	2: 2	Jesus Christ, and him **crucified**
	2: 8	not **have crucified** the Lord of
2C	13: 4	he **was crucified** in weakness,
Ga	3: 1	publicly exhibited as **crucified**
	5:24	Christ Jesus **have crucified** the
	6:14	the world **has been crucified** to
Re	11: 8	also their Lord **was crucified.**

4717   GO46 AG765 LN227 B1:391 K7:581 R4716
σταυροω, I CRUCIFY

Mt	20:19	flogged and **crucified;** and on
	23:34	**crucify,** and some you will flog
	26: 2	be handed over to be **crucified.**
	27:22	said, "Let him be **crucified!**"
	27:23	the more, "Let him be **crucified**
	27:26	handed him over to be **crucified**
	27:31	led him away to **crucify** him.
	27:35	And when they **had crucified** him
	27:38	Then two bandits **were crucified**
	28: 5	for Jesus who **was crucified.**
Mk	15:13	They shouted back, "**Crucify**
	15:14	shouted all the more, "**Crucify**
	15:15	handed him over **to be crucified**
	15:20	they led him out to **crucify** him
	15:24	And they **crucified** him, and
	15:25	morning when they **crucified** him
	15:27	And with him they **crucified** two
	16: 6	who **was crucified.** He has been
Lk	23:21	they kept shouting, "**Crucify,**
	23:21	shouting, "Crucify, **crucify** him
	23:23	he should be **crucified;** and
	23:33	they **crucified** Jesus there with
	24: 7	to sinners, and be **crucified,**
	24:20	to death and **crucified** him.
Jn	19: 6	**Crucify** him! Crucify him!
	19: 6	Crucify him! **Crucify** him!
	19: 6	him yourselves and **crucify** him;
	19:10	you, and power to **crucify** you?
	19:15	Away with him! **Crucify** him!
	19:15	Shall I **crucify** your King?
	19:16	over to them to be **crucified.**
	19:18	There they **crucified** him, and
	19:20	place where Jesus **was crucified**

4718   GO3 AG765 LN227
σταφυλη, CLUSTER OF RIPE GRAPES

Mt	7:16	Are **grapes** gathered from thorns
Lk	6:44	nor are **grapes** picked from a
Re	14:18	earth, for its **grapes** are ripe.

4719   GO5 AG765 LN227 B3:523
σταχυς, STALK OF GRAIN

Mt	12: 1	began to pluck **heads of grain**
Mk	2:23	began to pluck **heads of grain.**
	4:28	first the stalk, then the **head,**
	4:28	then the full grain in the **head**
Lk	6: 1	plucked some **heads of grain,**

4720   GO1 AG765 LN227
σταχυς, STACHYS

| Ro | 16: 9 | Christ, and my beloved **Stachys.** |

4721   GO3 AG765 LN227
στεγη, ROOF

Mt	8: 8	have you come under my **roof;**
Mk	2: 4	they removed the **roof** above him
Lk	7: 6	to have you come under my **roof;**

4722   GO4 AG765 LN227 B3:887 K7:585
στεγω, I ENDURE

1C	9:12	but we **endure** anything rather
	13: 7	all things, **endures** all things.
1Th	3: 1	Therefore when we could **bear** it
	3: 5	when I could **bear** it no longer,

4723   GO5 AG766 LN227
στειρα, STERILE

Lk	1: 7	Elizabeth was **barren,** and both
	1:36	her who was said to be **barren.**
	23:29	Blessed are the **barren,** and

Ga　4:27　Rejoice, you **childless** one,
He　11:11　Sarah herself was **barren**—

4724　ᴳᴼ2 ᴬᴳ766 ᴸᴺ227 ᴮ1:126 ᴷ7:588
στελλω, I AVOID
2C　8:20　We **intend** that no one should
2Th　3: 6　**to keep away** from believers

4725　ᴳᴼ1 ᴬᴳ766 ᴸᴺ227 ᴮ1:405
στεμμα, GARLAND
Ac　14:13　brought oxen and **garlands** to

4726　ᴳᴼ2 ᴬᴳ766 ᴸᴺ227 ᴮ2:423 ᴷ7:600 ᴿ4727
στεναγμος, GROANING
Ac　7:34　have heard their **groaning,** and
Ro　8:26　intercedes with **sighs** too deep

4727　ᴳᴼ6 ᴬᴳ766 ᴸᴺ227 ᴮ2:423 ᴷ7:600
στεναζω, I GROAN
Mk　7:34　he **sighed** and said to him,
Ro　8:23　**groan** inwardly while we wait
2C　5: 2　For in this tent we **groan,**
　　5: 4　we **groan** under our burden,
He　13:17　with joy and not with **sighing**
Ja　5: 9　Beloved, do not **grumble**
　　　　　against

4728　ᴳᴼ3 ᴬᴳ766 ᴸᴺ227 ᴮ2:807 ᴷ7:604
στενος, NARROW
Mt　7:13　Enter through the **narrow** gate;
　　7:14　For the gate is **narrow** and the
Lk　13:24　enter through the **narrow** door;

4729　ᴳᴼ3 ᴬᴳ766 ᴸᴺ227 ᴮ2:807 ᴷ7:604
στενοχωρεω, I AM ANGUISHED
2C　4: 8　but not **crushed;** perplexed,
　　6:12　There is no **restriction** in our
　　6:12　affections, but only in **yours.**

4730　ᴳᴼ4 ᴬᴳ766 ᴸᴺ227 ᴮ2:807 ᴷ7:604
στενοχωρια, ANGUISH, DISTRESS
Ro　2: 9　will be anguish and **distress**
　　8:35　or **distress,** or persecution,
2C　6: 4　hardships, **calamities,**
　　12:10　persecutions, and **calamities**

4731　ᴳᴼ4 ᴬᴳ766 ᴸᴺ227 ᴮ1:660 ᴷ7:609
στερεος, SOLID
2Ti　2:19　God's **firm** foundation stands,
He　5:12　You need milk, not **solid** food;

　　5:14　But **solid** food is for the
1P　5: 9　Resist him, **steadfast** in your

4732　ᴳᴼ3 ᴬᴳ766 ᴸᴺ227 ᴷ7:609 ᴿ4731
στερεοω, I MAKE STRONG, SOLID
Ac　3: 7　and ankles **were made strong.**
　　3:16　**has made** this man **strong,**
　　　　　whom
　　16: 5　the churches **were strengthened**

4733　ᴳᴼ1 ᴬᴳ766 ᴸᴺ227 ᴷ7:609 ᴿ4732
στερεωμα, SOLIDITY
Co　2: 5　morale and the **firmness** of your

4734　ᴳᴼ3 ᴬᴳ767 ᴸᴺ227
στεφανας, STEPHAN
1C　1:16　also the household of **Stephanas**
　　16:15　household of **Stephanas** were the
　　16:17　the coming of **Stephanas** and

4735　ᴳᴼ18 ᴬᴳ767 ᴸᴺ227 ᴮ1:405 ᴷ7:615
στεφανος, CROWN
Mt　27:29　thorns into a **crown,** they put
Mk　15:17　thorns into a **crown,** they put
Jn　19: 2　And the soldiers wove a **crown**
　　19: 5　wearing the **crown** of thorns and
1C　9:25　receive a perishable **wreath,**
Ph　4: 1　my joy and **crown,** stand firm
1Th　2:19　is our hope or joy or **crown** of
2Ti　4: 8　reserved for me the **crown** of
Ja　1:12　will receive the **crown** of life
1P　5: 4　you will win the **crown** of glory
Re　2:10　will give you the **crown** of life
　　3:11　no one may seize your **crown.**
　　4: 4　with golden **crowns** on their
　　4:10　they cast their **crowns** before
　　6: 2　a **crown** was given to him, and
　　9: 7　what looked like **crowns** of gold
　　12: 1　on her head a **crown** of twelve
　　14:14　with a golden **crown** on his head

4736　ᴳᴼ7 ᴬᴳ767 ᴸᴺ227
στεφανος, STEPHEN
Ac　6: 5　and they chose **Stephen,** a man
　　6: 8　**Stephen,** full of grace and
　　6: 9　up and argued with **Stephen.**
　　7:59　While they were stoning **Stephen**
　　8: 2　Devout men buried **Stephen** and
　　11:19　over **Stephen** traveled as far as
　　22:20　your witness **Stephen** was shed,

4737 GO3 AG767 LN227 B1:405 K7:615 R4735
στεφανοω, I CROWN

2Ti 2: 5 **is crowned** without competing
He 2: 7 **have crowned** them with glory
2: 9 now **crowned** with glory and

4738 GO5 AG767 LN227
στηθος, CHEST

Lk 18:13 beating his **breast** and saying,
23:48 home, beating their **breasts.**
Jn 13:25 while reclining **next** to Jesus,
21:20 reclined **next** to Jesus at the
Re 15: 6 sashes across their **chests.**

4739 GO10 AG767 LN227 K7:636
στηκω, I STAND

Mk 3:31 **standing** outside, they sent to
11:25 Whenever you **stand** praying,
Ro 14: 4 that they **stand** or fall. And
1C 16:13 Keep alert, **stand** firm in your
Ga 5: 1 **Stand** firm, therefore, and do
Ph 1:27 know that you **are standing** firm
4: 1 **stand** firm in the Lord in this
1Th 3: 8 if you continue to **stand** firm
2Th 2:15 **stand** firm and hold fast to the

4740 GO1 AG768 LN228 K7:653 R4741
στηριγμος, STRENGTHENING

2P 3:17 and lose your own **stability.**

4741 GO13 AG768 LN228 B1:660 K7:653
στηριζω, I STRENGTHEN

Lk 9:51 **set** his face to go to Jerusalem
16:26 a great chasm **has been fixed,**
22:32 back, **strengthen** your brothers.
Ro 1:11 spiritual gift to **strengthen**
16:25 who is able to **strengthen** you
1Th 3: 2 to **strengthen** and encourage you
3:13 And may he so **strengthen** your
2Th 2:17 **strengthen** them in every good
3: 3 **will strengthen** you and guard
Ja 5: 8 **Strengthen** your hearts, for the
1P 5:10 **strengthen,** and establish you.
2P 1:12 **are established** in the truth
Re 3: 2 **strengthen** what remains and is

4741a GO1 AG768 LN228
στιβας, LEAFY BRANCH

Mk 11: 8 spread leafy **branches** that they

4742 GO1 AG768 LN228 B2:572 K7:657
στιγμα, BRAND

Ga 6:17 for I carry the **marks** of Jesus

4743 GO1 AG768 LN228
στιγμη, POINT

Lk 4: 5 showed him in an **instant** all

4744 GO1 AG768 LN228 K7:665
στιλβω, GLISTENING

Mk 9: 3 and his clothes became
dazzling

4745 GO4 AG768 LN228 B1:68
στοα, COLONNADE

Jn 5: 2 which has five **porticoes.**
10:23 in the **portico** of Solomon.
Ac 3:11 called Solomon's **Portico,**
5:12 together in Solomon's
Portico.

4747 GO7 AG768 LN228 B1:104 K7:670 R4748
στοιχειον, ELEMENT

Ga 4: 3 enslaved to the **elemental**
4: 9 beggarly **elemental** spirits?
Co 2: 8 according to the **elemental**
2:20 died to the **elemental** spirits
He 5:12 the basic **elements** of the
2P 3:10 the **elements** will be dissolved
3:12 **elements** will melt with fire?

4748 GO5 AG769 LN228 B2:451 K7:666
στοιχεω, I WALK

Ac 21:24 you yourself **observe** and guard
Ro 4:12 follow the **example** of the faith
Ga 5:25 let us also **be guided** by the
6:16 As for those who **will follow**
Ph 3:16 Only **let** us **hold fast** to what

4749 GO9 AG769 LN228 B1:312 K7:687
στολη, LONG ROBE

Mk 12:38 to walk around in long **robes,**
16: 5 dressed in a white **robe,**
Lk 15:22 Quickly, bring out a **robe**—
20:46 walk around in long **robes,** and
Re 6:11 were each given a white **robe**
7: 9 **robed** in white, with palm
7:13 **robed** in white, and where have
7:14 washed their **robes** and made
22:14 wash their **robes,** so that they

4750   GO78 AG769 LN228 B2:726 K7:692
στομα, MOUTH

Mt	4: 4	comes from the **mouth** of God
	5: 2	of the heart the **mouth** speaks.
	13:35	I will open my **mouth** to speak
	15:11	what goes into the **mouth** that
	15:11	what comes out of the **mouth**
	15:17	whatever goes into the **mouth**
	15:18	But what comes out of the **mouth**
	17:27	when you open its **mouth,** you
	18:16	confirmed by the **evidence** of
	21:16	Out of the **mouths** of infants
Lk	1:64	Immediately his **mouth** was
	1:70	spoke through the **mouth** of his
	4:22	words that came from his **mouth.**
	6:45	the heart that the **mouth** speaks
	11:54	him in something he might **say.**
	19:22	judge you by your own **words,**
	21:15	for I will give you **words** and
	21:24	they will fall by the **edge** of
	22:71	it ourselves from his own **lips!**
Jn	19:29	hyssop and held it to his **mouth.**
Ac	1:16	the Holy Spirit **through** David
	3:18	what he had foretold **through**
	3:21	God announced long ago **through**
	4:25	by the Holy Spirit **through** our
	8:32	so he does not open his **mouth.**
	8:35	Then Philip began to **speak,** and
	10:34	Then Peter began to **speak** to
	11: 8	has ever entered my **mouth.**
	15: 7	I should be the one **through**
	18:14	Paul was about to **speak,** Gallio
	22:14	One and to hear his own **voice;**
	23: 2	him to strike him on the **mouth**
Ro	3:14	**mouths** are full of cursing and
	3:19	so that every **mouth** may be
	10: 8	on your **lips** and in your heart
	10: 9	confess with your **lips** that
	10:10	one confesses with the **mouth**
	15: 6	you may with one **voice** glorify
2C	6:11	our **heart** is wide open to you.
	13: 1	sustained by the **evidence** of
Ep	4:29	come out of your **mouths,** but
	6:19	so that when I **speak,** a message
Co	3: 8	language from your **mouth.**
2Th	2: 8	with the breath of his **mouth,**
2Ti	4:17	rescued from the lion's **mouth.**
He	11:33	shut the **mouths** of lions,
	11:34	escaped the **edge** of the sword,

Ja	3: 3	If we put bits into the **mouths**
	3:10	From the same **mouth** come
1P	2:22	deceit was found in his **mouth.**
2J	1:12	talk with you **face** to face, so
	1:12	talk with you face to **face,** so
3J	1:14	we will talk together **face** to
	1:14	will talk together face to **face**
Ju	1:16	they are **bombastic** in speech
Re	1:16	and from his **mouth** came a sharp
	2:16	them with the sword of my **mouth**
	3:16	to spit you out of my **mouth.**
	9:17	sulfur came out of their **mouths**
	9:18	coming out of their **mouths.**
	9:19	horses is in their **mouths** and
	10: 9	sweet as honey in your **mouth.**
	10:10	sweet as honey in my **mouth,** but
	11: 5	fire pours from their **mouth** and
	12:15	Then from his **mouth** the serpent
	12:16	woman; it opened its **mouth** and
	12:16	had poured from his **mouth.**
	13: 2	and its **mouth** was like a lion's
	13: 2	like a lion's **mouth.** And the
	13: 5	The beast was given a **mouth**
	13: 6	It opened its **mouth** to utter
	14: 5	and in their **mouth** no lie was
	16:13	frogs coming from the **mouth** of
	16:13	from the **mouth** of the beast,
	16:13	and from the **mouth** of the false
	19:15	From his **mouth** comes a sharp
	19:21	sword that came from his **mouth;**

4751   GO1 AG770 LN228
στομαχος, STOMACH

1Ti	5:23	for the sake of your **stomach**

4752   GO2 AG770 LN228 B3:958 K7:701 R4754
στρατεια, SOLDIERY

2C	10: 4	for the weapons of our **warfare**
1Ti	1:18	you may fight the good **fight,**

4753   GO8 AG770 LN228 B3:958 K7:701 R4754
στρατευμα, ARMY

Mt	22: 7	He sent his **troops,** destroyed
Lk	23:11	Even Herod with his **soldiers**
Ac	23:10	ordered the **soldiers** to go down
	23:27	I came with the **guard** and
Re	9:16	The number of the **troops** of
	19:14	And the **armies** of heaven,
	19:19	with their **armies** gathered to
	19:19	the horse and against his **army.**

4754   ᴳᴼ7 ᴬᴳ770 ᴸᴺ228 ᴮ3:958 ᴷ7:701
στρατευω, I SOLDIER
Lk	3:14	**Soldiers** also asked him, "And
1C	9: 7	for **doing military service?** Who
2C	10: 3	we do not **wage war** according to
1Ti	1:18	following them you **may fight**
2Ti	2: 4	No one **serving in the army** gets
Ja	4: 1	cravings that **are at war** within
1P	2:11	flesh that **wage war** against the

4755   ᴳᴼ10 ᴬᴳ770 ᴸᴺ228 ᴮ3:958 ᴷ7:701 ᴿ4754
στρατηγος, CAPTAIN
Lk	22: 4	chief priests and **officers** of
	22:52	the **officers** of the temple
Ac	4: 1	the **captain** of the temple, and
	5:24	Now when the **captain** of the
	5:26	Then the **captain** went with the
	16:20	before the **magistrates,** they
	16:22	**magistrates** had them stripped
	16:35	the **magistrates** sent the police
	16:36	The **magistrates** sent word to
	16:38	to the **magistrates,** and they

4756   ᴳᴼ2 ᴬᴳ770 ᴸᴺ229 ᴮ3:958 ᴷ7:701 ᴿ4754
στρατια, ARMY
Lk	2:13	multitude of the heavenly **host,**
Ac	7:42	them over to worship the **host**

4757   ᴳᴼ26 ᴬᴳ770 ᴸᴺ229 ᴮ3:958 ᴷ7:701 ᴿ4754
στρατιωτης, SOLDIER
Mt	8: 9	with **soldiers** under me; and I
	27:27	the **soldiers** of the governor
	28:12	sum of money to the **soldiers,**
Mk	15:16	Then the **soldiers** led him into
Lk	7: 8	with **soldiers** under me; and I
	23:36	The **soldiers** also mocked him,
Jn	19: 2	And the **soldiers** wove a crown
	19:23	When the **soldiers** had crucified
	19:23	one for each **soldier.** They also
	19:24	25 is what the **soldiers** did
	19:32	Then the **soldiers** came and
	19:34	Instead, one of the **soldiers**
Ac	10: 7	a devout **soldier** from the ranks
	12: 4	four squads of **soldiers** to
	12: 6	sleeping between two **soldiers,**
	12:18	among the **soldiers** over what
	21:32	Immediately he took **soldiers**
	21:32	tribune and the **soldiers,** they
	21:35	to be carried by the **soldiers.**
	23:23	with two hundred **soldiers,**
	23:31	So the **soldiers,** according
	27:31	centurion and the **soldiers,**
	27:32	Then the **soldiers** cut away the
	27:42	The **soldiers'** plan was to kill
	28:16	the **soldier** who was guarding
2Ti	2: 3	like a good **soldier** of Christ

4758   ᴳᴼ1 ᴬᴳ770 ᴸᴺ229 ᴮ3:958 ᴷ7:701
στρατολογεω, I ENLIST AS A SOLDIER
2Ti	2: 4	the **soldier's aim** is to please

4760   ᴳᴼ1 ᴬᴳ771 ᴸᴺ229 ᴮ3:958 ᴷ7:701
στρατοπεδον, SOLDIER CAMPS
Lk	21:20	Jerusalem surrounded by **armies,**

4761   ᴳᴼ1 ᴬᴳ771 ᴸᴺ229 ᴿ4762
στρεβλοω, I TWIST
2P	3:16	the ignorant and unstable **twist**

4762   ᴳᴼ21 ᴬᴳ771 ᴸᴺ229 ᴮ1:354 ᴷ7:714
στρεφω, I TURN
Mt	5:39	right cheek, **turn** the other
	7: 6	them under foot and **turn** and
	9:22	Jesus **turned,** and seeing her
	16:23	But he **turned** and said to
	18: 3	unless you **change** and become
	27: 3	repented and **brought back** the
Lk	7: 9	and **turning** to the crowd that
	7:44	Then **turning** toward the woman,
	9:55	But he **turned** and rebuked them.
	10:23	Then **turning** to the disciples,
	14:25	and he **turned** and said to them,
	22:61	The Lord **turned** and looked at
	23:28	But Jesus **turned** to them and
Jn	1:38	When Jesus **turned** and saw them
	12:40	with their heart and **turn**—
	20:14	she **turned** around and saw Jesus
	20:16	"Mary!" She **turned** and said to
Ac	7:39	in their hearts they **turned**
	7:42	But God **turned** away from them
	13:46	are now **turning** to the Gentiles
Re	11: 6	over the waters to **turn** them

4763   ᴳᴼ2 ᴬᴳ771 ᴸᴺ229 ᴿ4764
στρηνιαω, I LUXURIATE
Re	18: 7	**lived luxuriously,** so give her
	18: 9	**lived in luxury** with her, will

4764   GO2   AG771   LN229
στρηνος, LUXURY
Re   18: 3   from the power of her **luxury.**

4765   GO4   AG771   LN229   B1:173   K7:730
στρουθιον, SPARROW
Mt   10:29   Are not two **sparrows** sold for
     10:31   more value than many **sparrows.**
Lk   12: 6   Are not five **sparrows** sold for
     12: 7   more value than many **sparrows.**

4766   GO6   AG771   LN229
στρωννυω, I SPREAD
Mt   21: 8   A very large crowd **spread** their
     21: 8   from the trees and **spread** them
Mk   11: 8   Many people **spread** their cloaks
     14:15   large room upstairs, **furnished**
Lk   22:12   already **furnished.** Make
Ac   9:34   get up and **make your bed!"**
        And

4767   GO1   AG771   LN229
στυγητος, DESTESTABLE
Ti   3: 3   **despicable,** hating one another.

4768   GO2   AG771   LN229
στυγναζω, I AM GLOOMY
Mt   16: 3   the sky is red and **threatening.**
Mk   10:22   he **was shocked** and went away

4769   GO4   AG772   LN229   B3:795   K7:732
στυλος, PILLAR
Ga   2: 9   who were acknowledged **pillars,**
1Ti   3:15   **pillar** and bulwark of the truth
Re   3:12   I will make you a **pillar** in the
     10: 1   his legs like **pillars** of fire.

4770   GO1   AG772
στωικος, STOIC
Ac   17:18   Also some Epicurean and **Stoic**

4772   GO3   AG772   LN229   B1:194   K7:736   R4773
συγγενεια, RELATIVE
Lk   1:61   None of your **relatives** has
Ac   7: 3   your **relatives** and go to the
     7:14   **relatives** to come to him,

4773   GO11   AG772   LN229   B2:549   K7:736
συγγενης, RELATIVE
Mk   6: 4   among their own **kin,** and in

Lk   1:58   Her neighbors and **relatives**
     2:44   among their **relatives** and
     14:12   **relatives** or rich neighbors, in
     21:16   by **relatives** and friends; and
Jn   18:26   a **relative** of the man whose ear
Ac   10:24   called together his **relatives**
Ro   9: 3   **kindred** according to the flesh.
     16: 7   **relatives** who were in prison
     16:11   Greet my **relative** Herodion.
     16:21   and Sosipater, my **relatives.**

4773a   GO1   AG772   LN229
συγγενις, RELATIVE
Lk   1:36   now, your **relative** Elizabeth

4774   GO1   AG773   LN229   K1:716
συγγνωμη, CONCESSION
1C   7: 6   This I say by way of **concession**

4775   GO2   AG773   LN229   R4862,2521
συγκαθημαι, I SIT TOGETHER
Mk   14:54   he **was sitting with** the guards,
Ac   26:30   those who **had been seated**
        with

4776   GO2   AG773   LN229   K7:766   R4862,2523
συγκαθιζω, I SIT TOGETHER
Lk   22:55   **sat down together,** Peter sat
Ep   2: 6   and **seated** us **with** him in the

4777   GO2   AG773   LN230   B3:719   K5:936   R4862,2553
συγκακοπαθεω, I SUFFER BAD
     TOGETHER
2Ti   1: 8   but **join** with me **in suffering**
     2: 3   **Share in suffering** like a good

4778   GO1   AG773   LN230   R4862,2558
συγκακουχεομαι, I HAVE BAD WITH
He   11:25   to **share ill-treatment** with the

4779   GO8   AG773   LN230   K3:496   R4862,2564
συγκαλεω, I CALL TOGETHER
Mk   15:16   they **called together** the whole
Lk   9: 1   **called** the twelve **together** and
     15: 6   he **calls together** his friends
     15: 9   she **calls together** her friends
     23:13   Pilate then **called together** the
Ac   5:21   **called together** the council
     10:24   and **had called together** his
     28:17   he **called together** the local

4780 GO1 AG773 LN230 B2:212 K7:743 R4862,2572
συγκαλυπτω, I COVER TOGETHER
Lk 12: 2   Nothing **is covered up** that will

4781 GO1 AG773 LN230 R4862,2578
συγκαμπτω, I BOW TOGETHER
Ro 11:10   **keep** their backs forever **bent.**

4782 GO1 AG773 LN230 R4862,2597
συγκαταβαινω, I COME DOWN WITH
Ac 25: 5   **come down with** me, and if there

4784 GO1 AG773 LN230 R4862,2698
συγκαταθεσις, PACT
2C 6:16   What **agreement** has the temple

4784a GO1 AG773 LN230
συγκατατιθημι, I SET TOGETHER AGAIN
Lk 23:51   **had** not **agreed** to their plan

4785 GO1 AG773 LN230 K9:604
συγκαταψηφιζομαι, I COUNT TOGETHER
Ac 1:26   he **was added to** the eleven

4786 GO2 AG773 LN230 B1:69 R4862,2767
συγκεραννυμι, I MIX TOGETHER
1C 12:24   But God has so **arranged** the
He 4: 2   they **were** not **united** by

4787 GO1 AG773 LN230 R4862,2795
συγκινεω, I STIR TOGETHER
Ac 6:12   They **stirred up** the people as

4788 GO4 AG774 LN230 B3:491 K7:744 R4862,2808
συγκλειω, I CLOSE TOGETHER
Lk 5: 6   they **caught** so many fish
Ro 11:32   For God **has imprisoned** all in
Ga 3:22   the scripture **has imprisoned**
    3:23   we **were imprisoned** and guarded

4789 GO4 AG774 LN230 B2:295 K3:767 R4862,2818
συγκληρονομος, CO-INHERITOR
Ro 8:17   heirs of God and **joint heirs**
Ep 3: 6   become **fellow heirs,** members of
He 11: 9   who were **heirs with him** of the
1P 3: 7   they too are also **heirs** of the

4790 GO3 AG774 LN230 B1:639 K3:797 R4862,2841
συγκοινωνεω, I AM CO-PARTNER
Ep 5:11   **Take** no **part** in the unfruitful

Ph 4:14   it was kind of you **to share** my
Re 18: 4   that you **do** not **take part** in

4791 GO4 AG774 LN230 B1:639 K3:797 R4862,2844
συγκοινωνος, CO-PARTNER
Ro 11:17   **share** the rich root of the
1C 9:23   I may **share** in its blessings.
Ph 1: 7   all of you **share** in God's grace
Re 1: 9   I, John, your brother who **share**

4792 GO1 AG774 LN230 R4862,2865
συγκομιζω, I OBTAIN TOGETHER
Ac 8: 2   Devout men **buried** Stephen and

4793 GO3 AG774 LN230 B2:362 K3:953 R4862,2919
συγκρινω, I JUDGE TOGETHER
1C 2:13   **interpreting** spiritual things
2C 10:12   classify or **compare** ourselves
    10:12   and **compare** themselves with one

4794 GO1 AG775 LN230 R4862,2955
συγκυπτω, I BEND DOWN WITH
Lk 13:11   She **was bent over** and was quite

4795 GO1 AG775 LN230
συγκυρια, COINCIDENCE
Lk 10:31   **by chance** a priest was going

4796 GO7 AG775 LN230 K9:359 R4862,5463
συγχαιρω, I REJOICE TOGETHER
Lk 1:58   her, and they **rejoiced with** her
    15: 6   **Rejoice with** me, for I have
    15: 9   **Rejoice with** me, for I have
1C 12:26   all **rejoice together** with it.
    13: 6   but **rejoices** in the truth.
Ph 2:17   I am glad and **rejoice with** all
    2:18   must be glad and **rejoice with**

4797 GO5 AG775 LN230
συγχεω, I AM CONFUSED
Ac 2: 6   gathered and was **bewildered,**
    9:22   more powerful and **confounded**
    19:32   the assembly was in **confusion,**
    21:27   **stirred up** the whole crowd.
    21:31   all Jerusalem was in an **uproar.**

4798 GO1 AG775 LN230 R4862,5530
συγχραομαι, I MAKE USE TOGETHER
Jn 4: 9   **share things in common with**

4799 GO1 AG775 LN230 R4797
συγχυσις, CONFUSION
Ac 19:29 filled with the **confusion**

4800 GO3 AG775 LN230 B1:643 K7:766 R4862,2198
συζαω, I LIVE TOGETHER
Ro 6: 8 we **will** also **live with** him.
2C 7: 3 together and **to live together.**
2Ti 2:11 we **will** also **live with** him;

4801 GO2 AG775 LN230 B3:1160 R4862,2201
συζευγνυμι, I YOKE TOGETHER
Mt 19: 6 what God **has joined together,**
Mk 10: 9 what God **has joined together,**

4802 GO10 AG775 LN230 K7:747 R4862,2212
συζητεω, I DISPUTE
Mk 1:27 they **kept on asking** one another
 8:11 began **to argue** with him, asking
 9:10 **questioning** what this rising
 9:14 and some scribes **arguing** with
 9:16 What are you **arguing** about
 12:28 heard them **disputing** with one
Lk 22:23 Then they began **to ask** one
 24:15 talking and **discussing,** Jesus
Ac 6: 9 stood up and **argued** with
 9:29 He spoke and **argued** with the

4804 GO1 AG775 LN231 K7:748 R4802
συζητητης, DISPUTER
1C 1:20 Where is the **debater** of this

4805 GO1 AG775 LN231 B3:1160 K7:748 R4801
συζυγος, YOKE FELLOW
Ph 4: 3 my loyal **companion,** help these

4806 GO2 AG776 LN231 B1:643 K7:766 R4862,2227
συζωοποιεω, I MAKE ALIVE TOGETHER
Ep 2: 5 **made** us **alive together** with
Co 2:13 God **made** you **alive together**

4807 GO1 AG776 LN231 K7:758
συκαμινος, MULBERRY
Lk 17: 6 you could say to this **mulberry**

4808 GO16 AG776 LN231 B1:723 K7:751 R4810
συκη, FIG TREE
Mt 21:19 And seeing a **fig tree** by the
 21:19 the **fig tree** withered at once.
 21:20 How did the **fig tree** wither at

 21:21 has been done to the **fig tree,**
 24:32 From the **fig tree** learn its
Mk 11:13 distance a **fig tree** in leaf, he
 11:20 they saw the **fig tree** withered
 11:21 The **fig tree** that you cursed
 13:28 From the **fig tree** learn its
Lk 13: 6 A man had a **fig tree** planted
 13: 7 for fruit on this **fig tree,** and
 21:29 Look at the **fig tree** and all
Jn 1:48 I saw you under the **fig tree**
 1:50 I saw you under the **fig tree?**
Ja 3:12 Can a **fig tree,** my brothers and
Re 6:13 the **fig tree** drops its winter

4809 GO1 AG776 LN231 K7:758
συκομορεα, SYCAMORE
Lk 19: 4 climbed a **sycamore** tree to see

4810 GO4 AG776 LN231 K7:751
συκον, FIG
Mt 7:16 thorns, or **figs** from thistles?
Mk 11:13 it was not the season for **figs.**
Lk 6:44 **Figs** are not gathered from
Ja 3:12 or a grapevine **figs?** No more

4811 GO2 AG776 LN231 K7:759
συκοφαντεω, I ACCUSE FALSELY
Lk 3:14 threats or **false accusation,**
 19: 8 if I **have defrauded** anyone of

4812 GO1 AG776 LN231 B3:379
συλαγωγεω, I KIDNAP
Co 2: 8 one **takes** you **captive** through

4813 GO1 AG776 LN231 B3:379
συλαω, I ROB
2C 11: 8 I **robbed** other churches by

4814 GO6 AG776 LN231 R4862,2980
συλλαλεω, I SPEAK TOGETHER
Mt 17: 3 Moses and Elijah, **talking with**
Mk 9: 4 Moses, who **were talking with**
Lk 4:36 amazed and **kept saying to** one
 9:30 Moses and Elijah, **talking to**
 22: 4 he went away and **conferred with**
Ac 25:12 after he **had conferred with** his

4815 GO16 AG776 LN231 B1:343 K7:759 R4862,2983
συλλαμβανω, I TAKE TOGETHER
Mt 26:55 **arrest** me as though I were a

Mk 14:48 to **arrest** me as though I were
Lk 1:24 Elizabeth **conceived,** and for
1:31 And now, you **will conceive** in
1:36 **has** also **conceived** a son; and
2:21 before he **was conceived** in the
5: 7 come and **help** them. And they
5: 9 of fish that they **had taken;**
22:54 Then they **seized** him and led
Jn 18:12 Jewish police **arrested** Jesus
Ac 1:16 guide for those who **arrested**
12: 3 proceeded to **arrest** Peter also.
23:27 This man **was seized** by the Jews
26:21 Jews **seized** me in the temple
Ph 4: 3 **help** these women, for they have
Ja 1:15 when that desire **has conceived,**

4816 GO8 AG777 LN231 B2:33 R4862,3004
συλλεγω, I COLLECT
Mt 7:16 Are grapes **gathered** from thorns
13:28 want us to go and **gather** them?
13:29 No; for in **gathering** the weeds
13:30 **Collect** the weeds first and
13:40 Just as the weeds **are collected**
13:41 they **will collect** out of his
13:48 sat down, and **put** the good into
Lk 6:44 Figs are not **gathered** from

4817 GO1 AG777 LN231 R4862,3049
συλλογιζομαι, I REASON TOGETHER
Lk 20: 5 They **discussed** it with one

4818 GO1 AG777 LN231 K4:323 R4862,3076
συλλυπεω, I GREATLY GRIEVE
Mk 3: 5 **was grieved** at their hardness

4819 GO8 AG777 LN231
συμβαινω, I COME/GO TOGETHER
Mk 10:32 tell them what was **to happen** to
Lk 24:14 amazement at what **had happened**
Ac 3:10 what had **happened** to him
20:19 trials **that came** to me through
21:35 that he **had** to be carried by
1C 10:11 These things **happened** to them
1P 4:12 strange **were happening** to you.
2P 2:22 **has happened** to them according

4820 GO6 AG777 LN231 R4862,906
συμβαλλω, I THROW TOGETHER
Lk 2:19 and **pondered** them in her heart.

14:31 Or what king, going out to **wage**
Ac 4:15 while they **discussed** the matter
17:18 philosophers **debated** with him.
18:27 his arrival he greatly **helped**
20:14 When he **met** us in Assos, we

4821 GO2 AG777 LN231 B2:372 K1:564 R4862,936
συμβασιλευω, I AM KING TOGETHER
1C 4: 8 that we **might be kings with** you
2Ti 2:12 we **will** also **reign with** him; if

4822 GO7 AG777 LN231 K7:763
συμβιβαζω, I FORCE TOGETHER
Ac 9:22 by **proving** that Jesus was the
16:10 **being convinced** that God had
19:33 tried to **make a defense** before
1C 2:16 so as to **instruct** him?" But we
Ep 4:16 joined and **knit together** by
Co 2: 2 encouraged and **united** in love,
2:19 nourished and **held together** by

4823 GO4 AG777 LN231 B1:362 R4862,1011
συμβουλευω, I PLAN TOGETHER
Mt 26: 4 and they **conspired** to arrest
Jn 18:14 who **had advised** the Jews that
Ac 9:23 the Jews **plotted** to kill him,
Re 3:18 Therefore I **counsel** you to buy

4824 GO8 AG778 LN231 B1:362 R4825
συμβουλιον, COUNCIL
Mt 12:14 **conspired** against him, how to
22:15 **plotted** to entrap him in what
27: 1 **conferred together** against
27: 7 After **conferring together,** they
28:12 they **devised** a plan to give a
Mk 3: 6 immediately **conspired** with the
15: 1 **held a consultation** with the
Ac 25:12 conferred with his **council,**

4825 GO1 AG778 LN231 B1:362 R4862,1012
συμβουλος, COUNSELOR
Ro 11:34 Or who has been his **counselor?**

4826 GO7 AG778 LN231
συμεων, SIMEON
Lk 2:25 whose name was **Simeon;** this man
2:34 Then **Simeon** blessed them and
3:30 son of **Simeon,** son of Judah,

Ac 13: 1   Barnabas, **Simeon** who was called
    15:14   **Simeon** has related how God
2P   1: 1   **Simeon** Peter, a servant and
Re   7: 7   from the tribe of **Simeon** twelve

4827   GO1 AG778 LN231 K4:460 R4862,3101
συμμαθητης, CO-LEARNER
Jn 11:16   to his **fellow disciples,** "Let

4828   GO3 AG778 LN232 B3:1038 K4:508 R4862
συμμαρτυρεω, I TESTIFY TOGETHER
Ro   2:15   conscience also **bears witness;**
     8:16   Spirit **bearing witness with** our
     9: 1   my conscience **confirms** it by

4829   GO1 AG778 LN232 R4862,3307
συμμεριζω, I DIVIDE WITH
1C   9:13   **share in what is sacrificed** on

4830   GO2 AG778 LN232 K2:830 R4862,3353
συμμετοχος, CO-PARTAKERS
Ep   3: 6   **sharers** in the promise in
     5: 7   Therefore do not be **associated**

4831   GO1 AG778 LN232 B1:490 K4:659 R4862,3402
συμμιμητης, CO-IMITATOR
Ph   3:17   **join in imitating** me, and

4832   GO1 AG778 LN232 B1:705 K7:766 R4862,3444
συμμορφιζω, I CONFORM
Ph   3:10   sufferings by **becoming like** him

4833   GO2 AG778 LN232 B1:705 K7:766 R4832
συμμορφος, CONFORMED
Ro   8:29   predestined to be **conformed** to
Ph   3:21   that it may be **conformed** to the

4834   GO2 AG778 LN232 B3:719 K5:935 R4835
συμπαθεω, I SUFFER WITH
He   4:15   is unable to **sympathize** with
    10:34   For you **had compassion** for

4835   GO1 AG779 LN232 K5:935 R4841
συμπαθης, CO-SUFFERING
1P   3: 8   **sympathy,** love for one another,

4836   GO1 AG779 LN232 R4862,3854
συμπαραγινομαι, I COME ALONG WITH
Lk 23:48   who **had gathered** there for this

4837   GO1 AG779 LN232 R4862,3870
συμπαρακαλεω, I ENCOURAGE TOGETHER
Ro   1:12   be **mutually encouraged** by each

4838   GO4 AG779 LN232 R4862,3880
συμπαραλαμβανω, I TAKE ALONG WITH
Ac 12:25   **returned** to Jerusalem and
    15:37   Barnabas wanted to **take with**
    15:38   and **had** not **accompanied** them in
Ga   2: 1   **taking** Titus **along** with me.

4840   GO1 AG779 LN232 R4862,3918
συμπαρειμι, I AM PRESENT
Ac 25:24   all **here present with** us, you

4841   GO2 AG779 LN232 B3:719 K5:925 R4862,3958
συμπασχω, I SUFFER WITH
Ro   8:17   we **suffer with** him so that we
1C 12:26   all **suffer together** with it; if

4842   GO2 AG779 LN232 R4862,3992
συμπεμπω, I SEND TOGETHER
2C   8:18   **With** him we **are sending** the
     8:22   And **with** them we **are sending**

4843   GO1 AG779 LN232 R4862,4012,2983
συμπεριλαμβανω, I EMBRACE
Ac 20:10   **took** him **in his arms,** and said,

4844   GO1 AG779 LN232 R4862,4095
συμπινω, I DRINK TOGETHER
Ac 10:41   ate and **drank with** him after he

4844a   GO1 AG779 LN232
συμπιπτω, I FALL TOGETHER
Lk   6:49   immediately it **fell,** and great

4845   GO3 AG779 LN232 B1:736 K6:308 R4862,4137
συμπληροω, I FILL TOGETHER
Lk   8:23   the boat **was filling with** water
     9:51   When the days **drew near** for him
Ac   2: 1   the day of Pentecost **had come,**

4846   GO5 AG779 LN232 B1:226 K6:455 R4862,4155
συμπνιγω, I CHOKE TOGETHER
Mt 13:22   lure of wealth **choke** the word,
Mk   4: 7   thorns grew up and **choked** it,
     4:19   come in and **choke** the word, and
Lk   8:14   they **are choked** by the cares
     8:42   the crowds **pressed in** on him.

4847   GO1 AG780 LN232 B2:794 R4862,4177
συμπολιτης, CO-CITIZEN
Ep   2:19   are **citizens with** the saints

4848   GO4 AG780 LN232 R4862,4198
συμπορευομαι, I TRAVEL TOGETHER
Mk 10: 1   crowds again **gathered around**
Lk   7:11   a large crowd **went with** him.
     14:25   **were traveling with** him; and he
     24:15   came near and **went with** them,

4849   GO2 AG780 LN232
συμποσιον, BY GROUP
Mk   6:39   to sit down in **groups** on the
       6:39   in **groups** on the green grass.

4850   GO1 AG780 LN232 K6:651 R4862,4245
συμπρεσβυτερος, CO-ELDER
1P   5: 1   Now as an **elder myself** and a

4851   GO15 AG780 LN232 K9:69
συμφερω, IT IS ADVANTAGEOUS
Mt   5:29   **it is better** for you to lose
       5:30   **it is better** for you to lose
       18: 6   **it would be better** for you if a
       19:10   **it is better** not to marry.
Jn   11:50   **it is better** for you to have
       16: 7   **it is** to your **advantage** that I
       18:14   **it was better** to have one
Ac   19:19   **collected** their books and
       20:20   anything **helpful,** proclaiming
1C   6:12   not all things are **beneficial.**
       10:23   not all things are **beneficial.**
       12: 7   Spirit for the **common good.**
2C   8:10   **it is appropriate** for you who
       12: 1   nothing **is to be gained** by it,
He   12:10   disciplines us for our **good,** in

4852   GO1 AG780 LN232 R4862,5346
συμφημι, I SAY WITH
Ro   7:16   I **agree** that the law is good.

4852a   GO2 AG780 LN232
συμφορος, ADVANTAGE
1C   7:35   I say this for your own **benefit**
       10:33   not seeking my own **advantage,**

4853   GO1 AG780 LN232 R4862,5443
συμφυλετης, CO-TRIBESMAN
1Th   2:14   from your own **compatriots** as

4854   GO1 AG780 LN233 K7:766 R4855
συμφυτος, PLANTED TOGETHER
Ro   6: 5   For if we have been **united** with

4855   GO1 AG780 LN233 R4862,5453
συμφυω, I SPROUT TOGETHER
Lk   8: 7   and the thorns **grew with** it and

4856   GO6 AG780 LN233 K9:304 R4859
συμφωνεω, I AGREE
Mt   18:19   if two of you **agree** on earth
       20: 2   After **agreeing** with the
       20:13   did you not **agree** with me for
Lk   5:36   from the new **will not match** the
Ac   5: 9   you have **agreed together** to put
       15:15   This **agrees** with the words of

4857   GO1 AG781 LN233 K9:304 R4856
συμφωνησις, HARMONY
2C   6:15   What **agreement** does Christ

4858   GO1 AG781 LN233 K9:304 R4859
συμφωνια, MUSIC
Lk   15:25   he heard **music** and dancing.

4859   GO1 AG781 LN233 K9:304 R4862,5456
συμφωνος, AGREEMENT
1C   7: 5   except perhaps by **agreement** for

4860   GO1 AG781 LN233 K9:604 R4862,5585
συμψηφιζω, I CALCULATE TOGETHER
Ac   19:19   of these books **was calculated,**

4861   GO1 AG781 LN233 B3:687 R4862,5590
συμψυχος, TOGETHER IN SOUL
Ph   2: 2   **being in full accord** and of one

4862   GO128 AG781 LN233 B3:1206 K7:766
συν, WITH, TOGETHER [MULTIPLE
OCCURRENCES]

4863   GO59 AG782 LN233 B1:291 R4862,71
συναγω, I BRING TOGETHER
Mt   2: 4   and **calling together** all the
       3:12   **will gather** his wheat into the
       6:26   neither sow nor reap nor **gather**
       12:30   whoever **does** not **gather** with me
       13: 2   great crowds **gathered around**
       13:30   but **gather** the wheat into my
       13:47   **caught** fish of every kind;

	18:20	two or three **are gathered** in my
	22:10	**gathered** all whom they found,
	22:34	they **gathered together,**
	22:41	**were gathered together,** Jesus
	24:28	there the vultures **will gather.**
	25:24	and **gathering** where you did not
	25:26	**gather** where I did not scatter?
	25:32	the nations **will be gathered**
	25:35	a stranger and you **welcomed** me,
	25:38	stranger and **welcomed** you, or
	25:43	you **did** not **welcome** me, naked
	26: 3	elders of the people **gathered**
	26:57	and the elders **had gathered.**
	27:17	So after they **had gathered,**
	27:27	they **gathered** the whole cohort
	27:62	the Pharisees **gathered** before
	28:12	After the priests **had assembled**
Mk	2: 2	So many **gathered** around that
	4: 1	a very large crowd **gathered**
	5:21	a great crowd **gathered** around
	6:30	The apostles **gathered** around
	7: 1	Jerusalem **gathered** around him,
Lk	3:17	to **gather** the wheat into his
	11:23	whoever **does** not **gather** with me
	12:17	I have no place to **store** my
	12:18	there I **will store** all my grain
	15:13	son **gathered** all he had and
	22:66	**gathered together,** and they
Jn	4:36	**is gathering** fruit for eternal
	6:12	**Gather** up the fragments left
	6:13	So they **gathered** them up, and
	11:47	Pharisees **called a meeting** of
	11:52	**gather** into one the dispersed
	15: 6	such branches **are gathered,**
	18: 2	Jesus often **met** there with his
Ac	4: 5	scribes **assembled** in Jerusalem,
	4:26	rulers **have gathered together**
	4:27	**gathered together** against your
	4:31	**gathered together** was shaken;
	11:26	entire year they **met** with the
	13:44	whole city **gathered** to hear the
	14:27	they **called** the church **together**
	15: 6	elders **met together** to consider
	15:30	**gathered** the . . . **together,**
	20: 7	when we **met** to break bread,
	20: 8	upstairs where we **were meeting.**
1C	5: 4	When you **are assembled,** and my
Re	16:14	to **assemble** them for battle on
	16:16	And they **assembled** them at the

	19:17	Come, **gather** for the great
	19:19	armies **gathered** to make war
	20: 8	order to **gather** them for battle

4864   ᴳᴼ56 ᴬᴳ782 ᴸᴺ233 ᴮ1:291 ᴷ7:798 ᴿ4863
συναγωγη, SYNAGOGUE

Mt	4:23	teaching in their **synagogues**
	6: 2	in the **synagogues** and in the
	6: 5	pray in the **synagogues** and at
	9:35	teaching in their **synagogues,**
	10:17	flog you in their **synagogues;**
	12: 9	and entered their **synagogue;**
	13:54	the people in their **synagogue,**
	23: 6	best seats in the **synagogues,**
	23:34	flog in your **synagogues** and
Mk	1:21	entered the **synagogue** and
	1:23	in their **synagogue** a man with
	1:29	they left the **synagogue,** they
	1:39	in their **synagogues** and casting
	3: 1	Again he entered the **synagogue,**
	6: 2	began to teach in the **synagogue**
	12:39	best seats in the **synagogues**
	13: 9	beaten in **synagogues;** and you
Lk	4:15	teach in their **synagogues** and
	4:16	went to the **synagogue** on the
	4:20	eyes of all in the **synagogue**
	4:28	all in the **synagogue** were
	4:33	In the **synagogue** there was a
	4:38	After leaving the **synagogue**
	4:44	message in the **synagogues** of
	6: 6	entered the **synagogue** and
	7: 5	is he who built our **synagogue**
	8:41	a leader of the **synagogue.** He
	11:43	seat of honor in the **synagogues**
	12:11	you before the **synagogues,** the
	13:10	in one of the **synagogues** on the
	20:46	best seats in the **synagogues**
	21:12	hand you over to **synagogues** and
Jn	6:59	was teaching in the **synagogue**
	18:20	always taught in **synagogues** and
Ac	6: 9	belonged to the **synagogue** of
	9: 2	letters to the **synagogues** at
	9:20	Jesus in the **synagogues,** saying
	13: 5	in the **synagogues** of the Jews.
	13:14	went into the **synagogue** and sat
	13:43	the meeting of the **synagogue**
	14: 1	went into the Jewish **synagogue**
	15:21	every sabbath in the **synagogues**
	17: 1	was a **synagogue** of the Jews.

17:10　went to the Jewish **synagogue.**
17:17　So he argued in the **synagogue**
18: 4　argue in the **synagogue** and
18: 7　was next door to the **synagogue.**
18:19　went into the **synagogue** and had
18:26　speak boldly in the **synagogue;**
19: 8　He entered the **synagogue** and
22:19　in every **synagogue** I imprisoned
24:12　either in the **synagogues** or
26:11　in all the **synagogues** I tried
Ja　2: 2　comes into your **assembly,** and
Re　2: 9　but are a **synagogue** of Satan.
　　3: 9　the **synagogue** of Satan who say

4865　GO1　AG783　LN233　B1:645　R4862,75
συναγωνιζομαι, I CONTEND TOGETHER
Ro　15:30　to **join** me in earnest prayer to

4866　GO2　AG783　LN233　B1:645　K1:167　R4862,118
συναθλεω, I STRUGGLE WITH
Ph　1:27　**striving side by side** with one
　　4: 3　for they **have struggled** beside

4867　GO2　AG783　LN233
συναθροιζω, I GATHER TOGETHER
Ac　12:12　many **had gathered** and were
　　19:25　These he **gathered together,**

4868　GO3　AG783　LN233　R4862,142
συναιρω, I LIFT UP TOGETHER
Mt　18:23　wished to **settle accounts** with
　　18:24　When he began the **reckoning,**
　　25:19　came and **settled accounts** with

4869　GO3　AG783　LN233　K1:195　R4862,164
συναιχμαλωτος, CO-CAPTIVE
Ro　16: 7　who **were in prison with** me;
Co　4:10　Aristarchus my **fellow prisoner**
Pm　1:23　Epaphras, my **fellow prisoner** in

4870　GO3　AG783　LN233　B1:480　K1:216　R4862,190
συνακολουθεω, I FOLLOW WITH
Mk　5:37　He allowed no one to **follow** him
　　14:51　young man **was following** him,
Lk　23:49　the women who **had followed** him

4871　GO1　AG783　LN233　B3:449
συναλιζω, I TAKE SALT TOGETHER
Ac　1: 4　While **staying** with them, he

4871a　GO1　AG784　LN233
συναλλασσω, I CHANGE TOGETHER
Ac　7:26　tried to **reconcile** them, saying

4872　GO2　AG784　LN233　R4862,305
συναναβαινω, I GO UP TOGETHER
Mk　15:41　who **had come up with** him to
Ac　13:31　those who **came up with** him
　　　　　from

4873　GO7　AG784　LN233　K3:654　R4862,345
συνανακειμαι, I RECLINE TOGETHER
Mt　9:10　**were sitting with** him and his
　　14: 9　for the **guests,** he commanded
Mk　2:15　sinners **were** also **sitting with**
　　6:22　pleased Herod and his **guests;**
Lk　7:49　who **were at the table with** him
　　14:10　all who **sit at the table with**
　　14:15　One of the **dinner guests,** on

4874　GO3　AG784　LN233　K7:852
συναναμειγνυμι, I MIX UP TOGETHER
1C　5: 9　not **to associate with** sexually
　　5:11　not **to associate with** anyone
2Th　3:14　**have** nothing **to do with** them,

4875　GO1　AG784　LN233　R4862,373
συναναπαυομαι, I REST UP TOGETHER
Ro　15:32　with joy and **be refreshed** in

4876　GO6　AG784　LN233
συνανταω, I MEET
Lk　9:37　mountain, a great crowd **met**
　　　　　him
　　22:10　**will meet** you; follow him into
Ac　10:25　Peter's arrival Cornelius **met**
　　20:22　knowing what **will happen** to me
He　7: 1　**met** Abraham as he was returning
　　7:10　ancestor when Melchizedek **met**

4878　GO2　AG784　LN233　K1:375　R4862,482
συναντιλαμβανομαι, I HELP WITH
Lk　10:40　Tell her then **to help** me.
Ro　8:26　Likewise the Spirit **helps** us in

4879　GO3　AG784　LN234　R4862,520
συναπαγω, I LEAD OFF TOGETHER
Ro　12:16　but **associate with** the lowly;
Ga　2:13　even Barnabas **was led astray** by
2P　3:17　that you **are** not **carried away**

4880　GO3 AG784 LN234 K3:7 R4862,599
συναποθνησκω, I DIE TOGETHER
Mk 14:31　I must **die with** you, I will not
2C　7: 3　to **die together** and to live
2Ti　2:11　If we have **died with** him, we

4881　GO1 AG785 LN234 R4862,622
συναπολλυμι, I DESTROY WITH
He 11:31　did not **perish with** those who

4882　GO1 AG785 LN234 R4862,649
συναποστελλω, I DELEGATE TOGETHER
2C 12:18　and **sent** the brother **with** him.

4883　GO2 AG785 LN234 K7:855
συναρμολογεω, I JOIN TOGETHER
Ep　2:21　structure is **joined together**
　　4:16　**joined** and knit **together** by

4884　GO4 AG785 LN234 R4862,726
συναρπαζω, I SEIZE TOGETHER
Lk　8:29　(For many times it **had seized**
Ac　6:12　**seized** him, and brought him
　19:29　**dragging with** them Gaius and
　27:15　Since the ship **was caught** and

4885　GO1 AG785 LN234 R4862,837
συναυξανω, I GROW TOGETHER
Mt 13:30　Let both of them **grow together**

4886　GO4 AG785 LN234 B3:591 K7:856 R4862,1199
συνδεσμος, CO-CHAIN
Ac　8:23　and the **chains** of wickedness.
Ep　4: 3　unity of the Spirit in the **bond**
Co　2:19　its ligaments and **sinews**,
　　　　grows
　　3:14　which **binds** everything **together**

4887　GO1 AG785 LN234 R4862,1210
συνδεω, I AM BOUND WITH
He 13: 3　those who are **in prison**,

4888　GO1 AG785 LN234 B2:44 K2:253 R4862,1392
συνδοξαζω, I GIVE SPLENDOR TOGETHER
Ro　8:17　may also **be glorified with** him.

4889　GO10 AG785 LN234 B1:256 K2:261 R4862,1401
συνδουλος, CO-SLAVE
Mt 18:28　his **fellow slaves** who owed him
　18:29　Then his **fellow slave** fell down

18:31　When his **fellow slaves** saw
　　　　what
18:33　mercy on your **fellow slave,** as
24:49　his **fellow slaves,** and eats and
Co　1: 7　our beloved **fellow servant.** He
　4: 7　a **fellow servant** in the Lord.
Re　6:11　both of their **fellow servants**
　19:10　I am a **fellow servant** with you
　22: 9　I am a **fellow servant** with you

4890　GO1 AG785 LN234 R4936
συνδρομη, RUNNING TOGETHER
Ac 21:30　the people **rushed together.**

4891　GO3 AG785 LN234 K7:766 R4862,1453
συνεγειρω, I RAISE TOGETHER
Ep　2: 6　and **raised** us **up with** him and
Co　2:12　you were also **raised with** him
　3: 1　So if you **have been raised with**

4892　GO22 AG786 LN234 B1:363 K7:860
συνεδριον, COUNCIL
Mt　5:22　will be liable to the **council;**
　10:17　hand you over to **councils** and
　26:59　whole **council** were looking for
Mk 13: 9　hand you over to **councils;** and
　14:55　whole **council** were looking for
　15: 1　scribes and the whole **council.**
Lk 22:66　brought him to their **council.**
Jn 11:47　called a meeting of the **council**
Ac　4:15　leave the **council** while they
　5:21　called together the **council** and
　5:27　them stand before the **council.**
　5:34　But a Pharisee in the **council**
　5:41　As they left the **council,** they
　6:12　brought him before the **council.**
　6:15　And all who sat in the **council**
　22:30　the entire **council** to meet. He
　23: 1　looking intently at the **council**
　23: 6　he called out in the **council,**
　23:15　Now then, you and the **council**
　23:20　bring Paul down to the **council**
　23:28　him brought to their **council.**
　24:20　when I stood before the **council**

4893　GO30 AG786 LN234 B1:348 K7:898
συνειδησις, CONSCIENCE
Ac 23: 1　with a clear **conscience** before
　24:16　have a clear **conscience** toward
Ro　2:15　to which their own **conscience**

	9: 1	my **conscience** confirms it by
	13: 5	but also because of **conscience.**
1C	8: 7	their **conscience,** being weak,
	8:10	since their **conscience** is weak,
	8:12	wound their **conscience** when it
	10:25	on the ground of **conscience,**
	10:27	on the ground of **conscience.**
	10:28	for the sake of **conscience**—
	10:29	I mean the other's **conscience,**
	10:29	of someone else's **conscience?**
2C	1:12	the testimony of our **conscience**
	4: 2	ourselves to the **conscience** of
	5:11	well known to your **consciences.**
1Ti	1: 5	a good **conscience,** and sincere
	1:19	faith and a good **conscience.** By
	3: 9	faith with a clear **conscience.**
	4: 2	liars whose **consciences** are
2Ti	1: 3	worship with a clear **conscience**
Ti	1:15	very minds and **consciences** are
He	9: 9	cannot perfect the **conscience**
	9:14	purify our **conscience** from dead
	10: 2	longer have any **consciousness**
	10:22	clean from an evil **conscience**
	13:18	we have a clear **conscience,**
1P	2:19	**being aware** of God, you endure
	3:16	Keep your **conscience** clear, so
	3:21	to God for a good **conscience,**

4895   GO2 AG787 LN234 R4862,1510
συνειμι, I AM WITH
Lk   9:18   only the disciples **near** him,
Ac 22:11   those who **were with** me took my

4896   GO1 AG787 LN234
συνειμι, I COME TOGETHER
Lk   8: 4   When a great crowd **gathered** and

4897   GO2 AG787 LN235 B1:321 R4862,1525
συνεισερχομαι, I COME IN WITH
Jn   6:22   **had** not **got into** the boat **with**
     18:15   he **went with** Jesus **into** the

4898   GO2 AG787 LN235
συνεκδημος, COMPANION
Ac 19:29   were Paul's **travel companions.**
2C   8:19   by the churches to **travel with**

4899   GO1 AG787 LN235 R4862,1586
συνεκλεκτος, CO-ELECT
1P   5:13   **chosen together** with you, sends

4901   GO1 AG787 LN235 K4:508 R4862,1957
συνεπιμαρτυρεω, I TESTIFY TOGETHER ON
He   2: 4   while God **added** his **testimony**

4901a   GO1 AG787 LN235
συνεπιτιθημι, I PLACE TOGETHER
Ac 24: 9   The Jews also **joined** in the

4902   GO1 AG787 LN235
συνεπομαι, I ACCOMPANY
Ac 20: 4   He was **accompanied** by Sopater

4903   GO5 AG787 LN235 B3:1147 K7:871 R4904
συνεργεω, I WORK TOGETHER
Mk 16:20   while the Lord **worked with** them
Ro   8:28   all things **work together** for
1C 16:16   of everyone who **works** and toils
2C   6: 1   As we **work together** with him,
Ja   2:22   You see that faith **was active**

4904   GO13 AG787 LN235 B3:1147 K7:871 R4862,2041
συνεργος, CO-WORKER
Ro 16: 3   **work with** me in Christ Jesus,
     16: 9   our **co-worker** in Christ, and my
     16:21   Timothy, my **co-worker,** greets
1C   3: 9   **working together;** you are God's
2C   1:24   we are **workers with** you for
     8:23   partner and **co-worker** in your
Ph   2:25   my brother and **co-worker** and
     4: 3   rest of my **co-workers,** whose
Co   4:11   among my **co-workers** for the
1Th 3: 2   our brother and **co-worker** for
Pm   1: 1   our dear friend and **co-worker,**
     1:24   and Luke, my **fellow workers.**
3J   1: 8   **co-workers** with the truth.

4905   GO30 AG788 LN235 B1:320 K2:684 R4862,2064
συνερχομαι, I COME/GO TOGETHER
Mt   1:18   before they **lived together,** she
Mk   3:20   and the crowd **came together**
     14:53   and the scribes **were assembled.**
Lk   5:15   many crowds **would gather** to
     23:55   The women who **had come with**
Jn 11:33   the Jews who **came with** her also
     18:20   all the Jews **come together.** I
Ac   1: 6   So when they **had come together,**
     1:21   who **have accompanied** us during
     2: 6   the crowd **gathered** and was
     5:16   would also **gather** from the
     9:39   So Peter got up and **went with**

	10:23	from Joppa **accompanied** him.
	10:27	found that many **had assembled;**
	10:45	believers who **had come with**
	11:12	The Spirit told me **to go with**
	15:38	had not **accompanied** them in the
	16:13	to the women who **had gathered**
	19:32	know why they **had come together**
	21:16	also **came** along and brought us
	22:30	the entire council **to meet.** He
	25:17	So when they **met** here, I lost
	28:17	When they **had assembled,** he
1C	11:17	when you **come together** it is
	11:18	when you **come together** as a
	11:20	When you **come together,** it is
	11:33	when you **come together** to eat,
	11:34	so that when you **come together,**
	14:23	the whole church **comes together**
	14:26	When you **come together,** each

4906   GO5 AG788 LN235 R4862,2068
συνεσθιω, I EAT TOGETHER

Lk	15: 2	welcomes sinners and **eats with**
Ac	10:41	**ate** and drank **with** him after he
	11: 3	uncircumcised men and **eat with**
1C	5:11	Do not even **eat with** such a one
Ga	2:12	used to **eat with** the Gentiles.

4907   GO7 AG788 LN235 B3:130 K7:888 R4920
συνεσις, UNDERSTANDING

Mk	12:33	with all the **understanding,** and
Lk	2:47	amazed at his **understanding** and
1C	1:19	**discernment** of the discerning I
Ep	3: 4	perceive my **understanding** of
Co	1: 9	wisdom and **understanding,**
	2: 2	riches of assured **understanding**
2Ti	2: 7	will give you **understanding** in

4908   GO4 AG788 LN236 B2:555 K7:888
συνετος, UNDERSTANDING

Mt	11:25	**intelligent** and have revealed
Lk	10:21	wise and the **intelligent** and
Ac	13: 7	**intelligent** man, who summoned
1C	1:19	discernment of the **discerning** I

4909   GO6 AG788 LN236 R4862,2106
συνευδοκεω, I THINK WELL TOGETHER

Lk	11:48	you are witnesses and **approve**
Ac	8: 1	And Saul **approved** of their
	22:20	**approving** and keeping the coats
Ro	1:32	**applaud** others who practice

1C	7:12	she **consents** to live with him,
	7:13	he **consents** to live with her,

4910   GO2 AG789 LN236
συνευωχεομαι, I FEAST WITH

2P	2:13	while they **feast with** you.
Ju	1:12	they **feast with** you without

4911   GO1 AG789 LN236 R4862,2186
συνεφιστημι, I STOOD ON TOGETHER

Ac	16:22	The crowd **joined in** attacking

4912   GO12 AG789 LN236 B2:733 K7:877 R4862,2192
συνεχω, I HOLD TOGETHER

Mt	4:24	those who **were afflicted** with
Lk	4:38	**was suffering** from a high fever
	8:37	for they **were seized** with great
	8:45	Master, the crowds **surround**
	12:50	what **stress I am under** until it
	19:43	and **hem** you **in** on every side.
	22:63	Now the men who **were holding**
Ac	7:57	But they **covered** their ears,
	18: 5	**was occupied with** proclaiming
	28: 8	Publius lay **sick** in bed with
2C	5:14	the love of Christ **urges** us **on**
Ph	1:23	I am **hard pressed** between the

4913   GO1 AG789 LN236
συνηδομαι, I HAVE PLEASURE TOGETHER

Ro	7:22	For I **delight** in the law of God

4914   GO3 AG789 LN236
συνηθεια, CUSTOM

Jn	18:39	But you have a **custom** that I
1C	8: 7	some have become so **accustomed**
	11:16	we have no such **custom,** nor do

4915   GO1 AG789 LN236
συνηλικιωτης, CONTEMPORARY ONE

Ga	1:14	among my people of the **same age**

4916   GO2 AG789 LN236 B1:266 K7:766 R4862,2290
συνθαπτω, I BURY WITH

Ro	6: 4	**have been buried with** him by
Co	2:12	when you **were buried with** him

4917   GO2 AG790 LN236
συνθλαω, I CRUSH THOROUGHLY

Mt	21:44	**will be broken to pieces;** and
Lk	20:18	**will be broken to pieces;** and

4918 GO2 AG790 LN236 R4862,2346
συνθλιβω, I PRESS TOGETHER
Mk 5:24 followed him and **pressed in** on
      5:31 You see the crowd **pressing in**

4919 GO1 AG790 LN236
συνθρυπτω, I BREAK UP
Ac 21:13 weeping and **breaking** my heart?

4920 GO26 AG790 LN237 B3:130 K7:888
συνιημι, I UNDERSTAND
Mt 13:13 listen, nor do they **understand.**
      13:14 listen, but never **understand,**
      13:15 and **understand** with their heart
      13:19 does not **understand** it, the
      13:23 hears the word and **understands**
      13:51 **Have** you **understood** all this?
      15:10 them, "Listen and **understand:**
      16:12 Then they **understood** that he
      17:13 Then the disciples **understood**
Mk 4:12 but not **understand;** so that
      6:52 for they did not **understand**
      7:14 me, all of you, and **understand:**
      8:17 not perceive or **understand?** Are
      8:21 Do you not yet **understand?**
Lk 2:50 But they did not **understand**
      8:10 they may not **understand.**
      18:34 But they **understood** nothing
      24:45 their minds to **understand** the
Ac 7:25 kinsfolk would **understand** that
      7:25 but they did not **understand.**
      28:26 listen, but never **understand,**
      28:27 and **understand** with their heart
Ro 3:11 no one who has **understanding,**
      15:21 heard of him shall **understand.**
2C 10:12 they **do** not **show good sense.**
Ep 5:17 but **understand** what the will

4921 GO16 AG790 LN237 B1:166 K7:896
συνιστημι, I COMMEND
Lk 9:32 two men who **stood with** him.
Ro 3: 5 **serves to confirm** the justice
      5: 8 But God **proves** his love for us
      16: 1 I **commend** to you our sister
2C 3: 1 Are we beginning to **commend**
      4: 2 we **commend** ourselves to the
      5:12 We **are** not **commending**
            ourselves
      6: 4 **have commended** ourselves in
      7:11 At every point you **have proved**

10:12 of those who **commend** themselves
10:18 For it is not those who **commend**
10:18 those whom the Lord **commends.**
12:11 the ones **commending** me, for I
Ga 2:18 then I **demonstrate** that I am
Co 1:17 in him all things **hold together**
2P 3: 5 word of God heavens **existed**

4922 GO1 AG791 LN237 R4862,3593
συνοδευω, I JOURNEY TOGETHER
Ac 9: 7 The men who **were traveling with**

4923 GO1 AG791 LN237
συνοδια, CO-TRAVELER
Lk 2:44 in the **group of travelers,** they

4923a GO2 AG791 LN237 B1:348 K7:898
συνοιδα, I KNOW TOGETHER
Ac 5: 2 with his wife's **knowledge,** he
1C 4: 4 **I am** not **aware** of anything

4924 GO1 AG791 LN237 R4862,3611
συνοικεω, I HOUSE TOGETHER
1P 3: 7 wives in your **life together,**

4925 GO1 AG791 LN237 B2:249 K5:148 R4862
συνοικοδομεω, I BUILD TOGETHER 3618
Ep 2:22 **are built together** spiritually

4926 GO1 AG791 LN237 R4862,3656
συνομιλεω, I CONVERSE TOGETHER
Ac 10:27 And as he **talked with** him, he

4927 GO1 AG791 LN237
συνομορεω, I JOIN TOGETHER
Ac 18: 7 his house **was next door** to the

4927a GO2 AG791 LN237
συνοραω, I SEE TOGETHER
Ac 12:12 As soon as he **realized** this, he
      14: 6 the apostles **learned** of it and

4928 GO2 AG791 LN237 K7:886
συνοχη, ANGUISH
Lk 21:25 on the earth **distress** among
2C 2: 4 much distress and **anguish** of

4929 GO3 AG791 LN237 R4862,5021
συντασσω, I ORDER FULLY
Mt 21: 6 did as Jesus **had directed** them;

26:19   did as Jesus **had directed** them,
27:10   field, as the Lord **commanded** me

4930   G06 AG792 LN238 B2:59 K8:64 R4931
συντελεια, FULL COMPLETION
Mt   13:39   harvest is the **end** of the age,
     13:40   will it be at the **end** of the
     13:49   will be at the **end** of the age.
     24: 3   coming and of the **end** of the age
     28:20   always, to the **end** of the age.
He   9:26   at the **end** of the age to

4931   G06 AG792 LN238 B2:59 K8:62 R4862,5055
συντελεω, I COMPLETE FULLY
Mk   13: 4   are about **to be accomplished?**
Lk   4: 2   they **were over,** he was famished
     4:13   When the devil **had finished**
Ac   21:27   **were** almost **completed,** the Jews
Ro   9:28   for the Lord **will execute** his
He   8: 8   when I **will establish** a new

4932   G01 AG792 LN238
συντεμνω, I CUT
Ro   9:28   earth quickly and **decisively.**

4933   G03 AG792 LN238 K8:151 R4862,5083
συντηρεω, I KEEP TOGETHER
Mt   9:17   and so both **are preserved.**
Mk   6:20   and he **protected** him. When he
Lk   2:19   But Mary **treasured** all these

4934   G03 AG792 LN238 R4862,5087
συντιθημι, I AGREE
Lk   22: 5   greatly pleased and **agreed** to
Jn   9:22   for the Jews **had** already **agreed**
Ac   23:20   The Jews **have agreed** to ask

4935   G02 AG793 LN238
συντομως, CONCISELY
Mk   16: 8   they told **briefly** to those
Ac   24: 4   I beg you to hear us **briefly**

4936   G03 AG793 LN238 B3:947 R4862,5143
συντρεχω, I RUN TOGETHER
Mk   6:33   they **hurried** there on foot from
Ac   3:11   all the people **ran together** to
1P   4: 4   you no longer **join** them in the

4937   G07 AG793 LN238 K7:919
συντριβω, I BREAK

Mt   12:20   He will not break a **bruised**
Mk   5: 4   shackles he **broke in pieces;**
     14: 3   **broke open** the jar and poured
Lk   9:39   it **mauls** him and will scarcely
Jn   19:36   of his bones **shall be broken.**
Ro   16:20   God of peace will shortly **crush**
Re   2:27   as when clay pots **are shattered**

4938   G01 AG793 LN238 K7:919 R4937
συντριμμα, RUIN
Ro   3:16   **ruin** and misery are in their

4939   G01 AG793 LN238 R4862,5162
συντροφος, FED TOGETHER
Ac   13: 1   Manaen a **member of the court** of

4940   G01 AG793 LN238
συντυγχανω, I MEET TOGETHER
Lk   8:19   could not **reach** him because of

4941   G01 AG793 LN238
συντυχη, SYNTYCHE
Ph   4: 2   I urge **Syntyche** to be of the

4942   G01 AG793 LN238 K8:559 R4862,5271
συνυποκρινομαι, I AM HYPOCRITICAL TOGETHER WITH
Ga   2:13   **joined** him in this **hypocrisy,**

4943   G01 AG793 LN238
συνυπουργεω, I WORK TOGETHER
2C   1:11   as you also **join in helping** us

4944   G01 AG793 LN238 R4862,5271
συνωδινω, I SUFFER BIRTH PAINS TOGETHER WITH
Ro   8:22   been groaning **in labor pains**

4945   G01 AG793 LN238 R4862,3660
συνωμοσια, CO-OATH
Ac   23:13   who joined in this **conspiracy.**

4946   G01 AG794 LN238
συρακουσαι, SYRACUSE
Ac   28:12   put in at **Syracuse** and stayed

4947   G08 AG794 LN238
συρια, SYRIA
Mt   4:24   throughout all **Syria,** and they
Lk   2: 2   Quirinius was governor of **Syria**

Ac 15:23 **Syria** and Cilicia, greetings.
   15:41 went through **Syria** and Cilicia,
   18:18 sailed for **Syria,** accompanied
   20: 3 about to set sail for **Syria**
   21: 3 we sailed to **Syria** and landed
Ga 1:21 went into the regions of **Syria**

4948 GO1 AG794 LN238
συρος, SYRIAN
Lk 4:27 except Naaman the **Syrian.**

4949 GO1 AG794 LN238
συροφοινικισσα, SYROPHOENICIAN
Mk 7:26 of **Syrophoenician** origin. She

4950 GO1 AG794 LN238
συρτις, SYRTIS
Ac 27:17 they would run on the **Syrtis,**

4951 GO5 AG794 LN238
συρω, I DRAG
Jn 21: 8 **dragging** the net full of fish,
Ac 8: 3 **dragging** off both men and
       women
   14:19 **dragged** him out of the city,
   17: 6 they **dragged** Jason and some
Re 12: 4 His tail **swept** down a third of

4952 GO2 AG794 LN239 R4862,4682
συσπαρασσω, I CONVULSE
Mk 9:20 immediately it **convulsed** the
Lk 9:42 to the ground in **convulsions.**

4953 GO1 AG794 LN239 K7:269
συσσημον, SIGNAL
Mk 14:44 had given them a **sign,** saying,

4954 GO1 AG794 LN239 K7:1024 R4862,4983
συσσωμος, CO-BODY
Ep 3: 6 **members of the same body,** and

4956 GO1 AG795 LN239 R4921
συστατικος, COMMENDATION
2C 3: 1 letters of **recommendation** to

4957 GO5 AG795 LN239 B1:391 K7:766 R4862,4717
συσταυροω, I CRUCIFY TOGETHER
Mt 27:44 **were crucified with** him also
Mk 15:32 Those who **were crucified with**
Jn 19:32 who **had been crucified with** him

Ro 6: 6 **was crucified with** him so that
Ga 2:19 I **have been crucified with**

4958 GO2 AG795 LN239 K7:596 R4862,4724
συστελλω, I SEND TOGETHER
Ac 5: 6 The young men came and **wrapped**
1C 7:29 appointed time has **grown short;**

4959 GO1 AG795 LN239 K7:600 R4862,4727
συστεναζω, I GROAN TOGETHER
Ro 8:22 **has been groaning** in labor

4960 GO1 AG795 LN239 B2:451 K7:669
συστοιχεω, I LINE UP TOGETHER
Ga 4:25 **corresponds** to the present

4961 GO2 AG795 LN239 K7:701 R4862,4762
συστρατιωτης, CO-SOLDIER
Ph 2:25 **fellow soldier,** your messenger
Pm 1: 2 **fellow soldier,** and to the

4962 GO2 AG795 LN239 B2:33 R4862,4762
συστρεφω, I TURN TOGETHER
Mt 17:22 As they **were gathering** in
Ac 28: 3 Paul **had gathered** a bundle of

4963 GO2 AG795 LN239 R4962
συστροφη, COMBINATION
Ac 19:40 give to justify this **commotion.**
   23:12 joined in a **conspiracy** and

4964 GO2 AG795 LN239 R4862,4976
συσχηματιζω, I FASHION TOGETHER
Ro 12: 2 **Do** not **be conformed** to this
1P 1:14 **do** not **be conformed** to the

4965 GO1 AG795 LN239
συχαρ, SYCHAR
Jn 4: 5 Samaritan city called **Sychar,**

4966 GO2 AG795 LN239
συχεμ, SYCHEM (SHECHEM)
Ac 7:16 brought back to **Shechem** and
   7:16 the sons of Hamor in **Shechem.**

4967 GO3 AG795 LN239 K7:935 R4969
σφαγη, SLAUGHTER
Ac 8:32 he was led to the **slaughter,**
Ro 8:36 as sheep to be **slaughtered.**
Ja 5: 5 hearts in a day of **slaughter.**

4968 GO1 AG796 LN239 R4967
σφαγιον, SLAUGHTER
Ac 7:42 you offer to me **slain victims**

4969 GO10 AG796 LN239 B2:411 K7:925
σφαζω, I SLAUGHTER
1J 3:12 from the evil one and **murdered**
3:12 And why did he **murder** him?
Re 5: 6 as if it **had been slaughtered,**
5: 9 for you **were slaughtered** and by
5:12 Lamb that **was slaughtered** to
6: 4 that people would **slaughter** one
6: 9 those who **had been slaughtered**
13: 3 **have received** a death-**blow,** but
13: 8 the Lamb that **was slaughtered.**
18:24 all who **have been slaughtered**

4970 GO11 AG796 LN239 B2:846
σφοδρα, EXCEEDING
Mt 2:10 they were **overwhelmed** with joy.
17: 6 ground and were **overcome** by
17:23 they were **greatly** distressed.
18:31 they were **greatly** distressed,
19:25 they were **greatly** astounded and
26:22 And they became **greatly**
27:54 they were **terrified** and said,
Mk 16: 4 which was **very** large, had
Lk 18:23 sad; for he was **very** rich.
Ac 6: 7 increased **greatly** in Jerusalem,
Re 16:21 plague of the hail, so **fearful**

4971 GO1 AG796 LN239 R4970
σφοδρως, EXCEEDINGLY
Ac 27:18 storm so **violently** that on the

4972 GO15 AG796 LN239 B3:497 K7:939 R4973
σφραγιζω, I SEAL
Mt 27:66 made the tomb secure by **sealing**
Jn 3:33 **has certified** this, that God is
6:27 God the Father **has set** his **seal**
Ro 15:28 and **have delivered** to them what
2C 1:22 by **putting** his **seal** on us and
Ep 1:13 **were marked with the seal** of
4:30 **were marked with a seal** for the
Re 7: 3 we have **marked** the servants of
7: 4 who **were sealed,** one hundred
7: 4 **sealed** out of every tribe of
7: 5 twelve thousand **sealed,** from
7: 8 twelve thousand **sealed.**
10: 4 **Seal up** what the seven

20: 3 and locked and **sealed** it over
22:10 **Do** not **seal** up the words of

4973 GO16 AG796 LN239 B3:497 K7:939
σφραγις, SEAL
Ro 4:11 as a **seal** of the righteousness
1C 9: 2 are the **seal** of my apostleship
2Ti 2:19 bearing this **inscription:** "The
Re 5: 1 sealed with seven **seals;**
5: 2 scroll and break its **seals?**
5: 5 the scroll and its seven **seals.**
5: 9 scroll and to open its **seals,**
6: 1 open one of the seven **seals,**
6: 3 When he opened the second **seal,**
6: 5 When he opened the third **seal,**
6: 7 When he opened the fourth **seal,**
6: 9 When he opened the fifth **seal,**
6:12 When he opened the sixth **seal,**
7: 2 having the **seal** of the living
8: 1 Lamb opened the seventh **seal,**
9: 4 do not have the **seal** of God on

4974 GO1 AG797 LN239
σφυδρον, ANKLE
Ac 3: 7 immediately his feet and **ankles**

4975 GO3 AG797 LN239
σχεδον, ALMOST
Ac 13:44 next sabbath **almost** the whole
19:26 only in Ephesus but in **almost**
He 9:22 Indeed, under the law **almost**

4976 GO2 AG797 LN239 B1:708 K7:954
σχημα, SHAPE
1C 7:31 For the present **form** of this
Ph 2: 7 And being found in human **form,**

4977 GO11 AG797 LN239 B3:543 K7:959
σχιζω, I SPLIT
Mt 27:51 **was torn** in two, from top to
27:51 and the rocks **were split.**
Mk 1:10 saw the heavens **torn apart** and
15:38 curtain of the temple **was torn**
Lk 5:36 No one **tears** a piece from a
5:36 the new **will be torn,** and the
23:45 curtain of the temple **was torn**
Jn 19:24 **Let** us not **tear** it, but cast
21:11 so many, the net **was** not **torn.**
Ac 14: 4 **were divided;** some sided with
23: 7 and the assembly **was divided.**

4978 GO8 AG797 LN239 B3:543 K7:963 R4977
σχισμα, SPLIT

Mt	9:16	cloak, and a worse **tear** is made
Mk	2:21	old, and a worse **tear** is made.
Jn	7:43	So there was a **division** in the
	9:16	signs?" And they were **divided.**
	10:19	Again the Jews were **divided**
1C	1:10	there be no **divisions** among you
	11:18	there are **divisions** among you;
	12:25	that there may be no **dissension**

4979 GO2 AG797 LN240
σχοινιον, OF SMALL CORDS

| Jn | 2:15 | Making a whip **of cords,** he |
| Ac | 27:32 | soldiers cut away the **ropes** of |

4980 GO2 AG797 LN240
σχολαζω, I UNOCCUPY

| Mt | 12:44 | it finds it **empty,** swept, and |
| 1C | 7: 5 | **to devote** yourselves to prayer, |

4981 GO1 AG798 LN240
σχολη, LECTURE HALL

| Ac | 19: 9 | daily in the **lecture hall** of |

4982 GO107 AG798 LN240 B3:205 K7:965
σωζω, I DELIVER, I SAVE

Mt	1:21	for he will **save** his people
	8:25	Lord, **save** us! We are perishing
	9:21	cloak, I **will be made well.**
	9:22	your faith **has made** you **well.**
	9:22	the woman **was made well.**
	10:22	to the end **will be saved.**
	14:30	he cried out, "Lord, **save** me!"
	16:25	For those who want to **save**
	19:25	Then who can **be saved?**
	24:13	to the end **will be saved.**
	24:22	no one would **be saved;** but for
	27:40	**save** yourself! If you are the
	27:42	He **saved** others; he cannot
	27:42	he cannot **save** himself. He is
	27:49	Elijah will come to **save** him.
Mk	3: 4	to **save** life or to kill?" But
	5:23	so that she may **be made well,**
	5:28	clothes, I will **be made well.**
	5:34	your faith **has made** you **well;**
	6:56	all who touched it **were healed.**
	8:35	For those who want to **save**
	8:35	of the gospel, **will save** it.
	10:26	another, "Then who can **be saved**

	10:52	your faith **has made** you **well.**
	13:13	to the end **will be saved.**
	13:20	no one would **be saved;** but for
	15:30	**save** yourself, and come down
	15:31	He **saved** others; he cannot
	15:31	others; he cannot **save** himself.
	16:16	baptized **will be saved;** but the
Lk	6: 9	**to save** life or to destroy it?
	7:50	Your faith **has saved** you; go
	8:12	may not believe and **be saved.**
	8:36	by demons **had been healed.**
	8:48	your faith **has made** you **well;**
	8:50	believe, and she **will be saved.**
	9:24	For those who want **to save**
	9:24	life for my sake **will save** it.
	13:23	Lord, will only a few **be saved**
	17:19	your faith **has made** you **well.**
	18:26	said, "Then who can **be saved?"**
	18:42	your faith **has saved** you.
	19:10	seek out and **to save** the lost.
	23:35	He **saved** others; let him save
	23:35	He saved others; **let** him **save**
	23:37	King of the Jews, **save** yourself
	23:39	Messiah? **Save** yourself and us!
Jn	3:17	world might be **saved** through
	5:34	things so that you **may be saved**
	10: 9	enters by me **will be saved,** and
	11:12	asleep, he **will be all right.**
	12:27	world, but to **save** the world.
Ac	2:21	name of the Lord **shall be saved**
	2:40	**Save** yourselves from this
	2:47	those who **were being saved.**
	4: 9	how this man **has been healed,**
	4:12	by which we must **be saved.**
	11:14	entire household **will be saved.**
	14: 9	that he had faith **to be healed,**
	15: 1	Moses, you cannot **be saved.**
	15:11	believe that we **will be saved**
	16:30	what must I do **to be saved?**
	16:31	you **will be saved,** you and your
	27:20	all hope of our **being saved** was
	27:31	the ship, you cannot **be saved.**
Ro	5: 9	**will** we **be saved** through him
	5:10	reconciled, **will** we **be saved** by
	8:24	For in hope we **were saved.** Now
	9:27	remnant of them **will be saved;**
	10: 9	the dead, you **will be saved.**
	10:13	name of the Lord **shall be saved**
	11:14	and thus **save** some of them.

	11:26	And so all Israel **will be saved**
1C	1:18	but to us who **are being saved**
	1:21	**to save** those who believe.
	3:15	the builder **will be saved,** but
	5: 5	so that his spirit **may be saved**
	7:16	you **might save** your husband.
	7:16	you **might save** your wife.
	9:22	that I **might** by all means **save**
	10:33	so that they **may be saved.**
	15: 2	which also you **are being saved,**
2C	2:15	those who **are being saved** and
Ep	2: 5	by grace you **have been saved**—
	2: 8	by grace you **have been saved**
1Th	2:16	so that they **may be saved.** Thus
2Th	2:10	love the truth and so **be saved.**
1Ti	1:15	came into the world **to save**
	2: 4	desires everyone **to be saved**
	2:15	Yet she **will be saved** through
	4:16	in doing this you **will save**
2Ti	1: 9	who **saved** us and called us with
	4:18	every evil attack and **save** me
Ti	3: 5	he **saved** us, not because of
He	5: 7	to the one who was able **to save**
	7:25	able for all time **to save** those
Ja	1:21	the power **to save** your souls.
	2:14	works? Can faith **save** you?
	4:12	who is able **to save** and to
	5:15	The prayer of faith **will save**
	5:20	from wandering **will save** the
1P	3:21	**saves** you—not as a removal
	4:18	for the righteous **to be saved,**
Ju	1: 5	who once for all **saved** a people
	1:23	**save** others by snatching them

4983 GO142 AG799 LN240 B1:232 K7:1024
σωμα, BODY

Mt	5:29	than for your whole **body** to be
	5:30	than for your whole **body** to go
	6:22	eye is the lamp of the **body.** So
	6:22	your whole **body** will be full of
	6:23	your whole **body** will be full of
	6:25	about your **body,** what you will
	6:25	and the **body** more than clothing
	10:28	those who kill the **body** but
	10:28	destroy both soul and **body** in
	26:12	ointment on my **body** she has
	26:26	Take, eat; this is my **body.**
	27:52	many **bodies** of the saints who
	27:58	asked for the **body** of Jesus;

	27:59	So Joseph took the **body** and
Mk	5:29	she felt in her **body** that she
	14: 8	she has anointed my **body**
	14:22	said, "Take; this is my **body.**"
	15:43	asked for the **body** of Jesus.
Lk	11:34	eye is the lamp of your **body.**
	11:34	your whole **body** is full of
	11:34	your **body** is full of darkness.
	11:36	If then your whole **body** is full
	12: 4	those who kill the **body,** and
	12:22	about your **body,** what you will
	12:23	and the **body** more than clothing
	17:37	Where the **corpse** is, there the
	22:19	asked for the **body** of Jesus.
	23:55	tomb and how his **body** was laid.
	24: 3	in, they did not find the **body.**
	24:23	did not find his **body** there,
Jn	2:21	of the temple of his **body.**
	19:31	Jews did not want the **bodies**
	19:38	let him take away the **body** of
	19:38	let him take away the **body** of
	19:40	They took the **body** of Jesus and
	20:12	sitting where the **body** of Jesus
Ac	9:40	turned to the **body** and said,
Ro	1:24	degrading of their **bodies** among
	4:19	when he considered his own **body**
	6: 6	so that the **body** of sin might
	6:12	dominion in your mortal **bodies,**
	7: 4	through the **body** of Christ, so
	7:24	rescue me from this **body** of
	8:10	though the **body** is dead because
	8:11	life to your mortal **bodies** also
	8:13	to death the deeds of the **body,**
	8:23	the redemption of our **bodies.**
	12: 1	to present your **bodies** as a
	12: 4	For as in one **body** we have many
	12: 5	are one **body** in Christ, and
1C	5: 3	For though absent in **body,**
	6:13	The **body** is meant not for
	6:13	Lord, and the Lord for the **body**
	6:15	you not know that your **bodies**
	6:16	prostitute becomes one **body**
	6:18	commits is outside the **body;**
	6:18	sins against the **body** itself.
	6:19	that your **body** is a temple of
	6:20	glorify God in your **body.**
	7: 4	authority over her own **body,**
	7: 4	authority over his own **body,**

	7:34	they may be holy in **body** and
	9:27	I punish my **body** and enslave
	10:16	a sharing in the **body** of Christ
	10:17	we who are many are one **body,**
	11:24	This is my **body** that is for
	11:27	be answerable for the **body** and
	11:29	without discerning the **body,**
	12:12	For just as the **body** is one
	12:12	all the members of the **body,**
	12:12	are one **body,** so it is with
	12:13	all baptized into one **body**—
	12:14	Indeed, the **body** does not
	12:15	I do not belong to the **body,**
	12:15	I do not belong to the **body,**
	12:16	I do not belong to the **body,**
	12:16	it any less a part of the **body.**
	12:17	If the whole **body** were an eye,
	12:18	the members in the **body,** each
	12:19	where would the **body** be?
	12:20	are many members, yet one **body.**
	12:22	the members of the **body** that
	12:23	and those members of the **body**
	12:24	God has so arranged the **body,**
	12:25	no dissension within the **body,**
	12:27	Now you are the **body** of Christ
	13: 3	if I hand over my **body** so that
	15:35	With what kind of **body** do they
	15:37	you do not sow the **body** that is
	15:38	But God gives it a **body** as he
	15:38	each kind of seed its own **body.**
	15:40	There are both heavenly **bodies**
	15:40	bodies and earthly **bodies,** but
	15:44	It is sown a physical **body,** it
	15:44	it is raised a spiritual **body.**
	15:44	If there is a physical **body,**
2C	4:10	always carrying in the **body** the
	4:10	be made visible in our **bodies.**
	5: 6	we are at home in the **body** we
	5: 8	away from the **body** and at home
	5:10	what has been done in the **body,**
	10:10	but his **bodily** presence is weak
	12: 2	whether in the **body** or out of
	12: 2	or out of the **body** I do not
	12: 3	whether in the **body** or out of
	12: 3	or out of the **body** I do not
Ga	6:17	of Jesus branded on my **body.**
Ep	1:23	which is his **body,** the fullness
	2:16	both groups to God in one **body**

	4: 4	is one **body** and one Spirit,
	4:12	building up the **body** of Christ,
	4:16	from whom the whole **body,**
	4:16	promotes the **body's** growth in
	5:23	the **body** of which he is the
	5:28	as they do their own **bodies.**
	5:30	we are members of his **body.**
Ph	1:20	now as always in my **body,**
	3:21	He will transform the **body**
	3:21	be conformed to the **body** of his
Co	1:18	He is the head of the **body,** the
	1:22	reconciled in his fleshly **body**
	1:24	for the sake of his **body,** that
	2:11	by putting off the **body** of the
	2:17	the **substance** belongs to Christ
	2:19	from whom the whole **body,**
	2:23	severe treatment of the **body,**
	3:15	you were called in the one **body**
1Th	5:23	your spirit and soul and **body**
He	10: 5	but a **body** you have prepared
	10:10	offering of the **body** of Jesus
	10:22	**bodies** washed with pure water.
	13: 3	yourselves were **being** tortured.
	13:11	For the **bodies** of those animals
Ja	2:16	supply their **bodily** needs, what
	2.26	For just as the **body** without
	3: 2	able to keep the whole **body** in
	3: 3	us, we guide their whole **bodies**
	3: 6	it stains the whole **body,** sets
1P	2:24	bore our sins in his **body** on
Ju	1: 9	disputed about the **body** of
Re	18:13	slaves—and **human** lives.

4984　　GO2　AG800　LN240　K7:1024　R4983
σωματικος, BODILY
Lk	3:22	descended upon him in **bodily**
1Ti	4: 8	for, while **physical** training

4985　　GO1　AG800　LN240　R4984
σωματικως, BODILY
Co	2: 9	fullness of deity dwells **bodily**

4986　　GO1　AG800　LN240
σωπατρος, SOPATER
Ac	20: 4	He was accompanied by **Sopater**

4987　　GO2　AG800　LN240　K7:1094
σωρευω, I HEAP UP
Ro	12:20	for by doing this you **will heap**
2Ti	3: 6	**overwhelmed** by their sins and

4988 ᴳᴼ2 ᴬᴳ800 ᴸᴺ240
σωσθενης, SOSTHENES
Ac 18:17 all of them seized **Sosthenes,**
1C 1: 1 God, and our brother
Sosthenes,

4989 ᴳᴼ1 ᴬᴳ800 ᴸᴺ240
σωσιπατρος, SOSIPATER
Ro 16:21 and **Sosipater,** my relatives.

4990 ᴳᴼ24 ᴬᴳ800 ᴸᴺ240 ᴮ3:216 ᴷ7:1003 ᴿ4982
σωτηρ, DELIVERER, SAVIOR
Lk 1:47 rejoices in God my **Savior,**
   2:11 in the city of David a **Savior,**
Jn 4:42 this is truly the **Savior** of the
Ac 5:31 Leader and **Savior** that he might
   13:23 brought to Israel a **Savior,**
Ep 5:23 body of which he is the **Savior.**
Ph 3:20 we are expecting a **Savior,** the
1Ti 1: 1 God our **Savior** and of Christ
   2: 3 in the sight of God our **Savior,**
   4:10 who is the **Savior** of all people
2Ti 1:10 appearing of our **Savior** Christ
Ti 1: 3 the command of God our **Savior,**
   1: 4 and Christ Jesus our **Savior.**
   2:10 the doctrine of God our **Savior.**
   2:13 of our great God and **Savior,**
   3: 4 kindness of God our **Savior**
   3: 6 Jesus Christ our **Savior,**
2P 1: 1 our God and **Savior** Jesus
      Christ
   1:11 Lord and **Savior** Jesus Christ
   2:20 Lord and **Savior** Jesus Christ,
   3: 2 Lord and **Savior** spoken
      through
   3:18 of our Lord and **Savior** Jesus
1J 4:14 Son as the **Savior** of the world.
Ju 1:25 to the only God our **Savior,**

4991 ᴳᴼ46 ᴬᴳ801 ᴸᴺ240 ᴮ3:205 ᴷ7:965 ᴿ4990
σωτηρια, DELIVERANCE, SALVATION
Mk 16: 8 Proclamation of . . . **salvation**
Lk 1:69 has raised up a mighty **savior**
   1:71 that we would be **saved** from our
   1:77 to give knowledge of **salvation**
   19: 9 Today **salvation** has come to
Jn 4:22 for **salvation** is from the Jews.
Ac 4:12 There is **salvation** in no one
   7:25 God through him was **rescuing**
   13:26 message of this **salvation** has

13:47 you may bring **salvation** to the
16:17 to you a way of **salvation.**
27:34 it will help you **survive;** for
Ro 1:16 power of God for **salvation** to
   10: 1 them is that they may be **saved.**
   10:10 with the mouth and so is **saved.**
   11:11 their stumbling **salvation** has
   13:11 For **salvation** is nearer to us
2C 1: 6 your consolation and **salvation;**
   6: 2 on a day of **salvation** I have
   6: 2 now is the day of **salvation!**
   7:10 that leads to **salvation** and
Ep 1:13 the gospel of your **salvation,**
Ph 1:19 turn out for my **deliverance.**
   1:28 but of your **salvation.** And this
   2:12 work out your own **salvation**
1Th 5: 8 a helmet the hope of **salvation.**
   5: 9 but for obtaining **salvation**
2Th 2:13 first fruits for **salvation**
2Ti 2:10 obtain the **salvation** that is in
   3:15 instruct you for **salvation**
He 1:14 who are to inherit **salvation?**
   2: 3 neglect so great a **salvation?**
   2:10 pioneer of their **salvation**
   5: 9 the source of eternal **salvation**
   6: 9 things that belong to **salvation**
   9:28 to **save** those who are eagerly
   11: 7 an ark to **save** his household;
1P 1: 5 faith for a **salvation** ready to
   1: 9 of your faith, the **salvation** of
   1:10 Concerning this **salvation,** the
   2: 2 you may grow into **salvation**—
2P 3:15 of our Lord as **salvation.** So
Ju 1: 3 about the **salvation** we share, I
Re 7:10 **Salvation** belongs to our God
   12:10 Now have come the **salvation**
   19: 1 **Salvation** and glory and power

4992 ᴳᴼ5 ᴬᴳ801 ᴸᴺ240 ᴮ3:216 ᴷ7:1021 ᴿ4991
σωτηριος, DELIVERANCE, SALVATION
Lk 2:30 eyes have seen your **salvation,**
   3: 6 flesh shall see the **salvation**
Ac 28:28 that this **salvation** of God has
Ep 6:17 Take the helmet of **salvation,**
Ti 2:11 appeared, bringing **salvation** to

4993 ᴳᴼ6 ᴬᴳ802 ᴸᴺ240 ᴮ1:501 ᴷ7:1097 ᴿ4998
σωφρονεω, I THINK SOBERLY
Mk 5:15 clothed and in his **right mind,**

Lk	8:35	clothed and **in** his **right mind.**
Ro	12: 3	to think **with sober judgment,**
2C	5:13	we are **in** our **right mind,** it is
Ti	2: 6	men **to be self-controlled.**
1P	4: 7	**be serious** and discipline

4994   ᴳᴼ1 ᴬᴳ802 ᴸᴺ240 ᴷ7:1104 ᴿ4998
σωφρονιζω, I BRING TO
SOBER-MINDEDNESS, I ENCOURAGE
| Ti | 2: 4 | so that they may **encourage** the |

4995   ᴳᴼ1 ᴬᴳ802 ᴸᴺ240 ᴷ7:1104 ᴿ4994
σωφρονισμος, SOBER MIND
| 2Ti | 1: 7 | of love and of **self-discipline.** |

4996   ᴳᴼ1 ᴬᴳ802 ᴸᴺ240 ᴮ1:501 ᴿ4998
σωφρονως, SOBER-MINDEDLY
| Ti | 2:12 | lives that are **self-controlled,** |

4997   ᴳᴼ3 ᴬᴳ802 ᴸᴺ240 ᴮ1:494 ᴷ7:1097 ᴿ4998
σωφροσυνη, SOBERMINDEDNESS
Ac	26:25	I am speaking the **sober** truth.
1Ti	2: 9	decently in **suitable** clothing,
	2:15	love and holiness, with **modesty**

4998   ᴳᴼ4 ᴬᴳ802 ᴸᴺ240 ᴮ1:501 ᴷ7:1097
σωφρων, SOBER-MINDED
1Ti	3: 2	**sensible,** respectable,
Ti	1: 8	a lover of goodness, **prudent,**
	2: 2	temperate, serious, **prudent,**
	2: 5	to be **self-controlled,** chaste,

τ

4999   ᴳᴼ1 ᴬᴳ802 ᴸᴺ240
ταβερνη, TAVERN
| Ac | 28:15 | Three **Taverns** to meet us. On |

5000   ᴳᴼ2 ᴬᴳ802 ᴸᴺ241
ταβιθα, TABITHA
| Ac | 9:36 | disciple whose name was **Tabitha** |
| | 9:40 | "**Tabitha,** get up." Then she |

5001   ᴳᴼ1 ᴬᴳ802 ᴸᴺ241 ᴷ8:31 ᴿ5021
ταγμα, ORDER
| 1C | 15:23 | But each in his own **order:** |

5002   ᴳᴼ1 ᴬᴳ803 ᴸᴺ241 ᴿ5021
τακτος, ORDERED
| Ac | 12:21 | On an **appointed** day Herod put |

5003   ᴳᴼ1 ᴬᴳ803 ᴸᴺ241 ᴮ3:858 ᴿ5005
ταλαιπωρεω, I AM MISERABLE
| Ja | 4: 9 | **Lament** and mourn and weep. |

5004   ᴳᴼ2 ᴬᴳ803 ᴸᴺ241 ᴮ3:858 ᴿ5005
ταλαιπωρια, MISERY
| Ro | 3:16 | ruin and **misery** are in their |
| Ja | 5: 1 | weep and wail for the **miseries** |

5005   ᴳᴼ2 ᴬᴳ803 ᴸᴺ241 ᴮ3:858
ταλαιπωρος, MISERABLE
| Ro | 7:24 | **Wretched** man that I am! Who |
| Re | 3:17 | you are **wretched,** pitiable, |

5006   ᴳᴼ1 ᴬᴳ803 ᴸᴺ241 ᴿ5007
ταλαντιαιος, TALENT WEIGHT
| Re | 16:21 | **weighing about a hundred pounds** |

5007   ᴳᴼ14 ᴬᴳ803 ᴸᴺ241
ταλαντον, TALENT
Mt	18:24	owed him ten thousand **talents**
	25:15	to one he gave five **talents**
	25:16	received the five **talents** went
	25:20	received the five **talents** came
	25:20	bringing five more **talents,**
	25:20	handed over to me five **talents**
	25:20	have made five more **talents.**
	25:22	the one with the two **talents**
	25:22	handed over to me two **talents**
	25:22	I have made two more **talents**
	25:24	who had received the one **talent**
	25:25	I went and hid your **talent**
	25:28	So take the **talent** from him
	25:28	to the one with the ten **talents**

5008   ᴳᴼ1 ᴬᴳ803 ᴸᴺ241 ᴮ1:581
ταλιθα, TALITHA
| Mk | 5:41 | **Talitha** cum," which means |

5009   ᴳᴼ4 ᴬᴳ803 ᴸᴺ241
ταμειον, STOREROOM
Mt	6: 6	you pray, go into your **room**
	24:26	He is in the **inner rooms**
Lk	12: 3	whispered behind **closed doors**
	12:24	have neither **storehouse** nor

5010   ᴳᴼ9 ᴬᴳ803 ᴸᴺ241 ᴮ1:271 ᴿ5021
ταξις, RANK
| Lk | 1: 8 | and his **section** was on duty, |
| 1C | 14:40 | done decently and in **order.** |

Co　2: 5　rejoice to see your **morale**
He　5: 6　to the **order** of Melchizedek.
　　5:10　to the **order** of Melchizedek.
　　6:20　forever according to the **order**
　　7:11　to the **order** of Melchizedek,
　　7:11　according to the **order** of Aaron
　　7:17　to the **order** of Melchizedek.

5011　GO8　AG804　LN241　B2:259　K8:1
ταπεινος, HUMBLE
Mt　11:29　I am gentle and **humble** in heart
Lk　1:52　and lifted up the **lowly;**
Ro　12:16　but associate with the **lowly**
2C　7: 6　God, who consoles the **downcast**
　　10: 1　I who am **humble** when face to
Ja　1: 9　Let the believer who is **lowly**
　　4: 6　gives grace to the **humble.**
1P　5: 5　but gives grace to the **humble.**

5012　GO7　AG804　LN241　B2:259　K8:1　R5011,5424
ταπεινοφροσυνη, HUMBLEMINDEDNESS
Ac　20:19　Lord with all **humility** and with
Ep　4: 2　all **humility** and gentleness,
Ph　2: 3　in **humility** regard others as
Co　2:18　insisting on **self-abasement**
　　2:23　self-imposed piety, **humility**
　　3:12　compassion, kindness, **humility**
1P　5: 5　clothe yourselves with **humility**

5012a　GO1　AG804　LN241　B2:259　K8:1　R5012
ταπεινοφρων, HUMBLEMINDED
1P　3: 8　tender heart, and a **humble mind**

5013　GO14　AG804　LN241　B2:259　K8:1　R5011
ταπεινοω, I HUMBLE
Mt　18: 4　**becomes humble** like this child
　　23:12　themselves **will be humbled,**
　　23:12　**humble** themselves will be
Lk　3: 5　hill **shall be made low,**
　　14:11　themselves **will be humbled**
　　14:11　**humble** themselves will be
　　18:14　themselves **will be humbled**
　　18:14　who **humble** themselves will be
2C　11: 7　Did I commit a sin by **humbling**
　　12:21　I come again, my God **may humble**
Ph　2: 8　he **humbled** himself and became
　　4:12　know what it is **to have little**
Ja　4:10　**Humble yourselves** before the
1P　5: 6　**Humble yourselves** therefore

5014　GO4　AG805　LN241　B2:259　K8:1　R5013
ταπεινωσις, HUMILITY
Lk　1:48　favor on the **lowliness** of his
Ac　8:33　In his **humiliation** justice was
Ph　3:21　the body of our **humiliation**
Ja　1:10　the rich in **being brought low**

5015　GO18　AG805　LN241　B3:709
ταρασσω, I TROUBLE
Mt　2: 3　he **was frightened,** and all
　　14:26　they **were terrified,** saying
Mk　6:50　all saw him and **were terrified.**
Lk　1:12　he **was terrified;** and fear
　　24:38　Why are you **frightened,** and why
Jn　5: 7　when the water **is stirred up**
　　11:33　in spirit and deeply **moved.**
　　12:27　Now my soul **is troubled.**
　　13:21　saying this Jesus **was troubled**
　　14: 1　not **let** your hearts **be troubled**
　　14:27　not **let** your hearts **be troubled**
Ac　15:24　have said things to **disturb** you
　　17: 8　city officials **were disturbed**
　　17:13　to stir up and **incite** the
Ga　1: 7　are some who **are confusing** you
　　5:10　it is that **is confusing**
1P　3:14　do not **be intimidated,**

5017　GO2　AG805　LN241　B3:709　R5015
ταραχος, TROUBLE
Ac　12:18　no small **commotion** among the
　　19:23　no little **disturbance** broke out

5018　GO2　AG805　LN241
ταρσευς, OF TARSUS
Ac　9:11　**man of Tarsus** named Saul
　　21:39　I am a Jew, **from Tarsus** in

5019　GO3　AG805　LN241
ταρσος, TARSUS
Ac　9:30　and sent him off to **Tarsus.**
　　11:25　Then Barnabas went to **Tarsus**
　　22: 3　I am a Jew, born in **Tarsus.**

5020　GO1　AG805　LN241
ταρταροω, I SEND TO TARTARUS
2P　2: 4　but **cast** them **into hell** and

5021　GO8　AG805　LN241　K8:27
τασσω, I SET IN ORDER
Mt　28:16　which Jesus **had directed** them.

Lk	7: 8	am a man **set** under authority
Ac	13:48	**destined** for eternal life
	15: 2	**were appointed** to go up to
	22:10	has been **assigned** to you to do
	28:23	After they **had set** a day to
Ro	13: 1	have been **instituted** by God.
1C	16:15	they **have devoted** themselves

5022   GO4 AG806 LN242 B1:116
ταυρος, BULL

Mt	22: 4	my **oxen** and my fat calves have
Ac	14:13	brought **oxen** and garlands
He	9:13	if the blood of goats and **bulls**
	10: 4	blood of **bulls** and goats

5027   GO1 AG806 LN242 B1:263 R2290
ταφη, BURIAL

Mt	27: 7	as a **place to bury** foreigners.

5028   GO7 AG806 LN242 B1:263 R2290
ταφος, TOMB

Mt	23:27	you are like whitewashed **tombs**
	23:29	build the **tombs** of the prophets
	27:61	sitting opposite the **tomb.**
	27:64	command the **tomb** to be made
	27:66	made the **tomb** secure by sealing
	28: 1	Mary went to see the **tomb.**
Ro	3:13	throats are opened **graves**

5029   GO2 AG806 LN242 R5036
ταχα, PERHAPS

Ro	5: 7	though **perhaps** for a good
Pm	1:15	**Perhaps** this is the reason

5030   GO15 AG806 LN242 R5036
ταχεως, QUICKLY

Lk	14:21	Go out **at once** into the streets
	16: 6	sit down **quickly,** and make it
Jn	11:31	Mary get up **quickly** and go out
	13:27	Do **quickly** what you are going
	20: 4	other disciple **outran** Peter
Ac	17:15	as **soon** as possible, they left
1C	4:19	But I will come to you **soon,**
Ga	1: 6	you are so **quickly** deserting
Ph	2:19	to send Timothy to you **soon**
	2:24	not to be **quickly** shaken in
1Ti	5:22	Do not ordain anyone **hastily**
2Ti	4: 9	Do your best to come to me **soon**
He	13:19	be restored to you **very soon.**
	13:23	if he comes **in time,**

5031   GO2 AG807 LN242 B3:847 R5036
ταχινος, QUICK

2P	1:14	my death will come **soon**
	2: 1	bringing **swift** destruction on

5034   GO8 AG807 LN242 R5036
ταχος, QUICKNESS

Lk	18: 8	I tell you, he will **quickly**
Ac	12: 7	Get up **quickly."** And the chains
	22:18	get out of Jerusalem **quickly**
	25: 4	intended to go there **shortly**
Ro	16:20	will **shortly** crush Satan
1Ti	3:14	I hope to come to you **soon,**
Re	1: 1	what must **soon** take place
	22: 6	servants what must **soon** take

5036   GO13 AG807 LN242 B3:1169
ταχυς, QUICKLY

Mt	5:25	Come to terms **quickly** with your
	28: 7	Then go **quickly** and tell his
	28: 8	left the tomb **quickly** with fear
Mk	9:39	**soon afterward** to speak evil of
Lk	15:22	**Quickly,** bring out a robe
Jn	11:29	she got up **quickly** and went to
Ja	1:19	let everyone be **quick** to listen
Re	2:16	I will come to you **soon**
	3:11	I am coming **soon;** hold fast
	11:14	third woe is coming **very soon.**
	22: 7	See, I am coming **soon!** Blessed
	22:12	See, I am coming **soon**
	22:20	Surely I am coming **soon**

5037   GO215 AG807 LN242
τε, BOTH [MULTIPLE OCCURRENCES]

5038   GO9 AG808 LN242 B3:948
τειχος, WALL

Ac	9:25	through an **opening in the wall**
2C	11:33	through a window in the **wall**
He	11:30	By faith the **walls** of Jericho
Re	21:12	It has a great, high **wall** with
	21:14	And the **wall** of the city has
	21:15	city and its gates and **walls.**
	21:17	He also measured its **wall**
	21:18	The **wall** is built of jasper
	21:19	The foundations of the **wall**

5039   GO1 AG808 LN242 B3:571
τεκμηριον, CONVINCING PROOFS

Ac	1: 3	many **convincing proofs**

5040 GO8 AG808 LN242 B1:285 K5:636 R5043
τεκνιον, LITTLE CHILDREN
Jn	13:33	**Little children,** I am with you
1J	2: 1	**little children,** I am writing
	2:12	writing to you, **little children**
	2:28	And now, **little children,** abide
	3: 7	**Little children,** let no one
	3:18	**Little children,** let us love
	4: 4	**Little children,** you are from
	5:21	**Little children,** keep

5041 GO1 AG808 LN242 B1:187
τεκνογονεω, I BEAR CHILDREN
| 1Ti | 5:14 | widows marry, **bear children** |

5042 GO1 AG808 LN242 B1:187 R5041
τεκνογονια, CHILDBEARING
| 1Ti | 2:15 | be saved through **childbearing** |

5043 GO99 AG808 LN242 B1:284 K5:636
τεκνον, CHILD
Mt	2:18	Rachel weeping for her **children**
	3: 9	raise up **children** to Abraham.
	7:11	good gifts to your **children**
	9: 2	Take heart, **son;** your sins are
	10:21	a father his **child,**
	10:21	**children** will rise against
	15:26	take the **children's** food
	18:25	wife and **children** and all his
	19:29	mother or **children** or fields
	21:28	A man had two **sons;** he went
	21:28	**Son,** go and work in the
	22:24	If a man dies **child**less, his
	23:37	desired to gather your **children**
	27:25	on us and on our **children!**
Mk	2: 5	**Son,** your sins are forgiven.
	7:27	Let the **children** be fed first
	7:27	not fair to take the **children's**
	10:24	**Children,** how hard it is to
	10:29	father or **children** or fields
	10:30	mothers and **children,** and
	12:19	leaving a wife but no **child**
	13:12	a father his **child,** and
	13:12	**children** will rise against
Lk	1: 7	But they had no **children**
	1:17	of parents to their **children**
	2:48	**Child,** why have you treated
	3: 8	raise up **children** to Abraham.
	7:35	vindicated by all her **children**
	11:13	good gifts to your **children**

	13:34	gather your **children** together
	14:26	wife and **children,** brothers
	15:31	**Son,** you are always with me
	16:25	But Abraham said, '**Child**
	18:29	parents or **children,** for the
	19:44	you and your **children** within
	20:31	all seven died **child**less.
	23:28	and for your **children.**
Jn	1:12	to become **children** of God,
	8:39	you were Abraham's **children**
	11:52	the dispersed **children** of God.
Ac	2:39	**children,** and for all who are
	7: 5	even though he had no **child.**
	13:33	their **children,** by raising
	21: 5	wives and **children,** escorted us
	21:21	circumcise their **children** or
Ro	8:16	that we are **children** of God,
	8:17	and if **children,** then heirs
	8:21	glory of the **children** of God.
	9: 7	not all of Abraham's **children**
	9: 8	it is not the **children** of the
	9: 8	who are the **children** of God
	9: 8	but the **children** of the promise
1C	4:14	you as my beloved **children.**
	4:17	beloved and faithful **child**
	7:14	your **children** would be unclean
2C	6:13	I speak as to **children**
	12:14	**children** ought not to lay up
	12:14	but parents for their **children.**
Ga	4:19	My **little children,** for whom
	4:25	in slavery with her **children.**
	4:27	the **children** of the desolate
	4:28	are **children** of the promise
	4:31	**children,** not of the slave but
Ep	2: 3	by nature **children** of wrath
	5: 1	of God, as beloved **children,**
	5: 8	Live as **children** of light—
	6: 1	**Children,** obey your parents
	6: 4	do not provoke your **children**
Ph	2:15	and innocent, **children** of God
	2:22	how like a **son** with a father
Co	3:20	**Children,** obey your parents
	3:21	do not provoke your **children**
1Th	2: 7	caring for her own **children.**
	2:11	a father with his **children,**
1Ti	1: 2	To Timothy, my loyal **child**
	1:18	Timothy, my **child,** in
	3: 4	keeping his **children** submissive
	3:12	manage their **children** and their

	5: 4	If a widow has **children** or
2Ti	1: 2	To Timothy, my beloved **child**
	2: 1	You then, my **child,** be
Ti	1: 4	To Titus, my loyal **child** in the
	1: 6	whose **children** are believers
Pm	1:10	appealing to you for my **child**
1P	1:14	Like obedient **children,** do not
	3: 6	have become her **daughters** as
2P	2:14	in greed. Accursed **children!**
1J	3: 1	we should be called **children**
	3: 2	Beloved, we are God's **children**
	3:10	**children** of God and the
	3:10	**children** of the devil are
	5: 2	know that we love the **children**
2J	1: 1	the elect lady and her **children**
	1: 4	find some of your **children**
	1:13	**children** of your elect sister
3J	1: 4	**children** are walking in the
Re	2:23	I will strike her **children**
	12: 4	he might devour her **child**
	12: 5	her **child** was snatched away

5044   ᴳᴼ1 ᴬᴳ808 ᴸᴺ243 ᴮ1:187
τεκνοτροφεω, I NOURISH CHILDREN
1Ti   5:10   who has **brought up children**

5045   ᴳᴼ2 ᴬᴳ809 ᴸᴺ243 ᴮ1:279
τεκτων, CARPENTER
Mt   13:55   Is not this the **carpenter's** son
Mk   6: 3   Is not this the **carpenter,** the

5046   ᴳᴼ19 ᴬᴳ809 ᴸᴺ243 ᴮ2:59 ᴷ8:67 ᴿ5056
τελειος, COMPLETE

Mt	5:48	Be **perfect,** therefore, as your
	5:48	your heavenly Father is **perfect.**
	19:21	If you wish to be **perfect,** go
Ro	12: 2	good and acceptable and **perfect.**
1C	2: 6	among the **mature** we do speak
	13:10	but when the **complete** comes,
	14:20	but in thinking be **adults.**
Ep	4:13	to **maturity,** to the measure
Ph	3:15	those of us then who are **mature**
Co	1:28	we may present everyone **mature**
	4:12	you may stand **mature** and fully
He	5:14	solid food is for the **mature**
	9:11	the greater and **perfect** tent
Ja	1: 4	and let endurance have its **full**
	1: 4	so that you may be **mature** and
	1:17	every **perfect** gift, is from
	1:25	who look into the **perfect** law

	3: 2	is **perfect,** able to keep the
1J	4:18	**perfect** love casts out fear

5047   ᴳᴼ2 ᴬᴳ809 ᴸᴺ243 ᴮ2:59 ᴷ8:78 ᴿ5046
τελειοτης, COMPLETENESS
Co   3:14   together in **perfect harmony.**
He   6: 1   let us go on toward **perfection**

5048   ᴳᴼ23 ᴬᴳ809 ᴸᴺ243 ᴮ2:59 ᴷ8:79 ᴿ5046
τελειοω, I COMPLETE

Lk	2:43	When the festival **was ended**
	13:32	third day I **finish my work.**
Jn	4:34	sent me and **to complete** his
	5:36	Father has given me **to complete**
	17: 4	on earth by **finishing** the
	17:23	they may **become completely** one
	19:28	knew that all **was now finished**
Ac	20:24	I **may finish** my course and the
Ph	3:12	have already **reached the goal**
He	2:10	**make** . . . salvation **perfect**
	5: 9	and **having been made perfect**
	7:19	law **made** nothing **perfect**
	7:28	Son who **has been made perfect**
	9: 9	that cannot **perfect** the
	10: 1	**make perfect** those who approach
	10·14	he **has perfected** for all time
	11:40	apart from us, **be made perfect.**
	12:23	of the righteous **made perfect,**
Ja	2:22	**was brought to completion** by
1J	2: 5	of God **has reached perfection**
	4:12	his love is **perfected** in us.
	4:17	Love **has been perfected** among
	4:18	**has not reached perfection** in

5049   ᴳᴼ1 ᴬᴳ810 ᴸᴺ243 ᴮ2:63 ᴿ5046
τελειως, COMPLETELY
1P   1:13   set **all** your hope on the grace

5050   ᴳᴼ2 ᴬᴳ810 ᴸᴺ243 ᴮ2:59 ᴷ8:84 ᴿ5048
τελειωσις, COMPLETION
Lk   1:45   **fulfillment** of what was spoken
He   7:11   Now if **perfection** had been

5051   ᴳᴼ1 ᴬᴳ810 ᴸᴺ243 ᴮ2:59 ᴷ8:86 ᴿ5048
τελειωτης, COMPLETER
He   12: 2   pioneer and **perfecter** of our

5052   ᴳᴼ1 ᴬᴳ810 ᴸᴺ243 ᴿ5052,5342
τελεσφορεω, I BRING TO COMPLETION
Lk   8:14   their **fruit does** not **mature.**

5053 GO13 AG810 LN243 B1:429
τελευταω, I DIE

Mt	2:19	When Herod **died,** an angel of
	9:18	daughter **has** just **died;** but
	15: 4	mother **must** surely **die.**
	22:25	first married, and **died**
Mk	7:10	mother **must** surely **die.**
	9:48	where their worm never **dies**
Lk	7: 2	was ill and close **to death.**
Jn	11:39	sister of the **dead** man, said
Ac	2:29	he both **died** and was buried
	7:15	He himself **died** there as well
He	11:22	Joseph, **at the end of** his **life**

5054 GO1 AG810 LN243 B2:59 R5053
τελευτη, END

| Mt | 2:15 | remained there until the **death** |

5055 GO28 AG810 LN243 B2:59 K8:57 R5056
τελεω, I COMPLETE

Mt	7:28	Now when Jesus **had finished**
	10:23	you **will** not **have gone through**
	11: 1	Now when Jesus **had finished**
	13:53	When Jesus **had finished** these
	17:24	teacher not **pay** the temple tax
	19: 1	When Jesus **had finished** saying
	26: 1	When Jesus **had finished** saying
Lk	2:39	When they **had finished**
	12:50	until it **is completed!**
	18:31	prophets **will be accomplished.**
	22:37	scripture must **be fulfilled**
Jn	19:28	that all **was** now **finished**
	19:30	he said, "It **is finished**
Ac	13:29	When they **had carried out**
Ro	2:27	but **keep** the law will condemn
	13: 6	you also **pay** taxes, for the
2C	12: 9	power **is made perfect** in
Ga	5:16	**do** not **gratify** the desires
2Ti	4: 7	I **have finished** the race,
Ja	2: 8	you really **fulfill** the royal
Re	10: 7	of God **will be fulfilled**
	11: 7	When they **have finished** their
	15: 1	wrath of God **is ended.**
	15: 8	the seven angels **were ended.**
	17:17	words of God **will be fulfilled.**
	20: 3	the thousand years **were ended**
	20: 5	the thousand years **were ended.**
	20: 7	the thousand years **are ended**

5056 GO40 AG811 LN243 B2:59 K8:49
τελος, COMPLETION

Mt	10:22	endures to the **end** will be
	17:25	earth take **toll** or tribute?
	24: 6	but the **end** is not yet.
	24:13	the one who endures to the **end**
	24:14	and then the **end** will come.
	26:58	order to see how this would **end.**
Mk	3:26	cannot stand, but his **end** has
	13: 7	but the **end** is still to come.
	13:13	endures to the **end** will be
Lk	1:33	kingdom there will be no **end.**
	18: 5	not wear me out by **continually**
	21: 9	but the **end** will not follow
	22:37	about me is being **fulfilled.**
Jn	13: 1	he loved them to the **end.**
Ro	6:21	**end** of those things is death.
	6:22	The **end** is eternal life.
	10: 4	Christ is the **end** of the law
	13: 7	**revenue** to whom revenue is due
	13: 7	to whom **revenue** is due, respect
1C	1: 8	also strengthen you to the **end**
	10:11	on whom the **ends** of the ages
	15:24	Then comes the **end,** when he
2C	1:13	understand until the **end**—
	3:13	from gazing at the **end** of the
	11:15	**end** will match their deeds.
Ph	3:19	Their **end** is destruction
1Th	2:16	has overtaken them at **last.**
1Ti	1: 5	But the **aim** of such instruction
He	3:14	confidence firm to the **end.**
	6: 8	its **end** is to be burned over.
	6:11	of hope to the **very end,**
	7: 3	beginning of days nor **end** of
Ja	5:11	seen the **purpose** of the Lord
1P	1: 9	you are receiving the **outcome**
	3: 8	**Finally,** all of you, have unity
	4: 7	The **end** of all things is near
	4:17	what will be the **end** for those
Re	2:26	to do my works to the **end**
	21: 6	the beginning and the **end**
	22:13	last, the beginning and the **end**

5057 GO21 AG812 LN243 B3:755 K8:88
τελωνης, TAX COLLECTOR

Mt	5:46	Do not even the **tax collectors**
	9:10	many **tax collectors** and sinners
	9:11	teacher eat with **tax collectors**

	10: 3	Matthew the **tax collector**
	11:19	friend of **tax collectors** and
	18:17	a Gentile and a **tax collector.**
	21:31	the **tax collectors** and the
	21:32	but the **tax collectors** and the
Mk	2:15	many **tax collectors** and sinners
	2:16	sinners and **tax collectors**
	2:16	does he eat with **tax collectors**
Lk	3:12	Even **tax collectors** came to be
	5:27	saw a **tax collector** named Levi
	5:29	large crowd of **tax collectors**
	5:30	drink with **tax collectors** and
	7:29	including the **tax collectors**
	7:34	a friend of **tax collectors** and
	15: 1	Now all the **tax collectors** and
	18:10	and the other a **tax collector.**
	18:11	even like this **tax collector.**
	18:13	But the **tax collector,** standing

5058 ᴳᴼ3 ᴬᴳ812 ᴸᴺ243 ᴮ3:755 ᴿ5057
τελωνιον, TAX TABLE

Mt	9: 9	Matthew sitting . . . **tax booth**
Mk	2:14	sitting at the **tax booth**
Lk	5:27	sitting at the **tax booth**

5059 ᴳᴼ16 ᴬᴳ812 ᴸᴺ243 ᴮ2:633 ᴷ8:113
τερας, MARVEL

Mt	24:24	produce great signs and **omens**
Mk	13:22	produce signs and **omens,**
Jn	4:48	you see signs and **wonders**
Ac	2:19	show **portents** in the heaven
	2:22	with deeds of power, **wonders**
	2:43	many **wonders** and signs were
	4:30	and signs and **wonders** are
	5:12	Now many signs and **wonders** were
	6: 8	Stephen . . . did great **wonders**
	7:36	having performed **wonders** and
	14: 3	granting signs and **wonders** to
	15:12	**wonders** that God had done
Ro	15:19	power of signs and **wonders**
2C	12:12	patience, signs and **wonders**
2Th	2: 9	all power, signs, lying **wonders**
He	2: 4	testimony by signs and **wonders**

5060 ᴳᴼ1 ᴬᴳ812 ᴸᴺ243
τερτιος, TERTIUS

| Ro | 16:22 | I **Tertius,** the writer of this |

5061 ᴳᴼ2 ᴬᴳ813 ᴸᴺ243
τερτυλλος, TERTULLUS

| Ac | 24: 1 | attorney, a certain **Tertullus** |
| | 24: 2 | **Tertullus** began to accuse him |

5062 ᴳᴼ22 ᴬᴳ813 ᴸᴺ243 ᴮ2:689 ᴷ8:135 ᴿ5064
τεσσαρακοντα, FORTY

Mt	4: 2	He fasted **forty** days and forty
	4: 2	He fasted forty days and **forty**
Mk	1:13	He was in the wilderness **forty**
Lk	4: 2	for **forty** days he was tempted
Jn	2:20	construction for **forty**-six
Ac	1: 3	during **forty** days and speaking
	4:22	performed was more than **forty**
	7:30	Now when **forty** years had
	7:36	in the wilderness for **forty**
	7:42	sacrifices **forty** years in the
	13:21	who reigned for **forty** years.
	23:13	There were more than **forty** who
	23:21	**forty** of their men are lying in
2C	11:24	Jews the **forty** lashes minus one
He	3:10	for **forty** years. Therefore I
	3:17	whom was he angry **forty** years
Re	7: 4	sealed, one hundred **forty**-four
	11: 2	the holy city for **forty**-two
	13: 5	authority for **forty**-two months.
	14: 1	**forty**-four thousand who had his
	14: 3	**forty**-four thousand who have
	21:17	one hundred **forty**-four cubits

5063 ᴳᴼ2 ᴬᴳ813 ᴸᴺ244 ᴷ8:135 ᴿ5062,2094
τεσσαρακονταετης, FORTY YEARS

| Ac | 7:23 | When he was **forty years** old |
| | 13:18 | For about **forty years** he put |

5064 ᴳᴼ40 ᴬᴳ813 ᴸᴺ243 ᴮ2:688 ᴷ8:127
τεσσαρες, FOUR

Mt	24:31	elect from the **four** winds, from
Mk	2: 3	man, carried by **four** of them.
	13:27	gather his elect from the **four**
Lk	2:37	widow to the age of eighty-**four**
Jn	11:17	already been in the tomb **four**
	19:23	divided them into **four** parts
Ac	10:11	ground by its **four** corners.
	11: 5	lowered by its **four** corners
	12: 4	**four** squads of soldiers to
	21: 9	He had **four** unmarried daughters
	21:23	**four** men who are under a vow.
	27:29	**four** anchors from the stern
Re	4: 4	throne are twenty-**four** thrones

4: 4	twenty-**four** elders, dressed in
4: 6	**four** living creatures, full of
4: 8	And the **four** living creatures
4:10	the twenty-**four** elders fall
5: 6	between the throne and the **four**
5: 8	taken the scroll, the **four**
5: 8	twenty-**four** elders fell before
5:14	And the **four** living creatures
6: 1	**four** living creatures call out
6: 6	midst of the **four** living
7: 1	After this I saw **four** angels
7: 1	the **four** corners of the earth
7: 1	holding back the **four** winds of
7: 2	loud voice to the **four** angels
7: 4	forty-**four** thousand, sealed out
7:11	elders and the **four** living
9:13	**four** horns of the golden altar
9:14	Release the **four** angels who are
9:15	the **four** angels were released
11:16	twenty-**four** elders who sit on
14: 1	forty-**four** thousand who had his
14: 3	before the **four** living
14: 3	forty-**four** thousand who have
15: 7	Then one of the **four** living
19: 4	And the twenty-**four** elders
19: 4	**four** living creatures fell down
20: 8	nations at the **four** corners of
21:17	forty-**four** cubits by human

5065　ᴳᴼ2 ᴬᴳ813 ᴸᴺ243 ᴿ5064,2532,1182
τεσσαρεσκαιδεκατος, FOUR AND TEN
Ac 27:27　When the **fourteenth** night had
　　27:33　Today is the **fourteenth** day

5066　ᴳᴼ1 ᴬᴳ813 ᴸᴺ244 ᴷ8:127 ᴿ5064
τεταρταιος, FOURTH
Jn 11:39　he has been dead **four days.**

5067　ᴳᴼ10 ᴬᴳ813 ᴸᴺ244 ᴷ8:127 ᴿ5064
τεταρτος, FOURTH
Mt 14:25　**early** in the **morning** he came
Mk 6:48　**early** in the **morning,** walking
Ac 10:30　Cornelius replied, "**Four** days
Re 4: 7　**fourth** living creature like
　6: 7　When he opened the **fourth** seal
　6: 7　I heard the voice of the **fourth**
　6: 8　authority over a **fourth** of the
　8:12　**fourth** angel blew his trumpet
　16: 8　**fourth** angel poured his bowl
　21:19　agate, the **fourth** emerald,

5068　ᴳᴼ1 ᴬᴳ813 ᴸᴺ244 ᴿ5064,1137
τετραγωνος, FOUR-CORNERED
Re 21:16　The city lies **foursquare,** its

5069　ᴳᴼ1 ᴬᴳ813 ᴸᴺ244 ᴮ2:689
τετραδιον, GROUP OF FOUR
Ac 12: 4　**four squads** of soldiers to

5070　ᴳᴼ5 ᴬᴳ813 ᴸᴺ244 ᴮ2:699 ᴿ5064,5507
τετρακισχιλιοι, FOUR THOUSAND
Mt 15:38　had eaten were **four thousand**
　16:10　loaves for the **four thousand**
Mk 8: 9　were about **four thousand** people
　8:20　the seven for the **four thousand**
Ac 21:38　led the **four thousand** assassins

5071　ᴳᴼ4 ᴬᴳ813 ᴸᴺ244 ᴮ2:689 ᴿ5064,1540
τετρακοσιοι, FOUR HUNDRED
Ac 5:36　about **four hundred,** joined him
　7: 6　them during **four hundred** years.
　13:20　about **four hundred** fifty years
Ga 3:17　**four hundred** thirty years later

5072　ᴳᴼ1 ᴬᴳ813 ᴸᴺ244 ᴿ5064,3376
τετραμηνος, FOUR MONTHS
Jn 4:35　Do you not say, '**Four months**

5073　ᴳᴼ1 ᴬᴳ813 ᴸᴺ244
τετραπλους, FOUR TIMES
Lk 19: 8　pay back **four times as much**

5074　ᴳᴼ3 ᴬᴳ814 ᴸᴺ244 ᴿ5064,4228
τετραπους, FOUR FOOTED
Ac 10:12　were all kinds of **four-footed**
　11: 6　I saw **four-footed** animals
Ro 1:23　**four-footed** animals or reptiles

5075　ᴳᴼ3 ᴬᴳ814 ᴸᴺ244 ᴿ5064,758
τετραρχεω, I RULE ONE FOURTH
Lk 3: 1　Herod **was ruler** of Galilee
　3: 1　Philip **ruler** of the region of
　3: 1　Lysanias **ruler** of Abilene,

5076　ᴳᴼ4 ᴬᴳ814 ᴸᴺ244 ᴿ5075
τετραρχης, RULER OF FOURTH
Mt 14: 1　At that time Herod the **ruler**
Lk 3:19　But Herod the **ruler,** who had
　9: 7　Now Herod the **ruler** heard about
Ac 13: 1　of the court of Herod the **ruler**

5077   GO1 AG814 LN244
τεφροω, I COVER IN ASHES
2P   2: 6   **turning** . . . Gomorrah **to ashes**

5078   GO3 AG814 LN244 B1:279
τεχνη, CRAFT
Ac   17:29   image formed by the **art** and
     18: 3   by **trade** they were tentmakers.
Re   18:22   artisan of any **trade** will

5079   GO4 AG814 LN244 B1:279
τεχνιτης, CRAFTSMAN
Ac   19:24   business to the **artisans.**
     19:38   Demetrius and the **artisans**
He   11:10   whose **architect** and builder
Re   18:22   an **artisan** of any trade will

5080   GO1 AG814 LN244 B3:559
τηκω, I MELT
2P   3:12   elements **will melt** with fire?

5081   GO1 AG814 LN244
τηλαυγως, CLEARLY
Mk   8:25   he saw everything **clearly.**

5082   GO4 AG814 LN244
τηλικουτος, SO GREAT
2C   1:10   rescued us from **so deadly**
He   2: 3   we neglect **so great** a salvation
Ja   3: 4   ships: though they are **so large**
Re   16:18   **so violent** was that earthquake.

5083   GO70 AG814 LN244 B2:132 K8:140
τηρεω, I KEEP, I GUARD
Mt   19:17   life, **keep** the commandments
     23: 3   teach you and **follow** it; but
     27:36   there and **kept watch** over him.
     27:54   **were keeping watch** over Jesus
     28: 4   For fear of him the **guards**
     28:20   and teaching them to **obey**
Jn   2:10   **have kept** the good wine until
     8:51   whoever **keeps** my word will
     8:52   **keeps** my word will never taste
     8:55   him and I **keep** his word.
     9:16   he **does** not **observe** the sabbath
     12: 7   she **might keep** it for the day
     14:15   If you love me, you **will keep**
     14:21   **keep** them are those who love
     14:23   love me **will keep** my word, and
     14:24   not love me **does** not **keep** my

     15:10   If you **keep** my commandments
     15:10   just as I **have kept** my Father's
     15:20   if they **kept** my word, they
     15:20   they **will keep** yours also.   .
     17: 6   they **have kept** your word.
     17:11   Holy Father, **protect** them
     17:12   I **protected** them in your name
     17:15   **protect** them from the evil one
Ac   12: 5   While Peter **was kept** in prison
     12: 6   **were keeping** watch over the
     15: 5   ordered **to keep** the law of
     16:23   jailer **to keep** them securely.
     24:23   **to keep** him **in custody,** but to
     25: 4   Paul **was being kept** at Caesarea
     25:21   appealed **to be kept in custody**
     25:21   I ordered him **to be held** until
1C   7:37   **to keep** her as his fiancée
2C   11: 9   I **refrained** and will continue
     11: 9   **will continue to refrain** from
Ep   4: 3   making every effort **to maintain**
1Th   5:23   soul and body **be kept** sound
1Ti   5:22   **keep** yourself pure.
     6:14   **to keep** the commandment without
2Ti   4: 7   race, I **have kept** the faith.
Ja   1:27   **to keep** oneself unstained by
     2:10   For whoever **keeps** the whole law
1P   1: 4   unfading, **kept** in heaven for
2P   2: 4   darkness **to be kept** until the
     2: 9   **to keep** the unrighteous under
     2:17   darkness **has been reserved.**
     3: 7   **being kept** until the day of
1J   2: 3   if we **obey** his commandments.
     2: 4   does not **obey** his commandments
     2: 5   but whoever **obeys** his word
     3:22   we **obey** his commandments and do
     3:24   **obey** his commandments abide in
     5: 3   we **obey** his commandments
     5:18   was born of God **protects** them
Ju   1: 1   **kept safe** for Jesus Christ:
     1: 6   angels who **did** not **keep** their
     1: 6   he **has kept** in eternal chains
     1:13   darkness **has been reserved**
     1:21   **keep** yourselves in the love of
Re   1: 3   who **keep** what is written in it
     2:26   continues **to do** my works to the
     3: 3   heard; **obey** it, and repent
     3: 8   yet you **have kept** my word and
     3:10   Because you **have kept** my word
     3:10   I **will keep** you from the hour

12:17	**keep** the commandments of God
14:12	**keep** the commandments of God
16:15	who stays awake and is **clothed**
22: 7	**keeps** the words of the prophecy
22: 9	**keep** the words of this book

5084 GO3 AG815 LN244 B2:132 K8:146 R5083
τηρησις, A KEEPING PLACE

Ac	4: 3	put them in **custody** until the
	5:18	put them in the public **prison.**
1C	7:19	but **obeying** the commandments of

5085 GO3 AG815 LN244
τιβεριας, TIBERIAS

Jn	6: 1	also called the Sea of **Tiberias**
	6:23	Then some boats from **Tiberias**
	21: 1	**Tiberias;** and he showed

5086 GO1 AG815 LN245
τιβεριος, TIBERIUS

| Lk | 3: 1 | reign of Emperor **Tiberius,** when |

5087 GO100 AG815 LN245 B1:477 K8:152
τιθημι, I PUT, I PLACE, I SET

Mt	5:15	after lighting a lamp **puts** it
	12:18	I **will put** my Spirit upon him
	22:44	at my right hand, until I **put**
	24:51	**put** him with the hypocrites
	27:60	and **laid** it in his own new tomb
Mk	4:21	Is a lamp brought in **to be put**
	4:21	bed, **and** not **on** the lampstand?
	4:30	what parable will we **use** for it
	6:29	body, and **laid** it in a tomb.
	6:56	they **laid** the sick in the
	10:16	in his arms, **laid** his hands on
	12:36	until I **put** your enemies under
	15:19	and **knelt** down in homage to him
	15:46	linen cloth, and **laid** it in a
	15:47	saw where the body **was laid.**
	16: 6	is the place they **laid** him.
Lk	1:66	All who heard them **pondered**
	5:18	and **lay** him before Jesus;
	6:48	**laid** the foundation on rock
	8:16	or **puts** it under a bed
	8:16	but **puts** it on a lampstand, so
	9:44	**Let** these words **sink** into
	11:33	lamp **puts** it in a cellar, but
	12:46	**put** him with the unfaithful.
	14:29	when he has **laid** a foundation
	19:21	take what you **did** not **deposit**

19:22	I **did** not **deposit** and reaping
21:14	So **make up** your minds not to
22:41	throw, **knelt** down, and prayed,
23:53	**laid** it in a rock-hewn tomb
23:55	how his body **was laid.**
Jn	2:10	Everyone **serves** the good wine
	10:11	shepherd **lays down** his life
	10:15	**lay down** my life for the sheep
	10:17	because I **lay down** my life in
	10:18	but I **lay** it **down** of my own
	10:18	I have power to **lay** it **down**
	11:34	Where **have** you **laid** him
	13: 4	**took off** his outer robe
	13:37	I will **lay down** my life for you
	13:38	**Will** you **lay down** your life for
	15:13	**lay down** one's life for one's
	15:16	I **appointed** you to go and bear
	19:19	**put** on the cross. It read,
	19:41	no one had ever been **laid.**
	19:42	they **laid** Jesus there.
	20: 2	not know where they **have laid**
	20:13	not know where they **have laid**
	20:15	tell me where you **have laid** him
Ac	1: 7	Father **has set** by his own
	2:35	until I **make** your enemies your
	3: 2	People **would lay** him daily
		at the
	4: 3	So they arrested them and **put**
	4:35	They **laid** it at the apostles
	4:37	**laid** it at the apostles' feet.
	5: 2	**laid** it at the apostles' feet.
	5: 4	you **have contrived** this deed
	5:15	**laid** them on cots and mats
	5:18	**put** them in the public prison.
	5:25	whom you **put** in prison are
	7:16	**laid** in the tomb that Abraham
	7:60	Then he **knelt** down and cried
	9:37	they **laid** her in a room
	9:40	then he **knelt** down and prayed.
	12: 4	he **put** him in prison and handed
	13:29	and **laid** him in a tomb.
	13:47	I **have set** you to be a light
	19:21	Paul **resolved** in the Spirit
	20:28	Spirit **has made** you overseers
	20:36	he **knelt** down with them all
	21: 5	we **knelt** down on the beach and
	27:12	majority **was in** favor of
Ro	4:17	I **have made** you the father of
	9:33	I **am laying** in Zion a stone
	14:13	never **to put** a stumbling block

1C	3:10	I **laid** a foundation, and
	3:11	can **lay** any foundation other
	9:18	I **may make** the gospel free
	12:18	God **arranged** the members in the
	12:28	God **has appointed** in the church
	15:25	he **has put** all his enemies
	16: 2	**put** aside and save whatever
2C	3:13	not like Moses, who **put** a veil
	5:19	**entrusting** the message of
1Th	5: 9	For God **has destined** us not for
1Ti	1:12	and **appointed** me to his service,
	2: 7	I **was appointed** a herald and an
2Ti	1:11	For this gospel I **was appointed**
He	1: 2	**appointed** heir of all things
	1:13	until I **make** your enemies a
	10:13	enemies **would be made** a
1P	2: 6	See, I **am laying** in Zion a
	2: 8	as they **were destined** to do.
2P	2: 6	**made** them an example of what
1J	3:16	he **laid down** his life for us
	3:16	we ought **to lay down** our lives
Re	1:17	he **placed** his right hand on me
	10: 2	**Setting** his right foot on the
	11: 9	let them **be placed** in a tomb;

5088   GO18 AG816 LN245 B1:186
τικτω, I GIVE BIRTH

Mt	1:21	She **will bear** a son, and you
	1:23	conceive and **bear** a son
	1:25	until she **had borne** a son
	2: 2	child who **has been born** king
Lk	1:31	**bear** a son, and you will name
	1:57	Elizabeth to **give birth**
	2: 6	time came for her **to deliver**
	2: 7	she **gave birth** to her firstborn
	2:11	to you **is born** this day in the
Jn	16:21	When a woman is **in labor,** she
Ga	4:27	who **bear** no **children,** burst
He	6: 7	that **produces** a crop useful
Ja	1:15	it **gives birth** to sin, and that
Re	12: 2	in the agony of **giving birth.**
	12: 4	who was about **to bear a child**
	12: 4	child as soon as it **was born.**
	12: 5	And she **gave birth** to a son
	12:13	woman who **had given birth**

5089   GO3 AG817 LN245
τιλλω, I PICK

Mt	12: 1	they began **to pluck** heads of

Mk	2:23	disciples began **to pluck** heads
Lk	6: 1	disciples **plucked** some heads

5090   GO1 AG817 LN245
τιμαιος, TIMAEUS

Mk	10:46	Bartimaeus son of **Timaeus**

5091   GO21 AG817 LN245 B2:48 K8:169 R5093
τιμαω, I VALUE

Mt	15: 4	God said, '**Honor** your father
	15: 6	need not **honor** the father.
	15: 8	This people **honors** me with
	19:19	**Honor** your father and mother
	27: 9	on whom a **price had been set**
	27: 9	Israel **had set a price,**
Mk	7: 6	This people **honors** me with
	7:10	For Moses said, '**Honor** your
	10:19	**Honor** your father and mother
Lk	18:20	**Honor** your father and mother
Jn	5:23	so that all **may honor** the Son
	5:23	they **honor** the Father. Anyone
	5:23	who **does** not **honor** the Son
	5:23	honor the Son **does** not **honor**
	8:49	I **honor** my Father, and you
	12:26	the Father **will honor.**
Ac	28:10	They **bestowed** many honors on us
Ep	6: 2	**Honor** your father and mother
1Ti	5: 3	**Honor** widows who are really
1P	2:17	**Honor** everyone. Love the family
	2:17	Fear God. **Honor** the emperor.

5092   GO41 AG817 LN245 B2:48 K8:169
τιμη, VALUE

Mt	27: 6	since they are blood **money**
	27: 9	the **price** of the one on whom
Jn	4:44	prophet has no **honor** in the
Ac	4:34	brought the **proceeds** of what
	5: 2	kept back some of the **proceeds**
	5: 3	keep back part of the **proceeds**
	7:16	Abraham had bought for a **sum**
	19:19	when the **value** of these books
	28:10	They bestowed many **honors** on us
Ro	2: 7	glory and **honor** and immortality
	2:10	but glory and **honor** and peace
	9:21	one object for **special use**
	12:10	one another in showing **honor.**
	13: 7	**honor** to whom honor is due.
	13: 7	honor to whom **honor** is due.
1C	6:20	you were bought with a **price**
	7:23	You were bought with a **price**

	12:23	we clothe with greater **honor**
	12:24	giving the greater **honor** to
Co	2:23	no **value** in checking self-imposed
1Th	4: 4	own body in holiness and **honor,**
1Ti	1:17	be **honor** and glory forever
	5:17	worthy of double **honor**
	6: 1	worthy of all **honor,** so that
	6:16	to him be **honor** and eternal
2Ti	2:20	some for **special use,** some for
	2:21	will become **special** utensils
He	2: 7	them with glory and **honor,**
	2: 9	crowned with glory and **honor**
	3: 3	house has more **honor** than the
	5: 4	not presume to take this **honor**
1P	1: 7	praise and glory and **honor** when
	2: 7	who believe, he is **precious**
	3: 7	paying **honor** to the woman as
2P	1:17	For he received **honor** and glory
Re	4: 9	give glory and **honor** and thanks
	4:11	receive glory and **honor** and
	5:12	might and **honor** and glory and
	5:13	**honor** and glory and might
	7:12	**honor** and power and might
	21:26	and the **honor** of the nations.

5093　GO13　AG818　LN245　B3:391　R5092
τιμιος, VALUABLE

Ac	5:34	**respected** by all the people
	20:24	not count my life of any **value**
1C	3:12	gold, silver, **precious** stones
He	13: 4	Let marriage be held in **honor**
Ja	5: 7	farmer waits for the **precious**
1P	1:19	but with the **precious** blood
2P	1: 4	his **precious** and very great
Re	17: 4	with gold and **jewels** and pearls
	18:12	cargo of gold, silver, **jewels**
	18:12	articles of **costly** wood, bronze
	18:16	with **jewels,** and with pearls!
	21:11	like a **very rare** jewel, like
	21:19	adorned with every **jewel;** the

5094　GO1　AG818　LN245
τιμιοτης, MOST VALUABLE

| Re | 18:19 | grew rich by her **wealth!** For in |

5095　GO24　AG818　LN245
τιμοθεος, TIMOTHY

| Ac | 16: 1 | disciple named **Timothy,** the son |
| | 17:14 | Silas and **Timothy** remained |

	17:15	Silas and **Timothy** join him as
	18: 5	When Silas and **Timothy** arrived
	19:22	**Timothy** and Erastus, to
	20: 4	by **Timothy,** as well as by
Ro	16:21	**Timothy,** my co-worker, greets
1C	4:17	I sent you **Timothy,** who is my
	16:10	If **Timothy** comes, see that he
2C	1: 1	God, and **Timothy** our brother
	1:19	Silvanus and **Timothy** and I
Ph	1: 1	Paul and **Timothy,** servants of
	2:19	the Lord Jesus to send **Timothy**
Co	1: 1	will of God, and **Timothy** our
1Th	1: 1	Paul, Silvanus, and **Timothy**
	3: 2	we sent **Timothy,** our brother
	3: 6	But **Timothy** has just now come
2Th	1: 1	Paul, Silvanus, and **Timothy**
1Ti	1: 2	To **Timothy,** my loyal child
	1:18	these instructions, **Timothy**
	6:20	**Timothy,** guard what has been
2Ti	1: 2	To **Timothy,** my beloved child
Pm	1: 1	**Timothy** our . . . Philemon our
He	13:23	**Timothy** has been set free

5096　GO1　AG818　LN245
τιμων, TIMON

| Ac | 6: 5 | Nicanor, **Timon,** Parmenas, and |

5097　GO2　AG818　LN245
τιμωρεω, I PUNISH

| Ac | 22: 5 | to Jerusalem for **punishment.** |
| | 26:11 | By **punishing** them often in all |

5098　GO1　AG818　LN245　R5097
τιμωρια, PUNISHMENT

| He | 10:29 | How much worse **punishment** do |

5099　GO1　AG818　LN245
τινω, I PAY

| 2Th | 1: 9 | **will suffer** the punishment of |

5100　GO526　AG819　LN245
τις, SOME, ANY, A CERTAIN [MULTIPLE OCCURRENCES]

5101　GO555　AG818　LN245
τις, WHO, WHAT [MULTIPLE OCCURRENCES]

5101a　GO1　AG820　LN246
τιτιος, TITIUS

| Ac | 18: 7 | **Titius** Justus, a worshiper of |

5102   GO2 AG820 LN246 B1:392
τιτλος, NOTICE
Jn 19:19   Pilate also had an **inscription**
   19:20   the Jews read this **inscription**

5103   GO13 AG820 LN246
τιτος, TITUS
2C 2:13   find my brother **Titus** there
    7: 6   us by the arrival of **Titus,**
    7:13   still more at the joy of **Titus**
    7:14   boasting to **Titus** has proved
    8: 6   so that we might urge **Titus**
    8:16   who put in the heart of **Titus**
    8:23   As for **Titus,** he is my partner
   12:18   I urged **Titus** to go, and sent
   12:18   **Titus** did not take advantage of
Ga 2: 1   taking **Titus** along with me.
    2: 3   But even **Titus,** who was with
2Ti 4:10   gone to Galatia, **Titus** to
Ti 1: 4   To **Titus,** my loyal child in

5105   GO2 AG821 LN246
τοιγαρουν, CONSEQUENTLY
1Th 4: 8   **Therefore** whoever rejects this
He 12: 1   **Therefore,** since we are

5106   GO3 AG821 LN246
τοινυν, ACCORDINGLY
Lk 20:25   **Then** give to the emperor the
1C 9:26   **So** I do not run aimlessly
He 13:13   Let us **then** go to him outside

5107   GO1 AG821 LN246
τοιοσδε, SUCH
2P 1:17   when **that** voice was conveyed to

5108   GO57 AG821 LN246
τοιουτος, SUCH
Mt 9: 8   who had given **such** authority
   18: 5   Whoever welcomes one **such** child
   19:14   for it is to **such as these** that
Mk 4:33   many **such** parables he spoke the
    6: 2   **What** deeds of power are being
    7:13   you do many things **like this**
    9:37   welcomes one **such** child in my
   10:14   **such as these** that the kingdom
   13:19   suffering, **such as has** not been
Lk 9: 9   about whom I hear **such things**
   18:16   **such as these** that the kingdom
Jn 4:23   Father seeks **such as these** to

8: 5   to stone **such women.** Now what
9:16   is a sinner perform **such** signs
Ac 16:24   Following **these** instructions
   19:25   workers of the **same** trade
   22:22   Away with **such a fellow** from
   26:29   become **such** as I am
Ro 1:32   practice **such things** deserve
    2: 2   on those who do **such things**
    2: 3   judge those who do **such things**
   16:18   For **such people** do not serve
1C 5: 1   **of a kind** that is not found
    5: 5   you are to hand **this man** over
    5:11   Do not even eat with **such a one**
    7:15   **such a case** the brother or
    7:28   Yet **those who** marry will
   11:16   we have no **such** custom, nor
   15:48   are **those who** are of the dust
   15:48   are **those who** are of heaven.
   16:16   at the service of **such people**
   16:18   recognition to **such persons.**
2C 2: 6   is enough for **such a person;**
    2: 7   **he** may not be overwhelmed by
    3: 4   **Such** is the confidence that
    3:12   then, we have **such** a hope
   10:11   Let **such people** understand
   10:11   we will also **do** when present
   11:13   For **such boasters** are false
   12: 2   was caught **up** to the third
   12: 3   And I know that **such** a person
   12: 5   On behalf of **such a one** I will
Ga 5:21   things **like these.** I am warning
    5:23   is no law against **such things.**
    6: 1   restore **such a one** in a spirit
Ep 5:27   wrinkle or anything **of the kind**
Ph 2:29   joy, and honor **such people,**
2Th 3:12   Now **such persons** we command
Ti 3:11   that **such a person** is perverted
Pm 1: 9   do **this** as an old man, and now
He 7:26   should have **such** a high priest
    8: 1   we have **such** a high priest, one
   11:14   people who speak **in this way**
   12: 3   Consider him who endured **such**
   13:16   **such** sacrifices are pleasing to
Ja 4:16   all **such** boasting is evil.
3J 1: 8   we ought to support **such people**

5109   GO1 AG821 LN246 B3:948
τοιχος, WALL
Ac 23: 3   you whitewashed **wall!** Are you

5110　ᴳᴼ2 ᴬᴳ821 ᴸᴺ246 ᴮ3:1156
τοκος, INTEREST
Mt　25:27　what was my own with **interest.**
Lk　19:23　collected it with **interest.**

5111　ᴳᴼ16 ᴬᴳ821 ᴸᴺ246 ᴮ1:364 ᴷ8:181
τολμαω, I DARE
Mt　22:46　**did** anyone **dare** to ask him any
Mk　12:34　**dared** to ask him any question.
　　15:43　went **boldly** to Pilate and asked
Lk　20:40　For they no longer **dared** to ask
Jn　21:12　disciples **dared** to ask him
Ac　5:13　None of the rest **dared** to join
　　7:32　tremble and **did** not **dare** to
Ro　5: 7　**might** actually **dare** to die.
　　15:18　For I **will** not **venture** to speak
1C　6: 1　**do** you **dare** to take it to court
2C　10: 2　not show boldness by **daring**
　　10:12　We **do** not **dare** to classify or
　　11:21　whatever anyone **dares to boast**
　　11:21　I also **dare to boast** of that.
Ph　1:14　**dare** to speak the word with
Ju　1: 9　he **did** not **dare** to bring a

5112　ᴳᴼ1 ᴬᴳ822 ᴸᴺ246 ᴷ8:181 ᴿ5111
τολμηρως, MORE DARING
Ro　15:15　written to you **rather boldly** by

5113　ᴳᴼ1 ᴬᴳ822 ᴸᴺ246 ᴮ1:364 ᴷ8:181 ᴿ5111
τολμητης, BOLD
2P　2:10　**Bold** and willful, they are not

5114　ᴳᴼ1 ᴬᴳ822 ᴸᴺ246
τομος, SHARP
He　4:12　**sharper** than any two-edged

5115　ᴳᴼ1 ᴬᴳ822 ᴸᴺ246 ᴮ3:1002
τοξον, BOW
Re　6: 2　Its rider had a **bow;** a crown

5116　ᴳᴼ1 ᴬᴳ822 ᴸᴺ246 ᴮ3:396
τοπαζιον, TOPAZ
Re　21:20　the ninth **topaz,** the tenth

5117　ᴳᴼ94 ᴬᴳ822 ᴸᴺ246 ᴷ8:187
τοπος, PLACE
Mt　12:43　through waterless **regions**
　　14:13　to a deserted **place** by himself
　　14:15　This is a deserted **place,** and
　　14:35　After the people of that **place**

　　24: 7　earthquakes in various **places:**
　　24:15　standing in the holy **place**
　　26:52　sword back into its **place**
　　27:33　to a **place** called Golgotha
　　27:33　(which means **Place** of a Skull),
　　28: 6　see the **place** where he lay.
Mk　1:35　went out to a deserted **place**
　　1:45　stayed out in the **country**
　　6:11　If any **place** will not welcome
　　6:31　Come away to a deserted **place**
　　6:32　a deserted **place** by themselves.
　　6:35　This is a deserted **place,** and
　　13: 8　earthquakes in various **places**
　　15:22　to the **place** called Golgotha
　　15:22　means the **place** of a skull).
　　16: 6　is the **place** they laid him.
Lk　2: 7　no **place** for them in the inn.
　　4:17　found the **place** where it was
　　4:37　began to reach every **place** in
　　4:42　went into a deserted **place**
　　6:17　stood on a level **place,** with a
　　9:12　we are here in a deserted **place**
　　10: 1　**place** where he himself intended
　　10:32　came to the **place** and saw him,
　　11: 1　was praying in a certain **place**
　　11:24　through waterless **regions**
　　14: 9　Give this person your **place,**
　　14: 9　start to take the lowest **place.**
　　14:10　sit down at the lowest **place**
　　14:22　and there is still **room.**
　　16:28　come into this **place** of torment
　　19: 5　When Jesus came to the **place**
　　21:11　in various **places** famines and
　　22:40　When he reached the **place,**
　　23:33　**place** that is called The Skull
Jn　4:20　**place** where people must worship
　　5:13　in the crowd that was **there.**
　　6:10　deal of grass in the **place**
　　6:23　**place** where they had eaten the
　　10:40　**place** where John had been
　　11: 6　two days longer in the **place**
　　11:30　**place** where Martha had met him.
　　11:48　our holy **place** and our nation.
　　14: 2　I go to prepare a **place** for you
　　14: 3　And if I go and prepare a **place**
　　18: 2　knew the **place,** because Jesus
　　19:13　**place** called The Stone Pavement
　　19:17　The **Place** of the Skull, which
　　19:20　**place** where Jesus was crucified

	19:41	**place** where he was crucified
	20: 7	rolled up in a **place** by itself.
Ac	1:25	take the **place** in this ministry
	1:25	to go to his own **place.**
	4:31	**place** in which they were
	6:13	against this holy **place** and the
	6:14	will destroy this **place**
	7: 7	worship me in this **place.**
	7:33	**place** where you are standing
	7:49	what is the **place** of my rest?
	12:17	left and went to another **place.**
	16: 3	who were in those **places,** for
	21:28	our law, and this **place;** more
	21:28	has defiled this holy **place.**
	25:16	**opportunity** to make a defense
	27: 2	sail to the **ports** along the
	27: 8	**place** called Fair Havens, near
	27:29	we might run on the **rocks,** they
	27:41	But striking a **reef,** they ran
	28: 7	**place** were lands belonging to
Ro	9:26	And in the very **place** where
	12:19	leave **room** for the wrath of God
	15:23	But now, with no further **place**
1C	1: 2	in every **place** call on the name
	14:16	in the **position** of an outsider
2C	2:14	spreads in every **place** the
Ep	4:27	do not make **room** for the devil.
1Th	1: 8	every **place** your faith in God
1Ti	2: 8	in every **place** the men should
He	8: 7	need to look for a second **one.**
	11: 8	to set out for a **place** that he
	12:17	he found no **chance** to repent
2P	1:19	lamp shining in a dark **place**
Re	2: 5	your lampstand from its **place**
	6:14	was removed from its **place.**
	12: 6	where she has a **place** prepared
	12: 8	any **place** for them in heaven.
	12:14	**place** where she is nourished
	16:16	assembled them at the **place**
	18:17	all shipmasters and **seafarers**
	20:11	no **place** was found for them.

5118　　GO20　AG523　LN246
τοσουτος, SUCH

Mt	8:10	Israel have I found **such** faith.
	15:33	get **enough** bread in the desert
	15:33	desert to feed **so great** a crowd
Lk	7: 9	Israel have I found **such** faith
	15:29	**all these** years I have been

Jn	6: 9	what are they among **so many**
	12:37	performed **so many** signs in
	14: 9	Have I been with you **all this**
	21:11	**so many,** the net was not torn.
Ac	5: 8	sold the land for **such and such**
	5: 8	Yes, **that was the price.**
1C	14:10	doubtless **many** different kinds
Ga	3: 4	Did you experience **so much** for
He	1: 4	having become **as much** superior
	4: 7	saying through David **much** later
	7:22	**accordingly** Jesus has also
	10:25	**all the** more as you see the Day
	12: 1	surrounded by **so great** a cloud
Re	18: 7	a like **measure** of torment and
	18:17	For in one hour **all** this wealth

5119　　GO160　AG823　LN246　B1:282
τοτε, THEN

Mt	2: 7	**Then** Herod secretly called for
	2:16	**When** Herod saw that he had been
	2:17	**Then** was fulfilled what had
	3: 5	**Then** the people of Jerusalem
	3:13	**Then** Jesus came from Galilee
	3:15	**Then** he consented.
	4: 1	**Then** Jesus was led up by the
	4: 5	**Then** the devil took him to the
	4:10	**[Then]** Jesus said to him, "Away with
	4:11	**Then** the devil left him, and
	4:17	From **that time** Jesus began to
	5:24	**then** come and offer your gift.
	7: 5	**then** you will see clearly to
	7:23	**Then** I will declare to them, 'I
	8:26	**Then** he got up and rebuked the
	9: 6	he **then** said to the paralytic
	9:14	**Then** the disciples of John came
	9:15	and **then** they will fast.
	9:29	**Then** he touched their eyes
	9:37	**Then** he said to his disciples
	11:20	**Then** he began to reproach the
	12:13	**Then** he said to the man
	12:22	**Then** they brought to him a
	12:29	**Then** indeed the house can be
	12:38	**Then** some of the scribes and
	12:44	**Then** it says, 'I will return to
	12:45	**Then** it goes and brings along
	13:26	**then** the weeds appeared as well
	13:36	**Then** he left the crowds
	13:43	**Then** the righteous will shine
	15: 1	**Then** Pharisees and scribes

15:12	**Then** the disciples approached		26:74	**Then** he began to curse, and he
15:28	**Then** Jesus answered her, "Woman		27: 3	**When** Judas, his betrayer, saw
16:12	**Then** they understood that he		27: 9	**Then** was fulfilled what had
16:20	**Then** he sternly ordered the		27:13	**Then** Pilate said to him, "Do
16:21	From **that time** on, Jesus began		27:16	**At that time** they had a
16:24	**Then** Jesus told his disciples		27:26	**So** he released Barabbas for
16:27	**then** he will repay everyone for		27:27	**Then** the soldiers of the
17:13	**Then** the disciples understood		27:38	**Then** two bandits were crucified
17:19	**Then** the disciples came to		27:58	**then** Pilate ordered it to be
18:21	**Then** Peter came and said to him		28:10	**Then** Jesus said to them, "Do
18:32	**Then** his lord summoned him and	Mk	2:20	**then** they will fast on that day
19:13	**Then** little children were being		3:27	**then** indeed the house can be
19:27	**Then** Peter said in reply, "Look,		13:14	**then** those in Judea must flee
20:20	**Then** the mother of the sons of		13:21	says to you **at that time,** 'Look
21: 1	**[Then]** Jesus sent two		13:26	**Then** they will see 'the Son of
22: 8	**Then** he said to his slaves		13:27	**Then** he will send out the
22:13	**Then** the king said to the	Lk	5:35	**then** they will fast in those
22:15	**Then** the Pharisees went and		6:42	**then** you will see clearly to
22:21	emperor's." **Then** he said to		11:24	**it** says, 'I will return to my
23: 1	**Then** Jesus said to the crowds		11:26	**Then** it goes and brings seven
24: 9	**Then** they will hand you over		13:26	**Then** you will begin to say
24:10	**Then** many will fall away, and		14: 9	**then** in disgrace you would
24:14	and **then** the end will come.		14:10	**then** you will be honored in
24:16	**then** those in Judea must		14:21	**Then** the owner of the house
24:21	For **at that time** there will be		16:16	**then** the good news of the
24:23	**Then** if anyone says to you		21:10	**Then** he said to them, "Nation
24:30	**Then** the sign of the Son of Man		21:20	**then** know that its desolation
24:30	**then** all the tribes of the		21:21	**Then** those in Judea must flee
24:40	**Then** two will be in the field		21:27	**Then** they will see 'the Son of
25: 1	**Then** the kingdom of heaven will		23:30	**Then** they will begin to say to
25: 7	**Then** all those bridesmaids got		24:45	**Then** he opened their minds to
25:31	**then** he will sit on the throne	Jn	7:10	**then** he also went, not publicly
25:34	**Then** the king will say to those		8:28	**then** you will realize that I am
25:37	**Then** the righteous will answer		10:22	**At that time** the festival of
25:41	**Then** he will say to those at		11: 6	**after** having heard that Lazarus
25:44	**Then** they also will answer		11:14	**Then** Jesus told them plainly
25:45	**Then** he will answer them		12:16	**then** they remembered that these
26: 3	**Then** the chief priests and the		13:27	**After** he received the piece of
26:14	**Then** one of the twelve, who was		19: 1	**Then** Pilate took Jesus and had
26:16	from **that moment** he began to		19:16	**Then** he handed him over to them
26:31	**Then** Jesus said to them, "You		20: 8	**Then** the other disciple, who
26:36	**Then** Jesus went with them to a	Ac	1:12	**Then** they returned to Jerusalem
26:38	**Then** he said to them, "I am		4: 8	**Then** Peter, filled with the
26:45	**Then** he came to the disciples		5:26	**Then** the captain went with the
26:50	**Then** they came and laid hands		6:11	**Then** they secretly instigated
26:52	**Then** Jesus said to him, "Put		7: 4	**Then** he left the country of
26:56	**Then** all the disciples deserted		8:17	**Then** Peter and John laid their
26:65	**Then** the high priest tore his		10:46	extolling God. **Then** Peter said,
26:67	**Then** they spat in his face and			

	10:48	**Then** they invited him to
	13: 3	**Then** after fasting and praying
	13:12	**When** the proconsul saw what
	15:22	**Then** the apostles and the
	17:14	**Then** the believers immediately
	21:13	**Then** Paul answered, "What are
	21:26	**Then** Paul took the men, and the
	21:33	**Then** the tribune came, arrested
	23: 3	**At this** Paul said to him, "God
	25:12	**Then** Festus, after he had
	26: 1	**Then** Paul stretched out his
	27:21	**then** stood up among them and
	27:32	**Then** the soldiers cut away the
	28: 1	we **then** learned that the island
Ro	6:21	So what advantage did you **then**
1C	4: 5	**Then** each one will receive
	13:12	**then** we will see face to face.
	13:12	**then** I will know fully, even as
	15:28	**then** the Son himself will also
	15:54	**then** the saying that is written
	16: 2	**so** that collections need not be
2C	12:10	I am weak, **then** I am strong.
Ga	4: 8	**when** you did not know God, you
	4:29	**at that time** the child who was
	6: 4	must test their own work; **then**
Co	3: 4	**then** you also will be revealed
1Th	5: 3	**then** sudden destruction will
2Th	2: 8	And **then** the lawless one will
He	10: 7	**Then** I said, 'See, God, I have
	10: 9	**then** he added, "See, I have
	12:26	**At that time** his voice shook
2P	3: 6	world **of that time** was deluged

5121   GO3   AG824   LN246
τουναντιον, ON THE CONTRARY

2C	2: 7	**now instead** you should forgive
Ga	2: 7	**On the contrary,** when they saw
1P	3: 9	**on the contrary,** repay with a

5122   GO1   AG824   LN246
τουνομα, THE NAME

| Mt | 27:57 | from Arimathea, **named** Joseph |

5131   GO4   AG824   LN246   B1:114
τραγος, GOAT

He	9:12	with the blood of **goats** and
	9:13	if the blood of **goats** and bulls
	9:19	**goats,** with water and scarlet
	10: 4	**goats** to take away sins.

5132   GO15   AG824   LN247   B2:520   K8:209
τραπεζα, TABLE

Mt	15:27	fall from their masters' **table.**
	21:12	overturned the **tables** of the
Mk	7:28	dogs under the **table** eat the
	11:15	**tables** of the money changers
Lk	16:21	fell from the rich man's **table**
	19:23	put my money into the **bank?**
	22:21	his hand is on the **table.**
	22:30	eat and drink at my **table** in
Jn	2:15	overturned their **tables.**
Ac	6: 2	in order to wait on **tables.**
	16:34	set **food** before them; and he
Ro	11: 9	Let their **table** become a snare
1C	10:21	of the **table** of the Lord and
	10:21	Lord and the **table** of demons
He	9: 2	lampstand, the **table,** and

5133   GO1   AG824   LN247   R5132
τραπεζιτης, ONE AT TABLE

| Mt | 25:27 | my money with the **bankers,** and |

5134   GO1   AG824   LN247
τραυμα, WOUND

| Lk | 10:34 | bandaged his **wounds,** having |

5135   GO2   AG824   LN247   R5134
τραυματιζω, I WOUND

| Lk | 20:12 | they **wounded** and threw out. |
| Ac | 19:16 | of the house naked and **wounded.** |

5136   GO1   AG824   LN247   R5137
τραχηλιζω, I STICK OUT NECK

| He | 4:13 | **laid bare** to the eyes of the |

5137   GO7   AG825   LN247   B1:241
τραχηλος, NECK

Mt	18: 6	were fastened around your **neck**
Mk	9:42	were hung around your **neck** and
Lk	15:20	put his arms **around** him and
	17: 2	were hung around your **neck** and
Ac	15:10	**neck** of the disciples a yoke
	20:37	they **embraced** Paul and kissed
Ro	16: 4	risked their **necks** for my life

5138   GO2   AG825   LN247   B3:709
τραχυς, ROUGH

| Lk | 3: 5 | the **rough ways** made smooth; |
| Ac | 27:29 | we might run on the **rocks,** they |

5139 ᴳᴼ1 ᴬᴳ825 ᴸᴺ247
τραχωνιτις, TRACHONITIS
Lk 3: 1 Ituraea and **Trachonitis**

5140 ᴳᴼ69 ᴬᴳ825 ᴸᴺ247 ᴮ2:686 ᴷ8:216
τρεις, THREE
Mt 12:40 Jonah was **three** days and three
   12:40 **three** nights in the belly
   12:40 so for **three** days and three
   12:40 **three** nights the Son of Man
   13:33 mixed in with **three** measures of
   15:32 for **three** days and have nothing
   17: 4 I will make **three** dwellings
   18:16 of two or **three** witnesses.
   18:20 where two or **three** are gathered
   26:61 to build it in **three** days
   27:40 build it in **three** days, save
   27:63 After **three** days I will rise
Mk 8: 2 now for **three** days and have
    8:31 after **three** days rise again.
    9: 5 let us make **three** dwellings
    9:31 **three** days after being killed
   10:34 after **three** days he will rise
   14:58 in **three** days I will build
   15:29 build it in **three** days,
Lk 1:56 remained with her about **three**
    2:46 After **three** days they found
    4:25 heaven was shut up **three** years
    9:33 let us make **three** dwellings
   10:36 Which of these **three**, do you
   11: 5 lend me **three** loaves of bread;
   12:52 divided, **three** against two and
   12:52 two and two against **three**;
   13: 7 **three** years I have come looking
   13:21 mixed in with **three** measures of
Jn 2: 6 twenty or **thirty** gallons.
    2:19 in **three** days I will raise it
    2:20 raise it up in **three** days?
   21:11 a hundred fifty-**three** of them
Ac 5: 7 **three** hours his wife came in
    7:20 **three** months he was brought up
    9: 9 **three** days he was without sight
   10:19 **three** men are searching for you
   11:11 **three** men, sent to me from
   17: 2 on **three** sabbath days argued
   19: 8 **three** months spoke out boldly
   20: 3 he stayed for **three** months
   25: 1 **Three** days after Festus had
   28: 7 us hospitably for **three** days.

   28:11 **Three** months later we set sail
   28:12 stayed there for **three** days;
   28:15 **Three** Taverns to meet us.
   28:17 **Three** days later he called
1C 10: 8 twenty-**three** thousand fell in a
   13:13 these **three**; and the greatest
   14:27 at most **three**, and each in turn
   14:29 Let two or **three** prophets speak
2C 13: 1 evidence of two or **three**
Ga 1:18 after **three** years I did go up
1Ti 5:19 evidence of two or **three**
He 10:28 of two or **three** witnesses
Ja 5:17 **three** years and six months it
1J 5: 7 There are **three** that testify:
    5: 8 blood, and these **three** agree.
Re 6: 6 **three** quarts of barley for a
    8:13 **three** angels are about to blow
    9:18 By these **three** plagues a third
   11: 9 **three** and a half days members
   11:11 after the **three** and a half days
   16:13 **three** foul spirits like frogs
   16:19 great city was split into **three**
   21:13 on the east **three** gates, on the
   21:13 on the north **three** gates, on the
   21:13 on the south **three** gates, and on
   21:13 on the west **three** gates.

5141 ᴳᴼ3 ᴬᴳ825 ᴸᴺ247
τρεμω, I TREMBLE
Mk 5:33 in fear and **trembling**, fell
Lk 8:47 came **trembling**; and falling
2P 2:10 they are not **afraid** to slander

5142 ᴳᴼ9 ᴬᴳ825 ᴸᴺ247 ᴿ5160
τρεφω, I FEED
Mt 6:26 heavenly Father **feeds** them.
   25:37 **gave** you **food,** or thirsty and
Lk 4:16 where he **had been brought up**
   12:24 yet God **feeds** them. Of how much
   23:29 the breasts that never **nursed.**
Ac 12:20 on the king's country for **food.**
Ja 5: 5 you **have fattened** your hearts
Re 12: 6 **be nourished** for one thousand
   12:14 she **is nourished** for a time,

5143 ᴳᴼ20 ᴬᴳ825 ᴸᴺ247 ᴮ3:945 ᴷ8:226
τρεχω, I RUN
Mt 27:48 **ran** and got a sponge, filled it
   28: 8 **ran** to tell his disciples.
Mk 5: 6 he **ran** and bowed down before

	15:36	someone **ran,** filled a sponge
Lk	15:20	he **ran** and put his arms around
	24:12	got up and **ran** to the tomb
Jn	20: 2	So she **ran** and went to Simon
	20: 4	The two **were running** together
Ro	9:16	not on human will or **exertion**
1C	9:24	**runners** all compete, but only
	9:24	runners all **compete,** but only
	9:24	**Run** in such a way that you may
	9:26	So I do not **run** aimlessly, nor
Ga	2: 2	sure that I was not **running,** or
	2: 2	or had not **run,** in vain.
	5: 7	You were **running** well; who
Ph	2:16	I did not **run** in vain or labor
2Th	3: 1	may **spread rapidly** and be
He	12: 1	let us **run** with perseverance
Re	9: 9	with horses **rushing** into battle

5143a   GO1 AG826 LN247
τρημα, OPENING
Lk 18:25   through the **eye** of a needle

5144   GO11 AG826 LN247 R5140
τριακοντα, THIRTY

Mt	13: 8	some sixty, some **thirty.**
	13:23	sixty, and in another **thirty.**
	26:15	They paid him **thirty** pieces of
	27: 3	brought back the **thirty** pieces
	27: 9	they took the **thirty** pieces of
Mk	4: 8	yielding **thirty** and sixty and
	4:20	bear fruit, **thirty** and sixty
Lk	3:23	Jesus was about **thirty** years
Jn	5: 5	had been ill for **thirty**-eight
	6:19	rowed about **three or four** miles
Ga	3:17	four hundred **thirty** years later

5145   GO2 AG826 LN247 R5140,1540
τριακοσιοι, THREE HUNDRED
Mk 14: 5   for more than **three hundred**
Jn 12: 5   sold for **three hundred** denarii

5146   GO2 AG826 LN247 B1:726
τριβολος, THISTLE
Mt 7:16   thorns, or figs from **thistles?**
He 6: 8   it produces thorns and **thistles**

5147   GO3 AG826 LN247
τριβος, PATH
Mt 3: 3   Lord, make his **paths** straight

Mk 1: 3   make his **paths** straight
Lk 3: 4   Lord, make his **paths** straight.

5148   GO1 AG826 LN247 R5140,2094
τριετια, THREE YEARS
Ac 20:31   **three years** I did not cease

5149   GO1 AG826 LN247
τριζω, I GRIND
Mk 9:18   **grinds** his teeth and becomes

5150   GO1 AG826 LN247 R5140,3376
τριμηνον, THREE MONTHS
He 11:23   **three months** after his birth

5151   GO12 AG826 LN247 B2:686 K8:216 R5140
τρις, THREE TIMES

Mt	26:34	you will deny me **three** times
	26:75	you will deny me **three** times
Mk	14:30	you will deny me **three** times
	14:72	you will deny me **three** times
Lk	22:34	denied **three** times that you
	22:61	you will deny me **three** times
Jn	13:38	have denied me **three** times.
Ac	10:16	This happened **three** times
	11:10	This happened **three** times
2C	11:25	**Three** times I was beaten with
	11:25	**Three** times I was shipwrecked
	12: 8	**Three** times I appealed to the

5152   GO1 AG826 LN247 R5140,4721
τριστεγον, THIRD STORY
Ac 20: 9   fell to the ground **three floors**

5153   GO1 AG826 LN248 B2:699 R5151,5507
τρισχιλιοι, THREE THOUSAND
Ac 2:41   **three thousand** persons were

5154   GO56 AG826 LN248 B2:687 K8:216 R5140
τριτος, THIRD

Mt	16:21	on the **third** day be raised.
	17:23	**third** day he will be raised
	20: 3	went out about **nine** o'clock
	20:19	on the **third** day he will be
	22:26	so also the **third,** down to the
	26:44	prayed for the **third** time
	27:64	be made secure until the **third**
Mk	12:21	children; and the **third**
	14:41	He came a **third** time and said

	15:25	was **nine** o'clock in the morning
Lk	9:22	on the **third** day be raised.
	12:38	or **near dawn,** and finds them
	13:32	**third** day I finish my work.
	18:33	**third** day he will rise again.
	20:12	And he sent still a **third; this**
	20:31	and the **third** married her
	23:22	A **third** time he said to them
	24: 7	on the **third** day rise again.
	24:21	it is now the **third** day since
	24:46	the dead on the **third** day,
Jn	2: 1	**third** day there was a wedding
	21:14	This was now the **third** time
	21:17	**third** time, "Simon son of John
	21:17	**third** time, "Do you love me?"
Ac	2:15	it is only **nine** o'clock in the
	10:40	but God raised him on the **third**
	23:23	by **nine** o'clock tonight for
	27:19	and on the **third** day with their
1C	12:28	second prophets, **third** teachers
	15: 4	he was raised on the **third** day
2C	12: 2	was caught up to the **third**
	12:14	ready to come to you this **third**
	13: 1	This is the **third** time I am
Re	4: 7	the **third** living creature with
	6: 5	When he opened the **third** seal
	6: 5	When he opened the **third** sea
	8: 7	a **third** of the earth was burned
	8: 7	**third** of the trees were burned
	8: 8	**third** of the living
	8: 9	**third** of the living creatures
	8: 9	**third** of the ships were
	8:10	**third** angel blew his trumpet
	8:10	fell on a **third** of the rivers
	8:11	A **third** of the waters became
	8:12	**third** of the sun was struck
	8:12	and a **third** of the moon, and a
	8:12	a **third** of the stars, so that
	8:12	**third** of their light was
	8:12	a **third** of the day was kept
	9:15	kill a **third** of humankind.
	9:18	a **third** of humankind was killed
	11:14	The **third** woe is coming very
	12: 4	His tail swept down a **third**
	14: 9	Then another angel, a **third,**
	16: 4	The **third** angel poured his bowl
	21:19	the **third** agate, the fourth

5155 GO1 AG827 LN248 R2359
τριχινος, OF HAIR
| Re | 6:12 | black as **sackcloth,** the full |

5156 GO5 AG827 LN248 B1:622 R5141
τρομος, TREMBLING
Mk	16: 8	for **terror** and amazement had
1C	2: 3	in fear and in much **trembling.**
2C	7:15	him with fear and **trembling.**
Ep	6: 5	masters with fear and **trembling**
Ph	2:12	with fear and **trembling;**

5157 GO1 AG827 LN248
τροπη, TURNING
| Ja | 1:17 | or shadow **due to change.** |

5158 GO13 AG827 LN248 B2:781
τροπος, MANNER
Mt	23:37	**as** a hen gathers her brood
Lk	13:34	**as** a hen gathers her brood
Ac	1:11	will come in the **same way** as
	7:28	Do you want to kill me **as** you
	15:11	Lord Jesus, just **as** they will
	27:25	exactly **as** I have been told.
Ro	3: 2	Much, **in every way.** For in the
Ph	1:18	is proclaimed **in every way**
2Th	2: 3	no one deceive you **in any way**
	3:16	peace at all times **in all ways**
2Ti	3: 8	**As** Jannes and Jambres opposed
He	13: 5	**Keep** your lives free from the
Ju	1: 7	in the same **manner** as they

5159 GO1 AG827 LN248
τροποφορεω, I BEAR WITH MANNERS
| Ac | 13:18 | **he put up** with them in the |

5160 GO16 AG827 LN248 R5142
τροφη, FOOD
Mt	3: 4	his **food** was locusts and wild
	6:25	Is not life more than **food**
	10:10	laborers deserve their **food.**
	24:45	allowance of **food** at the proper
Lk	12:23	For life is more than **food,**
Jn	4: 8	ate their **food** with glad and
Ac	9:19	and after taking some **food**
	14:17	filling you with **food** and your
	27:33	to take some **food,** saying
	27:34	I urge you to take some **food**
	27:36	took **food** for themselves.
	27:38	they had satisfied their **hunger**

He   5:12   You need milk, not solid **food;**
      5:14   solid **food** is for the mature
Ja   2:15   naked and lacks daily **food,**

5161   GO3 AG827 LN248
τροφιμος, TROPHIMUS
Ac   20: 4   Tychicus and **Trophimus** from
     21:29   had previously seen **Trophimus**
2Ti   4:20   **Trophimus** I left ill in Miletus

5162   GO1 AG827 LN248 B1:282 R5142
τροφος, FEEDER
1Th   2: 7   like a **nurse** tenderly

5163   GO1 AG828 LN248
τροχια, TRACKS
He   12:13   make straight **paths** for your

5164   GO1 AG828 LN248 B1:182
τροχος, CYCLE
Ja   3: 6   sets on fire the **cycle** of

5165   GO2 AG828 LN248
τρυβλιον, DISH
Mt   26:23   dipped his hand into the
              bowl
Mk   14:20   dipping bread into the **bowl**

5166   GO3 AG828 LN248 B2:33
τρυγαω, I GATHER
Lk   6:44   grapes **picked** from a bramble
Re   14:18   **gather** the clusters of the vine
     14:19   **gathered** the vintage of the

5167   GO1 AG828 LN248 K6:63
τρυγων, TURTLEDOVES
Lk   2:24   a pair of **turtledoves** or

5168   GO1 AG828 LN248
τρυμαλια, EYE
Mk   10:25   **eye** of a needle than for

5169   GO1 AG828 LN248 R5168
τρυπημα, OPENING
Mt   19:24   through the **eye** of a needle

5170   GO1 AG828 LN248
τρυφαινα, TRYPHAENA
Ro   16:12   **Tryphaena** and Tryphosa.
              Greet

5171   GO1 AG828 LN248 R5172
τρυφαω, I INDULGE
Ja   5: 5   You **have lived** on the earth

5172   GO2 AG828 LN248
τρυφη, INDULGENCE
Lk   7:25   **live** in luxury are in royal
2P   2:13   pleasure to **revel** in the

5173   GO1 AG828 LN248
τρυφωσα, TRYPHOSA
Ro   16:12   Tryphaena and **Tryphosa.** Greet

5174   GO6 AG829 LN248
τρωας, TROAS
Ac   16: 8   they went down to **Troas.**
     16:11   We set sail from **Troas** and
     20: 5   were waiting for us in **Troas;**
     20: 6   we joined them in **Troas**
2C   2:12   I came to **Troas** to proclaim
2Ti   4:13   I left with Carpus at **Troas**

5176   GO6 AG829 LN248 B2:535 K8:236
τρωγω, I GNAW
Mt   24:38   they were **eating** and drinking
Jn   6:54   Those who **eat** my flesh and
      6:56   Those who **eat** my flesh and
      6:57   whoever **eats** me will live
      6:58   the one who **eats** this bread
     13:18   The one who **ate** my bread has

5177   GO12 AG829 LN248 K8:238
τυγχανω, I OBTAIN
Lk   20:35   considered worthy **of a place**
Ac   19:11   God did **extraordinary** miracles
     24: 2   we have long **enjoyed** peace
     26:22   To this day I **have had** help
     27: 3   friends to **be cared** for.
     28: 2   natives showed us **unusual**
1C   14:10   are **doubtless** many different
     15:37   **perhaps** of wheat or of some
     16: 6   **perhaps** I will stay with you
2Ti   2:10   **may** also **obtain** the salvation
He   8: 6   Jesus **has** now **obtained** a more
     11:35   to **obtain** a better resurrection

5178   GO1 AG829 LN248 R5180
τυμπανιζω, I TORTURE
He   11:35   Others **were tortured,** refusing

5178a ᴳᴼ1 ᴬᴳ829 ᴸᴺ249
τυπικως, BY EXAMPLE
1C 10:11 serve **as an example,** and they

5179 ᴳᴼ15 ᴬᴳ829 ᴸᴺ249 ᴮ3:903 ᴷ8:246
τυπος, EXAMPLE
Jn 20:25 **mark** of the nails in his hands
20:25 put my finger in the **mark** of
Ac 7:43 **images** that you made to worship
7:44 according to the **pattern** he had
23:25 wrote a letter to this **effect:**
Ro 5:14 who is a **type** of the one who
6:17 to the **form** of teaching to
1C 10: 6 occurred as **examples** for us,
Ph 3:17 live according to the **example**
1Th 1: 7 became an **example** to all the
2Th 3: 9 give you an **example** to imitate.
1Ti 4:12 **example** in speech and conduct
Ti 2: 7 in all respects a **model** of good
He 8: 5 according to the **pattern** that
1P 5: 3 but be **examples** to the flock.

5180 ᴳᴼ13 ᴬᴳ830 ᴸᴺ249 ᴮ3:903 ᴷ8:260
τυπτω, I BEAT
Mt 24:49 begins to **beat** his fellow
27:30 and **struck** him on the head.
Mk 15:19 **struck** his head with a reed
Lk 6:29 anyone **strikes** you on the cheek
12:45 if he begins to **beat** the other
18:13 **was beating** his breast and
23:48 home, **beating** their breasts.
Ac 18:17 **beat** him in front of the
21:32 they stopped **beating** Paul.
23: 2 him to **strike** him on the mouth.
23: 3 God **will strike** you, you
23: 3 law you order me **to be struck**
1C 8:12 **wound** their conscience when

5181 ᴳᴼ1 ᴬᴳ830 ᴸᴺ249 ᴮ2:372
τυραννος, TYRANNUS
Ac 19: 9 in the lecture hall of **Tyrannus**

5183 ᴳᴼ1 ᴬᴳ830 ᴸᴺ249
τυριος, TYRENEANS
Ac 12:20 people of **Tyre** and Sidon.

5184 ᴳᴼ11 ᴬᴳ830 ᴸᴺ249
τυρος, TYRE
Mt 11:21 had been done in **Tyre** and Sidon
11:22 more tolerable for **Tyre** and

15:21 the district of **Tyre** and Sidon.
Mk 3: 8 region around **Tyre** and Sidon.
7:24 to the region of **Tyre.** He
7:31 from the region of **Tyre,**
Lk 6:17 coast of **Tyre** and Sidon.
10:13 you had been done in **Tyre**
10:14 more tolerable for **Tyre**
Ac 21: 3 to Syria and landed at **Tyre,**
21: 7 finished the voyage from **Tyre**

5185 ᴳᴼ50 ᴬᴳ830 ᴸᴺ249 ᴮ1:218 ᴷ8:270 ᴿ5186
τυφλος, BLIND
Mt 9:27 two **blind** men followed him,
9:28 the **blind** men came to him;
11: 5 the **blind** receive their sight
12:22 who was **blind** and mute; and
15:14 they are **blind** guides of the
15:14 guides of the **blind.** And if
15:14 if one **blind** person guides
15:14 **another,** both will fall into
15:30 maimed, the **blind,** the mute
15:31 the **blind** seeing. And they
20:30 two **blind** men sitting by the
21:14 The **blind** and the lame came
23:16 Woe to you, **blind** guides,
23:17 You **blind** fools! For which is
23:19 How **blind** you are! For which
23:24 You **blind** guides! You strain
23:26 You **blind** Pharisee! First clean
Mk 8:22 people brought a **blind** man to
8:23 He took the **blind** man by the
10:46 son of Timaeus, a **blind** beggar
10:49 they called the **blind** man
10:51 **blind** man said to him, "My
Lk 4:18 recovery of sight to the **blind**
6:39 Can a **blind** person guide a
6:39 guide a **blind** person? Will
7:21 sight to many who were **blind.**
7:22 the **blind** receive their sight
14:13 the lame, and the **blind.**
14:21 crippled, the **blind,** and the
18:35 a **blind** man was sitting by the
Jn 5: 3 many invalids—**blind,** lame
9: 1 he saw a man **blind** from birth.
9: 2 that he was born **blind?**
9:13 man who had formerly been **blind**
9:17 said again to the **blind** man
9:18 he had been **blind** and had

9:19	who you say was born **blind?**	
9:20	and that he was born **blind;**	
9:24	the man who had been **blind**	
9:25	that though I was **blind,** now I	
9:32	eyes of a person born **blind.**	
9:39	who do see may become **blind.**	
9:40	Surely we are not **blind,** are we	
9:41	If you were **blind,** you would	
10:21	open the eyes of the **blind?**	
11:37	eyes of the **blind** man have kept	
Ac 13:11	you will be **blind** for a while	
Ro 2:19	you are a guide to the **blind**	
2P 1: 9	is nearsighted and **blind,** and	
Re 3:17	wretched, pitiable, poor, **blind**	

5186 GO3 AG831 LN249 K8:270 R5185
τυφλοω, I BLIND

Jn 12:40	He **has blinded** their eyes and	
2C 4: 4	world **has blinded** the minds of	
1J 2:11	**has brought on blindness.**	

5187 GO3 AG831 LN249
τυφοω, I PUFF UP

1Ti 3: 6	may be **puffed up** with conceit	
6: 4	**is conceited,** understanding	
2Ti 3: 4	**swollen with conceit,** lovers	

5188 GO1 AG831 LN249
τυφω, I SMOKE

Mt 12:20	quench a **smoldering** wick	

5189 GO1 AG831 LN249
τυφωνικος, TEMPEST

Ac 27:14	But soon a **violent** wind, called	

5190 GO5 AG831 LN249
τυχικος, TYCHICUS

Ac 20: 4	by **Tychicus** and Trophimus from	
Ep 6:21	**Tychicus** will tell you	
Co 4: 7	**Tychicus** will tell you all the	
2Ti 4:12	I have sent **Tychicus** to Ephesus	
Ti 3:12	Artemas to you, or **Tychicus,**	

υ

5191 GO1 AG831 LN249 R5192
'υακινθινος, OF HYACINTH

Re 9:17	color of fire and of **sapphire**	

5192 GO1 AG831 LN249 B3:396
'υακινθος, HYACINTH

Re 21:20	eleventh **jacinth,** the twelfth	

5193 GO3 AG831 LN249 B3:984 R5194
'υαλινος, OF GLASS

Re 4: 6	a sea of **glass,** like crystal.	
15: 2	appeared to be a sea of **glass**	
15: 2	beside the sea of **glass** with	

5194 GO2 AG831 LN249
'υαλος, GLASS

Re 21:18	is pure gold, clear as **glass.**	
21:21	pure gold, transparent as **glass**	

5195 GO5 AG831 LN249 B3:27 K8:295 R5196
'υβριζω, I ABUSE

Mt 22: 6	**mistreated** them, and killed	
Lk 11:45	you **insult** us too.	
18:32	mocked and **insulted** and spat	
Ac 14: 5	**mistreat** them and to stone them	
1Th 2: 2	shamefully **mistreated** at	

5196 GO3 AG832 LN249 B3:27 K8:295
'υβρις, ABUSE

Ac 27:10	voyage will be with **danger**	
27:21	avoided this **damage** and loss.	
2C 12:10	with weaknesses, **insults,**	

5197 GO2 AG832 LN249 B3:27 K8:295 R5195
'υβριστης, ABUSER

Ro 1:30	God-haters, **insolent,** haughty,	
1Ti 1:13	**man of violence.** But I received	

5198 GO12 AG832 LN249 B2:169 K8:308 R5199
'υγιαινω, I AM HEALTHY

Lk 5:31	Those who **are well** have no need	
7:10	found the slave in good **health.**	
15:27	got him back **safe and sound.**	
1Ti 1:10	contrary to the **sound** teaching	
6: 3	not agree with the **sound** words	
2Ti 1:13	standard of **sound** teaching	
4: 3	not put up with **sound** doctrine	
Ti 1: 9	preach with **sound** doctrine	
1:13	may become **sound** in the faith,	
2: 1	consistent with **sound** doctrine.	
2: 2	**sound** in faith, in love, and in	
3J 1: 2	may be in good **health,** just as	

5199　GO12 AG832 LN249 B2:169 K8:308
'υγιης, HEALTHY

Mt	12:13	was restored, as **sound** as the
	15:31	maimed **whole,** the lame walking
Mk	5:34	**be healed** of your disease.
Jn	5: 6	Do you want to be made **well?**
	5: 9	At once the man was made **well**
	5:11	man who made me **well** said to me
	5:14	you have been made **well!** Do not
	5:15	was Jesus who had made him **well.**
	7:23	I **healed** a man's whole body on
Ac	4:10	in good **health** by the name of
Ti	2: 8	and **sound** speech that cannot be

5200　GO1 AG832 LN249 B1:390
'υγρος, MOIST

| Lk | 23:31 | do this when the wood is **green** |

5201　GO3 AG832 LN249 R5204
'υδρια, WATERPOT

Jn	2: 6	six stone **water jars** for the
	2: 7	Fill the **jars** with water
	4:28	the woman left her **water jar**

5202　GO1 AG832 LN250 R5204,4095
'υδροποτεω, I DRINK WATER

| 1Ti | 5:23 | No longer **drink** only **water** |

5203　GO1 AG832 LN250
'υδρωπικος, DROPSY

| Lk | 14: 2 | there was a man who had **dropsy.** |

5204　GO78 AG832 LN250 B3:988 K8:314
'υδωρ, WATER

Mt	3:11	I baptize you with **water** for
	3:16	he came up from the **water**
	8:32	sea and perished in the **water.**
	14:28	me to come to you on the **water**
	14:29	started walking on the **water**
	17:15	fire and often into the **water.**
	27:24	took some **water** and washed his
Mk	1: 8	I have baptized you with **water**
	1:10	was coming up out of the **water**
	9:22	the fire and into the **water**
	9:41	gives you a cup of **water** to
	14:13	man carrying a jar of **water**
Lk	3:16	I baptize you with **water;** but
	7:44	you gave me no **water** for my
	8:24	the raging **waves;** they ceased
	8:25	even the winds and the **water**

	16:24	tip of his finger in **water**
	22:10	man carrying a jar of **water**
Jn	1:26	I baptize with **water.** Among
	1:31	I came baptizing with **water** for
	1:33	sent me to baptize with **water**
	2: 7	Fill the jars with **water."** And
	2: 9	steward tasted the **water** that
	2: 9	had drawn the **water** knew), the
	3: 5	being born of **water** and Spirit.
	3:23	because **water** was abundant
	4: 7	woman came to draw **water,** and
	4:10	have given you living **water.**
	4:11	do you get that living **water?**
	4:13	drinks of this **water** will be
	4:14	those who drink of the **water**
	4:14	**water** that I will give will
	4:14	spring of **water** gushing up to
	4:15	Sir, give me this **water,** so
	4:46	changed the **water** into wine.
	5: 7	when the **water** is stirred up
	7:38	flow rivers of living **water**
	: 5	poured **water** into a basin
	19:34	once blood and **water** came out.
Ac	1: 5	for John baptized with **water**
	8:36	**water;** and the eunuch said
	8:36	Look, here is **water!** What is
	8:38	went down into the **water**
	8:39	they came up out of the **water**
	10:47	**water** for baptizing these
	11:16	John baptized with **water,** but
Ep	5:26	washing of **water** by the word,
He	9:19	with **water** and scarlet wool and
	10:22	bodies washed with pure **water.**
Ja	3:12	No more can salt **water** yield
1P	3:20	were saved through **water.**
2P	3: 5	earth was formed out of **water**
	3: 5	water and by means of **water,**
	3: 6	time was deluged with **water**
1J	5: 6	one who came by **water** and blood
	5: 6	not with the **water** only but
	5: 6	with the **water** and the blood
	5: 8	Spirit and the **water** and the
Re	1:15	like the sound of many **waters.**
	7:17	springs of the **water** of life
	8:10	and on the springs of **water.**
	8:11	A third of the **waters** became
	8:11	many died from the **water**
	11: 6	authority over the **waters**
	12:15	serpent poured **water** like a

14: 2	like the sound of many **waters**
14: 7	sea and the springs of **water**
16: 4	**water,** and they became blood.
16: 5	heard the angel of the **waters**
16:12	its **water** was dried up in order
17: 1	who is seated on many **waters,**
17:15	**waters** that you saw, where the
19: 6	like the sound of many **waters**
21: 6	spring of the **water** of life.
22: 1	river of the **water** of life
22:17	the **water** of life as a gift.

5205   ᴳᴼ5 ᴬᴳ833 ᴸᴺ250 ᴮ3:1000
ʹυετος, RAIN

Ac	14:17	giving you **rains** from heaven
	28: 2	begun to **rain** and was cold
He	6: 7	drinks up the **rain** falling on
Ja	5:18	heaven gave **rain** and the
Re	11: 6	so that no **rain** may fall during

5206   ᴳᴼ5 ᴬᴳ833 ᴸᴺ250 ᴮ1:286 ᴷ8:397 ᴿ5207,5087
ʹυιοθεσια, ADOPTION AS SON

Ro	8:15	spirit of **adoption.** When we
	8:23	we wait for **adoption,** the
	9: 4	to them belong the **adoption**
Ga	4: 5	receive **adoption** as children.
Ep	1: 5	He destined us for **adoption**

5207   ᴳᴼ379 ᴬᴳ833 ᴸᴺ250 ᴮ1:286 ᴷ8:334
ʹυιος, SON

Mt	1: 1	Messiah, the **son** of David, the
	1: 1	of David, the **son** of Abraham.
	1:20	Joseph, **son** of David, do not be
	1:21	She will bear a **son,** and you
	1:23	conceive and bear a **son**
	1:25	until she had borne a **son**
	2:15	Egypt I have called my **son.**
	3:17	This is my **Son,** the Beloved
	4: 3	If you are the **Son** of God
	4: 6	**Son** of God, throw yourself down
	5: 9	will be called **children** of God.
	5:45	may be **children** of your Father
	7: 9	if your **child** asks for bread
	8:20	**Son** of Man has nowhere to lay
	8:29	to do with us, **Son** of God?
	9: 6	**Son** of Man has authority on
	9:15	wedding **guests** cannot mourn
	9:27	Have mercy on us, **Son** of David
	10:23	before the **Son** of Man comes.
	10:37	loves **son** or daughter more than

11:19	the **Son** of Man came eating and
11:27	no one knows the **Son** except the
11:27	knows the Father except the **Son**
11:27	whom the **Son** chooses to reveal
12: 8	For the **Son** of Man is lord of
12:23	Can this be the **Son** of David?
12:27	your own exorcists [**sons**] cast them
12:32	a word against the **Son** of Man
12:40	**Son** of Man will be in the heart
13:37	good seed is the **Son** of Man;
13:38	good seed are the **children** of
13:38	weeds are the **children** of the
13:41	The **Son** of Man will send his
13:55	Is not this the carpenter's **son**
14:33	Truly you are the **Son** of God.
15:22	Lord, **Son** of David; my daughter
16:13	people say that the **Son** of Man
16:16	Messiah, the **Son** of the living
16:27	For the **Son** of Man is to come
16:28	see the **Son** of Man coming in
17: 5	This is my **Son,** the Beloved
17: 9	**Son** of Man has been raised
17:12	**Son** of Man is about to
17:15	have mercy on my **son,**
17:22	**Son** of Man is going to be
17:25	From their **children** or from
17:26	Then the **children** are free.
19:28	when the **Son** of Man is seated
20:18	**Son** of Man will be handed over
20:20	mother of the **sons** of Zebedee
20:20	came to him with her **sons**
20:21	two **sons** of mine will sit
20:28	**Son** of Man came not to be
20:30	mercy on us, **Son** of David
20:31	Lord, **Son** of David!
21: 5	colt, the **foal** of a donkey.
21: 9	Hosanna to the **Son** of David
21:15	Hosanna to the **Son** of David
21:37	Finally he sent his **son** to
21:37	They will respect my **son.**
21:38	tenants saw the **son,** they said
22: 2	wedding banquet for his **son.**
22:42	Whose **son** is he?" They said to
22:45	Lord, how can he be his **son?**
23:15	twice as much a **child** of hell
23:31	you are **descendants** of those
23:35	Zechariah **son** of Barachiah
24:27	coming of the **Son** of Man.
24:30	sign of the **Son** of Man will

24:30	**Son** of Man coming on the clouds
24:36	nor the **Son,** but only the
24:37	the coming of the **Son** of Man.
24:39	coming of the **Son** of Man.
24:44	for the **Son** of Man is coming
25:31	**Son** of Man comes in his glory
26: 2	**Son** of Man will be handed over
26:24	The **Son** of Man goes as it is
26:24	whom the **Son** of Man is betrayed
26:37	Peter and the two **sons** of
26:45	**Son** of Man is betrayed into the
26:63	are the Messiah, the **Son** of God
26:64	**Son** of Man seated at the right
27: 9	**people** of Israel had set a
27:40	If you are the **Son** of God, come
27:43	he said, 'I am God's **Son**
27:54	Truly this man was God's **Son!**
27:56	mother of the **sons** of Zebedee.
28:19	of the Father and of the **Son**

Mk 1: 1　Jesus Christ, the **Son** of God.

1:11	You are my **Son,** the Beloved;
2:10	**Son** of Man has authority on
2:19	The wedding **guests** cannot fast
2:28	**Son** of Man is lord even of the
3:11	You are the **Son** of God!
3:17	that is, **Sons** of Thunder
3:28	**people** will be forgiven for
5: 7	**Son** of the Most High God?
6: 3	**son** of Mary and brother of
8:31	**Son** of Man must undergo great
8:38	**Son** of Man will also be ashamed
9: 7	This is my **Son,** the Beloved
9: 9	after the **Son** of Man had risen
9:12	written about the **Son** of Man
9:17	I brought you my **son;** he has a
9:31	**Son** of Man is to be betrayed
10:33	**Son** of Man will be handed over
10:35	James and John, the **sons** of
10:45	**Son** of Man came not to be
10:46	Bartimaeus **son** of Timaeus, a
10:47	Jesus, **Son** of David, have mercy
10:48	**Son** of David, have mercy on me
12: 6	beloved **son.** Finally he sent
12: 6	They will respect my **son.**
12:35	Messiah is the **son** of David?
12:37	how can he be his **son**
13:26	**Son** of Man coming in clouds
13:32	the **Son,** but only the Father.
14:21	For the **Son** of Man goes as it

14:21	whom the **Son** of Man is betrayed
14:41	**Son** of Man is betrayed into the
14:61	Messiah, the **Son** of the Blessed
14:62	**Son** of Man seated at the right
15:39	Truly this man was God's **Son!**

Lk 1:13　Elizabeth will bear you a **son**

1:16	He will turn many of the **people**
1:31	bear a **son,** and you will name
1:32	called the **Son** of the Most High
1:35	he will be called **Son** of God.
1:36	age has also conceived a **son**
1:57	give birth, and she bore a **son.**
2: 7	gave birth to her firstborn **son**
3: 2	word of God came to John **son**
3:22	You are my **Son,** the Beloved
3:23	was the **son** (as was thought)
4: 3	If you are the **Son** of God,
4: 9	If you are the **Son** of God,
4:22	Is not this Joseph's **son?**
4:41	You are the **Son** of God
5:10	**sons** of Zebedee, who were
5:24	**Son** of Man has authority on
5:34	cannot make wedding **guests** fast
6: 5	**Son** of Man is lord of the
6:22	on account of the **Son** of Man.
6:35	be **children** of the Most High
7:12	his mother's only **son,** and she
7:34	the **Son** of Man has come eating
8:28	**Son** of the Most High God? I beg
9:22	The **Son** of Man must undergo
9:26	**Son** of Man will be ashamed when
9:35	This is my **Son,** my Chosen
9:38	I beg you to look at my **son**
9:41	Bring your **son** here.
9:44	**Son** of Man is going to be
9:58	**Son** of Man has nowhere to lay
10: 6	**who shares** in peace, your peace
10:22	the **Son** is except the Father
10:22	the Father is except the **Son**
10:22	the **Son** chooses to reveal him
11:11	if your **child** asks for a fish
11:19	do your exorcists [**sons**] cast
11:30	**Son** of Man will be to this
12: 8	**Son** of Man also will
12:10	speaks a word against the **Son**
12:40	**Son** of Man is coming at an
12:53	divided: father against **son**
12:53	**son** against father, mother
14: 5	has a **child** or an ox that has

15:11	was a man who had two **sons.**	
15:13	younger **son** gathered all he had	
15:19	worthy to be called your **son**	
15:21	the **son** said to him, 'Father, I	
15:21	worthy to be called your **son.**	
15:24	for this **son** of mine was dead	
15:25	elder **son** was in the field	
15:30	this **son** of yours came back	
16: 8	**children** of this age are more	
16: 8	than are the **children** of light.	
17:22	one of the days of the **Son** of	
17:24	so will the **Son** of Man be in	
17:26	the days of the **Son** of Man.	
17:30	that the **Son** of Man is revealed	
18: 8	**Son** of Man comes, will he find	
18:31	**Son** of Man by the prophets will	
18:38	shouted, "Jesus, **Son** of David	
18:39	**Son** of David, have mercy on me!	
19: 9	he too is a **son** of Abraham.	
19:10	For the **Son** of Man came to seek	
20:13	I will send my beloved **son**	
20:34	**Those who belong** to this age	
20:36	like angels and are **children**	
20:36	**children** of the resurrection.	
20:41	the Messiah is David's **son?**	
20:44	so how can he be his **son?**	
21:27	**Son** of Man coming in a cloud	
21:36	to stand before the **Son** of Man	
22:22	**Son** of Man is going as it has	
22:48	are betraying the **Son** of Man?	
22:69	**Son** of Man will be seated at	
22:70	Are you, then, the **Son** of God	
24: 7	**Son** of Man must be handed over	
Jn 1:34	that this is the **Son** of God.	
1:42	You are Simon **son** of John.	
1:45	Jesus **son** of Joseph from	
1:49	Rabbi, you are the **Son** of God	
1:51	descending upon the **Son** of Man.	
3:13	from heaven, the **Son** of Man.	
3:14	the **Son** of Man be lifted up,	
3:16	he gave his only **Son,** so that	
3:17	not send the **Son** into the world	
3:18	name of the only **Son** of God.	
3:35	The Father loves the **Son** and	
3:36	believes in the **Son** has eternal	
3:36	disobeys the **Son** will not see	
4: 5	had given to his **son** Joseph.	
4:12	with his **sons** and his flocks	
4:46	whose **son** lay ill in Capernaum.	

4:47	come down and heal his **son,** for	
4:50	Go; your **son** will live	
4:53	Your **son** will live." So he	
5:19	**Son** can do nothing on his own	
5:19	Father does, the **Son** does	
5:20	The Father loves the **Son** and	
5:21	so also the **Son** gives life	
5:22	given all judgment to the **Son,**	
5:23	so that all may honor the **Son**	
5:23	does not honor the **Son** does not	
5:25	voice of the **Son** of God, and	
5:26	he has granted the **Son** also to	
5:27	because he is the **Son** of Man.	
6:27	which the **Son** of Man will give	
6:40	see the **Son** and believe in him	
6:42	**son** of Joseph, whose father and	
6:53	eat the flesh of the **Son** of Man	
6:62	see the **Son** of Man ascending	
8:28	lifted up the **Son** of Man, then	
8:35	**son** has a place there forever.	
8:36	So if the **Son** makes you free	
9:19	Is this your **son,** who you say	
9:20	this is our **son,** and that he	
9:35	Do you believe in the **Son** of	
10:36	I said, 'I am God's **Son'?**	
11: 4	**Son** of God may be glorified	
11:27	Messiah, the **Son** of God, the	
12:23	hour has come for the **Son** of	
12:34	**Son** of Man must be lifted up?	
12:34	Who is this **Son** of Man?	
12:36	may become **children** of light	
13:31	**Son** of Man has been glorified	
14:13	may be glorified in the **Son.**	
17: 1	glorify your **Son** so that the	
17: 1	so that the **Son** may glorify you	
17:12	except the **one** destined to be	
19: 7	claimed to be the **Son** of God	
19:26	Woman, here is your **son.**	
20:31	Messiah, the **Son** of God, and	
Ac 2:17	**sons** and your daughters shall	
3:25	You are the **descendants** of the	
4:36	means "**son** of encouragement	
5:21	whole body of the **elders** of	
7:16	the **sons** of Hamor in Shechem.	
7:21	brought him up as her own **son.**	
7:23	his relatives, the **Israelites.**	
7:29	became the father of two **sons.**	
7:37	said to the **Israelites,** 'God	
7:56	**Son** of Man standing at the	

	9:15	and before the **people** of Israel
	9:20	He is the **Son** of God.
	10:36	he sent to the **people** of Israel
	13:10	and said, "You **son** of the devil
	13:21	Saul **son** of Kish, a man of the
	13:26	My brothers, you **descendants**
	13:33	psalm, 'You are my **Son;** today
	16: 1	Timothy, the **son** of a Jewish
	19:14	Seven **sons** of a Jewish high
	23: 6	I am a Pharisee, a **son** of
	23:16	Now the **son** of Paul's sister
Ro	1: 3	the gospel concerning his **Son,**
	1: 4	was declared to be **Son** of God
	1: 9	gospel of his **Son,** is my witness
	5:10	through the death of his **Son**
	8: 3	by sending his own **Son** in the
	8:14	Spirit of God are **children** of
	8:19	of the **children** of God;
	8:29	to the image of his **Son**
	8:32	not withhold his own **Son**
	9: 9	Sarah shall have a **son.**
	9:26	they shall be called **children**
	9:27	number of the **children** of
1C	1: 9	fellowship of his **Son,** Jesus
	15:28	**Son** himself will also be
2C	1:19	the **Son** of God, Jesus Christ
	3: 7	**people** of Israel could not gaze
	3:13	keep the **people** of Israel from
	6:18	you shall be my **sons** and
Ga	1:16	to reveal his **Son** to me, so
	2:20	I live by faith in the **Son** of
	3: 7	who believe are the **descendants**
	3:26	you are all **children** of God
	4: 4	God sent his **Son,** born of a
	4: 6	And because you are **children**
	4: 6	Spirit of his **Son** into our
	4: 7	no longer a slave but a **child**
	4: 7	if a **child** then also an heir
	4:22	Abraham had two **sons,** one by
	4:30	out the slave and her **child**
	4:30	for the **child** of the slave will
	4:30	inheritance with the **child** of
Ep	2: 2	among **those** who are disobedient
	3: 5	was not made known to **humankind**
	4:13	knowledge of the **Son** of God
	5: 6	on **those** who are disobedient.
Co	1:13	the kingdom of his beloved **Son,**
	3: 6	on **those** who are disobedient.
1Th	1:10	wait for his **Son** from heaven

	5: 5	you are all **children** of light
	5: 5	**children** of the day; we are not
2Th	2: 3	**one** destined for destruction
He	1: 2	spoken to us by a **Son,** whom he
	1: 5	You are my **Son;** today I have
	1: 5	Father, and he will be my **Son**"?
	1: 8	the **Son** he says, "Your throne
	2: 6	are mindful of them, or **mortals**
	2:10	bringing many **children** to glory
	3: 6	over God's house as a **son**
	4:14	Jesus, the **Son** of God, let us
	5: 5	You are my **Son,** today I have
	5: 8	Although he was a **Son,** he
	6: 6	are crucifying again the **Son**
	7: 3	resembling the **Son** of God
	7: 5	And those **descendants** of Levi
	7:28	appoints a **Son** who has been
	10:29	have spurned the **Son** of God
	11:21	blessed each of the **sons** of
	11:22	the exodus of the **Israelites**
	11:24	refused to be called a **son** of
	12: 5	that addresses you as **children**
	12: 5	My **child,** do not regard lightly
	12: 6	chastises every **child** whom he
	12: 7	God is treating you as **children**
	12: 7	for what **child** is there whom a
	12: 8	illegitimate . . . **children.**
Ja	2:21	he offered his **son** Isaac on the
1P	5:13	greetings; and so does my **son**
2P	1:17	This is my **Son,** my Beloved
1J	1: 3	and with his **Son** Jesus Christ.
	1: 7	blood of Jesus his **Son** cleanses
	2:22	denies the Father and the **Son.**
	2:23	No one who denies the **Son** has
	2:23	confesses the **Son** has the
	2:24	will abide in the **Son** and in
	3: 8	**Son** of God was revealed for
	3:23	name of his **Son** Jesus Christ
	4: 9	God sent his only **Son** into the
	4:10	sent his **Son** to be the atoning
	4:14	sent his **Son** as the Savior of
	4:15	confess that Jesus is the **Son**
	5: 5	believes that Jesus is the **Son**
	5: 9	he has testified to his **Son.**
	5:10	who believe in the **Son** of God
	5:10	has given concerning his **Son.**
	5:11	this life is in his **Son.**
	5:12	Whoever has the **Son** has life
	5:12	not have the **Son** of God does

	5:13	believe in the name of the **Son**
	5:20	And we know that the **Son** of God
	5:20	who is true, in his **Son** Jesus
2J	1: 3	Jesus Christ, the Father's **Son**
	1: 9	has both the Father and the **Son**
Re	1:13	saw one like the **Son** of Man
	2:14	block before the **people** of
	2:18	words of the **Son** of God, who
	7: 4	tribe of the **people** of Israel
	12: 5	And she gave birth to a **son,**
	14:14	cloud was one like the **Son** of
	21: 7	and they will be my **children.**
	21:12	twelve tribes of the **Israelites;**

5208   GO1 AG836 LN250
'υλη, WOOD

Ja	3: 5	great a **forest** is set ablaze by

5211   GO2 AG836 LN250
'υμεναιος, HYMENAEUS

1Ti	1:20	among them are **Hymenaeus** and
2Ti	2:17	Among them are **Hymenaeus** and

5212   GO11 AG836 LN250
'υμετερος, YOUR

Lk	6:20	for **yours** is the kingdom of God
	16:12	will give you what is **your own?**
Jn	7: 6	but **your** time is always here.
	8:17	In **your** law it is written that
	15:20	they will keep **yours** also.
Ac	27:34	it will help **you** survive; for
Ro	11:31	mercy **shown to you,** they too
1C	15:31	as my boasting **of you**—a boast
	16:17	have made up for **your** absence;
2C	8: 8	genuineness of **your** love
Ga	6:13	may boast about **your** flesh.

5214   GO4 AG836 LN250 B3:668 K8:489 R5215
'υμνεω, I SING

Mt	26:30	When they **had sung the hymn,**
Mk	14:26	When they **had sung the hymn,**
Ac	16:25	praying and **singing hymns** to
He	2:12	congregation I **will praise** you.

5215   GO2 AG836 LN250 B2:874 K8:489
'υμνος, HYMN

Ep	5:19	as you sing psalms and **hymns**
Co	3:16	psalms, **hymns,** and spiritual

5217   GO79 AG836 LN250 K8:504
'υπαγω, I GO OFF

Mt	4:10	**Away with you,** Satan! for it is
	5:24	**go;** first be reconciled to your
	5:41	**go** also the second mile.
	8: 4	**go,** show yourself to the priest
	8:13	**Go;** let it be done for you
	8:32	**Go!"** So they came out
	9: 6	our bed and **go** to your
	13:44	he **goes** and sells all that he
	16:23	**Get** behind me, Satan! You are a
	18:15	**go** and point out the fault when
	19:21	**go,** sell your possessions, and
	20: 4	You also **go** into the vineyard
	20: 7	You also **go** into the vineyard.
	20:14	Take what belongs to you and **go**
	21:28	Son, **go** and work in the
	26:18	**Go** into the city to a certain
	26:24	The Son of Man **goes** as it is
	27:65	soldiers; **go,** make it as secure
	28:10	**go** and tell my brothers to go
Mk	1:44	**go,** show yourself to the priest
	2:11	take your mat and **go** to your
	5:19	**Go** home to your friends
	5:34	**go** in peace, and be healed of
	6:31	many were coming and **going,** and
	6:33	Now many saw them **going** and
	6:38	How many loaves have you? **Go**
	7:29	you may **go**—the demon has
	8:33	**Get** behind me, Satan! For you
	10:21	**go,** sell what you own, and give
	10:52	**Go;** your faith has made you
	11: 2	**Go** into the village ahead of
	14:13	**Go** into the city, and a man
	14:21	For the Son of Man **goes** as it
	16: 7	But **go,** tell his disciples and
Lk	8:42	As he **went,** the crowds pressed
	10: 3	**Go** on your way. See, I am
	12:58	when you **go** with your accuser
	17:14	**Go** and show yourselves to the
	19:30	**Go** into the village ahead of
Jn	3: 8	comes from or where it **goes**
	4:16	**Go,** call your husband, and
	6:21	toward which they **were going**
	6:67	Do you also wish to **go away?**
	7: 3	Leave here and **go** to Judea so
	7:33	I am **going** to him who sent me.
	8:14	come from and where I **am going**
	8:14	come from or where I **am going.**

	8:21	I **am going away,** and you will
	8:21	Where I **am going,** you cannot
	8:22	Where I **am going,** you cannot
	9: 7	**Go,** wash in the pool of Siloam
	9:11	**Go** to Siloam and wash.' Then I
	11: 8	are you **going** there again?
	11:31	she **was going** to the tomb
	11:44	Unbind him, and let him **go.**
	12:11	many of the Jews **were deserting**
	12:35	not know where you **are going.**
	13: 3	from God and **was going** to God,
	13:33	Where I **am going,** you cannot
	13:36	Lord, where **are** you **going?**
	13:36	I **am going,** you cannot follow
	14: 4	to the place where I **am going**
	14: 5	do not know where you **are going**
	14:28	I **am going away,** and I am
	15:16	appointed you to **go** and bear
	16: 5	But now I **am going** to him who
	16: 5	asks me, 'Where **are** you **going?'**
	16:10	I **am going** to the Father and
	16:17	I **am going** to the Father'?
	18: 8	looking for me let these men **go**
	21: 3	I **am going** fishing." They said
Ja	2:16	**Go** in peace; keep warm and eat
1J	2:11	does not know the way to **go**
Re	10: 8	**Go,** take the scroll that is
	13:10	captive, into captivity you **go**
	14: 4	the Lamb wherever he **goes.** They
	16: 1	**Go** and pour out on the earth
	17: 8	pit and **go** to destruction. And
	17:11	and it **goes** to destruction.

5218   GO15 AG837 LN250 B2:179 K1:224 R5219
ὑπακοη, OBEDIENCE

Ro	1: 5	bring about the **obedience** of
	5:19	by the one man's **obedience** the
	6:16	as **obedient** slaves, you are
	6:16	death, or of **obedience,** which
	15:18	win **obedience** from the Gentiles
	16:19	while your **obedience** is known
	16:26	about the **obedience** of faith—
2C	7:15	he remembers the **obedience** of
	10: 5	thought captive to **obey** Christ.
	10: 6	when your **obedience** is complete.
Pm	1:21	Confident of your **obedience**
He	5: 8	learned **obedience** through what
1P	1: 2	to be **obedient** to Jesus Christ

	1:14	Like **obedient** children, do not
	1:22	souls by your **obedience** to the

5219   GO21 AG837 LN250 B2:179 K1:223 R5259,191
ὑπακουω, I OBEY

Mt	8:27	the winds and the sea **obey** him
Mk	1:27	spirits, and they **obey** him
	4:41	the wind and the sea **obey** him
Lk	8:25	water, and they **obey** him?
	17: 6	the sea,' and it would **obey** you
Ac	6: 7	priests **became obedient** to the
	12:13	named Rhoda came **to answer.**
Ro	6:12	to make you **obey** their passions
	6:16	slaves of the one whom you **obey**
	6:17	**have become obedient** from the
	10:16	not all **have obeyed** the good
Ep	6: 1	Children, **obey** your parents in
	6: 5	Slaves, **obey** your earthly
Ph	2:12	as you have always **obeyed** me
Co	3:20	Children, **obey** your parents in
	3:22	Slaves, **obey** your earthly
2Th	1: 8	who do not **obey** the gospel
	3:14	note of those who do not **obey**
He	5: 9	salvation for all who **obey** him,
	11: 8	By faith Abraham **obeyed** when
1P	3: 6	Thus Sarah **obeyed** Abraham and

5220   GO1 AG837 LN250 R5259,435
ὑπανδρος, ONE UNDER A MAN

Ro	7: 2	Thus a **married** woman is bound

5221   GO10 AG837 LN250 B1:324 K3:625
ὑπανταω, I MEET

Mt	8:28	coming out of the tombs **met** him
	28: 9	Suddenly Jesus **met** them
Mk	5: 2	with an unclean spirit **met** him.
Lk	8:27	who had demons **met** him. For a
	14:31	ten thousand to **oppose** the one
Jn	4:51	his slaves **met** him and told
	11:20	she went and **met** him, while
	11:30	place where Martha had **met** him.
	12:18	that the crowd went to **meet** him
Ac	16:16	we **met** a slave-girl who had a

5222   GO3 AG837 LN250 B1:324 K3:625 R5221
ὑπαντησις, MEETING

Mt	8:34	town came out to **meet** Jesus;
	25: 1	went to **meet** the bridegroom.
Jn	12:13	**meet** him, shouting, "Hosanna!

5223   GO2 AG837 LN250 B2:845 R5225
ὕπαρξις, POSSESSION

Ac	2:45	**goods** and distribute the
He	10:34	you yourselves **possessed**

5225   GO60 AG838 LN250
ὑπάρχω, I EXIST

Mt	19:21	go, sell your **possessions**
	24:47	charge of all his **possessions.**
	25:14	entrusted his **property** to them
Lk	7:25	live in **luxury** are in royal
	8: 3	for them out of their **resources**
	8:41	**a** leader of the synagogue.
	9:48	all of you **is** the greatest.
	11:13	If you then, who **are** evil
	11:21	guards his castle, his **property**
	12:15	in the abundance of **possessions**
	12:33	Sell your **possessions,** and give
	12:44	charge of all his **possessions.**
	14:33	give up all your **possessions.**
	16: 1	was squandering his **property.**
	16:14	who **were** lovers of money
	16:23	he was **being** tormented, he
	19: 8	half of my **possessions,** Lord
	23:50	**was** a good and righteous man
Ac	2:30	Since he **was** a prophet, he
	3: 2	And **a** man lame from birth was
	3: 6	I **have** no silver or gold, but
	4:32	ownership of any **possessions**
	4:34	for as many as **owned** lands or
	4:37	He sold a field that **belonged**
	5: 4	the **proceeds** at your disposal?
	7:55	**filled** with the Holy Spirit
	8:16	they had only **been** baptized in
	10:12	**were** all kinds of four-footed
	16: 3	his father **was** a Greek.
	16:20	our city; they **are** Jews
	16:37	men who **are** Roman citizens
	17:24	he who **is** Lord of heaven and
	17:27	he **is** not far from each one of
	17:29	Since we **are** God's offspring
	19:36	you ought to **be** quiet and do
	19:40	since there **is** no cause that we
	21:20	**are** all zealous for the law.
	22: 3	**being** zealous for God, just as
	27:12	the harbor **was** not suitable
	27:21	they **had been** without food
	27:34	it will **help** you survive
	28: 7	**were** lands belonging to the

	28:18	**was** no reason for the death
Ro	4:19	**was** about a hundred years old
1C	7:26	it **is** well for you to remain as
	11: 7	he **is** the image and reflection
	11:18	there **are** divisions among you
	12:22	to be weaker **are** indispensable,
	13: 3	I give away all my **possessions**
2C	8:17	he **is** more eager than ever
	12:16	(you say) since I **was** crafty
Ga	1:14	I **was** far more zealous for the
	2:14	If you, **though** a Jew, live like
Ph	2: 6	who, though he **was** in the form
	3:20	citizenship **is** in heaven
He	10:34	plundering of your **possessions**
Ja	2:15	If a brother or sister **is** naked
2P	1: 8	For if these things **are** yours
	2:19	**are** slaves of corruption; for
	3:11	**to be** in leading lives of

5226   GO1 AG838 LN251
ὑπείκω, I YIELD

He	13:17	Obey your leaders and **submit**

5227   GO2 AG838 LN251
ὑπεναντίος, OVER AGAINST

Co	2:14	record that stood **against** us
He	10:27	will consume the **adversaries.**

5228   GO150 AG838 LN251 B3:1171 K8:507
ὑπέρ, ON BEHALF OF, OVER, BEYOND
[MULTIPLE OCCURRENCES]

5229   GO3 AG839 LN251 R5228,142
ὑπεραίρω, I LIFT BEYOND

2C	12: 7	keep me from **being too elated**
	12: 7	keep me from **being too elated.**
2Th	2: 4	**exalts** himself **above** every

5230   GO1 AG839 LN251 B2:587
ὑπέρακμος, BEYOND PEAK

1C	7:36	if his **passions** are strong

5231   GO3 AG840 LN251 R5228,507
ὑπεράνω, UP ABOVE

Ep	1:21	**far above** all rule and
	4:10	who ascended **far above** all the
He	9: 5	**above** it were the cherubim

5232   GO1 AG840 LN251 B2:128 K8:517 R5228,837
ὑπεραυξάνω, I GROW BEYOND

2Th	1: 3	faith is **growing abundantly**

5233 GO1 AG840 LN251 B3:583 K7:743
ὑπερβαινω, I GO BEYOND
1Th 4: 6   that no one wrong or **exploit** a

5234 GO1 AG840 LN251 K8:520 R5235
ὑπερβαλλοντως, EXCEEDINGLY
2C 11:23   with **countless** floggings, and

5235 GO5 AG840 LN251 K8:520 R5228,906
ὑπερβαλλω, I EXCEED
2C 3:10   glory because of the **greater**
    9:14   **surpassing** grace of God that
Ep 1:19   is the **immeasurable** greatness
    2: 7   show the **immeasurable** riches
    3:19   love of Christ that **surpasses**

5236 GO8 AG840 LN251 K8:520 R5235
ὑπερβολη, EXCESS
Ro 7:13   become sinful **beyond measure.**
1C 12:31   a still **more excellent** way.
2C 1: 8   we were so **utterly,** unbearably
    4: 7   this **extraordinary** power
    4:17   eternal weight of glory **beyond**
    4:17   glory beyond all **measure,**
    12: 7   **exceptional** character of the
Ga 1:13   I was **violently** persecuting

5238 GO1 AG840 LN251
ὑπερεκεινα, BEYOND
2C 10:16   good news in lands **beyond** you

5238a GO3 AG840 LN251 B1:728 K6:61
ὑπερεκπερισσου, EXCESSIVELY BEYOND
Ep 3:20   accomplish **abundantly** far
    more
1Th 3:10   and day we pray **most
    earnestly**
    5:13   esteem them **very highly** in love

5239 GO1 AG840 LN251 K2:465 R5228,1614
ὑπερεκτεινω, I STRETCH BEYOND
2C 10:14   For we were not **overstepping**

5240 GO1 AG840 LN251 R5228,1632
ὑπερεκχυννω, I POUR OUT EXCESSIVELY
Lk 6:38   shaken together, **running over,**

5241 GO1 AG840 LN251 B2:874
ὑπερεντυγχανω, I APPEAL URGENTLY
Ro 8:26   Spirit **intercedes** with sighs

5242 GO5 AG840 LN251,2:609 K8:523 R5228,2192
ὑπερεχω, I EXCELL
Ro 13: 1   be subject to the **governing**
Ph 2: 3   regard others as **better than**
    3: 8   because of the **surpassing
    value**
    4: 7   **surpasses** all understanding
1P 2:13   of the emperor as **supreme,**

5243 GO1 AG841 LN251 B3:28 K8:525 R5244
ὑπερηφανια, ARROGANCE
Mk 7:22   envy, slander, **pride,** folly.

5244 GO5 AG841 LN251 B3:27 K8:525
ὑπερηφανος, ARROGANT
Lk 1:51   scattered the **proud** in the
Ro 1:30   God-haters, insolent, **haughty**
2Ti 3: 2   boasters, **arrogant,** abusive,
Ja 4: 6   God opposes the **proud,** but
1P 5: 5   opposes the **proud,** but gives

5244a GO2 AG841 LN252
ὑπερλιαν, VERY BEYOND
2C 11: 5   inferior . . . **super**-apostles
    12:11   inferior . . . **super**-apostles

5245 GO1 AG841 LN252 B1:650 K4:942 R5228,3528
ὑπερνικαω, I CONQUER BEYOND
Ro 8:37   we are **more than conquerors**

5246 GO2 AG841 LN252
ὑπερογκος, OVERINFLATED
2P 2:18   speak **bombastic** nonsense
Ju 1:16   they are **bombastic** in speech

5246a GO1 AG841 LN252
ὑπεροραω, I OVERLOOK
Ac 17:30   While God has **overlooked** the

5247 GO2 AG841 LN252 K8:523 R5242
ὑπεροχη, EXCELLENCE
1C 2: 1   to you in **lofty** words or
    wisdom
1Ti 2: 2   who are in **high positions,** so

5248 GO2 AG841 LN252 B1:730 K6:58 R5228,4052
ὑπερπερισσευω, I EXCEED BEYOND
Ro 5:20   grace **abounded all the
    more,**
2C 7: 4   I am **over**joyed in all our

5249　GO1 AG842 LN252 B1:728 R5228,4057
ὑπερπερισσῶς, EXCEEDINGLY BEYOND
Mk　7:37　astounded **beyond measure**

5250　GO1 AG842 LN252 B2:130 K6:263 R5228,4121
ὑπερπλεοναζω, I INCREASE BEYOND
1Ti　1:14　grace of our Lord **overflowed**

5251　GO1 AG842 LN252 B2:200 K8:606 R5228,5312
ὑπερυψοω, I ELEVATE BEYOND
Ph　2: 9　God also **highly exalted** him

5252　GO1 AG842 LN252 B2:617 R5228,5426
ὑπερφρονεω, I THINK BEYOND
Ro 12: 3　**think** of yourself **more highly**

5253　GO4 AG842 LN252
ὑπερωος, UPSTAIRS ROOM
Ac　1:13　went to the **room upstairs**
　　9:37　laid her in a **room upstairs.**
　　9:39　took him to the **room upstairs.**
　 20: 8　many lamps in the **room upstairs**

5254　GO1 AG842 LN252
ὑπεχω, I HOLD UNDER
Ju　1: 7　by **undergoing** a punishment of

5255　GO3 AG842 LN252 B2:179 K1:224 R5219
ὑπηκοος, OBEDIENT
Ac　7:39　were unwilling to **obey** him
2C　2: 9　whether you are **obedient** in
Ph　2: 8　became **obedient** to the point

5256　GO3 AG842 LN252 B3:544 K8:530 R5257
ὑπηρετεω, I ASSIST
Ac 13:36　he **had served** the purpose of
　 20:34　own hands to **support** myself
　 24:23　friends from **taking care** of his

5257　GO20 AG842 LN252 B3:544 K8:530
ὑπηρετης, ASSISTANT
Mt　5:25　and the judge to the **guard,** and
　 26:58　he sat with the **guards** in order
Mk 14:54　he was sitting with the **guards**
　 14:65　**guards** also took him over and
Lk　1: 2　eyewitnesses and **servants** of
　　4:20　gave it back to the **attendant**
Jn　7:32　Pharisees sent **temple police**
　　7:45　**temple police** went back to the
　　7:46　The **police** answered, "Never has

　 18: 3　detachment of **soldiers** together
　 18:12　Jewish **police** arrested Jesus
　 18:18　**police** had made a charcoal fire
　 18:22　**police** standing nearby struck
　 18:36　my **followers** would be fighting
　 19: 6　**police** saw him, they shouted
Ac　5:22　But when the **temple police** went
　　5:26　**temple police** and brought them
　 13: 5　John also to **assist** them.
　 26:16　to appoint you to **serve** and
1C　4: 1　as **servants** of Christ and

5258　GO6 AG843 LN252 B1:441 K8:545
ὑπνος, SLEEP
Mt　1:24　When Joseph awoke from **sleep**
Lk　9:32　were weighed down with **sleep**
Jn 11:13　was referring merely to **sleep.**
Ac 20: 9　into a deep **sleep** while Paul
　 20: 9　Overcome by **sleep,** he fell
Ro 13:11　for you to wake from **sleep**

5259　GO220 AG843 LN252 B3:1171
ὑπο, UNDER, BY [MULTIPLE OCCURRENCES]

5260　GO1 AG843 LN252 R5259,906
ὑποβαλλω, I INDUCE
Ac　6:11　Then they **secretly instigated**

5261　GO1 AG843 LN252 B2:291 K1:772
ὑπογραμμος, PATTERN
1P　2:21　leaving you an **example,** so that

5262　GO6 AG844 LN252 B2:290 K2:32 R5263
ὑποδειγμα, EXAMPLE
Jn 13:15　For I have set you an **example,**
He　4:11　fall through **such** disobedience
　　8: 5　sanctuary that is a **sketch** and
　　9:23　**sketches** of the heavenly things
Ja　5:10　As an **example** of suffering and
2P　2: 6　made them an **example** of what is

5263　GO6 AG844 LN253 R5259,1166
ὑποδεικνυμι, I GIVE AN EXAMPLE
Mt　3: 7　Who **warned** you to flee from the
Lk　3: 7　**warned** you to flee from the
　　6:47　I **will show** you what someone
　 12: 5　But I **will warn** you whom to
Ac　9:16　I myself **will show** him how much
　 20:35　**have given** you **an example** that

5264 GO4 AG844 LN253 R5259,1209
'υποδεχομαι, I ENTERTAIN
Lk 10:38 Martha **welcomed** him
            into her
    19: 6 was happy to **welcome** him.
Ac 17: 7 **entertained** them **as guests.**
Ja   2:25 by works when she **welcomed**

5265 GO3 AG844 LN253 K5:310 R5259,1209
'υποδεω, I TIE DOWN
Mk   6: 9 but to **wear** sandals and not to
Ac 12: 8 belt and **put on** your sandals
Ep   6:15 As **shoes** for your feet **put on**

5266 GO10 AG844 LN253 K5:310 R5265
'υποδημα, SANDAL
Mt   3:11 worthy to carry his **sandals.**
    10:10 or two tunics, or **sandals**
Mk   1: 7 untie the thong of his **sandals.**
Lk   3:16 untie the thong of his **sandals.**
    10: 4 no purse, no bag, no **sandals**
    15:22 on his finger and **sandals** on
    22:35 a purse, bag, or **sandals,** did
Jn   1:27 untie the thong of his **sandal**
Ac   7:33 Take off the **sandals** from your
    13:25 untie the thong of the **sandals**

5267 GO1 AG844 LN253 K8:557
'υποδικος, ACCOUNTABLE
Ro   3:19 be held **accountable** to God.

5268 GO2 AG844 LN253
'υποζυγιον, YOKE ANIMAL
Mt 21: 5 colt, the foal of a **donkey**
2P   2:16 a speechless **donkey** spoke

5269 GO1 AG844 LN253
'υποζωννυμι, I BELT UNDER
Ac 27:17 measures to **undergird** the ship

5270 GO11 AG844 LN253 R5259,2736
'υποκατω, UNDERNEATH
Mt 22:44 your enemies **under** your feet
Mk   6:11 dust that is **on** your feet as
     7:28 dogs **under** the table eat the
    12:36 I put your enemies **under** your
Lk   8:16 or puts it **under** a bed, but
Jn   1:50 I saw you **under** the fig tree
He   2: 8 subjecting all things **under**
Re   5: 3 **under** the earth was able to

5:13 on earth and **under** the
6: 9 I saw **under** the altar the souls
12: 1 with the moon **under** her feet

5271 GO1 AG845 LN253 B2:468 K8:559 R5259,2919
'υποκρινομαι, I PRETEND
Lk 20:20 spies who **pretended** to be

5272 GO6 AG845 LN253 B2:468 K8:559 R5271
'υποκρισις, HYPOCRISY
Mt 23:28 of **hypocrisy** and lawlessness.
Mk 12:15 But knowing their **hypocrisy**
Lk 12: 1 that is, their **hypocrisy.**
Ga   2:13 led astray by their **hypocrisy.**
1Ti 4: 2 through the **hypocrisy** of liars
1P   2: 1 guile, **insincerity,** envy, and

5273 GO18 AG845 LN253 B2:468 K8:559 R5271
'υποκριτης, HYPOCRITE
Mt   6: 2 **hypocrites** do in the synagogues
     6: 5 do not be like the **hypocrites**
     6:16 dismal, like the **hypocrites**
     7: 5 You **hypocrite,** first take the
    15: 7 **hypocrites!** Isaiah prophesied
    22:18 me to the test, you **hypocrites**
    23:13 Pharisees, **hypocrites!** For you
    23:15 **hypocrites!** For you cross sea
    23:23 **hypocrites!** For you tithe mint
    23:25 **hypocrites!** For you clean the
    23:27 **hypocrites!** For you are like
    23:29 **hypocrites!** For you build the
    24:51 put him with the **hypocrites**
Mk   7: 6 rightly about you **hypocrites**
Lk   6:42 **hypocrite,** first take the log
    12:56 **hypocrites!** You know how to
    13:15 **hypocrites!** Does not each of

5274 GO5 AG845 LN253 B3:747 K4:15 R5259,2983
'υπολαμβανω, I TAKE UP
Lk   7:43 I **suppose** the one for whom he
    10:30 Jesus **replied,** "A man was
            going
Ac   1: 9 cloud **took** him out of their
     2:15 are not drunk, as you **suppose**
3J   1: 8 Therefore we ought **to**
            support

5274a GO1 AG845 LN253 B3:247 K4:194
'υπολειμμα, REMNANT
Ro   9:27 a **remnant** of them will be saved

5275 GO1 AG845 LN253 B3:247 R5259,3007
'υπολειπω, I LEFT UNDER
Ro 11: 3 I alone **am left,** and they are

5276 GO1 AG845 LN253 K4:254 R5259,3025
'υποληνιον, PIT (UNDER WINE PRESS)
Mk 12: 1 dug a **pit for the wine press,**

5277 GO1 AG845 LN253
'υπολιμπανω, I LEAVE BEHIND
1P   2:21 **leaving** you an example, so that

5278 GO17 AG845 LN253 B2:764 K4:581 R5259,3306
'υπομενω, I ENDURE
Mt 10:22 **endures** to the end will be
    24:13 But the one who **endures** to the
Mk 13:13 **endures** to the end will be
Lk   2:43 boy Jesus **stayed behind** in
Ac 17:14 and Timothy **remained behind.**
Ro 12:12 **be patient** in suffering
1C 13: 7 hopes all things, **endures**
2Ti 2:10 Therefore I **endure** everything
     2:12 if we **endure,** we will also
He 10:32 you **endured** a hard struggle
    12: 2 **endured** the cross, disregarding
    12: 3 Consider him who **endured** such
    12: 7 **Endure** trials for the sake of
Ja   1:12 Blessed is anyone who **endures**
     5:11 those who **showed endurance**
1P   2:20 **endure** when you are beaten for
     2:20 **endure** when you do right and

5279 GO7 AG846 LN253 B3:230 R5259,3403
'υπομιμνησκω, I REMIND
Lk 22:61 Peter **remembered** the word of
Jn 14:26 **remind** you of all that I have
2Ti 2:14 **Remind** them of this, and warn
Ti   3: 1 **Remind** them to be subject to
2P   1:12 I intend to keep on **reminding**
3J   1:10 I will **call attention** to what
Ju   1: 5 Now I desire to **remind** you

5280 GO3 AG846 LN253 B3:230 K1:348 R5279
'υπομνησις, REMINDER
2Ti 1: 5 I am **reminded** of your sincere
2P   1:13 body, to refresh your **memory,**
     3: 1 sincere intention by **reminding**

5281 GO32 AG846 LN253 B2:772 K4:581 R5278
'υπομονη, PATIENCE

Lk   8:15 fruit with **patient endurance.**
    21:19 By your **endurance** you will
Ro   2: 7 who by **patiently** doing good
     5: 3 suffering produces **endurance,**
     5: 4 **endurance** produces character,
     8:25 we wait for it with **patience.**
    15: 4 so that by **steadfastness** and
    15: 5 May the God of **steadfastness**
2C   1: 6 you **patiently endure** the same
     6: 4 through great **endurance,**
    12:12 among you with utmost
              patience
Co   1:11 you be prepared to **endure**
1Th 1: 3 labor of love and **steadfastness**
2Th 1: 4 **steadfastness** and faith during
     3: 5 to the **steadfastness** of Christ.
1Ti 6:11 faith, love, **endurance,**
2Ti 3:10 my **patience,** my love, my
Ti   2: 2 in love, and in **endurance.**
He 10:36 For you need **endurance,** so
    12: 1 let us run with **perseverance**
Ja   1: 3 your faith produces **endurance;**
     1: 4 let **endurance** have its full
     5:11 heard of the **endurance** of Job
2P   1: 6 self-control with **endurance**
     1: 6 and **endurance** with godliness,
Re   1: 9 **patient endurance,** was on the
     2: 2 your **patient endurance.**
     2: 3 you are **enduring patiently** and
     2:19 service, and **patient endurance**
     3:10 my word of **patient endurance**
    13:10 call for the **endurance** and
    14:12 **endurance** of the saints,

5282 GO3 AG846 LN253 K4:1017 R5259,3539
'υπονοεω, I SUPPOSE
Ac 13:25 What do you **suppose** that
              I am?
    25:18 the crimes that I **was**
              expecting
    27:27 midnight the sailors **suspected**

5283 GO1 AG846 LN253 K4:1017 R5282
'υπονοια, CONJECTURE
1Ti 6: 4 slander, base **suspicions,**

5284 GO2 AG846 LN253 R5259,4126
'υποπλεω, I SAIL UNDER
Ac 27: 4 **sailed under** the lee of Cyprus
    27: 7 **sailed under** the lee of Crete

5285 ᴳᴼ1 ᴬᴳ846 ᴸᴺ254 ᴿ5259,4154
ὑποπνεω, I BLOW BY
Ac   27:13   south wind began **to blow,** they

5286 ᴳᴼ7 ᴬᴳ846 ᴸᴺ254 ᴿ5259,4228
ὑποποδιον, FOOTSTOOL
Mt   5:35   for it is his **footstool,** or by
Lk   20:43   your enemies your **footstool**
Ac   2:35   your enemies your **footstool**
       7:49   earth is my **footstool.** What
He   1:13   your enemies a **footstool** for
      10:13   made a **footstool** for his feet
Ja   2: 3   or, "Sit at my **feet,**"

5287 ᴳᴼ5 ᴬᴳ847 ᴸᴺ254 ᴮ1:710 ᴷ8:572
ὑποστασις, SUBSTANCE
2C   9: 4   of you—in this **undertaking.**
      11:17   to this boastful **confidence**
He   1: 3   imprint of God's **very being**
       3:14   hold our first **confidence** firm
      11: 1   Now faith is the **assurance** of

5288 ᴳᴼ4 ᴬᴳ847 ᴸᴺ254 ᴷ7:597 ᴿ5259,4724
ὑποστελλω, I WITHDRAW
Ac   20:20   I **did** not **shrink** from doing
      20:27   for I **did** not **shrink** from
Ga   2:12   he **drew back** and kept himself
He   10:38   in anyone who **shrinks back.**

5289 ᴳᴼ1 ᴬᴳ846 ᴸᴺ254 ᴮ1:713 ᴷ7:599 ᴿ5288
ὑποστολη, WITHDRAWAL
He   10:39   not among those who **shrink back**

5290 ᴳᴼ35 ᴬᴳ847 ᴸᴺ254 ᴿ5259,4762
ὑποστρεφω, I RETURN
Lk   1:56   and then **returned** to her home.
       2:20   The shepherds **returned**
       2:43   started **to return,** the boy
       2:45   **returned** to Jerusalem to search
       4: 1   **returned** from the Jordan and
       4:14   **returned** to Galilee, and a
       7:10   who had been sent **returned** to
       8:37   got into the boat and **returned.**
       8:39   **Return** to your home, and
       8:40   Now when Jesus **returned,**
       9:10   On their **return** the apostles
      10:17   The seventy **returned** with joy
      11:24   I **will return** to my house
      17:15   **turned back,** praising God
      17:18   found to **return** and give praise

      19:12   for himself and then **return.**
      23:48   **returned** home, beating their
      23:56   they **returned,** and prepared
      24: 9   and **returning** from the tomb,
      24:33   **returned** to Jerusalem; and they
      24:52   worshiped him, and **returned** to
Ac   1:12   **returned** to Jerusalem from the
       8:25   they **returned** to Jerusalem,
       8:28   and **was returning** home; seated
      12:25   Saul **returned** to Jerusalem
      13:13   left them and **returned** to
      13:34   no more to **return** to corruption
      14:21   they **returned** to Lystra, then
      20: 3   decided to **return** through
      21: 6   and they **returned** home.
      22:17   had **returned** to Jerusalem
      23:32   they **returned** to the barracks.
Ga   1:17   I **returned** to Damascus.
He   7: 1   met Abraham as he **was returning**
2P   2:21   to **turn back** from the holy

5291 ᴳᴼ1 ᴬᴳ847 ᴸᴺ254 ᴿ5259,4766
ὑποστρωννυω, I SPREAD
Lk   19:36   people kept **spreading** their

5292 ᴳᴼ4 ᴬᴳ847 ᴸᴺ254 ᴮ1:347 ᴷ8:46 ᴿ5293
ὑποταγη, SUBJECTION
2C   9:13   glorify God by your **obedience**
Ga   2: 5   we did not **submit** to them even
1Ti   2:11   in silence with full **submission**
       3: 4   keeping his children **submissive**

5293 ᴳᴼ38 ᴬᴳ847 ᴸᴺ254 ᴷ8:39 ᴿ5259,5021
ὑποτασσω, I SUBJECT
Lk   2:51   and was **obedient** to them.
      10:17   even the demons **submit** to us
      10:20   the spirits **submit** to you, but
Ro   8: 7   it does not **submit** to God's law
       8:20   creation **was subjected** to
       8:20   will of the one who **subjected**
      10: 3   have not **submitted** to God's
      13: 1   Let every person **be subject**
      13: 5   Therefore one must **be subject**
1C   14:32   spirits of prophets **are subject**
      14:34   **be subordinate,** as the law also
      15:27   things are put in **subjection**
      15:27   this does not **include** the one
      15:27   things in **subjection** under him.
      15:28   When all things are **subjected**
      15:28   himself will also be **subjected**

	15:28	put all things in **subjection**
	16:16	**put** yourselves **at the service**
Ep	1:22	And he **has put** all things under
	5:21	**Be subject** to one another out
	5:24	church **is subject** to Christ, so
Ph	3:21	all things **subject** to himself.
Co	3:18	Wives, **be subject** to your
Ti	2: 5	**being submissive** to their
	2: 9	Tell slaves **to be submissive**
	3: 1	Remind them to **be subject**
He	2: 5	Now God **did** not **subject** the
	2: 8	**subjecting** all things under
	2: 8	Now in **subjecting** all things
	2: 8	see everything in **subjection**
	12: 9	more willing to **be subject**
Ja	4: 7	**Submit** yourselves therefore to
1P	2:13	**accept the authority** of every
	2:18	Slaves, **accept the authority**
	3: 1	**accept the authority** of your
	3: 5	by **accepting the authority** of
	3:22	powers **made subject** to him.
	5: 5	must **accept the authority** of

5294 GO2 AG848 LN254 R5259,5087
ὑποτίθημι, I SET UNDER (I RISK)
Ro 16: 4   and who **risked** their necks
1Ti 4: 6   If you **put** these instructions

5295 GO1 AG848 LN254 R5259,5143
ὑποτρεχω, I RUN UNDER
Ac 27:16   By **running under** the lee of a

5296 GO2 AG848 LN254 B3:903 K8:246 R5259,5179
ὑποτυπωσις, MODEL
1Ti 1:16   making me an **example** to those
2Ti 1:13   Hold to the **standard** of sound

5297 GO3 AG848 LN254 R5259,5342
ὑποφερω, I ENDURE
1C 10:13   that you may be able **to endure**
2Ti 3:11   What persecutions I **endured!**
1P 2:19   you **endure** pain while suffering

5298 GO2 AG848 LN254 R5259,5562
ὑποχωρεω, I WITHDRAW
Lk 5:16   would **withdraw** to deserted
   9:10   **withdrew** privately to a city

5299 GO2 AG848 LN254 B1:162 K8:590
ὑπωπιαζω, I WEARY

Lk	18: 5	she may not **wear** me **out** by
1C	9:27	should not be **disqualified.**

5300 GO1 AG848 LN254 B1:117
ὑς, PIG
2P 2:22   The **sow** is washed only to

5301 GO2 AG849 LN254
ὑσσωπος, HYSSOP
Jn 19:29   wine on a branch of **hyssop** and
He 9:19   scarlet wool and **hyssop**

5302 GO16 AG849 LN254 B3:952 K8:592 R5306
ὑστερεω, I LACK

Mt	19:20	what **do** I still **lack**
Mk	10:21	You **lack** one thing; go, sell
Lk	15:14	**did** you **lack** anything?" They
Jn	2: 3	They **have no** wine."
Ro	3:23	sinned and **fall short** of the
1C	1: 7	so that you **are** not **lacking**
	8: 8	We **are no worse off** if we do
	12:24	honor to the **inferior** member,
2C	11: 5	**least inferior** to these super-
	11: 9	I was with you and **was in need**
	12:11	for I **am** not **at all inferior**
Ph	4:12	plenty and of **being in need.**
He	4: 1	seem **to have failed** to reach
	11:37	**destitute,** persecuted,
	12:15	See to it that no one **fails**

5303 GO9 AG849 LN254 K8:592 R5302
ὑστερημα, LACK

Lk	21: 4	**poverty** has put in all she had
1C	16:17	have made up for your **absence;**
2C	8:14	abundance and their **need,** so
	8:14	abundance may be for your **need**
	9:12	not only supplies the **needs** of
	11: 9	my **needs** were supplied by the
Ph	2:30	that you **could not give** me.
Co	1:24	what **is lacking** in Christ's
1Th	3:10	**is lacking** in your faith.

5304 GO2 AG849 LN255 B3:952 K8:592 R5302
ὑστερησις, LACK
Mk 12:44   out of her **poverty** has put in
Ph 4:11   referring to being in **need**

5306 GO12 AG849 LN255 B3:952 K8:592
ὑστερος, LATER
Mt 4: 2   **afterwards** he was famished.

21:29	but **later** he changed his mind
21:32	even **after** you saw it, you did
21:37	**Finally** he sent his son to them
22:27	**Last** of all, the woman herself
25:11	**Later** the other bridesmaids
26:60	**At last** two came forward
Mk 16:14	**Later** he appeared to the eleven
Lk 20:32	**Finally** the woman also died.
Jn 13:36	but you will follow **afterward**
1Ti 4: 1	**later** times some will renounce
He 12:11	**later** it yields the peaceful

5307　GO1 AG849 LN255
'υφαντος, WOVEN

Jn 19:23　**woven** in one piece from the top.

5308　GO11 AG849 LN255 B2:198 R5311
'υψηλος, HIGH

Mt 4: 8	devil took him to a very **high**
17: 1	John and led them up a **high**
Mk 9: 2	led them up a **high** mountain
Lk 16:15	what is **prized** by human beings
Ac 13:17	with **uplifted** arm he led them
Ro 11:20	do not become **proud,** but stand
12:16	do not be **haughty,** but
He 1: 3	hand of the Majesty on **high,**
7:26	and **exalted above** the heavens.
Re 21:10	away to a great, **high** mountain
21:12	It has a great, **high** wall with

5309　GO1 AG850 LN255 B2:198 R5308,5426
'υψηλοφρονεω, I THINK HIGHLY

1Ti 6:17　command them not **to be haughty**

5310　GO13 AG850 LN255 B2:198 K8:614 R5311
'υψιστος, HIGHEST

Mt 21: 9	Hosanna in the **highest** heaven
Mk 5: 7	Jesus, Son of the **Most High** God
11:10	Hosanna in the **highest** heaven
Lk 1:32	Son of the **Most High,** and the
1:35	power of the **Most High** will
1:76	prophet of the **Most High**
2:14	Glory to God in the **highest**
6:35	be children of the **Most High**
8:28	Son of the **Most High** God?
19:38	glory in the **highest** heaven
Ac 7:48	**Most High** does not dwell
16:17	are slaves of the **Most High** God
He 7: 1	priest of the **Most High** God,

5311　GO6 AG850 LN255 B2:198 K8:602
'υψος, HEIGHT

Lk 1:78	dawn from on **high** will break
24:49	clothed with power from on **high**
Ep 3:18	length and **height** and depth,
4: 8	he ascended on **high** he made
Ja 1: 9	boast in being **raised up,**
Re 21:16	width and **height** are equal.

5312　GO20 AG850 LN255 B2:200 K8:606 R5311
'υψοω, I ELEVATE

Mt 11:23	will you **be exalted** to heaven?
23:12	All who **exalt** themselves will
23:12	themselves **will be exalted.**
Lk 1:52	and **lifted up** the lowly;
10:15	will you **be exalted** to heaven?
14:11	For all who **exalt** themselves
14:11	themselves **will be exalted.**
18:14	all who **exalt** themselves will
18:14	themselves **will be exalted.**
Jn 3:14	Moses **lifted up** the serpent
3:14	the Son of Man be **lifted up,**
8:28	have **lifted up** the Son of Man
12:32	I **am lifted up** from the earth,
12:34	must **be lifted up?** Who is this
Ac 2:33	Being therefore **exalted** at the
5:31	God **exalted** him at his right
13:17	**made** the people **great** during
2C 11: 7	that you **might be exalted**
Ja 4:10	Lord, and he **will exalt** you.
1P 5: 6	he **may exalt** you in due time.

5313　GO2 AG851 LN255 B2:198 K8:613 R5312
'υψωμα, HEIGHT

| Ro 8:39 | nor **height,** nor depth, nor |
| 2C 10: 5 | every **proud obstacle** raised up |

φ

5314　GO2 AG851 LN255 R2068
φαγος, EATER

| Mt 11:19 | Look, a **glutton** and a drunkard |
| Lk 7:34 | **glutton** and a drunkard, |

5314a　GO1 AG851 LN255
φαιλονης, COAT

| 2Ti 4:13 | When you come, bring the **cloak** |

5316 GO31 AG851 LN255 B2:487 K9:1
φαινω, I SHINE

Mt	1:20	Lord **appeared** to him in a dream
	2: 7	time when the star **had appeared**
	2:13	angel of the Lord **appeared** to
	2:19	**appeared** in a dream to Joseph
	6: 5	they **may be seen** by others.
	6:16	so as **to show** others that they
	6:18	that your fasting **may be seen**
	9:33	like this **been seen** in Israel
	13:26	then the weeds **appeared** as well
	23:27	on the outside **look** beautiful
	23:28	outside **look** righteous
	24:27	from the east and **flashes** as
	24:30	Son of Man **will appear** in
Mk	14:64	What is your **decision**
	16: 9	he **appeared** first to Mary
Lk	9: 8	some that Elijah **had appeared**
	24:11	words **seemed** to them an idle
Jn	1: 5	light **shines** in the darkness
	5:35	He was a burning and **shining**
Ro	7:13	sin **might be shown** to be sin
2C	13: 7	we **may appear** to have met the
Ph	2:15	in which you **shine** like stars
He	11: 3	things that **are** not **visible.**
Ja	4:14	mist that **appears** for a little
1P	4:18	what **will become** of the ungodly
2P	1:19	lamp **shining** in a dark place
1J	2: 8	true light is already **shining.**
Re	1:16	sun **shining** with full force.
	8:12	day was kept from **shining,**
	18:23	light of a lamp **will shine** in
	21:23	no need of sun or moon to **shine**

5317 GO1 AG852 LN255
φαλεκ, PHALEK (PELEG)

| Lk | 3:35 | son of **Peleg,** son of Eber, son |

5318 GO18 AG852 LN255 B3:317 K9:2
φανερος, EVIDENT

Mt	12:16	them not to make him **known.**
Mk	3:12	them not to make him **known.**
	4:22	secret, except to come to **light**
	6:14	Jesus' name had become **known.**
Lk	8:17	will not be **disclosed,** nor is
	8:17	become known and come to **light.**
Ac	4:16	For it is **obvious** to all who
	7:13	Joseph made himself **known**
Ro	1:19	can be known about God is **plain**
	2:28	not a Jew who is one **outwardly**
	2:28	circumcision something **external**
1C	3:13	builder will become **visible**
	11:19	**clear** who among you are genuine
	14:25	heart are **disclosed,** that
Ga	5:19	works of the flesh are **obvious:**
Ph	1:13	so that it has become **known**
1Ti	4:15	that all **may see** your progress.
1J	3:10	of the devil **are revealed** in

5319 GO49 AG852 LN255 B3:317 K9:3 R5318
φανεροω, I DEMONSTRATE

Mk	4:22	except **to come to light.**
	16:12	he **appeared** in another form
	16:14	Later he **appeared** to the eleven
Jn	1:31	he **might be revealed** to Israel
	2:11	**revealed** his glory; and his
	3:21	it **may be clearly seen** that
	7: 4	**show** yourself to the world."
	9: 3	works **might be revealed** in him
	17: 6	I **have made** your name **known** to
	21: 1	Jesus **showed** himself again to
	21: 1	he **showed** himself in this way.
	21:14	third time that Jesus **appeared**
Ro	1:19	because God **has shown** it to
	3:21	God **has been disclosed,** and is
	16:26	**is** now **disclosed,** and through
1C	4: 5	**will disclose** the purposes of
2C	2:14	through us **spreads** in every
	3: 3	**show** that you are a letter of
	4:10	Jesus may also **be made visible**
	4:11	Jesus **may be made visible** in
	5:10	all of us must **appear** before
	5:11	ourselves **are well known** to God
	5:11	we **are** also **well known** to your
	7:12	**might be made known** to you
	11: 6	**have made** this **evident** to you.
Ep	5:13	everything **exposed** by the light
	5:14	everything that **becomes visible**
Co	1:26	**has** now **been revealed** to his
	3: 4	who is your life **is revealed**
	3: 4	**will be revealed** with him in
	4: 4	that I **may reveal** it **clearly,**
1Ti	3:16	He **was revealed** in flesh,
2Ti	1:10	but it **has** now **been revealed**
Ti	1: 3	he **revealed** his word through
He	9: 8	**has** not yet **been disclosed**
	9:26	**has appeared** once for all at
1P	1:20	**was revealed** at the end of the
	5: 4	the chief shepherd **appears,** you

1J	1: 2	this life **was revealed,** and we
	1: 2	and **was revealed** to us—
	2:19	they **made** it **plain** that none of
	2:28	he **is revealed** we may have
	3: 2	**has** not yet **been revealed.**
	3: 2	when he **is revealed,** we will be
	3: 5	he **was revealed** to take away
	3: 8	Son of God **was revealed** for
	4: 9	God's love **was revealed** among
Re	3:18	your nakedness from **being seen**
	15: 4	judgments **have been revealed**

5320   GO2 AG853 LN255 B3:317 R5318
φανερως, OPENLY
Mk	1:45	no longer go into a town **openly**
Jn	7:10	he also went, not **publicly** but
Ac	10: 3	he **clearly** saw an angel of God

5321   GO2 AG853 LN255 B3:317 K9:6 R5319
φανερωσις, DEMONSTRATION
| 1C | 12: 7 | is given the **manifestation** of |
| 2C | 4: 2 | by the **open** statement of the |

5322   GO1 AG853 LN255 R5316
φανος, TORCH
| Jn | 18: 3 | with lanterns and **torches** and |

5323   GO1 AG853 LN256
φανουηλ, PHANUEL
| Lk | 2:36 | Anna the daughter of **Phanuel** |

5324   GO1 AG853 LN256 B3:317 K9:6 R5316
φανταζω, I APPEAR
| He | 12:21 | terrifying was the **sight** that |

5325   GO1 AG853 LN256 B3:891 R5324
φαντασια, FANTASY
| Ac | 25:23 | Bernice came with great **pomp** |

5326   GO2 AG853 LN256 B3:317 K9:6 R5324
φαντασμα, GHOST
| Mt | 14:26 | It is a **ghost!"** And they cried |
| Mk | 6:49 | thought it was a **ghost** and |

5327   GO1 AG853 LN256
φαραγξ, RAVINE
| Lk | 3: 5 | Every **valley** shall be filled |

5328   GO5 AG853 LN256
φαραω, PHARAOH

Ac	7:10	before **Pharaoh,** king of Egypt
	7:13	family became known to **Pharaoh.**
	7:21	**Pharaoh's** daughter adopted him
Ro	9:17	scripture says to **Pharaoh,** "I
He	11:24	a son of **Pharaoh's** daughter,

5329   GO3 AG853 LN256
φαρες, PHARES (PEREZ)
Mt	1: 3	Judah the father of **Perez** and
	1: 3	and **Perez** the father of Hezron
Lk	3:33	son of **Perez,** son of Judah,

5330   GO99 AG853 LN256 B2:810 K9:11
φαρισαιος, PHARISEE
Mt	3: 7	**Pharisees** and Sadducees coming
	5:20	**Pharisees,** you will never enter
	9:11	When the **Pharisees** saw this
	9:14	**Pharisees** fast often, but your
	9:34	**Pharisees** said, "By the ruler
	12: 2	When the **Pharisees** saw it,
	12:14	But the **Pharisees** went out
	12:24	But when the **Pharisees** heard
	12:38	**Pharisees** said to him, "Teacher
	15: 1	Then **Pharisees** and scribes came
	15:12	**Pharisees** took offense when
	16: 1	**Pharisees** and Sadducees came
	16: 6	yeast of the **Pharisees** and
	16:11	yeast of the **Pharisees** and
	16:12	teaching of the **Pharisees**
	19: 3	Some **Pharisees** came to him,
	21:45	**Pharisees** heard his parables
	22:15	**Pharisees** went and plotted to
	22:34	When the **Pharisees** heard
	22:41	**Pharisees** were gathered
	23: 2	**Pharisees** sit on Moses' seat;
	23:13	**Pharisees,** hypocrites! For you
	23:15	**Pharisees,** hypocrites! For you
	23:23	**Pharisees,** hypocrites! For you
	23:25	**Pharisees,** hypocrites! For you
	23:26	You blind **Pharisee!** First clean
	23:27	**Pharisees,** hypocrites! For you
	23:29	**Pharisees,** hypocrites! For you
	27:62	**Pharisees** gathered before
Mk	2:16	scribes of the **Pharisees** saw
	2:18	**Pharisees** were fasting; and
	2:18	disciples of the **Pharisees** fast
	2:24	**Pharisees** said to him, "Look
	3: 6	The **Pharisees** went out and
	7: 1	Now when the **Pharisees** and some

7: 3	**Pharisees,** and all the Jews, do
7: 5	**Pharisees** and the scribes asked
8:11	The **Pharisees** came and began to
8:15	yeast of the **Pharisees** and the
10: 2	Some **Pharisees** came, and to test
12:13	they sent to him some **Pharisees**

Lk
5:17	**Pharisees** and teachers of the
5:21	**Pharisees** began to question,
5:30	The **Pharisees** and their scribes
5:33	**Pharisees,** frequently fast and
6: 2	But some of the **Pharisees** said
6: 7	**Pharisees** watched him to see
7:30	**Pharisees** and the lawyers
7:36	One of the **Pharisees** asked
7:36	he went into the **Pharisee's**
7:37	eating in the **Pharisee's** house
7:39	**Pharisee** who had invited him
11:37	**Pharisee** invited him to dine
11:38	The **Pharisee** was amazed to see
11:39	**Pharisees** clean the outside
11:42	But woe to you **Pharisees**
11:43	Woe to you **Pharisees**
11:53	the scribes and the **Pharisees**
12: 1	the yeast of the **Pharisees**
13:31	some **Pharisees** came and said
14: 1	of a leader of the **Pharisees**
14: 3	asked the lawyers and **Pharisees**
15: 2	the **Pharisees** and the scribes
16:14	The **Pharisees,** who were lovers
17:20	asked by the **Pharisees** when
18:10	one a **Pharisee** and the other
18:11	**Pharisee,** standing by himself
19:39	Some of the **Pharisees**

Jn
1:24	been sent from the **Pharisees**
3: 1	was a **Pharisee** named Nicodemus
4: 1	learned that the **Pharisees**
7:32	The **Pharisees** heard the crowd
7:32	**Pharisees** sent temple police
7:45	the chief priests and **Pharisees**
7:47	Then the **Pharisees** replied
7:48	the **Pharisees** believed in him
8: 3	The scribes and the **Pharisees**
8:13	Then the **Pharisees** said to him
9:13	They brought to the **Pharisees**
9:15	Then the **Pharisees** also began
9:16	Some of the **Pharisees** said
9:40	Some of the **Pharisees** near him
11:46	went to the **Pharisees** and told
11:47	the **Pharisees** called a meeting

11:57	the **Pharisees** had given orders
12:19	The **Pharisees** then said to one
12:42	But because of the **Pharisees**
18: 3	chief priests and the **Pharisees**

Ac
5:34	But a **Pharisee** in the council
15: 5	to the sect of the **Pharisees**
23: 6	and others were **Pharisees**
23: 6	I am a **Pharisee,** a son of
23: 6	Pharisee, a son of **Pharisees**
23: 7	began between the **Pharisees**
23: 9	scribes of the **Pharisees'** group
26: 5	and lived as a **Pharisee**

Ph
3: 5	as to the law, a **Pharisee**

5331　　GO2　AG854　LN256　B2:552　R5332
φαρμακεια, MAGIC, SORCERY
Ga　5:20　idolatry, **sorcery,** enmities
Re　18:23　were deceived by your **sorcery**

5331a　　GO1　AG854　LN256　B2:552
φαρμακον, MAGIC, SORCERY
Re　9:21　murders or their **sorceries**

5333　　GO2　AG854　LN256　B2:552　R5332
φαρμακος, MAGICIAN
Re　21: 8　the fornicators, the **sorcerers**
　　22:15　are the dogs and **sorcerers**

5334　　GO1　AG854　LN256　R5346
φασις, NEWS
Ac　21:31　**word** came to the tribune

5335　　GO3　AG854　LN256
φασκω, I AFFIRM
Ac　24: 9　**asserting** that all this was
　　25:19　whom Paul **asserted** to be alive
Ro　1:22　**Claiming** to be wise

5336　　GO4　AG854　LN256　K9:49
φατνη, FEEDING TROUGH
Lk　2: 7　and laid him in a **manger**
　　2:12　cloth and lying in a **manger**
　　2:16　the child lying in the **manger**
　　13:15　or his donkey from the **manger**

5337　　GO6　AG854　LN256　B1:561
φαυλος, FOUL
Jn　3:20　all who do **evil** hate the light
　　5:29　and those who have done **evil**
Ro　9:11　had done anything good or **bad**

2C	5:10	the body, whether good or **evil**
Ti	2: 8	having nothing **evil** to say
Ja	3:16	be disorder and **wickedness**

5338   GO2 AG854 LN256 B2:484
φεγγος, LIGHT

Mt	24:29	moon will not give its **light**
Mk	13:24	moon will not give its **light**

5339   GO10 AG854 LN256
φειδομαι, I SPARE

Ac	20:29	not **sparing** the flock
Ro	8:32	**did** not **withhold** his own Son
	11:21	For if God **did** not **spare**
	11:21	perhaps he **will** not **spare** you
1C	7:28	and I **would spare** you that
2C	1:23	it was to **spare** you that I did
	12: 6	But I **refrain** from it
	13: 2	I will not **be lenient**
2P	2: 4	if God **did** not **spare** the angels
	2: 5	if he **did** not **spare** the ancient

5340   GO2 AG854 LN256 B1:214 R5339
φειδομενως, SPARINGLY

2C	9: 6	the one who sows **sparingly**
	9: 6	will also reap **sparingly**

5342   GO66 AG854 LN256 B3:1195 K9:56
φερω, I BEAR, I BRING, I CARRY

Mt	14:11	head **was brought** on a platter
	14:11	who **brought** it to her mother
	14:18	**Bring** them here to me
	17:17	**Bring** him here to me
Mk	1:32	they **brought** to him all
	2: 3	**bringing** to him a paralyzed
	4: 8	soil and **brought** forth grain
	6:27	orders to **bring** John's head
	6:28	**brought** his head on a platter
	7:32	**brought** to him a deaf man
	8:22	people **brought** a blind man
	9:17	I **brought** you my son
	9:19	**Bring** him to me
	9:20	they **brought** the boy to him
	11: 2	untie it and **bring** it
	11: 7	Then they **brought** the colt
	12:15	**Bring** me a denarius and let me
	12:16	And they **brought** one
	15:22	**brought** Jesus to the place
Lk	5:18	**carrying** a paralyzed man
	15:23	And **get** the fatted calf

	23:26	made him **carry** it behind Jesus
	24: 1	**taking** the spices that they
Jn	2: 8	**take** it to the chief steward
	2: 8	So they **took** it
	4:33	Surely no one **has brought** him
	12:24	it **bears** much fruit
	15: 2	every branch in me that **bears**
	15: 2	Every branch that **bears** fruit
	15: 2	he prunes to make it **bear** more
	15: 4	the branch cannot **bear** fruit
	15: 5	and I in them **bear** much fruit
	15: 8	that you **bear** much fruit
	15:16	appointed you to go and **bear**
	18:29	do you **bring** against this man
	19:39	**bringing** a mixture of myrrh
	20:27	**Put** your finger here and see
	20:27	**Reach out** your hand and put it
	21:10	**Bring** some of the fish
	21:18	**take** you where you do not wish
Ac	2: 2	like the **rush** of a violent wind
	4:34	**brought** the proceeds of what
	4:37	then **brought** the money
	5: 2	**brought** only a part and laid it
	5:16	**bringing** the sick and those
	12:10	the iron gate **leading** into the
	14:13	**brought** oxen and garlands
	25:18	they did not **charge** him with
	27:15	we **gave way** to it and were
	27:17	sea anchor and so **were driven**
Ro	9:22	**has endured** with much patience
2Ti	4:13	**bring** the cloak that I left
He	1: 3	and he **sustains** all things
	6: 1	let us **go on** toward perfection
	9:16	made it **must be established**
	12:20	For they **could** not **endure**
	13:13	and **bear** the abuse he endured
1P	1:13	that Jesus Christ **will bring**
2P	1:17	when that voice **was conveyed**
	1:18	this voice **come** from heaven
	1:21	because no prophecy ever **came**
	1:21	men and women **moved** by the Holy
	2:11	**do** not **bring** against them
2J	1:10	does not **bring** this teaching
Re	21:24	**will bring** their glory into it
	21:26	**will bring** into it the glory

5343   GO29 AG855 LN256 B1:558
φευγω, I FLEE

Mt	2:13	his mother, and **flee** to Egypt

	3: 7	**flee** from the wrath to come
	8:33	The swineherds **ran off**
	10:23	**flee** to the next
	23:33	**escape** being sentenced to hell
	24:16	then those in Judea must **flee**
	26:56	disciples deserted him and **fled**
Mk	5:14	swineherds **ran off** and told it
	13:14	then those in Judea must **flee**
	14:50	of them deserted him and **fled**
	14:52	linen cloth and **ran off** naked
	16: 8	went out and **fled** from the tomb
Lk	3: 7	Who warned you to **flee**
	8:34	they **ran off** and told it
	21:21	Then those in Judea must **flee**
Jn	10: 5	but they **will run** from him
	10:12	leaves the sheep and **runs away**
Ac	7:29	**fled** and became a resident
	27:30	tried **to escape** from the ship
1C	6:18	**Shun** fornication
	10:14	**flee** from the worship of idols
1Ti	6:11	man of God, **shun** all this
2Ti	2:22	**Shun** youthful passions
He	11:34	**escaped** the edge of the sword
Ja	4: 7	and he **will flee** from you
Re	9: 6	but death **will flee** from them
	12: 6	woman **fled** into the wilderness
	16:20	And every island **fled** away
	20:11	heaven **fled** from his presence

5344   GO9 AG846 LN256
φηλιξ, FELIX

Ac	23:24	safely to **Felix** the governor
	23:26	Excellency the governor **Felix,**
	24: 3	**Your Excellency,** because of
	24:22	But **Felix,** who was rather well
	24:24	Some days later when **Felix** came
	24:25	**Felix** became frightened
	24:27	**Felix** was succeeded by Porcius
	24:27	**Felix** left Paul in prison
	25:14	who was left in prison by **Felix**

5345   GO2 AG856 LN257 R5346
φημη, REPORT

Mt	9:26	And the **report** of this spread
Lk	4:14	and a **report** about him spread

5346   GO66 AG856 LN257 B3:341
φημι, I SAY

Mt	4: 7	Jesus **said** to him
	8: 8	The centurion **answered**
	13:28	He **answered**
	13:29	But he **replied**
	14: 8	by her mother, she **said**
	17:26	Jesus **said** to him
	19:21	Jesus **said** to him
	21:27	And he **said** to them
	22:37	He **said** to him
	25:21	His master **said** to him
	25:23	His master **said** to him
	26:34	Jesus **said** to him
	26:61	This fellow **said**
	27:11	Jesus **said**
	27:23	Then he **asked**
	27:65	Pilate **said** to them
Mk	9:12	He **said** to them
	9:38	John **said** to him
	10:20	He **said** to him
	10:29	Jesus **said**
	12:24	Jesus **said** to them
	14:29	Peter **said** to him
Lk	7:40	Jesus spoke up and **said**
	7:44	he **said** to Simon
	15:17	he came to himself he **said**
	22:58	else, on seeing him, **said**
	22:58	But Peter **said**
	22:70	He **said** to them
	23: 3	He **answered,** "You say so."
	23:40	the other rebuked him, **saying**
Jn	1:23	He **said**
	9:38	He **said**
	18:29	went out to them and **said**
Ac	2:38	Peter **said** to them
	7: 2	And Stephen **replied**
	8:36	and the eunuch **said**
	10:28	and he **said** to them
	10:30	Cornelius **replied**
	10:31	He **said**
	16:30	brought them outside and **said**
	16:37	But Paul **replied**
	17:22	of the Areopagus and **said**
	19:35	quieted the crowd, he **said**
	21:37	The tribune **replied**
	22: 2	Then he **said**
	22:27	And he **said,** "Yes."
	22:28	Paul **said**
	23: 5	And Paul **said**
	23:17	one of the centurions and **said**
	23:18	to the tribune, and **said**
	23:35	he **said**

	25: 5	"So," he **said,** "let those
	25:22	Tomorrow," he **said**
	25:24	And Festus **said**
	26: 1	Agrippa **said** to Paul
	26:24	Festus **exclaimed**
	26:25	But Paul **said**
	26:32	Agrippa **said** to Festus
Ro	3: 8	people slander us by **saying**
1C	6:16	For it is **said**
	7:29	I **mean,** brothers and sisters
	10:15	judge for yourselves what I **say**
	10:19	What do I **imply** then
	15:50	What I am **saying**
2C	10:10	For they **say**
He	8: 5	See **that** you make everything

5347 GO13 AG856 LN257
φηστος, FESTUS

Ac	24:27	was succeeded by Porcius **Festus**
	25: 1	days after **Festus** had arrived
	25: 4	**Festus** replied that Paul
	25: 9	But **Festus,** wishing to do
	25:12	Then **Festus,** after he had
	25:13	at Caesarea to welcome **Festus**
	25:14	**Festus** laid Paul's case
	25:22	Agrippa said to **Festus**
	25:23	Then **Festus** gave the order
	25:24	And **Festus** said
	26:24	this defense, **Festus** exclaimed
	26:25	most excellent **Festus**
	26:32	Agrippa said to **Festus**

5348 GO7 AG856 LN257 B2:932 K9:88
φθανω, I ARRIVE

Mt	12:28	kingdom of God **has come** to you
Lk	11:20	kingdom of God **has come** to you
Ro	9:31	**did** not **succeed** in fulfilling
2C	10:14	the first **to come** all the way
Ph	3:16	fast to what we **have attained**
1Th	2:16	God's wrath has **overtaken** them
	4:15	**will** by no means **precede** those

5349 GO6 AG857 LN257 B1:468 K9:93 R5351
φθαρτος, CORRUPTIBLE

Ro	1:23	for images resembling a **mortal**
1C	9:25	to receive a **perishable** wreath
	15:53	For this **perishable** body
	15:54	When this **perishable** body
1P	1:18	not with **perishable** things
	1:23	not of **perishable** but of

5350 GO3 AG857 LN257
φθεγγομαι, I SPEAK

Ac	4:18	not **to speak** or teach at all
2P	2:16	a speechless donkey **spoke**
	2:18	they **speak** bombastic nonsense

5351 GO9 AG857 LN257 B1:467 K9:93
φθειρω, I CORRUPT

1C	3:17	anyone **destroys** God's temple
	3:17	God **will destroy** that person
	15:33	Bad company **ruins** good morals
2C	7: 2	we have **corrupted** no one
	11: 3	thoughts will be **led astray**
Ep	4:22	**corrupt** and deluded by its
2P	2:12	they also **will be destroyed**
Ju	1:10	they **are destroyed** by
Re	19: 2	the great whore who **corrupted**

5352 GO1 AG857 LN257
φθινοπωρινος, LATE AUTUMN

Ju	1:12	**autumn** trees without fruit

5353 GO2 AG857 LN257 R5350
φθογγος, SOUND

Ro	10:18	Their **voice** has gone out to all
1C	14: 7	do not give distinct **notes**

5354 GO1 AG857 LN257 B1:557 R5355
φθονεω, I ENVY

Ga	5:26	another, **envying** one another

5355 GO9 AG857 LN257 B1:557
φθονος, ENVY

Mt	27:18	that it was out of **jealousy**
Mk	15:10	that it was out of **jealousy**
Ro	1:29	Full of **envy,** murder, strife
Ga	5:21	**envy,** drunkenness, carousing
Ph	1:15	Some proclaim Christ from **envy**
1Ti	6: 4	From these come **envy**
Ti	3: 3	days in malice and **envy**
Ja	4: 5	yearns **jealously** for the spirit
1P	2: 1	all guile, insincerity, **envy**

5356 GO9 AG858 LN257 B1:467 K9:93 R5351
φθορα, CORRUPTION

Ro	8:21	free from its bondage to **decay**
1C	15:42	What is sown is **perishable**
	15:50	nor does the **perishable**
Ga	6: 8	you will reap **corruption**
Co	2:22	to things that **perish** with use

2P 1: 4   may escape from the **corruption**
2:12   born to be caught and **killed**
2:12   those creatures are **destroyed**
2:19   are slaves of **corruption**

5357 GO12 AG858 LN257
φιαλη, BOWL
Re 5: 8   holding a harp and golden **bowls**
15: 7   golden **bowls** full of the wrath
16: 1   seven **bowls** of the wrath of God
16: 2   poured his **bowl** on the earth
16: 3   poured his **bowl** into the sea
16: 4   poured his **bowl** into the rivers
16: 8   poured his **bowl** on the sun
16:10   poured his **bowl** on the throne
16:12   poured his **bowl** on the great
16:17   poured his **bowl** into the air
17: 1   angels who had the seven **bowls**
21: 9   seven **bowls** full of the seven

5358 GO1 AG858 LN257 B2:549 K1:18 R5384,18
φιλαγαθος, LOVER OF GOOD
Ti 1: 8   **lover of goodness**, prudent,

5359 GO2 AG858 LN257 B2:550
φιλαδελφεια, PHILADELPHIA
Re 1:11   to Sardis, to **Philadelphia**
3: 7   church in **Philadelphia** write:

5360 GO6 AG858 LN257 B2:549 K1:144 R5361
φιλαδελφια, BROTHERLY LOVE
Ro 12:10   another with **mutual affection**
1Th 4: 9   **love of the brothers**
He 13: 1   Let **mutual love** continue.
1P 1:22   you have genuine **mutual love**
2P 1: 7   godliness with **mutual affection**
1: 7   **mutual affection** with love.

5361 GO1 AG858 LN257 B1:254 K1:144 R5384,80
φιλαδελφος, LOVER OF BROTHER
1P 3: 8   **love for one another**, a tender

5362 GO1 AG858 LN257 B2:549 R5384,435
φιλανδρος, LOVER OF MAN
Ti 2: 4   **love** their **husbands**, to love

5363 GO2 AG858 LN257 B2:547 K9:107 R5364
φιλανθρωπια, LOVE OF MAN
Ac 28: 2   showed us **unusual kindness.**
Ti 3: 4   goodness and **loving kindness**

5364 GO1 AG858 LN257 B2:550 K9:107 R5384,444
φιλανθρωπως, LOVING MEN
Ac 27: 3   Julius treated Paul **kindly**

5365 GO1 AG859 LN257 B1:138 R5366
φιλαργυρια, LOVE OF SILVER
1Ti 6:10   **love of money** is a root of all

5366 GO2 AG859 LN257 B2:550 R5384,696
φιλαργυρος, LOVER OF SILVER
Lk 16:14   who were **lovers of money,**
2Ti 3: 2   **lovers of money,** boasters,

5367 GO1 AG859 LN257 B2:550
φιλαυτος, LOVER OF SELF
2Ti 3: 2   will be **lovers of themselves**

5368 GO25 AG859 LN257 B2:538 K9:114 R5384
φιλεω, I LOVE
Mt 6: 5   they **love** to stand and pray
10:37   **loves** father or mother more
10:37   **loves** son or daughter more
       than
23: 6   **love** to have the place of honor
26:48   I **will kiss** is the man; arrest
Mk 14:44   I **will kiss** is the man; arrest
Lk 20:46   **love** to be greeted with respect
22:47   approached Jesus **to kiss** him;
Jn 5:20   The Father **loves** the Son and
11: 3   Lord, he whom you **love** is ill
11:36   See how he **loved** him
12:25   Those who **love** their life lose
15:19   world would **love** you as its
       own
16:27   the Father himself **loves** you
16:27   **loved** me and have believed
20: 2   the one whom Jesus **loved,**
21:15   Yes, Lord; you know that I **love**
21:16   Lord; you know that I **love** you
21:17   son of John, **do** you **love** me
21:17   third time, "Do you **love** me?"
21:17   you know that I **love** you
1C 16:22   has no **love** for the Lord.
Ti 3:15   those who **love** us in the faith
Re 3:19   discipline those whom I **love**
22:15   **loves** and practices falsehood.

5369 GO1 AG859 LN257 B1:468 K2:909 R5384,2237
φιληδονος, LOVER OF PLEASURE
2Ti 3: 4   **lovers of pleasure** rather than

5370 GO7 AG859 LN257 B2:538 K9:114 R5368
φιλημα, KISS
Lk	7:45	You gave me no **kiss,** but from
	22:48	Judas, is it with a **kiss** that
Ro	16:16	one another with a holy **kiss.**
1C	16:20	one another with a holy **kiss.**
2C	13:12	one another with a holy **kiss.**
1Th	5:26	sisters with a holy **kiss.**
1P	5:14	Greet one another with a **kiss**

5371 GO1 AG859 LN257 B2:550
φιλημων, PHILEMON
Pm	1: 1	To **Philemon** our dear friend and

5372 GO1 AG859 LN258 B2:550
φιλητος, PHILETUS
2Ti	2:17	them are Hymenaeus and
		Philetus,

5373 GO1 AG859 LN258 B2:538 K9:146 R5384
φιλια, LOVE
Ja	4: 4	**friendship** with the world is

5374 GO1 AG859 LN258 B2:550
φιλιππησιος, PHILIPPIAN
Ph	4:15	You **Philippians** indeed know

5375 GO4 AG860 LN258 B2:550
φιλιπποι, PHILIPPI
Ac	16:12	**Philippi,** which is a leading
	20: 6	but we sailed from **Philippi**
Ph	1: 1	**Philippi,** with the bishops and
1Th	2: 2	mistreated at **Philippi,** as you

5376 GO36 AG860 LN258 B2:550
φιλιππος, PHILIP
Mt	10: 3	**Philip** and Bartholomew;
		Thomas
	14: 3	Herodias, his brother **Philip's**
	16:13	district of Caesarea **Philippi**
Mk	3:18	and Andrew, and **Philip**
	6:17	Herodias, his brother **Philip's**
	8:27	villages of Caesarea **Philippi**
Lk	3: 1	brother **Philip** ruler of the
	6:14	**Philip,** and Bartholomew,
Jn	1:43	He found **Philip** and said to him
	1:44	**Philip** was from Bethsaida
	1:45	**Philip** found Nathanael
	1:46	**Philip** said to him, "Come and
	1:48	fig tree before **Philip** called

	6: 5	Jesus said to **Philip,** "Where
	6: 7	**Philip** answered him, "Six
	12:21	They came to **Philip,** who was
	12:22	**Philip** went and told Andrew;
	12:22	then Andrew and **Philip** went
	14: 8	**Philip** said to him, "Lord,
	14: 9	with you all this time, **Philip**
Ac	1:13	**Philip** and Thomas, Bartholomew
	6: 5	**Philip,** Prochorus, Nicanor
	8: 5	**Philip** went down to the city
	8: 6	**Philip,** hearing and seeing the
	8:12	But when they believed **Philip,**
	8:13	stayed constantly with **Philip**
	8:26	Lord said to **Philip,** "Get up
	8:29	Then the Spirit said to **Philip**
	8:30	**Philip** ran up to it and heard
	8:31	he invited **Philip** to get in and
	8:34	The eunuch asked **Philip,** "About
	8:35	Then **Philip** began to speak
	8:38	**Philip** and the eunuch, went
	8:39	Lord snatched **Philip** away
	8:40	**Philip** found himself at Azotus
	21: 8	house of **Philip** the evangelist

5377 GO1 AG860 LN258 B2:550 R5384,2316
φιλοθεος, GOD LOVER
2Ti	3: 4	rather than **lovers of God,**

5378 GO1 AG860 LN258 B2:550
φιλολογος, PHILOLOGUS
Ro	16:15	Greet **Philologus,** Julia,

5379 GO1 AG860 LN258 B2:550 R5380
φιλονεικια, FRIEND'S QUARREL
Lk	22:24	A **dispute** also arose among them

5380 GO1 AG860 LN258 B2:550
φιλονεικος, FRIEND OF QUARRELS
1C	11:16	is disposed to be **contentious**

5381 GO2 AG860 LN258 B1:686 K5:1 R5382
φιλοξενια, LOVE TO STRANGER
Ro	12:13	extend **hospitality to strangers**
He	13: 2	show **hospitality to strangers**

5382 GO3 AG860 LN258 B1:686 K5:1 R5384,3581
φιλοξενος, LOVE TO STRANGER
1Ti	3: 2	respectable, **hospitable,** an apt
Ti	1: 8	he must be **hospitable,** a lover
1P	4: 9	Be **hospitable** to one another

5383 GO1 AG860 LN258 B2:550 R5384,4413
φιλοπρωτευω, I LOVE FIRST
3J 1: 9 who **likes to put himself first**

5384 GO29 AG861 LN258 B2:547 K9:146
φιλος, FRIEND
Mt 11:19 a **friend** of tax collectors
Lk 7: 6 centurion sent **friends** to say
7:34 drunkard, a **friend** of tax
11: 5 Suppose one of you has a **friend**
11: 5 **Friend,** lend me three loaves of
11: 6 a **friend** of mine has arrived
11: 8 because he is his **friend,** at
12: 4 my **friends,** do not fear those
14:10 **Friend,** move up higher'; then
14:12 do not invite your **friends** or
15: 6 he calls together his **friends**
15: 9 she calls together her **friends**
15:29 might celebrate with my **friends**
16: 9 And I tell you, make **friends**
21:16 by relatives and **friends;** and
23:12 Herod and Pilate became
friends
Jn 3:29 **friend** of the bridegroom, who
11:11 Our **friend** Lazarus has fallen
15:13 one's life for one's **friends.**
15:14 You are my **friends** if you do
15:15 I have called you **friends**
19:12 are no **friend** of the emperor
Ac 10:24 his relatives and close **friends**
19:31 who were **friendly** to him, sent
27: 3 him to go to his **friends** to be
Ja 2:23 he was called the **friend** of God
4: 4 a **friend** of the world becomes
3J 1:15 Peace to you. The **friends** send
1:15 Greet the **friends** there, each

5385 GO1 AG861 LN258 B2:550 K9:172 R5386
φιλοσοφια, PHILOSOPHY
Co 2: 8 captive through **philosophy**
and

5386 GO1 AG861 LN258 B3:1034 K9:172 R5384,4680
φιλοσοφος, PHILOSOPHER
Ac 17:18 Stoic **philosophers** debated
with

5387 GO1 AG861 LN258 B2:538
φιλοστοργος, LOVINGLY AFFECTIONATE
Ro 12:10 **love one another** with mutual

5388 GO1 AG861 LN258 B2:550 R5384,5043
φιλοτεκνος, LOVER OF CHILDREN
Ti 2: 4 to **love** their **children,**

5389 GO3 AG861 LN258 B2:550 R5384,5092
φιλοτιμεομαι, I CONSIDER IT AN HONOR
Ro 15:20 **make** it my **ambition** to proclaim
2C 5: 9 **make** it our **aim** to please him.
1Th 4:11 to **aspire** to live quietly,

5390 GO1 AG861 LN258 B2:550 R5384,5424
φιλοφρονως, IN A FRIENDLY MANNER,
HOSPITABLE
Ac 28: 7 entertained us **hospitably** for

5392 GO7 AG861 LN258
φιμοω, I MUZZLE
Mt 22:12 And he was **speechless.**
22:34 he **had silenced** the Sadducees
Mk 1:25 **Be silent,** and come out of him
4:39 Peace! **Be still!"** Then the wind
Lk 4:35 **Be silent,** and come out of him
1Ti 5:18 You **shall** not **muzzle** an ox
1P 2:15 should **silence** the ignorance

5393 GO1 AG862 LN258
φλεγων, PHLEGON
Ro 16:14 Greet Asyncritus, **Phlegon**

5394 GO2 AG862 LN258 R5395
φλογιζω, I ENFLAME
Ja 3: 6 **sets on fire** the cycle of
3: 6 is itself **set on fire** by hell.

5395 GO7 AG862 LN258
φλοξ, FLAME
Lk 16:24 I am in agony in these **flames.**
Ac 7:30 the **flame** of a burning bush.
2Th 1: 8 in **flaming** fire, inflicting
He 1: 7 his servants **flames** of fire
Re 1:14 eyes were like a **flame** of fire
2:18 eyes like a **flame** of fire, and
19:12 His eyes are like a **flame** of

5396 GO1 AG862 LN258 R5397
φλυαρεω, I GOSSIP
3J 1:10 **spreading false charges** against

5397 GO1 AG862 LN258
φλυαρος, GOSSIP
1Ti 5:13 also **gossips** and busybodies

5398 GO3 AG862 LN258 B1:621 R5401
φοβερος, FEARFUL

He	10:27	**fearful** prospect of judgment
	10:31	It is a **fearful** thing to fall
	12:21	said, "I tremble with **fear**

5399 GO95 AG862 LN258 B1:621 K9:189 R5401
φοβεω, I FEAR

Mt	1:20	**do** not be **afraid** to take Mary
	2:22	he **was afraid** to go there.
	9: 8	they **were filled with awe,**
	10:26	**have** no **fear** of them; for
	10:28	**Do** not **fear** those who kill
	10:28	rather **fear** him who can destroy
	10:31	So **do** not **be afraid;** you are
	14: 5	he **feared** the crowd, because
	14:27	it is I; **do** not **be afraid**
	14:30	wind, he **became frightened**
	17: 6	and were **overcome by fear.**
	17: 7	Get up and **do** not **be afraid**
	21:26	we **are afraid** of the crowd
	21:46	they **feared** the crowds, because
	25:25	so I **was afraid,** and I went
	27:54	they **were terrified** and said
	28: 5	**Do** not **be afraid;** I know that
	28:10	**Do** not **be afraid;** go and tell
Mk	4:41	**were filled with great awe**
	5:15	legion; and they **were afraid**
	5:33	came in **fear** and trembling
	5:36	**Do** not **fear,** only believe.
	6:20	for Herod **feared** John, knowing
	6:50	it is I; **do** not **be afraid**
	9:32	and **were afraid** to ask him.
	10:32	who followed **were afraid.**
	11:18	they **were afraid** of him,
	11:32	they **were afraid** of the crowd
	12:12	they **feared** the crowd. So they
	16: 8	for they **were afraid.**
Lk	1:13	**Do** not **be afraid,** Zechariah,
	1:30	**Do** not **be afraid,** Mary,
	1:50	mercy is for those who **fear** him
	2: 9	and they **were terrified.**
	2:10	**Do** not **be afraid;** for see
	5:10	Simon, **"Do** not **be afraid;**
	8:25	They **were afraid** and amazed
	8:35	mind. And they **were afraid.**
	8:50	**Do** not **fear.** Only believe,
	9:34	they **were terrified** as they
	9:45	they **were afraid** to ask him
	12: 4	**do** not **fear** those who kill the
	12: 5	will warn you whom to **fear**
	12: 5	**fear** him who, after he has
	12: 5	Yes, I tell you, **fear** him
	12: 7	**Do** not **be afraid;** you are of
	12:32	**Do** not **be afraid,** little flock
	18: 2	neither **feared** God nor had
	18: 4	Though I **have** no **fear** of God
	19:21	for I **was afraid** of you,
	20:19	but they **feared** the people.
	22: 2	they **were afraid** of the people.
	23:40	**Do** you not **fear** God, since you
Jn	6:19	and they **were terrified.**
	6:20	It is I; **do** not **be afraid**
	9:22	**were afraid** of the Jews
	12:15	**Do** not **be afraid,** daughter
	19: 8	he **was** more **afraid** than ever.
Ac	5:26	they **were afraid** of being
	9:26	they **were** all **afraid** of him
	10: 2	He was a devout man who **feared**
	10:22	an upright and God-**fearing** man
	10:35	anyone who **fears** him and does
	13:16	and others who **fear** God, listen
	13:26	family, and others who **fear** God
	16:38	they **were afraid** when they
	18: 9	**Do** not **be afraid,** but speak
	22:29	tribune also **was afraid,**
	23:10	the tribune, **fearing** that they
	27:17	**fearing** that they would run on
	27:24	**Do** not **be afraid,** Paul; you
	27:29	**Fearing** that we might run on
Ro	11:20	proud, but **stand in awe.**
	13: 3	Do you wish to **have** no **fear** of
	13: 4	you should **be afraid,** for the
2C	11: 3	**am afraid** that as the serpent
	12:20	For I **fear** that when I come
Ga	2:12	kept himself separate for **fear**
	4:11	I **am afraid** that my work for
Ep	5:33	wife should **respect** her husband
Co	3:22	wholeheartedly **fearing** the Lord
He	4: 1	let us **take care** that none of
	11:23	**were** not **afraid** of the king's
	11:27	un**afraid** of the king's anger
	13: 6	helper; I **will** not **be afraid.**
1P	2:17	**Fear** God. Honor the emperor.
	3: 6	never let **fears** alarm you.
	3:14	**Do** not **fear** what they fear
1J	4:18	whoever **fears** has not reached
Re	1:17	**Do** not **be afraid;** I am the

2:10   **Do** not **fear** what you are about
11:18   all who **fear** your name, both
14: 7   **Fear** God and give him glory
15: 4   **will** not **fear** and glorify your
19: 5   all who **fear** him, small and

5400   GO1 AG863 LN258 B1:622 R5399
φοβητρον, FEARFUL
Lk   21:11   there will be **dreadful** portents

5401   GO47 AG863 LN258 B1:621 R9:189
φοβος, FEAR
Mt   14:26   And they cried out in **fear.**
28: 4   For **fear** of him the guards
28: 8   the tomb quickly with **fear**
Mk   4:41   were filled with great **awe**
Lk   1:12   and **fear** overwhelmed him.
1:65   **Fear** came over all their
2: 9   and they were **terrified.**
5:26   God and were filled with **awe**
7:16   **Fear** seized all of them
8:37   were seized with great **fear**
21:26   People will faint from **fear**
Jn   7:13   him for **fear** of the Jews.
19:38   of his **fear** of the Jews,
20:19   locked for **fear** of the Jews
Ac   2:43   **Awe** came upon everyone
5: 5   great **fear** seized all
5:11   **fear** seized the whole church
9:31   Living in the **fear** of the Lord
19:17   everyone was **awestruck;** and the
Ro   3:18   There is no **fear** of God before
8:15   fall back into **fear,** but you
13: 3   have no **fear** of the authority?
13: 7   **respect** to whom respect is due,
13: 7   **respect** is due, honor to whom
1C   2: 3   in weakness and in **fear** and in
2C   5:11   knowing the **fear** of the Lord,
7: 1   perfect in the **fear** of God.
7: 5   without and **fears** within.
7:11   what **alarm,** what longing, what
7:15   him with **fear** and trembling.
Ep   5:21   out of **reverence** for Christ.
6: 5   masters with **fear** and trembling
Ph   2:12   our own salvation with **fear** and
1Ti   5:20   the rest also may stand in **fear**
He   2:15   slavery by the **fear** of death.
1P   1:17   in reverent **fear** during the
2:18   masters with all **deference,** not

3: 2   purity and **reverence** of your
3:14   Do not fear what they **fear,** and
3:16   with gentleness and **reverence.**
1J   4:18   There is no **fear** in love, but
4:18   perfect love casts out **fear;**
4:18   **fear** has to do with punishment,
Ju   1:23   with **fear,** hating even the
Re   11:11   who saw them were **terrified.**
18:10   in **fear** of her torment, and say
18:15   in **fear** of her torment, weeping

5402   GO1 AG864 LN258
φοιβη, PHOEBE
Ro   16: 1   sister **Phoebe,** a deacon of the

5403   GO3 AG864 LN258
φοινικη, PHOENICIA
Ac   11:19   traveled as far as **Phoenicia,**
15: 3   both **Phoenicia** and Samaria,
21: 2   ship bound for **Phoenicia,** we

5404   GO2 AG864 LN259 B1:648
φοινιξ, PALM
Jn   12:13   branches of **palm trees** and went
Re   7: 9   **palm** branches in their hands.

5405   GO1 AG864 LN259
φοινιξ, PHOENIX
Ac   27:12   they could reach **Phoenix,** where

5406   GO7 AG864 LN259
φονευς, MURDERER
Mt   22: 7   destroyed those **murderers,** and
Ac   3:14   asked to have a **murderer** given
7:52   his betrayers and **murderers.**
28: 4   This man must be a **murderer;**
1P   4:15   suffer as a **murderer,** a thief,
Re   21: 8   the **murderers,** the fornicators,
22:15   **murderers** and idolaters, and

5407   GO12 AG864 LN259 B3:113 R5406
φονευω, I MURDER
Mt   5:21   'You **shall** not **murder';** and
5:21   whoever **murders** shall be liable
19:18   **shall** not **murder;** You shall not
23:31   those who **murdered** the prophets
23:35   **murdered** between the sanctuary
Mk   10:19   You **shall** not **murder**
Lk   18:20   You **shall** not **murder**
Ro   13: 9   You **shall** not **murder**

Ja	2:11	You **shall** not **murder**
	2:11	but if you **murder**
	4: 2	so you **commit murder**
	5: 6	**murdered** the righteous one

5408   GO9 AG864 LN259 R5407
φονος, MURDER

Mt	15:19	intentions, **murder,** adultery
Mk	7:21	fornication, theft, **murder**
	15: 7	rebels who had committed **murder**
Lk	23:19	the city, and for **murder**
	23:25	for insurrection and **murder**
Ac	9: 1	breathing threats and **murder**
Ro	1:29	Full of envy, **murder,** strife
He	11:37	they were **killed** by the sword
Re	9:21	not repent of their **murders**

5409   GO6 AG864 LN259 K9:83
φορεω, I BEAR

Mt	11: 8	Someone **dressed** in soft robes?
Jn	19: 5	**wearing** the crown of thorns
Ro	13: 4	**does** not **bear** the sword in vain
1C	15:49	**have borne** the image of the man
	15:49	we **will** also **bear** the image
Ja	2: 3	one **wearing** the fine clothes

5410   GO1 AG865 LN259
φορον, FORUM

Ac	28:15	as far as the **Forum** of Appius

5411   GO5 AG865 LN259 B3:752 K9:78
φορος, TAX

Lk	20:22	to pay **taxes** to the emperor
	23: 2	forbidding us to pay **taxes**
Ro	13: 6	same reason you also pay **taxes**
	13: 7	**taxes** to whom taxes are due
	13: 7	taxes to whom **taxes** are due

5412   GO2 AG865 LN259 B1:260 K9:86
φορτιζω, I PACK, I CARRY BURDENS

Mt	11:28	and are **carrying heavy burdens**
Lk	11:46	you **load** people with burdens

5413   GO6 AG865 LN259 B1:260 K9:84 R5412
φορτιον, PACK, BURDEN

Mt	11:30	and my **burden** is light
	23: 4	They tie up heavy **burdens**
Lk	11:46	you load people with **burdens**
	11:46	not lift a finger to ease **them**

Ac	27:10	not only of the **cargo**
Ga	6: 5	must carry their own **loads**

5415   GO1 AG865 LN259
φορτουνατος, FORUNATUS

1C	16:17	Stephanas and **Fortunatus** and

5416   GO1 AG865 LN259 B1:162 R5417
φραγελλιον, WHIP

Jn	2:15	Making a **whip** of cords

5417   GO2 AG865 LN259 B1:162
φραγελλοω, I WHIP

Mt	27:26	and after **flogging** Jesus
Mk	15:15	and after **flogging** Jesus

5418   GO4 AG865 LN259 B3:950
φραγμος, HEDGE

Mt	21:33	vineyard, put a **fence** around it
Mk	12: 1	vineyard, put a **fence** around it
Lk	14:23	into the roads and **lanes**
Ep	2:14	broken down the dividing **wall**

5419   GO1 AG865 LN259
φραζω, I EXPLAIN

Mt	15:15	**Explain** this parable to us

5420   GO3 AG865 LN259 B3:950
φρασσω, I STOP

Ro	3:19	every mouth **may be silenced**
2C	11:10	**will** not **be silenced** in the
He	11:33	**shut** the mouths of lions

5421   GO7 AG865 LN259 B3:986
φρεαρ, WELL

Lk	14: 5	ox that has fallen into a **well**
Jn	4:11	no bucket, and the **well** is deep
	4:12	Jacob, who gave us the **well**
Re	9: 1	the shaft of the bottomless **pit**
	9: 2	the **shaft** of the bottomless pit
	9: 2	and from the **shaft** rose smoke
	9: 2	with the smoke from the **shaft**

5422   GO1 AG865 LN259 R5423
φρεναπαταω, I DECEIVE A MIND

Ga	6: 3	they **deceive** themselves

5423   GO1 AG865 LN259 R5424,539
φρεναπατης, MIND-DECEIVERS

Ti	1:10	idle talkers and **deceivers**

5424 GO1 AG865 LN259
φρην, UNDERSTANDING
1C 14:20 be children in your **thinking**
      14:20 but in **thinking** be adults

5425 GO1 AG866 LN259
φρισσω, I QUIVER
Ja   2:19 demons believe—and **shudder**

5426 GO26 AG866 LN259 B2:616 K9:220 R5424
φρονεω, I THINK
Mt 16:23 **are setting** your **mind** not **on**
Mk   8:33 **are setting** your **mind** not **on**
Ac 28:22 to hear from you what you
            think
Ro   8: 5 **set** their **minds on** the things
      11:20 So do not **become** proud
      12: 3 highly than you ought to **think**
      12: 3 **to think** with sober judgment
      12:16 **Live in harmony** with one
      12:16 do not **be haughty**
      14: 6 Those who **observe** the day
      14: 6 **observe** it in honor
      15: 5 grant you to **live in harmony**
1C 13:11 I **thought** like a child
2C 13:11 **agree** with one another
Ga   5:10 you will not **think** otherwise
Ph   1: 7 It is right for me to **think**
      2: 2 be of the same **mind**
      2: 2 full accord and of one **mind**
      2: 5 Let the same **mind** be in you
      3:15 be of the same **mind**
      3:15 and if you **think** differently
      3:19 their **minds** are set on earthly
      4: 2 to be of the same **mind**
      4:10 you have revived your **concern**
      4:10 you were **concerned** for me
Co   3: 2 **Set** your **minds on** things

5427 GO4 AG866 LN259 B2:616 K9:220 R5426
φρονημα, THOUGHT
Ro   8: 6 To set the **mind** on the flesh
      8: 6 to set the **mind** on the Spirit
      8: 7 the **mind** that is set on the
      8:27 what is the **mind** of the Spirit

5428 GO2 AG866 LN259 B2:616 K9:220 R5426
φρονησις, THOUGHTFULNESS
Lk   1:17 to the **wisdom** of the righteous
Ep   1: 8 With all wisdom and **insight**

5429 GO14 AG866 LN259 B2:616 K9:220 R5424
φρονιμος, THOUGHTFUL
Mt   7:24 like a **wise** man who built
      10:16 so be **wise** as serpents
      24:45 is the faithful and **wise** slave
      25: 2 foolish, and five were **wise**
      25: 4 **wise** took flasks of oil with
      25: 8 The foolish said to the **wise**
      25: 9 But the **wise** replied
Lk 12:42 faithful and **prudent** manager
      16: 8 are **more shrewd** in dealing
Ro 11:25 may not claim to be **wiser**
      12:16 do not claim to be **wiser**
1C   4:10 but you are **wise** in Christ
      10:15 I speak as to **sensible** people
2C 11:19 being **wise** yourselves

5430 GO1 AG866 LN259 B2:617 R5429
φρονιμως, THOUGHTFULLY
Lk 16: 8 because he had acted **shrewdly**

5431 GO1 AG866 LN259 R5424
φροντιζω, I THINK
Ti   3: 8 **may be careful** to devote

5432 GO4 AG867 LN260 B2:134
φρουρεω, I GUARD
2C 11:32 **guarded** the city of Damascus
Ga   3:23 were imprisoned and **guarded**
Ph   4: 7 **will guard** your hearts
1P   1: 5 who **are being protected**

5433 GO1 AG867 LN260
φρυασσω, I RAGE
Ac   4:25 Why did the Gentiles **rage**

5434 GO1 AG867 LN260
φρυγανον, STICK BUNDLE
Ac 28: 3 gathered a bundle of **brushwood**

5435 GO3 AG867 LN260
φρυγια, PHYRGIA
Ac   2:10 **Phrygia** and Pamphylia, Egypt
      16: 6 through the region of **Phrygia**
      18:23 region of Galatia and **Phrygia**

5436 GO1 AG867 LN260
φυγελος, PHYGELUS
2Ti 1:15 from me, including **Phygelus**

5437   ᴳᴼ1 ᴬᴳ867 ᴸᴺ260 ᴮ1:558 ᴿ5343
φυγη, FLIGHT
Mt 24:20   **flight** may not be in winter

5438   ᴳᴼ47 ᴬᴳ867 ᴸᴺ260 ᴮ2:134 ᴷ9:241 ᴿ5442
φυλακη, GUARD, PRISON
Mt   5:25   you will be thrown into **prison**
     14: 3   put him in **prison** on account
     14:10   had John beheaded in the **prison**
     14:25   And early in the **morning**
     18:30   threw him into **prison**
     24:43   in what **part** of the night
     25:36   I was in **prison** and you visited
     25:39   we saw you sick or in **prison**
     25:43   sick and in **prison** and you did
     25:44   naked or sick or in **prison**
Mk   6:17   put him in **prison** on account
      6:27   beheaded him in the **prison**
      6:48   he came towards them **early**
Lk   2: 8   keeping **watch** over their flock
      3:20   during the **middle** of the night
     12:58   the officer throw you in **prison**
     21:12   to synagogues and **prisons**
     22:33   ready to go with you to **prison**
     23:19   who had been put in **prison**
     23:25   one who had been put in **prison**
Jn   3:24   yet been thrown into **prison**
Ac   5:19   opened the **prison** doors
      5:22   not find them in the **prison**
      5:25   the men whom you put in
              prison
      8: 3   he committed them to **prison**
     12: 4   he put him in **prison**
     12: 5   While Peter was kept in **prison**
     12: 6   keeping watch over the **prison**
     12:10   first and the second **guard**
     12:17   brought him out of the **prison**
     16:23   they threw them into **prison**
     16:24   put them in the innermost **cell**
     16:27   saw the **prison** doors wide open
     16:37   and have thrown us into **prison**
     16:40   After leaving the **prison**
     22: 4   and putting them in **prison**
     26:10   many of the saints in **prison**
2C   6: 5   beatings, **imprisonments**, riots
     11:23   far more **imprisonments**
He 11:36   even chains and **imprisonment**
1P   3:19   to the spirits in **prison**
Re   2:10   throw some of you into **prison**
     18: 2   a **haunt** of every foul spirit

     18: 2   a **haunt** of every foul bird
     18: 2   a **haunt** of every foul
     20: 7   be released from his **prison**

5439   ᴳᴼ1 ᴬᴳ868 ᴸᴺ260 ᴮ2:136 ᴿ5441
φυλακιζω, I SET UNDER GUARD
Ac 22:19   I **imprisoned** and beat those

5440   ᴳᴼ1 ᴬᴳ868 ᴸᴺ260 ᴮ2:136 ᴿ5442
φυλακτηριον, GUARD PLACE
Mt 23: 5   they make their **phylacteries**

5441   ᴳᴼ3 ᴬᴳ868 ᴸᴺ260 ᴿ5438
φυλαξ, GUARD
Ac   5:23   **guards** standing at the doors
     12: 6   **guards** in front of the door
     12:19   he examined the **guards**

5442   ᴳᴼ31 ᴬᴳ868 ᴸᴺ260 ᴮ2:134 ᴷ9:236
φυλασσω, I GUARD
Mt 19:20   I **have kept** all these
Mk 10:20   I **have kept** all these since
Lk   2: 8   **keeping watch** over their flock
      8:29   he was **kept under guard**
     11:21   fully armed, **guards** his castle
     11:28   the word of God and **obey** it
     12:15   **Be on** your **guard** against all
     18:21   I **have kept** all these since
Jn 12:25   **will keep** it for eternal life
     12:47   my words and **does** not **keep**
              them
     17:12   I **guarded** them, and not one
Ac   7:53   and yet you **have** not **kept** it
     12: 4   squads of soldiers **to guard** him
     16: 4   for **observance** the decisions
     21:24   observe and **guard** the law
     21:25   that they should **abstain**
     22:20   approving and **keeping** the coats
     23:35   that he be **kept under guard**
     28:16   the soldier who **was guarding**
Ro   2:26   **keep** the requirements of the
Ga   6:13   do not themselves **obey** the law
2Th 3: 3   strengthen you and **guard** you
1Ti 5:21   to **keep** these instructions
      6:20   **guard** what has been entrusted
2Ti 1:12   is able to **guard** until that day
      1:14   **Guard** the good treasure
      4:15   You also must **beware** of him
2P   2: 5   even though he **saved** Noah
      3:17   **beware** that you are not carried

1J   5:21   **keep** yourselves from idols
Ju   1:24   who is able to **keep** you

5443   GO31 AG868 LN260 B3:870 K9:245
φυλη, TRIBE
Mt   19:28   judging the twelve **tribes**
      24:30   all the **tribes** of the
Lk   2:36   Phanuel, of the **tribe** of Asher
      22:30   judging the twelve **tribes**
Ac   13:21   a man of the **tribe** of Benjamin
Ro   11: 1   member of the **tribe** of Benjamin
Ph   3: 5   of the **tribe** of Benjamin
He   7:13   belonged to another **tribe**
       7:14   in connection with that **tribe**
Ja   1: 1   To the twelve **tribes**
Re   1: 7   all the **tribes** of the earth
       5: 5   the Lion of the **tribe** of Judah
       5: 9   saints from every **tribe**
       7: 4   sealed out of every **tribe**
       7: 5   From the **tribe** of Judah
       7: 5   from the **tribe** of Reuben
       7: 5   from the **tribe** of Gad
       7: 6   from the **tribe** of Asher
       7: 6   from the **tribe** of Naphtali
       7: 6   from the **tribe** of Manasseh
       7: 7   from the **tribe** of Simeon
       7: 7   from the **tribe** of Levi
       7: 7   from the **tribe** of Issachar
       7: 8   from the **tribe** of Zebulun
       7: 8   from the **tribe** of Joseph
       7: 8   from the **tribe** of Benjamin
       7: 9   from all **tribes** and peoples
      11: 9   of the peoples and **tribes**
      13: 7   authority over every **tribe**
      14: 6   to every nation and **tribe**
      21:12   the names of the twelve **tribes**

5444   GO6 AG869 LN260 B3:865
φυλλον, LEAF
Mt   21:19   nothing at all on it but
                  leaves.
      24:32   puts forth its **leaves,** you
Mk   11:13   a fig tree in **leaf,** he went to
      11:13   he found nothing but **leaves**
      13:28   puts forth its **leaves,** you know
Re   22: 2   **leaves** of the tree are for the

5445   GO5 AG869 LN260 B3:917
φυραμα, MIXTURE
Ro   9:21   to make out of the same **lump**

      11:16   then the whole **batch** is holy
1C   5: 6   yeast leavens the whole **batch**
       5: 7   you may be a new **batch,** as you
Ga   5: 9   yeast leavens the whole **batch**

5446   GO3 AG869 LN260 B2:656 K9:251 R5449
φυσικος, NATURAL
Ro   1:26   exchanged **natural** intercourse
       1:27   giving up **natural** intercourse
2P   2:12   mere creatures of **instinct**

5447   GO1 AG869 LN260 B2:656 K9:251 R5446
φυσικως, NATURALLY
Ju   1:10   animals, they know by **instinct.**

5448   GO7 AG869 LN260 B2:422
φυσιοω, I PUFF UP
1C   4: 6   none of you **will be puffed up**
       4:18   to you, **have become arrogant.**
       4:19   the talk of these **arrogant**
       5: 2   And you are **arrogant!** Should
       8: 1   Knowledge **puffs up,** but love
      13: 4   envious or boastful or **arrogant**
Co   2:18   **puffed up** without cause by a

5449   GO14 AG869 LN260 B2:656 K9:251
φυσις, NATURE
Ro   1:26   intercourse for **unnatural,**
       2:14   **instinctively** what the law
       2:27   are **physically** uncircumcised
      11:21   not spare the **natural** branches
      11:24   by **nature** a wild olive tree
      11:24   contrary to **nature,** into a
      11:24   much more will these **natural**
1C   11:14   Does not **nature** itself teach
Ga   2:15   We ourselves are Jews by **birth**
       4: 8   that by **nature** are not gods.
Ep   2: 3   by **nature** children of wrath
Ja   3: 7   For every **species** of beast and
       3: 7   been tamed by the human
                  species
2P   1: 4   of the divine **nature.**

5450   GO1 AG870 LN260 R5448
φυσιωσις, PUFFING UP
2C   12:20   gossip, **conceit,** and disorder.

5451   GO1 AG870 LN260 B3:865 R5452
φυτεια, PLANT
Mt   15:13   Every **plant** that my heavenly

5452　GO11 AG870 LN260 B3:865 R5453
φυτευω, I PLANT

Mt	15:13	heavenly Father **has** not **planted**
	21:33	who **planted** a vineyard, put a
Mk	12: 1	A man **planted** a vineyard, put
Lk	13: 6	tree **planted** in his vineyard
	17: 6	uprooted and **planted** in the sea
	17:28	selling, **planting** and building,
	20: 9	**planted** a vineyard, and leased
1C	3: 6	I **planted,** Apollos watered
	3: 7	So neither the one who **plants**
	3: 8	The one who **plants** and the one
	9: 7	Who **plants** a vineyard and does

5453　GO3 AG870 LN260
φυω, I SPROUT

Lk	8: 6	it **grew up,** it withered for
	8: 8	when it **grew,** it produced a
He	12:15	root of bitterness **springs up**

5454　GO2 AG870 LN260
φωλεος, HOLE

Mt	8:20	Foxes have **holes,** and birds
Lk	9:58	Foxes have **holes,** and birds

5455　GO43 AG870 LN260 B3:113 K9:301 R5456
φωνεω, I CALL

Mt	20:32	Jesus stood still and **called**
	26:34	before the cock **crows,** you will
	26:74	At that moment the cock **crowed.**
	26:75	Before the cock **crows,** you will
	27:47	This man **is calling** for Elijah
Mk	1:26	**crying** with a loud voice, came
	9:35	He sat down, **called** the twelve
	10:49	**Call** him here." And they called
	10:49	they **called** the blind man,
	10:49	get up, he **is calling** you.
	14:30	before the cock **crows** twice,
	14:68	Then the cock **crowed.**
	14:72	cock **crowed** for the second time
	14:72	Before the cock **crows** twice,
	15:35	he **is calling** for Elijah
Lk	8: 8	he **called** out, "Let anyone with
	8:54	and **called** out, "Child, get up
	14:12	**do** not **invite** your friends or
	16: 2	So he **summoned** him and said to
	16:24	He **called** out, 'Father Abraham
	19:15	**to be summoned** so that he might
	22:34	cock **will** not **crow** this day
	22:60	still speaking, the cock **crowed**

	22:61	Before the cock **crows** today
	23:46	Jesus, **crying** with a loud voice
Jn	1:48	fig tree before Philip **called**
	2: 9	steward **called** the bridegroom
	4:16	Go, **call** your husband, and come
	9:18	until they **called** the parents
	9:24	**called** the man who had been
	10: 3	He **calls** his own sheep by name
	11:28	**called** her sister Mary, and
	11:28	Teacher is here and **is calling**
	12:17	when he **called** Lazarus out of
	13:13	You **call** me Teacher and Lord
	13:38	before the cock **crows,** you will
	18:27	at that moment the cock **crowed**
	18:33	**summoned** Jesus, and asked him
Ac	9:41	**calling** the saints and widows
	10: 7	**called** two of his slaves and a
	10:18	They **called** out to ask whether
	16:28	Paul **shouted** in a loud voice
Re	14:18	he **called** with a loud voice to

5456　GO139 AG870 LN261 B3:113 K9:278
φωνη, SOUND, VOICE

Mt	2:18	A **voice** was heard in Ramah,
	3: 3	**voice** of one crying out in the
	3:17	And a **voice** from heaven said,
	12:19	nor will anyone hear his **voice**
	17: 5	**voice** said, "This is my Son
	27:46	**voice,** "Eli, Eli, lema
	27:50	**voice** and breathed his last.
Mk	1: 3	the **voice** of one crying out
	1:11	And a **voice** came from heaven
	1:26	loud **voice,** came out of him.
	5: 7	shouted at the top of his **voice**
	9: 7	**voice,** "This is my Son, the
	15:34	loud **voice,** "Eloi, Eloi, lema
	15:37	loud **cry** and breathed his last
Lk	1:44	**sound** of your greeting
	3: 4	**voice** of one crying out in the
	3:22	**voice** came from heaven, "You
	4:33	he cried out with a loud **voice,**
	8:28	shouted at the top of his **voice**
	9:35	from the cloud came a **voice**
	9:36	When the **voice** had spoken,
	11:27	raised her **voice** and said to
	17:13	they **called** out, saying, "Jesus
	17:15	praising God with a loud **voice.**
	19:37	God joyfully with a loud **voice**
	23:23	demanding with loud **shouts**

	23:23	their **voices** prevailed.
	23:46	crying with a loud **voice,** said
Jn	1:23	I am the **voice** of one crying
	3: 8	you hear the **sound** of it, but
	3:29	at the bridegroom's **voice.** For
	5:25	dead will hear the **voice** of the
	5:28	graves will hear his **voice**
	5:37	his **voice** or seen his form,
	10: 3	sheep hear his **voice.** He calls
	10: 4	because they know his **voice.**
	10: 5	not know the **voice** of strangers
	10:16	they will listen to my **voice.**
	10:27	My sheep hear my **voice.** I know
	11:43	loud **voice,** "Lazarus, come out
	12:28	Then a **voice** came from heaven
	12:30	This **voice** has come for your
	18:37	the truth listens to my **voice.**
Ac	2: 6	And at this **sound** the crowd
	2:14	raised his **voice** and addressed
	4:24	their **voices** together to God
	7:31	came the **voice** of the Lord:
	7:57	loud **shout** all rushed together
	7:60	**voice,** "Lord, do not hold this
	8: 7	crying with loud **shrieks,** came
	9: 4	a **voice** saying to him, "Saul,
	9: 7	heard the **voice** but saw no one.
	10:13	**voice** saying, "Get up, Peter;
	10:15	The **voice** said to him again,
	11: 7	**voice** saying to me, 'Get up,
	11: 9	But a second time the **voice**
	12:14	On recognizing Peter's **voice**
	12:22	The **voice** of a god, and not of
	13:27	understand the **words** of the
	14:10	said in a loud **voice,** "Stand
	14:11	they **shouted** in the Lycaonian
	16:28	Paul shouted in a loud **voice**
	19:34	all of them **shouted** in unison
	22: 7	a **voice** saying to me, 'Saul,
	22: 9	not hear the **voice** of the one
	22:14	One and to hear his own **voice**
	22:22	**shouted,** "Away with such a
	24:21	unless it was this one **sentence**
	26:14	**voice** saying to me in the
	26:24	Festus **exclaimed,** "You are out
1C	14: 7	instruments that produce **sound**
	14: 8	bugle gives an indistinct **sound**
	14:10	kinds of **sounds** in the world
	14:11	not know the meaning of a **sound**
Ga	4:20	could change my **tone,** for I am

1Th	4:16	archangel's **call** and with the
He	3: 7	Today, if you hear his **voice**
	3:15	**voice,** do not harden your
	4: 7	Today, if you hear his **voice**
	12:19	**voice** whose words made the
	12:26	his **voice** shook the earth
2P	1:17	when that **voice** was conveyed to
	1:18	We ourselves heard this **voice**
	2:16	donkey spoke with a human **voice**
Re	1:10	a loud **voice** like a trumpet
	1:12	I turned to see whose **voice**
	1:15	his **voice** was like the sound
	1:15	like the **sound** of many waters.
	3:20	if you hear my **voice** and open
	4: 1	first **voice,** which I had heard
	4: 5	lightning, and **rumblings**
	5: 2	proclaiming with a loud **voice**
	5:11	heard the **voice** of many angels
	5:12	singing with full **voice,**
	6: 1	with a **voice** of thunder, "Come
	6: 6	**voice** in the midst of the four
	6: 7	heard the **voice** of the fourth
	6:10	**voice,** "Sovereign Lord, holy
	7: 2	loud **voice** to the four angels
	7:10	**voice,** saying, "Salvation
	8: 5	thunder, **rumblings,** flashes
	8:13	**voice** as it flew in midheaven
	8:13	earth, at the **blasts** of the
	9: 9	**noise** of their wings was like
	9: 9	like the **noise** of many chariots
	9:13	**voice** from the four horns of
	10: 3	a great **shout,** like a lion
	10: 3	the seven thunders **sounded.**
	10: 4	**voice** from heaven saying, "Seal
	10: 7	seventh angel is to **blow** his
	10: 8	Then the **voice** that I had heard
	11:12	Then they heard a loud **voice**
	11:15	loud **voices** in heaven, saying
	11:19	lightning, **rumblings,** peals of
	12:10	**voice** in heaven, proclaiming,
	14: 2	**voice** from heaven like the
	14: 2	**sound** of many waters and like
	14: 2	**sound** of loud thunder; the
	14: 2	**voice** I heard was like the
	14: 7	He said in a loud **voice,** "Fear
	14: 9	loud **voice,** "Those who worship
	14:13	And I heard a **voice** from heaven
	14:15	loud **voice** to the one who sat

14:18 **voice** to him who had the sharp
16: 1 **voice** from the temple telling
16:17 **voice** came out of the temple,
16:18 lightning, **rumblings,** peals
18: 2 **voice,** "Fallen, fallen is
18: 4 Then I heard another **voice** from
18:22 and the **sound** of harpists and
18:22 **sound** of the millstone will be
18:23 **voice** of bridegroom and bride
19: 1 **voice** of a great multitude in
19: 5 from the throne came a **voice**
19: 6 the **voice** of a great multitude
19: 6 like the **sound** of many waters
19: 6 **sound** of mighty thunderpeals,
19:17 loud **voice** he called to all
21: 3 And I heard a loud **voice** from

5457   GO73 AG871 LN261 B2:490 K9:310
φως, LIGHT

Mt 4:16 have seen a great **light**
4:16 of death **light** has dawned
5:14 You are the **light** of the world
5:16 let your **light** shine before
6:23 the **light** in you is darkness
10:27 tell in the **light;** and what
17: 2 clothes became **dazzling** white.
Mk 14:54 warming himself at the **fire.**
Lk 2:32 a **light** for revelation to the
8:16 who enter may see the **light.**
11:33 who enter may see the **light.**
11:35 consider whether the **light**
12: 3 dark will be heard in the **light**
16: 8 than are the children of **light.**
22:56 seeing him in the **firelight,**
Jn 1: 4 the life was the **light** of all
1: 5 **light** shines in the darkness
1: 7 witness to testify to the **light**
1: 8 He himself was not the **light**
1: 8 he came to testify to the **light**
1: 9 The true **light** which enlightens
3:19 **light** has come into the world
3:19 darkness rather than **light**
3:20 all who do evil hate the **light**
3:20 do not come to the **light,**
3:21 what is true come to the **light**
5:35 for a while in his **light.**
8:12 I am the **light** of the world
8:12 but will have the **light** of life
9: 5 I am the **light** of the world.

11: 9 see the **light** of this world
11:10 because the **light** is not in
12:35 The **light** is with you for a
12:35 Walk while you have the **light**
12:36 While you have the **light,**
12:36 believe in the **light,** so that
12:36 may become children of **light**
12:46 I have come as **light** into the
Ac 9: 3 suddenly a **light** from heaven
12: 7 a **light** shone in the cell.
13:47 set you to be a **light** for the
16:29 The jailer called for **lights**
22: 6 about noon a great **light** from
22: 9 saw the **light** but did not hear
22:11 brightness of that **light,**
26:13 saw a **light** from heaven
26:18 turn from darkness to **light**
26:23 proclaim **light** both to our
Ro 2:19 **light** to those who are in
13:12 put on the armor of **light;**
2C 4: 6 Let **light** shine out of darkness
6:14 between **light** and darkness?
11:14 himself as an angel of **light.**
Ep 5: 8 in the Lord you are **light**
5: 8 Live as children of **light**
5: 9 for the fruit of the **light**
5:13 exposed by the **light** becomes
5:14 that becomes visible is **light**
Co 1:12 of the saints in the **light.**
1Th 5: 5 you are all children of **light**
1Ti 6:16 dwells in unapproachable **light**
Ja 1:17 down from the Father of **lights**
1P 2: 9 into his marvelous **light.**
1J 1: 5 God is **light** and in him there
1: 7 but if we walk in the **light** as
1: 7 **light,** we have fellowship with
2: 8 true **light** is already shining.
2: 9 I am in the **light,**" while
2:10 sister lives in the **light,**
Re 18:23 **light** of a lamp will shine
21:24 nations will walk by its **light**
22: 5 they need no **light** of lamp or
22: 5 Lord God will be their **light**

5458   GO2 AG872 LN261 B2:490 K9:310 R5457
φωστηρ, LIGHT-GIVING BODY (STAR),
RADIANCE

Ph 2:15 shine like **stars** in the world.
Re 21:11 **radiance** like a very rare jewel

5459 GO1 AG872 LN261 B2:490 K9:310 R5457,5342
φωσφορος, LIGHT-BEARER
2P 1:19 **morning star** rises in your

5460 GO5 AG872 LN261 B2:490 K9:310 R5457
φωτεινος, LIGHTENED
Mt 6:22 body will be full of **light;**
  17: 5 **bright** cloud overshadowed them
Lk 11:34 whole body is full of **light**
  11:36 whole body is full of **light,**
  11:36 it will be as full of **light**

5461 GO11 AG872 LN261 B2:490 K9:310 R5457
φωτιζω, I LIGHT
Lk 11:36 lamp **gives** you **light** with its
Jn 1: 9 true light, which **enlightens**
1C 4: 5 who **will bring to light** the
Ep 1:18 eyes of your heart **enlightened**
  3: 9 and to **make** everyone **see** what
2Ti 1:10 life and immortality **to light**
He 6: 4 **have** once **been enlightened,**
  10:32 after you **had been enlightened**
Re 18: 1 earth **was made bright** with his
  21:23 glory of God **is** its **light,** and
  22: 5 Lord God **will be** their **light**

5462 GO2 AG873 LN261 B2:490 K9:310 R5461
φωτισμος, LIGHTENING
2C 4: 4 keep them from seeing the **light**
  4: 6 **light** of the knowledge of the

χ

5463 GO74 AG873 LN261 B2:356 K9:359
χαιρω, I REJOICE
Mt 2:10 they **were overwhelmed**
      with joy.
  5:12 **Rejoice** and be glad, for your
  18:13 he **rejoices** over it more than
  26:49 **Greetings,** Rabbi!" and kissed
  27:29 **Hail,** King of the Jews
  28: 9 **Greetings!"** And they came to
Mk 14:11 they **were greatly pleased,**
  15:18 **Hail,** King of the Jews
Lk 1:14 many **will rejoice** at his birth,
  1:28 **Greetings,** favored one! The
  6:23 **Rejoice** in that day and leap
  10:20 do not **rejoice** at this, that
  10:20 but **rejoice** that your names

13:17 entire crowd **was rejoicing** at
15: 5 his shoulders and **rejoices.**
15:32 we had to celebrate and **rejoice**
19: 6 he hurried down and **was happy**
19:37 began to praise God **joyfully**
22: 5 They were **greatly pleased**
23: 8 saw Jesus, he **was** very **glad,**
Jn 3:29 stands and hears him, **rejoices**
  4:36 reaper **may rejoice** together.
  8:56 Your ancestor Abraham
        rejoiced
  11:15 I **am glad** I was not there
  14:28 you would **rejoice** that I am
  16:20 world **will rejoice;** you will
  16:22 your hearts **will rejoice,**
  19: 3 **Hail,** King of the Jews!" and
  20:20 disciples **rejoiced** when they
Ac 5:41 they **rejoiced** that they were
  8:39 went on his way **rejoicing.**
  11:23 he **rejoiced,** and he exhorted
  13:48 **were glad** and praised the word
  15:23 Syria and Cilicia, **greetings.**
  15:31 **rejoiced** at the exhortation.
  23:26 the governor Felix, **greetings.**
Ro 12:12 **Rejoice** in hope, be patient
  12:15 **Rejoice** with those who rejoice
  12:15 who **rejoice,** weep with those
  16:19 I **rejoice** over you, I want
1C 7:30 who **rejoice** as though they
  7:30 they **were** not **rejoicing,**
  13: 6 **does** not **rejoice** in wrongdoing
  16:17 I **rejoice** at the coming of
2C 2: 3 who should **have made** me
  6:10 yet always **rejoicing;** as poor
  7: 7 so that I **rejoiced** still more
  7: 9 Now I **rejoice,** not because
  7:13 we **rejoiced** still more at the
  7:16 I **rejoice,** because I have
  13: 9 we **rejoice** when we are weak
  13:11 brothers and sisters, **farewell**
Ph 1:18 in that I **rejoice.** Yes, and I
  1:18 I will continue to **rejoice,**
  2:17 I **am glad** and rejoice with
  2:18 you also must **be glad** and
  2:28 you may **rejoice** at seeing him
  3: 1 **rejoice** in the Lord. To write
  4: 4 **Rejoice** in the Lord always;
  4: 4 again I will say, **Rejoice.**
  4:10 I **rejoice** in the Lord greatly
Co 1:24 I **am** now **rejoicing** in my

	2: 5	I **rejoice** to see your morale
1Th	3: 9	for all the joy that we **feel**
	5:16	**Rejoice** always,
Ja	1: 1	in the Dispersion: **Greetings.**
1P	4:13	But **rejoice** insofar as you are
	4:13	also **be glad** and shout for joy
2J	1: 4	I was **overjoyed** to find some
	1:10	**welcome** anyone who comes to you
	1:11	to **welcome** is to participate
3J	1: 3	I was **overjoyed** when some of
Re	11:10	**will gloat** over them and
	19: 7	**Let** us **rejoice** and exult and

5464   GO4 AG874 LN261 B3:1000
χαλαζα, HAIL

Re	8: 7	there came **hail** and fire, mixed
	11:19	earthquake, and heavy **hail.**
	16:21	huge **hailstones,** each weighing
	16:21	plague of the **hail,** so fearful

5465   GO7 AG874 LN261
χαλαω, I LOWER

Mk	2: 4	they **let down** the mat on which
Lk	5: 4	**let down** your nets for a catch
	5: 5	I **will let down** the nets
Ac	9:25	**let** him **down** through an opening
	27:17	they **lowered** the sea anchor
	27:30	had **lowered** the boat into the
2C	11:33	but I **was let down** in a basket

5466   GO1 AG874 LN261
χαλδαιος, CHALDEAN

Ac	7: 4	the country of the **Chaldeans**

5467   GO2 AG874 LN261 B1:419
χαλεπος, DIFFICULT

Mt	8:28	They were so **fierce** that no
2Ti	3: 1	in the last days **distressing**

5468   GO2 AG874 LN261
χαλιναγωγεω, I BRIDLE

Ja	1:26	**do** not **bridle** their tongues
	3: 2	**keep . . . in check with a bridle**

5469   GO2 AG874 LN261
χαλινος, BRIDLE

Ja	3: 3	**bits** into the mouths of horses
Re	14:20	as high as a horse's **bridle,**

5470   GO1 AG875 LN261 R5475
χαλκους, COPPER

Re	9:20	of gold and silver and **bronze**

5471   GO1 AG874 LN261 B2:96 R5475
χαλκευς, COPPERSMITH

2Ti	4:14	Alexander the **coppersmith**

5472   GO1 AG874 LN261 B3:396
χαλκηδων, CHALCEDON

Re	21:19	the third **agate,** the fourth

5473   GO1 AG874 LN261 B2:96 R5475
χαλκιον, COPPER THINGS

Mk	7: 4	cups, pots, and **bronze kettles**

5474   GO2 AG875 LN261 B2:97
χαλκολιβανον, POLISHED COPPER

Re	1:15	feet were like **burnished bronze**
	2:18	feet are like **burnished bronze:**

5475   GO5 AG875 LN261 B2:96
χαλκος, COPPER

Mt	10: 9	silver, or **copper** in your belts
Mk	6: 8	no bag, no **money** in their belts
	12:41	crowd putting **money** into the
1C	13: 1	I am a noisy **gong** or a clanging
Re	18:12	articles of costly wood, **bronze**

5476   GO2 AG875 LN261
χαμαι, ON GROUND

Jn	9: 6	he spat **on the ground** and made
	18: 6	back and fell **to the ground.**

5477   GO2 AG875 LN261
χανααν, CANAAN

Ac	7:11	throughout Egypt and **Canaan,**
	13:19	nations in the land of **Canaan**

5478   GO1 AG875 LN262
χαναναιος, CANAANITE

Mt	15:22	Just then a **Canaanite** woman

5479   GO59 AG875 LN262 B2:356 K9:359 R5463
χαρα, JOY

Mt	2:10	were overwhelmed with **joy.**
	13:20	receives it with **joy;**
	13:44	in his **joy** he goes and sells
	25:21	into the **joy** of your master.
	25:23	enter into the **joy** of your

	28: 8	with fear and great **joy,**
Mk	4:16	receive it with **joy.**
Lk	1:14	You will have **joy** and gladness
	2:10	good news of great **joy** for all
	8:13	receive it with **joy.** But these
	10:17	The seventy returned with **joy**
	15: 7	**joy** in heaven over one sinner
	15:10	there is **joy** in the presence
	24:41	**joy** they were disbelieving
	24:52	to Jerusalem with great **joy;**
Jn	3:29	rejoices **greatly** at the
	3:29	my **joy** has been fulfilled.
	15:11	my **joy** may be in you, and
	15:11	that your **joy** may be complete.
	16:20	your pain will turn into **joy.**
	16:21	**joy** of having brought a human
	16:22	no one will take your **joy** from
	16:24	that your **joy** may be complete
	17:13	may have my **joy** made complete
Ac	8: 8	So there was great **joy** in that
	12:14	she was so **overjoyed** that,
	13:52	disciples were filled with **joy**
	15: 3	brought great **joy** to all
Ro	14:17	peace and **joy** in the Holy
	15:13	fill you with all **joy** and
	15:32	I may come to you with **joy**
2C	1:24	workers with you for your **joy**
	2: 3	my **joy** would be the joy of all
	7: 4	I am **overjoyed** in all our
	7:13	still more at the **joy** of Titus
	8: 2	their abundant **joy** and their
Ga	5:22	is love, **joy,** peace, patience
Ph	1: 4	constantly praying with **joy** in
	1:25	progress and **joy** in faith,
	2: 2	make my **joy** complete: be of
	2:29	**joy,** and honor such people,
	4: 1	my **joy** and crown, stand firm
Co	1:11	with patience, while **joyfully**
1Th	1: 6	received the word with **joy**
	2:19	For what is our hope or **joy**
	2:20	Yes, you are our glory and **joy**
	3: 9	in return for all the **joy**
2Ti	1: 4	I may be filled with **joy.**
Pm	1: 7	I have indeed received much **joy**
He	10:34	you **cheerfully** accepted the
	12: 2	**joy** that was set before
	12:11	painful rather than **pleasant**
	13:17	do this with **joy** and not with
Ja	1: 2	consider it nothing but **joy,**

	4: 9	and your **joy** into dejection.
1P	1: 8	indescribable and glorious **joy,**
1J	1: 4	that our **joy** may be complete.
2J	1:12	that our **joy** may be complete.
3J	1: 4	I have no greater **joy** than this

5480   GO8 AG876 LN262 B2:573 K9:416
χαραγμα, MARK

Ac	17:29	an **image formed** by the art
Re	13:16	**marked** on the right hand or
	13:17	sell who does not have the **mark**
	14: 9	**mark** on their foreheads or on
	14:11	receives the **mark** of its name
	16: 2	had the **mark** of the beast and
	19:20	had received the **mark** of the
	20: 4	had not received its **mark**

5481   GO1 AG876 LN262 B2:288 K9:418
χαρακτηρ, REPRODUCTION

He	1: 3	**exact imprint** of God's very

5482   GO1 AG876 LN262 B3:951
χαραξ, RAMPART

Lk	19:43	enemies will set up **ramparts**

5483   GO23 AG876 LN262 B2:115 K9:372 R5485
χαριζομαι, I FAVOR

Lk	7:21	**given** sight to many who were
	7:42	he **canceled** the debts for both
	7:43	he **canceled** the greater debt
Ac	3:14	to have a murderer **given** to you
	25:11	no one can **turn** me **over** to them
	25:16	**hand over** anyone before the
	27:24	God **has granted** safety to all
Ro	8:32	also **give** us everything else?
1C	2:12	the gifts **bestowed** on us by God
2C	2: 7	now instead you should **forgive**
	2:10	Anyone whom you **forgive,** I also
	2:10	What I **have forgiven,** if I have
	2:10	I **have forgiven** anything, has
	12:13	**Forgive** me this wrong!
Ga	3:18	God **granted** it to Abraham
Ep	4:32	**forgiving** one another, as God
	4:32	God in Christ **has forgiven** you
Ph	1:29	For he has graciously **granted**
	2: 9	**gave** him the name that is above
Co	2:13	when he **forgave** us all our
	3:13	**forgive** each other; just as
	3:13	as the Lord **has forgiven** you
Pm	1:22	prayers **to be restored** to you.

5484   GO9   AG877   LN262

χαριν, ON ACCOUNT OF

Lk	7:47	**Therefore,** I tell you, her sins
Ga	3:19	added **because of** transgressions
Ep	3: 1	This is the **reason** that I Paul
	3:14	For this **reason** I bow my knees
1Ti	5:14	adversary **no occasion** to revile
Ti	1: 5	behind in Crete for this **reason**
	1:11	by teaching **for** sordid gain
1J	3:12	And **why** did he murder him?
Ju	1:16	people **to their own** advantage.

5485   GO156   AG877   LN262   B2:115   K9:372   R5463

χαρις, FAVOR

Lk	1:30	you have found **favor** with God.
	2:40	the **favor** of God was upon him.
	2:52	in divine and human **favor.**
	4:22	amazed at the **gracious** words
	6:32	what **credit** is that to you?
	6:33	what **credit** is that to you?
	6:34	what **credit** is that to you?
	17: 9	Do you **thank** the slave for
Jn	1:14	son, full of **grace** and truth.
	1:16	received, **grace** upon grace.
	1:16	received, grace upon **grace.**
	1:17	**grace** and truth came through
Ac	2:47	having the **goodwill** of all
	4:33	great **grace** was upon them all
	6: 8	Stephen, full of **grace**
	7:10	enabled him to win **favor** and
	7:46	who found **favor** with God
	11:23	When he came and saw the **grace**
	13:43	continue in the **grace** of God.
	14: 3	to the word of his **grace** by
	14:26	commended to the **grace** of God
	15:11	through the **grace** of the Lord
	15:40	commending him to the **grace**
	18:27	through **grace** had become believers
	20:24	good news of God's **grace.**
	20:32	the message of his **grace,**
	24:27	to grant the Jews a **favor**
	25: 3	and requested, as a **favor**
	25: 9	wishing to do the Jews a **favor**
Ro	1: 5	whom we have received **grace**
	1: 7	**Grace** to you and peace from
	3:24	justified by his **grace** as a
	4: 4	not reckoned as a **gift** but
	4:16	promise may rest on **grace**
	5: 2	obtained access to this **grace**

	5:15	have the **grace** of God and the
	5:15	the free gift in the **grace**
	5:17	**grace** and the free
	5:20	sin increased, **grace** abounded
	5:21	so **grace** might also exercise
	6: 1	in order that **grace** may abound?
	6:14	not under law but under **grace.**
	6:15	not under law but under **grace?**
	6:17	But **thanks** be to God that you,
	7:25	**Thanks** be to God through Jesus
	11: 5	is a remnant, chosen by **grace.**
	11: 6	But if it is by **grace,** it is no
	11: 6	otherwise **grace** would no longer
	11: 6	grace would no longer be **grace.**
	12: 3	For by the **grace** given to me
	12: 6	differ according to the **grace**
	15:15	because of the **grace** given me
	16:20	**grace** of our Lord Jesus Christ
1C	1: 3	**Grace** to you and peace from
	1: 4	because of the **grace** of God
	3:10	According to the **grace** of God
	10:30	If I partake with **thankfulness**
	15:10	But by the **grace** of God I am
	15:10	his **grace** toward me has not
	15:10	but the **grace** of God that is
	15:57	But **thanks** be to God, who
	16: 3	letters to take your **gift** to
	16:23	The **grace** of the Lord Jesus
2C	1: 2	**Grace** to you and peace from
	1:12	wisdom but by the **grace** of God
	1:15	you might have a double **favor;**
	2:14	But **thanks** be to God, who in
	4:15	so that **grace,** as it extends
	6: 1	accept the **grace** of God in vain
	8: 1	about the **grace** of God that has
	8: 4	earnestly for the **privilege**
	8: 6	this **generous undertaking** among
	8: 7	in this **generous undertaking.**
	8: 9	For you know the **generous act**
	8:16	But **thanks** be to God who put
	8:19	this **generous undertaking** for
	9: 8	every **blessing** in abundance
	9:14	surpassing **grace** of God that
	9:15	**Thanks** be to God for his
	12: 9	My **grace** is sufficient for
	13:13	The **grace** of the Lord Jesus
Ga	1: 3	**Grace** to you and peace from
	1: 6	called you in the **grace** of
	1:15	called me through his **grace**

	2: 9	recognized the **grace** that had
	2:21	not nullify the **grace** of God;
	5: 4	you have fallen away from **grace**
	6:18	May the **grace** of our Lord Jesus
Ep	1: 2	**Grace** to you and peace from God
	1: 6	praise of his glorious **grace**
	1: 7	to the riches of his **grace**
	2: 5	by **grace** you have been saved
	2: 7	riches of his **grace** in kindness
	2: 8	by **grace** you have been saved
	3: 2	commission of God's **grace**
	3: 7	gift of God's **grace** that was
	3: 8	this **grace** was given to me to
	4: 7	But each of us was given **grace**
	4:29	your words may give **grace** to
	6:24	**Grace** be with all who have an
Ph	1: 2	**Grace** to you and peace from God
	1: 7	share in God's **grace** with me
	4:23	The **grace** of the Lord Jesus
Co	1: 2	**Grace** to you and peace from
	1: 6	comprehended the **grace** of God.
	3:16	with **gratitude** in your hearts
	4: 6	your speech always be **gracious**
	4:18	**Grace** be with you.
1Th	1; 1	**Grace** to you and peace.
	5:28	The **grace** of our Lord Jesus
2Th	1: 2	**Grace** to you and peace from
	1:12	according to the **grace** of our
	2:16	through **grace** gave us eternal
	3:18	The **grace** of our Lord Jesus
1Ti	1: 2	**Grace,** mercy, and peace from
	1:12	I am **grateful** to Christ
	1:14	and the **grace** of our Lord
	6:21	**Grace** be with you.
2Ti	1: 2	**Grace,** mercy, and peace from
	1: 3	I am **grateful** to God
	1: 9	**grace** was given to us in Christ
	2: 1	be strong in the **grace** that
	4:22	**Grace** be with you.
Ti	1: 4	**Grace** and peace from God the
	2:11	the **grace** of God has appeared
	3: 7	justified by his **grace,** we
	3:15	**Grace** be with all of you.
Pm	1: 3	**Grace** to you and peace from God
	1:25	The **grace** of the Lord Jesus
He	2: 9	by the **grace** of God he might
	4:16	approach the throne of **grace**
	4:16	receive mercy and find **grace**
	10:29	outraged the Spirit of **grace?**

	12:15	fails to obtain the **grace** of
	12:28	let us give **thanks,** by which
	13: 9	to be strengthened by **grace,**
	13:25	**Grace** be with all of you.
Ja	4: 6	he gives all the more **grace**
	4: 6	but gives **grace** to the humble
1P	1: 2	May **grace** and peace be yours in
	1:10	who prophesied of the **grace**
	1:13	set all your hope on the **grace**
	2:19	For it is a **credit** to you if,
	2:20	what **credit** is that? But if
	3: 7	heirs of the **gracious** gift of
	4:10	stewards of the manifold **grace**
	5: 5	gives **grace** to the humble.
	5:10	the God of all **grace,** who has
	5:12	this is the true **grace** of God.
2P	1: 2	May **grace** and peace be yours
	3:18	But grow in the **grace** and
2J	1: 3	**Grace,** mercy, and peace will
Ju	1: 4	pervert the **grace** of our God
Re	1: 4	**Grace** to you and peace from
	22:21	The **grace** of the Lord Jesus be

5486   ᴳᴼ17 ᴬᴳ878 ᴸᴺ262 ᴮ2:115 ᴷ9:402 ᴿ5483
χαρισμα, FAVOR, GIFT

Ro	1:11	spiritual **gift** to strengthen
	5:15	But the free **gift** is not like
	5:16	And the free **gift** is not like
	6:23	free **gift** of God is eternal
	11:29	for the **gifts** and the calling
	12: 6	We have **gifts** that differ
1C	1: 7	lacking in any spiritual **gift**
	7: 7	has a particular **gift** from God
	12: 4	there are varieties of **gifts**
	12: 9	to another **gifts** of healing by
	12:28	then **gifts** of healing, forms of
	12:30	Do all possess **gifts** of healing
	12:31	strive for the greater **gifts**
2C	1:11	for the **blessing** granted us
1Ti	4:14	Do not neglect the **gift** that
2Ti	1: 6	rekindle the **gift** of God that
1P	4:10	one another with whatever **gift**

5487   ᴳᴼ2 ᴬᴳ879 ᴸᴺ262 ᴮ2:115 ᴷ9:372 ᴿ5485
χαριτοω, I FAVOR

Lk	1:28	Greetings, **favored one!** The
Ep	1: 6	grace that he freely **bestowed**

5488   ᴳᴼ2 ᴬᴳ879 ᴸᴺ262
χαρραν, CHARRAN (HARAN)

| Ac | 7: 2 | before he lived in **Haran,** |
| | 7: 4 | settled in **Haran.** After his |

5489 GO1 AG879 LN262
χαρτης, SHEET (OF PAPYRUS)

| 2J | 1:12 | rather not use **paper** and ink |

5490 GO1 AG879 LN262
χασμα, CHASM

| Lk | 16:26 | you and us a great **chasm** has |

5491 GO7 AG879 LN262 B2:740
χειλος, LIP

Mt	15: 8	honors me with their **lips,** but
Mk	7: 6	honors me with their **lips,** but
Ro	3:13	of vipers is under their **lips**
1C	14:21	strange tongues and by the **lips**
He	11:12	grains of sand by the **seashore**
	13:15	fruit of **lips** that confess his
1P	3:10	their **lips** from speaking deceit

5492 GO1 AG879 LN262 R5494
χειμαζω, I TOSS

| Ac | 27:18 | **were being pounded** by the storm |

5493 GO1 AG879 LN262 R5494,4482
χειμαρρος, WINTER FLOW

| Jn | 18: 1 | across the Kidron **valley** to a |

5494 GO6 AG879 LN262
χειμων, WINTER

Mt	16: 3	It will be **stormy** today, for
	24:20	flight may not be in **winter**
Mk	13:18	that it may not be in **winter.**
Jn	10:22	Jerusalem. It was **winter,**
Ac	27:20	no small **tempest** raged, all
2Ti	4:21	to come before **winter.**

5495 GO178 AG879 LN262 B2:148 K9:424
χειρ, HAND

Mt	3:12	winnowing fork is in his **hand**
	4: 6	On their **hands** they will bear
	5:30	right **hand** causes you to sin,
	8: 3	He stretched out his **hand** and
	8:15	he touched her **hand,** and the
	9:18	lay your **hand** on her, and she
	9:25	**hand,** and the girl got up.
	12:10	there with a withered **hand**
	12:13	Stretch out your **hand.**" He
	12:49	And **pointing** to his disciples

	14:31	reached out his **hand** and caught
	15: 2	they do not wash their **hands**
	15:20	unwashed **hands** does not defile
	17:22	to be betrayed into human **hands**
	18: 8	If your **hand** or your foot
	18: 8	than to have two **hands** or two
	19:13	he might lay his **hands** on them
	19:15	And he laid his **hands** on them
	22:13	Bind him **hand** and foot, and
	26:23	one who has dipped his **hand**
	26:45	is betrayed into the **hands** of
	26:50	they came and laid **hands** on
	26:51	put his **hand** on his sword,
	27:24	washed his **hands** before the
Mk	1:31	by the **hand** and lifted her up.
	1:41	Jesus stretched out his **hand**
	3: 1	who had a withered **hand.**
	3: 3	had the withered **hand,** "Come
	3: 5	Stretch out your **hand.**" He
	3: 5	and his **hand** was restored.
	5:23	Come and lay your **hands** on her
	5:41	He took her by the **hand** and
	6: 2	are being done by his **hands!**
	6: 5	he laid his **hands** on a few sick
	7: 2	were eating with defiled **hands**
	7: 3	thoroughly wash their **hands**
	7: 5	but eat with defiled **hands?**
	7:32	begged him to lay his **hand** on
	8:23	blind man by the **hand** and led
	8:23	laid his **hands** on him, he
	8:25	Then Jesus laid his **hands** on
	9:27	But Jesus took him by the **hand**
	9:31	betrayed into human **hands**
	9:43	If your **hand** causes you to
	9:43	two **hands** and to go to hell
	10:16	laid his **hands** on them, and
	14:41	betrayed into the **hands** of
	14:46	Then they laid **hands** on him
	16:18	pick up snakes in their **hands**
	16:18	lay their **hands** on the sick,
Lk	1:66	the **hand** of the Lord was with
	1:71	the **hand** of all who hate us.
	1:74	rescued from the **hands** of our
	3:17	winnowing fork is in his **hand**
	4:11	On their **hands** they will bear
	4:40	he laid his **hands** on each
	5:13	Jesus stretched out his **hand**
	6: 1	rubbed them in their **hands**
	6: 6	whose right **hand** was withered.

	6: 8	man who had the withered **hand**		9:41	He gave her his **hand** and helped
	6:10	Stretch out your **hand.**" He did		11:21	The **hand** of the Lord was with
	6:10	his **hand** was restored.		11:30	to the elders **by** Barnabas
	8:54	But he took her by the **hand**		12: 1	Herod laid violent **hands** upon
	9:44	to be betrayed into human **hands**		12: 7	chains fell off his **wrists.**
	9:62	puts a **hand** to the plow		12:11	rescued me from the **hands** of
	13:13	When he laid his **hands** on her		12:17	motioned to them with his **hand**
	15:22	put a ring on his **finger** and		13: 3	they laid their **hands** on
	20:19	they wanted to lay **hands** on him		13:11	**hand** of the Lord is against you
	21:12	they **will arrest** you		13:16	with a **gesture** began to speak
	22:21	and his **hand** is on the table.		14: 3	wonders to be done through **them**
	22:53	you did not lay **hands** on me.		15:23	with the following **letter:**
	23:46	Father, into your **hands** I		17:25	nor is he served by human **hands**
	24: 7	must be handed over to **sinners**		19: 6	When Paul had laid his **hands** on
	24:39	Look at my **hands** and my feet		19:11	miracles through **Paul,**
	24:40	he showed them his **hands** and		19:26	gods made with **hands** are not
	24:50	lifting up his **hands,** he		19:33	Alexander **motioned** for silence
Jn	3:35	placed all things in his **hands**		20:34	I worked with my own **hands** to
	7:30	no one laid **hands** on him,		21:11	bound his own feet and **hands**
	7:44	but no one laid **hands** on him.		21:11	will **hand** him over to the
	10:28	will snatch them out of my **hand**		21:27	They **seized** him,
	10:29	it out of the Father's **hand.**		21:40	**motioned** to the people for
	10:39	he escaped from their **hands.**		23:19	tribune took him by the **hand**
	11:44	dead man came out, his **hands**		26: 1	Paul stretched out his **hand**
	13: 3	given all things into his **hands**		28: 3	fastened itself on his **hand.**
	13: 9	but also my **hands** and my head		28: 4	creature hanging from his **hand**
	20:20	he showed them his **hands**		28: 8	praying and putting his **hands**
	20:25	mark of the nails in his **hands**		28:17	and **handed** over to the Romans.
	20:25	mark of the nails and my **hand**	Ro	10:21	I have held out my **hands** to
	20:27	here and see my **hands.** Reach	1C	4:12	from the work of our own **hands**
	20:27	Reach out your **hand** and put		12:15	Because I am not a **hand,** I do
	21:18	you will stretch out your **hands**		12:21	The eye cannot say to the **hand**
Ac	2:23	killed by the **hands** of those		16:21	this greeting with my own **hand.**
	3: 7	took him by the right **hand**	2C	11:33	and escaped from his **hands.**
	4: 3	So they **arrested** them and put	Ga	3:19	through angels by a **mediator.**
	4:28	to do whatever your **hand** and		6:11	I am writing in my own **hand!**
	4:30	while you stretch out your **hand**	Ep	4:28	honestly with their own **hands**
	5:12	people through the **apostles.**	Co	4:18	this greeting with my own **hand**
	5:18	**arrested** the apostles and put	1Th	4:11	and to work with your **hands**
	6: 6	laid their **hands** on them.	2Th	3:17	this greeting with my own **hand**
	7:25	God through **him** was rescuing	1Ti	2: 8	lifting up holy **hands** without
	7:35	through the **angel** who appeared		4:14	laying on of **hands** by the
	7:41	in the works of their **hands.**		5:22	Do not **ordain** anyone hastily
	7:50	Did not my **hand** make all these	2Ti	1: 6	the laying on of my **hands**
	8:17	Peter and John laid their **hands**	Pm	1:19	writing this with my own **hand**
	8:18	apostles' **hands,** he offered	He	1:10	are the work of your **hands;**
	8:19	on whom I lay my **hands** may		6: 2	baptisms, laying on of **hands**
	9:12	lay his **hands** on him so that		8: 9	I took them by the **hand** to lead
	9:17	He laid his **hands** on Saul and		10:31	to fall into the **hands** of the

	12:12	lift your drooping **hands**
Ja	4: 8	Cleanse your **hands,** you sinners
1P	5: 6	under the mighty **hand** of God
1J	1: 1	touched with our **hands,**
Re	1:16	In his right **hand** he held seven
	6: 5	a pair of scales in his **hand,**
	7: 9	palm branches in their **hands.**
	8: 4	from the **hand** of the angel.
	9:20	works of their **hands** or give up
	10: 2	little scroll open in his **hand**
	10: 5	raised his right **hand** to heaven
	10: 8	open in the **hand** of the angel
	10:10	little scroll from the **hand**
	13:16	be marked on the right **hand**
	14: 9	foreheads or on their **hands,**
	14:14	sharp sickle in his **hand!**
	17: 4	holding in her **hand** a golden
	19: 2	he has avenged on **her** the blood
	20: 1	holding in his **hand** the key
	20: 4	their foreheads or their **hands**

5496　GO2 AG880 LN262 K9:435 R5497
χειραγωγεω, I LEAD BY HAND

Ac	9: 8	they **led** him **by the hand** and
	22:11	**took** my **hand** and led me to

5497　GO1 AG880 LN262 K9:435 R5495,71
χειραγωγος, LEADING BY HAND

Ac	13:11	someone to **lead** him **by the hand**

5498　GO1 AG880 LN263 B3:1199 K9:435 R5495,1125
χειρογραφον, HAND-WRITTEN

Co	2:14	erasing the **record** that stood

5499　GO6 AG880 LN263 B3:185 K9:436 R5495,4160
χειροποιητος, HAND-MADE

Mk	14:58	that is **made with hands,** and in
Ac	7:48	in houses **made with human hands**
	17:24	in shrines **made by human hands,**
Ep	2:11	in the flesh **by human hands**
He	9:11	not **made with hands,** that is
	9:24	sanctuary **made by human hands**

5500　GO2 AG881 LN263 B1:478 K9:437
χειροτονεω, I STRETCH OUT HAND
(APPOINT)

Ac	14:23	they had **appointed** elders for
2C	8:19	**been appointed** by the churches

5501　GO11 AG881 LN263
χειρων, WORSE

Mt	9:16	cloak, and a **worse** tear is made
	12:45	state of that person is **worse**
	27:64	last deception would be **worse**
Mk	2:21	old, and a **worse** tear is made.
	5:26	better, but rather grew **worse.**
Lk	11:26	state of that person is **worse**
Jn	5:14	so that nothing **worse** happens
1Ti	5: 8	denied the faith and is **worse**
2Ti	3:13	go from bad to **worse,** deceiving
He	10:29	How much **worse** punishment do
2P	2:20	last state has become **worse** for

5502　GO1 AG881 LN263 B1:279 K9:438
χερουβ, CHERUB

He	9: 5	above it were the **cherubim** of

5503　GO27 AG881 LN263 B3:1073 K9:440
χηρα, WIDOW

Mk	12:40	They devour **widows'** houses and
	12:42	A poor **widow** came and put in
	12:43	this poor **widow** has put in more
Lk	2:37	then as a **widow** to the age of
	4:25	there were many **widows** in
	4:26	except to a **widow** at Zarephath
	7:12	only son, and she was a **widow;**
	18: 3	In that city there was a **widow**
	18: 5	yet because this **widow** keeps
	20:47	They devour **widows'** houses and
	21: 2	he also saw a poor **widow** put in
	21: 3	this poor **widow** has put in more
Ac	6: 1	because their **widows** were being
	9:39	All the **widows** stood beside him
	9:41	calling the saints and **widows,**
1C	7: 8	To the unmarried and the **widows**
1Ti	5: 3	Honor **widows** who are really
	5: 3	widows who are really **widows.**
	5: 4	If a **widow** has children or
	5: 5	The real **widow,** left alone, has
	5: 9	Let a **widow** be put on the list
	5:11	refuse to put younger **widows** on
	5:16	relatives who are really **widows**
	5:16	those who are real **widows.**
Ja	1:27	to care for orphans and **widows**
Re	18: 7	I am no **widow,** and I will never

5505　GO25 AG882 LN263 B2:697 K9:466 R5507
χιλιας, THOUSAND

Lk	14:31	with ten **thousand** to oppose the

	14:31	him with twenty **thousand?**
Ac	4: 4	numbered about five **thousand.**
1C	10: 8	twenty-three **thousand** fell in a
Re	5:11	myriads and **thousands** of
	5:11	and thousands of **thousands,**
	7: 4	one hundred forty-four **thousand**
	7: 5	twelve **thousand** sealed, from
	7: 5	tribe of Reuben twelve **thousand**
	7: 5	tribe of Gad twelve **thousand,**
	7: 6	tribe of Asher twelve **thousand,**
	7: 6	of Naphtali twelve **thousand,**
	7: 6	of Manasseh twelve **thousand,**
	7: 7	of Simeon twelve **thousand,**
	7: 7	tribe of Levi twelve **thousand,**
	7: 7	of Issachar twelve **thousand,**
	7: 8	of Zebulun twelve **thousand,**
	7: 8	tribe of Joseph twelve **thousand**
	7: 8	Benjamin twelve **thousand** sealed
	11: 3	prophesy for one **thousand** two
	11:13	seven **thousand** people were
	12: 6	nourished for one **thousand** two
	14: 1	one hundred forty-four **thousand**
	14: 3	one hundred forty-four **thousand**
	21:16	fifteen hundred miles [twelve **thousand** stadia]

5506　GO22　AG881　LN263　B2:699　R5507,757
χιλιαρχος, RULER OF THOUSAND

Mk	6:21	for his courtiers and **officers**
Jn	18:12	So the soldiers, their **officer,**
Ac	21:31	word came to the **tribune** of the
	21:32	When they saw the **tribune** and
	21:33	Then the **tribune** came, arrested
	21:37	he said to the **tribune,** "May I
	22:24	the **tribune** directed that he
	22:26	he went to the **tribune** and said
	22:27	The **tribune** came and asked Paul
	22:28	The **tribune** answered, "It cost
	22:29	and the **tribune** also was afraid
	23:10	the **tribune,** fearing that they
	23:15	notify the **tribune** to bring him
	23:17	this young man to the **tribune,**
	23:18	brought him to the **tribune,** and
	23:19	The **tribune** took him by the
	23:22	So the **tribune** dismissed the
	24:22	When Lysias the **tribune** comes
	25:23	the military **tribunes** and the
Re	6:15	magnates and the **generals** and
	19:18	flesh of **captains,** the flesh

5507　GO9　AG882　LN263　B2:697　K9:466
χιλιοι, THOUSANDS

2P	3: 8	one day is like a **thousand**
	3: 8	a **thousand** years are like one
Re	14:20	two hundred miles [one **thousand** six hundred stadia]
	20: 2	and bound him for a **thousand**
	20: 3	until the **thousand** years were
	20: 4	reigned with Christ a **thousand**
	20: 5	until the **thousand** years were
	20: 6	will reign with him a **thousand**
	20: 7	When the **thousand** years are

5508　GO1　AG882　LN263
χιος, CHIOS

Ac	20:15	we arrived opposite **Chios.**

5509　GO11　AG882　LN263
χιτων, SHIRT

Mt	5:40	take your **coat,** give your cloak
	10:10	or two **tunics,** or sandals, or a
Mk	6: 9	not to put on two **tunics**
	14:63	high priest tore his **clothes**
Lk	3:11	Whoever has two **coats** must
	6:29	do not withhold even your **shirt**
	9: 3	not even an extra **tunic.**
Jn	19:23	They also took his **tunic;** now
	19:23	now the **tunic** was seamless,
Ac	9:39	weeping and showing **tunics**
Ju	1:23	hating even the **tunic** defiled

5510　GO2　AG882　LN263
χιων, SNOW

Mt	28: 3	and his clothing white as **snow.**
Re	1:14	as white wool, white as **snow;**

5511　GO2　AG882　LN263
χλαμυς, ROBE

Mt	27:28	and put a scarlet **robe** on him,
	27:31	they stripped him of the **robe**

5512　GO1　AG882　LN263
χλευαζω, I JEER

Ac	17:32	some **scoffed;** but others said,

5513　GO1　AG882　LN263　B1:317　K2:876
χλιαρος, LUKEWARM

Re	3:16	So, because you are **lukewarm,**

5514 GO1 AG882 LN263 B2:27
χλοη, CHLOE
1C 1:11 by **Chloe's** people that there

5515 GO4 AG882 LN263 B1:205
χλωρος, GREEN
Mk 6:39 sit down in groups on the **green**
Re 6: 8 there was a pale **green** horse!
8: 7 all **green** grass was burned up.
9: 4 any **green** growth or any tree,

5517 GO4 AG883 LN263 B1:520 K9:472
χοικος, DUST
1C 15:47 a man of **dust;** the second man
15:48 As was the man of **dust,** so are
15:48 are those who are of the **dust;**
15:49 the image of the man of **dust,**

5518 GO2 AG883 LN263
χοινιξ, CHOINIX
Re 6: 6 A **quart** of wheat for a day's
6: 6 three **quarts** of barley for a

5519 GO12 AG883 LN263 B1:117
χοιρος, PIG
Mt 7: 6 pearls before **swine,** or they
8:30 Now a large herd of **swine** was
8:31 send us into the herd of **swine.**
8:32 came out and entered the **swine;**
Mk 5:11 great herd of **swine** was feeding
5:12 Send us into the **swine;** let us
5:13 and entered the **swine;** and the
5:16 the demoniac and to the **swine**
Lk 8:32 large herd of **swine** was feeding
8:33 entered the **swine,** and the herd
15:15 to his fields to feed the **pigs.**
15:16 pods that the **pigs** were eating;

5520 GO1 AG883 LN263 R521
χολαω, I AM BITTER
Jn 7:23 **are** you **angry** with me because

5521 GO2 AG883 LN263 B2:27
χολη, GALL
Mt 27:34 mixed with **gall;** but when he
Ac 8:23 are in the **gall** of bitterness

5523 GO2 AG883 LN263
χοραζιν, CHORAZIN
Mt 11:21 Woe to you, **Chorazin!** Woe to

Lk 10:13 Woe to you, **Chorazin!** Woe to

5524 GO2 AG883 LN263
χορηγεω, I SUPPLY
2C 9:10 bread for food **will supply**
1P 4:11 the strength that God **supplies,**

5525 GO1 AG883 LN263 B1:728
χορος, DANCING
Lk 15:25 he heard music and **dancing.**

5526 GO16 AG883 LN263
χορταζω, I AM SATISFIED
Mt 5: 6 for they **will be filled.**
14:20 And all ate and **were filled;**
15:33 desert **to feed** so great a crowd
15:37 ate and **were filled;** and they
Mk 6:42 And all ate and **were filled;**
7:27 **Let** the children **be fed** first,
8: 4 How can one **feed** these people
8: 8 They ate and **were filled;** and
Lk 6:21 you **will be filled.** "Blessed
9:17 And all ate and **were filled.**
15:16 He would gladly **have filled**
16:21 who longed to **satisfy** his
Jn 6:26 you ate your **fill** of the loaves
Ph 4:12 secret of **being well-fed** and
Ja 2:16 keep warm and **eat** your **fill,"**
Re 19:21 all the birds **were gorged** with

5527 GO1 AG884 LN263 B1:743 R5526
χορτασμα, SUSTENANCE
Ac 7:11 ancestors could find no **food.**

5528 GO15 AG884 LN263 B1:743
χορτος, GRASS
Mt 6:30 But if God so clothes the **grass**
13:26 So when the **plants** came up and
14:19 crowds to sit down on the
grass
Mk 4:28 first the **stalk,** then the head,
6:39 in groups on the green **grass.**
Lk 12:28 But if God so clothes the **grass**
Jn 6:10 there was a great deal of **grass**
1C 3:12 precious stones, wood, **hay,**
Ja 1:10 will disappear like a **flower** in
1:11 withers the **field;** its flower
1P 1:24 For "All flesh is like **grass**
1:24 glory like the flower of **grass.**
1:24 **grass** withers, and the flower

Re	8: 7	all green **grass** was burned up.
	9: 4	damage the **grass** of the earth

5529   GO1   AG884   LN264
χουζας, CHUZA

Lk	8: 3	of Herod's steward **Chuza,** and

5529a   GO2   AG884   LN264   B1:520
χους, DUST

Mk	6:11	shake off the **dust** that is on
Re	18:19	And they threw **dust** on their

5530   GO11   AG884   LN264
χραομαι, I USE

Ac	27: 3	Julius **treated** Paul kindly, and
	27:17	they **took measures** to undergird
1C	7:21	**make use** of your present
	7:31	and those who **deal** with the
	9:12	we **have** not **made use** of this
	9:15	But I have **made** no **use** of any
2C	1:17	Was I **vacillating** when I wanted
	3:12	we **act** with great boldness,
	13:10	I **may** not **have** to be severe in
1Ti	1: 8	if one **uses** it legitimately.
	5:23	but **take** a little wine for the

5532   GO49   AG884   LN264   B3:956   R5530
χρεια, NEED

Mt	3:14	I **need** to be baptized by you,
	6: 8	knows what you **need** before you
	9:12	who are well have no **need** of a
	14:16	Jesus said to them, "They **need**
	21: 3	'The Lord **needs** them.' And he
	26:65	Why do we still **need** witnesses?
Mk	2:17	who are well have no **need** of a
	2:25	were hungry and in **need** of food
	11: 3	The Lord **needs** it and will
	14:63	Why do we still **need** witnesses
Lk	5:31	who are well have no **need** of a
	9:11	healed those who **needed** to be
	10:42	there is **need** of only one thing
	15: 7	persons who **need** no repentance.
	19:31	say this, 'The Lord **needs** it.'
	19:34	They said, "The Lord **needs** it."
	22:71	further testimony do we **need?**
Jn	2:25	**needed** no one to testify about
	13:10	bathed does not **need** to wash,
	13:29	Buy what we **need** for the
	16:30	do not **need** to have anyone
Ac	2:45	to all, as any had **need.**

	4:35	to each as any had **need.**
	6: 3	we may appoint to this **task,**
	20:34	my own hands to **support** myself
	28:10	all the provisions we **needed.**
Ro	12:13	Contribute to the **needs** of the
1C	12:21	I have no **need** of you.
	12:24	do not **need** this. But God has
Ep	4:28	to share with the **needy.**
	4:29	as there is **need,** so that your
Ph	2:25	and minister to my **need;**
	4:16	help for my **needs** more than
	4:19	will fully satisfy every **need**
1Th	1: 8	so that we have no **need** to
	4: 9	you do not **need** to have anyone
	4:12	outsiders and be **dependent** on
	5: 1	do not **need** to have anything
Ti	3:14	in order to meet urgent **needs,**
He	5:12	you **need** someone to teach you
	5:12	You **need** milk, not solid food;
	7:11	what further **need** would there
	10:36	For you **need** endurance, so that
1J	2:27	so you do not **need** anyone to
	3:17	a brother or sister in **need** and
Re	3:17	I have prospered, and I **need**
	21:23	And the city has no **need** of sun
	22: 5	they **need** no light of lamp or

5533   GO2   AG885   LN264
χρεοφειλετης, BORROWER

Lk	7:41	creditor had two **debtors;** one
	16: 5	summoning his master's **debtors**

5534   GO1   AG885   LN264   B3:956
χρη, IT IS USEFUL

Ja	3:10	this **ought** not to **be** so.

5535   GO5   AG885   LN264   R5532
χρηζω, I NEED

Mt	6:32	knows that you **need** all these
Lk	11: 8	give him whatever he **needs.**
	12:30	knows that you **need** them.
Ro	16: 2	in whatever she **may require**
2C	3: 1	Surely we **do** not **need,** as some

5536   GO6   AG885   LN264   B2:845   K9:480
χρημα, WEALTH

Mk	10:23	for those who have **wealth** to
Lk	18:24	those who have **wealth** to enter
Ac	4:37	then brought the **money,** and
	8:18	hands, he offered them **money,**

8:20	obtain God's gift with **money!**
24:26	he hoped that **money** would be

5537　GO9　AG885　LN264　B3:324　K9:480
χρηματιζω, I WARN

Mt	2:12	And **having been warned** in a
	2:22	after **being warned** in a dream,
Lk	2:26	It **had been revealed** to him by
Ac	10:22	**was directed** by a holy angel to
	11:26	**were** first **called** "Christians."
Ro	7: 3	Accordingly, she **will be called**
He	8: 5	**was warned,** "See that you make
	11: 7	By faith Noah, **warned by God**
	12:25	one who **warned** them on earth,

5538　GO1　AG885　LN264　B3:324　K9:482　R5537
χρηματισμος, WARNING

| Ro | 11: 4 | But what is the **divine reply** to |

5539　GO1　AG884　LN264　R5540
χρησιμος, USEFUL

| 2Ti | 2:14 | which does no **good** but only |

5540　GO2　AG884　LN264　R5530
χρησις, USE

| Ro | 1:26 | **intercourse** for unnatural, |
| | 1:27 | giving up natural **intercourse** |

5541　GO1　AG886　LN264　B2:105　K9:491　R5543
χρηστευομαι, I AM KIND

| 1C | 13: 4 | Love is patient; love **is kind;** |

5542　GO1　AG886　LN264　B1:212　K9:492　R5543,3004
χρηστολογια, KIND WORD

| Ro | 16:18 | by **smooth talk** and flattery |

5543　GO7　AG886　LN264　B2:105　K9:483
χρηστος, KIND

Mt	11:30	For my yoke is **easy,** and my
Lk	5:39	but says, 'The old is **good.**'
	6:35	he is **kind** to the ungrateful
Ro	2: 4	realize that God's **kindness** is
1C	15:33	Bad company ruins **good** morals.
Ep	4:32	and be **kind** to one another,
1P	2: 3	tasted that the Lord is **good.**

5544　GO10　AG886　LN264　B2:105　K9:489　R5543
χρηστοτης, KINDNESS

| Ro | 2: 4 | riches of his **kindness** and |
| | 3:12 | no one who shows **kindness,** |

11:22	Note then the **kindness** and the
11:22	but God's **kindness** toward you,
11:22	continue in his **kindness;**
2C	6: 6	**kindness,** holiness of spirit,
Ga	5:22	peace, patience, **kindness,**
Ep	2: 7	his grace in **kindness** toward
Co	3:12	**kindness,** humility, meekness,
Ti	3: 4	loving **kindness** of God our

5545　GO3　AG886　LN264　B1:119　K9:493　R5548
χρισμα, ANOINTING

1J	2:20	But you have been **anointed** by
	2:27	As for you, the **anointing** that
	2:27	But as his **anointing** teaches

5546　GO3　AG886　LN264　B2:343　K9:493　R5547
χριστιανος, CHRISTIAN

Ac	11:26	were first called **"Christians."**
	26:28	me to become a **Christian?"**
1P	4:16	suffers as a **Christian,** do not

5547　GO531　AG886　LN264　B2:334　K9:493　R5548
χριστος, CHRIST

Mt	1: 1	genealogy of Jesus the **Messiah,**
	1:16	born, who is called the **Messiah**
	1:17	Babylon to the **Messiah,**
	1:18	birth of Jesus the **Messiah** took
	2: 4	where the **Messiah** was to be
	11: 2	what the **Messiah** was doing, he
	16:16	You are the **Messiah,** the Son
	16:20	anyone that he was the **Messiah.**
	22:42	do you think of the **Messiah?**
	23:10	one instructor, the **Messiah.**
	24: 5	'I am the **Messiah!**' and they
	24:23	'Look! Here is the **Messiah!**' or
	26:63	you are the **Messiah,** the Son of
	26:68	Prophesy to us, you **Messiah!**
	27:17	Jesus who is called the **Messiah**
	27:22	Jesus who is called the **Messiah**
Mk	1: 1	Jesus **Christ,** the Son of God.
	8:29	him, "You are the **Messiah.**"
	9:41	bear the name of **Christ** will by
	12:35	say that the **Messiah** is the son
	13:21	'Look! Here is the **Messiah!**' or
	14:61	Are you the **Messiah,** the Son
	15:32	Let the **Messiah,** the King of
Lk	2:11	who is the **Messiah,** the Lord.
	2:26	he had seen the Lord's **Messiah.**
	3:15	whether he might be the **Messiah**
	4:41	knew that he was the **Messiah.**

	9:20	answered, "The **Messiah** of God."		24:24	concerning faith in **Christ**
	20:41	that the **Messiah** is David's son		26:23	that the **Messiah** must suffer,
	22:67	If you are the **Messiah,** tell		28:31	Lord Jesus **Christ** with all
	23: 2	he himself is the **Messiah,** a	Ro	1: 1	Paul, a servant of Jesus **Christ**
	23:35	if he is the **Messiah** of God,		1: 4	the dead, Jesus **Christ** our Lord
	23:39	Are you not the **Messiah?** Save		1: 6	to belong to Jesus **Christ,**
	24:26	that the **Messiah** should suffer		1: 7	and the Lord Jesus **Christ.**
	24:46	that the **Messiah** is to suffer		1: 8	through Jesus **Christ** for all of
Jn	1:17	truth came through Jesus **Christ**		2:16	God, through Jesus **Christ,** will
	1:20	I am not the **Messiah.**		3:22	through faith in Jesus **Christ**
	1:25	if you are neither the **Messiah,**		3:24	redemption that is in **Christ**
	1:41	(which is translated **Anointed**).		5: 1	through our Lord Jesus **Christ,**
	3:28	I am not the **Messiah,** but I		5: 6	at the right time **Christ** died
	4:25	(who is called **Christ**). "When		5: 8	we still were sinners **Christ**
	4:29	He cannot be the **Messiah,** can		5:11	through our Lord Jesus **Christ,**
	7:26	know that this is the **Messiah?**		5:15	Jesus **Christ,** abounded for the
	7:27	but when the **Messiah** comes, no		5:17	the one man, Jesus **Christ.**
	7:31	When the **Messiah** comes, will		5:21	life through Jesus **Christ** our
	7:41	"This is the **Messiah."** But some		6: 3	baptized into **Christ** Jesus were
	7:41	Surely the **Messiah** does not		6: 4	just as **Christ** was raised from
	7:42	the **Messiah** is descended from		6: 8	But if we have died with **Christ**
	9:22	Jesus to be the **Messiah** would		6: 9	We know that **Christ,** being
	10:24	If you are the **Messiah,** tell us		6:11	alive to God in **Christ** Jesus.
	11:27	you are the **Messiah,** the Son of		6:23	eternal life in **Christ** Jesus
	12:34	the **Messiah** remains forever.		7: 4	law through the body of **Christ,**
	17: 3	Jesus **Christ** whom you have sent		7:25	through Jesus **Christ** our Lord!
	20:31	Jesus is the **Messiah,** the Son		8: 1	those who are in **Christ** Jesus.
Ac	2:31	resurrection of the **Messiah,**		8: 2	Spirit of life in **Christ** Jesus
	2:36	Lord and **Messiah,** this Jesus		8: 9	not have the Spirit of **Christ**
	2:38	in the name of Jesus **Christ** so		8:10	But if **Christ** is in you, though
	3: 6	of Jesus **Christ** of Nazareth,		8:11	he who raised **Christ** from the
	3:18	that his **Messiah** would suffer.		8:17	joint heirs with **Christ**—if,
	3:20	may send the **Messiah** appointed		8:34	Who is to condemn? It is **Christ**
	4:10	by the name of Jesus **Christ** of		8:35	from the love of **Christ?** Will
	4:26	Lord and against his **Messiah.**		8:39	from the love of God in **Christ**
	5:42	proclaim Jesus as the **Messiah.**		9: 1	speaking the truth in **Christ**—
	8: 5	proclaimed the **Messiah** to them.		9: 3	cut off from **Christ** for the
	8:12	name of Jesus **Christ,** they were		9: 5	comes the **Messiah,** who is over
	9:22	that Jesus was the **Messiah.**		10: 4	For **Christ** is the end of the
	9:34	Aeneas, Jesus **Christ** heals you		10: 6	(that is, to bring **Christ** down)
	10:36	preaching peace by Jesus **Christ**		10: 7	to bring **Christ** up from the
	10:48	in the name of Jesus **Christ.**		10:17	through the word of **Christ.**
	11:17	in the Lord Jesus **Christ,** who		12: 5	are one body in **Christ,** and
	15:26	sake of our Lord Jesus **Christ.**		13:14	put on the Lord Jesus **Christ,**
	16:18	in the name of Jesus **Christ** to		14: 9	For to this end **Christ** died and
	17: 3	necessary for the **Messiah** to		14:15	ruin of one for whom **Christ**
	17: 3	This is the **Messiah,** Jesus		14:18	The one who thus serves **Christ**
	18: 5	Jews that the **Messiah** was Jesus		15: 3	For **Christ** did not please
	18:28	that the **Messiah** is Jesus.		15: 5	in accordance with **Christ** Jesus

15: 6	of our Lord Jesus **Christ**.
15: 7	just as **Christ** has welcomed you
15: 8	For I tell you that **Christ** has
15:16	a minister of **Christ** Jesus to
15:17	In **Christ** Jesus, then, I have
15:18	anything except what **Christ** has
15:19	the good news of **Christ**.
15:20	not where **Christ** has already
15:29	of the blessing of **Christ**.
15:30	by our Lord Jesus **Christ** and by
16: 3	work with me in **Christ** Jesus,
16: 5	convert in Asia for **Christ**.
16: 7	were in **Christ** before I was.
16: 9	our co-worker in **Christ,** and
16:10	who is approved in **Christ**.
16:16	All the churches of **Christ**
16:18	do not serve our Lord **Christ,**
16:25	proclamation of Jesus **Christ,**
16:27	through Jesus **Christ,** to whom
1C 1: 1	be an apostle of **Christ** Jesus
1: 2	who are sanctified in **Christ**
1: 2	name of our Lord Jesus **Christ,**
1: 3	and the Lord Jesus **Christ**.
1: 4	given you in **Christ** Jesus,
1: 6	just as the testimony of **Christ**
1: 7	of our Lord Jesus **Christ**.
1: 8	day of our Lord Jesus **Christ**.
1: 9	Son, Jesus **Christ** our Lord.
1:10	name of our Lord Jesus **Christ,**
1:12	Cephas," or "I belong to **Christ**
1:13	Has **Christ** been divided? Was
1:17	For **Christ** did not send me to
1:17	that the cross of **Christ** might
1:23	we proclaim **Christ** crucified,
1:24	**Christ** the power of God and the
1:30	your life in **Christ** Jesus, who
2: 2	among you except Jesus **Christ,**
2:16	But we have the mind of **Christ**.
3: 1	the flesh, as infants in **Christ**
3:11	that foundation is Jesus **Christ**
3:23	and you belong to **Christ,** and
3:23	and **Christ** belongs to God.
4: 1	as servants of **Christ** and
4:10	fools for the sake of **Christ,**
4:10	but you are wise in **Christ**. We
4:15	thousand guardians in **Christ,**
4:15	in **Christ** Jesus I became your
4:17	remind you of my ways in **Christ**
5: 7	For our paschal lamb, **Christ,**

6:11	name of the Lord Jesus **Christ**
6:15	bodies are members of **Christ**?
6:15	take the members of **Christ** and
7:22	called is a slave of **Christ**.
8: 6	one Lord, Jesus **Christ,** through
8:11	believers for whom **Christ** died
8:12	is weak, you sin against **Christ**
9:12	the way of the gospel of **Christ**
9:21	but am under **Christ's** law) so
10: 4	them, and the rock was **Christ**.
10: 9	We must not put **Christ** to the
10:16	sharing in the blood of **Christ**?
10:16	sharing in the body of **Christ**?
11: 1	of me, as I am of **Christ**.
11: 3	understand that **Christ** is the
11: 3	and God is the head of **Christ**.
12:12	one body, so it is with **Christ**.
12:27	Now you are the body of **Christ**
15: 3	that **Christ** died for our sins
15:12	Now if **Christ** is proclaimed as
15:13	then **Christ** has not been raised
15:14	and if **Christ** has not been
15:15	that he raised **Christ**
15:16	then **Christ** has not been raised
15:17	If **Christ** has not been raised,
15:18	who have died in **Christ** have
15:19	we have hoped in **Christ,** we are
15:20	But in fact **Christ** has been
15:22	will be made alive in **Christ**.
15:23	in his own order: **Christ** the
15:23	those who belong to **Christ**.
15:31	a boast that I make in **Christ**
15:57	through our Lord Jesus **Christ**.
16:24	be with all of you in **Christ**
2C 1: 1	Paul, an apostle of **Christ**
1: 2	and the Lord Jesus **Christ**.
1: 3	of our Lord Jesus **Christ,** the
1: 5	the sufferings of **Christ** are
1: 5	is abundant through **Christ**.
1:19	**Christ,** whom we proclaimed
1:21	us with you in **Christ** and has
2:10	sake in the presence of **Christ**.
2:12	the good news of **Christ,** a door
2:14	who in **Christ** always leads us
2:15	For we are the aroma of **Christ**
2:17	in **Christ** we speak as persons
3: 3	you are a letter of **Christ,**
3: 4	that we have through **Christ**
3:14	since only in **Christ** is it set

4: 4	the glory of **Christ,** who is the
4: 5	proclaim Jesus **Christ** as Lord
4: 6	God in the face of Jesus **Christ**
5:10	the judgment seat of **Christ,** so
5:14	For the love of **Christ** urges us
5:16	we once knew **Christ** from a
5:17	So if anyone is in **Christ,**
5:18	himself through **Christ,** and has
5:19	that is, in **Christ** God was
5:20	ambassadors for **Christ,** since
5:20	entreat you on behalf of **Christ**
6:15	What agreement does **Christ** have
8: 9	act of our Lord Jesus **Christ,**
8:23	churches, the glory of **Christ.**
9:13	of the gospel of **Christ** and by
10: 1	and gentleness of **Christ**
10: 5	thought captive to obey **Christ.**
10: 7	that you belong to **Christ,**
10: 7	just as you belong to **Christ,**
10:14	with the good news of **Christ.**
11: 2	as a chaste virgin to **Christ.**
11: 3	and pure devotion to **Christ.**
11:10	As the truth of **Christ** is in me
11:13	as apostles of **Christ.**
11:23	Are they ministers of **Christ?** I
12: 2	I know a person in **Christ** who
12: 9	the power of **Christ** may dwell
12:10	for the sake of **Christ;** for
12:19	are speaking in **Christ** before
13: 3	you desire proof that **Christ** is
13: 5	not realize that Jesus **Christ**
13:13	of the Lord Jesus **Christ,** the

Ga	1: 1	through Jesus **Christ** and God
	1: 3	and the Lord Jesus **Christ,**
	1: 6	in the grace of **Christ** and are
	1: 7	to pervert the gospel of **Christ**
	1:10	not be a servant of **Christ.**
	1:12	a revelation of Jesus **Christ.**
	1:22	of Judea that are in **Christ;**
	2: 4	freedom we have in **Christ** Jesus
	2:16	through faith in Jesus **Christ.**
	2:16	have come to believe in **Christ**
	2:16	justified by faith in **Christ,**
	2:17	be justified in **Christ,** we
	2:17	is **Christ** then a servant of sin
	2:19	have been crucified with **Christ**
	2:20	but it is **Christ** who lives in
	2:21	then **Christ** died for nothing.
	3: 1	Jesus **Christ** was publicly

3:13	**Christ** redeemed us from the
3:14	in order that in **Christ** Jesus
3:16	to one person, who is **Christ.**
3:22	through faith in Jesus **Christ**
3:24	until **Christ** came, so that we
3:26	for in **Christ** Jesus you are all
3:27	were baptized into **Christ** have
3:27	clothed yourselves with **Christ.**
3:28	of you are one in **Christ** Jesus.
3:29	And if you belong to **Christ,**
4:14	as an angel of God, as **Christ**
4:19	of childbirth until **Christ** is
5: 1	For freedom **Christ** has set us
5: 2	**Christ** will be of no benefit to
5: 4	cut yourselves off from **Christ;**
5: 6	For in **Christ** Jesus neither
5:24	And those who belong to **Christ**
6: 2	will fulfill the law of **Christ.**
6:12	for the cross of **Christ.**
6:14	cross of our Lord Jesus **Christ,**
6:18	grace of our Lord Jesus **Christ**

Ep	1: 1	Paul, an apostle of **Christ**
	1: 1	are faithful in **Christ** Jesus:
	1: 2	and the Lord Jesus **Christ.**
	1: 3	of our Lord Jesus **Christ,** who
	1: 3	who has blessed us in **Christ**
	1: 5	through Jesus **Christ,** according
	1:10	to gather up all things in **him,**
	1:12	set our hope on **Christ,** might
	1:17	God of our Lord Jesus **Christ,**
	1:20	power to work in **Christ** when he
	2: 5	us alive together with **Christ**
	2: 6	the heavenly places in **Christ**
	2: 7	kindness toward us in **Christ**
	2:10	created in **Christ** Jesus for
	2:12	time without **Christ,** being
	2:13	But now in **Christ** Jesus you who
	2:13	near by the blood of **Christ.**
	2:20	with **Christ** Jesus himself as
	3: 1	Paul am a prisoner for **Christ**
	3: 4	of the mystery of **Christ.**
	3: 6	promise in **Christ** Jesus through
	3: 8	the boundless riches of **Christ,**
	3:11	carried out in **Christ** Jesus our
	3:17	and that **Christ** may dwell in
	3:19	and to know the love of **Christ**
	3:21	in the church and in **Christ**
	4: 7	to the measure of **Christ's** gift
	4:12	building up the body of **Christ,**

	4:13	of the full stature of **Christ.**
	4:15	who is the head, into **Christ,**
	4:20	not the way you learned **Christ!**
	4:32	God in **Christ** has forgiven you.
	5: 2	and live in love, as **Christ**
	5: 5	in the kingdom of **Christ** and of
	5:14	Rise from the dead, and **Christ**
	5:20	name of our Lord Jesus **Christ.**
	5:21	out of reverence for **Christ.**
	5:23	just as **Christ** is the head of
	5:24	subject to **Christ,** so also
	5:25	just as **Christ** loved the church
	5:29	just as **Christ** does for the
	5:32	I am applying it to **Christ** and
	6: 5	of heart, as you obey **Christ;**
	6: 6	but as slaves of **Christ,** doing
	6:23	and the Lord Jesus **Christ.**
	6:24	love for our Lord Jesus **Christ.**
Ph	1: 1	servants of **Christ** Jesus, To
	1: 1	To all the saints in **Christ**
	1: 2	and the Lord Jesus **Christ.**
	1: 6	by the day of Jesus **Christ.**
	1: 8	with the compassion of **Christ**
	1:10	so that in the day of **Christ**
	1:11	through Jesus **Christ** for the
	1:13	my imprisonment is for **Christ;**
	1:15	Some proclaim **Christ** from envy
	1:17	the others proclaim **Christ** out
	1:18	Just this, that **Christ** is
	1:19	Spirit of Jesus **Christ** this
	1:20	**Christ** will be exalted now as
	1:21	For to me, living is **Christ** and
	1:23	depart and be with **Christ,** for
	1:26	in your boasting in **Christ**
	1:27	worthy of the gospel of **Christ,**
	1:29	not only of believing in **Christ**
	2: 1	encouragement in **Christ,** any
	2: 5	you that was in **Christ** Jesus,
	2:11	confess that Jesus **Christ** is
	2:16	can boast on the day of **Christ**
	2:21	not those of Jesus **Christ.**
	2:30	for the work of **Christ,** risking
	3: 3	boast in **Christ** Jesus and have
	3: 7	as loss because of **Christ.**
	3: 8	value of knowing **Christ** Jesus
	3: 8	in order that I may gain **Christ**
	3: 9	comes through faith in **Christ,**
	3:12	because **Christ** Jesus has made
	3:14	heavenly call of God in **Christ**

	3:18	enemies of the cross of **Christ;**
	3:20	a Savior, the Lord Jesus **Christ**
	4: 7	and your minds in **Christ** Jesus.
	4:19	riches in glory in **Christ** Jesus
	4:21	Greet every saint in **Christ**
	4:23	grace of the Lord Jesus **Christ**
Co	1: 1	Paul, an apostle of **Christ**
	1: 2	brothers and sisters in **Christ**
	1: 3	Father of our Lord Jesus **Christ**
	1: 4	heard of your faith in **Christ**
	1: 7	a faithful minister of **Christ**
	1:24	what is lacking in **Christ's**
	1:27	which is **Christ** in you, the
	1:28	everyone mature in **Christ.**
	2: 2	that is, **Christ** himself,
	2: 5	of your faith in **Christ.**
	2: 6	have received **Christ** Jesus the
	2: 8	and not according to **Christ.**
	2:11	in the circumcision of **Christ;**
	2:17	the substance belongs to **Christ**
	2:20	If with **Christ** you died to the
	3: 1	raised with **Christ,** seek the
	3: 1	where **Christ** is, seated at the
	3: 3	is hidden with **Christ** in God.
	3: 4	When **Christ** who is your life
	3:11	but **Christ** is all and in all!
	3:15	And let the peace of **Christ**
	3:16	Let the word of **Christ** dwell
	3:24	you serve the Lord **Christ.**
	4: 3	declare the mystery of **Christ,**
	4:12	a servant of **Christ** Jesus,
1Th	1: 1	the Lord Jesus **Christ:** Grace to
	1: 3	hope in our Lord Jesus **Christ.**
	2: 7	demands as apostles of **Christ.**
	2:14	the churches of God in **Christ**
	3: 2	gospel of **Christ,** to strengthen
	4:16	the dead in **Christ** will rise
	5: 9	through our Lord Jesus **Christ,**
	5:18	the will of God in **Christ** Jesus
	5:23	coming of our Lord Jesus **Christ**
	5:28	grace of our Lord Jesus **Christ**
2Th	1: 1	and the Lord Jesus **Christ:**
	1: 2	and the Lord Jesus **Christ.**
	1:12	God and the Lord Jesus **Christ.**
	2: 1	coming of our Lord Jesus **Christ**
	2:14	glory of our Lord Jesus **Christ.**
	2:16	Now may our Lord Jesus **Christ**
	3: 5	to the steadfastness of **Christ.**
	3: 6	name of our Lord Jesus **Christ,**

	3:12	exhort in the Lord Jesus **Christ**
	3:18	of our Lord Jesus **Christ** be
1Ti	1: 1	an apostle of **Christ** Jesus by
	1: 1	and of **Christ** Jesus our hope,
	1: 2	God the Father and **Christ** Jesus
	1:12	I am grateful to **Christ** Jesus
	1:14	love that are in **Christ** Jesus.
	1:15	that **Christ** Jesus came into the
	1:16	Jesus **Christ** might display the
	2: 5	**Christ** Jesus, himself human,
	3:13	faith that is in **Christ** Jesus.
	4: 6	a good servant of **Christ** Jesus,
	5:11	alienate them from **Christ,**
	5:21	presence of God and of **Christ** Jesus
	6: 3	words of our Lord Jesus **Christ**
	6:13	and of **Christ** Jesus, who in his
	6:14	of our Lord Jesus **Christ,**
2Ti	1: 1	Paul, an apostle of **Christ**
	1: 1	of life that is in **Christ**
	1: 2	from God the Father and **Christ**
	1: 9	grace was given to us in **Christ**
	1:10	our Savior **Christ** Jesus, who
	1:13	love that are in **Christ** Jesus.
	2: 1	in the grace that is in **Christ**
	2: 3	like a good soldier of **Christ**
	2: 8	Remember Jesus **Christ,** raised
	2:10	salvation that is in **Christ**
	3:12	live a godly life in **Christ**
	3:15	through faith in **Christ** Jesus.
	4: 1	God and of **Christ** Jesus, who is
Ti	1: 1	an apostle of Jesus **Christ,** for
	1: 4	God the Father and **Christ** Jesus
	2:13	God and Savior, Jesus **Christ.**
	3: 6	through Jesus **Christ** our Savior
Pm	1: 1	Paul, a prisoner of **Christ**
	1: 3	and the Lord Jesus **Christ.**
	1: 6	good that we may do for **Christ.**
	1: 8	I am bold enough in **Christ** to
	1: 9	also as a prisoner of **Christ**
	1:20	Refresh my heart in **Christ.**
	1:23	prisoner in **Christ** Jesus, sends
	1:25	Lord Jesus **Christ** be with your
He	3: 6	**Christ,** however, was faithful
	3:14	partners of **Christ,** if only we
	5: 5	So also **Christ** did not glorify
	6: 1	basic teaching about **Christ,**
	9:11	But when **Christ** came as a high
	9:14	will the blood of **Christ,** who
	9:24	For **Christ** did not enter

	9:28	so **Christ,** having been offered
	10:10	the body of Jesus **Christ** once
	11:26	suffered for the **Christ** to be
	13: 8	Jesus **Christ** is the same
	13:21	through Jesus **Christ,** to whom
Ja	1: 1	of the Lord Jesus **Christ,** To
	2: 1	our glorious Lord Jesus **Christ?**
1P	1: 1	an apostle of Jesus **Christ,** To
	1: 2	be obedient to Jesus **Christ** and
	1: 3	Father of our Lord Jesus **Christ**
	1: 3	Father of our Lord Jesus **Christ**
	1: 7	and honor when Jesus **Christ** is
	1:11	that the Spirit of **Christ**
	1:11	sufferings destined for **Christ**
	1:13	grace that Jesus **Christ** will
	1:19	precious blood of **Christ,** like
	2: 5	to God through Jesus **Christ.**
	2:21	because **Christ** also suffered
	3:15	in your hearts sanctify **Christ**
	3:16	good conduct in **Christ** may be
	3:18	For **Christ** also suffered for
	3:21	resurrection of Jesus **Christ,**
	4: 1	Since therefore **Christ** suffered
	4:11	all things through Jesus **Christ**
	4:13	are sharing **Christ's** sufferings
	4:14	for the name of **Christ,** you are
	5: 1	of the sufferings of **Christ,**
	5:10	his eternal glory in **Christ,**
	5:14	to all of you who are in **Christ**
2P	1: 1	apostle of Jesus **Christ,**
	1: 1	God and Savior Jesus **Christ:**
	1: 8	of our Lord Jesus **Christ.**
	1:11	Lord and Savior Jesus **Christ**
	1:14	indeed our Lord Jesus **Christ**
	1:16	coming of our Lord Jesus **Christ**
	2:20	Lord and Savior Jesus **Christ,**
	3:18	Lord and Savior Jesus **Christ.**
1J	1: 3	and with his Son Jesus **Christ.**
	2: 1	Jesus **Christ** the righteous;
	2:22	denies that Jesus is the **Christ**
	3:23	name of his Son Jesus **Christ**
	4: 2	that Jesus **Christ** has come in
	5: 1	Jesus is the **Christ** has been
	5: 6	water and blood, Jesus **Christ,**
	5:20	in his Son Jesus **Christ.**
2J	1: 3	and from Jesus **Christ,**
	1: 7	confess that Jesus **Christ** has
	1: 9	abide in the teaching of **Christ**
Ju	1: 1	Jude, a servant of Jesus **Christ**

	1: 1	and kept safe for Jesus **Christ:**
	1: 4	Master and Lord, Jesus **Christ.**
	1:17	of our Lord Jesus **Christ;**
	1:21	mercy of our Lord Jesus **Christ**
	1:25	through Jesus **Christ** our Lord,
Re	1: 1	The revelation of Jesus **Christ,**
	1: 2	the testimony of Jesus **Christ,**
	1: 5	and from Jesus **Christ,** the
	11:15	of his **Messiah,** and he will
	12:10	the authority of his **Messiah,**
	20: 4	reigned with **Christ** a thousand
	20: 6	God and of **Christ,** and they

5548　GO5　AG887　LN264　B1:119　K9:493
χρίω, I ANOINT

Lk	4:18	he has **anointed** me to bring
Ac	4:27	Jesus, whom you **anointed,**
	10:38	how God **anointed** Jesus of
2C	1:21	you in Christ and **has anointed**
He	1: 9	**has anointed** you with the oil

5549　GO5　AG887　LN264　B3:839　R5550
χρονίζω, I SPEND TIME

Mt	24:48	My master **is delayed,**
	25: 5	As the bridegroom **was delayed,**
Lk	1:21	wondered at his **delay** in the
	12:45	My master **is delayed** in coming
He	10:37	will come and **will** not **delay;**

5550　GO54　AG887　LN264　B3:839　K9:581
χρόνος, TIME

Mt	2: 7	from them the exact **time**
	2:16	according to the **time** that he
	25:19	After a long **time** the master of
Mk	2:19	fast **while** the bridegroom
	9:21	**long** has this been happening to
Lk	1:57	Now the **time** came for Elizabeth
	4: 5	showed him in an **instant** all
	8:27	For a long **time** he had worn no
	8:29	(For many **times** it had seized
	18: 4	For a **while** he refused; but
	20: 9	another country for a long **time**
	23: 8	to see him for a long **time,**
Jn	5: 6	he had been there a long **time,**
	7:33	with you a little **while** longer,
	12:35	you for a little **longer.** Walk
	14: 9	been with you all this **time,**
Ac	1: 6	Lord, is this the **time** when
	1: 7	know the **times** or periods that
	1:21	all the **time** that the Lord

	3:21	until the **time** of universal
	7:17	But as the **time** drew near for
	7:23	When he was forty years **old,**
	8:11	because for a long **time** he had
	13:18	For about forty **years** he put up
	14: 3	they remained for a long **time,**
	14:28	the disciples for some **time.**
	15:33	been there for some **time,** they
	17:30	overlooked the **times** of human
	18:20	asked him to stay **longer,** he
	18:23	After spending some **time** there
	19:22	stayed for some **time** longer in
	20:18	the entire **time** from the first
	27: 9	Since much **time** had been lost
Ro	7: 1	during that person's **lifetime?**
	16:25	was kept secret for long **ages**
1C	7:39	A wife is bound as **long** as her
	16: 7	I hope to spend some **time** with
Ga	4: 1	as **long** as they are minors, are
	4: 4	But when the fullness of **time**
1Th	5: 1	Now concerning the **times** and
2Ti	1: 9	Christ Jesus before the **ages**
Ti	1: 2	promised before the **ages** began
He	4: 7	through David much **later,** in
	5:12	For though by this **time** you
	11:32	For **time** would fail me to tell
1P	1:17	reverent fear during the **time**
	1:20	at the end of the **ages** for your
	4: 2	earthly life no **longer** by human
	4: 3	spent enough **time** in doing what
Ju	1:18	In the last **time** there will be
Re	2:21	I gave her **time** to repent, but
	6:11	told to rest a little **longer,**
	10: 6	There will be no more **delay,**
	20: 3	be let out for a little **while.**

5551　GO1　AG888　LN264　B3:839
χρονοτριβέω, I CONTINUE TIME

Ac	20:16	he might not **have to spend time**

5552　GO18　AG888　LN265　B2:95　R5557
χρύσους, GOLD

2Ti	2:20	utensils not only of **gold** and
He	9: 4	In it stood the **golden** altar of
	9: 4	there were a **golden** urn holding
Re	1:12	I saw seven **golden** lampstands,
	1:13	with a **golden** sash across his
	1:20	the seven **golden** lampstands:
	2: 1	the seven **golden** lampstands:

4: 4	with **golden** crowns on their
5: 8	harp and **golden** bowls full of
8: 3	Another angel with a **golden**
8: 3	saints on the **golden** altar that
9:13	four horns of the **golden** altar
9:20	demons and idols of **gold** and
14:14	with a **golden** crown on his head
15: 6	with **golden** sashes across their
15: 7	seven angels seven **golden** bowls
17: 4	in her hand a **golden** cup
21:15	measuring rod of **gold** to

5553   GO12 AG888 LN264 B2:95 R5557
χρυσιον, GOLD

Ac	3: 6	I have no silver or **gold,** but
	20:33	no one's silver or **gold** or
1Ti	2: 9	with **gold,** pearls, or expensive
He	9: 4	overlaid on all sides with **gold**
1P	1: 7	more precious than **gold** that,
	1:18	things like silver or **gold,**
	3: 3	wearing **gold** ornaments or fine
Re	3:18	buy from me **gold** refined by
	17: 4	adorned with **gold** and jewels
	18:16	adorned with **gold,** with jewels,
	21:18	while the city is pure **gold,**
	21:21	street of the city is pure **gold**

5554   GO1 AG888 LN265 R5557,1146
χρυσοδακτυλιος, GOLD FINGERED
Ja   2: 2   For if a person with **gold rings**

5555   GO1 AG888 LN265 B3:396 R5557,3037
χρυσολιθος, GOLD STONE
Re   21:20   the seventh **chrysolite,**

5556   GO1 AG888 LN265 B3:396
χρυσοπρασος, CHRYSOPRASE
Re   21:20   the tenth **chrysoprase** the

5557   GO10 AG888 LN265 B2:95
χρυσος, GOLD

Mt	2:11	offered him gifts of **gold,**
	10: 9	Take no **gold,** or silver, or
	23:16	by the **gold** of the sanctuary is
	23:17	the **gold** or the sanctuary that
	23:17	that has made the **gold** sacred?
Ac	17:29	that the deity is like **gold,** or
1C	3:12	foundation with **gold,** silver,
Ja	5: 3	Your **gold** and silver have

Re	9: 7	looked like crowns of **gold;**
	18:12	cargo of **gold,** silver, jewels

5558   GO2 AG889 LN265 B2:95 R5557
χρυσοω, I MAKE GOLDEN

Re	17: 4	and **adorned** with gold and
	18:16	**adorned** with gold, with jewels,

5559   GO1 AG889 LN265
χρως, BODY SURFACE (SKIN)
Ac   19:12   touched his **skin** were brought

5560   GO14 AG889 LN265 B2:415
χωλος, LAME

Mt	11: 5	the **lame** walk, the lepers are
	15:30	bringing with them the **lame,**
	15:31	the maimed whole, the **lame**
	18: 8	enter life maimed or **lame** than
	21:14	The blind and the **lame** came to
Mk	9:45	enter life **lame** than to have
Lk	7:22	the **lame** walk, the lepers are
	14:13	the crippled, the **lame,** and the
	14:21	the blind, and the **lame.**
Jn	5: 3	blind, **lame,** and paralyzed.
Ac	3: 2	And a man **lame** from birth was
	8: 7	who were paralyzed or **lame** were
	14: 8	he had been **crippled** from birth
He	12:13	so that what is **lame** may not be

5561   GO28 AG889 LN265 B1:741
χωρα, COUNTRY

Mt	2:12	left for their own **country** by
	4:16	those who sat in the **region** and
	8:28	to the **country** of the Gadarenes
Mk	1: 5	whole Judean **countryside** and
	5: 1	to the **country** of the Gerasenes
	5:10	to send them out of the **country**
	6:55	that whole **region** and began to
Lk	2: 8	shepherds living in the **fields,**
	3: 1	Philip ruler of the **region** of
	8:26	**country** of the Gerasenes, which
	12:16	**land** of a rich man produced
	15:13	traveled to a distant **country,**
	15:14	throughout that **country,**
	15:15	citizens of that **country,** who
	19:12	went to a distant **country** to
	21:21	those out in the **country** must
Jn	4:35	see how the **fields** are ripe for
	11:54	Ephraim in the **region** near the

	11:55	many went up from the **country**
Ac	8: 1	throughout the **countryside** of
	10:39	all that he did both in **Judea**
	12:20	their **country** depended on the
	13:49	spread throughout the **region.**
	16: 6	They went through the **region**
	18:23	through the **region** of Galatia
	26:20	throughout the **countryside** of
	27:27	that they were nearing **land.**
Ja	5: 4	laborers who mowed your **fields,**

5562 GO10 AG889 LN265 B1:741
χωρεω, I MAKE ROOM

Mt	15:17	goes into the mouth **enters** the
	19:11	Not everyone can **accept** this
	19:12	Let anyone **accept** this who can.
	19:12	Let anyone accept this who **can.**
Mk	2: 2	there **was** no longer **room** for
Jn	2: 6	each **holding** twenty or thirty
	8:37	because there **is** no **place** in
	21:25	could not **contain** the books
2C	7: 2	**Make room** in your hearts for us
2P	3: 9	but all **to come** to repentance.

5563 GO13 AG890 LN265 B3:534
χωριζω, I SEPARATE

Mt	19: 6	together, **let** no one **separate.”**
Mk	10: 9	together, **let** no one **separate.”**
Ac	1: 4	ordered them not **to leave**
	18: 1	After this Paul **left** Athens
	18: 2	ordered all Jews **to leave** Rome.
Ro	8:35	Who **will separate** us from the
	8:39	will be able **to separate** us
1C	7:10	should not **separate** from her
	7:11	(but if she does **separate,** let
	7:15	unbelieving partner **separates,**
	7:15	separates, let it **be so;** in
Pm	1:15	he **was separated** from you
He	7:26	**separated** from sinners, and

5564 GO10 AG890 LN265 B1:93 R5561
χωριον, SMALL FIELD

Mt	26:36	to a **place** called Gethsemane;
Mk	14:32	to a **place** called Gethsemane;
Jn	4: 5	near the **plot of ground** that
Ac	1:18	(Now this man acquired a **field**
	1:19	so that the **field** was called in
	1:19	that is, **Field** of Blood.)

	4:34	for as many as owned **lands** or
	5: 3	of the proceeds of the **land?**
	5: 8	sold the **land** for such and such
	28: 7	**lands** belonging to the leading

5565 GO41 AG890 LN265 B2:446
χωρις, WITHOUT

Mt	13:34	things in parables; **without** a
	14:21	five thousand men, **besides**
	15:38	men, **besides** women and children
Mk	4:34	he did not speak to them **except**
Lk	6:49	**without** a foundation. When the
Jn	1: 3	**without** him not one thing came
	15: 5	because **apart** from me you can
	20: 7	rolled up in a place **by itself.**
Ro	3:21	But now, **apart** from law, the
	3:28	justified by faith **apart** from
	4: 6	righteousness **apart** from works:
	7: 8	**Apart** from the law sin lies
	7: 9	I was once alive **apart** from the
	10:14	how are they to hear **without**
1C	4: 8	Quite **apart** from us you have
	11:11	woman is **not independent** of man
	11:11	man or man **independent** of woman
2C	11:28	And, **besides** other things, I am
	12: 3	whether in the body or **out of**
Ep	2:12	were at that time **without**
Ph	2:14	Do all things **without** murmuring
1Ti	2: 8	lifting up holy hands **without**
	5:21	keep these instructions **without**
Pm	1:14	do nothing **without** your consent
He	4:15	as we are, yet **without** sin.
	7: 7	It is **beyond** dispute that the
	7:20	This was confirmed **with** an oath
	7:20	their office **without** an oath,
	9: 7	not **without** taking the blood
	9:18	was inaugurated **without** blood.
	9:22	and **without** the shedding of
	9:28	**not** to deal **with** sin, but to
	10:28	dies **without** mercy “on the
	11: 6	And **without** faith it is
	11:40	**apart** from us, be made perfect.
	12: 8	do **not** have that discipline in
	12:14	the holiness **without** which no
Ja	2:18	Show me your faith **apart** from
	2:20	that faith **apart** from works is
	2:26	For just as the body **without**
	2:26	faith **without** works is also

5566 GO1 AG891 LN265
χωρος, NORTHWEST
Ac 27:12   facing southwest and **northwest.**

5567 GO5 AG891 LN265 B3:670 K8:489
ψαλλω, I PSALM
Ro 15: 9   and **sing praises** to your name"
1C 14:15   I **will sing praise** with the
     14:15   I **will sing praise** with the
Ep   5:19   as you **sing psalms** and hymns
Ja   5:13   should **sing songs of praise.**

5568 GO7 AG891 LN265 B3:670 K8:489 R5567
ψαλμος, PSALM
Lk 20:42   in the book of **Psalms,** 'The
     24:44   the **psalms** must be fulfilled.
Ac   1:20   in the book of **Psalms,** 'Let his
     13:33   written in the second **psalm,**
1C 14:26   each one has a **hymn,** a lesson,
Ep   5:19   as you sing **psalms** and hymns
Co   3:16   your hearts sing **psalms,** hymns,

5569 GO2 AG891 LN265 B1:254 K1:144 R5571,80
ψευδαδελφος, FALSE BROTHER
2C 11:26   danger from **false brothers** and
Ga   2: 4   But because of **false believers**

5570 GO1 AG891 LN265 B2:472 K1:445 R5570,652
ψευδαποστολος, FALSE DELEGATE
2C 11:13   boasters are **false apostles,**

5571 GO3 AG891 LN265 B2:470 K9:594 R5574
ψευδης, FALSE
Ac   6:13   They set up **false** witnesses who
Re   2: 2   and have found them to be **false**
     21: 8   and all **liars,** their place will

5572 GO1 AG891 LN265 B3:766 K2:160 R5571,1320
ψευδοδιδασκαλος, FALSE TEACHER
2P   2: 1   will be **false teachers** among

5573 GO1 AG891 LN265 B2:472 R5571,3004
ψευδολογος, FALSE WORD
1Ti 4: 2   through the hypocrisy of **liars**

5574 GO12 AG891 LN265 B2:470 K9:594
ψευδομαι, I LIE

Mt   5:11   evil against you **falsely** on my
Ac   5: 3   filled your heart to **lie** to the
     5: 4   You did not **lie** to us but to
Ro   9: 1   I **am** not **lying;** my conscience
2C 11:31   knows that I **do** not **lie.**
Ga   1:20   before God, I **do** not **lie!**
Co   3: 9   **Do** not **lie** to one another,
1Ti 2: 7   I **am** not **lying),** a teacher of
He   6:18   God **would prove false,** we who
Ja   3:14   boastful and **false** to the truth
1J   1: 6   we **lie** and do not do what is
Re   3: 9   but **are lying**—I will make

5576 GO5 AG891 LN265 B3:1038 K4:513 R5571
ψευδομαρτυρεω, I TESTIFY FALSELY
Mt 19:18   shall not **bear false witness;**
Mk 10:19   shall not **bear false witness;**
     14:56   For many **gave false testimony**
     14:57   **gave false testimony** against
Lk 18:20   shall not **bear false witness;**

5577 GO2 AG892 LN265 B3:1038 K4:513 R5575
ψευδομαρτυρια, FALSE TESTIMONY
Mt 15:19   theft, **false witness,** slander.
     26:59   looking for **false testimony**

5577a GO2 AG892 LN265 B3:1038 K4:513 R5575
ψευδομαρτυς, FALSE TESTIFIER
Mt 26:60   though many **false witnesses**
1C 15:15   found **to be misrepresenting** God

5578 GO11 AG892 LN265 B3:74 K6:781 R5571,4396
ψευδοπροφητης, FALSE SPOKESMAN
Mt   7:15   Beware of **false prophets,** who
     24:11   And many **false prophets** will
     24:24   **false prophets** will appear and
Mk 13:22   **false prophets** will appear and
Lk   6:26   did to the **false prophets.**
Ac 13: 6   a Jewish **false prophet,** named
2P   2: 1   But **false prophets** also arose
1J   4: 1   many **false prophets** have
                 gone
Re 16:13   the mouth of the **false prophet.**
     19:20   with it the **false prophet** who
     20:10   beast and the **false prophet**

5579 GO10 AG892 LN265 B2:470 K9:594 R5574
ψευδος, LIE
Jn   8:44   he **lies,** he speaks according to
Ro   1:25   truth about God for a **lie** and

Ep 4:25 So then, putting away **falsehood**
2Th 2: 9 all power, signs, **lying** wonders
2:11 them to believe what is **false,**
1J 2:21 know that no **lie** comes from the
2:27 true and is not a **lie,** and just
Re 14: 5 and in their mouth no **lie** was
21:27 abomination or **falsehood,** but
22:15 loves and practices **falsehood.**

5580 GO2 AG892 LN266 B1:124 R5571,5547
ψευδοχριστος, FALSE CHRIST
Mt 24:24 For **false messiahs** and false
Mk 13:22 **False messiahs** and false

5581 GO1 AG892 LN266 B2:648 K5:282 R5571,3686
ψευδωνυμος, FALSELY NAMED
1Ti 6:20 is **falsely called** knowledge;

5582 GO1 AG892 LN266 K9:594 R5574
ψευσμα, LIE
Ro 3: 7 But if through my **falsehood**

5583 GO10 AG892 LN266 B2:470 K9:594 R5574
ψευστης, LIAR
Jn 8:44 he is a **liar** and the father of
8:55 I would be a **liar** like you. But
Ro 3: 4 everyone is a **liar,** let God be
1Ti 1:10 slave traders, **liars,** perjurers
Ti 1:12 Cretans are always **liars,**
1J 1:10 we make him a **liar,** and his
2: 4 is a **liar,** and in such a person
2:22 Who is the **liar** but the one who
4:20 are **liars;** for those who do not
5:10 made him a **liar** by not

5584 GO4 AG892 LN266
ψηλαφαω, I TOUCH
Lk 24:39 **Touch** me and see; for a ghost
Ac 17:27 perhaps **grope** for him and find
He 12:18 that can be **touched,** a blazing
1J 1: 1 looked at and **touched** with our

5585 GO2 AG892 LN266 K9:604 R5586
ψηφιζω, I CALCULATE
Lk 14:28 first sit down and **estimate** the
Re 13:18 with understanding **calculate**

5586 GO3 AG892 LN266 B2:674 K9:604
ψηφος, PEBBLE
Ac 26:10 I also cast my **vote** against

Re 2:17 I will give a white **stone,** and
2:17 I will give a white **stone,** and

5587 GO1 AG892 LN266 B3:346
ψιθυρισμος, WHISPERINGS
2C 12:20 slander, **gossip,** conceit, and

5588 GO1 AG893 LN266 B3:346 R5587
ψιθυριστης, WHISPERER
Ro 1:29 craftiness, they are **gossips,**

5589 GO2 AG893 LN266
ψιχιον, SMALL CRUMB
Mt 15:27 table eat the children's **crumbs**

5590 GO103 AG893 LN266 B3:676 K9:608
ψυχη, SOUL, LIFE
Mt 2:20 seeking the child's **life** are
6:25 worry about your **life,** what you
6:25 Is not **life** more than food, and
10:28 cannot kill the **soul;** rather
10:28 destroy both **soul** and body in
10:39 Those who find their **life** will
10:39 who lose their **life** for my sake
11:29 will find rest for your **souls.**
12:18 whom my **soul** is well pleased.
16:25 save their **life** will lose it,
16:25 those who lose their **life** for
16:26 world but forfeit their **life?**
16:26 give in return for their **life?**
20:28 give his **life** a ransom for many
22:37 with all your **soul,** and with
26:38 I am deeply grieved, even to
Mk 3: 4 to save **life** or to kill?" But
8:35 save their **life** will lose it,
8:35 those who lose their **life** for
8:36 world and forfeit their **life?**
8:37 give in return for their **life?**
10:45 to give his **life** a ransom for
12:30 and with all your **soul,** and
14:34 I am deeply grieved, even to
Lk 1:46 And Mary said, "My **soul**
2:35 will pierce your own **soul** too.
6: 9 to save **life** or to destroy it?
9:24 save their **life** will lose it,
9:24 lose their **life** for my sake
10:27 with all your **soul,** and with
12:19 And I will say to my **soul,**
12:19 **Soul,** you have ample goods
12:20 This very night your **life** is

	12:22	do not worry about your **life,**
	12:23	For **life** is more than food, and
	14:26	even **life** itself, cannot be my
	17:33	make their **life** secure will
	21:19	you will gain your **souls.**
Jn	10:11	down his **life** for the sheep.
	10:15	lay down my **life** for the sheep.
	10:17	I lay down my **life** in order to
	10:24	will you keep us in **suspense?**
	12:25	Those who love their **life** lose
	12:25	those who hate their **life** in
	12:27	Now my **soul** is troubled. And
	13:37	I will lay down my **life** for you
	13:38	Will you lay down your **life**
	15:13	lay down one's **life** for one's
Ac	2:27	abandon my **soul** to Hades, or
	2:41	about three thousand **persons**
	2:43	Awe came upon **everyone,** because
	3:23	And it will be that **everyone**
	4:32	were of one heart and **soul,** and
	7:14	to him, seventy-**five** in all;
	14: 2	poisoned their **minds** against
	14:22	strengthened the **souls** of the
	15:24	and have unsettled your **minds,**
	15:26	who have risked their **lives** for
	20:10	alarmed, for his **life** is in him
	20:24	But I do not count my **life** of
	27:10	the ship, but also of our **lives**
	27:22	will be no loss of **life** among
	27:37	two hundred seventy-six **persons**
Ro	2: 9	distress for **everyone** who does
	11: 3	and they are seeking my **life.**"
	13: 1	Let every **person** be subject to
	16: 4	risked their necks for my **life,**
1C	15:45	became a living **being**"; the
2C	1:23	God as witness against **me:** it
	12:15	spend and be spent for **you.** If
Ep	6: 6	the will of God from the **heart.**
Ph	1:27	side by side with one **mind** for
	2:30	risking his **life** to make up for
Co	3:23	put **yourselves** into it, as done
1Th	2: 8	God but also our own **selves,**
	5:23	your spirit and **soul** and body
He	4:12	piercing until it divides **soul**
	6:19	steadfast anchor of the **soul,** a
	10:38	My **soul** takes no pleasure in
	10:39	not grow weary or lose **heart.**
	13:17	keeping watch over your **souls**
Ja	1:21	the power to save your **souls.**

	5:20	save the sinner's **soul** from
1P	1: 9	the salvation of your **souls.**
	1:22	purified your **souls** by your
	2:11	that wage war against the **soul.**
	2:25	and guardian of your **souls.**
	3:20	eight **persons,** were saved
	4:19	will entrust **themselves** to a
2P	2: 8	tormented in his righteous **soul**
	2:14	They entice unsteady **souls.**
1J	3:16	he laid down his **life** for us—
	3:16	we ought to lay down our **lives**
3J	1: 2	as it is well with your **soul.**
Ju	1:15	to convict **everyone** of all the
Re	6: 9	I saw under the altar the **souls**
	8: 9	a third of the **living** creatures
	12:11	for they did not cling to **life**
	16: 3	every living **thing** in the sea
	18:13	slaves—and human **lives.**
	18:14	The fruit for which your **soul**
	20: 4	I also saw the **souls** of those

5591   G06 AG894 LN266 B3:676 K9:661 R5590
ψυχικος, SOUL-LIKE

1C	2:14	they are **spiritually** discerned.
	15:44	It is sown a **physical** body, it
	15:44	If there is a **physical** body,
	15:46	but the **physical,** and then the
Ja	3:15	but is earthly, **unspiritual,**
Ju	1:19	It is these **worldly** people,

5592   G03 AG894 LN266 B1:317
ψυχος, COLD

Jn	18:18	fire because it was **cold,** and
Ac	28: 2	begun to rain and was **cold,**
2C	11:27	often without food, **cold** and

5593   G04 AG894 LN266 B1:317 K2:876 R5594
ψυχρος, COLD

Mt	10:42	even a cup of **cold** water to one
Re	3:15	you are neither **cold** nor hot. I
	3:15	wish that you were either **cold**
	3:16	neither **cold** nor hot, I am

5594   G01 AG894 LN266 B1:317
ψυχω, I GROW COLD

Mt	24:12	the love of many **will grow cold**

5595   G02 AG894 LN266 R5596
ψωμιζω, I GIVE SMALL BITS

Ro	12:20	**feed** them; if they are thirsty,
1C	13: 3	I **give away** all my possessions,

5596   GO4 AG894 LN266

ψωμιον, SMALL BIT

Jn	13:26	I give this **piece of bread** when
	13:26	had dipped the **piece of bread,**
	13:27	he received the **piece of bread,**
	13:30	receiving the **piece of bread,**

5597   GO1 AG894 LN266

ψωχω, I RUB

Lk	6: 1	**rubbed** them in their hands, and

ω

5598   GO3 AG895 LN267 K1:1

ω, OMEGA

Re	1: 8	I am the Alpha and the **Omega,**
	21: 6	I am the Alpha and the **Omega,**
	22:13	I am the Alpha and the **Omega,**

5599   GO17 AG895 LN267

ω, O, OH

Mt	15:28	**Woman,** great is your faith!
	17:17	**You** faithless and perverse
Mk	9:19	**You** faithless generation, how
Lk	9:41	**You** faithless and perverse
	24:25	**Oh,** how foolish you are, and
Ac	1: 1	In the first book, **Theophilus,**
	13:10	**full** of all deceit and villainy
	18:14	Gallio said to the **Jews,** "If it
	27:21	**Men,** you should have listened
Ro	2: 1	**whoever** you are, when you judge
	2: 3	Do you imagine, **whoever** you are
	9:20	But who indeed are you, **a** human
	11:33	**O** the depth of the riches and
Ga	3: 1	**You** foolish Galatians! Who has
1Ti	6:11	But as for you, **man** of God,
	6:20	**Timothy,** guard what has been
Ja	2:20	Do you want to be shown, **you**

5602   GO61 AG895 LN267

ὡδε, HERE

Mt	8:29	Have you come **here** to torment
	12:41	greater than Jonah is **here!**
	12:42	greater than Solomon is **here!**
	14: 8	John the Baptist **here** on a
	14:17	We have nothing **here** but five
	14:18	he said, "Bring them **here** to me
	16:28	there are some standing **here**
	17: 4	it is good for us to be **here;**
	17: 4	will make three dwellings **here,**
	17:17	with you? Bring him **here** to me.
	20: 6	Why are you standing **here** idle
	22:12	how did you get in **here** without
	24: 2	will be left **here** upon another;
	24:23	'Look! **Here** is the Messiah!' or
	24:23	**'There** he is!'—do not
	26:38	remain **here,** and stay awake
	28: 6	He is not **here;** for he has been
Mk	6: 3	not his sisters **here** with us?
	8: 4	these people with bread **here** in
	9: 1	there are some standing **here**
	9: 5	it is good for us to be **here;**
	11: 3	it and will send it back **here**
	13: 2	Not one stone will be left **here**
	13:21	'Look! **Here** is the Messiah!' or
	14:32	Sit **here** while I pray.
	14:34	remain **here,** and keep awake.
	16: 6	he is not **here.** Look, there is
Lk	4:23	And you will say, 'Do **here** also
	9:12	we are **here** in a deserted place
	9:33	it is good for us to be **here;**
	9:41	with you? Bring your son **here."**
	11:31	greater than Solomon is **here!**
	11:32	greater than Jonah is **here!**
	14:21	bring **in** the poor, the crippled
	15:17	but **here** I am dying of hunger!
	16:25	now he is comforted **here,** and
	17:21	nor will they say, 'Look, **here**
	17:23	'Look there!' or 'Look **here!'**
	19:27	bring them **here** and slaughter
	22:38	They said, "Lord, look, **here**
	23: 5	he began even to **this place."**
	24: 6	He is not **here,** but has risen
Jn	6: 9	There is a boy **here** who has
	6:25	Rabbi, when did you come **here?**
	11:21	Lord, if you had been **here,** my
	11:32	Lord, if you had been **here,** my
	20:27	Put your finger **here** and see
Ac	9:14	and **here** he has authority from
	9:21	And has he not come **here** for
1C	4: 2	**Moreover,** it is required of
Co	4: 9	tell you about everything **here.**
He	7: 8	**In the one case,** tithes are
	13:14	For **here** we have no lasting
Ja	2: 3	Have a seat **here,** please,

Re   4: 1   Come up **here,** and I will show
11:12   "Come up **here!**" And they went
13:10   **Here** is a call for the
13:18   **This** calls for wisdom: let
14:12   **Here** is a call for the
17: 9   **This** calls for a mind that has

5603   GO7 AG895 LN267 B2:874 K1:164
ωδη, SONG
Ep   5:19   hymns and spiritual **songs** among
Co   3:16   and spiritual **songs** to God.
Re   5: 9   They sing a new **song:** "You are
14: 3   and they sing a new **song** before
14: 3   No one could learn that **song**
15: 3   And they sing the **song** of Moses
15: 3   and the **song** of the Lamb:

5604   GO4 AG895 LN267 B3:857 K9:667
ωδιν, BIRTH PAIN
Mt   24: 8   beginning of the **birth pangs.**
Mk   13: 8   beginning of the **birth pangs.**
Ac   2:24   having freed him from **death,**
1Th   5: 3   as **labor pains** come upon a

5605   GO3 AG895 LN267 B3:857 K9:667 R5604
ωδινω, I HAVE BIRTH PAINS
Ga   4:19   **in the pain of childbirth** until
4:27   you who **endure** no **birth pangs;**
Re   12: 2   crying out **in birth pangs,** in

5606   GO2 AG895 LN267
ωμος, SHOULDER
Mt   23: 4   lay them on the **shoulders** of
Lk   15: 5   he lays it on his **shoulders** and

5608   GO1 AG895 LN267 B3:144
ωνεομαι, I PAY PRICE
Ac   7:16   tomb that Abraham **had bought**

5609   GO1 AG896 LN267
ωον, EGG
Lk   11:12   Or if the child asks for an **egg**

5610   GO106 AG896 LN267 B3:845 K9:675
ωρα, HOUR
Mt   8:13   servant was healed in that **hour**
9:22   And **instantly** the woman was
10:19   be given to you at that **time;**
14:15   the **hour** is now late; send the
15:28   daughter was healed **instantly.**

17:18   the boy was cured **instantly.**
18: 1   At that **time** the disciples came
20: 3   went out about nine **o'clock,** he
20: 5   noon and about three **o'clock,**
20: 9   five **o'clock** came, each of them
20:12   last worked only one **hour,** and
24:36   But about that day and **hour** no
24:44   is coming at an unexpected **hour**
24:50   an **hour** that he does not know.
25:13   neither the day nor the **hour.**
26:40   stay awake with me one **hour?**
26:45   See, the **hour** is at hand, and
26:55   At that **hour** Jesus said to the
27:45   From **noon** on, darkness came
27:45   over the whole land until **three**
27:46   And about three **o'clock** Jesus
Mk   6:35   When it grew **late,** his
6:35   and the **hour** is now very late;
11:11   as it was already **late,** he went
13:11   is given you at that **time,** for
13:32   But about that day or **hour** no
14:35   the **hour** might pass from him.
14:37   you not keep awake one **hour?**
14:41   The **hour** has come; the Son of
15:25   It was nine **o'clock** in the
15:33   When it was **noon,** darkness came
15:33   until three in the **afternoon.**
15:34   At three **o'clock** Jesus cried
Lk   1:10   Now at the **time** of the incense
2:38   At that **moment** she came, and
7:21   Jesus had **just then** cured
10:21   At that same **hour** Jesus
12:12   teach you at that very **hour**
12:39   had known at what **hour** the
12:40   coming at an unexpected **hour.**"
12:46   at an **hour** that he does not
13:31   At that very **hour** some
14:17   At the **time** for the dinner he
20:19   hands on him at that very **hour,**
22:14   When the **hour** came, he took his
22:53   But this is your **hour,** and the
22:59   Then about an **hour** later
23:44   It was now about **noon,** and
23:44   until three in the **afternoon,**
24:33   That same **hour** they got up and
Jn   1:39   It was about four **o'clock** in
2: 4   to me? My **hour** has not yet come
4: 6   by the well. It was about **noon.**
4:21   Woman, believe me, the **hour** is

	4:23	But the **hour** is coming, and is
	4:52	So he asked them the **hour** when
	4:52	at one in the **afternoon** the
	4:53	this was the **hour** when Jesus
	5:25	I tell you, the **hour** is coming,
	5:28	for the **hour** is coming when all
	5:35	rejoice for a **while** in his
	7:30	his **hour** had not yet come.
	8:20	his **hour** had not yet come.
	11: 9	Are there not twelve **hours** of
	12:23	The **hour** has come for the Son
	12:27	Father, save me from this **hour**
	12:27	that I have come to this **hour.**
	13: 1	Jesus knew that his **hour** had
	16: 2	Indeed, an **hour** is coming when
	16: 4	so that when their **hour** comes
	16:21	because her **hour** has come. But
	16:25	The **hour** is coming when I will
	16:32	The **hour** is coming, indeed it
	17: 1	Father, the **hour** has come;
	19:14	and it was about **noon.** He said
	19:27	And from that **hour** the disciple
Ac	2:15	it is only nine **o'clock** in the
	3: 1	at three **o'clock** in the
	5: 7	interval of about three **hours**
	10: 3	about three **o'clock** he had a
	10: 9	About **noon** the next day, as
	10:30	at three **o'clock,** I was praying
	16:18	And it came out that very **hour.**
	16:33	At the same **hour** of the night
	19:34	for about two **hours** all of them
	22:13	In that very **hour** I regained my
	23:23	ready to leave by nine **o'clock**
Ro	13:11	how it is now the **moment** for
1C	4:11	To the present **hour** we are
	15:30	ourselves in danger every **hour?**
2C	7: 8	letter, though only **briefly).**
Ga	2: 5	to them even for a **moment,** so
1Th	2:17	for a **short** time, we were made
Pm	1:15	separated from you for a **while,**
1J	2:18	Children, it is the last **hour!**
	2:18	know that it is the last **hour.**
Re	3: 3	you will not know at what **hour**
	3:10	I will keep you from the **hour**
	9:15	held ready for the **hour,** the
	11:13	At that **moment** there was a
	14: 7	for the **hour** of his judgment
	14:15	the **hour** to reap has come,
	17:12	authority as kings for one **hour**

	18:10	in one **hour** your judgment has
	18:17	For in one **hour** all this wealth
	18:19	For in one **hour** she has been

5611   GO4 AG896 LN267 B3:845
'ωραιος, BEAUTIFUL

Mt	23:27	on the outside look **beautiful,**
Ac	3: 2	temple called the **Beautiful**
	3:10	alms at the **Beautiful** Gate of
Ro	10:15	How **beautiful** are the feet of

5612   GO1 AG897 LN267
ωρυομαι, I ROAR

1P	5: 8	Like a **roaring** lion your

5613   GO504 AG897 LN267
'ως, AS [MULTIPLE OCCURRENCES]

5614   GO6 AG899 LN267 B1:100 K9:682
'ωσαννα, HOSANNA

Mt	21: 9	**Hosanna** to the Son of David!
	21: 9	**Hosanna** in the highest heaven!
	21:15	**Hosanna** to the Son of David,
Mk	11: 9	**Hosanna!** Blessed is the one
	11:10	**Hosanna** in the highest heaven!
Jn	12:13	**Hosanna!** Blessed is the one

5615   GO17 AG899 LN267
'ωσαυτως, LIKEWISE

Mt	20: 5	three o'clock, he did **the same.**
	21:30	said **the same;** and he answered,
	21:36	treated them **in the same way.**
	25:17	**In the same way,** the one who
Mk	12:21	and the third **likewise;**
	14:31	all of them said **the same.**
Lk	13: 5	all perish **just as they did."**
	20:31	so **in the same way** all seven
	22:20	he did **the same** with the cup
Ro	8:26	**Likewise** the Spirit helps us in
1C	11:25	**In the same way** he took the cup
1Ti	2: 9	**also** that the women should
	3: 8	Deacons **likewise** must be
	3:11	Women **likewise** must be serious,
	5:25	**So also** good works are
Ti	2: 3	**Likewise,** tell the older women
	2: 6	**Likewise,** urge the younger men

5616   GO21 AG899 LN267
'ωσει, AS

Mt	3:16	descending **like** a dove and

	9:36	**like** sheep without a shepherd.
	14:21	those who ate were **about** five
Mk	9:26	the boy was **like** a corpse, so
Lk	3:23	Jesus was **about** thirty years
	9:14	were **about** five thousand men.
	9:14	down in groups of **about** fifty
	9:28	Now **about** eight days after
	22:41	**about** a stone's throw, knelt
	22:44	**like** great drops of blood
	22:59	Then **about** an hour later still
	23:44	**about** noon, and darkness came
	24:11	seemed to them **an** idle tale,
Ac	1:15	numbered **about** one hundred
	2: 3	Divided tongues, **as** of fire,
	2:41	**about** three thousand persons
	6:15	his face was **like** the face of
	10: 3	**about** three o'clock he had a
	19: 7	were **about** twelve of them.
Ro	6:13	brought **from** death to life,
He	1:12	**like** clothing they will be

5617 GO1 AG899 LN267
'ωσηε, HOSEA
Ro 9:25 he says in **Hosea,** "Those who

5618 GO36 AG899 LN267
'ωσπερ, AS INDEED

Mt	6: 2	**as** the hypocrites do in the
	6: 7	heap up empty phrases **as** the
	12:40	**just as** Jonah was three days
	13:40	**Just as** the weeds are collected
	18:17	to you **as** a Gentile and a tax
	20:28	**just as** the Son of Man came not
	24:27	For **as** the lightning comes from
	24:37	For **as** the days of Noah were,
	25:14	For it is **as** if a man, going
	25:32	**as** a shepherd separates the
Lk	17:24	For **as** the lightning flashes
	18:11	I am not **like** other people:
Jn	5:21	just **as** the Father raises the
	5:26	For just **as** the Father has life
Ac	2: 2	a sound **like** the rush of a
	3:17	**as** did also your rulers.
	11:15	just **as** it had upon us at the
Ro	5:12	just **as** sin came into the world
	5:19	just **as** by the one man's
	5:21	just **as** sin exercised dominion
	6: 4	just **as** Christ was raised from
	6:19	just **as** you once presented your

	11:30	Just **as** you were once
1C	8: 5	**as** in fact there are many gods
	10: 7	**as** it is written, "The people
	11:12	For just **as** woman came from man
	15:22	for **as** all die in Adam, so all
	16: 1	follow the directions **I** gave
2C	8: 7	Now **as** you excel in everything
Ga	4:29	But just **as** at that time the
1Th	5: 3	**as** labor pains come upon a
He	4:10	from their labors **as** God did
	7:27	**Unlike** the other high priests,
	9:25	**as** the high priest enters the
Ja	2:26	just **as** the body without the
Re	10: 3	shout, **like** a lion roaring. And

5619 GO1 AG899 LN267
'ωσπερει, AS INDEED IF
1C 15: 8 **as** to one untimely born, he

5620 GO83 AG899 LN267
'ωστε, SO THAT

Mt	8:24	so great **that** the boat was
	8:28	They were so fierce **that** no one
	10: 1	spirits, **to** cast them out, and
	12:12	**So** it is lawful to do good on
	12:22	**so that** the one who had been
	13: 2	him **that** he got into a boat and
	13:32	a tree, **so that** the birds of
	13:54	**so that** they were astounded and
	15:31	**so that** the crowd was amazed
	15:33	desert **to** feed so great a crowd
	19: 6	**So** they are no longer two, but
	23:31	**Thus** you testify against
	24:24	**to** lead astray, if possible,
	27: 1	**in order** to bring about his
	27:14	**so that** the governor was
Mk	1:27	**and** they kept on asking one
	1:45	**so that** Jesus could no longer
	2: 2	So many gathered around **that**
	2:12	**so that** they were all amazed
	2:28	**so** the Son of Man is lord even
	3:10	**so that** all who had diseases
	3:20	**so that** they could not even eat
	4: 1	**that** he got into a boat on the
	4:32	**so that** the birds of the air
	4:37	**so that** the boat was already
	9:26	**so that** most of them said, "He
	10: 8	**So** they are no longer two, but
	15: 5	**so that** Pilate was amazed.

Lk	4:29	**so that** they might hurl him off
	5: 7	**so that** they began to sink.
	12: 1	**so that** they trampled on one
	20:20	**in order** to trap him by what he
Jn	3:16	**that** he gave his only Son, so
Ac	1:19	**so that** the field was called
	5:15	**so that** they even carried out
	14: 1	spoke in such a way **that** a
	15:39	sharp **that** they parted company;
	16:26	earthquake, **so** violent that the
	19:10	**so that** all the residents of
	19:12	**so that** when the handkerchiefs
	19:16	**that** they fled out of the house
Ro	7: 4	**so that** you may belong to
	7: 6	**so that** we are slaves not under
	7:12	**So** the law is holy, and the
	13: 2	**Therefore** whoever resists
	15:19	**so that** from Jerusalem and as
1C	1: 7	**so that** you are not lacking in
	3: 7	**So** neither the one who plants
	3:21	**So** let no one boast about human
	4: 5	**Therefore** do not pronounce
	5: 1	**for** a man is living with his
	5: 8	**Therefore,** let us celebrate the
	7:38	**So then,** he who marries his
	10:12	**So** if you think you are
	11:27	**therefore,** eats the bread or
	11:33	**So then,** my brothers and
	13: 2	if I have all faith, **so as** to
	14:22	Tongues, **then,** are a sign not
	14:39	**So,** my friends, be eager to
	15:58	**Therefore,** my beloved, be
2C	1: 8	**that** we despaired of life
	2: 7	**so** now instead you should
	3: 7	**so that** the people of Israel
	4:12	**So** death is at work in us, but
	5:16	**therefore,** we regard no one
	5:17	**So** if anyone is in Christ,
	7: 7	**so that** I rejoiced still more.
Ga	2:13	**so that** even Barnabas was led
	3: 9	**For this reason,** those who
	3:24	**Therefore** the law was our
	4: 7	**So** you are no longer a slave
	4:16	**Have** I now become your enemy
Ph	1:13	**so that** it has become known
	2:12	**Therefore,** my beloved, just
	4: 1	**Therefore,** my brothers and
1Th	1: 7	**so that** you became an example

	1: 8	**so that** we have no need to
	4:18	**Therefore** encourage one another
2Th	1: 4	**Therefore** we ourselves boast of
	2: 4	**so that** he takes his seat in
He	13: 6	**So** we can say with confidence,
1P	1:21	**so that** your faith and hope are
	4:19	**Therefore,** let those suffering

5620a   GO2 AG900 LN268 K5:559
ωταριον, EAR

| Mk | 14:47 | priest, cutting off his **ear.** |
| Jn | 18:10 | and cut off his right **ear.** |

5621   GO3 AG900 LN268 K5:558 R3775
ωτιον, EAR

Mt	26:51	priest, cutting off his **ear.**
Lk	22:51	he touched his **ear** and healed
Jn	18:26	man whose **ear** Peter had cut off

5622   GO2 AG900 LN268 B3:137 R5624
ωφελεια, BENEFIT

| Ro | 3: 1 | is the **value** of circumcision? |
| Ju | 1:16 | people to their own **advantage.** |

5623   GO15 AG900 LN268 B1:463 R5622
ωφελεω, I BENEFIT

Mt	15: 5	Whatever **support** you might
	16:26	For what **will** it **profit** them if
	27:24	saw that he **could do** nothing,
Mk	5:26	she **was** no **better,** but rather
	7:11	Whatever **support** you might
	8:36	**will** it **profit** them to gain the
Lk	9:25	**does** it **profit** them if they
Jn	6:63	life; the flesh **is useless.**
	12:19	You see, you can **do** nothing.
Ro	2:25	Circumcision indeed **is of value**
1C	13: 3	not have love, I **gain** nothing.
	14: 6	how **will** I **benefit** you unless I
Ga	5: 2	Christ **will be of** no **benefit** to
He	4: 2	they heard **did** not **benefit** them
	13: 9	which **have** not **benefited** those

5624   GO4 AG900 LN268
ωφελιμος, HELPFUL

1Ti	4: 8	physical training is of some **value,**
	4: 8	**valuable** in every way, holding
2Ti	3:16	inspired by God and is **useful**
Ti	3: 8	excellent and **profitable** to